ENCYCLOPÆDIA
BRITANNICA

MICROPÆDIA

The Encyclopædia Britannica
is published with the editorial advice
of the faculties of the University of Chicago;
a committee of persons holding
academic appointments at the universities
of Oxford, Cambridge, London, and Edinburgh;
a committee at the University of Toronto;
and committees drawn from members of the faculties
of the University of Tokyo
and the Australian National University.

THE UNIVERSITY OF CHICAGO

"Let knowledge grow from more to more
and thus be human life enriched."

The New Encyclopædia Britannica

in 30 Volumes

MICROPÆDIA
Volume VII

Ready Reference
and
Index

FOUNDED 1768
15 TH EDITION

Encyclopædia Britannica, Inc.
William Benton, Publisher, 1943–1973
Helen Hemingway Benton, Publisher, 1973–1974
Chicago/Geneva/London/Manila/Paris/Rome
Seoul/Sydney/Tokyo/Toronto

First Edition	1768–1771
Second Edition	1777–1784
Third Edition	1788–1797
Supplement	1801
Fourth Edition	1801–1809
Fifth Edition	1815
Sixth Edition	1820–1823
Supplement	1815–1824
Seventh Edition	1830–1842
Eighth Edition	1852–1860
Ninth Edition	1875–1889
Tenth Edition	1902–1903

Eleventh Edition
© 1911
By Encyclopædia Britannica, Inc.

Twelfth Edition
© 1922
By Encyclopædia Britannica, Inc.

Thirteenth Edition
© 1926
By Encyclopædia Britannica, Inc.

Fourteenth Edition
© 1929, 1930, 1932, 1933, 1936, 1937, 1938, 1939, 1940, 1941, 1942, 1943, 1944, 1945, 1946, 1947, 1948, 1949, 1950, 1951, 1952, 1953, 1954, 1955, 1956, 1957, 1958, 1959, 1960, 1961, 1962, 1963, 1964, 1965, 1966, 1967, 1968, 1969, 1970, 1971, 1972, 1973
By Encyclopædia Britannica, Inc.

Fifteenth Edition
© 1974, 1975, 1976, 1977, 1978, 1979, 1980, 1981, 1982
By Encyclopædia Britannica, Inc.

Printed in U.S.A.

Library of Congress Catalog Card Number: 80-67750
International Standard Book Number: 0-85229-387-9

How to use this volume

This is one of the ten volumes of the *Ready Reference and Index*, or Micropædia (Volumes I through X).

Begin all reference searches here.

To satisfy a reference inquiry quickly.

To learn what *The New Encyclopædia Britannica* contains in its many articles.

Enter these volumes at any alphabetical point. The entries have been designed to provide information or to direct readers elsewhere in ways that are self-evident. But knowledge of a few editorial conventions will provide fuller understanding of what is offered:

1. Cross references appear often—identified by *see*, *see also*, or *q.v.* (*quod vide*, for "which see"), or as RELATED ENTRIES—and always refer to other entries in the *Ready Reference and Index* in alphabetical order (Volumes I-X).

> **ephedrine,** an alkaloid compound formerly derived from the leaves of several species of Chinese shrubs of the genus *Ephedra* of the family Ephedraceae (*q.v.*, order Gnetales), but now made synthetically. It is used as a decongestant drug (*q.v.*).

2. Entries are alphabetized as if they were one word, up to the comma, regardless of the number of words in the title. Thus *mountaineering* precedes *mountain goat*, whereas *charge, electron* precedes *chargé d'affaires*.

3. Directions, or *Index* references, are given to the page in the Macropædia (Volumes 1-19) on which a subject or aspect of a subject may be found in the longer articles.

   Volume and page numbers immediately following the title of an entry always refer to a comprehensive article in volumes 1 through 19.

> **Johnson, Samuel 10**:244 (b. Sept. 18, 1709, Lichfield, Staffordshire—d. Dec. 13, 1784, London), poet, essayist, critic, journalist, lexicographer, and conversationalist, is one of the outstanding figures of English 18th-century life and letters.

   All other volume and page references follow the text and cite *sections* of the longer (Macropædia) articles: the small, or lowercase, letters following page numbers—a, b, c, d, and e, f, g, h—identify the quarter of the column in which a reference begins. See marginal illustration.

> REFERENCES in other text articles:
> ·Addison's prose style and fame **1**:84a
> ·advertising criticism **1**:103h
> ·book publishing history **15**:228e
> ·Boswell's friendship and biographical work **3**:61h

a	e
b	f
c	g
d	h

   Another point about index references: *Major ref.* (for "major reference") followed by a volume and page number always cites a reference that is more comprehensive than the references following and should be considered the principal place to look for broad coverage of the topic under discussion.

   All other references carry brief descriptive phrases so that the reader may know what he may expect to find.

> **Anglo-Norman literature,** the writings in the French dialect of medieval England, also known as Norman-French or Anglo-French. Beginning effectively with the Norman Conquest (1066), it became the vernacular of the court, the law, the church, the schools and universities, Parliament, and, later, of municipalities and trade. *Major ref.* **10**:1105d.
> ·chansons de geste and the Tristan tale **15**:1021d *passim* to 1022g

   Index volume-and-page references are preceded by a small dot [·]. Underscored phrases are headings under which several index references are grouped.

Montpelier, capital of Vermont, U.S., and seat of Washington County (1811), on the upper Winooski River, 5 mi (8 km) northwest of Barre. It commands the main pass through the Green Mountains near the centre of the state. Named for Montpellier, Fr., the town (township) was chartered in 1781 by proprietors from Massachusetts and western Vermont. The first permanent dwelling was a log cabin built in 1787 by Col. Jacob Davis. Montpelier established a town meeting in 1791 and was named the state capital in 1805. The farming area was set off as East Montpelier in 1848. The capitol building (the third constructed on the site; completed in 1859) is built of Vermont granite. Within the portico is a marble statue representing Ethan Allen, American Revolutionary War hero.

Development of the granite industry in the area spurred the city's growth. Its present economy is based also on the business of state government, insurance companies, light manufacturing, and the nearby ski areas. Inc. village, 1828; city, 1895. Pop. (1980) 8,241.
44°16′ N, 72°35′ W

·map, United States **18**:908

Montpellier, capital of Hérault *département*, southern France, 7 mi (12 km) from the Mediterranean coast. An old university city, Montpellier is the chief administrative and commercial centre of the *bas* (low) Languedoc region. Situated in a fertile plain, the city has grown up around its old quarters, contained within boulevards on the site of the former city walls. It is famed for the terraced 17th- and 18th-century Promenade du Peyrou, which offers views of the Mediterranean and of the city's elegant mansions. The Botanical Gardens, founded by Henry IV in 1593, are the oldest in France. The Fabre Museum contains one of the richest French collections of paintings in existence. The 14th-century Gothic cathedral has been heavily restored.

A trading station for spice imports in the 10th century, Montpellier acquired a charter in 1141. Its school of medicine became important during the 11th century, the faculty of medicine being founded in 1221. The city's school of law dates from 1160. The University of Montpellier itself was founded by Pope Nicholas IV in 1289. Louis XIV (ruled 1643–1715) made Montpellier the administrative capital of the Languedoc region, famous for its wines. The modern city is the seat of the International Vine and Wine Fair. Its industries include food processing, metallurgy, and textile weaving. Latest census 152,105.
43°36′ N, 3°53′ E

·Huguenot possession under Henry IV **7**:631h
·map, France **7**:584
·Philip VI's acquisition for French crown **7**:623d; map 620

Montpellier I, II, et III, Universités de, English UNIVERSITIES OF MONTPELLIER I, II, AND III, coeducational, autonomous, state-financed institutions of higher learning at Montpellier, Fr. The three universities were founded in 1970 under France's 1968 Orientation Act, providing for reform of higher education. One of the provisions of this act empowered a university centre such as Montpellier to create one or more separate universities combining, as far as possible, arts and letters with sciences and technical studies, or, if preferred, concentrating on a particular field of specialization. Montpellier I, II, and III replaced the former University of Montpellier, which was founded in 1289, suppressed by the Revolution, and reconstituted as a university in 1896.

The structure of the new universities is based on academically and administratively independent teaching and research faculties called units. In the early 1970s total enrollment was about 18,000.

Montpellier faience, French tin-glazed earthenware made at factories in the city of Montpellier from the end of the 16th century into the 19th century. Its heyday was between 1570 and 1740. Much of the output consisted of drug jars (Montpellier was one of the oldest medical centres in Europe); but its wares from the beginning showed a certain individuality. Among the better decorations were the much copied naturalistic bouquets on a white or yellow background, instead of the traditional stylized flower arrangements.

Faience écuelle attributed to Montpellier, *c.* 1750; in the Victoria and Albert Museum, London

By courtesy of the Victoria and Albert Museum, London; photograph, EB Inc.

Montpellier snake, or LIZARD SNAKE (*Malpolon monspessulana*), of Mediterranean countries (except Italy) and Asia Minor, is a rear-fanged member of the family Colubridae. It is plain brown and as much as 2 metres (6½ feet) long. Found in stony arid land, it captures lizards, other snakes, and small mammals. Others of the genus are found in northern Africa and southwestern Asia.

Montpensier, Anne-Marie-Louise d'Orléans, duchesse de (b. May 29, 1627, Paris —d. April 5, 1693, Paris), princess of the royal house of France, prominent during the Fronde and the minority of Louis XIV (ruled 1643–1715); known as Mademoiselle because her father, Gaston de France, duc d'Orléans, lieutenant general of the realm, had the designation of Monsieur. From her mother, Marie de Bourbon-Montpensier, she inherited a huge fortune, including Eu and Dombes as well as Montpensier.

Tall and with a noble bearing, Mademoiselle set her heart on an exalted marriage, but the government would neither promise her the future Louis XIV in 1638 nor make a premature peace with the Habsburg powers in time for her to catch the Holy Roman emperor Ferdinand III in 1647. In 1651, during the first exile of the cardinal and statesman Jules Mazarin, Mademoiselle pulled her father along the path of collaboration with Louis II de Bourbon, prince de Condé.

In the third war of the Fronde, to overthrow the absolutism of royal government, she took command of the troops that occupied Orléans on March 27, 1652, against token opposition. Finally, she saved Condé's army from annihilation in the Battle of the Faubourg Saint-Antoine (July 2, 1652) by ordering the cannon of the Bastille fired against the royal troops. On Louis XIV's return to Paris (October 1652), Mademoiselle went into exile till 1657. She was again exiled from court from 1662 to 1664 for refusing to marry Afonso VI of Portugal.

To everyone's amazement, Louis XIV, on Dec. 15, 1670, consented to Mademoiselle's plea for permission to marry a low-ranking gentleman, the Comte de Lauzun, a captain in the King's bodyguard. Louis then retracted under pressure from outraged advisers and had Lauzun imprisoned. Mademoiselle finally obtained Lauzun's release in 1680 and, in return, ceded much of her estate to Louis's illegitimate son Louis-Auguste, duc du Maine. She and Lauzun were married secretly in 1681 or 1682 but were unhappy together and separated in 1684. Mademoiselle's *Mémoires* cover her life to 1688. She also left two short novels and literary "portraits."

Montpensier, Antoing, duc de (1824–90), son of Louis-Philippe.

·French influence on marriage to Luisa **3**:83e

Montpensier, Catherine, duchesse de (1552–96), sister of the 3rd Duke of Guise.

·Guise historical role and succession **8**:478b; table 477

Montpensier, Gilbert de Bourbon, comte de (1443–96), French military commander.

·Charles VIII's Italian wars **6**:1083c

Montreal 12:411, largest city and a major seaport of Canada and of Quebec province, located on Montreal Island at the confluence of the Ottawa and St. Lawrence rivers. Pop. (1971) city, 1,214,352; metropolitan area, 2,743,208.

The text article, after a brief survey of the city, covers its history and such aspects of the contemporary scene as the physical plan, people, economy, administration, transportation, educational and health services, and cultural life and institutions.
45°31′ N, 73°34′ W

REFERENCES in other text articles:
·aqueduct construction and history **1**:1039h
·botanical garden table **3**:64
·British fur-trade control and later influence **3**:738g
·Cartier St. Lawrence exploration **3**:971a
·establishment and economic growth **15**:330c
·fur auctions **7**:815b
·map, Canada **3**:716
·settlement and colonial importance **3**:735e
·St. Lawrence River freezing and navigation problems **16**:173c

Montreal Expos, professional baseball team in the eastern division of the National League; formed in an expansion of the major leagues in 1969.

·major-league-baseball franchise **12**:413g

Montreal group, coterie of poets who precipitated a renascence of Canadian poetry during the 1920s and '30s by advocating a break with the traditional picturesque landscape poetry that had dominated Canadian poetry since the late 19th century. They encouraged an emulation of the realistic themes, metaphysical complexity, and techniques of the U.S. and British poets Ezra Pound, T.S. Eliot, and W.H. Auden that resulted in an Expressionist poetry reflective of the values of an urban civilization. Based in Montreal, then Canada's most cosmopolitan city, the group included A.M. Klein; A.J.M. Smith, whose *Book of Canadian Poetry* (1943) and other anthologies contributed greatly to the raising of literary standards in Canada; Leo Kennedy; and Francis Reginald Scott; as well as two kindred spirits from Toronto, E.J. Pratt and Robert Finch. First brought together at McGill University in Montreal, these poets founded the *Canadian Mercury* (1928–29), a literary organ for young writers, and subsequently founded, edited, and wrote for a number of other influential journals—*e.g.*, the *McGill Fortnightly Review* and *Canadian Forum.*

Montréal-Nord, English MONTREAL NORTH, city, Montréal region, southern Quebec province, Canada, on the south shore of the Rivière des Prairies, north of Montreal city. A large residential and industrial suburb, it has grown rapidly since World War II. In 1959 it joined the newly established Montreal Metropolitan Corporation. Inc. town, 1915; city, 1959. Pop. (1971) 89,139.
45°35′ N, 73°38′ W

Montreuil, also called MONTREUIL-SOUS-BOIS, eastern industrial suburb of Paris, situated on a plateau 400 ft (120 m) high, in the Seine-Saint-Denis *département.* Located one mi (1.6 km) away from the city limits of the capital, it is connected to Paris by the Métro (subway). A centre for processing hides and skins, Montreuil also manufactures biscuits (cookies) and porcelain and produces chemicals for tanning. Peach trees, for which the locality was once famous, still grow there. In the centre of the old town the church of Saint-Pierre-Saint-Paul has a 12th-century choir. A wooded park on the edge of the plateau contains a museum of history. Latest census 95,714.

Montreux, comprises three resort communities (Le Châtelard-Montreux, Les Planches-Montreux, and Veytaux-Montreux; merged 1962) in Vaud canton, western Switzerland, extending 4 mi (6 km) along the eastern shore of Lake Geneva (Lac Léman). Its natural setting below mountains protecting it from northerly and easterly winds has made Montreux the lake's most fashionable health resort. The nearby 13th-century Château de Chillon, made famous by Lord Byron's poem "Prisoner of Chillon," is one of Switzerland's best known pieces of architecture. Montreux is on railway lines from Geneva and France to Italy via the Simplon Tunnel and is also a terminus of mountain railways. The tourist trade is important, while the villages (Caux, Chernex, Glion, Chamby, and Les Avants) on terraces above Montreux depend mainly on agriculture and viticulture. Pop. (1970) 21,331.
46°26′ N, 6°55′ E
·map, Switzerland **17**:868

Montreux Convention (1936): *see* Straits Question.

Montrose, royal burgh (chartered town) and North Sea port, county of Angus, Scotland, situated at the mouth of the South Esk River, on the Montrose Basin, a tidal lagoon. Montrose received its first charter from David I of Scotland (ruled 1124–53) and was created a royal burgh in 1352. It was there in 1296 that Edward I of England accepted the surrender of Scotland from John de Baliol. Montrose prospered as a market town and fishing port and by the 18th century had developed into a popular spa; trade links were established with the south (after the union of Scotland and England); and the Inchbrayock Bridge was built over the narrows of the Montrose Basin. That wooden bridge has since been replaced by a modern suspension bridge, seaward of which lie the harbour and wet dock. Jute processing and the making of jam from local and imported soft fruits are the main industries. Timber is imported, and local beer is shipped to Newcastle, in northeast England. The town, although no longer a spa, is a popular holiday resort. James Graham, 1st marquess of Montrose, Scotland's most famous soldier after Robert I the Bruce, was born there in 1612. Pop. (1971 prelim.) 10,178.
56°43′ N, 2°29′ W
·map, United Kingdom **18**:866

Montrose, city seat (1883) of Montrose County, western Colorado, U.S., on the Uncompahgre River. After the land was opened for settlement (1881), a railway depot was established on the site. The town that grew up around it was named by an early citizen, who was inspired by the 19th-century Scottish Romantic writer Sir Walter Scott's *Legend of Montrose*. By 1900, major canal projects irrigated about 75,000 ac (30,000 ha) of land for farming, and lumbering and mining (carnotite ores yielding uranium, vanadium, and radium) became important. In about 1909 water diverted from the Gunnison River through the Gunnison Tunnel, 6 mi long, increased irrigation facilities.

The city is now a busy trading centre, with food and wood processing industries. The area is part of the Upper Colorado River Storage Project. The Ute Indian Museum is nearby, and Montrose is a tourist base for Black Canyon of the Gunnison National Monument and the Uncompahgre and Gunnison national forests. Inc. town, 1882; city, 1906. Pop. (1980) 8,722.
38°29′ N, 107°53′ W
·map, United States **18**:908

Montrose, James Graham, 5th earl and 1st marquess of (b. 1612—d. May 21, 1650, Edinburgh), general who won a series of spectacular victories in Scotland for King Charles I of England during the English Civil War (1642–51) between the King and Parliament. He inherited the title earl of Montrose from his father in 1626. In 1637 Montrose signed a covenant promising to defend Scotland's Presbyterian religion against attempts by Charles I to impose Anglican forms of worship. Nevertheless, Montrose was still essentially a royalist, and, as such, he became the bitter enemy of Archibald Campbell, earl of Argyll, leader of Scotland's powerful anti-royalist party.

Marquess of Montrose, portrait miniature after a painting by W. Dobson (1610–46); in the Wallace Collection, London

By courtesy of the trustees of the Wallace Collection, London

Montrose served in the covenanter army that invaded and occupied part of northern England in August 1640, but he subsequently lost his political struggle with Argyll and was imprisoned by the Earl in Edinburgh from June to November 1641.

In 1644, when the covenanters invaded England to fight for Parliament against the King, Charles appointed Montrose lieutenant general in Scotland; three months later he was made a marquess. Going to the Scottish Highlands in August 1644, Montrose raised an army of Highlanders, and within a year his brilliance had brought him victories in major battles: at Tippermuir (Tibbermore), Aberdeen, Inverlochy, Auldearn, Alford, and Kilsyth. Charles made him lieutenant governor and captain general of Scotland.

But after the King's decisive defeat at Naseby in June 1645, Montrose's army melted away, and the small force remaining was routed at Philiphaugh in September. Montrose fled to the Continent in 1646 but returned to Scotland with about 1,200 men in March 1650. After suffering a defeat at Carbisdale on April 27, he was surrendered by Neil MacLeod of Assynt, with whom he had sought protection. He was hanged in the marketplace of Edinburgh in May. A biography of Montrose by John Buchan appeared in 1913 and one by C.V. Wedgwood in 1952.

Montrouge, also called LE GRAND-MONTROUGE, town, a southern suburb of Paris, in Hauts-de-Seine *département*, north central France. It has printing and bookbinding establishments and manufactures surgical instruments, radios and televisions, and perfume. The area, recorded as Mons Rubicus, from the local reddish soil, in ancient charters was divided in 1860—Le Petit Montrouge was absorbed into the 14th *arrondissement* (administrative division) of Paris and the remainder formed the commune of Montrouge. Latest census 44,788.

Mont-Royal (Quebec): *see* Mount Royal.

Monts, Pierre du Guast, Sieur de (1568–1630), French explorer.
·Champlain Nova Scotia settlement **3**:734c

Mont-Saint-Michel (France): *see* Le Mont-Saint-Michel.

Montserrado County, administrative division (since 1847) of western Liberia. Named for Cape Mesurado on the Atlantic, it has an area of 2,550 sq mi (6,605 sq km). Its seat, Monrovia (*q.v.*), is also the nation's capital, largest city, and chief port. The country's hinterland produces rubber, iron ore, cocoa, and coffee for export. Its chief inland towns are Careysburg, Harbel, Kakata, Kle, and Vaitown (*qq.v.*). Latest pop. est. 280,527.
·area and population table **10**:853
·map, Liberia **10**:852

Montserrat, an island of the Leeward Islands group of the Lesser Antilles (Caribbees) in the Caribbean Sea. It lies 27 mi (43 km) southwest of Antigua and is 11 mi long and 7 mi wide with an area of 39.5 sq mi (102.3 sq km). It consists of a serrated range of volcanic peaks rising in three main hill masses, the summits of which are forested. Chance Peak, 3,002 ft (915 m) in the southern hills above the still-active Soufrière Hills, is the highest point. The 1960 constitution provides for government through an administrator who heads an executive and a legislative council. Primary education is compulsory and free, and there is one government secondary school. In 1956 access to Montserrat was facilitated by the completion of Blackburne Airfield. Previously, visitors were dependent upon ships that sailed irregularly. The principal products are vegetables, limes, and sea island cotton.

Montserrat was discovered in 1493 by Christopher Columbus and named after the monastery in Spain; it was colonized by Irish settlers led by Sir Thomas Warner, in 1632. Between 1871 and 1956, it was a crown colony, a part of the (British) Federal Colony of the Leeward Islands. In 1958 Montserrat joined the Federation of the West Indies, which was dissolved in 1962. Subsequent attempts to form a federation of the Leeward and Windward islands were also abandoned in 1966. Its capital is Plymouth and its political status is that of a crown colony of the United Kingdom. Pop. (1971 est.) 13,076.
16°45′ N, 62°12′ W

Montserrat, mountain in northwestern Barcelona province, Catalonia, Spain, just west of the Río Llobregat and northwest of Barcelona city. The Mons Serratus (Saw-toothed) of the Romans and known to the Catalans as Montsagrat (Sacred Mountain), it is famous for its Benedictine monastery of Santa María de Montserrat and for the ancient wooden statue of the Virgin and Child, supposedly carved by St. Luke, brought to Spain by St. Peter, and hidden in a cave during the Moorish occupation. Found in 880, it has been venerated there since by numerous pilgrims, who attribute many miracles to the intercession of the Virgin Mary.

Jagged pinnacles (hence its name) rise from the mountain's huge base, and it is cloven by ravines; the monastery stands on the edge of the widest of these, the Valle Malo, at 2,400 ft (730 m). Remains indicate that the mountain was inhabited in prehistoric times. Christian hermits of Santa María were residing on Montserrat when in 888 the Benedictine monastery of Ripoll was granted jurisdiction over them. From the 11th to the early 15th century a regular priory flourished there and obtained independence as an abbey in 1410, which status it has held almost continuously ever since. The present basilica was begun in 1560 and the monastery in 1755, though these were extensively rebuilt after destruction by French troops during the Peninsular Campaign in 1812.
41°36′ N, 1°49′ E

Monts Mandara (Cameroon): *see* Mandara Mountains.

Montt, Manuel (b. Sept. 8, 1809, Petorca, Chile—d. Sept 20, 1880, Santiago), president of Chile, an enlightened despot who throughout his two terms (1851–61) angered Liberals and Conservatives alike, yet accomplished many constructive reforms.

After studying law at the Instituto Nacional, where he also served as rector (1835–40),

Montt was elected to the Chilean Congress in 1840. He served as minister of the interior and minister of justice under Pres. Manuel Bulnes (1841–51).

Manuel Montt, engraving by an unknown artist

By courtesy of the Library of Congress, Washington, D.C.

In 1851 Montt won the presidency, but the Liberals thought his election was fraudulent and instigated an armed revolt, which was quickly subdued. Montt represented the conservative oligarchy and was authoritarian and inflexible in his beliefs. He angered the Conservatives, however, both when he asserted the state's right of patronage in Chile's Roman Catholic Church and when he supported the abolition of restrictions on the sale or bequeathing of estates. In addition, his administration made outstanding advances in technology, commerce and banking, and legal codification, and it strongly promoted public education and immigration.

Near the end of his term, when he indicated a preference for Antonio Varas, his minister of the interior, to be his successor, Liberals again staged an armed uprising. Montt again subdued the revolt but pacified the Liberals by shifting his support to José Joaquín Pérez, a moderate. On giving up the presidency in 1861, Montt became president of the Supreme Court, a post he held at the time of his death.

·economic development role **4**:255h

Montt, Pedro (b. 1846, Santiago, Chile—d. Aug. 16, 1910, Bremen, now in West Germany), Chilean president (1906–10), whose Conservative government furthered railroad and manufacturing activities but ignored pressing social and labour problems.

The son of the former Chilean president Manuel Montt, Pedro Montt was graduated in law at the Instituto Nacional in 1870. He was elected a member of the Chamber of Deputies (1876) and became its president in 1885. He held two posts in the Cabinet of Pres. José Balmaceda but later (1891) took an active part in the revolution that overthrew him. He then went to the United States, first as an agent of the revolutionary junta and later (after U.S. recognition) as minister from Chile.

Unsuccessful in his first bid for the presidency (1901), Montt was elected by a large majority in 1906 as the candidate of the National Union ticket. His first action was to call out the army to suppress large-scale strikes (1907). His administration supported the construction of a railway that ran the length of the country and stimulated the production of nitrates and copper. It did little, however, to improve the living conditions of the people. In 1910 Montt left Chile for medical treatment in Germany, where he died.

Montúfar y Rivera Maestre, Lorenzo (b. March 11, 1823, Guatemala City—d. 1898), Central American statesman and historian, whose liberal political activities often resulted in his exile.

Receiving degrees in philosophy and law from the University of Guatemala in 1846, Montúfar began his career as a professor of civil law. He vigorously opposed the dictatorship of Rafael Carrera and was frequently exiled for his political opinions. While in exile in El Salvador, he was elected to the Guatemalan Congress, which proscribed Carrera, but on the dictator's return Montúfar was forced to flee to Costa Rica. Much later in his life he wrote the monumental *Reseña Historica de Centro America* (17 vol., 1878–88), which covers much of the Carrera era.

A Costa Rican exile, Montúfar assumed a career as a lawyer, magistrate, and publisher. Later, as foreign minister, he helped to organize the Central American defense against the U.S. adventurer William Walker, who in 1855–62 sought control of Nicaragua. At home in each of the Central American republics, Montúfar travelled extensively in Latin America, the United States, and Europe. As one of the leading advocates of Central American unity, he repeatedly urged that the distintegrated Federation of Republics be re-established. He held numerous government posts and negotiated treaties that settled some of the many Central American boundary disputes. In 1891 he was unsuccessful in his bid for the presidency of Guatemala.

Monumenta Germaniae Historica (MGH), a voluminous, comprehensive, and critically edited collection of sources pertaining to German history from *c.* AD 500 to 1500, begun in the early 19th century as a result of rising nationalistic feeling, which gave impetus to similar endeavours by historians in other European countries. The most important antecedent of the MGH was the *Monarchia romani imperii*, a collection of documents on German medieval history compiled by Melchior Goldast (died 1635). The initiator of the MGH was Karl Freiherr vom Stein (died 1831), leading early 19th-century German statesman and reformer, who, after retiring from politics in 1816, exercised his patriotic energies in stirring up interest in German history. He founded at Frankfurt am Main in 1819, the Gesellschaft für Deutschlands Ältere Geschichtskunde (Society for Earlier German History). The success of the MGH project was in large measure due to the scholarly capability and energy of a Hanoverian Georg Heinrich Pertz (died 1876), whom Stein enlisted as editor and put in charge of the work in 1823. Under Pertz's half century of editorship and collaboration with leading German scholars, 20 volumes of sources were published; 100 more were to follow, the last of which was issued in 1925. The documents in the MGH are classified according to the following categories: *scriptores*, *leges*, *diplomata*, *epistolae*, and *antiquitates*. The MGH was a seminal undertaking that set a high standard of scholarship for later generations of historians producing similiar collections.

·textual editing methodology **18**:194d

monumental axis, central core area of Brasília, in which federal government and other public buildings are located, running roughly perpendicular to the residential axis of the city.

·location and importance **3**:121d; map 120

monuments and memorials, broadly, terms inclusive of all objects of whatever size or nature that have been put on view for the primary purpose of recalling to mind or commemorating specific events or personages. Their production is a distinctive characteristic of societies that put value upon the individual human being and hold an objective view of historical events. *See also* funerary art; megalith; sculpture, sepulchral; tomb.

·ancient Greek art forms and styles **19**:287a
·ancient Near East visual art history **19**:259c
·Byzantine churches and architecture in Istanbul **9**:1071c; table 1069
·Delhi's composite architecture **5**:574c
·Dome of the Rock symbolism **9**:987f
·Donatello's classic debt and Gattamelata **5**:952d
·early Christian mosaic designs **19**:323e
·Egyptian tombs, pyramids, and temples **19**:250d
·hieroglyph origin in picture chronicles **8**:853d
·Indonesian temple complexes **9**:475c
·Javanese Buddhist and Hindu art **9**:479g
·medieval brass tomb engraving **11**:1101d
·Michelangelo's tombs **12**:98f
·museums out of historical monuments **12**:657e
·Neoclassical sculpture developments **19**:440d
·Orissa's Śaivite temple **13**:739e
·prehistoric megalith interpretations **14**:985f
·Roman visual art forms and styles **19**:305a *passim* to 311d
·Turkish mosques and architecture in Instanbul **9**:1071h; table 1069
·Verrocchio's Medici tomb and Colleoni **19**:93e
·Washington, D.C. trends **19**:626g

Monumentum Ancyranum (ancient inscription): *see* Ancyranum, Monumentum.

Monura, extinct order of insects (phylum Arthropoda).

·characteristics and taxonomy **1**:1023h

Monville, Hôtel de, Neoclassical style Parisian townhouse designed by Étienne-Louis Boullée and built *c.* 1770.

·Neoclassical architectural developments **19**:435f

Monywa, administrative headquarters of Lower Chindwin District (*q.v.*), Sagaing Division, west central Upper Burma. Latest census 26,172.
22°05′ N, 95°08′ E

·map, Burma **3**:505

Monza, city, Milano province, Lombardia (Lombardy) region, northern Italy, on the Lambro River, just northeast of Milan. The ancient Modicia, it was a village until the 6th century, when the Lombard queen Theodelinda established a residence and a monastery there. During the period of the communes, Monza was sometimes independent, sometimes subject to Milan. The Visconti family built a castle there in 1325; it withstood many sieges and was repeatedly plundered, notably by the troops of Charles V. King Umberto I of Italy was assassinated at Monza on July 29, 1900; an expiatory chapel was dedicated in 1910.

Monza is known for its cathedral, founded in 595 by Theodelinda and enlarged in the 13th century. The facade was erected in 1390–96 by Matteo da Campione, and the campanile dates from 1592–1606. Within the cathedral church is the iron crown (Corona Ferrea) of Lombardy, supposedly formed from one of the nails used at Christ's crucifixion and used after 1311 for the coronation of the Holy Roman emperors and of Napoleon at Milan in 1805; the church's rich treasury also contains the relics of Theodelinda and other crosses and reliquaries of the Lombard and Gothic periods. Also notable are the Church of Sta. Maria in Strada (1357) with a terra-cotta facade of 1393; the 13th-century communal palace, Arengario; and the Villa Reale (royal palace; 1777–80), used for art exhibitions.

Monza is a busy industrial centre manufacturing felt hats and carpets, textiles, machinery, furniture, glass, paint, and plastics. It is the site of the famous Autodromo (automobile-racing track), which, because of its elliptical shape and concrete banked curves, is claimed to be the fastest in the world. Pop. (1971 prelim.) mun., 116,257.
45°35′ N, 9°16′ E

·Grand Prix, speedway, and formula car racing **12**:566g *passim* to 571b
·map, Italy **9**:1088

Monzaemon, Chikeamatsu: *see* Chikamatsu Monzaemon.

monzonite, intrusive igneous rock that contains abundant and approximately equal amounts of plagioclase and potash feldspar; it also contains subordinate amounts of biotite and hornblende, and sometimes minor quantities of ortho-pyroxene. Quartz, nepheline, and olivine, which are occasionally present, pro-

duce quartz, nepheline, and olivene monzonite. In the type region of Monzoni, Italy, in the Italian Tirol, these minerals rarely occur as major constituents; moreover, in Monzoni the plagioclase is often calcium-rich (labradorite) and commonly shows prominent zoning. Rocks similar to those of the type area have been described from Norway (akerite), Montana (yogoite, shonkinite), Sakhalin Island off the Pacific coast of the Soviet Union, and other localities throughout the world. Monzonite is not a rare rock type, but it generally occurs in rather small, heterogeneous masses associated with (and perhaps gradational to) diorites, pyroxenites, or gabbros.
·classification and abundance **9**:212b; table 207
·crustal abundance, illus. 4 **9**:223
·mineralogical composition and relation to granite **9**:222e; table 221

mood, also called MODE, in grammar, speaker's attitude toward his utterance that may be marked by verb inflections or by variation of word order. The imperative (commanding), indicative (fact expressing), and subjunctive (wishing and contingency expressing) moods characterize many Indo-European languages but are not shown by separate forms in all. The subjunctive mood is indicated by a series of distinct verb endings in such languages as Spanish, French, and German. In English it is often shown by such words as "if," "might," "may," "should," and "would," along with a lack of ending, as "Should the rain fall" (but "The rain fall*s*"). The examples "be" and "were" in "If this be so" and "If I were you," not often used on an informal level of speech, are survivals of a once more extensive group of English subjunctive constructions. *See also* conjugation; inflection.
·Eskimo–Aleut derivation and inflection **6**:964c
·Hopi evidential verb forms **13**:211c

mood, in logic, the classification of categorical syllogisms according to the quantity (universal or particular) and quality (affirmative or negative) of their constituent propositions. There are four forms of propositions: *A* (universal affirmative), *E* (universal negative), *I* (particular affirmative), and *O* (particular negative). Because each syllogism has three propositions and each proposition may take four different forms, there are 64 different patterns (moods) of syllogisms.

Twenty-four of the 64 possible moods are valid, though only 19 were traditionally accepted as valid. Various mnemonic terms are employed to label these moods. The vowels of these terms represent the forms of propositions in the syllogism. For example, "Felapton" is the mnemonic term to signify the mood in which the major premise (the premise containing the predicate of the conclusion) of the syllogism is an *E* proposition, the minor premise (the premise containing the subject of the conclusion) is an *A*, and the conclusion is an *O*.
·classification by figure **11**:50h; tables
·classification of valid forms **17**:892f

Moodie, Susanna Strickland (b. Dec. 6, 1803, Bungay, Suffolk—d. April 8, 1885, Toronto), Canadian pioneer who wrote realistic, perceptive, and often humorous accounts of life in the wilderness. Her most important work is *Roughing It in the Bush; or, Life in Canada* (1852). She emigrated to the Upper Canadian wilderness in 1832 with her husband, a British army officer, and her sister, Catherine Parr Traill (*q.v.*), who was also an author. Moodie's initial distaste for the hardships of "roughing it" gradually changed to an earnest commitment to Canada's future.
·Canadian literature of the 19th century **10**:1192a

Moods, Cadenced and Declaimed (1926), volume of poetry by Theodore Dreiser.
·reception of Dreiser's works **5**:1015c

Moody, Dwight L(yman) (b. Feb. 5, 1837, East Northfield, Mass.—d. Dec. 22, 1899, Northfield), prominent U.S. evangelist who set the pattern for later evangelism in large cities.

Dwight L. Moody, detail from a drawing by Charles Stanley Reinhart; in *Harper's Weekly*, March 1876
By courtesy of the Library of Congress, Washington, D.C.

Moody left his mother's farm at 17 to work in Boston and there was converted from Unitarianism to Fundamentalist evangelicalism. In 1856 he moved to Chicago and prospered as a shoe salesman, but in 1860 he gave up business for missionary work. He worked with the Young Men's Christian Association (YMCA; 1861–73), was president of the Chicago YMCA, founded the Moody Church, and engaged in slum mission work.

In 1870 he met Ira D. Sankey, a hymn writer, and with him became noted for contributing to the development of the "gospel hymn." They made extended evangelical tours in Great Britain (1873–75, 1881–84). Moody shunned divisive sectarian doctrines, deplored "higher criticism" of the Bible, the social gospel movement, and the theory of evolution, and instead colourfully and intensely preached "the old-fashioned gospel," literally interpreting the Bible and the premillennial Second Coming.

Moody's mass revivals were financed by prominent businessmen who believed he would alleviate the hardships of the poor. Moody himself ardently supported various charities but felt that social problems could be solved only by the divine regeneration of individuals. In addition to conducting revivals, he directed annual Bible conferences at Northfield, Mass., where he founded a seminary for girls in 1879. In 1889 he founded the Chicago Bible Institute (now the Moody Bible Institute). His life and work are examined by James F. Findlay, Jr., in *Dwight L. Moody, American Evangelist: 1837–1899* (1969).
·Evangelicals in Northfield conferences **7**:778d
·Protestant revivalism **15**:116d

Moody, Helen Wills: *see* Wills, Helen (Newington).

Moody, William Vaughn (1869–1910), U.S. poet and playwright whose two most important plays are *The Great Divide* (1906) and *The Faith Healer* (1909). He also wrote a history of and an introduction to English literature.
·American literature of the 19th century **10**:1191b

Moody Bible Institute, original name CHICAGO BIBLE INSTITUTE, Fundamentalist Protestant institution founded in Chicago by Dwight L. Moody in 1889.
·modern Fundamentalist activities **7**:779f

Moog: *see* music synthesizer.

Mooleyser, Willem, 17th-century Dutch engraver known for his decoration of glass.
·diamond-point style **8**:186a

Moon 12:415, sole natural satellite of the planet Earth.

TEXT ARTICLE covers:
The motion of the Moon **12**:415a
The mass and gravity field of the Moon 418d
The physical nature of the Moon: selenology 419e
The origin and evolution of the Moon 429a

REFERENCES in other text articles:
·Arabian cults' astral pantheon **1**:1058a
·astronomical research methods **2**:248f
·biological rhythms affected **14**:69h
·catastrophic continental drift theory **5**:109c
·comparison of properties with Mercury **11**:917g
·Copernican theory in historical perspective **5**:145e
·cosmogony and evolution of planetary systems **18**:1010h
·crater sizes and number **12**:48d
·desert characteristics **5**:602g
·Earth rotation influence **6**:59c
·Earth's magnetic field variations **6**:31c
·eclipses and occultations **6**:188d *passim* to 197a
·element abundance and rock sampling **6**:701h; table 702
·Euler lunar motion theory **6**:1027d
·geological forms and features analysis **7**:1055c
·geological history and dating studies **5**:513d
·gravity investigation and properties **8**:287c
·heat flow and radioactivity **6**:24c
·Hipparchus' study of celestial movement **8**:941b
·history of astronomical theories **14**:384e *passim* to 388f
·impact and volcanic crater identification **12**:53h
·infrared source research **9**:582a
·interplanetary plasma interaction **9**:789b
·life possibility **10**:908a
·lunar exploration, illus., **17**:Space Exploration, Plates I and III
·lunar exploration findings **17**:373h
·mapping of features **2**:231g
·Mars crater comparison **11**:523b
·mineral formation factors **12**:244b
·Moon–Earth distance limitations **10**:625g
·motion on celestial sphere **2**:224e
·myths and folk traditions **12**:880f
·oceanic tide generation **13**:495d
·parallax measurement development **13**:994a; illus.
·planetary motion and stability **11**:760f
·planet composition similarity **4**:119g
·radio-wave emissions **15**:469c
·rare-earth element distribution **15**:516e
·seismograph station establishment **16**:492b
·silicate mineral occurrence **16**:764d
·solar studies during eclipses **17**:800d
·sound transmission by Moon reflection **16**:262f
·space exploration history **17**:365c
·surface composition and analysis **6**:86b
·tektite origin theories **18**:62g
·tidal effects mutuality with Earth **18**:383a; illus.
·time systems and units **18**:414a *passim* to 415e
·weather lore and forecasting **19**:706b

RELATED ENTRIES in the *Ready Reference and Index: for*
surface features: see Alphonsus; Copernicus; Fra Mauro; Linné; lunar bright rays; mascon; Moon, compass directions on the; Moon, craters of the; Moon, observed transient changes on the; Moon, seas of the; rille; Tycho; walled plain
appearance and motion: albedo; Cassini's laws; earthshine; evection; full moon; harvest moon; libration; lunation; month; new moon; nutation; phase

Moon, compass directions on the, directions that were redefined in 1961 to conform to terrestrial conventions. By these conventions, a person standing on the Moon and facing north (toward the pole of the Moon's rotation most closely aligned with Earth's North Pole) has lunar east on the right hand and west on the left, as on Earth.

This east–west convention for the Moon was adopted by the International Astronomical Union in 1961 because increasing numbers of persons who were not astronomers were involved in efforts toward lunar exploration and many of them objected to the previous directional convention used by astronomers, in which lunar east was at the eastern limb (edge) in the sky.

From the 17th century, when telescopic observation of the Moon began, astronomers found it most convenient to consider lunar east as coinciding with east in the sky of Earth; this corresponded to the direction on the left of a person actually on the Moon and facing north. A new difficulty arose from the use of maps made according to the revised 1961 rules, which showed north at the top, because most astronomical telescopes present inverted images to the eye. To an astronomer observing through a telescope from Earth's Northern Hemisphere, the south pole of the Moon appears approximately "on top." Since the 1960s, maps and pictures of the Moon commonly have north at the top; at the telescope, either the map with all its printing or the image must be reversed for comparison. Lunar longitude is measured from a point in the Sinus Medii (Central Bay), approximately in the centre of the side of the Moon turned toward Earth.

Moon, craters of the, ubiquitous, nearly circular features of the lunar surface, consisting of relatively smooth, level floors, usually surrounded by walls. They occur in many sizes, from less than 100 metres to more than 160 kilometres in diameter. Some are the result of meteorites striking the Moon, some were caused by eruptions of gas or lava from the lunar interior, and some were formed by a combination of the two.

The theory that craters are marks left by the eruption of material from the Moon's interior was suggested in 1665, by Robert Hooke, who thought that at least some of them were the solidified remnants of enormous bubbles. Hooke also performed experiments, dropping objects into wet plaster of Paris to determine whether he could simulate other lunar crater forms by impact.

The meteoric impact theory of crater formation was proposed later by several scientists in the 19th century and was still held by most astronomers in the early 1980s.

Hundreds of lunar craters have been named, primarily for scientists such as Galileo, Newton, Caroline Herschel, and Marie Skłodowska Curie. On the far side of the Moon, observed from spacecraft since 1959, craters have also been named for cosmonauts and astronauts (*e.g.*, Gagarin, Armstrong), rocket engineers (*e.g.*, Congreve), writers (*e.g.*, Chaucer, Dante, Omar Khayyam, Jules Verne), and mythical characters (*e.g.*, Daedalus).

·formation, occurrence, and statistical studies **12**:419c *passim* to 423a
·structures photographs **12**:421

Moon, maria of, dark areas thought by the first telescopic observers in the 17th century to be actual bodies of water and named maria (Latin: "seas") by Galileo. With improved instruments the maria were seen to be relatively smooth land areas, generally lower than the more rugged, lighter coloured parts of the surface, called the highlands, or terrae (Latin: "lands").

The maria occupy almost half the face of the Moon turned to Earth but only a small percentage of the far side. They are classified by shape into two categories: the regular (or circular) and the irregular. Whether the maria were formed during formation of the Moon itself or by the impact of great meteoric bodies or by the Moon's internal forces is still uncertain. (Whether lunar maria and lunar craters are essentially different except in size is also an unsolved question.)

Many scientists believe that the maria may have been formed by outflows of lava; the irregular maria are generally connected to the circular, in such a way that the former seem to represent overflows of lava from the latter. After hardening, the lava of the maria may have become pitted by craters and marked by occasional rilles, ridges, and rays and had their surface layers fragmented into soil, while still remaining smoother than the surrounding uplands.

The largest of the circular maria, Mare Imbrium (Sea of Rains), located in the Moon's northern hemisphere on the side turned toward Earth, is about 890,000 square kilometres (340,000 square miles) in area. Other prominent regular maria include Mare Serenitatis (Sea of Serenity) and Mare Crisium (Sea of Crises). The largest of the irregular maria is Oceanus Procellarum (Ocean of Storms), connected to the Mare Imbrium and about 2,000,000 square miles in extent, or the size of the Mediterranean Sea. The second and third U.S. Apollo manned lunar landings were made on the Oceanus Procellarum. The irregular Mare Tranquillitatis (Sea of Tranquillity), about 400,000 square kilometres (150,000 square miles) in area, was the site of the first manned landing in 1969. Other notable irregular maria include Mare Nubium (Sea of Clouds) and Mare Fecunditatis (Sea of Fertility).

On the Western limb (new style, post-1961) of the Moon is the circular Mare Orientale (Eastern Sea), which is ringed by two concentric mountain ranges (Montes Cordillera, the outer, and Montes Rook).

·basalt mineralogy **16**:764e
·formation and rock types **12**:428g
·gravity anomaly and mascons **12**:418g
·impact and volcanic crater identification **12**:53h
·Mars surface markings **11**:522f
·Moon, photograph 1 **12**:421

Moon, observed transient changes on the, various reported instances of apparent eruptive activity and temporary changes in craters, ridges, and other surface features of the Moon. No new craters are known to have been formed on the Moon since telescopic observations began in the early 17th century, but, because the number of craters registered on early maps was very small, such statements cannot be verified. In November 1969, U.S. Apollo 12 astronauts on the Moon examined the unmanned spacecraft Surveyor 3 at the point where it had landed and had photographed the surface 31 months earlier. Little or no detectable change had occurred during that period in the imprints made by Surveyor or in the lunar soil it had turned over.

Temporary changes in the light level, or glows, of small areas, such as craters, have been recorded several times even on the dark side of the Moon, and it is now clear that at least some of the many reports refer to real occurrences. Almost every lunar observer of note in the 19th century reported at least one case, and the records of such cases date back more than 400 years. The glows are now thought to be caused by the electrical discharge of small quantities of gas from below the surface.

·tidal forces, quakes, and transient events **18**:390h
·types and interpretations **12**:425d

Moon, William (1818–94), British inventor of a reading system for the blind.

·reading system for the blind **3**:110f

Moon and Sixpence, The (1919), novel, based on the life of Paul Gauguin, written by W. Somerset Maugham.

·fiction in biographical form **2**:1009d

moon bear: *see* Asiatic black bear.

moon cactus, also called NIGHT-BLOOMING CEREUS, the genus *Selenicereus*, of about 20 species, family Cactaceae, native to tropical and subtropical America including the West Indies. It and its hybrids are widely grown in suitable American climates and have escaped from cultivation. The genus is known for its large, usually fragrant, night-blooming white flowers, among the largest in the cactus family. Some species clamber along the ground; others cling with aerial roots to trees and other objects. *S. grandiflorus*, the popular night-blooming cereus, is difficult to grow.

Stems are ribbed, angled, or flattened. *S. hamatus*, often called queen of the night, or reina de la noche, has backward-projecting lobes that aid clinging.

mooneye, also called TOOTHED HERRING, North American freshwater fish of the family Hiodontidae. The mooneye is a spirited catch but is not greatly valued as food. Mooneyes are herring-like fishes with sharp teeth, large eyes, and deeply forked tail fins. Those of

Mooneye (*Hiodon tergisus*)
Painting by Richard Ellis

the species *Hiodon tergisus* are bright silvery and may be about 42.5 centimetres (17 inches) long. The goldeye, *H.* (sometimes called *Amphiodon*) *alosoides*, is blue-backed, silvery, and about 25 cm (10 in.) long; the southern mooneye (*H. selenops*) is a silvery fish about 30 cm (12 in.) long.

·reproduction and classification **13**:763g

moon face, term for an abnormally rounded, ruddy face, symptomatic, in humans, of adrenal cortex disturbances.

·Cushing's syndrome signs **5**:860b

moonfish, any of several unrelated fishes of the order Perciformes, such as *Vomer setapinnis* of the family Carangidae, and *Mene maculata*, the sole member of the family Menidae.

The carangid moonfish is thin, with an extremely deep body, a slender tail base, a forked tail, and slim, sickle-shaped pectoral fins. It is silver or golden in colour and grows to about 30 centimetres (12 inches). It inhabits the western Atlantic Ocean and, when young, is distinguished by long, threadlike rays extending from its dorsal and ventral fins. Related species, also deep-bodied and called moonfish, are the Pacific *Vomer declivifrons* and the lookdown (*Selene vomer*) of the Atlantic and Pacific.

The moonfish of the family Menidae is allied to the carangids. It is a thin, Indo-Pacific fish with a very deep, sharp-edged chest, a long anal fin, a forked tail, and an extended, long ray in each pelvic fin. It is silvery with darker spots and grows to about 20 centimetres (8 inches).

Other fishes sometimes called moonfish include the opah and platy (*qq.v.*).

·classification and general features **14**:53g

moonflower: *see* Ipomoea.

Moon god: *see* lunar deities.

moon guitar: *see* yüeh-ch'in.

Moonie, town, southeast Queensland, Australia. Moonie, located in a sheep-grazing district, is also the site of the nation's first (1964) commercially developed oil field. The oil, discovered in 1961, is piped 190 mi (306 km) east to Brisbane. There is a second field at Alton (60 mi southwest). Moonie lies at the intersection of the Moonie and Newell highways. Pop. (latest est.) less than 100 persons.
27°45′ S, 150°19′ E

Moonlight Sonata, popular name for PIANO SONATA IN C SHARP MINOR (1801), composition by Beethoven.

·dedication to Countess Giulietta **2**:798c

Moon of Bali, large cast bronze drum found on the island of Bali, a relic of the Southeast Asian Dong Son culture.
·style, age, and ritual use **17**:264g; illus.

Moon of the Caribbees, The (*c.* 1919), play by Eugene O'Neill.
·O'Neill's early plays **13**:572b

moonquake, seismic disturbance occurring on the Moon.
·tidal effects of Earth **18**:390h

moonrat (mammal): *see* gymnure.

moonseed, common name for about three species of woody vines constituting the genus *Menispermum* of the family Menispermaceae.

Canada moonseed (*Menispermum canadense*)
Richard Parker

They occur in East Asia, eastern North America, and Mexico. The flowers are greenish white and the seeds are crescent-shaped.
·alkaloid derivatives **1**:603h

moonstone, a gem-quality feldspar mineral, a mixed sodium and potassium aluminosilicate $(K,Na)AlSi_3O_8$ that shows a silvery or bluish iridescence. Nearly all commercial moonstones come from Dumbara District, Sri Lanka, where they occur in gem gravels and in acid granulites and pegmatites.

The term moonstone also has been applied to the plagioclase feldspars peristerite and labradorite, which also exhibit iridescence.
·composition and iridescence **7**:215g
·gemstone characteristics and value **7**:972a
·Sinhalese decorative use **17**:206d

Moonstone, The (1868), novel by Wilkie Collins about a diamond (the Moonstone) that mysteriously disappears, providing a problem for Sergeant Cuff, the first of a long line of detectives in English fiction.
·epistolary novel tradition **13**:286h

Moon Sun Myung (b. Jan. 6, 1920, Jung Joo, now in North Korea), founder of the Unification Church (in Korean called Tongil-gyo). He began to preach and prophesy in northern Korea in 1946 and two years later was excommunicated by the Presbyterian Church. Following imprisonment in North Korea, he moved to South Korea, where he founded the Unification Church in 1954. He began missionary operations in the U.S. in 1973. By the early 1980s, the church claimed a worldwide membership numbering in the millions and had accrued vast financial assets.

Moon's U.S. converts, popularly called "Moonies," were typically young single men and women recruited from college campuses. They lived communally and were required, upon becoming full members of the church, to give all possessions to the church. In 1981 the church's bid for U.S. tax-exempt status as a religious organization was denied when an appellate court ruled that the church's primary purpose was political rather than religious.

Moon type, system of written letters invented in 1845 by William Moon of Brighton, East Sussex, to enable blind people to read. Moon type partly retains the outlines of letters in the Latin alphabet. Easily learned by those who have become blind late in life, it is the only writing system for the blind based on the Latin alphabet that is still in use in the English-speaking world (although it has been largely superseded by Braille).
·non-Braille reading systems **3**:110f

moon white, cobalt glaze of pale blue.
·Ch'ing glazes and coloration **14**:923c

moon worship (religion): *see* lunar deities.

moonwort, species of fern of the family Ophioglossaceae (*q.v.*).

moor: *see in* swamps, marshes, and bogs.

Moore, city, Cleveland County, central Oklahoma, southern suburb of Oklahoma City. First settled in 1887, it was supposedly named for an engineer of the Santa Fe Railway. Its population remained small until the 1960s, when planned urban and industrial development began. Industries include the manufacture of aircraft parts, building materials, petroleum products, and processed foods. Inc. town, 1893; city, 1962. Pop. (1960) 1,783; (1970) 18,761; (1980) 35,063.
35°20′ N, 97°29′ W

Moore, Archie, original name ARCHIBALD LEE WRIGHT (b. Dec. 13, 1913, Benoit, Miss.), world light-heavyweight boxing champion from Dec. 17, 1952, when he defeated Joey Maxim in 15 rounds in St. Louis, Mo., until 1962, when he lost recognition as champion for failing to meet Harold Johnson, the leading 175-pound challenger. A professional boxer from the 1930s, Moore for many years was avoided by middleweight and light-heavyweight champions, who considered him too formidable. In attempts to win the heavyweight title, he was knocked out by Rocky Marciano in 1955 and by Floyd Patterson in 1956.

An exceptionally colourful and popular champion, Moore called himself "the Old Mongoose" and encouraged controversy about his age. He became a film actor, receiving critical praise for his portrayal of the slave Jim in *The Adventures of Huckleberry Finn* (1959). His autobiography, *The Archie Moore Story*, appeared in 1960.
·boxing champions in U.S. **3**:93h

Moore, Brian (b. Aug. 25, 1921, Belfast, N.Ire.), Irish novelist who emigrated to North America to reside alternately in Canada and the United States; he is best known for his first novel, *The Lonely Passion of Judith Hearne* (1955), which is considered a minor classic.

Moore's recurrent themes are the familiar Irish conflicts between sex and religion, drink and respectability, and self-confidence and blarney. *Judith Hearne* deals with an aging spinster whose crumbling pretensions to past and future gentility are gradually dissolved in alcoholism. His next novel, *The Feast of Lupercal* (1957), concerns a bachelor schoolteacher's sexual maladjustment. *The Luck of Ginger Coffey* (1960) portrays a middle-aged Irish failure who emigrates to Canada to charm his way to fortune; and *The Emperor of Ice Cream* (1965) deals with a rebellious and grandiose adolescent boy who is shocked into manhood by the bombing of Belfast in World War II.

Among a succession of later works, *Catholics* (1973) and *The Great Victorian Collection* (1975) attracted more favourable attention than *I am Mary Dunne* (1968), *Fergus* (1970), *The Revolution Script* (1971), and *The Doctor's Wife* (1976). Though they are interesting and provocative, none of his later novels is considered to match the superb control and relentless realism of *Judith Hearne*.
·Canadian novel tradition **13**:292d

Moore, Clement Clarke (b. July 15, 1779, New York City—d. July 10, 1863, Newport, R.I.), scholar of Hebrew and teacher, now chiefly remembered for his casually written but felicitous ballad that begins, " 'Twas the night before Christmas . . . ." The son of Benjamin Moore, a president of Columbia University and later second Episcopal bishop of New York, he had a lifelong interest in church matters, although he never took orders himself.

In 1809 he published a two-volume scholarly work, *A Compendious Lexicon of the Hebrew Language*. He donated his inherited New York property to assist in the establishment of General Theological Seminary, where he was later professor of Oriental and Greek literature.

He is said to have composed "A Visit from St. Nicholas" to amuse his children on Christmas, 1822, but, unknown to him, a house guest copied it and gave it to the press. First published anonymously in the *Troy* (N.Y.) *Sentinel*, Dec. 23, 1823, it became an integral part of Christmas celebration in the United States.

Moore, D(aniel) McFarlan (1869–1936), U.S. electrical engineer, inventor of the neon gas-discharge lamp in 1917.
·television systems development **18**:106d

Moore, George (Augustus) (b. Feb. 24, 1852, Ballyglass, County Mayo—d. Jan. 21, 1933, London), Irish novelist and man of letters best known for his novel *Esther Waters* (1894) and for his autobiographical trilogy, *Hail and Farewell* (1911–14).

George Moore, detail of a drawing by Sir William Rothenstein, 1896; in the National Gallery of Ireland, Dublin
By courtesy of the National Gallery of Ireland, Dublin

When he was 18, Moore, who came from a family of Irish landholders, left Ireland for France to become a painter. In Paris he became friendly with the avant-garde Impressionist group and particularly with Édouard Manet. Moore recorded his years in Paris in his first autobiography, *Confessions of a Young Man* (1888).

Deciding that he had no talent for painting, he returned to London in 1882 to write. His first novels, *A Modern Lover* (1883) and *A Mummer's Wife* (1885), introduced to the Victorian novel a new note of French Naturalism, and he later adopted the realistic techniques of Flaubert and Balzac. *Esther Waters*, his best novel, is a story of hardship and humiliation illumined by the novelist's compassion. It was an immediate success, and he followed it with two works written in a similar vein: *Evelyn Innes* (1898) and *Sister Teresa* (1901).

In 1901 Moore moved to Dublin, where he contributed notably to the planning of the Abbey Theatre. He also produced a volume of short stories, *The Untilled Field* (1903), and a short, poetic novel, *The Lake* (1905).

The real fruits of Moore's life in Ireland, however, came with *Hail and Farewell* (*Ave*, 1911; *Salve*, 1912; *Vale*, 1914). It is both a carefully studied piece of self-revelation and an acute (though not always reliable) portrait gallery of his Irish acquaintance, which included W.B. Yeats, Æ, and Lady Gregory.

The increasing narrowness of the Irish mind, politics, and clericalism had sent Moore back to England in 1911. After *Hail and Farewell* he made another literary departure: aiming at epic effect he produced *The Brook Kerith* (1916), an elaborate and stylish retelling of the Gospel story that is surprisingly effective despite some dull patches. He continued his attempts to find a prose style worthy of epic theme in *Héloïse and Abélard* (1921). Later works included *A Story-Teller's Holiday* (1918), a blend of autobiography, anecdote, Irish legend, and satire; *Conversations in Ebury Street* (1924), autobiography; *The Pastoral Loves of Daphnis and Chloe* (1924); and *Ulick and Soracha* (1926), an Irish legendary romance. From 1911 until his death he lived on Ebury Street, a legendary figure, though as the years went by, perhaps a slightly neglected one.

·intellectual biographical writings **2**:1010g
·Irish novel tradition **13**:291a
·Manet acquaintance and portrait **11**:442a

Moore, G(eorge) E(dward) (b. Nov. 4, 1873, London—d. Oct. 24 1958, Cambridge), influential Realist philosopher and professor whose systematic approach to ethical problems and remarkably meticulous approach to philosophy made him an outstanding modern British thinker.

Elected to a fellowship at Trinity College, Cambridge, in 1898, Moore remained there until 1904, during which time he published several journal articles, including "The Nature of Judgment" (1899) and "The Refutation of Idealism" (1903), as well as his major ethical work, *Principia Ethica* (1903). These writings were important in helping to undermine the influence on British philosophy of the Germans G.W.F. Hegel and Immanuel Kant. After residence in Edinburgh and London, he returned to Cambridge in 1911 to become a lecturer in moral science. From 1925 to 1939 he was professor of philosophy there, and from 1921 to 1947 he was editor of the philosophical journal *Mind*.

G.E. Moore, detail of a pencil drawing by Sir William Orpen (1878–1931); in the National Portrait Gallery, London
By courtesy of the National Portrait Gallery, London

Though Moore grew up in a climate of evangelical religiosity, he eventually became an agnostic. A friend of Bertrand Russell, who first directed him to the study of philosophy, he was also a leading figure in the Bloomsbury group, a coterie that included the British economist John Keynes and the British writers Virginia Woolf and E.M. Forster. Because of his view that "the good" is knowable by direct apprehension, he became known as an "ethical intuitionist." He claimed that other efforts to decide what is "good," such as analyses of the concepts of approval or desire, which are not themselves of an ethical nature, partake of a fallacy that he termed the "naturalistic fallacy."

To join the concepts of "good" and "right," or of value and obligation, Moore developed a doctrine later called Ideal Utilitarianism. This doctrine, expressed in *Principia Ethica*. identifies the assertion "I am morally bound to perform this action" with the assertion "This action will produce the greatest possible amount of good in the universe." Although he modified this doctrine slightly in his *Ethics* (1912) by changing the phrase " is identical with" to the weaker phrase "is logically equivalent to," he retained his stress on the utilitarian element, which refers to the usefulness of a given action.

He saw personal affection and aesthetic enjoyments as the most highly valued goods for most men.

Moore was also preoccupied with such problems as the nature of sense perception and the existence of other minds and material things. He was not as skeptical as those philosophers who felt that they lacked sufficient data to prove that objects exist outside their own minds, but he did believe that proper philosophical proofs had not yet been devised to overcome such objections.

Although few of Moore's theories achieved general acceptance, his unique approaches to certain problems and his intellectual rigour helped change the texture of philosophical discussion in England. His other major writings include *Philosophical Studies* (1922) and *Some Main Problems of Philosophy* (1953); posthumous publications were *Philosophical Papers* (1959) and the *Commonplace Book, 1919–1953* (1962).

Further information may be found in *The Philosophy of G.E. Moore* (P.A. Schillp, ed.) (1952), and A.P. White's, *G.E. Moore: A Critical Exposition* (1958).

·aesthetic theory of value **1**:158a
·analysis in Principia Ethica **14**:248f *passim* to 250a
·Analytic philosophy's development **1**:802d
·anti-Idealist Rationalism **6**:936g
·criticism of Idealism **9**:193d
·idealism refutation **9**:193d
·intuitionistic cognitivistic meta-ethics **6**:980d
·Mach's philosophy of science **16**:380h
·meta-ethics and noncognitivism **6**:986h
·metaphysics and common sense **12**:32c
·philosophy as analysis **14**:273b
·primacy of metaphysics **12**:14e
·Rational determination of morals **15**:530b
·Utilitarian nonhedonistic value system **19**:1h

Moore, George Foot (b. Oct. 15, 1851, West Chester, Pa.—d. May 16, 1931, Cambridge, Mass.), Old Testament scholar, theologian and orientalist, who had a knowledge and understanding of the rabbinical source literature extraordinary among Christians. Graduated from Yale college in 1872 and from Union Theological seminary in 1877, in 1878 he was ordained in the Presbyterian ministry and until 1883 was pastor of the Putnam Presbyterian church, Zanesville, O. He was Hitchcock professor of the Hebrew language and literature at Andover Theological seminary, 1883–1902. In 1902 he became professor of theology and in 1904 professor of the history of religion at Harvard university. Moore's chief critical work dealt both with the Hexateuch (the first six books of the Old Testament), and more particularly the Book of Judges. He was also the author of *The Literature of the Old Testament* (1913), *History of Religions* (2 vol., 1913–19), *Metempsychosis* (1914) and, perhaps his greatest work, *Judaism in the First Centuries of the Christian Era* (3 vol., 1927-30). He was a leading figure in the establishment of the *Harvard Theological Review*.

Moore, Henry **12**:432 (b. July 30, 1898, Castleford, Yorkshire), sculptor whose use of new and original means to continue the tradition of humanist sculpture into the 20th century won him an international reputation. His artistic concerns have been respecting the organic nature of his materials, the sculpting of spaces as well as solid masses, and the presentation of intense psychological content.

Abstract of text biography. The son of a coal miner, Moore studied at the Leeds School of Art (1919–21) and at the Royal College of Art in London (1921–24). In 1929 he married Irina Radetzky, a painting student. He taught sculpture part-time at the Royal College of Art (1925–32) and then at the Chelsea School of Art (1932–39). During this period he showed his work in six one-man shows and many small group exhibitions, and by 1939 he was already known to a small informed public as England's leading avant-garde sculptor. During World War II, he was an official war artist, and his drawings of people sheltering from the bombing in the London Underground provided the basis for his wider popularity. He had a retrospective exhibition at the Museum of Modern Art, New York City, in 1946; and in 1948 he was awarded the international sculpture prize at the Venice Biennale. Among his major commissions are sculptures for UNESCO headquarters in Paris (1957–58), for the Lincoln Center in New York City (1963–65), and for a memorial to the world's first self-sustaining nuclear reaction at the University of Chicago (1964–66).

REFERENCES in other text articles:
·abstract sculpture style **19**:481h
·creative process **2**:49a
·modern sculpture influence **19**:243b
·plasticity in drawings **5**:1002g; illus.
·spatial design and visibility **16**:432c
·wood carving technique illus. **16**:428
·20th-century British printmaking **14**:1095h

Moore, Sir John (b. Nov. 13, 1761, Glasgow, Lanark—d. Jan. 16, 1809, La Coruña, Spain), British lieutenant general who, during the Peninsular War (campaigns in the Iberian Peninsula against Napoleonic France), led a retreat (Dec. 24, 1808–Jan. 11, 1809) 250 miles over the snow-covered Cordillera Cantábria to La Coruña and died in battle there, although his army escaped by sea.

Sir John Moore, detail of an oil painting by Sir Thomas Lawrence (1769–1830); in the National Portrait Gallery, London
By courtesy of the National Portrait Gallery, London

After the outbreak of war with Revolutionary France (1793), Moore served on Corsica and in the West Indies, Ireland, the Netherlands, and Egypt. While commanding a corps at Shorncliffe Camp, Kent (1803–06), Moore, by his flexible system of tactics and his efficient, humane discipline, earned a reputation as one of the greatest trainers of infantrymen in military history.

Sent in 1808 to expel the French from Spain, Moore moved north from Salamanca to attack Marshal Nicolas Soult's French corps on the Carrión River, west of Burgos. Learning that Napoleon had cut off his route of withdrawal into Portugal, he retreated from Sahagún to the port of La Coruña (Corunna). On Jan. 16, 1809, while Moore's army was preparing to board British troopships, Soult launched an attack, which was repulsed, although Moore was mortally wounded. In Great Britain, Moore was unjustly excoriated for retreating. Strategically, he succeeded: he extricated his men from a trap, forced Napoleon to divert badly needed troops from Portugal and southern Spain, and delayed the French conquest of Spain for a year.

·Peninsular War tactics **19**:579d

Moore, John Bassett (b. Dec. 3, 1860, Smyrna, Del.—d. Nov. 12, 1947, New York City), known for his exhaustive codification of international law. His advice on matters pertaining to international adjudication was frequently sought by the U.S. government. Admitted to the Delaware bar in 1883, Moore in 1885 joined the Department of State, where he served until 1891. He then joined the faculty of Columbia University, retiring in 1924 as Hamilton Fish Professor of International Law and Diplomacy. From 1912 to 1938 he was a member of the Permanent Court of Arbitration, The Hague.

Among Moore's studies in international law is the monumental *Digest of International Law*, 8 vol. (1906). Between 1929 and 1933 he edited the eight-volume compendium of *International Adjudications, Ancient and Modern*.

Moore, Marianne (Craig) (b. Nov. 15, 1887, St. Louis, Mo.—d. Feb. 5, 1972, New York City), poet whose work distills moral and intellectual insights from the close and accurate observation of objective detail. A disciplined craftsman on guard against making a false response to the objects of her attention —whether animals, works of art, or sports figures—she won the admiration of fellow poets throughout her long career. T.S. Eliot, the American-born British poet and critic, who wrote a foreword to her *Selected Poems* (1935), called her one of the few producers of durable poetry in her time.

Marianne Moore, 1957
Imogen Cunningham

Miss Moore was graduated from Bryn Mawr (Pennsylvania) College in 1909, then studied commercial subjects and taught them at the U.S. Indian School in Carlisle, Pa. From 1921 to 1925 she was an assistant in the New York Public Library system. In 1925—already well-known as one of the leading new poets—she became acting editor of *The Dial*, an influential U.S. journal of literature and arts, until it was discontinued in 1929.

Her early poems were printed in college publications, but she did not publish in periodicals until about 1915. In 1921 her first book, *Poems*, was published in London by the Egoist Press. Her first U.S. volume, *Observations* (1924), won the Dial Award. These initial volumes already exhibit her conciseness and her creation of a mosaic of juxtaposed images leading unerringly to a conclusion that at its best is both surprising and inevitable. They contain some of her best known poems, including "To a Steam Roller," "The Fish," "When I Buy Pictures," "Peter," "The Labors of Hercules," and "Poetry." The last named is the source of her often quoted admonition that poets should present imaginary gardens with real toads in them.

After 1919, living in Brooklyn, N.Y., she devoted herself to poetry and criticism, contributing to many journals in the U.S. and England and publishing several books of verse. *Collected Poems* (1951) was awarded a Pulitzer Prize, a Bollingen Prize, and a National Book Award, as well as the Gold Medal for Poetry of the National Institute of Arts and Letters. Her translation of *The Fables of La Fontaine* was published in 1954, a volume of critical papers, *Predilections*, in 1955, and *Idiosyncrasy and Technique: Two Lectures*, in 1958.

Among the better known of Miss Moore's later poems are "Critics and Connoisseurs," "The Monkeys," "Spenser's Ireland," "What Are Years?" "In Distrust of Merits," "Tom Fool at Jamaica," and "Carnegie Hall: Rescued."

Moore, Nicholas (b. 1918, Cambridge, Cambridgeshire), one of the "new apocalypse" English poets of the 1940s who reacted against the preoccupation with social and political issues of the 1930s by turning toward romanticism. The son of G.E. Moore, classicist and Cambridge philosopher, he published an important literary review, *Seven* (1938–40), while a Cambridge undergraduate and was a conscientious objector during World War II. Most of his verse was published in the war years: *The Island and the Cattle* and *A Wish in Season* (both 1941); *The Cabaret, the Dancer, the Gentleman* (1942), and *The Glass Tower* (1944). *Recollections of the Gala: Selected Poems, 1943–1948* appeared in 1950. After editing poetry magazines in London, he became a horticulturalist and wrote little until an illness in 1963 provided the leisure for it. *Resolution and Identity* appeared in a limited edition in 1970.

Moore, Raymond Cecil (b. Feb. 20, 1892, Roslyn, Wash.), paleontologist known for his work on Paleozoic crinoids, bryozoans, and corals (invertebrate organisms ranging from 225,000,000 to 570,000,000 years in age). Moore was a member of the U.S. Geological Survey from 1913 until 1949; he became a professor at the University of Kansas (Lawrence) in 1919 and a principal geologist of the Kansas Geological Survey in 1954. Moore was the organizer and editor of the work *Treatise on Invertebrate Paleontology* (1953), the contributors to which included 150 of the world's specialists in the field. He wrote *Historical Geology* (1933), *Introduction to Historical Geology* (1949), and, with others, *Invertebrate Fossils* (1952).

Moore, Stanford (b. Sept. 4, 1913, Chicago), biochemist, shared the 1972 Nobel Prize for Chemistry for his contributions to establishing the molecular structures of proteins.

Moore received his Ph.D. degree from the University of Wisconsin in 1938 and joined the staff of the Rockefeller Institute for Medical Research (now Rockefeller University) in New York City in 1939, attaining the rank of professor in 1952. He is best known for his applications of the technique of chromatography to the analysis of amino acids and peptides obtained from proteins and biological fluids and for the use of those analyses in determining the structure of the enzyme ribonuclease.

Moore, Thomas (b. May 28, 1779, Dublin —d. Feb. 25, 1852, Wiltshire), poet, satirist, composer, and musician; the friend of Byron and Shelley. Moore's major poetic work, *Irish Melodies* (1807–34), earned for the author an income of £500 annually for a quarter of a century. They contained such still familiar titles as "The Last Rose of Summer" and "Believe Me If All Those Endearing Young Charms." The *Melodies*, a group of 130 poems set to the music of Moore and of Sir John Stevenson and performed for London's aristocracy, aroused sympathy and support for the Irish nationalists, among whom Moore was a popular hero.

Lalla Rookh (1817), a narrative poem set (on Byron's advice) in an atmosphere of oriental splendour, gave Moore a reputation among his contemporaries rivalling that of Byron and Scott. It was perhaps the most translated poem of its time, and it earned what was till then the highest price paid by an English publisher for a poem (£3,000). Moore's many satirical works, such as *The Fudge Family in Paris* (1818), portray the politics and manners of the Regency period.

Thomas Moore, detail of an oil painting by Sir Martin Archer Shee, 1818; in the National Portrait Gallery, London
By courtesy of the National Portrait Gallery, London

In 1824 Moore became a participant in one of the most celebrated episodes of the Romantic period. He was the recipient of Byron's memoirs, but he and the publisher John Murray burned them, presumably to protect Byron. Moore later brought out the *Letters and Journals of Lord Byron* (1830), in which he included a life of the poet.

·Byron's friendship **3**:545b
·English literature of the 19th century **10**:1187a

Moorea, formerly EIMEO, volcanic island, second largest of the Îles du Vent (Windward Group), Society Islands, French Polynesia, central southern Pacific, 12 mi (20 km) northwest of Tahiti. It is triangular (area 51 sq mi [132 sq km]), rugged and mountainous (highest peak Mt. Tohivea, 3,960 ft [1,207 m]), with 25 rivers and fertile soils. The chief village on the east coast, Afareai tu, is overlooked by Mt. Muaputa (2,723 ft). Baie de Cook (Paopao) and Baie de Papetoai (Oponu), divided by Mt. Rotui, are on the north coast; Haapiti is on the west. It was on Moorea, in the early 19th century, that the Rev. Henry Nott, companion of King Pomare II, translated the Bible into Tahitian. Chief crops are vanilla, copra, and coffee. The island is now a favoured tourist location. Pop. (1971) 4,842.

17°32′ S, 149°50′ W

·topography and location **7**:716g

Cook (Paopao) Bay indenting the east coast of Moorea
Richard A. Abeles

Moore's Creek Bridge, Battle of (Feb. 27, 1776), in the U.S. War of Independence, North Carolina Revolutionaries' defeat of a force of North Carolina Loyalists, in part thwarting a British invasion of the southern colonies. Gen. Donald McDonald, who had amassed some 1,600 Scottish Highlanders and

North Carolina Regulators, marched toward Wilmington, N.C., to join British troops coming by sea from Boston and England. A rebel militia, about 1,000 strong, under Cols. Alexander Lillington and Richard Caswell, was assembled and positioned at Moore's Creek Bridge, 18 miles northwest of Wilmington. The Loyalists attacked the rebel force at the bridge but were quickly defeated. The rebels, of whom only one was killed and one wounded, captured or killed more than half of the Loyalist forces and seized arms, supplies, and £15,000 sterling.

Moore space, generalization of the notion of metric space (*q.v.*) by the 20th-century U.S. mathematician Robert Moore sharing many of the properties of metric spaces.
·topological basis and metrizability **18**:513g

Moorestown, township, Burlington County, New Jersey, U.S., east of Camden. The early 18th-century Quaker settlements of Chestertown (for Chester, Cheshire) and Rodmantown amalgamated to form the village of Chester, which was renamed Moorestown about 1790, probably for Thomas Moore, who had laid out the town in 1722. The Moorestown Friends School was founded in 1785, and the Free Library began as the Library Association of Friends (Quakers), which was organized in 1853. Among historic landmarks is the red brick-timber Zelley House (1721). Truck and fruit farming, dairying, and poultry raising are local activities. Manufactures include wood and metal products, fungicides, and insecticides. Moorestown became a township in 1922. Pop. (1980) 15,596.
39°58′ N, 74°57′ W

Moorfields carpets: *see* Axminster carpets.

Moorhead, city, seat (1872) of Clay County, western Minnesota, U.S., on the Red River across from Fargo, N.D., in a mixed-farming area. Founded with the coming of the railroad in 1871, it was a natural transportation hub, with overland road and rail traffic meeting the barges and, later, steamboats on the river. Known first as Burbank, it was renamed for William G. Moorhead, a director of the Northern Pacific Railway. Moorhead State College (opened 1888) and Concordia College (1891) are there. Its agriculture-based economy depends chiefly on sugar-beet refining, dairying, potato processing, and farm-equipment manufacture. Inc. village, 1875; city, 1881. Pop. (1980) 29,998.
46°53′ N, 96°45′ W
·map, United States **18**:908

moorhen (bird): *see* gallinule.

Moorish idol (*Zanclus canescens*), deep-bodied, tropical reef fish, commonly placed alone in the family Zanclidae (order Perciformes). The Moorish idol is a striking-looking fish—thin, deeper than it is long, and with a protruding, beaklike mouth and a dorsal fin greatly extended in front. An Indo-Pacific fish, relatively common and found in shallow water, it is about 18 centimetres (7 inches) long and is boldly patterned with three vertical black stripes on a yellowish body.
·disruptive coloration patterns **4**:924g, illus., **4**:Coloration, Biological, Plate II

Moorish idol (*Zanclus canescens*)
Douglas Faulkner

Moorish Science Temple of America, a black American cult founded by Timothy Drew, later known as Noble Drew Ali, in 1913. The movement split in 1930 between a sect calling themselves the Moors and a sect, led by Wallace D. Fard, that was the forerunner of the Nation of Islām (Black Muslims).
·Black Muslim origins and tradition **2**:1093f
·Negro cults' history and beliefs **12**:943g

Moorish style (furniture): *see* Turkish style.

Moor language: *see* Moré language.

Moors, in English usage, a term often synonymous with Moroccans and sometimes descriptive of the former Muslims of Spain, of mixed Arab, Spanish, and Berber origins, who created the Arab Andalusian civilization and subsequently settled as refugees in North Africa between the 11th and 17th centuries. By extension (corresponding to the Spanish *moro*), it occasionally denotes Muslims in general, as in the case of the Moors of Sri Lanka (Ceylon) or of the Philippines.

The word Moors (from Latin *Mauri*) was first used by the Romans to describe the inhabitants of the Roman province of Mauretania, comprising the western portion of modern Algeria and the northeastern portion of modern Morocco. Modern Mauritanians are also sometimes referred to as Moors (as with the French *maure*); the Islāmic Republic of Mauritania, however, lies in the large Saharan area between Morocco and the republics of Senegal and Mali.
·art forms, illus., **9**:Islāmic Peoples, Arts of, Plate IV
·bullfighting influence in Spain **3**:476c
·furniture design and decoration **7**:798c
·invasion of Spain **17**:404e
·Jiménez' conversion technique's results **10**:223a
·location and lifestyle **16**:150b
·Mali population and language **11**:382c
·Mauritania's ethnic composition **11**:712h
·North African rule of Muslim Spain **13**:157h
·North African sedentary tribe emergence **13**:150a
·Plateresque style influence **19**:392c
·Portuguese crusades and conquests **14**:865e
·Portuguese racial influence **14**:858h
·Senegalese peoples and language **16**:535a
·Sénégal River populations **16**:540f
·Tunisian massive immigration **18**:747a

Moors and Christians (dance): *see* Morris dance.

moorwort (shrub): *see* bog rosemary.

moose, in North America, or elk in Europe, *Alces alces*, largest member of the deer family (Cervidae; order Artiodactyla). Moose are heavy, long-legged, short-necked ruminants, standing 1.5–2 metres (5–6½ feet) tall at the shoulder and weighing to about 820 kilograms (1,800 pounds). The back slopes downward to the hips, the tail is short, and the muzzle is somewhat inflated and pendulous. A fleshy dewlap (the bell) hangs from the throat. The brown coat is coarse and shaggy, becoming grizzled with age. The enormous antlers in the males (bulls) are characteristically palmate with projecting tines.

Moose occur in the northern parts of North America and Eurasia. They prefer being near water and often wade into forest-edged lakes and streams to feed on submerged aquatic plants. They also eat a variety of grasses, herbs, and bark. Usually solitary, moose in North America often assemble in small bands in winter and tramp the snow firm in a small area to form a "moose yard." Their normal gait is a stiff-legged, shuffling walk that enables them to cover ground with surprising speed. They sometimes trot but seldom run. Moose are usually shy, but they tend to be unpredictable and belligerent. They breed in autumn, the male then fighting fiercely for the female's favour. One to three ungainly young are born after gestation of about eight months. The female cares for the calf until the birth of another is imminent.

Bull moose (*Alces alces*)
Leonard Lee Rue III

Moose generally are hunted both for trophies—their huge antlers and head—as well as for their flesh, which is beeflike but somewhat dry and with strong-tasting fat. The pressure of hunting substantially reduced the numbers of moose and virtually eliminated them from the southern parts of their range, especially in the United States. They are now generally protected by law, both in North America and in Europe.
·predator–prey oscillations **14**:835c

Moose Factory, village, Cochrane District, northeastern Ontario, Canada, on Moose Factory Island, in the estuary of the Moose River, at the south end of James Bay. Originally established as a Hudson's Bay Company trading post by Pierre Esprit Radisson in 1672, it was captured by the French in 1686 and later destroyed. Since it was re-established, in 1730, the post has been in continuous operation, and the predominantly Cree Indian population is still dependent upon trapping as a livelihood. Moose Factory is the site of an Anglican mission and school (1850) and a large hospital constructed in the early 1950s. The Ontario Northland Railway serves the community from its northern terminus at nearby Moosonee. Latest census 800.
51°16′ N, 80°37′ W

Moosehead Lake, west central Maine, U.S. The largest lake in the state, its waters cover an area of 120 sq mi (310 sq km). At an altitude of 1,023 ft (312 m), the lake is dotted with numerous islands, the largest of which is Sugar Island. The lake is the source of the Kennebec River. Moosehead's irregularly shaped shoreline shelters numerous fishing and recreation coves; Greenville, on its southern end, is a centre for resort activities.
45°40′ N, 69°40′ W
·map, United States **18**:908

Moose Jaw, city, south central Saskatchewan, Canada, on Moose Jaw Creek, a tributary of the Qu'Appelle River. According to Indian legend, its name is derived from the moose jawbone-like appearance of the creek's course; another legend says it was "the place where the white man mended the cart wheel with the jawbone of the moose." Founded in 1882 with the arrival of the main line of the Canadian Pacific Railway, Moose Jaw grew as a rail terminus and distribution centre for a large wheat-growing area. The city is one of the most industrialized in Saskatchewan, with major oil refineries, flour-milling operations, large grain-storage facilities, extensive stockyards, and a slaughterhouse. Other industries include meat-packing, dairying, lumber and woolen milling, and garment making. Moose Jaw, located on the Trans-Canada Highway 45 mi (72 km) west of Regina, is the site of an

air force training base, a provincial technical school, a wild animal park, and a noted historical museum. Inc. 1884. Pop. (1971) 31,284.
50°23′ N, 105°32′ W
·map, Canada **3**:716
·population and importance **16**:259c

Moose River, Cochrane District, northeastern Ontario, Canada. Arising at the confluence of its two major headstreams, the Mattagami, 260 mi (420 km) long, and the Missinaibi, 265 mi long, it flows northeastward for more than 60 mi to James Bay. Though short in length, the Moose, along with its headstreams and tributaries, including the Abitibi River (340 mi), drains most of northeastern Ontario. Economic activities in the watershed include mining and pulp- and paper-milling operations powered by hydroelectric plants on the Abitibi and Mattagami rivers. The Ontario Northland Railway parallels the Abitibi Valley and terminates at Moosonee, opposite the historic island of Moose Factory (*q.v.*) in the river's mouth. Kapuskasing, Iroquois Falls, and Timmins are the chief towns in the basin.
51°20′ N, 80°24′ W

Moosonee, village, Cochrane District, northeastern Ontario, Canada, on the left bank of the Moose River, near its mouth on James Bay and opposite Moose Factory. Originating as an important fur-trading post, now belonging to the Hudson's Bay Company, the community became the northern terminus of the Ontario Northland Railway in 1832. Bi-weekly train service links it, the province's only saltwater port, with Cochrane, 155 mi (250 km) south. A meteorological station and a Roman Catholic bishopric are located in Moosonee, which is becoming popular with tourists and sportsmen; Hannah Bay, noted for its goose hunting, is 30 mi east. Latest census 1,110.
51°17′ N, 80°39′ W
·map, Canada **3**:716

moot (from Old English *gemot*), the common term for an assembly in Anglo-Saxon England, survives in the name "moot hall" given to some English town halls and as an adjective denoting a debatable point. An early compound was folkmoot, and by the 10th century there were shire, hundred (a division of the shire), and borough moots. The *witenagemot*, "moot of the wise men," was the term for the national council.

moot court, mock court in which law students argue cases for practice.
·legal education in England **10**:775b

moped: *see* motorcycle.

mopoke (bird): *see* morepork.

Mopsus, the name of two seers in Greek mythology.

Mopsus, a Lapith (a northern mountain people) from Thessaly, took part in the Calydonian boar hunt and accompanied the Argonauts, dying of a snake's bite in Libya.

Mopsus was the son of the Carian king Rhacius (or the god Apollo) and Manto, daughter of the Theban seer Tiresias. He was associated with the foundation of the oracles at Clarus near Colophon and Mallos in Cilicia and of other cities in Asia Minor, including Mopsuestia, or Mopsuhestia (meaning Mopsus' Hearth; modern Misis in southern Turkey), and Mopsucrene (meaning Mopsus' Spring). In 1947, 8th-century-BC hieroglyphic and Phoenician inscriptions were discovered at Karatepe, Tur., containing the name of Mopsus, suggesting that he may have been a historical person.
·Greek legend and historicity **1**:823c

Mopti, town and capital of Mopti administrative region in southern Mali, at the confluence of the Bani and Niger rivers, stands on three small islands connected by barrages. Mopti is a market town, chiefly for agricultural products, and has a lime-kiln and a tannery. There is an airfield. Latest pop. est. 33,990.
14°30′ N, 4°12′ W
·government structure, population, and area **11**:384b; table 382
·map, Mali **11**:384
·Niger River physiography and course **13**:97b; map 98
·physical geography, demography, and transportation **11**:381f *passim* to 384a

Moqrani, North African tribe.
·French control of Kabylie resistance **13**:163f

Moquegua, department of southern Peru, stretches inland from the Pacific Ocean and occupies an area of 6,245 sq mi (16,175 sq km). From its creation as a department in 1857 (reorganized in 1875 and 1936) until the mid-20th century, agriculture was the principal economic activity. Extensive vineyards and olive orchards are found in irrigated areas on the arid coast and lower mountain slopes. Alfalfa is grown for the llamas, alpacas, and other livestock pastured in the Andes of the north, where Indians practice subsistence agriculture. The capital city of Moquegua is the major urban centre; with the growth of the fish meal and copper industries, the seaport of Ilo is undergoing rapid development. The Pan-American Highway traverses the coastal area, but few roads penetrate the mountainous areas. Pop. (1972 prelim.) 74,573.
·area and population table **14**:131

Moquegua, capital of Moquegua department and Mariscal Nieto province, southern Peru, is located on the Río Moquegua at 4,626 ft (1,410 m) above sea level, a cool oasis in the coastal desert.

Founded in 1626 as Villa de Santa Catalina del Guadalcázar del Valle de Moquegua (Town of Saint Catherine of Guadalcázar of Moquegua Valley), it was granted city status in 1823. It is a tranquil, traditional city serving as a processing and agricultural centre. Olives, grapes, and cotton are principal crops, and cotton ginning, wine making, liquor distilling, and olive oil processing are among the city's industries.

On the Pan-American Highway, Moquegua is connected by rail to its seaport at Ilo, 37 mi (60 km) south, and can be reached by air. Pop. (1972 prelim.) 16,959.
17°20′ S, 70°55′ W
·map, Peru **14**:128

Mor, Anthonis (Dutch painter): *see* More, Sir Anthony.

mor: *see* humus.

Moraceae, the mulberry family of the flowering plant order Urticales, over 54 genera with more than 1,400 species of deciduous or evergreen trees and shrubs (rarely herbs), distributed mostly in tropical and subtropical regions. Plants of the family contain a milky latex and have alternate leaves and small, petalless male or female flowers; the fruits of many species are multiple because fruits from different flowers become joined together. Some genera produce edible fruits, such as mulberry (*Morus*), fig (*Ficus*), breadfruit and jackfruit (*Artocarpus*), and affon, or African breadfruit (*Treculia*); others are important for their timber and latex, such as *Antiaris*, *Ficus*, *Castilloa*, and *Musanga*. The latex of the upas tree (*Antiaris toxicaria*) of Java is used as an arrow poison; the latex of the cow tree (*Brosimum utile*) of tropical America is sweet and nutritious. The latex of *Cecropia* species yields caoutchouc, the main constituent of natural rubber.

The largest genus, *Ficus* (*q.v.*), contains the banyan and the India rubber plant; it has many species whose roots cling tightly to a host plant and sometimes strangle it. The bark of paper mulberry (*Broussonetia*) is used for the manufacture of paper products. Many genera, including fustic (*Chlorophora*), *Cudrania*, *Dorstenia*, and Osage orange (*Maclura*), are cultivated as ornamentals.
·Chlorophora excelsa features and economic importance **18**:1090a
·general features and classification **18**:1088d; illus. 1089

Morādābād, administrative headquarters, Morādābād district, Uttar Pradesh state, northern India, on a ridge along the Rāmganga River. Located at a major road and rail junction, it is a trade centre for agricultural products. Industries include cotton milling and weaving, metalworking, electroplating, and printing. The city houses four colleges of Āgra University. Morādābād was founded in 1625 by Rustam Khān, who built the fort north of the city and the Jāmiʿ Masjid, a large mosque.

Morādābād district, 2,288 sq mi (5,927 sq km) in area, consists of a level plain bounded by the Ganges River (west) and drained by the Rāmganga. Grains, cotton, and sugarcane are grown. Sugar milling and cotton weaving are the principal industries. Morādābād, Sambhal, Amroha, and Chandausi are the major urban areas. Pop. (1971 prelim.) city, 258,251; district, 2,431,587.

Moraga, José Joaquin, 18th-century Spanish colonist, military leader of the band of soldiers and settlers that established the first presidio and mission at San Francisco, in 1776.
·San Francisco history and settlement **16**:218b

moraine, accumulation of rock debris (till) carried or deposited by a glacier. The material, which ranges in size from blocks or boulders (usually faceted or striated) to sand and clay, is unstratified when dropped by the glacier and shows no sorting or bedding. Several kinds of moraines are recognized:

1. Ground moraine, irregular blanket of till deposited under a glacier. Composed mainly of clay and sand, it is the most widespread deposit of continental glaciers. Although seldom more than 5 metres (15 feet) thick, it may attain a thickness of 18.24 metres (60 feet).

2. Terminal or end moraine, ridgelike accumulation of glacial debris pushed forward by the leading glacial snout and dumped at the outermost edge of any given ice advance. It curves convexly down valley and may extend up the sides as lateral moraines. It may

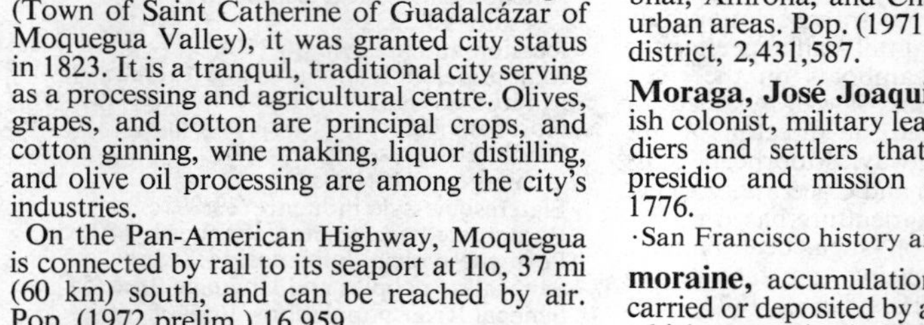

Lateral moraine of Victoria Glacier, Banff National Park, Alberta
Jerome Wyckoff

appear as a belt of hilly ground with knobs and kettles.

3. Lateral moraine, debris derived by erosion and avalanche from the valley wall onto the edge of a glacier and ultimately deposited as an elongate ridge when the glacier recedes.

4. Medial moraine, long, narrow line or zone of debris formed when lateral moraines join at the intersection of two ice streams; the resultant moraine is in the middle of the combined glacier. It is deposited as a ridge, roughly parallel to the direction of ice movement.

5. Recessional moraine, secondary terminal moraine deposited during a temporary glacial standstill. Such deposits reveal the history of glacial retreats up valley; in some instances ten or more recessional moraines are present in a given valley, and the ages of growing trees or other sources of dates provide a chronology of glacial movements.

·glacial margin mapping **8**:164g
·glaciation and climate indications **4**:731d
·North Sea floor topography **13**:249f
·types and formation **8**:173a; illus. 169
·waterfalls and glacial deposition **19**:642b

Morais, Prudente de (1841–1902), Brazilian political figure.

·presidency and military opposition **3**:146d

Morales, Cristóbal de (b. ?1500, Seville—d. 1553, Málaga?), composer who, with Tomás Luis de Victoria and Francisco Guerrero, was one of the three most important Spanish composers of the 16th century. His first post was as *maestro de capilla* at the cathedral at Ávila (1526–29). After a short stay at Plasencia he joined the papal choir in Rome (1535), where he remained for 10 years, during which time he published several collections of his compositions. His work and travels with the papal choir greatly advanced his fame. His health seems to have suffered during this period, and he returned to Spain in 1545, where he was appointed *maestro de capilla* at Toledo Cathedral the same year. He left after two years, and after a period at Marchena in the service of the duke of Arcos he was appointed *maestro de capilla* at Málaga in 1551.

He enjoyed remarkable fame during his lifetime, and his reputation continued to grow after his death. Apart from his numerous publications in Rome, including 16 of his Masses, his works were published widely during his lifetime and quickly found their way to cathedrals as far away as Cuzco in Peru. The earliest printed polyphony prepared for use in the New World was Morales' 1544 book of Masses, now part of the cathedral treasure of Pueblo, Mex.

Of his 21 Masses, 16 were published in Rome in 1544, under Morales' personal supervision. Morales was the first Spanish conposer to write Magnificats in all eight ecclesiastical modes. They were unquestionably the most popular of his works in the 16th century and were widely reprinted. Of his many motets, two have been repeatedly singled out for mention, *Lamentabatur Jacob* and *Emendemus in melius*, both in five parts. But there are frequently suspect grounds for contemporary popularity of particular works, and many of his other motets are equally fine. *Jubilate Deo omnis terra* (in six parts), commissioned by Pope Paul III to mark the peace treaty between Charles V and Francis I, was later parodied by Victoria in his Mass *Gaudeamus*, and Guerrero based his Mass *Sancta et immaculata* on Morales' motet. No less a figure than Palestrina parodied a Morales motet for his Mass *O sacrum convivium.*

Morales, Luis de, called EL DIVINO (b. *c.* 1509, Badajoz, Spain—d. May 9, 1586, Badajoz), painter who was the first Spanish artist of pronounced national character, considered to be the greatest native Mannerist painter of Spain. He is remembered for his emotional religious paintings, which earned him his sobriquet and greatly appealed to the Spanish populace.

"The Virgin and Child," panel by Luis de Morales (d. 1586); in the National Gallery, London

By courtesy of the National Gallery, London; photograph, A.C. Cooper

Morales may have studied with the Flemish painter Hernando Sturmio in Badajoz. He worked in Badajoz from 1546, leaving on occasional commissions but making his home there all his life. Summoned by King Philip II of Spain to help in the decoration of El Escorial, he painted a "Christ Carrying the Cross" that did not please the King and was removed to the church of San Jerónimo, Madrid.

Morales always worked on panels, often depicting such subjects as "Ecce Homo," Pietà," and "The Virgin and Child." Perhaps the best known of these panels are 20 on the life of Christ, painted for the church of Arroyo del Puerco (1563–68). All of his paintings are marked by their Leonardesque composition, detailed execution, and anguished asceticism. He remains an artist remarkably representative of his period and nation.

Moralia, also called ETHICA, 1st-century-AD collection of essays by Plutarch.

·stylistic influence on later essayists **14**:578e

moralism, in art, the view that the function of the arts is to promote or reinforce the moral beliefs and attitudes adhered to by the moralist.

·art as a means to moral improvement **2**:53e

morality, standard of human behaviour determined either subjectively or objectively and based on what is considered ethically right or wrong.

·ancestor cult moral significance **1**:837e
·Bergson's static–dynamic dichotomy **2**:844e
·Buddhist teaching on universal norms **3**:428h
·Bushman morality as humanly devised **10**:451c
·Christian essence in moral perfection **4**:461c
·Confucian concept of man **4**:416c
·Confucian moral thought **4**:1107b
·Confucius' moral theory **4**:1108h
·cosmic order functions **15**:35h
·Egyptian religion, society, and Amenhotep IV **6**:506c *passim* to 508h
·elderly persons and homogeneous values **13**:547d
·Hindu concept of ṛta **8**:930a
·Hindu emphasis on respect for life **8**:889e
·Islāmic moral theology **9**:915g
·Islāmic religious, legal, and moral code **9**:938c
·Jain precepts for ascetics and laity **10**:10e
·Japanese faith and works in Buddhism **10**:101f
·Jewish anthropological presuppositions **10**:289g
·Lutheran perspective **11**:200c
·Marlowe's drama as Christian tragedy **18**:583d
·Matthew Gospel and Jesus' broadening of Law **2**:954a
·metaphysical view of world **12**:13a
·mysticism contrasts in religion **12**:789e
·Near East ancient value system **12**:919f
·nonviolent conflict morality **13**:851f
·passage rites and moral inculcation **13**:1049d
·personality dynamics and social values **14**:116d
·philosophical inconsistency of religion **15**:595g
·philosophical–theological censorship **3**:1083g
·Plato's view of the good **14**:536d
·prayer integration with religiosity **14**:949c
·primitive religion's secular role **14**:1042b
·prophecy, institutionalism, and freedom **15**:62e
·Protestant movement feature in Reformation **15**:109d
·religious behavioral discipline **15**:593g
·religious experience and action **15**:648f
·religious ideal in Judaism **10**:302e
·Shintō virtues and attitudes **16**:673g
·Sophist attack on traditional codes **17**:12e
·Taoist moral doctrine origins **17**:1040h
·theological basis of social behaviour **18**:275e
·Vedic concept of evil as ritual impurity **8**:891f

morality plays, along with scriptural drama ("mystery plays") and saints' plays ("miracle plays"), one of the three principal kinds of vernacular drama of the Middle Ages. A morality play is a dramatized allegory, in which the characters are abstractions. The hero is Mankind, and the theme is his response to the temptations and moral forces of life and his possible salvation through the mercy of God at the moment of inevitable death.

No examples of the morality play are known earlier than the beginning of the 15th century. Possibly the earliest is a fragmentary play known as *The Pride of Life*, in which the King of Life challenges all comers including Death. He fights with Death, and, despite the presence of his companions Sanitas and Fortitude, he is overcome. The most important of the early moralities is *The Castle of Perseverance* (*c.* 1405), which is preserved with two other English plays in a manuscript known as the *Macro Morals* (so called after a former owner, Cox Macro) and which introduces most of the themes to be treated in later plays: the Good and the Bad Angel; the World, the Flesh, and the Devil; the Seven Deadly Sins; the Dance of Death; and the siege of a castle. Confession, Shrift, and Penitence appear; salvation is determined after a debate by the Four Daughters of God (Psalm 85: 10). The greatest and most famous example of a morality play is often considered to be *Everyman* (*q.v.*).

In Tudor times the morality play became much more elaborate and had a great influence on later dramatists. Its influence on the Elizabethan drama is strikingly evident in Christopher Marlowe's *The Tragicall History of D. Faustus*.

·allegory of personified abstractions **7**:134d
·Calderón's autos sacramentales **3**:594g
·Central Asian origin and performance **3**:1129g
·costume design in Middle Ages **17**:560h
·Marlowe's Doctor Faustus **11**:517g
·medieval dramatic literature **10**:1099h
·production organization system **18**:258e
·staging conventions of Middle Ages **17**:536f
·theatre development in Russia **17**:542h

Moral Man and Immoral Society, a book by Reinhold Niebuhr, published in 1932.

·context, theme, and impact **13**:74f

moral philosophy: *see* ethics.

Moral Re-armament (MRA), also known as BUCHMANISM or OXFORD GROUP, a modern, nondenominational revivalistic movement founded by U.S. churchman Frank N.D. Buchman (1878–1961). It has sought to deepen the spiritual life of individuals and has encouraged participants to continue as members of their own churches. Primarily a Protestant movement, it has been criticized and banned by some Catholic authorities and praised by others.

After his ordination as a Lutheran pastor in 1902, Buchman combined pastoral responsibilities with social work. Subsequently he worked with the YMCA at the Pennsylvania State University, as lecturer in personal evangelism at the Hartford Seminary Foundation at Hartford, Conn., and as an evangelist among college students. Following friction at Hartford, he resigned in 1922 to "live by faith" and launch a worldwide evangelistic campaign based on God's guidance, moral absolutes, and the "life-changing" of individuals through personal work. The centre of Buchman's operations was shifted to the campus of Princeton University, where he encountered opposition and where the authorities asked him to cease his work in 1926. He was subsequently successful in winning influential support at the University of Oxford in England, and the movement gradually became known as the Oxford Group (not to be confused with the Oxford Movement). During the next ten years the movement held increasingly successful conferences, often attended by thousands of people, in England, The Netherlands, the United States, South Africa, and other countries. In 1938 the name of the movement was changed to Moral Re-armament, and an attempt was made to widen its appeal to include all faiths. Buchman hoped that the world would avoid war if individuals experienced a moral and spiritual awakening. After World War II, MRA sent "task forces" to all corners of the free world to carry on its program, in part through plays emphasizing cooperation, honesty, and mutual respect between opposing groups. Buchman was honoured in many countries for his work of reconciliation.

The MRA has carried out its work by using various methods. A primary way has been the spiritual "house party," which is similar to a religious retreat. In the 1960s meeting places and training centres were located at Mackinac Island, Michigan (*q.v.*); Caux, Switz.; and Odawara, Japan. Though it has by no means exclusively cultivated the upper classes, MRA has always shown much interest in converting the influential and the rich, the "up-and-outs," as Buchman called them. It has steadfastly opposed Communism.

The theology of the movement has been primarily conservative and not complex. An individual is urged to confess his sins, to surrender to and accept Jesus Christ as his personal saviour, and to seek guidance from and share with others whose lives have been changed. Thus, a converted person can reach the four moral absolutes: purity, unselfishness, honesty, and love. Once a person has experienced conversion, he should be able to help others attain the experience.

The MRA publishes no membership figures. Those who decide to become part of the movement are not required to give any special pledges or promises. They attempt to live as converted persons, and they voluntarily give time and money to the organization. In the 1960s about 3,000 persons were serving MRA as full-time workers in many countries throughout the world, but the influence of the movement declined after the death of Buchman (1961) and his successor, Peter Howard (1965).

moral sense: *see* conscience; ethics.

moral tale, didactic story, commonly intended for children. *See also* fable, parable, and allegory.

·English juvenile literature's
development **4**:232h *passim* to 234a

moral theology, a Christian theological discipline frequently called Christian ethics, the systematic reflection on the principles for determining the quality of human behaviour in the light of Christian revelation. It is distinguished from the philosophical discipline of ethics, which relies upon the authority of reason and which can only call upon rational sanctions for moral failure. Moral theology appeals to the authority of revelation, specifically as found in the preaching and activity of Jesus Christ.

The moral teaching in Christian communities has varied in the different eras, regions, and confessional traditions in which Christianity has been professed. The Roman Catholic tradition has been inclined to emphasize the mediating role of ecclesiastical institutions in its approach to the authority of revelation. Protestant churches have often put great emphasis on the direct, or immediate, responsibility of the individual before God. The influence of the spiritual director for the individual Christian has been a significant aspect of Eastern Christianity.

Moral theology has at times seemed to have been restricted in its scope to a consideration of those thoughts, works, and actions that are viewed as offensive to God and spiritually harmful to men—that is, an enumeration of sins. It was thus seen as a negative complement of, or perhaps an anticipation of, the separate disciplines of ascetical and mystical theology, which both presuppose a more positive orientation of the individual toward God.

Many moral theologians, however, have believed that it is more faithful to the New Testament and to early theology not to separate moral teaching from religious anthropology (or the teaching about man) that is implicit in the message of the Gospels. This approach has been reflected in the traditional Eastern Christian emphasis on the divinization of man through his association with Jesus Christ and in the Protestant concern with the moral power of justification. Medieval and post-Reformation Roman Catholic moral theology tended to separate moral teaching from dogmatic theology.

The significance of the relation of moral teaching to divine revelation lies in the problem of determining the nature of the particular "highest good" that characterizes any ethical system. Without such a determination of the nature of this good, one could easily have the impression that morality is simply obedience to a set of rules or laws the observance of which has been labelled, more or less arbitrarily, good. In the light of revelation, sin is seen as a deterioration of the fundamental disposition of man toward God rather than as a breaking of rules or laws. Virtue is viewed as the tendency of man to respond freely and consciously to situations in a manner that reflects and intensifies his conformity to Jesus Christ. The moral theologian's evaluation of moral acts, whether sinful or virtuous, includes a discussion of the relation of motivation and circumstance.

Only when it has been possible to discern the nature of the moral act can the moral theologian attempt to aid the individual in determining the correct Christian response to concrete situations. In eras characterized by an uneducated clergy, the use of penitentials, or lists of moral offenses, was prevalent. Casuistry, an approach to the study of morality through a consideration of large numbers of cases, has tended to deprive the moral act of the spontaneous and unique character expected of a truly free and intelligent action. In recent centuries, several Roman Catholic systems of casuistry (*e.g.*, probabilism) have been developed that have been concerned with the degree of certainty required before an individual should proceed with an act that is of doubtful morality.

The diverse approaches to moral theology through the centuries have varied greatly in their recourse to logical reasoning and in the degree of their acceptance of general moral principles that are considered universally applicable. A recent tendency challenging the validity of such general principles is called situation ethics. Contemporary moral theology must confront problems resulting from modern technology, such as the moral issues related to the use of sophisticated instruments of warfare, individual responsibility in large corporate institutions, the demands of social justice, and recent developments in the biological sciences.

·asceticism as means to spiritual powers **2**:135c
·Bible as rule of conduct **7**:63e
·Christian affirmation of creation's
goodness **4**:561b
·Christian essence in moral perfection **4**:461c
·Christian interpretations of love **4**:524g
·Jesus' individual and social ethics **10**:152g
·philosophical–theological censorship **3**:1083g

Moran, Charles McMoran Wilson, 1st Baron (1882–1977), English physician and biographer of Winston Churchill.

·biography's ethical aspects **2**:1007e

Morand, Paul (1888–1976), French diplomat (1912–45) and author of outstanding short novels that capture the feverish tempo of the 1920s.

Morandi, Giorgio (b. July 20, 1890, Bologna, Italy—d. June 18, 1964, Bologna), painter and etcher whose simple, geometric still lifes of bottles, jars, and boxes were an important contribution to the development of formalism in 20th-century art. Morandi cannot be closely identified with a particular school of painting. He first exhibited in 1914 in Bologna with the Futurist painters, and in 1918–19 he was associated with Giorgio De Chirico and Carlo Carrà, leaders of the Surrealist *scuola metafisica* (Metaphysical School) of painting. He developed a contemplative approach to art that, directed by a highly refined formal sensibility, gave his quiet landscapes and disarmingly simple still-life compositions a characteristic delicacy of tone and extraordinary subtlety of design. His gentle, lyrical colours are subdued and limited to clay-toned whites, drab greens, and umber browns, with occasional highlights of terra-cotta. Morandi's paintings of bottles and jars convey a mood of contemplative repose reminiscent of the work of Piero della Francesca, an Italian Renaissance artist he admired.

"Still Life," oil on canvas by Giorgio Morandi, 1953; in the Phillips Collection, Washington, D.C.

By courtesy of the Phillips Collection, Washington, D.C.

As instructor of etching at the Academy of Fine Arts in Bologna from 1930 to 1956, Morandi had a profound influence on succeeding Italian graphic artists.

·style, subject, and popularity **9**:1111f
·20th-century Italian printmaking **14**:1095h

Morandi, Riccardo (1902–), Italian engineer, designer of the Urdaneta Bridge in Venezuela, built 1958–61.

·Gen. Rafael Urdaneta Bridge illus. **3**:189

Morant Bay, chief town of the Parish of St. Thomas, southeastern Jamaica, at the mouth of the Morant River, east-southeast of Kingston. It is a resort and a shipping point for bananas, coffee, pimiento, ginger, coconuts, copra, honey, and rum. Many of the early public buildings were burned during severe riots of 1865 in which the chief magistrate of the parish and 18 other white persons were killed. The ruthless suppression of the rioters under martial law led to indignation in England and the recall of the Jamaican governor, Edward John Eyre. Pop. (1970) 7,465.
17°50′ N, 76°25′ W

·British handling of riot **10**:17e
·map, Jamaica **10**:16

Morante, Elsa (b. Aug. 18, 1915, Rome), poet, short-story writer, and novelist known particularly for two prizewinning novels, *Menzogna e sortilegio* (1948; Eng. trans., *House of Liars*, 1951) and *L'isola di Arturo* (1957; Eng. trans., *Arturo's Island*, 1959).

Elsa Morante, former wife of novelist Alberto Moravia, fled with him from the Fascists during World War II and hid out for almost a year, waiting for the Allied advance—an experience reflected in Moravia's novel *La ciociara* (1957; Eng. trans., *Two Women*, 1958). Morante's fiction, unlike the grim and graphic Social Realism of Moravia's, is noted for its creative power, poetic beauty, and superbly wrought, subtle style.

Her highly acclaimed and widely translated first novel, *Menzogna e sortilegio*, won a divided Viareggio Prize in the year of its publication. Set in a painstakingly recreated Palermo in the mid-19th century, the novel mingles elements of the Gothic romance, intrigue, and the human dilemmas of love, deceit, and honour. Her second novel, *L'isola di Arturo*, won the Strega Prize in Italy, and critics abroad considered it even better than her first. She handles the story of the boy Arturo's growth from childhood dreams to the painful disillusion of adulthood with lyricism and perfect control, mingling an air of unreality with firm, realistic detail.

Elsa Morante has also published two volumes of short stories, *Il gioco segreto* (1941; "The Secret Game") and *Lo scialle andalusio* (1963; "The Andalusian Shawl"), as well as two volumes of poems, *Alibi* (1958) and *Il mondo salvato dei ragazzini e altri poemi* (1968).

morass: *see* swamps, marshes, and bogs.

Morat, Battle of (June 22, 1476), a major victory for the Swiss Confederation in its war of 1474–76 against Burgundy. It was won just outside Morat (or Murten), the town beside the lake of the same name, west of Bern and east of Lake Neuchâtel. The Swiss had been drawn into the war as allies of the Holy Roman emperor Frederick III and King Louis XI, who were opposed to the Burgundian duke Charles the Bold. Bern, a member state of the Swiss Confederation, hoped to make territorial gains at Charles' expense. Toward the end of 1475, both Frederick and Louis suspended hostilities against Charles, who thus became free to concentrate on the Swiss. After suffering a humiliating defeat at Grandson (March 2, 1476), Charles returned to the attack in the summer with 23,000 men and was besieging Morat, on his way toward Bern from Lausanne, when the Bernese, with late reinforcements from the other confederates, came forward to challenge him. The compact formations of the Swiss prevailed over the Burgundian army, of which more than one-third was annihilated.

Morata (Solomon Sea): *see* Goodenough Island.

Moratín, Leandro Fernández de: *see* Fernández de Moratín, Leandro.

Morava River, German MARCH, one of the important streams in Czechoslovakia. It gives its name to Moravia, an ancient region that covers most of the river's drainage basin, which is 15,000 sq mi (38,900 sq km) in area. For part of its length, the river divides Moravia from Slovakia and then Slovakia from Austria. Its western tributaries drain from the Českomoravská vysočina (Bohemian–Moravian Highlands); the eastern tributaries, of which the Bečva is the most significant, drain from the westernmost ranges of the Carpathians. The Morava rises on the south slope of Králický Sněžník in the Nízký and Hrubý Jeseníky mountains and follows a 227-mi (365-km) course south to enter the Danube just above Bratislava. The river valley has been important historically as one of Europe's natural corridors. A low pass between the Bečva and Odra (Oder)—the Moravian Gate—connects the Danube countries with the Nizina Śląska (Silesian Plain) and the Central Plain of Poland.
48°10′ N, 16°59′ E
·map, Czechoslovakia **5**:412

Morava River, Serbo-Croatian VELIKA MORAVA, in Serbia, Yugoslavia, formed by the confluence of the Južna (South) and Zapadna (West) rivers. It follows a 137-mi (221-km) course, mainly northerly, to enter the Danube River near Smederevo. North of Lapovo the Morava opens into the wide, meandering Pomoravlje valley, a fertile agricultural region. Total area of the Morava Basin is 14,457 sq mi (37,444 sq km), corresponding almost to the political definition of Serbia.

The Zapadna Morava originates in southern Serbia and Macedonia on the west-facing slope of Golija Mountain. Three hydroelectric stations are located along its 185-mi (298-km) course. The Južna Morava is 198 mi (318 km) long from its source at the union of the Binačka Morava and Moravica rivers. Lake Vlasina on the Vlasina, a tributary, provides water for four hydroelectric stations. The Nišava, another tributary, rises in western Bulgaria; its valley provides an important transportation route from Belgrade via Sofia to Turkey. The Morava and the Južna Morava together are a vital part of the Morava–Vardar (Axiós) corridor, the main road and rail route across eastern and southern Yugoslavia.
44°43′ N, 21°03′ E
·map, Yugoslavia **19**:1100

Moravia, central European region that was the centre of a major medieval kingdom, known as Great Moravia, before it was incorporated into the Kingdom of Bohemia (11th century); in the 20th century Moravia became part of the modern state of Czechoslovakia.

Located in the midst of Bohemia, Silesia, and Lower Austria, Moravia was inhabited from the 4th century BC by Celtic and then Germanic tribes. In the 6th and 7th centuries the Avars dominated the area, which was settled by Slavic tribes by the late 8th century. The Slavs, who took the name Moravians from the Morava River, developed a political community, which emerged under Prince Mojmír I (ruled 830–846) as a united kingdom that included a part of western Slovakia. Mojmír's successors Rostislav (ruled 846–870) and his nephew Svatopluk (ruled 870–894) extended their territory to include all of Bohemia, the southern part of modern Poland, and the western part of modern Hungary, thereby creating the state of Great Moravia. Rostislav also invited the Byzantine missionaries Cyril and Methodius (who arrived in 863) to spread Christianity in Bohemia and Moravia on the basis of their Slavonic translation of the chief liturgical texts. After Svatopluk died (894), however, Great Moravia disintegrated and was finally destroyed by a Magyar attack in 906.

The territories of Great Moravia were then contested by Poland, Hungary, and Bohemia. In 1029 Moravia (*i.e.*, the western portion of Great Moravia) was incorporated as a distinct province into the Bohemian kingdom, and thereafter it remained closely attached to Bohemia (with only a few brief intermissions) until after both regions had come under the rule of the Habsburgs (1526), who eventually separated them administratively; after the Revolution of 1848, the Habsburgs made Moravia a separate Austrian crown land.

In 1918 that crown land became a province of the new state of Czechoslovakia, and, although it was annexed by Germany just before the outbreak of World War II, it was restored to the reconstituted state of Czechoslovakia after the war. On Jan. 1, 1949, however, the Czechoslovak government dissolved Moravia into a number of smaller administrative units. In 1960 another administrative reorganization created the South Moravian (Jihomoravský) and North Moravian (Severomoravský) regions on the territory formerly known as Moravia-Silesia.

·Germanic settlement and expansion **2**:450c
·Hungarian historical domination **9**:30a
·linguistic composition and liturgy **16**:869b
·location and size **5**:411b
·pewter flagon motifs **11**:1108d
·political and ecclesiastical history **2**:1185e
·Svatopluk's reign **14**:638b

Moravia, Alberto, pseudonym of ALBERTO PINCHERLE (b. Nov. 28, 1907, Rome), journalist, short-story writer, and novelist known for his fictional portrayals of social alienation and loveless sexuality.

Moravia, 1969
Horst Tappe—EB Inc.

When he contracted tuberculosis at the age of 16, Moravia had to abandon his formal education. During two years in sanitoriums, however, he studied French and English; read Boccaccio, Ariosto, Shakespeare, and Molière; and began to write. One of his short stories, "Hiverno di un ragazzo malato" ("A Sick Boy's Winter"), describes his feelings during that period.

After his illness Moravia was a journalist for a time in Turin and a foreign correspondent in London. His first novel, a scathingly realistic study of the moral corruption of a middle-class mother and two of her children, was called *Gli indifferenti* (1929; 1st Eng. trans., 1932, best trans., *The Time of Indifference*, 1953). After the critic Giuseppe Borgese praised the novel in the Milan daily *Corriere della sera*, *Gli indifferenti* became a sensation, despite its divergence from the idealistic formalism demanded by the cultural establishment and the Fascist dictatorship. Moravia only gained wider renown in Italy and abroad with the changed political conditions after World War II.

During the Fascist years, Moravia continued to produce novels and collections of stories, most of them dealing with emotional aridity, isolation, and existential frustration, and expressing the futility of either sexual promiscuity or conjugal love as an escape. Some of his more important novels are *Agostino* (1944; Eng. trans., *Two Adolescents*, 1950); *La disubbidienza* (1948; *Disobedience*, 1950); and *Il conformista* (1951; *The Conformist*, 1952), all on themes of isolation and alienation. Moravia's best known book, *La romana* (1947; *The Woman of Rome*, 1949), a realistic and sympathetic story of a prostitute and her varied clientele, has been praised for avoiding the cliches of excessive eroticism and sentimentality. A later work, *La noia* (1960; *The Empty Canvas*, 1962), in which a painter is unable to find meaning either in love or work, won the Viareggio Prize in 1961.

Moravia has written several books of short stories: *Racconti romani* (1954; *Roman Tales*, 1956), winner of the Marzotto Prize in 1954; *Nuovi racconti romani* (1959; *More Roman Tales*, 1963); and *L'automa* (1962; "The Automaton"), the last a gathering of 41 stories about people so divorced from themselves and from reality that they function like robots. *Racconti di Alberto Moravia* (1968) is a collection of earlier stories.

Critics have praised Moravia's stark, unadorned style, his psychological penetration, his narrative skill, and his ability to create authentic characters and realistic dialogue, though some have become weary of the sameness of his themes. Moravia's views on literature and realism are expressed in a stimulating book of essays, *L'uomo come fine* (1963; *Man as an End*, 1966). He was married for a time to the novelist Elsa Morante.

·Italian literary role **10**:1238c

Moravian Brethren: *see* Unitas Fratrum.

Moravian Church 12:435, a Protestant communion founded in the 18th century but tracing its origin to the 15th-century Hussite Unitas Fratrum (Unity of Brethren) in Bohemia and Moravia. It is principally a product of German Pietism. Developing a communal piety centring in encounter and identification with the historical Jesus under the influence of Nikolaus Ludwig, Graf von Zinzendorf, on the estate of Berthelsdorf at a place later called Herrnhut, the Moravians—though numerically insignificant—spread to many parts of the world. They influenced modern Protestantism in worship, evangelism, missions, and theology.

The text article covers the history of the Moravians, including their origins, the Reformation period, the Moravian Church, its influence within Protestantism, and Moravians since the 18th century. The article concludes with a brief summary of Moravian beliefs, practices, and institutions.

REFERENCES in other text articles:

·Bohemian religious reform controversy **2**:1188d
·Comenius' Bohemian leadership **4**:967g
·Herrnhut Brethren under Zinzendorf **14**:457f
·Lutheranism and Pietism **11**:197g
·Schleiermacher's early training **16**:345g
·Wesley brothers' contacts in Georgia and England **19**:760a
·Zinzendorf's organizational development **19**:1155c

RELATED ENTRIES in the *Ready Reference and Index:*
Confessio Bohemica; Hussites; Taborites; Unitas Fratrum; Utraquists

Moravian dialects: *see* Czech language.

Moravian Gate (Czechoslovakia): *see* Morava River.

Moravian Karst, Czech MORAVSKÝ KRAS, in Jihomoravský *kraj* (South Moravia region), Czechoslovakia, one of several small disconnected karst areas. It is situated north of Brno, along the east bank of the Svitava River, and eastward along its underground tributaries, the Punkva and the Říčka. In area it is about 20 mi (32 km) north–south and 6–9 mi (10–15 km) east–west. The Devonian limestone contains a labyrinth of swallow holes, underground passages and lakes, caverns, and calcareous formations. In several places sites of prehistoric hunting settlements have been excavated. Czech archaeologists believe that only a small percentage of the karst features have been charted.

Moray, formerly ELGINSHIRE, until the reorganization of 1975 a county in northeastern Scotland. It is now largely in Moray (*q.v.*) district, of Grampian (*q.v.*) region. It had an area of 476 sq mi (1,234 sq km).

The area is divided into a lowland plain, the Laigh of Moray, in the north behind a 35-mi (56-km) coastline of sand dunes (the Culbin Sands) and the Hills of Cromdale in the Highlands, which rise to about 2,300 ft (about 700 m) in the south. The Hills of Cromdale are separated from the lower moorlands (750–1,300 ft) to the north by Strathspey, the broad valley of the River Spey, which runs northeastward to the North Sea. South of the postglacial raised beaches fringing the shore, the lowlands and river valleys are covered by fertile clay and fluvioglacial deposits; peat covers large stretches of moorland in the south. The Laigh of Moray has an annual rainfall of less than 30 in (750 mm), and the mountains in the south have about 50 in.

Archaeological evidence shows that the area was occupied by the Picts in prehistoric times and that Christianity was introduced before the Norse invasions of the 10th and 11th centuries. During the 13th century, Edward I of England occupied Elgin. Many villages were ravaged during the English Civil War in the mid-17th century. Moray was little affected by the industrial development of the 19th century.

The low rainfall, combined with sunny conditions and fertile soil, make the lowlands a productive agricultural region. Beef cattle and dairying are significant, and the wintering of sheep is the mainstay of the upland farms. Barley and seed potatoes for export are important crops. The intensive growing of fruit and vegetables increased after the establishment of a canning factory at Fochabers. Almost 20 percent of the area is forested. The Forestry Commission's plantations of larch and fir include stretches on the sandy wastes of the Culbin. Fishing for whitefish in the Moray Firth and for salmon at the mouths of the Spey and Findhorn remains productive. Moray's main industry, apart from agriculture, forestry, and fishing, is whisky distilling, especially in Strathspey. Elgin supports distilleries, woollen mills, iron foundries, and sawmills; Forres has distilleries, woollen mills, and chemical works.

Moray, district, Grampian (*q.v.*) region, northeastern Scotland; created by the reorganization of 1975, it includes most of the former counties of Moray and Banff (*qq.v.*). The district, area 754 sq mi (1,953 sq km), meets the Moray Firth on the north with beaches and sand dunes. The Spey and Findhorn rivers issue from the hills and peat moors in the south and cross the fertile coastal plain to reach the firth. On the far southern boundary rises the huge mountain block of the Cairngorms, attaining nearly 4,000 ft (1,220 m). Cereals and potatoes are grown and beef cattle bred in the plain; sheep graze on the hills, and there is sea fishing, especially at Buckie, forestry, and quarrying, with distilling and woollen mills at Forres and Elgin, the seat of the district authority. Pop. (1974 est.) 79,211.

Moray (MURRAY), **earls of,** a Scottish title held from 1581 to the present by descendants of James Stewart (died 1592, known as "the bonnie earl of Moray"), as a result of his marriage with the heiress of James Stewart (died 1570), created earl of Moray in 1562 by his half sister Mary, Queen of Scots. Moray was one of the traditional seven provinces of Scotland. Little is known of its earlier rulers, but the earldom was held (1312–46) by Thomas Randolph, a nephew of King Robert I, and his sons, and thereafter by the Dunbar family (earls of March) until it passed with an heiress to Archibald Douglas, who was forfeited in 1455. Later it was held briefly by George Gordon, 4th earl of Huntly.

Moray (MURRAY), **James Stewart, earl of** (b. *c.* 1531—d. Jan. 21, 1570, Linlithgow, West Lothian), half brother of Mary Stuart, Queen of Scots, who became regent of Scotland after her abdication. The illegitimate son of King James V, Stewart led the Protestant lords in their conflict with Mary Stuart's mother, the queen regent. When Mary Stuart assumed control of the government upon the death of her mother in 1560, however, he supported her, despite her Roman Catholicism. In 1562 she made him earl of Moray, but he lost her favour by supporting the Calvinist reformer John Knox and by opposing the Queen's marriage (July 1565) to Henry Stewart, Lord Darnley. From August to October 1565 Moray attempted to arouse Edinburgh citizens against Mary's authority. She personally led the force that drove him and his supporters across the border. The outlawed Moray fled to England but was pardoned and allowed to return to Scotland the following year. When Mary abdicated in 1567, Moray was appointed regent for her year-old son, King James VI. He suppressed her final effort to regain power when he routed her forces at Langside on May 13, 1568, and she, in turn, fled to England. A substantial portion of the nobility continued to maintain Mary's right to rule, however, and Moray had difficulty putting into practice his vigorously Protestant and pro-English policies. In January 1570 he was assassinated by James Hamilton

James Stewart, earl of Moray, detail of a portrait by Hans Eworth, 1561; in the Darnaway Castle Collection, Moray
By courtesy of the Darnaway Castle Collection

of Bothwellhaugh, who favoured Mary, while riding through Linlithgow. Moray's career is recounted in Maurice Lee's *James Stewart, Earl of Moray* (1953).

·John Knox and Scottish Reformation **10**:497c
·Mary Stuart's Scottish administration **11**:565a

Moray, Thomas Randolph, 1st earl of (d. July 20, 1332, Musselburgh, Midlothian), nephew of King Robert I the Bruce of Scotland and a leading military commander in Robert's successful struggle to gain independence from English rule; later he was regent for Robert's young son and successor, David II (ruled 1329–71).

Randolph was the son of one of Robert's sisters. When Robert revolted against the English and claimed the Scottish throne (1306), Randolph joined the insurgency, but he was soon thereafter taken prisoner at the Battle of Methven. He did homage to King Edward I of England and fought in the English army against Robert until captured by the Scottish commander Sir James Douglas in 1308. Submitting to Robert, Randolph quickly became a trusted commander and adviser. Robert made him earl of Moray in 1312. By a brilliant tactical manoeuvre Moray captured Edinburgh Castle from the English in March 1314, and three months later he distinguished himself in the spectacular Scottish victory over Edward II of England at Bannockburn.

With Douglas, Moray took Berwick-upon-Tweed from the English (1318), ravaged northern England (1319), and defeated an English army at Byland, Yorkshire (1322). In 1323 he persuaded Pope John XXII to recognize Robert's right to the Scottish throne. Five years later he played a major role in negotiating the treaty by which England recognized Robert as king of Scots. Robert died in June 1329, and Randolph was regent for David II until his death.

moray eel, any of 80 or more species of eels of the family Muraenidae, found in warm and tropical seas. Thick-bodied eels with no pectoral fins or scales, they live in shallow water among reefs and rocks and hide in crevices. They generally do not exceed a length of about 1.5 metres (5 feet), but one species, *Thyrsoidea macrura* of the Pacific, is known to grow about 3.5 metres long. Morays are usually vividly marked or coloured. Carnivorous and with large mouths and powerful teeth, they are apt to attack when disturbed;

Green moray eel (*Gymnothorax funebris*)
Carleton Ray—Photo Researchers

large morays are considered dangerous to human beings. Morays are eaten in some areas, but their flesh is sometimes toxic and can cause illness or death.
·habitat and classification 1:899e; illus. 898
·poisonous animals, table 6 14:612

Moray Firth, triangular-shaped inlet of the North Sea in northeast Scotland. The apex of the triangle is at Inverness, the firth there being called the Firth of Inverness. Its extreme limits are, in the north, Duncansby Head, north of Wick, and, in the south, Kinnaird's Head, where the town of Fraserburgh is located. The northwest shore is indented by the Cromarty and Dornoch firths. Fish are very plentiful in the Moray Firth, and prosperous fishing villages (notably Lossiemouth, Buckie, and Macduff) line the shores.
57°50′ N, 3°30′ W
·map, United Kingdom 18:866

Morazán, department, eastern El Salvador, bordered by Honduras, has an area of 519 sq mi (1,344 sq km). Formed in 1875, it is composed of deep valleys and rugged mountains, the highest being Cacaguatique Volcano (5,417 ft [1,651 m]). Except in the northeast, which is sparsely settled, the population is evenly distributed in the valleys and on the lower mountain slopes. The economy is basically agricultural; henequen (more than one-third of the national production of this twine fibre), sugarcane, and fruit are the main products. Gold and silver are mined in small quantities. The departmental capital was moved from Osicala to San Francisco Gotera in 1887. Pop. (1971) 156,052.
·area and population table 6:733

Morazán, Francisco (b. Oct. 16, 1792, Tegucigalpa, Honduras—d. Sept. 15, 1842, San José, Costa Rica), president of the United Provinces of Central America (1830–40) who was the outstanding military and political hero of Central America from 1827 until his death.

Francisco Morazán, detail of an engraving by A. Demarest
By courtesy of the Library of Congress, Washington, D.C.

Self-educated, Morazán began his political career in his native Honduras. When he was 35 years old (1827), he led the Liberal Party's forces in a revolt against Manuel José Arce, first president of the United Provinces, which had been set up in 1823. He defeated the Conservative army (1829) at Guatemala City, the capital, and in 1830 was elected president. During his presidency he introduced many reforms designed to limit the power of the Roman Catholic Church, but his administration aroused the anger of Conservatives and he had to devote most of his energy to putting down revolts.

By the end of Morazán's second term (1839), most of the member states had deserted the federation. A Conservative-backed rebel army under Rafael Carrera defeated Morazán at Guatemala City in March 1840, and the former president went into exile. In 1842 he returned to attempt the restoration of the federation. He attacked and defeated the forces of the Costa Rican dictator Braulio Carillo, but, when he tried to follow up this triumph, his forces were quickly routed. Betrayed and captured, Morazán was executed by a firing squad. *See also* Central America, United Provinces of.
·Central American federation presidency 3:1109g

Morbihan, *département* in northwestern France, created from a part of western Brittany. It takes its name from the practically landlocked Morbihan (Breton: "Little Sea") Gulf. With an area of 2,611 sq mi (6,763 sq km), it covers the south coast of the Breton peninsula bordering the Atlantic Ocean. The ancient towns of Auray and Vannes (*q.v.*), the capital, are situated on estuaries opening southward onto the gulf. West of the gulf, the coast juts out to the Quiberon Peninsula, then, turning northwestward, passes the mouth of the three estuaries on which Lorient, a naval port, is situated, and extends to the estuary of the Leita River, which divides Morbihan from Finistère. East of the gulf, the coast, indented by estuaries and creeks, extends to the mouth of the Vilaine River and to the border of Loire-Atlantique *département*. Belle-Île-en-Mer, south of Quiberon, and other small islands are included in Morbihan.

The highest point is in the Montagnes Noires (970 ft [296 m]), a range that forms the northwestern boundary. The main ranges of hills and the central plateau of the Landes de Lanvaux heath run west-east, parallel to the coast, across nearly the entire *département*. Rivers in the west, including the Scorff and the Blavet, flow southward, but the main streams in the east, such as the Oust and the Arz, flow eastward to join the Vilaine. The climate is predominantly oceanic, with frequent and abundant rain at all seasons. Agriculture and fishing are the principal activities, and oysters are cultivated in the gulf. Light industries have been established at Vannes, submarines are built at Lorient, and there is some canning in the harbour towns of Port-Louis, Étel, Quiberon, and Groix.

Morbihan has more prehistoric stone monuments than any other *département* of France, with several thousand megaliths in the Carnac-Locmariaquer area west of the gulf. Breton is still spoken in the west, and traditional folklore remains very much alive. The medieval towns and villages are major tourist attractions. The *département* is divided into the *arrondissements* of Vannes, Lorient, and Pontivy. It is in the educational division of Rennes. Pop. (1975 prelim.) 567,000.
·area and population table 7:594

Morchella (morel): *see* cup fungus.

Mordaciidae, family of fishes of the class Agnatha.
·classification and general features 1:311c

Mordano, Dino Grandi, conte di (Italian Fascist): *see* Grandi, Dino, conte di Mordano.

mordant dye, colorant that can be bound to a material for which it has little or no affinity by the addition of a mordant, a chemical that combines with the dye and the fibre. As the principal mordants are dichromates and chromium complexes, mordant dye usually means chrome dye. Most mordant dyes yield different colours with different mordants.
·dye manufacturing and methods of application 5:1099e
·dyestuff affinity to natural fibres 5:1106c
·fabric type and treatment 18:186f

Mordecai, in the Old Testament Book of Esther, a relative of Queen Esther who thwarted a plot against the Jews.
·Book of Esther's sanctioning of Purim 2:928g

Mordell, Louis Joel (1888–1972), mathematician, contributed important proofs to the theory of Diophantine analysis and the theory of numbers, of which Diophantine analysis is a branch.

Mordellidae (order of insects): *see* tumbling flower beetle.

Morden, town, southern Manitoba, Canada, on Dead Horse Creek, just north of the North Dakota (U.S.) border. Named for Alvey Morden, who moved there from Walkerton, Ont., in 1874, the town was built when the Canadian Pacific Railway reached the site in 1881, bypassing Nelson to the northwest and Mountain City to the south.

A farming and livestock-marketing centre, it is the site of a dominion horticulture-experimental station. Canned foods, dressed poultry, processed potatoes, clothing, and farm machinery are the chief products. Water is provided by Lake Minnewasta, formed by a large dam on Dead Horse Creek. Inc. 1882. Pop. (1971) 3,266.
49°11′ N, 98°05′ W
·map, Canada 3:716

mordenite, a sodium, potassium, and calcium aluminosilicate mineral, $(Na_2,K_2,Ca)Al_2Si_{10}O_{24}\cdot 7H_2O$, in the zeolite family. It commonly occurs as white, glassy needles filling veins and cavities in igneous rocks; it also is found in marine sediments, as in the Urals, and in dikes where water has attacked and altered volcanic glasses, as on the Isle of Arran in Scotland. Mordenite's molecular structure is a framework containing chains of five-membered rings of linked silicate tetrahedra (four oxygen atoms arranged at the points of a triangular pyramid about a central silicon atom). For detailed physical properties, *see* table under zeolites.

Mordvin, also called MORDVA, MORDVINIAN, and MORDOVIAN, the name of a people and of their language, one of the Finno-Ugric group of the Uralic family. The Mordvins live mainly in the Middle Volga region of the Russian Soviet Federated Socialist Republic. Under the Soviet government they were given some autonomy in 1928, and the Mordvinian Autonomous Soviet Socialist Republic (*q.v.*), with its capital at Saransk, was created in 1934. Mordvins numbered some 1,263,000 in 1970, with about a third living in the republic (where they were far outnumbered by Russians) and the remainder distributed in other parts of the Soviet Union. They are divided into two dialectal groups, the Moksha and Erzya (*see* Mordvin language).

Traditionally agricultural, the Mordvins are noted as master beekeepers. The old national costume still may be seen, especially among the women, whose profusely embroidered skirts, large earrings, and numerous necklaces distinguish them from Russians. Although many modern Mordvins cannot speak the original tongue, there exists a considerable Cyrillic literature of Mordvin songs and legends, some recounting the feats of their king Tushtyan, who was a contemporary of Ivan IV the Terrible. Mordvin religion consists of a Christian veneer over more traditional beliefs. The practice of pretending to kidnap brides in the face of mock resistance has been reported to persist.

·Iranian religious loans **16**:875b
·religiocultural history 7:310d *passim* to 312d
·Soviet Union nationalities distribution, table 3 **17**:338

Mordvinian Autonomous Soviet Socialist Republic, administrative division of the central European Russian Soviet Federated Socialist Republic, in the middle Volga Basin, covering an area of 10,100 sq mi (26,200 sq km). The capital is Saransk.

A gently rolling plain crossed by the broad, shallow, and often swampy valley of the Moksha River in the west and the Sura, a direct tributary of the Volga, in the east, the republic has a climate that is markedly continental. The average January temperature is 10° F (−12° C), but incursions of cold air from the north can drop the temperature to −40° F (−40° C). The average July temperature is 68° F (20° C). Annual rainfall (summer maximum) ranges from 20 in. (500 mm) in the west to 16 in. (400 mm) in the east; it is, however, extremely variable, and periods of drought occur. Most of the original vegetation, including the mixed forests (oak, lime, maple, ash, and birch) and the wooded steppe, has been cleared for agricultural purposes. Soils are usually of the leached or degraded chernozem (black earth) or gray forest type, with belts of floodplain meadows along the rivers.

The Mordvin, representing about 35 percent of the republic's population, are of Finno-Ugrian origin and related to the nearby Mari and Udmurts. They are composed of two groups distinguished by language differences: the Erzya-Mordvin of the east, and the Moksha-Mordvin of the west and north. Russians, who form the majority of the population, penetrated the area as early as the 12th century, but it was not until the overthrow of the Kazan Khanate, or empire, in the late 16th and 17th centuries that the area came under Russian control. In 1930 it was made an autonomous *oblast*, (administrative region), and in 1934 it received its present status. The chief cities are the capital, Saransk (*q.v.*), Ardatov, Ruzayevka, and Kovylkino.

Mainly agricultural, the republic plants 65 percent of its cropped area in grains—winter rye, spring wheat, oats, millet, buckwheat, and corn (maize) for silage. Hemp, *makhorka* (tobacco), and vegetables are also grown; draft horses are bred; beekeeping is widespread; and some raising of sheep, goats, cattle, and pigs is carried on. Industrial activity includes timber working, tannin extraction, metalworking, light manufacturing, food and textile processing, cement making, and the production of paper, wooden crates, and prefabricated housing materials. Machine-building enterprises produce instruments and heavy engineering, electrical, and chemical equipment. Peat is dug to supply the Saransk peat-burning electric power station. Natural gas from the Saratov–Gorky pipeline that passes through Saransk is the basis of a developing chemical industry. The Mowcow–Ryazan–Kuybyshev trunk railway crosses the republic from west to east, while lines from Gorky and Kazan to Penza traverse it from north to south. Highways link Saransk with Gorky, Ulyanovsk, and Penza. Pop. (1970 prelim.) 1,030,000.

·location and features **17**:330g

Mordvin language, member of the Finno-Ugric group of the Uralic language family, spoken by over 1,000,000 persons, about half of whom live in the Mordvinian A.S.S.R. of the U.S.S.R. The third largest Uralic language in number of speakers, ranking after Hungarian and Finnish, it has two major dialects: Erza, spoken in the northwest portion of the Mordvinian A.S.S.R. and the surrounding territory; and Moksha, spoken in the southeast. Both dialects are currently written and have official status. Mordvin is most closely related to the Mari language, with which it makes up the Volga-Finnic subgroup of the Finnic languages of Finno-Ugric. For linguistic characteristics, *see* Finno-Ugric languages.

·history and dialects **18**:1026h; map 1023

More, Sir Anthony, known as ANTONIO MORO, originally ANTHONIS MOR (b. 1512 or 1525, Utrecht, Neth.—d. 1575, Antwerp, Belg.), Dutch portrait painter. He studied his art under Jan Schoreel, and after making a professional visit to Italy he began to paint portraits in the style of Hans Holbein. His rise to eminence was rapid. In 1552 (or 1542?) he was invited to Madrid by the emperor Charles V. In 1554 he was in London painting the portrait of Queen Mary for her bridegroom, Philip II of Spain. This picture (at the Prado in Madrid) is his masterpiece. For it an annual salary and, supposedly, the honour of knighthood were conferred upon him.

·Alba oil portrait illus. **1**:416
·Mary I portrait illus. **11**:563

More, Hannah (b. Feb. 2, 1745, Stapleton, Gloucestershire—d. Sept. 7, 1833, Bristol, Eng.), best known as a writer of popular religious tracts and as an educator of the poor. As a young woman with literary aspirations, Miss More made the first of her triumphal visits to London in 1773–74. She was welcomed into a circle of Bluestocking wits and was befriended by Sir Joshua Reynolds, Dr. Johnson, Edmund Burke, and, particularly, by David Garrick, who produced her plays (*The Inflexible Captive*, 1775; *Percy*, 1777). After Garrick's death (1779), she forsook writing for the stage, and her strong piety and Christian attitudes, already intense, became more marked.

Hannah More, detail of an oil painting by Sir Henry Raeburn (1756–1823); in the Louvre, Paris

Cliche Musees Nationaux

Through her friendship with the abolitionist philanthropist William Wilberforce, she was drawn to the Evangelicals. From her cottage in Somerset, she began to admonish society in a series of treatises beginning with *Thoughts on the Importance of the Manners of the Great to General Society* (1788). In the climate of alarm over the French Revolution, her fresh and forceful defense of traditional values met with strong approval.

Village Politics (1792; under the pseudonym of Will Chip), written to counteract Thomas Paine's *Rights of Man*, was so successful that it led to the production of a series of "Cheap Repository Tracts." Produced at the rate of three a month for three years with the help of her sisters and friends, the tracts sold for a penny each, 2,000,000 being circulated in a single year. They advised the poor in ingeniously homely language to cultivate the virtues of sobriety and industry and to trust in God and in the kindness of the gentry.

Like most of her educated contemporaries, Miss More believed that society was static and that civilization depended upon a large body of the poor, for whom the best education was one that reconciled them to their fate. Hence she established clubs for women and schools for children, in which the latter were taught the Bible, catechism, and skills thought to befit their station. She persevered in her efforts in spite of much opposition and abuse from country neighbours, who thought that even the most limited education of the poor would destroy their interest in farming, and from the clergy, who accused her of Methodism.

Her final popular success as a writer was her didactic novel *Coelebs in Search of a Wife* (1808). *See also* Bluestocking.

More, Henry (b. 1614, Grantham, Lincolnshire—d. Sept. 1, 1687, Cambridge, Cambridgeshire), poet and philosopher of religion whose affinity for the metaphysics of Plato places him among the group of thinkers known as the Cambridge Platonists.

Henry More, engraving by D. Loggan, 1679

By courtesy of the trustees of the British Museum; photograph, J.R. Freeman & Co. Ltd.

Reared a Calvinist, More became an Anglican as a youth. At Christ's College, Cambridge, he encountered such Platonists as Edward Fowler and John Worthington and came under the influence of Joseph Mead (or Mede), the mystic who wrote *Clavis Apocalyptica* (1627; "The Key to the Apocalypse"). In 1639 he was elected to a fellowship at Cambridge. Among his pupils was Lady Anne Conway, whose religious enthusiasm influenced More and at whose request he later wrote *Conjectura Cabbalistica* (1653).

In close touch with the leading philosophers and scientists of his time, More gradually abandoned his admiration for the thought of the French Rationalist René Descartes, which separated mind and matter, and came to see mechanical naturalism and atheism as the inevitable result of Cartesian philosophy. In their correspondence of 1648–49, published as *The Immortality of the Soule* (1659), and in his major metaphysical work, *Enchiridion Metaphysicum* (1671), More argued against Descartes' skepticism and maintained his own spiritualist views. In a similar fashion, he sought to refute the claim of the English philosopher Thomas Hobbes that theism is impossible because the human mind cannot know an immaterial substance.

More's early poetry, written in a style akin to that of the English lyricist Edmund Spenser, treated metaphysical subjects and included satirical sketches of the Puritan religion, against which he had rebelled. His religious views, most fully expressed in *An Explanation of the Grand Mystery of Godliness* (1660) and *Divine Dialogues* (1668), centred on his idea that "there is no real clashing at all betwixt any genuine point of Christianity and what true Philosophy and Right Reason does determine or allow." His ethical writings include *Enchiridion Ethicum* (1667); his work *An Antidote against Atheism* (1652) is curiously devoted, in large part, to witch and ghost stories. His poetry is published in Alexander Balloch Grosart's *Complete Poems of Henry More* (1878). Excerpts from his philosophical writings appear in Flora Isabel MacKinnon's *Philosophical Writings of Henry More* (1925).

BIBLIOGRAPHY. Richard Ward, *The Life of the Learned and Pious Dr Henry More* (1710); Marjorie Nicolson (ed.), *The Conway Letters* (1930).
·Newton and Hermetic tradition **13**:17e

More, Paul Elmer (b. Dec. 12, 1864, St. Louis, Mo.—d. March 9, 1937, Princeton, N.J.), scholar and conservative critic, one of the leading exponents of the New Humanism in literary criticism. He was educated at Washington University and at Harvard, where he met Irving Babbitt and where, from 1894 to 1895, he was assistant in Sanskrit. In 1895–97 he was associate in Sanskrit and classical literature at Bryn Mawr College. He served as literary editor of *The Independent* (1901–03) and the *New York Evening Post* (1903–09) and as editor of *The Nation* (1909–14). More, like his associate and fellow leader of the New Humanists, Babbitt, was an uncompromising advocate of traditional critical standards and classical restraint in a time that saw the emergence of the Naturalists: such writers as Theodore Dreiser and Sinclair Lewis whose novels dealt with social issues. As a consequence he drew considerable critical fire, in particular from H.L. Mencken, who led the attack on More, Babbitt, and their disciple, Norman Foerster.

More's best known work is his *Shelburne Essays* (11 volumes, 1904–21), a collection of articles and reviews, most of which had appeared in *The Nation* and other periodicals. Also notable among More's writings are his *Life of Benjamin Franklin* (1900); *Nietzsche* (1912); *Platonism* (1917); *The Religion of Plato* (1921); *Hellenistic Philosophies* (1923); *New Shelburne Essays* (1928–36); and his biography and last published work, *Pages from an Oxford Diary* (1937). His monumental *Greek Tradition* (5 volumes, 1924–31) is generally thought to be his finest work.
·essay use in societal redefinition **10**:1078e

More, Sir Thomas **12**:437 (b. Feb. 7, 1477, London—d. July 6, 1535, London), Humanist and statesman who was put to death for refusing to accept King Henry VIII as head of the Church of England. He is recognized as a saint by the Roman Catholic Church.

Abstract of text biography. More studied law and in 1501 became a barrister. A friend of the Dutch Humanist Erasmus, More campaigned for Erasmus' religious and cultural program (1515–20). In 1516 More published his great speculative political book, *Utopia*. In the 1520s he began attacking Martin Luther's dogmas and served as a representative of the king. More became chancellor of England in 1529, retiring in 1532. His refusal to attend the coronation as queen of Anne Boleyn, whom Henry had married after divorcing Catherine of Aragon, earned him the King's wrath. Tried and sentenced to death for refusing to recognize Henry as head of the English Church, More was beheaded on Tower Hill.

REFERENCES in other text articles:
·Agricola's literary association **1**:314g
·biographical writings **2**:1011e
·Communism in distribution **1**:809f
·Erasmus' influence **6**:952d
·Henry VIII's politico-religious problems **8**:770f *passim* to 771g
·Holbein's portraits **8**:991c
·satire in utopian literature **16**:270f

Morea, Despotate of, autonomous Byzantine principality located on the Greek Peloponnese (Morea); established in the mid-14th century by the Byzantine emperor John VI Cantacuzenus (1347–54) as an appanage for his son Manuel.

Manuel Cantacuzenus consolidated his territory against the claims of Latins (Western Europeans) and the inroads of Turks, but after his death (1380) the Palaeologians seized Byzantine territory in the Morea from Manuel's heirs. Theodore I Palaeologus (reigned 1383–1407), son of Byzantine emperor John V Palaeologus, ruled in the Morea from his capital at Mistra (Mistras, Greece). He consolidated Byzantine rule by recognizing Turkish suzerainty and settling Albanians in the territory to bring new blood and workers into the despotate, which, his successor, became a bastion of Byzantine strength in the midst of a crumbling empire.

Mistra, near the site of ancient Sparta, was the residence of the despots. Their tombs were located there, and an important cultural centre grew up within the castle walls. Educated Greeks, scholars, and artists flocked there in the 14th century.

By the mid-15th century the despotate of Morea had incorporated the remaining Latin possessions on the Peloponnese. But the Turks destroyed the Hexamilion wall built across the Isthmus of Corinth to protect southern Greece and overran the despotate in 1460 to incorporate it into the Ottoman Empire.
·Byzantine control of the Balkans **2**:617d
·Byzantine cultural survivals **3**:570f; map
·geology, area, and population **8**:313b; table 318
·map, Greece **8**:314
·Ottoman Empire historical relation **13**:774g

Moréas, Jean, pseudonym of YÁNNIS PAPADIAMANTÓPOULOS (b. April 15, 1856, Athens—d. March 31, 1910, Paris), poet who played a leading part in the French Symbolist movement. In 1879 he went to Paris, where he became a familiar literary figure. His *Syrtes* (1884) were Parnassian in form, but *Les Cantilènes* (1886), and especially *Le Pèlerin passionné* (1891), were heralded as masterpieces of the newly founded Symbolist school. The Parnassians attached great importance to severe objectivity in descriptive poetry and purity of form, while Symbolist poetry was evocative and impressionistic.

Moréas
Harlingue—H. Roger-Viollet

Moréas was the first to formulate the principles of Symbolism in the magazine *XIXe siècle* (Aug. 11, 1885), and in September 1886 he published an important manifesto in the literary supplement of *Figaro*. He founded a periodical, *Le Symboliste* (1886). But in 1891 he forsook Symbolism and founded the *école romane*, which attempted to revive the Greek and Latin classical traditions that had governed French poetry in the 16th and 17th centuries. The chief members of this group were the young French poets Raymond de la Tailhède, Maurice du Plessys, Ernest Raynaud, and Charles Maurras. He abandoned the *vers libre* (free verse) typical of his Symbolist work and returned to traditional French versification and classical sources of inspiration. The new aesthetic found expression in *Énone au clair visage* (1893), *Eriphyle* (1894), and *Sylves* (1896). In his last and finest work, *Stances* (1899–1905), he retained the best of his earliest Symbolist venture in verse of classical perfection and purity. The mood of his poetry is one of pagan resignation. In the same melancholy vein, and with equal lyrical power, he wrote a play, *Iphigénie* (published 1904), closely inspired by Euripides, which met with considerable success when presented in the *théatre antique* of Orange and subsequently on the stage of the Odéon in Paris.
·French literature of the 19th century **10**:1195f

Moreau, Gustave (b. April 6, 1826, Paris—d. April 18, 1898, Paris), Symbolist painter

"L'Apparition," oil painting by Gustave Moreau, *c.* 1876; in the Fogg Art Museum, Harvard University, Cambridge, Mass.
By courtesy of the Fogg Art Museum, Harvard University, Grenville L. Winthrop Bequest

known for his erotic paintings of mythological and religious subjects. The only influence that really affected Moreau's development was that of his master, Chassériau (1819–56), an eclectic painter whose enigmatic sea goddesses deeply impressed his student. Moreau's first picture was a "Pietà" (1852), now in the cathedral at Angoulême. In the Salon of 1853 he exhibited a "Scene from the Song of Songs" and the "Death of Darius," both conspicuously under the influence of Chassériau.

His "Oedipus and the Sphinx" (1864; Metropolitan Museum of Art, New York) and his "L'Apparition" (*c.* 1876; Fogg Art Museum, Cambridge, Mass.) and "Dance of Salome" (*c.* 1876, Musée Gustave Moreau, Paris) show that his work became increasingly concerned with exotic eroticism and violence, and his richly crowded canvases made greater use of dramatic lighting to heighten his brilliant, jewel-like colours. His last work, "Jupiter and Sémélé" (1896; Musée Gustave Moreau, Paris), is the culmination of such tendencies. The entirety of this huge work is crowded with figures and decorative surfaces precisely rendered. His art has often been described as decadent. He made a number of technical experiments, including scraping his canvases; and his nonfigurative paintings, done in a loose manner with thick impasto, have led him to be called a herald of Abstract Expressionism.

Moreau succeeded Elie Delaunay as professor at the École des Beaux-Arts, and his teaching was highly popular. He was the teacher of some of the artists of the Fauve movement, including Matisse and Rouault. At his death, Moreau left to the state his house and about 8,000 works, which now form the Musée Gustave Moreau in Paris.
·artistic style and teaching influence **11**:699a
·Impressionist use of colour and detail **19**:474g
·Rouault as student and curator **15**:1166f

Moreau, (Jean-) Victor (-Marie) (b. Feb. 14, 1763, Morlaix, Fr.—d. Sept. 2, 1813, Lahn, now in Czechoslovakia), a leading French general of the French Revolutionary Wars (1792–99); he later became a bitter opponent of Napoleon Bonaparte's regime.

The son of a lawyer, Moreau studied law at Rennes, where, in 1788, he led a student riot in protest against King Louis XVI's attempts to restrict the authority of the *parlements* (high courts of justice). Moreau welcomed the outbreak of the Revolution in the following year and immediately organized a unit of the national guard at Rennes. Elected lieutenant colonel of a battalion of volunteers in 1791, he joined Gen. Charles-François du Périer Dumouriez's Army of the North after France went to war with Austria and Prussia in 1792. Appointed general of a division in April 1794, Moreau helped Gen. Charles Pichegru conquer the Austrian Netherlands, and in March 1795 he replaced Pichegru as commander of the Army of the North.

On March 14, 1796, Moreau was given command of the armies of the Rhine and Moselle. He crossed the Rhine into Germany on June 24 and advanced toward Munich. Confronted with overwhelming opposition, he made a brilliant tactical retreat through the Black Forest, arriving in Alsace in the autumn. In April 1797, he discovered documents indicating that his friend Pichegru had been conspiring with the French émigrés (nobles in exile). He delayed in presenting this evidence to the republican government in Paris, and, as a result, he was relieved of his command on September 9, five days after the royalists had been expelled from the government (and Pichegru arrested) in a coup d'etat.

Victor Moreau, engraving by Anthony Cardon, 1802

H. Roger-Viollet

Nevertheless, Moreau was made commander of the Army of Italy in April 1799. Returning to Paris in October, he played a minor role in the military coup d'etat of 18 Brumaire (Nov. 8, 1799) that brought Bonaparte to power. Bonaparte rewarded him with the command of the Army of the Rhine and troops in the Helvetic Republic, and on Dec. 3, 1800, Moreau decisively defeated the Austrians at Hohenlinden. The victory forced Austria to sue for peace, but it also aroused Bonaparte's jealousy. The dictator's wife, Joséphine, made no attempt to hide her contempt for Moreau, and, as a result, Moreau renewed his relations with Pichegru, who was plotting to overthrow Bonaparte's regime. On Feb. 5, 1804, Moreau was arrested. Banished by Bonaparte, he emigrated to the United States. Moreau returned to Europe in 1813 on the invitation of French royalists and joined the allied forces arrayed against France. Wounded at the Battle of Dresden on August 26–27, he died several weeks later.

·conspiracy trial and conviction **13**:56d
·French Revolution territorial defense **7**:721h

Moreau River, formed by the confluence of several headstreams in Perkins County, South Dakota, U.S., flows about 290 mi (470 km) east through the Cheyenne River Indian Reservation, where it receives several north-bank tributaries (including Thunder Butte and Little Moreau), to the Missouri River south of Mobridge. The lower Moreau Basin was inundated by the Oahe Dam, a major flood-control unit of the Missouri River Basin project. The river was named for an early French trader.
45°18′ N, 100°43′ W
·map, United States **18**:908

Morecambe and Heysham, borough (1902), resort, and Irish Sea port in Lancashire, England, on Morecambe Bay. The town, whose economy is based upon the tourist industry, has a 4½-mi (7-km) promenade, a quay, and two piers. From Heysham Harbour important ferries connect with the Isle of Man and Belfast, N.Ire. Pop. (1971 prelim.) 41,863.
54°04′ N, 2°53′ W

Morecambe Bay, Irish Sea inlet bounded on the north by the county of Cumbria (until 1974 by Westmorland), England, and on the south by Lancashire. The towns of Barrow-in-Furness and Morecambe and Heysham are situated to the north and south of the entry to the bay, respectively. Much of the Lake District massif drains into the bay. In the early 1970s there were plans to construct a barrage (dam) across the bay that would create a reservoir with a capacity of 66,000,000,000 gal (2,500,000,000 hl). The water thus stored would be sufficient to supply the Greater Manchester region and similar urban areas with 500,000,000 gal of water per day.
54°07′ N, 3°00′ W

Moree, town, north New South Wales, Australia, on the Gwydir River, in the Western Slopes district. Originating in 1848 as a livestock station, it became a village (1852), a town (1862), and a municipality (1890). Its name comes from an Aboriginal word for "rising sun," "long spring," and "water hole." At the junction of the Gwydir and Newell highways, with regular air and rail service to Sydney (319 mi [513 km] southeast), Moree serves an area of pastoralism and grain farming. It is also known as a health spa, based on artesian mineral water drawn from a bore 3,000 ft (900 m) deep made in 1895. Broadwater Creek, a local stream, is a rare phenomenon; flowing into the Gwydir River during times of high water, it reverses itself at low water to flow into the Mehi River. Flooding is an occasional problem. Pop. (1971 prelim.) 9,114.
29°28′ S, 149°51′ E
·map, Australia **2**:400

Morehead, town, seat of Rowan County, northeastern Kentucky, U.S., at the edge of the Daniel Boone National Forest. Morehead is the centre of a mountain resort area and an agricultural and timber shipping point. There is some light manufacturing. It is the seat of Morehead State University (1922). Pop. (1980) 7,789.
38°11′ N, 83°25′ W
·map, United States **18**:908

Morehead, city, North Carolina, U.S. Pop. (1970) 5,233.
34°43′ N, 76°43′ W
·North Carolina port facilities **13**:232h

Morehouse, Comet (1908 III), named after Daniel Walter Morehouse (1876–1941), U.S. astronomer, was observed in 1908 and was remarkable for variations in the form and structure of its tail. This on several occasions appeared to break into fragments and to be completely separated from the head. Also, its tail became visible at twice the Earth's distance from the Sun (2 astronomical units), whereas most comets start to produce a visible tail only at about 1.5 astronomical units from the Sun.
·tail movement direction and velocity **4**:974g; illus.

morel: *see* cup fungus.

Moré language, also known as MÕÕRE, MOLE, MOSSI, and MOSHI, Niger-Congo language belonging to the Voltaic, or Gur, subgroup; is spoken by the Mossi people (and the majority of the population) of Upper Volta and by groups in Togo and Ghana.
·Togo culture and peoples **18**:472d
·Upper Volta cultural environment **18**:1019g

Morelia, capital, Michoacán state, west central Mexico. It lies between the Chiquito and Grande rivers, at the southern extreme of the central plateau, at an altitude of 6,368 ft (1,941 m). Originally known as Valladolid, the city was founded in 1541. The site was already inhabited by Tarascan Indians, and people of Indian descent still predominate. In the colonial period the city had the reputation of being an intellectual and art centre, stimulated by the Colegio San Nicolás (founded in 1540 in Pátzcuaro and moved to Morelia in 1580), claimed to be the oldest institution of higher learning in Mexico. The Baroque cathedral, completed in 1744, is an outstanding example of Spanish Renaissance church architecture,

Cathedral and plaza gardens, Morelia, Mexico

Carl Frank—Photo Researchers

and the colonial governor's palace is also an imposing structure. The 3-mi (5-km) aqueduct, carried on arches, was built in 1785 as a famine-relief project. During the Mexican wars for independence, the city served briefly as the base of operations for the revolutionary leader Miguel Hidalgo y Costilla (*q.v.*). In 1828 the city was renamed in honour of José María Morelos y Pavón, a locally born leader of the independence movement. Since 1582, when it replaced Pátzcuaro as the capital of Michoacán, Morelia has served as a commercial and processing centre for an extensive agricultural region that yields principally corn (maize), beans, fruit, sugarcane, and cattle. The Michoacana University of San Nicholás of Hidalgo (1957), which includes the original college, and the University of Michoacán (1939) are located in Morelia. The city has rail, highway, and air connections with all major Mexican urban centres. Pop. (1970) 161,040.
19°42′ N, 101°07′ W
·map, Mexico **12**:68

Morellet, André (b. March 7, 1727, Lyons—d. Jan. 12, 1819, Paris), economist and man of letters. Although he had trained for the priesthood and had taken holy orders, there was little of the religious in his nature. He had a reputation as a wit and as the author of acid pamphlets. His interest in economics led to works on such matters as the control of the corn trade and the exploitation of colonies. His *Mémoires sur le XVIII*[e] *siècle et la Révolution* (published posthumously in 1821) are a valuable record of recent upheavals by a man who remained to the end essentially a typical 18th-century Philosophe.

Morelli, Giovanni (b. Feb. 25, 1816, Verona, Italy—d. Feb. 28, 1891, Milan), patriot and art critic whose methods of direct study became basic for subsequent art criticism. As a Protestant, he was sent to Munich University where he acquired so great a command of German as to write his principal works in that language. He studied medicine but never practiced; and he took part in the war of 1848, after which he devoted much of his time to politics. In 1861, although a Protestant, he was elected deputy for Bergamo in the first free Italian parliament. Later, he became alarmed by increasingly democratic tendencies and in 1870 resigned his seat, but he was made a senator in 1873.

His principal achievement was to secure the passing of an act (named after him) prohibiting the sale of works of art from public or religious institutions and the appointment of a commission to nationalize and conserve all major works that could be regarded as public property, thus undoubtedly saving many masterpieces. Morelli had a tendency to sarcasm which, in his books, made him many enemies.

His first book, *Italian Masters in German Galleries* (1880; Eng. trans., 1883), marks an

epoch in 19th-century art criticism. The so-called "Morellian method" was followed in this and his later *Critical Studies;* essentially 19th century in its scientific rigorousness, it consisted of the apparently simple thesis that the evidence presented by the pictures themselves is superior to all other evidence, whether documentary or traditional. Further, the crux of the method was that all painters, however great, tend to fall back on a formula for rendering such details as the ear or the fingernails, and that these minor details were therefore the most characteristic parts of a picture and the surest guide to attribution. Both Morelli himself and his principal follower, Bernard Berenson, corrected hundreds of false attributions; but the limitations of his method did not pass unnoticed at the time.
·stylistic theory of artist's mastery **2**:129a

Morelly (fl. 18th century), French philosopher whose writings influenced Communist doctrine. His works, which frequently delineate a utopian society based on Communist principles, include *Essai sur l'esprit humain* (1743; "Essay on the Human Spirit"), *Essais sur le coeur humain ou principes naturels de l'éducation* (1745; "Essays on the Human Heart, or Natural Principles of Education"), and *Le Code de la nature* (1755; "The Law of Nature").
·anti-property proposals **6**:893d
·French literature development **10**:1171d

Morelos, inland state, central Mexico. It is bordered by the Federal District on the north and by the states of Puebla on the east and southeast and Guerrero on the south and southwest and by México on the west. Its 1,908-sq-mi (4,941-sq-km) territory lies on the southern slope of the central Mexican Plateau, its surface roughly broken by mountain ranges. The valleys thus formed give Morelos a variety of climates and vegetation types. It is drained by the Río Amacuzac, a northern tributary of the Mescala, or Balsas. The state is named after José María Morelos y Pavón (*q.v.*), one of the heroes of Mexico's war for independence. Morelos is one of the most flourishing agricultural states of Mexico, producing sugarcane, rice, corn (maize), wheat, fruits, and vegetables. Although the state is supposed to have several of the minerals found in that part of Mexico (silver, cinnabar, iron, lead, gold, petroleum, and coal), its mining industries have not been developed. Railways and a superhighway cross the state, linking Cuernavaca (*q.v.*), the state capital, with Mexico City and Acapulco. The population includes a large percentage of Indians and mestizos. Pop. (1970) 616,119.
·area and population table and map **12**:71

Morelos (y Pavón), José María (b. Sept. 30, 1765, Valladolid, now Morelia, Michoacán, Mex.—d. Dec. 22, 1815, San Cristóbal), revolutionary priest who assumed leadership of the Mexican independence movement after Miguel Hidalgo's 1810 rebellion and subsequent execution.

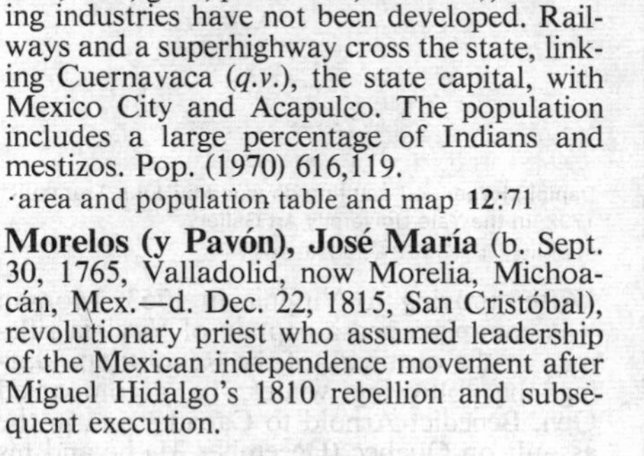

José María Morelos, detail of a portrait by an unknown artist, 19th century
By courtesy of the Instituto Nacional de Antropologia e Historia, Mexico City

Born in poverty, Morelos worked as a muleteer and cowhand until at the age of 25 he began study for the priesthood at the Colegio de San Nicolás in Valladolid. He held several obscure curacies serving mostly Indians and mestizos. Early in 1811 he joined Miguel Hidalgo's insurrection, and, after Hidalgo's death (July 31), took command of the movement in southern Mexico. Between 1812 and 1815 he controlled most of Mexico southwest of Mexico City, holding at one time or another Acapulco, Oaxaca, Tehuacán, and Cuatla. Lacking manpower to consolidate control over all the region after his victories, he turned increasingly to guerrilla tactics.

Morelos called the Congress of Chilpancingo in 1813 to form a government and draft a constitution. In November the congress declared Mexico's independence, and in October 1814, at Apatzingán, it promulgated an egalitarian constitution. The congress was safe, however, only so long as it moved from place to place under the protection of Morelos' nomadic army. Finally, royalist forces caught up with the insurgents, but Morelos fought a rearguard action allowing most of the revolutionary government to escape. He was captured, however, and, after being defrocked, was shot as a traitor.
·Hidalgo cause continuation **12**:79g
·revolution leadership and fate **10**:705d

Moremi Wildlife Reserve, Botswana, contains all major species of central African wildlife.
·Okavango delta wildlife representation **13**:541b

Morena, or PECH MORENA, town and headquarters of Morena district, Gwalior division, Madhya Pradesh state, India. An agricultural trade centre, it is connected by rail and national highway with Gwalior and Āgra. Oilseed milling and cotton weaving are the chief industries, and a college there is affiliated with Jiwaji University.

Morena district (area 4,488 sq mi, or 11,625 sq km) constituted in 1948, comprises the former Sheopur and Tonwarghar princely states. In the lower Chambal Basin, it consists of an alluvial tract in the north, cut by numerous ravines, and a forested area toward the south. Wheat and oilseeds are the main crops; building stone is quarried. The district has one cement factory, and Sheopur (*q.v.*) is an important trade centre. Pop. (1971 prelim.) town, 44,902; district, 984,461.

Morena, Sierra, mountain range, central Spain, forms the southern edge of the Meseta Central (*q.v.*), stretching for about 200 mi (320 km) from the Sierra de Alcaraz (5,896 ft [1,797 m]) in the east to the Portuguese border in the west. It includes many minor ranges that run transversely: *e.g.*, the Sierras Madrona, Sur de Alcudia, and de Aracena. The Sierra Morena, which forms the main watershed between the Guadiana and Guadalquivir rivers, is mostly wild desolate country thickly covered with dense evergreen bushes and shrubs. Its great breadth has long made it a formidable barrier in the history of Spain. Silver, lead, and copper are mined in the Linares region; mercury at Almadén; and copper at Riotinto and at Tharsis in the Sierra de Aracena. The chief communications route is via the Destiladero (pass) de Despeñaperros, which links Andalusia with Castile.
38°00′ N, 5°00′ W
·map, Spain **17**:382

morenada, Bolivian dance.
·symbolic meaning **3**:8h

Morenci (Arizona): *see* Clifton–Morenci.

More Nehukhim (theological treatise): *see* Guide of the Perplexed, The.

Moreno, Mariano (b. Sept. 3, 1778, Buenos Aires—d. 1811, at sea), patriot who was the intellectual and political leader of Argentina's movement for independence. After practicing law in Buenos Aires and holding several posts in the Spanish colonial bureaucracy, Moreno came to public attention in September 1809 with his tract *Representación de los hacendados* ("Landowners' Petition"). His argument attacking the restrictive Spanish Navigation Acts and urging that Argentines be free to trade with other nations induced concessions by the viceroy two months later.

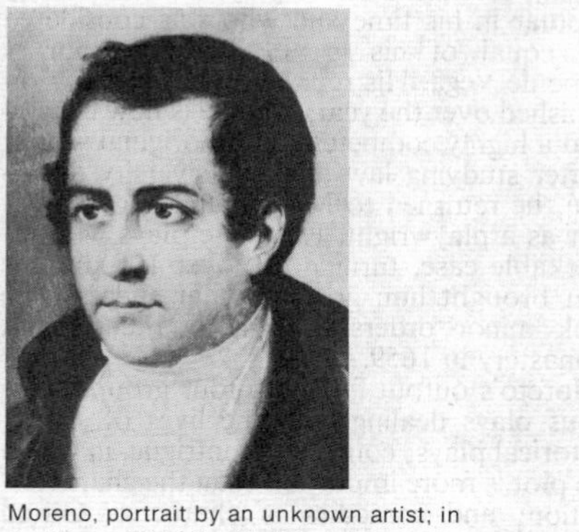

Moreno, portrait by an unknown artist; in the Museo Histórico Nacional, Buenos Aires
By courtesy of the Archivo General de la Nacion, Buenos Aires

In May 1810 a provisional junta replaced the Spanish officials in Buenos Aires, and Moreno became its secretary of military and political affairs. His ability and energy soon made him the leader of the junta. Among the decisions in which he was prominent were those to exile the viceroy and to take aggressive action to extend the revolution from Buenos Aires into the provinces. He also founded the national library and established and edited the government newspaper, *La Gaceta de Buenos Aires.* Moreno led in advocating complete separation from Spain, a course too radical for some members of the junta. (Independence was not declared until 1816.) Conservative opposition to him grew and finally forced his resignation at the end of 1810. He accepted a diplomatic mission to Brazil and Great Britain, but died at sea on his way to London.

Møre og Romsdal, *fylke* (county), of western Norway facing the Norwegian Sea. It includes the Stadlandet Peninsula in the south and extends northward to Trondheimsfjorden. The county seat is Molde. The bleak Dovrefjell (Dovre Mountains) embrace an island corner of its terrain that is characterized by a fjord-indented coastline, rugged peaks, deep valleys, and many offshore islands. About one-half of the inhabitants live on the islands. The county has an area of 5,821 sq mi (15,076 sq km) and comprises three regions: Sunnmøre (South Møre) in the south, around the port of Ålesund; Romsdalen (Romsdal Valley), in the centre, with many scenic waterfalls and the port of Åndalsnes; and Nordmøre (North Møre), in the north around the fishing port of Kristiansund. The economy is based on the coastal fisheries, tourism, and on scattered farming; there is small-scale manufacturing in the larger towns. Pop. (1971 est.) 223,709.
·area and population table **13**:265
·map, Norway **13**:266

morepork, or MOPOKE, imitative name in Australia for a bird, the tawny frogmouth (*see* frogmouth), and in Australia and New Zealand for the boobook owl.

More Pricks than Kicks (1934), collection of stories by Samuel Beckett.
·Beckett's literary development **2**:789d

mores (sociology): *see* folkways.

Moresnet, small area (1.2 sq mi [3.1 sq km]) in Liège province, Belgium, on the German border, formerly neutral territory. *See* Eupen-et-Malmédy.

moresque: *see* Morris dance.

More Stately Mansions (1964), play by Eugene O'Neill.
·posthumous publication and production **13**:573a

Moreto (y Cabaña), Agustín (b. April 1618, Madrid—d. October 1669, Toledo, Spain), dramatist whose plays were extremely popular in his time and who was considered the equal of his great near-contemporary Lope de Vega. His reputation has steadily diminished over the years, and he is now considered a highly competent but unoriginal writer.

After studying law at the University of Alcalá, he returned to Madrid and began a career as a playwright. He wrote plays with remarkable ease, turning out over 100 dramas that brought him great popular success. He took minor orders in 1642 and entered a monastery in 1659.

Moreto's output falls into four groups: religious plays dealing with the lives of saints; historical plays; comedies of intrigue, in which the plot is more important than the characterization; and comedies of character. Gifted with a sense for stagecraft, he made old stories come alive on stage. His masterpiece, *El desdén con el desdén* ("Contempt with Contempt"), based on parts of four plays of Lope, is marked, as are all his best plays, by its elegance and faithfulness to real life.

Moreton Bay, shallow inlet of the Pacific Ocean, indenting southeast Queensland, Australia. Sheltered on the north by Bribie Island and on the east and south by Moreton and Stradbroke islands, the bay measures 65 mi (105 km) by 20 mi. It is filled with numerous shoals, and some low islands lie to the south. In 1770, the British navigator Capt. James Cook discovered South Passage between the main offshore islands leading to the bay, which he named after James Douglas, 14th earl of Morton. This name was also originally applied to the mainland area that eventually became Queensland. The bay, explored (1823) by John Oxley, was the site of the state's first settlement (1824), a penal colony at Redcliffe. Receiving the Brisbane River, the bay is the gateway to the port of Brisbane, with the primary shipping channel passing between Bribie and Moreton. Its waters yield game and commerical fish.
27°20′ S, 153°15′ E

Moreton Bay pine, also called HOOP PINE, COLONIAL PINE, WHITE PINE, or RICHMOND RIVER PINE (*Araucaria cunninghamii*), a large evergreen timber conifer of the family Araucariaceae, native to the Great Dividing Range of southeastern Australia and the Pegunungan Arfak (Arfak Mountains) of western New Guinea. The tree reaches a height of about 60 metres (200 feet); its branches are horizontal and bear dense tufts of branchlets near the tips. The leaves are dagger shaped or triangular.
·longevity comparison, table 2 **10**:914
·New Hampshire importance and use **12**:1093a
·rust life cycle and control measures **16**:294g
·taxonomic features of conifers **5**:8h

Moreton Island, lies across Moreton Bay from Brisbane, off the southeast coast of Queensland, Australia. It is about 25 mi (40 km) long by 5 mi (8 km) wide and has an area of 71 sq mi (184 sq km). The island's sand dunes, originally wind formed but now fixed by vegetation, may be the world's loftiest, rising to 914 ft (279 m) at Mt. Tempest. In 1770 Capt. James Cook, the British navigator, visited the island, which he thought to be a peninsula, and named its northwest extremity Cape Moreton. The British navigator who surveyed the entire coast of Australia, Matthew Flinders, determined its insular characteristics in 1799. Site of the state's first lighthouse (1857), Moreton also had a short-lived (1952) whaling station at Tangalooma. A ferry links the island to Brisbane.
27°10′ S, 153°25′ E

Moretto, in full MORETTO DA BRESCIA, originally ALESSANDRO BONVICINO or BUONVICINO (*c.* 1498–1554), leading Italian painter of the Brescian school, whose distinctive style is characterized by a cool, silvery tone.

Morgagni, Giovanni Battista (b. Feb. 25, 1682, Forlì, Italy—d. Dec. 5, 1771, Padua), anatomist whose *Adversaria Anatomica* (1706–19) made pathological anatomy a science. He is credited, through his *De Sedibus et Causis Morborum per Anatomen Indagatis* (1761; *On the Seats and Causes of Diseases as Investigated by Anatomy*, 1769), as a founder of morbid anatomy. With Antonio Valsalva he prepared *De Aure Humana* (1704; *Anatomy and Diseases of the Ear*).

Morgagni, engraving by Giovanni Volpato (1733–1803)
Archiv fur Kunst und Geschichte

Morgagni held the chair of anatomy at Padua during most of his career. He was among the first to demonstrate the necessity for basing diagnosis, prognosis, and treatment on knowledge for anatomical conditions.
·autopsy's history as diagnostic method **2**:536d
·medicine in the 18th century **11**:830h

Morgan, breed of horse, once the most famous and widely disseminated breed in the United States; it declined in popularity, and for a while breeding was supervised by the government. The breed was founded by a horse known as Justin Morgan, after his owner. Though the horse died in 1821, his individual stamp still persists. He stood about 14 hands (56 inches, or 142 centimetres) high and was a compact, active, virile, and stylish little horse whose pedigree was probably a blend of Thoroughbred and Arabian, with some other elements. The modern Morgans average about 15 hands in height and from 900 to 1,100 pounds (408–499 kilograms) in weight. They are stylish and attractive, with smooth lines, small ears, expressive eyes, and a nicely crested neck. They are an all-purpose horse though they lean toward the riding-horse type more than formerly. The *American Morgan Horse Register* was first published in 1894 by Colonel Battell of Middlebury, Vermont, who traced Justin Morgan's descendants and encouraged Morgan breeding. The Morgan Horse Club was organized in 1909 and took over the *Register*.

Morgan
Paul Quinn

·breeding and general features **10**:1284b
·origin, characteristics, and uses **8**:1091f

Morgan, Charles (Langbridge) (b. Jan. 22, 1894, Bromley, Kent—d. Feb. 6, 1958, London), novelist, playwright, and critic, a distinguished writer of a refined prose who stood apart from the main literary trends of his time. His early novel *My Name Is Legion* (1925) shows his preoccupation with the conflict between the spirit and the flesh and his predilection for a form of secular mysticism. *Portrait in a Mirror* (1929) and subsequent novels—*The Fountain* (1932), *Sparkenbrooke* (1936), *The Voyage* (1940), *The Empty Room* (1941), and *The Judge's Story* (1947)—exhibit his subtle analysis of motive and character, as well as his narrative skill. Morgan also wrote three successful plays—*The Flashing Stream* (1938), *The River Line* (1952), and *The Burning Glass* (1953).

Morgan, Conwy Lloyd (1852–1936), British zoologist and psychologist, sometimes called the founder of comparative psychology. He was successively professor, principal, and vice chancellor of the University of Bristol.
·theoretic contributions to ethology **19**:1168a

Morgan, Daniel (b. 1736, Hunterdon County, N.J.—d. July 6, 1802, Winchester, Va.), general in the American Revolution (1775–83) who won an important victory against the British at the Battle of Cowpens (Jan. 17, 1781).

Daniel Morgan, oil painting on wood by John Trumbull, 1792; in the Yale University Art Gallery
By courtesy of the Yale University Art Gallery

After moving to Virginia in 1753, Morgan was commissioned a captain of Virginia riflemen at the outbreak of the Revolution. During the following winter, he accompanied Gen. Benedict Arnold to Canada, and in the assault on Quebec (December 31) he and his riflemen penetrated well into the city, where he was hemmed in and forced to surrender. Late in 1776 he was released, however, and soon commissioned colonel. In September 1777 he joined Gen. Horatio Gates and took part in both Battles of Saratoga (N.Y.) that fall.

Partly because of ill health, Morgan resigned from the army in 1779 and retired to Virginia. After the disastrous U.S. defeat at the Battle of Camden, S.C. (1780), however, he agreed to join Gates at Hillsborough, N.C., where he took command of a corps and was made brigadier general. Aiming at slowing Lord Cornwallis' advance in the South, Morgan gradually retired northward and then turned suddenly at Cowpens to confront the enemy with a force of fewer than 1,000 men. Mainly because of his effective use of cavalry, Morgan won a brilliant and unexpected victory over a larger force under Col. Banastre Tarleton. He then escaped Cornwallis and rejoined his command.

In 1794 Morgan led federal troops into western Pennsylvania to suppress the Whiskey Rebellion. He was a Federalist representative in Congress from 1797 to 1799.

·Greene's clash with Cornwallis **19**:604g; map 605
·musket substitution for rifles in Morgan's battalion **16**:896h

Morgan, Sir Henry (b. 1635, Llanrhymney, Glamorgan—d. Aug. 25, 1688, probably Lawrencefield, Jamaica), Welsh buccaneer,

Henry Morgan, detail of an engraving by an unknown artist

By courtesy of the trustees of the British Museum; photograph, J.R. Freeman & Co. Ltd.

most famous of the adventurers who plundered Spain's Caribbean colonies during the late 17th century. Operating with the unofficial support of the English government, he seriously undermined Spanish authority in the West Indies.

Morgan's origins and early career are obscure. He was probably a member of the expedition that in 1655 seized Jamaica from the Spanish and converted it into an English colony. He may have participated in an expedition against Cuba in 1662; and during the second Anglo-Dutch War (1665–67), he was second in command of the buccaneers operating against Dutch colonies in the Caribbean.

Selected commander of the buccaneers in 1668, Morgan quickly captured Puerto Príncipe (now Camagüey), Cuba, and—in an extraordinarily daring move—stormed and sacked the well-fortified city of Portobelo on the Isthmus of Panama. In 1669 he made a successful raid on wealthy Spanish settlements around Lake Maracaibo on the coast of Venezuela. Finally, in August 1670 Morgan, with 36 ships and nearly 2,000 buccaneers, set out to capture Panamá, one of the chief cities of Spain's American empire. Crossing the Isthmus of Panama, he defeated a large Spanish force (Jan. 18, 1671) and entered the city, which burned to the ground while his men were looting it. On the return journey he deserted his followers and absconded with most of the booty.

Because Morgan's raid on Panamá had taken place after the conclusion of a peace between England and Spain, he was arrested and transported to London (April 1672). Nevertheless, relations with Spain quickly deteriorated, and in 1674 King Charles II knighted Morgan and sent him out again as deputy governor of Jamaica, where he lived as a wealthy and respected planter until his death.

An exaggerated account of Morgan's exploits, written by one of his crew, created his popular reputation as a bloodthirsty pirate.

Morgan, John (b. June 10, 1735, Philadelphia—d. Oct. 15, 1789, Philadelphia), pioneer of U.S. medical education, surgeon general of the Continental armies during the U.S. War of Independence, founded the United States' first medical school. A colonial army surgeon during the French and Indian War (1757–60), he studied at the University of Edinburgh (M.D. 1763), at Paris, and in Italy. His doctoral thesis, *De Puopoiesi* ("Concerning the Formation of Pus"), maintained that pus is secreted by the blood vessels, a fact established by the German pathologist Julius Cohnheim a century later.

Returning to the colonies in 1765, he founded their first medical school at the College of Philadelphia (now the University of Pennsylvania) and there was appointed North America's first professor of medicine. His policies of requiring a liberal education for medical students and the separation of medicine, surgery, and pharmacology into distinct disciplines, outlined in his *Discourse upon the Institution of Medical Schools in America* (1765), met with widespread opposition from colonial physicians and failed to gain acceptance.

Although he had written one of the *Four Dissertations on the Reciprocal Advantages of a Perpetual Union Between Great Britain and Her American Colonies* (1766), Morgan became an ardent patriot and was appointed "Director-General to the Military Hospitals and Physician-in-Chief to the American Army" by the Continental Congress in 1775. A violent quarrel immediately erupted between him and William Shippen, who had joined Morgan in founding the Philadelphia Medical School, but who then headed a faction seeking to oust him from office.

Morgan failed to bring autonomous regimental surgeons under general army control and in 1777 was dismissed from his post by Congress. He immediately published *Vindication*, attacking Shippen, and refused to reassume his chair at the medical school, where Shippen continued to serve as professor of anatomy and surgery. Although Gen. George Washington and Congress vindicated Morgan in 1779, he never recovered from his disgrace and died an impoverished recluse 10 years later. One of the first U.S. physicians to adopt the English physician Edward Jenner's method of inoculation against smallpox, Morgan also wrote *A Recommendation of Inoculation* (1776).

Morgan, J(ohn) P(ierpont) (b. April 17, 1837, Hartford, Conn.—d. March 31, 1913, Rome), U.S. financier and industrial organizer, one of the world's primary financial figures during the two pre-World War I decades. He reorganized several major railroads and consolidated the United States Steel, International Harvester, and General Electric corporations.

The son of a successful financier, Junius Spencer Morgan (1813–90), John Pierpont became a partner in 1871 of the New York City firm of Drexel, Morgan and Company, which soon became the predominant source of U.S. government financing. Renamed J.P. Morgan and Company in 1895, the firm became one of the most powerful banking houses in the world.

Morgan began reorganizing railroads in 1885, when he arranged for the merger of the New York Central, owned by railway magnate William H. Vanderbilt, with competing New York lines. Between 1885 and 1888 he extended his influence to lines based in Pennsylvania and Ohio, and after the financial panic of 1893 he was called upon to rehabilitate several major lines, including the Southern Railway, the Erie, and the Northern Pacific.

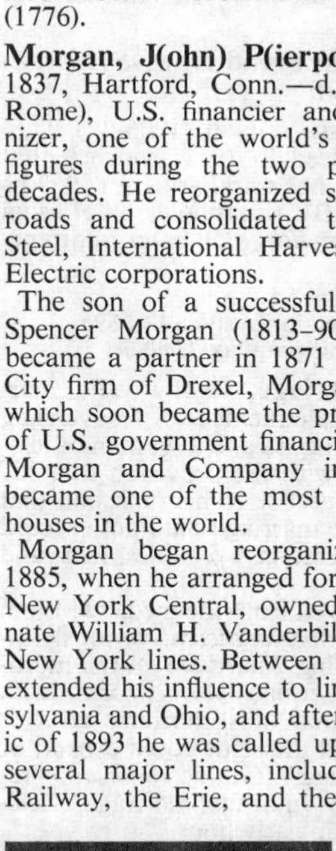

J.P. Morgan, 1902

By courtesy of the Library of Congress, Washington, D.C.

He helped to achieve railroad rate stability and discourage overly chaotic competition in the East. By gaining control of much of the stock of the railroads that he influenced, he became one of the world's most powerful railroad leaders by 1900.

In 1895 Morgan formed a syndicate to resupply the government's depleted gold reserve and relieve a Treasury crisis. Three years later he began financing industrial consolidations, forming the Federal Steel Company and, in 1901, the United States Steel Corporation, the largest corporation in the world at that time. He then financed International Harvester and the International Merchant Marine, an amalgamation of a majority of the transatlantic shipping lines, in 1902.

Morgan played a key role in the financial crisis of 1907, using his banking house and affiliated banks to take in large government deposits and dominating the decisions on how the money was to be used for financial relief.

In 1912 a committee of the U.S. House of Representatives investigated his operations. Morgan had become a symbol of the "money trust" and its top-heavy concentration of economic power in the nation's leading corporations and financial institutions. Also a renowned art collector, he donated many works to the Metropolitan Museum of Art in New York City.

His son, John Pierpont Morgan, Jr. (1867–1943), who became head of the banking house of Morgan in 1913, helped finance the Allies' supply and credit needs during World War I

J.P. Morgan, Jr.

By courtesy of the Morgan Guaranty Trust Co.

and, after the war, floated $1,700,000,000 in loans for European reconstruction. He was the last Morgan to head the family banking house.

·Tesla's broadcasting tower project **18**:162b

Morgan, Lewis Henry (b. Nov. 21, 1818, near Aurora, N.Y.—d. Dec. 17, 1881, Rochester), ethnologist and a principal founder of scientific anthropology, known especially for establishing the study of kinship systems and for his comprehensive theory of social evolution.

An attorney by profession, Morgan practiced law at Rochester (1844–62) and served in the New York State Assembly (1861–68) and Senate (1868–69). In the early 1840s he developed a deep interest in American Indians and over his lifetime championed the Indian struggle against white oppression. While making an exhaustive survey of the history, social organization, and material culture of the Iroquois Indians, he was adopted by the Seneca tribe (1846), the object of his particular interest. Results of his observations appeared in *The League of the Ho-dé-no-sau-nee, or Iroquois* (1851).

About 1856, Morgan's interest turned to the Seneca way of designating relatives, which differed markedly from Anglo-American convention. Upon discovering virtually identical designations among the Ojibwa of northern Michigan, he conjectured that if the system were also to be found in Asia, the Asiatic origin of the American Indians might be shown. Embarking on far-flung field research in the Hudson Bay region of Canada, the Great Plains, and the Southwest region of the U.S., he also sent questionnaires abroad in his effort to substantiate whether the American Indians had migrated from Asia to North America. In his influential pioneer elaboration of kinship, *Systems of Consanguinity and Affinity of the Human Family* (1871), he contended that kinship terminology in a part of India positively corroborated his migration theory. Also attracted to Australian ethnology, he published the first anthropological study of Australian kinship (1872) and was also the mentor of other efforts in Australian ethnology.

Morgan's kinship study led him to develop his theory of cultural evolution, advanced in *Ancient Society, or Researches in the Lines of Human Progress from Savagery through Barbarism to Civilization* (1877). This was the first major scientific account of the origin and evolution of civilization, with illustrations of developmental stages drawn from various cultures. Though his view on the evolution of the family has long been held obsolete, many of his other observations remain valid and significant, including his distinction between primitive and civil society; his assessment of cultural evolution in technology; and his attention to cultural survivals, institutions persisting in later cultural stages with evidence of their earlier origins. Morgan's emphasis on property in cultural evolution, his consideration of the revolutionary character of social change, and his prediction of a more equitable social order attracted the attention of Karl Marx and Friedrich Engels. That *Ancient Society* became a Marxist classic was largely the result of the importance that Marx and Engels attached to it, because Morgan's own social allegiance was to the industrial and commercial middle class and its achievements. For a number of years Morgan remained the dean of U.S. anthropology. Among his other works is *The Indian Journals, 1859–1862* (1959). There is a biography, *Lewis Henry Morgan: American Scholar* (1960), by Carl Resek.

·anthropological evolutionism **1**:971a
·cultural stages of evolution **4**:657h
·culture development similarity theory **8**:1155f
·kinship relationship studies **10**:478c
·social evolution theory **16**:985f
·sociocultural change theory influence **16**:920b

Morgan, Lady Sydney, *née* OWENSON (b. Dec. 25, 1776, Dublin—d. April 16, 1859, London), better remembered for her personality than for her many successful novels. Established as a popular novelist with *The Wild Irish Girl* (1806), a paean of praise of Ireland in a fictional guise, she took London by storm. The Marquess of Abercorn made her his "companion," but in 1812 married her off to her own surgeon, Sir Thomas Charles Morgan, for whom he had prudently arranged a knighthood.

After marriage she continued her output of novels, verse, and essays. *O'Donnel* (1814), considered her best novel for its realistic treatment of Irish peasant life, was followed by *France* (1817), a survey of French society and politics in a breezy, journalistic style, which was savagely attacked by the influential Tory *Quarterly Review* for its praise of the French Revolution. Lady Morgan struck back with *Florence McCarthy* (1816), a novel in which a *Quarterly* reviewer is subtly caricatured.

Morgan, Thomas Hunt 12:440 (b. Sept. 25, 1866, Lexington, Ky.—d. Dec. 4, 1945, Pasadena, Calif.), geneticist and embryologist, is famous for experimental research with the fruit fly (*Drosophila*) and establishment of the chromosome theory of heredity.

Abstract of text biography. Morgan showed an interest in natural history early in life and earned a doctorate in zoology in 1890 from Johns Hopkins University. He began an elaborate series of experiments that illustrated the validity of Mendelism and the cell basis for it.

He and his collaborators Sturtevant, Bridges, and Muller wrote the influential book *The Mechanism of Mendelian Heredity* (1915). Morgan received many awards and honours, including the Nobel Prize for Physiology or Medicine in 1933.

REFERENCES in other text articles:
·biological sciences development **2**:1025b
·experimental genetics contributions **12**:614d
·gene and chromosome research **19**:1167b
·gene linkage and recombination **7**:982h
·heredity theories **8**:806c

Morgan, William (b. *c.* 1545, Caernarvon, Caernarvonshire—d. Sept. 10, 1604, St. Asaph, Flintshire), Anglican bishop of the Reformation whose translation of the Bible into Welsh helped standardize the literary language of his country. Ordained in 1568, he became a parish priest at Llanrhaeadr ym Mochnant, Denbighshire, ten years later and was appointed bishop of Llandaff in 1595 and of St. Asaph in 1601. His translation of the Bible and the Apocrypha, published in 1588, was meant to complete the work of the Welsh writer William Salesbury, whose translation of the New Testament and *The Book of Common Prayer* appeared in 1567.

In his dedication to Queen Elizabeth I, Morgan acknowledges the assistance given him in translation by the Welsh scholar Edmund Prys, archdeacon of Merioneth and author of a version of the Psalms in the metre of the Welsh ballad style. Morgan's adaptation of the diction and style of earlier literature was further affirmed in the revised translation by the Welsh bishop John Davies in 1620. The literary Welsh thus established was subsequently taught to the Welsh public for more than 200 years; Davies' revision of Morgan's Bible remained in use in Wales into the 20th century.

Morgan, William Frend De: *see* De Morgan, William Frend.

Morgan, William Wilson (1906–), U.S. astronomer, adduced in 1951 evidence that the Earth's galaxy has spiral arms. In 1953 he established the UBV (ultraviolet blue visual magnitudes) system for wide-band photometry.

·galaxy classification **7**:829b
·luminosity classification system **17**:589c
·stellar spectroscopic parallax **13**:996e

morganatic marriage, legally valid marriage between a male member of a sovereign, princely, or noble house and a woman of lesser birth or rank, with the provision that she shall not thereby accede to his rank and that the children of the marriage shall not succeed to their father's hereditary dignities, fiefs, and entailed property.

The name is derived from the medieval Latin *matrimonium ad morganaticum*, variously interpreted as meaning "marriage on the morning gift" (from German *Morgengabe*), with the implication that this morning gift, or dowry, was all that the bride could expect; or "restricted marriage" (Gothic *maurjan*, "restrain"); or simply "morning marriage," celebrated quietly at an early hour.

Essentially a German institution, it was adopted by some dynasties outside Germany but not by those of France or England. The practice ensues from the German notion of *Ebenbürtigkeit* or *Gleichbürtigkeit* (evenness or equality of birth), which in the Middle Ages had a widespread application in German law. It required parties to many sorts of transaction to be of the same standing or estate but could not be an impediment to marriage in the law of the church.

Morgan City, St. Mary Parish, southern Louisiana, U.S., on Berwick Bay (bridged to Berwick) of the Atchafalaya River (there widened into Six Mile Lake), and on the Gulf Intracoastal Waterway. Founded in 1850, it was incorporated (1860) as Brashear City but was renamed in 1876 to honour Charles Morgan, president of the New Orleans, Opelousas and Great Western Railroad, which established its western terminus there. During the Civil War, the city was a strategic point as the locale for forts and gunboats. Morgan City is headquarters for offshore oil drilling and is the base of a large shrimp fleet. Manufactures include chemicals, machinery, and metal and seafood products. Nearby waterways, forests, and rice fields provide excellent hunting for small game and ducks. Pop. (1980) 16,114. 29°42′ N, 91°12′ W

·map, United States **18**:908

morganite, gem-quality beryl (*q.v.*) whose lovely pink or rose-lilac colour is due to the presence of cesium. It is often found with peach, orange, or pinkish-yellow beryl (also called morganite); these colours transform to pink or purplish with high-temperature heat treatment. Morganite crystals often show colour banding: blue near the base, through nearly colourless in the centre, to peach or pink at the terminations. This colour change is probably caused by differences in the composition of the solution from which the crystal grew. Typical occurrences are as squat, tabular crystals in lithia pegmatites, as in southern California and New England.

·gem characteristics and value **7**:970a
·jewelry-making materials and sources **10**:165a

Morgan le Fay, a fairy enchantress of Arthurian legend and romance linked with various personages in Celtic mythology. Geoffrey of Monmouth's *Vita Merlini* (*c.* 1150) named her as the ruler of Avalon, a marvellous island where King Arthur was to be healed of his wounds, and it described her as skilled in the arts of healing and of changing shape. In Chrétien de Troyes's romance of *Erec* (*c.* 1165), she first appeared as King Arthur's sister. In 12th–13th-century elaborations of Arthurian legend two themes, healing and hostility (due to unrequited love), were developed: in the early-13th-century Vulgate cycle (*see* Arthurian legend), for example, she was responsible for stirring up trouble between Arthur and his queen, Guinevere, yet finally appeared as a beneficent figure conveying Arthur to Avalon. Her magic powers were explained as learned from books and from the enchanter Merlin. Although later versions of the legend placed Arthur's death in a Christian context, traditions of a living Arthur being tended by Morgan le Fay (until the time should come for him to return to his kingdom) survived in some 13th–14th-century texts, many of them associated with Sicily—perhaps taken there by Norman conquerors—where the term Fata Morgana is still used, to designate a mirage sometimes seen in the Strait of Messina.

Morgannwg, ancient Welsh principality.

·Welsh history to 1536 **3**:229e

Morgantown, city, north central West Virginia, U.S., seat (1782) of Monongalia County, on the Monongahela River. The first settlement (1758), near the Scioto-Monongahela Trail, fell to an Indian raid. Zackquill Morgan, son of West Virginia's first permanent settler, Morgan ap Morgan, founded a new community in 1766. The first steamboat arrived in 1826, and since then a large river traffic has developed; coal (mined since 1833) is shipped from the Scott's Run bituminous field. Limestone is quarried nearby, and a variety of goods are manufactured, including glass, plumbing supplies, and textiles.

West Virginia University (chartered as an agricultural college in 1867) is in the city and maintains experimental farms and forests nearby. The Morgantown Research Center, 4 mi northwest, is maintained by the U.S. Bureau of Mines. The Cheat River is dammed northeast of Morgantown to form Cheat Lake, site of Mont Chateau State Park.

Coopers Rock State Forest is nearby. Inc. town, 1786; city, 1905. Pop. (1980) 27,605.
39°38′ N, 79°57′ W

Morganucodon, fossil genus of early, primitive mammals found in Late Triassic fissure fillings of Europe and eastern Asia (the Triassic Period began 225,000,000 years ago and lasted 35,000,000 years). The skull and lower jaw show resemblances to those of the therapsids, advanced mammal-like reptiles. Forms apparently related to *Morganucodon* have also been found in South Africa.

Morgarten, Battle of (Nov. 15, 1315), the first great military success of the Swiss Confederation in its struggle against the Austrian Habsburgs. When the men of Schwyz, a member state of the confederation, raided the neighbouring abbey of Einsiedeln early in 1314, the Habsburg duke Leopold I of

The Battle of Morgarten, 1315, illumination from Diebold Schilling's chronicle of Bern, 1484; in the Burgerbibliothek, Bern
By courtesy of the Burgerbibliothek, Bern

Austria, who claimed jurisdiction in the area, raised an army of knights for an invasion of Schwyz from Zug by way of the Morgarten Pass alongside Lake Egeri (Ägerisee). The men of Schwyz, however, and some confederates from Uri caught the Austrians before they were out of the pass, killed some 1,500 of them outright, drove others in the lake, and put the rest to flight. The victory ensured the survival of the confederation, which was formally renewed less than a month later (Pact of Brunnen, Dec. 9, 1315). Because of the prestige won by Schwyz in this battle, the confederation as a whole is still known to foreigners as Schweiz, Suisse, or Switzerland.
·Swiss Confederation victory **17**:879h

morgen, Prussian unit of area, equivalent to 0.631 acre (0.255 hectare); in South Africa and formerly in the Netherlands, equivalent to 2.117 acres (0.857 hectare).
·weights and measures, table 5 **19**:734

Morgenstern, Christian (b. May 6, 1871, Munich—d. March 31, 1914, Meran, now Merano, Italy), German poet famous for his nonsense verse, which nevertheless carries a deeper meaning. His humour relies mainly on the incongruous juxtaposition of human experiences and on the subtle but skeptical exploration of the possibilities of language. His collections of lyric poetry are *Galgenlieder* (1905), *Palmström* (1910), *Palma Kunkel* (1916), *Der Gingganz* (1919).
·nondidactic poetry **4**:238a

Morgenstern, Oskar (b. Jan. 24, 1902, Görlitz, now in East Germany—d. July 26, 1977, Princeton, N.J.), German-born U.S. economist, professor at the University of Vienna (1929–38) and at Princeton (1938–70) and New York (1970–77) universities. With John von Neumann he wrote *Theory of Games and Economic Behavior* (1944), applying Neumann's theory of games of strategy (published 1928) to competitive business. Among his other books are *On the Accuracy of Economic Observations* (1950; for the U.S. Office of Naval Research), *Prolegomena to a Theory of Organization* (1951; for the U.S. Air Force), and *Predictability of Stock Market Prices* (1970; with C.W.J. Granger).
·game theory in economic
measurement **11**:740d
·optimization theory and method **13**:622d

Morgenthau, Hans J(oachim) (b. Feb. 17, 1904, Coburg, now in West Germany—d. July 19, 1980, New York City), political scientist and historian noted as a leading analyst of power in international politics.

Educated at the universities of Berlin, Frankfurt, and Munich, Morgenthau did postgraduate work at the Graduate Institute for International Studies at Geneva. He was admitted to the bar in 1927 and served as acting president of the Labour Law Court in Frankfurt. In 1932 he went to Geneva to teach public law for a year but, because of Hitler's rise to power in Germany in 1933, stayed on until 1935. In 1935–36 he taught in Madrid and then in 1937 took up residence in the United States (naturalized 1943), serving on the faculties of Brooklyn (N.Y.) College (1937–39), the University of Kansas City, Mo. (1939–43), the University of Chicago (1943–71), the City College of the City University of New York (1968–74), and, from 1974, the New School for Social Research.

In 1948 Morgenthau published *Politics Among Nations*, a highly regarded study of international relations that became a leading textbook, presenting a modern realist approach to international politics. Central to Morgenthau's theory is the concept of power as the dominant goal in international politics and the definition of national interest in terms of power. He points out the need for recognition of the nature and limits of power and for the use of traditional methods of diplomacy, including compromise.

A contributor to numerous scholarly periodicals and journals of opinion, Morgenthau is also the author of *Scientific Man vs. Power Politics* (1946), *In Defense of the National Interest* (1951), *Dilemmas of Politics* (1958), *The Purpose of American Politics* (1960), *Politics in the Twentieth Century* (3 vol., 1962), *Vietnam and the United States* (1965), *Truth and Power* (1970), and *Science: Master or Servant?* (1972).
·power politics in international relations **9**:781f

Morgenthau, Henry, Jr. (b. May 11, 1891, New York City—d. Feb. 6, 1967, Poughkeepsie, N.Y.), U.S. secretary of the treasury who,

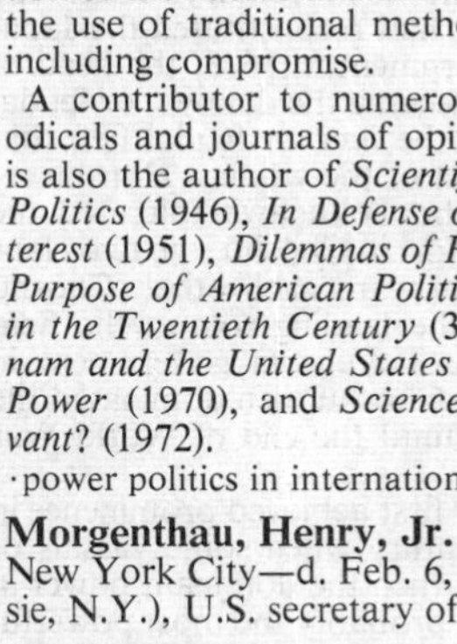

Henry Morgenthau, Jr.
By courtesy of the Library of Congress, Washington, D.C.

during his 12 years in office (1934–45) under Pres. Franklin D. Roosevelt, supervised without scandal the spending of $370,000,000,000—three times more money than had passed through the hands of his 50 predecessors combined. Editor of a farm journal, *American Agriculturist*, from 1922 to 1933, Morgenthau became a close friend of Roosevelt, whose Hyde Park estate was near Morgenthau's farm in Dutchess County, New York. During Roosevelt's governorship of New York (1929–33), Morgenthau served as state conservation commissioner and as chairman of the governor's agricultural advisory committee.

In 1933 Morgenthau accompanied Roosevelt to Washington, where, before being appointed to the treasury office in January 1934, he served in several offices. Conservative and orthodox in his economic views, he was frequently torn between his intense loyalty to the President and his conviction that a balanced budget was essential to the national welfare. In the end, he wholeheartedly supported financing the ambitious New Deal domestic program and the nation's enormous responsibilities in World War II. He formulated the Morgenthau Plan, which aimed at crippling German industrial potential after the war but was never put into effect. He resigned shortly after Roosevelt's death (April 1945).

After retirement, Morgenthau devoted himself to his farm, to philanthropic interests, and to foreign travel. His official records, filling more than 800 bound volumes, were turned over to the Franklin D. Roosevelt library at Hyde Park.
·Octagon Conference occupation
policy **19**:1008f

Morhange, Charles-Henri Valentin: *see* Alkan.

Moriah, Mount (Jerusalem): *see* Temple Mount.

Mori Arinori (b. 1847, Kagoshima Prefecture, Kyushu, Japan—d. 1899, Ise, Honshu), one of the most influential and iconoclastic proponents of Western ideas in Japan during the late 19th century.

Mori early developed an interest in Western studies, and in 1865 he was among the first Japanese to go abroad (to London University) for an education. He returned to Japan after the Meiji Restoration in 1868 and in 1870 was invited to join the new imperial government. He was appointed an investigator of parliamentary and educational systems and deputy minister to the U.S.

In 1873 Mori, together with 15 other prominent intellectuals—including Fukuzawa Yukichi—formed the Meirokusha (Sixth Year of Meiji Society), to popularize Western ideas. Mori, one of the most vigorous westernizers of the group, wore Western clothing, engaged in ballroom dancing, and even advocated the writing of Japanese in the Latin alphabet.

After the Meirokusha was dissolved in 1875, Mori continued to serve in the new government, where he gained increasing influence. In 1885 he was appointed the first minister of education. He helped develop a new centralized educational system, from primary school to national university education. These schools not only educated the elite in Western subjects but also indoctrinated the general populace with Confucian ethics and patriotic fervour. Mori's iconoclasm, however, resulted in his death; he was assassinated by a religious fanatic when he supposedly desecrated the Ise Shrine, one of the holy places of the Shintō religion.
·Korean policy mission in China **4**:363c
·Meiji educational reform **6**:371e

moribana (Japanese: "heaped up flowers," referring to piles of flowers in a bowl), in Japanese floral art, a style of arrangement in which naturalistic landscapes are constructed in low, dishlike vases. Developed in the early 20th century by the floral master Ohara Unshin, *moribana* breaks with the rigid structural rules of classical floral art; it may incorporate flowers imported from Western countries and uses the triangular principle of floral art

Moribana arrangement
By courtesy of Houn Ohara

in a three-dimensional (foreground, middle ground, and distance) rather than a vertical way.

In *moribana* the arranger conceives of the flat vase as four separate quarters: the part facing the room represents the south and summer; farthest away is the north and winter; the quarter to the right is the east and spring; to the left is west and autumn. He positions the arrangement in the dish according to the season represented; *e.g.*, a winter arrangement of dried flowers is placed in the "winter" quarter, with the three remaining sections holding only water. One of the most popular branches of the Moribana school is *bonkei*, the art of creating miniature landscape gardens.

·floral decoration style development **7**:418g

Móricz, Zsigmond (b. June 29, 1879, Csécse, Austria-Hungary, now in Hungary—d. Sept. 4, 1942, Budapest), realist novelist who wrote of villages and country towns. While working as a journalist, he published his first story (1908) in the review *Nyugat* ("The West"), which he later came to edit. In his many novels and short stories, finely characterized men and women of various social classes come into collision, and their fierce energies collapse or degenerate into a murderous passion. Some of his works are veritable dances of death of the morbid and doomed elements of society.

Móricz
Interfoto MTI

Móricz's greatest works include his first novel, *Sárarany* (1910; "Gold in the Mire"), and *A boldog ember* (1935; "The Happy Man"), which portray individualist peasant characters against the collective life of a village. *Kivilágos kivirradtig* (1924; "Till the Small Hours of Morning") and *Rokonok* (1930; "Relatives") deal with the life of the decaying provincial nobility. In Móricz's world, marriage and family life are fraught with bitter conflicts; but he also evokes pure, even idyllic, love as in *Légy jó mindhalálig* (1920; "Be Good Till Death"), often considered the finest book about children written in Hungarian, and in *Pillangó* (1925; "Butterfly"). He also wrote monumental historical novels, *Erdély trilógia* (1922–35; "Transylvania, a Trilogy") and *Rózsa Sándor* (1940–42). He was a master of Hungarian, his style absorbing elements of both the old language and the dialects.

Morier, James Justinian (b. *c.* 1780, Smyrna, modern Izmir, Tur.—d. March 19, 1849, Brighton, Sussex), English diplomat and writer whose fame depends on *The Adventures of Hajji Baba of Ispahan* (1824), a picaresque romance of Persian life that long influenced English ideas of Persia; its Persian translation (1905) led to the development of the modern Persian novel of social criticism. The first of a series of novels written by Morier after he retired, it drew on his knowledge of Persia and its people, acquired on the British embassy staff at Tehrān (1809–15) and in journeys described in two travel books. It pleased a public with a taste for Oriental tales and is still

Morier, portrait by an unknown artist
Radio Times Hulton Picture Library

read—although Morier's other works are forgotten—for its authentic account of everyday life in early-19th-century Persia and for its entertaining incidents and sparkling narrative style.

Mōri family, a clan that dominated the strategic western Honshu region of south central Japan from early in the 16th century to the middle of the 19th century. After the Tokugawa family had reconstituted the Japanese central government in 1603, the head of the Mōri family became the daimyo, or feudal lord, of Chōshū, the *han*, or feudal fief, that encompassed most of the western Honshu region. Although the Tokugawa tolerated the existence of the Mōri in Chōshū, the two clans remained hostile toward each other. Chōshū warriors played the leading role in the final overthrow of the Tokugawa government in 1867, after which Chōshū men dominated the new government until the end of World War II.

The Mōri family first achieved prominence in the early 16th century when some vassals of the Ōuchi family, then the dominant power in west Honshu and probably the most powerful warriors in all Japan, revolted against the Ōuchi's autocratic rule. Under the leadership of Mōri Motonari (1497–1571) his family, though not directly involved in the uprising, was able to profit by the revolt, and in 1557 he became the new overlord of west Honshu.

Motonari's grandson, Mōri Terumoto (1553–1625), became the major opponent of Oda Nobunaga (1534–82) when that great warrior made his bid to reunify Japan. After Oda was assassinated in 1582, however, Terumoto made peace with Oda's successor, Toyotomi Hideyoshi (1537–98), whose trusted general he became. Before Hideyoshi died in 1598, he named Terumoto as one of the five regents who were to govern the country for his infant son, Hideyori (1593–1615). When fighting erupted among the regents, Terumoto sided against Tokugawa Ieyasu (1542–1616), the eventual victor. Because Terumoto's resistance had been minimal, the Mōri family was permitted to retain almost half of its Chōshū domain.

Nevertheless, throughout the Tokugawa period (1603–1867) the Mōri family indoctrinated their warriors with hatred of the Tokugawa family and respect for the emperor, whose power the Tokugawa usurped in 1603. When Chōshū warriors led the fight to overthrow the Tokugawa in 1867, they did so under the banner of restoring power to the emperor.

Moriguchi, city, Ōsaka Urban Prefecture (*fu*), Honshu, Japan, on the southern bank of the Yodo-gawa (Yodo River). A prosperous post town on the Ōsaka–Kaida road during the Tokugawa era (1603–1867), it rapidly industrialized with the opening of a railway to Ōsaka in 1910. Manufactures include electrical machinery and appliances, textiles, and processed foods. The city is also a residential suburb of Ōsaka. The rural area north of Moriguchi is famous for its radishes, while the southern outskirts are known for lotus flowers. Pop. (1970) 184,446.
34°44′ N, 135°34′ E

Mörike, Eduard Friedrich (b. Sept. 8, 1804, Ludwigsburg—d. June 4, 1875, Stuttgart), one of Germany's greatest lyric poets, some critics putting him next to his master Goethe. After studying theology at Tübingen (1822–26), Mörike held several curacies before becoming, in 1834, pastor of Cleversulzbach, the remote Württemberg village immortalized in *Der alte Turmhahn*, where inhabitants and pastor are seen through the whimsical but percipient eyes of an old weathercock. All his life Mörike suffered from psychosomatic illnesses, no doubt intensified by unconscious conflict between humanism and church dogmas. When only 39, Mörike retired on a pension, but after his marriage to Margarete von Speeth in 1851, he supplemented his pension by lecturing on German literature at a girls' school in Stuttgart. After happy years of rich literary achievement, tensions caused by Margarete's jealousy of Clara, Mörike's sister who lived with them, almost killed his creative urge. Mörike spent his last two years with Clara and his younger daughter, separated from Margarete, and died poor and unhappy.

The variety of Mörike's small output is astonishing. Everything he wrote has its distinctive flavour, but in his early days romantic influences preponderate. His novel, *Maler Nolten* (1832), in addition to its stylistic perfection and psychological insight into mental unbalance, explores the realm of the subconscious and the mysterious forces linking Nolten and his early love even beyond the grave. Mörike's poems in folk-song style and his fairy tales also smack of German romanticism, though his best folk tale, *Das Stuttgarter Hutzelmännlein* (1853), is peculiarly his own, with its Swabian background and humour. In his *Novelle, Mozart auf der Reise nach Prag* (1856), Mörike penetrates deeper into Mozart's personality than do many longer studies. It is, however, as a lyric poet that Mörike is supreme. Mörike handled free rhythms, sonnets, regular stanza forms and, more particularly in his later poems, classical metres, with equal virtuosity. The "Peregrina" poems, immortalizing a youthful love of his Tübingen days, and the sonnets to Luise Rau, his one-time betrothed, are among the most exquisite German love lyrics.

·German literature of the 19th century **10**:1196h

Morin, Jean, in Latin JOANNES MORINUS (b. 1591, Blois, Fr.—d. 1659), French theologian whose fame rests on his *editio princeps* of the Samaritan Pentateuch and Targum. Born a Protestant, he was converted to Roman Catholicism, reputedly by Cardinal Duperron. In 1618 Morin joined the Congregation of the Oratory and in due course took priest's orders. In 1625 he visited England in the train of Henrietta Maria; in 1640 he was at Rome, on the invitation of Cardinal Barberini, and was received with special favour by Pope Urban VIII. He was soon recalled to Paris by Richelieu, and the rest of his life was spent in incessant literary labour. The *Histoire de la deliv-*

rance de l'église chrétienne par l'emp. Constantin (1630), gave great offense at Rome, and a *Déclaration* (1654), directed against faults in the administration of the Oratory, was strictly suppressed. So, too, his great work on penance gave equal offense to the Jesuits and to Port-Royal; even after his death, the polemical vehemence of his *Exercitationes biblicae* long led Protestants to neglect his work in which he destroyed the current theory of the integrity of the Hebrew text of the Scriptures. Morin's edition of the Samaritan Pentateuch and Targum, which appeared in the Paris Polyglott Bible in 1645, gave the first impulse in Europe to the study of this dialect. He learned it without a teacher (framing a grammar for himself) from manuscripts then newly brought to Europe.

Morin, Jean (1600–50), French engraver.
·Jansen engraving illus. **10**:33

Morin, Paul (d'Equilly) (b. April 6, 1889, Montreal—d. July 17, 1963, Beloeil, Que.), French-Canadian poet whose evocative descriptions of exotic countries and of the splendour of pagan antiquity set him apart from Canadian literary tradition. A lawyer with a Ph.D. in literature (University of Paris, 1912), Morin travelled widely in Europe and the Near East. He was professor of French literature at various colleges in the United States and Canada, and, in 1913, taught French in Istanbul. Returning to Montreal in 1917, he opened a translation service and occasionally published verse in Canadian periodicals. Morin's poetry, although praised for its rich imagery and technical competence, at first shocked Canadian society, which considered it hedonistic and immoral. Collections include *Le Paon d'émail* (1911; "The Enamel Peacock"), *Poèmes de cendre et d'or* (1922; "Poems of Ashes and Gold"), and *Oeuvres poétiques* (1961; "Poetic Works").

Morina (plant): *see* Dipsacaceae.

Moringa oleifera (botany): *see* drumstick tree.

Moringuidae, family of eel worms of the fish order Anguilliformes.
·characteristics and classification **1**:900b

Morini, ancient Celtic people.
·Caesar's Gallic military conquests **3**:577h
·Low Countries early inhabitants **11**:132e

Morinigo, Higinio (1887–), Paraguayan army officer and politician.
·Paraguayan party politics **13**:991e

Mori Ōgai, pseudonym of MORI RINTARŌ (b. 1862—d. 1922), one of the creators of modern Japanese literature. The son of a physician of the aristocratic warrior (samurai) class, Mori Ōgai studied medicine, at first in Tokyo and from 1884 to 1888 in Germany. In 1889 he published *Maihime* ("The Dancing Girl"), an account closely based on his own experience of an unhappy attachment between a German girl and a Japanese student in Berlin. It represented a marked departure from the impersonal fiction of preceding generations and initiated a vogue for autobiographical revelations among Japanese writers. Ōgai's most popular novel, *Gan* (1911–13; part translation: *The Wild Goose* by B. Watson in *Modern Japanese Literature*, ed. Donald Keene, 1956), is the story of the undeclared love of a moneylender's mistress for a medical student who passes by her house each day. Ōgai also translated Hans Christian Andersen's autobiographical novel *Improvisatoren*.

In 1912 Ōgai was profoundly moved by the suicide of Gen. Nogi Maresuke, following the death of the Emperor Meiji, and he abandoned fiction in favour of historical works depicting the samurai code. The heroes of several of his works are warriors, who, like General Nogi, commit suicide in order to follow their masters to the grave. Despite his early confessional writings, Ōgai came to share with his samurai heroes a reluctance to dwell on emotions. His detachment made his later works seem cold, but their strength and integrity were strikingly close to the samurai ideals he so admired.
·styles and use **10**:1072e

Morioka, capital, Iwate Prefecture (*ken*), northeastern Honshu, Japan, on the Kitakami-gawa (Kitakami River), southeast of the volcanic cone of Iwate-yama (Iwate Mountain). Although the largest city of the prefecture, it retains the atmosphere of the feudal period, when it was the Nambu fief castle town. Now primarily a commercial, railway, and cultural centre, it is known for its traditional ironware and its annual horse fairs. Pop. (1970) 196,036.
39°42′ N, 141°09′ E
·map, Japan **10**:36

Moriori, the aboriginal inhabitants of the Chatham Islands of New Zealand. They were a Polynesian people whose language was related to that of the Maori (*q.v.*) of South Island; their culture was allied to, but less highly developed than, that of the Maori. They lived on fern root, eels, fish, *karaka* berries, and birds. Albatrosses were obtained by perilous expeditions to the outlying rocks where they nested. The clothing of the Moriori was of sealskin and rudely woven flax. Their social organization was similar to that of the Maori. Estimated to number more than 1,000 when discovered in the late 18th century, they were easily conquered and enslaved by a party of Maori in 1835 and were gradually assimilated. The last pureblood Moriori died in 1933; the majority of the Polynesians in the Chatham Islands in the 1970s are of mixed Maori–Moriori–European stock.

morisco (ritual dance): *see* Morris dance.

Moriscos, name given to those Spanish Muslims and their descendants who became baptized Christians, from the pejorative form of Spanish *moros*, "Moors" or "Muslims."

During the Christian reconquest of Muslim Spain, surrendering Muslim (Mudejar) communities in Aragon (1118), Valencia (1238), and Granada (1492) were usually guaranteed freedom of religion by treaty. This tolerant policy was abandoned in the late 15th century, when Christian authorities began to make conversions and ordered the destruction of Islāmic theological books. The Muslims of Granada rebelled. In 1502, offered the choice of Baptism or exile, many of them were baptized and continued to practice Islām secretly; in 1526 the Muslims of Valencia and Aragon were similarly forced to convert. Thereafter, Islām was officially prohibited in Spain.

The Moriscos, however, did not prove to be assimilable. Though they were racially indistinguishable from their Old Christian neighbours (Christians who had retained their faith under Muslim rule), they continued to speak, write, and dress like Muslims. The Old Christians suspected the Moriscos of abetting the Algerians and the Turks, both enemies of Spain, and were fearful of their holy wars (*jihāds*), which terrorized whole districts. Subjected to discriminative taxation while their staple industry, the silk trade, was reduced by a misguided fiscal policy, ill-taught in their new faith, yet punished for ignorance by church and inquisition, the Moriscos turned outside Spain for Muslim support. They obtained legal opinions (*fatwās*) that assured them that it was permissible to practice Islām in secret (*taqīyah*), then produced books known as *aljamiados*, written in Spanish, using the Arabic alphabet, to instruct fellow Moriscos in Islām.

In 1566, Philip II issued an edict forbidding the Granada Moriscos their language, customs, and costume. They revolted in 1569; after two years of war they were removed en masse from Granada and scattered throughout northern Spain. Evidence of their continued political and religious infidelity led to a royal order for deportation on Sept. 22, 1609; their expulsion was completed some five years later. An estimated 300,000 Moriscos relocated mainly in Algeria, Tunisia, and Morocco, where again they found themselves an alien element. They were assimilated after several generations, but something of their Spanish heritage has survived into modern times.
·cultural status and resulting problems **17**:423g
·political and economic suppression **17**:426g

Morison, James (b. Feb. 14, 1816, Bathgate, Linlithgowshire—d. Nov. 13, 1893, Glasgow), theologian and founder of the Evangelical Union, whose followers were also called Morisonians.

Licensed to preach in 1839, he won many converts to his view that Christ's atonement saved not only believers but all men as well. This universalism, contrary to the Westminster Confession (a statement of beliefs based on the Reformation theology of John Calvin), led to a charge of heresy against Morison. In 1840 he was called to Kilmarnock, Ayrshire, where he became famous as an evangelist, but in 1841 the synod of the United Secession Church removed his name from its ministerial roll because of his beliefs. Morison and his father, Robert, with two others who shared his condemnation, became associates in a new denomination founded at Kilmarnock on May 16, 1843. Called the Evangelical Union, it trained its ministers first at Kilmarnock and then in Glasgow in a college that Morison served as president. In 1897 the Evangelical Union and the Scottish Congregationalists, totalling more than 90 congregations, united as the Congregational Union of Scotland. Morison, who also gained a reputation as a scholar, was the author of biblical commentaries and several books on Christian doctrine, including *The Nature of the Atonement* (1841).

Morison, Stanley (b. May 6, 1889, Wanstead, Essex—d. Oct. 11, 1967, London), typographer, scholar, and historian of printing, particularly remembered for his design of Times New Roman, later called the most successful new typeface of the first half of the 20th century. Following an elementary school education, he became, in 1905, a clerk in the London City Mission, where he remained for seven years.

After reading a printing supplement in *The Times* in 1912, he became interested in the study of typography and type design. The supplement also contained an advertisement for a new periodical, *The Imprint*, the purpose of which was to raise the standards of printing. Answering an advertisement in the first issue, Morison joined the publication, which, although short-lived, gave him important typographic experience and led to his employment by the publishers Burns and Oates. There, from 1913 to 1917, he had an opportunity to design books and publicity material. Periods with the Pelican Press (1919–21) and Cloister Press (1921–22) gave him further printing and typographic experience.

In 1923 Morison was appointed typographic adviser to the Monotype Corporation, where he was instrumental in having many important type faces of the past adapted to machine composition. For three years (1923–25) he was also a writer and an editor on the staff of the *Penrose Annual*, which he helped to broaden from its former stress on technical processes in the graphic arts. In 1923 he was appointed typographic adviser to Cambridge University Press, a position he held until 1959. From 1926 to 1930 he was editor of *The Fleuron*, an influential typographic journal.

In 1929 Morison joined the staff of *The Times*, for which he designed a new face, Times New Roman, which appeared for the first time on Oct. 3, 1932. He continued to serve *The Times* in various capacities until his retirement in 1960. He was editor of *The Times Literary Supplement* from 1945 to 1947.

Morison's extensive and influential writings include *Four Centuries of Fine Printing* (1924) and *First Principles of Typography* (1936). He was the major author of *History of The Times* (4 vol., 1935, 1939, 1947, and 1952). He was a member of the Board of Editors of *Encyclopædia Britannica* and a contributor to its 14th edition (1929).
·typography development role **18**:822f

Morisot, Berthe (b. Jan. 14, 1841, Bourges, Fr.—d. March 2, 1895, Paris), painter and printmaker who exhibited regularly with the Impressionists and, despite the protests of friends and family, continued her participation in their struggle for recognition. The daughter of a high government official (and a granddaughter of the important Rococo painter Jean-Honoré Fragonard), she decided early to

"The Artist's Sister, Mme Pontillon, Seated on the Grass," oil on canvas by Berthe Morisot, 1873; in the Cleveland Museum of Art, Ohio
By courtesy of the Cleveland Museum of Art, gift of Hanna Fund

be an artist and pursued her goal with seriousness and dedication. From 1862–68 she worked under the guidance of Corot. In 1868 she met Manet, who was to exert a tremendous influence over her work. He did several portraits of her (*e.g.*, "Repose," *c.* 1870; Rhode Island Museum of Art, Providence, R.I.). Manet had a liberating effect on her work, and she in turn aroused his interest in outdoor painting. Morisot's work never lost its Manet-like quality—an insistence on the design of the painting. Never as involved in colour-optical experimentation as her fellow Impressionists, Morisot's work is distinguished by the fresh, original quality of its design. Her paintings frequently included members of her family, particularly her sister, Edma (*e.g.*, "The Artist's Sister, Mme. Pontillon, Seated on the Grass," 1873; Cleveland Museum of Art and "The Artist's Sister Edma and Their Mother," 1870; National Gallery of Art, Washington, D.C.). Delicate and subtle, exquisite in colour—often with a subdued emerald glow—they won her the admiration of her Impressionist colleagues. Like the other Impressionists, her work was ridiculed by many critics. A woman of great culture and charm, Mallarmé, Degas, Renoir and Monet were among her close friends. She married Édouard Manet's brother, Eugène.
·Manet friendship and portraits **11**:441b

Mori Terumoto (1553–1625), Japanese warrior.
·Toyotomi Hideyoshi's encounter **18**:537d

Moritz (duke of Saxony): *see* Maurice.

Moritz, Karl Philipp (b. Sept. 15, 1757, Hameln, Hanover—d. July 26, 1793, Berlin), novelist whose most important works are his two autobiographical novels, *Andreas Hartknopf* (1786) and *Anton Reiser* (4 vol., 1785–90). The latter is, with Goethe's *Wilhelm Meister*, the most mature 18th-century German novel of contemporary life. He was also an influential writer on aesthetics. In 1786 he travelled to Italy, where he met Goethe, whom he later advised on artistic theory. After his return to Berlin in 1789 he became professor of aesthetics and archaeology at the Academy of Arts.

Morkinskinna (*c.* 1220), Icelandic saga that deals with the kings of Norway from 1047 to 1177.
·content and features **16**:146b

Morlaix, or VILLE DE BRETAGNE, seaport, Finistère *département*, western France, situated on the Dossen Estuary, a tidal inlet of the English Channel, northeast of Brest. Coins found in the vicinity suggest Roman occupation of the site (possibly Mons Relaxus). The counts of Léon held the lordship in the 12th century, but this was disputed by the dukes of Brittany. Morlaix was captured by the English in 1187 and 1522. It has several 15th–16th-century houses (notably Maison de la Reine Anne) and the 15th-century Gothic Church of Saint-Melaine. The town is dominated by a two-storied railway viaduct (built 1861–64, partially destroyed by the Royal Air Force in 1943) that spans the valley 200 ft (60 m) above the quays. A French revolutionary general, J.V. Moreau, was born there in 1763. Pop. (1968) 16,750.
48°35′ N, 3°50′ W
·map, France **7**:584

Morland, George (b. June 26, 1763, London—d. Oct. 29, 1804, London), genre, landscape, and animal painter whose style and works were much imitated in England during the late 18th and early 19th centuries. At the age of ten, Morland exhibited sketches at the Royal Academy and was apprenticed from 1777 to 1784 to his father Henry Robert Morland, a painter and picture restorer. He drew from the antique and copied from George Stubb's "Anatomy of the Horse," as well as works of the English painters Thomas Gainsborough and Sir Joshua Reynolds and the pictures of the French landscapist Joseph Vernet. In 1780 his first signed engraving was published, and a year later his first oil painting, "A Hovel With Asses," was exhibited at the Academy; then also he began, unknown to his father, to paint *galanteries* (scenes of love and compliment) for a Drury Lane publisher and to associate with the demimonde.

After his apprenticeship had expired, he studied briefly at the Royal Academy schools and held his first one-man show of paintings on private premises. Throwing off parental restraint, in 1785 he visited Calais and St. Omer, and rode as an amateur jockey at Margate, Kent. In July 1786 he married Anne Ward, sister to William, the engraver. Settled in London, Morland painted the series "Laetitia, or Seduction," and in 1787 he abandoned portraiture for sentimental rustic genre, which, through Ward's engravings, satisfied a steady public demand for the picturesque. Morland's deliberate flouting of commissioned work in which the patron dictated the subject, scale, and medium and his policy of selling through an intermediary anticipated the situation whereby artists sought to please a wide public with unexceptional, easily comprehensible works.

Morland's best work occurs between 1787 and 1794 and a typical example is the "Inside of a Stable" (Tate Gallery, London) exhibited at the 1791 Academy, the year in which the artist's extravagances forced him, despite his successes, to flee his creditors. After 1794 his painting deteriorated, and he alternated between periods of dissipation and concentrated work until his arrest for debt in 1799. Released by the Insolvent Act, 1802, of feeble health and still pursued by creditors, he escaped to his brother Henry's house in Soho. This same Henry had, during the previous eight years, unscrupulously exploited him, selling nearly 500 of his paintings. Arrested again on Oct. 19, 1804, Morland died of a brain fever ten days later.

Morley, borough (chartered in 1885) in the metropolitan county of West Yorkshire, England, lying 5 mi (8 km) southwest of Leeds. In the neighbourhood are the ruins of Howley Hall (1580). The town's chief industries are woollen textiles, coal mining, stone quarrying, and glassmaking. Pop. (1971 prelim.) 44,340.
53°46′ N, 1°36′ W

Morley, John Morley, Viscount (b. Dec. 24, 1838, Blackburn, Eng.—d. Sept. 23, 1923, Wimbleton), English Liberal party statesman who was friend and official biographer of W.E. Gladstone and who gained fame as a man of letters, particularly as a biographer. As a long-time member of Parliament (1883–95; 1896–1908), he was chief secretary for Ireland (1886; 1892–95) and secretary of state for India (1905–10), and was raised to the peerage in 1908. Among his published works are *Edmund Burke* (1867), *Voltaire* (1872), *Rousseau* (1873), *Diderot and the Encyclopaedists* (1878), *The Life of Richard Cobden* (1881), *Ralph Waldo Emerson* (1884), *Studies in Literature* (1891), *Oliver Cromwell* (1900), *Life of Gladstone* (1903), *Critical Miscellanies* (1908), and *Recollections* (1917).
·Gladstone's Irish policies **3**:272e
·liberal reforms in India **9**:415b

Morley, Christopher Darlington (1890–1957), novelist, poet, and essayist who produced more than 50 volumes. His novels include *Where the Blue Begins* (1922) and *Kitty Foyle* (1939). Collections of his essays include *Shandygaff* (1918), *Mince Pie* (1919), and *Forty-Four Essays* (1925); his verse appears in *Poems* (1929).

Morley, Edward Williams (1838–1923), U.S. chemist who with A.A. Michelson conducted a famous experiment (1887) that indicated the absence in the universe of a stationary luminiferous ether and served as an experimental basis for Albert Einstein's special theory of relativity (*q.v.*).
·atomic weight determination **2**:344d
·ether theory disproof **6**:647d
·Michelson–Morley Earth velocity study **12**:104b
·relativity theory development **15**:582e
·velocity-of-light experiment **10**:951e

Morley, Thomas (b. 1557/1558—d. 1603?), composer, organist, and theorist, and first of the great English madrigalists. He held a number of church musical appointments, first as master of the children at Norwich Cathedral (1583–87), then by 1589 as organist at St. Giles, Cripplegate, in London, and by 1591 at St. Paul's Cathedral. In 1592 Morley was sworn in as a gentleman of the Chapel Royal. By 1597 he was in ill health, and his place at the Chapel Royal was filled in 1603. Since the appointment as gentleman was normally made for life, it seems likely that he died earlier that year.

It is highly probable that Morley became a Roman Catholic early in life, perhaps under the influence of his master, William Byrd, who remained a Catholic until his death. By 1591 Morley had defected, for in that year he engaged in espionage work among the English Catholics in the Netherlands. The mission nearly cost him his life, but he obtained useful information against the Catholic party in England.

About that time, Morley evidently began to realize the possibilities offered by the new popularity of Italian madrigals fitted with English texts, for he began publishing sets of madrigals of his own composition. Morley published 25 canzonets ("little short songs" as he called them) for three voices in 1593; in 1597 he published 17 for five voices; and four canzonets for six voices in the same year. His first madrigals—a set of 22—appeared in 1594; and 20 ballets, modelled on the balletti of Giovanni Giacomo Gastoldi but with more elaborate musical development and a stronger sense of harmonic direction, came out in 1595. In fact Morley excelled in the lighter and more cheerful types of madrigal or canzonet.

Among the works are a considerable proportion of Italian madrigals reworked and published by Morley with no acknowledgement of the original composers—a practice not uncommon at the time. In 1598 Morley brought out a volume of English versions of selected Italian madrigals; and in that same year he was licensed to print music in England for 21 years (a monopoly, originally granted to Byrd and Thomas Tallis in 1575, had expired in 1596). His textbook, *A Plaine and Easie Introduction to Practicall Musicke* (1597), provides knowledge of the theoretical basis of composition of Morley's own time and that of earlier generations.

Morley's compositions are written in two distinct styles that may be chronologically separated. As a pupil of Byrd he was brought up in the pre-madrigalian English style of broad and strong polyphony. In 1576 he wrote two of a number of Latin motets that survive in manuscript sources; all may well belong to his earlier period of presumed Catholicism. On the other hand, his madrigal volumes of the 1590s employ the style of the Italian madrigal, characterized by a direct effectiveness, gentle harmonic warmth, springy rhythms, and clarity of texture.

Morley edited *The Triumphes of Oriana* (published 1603), a collection of 25 madrigals by various composers in praise of Oriana, who may or may not be identified with Queen Elizabeth I. His last volume of original compositions was *The First Booke of Ayres* (1600). The six-voice motets, "Laboravi in gemitu meo" and "De profundis clamavi," are considered among his best works.

·Italian forms as stylistic influence **12**:708d

Morley's theorem, in metalogic, the statement propounded in 1963 by the U.S. mathematician Michael Morley that a theory that is categorical in one uncountable cardinality is categorical in every uncountable cardinality.

·model theory proof **11**:1085b

mormaor, also spelled MORMAER (Gaelic *mor*, "great"; *maor*, or *maer*, "steward," or "bailiff"), a title of the rulers of the seven provinces into which Celtic Scotland (*i.e.*, the part of the country north of the Forth and the Clyde) was divided. This Celtic title was rendered *jarl* by the Norsemen and after the 12th century, under Anglo-Norman influence, "earl." The seven mormaorships, or original "earldoms," of Scotland were Angus, Atholl with Gowrie, Caithness with Sutherland, Fife, Mar with Buchan, Moray with Ross, and Strath Earn with Menteith.

Mormon, Book of, work accepted as holy scripture, in addition to the Bible, in the Church of Jesus Christ of Latter-day Saints. First published in 1830 in Palmyra, N.Y., it was thereafter widely reprinted and translated. Mormons hold that it is a divinely inspired work revealed to and translated by Joseph Smith.

It relates the history of a group of Hebrews who migrated from Jerusalem to America about 600 BC, led by a prophet, Lehi. They multiplied and eventually split into two groups. One group, the Lamanites, forgot their beliefs, became savages, and were the ancestors of the American Indians. The other group, the Nephites, developed culturally and built great cities but were eventually destroyed by the Lamanites about AD 400. Before this occurred, however, Jesus had appeared and taught the Nephites (after his ascension). The history and teachings were abridged and written on gold plates by the prophet Mormon. His son, Moroni, made additions and buried the plates in the ground, where they remained about 1,400 years, until Moroni, a resurrected being or angel, delivered them to Joseph Smith; subsequently they disappeared.

Non-Mormon critics disagree in their opinions as to the origin of the book. Some have claimed that it was based on the lost manuscript of a novel by a clergyman, Solomon Spaulding, but this theory has never been proved. Other critics believe that it was written solely by Joseph Smith.

·Mormon translation and religious beliefs **12**:442d

Mormon cricket (*Anabrus simplex*): *see* shield-backed grasshopper.

Mormonism 12:442, formally CHURCH OF JESUS CHRIST OF LATTER-DAY SAINTS, a religion founded by Joseph Smith, Jr., in the United States in 1830. Proclaiming a new dispensation, the restoration of the priesthood and rituals of the "true church," and the eligibility for the attainment of deity by all Mormons, the Latter-day Saints, who originated in the millennial enthusiasm of the 19th century, eventually migrated to Utah (their headquarters are in Salt Lake City). Though the majority of Mormons live in the United States, the church has also spread to Latin America, Canada, Europe, and parts of Oceania.

The text article covers the history, scriptures, doctrines, and institutions and practices of the church. It includes a summary of the structure of the church, views and practices of the Reorganized Church of Jesus Christ of Latter Day Saints (headquarters in Missouri), and a brief description of Mormon splinter groups.

REFERENCES in other text articles:

·anti-Mormon sentiment results in Idaho **9**:187f
·Christian covenantal theocracy ideology **4**:512e
·Church continuity concept **4**:465h
·distinctive cultural orientation **18**:926d
·folklore as essential part of devout life **7**:464h
·Iowa settlement by religious groups **9**:818b
·Missouri settlement and emigration **12**:285c
·postmillennialist expectations **1**:101d
·Protestant apocalyptic groups **15**:116f
·Utah settlement and subsequent growth **18**:1101e *passim* to 1105h
·Wyoming settlement location **19**:1053c

RELATED ENTRIES in the *Ready Reference and Index:*
Aaronic priesthood; Melchizedek priesthood; Mormon, Book of; Moroni; Mountain Meadows massacre

Mormon Station, also called GENOA, village, Nevada, U.S. Pop. (1970) 115.
39°00′ N, 119°51′ W

·settlement in 1849 **12**:1076h

Mormon Tabernacle (1867), meetinghouse of the Church of Jesus Christ of Latter-day Saints in Salt Lake City, Utah. It contains one of the finest organs in the world and is the base of the Mormon Tabernacle Choir, a group of 375 trained singers.

·architectural individuality and choir activity **18**:1105f

Mormon tea bush (plant): *see* Ephedraceae.

Mormon war (1857): *see* Utah war.

Mormoopidae, family of bats of the mammalian order Chiroptera.

·classification and general features **4**:435f

Mormotomyiidae, family of flies of the insect order Diptera.

·classification and features **5**:824d

mormyr, or MORMYRID, slimy freshwater African fish usually found in sluggish, muddy water. Mormyrs are soft-rayed bony fishes with abdominal pelvic fins, forked tail fins, small

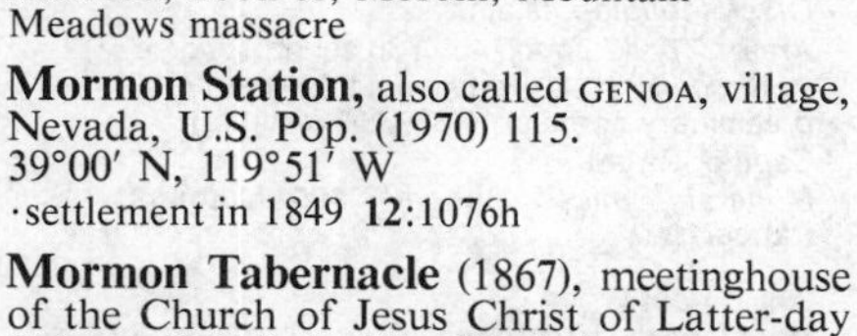

Scaly mormyr (*Gnathonemus*)
Russ Kinne—Photo Researchers

mouths and eyes, restricted gill openings, and small scales. The brain is proportionately very large, comparable to that of man in relation to body weight; enlarged areas of the brain indicate well-developed senses. A loosely attached bony plate on each side of the head covers a vesicle that communicates with the internal ear. Paired electric organs of mild power, present in the tail, set up a continuous electric field around the fish, acting as a sensory screen. Most mormyrs feed on small prey, aquatic vegetation, or organic debris. More than a hundred species of unusual appearance are placed in about 11 genera. The "elephant-nosed" species of *Gnathonemus* have the mouth at the end of a long, trunklike snout. Other mormyrs have narrow heads, protruding lower lips, or short, rounded snouts. The Nile species of *Mormyrus* are represented in ancient Egyptian mural paintings and hieroglyphics. Mormyrs range from 9 to 50 cm (3.5 to about 20 in.) in length. Mormyrs are of the family Mormyridae and the order Mormyriformes.

·bioelectric field generation **2**:1000c
·classification and general features **13**:765d
·electric organs and shocks **11**:804c
·elephant-nosed fish ear mechanism and development **17**:44a

morna, Cape Verde song and dance.

·Cape Verde Islands practices **3**:798e

Mornay, Philippe de, seigneur du Plessis-Marly, usually known as DUPLESSIS-MORNAY (b. Nov. 5, 1549, Buhy, Normandy, Fr.—d. Nov. 11, 1623, La Forêt-sur-Sèvre), diplomat who was one of the most outspoken and well-known publicists for the Protestant cause during the French Wars of Religion (1562–98).

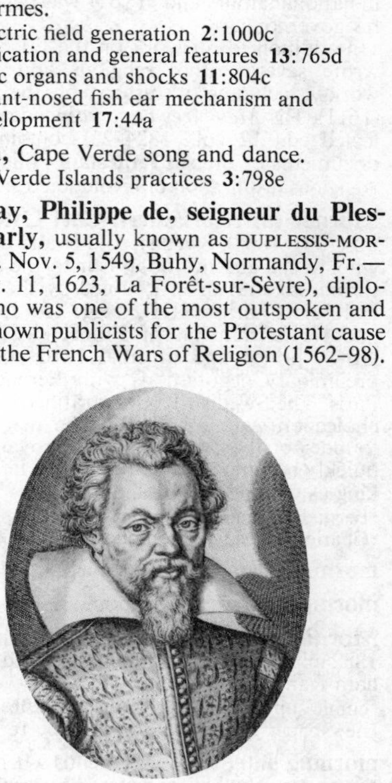

Mornay, engraving by L. Gaultier (1561–1641)
By courtesy of the Bibliotheque Nationale, Paris

Because of his mother's influence, Mornay received a Protestant education, studying Hebrew, law, and German at Heidelberg. While at Cologne (1571–72), he wrote two "Remonstrances" urging the people of the Netherlands to resist Spanish rule. In Paris at the time of the massacre of Protestants on St. Bartholomew's Day (Aug. 24, 1572), Mornay narrowly escaped death.

During the next four years he wrote numerous political tracts, including *Discours au roi Charles* (1572; "Discourse to King Charles") and *Remonstrances aux estats pour la paix* (1576; "Remonstrances on the Conditions for Peace"). Scholars have disputed whether the *Vindiciae contra tyrannos* (1579; "A Defense of Liberty Against Tyrants"), the most famous tract of Protestant political thought of the time, should be attributed to Mornay or to his friend Hubert Languet. The *Vindiciae* acknowledges a contract between a sovereign and his people: if the sovereign becomes a tyrant, the contract is broken and the people have the right to depose him.

Fighting for the Huguenots, he was captured in 1575, but by concealing his identity he was able to secure release for only a small ransom. In 1576 he married Charlotte Arbaleste, whose memoirs are a major source for the events of her husband's life. Mornay became a valued counsellor of Henry of Navarre (later King Henry IV of France) and negotiated the reconciliation between Navarre and Henry III of France in April 1589. He conducted many important embassies for the Protestant cause and for Henry IV both before and after Henry's accession to the throne. During this time he was appointed governor of Saumur.

Henry IV's reconciliation with the Catholic Church (1593) ended their collaboration, and the publication of Mornay's *De l'institution . . . de l'Eucharistie* (1598), in which he used scriptural quotations to attack Catholic eucharistic doctrine, increased the breach. At a public disputation at Fontainebleau in 1600 with Jacques Davy Duperron, bishop of Évreux, it became clear that Mornay had lost Henry IV's favour. He played no further part in national affairs and in 1621 was deprived of his governorship.

In addition to his work on the Eucharist he wrote several other religious and polemic works, including a history of the papacy (1611). His *Mémoires et correspondance* (collected ed., 12 vol., 1824–25) contains many documents of French Protestant policy.

·religious justification of revolution **15**:558a

Mörner (af Morlanda), Carl Otto, Baron (1781–1868), Swedish soldier and diplomat who, in the absence of an heir to the Swedish throne (at that time occupied by the elderly, childless Charles XIII), suggested Jean Bernadotte, a marshal of France, as a likely crown prince and in June 1810 conducted preliminary negotiations with Bernadotte in Paris. The Swedish Riksdag ratified Mörner's choice on Aug. 21, 1810. The new prince, founder of the present Swedish royal family, quickly became regent, and in 1818 he became king as Charles XIV John.

·Bernadotte and the Swedish princeship **4**:60a
·Charles XIII succession question **16**:323e

morning drop: *see* gonorrhea.

morning glory: *see in* Ipomoea.

Morning Journal, newspaper founded in 1882 in New York City and purchased by William Randolph Hearst in 1895.

·comic supplement appearance **3**:920b
·newspaper publishing history **15**:241e

morning star, the planet Venus when seen in the eastern sky before dawn. As morning star, Venus was identified in classical mythology with Lucifer, or Phosphoros. Other planets visible to the naked eye and bright stars seen near the horizon near sunrise are sometimes also called morning stars. *Compare* evening star.

Mornington, shire, formerly part of Mornington-Balcombe urban area, now absorbed by the city of Melbourne, southern Victoria, Australia, on Mornington Peninsula. The shire, a popular seaside resort in the neighbourhood of southern Melbourne, also has light manufacturing. The peninsula, named for an Irish town, is a boot-shaped promontory occupying 125 sq mi (325 sq km) and almost enclosing Port Phillip Bay (northwest), which it separates from Western Port Bay (southeast). While its coastal towns are virtually suburbs of Melbourne, the peninsula's interior is devoted to agriculture. Pop. (1976 prelim.) shire, 20,166.
38°13′ S, 145°03′ E

·Melbourne's expansion **13**:871d; map inset 872

Mornington, Richard Colley Wellesley, 2nd earl of: *see* Wellesley (of Norragh), Richard Colley Wellesley, Marquess.

Mornington Island, one of the Wellesley Islands (*q.v.*) in the Gulf of Carpentaria, off the coast of Queensland, Australia. Pop. (1976 est.), Aborigines only, 681.
16°33′ S, 139°24′ E

Morny, Charles-Auguste-Louis-Joseph, duc de (b. Oct. 21, 1811, Paris—d. March 10, 1865, Paris), political and social leader during the Second Empire who played an important part in the coup d'etat of Dec. 2, 1851, which ended the Second Republic and led to the establishment of Charles-Louis-Napoléon Bonaparte, Morny's half brother, as Emperor Napoleon III.

Morny, the illegitimate son of Hortense de Beauharnais (the estranged wife of Louis Bonaparte, a brother of Napoleon I) by Charles-Joseph, comte de Flahaut, began his career as a lieutenant in the French army, serving mainly in Africa (1832–36). Above all addicted to social pleasures, he resigned his commission and devoted himself to Parisian society and to making a fortune by speculation and by manufacturing beet sugar. He was elected to represent Clermont-Ferrand in the Chamber of Deputies in 1842 and again in 1846 but did not reach the first rank in politics until his half brother, Louis-Napoléon, was elected president of the republic in 1848. He was elected deputy for Puy-de-Dôme in 1849.

Becoming minister of the interior on the day of Louis-Napoléon's coup, Morny organized the plebiscite that made Louis-Napoléon dictator. Soon resigning his ministry, he served briefly as ambassador to Russia (1856) and then became president of the legislature. In this office he abandoned his formerly reactionary role and tried to persuade Napoleon III to mitigate his authoritarianism. He saw that Napoleon's dictatorial power could not last and urged him to yield it voluntarily rather than be compelled to do so.

·Bernhardt theatrical patronage **2**:862e
·Napoleon III's liberal influence **12**:841a

Moro, Aldo (b. Sept. 23, 1916, Maglie, Italy —d. May 9, 1978), law professor, statesman, and secretary of the Christian Democrat Party (1959–63), to which he demonstrated the necessity of cooperating with the left. Consequently, he became the first prime minister (1963–68) to preside over an Italian coalition government representing both Christian Democrats and Socialists.

A professor of law at the University of Bari, Moro published several books on legal subjects, serving also as president of the Federation of Italian University Catholics (1939–42) and the Movement of Catholic Graduates (1945–46).

Elected deputy to the Constituent Assembly after World War II, and then to the parliament, Moro held a series of Cabinet posts, including those of undersecretary of foreign affairs (December 1947–May 1948), minister of justice (1955–57), and minister of public instruction (1957–59).

Moro took office as secretary of the Christian Democrats during a crisis that threatened to split the party (March 1959). Although he was the leader of the Dorothean, or centrist, group of the Christian Democrats, he favoured forming a coalition with the Socialists and helped bring about the resignation of the conservative Christian Democrat prime minister Fernando Tambroni (July 1960).

MOROCCO

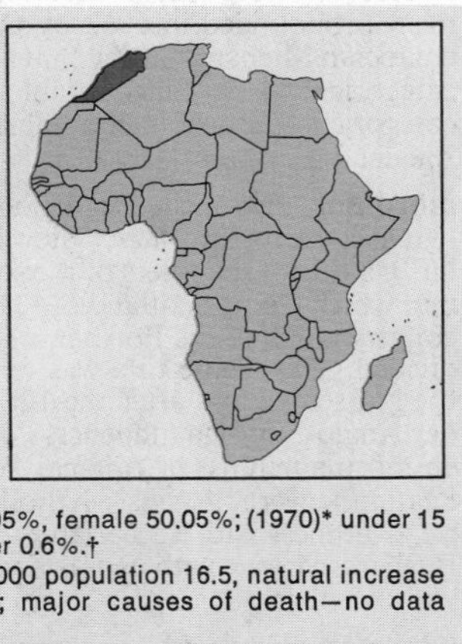

Official name: al-Mamlakah al-Maghribīyah (Kingdom of Morocco).
Location: northern Africa.
Form of government: constitutional monarchy.
Official language: Arabic.
Official religion: Islām.
Area: 177,117 sq mi, 458,730 sq km.
Population: (1960 census) 11,626,232; (1971 preliminary census) 15,379,259 (de jure).
Capital: Rabat.
Monetary unit: 1 dirham = 100 Moroccan francs.

Demography

Population: (1971 census) density 86.8 per sq mi, 33.5 per sq km; (1970) urban 32.5%, rural 67.5%; (1970)* male 49.95%, female 50.05%; (1970)* under 15 46.4%, 15–29 25.8%, 30–44 15.0%, 45–59 8.5%, 60–74 3.6%, 75 and over 0.6%.†
Vital statistics: (1965–70) births per 1,000 population 49.5, deaths per 1,000 population 16.5, natural increase per 1,000 population 33.0; (1965–70) life expectancy at birth—50.5; major causes of death—no data available.
Ethnic composition (1969): Moroccan Arab 98.6%, French 0.6%, Spanish 0.3%, Moroccan Jew 0.3%, other 0.2%. *Religious affiliation* (1971): Muslim 99.1%, Jewish 0.2%, other 0.7%.

National accounts

Budget (1970). Revenue: 3,575,000,000 dirhams (domestic revenue 90.3%, of which, sales tax 31.8%, income tax 15.4%, customs duties 15.1%; government enterprise surplus used for capital outlay 9.7%). Expenditures: 4,042,000,000 dirhams (agriculture 18.2%, education 16.9%, defense 11.8%, industry and power 5.9%, health 5.8%, interest 5.3%, transportation 3.6%). *Total national debt* (1969): 4,014,446,807 dirhams. *Tourism* (1970). Receipts from visitors: U.S. $136,400,000. Expenditures by nationals abroad: U.S. $62,000,000.

Domestic economy

Gross national product (GNP; at current market prices, 1970): U.S. $3,600,000,000 (U.S. $230 per capita).

Origin of gross domestic product (at 1960 market prices):	1960				1970			
	value in 000,000 dirhams	% of total value	labour force	% of labour force	value in 000,000 dirhams	% of total value	labour force	% of labour force
agriculture, forestry, hunting, fishing	2,650	32.3	1,833,759	56.3	3,720	31.0	...	...
mining, quarrying	540	6.6	39,387	1.2	620	5.2	...	...
manufacturing	1,100	13.4	266,303	8.2	1,700	14.2	...	...
construction	320	3.9	56,153	1.7	700	5.8	...	...
electricity, gas, water	180	2.2	8,173	0.3	350	2.9	...	...
transport, storage, communication	‡	...	80,073	2.5	‡	...	...	...
trade	1,910	23.3	238,949	7.3	2,730	22.7	...	...
banking, insurance, real estate	‡	...	...	...	‡	...	...	...
ownership of dwellings	‡	...	...	...	‡	...	...	...
public administration, defense	...	...	...	...	...	...	...	...
services	1,500‡	18.3	322,278	9.9	2,190‡	18.2	...	...
other	...	...	409,304	12.6	...	...	...	...
total	8,200	100.0	3,254,379	100.0	12,010	100.0	...	...

Production (metric tons except as noted, 1970). Agriculture, forestry, hunting, fishing: barley 2,032,000, wheat 1,700,000, oranges and tangerines 816,000, olives 165,000,§ maize (corn) 456,000, tomatoes 250,000,§ grapes 140,000,§ dry broad beans 160,000, chick-peas 59,000, potatoes 300,000, watermelons 110,000,§ raw milk 965,000, sheep 14,500,000 head,‖ cattle 3,600,000 head,‖ fish catch 256,000. Mining, quarrying: phosphate rock 11,399,455, iron ore 872,476, lead ore 120,911. Manufacturing: flour 818,000, refined sugar 399,000, cement 1,421,000, soft lead 24,901, metal containers 28,581, phosphates 179,697, carpets 471,360 sq m. Construction (square metres): residential 1,653,600, nonresidential 481,200.

Invited to form his own government (December 1963), Moro assembled a Cabinet that included some Socialists, participating in the government for the first time in 16 years. He resigned after a defeat on a budget issue (June 26, 1964) but in July formed a new Cabinet much like the old one. In 1965 he temporarily became his own foreign minister, renewing Italian pledges to NATO and the United Nations.

Italy's inflation and failing industrial growth prevented Moro from initiating many of the reforms he had envisaged, and this angered the Socialists, who effected his defeat in January 1966. He succeeded, however, in forming a new government on February 23. After the general elections in 1968, Moro, as is customary, resigned (June 5). He was foreign minister during 1970–72. In November 1974 he became premier with a coalition government, the second party being the Republican, but this government fell on Jan. 7, 1976. He was again premier in 1976, from February 12 to April 30, remaining in office as head of a caretaker government till July 9.

On March 16, 1978, Moro was kidnapped by terrorists, who demanded the release of other terrorists held in Italian prisons in exchange for his life. The government refused to bargain with the kidnappers, and on the afternoon of May 9 Moro's body was found in a car parked in the centre of Rome.

·Paul VI's early relationship **13**:1088h
·political opening to the left **9**:1172b

Moro, Antonio: *see* More, Sir Anthony.

Moro, Il: *see* Sforza, Ludovico.

Morobe, province (until 1976 called Morobe District), Papua New Guinea, southwest Pacific. Its area of 13,300 sq mi (34,500 sq km) curves around Huon Gulf, rising to 13,000 ft (4,000 m) in the Saruwaged Range on the Huon Peninsula (north) and to 10,000 ft in the Kuper Range (south). The mountains rise precipitously from the coast, and the rivers, some of which drop several thousand feet within a few miles and then spread out over the coastal plain in a fan of small channels, are unnavigable. Even the largest, the Markham River, which runs east to west across the province, is navigable by canoe only for short periods of the year. The country's most populous province, Morobe produces coffee, beef, dairy products, peanuts, and copra; the cultivation of sorghum in the Markham Valley is expanding, and spice crops, such as pepper, have been grown on an experimental basis. Gold mining, once important to the towns of Wau, Bulolo, and Mumeng in the Bulolo Valley, has been replaced by a vigorous forestry and plywood industry.

The town of Morobe, on Morobe Harbour, was originally a German settlement and was capital of the district until the 1920s. At that time the headquarters were moved to Salamaua, on the south side of the Huon Gulf. The present headquarters are at Lae, on the northwest side of the Huon Gulf near the mouth of the Markham; founded in the late 1920s when air service to the goldfields was begun, Lae is the principal port of the province and is linked by trunk roads to Wau and Bulolo. Finschhafen, also originally a German settlement, is situated on a good harbour of the Huon Peninsula. Pop. (1977 est.) 294,500.

·area and population table **12**:1091

Moroccan crises: *see* Algeciras Conference; Agadir incident.

Morocco 12:444, constitutional monarchy in northwest Africa, lying along the Mediterranean and Atlantic coasts and bordered by Algeria (east and southeast) and Western Sahara (southwest).

The text article, after a brief survey of the nation, covers its natural and human landscape, people, economy, administration and social conditions, cultural life and institutions, and prospects.

REFERENCES in other text articles:
·African political divisions map **1**:208; table 209
·armed forces statistics table **2**:16
·Atlas Mountains **2**:304c *passim* to 306h
·Casablanca's economic importance **3**:976d
·China's trade relationship, table 5 **4**:280
·Christian denominational demography map **4**:459
·coal production and reserves, table 5 **4**:781
·educational modernization and universities **6**:400e
·Hamito-Semitic languages map **8**:590
·jewelry forms and Byzantine influence **10**:171g
·map, Africa **1**:179
·newspaper publishing statistics table **15**:237
·petroleum production statistics, table 1 **14**:176
·petroleum reserves of the world table **14**:175
·phosphorite reserve table **14**:290
·railway systems data table **15**:482
·spice import, export, and value, table 3 **17**:506
·urban population ratio table **16**:26

morocco, also called MOROCCO LEATHER, firm, flexible leather made from goatskin or an imitation of it made from sheepskin or lambskin. *See* leather and hides.

Morococcyx: *see in* ground cuckoo.

Morogoro Region, administrative unit (established 1963), eastern Tanzania, with an area of 28,200 sq mi (73,038 sq km). Its northern section contains the isolated Uluguru Mountains (8,681 ft [2,646 m]), part of the Nguru Mountains (6,923 ft), and the Okaguru (7,432 ft) and Usagara mountains along the plateau escarpment, and is drained by the Wami and Ruvu rivers. South of the Great Ruaha River lie the Kilombero Valley, the Mahenge Plateau, and part of the Selous Game Reserve. The southern rivers are tributaries of the Rufiji, which, with the Mbarangandu, forms part of Morogoro's eastern boundary.

Cash crops include sisal, kapok, cotton, rubber, vegetables, coffee, peanuts (groundnuts), papain, castor beans, sunflower seeds, sugarcane, and tobacco. Mica is mined near the capital, Morogoro town, and cattle are raised on the Mkata Plain in spite of infestation with tsetse flies. The Luguru, Nguru, Sagara, Pogoro, Mbunga, Ndamba, Kaguru, Vidunda, and Kutu are among the region's larger ethnic groups. Pop. (1976 est.) 818,000.

·area and population table **17**:1030
·map, Tanzania **17**:1027

Moroleón, city, southern Guanajuato state, north central Mexico. It lies at 5,814 ft (1,772 m) above sea level in the Bajío region. Moroleón is the commercial and manufacturing centre for the surrounding farms and ranches. Corn (maize), beans, alfalfa, wheat, chick-peas, and onions thrive in the cool climate, and livestock raising is widespread. Shoes and *rebozos* (shawls) are the principal manufactures. The city is situated on a high-

Energy: (1973) installed electrical capacity 821,950 kW, (1973) production 2,705,900,000 kWhr (166 kWhr per capita).

Persons economically active (1971): 3,980,518 (26.3%), unemployed 348,939 (2.2%).

Price and earnings indexes (1970 = 100):	1971	1972	1973	1974
consumer price index¶	104.2	108.1	112.5	128.7

Land use (1966): total area 44,505,000 hectares (agricultural and under permanent cultivation 17.7%; meadows and pastures 17.2%; forested 11.6%; built-on, wasteland, unused but potentially productive, and other 53.5%).

Foreign trade

Imports (1973): 4,683,568,000 dirhams (vegetable products 15.6%, of which, cereals 11.1%, coffee, tea, and spices 2.8%; engines and mechanical apparatus 10.7%; chemical products 7.9%, of which, chemicals 2.5%, pharmaceuticals 1.2%, paints and varnish 1.1%; iron and steel bars 7.3%; automobiles, tractors, and cycles 7.0%; prepared food products 6.7%, of which, sugar and honey 5.3%; mineral oils and fuels 6.5%; textiles, artificial 5.5%; fats, oils, and waxes 4.1%; electrical machinery 4.0%; wood 3.1%; plastics and artificial materials 2.2%). *Major import sources:* France 31.8%, United States 10.6%, West Germany 8.2%, Spain 5.0%, Italy 4.6%, Soviet Union 3.9%, United Kingdom 3.4%, The Netherlands 3.2%.

Exports (1973): 3,745,947,000 dirhams (vegetable products 33.2%, of which, edible fruit 15.2%, leguminous vegetables 14.6%; nonmetallic minerals, metals, and ores 27.7%, of which, clay, cement, and gypsum 21.5%, metallurgical ores 5.7%; prepared food products 15.2%, of which, meat and fish 5.1%, legumes and fruit, processed 4.4%, beverages, alcohol, and vinegar 2.6%; chemicals 3.1%, of which, fixed vegetable oils, soft 2.2%; textiles 7.9%, of which, velours, ribbons, brocades, etc. 2.3%). *Major export destinations:* France 33.7%, West Germany 9.7%, Italy 6.9%, Spain 4.8%, United Kingdom 4.7%, Belgium–Luxembourg 4.2%, The Netherlands 4.2%.

Transport and communication

Transport. Railroads (1973): length 1,091 mi, 1,756 km; passenger-mi 390,000,000, passenger-km 628,000,000; short ton-mi cargo 2,269,000,000, metric ton-km cargo 3,312,000,000. Roads (1973): total length 32,180 mi, 51,790 km (paved 11,203 mi, 18,030 km; earth, graded and drained 3,244 mi, 5,221 km; unimproved 17,733 mi, 28,539 km). Vehicles (1972): passenger cars 254,953, trucks and buses 92,485. Merchant marine (1974): vessels (100 gross tons and over) 43, total deadweight tonnage 63,139. Air transport: (1973) passenger-mi 407,100,000, passenger-km 655,200,000; short ton-mi cargo 5,269,000, metric ton-km cargo 7,692,000; (1974) airports with scheduled flights 8.

Communication. Daily newspapers (1972): total number 11, total circulation 234,000,♀ circulation per 1,000 population 15.♀ Radios (1972): total number of receivers 1,500,000 (1 per 11 persons). Television (1972): receivers 225,000 (1 per 70 persons); broadcasting stations 9. Telephones (1974): 181,000 (1 per 88 persons).

Education and health

Education♂ (1970–71):	schools	teachers	students	student-teacher ratio
primary (age 7 to 12)	1,548	34,277	1,175,277	34.3
secondary (age 14 to 21)	...	19,542	298,880	15.3
vocational	...	911	13,772	15.1
teacher training□	...	104	1,771	17.0
higher	...	512	10,908	21.3

College graduates (per 100,000 population, 1964): 6.9.* *Literacy* (1971): total population literate (15 and over) 22.2%; males literate 33.6%, females literate 11.1%.

Health: (1970) doctors 1,163 (1 per 13,345 persons); (1971) hospital beds 22,727 (1 per 670 persons); (1967) daily per capita caloric intake 2,180 calories (FAO recommended minimum requirement 2,340 calories).

*Excluding Ifni. †Percentages do not add to 100.0 because of rounding. ‡Services include banking, insurance, real estate, transport, storage, communication, ownership of dwellings. §1969. ‖1969–70. ¶For Casablanca only. ♀Refers to 8 dailies only. ♂Figures for vocational, teacher training, and higher are for 1968–69 and exclude Ifni. □Secondary level only.

way linking Salamanca, to the north, and Morelia, the capital of Michoacán state, to the south. Pop. (1970) 25,620.
20°08′ N, 101°12′ W

moro-moro, earliest known form of organized theatre in the Philippines.
·Philippine Christian–Muslim theme **17**:249e; illus.

moron, person with a mild degree of mental retardation. According to a classification system no longer much used, morons have an intelligence quotient (IQ) of between about 50 and 70 and rank above idiots and imbeciles in a classification of mentally deficient persons. Many morons are able to learn to read and write, but their mental development stops roughly at the equivalent of an 8- to 12-year-old child's. Some can earn a living at simple jobs, and some marry and have children. Morons are not always easily distinguishable from persons not classed as mentally deficient; the development of a moron depends a great deal upon environmental factors. Morons make up the largest group of the mentally deficient.
·eugenic interpretation of IQ levels **6**:1023h
·incidence of retardation in the U.S. **9**:673f

Morón, city, northeastern Buenos Aires province, east central Argentina. The settlement grew up in the 16th century around the chapel of Nuestra Señora del Buen Viaje (Our Lady of the Safe Journey) as a way station for travellers en route to or from present-day Chile and Peru.

From 1930 to 1943 Morón was known as Seis de Septiembre in honour of a military uprising of Sept. 6, 1930. Horticulture, agriculture (grains and alfalfa), and livestock raising are widespread in the outlying rural areas. It is now an important industrial centre, with meat-packing, dairying, food canning, tanning, and varied manufacturing plants. With the growth of the national capital, Morón has merged into the suburban area of greater Buenos Aires, 16 mi (26 km) to the east-northeast, to which it is linked by roads and rail. Morón has an airport. Pop. (1970 prelim.) 485,983.
34°39′ S, 58°37′ W

Morón, city, northern Ciego de Avila province, east central Cuba. It is situated in the swampy coastal plain just south of the Laguna de Leche.

Morón is an important regional transportation and manufacturing centre. From the hinterland come sugarcane, tobacco, cacao, coffee, fruit, cattle, and timber to be processed in the city. Asphalt and chromite are found in the vicinity. Morón is linked by railroad and highway to other urban centres along the northern coast and has an airfield. Pop. (1970) 28,997.
22°06′ N, 78°38′ W
·map, Cuba **5**:351

Morón, town, in the central highlands of Carabobo state, north central Venezuela. In 1950 the site was selected for development under the government's policy of using the revenues from the petroleum industry to foster domestic production of as many goods as possible.

The town is close to raw materials (petroleum, natural gas, salt, pyrite, phosphate, and limestone); to the country's principal population centres; to Puerto Cabello (14 mi [23 km] west), Venezuela's second most important port; and to a major railway and highway. It has facilities to refine petroleum and to manufacture synthetic rubber, detergents, plastics and plastic derivatives, pharmaceuticals, nylon, caustic soda, chlorine, ammonia, urea, herbicides, insecticides, explosives, and fertilizers. The industrial complex was originally intended to remain entirely in the hands of the Venezuelan Institute of Petrochemicals (IVP), an autonomous government agency, but by the late 1960s private capital accounted for 25 to 28 percent of the total investment. Pop. (1950) 1,203; (1961) 7,079; (1971) 19,451; (1977 est.) 24,000.
10°29′ N, 68°11′ W
·manufacturing activities **19**:65g
·map, Venezuela **19**:60

Morona-Santiago, province, southeast Ecuador, bounded by Brazil on the southeast. It covers two distinct natural regions: in the west is the high Cordillera Oriental of the Andes, rising to 17,158 ft (5,230 m) in Sangay, one of Ecuador's highest volcanoes; the eastern part of the province drops off into the flat, tropical rain forest of the headwaters of the Amazon. The boundaries have not been precisely surveyed.

The province was established in 1953 from part of former Santiago-Zamora province. The forested portions, not fully integrated into the national economy, are chiefly inhabited by Jívaro Indians and yield hardwoods, medicinal and insecticidal plants, and wild rubber. The provincial capital, Macas (*q.v.*), is a Salesian missionary centre. Pop. (1977 est.) 62,200.
·area and population table **6**:288
·map, Ecuador **6**:286

Morón de la Frontera, city, Sevilla province of Andalusia, in southwestern Spain, in the valley of the Río Guadalquivir, near the northwestern foothills of the Penibético Mountain System. Founded by the Phoenicians, the place was settled by the Romans, who called it Arunci. The Arabs later gave it a hybrid name: the Hebrew *moram*, meaning "elevated site," and the Spanish *frontera*, referring to its 250-year position at the border of the Muslim kingdom of Granada. Reconquered by Melén Rodríguez Gallinato for Ferdinand III of Leon and Castile, it was ceded to Seville for repopulation.

On a hill above the city stand the ruins of a Moorish castle, abandoned in the 17th century and partly destroyed by the French in 1812. Basically an agricultural community, Morón produces olives, oil, wheat, and liquors, as well as construction materials. Pop. (1970) 29,488.
37°08′ N, 5°27′ W
·map, Spain **17**:382

Morone, Giovanni (b. Jan. 25, 1509, Milan—d. Dec. 1, 1580, Rome), cardinal, one of the greatest diplomats of the Reformation, and the last president of the Council of Trent—the 19th ecumenical council of the Roman Catholic Church—convened between 1545 and 1563 at Trento, Italy, to restore church morale and doctrines challenged by the Reformation. He was named bishop of Modena, Italy, in 1529. In 1536 Pope Paul III sent him as ambassador to Germany, where he encouraged theological discussions while working toward a general council that would bring peace to Christian countries. His efforts won the approval of the Germans. He assisted at the German diets of Hagenau (1540), Ratisbon (now Regensburg; 1541), and Speyer (1542).

He returned to Rome in 1542 and was made cardinal. He was appointed as Paul's emissary to the Council of Trent to be opened Nov. 1, 1542. When the council was postponed (until 1545), Paul made Morone governor of Bologna in 1544. Under Pope Julius III, Morone became bishop of Novara (1553–60). In 1557 Paul IV imprisoned him at Rome on suspicion of heresy, but he was released on Paul's death (1559) and was absolved by Pius IV, who in 1563 appointed him president of the council.

Morone's diplomacy saved the council from disaster when a large international body of bishops pressed for a statement that episcopal jurisdiction came to each bishop directly from God and not through the pope. Opposition by the Roman delegation resulted in a deadlock. Morone secured the surrender of the extremists on both sides, and the council finally accepted the statement that bishops were assigned by the Holy Ghost to rule the church. Thus he brought the council's last period to a successful conclusion.

Morone was made bishop of Ostia in 1570 and spent his last years administering the English College in Rome.

Moroni, according to the teaching of the Church of Jesus Christ of Latter-day Saints, an angel or resurrected being who appeared to Joseph Smith on Sept. 21, 1823, to inform him that he had been chosen to restore God's church on earth. Four years later Smith received plates of gold from Moroni, who, as last of the ancient prophets, had buried them in a hill called Cumorah (near Palmyra, N.Y.) some 14 centuries earlier. After Smith had produced the *Book of Mormon*, using information about ancient American prophets and peoples contained on these plates, Moroni took them away.
·revelations through golden plates **12**:442f

Moroni, capital of the Comoros, on southwestern Grande Comore. It is the largest settlement of the islands, which became independent in 1975. Despite the presence of modern office buildings, Moroni retains its Arabic cultural flavour. It is a port and trading centre for vanilla, cocoa, and coffee. There is a daily market for agricultural produce of the surrounding area. Of the many mosques, Chiounda is a pilgrimage point. Pop. (1976 est.) 18,330.
11°41′ S, 43°16′ E

A mosque along the waterfront at Moroni, Comoros
Gerald Cubitt

Moroni, Giovanni Battista (b. *c.* 1525, Albino, Venetia—d. Feb. 5, 1578, Bergamo),

"The Tailor," oil on canvas by Giovanni Battista Moroni; in the National Gallery, London
By courtesy of the trustees of the National Gallery, London; photograph, J.R. Freeman & Co. Ltd.

painter unique among artists of the Italian Renaissance for confining his work almost exclusively to portraiture. His portraits were principally of the petty aristocracy and bourgeois of Bergamo, such as "Portrait of a Man" ("The Tailor"; National Gallery, London). These likenesses emphasize a sense of life and the sitter's individuality of personality.

Moronidae (fish family): *see* sea bass.

Moropus, extinct genus of the chalicotheres, a group of very unusual mammals related to the horse. *Moropus* occurs as fossils in Miocene deposits in North America and Asia (the Miocene Epoch began 26,000,000 years ago and lasted 19,000,000 years). *Moropus* was as large as a good-sized modern horse, but unlike other horselike forms, the perissodactyls, it had claws instead of hoofs. The forelimbs were longer than the hind limbs, and the back sloped downward to the hindquarters. The teeth possessed low crowns; the molars were large and the premolars small. It is likely that

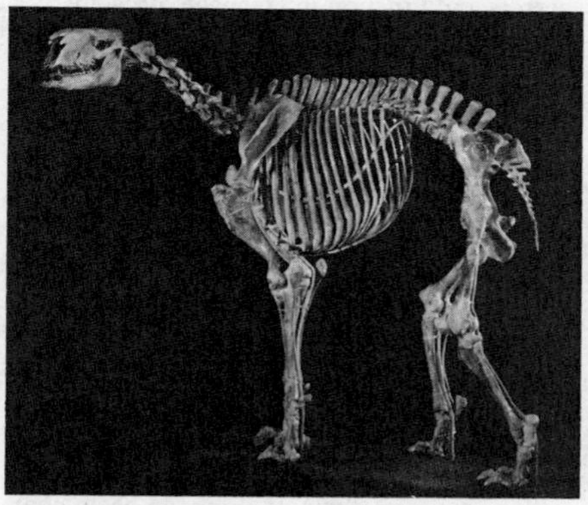

Moropus skeleton
By courtesy of the American Museum of Natural History, New York

Moropus did not browse or graze as did other horselike forms and, instead, probably used its large claws to dig up roots and tubers more suited to its type of dentition than grasses.
·horse relatives' evolution **14**:87h;
illus. 85

Moro reflex, a startle reflex of an infant in which the arms are thrown outward.
·disorders of amino acid
metabolism **11**:1054d

Morosini, noble Venetian family that gave four doges and several generals and admirals to the Republic as well as two cardinals and many other prelates to the church. The Morosini first achieved prominence in the 10th century when they destroyed the rival Caloprino family for planning to surrender Venice to the Holy Roman emperor Otto II.

Domenico Morosini (died 1156), elected doge in 1148, consolidated and extended Venetian power in Istria, Dalmatia, and the Adriatic. Marino was doge from 1249 to 1253. Roger served as admiral in the war against Genoa that ended with the Genoese victory at the battle of Curzola (1298). Michele, doge in 1382, played a conspicuous part in the peace negotiations with Genoa of that year. Antonio (*c.* 1366–*c.* 1434) used his seat in the grand council as an observation post to assist in compiling a history of Venice. His chronicling of the events of his own time was more scrupulous than suited the government, which forced him to amend his text. By contrast, a later Morosini, Andrea (1558–1618), was commissioned by the Senate to contribute to an official history of the republic for the years 1521–1615. Andrea's history, while acceptable to the lay authorities, displeased the church.

The most illustrious member of the family, Francesco Morosini (1618–94), rose in the prolonged wars with the Turks in the 17th century to become one of the greatest captains of his time. Commander in chief of the Vene-

Francesco Morosini, engraving by an unknown artist
Microfoto 35

tian fleet in 1657, he conducted several successful campaigns before he was recalled through the intrigues of a rival. Sent to relieve besieged Candia (Crete) in 1667, he was unable to save the city from surrender but was absolved of blame and, on the renewal of the war in 1684, again was appointed commander in chief. After several brilliant victories he reconquered the Peloponnesus and Athens; on his return to Venice he was loaded with honours and given the title "Peloponnesiaco." Elected doge in 1688, five years later, at the age of 75, he once more assumed command of the fleet against the Turks; such was the respect of the Turks for his prowess that their fleet, cruising in the Venetian archipelago, withdrew at his approach.
·Byzantine administration under
Venice **5**:306e

Morotai, or MORTY, island in Maluku Utara (North Moluccas) district (*daerah tingkat* II), Maluku province (*daerah tingkat* I), Indonesia, northeast of Halmahera. With an area of 700 sq mi (1,800 sq km), it is mountainous and wooded, with swampy areas in the southwest; the chief products are resin and timber. There are some Muslims and Christians and a leper colony in Bidoho on the east coast. During World War II, it was an important Japanese military base; captured by Allied forces (1944), it was developed into a strategic air base, and an operational airfield still exists. Latest census 19,523.
2°20′ N, 128°25′ E
·map, Indonesia **9**:460

Moroto, mountain, Northern Province, Uganda, rises to 10,000 ft (3,000 m).
2°32′ N, 34°46′ E
·Ugandan physical geography **18**:825h

Morovis, town and municipality, north central Puerto Rico. The town, about 23 mi (37 km) southwest of San Juan, is in a sugarcane and fruit growing region. Caves and fossil remains are in the vicinity. Pop. (1980 prelim.) town, 2,636.
18°20′ N, 66°24′ W
·area and population table **15**:261
·map, Puerto Rico **15**:262

Moro Wars (1901–13), a series of scattered battles between American troops and Muslim bands on Mindanao, Philippines. The Moros fought for religious rather than political reasons, and their actions were unconnected with the Philippine Insurrection (*q.v.*) against American rule.

When sovereignty over the Philippines passed to the United States in 1898 after the Spanish–American War, a new policy toward the Moros emerged. Spain had been content to leave them alone, but the Americans tried to assimilate the Moros into the Philippine nation and to curb some feudal practices such as slave trading. The result was intransigence and rebellion.

Sporadic fighting began in 1901 and in spring 1903. American troops were attacked near Lake Lanao in the interior of Mindanao. The most famous of the U.S.–Moro battles occurred in March 1906 at the top of Mt. Dajo on the island of Jolo. Six hundred Moros inside a large volcanic crater were killed by troops under Gen. Leonard Wood. Because a number of women and children were killed in the fight, Wood came under severe criticism in Congress but was absolved of any wrongdoing by Pres. Theodore Roosevelt.

Outbreaks occurred again in September 1911 and June 1913.

moroxite (mineral): *see* apatite.

Morozov, Boris Ivanovich (1590–1662), tutor and, after 1648, brother-in-law of Tsar Alexis of Russia; having assumed the direction of state affairs at the beginning of Alexis' reign (1645), Morozov was temporarily sent into exile after he increased the salt tax (1646) and thereby provoked violent popular disorders in Moscow (1648).
·regency economic reforms **16**:48a

Morpeth, market town and borough in the county of Northumberland, England, on the River Wansbeck.

The town grew up around Morpeth Castle, a Norman fortress guarding the river crossing on the main east-coast route to Scotland in the north. Only the 14th-century gatehouse remains. There are a number of small industries, but the town primarily functions as a service centre for the surrounding rural area and the settlements of the Northumberland coalfield. Close by are the ruins of Newminster Abbey, a Cistercian foundation of the 12th century. Pop. (1971 prelim.) 14,055.
55°10′ N, 1°41′ W
·map, United Kingdom **18**:866

morphallaxis, a process of tissue reorganization seen frequently in lower animals following severe injury, such as bisection of the animal, and involving the breakdown and reformation of cells, movement of organs, and redifferentiation of tissues. The result is usually a smaller but complete individual, derived entirely from the tissues of part of the original animal.
·regeneration in plants and
coelenterates **15**:577a

morpheme, in linguistics, the smallest grammatical unit of speech; it may be a word, like "place" or "an," or an element of a word, like *re-* and *-ed* in "reappeared." Some languages, such as Vietnamese, have a one-to-one correspondence of morphemes to words; *i.e.*, no words contain more than one morpheme. Variants of a morpheme are called allomorphs; the ending *-s*, indicating plural in "cats," "dogs," the *-es* in "dishes," and the *-en* of "oxen" are all allomorphs of the plural morpheme. The word "talked" is represented by two morphemes, "talk" and the past-tense morpheme, here indicated by *-ed*. The study of words and morphemes is morphology (*q.v.*).
·definition, analysis, and theories **10**:997g
·definition in contrast to word **8**:271h
·stratificational concepts of analysis **10**:1004h

Morpheus, in Greek mythology, one of the sons of Somnus, the god of sleep. He sends human shapes (Greek *morphai*) of all kinds to the dreamer, while his brothers Phobetor (or Ikelos) and Phantasus send the forms of animals and inanimate things. It is possible, although not very probable, that his name actually meant Dark (from Greek *morphnos*).

morphine, the principal alkaloid of opium, is a narcotic analgesic drug used in medicine in the form of its hydrochloride, sulfate, acetate, and tartrate salts. Morphine was isolated by the German chemist F.W.A. Sertürner in 1806. It relieves pain and produces a deep sleep. In its power to relieve pain it has no rival among naturally occurring compounds, being of use in the treatment of severe pain of gallstone, renal colic, and metastatic cancer and in cases where other analgesics have failed.

It also has a calmative effect that protects the system against exhaustion in traumatic shock, internal hemorrhage, congestive heart failure, and debilitated conditions (as certain forms of typhoid fever). It is most frequently administered by injection to insure rapid action, but it is also effective when given orally.

Morphine has a euphoric effect and many undesirable side actions that are manifested on the respiratory, circulatory, and gastrointestinal systems. It also has an emetic effect and is a general depressant. The most serious drawback to the drug is its addiction liability.

Morphine can be converted into a diacetyl derivative known as heroin that shows a considerably higher euphoric effect and has such a powerful addicting capacity that its manufacture is prohibited. Other derivatives of morphine include the analgesics ethylmorphine, dihydrocodeinone, and dihydromorphinone, and the emetic apomorphine.

The structure of morphine proposed in the 1920s by J.M. Gulland and R. Robinson was confirmed in 1952 by its total synthesis, accomplished by M. Gates and G. Tschudi. Starting with Schaeffer's acid, a coal tar intermediate, they succeeded in preparing morphine by a 27-step process, a synthesis much too long and complicated to be feasible commercially. Synthetic organic chemistry also has provided a number of compounds (as meperidine, methadone, and pentazocine) that have in part supplanted morphine in medical use.

Morphine is extracted from the dried milky exudate of the unripe seed capsule of the opium poppy (*Papaver somniferum*). It occurs as colourless crystals or a white crystalline powder. The anhydrous alkaloid melts at 254° C. One gram of the alkaloid dissolves in about 5,000 millilitres (ml) of water, about 1,100 ml boiling water, 210 ml alcohol, and 1,220 ml of chloroform. It is freely soluble in alkalies because of its acidic character. It is also a monoacidic base, forming salts that crystallize readily. The most commonly used are the sulfate, $(C_{17}H_{19}NO_3)_2 \cdot H_2SO_4 \cdot 5H_2O$, and the hydrochloride, $C_{17}H_{19}NO_3 \cdot HCl \cdot 3H_2O$.

·analgesic effect on nervous system **18**:283a
·childbirth drug therapy complications **13**:1038b
·codeine synthesis by methylation **14**:194e
·disease causation mechanism **5**:852e
·early isolation and structure **1**:595c
·effects on nervous system **12**:992d
·narcotic source, use, and importance **12**:842; table
·overdose treatment with caffeine **17**:695a
·Papaverales opium derivatives and use **13**:963f
·respiratory disease treatment **18**:283h
·tolerance, control attempts, and addiction therapies **5**:1050c
·toxicity rating for drugs, table 2 **14**:619

morphogenesis, the shaping of an organism by embryological processes of cellular differentiation, histogenesis, organogenesis (*qq.v.*), and development of organ systems according to the genetic "blueprint" of the potential organism and environmental conditions.

Plant morphogenesis is brought about chiefly through differential growth. Permanent embryonic tissue results in a morphogenetic potential that varies greatly with the environment and continues to produce new organs throughout the life of the plant. Animal morphogenesis is accomplished by growth and by cell movement. A fixed pattern is established early; the organism is determined as to shape, size, and organ complement. Once organs are formed, no new ones (with few exceptions) are produced.

·Acetabularia use in experimentation **1**:494f
·biological development processes **5**:646f
·embryonic development of animals **5**:626d
·embryonic differentiation and body form **6**:746a
·muscles in aquatic and terrestrial embryos **12**:645d
·philosophical aspects of biology **16**:381g

morphogenetic region, theoretical area devised by geomorphologists to relate climate, geomorphic processes, and landforms. Morphogenetic classification was first proposed by Julius Büdel, the German geographer, in 1945. The morphogenetic concept asserts that under a particular climatic regime, certain geomorphic processes will predominate and produce a characteristic topographic expression. Proponents of the concept say that climatic controls outweigh rock type as a landform factor because the resistance of a rock type to erosion is dependent on the climate to which it is subjected. Present knowledge, however, indicates that landforms result from the interaction of climate, rock type, and physical processes.

·landform evolution theories **10**:624g; illus. 627

Morphoidae, family of New World tropical butterflies, sometimes considered a subfamily of the brush-footed butterfly (*q.v.*) family Nymphalidae (order Lepidoptera). Microscopic ridges on the wing scales break up and reflect light, producing the iridescent blue of some male *Morpho* species and the dull

Morpho nestira
Appel Color Photography

browns (brightened by contrasting eye spots on the wing undersurfaces) of male *Caligo* species. The generally duller coloured females have broader, less graceful wings than the males. The hairy larvae feed on plants and live and pupate in a communal web. Some *Morpho* species have poisonous hairs that cause a rash on human skin, but they are bred commercially in South America for use in jewelry, lampshades, pictures, and tray inlays. The adults of some species live in the tops of forest trees, rarely coming near the ground.

morphological theory of personality: *see* constitutional theory of personality.

morphology 12:451, the study of the size, shape, and structure of animals, plants, and micro-organisms and the relationships of their internal parts.

The text article includes a section on the historical background and the future trends of morphology. The concepts of homology and analogy are explained, and the associated disciplines of anatomy, histology, cytology, and embryology are defined. Chemical and microscopic techniques of morphology are also surveyed.

REFERENCES in other text articles:
·aging effects on body structure **1**:303a
·biological sciences classification **2**:1014g
·classification by domain **4**:692d
·Goethe's foundation of scientific study **8**:229h
·history of theoretic orientation **19**:1164g
·modes of studying botany **3**:67c

RELATED ENTRIES in the *Ready Reference and Index:*
anatomy; embryology; histology

morphology, in linguistics, study of the internal construction of words. Languages vary widely in the degree to which words can be analyzed into word elements, or morphemes (*q.v.*). In English, there are numerous examples, such as "replacement," which is composed of *re-*, "place," and *-ment*, and "walked," from the elements "walk" and *-ed*. Many American Indian languages have a highly complex morphology; other languages, such as Vietnamese or Chinese, have very little or none. Morphology includes the grammatical processes of inflection (*q.v.*) and derivation. Inflection marks categories such as person, tense, and case; *e.g.*, "sings" contains a final *-s*, marker of the 3rd person singular, and German *Mannes* consists of the stem *Mann* and the genitive singular inflection *-es*. Derivation is the formation of new words from existing words; *e.g.*, "singer" from "sing" and "acceptable" from "accept." Derived words can also be inflected: "singers" from "singer." *Major ref.* **10**:997f

·definition in contrast to syntax **8**:265g
·pidgin language simplification **14**:453b
·system and function in language **10**:645b

morphometric analysis, quantitative description and analysis of landforms as practiced in geomorphology that may be applied to a particular kind of landform or to drainage basins and large regions generally. Formulas for right circular cones have been fitted to the configurations of alluvial fans, logarithmic spirals have been used to describe certain shapes of beaches, and drumlins, spoon-shaped glacial landforms, have been found to accord to the form of the lemniscate curve. With regard to drainage basins, many quantitative measures have been developed to describe valley side and channel slopes, relief, area, drainage network type and extent, and other variables. Attempts to correlate statistically parameters defining drainage basin characteristics and basin hydrology, as in studies of sediment yield, are generally designated as morphometric analyses.

morphophonemics, in linguistics, study of the relationship between morphology (the internal construction of words) and phonology (the sound systems). Morphophonemics involves an investigation of the phonological variations within morphemes, usually marking different grammatical functions; *e.g.*, the vowel changes in "sleep" and "slept," "bind" and "bound," "vain" and "vanity," and the consonant alternations in "knife" and "knives," "loaf" and "loaves." Morphophonemics also includes the study of permissible sound combinations in a language. For example, in English a word cannot begin with the *ng* sound in "sing," nor the *z* sound in "azure," and only certain initial-consonant clusters, such as *tr*, *pr*, *pl*, *spl*, and *str*, appear. *See also* phonology; morphology. *Major ref.* **10**:998b

morphosyntax, grammatical discipline studying the rules underlying construction of words from morphemes and sentences and phrases from words.

·grammar's sub-disciplines **8**:265g

Morphy, Paul Charles (b. June 22, 1837, New Orleans—d. July 10, 1884, New Orleans), Chess master during his public career of less than two years, during which he became the world's leading player. Acclaimed by some as the most brilliant player of all time, he was first to rely on the now established principle of development before attack. Morphy learned Chess at the age of 10. At 19 he was admitted to the Louisiana bar, on condition that he not practice until coming of age.

After winning an important New York tournament in 1857, he travelled to Europe, where he defeated Adolf Anderssen of Germany, who had been regarded as the world's best player, and every other master who would face him—English player Howard Staunton avoided a match. Several times Morphy won games blindfolded against eight strong players who opposed him simultaneously.

He returned to the U.S. in 1859 and issued a challenge, offering to face any player in the world at odds of Pawn and move. When there was no response, Morphy abandoned his public Chess career. After an unsuccessful attempt to practice law, he gradually withdrew into a life of seclusion, marked by eccentric behaviour and delusions of persecution.

·development of modern chess **4**:198c

Morquio's syndrome, also known as MUCOPOLYSACCHARIDOSIS IV, uncommon disorder of intracartilaginous bone development that results in severe malformation of the skeleton and dwarfing. The disease is heritable (autosomal recessive); it is recognized within the first two years of life; and it is usually progressive until bone growth ceases in late adolescence. The vertebral bodies are wedge shaped and flattened, and back deformity is usual. The heads of the thighbones are small and malformed, sometimes resulting in dislocation of the hip; knock-knees and asymmetrical development of paired bones are also common. Associated findings include clouded corneas, circulatory malformations, and a tendency to compression of the spinal cord when back deformity is severe, but intelligence and life expectancy are apparently unaffected.

·joint disease affecting vertebrae **10**:263c
·mucopolysaccharide disease table **11**:1059

Morrell, Lady Ottoline (b. June 16, 1873, London—d. April 21, 1938, Tunbridge Wells, Kent), hostess and patron of the arts who brought together some of the most important writers and artists of her day. A woman of marked individuality and discernment, she was often the first to recognize a talent and assist its possessor—although not a few such relationships ended in quarrels.

The daughter of a general, she broke with her conventionally upper-class background when she built her circle of artists and intellectuals, which included, among others, D.H. Lawrence, Virginia Woolf, Aldous Huxley, Bertrand Russell, and Augustus John. She and her husband, Philip, Liberal member of Parliament, lived in London from 1902 until 1913, when they settled at Garsington Manor, Oxfordshire. Their home became a refuge for conscientious objectors during World War I, since the Morrells were pacifists. They lived in the Bloomsbury section of London from 1924. A collection of her writings, *Ottoline*, was edited by R. Gathorne-Hardy in 1963.

·D.H. Lawrence in magazine collaboration **10**:722g

Morrígan (Celtic: Queen of Demons), one of three Celtic war goddesses; the other two members were known as Badb (Crow or Raven) and Nemain (Frenzy) or, alternatively, Macha (*q.v.*). Sometimes the three were called Macha. The heads of those slain in battle were offered up to this sinister group and were known as *mesrad Machae* ("Macha's mast"). Sometimes the group was referred to as the three Morrígan, showing that the goddesses were in fact a triplication of a single deity, a common Celtic characteristic. The goddesses were able to take the form of a crow or raven at will and possessed great powers of prophecy; they could also influence the outcome of battle by magical means. They were similar in many respects to the Gaulish Nantosuelta (*q.v.*).

The goddess Morrígan mated with the Irish god Dagda. She clearly had aquatic associations, for she not only had sexual relations with the Dagda beside a river, but she also appeared in the guise of Washer at the Ford, washing the garments and weapons of those about to be killed in battle and prognosticating their fate. Morrígan survives in Arthurian legend as the enchantress Morgan le Fay (Fata Morgana).

Morrill, Justin S(mith) (b. April 14, 1810, Strafford, Vt.—d. Dec. 28, 1898, Washington, D.C.), Republican legislator who established a record for longevity by serving 43 years in both houses of the U.S. Congress; his name is particularly associated with the first high protective tariff and with federal support of land-grant colleges.

Following a modest career in local business, Morrill became active in Whig politics in the 1850s. Struck by the internal dissension within the party, he devoted himself afterward to preserving harmony within the Republican Party, which he helped found in Vermont (1855). He then went on to serve 12 years in the U.S. House of Representatives (1855–67) and 31 years in the Senate (1867–98).

Morrill
By courtesy of the Library of Congress, Washington, D.C.

A conservative in financial matters, Morrill sponsored the Tariff Act of 1861 and succeeding years, usually referred to as the Morrill tariffs, which inaugurated the policy of high import duties not for the traditional purpose of national revenue but to protect American industry from overseas competition. A consistent champion of "sound" currency, he opposed the resort to legal tender-paper money during and after the U.S. Civil War (1861–65). He also opposed the various proposals for the use of silver as a monetary standard. For special needs and to supplement tariff receipts, he favoured internal-revenue taxes.

Many considered that Morrill's most important legislative contribution lay in the area of federal aid to education. The Morrill Act of 1862 first provided grants of land to state colleges in which the "leading object" would be to teach subjects "related to agriculture and the mechanic arts," without excluding the general sciences and classical studies. It also provided for training in military science. (This aid was supplemented in 1890 by a monetary grant.) Morrill was henceforth called the "Father of the Agricultural Colleges," many of which have become leading educational institutions.

Morrill Tariff: *see* tariffs, U.S.

Morrilton, city, seat of Conway County, central Arkansas, U.S., in the Arkansas River Valley. Lewisburg, founded in 1819 as a trading post by Stephen Lewis and once a river port on Point Remove Creek, was relocated 1 mi north in 1872 to be on the Little Rock and Fort Smith (now Missouri Pacific) Railroad. The community, renamed to honour Henry Morrill, a Lewisburg resident, developed as an agricultural trade-processing centre, especially for poultry. Some light manufactures subsequently were established. Petit Jean State Park and Winrock Farm (owned by Winthrop Rockefeller and noted for the breeding of Santa Gertrudis cattle) lie to the southwest. Inc. 1880. Pop. (1980) 7,355.
35°09′ N, 92°45′ W

Morris, Edward Patrick Morris, 1st Baron (b. May 8, 1859, St. John's, Nfd.—d. Oct. 24, 1935, London), statesman, prime minister of Newfoundland from 1909 to 1918, and member of the British House of Lords from 1918.

Morris was called to the bar in 1885 and was made queen's counsellor in 1896. He represented St. John's West in the Newfoundland house of assembly from 1885 to 1918, originally as an Independent. From 1890 to 1895 he served as acting attorney general for Newfoundland under a Liberal administration, and he was director of the Newfoundland Savings Bank from 1893 to 1906. He left the Liberal Party in 1898 and led first the Independent Liberals (1898–1908) and then the People's Party (1908–19). He was attorney general again in 1902 and later became minister of justice in Sir Robert Bond's Liberal government. He resigned in 1907, however, because he considered Bond's social policies to be overly cautious. He then joined with the Conservatives to lead the new People's Party, becoming prime minister in 1909.

Under Morris' leadership, many social improvements were begun, and help was given to the British war effort during World War I (1914–18). Morris attended several imperial councils, and he joined the privy council in 1911 and the imperial war cabinet in 1916. He persuaded the Liberal Party and Fisherman's Union to join him in a National government in 1917. He resigned in 1918, retiring to England and entering the House of Lords, having been made a peer.

·Coaker rivalry submerged by war effort **12**:1084g

Morris, Alexander (b. March 17, 1826, Perth, Upper Canada, now Ontario—d. Oct. 28, 1889, Toronto), statesman and an advocate of Confederation who served as lieutenant governor of Manitoba and the Northwest Territories in 1872–77.

After studying at McGill University in Montreal, Morris was called to the bar in 1851. He entered politics 10 years later, when he was elected to the legislature of the United Province of Canada as Conservative member for Lanark, a seat he held through Confederation (1867) until 1872. He was an advocate of Confederation and wrote pamphlets supporting it. In 1869–72 he served as the dominion's minister of inland revenue in Sir John A. Macdonald's administration. In 1872 he was appointed chief justice of the Manitoba Court of Queen's Bench. Later that year he was made lieutenant governor of Manitoba and the Northwest Territories, in which post he served for five years before returning to Ontario. In 1878–86 he represented East Toronto in the Ontario legislature.

Morris, Charles William (1901–), U.S. philosopher, studied the development of philosophical Pragmatism and Neopositivism in the U.S., and investigated the semantic and linguistic significance of symbols. In addition to editing (1934–38) the works of the U.S. Pragmatic philosopher George Herbert Mead, he wrote *Six Theories of Mind* (1932); *Logical Positivism, Pragmatism, and Scientific Empiricism* (1937); *Signs, Language, and Behaviour* (2nd ed., 1955); and *The Pragmatic Movement in American Philosophy* (1970).

·linguistic semantic study range **16**:510d
·metalogical study of semiotic **11**:1079d
·three divisions of semiotic **14**:881h

Morris (MORRISON), **Clara** (b. March 17, 1846/48, Toronto—d. Nov. 20, 1925, New Canaan, Conn.), actress known for her realistic portrayal of unfortunate women in melodrama. She began her stage career in Cleveland in her early teens. In 1869 she joined a company in Cincinnati and a year later was engaged by producer Augustin Daly for his theatre in New York City to portray Anne Sylvester in Wilkie Collins' *Man and Wife*, a part that brought her immediate popularity. One of her most remembered roles was as Miss Multon (1876), an Americanized version of a French translation of *East Lynne*, from the novel by Mrs. Henry Wood. At the peak of her career her health failed, and from about 1900 she wrote books and stories about the theatre. In 1904 she returned to the stage in a revival and after 1905 appeared occasionally in vaudeville.

Morris, Gouverneur (b. Jan. 31, 1752, Morrisania, now in New York City—d. Nov. 6, 1816, Morrisania), statesman, diplomat, and financial expert who helped plan the U.S. decimal coinage system. Morris distrusted the democratic tendencies of colonists who wanted to break with England, but his belief in independence led him to join their ranks. He served in the New York Provincial Congress (1776–77), where he distinguished himself by a successful fight to include a provision for religious toleration in the first state constitution. He became an important advocate of a strong executive and a strong central government, and he sat in the Continental Congress (1778–79), where he was a leading supporter of George Washington, commander in chief of the Continental Army.

Following his defeat for reelection to Congress in 1779, Morris settled in Philadelphia as a lawyer. His series of essays on finance (published in the *Pennsylvania Packet*, 1780) led to his serving under the Articles of Confederation as assistant to the superintendent of finance, Robert Morris (to whom he was not related), from 1781 to 1785. In this office he prepared the report on a decimal coinage, suggesting the use of the terms dollar and cent. His plan, with some modifications by Thomas Jefferson, forms the basis of the present monetary system of the U.S. During the Constitutional Convention (1787), Morris was a member of the revision committee, where his literary skill was employed to give final form to the Constitution.

Gouverneur Morris, detail of a portrait by Ezra Ames; in the New York Historical Society collection

By courtesy of the New York Historical Society

Morris was appointed minister to France in 1792; he openly disapproved of the radical course of the French Revolution and sought to aid King Louis XVI to flee the country. His hostility led the French Revolutionary government to request his recall in 1794. He ended his active participation in politics after a brief term in the U.S. Senate (1800–03). Out of sympathy with the forces of republicanism, he allied himself with the extreme Federalists, who hoped to create a northern confederation during the War of 1812. From 1810 he was chairman of the commission in charge of the construction of the Erie Canal.

·Constitutional Convention leadership **18**:957b

Morris, Margaret (1891–1980), English dancer and teacher, who developed a system of dance notation in 1928 and encouraged the application of dance techniques to physical rehabilitation and to sports training.

·dance notation study **4**:456a

Morris, Michael, 3rd Baron Killanin: *see* Killanin, Michael Morris, 3rd Baron.

Morris, Robert (b. Jan. 31, 1734, Liverpool —d. May 7, 1806, Philadelphia), merchant and banker who came to be known as the financier of the American Revolution (1775–83). He left England to join his father in Maryland in 1747, entered a mercantile house in Philadelphia, and at the age of 20 became a member of a firm in which he later became a partner. During the Revolution, Morris joined the patriots and associated himself with their more conservative wing in Pennsylvania. He was vice president of the Pennsylvania Committee of Safety (1775–76) and was a member of both the Continental Congress (1775–78) and the Pennsylvania legislature (1778–79, 1780–81). He delayed signing the Declaration of Independence until several weeks after its adoption, hoping for reconcilation with Britain.

Robert Morris, portrait by Bass Otis and Thomas Sully; in the Historical Society of Pennsylvania collection, Philadelphia

By courtesy of the Historical Society of Pennsylvania

As chairman or member of various committees of the Continental Congress, Morris practically controlled the financial operations of the Revolution from 1776 to 1778. He raised the funds that made it possible for Gen. George Washington to move his army from the New York area to Yorktown, where Lord Cornwallis surrendered (1781). Morris had borrowed from the French, requisitioned from the states, and also advanced money from his own pocket. That same year, in Philadelphia, Morris established the Bank of North America, chartered at first by Congress and later by the state of Pennsylvania.

After the war Morris served as superintendent of finance under the Articles of Confederation (1781–84), and he directed the navy department as agent of marine during the same period. He served in the U.S. Senate (1789–95). Meanwhile, he had disposed of his mercantile and banking investments and had plunged heavily into land speculation. When returns from his lands slowed, he fell into bankruptcy and was confined in a debtors' prison for more than three years before his release in 1801.

Morris, Tom, name of two golfers popularly known as "Old Tom" and "Young Tom" (respectively b. June 16, 1821, St. Andrews, Fifeshire—d. May 24, 1908, St. Andrews; b. *c.* 1851—d. Sept. 25, 1875), father and son, each of whom won the British Open tournament four times. The father spent most of his life at St. Andrews as professional and greenskeeper and during his lifetime became an almost legendary figure in golf. He won in 1861, 1862, 1864, and 1867 the contest that was later called the British Open. "Young Tom" won the Open four consecutive times (1868–70 and 1872, there being no contest in 1871).

·British Open record **8**:246e
·club innovation, test, and competition **8**:245f
·gutta-percha ball acceptance **8**:245b

Morris, William 12:456 (b. March 24, 1834, Walthamstow, near London—d. Oct. 3, 1896, Hammersmith), designer, craftsman, poet, and early Socialist, whose designs for the decorative arts revolutionized Victorian taste and whose work was credited with dignity, a sense of purpose, and a vigorous freshness of approach.

Abstract of text biography. Morris was a member of a wealthy family and attended Exeter College at Oxford; he became associated with the painter Edward Burne-Jones and the poet Dante Gabriel Rossetti. In 1861 he founded with friends the firm of Morris, Marshall, Faulkner & Company, an association of "fine art workmen" designing and making furniture, fabrics, stained glass, wallpaper and similar products. Thirty years later he started the Kelmscott Press, which printed fine books in new typefaces of Morris' design based on medieval fonts.

REFERENCES in other text articles:
·architecture preservation activities **2**:57b
·art education criticism **2**:95b
·arts and crafts improvement program **13**:875a
·Arts and Crafts movement initiation **6**:1078d
·British Marxism **16**:968b
·calligraphy revival **3**:660f; illus.
·development in architectural ornament **1**:1109g
·improvement in ceramics quality **14**:916d
·medieval and Oriental influenced design **9**:723a; illus. 42
·medieval craftsmanship advocacy **9**:513g *passim* to 515e
·Rossetti's influence **15**:1156f
·tapestry design contributions **17**:1065e; illus.

Morris, William (b. 1873, Schwarzenau, Ger.—d. Nov. 2, 1932, New York City), theatrical agent and manager who opposed the attempted monopoly of vaudeville talent in the early 20th century. Morris was hired by Klaw and Erlanger, heads of a legitimate theatre trust, to book vaudeville acts for their theatre chain. This put him in conflict with the Keith-Albee United Booking Office, which sought to monopolize variety talent. Though Keith-Albee was forced to buy out Klaw and Erlanger, stipulating that they stay out of vaudeville for 10 years, the independent Morris was still free to harass them. He continued to manage theatrical acts, with the popular Harry Lauder as his chief attraction. When theatres were closed to Lauder, Morris appealed to Pres. Theodore Roosevelt, who requested that Lauder be allowed to appear in Washington, D.C., and who personally attended the consequent performance.

Morris, with strong support from the theatrical trade paper *Variety*, finally won his case against the theatrical monopolies. He founded the William Morris Agency, one of the foremost theatrical agencies in the country. His son, William Morris, Jr. (born Oct. 22, 1899, New York City), later became president of the agency (1932–52) and from 1952 served as a director.

Morris, William (1913–) U.S. editor, newspaper columnist, and lexicographer.

·American Heritage Dictionary **5**:718a

Morris, William Richard, 1st Viscount Nuffield: *see* Nuffield, William Richard Morris, 1st Viscount.

Morris, Wright (b. Jan. 6, 1910, Central City, Neb.), prolific novelist whose works are regarded by some as important for their treatment of the conflict between rural midwestern characters and urban sophisticates. His first novel, *My Uncle Dudley* (1942), concerned a man and a boy travelling westward; the restlessness suggested in this novel occurs repeatedly in Morris' later novels.

His better known works include *The Home Place* (1948); *The Works of Love* (1951); *The Field of Vision* (1956), for which he received the National Book Award; *Love Among the Cannibals* (1957); *Fire Sermon* (1971); and *Earthly Delights, Unearthly Adornments* (1978).

Morris chair, named for William Morris, the English poet, painter, polemicist, and craftsman, who in the 19th century pioneered the production of light, functional furniture of a traditional rural type. The Morris chair is of the "easy" variety, with padded armrests and

Morris chair of ebonized wood with turned decoration, designed by Phillip Webb, 1861, made by Morris & Co. from 1866; in the Victoria and Albert Museum, London

By courtesy of the Victoria and Albert Museum, London, Crown copyright

detachable cushions on the seat and back. The wooden structure of the chair usually makes much use of turned (*i.e.*, shaped on a lathe) spindle elements.

Morris dance, ritual folk dance performed in rural England by groups of specially chosen and trained men; less specifically, a variety of related customs, such as mumming, as well as some popular entertainments derived from them. Similar customs are widespread throughout Europe and extend to the Middle East, India, and parts of Central and South America. Notable examples are the *Perchten* dancer-masqueraders of Austria; and ritual dances such as the moriscos, *santiagos*, *matachinas* and Moors and Christians of the Mediterranean and Latin America, and the *călușari*, a Romanian dance of healing and fertility. The wide distribution of such dances suggests an ancient Indo-European origin. A common feature of many of them is that of a group of dancing men attendant on a pagan god who celebrates his revival after death (as in the *călușari* dance); or of battle between opposing forces of good and evil (as in the Moors' and Christians' dances). Often the dancers wear white clothes and dance with bells fastened to the legs or body. A feeling that the dances have magic power or bring luck persists wherever they are traditionally performed.

The central figure of the dances, usually an animal-man, varies considerably in importance. In some cases, he may dominate the rite; in others—as in many English Morris dances—the young men in the *corps d'élite* may dominate, with the animal-man and other dramatic characters either relegated to the subsidiary role of comics or omitted.

The name Morris is also associated with the horn dance held each year at Abbots Bromley, Staffordshire. This dance-procession includes six animal-men bearing deer antlers, three white and three black sets; a man-woman, or Maid Marian, and a fool, both carrying phallic symbols; a hobby horse; and a youth with a crossbow who shoots at the leading "stags" whenever possible.

A comparable surviving animal custom is the May Day procession of a man-horse, notably at Padstow, Cornwall. There, the central figure, "Oss Oss," is a witch doctor disguised as a horse and wearing a medicine mask. The dancers are attendants who sing the May Day song, beat drums, and in turn act the horse or dance in attendance.

The name Morris is also associated with groups of mummers who act, rather than dance, the death-and-survival rite at the turn of the year.

Throughout history, the Morris seems to have been common. It was imported from village festivities into popular entertainment after the invention of the court masque by Henry VIII. The word Morris apparently derived from "morisco," meaning "Moorish." Cecil Sharp, whose collecting of Morris dances preserved many from extinction, suggested that it might have arisen from the dancers' blacking their faces as part of the necessary ritual disguise.

Among specific Morris dances are Bean Setting, Leap Frog, and Laudnum Bunches. The few solo Morris dances are called Morris jigs; an example is the Shepherds' Hey. The name Morris dance is sometimes loosely applied to sword dances (*q.v.*) in which a group of men weave their swords into intricate patterns. Such dances are closely related to dances of the Morris family.

·folk dance functional variation **7**:449e
·form and popularity **5**:462h
·Middle American variants and ritual use **1**:665h; illus. 672

Morris dancers, replica of the stained glass window in the house of George Tollet, Betley, Eng., early 15th century; in the Kingston-upon-Thames Museum and Art Gallery, London

Kingston Photographic Services Ltd.

Morris Jesup, Cape, next to Kaffeklubben Island (*q.v.*), the world's northernmost point of land, in the Peary Land region, at the northernmost extremity of Greenland, on the Arctic Ocean, 440 mi (710 km) from the North Pole. It was reached in 1900 by Robert E. Peary, the U.S. Arctic explorer, and was named for Morris Ketchum Jesup, a merchant-banker who had financed several polar expeditions.

83°39.7′ N, 33°25′ W

·map, Greenland **8**:412

Morris-Jones, Sir John (b. Oct. 17, 1864, Llandrygarn, Anglesey—d. April 16, 1929, Bangor, Carnarvonshire), teacher, scholar, and poet who revolutionized Welsh literature. By insisting—through his teaching and his writings and his annual adjudication at national eisteddfodau (poetic competitions)—that correctness was the first essential of style and sincerity the first essential of the literary art, he helped restore to Welsh poetry its classical standards. The eldest son of Morris Jones, a shopkeeper, he gave up the study of mathematics to devote his entire time to Welsh language and literature. After graduation from Oxford, he became the first professor of Welsh at the University College of North Wales, Bangor.

His works include *A Welsh Grammar, Historical and Comparative* (1913), *Cerdd Dafod* (1925; "The Art of Poetry"), *Orgraff yr Iaith Gymraeg* (1928; "The Orthography of the Welsh Language"), and an unfinished study of syntax (1931), published posthumously under the title *Welsh Syntax*. He also translated a collection of poems (1907), the most notable being that of the *Robāʿiyāt* of Omar Khayyam directly from the Persian.

Morris-Jones, oil painting by Christopher Williams, 1924; in the National Museum of Wales, Cardiff

By courtesy of the National Museum of Wales, Cardiff

Morrison, Arthur (b. Nov. 1, 1863, Kent, England—d. Dec. 4, 1945, Chalfont St. Peter, Buckinghamshire), writer noted for novels and short stories describing slum life in London's East End at the end of the Victorian era that were so vividly written that they helped bring about changes in British housing legislation. These include *Tales of Mean Streets* (1894), a collection of short stories that had originally appeared in the London *National Observer*, and *A Child of the Jago* (1896), a novel credited with precipitating the clearance of the worst London slum of that time. His realistic novels and stories are sober in tone, but the characters are portrayed with a Dickensian colourfulness. His attitude toward the people he described was paternalist, rather than radical, and he opposed Socialism and the trades union movement. He also wrote detective fiction that featured the lawyer-detective Martin Hewitt. Although not particularly baffling, these mysteries, such as *Martin Hewitt: Investigator* (1894) and *The Red Triangle* (1903), kept the detective genre alive during the post-Sherlock Holmes period.

An authority and collector of Chinese and Japanese art, Morrison also published the authoritative *Painters of Japan* (1911).

Morrison, Clara: *see* Morris, Clara.

Morrison, DeLesseps S(tory) (1912–64), mayor of New Orleans (1946–62), effected physical rehabilitation of the city; he was U.S. ambassador to the Organization of American States (1961–63).

·New Orleans municipal improvements **13**:8c

Morrison, Herbert, in full HERBERT STANLEY MORRISON, BARON MORRISON OF LAMBETH (1888–1965), British Labour statesman who played a leading role in London local government for 25 years and was a prominent member of the coalition government during World War II and of the postwar Labour governments.

Morrison, Robert (b. Jan. 5, 1782, Buller's Green, Northumberland—d. Aug. 1, 1834, Canton, China), Presbyterian minister, translator, and the London Missionary Society's first missionary to China; he is considered the father of Protestant mission work there.

After studies in theology and Chinese, he was ordained in 1807 and was immediately sent by the society to Canton. In 1809 he became translator to the East India Company, a post he held until his death. Only 10 converts were baptized during the 27 years of his service in China, but each proved faithful. Admission of the convert Liang A-fa to the office of evangelist was the first Protestant ordination performed in China. With his colleague William Milne, Morrison founded the Anglo-Chinese College in Malacca (moved to Hong Kong in 1843) for "the cultivation of English and Chinese literature in order to encourage the spread of the Gospel of Jesus Christ." With Milne he also translated the New Testament into Chinese (1813), his own contribution being the Gospels, the Letter to the Hebrews, and the Revelation to John. Their translation of the entire Bible appeared in 1821. Among Morrison's other works are a *Grammar of the Chinese Language* (1815) and a *Dictionary of the Chinese Language, in Three Parts* (1815–23). After his death another school for Chinese youth, located first in Macau (1838) and later in Hong Kong (1842), was established by the newly founded Morrison Education Society.

·non-European Bible versions **2**:895e

Morrison Formation, division of Upper Jurassic rocks in the U.S. (The Jurassic Period began about 190,000,000 years ago and lasted about 54,000,000 years.) The formation was named for exposures studied near Morrison, Colo., whose rocks consist of shales, siltstones, sandstones, and local conglomerates that are frequently highly coloured. The Morrison Formation is of nonmarine origin and occurs from Arizona to Montana. Before erosion stripped much of it away, it covered some 1,300,000 square kilometres (500,000 square miles) of the western interior of the U.S. It is no more than 120 metres (400 feet) in thickness. At the time of its deposition, the area consisted of a low alluvial plain across which sluggish streams flowed; highlands existed to the south and west, and swamps and lakes frequently interrupted the courses of streams. The land was covered by lush vegetation, and animal life was plentiful. The large Jurassic dinosaurs that have been found in the United States occur in the Morrison—no fewer than 69 species have been recovered in its deposits, as well as 25 species of small, primitive mammals. Dinosaur species similar to those of the Morrison occur in East Africa.

Morris Plan, U.S. loan and investment method initiated in 1910.

·consumer credit in U.S. **5**:99d

Morristown, town, seat (1740) of Morris County, New Jersey, U.S., on the Whippany River, west of New York City. Founded as West Hanover in 1710 when a forge was established to exploit local iron ore, it was renamed in 1740 for Lewis Morris, then governor of the colony.

Wick House (18th century, restored) in Jockey Hollow Area, Morristown National Historical Park, New Jersey
George E. Jones III—Photo Researchers

The Morristown National Historical Park, established in 1933, includes Jockey Hollow, in which U.S. troops spent the winter of 1779–80; Wick House, a restored farmhouse of the Revolutionary era; Ford mansion, which served as George Washington's headquarters; and the site of Ft. Nonsense, a low earthworks built by troops in 1777. The historical museum has a collection of relics, books, and manuscripts pertaining to Washington and the Revolution. Benedict Arnold was court-martialed in the Dickerson Tavern (now demolished), and Samuel F.B. Morse and Alfred Vail developed the telegraph at a local ironworks. In the late 19th century, Morristown was home to such notable persons as the writers Bret Harte and Frank R. Stockton and the cartoonist Thomas Nast. It was also surrounded by the estates of wealthy persons.

Morristown is now largely a residential community, many of whose citizens commute to New York and to Newark to work; it is also a centre for chemical production and research laboratories. There are several private schools and a junior college and Seeing Eye, Inc., which trains guide dogs for the blind. Inc. 1865. Pop. (1980) 16,614.
40°48′ N, 74°29′ W

Morristown, city, seat (1870) of Hamblen County, northeastern Tennessee, U.S., northeast of Knoxville; it lies in a valley bounded on the north and west by the Clinch Mountains and on the southeast by the Great Smoky Mountains National Park. The community was named for Gideon Morris, who settled the site in 1787. The boyhood home of Davy Crockett, pioneer frontiersman, has been reproduced as a tavern–museum. A cavalry action of the Civil War known as Gilliam's Stampede was fought in the vicinity on Nov. 12, 1864.

Local industries produce nylon, rayon, furniture, and metals. The chief agricultural products are tobacco, corn (maize), hay, and soybeans. Morristown College was founded in 1881, and the city is the site of a state area vocational–technical school. Cherokee and Douglas lakes, upper reservoirs of the Tennessee Valley Authority system, are nearby. Inc. 1885. Pop. (1980) 19,683.
36°13′ N, 83°18′ W

Morro, Castillo del, English MORRO CASTLE, fort at the entrance to Havana harbour.

·lighthouse addition and importance **8**:669g; map and photograph 670

Morrone, Pietro da: *see* Celestine V, Saint.

Morrow, Dwight W(hitney) (1873–1931), U.S. lawyer, financier, and statesman.

·Mexican–U.S. diplomatic expertise **12**:86d

Morrowan Series, major division of Pennsylvanian rocks and time in the U.S. (the Pennsylvanian Period began about 325,000,000 years ago and lasted about 45,000,000 years). It was named for exposures studied in Arkansas and Texas, especially well developed near Morrow, Ark., and is the oldest Pennsylvanian series. It underlies rocks of the Atokan Series and consists predominantly of sandstones, shales, and some limestones; conglomerates also occur.

Late in the preceding Mississippian Period, uplift began to affect the areas along the Gulf borders south of the Ouachita Geosyncline. Early in the Morrowan, mountain-building activity extended northward and formed a mountain system, the Oklahoma mountains of the Pennsylvanian and following Permian periods, in southern Oklahoma and the Texas Panhandle.

Morse, Edward Sylvester (1838–1925), U.S. zoologist.

·Japanese Neolithic culture name **19**:216g

Morse, Jedidiah (b. Aug. 23, 1761, Woodstock, Conn.—d. June 9, 1826, New Haven), Congregational minister, known in his time as the father of American geography and author of the first textbook on the subject published in the U.S., *Geography Made Easy* (1784). His geographical writings dominated the field in the U.S. until his death.

While a young man teaching school in New Haven, he developed an interest in U.S. geography because, as he wrote, "so imperfect are all the accounts of America hitherto published . . . that from them very little knowledge of this country can be gained." The success of *Geography Made Easy* (25 editions during his lifetime) encouraged him to produce the work that firmly established his reputation, *The American Geography* (1789), known in later editions as *The American Universal Geography*. This book was followed by

Jedidiah Morse, watercolour miniature by Nathaniel Hancock (1790–1802); in the Mabel Brady Garvan Collection, Yale University Art Gallery
By courtesy of Yale University Art Gallery, Mabel Brady Garvan Collection

a work for children, *Elements of Geography* (1795), *The American Gazetteer* (1797), and *A New Gazetteer of the Eastern Continent* (1802). The inventor Samuel F.B. Morse was his eldest son.

Morse, (Harold) Marston (1892–1977), U.S. mathematician.

·functional analysis fundamentals **1**:762d

Morse, Samuel F(inley) B(reese) **12**:458 (b. April 27, 1791, Charlestown, Mass.—d. April 2, 1872, New York City), portrait painter and inventor of the electric telegraph.

Abstract of text biography. Morse, son of the distinguished geographer Jedidiah Morse, graduated from Yale College in 1810 and became a clerk for a Boston book publisher. In 1811 he went to England to study painting. After returning to the U.S. in 1815, he became an itinerant portrait painter in New England, New York, and South Carolina. He settled in New York City in 1825. In 1827 he helped launch the New York *Journal of Commerce*. He was a founder of the National Academy of Design and served as its first president (1826–45). He conceived the idea of the telegraph in 1832 and probably had completed his first working model by 1835. By 1837 he turned his full attention to the new invention and in 1838 developed the Morse Code. The first telegraph line in the U.S. was established between Baltimore and Washington. A Supreme Court decision established his patent rights in 1854.

REFERENCES in other text articles:
·technology development **18**:44g
·telegraph and code development **18**:69a; illus.
·Whitney portrait illus. **19**:822

Morse Code, a system of signals in which dots and dashes are combined to represent letters of the alphabet, developed in 1838 by Samuel F.B. Morse of the U.S., for use in electric telegraphy. Highly successful, it continued to be used in telegraphy till the 1920s, when it was supplanted by the Baudot code. Morse continues to be used in radiotelegra-

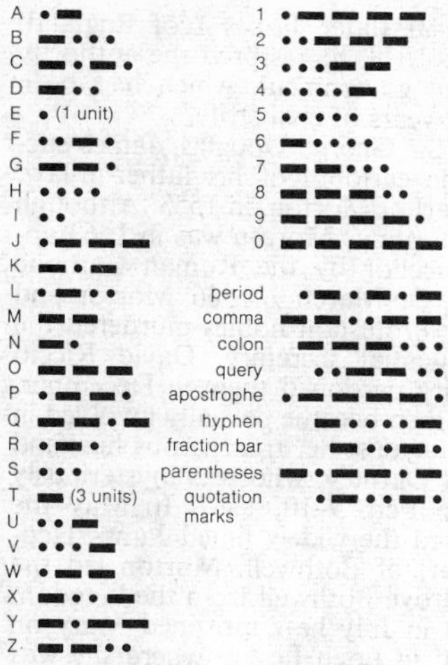

International Morse Code

phy, in submarine cable systems, and when simple mobile apparatus is required.
·Morse's invention of telegraph **12**:458e
·specialized forms of writing **19**:1040d
·technology development **18**:44g
·telegraph development **18**:69a; illus.

Morse theory, study of the critical points of functions, with particular attention to the implied topological aspects of the domain space.
·functional analysis fundamentals **1**:764f
·topological group theory **18**:497b

Morsztyn, Jan Andrzej (1613–93), Polish author.
·literary style and contributions **10**:1162d

Morsztyn, Zbigniew (1627–89), Polish author.
·Polish Baroque literature **10**:1162d

mortality, human, in demographic usage, the frequency of death in a population. Determinants of death are biological, social, and economic.

Individual factors in mortality include heredity, sex differences, and age. In general, the risk of death at any given age is less for females than for males, except during the childbearing years (and in Western societies females have a lower mortality even during those years). The risk of death is high immediately after birth, diminishing during childhood and reaching a minimum at 10 to 12 years of age. The risk then rises again, until at late ages it surpasses that of the first year of life. The expectation of life at birth is the most efficient index of the general level of mortality of a population. In ancient Greece and Rome the average life expectancy was about 28 years; in the Western world it was about 70 years at the beginning of the 1970s.
·aging process effects **1**:299g
·biological population factors **14**:830a
·cancer's worldwide effect **3**:763f; table 767
·demographic analysis of death rates **5**:576b; table 577
·disease classification systems **5**:862g
·eugenic study of changes **6**:1025g
·heart attack survival rates **3**:889c
·industrial medicine applications **9**:528f
·infant and maternal death risk in abnormal childbirth **13**:1037f
·population growth theory **14**:816a; table 2
·rheumatic fever's declining lethality **3**:890c
·Semmelweis' influence on antisepsis **16**:529f
·sex differences during life-span **7**:998c
·snakebite likelihood and incidence **16**:559g

mortar, material used in building construction to bond brick, stone, tile, or concrete blocks into a structure. Mortar consists of inert siliceous (sandy) material mixed with cement in such proportions that the resulting substance will be sufficiently plastic when wet to flow readily under the weight of the masonry units and the tap of the mason's trowel. Cement is the most costly ingredient and is held to the minimum consistent with desired strength and watertightness.

Mortar is combined with water before use to form a plastic substance, which, after application, hardens into a stonelike mass. By fully bedding the masonry units, the mortar distributes the load of the structure uniformly over their entire bonding surfaces and provides a weathertight joint.
·aluminum refractory production and uses **1**:646g
·building construction development **3**:453h
·calcium hydroxide setting reaction **3**:586b
·cement production processes and uses **3**:1075h
·masonry construction methods **11**:588h
·mosaic art setting techniques **12**:465a
·Roman roadway construction methods **15**:894a; fig. 892

mortar, short-range military firearm with short barrel, low muzzle velocity, and high arched trajectory. Large types have been used against fortifications since medieval times; portable models became standard 20th-century infantry weapons, especially for trench or mountain warfare. *Major ref.* **8**:495d
·siege artillery of 1600s to 1800s **19**:684d
·small arms design and operation **16**:902a
·weapons design trends **19**:696d
·World War I improvements **19**:687b

mortar and pestle, ancient device for milling by pounding. Together with the saddle quern

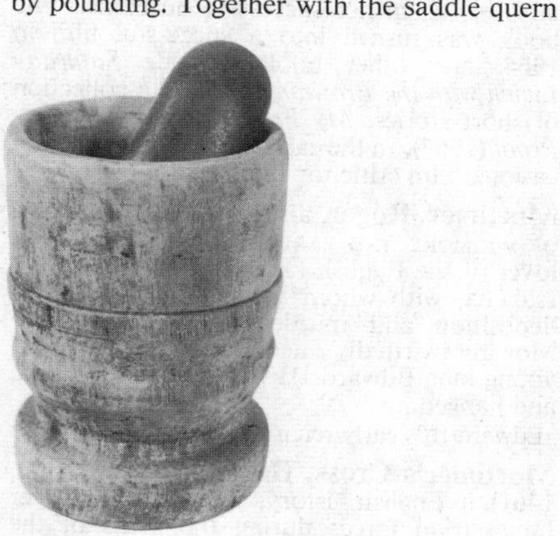
Wooden mortar and pestle from Ontario, Canada

Shackleton—Miller Services Ltd.

(a round stone rolled or rubbed on a flat stone bed), it was the first means known for grinding grain; the grain was placed in a shallow depression in a stone, the mortar, and pounded with a rodlike stone, the pestle. Refined versions of the mortar and pestle have continued to find use in kitchens for preparing pastes and other finely ground elements of cuisine, in pharmacy for preparing medicines, and in chemical laboratories.
·oil extraction with ghani **13**:528b

Mort d'Ancestor, assize of, law made during the reign of Henry II of England which established procedure for dealing with cases of property rights.
·Henry II's legal reform **8**:766c

Mort de Socrate (1823), poem by Alphonse de Lamartine.
·publication and metaphysical theme **10**:618e

Morte Darthur, Le, the first account of the Arthurian legend (*q.v.*) in modern English prose, completed by Thomas Malory (*q.v.*) *c.* 1470 and printed by William Caxton in 1485. It retells the adventures of the knights of the Round Table in chronological sequence from the birth of Arthur. Based on French romances, Malory's account differs from his models in its emphasis on the brotherhood of the knights rather than on courtly love and on the conflicts of loyalty (brought about by the adultery of Lancelot and Guinevere) that finally destroy the fellowship.
·chivalric–barbaric mood **10**:1048e
·literary significance **10**:1110g

Mortes River, Portuguese RIO DAS MORTES, also called RIO MANSO, river in central Brazil, rises east of Cuibá, and flows east-northeastward across the Planalto (plateau) do Mato Grosso. East of the Serra do Roncador and above São Félix across from Bananal Island, it turns north-northeastward and empties into the Araguaia River (*q.v.*), a principal affluent of the Tocantins. Its total length is about 500 mi (800 km). There is some diamond washing along its banks.
11°45′ S, 50°44′ W

mortgages, law of **12**:459, rules of law applying to the transfer of a property interest by a debtor (mortgagor) to his creditor (mortgagee), to be held as security for the performance of an obligation.

The text article covers the development of the law of mortgage since Roman times, in both civil and common law systems.

REFERENCES in other text articles:
·French civil code registration system **4**:663h
·life and term insurance protection **9**:651f
·maritime law concerning liens on ships **11**:501g

Mortier, Édouard-Adolphe-Casimir-Joseph, duc de Trévise (b. Feb. 13, 1768, Cateau-Cambrésis, Fr.—d. July 28, 1835, Paris), French general, one of Napoleon's marshals, who also served as prime minister and minister of war during the reign of King Louis-Philippe.

Mortier fought in the wars of the French Revolution, serving in the Army of the North, the Army of the Danube, and the Army of Helvetia. Promoted to general in 1799, he became in May 1800 commander of the 10th military division, in charge of Paris. In April 1803 he occupied Hanover after the collapse of the peace of Amiens and in May 1804 was named one of the 18 marshals of the empire by Napoleon. In November 1805 he was defeated at Dürnstein in Austria by the Russian general Mikhail Kutuzov. He served in the Prussian campaign in 1806 and 1807 and fought in Spain in 1808, taking part in the siege of Saragossa and defeating 60,000 Spanish troops in the Battle of Ocaña. He commanded the Young Guard in the Russian campaign of 1812 and attempted to hold off the onslaught of the Allied armies outside Paris in 1814.

Mortier, detail from a portrait by Charles-Philippe de Larivière (1798–1876); in the Musée National de Versailles et des Trianons, France

H. Roger-Viollet

At the first restoration of the Bourbons (1814), Mortier was recognized as a peer, but during the Hundred Days, in which Napoleon tried to reconquer his empire, Mortier rejoined him. After the second return of the Bourbons, he was in disgrace until 1819, when his peerage was restored. After the Revolution of July 1830, in which Charles X was replaced by Louis-Philippe, he served as ambassador to St. Petersburg (now Leningrad) and was prime minister and minister of war from November 1834 to March 1835. He was killed in Giuseppe Fieschi's assassination attempt on the life of King Louis-Philippe.
·Prussian campaign strategy **7**:726f

Mortillet, (Louis-Laurent-Marie) Gabriel de (b. Aug. 29, 1821, Meylan, Fr.—d. Sept. 25, 1898, Saint-Germain-en-Laye), archaeologist who formulated the first chronological classification of the epochs of man's prehistoric cultural development. His ordering of the Paleolithic (Stone Age) epochs into Chellean, Acheulean, Mousterian, Solutrean, Magdalenian, etc., continued into the 20th century as the basis for anthropological classification.

Mortillet, engraving by L. Coutil, 1895
J.P. Ziolo

Mortillet's early studies of the geology and paleontology of the Alps were summarized in his *Géologie et minéralogie de la Savoie* (1858; "Geology and Mineralogy of Savoie"). He joined the staff of the Museum of National Antiquities, Saint-Germain-en-Laye (1868), was assistant curator for 17 years, and was professor of prehistoric anthropology at the School of Anthropology in Paris (1876–98). His classifications, elaborated in *Le Préhistorique: antiquité de l'homme* (1882; "The Prehistoric: Man's Antiquity"), were revised in subsequent editions of the work.

Mortimer, the name of an Anglo-Norman family, afterward earls of March and Ulster, which wielded great power on the Welsh marches, attained political eminence in the 13th and 14th centuries, and in the 15th possessed a claim to the English throne. Among the most notable members of the family were Roger Mortimer (*q.v.*; d. 1330), earl of March; Edmund (d. 1381), 3rd earl, whose marriage to Philippa, daughter and heiress of Lionel of Antwerp, duke of Clarence (second surviving son of Edward III), later brought the family a claim to the throne; and Edmund (d. 1428), 5th earl, son of the 3rd earl and Philippa, had by the laws of ordinary descent a better claim to the throne than Henry IV, son of Edward III's third surviving son, John of Gaunt, duke of Lancaster, but nevertheless remained loyal to him.

Mortimer, John (Clifford) (b. April 21, 1923, Hampstead, London), dramatist whose plays reveal the influence of the 19th-century Russian playwright Anton Chekhov, but whose work also reflects the contemporary concern for the want of communication between people. His comedy focusses on the lonely, the neglected, and the unsuccessful.

Educated at Harrow, Brasenose College, Oxford, Mortimer began writing before he was called to the bar (1948). The following year he married Penelope Ruth Fletcher (the novelist Penelope Mortimer).

Mortimer, too, began his writing career as a novelist, with *Charade* (1947). Not until 1958, with his play *The Dock Brief*—which formed a double bill with his family comedy *What Shall We Tell Caroline?*—was his reputation established.

Mortimer's other plays include *The Wrong Side of the Park* (performed 1960), *Two Stars for Comfort* (performed 1962), and *The Judge* (performed 1967). In 1965 Mortimer successfully adapted the farce, *A Flea in Her Ear*, from the French of Georges Feydeau. In a change of pace, he wrote a highly personal and autobiographical play on his relationship with his blind father, *A Voyage Round My Father* (1970). He then returned to translation in 1971 with a free rendition of Carl Zuckmayer's satire on Prussian militarism, *The Captain of Köpenick*. Mortimer also did the screenplay for the film *John and Mary* (1970).

Mortimer, John Hamilton, 18th-century English painter.
·Romanticism style development **19**:454e

Mortimer, Penelope (Ruth), *née* FLETCHER (b. 1918, Rhyl, North Wales), mid-20th century journalist and novelist noted for her intense style of writing depicting a nightmarish world of neuroses and broken marriages.

After her graduation from London University, she began to write—poetry, book reviews, and short stories. In 1949 she married the playwright John Mortimer, with whom she later collaborated on the book *Daddy's Gone A-Hunting* (1958). She is perhaps best known for her novel *The Pumpkin Eater* (1962), a disturbingly vivid story of a woman whose compulsive anxiety to bear children gradually isolates her from her successive husbands. The book was turned into a successful film in 1964. Her other books include *Saturday Lunch with the Brownings* (1960), a collection of short stories, *My Friend Says It's Bullet-Proof* (1967). In the early 1970s she was an occasional film critic for the London *Observer*.

Mortimer, Roger, also known as 8TH BARON OF WIGMORE AND EARL OF MARCH (d. 1330), lover of the English king Edward II's queen, Isabella, with whom he contrived Edward's deposition and murder (1327). Thereafter Mortimer virtually ruled England. In 1330 the young king Edward III had him seized, tried, and hanged.
·Edward III's early reign **6**:436h

Mortimer's Cross, Battle of (February 2, 1461), in English history, Yorkist victory over Lancastrian forces during the Wars of the Roses.

mortise and tenon, joint used in carpentry to fasten timbers and joists together at right angles. The end of one timber is reduced to about one-third normal size, forming the tenon, and a hole or mortise is cut in the other timber, into which the tenon fits.
·carpentry construction and use **3**:953c; illus.
·furniture constructional uses **7**:783d
·furniture technology and construction **7**:807f
·Maurya period stūpa construction **17**:173f

mortmain, in English law, the state of land being held by the "dead hand" (French *mort main*) of a corporation. In feudal days a conveyance of land to a monastery or other corporation deprived the lord of many profitable feudal incidents, for the corporation was never under age, never died, and never committed felony or married. Statutes were consequently passed between the 13th and 16th centuries prohibiting alienation into mortmain without license from the crown. The modern law was contained in the Mortmain and Charitable Uses acts, 1888 and 1891, and in a number of acts that authorized limited companies and some other corporations to hold land without license in mortmain. An unauthorized conveyance into mortmain made the land liable to forfeiture to the crown. The law of mortmain was out of accord with modern ideas, however, and so it was abolished in Britain in 1960.

Mortmain legislation exists in some other jurisdictions in the British Commonwealth and in the United States.
·Statute of 1279 under Edward I **3**:211e

Morton, James Douglas, 4th earl of (b. *c.* 1516—d. June 2, 1581, Edinburgh), Scottish lord who played a leading role in the overthrow of Mary, Queen of Scots (ruled 1542–67). As regent of Scotland for young King James VI (later James I of England) from 1572 to 1578, he restored the authority of the central government, which had been weakened by years of civil strife.

The son of Sir George Douglas, James succeeded to the earldom of his father-in-law, James, 3rd earl of Morton, in 1553. Although he was a Protestant, Morton was in 1563 appointed chancellor by the Roman Catholic Mary Stuart. On March 9, 1566, Morton and several other Protestant nobles murdered the Queen's influential secretary, David Riccio (Rizzio). Mary pardoned them in December, and Morton then became partially involved in a conspiracy against her treacherous husband Henry, Lord Darnley, who was mysteriously murdered on Feb. 9–10, 1567. In May the Queen married the widely hated James Hepburn, 4th earl of Bothwell. Morton led the forces that drove Bothwell from the kingdom in June, and in July he imprisoned Mary on Castle Island in Loch Leven, where she was forced to abdicate in favour of her infant son James (King James VI). The Queen escaped on May 2, 1568, but Morton decisively defeated her army at Langside, near Glasgow, 11 days later. She then fled to England.

During the ensuing civil war between the supporters of Mary and of James, Morton was an able ally of the regent, James Stewart, earl of Moray (died 1570). Upon becoming regent in 1572, Morton completed the suppression of the rebels, restored the rule of law, and introduced a reformed episcopacy. Nevertheless, the nobles resented the efficiency of his administration, and the Presbyterians rejected the episcopacy. His opponents forced him to resign the regency in 1578; three years later he was charged with complicity in Darnley's murder and executed.
·regency and execution **10**:21h

Morton, Charles, 17th-century Puritan divine and educator.
·teaching greatness and Defoe's training **5**:551a

Morton, Jelly Roll, real name FERDINAND JOSEPH LA MENTHE MORTON (b. Sept. 20, 1885, Gulfport, La.—d. July 10, 1941, Los Angeles), composer and pianist who claimed to have invented jazz.

He was one of the most enigmatic of all jazz figures, largely because of the wide disparity of opinion as to his ability and the vast gulf between his pretensions and his achievements. He learned the guitar and piano as a child and from 1902 was a professional pianist in the bordellos of New Orleans, La. Drifting northward and living an itinerant life, he made his recording debut in 1923; and from 1926 to 1930 he made, under the name of Morton's Red Hot Peppers, the series of recordings on which his reputation rests. He made a partial comeback with some recordings in New York in 1939.

Something of a primitive pioneer in the art of inducing jazz musicians to produce prearranged, semi-orchestrated effects, he was probably overrated as both a pianist and a composer. His famed braggadocio, a quality that so enraged his contemporaries, seems to have endeared him to posterity. His survival as a character is assured by Alan Lomax's *Mister Jelly Roll* (1950).
·evolution of orchestral jazz **10**:124d

Morton, John (b. *c.* 1420, Bere Regis or Milborne St. Andrew, Dorset—d. Oct. 12, 1500, Knole, Kent), archbishop of Canterbury and cardinal, one of the most powerful men in England in the reign of King Henry VII (1485–1509). During the Wars of the Roses (1455–85) between the Houses of York and Lancaster, Morton favoured the Lancastrian cause. He received minor ecclesiastical posts under the Lancastrian monarch Henry VI, but upon the accession of the Yorkist Edward IV, in 1461, he was declared a traitor. In 1470 Morton helped assemble the coalition of Lancastrians and disaffected Yorkists that drove Edward IV from the country. Nevertheless, after Edward regained his throne in 1471, Morton was given ambassadorial posts and appointed bishop of Ely (1479). When Edward's brother seized the throne as King Richard III in 1483, Morton became one of Richard's bitterest enemies. While imprisoned by Richard in Brecon castle, the Bishop helped plot the unsuccessful uprising led by Henry Stafford, 2nd duke of Buckingham (October 1483). Morton then escaped to Flanders. Returning to England after the Lancastrian Henry VII assumed the throne in 1485, he became one of the most trusted and influential royal advisers. He was made archbishop of Canterbury in 1486, lord chancellor in 1487, and cardinal in 1493. Traditionally, Morton has been known as the inventor of "Morton's Fork," a sophistical dilemma imposed on both rich and poor by Henry's tax commissioners in order to extort funds for the crown. The rich were told that they could afford to contribute, and the poor were accused of having concealed wealth.

Morton, Levi Parsons (b. May 16, 1824, Shoreham, Vt.—d. May 16, 1920, Rhinebeck, N.Y.), influential Eastern banker who became prominent in Republican politics, serving as vice president of the United States from 1889 to 1893; his prestige in New York business circles lasted from the Civil War until after the Panic of 1907.

Levi Morton
By courtesy of the Library of Congress, Washington, D.C.

Gaining early experience as a merchant in Hanover, N.H. and in Boston, Morton moved to New York in the mid-1850s to become a partner in a dry goods store. In 1863 he established the banking house of L.P. Morton and Company (dissolved 1899).

Turning to politics, Morton won election to the U.S. House of Representatives (1879–81), after which he accepted appointment as minister to France (1881–85). He was elected vice president under Pres. Benjamin Harrison. Following 12 years of Democratic administration in New York, he was elected governor (1895–96), lending support to civil service reform.

At the end of his term in office, Morton strongly upheld the gold standard plank in the national Republican platform of 1896. He remained active in banking until his death.

Morton, Oliver H(azard) P(erry) T(hrock) (b. Aug. 4, 1823, Salisbury, Ind.—d. Nov. 1, 1877, Indianapolis), political leader and governor of Indiana during the Civil War. He achieved fame through his vigorous handling of political forces bent on disunion. Faced with a hostile legislature in 1863, he governed for two years virtually by fiat, raising the necessary funds through private appeals. After the war, as a member of the U.S. Senate, he emerged as a leader of the radical forces in Congress, voting for President Johnson's impeachment and urging immediate Negro suffrage. He was a prominent, though unsuccessful, candidate for the Republican nomination for the presidency in 1876.

Morton, Thomas (b. *c.* 1590—d. *c.* 1647, Maine), one of the most picturesque of the early settlers in colonial America, who ridiculed the strict religious tenets of the Pilgrims and the Puritans. He arrived in Massachusetts in 1624 as one of the owners of the Wollaston Company, which established a settlement within the limits of modern Quincy. In 1626, when Wollaston and most of the settlers moved to Virginia, Morton stayed on and took charge of the colony and named it Merry Mount. Inevitably this free-living, prospering, sharp-tongued Anglican conflicted with his pious neighbours. He erected a maypole, encouraged conviviality and merriment, wrote bawdy verse, poked fun at his saintly neighbours, conducted religious services using the Book of Common Prayer, monopolized the beaver trade, and sold firearms to the Indians. The Pilgrims cut down the maypole, arrested Morton, and exiled him to the Isle of Shoals from whence he escaped to England. He returned within two years and his troubles were resumed, this time with John Endecott as well as William Bradford, governors of Massachusetts. Morton was taken into custody again (1630) and his property confiscated. Exiled to England, he spent several years in collaborating unsuccessfully with the enemies of Massachusetts in an attempt to get the charter of the Puritans revoked and in writing an account of the colonies under the title *New English Canaan*. Upon his return to America in 1643, he was imprisoned again, fined, and exiled to Maine.

Morton has persisted as the epitome of the anti-Puritan; he appears as a character in a short story by Nathaniel Hawthorne, "The Maypole of Merrymount," and two novels by John Lothrop Motley, *Morton's Hope* (1839) and *Merry Mount* (1849). The settlement is the subject of an opera, *Merry Mount* (1934), by the U.S. composer Howard Hanson.

Morton, William Thomas Green (b. Aug. 9, 1819, Charlton, Mass.—d. July 15, 1868, New York City), dental surgeon who in 1846 was the first to demonstrate to the medical and dental professions the use of ether during surgery. He is credited with gaining the medical world's acceptance of surgical anesthesia. Morton began dental practice in Boston in 1844. Formerly a partner of the Hartford (Connecticut) dentist Horace Wells, he was present at Massachusetts General Hospital, Boston, in January 1845, when Wells attempted unsuccessfully to demonstrate the anodyne properties of nitrous oxide gas. Determined to find a more reliable pain-killing chemical, Morton consulted the Boston chemist Charles Jackson, who, although skeptical, suggested to him the use of ether. Morton first used it with success in extraction of a tooth on Sept. 30, 1846. A month later he successfully demonstrated its use, administering ether to a patient undergoing a tumour operation in the same theatre where Wells had failed nearly two years earlier.

Unfortunately, Morton attempted to obtain exclusive rights to the use of ether anesthesia, spending the remainder of his life engaged in a costly contention with Jackson for recognition as the discoverer of anesthesia, despite official recognition of priority accorded to Wells and the U.S. physician Crawford Long.

·anesthetic use of ether in 1846 **1**:867c
·history of medicine and surgery **11**:832d

Morton National Park, in eastern New South Wales, Australia, lies in the coastal range 100 mi (160 km) south of Sydney. It has an area of 70 sq mi (180 sq km). Established in 1938, it was named for Mark Morton, member of the state legislative assembly who campaigned vigorously for the reserve. The park is drained by the Shoalhaven and Kangaroo rivers and by several creeks. A notable feature is Fitzroy Falls. The sandstone summits in the park are covered with bloodwood-scribbly gum forest, and the sides and floors of the gorges are clothed in rain forest and hardwood trees. The most common forms of wildlife are platypus and native fish. Trails and rough roads lead from highways skirting the park.

mortuary profession, or UNDERTAKING, the preparation of the bodies of dead persons for burial or cremation for a fee.

·history of embalming techniques **6**:737b

mortuary temple, in ancient Egypt, places of worship of deceased kings as well as places where services were held to deliver food and objects to the dead monarch. In the Old and

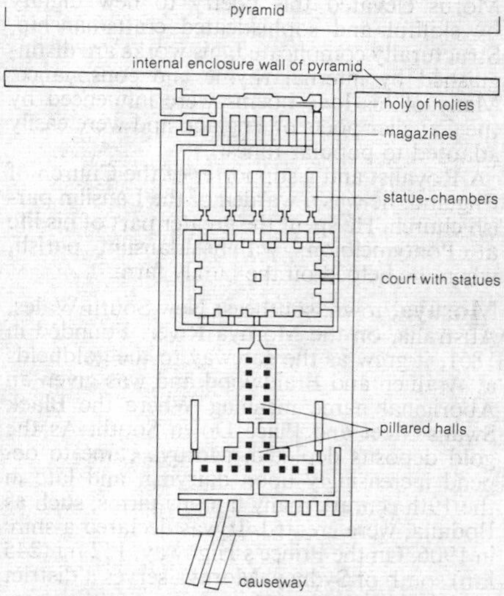

Mortuary temple of the pharaoh Khafre at Giza (4th dynasty)
Taken from *The Art of Egypt* by Irmgard Woldering. © 1962 by Holle Verlag G.m.b.H. Used by permission of Crown Publishers, Inc.

Middle Kingdoms (*c.* 2686–2160 BC; and *c.* 2040–1786 BC), the mortuary temple usually adjoined the pyramid and had an open, pillared court, storerooms, five elongated shrines, and a chapel containing a false door and an offering table. In the chapel, priests performed the daily funerary rites and presented the offerings to the dead king's *ka* (protective spirit). In the New Kingdom (1567–1085 BC) the kings were buried in rock-cut tombs, but separate mortuary temples continued to be built nearby. All were provided with a staff of priests and assured of supplies through endowments of estates and lands to ensure religious services and offerings in perpetuity.

·ancient Egyptian monument construction **19**:250g

Morty (Indonesia): *see* Morotai.

morula, solid mass of cells (blastomeres) resulting from a number of cleavages of a zygote, or fertilized egg. Its name derives from its resemblance to a mulberry (Latin *morum*). A morula is usually produced in those species the eggs of which contain little yolk and, consequently, undergo complete cleavage. Those blastomeres on the surface of the morula give rise to extraembryonic parts of the embryo. The cells of the interior, the inner cell mass, develop into the embryo proper.

·placental mammal embryology **5**:630g
·prenatal growth and cavity formation **6**:744a
·tunicate cell structure and function **18**:740a
·zygote's early development **14**:968e

Moru-Madi, a people of The Sudan.

·Sudan ethnic composition map **17**:762

Moru-Madi languages: *see* Central Sudanic languages.

Morung, communal house of the Nāgās of India.

·Nāga communal use and decor **12**:808a

Morungen, Heinrich von: see Heinrich von Morungen.

Morungole, mountain, Uganda, East Africa. 3°49′ N, 34°02′ E

·Ugandan physical geography **18**:825h

Morus (plant genus): *see* mulberry.

Morus, Huw, called EOS CEIRIOG (b. 1622, probably at Llangollen, Denbighshire—d. August 1709, Llansilin, Denbighshire), considered one of the finest Welsh poets of the 17th century.

He wrote during the period when the strict bardic metres were in decline and the free metres of popular poetry were on the rise. Morus elevated this poetry to new dignity by skillful and sophisticated craftsmanship. Structurally complicated, his works are distinguished by internal rhyme and consonance. Many of his love poems were influenced by the Cavalier poets of England and were easily adapted to popular tunes.

A Royalist and a supporter of the Church of England, he was a warden of the Lansilin parish church. He spent the greater part of his life at Pontymeibion, within Llansilin parish, where he helped on the family farm.

Moruya, town, southeast New South Wales, Australia, on the Moruya River. Founded in 1851, it grew as the gateway to the goldfields at Araluen and Braidwood and was given an Aboriginal name meaning Where the Black Swans Meet and Place Down South. As the gold deposits depleted, Moruya came to depend increasingly upon dairying, and late in the 19th century many famous farms, such as Bodalla, were created. It was declared a shire in 1906. On the Prince's Highway, 152 mi (245 km) south of Sydney, Moruya serves a district of dairying, lumbering, granite quarrying, arsenic and gold mining, and oyster farming; it has sawmills, freezing works, and butter and cheese factories. Tourism, based on local lakes and beaches, is an added source of income. Pop. (1971 prelim.) 1,656.
35°55′ S, 150°05′ E

Morvan, highland region, central France, forming a northeastern extension of the Massif Central in the direction of the Paris Basin. The headwaters of the Yonne and Armançon rivers, tributaries of the Seine River, drain the northern part of the region. The Aroux River, a tributary of the Loire River, drains the more southerly parts. The Morvan is thickly wooded and has large stretches of heathland. Covering an area of about 1,350 sq mi (3,500 sq km), it extends north–south approximately from Avallon to Saint-Léger-sous-Beuvray and east–west from the Saulieu Hills to Corbigny. Its rounded heights rise to the south to nearly 3,000 ft. The Signal du Bois-du-Roi massif culminates in the peak called the Haut-Folin at 2,956 ft (901 m). Mont Beuvray, 2,661 ft (811 m), was the site of the 18th-century BC entrenched Gaulish camp of Bibracte. In modern times, some areas have been deforested, while some of the marshy areas have been reclaimed; these lands have then been fertilized for pasturage. Beauty spots in the Morvan attract Parisians for weekend and summer holidays.
·map, France 7:584

Morvi, town, Rājkot district, Gujarāt state, west central India, in the lowlands of the Kāthiāwār Peninsula, south of the Little Rann of Kutch. Once the capital of the former princely state of Morvi, it is now a trade centre for agricultural produce with cotton processing and various manufacturing industries. Morvi is also a rail and road junction. Pop. (1971 prelim.) 61,161.
22°50′ N, 70°50′ E
·map, India **9**:278

Morwell, town, southeast Victoria, Australia, in the La Trobe Valley of west Gippsland. Founded in 1861, near the short Morwell River, and gazetted a shire in 1892, its name was probably derived from an uncertain Aboriginal term, *moorwillie*. After 1916, with the development of the valley's vast open-cut brown-coal deposits, Morwell was transformed from a small rural settlement into an industrial town (one of a series in the valley, including Moe, Yallourn, and Traralgon) that produces electrical power, gas, and briquettes. Other manufactures include wood pulp and paper, textiles, clothing, and shoes. The hinterland supports beef, dairy, and sheep farming. The town is connected by rail to Melbourne, 85 mi (137 km) to the northwest, and is the junction of the Midland and Prince's highways. Pop. (1971 prelim.) 16,827.
38°14′ S, 146°24′ E

Morzin, Ferdinand Maximilian von, 18th-century Bohemian count under whose sponsorship Haydn wrote his first symphony.
·Haydn's direction of estate orchestra **8**:681g

Mosaddeq (MOSSADEGH, MASADDIQ), **Mohammad** (b. 1880, Tehrān—d. March 5, 1967, Tehrān), Iranian political leader who nationalized the huge British oil holdings in Iran and, as premier in 1951–53, almost succeeded in deposing the Shah.

Mosaddeq
UPI Compix

The son of an Iranian public official, Mosaddeq grew up as a member of Iran's ruling elite. He received a doctor of law degree from the University of Lausanne in Switzerland and then returned to Iran in 1914 and was appointed governor general of the important Fars province. He remained in the government following the rise to power of Reza Shah in 1919 and served as minister of finance and then briefly as minister of foreign affairs. Mosaddeq was elected to the Majles (parliament) in 1923. When Reza Shah assumed full dictatorial powers in 1925, however, Mosaddeq opposed the move and retired to private life.

Mosaddeq re-entered public service in 1944, following Reza Shah's forced abdication and was elected again to the Majles. An outspoken advocate of nationalism, he soon played a leading part in successfully opposing the grant to the Soviet Union of an oil concession for northern Iran similar to an existing British concession in southern Iran. He built considerable political strength, based largely on his call to nationalize the huge British-owned Anglo-Iranian Oil Company. In March 1951 the Majles passed his oil nationalization act, and his power had grown so great that the shah, Mohammad Reza Pahlavi, was virtually forced to appoint him premier.

The nationalization resulted in a deepening crisis in Iran, both politically and economically. Mosaddeq and his National Front Party continued to gain power but alienated many supporters, particularly among the ruling elite and in the Western nations, since he refused to deal with the British. The British soon withdrew completely from the Iranian oil market, and economic problems increased when Mosaddeq could not readily find alternate oil markets.

A continuing struggle for control of the Iranian government developed between Mosaddeq and the Shah. In August 1953, when the Shah attempted to dismiss the Premier, mobs of Mosaddeq followers took to the streets and forced the Shah to leave the country. Within a few days, however, Mosaddeq's opponents, probably with U.S. support, overthrew his regime and restored the Shah to power. Mosaddeq was sentenced to three years' imprisonment for treason and, after he had served his sentence, was kept under house arrest for the rest of his life. The Iranian oil-production facilities remained under control of the Iranian government.

Mosaddeq's personal behaviour, which included wearing pajamas for numerous public appearances; speeches to the Majles from his bed, which was brought into the chambers; and frequent bouts of public weeping, helped focus world attention upon him during his premiership. Supporters claim the behaviour was a result of illness; detractors say he had a shrewd sense of public relations.
·expropriation move and Western clash **9**:761b

Mosāferids, also called SALLĀRIDS and KANGARIDS, an Iranian dynasty that ruled in northwestern Iran *c.* 916–*c.* 1090.

The founder of the dynasty was Moḥammad ebn Mosāfer (ruled *c.* 916–941), military commander of the strategic mountain fortresses of Ṭārom and Samīrān in Daylam, in northwestern Iran. With the increasing weakness of the Justānid dynasty that ruled the region, Moḥammad increased his power and gained control of most of Daylam. After Moḥammad's death in 941, his domains were divided between his two sons, Marzobān I (ruled 941–957) and Vahsūdān (ruled 941–957). Vahsūdān ruled over the fortresses of Ṭārom and Samīrān. Marzobān I expanded northward and westward and captured Azerbaijan and east Transcaucasia; these territories, however, were lost by the Mosāferids by 984.

Ebrāhīm II (ruled 997–*c.* 1030) was able to re-establish Mosāferid control over Daylam and to expand southward as far as Zanjān. After Ebrāhīm's death, however, the history of the dynasty becomes fragmentary; Ebrāhīm's descendants ruled in Daylam, first as vassals of the Ghaznavids and then of the Seljuqs. At the end of the 11th century the Mosāferids were extinguished by the Ismāʿīlīs of Alamūt.

mosaic 12:462, art of decorating a surface with designs made up of closely set, usually variously coloured, small pieces of material such as stone, glass, tile, or shell.

The text article covers principles of design, materials, techniques, and history.

REFERENCES in other text articles:
·ancient British craft development **3**:197a
·ancient Greek visual art history **19**:297c
·ancient Near East visual art history **19**:259d
·Antioch relics **1**:993a
·arms and armour decoration **2**:32g
·Byzantine visual art forms and styles **19**:327f; illus. 325
·Christian substitute for sculpture **4**:519d
·Classical domestic interior styles **9**:704e
·early Christian forms and styles **19**:323a
·floor covering history and development **7**:406e
·Ravenna's Byzantine and Arian treasures **15**:534h; illus.
·Roman and Byzantine decorative use **11**:587c
·Roman floral arrangement **7**:414h; illus. 415
·Roman forms and styles **19**:315g
·stained glass foundation in earlier art forms **17**:568a
·synagogue floor mosaic style and motif **10**:203f; illus.
·Uccello's artistic development **18**:824g
·visual arts development in West **19**:247a

RELATED ENTRIES in the *Ready Reference and Index*: *for*
materials: see pietra dura; sottosquadra; tesserae
pavement mosaics: Alexandrinum, opus; mosaic, pebble; opus signium
other: commesso; Cosmati work; emblēma; opus sectile; opus tessellatum; vermiculatum, opus

mosaic, plant disease caused by several hundred strains of virus. Symptoms are variable but commonly include irregular leaf mottling (light and dark green or yellow patches or streaks). Leaves are commonly stunted, curled, or puckered; veins may be lighter than normal or banded with dark green or yellow. Plants are often dwarfed, with fruit and flowers fewer than usual, deformed, and stunted.

Flowers may be blotched or streaked (flower breaking), a condition appreciated in certain tulips, often termed Rembrandt tulips, for their attractive and colourful streaking. Mosaic symptoms may be masked or latent, especially at temperatures above 27° C (81° F), and are sometimes confused with nutrient deficiency or herbicide injury. The causal viruses are spread by aphids and other insects, mites, fungi, nematodes, and contact; pollen and seeds can carry the infection as well.

Mosaic can be avoided by using virus-free seeds and plants, growing resistant varieties, separating new from old plantings, rotating annuals, observing stringent sanitation and weed control measures, and judiciously applying contact insecticides to combat insect invasions.

·abaca production in Philippines **7**:281g
·sugarcane disease and industry decline **17**:771a

mosaic, pebble, a type of mosaic work that uses natural pebbles arranged to form decorative or pictorial patterns. Used only for pavements, pebble mosaics were the earliest type of mosaic in all areas of the eastern Mediterranean, appearing in Asia Minor in excavated floors from the 8th and 7th centuries BC. The first pebble mosaics had rough geometric designs, but by the 5th-century-BC artists in Greece had achieved a degree of technical

Bellerophon, mounted on Pegasus, fighting the chimera, detail of a Greek pebble mosaic from Olynthus, Greece, *c.* 400 BC

By courtesy of the University of Mississippi; photograph, David Moore Robinson

proficiency that allowed them to create designs and figures with delicacy and considerable detail, as in a series of black-and-white mosaic floors depicting mythological scenes at Olynthus in northern Greece (*c.* 400 BC). Most pebble mosaics were made simply with dark and light patterns, but a few were multicoloured, such as the magnificent floors from the late 4th century BC found at Pella in Macedonia, which show monumental figures of people and animals rendered with impressive naturalism and grace. Pebble mosaics persisted as the major form of mosaic decoration until about the 3rd century BC, when they began to be replaced with mosaics of cut stone cubes, or tesserae (*q.v.*). The later pebble mosaics, including those at Pella, were increasingly supplemented with stone tesserae chosen for colour intensity and with lead or terracotta strips for delineation of detail.

Mosaic Atrium, House of the, building in Herculaneum.

·excavations in the 18th century **14**:791b

mosaic evolution, pattern in evolution characterized by the retention of primitive features while at the same time advanced features are appearing, so that a mixture of ancestral and modern aspects can be seen. An example is the transition from reptile to bird. The bird retains reptilian traits such as scaly legs, small brain, and free fingers, while exhibiting innovations such as feathers and wings.

·human bipedalism and brain **11**:425a
·transitional stages in vertebrates **7**:19d

mosaic glass, vessel produced by one of the oldest known glassmaking techniques, western Asiatic examples of which survive from the 15th century BC. In the basic procedure, rods of different-coloured glass are fused together in bundles and the resultant multicoloured strip cut into sections. These sections are then used to build up a vessel or are otherwise embedded in a matrix; in this way the slices appear as small identically repeating motives. The so-called millefiori ("thousand flowers") technique is a kind of mosaic. Mosaic was used by Egyptian glassmakers in the late Ptolemaic period (1st century BC) and by Roman glassmakers during the same period and after. It is distinct from opus sectile, in which little squares of glass (tesselae) were embedded in cement for pavements and other surfaces.

·technique and decorative use **8**:182a

mosaic gold (metal alloy): *see* ormolu.

mosaicism, appearance in one individual of cells differing in chromosome structure or number, resulting in sectors of tissue that may be radically different, as in the case of a gynandromorph, an organism that has sectors of male and female tissue caused by an early developmental mishap.

·human hereditary disease basis **7**:1001b
·radiation-induced somatic mutations **15**:381d

Mosaic Law: *see* Torah.

Mosander, Carl Gustaf (b. Sept. 10, 1797, Kalmar, Swed.—d. Oct. 15, 1858, Angsholmen), chemist whose work on rare earths revealed the existence of numerous rare earth elements with closely similar chemical properties.

In 1826 Mosander was placed in charge of the chemical laboratory of the Caroline Medical Institute, Stockholm, and in 1832 became professor of chemistry and mineralogy. While studying a compound of cerium, he discovered the element lanthanum in 1839. He pursued his investigations of the rare earths and in 1843 reported discovery of the elements erbium, terbium, and didymium. In 1885 the Austrian chemist Baron Carl Auer von Welsbach found that didymium was in reality a mixture of two elements: neodymium and praseodymium.

·rare-earth discovery and properties **15**:515f

Mosan school, regional style of Romanesque manuscript illumination, metalwork, and enamelwork that flourished in the 11th and 12th centuries and was centred in the Meuse River valley, especially at Liege and the Benedictine monastery of Stavelot. Two of the most important artists associated with the Mosan school were Godefroid de Claire (*q.v.*), a goldsmith from Huy, and Nicholas of Verdun (*q.v.*), who also was a goldsmith, as well as one of the most renowned enamellers of the Middle Ages. Among the major examples of Mosan art are the Stavelot Bible (1093–97; British Museum, London); the Reliquary Triptych of the Holy Cross (*c.* 1150; Pierpont Morgan Library, New York City); the gilded bronze cross from the Abbey of St. Bertain (*c.* 1170; Musée de Saint-Omer, France), and the portable Altar of Stavelot (c. 1150; Musées Royaux d'Art et d'Histoire, Brussels).

·enamelwork tradition of the Middle Ages **6**:776e

mosasaur, a family of extinct aquatic lizards closely related to the present-day Oriental and African monitor lizards. They attained a high degree of adaptation to the marine environment and became distributed around the world during Cretaceous time (from 136,000,000 to 65,000,000 years ago). The mosasaurs competed with other marine reptiles—the plesiosaurs and ichthyosaurs—for food, which consisted largely of fish and cuttlefish. Many of the Late Cretaceous forms were large animals, exceeding 9 metres (30 feet) in length; but the most common ones were no larger than most of the porpoises of today.

The mosasaurs had elongated, snakelike bodies, with large skulls and long snouts. Fore and hind limbs were modified as paddles, having shortened limb bones and a modest-to-great increase in the number of finger and toe bones. The tail region of the body was long, and its end was slightly downcurved in a manner similar to that of the early ichthyosaurs. The backbone consisted of more than 100 vertebrae. The construction of the skull was very similar to that of the modern monitors. The jaws bore many conical, slightly recurved teeth set in individual sockets. The jawbones are noteworthy in that they were jointed near mid-length, as in some of the advanced monitors, and connected in front by ligaments only. This arrangement enabled the animals not only to open the mouth by lowering the mandible but also to extend the lower jaws sidewise while feeding on large prey.

·fossil era and traits **7**:570e

Mosbach faience, German tin-glazed earthenware produced in Baden in the late 18th century. Like most German faience, it is largely derivative though competent. It was founded in 1770 by an itinerant French potter, Pierre Berthevin, whose known career started at Mennecy outside Paris.

Mosby, John Singleton (1833–1916), U.S. Confederate cavalry officer.

·guerrilla raids in northern Virginia **8**:459d

Mosca, Gaetano (b. April 1, 1858, Palermo—d. Nov. 8, 1941, Rome), jurist and political theorist who, by applying a historical method to political ideas and institutions, elaborated the concept of a ruling minority (*classe politica*) present in all societies. His theory seemed to have its greatest influence on apologists for Fascism who misunderstood or scarcely read his works. Although he insisted, for example, on the importance of education and the separation of church and state, his writings were invoked to justify clerical-aristocratic rule over an ignorant majority, quite opposed to the 19th-century liberalism he favoured.

Educated at the University of Palermo, Mosca taught constitutional law there (1885–88) and at the universities of Rome (1888–96) and Turin (1896–1908). A member of the Italian chamber of deputies from 1908, he served as undersecretary of state for the colonies from 1914 to 1916 and was made a senator for life by King Victor Emmanuel III in 1919. His last speech in the Senate was an attack on Benito Mussolini.

Mosca's *Teorica* (*Sulla teorica dei governi e sul governo parlamentare*, 1884; 2nd ed., *Teorica dei governi e governo parlamentare*, 1925; "Theory of Governments and Parliamentary Government") was followed by *Elementi di scienza politica* (1896, 4th ed. 1939; Eng. trans., *The Ruling Class*, rev. ed. 1939). In these and other writings, but especially in the *Elementi*, he asserted, contrary to theories of majority rule, that societies are necessarily governed by minorities: by military, priestly, or hereditary oligarchies or by aristocracies of wealth or of merit. He showed an impartial indifference to the most diverse systems. For him the will of God, the will of the people, the sovereign will of the state, and the dictatorship of the proletariat were all mythical.

Sometimes called "Machiavellian," Mosca actually considered most of Niccolò Machiavelli's political ideas impractical. He opposed the racist elitism preached in Nazi Germany; condemned Marxism, which in his view expressed the hatred within Karl Marx; and mistrusted democracy, seeing the greatest threat to liberal institutions in "the extension of the suffrage to the most uncultured strata of the population." To him the most enduring social organization was a mixed government (partly autocratic, partly liberal) in which "the aristocratic tendency is tempered by a gradual but continuous renewal of the ruling class" by the addition of men of lower socio-economic origin who have the will and the ability to rule.

Studies of Mosca include James H. Meisel's *Myth of the Ruling Class: Gaetano Mosca and the "Elite"* (1958).

·analysis of political myths **14**:694c
·Fascist roots in theory of elitism **7**:184b
·Marxist theory criticism **16**:948c
·typologies of government **14**:713h

Moscheles, Ignaz, first name also spelled ISACK (b. May 23, 1794, Prague—d. March 10, 1870, Leipzig), one of the outstanding pianists of his era. He studied at the Prague Conservatory and later at Vienna under J.G. Albrechtsberger and A. Salieri. In 1814, commissioned by Artaria & Co., publishers, he made the first piano arrangement of Beethoven's *Fidelio*, under the composer's supervision. After giving piano recitals in Germany and France, he settled in London in 1821. In 1829 he took part in the first London performance of the *Concerto for Two Pianos* by Mendelssohn, who had been his pupil. He conducted the first English performance of Beethoven's *Missa Solemnis* and later conducted Beethoven's *Ninth Symphony* at the Philharmonic Society, of which he was a regular conductor from 1845. From 1846 he was principal professor of piano at the Leipzig Conservatory, and his reputation and skill as a teacher were important factors in the continued success of that institution.

Moscheles belonged to a conservative school of piano playing that did not lend itself to the works of Chopin and Liszt; of the younger composers of his day, he leaned more toward Mendelssohn and Schumann. Nevertheless, his explorations of the gradations of tone colour influenced Liszt as well as Schumann. He was also admired for his brilliant extempore performances. His compositions include eight piano concerti, studies, and chamber works.

moschellandsbergite (mineral): *see* amalgam.

Moscherosch, Johann Michael, pen name PHILANDER VON SITTEWALD (b. March 5, 1601, Willstätt, now in West Germany—d. April 4, 1669, Worms), Lutheran satirist whose bitterly brilliant but partisan writings graphically describe life in a Germany ravaged by the Thirty Years' War (1618–48). His satires, which at times are tedious, also show an overwhelming moral zeal added to a sense of mission. Moscherosch was educated at Strassburg and was for some years tutor in the family of the Count of Leiningen-Dagsburg. He held various government offices, including those of president of the chancellery and counsellor to the chamber of finances (1656) to the Count of Hanau and privy councillor to the Countess of Hesse-Kassel.

Moscherosch's most famous work, *Wunderliche und wahrhafftige Gesichte Philanders von Sittewald* (1641–43; "Peculiar and True Visions of Philander von Sittewald"), displays his satirical ability; modelled on *Los sueños* (1627; "Visions") of Francisco de Quevedo y Villegas, it lampoons the customs and culture of his day from the standpoint of a Lutheran patriot. Almost of equal excellence is the *Insomnis Cura Parentum* (1643), a religious work addressed to his family that reflects his strict Lutheran piety. Moscherosch was also a member of the Fruchtbringende Gesellschaft ("Productive Society"), founded for the purification of the German language and the fostering of German literature.

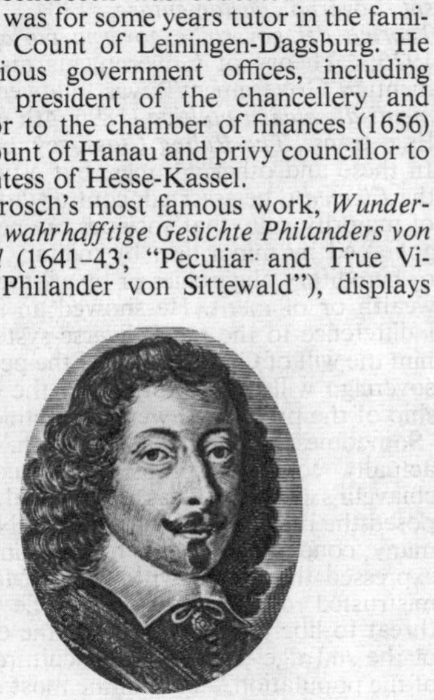

Moscherosch, detail from an engraving by an unknown artist
Bavaria-Verlag

Moschopoulos, Manuel (fl. late 13th–early 14th century, Constantinople), Byzantine grammarian and critic during the reign (1282–1328) of Andronicus II Palaeologus. Little is known of his life except what can be gathered from his correspondence and a reference in a letter of one Maximus Planudes, who describes him as his pupil. Moschopoulos is a prominent representative of those Humanist scholars active during the last revival of classical learning in Byzantium and is best remembered for his *Erotemata grammatika* ("Grammatical Questions," first printed in Milan, 1493), a handbook of Greek in the form of question and answer, which enjoyed great popularity among Western Humanists of the early Renaissance. He also compiled a lexicon of Attic Greek (*Sylloge onomaton Attikon*) and wrote treatises on mathematics and theology. He studied the works of several Greek poets and wrote commentaries on them; but his most important contribution to classical scholarship is his recension of three Sophoclean tragedies (*Ajax*, *Electra*, *Oedipus Tyrannus*), in which he displays awareness of metrical problems and considerable critical acumen.

Moschops, extinct genus of mammal-like reptiles found as fossils in rocks of Middle Permian age in southern Africa (the Permian Period began 280,000,000 years ago and lasted 55,000,000 years). *Moschops*, which is representative of a group of mammal-like reptiles (*see* therapsid) that became adapted to a diet of plant food, was a relatively large animal, about 2.6 metres (about 8 feet) long. The body was massive, no doubt to accommodate the large amounts of plant material *Moschops* consumed to maintain itself. The skull was relatively high and shortened front to back. Numerous peglike teeth, suited to plant food, were present in the jaws. The back characteristically sloped downward from the front to the back in giraffe-like fashion. The limb girdles or supports were massive, especially in the shoulder region, in order to support the animal's relatively great bulk. The bone on the top of the skull was greatly thickened and perhaps employed for butting. *Moschops* probably inhabited drier upland regions of the Permian Period.

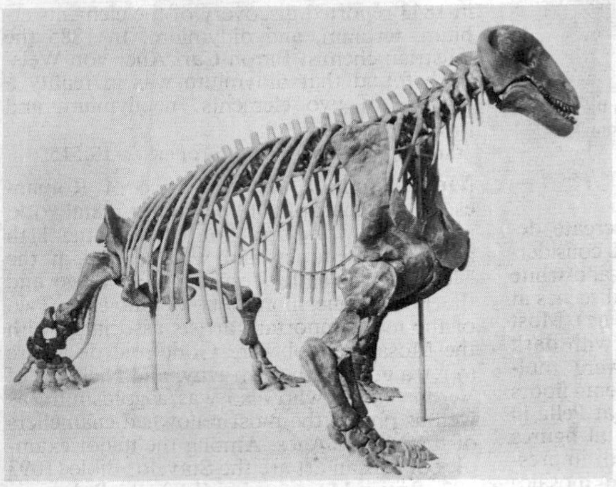

Moschops, skeleton
By courtesy of the American Museum of Natural History, New York

Moschus (fl. *c.* 150 BC), Greek pastoral poet and grammarian from Syracuse, in Sicily, whose only surviving works are three short extracts from his *Bucolica*, a longer piece translated as *Love the Runaway*, and an elegiac piece on love as a plowman. The attractive short epic poem *Europa* is perhaps correctly attributed to him; the *Lament for Bion*, considered an excellent work, less certainly so. No traces of his activity as a grammarian survive, with the possible exception of a reference by the Greek grammarian Athenaeus to a Moschus who wrote a work on Rhodian words.

Moschus, John (b. *c.* 550, probably Damascus, Syria—d. 619, Rome), Byzantine monk and writer whose work *Pratum spirituale* ("The Spiritual Meadow"), describing monastic spiritual experiences throughout the Middle East, became a popular example of ascetic literature during the medieval period and was a model for similar works.

Moschus began his monastic life at St. Theodosius monastery near Jerusalem *c.* 565. After observing monastic practices among hermits along the Jordan River, followed by sojourns in Egypt, the Sinai Desert, Cyprus, and Antioch, he settled at Rome and composed a personal narrative of his monastic encounters, augmenting it from other sources. "The Spiritual Meadow," or "The New Paradise" (a translation of its Greek title), contains more than 300 tales of religious practices in simple language, replete with details of the life and beliefs of the times.

Abounding in reports of miracles and spiritual ecstasies and lacking any critical standards, "The Spiritual Meadow" nevertheless provides singular data on the modes of worship, ceremonies in 6th- and 7th-century monasticism, devotion to the Virgin Mary, political circumstances (including accounts of Persian and Arabic invasions), and criticism of prevailing heresies.

Moschus moschiferus (deer species): *see* musk deer.

Mościcki, Ignacy (b. Dec. 1, 1867, Mierzanów, Pol.—d. Oct. 2, 1946, Versoix, Switz.), statesman, scholar, and scientist, who, as president of the Polish republic, was a strong supporter of the dictatorship of Józef Piłsudski.

Mościcki was educated as a chemist. He joined the nationalistic Polish Socialist Party in the early 1890s and was involved in an attempt on the life of the governor general of Warsaw. Sought by the Russian police for that involvement, Mościcki fled to England (1892), where he met Piłsudski.

Returning to the continent, in 1897 Mościcki began to teach at the Catholic university in Freibourg, Switz. In 1912 he was given the professorship of electrochemistry at Lemberg,

Mościcki, *c.* 1937

By courtesy of Mrs. Marya Moscicka

Lvov) in Austrian Galicia. After World War I Mościcki served the new Polish state by restoring synthetic nitrogen production at Królewska Huta (now Chorzów), Upper Silesia, in a plant that had been stripped by the Germans. After the Piłsudski coup d'état in May 1926, Mościcki was installed as president of the republic in June, in which post he served Piłsudski faithfully. With the German occupation of Poland in September 1939, Mościcki fled to Romania, where he was interned briefly, and thence to Switzerland.

·presidency of Polish government **14**:464h

Mosconi, Willie, byname of WILLIAM JOSEPH MOSCONI (b. June 21, 1913, Philadelphia), U.S. billiards player who won the men's world pocket billiards open championship 15 times from 1941 to 1957. His publications include *Winning Pocket Billiards* (1965). *See* sporting record.

·prominent billiards players **2**:993a

Moscow, Russian MOSKVA, *oblast* (administrative region), Russian Soviet Federated Socialist Republic, that occupies an area of 18,150 sq mi (47,000 sq km) surrounding the city of Moscow, the capital of the Soviet Union. Moscow *oblast* was formed in 1929. The main feature of its relief is the Klin-Dmitrov Ridge, which stretches roughly east–west across the *oblast* north of Moscow city, and reaches a height of 1,000 ft (300 m) with a steep northern slope to the boulder clay plain of the upper Volga River. South of the ridge is the broad, level plain of the Oka and its major tributary, the Moskva, on which the capital stands. In the southeast the plain gradually drops to the Meshchera Lowland, an area of extensive swamps. South of the Oka the land rises toward the northern edge of the Central Russian Upland.

The climate is continental; average annual precipitation ranges from 18 in. (450 mm) in the southeast to 26 in. (650 mm) on the Klin-Dmitrov Ridge, with the maximum precipitation in the summer. The natural vegetation of mixed forest, dominated by spruce, pine, oak, and birch, now survives over only 40 percent of the surface, but almost all remaining forest has been put under protective regulation for preservation.

The *oblast* is the heavily industrialized core of the Central Industrial region. The area retains its historic importance, dating back to the late 17th century, as Russia's chief producer of textiles, especially of cotton and woollen cloth. Artificial textiles, silk, linen, clothing, and knitwear are made. The second major branch of industry, engineering, produces a wide range of heavy machinery, machine tools, locomotives, and buses. A steadily growing chemical industry produces artificial fibres, plastics, and fertilizers. Old established glass and chinaware industries still flourish, especially in the north. Lignite (brown coal) and phosphorite are mined in the south, and peat is extensively dug to supply peat-burning power stations, especially in the east around Shatura. Local fuel resources are supplemented by natural-gas pipelines from the northern Caucasus, the western Ukraine, and from Saratov to the south; a high-tension grid transmits power from the Volga River hydroelectric stations.

The *oblast* is highly urbanized; of its 1979 population, 75 percent lived in more than 140 cities. Greater Moscow (8,099,000) and the satellite towns within its surrounding "forest-park" greenbelt dominate the urban scene: many workers commute into the city from adjacent areas. Moscow, although the administrative centre of the *oblast*, is itself independently administered.

Agriculture plays a relatively minor role in the economy, engaging only one-fifth of the employed population; only 25 percent of the area is under the plough. Throughout the *oblast*, but especially around Moscow, dairying and market gardening are well developed to serve the city. In the east the emphasis is on dairy and beef cattle, and pig keeping and poultry farming are widespread.

Communications throughout the *oblast* are excellent. Eleven trunk railways from all parts of the Soviet Union focus on Moscow, and a network of electrified lines runs to the city's suburbs. The *oblast* has the highest proportion of asphalt-surfaced roads in the country. It is also served by waterways, including the Moscow Canal from the capital north to the Volga, the canalized Moskva for smaller craft, and the Oka, all of which give access to the Volga system. Pop. (1980 est.) 14,509,000.

Moscow 12:474, Russian MOSKVA, capital and largest city of the Soviet Union and of the Russian Soviet Federated Socialist Republic, situated on the Moskva River, near the confluence of the Oka and Volga rivers. It is the administrative headquarters of Moscow *oblast* (administrative region) and the leading Soviet political, scientific, cultural, and industrial centre. Pop. (1980 est.) city, 7,915,000; metropolitan area, 8,099,000.

The text article covers the city's physical environment; history; layout and architecture; administration and government; economy; and education, cultural life, and social services.

55°45′ N, 37°35′ E

REFERENCES in other text articles:

·appanage expansion and institutions **16**:42e; map 80
·botanical garden table **3**:64
·Byzantine architectural developments **19**:339h
·department store operations **11**:507c
·destruction during Napoleonic war **1**:474h
·expansion, culture, and institutions **16**:44a
·geographic and social features **17**:330a
·Le Corbusier Centrosoyus design **5**:169f
·Lithuanian post-Mongol rivalry **6**:154f
·map, Soviet Union **17**:322
·medieval literary traditions **10**:1129b
·third Rome concept formative influence **4**:469g

Moscow, city, seat (1888) of Latah County, northwestern Idaho, U.S., on Paradise Creek, in the Palouse country, near the Washington border. It was founded as a stagecoach station (1871) and probably named by J. Neff, a homesteader, who had lived near communities named Moscow in Iowa and Pennsylvania. The establishment of the University of Idaho (1889) was a major factor in its development. The state Bureau of Mines and Geology has its headquarters on the campus, and the colleges of agriculture and forestry maintain research stations in the area. Agriculture (peas and wheat) and lumbering are economic factors. St. Joe National Forest is to the northeast. Inc. town, 1877; city, 1893. Pop. (1980) 16,513.

46°44′ N, 116°60′ W

·map, United States **18**:908

Moscow, Grand Principality of, also called MUSCOVY, Russian MOSKOVSKOYE VELIKOYE KNAZHESTVO, medieval principality that, under the leadership of a branch of the Rurik dynasty, was transformed from a small settlement in the Rostov-Suzdal principality into the dominant political unit in northeastern Russia.

Muscovy became a distinct principality during the second half of the 13th century under the rule of Daniel, the youngest son of Alexander Nevsky. Located in the midst of forests and at the intersection of important trade routes, it was well protected from invasion and well situated for lucrative commerce. In 1326 it became the permanent residence of the Russian metropolitan of the Orthodox Church; Muscovy attracted many inhabitants and its princes collected large revenues in customs and taxes. After a short period of rivalry with the princes of Tver during the reign of Daniel's son Yury (died 1326), the princes of Muscovy received the title of grand prince of Vladimir from their Tatar overlords (1328). That title enabled them to collect the Russian tribute for the Tatar khan and, thereby, to strengthen the financial and political position of their domain.

The Muscovite princes also pursued a policy of "gathering the Russian lands." Yury extended his principality to include almost the entire Moscow basin; and Ivan I Kalita (reigned 1328–41), followed by his sons Semyon (reigned 1341–53) and Ivan II (reigned 1353–59), purchased more territory.

Dmitry Donskoy (reigned as prince of Moscow from 1359, grand prince of Vladimir 1362–89) increased his holdings by conquest; he also won a symbolically important victory over the Tatars (Battle of Kulikovo, 1380). Dmitry's successors Vasily I (reigned 1389–1425) and Vasily II (reigned 1425–62) continued to enlarge and strengthen Moscow despite a bitter civil war during the latter's reign.

Ivan III (reigned 1462–1505) completed the unification of the Great Russian lands, incorporating Ryazan, Yaroslavl (1463), Rostov (northwest of Vladimir and southeast of Yaroslavl; 1474), Tver (1485), and Novgorod (1478) into the Muscovite principality. By the end of Ivan's reign, the prince of Moscow was, in fact, the ruler of Russia proper. *See also* Rurik dynasty.

·educational organization and development **6**:331f
·Ivan III's territorial expansion **9**:1178c
·medieval literary traditions **10**:1129b
·Moscow history **12**:477a
·opposition to Lithuanian expansion **1**:573b
·Orthodox leadership in emerging Russia **6**:154f
·patriarchate and imperial ideology **6**:156g
·Russian history **16**:42g

Moscow, Treaty of (July 12, 1920), peace settlement that was agreed upon by Lithuania and Soviet Russia. *See* Baltic War of Liberation.

Moscow, Treaty of (March 16, 1921), pact concluded at Moscow between the nationalist government of Turkey and the Soviet Union that fixed Turkey's northeastern frontier and established friendly relations between the two nations. With the advent of the Bolshevik Revolution (October 1917), Russia withdrew from World War I and ceased hostilities against the Ottoman Empire. The new Soviet regime found itself allied against the West with the Turkish nationalists, who were fighting simultaneously against Western domination and the Ottoman government that had capitulated to the Western Allies. Diplomatic relations between the nationalists and the Soviets began in August 1920 and led to the Treaty of Moscow, which settled border disputes by giving Kars and Ardahan to Turkey and Batumi to Russia. By the treaty, the Soviets recognized the nationalist leadership under Mustafa Kemal (later styled Kemal Atatürk) as the only government in Turkey. As a result of the treaty, the Soviets supplied the nationalists with weapons and ammunition, which the Turks used successfully in a war against Greece in 1921–22.

Moscow Art Theatre, outstanding Russian theatre of theatrical naturalism founded in 1898 by two teachers of dramatic art, Konstantin Stanislavsky and Vladimir Nemirovich-Danchenko. Its purpose was to establish a theatre of new art forms, with a fresh approach to its function. Sharing similar theatrical experience and interests, the co-founders met to plan the new venture, and by the time the meeting was concluded, it was agreed that Stanislavsky was to have absolute control over stage direction while Nemirovich-Danchenko was assigned the literary and administrative duties. The original ensemble was made up of amateur actors from the Society of Art and Literature and from the dramatic classes of the Moscow Philharmonic Society, where Stanislavsky and Nemirovich-Danchenko taught, respectively. Influenced by the Meiningen Company, a German theatre company that emphasized stage realism through ensemble acting, Stanislavsky began to develop a system of training for actors that would guide them through all phases of work. This system, or "Method," as it has come to be called, was an attempt to eliminate stereotyped mannerisms, commercialism, and theatricalism from the stage by concentrating on the inner truth of feelings, moods, and emotions. As a technique, it called for an introspective approach to characterization and an internal, psychological development of the role.

After some 70 rehearsals, the Moscow Art Theatre opened with Aleksey Tolstoy's *Tsar Fyodor Ioannovich* in October 1898. For its fifth production it staged Chekhov's *Seagull*, a play that had failed in its first production. With its revival of *The Seagull*, the Art Theatre not only achieved its first major success but also began a long, artistic association with one of Russia's most celebrated playwrights: in Chekhov's artistic realism, the Art Theatre discovered a writer suited to its aesthetic sensibilities. In *The Seagull*, as in all of Chekhov's plays, the Art Theatre emphasized the sub-text, the underlying meaning of the playwright's thought. Dialogue and action were of secondary importance; what mattered was man's inner feelings and experiences as revealed in the "play" that lay beneath the surface. Artistically, the Art Theatre tried all that was new. Its repertoire included works of Gorky, Andreyev, Tolstoy, Maeterlinck, and Hauptmann, among others, and it staged works of political and social significance as well as satires, fantasies, and comedies.

After the Russian Revolution, it received crucial support from Lenin and Lunacharsky, first commissar of education in the Soviet Union, and in 1922 the Art Theatre toured Europe and the U.S., winning critical acclaim wherever it performed. Returning to Moscow in 1924, it continued to produce new Soviet plays and Russian classics until its evacuation in 1941. Two successful tours of London in the late 1950s and early 1960s re-established its pre-eminence in world theatre. The Art Theatre has exercised a tremendous influence on theatres all over the world. It fostered many experimental studios (*e.g.*, Vakhtangov Theatre, Realistic Theatre, Habima Theatre, Musical Studio of Nemirovich-Danchenko). Today, virtually all professional training in acting uses some aspects of Konstantin Stanislavsky's Method.

·direction of Chekhov plays **5**:827b
·formation and directing theories **18**:228e
·naturalistic staging of realistic drama **17**:548b
·Soviet Union cultural history **17**:354f
·Stanislavsky's creation of people's theatre **17**:581c

Moscow Ballet: *see* Bolshoi Ballet.

Moscow Canal, ship waterway linking Moscow to the Volga River at Ivankovo, north of Moscow. Built between 1932 and 1937, the canal replaced the canalized Moskva River, which can take only small craft, as the main water access to Moscow. The water journey to the important industrial centre of Gorky was shortened by 75 mi (120 km). Along the Moscow Canal's length of 80 mi (128 km) there are 11 locks. The minimum depth is 18 ft (5.5 m), whereas lock dimensions are 950 by 100 ft (290 by 30 m), making possible the passage of seagoing ships.

Moscow Conferences (1942, 1943, 1944, and 1945), three Allied strategy meetings during World War II and a postwar conference on the problem of Korean unification.

·Allied strategy formulation in 1941 **19**:988g
·Churchill's division of Europe in 1944 **19**:1008f
·Korean trusteeship controversy in 1945 **10**:512g

Moscow Declaration (1943), declaration in which the Big Four (U.S., U.S.S.R., Britain, and China) announced the need for an international organization.

·war crimes definition and punishment **19**:555b

Moscow Main Botanic Garden, Moscow, a 356-hectare (880-acre) garden affiliated with the Academy of Sciences of the U.S.S.R. It has about 8,300 plant types, including outstanding collections of native flora, decorative flowers, economic and medicinal plants, and tropical and subtropical plants.

Moscow school, major school of late medieval Russian icon and mural painting that flourished in Moscow from *c.* 1400 to the end of the 16th century, succeeding the Novgorod school (*q.v.*) as the dominant Russian school of painting and eventually developing the stylistic basis for a national art. Moscow began a local artistic development parallel to that of Novgorod and other centres as it rose to a leading position in the movement to expel the Mongols, who had occupied most of Russia since mid-13th century. The autocratic tradition of the city fostered from the beginning a preference for abstracted spiritual expression over practical narrative.

"The Savior," icon painted on panel by Andrey Rublyov, Moscow school, 1411; in the Tretyakov Art Gallery, Moscow

Novosti—Sovfoto

The first flowering of the Moscow school occurred under the influence of the painter Theophanes the Greek, who was born and trained in Constantinople, assimilated the Russian manner and spirit at Novgorod, and moved from Novgorod to Moscow in about 1400. Theophanes went far beyond contemporary models in complexity of composition, subtle beauty of colour, and the fluid, almost impressionistic rendering of his deeply expressive figures. His achievements instilled in Muscovite painting a permanent appreciation of curving planes. Theophanes' most important successor was the most distinguished of Russia's medieval painters, a monk, Andrey Rublyov, who painted pictures of overwhelming spirituality and grace in a style that owes almost nothing to Theophanes except a devotion to artistic excellence. He concentrated on delicacy of line and luminous colour; he eliminated all unnecessary detail to strengthen the impact of the composition, and he constructed remarkably subtle and complex relationships among the few forms that remained. Elements of Rublyov's art are reflected in most of the finest Moscow paintings of the 15th century.

The period from the time of Rublyov's death, in about 1430, to the end of the 15th century was marked by a sudden growth in Moscow's prestige and sophistication. The Grand Dukes of Moscow finally drove out the Mongols and united most of the cities of central Russia, including Novgorod, under their leadership. With the fall of Constantinople to the Turks in 1453, Moscow, for some time the centre of the Russian Orthodox Church, became the virtual centre of Eastern Orthodoxy. An artist whose career reflected the new sophistication was the major painter Dionisy, a layman. Dionisy's compositions, based more on intellect than on an instinctive expression of spirituality, are more arresting than either Theophanes' or Rublyov's. His figures, only slightly taller than was conventional in Russian painting, nevertheless convey an effect of extreme elongation and buoyancy through a drastic reduction, by simplified drawing, to silhouette and through a disparate spacing that spreads them out in a processional effect, breaking with the earlier Russian predilection for tight composition. There is a subtle colour scheme of turquoise, pale green, and rose against darker blues and purples. Perhaps the most significant quality of Dionisy's painting was his ability to emphasize the mystical over the dramatic content of narrative scenes, to take them beyond a specific time or place.

The new prestige of the Russian Orthodox Church led to an unprecedented seriousness in the mystical interpretation of traditional subject matter; by mid-16th century there were specific directives from the church based on a new didactic iconography that expounded mysteries, rites, and dogmas. The general stylistic traditions already established were followed throughout the 16th and 17th centuries, but icons became smaller and crowded in composition and steadily declined in quality. By the late 16th century much of the former spirituality had been lost, replaced by decorative enrichment and elegance.

At the beginning of the 17th century the so-called Stroganov school (*q.v.*) of accomplished Moscow artists assumed the leadership of the last phase of Russian medieval art.

Moscow State University, more fully MOSCOW M.V. LOMONOSOV STATE UNIVERSITY, coeducational state-controlled institution of higher learning at Moscow, Soviet Union, first and largest Russian university, founded in 1755 by the linguist M.V. Lomonosov. It was modelled after German universities, and its faculty was originally primarily German. Since its inception, tuition has been free and students living in university quarters have been maintained at government expense. Before the October Revolution (1917), the university had about 10,000 students. By the early 1970s enrollment was almost 30,000. Among the faculties are physics, chemistry, mathematics, biology, geography, history and philosophy.

·campus, enrollment, and history **12**:485a; map 476
·Lomonosov founding and development role **11**:89f
·Table of Ranks requirements fulfillment **16**:53e

Moscow Zoo, Russian MOSKOVSKY ZOOPARK, largest zoo in the Soviet Union, exhibiting an outstanding collection of northern animals and many exotic species. Founded by a public society in 1864, the zoo later was privately owned. In 1919 it was declared the property of Soviet Russia and in 1923 was put under the Moscow City Soviet (council). It incorporates 16.5 hectares (41 acres) and includes small, unbarred enclosures as well as large paddocks for herds. The Moscow Zoo remained open during World War II, though annual attendance fell from 2,500,000 to 435,000, and much of the park was destroyed. The zoo contains 2,970 specimens of 585 species. Annual attendance is 3,200,000.

·map, Moscow **12**:476

Moseley, Henry Gwyn Jeffreys (b. Nov. 23, 1887, Weymouth, Dorset—d. Aug. 10, 1915, Gallipoli, Tur.), physicist who experimentally demonstrated that the major properties of an element are determined by the atomic number, not by the atomic weight, and firmly established the relationship between atomic number and the charge of the atomic nucleus. The atomic number is now known to be the number of protons in the nucleus; the atomic weight is an average of the naturally occurring isotopes of an element.

Educated at Trinity College, Oxford, Moseley in 1910 was appointed lecturer in physics at Ernest (later Lord) Rutherford's laboratory at the University of Manchester, where he worked until the outbreak of World War I, when he entered the army. His first researches were concerned with radioactivity and beta radiation in radium. He then turned to the study of the X-ray spectra of the elements (the characteristic X-rays emitted by an element when bombarded with electrons). In a brilliant series of experiments he found a relationship between the frequencies of corresponding lines in the X-ray spectra. In a paper published in 1913, he reported that the frequencies are proportional to the squares of whole numbers that are equal to the atomic number plus a constant.

Known as Moseley's law, this fundamental discovery concerning atomic numbers was a milestone in advancing the knowledge of the atom. In 1914 Moseley published a paper in which he concluded that there were three unknown elements between aluminum and gold. He also concluded that there were only 92 elements up to and including uranium.

Moseley's death at the Battle of Suvla Bay (in Turkey) at the age of 27 deprived the world of one of its most promising experimental physicists.

·atomic structure research **2**:337c
·periodic law and atomic number assignment **14**:76g
·rare-earth property similarities **15**:516d
·X-ray line spectra research **19**:1060h

Moseley's law: *see* X-ray, characteristic.

Moselle, *département*, northeastern France, established in 1790 from territories of Lorraine (*q.v.*) and the city of Metz (*q.v.*). It was annexed by Germany after the Franco-German War (1870–71) and restored to France in 1919 after World War I. Germany annexed it again in World War II and held it until 1944. The *département*, which contains one of the most important concentrations of heavy industry in France, occupies an area of 2,399 sq mi (6,214 sq km) between the eastern border of Meurthe-et-Moselle and the western border of the West German Saarland. It extends from the forested Vosges massif in the southeast, across the Plateau Lorrain (altitude about 600 ft [180 m]), to the Luxembourg border in the north. The Moselle River (*q.v.*) crosses the northwest region, flowing north through Metz, capital of Moselle, and alongside the iron-ore fields of Côtes de Moselle and Thionville. The Lorraine coalfield, a prolongation of the Saar Basin, is situated near the German border east of the industrial complex. In the southeast the *département* is watered by the Sarre River, flowing north through Sarrebourg past salt mines and chemical works. Modernized canals link the Moselle and Saar industrial regions and connect them with the Paris Basin. Communications through Metz to Nancy, the Saar, and Luxembourg are being improved with the construction of motorways.

Moselle has warm summers and severe winters. The agricultural population, which has declined steadily with industrialization, tends to concentrate on cattle raising and dairy farming for local markets. The Moselle iron-ore fields are among those worked earliest in the world, but they still contain substantial reserves. The Moselle Valley near Thionville, and the valleys of Fentsch and Orne, are lined with scores of blast furnaces, iron and steel works, and coking plants. The *département* accounts for more than one-third of France's total output of coal, iron, and steel. Gas produced as a by-product is fed to the Paris region by pipeline. Moselle has nine *arrondissements*—Boulay-Moselle, Château-Salins, Forbach, Metz-Ville, Metz-Campagne, Sarrebourg, Sarreguemines, Thionville-Est, and Thionville-Ouest. It is in the educational division of Strasbourg. Pop. (1974 est.) 1,035,000.

·area and population table **7**:594

Moselle (German MOSEL) **River,** left-bank tributary of the Rhine River, flows for 339 mi (545 km) across northeastern France and West Germany. Rising on the forested slopes of the Vosges massif, the river meanders past Épinal, Pont-Saint-Vincent, Toul, Frouard, Metz, and Thionville before leaving France to form the frontier between West Germany and Luxembourg for a short distance. The river enters West Germany and flows past Trier to its confluence with the Rhine at Koblenz. In this sector of the valley (German Moseltal) are the vineyards from which the famous Moselle wines are produced. The chief tributaries are the Madon, Orne, and Sauer (French Sûre) on the left, and the Meurthe, Seille, and Saar (French Sarre) on the right. Above Metz the Moselle has been navigable to 300-ton barges since the 19th century. It connects at Toul and Frouard with the Rhine–Marne Canal. From Metz to Thionville the river has been navigable by 300-ton barges since 1932; below Thionville it was not navigable until the inauguration in 1964 of the Moselle Canal from Metz to Koblenz, built to take barges up to 1,500 tons. The canal is administered by a tripartite authority representing France, West Germany, and Luxembourg. There are several iron and steel plants and power stations along the waterway.
50°22′ N, 7°36′ E

·international navigation control **15**:806h; map
·Luxembourg farming and animal raising **11**:203a

maps
·Federal Republic of Germany **8**:47
·France **7**:585
·Luxembourg **11**:203

Möser, Justus (b. Dec. 14, 1720, Osnabrück, now in West Germany—d. Jan. 8, 1794, Osnabrück), political essayist and poet who was a forerunner of the *Sturm und Drang* ("Storm and Stress") movement of rebellious young German writers.

Trained in jurisprudence at the universities of Jena and Göttingen, Möser was named state's attorney at Osnabrück (1747), a Protestant prince-bishopric, and from 1764 he was virtually head of the government there. Möser also served as chief justice of the criminal court (1762–68), privy councillor of justice (1768), and councillor of justice (1783).

In Möser's collection of weekly papers, *Patriotischen Phantasien* (1774–76; "Patriotic Ideas"), he called for the national organic development of a state rather than a system of arbitrary laws imposed by a sovereign; Goethe compared the *Phantasien* to analogous writings by Benjamin Franklin. Möser's *Osnabrücke Geschichte* (2 vol., 1768; "History of Osnabrück") was a pioneer work, showing the influence of folk traditions on the customs and government of a community. His complete writings, including essays, poems, and a tragedy, are available in *Sämtliche Werke* (10 vol., 1842–44; "Collected Works").

Moses 12:487, Hebrew MOSHE (fl. *c.* 14th–13th century BC), Hebrew prophet, teacher, and leader who delivered his people from Egyptian slavery and founded the religious community known as Israel, based on a Covenant relationship with God.

Abstract of text biography. According to the biblical account, in Exodus and Numbers, Moses, a Hebrew foundling adopted and reared in the Egyptian court, somehow learned that he was a Hebrew and killed an Egyptian taskmaster who was beating a Hebrew slave. He fled to Midian (mostly in northwest Arabia), where he became the shepherd and eventually the son-in-law of a Midianite priest, Jethro. While tending his flocks he had the experience of seeing a burning bush that remained unconsumed and of a call there from the God—thereafter to be called Yahweh—of Abraham, Isaac, and Jacob to deliver his people the Hebrews from Egypt. Because Moses was a stammerer, his brother Aaron was to be spokesman, but Moses would be Yahweh's representative.

Ramses II (reigned 1304–1237 BC) was probably the pharaoh at the time. Regarding himself as divine, he rejected the demand of this unknown God through Moses and Aaron and responded by increasing the oppression of the Hebrews. During the ensuing contest, Moses used plagues sent by Yahweh to bend Ramses' will. Whether the Hebrews were finally permitted to leave or simply fled is not clear; but in any case, according to the biblical account, Pharaoh's forces pursued them eastward to the Sea of Reeds, a papyrus lake (not the Red Sea), which the Hebrews crossed safely but in which the Egyptians were engulfed. Moses then led the people to Mt. Sinai (Horeb) at the southern tip of the Sinai Peninsula. The appearance of Yahweh in a terrific storm there, in the biblical narrative, was a revelatory experience for Moses, as the burning bush had been. Out of this came the Covenant between Yahweh and the people of Israel, including the Ten Commandments; and Moses began issuing ordinances for specific situations, instituted a system of judges and hearings in civil cases, and regulated the cult.

After leaving Mt. Sinai and continuing the journey toward Canaan, Moses faced increasing resistance and frustration and once got so angry at the people that, according to tradition, God accounted it a lack of faith and denied him entrance into Canaan. As his last official act, Moses renewed the Sinai Covenant with the survivors of the wanderings, then climbed Mt. Pisgah to look over the land that he would not enter. The Hebrews never saw him again, and the circumstances of his death and burial remain shrouded in mystery.

TEXT BIOGRAPHY covers:
Historical views of Moses **12**:487d
The date of Moses 487f
The formative years 487h
Moses in Midian 488c
Moses and Pharaoh 488f
From Goshen to Sinai 489b
The Covenant at Sinai 489e
From Sinai to Transjordan 490a
Moses the man 490d

REFERENCES in other text articles:
·Aaron's secondary position **1**:2e
·biblical account of Hebrew history **2**:900e
·biographical parallels in various myths **10**:192a *passim* to 193g
·Islām and prophetic messengers **9**:914a
·Joshua–Moses role comparison **2**:907c
·Lord's call for intelligence operation **9**:680g
·Maimonides' and Spinoza's views about prophecy **10**:212b
·miracles and religious founders **12**:271a
·page illumination from Bury Bible, illus., **19**:Visual Arts, Western, Plate V
·patriarchal relationship with Yahweh **10**:303g *passim* to 304g

·personal encounter and transcendent God **18**:265f
·religious founders' roles **15**:651e
·St. Paul's argument on impermanence of Law **2**:963b

Moses (1505–45), sculpture by Michelangelo.
·symbolism and quality of terror **12**:100a

Moses, Assumption of, a pseudepigraphical work (a noncanonical writing that in style and content resembles authentic biblical literature), originally written in Hebrew or Aramaic, although the only extant text is a Latin translation made from a previous Greek translation. The book does not mention the actual ascension of Moses, but the Letter of Jude, when discussing the battle between Satan and the archangel Michael for possession of Moses' body, refers to the *Assumption of Moses*. It is thus clear that this work must have described the actual assumption in chapters that have been lost. Several passages, moreover, are incomplete.

References to the death of King Herod the Great and other events of the year 4/3 BC indicate that the book was written in that year or shortly thereafter, probably in Palestine. The unknown Jewish author set forth an apocalyptic view of the history of the Jews, using as a framework Moses' predictions and instructions to Joshua. The tone of the work is decidedly negative toward the fusion of politics with religion and condemns the Hasmonean leaders who ruled Judaea after the Maccabean revolt of 168–161 BC. This ascetic and purist theological stand and the mention of a prophetic figure similar to the "supervisor" in the *Damascus Document* of the Essene community at Qumrān possibly indicate that the *Assumption of Moses* was written by a sympathizer or member of the Essene sect, the members of which deplored the introduction of nationalism into Judaism and were characterized by strict observance of Mosaic Law and a heightened interest in messianism. The author portrays Moses as a culture hero who was the prime mediator between God and the Jews before, during, and after his life. A long section describes the messianic age, which is presaged by catastrophic upheavals in the physical world, after which the Jews will ascend to heaven to watch the punishment of their adversaries on earth. *Major ref.* **2**:936d

Moses, Grandma, real name ANNA MARY ROBERTSON MOSES (b. Sept. 7, 1860, Greenwich, N.Y.—d. Dec. 13, 1961, Hoosick Falls, N.Y.), folk painter, internationally popular for her documentary primitives of U.S. rural life in the late 19th and early 20th centuries. At 12 she left her parents' farm and was a hired girl until she married Thomas Moses in 1887. They first farmed in the Shenandoah Valley near Staunton, Va., and in 1905 moved to a farm at Eagle Bridge, N.Y., near the place where she had been born. Thomas died in 1927, and Anna continued to farm with the help of her youngest son until advancing age forced her to retire to a daughter's home in 1936.

As a child Grandma Moses had drawn pictures and coloured them with the juice of berries and grapes. After her husband died she created worsted embroidery pictures, and when her arthritis made manipulating a needle too difficult, she turned to painting.

Her first works, done around 1938, were copies of prints by Currier & Ives and picture postcards. She soon turned to painting her memories of what she called "old-timey" farm life in New York and Virginia. The titles of these pictures alone are nostalgic reminders of an America past: "Catching the Thanksgiving Turkey," "Out for the Christmas Trees," "Over the River to Grandma's House," and "Sugaring-off in the Maple Orchard." Her works are characteristically composed as panoramic views of a landscape or interior with lively small figures and animals engaged in daily or seasonal tasks and recreations. Precisely painted, they are drawn with a naïve sense of perspective resulting in patterns of flattened forms.

Painting on masonite, Grandma Moses would size the board with three coats of flat white paint to make her colours more brilliant. Usually working in her bedroom, she would lay three or four boards flat on a table and paint them simultaneously—first painting the skies, then the mountains and foreground landscapes, and finally adding the figures.

Her first pictures sold in a drugstore in Hoosick Falls. By 1939, however, her pictures were exhibited throughout the United States and Europe (where she had 15 one-man shows). Her two honourary doctorates and the commemoration of her 100th and 101st birthdays as "Grandma Moses Day" by the governor of New York also attest to her popularity. In 1952 she wrote in the bright style of her pictures an autobiography, *My Life's History*.
·hobby inspiration in primitive painting **8**:974g

"Out for the Christmas Trees," oil on masonite by Grandma Moses, 1946; in the Galerie St. Etienne, New York City
By courtesy of the Galerie St. Etienne, New York; © Grandma Moses Properties, Inc., New York

Moses and Monotheism, English translation of DER MANN MOSES UND DIE MONOTHEISTISHE RELIGION, a book by Sigmund Freud, published in German in 1939 and in English in 1964.
·psychoanalysis of religious history **15**:621e

Moses ben Maimon: *see* Maimonides, Moses.

Moses ben Samuel ibn Tibbon: *see* ibn Tibbon, Moses ben Samuel.

Moses (ben Shem Tov) de León (b. 1250, León, Spain—d. 1305, Arevalo), Jewish Kabbalist and presumably the author of the *Sefer ha-zohar* ("The Book of Splendour"), the most important work of Jewish mysticism; for a number of centuries its influence rivalled that of the Old Testament and the Talmud, the rabbinical compendium of law, lore, and commentary. The details of Moses de León's life, like those of most Jewish mystics, are obscure. Until 1290 he lived in Guadalajara (located in Castile, the Spanish centre of adherents of the Kabbala, the accumulated body of important Jewish mystical writings). He then travelled a great deal and finally settled in Ávila. On a trip to Valladolid, he met a Palestinian Kabbalist, Isaac ben Samuel of Acre; to him (as recorded in Isaac's diary), Moses confided that he possessed the centuries-old, original manuscript of the *Zohar*, copies of which he had been circulating since the 1280s. He promised to show it to Isaac at his home in Ávila. Because the authorship of the *Zohar* was ascribed to the 2nd-century Palestinian rabbinic teacher Simeon ben Yoḥai (a reputed worker of miracles), the original manuscript would have been of incomparable interest and value. Unfortunately, Moses died before he could fulfill his promise, and Isaac subsequently heard rumours that Moses' wife had denied the existence of this manuscript, claiming rather that Moses himself was the author of the *Zohar*.

The *Zohar*, written for the most part in a strange, artificial, literary Aramaic, is primarily a series of mystical commentaries on the Pentateuch (the Five Books of Moses), in manner much like the traditional Midrashim, or homilies based on Scripture. Against the backdrop of an imaginary Palestine, Simeon ben Yoḥai and his disciples carry on a series of dialogues. In them, it is revealed that God manifested himself in a series of 10 descending, or *sefirot*, emanations (*e.g.*, "love" of God, "beauty" of God, and "kingdom" of God). The spheres, however, do not reveal God's unknowable inner self or *En Sof* (the Infinite). This doctrine of the *sefirot* is in the mode of Neoplatonism, a philosophy in which the material world is seen as the faintest of the emanations of the completely noncorporeal One. In addition to the influence of Neoplatonism, the *Zohar* also shows evidence of the influence of Joseph Gikatilla, a medieval Spanish Kabbalist thought to have been a friend of Moses de León. Gikatilla's work *Ginnat ʾegoz* ("Nut Orchard") provides some of the *Zohar*'s key terminology, including that used to describe the mystic "primordial point," the seminal manifestation of God's wisdom.

These influences, although cunningly disguised, were discerned by Gershom Scholem, one of the great 20th-century scholars of Jewish mysticism, and he became convinced that the *Zohar* was a medieval work. He was able to demonstrate, further, that the Aramaic in which the *Zohar* is written is in both vocabulary and idiom the work of an author whose native language was Hebrew. Finally, by comparing the *Zohar* with the Hebrew works of Moses de León, Scholem identified León as the *Zohar*'s author. Scholem theorized that the *Zohar* was León's attempt to combat the rise of rationalism among Spanish Jewry and the resultant laxity in religious observance. With the *Zohar*, according to Scholem, Moses de León attempted to reassert the authority of traditional religion (Kabbala itself means "tradition") by simultaneously giving its doctrines and rituals a fresh, compelling reinterpretation and ascribing this reinterpretation to an old, mythically revered authority.

Many orthodox scholars, nevertheless, still hold that Simeon ben Yoḥai wrote the *Zohar*.
·antiphilosophic Talmudic pseudepigrapha **10**:188a
·fundamentalist mysticism and philosophy **10**:320h

Moses ibn Ezra: *see* ibn Ezra, Moses (ben Jacob ha-Sallaḥ).

Moses Lake, city, Grant County, central Washington, U.S., on the northeast shore of

Moses Lake (16 mi [26 km] long). The town was settled in 1897 and was laid out in 1910 as Neppel; it was incorporated in 1938 and renamed for the Indian chief Moses. The city, located in the Columbia Basin, serves as the trade centre of an irrigated farm region producing sugar beets, alfalfa, cereals, potatoes, and livestock. The impounded waters of Grand Coulee Dam (60 mi [97 km] north) have raised the water table and created numerous lakes. Tourism and food processing are the main economic factors. Nearby Larson Air Force Base (1943–66) is now used as an industrial park. Moses Lake is the home of Big Bend Community College (1962). Pop. (1980) 10,629.
47°08′ N, 119°17′ W

Moses of Khoren, Armenian MOVSES KHORENATZI, known as the father of Armenian literature. He is traditionally believed to be a 5th-century author, but he has also been dated as late as the 9th century. Nothing is known of his life apart from alleged autobiographical details contained in the *History of Armenia*, which bears his name as author. His claims to have been the disciple of St. Sahak (Isaac) and St. Mesrop, to have studied in Edessa and Alexandria after the Council of Edessa (431), and to have been commissioned to write his *History* by the governor Sahak Bagratuni, have been rejected by most serious scholars, in large part because of anachronisms in his text. He is the only early Armenian historian to treat of events in his country long before its conversion to Christianity.

Moses (ben Joshua) of Narbonne, also called MOSES NARBONI (d. 1362), French-Jewish philosopher and physician. He was the author of about 20 works, including commentaries on works by the Muslim philosophers al-Ghazālī and Ibn Ṭufayl, supercommentaries on Averroës' commentaries on Aristotle's works, and, especially, a commentary on Maimonides' *Guide of the Perplexed*.
·Jewish philosophy and commentaries **10**:213a

Moses und Aron, unfinished opera (begun 1930) by the Austrian composer Arnold Schoenberg.
·allegoric and expressive qualities **16**:351c

Mosharref od-Dīn: *see* Saʿdī.

moshav (Hebrew: "settlement"; pl. *moshavim*), in Israel, a type of cooperative agricultural settlement. The *moshav*, which is generally based on the principle of private ownership of land, self-labour (avoidance of hired labour), and communal marketing, represents an intermediate stage between privately owned settlements and the complete communal living of the kibbutz. *Moshavim* are built on land belonging to the Jewish National Fund or to the state. The commonest type, the *moshav ʿovdim* ("workers' settlement"), consists of privately farmed agricultural plots. In a newer variant, the *moshav shitufi* ("partnership settlement"), the land is farmed as a single large holding, but contrary to practice in the kibbutz, households are independently run by their members.

Moshavim ʿovdim were first established before World War I but did not last; the first successful settlements of this type were Nahalal and Kefar Yeḥezqel, founded in 1921 in the Plain of Esdraelon. The first *moshavim shitufiyyim* were Kefar Ḫittim (1936) and Bene Berit (Moledet; 1938), both in lower Galilee.

In the period of immigration that followed the creation of Israel (1948), the *moshav* was found to be an ideal settlement form for the immigrants, few of whom were accustomed to communal living. In the late 1970s some 136,500 persons lived in *moshavim ʿovdim*, and about 7,000 in *moshavim shitufiyyim*.
·farm management methods **7**:180c
·Israel's pioneering in rural development **9**:1060d

Moshe (Hebrew prophet): *see* Moses.

Mosheim, Johann Lorenz von (b. Oct. 9, 1694, Lübeck, now in West Germany—d. Sept. 9, 1755, Göttingen), Lutheran theologian who founded the pragmatic school of church historians, which insisted on objective, critical treatment of original sources. In 1723 he became professor at Helmstedt and in 1747 was made professor of divinity and chancellor of the university at Göttingen.

Mosheim departed from the established method of writing history as simple narration of unquestioned events and called instead for fresh attention to wide historical movements and pervasive themes. Among his 85 works, written in Latin and German, on church history is *Institutiones Historiae Ecclesiasticae Antiquae et Recentioris* (1755; *Institutes of Ecclesiastical History*, 1832).

Moshesh (Sotho leader): *see* Mshweshwe.

Moshi, capital of Kilimanjaro Region, northeast Tanzania, eastern Africa, at the southern foot of Mt. Kilimanjaro. The town is a centre for processing coffee and sisal that is grown in the area. Pop. (1972 est.) 37,826.
3°21′ S, 37°20′ E
·map, Tanzania **17**:1027
·population density map **17**:1030

Moshi language: *see* Moré language.

Moshoeshoe (Sotho leader): *see* Mshweshwe.

Mosi (people): *see* Mossi.

Moṣībat-nāmeh ("Book of Affliction"), mystical poem by the Persian poet Farīd od-Dīn ʿAṭṭār.
·mystical theme and imagery **9**:963h

Moskenesøya (Norway): *see* Lofoten.

Moskenstraumen (Norway): *see* Maelstrøm.

Moskowa, Michel Ney, prince de la (marshal of France): *see* Ney, Michel.

Moskva (Soviet Union): *see* Moscow.

Moskva, Soviet ship, designed as a cruiser and a helicopter cruiser, that was commissioned in 1967; a sister ship, the "Leningrad," followed in 1968. The "Moskva" could carry 18 helicopters and was armed with two surface-to-air systems of twin missile launchers, one twin missile launcher possibly for antisubmarine missiles, four 57-millimetre guns, two 12-tube mortars, and two torpedo tubes.
·naval craft design history **12**:898c

Moskva River, river in Moscow *oblast* and part of Smolensk *oblast*, Russian S.F.S.R. It rises in the Smolensk-Moscow Upland and flows for 312 mi (502 km) generally southeast through the city of Moscow, and drains an area of 6,800 sq mi (17,600 sq km). It is also a left tributary of the Oka River in the Volga basin.
55°05′ N, 38°50′ E
·Moscow's topography **12**:474h

Moṣleḥ od-Dīn Saʿdī (Persian poet): *see* Saʿdī.

Moslem . . . : For terms beginning so, *see under* Muslim; for discussion of the religion, *see* Islām.

Mosley, Sir Oswald (Ernald), 6th Baronet (b. Nov. 16, 1896, London—d. Dec. 3, 1980, Orsay, Fr.), politician who was the leader of the British Union of Fascists from 1932 to 1940 and of its successor, the Union Movement, from 1948 until his death. These groups were known for distributing anti-Semitic propaganda, conducting hostile demonstrations in the largely Jewish sections of east London, and wearing Nazi-style uniforms and insignia.

Serving in the House of Commons from 1918 to 1931, Mosley was successively a Conservative, an Independent, and a Labour Party member. In 1931 he tried to form a socialist party but was defeated for reelection to Parliament. The next year he founded the British Union of Fascists, for which some enthusiasm was generated by his own powerful oratory and by the support of the newspaper publisher Viscount Rothermere. Mosley was interned after the outbreak of World War II but was released in 1943 because of illness. On Feb. 7, 1948, he launched the Union Movement, which he described as an amalgam of 51 organizations; however, he never regained his earlier prominence.
·Fascist movement in England **7**:187f

Moso (ethnolinguistic group): *see* Yi.

mosque, Arabic MASJID, place of prayer in Islām, serving primarily as the centre of community worship in which all men are equal before God. The mosque has historically been used for many public functions—military, political, social, and educational. Schools and libraries were often attached to medieval mosques, most notably to al-Azhar in Cairo. The mosque also functioned as a court of justice until the introduction of secular law into many Islāmic countries in modern times.

The first mosques were modelled on the place of worship of the Prophet Muḥammad—the courtyard of his house at Medina—and were simply plots of ground marked out as sacred. Though the architecture of the mosque developed under the influence of local styles, the building remained essentially an open space, generally roofed over, with a minaret sometimes attached to it. A mosque is entered from the north; within, the *miḥrāb*, a semicircular niche reserved for the prayer leader (*imām*), points to the *qiblah*, the direction of Mecca; the *minbar*, a seat at the top of steps placed at the right of the *miḥrāb*, is used by the preacher (*khaṭīb*) as a pulpit. Occasionally there also is a *maqsūrah*, a box or wooden screen near the *miḥrāb*, used to shield a worshipping ruler. Mats or carpets cover the floor of the mosque, where the ritual prayer (*ṣalāt*) is performed by rows of barefoot men, who bow and prostrate themselves under the *imām*'s guidance. Professional chanters (*qurrāʾ*) may chant the Qurʾān (Koran; Islāmic sacred scriptures) according to rigidly prescribed systems taught in special schools, but no music or singing is allowed. Statues, ritual objects, and pictures are also proscribed. Friday services generally take place in the *masjid jāmiʿ*, a mosque theoretically large enough to accommodate an entire community.

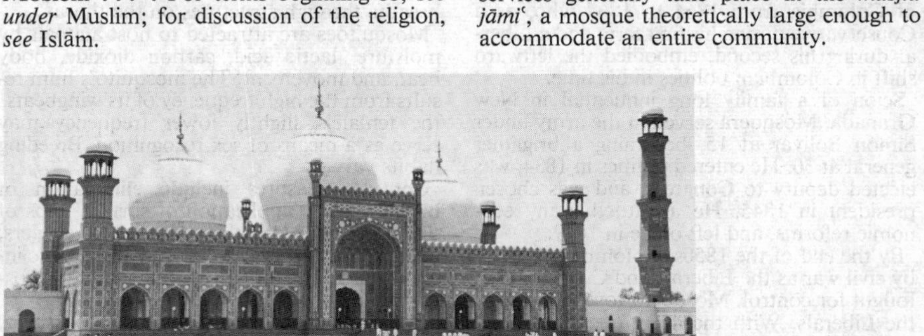

The Bādshāhī Mosque at Lahore, Pakistan
Frederick Ayer III—Photo Researchers

Outside the mosque stands the minaret (*q.v.*; *ma'dhanah*), originally any elevated place but now usually a tower; it is used by the *mu'adhdhin* (muezzin, "crier") to proclaim the call to worship (*adhān*) five times each day. A place for ablution, containing running water, is usually attached to the mosque but may be separated from it.

Whereas many social, educational, and political functions of the mosque have been taken over by other institutions in modern times, it remains a religious centre of influence. In some cases a *maktab* (elementary school) is attached, mainly for the teaching of the Qur'ān. On certain occasions the *'ulamā'* (religious scholars) give public lectures there.
·architectural origins and development **9**:983h
·architectural history **9**:924c; illus. 919
·design components and variations **9**:952e
·footwear regulations **15**:638c
·Hagia Sophia architecture and art **9**:1071f
·Ḥasan facade and minarets illus. **3**:581
·increase and distinction **6**:332g
·Islāmic religious institutions **9**:920a
·worship site criteria **19**:1017d

mosque of Islam, also called TEMPLE OF ISLAM, primal community institution in the evolution of the World Community of al-Islām in the West (formerly, the Nation of Islam, or Black Muslims). The mosque (Arabic, *masjid*) has played a central role in Muslim life under the leadership of Elijah Muhammad (1930–75) and his son, Warith Deen Muhammad (1975–). A series of changes in the social, intellectual, and spiritual direction and development of the community were effected in the late 1970s. As a result, the Fruits of Islam (FOI; a male auxiliary group) and the Muslim Girls Training and General Civilization Class (MGTGCC; a female auxiliary group) were disbanded; all forms of colour-consciousness and racism were repudiated; and a new name for the organization was adopted.

The mosque functions under Qur'ānic principles as a place of prayer and worship and as a centre of community activities. Mosques have been established throughout the U.S. and in the Caribbean region. Each mosque is overseen by an imām (a leader of prayer), who is chosen by the mosque's members.

The primary concerns of the mosque membership are religious propagation, education, and family and community development. In most large cities, certified elementary and secondary schools—called the Sister Clara Muhammad Elementary and Secondary schools—are affiliated with the mosques; their courses of instruction include Islāmic studies, Arabic, English, and history as well as reading, writing, and mathematics. Mosque meetings take place on Fridays and Sundays. Attendance and membership are open to all and are no longer restricted as they once were. *Major ref.* **2**:1094f

Mosquera, Tomás Cipriano de (b. Sept. 20, 1798, Popayán, New Granada, now Colombia—d. Oct. 7, 1878, Coconuco), president of New Granada from 1845 to 1849 and of Colombia from 1864 to 1867 who, as a Conservative during his first term and a Liberal during his second, embodied the leftward shift in Colombian politics in his time.

Scion of a family long influential in New Granada, Mosquera served in the army under Simón Bolívar at 15, becoming a brigadier general at 30. He entered politics in 1834, was elected deputy to Congress, and was chosen president in 1845. He instituted many economic reforms, and left office in 1849.

By the end of the 1850s, Colombia was torn by civil war as the Liberals and Conservatives fought for control. Mosquera took the side of the Liberals. With the army under his command he took Bogotá (July 1861) and declared himself president. He ruled as a dictator until the adoption of a new constitution (1863), which provided for a two-year presidential term and changed the name of the country to the United States of Colombia. Not fully trusting Mosquera, the Liberals limited his first term to one year (1864–65). But he was re-elected in 1865 and imposed a dictatorship. Overthrown in 1867, he was exiled for two years. He returned to Colombia to serve as president of the state of Cauca and as senator, retiring from public life in 1876.
·Colombian tobacco trade expansion **4**:875d

Mosquito, also spelled MISKITO OR MOSTIQUE, Central American Indians of the Caribbean lowlands of northeastern Nicaragua. They were discovered by Columbus on his fourth voyage and have been in steady European contact since the mid-17th century. In the 20th century five subgroups existed, with a total population estimated at 45,000 to 80,000.

The Mosquito are agricultural, their staple crop being sweet manioc (yuca). They keep poultry, cattle, and other farm animals. Their culture has been influenced by European contacts and by intermarriage with Africans brought there as slaves. In colonial times it was similar to that of the neighbouring Sumo (*q.v.*).
·cinerary urn burial customs **3**:1180e
·colonial and modern relationships **3**:1108h; map 1107
·Nicaragua's early history **3**:1114d

mosquito, any of the familiar insects of the family Culicidae (order Diptera), numbering about 2,500 species, important in public health because of the bloodsucking habits of the females. Mosquitoes are known to transmit such serious diseases as yellow fever, malaria, filariasis, and dengue.

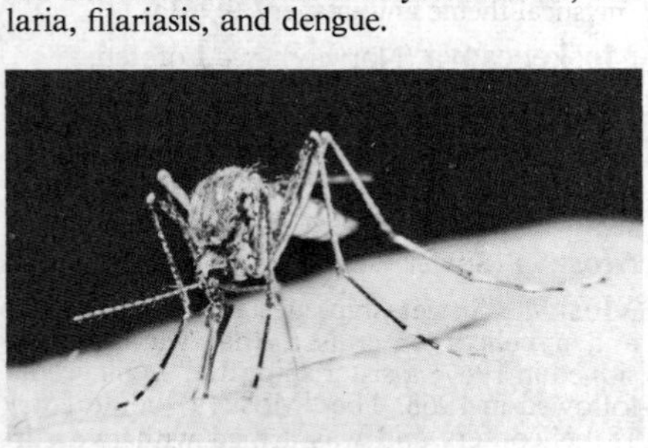

Mosquito (*Theobaldia anulata*)
N.A. Callow—EB Inc.

The slender elongated body of the adult is covered with scales; in addition, the mosquito is characterized by its long, fragile-looking legs and its mouthparts, which are contained in an elongated proboscis. The threadlike antennae of the male are generally bushier than those of the female. The males, and sometimes the females, feed on nectar and other plant juices; most females require a blood meal in order to mature their eggs, which are laid on the surface of water. Eggs hatch into aquatic larvae, or wrigglers, which swim with a jerking, wriggling movement and feed on algae and organic debris; a few are predatory and may even feed on other mosquitoes. Unlike most insects, mosquitoes in the pupal stage, called tumblers, are active. They breathe through structures on the thorax.

Mosquitoes are attracted to host animals by moisture, lactic acid, carbon dioxide, body heat, and movement. The mosquito's hum results from the high frequency of its wingbeats; the female's slightly lower frequency may serve as a means of sex recognition. Breeding habits vary.

Control measures include elimination of breeding sites, application of surface films of oil to clog the breathing tubes of wrigglers, and the use of larvicides. Synthetic organic insecticides may be used to destroy adult mosquitoes indoors.

There are three important mosquito genera. *Anopheles*, the only known carrier of malaria, also transmits filariasis and encephalitis. *Anopheles* mosquitoes are easily recognized in their resting position, in which the proboscis, head, and body are held on a straight line to each other but at an angle to the surface. The spotted colouring on the wings results from coloured scales. The female deposits her eggs singly on the water surface. *Anopheles* larvae lie parallel to the water surface and breathe through posterior spiracular plates on the abdomen instead of through a tube, as do most other mosquito larvae. Breeding usually occurs in water containing heavy vegetation. The life cycle is from 18 days to several weeks.

The genus *Culex* is a carrier of viral encephalitis and, in tropical and subtropical climates, of filariasis. It holds its body parallel to the resting surface, and its proboscis is bent downward relative to the surface. The wings, with scales on the veins and the margin, are uniform in colour. The tip of the female's abdomen is blunt and has retracted cerci (sensory appendages). The long and slender *Culex* larvae have breathing tubes that contain hair tufts; they lie head downward at an angle of 45° from the water surface. Breeding may occur on almost any body of freshwater, including standing polluted water. The eggs, which float on the water, are joined in masses of 100 or more. The life cycle, usually 10 to 14 days, may be longer in cold weather. *C. pipiens pipiens* is the most abundant house mosquito in northern regions; *C. pipiens quinquefasciatus* is abundant in southern parts.

The genus *Aedes* carries yellow fever, dengue, and encephalitis. Like *Culex*, it holds its body parallel to the surface with the proboscis bent down. The wings are uniformly coloured. *Aedes* may be distinguished from *Culex* by its silver thorax with white markings and posterior spiracular bristles. The tip of the female's abdomen is pointed and has protruding cerci. The short, stout larvae have a breathing tube containing a pair of tufts; the larvae hang head down at a 45° angle from the water surface. *Aedes* usually breeds in floodwater, rain pools, or salt marshes, the eggs being capable of withstanding long periods of dryness. The life cycle may be as short as 10 days or, in cool weather, as long as several months. *A. aegypti*, the important carrier of yellow fever, has white bands on its legs and spots on its abdomen and thorax. This domestic species breeds in almost any kind of container. *A. sollicitans*, *A. taeniorhynchus*, and *A. dorsalis* are important salt-marsh mosquitoes. They are prolific breeders, strong fliers, and irritants to animals, including man. *Major ref.* **5**:819b; illus.
·disease causation and control **11**:836f
·dormancy for survival and reproduction **5**:961c
·flight muscles' special cycle **12**:643h
·food storage mechanism **5**:783h
·hearing organ and mating use **17**:40e; illus. 41
·malaria transmission and life cycle **9**:557d
·mouthpart feeding modifications **9**:614g
·nematode invasion of larva illus. **14**:145
·prey location **4**:182c
·rain forest disease carriers **10**:344g
·thermoreception in invertebrates **18**:329b
·transmission of viral infections **5**:912h
·yellow fever transmission **15**:547a

Mosquito, Italian antitank rocket used in World War II.
·design characteristics, table 1 **15**:932

Mosquito, British bomber and reconnaissance plane used in World War II.
·British bomber strength **19**:999b
·design and military capabilities **1**:389b

Mosquito (MISKITO) **Coast,** Spanish COSTA DE MOSQUITOS, region of Nicaragua and Honduras. It comprises a band approximately 40 mi (65 km) wide of coastal lowland that skirts the Caribbean Sea for approximately 225 mi. Although it was visited by Columbus in 1502, the area had little contact with Europeans until the rise of the buccaneers in the 17th century, after which the English established a protectorate over the Mosquito Indians for whom the region is named. Spain, Nicaragua, and the U.S. disputed this claim until the matter was finally settled by the occupation of the Mosquito Coast by the Nicaraguan government and by the Clayton–Bulwer Treaty of 1850 between the U.S. and Great Britain.

The Mosquito Coast of Nicaragua is divided between Río San Juan and Zelaya departments. Its principal city is Bluefields (*q.v.*), capital of Zelaya, an important seaport. Other centres are Puerto Cabezas and San Juan del Norte (*q.v.*). Pop. (1971 est.) 56,000.
13°00′ N, 83°45′ W

Mosquitoes (1927), novel by William Faulkner.
·Faulkner's satire on literary circles **7**:196a

mosquito fern, common name for species of aquatic ferns of the family Azollaceae.
·fern characteristics and classification **7**:247f

mosquito fish (*Gambusia affinis*), live-bearing topminnow of the family Poeciliidae (*see* live-bearer), native to freshwaters of the

Mosquito fish (*Gambusia affinis*)
Gene Wolfsheimer

southeastern United States but widely introduced in other parts of the world for mosquito control. The hardy mosquito fish, which has a prodigious appetite for mosquito larvae, is usually light grayish, but may be spotted or blotched with black. The female reaches a length of about 6.4 centimetres (2½ inches), the male about 4 centimetres.

Moss, town, Østfold *fylke* (county), southeastern Norway, on the eastern shore of Oslofjorden. Founded in the 16th century, Moss was the site of the signing of the Convention of Moss, which united Norway and Sweden, in 1814.

Moss is a port city with paper and cotton mills, metalworks, shipyards, textile factories, breweries, and facilities for cement, asphalt, and tar production. The harbour is protected by adjacent Jeløya (island), called the "Pearl of Oslofjorden" for its fine resort area and many large estates. The Mosselva (river) drains Vannsjø (lake), the largest lake in the *fylke*, and flows through the town and into Oslofjorden. Moss has ferry, bus, and railroad connections to the rest of Norway. Pop. (1974 est.) 25,522.
59°26′ N, 10°42′ E
·map, Norway **13**:267

moss, any member of the class Bryopsida, or Musci (division Bryophyta), which contains about 15,000 species in more than 600 genera, distributed throughout the world except in salt water. Granite mosses constitute the order Andreaeales, and peat mosses the order Sphagnales; all other species, often called true mosses, are members of the order Bryales.

The "moss" found on the north side of trees is the green alga *Pleurococcus;* Irish moss is a red alga. Beard lichen (beard moss), Iceland moss, oak moss, and reindeer moss are lichens. Spanish moss is a common name for both a lichen and an air plant of the pineapple family (Bromeliaceae). Club moss is an evergreen herb of the family Lycopodiaceae, and flowering moss is an evergreen plant of the family Diapensiaceae.

Mosses may range in size from microscopic forms to plants more than one metre (40 inches) long. They differ primarily in the structure and specialization of their capsules (spore cases). The stemlike and leaflike structures of moss plants are organs of the gametophytic (sexual) generation rather than of the sporophytic (asexual) generation as in higher plants.

Mosses break down exposed substrates, releasing nutrients for the use of more complex plants that succeed them; they aid in erosion control by providing surface cover and absorbing water. Mosses also provide clues to past floras and are useful in plant physiology studies. The only economically important species are those in the genus *Sphagnum* that form peat.

Mosses existed as early as the Permian Period (225,000,000 years ago), and more than 100 species were present during the Tertiary Period (2,500,000 to 65,000,000 years ago). *Muscites*, *Protosphagnum*, *Palaeohypnum*, and other fossil mosses are similar in structure to modern genera. *Major ref.* **3**:351f
·bog types and floras **17**:837a
·flower mimicry in spore dispersal **12**:218g
·life-span and age indications **10**:915a
·permafrost thawing **12**:117g
·phylogenic position and traits **14**:379g
·polar biotic elements **14**:655h *passim* to 657c
·reproduction and life cycle **15**:678d
·reproductive system **15**:716d; illus. 718
·tissue and organ types **13**:733f

RELATED ENTRIES in the *Ready Reference and Index: for*
common mosses: see apple moss; brook moss; bug-on-a-stick; carpet moss; cord moss; cushion moss; extinguisher moss; feather moss; fern moss; fringe moss; granite moss; horn-tooth moss; luminous moss; peat moss; pigeon wheat; rose moss; screw moss; stair-step moss; tree moss; turkish-slipper moss; urn moss; wind-blown moss
genera of mosses: Atrichum; Brachythecium; Bryum; Mnium; Pogonatum
other: Bryales; calyptra; caulid; phyllid; protonema

Moss, Convention of (1814), agreement by which Norway was united with Sweden under King Charles XIII.
·Charles John and the defeat of Norway **4**:60d

Moss, Stirling (b. Sept. 17, 1929), English automobile racing driver and writer on auto racing, was generally considered the world's best driver after the retirement of Juan Manuel Fangio in 1958. Moss won the British Grand Prix in 1955 and 1957, the Monaco Grand Prix in 1956, 1960, and 1961, and numerous others. Driving for Mercedes-Benz in 1955, he became the first Englishman to win the Italian Mille Miglia. He retired after being critically injured on the Goodwood course in England in 1962. In addition to writing for periodicals, he wrote several books, including *Stirling Moss's Book of Motor Sport* (1955) and *All But My Life* (1963). A biography, *Stirling Moss*, by Robert Raymond, was published in 1953.

Mossadegh, Mohammad (Iranian politician): *see* Mosaddeq, Mohammad.

moss agate, or MOCHA STONE, grayish to milky-white agate (*q.v.*), a variety of the silica

Polished nodules of moss agate
B.M. Shaub

mineral quartz that contains opaque, dark-coloured inclusions the branching forms of which resemble ferns, moss, or other vegetation. The included materials, mainly manganese and iron oxides, are of inorganic origin. Most moss agates are found as fragments weathered from volcanic rocks. Long used for ornamental purposes, they are obtained chiefly from India, Brazil, Uruguay, the Soviet Union, central Europe, and the western United States. The best stones are cut in flat or rounded form, and some are dyed to improve their colour. Its properties are those of quartz (*see* table under silica minerals).
·chalcedony formation and properties **16**:753f

Mossamedes (Angola): *see* Moçâmedes.

moss animal, common name for any member of the aquatic invertebrate phylum Bryozoa. About 3,500 species are known; most live in marine waters. Saltwater species live in colonies on submerged objects and on seaweed. They are common in shallow coastal waters.

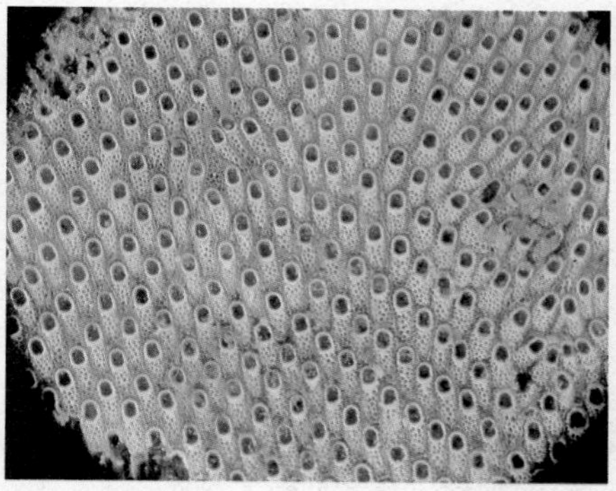

Moss animal (*Membranipora*)
Grant Heilman—EB Inc.

Bryozoans range in size from about 1 to 1,000 millimetres (about 0.04 inch to 40 inches) or more. Some appear mosslike, hence their common name; others grow in twiglike or fanlike colonies. Many colonies are white or pale in colour. Some, such as *Flustra*, resemble seaweed. *Membranipora* grows in lacelike sheets.

Each individual (zooid) of a moss-animal colony has tentacles at one end that are used to gather food particles into the mouth. When disturbed, the animal withdraws its tentacles.

Moss animals are of little economic importance except as fouling organisms on ships' hulls. Some freshwater species, such as *Pectinatella magnifica*, clog water pipes. *Major ref.* **3**:354h
·asexual reproduction considerations **5**:625d
·calcium carbonate skeleton table **6**:714
·Cenozoic evolutionary forms **3**:1082e
·circulatory system anatomy **4**:623g
·Devonian representatives **5**:675d
·fossil occurrence, illus. 3 **17**:721
·fossils and evolution **7**:562g; illus. 563
·Jurassic forms and habitats **10**:356h
·Lower Paleozoic appearance **13**:917h
·Ordovician evolution **13**:658d *passim* to 659f
·Silurian evolution **16**:772b
·social behaviour patterns **16**:939e
·statoblast formation for survival **5**:960h
·Triassic Canadian fossil **18**:695b

RELATED ENTRIES in the *Ready Reference and Index:*
cheilostomate; gymnolaemate; phylactolaemate; stenolaemate

Mössbauer, Rudolf Ludwig (b. Jan. 31, 1929, Munich), winner, with Robert Hofstadter of the United States, of the Nobel Prize for Physics in 1961 for his discovery of the Mössbauer effect. This effect has found applications in verifying Albert Einstein's theory of relativity and is also used for the measurement of the magnetic field of atomic nuclei and the study of other properties of solid materials.

Mössbauer discovered the effect in 1957, one year before he received his doctorate from the Technische Hochschule of Munich. He became professor of physics at the California Institute of Technology, Pasadena, in 1961. Three years later he returned to Munich to become professor of physics at the Technische Hochschule.

·gamma ray resonance absorption **12**:491a

Mössbauer effect 12:491, also called RECOIL-FREE GAMMA-RAY RESONANCE ABSORPTION, a phenomenon resulting from the interaction of atomic nuclei and gamma rays such that the full energy of the ray is emitted or absorbed without the nucleus undergoing a recoil. The Mössbauer effect can be used with unexcelled precision in measuring small energy changes in nuclei, atoms, and crystals induced by gravitational, electrical, and magnetic fields.

The text article covers in detail the nature of the phenomenon and shows how the effect may be used as a scientific tool in studying diverse topics in the physical sciences. The concepts of Doppler shift, recoil energy loss, and gamma-ray resonance are treated in the opening section to explain recoil-free gamma-ray resonance absorption and the use of Doppler shift to measure small energy changes. A brief history relates Mössbauer's investigation that led to his winning the Nobel Prize. Applications are described in relativity studies, nuclear physics, solid-state physics, and chemistry. The article ends with a discussion of the Mössbauer effect as a quantum mechanical phenomenon.

REFERENCES in other text articles:
·iron compound study **18**:615c
·time dilation investigation **8**:290d

Mossbunker (fish): *see* Menhaden.

Mosse, Bartholomew (1712–59), Irish physician and philanthropist.
·Dublin's Lying-In Hospital foundation **5**:1074d

Mosses From an Old Manse (1846), collection of tales and sketches by Nathaniel Hawthorne.
·Melville's review **8**:680b

Mossi, also spelled MOSI, people of the Republic of Upper Volta, numbering approximately 1,800,000 in the 1970s. An estimated 500,000 live in other parts of West Africa. The Mossi language belongs to the Gur group and is akin to that spoken by the Mamprusi and Dagomba of northern Ghana, from whom the Mossi ruling class trace their origin.

The Morho Naba, or paramount chieftain of the Mossi tribe, attended by a servant

Marc and Evelyne Bernheim—Rapho Guillumette

The Mossi are sedentary farmers, growing millet and sorghum as staples. Some artisans, such as smiths and leatherworkers, belong to despised castes.

Mossi society, which is organized on the basis of a feudal kingdom, is divided into royalty, nobles, commoners and, formerly, slaves. Each village is governed by a chief who, in turn, is subordinate to a divisional chief. At the top of the hierarchy is the paramount ruler, the Morho Naba (Big Lord) of Ouagadaougou. Divisional chiefs serve as advisers to the Morho Naba and theoretically choose his successor. Usually, however, the paramount chief's eldest son succeeds.

Prior to its modernization during the latter part of French rule and since independence (1960) the Mossi kingdom provided an example of a typical African despotism. The king's elaborate court, in addition to nobles and high officials, contained numerous bodyguards, page boys, and eunuchs; his wives lived in special villages, all of whose male inhabitants were eunuchs.

Most Mossi are pagan, placing emphasis on an ancestor cult and a cult of the Earth. Islām and Christianity are minority religions.
·habitation area and numbers **19**:796e
·mask form of Wango society **1**:259d
·origin theory and location **19**:764h; map 762
·Upper Volta cultural environment **18**:1019d

Mossi language: *see* Moré language.

Mossi states, complex of pagan independent West African kingdoms (flourished *c.* 1500–1895) around the headwaters of the River Volta (within the modern republics of Upper Volta and Ghana) comprising in the south Mamprusi, Dagomba, and Nanumba, and in the north Tenkodogo, Wagadugu, Yatenga, and Fada-n-Gurda.

Though Mossi traditions held that ancestors came from the east—perhaps in the 13th century—the origins of the kingdoms are obscure. The Mossi, unlike their forest neighbours, relied on long-ranging light cavalry with which they harassed the empire of Mali to the north, and that of Songhai with which they vied for control of the Middle Niger. From about 1400 they acted as trading intermediaries between the forest states and the cities of the Niger. Confined by Songhai after 1600 to a more southerly region, they nevertheless remained independent until the French invasions of the late 19th century.
·origin theory and location **19**:763e; map 762

Mossoró, formerly SANTA LUIZA DE MOSSORÓ, city, northwestern Rio Grande do Norte state, northeastern Brazil, on the Rio Apodi (also known as the Mossoro), 30 mi (48 km) from its mouth on the Atlantic coast, at 66 ft (20 m) above sea level. It was given city status in 1870 and is now the state's second largest community. Salt and clay are the most important products of the region, but cotton is also widely cultivated. Textiles, carnauba wax, and oil of oiticica are produced in Mossoró, which is accessible by highway from Natal, the state capital (200 mi [320 km] east-southeast), and other communities in Rio Grande do Norte and Ceará states and by railroad from Grossos. Pop. (1970 prelim.) 77,251.
5°11′ S, 37°20′ W
·map, Brazil **3**:124

Mossovet, formally MOSCOW CITY SOVIET OF WORKERS' DEPUTIES, responsible for the Moscow municipal administration and for the political, economic, cultural, and social institutions in the city.
·Moscow's administration **12**:484f

moss pink (plant): *see* Phlox.

Moss Point, city, Jackson County, southeastern Mississippi, U.S., at the juncture of the Escatawpa and Pascagoula rivers. Settled by Andrew Jackson's soldiers after the Battle of New Orleans (Jan. 8, 1815) and named (1867) for the moss-laden oaks leading to a point on the riverbank, it developed as a sawmilling centre. The Civil War brought occupation by Federal troops and the temporary shutdown of logging operations. During World War I two emergency shipyards at Moss Point constructed wooden "Liberty Ships." Pine-pulp paper, lumber, and fish meal and oil are now its economic mainstays. Pop. (1980) 18,998.
30°25′ N, 88°29′ W

Moss Vale, town, east New South Wales, Australia, in the Southern Highlands, 65 mi (105 km) southwest of Sydney. Founded in the mid-1830s as Sutton Forest, it was proclaimed a village in 1853 and was later renamed for Jemmy Moss, an early resident. Made a town (1861) and a municipality (1888), Moss Vale was gazetted a shire in 1906. On the main Sydney–Melbourne rail line and the Highland Way (connecting the Prince's and Hume highways), it lies in rolling countryside supporting livestock, fruit, and vegetable farming, limestone and granite quarrying, and coal mining. Industries include a cement works and agricultural-lime and dairy factories. Moss Vale is close to Moreton National Park and has many weekend and vacation homes. Pop. (1971 prelim.) 3,233.
34°33′ S, 150°23′ E

Most, town, Severočeský *kraj* (Northern Bohemia region), Czechoslovakia, on the Bílina River, southwest of Útsí nad Labem. It was mentioned in early 11th-century German documents as Brux, which means Bridge, as does its Czech name. This probably refers to an ancient structure spanning marshy ground near the old town. Medieval buildings include the Renaissance belfry in the town centre and the late- Gothic church of St. Mary. Most is the heart of the north Bohemian coalfield and the headquarters of the state lignite mining authority. The production of steel, chemicals, and ceramics is also important, and there is a synthetic-fuel plant at nearby Záluží. Pop. (1970 est.) 55,364.
50°32′ N, 13°39′ E
·map, Czechoslovakia **5**:412

Mostaert, Jan (b. *c.* 1475, Haarlem, Neth. —d. 1555/56), painter of portraits and reli-

"Portrait of a Man," painting by Jan Mostaert; in the Musées Royaux des Beaux-Arts, Brussels

By courtesy of the Musees Royaux des Beaux-Arts, Brussels

gious subjects. Little is known about his life. According to one account, he spent 18 years in Brussels and Mechelen as court painter to Margaret of Austria, regent of the Netherlands, but other evidence suggests that he worked chiefly in Haarlem. His best known work is a "Deposition" triptych in the Musées Royaux des Beaux-Arts, Brussels. Other works include "The Adoration of the Kings" (Rijksmuseum, Amsterdam), a "Tree of Jesse," and a West Indian landscape, both in private collections. Although he was a contemporary of the Flemish artists Quentin Massys and Joachim de Patinir, Mostaert's style was essentially conservative, exhibiting the careful detail, smooth finish, and crystalline brightness of an older generation of Dutch painters.

Mostaganem, *wilāyah* (province), northwestern Algeria. With an area of 4,290 sq mi (11,110 sq km), it extends southward from the Mediterranean to the Tell Atlas. Main towns include Mostaganem (*wilāyah* capital), Mascara, and Ighil Izane (*qq.v.*). Pop. (1970 est.) 874,000.
·area and population
table **1**:563
·map, Northern Algeria **1**:560

Mostaganem, port and capital of Mostaganem *wilāyah* (province), Algeria, on the Gulf of Arzew. Known as Murustuge in the 11th century, it contains al-Mehal (the old citadel) attributed to the 11th-century Almoravid amir Yūsuf ibn Tāshufīn. Captured in 1516 by the sea rover Khayr ad-Dīn (Barbarossa), the town passed to his brother, enjoyed great commercial prosperity, and then declined. It was garrisoned by the French in 1833.

Divided by the ravine of the Oued Aïn Sefra, the modern quarter lies on the left bank and the compact Muslim sector of Tidgit on the right. The port area and bathing beaches at La Salamandre and Les Sablettes are to the southwest. Wine, fruit, vegetables, and porous diatomite are exported. Mostaganem receives a natural gas pipeline from Hassi R'Mel in the Sahara. Latest census 63,297.
35°56′ N, 0°05′ E
·map, Algeria **1**:564

Mostar, town in Bosnia and Hercegovina, Yugoslavia, in mountainous country on the Neretva River. It is on the Sarajevo–Ploče rail line. First mentioned in 1452, Mostar became a Turkish garrison town in the 16th century.

Stone arch bridge across the Neretva River at Mostar, Yugos.
E.P.A. Inc.—EB Inc.

In 1566, the Turks replaced the Neretva bridge with a stone arch, whence the name Mostar (Serbo-Croatian: Old Bridge). The town was a centre for crafts and trade, and the reconstructed coppersmith's bazaar is a present-day attraction. In 1875, the Hercegovinians began an uprising against the Turks that culminated in Austrian annexation. Under Austrian rule (1878–1918), Mostar was a centre for Serbian scholars and poets and for a strong nationalistic movement.

The region is particularly noted for its quality wines, tobacco, fruit, and vegetables. Počitelj, just south of Mostar, is also famous for its Muslim-inspired architecture. Pop. (1971) 47,600.
43°20′ N, 17°49′ E
·map, Yugoslavia **19**:1100

most-favoured-nation treatment, guarantee of trading opportunity equal to that accorded to the most favoured nation; essentially a method of establishing equality of trading opportunity among states by making originally bilateral agreements multilateral. As a principle of public international law it establishes the sovereign equality of states with respect to trading policy; as an instrument of economic policy it provides a treaty basis for competitive international transactions.

Attempts to guarantee such equality of trading opportunity were incorporated into the provisions of commercial treaties and agreements as early as the beginning of the 17th century. The Anglo-French treaty negotiated in 1860 by Richard Cobden and Michel Chevalier became the model for many subsequent agreements. They established a set of interlocking tariff concessions that were extended by most-favoured-nation treatment throughout the world.

Such treatment has always applied primarily to the duties charged on imports, but specific provisions have extended the most-favoured-nation principle to other areas of international economic contact—for example, the establishment of enterprises of one country's nationals in the territory of the other; navigation in territorial waters; real and personal property rights; intangible property rights such as patents, industrial designs, trademarks, copyrights, and literary property; government purchases; foreign exchange allocations; and taxation.

There are two forms of most-favoured-nation treatment: conditional and unconditional. The conditional form grants gratuitously to the contracting party only those concessions originally made gratuitously to a third party and grants concessions originally obtained as part of a bargain only under equivalent conditions or in return for equivalent gains. Under the unconditional form, any tariff concession granted to a third party is granted to the contracting party, a principle that was included in the 1948 General Agreement on Tariffs and Trade (GATT).

Application of most-favoured-nation treatment has been limited in the past by the practice of granting concessions to the principal supplier country in an effort to obtain reciprocal concessions or by reclassifying and minutely defining items in the customs tariff so that a duty concession, while general in form, applies in practice only to one country.

International concern with most-favoured-nation treatment decreased as new devices of trade regulation (import quotas, exchange control, and state trading) became greater obstacles to trade than tariffs. The discretionary and often arbitrary nature of such regulations rendered any specific guarantee of equal trading opportunity impossible. Most-favoured-nation treatment came under concerted attack with the rise of the European Economic Community, which reduced duties among its members only. In the 1960s many of the less developed countries sought preferential treatment for their exports. *Major ref.* **5**:376d
·Opium War's demoralizing
consequence **4**:358h

Mostique (people): *see* Mosquito.

Mostowski, Andrzej (1913–), Polish mathematician.
·decidability degrees in
arithmetic **11**:638h

Mosu, or MOSO (ethnic group): *see* Yi.

Mosul, Arabic AL-MAWṢIL, capital of Nīnawā *muḥāfaẓah* (governorate), northwestern Iraq. Located on the Tigris River across from the ruins of the ancient Assyrian city of Nineveh, it is Iraq's third largest city and the commercial centre of the *muḥāfaẓah.* Mosul once produced fine cotton goods, from which the name "muslin" is derived; it is now a centre of cement, textile, sugar, and other industries, and a marketplace for agricultural products. The city has road and rail connections with Baghdad and other Iraqi cities and with nearby Syria and Turkey, and it has an airport.

Jāmiʿ al-Kabīr (Great Mosque), with leaning minaret in background, Mosul, Iraq
Editorial Photocolor Archives, New York

Mosul contains many ancient buildings, some dating from the 13th century. These include the Red Mosque and other mosques, shrines, and Christian churches. Since World War II the city has been enlarged several times in area by new construction. A university and a hospital are among the modern buildings.

Mosul, founded on the site of much earlier settlements, became by the 8th century AD the principal city of northern Mesopotamia. In succeeding centuries a number of independent dynasties ruled the city and surrounding country during a period of relative prosperity and stability. This situation ended in 1258 when the Mongol ruler Hülagü ravaged the entire region, after which there was little effective government until the Persian Esmāʿīl I occupied it in 1508.

He was followed by the Ottoman Turks, who ruled from 1534 to 1918; Mosul became a trade centre of their empire, and the headquarters of a political subdivision. Following World War I and Iraqi independence from Turkey, the city's commercial importance declined because it was cut off from the rest of the former Ottoman Empire. Turkey continued to claim the Mosul area until 1926. Mosul has since grown more prosperous with increased trade and the development of nearby important oil fields. Pop. (1970 est.) 293,079 (mainly Arab, Kurd, and Turkmen).
36°20′ N, 43°08′ E
·map, Iraq **9**:874
·oil and manufacturing industries **9**:878b

Mosul rugs: *see* Hamadan rugs.

Mosul school, in metalwork, group of 13th-century metal craftsmen, centred in Mosul, Iraq, who for centuries to follow influenced the metalwork of the Islāmic world from North Africa to eastern Iran. Under the active patronage of the Zangid dynasty (*see* Zangid art), the Mosul school developed an extraordinarily refined technique of inlay—particularly in silver—far overshadowing the earlier work of the Sāmānids in Persia and the Būyids in Iraq (*see* Sāmānid art; Būyid art).

Mosul craftsmen used both gold and silver for inlay on bronze and brass. After delicate engraving had prepared the surface of the piece, strips of gold and silver were worked so carefully that not the slightest irregularity appeared in the whole of the elaborate design. The technique was carried by Mosul metalworkers to Aleppo, Damascus, Baghdad, Cairo, and Persia; a class of similar metalwork from these centres is called Mosul bronzes.

Among the most famous surviving Mosul pieces is a brass ewer inlaid with silver (1232; British Museum); the artist was Shujāʿ ibn Mana. The ewer features representational as well as abstract design, depicting battle scenes, animals, and musicians within medallions. Mosul metalworkers also created pieces for Eastern Christians. A candlestick of this variety (1238; Musée des Arts Décoratifs, Paris), attributed to Dā'ūd ibn Salamah of Mosul, is bronze with silver inlay. It displays the familiar medallions but is also engraved with scenes showing Christ as a child. Rows of

Mosul brass ewer, 1223; in the Cleveland Museum of Art

By courtesy of the Cleveland Museum of Art; purchase, John L. Severance Fund

standing figures, probably saints, decorate the base. The background is decorated with typically Islāmic vine scrolls and intricate arabesques, giving the piece a unique flavor.

·description and vessel example **11**:1095b

Mosul school, in painting, a style of miniature painting that developed in northern Iraq in the late 12th to early 13th century under the patronage of the Zangid dynasty (1127–1222). *See* Zangid art.

In technique and style, the Mosul school was similar to the painting of the Seljuq Turks, who controlled Iran at that time, but the Mosul artists had a sharper sense of realism based on the subject matter and degree of detail in the painting rather than on representation in three dimensions, which did not occur. Most of the Mosul iconography was Seljuq; for example, the use of figures seated cross-legged in a frontal position. Certain symbolic elements, such as the crescent and serpents, derived, however, from the classical Mesopotamian repertory.

Most Mosul paintings were illustrations of manuscripts—mainly scientific works, animal books, and lyric poetry. A frontispiece painting (Bibliothèque Nationale, Paris) from a late-12th-century copy of Galen's medical treatise, the *Kitāb al-diriyak* ("Book of Antidotes"), is a good example of the earlier work of the Mosul school. It depicts four figures surrounding a central, seated figure who holds a crescent-shaped halo. The painting is in a variety of solid colours: reds, blues,

"Physician Andromachus Watching Labourers," Mosul miniature from the *Kitāb al-diriyak* ("Book of Antidotes"), 1199 (Bibliothèque Nationale, Paris, MS. arabe 2964, fol. 22)

By courtesy of the Bibliotheque Nationale, Paris

greens, and gold. The Kūfic lettering is blue. The total effect is best described as majestic. A mid-13th-century frontispiece (Nationalbibliothek, Vienna) to another copy of the same text suggests the quality of later Mosul painting. There is realism in its depiction of the preparation of a ruler's meal and of horsemen engaged in various activities, and the painting is as colourful as that of the early Mosul school; yet it is somehow less spirited. The composition is more elaborate but less successful. By this time the Baghdad school, which combined the styles of the Syrian and early Mosul schools, had begun to dominate. With the invasion of the Mongols in mid-13th century, the Mosul school came to an end.

Moszkowski, Moritz (b. Aug. 23, 1854, Breslau, Ger.—d. March 4, 1925, Paris), pianist and composer known for his Spanish dances. He studied piano at Dresden and Berlin, where he gave his first concert in 1873. In 1879 he settled in Paris. His two books of *Spanische Tänze*, Opus 12, were published in 1876 for piano duet and later in many different arrangements. They were long popular as examples of national music in a light style. Other attempts with national idioms were less successful. His opera *Boabdil* (1892) was known chiefly for its ballet. He also wrote concerti and chamber music.

Mot (from Hebrew *met*, "death"), ancient West Semitic god of the dead and of all the powers that opposed life and fertility; he was the favourite son of the god El, and the most prominent enemy of the god Baal. Mot was the god of sterility and the master of all barren places. Traditionally, Mot and Baal (a god of springs, sky, and fertility) were perpetually engaged in a seasonal struggle in which Baal, like many similar harvest deities, was annually vanquished and slain. Mot, however, was also annually killed by Baal's sister Anath, who thus aided Baal's resurrection.

Motacillidae (bird family): *see* pipit; wagtail.

Motagua River, eastern Guatemala, rising in the central highlands near Chichicastenango, in southern Quiché department. The Motagua is Guatemala's longest river, measuring approximately 250 mi (400 km). Flowing generally eastward and northeastward through Chimaltenango, El Progreso, Zacapa, and Izabal departments, it empties into Omoa Bay off the Gulf of Honduras at the Honduran border. The Sierra de Chuacús, Sierra de las Minas, and Cerro de San Isidro rise from the left bank of the Motagua; the major tributaries, including the Chiquimula, flow from the south. Navigable for approximately 125 mi (200 km) upstream from its mouth, the Motagua is a major transportation artery for the bananas, coffee, and other fruits raised in its valley. There is some placer gold mining along its course. The Puerto Barrios–Guatemala City railroad and highway follow the river valley upstream as far as El Progreso.

15°44′ N, 88°14′ W

·map, Guatemala **8**:454

·navigability and flow **8**:455f

Motala, town, in Östergötland *län* (county), southern Sweden, on Lake Vättern, at the efflux of the Motala Ström (Motala Stream). The town, incorporated in 1881, is a centre of heavy industry and the site of a hydroelectric plant and a transmitting station, as well as being a summer resort, with open-air bathing at Varamon on Lake Vättern. Motala is the eastern terminus of the Göta Kanal and has good road and rail connections with the rest of Sweden. Pop. (1970) 37,965.

58°33′ N, 15°03′ E

·map, Sweden **17**:848

motel (from "motor hotel"), originally a hotel designed for persons travelling by automobile, with convenient parking space provided. Also called motor lodges, motor courts, tourist courts, and motor inns, motels serve commercial and business travellers and persons attending conventions and meetings as well as vacationers and tourists. The automobile became the principal mode of travel by 1950 in the United States and by the 1960s in Europe and Japan; and motels were built as near as possible to interstate highways, just as hotels had been built as near as possible to railroad stations. Most motels provide an informal atmosphere compared to hotels; many have swimming pools, and most rooms contain a television set.

Motels originated as a series of separate or attached roadside cabins, independently operated; but when professional management took over, their size increased, and the chain concept became popular. Franchising operations, in which an individual is allowed to go into business for himself while reaping the advantages of chain operations, has achieved remarkable growth for several chains.

In the 1970s there were more motels in North America than elsewhere, but significant expansion was taking place in Great Britain, Europe, the Caribbean, and Japan.

·history and development **8**:1118c

motel industry: *see* hotel and motel industry.

Moten, Bennie (b. Nov. 13, 1894, Kansas City, Mo.—d. 1935), pianist, one of the earliest known organizers of bands in the Midwest in the emergent years of jazz.

He became a bandleader in and around his home town in 1922 and remained so until his death. His recording debut was in 1923; and, although many of his recordings sound unremarkable, he is regarded as a figure of great importance in the development of the larger jazz orchestra, his achievement being verified when, after his death, the remnants of his group were taken up by his second pianist, Count Basie, and fashioned into a new, far more streamlined orchestra, destined to become one of the outstanding orchestras in jazz history.

·early jazz bands of Henderson following **10**:124f

motet (from French *mot*, "word"), style of vocal composition that has undergone numerous transformations through several centuries; typically, it is a Latin religious choral composition, yet it can be a secular composition or a work for soloist(s) and instrumental accompaniment, in any language, with or without a choir.

The motet began in the early 13th century as

an application of a new text (*i.e.*, "word") to older music. Specifically, the text was added to the wordless upper voice parts of discant clausulae. These were short sections of organum, a 13th-century and earlier form consisting of a plainchant melody in the tenor, above which were added one, two, or three simultaneous melodies; in discant clausulae, as opposed to other organum, all the voice parts were set in short, repeated rhythmic patterns called rhythmic modes.

In forming motets from discant clausulae, two or even three parts were each given a text. Although the earliest motets were usually in Latin and intended for church use, there later arose bilingual motets (French–Latin, English–Latin) on secular and sacred texts or combinations of both. Particularly during the late 13th century, the motet was secular in its added texts, which were often all in French. Tenors were sometimes chosen from French popular songs, rather than from plainchant. Rhythmic patterns became freer and more varied, and the rhythmic modes fell into disuse. Instruments apparently played the lower voice parts as accompaniment to a singer's performance of the upper part, so that the motet became an accompanied solo song.

In the 14th century secular motets were largely serious in content (*e.g.*, on historical topics) and were used for ceremonial occasions. Both sacred and secular motets often used the technique of isorhythm: the repetition of an often complex rhythmic pattern throughout the composition. This pattern often overlapped but did not always coincide with the repetition of a melody.

By the second half of the 15th century, motets were normally sung in all voice parts. Nearly always all parts now shared the same text. The musical texture was largely contrapuntal (*i.e.*, consisting of interwoven melodies). Syllables and words were not always sung simultaneously in the different voice parts except in contrasting sections based on chords. The tenor melodies were largely chosen from plainchant, and sacred texts predominated.

Motets were frequently written for a particular holy day and were sung at mass between the Credo and Sanctus or at Vespers in the Divine Office. Such motets were often based on plainchants associated with their texts. The music of the mass might also be founded on the same musical themes, giving the entire service a musical unity not approached in any later church music, even under J.S. Bach. Even when a motet was not founded on a plainchant fragment, it was possible for a composer to design a motet and a mass setting on the same themes. Titles of 16th-century masses often indicate either the motet or the plainchant on which they are founded. Thus, the *Missa nos autem gloriari* by the Roman composer Francesco Soriano was based on the motet *Nos autem gloriari* by Giovanni da Palestrina. When a motet was in two movements, or self-contained sections, the second movement usually ended with the last musical phrases and text of the first.

After about 1600 the term motet came to indicate any composition setting a serious nonliturgical but often sacred text. In the late 16th century, Venetian composers such as Giovanni Gabrieli wrote motets for multiple choirs and contrasting instruments. In the 17th and 18th centuries, the musical style varied from instrumentally accompanied motets for solo voice to the large choral motets of Bach, which may have been sung with instrumental accompaniment. In Lutheran Germany motets were based on the texts, and often the melodies, of chorales (German hymns). In England motets with English texts for use in Anglican services were called anthems (*q.v.*). They were either for chorus (full anthems) or for soloist(s) and chorus (verse anthems). Instrumental accompaniment was common in both types. After the end of the Baroque era in the mid-18th century, the motet became a less prominent form. Motets continued to be written; *e.g.*, by Mozart in the 18th century, Brahms in the 19th century, and in the 20th century by the German Hugo Distler and the French composer Francis Poulenc.

·concerto evolution from vocal forms **4**:1065g
·counterpoint of contrasting rhythms **5**:214b
·evolution as choral medium **4**:444b
·instrumental accompaniment **19**:858g
·language content and performance genre **12**:716h
·medieval and Renaissance forms **12**:705e
·Palestrina's liturgical style **13**:932d
·symbolism in musical structure **17**:905f
·through-compositional form **12**:727b

moth: *see* Lepidoptera.

Mothe-Fénelon, François de Salignac de la: *see* Fénelon, Francois de Salignac de la Mothe-.

Mother (1926), Soviet film by Pudovkin.
·plot and techniques **12**:525h

Mother Church: *see* First Church of Christ, Scientist.

Mother Courage and Her Children (first performed 1949), translation of MUTTER COURAGE UND IHRE KINDER (first performed 1941), epic drama by Bertolt Brecht, a chronicle play of the Thirty Years' War, about an old woman whose living depends on the military, which she follows, selling goods to the soldiers. Her three children die violent deaths, and at the end she is left alone, trudging on.
·Brecht's artistic maturation **3**:153c

mother goddess, a widely used term to designate a variety of feminine deities and maternal symbols of creativity, birth, fertility, sexual union, nurturing, and the cycle of growth. The term also has been applied to figures as diverse as the so-called Stone Age Venuses and the Virgin Mary. Because motherhood is one of the basic human realities, there is no culture that has not employed some maternal symbolism in depicting its deities. Because of the wide variations concerning maternal figures, there is a pressing, but as yet unmet, need for a more complex and useful typology of mother goddesses and maternal motifs based on meaning, symbolism, and function.

Mother goddesses, as a specific type, should be distinguished from the Earth Mother (*q.v.*), with which they have often been confused. Unlike the mother goddess, who is a specific source of vitality and who must periodically undergo intercourse, the Earth Mother is a cosmogonic figure, the eternally fruitful source of everything. She is simply the Mother. All things come from her, return to her, and are her. The totality of the cosmos is her body, she gives birth to everything from her womb, and she nourishes all from her breasts. There is no essential change or individuation. Each separate being is a manifestation of her; all things share in her life through an eternal cycle of birth and rebirth.

Diana of Ephesus, alabaster and bronze figure, Roman copy of a Hellenistic original, AD 2nd century; in the Museo Archeologico Nazionale, Naples
Alinari

In contrast, mother goddesses are individual, possess distinct characters, are young, are not cosmogonic, and are highly sexual. Although the male plays a relatively less important role, being frequently reduced to a mere fecundator, Mother goddesses are usually part of a divine pair, and their mythology narrates the vicissitudes of the goddess and her (frequently human) consort.

The essential moments in the myth of most mother goddesses are her disappearance and reappearance and the celebration of her divine marriage. Her disappearance has cosmic implications. Sexuality and growth decline. Her reappearance, choice of a male partner, and intercourse with him restore and guarantee fertility, after which the male consort is frequently set aside or sent to the underworld to be replaced the next year (this has led to the erroneous postulation of a dying–rising deity).

The other major form of the mother goddess emphasizes her maternity. She is the protector and nourisher of a divine child and, by extension, of all mankind. This form occurs more frequently in iconography—a full-breasted (or many-breasted) figure holding a child in her arms—than in myth.
·Buddhist major feminine divinities **3**:423f
·Hindu cults and Tantric association **8**:914a
·religiocultural importance **15**:619e
·women's status in ancient times **19**:909d

Mother Goose, fictitious old woman, reputedly the source of the body of traditional songs and verses told to young children, which are known as "nursery rhymes" in England but are generally called "Mother Goose rhymes" in the U.S. She is often pictured as a beak-nosed, sharp-chinned granny riding on the back of a flying gander. "Mother Goose" was first associated with nursery rhymes in an early collection of "the most celebrated Songs and Lullabies of old British nurses," *Mother Goose's Melody; or Sonnets for the Cradle* (1781), published by the successors of one of the first publishers of children's books, John Newbery. The oldest extant copy dates from 1791, but it is thought that an edition appeared, or was planned, as early as 1765, and it is likely that it was edited by Oliver Goldsmith, who may also have composed some of the verses. The Newbery firm seems to have derived the name "Mother Goose" from the subtitle of Charles Perrault's fairy tales, *Contes de ma mère l'oye* (1697; "Tales of Mother Goose"), a French folk expression roughly equivalent to "old wives' tale."

The persistent legend that Mother Goose was an actual Boston woman, Elizabeth Goose (Vergoose or Vertigoose), whose grave in Boston's Old Granary Burying Ground is still a tourist's attraction, is false. No evidence of the book of rhymes she supposedly wrote in 1719 has ever been found. The first U.S. edition of Mother Goose rhymes was a reprint of the Newbery edition published by Isaiah Thomas in 1785.

Mother Hubberd's Tale (1591), story by Edmund Spenser.
·Spenser's use of the beast fable **7**:135f

Mother-in-Law, The, also called HECYRA (165 BC), play by Terence.
·Terence's career as dramatist **18**:143a

mother-of-pearl: *see* pearl.

mother-of-pearl cloud: *see* nacreous cloud.

Mother of Us All, The, opera by Virgil Thomson to a libretto by Gertrude Stein on the subject of the woman suffrage movement, first performed in New York City in 1947.
·unique niche in American opera **13**:593b

mother roasting, the practice, among some Southeast Asian and Indonesian tribes, of placing a new mother over or near a fire for several days, as a protection against harmful supernatural influences.
·Southeast Asian practice and beliefs **13**:1050b

Motherwell, district, Strathclyde (*q.v.*) region, southwestern Scotland; created by the reorganization of 1975, it is part of the former county of Lanark (*q.v.*). The district, area 69 sq mi (179 sq km), lies in the valley of the River Clyde and contains the large industrial burgh of Motherwell and Wishaw, the seat of the district authority. Founded on coal and iron resources, Motherwell is a centre of the Scottish steel industry. Pop. (1974 est.) 160,865.

Motherwell, Robert (b. Jan. 24, 1915, Aberdeen, Wash.), painter, one of the founders and principal exponents of Abstract Expressionism (*q.v.*), who was among the first U.S. artists to cultivate accidental elements in his work.

Motherwell, photograph by Arnold Newman, 1959
© Arnold Newman

A precocious youth, Motherwell received a scholarship to study art when he was 11 years old. He preferred academic studies, however, and eventually took degrees in aesthetics from Stanford and Harvard universities.

Motherwell decided to become a serious artist only in 1941. Although he was especially influenced by the Surrealist artists Max Ernst, Yves Tanguy, and André Masson, he remained largely self-taught. "The Little Spanish Prison" (1941–44; Robert Motherwell Collection, New York City) and the collage painting "Pancho Villa, Dead and Alive" (1943; Museum of Modern Art, New York City) show that his early work followed no single style but already contained motifs from which much of his later art grew. More importantly, his deep interest in Freudian psychoanalysis led him to adopt the Surrealists' technique of "automatism," the use of spontaneous drawing to stimulate the flow of images from the artist's unconscious mind. Through automatism, he explored the creative potential of intuition and accident.

In the mid-1940s Motherwell painted numerous abstract figurative works and "hard-edged," nonobjective pieces that contributed to the formation of Abstract Expressionism. But in 1949 he painted "At Five in the Afternoon" (Robert Motherwell Collection), the first in a series of paintings collectively entitled "Elegy to the Spanish Republic." He painted more than 100 versions of these "Elegies" in the next decade. These Abstract Expressionist paintings show the continuous development of a limited repertory of simple forms applied in black and white to the picture plane with a heavily loaded brush that often is allowed to drip or spatter wildly.

In 1958 Motherwell married the U.S. painter Helen Frankenthaler. During the following decade the design and execution of his work became more controlled, so that such paintings as "Africa" (1964–65; Baltimore Museum of Art) look like enlarged details of elegant calligraphy, while "Indian Summer, #2" (1962–64; Robert Motherwell Collection) combines the bravura brushwork typical of Abstract Expressionism with the broad areas of evenly applied colour characteristic of the then emerging Colour Field Painting. By the end of the decade, paintings in his "Open" series (1967–69) had abandoned Abstract Expressionism in favour of the new style.

Motherwell and Wishaw, large industrial burgh in the district of Motherwell, Strathclyde region (until 1975 in the former county of Lanark), Scotland, on the southeast periphery of the metropolitan complex centred at Glasgow. Coal and ironworks became important in the 19th century, and the large modern steelworks of Ravenscraig emphasizes and continues this tradition. Pop. (1974 est.) 73,116.
55°48′ N, 4°00′ W
·map, United Kingdom **18**:866

moth fly, any member of the family Psychodidae (order Diptera), commonly found around the openings of drain pipes. No more than 5 millimetres (0.2 inch) long, these flies, with broad hairy wings that are held rooflike over the body when at rest, resemble tiny moths. The larvae, which feed on decaying matter, inhabit drain pipes regardless of the temperature of the entering water. Most species are harmless, but there are bloodsucking members, sometimes classified separately as the family Phlebotomidae, commonly called sand flies (*see* sand fly).
·classification and features **5**:823e; illus. 819

Moth fly (Psychodidae)
William E. Ferguson

moth orchid, common name for plants of the genus *Phalaenopsis*, family Orchidaceae, to which belong about 40 species native to southeastern Asia and part of Australia. A moth orchid has a very short stem that bears several broad, leathery leaves. The flower spike arises from the base of the plant and has one to several long-lasting flowers. Some species are cultivated for the commercial flower trade and are crossed to produce hybrids with beautiful white, purple, and pink flowers.
·diversity of orchids illus. **13**:648

Moth orchid (*Phalaenopsis violacea*)
Walter Chandoha

moth owl (bird): *see* owlet frogmouth.

Mo Ti (Chinese philosopher): *see* Mo-tzu.

Motīhāri, administrative headquarters of Champaran district, Bihār state, northeastern India. A major road centre, the town trades in oilseeds and has sugar-milling and cotton-weaving industries. On the east bank of a lake, it houses three colleges affiliated with the University of Bihār. Motīhāri was constituted a municipality in 1869. Pop. (1971) 37,032.
26°39′ N, 84°55′ E

Motilón, plural MOTILONES, Spanish for HAIRLESS ONE(s), collective name loosely applied by the Spaniards to various highland and lowland American Indian peoples who lived in and about the Colombian and Venezuelan Andes and Lake Maracaibo. Chief among them were the Chaké and the Mape, who were agricultural and forest dwelling and hostilely resisted white encroachments well into the 20th century.
·hunting and fishing economy and tribal distribution map **3**:1107c
·music characteristics and use **1**:668f

motion, change of position of a body relative to another body. All motions take place on definite paths, and the nature of these paths determines the character of the motions. If all points in a body have similar but not necessarily straight paths relative to another body, the first body has motion of translation relative to the second body. If the paths are straight, it is called rectilinear translation. In both cases all points in the body have the same velocity (directed speed) and the same acceleration (time rate of change of velocity).

If all points in a body have different paths on another body, the motion of the first body relative to the second is a combination of translation and rotation. Rotation occurs when any line on a body changes its orientation relative to a line on another body. For example, on a reciprocating engine, one end of the connecting rod is attached by a hinge-type joint (the wrist pin) to the piston and moves with it on a straight path relative to the cylinder block, while the other end of the rod is attached by a hinge-type joint (the crankpin) to the crankshaft and moves with it on a circular path relative to the block.

Bodies connected by hinges can only rotate relative to one another. Consequently, the motion of the connecting rod relative to the piston and relative to the crankshaft is pure rotation. Relative to the block, the motion is a combination of translation and rotation, which is the most general type of plane motion; *i.e.*, motion in parallel planes relative to the block.

All motions are relative, but the term relative motion is usually reserved for motion relative to a moving body; *i.e.*, motion on a moving path. Strictly speaking, Newton's laws of motion are valid only for motions on paths that are fixed to the centre of the solar system. These are known as absolute paths, and, because the Earth rotates and moves around the Sun, motion relative to Earth is not absolute motion. In most cases, however, the effects of the Earth's motion on calculations involving Newton's laws are small and can be neglected. Motions relative to the Earth or to any body that is fixed to the Earth are assumed to be absolute.

In addition to rotating about moving axes, like the connecting rod, or about a fixed axis,

like the crankshaft, a body can also rotate about a fixed point. This is the type of motion that a spinning top executes. *Major ref.* **11**:767a
·Aristotelian physical universe **1**:1168a
·ballistics theory and equations **2**:655h
·biological systems application **7**:543a
·Cartesian conservation of motion **3**:969e
·celestial mechanics foundation **11**:758a
·centrifugation principles **3**:1144a
·classical mechanics concepts **11**:763c
·Eleatic and Parmenidean theories **14**:251d *passim* to 252b
·electromagnetic radiation theory **6**:656d
·energy interconversion through motion **6**:854h
·Epicurean Atomistic explanation **6**:911g
·Galileo's work with falling bodies **7**:851h
·gas particle behaviour and statistics **7**:916h
·gravitational laws and acceleration **6**:19c
·Hobbes's materialist analysis **8**:970c
·Leibniz' metaphysical theories **10**:786b *passim* to 787g
·mathematical concepts and formulations **14**:392f
·mechanics principles and development **14**:424e
·Newtonian system development **13**:19d
·physics and astronomy theories **14**:384d *passim* to 387c
·Plato's formulation of theistic concept **18**:265h
·relativity theory principles **15**:582a
rotation
·Earth influencing factors **6**:59b; table
·galaxy and planet rotation origins **18**:1009d
·Galaxy motions and theories **7**:846b
·ionosphere variations with solar energy **9**:811b
·Mercury study techniques and results **11**:917d *passim* to 921g
·Neptune spectroscopic observation **12**:964d
·physical constants in proton **5**:77f
·satellite spin for altitude–orbit control **16**:263f
·sensory perception of equilibrium **16**:551d
·Venus peculiarities **19**:77g
·weather forecasting and wind effect **19**:699a
·vibration principles and applications **19**:99d
·wave motion theory development **19**:665b

motion, in parliamentary rules of order, procedure by which proposals are submitted for the consideration of deliberative assemblies. If a motion is in order and properly seconded (endorsed by another member), it then becomes subject to the action of the assembly. (A second is generally not required in legislative proceedings.) A motion may be characterized as a main (or principal) motion, which is used to introduce a proposition, or as a secondary (or ancillary) motion, designed to affect the pending main motion or its consideration. A main motion is entertained by the deliberative body only when there is no other business before the assembly and yields in precedence to all other questions.

Secondary motions are further subdivided into subsidiary, incidental, and privileged motions. Subsidiary motions are submitted for the purpose of modifying the principal issue or affecting its disposition. Action on a subsidiary motion takes precedence to the consideration of the main motion to which it applies but yields to the determination of privileged and incidental motions. Incidental motions embrace questions arising incidentally in the consideration of other proposals and are decided prior to the disposition of the issue to which they are incident. They are usually not debatable. In the absence of contrary provision, an incidental motion requires a two-thirds vote of those present for passage. Privileged motions relate to the needs and interests of the assembly and its members in matters of such paramount importance as temporarily to supersede pending business. They take precedence over all other motions and may be submitted while other motions are awaiting disposition. Included in this category are the motions to fix a time at which to adjourn, to adjourn, and to take a recess, all of which are undebatable by the general assembly.

motion, in procedural law, an application to a court or judge for a ruling or order. Generally speaking, a motion is an oral application, as opposed to a petition, which is written.
·criminal procedure grounds for motion **5**:280g
·types in civil action procedure **15**:9e

motion, Newton's laws of: *see* Newton's laws of motion.

Motion Picture Arts and Sciences, Academy of, honorary association of motion-picture industry personnel. Membership is based on outstanding contribution to the film industry and includes actors, administrators, art directors, cinematographers, directors, executives, film editors, producers, writers, musicians, public relations experts, and sound technicians. The organization was formed in 1927 by Louis B. Mayer, the executive head of Metro-Goldwyn-Mayer production studio, and a group of leading motion-picture personalities to raise standards of the arts and sciences in motion-picture production. It quickly became best known, however, for its annual presentation of the Academy Awards of Merit, gold-plated statuettes (traditionally called "Oscars") symbolizing recognition for excellence in acting, directing, and other activities in films released during the previous calendar year. Nominations for the awards are made by members of the appropriate craft (such as actors, film editors, or sound technicians), while the final balloting is conducted among the entire membership of the academy.

The academy also keeps official records of screen credits, maintains a film archive, a library, and a theatre at its headquarters in Los Angeles, and publishes trade journals.
·Oscars and artistic judgment **12**:496f

Motion Picture Association of America (MPAA), in the United States, organization of the major motion-picture studios that censors and rates films for suitability to various kinds of audiences, aids the studios in international distribution, advises them on taxation, and carries on a nationwide public relations program for the film industry. The MPAA, originally called the Motion Picture Producers and Distributors of America (MPPDA), was established in 1922 by the major Hollywood production studios in response to a threat of government censorship of films that arose from the general public outcry against indecency on the screen. The MPPDA, popularly called the Hays Office for its first director, Will H. Hays (*q.v.*), codified the complaints of local censoring boards and informed producers of the compiled views. In 1930 the Hays Office adopted the Motion Picture Production Code, a detailed description of what was morally acceptable on the screen.
·Hollywood public image **12**:521a

motion-picture camera, any of a variety of complex photographic cameras designed to record a succession of images on a reel of film that is automatically repositioned after each exposure. Commonly, exposures are made at the rate of 24 or 30 frames per second on 8-, 16-, 35-, or 70-millimetre film. *Major ref.* **12**:544c

motion-picture industry **12**:493, business of producing theatrical motion pictures as mass entertainment for national or international markets, distinct from industrial, educational, amateur, and semiprofessional filmmaking.

The text article covers the relationship of the motion-picture industry to society and the industry's economics, peripheral activities, and festivals and awards.

REFERENCES in other text articles:
·adaptation of the novel to film **13**:297b
·artistic elements **12**:497b
·Bengali films' stylistic contributions **19**:788f
·Berlin postwar managerial weakness **2**:854d
·Buñuel's stylistic contributions **3**:479h
·Cartier-Bresson's photographic overview **3**:971h
·corporation history in U.S. **5**:185c
·dance importance in Indian film **17**:159e
·fan magazine publication **15**:255g
·Hollywood's first movie studio **11**:109d
·motion pictures evaluation **12**:511g
·music in commercial and artistic use **12**:667d
·production and development in New York **13**:41f
·rare-earth fluorides industrial uses **15**:526d
·theatrical performance's decline **18**:249h
·U.S. decline and re-direction attempts **18**:942g

RELATED ENTRIES in the *Ready Reference and Index: for*
Japanese producers: see Daiei Motion Picture Company; Nikkatsu Motion Picture Company; Shintoho Motion Picture Company; Shochiku Motion Picture Company; Toei Motion Picture Company; Tōhō Motion Picture Company
U.S. producers: Biograph Company; Columbia Pictures, Inc.; Metro-Goldwyn-Mayer, Inc.; Motion Picture Patents Company; Paramount Pictures Corporation; RKO Radio Pictures, Inc.; 20th Century-Fox Film Corporation; United Artists Corporation; Universal Pictures Company; Warner Brothers Pictures, Inc.
other producers: Cinecittà; Ealing Studios; Svensk Filmindustri; Ufa
organizations: Academy of Motion Picture Arts and Sciences; Motion Picture Association of America; National Film Board of Canada

Motion Picture Patents Company, trust of nine film producers and distributors who attempted to gain complete control of the industry in the U.S. from 1909 to 1912. The original members were the U.S. companies Edison, Vitagraph, Biograph, Essanay, Selig, Lubin, and Kalem, and the French companies Pathé and Méliès. The company, which was sometimes called the Movie Trust, possessed most of the available motion-picture patents, especially those of Thomas A. Edison, for camera and projection equipment. It entered into a contract with Eastman Kodak Company, the largest manufacturer of raw film stock, to restrict the supply of film to licensed members of the company.

The company was notorious for enforcing restrictions that limited the supply of equipment to uncooperative filmmakers and theatre owners. It limited the length of films to one and two reels (10 to 20 minutes) because movie audiences were believed incapable of enjoying more protracted entertainment. It also forbade identification of actors because it feared that popular entertainers might demand higher salaries. By 1912, however, the success of European and independent producers and the opposition of filmmakers outside the company weakened the Movie Trust, which in 1917 was dissolved by court order.
·commercial film monopoly attempt **12**:515a

Motion Picture Producers and Distributors of America: *see* Motion Picture Association of America.

Motion Picture Production Code (1930), formulated by the Motion Picture Association of America to describe what was morally acceptable in motion pictures. The code was liberalized in 1966.

motion pictures, art of **12**:497, creative aspects of motion-picture making.

The text article covers the essential characteristics of motion pictures; their expressive elements, styles, and types; and their study and appreciation.

REFERENCES in other text articles:
·acting skills and qualifications **1**:64a
·advertising design in moving media **1**:109c
·animation potentialities **1**:918h; illus. 919
·Bergman's writing–directing objective **2**:841g
·Buñuel and film **3**:479h
·Cartier-Bresson's photographic overview **3**:972a
·Chaplin's comic contribution **4**:32b
·comic style in America and Europe **4**:966g
·Czechoslovakia's film expertise **5**:420a
·dancing art accessibility **5**:468e
·directing technique development **5**:829c
·Disney's animated cartoon pioneering **5**:896b

·dramatic literature's role in cinema **5**:988d
·Duchamp machine-like films **5**:1080b
·Eisenstein's montage theory **6**:516g
·Fellini's writing–directing creativity **7**:223a
·Godard's contribution to cinéma vérité **8**:221c
·Griffith's technical innovations **8**:426e
·Indian film music sources **17**:151b
·Italian contemporary industry and style **9**:1112b
·Jean Renoir's contribution **15**:673d
·Kabuki theatre influence on cinematic montage **10**:370c
·literature and film interdependence **10**:1047f
·lively arts classification **2**:82f *passim* to 83d
·Marey and the single camera **12**:512c
·mass adulation of film star **2**:99h
·media–subject matter relationships, table 2 **18**:125
·musical enhancement and synthesis **12**:667d
·musical sources and visual interaction **12**:698c
·popular literature value decline **14**:805b
·professional and artistic training **2**:96e
·René Clair's avant-garde films **4**:681g
·Resnais' philosophy and contributions **15**:744c
·satirical content in film **16**:271b
·Satyajit Ray's film career **15**:537f
·television audience impact comparison **18**:124e
·theatre–cinema contrast **18**:255a
·United Kingdom cultural life **18**:890h

RELATED ENTRIES in the *Ready Reference and Index: for*
equipment: see frame; Cinematographe; Kinetoscope; projector, film; reel; screen, projection; Vitascope
film types: documentary film; horror film; musical film; newsreel; western
processes: CinemaScope; Cinerama; 3-D
story and technique: scenario; script
style: auteur theory; cinéma vérité; Neorealist films; New Wave; street film; underground film
technique: dubbing; montage; pan; tracking

motion pictures, history of 12:511, deals with the development of the motion picture from its origins in the 19th century.

TEXT ARTICLE covers:
Origins: 1815–95 **12**:511g
Filmstrip and "one reelers": 1896–1907 513f
The silent feature: 1908–28: United States, Europe 515g
The sound era: 1928 to 1945: United States, Italy, France, Sweden, Britain, Eastern Europe, Japan, and India 526g
Recent trends 538b

REFERENCES in other text articles:
·animation techniques and production **1**:918h; illus. 919
·Antonioni's contribution to film making **1**:999a
·Bergman's world and Swedish influence **2**:841g
·Buñuel and his themes **3**:479h
·Cartier-Bresson's photographic overview **3**:971h
·Chaplin's comic contribution **4**:32b
·directing technique development **5**:829c
·Disney's animated cartoon pioneering **5**:896b
·Eisenstein's theory and technique **6**:516g
·Fellini's writing and directing roles **7**:223a
·German contribution evaluation **8**:67e
·Griffith's life and works **8**:426a
·Jean Renoir's contribution **15**:673d
·Kurosawa's film career **10**:546b
·motion picture development as art form **12**:497d
·musical sources and uses **12**:698d
·René Clair's contribution **4**:681g
·Satyajit Ray's film career **15**:537f
·silent era **12**:213e
·theatrical production growth in U.S. **18**:231g
·theatrical realism decline **18**:213h
·Truffaut's leadership of the New Wave **18**:723e

RELATED ENTRIES in the *Ready Reference and Index: for*
equipment: see frame; Cinematographe; Kinetoscope; projector, film; reel; screen, projection; Vitascope
processes: CinemaScope; Cinerama; 3-D
story: scenario; script
style: auteur theory; cinéma vérité; Neorealist films; New Wave; street film; underground film
technique: dubbing; montage; pan; tracking
film types: documentary film; horror film; musical film; newsreel; western film
Japanese producers: Daiei Motion Picture Company; Nikkatsu Motion Picture Company; Shintoho Motion Picture Company; Shochiku Motion Picture Company; Toei Motion Picture Company; Tōhō Motion Picture Company
U.S. producers: Biograph Company; Columbia Pictures, Inc.; Metro-Goldwyn-Mayer, Inc.; Motion Pictures Patent Company; Paramount Pictures Corporation; RKO Radio Pictures, Inc.; 20th Century-Fox Film Corporation; United Artists Corporation; Universal Pictures Company; Warner Brothers Pictures, Inc.
other producers: Cinecitta; Ealing Studios; Svensk Filmindustri; Ufa
organizations: Academy of Motion Picture Arts and Sciences; Motion Picture Association of America; National Film Board of Canada

motion pictures, technology of 12:540, all the technical (as opposed to artistic) means and devices by which motion pictures are produced.

TEXT ARTICLE covers:
Early history of motion pictures **12**:540b
Introduction of sound 541d
Introduction of colour 542d
Wide-screen and stereoscopic pictures 542g
Professional motion-picture photography 544c
Special effects 549h
Production techniques and equipment 550c
Animation 551f
Time-lapse cinematography 552e
High-speed cinematography 552f
Amateur motion-picture photography 553h

REFERENCES in other text articles:
·De Forest's sound-on-film development **5**:553f
·Edison's operational improvements **6**:310c
·flicker reduction method **18**:108d
·Marey and the single camera **12**:512c
·mass communication technology effects **4**:1009b
·sound recording on optical track **17**:57d
·television and film **18**:125e

RELATED ENTRIES in the *Ready Reference and Index:*
CinemaScope; Cinématographe; Cinerama; Kinetoscope; projector, film; screen, projection; sound track

motion sickness 12:555, symptoms resulting from sudden exposure to periodic unnatural accelerations.

The text article describes the effect upon the vestibular systems (in the inner ear) of sudden exposure to unnatural accelerations and reviews the mechanisms and manifestations of motion sickness, secondary influences upon motion sickness, and its prevention.

REFERENCES in other text articles:
·causes, symptoms, and prevention **1**:143g
·movement perception and vestibular damage **14**:46d
·neural causative mechanisms **12**:1004d

motion study: *see* time and motion studies.

motivation 12:556, factors popularly understood to be the causes of the behaviour of human beings and other animals.

The text article reviews the history of such terms as motive, instinct, and drive. Theories of motivation are represented by examples. These include the psychoanalytic emphases of Sigmund Freud on inborn strivings toward life, death, and destruction; considerations of body physiology by the U.S. physiologist Walter B. Cannon; and concepts that derive from the study of learning processes. Applications to industrial and social problems are summarized. *See also* drive; libido.

REFERENCES in other text articles:
·addiction and abuse of drugs **5**:1048e
·advertising research focus **1**:106a
·aggressive behaviour in animals **1**:296a
·alienation for lack of intrinsic rewards **1**:575b
·animal behaviour patterns **2**:807a
·animal displays as motivational indices **4**:1014a
·attitudinal functions and attributes **2**:360g
·behaviour development in children **8**:1142d
·collective behaviour theory of participation **4**:851c
·cross-cultural comparisons of work motive **9**:499f
·development of motivation in children **8**:1142e
·egoist ethical theories **6**:995d
·emotion and its objective indicators **6**:757e
·faith and Roman Catholicism **15**:992g
·fatigue in nonexertional situations **7**:189b *passim* to 190b
·feeding behaviour and hunger **7**:209g
·group performance influence **16**:962h
·human and animal learning contrast **6**:408h
·intentionality as mind criterion **12**:225d
·learning performance and practice **10**:758a
·mind's volitional faculty and acts **12**:231f
·motivation and the power of conditioning **12**:561a
·pedagogic objectives and methods **13**:1099e
·perceptual difference factors **14**:44f
·personnel departments and worker morale **14**:121f
·persuasion and credibility of source **14**:124b
·political power as a goal **14**:700e
·prayer and autonomy of spiritual drive **14**:949b
·primary and secondary motives **15**:149c
·primitive group belligerence **13**:846a
·psychomotor learning factors **10**:752c
·psychophysiological theories **15**:161a
·second-language learning factors **10**:657h
·sensory reception of pain and pleasure **16**:548e
·Soviet economic system **6**:276d
·thinking and symbolic gratification **18**:357d
·thought processes and direction of learning **18**:354b
·time estimation variation **18**:423e
·Utilitarian philosophic interpretation **19**:1d
·wage structure of straight piece rates **10**:566f
·worker–manager relations and incentive **9**:503g
·work incentive in cross-cultural comparison **9**:499f

motive (music): *see* melody.

Motley, John Lothrop (b. April 15, 1814, Boston—d. May 29, 1877, Dorchester, Dorset), diplomat and historian best remembered for *The Rise of the Dutch Republic* (1856), a remarkable work of amateur scholarship that familiarized readers with the dramatic events of the Dutch revolt against Spanish rule in the 16th century, though it was superseded by later scholarship. The conflict seemed to him essentially between a democratic, tolerant, and rational Protestantism and the persecuting absolutism of Catholic Spain. Later historical analysis modified Motley's religious basis of the revolt to include constitutional and economic factors.

Motley
By courtesy of the Library of Congress, Washington, D.C.

After studying law in Germany, Motley was appointed secretary to the U.S. legation in St. Petersburg (now Leningrad) in 1841 and was later minister to Austria (1861–67) and Great Britain (1869–70). At the time of his death he had completed only part of his planned history to 1648, *The History of the United Netherlands, 1584–1609* (1860–67), and *The Life and Death of John of Barneveld* (1874).

motmot, general name for eight species of tropical American birds that make up the family Momotidae of the order Coraciiformes. Most are notably long-tailed, and in six species the two central feathers are elongated and become racket-tipped as very brittle barbs (branches) along the shaft snap off in preening. About 17 to 50 centimetres (6½ to 20 inches) long, motmots are mostly brownish green, often with touches of bright blue on the head or wings.

Motmot (*Eumomota superciliosa*)
Anthony Mercieca from Root Resources—EB Inc.

Motmots take flying insects and pluck a variety of other invertebrates and small vertebrates from branches. When perched, a motmot often swings the tail from side to side or holds it askew. The nest is a hole dug with the downcurved bill in a sandbank or tree. *Major ref.* **5**:157a

MOTNE, acronym for METEOROLOGICAL OPERATIONAL TELECOMMUNICATIONS NETWORK EUROPE, agency that collects and distributes weather reports to major airports in Europe.
·weather information distribution **18**:643f

moto-cross, a form of motorcycle racing in which cyclists compete on a course marked out over open and often quite rough terrain. Courses vary widely, but must be 1.5 to 5 kilometres (1–3 miles) in length in international competition, with steep uphill and downhill grades, wet or muddy areas, and many left and right turns of varying difficulty. Moto-cross is probably the most physically demanding motorcycle sport, although its races are quite short—40 minutes or less for each of the two heats of a race. Riders must use the same motorcycle throughout a race, with repairs made between heats if necessary. A cotton jersey, leather pants padded at the knee and thigh, padded boots, a helmet and goggles, and a kidney belt for support constitute the moto-cross cyclist's usual outfit. For international competition, under supervision of the Fédération Internationale Motocycliste, motorcycles are grouped in three classes according to engine displacement limits of 125, 250, and 500 cubic centimetres. A world championship series of races in each class is held annually. Moto-cross competition has been organized in Europe since the early 1950s. Other amateur and professional racing is also concentrated in Europe, although moto-cross events are held in other parts of the world.
·motorcycling history and race locations **12**:569g; illus. 576

Motoda Eifu (b. 1818, Kumamoto, Japan—d. 1891, Tokyo), Imperial tutor responsible for the conservative tone of the famous Japanese Imperial Rescript on Education (Oct. 30, 1890). Placed in every school throughout Japan until 1945, it started the trend toward political indoctrination of the nation's young people.

Motoda was a Confucian instructor who joined the Imperial household in 1870. He became a tutor and then councillor to the emperor Meiji (reigned 1868–1912), on whom he exerted great influence. He insisted on the Confucian tone of the rescript, emphasizing values of filial piety, social harmony, and loyalty to the Emperor.
·Japanese imperial constitution **10**:80e

Motol Beds (geology): *see* Liten Beds.

Moto-ori Norinaga (b. 1730, Matsuzaka, Japan—d. Sept. 29, 1801, Matsuzaka), the most eminent scholar in Shintō and Japanese classics. His father, a textile merchant, died when Norinaga was 11 years old, but with his mother's encouragement he studied medicine in Kyōto and became a physician. In time he came under the influence of the National Learning (*Koku-gaku*) movement, which emphasized the importance of Japan's own literature. Moto-ori applied careful philological methods to the study of the *Kojiki*, the *Tale of Genji*, and other classical literature, and stressed *mono-no-aware* (sensitiveness to beauty) as the central concept of Japanese literature.

Moto-ori's study of Japanese classics, especially the *Kojiki*, provided the theoretical foundation of the modern Shintō revival. Rejecting Buddhist and Confucian influence on the interpretation of Shintō, he traced the genuine spirit of Shintō to ancient Japanese myths and the sacred traditions transmitted from antiquity. His definition of the ancient idea of *kami* is somewhat analogous to the theory of the nonrational factor in the idea of the divine put forth by Rudolf Otto in 1917. *Kami*, according to Moto-ori, was "anything whatsoever which was outside the ordinary, which possessed superior power or which was awe-inspiring." Moto-ori also reaffirmed the ancient Japanese concept of *musubi* (the mysterious power of all creation and growth), which has become one of the main tenets of modern Shintō. Moto-ori revered the sun-goddess Amaterasu Omikami as the supreme deity. While he accepted ethical dualism, he believed that evil existed for the sake of good, as an antithetic element of the dialectical higher good. In his view, life in this world is eternally developing, and history has no end. He accepted the world as it is as pure and meaningful, and affirmed the importance of here and now. Conversely, he held that after this life every man, whether virtuous or evil, and not as a consequence of retribution, is destined to go to an eternal state of darkness. To him, faith in Shintō meant living every moment with absolute reliance on the will of the *kami*, accepting the joy of life and the sadness of death.

Moto-ori's 49-volume commentary on the *Kojiki* (*Kojiki-den*), completed in 1798 after 35 years of effort, is incorporated in the *Moto-ori Norinaga zenshū* ("Complete Works of Moto-ori Norinaga," 12 vol., 1926–27).
·aesthetic value concept **1**:161b
·Japanese social change **10**:1049d
·Shintō philosophical revival **10**:106d
·Shintō religio-nationalistic revival **10**:113c
·Shintō revival emphasis on musubi **16**:672h

motor, electric: *see* electric motor.

motor, linear, power source providing electric traction in a straight line, rather than rotary, as a conventional motor; useful in such applications as high-speed ground transportation. In one form designed for rail vehicles, a continuous stationary conductor is fastened to the roadbed and a double stator is suspended between the wheels in the centre of the vehicle, straddling the stationary conductor. Power is generated on the vehicle or is picked up by trolley from a power line paralleling the track. This power is fed to the double stator to produce traction in a linear direction.

In addition to railway applications, linear motors are used for belt conveyors, as shuttles in textile looms, for curtain rods, for aircraft launchers, and in electromagnetic pumps where the solid conductor is replaced by a conducting fluid such as a liquid metal. The force on the conducting fluid produces the pumping action. *Major ref.* **6**:612h; illus. 613
·hydraulic power transmission system **9**:78b

motor, rotary hydraulic, device that converts the kinetic energy of a stream of flowing liquid into continuous rotary motion and mechanical turning force, or torque. Hydraulic motors are similar to pumps in construction but opposite in action. There are three main types of rotary hydraulic motors: gear, vane, and piston. The pressurized liquid supplied to the motor acts on the surfaces of the gear teeth, vanes, or pistons and creates a force that produces a torque on the output shaft. Hydraulic motors can be made that are only one-tenth the size of their electrical counterparts of the same power and that have wide ranges of speed variation. *Major ref.* **9**:78b

motor aphasia (biology): *see* aphasia.

motor area, in biology, an area of the brain that controls the skeletal muscles.
·injury consequences **12**:1002b; illus.
·oral speech muscle control **17**:485d
·structure and function **12**:982g

motorboat, watercraft propelled by an internal-combustion or electric engine. The two most common types are classified by the manner in which the engine is installed: an inboard motorboat has the engine permanently mounted within the hull with the drive shaft passing through the hull; an outboard motorboat has a portable, detachable motor, incorporating drive shaft and propeller, clamped or bolted to the stern or in a well within the hull.

While the motorboat engine usually turns a propeller, variations for use in shallow water are the paddle wheel, airscrew, and water jet pump. The aircraft jet engine and the planing hull (*see* hydrofoil) have been applied in the quest for speed. Motorboats range in size from miniature craft designed to carry one lightweight person to seagoing vessels of 100 feet (30 metres) or more. Most motorboats, however, have space for six passengers or fewer.
·history, competitive events, and clubs **2**:1170h

RELATED ENTRIES in the *Ready Reference and Index:*
canoe; launch; lifeboat; tugboat; yacht.

motorboating, recreational or competitive use of boats powered by internal-combustion engines. Recreational activities, in which most motorboats are employed, include short- and long-distance cruising, fishing, swimming, skin diving, water-skiing, sunbathing, and entertaining.

Motorboat racing is governed by the Union of International Motorboating through its member national organizations. Boats with inboard and outboard engines generally compete separately in various classes based on hull type and engine displacement. Some of the smaller craft are barely large enough to hold the driver, whereas the unlimited class hydroplanes used in competition for the prized Gold Cup weigh nearly four tons. For selected world and Gold Cup speed records, *see* sporting record. *Major ref.* **2**:1170h

RELATED ENTRIES in the *Ready Reference and Index:*
Gold Cup; Harmsworth Trophy; predicted-log contest; Union of International Motorboating; yacht club

motorcar: *see* automobile.

motorcycle, bicycle or tricycle propelled by an electric or internal-combustion engine. The driving motors on minibikes, scooters, and mopeds, or motorized velocipedes, are usually air-cooled and range from 25 to 250 cubic centimetres in piston displacement;

(Top) Honda Motosport 70 (SL-70), designed for trail riding; (bottom) Harley-Davidson Electra Glide, a touring cycle

By courtesy of (top) American Honda Motor Co., Inc., (bottom) Harley-Davidson Motor Co. Inc.

the multiple-cylinder motorcycles have displacements of up to 1,200 cubic centimetres. The European method of rating an engine is by the volumetric displacement of the pistons in cubic centimetres. The horsepower method of rating is used in some countries, including the U.S. A rough rating equivalent is 8 to 10 horsepower per 100 cubic centimetres.

The first motor tricycle was built in 1884 by an Englishman, Edward Butler. The first gasoline-engined motorcycle to appear publicly was built by Gottlieb Daimler, of Bad Cannstatt, Ger., in 1885. The first practical engines and motorcycles were designed by the French and Belgians, followed by British, German, Italian, and U.S. makers.

Popularity of the vehicle grew, especially after 1910. During World War I the motorcycle was used by all combatants, principally for dispatching. After the war it enjoyed a sport vogue until the economic depression that began in 1929. During World War II, motorcycles were again used by the military, but for many applications they were displaced by small automobiles. The postwar revival of interest in motorcycles, scooters, and mopeds extended into the 1970s, with the vehicle being used for high-speed touring and sport competitions. In several countries the restoration of vintage motorcycles is a hobby.

Single-cylinder motorcycles, long dominant in the market, usually have four-stroke gasoline engines; but many smaller machines, both European and Japanese, utilize two-stroke engines below 250 cubic centimetres, which are more economical to run but need more frequent decarbonization. The most popular motorcycle is a Japanese four-stroke; the most popular two-stroke is also Japanese, a 500-cubic-centimetre cycle.

In many two-strokes, the fuel consists of a mixture of oil and gasoline. Most large modern machines use coil-ignition electrical systems, but magneto ignition is common on lightweight two-strokes. Transmission is normally through chain or gearing between engine and a two- to six-speed gearbox and then by primary chain to the rear-wheel sprocket. In some more advanced machines the final drive is via a shaft and bevel-gear system.

Controls on handlebar grips govern the throttle action and often the front-wheel brake system as well; the rear-wheel brake is usually controlled by foot pedal, but these systems vary. Modern braking systems utilize antifriction linings, which expand internally on drums. A sidecar increases stability, but motorcycle sidecars declined in popularity during the 1950s and '60s. Three-wheeled motorcycles with radio equipment located in a trunk mounted between the two rear wheels are used to a considerable extent in the U.S. by police departments.

The practice of attaching auxiliary engines to bicycles in western Europe and parts of the U.S. led to the development in the 1950s of a new type of light motorcycle, the moped. Originating in Germany as a 50-cubic-centimetre machine with simple controls and low initial cost, it was largely free of licensing and insurance regulations except in Britain.

The more sophisticated motor scooter originated in Italy soon after World War II, led by manufacture of a 125-cubic-centimetre model. Despite strong competition from Germany, France, Austria, and Britain, the Italian scooters maintained the lead in the diminishing market. The scooter has small wheels from 8 to 14 inches (20 to 36 centimetres) in diameter, and the rider sits inside the frame. Power units are placed low and close to the rear wheel, which is driven by bevel gearing or chain. Capacities vary from 50 to 225 cubic centimetres, and four-speed gearing is common.

motorcycle sport, recreational and competitive use of motorcycles, practiced throughout the world in various forms, including road, track (speedway), and cross-country (moto-cross) racing, drag racing, hill climbs, speed-record trials, and rallies. The international governing body for motorcycle sports is the Fédération Internationale Motocycliste (FIM), founded in 1904. The FIM groups racing motorcycles into classes according to engine displacement, with limits of 50, 125, 250, 350, and 500 cubic centimetres. In some events there are also separate classes for motorcycles with sidecars. Full-scale racing requires motorcycles of proved reliability with top-grade tuning and drivers. While primarily a young man's sport, it is not unusual for men in their 40s and 50s to ride. After World War II, world championship titles were generally shared by riders of German, Italian, and Japanese machines. *See also* moto-cross; speedway; sporting record.

·racing development and regulation **12**:569c; illus. 576

motor-generator set, apparatus for transforming or converting electric power from ac to dc and vice versa, consisting of one or more motors coupled to and driving one or more generators. The motors operate from the power source available, and the generators provide power of the desired characteristics. For example, a set may be designed to convert commercially available alternating current (ac) to direct current (dc); or it may, from the same commercial source, provide high-frequency ac power for induction heating or other purposes. Such a combination is often termed a dynamotor.

The term motor-generator is also applied to a combination of electric generator and a driving motor, such as a gasoline or diesel engine.

motor hotel: *see* motel.

motor lorry: *see* trucks and buses.

motor neuron, nerve cell that transmits impulses from a central area of the nervous system to an effector such as a muscle.

·brain anatomy and physiology **12**:1000f
·cell anatomy **12**:976g; illus. 977
·cranial nerve functions **12**:1018e
·growth pathway and termination **12**:996b
·impulse conduction along specific path **12**:968g
·neural tube origins and nerve processes **6**:750g
·peripheral nervous system organization **12**:988c
·respiratory mechanism control reflexes **15**:761f; illus.
·spinal cord structures and functions **12**:1010a

motor-paced race, in bicycle racing, a form of competition in which each bicycle racer competes behind a motorbike or motorcycle. (Originally, racers followed tandem bicycles or multicycles.) The bicycles used have small front wheels, enabling the rider to move close to a freely moving roller on a bar projecting from the rear of the pacing motorbike and

Motor-paced race

Geoffrey Magnay

thus to take full advantage of the air currents created by the motorbike's passage. The technique requires excellent teamwork by both the motorcyclist and the racer to keep from becoming separated and thereby losing ground. Speeds may average better than 60 kilometres (40 miles) per hour in a 100-kilometre (60-mile) race.

·cycling competition features **5**:391h

motor rally: *see* rally.

motor root of spinal nerve, also called VENTRAL, or FORWARD, ROOT OF SPINAL NERVE, the bundle of nerve fibres carrying impulses away from the spinal cord to muscles and other structures; it joins the dorsal, or posterior, root of a spinal nerve, which is a bundle of nerve fibres carrying impulses to the spinal cord. The motor root and the dorsal root are the components of a spinal nerve.

·components and structural contributions **12**:1021h; illus. 1011

motor scooter: *see* motorcycle.

motor sports 12:565, a wide variety of recreational and competitive activities requiring the use of motor vehicles.

The text article covers the history and current scope and status of the major automobile and motorcycle sports, including sections on racing, rallies, hill climbs and trials, speed-record trials, and other events.

REFERENCES in other text articles:
·auto racing growth due to sponsorship **17**:515e
·Monaco automobile race significance **12**:335g
·Stanley Steamer racing success **17**:630e

RELATED ENTRIES in the *Ready Reference and Index:* for

car racing: see automobile racing; drag racing; hill climb; hot rod; karting; midget-car racing; off-road racing; rally; sports-car racing; stock-car racing

car-racing championships: Canadian-American Challenge Cup; Grand Prix; Indianapolis 500; Tasman Championship; Trans-American Sedan Championship

motorcycling: Fédération Internationale Motorcycliste; moto-cross; motorcycle sport; speedway

other: automobile club; concours d'élégance; Fédération Internationale de l'Automobile; gymkhana; veteran car club

motor tract (DESCENDING TRACT) **of the spinal cord,** one of the bundles of nerve fibres in the spinal cord conducting impulses headed away from the central nervous system.

·anatomic relationships and functions **12**:1010a

motor vehicle insurance, a contract by which the insurer assumes the risk of any loss the owner or operator of a motor vehicle may incur through damage to property or persons as the result of an accident. There are many specific forms of motor vehicle insurance, varying not only in the kinds of risk that they cover but also in the legal principles underlying them.

Liability insurance pays for damage to someone else's property or for injury to other persons resulting from an accident for which the insured is judged legally liable; collision insurance pays for damage to the insured car if it collides with another vehicle or object; comprehensive insurance pays for damage to the insured car resulting from fire or theft and also from many other causes; medical-payment insurance covers medical treatment for the policyholder and his passengers.

In many countries, and increasingly in the U.S., other approaches to automobile accident insurance have been tried. These include compulsory liability insurance on a no-fault basis and loss insurance (accident and property insurance) carried by the driver or owner on behalf of any potential victim, who would recover without regard to fault.

·economic analysis of common and proposed types **14**:1006b
·insurance coverage and underwriting **9**:647g *passim* to 654a
·tort law in various countries **18**:525c

Mototsune (Japanese regent): *see* Fujiwara Mototsune.

Motril, city, Granada province, Andalusia, southern Spain. It lies south of Granada city and just north of El Verdadero, its port on the Mediterranean Sea. Settled since Roman times, Motril flourished under the Moors and was united to Christian Spain in 1489. Its chief industry is processing sugar from locally grown cane and beets. Flowers, especially carnations, are also a specialty. Zinc, lead, and copper are mined in the area. Pop. (1970) 25,121.
36°45′ N, 3°31′ W
·map, Spain **17**:383

Mots, Les, (1963), Eng. trans., THE WORDS (1964), autobiography by Jean-Paul Sartre.
·Sartre's early life **16**:256d

Motse (Chinese philosopher): *see* Mo-tzu.

Mott, John R(aleigh) (b. May 25, 1865, Livingston Manor, N.Y.—d. Jan. 31, 1955, Orlando, Fla.), Methodist layman and evangelist who shared the 1946 Nobel Peace Prize (with the U.S. sociologist-economist Emily Greene Balch) for his work in international church and missionary movements. Mott was student secretary (1888–1915) of the International Committee of the Young Men's Christian Association and was one of the organizers of the World Missionary Conference (Edinburgh, 1910), which marked the beginning of the modern ecumenical movement. He was chairman of the Student Volunteer Movement for Foreign Missions (1915–28) and of the International Missionary Council (1921–42) and president of the World's Alliance of YMCA's (1926–37). Mott's many writings include *The Future Leadership of the Church* (1909) and *The Larger Evangelism* (1944).

John R. Mott, 1930
By courtesy of the National Council of the Young Men's Christian Association, New York

·inspiration for all Christian missions **4**:504d
·Protestant ecumenical organization **15**:119f

Mott, Lucretia, *née* COFFIN (b. Jan. 3, 1793, Nantucket, Mass.—d. Nov. 11, 1880, near Abington, Pa.), pioneer reformer who, with Elizabeth Cady Stanton, founded the organized women's rights movement in the U.S. At the age of 13 she was sent to a Friends' boarding school near Poughkeepsie, N.Y., where two years later she was engaged as an assistant and later as a teacher. It was then that her interest in women's rights began. Solely because of her sex, she was paid only half the salary male teachers were receiving.

Lucretia Mott
By courtesy of the Library of Congress, Washington, D.C.

After her marriage in 1811 to James Mott, also a teacher at the school, the couple moved to Philadelphia. Both were members of the Society of Friends, and Lucretia became a Quaker minister in 1821. Later they associated themselves with the "Hicksite" Friends branch, which tended toward a quasi-Unitarian position. The Motts were active in the campaign against slavery, and, after the passage of the Fugitive Slave Law of 1850, their home became a sanctuary for runaway slaves.

In 1848, taking up the cause of women's rights (*see* woman suffrage), she and Elizabeth Stanton called a convention at Seneca Falls, N.Y., the first of its kind, "to discuss the social, civil, and religious rights of women." The convention issued a "Declaration of Sentiments" modelled on the Declaration of Independence; it stated that "all men and women are created equal. . . ." From that time Mott devoted most of her attention to the women's rights movement. She wrote articles, lectured widely, was elected president of the 1852 convention at Syracuse, N.Y., and attended almost every annual meeting thereafter. After the Civil War (1861–65) she also worked for voting rights and educational opportunities for freedmen. Until her death at 87, she was considered one of the most effective reformers in the country.

Mott, Sir Nevill (Francis) (b. Sept. 30, 1905, Leeds, Eng.), authority on solid state physics who devised the theoretical description of the effect light has on a photographic emulsion at the atomic level. Mott became lecturer at Manchester University in 1929, professor of theoretical physics at the University of Bristol in 1933, director of the Henry Herbert Wills Physical Laboratories at Bristol in 1948, and Cavendish professor of experimental physics at Cambridge University in 1954. He wrote numerous books and papers on atomic physics, metals, and photographic emulsions. He was knighted in 1962 and shared the Nobel Prize for Physics in 1977.

Motta, Giuseppe (b. Dec. 29, 1871, Airolo, Switz.—d. Jan. 23, 1940, Bern), Swiss political leader, long-time head of the federal political department and five times president of the confederation; between 1920 and 1940 he served as the chief Swiss delegate to the League of Nations.

A lawyer of clerical and conservative leanings from the canton of Ticino, he was Nationalrat (National Council) assemblyman from 1899 to 1911. In December 1911 Motta became the first member of the Bundesrat (Federal Council) from the Italian part of Switzerland since 1864. Director of the department of finance from 1912 to 1919, he became head of the political department in 1920, holding the position until his death. First achieving the federal presidency in 1915, he occupied the office subsequently in 1920, 1927, 1932, and 1937. A consummate diplomat, he assumed control of Swiss foreign policy during the interwar period, often leaning favourably toward the Fascist powers. He was named honorary president of the first League of Nations assembly (1920) and president of the fifth assembly (1924).

motte and bailey castle: *see* castle.

Mottelson, Ben Roy (b. July 9, 1926, Chicago), Danish physicist who shared the Nobel Prize for Physics in 1975 for his work on the development of the theory of the structure of the atomic nucleus. A graduate of Purdue University with a doctorate from Harvard University, Mottelson won a fellowship to the Institute of Theoretical Physics (1950–51) in Copenhagen, later (from 1957) becoming a professor there (now called the Nordic Institute of Atomic Physics). He became a Danish citizen in 1971.

Motteux, Peter Anthony, original name PIERRE ANTOINE MOTTEUX (1660/63–1718), French-born English translator, journalist, and dramatist who founded and edited the *Gentleman's Journal* and is remembered for his versions of Rabelais and of Cervantes' *Don Quixote*.
·magazine publishing history **15**:248c

Motteville, Françoise Bertaut, dame de (*c.* 1621–89), French memorialist (and lady-in-waiting to Anne of Austria), whose *Mémoires* (1723; Eng. trans. 1725–26) are clearly narrated, informative, and express disapproval of all troublemakers.

Mottl, Felix (b. Aug. 24, 1856, Unter-St.-Veit, Austria—d. July 2, 1911, Munich), conductor known for his performances of Richard Wagner. He studied at the Vienna Conservatory and took part in the first Bayreuth festival in 1876, later conducting *Tristan und Isolde* there in 1886. From 1881 to 1903 he directed the opera at Karlsruhe, which he developed into one of the finest opera companies in Germany. There he was noted for his performances of the operas of Hector Berlioz and Wagner. He conducted Wagner's *Ring* at London's Covent Garden in 1898 and *Parsifal* at the Metropolitan Opera, New York City, in 1903–04. Mottl was appointed director of opera at Munich in 1907. He also conducted symphonic repertoire; composed three operas, a string quartet, and songs; edited and orchestrated works by Wagner, Berlioz, Emmanuel Chabrier, and Peter Cornelius' opera *Der Barbier von Bagdad*.

mottramite (mineral): *see* descloizite.

Motuan Stage (geology): *see* Clarence Series.

motu proprio (Latin: "on one's own initiative"), in the Roman Catholic Church, papal document personally signed by the pope to signify his special interest in the subject, less formal than constitutions and carrying no papal seal. Its content may be instructional (*e.g.*, on the use of plainchant), administrative (*e.g.*, concerning a church law or the establishment of a commission), or merely to confer a special favour. The words *motu proprio* always introduce the document.

Mo-tzu 12:577, Pin-yin romanization MO-ZU, born MO TI, also spelled MOTZE, MOTSE, MICIUS (b. 470? BC, China—d. 391? BC, China), philosopher whose fundamental doctrine of universal love challenged Confucianism for several centuries and became the basis of a long since defunct religious movement.

Abstract of text biography. Mo-tzu was first a Confucianist but experienced a growing desire for a life of simplicity. He devoted most of his adult life to travelling from one feudal state to another in the hope of meeting a prince who would allow him to put his teaching into practice. Mo-tzu's doctrine was attacked as incompatible with the special claims of one's parents. After centuries of obscurity and neglect, Mo-tzu is again being studied with renewed interest.

REFERENCES in other text articles:
·Confucianism as primary influence **4**:306f
·religious basis of Moism philosophy **4**:417c
·writing style **10**:1052h

Mo-tzu, principal work of the Chinese philosopher Mo-tzu (470?–?391 BC).
·philosophy and teaching of Mo-tzu and followers **12**:577c

mou, Chinese unit of area that varies with location but is commonly 806.65 square yards (666.5 square metres). Based on a ch'ih (*q.v.*) of 14.1 inches, the mou by customs treaty is 920.417 square yards.
·Chinese linear measurement system **19**:728h
·weights and measures, table 5 **19**:734

Mouanda, town and district, in Haut-Ogooué *région*, southeastern Gabon, at the intersection of roads from Mounana, Franceville, and Mossendjo in Congo (Brazzaville). After large manganese deposits were discovered

Manganese mining operations at Mouanda, Gabon, showing the cable railway for carrying the ore
Agence HOA-QUI

near the town in 1938, exploitation began in 1951; reserves estimated at about 1,000,000,000 tons of ore are among the world's largest. A cable railway carries the ore 48 mi (77 km) south-southwest across the foothills of the Chaillu Mountains to the border with Congo (Brazzaville), and eventually to the Congo-Océan railway for shipment to Pointe-Noire. Since 1964 COMILOG (Compagnie Minière de L'Ogooué), a consortium of U.S and French mining interests, has been building a plant for producing manganese dioxides, as well as schools, roads, airfields, two hospitals, and several dispensaries. The company also has facilities for training skilled workers, draftsmen, and chemists and promotes literacy classes. An influx of workers from neighbouring districts (primarily the Duma [Adouma] people) has caused a population explosion in Mouanda and Bakamba, at the end of the cable line. Pop. (1970 prelim.) town, 6,499; district, 13,380.

moucharaby, Arabic MASHRABĪYAH or MUSHRABĪYAH, Islāmic architectural element: an oriel, or projecting second-story window of latticework. This element also appears in French architecture, in which it is known as *moucharabieh*. The moucharaby is a familiar

Muslim house with a moucharaby, Cairo
A.A.A.—FPG

feature of residences in such cities as Cairo. These windows are characterized by the use of grills or lattices to replace glass and shutters. The grills are comprised of small, turned (shaped on a lathe) wooden bobbins put together in intricate geometric patterns. Delicate and beautiful, moucharaby work provides the interior with light and air as it shades it from the hot African sun. It also permits those within to observe the street below and at the same time maintain their privacy, which was particularly important for the women of the segregated Muslim harem.

Mouche, translated FLY (1890), short story by Guy de Maupassant.
·Maupassant's obsession with prostitutes **11**:707g

Moúdhros, Armistice of (1918), agreement concluded between Turkey and the European Allies of World War I.
·Mustafa Kemal's military strategy **2**:255h

mouflon (*Ovis musimon*), small wild sheep, family Bovidae (order Artiodactyla), of Corsica and Sardinia. The mouflon stands about 70 centimetres (27–28 inches) at the shoulder and is reddish brown with white underparts. The male has a light, saddle-shaped mark on its back and bears large, curving horns with

Mouflon (*Ovis musimon*)
Anthony Merceica from Root Resources—EB Inc.

the tips turned outward. The female is hornless. The mouflon has been introduced into parts of Europe. It is thought by some to be one of the animals from which the domestic sheep (*Ovis aries*) was derived.
·Cyprus conservation program success **5**:402g

Mougel, E., also called MOUGEL BEY, 19th-century French engineer and surveyor.
·Suez canal plans **10**:837f

Mouhot, (Alexandre-)Henri (b. May 15, 1826, Montbéliard, Fr.—d. Nov. 10, 1861, near Luang Prabang, Laos), French naturalist and explorer who rediscovered the ruins of Angkor, capital of the ancient Khmer civilization of Cambodia.

Mouhot went to Russia as a young professor of philology in the 1850s and travelled throughout Europe with his brother Charles, studying photographic techniques developed by Louis Daguerre. In 1856 the two went to England, where Henri devoted himself to zoological studies. British academic societies proved sympathetic to Mouhot's interest in natural history and foreign travel and he received support from the Royal Geographical Society and the Zoological Society of London for a zoological mission to Indochina in 1858.

While exploring the tributaries of the Mekong River in Siam, Cambodia, and Laos in 1858, Mouhot came upon Angkor. He was the second European to visit the site; a 17th-century missionary had preceded him, but it was through Mouhot that Angkor became known to Western scholars as an important archaeological site.

Mouhot was a tireless explorer, dedicated, as he wrote, "with the sole object of being useful to his fellow-men, or of discovering some insect, plant, or unknown animal, or verifying some point of latitude, crosses the ocean, and sacrifices family, comfort, health, and, too often, life itself." He was warmly received by the sovereigns of the several kingdoms and tribes he visited. In October 1861 Mouhot was overcome by jungle fever, and he succumbed to it just a few weeks later. He continued to write entries in his journal until the very end. His papers and personal effects were forwarded to the French consul in Bangkok, and he was buried three kilometres from Luang Prabang, capital of northern Laos, where in 1867 a tomb was erected in his honour by the French.

Mouhot's passion for exploration and his deep respect and admiration for the peoples he visited, as well as his insights into French expansionist rationale, are preserved in his *Voyage dans les royaumes de Siam, de Cambodge, de Laos et autres parties centrales de l'Indo-Chine* (1863; Eng. trans., *Travels in the Central Parts of Indo-China, Cambodia and Laos During the Years 1858, 1859, and 1860*, 1864).

Mouila, capital of Ngounié *région*, southwestern Gabon, on the Ngounié River and on the road from Lambaréné to Ndendé. It is connected by air with Tchibanga, Lambaréné, Port-Gentil, and Libreville (190 mi [306 km] north-northwest). The town is a trading centre in cassava, bananas, yams, groundnuts (peanuts), and maize (corn) for the Puno (Bapouno), Vungo (Bavoungo), and Shogo (Mitchogo) peoples. Coffee and palm oil are important exports, and there is a cooperative palm oil mill at Moabi, 35 mi southwest. Diamonds are found at nearby Makongonio and gold at Ekété, but production of both is small. Mouila has a Catholic mission and teachers' college, a Protestant mission, a hospital, and a government secondary school. The town of Ndendé, 44 mi south-southwest, has a game reserve nearby and is known as a base for hunters. Pop. (1969–70) 9,034.
1°52′ S, 11°01′ E
·map, Gabon **7**:820

Moulay Abd al-Hafid (*c.* 1875–1937), sultan of Morocco, 1908–12, was the brother of sultan Abd-al-Aziz IV, against whom he revolted in 1907. With Marakkesh, the southern capital, his, Abd al-Hafid routed his brother's forces and pensioned off the sultan. Recognized as sultan by the western powers (1909), Abd al-Hafid invoked French aid against another pretender in 1912 and then abdicated in the same year, having been forced to recognize a French protectorate over Morocco.
·Moroccan rejection of European example **13**:168h

mould (fungus): *see* mold.

moulin (French: "mill"), nearly cylindrical, vertical shaft that extends through a glacier and is carved by meltwater from the glacier's surface. Postglacial evidence of a moulin, also called a glacial mill, is a giant kettle, or, more properly, a moulin pothole, scoured to great depth in the bedrock by the rocks and boulders transported by the falling water. A moulin pothole in Lucerne, Switz., was scoured to a depth of 8 metres (27 feet). Although the process of formation is thought to be approximately the same as that of a fluvial pothole, the moulin pothole can be distinguished by its location. Moulin potholes have been found on hilltops and steep slopes and may occur scattered over a valley floor, without the kind of alignment that occurs when streams are involved. A moulin is noted for the thunderous sound of the meltwater that funnels into it.

Moulin, Jean (b. June 20, 1899, Béziers, Fr. —d. July 8, 1943, Metz), civil servant and hero of the Resistance during World War II.

Moulin, *c.* 1940

H. Roger-Viollet

After studying law at Montpellier, he entered the civil service. In 1930 he became the youngest subprefect (in charge of an *arrondissement*) and in 1937 the youngest prefect (of the Eure-et-Loir *département*). When the Germans occupied his *département* in 1940, he refused to sign a document describing atrocities alleged to have been committed by the French Army and tried to commit suicide.

After being removed from his prefecture, he joined the Resistance and escaped to England, later returning to France as Gen. Charles de Gaulle's delegate general for the unoccupied zone. He played a leading part in the organization of the *maquis* (French guerrillas who fought the Germans) and in the development of the National Council of the Resistance, which coordinated the various movements, becoming first chairman (May 27, 1943). As "Max" he became a legendary figure. In June 1943 the Gestapo arrested him at Caluire, near Lyon. Tortured in one prison after another, he died in Metz.

Moulin de la Galette, dance hall in the Montmartre section of Paris that was immortalized by such painters as Pierre-Auguste Renoir and Pablo Picasso.

·Impressionism's early forms **19**:475f;
 illus. **19**:Visual Arts, Western, Plate 23
·Renoir's style development **15**:675b

Moulin Rouge, (Bal du), dance hall (opened 1889) in the Montmartre district of Paris that was immortalized in paintings and posters by Henri de Toulouse-Lautrec.

·Toulouse-Lautrec poster promotion **18**:535a

Moulins, capital of Allier *département*, central France, northwest of Lyon, situated on the right bank of the Allier River.

The 16th- to 17th-century flamboyant Gothic cathedral of Notre-Dame houses a famous triptych by the 15th-century Dutch painter referred to as the Master of Moulins (*q.v.*). The cathedral has some fine 15th- and 16th-century stained-glass windows. The nearby

Jaquemart (or jack) clock and tower in Moulins, Fr.; in the background are the steeples of the cathedral of Notre-Dame

Editions Modernes "Theojac"

15th-century tower has a quaint *jaquemart* clock with automatons that strike the quarters. The municipal library opposite contains the 12th-century Bible of Souvigny, a magnificent illuminated manuscript from Souvigny Priory, 7 mi (12 km) southeast of Moulins. Part of the ancient castle of the dukes of Bourbon currently serves as a prison. The town, which has some fine old houses, reached a high state of prosperity in the 15th and 16th centuries. Today it has light industries (footwear and electromechanical appliances) and food processing; it is also a market town for a prosperous agricultural region. Pop. (1975) 25,856.

46°34′ N, 3°20′ E

·map, France **7**:584

Moulins, Master of (fl. *c.* 1480–*c.* 1500), anonymous painter and miniaturist, considered the most significant artist of the French school of late Gothic painting. His anonym derives from his most notable work, a triptych

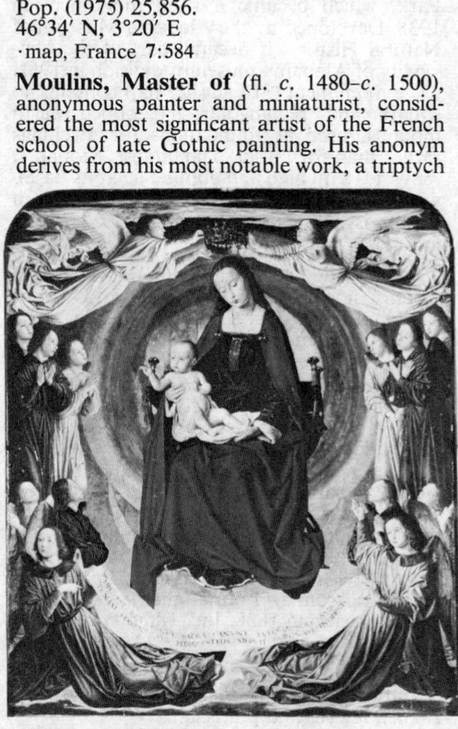

"Madonna and Child Surrounded by Angels," central panel of the triptych by the Master of Moulins, *c.* 1498; in the cathedral of Notre-Dame, Moulins, Fr.

Telarci–Giraudon

(*c.* 1498) in the cathedral of Notre-Dame at Moulins. While the brittle draperies, explicit detail, and enamel-like colours of this work reveal the artist's lifelong affinity for Flemish art (especially with that of Hugo van der Goes, under whom he may have studied), his style is unmistakably rooted in French artistic traditions, particularly those of Bourges and the Bourbonnais schools. The modelling of the faces suggests that he may also have been familiar with Italian art.

Other paintings, such as the well known "Nativity with Cardinal Rolin" (*c.* 1480; Musée Rolin, Autun, Fr.), "Portrait of a Praying Child" (*c.* 1495; Louvre, Paris), and the "Female Donor with St. Magdalen" (*c.* 1495–1500; Louvre, Paris), are attributed to the Master of Moulins on the basis of their stylistic relationship to the Moulins triptych. These works and others attributed to him indicate that he worked primarily for King Charles VIII, the Bourbon family, and the archduchess Margaret of Austria.

A number of attempts have been made to identify the Master of Moulins. One hypothesis, based on the sitters of his portraits, identifies him as Jean Perréal, official painter of Charles VIII and of Margaret of Austria; another, based only on a strong similarity of style, with Jean Hay of Flemish origin, the painter of an "Ecce Homo" (1494) in the Musée d'Art Ancien, Brussels.

Moulins faience, tin-glazed earthenware produced in Moulins, Fr., at first a slavish copy of the wares of neighbouring Nevers. It is distinguished only by its use of an iron red that is not found on the Nevers ware. Later, Moulins showed more originality, especially in its ware decorated in Chinese style. Typical Moulins themes in this style are a Chinese standing near a large flowered plant and holding a parasol; the so-called Chinese music lover; and the Tatar rider.

Moulis, Laboratoire Souterraine de, cave system near Moulis, in the Pyrenees in the south of France, with a laboratory established in 1948 by the Centre National de la Recherche Scientifique for the study of cave life.

·cave system research **3**:1022b

Moulmein, administrative headquarters of Amherst District (*kayaing*) and of Tenasserim Division (*taing*), Lower Burma. An important port on the Gulf of Martaban near the mouth of the Salween River, Moulmein was the chief town of British Burma from the Treaty of Yandabo (1826) until the annexation of Pegu in 1852. Sheltered by Bilugyun Island, it is approached from the south and lies opposite Martaban at the confluence of the Gyaing and Ataran rivers. The low hills that flank the town on the east and west are dotted with pagodas, including the Kyaikthanlan, renowned for its view, and Uzina with life-sized figures representing the four events that influenced the Buddha to become a hermit.

Moulmein has a ferry service to Martaban, the railhead for a line to Rangoon. Another rail line begins at Moulmein and ends at Ye to the south. River steamers ply the Salween and several of its major tributaries. Teak and rice are floated downriver for export, and there are several steam-powered rice mills and sawmills. Moulmein was once a busy shipbuilding centre; it has an airport, a diesel electric plant, a museum, and is noted for its gastronomy. Moulmein College is affiliated with the Arts and Science University, Rangoon. Pop. (1973) 171,970.

16°30′ N, 97°38′ E

·climate and population distribution **3**:503f
·map, Burma **3**:505

Moulouya, Oued, chief river of northeastern Morocco. Rising in the Haut (High) Atlas in central Morocco, it flows northeastward through a semi-arid valley to the Mediter-

ranean Sea just west of the Algerian border. Although not navigable, it has been harnessed by a dam (completed 1967) at Mechra Klila to provide electricity for the towns of northern Morocco. Lead and manganese deposits are worked in the river valley.
35°05′ N, 2°25′ W
·drainage and flow **12**:445d
·map, Morocco **12**:446

moulting (biology): *see* molt.

Moulton, Alexander (1920–), British engineer and industrialist.
·bicycle innovations and development **2**:982h; illus.

Moultrie, William (b. Dec. 4, 1730, Charleston, S.C.—d. Sept. 27, 1805, Charleston), general who resisted British incursions into the South during the U.S. War of Independence (1775–83).

Elected to the provincial assembly of South Carolina (1752–62), Moultrie gained early military experience fighting against the Cherokee Indians. A member of the provincial congress (1775–76) at the outbreak of the Revolution, he sided with the patriot cause and took command (March 1776) of a fort he had built of sand and palmetto logs on Sullivan's Island off Charleston. He held the fort against heavy British attack on June 28, and it was named Ft. Moultrie in his honour. He received the thanks of the federal Congress and was made a brigadier general in the Continental Army that September.

Moultrie, oil painting on wood by John Trumbull, 1791; in Yale University Art Gallery
Yale University Art Gallery

Moultrie went on to campaign in Georgia and dislodged the British from Beaufort, S.C. (February 1779), but surrendered with the fall of Charleston (May 1780). He was a prisoner on parole until February 1782, when he was exchanged, and he then served until the end of hostilities. After the war he served two terms as governor of his state (1785–87, 1792–94) and in the state senate between terms. He was also a member of the state convention that ratified the federal constitution.

Mounana I, town, Haut-Ogooué *région*, southeastern Gabon, on the road from Lastoursville to Franceville. After uranium was discovered in 1956, exploitation began in 1961, and in 1968 mining changed from quarry to underground. The ore, which is of a superior grade, is sold exclusively to the French Atomic Energy Commisariat for processing, although Mounana I has its own processing plant for uranium concentrates. Extensive manganese deposits are mined at Mouanda, 13 mi south.
1°37′ S, 12°57′ E
·map, Gabon **7**:820

Mound City Group National Monument, in south central Ohio, U.S., on the Scioto River, just northwest of Chillicothe was established in 1923 and includes a group of 24 cone-shaped ceremonial burial mounds of the Hopewell Indians, dating from about AD 1000. Numerous pottery utensils, copper or-

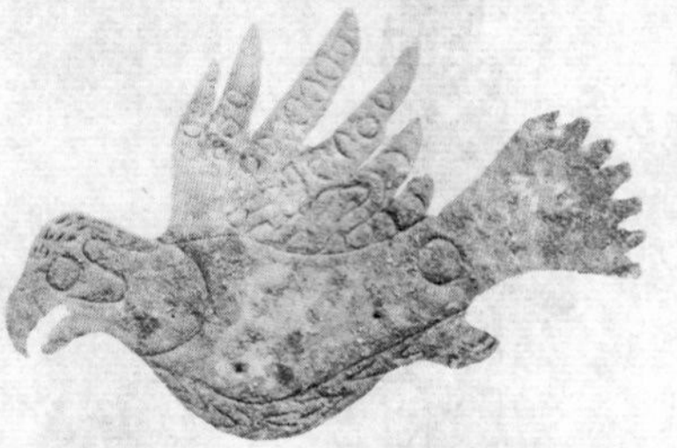

Hopewell copper ornament in the shape of a flying eagle; from the Mound City Group National Monument, Ohio
By courtesy of the Ohio Historical Society

naments, and other artifacts have been recovered from the site, which was first explored in 1846. The monument occupies an area of 68 ac (28 ha).

Moundou, capital of Logone *préfecture*, southeastern Chad, Central Africa, on the Logone Occidental River. With a warm, seasonally wet climate, it lies in the centre of the nation's cotton-growing region and is the site of a cotton research institute established in 1939. It is also the site of one of Chad's largest commercial enterprises, Brasseries du Logone, a brewery established in 1964. Moundou has a secondary school branch, a hospital, an electrical power supply, and a local air service. Pop. (1972 est.) 39,600.
8°34′ N, 16°05′ E
·map, Chad **4**:13
·rainfall seasonal average **4**:14d

Mound State Monument, habitation site (from AD 1200 to 1500) of Indian village farmers and pottery makers, near Moundville, western Alabama, U.S., on a plain above the Black Warrior River, 17 mi (27 km) south of Tuscaloosa. Archaeological excavations, started in 1906 by Clarence B. Moore, led to the establishment (1933) of Mound State Park, which became a state monument in 1938. Developed by the Alabama Museum of Natural History, it became part of the University of Alabama museums division in 1961.

The monument (315 ac [127 ha]) contains 40 square and rectangular flat-topped earth mounds, used as foundations for dwellings rather than for burial. The largest, Mound B (58½ ft [18 m] high and about 2 ac at its base), was the foundation of a temple. A museum (1939) is built partly over exposed burial grounds.

Moundsville, city, seat (1835) of Marshall County, northwestern West Virginia, U.S., on the Ohio River, just south of Wheeling. The original settlement, known in 1771 as Grave Creek for the large Indian burial mound (now within city limits), was renamed Elizabethtown in 1798. Mound City was established nearby in 1831, and the two communities were consolidated as Moundsville in 1865. The city is in a rich coal-mining area and has diversified manufactures. It is the site of the state penitentiary. Grave Creek Mound, one of the nation's largest conical mounds, is 79 ft (24 m) high, 50 ft across the top, and 900 ft in circumference. Numerous relics have been recovered from two burial chambers in excavations begun in 1838. Inc. 1865. Pop. (1980) 12,419.
39°55′ N, 80°44′ W

Mounier, Jean-Joseph (1758–1806), French lawyer and politician.
·Monarchical leadership and failure **7**:651h

Mount, Shepard: *see* Mount, William Sidney.

Mount, William Sidney (b. Nov. 26, 1807, Setauket, Long Island, N.Y.—d. Nov. 19, 1868), Romantic painter of idyllic genre scenes primarily depicting rustic life in his native Long Island.

A farm boy until the age of 17, Mount apprenticed himself to his older brother, Henry, a sign painter working in New York. They were joined by their younger brother, Shepard Alonzo (1804–68), who eventually became a portrait painter. In 1826, when the National Academy of Design opened drawing classes, Mount was one of the first students to enroll. He stayed only a year before he returned to Setauket, where he continued painting and exhibiting his work. He became an associate member of the design academy in 1832 and a full member in 1833.

Mount, one of the first and best of the 19th-century American anecdotal painters, began by painting historical subjects. His first genre painting, "The Rustic Dance" (1830), was an immediate success, and Mount never departed from this vein. His genial portrayals of country life—a blend of affection and humour—are a valuable record of a bygone agrarian

"Eel Spearing at Setauket," oil on canvas by William Sidney Mount, 1845; in the New York State Historical Association, Cooperstown
By courtesy of the New York State Historical Association, Cooperstown

age. The recognizable situations and the detailed representational character of Mount's paintings struck a responsive chord in Victorian America. Mount did not sentimentalize but portrayed the relationship of his subjects with naturalness and simplicity.
·Hudson River school **19**:458c

Mount Abu, town and mountain, Sirohi district, Rājasthān state, India. The mountain, an isolated feature of the Arāvalli Range, is detached from the chain by a valley seven miles across, in which flows the western Banās. It has several peaks, one of which, Guru Sikhar (5,650 ft [1,722 m]), to the north, is the highest peak of the Arāvalli Range. Mount Abu, covered with numerous Jain temples, shrines, and tombs, has been a place of pilgrimage for more than 2,000 years and is mentioned in the *Mahābhārata* (the great Sanskrit epic of India) as Ārbuda ("the hill of wisdom").

Mount Abu town is a noted hill resort; the Jain temples at nearby Dilwara, built of white

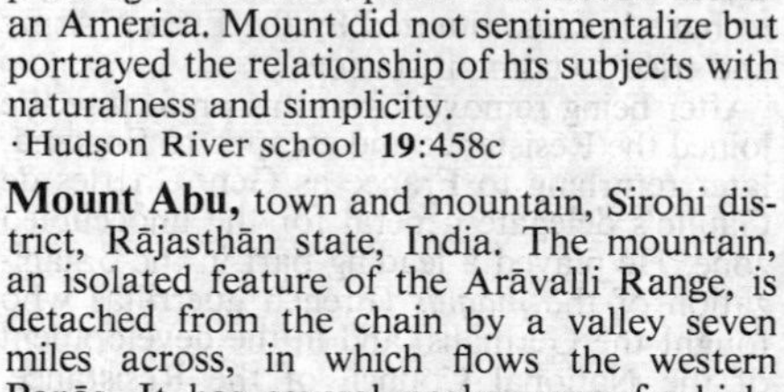

White marble Jain temple at Dilwāra, near Mount Abu, Rājasthān, India
Paolo Koch—Rapho Guillumette

marble, are famous. Tejpāl temple, built *c.* 1200, is known for the delicacy and richness of its carving, especially for that on the underside of its dome. The earlier Vimala Sahī temple, built *c.* 1031, is simpler and bolder in style. Mount Abu town was the headquarters of the British Rājputāna States Agency and has a police training college. Pop. (1971) 9,840.
24°41′ N, 72°50′ E
·temples' elaborate decoration **17**:178f

Mountague, Richard (Anglican bishop): *see* Montagu, Richard.

mountain, landform that rises prominently above adjacent land, exhibiting a confined or narrow summit area and considerable local relief. Mountains generally are understood to be larger than hills, but the term has no standardized geographic meaning. Most of the larger and more prominent mountains are concentrated within two huge mountainous bands. One band forms an interrupted ring around the Pacific Ocean. The second extends eastward across the general area of the Mediterranean into Asia Minor and Asia. There are other long chains of mountains beneath the oceans, some of which form the greatest irregularities found on the solid surface of this planet.

All mountains have been elevated above adjacent areas quite recently, with respect to geological time; the processes of surface weathering and erosion, if given sufficient time, will reduce them to comparatively low levels. Mountains may be formed by folding, faulting, or volcanic activity. The shape or topography of a mountain is influenced by its structure, the kinds of rock from which it is made, and the climate in which it occurs. *Major ref.* **12**:588d
·life-form evolution **18**:144d
·mapping techniques **11**:477c
·origin, tectonism, and deformation **12**:577h; illus. 578
·tundra's flora and fauna **18**:734c

mountain and valley winds, local winds that reverse their direction diurnally in mountainous regions. Rapid daytime warming of a valley floor causes air to expand and flow up the slopes as a valley wind; the rising currents sometimes trigger thunderstorms. Nighttime radiation then cools the slopes and causes cold, dense air to drain into the valley as a mountain wind. This wind may attain high velocities if it is funnelled through a narrow, constricting gorge.
·cloud formation and air motion **4**:758g
·microclimates and wind motion **12**:116f

Mountain Ash, Welsh ABERPENNAR, township group, county of Mid Glamorgan (until 1974 it was in the former Glamorganshire), Wales, in the Cynon Valley. Its growth dates almost entirely from *c.* 1850 with the exploitation of rich reserves of coal, and only after about 1945 were factory industries significantly introduced to offset the serious fall in local mining employment. It contains a huge pavilion, built in 1906 for the national eisteddfod (Welsh festival of the arts) and used later for music festivals and other community purposes.

The township group also includes other former mining villages, such as Abercynon and Ynysybwl. Pop. (1973 est.) 27,710.
51°42′ N, 3°24′ W

mountain ash, any of several trees of the genus *Sorbus* within the rose family (Rosaceae). They are widely distributed throughout the North Temperate Zone. Many species are grown as ornamentals for their handsome red berry-like fruits. *S. aucuparia,* commonly called European mountain ash, or rowan tree, is one of the most commonly cultivated species. It grows to about 13 metres (about 45 feet) tall.

The leaves are pinnately compound (feather-

Mountain ash (*Sorbus americana*)
Grant Heilman—EB Inc.

formed), and the tiny, white flowers grow in clusters 10–15 centimetres (4–6 inches) broad. The round, bright-red fruits are about one centimetre in diameter.
·general features and importance **15**:1150b

mountain beaver (rodent): *see* sewellel.

Mountain Brook, city, Jefferson County, central Alabama, U.S.; it is a southeastern suburb of Birmingham and was founded and incorporated in 1942. Pop. (1980) 17,400.
33°29′ N, 86°46′ W

mountain-building processes 12:577, the physical processes that are responsible for orogenesis, or mountain building.

The text article covers the distribution of mountain belts, tectonic mountain belts, theories of orogenesis (with emphasis on the geosynclinal hypothesis), and development of mountain systems.

REFERENCES in other text articles:
·African geological history **1**:182a; map 181
·Alpine origin theory development **1**:633e
·Andes geological history **1**:857g
·Apennine rocks and origin **1**:1011c
·Appalachian, Northern Rockies, and Sierra Nevada formation **18**:907c *passim* to 914h
·Appalachian geological development **1**:1016d
·Asian geological history **2**:147g
·Atlas Mountains development **2**:304f
·block faulting in western United States **14**:529d
·Carboniferous ocean basins and tectonism **3**:853f
·catastrophic development theory **18**:857e
·Caucasus Mountains origin **3**:1016c
·classification and characteristics **6**:62d
·climatic and topographic changes **4**:741b
·conglomerate deposits and uplift **4**:1112f
·Cretaceous tectonism and orogenic areas **5**:250c
·Dana's major chain development theory **5**:451b
·Death Valley thrust and block faults **5**:539d
·Devonian orogeny and rock deformation **5**:672e
·Earth geological history **6**:8e
·extrusive igneous rock formation **9**:215h
·folded mountains in geosynclinal areas **5**:121f
·geologic dating and orogenic episodes **7**:1069e
·geosyncline deformation **6**:10f
·graywacke in geosynclines and tectonism **8**:299d
·Great Basin faulting and development **2**:750c
·heat flow importance **6**:26d
·landform evolution theories **10**:626g
·mechanism theories **6**:41e
·Mesozoic orogeny and volcanism **11**:1016h
·metamorphism under crustal stresses **15**:948e
·mountain range and belt formation **12**:588d; illus. 589
·Mt. Everest's geological formation **6**:1139h
·New Guinea mountain range formation **12**:1088f
·North American continent evolution **13**:180f
·Norwegian mountain system formation **13**:263e
·Pacific Coast Range formation **13**:824h
·Pacific island arcs and fault zones **13**:837e
·Permian orogeny **14**:99c
·Precambrian events and mountain roots **14**:958g
·pre-Silurian rock deformation **16**:769c
·Pyrenees structure and formation **15**:316c
·Rocky Mountain geosynclines and faults **15**:966a *passim* to 968a
·sandstone correlation with peak height **16**:216c
·tectonism's physiographic effects **14**:434a
·Tertiary Period tectonic activity **3**:1080d
·Tertiary worldwide activity **18**:151f
·Triassic and Late Paleozoic activity **18**:696f
·uplift rates and erosion **8**:874b
·Upper Paleozoic continental convergence **13**:929e
·vertical movement theories **6**:82g

RELATED ENTRIES in the *Ready Reference and Index:*
Gondwanaland; orogeny; plate tectonics; subduction zone; tectogene

mountain climate: *see* highland climate.

mountain cork (mineralogy): *see* actinolite.

mountaineering 12:584, the sport of climbing mountains, including the basic elements of hiking, rock-climbing, and negotiating snow and ice.

The text article covers the background and origins of mountain climbing and the history of mountain climbing as a sport since its relatively recent emergence, in the 18th century, through the conquest of the world's highest peaks in Europe, North and South America, Africa, and Asia. A table of some of these peaks and the dates of their first successful climbing is included. Also covered are the essential characteristics and organization of the sport, hazards and safety precautions, and the basic principles of rock-climbing, rope handling, and climbing on snow and ice.

REFERENCES in other text articles:
·climatic influence on man **4**:729c
·Gesner's historic records **8**:131f
·Humboldt climbing record **8**:1190e
·Mount Everest expeditions **6**:1141a
·oxygen-breathing apparatus **10**:917h

mountain fever: *see* Colorado tick fever.

mountain forest: *see* cloud forest.

mountain glacier: *see* alpine glacier.

mountain goat, also called ROCKY MOUNTAIN GOAT (*Oreamnos americanus*), North Ameri-

Mountain goat (*Oreamnos americanus*)
Earl Kubis—Root Resources

can ruminant, family Bovidae (order Artiodactyla). Mountain goats occur from the Yukon to the northern U.S. Rockies. Although goatlike, they are more closely related to antelopes than to true goats. Stocky, and with a slight hump at the withers, mountain goats stand about one metre (39 inches) at the shoulder. Members of both sexes bear short, hollow, slightly backward curving horns. The hair is coarse, white, and shaggy over a thick, woolly underfur, and a beard frames the slender muzzle. The blackish hooves and horns stand out in contrast.

Surefooted relatives of the chamois, mountain goats live among rugged, craggy mountain peaks, usually above the timberline. They excel even the bighorn in climbing rocky precipices. Mountain goats live in small bands. They mate in November, and the males fight for possession of the females. A single kid, rarely two, is born in late spring in a nursery group. A few minutes later it walks about and nurses. Mountain goats eat a variety of plants—moss, lichen, scrub foliage—and seemingly require little. Their slow gait is a stiff-legged walk. They are agile climbers and are capable of leaping more than 3.5 metres (11.5 feet).

·social behaviour **2**:72d

Mountain Home, town, seat of Baxter County, northern Arkansas, U.S., in the Ozarks. It is located between Bull Shoals Lake and Norfork Lake, which were impounded (1952) by hydroelectric projects on the White River. The town is the hub of the state's most popular recreation area. The Norfork National Fish Hatchery is 11 mi (18 km) southeast. Pop. (1980) 7,447.
36°20′ N, 92°23′ W

mountain laurel (shrub): *see* Kalmia.

mountain leather (mineralogy): *see* actinolite.

mountain lion: *see* puma.

mountain mahogany, any of several western North American shrubs in the genus *Cercocarpus*. The heartwood is very hard and valued for carving.

·Rosales poisonous plants **15**:1152h

Mountain Meadows Massacre (September 1857), slaughter of a band of Arkansas emigrants passing through Utah on their way to California by a party of Paiute Indians and Mormon settlers led by John Doyle Lee. Lee was convicted of first degree murder and on March 23, 1877, was shot at the site of the massacre.

·Mormon federal defiance and persecution of non-Mormon settlers **12**:442h

mountain men, pioneers of the U.S. Rocky Mountain West who went first as fur trappers. Attracted by beaver in virgin streams, the trappers became the explorers of the Far West. The most experienced trappers were the French, who joined American and Spanish fur traders, with St. Louis as a base for trading parties and trading company caravans early in the 19th century. Mingling extensively with Indians, the mountain men adopted many of the natives' manners of life, morals, beliefs, and love of adornment. The summer rendezvous, especially at Green River, Wyo., became an institution of the mountain men, combining trade with recreation. As permanent settlers arrived, many mountain men served as scouts and guides, but their way of life was gradually eliminated by advancing civilization.

Mountain Nile (The Sudan): *see* Baḥr al-Jabal.

mountain nyala (*Tragelaphus buxtoni*): *see* nyala.

Mountain of Iron (South Africa): *see* Thabazimbi.

Mountain Province, north central Luzon, Philippines, largest province in the republic until 1966, when the elevation of four subprovinces (Kalinga, Apayao, Ifugao, and Benguet) to provincial status reduced its size to

Rice terraces near Banaue in Mountain Province, Luzon, Phil.
Ted Spiegel—Rapho Guillumette

810 sq mi (2,097 sq km). Filipinos still speak of Mountain Province as the larger area. Almost wholly mountainous (Cordillera Central), with Mt. Cauitan (8,508 ft [2,594 m]) as the highest point, it is a tourist region and site of the famous Ifugao rice terraces, located near Sagada and between Bontoc (the capital) and Banaue in Ifugao. Rice, corn, and camote are major crops. Pop. (1975) 94,096.

·area and population table **14**:236

mountain ranges and mountain belts **12**:588, elongated chainlike groupings of mountains on the Earth's surface.

The text article briefly treats the various types of mountains, including dome mountains, block mountains, fold mountains, fold-fault mountains, volcanic mountains, island arcs, Alpine-type mountains, and residual mountains. It also deals with the world's mountain systems, in particular the two principal ones: the Tethyan Mountain System, which separates the continental platforms of Eurasia from Africa and India; and the Circum-Pacific Mountain System, which consists of three dissimilar mountain belts that ring the Pacific Ocean—*i.e.*, the North American Cordillera and the mountain belts of eastern Siberia, the South American Cordillera, and the west Pacific island arcs.

REFERENCES in other text articles:

·Alaskan Mountain geological formation **1**:414d
·alluvial fan formation and properties **1**:612b
·Andes' course, formation, and elevation **1**:856b
·Appalachian and Western Cordillera features and formation **18**:907b
·Asian geography and geology **2**:155h; map
·Asian soil zones **2**:166g
·Caledonian System northern continuation **13**:263e
·California's Coast and Sierra Nevada ranges and features **3**:615d
·Caucasus Mountains description **3**:1015b
·Cenozoic floral belt movement **3**:1081h
·climatic variations and local effects **4**:723c
·conglomerate deposition in troughs **4**:1112g
·Cretaceous orogenic systems **5**:250c
·Cyprus' geological formation **5**:402d
·Death Valley bounds and formation **5**:539b
·desert landforms **5**:611g
·Devonian orogeny and rock deformation **5**:672e
·evolution and erosion theories **6**:83a
·geological forms and transformations **7**:1055f
·geological study with gravity meters **8**:289a
·glacial valley formation and features **8**:168h
·Himalayan formation and characteristics **9**:277b
·Karakorams' physiography and geology **10**:402f
·North American geological history **13**:180f
·origin, tectonism, and deformation **12**:577h; illus. 578
·Pacific Coast Range geological history **13**:824d
·Pacific continental and volcanic islands **13**:826f
·paleoclimates and paleogeography **13**:910a
·physiography of the continents **6**:45c
·Pleistocene and modern glaciation **8**:164b
·Precambrian rock types and formations **14**:953f
·Rocky Mountain ranges and formations **15**:964g; illus. 965
·Shensi southern region divisions and features **16**:665f
·thunderstorm generation **18**:62b
·volcano location and activity **19**:502f
·Yugoslav topography **19**:1098h

RELATED ENTRIES in the *Ready Reference and Index:*
cordillera; dome mountain; fault-block mountain; folded mountain; mountain

Mountain region, Kentucky, U.S., eastern quarter of the state of Kentucky, a region of narrow valleys and sharp ridges belonging to the plateau of the Allegheny Mountains. It includes the Cumberland and Pine mountains.

·landform features and coal source **10**:420d

mountain sheep: *see* bighorn.

mountain spectre (optical phenomenon): *see* Brocken bow.

Mountain Tadzhiks: *see* Yaghnābīs.

Mountain View, city, Santa Clara County, California, U.S., on the southwest shore of San Francisco Bay. Settled in 1852 as a stagecoach station, it became a shipping point for fruit and grain and a centre of religious book publishing. In 1929 Moffett Field Naval Air Station was established there, and in 1940 the Ames Laboratory of the National Advisory Committee for Aeronautics was located on the site. These facilities influenced the development of the city's aerospace and electronics industries. Inc. 1902. Pop. (1950) 6,563; (1970) 54,132; (1980) 58,655.
37°23′ N, 122°04′ W

mountain wood (mineralogy): *see* actinolite.

Mountain Zebra National Park, eastern Cape Province, South Africa, in the Great Karoo region, northwest of Cradock. It has an area of 25 sq mi (65 sq km) and was founded in 1937 primarily to protect the diminishing mountain zebra, which differ from common zebra in having a short, stocky conformation and a distinctive stripe pattern (*see* zebra). The park also supports black wildebeests, elands, and several other species of antelopes.
32°16′ S, 25°29′ E

·map, South Africa **17**:63

Mount Barker, town, southwest Western Australia, at the base of 829-ft (253-m) Mt. Barker, which was sighted in 1829 and named after Capt. Collett Barker, the last military commandant at Albany on the coast, 35 mi (56 km) south. The town, proclaimed in 1899, is the administrative headquarters of Plantagenet shire. Situated on the Great Southern Railway and Albany Highway to Perth (210 mi northwest), it is a processing centre for a region of beef, sheep, grain, apple, and vegetable farming and manufactures concrete pipe. Mount Barker is a base for excursions to the scenic Porongorup and Stirling ranges. Pop. (1976 prelim.) 1,562.
34°38′ S, 117°40′ E

Mountbatten, Louis Alexander: *see* Milford Haven, Louis Alexander Mountbatten, 1st marquess of.

Mountbatten of Burma, Louis Mountbatten, 1st Earl (b. June 25, 1900, Frogmore House, Windsor, Eng.—d. Aug. 27, 1979, Donegal Bay, off County Sligo, Ireland), British statesman, naval leader, and last viceroy of India. He had an international royal family background; his career involved extensive naval commands, the diplomatic negotiation of independence for India and Pakistan, and the highest military defense leaderships.

Christened Louis Francis Albert Victor Nicholas of Battenberg, he was the fourth child of Prince Louis of Battenberg, afterward marquess of Milford Haven, and his wife, Princess Victoria of Hesse-Darmstadt, granddaughter of England's Queen Victoria. He en-

1st Earl Mountbatten of Burma

tered the Royal Navy in 1913 and had various naval assignments before becoming aide-de-camp to the Prince of Wales (1921). In 1922 he married Edwina Ashley (who died in 1960 in North Borneo while on tour as superintendent-in-chief of the St. John Ambulance Brigade). In 1932 he was promoted to captain and the next year qualified as an interpreter in French and German. In command of the destroyer "Kelly" and the 5th destroyer flotilla at the outbreak of World War II, he was appointed commander of an aircraft carrier in 1941. From a post as a comparatively junior naval officer he was appointed supreme allied commander for Southeast Asia (1943–46), prompting complaints of nepotism against his cousin the king. He successfully conducted the campaign against Japan that led to the recapture of Burma. As viceroy of India (March–August 1947) he administered the transfer of power to India and Pakistan at the Aug. 15, 1947, partition of the subcontinent, with his reputation less esteemed in the latter area. While governor general of India (August 1947–June 1948) he helped persuade Indian princes to merge their states into the Republic of India or into Pakistan. He was created viscount in 1946 and earl in 1947.

Mountbatten was fourth sea lord in 1950–52, commander in chief of the Mediterranean fleet in 1952–54, and first sea lord in 1955–59. He became an admiral of the fleet in 1956 and served as chief of the United Kingdom Defense Staff and chairman of the Chiefs of Staff Committee in 1959–65.

Lord Mountbatten was killed by an explosion on his boat in Donegal Bay. The assassination was claimed by the Irish Republican Army as part of its campaign against British rule in Northern Ireland.

·Burmese alliance formation **3**:515c
·Indian viceregal policies **9**:422c

Mountbatten Plan (1947), plan under which India and Pakistan became independent.

·Gandhi's opposition to partition **7**:877g
·Indian subcontinent history **9**:422e

Mount Buller, resort, east central Victoria, Australia, on the slopes of Mt. Buller (5,928 ft [1,807 m]). It is the most fully developed tourist centre in the Victorian Alps, offering skiing from June to September. Pop. (latest census) about 100 persons.
37°10′ S, 146°27′ E

Mount Carmel, borough, Northumberland County, east central Pennsylvania, U.S., at the head of Shamokin Creek. Settled about 1775, it was laid out in 1848 and became an anthracite coal mining town. The economic mainstay is now light manufacturing. Inc. 1862. Pop. (1980) 8,190.
40°48′ N, 76°25′ W
·map **18**:United States of America, Plate 15

Mount Carmel fossils, remains of a dozen or more humans, discovered in 1931 and 1932 in two caves, Maghārat at-Tabūn and Maghārat as-Skhūl, 15 miles south of Haifa, Israel. Material from Skhūl (seven adults, three immature individuals, and several miscellaneous fragments) presents a mosaic of Neanderthal and modern characters. In the Tabūn cave were found a nearly complete skeleton of an adult woman and the jaw of a man; these finds resemble the classic Neanderthals of Europe, except that the mandible has a small chin. Acheulian through upper Mousterian artifacts were found at Tabūn; at Skhūl (a much shallower site) only Mousterian artifacts were present. A carbon-14 dating suggests that Tabūn was occupied approximately 41,000 years ago; Skhūl is 5,000–10,000 years later.

Four interpretations of the fossils have been advanced: (1) hybridization between Neanderthal man and populations of the modern type; (2) a population in the throes of rapid evolution in a modern direction but developing too late to be ancestors of modern man—the Mt. Carmel people being superseded by fully modern men entering from the east; (3) members of one of a series of locally interrelated populations from which all later forms of man have descended; (4) Tabūn as the Neanderthal stage of evolution in the Middle East and Skhūl as their descendants evolving toward modern man. Recent thought favours the fourth hypothesis; in any case, the mixture of characteristics observed among the Mt. Carmel fossils assures them an important place in the study of human evolution.

·Asian Neanderthal fossils **2**:201d; map 202
·characteristics and significance **11**:426g

Mount Clemens, city, seat of Macomb County, southeastern Michigan, U.S., on the Clinton River, near its mouth on Lake St. Clair. Permanent settlement dates from 1795, and Christian Clemens made the first plat in 1818. Cooperage and glassmaking were early economic endeavours, and since 1873 local sulfurous health springs have attracted bathers. Mount Clemens is noted for its pottery and is one of the nation's largest producers of roses under glass. At Grand Trunk Station, Thomas Edison first learned telegraphy. Inc. village, 1837; city, 1879. Pop. (1980) 18,806.
42°36′ N, 82°53′ W
·map **18**:United States of America, Plate 14

Mount Darwin, town, North Mashonaland Province, northern Zimbabwe, administrative headquarters for the Tribal Trust Lands areas set aside for African occupation. It is also an agricultural and mining (gold, asbestos) centre. To the southeast, Mt. Darwin, named for the naturalist Charles Darwin, rises 4,951 ft (1,509 m) above sea level. Pop. (latest census) 900.
16°48′ S, 31°30′ E

Mount Desert Island, Hancock County, southeastern Maine, U.S., in Frenchman Bay of the Atlantic Ocean. With an area of 108 sq mi (280 sq km), the island is 15 mi (24 km) long and about 8 mi wide. Somes Sound, a 6-mi-long, narrow fjord, divides it into eastern and western segments. The island was discovered in September 1604 by Samuel de Champlain while he was exploring the Acadian Coast from St. Croix westward and was named by him for the bare-rock summits of its mountains. A bridge connects the mainland and the island's network of excellent roads, bridle paths, and foot paths, which join the towns on the island, including Bar Harbor, Mount Desert, Southwest Harbor, Northeast Harbor, Seal Harbor, and Tremont.

In 1947 the island was swept by a tremendous fire that destroyed many buildings and natural attractions. Mount Desert Island's bare-rock summits, including Cadillac Mountain (1,530 ft [466 m]), are the highest on the Atlantic Coast north of Rio de Janeiro.

The first eastern national park in the United States, Acadia National Park, was established on the island in 1919; the park also includes picturesque Schoodic Point on the mainland and part of Isle au Haut.
44°20′ N, 68°20′ W
·map **18**:United States of America, Plate 16

Mount Gambier, city, southeast South Australia, southeast of Adelaide, with which it is connected by road, rail, and air. It lies at the foot of Mt. Gambier (623 ft [190 m]), an extinct volcano with four crater lakes sighted (1800) by Lieut. James Grant of the Royal Navy, who named it after Admiral James (later Lord) Gambier. Stephen Henty surveyed the area in 1839, climbed the mountain, and established a livestock station in 1841. A private settlement called Gambier Town was founded (1854) there by Hastings Cunningham and was proclaimed a municipality in 1876. Now the state's third largest city, Mount Gambier is the centre of a mixed farming area (cereals, potatoes, onions, livestock) and processes dairy foods, meats, and flour; it manufactures woollens, cellulose, and concrete pipes. Local plantations of pine trees supply a timber industry, and coralline limestone, dolomite, and diatomite are mined in the vicinity. Pop. (1976 prelim.) 19,292.
37°50′ S, 140°46′ E
·map, Australia **2**:401

Mount Hagen, town, administrative headquarters of the Western Highlands province and Hagen district, Papua New Guinea, east central New Guinea island, southwest Pacific. The town, established as a patrol post in 1936, is near the Wahgi River, a tributary of the Purari. It takes its name from a 12,392-ft (3,777-m) peak in the Hagen Range of the central highlands (15 mi [24 km] northwest). (The name Hagen comes from the president of the former German New Guinea Company.) It is believed that the mountain, an extinct volcano, once stood 6,000 ft higher but was reduced by an ancient cataclysmic eruption.

The town is on the important trucking highway leading 380 mi (610 km) east to Lae (on the coast) and subsidiary roads running northwest to Wabag, north to Baiyer River, and south to Mendi. It has plants processing locally grown tea, coffee, and pyrethrum; timber mills; and a cordial factory. Its airport, built during World War II, has regularly scheduled flights. The town holds a large biennial agricultural show and is becoming an increasingly popular resort because of its mile-high elevation. Pop. (1971) 10,621.
5°50′ S, 144°15′ E
·map, New Guinea **12**:1089

Mount Holly, township, seat (1795) of Burlington County, south central New Jersey, U.S., on Rancocas Creek. Established by Quakers in 1677 and incorporated in 1688, it was known successively as Northampton and Bridgetown, until it was renamed for the holly-covered hill on which it was built. A temporary capital of New Jersey during the American Revolution, it was raided several times by the British. Surviving 18th-century buildings include the County Court House; the Friends Meeting House; the Stephen Girard House, home of the founder of Girard College; the original building of the Relief Fire Company, one of the oldest volunteer fire companies in the U.S.; and the Woolman Memorial, honouring John Woolman (1720–72), Quaker reformer and abolitionist. It is an agricultural trade centre with some light manufacturing. Pop. (1980) 10,818.
39°60′ N, 74°47′ W

Mount Hood National Forest, northwestern Oregon, U.S., extending along the Cascade Range southward from the Co-

Punch Bowl Falls, Mount Hood National Forest, Oregon

B. Nelson—Shostal

lumbia River. Established in 1911 and formerly called Oregon National Forest, it covers an area of 1,170,782 ac (473,815 ha). The forest provides timber, water, forage, wildlife habitat, and recreation; it is drained by the Columbia, Sandy, Clackamas, Hood, and White rivers and their tributaries. Mt. Hood (11,235 ft [3,424 m]), near the centre of the forest, is Oregon's highest point. Features include Mount Hood Wilderness Area; Timberline Lodge; Multnomah Falls (605 ft); Austin and Bagby hot springs; Timothy Lake; and Eagle Creek Trail, leading through a region of waterfalls. Recreational activities include hunting, fishing, skiing, mountain climbing, and hiking. Headquarters are at Portland.

Mount Hope Bay, Rhode Island, U.S., northeast arm of Narragansett Bay, south of the city of Fall River, Mass. It is crossed by Mount Hope Bridge (built 1929), one of the largest in New England.
41°43′ N, 71°09′ W
·Narragansett Bay description **15**:809c

Mounties: *see* Royal Canadian Mounted Police.

Mount Isa, city and mining centre, Queensland, Australia, flanked east and west by peaks

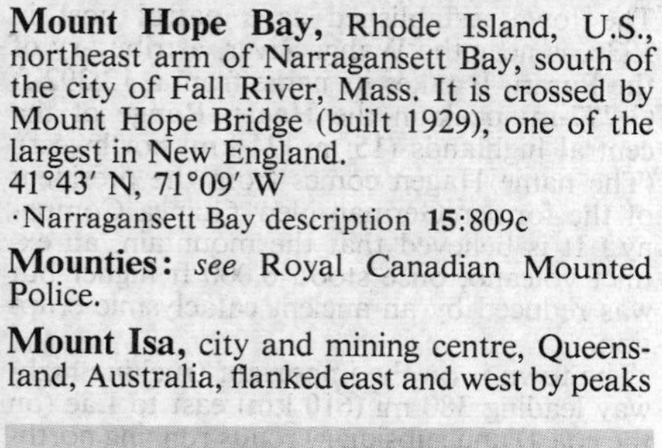

Lead smelter at Mount Isa Mines, Queensland

By courtesy of the Australian News and Information Bureau

(2,000 ft [600 m]) of the Selwyn Range. The name is attributed to John Campbell Miles, who in 1923 discovered deposits of silver-lead ore and named one of his leases after his sister Isabelle. Subsequently Mount Isa Mines, Ltd., the principal leaseholder, developed the minefields, which are Australia's main source of copper and also yield silver, lead, and zinc. Cattle are raised in the district, and there is an annual rodeo. Nearby damming created Lake Moondarra (1958) and Lake Julius (1976) as local water reservoirs. The former shire became a city (one of the world's largest in area at nearly 16,000 sq mi [41,000 sq km]) in 1968. Pop. (1976 prelim.) 25,377.
20°44′ S, 139°30′ E
·map, Australia **2**:401

Mountjoy, William Blount, 4th baron of (d. 1534), British statesman and patron of learning.
·Erasmus' first English sojourn as tutor **6**:952c

Mountjoy, Charles Blount, 8th Baron, afterward EARL OF DEVONSHIRE (b. *c.* 1562—d. April 3, 1606, London), soldier, English lord deputy of Ireland, whose victory at Kinsale, County Cork, in 1601 led to the complete conquest of Ireland by English forces.

After fighting in the Low Countries against Spain, Mountjoy in 1597 accompanied the 2nd Earl of Essex and Sir Walter Raleigh on an expedition to the Azores against Spanish treasure ships. After the defeat of Sir Henry Bagnal's English army in Ireland (August 1598), Mountjoy was expected to assume command there. Essex, who was sent instead, also failed and was subsequently dismissed from office in June 1600, when Mountjoy was appointed lord deputy.

Spanish troops landed at Kinsale in 1601, and the Irish leader, Hugh O'Neill, 2nd earl of Tyrone, marched southward from Ulster to join them. Mountjoy waited outside Kinsale,

8th Baron Mountjoy, detail of an engraving by Valentine Green (1739–1813) after a portrait by Paul Van Somer (1576–1621)

By courtesy of the trustees of the British Museum; photograph, J.R. Freeman & Co. Ltd.

and on Dec. 24, 1601, his cavalry routed the Irish army. The Spanish evacuated Kinsale, and Ulster thus was left open to English invasion. Mountjoy received Tyrone's submission in 1603 and was able to win moderate treatment for him from King James I of England. In the same year Mountjoy was created earl of Devonshire.

Mountlake Terrace, city, Snohomish County, northwest Washington, U.S. A residential suburban community between Everett and Seattle, it was developed in the late 1940s. Inc. 1954. Pop. (1960) 9,122; (1980) 16,534.
47°47′ N, 122°18′ W

Mount Lofty Ranges, series of hills in southeastern South Australia, east of Ade-

Cascade in the Morialta Falls Reserve situated in a gorge on the western side of the Mount Lofty Ranges, South Australia

By courtesy of the South Australian Government Tourist Bureau

laide. A southerly continuation of the Flinders Range, they extend southward from Peterborough for 200 mi (320 km) to Cape Jervis. Averaging 15 to 20 mi wide, the ranges are divided at the Barossa Valley into northern and southern segments. The former is higher and rises to Mt. Byron (3,063 ft [934 m]); the latter has peaks generally below 2,000 ft with a high point at Mt. Lofty (2,384 ft). Most of the permanent rivers that originate in these hills, including the Onkaparinga, Gawler, Light, and Torrens, flow down the western slopes to the Gulf St. Vincent.

The ranges were discovered and named by Matthew Flinders, an explorer who viewed them offshore from Kangaroo Island (*q.v.*) in 1802. To Adelaide they are important as sources of food (orchards, truck gardens, and dairy farms in the valleys and hills), water, and recreation. Belair National Park, in the ranges, has been comprehensively developed.
35°15′ S, 138°50′ E
·formation and relief **2**:389f; illus. 388

Mount Lyell, mining area, western Tasmania, Australia. The site, discovered in the 1880s, derives its name from a 2,900-ft (880-m) peak in the west coast range, which was named after Charles Lyell, a 19th-century English geologist. First mined for gold, then silver, it currently yields more than 90 percent of the state's copper, mostly from low-grade open-cut deposits such as at West Lyell. After 1968, vast new underground deposits were developed. Most of the workers reside nearby in Queenstown. The ore is sent northward to the port of Burnie, from which 80 percent is shipped to Japan and the remainder sent to Port Kembla, New South Wales.
42°03′ S, 145°38′ E

Mount McKinley National Park, south central Alaska, U.S., established in 1917 and enlarged twice to its present 1,939,493 ac (784,886 ha). It contains a spectacular portion of the Alaska Range (*q.v.*), including Mt. McKinley, 20,320 ft (6,193 m) high, the highest mountain in North America. Glaciers and vast snowfields cover much of the range, and wet tundra, trees, shrubs, and herbs are found on the rest. The park's wildlife is varied and includes some rare species. Dall sheep, caribou, bears, and moose are the largest animals. Birds are common, some from winter homes as far away as Hawaii and Asia. Fish abound in Wonder Lake and the clearer streams. *See also* McKinley, Mount.
·wildlife species present **1**:413d

Mount Marion Sandstone Formation: *see* Cazenovian Stage.

Mount Morgan, mining town, eastern Queensland, Australia, in the Dee Range. One of Australia's most important gold strikes, called the "mountain of gold," was made there in 1882 by Edward Morgan. Although there were early difficulties in mining and treating the ore, the "Glory Hole" (½ mi [1 km] in diameter and 850 ft [260 m] deep) has already yielded more than 100 tons of gold, 250,000 tons of copper, and iron pyrites. This open-cut excavation has created a gaping, terraced crater in the mountain overlooking the town on the Dee River flats below. Declared a town in 1890, Mount Morgan was merged with the shire of Calliungal in 1931. It is linked by rail and the Burnett Highway to Rockhampton (22 mi [35 km] north) and Brisbane (313 mi southeast). Pop. (1976 prelim.) 3,246.
23°39′ S, 150°23′ E
·map, Australia **2**:401

Mount of Olives, Arabic JABAL AṬ-ṬŪR, Hebrew HAR HA-ZETIM, multi-summited limestone ridge just east of the Old City of Jerusalem and separated from it by the Kidron Valley. Frequently mentioned in the Bible and later religious literature, it is holy both to Judaism and to Christianity. Politically, it is part of the municipality of Greater Jerusalem placed under direct Israeli administration following the Six-Day War of 1967; it is not part of the West Bank (Judaea and Samaria) territory.

The peak usually regarded as the Mount of Olives proper is the southern summit, 2,652 ft (808 m) above sea level. The middle peak (2,645 ft) is crowned by the Augusta Victoria Hospital; at the north is the highest peak, commonly called Mount Scopus (Hebrew Har ha-Ẕofim, Arabic R'as al-Mashārif [2,684 ft]).

First mentioned in the Bible as the "ascent of the Mount of Olives" (2 Sam. 15); it is referred to in the book of Zechariah in the prophecy of the end of days (Zech. 14). During the Second Temple period (516 BC–AD 70), signal fires were lit on the mountaintop to indicate the date of the New Moon.

The Mount of Olives is often mentioned in the New Testament; from it, Jesus entered Jerusalem at the beginning of the last week of his life (Matt. 21:1; Mark 11:1); his prophecies of the apocalyptic fall of Jerusalem were delivered there. The traditional site of the Garden of Gethsemane, where he prayed just before his betrayal by Judas Iscariot (Matt. 26; Mark 14), is shown on the western slopes. One of the traditional sites of the Ascension is on the mountain (Acts 1:12). From at least the 4th century AD, Christian churches and shrines have been built there; many denominations are now represented.

So-called Tomb of Absalom on the southern slope of the Mount of Olives, Jerusalem

Patellani—Publix

According to ancient Jewish tradition, the messianic era will commence on the Mount of Olives; for this reason, its slopes have been the most sacred burial ground in Judaism for centuries. In modern times, the south and central peaks were on the Jordanian side of the Israel–Jordan armistice line after Israel's War of Independence (1948–49).

On Mount Scopus (north), the cornerstone of the Hebrew University was laid by Chaim Weizmann in 1918; the campus was opened by Lord Balfour in 1925. By 1948, many buildings had been built, including the Jewish National and University Library (1929), and the Rothschild-Hadassah University Hospital (1934), one of the largest in the Middle East. After the 1948–49 war, the university area on Mount Scopus was an exclave (detached portion) of sovereign Israeli territory, separated from Israeli Jerusalem by Jordan. The armistice agreement provided for free Israeli access to the scholastic and medical facilities on the mountain; contrary to this, however, Jordan allowed only a skeleton force of Israeli caretakers in the buildings, and the university was forced to build a new campus in the Giv'at Ram section of west Jerusalem. After the Six-Day War (June 1967), the entire Mount of Olives came under Israeli rule; by the early 1970s, the Mount Scopus complex was repaired and was in use by various university faculties. The Christian holy places were undamaged in the war; careful efforts have been made to restore the ancient Jewish cemetery, desecrated by the Jordanians.
31°47′ N, 35°15′ E
·mortuary significance **10**:141h

Mount Palomar Observatory: *see* Hale Observatories.

Mount Pearl, town, southwestern residential suburb of St. John's, Newfoundland, Canada. The site, originally granted to Sir James Pearl by the British government in 1834, was successively used for horse racing, for a naval radio station during World War I, and as an airfield during the early 1930s. Prior to World War II, it was a summer colony; after the war, permanent homes were built. Incorporated as Mount Pearl Park-Glendale in 1955, it was renamed Mount Pearl in 1958. Pop. (1971) 7,211.
47°31′ N, 52°47′ W

Mount Pleasant, city, seat (1836) of Henry County, southeastern Iowa, U.S., near the Skunk River. Settled in 1834, it was surveyed in 1837 and named for its commanding elevation and pleasant shade trees. In 1839 it became the site of the state's first courthouse. The city's early machine shop, foundry, and wagon industries are reflected in its annual Midwest Old Settlers and Threshers Reunion, a steam-engine and antique show. It is now a livestock shipping point with some light industry, including the manufacture of bus bodies.

It is the home of Iowa Wesleyan College (1842); the Harlan–Lincoln Museum on the campus was formerly the home of Sen. James Harlan, whose daughter Mary married Robert Todd Lincoln. The P.E.O. Sisterhood, which provides financial aid for the education of young women, was founded there in 1869 (the initials remain a secret). Mt. Pleasant is the birthplace of the astrophysicist James A. Van Allen. Inc. 1842. Pop. (1980) 7,322.
40°58′ N, 91°33′ W

Mount Pleasant, city, seat of Isabella County, central Michigan, U.S., on the Chippewa River. It was an Indian trading post and lumber camp in the 1850s, later becoming a farming centre. Its development was sustained by the arrival of the railroad (1879) and the foundation of a normal school (1892; since 1959, Central Michigan University) and of a Federal Indian Industrial School (closed 1934). After the discovery of oil in the vicinity (1927), the city became the state's "oil capital." Its economy is now balanced between diversified agriculture, industry, and educational interests. Inc. village, 1875; city, 1889. Pop. (1980) 23,746.
43°35′ N, 84°47′ W
·map, United States **18**:908

Mount Pleasant, town, Charleston County, southeastern South Carolina, U.S., on the Atlantic Intracoastal Waterway, overlooking Charleston Harbor and linked to Charleston (west) by the Cooper River (John P. Grace) Bridge. Settled in the 1690s, the town originated around Jacob Motte's plantation as a resort for island planters. Gen. William Moultrie was detained on parole by the British at Hibben House during the American Revolution. Nearby Sullivan's Island, site of Ft. Moultrie (1776), was the setting for Edgar Allen Poe's "The Gold Bug." Economic activities focus on pulp and paper, aircraft assembly, the Shem Creek shipyards, and the seafood industry. Inc. 1837. Pop. (1970) 6,879; (1980) 13,838.
32°46′ N, 79°52′ W

Mount Rainier National Park, in Washington, U.S., created in 1899 to preserve 241,781 ac (97,845 ha) of the Cascade Range, including Mt. Rainier, a dormant volcano 14,410 ft (4,392 m) high. This peak is sculptured by ice and 41 glaciers remain around the summit. During the warm months, the park and the mountain are largely covered with wild flowers that bloom progressively higher up the slopes as the summer passes. The lower areas also have dense forests.

The park's wildlife is likewise abundant and varied. Deer, elk, bears, and mountain goats are the largest animals; there are also raccoons, squirrels, and other smaller mammals. Small birds are also numerous. *See also* Rainier, Mount.

Mount Revelstoke National Park, southeastern British Columbia, Canada, occupying the western slope of the Selkirk Mountains, above the city of Revelstoke, which lies at the junction of the Columbia and Illecillewaet rivers. Established in 1914, it covers an area of 100 sq mi (260 sq km). An 18-mile-long road leads from the Trans-Canada Highway to the Summit (6,375 ft [1,943 m]), which affords a spectacular view of three mountain ranges (Monashee, Selkirk, Purcell). Below is a mountain-top plateau with rolling alpine landscape and steep-banked mountain lakes. Besides hiking trails, the park has a downhill ski course (named for skier Nels Nelson) 1¼ mi long, with a drop of 2,500 ft.

Mount Royal, French MONT-ROYAL, town, Île de Montréal (Montreal Island), Quebec province, Canada; it is chiefly a residential suburb of Montreal city, between Outremont and Saint-Laurent. It lies on the northwestern slope of Mount Royal (764 ft [232 m]), one of the Monteregian Hills (*q.v.*); and an electrified double-track tunnel through the mountain provides a fast and direct train route to the centre of Montreal. This transport facility played an important part in opening up the suburban area beyond the mountain. The industrial section is limited to the extreme eastern and western ends of the town. About 75 percent of the residents speak English. Inc. town, 1912. Pop. (1971) 21,561.
45°31′ N, 73°39′ W
·Montreal founding, growth, and sports **12**:411g *passim* to 415a

Mount Rushmore National Memorial, in southwestern South Dakota, U.S., 25 mi (40 km) southwest of Rapid City, is a huge sculpture of the heads of Presidents George Washington, Thomas Jefferson, Abraham Lincoln, and Theodore Roosevelt, carved in granite on the northeast side of Mt. Rushmore. The four heads, each about 60 ft (18 m) high, represent, respectively, the nation's founding, political philosophy, preservation, and expansion and conservation.

The memorial, first suggested by Jonah Robinson of the South Dakota State Historical Society, was dedicated in 1925. Work began in 1927 under Gutzon Borglum and was finished

Mount Rushmore National Memorial, S.D.

By courtesy of the American Forest Products Industry

in 1941, after 6½ years of actual work. The federal government paid most of the costs. About 1,000,000 persons visit the memorial each year.
43°50′ N, 103°24′ W

Mount Sinai Holy Church of America, Inc., an independent denomination founded in Philadelphia, Penn., in 1924.
·founding and membership **12**:940h

Mount Sterling, city, seat (1796) of Montgomery County, eastern Kentucky, U.S., at the edge of the Bluegrass region. The site, near "Little Mountain" (one of many burial mounds in the vicinity dating from Adena times, AD 400), was settled *c.* 1790. The town was established in 1792 and named for Stirling, Scot. (it was later spelled with an *e*). During the Civil War (1863), it was captured by Confederate cavalry under Col. R.S. Cluke. It developed as a market centre for tobacco, grain, livestock, and poultry, with light manufacturing. Natural Bridge State Park lies to the southeast in the Daniel Boone National Forest. Declared a city, 1950. Pop. (1980) 5,820.
38°04′ N, 84°56′ W

Mount Vernon, city, seat (1819) of Jefferson County, southern Illinois, U.S. Founded in 1819 by settlers from Virginia and the Carolinas, it was named for George Washington's birthplace. The Illinois Supreme Court was located in Mt. Vernon (1856–96), and there in 1859 Abraham Lincoln argued and won a tax case. The city is an agricultural, manufacturing, and distributing centre and coal and oil are produced in the area. Mt. Vernon is the site of Rend Lake (junior) College, a state tuberculosis sanitarium, and the Methodist Children's Home. Inc. town, 1837; city, 1872. Pop. (1980) 16,995.
38°19′ N, 88°55′ W
·map, United States **18**:908

Mount Vernon, city, Westchester County, New York, U.S., on the Bronx and Hutchinson rivers, adjacent to the Bronx, New York City (south). It was settled in 1664 near the site where religious dissenter Anne Hutchinson (banished from the Massachusetts Bay Colony) was killed in 1643 by Indians. It became a farm village (considered part of Eastchester Township) the meeting house of which was the scene of the election of Lewis Morris to the provincial assembly in 1773. Morris' subsequent removal from office by Gov. William Cosby increased support of the antigovernment newspaper of John Peter Zenger, whose trial for sedition ultimately established the principle of freedom of the press. The area, scene of several Revolutionary War battles, was where a delaying action by Glover's Brigade on Oct. 18, 1776, probably saved Washington's army from defeat by Gen. William Howe. Growth as a suburban community was assured when the Industrial Home Association, a cooperative group seeking relief from high New York City rents, purchased land for home sites there in 1851 and named the community for Washington's home. Diversified industrial development includes book publishing and the manufacture of clothing, electrical instruments, and chemicals. A dredged portion of the Hutchinson River serves as a port, and the city is a major petroleum-storage centre.

St. Paul's Church, Mount Vernon, N.Y.
Milt and Joan Mann from CameraMann

St. Paul's Church (1761), used during the Revolutionary War as a British military hospital, was dedicated a national historic site in 1943 and commemorates the Zenger affair and the Bill of Rights. Inc. village, 1853; city, 1892. Pop. (1980) 66,713.
40°54′ N, 73°50′ W

Mount Vernon, city, seat of Knox County, central Ohio, U.S., on the Kokosing River. Johnny Appleseed (John Chapman) owned several lots in the original plot laid out in 1805 by Benjamin Butler, Thomas Patterson, and Joseph Walker. The settlement was incorporated as a city in the same year and named for George Washington's estate in Virginia. Mount Vernon is the service centre for an area of general farming and of oil and gas production. A livestock auction is held regularly in the city. Manufactures include internal combustion engines, glass and paper products, and bridge sections. Daniel (Dan) Emmett (1815–1904), the composer of "Dixie" and other well-known songs, was born in Mount Vernon. The village of Gambier 5 mi (8 km) east of the city is the site of Kenyon College (1824). Pop. (1980) 14,380.
40°23′ N, 82°29′ W

Mount Vernon, home and burial place of George Washington, in Fairfax County, Virginia, U.S., on the Potomac River, 15 mi (24 km) below Washington, D.C. The 18th-century mansion, which overlooks the river, is built of wood; but the siding is of wide, thick boards so panelled as to give the appearance of cut and dressed stonework. The rooms have been restored as they were when occupied by Washington and his family; most of the pieces on the first floor and all of those in Washington's bedchamber are the originals. Other furniture has been replaced by pieces of the period. Additional articles relating to Washington are housed in a separate museum building.

From each end of the house, a curved colonnade leads to a row of outbuildings. A spacious lawn surrounds the mansion, with shaded drives, walks, and gardens. A short distance southwest of the mansion is a plain brick tomb built at Washington's direction on a site chosen by himself. It contains the remains of Washington and his wife (removed to this tomb from the old family vault in 1831) and of a number of other members of the family.

The estate, originally called Little Hunting Creek Plantation, consisted of about 5,000 ac (2,000 ha). It descended by inheritance from John Washington, the first of the family in America, to his son Lawrence, who in turn devised it to his daughter Mildred. From Mildred it was purchased in 1726 by her brother Augustine, George Washington's father and in 1735, when George was three years old, the family settled on the estate and lived there for several years. It is believed that the central part of the house was built during this time. In 1740, Augustine conveyed the plantation to

Mount Vernon
By courtesy of the Washington Convention and Visitor's Bureau

his son Lawrence, elder half brother of George; and Lawrence settled there three years later. He renamed the plantation Mount Vernon in honour of his former commander, Adm. Edward Vernon, under whom he had served in the Caribbean. Augustine Washington died in 1743; young George, after his father's death, spent part of his youth at Mount Vernon with Lawrence.

After Lawrence's death in 1751, George Washington inherited the property; but because of military service he did not take up residence at Mount Vernon until January 1759 when he married Martha (Dandridge) Custis. During the next 15 years he made improvements, including the enlargement of the house, the addition of the smaller wings, the erection of several of the outbuildings, and the expansion of the gardens. Again called into public service, it was not until December 1783, when he tendered his resignation to Congress as commander in chief of the Continental Army, that he again settled at Mount Vernon. But in 1789 his plantation life was again interrupted when he became the first president of the United States and was home rarely for eight years. From 1797 until his death (Dec. 14, 1799) he lived at Mount Vernon. At his death, a life interest in Mount Vernon went to his widow; and the estate passed to his nephew, Bushrod Washington; from Bushrod it descended to John Augustine Washington, Jr., who was authorized by will to sell it to the U.S. government. The government refused to buy the property.

In 1858, through the efforts of the Mount Vernon Ladies' Association of the Union, the house and 200 ac of the original estate were purchased. The association, under its charter, bound itself to restore the estate and to keep it sacred to the memory of Washington; the state of Virginia agreed to exempt it from taxation so long as these terms were fulfilled. The association became an influential pioneer in the restoration of historic places.
·colonial architecture preservation **19**:157d
·garden design in United States **7**:898b; illus. 886
·historical monument museums **12**:655d
·Washington's estate management **19**:610g

Mount Washington Glass Company, American glass company, at New Bedford, Mass., active from 1869 until 1900, and known for its coloured art glasses, particularly the so-called Burmese glass, a delicately coloured glass with a dull finish, shading from yellow to coral pink, much admired by Queen Victoria, and the Peachblow glass (*q.v.*). The company was also renowned for its cut glass, having been the only glass company in the United States to have produced complete chandeliers made of cut glass.

Mount Wilson Observatory: *see* Hale Observatories.

Moura, town, east Queensland, Australia, on the Dawson River. Together with its neighbouring town, Kianga (*q.v.*), Moura is the focus of a 350-sq-mi (910-sq-km) coalfield from which coking coal is mined for export to Japan. Local farms are supplied from Moura Weir, part of the Dawson Valley's irrigation system. Moura is served by the Dawson High-

way from Brisbane, 460 mi (740 km) south-southeast. Pop. (1971 prelim.) 1,877.
24°34′ S, 150°01′ E

Mouret, Jean-Joseph (1682–1738), French composer of divertissements, other instrumental music, cantatas, motets, and a mass. His opera-ballets occupy an important place in the music of the period.

Mourne, River, part of the Strule–Foyle river system in County Tyrone, N. Ire., formed by the junction of the Rivers Strule and Glenelly at Newton-Stewart. It flows north-northwest for about 10 mi (16 km) to a point west of Strabane, where it joins with the River Finn to form the Foyle.
54°45′ N, 7°28′ W

Mourne Mountains, County Down, Northern Ireland, a compact range of granite peaks rising abruptly from the Irish Sea at Carlingford Lough and extending for 9 mi (14.5 km) between Newcastle and Rostrevor. Their oval

Part of the Mourne Mountains in County Down, Northern Ireland
G.F. Allen—Bruce Coleman

outline reflects the extent of five overlapping granite intrusions into Silurian (about 400,000,000 years old) shales in later Tertiary times. Slieve Donard rises to 2,796 ft (852 m) within 2 mi of the sea. A dozen other peaks, including Slieve Bearnagh and Slieve Bingian, exceed 2,000 ft. The hills are used economically for reservoirs that supply Belfast, Portadown, and Banbridge. There is also some sheep raising. The lower hillslopes are extensively reafforested. The historic kingdom of Mourne, a crescent-shaped lowland now famous for potatoes, separates the mountains from the sea. The small coastal towns of Newcastle, Annalong, Kilkeel, and Rostrevor, once engaged in exporting dressed granite, are now fishing and tourist centres. Ruined castles at Greencastle and Dundrum attest the efforts of the Anglo-Norman settlers to hold this difficult coast. Between Newcastle and Castlewellan is the Tollymore Forest Park.
54°10′ N, 6°04′ W
·map, United Kingdom **18**:866
·United Kingdom physical geography **18**:865f

mourning, formal demonstration of grief at the death of a person, practiced in most societies. Mourners are usually relatives, although they may be friends or merely members of the community. Mourning rites, which are of varying duration and rationale, usually weigh more heavily on women than on men. Mourners may deny themselves certain amusement, ornaments, or food. They may practice sexual continence or keep vigil over the body of the deceased. Changes in garb, such as black robes, and alterations in hairstyle may distinguish mourners, but such evidences of mourning have declined in many societies.
·Chinese funeral professionalism **4**:425e
·customs in various cultures **5**:536c
·Iranian extremes in ritual grief **9**:869b
·Mesopotamian laments for god, temple, or city **11**:1007d
·North American Plateau Indian practices **13**:229b
·ritual ceremonies and institutions **13**:1051h
·Scythian burial customs **16**:440g

Mourning Becomes Electra (produced and published 1931), play by the U.S. dramatist Eugene O'Neill. The work is a Greek-inspired tragedy, transposed to the New England of the Civil War era.
·Aeschylean mood **1**:149e
·setting and tragic theme **13**:572e
·tragedy of Greece and Freudian psychology **18**:587b

mourning bride (plant): *see* scabious.

mourning cloak: *see* brush-footed butterfly.

mourning dove (*Zenaidura macroura*), a member of the pigeon order Columbiformes, the common wild pigeon of North America having a long pointed tail and violet and pink on the sides of the neck. This game bird may live up to 16 years in captivity; however, most mourning doves live only 4 or 5 years in the wild. First year mortality is about 80 percent. These doves migrate south in the winter; the most northward-living ones migrate the farthest south.
·feeding behaviour and migration **4**:933e

Mouron, Adolphe Jean-Marie: *see* Cassandre.

Mousai (Greek religion): *see* Muses.

mouse, any of many small, scampering rodents but often meant to apply to the house mouse (*Mus musculus*), family Muridae (order Rodentia). The term mouse, like the term rat, has no scientific definition; it is used simply to designate any of numerous ratlike, but small, rodents. Many species of the large family Cricetidae are called mice, as are members of the families Muridae (Old World mice and rats), Heteromyidae (pocket mice), and Zapodidae (jumping mice and birch mice). The marsupial mouse (*see* Dasyuridae) is a mouselike relative of the kangaroos.

Mice are common and are indigenous to almost every land area. They eat various foods, including grain, roots, fruit, grass, insects, and in some instances human foodstuffs. Many species seem to prefer dwelling in man-made structures and can become serious pests by destroying food, gnawing all types of materials, and, possibly, harbouring such disease-producing organisms as murine typhus and plague. Mice living in the wild may be so numerous as to become serious, although usually temporary, agricultural pests. Except in abnormal circumstances, however, mice are beneficial to man because they form the bulk of the diet of most furbearers and of predators that otherwise would take more valuable animals, including livestock. Serious household infestations of mice may require the services of trained exterminators, but minor infestations can be handled adequately and most safely by trapping.

The house mouse, the mouse most often en-

House mouse (*Mus musculus*)
Ingmar Holmasen

countered in buildings, has been distributed by man from Eurasia to all inhabited areas of the world. It usually seeks shelter and food in human dwellings. A brown or gray rodent, it grows up to 20 centimetres (8 inches) long, including a 10-centimetre (4-inch) tail. It consumes almost anything edible, even sampling soap, paste, and glue. It matures quickly, being ready to mate two to three months after birth. Litters consist of as many as 12 young; gestation takes about three weeks. In warm areas or heated buildings, breeding occurs throughout the year.

The common white laboratory mouse is a domesticated form of the house mouse, widely used in medical experiments and also commonly kept as a pet. Various other strains of house mice include: piebald mice; singing mice, which emit faint twitterings; and waltzing mice, which cannot move normally because of an inherited, defective sense of balance.
·aging and heredity relationships **1**:301c
·beekeeping pests and hive destruction **2**:794g
·biological development and evolution **5**:650c
·daily rhythm's dependence on light **14**:74e
·diseases of animals, tables 1, 2, 8, and 9 **5**:866
·embryonic gonads and germ cells **5**:638b; illus.
·growth factor experimentation **12**:1033a
·human pregnancy tests **14**:968h
·longevity comparison, table 1 **10**:913
·monocytic origins in bone marrow **2**:1119b
·oxygen consumption comparison, table 1 **15**:751
·pet ownership possibilities **14**:151b
·radiation effects in germplasm **15**:380d
·radiation-induced congenital defects **15**:385e
·reproductive hormone cycle type **2**:814a
·tissue culture illus. **18**:439
·tumour growth rate table **8**:442

RELATED ENTRIES in the *Ready Reference and Index:*
birch mouse; field mouse; grasshopper mouse; harvest mouse; jumping mouse; pocket mouse; Selevin's mouse; spiny mouse; white-footed mouse

mousebird: *see* coly.

mouse deer: *see* chevrotain.

mouse-eared bat: *see* brown bat.

mousehare: *see* pika.

Mouseion, originally a Greek temple dedicated to the Muses or a place where the arts were studied or practiced. Specifically it refers to the Mouseion (Museum) of Alexandria, Egypt. This centre of classical learning (especially noted for its scientific and literary scholarship) was built near the royal palace either by Ptolemy II Philadelphus *c.* 280 BC or by his father Ptolemy I Soter (ruled 323–285/283 BC). The best surviving description is by the Greek geographer and historian Strabo who mentions that it was a large complex of buildings and gardens with richly decorated lecture and banquet halls linked by porticos or colonnaded walks. Organized in faculties with a president-priest at the head, the salaries of the scholars on the staff were paid by the Egyptian king and later by the Roman emperor. In AD 270 the buildings of the Mouseion were probably destroyed by Zenobia, the queen of Palmyra, although the educational and research function of the institution seems to have continued until the 5th century AD.
·endowment and instruction type **6**:326c
·foundation and functions **15**:181h
·humanistic scholarship's beginnings **8**:1172d
·library founding, purpose, and staff **10**:857b
·Ptolemaic Hellenic cultural activity **6**:482d

mousetail, common name for about 15 species of small, annual, herbaceous (nonwoody) plants constituting the genus *Myosurus* of the buttercup family (Ranunculaceae). They occur in the Temperate Zones of both the Northern and Southern Hemispheres. Mousetails are so named for a long, slender column

Mousetail (*Myosurus*)
Ron Foord from the Natural History Photographic Agency—EB Inc.

covered with pistils (female seed-bearing organs) that arises from the centre of the flower.

mouse-tailed bat, any of the four species of the genus *Rhinopoma* (family Rhinopomatidae), found in northeast Africa and southwest Asia. Sometimes called rat-tailed bats, they have long tails and live in caves, rock crevices, or buildings, where they cling with all four feet. They prefer arid regions.
·classification and general features **4**:435a

Mousetrap, U.S. rocket-powered antisubmarine weapon.
·research and development program **15**:928f

Mousetrap, The (1952), play by Agatha Christie.
·performance run **18**:259b

Mouskos, Mikhail Khristodolou: *see* Makarios III.

Mousnier, Roland (1907–), French historian.
·view of 17th-century French uprisings **7**:633h

moustache, also spelled MUSTACHE, hair grown on the upper lip. The wearing of moustaches, like beards, has been since antiquity a reflection of such factors as climate (local or temporal), custom, religious belief, and personal taste. It was usual in the past to make no distinction between a moustache and other facial hair such as a beard or whiskers, as these were usually worn together. As early as *c.* 2650 BC, however, Egyptian artifacts show a pencil-line moustache with no beard.

Throughout history controversies have raged over the subject of facial hair. When clean-shaven faces were stylish, moustaches and beards were considered eccentric and often were forced by law to be shaved. The Romans considered the Gauls' wearing of moustaches with no beards to be the epitome of barbarism. In 1447 an English act was passed forcing men to shave their upper lip, but, some 400 years later, English soldiers were forbidden to shave their upper lip. The French military, the Prussian guard, and the Hussars sported the moustache in the early 19th century, but in 1838 the King of Bavaria forbade the wearing of mustaches in his military. Whenever moustaches have been sanctioned in fashionable circles, they have taken on a variety of forms. Regulations still govern facial hair, usually in the military, but moustaches are generally acceptable and determined by personal taste.

Mousterian tool industry, traditionally associated with Neanderthal man in Europe during the early Fourth (Würm) Glacial Period (*c.* 40,000 BC). The Mousterian tool assemblage is believed to have developed mainly from the Clactonian flake industry, but it also shows Acheulean and Levalloisian elements (*e.g.*, hand axes); it existed contemporarily with the Levalloisian industry. Tools included small hand axes made from disk-shaped cores; flake tools, such as well-made side-scrapers and triangular points, probably used as knives; denticulate (toothed) instruments produced by making notches in a flake, perhaps used as saws or shaft straighteners; and round limestone balls, believed to have served as bolas (weapon of a type used today in South America, consisting of three balls on the end of a thong, which is hurled at an animal, wraps itself around its legs, and trips it). Wooden spears were used to hunt large game such as mammoth and woolly rhinoceros. Mousterian "tool kits" often have quite different contents from site to site. Some investigators explain this by suggesting that different groups of Neanderthal men had varying toolmaking traditions; other workers believe the tool kits were used by the same peoples to perform different functions (*e.g.*, hunting, butchering, food preparation). Mousterian implements disappear abruptly from Europe with Neanderthal man; some evidence suggests, however, that the later Solutrean tool industry was in some respects influenced by the Mousterian.
·archaeological time scale **5**:501e; illus. 500
·Asian flake tool traditions **2**:204a
·Iranian civilization distinctions **9**:830b
·Neanderthal cultural manifestations **12**:912e
·Neanderthal fossil remains analysis **8**:1046c
·tools and toolmaking technique **8**:609a; illus. 608

Moustiers faience, French tin-glazed earthenware produced by factories in the town of

Moustiers faience plate decorated with a scene after an engraving by Antonio Tempesta, the Clérissy factory, *c.* 1700; in the Victoria and Albert Museum, London
By courtesy of the Victoria and Albert Museum, London; photograph, EB Inc.

Moustiers from about 1679 into the 19th century. The wares manufactured in the 17th and 18th centuries were so distinctive and of such high quality that they were extensively copied at other faience centres in France.

According to tradition, a monk, originally from Faenza, a major Italian centre for the production of maiolica, gave the secret of faience making to a local potter named Antoine Clérissy, who established the most important factory in Moustiers and founded a dynasty of *faïenciers* active until the late 18th century. Characteristic Clérissy faience, which is blue and white, falls into two periods: in the early period (1680–1710), decoration was inspired by the engravings of Antonio Tempesta (died 1630); in the later period (1710–40), by the engravings of Jean Berain (died 1711), whose designs greatly influenced French decorative art at the time. Wares in the Berain style, for which Moustiers is probably most famous, are delicate and fanciful; large dishes, for example, are decorated with a spidery net, made up of arabesques, architectural motifs, birds, vases of flowers, and the like, which serves as a frame for a classical scene.

Another important Moustiers factory was that of Joseph Olerys, founded in 1738 and active until *c.* 1793. Olerys introduced polychrome underglaze colours, producing faience in the Berain style painted in purple, soft green, and orange as well as blue. Other polychrome faience wares produced by this factory were decorated with such designs as chinoiseries (designs in the Chinese manner), military motifs, medallions, and a so-called potato flower motif.

Overglaze painted decoration was introduced in the late 18th century by yet another Moustiers factory.

Nineteenth-century Moustiers faience consisted of reproductions of earlier wares.

mouth, in zoology, the opening of the body of an animal through which food enters.
·animal tissue comparisons **18**:443h
·arthropod modification and evolution **2**:68c
·bivalve anatomical features **2**:1090e; illus. 1089
·fish anatomy comparison, illus. 3 **7**:334
human
·cranial nerve distribution **12**:1019a; illus. 1017
·digestion and mastication of food **5**:771h
·digestion disorder symptoms **5**:768a
·digestion disturbances due to oral lesions **5**:796h
·digestive system anatomy **5**:789d
·ectodermal and endodermal origins **6**:750a
·infectious local diseases **9**:543c
·respiratory function **15**:764g
·tooth structure and development **18**:55g; illus. 56
·lepidopteran evolutionary reductions **10**:824h; illus. 820
·phonetic study of speech production **14**:276a; illus. 275
·piercing-sucking mouth parts of Heteroptera and their taxonomic significance **8**:848f; illus.
·respiration in fish and amphibians **15**:756b; illus. 757
·rotifer digestive system **2**:141a; illus. 139
·vertebrate embryonic formation **5**:639c

mouth bow (musical instrument): *see* musical bow.

mouthbreeder, any fish that breeds its young in the mouth. Examples include certain catfishes, and cardinal fishes. The male of the sea catfish *Galeichthys felis* places up to 50 fertilized eggs in its mouth and retains them until they are hatched and the young are two or more weeks old. The cardinal fish *Apogon imberbis* incubates the eggs in the pharynx. Both the male and female *Symphysodon discus* take turns mouthing the eggs.
·chemoreception and offspring identification **4**:185d
·fertilization in behavioral extreme **12**:218h
·fertilization of eggs **2**:806e

mouth fungus, fish disease caused by bacteria that attack the fish's mouth and produce a fuzzy cotton-like growth, which hinders breathing and eats away the jaws. No remedy for this contagious fish disease has been found, although a suggested cure involves dousing the diseased fish with a hydrogen peroxide solution.
·common diseases of fish, table 7 **5**:875

mouth organ, free-reed wind instrument blown by the player. *See* sheng; harmonica.

mouth-to-mouth resuscitation, method of artificial respiration in which the rescuer uses his breath to inflate the patient's lungs.
·respiratory ventilation technique **15**:745e

mouton, processed sheepskin sheared and dyed to resemble beaver or seal, used especially for coats.
·origin and pelt characteristics **7**:814e; table

Mouton, Gabriel (1618–94), French mathematician who proposed a method of measurement similar to the metric system.
·metric system proposal **19**:730c

Mouton, Jean (b. *c.* 1459, Haut-Wignes, Fr.—d. Oct. 30, 1522, Saint-Quentin), composer in the Franco-Flemish style of the early 16th century known for his sacred music. He was a chorister in Nesle (1477–83) and worked in Amiens and Grenoble from 1500 to 1502 before joining the French royal chapel under Louis XII and Francis I. He apparently studied with Josquin des Prez, and he taught Adriaan Willaert. His music leads away from the older style, which falls into clear sections, and emphasizes continuous flow of vocal lines from beginning to end, with pervasive melodic imitation. He was a master of the technique of canon. His output is largely masses and motets, published during his life by printers such as Petrucci and Attaignant.

Mouvement Démocratique de la Rénovation Malgache (MDRM), Madagascar nationalist movement organized in the 1940s.
·Madagascar nationalist movements **11**:278g

Mouvement d'Evolution Sociale en Afrique Noire (MESAN), Central Africa political party organized by Barthélemy Boganda in the 1950s.
·CAR independence role **3**:1100d

Mouvement National Congolais, Congolese nationalist party organized by Patrice Lumumba in the 1950s.
·extent and influence **3**:1098c

Mouvement Populaire de la Révolution (MPR), political organization of Zaire, led by Pres. Mobutu Sese Seko.
·Zairian political institute **19**:1125c

Mouvement pour le Triomphe des Libertés Démocratiques (MTLD), English MOVEMENT FOR THE TRIUMPH OF DEMOCRATIC LIBERTIES, chief Algerian nationalist organization prior to the outbreak of the Algerian revolt against French rule (Nov. 1, 1954). It was originally founded in 1937 as the Parti Populaire Algérien (PPA; Algerian People's Party) by Messali Hadj, who reorganized it under its later name in 1946. In the elections of 1947 the MTLD won a third of the seats in Algeria's city councils but was subsequently less successful as French control of the electoral machinery tightened. Its program of street demonstrations, attacks on the French parliamentary system, and sporadic acts of terrorism led to periodic arrests of MTLD members; rioting followed in the wake of Messali's public addresses; and in May 1952, after organizing the Front of North African Unity and Action, a coalition of Moroccan, Algerian, and Tunisian nationalist leaders, Messali Hadj was deported to France. In his absence the movement split into three factions: the Messalists, who favoured the increasingly autocratic leadership of Messali; the Centralists; and the CRUA (Comité Révolutionnaire d'Unité et d'Action), a group of young militants. In the early days of the revolution the Centralists and CRUA reappeared in the Front de Libération Nationale (FLN), which then assumed the leadership of the independence struggle, while Messali's organization continued to exist for a time as the Mouvement National Algérien.
·Algerian nationalism growth **13**:164g

Mouvement Républicain Populaire (MRP), called in English POPULAR REPUBLICAN MOVEMENT, French social reform party whose policies correspond largely to the European Christian Democratic tradition.

Founded on Nov. 26, 1944, just after the German occupation of France during World War II, the MRP consistently won some 25 percent of the vote in the elections of the remainder of the 1940s, and it served as a bulwark of the early governments of the Fourth Republic. As a centre party, however, the MRP lost votes to both the right and the left as political opinions began to polarize during the East–West Cold War; in the 1951 elections it won only 12.6 percent of the votes cast and never regained its former popularity.

In October 1965 the MRP joined other right-centre parties to support the presidential candidacy of Jean Lecanuet, who came in a poor third to Gen. Charles de Gaulle and the candidate of the left, François Mitterrand. Lecanuet attempted to solidify the parties that supported him, including the MRP, into a centre party, the Centre Démocrate, founded in February 1966. Legislative elections in 1967 and 1968, however, brought fresh defeats for the centre, which failed to win more than 13 percent of the vote in either election. By the end of 1967 the MRP had become little more than a political club.
·Christian Democratic Party constitution proposals **7**:677c
·presidential elections of 1965 and 1969 **7**:605h

Mouvement Socialist Africain (MSA), Congolese socialistic political party organized in the 1950s.
·independence parties' comparison **3**:1100f

Mou-yü, 8th-century Uighur leader, reigned 759–80.
·Manichaeism conversion repercussions **9**:598e

movable bridge, either a drawbridge, a vertical-lift bridge, or a swing (pivot) bridge. The drawbridge, or bascule, is the best known. It originated in medieval Europe, probably Normandy, as a defensive feature of castles and towns. It was operated by a counterweight and winch. The drawbridge that formed one span of Old London Bridge was occasionally raised to permit passage of a boat having masts too tall to pass under and a hull narrow enough to go between the piers at this point. In the late 19th century drawbridges began to be built specifically for navigation; the Tower Bridge, London, and the Van Buren Street Bridge, Chicago, were built almost simultaneously. Both were double-leaf bascules, and their success led to wide imitation; more than 20 were built to span the Chicago River alone, including several double-decked. Bascules may be single as well as double leaf.

Single-leaf bascule (drawbridge)
De Cou—Ewing Galloway

At the same time, another movable bridge was pioneered in Chicago: the vertical lift, designed by J.A.L. Waddell. For several years it was unimitated; later, when its great strength for railroad loading was appreciated, it was repeated widely, in increasing span lengths, many exceeding 500 feet (152 metres). The vertical lift also relies on counterweights; the entire bridge roadway is elevated by counterweights and machinery in two towers.

For exceptionally long spans, the pivot, or swing bridge, which turns on a table, is suitable. Several of over 500 feet (152 metres) have been built in the U.S., but the turntable obstructs the river, limiting its use.
·bridge construction history **3**:180h; illus. 181
·siege tactics in weaponry history **19**:682c
·spans of longest bridges, table 1 **3**:181

movables and immovables, in later Roman and modern civil-law systems, the basic division of things subject to ownership. In general, the distinction rests on ordinary conceptions of physical mobility: immovables would be such things as land or buildings, which are thought to be stationary in space; movables would be such things as cattle or personal belongings, which can either move themselves or be moved in space. The definition is by no means rigid, however; the law may be so written as to place a specified thing in one category or the other for the sake of legal convenience or utility, even though the thing may seem illogically categorized in the layman's mind. Thus, in French law, standing crops are movables; farm implements and animals are immovables (largely because they are thought to serve the land and be components of it). In German law, the distinction is somewhat clearer: immovables are tracts of land and their component parts; movables are everything else.
·property classifications **15**:51a
·Roman property law and possession means **15**:1057f

movement, in music, one of a number of separate compositions in the same or related keys and self-sufficient or nearly so, comprising a larger work such as a symphony, sonata, or suite.
·tonality as unifying device **12**:727c

Movere, Panamanian dialect of the Guaymi language.
·Panama dialect usage **13**:942e

Movete al mio bel suon, translated YOU MOVE TO MY BEAUTIFUL SOUND (1638), ballet by Monteverdi.
·text painting of composition **4**:446a

Movietone, sound-on-film process developed in the 1920s that recorded static performances of talking and singing.
·cinema sound era origins **12**:527a

Movimento Democrático Brasileiro (MDB), official opposition political party created by Brazil's military government in 1965.
·foundation and support **3**:150b

Movimento Popular de Libertação de Angola (MPLA), Marxist-oriented Angolan political movement organized in the early 1950s.
·organization, suppression, and revival **17**:298c

Movimento Sociale Italiano (MSI), called in English ITALIAN SOCIAL MOVEMENT, neo-Fascist party appealing to anti-Communist and nationalist sentiments; its presence on the extreme right of Italian political life harassed Italian moderates after 1949.

The MSI was formed in 1948 from elements of the defunct Uomo Qualunque (Average Man) Party that had appeared in 1945. In the early 1950s MSI's electoral success worried moderates until they saw that the right-wing party was not gaining a substantial number of votes. The moderates' occasional need for MSI votes, however, proved embarrassing; in 1960, when the MSI formed a necessary part of a parliamentary majority, protest riots led to the fall of the Christian Democratic government. In some 1971 local elections, MSI won 13.9 percent of the popular vote.
·affiliation and appeal **9**:1108d

Movimiento de Acción Popular Unitario (Chilean political group): *see* Popular Unity.

Movimiento Nacionalista Revolucionario (MNR), middle-class Bolivian political party formed in the late 1930s. The MNR, now one of many Bolivian political parties, governed the country from 1952 to 1964, largely under the leadership of Víctor Paz Estenssoro.
·party program and support **3**:8d
·popular support and social reforms **3**:12b

moving-average map, cartographic representation of data in a "smoothed" form; the map is produced by arbitrarily averaging a fixed number of data points or contour lines to produce a series of "new" data points or lines that are averages of the original sets. The moving-average map is a useful device in any study that has as its goal determination of regional trends, because the averaging procedure tends to reduce the largest high and low values that serve to obscure regional trends.

moving sidewalk: *see* escalator.

moving-target-indicator, method whereby a target moving radially can be traced by radar using the Doppler shift phenomenon to trace its motion.
·radar and Doppler shift **15**:372c

Movius's Line, geographic transitional zone in India between two middle Pleistocene stone-tool traditions. The bifacial hand-ax and cleaver-tool tradition is found west of Movius's Line and the chopper-chopping-tool tradition is found east of it.
·Asian stone tool tradition distinctions **2**:203g
·Pleistocene stone tool cultures **14**:840b; illus.

Movses Khorenatzi: *see* Moses of Khoren.

Mowat, Sir Oliver (1820–1903), Canadian jurist and statesman.
·Ontario area increase **13**:573h

Mowatt, Anna Cora, *née* OGDEN (b. March 5, 1819, Bordeaux, Fr.—d. July 21, 1870, London), U.S. playwright and actress, author of the satirical play *Fashion.* A precocious child, she acted at the age of five and had read all of Shakespeare's plays before she was ten.

Anna Cora Mowatt, engraving from a daguerreotype
By courtesy of the Library of Congress, Washington, D.C.

Her marriage at 15 to James Mowatt, a New York lawyer, gave her ample opportunity to continue dabbling in the arts. In 1841, after her husband lost his wealth, she turned to performing and writing in earnest, giving poetry readings and writing articles for the popular magazines. In 1845 she wrote *Fashion,* the play with which she has since been associated. A devastating social satire, *Fashion* expressed the growing feeling in the United States against emulation of European manners. In June 1845 Mrs. Mowatt made a successful debut as an actress and entered another phase of her many-sided career. In addition to *Fashion,* she wrote the plays *Gulzara* (1841) and *Armand* (1847) and, in 1854, her *Autobiography of an Actress.* James Mowatt having died in 1851, she married William F. Ritchie in 1854 and retired from the stage.

Mowbray, the name (derived from Montbray near Saint-Lô in Normandy) of a medieval English baronial family that achieved eminence in the late 14th century when Thomas Mowbray (died 1399), a favourite of King Richard II, was made duke of Norfolk (his father having married the hieress of the last earl of Norfolk). The line became extinct in 1476.

Mowbray, George (1814–91), U.S. chemist and industrialist.
·nitroglycerin production and handling **7**:85a

Mowbray, Thomas, 1st duke of Norfolk: *see* Norfolk, Thomas Mowbray, 1st duke of.

mower: *see* haymaking and forage machinery.

Mowinckel, Sigmund (Olaf Plytt) (b. Aug. 4, 1884, Kjerringy, Nor.—d. June 4, 1965, Oslo), a biblical scholar especially noted for his analysis and interpretation of the Old Testament book of Psalms. Influenced by German linguistic research in the worship of ancient Israel, he wrote *Psalmenstudien,* 6 vol. (1921–24; "Studies in the Psalms," later popularized as *The Psalms in Israel's Worship,* 1962), one of the 20th-century's major works of biblical commentary. Depicting the psalms in their concrete cultural milieu, he emphasized the cultic nature of their origin and development. More specifically, he claimed, despite some criticism, to have discovered a class of "enthronement psalms" that originated in a particular festival Israel celebrated to their god Yahweh. Among his other important writings are *Prophecy and Tradition* (1946), a study of Israel's prophets, and *He That Cometh* (1956), a significant contribution to the Judeo-Christian concept of eschatology (a religious belief in an evolving, climactic plan of salvation).
·biblical multi-source theory **1**:3b
·cultic origination of psalms **2**:924e

Mowlanā Nūr od-Dīn ʿAbd or-Raḥmān ebn Aḥmad: *see* Jāmī.

moxa treatment, or MOXIBUSTION, traditional medical practice that originated in China and thence spread to Japan and other Asian countries. It is performed by burning small cones of dried leaves on certain designated points of the body, generally the same points as those used in acupuncture.

The term derives from the name of the wormwood plant most frequently used, *Artemisia moxa* or (Jap.) *A. mogusa.* Acupuncture and moxibustion are sometimes used in combination for the treatment of disease and for anesthesia purposes.

As early as the Stone Age, the Chinese learned that burning or heating certain points on the body increased circulation "full-bloodedness" and relieved pain. It is assumed, however, that acupuncture with stone needles is older than moxibustion. Generally, points near large blood vessels, eyes, and ears are treated by moxa, as puncture is inadvisable.

This process was developed in northern China and probably was first used to relieve the pains of rheumatism. In ancient times the points on the skin were actually blistered by burning, but now the areas to be stimulated are warmed. Hot rods were replaced by rolled leaves of the mugwort, mulberry, ginger, and aconite plants.

In modern practice the herb is usually crushed, wrapped in special paper, and when lit is held above the point to be warmed or placed on the skin and removed before overheating occurs. The Japanese developed small tubes, fitted with handles, in which the powdered plant is burned away and heating is controlled by the therapist. A moxa stick burns for four or five minutes; it is used to relieve pain, congestion, and to provide an anesthetic effect. Toning skin is accomplished by lightly tapping the surface with a glowing stick. Pieces of heated ginger are used to treat stomachache, vomiting and diarrhea, and rheumatic pain; garlic is applied in respiratory disorders; and salt is used to stimulate hypofunction of abdominal organs. Chinese practitioners emphasize the importance of correct body positioning for best results.

Attempts have been made to correlate acupuncture–moxa skin area counterirritant treatment with accepted Western treatment for specific ailments. Although stimulation of points on the body by moxa is believed to affect the autonomic nervous system, no physiological basis for moxibustion is known.
·Chinese therapeutic technique **11**:825g

Moxeke, archaeological site or Coast Chavín culture in Casma Valley, Peru.
·Chavín pyramid architecture **1**:842h

Moxico, eastern district of the Portuguese West African overseas province of Angola, occupies an area of 77,137 sq mi (199,786 sq km). The capital is Luso. The district is served by the Benguela Railway, which runs from the coast completely across Moxico and into the copper-producing region of Shaba (formerly Katanga) in Zaire. Forestry is important, and there is local copper extraction. Rudimentary crude rubber, wax, and honey are produced, and the Dilôlo *concelho* (municipality) is rich in fish and game. Pop. (1970 prelim.) 213,119.
·area and population table **1**:892

Moyamba, town, Southern Province, southwestern Sierra Leone, on the government railway. It is the nation's major collecting centre for ginger (a cash crop exported from Freetown, 59 mi [95 km] west-northwest) and a local trade centre in rice, kola nuts, and palm oil and kernels among the Mende people. Several mission secondary schools (Methodist and Catholic) and a government hospital are located in the town, which is the administrative headquarters of the Moyamba District. Latest census 4,564.
8°10′ N, 12°26′ W
·map, Sierra Leone **16**:734

Moyano, Sebástian: *see* Belalcázar, Sebastián de.

Moyen Atlas, or MIDDLE ATLAS, mountain range in central Morocco, Africa, lies between a plateau and plain region (northwest) and the main part of the Atlas Mountains (southeast). Many peaks exceed 8,000 ft (2,000 m), with the highest being Adrar Bou Nasser (Djebel Bou Naceur; 10,958 ft [3,340 m]). Covered by cedar forests, the mountains form a fishing, hunting, and skiing area.
33°30′ N, 5°00′ W
·High Atlas relationship **12**:445b
·map, Morocco **12**:446

Moyen-Chari, prefecture, Chad, Africa.
·population growth 1963–70 table **4**:15

Moyen-Congo (French: Middle Congo), one of the four territories comprising French Equatorial Africa, the origins of which derive from the establishment before 1880 by the explorer Pierre Savorgnan de Brazza of a station at Ntamo. From 1912 to 1919 its area was reduced by the cession to Germany of a strip of land on its northwestern periphery. From 1934 it was directly administered by the governor general of French Equatorial Africa. It was granted independent status as the Congo Republic in 1960 and was subsequently renamed the People's Republic of the Congo, abbreviated Congo (Brazzaville).

Moyen-Ogooué, administrative *région,* Gabon, western Africa. Lambaréné is the capital.
·area and population table **7**:819
·map, Gabon **7**:820

Moyne Commission, appointed in 1938 by the British Parliament to investigate conditions in the British West Indies.
·West Indies riot investigation results **2**:718d

Moyobamba, capital of San Martín department and Moyobamba province, north central Peru. The city sits on a bluff overlooking the Río Mayo, at 2,820 ft (860 m) above sea level, in the humid, tropical region known as the selva.

The second oldest Spanish town east of the Andes, Moyobamba (from the Quechua Indian *mayupampa,* "a circular plain") was founded on the site of an Inca settlement and was named Santiago de los Valles de Moyobamba (Saint James of the Moyobamba Valleys). An important commercial centre during the colonial era (1533–1821), it was given city status in 1857. It is now the centre of a large agricultural region, producing cotton, sugarcane, tobacco, cocoa, and rice. Alcohol, liquor, wines, and straw hats are produced in the city. Hot springs, gold, and some petroleum are found nearby.

Moyobamba's isolation was being alleviated in the mid-1970s with the construction of the Marginal Highway, which will link settlements in the Amazon Basin and on the eastern Andean slopes. The city possesses an airport. Pop. (1972 prelim.) 10,004.
6°02′ S, 76°58′ W
·map, Peru **14**:129

Mozabites (people): *see* Mzab.

Moẓaffar ʿAlī (fl. 16th century, Iran), notable Persian artist who painted during the great flowering of Persian art in the 16th century.

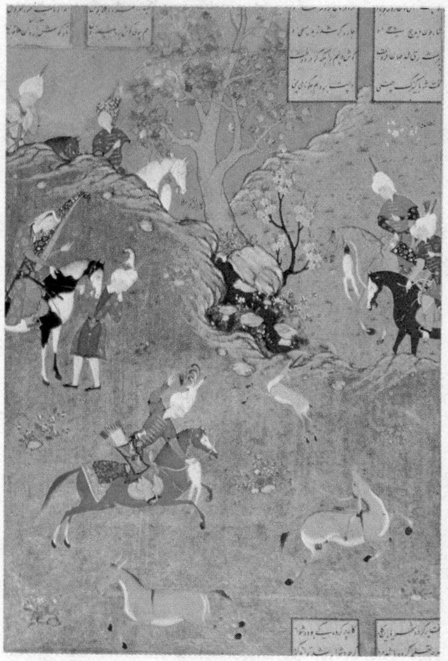

Bahrām Gūr hunting, miniature by Moẓaffar ʿAlī in the *Khamseh* of Neẓāmī done for Shah Ṭahmāsp I, 1539–43; in the British Museum (OR MS. 2265 fol 211r)

By courtesy of the trustees of the British Museum

Very little is known about his life except that he was a pupil of Behzād, the greatest of the Persian painters, and that he died shortly after the year 1576. He was particularly noted as a portrait painter. Moẓaffar ʿAlī worked together with the other important painters of the day on a series of 17 illustrations for a manuscript of the works of the Persian poet Neẓāmī produced in the years 1539 to 1543 at the direction of the Ṣafavid Shah Ṭahmāsp I. The illustrations are of high excellence.

In addition to painting miniatures, Moẓaffar ʿAlī designed and for the most part executed a series of decorative paintings for the walls of the royal palaces and the Chehel Sotūn (Hall of 40 Columns) in Isfahan.

Moẓaffarids, an Iranian dynasty that ruled over southern Iran *c.* 1314–93. The founder of the dynasty was Sharaf od-Dīn Moẓaffar, a vassal of the Il-Khanid rulers of Iran, who was governor of Meybod, a city lying between Isfahan and Yazd. In 1314 his son Mobārez od-Dīn Moḥammad was made governor of Fārs and Yazd by Abū Saʿīd, the Il-Khanid ruler. After Abū Saʿīd's death, Moḥammad expanded his possessions. In 1340 he married the only daughter of Shāh Jahān, the last ruler of the Qutlugh dynasty in Kermān, thus gaining possession of that region. By 1356, after a series of campaigns, Moḥammad had become the undisputed ruler of southern Iran. In 1356 he attacked and captured Tabrīz, but he was unable to hold it. In 1358 he was deposed by his two sons, Qoṭb od-Dīn Shāh Maḥmūd (ruled 1358–75) and Jalāl od-Dīn Shāh Shojāʿ (ruled 1358–84), who divided the Moẓaffarid territories between them.

Shortly before his death in 1384, Shāh Shojāʿ divided his possessions among his three sons. The Moẓaffarid power was thus fragmented, and Shāh Shojāʿ's sons were forced to become vassals of Timur, who in 1393 extinguished the dynasty by defeating and killing its last ruler, Manṣūr (ruled 1384–93).

Moẓaffar od-Dīn Shāh (b. 1852, Tehrān—d. Jan. 9, 1907, Tehrān), Persian ruler of the Qājār dynasty whose incompetence precipitated a constitutional revolution in 1906.

The son of the Qājār ruler Naṣer od-Dīn Shāh, Moẓaffar od-Dīn was named crown prince and sent as governor to the northern province of Azerbaijan in 1861. He spent his 35 years as crown prince in the pursuit of pleasure; his relations with his father were often strained, and he was not consulted in important matters of state. Thus, when he ascended the throne in May 1896, he was unprepared for the burdens of office. Ill health, an indecisive nature, and coarseness of taste also failed to recommend him for ruling. At Moẓaffar's accession Iran faced a growing financial crisis, with annual governmental expenditures far exceeding revenues. He had to make up this deficit by contracting unpopular loans from Russia, which exacted political concessions in return.

Increased influence of Russia and Moẓaffar's squandering of the loans on extravagant European trips in 1900, 1902, and 1905 raised strong domestic opposition. The Shāh's capricious rule, his court's corruption, and his inability to come to grips with Iran's financial crisis brought demands for constitutional limits to his rule. Widespread popular disturbances in 1906 forced him to convene a Majles (National Consultative Assembly) that October and to grant two months later, in December, a constitution modelled on that of Belgium. The political crisis may have precipitated the heart attack from which he died.
·economic aspects of political shift **9**:860g

Mozambique 12:592, formal name PEOPLE'S REPUBLIC OF MOZAMBIQUE, formerly PORTUGUESE EAST AFRICA, from June 25, 1975, an independent country of Africa, was prior to independence an overseas dependency of Portugal. Located on the southeast coast of Africa, it is bounded by Tanzania (north), by Malawi, Zambia, Rhodesia, and the Transvaal province of South Africa (west), and by Natal province of South Africa and Swaziland (south).

The text article covers its landscape, climate, vegetation and animal life, traditional regions, human settlement, people and population, demography, national economy, resources, sources of national income, management of the economy, transportation, administration, social services, living conditions, and cultural life and institutions. (For statistical details, *see* p. 74.) *See also* southern Africa, history of.

REFERENCES in other text articles:
·African political divisions map **1**:208
·African states population table **1**:209
·Christian denominational demography map **4**:459
·Congo ethnic groups and sociality **4**:1118g
·East African peoples' socio-economic patterns **6**:109e
·lake geography and industry **6**:116c; map 119
·newspaper publishing statistics table **15**:237
·railway systems data table **15**:482
·South Africa electric power purchase **17**:68e
·spice import, export, and value, table 3 **17**:506
·visual art of Lunda-Luba zone **1**:269h
·world coal production and reserves, table 5 **4**:781
·Zambezi River hydroelectric projects **19**:1128d; map

Mozambique Channel, Portuguese CANAL DE MOÇAMBIQUE, passage of the western Indian Ocean, threading between the island nation of the Malagasy Republic on the east and Mozambique on the African mainland (west). About 1,000 mi (1,600 km) long, it varies in width from 250 to 600 mi and reaches a maximum depth of 10,000 ft (3,000 m). The Comoro Archipelago marks the northern entrance, and the islands of Bassas da India and Europa lie in the south. An important route for shipping in East Africa, it receives all major Malagasy rivers and has the ports of Majunga and Tuléar on the same coast. Along the opposite coast are the mouth of the Zambezi River and the ports of Maputo (formerly Lourenço Marques), Moçambique, and Beira. The Mozambique Current passes through the strait.
19°00′ S, 41°00′ E
·map, Mozambique **12**:594

Mozambique Convention, agreement concerning relations between South Africa and the then Portuguese colony of Mozambique. The initial convention, concluded between Portugal and the Transvaal republic in 1875, provided for commercial relations between the parties and the building of a railroad between Lourenço Marques in Mozambique and the Transvaal. After the annexation of the Transvaal by Great Britain in 1877, the convention was recognized by Britain and Portugal in 1882 and reaffirmed in 1901. A new convention, in 1909, between Portugal and the governor of the Transvaal, included provisions for the recruitment of labourers in Mozambique for work in the Transvaal mines. These provisions were revised in a convention of 1928 between Portugal and the Union of South Africa. Further revisions were made later, notably in 1934 and 1964.

Mozambique Current, relatively warm drift of the western Indian Ocean. The southeast trade winds move the Indian South Equatorial Current toward the east coast of Africa, off which, because of the Earth's rotation, it is directed south to follow the outline of the mainland and its continental shelf. While some of this flow passes east of the island of Madagascar, the rest funnels to the west through the Mozambique Channel, bringing with it strong influences on the climate of the island and mainland. South of Madagascar both streams feed into the Agulhas Current.

Mozambique Fracture Zone, submarine feature, Indian Ocean, off the coast of South Africa.
39°00′ S, 34°00′ E
·South Polar sea floor features map **1**:957

Mozarab, general term applied to those Spanish Christians living under Muslim rule (8th–11th century), who, while unconverted to Islām, adopted Arabic language and culture. Separate Mozarab enclaves were located in the large Muslim cities, especially Toledo, Córdoba, and Seville, where they formed prosperous communities ruled by their own officials and were subject to a Visigothic legal code. They also maintained their own bishoprics, churches, and monasteries and translated the Bible into Arabic. The Mozarabs eventually relocated in the north of the Iberian Peninsula, bringing with them the architectural style of Islāmic Córdoba, characterized by the horseshoe arch and the ribbed dome (*see also* Mozarabic art).

The word Mozarab was a Spanish corruption (Mozárabe) of the Arabic *mustaʿrib*, meaning "arabicized," a term used by early Arab genealogists to identify tribes that were not Arab by birth.
·Alfonso I's liberation and resettlement **17**:408g
·Christianity in Muslim Spain **3**:629e

Mozarabic art, artistic tradition of the Mozarabs, Christians who lived in the Iberian Peninsula after the Arab invasion of 711. The conquered Christians were tolerated, although called *mustaʿrib* ("arabicized," from which "Mozarab" is derived), and maintained their traditional religion. Exposure to Islāmic culture and art forms proved to be very influential, however, and their art became a synthesis of the two traditions. The subject matter is Christian, but the style shows the assimilation of Islāmic decorative motifs and forms. Even those who emigrated to reconquered territory or to other countries continued to produce art and architecture in the Mozarabic style, and it was in part the result of these movements that Arabic influences spread northward into Europe.

The Mozarabic style is identifiable only in religious art; in the minor arts, especially textiles, ceramic tiles, and pottery, the style is so close to contemporary Islāmic work that only by the Christian subject matter is it known that the artists were not Arabs. Among the most characteristic Mozarabic productions was a series of manuscripts called the Beatus Apocalypses, brightly illustrated copies of commentaries on the Book of Revelation by the monk Beatus of Liébana.

"St. Luke," illuminated page from the Beatus Apocalypse, Mozarabic, 975; in the Gerona cathedral

Archivo Mas, Barcelona

Mozarabic architecture also shows the influence of Islāmic style, especially in its use of the horseshoe-shaped arch and the ribbed dome. Restrictions on building and restoring their shrines inhibited the Mozarabs still living under Muslim rule, but a large number of churches built in the Mozarabic style by monks who emigrated to the non-Islāmic territories of northern Spain survive from the late 9th to early 11th century. San Miguel de Escalada, near León, for example, the largest surviving example of Mozarabic architecture, was founded by monks from Córdoba and consecrated in 913.

·examples of Muslim influence 9:1001d

Mozarabic chant, music of the Latin liturgy of the Roman Catholic Church in Spain. By the 5th century, Spain had its own religious and liturgical traditions, which reached a full flowering under the Visigoths in the 6th and 7th centuries. The term Mozarab, for Christians under Muslim rule, came into use after the Iberian Peninsula was invaded by the Moors (711) and eventually came to designate the Spanish liturgy before, during, and after the Moorish domination, which ended in 1085.

The earliest extant manuscripts of Mozarabic chant (8th–11th century) preserve the musical notation and texts of the entire church year. The notation consists of neumes, or signs showing one or more notes; but it lacks a musical staff, which alone could give the exact pitches of the notes.

In the 11th century Pope Gregory VII, desiring to unify liturgical practice, suppressed the Mozarabic rite in favour of the Roman. Only six parishes in Toledo and some monasteries were allowed to continue using it. In the early 16th century, Cardinal Francisco Jiménez de Cisneros tried to revive the Mozarabic chant, but by this time the key to the transcription of the neumes had been lost.

The Mozarabic liturgy contains one element found in no other liturgy of equal antiquity. This is a Clamor ("Shout") in the mass, added on feast days to the Psallendum, a chant that follows the scriptural readings, in order to elicit religious fervour. Musically, Mozarabic chant contains not only influences of Eastern Church chant—such as the long melismata of the Alleluia (prolongations of one syllable over many notes)—but it also has affinities to the Gallican (Frankish) and Ambrosian (Milanese) rites and chants.

·Gregory VII's attempt to discourage use 8:417h

MOZAMBIQUE

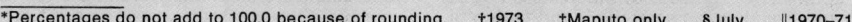

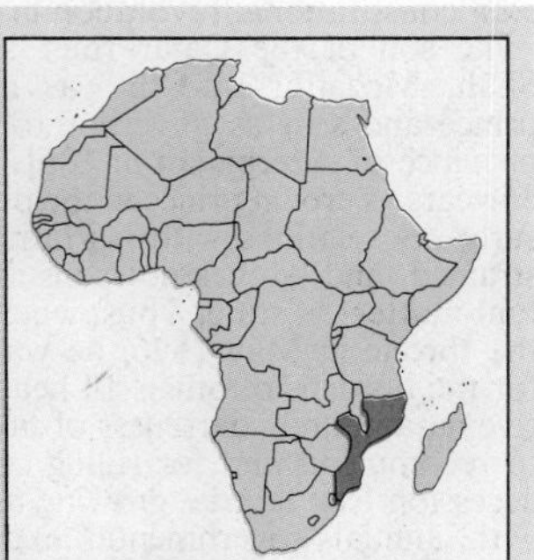

Official name: República Popular de Moçambique (People's Republic of Mozambique).
Location: eastern Africa.
Form of government: republic.
Official language: Portuguese.
Official religion: none.
Area: 308,642 sq mi, 799,380 sq km.
Population: (1975 estimate) 9,239,000.
Capital: Maputo.
Monetary unit: 1 escudo = 100 centavos.

Demography

Population: (1975 estimate) density 30.8 per sq mi, 11.9 per sq km; urban 6.3%, rural 93.7%; male 48.40%, female 51.60%; (1970) under 15 43.4%, 15–29 24.4%, 30–44 19.1%, 45–59 9.1%, 60–74 3.8%, 75 and over 0.3%.*
Vital statistics: (1970–75) births per 1,000 population 43.1, deaths per 1,000 population 20.1, natural increase per 1,000 population 23.0; life expectancy at birth—male 41.9, female 45.1; (1974) major causes of death (number of events)—senility without mention of psychosis, ill-defined and unknown causes 3,774; pneumonia 1,080; gastritis, duodenitis, enteritis, and colitis, except diarrhea of the newborn 1,012; malaria 973; tuberculosis of respiratory system 830; malignant neoplasms 691. *Ethnic composition* (1970): African 97.1%, white 2.0%, mixed 0.6%, Indian 0.3%. *Religious affiliation* (1970): traditional beliefs or no religion 49.6%, Roman Catholic 22.3%, Muslim 13.6%, Protestant 4.5%, Buddhist 0.1%, other 9.8%.*

National accounts

Budget (1974). Revenue: 14,359,855,000 escudos (consigned receipts 42.2%, extraordinary revenue 16.1%, direct taxes 15.5%, indirect taxes 12.7%, special taxes on industries 5.8%). Expenditures: 6,442,597,000 escudos (ordinary expenditure 77.1%, of which, fiscal and general administration 27.7%, defense 12.9%; extraordinary expenditure 22.9%). *Total national debt* (1972): 5,796,882,000 escudos.

Domestic economy

Gross national product (GNP; at current market prices, 1974): U.S. $3,590,000,000 (U.S. $420 per capita).

Origin of gross domestic product (at constant prices of 1970):	1960				1970			
	value in 000,000 U.S. $	% of total value	labour force	% of labour force	value in 000,000 U.S. $	% of total value	labour force	% of labour force
agriculture	591.6	54.8	2,984,630	71.4	731.2	43.4	2,134,972	73.4
mining, quarrying	4.0	0.4	161,516	3.9	6.9	0.4	123,772	4.3
manufacturing, electricity	88.7	8.2	124,811	3.0	221.0	13.1	158,524	5.5
construction	4.6	0.4	70,403	1.7	26.8	1.6	81,469	2.8
services, other	390.0	36.1	841,200	20.1	697.3	41.4	407,180	14.0
total	1,078.9	100.0*	4,182,560	100.0*	1,683.2	100.0*	2,905,917	100.0

Production (metric tons except as noted, 1974): Agriculture, forestry, hunting, fishing: sugarcane 3,100,000, corn (maize) 550,000, cassava 2,160,000, cashew nuts 204,000, peanuts (groundnuts) 160,000, copra 63,000, coconuts 416,000, bananas 68,000, sorghum 215,000, sweet potatoes 38,000, potatoes 18,000, tea 18,795; livestock (number of live animals): cattle 2,250,000, goats 910,000, pigs 280,000, sheep 250,000; roundwood 9,075,000 cu m†; fish catch 9,012,000. Mining, quarrying: limestone 682,000, copper concentrates 2,500, bauxite 2,405. Manufacturing: crude oil refining 485,068; cement 465,094; coal 425,841; sugar 265,546; fuel oil 241,299; diesel oil 126,882; wood 111,595 cu m; gasoline 70,721; wheat flour 81,568; beer 808,170 hectolitres. Construction: residential 21,000 sq m, nonresidential 12,000 sq m. *Energy:* (1971) installed electrical capacity 365,000 kW; (1974) production 586,776,000 kWhr (65 kWhr per capita).

Price and earnings indexes (1970 = 100):	1971	1972	1973	1974	1975
consumer price index‡	115.7	123.9	130.6	159.0	166.4§

Land use (1970): total area 78,303,000 ha (meadows and pastures 56.2%; forested 24.8%; agricultural and under permanent cultivation 3.8%; built-on, wasteland, and other 15.2%).

Foreign trade

Imports (1973): 11,415,260,000 escudos (machines and electrical equipment 27.3%, transport equipment 13.4%, base metals and products 12.1%, textiles 9.4%, crude oil 4.1%, wheat 2.9%, paper products 2.7%). *Major import sources:* South Africa 20.3%, Portugal 19.2%, West Germany 13.5%, France 8.4%, United Kingdom 7.6%, Japan 5.1%, United States 4.9%, Iraq 4.1%, Italy 2.7%, Switzerland 2.4%, Angola 2.0%.
Exports (1973): 5,540,628,000 escudos (textiles 25.4%, cashew nuts 22.1%, raw cotton 20.1%, sugar 10.0%, vegetable oils 5.1%, wood 5.0%, tea 4.2%). *Major export destinations:* Portugal 35.6%, United States 13.6%, South Africa 9.3%, United Kingdom 5.7%, Angola 3.5%, West Germany 3.1%, The Netherlands 2.7%, Italy 2.4%, Spain 2.1%, Japan 2.0%, France 1.9%, Belgium-Luxembourg 1.2%.

Transport and communications

Transport. Railroads: (1974) length 2,550 mi, 4,104 km; (1973) passenger-mi 246,100,000, passenger-km 396,000,000; short ton-mi cargo 2,326,100,000, metric ton-km cargo 3,396,000,000. Roads (1974): total length 24,340 mi, 39,173 km (primary 7,397 mi, 11,905 km; secondary 9,143 mi, 14,715 km; other 7,800 mi, 12,553 km). Vehicles (1975): passenger cars 95,795, trucks and buses 19,616. Air transport: (1974) cargo handled 9,157 short tons, 8,307 metric tons; (1976) airports with scheduled flights 7.
Communications. Daily newspapers (1973): total number 5, total circulation 42,000, circulation per 1,000 population 5. Radios (1973): total number of receivers 176,000 (1 per 50 persons). Television (1974): total number of receivers 1,000 (1 per 9,030 persons). Telephones (1975): 55,708 (1 per 166 persons).

Education and health

Education (1971–72):	schools	teachers	students	student/teacher ratio
primary (age 6–11)	4,088‖	10,800	605,000	56.0
secondary (age 10–15)	91‖	2,000	17,831‖	. . .
vocational	25‖	292	2,754	9.4
higher	9‖	200	2,300	11.5

College graduates (per 100,000 population, 1968): 0.7. *Literacy* (early 1970s): about 10% literate.
Health: (1971) doctors 510 (1 per 16,392 persons); (1967) hospital beds 13,102 (1 per 549 persons); (1974) daily per capita caloric intake 2,190 calories (FAO recommended minimum requirement 2,330 calories).

*Percentages do not add to 100.0 because of rounding. †1973. ‡Maputo only. §July. ‖1970–71.

Mozarabic language, archaic dialect of Spanish that was spoken in those parts of Spain under Arab occupation from the early 8th century until *c.* 1300. Mozarabic retained many archaic Latin forms and borrowed many words from Arabic; although almost completely overshadowed by Arabic during the period of Muslim domination, Mozarabic nevertheless maintained a completely Romance sound system and typically Romance grammar. The dialect is known almost entirely from refrains, known as *kharjah*s, added to Arabic and Hebrew poems of the 11th century. These refrains are written in Arabic characters that lack most vowel markings and are often rather difficult to decipher. *See also* Spanish language.

·medieval literary evidence **10**:1122c
·textual remains and range of use **15**:1027b

Mozart, (Johann Georg) Leopold (b. Nov. 14, 1719, Augsburg, Ger.—d. May 28, 1787, Salzburg, Austria), violinist, teacher and composer; the father and only teacher of Wolfgang Amadeus Mozart, whom he exhibited throughout Europe as a child prodigy. A violinist at the court of the prince-archbishop of Salzburg, Leopold Mozart became court composer (1757) and also (1762) vice kapellmeister (conductor).

His method of teaching, *Versuch einer gründlichen Violinschule* (1756; trans. by Editha Knocker, *A Treatise on the Fundamental Principles of Violin Playing*, 1948), was long a standard text and was widely reprinted and translated. Among his works are concerti for various instruments, symphonies, and other pieces; he is sometimes credited with the *Toy Symphony*.

In 1763 he began the first of many triumphant and highly publicized exhibitions of his two prodigiously talented children (the other five of his seven children did not survive infancy): Maria Anna (Nannerl; 1751–1829), an accomplished clavierist and Wolfgang Amadeus who, at age six, performed his own and others' works on several instruments, improvised, and played at sight difficult, unfamiliar compositions. Although often criticized for exploiting his son and commercializing his talents, Leopold Mozart sincerely felt it was his God-given obligation to develop such abilities and to exhibit them to the world. Some of the extensive correspondence of father and son is contained in *The Letters of Mozart and His Family* (1963), by E. Anderson.

·son's early instruction **12**:600g

Mozart, Wolfgang Amadeus 12:600 (b. Jan. 27, 1756, Salzburg, Austria—d. Dec. 5, 1791, Vienna), composer who, together with Joseph Haydn, represents the climax of the late-18th-century Viennese Classical style and by virtue of the extraordinary quality of his broad achievements in opera, chamber music, symphonies, and piano concerti is regarded as one of the greatest musical geniuses of all time.

Mozart began to compose when he was five and soon became proficient on the harpsichord and violin; he concentrated later on the pianoforte and was taken with his sister on tours of Europe by his father. He continued to compose while on his travels. From 1775 he was at Salzburg in the service of the archbishop there until his break with him in 1781. The first of his mature operas, *Idomeneo*, was written for Munich in 1781. He settled in Vienna, and after years of waiting was engaged by the emperor Joseph II as chamber composer in 1787. Meanwhile, he continued to compose as a "freelance," producing many of his most famous quartets and symphonies. Despite successes, such as the operas *The Marriage of Figaro* in 1786 and *Don Giovanni* in 1787, he fell increasingly into debt. A concert tour in 1789 did little to improve his position; nor did *Die Zauberflöte* (1791; *The Magic Flute*). In that year Mozart's health failed, and he died in the autumn, in poverty.

TEXT BIOGRAPHY covers:
The first tours **12**:601a
The Italian tours 601c
Vienna, Salzburg, and Munich (1773–77) 601f
The journey to Paris (1777–79) 602a
Later life and works 602f
Assessment 603g

REFERENCES in other text articles:
·Beethoven's musical training **2**:795f
·chamber music and influence on Haydn **4**:23c
·choral style of mass settings **4**:443f
·Classical period and style **12**:710g
·C major string quartet's harmonic blurring and chromaticism **8**:651d
·C major string quintet's expressive and dramatic qualities **4**:26f
·comic style in opera **4**:966e
·concertos and sinfonia concertante **4**:1070c
·contrapuntal elements and influences **5**:215d
·creative process **2**:48g
·fugues inspired by Bach **7**:770d
·harmonic plan of sonata form **8**:650e
·Haydn friendship and influence **8**:681a *passim* to 682g
·incidental music composition **12**:702g
·Near-East popular music influence **14**:808b
·operas in Italian and German styles **13**:581c
·orchestration in Classical period **13**:646a
·rebellion against artist's inferior status **2**:99b
·sonata form outline **17**:5f
·symphonic style evolution **17**:913d
·variation techniques in Duport **19**:29f

Mozelekatse (South African king): *see* Mzilikazi.

Mozhaysky, Aleksandr, 19th-century Russian airplane designer.

·aircraft propulsion by steam power **7**:385b

Mozo, Eli: *see* Herrera, Francisco de, the Younger.

Mo-zu (Chinese philosopher): *see* Mo-tzu.

Mozyr, centre of a *rayon* (district), Gomel *oblast* (administrative region), Belorussian Soviet Socialist Republic, on the high bank of the Pripyat River. It dates from at least the 12th century, and from the 18th century it was a centre of trade and handicrafts. The city was a woodworking centre in the early Soviet period but now also has an important engineering industry as well as clothing and food industries. There is a teacher-training institute and a medical school. Pop. (1970) 49,000.
52°03′ N, 29°14′ E

mozzetta, a nonliturgical vestment worn over the rochet by Roman Catholic dignitaries for processionals and ceremonial occasions. It is a short wool or silk shoulder cape, has a miniature hood, and is fastened down the front with buttons. The colour depends upon the rank of the wearer: white for the pope, red for cardinals, purple for bishops, and the colour of the religious habit for abbots. Derived from the cope, it was in use by the 12th century.

MP-44, German submachine gun used in World War II.

·development and accuracy **16**:900d

Mpadi, Simon-Pierre (b. *c.* 1900, Madimba territory, Belgian Congo, now Zaire—d. unknown), messianic Congolese religious leader and the organizer of a militant, separatist African church. Mpadi exploited African bitterness over the racism of the white Christian missions to create a movement that, though short-lived, had significant effects on the growth of nationalist political and cultural feelings in the Belgian and French Congos.

A former officer in the Salvation Army, Mpadi separated himself from the white missions in 1936 and became a follower of Simon Kimbangu, the founder of a Christian movement called Gounzism (from the Swahili word *gounza*, "messiah"). Mpadi gave the movement organizational form and extended its range and influence. When he called himself Chief of the Apostles, his names (Simon-Peter) were seen as confirmation of his tie with Kimbangu and his position as an apostle.

In 1939 Mpadi created a subsidiary organization for the church, called Mission des Noirs (Blacks' Mission). He twice fled to the French Congo and was twice deported, in 1943 and 1944; he eventually disappeared, and the movement lost strength and cohesion by the early 1950s.

MPAJA: *see* Malayan People's Anti-Japanese Army.

Mpezeni (b. *c.* 1830—d. Sept. 21, 1900, near Fort. Jameson, northeastern Rhodesia, now in Zambia), South African chief, a son of the great Ngoni king Zwangendaba. Mpezeni found himself in the middle of European competition for control of southeastern Africa, and his unwillingness to grant land and mineral concessions to European colonists earned him their enmity. He was eventually defeated by the British.

At Zwangendaba's death in 1848, the immense Ngoni kingdom split into five major groups under different sons of the old king. Mpezeni led his group to what is now southern Zambia, where they were undisturbed by external threats until the closing years of the 19th century. From 1889, however, Germany, Portugal, and Britain attempted to gain control of his territory. Mpezeni tried to play off the European powers against each other, but by 1896 his waiting policy began to cause dissension among his own people, and in 1897 he reluctantly consented to an attack on British settlements in the Nyasaland Protectorate (now Malawi). The British counterattacked in force, and in February 1898 Mpezeni was forced to surrender.

Mphahlele, Ezekiel (b. 1919, Pretoria, S.Af.), novelist, essayist, short-story writer, and teacher whose autobiography, *Down Second Avenue* (1959), has become a South African classic. It combines the story of a young man's growth into adulthood with penetrating social criticism of the conditions forced upon black South Africans by apartheid. Mphahlele grew up in Pretoria and, through the sacrifice of relatives, was able to attend the well-known St. Peter's Secondary School in Johannesburg and then Adams College in Natal. His career as a teacher of English and Afrikaans was cut short by the government because of his strong opposition to the highly restrictive Bantu Education Act. After working for some time as reporter and fiction editor of *Drum* magazine in Pretoria and qualifying for an M.A. with distinction from the University of South Africa, he chose exile in Nigeria (1957) to fighting government repression of black writers at home.

Mphahlele held a number of positions in Africa, Europe, and the U.S. He lectured in English at the University of Ibadan, Nigeria; the University of Zambia; University College, Nairobi; and the University of Denver. He served as director of the African program at the Congress for Cultural Freedom in Paris. He was co-editor (1960–64) with Ulli Beier and Wole Soyinka of the influential literary periodical *Black Orpheus*, published in Ibadan, Nigeria; founder and director of Chemchemi, a cultural centre in Nairobi for artists and writers (1963–65); and editor of the periodical *Africa Today* (1967).

His critical writings range from *The African Image* (1962), essays treating Negritude, the African personality, nationalism, and the black and white man's literary image of Africa, to book reviews and articles in magazines and periodicals. He has edited two anthologies, *Modern African Stories* (1964) and *African Writing Today* (1967), both intended to acquaint his audience with major themes and styles of modern African writers. He has also published several books of short stories and a second autobiographical novel, *The Wanderers* (1970), which won first prize in the 1968 *African Arts* literary competition. His work has been praised for moving beyond a journalistic treatment of the themes of pover-

ty and oppression to a broader perspective that enables him to accept (with irony) as well as to protest native life in South Africa.
·contribution and distinction **1**:241b

MPLA (Angolan political movement): *see* Movimento Popular de Libertação de Angola.

Mqhayi, Samuel E(dward) K(rune) (b. Dec. 1, 1875, near Gqumahashe, S.Af.—d. July 29, 1945, Berlin, S.Af.?), poet, historian, journalist, biographer, and translator who, by the 1920s, had earned the name "Imbongi Yesizwe Jikelele" ("Xhosa Poet Laureate"). His many publications helped to stabilize and purify the Xhosa language, and he dominated the Xhosa literary scene, serving as a model for young writers until his death in 1945.

Mqhayi began his career as a teacher, but he was soon writing and editing newspapers. By 1910 he had worked on the Xhosa Bible Revision Board, published *U-Samson*, his version of the biblical story, and had devoted his energy to the task of standardizing Xhosa orthography and of writing down the rules of grammar and syntax.

His most prolific period followed. *Ityala lamaWele* (1914; "The Lawsuit of the Twins") brought him immediate fame and is considered a Xhosa classic. It is based on his experiences as a youth at the Great Place (court) of Chief Nzanzana. While a teacher at Lovedale, S.Af., in the 1920s, he wrote several biographies and in 1927 a book of verse called *Imihobe nemi-Bongo*, the first published collection of Xhosa poems, many of which celebrate current events or important figures. He also wrote *U-Don Jadu* (1927), a record of his early travels and adventures, and finally the autobiography *U-Mqhayi wase- Ntab' ozuko* (1939), which traces his mental and spiritual growth, giving at the same time a vivid picture of late 19th-century Bantu life.

The last years of his life Mqhayi spent as a bard living among his people, always willing to recite the praises of chiefs and notables at celebrations and gatherings. His collected poems, *Inzuzo* ("Cain"), appeared in 1943.

MRA (revivalistic movement): *see* Moral Re-armament.

Mṛcchakaṭikā, 4th-century play in Sanskrit by Śūdraka.
·plot structure and importance **17**:138a

mṛdaṅga, two-headed drum played in the classical music of South India. It is made of wood in an angular barrel shape, having an outline like an elongated hexagon. Thong hoops around each end of the drum, leather thong lacing, and small wooden dowels slipped under the lacings control the skin tension. A disk of black tuning paste is affixed to each end, giving the drum a definite pitch. The paste is removable from the left head, which is usually tuned an octave lower than the right. The drum is held across the lap and played on both ends by the fingers and wrists.

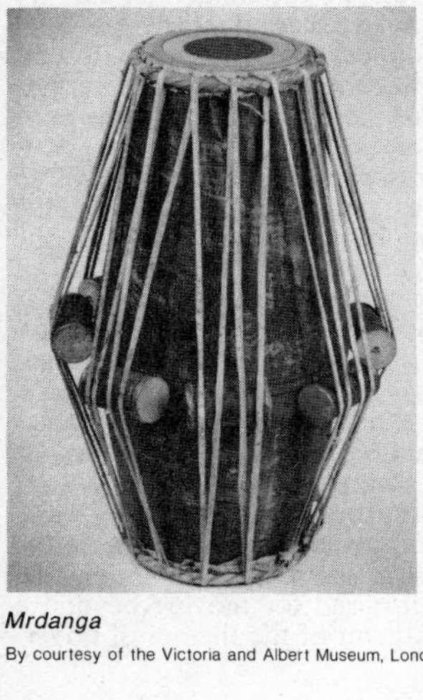

Mrdanga
By courtesy of the Victoria and Albert Museum, London

mRNA (messenger ribonucleic acid): *see* ribonucleic acid.

Mrohaung, Arakanese Kingdom of, in Lower Burma, state whose longevity (1433–1785) provided a strong tradition of independence for Arakan (*q.v.*), a coastal strip on the Bay of Bengal.

King Narameikhla founded a strong, stable kingdom in 1433. In 1531 the first European ships appeared in the region, and Portuguese freebooters began to settle at Chittagong. Under King Minbin, Mrohaung's navy, with Portuguese assistance, was the terror of the Ganges region. Arakan's neighbour and traditional antagonist, Bengal, was weak; the freebooters raided there at will, carrying hundreds of slaves off to Arakan. For almost a century Mrohaung retained its naval power.

The slave markets at Mrohaung attracted the attention of Dutch traders, who purchased slaves from the Arakanese. To stop the depopulation of coastal Bengal, in 1629 the Mughal emperor Shāh Jahān wiped out a Portuguese pirate nest on the Chittagong coast; but not until 1666 was the naval power of Mrohaung broken and the coastal area annexed to Bengal.

When King Sandathudamma died in 1684, the country became prey to internal disorder. Another 25 kings came to the throne, however, before the armies of the Burmese king Bodawpaya invaded the kingdom and deposed the last king, Thamada, in 1785.

Mrożek, Sławomir (1930–), Polish playwright and author of short stories.
·themes of major works **10**:1254f

MRP (French political party): *see* Mouvement Républicain Populaire.

MSA (Congolese political party): *see* Mouvement Socialist Africain.

Msaken, also transliterated MASĀKIN, town in Sousse (Sūsah) *wilāyah* (governorate), eastern Tunisia, on the Sahel (coastal strip), 7 mi (11 km) from the sea. A road and rail junction, the town is also a centre for olive growing and processing, flour milling, and weaving. Its buildings, typical of the area, are constructed mostly of beaten earth. Pop. (latest census) 28,130.
35°44′ N, 10°35′ E
·map, Tunisia **18**:746

MSBS, French submarine-launched rocket.
·design characteristics, table 1 **15**:932

MSG (flavouring agent): *see* monosodium glutamate.

Mshattā, Umayyad desert palace in Jordan.
·architecture, function, and stone relief **9**:989a *passim* to 991e

Mshweshwe, also MOSHOESHOE, or MOSHESH (b. *c.* 1786, near the upper Caledon River, northern Basutoland—d. March 11, 1870, Thaba Bosiu, Basutoland, now Lesotho), first paramount chief of the Sotho (Basuto, Basotho) nation that he founded. Son of a lesser chieftain, he won a reputation for leadership as a young man by conducting daring cattle raids and was given the name Mshweshwe, an imitation of the sounds made by a knife in shaving. By employing superior military tactics and skillful diplomacy, Mshweshwe eventually united the various small groups to form the Sotho nation called by English-speaking persons Basutoland. Ruling from his impregnable stronghold, Thaba Bosiu (*q.v.*; Mountain of the Night), he pursued a policy of peace and prosperity.

In 1833 the Sotho chief welcomed French missionaries. Though he encouraged them in their activities, he continued to support the old customs and religion. (Not until he lay dying did Mshweshwe convert to Christianity.) He relied heavily on the missionaries for advice in dealing with Europeans, who were coming north into his lands. With characteristic temporizing, Mshweshwe maintained his power, often playing off British and Boer against one another, until 1843, when he allied himself with the British. Five years later most of his lands were annexed by Britain, and soon disputes led to a war in which the overconfident British were defeated.

After the British abandoned the territories beyond the Orange River, Mshweshwe became involved in a series of wars with the Orange Free State. When that conflict began to go against him, Mshweshwe succeeded in getting the British to annex Basutoland in 1868. But in a British–Free State treaty negotiated the following year, the frontiers of Basutoland were delimited and soon afterward it was handed over to the Cape again. After a war with the Sotho, the Cape gave the territory back to Britain in 1884, and British it remained until 1966, when it became independent, as Lesotho. Though Mshweshwe's power waned in the last years of his life, his people continue to venerate his name.
·Basutoland–Boer conflict leadership **17**:285b
·Sotho emotional influence **10**:836g
·Zulu refugee kingdom creation **17**:282c

MSI (Italian political party): *see* Movimento Sociale Italiano.

Msiri, also called NGELENGWA or MWENDA (b. near Tabora, now in Tanzania—d. Dec. 20, 1891, Katanga, now in Zaire), African ruler, one of the most successful of the 19th-century immigrant adventurers and state builders in Central Africa. About 1856 he settled in southern Katanga with a few Nyamwezi followers, and by about 1870 had succeeded in taking over most of this valuable copper region from its previous Lunda rulers. During the height of his power in the mid-1880s Msiri not only ruled directly a very large kingdom but also received tribute from neighbouring areas. His prosperity was largely based on the copper trade, though he dealt in slaves and ivory as well; thus his basic policy was to keep trade routes open toward both the east and west coasts. In the 1870s he began to trade with the Arab trader and state builder Tippu Tib. Like many African rulers, Msiri was especially interested in buying rifles, which he saw as absolutely necessary to his military strength.

Missionaries first entered Msiri's kingdom in 1886. Of greater consequence, however, was the realization by other Europeans that Katanga was rich in minerals. Msiri refused to negotiate with the British South African Company, but in 1891 more importunate expeditions arrived from the Belgian king Leopold II's Congo Independent State. One tried to encourage rebellion against Msiri, who was fatally shot while negotiating with another expedition.

Though Msiri adopted older patterns of indigenous Lunda state building, he also introduced new political titles and ceremonies and made some changes in customary law. Of at least equal importance was the introduction by the Nyamwezi into Katanga of the sweet potato, smallpox vaccination, and a technique for making copper wire.

Mswati, or MSWAZI (b. *c.* 1820, near Manzini, Swaziland—d. 1868, Swaziland), South African chief and son of Sobhuza I (*q.v.*; founder of Swaziland); he was the greatest of the Ngwane kings, and the Swazi (as the Ngwane came to be called) take their name from him. Mswati extended the kingdom he inherited northward into Rhodesia, including territory since lost by the Swazi.

Mswati became king in 1840 and established control over the Bantu tribes in eastern South Africa. Reorganizing the Ngwane along the lines of the successful Zulu regimental castes, he made them one of the most powerful nations of southern Africa. In 1860 a disputed succession in the Shangane kingdom to the north enabled Mswazi to extend his influence into southern Rhodesia and Mozambique. In 1845 he ceded some territory to Boer settlers in the Transvaal, South Africa, and in 1864 he aided them in conquering the Poko tribe. Apparently unaware of the dangers involved, Mswazi encouraged contact with the Boers, though this eventually led to the loss of Swazi independence in 1894.

Mtetwa (MTHETHWA) **Empire,** one of the larger territorial units that arose in northern Zululand, in South Africa, at the end of the 18th century, probably in response to the increased trading opportunities in Delagoa Bay, and possibly also because of population and an increasing need for grazing land. Under the rule of Dingiswayo (d. 1817) many of the military and administrative innovations, including the system of age-regiments that later characterized the Zulu Empire, were initiated, and it was in the Mtetwa armies that the Zulu chieftain Shaka first rose to fame. On Dingiswayo's death the Mtetwa were absorbed by the Zulu Empire. *See* Mfecane.

MTLD (Algeria): *see* Movement for the Triumph of Democratic Liberties.

MTS (Soviet institution): *see* machine-tractor station.

Mtsinkvari, also called KAZBEK, extinct volcano in the Caucasus Mountains of the Soviet Union.
42°42′ N, 44°31′ E
·location and height **7**:1132e

Mtskheta, town, Georgian Soviet Socialist Republic, at the confluence of the Kura and Aragvi rivers, just northwest of Tbilisi. One of the oldest settlements of Transcaucasia, Mtskheta was the capital of Georgia from the 2nd to the 5th century AD. Survivals of historic and architectural interest are the magnificent Cathedral of Sveti-Tskhoveli, the Samtavro Convent, the Dzhvari Church, and, on a hilltop outside the town, the ruins of the Armaz-Tsikhe Castle, seat of the 2nd–5th-century kings. Latest pop. est. 2,000.
41°51′ N, 44°43′ E

Cathedral of Sveti-Tskhoveli, dating from the 4th century, in Mtskheta, Georgian S.S.R.
Alexander M. Chabe

Mtwara Region, administrative unit (formed 1963), southeastern Tanzania, with an area of about 31,950 sq mi (82,751 sq km) and bordered east by the Indian Ocean and south by Mozambique. The hilly terrain, mostly below 3,000 ft (900 m), is drained by the Ruvuma (part of the southern boundary), Rufiji and Mbarangandu (part of the western boundary), Matandu, Mbwemburu, and Lukuledi rivers. The annual rainfall exceeds 30 in. (760 mm) but is unreliable. Miombo woodland and savanna with baobabs dominate inland, bush with coconuts and casuarinas at the coast, and mangrove swamp south of the Rufiji Delta.

The region is the nation's largest producer of cashew nuts and sesame seeds; but copra, kapok, cassava, sisal, and peanuts are also leading cash crops. Wild rubber, beeswax, roll tobacco, and gums are important inland. Mica, salt, gypsum, and rock salt are exported; there are also deposits of copal, garnet, and beryl. Ports include Mtwara (the regional capital), Lindi, and Kilwa Masoko. Most of the region's inhabitants, mainly Makonde (noted for their contemporary wood sculptures), Machinga, Matumbi, Mwera, Ngindo, Makua, Mawia, Yao, and Matambwe tribesmen, live near the coast and in the south. Pop. (1972 est.) 1,167,000.
·area and population table **17**:1030
·map, Tanzania **17**:1026

muahiset (mythology): *see* maa-alused.

Muʿallaqāt, al-, a collection of seven pre-Islāmic Arabic odes (*qaṣīdahs*), each considered the best piece by its author. Since the authors themselves are among the dozen or so most famous poets of the 6th century, the selection enjoys a unique position in Arabic literature, representing the finest of early Arabic poetry.

Ḥammād ar-Rāwiyah, an 8th-century collector of early poetry, is the acknowledged compiler of the *Muʿallaqāt*. The origin of the name of the collection, however, is obscure. Ḥammād himself seems to have referred to it as the "seven renowned ones" (*as-sabʿ al-mashhūrāt*), or simply "the renowned ones" (*al-mashhūrāt*). The name *Muʿallaqāt* appears *c.* 900 to distinguish the seven poems as the finest in a larger collection. Legends abound, and modern scholars proffer their own theories, but there is no conclusive explanation of the name.

The precise poems included the *Muʿallaqāt* present another puzzle. The list usually accepted as standard, the one recorded by Ibn ʿAbd Rabbihi, names poems by Imruʾ al-Qays, Ṭarafah, Zuhayr, Labīd, ʿAntarah, ʿAmr ibn Kulthum, and al-Ḥārith. Such authorities as Ibn Qutaybah, however, count ʿAbid ibn al-Abras as one of the seven, while Abū ʿUbaydah replaces the last two poets of Ibn ʿAbd Rabbini's list with Nābighah and al-Aʿshah.

Of the authors of the *Muʿallaqāt*, the earliest is Imruʾ al-Qays, who lived in the early part of the 6th century. The others belong to the latter half of that century. Zuhayr and Labid are said to have survived into the time of Islām, but their poetic output belongs to the pre-Islāmic period.

The *Muʿallaqāt* odes are all in the classical *qaṣīdah* pattern, which some Arab scholars believed to have been created by Imruʾ al-Qays. The main theme of the *qaṣīdah* (the *madīḥ*, or panegyric, the poet's tribute to himself, his tribe, or his patron) is often disguised in the vivid descriptive passages that are the chief glory of the *Muʿallaqāt*. Their vivid imagery, exact observation, and deep feeling of intimacy with nature as it manifests itself in the Arabian Desert contribute to the *Muʿallaqāt*'s standing as a masterpiece of world literature.

While little in the way of historical data can be gleaned from the actual texts of the *Muʿallaqāt*, they do provide a picture of Bedouin life, manners, and modes of thought.
·pre-Islāmic literary history **9**:957e

Muan, the 15th month of the Mayan solar calendar.
·Mayan ceremonial year **11**:722d

Muar, or BANDAR MAHARANI, port, northwestern Johor (formerly Johore), West Malaysia (Malaya), on the Strait of Malacca at the mouth of the Sungai (River) Muar. While many of its residents are fishermen, the town is also an administrative centre and an agricultural (rubber, coconuts, bananas) depot. The Sungai Muar is navigable for native boats for much of its 100-mi (160-km) course and during the 15th and 16th centuries was part of a portage route between the sultanates of Malacca and Pahang. Pop. (1970 prelim.) 61,218.
2°02′ N, 102°34′ E
·map, Malaysia **11**:370

Muara, settlement, western Brunei, northwestern Borneo. Pop. (latest census) 923.
5°02′ N, 115°02′ E
·location and vegetation **3**:342a; map

Muav Limestone Formation, Middle Cambrian carbonate rocks that occur in the Grand Canyon region of northern Arizona (the Cambrian Period began about 570,000,000 years ago and lasted about 70,000,000 years). The Muav Limestone was named for exposures studied in Muav Canyon, in the Grand Canyon region, and consists of about 136 metres (450 feet) of bluish-gray limestones that are thinly bedded. A characteristic mottled appearance is imparted to the Muav by many thin bands of greenish to tan shaly material. The Muav underlies the Redwall Limestone and overlies the Bright Angel Shale Formation.

Muʿāwiyah I **12**:604, more complete name MUʿĀWIYAH IBN ABĪ SUFYĀN, (b. *c.* 602, Mecca, now in Saudi Arabia—d. 680, Damascus), early Islāmic leader and founder of the great Umayyad dynasty of caliphs.

Abstract of text biography. Muʿāwiyah became a Muslim after Muḥammad's conquest of Mecca and reconciliation with his former enemies. Appointed governor of Damascus (640), Muʿāwiyah conducted military campaigns against the Byzantines. He fought against the fourth caliph, ʿAlī (Muḥammad's son-in-law), seized Egypt, and assumed the caliphate after ʿAlī's assassination in 661. He introduced administrative procedures that increased the central organization of the government and sent further expeditions against the Byzantines but failed to take Constantinople.

REFERENCES in other text articles:
·ʿAlī's reluctant arbitration **1**:573g
·Averroës' political criticism **2**:539h
·caliphal accession and policies **3**:626f
·caliph succession and Ali's defeat **1**:1047d
·Iraq under the caliphate **11**:991a
·Islāmic expansion and caliphal politics **9**:929c
·Syrian-based rule **17**:952b

Muʿāwiyah II (d. 684), Muslim caliph.
·Yazīd I's troubled heritage **3**:628a

mubālaghah (Arabic: "hyperbole"), a literary device used in classical Islāmic literature to satisfy the need for getting away from the starkly real without creating an actual falsehood.
·Islāmic art and religious restrictions **9**:924b

Mubārak, ʿAlī Pasha (b. *c.* 1823, Birinbāl, now Birimbāl, Egypt—d. Nov. 14, 1893, Cairo), administrator and author, who was responsible for the creation and modernization of a unified system of education in Egypt.

A product of the military schools created by Muḥammad ʿAlī Pasha (ruled 1805–48), Mubārak was sent in 1844 to France to complete his education, and on his return in 1849/50 was appointed to the ministry of war. Shortly afterward he became the head of the military training college at Mafruza. During the reign of Muḥammad Saʿīd (ruled 1854–63) he found himself out of favour and was dismissed from office.

With the accession of Ismāʿīl Pasha (ruled 1863–79), Mubārak joined the government as a member of the Public Works Commission and worked, among other projects, on a scheme for the beautification of Cairo. In his next post as assistant director of education (1867) he separated the military schools from the government-operated civilian schools. In 1870 he created the *Dār al-ʿulūm* ("The Abode of Learning"), a teacher training college modelled on the French École Normale Supérieure. He also improved conditions in the village schools, changed the curriculum of the traditional religious schools to emphasize foreign languages and science, and encouraged the translation, publication, and adaptation of technical textbooks. After serving another five years as minister for public works, he became minister of education (1888–91) and succeeded in unifying Egypt's system of education, integrating all military, secular, and religious schools under the responsibility of the minister of education.

Mubārak's most famous work was *Khiṭaṭ at-tawfīqīyah al-jadīdah* (20 vol., 1886), an encyclopedia which dealt with all aspects of Egyptian culture and history.

Mubarrad, al- (b. ABŪ AL-ʿABBĀS MUḤAMMAD IBN YAZĪD, March 25, 826, Basra, now in Iraq—d. Oct. 898, Baghdad), Arab grammarian and literary scholar whose *al-Kāmil* ("The Perfect One") is a storehouse of linguistic knowledge.

After studying grammar in Basra, al-Mubarrad was called to the court of the ʿAbbāsid caliph al-Mutawakkil at Sāmarrāʾ in 860. When the Caliph was killed in the following year, al-Mubarrad went to Baghdad, remaining there most of his life as a teacher. Excerpts from poetry and proverbs, from history and Ḥadīth (traditions of the prophet Muḥammad) are given in *al-Kāmil* and subjected to grammatical and literary scrutiny.

Mubende, town and administrative district, south central Uganda, northwest of Kampala. The town is on a main road, connecting it with Kampala and Fort Portal. It is a trading centre for agricultural products, notably cotton, coffee, bananas and corn (maize). Deposits of tungsten, beryl, and tantalite are found nearby. Latest census town, 6,004.
0°35′ N, 31°23′ E
·area and population table and map **18**:828
·map, Uganda **18**:826

Mubi, capital and largest town of Sardauna Province, North-Eastern State, northeastern Nigeria. It lies on the Yedseram River, a stream the waters of which feed Lake Chad; a bridge was built at Mubi in 1953. It has road connections to Maiduguri, Yola, Biu, and Garua (Cameroon). Probably founded in the late 18th century in Bata tribal territory by the Ilaga'en clan of the Fulani people, it remained under the jurisdiction of the sultanate of Mandara, a mountainous region to the north, until it was conquered in the Fulani *jihād* ("holy war") by Modibbo Adama. By the 1820s, the peoples (the "Fali of Mubi" [Gude], the Bata, and the Ilaga'en) of Mubi and its environs were incorporated into Adama's Fulani kingdom of Fumbina, later called Adamawa; in the 1890s, they were subjected to slave raids by Adamawa's Lamido (Emir) Zubeiru.

The town was taken by German forces in 1903 and served as a frontier post and administrative centre of German Kamerun until its capture by the British in 1914. Mubi district was placed in the British Cameroons by a League of Nations mandate in 1922 and administered as part of Yola (later Adamawa) province; after the plebiscite of 1961, the district became part of Nigeria's newly created Sardauna province, and Mubi town became the provincial capital.

Mubi also serves as a collecting point for peanuts (groundnuts) and cattle and as a local market centre for guinea corn, millet, peppers, rice, and cotton. A government hospital (1954), a health office, a dispensary, and a teacher-training college are in the town. The Khumtla shrine of the Margi (Marghi) people is 30 mi (50 km) northeast at the foot of Kamale (Chirgi), a granite pinnacle 700 ft (210 m) tall that dominates the upper Yedseram valley. Pop. (1972 est.) 35,084.
10°18′ N, 13°20′ E
·map, Nigeria **13**:86

Mucha, Alphonse, original name ALFONS MARIA MUCHA (b. Aug. 24, 1860, Ivančice, Moravia, now in Czechoslovakia—d. July 14, 1939, Prague), Art Nouveau illustrator and painter who first became prominent as the principal advertiser of the actress Sarah Bernhardt in Paris and later enjoyed popularity in the United States.

After early education in Brno, Moravia, and work for a theatre scene-painting firm in Vienna, he studied art in Munich (1883–88) and in Paris (1888–89). Remaining in Paris, he became a friend of the painter Paul Gauguin, the dramatist August Strindberg, the astronomer Camille Flammarion, and many other artists and intellectuals. Late in 1894 he was commissioned to design a poster advertising the actress Sarah Bernhardt in Victorien Sardou's *Gismonda*. The box office success of this play induced her to give Mucha a six-year contract for other posters, costumes, stage sets, and jewelry. He also received poster commissions from several business firms and produced many magazine illustrations. His representations of idealized women were largely free of the sexual ambivalence and morbidity perceptible in much Art Nouveau work.

Between 1903 and 1922 Mucha made four trips to the U.S., where he attracted another major patron—Charles Richard Crane, a Chicago industrialist and Slavophile, who subsidized Mucha's "Slav Epic" series of 20 large paintings (1912–30). Mucha's one-man show in Brooklyn, N.Y. (1921–22), drew large crowds. After 1922 he lived in Czechoslovakia, for which nation he designed banknotes and postage stamps.
·Art Nouveau jewelry design **10**:177f; illus. 178

Much Ado About Nothing (first performed 1598/99), romantic comedy by Shakespeare in which the battle of the sexes is waged in a series of witty skirmishes between the reluctant lovers Beatrice and Benedick.
·comedy and lack of self-knowledge **4**:961e
·dramatic devices and analysis **16**:623h
·literature of the Renaissance **10**:1141e

Mu-ch'a T'i-p'o (Buddhist scholar): *see* Hsüan-tsang.

Mu-ch'i Fa-ch'ang (fl. 13th century), one of the most famous of Chinese Ch'an (in Japanese Zen) Buddhist painters whose works have been very influential in Japan. Toward the end of the Sung dynasty (960–1279), Mu-ch'i found himself in political trouble and fled to a monastery near the capital city of Hang-chou. His paintings on Ch'an themes have stimulated many copies in Japan, and it is there that paintings of any authenticity are now found, though a Japanese painter, Mokuan (died *c.* 1345), travelled to Mu-ch'i's monastery and is said to have received two of Mu-ch'i's seals from the then abbot of the temple, making the paintings in Japan somewhat suspect. Mu-ch'i, like many other Chinese painters, painted a variety of subjects—including landscapes, flowers, still lifes, and more orthodox iconographic subjects. While there are various examples of each extant, which indicate his diverse interests and styles, the most famous paintings associated with Mu-ch'i include "Six Persimmons" and a triptych with a white-robed Kuan-yin at the centre flanked on either side by a scroll of monkeys and a crane (all in the Daitoku-ji, Kyōto), and a surviving set of four sections (in various Japanese collections) of an original set of "Eight Views of the Hsiao and Hsiang Rivers." However different the paintings in style and subject matter, there is throughout an appropriate sense of immediate vision and creation and a totally responsive hand, expressed with broad and evocative washes of ink.
·Buddhist style influence and range **19**:195e

"Six Persimmons," ink painting on paper by Mu-ch'i; in the Daitoku-ji, Kyōto
By courtesy of the International Society for Educational Information, Tokyo

Much Wenlock, residential area in the county of Salop, England (until 1974 called Shropshire or Salop). The community is situated at the northeastern end of the sharp limestone ridge of Wenlock Edge and about 6 mi (10 km) south of the isolated hill of the Wrekin (1,335 ft, or 407 m). From 1966 until 1974, after the dissolution of the former municipal borough of Wenlock, Much Wenlock was included in the new rural district of Bridgnorth. The Cluniac Priory of St. Mildburg, refounded in 1017 on the site of a 17th-century foundation, gave Much Wenlock its importance in the past, but it was dissolved in 1539; considerable remains are left, including the prior's house with Norman and 15th-century work. By the 16th century Much Wenlock was a flourishing market town with a trade in limestone, a function it continues to fulfill. It possesses a 12th-century church, 16th-century buildings such as its timbered Guildhall, and a Tudor manor house.
52°30′ N, 2°40′ W

Mucianus, Publius Licinius Crassus Dives: *see* Crassus Dives Mucianus, Publius Licinius.

mucilage, aqueous solution of gum used as an excipient in pharmacy.
·pharmaceutical preparation methods **14**:198h

muckrakers, group of U.S. writers, identified with pre-World War I reform and exposé literature. The name was given to them pejoratively from Pres. Theodore Roosevelt's speech of April 14, 1906, in which, borrowing a passage from John Bunyan's *Pilgrim's Progress*, he denounced "the Man with the Muckrake . . . who could look no way but downward." But "muckraker" also took on favourable connotations of social concern and courageous exposition.

The muckrakers' work grew out of the yellow journalism of the 1890s, which whetted the public appetite for news arrestingly presented, and of popular magazines, established by John Brisben Walker, Cyrus H.K. Curtis, and especially S.S. McClure, Frank A. Munsey, and Peter F. Collier. The emergence of muckraking was heralded in the January 1903 issue of *McClure's Magazine* by articles on municipal government, labour, and trusts, written by Lincoln Steffens, Ray Stannard Baker, and Ida M. Tarbell.

The intense public interest aroused by articles critical of political and financial rings, housing, labour, insurance, and other problems rallied writers, editors, and reformers. Charles Edward Russell led the reform writers with exposés ranging from *The Greatest Trust in the World* (1905) to *The Uprising of the Many* (1907), the latter reporting methods being tried to extend democracy in other countries. Brand Whitlock, who wrote *The Turn of the Balance* (1907), a novel opposing capital punishment, was also a reform mayor

of Toledo, Ohio. Thomas W. Lawson, a Boston financier, in "Frenzied Finance" (*Everybody's*, 1904–05), provided a major exposé of corporate irresponsibility. Edwin Markham's *Children in Bondage* was a major attack on child labour. Upton Sinclair's novel *The Jungle* (1906) and Samuel Hopkins Adams' *Great American Fraud* (1906), combined with the work of Harvey W. Wiley and Sen. Albert J. Beveridge, brought about passage of the Beef Inspection Act and the Pure Food and Drug Act. David Graham Phillips' series "The Treason of the Senate" (*Cosmopolitan*, 1906), which inspired President Roosevelt's speech in 1906, was influential in leading to the passage of the Seventeenth Amendment to the Constitution, providing for popular senatorial elections. Muckraking as a movement largely disappeared between 1910 and 1912.
·newspaper publishing history **15**:242h
·Progressive Movement role **18**:983g
·U.S. magazine history **15**:252d

mucopolysaccharidoses, group of inherited disorders characterized by abnormal production and storage, and excretion, of one or more mucopolysaccharides, the complex carbohydrates that are the chief constituents of the substance—the so-called ground substance—filling the spaces between the cells and fibres of the connective tissues. Persons with Hurler's syndrome (*q.v.*), also called mucopolysaccharidosis I, usually fail to survive beyond childhood. Hunter's syndrome, or mucopolysaccharidosis II, affects only males. The other disorders of the group are Sanfilippo's syndrome, or mucopolysaccharidosis III; Morquio's syndrome (*q.v.*), or mucopolysaccharidosis IV; Scheie's syndrome, or mucopolysaccharidosis V; and Maroteaux–Lamy syndrome, or mucopolysaccharidosis VI. None of the six types becomes evident unless inherited from both parents.

Skeletal deformities—including dwarfism and a grotesque facial appearance—mental deficiency, heart defects, enlargement of the liver and the spleen, opacity of the corneas, and deafness are present in Hurler's syndrome; and one or more of these features is present in each of the other mucopolysaccharidoses. Morquio's syndrome closely resembles Hurler's. Stiff joints and clouding of the corneas characterize Scheie's syndrome; restlessness and rapidly progressing mental deficiency, Sanfilippo's syndrome. In the Maroteaux–Lamy syndrome, most of the physical features of Hurler's syndrome are present, but the mental development is normal. Hunter's syndrome differs from Hurler's in that it affects only males, is milder, does not cause corneal opacity, and involves less severe mental retardation.
·genetic cause **11**:1059; table
·types, symptoms, and causation **5**:19b

mucous cell, a cell that secretes mucus.
·human digestive system anatomy **5**:793b

mucous glands: *see* salivary glands.

mucous membrane, membrane lining many tracts and structures of the body, including the passages of the digestive system, the nose, the eyelids, the windpipe and bronchi, and the ureters, urethra, and urinary bladder. The membranes are called mucous because they contain cells that secrete mucin, a mucopolysaccharide (*see* polysaccharide) that is the principal constituent of mucus.
·animal tissue comparisons **18**:444a
·chemoreceptive structures of
  vertebrates **4**:184d
human
·air ionization effects of air conditioning and
  heating systems tab **8**:727
·digestive system anatomy **5**:789e
·digestive tract disease symptoms **5**:797a
·gastrointestinal hormone source **6**:814f
·industrial environment hazards **9**:529b
·pain sensations in oral cavity **16**:550c
·respiratory system anatomy **15**:764c
·urinary bladder anatomy **7**:54a
·vocal apparatus function **17**:480b
·infectious diseases of the mouth, nose, eye,
  and genital tract **9**:542h

mucoviscidosis (metabolic disorder): *see* cystic fibrosis of the pancreas.

Mucrospirifer, genus of extinct brachiopods (lampshells) found as fossils in Middle and Upper Devonian marine rocks (the Devonian Period began 395,000,000 years ago and lasted 50,000,000 years). *Mucrospirifer* forms are

Mucrospirifer mucronatus, collected from the Hamilton Group, Thedford, Ontario
By courtesy of the Buffalo Museum of Science

characterized by an extended hinge line of the two valves, or shells, of the brachiopod and a prominent fold and sulcus—a bow-shaped ridge and depressed trough, respectively. The many species of *Mucrospirifer* are abundant Devonian fossils; evolutionary trends within the genus and related forms are relatively well-known and studied.
·body plan, illus. 1 **3**:98

mucus, slimy fluid exuded by living organisms to conserve moisture or to protect and lubricate surfaces. In mammals it is a fluid composed principally of water and mucin, a mucopolysaccharide (*see* polysaccharide) secreted by certain cells of the mucous membrane.
·animal disease and degeneration **5**:870h
·animal tissues and fluids comparisons **18**:444a
·feeding behaviour in animals **7**:208d
human
·gastric juice composition and
  functions **5**:774c
·immunoglobulin content **9**:252h
·lubrication of nasal passages and
  sinuses **16**:807c
·locomotion of flatworms and protozoa **11**:16f
·protective function on fish skin **7**:333d
·snail and slug multiple uses **7**:949c *passim*
  to 953b
·source and lubrication properties **9**:668a

mud, Netherlandic unit of measure equal to one hectolitre.
·weights and measures, table 5 **19**:734

mud, marine, unconsolidated mixture of seawater with clay, with or without silt and less common larger particles, occurring on the sea floor. The term has no compositional restrictions and embraces the entire spectrum of organic and inorganic chemical and mineralogic material occurring in particulate form.

Müdafaa-ı Hukuk Cemiyetleri (Turkey): *see* Associations for the Defense of Rights.

mudang (Korean: "female shaman"), a Korean priestess who employs magic to effect cures, to tell fortunes, to soothe spirits of the dead, and to repulse evil. Her counterpart, the male shaman, is called a *paksu;* both, however, are also known by numerous other names in various parts of Korea.

Hereditary *mudang*, especially in former times, formed a separate religious group of low social standing and seldom married into families on a higher social level. Daughters of such shamans became either *mudang* after proper training or *kisaeng*, waitresses at Korean drinking houses. Sons of hereditary shamans usually became singers of *p'ansori*, the one-man opera of Korea, or musicians accompanying shamanistic rituals. Less gifted boys frequently became acrobats.

Certain *mudang* are believed to possess exceptional power and effectiveness because of a guardian spirit; they are professionally trained, are highly respected, and are the Korean shamans *par excellence*. (Most modern *mudang* are motivated by economic gain and are little respected.)

A *mudang* functions mainly during a *kut* (shamanistic séance), dancing and singing traditional songs during a ritual that invites happiness and repels evil. A *kut* generally consists of 12 *kŏri* (procedures), each of which is addressed to such specific gods or spirits as the god of childbirth, good harvest, and property or the goddesses in control of specific diseases or the patron spirit of shamans or the protector god of households. Before the *kut* begins, an altar is set on the floor and offerings are made. As the ritual progresses, the *mudang* goes into a trance during which the god is said to arrive, to be placated, and then to communicate a message to the client through the *mudang*.

A *kut* may be sponsored by a family, a village, or the state and is often motivated by a desire to avoid evil, recover from illness, or gain prosperity. The ultimate purpose of a *kut*, however, is the final goal of shamanism itself: the possession of happiness, fame, security, safety, and so on.

Mu-dan-jiang (China): *see* Mu-tan-chiang.

Mudanya, Armistice of (Oct. 11, 1922), agreement concluded between the European Allies and Turkey.
·Turkish territorial gains **13**:791a

mud crack: *see* sedimentary structure.

mud dauber: *see* thread-waisted wasp.

Muddiman, Henry, 17th-century English journalist.
·newspaper publishing history **15**:238c

Mudejars, Spanish MUDÉJARES (from Arabic *mudajjan*, "permitted to remain"), those Muslims who remained in Spain after the Christian reconquest (11th–15th centuries AD) of the Iberian Peninsula. In return for the payment

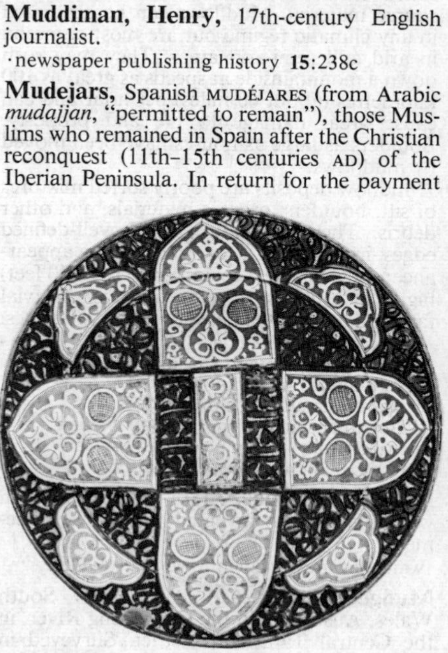

Hispano-Moresque dish, early 15th century, from Valencia; in the Victoria and Albert Museum, London
By courtesy of the Victoria and Albert Museum, London

of a poll tax, the Mudejars were a protected minority, allowed to retain their own religion, language, and customs. Headed by leaders assigned by the local Christian princes, they formed separate communities and quarters in larger towns, where they were subject to their own Muslim laws. By the 13th century the Mudejars, most of whom converted to Islām after the Arab invasion of Spain, began to abandon their Arabic for the Spanish spoken by the Christians—though they always wrote it in Arabic characters, giving rise to their characteristic *aljamiado* literature.

As highly skilled craftsmen, the Mudejars were also responsible for an extremely successful blending of Arabic and Spanish artistic elements: a Mudejar style, marked by the frequent use of the horseshoe arch and the vault, distinguishes the church and palace architecture of Toledo, Córdoba, Seville, and Valencia. The Mudejar hand is also evident in the ornamentation of wood and ivory, metalwork, ceramics, and textiles, and their lustre pottery is second only to that of the Chinese.

With the fall of Granada, the last Muslim stronghold in Spain (1492), however, the situation of the Mudejars rapidly deteriorated. They were dubbed Moriscos (Spanish: Little Moors) and forced to leave the country or convert to Christianity; thus, by 1614 the last of an estimated 3,000,000 Spanish Muslims were expelled from Spain.

·examples of Muslim influence **9**:1001c
·furniture design and decoration **7**:798c
·Gaudí's Barcelona designs **7**:957e
·reconquest settlement and governance **17**:410c
·Sevillian architectural heritage **16**:581d
·Spanish interior design features **9**:714c

mudfish: *see* bowfin.

mud flat: *see* playas, pans, and saline flats.

mudflow, flow of water that contains large amounts of suspended particles and silt. It has a higher density and viscosity than a streamflow and can deposit only the coarsest part of its load; this causes irreversible sediment entrainment. Its high viscosity will not allow it to flow as far as a water flow.

Mudflows occur on steep slopes where vegetation is not sufficient to prevent rapid erosion but can occur on gentle slopes if other conditions are met. Other factors are heavy precipitation in short periods and an easily erodible source material. Mudflows can be generated in any climatic regime but are most common in arid and semi-arid areas. They may rush down a mountainside at speeds as great as 100 kilometres (about 60 miles) per hour and can cause great damage to life and property. Boulders as large as houses have been moved by mudflows.

Mudflow deposits are poorly sorted mixtures of silt, boulders, organic materials, and other debris. They have abrupt and well-defined edges, irregular surfaces, and a lobate appearance; they may be 3 to 6 metres (10 to 20 feet) high. Such deposits are extensive on alluvial fans and around the bases of many volcanoes.

·alluvial fan flow regimes **1**:616b
·breccia formation and chacteristics **4**:1112c
·desert landform evolution **5**:610h
·earth movements on slopes **6**:65h
·sediment accumulation by runoff **8**:434h
·tectonism physiographic effects **14**:435a
·water content and plasticity **16**:636d

Mudge, Thomas, 18th-century English watchmaker who invented the lever escapement.

·watch lever escapement invention **4**:748d

Mudgee, town, east central New South Wales, Australia, on the Cudgegong River, in the Central Tableland district. Surveyed in 1836, it grew with gold mining in the 1850s and was gazetted a municipality in 1860. Mudgee is derived from an Aboriginal word meaning "nest among the hills." Linked to Sydney (130 mi [209 km] southeast) by air and rail, it serves a region yielding high quality merino sheep and wool, cereals, cattle, fodder, wine grapes, and dairy products. Industries include the manufacture of textiles, wine making, brewing, and sawmilling. The town celebrates a floral festival (September) to honour the author-poet Henry Lawson, whose boyhood home was at nearby Eurunderee. Pop. (1971 prelim.) 5,583.
32°36′ S, 149°35′ E

mud hen (bird): *see* coot.

muditā (Sanskrit: "joy," especially participation in the joy of others), one of the four noble practices (*brahmavihāra*) of Buddhism.

·Buddhist philosophy summary **3**:390g

mudlark (bird): *see* Grallinidae.

mudminnow, hardy fish, family Umbridae, found in cool, mud-bottomed ponds, lakes, and streams of Europe and North America.

Mudminnow (*Umbra*)
E.R. Degginger

Somewhat pikelike fishes with rounded snouts and tails, mudminnows are about 7.5 to 15 centimetres (3 to 6 inches) long. They frequently bury themselves, tail first, in the mud; they can survive in water too low in oxygen to support other fishes. The several species are of the genera *Umbra* and *Novumbra*. In North America the eastern mudminnow (*U. pygmaea*) is sometimes called rockfish and the central mudminnow (*U. limi*) mudfish or dogfish. Mudminnows are often used as bait or kept in home aquariums.

·classification and general features **16**:191d

mudnest builder (bird): *see* Grallinidae.

mudor šuan, a ceremony held by the Votyaks to consecrate a new family or clan shrine, *kuala*, and a sacred container, *voršud*, kept on a shelf within the shrine. *Mudor* itself means "ground," so that the ceremony in fact was the blessing of a new site taken over by people breaking off from the ancestral lineage when it expanded past a critical point. The main ceremony of the *mudor šuan*, or *mudor* "wedding," consisted of taking ashes from the hearth of the ancestral shrine with some appropriate formula such as "I am taking the lesser and leaving the greater" and transferring them to the shrine in a new location, which would then stand in a subordinate position in relation to the greater ancestral *kuala*.

mud plantain, common name for aquatic annual or perennial plants of the genus *Heteranthera* of the pickerelweed family (Pontederiaceae), about 10 species, distributed primarily in tropical America. The broad or ribbonlike leaves have leafstalks that form sheaths around the long stems. Water star grass (*H. dubia*) is widely distributed throughout North America; it has yellow star-shaped flowers. Some species of *Heteranthera* grow below the water; others float or are rooted on muddy stream banks and lakeshores.

mud puppy, common name for any of five species of salamanders of the genus *Necturus* (family Necturidae, order Urodela). Some zoologists recognize one species, *Necturus maculosus*, and several subspecies. The popular name derives from the mistaken belief that, like puppies, they are able to bark. They are found in lakes, rivers, and swamps of eastern North America. Those of southern United States are commonly called water dogs.

Adults range from about 18 to 43 cm (7 to 17 in.). The body is gray or brown and usually has a scattering of blurry dark spots. The tail fins have an orange tint. The external gills, retained throughout life, are bright red. The short, weak legs have four toes.

Mud puppies usually hide during the day under stones or buried in mud. They eat small animals and the eggs of other aquatic animals. Fertilization is internal. The female lays eggs but sometimes gives birth to live young.

·classification and general features **18**:1088c
·red blood cell characteristics **4**:632g
·reproductive system, illus. 4 **15**:709

mudrā (Sanskrit: "gesture, posture, seal"), symbolic gestures of the hands and fingers, used extensively in Indian ritual, iconography, recitation, and dance.

The position of one or both hands has innumerable combinations and variations, each with its own name indicating its meaning. In ritual, the involvement of the body reinforces speech and mental image to intensify and enrich the total religious experience. In iconography, the positions of the hands in a statue or a painting often symbolize a mythical episode associated with the god or an attitude. The gestures of the Buddha most commonly depicted in art are the *abhaya-mudrā* ("do not fear"—right hand held up at shoulder height, palm out); *dharmacakra-mudrā* ("the preaching of the law"—both hands raised in front of the chest); *dhyāna-mudrā* ("meditation"—right hand lying loosely on palm of left hand); and the *bhūmisparśa-mudrā* ("calling the earth to witness"—right hand, palm out, pointing at the ground).

*Mudrā*s are characteristic of all the classical styles of Indian dance but are most highly developed in the dance-drama of the Malabar coast, *kathākali*, in which the dancers mime the text as it is sung, from time to time elaborately improvising on a single phrase, such as "a budding lotus."

Buddha with his hands in the *dharmacakra-mudrā*, to symbolize preaching of the law, 5th century sculpture from the Sārnāth Museum, Sārnāth, Uttar Pradesh, India
Pramod Chandra

As Hinduism and Buddhism expanded to countries beyond India, the use of *mudrā*s spread also. This is particularly evident in the dance, drama, religious ritual, and art of Southeast Asia and Tibet.

·Asian dance gesture stylization **5**:470a
·Buddhist art and ritual **3**:395g *passim* to 396h
·Buddhist mystical significance **3**:415g
·dance and communication **5**:453d
·folk dance in India **7**:451h
·Hindu symbolic theology **8**:905h
·Southeast Asian theatrical adaptations **17**:242h

Mudrārākṣasa, 9th-century Indian drama by Viśākhadatta.

·political and historical theme **17**:138a

Mudros, Armistice of (Oct. 30, 1918), pact signed at the port of Mudros, on the Aegean island of Lemnos, between the Ottoman Empire and Great Britain (representing the Allied powers) marking the defeat of the Ottoman Empire in World War I (1914–18).

Under the terms of the Armistice, the Ottomans surrendered Hejaz, Yemen, Syria, Mesopotamia, Tripolitania, and Cyrenaica; the Allies were to occupy the Straits of the Dardanelles and the Bosporus, Batum (now in southwest Georgia, U.S.S.R.), and the Taurus tunnel system; and the Allies won the right to occupy "in case of disorder" the six Armenian provinces in Anatolia and to seize "any strategic points" in case of a threat to Allied security. The Ottoman Army was demobilized and ports, railways, and natural resources were surrendered to the Allies.
·Ottoman concessions to Allies **19**:964d

mud skipper, any of about six species of small, tropical gobies of the family Periophthalmidae (order Perciformes). Mud skippers are found in the Indo-Pacific, from Africa to Polynesia and Australia. They live in swamps and estuaries and on mud flats and are noted for their ability to climb, walk, and skip about out of water. Elongated fishes, they range up to about 30 centimetres (12 inches) long. They have two dorsal fins, and their pelvic fins are placed forward under the body, either partly or completely fused. Their blunt heads are topped by large, movable, close-set, and protuberant eyes, and their strong, leglike pectoral fins aid them in movements on land. Out of water, they breathe air and moisture trapped in their gill chambers. They prey on crustaceans and other small animals.

Mud skippers (*Periophthalmus*)
Ivan Polunin from Natural Historic Photographic Agency—EB Inc.

·classification and general features **14**:57f; illus. 52
·escape method and habitat **7**:332h

mud snake: *see* hoop snake.

mud snapper, marine sediment-sampling machinery.
·size and operation **18**:851c

mudstone, sedimentary rock composed primarily of clay- or silt-sized particles (less than 1⁄16 millimetre in diameter); it is not laminated or easily split into thin layers. Some geologists designate as mudstone any similar rock that is blocky or massive; others, however, prefer a broader definition that includes all of the members of the shale group.
·feldspar weathering and deposition **6**:706a
·graywacke sequences and shale **8**:298b
·mountain building and rock deposition **12**:582g
·sedimentary rock classification **16**:465b; table 464
·Silurian platform rocks **16**:769g

mud turtle, any of about a dozen species of freshwater turtles belonging to the genus *Kinosternon*, family Kinosternidae. Mud turtles are highly aquatic and are found in North and South America. Like the related musk turtles (*Sternotherus*), they are small animals (usually 15 centimetres [6 inches] or less in shell length) with fleshy barbels on the chin and the ability to exude a strong, musky odour. They differ in having a broad lower shell with a hinged section at either end. The hinged portions of the shell can be pulled up to cover and protect the head, legs, and tail of the turtle. Little is known of the habits of most mud turtles. The common, or eastern, mud turtle (*Kinosternon subrubrum*) of the eastern United States lives in shallow, often brackish, water; in captivity it takes almost any type of food.
·locomotion in water **11**:18f

Mudugh, administrative region, central Somalia (in Eastern Africa). It is a hot, arid plain with sand dunes along the Indian Ocean coast to the east. The capital is Galka'- yo.
·map, Somalia **16**:1058
·population groups and character **16**:1058e

mud volcano, mound of mud heaved up through overlying sediments. The craters are usually shallow and may intermittently erupt mud. These eruptions continuously rebuild the cones, which are eroded relatively easily.

Some mud volcanoes are due to hot-spring activity where large amounts of gas and small amounts of water react chemically with the surrounding rocks and form a boiling mud. Variations are the porridge pot (a basin of boiling mud that erodes chunks of the surrounding rock) and the paint pot (a basin of boiling mud that is tinted yellow, green, or blue by minerals from the surrounding rocks).

Other mud volcanoes, entirely of a nonigneous origin, occur only in oil-field regions that are relatively young and have soft unconsolidated formations. Under compactional stress, methane and related hydrocarbon gases mixed with mud force their way upward and burst through to the surface spewing mud into a conelike shape. Because of the compactional stress and the depth from which the mixture comes, the mud is often hot and may have an accompanying steam cloud.

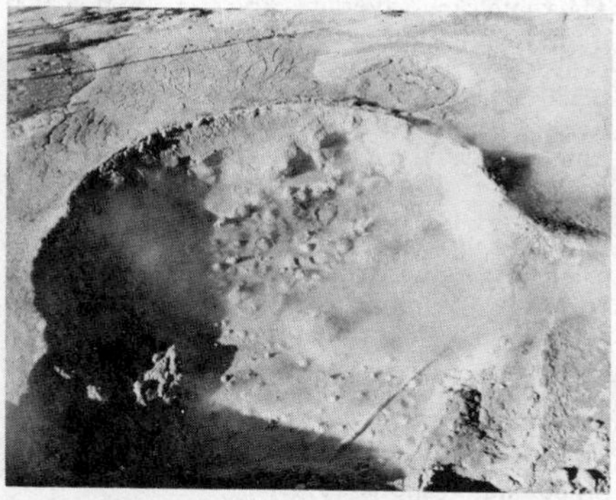

Crater of the Sulphur Cauldron, an active mud volcano, in Yellowstone National Park, Wyoming
Josef Muench

·petroleum occurrence and distribution **14**:172h

Muehlenbeckia platyclados (plant): *see* Polygonales.

Mueller (German MÜLLER), **Ferdinand (Jakob Heinrich), Baron von** (b. June 30, 1825, Rostock, now in East Germany—d. Oct. 10, 1896, Melbourne, Australia), botanist and explorer famous for his pioneer studies of the plants of Australia.

An apprenticeship as a chemist ended for Mueller when he passed the pharmaceutical examination and began the study of botany at the University of Kiel. Soon after receiving his Ph.D. he left Germany for Adelaide, South Australia (1847), where for some time he worked as a chemist (pharmacist). The same year he started writing a series of papers on the flora of southern Australia. Appointed as a foundation government botanist in 1853, he moved to Melbourne and travelled throughout the surrounding area conducting extensive botanical studies.

In 1857 Mueller was appointed director of the botanical gardens at Melbourne, where he had built what is now the national herbarium. He continued to make numerous explorative trips throughout Australia. In 1858 the first volume of his *Fragmenta Phytographiae Australiae* (12 vol., 1858–82) appeared. With the British botanist George Bentham he wrote a systematic monograph on the flora of Australia, *Flora Australiensis: A Description of the Plants of the Australian Territory* (1863–78). His most popular book was *Select Plants Readily Eligible for Industrial Culture or Naturalization in Victoria* (1876). In recognition of his outstanding contributions to botany, Mueller was elected to membership in the Royal Society of London at the age of 36.

Muenster, semi-soft cheese, bland or sharp depending on length of cure.
·characteristics and classification **5**:432h

Muette de Portici, La (French: "The Mute Girl of Portici"), also called MASANIELLO, opera by Daniel Auber.
·popularity in 19th century **13**:586c

muezzin, Arabic MUʾADHDHIN, in Islām, the official who proclaims the call (*adhān*) to public worship on Friday and to the five daily prayers (*ṣalāts*). The muezzin is the servant of the mosque chosen for his good character, who either stands at the door or at the side of a small mosque or on the minaret of a large one and cries the set formula.

Muezzin giving the call to prayer from the minaret of a mosque in Cairo
Ewing Galloway

·Islāmic ritual practices **9**:918f
·unifying effects of common prayer times **19**:1014g

Mufaḍḍalīyāt, al-, an anthology of ancient Arabic poems, compiled by al-Mufaḍḍal ibn Muḥammad ibn Yaʿlah between 762 and 784; it is of the highest importance as a record of the thought and poetic art of Arabia in the last two pre-Islāmic centuries. Not more than five or six of the 126 poems appear to have been composed by poets born under Islām, and, while a certain number converted to Islām, their work bears few marks of it. The ancient virtues alone—hospitality to the guest and to the poor, profuse expenditure of wealth, valour in battle, faithfulness to the cause of the tribe—were praised.

The 126 pieces are distributed among 68 poets, and the work represents a selection from the composition of those called *al-muqillūn*, "authors of whom little has survived," rather than the famous poets whose works had been collected in *dīwān*s. Not all poems of *al-Mufaḍḍaliyāt* are complete, many are mere fragments and even in the longest there are often gaps. Al-Mufaḍḍal, however, always tried to present complete poems and evidently set down all that he could collect of a poem from the memory of a *rāwī* (professional reciter).

Despite the sparseness of their extant work, several of the poets of *al-Mufaḍḍaliyat* are well-known and highly respected, such as ʿAlqamah ibn ʿAbadah, Mutammim ibn Nuwayrah, Salamah ibn Jandal, Shanfarā, ʿAbd Yaghuth, and Abu Dhuʿayb. Al-Ḥārith was already celebrated for his ode in the *Muʿallaqāt* collection.

muff, a cylindrical covering of fur, fabric, feathers, or other soft material with open ends into which the hands are placed to keep them warm. Originally a purse and hand warmer in one, the muff was first introduced by ladies of

Woman carrying a fur muff, "November," an engraving by Robert Dighton, *c.* 1785–90

By courtesy of the Victoria and Albert Museum, London

fashion in 1570, when all kinds of fur trimming were becoming popular. In the 19th century, muffs were considered an essential accessory of dress and ranged from large down muffs to small fur or velvet ones matching the trim on a lady's dress.

Muffat, Georg (baptized June 1, 1653, Megève, Savoy, in modern France—d. Feb. 23, 1704, Passau, Ger.), composer whose concerti grossi and instrumental suites were among the earliest German examples of those genres. He held positions as organist at Molsheim and Strasbourg cathedrals and in 1678 became organist to the archbishop of Salzburg. In 1681 he went to Italy and in Rome studied with Corelli and Pasquini. He spent about six years in Paris, where he acquainted himself thoroughly with the music of Lully. He became organist to the bishop of Passau in 1687, chapelmaster in 1690. His most famous work, 12 orchestral suites, *Florelegia* (two sets, 1695 and 1698), was one of the earliest German collections of suites in the French manner, utilizing dance movements influenced by those of Lully's stage works. The *Florelegia* also contains valuable information about French performance practices in the late 17th century. His *Ausserlesene . . . Instrumental-Music* (1701) was an early collection of concerti grossi in the style developed by Corelli. Among his other works are the *Armonico tributo*, a set of five-part trio sonatas, and the *Apparatus musico-organisticus*, toccatas for organ.

His son Gottlieb Muffat (1690–1770) became organist to the emperor. His most important works were *Versetten oder Fugen* for organ (1726) and *Componimenti musicali* (*c.* 1739), from which Handel borrowed heavily.

·concerto grosso style and performance **4**:1067f

muffler, device through which the exhaust gases from an internal-combustion engine are passed to suppress the airborne noise. To be efficient as a sound silencer, a muffler must decrease the velocity of the exhaust gases and either absorb the sound waves or cancel them by interference with reflected waves coming from the same source.

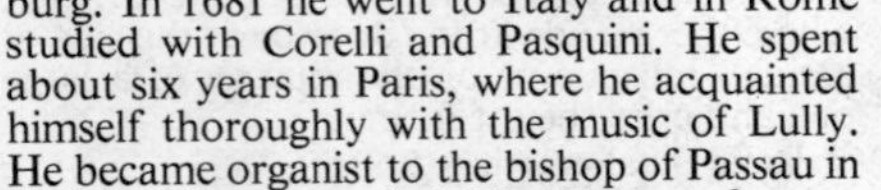

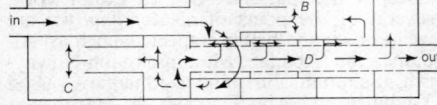

Noise flow through a typical muffler

From C.M. Harris (ed.), *Handbook of Noise Control* (copyright 1957); used with permission of McGraw-Hill Book Company

A typical sound-absorbing material is a thick layer of fine fibres; the fibres are caused to vibrate by the sound waves, thus converting the sound energy to heat. Muffler configurations that cancel sound waves by interference usually separate the waves into two components that follow different paths and come together again out of phase (out of step).

In the typical muffler shown schematically in the illustration, the heavy arrows indicate the gas flow and the light arrows the acoustic flow. The chambers *B* and *C* are known as resonators and are of such dimensions that they cancel sound waves of specified frequencies. The discharge tube *D* is surrounded by small annular (ringlike) chambers; sound enters these chambers through small holes in the discharge tube and is absorbed.

Mufflers of the straight-through type have a single tube with small holes connecting with annular chambers that are frequently stuffed with a sound-absorbing material.

·acoustical control of noise **1**:55d
·gasoline engine construction **7**:936h

Mufīd, al- (*c.* 10th–11th centuries), Muslim theologian.

·Muʿtazilite theology in Shīʿism **9**:1017e

Mu-fou Mountains, Wade-Giles romanization MU-FOU SHAN, Pin-yin romanization also MU-FOU SHAU, range in northern Hunan and Kiangsi provinces (*sheng*), China. The Mu-fou extend for more than 125 mi (200 km), from near P'ing-chiang in Hunan, northeastward to the Yangtze River Valley west of Chiu-chiang. The main range averages about 3,300 ft (1,000 m) in height; but Mt. Mu-fou itself, the great peak from which the range takes its name, reaches 5,236 ft (1,596 m), and San-feng Shan, further east, reaches 5,489 ft (1,673 m). The range divides the Yangtze Valley from the valley of the Hsiu Shui (stream), which drains into Po-yang Hu (lake). To the north of the main range is an area of low ridges and hills stretching down to the Yangtze Delta. The Mu-fou Mountains are extremely rugged and are forested. The range is a source of timber, wood oil, and other forest products; some areas are famous for their red tea.
29°00′ N, 114°00′ E

·Kiangsi geography and communications **10**:458h

muftī, anglicized MUFTI, an Islāmic canon lawyer who gives an opinion (*fatwā*) in answer to an inquiry by a private individual or judge. A *fatwā* usually requires knowledge of the Qurʾān and Ḥadīth (tradition), as well as knowledge of exegesis and collected precedents, and might be a pronouncement on some problematic legal matter. Under the Ottoman Empire, the *muftī* of Istanbul, the *shaykh al-islām* (in Turkish *şeyhülislâm*), ranked as Islām's foremost legal authority, theoretically presiding over the whole judicial and theological hierarchy. Development of civil codes in most Islāmic countries, however, tends to restrict the office of *muftī* to cases involving personal status, such as inheritance, marriage, and divorce; and even in this area, the prerogatives of the *muftī* are circumscribed by modern legislation.

Mufulira, town, Copperbelt Province, north central Zambia, just southwest of the Zaire frontier. It is one of the country's chief copper-mining centres, and rich local deposits have been exploited for many years. Smelting and electrolytic refining of copper is the only surface industry. Latest pop. est. 101,000.
12°33′ S, 28°14′ E

Mugano-Salyany, region, Azerbaijan Soviet Socialist Republic.

·economic aspects and prospects **2**:546a

Muggins, also known as ALL FIVES, Domino game similar to the draw game (*see* Dominoes) except for the rule that, if a player can play such a bone (domino) as makes the sum of the open-end pips on the layout a multiple of five, he scores that number. Each player takes five bones. If the leader poses either 5-5 (double-five), 6-4, 5-0, or 3-2, he scores the number of pips that are on the bone. If the leader does not score and to 2-4 the next player plays 4-3, the second player scores 5 (2+3); if to 2-4 he can play 4-4, he scores ten because a doublet scores its whole value. He must play if he can match; if he cannot, he draws until he can. Scores made during play (Muggins scores) are called and taken immediately. By prior agreement, if a player overlooks a score, his opponent may call "Muggins" (meaning simpleton) and take the score for himself. The first player to play all his bones scores in points the multiple of five that is nearest to the number of pips on bones remaining in his adversary's hand; *e.g.*, he scores 25 if his adversary has 27 pips, 30 if he has 28. If neither hand can match, the lowest number of pips wins, and the score is taken as before. Winner is the first to reach a total of 200 points.

The game All Threes is played in the same manner as Muggins, save that three or some multiple of three is aimed at.

Another game, Threes and Fives, is similar, but only one point is scored for each five or three made at the two ends, though they can be scored in combination. Thus A plays 6-5, B 1-6; B scores two points for 5-1 (two threes). A plays 1-5, B 5-5; B now scores eight more points, five points for five threes and three points for three fives because a doublet scores its whole value.

Sniff, a very popular domino game in the U.S., lends itself to skillful play. It is essentially Muggins, but the first double played is called Sniff and may be put down endwise or sidewise (*à cheval*), at the holder's option. Thereafter one may play to this bone both endwise and sidewise, so that there are usually four open ends with which to reckon.

Muggleton, Lodowick (b. July 1609, London—d. March 14, 1698, London), Puritan religious leader and anti-Trinitarian heretic whose followers, known as Muggletonians, believed he was a prophet. After claiming to

Muggleton, detail of an oil painting by W. Wood, 1674; in the National Portrait Gallery, London

By courtesy of the National Portrait Gallery, London

have had spiritual revelations, beginning in 1651, he and his cousin John Reeve announced themselves as the two prophetic witnesses referred to in Rev. 11:3. Their book, *A Transcendent Spiritual Treatise upon Several Heavenly Doctrines*, was published in 1652. They further expounded their beliefs in *A Divine Looking-Glass* (1656), maintaining that the traditional distinction between the three Persons of the Triune God is purely nominal, that God has a real human body, and that he left the Old Testament Hebrew prophet Elijah, who had ascended to heaven, as his vice regent when he himself descended to die on the Cross.

According to Muggleton and Reeve, the unforgivable sin was disbelief in them as true prophets. Although some notable men became Muggletonians, the group's notions provoked much opposition. Muggleton was imprisoned for blasphemy in 1653, and his own followers temporarily repudiated him in 1660 and again in 1670. His attack on the Quakers led their leader, William Penn, to write *The New Witnesses Proved Old Heretics* (1672). Tried for blasphemy in 1677, Muggleton was convicted and fined £500. George C. Williamson's *Lodowick Muggleton* (1919) also deals with his sect, which survived until the early 20th century.

Mughal carpets, handwoven in India in the 16th and 17th centuries for the Mughal emperors and their courts. Aside from patterns in the Persian manner (*see* Indo-Isfahan carpets), a series of distinctively Indian designs were developed, including scenic and landscape carpets; animal carpets with spirited chases backward and forward across the field;

Mughal carpet from India, 17th century; in the Textile Museum, Washington, D.C.

Textile Museum Collection, Washington, D.C.; photograph, Otto E. Nelson—EB Inc.

elaborate architectural latticeworks in the Italian manner, with floral content; and several magnificent prayer rugs with a prominent central flowering plant. Characteristic of the floral patterns is common use of trailing racemes such as wisteria or elongated bunches of grapes. Possibly of a later date, many rugs, including a series of prayer rugs that may have been produced in Kashmir, have densely packed millefleurs patterns. Fine quality Mughal carpets, with the warp in bands of contrasting colours and with pile of such extremely fine wool that it is sometimes taken for silk on a silken foundation, have the tightest and most delicate knotting found among antique Oriental rugs. The prayer rugs with a central flowering plant motif, for example, have approximately 2,000 knots to the square inch (300 per square centimetre) and a fragmentary lattice rug in the Textile Museum, Washington, D.C., has more than 2,500. Most Mughal rugs, however, have a foundation of cotton. Mughal carpets are thought to have been made in Lahore, Agra, and perhaps Fatehpur Sīkri. One of the most noted is the Girdlers' Carpet, in Girdlers' Hall, London.

Mughal, also spelled MOGUL, **dynasty,** the Arabic and Persian form of the word Mongol. It is conventionally used to describe the Muslim dynasty that ruled large parts of India from the early 16th to the mid-18th century. The dynasty was founded by Bābur (reigned 1526–30), a descendant of the Turkish conqueror Timur (Tamerlane) and of Chagatai, second son of the Mongol ruler Genghis Khan. The dynasty is notable for about two centuries of effective rule over much of India, for the ability of its rulers, who through seven generations maintained a record of unusual talent, and for its administrative organization. A further distinction was the attempt of the Mughals to integrate Hindus and Muslims into a united Indian state. Bābur's grandson Akbar (reigned 1556–1605) consolidated and transformed the Mughal state, extending its limits from Afghanistan to the Bay of Bengal and southward to Gujarāt and the northern Deccan. The empire was maintained by Akbar's son Jahāngīr (reigned 1605–27) and his grandson Shāh Jāhān (reigned 1627–58). Shāh Jāhān's son Aurangzeb (reigned 1658–1707) annexed the Muslim Deccan kingdoms of Bijāpur and Golconda. During the reign of Muḥammad Shāh (1719–48), the empire began to break up; by the second half of the 18th century, the Mughals ruled only a small area around Delhi, which passed under Marāthā (1785) and then British control (1803). The last Mughal, Bahādur Shāh II (reigned 1837–57), was exiled to Rangoon by the British after his involvement with the mutiny and revolt of 1857.

·Afghanistan origins of Bābur **1**:174c
·agricultural crops and technology **1**:330a
·Akbar's career and achievements **1**:399h
·Albuquerque's Indian conquest **1**:431a
·annexation of Mālwa **11**:279f
·annexation of Muslim states **9**:373e; map 383
·Aurangzeb's reign and significance **2**:372g
·Bābur's conquest of India **2**:553d
·British claim to legal rule of Bengal **8**:665h
·defense of British in Calcutta **3**:586h
·Delhi's shifting status as capital **5**:571b
·French colonialization progress **4**:887a
·Ganges Plain historical past **7**:881a
·Hyderābād's conquest and decline **9**:76c
·Ibn Baṭṭūṭah in Muḥammad's court **9**:144f
·Indian education organization **6**:339g
·Indian garden design **7**:893b; illus. 901
·Indian philosophical developments **9**:333a
·Islāmic architecture revival **17**:182g
·Islāmic cultural history **9**:935c
·Islāmic effect on Hinduism **8**:914h
·Islāmic visual arts **9**:1008b
·Jain prestige and mutual influences **10**:14c
·Lahore's cultural history **10**:599a
·landscape design development **7**:893b; illus. 901
·military and political history **9**:378c
·Mysore exploitation of empire turmoil **12**:777c
·Nāden Shāh victory at Karnāl **8**:663d
·Orissa's transition from Afghān rule **13**:739f
·prince and dervish illus. **9**:935
·Punjabi cultural history **15**:288b
·Rājasthān conquest and rule **15**:495f
·Sayyid Ahmad's cultural inheritance **1**:369a
·Sikh battles in 18th century **16**:744f
·Śivajī as obstruction to expansion **16**:812a
·Ṣūfī reaction to attempted syncretism **9**:944b

Mughal glass, made in India during the Mughal period (1556–1707). Because imported Persian craftsmen were patronized by the Mughal court, Mughal glass of the 17th and 18th centuries shows an obvious indebtedness to Persian influences. Floral arabesques and sprays and, to a lesser extent, geometrical motifs were popular with Mughal glassmakers. Bottles, hooka bowls, dishes, and spittoons were made in various fanciful and elegant shapes, the use of coloured glass with painted designs becoming increasingly frequent. In addition to Delhi and the provincial Mughal capitals, Kapadvanj, in Gujarāt, was an important centre of production.

Hookah bowl of blue glass painted with gold, Mughal, 18th century; in the Prince of Wales Museum of Western India, Bombay

M. Chandra

Mughalistan, 14th-century Chagatai khanate.

·Chagatai khanate disintegration **18**:794c

Mughal painting, a style of painting, confined mainly to book illustration and the production of individual miniatures, that evolved in India during the reigns of the Mughal emperors (16th to 19th centuries). In its initial phases it showed some indebtedness to the Safavid school of Persian painting but rapidly moved away from Persian ideals.

Bird perched on rocks, Mughal painting, *c.* AD 1610; in the State Museum, Hyderābād, Andhra Pradesh, India

P. Chandra

Mughal painting was essentially a court art; it developed under the patronage of the ruling Mughal emperors and began to decline when the rulers lost interest. The subjects treated were generally secular, consisting of illustrations to historical works and Persian and Indian literature, portraits of the emperor and his court, studies of natural life, and genre scenes.

The school had its beginnings during the reign of the emperor Humāyūn (1530–40 and 1555–56), who invited two Persian artists, Mīr Sayyid ʿAlī and Khwāja ʿAbd-uṣ-Ṣamad, to join him in India. The earliest and most important undertaking of the school was a series of large miniatures of the *Dāstān-e Amīr-Ḥamzeh* undertaken during the reign of Akbar (1556–1605), which when completed numbered some 1400 illustrations of an unusually large size (22 by 28 inches [56 by 71 centimetres]). Of the 200 or so that have survived, the largest number are in the Österreichisches Museum für Angewandte Künst, Vienna.

Though retaining the upright format, general setting, and flat aerial perspective of Persian painting, the Indian artists of Akbar's court exhibited an increasing naturalism and detailed observation of the world around them. Akbar's fondness for history resulted in his commissioning of such dynamic illustrated histories as the *Akbar-nāmeh* in the Victoria and Albert Museum, London. An empathy for animals is evident in the illustrations of the animal fables, particularly the *Kalīlah wa Dimnah* and the *Anwār-e Suhaylī*. Other outstanding series are the illustrations of the *Razm-nāmeh* (the Persian name for the Hindu epic, the *Mahābhārata*) in the City Palace Museum, Jaipur, and the *Dīvān* of Ḥāfeẓ in the Reza Library, Rāmpur. Outstanding painters of the period were Dasvant and Basāvan.

The Mughal artists gained knowledge of Western technique from engravings and illuminated manuscripts introduced into the court from 1580 onward by Jesuit missionaries and other European visitors. In turn, Western artists such as Rembrandt saw and made copies of samples of Mughal painting.

Less emphasis was given to book illustration during the period of Jahāngīr (1605–27). Instead, Jahāngīr preferred court scenes, portraits, and animal studies. The style shows technical advancement in the fine brushwork; the compositions are less crowded, colours are more subdued, and movement is much less dynamic. The artist of the Jahāngīr period exhibited a sensitive understanding of human nature and an interest in the psychological subtleties of portraiture. Noted painters of the period were Abū al-Ḥasan, called the "wonder of the age"; Bishandās, praised for his portraiture; and Ustād Mansūr, who excelled in animal studies.

The elegance and richness of the Jahāngīr period style continued during the reign of Shāh Jahān (1628–58) but with an increasing tendency to become cold and rigid. Genre scenes—such as musical parties, lovers on a terrace, or ascetics gathered around a fire—became frequent, and the trend continued in the reign of Aurangzeb (1659–1707). Despite a brief revival during the reign of Muḥammad Shāh (1719–48), Mughal painting continued to decline, and creative activity ceased during the reign of Shāh ʿĀlam II (1759–1806).

The technique of Mughal painting, in the initial phases, often involved a team of artists, one determining the composition, a second doing the actual colouring, and perhaps a specialist in portraiture working on individual faces. Fine brushes were made from the tail hairs of the gray squirrel. The paper, at first imported from Iran, was later produced in India from bamboo, jute, and cotton. Pigments were prepared from minerals and vegetables, diluted with water, and the brushing medium consisted of a glue such as gum arabic. The enamel-like brilliance was produced by burnishing the completed picture with a piece of polished agate.

·ʿAbbās I portrait, illus. **1**:4
·dervish and devotee illus. **9**:935
·17th-century drawing illus. **5**:1010
·style, technique, and major works **17**:198h; illus. 201
·style characteristics, illus., **17**: South Asian Peoples, Arts of, Plates 7 and 8

Mughal style, Indo-European style of furniture that originated during the 16th century with the introduction of Portuguese furniture into northern India.
·materials and Renaissance influence **7**:806h

Mughīrah ibn Shuʿbah, al-, 7th-century Umayyad governor of Kūfah, Iraq.
·Muʿāwiyah and his administrators **3**:627c

Mu Gia (MUGIA) **Deo,** pass in the Chaîne Annamitique between northern Vietnam and Laos, 55 mi (90 km) northeast of Donghoi in Binh Tri Thien province (*tinh*), northern Vietnam. The pass lies 1,371 ft (418 m) above sea level and carries the road from Tan Ap, Vietnam, to Thakhek, Laos, the seat of Khammouane province (*khoueng*) on the Mekong River. On its eastern approach a cable railway runs parallel with the pass.
17°40′ N, 105°47′ E
·map, Laos **10**:675
·map, Vietnam **19**:134

Mugilidae (fish family): *see* mullet.

Mugiloididae, family of fishes of the order Perciformes.
·classification and general features **14**:55b; illus. 49

Muğla, town and *il* (province), southwestern Turkey. Muğla town was a favourite residence of the emirs of the 14th-century Turkmen Menteşe principality and was annexed to the Ottoman Empire in 1425. It lies on the edge of a small plain and serves as capital of the *il* and as a local market for agricultural products. It is linked by road with Izmir and Denizli.

Muğla *il*, with an area of 4,828 sq mi (12,504 sq km), borders on both the Aegean and the Mediterranean coasts, extending from the Menteşe massif eastward into the western Taurus ranges. Within the hills and mountains that predominate are extensively cultivated, small, enclosed basins. Citrus fruits are grown on the coastal strip, and cereals, cotton, and tobacco are cultivated in the hinterland; vines are grown in the fertile basin below Muğla town. The *il*, lying in the region of ancient Caria, is rich in historical sites. Its harbour towns of Bodrum (ancient Halicarnassus), Marmaris, and Fethiye are the focus of the province's tourist trade. The Fethiye *ilçe* (district) is rich in chromium mines. Pop. (1980) town, 27,162; *il*, 436,959.
37°12′ N, 28°22′ E
·map, Turkey **18**:785
·province area and population, table 2 **18**:787

Mugodzhar Hills, extension of the Ural Mountains in the Kazakh Soviet Socialist Republic.
49°00′ N, 58°40′ E
·geography, climate, and vegetation **18**:1032d
·Kazakh S.S.R. physical geography **10**:407g

mugwort (plant): *see* wormwood.

mugwump, in U.S. political history, slang term for an independent voter or, specifically, for the group of independent Republican Party reformers that refused to support the candidacy of James G. Blaine for the presidency in 1884. Their leaders included Theodore Roosevelt, George Curtis, and Henry Cabot Lodge. The term, first used by Charles A. Dana in the New York *Sun*, was derived from the Algonkian Indian word *mogkiomp* ("great man" or "big chief"); it was later used in England to signify one who remains politically neutral and votes for no party.

Muhājir, al-, also called AḤMAD IBN ʿĪSĀ, 10th-century Arabian political leader who founded the house of ʿAlawī Sayyid at Ḥaḍramawt.
·ʿAlawī dynasty foundation **1**:1048d

muhājirūn (Arabic: "emigrants"), in Islām, term first used to signify the earliest converts to Islām who accompanied the prophet Muḥammad in his *hijrah* ("emigration") from Mecca to Medina (AD 622). In later years the term was applied broadly to any Muslim group forced to emigrate en masse. *See also* hijrah.
·early Muslim history in Medina **3**:624c
·Muḥammad and followers' Medina status **12**:607f
·Muḥammad's support from Quraysh **1**:1046h

Muhamadi, epic poem, written in Swahili, that tells the life of Muḥammad.
·African literary distinction **1**:242e

Muḥammad 12:605, in full ABŪ AL-QĀSIM MUḤAMMAD IBN ʿABD ALLĀH IBN ʿABD AL-MUṬṬALIB IBN HĀSHIM (b. *c.* 570, Medina, now in Saudi Arabia—d. June 8, 632, Medina), founder of the religion of Islām and of the Arab Empire who initiated religious, social, and cultural developments of monumental significance in the history of mankind.

During his early life in Mecca his merchant activities resulted in his marriage, in about 595, to the wealthy widow Khadījah. He received his prophetic call in about 610 and began his religious activities among his friends and members of his own family. He began preaching publicly in about 613. The rise of Meccan opposition in about 615 and the withdrawal of his clan's protection in about 619 caused him to seek aid elsewhere. In 620 he began negotiations with clans in Medina, leading to his *hijrah* (Arabic: "emigration") there in 622. He eventually went to battle with his Meccan opponents and achieved, at the battle near Badr (624), his first military victory, which he interpreted to be a divine vindication of his prophethood. He again engaged his Meccan opponents at Uḥud (625) and lost, but in outwitting them at the siege of Medina (627) he further strengthened his position. The Treaty of al-Ḥudaybiyah (628) forced the Meccans to acknowledge his political authority and grant him concessions. His following was meanwhile growing; and in January 630 he entered Mecca with 10,000 men. As he had also formed alliances with nomadic tribes scattered throughout the peninsula, he left, on his death, most of Arabia united and ready for spreading the faith in Syria and Iraq.

TEXT BIOGRAPHY covers:
Early life **12**:606a
Prophetic call and early religious activities 606b
Opposition at Mecca 606g
The winning of the Meccans 608d
The unification of Arabia 608h
March to the Syrian border 609e
Character and achievements 609b

REFERENCES in other text articles:
·ʿAli's relationship **1**:573d
·Arabian conflict and acceptance of Islām **1**:1046g
·Averroës' affirmation of prophetic powers **2**:540c
·community leadership in early Islām **3**:624b
·criticism of miracles **12**:273d
·dietary laws and Muslim unity **5**:733c
·educational role in Islām **15**:645g
·Ethiopian Christian contacts **6**:1008b
·Ḥadīth and Qur'ān origins **8**:536a
·house in Medina **9**:984a
·Islām and Arab history **9**:927f; illus. 928
·Islāmic law in historical development **9**:938e
·Islāmic religious and social practices **9**:911h
·Meccan activities **11**:753e
·miracle performance in Islāmic legends **9**:949b
·Muʿāwiyah I reconciled to Islām **12**:605a
·music sanctions in early Islām **9**:975e
·prophetic doctrine and character **15**:66e
·Qur'ān revealed to the Prophet **15**:342a
·revelations as foundation of Islām **15**:784h
·salvation through submission **16**:204a
·secular and religious unity **4**:591a
·Seraglio palace sanctuary and relics **9**:1072c
·slavery and attitudes toward servitude **16**:858h
·Ṣūfī Muḥammad-mysticism **9**:945c
·theology of Christianity and Judaism **10**:300b

Muḥammad, Seljuq ruler of Iran, who reigned from 1105 to 1118.
·Seljuq control in Iran collapses at death **16**:505a

Muḥammad I, Umayyad emir of Córdoba who reigned from 852 to 886.
·*muwallad* and Banū Qasī revolts **17**:415d

Muḥammad I ibn al-Aḥmar (1203–1273), Muslim king of Granada from 1238 until his death; he commissioned the earliest construction of the palace of the Alhambra.
·Castilian alliance and vassalage **17**:417g

Muḥammad II al-Muʿtamid (ʿAbbādid ruler): *see* Muʿtamid, al-.

Muḥammad II, sultan of the Bahmanī dynasty in India who reigned from 1378 to 1397.
·Bahmanī political history **9**:371b

Muḥammad III (1454–82), sultan of the Bahmanī dynasty of India (reigned 1463–82).
·execution of Maḥmūd Gāwān **9**:372e

Muhammad V, original name SIDI MUHAMMAD BEN YUSUF (b. Aug. 10, 1909, Fès, Mor.—d. Feb. 26, 1961, Rabat), sultan of Morocco (1927–57) who became a focal point of nationalist aspirations, secured Moroccan independence from French colonial rule, and then ruled as king from 1957 till 1961.

Muhammad was the third son of Sultan Moulay Yusuf; when his father died in 1927, French authorities chose him to be successor, expecting him to be more compliant than his two older brothers. The first indication of Muhammad's nationalist feelings occurred in 1930, when he forced the French to abandon legislation that would have established different legal systems for the two Moroccan ethnic groups, Berbers and Arabs—a policy resented by both groups. Moroccan nationalists then organized the Fête du Trône, an annual festival to commemorate the anniversary of Muhammad's assumption of power. On these occasions he gave speeches that, though moderate in tone, encouraged nationalist sentiment. In 1934 the French reluctantly agreed to make the festival an official holiday. For the next 10 years Muhammad remained above nationalist agitation but gave it his tacit support.

During World War II Muhammad supported the Allies, and in 1943 he met with U.S. Pres. Franklin D. Roosevelt, who encouraged him to seek independence. Muhammad's determination increased in January 1944, when French authorities arrested a number of nationalists. In 1947 he visited Tangier and made a speech stressing Moroccan links with the Arab world, making no mention of France. He found an effective means of resistance in refusing to sign, and thus make legally binding, the decrees of the French resident general.

In 1951 the French encouraged a tribal rebellion against him, and on the pretext of protecting him they surrounded his palace with troops. Under these conditions he was induced to denounce the nationalist movement. In August 1953 the French deported the Sultan to Corsica and then to Madagascar. Acts of terrorism multiplied during Muhammad's absence, and his prestige soared. The French government, already faced with rebellion in Algeria, allowed him to return in November 1955, and in March 1956 he negotiated a treaty securing full independence.

Thereafter Muhammad asserted his personal authority in the affairs of the central government, ruling with moderation. He took the title of king in 1957. His son Hassan (*see* Hassan II) resented the slow pace of government, and in May 1960 Muhammad made him deputy prime minister and relinquished active direction of the country.
·Morocco leaders' rejection of French rule **13**:169e

Muḥammad XI, in full ABŪ ʿABD ALLĀH MUḤAMMAD XI, Spanish BOABDIL (d. 1527), last Naṣrid sultan of Granada. His reign (1482–92) was marked by incessant civil strife and the fall of Granada to Ferdinand and Isabella of Aragon and Castile.

Instigated by his mother, a jealous wife, Boabdil rebelled against his father, the sultan Abū al-Ḥasan ʿAlī (called in Spanish sources Muley Hacén, or Alboacen), and with the aid of the Abencerrajes family seized the Alhambra in 1482 and was recognized as sultan. Abū al-Ḥasan succeeded in recapturing the capital but was deposed by his brother az-Zaghall (Abū ʿAbd Allāh Muḥammad az-Zaghall). On Boabdil's first military venture (1483) against the Castilians, he was captured and to obtain his release signed the Pact of Córdoba, promising to deliver to the Castilians that part of his domain that was in the control of az-Zaghall in return for their help in recovering the part that was held by Abū al-Ḥasan; the death of his father in 1485 enabled Boabdil to reoccupy the Alhambra. In 1491 az-Zaghall, after stiff resistance, was forced to surrender the territory under his command (eastern Granada and the district of Almería) to the Castilians and emigrated. Boabdil, holding only the town of Granada, was now in a hopeless position. After a siege that began in 1491, he too surrendered, on Jan. 2, 1492, bringing an end to Muslim rule in Spain and the completion of the Christian Reconquista.

Boabdil was granted a small territory in the Alpujarras district of southern Spain. In 1493 he went into exile in Morocco and entered the service of the Marīnid ruler of Fès. Called *el rey chico* ("the little king") by the Castilians and *al-zogoybi* ("the poor devil") by his own subjects, Boabdil emerges as a tragic figure, victimized by his ambitious mother and his own weak nature. His life story, interwoven with legend, survives in folktales, such as those collected by Washington Irving in *The Alhambra* (1832).
·rebellion against Muley Hacén **17**:418h

Muhammad, Elijah, original name ELIJAH POOLE (1897–1975), U.S. leader of the Nation of Islam (Black Muslims).
·Black Muslim history and leadership **2**:1093c

Muḥammad, Mīrzā (ruler): *see* Sirāj-ud-Dawlah.

Muhammad, Wallace Fard: *see* Fard, Wallace D.

Muhammad Abdille Hassan, Sayyid: *see* Ḥasan, Sayyid Muḥammad ibn ʿAbd Allāh.

Muḥammad ʿAbduh (Egyptian reformer): *see* ʿAbduh, Muḥammad.

Muḥammad ʿĀdil Shāh Sūr, original name MUBĀRIZ KHĀN, 16th-century Afghan ruler of the Sūr dynasty in India.
·background to Humāyūn's reconquest **9**:379d

Muḥammad Aḥmad ibn as-Sayyid ʿAbd Allāh (Sudanese prophet): *see* Mahdī, al-.

Muḥammad ʿAlī, 18th-century governor of Trichinopoly, in India, and claimant to the nawabship of the Carnatic.
·British support in succession war **9**:395b

Muhammad Ali, original name CASSIUS MARCELLUS CLAY, (b. Jan. 17, 1942, Louisville, Ky.) professional boxer, widely recognized as world heavyweight champion after knocking out Charles ("Sonny") Liston in seven rounds at Miami Beach, Fla., Feb. 25, 1964, and universally recognized after outpointing Ernie Terrell (World Boxing Association champion) in 15 rounds in Houston, Texas, Feb. 6, 1967.

Ali proclaimed his invincibility, often in doggerel verse, and made the boast "I am the greatest!" his personal slogan. His joining the Nation of Islam (Black Muslims) and adopting a Muslim name led to his refusal, on religious grounds, to submit to induction into the armed forces in 1967. He was convicted of violating the Selective Service Act, stripped of his title, and barred from the ring. The conviction was appealed and ultimately reversed by the U.S. Supreme Court in 1971. He had meanwhile resumed boxing in 1970 and had defeated two other title contenders, Jerry Quarry and Oscar Bonavena, but in New York City on March 8, 1971, he lost a 15-round decision to the heavyweight champion, Joe Frazier (*q.v.*). For nearly three years he fought other title contenders, including Quarry, Floyd Patterson, Bob Foster, Joe Bugner, and Ken Norton (who, in the first of two meetings in 1973, broke Ali's jaw and won a split decision). Finally Ali won a unanimous decision over Frazier in New York on Jan. 28, 1974, that led to his meeting with the new champion, George Foreman, on Oct. 30, 1974, in Kinshasa, Zaire. His eighth-round knockout of Foreman regained for Ali the world heavyweight title, along with half of the record $10,000,000 purse. In succeeding years he continued to defeat challengers (including Frazier and Norton) until Feb. 15, 1978, in Las Vegas, Nev., when he lost the title to Leon Spinks. Seven months later, in New Orleans, La., he defeated Spinks, by unanimous decision, in 15 rounds, and became the first heavyweight in history to capture the title three times.

As an amateur boxer, Ali in 1960 won Amateur Athletic Union, Golden Gloves, and Olympic Games championships. His candid autobiography, *The Greatest: My Own Story* (written with Richard Durham), was published in 1975.
·boxing record and appraisal **3**:96e

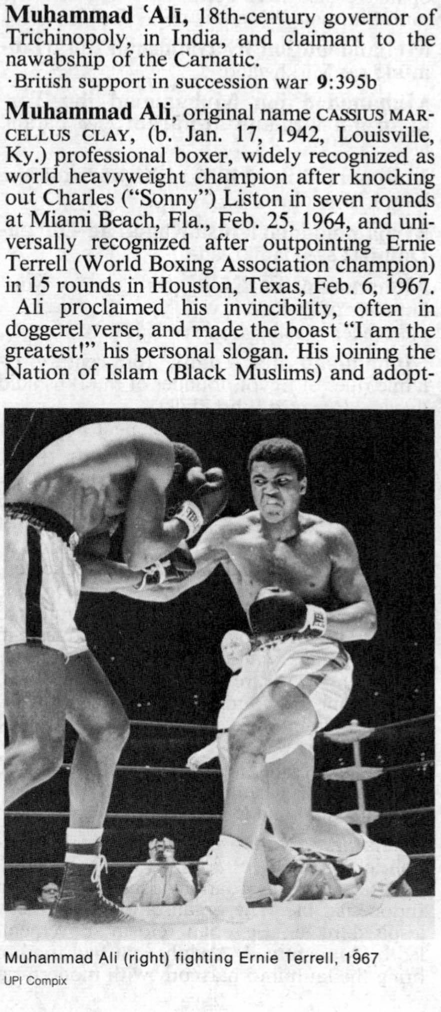

Muhammad Ali (right) fighting Ernie Terrell, 1967
UPI Compix

Muḥammad ʿAlī Pasha 12:609 (b. 1769, Kavala, Macedonia, now in Greece—d. Aug. 2, 1849, Alexandria, Egypt), founder of the dynasty that ruled Egypt from the beginning of the 19th century to the middle of the 20th, encouraged the emergence of the modern Egyptian state.

Abstract of text biography. Appointed as the Ottoman sultan's viceroy in Egypt (1805), Muḥammad ʿAlī built up his military and naval strength and conducted campaigns in support of the Sultan in Arabia and Greece and invaded the Nilotic Sudan. Then he challenged the Sultan (1831–33) and gained control of Syria. In 1838–41 he defeated the Ottomans, which brought about European intervention to prevent his gaining independence. He and his family were granted the hereditary right to rule Egypt and the Sudan, but the Sultan remained his suzerain. During his reign Muḥammad ʿAlī promulgated many economic and social reforms. Though they were aimed at self-aggrandizement, and many were abandoned after his death, they cleared the path for creation of an independent Egyptian state.

REFERENCES in other text articles:
·Alexandria's history and monuments **1**:480a *passim* to 482c
·Damascus' growth under rule **5**:448b
·Egyptian expansion and reorganization **6**:493f; map 495
·Europe's relation to Eastern powers **6**:1106e
·Greek Independence War **2**:625d
·internal reforms and autonomy **13**:785c
·international health conference of 1833 **8**:699d
·Islām and European colonialism **9**:936f
·Palmerston opposition to aggrandizement **13**:937d
·Turkish conquest of Sudan **13**:111d

Muḥammad (al-Amīn) al-Kanamī (d. 1835), scholar, diplomat, and warrior of Kanem-Bornu (*q.v.*), in West Africa, who successfully opposed the expansion of Fulani power and restored independence to Bornu (*q.v.*).
·Fulani opposition and state establishment **19**:773c

Muḥammad al-Mahdī al-Ḥujjah, also called MUḤAMMAD AL-MUNTAẒAR (disappeared 878), 12th and last *imām*, venerated by the Ithnā ʿAsharīyah (*q.v.*), the main body of Shīʿah Muslims, who believe that he has been concealed by God (*see* ghaybah) and will reappear in time as the *mahdī*.

Muḥammad al-Munsif (1881–1948), bey of Tunis.
·Tunisian nationals' oppression by France **13**:167g

Muhammadan Anglo-Oriental College: *see* Alīgarh Muslim University.

Muḥammad Bāqir Bihbihānī (d. 1803), Muslim religious leader in Iraq and Iran.
·Islāmic religious reform movements **9**:936e

Muhammad Bello (fl. early 19th century), West African Fulani ruler, son of the Islāmic reformer Usman dan Fodio. After his father's death (1817) Bello inherited the recently acquired eastern provinces of the Fulani empire, which he administered from Sokoto (in present-day Nigeria).
·government of Fulani empire **19**:773c
·ʿUmar Tal's early travels **8**:552h
·Usman dan Fodio's influence **18**:1100e

Muḥammad Ghūrī: *see* Muʿizz-ud-Dīn Muḥammad of Ghūr.

Muhammad Hashim Maiwandwal (1921–), Afghan prime minister, 1965–67.
·Afghanistan international diplomacy **1**:176h

Muḥammad ibn ʿAbd al-Karīm al-Khaṭṭābī: *see* Abd el-Krim.

Muḥammad ibn ʿAbd Allāh (the Mad Mullah): *see* Ḥasan, Sayyid Muḥammad ibn ʾAbd Allāh.

Muḥammad ibn ʿAbd Allāh al-Lawātī at Ṭanjī ʿAbd Allāh: *see* Ibn Baṭṭūṭah.

Muḥammad ibn ʿAbd al-Malik ibn Muḥammad ibn Muḥammad ibn Ṭufayl al-Qaysī: *see* Ibn Ṭufayl.

Muḥammad ibn ʿAbd al-Wahhāb: *see* Wahhāb, Muḥammad ibn ʿAbd al-.

Muḥammad ibn Abū Amīr al-Manṣūr: *see* Manṣūr, Abu ʿĀmir al-.

Muḥammad ibn Aḥmad al-Maqdisī: *see* Maqdisī, al-.

Muḥammad ibn al-Ḥanafīyah (b. 637—d. 710, Medina, Arabia), Muslim religious figure who many thought was the legitimate caliph (the titular leader of the Islāmic community). He was a son of ʿAlī, the fourth caliph, but not by his wife, Fāṭimah, who was the daughter of the Prophet Muḥammad. By nature, Muḥammad ibn al-Ḥanafīyah was retiring and inclined to avoid partisan strife; he acted with much caution despite the support of various factions that would have made him caliph. He eventually pledged allegiance to the Umayyad caliph ʿAbd al-Malik, from whom he received a large annual pension.

Muḥammad ibn ʿAlī, 8th-century head of the ʿAbbāsid family.
·ʿAbbāsid use of ʿAlid sympathies **3**:631g

Muḥammad ibn al-Qāsim, early 8th-century Muslim military leader in India.
·Muslim expansion into India **3**:629g

Muḥammad ibn Barakat, Mamlūk *sharīf* of Mecca, reigned 1452–53.
·Arabian economic tie with Mamlūks **1**:1048h

Muḥammad ibn Dāniyāl, *c.* 13th-century Egyptian physician and playwright.
·early shadow plays **9**:980c

Muḥammad ibn Dāʾūd Alp-Arslan: *see* Alp-Arslan.

Muḥammad ibn Falāh (b. *c.* 1400, Wāsiṭ, Iraq—d. 1461, Hoveyzeh, Iran), Muslim theologian who founded the extremist Mushaʿshaʿ sect of Shīʿism.

Muḥammad ibn Falāh was reputed to be descended from the seventh Shīʿite *imām*, Mūsā al-Kāẓim. He received a traditional Islāmic religious education in al-Ḥillah, a famous centre for Shīʿite studies. As a student he was noted for his extremist religious views, which bordered on heresy, and he was excommunicated from the faith by his teacher, himself a noted Shīʿite theologian.

From 1436 onward Muḥammad ibn Falāh actively propagated his views among Arab tribesmen, trying to create a coalition of discontented Arab tribes on what is now the border between Iraq and Iran. This coalition was held together by his contention that he was a prophet and the representative of ʿAlī (whom the Shīʿites regarded as the legitimate successor to the Prophet Muḥammad). In 1440 he and his followers were defeated in a clash with the authorities, but in February 1441 they managed to capture the city of Hoveyzeh, which became the seat of the Mushaʿshaʿ movement. Warfare persisted for the next 10 years, during which time Muḥammad ibn Falāh was able to consolidate his power in the vicinity of Hoveyzeh and the Tigris River. He owed his success as much to the weakness and division of his opponents as to his own messianic zeal and doctrinal propaganda.

The doctrinal foundations of the Mushaʿshaʿ are found in Muḥammad ibn Falāh's *Kalām al-mahdī* ("The Words of the Mahdī"). Written in the style of the Qurʾān, the book contains a rigid code of conduct regulating the affairs of the community. Besides acting as the spiritual leader of the Mushaʿshaʿ, he was also the military and temporal ruler of the movement. On his death he was succeeded by his son ʿAlī as the head of the movement.

Muhammad ibn Hūd, Almohad caliph in Spain (reigned 1228–38).
·anti-Christian resistance policy **17**:417g

Muḥammad ibn Khāvandshāh ibn Maḥmūd: *see* Mīrkhwānd.

Muḥammad ibn Muḥammad ibn Ṭarkhān ibn Uzalagh al-Fārābī: *see* Fārābī, al-.

Muḥammad ibn Mūsā al-Khwārizmī: *see* Khwārizmī, al-.

Muḥammad ibn Mūsā Kamāl ad-Dīn ad-Damīrī: *see* Damīrī, ad-.

Muḥammad ibn Rāʾiq, 10th-century Muslim *amīr* of Basra.
·surrender of caliphal power **3**:638h

Muḥammad ibn Ṭughj, 10th-century Islāmic ruler of Egypt, founder of the Ikhshīdid dynasty (*see also* Ikhshīdids).
·Egyptian autonomy reestablishment **6**:489d

Muḥammad ibn Tughluq 12:610 (b. *c.* 1290, Delhi, India—d. March 20, 1351, Sondaha, now in Pakistan), Indian ruler, briefly extended the rule of the Delhi sultanate of north India over most of the subcontinent.

Abstract of text biography. Well educated, Muḥammad succeeded his father to the throne in 1325. He transferred the capital to Deogir (1327) to consolidate his conquests in southern India and launched several military campaigns to secure the sultanate's frontiers. His administrative measures failed, however, and the sultanate began to decline in power at the end of his reign.

REFERENCES in other text articles:
·Ibn Baṭṭūṭah's meetings and dealings **9**:144e
·military gains and losses **9**:368f

Muhammadiyah, a socio-religious organization in Indonesia, established in 1912 at Jogjakarta, aimed at adapting Islām to modern Indonesian life. The organization was chiefly inspired by an Egyptian reform movement, led by Muḥammad ʿAbduh, that had tried to bring the faith into harmony with modern rational thought. The Muhammadiyah advocated the abolition of all superstitious customs, mostly relics of pre-Islāmic times, and the loosening of the stiff traditional bonds that tended to strangle cultural life. To achieve these aims, the Muhammadiyah employed many methods of the Christian missionaries. It established schools along modern lines, where Western subjects (including Dutch) as well as religion were taught. It even set up orphanages, hospitals, and other social services. The Muhammadiyah was willing to cooperate with the colonial government, and its schools were qualified to receive government financial assistance. It was therefore criticized by radical Indonesian nationalists, who had adopted a non-cooperation policy toward the Dutch authorities. The membership of the Muhammadiyah increased steadily, however, and by 1937 there were 913 branches, although more than half of them were in the outer islands. It was paralyzed by the Japanese occupation during World War II and never really recovered afterward.

Muḥammad Khwārezm-Shāh: *see in* Khwārezm-Shāhs.

Muḥammad of Ghūr: *see* Muʿizz-ud Dīn Muḥammad of Ghūr.

Muḥammad Qāsim Hindūshāh: *see* Firishtah.

Muḥammad Qulī Quṭb Shāh, 16th–17th-century Muslim ruler of Golconda.
·Hyderābād's founding and design **9**:75h

Muḥammad Rezā Khān, 18th-century Persian officer in India.
·career as deputy nawab **9**:397b

Muḥammad Shāh, in full NĀṢIR-UD-DĪN MUḤAMMAD SHĀH (b. Aug. 7, 1702, Ghaznī, Afg.—d. April 6, 1748, Delhi, India), ineffective, pleasure-loving Mughal emperor of India from 1719 to 1748. The son of Shāh Jahān (who was the fourth son of Bahādur Shāh I), he was made emperor in 1719 by the powerful Sayyid brothers, ʿAbdullāh and Ḥusayn ʿAlī, who had killed the emperor Farrukh-Siyar.

In 1720 the assassination of Ḥusayn ʿAlī and the defeat of ʿAbdullāh at the battle of Hasanpur (southwest of Delhi) liberated Muḥammad Shāh from effective Sayyid control. In 1721 he married the daughter of Farrukh-Siyar. After Niẓām-ul-Mulk Āṣaf Jāh, who was the court-appointed vizier, had left court in disgust in 1724, the provinces steadily slipped out of imperial control: Sādāt Khān became practically independent in Oudh; the Afghan Rohilla tribesmen made themselves masters of Rohilkhand (southeast of Delhi); Bengal paid only an annual tribute to Delhi; the leaders of the Marāthās, under the peshwa Bājī Rāo, made themselves lords of the regions of Gujarāt, Mālwa, and Bundelkhand and, in 1737, raided Delhi.

In 1739 Nāder Shāh of Persia took advantage of Mughal neglect of the Northwest Frontier areas (now in Pakistan) to rout the Mughals at Karnāl and occupy Delhi. In March 1748 Muḥammad Shāh defeated the Afghan ruler Aḥmad Shāh Durrānī at Sirhind, a success in his last years.
·weak rule and Mughal disintegration **9**:385e

Muḥammad Shāh I, sultan of the Bahmanī kingdom in southern India (reigned 1358–75).
·wars with neighbouring states **9**:371a

Muḥammad Shaybānī, also called SHAYBĀNĪ KHĀN UZBEK (1451–1510), Uzbek ruler of the Shaybānid branch of the descendants of Genghis Khan, who wrested Bukhara and Herāt from his Timurid cousins. In 1501 he decisively defeated Bābur, the first Mughal ruler in India, capturing Samarkand and Fergana from him. Muḥammad's descendants ruled in Bukhara until 1599.
·Bābur's loss of Samarkand **2**:553h
·Uzbek unification and expansion **18**:794h

Muhammed bin Hamid: *see* Tippu Tib.

Muḥammed ibn Tekesh, 13th-century Khwārezm-Shāh.
·caliphate conflict with Khwārezm-Shāh **11**:994a

Muhan, Asian Turk leader, son of Bumin, reigned 553 to 572.
·Turk Empire partition **9**:598a

Muḥarraq, al- (Bahrain): *see* al-Muḥarraq.

Muharrem, Decree of (1881), Ottoman governmental financial reform measure.
·Ottoman financial control initiation **13**:787g

Muḥāsibī, al- 12:611, in full ABŪ ʿABD AL-LĀH AL-ḤARITH IBN ASAD AL-ʿANAZĪ AL-MUḤASIBĪ (b. *c.* 781, Basra, Iraq—d. 857, Baghdad), eminent Muslim mystic (Ṣūfī) and theologian renowned for his psychological refinement of pietistic devotion and his role as a precursor of the doctrine of later Muslim orthodoxy.

Abstract of text biography. Though Muḥāsibī outwardly appeared to be bourgeois, his life was permeated by an otherworldly spirituality. From 833 to 851 he was involved in the theological inquisition. His main work was *Ar-rī ʿāyah li-ḥuqūq Allah*, in which he acknowledges asceticism to be valuable as an act of supererogation but always to be tempered by inner and outer duties toward God. He stressed the importance of reason far beyond the normal practice of mystics and advocated the use of *muḥāsabah*, the anticipation of the Last Judgment through constant self-examination.

Muḥaṣṣal afkār al-mutaqaddimīn wa-al-muta'akhkhir (Arabic: "Collection of the Opinions of Ancients and Moderns"), a work by the Muslim scholar Fakhr ad-Dīn ar-Rāzī, who died in 1209.
·ar-Rāzī's theological career **7**:144h

Muhavura, or VOLCAN MUHAVURA, extinct volcano at the easternmost end of the Virunga Mountains in east central Africa. It lies northeast of Lac Kivu on the border between Uganda and Rwanda. It is more than 10,000 ft high, and its crater contains a lake.
1°23′ S, 29°40′ E
·formation, location, and activity **19**:162f
·map, Uganda **18**:826
·Ugandan physical geography **18**:825h

Muḥī-ud-Dīn Muḥammad (Mughal emperor): *see* Aurangzeb.

Mühlberg, Battle of (1547), Duke of Alba's victory over the Schmalkaldic League.
·Alba's victory for Charles V **1**:416f

Muhlenberg, German-American family that led the Lutheran community in Pennsylvania throughout the 18th and 19th centuries, and contributed public figures in education, the military, and government.

Henry Melchior Mühlenberg (1711–87), German-born Lutheran pastor (1742) at New Providence (now Trappe, Pa.), organized the first Lutheran synod in America (1748).

John Peter Gabriel Muhlenberg (1746–1807), son of Henry Melchior, Lutheran minister and brigadier general in the Continental army (1777), commanded infantry at the battle of Yorktown.

Frederick Augustus Conrad Muhlenberg (1750–1801), brother of John Peter Gabriel, Lutheran clergyman, served as a member of the Continental Congress and first speaker of the national house of representatives.

Gotthilf Henry Ernest Muhlenberg (1753–1815), brother of Frederick Augustus Conrad, minister, botanist, was first president of Franklin College, Lancaster, Pa. (1787).

Henry Augustus Philip Muhlenberg (1782–1844), son of Gotthilf Henry Ernest, Lutheran pastor, was appointed the first U.S. minister to Austria (1838–40).

William Augustus Muhlenberg (1796–1877), grandson of Frederick Augustus Conrad, Episcopal priest, ecumenical theologian and hymnologist, founded St. Paul's College, Flushing, Long Island (1838); St. Luke's Hospital, New York City (1858); and the first American order of Episcopal deaconesses (1852), to realize his understanding of Christianity as essentially expressed by social service.

Frederick Augustus Muhlenberg (1818–1901), grandson of Gotthilf Henry Ernest, Lutheran minister, joined in establishing several Pennsylvania colleges and became the first president of Muhlenberg College, Allentown, Pa. (1867).
·Lutheranism organized in America **11**:198f
·Pietist beginnings in the U.S. **14**:458g

Mühlhausen, also called MÜHLHAUSEN IN THÜRINGEN, city, Erfurt *Bezirk* (district), southwestern East Germany, on the Unstrut River, northwest of Erfurt city. Originally a Germanic village and later a Frankish settlement, it was first documented in 775. It was granted royal privileges and was where Philip of Swabia was elected German king in 1198. Created a free imperial city after 1256, it joined the Hanseatic League *c.* 1420. After the Reformation, it became a centre of the people's reform movement, and during the Peasants' War (1523–25) against the feudal princes it was associated with the peasant leader Thomas Müntzer, who was executed there after the Battle of Frankenhausen. The city was subsequently deprived of its privileges but regained its independence under the supremacy of the German Empire in 1548. From 1802 to 1945 it was in the former Prussian province of Saxony, except from 1807 to 1815, when it was attached to Westphalia. Notable medieval buildings include the Church of St. Mary on the site of a Romanesque basilica, St. Blasius' Church (with an organ constructed to the plans of Johann Sebastian Bach), and the Gothic town hall. There are remains of medieval fortifications. Mühlhausen has a teachers' training college, a school for agriculture, and a folklore museum.

Industries include the manufacture of textiles, leather, machinery, electrical and radio equipment, wood products, and chemicals. Pop. (1971 prelim.) 45,200.
51°12′ N, 10°27′ E
·map, German Democratic Republic **8**:8

muhly, common name for about 125 species of range grasses constituting the genus *Muhlenbergia* (family Poaceae), native principally to North and South America. Some species are less than 30 centimetres (one foot) tall and bushy, others are highly branched and matlike, and still others are taller (up to one metre, or about three feet) and grow in tufts. Most are perennials, and all species have only one floret on each branch, or subdivision, within a panicle (flower cluster). Some species are used for fodder. Bush muhly (*M. porteri*) is so palatable to browsing animals that it is rarely found where livestock has access to it.

Muhly (*Muhlenbergia torreyi*)
Grant Heilman—EB Inc.

muḥtasib, Muslim censor of morals.
·Aurangzeb's religious orthodoxy **2**:373f

Muḥyī' ad-Dīn (Iraqui ruler): *see* Abū Kālījār al-Marzubān ibn Sulṭān ad-Dawlah.

Muḥyi ad-Dīn ʿArabī (Muslim mystic): *see* Ibn al-ʿArabī.

Muileann Cearr (Ireland): *see* Mullingar.

Muineachan (Ireland): *see* Monaghan.

Muir, Edwin (b. May 15, 1887, Deerness, Orkney, Scot.—d. Jan. 3, 1959, Cambridge, Eng.), literary critic translator, and one of the chief Scottish poets of his day writing in English. The son of a crofter, Muir received his education in Kirkwall. After his marriage (1919) to Willa Anderson, Muir went to London where he wrote literary reviews; he later taught English on the Continent.

His stature as a poet did not become widely recognized until the publication of *The Voyage* (1946) and *The Labyrinth* (1949). His *Collected Poems*, which reveal his meditative and myth-haunted vision, appeared in 1960. His works have been noted for their awareness of contemporary evils but also of the possibilities of innocence and regeneration. The critical work *Latitudes* (1924) and *Transition* (1927) were notable for their appreciation of D.H. Lawrence.

Of greater influence than his criticism, however, were the translations of Kafka, done in collaboration with his wife, that appeared during the 1930s and established Kafka's reputation in Britain. Affinities with Kafka have been discerned in Muir's novel, *The Marionette* (1927), which tells of the relationship of an idiot child and his father. He also translated works of Sholem Asch, Hermann Broch, and Lion Feuchtwanger. Muir's *Autobiography* was published in 1954.

Muir, John (b. April 21, 1838, Dunbar, East Lothian—d. Dec. 24, 1914, Los Angeles),

John Muir
By courtesy of the Library of Congress, Washington, D.C.

naturalist, advocate of U.S. forest conservation, was largely responsible for the establishment of such national parks as Sequoia and Yosemite, both in California.

Muir emigrated from Scotland with his family to a farm near Portage, Wis., in 1849. After attending the University of Wisconsin, Madison, he worked on mechanical inventions, but in 1867, when an industrial accident nearly cost him an eye, he abandoned that career and devoted himself to nature. He walked from the Middle West to the Gulf of Mexico, keeping a journal (published 1916) as he went. In 1868 he went to the Yosemite Valley, California, from which he took many trips into Nevada, Utah, Oregon, Washington, and Alaska, inspired by his interest in glaciers and forests. He was the first to attribute the spectacular Yosemite formations to glacial erosion, now generally accepted as the cause.

As early as 1876, Muir urged the federal government to adopt a forest conservation policy. The Sequoia and Yosemite national parks were established in September–October 1890. Early in 1897, Pres. Grover Cleveland designated 13 national forests to be preserved from commercial exploitation; business interests induced Congress to postpone the effect of that measure, but two eloquent magazine articles (June and August 1897) by Muir swung public and Congressional opinion in favour of national forest reservations. He also influenced the large-scale conservation program of Pres. Theodore Roosevelt, who in 1903, during his first term in office, accompanied Muir on a camping trip to the Yosemite region.

Muir's writings (10 vol., 1916–24) were edited by William Frederic Badè, who also wrote *The Life and Letters of John Muir* (2 vol., 1923–24). Linnie Marsh Wolfe edited Muir's previously unpublished journals as *John of the Mountains* (1938) and wrote a biography, *Son of the Wilderness* (1945). In 1908, during Muir's lifetime, the government established the Muir Woods National Monument, in Marin County, California, enclosing a virgin stand of redwood trees.

·California's environment and importance **3**:619e
·Sierra exploration accounts **16**:740b
·wilderness and national park system **5**:43b

Muir Woods National Monument, near the Pacific Coast of California, U.S., 15 mi (24 km) northwest of San Francisco at the foot of Mt. Tamalpais, contains one of the two virgin stands of coastal redwoods (*Sequoia sempervirens*) in the National Park Service. Some of these trees are more than 300 ft (90 m) high and 15 ft in diameter and are more than 2,000 years old. The forest, established in 1908 with an area of 503 ac (204 ha), was a gift of Congressman and Mrs. William Kent and was named in honour of John Muir (1838–1914).

Muisca (people): *see* Chibcha.

Muitanzige (Africa): *see* Albert, Lake.

Mu'izz, al- (reigned AD 953–75), Fāṭimid caliph who enjoyed acknowledged authority over most of the area that now comprises Morocco, Algeria, Tunisia, and Sicily. Under him Fāṭimid rule reached the Atlantic Ocean. He sent his general Jawhar westward to reduce Fez (958–959), which had rejected the Fāṭimid caliph's authority.

·Fāṭimid early expansion **7**:193g; map

Muʿizz ad-Dawlah, real name AḤMAD EBN BŪYEH (fl. 10th century), Iran *amīr* who in 945 established the dominance of his house (the Būyids) over the ʿAbbāsid caliphs.

·Būyid domination of the ʿAbbāsids **3**:639a
·Būyid influence and recognition **9**:855d
·Iraq under Būyid dynasty **11**:993b

Muʿizz ibn Bādīs (*c.* 12th century), Muslim ruler in North Africa.

·Muslim conflicts in North Africa **9**:931g

Muʿizz-ud-Dīn Muḥammad of Ghūr, more complete name MUʿIZZ-UD-DĪN MUḤAMMAD IBN SĀM, also known as MUḤAMMAD GHŪRĪ and SHIHĀB-UD-DĪN MUḤAMMAD GHŪRĪ (d. March 15, 1206, Damyak, now in Pakistan), the Ghūrid conqueror of the north Indian plain; he was one of the founders of Muslim rule in India. Muʿizz-ud-Dīn's elder brother, Ghiyaṣ-ud-Dīn, acquired power east of Herāt in the region of Ghūr (Ghowr, in present Afghanistan) *c.* 1162. Muʿizz-ud-Dīn always remained his brother's loyal subordinate. Thus Muʿizz-ud-Dīn expelled the Oğuz Turkmen nomads from Ghazna (Ghaznī) in 1173 and came as required to his brother's assistance in his contest with Khwārezm for the lordship of Khorāsān. After Ghiyaṣ-ud-Dīn's death in 1202, the rivalry between the two powers came to a head with Muʿizz-ud-Dīn's attack in 1204 on the Khwārezmian capital, Gurganj (in present Uzbek S.S.R.). In Hindustān, Muʿizz-ud-Dīn captured Multān and Uch in 1175, and annexed the Ghaznavid principality of Lahore in 1186. After being defeated by a coalition of Rājput kings at Tarā' in 1191, he returned the next year with an army of mounted archers and won a great victory over them on the same field, opening the way for his lieutenants to occupy most of northern India in the years that followed. Muʿizz-ud-Dīn was assassinated, according to some by Hindu Khokars, according to others by Ismāʿīlīs.

mujaddid (Arabic: "renewer"), in Islāmic tradition, one of a succession of historical figures who, though less important than prophets, bring about an upsurge of faith and keep religious values alive in the interim between prophetic advents.

·ar-Rāzī's historical impact **7**:145c

mujāhadah (Arabic: "striving"), a Ṣūfī (Muslim mystic) term meaning self-mortification. The term comes from the root *jahada* ("to strive," "to struggle"), from which the word *jihād* (holy war) is also derived. The Ṣūfīs regard self-mortification and the painful training that they undertake to purify their souls and rise above the temptations of the material world as superior to participation in holy wars. They thus refer to *mujāhadah* as *al-jihād al-akbar* (the greater war) in contrast to *al-jihād al-aṣghar* (the minor war), which is waged against unbelievers.

Mujāhadah is one of the major duties that a Ṣūfī must perform throughout his mystical journey toward union with God. The Ṣūfīs maintain that God can be satisfied only through the believer's disregard of his carnal self. Thus, all acts of penance and austerity, such as prolonged fasts and abstinence from the comforts of life, have become part of the *mujāhadah* doctrine. Circles that practice *dhikr* (repetition of divine names) are frequently convened by Ṣūfīs to help those who have recently entered the mystical path to practice *mujāhadah*. In protracted sessions, they repeat God's name over and over as a means of remembering him and denying the self. Some Ṣūfīs have gone beyond mere bodily torture to the extreme of self-immolation. Such excesses, however, are frowned upon by most Ṣūfīs as a sign of failure and weakness, not of strength. The purpose of *mujāhadah* is to conquer the temptations of the self in order to purify one's soul and bring one's soul to a state of readiness to receive the divine light.

The term *mujāhadah* is also used to characterize the effort that the Ṣūfī makes to progress from one *maqām* (stage) to the next on the way toward the vision of God, and it is through *mujāhadah* that the Ṣūfī may succeed in transforming his transitory *aḥwāl* (states) into permanent stages.

Mujib, Sheikh (president of Bangladesh): *see* Rahman, Mujibur.

muʿjizah (Arabic: "miracle," plural *muʿjizat*), in Islām, the technical term used for miraculous phenomena.

·saint prodigies and Muḥammad's miracles **16**:166f

mujtahid (Islam): *see* ijtihād.

Mu-jung, Hsien-pei tribe that settled around Peking in the 3rd century.

·Chinese dynastic wars **11**:435f

Mu jung Hui, 3rd-century Chinese warlord.

·Chinese dynastic wars **11**:435f

Mujur rugs, prayer rugs handwoven in Mucur (also Mujur or Mudjar), a village near Kırşehir in central Anatolia. The characteristic design in older examples, from the 19th century, is a prayer niche with a stepped arch crowned by a little turret form that is echoed in the crenellations of a narrow cross panel above. The niche is soft red and may contain a skeleton tree or be perfectly plain except for

Mujur prayer rug from Anatolia, 19th century; in a New York state private collection

New York state private collection; photograph, Otto E. Nelson—EB Inc.

an edging of small triangular indentations. The green spandrels (spaces between the exterior curves of the arch and the enclosing right angle) display stylized ewers. The broad stripe of the border is composed of varicoloured, carefully detailed squares, reminiscent of tilework; and the soft blue inner stripe has a diamond pattern. Like Makri rugs (*q.v.*), Mujur prayer rugs have been likened to the medieval stained glass windows of European churches.

Mukachovo, Hungarian MUNKÁCS, city, Zakarpatskaya *oblast* (administrative region), Ukrainian Soviet Socialist Republic, on the Latoritsa River. Its location controls the southern approach to the Veretsky Pass across the Carpathians, today followed by road and rail. This position has given Mukachovo a key fortress role in sub-Carpathian Ruthenia since its foundation in the 10th century—mainly during its period of Hungarian rule (1018–1920). Modern Mukachovo has light engineering, food-processing, and timber-working industries. It is also a significant tourist centre. Pop. (1970) 57,000.
48°27′ N, 22°45′ E

mukallit, also called MEDDAH, imitator or eulogist in the Turkish mime theatre.

·theatrical skills and popularity **9**:978f

Mukammas, David al-, in full DAVID ABŪ SULAYMĀN IBN MARWĀN AR-RAQQĪ AL-MUKAMMAS, also called DAVID HA-BAVLI (b. Raqqah, now in Syria; fl. 900), philosopher and polemicist, regarded as the father of Jewish medieval philosophy.

A young convert to Christianity, he studied at the Syriac academy of Nisibis but became disillusioned with its doctrines and wrote two famous polemics against the Christian religion. While considered a Jewish scholar by both Jews and Muslims, it is not entirely clear whether al-Mukammas returned fully to Judaism. Faulting Christianity for the impurity of its monotheism, he also attacked Islām; he maintained that the style of the Qur'ān did not prove its divine origin.

Al-Mukammas was almost unknown until the late 19th century, and the details of his life remain uncertain. The publication in 1885 of a commentary included a Hebrew translation from the Arabic of a small segment of al-Mukammas' *ʿIshrūn maqālāt* ("Twenty Treatises"). Then in 1898, 15 of the 20 tracts were discovered in the Imperial Library of St. Petersburg (now Leningrad).

Al-Mukammas was the first Jewish thinker to introduce the methods of *kalām* (Arab religious philosophy) into Judaism and the first

Jew to mention Aristotle in his writings. He cited Greek and Arab authorities, but his own Jewishness was not apparent in his writings, for he never quoted the Bible. God's attributes, he argued, reflecting the influence of *kalām*, are to be understood as negations; they are to be interpreted not as what he is but as statements of what he is not. The attributes are identical with each other and with the essence of God; thus, to superadd them to his essence, he argued, would undermine the oneness of the Almighty. It is only the limitations of language that necessitate man's making use of a multiplicity of terms in an attempt to describe the Divine Being.

Among other subjects presented in *ʿIshrūn maqālāt* are a proof of God's existence and his creation of the world, a discussion of the reality of science, the substantial and accidental composition of the world, the utility of prophecy and prophets, and the signs of true prophets and prophecy. Al-Mukammas also wrote on Jewish sects and is believed to have written commentaries on the biblical books of Genesis and Ecclesiastes.

mukarrib, 2nd-century-BC Sabaean politico-religious leaders.
·Arabian state and religion integration **1**:1044e

Mukasa (Balikuddembe), Saint Joseph: *see in* Uganda, Martyrs of.

mukataʿa, 14th-century Ottoman governmental institution.
·Ottoman administration evolution **13**:775g

Mukden 12:612, Manchu name of the city known in Chinese as SHEN-YANG, capital of Liaoning Province, China, and the largest city in the Northeast (Manchuria). It is one of China's largest industrial centres. Pop. (1975 est.) 4,012,000.

The text article covers the city's history, the city site and plan, transportation, demography, economic life, and education and culture.
41°48′ N, 123°27′ E

REFERENCES in other text articles:
·major industries **10**:843g *passim* to 845e
·map, China **4**:263
·population, table 2 **4**:270
·railway network statistics **4**:284f

Mukden Incident, seizure of the Manchurian city of Mukden by Japanese troops on the night of Sept. 18–19, 1931. This incident was followed by the Japanese invasion of all of Manchuria (Northeast) and the establishment of the Japanese-dominated state of Manchukuo in the area.

Throughout the 20th century the Japanese had maintained special rights in Manchuria, and they had felt that the neutrality of the area was necessary for the defense of their colony in Korea. They were thus alarmed when their position in Manchuria was threatened by the increasingly successful unification of China in the late 1920s by Chiang Kai-shek, at the same time that Soviet pressures on Manchuria increased from the north. Responding to this pressure, officers of the Japanese Kwangtung Army, which was stationed in Manchuria, initiated an incident in Mukden without the approval of the civil government of Japan.

On the night of September 18, Japanese troops used the pretext of an explosion along the Japanese-controlled South Manchurian Railway to occupy Mukden. On September 21, Japanese reinforcements arrived from Korea, and the army began to expand throughout northern Manchuria. In Tokyo the impotent civil Cabinet collapsed, and the new Japanese government reacted to a growing tide of public opinion by sanctioning the invasion. Within three months Japanese troops had spread throughout Manchuria. The Kwangtung Army met little resistance, because Chiang Kai-shek, intent on establishing his control over the rest of China, ordered the commander of the Chinese forces in Manchuria, Chang Hsüeh-liang, to pursue a policy of nonresistance and withdrawal. The League of Nations, Chiang announced, would determine the outcome of the case. The Lytton Commission, appointed by the League to investigate the situation, labelled Japan the aggressor, but Japan withdrew from the League and continued to occupy Manchuria until 1945.
·Japanese militarism in Manchuria **11**:438a
·Japanese militarist extremism **10**:83g
·purpose and effects on Mukden **12**:612h

Mukha (Yemen [Ṣanʿāʾ]): *see* Mocha.

Mukhina, Vera Ignatyevna (1889–1953), Soviet sculptor.
·Soviet Union cultural history **17**:354c

Mukhtār, Sīdī (d. 1811), Kunta tribal leader in western Sudan.
·West African politico-religious role **19**:772c

Mukhtār ibn Abū ʿUbayd, al- (d. AD 687), Muslim leader who in 686 championed Muḥammad ibn al-Ḥanafīyah, a son of ʿAlī (the fourth caliph), as leader of the Islāmic community in opposition to the Umayyad house. When his candidate died, Mukhtār taught that the *mahdī* ("the [divinely] guided one") Muḥammad ibn al-Ḥanafīyah was still alive and would appear to vanquish enemies. The idea remains important in the Shīʿite sect of Islām.
·popular revolt in al-Kūfah **3**:628e
·revolt leadership and failure **11**:991e

Muktafī, al-, ʿAbbāsid caliph (reigned AD 902–908), who defeated the Qarmaṭians in Syria (904) and recovered Egypt from the Ṭūlūnids (905) but was unable to prevent the occupation of Tunisia by the Fāṭimids.
·caliphal policies and dynastic decline **3**:638f
·Qarmaṭian movement suppression **11**:992h

Mukteśvara, 10th-century temple in Bhuvaneśvara, India.
·roof style and enclosing wall **17**:176e; illus. 177

mukti (Indian religion): *see* mokṣa.

Mūlamadhyamakakārikā (Sanskrit: "Fundamentals of the Middle Way"), Buddhist text by Nāgārjuna, the exponent of the Mādhyamika (Middle Way) school of Mahāyāna Buddhism. It is a work that combines stringent logic and religious vision in a lucid presentation of the doctrine of ultimate "emptiness."

The work of Nāgārjuna, apparently a South Indian Brahmin in origin, makes use of the classifications and analyses of the Theravāda (Way of the Elders) *Abhidharma*, or scholastic, literature; it takes them to their logical extremes and thus reduces to ontological nothingness the various elements, states, and faculties dealt with in *Abhidharma* texts. His basic philosophy, on the other hand, comes out of the *Prajñāpāramitā* ("Perfection of Wisdom") tradition, and the *Mūlamadhyamakakārikā* systematically sets forth the vision of the void that informs the *Prajñāpāramitā-sūtra*s. In some 450 verses the *Mūlamadhyamakakārikā* develops the doctrine that nothing, not even the Buddha or Nirvāṇa, is real in itself. It ends by commending to spiritual realization the ultimate identity of the transitory phenomenal world and Nirvāṇa itself.

Mulanje, formerly MLANJE, administrative headquarters of Mulanje District, southern Malawi. At the southwestern foot of Sapitwa (Mulanje) Peak, it lies near the railway to Blantyre and is the area's commercial centre. The district (area 1,329 sq mi [3,442 sq km]) is divided between the Shire Highlands and the Mulanje Mountains. Intensive agriculture produces tea, tung, and tobacco, and there is limited softwood afforestation. Pop. (latest census) town, 1,225; district, 398,881.
16°02′ S, 35°30′ E
·district area and population table **11**:362
·map, Malawi **11**:361

Mulanje Mountains, in Mulanje District, southeast Malawi, rise abruptly from the surrounding plateau in an almost rectangular syenite mass measuring 12 mi (19 km) across and overlook the Lake Chilwa-Phalombe Plain to the northeast. Sapitwa (Mulanje) Peak reaches a height of 9,842 ft (2,953 m), the highest point in Malawi; other peaks include Manene (8,695 ft), Chinzama (8,391 ft), and Chambe (8,385 ft). Two outliers, Mchese to the northeast and Chambe to the northwest, are both eroded ring structures. Characteristic erosional features include plateaus, deep narrow clefts, and crater-like hollows. The numerous mountain streams drain into the Ruo River system and Lake Chilwa. Red soils support a dense canopy of short, broad-leaved trees crowned by stands of Mulanje cedar (*Widdringtonia whytei*) at its northernmost occurrence in Africa. These trees grow on steep slopes and ravine walls and often reach heights of more than 100 ft and base diameters of 6 ft. Although access is difficult, they are an important factor in the forestry industry. Bauxite deposits occur on the plateaus, and the southern slopes support tea plantations.
15°58′ S, 35°38′ E
·map, Malawi **11**:361

Mula Sankara (Hindu reformer): *see* Dayananda Sarasvati.

Mūla-Sarvāstivāda, a branch of the Sarvāstivāda, a widespread Indian Buddhist school that originated in the 3rd century BC.
·Buddhist school derivations **3**:378f

mulatto, Spanish MULATO, a person of mixed European and Negro ancestry. Originally it denoted only the first-generation offspring of a white and a black person.
·Haitian racial and social elite **8**:548b
·South American distribution **17**:95c

Mulaydah, Battle of al-, decisive victory (1891) for Ibn Rashīd, the ruler of the Rashīdī kingdom centred on Ḥāʾil, in Jabal Shammar in Najd, northern Arabia, over allies of ʿAbd ar-Raḥmān, the head of the Wahhābī (fundamentalist Islāmic) state in Najd; it marked the end of the second Wahhābī empire.

The Wahhābī prince ʿAbd Allāh had allowed to dissipate under his ineffectual rule the territories that his father, Fayṣal (reigned 1834–65), had acquired by conquest following the collapse of the first Wahhābī empire (1818). In 1885 ʿAbd Allāh was "invited" to Ḥāʾil to be the "guest" of Ibn Rashīd, the dominant figure in Arabian politics at the time, while a representative of Ibn Rashīd was appointed governor of Riyadh, the Wahhābī capital.

Although ʿAbd Allāh was restored to the Wahhābī throne in 1889, he died the same year, and his youngest brother, ʿAbd ar-Raḥmān, soon became embroiled in hostilities with Ibn Rashīd and assembled against him an alliance of tribes in al-Qaṣīm. Ibn Rashīd promptly marched on Riyadh but, unable to take it, stationed himself at al-Mulaydah, on the edge of ad-Dahnāʾ desert, where he engaged and defeated the rebellious tribesmen of al-Qaṣīm in 1891. ʿAbd ar-Raḥmān, having missed the battle, fled Riyadh with most of his family and after some difficulty was able to take refuge in Kuwait. Ibn Rashīd, meanwhile, annexed the Wahhābī realm to his own empire.

mulberry, common name for ornamental fruit-bearing trees comprising the genus *Morus* of the family Moraceae (*q.v.*), about 12 to 15 species native to temperate Asia and North America. The paper mulberry (*Broussonetia papyrifera*), of the same family, produces bast fibres used for coarse fabrics; its bark is used in papermaking.

A true mulberry has toothed leaves and blackberry-like fruits; each fruit develops from an entire flower cluster. Red mulberry (*Morus rubra*), of eastern North America, has

(Top) Paper mulberry (*Broussonetia papyrifera*), (bottom) Red mulberry (*Morus rubra*)

(Top) Douglass David Dawn, (bottom) John H. Gerard

two-lobed, three-lobed, or unlobed leaves and dark-purple, edible fruits. White mulberry (*M. alba*), native to Asia, bears white fruits; its leaves are used as food for silkworms. It is naturalized in eastern North America. Russian mulberry (*M. alba* variety *tartarica*) has been introduced into western North America for shelterbelts and local timber use. Black mulberry (*M. nigra*), native to western Asia but also an introduced species in North America, has large, juicy black fruits.

·domesticated plant origins **5**:938b
·drawing paper from bark **5**:995h
·silkworm growth and development **7**:288a
·species and general features **18**:1088h; illus. 1089

Mulcahy, Richard James (b. May 10, 1886, Waterford, County Waterford—d. Dec. 16, 1971, Dublin), Irish Republican Brotherhood soldier, afterward (1944–59) leader of Fine Gael (United Ireland), the major political party in opposition to Eamon de Valera's Fianna Fáil (Republican Party). Imprisoned for fighting in the Irish rebellion of 1916, he later (December 1918) was elected to the British House of Commons as a member of the Irish nationalist Sinn Féin (We Ourselves) Party. In the same year he became chief of staff of the Irish Volunteers. Although he fought against the British until the truce of July 1921, he came to consider the Irish military situation hopeless, and he supported the Anglo-Irish Treaty of Dec. 6, 1921, by which the Irish Free State was established with British dominion status.

Mulcahy was minister of defense (1922–24) under the first two Free State presidents, Arthur Griffith and William T. Cosgrave, and subsequently (1927–32) was minister for local government and public health, also under Cosgrave. From August 1922 he was commander in chief of the Free State armed forces, directing operations against the irregular Irish Republican Army (IRA) in the civil war. Succeeding Cosgrave as president of the Fine Gael Party in January 1944, he resigned in October 1959 in favour of James Dillon. He was minister of education in John A. Costello's interparty governments of 1948–51 and 1954–57.

Mulcaster, Richard (b. 1530?, possibly Cumberland—d. April 15, 1611, Essex, Eng.), English schoolmaster, many of whose pedagogical theories were not generally accepted until at least 250 years after his death.

He was educated at Eton, Cambridge, and Oxford. In 1561 he became the first headmaster of the Merchant-Taylors' School, later acting as high master at St. Paul's.

Mulcaster's fame rests mainly upon his two books *Positions* and *The First Part of the Elementarie.* He recommended special university training for teachers, comparable to that for doctors or lawyers, careful selection of teachers and adequate salaries, assignment of the best teachers to the lowest grades, and close association between teachers and parents. He emphasized the importance of individual differences in children, the adjustment of the curriculum to these differences, and the use of readiness rather than age in determining progress.

·teaching philosophy and experience **6**:347a

mulching, applying a porous or nonporous material to the surface of the soil around plants to conserve moisture, retard the growth of weeds, and otherwise enhance growth. Porous mulch can be any vegetable matter, such as grass clippings, peat moss, and shredded leaves. When partially decayed, such material is usually called compost. Non-porous material usually consists of plastic sheet.

·agricultural innovations and benefits **1**:349h
·fruit farming and soil improvement **7**:763d
·hydrologic element conservation **9**:107b
·temperature control for plants **8**:1108b

Muldenstil, in Gothic sculpture, a style characterized by graceful, curving figures and soft, looping drapery.

·Gothic sculpture developments **19**:366g; illus. 368

Mulde River, tributary of the Elbe River in central East Germany, is formed 2 mi (3 km) north of Colditz by the confluence of the 63-mi-long Freiberger Mulde and the 80-mi Zwickauer Mulde. It flows generally northward past Grimma, Wurzen, Eilenburg, and Bitterfeld until reaching the Elbe near Dessau after a course of 77 mi.
51°52′ N, 12°15′ E

·map, German Democratic Republic **8**:8

The Zwickauer Mulde flowing past the castle of Rochlitz, East Germany

Wolfgang Krammisch—Bruce Coleman Inc.

mule, the hybrid offspring of a male ass (jackass, or jack) and a female horse (mare). The less frequent cross between a female ass and a male horse results in a hinny, or hinney, which is smaller than a mule. Mules were beasts of burden in Asia Minor at least 3,000 years ago and are still used today in many parts of the world because of their ability to withstand hardships and perform work under conditions too severe for many other draft and pack animals. Mules are usually sterile.

The mule resembles the horse in height, uniformity of coat, and shape of neck and croup. It resembles the ass in its short, thick head, long ears, thin limbs, small hoofs, and short mane. The colour of the coat is usually brown or bay. The largest mules range from 16 to 17½ hands (a hand equals four inches or about 10 centimetres) in height and from 1,200 to 1,600 pounds (550 to 700 kilograms) in weight, while the smallest types range from 12 to 16 hands in height and from 600 to 1,350 pounds (270 to 600 kilograms) in weight.

Spain and the U.S. have the finest mules, followed by Portugal and Italy. As farming has become more mechanized, interest in mules has declined.

·African livestock practices **1**:203h
·breeding and general characteristics **10**:1285b
·diseases of animals, tables 2 and 10 **5**:867
·draft work suitability in mountainous terrain **5**:970h
·hybridization and sterility **8**:815g

mule deer (*Odocoileus hemionus*), so called because of its large ears, inhabits western North America from Alaska to Mexico; it is of the family Cervidae (order Artiodactyla). A valued game animal, the mule deer lives alone or in small groups, sometimes gathering in larger herds in winter, in rough, mountainous terrain, and also in desert regions.

Mule deer buck (*Odocoileus hemionus*)

Harry Engels—National Audubon Society

The mule deer is stockier than the related white-tailed deer (*O. virginianus*). It stands 90–105 centimetres (3–3½ feet) at the shoulder and is yellowish to reddish brown in summer, grayish brown in winter. The tail is white with a black tip, except in the black-tailed deer (*O. h. columbianus*), a subspecies of the Pacific Northwest in which the tail is black on the entire upper surface. The male has antlers that fork twice above a short tine near the base; a mature male normally bears five tines on each antler.

·migration and reproductive behaviour **2**:72a
·predator–prey oscillations **14**:835b
·seasonal migration of herds **12**:181h

Muley Hacén, also known as ABU AL-HASSAN ʿALĪ, 15th-century Nasrid king of Granada, dethroned by his son Boabdil in 1482.

·Zahara seizure and Islāmic defeat **17**:418h

mulga snake, species of black snake (*q.v.*).

Mülhausen (France): *see* Mulhouse.

Mülheim an der Ruhr, city, Nordrhein-Westfalen (North Rhine-Westphalia) *Land* (state), northwestern West Germany, just southwest of Essen. First mentioned in 1093, it was early associated with the counts of Broich, whose medieval castle still overlooks the city. It later belonged to the duchy of Berg, which passed to Prussia in 1814. It was chartered in 1808. Between 1878 and 1929 it absorbed a number of neighbouring towns, including Broich and Heissen. Historical buildings include St. Peter's Church (11th century, now entirely rebuilt); Styrum Castle and the former Cistercian convent of Saarn (both 13th century); and the house of Gerhard Tersteegen (died 1769), a pious braid maker and hymn writer.

Mülheim is a hub of rail and road traffic and a Rhine-Ruhr port. The location of its heavy industry is regulated by ordinance. Well-planned modern sections were reconstructed after World War II, and there are many open-air recreational facilities including the Raffelberg racecourse and spa. Heavy industry includes iron foundries, blast furnaces, tube and rolling mills, and machine works. Electrical machinery, leather, steel wire, paper, beer, and cement are also manufactured. Mülheim is an important coal-mining and coal-distributing centre. In the city is the Max Planck Institute for Coal Research, where the Fischer-Tropsch process for liquefying coal and the Ziegler process for the production of polyethylene plastics were discovered. Pop. (1977 est.) 187,677.
51°24′ N, 6°54′ E

Mulhouse, German MÜLHAUSEN, industrial town, Haut-Rhin *département*, northeast France, located in the plain of Alsace between the Vosges and Jura mountains. Situated on the Ill River and on the Canal du Rhône au Rhin, it lies 12 mi (19 km) southwest of the Rhine and 21 mi (33 km) northwest of Basel, Switz. Its most noteworthy ancient building is the 16th-century Hôtel de Ville, covered with mural paintings. A reproduction of the Klapperstein, the evil gossips' stone, hangs on the southwest facade; the original Klapperstein, in the historical museum, is a stone weighing more than 25 lb (12 kg), which was hung around the necks of malicious prattlers on fair days, a practice that persisted until 1781. The 19th-century Protestant church of Saint-Étienne has its original 14th-century stained-glass windows. The restored 13th-century St. John chapel, built by the Knights of Malta, has notable wall paintings.

Textile industries, which developed in the 19th century and specialized in printing designs on calico, brought prosperity to the town, which also has potash and mechanical industries. Mulhouse, first mentioned in the 9th century, became a free imperial city in 1308. It entered into defensive alliances with the Swiss in the 16th century. In 1798 it joined the French Republic. It passed to Germany after the Franco-Prussian War (1871), and was reunited to France in 1918. Pop. (1975) 116,494.
47°45′ N, 7°20′ E
·map, France **7**:585

mulita, common name sometimes used for the nine-banded armadillo (*q.v.*).

Mull, largest island of the Inner Hebrides group, district of Argyll and Bute, Strathclyde region, off the west coast of Scotland, separated from the mainland by the Sound of Mull and the Firth of Lorn. Its coast is much indented, and the island is mountainous, reaching 2,289 ft (698 m) in Creachben and 3,169 ft (966 m) in Ben More. Its restricted farmland is mainly devoted to pasture for sheep and cattle. Granite and silica sand are worked. There are several ancient castles, including Aros and Duart (restored in 1912 and again the seat of the clan Maclean). The largest settlement is Tobermory (*q.v.*), founded in 1788 as a fishing village, which is the chief link with the mainland and has developed as a summer resort and boating centre. Pop. (1974 est.) 1,499.
56°27′ N, 6°00′ W
·map, United Kingdom **18**:866

mull, type of humus (*q.v.*).

mullah, Arabic MAWLĀ, meaning "tutor," or "master," English form of a title given in Muslim countries to religious leaders, teachers in religious schools, those versed in the canon law, leaders of prayer in the mosques (*imāms*), or reciters of the Qur'ān (*qurrā'*). There are no formal requirements for acquisition of the title, but normally persons called by it have had some training in a *madrasah*, or religious school. The word is often used to designate the entire class that upholds the traditional interpretation of Islām.
·Muslim secular–religious function **17**:130c

Mullā Sadrā, also called ṢADR AD-DĪN ASH-SHĪRĀZĪ (b. *c.* 1571 Shīrāz, Iran—d. 1640, Basra, Iraq), philosopher, who led the Iranian cultural renascence in the 17th century.

A scion of a notable Shīrāzī family, Mullā Sadrā completed his education at Isfahan, then the leading cultural and intellectual centre of the country. After studying with scholars there, he produced several works, the best known of which was his *Asfār* ("Journeys"). *Asfār* contains the bulk of his philosophy, which was influenced by a personal mysticism bordering on the ascetic that he experienced during a 15-year retreat at Kahak, a village near Qom.

Expounding his theory of nature, Mullā Sadrā argued that the entire universe—except God and His Knowledge—was originated both "eternally" and "temporally." Nature, he asserted, is the substance of all things and is the cause for all movement. Thus, nature is permanent and furnishes the continuing link between the eternal and the originated.

Toward the end of his life, Mullā Sadrā returned to Shīrāz to teach. His teachings, however, were considered heretical by the orthodox Muslim theologians, who persecuted him, though his powerful family connections permitted him to continue to write. He died on a pilgrimage to Arabia.
·philosophical speculations **9**:1024e

mullein, the 300 species of the genus *Verbascum* (family Scrophulariaceae, *q.v.*), large perennial herbs native to northern temperate regions, especially eastern Eurasia. The common mullein (*V. thapsus*) grows 0.6 to 2 metres (2 to 7 feet) tall, has a single, unbranched stem with large, thick, densely velvety leaves, and has pale-yellow, slightly irregular flowers about one inch across in a crowded terminal spike. Mulleins, often troublesome weeds in pastures and common in disturbed areas and along roadsides, have also found uses in the garden.

Mullein (*Verbascum*)
G.J. Chafaris—EB Inc.

muller, in painting, an instrument used in conjunction with a slab to grind artists' colours by hand. The modern muller and slab are made from glass, although from ancient Egyptian times until the 18th century porphyry was invariably used. After the introduction of the mechanical paint mill in the middle of the 19th century, the muller and slab became obsolete except when small quantities of pigment had to be ground.

Müller, Erwin Wilhelm (b. June 13, 1911, Berlin—d. May 17, 1977, Washington, D.C.), German-U.S. physicist who originated field emission microscopy. Besides working on solid surface phenomena and gas discharge, Müller studied field electron and field ion emissions, inventing the field emission microscope (1937) and the field ion microscope (1955), which for the first time made it possible to make pictures of atoms. A research physicist for certain German firms (1935–45), he joined the Kaiser Wilhelm Institute for Physical Chemistry in Göttingen, then the Free University of Berlin, and finally (1951) went to the U.S., becoming in 1952 professor of physics at Pennsylvania State University, where he taught until his retirement in 1976. He was naturalized in 1962.

Müller, Friedrich, also called MALER MÜLLER, (b. Jan. 13, 1749, Kreuznach, now in West Germany—d. April 23, 1825, Rome), poet, dramatist, and painter (the German word *maler* means "painter") who is best known for his slightly sentimental prose idylls on country life.

After studying painting at Zweibrücken, Müller was appointed court painter at Mannheim (1777) but left the next year for Italy. He abandoned painting soon after his arrival and devoted himself to the history of art. He remained in Italy until his death. The years 1774–78 were primarily devoted to literature, and his writing shows the influence of the *Sturm und Drang* ("Storm and Stress") movement of young literary rebels. His principal works include *Niobe* (1778), a lyric drama; *Fausts Leben dramatisiert* (1778; "Faust's Life Dramatized"); *Golo und Genoveva* (begun 1776; published 1811), a skillful imitation of Goethe's *Götz von Berlichingen;* and the idylls *Die Schafschur* (1775; "The Sheepshearing") and *Das Nusskernen* (1811; "The Nut Kernel"), reproducing scenes, some satirical, from German peasant life.

Müller, Friedrich (1834–98), Austrian philologist.
·African language classification **1**:219e

Müller, Fritz (1821–97), German-born Brazilian zoologist.
·mimicry discovery and importance **12**:214e

Müller, Georg Elias (b. July 20, 1850, Grimma, now in East Germany—d. Dec. 23, 1934, Göttingen, now in West Germany), psychologist who was probably second only to his colleague Wilhelm Wundt in influencing the early development of experimental psychology. Director (1881–1921) of one of the major centres of psychological research at the University of Göttingen, he contributed to the advancement of knowledge of sensations, memory, learning, and colour vision.

Müller received a Ph.D. from Göttingen (1873) for his basic analysis of sensory attention, a work that continued to be cited for 35 years. He was appointed *Privatdozent* at Göttingen in 1876 and two years later published *Toward a Foundation of Psychophysics* (1878), in which he dealt primarily with Weber's law concerning the stimulus–sensory intensity relationship. That work helped to establish him as a new leader in the field and obtained him a professorship. Initially he concerned himself mainly with perceptual thresholds. A noteworthy outcome was the knowledge that day-to-day fluctuations in individual thresholds are the result of individual variations in sensitivity.

Many of his papers on sensory discrimination are considered classics. That on weights (1899), revealing the effect of anticipation on discrimination, may also be viewed as one of the early experimental studies of attitude.

By the mid-1890s Müller began extending the pioneer efforts of the psychologist Hermann Ebbinghaus on memory and learning and exploring also the stimulus–response relation in vision. He made a thorough analysis of Ebbinghaus' methods and began to distinguish the active processes, such as conscious organization, in learning. He showed that learning is not mechanical and is not accounted for by contiguous associations. He also suggested that there is an active effort to find relations and that judgment involves such components as anticipated sensations and feelings, as well as doubt, hesitation, and readiness. In his work on colour vision he suggested that the brain adds a gray to retinally induced colours. He established principles relating neural events within the brain to corresponding perceptual events. Though these principles were later adopted by Gestalt psychology, which examines the structured wholes of mental life, Müller declared his opposition to the Gestalt approach in 1923. His *Outline of Psychology* (1924) was among his final works.

Müller, Hermann (b. May 18, 1876, Mannheim, now in West Germany—d. March 20, 1931, Berlin), Sozialdemokratische Partei Deutschlands (German Social Democratic Party) leader and statesman, twice chancellor of coalition governments during the Weimar Republic. Unable to avert the disastrous effects of the 1929 world economic crisis on Germany, he was forced to resign his second chancellorship.

Of middle class origin, Müller became editor of the Social Democratic paper *Görlitzer Zeitung* in 1889. Elected to the executive committee of the German Social Democratic Party in 1906, he steered a moderate course between the left and right wings. In July 1914 he was sent on an abortive mission to France to coordinate Socialist opposition to the impending World War I. Müller became a member of the Reichstag (federal lower house) in 1916, and, after the revolution of November 1918, entered the new provisional government. As foreign minister, he signed the Treaty of Versailles for Germany. After the failure of the Kapp Putsch (March 1920), he assumed office as chancellor until the June 1920 elections. From 1920 on, Müller headed his party. After the success of the Social Democrats in the 1928 elections, he formed a coalition government with the moderate parties. Under his administration, Germany began a naval construction program and negotiated the Young Plan, which reduced the reparations payments stipulated by the Treaty of Versailles. The advent of the depression, however, led to the breakup of the coalition, and Müller, whose party wished to increase unemployment benefits for the workers, was forced to resign on March 27, 1930.

·Weimar parliament instability **8**:117c

Muller, Hermann Joseph 12:614 (b. Dec. 21, 1890, New York City—d. April 5, 1967, Bloomington, Ind.), geneticist, is remembered for his demonstration that X-rays speed up the natural process of mutation and his theoretical idea of a sperm "bank" to "conserve genius."

Abstract of text biography. Muller studied with several famous biologists of his day, including T.H. Morgan, who had just introduced the fruit fly (*Drosophila*) to genetics research. After obtaining his doctorate in 1916, Muller taught and continued his research on mutations. A confluence of events—including his despair at social conditions during the Depression—precipitated a nervous breakdown, and Muller travelled to Europe, working in Berlin and in Russia. Lysenkoism and its aberrant doctrines forced Muller to leave Russia. After several teaching posts elsewhere, he assumed a professorship at Indiana University. He won a Nobel Prize for Physiology or Medicine in 1946.

REFERENCES in other text articles:
·analysis of radiation-induced mutations **15**:387b
·eugenic insemination proposals **6**:1026e
·gene linkage and recombination studies **7**:982h
·induced mutation experiments **12**:755b
·Morgan's fruit fly heredity experiments **12**:441e
·radiation induction of mutations **19**:1167b

Müller, Johann: *see* Regiomontanus.

Müller, Johannes Peter 12:615 (b. July 14, 1801, Koblenz, now in West Germany—d. April 28, 1858, Berlin), comparative physiologist and anatomist, was one of the great natural philosophers of the 19th century.

Abstract of text biography. Müller studied at the University of Bonn and taught there from 1824 until 1833, when he accepted a chair at the University of Berlin. Müller was widely respected for his painstaking research in physiology, pathology, and comparative anatomy. He suffered severe depressions that interfered with his work for extended periods and may have taken his own life.

Müller's most notable work was *Handbuch der Physiologie des Meuschen fur Vorlesungen* (1834–40; Eng. trans., *Elements of Physiology*, 1837–42).

REFERENCES in other text articles:
·Helmholtz' association and disagreement **8**:752b
·history of medicine in the 19th century **11**:831e
·physiology during 19th century **14**:436d
·sensory reception and the nervous system **15**:160b
·specific energy of nerves **15**:154h

Müller, Johannes von, sometimes known as THE SWISS TACITUS (b. Jan. 3, 1752, Schaffhausen—d. May 29, 1809, Kassel, now in West Germany), the most important Swiss historian of the 18th century. Müller's life was marked by the tension between his work as scholar and his activity as diplomat and political journalist at the court of the archbishop of Mainz (1786–92) and in the imperial chancery at Vienna (1793–98). In the last years of his life he entered the service of Napoleon as director of education for the kingdom of Westphalia, and his posthumous reputation was long clouded by what was unjustly interpreted as a betrayal of the idea of freedom.

His most important work was *Geschichten Schweizerischer Eidgenossenschaft* (1786–1808; unfinished, up to 1489). In it he combined comprehensive knowledge of chronicle sources (especially Aegidius Tschudi) with a terse elegance that earned him the title of the Swiss Tacitus; Tacitus, the 1st-century-AD Roman historian, was indeed his model. His idealistic and patriotic picture of the ancient Swiss constitution profoundly influenced the 19th-century European view of Switzerland. (Among other things, it was the source for Schiller's *Wilhelm Tell.*) Müller's attempt at universal history, the *24 Bücher allgemeiner Geschichten* (1810 *et seq.;* Eng. trans., *The History of the World*, 1840), is indebted to the historical outlook of the Enlightenment, but points forward to Leopold von Ranke in its religious conception. In *Fürstenbund* (1787) and *Reisen der Päpste* (1782), which are political journalism, Müller appears as an important theorist of the European balance of power.

As a Swiss and declared enemy of despotism, he supported the idea of the small state; as a representative of a mediating Switzerland and as a cosmopolitan of the Enlightenment, he tried to unite the spiritual heritage of Rome with the German origins of his civilization. The classics and Christianity coloured by pietism went to make up this remarkably gifted personality whom German classicism—Herder, Goethe, and Schiller—claimed as its own historian.

·literary works and influence **10**:1172b

Müller, Karl Otfried (b. Aug. 28, 1797, Brieg, Silesia, now in Poland—d. Aug. 1, 1840, Athens), German professor and scholar of classical Greek studies whose considerations of ancient Greece in a broad historical and cultural context began an important era in the development of Hellenic scholarship.

Müller was a pupil of August Boeckh, founder of a famous school of philology. His first published work, *Aegineticorum liber* (1817; "On the Isle of Aegina"), was of such brilliance that within two years he was made adjunct professor of ancient literature at the University of Göttingen (1819), where he lectured on archaeology and the history of ancient art. His most important work, *Geschichten hellenischer Stämme und Städte* (1820; "History of Greek Cities and Peoples"), provides a cultural history of the civilizations of ancient Greece and emphasizes the study of myths, successfully combining the historical and allegorical methods. His other works include numerous archaeological papers, historical surveys on the Dorians and Etruscans, and valuable methodological studies. Among the more noteworthy are his *Prolegomena zu einer wissenschaftlichen Mythologie* (1825; "Prolegomena to a Scientific Mythology"), which prepared the way for the scientific investigation of myths, and his edition of Aeschylus' *Eumenides* (1833), in which he attacks the prevalent philological criticisms of the classics. As political troubles made his position at Göttingen difficult, Müller left Germany for archaeological visits in Greece, where he succumbed to fever.

Müller, Lucas: *see* Cranach, Lucas, the Elder.

Müller, (Friedrich) Max (b. Dec. 6, 1823, Dessau, now in East Germany—d. Oct. 28, 1900, Oxford), Orientalist and language scholar whose works stimulated widespread interest in the study of linguistics, mythology, and religion. His principal achievement was the editing of *The Sacred Books of the East* (51 vol., 1879–1904). Originally a student of Sanskrit, he turned to comparative language studies, and around 1845 he began studying the Avesta, the Zoroastrian sacred scripture written in Old Iranian. This interest led him to the study of comparative religion and the editing

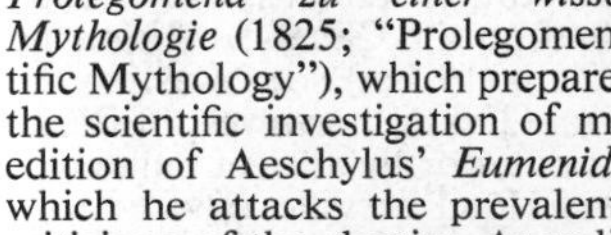

Max Müller

By courtesy of the Curator of the Senior Common Room, Christ Church, Oxford of the most ancient of Hindu sacred hymns, the Ṛgveda, which was published after he had settled in Oxford (1849–75). There he was appointed deputy professor of modern languages (1850) and professor of comparative philology (1868). He sought to popularize comparative Indo-European language studies.

Müller's essays on mythology are among his most appealing writings. His exploration of mythology also led him further into comparative religion and to the publication of *The Sacred Books of the East*, begun in 1875. Of the 51 volumes, including indexes, of translations of major Oriental, non-Christian scriptures, all but three appeared under his superintendence during his lifetime. In Müller's later years, he also wrote on Indian philosophy and encouraged the search for Oriental manuscripts and inscriptions. Among such discoveries were early Indian Buddhist scriptures written in Japan.

·ethnographic classification of religion **15**:629d
·folklore and cultural origins **7**:462f
·historical investigations of religions **15**:617e
·India and Western scholarship **9**:344e

Müller, Otto (b. 1874, Liebau, Ger., now Lubawka, Poland—d. Sept. 24, 1930, Breslau, Ger., now Wrocław, Poland), painter and printmaker of the German Expressionist movement, especially known for his paintings of nudes and gypsy women. When, in 1910, he joined Die Brücke (*see* Brücke, Die), a Dresden-based group of Expressionist artists, his work still displayed the early influence of the curvilinear art of Jugendstil (*q.v.*), the German Art Nouveau movement, as can be seen in "The Judgment of Paris" (*c.* 1910–11; Nationalgalerie, West Berlin). But his radically elongated figures reveal his affinity for the work of the Expressionist sculptor Wilhelm Lehmbruck.

Subsequent works, such as "The Large Bathers" (*c.* 1910–14; Kunsthalle der Stadt Bielefeld, now in West Germany) and "Self-Portrait" (1921; Morton D. May Collection, St. Louis, Mo.), show little stylistic change and retain the linearity and the muted colours

Self-portrait, oil painting by Otto Müller, 1922; in the Klaus Gebhard Collection, Munich

By courtesy of Klaus Gebhard; permission S.P.A.D.E.M. 1973 by French Reproduction Rights, Inc.; photograph, Gertrud Bingel

of his early paintings. He taught at the Breslau Academy from 1919 until his death. Like the work of many other modern German artists, his was declared "decadent" when the Nazis gained power in Germany in 1933.

Müller, Paul Hermann (b. Jan. 12, 1899, Olten, Switz.—d. Oct. 12, 1965, Basel), chemist, received the 1948 Nobel Prize for Medicine or Physiology for discovering the potent toxic effects on insects of DDT—with its chemical derivatives, the most widely used insecticide for more than 20 years and a major factor in increased world food production and the suppression of insect-borne diseases.

A research chemist at the J.R. Geigy Company, Basel (1925–65), Müller began his career with investigations of dyes and tanning agents. In 1935 he began his search for an "ideal" insecticide, one that would show rapid, potent toxicity for the greatest possible number of insect species, but would cause little or no damage to plants and warm-blooded animals. He also required that it be a substance possessing a high degree of chemical stability, so that its effect would persist for long periods of time and that its manufacture be economical. Four years later, after exhaustive but fruitless investigations, Müller synthesized and tested a substance known as dichlorodiphenyltrichloroethane (DDT) and found that it satisfied the requirements he had originally set down. The German chemist Othmar Zeidler had first synthesized the compound in 1874, but had failed to realize its value as an insecticide.

Paul Müller

EB Inc.

In 1939, DDT was tested successfully against the Colorado potato beetle by the Swiss government, and by the U.S. Department of Agriculture in 1943. In January 1944, DDT was used to quash an outbreak of typhus carried by lice in Naples, the first time a winter typhus epidemic had been stopped.

Although Müller had required his ideal insecticide to be relatively nontoxic to warm-blooded animals, the widespread use and persistence of DDT (in 1968 it was estimated that 1,000,000,000 pounds of the substance remained in the environment) has made it a hazard to animal life, and it has shown signs of disrupting ecological food chains. By 1970 DDT was rapidly being supplanted by more quickly degraded, less toxic agents; its use has been banned in Sweden, Ontario, and the U.S.

·pesticide research in 20th century **1**:345b

Müller, Sophus Otto (b. May 24, 1846, Copenhagen—d. Feb. 23, 1934, Copenhagen), one of the foremost paleontologists of his generation, who, during the late 19th century, discovered the first of the Neolithic battle-ax (single-grave) cultures in Denmark. Assistant (1878) and inspector (1885) at the Museum of National Antiquities, Copenhagen, he became co-director of the Danish prehistoric and ethnographic collections at the National Museum, Copenhagen, when it was established in 1892. His discovery in central Jutland of single burial graves enclosed within barrows (burial mounds) was the first evidence of the later Middle Neolithic Periods in Scandinavia. Excavations uncovered chronological sequences of graves containing well-proportioned battle-axes, flint axes, amber beads, beakers, and cups. These findings ended the association of barrows with only the succeeding period, the Bronze Age.

Müller developed new techniques of excavation and monument preservation, opposed rigid classification of prehistoric chronology, and supported the principle of the influence

Sophus Müller

By courtesy of the Royal Danish Embassy, London

of Mediterranean civilization on northern Europe. His writings include *Vor oldtid* (1897; "Our Antiquity"), *Ordning af danmarks oldsager* (3 vol., 1888–95; "System of Danish Antiquities"), and *Oldtidens kunst i danmark* (3 vol., 1918–33; "Ancient Art of Denmark").

Müller, Wilhelm (b. Oct. 7, 1794, Dessau, now in East Germany—d. Sept. 30, 1827, Dessau), poet known both for his lyrics that helped to arouse sympathy for the Greeks in their struggle for independence from the Turks and for his cycles "Die Schöne Müllerin" and "Die Winterreise," which were set to music as lieder by Schubert.

After studying philology and history at the University of Berlin, Müller volunteered in the Prussian uprising against Napoleon (1813–14). On his return from a trip to Italy (1817), he was appointed teacher of classics (1818) and librarian at the ducal library in Dessau.

Müller's reputation was established by the *Gedichte aus den hinterlassenen Papieren eines reisenden Waldhornisten* (2 vol., 1821–24; "Poems from the Bequeathed Papers of a Travelling Bugler"), folk lyrics that attempt to display emotion with complete simplicity, and *Lieder der Griechen* (1821–24; "Songs of the Greeks"), a collection that succeeded in evoking German sympathy for the Greek cause. His other works include *Neugriechische Volkslieder* (2 vol., 1825; "Modern Greek Folk Songs") and *Lyrische Reisen und epigrammatische spaziergänge* (1827; "Lyrical Travels and Epigrammatical Walks"). He also wrote a book, *Homerische Vorschule* (1824; "Homeric Preparatory School"), and made a translation of Marlowe's *Dr. Faustus*.

Müller, William John (1812–45), English landscape and figure painter, worked on the scenery of Gloucestershire and Wales and later made continental tours.

Müller-Brockmann, Josef (b. May 9, 1914, Rapperswil, Switz.), graphic artist, known for the originality and experimental nature of his poster designs. After studying subjects as diverse as architecture and anatomy at the University of Zürich, he became an apprentice to a graphic designer in Zürich until he opened his own studio in 1936. He specialized in exhibition design, commercial art, and photography, but he also designed stage sets and made puppets for the Zürich Marionette Theatre. His advertisement designs won many honours, and he taught graphic design at several notable schools, such as the Kunstgewerbeschule (School of Arts and Crafts) in Zürich and the Naniwa College in Ōsaka, Japan.

·lithograph poster illus. **1**:111

Müllerian mimicry, a form of biological resemblance in which two or more unrelated noxious, or dangerous, organisms exhibit closely similar warning systems, such as the same pattern of bright colours. According to the widely accepted theory advanced in 1878 by the German naturalist Fritz Müller, this resemblance, although differing from the better known Batesian mimicry (*q.v.*), in which one organism is not noxious, should be considered mimicry nonetheless, because a predator that has learned to avoid an organism with a given warning system will avoid all similar organisms, conferring an advantage to the resemblance.
·biotic interaction types **2**:1050e
·butterfly coloration patterns, illus., **12**:Mimicry, Plate I
·conditioned response to models **2**:811a
·examples, evolutionary mechanism, and behavioral bases **12**:214d
·nature and development **14**:775h

Müller-Lyer illusion, visual illusion in which one line segment with arrowheads pointing away from each other appears shorter than another with arrowheads pointing toward each other, though both segments are actually of equal length. The figure is named for the German psychiatrist and sociologist Franz Müller-Lyer (1857–1916), who described it in 1889.
·visual illusions and ambiguous drawings **9**:241h; illus. 242

Müller's muscle, name of three small muscles; (1) the circular fibres of the muscle that changes the shape of the lens of the eye; (2) a thin muscle layer that bridges an opening (the inferior orbital fissure) in the eye socket; and (3) a muscle in the upper eyelid.
·structure and function in human eye **7**:97d; illus. 93

mullet, any of the abundant, commercially valuable, schooling fishes of the family Mugilidae (order Perciformes) unrelated to the red mullet, or goatfish (*q.v.*) family. Mullets number fewer than 100 species, found throughout tropical and temperate regions. They generally inhabit saltwater or brackish water and frequent shallow, inshore areas, commonly grubbing about in the sand or mud for microscopic plants, small animals, and other food. They are silvery fishes 30–90 centimetres (1–3 feet) long, with large scales; relatively stocky, cigar-shaped bodies; forked tails; and two distinct dorsal fins, the first containing four stiff spines. Many have strong, gizzard-like stomachs and long intestines capable of handling a largely vegetarian diet. The common, or striped, mullet (*Mugil cephalus*), cultivated in some areas because of its rapid growth rate, is a well-known species found worldwide; it attains a length and weight of about 90 centimetres (35½ inches) and 7 kilograms (15 pounds).
·classification and general features **14**:51d; illus. 47

mullet, in heraldry, figure of a usually five-pointed star.
·heraldic cadency marks **8**:790h; illus. 791

Mullidae (fish family): *see* goatfish.

Mulligan, Gerry, real name GERALD JOSEPH MULLIGAN (b. April 6, 1927, New York City), outstanding member of the generation of white jazz musicians who emerged after World War II. Always a sophisticated and technically accomplished musician, he was one of many who helped give the lie to the old idea of the jazz musician as a purely intuitive performer. His first important work was with the Gene Krupa orchestra as musician and writer in 1947; and in the following year he composed and orchestrated several pieces for the highly influential Miles Davis nine-piece group.

Moving to California in 1952, Mulligan began experimenting with a pianoless quartet; this eccentric instrumentation created a disembodied, slightly ghostly sound that dovetailed beautifully with the restrained sonority of his own saxophone playing. The quartet was one of the few jazz groups to win commercial fame. Less active as a musician later, he occasionally toured with the Dave Brubeck group, remaining one of the cleverest musical thinkers of his generation. His motion pictures include *Jazz on a Summer's Day, I Want to Live* (1958), and *The Subterraneans* (1960).

Mulligan River, also called EYRE CREEK, intermittent stream in east central Australia; it rises as the Georgina River on the Barkly Tableland (Northern Territory) and flows south and west into Queensland, past Marion Downs, near Breadalbane (becoming Mulligan River), to enter Lake Machattie. It then crosses the South Australian border, joins with the Diamantina, and flows into Goyder's Lagoon after a course of 700 mi (1,100 km) before reaching Lake Eyre via the Warburton River. Principal tributaries are the Wills and Moonah creeks and the Burke River. Mulligan River, discovered (1845) by Charles Sturt and named by him after the explorer Edward John Eyre, crosses the pastoral Channel Country (*q.v.*) and may be in flood for six months at a time.
26°40′ S, 139°00′ E

Mulliken, Robert Sanderson (b. June 7, 1896, Newburyport, Mass.), chemist and physicist who received the 1966 Nobel Prize for Chemistry for "fundamental work chemical bonds and the electronic structure of molecules."

Mulliken, 1966
By courtesy of the Nobel Foundation, Stockholm

A graduate of Massachusetts Institute of Technology, Cambridge, Mulliken worked, during World War I and for a few years afterward, in government chemical research, and then he studied under the physicist Robert A. Millikan at the University of Chicago. He taught at New York University (1926–28) and then joined the faculty of the University of Chicago.

Mulliken began working on his theory of molecular structure in the 1920s. He theoretically systematized the electron states of molecules in terms of molecular orbitals. Departing from the idea that electron orbitals for atoms are static and that atoms combine like building blocks to form molecules, he proposed that, when molecules are formed, the atoms' original electron configurations are changed into an overall molecular configuration. Further extending his theory, he developed (1952) a quantum-mechanical theory of the behaviour of electron orbitals as different atoms merge to form molecules.

During World War II Mulliken worked on the Plutonium Project, part of the development of the atomic bomb, at the University of Chicago. In 1955 he served as scientific attaché at the U.S. embassy in London. Retaining his position at the University of Chicago, he joined (1965) the Institute of Molecular Biophysics at Florida State University, Tallahassee.
·molecular orbital theory development **4**:88h

Mullingar, Irish MUILEANN CEARR, county town (seat) of County Westmeath, Ireland, on the River Brosna. It is a major road and rail junction and the centre of a cattle-raising area. The Royal Canal almost encircles the town, which has a Roman Catholic cathedral. Principal industries are the manufacture of furniture and pencils. Pop. (1971) 6,790.
53°32′ N, 7°20′ W
·map, Ireland **9**:882

Mullins, city, Marion County, northeast South Carolina, U.S., on the Little Pee Dee River. Established in 1853 as a stop for the Wilmington and Manchester Railroad, it was named for Col. William Mullins, who helped plan the railroad. The community's development began in 1894 with the introduction of tobacco culture into the area. Tobacco remains the chief crop. Other agricultural products include corn (maize), soybeans, cotton, pecans, grapes, and watermelons. Industrial activities include the manufacture of textiles, furniture, lumber, metal and concrete products, and fertilizer. Inc. 1872. Pop. (1980) 6,068.
34°12′ N, 79°15′ W

mullite, aluminum silicate, $3Al_2O_3 \cdot 2SiO_2$, that is rarely found as a mineral in nature. It is formed from firing aluminosilicate raw materials and is the most important constituent of ceramic whiteware, porcelains, and high-temperature insulating and refractory materials. Mullite keeps the aluminum content of ceramics and refractories high, a proportion desirable for thermal stability because compositions having an alumina–silica ratio of at least 3:2 will not melt below 1,810° C (3,290° F), whereas those with a lower ratio partially melt as low as 1,545° C (2,813° F).

Natural mullite was discovered as white, elongated crystals on the Island of Mull, Inner Hebrides, Scotland. It has been recognized only in fused argillaceous (clayey) enclosures in intrusive igneous rocks, which suggests very high temperatures of formation. For mineralogic properties, *see* table under silicate minerals.
·clay mineral response to heat **4**:704a
·formation and economic use **16**:758g
·formula and metamorphic occurrence **12**:6h; table

Mulready, William (1786–1863), English painter who excelled in cottage, schoolroom, and romantic scenes, best known for his "Interior of an English Cottage" (1828), also designed (1840) the first penny postage envelope.
·Romantic style of genre painting **19**:455c

Mul Shankar (Hindu social reformer): *see* Dayananda Sarasvati.

Multān, city, district, and division, Punjab Province, Pakistan. The city, the district and division headquarters, is built on a mound just east of the Chenāb River. A commercial and industrial centre, it is connected by road and rail with Lahore and Karāchi and by air with Karāchi, Quetta, and Lyallpur. Industries include fertilizer and glass factories; foundries; cotton, woollen, and silk textile mills; flour, sugar, and oil mills; and a thermal power station. It is famous for its handicrafts and cottage industries.

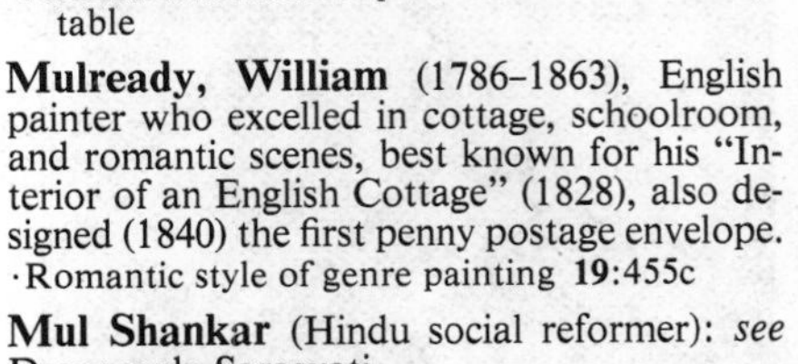
A cotton factory, Multān, Pak.
Frederic Ohringer from the Nancy Palmer Agency—EB Inc.

Multān was constituted a municipality in 1867. There are two hospitals, public gardens, and five colleges affiliated with the University of the Punjab. Large, irregular suburbs have grown outside the old walled town, and the city now covers an area of 9 sq mi (23 sq km); two satellite towns have been set up. Modern buildings include the town hall and the Nishtar Medical College and hospital. The numerous shrines within the old city offer impressive examples of workmanship and architecture. The Shams-e Tabriz shrine is built almost entirely of turquoise or sky-blue engraved glazed bricks. That of Shāh Rukn-e ʿAlam (Tughluq period) has one of the biggest domes in Asia. The shrine of Shaykh Yūsuf Gardēz is a masterpiece of the Multāni style. Other shrines include the Pahlādpurī Temple, the ʿIdgāh (1735), and the Walī Muḥammad Mosque (1758). On the site of the old fort is a public park, a stadium, a swimming pool, and a small museum.

The chief seat of the Malli, Multān was subdued by Alexander the Great in 326 BC and fell to the Muslims c. AD 712; for three centuries it remained the outpost of Islām in India. In the 10th century it became a centre of the Qarmaṭian heretics. The commercial and military key to the southern route into India, it suffered several sacks and sieges over the centuries. Subject to the Delhi sultanate and the Mughal Empire, it was captured by the Afghans (1779), the Sikhs (1818), and the British (1849). Formerly called Kashtpur, Hanspur Bāgpur, Sanb (or Sanābpur), and finally Mulasthān, it derives its name from that of the idol of the sun-god temple, a wealthy shrine from the pre-Muslim period.

Multān District (area 5,630 sq mi [14,582 sq km]) occupies an irregular triangle within the Bāri Doāb, a tract between the Sutlej, Rāvi, and Chenāb rivers, and extends northwestward across the Rāvi. The climate is arid, large portions being desert, and irrigation is by means of inundation from the Lower Bāri Doāb Canal system. The chief crops are wheat, millet, cotton, barley, legumes, and dates. There are cotton-ginning and cotton-pressing factories.

Multān Division (area 24,826 sq mi [64,300 sq km]) was constituted in 1960 to include Multān, Dera Ghāzi Khān, Muzaffargarh, and Sāhiwāl districts. The whole area is flat except for the Sulaimān Range, in the western part of Dera Ghāzi Khān District. Pop. (1972 prelim.) city, 544,000; district, 4,010,000; division, 9,495,000.

·map, Pakistan **13**:893

Multani dialect, important dialect of the Lahnda language, an Indo-Aryan language of the border region between India and Pakistan.

·Indian scripts and alphabets, table 3 **1**:623

Multatuli, real name EDUARD DOUWES DEKKER (b. March 2, 1820, Amsterdam—d. Feb. 19, 1887, Ingelheim-Mitte, now in West Germany), one of The Netherlands' greatest writers, whose radical ideas and freshness of style eclipsed the mediocre, self-satisfied Dutch literature of the mid-19th century.

Multatuli became internationally known with his most important work, the novel *Max Havelaar* (1860; Eng. trans., 1927). Partly autobiographical, it concerns the vain efforts of an enlightened official in Indonesia to expose the Dutch exploitation of the natives. The frame structure of the novel enabled him both to plead for justice in Java and to satirize unsparingly the Dutch middle class mentality. The conversational style and type of humour were far in advance of Multatuli's time, and the book long remained a solitary phenomenon.

Apart from *Minnebrieven* (1861; "Love Letters"), a fictitious romantic correspondence between Multatuli, his wife, and Fancy, his ideal soul mate, his main work was *Ideeën* (7 vol., 1862–77; "Ideas"), in which he gives his anachronistically radical views on woman's position in society and on education, national politics, and other topics from religion to roulette.

Included in the *Ideeën* is his autobiographical novel *Woutertje Pieterse* (Eng. trans., 1904), in which he anticipates the style of the later Realist school.

·Dutch literature of the 19th century **10**:1199c
·Indonesian organizational nationalism **9**:487h

mültezim, collector or tax farmer in the Ottoman Empire who assumed responsibility for collecting state revenue and paying a fixed amount to the state treasury, while keeping a portion of the taxes collected for his own use. The auctioning of the state tax farms (*iltizams*) to the highest bidder freed the central government from actual collection of taxes and insured a steady flow of funds into the treasury. The system, which had its beginnings during the reign of Sultan Mehmed II (1451–81), was officially abolished in 1856, but continued in various forms until the end of the empire in the early 20th century.

·Balkan colonial rule **2**:622e
·Ottoman administration and tax structure **13**:781b

multicellular organism, an organism composed of more than one cell. Multicellular organisms differ from aggregations of unicellular, or single-celled, organisms in that cells of the former are differentiated and interdependent; each cell in an aggregation of cells, on the other hand, is ordinarily self sufficient. The development of multicellular organisms is accompanied by cellular specialization and division of labour: cells become efficient in one process and are dependent upon other cells for the necessities of life.

Specialization in single-celled organisms exists at the subcellular level; *i.e.*, the basic functions that are divided among the cells, tissues, and organs of the multicellular organism are collected within one cell. Some biologists consider the single-celled organism to be acellular because, according to the cell theory, all living organisms are composed of cells. Unicellular organisms are sometimes grouped together and classified as the kingdom Protista. *See* protist.

multidimensional space, in higher mathematics, the general designation for abstract concepts of space—*i.e.*, space of the fourth dimension or greater.

·abstract geometry propositions **7**:1124e
·algebraic topology fundamentals **18**:505a
·chemical kinetics mathematical model **4**:141h
·elementary algebra principles **1**:504a
·elliptic geometry development and use **7**:1114d
·Euclidean basis in differential geometry **7**:1098b
·Euclidean geometry principles **7**:1110b
·historical development of geometry **11**:656c
·linear and multilinear algebra theory **1**:509c
·mathematics history from antiquity **11**:645c
·number theory principles **13**:375g
·probability theory and method **14**:1104f
·topological basis and construction **18**:510h

multilateral aid, foreign aid by international agencies, such as the International Bank for Reconstruction and Development, consisting of transfers of capital, goods, or services to other nations and their citizens.

·foreign aid through multilateral agencies **7**:524f; table 525

multilinear algebra: *see* algebra, linear and multilinear.

multilinear evolution, theory of culture change that deals with the evolution of particular cultures and with the parallels and similarities of form, function, and sequence among different cultures. The theory, formulated by the U.S. anthropologist Julian Steward, represents an attempt to develop an evolutionary approach that is distinct from unilinear evolutionism (concerned with the placement of particular societies at stages of one supposedly universal sequence from "primitive" to "modern") and from universal evolutionism (concerned with a supposedly generic evolution of all culture). Steward also disagrees, however, with the theory of cultural relativism, which views development of cultures as essentially divergent and not subject to comparison. He uses the approach of human ecological adaptation to study questions of specific, limited cultural differences and similarities, recurrent forms, processes, and functions but not to search for vague, universal laws.

The theory rests on the assumptions that parallels of form and function develop in historically independent cultural traditions and that these parallels can be explained by identical and independent causes. It faces the problem of identifying and classifying the recurrent phenomena with which it deals. For example, the category of hunting-and-gathering societies is too broad for analysis of concrete characteristics and processes. Narrower and more useful categories based on ecological adaptation and level of sociocultural integration (organizational level) are the patrilineal band or the nomadic bilateral band of hunters and gatherers. There are an undetermined number of cultural types, and not all hunters and gatherers may be classifiable into types that are crossculturally significant. Some may be unique except for parallels in limited features, such as the development of clans.

multilinear function, in linear and multilinear algebra, a function f that assigns to a matrix a scalar and that, when applied to the matrix

$$\begin{pmatrix} a_{11} \cdots a_{1n} \\ \vdots \\ a_{i1} + cb_{i1} \cdots a_{in} + cb_{in} \\ \vdots \\ a_{n1} \cdots a_{nn} \end{pmatrix},$$

equals the sum of f applied to the matrix

$$\begin{pmatrix} a_{11} \cdots a_{1n} \\ \vdots \\ a_{i1} \cdots a_{in} \\ \vdots \\ a_{n1} \cdots a_{nn} \end{pmatrix}$$

and the product of c and f applied to the matrix

$$\begin{pmatrix} a_{11} \cdots a_{1n} \\ \vdots \\ b_{i1} \cdots b_{in} \\ \vdots \\ a_{n1} \cdots a_{nn} \end{pmatrix}.$$

multiple fission, in biology, the division of a cell into more than two parts.

·cell reproduction processes **15**:677a
·Protozoan asexual reproductive patterns, illus. 2 **15**:123

multiple independently targeted re-entry vehicle: *see* MIRV.

multiple integral, in mathematics, integral of a function of two or more independent variables. Given a function $f(x, y)$ and a region A of the xy plane, the multiple integral

$$\iint_A f(x, y)\, dxdy$$

(*see* integration [for symbol]) is defined in a

manner analogous to the definite (Riemann) integral (*see* integral); its value is the volume of the solid under the surface $y = f(x, y)$ with vertical sides and A as its base. In practice the double integral is calculated by the use of iterated integrals:

$$\iint_A f(x, y)\,dxdy = \int_{x_1}^{x_2} \left[\int_{y_1(x)}^{y_2(x)} f(x, y)\,dy \right] dx$$

x_1 and x_2 are the least and greatest values of x in A and $y_1(x)$ and $y_2(x)$ describe the boundaries of A as functions of x.

·functional analysis fundamentals **1**:764a

multiple myeloma, also known as PLASMA CELL MYELOMA or MYELOMATOSIS, common malignant tumour of bone marrow, usually occurring in middle age and later. It is slightly more common in males and affects mostly the flat bones (*e.g.*, vertebrae, skull, pelvis, shoulder blade). Hyperplasia (increase in number) of certain marrow cells leads to an excess of protein in the circulation, which in turn causes kidney damage. The bone destruction also frees calcium into the circulation, which may be redeposited in abnormal places, such as the kidney. Symptoms and signs include pain, anemia, weakness, a tendency to hemorrhage, and kidney insufficiency. Pathological fractures occur, and neurological symptoms may follow collapse of affected vertebrae. The disease is progressive, and most patients die within two years of diagnosis. In the presence of multiple lesions, only symptomatic treatment is possible; when only one lesion is present, surgery or irradiation may arrest or cure the disease. *See also* tumours, bone-related.

·anemia and related blood changes **2**:1142a
·biomedical models, table 1 **5**:866
·immunoglobulins in blood and urine **9**:253c

multiple personality, a rare psychiatric disorder in which two or more distinct personalities are found in one individual. Each of these alter egos has its own characteristic behaviour patterns, often quite different or opposite from those of its fellows. The personalities may take different names and exhibit different handwriting, electroencephalograms, and performance on projective tests. They may be unaware of one another and amnesic about the actions of the others, although in cases in which one is dominant the subordinates may comment upon and criticize the dominant personality as if it were another person.

The condition is extremely rare, though highly publicized (*e.g.*, the case of Eve White, reported in the 1950s and made into a motion picture, *The Three Faces of Eve*); only about 100 genuine cases have been reported. Therapy generally is directed towards making the separate personalities aware of one another and toward acceptance by the individual of the conflicting tendencies implied by these personalities. *See also* hysteria.

·hypnosis as a related phenomenon **9**:134g
·symptoms and prevalence **15**:168h

multiple proportions, law of, in chemistry, states that, when two elements combine with each other to form more than one compound, the weights of one element that combine with a fixed weight of the other are in a ratio of small whole numbers. For example, there are five distinct oxides of nitrogen, and the weights of oxygen in combination with 14 grams of nitrogen are, in increasing order, 8, 16, 24, 32, and 40 grams, or in a ratio of 1, 2, 3, 4, 5. The law was announced (1804) by the English chemist John Dalton, and its confirmation for a wide range of compounds served as the most powerful argument in support of Dalton's theory that matter consists of indivisible atoms.

multiple-purpose water project, in the utilization of water resources, a project planned to serve more than one purpose, such as those designed for flood control, hydroelectric, and recreational purposes, as well as water storage and irrigation facilities. The long list of possible uses includes water management, fish and wildlife preservation, sediment and pollution control, and employment in depressed areas in need of reclamation facilities.

multiple sclerosis, a disease of the brain and spinal cord caused by an unknown agent that attacks the covering (myelin) sheath of nerve fibres, resulting in a temporary interruption of nervous impulses, particularly in pathways concerned with vision, sensation, and the use of limbs. The hard (sclerotic) patches produced by the disease eventually result in permanent paralysis.

Multiple sclerosis has a worldwide distribution, mainly in the Northern Hemisphere. The highest incidence is in persons in the third decade of life. Diagnosis is hampered by the varying nature and duration of early symptoms, of which the following may appear alone or in combination: temporary mistiness or loss of vision, disturbances of sensation, weakness of a lower limb, unsteadiness in walking, giddiness, double vision, and defective control of the bladder. Early symptoms tend to clear up (remission) but are followed by relapses at intervals of months or years, with an increasing risk of permanent paralysis. Occasionally, however, the disease runs a benign course.

The cause of multiple sclerosis remains uncertain, and, thus, medicinal treatment is unsatisfactory. Following a relapse, a period of rest in bed and the avoidance of overfatigue and mental stress are advised. Attempts to isolate a living micro-organism as a cause of the disease have failed. A form of allergy may be an important causal factor.

·cerebrospinal fluid diagnosis, table 2 **3**:1173
·symptoms, causation, and incidence **12**:1054b
·visual symptoms **7**:121e

multiple seismic reflections, several reflections from a natural or artificial seismic pulse that usually indicate more than one interface or at least more than one reflection event in the Earth's subsurface structure. If a single pulse of seismic energy is sent out and several pulses return to a single seismometer at successively increasing times, the later pulses must have travelled farther before they were reflected and refracted back. Two interfaces can sometimes give rise to many reflections because of multiple internal reflections between the interfaces.

·wave motion and recording **6**:70e; graph

multiple setting, or SIMULTANEOUS SETTING, called in France DÉCOR SIMULTANÉ, a staging technique used in medieval drama, in which all the scenes were simultaneously in view, the various locales being represented by small booths known as "mansions," or "houses," arranged around an unlocalized acting area, or *platea*. To change scenes, actors simply moved from one mansion to another; by convention, the audience regarded the *platea* as part of the mansion in use and ignored the other booths.

Multiple setting had its beginnings in liturgical drama, in which the performers, usually members of the clergy, indicated changes in scene by moving from place to place in the church. In the 12th century the plays were moved out of the churches into churchyards and market places, and the settings became increasingly elaborate, with booths that quite graphically represented such locales as palaces, temples, city gates, and even ships at sea. Heaven and hell were represented by mansions at either end of the stage. The most elaborate and ingenious mansion was usually the hellmouth, a booth in the shape of a monster's jaws, from which smoke and fireworks issued and actors dressed as devils appeared.

Multiple setting largely died out during the Renaissance, when dramas began to be acted in the more restricted space of indoor theatres, and movable scenery was perfected. The technique of multiple setting has been revived occasionally for modern plays.

·South Asian folk theatre use **17**:165h
·staging methods in 17th-century France **17**:538e

multiple souls, a widely distributed notion, especially in central and northern Asia and Indonesia, that an individual's life and personality are made up of a complex set of psychic interrelations. In some traditions the various souls are identified with the separate organs of the body; in others they are related to character traits. Each of the different souls making up a single individual has a different destiny after death. Among many northern Asian peoples, for example, one soul remains with the corpse, one soul descends to the underworld, and one soul ascends to the heavens.

The most famous example of multiple souls is the belief of the Apapocuva Guaraní of Brazil that a gentle vegetable soul comes, fully formed, from the dwelling place of the gods and joins with the infant at the moment of birth. To this is joined, shortly after birth, a vigorous animal soul. The type of animal decisively influences the recipient's personality: a gentle person has received a butterfly's soul; a cruel and violent man, the soul of a jaguar. Upon death, the vegetable soul enters paradise, and the animal soul becomes a fierce ghost that plagues the tribe.

Multiple stage setting designed by Jo Mielziner for Arthur Miller's *Death of a Salesman*, 1949, in which several rooms are visible simultaneously

Eileen Darby—Graphic House, Inc.

multiplexing, simultaneous electronic transmission of two or more messages in one or both directions over a single transmission path, with signals separated in time or frequency. In time-division multiplexing, different time intervals are employed for different signals. Two or more different signals may be transmitted in time sequence: the instantaneous amplitude of each signal is sampled and transmitted in sequence. When all signals have been sampled, the process is repeated. The sampling process is carried out rapidly enough to avoid loss of essential information in the signal.

In frequency-division multiplexing, each message is identified with a separate subcarrier frequency; all of these subcarriers are then combined to modulate the carrier frequency. For wire transmission, the modulated subcarriers may be transmitted directly without the introduction of a carrier frequency.

The subcarriers are separated at the receiver terminal by frequency selection and the original message signal recovered from the subcarrier.

·automata theory **2**:499g *passim* to 501c
·computer central processing unit **4**:1052g
·early telegraphy development **18**:83h
·electronic signal transmission and separation **6**:686e
·radiotelegraph transmission channels **15**:429f
·telegraph time-division multiplex system **18**:71h; illus. 72
·telemetry data transmission **18**:81a
·telemetry multiple channel transmission **18**:80h
·telephone message density **18**:86c; illus. 93

multiplication, in arithmetic, simplest form, repetition of addition (*q.v.*) to obtain the number of elements in *n* sets of *m* elements each in which *n* and *m* are integers. For example, 6 sets with 5 elements in each set are equal to 30 elements. There are also generalizations on this operation.

·algebraic geometry fundamentals **7**:1070e
·algebraic structure theory **1**:533a
·arithmetic laws and principles **1**:1172b
·binary arithmetic operation **4**:1050a
·elementary algebra principles **1**:499g
·history of calculatory device and table **11**:650c
·mathematical calculation theory and use **11**:672b
·real analysis principles **1**:774d
·vector and tensor analysis principles **1**:791d

multiplication table, square with numbers, such as 1 to 10, on the top and side and corresponding products, such as 1 to 100, in the square. To find an answer to a multiplication problem, one would look up the numbers to be multiplied on the top and the side.

×	1	2	3	4	5	6	7	8	9	10
1	1	2	3	4	5	6	7	8	9	10
2	2	4	6	8	10	12	14	16	18	20
3	3	6	9	12	15	18	21	24	27	30
4	4	8	12	16	20	24	28	32	36	40
5	5	10	15	20	25	30	35	40	45	50
6	6	12	18	24	30	36	42	48	54	60
7	7	14	21	28	35	42	49	56	63	70
8	8	16	24	32	40	48	56	64	72	80
9	9	18	27	36	45	54	63	72	81	90
10	10	20	30	40	50	60	70	80	90	100

Multiplication table

multiplicity, in physics, subdivision of energy levels of an atom, a molecule, or a nucleus arising from different values of the total spin (*q.v.*) of its electrons or nuclear particles; the multiplicity (m) is one more than twice the spin (s); *i.e.*, $m = 2s + 1$. Singlet, doublet, triplet, quartet, and quintuplet energy states refer to multiplicities of 1, 2, 3, 4, and 5, which correspond to spin values of 0, ½, 1, 3/2, and 2, respectively.

multiplier, in mathematics, the number by which another number is multiplied.

·arithmetic laws and principles **1**:1172b

multiplier, in economics, numerical coefficient showing the effect of a change in total national investment on the amount of total national income; it equals the ratio of the change in total income to the change in investment.

If, for example, the total amount of investment in an economy is increased by $1,000,000, a chain reaction of increases in consumption expenditures is set off. Producers of raw materials that are used on directly affected investment projects and workers employed in such projects receive the $1,000,000 as increases in their incomes. If they spend on the average 3/5 of that additional income, $600,000 will be added to the incomes of others. At this point in the process, total income will have been raised by (1 × $1,000,000) + (3/5 × $1,000,000), or the amount of the initial expenditure on investment plus the additional expenditure on consumption.

It will continue to increase as the producers of the additional consumption goods realize an increase in their incomes, of which they in turn spend 3/5 on consumption goods. The increase in total income will then be (1 × $1,000,000) + (3/5 × $1,000,000) + (3/5 × 3/5 × $1,000,000). The process continues indefinitely; the amount by which total income increases may be computed by means of the algebraic formula for such progressions. In this case it equals 1/ (1 − 3/5) or 2.5. This means that a $1,000,000 increase in investment has effected a $2,500,000 increase in total income.

The concept of the multiplier process became important in the 1930s when the British economist J.M. Keynes suggested it as a means of measuring the amount of government spending needed to compensate for a shortage of private investment in reaching a level of income at which full employment would prevail. The basic concept has since been applied to the cumulative effect of changes in many other variables on total income, such as changes in imports.

·business-cycle mechanics **3**:538b
·economic growth theory of investment **6**:218a
·economic study of growth theory **6**:272e
·income determination theory and model **9**:265e

multiplier phototube (electronics): *see* photomultiplier tube.

Multipoint, cold-type typesetting machine.

·calculation of justified spaces **14**:1062d

multipole, system involving two or more pairs of electric or magnetic dipoles.

·parity of electric and magnetic fields **6**:655c

multituberculate, an extinct, small, superficially rodent-like mammal that existed from the Jurassic Period (about 160,000,000 years ago) of the Mesozoic Era through the early part of the Cenozoic Era (the last 65,000,000 years of Earth history). During most of this span (about 100,000,000 years), they were by far the most abundant mammals; but relatively little evolutionary diversification occurred throughout their long history. These small herbivores were characterized by molar teeth with 2 or 3 longitudinal rows of cusps, 5 or 6 cusps in primitive forms, and up to 30 in advanced genera. They had a single large lower incisor and three upper incisors, with one enlarged. In most genera the lower premolars were large, compressed, shearing teeth. The multituberculates are not closely related to any other mammals. They apparently arose from the mammal-like reptiles and did not give rise to any other types.

·evolution and mammalian relationships **11**:413a
·fossil traits and era **7**:572d; illus.

Multnomah Falls, on a short tributary of the Columbia River that rises in the Larch Mountains (4,100 ft [1,219 m]) in northwestern Oregon, U.S., are located near the Columbia River Highway about 9 mi (15 km) west-southwest of Bonneville. The scenic upper and lower falls plunge into the Columbia River gorge and have a combined height of 850 ft, the highest single drop being 620 ft.

Mūlūd, celebration of the birth of the prophet Muḥammad.

·Berber annual celebrations **11**:296g

mulūk aṭ-ṭawā'if, Arabic name for the numerous "party kings" (called *reyes de taifas* in Spanish) who appeared in Muslim Spain in a period of great political fragmentation early in the 11th century. The dissolution of the central authority of the Umayyad caliphate of

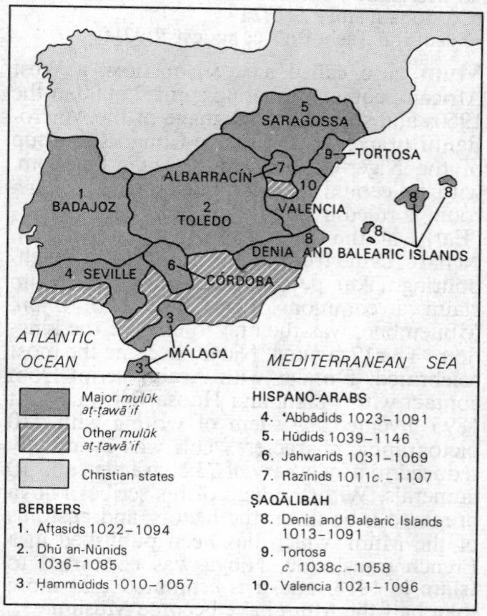

The *mulūk aṭ-ṭawā'if*, or "party kings," in Muslim Spain in 1050 (the kingdoms are named on the map; the "party kings" and the years of their rule are indicated on the numbered legend)

Adapted from Claudio Sanchez-Albornoz y Menduina, *La Espana Musulmana*, vol. 2

Córdoba after the dictatorship of al-Muẓaffar (reigned 1002–08) signalled the release of animosities between the three major parties, or factions (*ṭā'ifahs*), of the Muslim state: the Hispano-Arabs, or Andalusians; the Berbers, and the Ṣaqālibah (Slav mercenaries). Civil war reduced the caliphate to a puppet institution and allowed the various *ṭā'ifahs* to establish themselves in independent and short-lived kingdoms throughout the peninsula. There were at least 23 such states between 1009 and their final conquest by the Almoravids of North Africa in 1091. Thus, the Berbers counted in their party, the Afṭasids (*q.v.*) of Badajoz, the Dhū an-Nūnids (*q.v.*) of Toledo, and the Ḥammūdids (*q.v.*) of Málaga, who briefly helped the Córdoban caliphate, while the ʿAbbādids (*q.v.*) of Seville, the Jahwarids (*q.v.*) of Córdoba, and the Hūdids of Saragossa were prominent Andalusian dynasties. The Ṣaqālibah did not form dynasties but created such kingdoms as Tortosa, Denia, and Valencia (*q.v.*).

Wars between the various states never ceased. The states had few scruples in asking for Christian support against rival Muslim kings or in turning to the North African kingdoms for aid against Christian princes. Such lack of unity and consistency made the kingdoms of the *ṭā'ifahs* fair targets for the growing forces of Christian reconquest; soon Badajoz, Toledo, Saragossa, and even Seville were paying tribute to the Christian Alfonso VI of Leon and Castile.

Despite their political incompetence, however, the *mulūk aṭ-ṭawā'if* fostered a period of brilliant Islāmic cultural revival. In the manner of the caliphal courts, they entertained poets, promoted the study of philosophy, natural science, and mathematics and produced such noted figures as the poet-king al-Muʿtamid of Seville and his vizier Ibn ʿAmmār, the poets Ibn Zaydūn and Wallādah of Córdoba, and Ibn Ḥazm, the poet-philosopher-scholar.

In 1085 Alfonso took Toledo. At the invitation of several party kings, the Almoravid Yūsuf ibn Tāshufīn entered Spain and defeated Alfonso at the Battle of Zallāqah, near Badajoz, in 1086. When Muslim fortunes in Spain did not improve, Yūsuf returned in 1088; he dissolved the party kingdoms (1090–91) and extended the Almoravid Empire into Spain. *Major ref.* **17**:416c

·Alfonso VI's measures and aims **1**:485d
·al-Muʿtamid's decision and defeat **16**:581b
·Córdoba history **5**:172a
·Yūsuf ibn Tāshufīn's conquest **9**:931f

Mum, also called BAMUM, or MOM, a West African people numbering some 75,000 in the 1960s and speaking a language of the Macro-Bantu branch of the Benue-Congo subgroup of the Niger-Congo family. Their kingdom, with its capital at Foumban (*q.v.*) in Cameroon, is ruled over by a king (*mfon*).

Early in the 18th century the first *mfon*, Nchare, came from the territory of the neighbouring Tikar people, with whom the Mum claim a common origin. The 11th *mfon*, Mbuembue, was the first to enlarge the kingdom. The 17th *mfon*, Njoya, became the most celebrated. Familar with Arabic script from contact with Fulani and Hausa, Njoya about 1895 invented a system of writing with 510 pictographic characters. This was eventually reduced to a syllabary of 73 characters and 10 numerals. With the help of his scribes Njoya prepared a book on the history and customs of the Mum, which has been published in a French translation. Njoya was converted to Islām in 1918, and it is estimated that more than half the Mum have become Muslim.

The Mum are noted craftsmen. The economy rests on sedentary agriculture, supplemented by fishing and hunting.

·Congo sociocultural groupings **4**:1119a; map
·sculpture forms and techniques **1**:262c; illus.
·writing system development **19**:1040b

Muma (Ireland): *see* Munster.

Mumetal, any of a series of alloys that are highly permeable to magnetic fields. The alloys usually contain 75–78 percent nickel, 14–17 percent iron, and small proportions of copper, chromium, and molybdenum. *See also* permalloy; permeability, magnetic.

·magnetic properties, table 2 **11**:336

Mumford, Lewis (b. Oct. 19, 1895, Flushing, Long Island, N.Y.), U.S. social critic and teacher, whose numerous writings on architecture and urban planning reflect a faith in man's capacity to renew his world. Early writings, both in periodicals and in books, established him as a writer on architecture and the city, but his writing always was within a larger context, from *Sticks and Stones* (1924) and *The Brown Decades: A Study of the Arts in America, 1865–1895* (1931) to *The City in History* (1961) and *Roots of Contemporary Architecture* (1972). Mumford also taught or held research positions at Stanford University (California) from 1942 to 1944, the University of Pennsylvania (1951–59), Massachusetts Institute of Technology (1957–60), and Wesleyan University (Connecticut; 1963–64).

·city development through history **18**:1075a
·comment on mass production quality **9**:513f
·humanist political philosophy **14**:693h
·science's social relevance **16**:391g

Mummer's Wife, A (1885), novel by George Moore.

·Irish novel tradition **13**:291b

Mummery, Albert Frederick (1855–95), British mountaineer.

·rock climbing as a sport **12**:585h

mumming play, a traditional dramatic entertainment, still performed in a few villages of England and Northern Ireland, in which a "champion" is killed in a fight and is then brought to life by a doctor. It is thought likely that the play has links with primitive ceremonies held to mark important stages in the agricultural year. The name has been connected with words such as mumble and mute; with the German *mumme* ("mask," "masker"); and with the Greek *mommo* (denoting a child's bugbear, or a frightening mask).

Mummers were originally bands of masked persons who during winter festivals in Europe paraded the streets and entered houses to dance or play dice in silence. "Momerie" was a popular (and frequently licentious) amusement between the 13th and 16th centuries. In the 16th century it was absorbed by the Italian carnival masquerading (and hence was a forerunner of the courtly entertainment known as masque).

It is not known how old the mumming play is. Although contemporary references to it do not begin to appear until the late 18th century, the basic narrative framework is the story of St. George and the Seven Champions of Christendom, which was first popularized in England toward the end of the 16th century. It is possible that there was a common (lost) original play, which widely separated communities in England, Ireland, and Scotland modified to their own use. The plot remained essentially the same: St. George, introduced as a gallant Christian hero, fights an infidel knight, and one of them is slain. A doctor is then presented, who restores the dead warrior to life. Other characters include a presenter, a fool in cap and bells, and a man dressed in woman's clothes. Father Christmas also appears. It is likely that the basic story of death and resurrection was grafted onto an older game that stemmed from primitive ritual. Sir E.K. Chambers' *English Folk-Play* (1933), contains a basic study of the mumming play.

·pageantry games of Richard II of England **13**:862g
·theatre's development in Russia **17**:542g

RELATED ENTRIES in the *Ready Reference and Index:*
carnival; masque; Seven Champions of Christendom

Mummius Achaicus, Lucius (fl. mid-2nd century BC), Roman statesman and general who crushed the uprising of the Achaean League against Roman rule in Greece. As praetor in 153, Mummius defeated the rebellious Lusitanians in southwestern Spain; the following year he celebrated a triumph at Rome. As consul in 146, he was appointed commander of the war against the Achaean League. He defeated the Greek forces at Leucopetra on the Isthmus of Corinth and captured and destroyed Corinth. The Roman Senate then dissolved the Achaean League. For his services Mummius was given the surname Achaicus ("the Achaean").

·Critolaus' defeat and fall of Corinth **15**:1095d
·religious epigraphic recording **6**:923d
·Roman entrance to Hellenistic affairs **8**:385c
·Scipio Aemilianus' opposition **16**:395c

Mummu, in the Mesopotamian creation epic *Enuma elish*, the personification of the "original [watery] form" created when the freshwaters underground (Apsu) and the sea (Tiamat) came together; Mummu served as the page of Apsu.

·Babylonian political allegory of Enuma elish **11**:1010h

mummy, a body embalmed or treated for burial with preservatives after the manner of the ancient Egyptians. The process varied from age to age in Egypt, but it always involved removing the internal organs (though in a late period they were replaced, after treatment), treating the body with resin, and wrapping it in linen bandages. Among the many other peoples who practiced mummification were the Guanches of the Canary Islands; the people living along the Torres Strait, between New Guinea and Australia; and the Incas of South America.

There was a widespread belief that Egyptian mummies were prepared with bitumen (the word comes from the Arabic *mūmiyah*, "bitumen"), which was supposed to have medicinal value. Throughout the Middle Ages "mummy," made by pounding mummified bodies, was a standard product of apothecary shops. In course of time it was forgotten that the virtue of mummy lay in the bitumen, and spurious "mummy" was made from the bodies of felons and suicides. The traffic in mummy continued in Europe till the 18th century.

·bases for belief in reanimation **5**:535e
·Egyptian provisions for afterlife **6**:506d
·embalming methods in ancient Egypt **6**:736b

mumps, also known as EPIDEMIC PAROTITIS, acute contagious disease caused by a virus and characterized by inflammatory swelling of the salivary glands. It frequently occurs as an epidemic and most commonly affects young persons. The incubation period is about 17–21 days after contact; danger of transfer begins one week before the affected person feels sick and lasts about two weeks. Mumps generally sets in with symptoms of a slightly feverish cold, soon followed by swelling and stiffening in the region of the parotid salivary gland in front of the ear. The swelling rapidly increases and spreads toward the neck and under the jaw, involving the numerous glands there. The condition is often found on both sides. Pain is seldom severe, nor is there much redness or any tendency to discharge pus; there is, however, interference with chewing and swallowing. After four or five days the parts return to their normal condition. During convalescence in patients past puberty there occasionally occur swelling and tenderness in other glands, such as the testicles in males (orchitis) and the breasts (mastitis) or ovaries (oophoritis) in females and rarely involvement of the pancreas, but these are of short duration and usually of no serious significance. The testicles may become atrophied, but sterility from this cause is very rare. Meningoencephalitis (inflammation of the brain and its membranous covering) is a fairly common concomitant of mumps, but the outlook for recovery is favourable. Mumps itself requires no special treatment. The use, especially in adult patients, of gamma globulin has tended to reduce the incidence of complications.

·cause, symptoms, and complications **4**:222h

Mumu (1852), story by Ivan Turgenev.

·Turgenev's early novels **18**:779f

Mumuye, a people of Nigeria and Cameroon speaking a language that belongs to the Adamawa-Eastern subgroup of the Niger-Congo family of languages.

·figurative art forms **1**:261h

Mun, (Adrien-)Albert(-Marie), comte de (b. Feb. 28, 1841, Lumigny, Fr.—d. Oct. 6, 1914, Bordeaux), Christian Socialist leader and orator who was keenly aware of the workers' misery and advocated Catholicism as an instrument of social reform.

After leaving the military school at Saint-Cyr, Mun saw active service in Algeria (1862) and in the Franco-German War and later

Albert de Mun, *c.* 1880
Harlingue—H. Roger-Viollet

fought against the Paris Commune. From the end of 1871, however, he devoted himself to the formation of Catholic workers' clubs throughout France. Elected to the Chamber of Deputies, he allied himself with the Monarchists for many years. In obedience, however, to Pope Leo XIII's encyclical of 1892, he declared his readiness to rally to the Republican regime provided that it respected religion. Catholic support of the republic failed to create a conservative republican party, but it did further the cause of social Catholicism and Catholic trade unionism.

Mun, Mae Nam, main river system (*mae nam,* "river") of the Khorat Plateau, in eastern Thailand. The Mun rises in the San Kamphaeng Range northeast of Bangkok and flows east for 418 mi (673 km), receiving the Lam Nam Chi, its main tributary, and entering the Mekong at the Laotian border. Navigable from April to November below Tha Chang, the river is used for irrigation. Nakhon Ratchasima Korat and Ubon Ratchathani are the chief towns on its banks.
15°19′ N, 105°31′ E
·map, Thailand **18**:199

Mun, Thomas (baptized June 17, 1571, London—d. *c.* July 21, 1641), English writer on economics who gave the first clear and vigorous statement of the theory of the balance of trade. He came into public prominence with the depression of 1620. Many people held the East India Company responsible because it exported £30,000 in bullion on each voyage to finance its trade. Although the royal charter stipulated that the company had to import an equal amount of bullion within six months, it was charged that the company imported Indian goods valued in excess of British exports to the Indies.

In *A Discourse of Trade, from England unto the East Indies* (1621), Mun argued that so long as England's total exports exceeded its total imports, the export of bullion was not harmful. He pointed out that the money earned on the sale of re-exported East Indian goods was in excess of the amount of originally exported bullion with which those goods were purchased. He was a member of the committee of the East India Company and of the standing commission on trade, appointed in 1622. In his most important work, *England's Treasure by Forraign Trade*, published posthumously in 1664, Mun developed these ideas.
·balance of trade theory **6**:227d

Muna Island, Indonesian PULAU MUNA, formerly spelled MOENA, island, Sulawesi Tenggara (Southeast Celebes) province, Indonesia, south of the southeastern arm of Celebes. With an area of 658 sq mi (1,704 sq km), it has a hilly surface, rising to 1,460 ft (445 m). The north and northeast have teak forests. The Muna, a Muslim people speaking an Austronesian language, practice a simple agriculture, its principal products including teak, rice, sago starch, and sea cucumber. The hog-like babirusa and the marsupial cuscus are found on the island. The main town and principal port is Raha, on the northeastern coast. Pop. (1971 prelim.) 154,024.
5°00′ S, 122°30′ E

munāfiq, a term applied in the Qur'ān to those Muslim converts from Medina whose fidelity could not be entirely relied upon. It is usually translated "hypocrite," but in context "waverer" or "doubter" is generally more appropriate.
·Muḥammad's Medina opposition **12**:607h

Munakata Shikō (1903–75), Japanese wood-block artist whose works, many of which have Buddhist overtones, are known for their boldness and vividness of expression.
·Japanese woodcut printing **19**:243c; illus.

Munastīr (Tunisia): *see* Monastir.

Munch, Charles (b. Sept. 26, 1891, Strasbourg, Fr.—d. Nov. 6, 1968, Richmond, Va.), conductor known for his interpretations of works by Brahms, Debussy, and Ravel. After studying violin in Paris and Berlin, he became professor of violin at the Strasbourg Conservatoire, leader of the Strasbourg Orchestra

Charles Munch
By courtesy of the Boston Symphony Orchestra

(1919–25), and later leader of the Gewandhaus orchestra at Leipzig. He appeared as conductor of the Straram Orchestra in Paris in 1932 and in 1935 helped found the Paris Philharmonic Orchestra. As its conductor (1935–38) he gave much attention to the performance of modern French works. He conducted the Boston Symphony Orchestra from 1949 to 1962, directing 39 world and 17 U.S. premieres. From 1951 to 1962 he directed the Berkshire Music Center at Tanglewood, near Lenox, Mass. He wrote an autobiography, *I Am a Conductor* (Eng. trans. by L. Burkat, 1955).

Munch, Edvard 12:616 (b. Dec. 12, 1863, Löten, Nor.—d. Jan. 23, 1944, Oslo), painter and printmaker who was concerned with psychological and symbolic themes dealing primarily with love and death, which were given an Expressionistic form and colour. These highly evocative works were influential on the development of German Expressionism in the early 20th century.

Abstract of text biography. Death and illness haunted Munch's early life and became a dominant theme of his works. He received little formal training, and after his first trip to Paris (1885) such pictures as "The Evening Hour" were done in an Impressionistic manner. Later he was influenced by the Postimpressionists, and his transition to Expressionism is marked by "Evening on Karl Johan Street" (1892). In 1892 he was invited to exhibit in Berlin, where the emotionalism and unconventional imagery of his work created a furor that developed into a struggle over freedom of artistic expression. He began to make prints in 1894. Continuing to live and work mainly in Berlin and Paris, he had a nervous breakdown in 1908 and in 1910 returned to Norway. He abandoned printmaking but continued to paint until his death.

REFERENCES in other text articles:
·fin de siècle painting **19**:477f
·Ibsen lithograph illus. **9**:152
·Strindberg portrait illus. **17**:737
·"The Cry" (oil and tempera on wood), illus., **19**:Visual Arts, Western, Plate 23
·20th-century printmaking **14**:1094h; illus.

Munch, Peter Andreas (b. Dec. 15, 1810, Christiania, now Oslo—d. May 25, 1863, Rome), historian and university professor who was one of the founders of the Norwegian nationalist school of historiography.

Writing during the period of romantic nationalism, Munch, along with Jakob Rudolf Keyser, promoted the idea that the Norwegians, as opposed to the Danes and Swedes, arrived in Scandinavia from the north and thus represented the pure Nordic racial type; and that the Old Norse language was a product of Norwegian, and not general Scandinavian, culture. A lifetime of scholarship failed to prove the first idea but established the second beyond doubt. Munch's work influenced the philologist Ivar Aasen in his efforts to rehabilitate the Norwegian language and cleanse it of its Danish elements. Munch's multivolume *Det norske Folks Historie* (1852–63; "History of the Norwegian People") inspired many Norwegian artistic and literary works, among them Ibsen's *Peer Gynt*.

Munch, Peter Rochegune (b. July 25, 1870, Redsted, Den.—d. Jan. 12, 1948, Copenhagen), historian and politician who as Danish foreign minister in the 1930s attempted to maintain Danish neutrality and independence during the dictatorship of Adolf Hitler in Germany.

After a career as a historian of modern Europe, Munch entered the Danish Parliament in 1909 as a member of the Radical Party. In the same year he became minister of the interior in the Radical government of C.T. Zahle (1909–10). In the second Zahle government (1913–20) he served as minister of defense. While he was foreign minister in the Social Democratic–Radical government of Thorvald Stauning (1929–42), Munch's most difficult task was to induce Hitler to recognize the 1920 border between Denmark and Germany, traversing the ethnically mixed area of Schleswig. Although he failed in this undertaking, he succeeded in avoiding an open breach with Germany. At the time the Germans occupied Denmark in 1940, Munch was made a public scapegoat and resigned his post.
·Radical party leadership **16**:329e

München (West Germany): *see* Munich.

München Gladbach (West Germany): *see* Mönchengladbach.

Münchhausen, Karl Friedrich Hieronymus, Freiherr von (b. May 11, 1720, Bodenwerder, now in West Germany—d. Feb. 22, 1797, Bodenwerder), soldier who served with the Russians against the Turks, retiring to his estates in 1760. He became famous around Hanover as a raconteur of extraordinary tales about his life as a soldier, hunter, and sportsman. A collection of such tales appeared in *Vademecum für lustige Leute* (1781–83), all of them attributed to the Baron, though several can be traced to much earlier sources.

Münchhausen, however, was launched as a "type" of tall-story teller by Rudolph Erich Raspe (*q.v.*), who used the earlier stories as basic material for a small volume published (anonymously) in London in 1785. Later and much enlarged editions, none of them having much to do with the historical Baron Münchhausen, became widely known and popular in many languages. They are generally known as the *Adventures of Baron Münchhausen*, and the English edition of 1793 is now the usual text.

Münchner illustrierte Zeitung, 20th-century German photographic periodical.
·photojournalism development **14**:323e

Muncie, city, seat of Delaware County, eastern Indiana, U.S., on the White River. It is the average American town of the classic sociological study *Middletown*, published in 1929 by Robert S. and Helen M. Lynd. The name (originally Munseetown) commemorates the Munsee clan of Delaware Indians who lived there before selling the land to the U.S. government and moving west in 1820. The town was founded in 1827, when Goldsmith C. Gilbert, a trader, donated land for the county seat. The first railroad (1852) and the discovery of natural gas (1886) contributed to the city's industrial growth. When gas failed in the late 1890s, the city was economically strong and continued to grow. It is a trading and industrial centre and is the seat of Ball State University (1918). The Lynd studies (*Middletown in Transition* appeared in 1937) were at first resented; since that time, however, Muncie has come to be proud of its "typical American" title.

Inc. town, 1847; city, 1865. Pop. (1980) city, 77,216; metropolitan area (SMSA), 128,587. 40°11′ N, 85°23′ W
·map, United States **18**:908

mund, in Germanic law, the right of protection and guardianship over one's property, household, and family.
·Germanic legal and social organization **8**:32d

Munda, Battle of (45 BC), ended the ancient Roman civil war between the forces of Pompey the Great and those of Julius Caesar. The late Pompey's sons, Gnaeus and Sextus, had seized Córdoba in Spain, and Caesar came with an army to end the revolt. After a long series of withdrawals, the Pompeians took up a position on the high ground at Munda, near Urso (modern Osun). Caesar halted, luring the Pompeians down into battle. The fight raged for hours, Caesar himself entering the fray to bolster his veteran 10th Legion. A tactical shift of troops by Gnaeus to meet a Roman cavalry attack was misunderstood by the rest of his army. Thinking a retreat had begun, they broke, and Caesar won the day and the war.
·Caesar's conquest of Spain **17**:404c
·Pompeiian army's defeat in Spain **15**:1106a

Munda languages, Austro-Asiatic languages spoken by about 6,000,000 people (the Mundas) in northern and central India. Some scholars divide the languages into a northern group (spoken in the Chota Nāgpur Plateau of Bihār, Bengal, and Orissa) including Santali, Mundari, Bhumij, Ho, Birhor, Koda, Turi, Asuri, Korwa, and Kharia; a southern group (spoken in central Orissa and along the border between Andhra Pradesh and Orissa) including Juang, Sora (also called Saora or Savara), and Gadaba; and a western group, spoken in the Mahādeo Hills of Madhya Pradesh and including only the Korku language. Other specialists place Kharia in the southern group and Korku in the northern group.

Northern Munda (of which Santali is the chief language) is the more important of the two groups; its languages are spoken by about 88 percent of Munda speakers. After Santali, the Mundari and Ho languages rank next in number of speakers, followed by Sora and Korku. The remaining Munda languages are spoken by small, isolated groups of people and are little known. The northern Munda languages (except for Kharia and Korku) are sometimes grouped together as the Kherwari languages. Some scholars also include the Nahali language, spoken in an area north of the Korku speech area, among the Munda languages, classifying it as the only member of a separate branch.

Characteristics of the Munda languages include three numbers (singular, dual, and plural), two gender classes (animate and inanimate) for nouns, and the use of either suffixes or auxiliaries for indicating the tenses of verb forms. In Munda sound systems, consonant sequences are infrequent, except in the middle of a word. Except in Korku, where syllables show a distinction between high and low tone, accent is predictable in the Munda languages.
·Austro-Asiatic language distribution map **2**:484
·Austro-Asiatic membership and features **2**:480g *passim* to 483e
·South Asian ethnolinguistic pattern **2**:196g
·South Asian language area survey **10**:665a

Munda peoples, 10 more or less distinct tribal groups inhabiting a broad belt in central and eastern India and speaking various Munda languages of the Austro-Asiatic family. They numbered approximately 5,000,000 in the 1970s. In the Chota Nāgpur Plateau in southern Bihār, adjacent parts of West Bengal and Madhya Pradesh, and the hill districts of Orissa, they form a numerically important part of the population. No marked differences in physical type distinguish the Munda peoples from other Indian groups.

Munda history and origins are matters of conjecture. The territory they now occupy was until recently relatively difficult to reach and marginal to the great centres of Indian civilization; it is hilly, forested, and relatively poor for agriculture. It is believed that the Munda were once more widely distributed but retreated to their present homelands with the advance and spread of peoples having a more elaborate culture. Nevertheless, they have not lived in complete isolation and share (with some tribal variation) many culture traits with other Indian peoples. Most Munda peoples are agriculturists, but the Birhor, a small and dwindling group in Chota Nāgpur, are hunters and food-gatherers who supplement a meagre livelihood by selling forest products; a few tribes or tribal segments in Orissa practice slash-and-burn (*jhum*) cultivation. Along with their language all these groups have tended to preserve their own beliefs, values, and a sense of separate identity. The government of India is currently encouraging Munda assimilation to the larger Indian society.
·Australoid ethnolinguistic relationship **17**:125h; map 126
·Indian racial groups and distribution **14**:846f
·Orissa's tribal units and assimilation **13**:740a
·revolt against British and religion **2**:985b

Munday, Anthony (b. 1560?, London—buried Aug. 9, 1633, London), English poet, dramatist, pamphleteer, and translator, and an important predecessor of Shakespeare. Munday had some experience as an actor before he was 16, when he was apprenticed to a well-known printer. Soon afterward he commenced to write, but no copy has survived of his first publications, which included the romance of *Galien of France*, probably a translation, in 1578. After 1579 his writings streamed from the press; they included popular ballads, some original lyrics of great charm, much moralizing in verse, translations of many volumes of French and Spanish romances, prose pamphlets (some of which are still of historical interest), a number of edifying or moral works, but only two of his many plays.

In 1578 he was abroad, evidently as a secret agent sent to discover the plans of English Catholic refugees in France and Italy. Under a false name he obtained admission to the English College at Rome, remaining for several months as one of "the pope's scholars" in training for the reconversion of England. On his return he renewed his connection with the stage. In 1581–82 he was prominent in the capture and trials of the Jesuit emissaries, many of whom he had known at Rome, who followed the martyr Edmund Campion to England. He also wrote several pamphlets, apparently with official approval, justifying the persecution of the Jesuits and incidentally giving valuable autobiographical information. Critics have found his *English Romayne Lyfe* (1582) of permanent interest as a detailed and entertaining, though hostile, description of life and study in the English College at Rome. By 1586 he had been appointed one of the "messengers of her majesty's chamber," a post he seems to have held for the rest of Elizabeth I's reign.

Little is known about Munday's career as actor and playwright, except that after his journey to Rome he made some attempts to act extempore like the Italian players. He was writing successfully for the theatre before any of the so-called University Wits (a group of Oxonians living just outside London who were experimenting with poetic metre) except John Lyly and George Peele. His *Fedele and Fortunio* (1584 at latest) is an adaptation of Luigi Pasqualigo's *Il Fedele*; played at court, it was printed in 1585. *John a Kent and John a Cumber*, his earliest surviving original play, was probably written before the middle of 1589. He was apparently the only early Elizabethan dramatist whose popularity continued after Shakespeare's rise in the mid-1590s, and he was still receiving commissions from Philip Henslowe in 1602. Special interest attaches to the fact that most of the original manuscript of *Sir Thomas More* was in his hand, with a three-page addition widely believed to be Shakespeare's. From the late 1590s until at least 1623, he wrote many of the pageants with which lord mayors of London celebrated their entry into office.

Mundelein, village, northern suburb of Chicago, Lake County, Illinois, U.S. Founded in 1835, it was successively known as Mechanics Grove, Holcomb, Rockefeller, and Area (for Ability, Reliability, Endurance, and Action). In 1926 it was renamed in honour of Cardinal George Mundelein, archbishop of Chicago (1915–39), who was host to the Eucharistic Congress held at St. Mary-of-the-Lake Seminary (opened in 1921), which borders the village on the north. Mundelein is mainly residential with some light manufacturing. Inc. 1909. Pop. (1980) 17,053. 42°16′ N, 88°00′ W

Mundelein, George William (1872–1939), U.S. cardinal and archbishop of Chicago, and a prominent figure at the Eucharistic congress held in Chicago in June 1926. Mundelein, Ill., a town near Chicago, was named in his honour.

Mundhir, al-, 5th-century Arab prince of al-Ḥīrah.
·Sāsānian support of royalty **9**:850g

Mundhir, al-, 9th-century Umayyad caliph of Córdoba, reigned 886 to 888.
·muwallad and Banū Qasī revolts **17**:415d

Mundigak, prehistoric site in Afghanistan.
·early settlement evidence **9**:336h

Mundurukú, also spelled MUNDURUCÚ, South American Indian people of the Amazon tropical forest. The Mundurukú speak a language of the Tupian group. They inhabit the southwest part of the state of Pará and the southeastern corner of the state of Amazonas, Brazil. Formerly, they were an aggressive, warlike tribe that expanded along the Tapajóz River and its environs and were widely feared by neighbouring tribes. By the beginning of the 19th century, Brazilian colonists had pacified the Mundurukú and annexed their territory.

The Mundurukú economy was that of the tropical forest: a combination of farming, hunting, fishing, and gathering. Males were warriors, hunters, and fishermen, leaving cultivation to the women. The men lived in a separate house, visiting their family dwellings for brief intervals.

Mundurukú society was organized in clans and moieties (dual divisions). Clans were patrilineal (descent reckoned in the male line), and marriage was permitted only with those in other clans and in the other moiety.

The modern Mundurukú population has made a livelihood of collecting latex from wild rubber trees and exchanging it for manufactured goods. Their dependence on the Brazilian economy has led to the transformation of Mundurukú life. Most of the old village institutions are now practically extinct, and families, living in isolation with their rubber trees, are related to each other through the trading post. Only their isolation in the Amazon forest has prevented them from becoming assimilated into Brazilian life.
·geographic distribution and socioeconomic structure **17**:116h; map 117
·social organization **17**:122c; map 121

Mundy, John (b. between 1550 and 1554—d. 1630, Windsor, Eng.), organist and composer of choral and keyboard music. The son of the composer William Mundy, he was organist of Eton Chapel (1585) and organist at St. George's Chapel, Windsor. He received the bachelor of music at Oxford in 1586 and the doctorate in 1624.

Of his music, a few Latin works survive (apparently incomplete), which are often deeply expressive. About 20 English anthems survive (many incomplete). Some of his best known works, printed in *Songs and Psalmes* (1594), are pleasant and fluent. His instrumental works include four works in the *Fitzwilliam Virginal Book.*

Mundy, William (b. *c.* 1529—d. *c.* 1591), English composer of polyphonic sacred music. In 1543 he was head chorister of Westminster Abbey. He became vicar choral of St. Paul's Cathedral, London, and from 1564 was a gentleman of the Chapel Royal. Most of his surviving music—about 22 motets and 2 masses—is set to Latin texts. The motets are written in the broad polyphonic style of English music before the madrigal. His surviving English church music includes two services and six anthems, of which "O Lord, the Maker of All Things" is particularly well-known. William Mundy was the father of the organist and composer John Mundy.

Müneccimbaşı, Ahmed Dede (b. 1631, Thessaloníki, Greece—d. Feb. 27, 1702, Mecca, Arabia), Ottoman historian who wrote an outstanding general history. After 15 years with the Mevleviya (Mawlawīyah) dervishes, he took up astronomy and astrology and in 1665 became the *müneccimbaşı* (court astrologer, hence his name) to Sultan Mehmed IV. Falling out of favour with the court in 1687, however, he was exiled to Egypt and from there went to Mecca and Medina, where he spent the rest of his life.

Müneccimbaşı's great work, written in Arabic, was titled *Jāmiʿad-duwal* ("The Compendium of Nations"). *Sahaif-ül-Ahbar . . .* ("The Pages of the Chronicle . . . "), a Turkish summary translation made by the poet Ahmed Nedim, is the only published version. The work is a universal history that starts with Adam and ends in the year 1672. It covers in detail the Muslim dynasties, particularly the Ottoman house, but it also treats pre-Muslim and non-Muslim dynasties. Müneccimbaşı's pre-Muslim accounts suggest that he used Roman and Jewish sources, and his chapter on the Franks indicates that he made use of European chronicles. Furthermore, he touched upon dynasties never before dealt with by Islāmic historiographers, such as the Babylonians, the Seleucids, and the Assyrians. He tells of his use of Armenian chronicles for his discussion of the Armenian kings and even includes sections on India and China. Müneccimbaşı also wrote commentaries on the Qur'ān, translated the works of Persian writers, and composed a *Divān* ("Collected Poems") in Turkish on mystical themes under the pen name of Âşık.

mung bean, Asian bean (*q.v.*) used chiefly for sprouts.

Mungir (India): *see* Monghyr.

Mungo, department, Cameroon.
·area and population table **3**:698

Mungo, Saint: *see* Kentigern, Saint.

muni, in ancient India, a religious ascetic who observed silence (*mauna*). A *muni* was both respected and feared for his supernatural powers, attained after the severest disciplines (*tapas*), such as meditating between fires or fasting. In modern India, *muni* is used to refer to any pious hermit or holy man and is commonly employed for ascetics of the Jaina faith.

Muni, Paul, original name MUNI WEISENFREUND (b. Sept. 22, 1895, Lemberg, Austria—d. Aug. 25, 1967, Santa Barbara, Calif.), U.S. actor. Trained in the Yiddish Art Theatre in New York City, Muni went to Hollywood in 1929. He was famous for his roles in biographical motion pictures such as *The Story of Louis Pasteur* (1935; Academy Award, 1936) and in stage plays, including *Inherit the Wind* (1955; Antoinette Perry Award, 1956).

munia, name of several small finchlike Asian birds of the mannikin and waxbill (*qq.v.*) groups (family Estrildidae, order Passeriformes). The black-headed munia, or chestnut

Black-headed munia (*Lonchura malacca*)
John Markham

mannikin (*Lonchura malacca*, including *atricapilla* and *ferruginosa*), is a pest in rice fields from India to Java and the Philippines; as a cage bird it is often called tricolour nun. Others kept as pets include the white-headed munia (*L. maja*) of Thailand to Java and the green munia, or green tiger finch (*Amadava formosa*), of India. For red munia *see* avadavat; for white-throated munia *see* silverbill.

Munich 12:617, German MÜNCHEN, capital and largest city of the *Land* (state) of Bayern (Bavaria) and the second largest city in West Germany (not including Berlin), on the Isar River, about 30 mi (48 km) north of the edge of the Alps. Pop. (1977 est.) city, 1,314,600; (1970) metropolitan area, 1,833,400.

The text article deals with the history, location and boundaries, architectural features, the people, economic life, transportation, government, education and cultural life, and recreation of Munich.

REFERENCES in other text articles:
·founding as market by Henry the Lion **8**:776g
·map, Federal Republic of Germany **8**:47
·population and economy **2**:775d
·population change from 1870 to 1925, map **6**:237
·transportation and culture **8**:60a
·1972 Olympic Games events **2**:279f

Munich, University of: *see* Ludwig-Maximilians-Universität München.

Munich Agreement (Sept. 30, 1938), by Germany, Britain, France, and Italy, permitted German annexation of the Sudetenland of western Czechoslovakia. *Major ref.* **19**:978g
·Chamberlain's diplomatic failure **3**:278d
·Churchill's opposition to Chamberlain **4**:598a
·French resultant dissension **7**:674b
·Soviet diplomatic reaction **16**:78a
·Sudetenland cession to Germany **8**:120e
·Sudetenland crisis negotiations **2**:1196g

Munich Putsch, also called BEER HALL PUTSCH (Nov. 8–9, 1923), Adolf Hitler's attempt to start an insurrection in Germany against the Weimar Republic (*Putsch*, "armed rising," or "riot"). Hitler and his small Nazi Party associated themselves with Gen. Erich Ludendorff, a racist right-wing military leader of World War I. Forcing their way into a right-wing political meeting in a beer hall in Munich, Hitler and his men obtained agreement that the leaders there should join in carrying the "revolution" to Berlin (after the pattern of Mussolini's march on Rome in the preceding year); they later abandoned the project on learning that the government was prepared to counter the effort with force. At the subsequent trial in a sympathetic Bavarian court, Ludendorff was released, and Hitler was given a minimum sentence for treason—five years' imprisonment. He actually served less than nine months, in comfort, in the fortress of Landsberg, where he wrote much of his testamentary *Mein Kampf* ("My Struggle"). The abortive *Putsch* led Hitler to decide to achieve power by legal means.
·Göring's wound and escape **8**:254f
·Hitler and the postwar crisis **8**:118a
·Hitler's early power struggles **8**:966h
·Munich's history **12**:617e
·Stresemann's leniency toward rightists **17**:733c

Munich Zoo: *see* Hellabrunn Zoo.

Municipal Corporations Act (1835), British legislation reforming local governments.
·reform movement issues and results **3**:265h

municipality, in the United States, an urban unit of local government, a political subdivision of a state within which a municipal corporation has been established to provide general local government for a specific population concentration in a defined area. A municipality may be designated as a city, borough, village, or town, except in the New England states, New York, and Wisconsin, where the term town signifies a subdivision of the county or state by area.

In many European countries, the law provides for types of local government unit to which the term municipality may be applied—as in France (*commune*), Italy (*comune*), the Low Countries (*gemeente*), and most of the Scandinavian countries. Several other European countries, notably Great Britain and Germany, have a diversified system of local government in which several different categories exist. In Great Britain the term municipality is in general used only for the large boroughs (municipal corporations).
·system variety, development, and functions **4**:645b
·urban planning growing role **18**:1082g

municipal law, the law of a nation or state (and its subdivisions), as distinguished from international law, or the law of nations. Only in a narrower, more popular sense does it refer solely to the law of a city or town and its local government.
·nation-state system and international law **9**:744c

municipio, in the Iberian Peninsula and Latin America, a local civil administrative subdivision recognized by the national government. It may comprise one village or community, as is usual in Guatemala, or a number of separate communities, as is usual in Mexico. A *municipio* of several villages always has a head village, or *cabecera*, in which is centred the national government's local offices and the Roman Catholic local hierarchy.
·Meso-American territorial organization **11**:954g

municipium, a community under ancient Roman dominion whose residents shared the rights of commerce and intermarriage with residents of Roman origin. The *municipium* was completely autonomous, except in foreign policy decisions, and supplied soldiers to the Roman army. Only the residents, or *municipes*, who permanently settled in Rome qualified for Roman citizenship (*see* jus Latium). All Latin and Italian communities became *municipia* as a result of the Social War (90–89 BC). The *municipium* system prevailed largely in the Latin-speaking provinces and seldom occurred in the north or in the Greek-speaking eastern provinces. Chief sources of income for the *municipia* were donations from wealthy *municipes*, export and import taxes, and revenue from city lands. Local politics and finances were supervised by the council, or *ordo* (*see* decurio), which surpassed the powers of the magistrate and the assembly (*Comitia Curiata*).
·corporation rights under Roman law **15**:1057e
·nome organization in Severus' Egypt **6**:486f
·urban social mobility **15**:1109b

Munʿim Khān, 16th-century general in India, in the service of the Mughal emperor Akbar.
·victories in Bengal and Bihār **9**:380g

Munk, Kaj (Harald Leininger) (b. Jan. 13, 1898, Maribo, Den.—d. Jan. 4, 1944, near Silkeborg), playwright, priest, and patriot who was a rare exponent of religious drama with a strong sense of the theatre. He revived

Kaj Munk
By courtesy of the Royal Danish Ministry for Foreign Affairs, Copenhagen

the "heroic" Shakespearean and Schillerian drama with writing whose passionate quality is not often found among his fellow countrymen. He studied at the University of Copenhagen, where he began his first produced play, *En idealist* (1928; *Herod the King*, 1953). This was originally misunderstood by the critics, although it was acclaimed 10 years later.

In 1931 he achieved success with *Cant* (on the rise and fall of Anne Boleyn), and the impression made by *Ordet* (1932; *The Word*, 1955), a miracle play set among Jutland peasants, established him as Denmark's leading dramatist. *Ordet* later was made into a motion picture. For his principal character, Munk often chose a dictator or "strong man" struggling in vain against God.

En idealist, *Ordet*, and *Han sidder ved smeltediglen* (1938; *He Sits at the Melting-Pot*, 1944), a drama of Hitler's Germany, are his three best plays, though several others, such as *Cant*, *Kaerlighed* (1926), and *I Braendingen* (1929), remain popular. *Five Plays* by Kaj Munk, with preface and translations, was published in 1953.

Kaj Munk was a conscientious and much-loved parish priest, and during World War II his outspoken sermons drew large numbers of persons to the ranks of the Resistance and led to his being killed by the Nazis.
·Danish 20th-century drama **10**:1248h

Munk, Walter Heinrich (b. Oct. 19, 1917, Vienna), geophysicist and oceanographer who conducted numerous theoretical investigations of the wind-driven ocean circulation, the generation and propagation of ocean waves, and the rotation of the Earth. In 1947 Munk received his doctor's degree for work done mainly at the Scripps Institution of Oceanography in La Jolla, Calif., where he became professor of geophysics in 1954. He also served as a director of the Institute of Geophysics and Planetary Physics of the University of California.
·ocean currents' westward motion **13**:439e
·wave forecasting **6**:87g

Munkács (Ukrainian S.S.R.): *see* Mukachovo.

Munkar and Nakīr, in Islāmic eschatology, two angels who test the faith of the dead in their tombs. After death, the deceased is placed upright in the grave by Munkar and Nakīr and asked to identify Muḥammad. The righteous will know that he is the messenger of God (*rasūl Allāh*) and be allowed to rest in peace until the Judgment Day (*yawm ad-dīn*). Infidels and sinners, however, not being able to reply, will be beaten by the two angels every day except Friday for as long as God deems necessary.
·judgment of the dead **5**:537c

Munku-Sardyk, highest peak of the eastern Sayan Mountains (*q.v.*), Central Siberia, Russian Soviet Federated Socialist Republic. 51°45′ N, 100°32′ E
·Yenisey basin topography **19**:1089c

Münnich (MINIKH), **Burkhard Christoph, Graf von** (b. May 19 [May 9, old style], 1683, Neuenhuntorf, Oldenburg, now in West Germany—d. Oct. 27 [Oct. 16, O.S.], 1767, St. Petersburg, now Leningrad), military officer and statesman who was one of the major political figures in Russia during the reign of Empress Anna (ruled 1730–40) and who led the Russian Army to victory in the Russo-Turkish War of 1736–39.

Münnich entered the service of Peter I the Great of Russia in 1721 and participated in the construction of the Ladoga Canal. In 1728 he was appointed commander in chief of the Russian Army by Peter II and was subsequently made a field marshal and president of the war council (1732) by Anna (Ivanovna) (*q.v.*), whose government was dominated by German advisers. During the War of the Polish Succession (1733–35), Münnich captured Gdańsk (1734), and then, after persistently advocating an aggressive policy toward the Ottoman Empire, he led the Russian Army into the Crimea and Moldavia to fight the Turks. Despite complications resulting from fighting a war at a great distance from the political centre of Russia, Münnich conquered Perekop, Ochakov, and Azov (1736–38), won a major victory at Stavuchany near Khotin in northern Bessarabia (1739), and earned a reputation as an outstanding military leader.

At the conclusion of the war (September 1739), he returned to St. Petersburg and resumed his influential position in the government. But when Anna died (Oct. 28 [Oct. 17, O.S.], 1740), leaving her throne to her infant grandnephew Ivan VI and naming her favourite and chief adviser Ernst Johann Biron (*q.v.*) as regent, Münnich feared that Biron's widespread unpopularity would cause the entire ruling German clique to lose power. He, therefore, arrested Biron in the middle of the night of Nov. 19–20 (Nov. 8–9, O.S.), 1740, and sent him to Siberia. Münnich made Ivan's mother, Anna (*q.v.*) Leopoldovna, regent and personally assumed the role of first minister. A year later, however, he and Anna Leopoldovna were deposed by Elizabeth, daughter of Peter the Great, and Münnich was exiled to Siberia. After Peter III released him in 1762, he served Catherine II the Great as director general of the Baltic ports.
·Biron's role and fall **16**:53a

Münnich, Ferenc (1886–1967), Hungarian statesman.
·Hungarian Revolution suppression **9**:43a

Munn v. Illinois (1877), case leading to a decision by the U.S. Supreme Court that public utilities are a separate category of business requiring governmental regulation.
·price control in the public interest **15**:217h

Muñoz, Gil Sánchez (antipope): *see* Clement VIII.

Muñoz Marín, Luis (b. Feb. 18, 1898, San Juan, P.R.—d. April 30, 1980, San Juan), statesman who served four four-year terms as the elected governor of Puerto Rico; early in his career he advocated independence for the island but later worked for its social and economic progress under U.S. guidance.

Son of the publisher-patriot Luis Muñoz Rivera, Muñoz Marín was educated in the United States, where his father served as resident commissioner (1910–16). After serving as secretary to the commissioner (1916–18), studying law, and writing two books, he returned to Puerto Rico (1926) and edited the newspaper *La Democracia*, founded by his father. Elected to the Puerto Rican Senate (1932), he aligned himself with the radicals in advocating complete independence from the U.S. As a result, he was expelled from the Liberal Party (1937). In 1938 he organized the Partido Popular Democrático (Popular Democratic Party), which won its first victory in 1940 and made Muñoz Marín president of the Senate, a post he held until 1948.

Changing his mind about independence, Muñoz Marín worked closely with the U.S.-appointed governor, Rexford G. Tugwell, to improve housing, farming, and industrial conditions. His Operation Bootstrap was successful as a program for rapid economic growth. When the U.S. granted Puerto Rico the right to elect its own governor (1948), Muñoz Marín was overwhelmingly elected and then reelected in 1952, 1956, and 1960. During his governorship, he succeeded in changing Puerto Rico's status to that of a commonwealth. In 1963 he received the U.S. Presidential Medal of Freedom. He refused to run for a fifth term as governor in 1964, and reentered the Senate of Puerto Rico.
·Popular Democratic Party formation **15**:260c

Muñoz Rivera, Luis (b. July 17, 1859, Barranquitas, P.R.—d. Nov. 15, 1916, San-

Muñoz Rivera
By courtesy of the Organization of American States

turce), statesman, publisher, and patriot who devoted his life to obtaining Puerto Rico's autonomy.

In 1889 Muñoz Rivera founded the newspaper *La Democracia*, which crusaded for Puerto Rican freedom from Spanish domination. He became a leader of the autonomist parties, and in 1897 he was instrumental in obtaining Puerto Rico's charter of home rule from Spain. He soon became secretary of state and later president of the first autonomist Cabinet. He resigned in 1899 after the United States ended Puerto Rico's short-lived home rule.

Spending the remainder of his life primarily in the United States, Muñoz Rivera continually advocated the cause of Puerto Rico's independence. He published a magazine in New York City to acquaint North Americans with the plight of his homeland. In 1910 he became Puerto Rico's resident commissioner in Washington, D.C. He died just before passage of the Jones Bill, for which he had fought and which gave Puerto Rico a large measure of self-government. Muñoz Rivera's son Luis Muñoz Marín was governor of Puerto Rico from 1949 to 1965.
·Puerto Rico's political status **15**:260b

Munro, H(ector) H(ugh), pseudonym SAKI (b. Dec. 18, 1870, Akyab, Burma—d. Nov. 14, 1916, near Beaumont-Hamel, Fr.), Scottish writer whose stories depict the Edwardian social scene with a flippant wit and power of fantastic invention used both to satirize social

pretension, unkindness, and stupidity and to create an atmosphere of horror. Born the son of an officer in the Burma police, he was sent at the age of two to aunts near Barnstaple, north Devon. He took revenge on their strictness and lack of understanding by portraying tyrannical aunts in many of his stories about children. Educated at Exmouth and at Bedford grammar school, in 1893 he joined the Burma police but was invalided out. Turning to journalism, he wrote political satires for the *Westminster Gazette* and in 1900 published *The Rise of the Russian Empire*, a serious historical work. After acting as foreign correspondent for *The Morning Post* in the Balkans, Russia, and Paris, in 1908 he settled in London, writing short stories and sketches: *Reginald* (1904), *Reginald in Russia* (1910), *The Chronicles of Clovis* (1912), and *Beasts and Super-Beasts* (1914). Written in a style studded with epigrams and with well-contrived plots often turning on practical jokes or surprise endings, his stories reveal a vein of cruelty in their author and a self-identification with the *enfant terrible*. Among his most frequently anthologized works are *Tobermory*, *The Open Window*, *Sredni Vashtar*, *Laura*, and *The Schartz-Metterklume Method*. His novel *The Unbearable Bassington* (1912) describes the adventures of a fastidious and likable but maladjusted hero, in a manner anticipating that of the early Evelyn Waugh. Munro was killed in action in World War I.
·novel of manners tradition **13**:286g

Munro, Thomas (1897–   ), U.S. aesthetician.
·aesthetic theory's scientific approach **1**:153c

Munsell colour system, method of designating colours first presented in 1915 by Albert H. Munsell of the United States with the publication of the *Atlas of the Munsell Color System*. The Munsell system has been the standard method of specifying the colour of surfaces and is indispensable to paint chemists. Several hundred colour chips, small rectangular slips of paper painted with watercolour paints of considerable permanence, are arranged logically in the *Atlas*, based on three parameters: hue (dominant wave length), value (lightness or brightness), and chroma (strength or purity).

A three-dimensional representation of the system, called the colour tree of Munsell, is shown in the Figure. The value of a colour, its lightness or darkness (corresponding to the amount of gray it contains), is indicated by its position on the vertical axis of the tree, which ranges from black at the bottom to white at the top. All the colours in a horizontal row have the same amount of gray, or the same value.

Five basic hues (red, yellow, green, blue, and purple) and five intermediate hues (yellow red, green yellow, blue green, purple blue, and red purple) are assigned positions around the vertical axis of the colour tree. The darker the shade of colour, the lower down, and closer to the black end of the tree trunk is its position; the lighter the shade of colour, the higher up and closer to the white end of the tree trunk is its position.

The farther out a colour's position from the neutral black–gray–white axis of the tree, the higher the chroma, or the less gray it contains, and the stronger, or purer, the colour is said to be. All the colours in a vertical column have the same chroma (colour strength). Any colour can be specified according to its location in the tree by three coordinates.

After Munsell's death, a new edition of the *Atlas*, the *Munsell Book of Colour* was issued (1929). Superficially, the two editions are similar; but the philosophies underlying their construction were different. In the original system, Munsell divided the range between black and white into 10 equal steps on a scale of the square root of the reflectance. (Had he used a scale of the reflectance itself, the colours would have appeared to be too closely spaced in the upper range and too far apart in the lower range.) Although his original scale approximates psychologically equal spacing, the new edition is a closer approximation. Each system has advantages, the *Atlas* because of its fixed rules for assignment of positions and the *Book of Colour* because of its perceptual uniformity in spacing under standard viewing conditions.

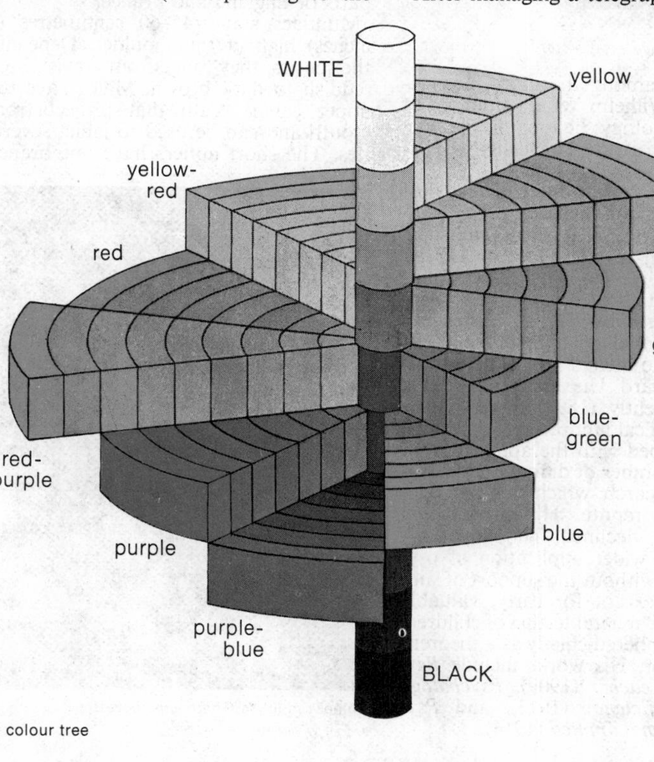

Munsell colour tree

Munsey, Frank Andrew (b. Aug. 21, 1854, Mercer, Maine—d. Dec. 22, 1925, New York City), newspaper and magazine publisher, a dominant figure in the trend toward journalistic consolidation in the U.S. Viewing his publications purely as moneymaking enterprises, he administered them in detail, maintained an inoffensive and colourless editorial policy, and acquired numerous papers in order to suppress them in favour of stronger competitors also owned by him.

After managing a telegraph office in Augusta, Maine, he went to New York City in 1882 and immediately founded the *Golden Argosy*, a magazine for children. Six years later it was renamed the *Argosy Magazine* and converted into an adult magazine. *Munsey's Magazine* (founded 1889; called *Munsey's Weekly* until 1891) was the first cheap (originally ten cents a copy) general-circulation, illustrated magazine in the U.S. His most important newspaper purchases were the *Baltimore News* (1908) and several papers in New York City: the *Star* (1891), the *Press* (1912), *The Sun* and the *Evening Sun* (1916), the *Herald* and its associate, the *Evening Telegram* (1920), and *The Globe* (1924); between 1916 and 1924 some of these disappeared in a series of profitable mergers. On his death most of his fortune (estimated at $20,000,000) went to the Metropolitan Museum of Art, New York City.
·magazine publishing history **15**:249e
·publishing and newspaper chains **15**:243f

Munsey
By courtesy of the Library of Congress, Washington, D.C.

Munshi, Kanaiyalal (1887–1971), Indian Gujarati novelist.
·modern Gujarati literary currents **17**:148d

Munster, Old Irish MUMA, the southwestern province of the Republic of Ireland, comprising the countries of Clare, Cork, Kerry, Limerick, Tipperary, and Waterford, and historically, one of the "fifths" (ancient provinces or kingdoms) of Ireland. Geographically, the area is divided by the Sliabh Luachra Mountains into Desmond to the south and Thomond to the north. The power of the kingdom originally lay in the south, where the ruling Érainn clan had their chief fortress at Temuir Érann in the Ballyhoura Hills. Inroads into northern Munster made by the neighbouring men of Leinster were fought off by a people known as the Eoganacht, who became rulers of Munster from *c.* AD 400. They later unsuccessfully challenged the Leinster high kings and in the 10th century failed to defend their own land against Viking raiders who settled in Waterford and Limerick. After the Anglo-Norman invasion of the mid-12th century, the feudal families of Fitzgerald, earls of Desmond, and Butler, earls of Ormonde, became all-powerful in the province.
·county area and population table **9**:884
·Ireland's history and cultures **3**:284a

Munster, town, Lake County, extreme northwestern Indiana, U.S., just south of Hammond. It is a shipping centre for garden produce and nursery stock to the Chicago metropolitan area. Pop. (1980) 20,671.
41°34′ N, 87°30′ W

Münster, city, Nordrhein-Westfalen (North Rhine-Westphalia) *Land* (state), northwestern West Germany, on the small Münster-Aa River and the Dortmund-Ems-Kanal. First mentioned as Mimigernaford (ford over the Aa) when Liudger (Ludger), a missionary sent by Charlemagne, founded a bishopric there in 804, it was renamed Münster in 1068 and was chartered in 1137. Its favourable position at the intersection of long-distance trade routes and its wool trade with England gave it early economic importance and contributed to its strong position in the Hanseatic League in the 13th and 14th centuries. The Anabaptists, who comprised the fanatical wing of the Reformation, founded their "kingdom of a thousand years" there in 1534; in 1535 the town was captured and their "king," John of Leiden (Jan Beuckelson), was executed with two of his accomplices in 1536; the iron cages in which their bodies were exhibited still hang in the Gothic tower of St. Lambert's Church. A neutralized Münster was the scene of the peace congress (1645–48) that resulted in the Treaty of Westphalia. In 1815 it became the capital of Prussian Westphalia.

There was widespread destruction in World War II, but most of the historic buildings have been restored or rebuilt, including the gabled houses and arcades of the Prinzipalmarkt, the Gothic town hall (1335) with its Friedenssaal (Peace Hall of 1648), the cathedral (1225–65), St. Ludger's, St. Lambert's, the Church of Our Lady, St. Martin's, and St.

Former Episcopal palace, now the Westfälische Wilhelms-Universität, Münster, W. Ger.

K. Praedel—ZEFA

Maurice's (all 13th–15th century). The work of Johann Conrad Schlaun, the Westphalian master architect of the Baroque period, is evident in the Westfälische Wilhelms-Universität (founded 1773, a full university from 1902; in the 18th-century former episcopal palace), the bailiff's high court, and several churches. Notable modern structures include the *Land* Chamber of Commerce building, municipal administrative offices, the theatre, the railway station (1956), and the Münsterland Hall. The centre of Westphalian culture, Münster has *Land*, geological, and diocesan museums and archives, a teachers' training college, and schools of engineering, music, and art. The birthplace (Haus Hülshoff) and the residence (Rüschhaus, 1748) of the poet Annette von Droste-Hülshoff are preserved. Industries include the manufacture of machinery and textiles and building construction. Münster is the centre of the Westphalian cattle-breeding market. Pop. (1970 est.) 204,600.
51°57′ N, 7°37′ E

·map, Federal Republic of Germany **8**:46
·Nordrhein-Westfalen's structured administration **13**:144c
·Radical Reformation millenialist community **15**:552e

Münster, Sebastian (b. 1489, Ingelheim, Palatinate, now in West Germany—d. May 23, 1552, Basel, Switz.), Hebrew scholar, mathematician, cartographer, and cosmographer whose *Cosmographia* (1544; "Cosmography") was the earliest German description of the world and a major work in the revival of geographic thought in 16th-century Europe. Appointed professor of Hebrew at the University of Basel in 1527, he edited the Hebrew Bible (2 vol., 1534–35), which was accompanied by a literal Latin translation and a number of annotations. In 1540 he published a Latin edition of Ptolemy's *Geographia*, illustrated with 27 woodcut maps after Ptolemy and 21 of Münster's own design. Of about 40 editions of the *Cosmographia* printed in Germany, the 1550 edition, containing views of the city and costume illustrations as well, is

Münster, detail from an engraving by an unknown artist, *c.* 1550

Historia-Photo

the most valued. His other works include *Dictionarium trilingue* (1530; "Trilingual Dictionary"), in Latin, Greek, and Hebrew, and *Mappa Europae* (1536; "Map of Europe").

·historiographic writings **8**:953d
·maps in "Cosmographia" **11**:473g

Munster and Osnaburg, Peace of: *see* Westphalia, Peace of.

Münsterberg, Hugo (b. June 1, 1863, Danzig, Prussia, now Gdansk, Pol.—d. Dec. 16, 1916, Cambridge, Mass.), psychologist and philosopher frequently regarded as the founder of applied psychology, particularly for extending psychology into law, business, industry, medicine, teaching, and sociology. At the University of Leipzig (now in East Germany),

Münsterberg

By courtesy of Harvard University Archives

Münsterberg was among the more independent students of Wilhelm Wundt, founder of experimental psychology; he took his Ph.D. in 1885 and his M.D. at the University of Heidelberg in 1887.

Appointed instructor at the University of Freiburg, where he established a psychological laboratory, Münsterberg began publishing original research in his *Beiträge zur experimentellen Psychologie* (1889–92; "Contributions to Experimental Psychology"). His work was harshly criticized by German colleagues but won the approval of U.S. psychologist William James, who invited him to be visiting professor at Harvard University (1892–95). Returning permanently (1897) to direct the Harvard psychological laboratory, he became increasingly absorbed with the application of psychology to a number of different areas, including psychic research, which won him considerable popular repute. His professional standing, however, declined. Though he argued the case for wider application of psychology, he did so without the support of substantial research, except for early, valuable contributions to the mental testing of children. Hence, he is remembered chiefly as a theoretician and originator. His works include *Psychology and the Teacher* (1909), *Psychology and Industrial Efficiency* (1913), and *Psychology: General and Applied* (1914).

Münsterland, lowland region in Nordrhein-Westfalen (North Rhine-Westphalia) *Land* (state), northwestern West Germany, extends between the Lippe River (south), the Emsland (north), the forested Teutoburger Wald (east), and the Lower Rhine River and the Dutch–German border (west). The region was the territory ruled by the bishops of Münster (until 1803). It is predominantly agricultural, and, with the exception of Münster in the centre, there are no large cities except on its outer fringes. Wild horses roam the Merfelder Bruch, a swampland near Dülmen, in the west central part of the region.

Muntaṣir, al-, 9th-century Muslim caliph, reigned 861 to 862.

·military control of the caliphate **3**:637f

Munthe, Axel Martin Fredrik (b. Oct. 31, 1857, Oskarshamn, Kalmar, Swed.—d. Feb. 11, 1949, Stockholm), physician, psychiatrist, and writer whose book, *The Story of San Michele* (1929), an account of his experiences as a doctor in Paris, Rome, and in semiretirement at the villa of San Michele on Capri, achieved immense popularity in its original English version and in many translations. Its lasting success may be attributed to its intimate revelation of an unusually vital personality and its sympathetic description of suffering. Munthe studied at Uppsala, Montpellier, and Paris, where he worked under Jean-Martin Charcot, the pioneer neurologist. After practicing in Paris and Italy (where he was awarded a gold medal for his work during the Messina earthquake), he became in 1908 physician-in-ordinary to the Swedish royal family. His other books of reminiscences, *Memories and Vagaries* (1898) and *Letters From a Mourning City* (1887; about a cholera outbreak in Naples) never achieved the success of *San Michele*.

Munthe, Gerhard (1849–1929), Norwegian painter.

·tapestry innovation in Norway **17**:1065h

Muntiacus (deer): *see* muntjac.

muntjac, OR BARKING DEER (*Muntiacus*), any of about four species of small Asiatic deer, family Cervidae (order Artiodactyla).

Called barking deer because of their cry, muntjacs are solitary, nocturnal, and usually live in areas of thick vegetation. They are native to India, southeastern Asia, and southern China, and some have become established in parts of England and France.

Muntjacs stand 45–60 centimetres (18–24 inches) high at the shoulder. Depending on the species, they range from grayish brown or reddish to dark brown. Males have tusklike upper canine teeth that project from the mouth and can be used to inflict severe injuries. The short antlers have one branch and

Chinese muntjac (*Muntiacus reevesi*)

Kenneth W. Fink—Root Resources

are borne on long bases from which bony ridges extend onto the face (hence another common name, rib-faced deer); the female has small knobs in place of antlers.

Muntjacs were formerly placed in the genus *Cervulus*.

·scent glands and classification 2:80b

Munttoren, tower, Amsterdam.

·Amsterdam's historical landmarks 1:712g; map 711

Müntzer, Thomas 12:619 (b. sometime before 1490, Stolberg—d. May 27, 1525, Mühlhausen, both now in East Germany), a leading radical Reformer during the Protestant Reformation, an exponent of the supremacy of the inner light as against the authority of the Scriptures.

Abstract of text biography. Müntzer studied at the University of Leipzig and in 1512 at the University of Frankfurt an der Oder, where he earned master of arts and bachelor of theology degrees. From 1513 to 1518 he was a clergyman and teacher and a prior at Frohse monastery at Aschersleben. In 1518 he was attracted to Martin Luther and his ideas of reform. From 1519 to 1520 he pursued literary studies at the monastery of Beuditz at Weissenfels, where he developed his ideas of the Reformation as a revolution. A pastor in Zwickau (1520–21), he was forced to leave that city and travelled to various cities in Germany, where he preached and won followers. In 1522 he broke with Luther and his followers. In 1523 he became pastor of a Saxon community in Allstedt but left there in 1524. In Mühlhausen he organized the working classes and, after additional travels, led the Peasants' Revolt (1524–25). When the revolt collapsed, he was taken prisoner and executed.

Müntzer remains a controversial figure because his movement became a symbol for revolutionary movements, and his work has been interpreted in various ways. His writings included religious, liturgical, and political works.

REFERENCES in other text articles:
·peasant revolt in name of God 11:193g
·Philip of Hesse's defeat and its result 14:230e
·Radical Reformation community of elect 15:552g

Muntz metal, variety of brass consisting of an alloy 60 percent copper and 40 percent zinc, named after the English businessman George F. Muntz, who patented it in 1832. It is also known as yellow metal, because of its colour resulting from the high zinc content, Muntz metal can be forged and is used to make machine parts exposed to corrosion.

muon, subatomic particle similar to the electron though 207 times heavier; it has two forms, the negative muon and its positive antiparticle. Discovered independently (1936) by C.D. Anderson and S.H. Neddermeyer and by J.C. Street and E.C. Stevenson while studying cosmic rays using cloud chamber photographs, the muon was at first thought to be the meson (particle with mass intermediate between electron and proton) predicted by H. Yukawa (1935) to explain the strong interaction that binds protons and neutrons together in atomic nuclei. Unlike mesons, however, a muon never reacts with nuclei or other particles through the strong interaction but decays by the weak (radioactive) interaction into an electron and two kinds of neutrinos; the positive muon, for example, in about a millionth of a second becomes a positron, an electron neutrino, and a muon antineutrino. Because they are charged, muons before decaying lose energy by forcing electrons out of atoms (ionization). Since ionization dissipates energy in relatively small amounts, muons are very penetrating, making up that part of cosmic rays that penetrates several miles below the earth's surface. Muons, and the weak interaction associated with their behaviour, still perplex physicists.

·cosmic particle interactions 5:205b *passim* to 208b
·electron peculiar similarity 6:668h
·spin, mass, and lepton number conservation 5:37g; table 34
·subatomic particle properties 13:1024d; tables

Muong, a people of northern Vietnam who speak a language closely related to Vietnamese. Traditionally they were an agricultural people, growing chiefly wet rice. Their religion is centred on spirits associated with natural objects. They reckon descent through the male line.

·Vietnamese legendary ancestors 19:121a
·Vietnam's ethnic relationship 19:133a

Muong Swa, 13th-century Thai principality in Laos.

·Laotian rule by Thai leaders 10:677e

muonium, short-lived quasi-atom composed of a positive muon (an antiparticle), as nucleus, and an ordinary negative electron, formed when positive muons capture atomic electrons after being shot into, and slowed down by, a gas under pressure. Muonium forms a few compounds with gases such as nitrogen dioxide and ethylene. Muonium research throws some light on the puzzling nature of muons (essentially heavy electrons) and their relation to ordinary electrons.

Muqaddasī, al- (Arab geographer): *see* Maqdisī, al-.

Muqaddimah, The, Arabic AL-MUQADDIMAH, a pioneer work on the sociological approach to the philosophy of history by the Muslim historian and philosopher Ibn Khaldūn (1332–1406); it is the introduction to his universal history (*Kitāb al-ʿibar*). In analyzing the patterns of the rise and decline of civilizations and dynasties it stresses Ibn Khaldūn's central concept of *ʿaṣabīyah* ("social cohesion"), which arises spontaneously in tribes and other small kinship groups and provides the motive force that carries groups to power. Inevitably a complex combination of psychological, sociological, economic, and political factors herald the decline of the civilization (or dynasty), whereupon another group with a stronger *ʿaṣabīyah* comes forward to start the process anew.

·historical objectives and impact 9:962b
·sociological and historical theory 9:148e

Muqannaʿ, al- (meaning the Veiled One), name given to HASHIM IBN HAKIM (d. AD 779), religious leader, originally a fuller from Merv, now Mary, Turkmen S.S.R., who led a revolt in Khorāsān against the ʿAbbāsid caliph al-Mahdī. Preaching a doctrine combining elements of Islām and Zoroastrianism, al-Muqanna' carried on warfare for about three years in the field and for two years longer in his fortress of Sanam before he was eventually defeated and committed suicide. He was the hero of *Lalla Rookh* (1817) by the early-19th-century Irish poet Thomas Moore.

muqarnas, stalactite niche, an important element of Islāmic architectural ornamentation.

·early use and later development 9:991a

muqāṭaʿah (land tenure): *see* iqṭāʿ.

Muqlah, Ibn (d. 939), Islāmic calligrapher and one of the developers of the *naskhī* script.

·calligraphic naskhī script 3:664b

Muqtadir, al-, 10th-century Muslim ʿAbbāsid caliph, reigned 908 to 932.

·caliphal political instability 3:638g

Muqtafī, al- (b. April 1096, Iraq—d. 1160, Iraq), an ʿAbbāsid caliph (titular leader of the Islāmic empire) during the later years of Seljuq influence in Iraq. In his younger years al-Muqtafī led an undistinguished life at the ʿAbbāsid court in Baghdad. He became caliph in 1136 and soon embarked upon a policy of strengthening his political authority vis-à-vis the Seljuqs, whose princes at the time were feuding among themselves, and in Iraq al-Muqtafī was able to annex one district after another. In 1156 he recognized the Seljuq prince Sulaymānshāh as sultan, provided that the latter would respect Muqtafī's autonomy in Iraq. Muqtafī even supported him in some military campaigns, but, when the Sultan was defeated, Muqtafī himself was besieged in Baghdad. The siege was lifted after several months, but it demonstrated Muqtafī's inability to control military and political affairs in Iraq and the surrounding regions.

·caliphal resurgence and Seljuq decline 3:641a

Mura, South American Indian people of the Amazon tropical forest. The Mura originally inhabited the right bank of the lower Madeira River near the mouth of the Jamari River. Contact with whites led them to adopt guerrilla tactics; they spread downstream to the Purus River, raiding sedentary farmers along the way. By 1774 the Mura expansion had been countered by a local Brazilian campaign of extermination. In 1786, weakened by disease and by losses suffered at the hands of the Mundurukú (*q.v.*), the Mura made peace with the whites.

The Mura are primarily fishermen of the rivers, admired for their skill. Villages are very small, numbering from 15 to 120 persons, without much organization. A family spends much of its time in its canoe.

The Mura of today are fast approaching extinction as an ethnic group. They now speak Portuguese, and few of them remember the Mura language. They are nominally Christian, but their rituals include the use of a narcotic made from the parica tree, flagellation rites, and shamanism.

·geographic distribution map 17:113
·housing and economy 17:123a; map 121

murābit (Islam): *see* marabout.

Murābiṭūn, al- (Berber tribal confederation): *see* Almoravids.

Murad I (b. 1326?—d. 1389, Kosovo, now in Yugoslavia), Ottoman sultan in 1360–89 whose reign witnessed rapid Ottoman expansion in Anatolia and the Balkans and the emergence of new forms of government and administration to consolidate Ottoman rule in these areas.

Shortly after Murad's accession, his forces penetrated western Thrace and took Adrianople and Philippolis and forced the Byzantine emperor John V Palaeologos to become a vassal. Adrianople was renamed Edirne, and it became Murad's capital in 1362. In 1366 a crusade commanded by Amadeus VI of Savoy rescued the Byzantines and occupied Gallipoli on the Dardanelles, but the Turks recaptured the town the next year. In 1371 Murad crushed a coalition of southern Serbian princes at Cirnomen on the Marica River, took the Macedonian towns of Dráma, Kavála, and Seres (Sérrai), and won a significant victory over a Bulgarian–Serbian coalition at Samakow (now Samokovo). These victories brought large territories under direct Ottoman rule and made the princess of northern Serbia and Bulgaria, as well as the Byzantine emperor, Murad's vassal.

In the 1380s Murad resumed his offensive in the west, conducting raids in Bosnia, Epirus, and Albania. Sofia was taken in 1385 and Niš in 1386. Meanwhile, in Anatolia, Murad had extended his power as far as Tokat and consolidated his authority in Ankara. Through marriage, purchase, and conquest he also acquired territories from the principalities of Germiyan, Tekke, and Hamid. A coalition of Turkmen principalities led by the Karaman was formed to stem Ottoman expansion, but it was defeated at Konya (1386).

In 1388 a coalition of northern Serbian princes and Bosnians stopped the Ottomans at Plocnick, but the next year Murad soundly defeated them at the Battle of Kosovo, where he himself fell dead on the battlefield.

Under Murad I the seeds of some of the basic Ottoman imperial institutions were sown. The administrative military offices of *kadıasker* (military judge), *beylerbeyi* (commander-in-chief), and grand vizier crystallized and were granted to persons outside the family of Osman I, founder of the dynasty. The Ottoman land-tenure system began to be applied in the Balkans. More significantly, the origin of the Janissary corps (elite forces) and the *devşirme* (child-levy) system through which the Janissaries were recruited are traced to Murad's reign.

·encroachment on Byzantine lands **3**:570c
·Ottoman administration and expansion **13**:771f *passim* to 772h

Murad II (b. June 1404, Amasya, Tur.—d. Feb. 3, 1451, Edirne), Ottoman sultan in 1421–51 who expanded and consolidated Ottoman rule in the Balkans and pursued a policy of restraint in Anatolia.

Early in his reign, Murad had to overcome several claimants to the Ottoman throne who were supported by the Byzantine emperor Manuel II Palaeologus and by many of the Turkmen principalities in Anatolia. By 1425 Murad had eliminated his rivals, had re-established Ottoman rule over the Turkmen principalities of western Anatolia, and had once again forced Byzantium to pay tribute. He then turned his attention to the Balkans. In 1430, after a five-year struggle, he captured Salonika (modern Thessaloníki), in northern Greece, which had been under Venetian control. At first the Ottoman armies were successful against a Hungarian–Serbian–Karaman alliance; but after 1441, when the alliance expanded to include German, Polish, and Albanian forces, the Ottomans lost Niš and Sofia (1443) and were soundly defeated at Jalowaz (1444). After signing a peace treaty at Edirne (June 12, 1444), Murad abdicated in favour of his 12-year-old son, Mehmed II.

European powers, under the auspices of Pope Eugenius IV, soon broke the truce; and Murad, leading the Ottoman army, inflicted a severe defeat on the Christian forces at Varna in November 1444. Under pressure from court notables and faced with external threats, Murad reassumed control of the state in 1446. In 1448 he defeated the Hungarians at the second Battle of Kosovo (October 17).

In Anatolia, Murad pursued a policy of caution because of the westward advance of the Timurid Shāh Rokh, who posed as protector of the Turkmen principalities. The Ottomans gained suzerainty over the Turkmen rulers in the Çorum-Amasya region and in western Anatolia, but the principality of Karaman, which through its alliances with the Balkan Christian rulers was a major threat to the Ottomans, was left autonomous.

During Murad's reign the office of grand vizier became increasingly dominated by the Çandarlı family. The Janissary corps (elite forces) gained in prominence, and the hereditary Turkish frontier rulers in the Balkans often acted independently of the sultan.

·European invasion and victory at Varna **9**:54f
·Islām and Ottoman politics **9**:934e
·Istanbul and Turkish siege **9**:1070f
·Mehmed's accessions to throne **11**:859h
·siege of Constantinople **3**:570g
·territorial expansion and internal reforms **13**:773e

Murad III (b. July 4, 1546, Manisa, Tur.—d. Jan. 16/17, 1595, Istanbul), Ottoman sultan in 1574–95 whose reign saw lengthy wars against Iran and Austria and social and economic deterioration within the Ottoman state.

Externally Murad continued the military offensive of his predecessors. He took Fez (now Fès, Morocco) from the Portuguese in 1578. He fought an exhausting war against Iran (1578–90), which extended his rule over Azerbaijan, Tiflis (now in Georgian S.S.R.), Nehāvand, and Hamadan (now in Iran). In Europe he began a long war against Austria (1593–1606), which saw an alliance in 1594 of the Ottoman vassal rulers of Moldavia, Transylvania, and Walachia with Austria in defiance of Ottoman authority.

Murad came under the influence of the women in his harem and of his courtiers, and he ignored the advice of the brilliant grand vizier Mehmed Sokullu, who was assassinated in 1579. Under Murad, nepotism, heavy taxes necessitated by the long wars, and inflation, aggravated by the influx of cheap South American silver from Spain, all contributed to the decline of the major Ottoman administrative institutions. The *tımar* (fief) system suffered dislocation when the peasants, because of high taxes, were forced to leave their lands. The highly effective Janissary corps (elite forces), because of a policy of indiscriminate recruitment, degenerated into a body of ruffians that threatened the urban and rural populations. In 1583 Murad weakened the empire economically by granting commercial privileges to England.

·European diplomatic intrigues **6**:1088h
·grand viziers' social decline **13**:782a

Murad IV, in full MURAD OGLU AHMED I (b. July 27, 1612, Istanbul—d. Feb. 8, 1640, Istanbul), Ottoman sultan from 1623 to 1640 whose heavy-handed rule put an end to prevailing lawlessness and rebelliousness and who is renowned as the conqueror of Baghdad.

Murad, who came to the throne at age of 11, ruled for several years through the regency of his mother, Kösem, and a series of grand viziers. Effective rule, however, remained in the hands of the turbulent *sipahis* (quasi-feudal cavalry) and the Janissaries, who more than once forced the execution of high officials. Corruption of government officials and rebellions in the Asiatic provinces, coupled with an empty treasury, perpetuated the discontent against the central government.

Embittered by the excesses of the troops, Murad was determined to restore order both in Istanbul and in the provinces. In 1632 the *sipahis* had invaded the palace and demanded (and got) the heads of the grand vizier and 16 other high officials. Soon thereafter Murad gained full control and acted swiftly and ruthlessly. He suppressed the mutineers with a bloody ferocity. He banned the use of tobacco and closed the coffeehouses and the wineshops (no doubt as nests of sedition); violators or mere suspects were executed.

In his foreign policy Murad took personal command in the continuing war against Iran and set out to win back territories lost to Iran earlier in his reign. Baghdad was reconquered in 1638 after a siege that ended in a massacre of garrison and citizens alike. In the following year peace was concluded.

A man of courage, determination, and violent temperament, Murad did not follow closely the precepts of the Sharīʿah (Islāmic law) and was the first Ottoman sultan to execute a *shaykhal-Islām* (the highest Muslim dignitary in the empire). He was able to restore order, however, and to straighten out state finances. A warrior and man of powerful physique, Murad's untimely death was caused by his addiction to alcohol.

·social and economic reforms **13**:782g
·war of succession **9**:384d

Murad V (b. Sept. 21, 1840, Istanbul—d. Aug. 29, 1904, Istanbul), Ottoman sultan from May to August 1876, whose liberal disposition brought him to the throne after the deposition of his autocratic uncle Abdülaziz.

A man of high intelligence, Murad received a good education and was widely read both in Turkish and European literature. In 1867 he accompanied Abdülaziz on his European tour and made a favourable impression; during the tour he secretly contacted exiled nationalist–liberal Young Turks, for which Abdülaziz placed him under close surveillance.

Upon Abdülaziz' deposition by a group of ministers led by Midhat Paşa, the great advocate of constitutional government, Murad was brought to the throne. The new sultan was determined to introduce constitutional reforms, but, under the impact of Abdülaziz' suicide and the murder of some of his key ministers, Murad suffered mental collapse. After declaration by Turkish and foreign doctors that his illness was incurable, Murad was deposed by the same men who had brought him to the throne. During the reign (1876–1909) of his brother Abdülhamid II, several attempts to restore him to the throne failed, and he spent the remaining years of his life confined in the Çiragan Palace.

·installation and deposition **13**:788c

Muraenesocidae, family of conger pike eels of the fish order Anguilliformes.

·characteristics and classification **1**:900c

Muraenidae: *see* moray eel.

mural painting, branch of painting having to do with the decoration of the walls and ceilings of buildings. The term may properly include painting on fired tiles but is incorrectly used when it includes mosaic decoration.

Mural painting is inherently different from all other forms of pictorial art in that it is organically connected with architecture. The use of colour, design, and thematic treatment can radically alter the sensation of spatial proportions of the building; in this sense mural is the only form of painting that is truly three-dimensional, since it modifies and partakes of a given space. Byzantine mosaic decoration evinced the greatest respect for organic architectural form. The great artists of the Renaissance on the other hand attempted to create an illusionistic feeling for space; and the masters of the subsequent Baroque period obtained such radical effects as to seem to dissolve almost entirely the walls or ceilings. Apart from its organic relation to architecture, a second characteristic of mural painting is its broad public significance. The mural artist must conceive pictorially a social, religious, or patriotic theme on the appropriate scale in reference both to the structural exigencies of the wall and to the idea expressed.

In the history of mural painting many techniques have been used: encaustic painting, tempera painting, fresco painting (*qq.v.*), ceramics, oil paint on canvas, and more recently liquid silicate and fired porcelain enamel. In classical times the most common medium was encaustic, in which colours are

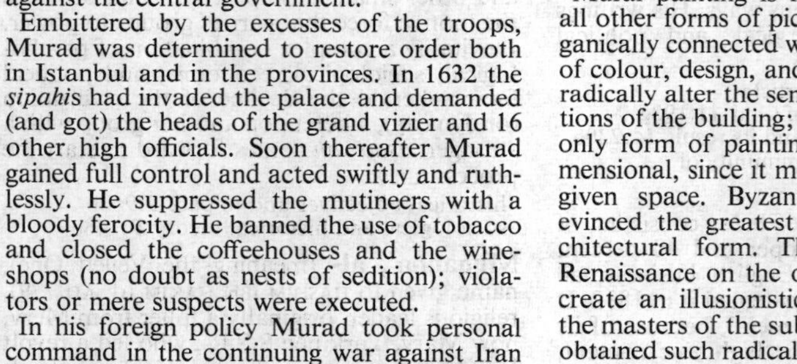

"Construction of the Dam," mural painting by William Gropper (1897–); in the Department of the Interior Building, Washington, D.C.

By courtesy of the Section of Fine Arts, Public Buildings Administration ground in a molten beeswax binder and applied to the painting surface while hot. Fresco, or painting applied to fresh wet plaster, dates back at least to the Greco-Roman paintings at Pompeii. Tempera painting (executed with pigment ground in a water-miscible medium) was probably practiced from the earliest times. In the 16th century, oil paint on canvas came into general use for murals. The fact that it could be completed in the artist's studio and later transported to its destination and attached to the wall was of practical convenience. Yet oil paint is the least satisfactory medium for murals: it lacks both brilliance of colour and surface texture, many pigments are yellowed by the binder or are affected by atmospheric conditions, and the canvas itself is subject to rapid deterioration.

·ancient Greek visual arts **19**:293b
·ancient Near Eastern and Roman styles **9**:703a; illus.
·ancient Near East visual art history **19**:259e
·Byzantine productions and restoration **4**:519e
·Byzantine wall decoration **19**:332f
·Correggio's early work **5**:190f
·early Christian subjects and styles **19**:322c
·Egyptian tombs and temples **18**:263e
·fragment of wall painting from Bezelik, illus., **3**:Central Asian Peoples, Arts of, Plate I
·fresco preservation techniques **2**:62a
·Georgian church decoration **19**:342b
·Ghirlandajo fresco and tempera styles **8**:150d
·history and technical development **13**:881a
·Iberian culture and art **17**:403e
·Mantegna's technique and accomplishment **11**:462a
·Monet's environmental innovation **12**:349c
·Orozco's Mexican public art movement **13**:741f
·Ottonian visual art developments **19**:352d
·rock-cut cave temple decoration **17**:197f
·Romanesque mural painting developments **19**:361a
·Roman forms and styles **19**:314e
·synagogue themes and style **10**:203f
·Turkistan discoveries and religious themes **3**:1134e
·visual arts of ancient Egypt **19**:249g

Muralt, Béat-Louis de (b. Jan. 9, 1665, Bern—d. Nov. 19, 1749, Colombier, Switz.), Swiss moralist who interpreted England to the French and the Swiss. He resigned his commission in the French Army to travel about England (1694–95) and then returned to Bern but was banished in 1701 because of his Pietism. His *Lettres sur les Anglais et les Français* and *Lettres sur les Voyages* (both 1725; Eng. trans., 2 parts, 1726) were written to friends, and he only agreed to their being published after much hesitation. *Lettres sur les Anglais* influenced Voltaire and Jean-Jacques Rousseau to some extent, introducing them to English thought and English institutions. *Lettres sur les Français* shocked France but strengthened English influences in Switzerland, which were very strong in the 18th century, at the expense of those (whether Catholic or materialist) from France. *Les Lettres fanatiques* demonstrate Muralt's mystical rationalism, whereas his *Instinct divin recommandé aux hommes* (1727; Eng. trans., 1751) is a work of visionary Illuminism mingled with Pietism.

Muramvya, or MURAMVIA, town and province, western Burundi. Cinchona plantations are in the vicinity. Latest census town, 9,899.

·map, Burundi **3**:528
·population growth 1965–70 table **3**:529

Murano, northern environ of Venice in Veneto region, northeastern Italy, on five islets (area of 1,134 ac [459 ha]) in the Laguna Veneta (Venice Lagoon). Founded between the 5th and 7th centuries, it experienced its major development after 1292, when glass furnaces were moved there from Venice. It became the manufacturing centre for Venetian glass, exported in large quantities to all Europe. Its high point was in the 16th century, when it had more than 30,000 inhabitants; glass-making continues but on a considerably reduced scale. A record of this aspect of Murano's history is found in the Museum of Glass Art in the Giustinian Palace. Notable landmarks are the basilica of SS. Maria e Donato (founded 7th century, rebuilt 9th and 12th), with Byzantine floor mosaics, and the S. Pietro Martire Church (14th century, rebuilt 1509), with paintings by Giovanni Bellini, Paolo Veronese, and Tintoretto. Latest census 7,844.

The basilica of SS. Maria e Donato, Murano, in the Venice region
Marzari—SCALA, New York

·glassmaking in Middle Ages **8**:199d
·glassmaking origins and development **8**:184e

Murano Tōgo (b. 1891, Saga Prefecture, Japan), architect particularly noted for the construction of large department stores with solid external walls. Trained in traditional Japanese styles, Murano was gradually drawn to European modern and by the 1930s was earning a reputation for his large stores, such as the Sogō store at Ōsaka (1935), the Sogō store at Tokyo (1957), Takashimaya in Tokyo, the Maruei Hotel at Nagoya, and Daimaru department store in Kōbe. In the New Kabuki Theatre in Ōsaka (1958), Murano combined construction in concrete with traditional pagoda-like curves. Other works include the town hall at Yonago, the town centre at Yawata, the office building for Chiyoda Insurance Company (1966), and the Takarazuka Catholic Church (1967).

Chiyoda Insurance Company Building, Tokyo, by Murano Tōgo, 1966
Saburo Ohmachi

Murasaki Shikibu (b. 978?—d. 1026?), court lady, author of the *Genji monogatari* (*Tale of Genji*), generally considered the greatest classic of Japanese literature, which is thought to be the world's first novel. Her real name is unknown; it is conjectured that she acquired the sobriquet of Murasaki from the name of the heroine of her novel. The main source of knowledge about her life is the diary she kept between 1007 and 1010. This work possesses considerable interest for the delightful glimpses it affords of life at the court of the Empress Akiko, whom Murasaki Shikibu served.

Some critics believe she wrote the entire *Tale of Genji* between 1001 (the year her husband Fujiwara Nobutaka died) and 1005, when she began serving at court. More probably, however, the composition of this extremely long and complex novel extended over a much greater period.

The *Tale of Genji* is not only the oldest full novel written anywhere in the world but also one of the finest. It captures the image of a unique society of ultrarefined and elegant aristocrats, whose indispensable accomplishments were skill in poetry, music, calligraphy, and courtship. Much of it is concerned with the loves of Prince Genji and the different women in his life, all of whom are exquisitely delineated. If the novel is lacking in scenes of powerful action, it is permeated with a sensitivity to human emotions and to the beauties of nature hardly paralleled elsewhere. The tone of the novel darkens as it progresses, indicating perhaps a deepening of Murasaki Shikibu's Buddhist conviction of the vanity of the world. Some, however, believe its last 14 chapters are written by another hand. The translation of *The Tale of Genji* (1935) by Arthur Waley (1889–1966) is a classic of English literature. *Diaries of Court Ladies of Old Japan*, which includes that of Murasaki Shikibu, was translated by Omori and Doi in 1935.

Murasaki Shikibu, wood-block print by an unknown artist
By courtesy of the International Society for Educational Information Tokyo, Inc.

·Heian period musical life of Japan **12**:682c
·influence in history **10**:1067e
·Japanese aesthetic theories **1**:161a
·Japanese novel development **13**:295g
·satiric and philosophical themes in works **10**:1044b
·Tales of Genji origin, segment remains, and deposition **19**:228c
·works and style **10**:1067h

Murat, Joachim (b. March 25, 1767, La Bastide-Fortunière, Fr.—d. Oct. 13, 1815, Calabria, Italy), brilliant cavalry leader who was one of Napoleon's most famous marshals and who as king of Naples (1808–15) lent stimulus

Murat, detail of a drawing by Antoine-Jean Gros (1771–1835); in the École des Beaux-Arts, Paris
Cliche Musees Nationaux, Paris

to Italian nationalism. The son of an innkeeper, he studied briefly for a career in the church but enlisted in a cavalry regiment in 1787 and, when war broke out in 1792, won rapid promotion. In October 1795 he was on hand in Paris at the moment that Napoleon Bonaparte was entrusted with the mission of suppressing a royalist insurrection; Murat's contribution in bringing up cannon won him a place as aide-de-camp to Bonaparte for the Italian campaign of 1796–97. In Italy and later in Egypt (1798–99) he established his reputation as a gifted and daring leader of cavalry, and he again served his chief well in the coup d'etat of 18 Brumaire (Nov. 9, 1799) by which Bonaparte seized power as first consul. Murat's reward was the hand of Napoleon's youngest sister, Caroline.

In the Italian campaign of 1800 Murat helped win the decisive Battle of Marengo, and in 1801 he rapidly concluded the campaign against Bourbon-ruled Naples by imposing the Armistice of Foligno. As governor of Paris in 1804, he was included among the first generals promoted to the rank of marshal after Napoleon's coronation as emperor on December 2. In 1805 he played a conspicuous role in the Austerlitz campaign, both in long-distance reconnaissance and tactically, helping to pin the Austrian Army in Ulm, where it was forced to surrender, and defeating Austrian and Russian cavalry on the field of Austerlitz. At Jena in 1806 his energetic pursuit completed destruction of the Prussian Army, and at Eylau in 1807 his headlong charge saved a desperate tactical situation.

Rewarded with the title of grand duke of Berg and Clèves, Murat began to have dreams of sovereignty, and when he was sent to act as Napoleon's lieutenant in Spain he tried to gain possession of the unoccupied Spanish throne. His intrigues led instead to Spanish opposition and a rising in Madrid that, though quelled (May 2, 1808), ended his hopes. Though Napoleon gave the Spanish throne to his brother Joseph, he rewarded Murat with Joseph's former place as king of Naples.

In Naples Murat not only satisfied his own vanity by a lavish court display but also carried out important reforms, breaking up the vast landed estates and introducing the democratic Code Napoléon. The administration was opened to advancement by merit, cotton growing was encouraged, and effective measures were taken against the chronic Neapolitan brigandage. Murat even foresaw the unification of Italy, a development at whose head he sought to place himself through the encouragement of secret societies that eventually played a major role in the Risorgimento.

In 1812 Murat took part in Napoleon's Russian campaign and once more distinguished himself at Borodino; but, left in charge of the shattered Grand Army during the retreat from Moscow, he abandoned it to try to save his kingdom of Naples. In 1813 he wavered between loyalty to Napoleon and negotiation with the Allies. The Austrians signed a treaty with him, but the former Bourbon rulers of Naples raised objections and his situation was in doubt when Napoleon returned to France in 1815. He now staked his hopes on an appeal to Italian nationalism, but his Neapolitans were defeated by the Austrians at Tolentino, and he was forced to flee to Corsica. In October he made a last, hopeless attempt to recover Naples virtually unaided, and was taken prisoner and shot.

·judicial and land reforms **9**:1157g
·Napoleon I's empire and downfall **12**:836a

Muratori, Lodovico Antonio (b. Oct. 21, 1672, Vignola, duchy of Modena, now Italy—d. Jan. 23, 1750, Modena), scholar and pioneer of modern Italian historiography. After studying at Modena under the Benedictine Benedetto Bacchini, who introduced him to the historical-critical methods of the French Maurists, in 1694 he was ordained priest and employed in the Ambrosian library at Milan. There he published the *Anecdota* (2 vol., 1697–98; two further volumes added, 1713), a selection of texts that he had discovered among the manuscripts belonging to the library. In 1700 he went to Modena as librarian for Duke Rinaldo I. Legal disputes between the Este family and the Holy See over the ownership of the territory of Comacchio led Muratori to study, in the original documents, some of the juridical and ideological problems of the Italian middle ages, and he came to see in that period the origin of the modern states, although as a man of the 18th century he still considered it a "barbarous" epoch. As a result he undertook a documentary study, and, with the active collaboration of local correspondents, he collected together in his *Rerum Italicarum Scriptores* (28 vol., 1723–51; "Writers on Italian Affairs") chronicles, diaries, and legal documents illustrating the history of medieval Italian society.

Muratori, engraving by I.I. Haid

By courtesy of the Bibliotheque Nationale, Paris

At the same time Muratori was working on his 75 dissertations, published in the *Antiquitates Italicae Medii Aevi*, 6 vol. (1738–42; "Antiquities of the Italian Middle Ages"), which includes the Muratorian Canon (*q.v.*), a 2nd-century list of the books of the New Testament. These constitute his most lively and acute historical work, and are made up of detailed and penetrating studies on such subjects as the history of institutions, of economics, of religion, and of social customs. Particularly acute is the analysis of relationships between social events and religious traditions, relationships that he establishes with independent critical judgment. In 1744 he began the publication of the *Annali d'Italia* (12 vol., 1744–49), a work of some significance because in it Muratori attempted to narrate the history of the Italian peninsula as a unified whole. As a work of historiography, however, the *Annali*, except for brief passages, are a failure. His analytical approach seems to be used to hide the absence of a central theme and the biographical sketches lack penetration and psychological insight. It would seem that Muratori had more understanding of the people and their needs than of individuals.

Muratori was not only a historian. As a man of letters he was sensitively aware of the connections between culture and morals and he believed that it was the duty of the critic to point them out, as can be seen from *Riflessioni sopra il buon gusto* (1708; "Reflections on Good Taste"). As a priest he fought against superstition and against medieval scholasticism, as revived by the Jesuits, for cultural as well as moral reasons. He was even accused of Jansenism, a Roman Catholic religious movement of non-orthodox tendencies—an accusation that, although unjust in itself, was based on the apparent affinity between his own advocacy of a moral rebirth and that of the Jansenists. He was further linked to them by his definite acceptance of jurisdictional theories, because of his own preferences and the influences of the Maurists.

·nationalistic aspects of historiography **8**:956f
·textual editing methodology **18**:194d

Muratorian Canon, a late 2nd-century-AD Latin list of New Testament writings regarded as canonical (scripturally authoritative), named for its discoverer Lodovico Antonio Muratori, an Italian scholar who published the manuscript in 1740. Included in the canon are the four Gospels (Matthew, Mark, Luke, and John), the book of Acts, 13 letters of the Apostle Paul, the three Pastoral Letters (I and II Timothy and Titus), Philemon, the Letter of Jude, two letters of John, the Wisdom of Solomon, and the apocalypses of John and of Peter. The *Shepherd of Hermas* was listed as a book for private devotions.

·Christian canons of late 2nd century **2**:940b
·early Christian Latin texts **13**:1081d
·Pastoral Letters' inclusion **2**:966c
·Saint Luke's identity clarification **11**:178a

Murat River, Turkish MURAT NEHRI, sometimes spelled MURAD, ancient ARSANIAS, major headstream of the Euphrates River; it rises north of Lake Van near Mt. Ararat, in eastern Turkey, and flows westward for 449 mi (722 km) through a mountainous region to unite with the Karasu Çayı and form the Upper Euphrates near Malatya.

Turkey's largest dam, the Keban, west of Elâzığ, completed in 1974, eventually will provide 1,240 MW of electric power and aid flood control and the irrigation of additional cropland. Agriculture in the valley now consists primarily of the cultivation of grains, fruits, vegetables, and cotton.

38°52′ N, 38°48′ E

·map, Turkey **18**:785

Muravyov, Mikhail Nikolayevich, Count (b. April 19 [April 7, old style], 1845, Grodno, Belorussia—d. June 21 [June 8, O.S.], 1900, St. Petersburg, now Leningrad), diplomat and statesman who at the end of the 19th century directed Russia's activities in the Far East and played a major role in developments leading to the outbreak of the Russo-Japanese War (1904–05). The grandson of Mikhail Nikolayevich Muravyov, known as the "hangman of Wilno" for his brutal suppression of the Polish uprising of 1863 in the Lithuanian provinces, and the son of the Governor of Grodno, the younger Mikhail Nikolayevich entered the Russian foreign ministry in 1864. After serving in various legations throughout Europe, he was appointed Russian minister to Denmark (1893) and then minister of foreign affairs (1896).

An advocate of Russian expansion into Manchuria, Muravyov recommended that the Russian Navy seize Port Arthur (Lüshun Kow) and Dalny (Talien) on the Liaotung Peninsula. After this was accomplished (December 1897), he concluded an agreement with China (March 1898) that gave Russia control of the entire peninsula for 25 years and also allowed Russia to build a railroad from Port Arthur to Harbin (now in Heilungkiang Province, China), which was connected with the Russian port of Vladivostok by the Russian-operated Chinese Eastern Railroad. Russia's gains in southern Manchuria antagonized Great Britain, which feared that Russia would encourage the Chinese government to adopt anti-British policies, and Japan, which had been forced by Russia, Great Britain, and France to abandon the Liaotung Peninsula in 1895 and now feared that Russia would challenge Japanese authority in Korea.

Muravyov improved relations with Great Britain by concluding an agreement (April 1899) in which the two nations defined and recognized their respective spheres of influence in China. By order of the Russian emperor Nicholas II, Muravyov also called for the convocation of a disarmament conference (Jan. 11, 1899), which assembled at The Hague (May–July 1899), but he was unable to control the increasingly hostile conflict developing between Russia and Japan, which after his death erupted into the Russo-Japanese War.

Muravyov, Nikolay Nikolayevich (1809–81), Russian diplomat and governor-general of Siberia.
·Ch'ing dynasty territory concessions **4**:359d

Muravyov-Amur Peninsula, Far Eastern U.S.S.R.
·location and geographical features **19**:496d

Muravyov-Apostol, Sergey Ivanovich (1796–1826), Russian army officer and republican, executed for his leading role in the Decembrist uprising of 1825–26.

mūrchanā, seven-degree scale of paired notes used in South Asian music.
·Western scale comparison and types **17**:152f

Murchison, Sir Roderick Impey (b. Feb. 19, 1792, Tarradale, Ross-shire, modern Ross and Cromarty—d. Oct. 22, 1871, London), geologist who first established the geologic sequence of Early Paleozoic (395,000,000 to 570,000,000 years old) strata. A British soldier from the age of 15, he retired at the conclusion of the Napoleonic Wars, married, and devoted himself to leisurely pursuits, principally fox hunting. In 1824 he turned to serious diversions, partly because of the influence of the noted British chemist Sir Humphry Davy, and moved to London.

Murchison joined the Geological Society in 1825 and in the following five years explored Scotland, France, and the Alps and collaborated alternately with the British geologists Adam Sedgwick and Sir Charles Lyell.

In 1831 he was elected president of the Geological Society, after serving as secretary for five years. In that same year he began his studies of the Early Paleozoic rocks in South Wales. His findings were embodied in the monumental work *The Silurian System* (1839). Following the establishment of the Silurian System, Murchison and Sedgwick founded the Devonian System, based on their research of the geology of southwest England and the Rhineland. Murchison then went on an expedition to Russia and wrote, with others, *The Geology of Russia in Europe and the Ural Mountains* (1845). In 1841 he proposed the establishment of the Permian System (280,000,000 to 225,000,000 years ago), based upon his Russian explorations. Knighted in 1846, Murchison was appointed director general of the Geological Survey and director of the Royal School of Mines and the Museum of Practical Geology, London, in 1855. He prepared successive editions of his work *Siluria* (1854, 5th ed. 1872), which presented the main features of the original *Silurian System* along with information on new findings. In addition, he fought unsuccessfully against the splitting of his original Silurian System into three parts: the Silurian Period (430,000,000 to 395,000,000 years ago), the Ordovician Period (500,000,000 to 430,000,000 years ago), and the Cambrian Period (570,000,000 to 500,000,000 years ago). In 1871 he founded a chair of geology and mineralogy at the University of Edinburgh, and in his will he provided for the establishment of the Murchison Medal and Geological Fund to be awarded annually by the Geological Society.

Murchison
The Mansell Collection

·Cambrian boundary controversy **3**:689h
·Cambrian-Silurian study **17**:723b
·Central African theory confirmation **3**:1095b
·Devonian rock correlation **5**:671g
·geological time scale and Silurian period development **7**:1067f
·Permian rock correlation **14**:96a
·Silurian rock correlation **16**:769a

Murchison Falls, waterfall on the lower Victoria Nile River in northwest Uganda, east central Africa, 20 mi (32 km) east of Lake Albert. The Victoria Nile passes through many miles of rapids before narrowing to a width of 17 ft (5 m) and dropping about 400 ft in a series of three cascades. The initial fall of 130 ft is generally recognized as Murchison Falls. The cataract forms the central feature of the Kabarega (formerly Murchison Falls) National Park (established 1952) and is one of the most famous waterfalls in Africa. The English explorer Sir Samuel White Baker discovered the falls in the mid-1860s and named them for the geologist Sir Roderick Murchison.

Murchison Falls on the lower Victoria Nile in Uganda
Gerald Cubitt

·map, Uganda **18**:826
·Nile River system physiography **13**:103f; map
·rift lake geography and fauna **6**:116e; map 119

Murchison River, Western Australia, rising north of Meekatharra on Peak Hill in the Robinson Ranges and fed by its tributaries the Sandford and Roderick; it flows sporadically west, south, and west to enter the Indian Ocean at Gantheaume Bay, north of Geraldton, after a course of 440 mi (710 km). Reached (1839) by the explorer Sir George Grey on a forced march from Shark Bay to the Swan River, it was named by him after the British scientist Sir Roderick Murchison. Reefs in its estuarine mouth, which is a good fishing ground, prevent navigation. Flowing principally during the winter, the Murchison is crossed by the North West Coastal Highway at Galena.

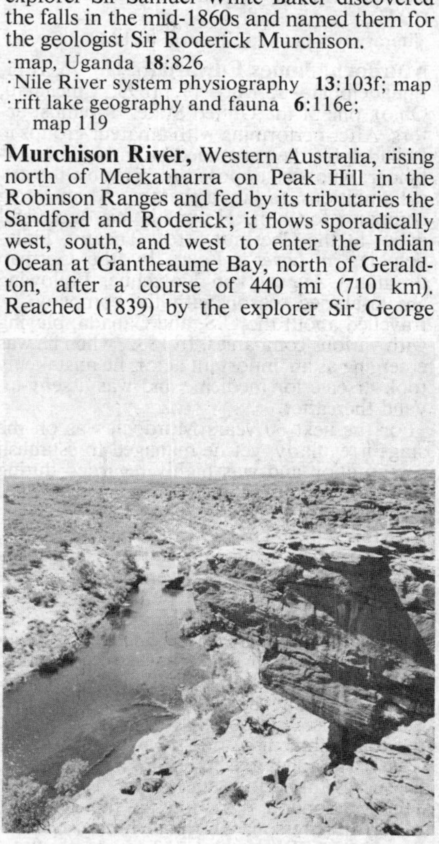
Hawke Head Lookout on the Murchison River, Western Australia
J. Yates—Shostal

In 1891, the stream gave its name to one of Australia's richest goldfields. The original find was followed by the East Murchison (1895) and Peak Hill (1897) fields. Although production has declined sharply, the fields still produce about 6 percent of the state's gold output. The area also yields wheat and sheep and is being actively prospected for mineral and petroleum deposits.
27°42′ S, 114°09′ E
·map, Australia **2**:400

Murcia, province of southeastern Spain, in the southern part of the old kingdom of Murcia; situated mainly in the Sistema (mountain system) Penibético, it has an area of 4,369 sq mi (11,317 sq km). Although noted for lack of rainfall, the province is, because of irrigation of the Murcian plain by the Río Segura, one of Spain's most productive agricultural regions. Principal crops include lemons, oranges, esparto grass, hemp, cotton, saffron, and olives. There are also rich deposits of minerals, including zinc, lead, sulfur, copper, and tin. A large oil refinery is at Escombreras on the coast. Other industries include the manufacture of chemicals and vegetable canning. Aside from Murcia city, the provincial capital, the main population centres are Cartagena, Lorca, Yecla, Cieza, and Caravaca. Ports include the naval base at Cartagena (*q.v.*), with the Bazan shipyards, and the fishing port of Mazarrón. There is a paratroop training base at Alcantarilla. Pop. (1970) 832,313.
·area and population table **17**:389
·map, Spain **17**:382

Murcia, capital of Murcia province, in southeastern Spain at the confluence of the Segura and Guadalentín (Sangonera) rivers in a fertile, irrigated area known as the *huerta* (orchard), northeast of Granada city. The site was settled before the Roman occupation of southern Spain in the 3rd century BC, but its name even during the Roman rule is unknown, although some have tried to identify it with the Roman town Vergilia. As Mursiyah it was first mentioned in the histories and chronicles of the Muslims. According to the Arab geographer Yāqūt it was founded in 825 by the Umayyad amīr of Córdoba, ʿAbd ar-Raḥmān II, who made it the capital of the province. After the fall of the caliphate of Córdoba in 1031, it came under the control of Almería and then of Valencia, until in 1063 its

Santa María cathedral in Cardenal Belluga Square, Murcia, Spain
FISA

ruler ʿAbd ar-Raḥmān ibn Ṭāhir, declared himself independent.

The Río Segura divides the city into an older, northern sector and a more modern, southern sector. The Gothic cathedral of Santa María dates from the 14th century and was restored in the 18th. It contains the fine chapel of the Vélez family (1507). In the Ermita de ("hermitage of") Jesús are the majority of the Passion sculptures of Francisco Salcillo, which attract many visitors during Holy Week. The University of Murcia was founded in 1915.

Murcia is a communications and agricultural trade centre for citrus fruits, almonds, cereals, olive oil, and pepper. The silk industry, which dates from Moorish times, is still carried on; manufactures include woollen, linen, and cotton goods, saltpetre, flour, leather, aluminum products, furniture, and hats. Pop. (1970) 243,759.

37°59′ N, 1°07′ W

·map, Spain **17**:382

Murcia, Kingdom of, independent Muslim (Moorish) kingdom centred around the city of Murcia (Arabic: Mursiyah), Spain, first in the 11th century, following the disintegration of the Spanish ʿUmmayad Caliphate; and again in the 12th century, as part of the Spanish Muslim reaction against the rule of the North African Almoravids. The kingdom's very complicated history is consistent in representing a nationalistic interpretation of Islām. Its ruler, ʿAbd-ar-Raḥmān ben Ṭāhir, declared himself independent in 1063, though to preserve the fiction of the unity of the ʿUmmayad Caliphate he took the title not of king (*malik*) but of minister (*hachib*).

Murcia then played an intermediary role between the Almoravids and the Castilians, but in the end religious sympathies inclined it to the Almoravids. Then their caliph Yusuf ibn Tashfin, who had brought the quarrelling states of Muslim Spain under his control, took possession of Murcia in 1092, incorporating it into his empire. General discontent under the Almoravids led to a rising under Abu Ch'afar ben Hud in 1144, and the re-establishment of Murcian independence. The kingdom was then united with Valencia.

After 1168, Murcia came under the rule of the North African Almohads. In spite of this, it retained an autonomous administrative system that was conserved by the Christian Castilians when they took possession of the territory, almost without a struggle, in 1243.

murder: *see* homicide.

Murder in the Cathedral (first performed 1935), verse drama by English poet, dramatist, and critic T.S. Eliot about the martyrdom of Thomas Becket, 12th-century Archbishop of Canterbury. In it Eliot examines the motives lying behind Becket's death, and relates the issues involved to the 20th century—explicitly in his use of tempters in the first act and of knight-murderers in the second to express modern attitudes in modern idiom. A striking feature of the play is a chorus used in the traditional Greek manner to make the meaning of the heroic action apprehensible to common humanity.

·tragic theme **6**:725d

Murders in the Rue Morgue, The (1841), short story by U.S. author Edgar Allan Poe which first appeared in *Graham's Magazine*. An amateur detective, C. Auguste Dupin, solves the mystery of who committed the brutal murders of a mother and her daughter.

·detective novel tradition **13**:288e

Mur des Fédérés, wall, Père-Lachaise Cemetery, Paris.

·Commune fight and pilgrimages **13**:1018c

Murdoch, (Jean) Iris, married name MRS. J.O. BAYLEY (b. July 15, 1919, Dublin), British writer and university lecturer, who by 1958 had attained general recognition as one of the foremost novelists of her generation. After an early childhood spent in London, where she attended the Froebel Educational Institute, she went to Badminton School, Bristol, and, from 1938–42, studied at Somerville College, Oxford. Between 1942 and 1944 she worked in the British Treasury and then for two years as

Iris Murdoch

Cecil Beaton—Camera Press from Publix

an administrative officer with UNRRA. In this connection she visited Belgium and Austria and finally worked for some time in a camp for displaced persons. After the end of World War II she held the Sarah Smithson studentship in philosophy at Newnham College, Cambridge, and in 1948 was elected a fellow of St. Anne's College, Oxford, where she remained as fellow and tutor in philosophy. Murdoch's first published work was a critical work, *Sartre, Romantic Rationalist* (1953), which was followed by two novels, *Under the Net* (1954) and *The Flight from the Enchanter* (1956). These were admired for their intelligence, wit, and high seriousness, qualities that—along with a rich comic sense and gift for analyzing the tensions and complexities in human relationships—have continued to distinguish her work. After *A Severed Head* (1961), Miss Murdoch published a novel almost every year—these include *The Red and the Green* (1965), *The Nice and the Good* (1968), *An Accidental Man* (1971), and *The Black Prince* (1973).

·literary works and influence **10**:1222a

Murdoch, James Edward (b. Jan. 25, 1811, Philadelphia—d. May 19, 1893, Cincinnati, Ohio), one of the United States' foremost actors. After performing with amateur groups in Philadelphia, he persuaded his father, a bookbinder, who was opposed to his son's theatrical ambitions, to hire a theatre and an acting company for him. He made his successful debut at the Chestnut Street Theatre, Philadelphia, in *Lover's Vows*, by the German dramatist August von Kotzebue. Following an unsalaried season with the company, he travelled about the U.S. and Canada, playing with various companies. In 1832, when he was emerging as an important actor, he mistakenly took arsenic for medicine and was a semi-invalid thereafter.

For the next 60 years Murdoch was on the stage irregularly, yet he managed to establish a reputation and was highly regarded during the 19th century as both tragedian and comedian. In 1833 he played again at the Chestnut Street Theatre, with Fanny Kemble, one of England's leading actresses, who was then on tour in the U.S. Twenty years later he performed with Joseph Jefferson, one of the outstanding figures of the U.S. stage, in Richard Sheridan's masterpiece *School for Scandal;* in such plays Murdoch was considered to be the finest light comedian of his day. His appearance at the new Metropolitan Theatre, San Francisco, about that same time helped the establishment of fine theatre on the West Coast. He appeared in England in 1856, and his successful performances at the Haymarket Theatre, London, were noted in the *Autobiography* of Jefferson, who paid him great tribute. His style was marked by superb elocution, strong finesse, and naturalness.

Murdoch came out of retirement in 1861 to entertain and perform benefits for the American Civil War wounded. His last appearance was at a dramatic festival in Cincinnati in 1883. Among his most popular roles were Mirabell (in William Congreve's *Way of the World*), Mercutio and Orlando (in Shakespeare's *Romeo and Juliet* and *As You Like It*, respectively). His nephew Frank H. Murdock (d. 1872), was an actor and the author of the popular frontier play *Davy Crockett. The Stage* by J.E. Murdock was published in 1880.

Murdochville, town in Bas-Saint-Laurent-Gaspésie region, eastern Quebec province, Canada, in the centre of the Gaspé Peninsula, just east of Gaspesian Provincial Park, one of the few settlements more than a few miles from the coast. Named after James Murdoch, president of the Noranda Mines, Ltd., it was developed in 1952 by that company's affiliate, Gaspé Copper Mines. Murdochville is now the chief centre of a rich copper-mining area; its main industry is copper smelting. Pop. (1971 prelim.) 2,858.

48°57′ N, 65°30′ W

Murdock, G(eorge) P(eter) (b. 1897), U.S. anthropologist noted for his work on social structure and cross-cultural comparisons and for his works classifying and indexing cultures of the world. His publications include *Outline of Cultural Materials* (4th rev. ed. 1965, with others), *Outline of World Cultures* (3rd ed. 1963), *Ethnographic Bibliography of North America* (3rd ed. 1960), *Social Structure* (1949), *Africa: Its People and Their Culture History* (1959), and *Culture and Society* (1965).

·African peoples' classification **1**:279e
·Central African Bantu expansion theory **3**:1091c
·family structure research **7**:155h
·sexual behaviour controls **16**:599a

Murdock, William (b. Aug. 21, 1754, Auchinleck, Ayrshire—d. Nov. 15, 1839, Birmingham, Warwickshire), inventor, the first to make extensive use of coal gas for illumination, and pioneer in the development of steam power. In 1777 he entered the engineering firm of Matthew Boulton and James Watt in their Soho works at Birmingham and about two

William Murdock, bust by an unknown artist; in the Science Museum, London

By courtesy of the Science Museum, London

years later was sent to Cornwall to superintend the fitting of Watt's steam engines. At his home in Redruth, Cornwall, he experimented in distilling coal; and in 1792, by producing coal gas in large iron retorts and conveying it 70 feet through metal pipes, he lighted his cottage and offices with gas. After returning to Birmingham about 1799, he perfected further practical methods for making, storing, and purifying gas. In 1802 part of the Soho factory's exterior was lighted with gas in celebration of the Peace of Amiens, and in 1803 the factory interior also was lighted with gas. Other places nearby, such as the Phillips and Lee cotton mill, began to use gas lighting, and in February 1808 Murdock read a paper before the Royal Society detailing his discovery.

Murdock also made important improvements in the steam engine. He was the first to devise an oscillating engine, of which he made a model about 1784; in 1786 he was busy—to the annoyance of Boulton and Watt, who considered it unfruitful—with a steam carriage or road locomotive that was unsuccessful; and in 1799 he invented the long D slide valve. He is generally credited with devising the so-called sun and planet motion, a means of making a steam engine give continuous revolving motion to a shaft provided with a flywheel. Watt, however, patented this motion in 1781. Murdock also experimented with compressed air and in 1803 constructed a steam gun. He retired from business in 1830.

·coal gas illumination experiments **10**:958b
·steam carriage development **2**:515d
·theatrical use of gas lighting **17**:554b
·town gas development **4**:782h

Murena, Lucius Licinius, 1st-century-BC Roman general in Mithridatic Wars.
·Mithradates VI's military opponents **12**:288d

Murena, Varro, 1st-century-BC Roman noble.
·conspiracy against Augustus **11**:291g

Mureş Magyar Autonomous Region, Romanian REGIUNEA MUREŞ-AUTONOMĂ MAGHIARĂ, a former administrative and economic region (*regiune*) in north central Romania (in the eastern part of Transylvania), came into being in 1952, when the Romanian constitution was redrawn and the regions of the country were redefined; in 1968, when the administrative regions were abolished, it was divided into two districts (*judeţe*), Mureş and Harghita. The population of the region, which comprised part of the Transylvania Plain in the west and the eastern Carpathian Gurghiu, Ciuc, and Harghita mountains in the east, was less than 20 percent Romanian, being a mixture of Szeklers, Magyars (*q.v.*), and Germans. A special article of the 1968 constitution guaranteed full equality of rights to all citizens regardless of nationality.
·area and population, table 1 **15**:1051

Mureşul River, Hungarian MAROS, in Romania, rising in the Munţii (mountains) Giurgeului in the Moldavian Carpathians. It cuts a gorge between the Călimanului and Gurghiului ranges, crosses the Transylvanian Basin flowing southwest, and then cuts across the Western Carpathians between the Munţii Poiana Ruscă and the Munţii Bihorului and emerges onto the Tisa Plain to join the Tisa (Hungarian, Tisza) River at Szeged, Hungary, after a course of 499 mi (803 km). It is the most important tributary of the Tisa with respect to its quantity of water. The large area of its basin, its length, and its diagonal cut across the Transylvanian Basin make it a significant traffic route. It is navigable for small craft below Deva and is followed by road and rail arteries; several important towns lie along its course.
46°15′ N, 20°13′ E
·map, Romania **15**:1048
·Romanian physical geography **15**:1047c

Muret, Battle of (Sept. 12, 1213), military engagement of the Albigensian Crusade; played a significant role in ending Aragonese interests in territories north of the Pyrenees and in bringing the province of Languedoc under the influence of the French crown. French Crusaders led by Simon de Montfort, seeking to destroy the Cathar religious sect based in southern France, were opposed by Count Raymond VI of Toulouse. In 1213 Simon came westward from Muret, a town 13 miles southwest of Toulouse, in Languedoc, and attacked the camp of Raymond's ally, Peter II of Aragon, killing him and causing a general flight of Raymond and his forces. Subsequent negotiations between Simon and Toulouse resulted in the submission of the town (1214–15).

Muretus, also called MARC-ANTOINE MURET (1526–85), progressive Humanist and classical scholar who had to leave France and take refuge in Italy because of charges of heresy.

murex, general name for marine snails comprising the family Muricidae (subclass Prosobranchia of the class Gastropoda). Typically the elongated or heavy shell is elaborately spined or frilled. The family occurs worldwide, mainly in the tropics. The many muricids that live in rocky shallows are called rock shells or rock whelks.

Oyster drill (*Urosalpinx cinerea*)
Grant Heilman—EB Inc.

The animal feeds by drilling a hole in the shell of another mollusk and inserting its long proboscis. Most species exude a yellow fluid that, when exposed to sunlight, becomes a purple dye. An example of the most important genus is the 15-centimetre (6-inch) Venus comb (*Murex pecten*), a white, long-spined species of the Indo-Pacific region. The dye murex (*M. brandaris*) of the Mediterranean was once a source of royal Tyrian purple.

Other members of the Muricidae include small, modestly ornamented shells given various names. The oyster drill (*Urosalpinx cinerea*) and dwarf tritons (genus *Ocenebra*) are pests in oyster beds. Drupes (*Drupa*, *Acanthina*) are colourful Indo-Pacific shells. Dogwinkles (*Nucella*) resemble periwinkles.

Murfreesboro, town, seat of Pike County, southwestern Arkansas, U.S. The nearby Crater of Diamonds State Park is the site of the nation's only diamond mine, which was worked commercially from 1906 to 1919. Pop. (1980) 1,883.
34°04′ N, 93°41′ W

Murfreesboro, city, seat (1811) of Rutherford County, southeast of Nashville, Tenn. U.S., on the West Fork of the Stones River. The community was established in 1811 on a land tract donated by a Revolutionary War soldier, Col. William Lytle, and named for his friend Col. Hardy Murfree. From 1819 to 1825, Murfreesboro served as the state capital. One of the most bitter encounters of the Civil War took place 3 mi (5 km) northwest of the city (Dec. 13, 1862–Jan. 2, 1863), in which the Federal forces under Gen. William S. Rosecrans won a strategic victory over the Confederates under Gen. Braxton Bragg. Stones River National Battlefield commemorates the battle.

The city has a mixed economy. Dairy and beef cattle are raised in the area, which is also noted for Tennessee Walking Horses, gaited horses, ponies, and racehorses. Dairy foods are processed. Manufactures include electric heating elements, electric motors, furniture, and cedar woodenware. Middle Tennessee State University (1911), located in the city, and Sewart Air Force Base near Smyrna to the northwest are important factors in the economy. Inc. 1817. Pop. (1980) 32,845.
35°51′ N, 86°23′ W
·Civil War tactics and Union army effect **4**:677d; map 679
·map, United States **18**:908

Murgab, town, Tadzhik Soviet Socialist Republic, on the Murgab River.
38°10′ N, 73°59′ E
·mean and record January temperatures **17**:985h

Murgab River, Afghan DARYĀ-YE MORGHĀB, rising in northeastern Afghanistan in a basin bounded on the north by the Band-e Torkistān Range and on the south by the Paropamisus Mountains. The course of the river is generally westward as far as Lukh-e Sorkh, where it turns north, passing through the town of Bālā Morghāb, just beyond which it forms the border between Afghanistan and the Turkmen Soviet Socialist Republic, for 10 mi (16 km). It is joined by its only important tributary, the Kushka, at Tashkepri. Dams control irrigation water at Tashkepri and Iolotan. At Mary (formerly Merv) it is crossed by the Transcaspian Railway, from which a branch runs southward along the Murgab and Kushka to the town of Kushka. North of Mary the river ends in the Kara-Kum Desert after a course of more than 530 mi.
38°10′ N, 73°59′ E
·Turkmen S.S.R. physical geography **18**:798h *passim* to 801a

Murgantia histrionica (insect): *see* harlequin cabbage bug.

Murger, (Louis-)Henri (1822–61), novelist who first depicted Bohemian life, notably in *Scènes de la vie de bohème* (1847–49), which was dramatized (1849) by Théodore Barrière and used as the basis of operas by Leoncavallo and Puccini.

Muri, town and emirate, Adamawa Province, North-Eastern State, eastern Nigeria. The town lies on the road from Zurak to K. Lamido town and is served by the minor Benue River port of Wuzu, 11 mi (18 km) east-southeast.

Originally part of the 17th-century Jukun kingdom called Kororofa, the region now known as Muri emirate was conquered in the 1804 *jihād* ("holy war") conducted by the Fulani people. By 1817, Hamman Ruwa, a brother of the emir of Gombe, an emirate to the north, had consolidated Fulani control over the native non-Muslim peoples and placed his territory under Gombe's jurisdiction. After Ruwa was put to death in 1833 by Gombe's Emir Buba Yero, the Fulani of the region requested independence from Gombe. Thus founded as an independent emirate in 1833, Muri, which was also known as the Hammaruwa kingdom, was ruled by Ruwa's descendants from Muri town (often called Hammaruwa) until 1893. Throughout this period, the kingdom paid tribute in slaves to the Sultan of Sokoto (the capital of the Fulani Empire, 464 mi west-northwest). William Balfour Baikie, the Scottish explorer, visited Muri in 1854 and described it in his *Narrative of an Exploring Voyage up the Rivers Kwo'ra and Binue* (1856).

Although Emir Muhammadu Nya signed a treaty in 1885 permitting the British Royal Niger Company (1886) to build a trading post at Ibi (104 mi southwest of Muri town), troubles with the company and the non-Muslim Jibu people led him to place the emirate under the short-lived (1892–93) French protectorate of Muri. Emir Nya also moved the emirate headquarters in 1893 to Jalingo (40 mi east-southeast), a war camp from which he sent sorties against the Mumuye tribesmen. The British established firm control over the region in 1900, and Muri emirate was incorporated as the Lau division of Muri Province (1900–26). Although Lau town (27 mi east) served as the emir's residence to 1910 and Mutum Biyu (Biu, 42 mi south) to 1917, Jalingo has been the emirate's capital and the headquarters of Muri division (1915) since 1917.

Muri division (area 11,014 sq mi [28,526 sq km]), which lies on both sides of the Benue River and is also drained by the Benue's Taraba and Pai tributaries, is now mainly inhabited by the Mumuye, Fulani, Wurkum, and Jukun peoples; but there is also a sizable

group of Hausa traders. Most of its inhabitants are engaged in farming—staple foods are guinea corn and millet—and in raising cattle, sheep, and goats. Cotton and peanuts (groundnuts) are the chief cash crops cultivated in the north, and soya beans and yams are important in the south. There is considerable fishing along the Benue. Salt extraction is a traditional occupation of the women near Muri town, but imported European salt has reduced its significance. There is lead mining near Muri town around Zurak (21 mi west), a town just outside the Muri boundary in Wase emirate. Besides Muri town, which has a government health office, and Jalingo, which has a noted mosque, the chief settlements of the emirate are Lau, Mutum Biyu, and Gassol. Pop. (1972 est.) 10,951.
·map, Nigeria **13**:86

Muria, people of the Madhya Pradesh region of India.
·bison-horn dance performance **17**:163g

Muricidae (snail family): *see* murex.

Muridae, large family of rodents (order Rodentia) containing about 100 genera and 460 living species, among them the common household rats and mice (*Rattus* and *Mus*). The family, known collectively as the Old World rats and mice, is basically Asian, but the household rats and mice have been introduced almost worldwide by man. For well-known or economically important members of the family *see* bandicoot rat; cloud rat; field mouse; harvest mouse; mouse; pouched rat; rat; spiny mouse; water rat.
·classification and general features **15**:978e

Murillo, Bartolomé Esteban (baptized Jan. 1, 1618, Seville, Spain—d. April 3, 1682, Seville), the most popular Baroque religious artist of 17th-century Spain, noted for his idealized, sometimes precious manner. Murillo, like most Spanish painters of his time outside the court, devoted himself mainly to religious subjects. Among his chief patrons were the religious orders, especially the Franciscans, and the confraternities in Seville and Andalucia.

Among Murillo's earliest works is the "Virgin of the Rosary" (*c.* 1642; Archbishop's Palace, Seville). In the vestigial style of his artistically conservative Sevillian master, Juan del Castillo, this early work combines 16th-century Italian mannerism and Flemish realism. The 11 paintings that originally hung in the small cloister of San Francisco in Seville—*e.g.*, the "Ecstasy of St. Diego of Alcalá" (1646; Louvre)—are executed in the more contemporary naturalistic style of the Sevillian school, established by Velázquez and continued by Zurbarán. That series is characterized by realism and tenebrism (contrasting light and shade) and use of commonplace models, with an emphasis on genre or scenes of everyday life, in the Andalucian tradition of painting *bodegónes* (*q.v.*).

In the 1650s a striking transformation of style occurred, usually attributed to a visit to Madrid, where Murillo undoubtedly met Velázquez and studied the works of Titian, Rubens, and Van Dyck in the royal collections. The softly modelled forms, rich colours, and broad brushwork of the 1652 "Immaculate Conception" (Seville) reflect direct visual contact with the art of the 16th-century Venetians and the Flemish. The "St. Leandro" and "St. Isidoro" (1655; sacristy of Seville Cathedral) are even further removed from the simple naturalism of his earlier Franciscan saints. These seated figures, more than life size, are in the grand manner of Baroque portraiture, which had become fashionable at the Spanish court.

The "Vision of St. Anthony" (1656; Seville Cathedral), one of Murillo's most celebrated pictures, is an early example of his so-called "vaporous" style, which was derived from Venetian painting. The compositional elements of this work apparently were influenced by the late Roman Baroque style, which had been introduced into Seville by Francisco Herrera the Younger. But, unlike Herrera and his other Sevillian contemporary, Juan de Valdés Leal, Murillo never adopted its more exaggerated elements: crowded space, violent movement, and excited gesture.

Increasingly a painter of mystic event and emotion, he retained his early interest in genre and narrative. Murillo's religious images, though idealized and often sentimental, are based on popular local types. The prominence he gives to homely accessory figures, particularly children, and to familiar details of everyday life, give an intimate character to his spiritual subjects.

"The Two Trinities," oil on canvas by Bartolome Esteban Murillo, *c.* 1681; in the National Gallery, London

By courtesy of the trustees of the National Gallery, London; photograph, J.R. Freeman & Co. Ltd.

In 1660 Murillo was one of the founders and first president of the Academy of Painting in Seville. During the two following decades he executed several important commissions, including the series of pictures for the Sevillian churches of Santa María la Blanca (completed 1665) and the Hospital de la Caridad (completed 1674), and 22 pictures for the Capuchins (completed 1676). Those works are characterized by masterful technique, attention to detail, and the frequent use of romantically conceived settings. Generally they represent dramatized genre on a grand scale, especially the paintings for the Hospital de la Caridad.

From 1678 onward Murillo worked on another series of paintings for the Hospicio de Venerables Sacerdotes in Seville, which included the celebrated "Soult Immaculate Conception" (1678; Louvre). Murillo's late style is exemplified by his unfinished works for the Capuchin church at Cadíz and the "Two Trinities" (popularly known as the "Holy Family"). The often mystical significance of his subjects is countered by the idealized reality of his figures based on familiar human archetypes, with natural gestures and tender, devout expressions, creating an effect of intimate rather than exalted religious sentiment.

Murillo's religious art, with its manifest appeal to popular piety, illustrates the teaching of the Counter-Reformation church. His paintings principally depict acts of faith and charity, mystical experiences, and the Virgin, above all the "Immaculate Conception," a cult that was enormously popular in Spain, especially Andalucia. His idealized infant "portraits" of Christ and St. John the Baptist, have their secular counterparts in his numerous rustic scenes with picaresque beggar children, though the latter have the features and expressions of individual Andalucian models; *e.g.*, "The Young Beggar" (Louvre) or "The Pie Eater" (*c.* 1670–75; Alte Pinakothek, Munich). His few portraits give an impression of unaffected likeness. The "Self-Portrait" (*c.* 1675; National Gallery, London) shows him in middle age, with an aspect as gentle and tranquil as is the nature of his art.

Murillo had many pupils and innumerable followers. His paintings were copied and imitated throughout Spain and its empire. He was the first Spanish painter to achieve widespread European fame, and until the 19th century he was the only Spanish artist whose works were widely known outside the Hispanic world. Formerly ranked as one of the greatest masters of painting, his usually facile technique, melodramatic spirituality, and sweet sentimentality did not appeal to 20th-century taste, and he lost popularity.
·Baroque painting developments **19**:425d
·"Boys Eating Grapes and Melon," oil painting, illus., **19**:Visual Arts, Western, Plate XVIII
·Carracci's stylistic influence **3**:958b

Murillo, Gerardo, also called DR. ATL (1875–1964) painter, writer, and revolutionary who was one of the pioneers in Mexico of the movement for artistic nationalism (*Méxicanismo*) and of the mural painting renaissance. From his student days at the Academia de San Carlos in Mexico City Murillo was passionately interested in the native art of Mexico, the creation of an indigenous modern artistic style or expression, and with the depiction of the Mexican landscape—his most famous paintings and drawings being of the Valley of Mexico and the volcanoes of Popocatépetl and Ixtacihuatl. Murillo is most commonly known by his Aztec name Atl (the Náhuatl word for "water") which he adopted as a repudiation of his Spanish heritage and as a demonstration of his pride in his Mexican Indian ancestors and their culture. Atl colours, a type of crayon made of wax, resin, oil, and pigment, were invented and used by him for both drawings and murals.
·cultural nationalism movement **13**:741h

murine typhus, or ENDEMIC TYPHUS, an infectious disease caused by *Rickettsia mooseri* (or *typhi*). Rat fleas, *Xenopsylla cheopis*, and the rat louse *Polyplax spinulosa* transmit the disease from rats to man.
·host-parasite relationships **9**:558b
·rodent disease transmission **15**:971b

Muris, Jean de (b. *c.* 1290, Normandy?—d. *c.* 1351, Paris), philosopher and mathematician who was a leading proponent of the new musical style of the 14th century. In his treatise *Ars novae musicae* (1319; "The Art of the New Music") he enthusiastically supported the great changes in musical style and notation occurring in the 14th century and associated with the composer and theorist Philippe de Vitry, whose book, *Ars Nova* (1320; "The New Art"), gave its name to the style of 14th-century music. De Muris was long believed to be the author of the important treatise *Speculum Musices*, an attack on these innovations now known to be by Jacques de Liège. De Muris, who taught at the Sorbonne, knew many of the great composers of his day and corresponded with De Vitry. Apparently he composed no music. In his treatise, translated in part in W.O. Strunk's *Source Readings in Music History* (1950), he argues for the acceptance of divisions and subdivisions of musical metre, which were not recognized in earlier music theory but became common in musical practice and notation.

Mu River, in north central Burma, flows south through Katha and Shwebo districts to

the Irrawaddy River west of Sagaing. The Mu, about 170 mi (274 km) long, has been used for irrigation in the Dry Zone since the 9th century; the current Mu Valley Irrigation Project is the largest in Burma.
21°56′ N, 95°38′ E
·Irrawaddy River irrigation for Dry Zone **9**:899d
·map, Burma **3**:505

Murji'ah (sing. Murji'; hence Murjites, Arabic, "Those Who Postpone"), one of the earliest Islāmic sects to believe in the postponement (*irjā'*, whence Murji'ah) of judgment on committers of serious sins, recognizing God alone as being able to decide whether or not a Muslim had lost his faith.

The Murji'ah flourished during the turbulent period of Islāmic history that began with the murder of ʿUthmān (third caliph) in AD 656, and ended with the assassination of ʿAlī (fourth caliph) in AD 661 and the subsequent establishment of the Umayyad dynasty (ruled until AD 750). During that period the Muslim community was divided into hostile factions, divided on the issue of the relationship of *islām* and *īmān* or works and faith. The most militant were the Khārijites, who held the extreme view that serious sinners should be ousted from the community and that *jihād* (holy war) should be declared on them. This led the adherents of the sect to revolt against the Umayyads, whom they regarded as corrupt and unlawful rulers. The Murji'ah took the opposite stand asserting that no one who once professed Islām could be declared *kāfir* (infidel), mortal sins notwithstanding. Revolt against a Muslim ruler, therefore, could not be justified under any circumstances. The Murji'ah remained neutral in the disputes that divided the Muslim world and called for passive resistance rather than armed revolt against unjust rulers. This point of view was blessed and encouraged by the Umayyads, who saw the political quietism and religious tolerance of the Murji'ah as support for their own regime. The Murji'ah, however, regarded their tolerance of the Umayyads as accidental and based only on religious grounds and on the recognition of the importance of law and order.

The Murji'ah were the moderates and liberals of Islām, who emphasized the love and goodness of God and labelled themselves *ahl al-waʿd* (the adherents of promise). To them external actions and utterances did not necessarily reflect an individual's inner beliefs. Some of their extremists, such as Jahm ibn Ṣafwān (d. AD 746), regarded faith as purely an inward conviction, thus allowing a Muslim outwardly to profess other religions and remain a Muslim, since only God could determine the true nature of his faith.
·doctrine of postponement **9**:1013g

Murle, Chari-Nile-speaking people of the Ethiopia–Sudan border; they number about 40,000. The Murle are seminomadic pastoralists.
·peoples of the eastern Sudan map **6**:165
·Sudan ethnic composition map **17**:762

Murle-Didinga languages, group of closely related Chari-Nile languages spoken on both sides of the Sudan–Ethiopia boundary.

Murmansk, *oblast* (administrative region), northwestern Russian Soviet Federated Socialist Republic, with an area of 55,950 sq mi (144,900 sq km) occupying the Kola Peninsula between the White and Barents seas. Its upland blocks and mountain massifs, rising to 3,907 ft (1,191 m) in the Khibiny Mountains, are covered by tundra in the north and swampy forest, or taiga, in the south. The economy is dominated by mineral exploitation, principally apatite, nephelinite, iron, and nickel; fishing is important along the coasts. Its administrative centre is Murmansk town. Pop. (1970) 799,000.
·location and features **17**:330c

Murmansk, seaport and centre of Murmansk *oblast* (administrative region), northwestern Russian Soviet Federated Socialist Republic, lying on the eastern shore of the long, narrow Kola inlet, 30 mi (50 km) from the ice-free Barents Sea. The town, founded in

Harbour at Murmansk, Russian S.F.S.R.
Bavaria-Verlag/IDF

1915 as a supply port in World War I, was a base for the British, French, and American expeditionary forces against the Bolsheviks in 1918. In World War II Murmansk served as the main port for Anglo-American convoys carrying war supplies to the U.S.S.R. through the Arctic Ocean. The ice-free harbour has ship repair yards and is a large fishing base. Education and research establishments include a teacher-training institute and a research institute of marine fisheries and oceanography. Murmansk is the largest town in the world north of the Arctic Circle. Pop. (1970) 309,000.
68°58′ N, 33°05′ E
·Barents Sea fishing and air temperature **2**:722b
·map, Soviet Union **17**:322

Murmansk Rise, submarine feature, Arctic Ocean.
75°00′ N, 37°00′ E
·Arctic Ocean floor features map **1**:1120

Murmean Sea (Arctic): *see* Barents Sea.

Murmur of the Heart (1971), film by Louis Malle.
·plot and theme **12**:536h

Murnau, F. W., pseudonym of FRIEDRICH WILHELM PLUMPE (b. Dec. 28, 1889, Bielefeld, Ger.—d. March 11, 1931, Hollywood), motion-picture director who revolutionized the art of cinematic expression by using the camera subjectively to interpret the emotional state of a character. He was educated at the Universities of Heidelberg and Berlin, where he was greatly influenced by the theatrical innovations of Max Reinhardt, the famous German stage director. During World War I service, Murnau assisted in the making of propaganda films. After the war he made a number of films, including *Der Januskopf* (1920; released in the U.S. as *Dr. Jekyll and Mr. Hyde*), a version of the Dr. Jekyll and Mr. Hyde legend; *Schloss Vogelöd* (1921; "Vogelod Castle"); and *Der brennender Acker* (1922; "The Burning Soil"), in which he employed close-ups to further the action. All contained the beginnings of an Expressionist style and his initial experimentation with the camera. Murnau's first important picture was *Nosferatu* (1922), an early film treatment of the vampire legend that incorporated technical effects such as white trees against a black sky.

The Last Laugh (*Der letzte Mann*, 1924), a collaboration between Murnau and the creative scriptwriter Carl Mayer, established his reputation as one of the foremost German directors. Its mobile camera style and the interpretive use of the camera to record the emotions of the aging doorman, made an international impact on the cinema. The camera moved through city streets, crowded tenements and hotel corridors, playing an integral role in the film by recording people and incidents through a limited point of view.

Murnau's next two films, *Tartuffe* (1925) and *Faust* (1926), were followed by the Hollywood-made films *Sunrise* (1927), *Four Devils* (1928), and *City Girl* (1930). His final film was *Tabu* (1931), an idyllic study of the South Seas, codirected with Robert Flaherty, the pioneer documentary film maker.
·camera tricks and devices **12**:524b

Murner, Thomas (1475–1537), German Franciscan friar, was an opponent of the Reformation. His fame rests on a number of satirical poems attacking the corruption of the age.

Muro Kyūsō (b. 1658, Edo, now Tokyo—d. 1734, Edo), noted Japanese Confucian scholar who, as a leading government official, helped propagate the philosophy of the famous Chinese Confucian thinker Chu Hsi (1130–1200). Muro interpreted Chu Hsi's emphasis on loyalty to one's ruler to mean loyalty to the Tokugawa shogun, the hereditary military dictator of Japan, rather than loyalty to the Japanese emperor, whom the shogun had relegated to no more than a symbolic role in the Japanese government. Muro thus helped establish the philosophical underpinning to the Tokugawa shogunate (1603–1867).

The son of a physician, Muro acquired his own belief in Chu Hsi only after prolonged and intense personal struggle. He was appointed to high office by the reformist shogun Tokugawa Yoshimune (reigned 1716–45) at a time when unorthodox views had become widely prevalent and the shogun's role in the government had begun to be questioned. Muro helped enforce orthodox thought, emphasizing the necessity of righteous behaviour, including duty to parents and to the shogun. Moreover, in keeping with the Confucian bias against commerce, he attempted to slow the rapid social and economic changes occurring in Japan.

Murom, town, Vladimir *oblast* (administrative region), western Russian Soviet Federated Socialist Republic, on the Oka River. It is one of the oldest Russian towns, first mentioned in 862. Surviving historic buildings include the Trinity and Annunciation monasteries and the churches of the Resurrection and Transfiguration, all from the 17th century. The contemporary town has engineering, textile, and sawmilling industries. Pop. (1970) 99,000.
55°34′ N, 42°02′ E

Muromachi period, in Japanese cultural history, the period of the Ashikaga shogunate (1338–1573); so-called because the shoguns' capital was at Kyōto, in the Muromachi district.
·development in Kyōto **10**:561c
·dress styles of samurai women **5**:1037h
·Japanese visual arts features and development **19**:232a; illus. 233
·lacquer ritual objects **10**:578b
·literary developments **10**:1069b
·pottery styles and decoration **14**:926h
·sectarian activity **10**:110f
·tsuba design, illus., **11**:Metalwork, Plate IV

Muromets, Ilya: *see* Ilya of Murom.

Muroran, city, southern Hokkaido, Japan, on the Chikyū-misaki (Cape Chikyū) at the entrance to Uchiura-wan (Uchiura Bay). It is a major industrial centre known for its iron and steel production. The port handles coal, wood and wood pulp, and marine products.

Iron mill in Muroran, Japan
Imperial Press—FPG

Muroran is connected by rail to other Hokkaido cities. Pop. (1976 est.) 158,717.
42°18′ N, 140°59′ E
·map, Japan **10**:36

Murovdag, mountain, Azerbaijan S.S.R.
40°18′ N, 46°19′ E
·Azerbaijan's relief features **2**:544c

Murphy, Charles Francis (1858–1924), New York politician.
·New York City political history **13**:37e

Murphy, Frank, original name WILLIAM FRANCIS MURPHY (b. April 13, 1890, Harbor Beach, Mich.—d. July 19, 1949, Detroit), associate justice of the Supreme Court of the United States from 1940 until his death, noted for his militant defense of individual liberties and civil rights and for his insistence on doing substantial justice irrespective of legal technicalities.

As mayor of Detroit (1930–33), Murphy gained national prominence for his efforts to aid the unemployed. Appointed by Pres. Franklin D. Roosevelt, he served as governor general (1933–35) and U.S. high commissioner (1935–36) in the Philippines, where he supported the independence movement. As governor of Michigan (1937–38), he earned the admiration of organized labour and the hatred of some industrialists (who brought about his defeat for re-election) by refusing to employ troops to break sit-down strikes by automobile workers. While serving as U.S. attorney general (1939–40), he established the Civil Rights Unit (now Division) of the Department of Justice. Perhaps Murphy's greatest judicial opinion was his dissent in *Korematsu* v. *United States* 323 U.S. 214 (1944), in which he denounced as "legalization of racism" the government's wartime internment of Japanese-American residents of the West Coast. His dissent in *Wolf* v. *Colorado* 338 U.S. 25 (1949), in which the court held that illegally seized criminal evidence was admissible in state (though not in federal) courts, was vindicated when a later court overruled the *Wolf* decision (*Mapp* v. *Ohio*, 1961).

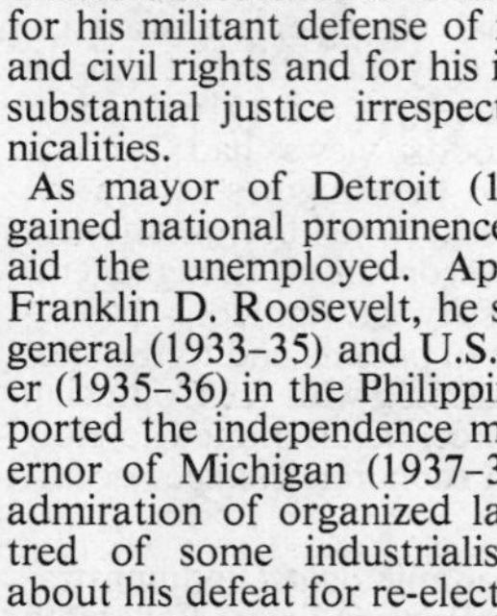

Frank Murphy
By courtesy of the Library of Congress, Washington, D.C.

Murphy, Isaac (b. 1856, Fayette County, Ky.—d. Feb. 12, 1896), outstanding jockey in U.S. Thoroughbred racing, the first to ride three Kentucky Derby winners (1884, 1890, 1891). He was the best known of a number of black jockeys who performed successfully in the late 19th century (black jockeys won 13 of the first 28 Kentucky derbies, 1875–1902) until racial discrimination forced them off the tracks. In his long career (1873–96), Murphy rode 628 winners in 1,412 recorded races. He scored victories in four of the first five American derbies (1884–86 and 1888). In 1955 he was elected to the National Museum of Racing Hall of Fame, Saratoga Springs, N.Y., and the next year he was chosen a member of the Jockeys' Hall of Fame, Pimlico, Md.
·horse racing record **8**:1098f

Murphy, John B(enjamin) (b. Dec. 21, 1857, Appleton, Wis.—d. Aug. 11, 1916, Mackinac Island, Michigan), surgeon who introduced and popularized early removal of the appendix in all cases of suspected appendicitis. He served as professor of surgery at Rush Medical College, Chicago (1905–08), and at the Northwestern University medical school, Chicago (1901–05, 1908–16).

In 1889 he established a pattern of early symptoms for appendicitis and strongly urged immediate removal of the appendix when this pattern appeared. Although Murphy's program first met with incredulity and derision from his colleagues, his more than 200 successful appendectomies over the next several years provided ample evidence to make the operation common medical practice.

He also introduced (1892) the anastomosis (Murphy's) button to join segments of the intestine without sutures and was first in the U.S. to induce (1898) artificial immobilization and collapse of the lung in treatment of pulmonary tuberculosis.

Murphy, Robert D(aniel) (1894–1978), U.S. diplomat.
·Allied North African invasion **19**:996f

Murphy, William Francis: *see* Murphy, Frank.

Murphy, William P(arry) (b. Feb. 6, 1892, Stoughton, Wis.), physician who with George R. Minot in 1926 reported success in the treatment of pernicious anemia with liver diet. Their discovery culminated in 1948 in vitamin B_{12} therapy, by which a previously fatal disorder became amenable to treatment. The Minot–Murphy research was suggested by George H. Whipple's demonstration that liver is essential for blood formation in animals. In 1934 the Nobel Prize for Physiology or Medicine was awarded jointly to the three.

Murphy received his M.D. from Harvard University (1920). He joined the staff of Peter Bent Brigham Hospital in Boston in 1923, becoming consultant in hematology in 1958. From 1923 to 1958, when he became lecturer emeritus, he also taught at Harvard. He was the recipient of many other honours in addition to the Nobel Prize. His textbook *Anemia in Practice* was published in 1939.
·pernicious anemia therapy **11**:836a

Murray, city, seat (1842) of Calloway County, southwestern Kentucky, U.S., on the East Fork of Clarks River, west of Kentucky Lakes State Park and Land Between the Lakes Recreation Area. Founded in the 1830s and named for Congressman John L. Murray, it developed as an agricultural service centre. Its economic base was subsequently broadened by light manufacturing, notably of kitchen ranges. Clay and silica are worked locally. Murray State University was founded in 1922. Inc. city, 1844. Pop. (1980) 14,248.
36°37′ N, 88°19′ W
·map, United States **18**:909

Murray, city, Salt Lake County, north central Utah, U.S., on the Jordan River, near the Wasatch Range. Founded by Mormons in 1847, it was named for Eli H. Murray, governor of the Territory of Utah. An extension of the Union Pacific Railroad (1870) through the site aided the development of Murray as a smelting centre for nearby mining operations. It is also a trading and shipping outlet for irrigated farm produce (sugar beets, alfalfa, and potatoes). Inc. 1903. Pop. (1980) 25,750.
40°40′ N, 111°53′ W

Murray, Bruce C (1931–), U.S. geologist and planetary scientist.
·thermal properties of Martian surface **11**:524b

Murray, Donald, English developer of a time-division multiplex system of telegraphy in 1903.
·teletypewriter development **18**:72d

Murray, F(rancis) J(oseph) (1911–), U.S. mathematician.
·functional analysis fundamentals **1**:762a

Murray, Lord George (b. Oct. 4, 1694, Huntingtower, Perth—d. Oct. 11, 1760, Medemblik, Holland), Scottish Jacobite, one of the ablest of the generals who fought for Charles Edward the Young Pretender, the Stuart claimant to the English throne, in the Jacobite rebellion of 1745–46. Murray joined the English army in 1712 but aided the Jacobites in their unsuccessful rebellion of 1715. When Charles Edward invaded Scotland in 1745, Murray became a lieutenant general in the Jacobite army. He was largely responsible for the overwhelming Jacobite victory at Prestonpans, East Lothian, on September 21, and he skillfully directed the Jacobite retreat from Derby, Derbyshire, into Scotland in December. On Jan. 17, 1746, Murray defeated an English army at Falkirk, Stirling. He opposed Charles Edward's decision to make a stand at Culloden; after the Jacobite forces were defeated there on April 16, Murray withdrew to Ruthven. The Pretender then abandoned the enterprise and dismissed him. Murray escaped to the Continent, where he died.

Murray, Lord George (1761–1803), English bishop of St. David's from 1801; interested in mechanical contrivances, he became director of the telegraph (*i.e.*, semaphore) at the Admiralty in 1796.
·semaphore telegraph development **18**:67g; illus.

Murray, (George) Gilbert (Aimé) (b. Jan. 2, 1866, Sydney—d. May 20, 1957, Oxford), classical scholar whose translations of the masters of ancient Greek drama—Aeschylus, Sophocles, Euripides, and Aristophanes—brought their works to renewed popularity on the contemporary stage. Between 1904 and 1912 he personally directed many of the productions that made Greek theatre once more a living art. By translating into rhymed rather than blank verse, he attempted to revive the rhythmic quality of Greek poetry. Murray also applied insights from the then-new science of anthropology to his other scholarly studies. Hence he was able to increase understanding of Homer and of the older forms of Greek religion. Among his many works in this vein are *The Rise of the Greek Epic* (1907) and *Five Stages of Greek Religion* (2nd ed.; revised and enlarged, 1925).

Murray became professor of Greek at Glasgow University at the age of 23 and regius professor of Greek at Oxford in 1908, where he remained until his retirement in 1936.
·evaluation of Gandhi **7**:876g

Murray, Gordon (1896–1976), Canadian surgeon.
·heart defect surgery **11**:840d

Murray, Grover Elmer (b. Oct. 26, 1916, Maiden, N.C.), geologist known for his research on the Tertiary stratigraphy (rock layers 2,500,000 to 65,000,000 years old) of the southern U.S. and the general occurrence of petroleum.

Murray was professor of geology at Louisiana State University (Baton Rouge) from 1948 to 1966 (Boyd professor from 1955), when he became president of Texas Technological University (Lubbock); in 1969 he became president of the School of Medicine of that university. He studied the salt domes and petroleum geology of the Gulf, the Atlantic coastal plains, and Australia and conducted research concerning rock and time-rock geologic units in stratigraphy. He was the author of *Geology of the Atlantic and Gulf Coastal Province of North America* (1961).

Murray, G(eorge) W(illiam) (1885–1966), British anthropologist.
·Nilotic family's wider relationships **1**:227e

Murray, H(arold) J(ames) R(uthven) (1868–1955), historian of Chess.
·Chess origins and history **4**:195h

Murray, Henry Alexander (1893–), U.S. psychologist who made valuable contributions to the study of human motivation and who advanced a theory of personality in which the concept of need was made pivotal. With C.D. Morgan he developed the Thematic Apperception Test, with which they attempted to determine personality dynamics both in the momentary cross section and from the longitudinal life history. He wrote *Explorations in Personality* (1938).
·motivational theory and human needs **12**:562a
·personality measurement and research **14**:117b

Murray, James (b. Jan. 21, 1721, Ballencrief, East Lothian—d. June 18, 1794, near Battle, Sussex), soldier who was military and civilian governor of Quebec from 1760 to 1768.

Murray joined the army in 1740 and served in the West Indies and Europe. Sent to North

Gen. James Murray (d. 1794), detail of a portrait by an unknown artist
By courtesy of the Archives Nationales du Quebec

America in 1757 as a lieutenant colonel during the Seven Years' War, in 1758 he commanded a brigade during the successful British siege of Louisbourg, in what is now Nova Scotia, under Lord Amherst. He was one of Gen. James Wolfe's three brigadiers in the British expedition against Quebec in 1759. After the British captured the city, Murray was made its military governor. When the French capitulated in 1760, he became military governor of Quebec district; he became the first civil governor of Quebec after its formal cession to Great Britain in 1763.

As governor, Murray opposed repressive measures against French-Canadians, and his conciliatory policy led to charges against him of partiality. Although exonerated, he left his post in 1768 and was appointed governor of Minorca in 1774. He surrendered to French and Spanish troops there in 1782, for which he was court-martialled in England; after being acquitted, he was made a general.
·French-Canadian sympathy and fate **3**:737c

Murray, Sir James (Augustus Henry) (b. Feb. 7, 1837, Denholm, Roxburgh—d. July 26, 1915, Oxford), lexicographer and editor of *A New English Dictionary on Historical Principles*, now known as *The Oxford English Dictionary* (the *OED*). He was a grammar school teacher from 1855 to 1885, during which time he also wrote a famous article on the English language for *Encyclopædia Britannica* (1878) and served as president of the Philological Society (1878–1880, 1882–1884). He undertook the editing of a vast dictionary that was intended as an inventory of words used in English from the mid-12th century and, in some instances, from earlier dates. Construction of the dictionary was to be grounded on strict historical and descriptive principles, and each definition was to be accompanied by an example, including date, of usage. The first section, A–Ant, appeared in 1884, printed at the Clarendon Press, Oxford. From 1885 until his death, Murray lived at Oxford, working with a staggering volume of materials and completing about half of the dictionary, sections A–D, H–K, O, P, and T. It was his organization that made completion of the great undertaking possible.
·English dictionary development **6**:883d

Murray, James Stewart, earl of (Scottish regent): *see* Moray, James Stewart, earl of.

Murray, Sir John, Baronet, called MURRAY OF BROUGHTON (b. 1715—d. Dec. 6, 1777, Cheshunt, Hertfordshire), Scottish Jacobite, secretary to Prince Charles Edward (the Young Pretender) during the rebellion of 1745–46. He damaged the rebels' cause by his nervous collapse in March 1746 and later by his incrimination of other leading supporters of the Stuart claim to the British throne.

Murray served from 1741 as a Jacobite agent. After going to Rome to offer his services to Charles Edward, he proved himself—until his breakdown—an efficient aide to the Young Pretender. His incapacity caused the rebels' commissariat to become seriously disorganized. Subsequently, he was accused, perhaps unjustly, of fomenting trouble between Charles Edward and Lord George Murray, one of the best Jacobite generals. Murray then turned king's evidence, incriminating chiefly those who, in his judgement, had failed the Jacobite cause. Pardoned in 1748, Murray was shunned as a traitor and became insane.

Murray, John (1808–92), member of a family firm of London publishers, began in 1836 the famous series of guidebooks called "Murray's Handbooks" or "Murray's Red Guides," the first of their kind in assembling practical information. Murray wrote several volumes himself.
·Byron's publishing experiences **3**:545b
·collaboration with Disraeli **5**:898e
·publication of Melville's writings **11**:873h
·Quarterly Review publication **15**:250f

Murray, Sir John (b. March 3, 1841, Cobourg, Ont.—d. March 16, 1914, near Kirkliston, West Lothian), one of the founders of oceanography, whose particular interests were ocean basins, deep-sea deposits, and coral-reef formation. In 1868 he began collecting marine organisms and making a variety of oceanographic observations during an expedition to the Arctic islands of Jan Mayen and Spitsbergen, off Norway. He did much to organize the "Challenger" Expedition (1872–76), which made extremely valuable contributions in charting, surveying, and biological investigation, and to outfit it with equipment for conducting oceanographic studies. As a naturalist with the expedition, he was placed in charge of the biological specimens collected. Kept at Edinburgh, they attracted the attention of marine biologists from around the world for 20 years. After the death of the expedition's leader, Sir Wyville Thomson (1882), Murray completed the publication of the 50-volume *Report on the Scientific Results of the Voyage of H.M.S. Challenger* (1880–95). He also directed biological investigations of Scottish waters (1882–94), surveyed the depths of Scottish lakes (1906), and took part in a North Atlantic oceanographic expedition (1910). He was knighted in 1898. His writings include the paper "On the Structure and Origin of Coral Reefs and Islands" (1880) and, with Johan Hjort, *The Depths of the Ocean* (1912).
·Challenger Expedition **6**:83h

Murray, John Courtney (1904–67), Roman Catholic Jesuit priest and theologian who was a principal author of the Declaration on Religious Liberty at the Second Vatican Council.

Murray, Margaret (Alice) (1863–1963), British archaeologist and Egyptologist, made her first archaeological expedition to Egypt in 1902–04. She excavated in Malta and the Balearic Islands in 1921–23, in Petra in 1937, and in Palestine in 1938. She was the author of many books, including several on Egypt, and two (both often re-issued) on *The Witch-Cult in Western Europe* (1921) and *The God of the Witches* (1933). In 1963, the year of her death, she published two books, *My First Hundred Years* and *The Genesis of Religion.*
·accounting for present witch beliefs **19**:897d

Murray, Matthew (1765–1826), British designer of steam locomotives.
·steam-locomotive design **18**:653e

Murray, Philip (b. May 25, 1886, Blantyre, Lanark—d. Nov. 9, 1952, San Francisco), U.S. labour leader who organized the United Steelworkers of America (USWA) from 1936 and played a prominent part in the Congress of Industrial Organizations (CIO) through its early years, serving as its president from 1940 until his death.

Emigrating to the U.S. from his native Scotland in 1902, Murray became a coal miner in Pennsylvania and joined the United Mine Workers of America (UMWA). A member of the union's international board from 1912, he served as vice president from 1920 to 1942. In 1936, when John L. Lewis, UMW president, became the first president of the newly formed CIO, he gave Murray the responsibility for creating an industry-wide steelworkers' union. Murray was chairman of the Steelworkers Organizing Committee until 1942, when he

Philip Murray, 1945
By courtesy of the United Steelworkers of America

became president of its successor, the USWA, which in his lifetime grew to include 2,500 local unions. Earlier, on Nov. 22, 1940, he had replaced Lewis as CIO president.

Although Murray otherwise supported the U.S. effort in World War II, he opposed Pres. Franklin D. Roosevelt's plan (proposed in 1944 but never put into effect) for compulsory civilian labour in war industries. In 1949–50 he forced the expulsion of several Communist-dominated unions from the CIO.

Murray, William, 1st earl of Mansfield (British jurist): *see* Mansfield, William Murray, 1st earl of.

Murray Bridge, town, southeast South Australia, on the Murray River southeast of

Adelaide. Originally a stop for cattle drovers, the town was organized in 1860 as the Hundred of Mobilong and grew as a river port. A bridge across the Murray (1879) was followed by a rail span in 1886. In the early 1900s, swamps along the river were drained for farming, and the district now yields wheat, fruits, dairy produce, vegetables, and poultry. Proclaimed a municipality in 1924, the community was renamed Murray Bridge. It is now a food-processing centre, with some light manufactures and resort facilities. Pop. (1971 prelim.) 7,400.
35°07′ S, 139°17′ E
·map, Australia **2**:400

Murray Fracture Zone, long mountainous lineation on the North Pacific sea floor, trending east-northeast for 3,000 kilometres (1,900 miles) from 28° N latitude, 155° W longitude (north of the Hawaiian Islands) to the base of the continental slope off Los Angeles. Maximum relief of the feature is about 2,000 metres (6,600 feet). The fracture zone has an irregular topography composed of parallel asymmetric ridges, scarps, and elongate depressions. Regional depths of the sea floor north of the fracture zone are several hundred metres greater than those to the south. The patterns of magnetic intensity of the sea-floor rocks in the area appear to be displaced laterally by 150 to 680 kilometres, and rocks of the northern block are tens of millions of years older than adjacent rocks south of the fracture zone. This eastward displacement of the sea floor north of the fracture zone is only apparent, resulting from sea-floor spreading at a midocean ridge that was active from about 80,000,000 to about 10,000,000 years ago. Neither earthquakes nor volcanic activity occur along the fracture zone at present.
·Pacific Ocean floor features map **13**:838

Murray of Broughton: *see* Murray, Sir John, Baronet.

Murray Ridge, submarine feature, Arabian Sea.
21°45′ N, 61°50′ E
·Arabian Sea submarine topography **1**:1060c

Murray River, principal stream of Australia, flowing 1,609 mi (2,589 km) across southeast Australia from the Snowy Mountains to the Indian Ocean. Although it has a total catchment area of 414,253 sq mi (1,072,905 sq km), its average annual discharge is only 12,000,000 ac-ft (1,500,000 ha-m), and in places it has dried up on at least three occasions. Named after Colonial Secretary Sir George Murray, the river rises on The Pilot (a mountain), near Mt. Kosciusko in southeast New South Wales. It flows west and northwest, forming much of the boundary between New South Wales and Victoria, and passes through Hume Reservoir above Albury. At Morgan, South Australia, it bends sharply southward to flow through Lake Alexandrina to Encounter Bay on the Indian Ocean. For most of its course through South Australia (250 mi), the river is bordered by a narrow floodplain and flows between cliffs 100 ft (30 m) high. Its upper 200 mi cut through mountainous terrain. The central section, however, lies on a broad and mature floodplain, with the Riverina plains of New South Wales to the north and the plains of northern Victoria to the south. Its principal tributaries are the Darling, Lachlan, Murrumbidgee (*qq.v.*), Mitta Mitta, Ovens, Goulburn, Campaspe, and Loddon rivers.

The Murray Valley is of immense economic significance, lying across the great wheat-sheep belt in its climatically most reliable section. During the second half of the 19th century, river shipping was of great importance, but, with growing competition from railways and demand for irrigation water (first used at Mildura, 1886), navigation practically ceased.

Murray River near Tintalba, New South Wales
Picturepoint—Publix

The valley has by far the most considerable irrigation, both actual (more than 1,000,000 ac [400,000 ha]) and potential, of the continent. Its chief products are cattle, sheep, grains, fruit, and wine. In 1915 the River Murray Commission, comprising representatives from the three state governments and the commonwealth, was established to regulate utilization of the river's waters. Its largest works are the Hume Reservoir and Lake Victoria (at the South Australia border). The multipurpose Snowy Mountains scheme, a 30-year project, was begun in 1949 to make much more water available for irrigation. Principal towns in the valley are Albury, Echuca, Swan Hill, Mildura, Renmark, and Murray Bridge.
35°22′ S, 139°22′ E
·delta, tides, and discharge table **15**:868
·drainage area and discharge table **15**:877
·map, Australia **2**:400
·map, Australian External Territories **2**:433
·New South Welsh drainage **13**:12a
·Sturt course exploration **7**:1044h
·water supply and scarcity **17**:209c

Murray Valley encephalitis virus, virus responsible for a form of encephalitis (brain tissue inflammation) that occurs in various regions of Australia. The disease is also called Australian X disease.
·disease transmission and bird migration **9**:538h

murre (*Uria*), black and white seabird of the auk family (Alcidae, order Charadriiformes).

Common murre (*Uria aalge*), ringed phase at left
R.J. Tulloch—Bruce Coleman Inc.

In British usage the two species of *Uria* are called guillemots, along with *Cepphus* species. Murres are about 40 centimetres (16 inches) long. They nest in vast numbers on sheer cliffs, each pair laying a single egg, The chick matures rapidly; when half-grown it enters the sea, in parental company, to escape marauding gulls and skuas. In autumn the birds travel south by swimming.

The common murre (*U. aalge*) breeds from the Arctic Circle south to Nova Scotia, Portugal, British Columbia, and Korea. Atlantic populations include the so-called bridled, or ringed, murre, a mutation that shows, in breeding season, a ring around the eye and a thin, white stripe behind the eye. This characteristic is nearly absent in murres of Portugal but increases toward the northwest and is seen in 70 percent of Icelandic murres. Beyond Iceland bridling is uncommon, and it does not occur in Pacific populations.

The thick-billed, or Brünnich's, murre (*U. lomvia*), with a somewhat heavier beak, nests farther north, to Ellesmere Island and other islands within the Arctic Circle, where the common murre is absent.
·characteristics and classification **4**:33d; illus. 40

Murree, town and hill station, Rāwalpindi Division, Punjab Province, Pakistan, lies at 7,517 ft (2,291 m) above sea level in the Murree Hills and is connected by road with Rāwalpindi, Islāmābād, and Muzaffarābād. In 1850 it was created a municipality. It was the summer residence of the British Punjab government and is developing into the summer capital of Pakistan. It is a cottage-industries development centre and has a brewery. Latest census 6,954.
33°54′ N, 73°24′ E
·map, Pakistan **13**:893
·Punjabi climate and geography **15**:288d

murrelet, small, black and white diving bird of the North Pacific coasts. There are six species, belonging to the auk family (Alcidae, order Charadriiformes). Murrelets are about 20 centimetres (8 inches) long, thin billed and plain plumaged. They are sometimes called sea sparrows, as are auklets. They nest in crevices or burrows above high water. In some species the young go to sea when only two days old. Their webbed feet are nearly full sized at hatching.

Marbled murrelet (*Brachyramphas marmoratus*)
Painting by Gene M. Christman

Breeding in Alaska are the marbled murrelet (*Brachyramphus marmoratus*), seen as far south as California, and Kittlitz's murrelet, (*B. brevirostris*), which reaches Japan. Most southerly is Xantus's murrelet (*Endomychura hypoleucus*), which nests on the hot coast of Baja California and (like some gulls of the region) travels north in winter.
·characteristics and classification **4**:35d

Mürren, Alpine village, Bern canton, south central Switzerland, high above the Lauter-

Mürren, Switz., with the north face of Eiger, a peak in the Bernese Alps
Ewing Galloway

brunnen Valley in the Bernese Oberland, opposite the Jungfrau (13,642 ft [4,158 m]). It is the highest village in the canton (altitude 5,450 ft) that is inhabited all the year round. A noted health and international winter sports resort, it is also a ballooning centre with an annual international ballooning week. The Kandahar Ski Club was founded there in 1924. Since 1891 the main access has been by a mountain railway from Lauterbrunnen. An automobile road up the valley was under construction in the 1970s. Pop. (1970) 460.
46°34′ N, 7°54′ E
·map, Switzerland **17**:868

murrey, sanguine, a colour used in heraldry.
·heraldic colour usage **8**:787d

murrine, a streaky semiprecious stone mentioned by the natural historian Pliny the Elder (AD 23–79) and possibly either agate or fluorspar. Pliny referred to murrine vessels (*i.e.*, made from the stone known as murra) and also to murrine glass, by which he probably meant glass simulating murra. Marbled glass that has survived from Pliny's time and earlier accords well with his descriptions.

Murrow, Edward (Egbert) R(oscoe) (b. April 25, 1908, Greensboro, N.C.—d. April 27, 1965, Pawling, N.Y.), U.S. broadcast journalist and director of the United States Information Agency (USIA).

Murrow graduated from Washington State College (now University), Pullman; from 1930 to 1932 he served as president of the National Student Association, assistant director of the Institute of International Education from 1932 to 1935, and secretary of the Emergency Commission of Displaced German Scholars (1933–34).

He joined the Columbia Broadcasting System (CBS) in 1935 as director of Talks and Education. Sent to London in 1937 to head the network's European Bureau, he covered the German occupation of Austria and the Munich Conference in 1938, the take-over of Czechoslovakia in 1939, and major developments in Great Britain, especially after the outbreak of World War II.

Back in the U.S. after the war, he became CBS vice president in charge of all news, education, and discussion programs. He returned to broadcasting in September 1947 with a weeknight newscast. Over the next 13 years he produced a series of highly acclaimed programs: with Fred W. Friendly he produced *Hear It Now*, an hour-long weekly news digest, and a comparable television series, *See It Now*, starting in 1951, with Murrow as the anchor man; and in 1954 he produced a notable exposé of Sen. Joseph McCarthy, who had gained prominence with largely undocumented charges of Communist infiltration of the U.S. Department of State and other government agencies. Murrow was also producer and host of *Person to Person* (1953–60) and *Small World* (1958–60). In 1960 he produced "Harvest of Shame," a special documentary for CBS News on the plight of the migratory farm workers.

Appointed in 1961 by Pres. John F. Kennedy as director of the U.S. Information Agency, Murrow did much to give a balanced picture of the U.S. to the world and to restore personnel who had been removed during the McCarthy era. Often televised while smoking a cigarette, he resigned in December 1963, suffering from lung cancer.

Murrumbidgee River, major right-bank tributary of the Murray, rises on the west slope of the Eastern Highlands (20 mi [32 km] north of Kiandra), in southeast New South Wales, Australia. It flows at first southeastward and then, after a remarkable fishhook bend, directly northward through the Australian Capital Territory. At Yass it trends westward, being joined by the Lachlan between Maude and Balranald, and enters the Murray 140 mi from the Victoria border, after a course of 1,050 mi. Explored by Charles Sturt (1829–30), its Aboriginal name means Big Water or Overflowing.

The river's drainage basin occupies 10,700 sq mi (27,700 sq km), and the Murrumbidgee Irrigation Area, roughly around the mid-course and its adjoining plains, is a highly organized and productive undertaking involving more than 1,000 sq mi of farmland. Established in 1912, the irrigation project was expanded to include the resettlement of former soldiers after World War I. It supports livestock pastures, grapes, citrus fruits, wheat, and cotton, and its rice yields are among the world's highest. Chief sources of irrigation water are the Burrinjuck and Berembed reservoirs. Water is also diverted across the divide into the Murrumbidgee's headstreams as part of the complex Snowy Mountains irrigation-hydroelectric development scheme. Important valley towns include Canberra (the federal capital), Yass, Wagga Wagga, Narrandera, Hay, and Balranald.
39°43′ S, 143°12′ E
·map, Australia **2**:400

Murry, John Middleton (b. Aug. 6, 1889, London—d. March 13, 1957, Bury St. Edmonds, Suffolk), journalist and critic whose romantic and biographical approach to literature ran counter to the leading critical tendencies of his day. He wrote at least 40 books and a large body of journalistic works in which his pronounced—though changeable—views on social, political, and religious questions were constantly before the public. He was the husband of short-story writer Katherine Mansfield and a close associate of D.H. Lawrence, both of whom influenced his development as a writer. During World War I the Murrys and Lawrences were neighbors in Cornwall, and something of the relationship between the two couples appears in Lawrence's *Women in Love*. Murry also appears, harshly lampooned, as the character Burlap in Aldous Huxley's *Point Counter Point*.

Murry began his career as editor of *Rhythm* while at Brasenose College, Oxford. He was editor of *Athenaeum* (1919–1921) and founding editor of *Adelphi* (1923–48), both literary magazines. As a pacifist, he edited *Peace News* during World War II and ran a Christian community on a farm near Colchester with the help of conscientious objectors. After the war, however, learning of the Nazi concentration camp atrocities, he renounced his former total pacifism. Among his numerous critical works are studies of Mansfield (*Katherine Mansfield and Other Literary Portraits*, 1949) and Lawrence (*Son of Woman, the Story of D.H. Lawrence*, 1931), as well as several works on Keats. As a man who believed that knowledge of a writer's private life was necessary to an understanding of his works, Murry made his autobiographical *Between Two Worlds* (1935) strikingly revealing about his own.
·Lawrence friendship and quarrels **10**:722g

Murry, Kathleen: *see* Mansfield, Katherine.

Mursa, Battle of (Sept. 28, AD 351), defeat of the usurper Magnentius by the Roman emperor Constantius II. Known as the bloodiest battle of the century, Mursa entailed losses on both sides that severely hurt the military strength of the Roman Empire. It was also the first defeat of Roman legionaries by heavy cavalry.

In 350, having deposed the emperor Constans in the western provinces and the self-proclaimed emperor Nepotanius in Rome, Magnentius failed to gain Constantius' recognition in the eastern provinces. Constantius organized Germans on the Rhine frontier but was defeated in 351 at Atrans (modern Trojane, Yugos.). Refusing Constantius' offer of compromise and suffering setbacks at Siscia (modern Sisak, Yugos.) and Sirmium (modern Sremska Mitrovica, Yugos.), Magnentius pursued Constantius to Mursa (modern Osijek, Yugos.). Constantius was outnumbered but managed to defeat Magnentius after prolonged savage fighting. Losses suffered by the victors (30,000) exceeded those of the routed force (24,000).
·Roman civil war massacre **15**:1127c

Murshidābād, historic town and district, Jalpaiguri division, West Bengal state, India. The town, lying just east of the Bhāgīrathi River, is an agricultural trade and silk-weaving centre. Originally called Makhsudābād, it was reputedly founded by the Mughal emperor Akbar in the 16th century. In 1704 the nawab Murshid Qulī Khān transferred the capital there from Dacca and renamed the town Murshidābād. It continued to be the capital under the British until 1790 and is still the seat of the prominent descendants of the nawabs of Bengal.

Of historic interest are Niẓāmat Kila (the palace of the nawabs), built in the Italianate style in 1837; Pearl Lake (Moti Jhīl) just to the south, with Murādbāgh Palace; and Khushbāgh Cemetery, containing the tombs of ʿAlī Vardī Khān, the last great nawab, and Siraj-ud-Dawlah, his grandson, who was defeated by the British at the Battle of Plassey. Constituted a municipality in 1869, Murshidābād has two colleges affiliated with the University of Calcutta.

Murshidābād district (area 2,056 sq mi [5,325 sq km]) comprises two distinct regions separated by the Bhāgīrathi River (*q.v.*). To the west lies the Rārh, a high undulating continuation of the Chota Nāgpur Plateau. The eastern portion, the Bagri, is a fertile, low-lying alluvial tract, part of the Ganges Delta. The district is drained by the Bhāgīrathi and Jalangi rivers and their tributaries. Rice, jute, legumes, oilseeds, wheat, barley, and mangoes are the chief crops in the east; extensive mulberry cultivation is carried out in the west. District headquarters are in Berhampore (*q.v.*). The district became part of the Gaur kingdom in 1197 and passed to the British East India Company in the 18th century. Pop. (1971 prelim.) town, 16,618; district, 2,942,125.
·West Bengal's industrial population **19**:787g

Mursilis (MURSHILISH) **I,** Hittite king (reigned *c.* 1620–*c.* 1590 BC) during the Old Kingdom. Succeeding his grandfather, Hattusilis I, on the throne, Mursilis first continued his predecessor's campaigns in northern Syria, destroying Halap (Aleppo) and delivering the final blow to Mari. He then turned eastward, and by raiding Babylon he put an end to the Amorite dynasty there. This event, recorded in Babylonian sources, firmly linked Hittite chronology with that of Babylonia. Mursilis also fought the Hurrians on the upper Euphrates River and returned to his capital, Hattusas (modern Boğaköy, in Turkey), with rich booty and many captives. Soon after his return, however, he was killed in a palace conspiracy planned by his brother-in-law Hantilis.
·Babylonian campaign against Hurrians **1**:817f
·invasion of Syria **17**:935d

Mursilis II, also spelled MURSHILISH, Hittite king (reigned *c.* 1334–*c.* 1306 BC) during the New Kingdom. Son of the great Hittite conqueror Suppiluliumas, he succeeded his father after the brief reign of his older brother Arnuwandas III. Mursilis renewed the allegiance of North Syria, particularly Carchemish (controlled by his brother Shar-Kushukh) and the kingdom of Amurru; he also conducted a successful campaign against the western kingdom of Arzawa, one of the main threats to the Hittite realm. Chronic trouble with the Kaska in the north necessitated almost annual pacification operations (10 in all), and the region of Azzi-Hayasa (east of the Kaska) also had to be reconquered by Mursilis in a number of campaigns. A prolific personal annalist, Mursilis also edited an account of his father's exploits; his detailed descriptions of his own

campaigns have yielded valuable information about Hittite military strategy.
·Babylonian epigraphic recording 6:917d
·Hittite stabilization of empire 1:818g

Murtaḍā, al-, 11th-century Islāmic Shīʿite theologian.
·Muʿtazilite theology in Shīʿism 9:1017f

Murtaḍā, Muḥammad al- (d. *c.* 1790), Yemenite Muslim scholar and exponent of the thought of the 12th-century Arabic philosopher al-Ghazālī, contributed to the intellectual orthodox Muslim reform that paralleled the sudden Wahhābī Islāmic revival throughout the Ottoman Empire and India during the 18th and 19th centuries.
·Islāmic reform and renewal 9:936f
·literary achievements 9:967g

Murtana (Turkey): *see* Perga.

Murtazā (d. 1588), ruler of Ahmadnagar, India.
·Ahmadnagar's political decline 9:373e

mūrti (Sanskrit: "image"), in Hindu sculpture, the conventional stance of a deity.
·Hindu hieratic conventions in sculpture 8:928f

Murtzuphlus, Alexius Ducas: *see* Alexius V.

Murugan, chief deity of the ancient Tamils of South India, later identified in part with the Hindu god Skanda. He probably originated as a fertility god, and his worship is said to have included orgiastic dancing. He is described as joining his fierce mother, Korravai, in cannibal feasts on the battlefield, a practice that authorities use to explain his association with the North Indian war god Skanda. His favourite weapon was the trident, or spear, and his banner carried the emblem of a wild fowl. The *Tirumurukārruppaṭai*, a "guide to the worship of the god Murugan," is a description of the chief shrines of the god that the worshipper is encouraged to visit and was probably written prior to the 7th century AD.
·Sanskritization of Tamil deities 8:912g

Mururoa Atoll, one of the Gambier Islands, French Polynesia, in the central South Pacific, 800 mi (1,300 km) southeast of Tahiti. It was chosen (1963) as the site for French nuclear weapons tests (the first explosion took place July 3, 1966). An uninhabited atoll once used to grow coconuts, it is served by a jet air strip on nearby Hao Atoll.
21°52′ S, 138°55′ W

Murwāra, town, Jabalpur district, Madhya Pradesh state, central India, just south of the Katnī Nadī (Katnī River). Sometimes called Katni, the town is a rail junction and a leading trade centre. Major industries include rice and flour milling, fuller's-earth processing, and various manufactures. Important bauxite and limestone works are nearby. Murwāra was constituted a municipality in 1874 and houses an industrial school and two constituent colleges of Jabalpur University. Pop. (1971 prelim.) 62,677.
23°50′ N, 80°24′ E
·map, India 9:278

Murwillumbah, coastal town, northeast New South Wales, Australia, 20 mi (32 km) above the mouth of the Tweed River, near the Queensland border. Surveyed in 1872, development was slow until the town was reached (1894) by a rail extension from Lismore. Murwillumbah, an Aboriginal term meaning either Campsite or Place of Many Possums, has had a history marked by disaster. It was destroyed by fire in 1907 and ravaged by floods in 1947, 1954, and 1956. On the Pacific Highway, it is a processing and service centre for a district of banana, sugarcane, and dairy farming. A banana festival is celebrated in August–September. Pop. (1971 prelim.) 7,374.
28°19′ S, 153°24′ E

Muryōju-kyō (Buddhist text): *see* Sukhāvatī-vyūha-sūtra.

Murzuk (Libya): *see* Marzūq.

Mürzzuschlag, city, Steiermark (Styria) *Bundesland* (federal state), east central Austria, at the junction of the Fröschnitz and Mürz rivers, northeast of Bruck an der Mur. First mentioned in 1227, it was chartered in 1318 and has been an ironworking centre since the 14th century. It has medieval houses and a former Cistercian abbey with a church from 1496 and beautiful cloisters. An Alpine summer and winter resort of the Semmering region, Mürzzuschlag is a noted skiing centre with a winter-sports museum and a chair lift up the Glanz Berg (2,887 ft [880 m]). Pop. (1971 prelim.) 48,412.
47°36′ N, 15°41′ E

Muş, capital of Muş *il* (province), eastern Turkey, lies at the mouth of a gorge on the slopes of the Kurtik Dağı, at the south side of a wide plain in the Murat Valley. The surrounding hills are covered with vineyards and oak scrub. Reputedly, the town and its castle, now in ruins, were founded by the Armenian king Mushel II Mamikonian in the 6th century. Later called Tarun by the Arabs, it came under Ottoman domination in 1515. The major part of the town was destroyed by an earthquake in 1966. Muş lies on the Elâzığ–Tatvan railway and is also linked by road to Erzurum (85 mi [137 km] north), Bitlis (east-southeast), and Bingöl (northwest).

Muş *il* (3,164 sq mi [8,196 sq km]), bordered on the north by the Bingöl Dağları (mountains), is rugged, with small basins of scarce arable land. The *il* has a large Kurdish population. Malazgirt (ancient Manatzikert), northeast of Muş town, is the site of the famous Seljuq victory (1071) over Byzantium, which gave the Turks access to the whole of Asia Minor. Pop. (1970 prelim.) town, 44,094; *il*, 233,919.
38°44′ N, 41°30′ E
·map, Turkey 18:784
·province area and population, table 2 18:787

Mus, Paul (b. 1902?, Bourges, Fr.—d. Aug. 9, 1969, Avignon), scholar of Southeast Asian civilizations, was a specialist on Vietnamese society and culture.

Brought to Vietnam as a small child, Mus grew up in Hanoi, where he attended high school with upperclass Vietnamese students, an experience that proved the basis for a keen perception of Vietnamese life that is reflected in his writings. He attended the University of Paris, where he became an accomplished Southeast Asian scholar, and returned to Hanoi in 1927 as a secretary and librarian with the Research Institute of the French School of the Far East until 1940. He participated in archaeological expeditions and explored the ruins of the ancient kingdom of Champa, in southernmost Vietnam; his book *Barabudur* (1935), a treatise on the origins of Buddhism and the Hindu-based cultures of Southeast Asia, resulted from those investigations.

After a variety of World War II assignments, Mus joined a British intelligence unit in India. His mission was to return to Vietnam and develop resistance there against the Japanese; he landed by parachute in the Hanoi area in 1945, shortly before the Japanese completely routed the last remnants of the French administration. He fled to the mountains and Dien Bien Phu, where he was met by a rescue plane and taken to China.

Upon his return to Vietnam in September, after the war, as political adviser to Gen. Philippe Leclerc, he was sent to negotiate with Ho Chi Minh, who had proclaimed an independent Vietnam in the north. The inflexible terms Mus had to offer the Viet-Minh leader proved unacceptable, and the guerrilla war continued. He returned to Paris, where he was appointed director of the French School for Overseas Administration and also received a professorship at the Collège de France.

Mus became a visiting lecturer at Yale University in 1950 and two years later a full professor of Southeast Asian civilizations. In his *Viet-Nam: sociologie d'une guerre* (1952; "Vietnam: Sociology of a War"), he tried to communicate his understanding of the Vietnamese to the French, who were then engaged in the Viet Minh war. He strongly influenced the large group of young Southeast Asian scholars that emerged in the United States. His and John McAlister's *The Vietnamese and Their Revolution* was published in 1970.

Musa: *see* Phraates V.

Mūsā, Mansa: *see* Mansa Mūsā of Mali.

Mūsā al-Kāẓim (d. 799), Islāmic religious leader, accepted as the seventh *imām* of the Twelver sect of Shīʿism.
·Shīʿite sects and their influence 9:917e

Muṣʿab (d. AD 691), governor of Basra, now in Iraq, supported his brother ʿAbd Allāh ibn az-Zubayr, a claimant to the caliphate.
·ʿAbd al-Malik's Umayyad victory 1:5d
·Mukhtar rebellion suppression 11:991e
·opposition to Umayyad rule 3:628e

Mûsa Bey (d. 1413), son of Bayezid I, Ottoman military commander in the Balkans.
·sultanate succession settlement 13:773d

Musaceae, the banana family (order Zingiberales), consisting of two genera, *Musa* and *Ensete*, with about 50 species native to Africa, Asia, and Australia. The common banana (*M. sapientum*) is a subspecies of the plantain (*M. paradisiaca*). Both are important food plants.

The slender or conical false trunk of Musaceae herbs may rise to 15 metres (50 feet). The trunk is formed by the leaf sheaths of the spirally arranged leaves, which form a crown at the top. The large leaves may be one metre long and half a metre wide. The prominent midrib of the leaf is joined at right or slightly oblique angles with parallel veins. When the plant grows in an unsheltered place, wind and rain easily tear the leaves between the veins, giving the leaves a fringed or ragged appearance. The large, leathery bracts (leaflike structures) are red to purple. The yellow flowers have five fertile stamens and are rich in honey.

Some species of wild bananas, such as *M. coccinea*, have ornamental scarlet flowers but inedible fruit. The Koae variety, named after the Koae bird, whose plumage grays prematurely, has green and white stripes on the leaves, trunk, and fruit.

M. textilis from the Philippines furnishes Manila hemp, also called abaca fibre.

The genus *Ensete* of Africa produces no edible bananas, but the flower stalk of one species, *E. ventricosa*, is edible after cooking. Species of *Ensete* are distinguished from those of *Musa* by their larger seeds. *See also* abaca; banana; plantain.
·classification and general features 19:1154d; illus. 1152
·Ethiopia's staple crops 6:1002e
·fibre properties and production 7:281a

musaf (Hebrew: "additional sacrifice"), in Jewish liturgy, the "additional service" recited on sabbaths and on festivals in commemoration of the additional sacrifices that were formerly offered in the Temple of Jerusalem (Num. 28, 29). The *musaf*, which usually follows the recital of the morning prayers (*shaḥarit*) and the reading of the Torah, is an added *ʿamida* (generally, seven blessings, recited standing), first recited privately by each worshipper, then repeated aloud by the official reader. Elements of the *musaf* vary, depending on the festival that is being celebrated and on the rite that is followed.

Mūsā ibn Nuṣayr (fl. early 8th century AD), Arab leader who extended Muslim power across North Africa and into Spain.
·African annexations and Berber campaign 17:414a
·Muslim conquest of the Berbers 3:629c

Musala Peak, southwest Bulgaria, highest point (9,596 ft [2,925 m]) in the Rhodope Mountains.
42°11′ N, 23°34′ E
·map, Bulgaria **3**:471
·relief and scenery **3**:468g

muṣallā (Arabic: "place of prayer"), enclosed sanctuary used by early Islāmic communities.
·location, design, and religious use **9**:984b

musāmarah (Arabic: "conversation at night"), early Arabic literary form in which the listener is carried from topic to topic by verbal associations.
·structure in Islāmic poetry and prose **9**:958c

Musandam Peninsula, portion of the Arabian Peninsula separating the Persian Gulf from the Gulf of Oman.
26°18′ N, 56°24′ E
·map, Oman **13**:567
·map, United Arab Emirates **18**:863

muṣannaf (Islām): *see in* isnād.

Musa paradisiaca: *see* plantain.

Musar Movement, a religious development among Orthodox Jews of Lithuania during the 19th century that emphasized personal piety as a necessary complement to intellectual studies of the Torah (*i.e.*, the Pentateuch, or first five books of the Bible) and Talmud. Though the Hebrew word *musar* means "ethics," the movement was not directed toward exposition of ethical principles or study of personal virtues. Its goal was rather to mold the lives of rabbinic students along pietistic lines. Rabbi Israel Salanter, later Israel Lipkin, who initiated the movement as head of the yeshiva at Vilnius, thus drew a sharp distinction between intellectual knowledge and personal behaviour.

The establishment of "Musar houses," where devout persons could join scholars in daily meditation and exercises of piety, helped to popularize the movement and guarantee its continued influence. The Musar literature that Salanter and others collected and reprinted was used to foster peace of mind, humility, tolerance, thoughtful consideration of others, self-examination, and purity of mind. Yeshivas throughout the world have since made Musar readings part of their standard curriculum.
·Jewish ethical doctrines **10**:292a

Musashi, ancient province, Japan.
·imperial consolidation and importance **18**:476c

Musashino, city, Tōkyō Metropolis (*to*), Honshu, Japan, bordered (east) by Tokyo city. Kichijōji, the centre of the city, was founded in 1659. Musashino grew as a farming village, and was served by a railway station on the Chūō Main Line.

Its rural character did not change until after the destructive Kantō earthquake of 1923, when Musashino became a residential suburb of Tokyo. The munitions factories established in the city during World War II were later replaced by electrical machinery plants. Pop. (1976 est.) 139,204.
35°42′ N, 139°34′ E
·Tokyo–Yokohama area map **18**:477

Muṣaṣir, also spelled MUSSASSIR, also called MUṢRI, ancient site probably located near the upper Great Zab River between Lake Urmia and Lake Van in what is now Turkey. Muṣaṣir was particularly important during the first half of the 1st millennium BC and is known primarily from reliefs and inscriptions of the Assyrian king Sargon II, who captured it in 714. According to the inscription, Sargon first plundered the palace storerooms of Urzana, king of Muṣaṣir, and then seized the even richer contents of the temple of the god Haldi.

Sargon's list, which describes the confiscated treasure in detail, is especially valuable for a study of the artistic and cultural development of the region. In addition, Sargon's relief portrays the Muṣaṣir temple, which scholars now believe is the oldest known temple with a pediment and a colonnade—elements that were widely used in Anatolia but apparently foreign to Mesopotamian temple architecture.
·Urartian territorial expansion **18**:1039f; map

Musa textilis: *see* abaca.

Musäus, Johann Karl August (b. March 29, 1735, Jena, now in East Germany—d. Oct. 28, 1787, Weimar), satirist and writer of fairy tales, remembered for his graceful and delicately ironical versions of popular folktales.

Musäus studied theology at Jena but turned instead to literature. His first book, *Grandison der Zweite* (3 vol., 1760–62; "Grandison the Second"), revised as *Der deutsche Grandison* (1781–82; "The German Grandison"), was a satire on Samuel Richardson's hero Sir Charles Grandison, who had many sentimental admirers in Germany. In 1763 Musäus was made master of the court pages at Weimar and later (1770) became professor at the Weimar Gymnasium.

A second book, *Physiognomische Reisen* (4 vol., 1778–79; "Physiognomical Travels"), a satire on Johann Lavater's work linking physiognomy to character, had many enthusiasts in Europe. His *Volksmärchen der Deutschen* (5 vol., 1782–86; "Fairy Tales of the Germans"), because it is written in a satirical vein, is not considered genuine folklore.

Musayʿīd, commonly and incorrectly called UMM SAʿĪD, urban settlement and port, Qatar, on the east coast of the Qatar Peninsula and on the Persian Gulf. It was established in 1949 as a tanker terminal by the Qatar Petroleum Company, Ltd., on an inhospitable, previously uninhabited site.

Qatar's onshore petroleum fields, the Dukhān formations, lie on the opposite (west) coast of the peninsula, along the Baḥr as-Salwá or Dawḥat Salwah, the bay separating Qatar from the main landmass of Arabia. Because coral reefs at the mouths of the bay prevented access by oceangoing tankers, the company laid a pipeline, 49 mi (79 km) long, across the peninsula to Musayʿīd, where tank farms and an artificial deepwater port were built.

Musayʿīd, the only deepwater port in Qatar for more than 20 years, handled not only the export of oil but the import of basic construction and industrial equipment, as well as consumer goods. The opening of the deepwater port at the capital city of ad-Dawḥah (*q.v.*) in the early 1970s lessened dependence on Musayʿīd as a general port. Modern industrial development there includes a plant producing ammonia and nitrogen fertilizers and a fully automated flour mill. Pop. (1971 est.) 7,000.
24°59′ N, 51°32′ E

Musaylimah (d. AD 633), Arab leader, was the chief opponent of Abū Bakr, the first Muslim caliph, during the political troubles following the death (June 632) of the Prophet Muḥammad. The struggle between them took place on the frontier of Yamāmah (now al-Kharj, in the eastern Najd in Arabia), and he eventually died in battle in that region.
·early Islām and rival sects **3**:625e
·Islām and Arab dissent **9**:925h

Musca (Latin: Fly), constellation of the southern sky.
·constellation table **2**:226

Musca domestica: *see* housefly.

Muscardinus avellanarius, the common dormouse (*q.v.*).

muscarine, one of several poisonous alkaloids found in the mushroom known as fly agaric, or *Amanita muscaria*. Muscarine causes general and sometimes fatal stimulation of the parasympathetic nervous system.
·autonomic system effects **12**:1035b
·poisonous mushrooms, table 3 **14**:609

Muscat, also transliterated MASQAṬ, the national capital of the Sultanate of Oman. The city long gave its name to the country, which was called Muscat and Oman until 1970. Located on the Gulf of Oman, it is isolated from the interior by a range of hills. Muscat first came in contact with Europeans in 1508, when the Portuguese gained control of the town and the adjacent coast. They maintained a trading post and naval base there until 1650; the present dynasty has ruled since 1741.

Muscat is no longer the most important port of the nation, having been surpassed by Maṭraḥ, its suburb to the northwest. Mīnāʾ al-Fahal, a few miles west of the capital, has an oil-loading terminal; oil is piped there from fields in the interior. In 1973 a new international airport was opened at as-Sīb, near Muscat. Pop. (early 1970 est.) 18,000; (1973 est.) capital area, 50,000.
23°37′ N, 58°35′ E
·Arabian, Portuguese, and Persian rule **1**:1049d
maps
·Asia **2**:148
·Oman **13**:567
·Persian Gulf **14**:107
·population, economy, and importance **13**:567d

Muscat and Oman (Arabia): *see* Oman.

muscatel, sweet dessert wine, golden to dark amber in colour, made from muscat grapes.
·wine classification **19**:877g

Muscatine, city, seat (1836) of Muscatine County, eastern Iowa, U.S., on the Mississippi River. Founded as a trading post in 1833, it was first called Bloomington but was renamed (1850), probably for the Mascoutin Indian word meaning "burning island" or "fiery nation." Industry is diversified; until 1971 the most distinctive was the making of pearl buttons from mussel shells found in the Mississippi's tributaries. Fairport National Fish Hatchery is 8 mi (13 km) east. Inc. town, 1839; city, 1851. Pop. (1980) 23,467.
41°25′ N, 91°03′ W
·map, United States **18**:909

Muschelkalk (German: "shell limestone"), Triassic rock sequences in Germany.
·Middle Triassic correlation **18**:693e; table

Muscheln (German: "mussels"), German stoneware pattern.
·Meissen stoneware styles **14**:909f

Musci (plant class): *see* Bryopsida.

Muscicapa, the main genus of flycatcher (*q.v.*).

Muscicapidae, songbird family that traditionally included the Old World flycatchers and monarch flycatchers (sometimes also the whistlers and fantails) but now is often broad-

Pied flycatcher (*Muscicapa hypoleuca*)
John Markham

ened to include the thrushes, Old World warblers, babblers, and several smaller groups, in addition to the flycatchers. Thus considered, the family contains some 1,400 species, roughly one-fourth of the order Passeriformes, or perching birds. Members of this group share a number of anatomical features including the presence of a 10th primary feather in the wing and adaptations for insect eating. Muscicapid taxonomy is controversial, chiefly because the subgroups intergrade and because no character is taxonomically useful throughout the wide family. A number of the subgroups are frequently ranked as families in their own right, especially the thrushes (*q.v.*; Turdidae), warblers (*q.v.*; Sylviidae), and babblers (*q.v.*; Timaliidae). Even when considered in the narrow sense, the family Muscicapidae presents many problems, for authorities disagree on which of the flycatching groups should be included.

The broader meaning of the family was adopted by the international committee that continued the authoritative *Check-List of Birds of the World*, following the death of the original author, James L. Peters. This check-list recognizes the following subfamilies:

Turdinae (thrushes)
Orthonychinae (rail-babblers)
Timaliinae (typical babblers)
Panurinae (parrotbills)
Picathartinae (rockfowl)
Polioptilinae (gnatwrens and gnatcatchers)
Sylviinae (warblers)
Malurinae (fairy wrens)
Muscicapinae (typical flycatchers)
Platysteirinae (wattle-eyes)
Monarchinae (monarch)
Pachycephalinae (whistlers)

Muscidae, fly family within the order Diptera. For *Musca domestica*, *see* housefly; for *Stomoxys calcitrans*, *see* stable fly; for *Haematobia irritans*, *see* horn fly; for *Glossina*, *see* tsetse fly.

muscle, a contractile tissue, found in animals, the function of which is to produce motion. The individual cells of muscle tissue are elongated and specialized to develop tension along the long axis, thus shortening the cell (isotonic contraction) or increasing the tension without shortening (isometric contraction). The contractile organelles, or elements, within the cell are threadlike myofilaments, often in bundles called myofibrils and myonemes. A myofilament is composed of protein complexes, notably actomyosin. Vertebrate muscle tissue is classed as striated or smooth, depending on the presence or absence of microscopic cross striations, or bands. Each striated muscle is enclosed in a sheath (sarcolemma).

·aging processes and effects **1**:301g
·biological development processes **5**:647f
·contraction structures and mechanisms **12**:621e; illus. 622
·intracellular ion concentration table **7**:429
·invertebrate skeletal relationships **16**:819a; illus. 821
·meat texture and quality **11**:746f
·morphologic classification criteria **12**:454d
·tonic muscle function **12**:638e; illus. 639
·vertebrate skeletal relationships **16**:822d

muscle cell, also called MUSCLE FIBRE, an elongated cell specialized as a contractile unit consisting of a nucleus and cell fluid (cytoplasm) called sarcoplasm. Within the sarcoplasm is a highly organized fibrillar system consisting of minute threads called myofilaments, which are often grouped into larger fibrils called myonemes and myofibrils.

·diseased tissue changes **12**:634d

myofibril
·animal tissue comparisons **18**:449a
·contraction structures and mechanisms **12**:629e
·physical properties of components **12**:622f; illus.

myoneme
·invertebrate muscle systems, illus. 5 **12**:641
·protozoan cilia structure and function **15**:125h
·Vorticella nervous system responses **12**:976d
·prenatal and postnatal growth in man **5**:651h

sarcoplasm
·anatomic relationships and function **12**:623a; illus. 622
·bioelectric responses to stimuli **3**:1050b
·contraction structures and mechanisms **12**:622c
·muscle cell structure and function **3**:1061h
·muscle fibre composition **12**:640b
·spinal reflex stimulation **12**:1011g
·structure and function in different types of muscle **12**:638d
·tonic muscle fibre contraction **12**:625b

muscle contraction **12**:620, the movement of animal organs composed of contractile tissue.

TEXT ARTICLE covers:
Primitive contractile systems **12**:621a
Muscle in higher animals 621e
The nature and properties of striated muscle 621g
The nature and properties of cardiac muscle 630d
The nature and properties of smooth muscle 631g

REFERENCES in other text articles:
·active transport of calcium ions **11**:883c
·animal tissue comparisons **18**:449a
·annelid locomotion events **1**:931a
·bioelectric responses to stimuli **3**:1050b
·bioelectric triggering **2**:999a
·energy conversion principles **6**:856h
·energy production in glycolysis **14**:437d
·fatigue from muscle activity **7**:189f
·Galvani's pioneering electrical studies **7**:859h
·heartbeat initiation mechanisms **4**:620d
·heat generation study by Hill **2**:1036e
·histamine effect on smooth muscle **8**:945b
·historical experimental studies **2**:1034h

human
·circulation and specialized muscle functions **2**:1126c
·digestive disorder causes and symptoms **5**:768e *passim* to 771d
·ear reflex action **5**:1126b
·eye coordination **7**:98e
·heartbeat regulation mechanism **3**:879b
·intestinal peristaltic motion **5**:776b
·spinal cord influences **12**:1011f
·tetany and tetanus symptoms **12**:634c
·initiation at myoneural junction **2**:999h
·insect wing-beat rate mechanism **9**:615d
·intestinal movements during digestion **5**:788f
·isotonic–isometric comparison, illus. 2 **12**:638
·mammalian breathing mechanism **11**:409c
·myosin properties and characteristics **15**:91c
·physics, mechanisms, controls, and special muscle types **12**:638c
·spasm in cricopharyngeal muscle **17**:479b
·spontaneous rhythm and coordination **2**:814e
·stretch receptors and control reflexes **15**:761d; illus.
·voluntary and involuntary movement **11**:805d
·wave form in fish swimming **16**:822e

muscle diseases **12**:633, disorders of the muscles (bodily tissues that by the contraction of their fibres perform mechanical functions such as those concerned with movement, sustaining weight, balancing, or narrowing the bore of blood vessels).

The text article considers common indications of diseases of the muscles and the types of muscle disease.

REFERENCES in other text articles:
·aging and muscle atrophy **1**:309e
·atrophy and loss of strength **2**:352e
·biomedical models, table 1 **5**:866
·birth defects of the musculoskeletal system **2**:1074e
·diagnosis of referred pain **5**:686b
·diagnostic symptoms of disorders **5**:687h
·drug action on smooth and skeletal muscles **5**:1045b
·endocrine system disorders **6**:818e
·epidemic pleurodynia infection **2**:1179c
·headache and neck muscle strain **8**:684h
·industrial environment perils **9**:529h
·neural symptoms of muscle disorders **12**:1056e
·nutritional mineral deficiencies **13**:418h
·physical therapy for atrophy **18**:286e
·polymyositis symptoms and treatment **5**:21d
·tetanus convulsions and spasms **9**:556c
·toxins' effects on heart **14**:621g
·tranquilizers and muscle spasm relief **18**:596d

RELATED ENTRIES in the *Ready Reference and Index*:
familial periodic paralysis; hernia; muscle tumours; muscular dystrophy; myasthenia gravis; myositis; myotonia

Muscle Shoals, a shoal section of the Tennessee River, northwestern Alabama, U.S., formerly a navigation hazard. Flinty, jagged rocks occurred near the surface, and rapids resulted from the fact that the fall of the river was about 130 ft (40 m) in 37 mi (60 km). The worst of the shoals and other obstructions in the "great bend" of the river lay to the east of the cities of Sheffield and Florence. The name Muscle Shoals is probably a variation in the spelling of mussells, which were abundant in the area.

With the advent of steamboating in the early 1800s, the Tennessee River became a major channel of transportation, extending about 650 mi from Knoxville, Tenn., about 300 mi above the shoals, to the Ohio River in Kentucky, and connecting with the Mississippi River. For 100 years, however, Muscle Shoals defied repeated efforts to make them safe for navigation. Canals, completed in 1836 and in 1890, proved unsuccessful. Early 20th-century efforts by private companies to build dams, which could also be used for hydroelectric power, were thwarted (1903) by Pres. Theodore Roosevelt, who recognized the need to preserve public control of the power resources of the river.

Concerned with the supply of nitrate following the outbreak of World War I in Europe, the U.S. Congress authorized (1916) the construction and operation of two nitrate plants and a dam for electric power as a national defense measure. Pres. Woodrow Wilson chose Muscle Shoals as the site of the dam, which was later named for him. From 1921 to 1933 a national controversy over public vs. private ownership raged. The argument was finally resolved when all the Muscle Shoals properties were turned over to the Tennessee Valley Authority (TVA), an independent government corporation created (1933) by Congress to promote navigation, flood control, reforestation, and other improvements for the entire Tennessee Valley.

The later completion of Wheeler Dam, 16 mi above Wilson, and Pickwick Landing Dam, 52 mi below Wilson, completely eliminated the Muscle Shoals' hazard. The term is still sometimes used in referring to the TVA complex of operations centring in the Wilson Dam area.

muscle system, human **12**:636. The text article is primarily concerned with the changes that occurred in the muscular system of man as a result of the long evolutionary process involving his assumption of the upright posture. It covers general trends and major changes in muscles of the lower limbs, upper limbs, head and neck, and trunk.

REFERENCES in other text articles:
·adolescent spurt in strength **5**:654d
·aging processes and effects **1**:301g
·alkaloid physiological effects **1**:596e
·anesthesia and neuromuscular blockers **1**:867a *passim* to 868f
·animal tissue comparisons **18**:448h
·Australopithecine anatomical posture adaptations and comparison **2**:438b
·autonomic system innervations **12**:1025d; illus. 1026
·brain role in speech mechanism **17**:484h
·brainstem mediation of contraction **12**:1005a
·cardiac fibre contraction mechanism **3**:879b
·cell adaptations to stress **5**:844e
·circulation and cardiac rhythm **2**:1125h
·circulation and muscle contraction **2**:1132a
·cranial nerve distributions **12**:1018e; illus. 1017
·digestion and mastication processes **5**:771h
·digestive motor disturbances **5**:768a *passim* to 771d
·digestive system relationship **5**:789d *passim* to 795d
·disease causes, symptoms, and treatment **12**:633g

RELATED ENTRIES in the *Ready Reference and Index: for*

muscle systems 12:637, groups of muscles so arranged in an animal body that they function together in a coordinated fashion.

The text article covers the definitions and distinctions, significance, arrangement, and gross function of muscle tissue; describes muscle contractile systems and contraction, and invertebrate and vertebrate muscle systems; and reviews the function and regulation of muscle action and electric organs.

REFERENCES in other text articles:

muscle tone, normal ability of a muscle to resist stretching for a considerable period of time. A healthy state, it is marked by a capability for vigorous performance. Muscle tone is generally maintained through proper diet, rest, and exercise.

muscle tumours, abnormal tissue growths located in or originating from muscle tissue. Tumours may either arise in muscle tissue or spread to it. Three major tumour types may appear; they are known as leiomyomas, rhabdomyomas, and rhabdomyosarcomas.

The leiomyoma is a tumour of smooth muscles (such as those in the walls of the intestines and of blood vessels). It is most frequently located in the uterus (womb). Leiomyomas have been found in the ovaries, the fallopian tubes, the alimentary canal, the bladder, and the ureters. The tumour is hard or firm, encapsulated, and easily removed. The inside of the leiomyoma appears whorled when cut; there are numerous bundles of muscle fibres interlacing in various planes. The tissue may contain crystals or may become totally calcified so that it is converted into a mass of stone. Although part of the tumour has been known to become malignant, it usually does not spread out of the uterus or recur once it is removed.

The rhabdomyoma is a tumour of striated (striped) muscles. Its commonest location is the heart. Some forms of the tumour do spread: metastases (secondary tumours at distant sites) have been found in the uterus, the bladder, the prostate, the esophagus, the digestive tract, the sex glands, and the kidneys. The tumour may be in nodes, flat masses, round clusters, or polyps. Sometimes it is closely contained in the tissue, and at other times it may be diffuse and difficult to remove. The tissue of the rhabdomyoma is soft and gray, with strands of white fibres; some tumours take on a reddish-yellow appearance. The cells are generally large with a spider- or spindle-shaped appearance.

Rhabdomyomas of the heart grow in the wall and may project into the heart cavities. The tissue invaded is loose and vacuolated (with large spaces). It is thought that the tumour is a result of an embryologic disorder in the development of the heart. Rhabdomyomas affecting other parts of the body commonly involve both the smooth and the striated muscles. Many of the mixed tumours are likely to be malignant and may grow to great proportions. Tumours of this type appearing in the uterus, the vagina, or the prostate are large and polyp-shaped masses that protrude from these structures; occasionally they rupture, giving off blood and malodorous discharges. In the prostate they may obstruct the bladder. The prostate tumours may be found at birth, in early childhood, or, more rarely, in the adult. Their symptoms are fever, difficulty in urinating, and a general wasting away. They tend to invade the adjacent pelvic tissue.

The rhabdomyosarcoma is extremely malignant; it arises in the skeletal muscles of the body. Most tumours of this type are located in the leg or arm muscles. The rhabdomyosarcoma usually recurs even after amputation of the involved extremity.

The tumour itself is generally the only clinical symptom; it appears most often in the fifth or sixth decade of life. It is soft and often necrotic (showing degeneration) or hemorrhagic. The amount of bleeding determines the colour, which varies from pale yellow to pink or dark red. The tumour is removed as soon as it is found. Radiation does not seem to be of much help. The tumour has been estimated to grow 10 or more years in most cases before it is discovered.

muscovite, also known as COMMON MICA, POTASH MICA, OR ISINGLASS, an abundant silicate mineral that contains potassium and aluminum; a member of the common mica group. It is economically important because its low iron content makes it a good electrical and thermal insulator. Muscovite typically occurs in metamorphic rocks, where it forms crystals and plates. It also occurs in granites, in fine-grained sediments, and in some highly siliceous rocks. When fine-grained, muscovite is called sericite or white mica. For chemical formula and detailed physical properties, *see* table under micas.

Muscovy (medieval principality): *see* Moscow, grand princes of.

Muscovy Company, OR RUSSIA COMPANY, a body of English merchants trading with Russia. The company was formed in 1555 by the navigator and explorer Sebastian Cabot and various London merchants and was granted a monopoly of Anglo-Russian trade; it was the first English joint-stock company in which the capital remained regularly in use instead of being repaid after every voyage. In 1553 Sir Hugh Willoughby and Richard Chancellor had sailed to seek out a Northeast Passage to China and the East Indies. Willoughby's ship was lost, but Chancellor reached Archangel (Arkhangelsk) in the White Sea and established trade links with Moscow.

The original aim of the Muscovy Company was to exploit these contacts, as well as to continue the search for the Northeast Passage. In about 1630 the company ceased to function on a joint-stock basis and became a regulated company, in which, subject to various rules, merchants traded on their own account. Exports to Russia included woollen cloth, metals, and Mediterranean goods; the English traders brought back, through Archangel, hemp, wax tallow, cordage, and other Russian products.

Although the tsar Alexis ended the company's privileges in 1649, and at home it lost its monopoly of the Russian trade in 1698, it survived as an influential City of London institution and shared in the 18th-century revival of Anglo-Russian trade.

Muscovy duck (waterfowl): *see* perching duck.

muscular atrophy, progressive (disease): *see* amyotrophic lateral sclerosis.

muscular dystrophy, inherited disease that causes increasing weakness in muscle tissue.

The muscles affected are the skeletal muscles and, occasionally, the muscles of the heart. Of the several types of dystrophy, the more common are Duchenne's, facioscapulohumeral (dystrophy related to the face, the shoulder blade, and the upper arm), Becker's, limb-girdle, and myotonic dystrophy (*see* myotonia). In all of these the muscle tissue seems to be affected in a random fashion. There is usually early evidence of first degeneration and then regeneration of some fibres. Those that regenerate become larger than normal, and eventually the muscles are totally replaced by fibrous scar tissue and fat. All forms of dystrophy have muscular weakness in common.

Duchenne's dystrophy affects only young male children. There are no obvious symptoms in the first year of life. When the child begins to walk there are minor abnormalities in his gait: he tends to waddle and to walk on the toes, and has difficulty in getting up once he has fallen and in raising his knees, which prevents running. The symptoms become more obvious as the child ages; by the age of five years there is enlargement of the calf muscles, difficulty in getting up, inability to run, and disappearance of a normal knee or ankle jerk. Stairs eventually become impossible to climb. The arms are next affected. By early adolescence the child is unable to walk. Ultimately breathing becomes shallow, and pulmonary infections become a constant hazard. Infections usually bring about death before age 30.

Becker's dystrophy is much like Duchenne's, but it begins in later childhood or adolescence, and it is generally not so devastating. Some affected persons can function well into adult life with certain limitations. The symptoms are otherwise the same. Limb-girdle dystrophy (dystrophy of the pelvic or the shoulder muscles) affects both sexes. The first symptoms are manifest in the pelvic region, starting in late childhood. There are frequent falls, difficulty in climbing, and a waddling gait.

The facioscapulohumeral dystrophy starts in adolescence. The affected person may be mildly affected or may be totally disabled. The first symptom may be difficulty in raising the arms. Weakness can also affect the legs and pelvic girdle. The main effect on the facial muscles is difficulty in closing the eyes.

Muscular dystrophy may be confused initially with endocrine disorders, nervous system diseases, and orthopedic problems. Sometimes the child is thought to be merely clumsy. There is no specific treatment. Physical therapy, exercises, splints, braces, and corrective surgery may help. *Major ref.* **12**:635d
·progressive form's symptoms and incidence **12**:1056g

musculus (Latin: "muscle"): for individual muscles, *see* English names.

Musée de Cluny, English CLUNY MUSEUM, in Paris, museum of medieval arts and crafts housed in the Hôtel de Cluny, a Gothic mansion built *c.* 1490 as the town residence of the abbots of Cluny. The collection assembled by Alexandre du Sommerard, owner of the mansion from 1833, was the basis of the museum. The French government acquired the property on du Sommerard's death in 1842. The collection was reorganized in the early 1950s to present a coherent history of medieval civilization and includes gold- and silverwork, stained glass, sculpture, jewelry, textiles, and such everyday articles as eating utensils.
·Gothic style and medieval collection **13**:1017a

Musée de l'Homme, English MUSEUM OF MAN, in Paris, museum and library of ethnography and anthropology, founded in 1878 and supported by the state. The institution is attached to the Muséum National d'Histoire Naturelle and has a professional staff that engages in postgraduate instruction and supervision of research.
·location in Paris **13**:1008d

Musée des Arts Décoratifs, English MUSEUM OF DECORATIVE ARTS, in Paris, museum of Western and Oriental decorative arts established in 1880 and housed in a wing of the Louvre.
·Louvre history and description **13**:1009h
·Rodin's bronze door **15**:982e

Musée des Monuments Français, English MUSEUM OF FRENCH MONUMENTS, in Paris, historical museum in the Palais de Chaillot, established by Alexandre Lenoir in 1795. The holdings of the museum include a collection of more than 200,000 photographs belonging to the Archives des Monuments Historiques.
·Neo-Gothic influence on the Romantics **19**:450d
·Palais de Chaillot description **13**:1008d
·preservation of historical past **12**:659h

Musée d'Art Moderne de la Ville de Paris, English MUSEUM OF MODERN ART OF THE CITY OF PARIS, comprehensive collection of primarily 20th-century art by French and non-French artists associated with modern French movements and schools of art. The museum was briefly opened to the public in 1942–43, reorganized after World War II, and reopened in 1947.
·creative ability stimulation **12**:650a

Muse Française, La (1823–24; "The French Muse"), French literary review founded by Victor Hugo.
·Hugo's foundation and literary endowment **8**:1133a

Muselo River, Mozambique, Africa, one of the main channels of the Zambezi River delta. 19°00′ S, 36°10′ E
·Zambezi River distributaries **19**:1127e

Museo Argentino de Ciencias Naturales "Bernardino Rivadavia" (Buenos Aires): *see* Argentine Museum of Natural Sciences.

Museo e Gallerie Nazionali di Capodimonte, English CAPODIMONTE NATIONAL MUSEUM AND GALLERY, art museum in Naples, occupying the mid-18th-century Palazzo di Capodimonte and comprising the private collections of Charles III, the Bourbon king of Naples and later of Spain. As well as presenting a representative survey of Italian painting from the 13th through 17th century, the museum maintains collections of arms, armour, gold- and silverwork, and examples of other decorative arts, including Capodimonte porcelain (*q.v.*).
·construction and collections **12**:831b

Museo Nacional de Antropología, English NATIONAL MUSEUM OF ANTHROPOLOGY, in Mexico City, founded 1825. Since 1964 the museum has been housed in a new building, designed by Pedro Ramírez Vázquez and Rafael Mijares, who followed classical Mayan tradition in integrating the building with open spaces on the 11-acre site. The chief structural material is a native pink and black stone, blended with metals, concrete, and Mexican hardwoods. The museum displays the arts and crafts of the past and present cultures of the varied regions that make up modern Mexico.
·Mexico City cultural life **12**:92e
·mushroom column and fountain illus. **1**:1098

Muses, Greek MOUSAI, or MOISAI, in Greek religion, group of goddesses of ancient and obscure origin, whose chief cult centre was Mt. Helicon in Boeotia. Their festival occurred at four-year intervals at Thespiae, near Helicon. At first the Muses were probably the patrons of poets. Later their range was extended to include all liberal arts and sciences.

There were nine Muses as early as the *Odyssey,* although apparently they were at first an undifferentiated group of deities. Differentiation began with Hesiod, who mentioned the names of Clio, Euterpe, Thalia, Melpomene,

The Muses Calliope, Thalia, and Erato, classical relief; in the Louvre
Alinari

Terpsichore, Erato, Polymnia, Urania, and Calliope, who was their chief. Their mother was Mnemosyne (Memory). Although Hesiod's list became canonical in later times, it was not the only one. All the Hesiodic names are significant; thus, for example, Clio is approximately "the proclaimer," Calliope "she of the beautiful voice."

The Muses were often spoken of as virgins, or at least as unmarried, but were repeatedly referred to as the mothers of more or less famous sons, such as Orpheus, Rhesus, Eumolpus, and others connected somehow either with poetry and song, or with Thrace and its neighbourhood, or both. Statues of the Muses were a popular decoration; sculptors gave each a different attribute, such as a lyre or scroll. That practice may have contributed to the fanciful distribution of the individual Muses among the different arts and sciences; *e.g.,* Clio as Muse of history, Erato of love poetry, Urania of astronomy. The existing lists, however, are all late and disagree widely.
·folklore and mythology **8**:405b

RELATED ENTRIES in the *Ready Reference and Index:*
Calliope; Clio; Erato; Euterpe; Melpomene; Polymnia; Terpsichore; Thalia; Urania

Muses, Hill of the, Athens, Greece. 37°58′ N, 23°44′ E
·Athens' topography **2**:265a

Muses, Temple of the (Alexandria, Egypt): *see* Mouseion.

Muses Modeller, 18th-century anonymous British artist and ceramist, originator of an amusing and primitive class of Bow figures.
·Bow factory ceramics production **14**:914d

Muset, Colin (trouvère): *see* Colin Muset.

musette, small, elegant bagpipe fashionable in French court circles in the 17th and 18th centuries; also a musical composition.

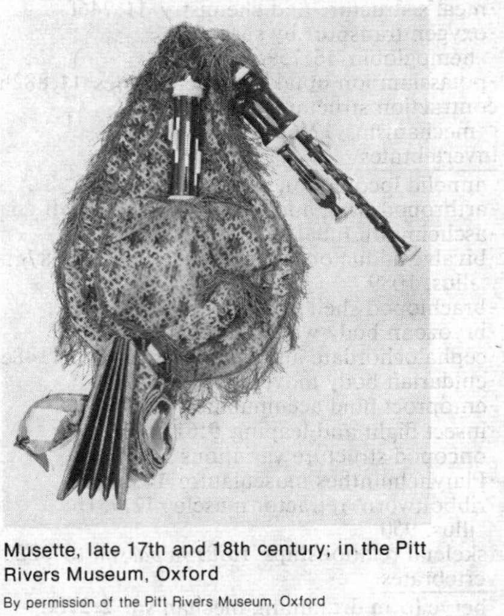

Musette, late 17th and 18th century; in the Pitt Rivers Museum, Oxford
By permission of the Pitt Rivers Museum, Oxford

The bagpipe was bellows-blown with a small, cylindrical double-reed chanter beside which the instrument maker Jean Hotteterre, *c.* 1650, placed a short stopped chanter with six keys giving notes above the main chanter compass. It employed a "shuttle" drone: a short cylinder with about 12 narrow channels variously connected in series to supply four drones, each sounded with a double reed and tuned or silenced by slider keys moving in the slots through which the bores vented to the exterior. The bag was typically covered with silk or velvet; the pipes were of ivory.

As a composition, the musette is a slow, pastoral dance with delicate figurations played over a pedal bass, or drone. It was originally played on the musette accompanied by the *vielle à roue* (hurdy-gurdy) and, later, on other instruments.

·development and cultural context **19**:852c

museum 12:649, institution that collects, studies, exhibits, and conserves objects for cultural and educational purposes. Museums and their collections may be of several kinds: art (including picture galleries), historical, scientific (including natural history), open-air, specialized (including industrial and commercial), and regional.

TEXT ARTICLE covers:
Social role of museums **12**:649f
Service to the community 650a
Educational and cultural roles 650e
Museum procedure 651h
Art museums 654f
Historical museums 655b
Science museums 655f
Specialized museums: Open-air museums, Regional museums, Other institutions functioning as museums 656b
Architecture: temple or palace museums 657b
Monuments transformed into museums 657e
Recently constructed museums 657h
Theory of museum architecture 658d
Aesthetic and functional architectures 658f
History of museums 659a

REFERENCES in other text articles:
·architectural development **1**:1092g; illus. 1093
·art social control and representation **2**:114g
·attendance and modern art trends **2**:120f
·Bangkok's cultural collections **2**:687c
·Boston's collections **3**:59h
·Bucharest Village Museum **3**:363h
·Istanbul churches and mosques **9**:1071g
·Lamarck and modern systematization **10**:617b
·Nürnberg's collections **13**:395d
·temperature control systems **13**:876d
·Vienna's art and music collections **19**:119h

Museum Computer Network, consolidation of information services of more than 20 U.S. museums, centred in New York City.

·museum research programs **12**:651e

Museum of Alexandria: *see* Mouseion.

Musgrave Ranges, series of granite hills, northwest South Australia, running parallel to the Northern Territory border for 130 mi (210 km). Their bare rock surfaces rise to numerous peaks exceeding 3,500 ft (1,100 m), including Mt. Woodruffe (4,970 ft), the state's highest point. Discovered (1873) by the English explorer William C. Gosse and crossed in that year by Gosse and Ernest Giles, they were named after Sir Anthony Musgrave, then lieutenant governor of South Australia. Lying within the arid Central Australian Aboriginal Reserve, the ranges are the source of many intermittent streams.
26°10′ S, 131°50′ E

·map, Australia **2**:400

mushāhadah, also SHUHUD (Arabic: "vision," "witness"), in Ṣūfī (Muslim mystic) terminology, the vision of God obtained by the illuminated heart of the seeker of truth (*ruʾyat al-qalb*). Through *mushāhadah*, the Ṣūfī acquires *yaqīn* (real certainty), which cannot be achieved by the intellect or transmitted to those who do not travel the Ṣūfī path. The Ṣūfī has to pass various ritual stages before he can attain the state of *mushāhadah*, which is eventually given to him only by an act of sheer grace of God. *Mushāhadah*, therefore, cannot be reached through good works or *mujāhadah* (self-mortification). Further, it is bestowed by God upon whom he pleases. A Ṣūfī can only strive to purify himself and attain the state of *qurb* (nearness to God), after which he must patiently await the divine gift.

Mushāhadah is the goal of every Ṣūfī who aspires to the ultimate vision of God; its opposite, *ḥijāb* (veiling of the divine face), is the most severe punishment that a Ṣūfī can imagine. The Ṣūfīs say that if God revealed himself to those in the depths of hellfire, sight of him would bring such overwhelming joy that suffering bodies would feel no more pain. Similarly, paradise becomes a tormenting affliction if God's face is not revealed.

A Ṣūfī who attains *mushāhadah* not only sees God but develops a supernatural power of discernment, called *firāsah*. The Ṣūfīs claim that Muḥammad alluded to this in the famous *ḥadīth* (saying): "Beware of the discernment of the true believer, for he sees by the light of Allah."

Many Qurʾānic (Islāmic scriptural) verses have been interpreted by the Ṣūfī in such a way as to reconcile their pantheistic doctrines with those of orthodox religion. *Mushāhadah* was thus explained in the light of the religious texts. Ṣūfīs maintain that *mushāhadah* is related to *shahādah* (a Muslim formula summarizing their profession of faith: "There is no God but God"). The highest level of realizing the oneness of God, the Ṣūfīs explain, is that which comes through the direct vision of God, which is granted only to those whose hearts are rightly disposed and duly prepared to receive it. The Qurʾānic verse "Tell the believers to close their eyes" is interpreted by Ṣūfīs to mean a command from God to believers not so much to close their eyes to bodily lusts as to close their minds to earthly thoughts and open their spiritual eyes to the beauty of divine Truth. For if "any one shuts his eyes to God for a single moment, he will never be rightly guided all his life long."

Ṣūfīs regard their life before attaining *mushāhadah* as having been wasteful. According to one anecdote, when the famous mystic Bāyazīd ol-Besṭāmī (died 874) was asked how old he was, he replied "four years." When asked for an explanation, he answered, "I have been veiled from God by this world for seventy years, but I have seen Him during the last four years; the period in which one is veiled does not belong to one's life."

Mushanga, Mucu, 27th king of the kingdom of Kuba in the Congo region of Africa.

·bark cloth clothing and fire invention **1**:274c

Mushanokōji Saneatsu (b. May 12, 1885, Tokyo), writer and painter noted for a lifelong philosophy of humanistic optimism. The eighth child of an aristocratic family, he went to the Peers' School and entered Tokyo Imperial University in 1906. He left without graduating to join his writer friends Shiga Naoya, Arishima Takeo, and Satomi Ton in founding the influential literary journal *Shirakaba* ("White Birch"). In high school he had first started reading Tolstoy and the Bible, which had great influence on the development of his humanitarian ideology. His early writings, of which *Omedetaki hito* (1911; "The Good-Natured Soul") is an example, are characterized by a bursting self-confidence. He was praised by the novelist Akutagawa Ryūnosuke for having "opened a window" to let light into a literary world dominated by dreary naturalist writing. His humanism reached out into the social sphere when he bought land in southern Japan and founded in 1918 his Atarashii Mura, the New Village, an experiment in communal living that ultimately failed. In later years he turned to painting but continued to make pronouncements affirming his optimism and his faith in mankind.

Musha ʿshaʿ, 15th-century Islamic religious faction in Iraq.

·challenge to Turkmen rule **11**:994c

Mushegh, 10th-century king of Kars, brother of Ashot III.

·Armenian independent rulers **18**:1042g

Mushezib-Marduk, 7th-century-BC Chaldean military leader.

·Sennacherib's wars with the Chaldeans **16**:542c

Mushfiqī, also known as NASRETTIN HOCA or JUḤĀ, comic character in Islāmic literature.

·role in popular literature **9**:966h

Mushin, town, Ikeja Province, Lagos State, southwestern Nigeria; it lies on the railway from Lagos, of which it is a southeastern suburb, and at the intersection of roads from Lagos, Shomolu, and Ikeja. Its inhabitants are predominantly Yoruba people. The town's continuing expansion since 1950 has led to problems of overcrowding, inadequate housing, and poor sanitation. Mushin is the site of a large industrial estate. Commercial enterprises include spinning and weaving cotton, shoe manufacturing, bicycle and motorized-cycle assembly, and the production of powdered milk. Agricultural produce is brought for sale to the large central market. The town is served by a secondary school and a private commercial institute. Pop. (1972 est.) 180,949.
6°32′ N, 3°22′ E

·map, Nigeria **13**:86
·theatrical music development **12**:695g
·18th–20th-century encyclopaedia specialization **6**:792b

mushrabīyah (Islāmic architecture): *see* moucharaby.

mushroom, in general refers to the conspicuous umbrella-shaped fruiting body (sporophore) of certain fungi mostly of the order Agaricales (*q.v.*) in the class of club fungi, the Basidiomycetes (*q.v.*), but also of some other groups. In a very restricted sense, mushroom indicates the common edible fungus of fields and meadows (*Agaricus campestris* or *Psalliota campestris*). A very closely related species, *A. bisporus*, is the mushroom grown commercially and seen in markets. Popularly, the term mushroom is used to identify the edible sporophores; the term toadstool is often reserved for the inedible or poisonous sporophores. There is, however, no scientific distinction between the two names, and either can be properly applied to any fleshy fungus fruiting structure.

Umbrella-shaped sporophores are found chiefly in the agaric family (Agaricaceae), members of which bear thin bladelike gills on the undersurface of the cap from which the spores are shed. The sporophore of an agaric consists of a cap (pileus) and stalk (stipe). The sporophore emerges from an extensive underground network of threadlike strands (mycelium). An example of an agaric is the honey mushroom (*Armillaria mellea*). Mushroom mycelia may live hundreds of years or die in a few months, depending on the available food supply. As long as nourishment is available and temperature and moisture are suitable, a mycelium will produce a new crop of sporophores each year during its fruiting season.

Fruiting bodies of some mushrooms occur in arcs or rings called fairy rings. The mycelium starts from a spore falling in a favourable spot and producing strands (hyphae) that grow out in all directions, eventually forming a circular mat of underground hyphal threads. Fruiting bodies, produced near the advancing edge of this mat, may widen the ring for hundreds of years.

A few mushrooms belong to the family Boletaceae (*q.v.*), which bear pores in an easily detachable layer on the underside of the

Meadow mushroom (*Agaricus campestris*)

Ellen Trueblood

cap. The agarics (*see* Agaricales) and boletes (*see* Boletaceae) include most of the forms known as mushrooms. Other groups of fungi, however, are considered to be mushrooms, at least by laymen. Among these are the hydnums or hedgehog mushrooms, which have teeth, spines, or warts on the undersurface of the cap (*e.g., Dentinum repandum, Hydnum imbricatum*) or at the ends of branches (*e.g., Hydnum coralloides, Hericium caput-ursi*). The polypores, shelf fungi, or bracket fungi (order Polyporales; *q.v.*) have tubes under the cap as in the boletes, but they are not present in an easily separable layer. Polypores usually grow on living or dead trees, sometimes as destructive pests. Many of them renew growth each year and thus produce annual growth layers by which their age can be estimated. Examples include the dryad's saddle (*Polyporus squamosus*), the beefsteak fungus (*Fistulina hepatica*), the sulfur fungus (*Polyporus sulphureus*), the artist's fungus (*Ganoderma applanatum*), and species of the genera *Fomes* and *Trametes*. The clavarias, or club fungi (*e.g., Clavaria, Ramaria*), are shrublike, clublike, or coral-like in growth habit. One club fungus, the cauliflower fungus (*Sparassis crispa*), has flattened clustered branches that lie close together, giving the appearance of the vegetable cauliflower. The cantharelloid fungi (*Cantharellus* and its relatives) are club-, cone-, or trumpet-shaped mushroom-like forms with an expanded top bearing coarsely folded ridges along the underside and descending along the stalk. Examples include the highly prized edible chantrelle (*C. cibarius*) and the horn-of-plenty mushroom (*Craterellus cornucopoides*).

Puffballs (order Lycoperdales; *q.v.*), stinkhorns (*q.v.*), earthstars (a kind of puffball), and bird's nest fungi are usually treated with

Honey mushroom (*Armillaria mellea*)

H.R. Allen from the Natural History Photographic Society—EB Inc.

the mushrooms. The morels (*Morchella, Verpa*) and false morels, or lorchels (*Gyromitra, Helvella*), of the class Ascomycetes (*q.v.*) are popularly included with the true mushrooms because of their shape and fleshy structure; they resemble a deeply folded or pitted cone-like sponge at the top of a hollow stem. Some are among the most highly prized edible fungi (*e.g., Morchella esculenta*). Another group of Ascomycetes includes the cup fungi (*see* cup fungus), or pezizas, with a cuplike or dishlike fruiting structure, sometimes highly coloured.

Examples of other unusual forms, not closely related to the true mushrooms but often included with them, are the jelly fungi (*Tremella* species), the ear fungus, or Jew's ear (*Auricularia auriculara-judae*), and the edible truffle (*q.v.*; *Tuber* species).

Mushrooms have insignificant nutritive value. They are esteemed as a succulent specialty food of delicate, subtle flavour and agreeable texture. By fresh weight, the common commercially grown mushroom is more than 90 percent water, less than 3 percent protein, less than 5 percent carbohydrate, less than 1 percent fat, and about 1 percent mineral salts and vitamins.

Poisoning by wild mushrooms is common and may be fatal or produce merely mild gastrointestinal disturbance or slight allergic reaction. It is important that every mushroom intended for the table be accurately identified, and collectors are to be discouraged from eating unknown or guessed-identity specimens (*see* mushroom poisoning).

·fungal features and classification **12**:756e
·hallucinogenic substances and effects **5**:1055c
·life-span features **10**:914f
·poisonous plant toxins **14**:608f; table 609
·spore dispersal via lured insects **12**:218g

mushroom fly: *see* fungus gnat.

mushroom poisoning, toxic, sometimes fatal effect of eating certain mushrooms (toadstools). There are some 70 to 80 species of mushrooms that are poisonous to human beings; many of them contain toxic alkaloids (muscarine, agaricine, phalline).

Among the mushrooms that most commonly cause poisoning are *Amanita muscaria* and *A. phalloides*. The ingestion of *A. muscaria* (fly agaric), which contains muscarine and other toxic alkaloids, is soon followed by nausea, vomiting, diarrhea, excessive salivation, perspiration, watering of the eyes, slowed and difficult breathing, dilated pupils, confusion, and excitability. Illness usually begins within six hours after eating the mushrooms, and recovery takes place within 24 hours.

A. phalloides, the death cup, or death cap, is far deadlier than the muscarine type; it contains heat-stable peptide toxins, phalloidin, and two amanitins, that damage cells throughout the body. Within 6 to 12 hours after eating the mushrooms, severe abdominal pain, vomiting, and bloody diarrhea appear, causing rapid loss of fluid from the tissues and intense thirst. Signs of severe involvement of the liver, kidneys, and central nervous system soon appear; these effects include a decrease in the output of urine and in the concentration of blood sugar, leading to coma that, in more than 50 percent of the incidents, ends in death.

The species *Gyromitra (Helvella) esculenta* contains a toxin that is ordinarily removed during cooking, but a few persons are highly susceptible to it. The chemical nature of the toxin has not been determined, but is a source of monomethylhydrazine, which affects the central nervous system and induces hemolytic jaundice.

The treatment of mushroom poisoning is aimed at removing the toxic material from the body (gastric lavage, enema) and at relieving the symptoms. Prevention rests upon the avoidance of all wild mushrooms. *See also* psilocin and psilocybin.

·poisonous plants **14**:608f; table 609

mushroom rock: *see* perched rock.

Musial, Stan(ley Frank) (b. Nov. 21, 1920, Donora, Pa.), professional baseball player who, in 22 years with the St. Louis Cardinals,

Musial

Pictorial Parade

won seven National League batting championships and in other ways established himself as one of the game's greatest hitters. He retired after the 1963 season with a career batting average of .331. His totals of times at bat (10,972), hits (3,630), and runs scored (1,949) have been surpassed only by Hank Aaron and Ty Cobb, his total of runs batted in (1,951) was exceeded only by Aaron, Babe Ruth, and Lou Gehrig; his number of 1,377 extra-base hits has been broken only by Aaron. From 1952 to 1957 he played in 895 consecutive games, a league record until 1969.

A left-handed batter and thrower, Musial began his professional career as a pitcher but developed a sore arm and switched to the outfield while still in the minor leagues. In the 1940s, Musial, Terry Moore, and Enos Slaughter formed one of the finest offensive and defensive outfield combinations in baseball history. Musial also proved adept at playing first base. When his career as a player ended, he became an executive of the Cardinals. In 1969 he was elected to the Baseball Hall of Fame.

Music V, process of digital-to-analog conversion for computer sound synthesis developed in the 1960s. *Cf.* computer music.

·electronic music composition **6**:677c

music, art of 12:662, expression in musical form, from the simplest to the most sophisticated, in any musical medium.

The text article covers speculations on the nature of music, from the ancient Greek to the modern, including non-Western theory; problems of musical meaning, including origins of modern theories, conflicting views about meaning, and considerations about performance practice; and music today, covering music and the mass media and discriminations among folk music, popular music, and jazz.

REFERENCES in other text articles:
·amateur instruction and participation **8**:975a
·art song development in West **19**:498f
·Bach and compositional methodology **2**:559a
·Beethoven's development of musical form **2**:799f
·Byzantine exclusion of instruments **4**:519h
·Cambodian cultural forms **3**:680f
·comic spirit and comic effect **4**:966d
·critical and aesthetic approaches **2**:43c
·dramatic import and use of music **5**:986g
·folk music development from special technique **7**:456b
·folk music forms and techniques **7**:466g
·humour hindered by nonverbal mode **9**:9g
·Islāmic art and religious restrictions **9**:923h
·Islāmic vocal and instrumental music **9**:973b
·jazz styles' reflection of societal conditions **10**:126d
·Jewish forms and performance **10**:205g
·Marxist-inspired Chinese folk music **12**:677f
·motion-picture elements and techniques **12**:497d
·musical sound's traditional limitation **17**:34g
·music criticism nature **12**:722a
·mythological basis of music **12**:799b

·Nietzsche theory of tragedy and opera **18**:592e
·opera criticism pro and con **13**:578f
·professional training and schools **2**:95g
·Rameau's life and works **15**:500b
·recording's importance and influence **12**:691f
·Roman attitude and educational decline **6**:327h
·Romantic style development **6**:1070d
·Scarlatti style and keyboard techniques **16**:338d
·solo-ensemble nature of jazz **10**:121e
·South Asian folk and classical music **17**:150b
·Southeast Asian traditional forms **17**:237a
·status in art classifications **2**:82d *passim* to 84g
·stylistic movements in the 19th century **6**:1076e
·symbolic and religious use **17**:905e
·visual arts relation to other arts **19**:246d
·Wagnerian impact on composition **19**:517c
·Zairian cultural life **19**:1126e

RELATED ENTRIES in the *Ready Reference and Index: for*
compositional style: see concertato style; empfindsamer Stil; Expressionism; gallant style; Gebrauchsmusik; Impressionism; Neoclassicism; Neoromanticism; Postromantic music
compositional technique: aleatoric music; cyclic technique; fauxbourdon; in nomine; isorhythm; microtonal music; organum; program music; quodlibet; twelve-tone music; variations, musical
musical form: Bar form; binary form; rondo; ternary form
musical rhythm: aksak; colotomic structure; iqaʿ; isorhythm; modes, rhythmic; tala
musical notation: accidental; bar; clef; mensural notation; neume; shape-note hymnals; staff; tablature; time signature
musical performance: accompaniment; cadenza; improvisation; obbligato; ornamentation

music, East Asian **12**:669, music of regional cultures as far south and west as Vietnam, Tibet, and Central Asia, north to Mongolia, Manchuria (Northeast Provinces), and Korea, and east to Japan.

The text article covers East Asian music from as early as 2000 BC to the present, concentrating on China, Korea, and Japan.

REFERENCES in other text articles:
·chamber music ensembles **17**:743b
Chinese music
·classical and modern theatre music **12**:700e
·idiophone types and functions **14**:61c *passim* to 62b
·metaphysical and numerical basis **12**:746g *passim* to 748a
·symbolic qualities **12**:746g
·drums in cult and ceremony **14**:65a
·expression in Western notation **2**:83g
·harmony's unimportance **8**:647b
·idiophone types and history **14**:61b
·Islāmic influences **9**:975b
Japanese music
·function of rhythm in gagaku music **12**:728f
·idiophone types and functions **14**:61c
·Nō and Kabuki theatre music **12**:700f
·Nō theatre's musical base **13**:272g
·Peking opera instrumentation and vocal style **12**:744c
·symbolic qualities **12**:746g *passim* to 748a
·traditions and changes **10**:55f
·Korean folk tradition preservation **10**:527e
·musical rhythm limited by harmony **12**:746d
·music in Confucian philosophy **12**:662h
·performing arts' aesthetic unity **5**:469a
·pitch representation in oral tradition **12**:736h
·poetry history **10**:1051c
·Shintō entertainment for gods **16**:675f
·Western popular music's development **14**:811g
·wind instrument varieties and influence **19**:858b

RELATED ENTRIES in the *Ready Reference and Index: for*
flutes: see shakuhachi; ti
idiophone percussion: stone chimes
membranophone percussion: changko; taiko; tsuzumi
performance genre: gagaku; hayashi; joruri; nagauta; opera, Chinese
reed wind instruments: hichiriki; sheng
zithers: ch'in; cheng; kayakeum; koto; wagon
other: lü pipes; shomyo

music, electronic: *see* electronic music and instruments.

music, primitive, concept usually understood to refer to vocal and instrumental sounds produced in primitive societies. Its meaning cannot be precise because usage of the words "primitive" and "music" has undergone changes. These shifting conditions reflect the evolution of new interests and attitudes, in relation to these sounds, among Western observers and in illiterate societies. Anthropologists have come to suspect the term primitive of being too ambiguous and to avoid it because of its pejorative associations. Western musicians doubt whether their concept of music, which refers to the music of artists, can legitimately be applied to the "sound making" of so-called primitives. The impasse has been partly overcome by art historians. They think of primitive music as a process and speak of premusical sounds—organized for rhythmization of work and ritual, for stimulation, and perhaps for magical purposes—and of a long premusical period in which "the elementary *materials* of music became established" (S.K. Langer).

Primitive music was found to be more diverse and complex than the lexicographic meanings of the word primitive suggest, a not surprising situation. Sound enters into and emanates from most human and other animal activities. Gibbon monkeys use stereotyped vocalizations that produce characteristic reactions in their fellows, and expression is given to "aggressive or defensive behaviour" (C.R. Carpenter). Chimpanzees form a circle, deck themselves out with twigs and leaves, and make rhythmic noises by stamping on the ground. Man's acoustic utterance, however, is invested with yet another quality: the supernatural. According to students of primitive religion, the supernatural took different forms at different stages of prehistory; but whatever the form, it was acted out and danced out. Elementary materials of music were thus nurtured and became established.

To speculate on the place of primitive music within the supernatural is not the same as speculating on the origin of music itself. The following have been held responsible for the genesis of music: competition in courting; imitation of bird calls; rhythms demanded by work; lulling an infant; release of passion; patterns of speech, or, more specifically, a primeval tonal communication that gave rise to both language and music; and calling from a distance, which requires an essentially musical treatment so that the voice may carry.

Among the inhabitants of Tierra del Fuego in South America, no known instruments are especially designed for sound. "Instead they blow into the windpipe of a newly killed duck or at their death dances they pound the earth with pairs of thick, long poles or drum on a rigid rolled piece of hide. Men bellow into the hollow of their hands placed against the earth, knock sticks and branches against the frame of the festival hut for rhythm, or simply beat the floor of the hut with bare fists" (E.M. Hornbostel).

The acoustic devices in these early instruments are manifold. The lowest (Paleolithic) levels show man stamping, shaking, rubbing, scraping, and blowing, armed with common objects turned to musical purpose ad hoc and, later, employing rattles, bull roarers, and flutes without finger holes. The later prehistoric levels add to these the slit drum, stamping tubes, flutes with finger holes, trumpets, and the earliest stringed instruments, including the musical bow.

With the invention of the bow, man succeeded in concentrating and controlling energy. To a 20th-century person it may be plausible that this must have been for shooting an arrow; to Neolithic man it may have been equally plausible to use the energy of the bow for communicating with the supernatural by making sounds. A prehistoric cave painting at Les Trois Frères in France shows the bow thus used in ritual.

The difficulty is understandable in identifying any survivals of rhythm from the lowest levels of the premusical period. Western civilization has a striking example of such survival in its children's rhymes. They are built to an underlying scheme of eight values, arranged in four pairs of two quavers, each pair read in $\frac{2}{8}$ time. Widely differing structures in many languages have been found to adapt their individual features to this scheme. The children's rhymes of Europe correspond to examples of adult singing among the Kabyle, Tuareg, the Negroes of Senegal, Dahomey, and The Sudan, and the indigenous peoples of Taiwan. *See* melody.

·African cultural impact **1**:244a
·shamanic ritual songs **16**:640f
·wind instrument ritual use **19**:851e

music, recording of **12**:691, physical reproduction of music by mechanical, acoustical, or electrical means.

The text article covers the impact of recording on composition, teaching, criticism, concerts, and musicology; the role of the producer; and the development of musical recording.

REFERENCES in other text articles:
·Amerindian musicology use **1**:669b
·appreciation of Berlioz' music **2**:856h
·audience dictation of mass music style **2**:108b
·automata and mechanical music box art **2**:494f
·automatic performance media **2**:83d
·basic technology and methods **17**:51g
·motion picture dubbing technique **12**:549g
·motion pictures and sound tracks **12**:504f

music, theatrical **12**:695, music composed to govern, enhance, or support a theatrical conception.

The text article covers the types of theatrical music and its historical development.

REFERENCES in other text articles:
·art song development in Spain **19**:501g
·ballet composition **4**:453f
·ballet score composition **2**:646f
·Beethoven's connection with theatre **2**:797f
·Cage philosophy and composition **18**:942d
·Central Asian religious ritual accompaniment **3**:1127f
·dance accompaniment and choreography **5**:454b
·drama's role in performing arts **5**:988b
·dramatic import and use of music **5**:986g
·East Asian performing arts **5**:469a
·Greek and Christian origins and impact **18**:220b
·humour analysis problems **9**:9h
·Italian literary influence **10**:1159f
·motion picture developments and effects **12**:504e
·motion picture elements and techniques **12**:497d
·motion-picture industry and song exposure **12**:496d
·popular theatre music from antiquity to musical comedy **14**:807f *passim* to 810c
·popular theatre's musical element **14**:813f
·puppet theatre's use of music **15**:295h
·Purcell's compositions and influence **15**:297f
·South Asian performance accompaniment **17**:152e
·Tibetian 'cham performance **3**:1127a
·Venetian historic opera presentations **19**:75b
·Vivaldi's operatic compositions **19**:494f
·wind instrument historical utilization **19**:852d

RELATED ENTRIES in the *Ready Reference and Index:*
incidental music; intermezzo; minstrel show; musical comedy; music hall and variety; operetta; vaudeville

music, Western **12**:704, music of Western civilizations.

TEXT ARTICLE covers:
Roots in antiquity **12**:704b
The Middle Ages 704g
The Renaissance period 706b
The Baroque era 708g
The Classical period 710d
The Romantic period 712e
Modern period 714d

REFERENCES in other text articles:
·African cross-cultural influences **1**:243d

Musica, De, treatise by St. Augustine.
·musical feet added **12**:745f

Musica enchiriadis (*c.* 900), treatise on music by Pseudo Hucbald (*see* Hucbald).
·polyphony's origin and development **12**:705b

musica ficta, or MUSICA FALSA, in medieval and Renaissance music, insertion, for theoretical or aesthetic reasons, of unnotated chromatic notes (notes not belonging to the mode of a piece) into music during performance—that is, the addition by performers of unwritten sharps and flats. This practice was responsible for the introduction of accidentals (sharps, flats, naturals) into musical notation. It also influenced the evolution of the major and minor keys on which most Western music came to be based, for it modified the medieval church modes to resemble the major and minor scales.

Musica ficta occurs both in the purely melodic music of plainchant and in polyphony, or many-voiced music. While the rules of its usage are known, medieval and Renaissance music theorists disagreed about details; their views lagged behind changes in performance practice; and modern scholars differ in their opinions as to how extensively the practice was carried out. Musical manuscripts offer some clues, but accidentals were frequently omitted, for they were often considered an insult to the performer. Consequently two modern editions of the same Renaissance piece may show slight differences in their notation of the musica ficta for the modern performer. In modern editions the editorial insertions of musica ficta are indicated by small accidental signs placed above the notes affected.

Certain rules of musica ficta are believed to have been commonly applied. Generally the tritone, for example, f–b, was avoided both in melodies and between the voices of polyphonic music, with, in this case, f♯ or b♭ substituted as appropriate. The "leading tone" was often used: the seventh tone of the mode was raised a half step (for example, f might become f♯) when it led, or ascended, to the final note of the mode (in this case, g). For purely aesthetic reasons an upper neighbour note might be altered (for example, a–b–a might become a–b♭–a). Other rules were applied in other instances. For example, the final chord of a piece was altered if it would not otherwise be a major triad (for example, the chord, or triad, c–e♭–g became c–e–g), considered a more appropriate conclusion to a composition.

musical bow, stringed instrument found in most archaic cultures. It consists of a flexible stick 1.5 to 10 feet (0.5 to 3 metres) long, strung end to end with a taut cord that the player plucks or taps to produce a weak fundamental note. The player may produce other notes by stopping the string with finger and thumb; by lightly touching the string to produce faint-sounding overtones; by tying the string to the stick to form two taut segments; or, on a mouth bow, by using his mouth as a resonator, varying its cavity in order to isolate overtones. In a gourd bow a truncated gourd attached to the stick serves as a resonator. Other musical bows may have separate resonators, as a gourd or pot.
·instrument origins and development **12**:730a
·stringed instrument resonator shape **17**:740b

musical colour: *see* timbre.

musical comedy, also called MUSICAL, dramatized production that is characteristically sentimental and amusing in nature, with a simple but distinctive plot, and offering music, dancing, and dialogue.

Since its beginnings in the middle of the 19th century, musical comedy has assumed diverse forms. The roots of this theatrical genre go back to public entertainments such as pantomime, variety shows (later to become vaudeville), minstrelsy, and extravaganza. These entertainments in time either fused into a single offering or, as in the case of pantomime, became shows unto themselves. These very early antecedents to musical comedy tended to blend the traditions of French ballet with toe dancing, acrobatics, aerial acts, and dramatic interludes—all very much like the television variety show of the mid-20th century.

On Sept. 12, 1866, a musical play, *The Black Crook*, opened in New York City. It has been described as a combination of French Romantic ballet and German Romantic melodrama, and it successfully attracted patrons of opera and serious drama and the devotees of the burlesque shows thriving in New York City's Bowery. In 1874 Johann Strauss the Younger produced his operetta *Die Fledermaus* in Vienna and in 1878 W.S. Gilbert and Arthur Sullivan their *H.M.S. Pinafore* in London. The latter was a production that combined a literate libretto with distinctive music and stylized acting, a milestone in musical theatre. In the late 1890s the British showman and entrepreneur George Edwardes brought his London Gaiety Girls to New York, calling his production musical comedy to distinguish it from his previous burlesques. From all these traditions, and with the addition of a native drive and ingenuity, U.S. musical comedy began to develop.

The European composers Victor Herbert, Rudolf Friml, and Sigmund Romberg brought to the United States a form of operetta that was, in every sense, the generic source for musical comedy; it was sentimental and melodious and established a tradition of the play based on musical numbers and songs. Romberg's works, such as *The Student Prince* and *The Desert Song*, were also successful motion pictures. Such works depended for their appeal largely on romance set in faraway times and lands and on memorable songs that resembled the operatic aria insofar as they furthered the plot with dialogue set to music.

During the 1920s and 1930s, musical comedies tended to dwell on the tribulations and successes of show business, with rags-to-riches plots that served as wish fulfillments for the audience. These productions were created by some of the most notable composers and writers in the United States, such as Richard Rodgers and Lorenz Hart, Rodgers and Oscar Hammerstein II, Harold Arlen, Jerome Kern, and George Gershwin. Vincent Youmans' and Irving Caesar's *No, No, Nanette*, which opened in Detroit in 1925, had a highly successful and nostalgic return to Broadway in 1971.

In the 1940s the musical comedy genre evolved into a form that laid more stress on the story, making the music more organic to the play, with dances that were carefully choreographed. Two prime examples of this trend were Rodgers and Hammerstein's *Oklahoma!*

(1943) and *South Pacific* (1949). Their show *Carousel* (1945) introduced an element of tragedy and death, along with eloquent music, which brought it very close to a folk opera.

In addition to reviving sentimental favourites such as *No, No, Nanette*, musical theatre in the 1970s became a vehicle for social comment. Most notable was the rock musical *Hair*, which blended amplified rock music, stroboscopic lighting, a degree of audience participation, youthful irreverence, and nudity.

Although the musical as it flourished in the period 1920–60 seemed by the 1970s to be on the wane, its descendants, such as *Hair* and *Jesus Christ Superstar*, showed the continuing development of the genre. *See also* operetta. *Major ref.* **12**:697d

·costume designer's task **17**:563h
·German adoption and popularity **8**:66h
·popular music style and examples **14**:810c
·popular theatre's musical element **14**:813g

musical composition 12:715, either the process of "putting together" a piece of music or the finished product susceptible to repeated rendition.

The text article covers the process of composition and the varying approaches to composition during different periods of Western music.

REFERENCES in other text articles:
·African structure and language influence **1**:243h *passim* to 246c
·ballet score composition **2**:646f
·chamber music origins **4**:22c
·choral writing refinement **4**:442e
·compositional aspect of counterpoint **5**:213e
·concerto forms **4**:1064g
·counterpoint as Western technique **5**:213d
·early symphony and theme manipulation **17**:911a
·East Asian musical rhythm organization **12**:685c
·electronic music composition **6**:675c
·European culture evaluation **6**:1070e
·fugue form dictated by composer's needs **7**:769b
·harmony succession importance in music **8**:647a
·instrumentation and ensembles **13**:644a *passim* to 647e
·jazz structural principle **10**:119g
·jazz structures **14**:810f
·Jewish temple music **10**:207a
·modal basis of non-Western music **12**:298a
·musical criticism principles **12**:722h
·musical form types and structure **12**:725a
·musical theory **12**:746g *passim* to 748g
·music in the Western world **12**:704a
·organ literature development **13**:680c
·performer's alienation from composer **2**:100a
·recording as influence and medium **12**:692c
·sound components as elements **12**:662f
·South Asian classical music development **17**:150h
·stringed instrument history and use **17**:742b
·text imagery in music allegory **7**:134g
·vocal music and prosody **19**:498b *passim* to 499a

RELATED ENTRIES in the *Ready Reference and Index:*
aleatoric music; homophony; improvisation; melody; monody; period; polyphony

musical criticism 12:722, branch of aesthetics concerned with making value judgments about either musical composition or performance or both.

The text article covers the function of musical criticism, proposes a definition of the practice, propounds a theory of musical criticism, and relates criticism to the form, content, and meaning of compositions. The article then treats criticism in relation to performance and concludes with a brief survey of the development of musical criticism.

REFERENCES in other text articles:
·criticism's nature and purpose **2**:85c
·Islāmic medieval writings **9**:974a
·jazz orchestra as self-contradiction **10**:124e
·records' effect on critical viewpoint **12**:692f

musical film, motion picture consisting of musical numbers and with a generally sentimental or lightly humorous plot. Although usually considered a U.S. genre, musical films from Japan, Italy, France, Great Britain, and Germany have contributed to the development of the type. The first sound picture was *The Jazz Singer* (1927), starring Al Jolson. It was followed by a series of musicals hastily made to capitalize on the novelty of sound. One of the few outstanding films of this early period was *Broadway Melody* (1929), which won the Academy Award for best picture of 1928–29.

In the early 1930s the German director G.W. Pabst presented a serious musical film, *The Threepenny Opera* (*Die Dreigroschenoper*, 1931), from the ballad opera by Bertolt Brecht and Kurt Weill. The most popular films of this period, though, were the extravagantly imaginative U.S. films of Busby Berkeley (1895–1976), a former Broadway dance director who presented elaborately staged dance sequences within the framework of well-worn stories. The Berkeley spectaculars such as the Gold Diggers productions (1933–37), *Footlight Parade* (1933), and *Forty-second Street* (1933) often starred Joan Blondell, Ruby Keeler, or Dick Powell, all of whom became well-known musical performers.

The films of the singing and dancing teams of the mid-1930s—*e.g.*, Fred Astaire and Ginger Rogers, the best known couple; Maurice Chevalier or Nelson Eddy and Jeanette MacDonald—gradually superseded the Berkeley spectacles in popularity.

The musicals of the late '30s and early '40s, including *The Wizard of Oz* (1939), *Babes on Broadway* (1941), *Meet Me in St. Louis* (1944), all starring Judy Garland, and the frankly sentimental *Going My Way* (1944) and *The Bells of St. Mary's* (1945), both starring the popular singer Bing Crosby, showed evidence of the trend toward more realistic unification of plot and music. Well-remembered films from the immediate post-World War II period are *Easter Parade* (1948); *An American in Paris* (1951) and *Singin' in the Rain* (1952), both starring Gene Kelly; and *Kiss Me Kate* (1953).

By the mid-1950s the demand for original musical films was declining, although film adaptations of Broadway hits such as *Oklahoma!* (1955), *Guys and Dolls* (1955), *South Pacific* (1958), *The King and I* (1956), *West Side Story* (1961), *The Sound of Music* (1965), and *My Fair Lady* (1964) were great box office successes.

There was also a growing subtlety in musicals, as in the French film *The Umbrellas of Cherbourg* (*Les Parapluies de Cherbourg*, 1964); a tendency to use the musical to exploit the appeal of a popular singing star, as in the many films of Elvis Presley; and experimentation with the merging of innovative popular music and film-making techniques, as in the pictures of the English singing group the Beatles.

·Indian film music sources **17**:151b
·motion picture popularity in U.S. **12**:508f

musical form 12:725, the structure, or shape, of a musical composition; that is, the arrangement of individual elements so as to constitute a whole.

The text article covers the principles of musical form, formal types, Western compound forms, and non-Western forms.

REFERENCES in other text articles:
·African song formula and function **1**:244d
·Amerindian song and dance patterns **1**:664b *passim* to 669b
·Cambodian and Western comparison **3**:680f
·Central Asian folk structure **3**:1124g
·chamber music stylistic evolution **4**:23d
·Christian 4th-century hymn elaboration **4**:541e
·concerto and concerto grosso **4**:1064g
·folk music structures **7**:468b
·fugue form arrangement **7**:769b
·harmony as determinant **8**:655b
·Islāmic musical structures **9**:974e
·jazz composition **10**:119g
·musical composition growth **12**:715e
·musical criticism principles **12**:722h
·organ literature development **13**:680c
·popular music forms **14**:807g *passim* to 811e
·South Asian classical music structure **17**:150g
·symphony evolution **17**:909f
·tripartite structure in Japanese music **12**:681b
·vocal art music development in the West **19**:497f

RELATED ENTRIES in the *Ready Reference and Index: for*
medieval derivation: see conductus; fanfare
Renaissance derivation: capriccio; fantasia; march; suite; toccata
Baroque derivation: barcarole; chorale prelude; concerto; fugue; invention; opera; sonata; symphony
Classical era derivation: étude; serenade; string quartet
Romantic era derivation: berceuse; brindisi; impromptu; nocturne
units and types: Bar form; binary form; coda; movement; ritornello; rondo; ternary form
compositional technique: aleatoric music; cyclic technique; fauxbourdon; in nomine; isorhythm; organum; quodlibet; serialism; twelve-tone music; variations, musical
dance forms: afterdance; allemande; basse danse; bergamasca; bourrée; branle; chaconne; contredanse; country dance; courante; écossaise; estampie; galliard; galop; gavotte; gigue; hornpipe; ländler; mazurka; minuet; passacaglia; passepied; pavane; polka; polonaise; rigaudon; saltarello; sarabande; schottische; volta; waltz
other: cadence; canon; character piece; choral music; clausula; finale; hocket; humoresque; vocal music

musical instruments 12:729, objects or artifacts used to produce musical sound, whether used for ritual or ceremonial purposes or to create music for its own sake.

The text article covers the production of sound by instruments, their technical development and the craftsmanship of their manufacture, and their ritual and ceremonial use. It further deals with their classification and history.

REFERENCES in other text articles:
·African intertribal relations **1**:235c
·African types, construction, and use **1**:248f
·Amerindian types and use **1**:664d
·ancient Chinese classification system **12**:673b
·ancient religious literary references **10**:206g
·Byzantine absence for religious reasons **4**:519h
·Central Asian variety and uses **3**:1124f
·folk instrument construction and design **7**:473e
·folklore and early musical sound **7**:457e
·folk uses and geographical types **7**:469a
·improvement in early 19th century **6**:1070f
·instrumental music development **12**:666e
·instrumental music since Renaissance **12**:707b
·Islāmic instrumental types **9**:974f
·keyboard instrument development **10**:436g
·Melanesian native accompaniment **11**:869f
·metalwork art in chung bells **11**:1116c
·musical sound production **17**:38c
·music criticism principles **12**:723b
·music since the Renaissance **12**:704c
·19th–20th-century instrumental techniques **4**:25c
·Oceanian music developments **13**:457h
·opera use **13**:579h *passim* to 581g
·organ history and construction **13**:676a
·percussion instrument classification **14**:58d
·sound production methods **17**:33e
·Southeast Asian traditions and use **17**:237b
·string history, construction, and use **17**:738h
·Sumerian culture's types and function **12**:740c *passim* to 743b
·wind instrument design, development, and use **19**:847d; illus. 851

RELATED ENTRIES in the *Ready Reference and Index:*
aerophone; chordophone; electrophone; idiophone; membranophone; musical instruments, mechanical; musical instruments, transposing

musical instruments, mechanical, instruments sounded by automatic arrangements, as the pinned cylinder and clockwork of a music box. Other examples include the barrel organ, barrel piano, and player piano (*qq.v.*).
·keyboard automatic instruments **10**:445g

musical instruments, transposing, instruments that produce a higher or lower pitch than indicated in music written for them. Examples include clarinets, the English horn, and saxophones. Musical notation written for transposing instruments shows the relative pitches, rather than the exact pitches produced. Writing in this manner is a historical convention that often allows players to switch from a given instrument to a related one without relearning fingerings and other techniques (as from E♭ clarinet to B♭ clarinet or from English horn to oboe). The instrument name, as in the case of B♭ clarinet, often indicates the pitch resulting when the player sounds the note written as C. If the actual pitch is lower (or higher) than the notated pitch—say, by one step—the written music must be adjusted upward (or downward) by the same amount. Thus, in the key of C major the music for the B♭ clarinet must be written in the key of D major.
Although most transposing instruments belong to the woodwind and brass families, transposing keyboard instruments have also been built. The piccolo, contrabassoon, and other instruments whose parts are written an octave above or below the actual pitch (as c′ above c) are not considered transposing instruments.

musical notation **12**:732, a visual record of musical sound (heard or imagined) or a set of visual instructions for performance of music that helps shape a composition in a way impossible by oral means and serves to preserve music for performance, study, and analysis. Its main elements are pitch (location of musical sound in the scale), duration, timbre, and volume.
The text article deals with the general principles of Western staff notation and its evolution; other systems of notation, including verbal, alphabetical, numerical, graphic, and tablatures. These latter sections include a full description of several ancient and several non-Western forms of notation.

REFERENCES in other text articles:
·advent of performer's interpretive role **12**:738f
·African musical interlocking relation **1**:248a
·Amerindian musicology methods **1**:669c
·Chinese ch'in zither system **12**:676f
·church mode structure in Middle Ages **12**:297f
·development and use **2**:120d
·early Japanese systems **12**:682e
·importance for choral music development **4**:443a
·Islāmic music and oral transmission **9**:974a
·Jewish 12th-century documents **10**:206h
·Korean mensural system **12**:679h
·mathematical relations in scale **12**:748a
·musical rhythm representation **12**:745b
·music as notational art **2**:83g
·Shostakovich four-note cell **16**:717g
·sound recording as alternative **12**:691f
·South Asian music's limited use **17**:151d
·Tibetan Buddhist distinction **3**:1126h

RELATED ENTRIES in the *Ready Reference and Index:*
accidental; bar; clef; mensural notation; neume; note; staff; tablature; time signature

musical performance **12**:738, the realization of musical ideas by instrumental, vocal, or other means and their transmission to listeners.
The text article covers aspects of musical performance, including the performer as interpreter, mediums of performance, artistic temperament, national characteristics, and historical classifications of performance; and the history of musical performance through the historical periods in the West as well as outside the West.

REFERENCES in other text articles:
·acoustical design features **1**:56f
·Amerindian vocal-accompaniment rhythms **1**:664a *passim* to 669b
·art music tradition **12**:670f
·Baroque emergence of instrumental idiom **12**:718b
·Beethoven's piano virtuosity **2**:796g
·big band era **10**:124d
·chamber music audience growth **4**:28g
·choral arrangement of solo music **4**:442f
·concertos as concert showpieces **4**:1070d
·concerto soloist's virtuoso role **4**:1065a
·considerations relating to music's nature **12**:662g *passim* to 663c
·Corelli's development and style **5**:172h
·Couperin's distinction as harpsichordist **5**:217e
·criticism and artistic identity **2**:85g
·cross-cultural vocal trait study **16**:791a
·developing function in jazz **10**:122a
·drumming techniques and innovations **14**:64h
·electronic music developments **6**:674b
·emergence of monodic style **16**:789g *passim* to 793g
·improvisation in jazz and Indian music **12**:668h
·Islāmic vocal presentation **9**:974b
·Japanese musician's traditional recognition **12**:681e
·Japanese tradition in present-day performance **12**:691c
·jazz working definition **10**:119h
·Lester Young's contribution to performance art **10**:124g
·Liszt's piano virtuosity **10**:1034d
·Mahler's influence as conductor **11**:349f
·media growth with art singing rise **16**:790d
·Micronesian music and dance **13**:459d
·musical criticism requirements **12**:724b
·musical rhythm and tempo **12**:745a
·music as autonomous art **12**:666d
·opera as museum art **13**:593c
·organ building style influences **13**:679d
·organ Romantic revival **13**:681d
·rāga instrumentation and execution **12**:728h
·recording and live music **12**:692f
·Renaissance popular theatre music **14**:808d
·reverberation time optimum **17**:33b
·South Asian classical music performance **17**:151a
·stringed instrument history and use **17**:742b
·television adaptation from stage **18**:126g
·tuning's musical importance **18**:741a
·variation as performance technique **19**:30e
·Venetian historic opera presentations **19**:75b
·Vienna as musical centre **19**:117a
·virtuoso as object of public esteem **2**:100a
·virtuoso writing for chamber groups **4**:25b
·vocal registers in singing **17**:480h

RELATED ENTRIES in the *Ready Reference and Index: for*
musical training: see conservatory, musical; metronome
soloistic expression: cadenza; improvisation; obbligato
other: accompaniment; expression, musical; musical societies and institutions; music festival; ornamentation

musical rhythm **12**:744, the ordered alternation of contrasting elements within the musical medium.
The text article covers elements of rhythm, time, metre, and the notion of a rational framework encompassing the elements of musical rhythm.

REFERENCES in other text articles:
·African dance accompaniment **1**:253a
·African forms, structure, and notation **1**:244f
·African rhythm forms and structure **1**:245e
·Amerindian rhythmic variation **1**:664a
·Amerindian song and dance patterns **1**:663h *passim* to 669b
·ballad and folk song music **2**:643b
·ballroom dance relationship **14**:800g
·basis of Western music **12**:747a
·Central Asian folk structure **3**:1124h
·dominant function in East Asian music **12**:675h
·folk dance music **7**:453a
·folk music patterns **7**:468g
·formal organization of music **12**:726c
·function in early and later Baroque **12**:718d
·Gregorian chant's performance practice **12**:741c
·Islāmic musical modes **9**:974d
·jazz formalities and subtleties **10**:119h
·motion pictures and manipulation of pace **12**:504a
·notational rate of pitch succession **12**:733d
·origin as verbal indicators **12**:735c
·percussion instrument classification **14**:58e
·polymetre in Korean shaman ritual music **12**:678d
·processes of architectural composition **1**:1106c
·relation of compositional elements **12**:716a
·rhythmic modes in medieval counterpoint **5**:213f
·South Asian classical music variations **17**:151a
·staff notation and Western music **12**:733e
·style and analysis of formal elements **2**:126e
·time and movement in painting **13**:873f
·Western music history through Renaissance **12**:704f *passim* to 707a

RELATED ENTRIES in the *Ready Reference and Index: for*
rhythmic patterns: see aksak; colotomic structure; iqa; isorhythm; modes, rhythmic; tala
tempo indication: beat; metre; rubato
other: accent; cross rhythm; polyrhythm; syncopation

musical scales: *see* scales, musical.

musical societies and institutions, organizations formed for the promotion or performance of music, usually with some common factor. The German guilds of Meistersingers (master singers) flourished from the 14th to the 16th century, and the earlier French guilds of troubadours were associated with secular music, whereas groups such as the Compagnia de Gonfalone (Rome, 1264) and the Confrérie de la Passion (Paris, 1402) were formed for the performance of sacred music. During the Renaissance in France and Italy, academies were formed for the encouragement of poetry and music, the best known being in Paris, Florence, Venice, and Bologna; Florentine Camerata were responsible for the production of the first operas.
In the 17th and 18th centuries the institution of the Collegium Musicum, deriving from an earlier institution, the Convivia Musica, was associated with German and Swiss universities; its aim was to organize public concerts. Early concert societies in London were the Academy of Ancient Music (1710), the Anacreontic Society (1766), and the Catch Club (1761). In Paris the most important concert-giving society in the 18th century was Le Concert Spirituel, founded by the French composer Anne Philidor in 1725. Its rival, the Concerts des Amateurs, was founded in 1770. In Vienna the Tonkünstler Societät was formed in 1771. Choral music was fostered by the foundation of the Singakademie (Berlin, 1791). Concert societies were also formed in Bergen, Nor.; Stockholm; and Copenhagen during the 18th century.
During the 19th century, music societies expanded considerably. They included concert societies such as the Gesellschaft der Musikfreunde (Society of Friends of Music), founded 1812 in Vienna; the Parisian Société Philharmonique, founded by the composer Hector Berlioz in 1850; and the Société des Concerts du Conservatoire, founded in 1828. Amateur choir societies sprang up in England during the century; the most important were the Royal Choral Society (1871) and the Bach Choir (1875).
In the mid-19th century, scholars began to publish editions of earlier composers. Societies were formed to study and perform the work of particular composers (*e.g.*, the Bach-Gesellschaft, 1850; the Purcell Society, 1876), whose music was produced in authoritative and authentic editions.
With the rise of nationalism in the middle of

the 19th century, societies came into existence that promoted the printing and performance of national music. The study of folk music was allied to this, and such institutions as the International Folk Music Council came into being. The promotion of new music was fostered by such organizations as the International Society for Contemporary Music, formed in 1922. Musicological research was published by organizations such as the Royal Musical Association (England, 1874) and the American Musicological Society (1934). Groups such as the American Society of Composers, Authors, and Publishers (ASCAP) protect the copyrights of authors and composers. The American Society of Ancient Instruments (1922), the Society of Recorder Players (England, 1937), and other organizations promote interest in older music.

musical sound: *see* sound, musical.

Music and Musical Criticism: A Discourse on Method, essay by Sir Henry Hadow (1859–1937).
·music criticism on rational footing **12**:722b

Music as Metaphor (1960), book by Donald Ferguson.
·expressivity of musical references **12**:665a

music box, mechanical musical instrument sounded when a revolving brass cylinder with properly spaced pins (small projections) plucks graduated steel tongues cut in a comb or flat plate. Harmonics (component tones contributing to the characteristic sound) are generated in the solid steel back of the comb.

German music box, with disk in playing position, from Leipzig, *c.* 1900

By courtesy of the Musical Wonder House, Wiscasset, Maine; photograph, John Spinks

A spring and clockwork move the cylinder, and a fly regulator governs the rate. Probably invented *c.* 1770 in Switzerland, the music box was a popular domestic instrument in the 19th century until displaced by the phonograph and player piano. Large models were sometimes made, the teeth being plucked by projections on the lower side of a brass disk about 2½ feet (75 centimetres) in diameter. The disks could be changed to allow different selections, as could the cylinders on some instruments of the other type.
The music box is one of several idiophones (instruments the sounding parts of which are resonant solids) that are plucked rather than vibrated by percussion.
·automata with music making figures **2**:494f
·mechanical music reproduction history **12**:692a
·origins and erstwhile popularity **14**:60f

Music Center of Los Angeles County, in Los Angeles, established in the 1960s, comprises a number of auditoriums.
·seating capacities **11**:112h; illus.

music drama, type of serious musical theatre first advanced by Richard Wagner in his book *Oper und Drama* (1850–51; "Opera and Drama"), that was originally referred to as simply "drama" (Wagner himself never used the term music drama, which was a term later adopted by his successors and critics and scholars). This new type of work was intended as a return to the Greek drama as Wagner understood it—the public expression of national human aspirations in symbolic form by enacting racial myths and using music for the full expression of the dramatic action. Wagner's emphasis on opera as drama merely resumed and developed the ideas of Monteverdi and Gluck. He envisaged the disappearance of the old type of opera with its libretto provided by a hack versifer as an opportunity for the composer to make a "setpiece" opera out of purely musical forms separated by a recitative. Briefly put, the new art form would be created by a single artist, who would write a poetic drama that should find full expression as a musical drama when it was set to a continuous vocal-symphonic texture. This texture would be woven from basic thematic ideas, called leitmotivs (*q.v.*; "leading motives"); these would arise naturally as expressive vocal phrases sung by characters at crucial emotional points of the drama and would then be developed by the orchestra as "reminiscences" in accordance with the expressive need of the dramatic and psychological development of the action. This conception found full embodiment in *Der Ring des Nibelungen* (*q.v.*), a cycle of four operas first performed in 1876; the only variation from Wagner's theory was that the leading motives in *The Ring* did not always arise as vocal utterances, but were often introduced by the orchestra to portray characters, emotions, or events in the drama.
·art film and Wagnerian ideal **12**:667f
·contrapuntal accompaniment of leitmotifs **5**:216a
·harmony and dramatic expressivity **8**:650g
·maturation of Wagner's aesthetic ideas **13**:588d
·staging and Wagner's myth-Romanticism **17**:544c
·Verdi's independent development **19**:82d
·Wagner's opera form innovations **12**:728b
·Wagner's operas and writings **19**:517b

music festival, usually a series of performances at a particular place and inspired by a unifying theme, such as national music, modern music, or the promotion of a prominent composer's works. It may also take the form of a competition for performers or composers.
Series of religious services associated with a given feast early established the idea of the music festival in the church. The term festival in its modern sense, however, was first used in England. The Festival of the Sons of the Clergy, originally an annual charity sermon, was first given at St. Paul's Cathedral, London, in 1655; it took on a musical character in 1698.
The famed Three Choirs Festival was established in 1724 (an earlier form existed in 1715) and continues to take place annually and in rotation at the cathedral cities of Gloucester, Worcester, and Hereford. Harp festivals were held in Ireland toward the end of the 18th century.
Festivals of secular music in England came into being in the 18th century; the first devoted to Handel was held in 1784 in Westminster Abbey. Handel festivals continued almost without interruption well into the 20th century, including the triennial Handel Festivals held at the Crystal Palace, London, from 1857 until the building burned in 1936. The Birmingham Festival (1768, triennial from 1769 until 1912) was originally devoted to Handel's music but extended to other composers in the 1800s. During the 18th and 19th centuries, festivals, mostly choral, were developed in various cities in England; they include the Leeds Festival (triennial). The Glyndebourne Festival (for opera) was established in 1934 in Sussex, and the Edinburgh International Festival of Music and Drama was inaugurated in 1947; the Cheltenham Festival, initiated in 1945, is devoted to modern music.
In the U.S., several large-scale choral festivals on the English model were held in the 19th century. In 1869 and 1872 the celebrated bandmaster Patrick Gilmore organized two Peace Jubilee festivals, featuring choirs of 20,000 and orchestras of 1,000, plus artillery firing and bells.
Annual chamber-music festivals, performing specially commissioned works, were established by Elizabeth Sprague Coolidge (Pittsfield, Mass., 1918), and more specialized ones followed in the 20th century. In 1937 the conductor Serge Koussevitzky inaugurated the Berkshire Festival at Tanglewood, near Lenox, Mass.; both became events of notable musical importance. The annual Newport, R.I., jazz festival (1954) also became a prominent gathering. Numerous festivals of rock music were held in the 1960s and 1970s. In Puerto Rico the Spanish cellist Pablo Casals established a noted festival in 1957. Other Latin American festivals have been held in Caracas; Santiago, Chile; and Buenos Aires.
Numerous festivals were given annually in German cities during the 19th century. The Bayreuth Festival was inaugurated by the German composer Richard Wagner in 1876 to present his operas and music dramas in an opera house especially built for this purpose. In Salzburg, Austria, Mozart's birthplace, the first Mozart festival was held in 1877. Later including works by many composers, it became an annual summer event from 1920. Especially important among European opera festivals is that held in Munich (established 1901), devoted mainly to the work of Mozart, Richard Strauss, and Wagner. Other prominent European festivals include the Maggio Musicale Fiorentino (Florence Musical May), held annually from 1933; the Spoleto, Italy, festival, inaugurated by the composer Gian Carlo Menotti (1958); and the festivals held at Besançon and Aix-en-Provence, Fr., from 1948. Adventurous modern works, including electronic music, are heard each summer at the Darmstadt, W.Ger., festivals (1946). In the U.S.S.R., festivals of Soviet music are held annually on the November anniversary of the Bolshevik Revolution.
The International Society for Contemporary Music promotes modern works of novel nature; formed in 1922, it has held summer festivals in various European and U.S. cities. The first festival of music and drama at Ōsaka, Japan, was held in 1958.
Contests of artistic skill, including music, are ancient; musical competitions were part of the 6th-century-BC Pythian Games at Delphi. The eisteddfod (*q.v.*) in Wales had its beginnings in the 12th century or earlier, and in the 12th century the troubadours held musical competitions, the *puys*, at Puy Notre Dame, near Saumur, in France. The song contest organized by the Meistersingers at Wartburg, Ger., dates from the 13th century.
In 18th-century England local singing competitions were held by groups of singers at taverns. In the 19th century, singing and brass band competitions between amateur musicians became popular and were adjudicated by prominent figures.
In the U.S. in 1790, singers from Dorchester and Stoughton, Mass., competed at Dorchester. Similar amateur activity among students was later encouraged; and in the 20th century band, choral, and orchestral competitions among schools and colleges were organized on a large scale.
In the 20th century a new form of international competition was organized to promote the careers of professional performers. Such competition festivals include the Chopin International Competition for Pianists (begun 1927, Warsaw); the Queen Elizabeth of Belgium prize for violinists and pianists (begun 1927, Brussels); and the Tchaikovsky competition for pianists, violinists, and cellists (begun 1958, Moscow).
·Vermont cultural sponsorship **19**:90g

Music for the Royal Fireworks (1749), a series of pieces by George Frideric Handel, performed at the fireworks given in London to celebrate the Treaty of Aix-la-Chapelle.
·inspiration and rehearsal **8**:604f

music hall and variety, popular entertainment that features successive acts starring singers, comedians, dancers, and actors and sometimes jugglers, acrobats, and magicians. Derived from the taproom concerts given in city taverns in England during the 18th and 19th centuries, music hall entertainment was eventually confined to a stage, with the audience seated at tables; liquor sales paid the ex-

"An Anti-Idiotic Entertainment Company" from *The Wilds of London,* featuring an imaginary music hall called the Grampion, lithograph by Alfred Concanean, 1874

By courtesy of the Mander and Mitchenson Theatre Collection, London

penses. To discourage these entertainments, a licensing act was passed in 1751. The measure, however, had the contrary effect; the smaller taverns avoided obtaining licenses by forming music clubs, and the larger taverns, reacting to the added dignity of being licensed, expanded by employing musicians and installing scenery. These eventually moved from their tavern premises into large, plush, and gilt palaces where elaborate scenic effects were possible. By the early 19th century, the unlicensed "musick" houses changed into "burletta" houses—*e.g.*, theatres where the entertainment consisted of plays that by law included a certain number of songs. "Saloon" became the name for any place of popular entertainment; "variety" was an evening of mixed plays; and "music hall" meant a concert hall that featured a mixture of musical and comic entertainment.

During the 19th century the demand for entertainment was intensified by the rapid growth of urban population. By the Theatre Regulations Act of 1843, although drinking and smoking were banned from the legitimate theatres, they were permitted in the music halls. Tavern owners, therefore, often annexed buildings adjoining their premises as music halls. The low comedy of the halls, designed to appeal to the working class and to males of the middle class, caricatured events familiar to the patrons—*e.g.*, weddings, funerals, seaside holidays, large families, and wash day. Space also was found in the protracted programs for ballads of domestic tragedy and patriotic heroism. Some outstanding performers were Marie Lloyd, Dan Leno, Vesta Tilley, and "Little Tich" (Harry Relph). In 1891 Albert Chevalier, an actor from a fashionable theatre who appeared in the music halls, broke with the taproom humour and introduced songs of street life that earned him the title of "costers laureate." Harry Lauder's Highland love songs and Will Fyffe's nostalgic songs of sea and mountains added an idyllic note. It later became acceptable for "respectable" theatres such as the Drury Lane to occasionally feature music hall entertainment.

In the early 20th century, music halls were dwarfed by large-scale variety palaces. London theatres, such as the Hippodrome, displayed aquatic dramas, and the Coliseum presented re-enactments of the Derby and chariot races of ancient Rome. These were short-lived, but other ambitious plans kept variety prosperous after the real music hall had been killed by the competition of the cinema.

Celebrities such as Sarah Bernhardt, Sir George Alexander, and Sir Herbert Beerbohn Tree put on one-act plays or the last acts of plays; musicians such as Pietro Mascagni and Sir Henry Wood gave performances with their orchestras; popular singers of the 1920s, such as Nora Bayes, Sophie Tucker, and Gracie Fields, elicited great enthusiasm; Diaghilev's ballet, at the height of its fame, appeared in 1918 at the Coliseum on a program that included comedians and jugglers.

The advent of the talking motion picture in the late 1920s caused variety theatres throughout Great Britain to be converted into cinemas. To keep comedians employed, a mixture of films and songs called cine-variety was introduced, and there were attempts to keep theatres open from noon to midnight with nonstop variety. Except for the Windmill Theatre near Picadilly Circus, London, and the prosperous Radio City Music Hall in New York City, only a few survivors remained after World War II from what had been hundreds of music halls.

·development resulting from theatre laws **12**:699f
·origins and influence on popular music **14**:809e
·popular theatre's erotic element **14**:812h

Musicians Seamounts, submarine feature, Pacific Ocean.
31°00′ N, 162°00′ W
·Pacific Ocean floor features map **13**:838

Music of Changes (1951), composition for piano by John Cage.
·notational adaptation to modern music **12**:735f

music of indeterminancy: *see* aleatoric music.

Music of Time, The, series of novels by Anthony Powell, the first of which was published in 1951.
·literary style and theme **10**:1222d

Musicomp, acronym for MUSIC SIMULATOR-INTERPRETER FOR COMPOSITIONAL PROCEDURES, uncompleted computer language of basic compositional operations attempted by composer Lejaren Hiller.
·electronic music composition **6**:676f

music synthesizer, also called ELECTRONIC SOUND SYNTHESIZER, highly complex and flexible computerized instrument used specifically for the composition of electronic music. The

Moog electronic sound synthesizer

Allen H. Kelson

synthesizer, like the digital computer, accepts coded data from the composer, processes it, and translates the data into sound. The information fed to the synthesizer is coded on a punched paper tape, which is then subjected to the functions of thousands of sound-generating devices, such as oscillators, circuits, and vacuum filters, that are capable of producing effects far beyond the range and versatility of conventional musical instruments.

The intricate apparatus of the synthesizer generates simple wave forms and then subjects them to alteration in intensity, duration, frequency, and timbre, as programmed by the composer. The aural product is usually recorded on magnetic tape, to be played back, edited, or modified as desired.

The first electronic sound synthesizer was developed by U.S. acoustical engineers Harry Olson and Herbert Belar in 1955 at the Radio Corporation of America (RCA) laboratories at Princeton, N.J. Designed for research into the properties of sound, it attracted composers seeking to extend the range of available sound or to achieve total control of their music (because no performer is necessary).

The earliest synthesizer was an instrument of awesome dimensions. During the 1960s synthesizers of more compact design were produced; first the Moog, and, soon after, others, including the Buchla and Syn-Ket, the last approximately the size of an upright piano. Many newer synthesizers have keyboards or some modification of traditional performing mechanisms. The Syn-Ket has two three-octave keyboards. Compositions for it include the *Microtonal Fantasy* recorded in 1968 by composer-pianist John Eaton.

The Moog III, developed by the U.S. physicist Robert Moog, has two five-octave keyboards that control voltage changes (and thus pitch, timbre, attack, decay of tone, and other aspects of sound), allowing the composer an almost infinite variety of tonal control. A notable use of the Moog is in Alwin Nikolais' television ballet *The Relay*.

The Buchla synthesizer, developed by the U.S. scientist Donald Buchla, is activated by a "keyboard" that is a touch-sensitive metal plate without movable keys, comparable to a violin fingerboard. It has been used in such works as Morton Subotnick's *Silver Apples of the Moon* (1967) and *The Wild Bull* (1968).

The above small synthesizers use subtractive synthesis—removing unwanted components from a signal containing a fundamental tone and all related overtones (sawtooth-wave signals). The harmonic tone generator developed by James Beauchamp at the University of Illinois, in contrast, uses additive synthesis—building tones from signals for pure tones; *i.e.*, without overtones (sine-wave signals)—and offers certain advantages in the nuances of tone colours produced.

·electronic music developments **6**:675f

music theory 12:746, theory encompassing acoustics, aesthetics, and stylistic practice.

The text article covers the origins and history of western European music theory and the application of mathematics to music.

REFERENCES in other text articles:
·aesthetics of theme and variation **1**:151f
·Chinese tonal system **12**:672d
·counterpoint as vertical element **5**:213e
·diverse theories of musical meaning **12**:664b
·fugue parts and structure **7**:769g
·Greek esteem for musical profession **2**:97g
·Islāmic musical modes **9**:974b
·Korean Akhak kwebon document **12**:679d
·medieval codification of notation **12**:734f
·Middle Age scientific status **12**:715h
·mode history, construction, and use **12**:295e
·musical form types and structure **12**:725a
·Rameau's harmonic studies **15**:500e
·recording's aid to musicology **12**:692h
·South Asian classical music development **17**:150g
·style and analysis of formal elements **2**:127f
·systems of major literate cultures **12**:670g

RELATED ENTRIES in the *Ready Reference and Index:* for
aesthetic principles: see affections, doctrine of the
compositional technique: aleatoric music; cyclic technique; fauxbourdon; in nomine; isorhythm; microtonal music; organum; program music; quodlibet; twelve-tone music; variations, musical
musical form: Bar form; binary form; rondo; ternary form
musical notation: accidental; bar; clef; mensural notation; neume; staff; tablature; time signature
musical performance: improvisation; ornamentation
musical rhythm: aksak; colotomic structure; iqa; isorhythm; modes, rhythmic; tala

Musil, Robert (1880–1942), writer chiefly renowned for his unfinished work *Der Mann ohne Eigenschaften*, 3 vol. (1930–1943; Eng. trans., *The Man Without Qualities*, 1953), an ironic analysis of the ills of the age.
·social themes and major works **10**:1243b
·tragicomic view of human nature **4**:965d

musique concrète (French: "concrete music"), experimental technique of musical composition using as raw material recorded sounds and developed around 1948 by the French composer Pierre Schaeffer and his associates at the Studio d'Essai (Experimental Studio) of the French radio system. The fundamental principle of *musique concrète* lies in the assemblage of various natural sounds recorded on tape (or, originally, on discs) to produce a montage of sound. During the preparation of such a composition, the sounds selected and recorded may be modified in any way desired: played backward, cut short or extended, subjected to echo-chamber effects, varied in pitch, intensity, and other characteristics. The finished composition thus represents the combination of varied auditory experiences into an artistic unity.

A precursor to the use of electronically generated sound, *musique concrète* was among the earliest uses of electronic means to extend the composer's sound resources. The experimental use of machinery in *musique concrète*, the random use of ingredients, and the absence of the traditional composer-performer roles characterize the technique as a pioneering effort that led to further developments in electronic and computer-produced research in music.

Compositions in *musique concrète* include *Symphonie pour un homme seul* (1950; *Symphony for One Man Only*), by Schaeffer and Pierre Henry; and *Déserts* (1954), for tape and instruments, and *Poème électronique* (performed by 400 loudspeakers at the 1958 Brussels World's Fair), both by French-American composer Edgard Varèse.
·electronic transformation of sound **12**:714h
·origin and characteristics **6**:674d

musique mesurée, style of late 16th-century French vocal music in which the duration of the notes reflected the metre of the poetic text. *Musique mesurée* was one of several late 16th-century attempts to emulate the unity of verse and music supposedly achieved in classical antiquity. It was associated with *vers mesurés à l'antique*, poetry written to classical quantitative metres (based on long and short syllables).

Musique mesurée was largely the product of a circle of poets and musicians, the Académie de Poésie et de Musique, founded in 1570 by Jean-Antoine de Baïf, one of the members of the Pléiade, a prominent group of poets who drew inspiration from classical literature; also associated with the Académie was the principal poet of the period and the most influential member of the Pléiade, Pierre de Ronsard. To forward the cause of *musique mesurée*, the Académie sponsored concerts, many attended by its patron, King Charles IX.

Songs in *musique mesurée* were generally set for five voices and were at first sung unaccompanied; instruments were later permitted. Long syllables were set to notes twice as long as short syllables; all voice parts shared the same text, so that the music moved in chords and in flexible rhythms determined by the accentuation of the text. This rhythmic freedom influenced another important genre, the *air de cour* (solo song with lute accompaniment).

Musique mesurée imposed restricting limitations on the composer, but the technique was utilized with unusual flexibility and effectiveness by Claude Le Jeune, one of the truly masterful musicians of the period. Jacques Mauduit and Eustache Du Caurroy were also prominent composers of *musique mesurée*.
·polyphonic chanson style **12**:708f
·vocal music and prosody **19**:498g

Musi (MOESI) **River,** main stream of southern Sumatra, Indonesia, is about 325 mi (525 km) long and drains an area of 24,500 sq mi (63,500 sq km). It rises near Gunung (mount) Dempo in the Pegunungan (mountains) Barisan at 2,200 ft (670 m), and flows first south-southeast, then northeast, breaking through the mountains in the upper Palembang district to enter the Tertiary hill zone at Tebingtinggi. In the rainy season the river is navigable upstream as far as the Air (river) Rawas. The Musi joins the Ogan and Komering rivers at Palembang, 50 mi downstream from which it passes through a large delta before entering the Selat (strait) Bangka. It has depth enough for ocean vessels below Palembang.
2°20′ S, 104°56′ E

musk, substance obtained from the male musk deer and having a penetrating, persistent odour; it is used in the highest grades of perfume because of its odour characteristics, ability to remain in evidence for long periods of time, and its ability to act as a fixative. Its quality varies according to the season and the age of the animal from which it is obtained. In India and other parts of the Far East, aphrodisiac, stimulant, and antispasmodic effects have been attributed to musk.

Musk is obtained from pods contained in a pouch, or sac, under the skin of the abdomen of the male musk deer. Fresh musk is semiliquid but dries to a grainy powder. It is usually prepared for use in perfumes by making a tincture of 3 percent grain in pure alcohol. After standing for several months, this solution imparts character, strength, and tenacity to perfume.

The odorous principle of musk is muscone (muskone), $CH_3C_{15}H_{27}O$, or 3-methylcyclopentadecanone. Chemical compounds that produce musk odour in at least six different structural classes including muscone have been synthesized and used in perfumes.
·source and commercial use **16**:555c

Muskabad carpets: *see* Ferahan carpets; Sarūk carpets.

musk deer (*Moschus moschiferus*), small, compact deer, family Cervidae (order Artiodactyla). A solitary, shy animal, the musk

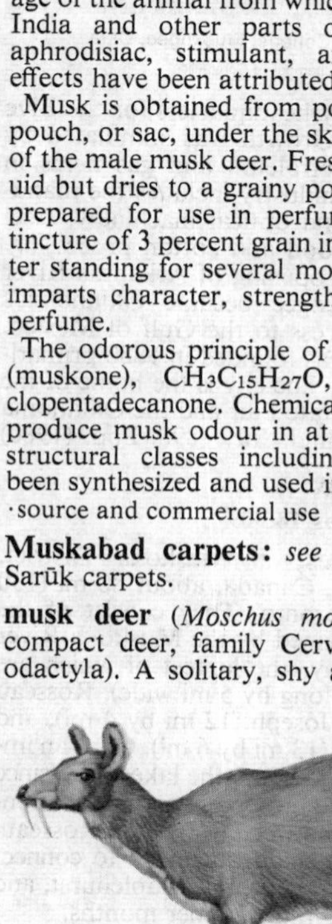

Musk deer (*Moschus moschiferus*)
Painting by Donald C. Meighan

deer lives in mountainous regions from Siberia to the Himalayas. It has large ears, a very short tail, no antlers and, unlike all other deer, a gall bladder. Grayish-brown, with long, coarse, brittle hair, the musk deer stands 50–60 centimetres (20–24 inches) at the shoulder, slightly higher at the rump. The male has long upper canine teeth that project downward from the mouth as tusks and has a musk-producing organ, the musk pod, on its abdomen. The musk from this organ is valued for use in perfumes and soaps.
·scent glands and classification **2**:77g

muskeg, bog type characteristic of far northern regions.
·bog types and characteristics **17**:837a

Muskegon, city, seat (1859) of Muskegon County, western Michigan, U.S., on Lake Michigan at the mouth of the Muskegon River, there forming Muskegon Lake. The largest port on Lake Michigan's eastern shore, it has auto and railroad ferry connections with Milwaukee. Laid out in 1849 on the site of a trading post (established in 1812), Muskegon (Indian: "river with marshes") became a sawmill centre and shipping point for lumber to Chicago. With depletion of the forests it turned to diversified manufacturing including aircraft engines, office furniture, auto parts, bowling equipment, and oil refining.

An Indian burial ground is in the centre of the city. Muskegon County Community College (1926) and Muskegon Business College (1885) are there. The Seaway Festival is an annual event. Inc. village, 1861; city, 1869. Pop. (1980) 40,823.
43°14′ N, 86°16′ W
·map, United States **18**:908

Muskegon Heights, city, Muskegon County, southwestern Michigan, U.S., just south of Muskegon city. Inc. village, 1891; city, 1903. Pop. (1980) 14,611.
43°12′ N, 86°12′ W

muskellunge (*Esox masquinongy*), solitary and somewhat uncommon pike (*q.v.*) valued

Muskellunge (*Esox masquinongy*)
By courtesy of the New York Zoological Society

as a fighting gamefish and, to a lesser extent, as a food fish. It inhabits weedy rivers and lakes of the North American Great Lakes region.

Largest of the pike family, the muskellunge averages about nine kilograms (20 pounds) in weight but may be 1.8 metres (6 feet) long and weigh 36 kilograms (80 pounds) or more. It is recognized by the elongate body and by the absence of scales on the lower part of the cheeks and gill covers.
·body plan, illus. 1 **16**:186
·Kentucky and natural habitat **10**:420c

muškēnum (2nd millennium), Assyrian palace officials.
·legal status and rights **11**:978h

musket, smoothbore shoulder firearm, evolved in 16th-century Spain as a larger version of the harquebus (*q.v.*). It was replaced in the 19th century by the rifle. Muskets were matchlocks until flintlocks were developed late in the 17th century. Most were muzzleloaders.

Early muskets were often handled by two men and fired from a portable rest. Such a weapon was typically 5.5 feet (1.7 metres) long and weighed 20 pounds (9 kilograms). It fired a two-ounce ball, with little accuracy, to

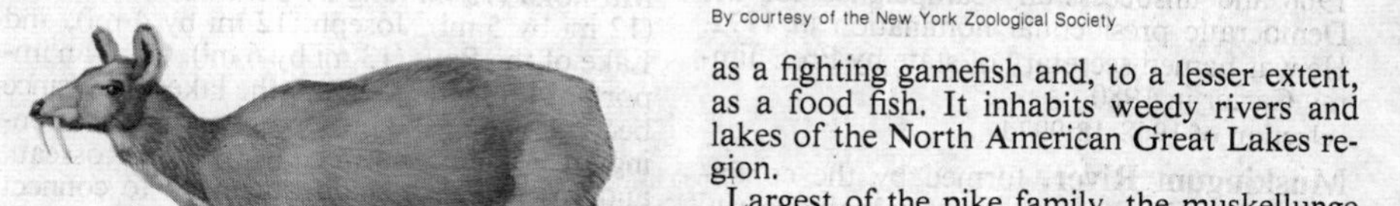

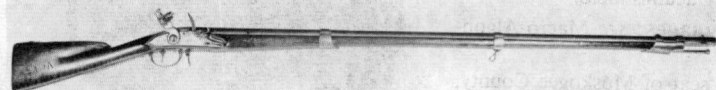

French Charleville musket *c.* 1779
By courtesy of the West Point Museum Collections, United States Military Academy

a range of about 175 yards (160 metres). Later types were smaller and lighter and accurate enough to hit a man-sized target at 80–100 yards. These had calibres ranging from 0.69 to more than 0.75.

·explosive ignition process **7**:84a
·Kentucky rifle and musket comparison **19**:578h
·shoulder weapons development **19**:684f
·small arms history and operation **16**:894h

Musketeers of Pig Alley, The (1912), motion picture by D.W. Griffith.

·gangster films **12**:508e
·social justice themes **12**:516e

Muskie, Edmund S(ixtus) (b. March 28, 1914, Rumsford, Maine), U.S. Democratic

Muskie
Fred Ward—Black Star

senator from Maine. The son of a Polish immigrant, he served as governor of Maine from 1954 to 1958, when he was elected to the U.S. Senate. He ran for the vice presidency on the Democratic ticket with Hubert Humphrey in 1968 and unsuccessfully campaigned for the Democratic presidential nomination in 1972. He was named secretary of state by Pres. Jimmy Carter in 1980.

·election of 1968 **18**:997d

Muskingum River, formed by the confluence of the Tuscarawas and Walhonding rivers at Coshocton, central southeastern Ohio, U.S. It flows about 115 mi (185 km) southward past Dresden, Zanesville, Duncan Falls, and McConnelsville to the Ohio River at Marietta. Licking River, which joins the Muskingum at Zanesville, is the chief tributary. A series of locks, dams, and short canals control flooding and make the river navigable.
40°03′ N, 81°59′ W

·map **18**:United States of America, Plate 14

musk mallow, also called ABELMOSK (*Hibiscus moschatus* or *H. abelmoschus*), annual or biennial plant of the mallow family (Malvaceae, *q.v.*), native to India. It grows 0.6–1.8 metres (2–6 feet) tall and bears large yellow flowers with a red centre. The plant is cultivated for its seeds, which are used in perfumes. The plant also yields a fibre used locally for clarifying sugar.

Musk mallow also refers to *Malva moschata*, a perennial European plant with pink or white flowers, deeply cut upper leaves, and kidney-shaped basal leaves. It has hairy black fruits.

muskmelon: *see* Cucumis melo.

Muskogean languages: *see* Macro-Algonkian languages.

Muskogee, city, seat of Muskogee County, east central Oklahoma, U.S., near the confluence of the Verdigris, Grand, and Arkansas rivers, surrounded by lakes. Founded in 1872 on the Missouri–Kansas–Texas Railroad and named for the Muskogee (Creek) Indians, it

The chapel of Bacone College, Muskogee, Okla.
By courtesy of the Muskogee Chamber of Commerce

became the agency headquarters for the Five Civilized Tribes. Growth was stimulated by the opening of petroleum and gas fields in 1904. Diversified industry includes the manufacture of glass and optical machinery, steel fabrication, and food and cotton processing. In 1970, with the opening of Arkansas River navigation, Muskogee became Oklahoma's first port with access to the Gulf of Mexico. Bacone College was founded in 1880 primarily for the Indians. The city is the home of the Oklahoma Free State Fair and the Oklahoma School for the Blind. Inc. 1898. Pop. (1980) 40,011.
35°45′ N, 95°22′ W

·map, United States **18**:909

Muskoka Lakes, in Muskoka District, southern Ontario, Canada, about 80 mi (130 km) north of Toronto. They consist of the chain of lakes drained by the Muskoka River into Georgian Bay, the largest of which are Muskoka (15 mi long by 5 mi wide), Rosseau (12 mi by 5 mi), Joseph (12 mi by 4 mi), and Lake of the Bays (13 mi by 6 mi). Once an important lumbering region, the lakes have since become one of the province's major vacationing areas. Locks between Muskoka, Rosseau, and Joseph lakes enable steamers to connect such resorts as Gravenhurst, Maplehurst, and Port Cockburn during summer months.

·location and resort area significance **13**:574d

musk-ox (*Ovibos moschatus*), shaggy-haired Arctic ruminant of the family Bovidae (order Artiodactyla).

Musk-oxen are stocky and have large heads, short necks, and short, stout legs. They have a musky odour. Bulls stand about 1.5 metres (5 feet) at the shoulder and weigh about 400 kilograms (880 pounds); cows are smaller. Horns, to about 60 centimetres (2 feet) long in old males, are present in both sexes. In males, they are broad based and proceed sideways from the midline of the skull, dipping downward at the sides of the head and curving upward at the ends. Females and the young have smaller horns. The coat of musk-oxen is of long, dark brown hair that reaches nearly to the feet, conceals the short tail, and nearly covers the small ears. Shorter hair covers the face. Underneath the shaggy coat is a thick wool, shed in summer.

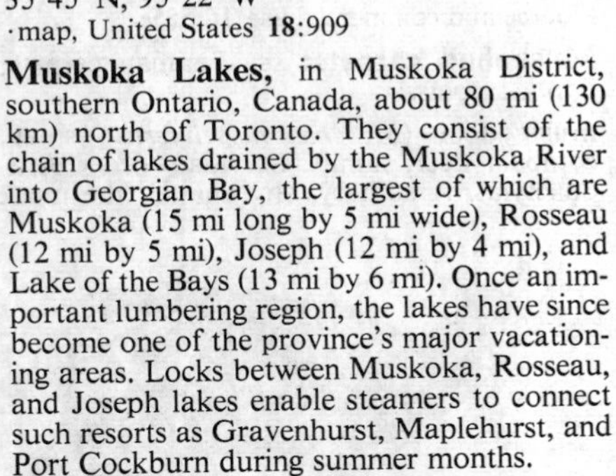

Musk-ox (*Ovibos moschatus*)
Authenticated News International

Musk-oxen travel in herds, often of 20 to 30 individuals. They are not aggressive but, when attacked, form a circle with the young inside and the larger animals presenting a formidable front of horns. Musk-oxen feed on grass and low-growing plants such as lichens and willows. Some authorities, who consider musk-oxen as Arctic cattle, urge their domestication in suitable areas.

In the Pleistocene Epoch (about 2,500,000 to 10,000 years ago) musk-oxen were circumpolar in distribution. They are now found from northern Canada to Greenland, and, since the advent of firearms to the Arctic, their range is thought to be even further restricted. In 1929 a group of musk-oxen was shipped from Greenland and introduced on Nunivak Island, near Alaska; from there a group was re-introduced to Siberia in 1975.

·Bovoidea superfamily classification **2**:80e
·tundra cold adaptation **18**:735b

muskrat, also called MUSQUASH (*Ondatra zibethica*), ratlike, semiaquatic rodent of the family Cricetidae (order Rodentia), found over most of North America except the tundra, and introduced into parts of Europe. The

Muskrat (*Ondatra zibethica*)
John H. Gerard

muskrat is a compact, heavy-bodied rodent about 30 centimetres (12 inches) long without the long, scaly tail that is flattened from side to side. The eyes and ears are small; the hind feet, used in swimming, are partially webbed and fringed with stiff bristles. The musky secretion for which the muskrat is named comes from musk sacs in the anal region. The fur, a basic commodity of the fur industry, is medium to dark blackish brown and consists of a dense, soft underfur heavily overlaid with long, stiff, glossy guard hairs.

The muskrat lives in marshes, shallow lakes, and streams, sheltering either in a burrow dug in a bank or in a reed and rush mound constructed in the water. Its food consists of a variety of sedges, reeds, roots—mostly of water plants—and occasional freshwater mussels, crayfish, salamanders, and fish. One or more litters of one to 11 young are produced each year after three to four weeks' gestation. The muskrat sometimes damages corn or burrows into earthen structures. It is edible and its flesh is sold as "marsh rabbit."

The round-tailed muskrat, or Florida water rat (*Neofiber alleni*), is another semiaquatic member of the family Cricetidae. It resembles a small muskrat about 36 centimetres (14 inches) in total length but is distinguished by its round, rather than flattened, tail. It is less aquatic than the muskrat and usually lives in heavily planted, watery areas, especially bogs.

·acclimatization to new environments **1**:32f
·diving ability comparison, table 2 **15**:762
·fur origin and characteristics table **7**:814
·fur source, habitat, migratory behaviour, and reproductive rate **15**:969h; table 975
·Mackenzie River Delta habitat area **11**:266f

musk turtle, any of the small freshwater turtles of the genus *Sternotherus*, family Kinosternidae. Musk turtles are named for the strong, musky odour they emit when disturbed. They are found in eastern North America, usually in quiet waters. Highly aquatic animals, they seldom emerge onto land. They take bait readily and are often caught by fishermen. Similar to small snapping turtles in appearance and pugnacious temperament, musk turtles are characterized

Musk turtle (*Sternotherus*)
Hugh Spencer

by a small lower shell and by small, fleshy barbels on the chin. Their upper shell is oval, dull in colour, and usually about 8–13 centimetres (3–5 inches) long. There are two or three generally recognized species of musk turtles. The stinkpot, or common musk turtle (*S. odoratus*), is an abundant form with two yellow stripes on each side of its head. It is the only member of the genus found in both the northeastern and southern United States.
·locomotion in water **11**:18f
·S. odoratus sexual maturation and size **15**:729g

Muslim Brotherhood, Arabic AL-IKHWĀN AL-MUSLIMŪN, religio-political organization founded in 1928 at Ismāʿīlīyah, Egypt, by Ḥasan al-Bannāʾ; it advocated a return to the Qurʾān and the Ḥadīth as guidelines for a healthy, modern Islāmic society. The brotherhood spread rapidly throughout Egypt, the Sudan, Syria, Palestine, Lebanon, and North Africa. Everywhere it set up schools, small industries, medical clinics, classes in military training, and an intelligence department.

After 1938 the Muslim Brotherhood began to politicize its outlook. In demanding purity of the Islāmic world, it rejected all direct foreign intervention and influence through Westernization, secularization, and modernization. A terrorist arm was organized, and, when the Egyptian government seemed to weaken in the mid-1940s, the brotherhood posed a real threat to the monarchy and the ruling Wafd Party. With the advent of the revolutionary regime in 1952, all political parties were dissolved. The brotherhood, however, simply retreated underground. After it had fomented disturbances among students, it was again prohibited in January 1954, but it continued to exist. An attempt to assassinate Nasser in Alexandria on Oct. 26, 1954, led to its forcible suppression. In the mid-1960s, however, it was again suspected of organizing anti-government demonstrations, and arrests and trials again ensued.
·attempt to assassinate Nasser **12**:844g
·modernism and tradition in Islām **9**:925c
·terrorist activities and suppression after 1952 revolution **6**:499c

Muslim (ISLAMIC) **calendar,** dating system based on a year of 12 months, each month beginning approximately at the time of the New Moon. The year has either 354 or 355 days, depending on whether the month Dhū al-Ḥijjah has 29 or 30 days. No months are intercalated, so that the named months do not remain in the same seasons but retrogress through the entire solar, or seasonal, year (of about 365¼ days) every 32½ solar years. The months are alternately 30 and 29 days long except for the 12th, Dhū al-Ḥijjah, the length of which is varied in a 30-year cycle intended to keep the calendar in step with the true phases of the Moon. In 11 years of this cycle, Dhū al-Ḥijjah has 30 days, and in the other 19 years it has 29. *Major ref.* **3**:600e
·chronology of Muslim history **4**:580e
·origin and sacred days **9**:920b

Muslim civil wars, major struggles for power that disrupted the Umayyad, ʿAbbāsid, and Spanish Umayyad caliphates.

The first civil war, or "great *fitnah*" (*q.v.*; AD 656–661), precipitated by the murder of the third caliph, ʿUthmān, was a contest for the caliphate between ʿAlī, the fourth caliph, and Muʿāwiyah, head of the Umayyad family. It not only propelled the Umayyads into a caliphate that became uniquely Arab and secular but also irrevocably split Islām into two factions: the Sunnī, who supported the Umayyads, and the Shīʿī, who believed in the divine right of ʿAlī and his successors to the caliphate.

The Umayyad dynasty, established in Damascus, was itself disrupted by civil war (683–692) when ʿAbd Allāh ibn az-Zubayr claimed the caliphate in Medina, and animosities between the northern (Qaysī) and southern (Kalbī) Arab tribes flared into open warfare. After the death of Caliph Yazīd I (683), the Qays, controlling most of Syria, including Damascus, declared for Ibn az-Zubayr; Syria was soon followed by Arabia, Iraq, and Egypt. Meanwhile, in Damascus, the Kalb recognized as caliph the Umayyad Marwān ibn al-Ḥakam (June 684). Kalbī and Qaysī armies met in July 684 on the plain of Marj Rāhiṭ, outside Damascus, and in a bloody 20-day battle Marwān defeated and killed 3,000 Qaysīs and their leader, aḍ- Ḍaḥḥāk ibn Qays. The blood feuds that ensued from the confrontation eventually destroyed Umayyad power, but at Marj Rāhiṭ the Umayyads achieved a decisive victory and re-established their rule over most of Syria. The next Umayad caliph, ʿAbd al-Malik ibn Marwān, was wholly occupied for several years with the restoration of tribal unity in Syria and the organization of a strong army. By 692 he had little difficulty in defeating the forces of Muṣʿab, Ibn az-Zubayr's brother and governor of Basra, and reoccupying Iraq, which had been weakened by internal Shīʿī rebellion. In the same year a Syrian force besieged Mecca for six months and killed Ibn az-Zubayr in the final assault.

Civil war broke out in the ʿAbbāsid empire after the death in 809 of Hārūn ar-Rashīd, as his designated successors struggled for control of the caliphate. In 802 Hārūn had issued the so-called Meccan documents, two measures that formally designated Muḥammad al-Amīn, his son by an Arab wife, as his successor and assigned the government of Khorāsān (modern northeastern Iran) exclusively to his second heir, ʿAbd Allāh al-Maʾmūn, a son by a Persian concubine. Relations between al-Amīn (reigned 809–813) and al-Maʾmūn were strained from the start, however, as the Khorāsānian guard, whom Hārūn had forced to swear allegiance to al-Maʾmūn, broke their oath and returned to Baghdad, the ʿAbbāsid capital. When al-Amīn indicated in 810 that his son Mūsā was to succeed him, open war between the brothers followed (811). Al-Maʾmūn, supported by a strong following in Khorāsān and a new Khorāsānian army, refused further allegiance to Baghdad. Al-Amīn's old Khorāsānian guard, sent to do battle with the deposed al-Maʾmūn, was repeatedly defeated, and Syria itself rose in revolt against the caliph. Al-Amīn was finally besieged in Baghdad, where after nearly two years of resistance his troops gave way, and he was captured and killed. The brothers' struggle had become a contest for supremacy between Iraq and Iran. Al-Maʾmūn, choosing to keep the caliphate in Iraq in spite of his Iranian allegiances, weakened ʿAbbāsid strength in the east; thenceforth, numerous semi-autonomous Iranian dynasties began to appear.

Between 1008 and 1031 the Umayyads, established since 756 in Córdoba, Spain, once again experienced civil war. Following the reign of al-Muẓaffar (1002–08), central authority in the Spanish Muslim state collapsed, and the period of the *mulūk aṭ-ṭawāʾif* (*q.v.*; "party kings") began (1009–91). Berber mercenaries and Slavonians (European slaves) occupied Córdoba and made and unmade caliphs; numerous Umayyad pretenders struggled for control, while most of Muslim Spain threw off Umayyad allegiance and became partitioned among petty rulers. The Spanish caliphate was abolished in 1031.
·caliphate internal conflicts **3**:626e
·Iraq under the caliphate **11**:991a
·Spanish Muslim political history **17**:416c

Muslim ibn al-Ḥajjāj, in full ABŪ AL-ḤUSAYN MUSLIM IBN AL-ḤAJJĀJ AL-QUSHAYRĪ (b. *c.* 817, Nīshāpūr, Iran—d. 875, Naṣrābād), scholar who was one of the chief authorities on the Ḥadīth, accounts of the sayings and deeds of the Prophet Muḥammad.

Muslim travelled widely; his great work the *Ṣaḥīḥ* ("The Genuine") is said to have been compiled from about 300,000 traditions, which he collected in Arabia, Egypt, Syria, and Iraq. The *Ṣaḥīḥ* has been unanimously acclaimed as authoritative and is one of the six canonical collections of Ḥadīth. Muslim was careful to give a full account of the *isnād*s (links in the chain of transmission) for each tradition and to record textual variations. The collection begins with an introduction dealing with all the subjects treated in the Ḥadīth; it ends with a discussion of the Qurʾān, which Muslim, like al-Bukhārī, another authoritative compiler of Ḥadīth, believed to be the creation of an inspired prophet and not a transcript of eternal divine law.

Muslim League, originally ALL-INDIA MUSLIM LEAGUE, political group in British India founded in 1906 to safeguard the rights of Indian Muslims. Encouraged by the British and generally favourable to their rule, the League adopted a nationalist program only in 1940, when it advocated the formation of an independent Muslim state separate from the projected independent nation of India, which the League feared would be dominated by Hindus. After the partition of India and formation of Pakistan in 1947, the League became Pakistan's dominant political party. In the late 1960s, it split into three groups: the Qayyum Muslim League, the Council Muslim League, and the Convention Muslim League.
·Congress Party's failure to reconcile **12**:945e
·Jinnah's political activities **10**:224a
·origins and political history **9**:414h
·Pakistan and Bangladesh founding role **13**:903e

Muslim Rebellion, uprising begun in 1862 by the Muslim populations of Kansu and Shensi in northwest China against the rule of the declining Ch'ing dynasty. The main rebel force was crushed in 1873, but the entire disturbance did not settle until 1878.
·background and effects **4**:360f
·Shensi effect and deaths **16**:665a
·suppression by Tso Tsung-t'ang **10**:387e

muslin, plain-woven cotton fabric made in various weights from very sheer to heavy sheetings. The better qualities are fine and smooth in texture, woven from evenly spun warps and wefts. They are given a soft finish, bleached or piece dyed, and sometimes patterned in the loom or printed. The coarser varieties are often of irregular yarns and textures, bleached, unbleached, or piece-dyed and generally finished by the application of sizing. Varieties of muslin are known under such names as book, mull, swiss, and sheeting.

The material was first made in the city of Mosul (now in Iraq). Early Indian muslins were handwoven of extremely fine handspun yarns and were very costly. They were imported into Europe in the 17th century and later manufactured in Scotland and England.

Mus musculus (house mouse): *see* mouse.

musnad (Islām): *see* isnād.

Musophagidae (bird family): *see* turaco.

Muspelheim, Old Norse MÚSPELL, in Norse mythology, a hot, bright, glowing land in the south, guarded by Surt, the fire giant. In the beginning, according to one tradition, the warm air from this region melted the ice of the opposite region, Niflheim, thus giving form to Ymir, the father of the evil giants. Sparks from Muspelheim became the Sun, Moon, and stars. At the doom of the gods (Ragnarök), the sons of Múspell, led by Surt, will arise and destroy the world by fire.

musquash (rodent): *see* muskrat.

Mussassir (ancient site): *see* Muṣaṣir.

Mussato, Albertino (b. 1261, Padua, Italy—d. May 31, 1329, Chioggia), statesman and writer outstanding both as a poet and as a historian of the 14th century.

Orphaned at an early age, Mussato earned his living as a copyist while studying for the profession of notary. He was knighted in 1296 and, after becoming a member of the Council of Padua, was sent in 1302 as ambassador to Pope Boniface VIII. In 1311 he was a member of an embassy from Guelf (pro-papal) Padua to Emperor Henry VII in Milan, and during a long war between Padua and Vicenza he often served as a negotiator between Padua and the Emperor. Fighting near Vicenza, Mussato was wounded and became the prisoner of Cangrande I della Scala, lord of Verona. After his release in November 1314, he returned to Padua to be crowned as a poet before the Senate and the university. In 1325 a quarrel with Marsilio da Carrara, lord of Padua, drove him into permanent exile.

Mussato's *Historia Augusta* ("Augustan History"), a chronicle of Henry VII's actions in Italy, and his *De gestis Italicorum post Henricum VII Caesarem* ("Concerning the Deeds of the Italians after Emperor Henry VII") are important sources for the history of 14th-century Italy, and his Latin poems and tragedy *Ecerinis*, modelled after Seneca's plays and based on the life of the Veronese tyrant Ezzolino da Romano, foreshadow Italian Humanism.

·Paduan literary tradition **15**:664b

Musschenbroek, Pieter van (1692–1761), Dutch mathematician and physicist, discoverer the principle of the Leyden jar (*q.v.*) about the same time (1745) as E.G. von Kleist of Pomerania.

mussel, common name for bivalve mollusks belonging to the marine family Mytilidae and to the freshwater superfamily Unionacea.

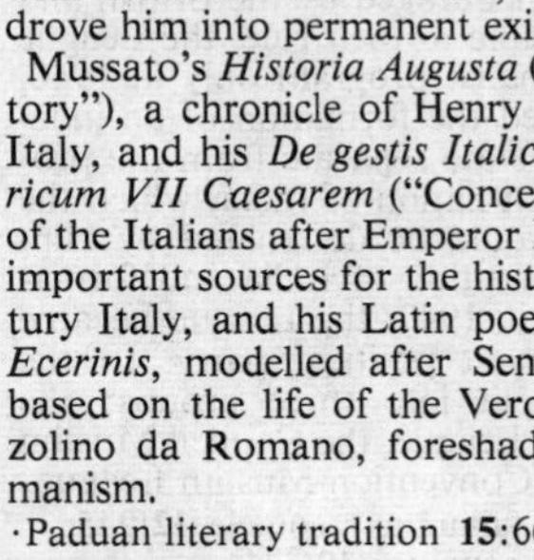

Blue mussel (*Mytilus edulis*) attached to a rock by byssus threads
Ralph Buchsbaum

Worldwide in distribution, they are commonest in cool seas. Freshwater mussels, also known as naiads, include about 1,000 known species inhabiting streams, lakes, and ponds over most of the world.

Marine mussels are usually wedge-shaped or pear-shaped and range in size from about 5 to 15 centimetres (about 2 to 6 inches). They may be smooth or ribbed and often have a hairy covering, the periostracum. The shells of many species are dark blue or dark greenish-brown on the outside; on the inside they are often pearly. The mollusks attach themselves to solid objects or to one another by strands called byssus threads and often occur in dense clusters. Some burrow into soft mud or wood. Principal enemies of the mussel are vertebrates such as walruses, birds (*e.g.*, herring gulls, oystercatchers, ducks), and flounders; and the invertebrate starfishes.

Some species (*e.g.*, the blue mussel, *Mytilus edulis*) are important as food in Europe and are raised commercially. *M. edulis*, which attains lengths of up to 11 centimetres (4 inches) and is usually blue or purple, has been cultivated in Europe since the 13th century. Mussels are collected from deep water by means of dredges or rakes. They spoil quickly after removal from the water and are therefore seldom shipped.

The California mussel (*Mytilus californianus*) is a tan or brown species occurring in waters from Alaska to California. The capax horse mussel (*Modiolus capax*) has a bright orange-brown shell under a thick periostracum; its range in the Pacific Ocean extends from California to Peru. The Atlantic ribbed mussel (*Modiolus demissus*), which has a thin, strong, yellowish-brown shell, occurs from Nova Scotia to the Gulf of Mexico. The tulip mussel (*Modiolus americanus*), from North Carolina to the Caribbean Sea, attaches itself to broken shells and rocks; its smooth, thin shell is usually light brown but sometimes has rosy or purple rays. The yellow mussel (*Mytilus citrinus*), from southern Florida to the Caribbean, is a light brownish-yellow. The hooked, or bent, mussel (*M. recurvus*), from New England to the Caribbean, attains lengths of about 4 centimetres (1½ inches) and is greenish-brown to purplish black. The scorched mussel (*M. exustus*), from North Carolina to the Caribbean, is bluish-gray and about 2.5 centimetres long.

The largest family of freshwater mussels is Unionidae, with about 750 species, the greatest number of which occur in the United States. Many species also live in Southeast Asian waters. The Indians of North America once ate the mussel flesh, now used as poultry and livestock feed. The shells are often made into buttons. *Major ref.* **2**:1085b

·anaerobic respiration at low tide **15**:754a
·byssus retractor muscle action **12**:644e
·cultivation area and method **7**:361h
·dinoflagellate role in aquatic ecosystem **15**:120f
·estuary growth and faunal sequence **6**:974b
·lacustrine environment adaptation **10**:615e
·Leeuwenhoek's scientific research **10**:773f
·paralytic shellfish poisoning **14**:609h
·reproductive system anatomy **15**:704b

Musselburgh, small burgh (town) of the county of Midlothian, Scotland, on the south shore of the Firth of Forth, an inlet of the North Sea. Archaeological remains indicate that there may have been a port on this site in Roman times. Musselburgh was made a royal burgh in 1632; and a chapel to Our Lady of Loretto had been founded as early as 1534, only to be destroyed, along with part of the town, in 1544 by the forces of the English Earl of Hertford. Musselburgh has become a suburb of Edinburgh, the Scottish capital (6 mi [10 km] to the west), but has retained many of the historic buildings of its High Street. The adjacent small village of Fisherrow was previously important for fishing and the manufacture of cloth, which have now been replaced by papermaking. Other main industries are the manufacture of wire rope, twine, and fishing nets. There also are some brewing and market gardening. Pop. (1973 est.) 17,045.
55°57′ N, 3°04′ W

·early golf club and course re-location **8**:243g

Musselshell River rises in the Crazy Mountains, in Meagher County, central Montana, U.S., and flows 292 mi (470 km) east and north past Harlowton and Roundup to Fort Peck Reservoir in the Missouri River, in northwest Garfield County. A small headstream is impounded near Martinsdale to form an irrigation reservoir. According to some sources, the river, originally known as the Dried Meat River, was renamed Musselshell by the explorers Meriwether Lewis and William Clark in 1805, when they found freshwater mussels on its banks.
47°21′ N, 107°58′ W

mussel shrimp, or SEED SHRIMP, any crustacean of the subclass Ostracoda, a widely distributed group. The name mussel shrimp derives from the resemblance to a mussel, or bivalve mollusk; in both cases the carapace, or body shield, covers much of the body. Mussel shrimp differ from most crustaceans in having a very short trunk that has lost its external segmentation, or divisions. The 2,000 living species include marine, freshwater, and terrestrial forms.

Approximately 10,000 extinct species are known, fossil ostracods ranging from Late Cambrian (about 520,000,000 years ago) to Recent (the last 10,000 years) in age. They are of particular stratigraphic significance in nonmarine marls, limestones, and shales, often serving as index fossils because of their abundance, widespread geographic occurrence, and limited vertical range. Certain genera are commonly used as guides in subsurface petroleum exploration, in a manner analogous to that of foraminifera (*q.v.*) in marine strata.

Ostracods are about 1 millimetre (about 0.04 inch) long. The largest is *Gigantocypris agassizi*, a Pacific species, which grows to 23 millimetres (about 1 inch). Most mussel shrimp live on or about the sea bottom. Some feed on micro-organisms and organic debris; others are predators on small invertebrates; and a few are parasitic. Most prefer shallow water, but some have been collected at depths of 2,000 metres (about 6,600 feet). *Major ref.* **5**:312e

·Cypridina bioluminescence mechanism **2**:1028g; illus. 1029
·Devonian crustacean evolution **5**:675f
·fossil occurrence, illus. 3 **17**:721
·fossils, characteristics, and evolution **7**:565d; illus. 564
·Jurassic index and Crustacea evolution **10**:358g
·Ordovician abundance **13**:658c
·reproductive system anatomy **15**:704e
·Silurian invertebrate life **16**:772c

mussel worm (genus *Nereis*): *see* rag worm.

Musset, (Louis-Charles-) Alfred de (b. Dec. 11, 1810, Paris—d. May 2, 1857, Paris), one of the most distinguished poets and playwrights of the French Romantic movement. His autobiographical *La Confession d'un enfant du siècle* (1836), if not entirely trustworthy, presents a striking picture of Musset's youth as a member of a noble family, well educated but ruled by his emotions in a period when all traditional values were under attack. While still an adolescent he came under the influence of the leaders of the Romantic movement, Charles Nodier, Alfred de Vigny, and Victor Hugo, and produced his first work, *Contes d'Espagne et d'Italie*, in 1830. At the same time he became a dandy, one of the elegant Parisian imitators of "Beau" Brummell, and embarked on a life of hectic sexual and alcoholic dissipation that seriously undermined his health.

After the failure of his play *La Nuit vénitienne* (1830), Musset refused to allow other plays to be performed but continued to publish historical tragedies—*e.g.*, *Lorenzaccio* (1834)—and delightful comedies—*e.g.*, *Il ne faut jurer de rien* (1836). Musset's plays are now performed regularly, while the other Romantic dramas by his contemporaries have been dropped from the standard repertory.

Above all, Musset is remembered for his poetry. He was extraordinarily versatile, writing light satirical pieces and poems of dazzling technical virtuosity as well as lyrics, such as *La Nuit d'octobre* (1837), which express with passion and eloquence all his fervent and complex emotions. Though always associated with the Romantic movement, Musset often poked fun at its excesses. His *Lettres de Dupuis et Cotonet* (1836–37), for example, contain a brilliant and illuminating satire of the literary fashions of the day.

Musset, oil painting by Charles Landelle (1821–1908); in the Louvre, Paris

Cliche Musees Nationaux, Paris

A love affair with the novelist George Sand (real name, Amandine-Lucile-Aurore Dudevant, *née* Dupin) that lasted intermittently from 1833 to 1839 inspired some of his finest lyrics, as is recounted in his *Confessions*.
·French literature of the 19th century **10**:1193a

Mussolini, Benito (Amilcare Andrea) **12**:749 (b. July 29, 1883, Predappio, Italy—d. April 28, 1945, near Azzano), Italian prime minister, was the first of Europe's Fascist dictators and ruled Italy for more than 20 years, leading his nation to defeat in World War II.

Abstract of text biography. As a young man Mussolini was a prominent Socialist, opposing Italy's entry into World War I, but he abruptly changed his views and went to fight in the war. In 1919 he founded the Fascist Party in Milan, and in 1922 the Fascist militia conducted the march on Rome that brought Mussolini to power as prime minister. He was soon accepted and respected at home and abroad, until the first of his foreign adventures, the conquest of Abyssinia (Ethiopia) in 1935–36. When World War II began, Mussolini joined forces with Hitler, and on Italy's defeat he was first expelled from office (1943) and then shot by his own countrymen.

REFERENCES in other text articles:
·African aggression and Balkan intrigue **19**:972g
·African empire ambitions **4**:903d
·Balkan expansion program **2**:635e
·Dollfuss' visit for security **2**:478b
·encyclopaedia contribution on ideology **6**:784b
·Fascist coup and career **9**:1167g *passim* to 1170a
·Fascist philosophy and Italian regime **7**:182g
·Hitler's military strategy **8**:968c
·Roman reconstruction and modernization **15**:1071c
·theatre construction motivation **18**:237f
·World War II origins and development **19**:978f

Mussoorie, town, Dehra Dūn district, Uttar Pradesh state, northern India, north of Dehra Dūn city. On a ridge of the Himalayan foothills, it is a popular summer resort for residents of Delhi and the plains south of the mountains. A number of residential schools are located in the town, which is also a brewing centre. Pop. (1971 prelim.) 18,047.
30°27′ N, 78°05′ E
·map, India **9**:278

Summer resort in Mussoorie, Uttar Pradesh, India

Harrison Forman

Mussorgsky, Modest (Petrovich) **12**:752 (b. March 21 [March 9, old style], 1839, Karevo, Russia—d. March 28 [March 16, O.S.], 1881, St. Petersburg, now Leningrad), composer noted particularly for his opera *Boris Godunov* (final version first performed 1874) and his songs, all of which show his gift for melody and clever characterization. Few 19th-century composers were less derivative, more original and bold in their musical style than was Mussorgsky.

Abstract of text biography. After piano lessons with his mother, he studied with Anton Gerke, future professor at the St. Petersburg Conservatory. He trained for a military career but, after becoming an officer, abandoned his commission for a post in the civil service so that he would have time to compose. But his unstable character, which led to heavy drinking, was not conducive to steady work habits, and many of his compositions, therefore, were left unfinished at his death. Nevertheless, what he did leave—particularly *Boris Godunov*, the historical opera *Khovanshchina*, the piano piece *Pictures from an Exhibition* (1874; later orchestrated by Maurice Ravel), and his songs—richly displays his individual style.

REFERENCES in other text articles:
·Boris Godunov and other operas **13**:590g
·new life in worn-out Western harmony **12**:720f
·Rimsky-Korsakov and Five **15**:852a
·Tchaikovsky's style in comparison **18**:2f

mussurana, also spelled MUSURANA (*Clelia clelia*), tropical American rear-fanged snake of the family Colubridae is almost exclusively a serpent-eater. It is largely immune to the venom of members of the genus *Bothrops* (fer-de-lance and allies), its chief prey. The mussurana may be 2.1 metres (about 7 feet) long. Adults are blue-black, with a white belly stripe; the young are pink, with dark head and collar.

Mu-ssu-t'a-ko-a-t'e Shan, Pin-yin romanization MU-SU-TA-GO-A-TE SHAN, also known as MUZTAGH ATA, or KASHGAR RANGE, in westernmost Sinkiang Province (*sheng*), China; it extends 200 mi (322 km) in a north-northwest and south-southeast axis parallel to the eastern edge of the Pamir mountainous area, and rises to 25,146 ft (7,360 m) in the Kungur massif. The peak of Mu-ssu-t'a-ko-a-t'e (24,388 ft) is about 100 mi southwest of Kashgar.
38°00′ N 75°25′ E
·map, China **4**:262
·mountaineering record and data table **12**:585

must, juice of grapes or other fruit before and during fermentation.
·wine making process and juice separation **19**:878h

mustache: *see* moustache.

mustache shrimp, any member of the crustacean subclass Mystacocarida, a small group of primitive, free-living marine animals. Of the few species known, the first was discovered near Woods Hole, Mass., in 1943.

The rather tubular body includes a long abdomen; thick, bristly antennules extend about two-thirds the length of the body. The largest species, *Derocheilocaris galvarina*, which attains lengths to 0.5 millimetres (about 0.02 inch), occurs on the Pacific coast of South America in the intertidal zone and on sandy bottoms in shallow waters. *D. typicus* occurs on the Atlantic coast of northeastern United States. *D. remani* is found on the coasts of Europe and Africa.
·classification and general features **5**:317g; illus. 311

Mustafa I (b. 1591, Manisa, Tur.—d. Jan. 20, 1639, Constantinople, now Istanbul), Ottoman sultan in 1617–18 and in 1622–23, a man of weak mental faculties who was deposed from the throne in 1618, but was reinstalled in 1622 by the Janissaries (elite troops), who dethroned Osman II.

Mustafa's reign, under the influence of his mother, witnessed continuous interference of the Janissaries in the administration and a revolt in Anatolia of Abaza Mehmed Paşa, who sought to avenge Osman II's death.

Mustafa II, in full MUSTAFA OGLU MEHMED IV (b. June 5, 1664, Edirne, Tur.—d. Dec. 31, 1703, Istanbul), Ottoman sultan from 1695 to 1703, whose determination to regain territories lost after the unsuccessful attempt to take Vienna in 1683 led to the continuation of the war against the Holy League (Austria, Poland, and Venice) and the Treaty of Carlowitz (1699), which radically reduced Turkey's Balkan holdings. Mustafa's campaigns met with early success. After recovering the island of Chios from Venice, he made gains against Austria in 1695 and 1696. The Russians occupied Azov (at the mouth of the Don) in 1696, however, and he was defeated by the Austrians at Senta (now in Yugoslavia) in 1697.

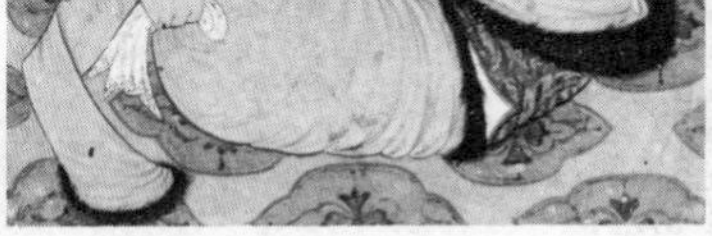

Mustafa II, miniature by C. Levni, *c.* 1700; in the Topkapı Saray Museum, Istanbul

By courtesy of the Topkapi Saray Museum, Istanbul

Internally, the continued warfare caused social and economic dislocations. Heavy taxes drove many cultivators off the land; the government's exclusive preoccupation with Europe resulted in local revolts in eastern Anatolia and among the Arab tribes of Syria and Iraq. Disillusioned by the defeat at Senta, Mustafa left most matters of state to the leader of the Muslim hierarchy, Feyzullah, while he himself devoted his last years to hunting. A military mutiny deposed Mustafa on Aug. 22, 1703.

Mustafa III (b. Jan. 28, 1717, Istanbul—d. Jan. 21, 1774, Istanbul), Ottoman sultan 1757–74 who attempted governmental and military reforms to halt the empire's decline and who declared a war on Russia that (after his death) culminated in a disastrous defeat. Though Mustafa and his able grand vizier, Ragib Mehmed Paşa, understood the necessity for reform, their efforts were directed toward the results, not the causes, of the Ottoman decline. They were unable to curb tax

Mustafa III, miniature; in Istanbul University Library (MS. Yildiz 8647/17)

By courtesy of Istanbul University Library

abuses, hence their fiscal reforms proved ineffective. Administrative reforms foundered on the central government's inability to extend its authority over the local rulers (*ayans*) of its provinces in Europe and Asia. Assisted by Baron François de Tott, a French artillery officer of Hungarian origin, they were more successful in their military reforms: the artillery corps was reorganized, an engineering school closed by the Janissaries in 1747 was reopened, and a school of mathematics for the navy was founded (1773).

In his foreign policy Mustafa was determined to maintain the peace established by the Treaty of Belgrade (1739). In spite of urgings by the French and by Frederick the Great of Prussia, the Ottomans were reluctant to join the European scheme of alliances and counteralliances. Later, however, Russian ambitions in Poland and in the Crimea compelled Mustafa to declare war on Russia (1768). Following a few initial unimportant successes, the Ottomans suffered a series of defeats on the Danube and in the Crimea that culminated in the destruction of the Ottoman fleet at Çeşme (1770) in the Aegean.

A poet and a scholar, Mustafa, during the years of his seclusion before his accession, had studied astrology, literature, and medicine. As a sultan who struggled to revive the empire and failed, he placed his sole hope with his son Selim (later Selim III), whom he educated with utmost care but who did not become sultan until 1789.

Mustafa IV (b. Sept. 8, 1779, Istanbul—d. Nov. 17, 1808, Istanbul), Ottoman sultan from 1807 to 1808 who participated in the reactionary conservative coalition that overthrew his reforming cousin Selim III.

A man of low intelligence, fanatical and ambitious, Mustafa, under the influence of the *shaykh al-islām* (head of the Muslim religious hierarchy) and the Janissaries, ended Selim's reforms and killed most of the reformers. Meanwhile Bayrakdar Mustafa Paşa of Rusçuk (modern Ruse, Bulg.), a reformist supporter, marched to Istanbul to restore Selim III. Mustafa, informed of Bayrakdar's intentions, killed Selim. He himself was immediately deposed (July 28, 1808) and lived in confinement until he was strangled on orders from his brother, who succeeded him as Mahmud II.

·reactionary repressive policies **13**:784g

Mustafa, Kara: *see* Kara Mustafa Pasa.

Muṣṭafā Kāmil (1874–1908), Egyptian lawyer and journalist.

·nationalist cause in British Egypt **6**:497c

Mustafa Kemal: *see* Atatürk, Kemal.

Mustafa Oğlu Mehmed IV: *see* Mustafa II.

Mustafa Reşid Paşa: *see* Reşid Paşa, Mustafa.

Mustaʿlī, al- (reigned 1094–1101), caliph of the Islāmic Fāṭimid Empire of Egypt.

·Shīʿite internal conflicts **9**:932e

Mustaʿlīs (Islāmic sect): *see* Ismāʿīlīyah.

mustang (horse): *see* cayuse.

Mustanṣir, al- (b. July 2, 1029, Egypt—d. Jan. 10, 1094, Cario), eighth Fāṭimid caliph (a dynasty of Muslim rulers based in Egypt). He inherited the rule of the most powerful Muslim state of the time, but during his reign, which was the longest of any Muslim ruler, the Fāṭimid government suffered decisive and irrevocable setbacks. He became caliph in 1036, when he was only seven years old, and real authority had to be wielded by his father's wazīr (prime minister) and, after the death of the latter, by al-Mustanṣir's mother. During this time Egypt was frequently the scene of pitched battles between bodies of soldiery, usually ethnic groups, such as the Sudanese, who supported various politicians. Al-Mustanṣir had neither the political or military influence to shape the direction of these events, although there were times when he personally led troops in battle. By 1073 he was reduced to desperation and secretly offered supreme military authority in Egypt to the governor of Akka, the Armenian general Badr al-Jamali. Badr accepted but insisted that he bring his own troops with him. In a series of brutal and swift-moving actions, Badr defeated the various military factions, executed a large number of Egyptian politicians, and thus brought a return of relative peace and prosperity. Al-Mustanṣir strengthened his relations with him by securing the marriage of his youngest son to Badr's daughter. He had, however, made a fateful decision, for real power now passed to Badr and after him to a series of other military commanders. Fāṭimid influence outside Egypt shrank, areas in North Africa slipped from al-Mustanṣir's control, and conditions in Syria were so chaotic that it was impossible to offer effective resistance to the Seljuq Turks, who were advancing from the east. Through most of his reign al-Mustanṣir lived in great luxury, the source of which was profitable commercial relations with Indian Ocean powers and with Constantinople.

·Fāṭimid caliphate disintegration **7**:194g
·Fāṭimid military power **9**:932e

mustard, any of several herbs of the genus *Brassica* or the condiment made from its pungent-tasting seeds. Mustard leaves are used as greens or pot herbs. Both white, or yellow mustard, *Brassica hirta*, and black, or brown mustard, *Brassica nigra*, originating in the Mediterranean region or western temperate Asia, have been cultivated for at least 2,000 years and have spread throughout most of the temperate regions of the world. Mustard plants are mentioned frequently in Greek and Roman writings and in the Bible; the seed is a symbol of faith in the Bible. Mustard seed was used medicinally by Hippocrates.

Mustard (*Brassica nigra*)

F.K. Anderson—EB Inc.

Indian mustard, *Brassica juncea*, may have originated in Africa, but it has been extensively cultivated in Asia since an early date. Wild mustard plants were biennial, but selection has developed annual strains, the only types cultivated. Black mustard is a troublesome weed in parts of Great Britain and California.

Mustard plants may reach about 15 feet (4 metres) high. Plants raised for leaves are grown in the spring or fall, because only basal leaves from fast-growing plants are suitable as pot herbs. Plants raised for seeds are grown in summer, when flowering occurs early and few leaves appear. Both cultures are practiced in Asia, Europe, and North America. Mustard is sometimes grown as a cover crop, for stock feed, and as a green manure in orchards.

Mustard seeds, white and black, are nearly globular in shape, finely pitted, odourless when whole, and have a pungent taste. White mustard seeds are yellowish in colour and about 0.1 inch (2 millimetres) in diameter; black mustard seeds are dark, reddish brown in colour, about 0.075 inch (1½ millimetres) in diameter, and give off a sharp, irritating odour when crushed in water. Mustard seeds contain about 30 percent of a fixed oil that may be extracted by the cold press method. The oil is edible but is used mainly as an illuminant, a lubricant, an ingredient in soapmaking, and other technical uses. When the seeds are ground and the resulting flour treated with water, a different oil is obtained. The water causes a chemical reaction between two constituents, an enzyme and a glucoside, producing an oil not present as such in the plant. In black mustard, the enzyme myrosin acts on the glucoside sinigrin (potassium myronate) in the presence of water to yield allyl isothiocyanate, the volatile oil of mustard, which has a pungent, irritating odour and an acrid taste. In white mustard the same enzyme acts on a different glucoside, sinalbin, in the presence of water to yield sinalbin mustard oil, a nonvolatile oil that has very little odour but a pungent taste that is less irritating than the oil from black mustard. Sinalbin mustard oil is a powerful rubefacient. Many species of *Brassica* have similar enzyme-and-glucoside systems in the seeds and, to a lesser degree, in the leaves. Boiling destroys the enzyme, so greens made from *Brassica juncea* are boiled twice, the first water being discarded to reduce the biting taste. The condiment is sold in three forms: as seeds, as dry powder that is freshly mixed with water for each serving to obtain the most aroma and flavour, and as a paste or cream sauce blended with other spices, vinegar or wine, and starch or flour to tone down the sharpness. Mustard is used to spice various foods, particularly cold meats, sausages, and salad dressings. On the continent of Europe table mustard made from the seeds of black mustard is preferred. In England, that made from white mustard is preferred. In the U.S. the condiment is usually a mixture of the two seeds and sometimes includes a small quantity of *Brassica juncea* seeds as well. Either dry or moist mustard loses its potency because of oxidation unless it is hermetically sealed. When eaten it stimulates salivary secretions and peristaltic action of the stomach. It is sometimes administered medicinally for this purpose.

In medicine, mustard plasters have long been used for their counterirritant properties in treating chest colds; hot mustard baths are considered relaxing.

·genetic changes and flax contamination **8**:814h
·radiation induced improvement table **7**:482
·spice history, use, production, and region of origin **17**:506d; tables 504

mustard gas: *see* chemical warfare; thioether.

mustard oil, common name for any of the isothiocyanates, a group of organic compounds containing sulfur and nitrogen and having the general formula RN = C = S, in which R is a grouping of carbon and hydrogen atoms. The name arises from the fact that several members of the group occur in the oils obtained from mustard seeds. The best known isothiocyanate is allyl isothiocyanate ($CH_2 = CHCH_2NCS$), the principal component of the volatile irritating oil prepared from black mustard seeds (*Brassica nigra*), used medicinally as a counter-irritant and an emetic for poisoning cases. The seeds contain a glycoside called sinigrin and an enzyme called myrosin; when the seeds are ground and treated with water, the enzyme acts on the glycoside to form the isothiocyanate. Allyl isothiocyanate can also be prepared synthetically by heating allyl bromide, allyl chloride, or allyl iodide with potassium thiocyanate.
·nitrogen compound preparation **13**:698d

mustard pot and spoon, pottery or glass-lined metal container for mustard, to be used at the table. A French pewter mustard pot is

Silver mustard pot and spoon, English, 1790
Helga Studio photo for S.J. Shrubsole Corp., New York City

mentioned in a 14th-century document, but the earliest surviving metal examples, with domed lids and pedestal bases, date from the 17th century. This type was largely supplanted in mid-18th century by the familiar barrel-shaped type. The earliest surviving silver mustard spoons, with characteristic almond-shaped bowls, date from mid-18th century.

mustaʿrib (Arab geneology): *see* Mozarab.

Mustaʿṣim, al- (1221–58), the last of the ʿAbbāsid caliphs, who reigned from 1242. He was defeated and put to death at Baghdad by Hülegü, grandson of Genghis Khan.
·fall of the ʿAbbāsids **3**:641c
·Hülegü's conquest of Iran **11**:994b
·Iraq under the caliphate **11**:992f
·Islām and the Mongol invasions **9**:933a
·military and political policies **3**:637b

Mustelidae, family of fur-bearing carnivores that includes the weasels, skunks, badgers, and others (about 25 existing genera with about 70 species, and 47 to 73 extinct genera); characteristically possessing well-developed anal scent glands. Mustelids evolved from North American and Eurasian forms in the early Oligocene and inhabit terrestrial and aquatic regions throughout the world, except Australia and most ocean islands. Their limbs are short in relation to their usually long bodies of variable size (females are generally smaller than males). Many species are trapped or raised commercially for their pelts, which differ in length, quality, and coloration.
·defenses against predation **1**:299d
·examples, traits, and anatomy **3**:931g; illus.
RELATED ENTRIES in the *Ready Reference and Index:*
badger; ermine; ferret; fisher; grison; kolinsky; marten; mink; otter; polecat; ratel; sable; skunk; stoat; tayra; weasel; wolverine; zorille

Mustelus canis (shark): *see* dogfish.

must (MUSTH) **gland,** gland above the eyes of a bull elephant that exudes a brown odorous substance.
·secretion initiation and function **15**:2e

musubi, the power of becoming or creation, a central concept in the Shintō religion of Japan. A number of deities are associated with *musubi*. In the legendary accounts of the creation of heaven and Earth given in the *Koji-ki* ("Records of Ancient Matters"), the three deities first named are Taka-mi-musubi-no-kami ("Exalted *musubi* Deity"), who is later related to the gods of the heaven; Kami-musubi-no-kami ("Sacred *musubi* Deity"), related to the gods of the Earth; and Ame-no-mi-naka-nushi-no-kami ("God Ruling the Centre"). Some Shintō scholars hold that all Shintō deities are in reality manifestations of the one deity, Ame-no-mi-naka-nushi. According to some Shintō sects, these three deities, together with the sun goddess Amaterasu (*q.v.*), are considered to be paramount deities.
·Shintō ethics of progress **16**:673a

musurana (snake): *see* mussurana.

Muswellbrook, town, east New South Wales, Australia, in the upper Hunter River Valley. Founded in 1827 and called Muscle Brook (after mussels found in a local stream), its name has been further corrupted to Muswellbrook. Proclaimed a town (1833), it became a municipality in 1870. A rail junction on the New England Highway, 70 mi (113 km) northwest of Newcastle, it serves a district of coal mining (open-pit and shaft) and farming. Numerous small irrigation developments are on tributaries of the Hunter. Coal mining is the economic mainstay, and the state mine at nearby Liddell is also the site of the nation's largest thermal power station, with a planned capacity of 2,000,000 kW. Pop. (1971 prelim.) 8,082.
32°16′ S, 150°54′ E

Mut, in Egyptian religion, a sky goddess and great divine mother. Originally she was a vulture goddess of Thebes; but during the 18th dynasty she was married to the god Amon

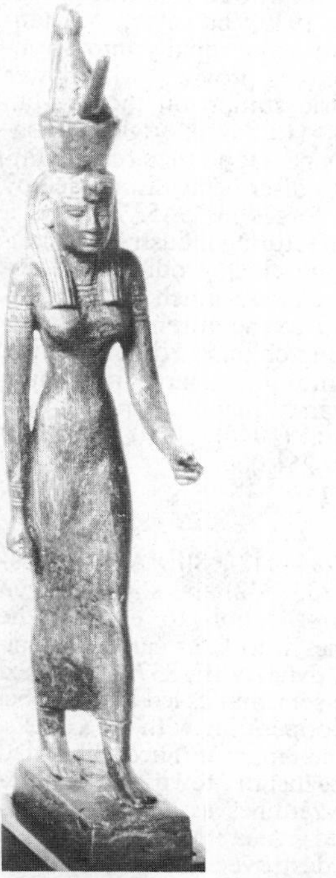

Mut, wearing double crown and vulture's head on forehead, bronze statuette; in the Oriental Institute, the University of Chicago
By courtesy of the Oriental Institute, the University of Chicago

and as such became, with their adopted son Khons, a member of the Theban Triad. During the New Kingdom the marriage of Amon and Mut became one of the great celebrations held annually at Thebes.

In her role as a sky goddess Mut often appeared as a cow, standing behind Amon as he rose from the primeval sea Nu to his place in the heavens. Mut became identified with other important goddesses, such as Bast and Sekhmet, and was usually represented as a woman with the head of a vulture or a lioness, on which was placed the Double Crown of Upper and Lower Egypt.

Mutabilitie Cantos, cantos of the unfinished Book VII of Edmund Spenser's poem *The Faerie Queene* (1609).
·references to Irish scene **17**:495c

Muʿtaḍid, al- (d. 902), 13th ʿAbbāsid caliph of Baghdad, son of al-Muwaffaq, forced his predecessor al-Muʿtamid to disinherit his son, reorganized the administration, and reformed the financial system. Al-Muʿtaḍid was skillful in dealing with the various provincial dynasties that were establishing themselves in different parts of the ʿAbbāsid realm but finally died following his defeat by the Qarmaṭians under Abū Saʿīd al-Jannābī.
·chronology of Islāmic history **4**:581a
·religious and military policies **3**:638f

mutagen, a substance or energy form that is capable of altering the genetic constitution of a cell by changing the structure of the hereditary material, deoxyribonucleic acid (DNA). Many forms of electromagnetic radiation (*e.g.*, cosmic rays, X-rays, ultraviolet light) are mutagenic, as are a variety of chemical compounds. The effects of some mutagens are potentiated (increased) or suppressed in some organisms by the presence of certain other, nonmutagenic substances; oxygen, for example, makes cells more sensitive to the mutagenic effects of X-rays.
·alkaloid toxicity considerations **1**:603a
·antibiotics and cellular change **1**:989e
·LSD and other drugs **5**:1056d
·physical and chemical sources **12**:755b
·radiation and chromosome breakage **15**:420d
·radiation effects in germplasm **15**:380a
·types and consequences **7**:1005b

mutʿah (Arabic: "pleasure"), in Islām, a temporary marriage, allegedly referred to in the Qurʾān (Muslim scriptures) in these words: "And you are allowed to seek out wives with your wealth in decorous conduct, but not in fornication, but give them their reward for what you have enjoyed of them in keeping with your promise" (4:24). Partners who engage in *mutʿah* must do so freely and must predetermine the conditions and duration of the contract. The woman, consequently, has no right to food or shelter, much less inheritance, unless such things have previously been agreed upon. No extension of the *mutʿah* is allowed, but cohabitation may resume if a new agreement is concluded. Many Muslim leaders have denounced *mutʿah* as simple prostitution, and numerous pious Muslims repudiate it as yielding to man's lowest passions. Others countenance it only if the duration of the marriage contract extends well beyond the normal lifetime of the individuals. Nonetheless, many *mutʿah* marriages reportedly have taken place in Mecca during pilgrimages when men are temporarily separated from their wives. Similarly, men away from home and military men on duty have found it advantageous. Those who interpret the Qurʾānic text to mean support and kindness due to a wife (not a sum of money) further affirm that Muḥammad forbade *mutʿah* in the specific case of a woman who, when two men offered her their cloak for a three-night marriage, chose the younger man with the shabbier cloak.
·Shīʿite marriage laws **9**:917b

mutakallimūn, also called LOQUENTES, theologians of Arabic philosophy.
·Averroës' opposition to doctrines **2**:538f
·Jewish philosophical thought **10**:209a
·secular education aim **6**:332c

Muʿtamid, al-, more complete name MUḤAMMAD II AL-MUʿTAMID (b. 1027, Spain—d. 1095, Morocco), third and last member of the ʿAbbādid dynasty of Seville, and the epitome of the cultivated Muslim Spaniard of the Middle Ages,—liberal, tolerant, and a patron of the arts. At the age of 13 he commanded a military expedition that had been sent against the city of Silves. The venture was successful, and he was appointed governor of this and another district. In 1069 his father died, and al-Muʿtamid acceeded to the throne of Seville. He was destined to rule in difficult times: neighbouring princes were resuming the inexorable advance that in time would bring all of Spain once again under Christian rule. Yet his first efforts were crowned with success. In 1071 he conquered and annexed the principality of Córdoba, although his rule was not effectively secured until 1078. During the same years he also brought the kingdom of Murcia under his rule.

But in 1085 the Alfonso VI, king of Leon and Castille captured the city of Toledo. This was a crippling blow to Spanish Islām. Al-Muʿtamid had already been forced to pay tribute to Alfonso, and, when he dared to refuse a payment, Alfonso invaded his kingdom and sacked various towns. Soon Alfonso also began making demands for territorial concessions. Al-Muʿtamid recognized that he could not stay the Christian advance with his own resources, and, acting as leader of a number of Muslim princes, he reluctantly sought the aid of Yūsuf ibn Tāshufīn. The latter, as the reigning Almoravid sultan, had just conquered all of Morocco and had powerful military forces at his disposal. In 1086 Yūsuf crossed the Strait of Gibraltar and at Zallaka inflicted a crushing defeat upon the Christian forces. Yet he had to return to Morocco before he could follow up his victory. Al-Muʿtamid now had a respite from Christian military pressure, but soon found himself again unable to defend his borders. This time he went in person to seek Yūsuf's aid, and in 1090 another Almoravid army invaded Spain. Now, however, Yūsuf decided to carry on the *jihād* ("holy war") in his own name and proceded to dethrone those who had invited him. Seville was captured, and al-Muʿtamid was sent to Morocco as a prisoner, where he remained until his death.
·Sevillian literary productivity **16**:581a

Mu'tamin, al-, 11th-century Muslim ruler of Saragossa (Zaragoza), Spain.
·El Cid defense offer and experiences **4**:615f

Mutanabbī, al-, in full ABŪ AṬ-ṬAYYIB AḤMAD IBN ḤUSAYN AL-MUTANABBĪ (b. 915, al-Kūfah, Iraq—d. August 965, near Dayr al-ʿĀqul), regarded by many critics as the greatest poet of Islāmic times. He influenced Arabic poetry until the 19th century.

Al-Mutanabbī was born into a poor family of noble and ancient southern Arabian descent. He received a thorough education, especially in Arabic, studying in Damascus and with the Bedouin of the desert, fabled for the purity of their language. An adventurous young man, he became involved in a series of wild escapades, most notably in 932, when he joined a heretical revolutionary movement among the nomad tribes of the Syrian Desert; there he is alleged to have declared himself their "prophet," earning himself the cognomen al-Mutanabbī (the Would-be Prophet). The revolt failed, however, and he spent two years in prison, thereafter returning to his poetry.

He had already begun to write panegyrics in the tradition established by the poets Abū Tammām (died 845) and al-Buḥturī (died 897). When he attached himself to the brilliant Ḥamdānid prince of northern Syria Sayf ad-Dawlah in 948, al-Mutanabbī had for the first time a patron whom he could admire. During their nine-year association he wrote in praise of Sayf ad-Dawlah panegyrics that rank as masterpieces of Arab poetry. The latter part of this period was clouded with intrigues and jealousies, which somehow culminated in al-Mutanabbī's leaving Syria for Egypt, then ruled in name by the Ikhshīdids. Al-Mutanabbī attached himself to the actual ruler, the Negro eunuch Kāfūr. By 960, however, having bitterly offended Kāfūr with scurrilous satirical poems, he fled Egypt and returned to Iraq. After four years of wandering in search of another patron, he was killed by bandits during a journey.

Al-Mutanabbī's pride and arrogance set the tone for much of his verse, which is ornately rhetorical, yet crafted with consummate skill and artistry. He had chosen, as had Abū Tammām and al-Buḥturī before him, to buoy up the worn spontaneity of the ancient *qaṣīdah*, or ode, through literary artifice and succeeded in producing poetry, mainly panegyric, of the highest quality.
·extravagant literary style **9**:960a
·popularity and influence **3**:644h

Mu-tan-chiang, Pin-yin romanization MU-DAN-JIANG, city in southeastern Heilungkiang Province (*sheng*), China, an autonomous sub-provincial level municipality, and also the administrative seat of the extensive border area of the Mu-tan-chiang Area (*ti-ch'ü*). Situated on the upper reaches of the Mu-tan Chiang (river), a tributary of the Sungari River in the mountains of eastern Manchuria (Northeast Provinces), Mu-tan-chiang was until the 1920s little more than a large village, overshadowed by the nearby county town of Ning-an.

The area was first settled after the completion of the Chinese Eastern Railway in 1908, when both Chinese settlers and a considerable Russian colony established themselves there. Substantial growth occurred in the 1930s under the Japanese occupation, when Mu-tan-chiang became a military and administrative centre, after the construction in 1935 of a rail link to Harbin and to Chia-mu-ssu. At that time some industry (light engineering, lumbering, and food processing) was established. After 1949, however, Mu-tan-chiang continued to grow rapidly into an industrial city. The city is provided with power from a hydroelectric station on the Mu-tan Chiang at Ching-po Hu (lake), originally constructed by the Japanese, and then rehabilitated in the early 1950s after being dismantled by Soviet occupation forces in 1945. There is a large rubber-manufacturing industry. Mu-tan-chiang is one of the chief producers of automobile tires in China; much of its production is delivered to the automotive industry centred in Ch'ang-ch'un in Kirin Province. It is also the centre of a large aluminum smelting plant, and manufactures asbestos products. Pop. (1948) 200,000; (1953) 151,000; latest est. 251,000.
44°35′ N, 129°36′ E
·map, China **4**:262

Muʿtaṣim, al- (794–842), 8th ʿAbbāsid caliph of Baghdad (833–842) and son of Hārūn ar-Rashīd; the first caliph to employ the Turkish mercenaries who later came to doninate the ʿAbbāsid dynasty. In 837 he crushed a revolt of Persian schismatics led by the rebel Bābak, who was cooperating with the Greeks. After the Byzantine emperor Theophilus had lain waste the Muslim town of Zibaṭra (known to the Byzantines as Sozopetra), al-Muʿtaṣim invaded Asia Minor, defeated Theophilus, and destroyed the fortresses of Ancyra (Ankara) and Amorium (August 838).
·ʿAbbāsid theological disputes **9**:930c
·Mamlūk slave origin and armies **11**:399d

mutation 12:754, an alteration in the genetic constitution of a cell that is transmitted to the cell's offspring. Mutations may be spontaneous (the results of accidents in the replication of genetic material) or induced by external factors (*e.g.*, electromagnetic radiation, certain chemicals).

The text article examines the nature of mutations, their causes, and their evolutionary significance.

REFERENCES in other text articles:
artificial and natural selection
·adaptation and mutation spread **10**:897g
·adaptive radiation and natural selection **14**:383f
·Asterales double-flower forms **2**:215h
·domesticated plant and animal forms **5**:941e
·evolution and heritable variation **7**:12f
·evolutionarily significant types in man **11**:428c
·evolutionary biology and teleology **12**:874e
·fruit plant breeding **7**:761g
·human genetic consequences **7**:1004e
·influenza viral strain mutations **9**:548e
·polymorphism and heterozygous advantage **14**:774h *passim* to 776a
·population genetic differences **14**:827a
·racial differentiation causes **1**:974f
·radiation and crop improvement **7**:483a; table 482
·radiation and plant disease resistance **15**:456d
·sex as source of moderate variability **16**:586f
·sexual reproduction evolutionary value **5**:625g
·silver fox and mink mutant colours **7**:812h
mechanisms
·aging and genetic mutation **1**:305c
·aging influences in tissue cultures **1**:302h
·amino acid sequence alteration **2**:1122g
·antibiotics and cellular change **1**:989e
·bacteria genotypic changes **2**:576d
·biological development regulation **5**:649c
·blood type inheritance patterns **2**:1148b
·Dobzhansky's research in genetics **5**:926b
·gene changes and hereditary importance **8**:811b
·gene structure and function **7**:983f; illus. 4
·genetic aberrations and early beliefs **7**:12a
·genetic concepts in 20th century **7**:994d
·life defined genetically **10**:893h
·metabolic pathway research **11**:1025h
·oxytocin and vasopressin derivation **8**:1078a
·phage recombination experiments **7**:986g
·photosynthetic path change by mutation **14**:368g
·pre-living systems in evolution **14**:377e
·radiation's effects on man **15**:416b
·viral-induced transduction **19**:167g
negative changes
·birth defects from gene abnormalities **6**:749d
·disease causes and classification **5**:848a
·genetic counselling implications of mutational load **7**:1005h
·nutrient biosynthesis path losses, results, and examples **13**:402h
·origin of hereditary defects **6**:1024g
·Pauling's work on sickle cell anemia **13**:1095b
·polarity reversal and organism extinction **15**:946c
·radiation-induced lethal genes **15**:387b
·radiologic damage control **15**:460h

RELATED ENTRIES in the *Ready Reference and Index:*
germinal mutation; mutagen; somatic mutation

mutation (language): *see* umlaut.

mutation rate, the frequency with which gene changes (mutations) occur within a given species per generation.
·aging related influences **1**:303d
·genetic equilibrium and selection **8**:813f
·gradual accumulation of variations **7**:13c
·human genetic change frequency **7**:1004h
·radiation-induced changes and doubling-dose variations **15**:380c

mutation stop, pipe-organ stop sounding pitches other than those indicated by the notes or one of their octaves (as a fifth, a twelfth).
·organ chorus configuration and use **13**:678h

Mutawakkil, al- (b. March 822, Iraq—d. December 861, Sāmarrāʾ, Iraq), an ʿAbbāsid caliph (leader of the Islāmic community) who, as a young man, held no political or military positions of importance but took a keen interest in the central religious debates of the day, debates that had far-reaching political importance. When he became caliph, al-Mutawakkil reverted to a position of Islāmic orthodoxy and began a persecution of all non-orthodox or non-Muslim groups. Synagogues and churches in Baghdad were torn down, while the shrine of al-Ḥusayin ibn ʿAlī (a Shīʿī martyr) in Karbalāʾ was razed, and further pilgrimages to the town were forbidden. Old regulations prescribing special dress for Christians and Jews were reinstated with new vigour.

Al-Mutawakkil was less successful in dealing with external enemies. He constantly had to dispatch expeditions to deal with rebellions in the provinces, although he suffered no important losses of territory. Warfare against the Byzantines continued its intermittent course and was likewise indecisive. Al-Mutawakkil continued the dangerous policy of depending upon Turkish soldiers, who eventually murdered him at the instigation of his eldest son, who had become estranged from him and feared to lose the succession.

·conservative religious policies **3**:637e
·Muḥāsibī's anathematization **12**:612b
·politico-religious policies **11**:992g

mutawallī (Arabic: "person endowed with authority"), in Islāmic countries, the title of an official in charge of holy shrines.

·Islāmic pilgrimage places and shrines **9**:920a

Muʿtazilah, al- (Arabic: Those Who Withdraw or Stand Apart), general Arabic term for political or religious neutralists; by the 10th century, used specifically of an Islāmic school of speculative theology that flourished in Basra and Baghdad (8th–10th centuries AD).

The name first appears in early Islāmic history in the dispute over ʿAlī's leadership of the Muslim community after the murder of the third caliph, ʿUthmān (656). Those who would neither condemn nor sanction ʿAlī or his opponents but took a middle position were termed al-Muʿtazilah.

The theological school is traced back to Wāṣil ibn ʿAṭāʾ (699–749), a student of al-Ḥasan al-Baṣrī, who by stating that a grave sinner (*fāsiq*) could not be classed as believer or unbeliever but was in an intermediate position (*al-manzilah bayna manzilatayn*), withdrew (*iʿtazala*, hence the name al-Muʿtazilah) from his teacher's circle. (The same story is told of ʿAmr ibn ʿUbayd [died 762].) Variously maligned as free thinkers and heretics, the Muʿtazilah, in the 8th century AD, were the first Muslims to use the categories and methods of Hellenistic philosophy to derive their three major and distinctive dogmatic points.

First, they stressed the absolute unity or oneness (*tawḥīd*) of God: all his many attributes (*al-asmāʾ al-ḥusnā*) were acknowledged insofar as they were part of his very being, but no separate, hypostatic existence was allowed them. From this it was logically concluded that the Qurʾān could not be technically considered the word of God (the orthodox view), as God has no separable parts, and so had to be created and was not coeternal with God. Under the ʿAbbāsid caliph al-Maʾmūn, this doctrine of the created Qurʾān was proclaimed (827) as the state dogma, and in 833, a *miḥnah* or tribunal was instituted to try those who disputed the doctrine (notably the theologian Aḥmad ibn Ḥanbal); the Muʿtazilī position was finally abandoned by the caliphate under al-Mutawakkil *c.* 849. The Muʿtazilah further stressed the justice (*ʿadl*) of God as their second principle. While the orthodox were concerned with the awful will of God to which each individual must submit himself without question, the Muʿtazilah posited that God desires only the best for man, but through free will man chooses between good and evil and thus becomes ultimately responsible for his actions. So in the third doctrine, the threat and the promise (*al-waʿd wa al-waʿīd*), or paradise and hell, God's justice becomes a matter of logical necessity, without the emotional Qurʾānic properties of mercy and grace: God *must* reward the good (as promised) and *must* punish the evil (as threatened).

Among the most important Muʿtazilī theologians were Abū al-Hudhayl al-ʿAllāf (d. *c.* 841) and an-Naẓẓām (d. 846) in Basra and Bishr ibn al-Muʿtamir (d. 825) in Baghdad. It was al-Ashʿarī (died 935 or 936), a student of the Muʿtazilī al-Jubbāʾī, who broke the force of the movement by refuting its teachings with the same Hellenistic, rational methods first introduced by the Muʿtazilah.

·ʿAbbāsid policy and orthodox reaction **3**:643f
·Al-Maʾmūn's attempted reforms **11**:418b
·Iraq's status as theological centre **11**:992d
·Islāmic theological positions **9**:915e
·Jewish and Islāmic philosophy **10**:209a
·Jewish theology and Muslim influence **16**:111e
·monotheistic austerity **2**:143d
·Muḥāsibī's opposition and diplomacy **12**:612a
·Qurʾān's unorthodox interpretation **15**:344c
·reason and revelation in doctrine **1**:368b
·theology and historical origins **9**:1013e

Muʿtazilites (Islāmic philosophical school): *see* Muʿtazilah, al-.

Mute, unfinished 19th-century U.S. submarine designed by Robert Fulton.

·submarine left unfinished by Fulton **17**:747h

mute, device used on a musical instrument to reduce, soften, or muffle its tone.

·technique for various instruments **13**:644g

Müteferrika, Ibrahim, 18th-century Hungarian-born Muslim convert who began printing the first Turkish language books in 1727.

·Ottoman westernization process **13**:784c

Mute Girl of Portici, The, French LA MUETTE DE PORTICI, or MASANIELLO, opera by Daniel Auber.

·phenomenal popularity in 19th century **13**:586c

Mutesa I, in full MUTEESA WALUGEMBE MUKAABYA (b. *c.* 1838—d. October 1884, Nabulagala, Buganda), autocratic but progressive *kabaka* (ruler) of the African kingdom of Buganda (now in Uganda) at a crucial time in its history, when extensive contacts with Arabs and Europeans were just beginning.

Mutesa has been described as both a ruthless despot and a highly skilled politician. Although his position during his first six years in office was extremely precarious and resulted in much bloodshed, he was soon able to consolidate his kingdom into a bureaucratic autocracy in which traditional priests and clan leaders had little power but in which, at least to some extent, talent was recognized. He also reformed the military system and expanded his fleet of war canoes on Lake Victoria.

Under him Buganda's chief wealth came from raids into neighbouring states, although he made no attempt to extend his direct political control. Slaves and ivory seized on these raids or paid to Buganda as tribute were traded to Arabs for guns and cotton cloth, but Mutesa kept both this trade and the Arabs themselves under strict control. He was apparently influenced enough by Islām to observe Ramaḍān (the month of fasting observed by all Muslims) from 1867 to 1877, but, wishing to use European influence as a counterweight to an Egyptian threat from the north, he also welcomed Christian missionaries in 1877.

Mutesa II, also known as SIR EDWARD FREDERICK MUTESA (b. Nov. 19, 1924—d. Nov. 21, 1969), *kabaka* (king) of the East African state of Buganda (now part of Uganda) in 1939–53, 1955–66; but he was deposed in 1953 by the British and again in 1966 by Milton Obote, president of independent Uganda.

During the 1940s Mutesa was essentially controlled by the British resident and his *katikiro* (prime minister) and was personally rather unpopular. In the "Kabaka crisis" of 1953, when the loss of the separate privileged position of the Kingdom of Buganda within the protectorate of Uganda seemed imminent, he had to take an unyielding stand in meetings with the governor of Uganda or completely alienate a large number of his increasingly suspicious and anti-British subjects. His key demands were for the separation of Buganda from the rest of Uganda and a definite promise of independence. When he refused to communicate British formal recommendations to his Lukiko (parliament), he was arrested and deported. Buganda leaders were able to engineer his return in 1955, legally as a constitutional monarch, but with in fact a great deal of influence in the Buganda government.

When Uganda became independent, Prime Minister Obote first hoped to placate the Ganda by encouraging Mutesa's election as president (a nonexecutive post) in 1963. A conflict over the role and over the continued integrity of the Buganda kingdom within Uganda followed. When Mutesa tried to foment discontent within Obote's Uganda People's Congress between the traditionally stateless northerners and the southern "kingdom" members, Obote suspended the constitution. The conflict escalated rapidly, and Mutesa was forced to flee to Britain in 1966, where he died in exile.

mutilation and deformation, permanent or semipermanent modifications of the living human body. Mutilation implies a technique that breaks the skin (or removes hair, nails, or part or all of a tooth), whereas deformation refers to changes in shape; techniques of both kinds frequently are combined in intentional modifications. The methods used, either singly or in combination, are incision, perforation, complete or partial removal, cautery, abrasion, adhesion, insertion of foreign bodies or materials, compression, distention, diversion, enlargement, and staining.

Motives for intentional changes are exceedingly varied. Modifications are frequently performed for magical and medical purposes, but cosmetic (aesthetic) motives such as those underlying much modern plastic surgery are perhaps the most common; the variability of the results in different cultures is an excellent indication of the relativity of ideals of beauty. Other motives are concerned with religion (sacrifice, ascetic mortification), magical protection, mourning, the indication of status or rank or group membership (*e.g.*, tribal marks, initiation mutilations), bravado, and punishment. Intentional mutilations and deformations are widespread. In cross-cultural perspective, the most commonly modified parts of the body are various parts of the head and the genitalia; this is also the case among modern Euramerican peoples.

·Homo erectus rituals **8**:1034e
·passage rite insignias **13**:1047a

RELATED ENTRIES in the *Ready Reference and Index:*
ear plug; lip ring, lip plug, and lip plate; mutilation and deformation of the genitalia; mutilation and deformation of the head; mutilation and deformation of the limbs; mutilation and deformation of the skin; mutilation and deformation of the torso; nose ring; tattoo.

mutilation and deformation of the genitalia, intentional permanent modification of the genitalia. The best known and most widespread genital mutilation is circumcision (*q.v.*). Subincision (opening the urethra along the inferior surface of the penis for a varying distance between the urinary meatus and the scrotum) is a common practice at puberty initiations among Australian Aborigines and is recorded as a therapeutic measure among Fijians, Tongans, and Amazonian Indians. Customary unilateral castration (monorchy) is known in central Algeria, among the Beja (Egypt), Sidamo (Ethiopia), Bushmen and Hottentot (southern Africa), and some Australian Aborigines, and on Ponape Island (Micronesia). Bilateral castration was common to produce eunuchs for Muslim harem attendants; for several centuries (until prohibited by Pope Leo XIII in the late 19th century) to produce male sopranos or contraltos called castrati (*see* castrato) for ecclesiastical chants in the Roman Catholic Church; for religious reasons among Russian Skoptsy, an 18th-century sect stressing celibacy; and as practiced on slaves, royal servants, or priests in several ancient Mediterranean lands and Mesopotamia, in Byzantium, and in China. Bilateral castration is mentioned as punishment for adultery among the Azande (central Africa), Babylonians, ancient Egyptians, ancient Chinese, and elsewhere. Among the Toradja and Sadang (Celebes) and some Dayak groups (Borneo), many or most adult men wore a penis pin, knobbed on each end and averaging about one and a half inches (four centimetres) long, in a permanent perforation through the glans, to increase pleasure in their sexual partners. The Alfur (Celebes) inserted pebbles under the skin of the glans for the same purpose. Female mutilations include excision (of part or all of the clitoris—clitoridectomy, female circumcision—and sometimes also of the labia, mons, or both), in much of Africa, ancient Egypt, India, Malaysia, and Australia, and among the Russian Skoptsy; incision (of the external genitalia, without removal of any part) among the Totonac (Mexico) and tropical South American Indians; infibulation (induced adhesion of the labia minora, leaving only a small orifice, to prevent sexual intercourse until the orifice is reopened by incision) in east Africa and among some Arabs; dilatation (of the vaginal orifice, often with incision) among some Australian Aborigines; elongation of the labia (*tablier*), recorded for southern Africa (and doubtfully elsewhere in Africa) and the Caroline Islands (on Truk, where it is combined with suspension of rattling objects from perforations in the distended labia minora); and artificial defloration (among Australian Aborigines and elsewhere).

mutilation and deformation of the head, intentional modification of the skull, lips, teeth, tongue, nose, eyes, or ears. Cephalic deformation is the best documented form of deformation or mutilation, largely because archaeological skeletal remains clearly show its presence. Tabular deformations are produced by constant pressure of small boards or other flattened surfaces against the infant's head, and annular deformations are produced by a constricting band; each kind is subdivided according to the resulting head shapes, which are often strikingly different from the normal. Cranial deformation is known from all continents except Australia and from Oceania. It is rather rare in Africa south of the Sahara and apparently absent from south India, northern North America (except the North Pacific coast), and most of northern Eurasia (except Kamchatka and Scandinavia). The practice survived into the 20th century in France, Indonesia, Melanesia, North Africa, and probably elsewhere.

Perforation of the lower lip (or less often the upper) for insertion of a decorative plug or other ornament is widespread in Africa and among lowland South American Indians and was formerly common among Indians of the northwest North American coast and the Eskimo. The most striking instance is that of the women of the Sara tribe of central Africa (commonly known as Ubangi after the name erroneously applied in P.T. Barnum's publicity), whose lips are slit and then stretched by saucer-shaped plugs averaging about 4 inches (10 centimetres) in diameter in the upper lip and seven inches (18 centimetres) in the lower and sometimes reaching 9 or 10 inches (up to 25 centimetres) in the lower. Men of the Botocudo tribe of Brazil wear a similar disk about 4 inches in diameter in the lower lip. Perforations in the cheeks for insertion of ornaments are much rarer.

Dental mutilations take the form of removal, usually of one or more incisors (ancient Peru, most Australian Aborigines, some groups in Africa, Melanesia, and elsewhere); pointing in various patterns by chipping (Africa) or filing (ancient Mexico and Central America); filing of the surface, sometimes into relief designs (Indonesia); incrustation with precious stones or metal (Southeast Asia, India, ancient Mexico, and Ecuador); insertion of a peg between the teeth (India); and blackening (south India, hill peoples in Burma, some Malaysian groups). Modern Euramerican dentistry in filling, capping, replacing, and straightening teeth provides other examples.

Ancient Aztec and Maya Indians drew a cord of thorns through the tongue as a form of sacrifice; some Australian tribes draw blood from gashes under the tongue at initiation rites; removal of the tongue as punishment is known from historic cultures (Europe, Africa).

For the insertion of decorative objects, perforation of the septum, or one or each of the nasal alae (or both procedures combined), is widespread among South American Indians, Melanesians, and inhabitants of India and Africa; it is sporadic elsewhere (*e.g.*, Polynesians, North American Indians). The nose was cut off as a punishment for adultery among Indians of central and southern Mexico. In modern plastic surgery, the nose is mutilated for aesthetic reasons.

The ancient Maya Indians considered cross-eyes beautiful and induced the condition by hanging an object between a baby's eyes. In Japan in the 1950s, a fad for a Caucasoid appearance led some women to undergo a simple operation to remove the internal epicanthic fold. Blinding as punishment is known from historic cultures.

Perforation of the earlobe for insertion of an ornament is exceedingly widespread. Sometimes the hole is gradually stretched to carry a larger ornament or to yield a greater distended pendant margin (Malaysia, Melanesia, Tonga, Easter Island, Palau, India, and among many American Indian and African tribes). More rarely, ornaments are inserted in holes along the auricular margin (eastern North American Indians and some African and tropical South American groups). Ears were mutilated or removed as punishment for adultery by the Mixtec (Mexico) and many North American tribes.

mutilation and deformation of the limbs, intentional modification of arms, legs, feet, or digits.

Constriction of the arms or legs by tight bands may cause permanent enlargement of the unconstricted area. The custom occurs among several east African and tropical South American peoples and also sporadically in Nigeria, southeast Asia, and Melanesia.

From the T'ang dynasty (AD 618–907) until the 20th century, many Chinese women had their feet tightly bound in early childhood, forming the famous "golden lily" feet, much reduced in size and deformed to match the aesthetic ideal. A similar but much less severe deformation is mentioned for the Kutchin Indians (Alaska).

Amputation of a phalanx or whole finger, usually as a form of sacrifice or in demonstration of mourning, was common among North American Indians, Australian Aborigines, Bushmen and Hottentots, Nicobarese, Tongans, Fijians, and some groups in New Guinea, South America, and elsewhere. Outlines of hands missing digits or parts of digits found among European Paleolithic cave paintings may indicate the presence of a similar custom at that period. Amputation of the toes is less common but occurred in Fijian mourning.

mutilation and deformation of the skin, intentional modification of the skin, primarily by tattooing (*q.v.*) and cicatrization. In the former, colour is introduced under the skin; in the latter, raised scars (keloids) are produced, usually in decorative patterns. Cicatrization is customary among darker skinned peoples (among whom tattooing would not be so obvious); it has been practiced in much of Africa, among Australian and Tasmanian Aborigines, and in many Melanesian and New Guinea groups. Usually an incision is made and an irritating substance is introduced to delay healing and produce a more marked scar. Sometimes scars have been produced by burning, as in Timor and northern Australia and among the Seminole Indians. Cicatrization also occurs sporadically elsewhere; *e.g.*, facial scars intentionally produced in German students' duels and light scars from chest and limb scratching for magical, medical, and disciplinary purposes among Indians of southeastern North America. Another form of skin mutilation is the introduction of objects under the skin: diamonds smuggled by South African miners; jewelry concealed under the skin of chest or neck by Yünnanese travellers; and various magical protective amulets inserted under the skin by some Burmese.

·Melanesian tatoos and cicatrization **11**:867a

mutilation and deformation of the torso, intentional modification of the neck, trunk, and breasts.

The Padaung women of Burma are famous for necks stretched by a coiled brass neck ring to a length of about 15 inches (38 centimetres), with about four thoracic vertebrae pulled up into the neck.

Well into the 19th century, European women's tight corsets caused permanent and often deleterious deformations of the rib cage and internal organs.

The shape of the breasts has sometimes been customarily altered for aesthetic reasons by compression (*e.g.*, in the Caucasus, in 16th–17th century Spain) or distention (*e.g.*, among the Payagua of Paraguay). Mutilations are also known: removal of the right breast by the Amazons of classical legend; removal of both nipples or both breasts for religious reasons by the Skoptsy (a Russian Christian sect); amputation of the breasts as punishment under Hammurabi's Code.

Among several African peoples (Efik, Ganda, Nyoro, and others) girls were secluded at puberty for several months and fattened with special diets. Women in Near Eastern harems were also artificially fattened for aesthetic reasons.

Mutillidae (insect family): *see* velvet ant.

Mutina (city, Italy): *see* Modena.

Mutinus (fungi): *see* stinkhorn.

mutiny, any overt act of defiance or attack upon military (including naval) authority by two or more persons subject to such authority. The term is occasionally used to describe nonmilitary instances of defiance or attack—such as mutiny on board a merchant ship or a rising of slaves in a state in which slavery is recognized by law or custom. Mutiny should be distinguished from revolt or rebellion, which involve a more widespread defiance and which generally have a political objective.

Historically, mutiny has always been regarded as a most serious offense, especially aboard ships at sea. Because the safety of the ship has been thought to depend upon the submission of all persons on board to the will of the captain, wide disciplinary powers have traditionally been given to the commanding officer, including the power to inflict the death penalty without waiting for a return to port and a court-martial. With the development of radio communications, however, such stringent penalties have become less necessary, and, under many current military codes, sentences for mutiny can be passed only by court-martial.

·Alexander the Great and opposition in army **1**:471d

·Magellan's suppression of crew's revolt **11**:293a

Mutis, José (Celestino Bruno) (b. April 6, 1732, Cádiz, Spain—d. Sept. 11, 1808, Bogotá), botanist who initiated one of the most important periods of botanical exploration in Spain.

After receiving the bachelor's degree from the University of Seville in 1753, Mutis studied medicine and in 1757 became physician to the royal household of Ferdinand VI. One of the first Spanish disciples of the Swedish botanist Carolus Linnaeus, Mutis studied botany in his spare time until 1760, when he was appointed physician to the viceroy of the Spanish kingdom of New Granada (now the Republic of Colombia, South America). In 1764, three years after arriving in Bogotá, Mutis requested financial support to establish

Mutis, detail from an engraving by an unknown artist

By courtesy of the Ashmolean Museum, Oxford

a botanical garden but was refused because of a lack of funds. Two years later he took up residence in the Andes at Pamplona, where he reorganized the teaching of medicine, developed modern mining methods, taught the use of platina, and discovered quinine near Bogotá. He also taught botany and botanical drawing, and he cultivated plants for medicinal and agricultural uses.

With the arrival of a new viceroy in 1782, Mutis was named first botanist and astronomer of the botanical expedition of northern America and granted a budget and salary to build a botanical garden in the town of Mariquita. At the same time, botanical explorers were sent by the Spanish government to Peru, Cuba, Mexico, Argentina, Uruguay, and Paraguay. Meanwhile, Mutis built one of the finest botanical libraries in the New World. Along with his staff of artists, zoologists, and botanists, he assembled thousands of drawings, a collection of bird and animal skins, and a herbarium containing more than 24,000 plants. He wrote hundreds of botanical papers, but his largest work, *Flora de Bogotá o de Nueva Granada*, ("The Flora of Bogotá or of New Granada") containing more than 6,000 illustrations, was so massive that the Spanish government could not afford to print it.

In 1791 the botanical expedition moved to Bogotá, where, some years later, it built the first conservatory to be constructed in South America.

muton, the smallest portion of a chromosome or gene which, by mutation, can give rise to a new trait.
·gene definition and rII mutant maps **7**:987e

Muṭrān, Khalīl (d. 1949), Muslim poet.
·romantic approach to poetry **9**:969f

Mu Tsung (1537–72): *see* Lung-ch'ing.

Mu Tsung (1856–75): *see* T'ung-chih.

Mutt and Jeff, comic strip feature created by Harry C. Fisher (*q.v.*).

mutton: *see* lamb and mutton.

muttonbird, any of several shearwaters (*q.v.*) whose chicks are harvested commercially for meat and oil. The species principally utilized are the short-tailed, or slender-billed shearwater (*Puffinus tenuirostris*), in Australia and Tasmania, and the sooty shearwater (*P. griseus*), in New Zealand. Certain of the large petrels (*Pterodroma* species) are also harvested occasionally.
·commercial use and name origin **15**:14g

muttonchops, also called PICCADILLY WEEPERS, DUNDREARIES, BURNSIDES, or SIDEBURNS, side-whiskers that are narrow at the temple and broad and round by the lower jaws.
·period of popularity and name origin **5**:1032a

mutton grass: *see* bluegrass.

Muttra (India): *see* Mathura.

Mutual Aid: A Factor in Evolution (1902), book by Peter Kropotkin, one of the classics of anarchist and socialist thought. Kropotkin maintained that cooperation rather than conflict is the chief factor in the evolution of animal species, including man. He endeavoured to show that, despite the Darwinian concept of the struggle for survival, sociability is a dominant feature at every level of the animal world. The trend of modern history, he believed, was toward decentralized, nonpolitical, cooperative societies.
·cooperation as society's natural basis **1**:809g
·sociability dominant in animal and man **10**:537g

Mutual Assistance, Draft Treaty of (1923), European defensive alliance presented to the League of Nations by France but never adopted.
·interwar peace efforts **19**:971h

Mutual Economic Assistance, Council for (CMEA), or COMECON, organization established in January 1949 to facilitate and coordinate the economic development of the member countries, which originally included the Soviet Union, Bulgaria, Czechoslovakia, Hungary, Poland, and Romania, through centralized arrangements for trade, credit, and technical assistance among its members. Albania joined in February 1949 but ceased taking an active part at the end of 1961. The German Democratic Republic became a member in September 1950 and the Mongolian People's Republic in June 1962. In 1964 an agreement was concluded enabling Yugoslavia to participate on equal terms with Comecon members in the areas of trade, finance, currency, and industry. Cuba, in 1972, became the ninth full member of Comecon. In 1969 more than 60 percent of member countries' total foreign trade was conducted with other Comecon countries.

Between 1949 and Stalin's death in 1953 the activities of Comecon were restricted chiefly to the registration of bilateral trade and credit agreements among member countries. During the late 1950s the first systematic efforts were made to promote industrial specialization among the member countries, thus reducing "parallelism" in their economies.

In June 1962 a meeting in Moscow recommended that individual development plans be coordinated at their draft stages when they could still be subjected to fundamental adjustments. It also called for a network of multilateral payments to replace the system of balanced bilateral accounts on planned transactions. In 1963 the International Bank for Economic Cooperation was founded under Comecon auspices to finance investment projects undertaken in common by two or more members, as well as to facilitate multilateral clearings in transferable rubles (currency usable only for international trade among Comecon countries); the bank became operative in 1964.

The economic integration envisaged in the conference's "basic principles for the international socialist division of labour" has met with opposition, most notably from Romania. The Romanians expressed the fear that integration would hold back Romania's industrial development by favouring the industries of more developed members. Even among the members nominally in favour of economic integration, differences have arisen. Some of the more developed countries, such as East Germany and Hungary, have pressed for greater national specialization to widen the markets for their own manufactured products; others, notably Poland, have called for a better distribution of investment funds among the members.

Observers of Comecon have noted that in order to reap the benefits of a large single market the members will have to break away from past bilateral patterns of trade; they will also have to adopt a system of pricing that more adequately reflects real economic costs. So far the transferable rubles used for Comecon trade have not been convertible into gold or other currencies; this policy has hindered any advance toward multilateralism because member countries have no incentive to acquire ruble balances.

In a special summit session of the council held in Moscow in April 1969, a decision was made to establish an investment bank that would make medium- and long-term loans; some hoped that the bank, by its encouragement of capital flows among member countries, would also be a step toward trading with convertible currency. *Major ref.* **5**:383g
·economic planning and trade problems **6**:258d
·formation and effectiveness **9**:756b
·functions and prospects **6**:1056a
·international trade influenced by Soviet involvement **18**:557g

regional effects
·Bulgarian accelerating economic growth **3**:468e *passim* to 474b
·Czechoslovakia's economic role **5**:415g
·East German economic structure **8**:125d
·German Democratic Republic's oil supply **8**:12c
·Hungarian industrial development **9**:29g
·Polish foreign trade **14**:632h
·Romanian industrialization program **2**:638f
·Romanian trade expansion **15**:1053e
·role and effect **4**:1024d

mutual fund, investment company that pools the funds of its shareholders and invests them in securities, which it selects. It is able to hold a diversified portfolio and make its investment choices on the basis of expert professional advice. It offers the advantages of safety, diversification, and convenience to the small investor.

In contrast to closed-end investment companies, which have a fixed capitalization and whose shares are bought and sold by the investor in the market, mutual, or open-end, funds make a continuous offering of new shares at net asset value (plus a sales charge) and redeem their shares on demand at net asset value, determined daily by the market value of the securities they hold.

The purpose of the fund may be to secure long-term capital appreciation, current income, or some combination of the two.
·securities trading and investment trusts **16**:452f

mutualism, a term used by the French anarchist thinker Pierre-Joseph Proudhon to mean the organization of society on an egalitarian basis. He envisioned factories run by associations of workers, linked by a system of mutual credit founded on people's banks. The various industrial associations and local communities would be bound by contract and mutual interest rather than by laws.
·anarchist theoretical development **1**:808h
·Proudhon's use of term and theory **15**:130d

mutualism, close relationship between two species of plants or animals in which each benefits from the association. The mutual association is said to be facultative if the species involved can survive independent of one another. An example is lichens, in which case algae and fungi form a mutual association.

If the facultative mutualism is either general or indirect (*e.g.*, between soil bacteria and higher plants), the relationship is referred to as protocooperation. A form of protocooperation known as cleaning symbiosis is seen in many animals, especially in birds and fishes. The cleaner fish (*Labroides*) is known for its role in removing external parasites from larger fishes without endangering itself.

Another type of mutualism involves a relationship in which one species cannot survive without the other, as in the case of the bacteria that help digest cellulose in the digestive tract of ruminants. This type of mutualism is referred to as obligative mutualism.

Mutualists, 19th-century secret society of weavers in Lyons, Fr.

Mutual Responsibility and Interdependence in the Body of Christ (1963), a document of the Anglican Communion.

mutual savings bank, savings institution popular in the North and Middle Atlantic United States that is operated solely for the benefit of its depositors rather than for the profit of shareholders. Mutual savings banks invest funds received from depositors to earn a return that is paid out as dividends. They are managed by self-perpetuating boards of trustees. *See* savings bank.

Muwaffaq, al- (d. 891), soldier and regent for his brother the ʿAbbāsid caliph al-Muʿtamid. He restored order in Iraq, defeated a Ṣaffārid attempt to march on Baghdad (876), and overcame negro rebels near Basra (883).

Muwaḥḥidūn, al- (Muslim dynasty): *see* Almohads.

muwallads, Spanish Muslims who revolted against Umayyad rule in the 9th century.

muwashshaḥ, an Arabic poetical genre in strophic form developed in Muslim Spain in the 11th and 12th centuries that, from the 12th century onward, spread to North Africa and the Muslim East.

The *muwashshaḥ* is written in Classical Arabic, and its subjects are those of classical Arabic poetry—love, panegyric, wine. It sharply differs in form, however, from classical poetry, in which each verse is divided into two metric halves and a single rhyme recurs at the end of each verse. The *muwashshaḥ* is usually divided into five strophes or stanzas, each numbering four, five, or six lines. A master rhyme appears at the beginning of the poem and at the end of the strophes, somewhat like a refrain; it is interrupted by subordinate rhymes. A possible scheme is *ABcdcdABefefABghghABijijABklklAB*. The last *AB*, called *kharjah* or *markaz*, is usually written in vernacular Arabic or in the Spanish Mozarabic dialect; it is normally put into the mouth of a girl and expresses her longing for her absent lover. These verses—the earliest examples of lyric poetry in a Romance language—make it probable that the *muwashshaḥ* was influenced by some kind of Romance oral poetry or song. Jewish poets of Spain also wrote *muwashshaḥ*s in Hebrew, with *kharjah*s in Arabic and Spanish.

Muwatallis, also spelled MUWATALLISH, Hittite king (reigned *c.* 1306–*c.* 1282 BC) during the New Kingdom; he was the son and successor of Mursilis II. Although Muwatallis' accession was unmarred by the customary flurry of revolts among the Hittite vassal states, a struggle with resurgent Egypt for domination of Syria became imminent after Egypt reconquered Palestine and made the Orontes River in Syria the Egyptian–Hittite frontier. One of the great battles of the ancient world was fought at Kadesh (modern Tall an-l Nabī Mind) on the Orontes in 1299. Although the Egyptian king Ramses II claimed a great victory, the outcome was actually indecisive.

During his protracted Syrian operations, Muwatallis had transferred his capital from Hattusas (Boğazköy in modern Turkey) to the more southerly city of Dattassa. In the meantime, his brother Hattusilis fought with the Kaska in the north (the only troublesome Hittite satellite during Muwatallis' reign) and was installed as viceroy of the "Upper Country" east of Hattusas. Later, after Muwatallis' son, Urhi-Teshub (Mursilis III), succeeded him, Hattusilis revolted and seized the throne.

Muybridge, Eadweard (b. April 9, 1830, Kingston-on-Thames, Eng.—d. May 8, 1904, Kingston-on-Thames), photographer important for his pioneering work in photographic studies of motion and in motion-picture projection. He adopted the name Eadweard Muybridge, believing it to be the original Anglo-Saxon form of his real name, Edward James Muggeridge. He emigrated to the U.S. as a young man but remained obscure until 1868, when his large photographs of Yosemite Valley, California, made him world famous. These photographs, signed "Helios—the Flying Studio," were composite pictures (photographic prints made from parts of several different photographs).

Muybridge's experiments in photographing motion began in 1872, when the railroad magnate Leland Stanford hired him to prove that during a particular moment in a trotting horse's gait all four legs were off the ground simultaneously. His first efforts were unsuccessful because his camera lacked a fast shutter, and he was forced to abandon the project temporarily while he was being tried for the murder of his wife's lover. Although he was acquitted, he found it expedient to travel for a number of years in Mexico and Central America, making publicity photographs for the Union Pacific Railroad, a company owned by Stanford.

In 1877 he returned to California and resumed his experiments in motion photography, using a battery of from 12 to 24 cameras and a special shutter he developed that gave an exposure of 2⁄1000 of a second. This arrangement gave satisfactory results and proved Stanford's contention.

The results of Muybridge's work were widely published, most often in the form of line drawings taken from his photographs. They were criticized, however, by those who thought that horse's legs could never assume such unlikely positions. To counter such criticism, Muybridge gave lectures on animal locomotion throughout the U.S. and Europe. These lectures were illustrated with a zoopraxiscope, a lantern he developed that projected images in rapid succession onto a screen from photographs printed on a rotating glass disc, producing the illusion of moving pictures. The zoopraxiscope display, an important predecessor of the modern cinema, was a sensation, and a special hall was built for its use at the World's Columbian Exposition of 1893 in Chicago.

Muybridge made his most important photographic studies of motion from 1884 to 1887 under the auspices of the University of Pennsylvania. These studies consisted of a vast number of photographs of various activities of human figures, clothed and naked, which were to form a visual compendium of human movements for the use of artists and scientists. Many of these photographs were published in 1887 in the portfolio, "Animal Locomotion, An Electro-Photographic Investigation of Consecutive Phases of Animal Movement." Despite their high cost, the wide sale of these photographs was ensured by the fact that the largest single category of pictures was of nude women engaged in such activities as falling face down onto a mattress and throwing bucketsfull of water onto one another. Muybridge continued to publicize and publish his work until 1900, when he retired to his birthplace.

Men playing leapfrog, motion study by Eadweard Muybridge
By courtesy of George Eastman House, Rochester, New York

Muyinga, town and province, northeastern Burundi. Pop. (latest census) town, 18,458.
·map, Burundi **3**:528
·population growth 1965–70 table **3**:529

Muzaffarābād, capital of the Pakistani sector of Jammu and Kashmir, in the western Punjab Himalayas, at the confluence of the Jhelum and Kishanganga rivers. It is a trade centre for the grain-producing hinterland. The town was damaged during the India–Pakistan conflict (1947–48).
34°22′ N, 73°28′ E

Muẓaffar al- (975–1008), Umayyad caliph of Spain.
·military policy successes **17**:416c

Muẓaffar ʿAlī (fl. *c.* 1540—*c.* 1576), Persian artist best known for his portraits, who painted during the great flowering of Persian painting under the Ṣafavid shahs. Very little is known about his life except that he was a pupil of Behzād, the greatest Persian painter of the period, and that he died shortly after 1576. Muẓaffar ʿAlī, together with other important miniaturists, worked on a series of 17 illustrations for a manuscript of the works of the Persian poet Neẓāmī that was produced (from 1539–43) at the direction of Ṭahmāsp I. In addition to painting miniatures, he designed, and for the most part executed, decorative wall paintings for the royal palace and the Cihīl Sutūn (Hall of Forty Columns) in Isfahan.

Muzaffargarh, town and district, Multān Division, Punjab Province, Pakistan. The town, the district headquarters, was founded in 1794. It is connected by road with Multān, Dera Ghāzi Khān, and Quetta and has cotton textile factories. In 1873 it was constituted a municipality. Institutions include a fort and mosque, a hospital, and a government college affiliated with the University of the Punjab.

Muzaffargarh District (area 5,613 sq mi [14,538 sq km]) is a narrow wedge of land bordered on the west by the Indus River and on the east by the Chenāb. It consists of the Indus and Chenāb valleys in the north, a central arid plateau (Thal), and a southern riverine tract subject to inundation. The Muzaffargarh Canal from the Taunsa Barrage on the Indus is planned to cultivate an area half of which will be reclaimed wasteland. Wheat, rice, legumes, cotton, mangoes, and dates are the chief crops. Pop. (latest census) town, 14,474; (1972 prelim.) district, 1,548,000.

Muẓaffar Jang (d. 1751), third viceroy of Hyderābād.
·French support in succession war **9**:395a

Muzaffarnagar, administrative headquarters, Muzaffarnagar district, Uttar Pradesh state, northern India, north-northeast of Delhi, with which it is connected by road and rail. An agricultural marketplace, it also has some light industry. Two colleges are located in the town. Muzaffarnagar was founded about 1633 by Khān-e Jahān, who named it after his father, Muẓaffar Khān.

Muzaffarnagar district, 1,683 sq mi (4,359 sq km) in area, stretches between the Ganges and Yamuna (Jumna) rivers, near the Himalayan foothills. It is irrigated by the Upper Ganges and Eastern Yamuna canals; crops include grains, sugarcane, and cotton. There is dhak forest in the northwest and a hydroelectric station east-northeast of Muzaffarnagar town. Pop. (1971 prelim.) town, 114,859; district, 1,801,428.
·map, India **9**:278

Muzaffarpur, administrative headquarters, Muzaffarpur district, Bihār state, northeastern India, just south of the Burhi Gandak River. A major road and rail hub, it is a trade centre on the Patna–Nepal route. Rice and sugar milling and cutlery manufacture are the chief industries. The city was founded by Muẓaffar Khān in the 18th century. It was constituted a municipality in 1864 and is the seat of the University of Bihār.

Muzaffarpur district (area 3,024 sq mi [7,831 sq km]), constituted in 1875, comprises parts of the alluvial plain of the Ganges River system.

Grains, tobacco, and sugarcane are the principal crops. The district has several power stations. Vaiśālī is said to be the birthplace of the Jain saint Mahāvīra and has an Aśokan *stūpa* and pillar. Pop. (1971 prelim.) city, 127,045; district, 4,836,516.
·map, India **9**:278

Muzaffar Shah, sultan of Malacca (now in Malaysia) from 1445 through 1459?, under whose leadership the city-state of Malacca became a major commercial and territorial power in Southeast Asia. After his accession, Muzaffar Shah refused to pay the customary tribute to Siam, and Malacca's forces repelled two Siamese punitive expeditions in 1445 and 1456. Malacca then began to thrive as a major trade centre between China to the east and the Muslim traders of India and Arabia to the west. Under Muzaffar Shah, Malacca also first became a territorial power, acquiring Selangor to the northwest as a source of food and taking control of strategic portions of the Sumatra coast across the Strait of Malacca. After the death of Muzaffar Shah and until its capture by the Portuguese in 1511, Malacca continued to be the pre-eminent trade centre in Southeast Asia.

Mužáková, Johanna, pen name KAROLINA SVĚTLÁ (1830–1899), novelist.
·Czechoslovak 19th-century literature **10**:1211d

Múzquiz, in full MELCHOR MÚZQUIZ or CIUDAD MELCHOR MÚZQUIZ, city, north central Coahuila state, northeastern Mexico. It lies on a small tributary of the Río Sabinas, 1,654 ft (504 m) above sea level and southwest of Piedras Negras, on the United States border. The hot, dry climate has great temperature ranges. Cattle and goats are raised in the area, which also yields wheat and nuts. Roads run eastward to connect with the main highway and railroad from Piedras Negras to Mexico City. Pop. (1970) 18,868.
27°53′ N, 101°31′ W

Muztagh Tower, mountain, Singkiang Uighur, China.
38°17′ N, 75°07′ E
·mountaineering record and data table **12**:585

MVD (Soviet police organization): *see* MGB.

Mwadui, mining centre, Tanzania. Latest census 7,399.
3°33′ S, 33°36′ E
·diamond mining and exporting **17**:1031e

Mwanga (b. 1866—d. 1901), *kabaka* (ruler) of the African kingdom of Buganda, whose short but turbulent reign included a massacre of Ganda Christians, spasmodic civil war, and finally an unsuccessful uprising against the British in which Mwanga had only limited support from his own people.

Only 18 when he came to the throne in 1884, Mwanga was characterized as inexperienced and erratic. Unlike his father, Mutesa I, he saw the increasing number of Christian converts among his people, the Ganda, as a possible threat to his power; in 1885 he killed three young Ganda Christians and openly declared his opposition to missionaries. In 1886 about 30 Ganda Christians were burned alive, but their martyrdom did nothing to diminish the appeal of Christianity.

Meanwhile, a new ruling elite was developing, divided by religion into Catholic, Protestant, and Muslim factions. In 1888 the Muslim party deposed Mwanga, and several years of instability and intermittent civil war followed. By the time Mwanga was able to regain his capital in early 1890 with the aid of the Christian parties, the Christian chiefs could successfully challenge the royal power. In the early 1890s the main conflict was between the Protestant (pro-British) and Catholic (pro-French) parties, but Mwanga was in too precarious a position to mediate between them. In 1893 and 1894 he was forced to sign agreements putting Buganda under British protection, and by this time the Christian oligarchy had reduced his power to that of a constitutional monarch. In 1897 he rebelled against the British but received almost no support. Forced to flee, he died in exile.

Mwanza Gulf, Lake Victoria, northern Tanzania, Africa.
2°31′ S, 32°54′ E
·Victoria geography and hydrography **6**:116g

Mwanza Region, administrative unit (established 1963), northwestern Tanzania, with an area of about 13,850 sq mi (35,872 sq km). The gently undulating land between 3,000 and 4,500 ft (900–1,400 m), dotted with hills and tors, is part of the Tanganyikan Central Plateau. The Moame River drains to Lake Victoria (north) at Mwanza (a port and the regional capital), but 12 mi (19 km) south of the lake a low watershed separates streams draining south to the Malagarasi River and Lake Tanganyika. Miombo woodland and savanna are characteristic, with wide areas of derived grassland and natural grassland in the poorly drained areas south of the lake. The region is the nation's largest producer of cotton; but citrus fruits, cassava, rice, and sweet potatoes are also significant cash crops.

Gold mining site at Geita in the Mwanza Region of Tanzania
W. Guiver—Shostal

Population is densest in the Mwanza and Kwimba districts where the Sukuma (Usukumu) are known for their cooperatives and intensive mixed farming. The Zinza (Zinga) tribe occupies Geita District, where gold mining is important. In spite of the tsetse fly, there is considerable trade in livestock. Pop. (1972 est.) 1,200,000.
·area and population table and map **17**:1030
·map, Tanzania **17**:1026

Mwata Yamvo, Lunda royal house of Central Africa, adopted generic name for dynastic title in the 18th century.
·Lunda origin and growth **3**:1092d

Mwenda (African ruler): *see* Msiri.

Mwene Matapa (Ravager of the Lands), alternate spelling MONOMOTAPA, title borne by a line of kings ruling a southeast African territory between the Zambezi and Limpopo rivers, in what is now Rhodesia and Mozambique, from the 14th to the 17th century. Their domain was often called the empire of the Mwene Matapa, and is associated with the site known as Zimbabwe (or Great Zimbabwe) in southwestern Rhodesia.

Oral traditions ascribe the dynasty's foundation to Mbire, a semimythical ruler of the 14th century. His great-great grandson Nyatsimba, who ruled in the late 15th century, was the actual creator of the empire and the first to bear the title Mwene Matapa. During his reign the centre of the state was shifted from Zimbabwe north to Mt. Fura on the Zambezi River.

In the 16th century the Mwene Matapa's realm was invaded by the Portuguese, who

moved in from the east coast beginning in the 1530s. When the reigning Mwene Matapa attempted to expel them in 1629, they deposed him and forced his successor to grant them extensive trading and mining privileges. By the late 17th century, the power of the Mwene Matapa was overshadowed by the Rowzi kingdom of southwestern Rhodesia.
·origin and gradual power loss **17**:276e *passim* to 278b

Mweru, Lake, in central Africa, bordered east by Zambia and west by Zaire. The name is Bantu for "lake." A part of the Congo River system, it lies in the northwest of the Mweru-Luapula-Bangweulu plain, its surface being about 3,010 ft (917 m) above sea level. Its greatest length (south-southwest–north-northeast) is 76 mi (122 km), its average width 31 mi, and its surface area 1,900 sq mi (4,920 sq km). The lake's margins are generally flat, except on the rocky west coast. The Luapula River enters Mweru on the south, and the Luvua leaves it on the north, west of the town of Pweto, flowing northwest to join the Lualaba. Kilwa and Sokwe islands are in the southern part of the lake.
9°00′ S, 28°45′ E
·map, Zaire **19**:1121
·map, Zambia **19**:1131
·Zambia's geographical configuration **19**:1129b

Mya arenaria (soft-shell clam): *see* clam.

Myalina, extinct genus of clams found in rocks of Mississippian to Permian age (345,000,000 to 225,000,000 years ago).

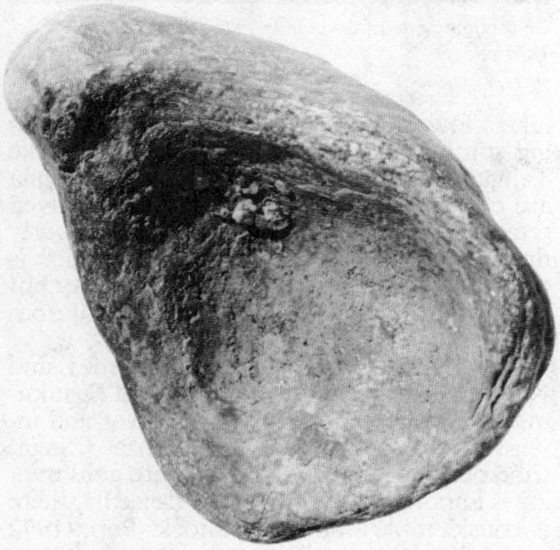

Myalina, collected in Dallas, Texas
By courtesy of the Buffalo Museum of Science, Buffalo, New York

Myalina belongs to an ancient group of clams, the Mytilacea, that first appeared in the earlier Ordovician Period, which began 500,000,000 years ago. As compared to other mytiacids, the shell of *Myalina* is relatively thick. *Myalina* was a sedentary clam, and it probably preferred shallow water. Abundant in many rock formations, it is important for stratigraphic correlations.

myall (*Acacia pendula*), a small, silver-gray tree of western New South Wales and Queensland, Australia. The name, of Aboriginal origin, is sometimes applied to other trees of the genus *Acacia* (*q.v.*), including *A. homalophylla* and the coast myall, *A. glaucescens*.

myasthenia gravis, chronic disorder that causes variable degrees of muscular weakness after the muscle has been exercised. The muscles initially affected are those concerned with eye movements, facial expression, chewing, swallowing, and respiration. The heart is not usually involved. The disease spreads to the neck, trunk, and limb muscles; respiratory difficulties or respiratory arrest may occur in severe cases. Muscles first fail to contract after prolonged use; they seem to become weaker with repeated mild activities but then regain their strength after rest. Eventually, even after periods of rest, muscular paralysis may remain and degeneration of muscle fibres and infiltration of lymph cells may occur.

The disorder is attributed to a breakdown in the linkage between the nervous system's stimulation of a muscle and the muscle's response. The cause of this functional failure is unknown. There are no distinct lesions to be found in either the nervous system or the muscle that can be correlated to the weakness.

Myasthenia gravis can occur at any age, but it is rarely seen initially before the age of 10 years or after 70. There is a tendency for the condition to be more prevalent in some families. Some symptoms show sudden onset, while others may be present for 10 to 20 years without becoming any worse; this is especially true of visual problems such as double vision, drooping eyelids, and eye wandering.

The affected person may have problems in climbing stairs, in rising from chairs, in lifting objects, or in raising the arms over the head. There is no change in mental attitude or faculties, nor are there pain, cramps, or muscle twitching. The inability to swallow and chew may lead to loss of weight. All of the lower facial muscles may become involved, so that speech takes on a nasal quality, and the affected person may even have to support the chin with one hand in order to talk. Neck weakness may be mild or so severe that the head cannot be held erect. Weakness of the legs may prevent walking or even turning in bed. Each affected person seems to manifest his own set of difficulties; he may be perfectly mobile and yet have difficulty in breathing, or he may be bedridden but free of any respiratory problems.

Symptoms may be suppressed with the aid of drugs. They also may regress spontaneously for several years. Some persons die from sudden respiratory arrest, but in most cases death is from some cause unrelated to the myasthenia. *Major ref.* **12**:635g
·fatigue causes and relief **7**:191f
·incidence and neurological signs **12**:1057c

Myaungmya, administrative headquarters of Myaungmya district (*kayaing*), Irrawaddy division (*taing*), Lower Burma. Lying on a distributary of the Irrawaddy River, it is a steamer landing and a rice-collecting centre. A government agricultural research and demonstration farm are nearby.

The district (area 2,835 sq mi [7,343 sq km]) occupies part of the Irrawaddy Delta between the Bassein (west) and Irrawaddy (east) rivers and has a southern coastline on the Andaman Sea. It is a fertile rice-growing region. Communication is mainly by water, and villages such as Wakema, Moulmeingyun, and Labutta are strung along the river banks. Pop. (latest census) town, 24,532; district, 85,027.
·map, Burma **3**:505

Myazedi inscription, epigraph written in 1113 in the Pāli, Pyu, Mon, and Burmese languages that provided a key not only to the Pyu language but also to the dates of the early days of the kingdom of Pagan. The inscription, engraved on a stone found at the Myazedi pagoda near Pagan, tells the story of King Kyanzittha's deathbed reconciliation with his estranged son, whom he had disinherited by a peace-producing compromise of 1084 that had helped end the bloodletting between the Pagan and Mon kingdoms.

The period described by the Myazedi stone saw the gradual transition from the Pāli and Mon languages to the Burmese language, which was reaching maturity as a medium of literary expression, using Mon script. The later decades of the Pagan period marked the ascendancy of Burmese cultural traits at the expense of Mon tradition. The Myazedi inscription was a benchmark from which to chronicle the development of a peculiarly Burmese culture.

My Brilliant Career (1901), novel by Miles Franklin.
·Australian novel tradition **13**:292e

Mycale, Battle of (August 479 BC), Greek victory over the Persians on the Aegean coast of present Turkey, opposite the island of Samos; with the simultaneous victory at Plataea, it ended the second Persian invasion of Greece.
·events and effects **8**:350d
·Persian reticence and Greek victory **8**:311e

Mycelia Sterilia (order of fungi): *see* Deuteromycetes.

mycelium, the mass of branched, tubular filaments (hyphae) of fungi (division Mycota).

Mycelium
William H. Amos—Helen Wohlberg, Inc.

The mycelium makes up the thallus, or undifferentiated body, of a typical fungus. It may be microscopic in size or developed into visible structures, such as brackets, mushrooms, puffballs, rhizomorphs (long strands of hyphae cemented together), sclerotia (hard, compact masses), stinkhorns, toadstools, and truffles. At a certain stage it produces spores, directly or through special fruiting bodies. *Major ref.* **12**:758b
·fungal plant disease transmission **5**:890c
·lichen structures and functions **10**:882e
·mushroom plant aging **10**:914f

Mycena (genus of fungi): *see* Agaricales.

Mycenae, prehistoric Greek city in the Argolid, capital of the Achaean Greeks and the home of Agamemnon. Since the discoveries of Heinrich Schliemann in the 1870s, Mycenae has been the chief Late Bronze Age site in mainland Greece. The ruins and artifacts uncovered there have lent the name Mycenaean to the race of Greeks that dominated the Aegean from the conquest of Crete (*c.* 1450 BC) to the time of the Dorian invasions (*c.* 1100 BC). Greek settlement in Mycenae appears as early as the 2nd millennium. By the

Royal tomb circle of Mycenae seen from the northeast
Foto Marburg

end of the Middle Helladic, or Middle Bronze Age (*c.* 1600), Mycenaean tomb architecture shows an increased sophistication with heavy borrowings from Minoan Crete. The richest architectural finds, including the "Treasury of Atreus" and the "Tomb of Clytemnestra,"

date from the latter part (*c.* 1400–*c.* 1200) of the Late Helladic, the acme of Mycenaean civilization. *Major ref.* **1**:111g
·clothing styles and ornaments **5**:1020e
·epigraphic record and cultural details **6**:922d
·jewelry-making development **10**:168d
·Schliemann's theory and discoveries **16**:348g
·visual art of Metal Age cultures **19**:276g; illus. 277

Mycenaean (or LATE HELLADIC) **civilization** (*c.* 1450–*c.* 1100 BC), the Late Bronze Age (Aegean) culture of mainland Greece in general and often of the Greek islands except Crete. It is named for Mycenae (*q.v.*), an ancient fortress-city in the Peloponnese, the site of its most important remains. In the 1870s Heinrich Schliemann made systematic excavations of its extensive and important ruins. Tiryns (*q.v.*) and Pylos are other important Mycenaean sites. *Major ref.* **1**:111g
·archaeological excavation **1**:1078g
·archaeology and Greek myths **8**:403d
·bronze, silver, gold, and lead art work **11**:1096d; illus. 1102
·clothing styles and ornaments **5**:1020f
·epigraphic record significance **6**:922d
·influence on Archaic Greece **8**:326b
·jewelry forms and historic development **10**:168d; illus. 169
·metalwork and weaponry illus., **11**:Metalwork, Plate 3
·pottery styles **14**:898d
·visual art of Late Bronze Age **19**:275d; illus. 277

Mycenaean Greek, the most ancient form of the Greek language that has been discovered. It was a chancellery language, used mainly for perishable records and inventories of royal palaces and commercial establishments. Written in a syllabic script known as Linear B, it has been found mostly on clay tablets discovered at Knossos in Crete and at Pylos in Messenia, as well as in inscriptions on pots and jars from Thebes, Mycenae, Tiryns, Eleusis, and Boeotian Orchomenos.

Because Mycenaean Greek shows more points of agreement with Arcado-Cypriot than with any other pre-Doric dialect group, it is classified by some scholars as an Arcado-Cypriot dialect.

One of the chief archaic characteristics of Mycenaean Greek is that it differentiates the labiovelars (consonant sounds formed by simultaneous contact of the back of the tongue with the soft palate and lip-rounding) from the labials (consonants articulated with the lips) and the dentals (consonants articulated with the tip of the tongue and the upper teeth or the gum ridge).
·range, uniformity, and artificiality **8**:393e

mycetocyte, in certain insects, a cell in the alimentary tract harbouring symbiotic micro-organisms that supply the insect with essential nutrients that it cannot synthesize from components of its diet.
·insect digestive symbiosis **9**:615f

mycetoma (disease): *see* Madura foot.

Mycetophagidae (beetle family): *see* hairy fungus beetle.

Mycetophilidae (fly family): *see* fungus gnat.

Mycetozoa (alternative name of division Myxomycophyta): *see* slime mold.

Mycobacterium, genus of bacteria of the family Mycobacteriaceae (order Actinomycetales), the most important species of which, *M. tuberculosis* and *M. leprae,* cause tuberculosis and leprosy, respectively, in man. *See* actinomycete; tubercle bacillus.

mycobiont, the fungous element of a lichen, the other element being algae (the phycobiont).
·lichens as associations of fungi and algae **10**:882e

mycology, the study of fungi, a group that includes the mushrooms, molds, yeasts, and actinomycetes. Many fungi are useful in medicine and industry. Mycological research has led to the development of such antibiotic drugs as penicillin, streptomycin, and tetracycline. Mycology also has important applications in the dairy, wine, and baking industries and in the production of dyes and inks. Medical mycology is the study of fungous organisms that cause disease in man.
·microbiology study **12**:110h

mycoplasma, micro-organisms of the order Mycoplasmatales, usually considered bacteria (class Schizomycetes). About 15 species are known, all placed in the genus *Mycoplasma;* new species are still being discovered. Most are parasites of birds or mammals, some occurring regularly in man; a few are free-living in stagnant or enriched water. Because *M. mycoides,* the agent of pleuropneumonia in cattle, was known long before most other species, the general name pleuropneumonia-like organism (frequently abbreviated as PPLO) is often applied to all the mycoplasmas.

Mycoplasmas are the smallest of bacterial organisms, some stages of certain species being less than 0.2 micron (a micron is 0.001 millimetre) in diameter. The cell shape is extremely variable within a single species. Colonies consist of threadlike, branching networks (mycelia) with spherical or bulbous inclusions of various sizes.

The relationships of mycoplasmas to diseases are poorly known. Many *Mycoplasma* species are found in the respiratory, genital, or digestive tracts of ruminants, carnivores (usually the domestic dog), rodents, and man, and some have been linked to diseases of infected organs. *M. pneumoniae* causes a widespread but rarely fatal pneumonia in man.
·antibiotic action of chloramphenicol **1**:989a
·classification and general features **2**:577c
·diseases of laboratory animals, table 8 **5**:876
·metabolic life cycle limitations in pleuropneumonia-like organisms **10**:897c
·M. hominis reproductive features, illus. 3 **2**:570
·plant disease-causing agents **5**:888f
·procaryotic cell characteristics **3**:1048d
·respiratory disease of bacterial origin **15**:770f
·size, structure, and growth habit **9**:533b

mycorrhiza, or MYCORHIZA, association between the branched, tubular filaments (hyphae) of a fungus (division Mycota) and the roots of higher plants. The association can be of mutual benefit (symbiotic), but it may also be a limited parasitic attack by the fungus on the host (the higher plant). The growth of certain plants, such as citrus trees, orchids, and pine trees, is dependent on the fungus.
·conifer root function and symbiotic relationship **5**:4f
·ecosystem structure and components **6**:284f
·Ericales symbiotic relationships **6**:955h
·fungal plant associations **12**:763h
·Gentianales growth relationships **7**:1018h
·Iridales mycotrophic relationships **9**:891b
·orchid germination and symbiosis **13**:650g
·root structure modifications **13**:730h

mycosis, in domestic animals and man, a fungous infection of deep tissue that develops slowly, takes a long course, and is difficult to eradicate. Numerous animal diseases are mycoses. Actinomycosis, caused by *Actinomyces bovis,* includes lumpy jaw of cattle and other chronic abscesses of swine and horses; *A. israelii* affects man. Nocardiosis, caused by *Nocardia asteroides,* chiefly attacks the lymph systems of dogs, cattle, poultry, and man. Histoplasmosis, marked by respiratory and digestive distress, is caused by *Histoplasma capsulatum;* it is the commonest mycosis in dogs and man. Coccidioidomycosis, from *Coccidioides immitis,* primarily attacks the lymph systems of cattle, sheep, horses, dogs, cats, and man. *See also* actinomycosis; histoplasmosis; nocardiosis.

mycostatin (medicine): *see* nystatin.

Mycota **12**:756, the fungi, about 50,000 species described, including mushrooms, yeasts, rusts, smuts, mildews, and molds.

The text article covers the importance of Mycota to man, their general features, natural history, form and function, and evolution and phylogeny; an annotated classification of the phylum is included.

REFERENCES in other text articles:
·antibiotic syntheses from soil organisms **1**:986a
·biological classification complications **4**:690c
·biotoxin classification and features **14**:608f; tables 609
·cereal crop damage patterns **3**:1161e
·Ericales mycorrhizal relationships **6**:955h
·flax fibre retting process **7**:278g
·fungicides and uses **14**:141e; table 140
·humidity and growth of pathogens **9**:5a
·Iridales mycotrophic relationships **9**:891b
·lichen associations of fungi and algae **10**:882e
·microbiology study development **12**:110h
·mushroom age possibility **10**:914f
·nutritional mutualisms of yeasts **13**:407e
·orchid symbiosis and germination **13**:650f
·plant disease-causing agents **5**:890b; illus.
·polar biotic components **14**:655h
·protozoan phylogenic links **14**:379e
·survival through spore formation **5**:959e
·symbioses on weevil backs **4**:832b

RELATED ENTRIES in the *Ready Reference and Index: for*
classes: see Ascomycetes; Basidiomycetes; Chytridiomycetes; Hyphochytridiomycetes; Oomycetes; Plasmodiophoromycetes; Zygomycetes
common names: cup fungus; fairy ring mushroom; fungus; inky cap; mildew; mold; mushroom; stinkhorn; toadstool; truffle; water mold; yeast
family: Boletaceae
genera: Amanita; Aphanomyces; Arthrobotrys; Aspergillus; Dactylella; Penicillium
orders: Agaricales; Hymenogastrales; Lycoperdales; Polyporales
structures: acervulus; aecium; ascocarp; ascus; basidium; basidiocarp; chlamydospore; conidium; hymenium; mycelium; oidium; plasmodium; pycnidium; rhizoid; rhizomorph; sclerotium; stroma; teliospore; urediospore; zygospore
other: Deuteromycetes; Discomycetes; Gasteromycetes; heterothallism; homothallism; Hymenomycetes; Laboulbeniomycetes; mycorrhiza; Plectomycetes; Pyrenomycetes; Trichomycetes

mycotrophy, the obtaining of food by association with a fungus. *See* mycorrhiza.
·Iridales nutritional features **9**:891b

Myctophidae (fish family): *see* lantern fish.

Myctophiformes, order of bony fish including both shallow-water and deep-sea forms. Among the members of the group are the barracudina, Bombay duck, lancet fish, lantern fish, and lizardfish (*qq.v.*).
·characteristics and classification **7**:343g

Mydaus javanensis (mammal): *see* badger.

Mydelton, Sir Hugh (1560?–1631), a Welsh merchant and a member of Parliament who built the New River water supply system for London (1609–13) by extending a canal for 38 miles from springs in Hertfordshire.
·aqueducts and formation of New River Company **1**:1039c
·enterprises and accomplishments **6**:222b

myelin, white, insulating sheath on the axon of many nerve fibres. It is composed of fatty materials, protein, and water. The myelin sheath is deposited by Schwann cells in layers surrounding the nerve fibres (*q.v.*) of the central and peripheral nervous systems of many animals. Nerve fibres containing myelin sheaths are white. Nonmyelinated nerve fibres form gray nerves, which are common in invertebrates and in the vertebrate sympathetic nervous system.
·demyelinating diseases and incidence **12**:1054a
·impulse transmission function **12**:997c
·neuron structure and function **12**:978b; illus.

·neurophysiological consequences of myelinization **12**:969f; illus. 971
·origin, composition, and function **12**:997c, illus. 1025
·pain and myelinated fibre relationship **13**:866e
·sensory reception and nerve impulse **16**:549d

myelinoclastic disease, disease marked by destruction of the fatty sheath (myelin) around certain nerve fibres.
·symptoms, causation, and incidence **12**:1054b

myelinosis, central pontine, loss of the sheathing substance (myelin) from the nerve fibres of the pons of the brain.
·causation, course, and incidence **12**:1052b

myeloblast, immature cell, found in bone marrow, believed to give rise to white blood cells of the granulocytic series (characterized by granules in the cytoplasm, as neutrophils, eosinophils, and basophils), via an intermediate stage called a myelocyte (*q.v.*). Some authorities equate the myeloblast with another immature cell stage, the hemocytoblast (*q.v.*) and consider it a multipotential cell—precursor to granulocytes, normoblasts, monocytes, and megakaryocytes (*qq.v.*). The myeloblast nucleus is large and round or oval; its membrane is thin, and the contained chromatin (readily stainable nuclear material) is dispersed in fine strands or tiny granules. Several nucleoli are present; there is relatively little cytoplasm. Cells vary in size and are capable of ameboid movement; they are difficult to distinguish in the laboratory from lymphoblasts, or immature lymphocytes, another white blood cell type.
·animal tissue comparisons **18**:450d
·blood cell changes in leukemia **2**:1140h
·granulocytic origins and development **2**:1118g

myelocele, or MYELOMENINGOCELE, protrusion of the spinal cord substance through an opening of the vertebral enclosure.
·birth defects involving spinal disorders **2**:1074g

myelocyte, stage in the development of the granulocytic series of white blood cells (leukocytes) in which granules first appear in the cell cytoplasm. The myeloblast, a precursor, develops into a promyelocyte, identified by a slightly indented nucleus displaced to one side of the cell. The myelocyte stage follows when the promyelocyte cytoplasm becomes filled with numerous granules, which may hide the nucleus. Three types of myelocytes—called eosinophilic, basophilic, and neutrophilic for the dyes the granules take—are distinguished; these in turn give rise to leukocytes called, respectively, eosinophils, basophils, and neutrophils (*qq.v.*).
·leukemic blood changes **2**:1141a

myelocytic leukemia (disease): *see* granulocytic leukemia.

myelography, procedure for examining the spinal cord, in which an injected contrast medium such as iophendylate or oxygen can be manoeuvred under fluoroscopic control into all parts of the spinal canal from the tip of the caudal sac in the lumbosacral region up to (but not into) the cisterna at the base of the brain. It is especially helpful in diagnosing ruptured lumbar and cervical disks and tumours. Existent abnormalities, however, cannot always be recognized in the films taken. After myelography a patient may suffer briefly from irritations caused by the contrast medium.
·radiologic methodology and applications **15**:463f

myeloid tissue: *see* bone marrow.

myeloma protein, in medicine, an abnormal immunoglobulin (protein with antibody activity) produced in persons (sometimes detected in other animals) suffering from multiple myeloma, or multiple myelomatosis. The disease is typified by the proliferation of cells that produce, in most cases, large quantities of one kind of immunoglobulin molecule; the myeloma proteins from different persons are not the same. Except for the fact that few myeloma proteins have been shown to combine specifically with an antigen, they are apparently typical immunoglobulins (*q.v.*) in other respects. They have been of value as a source of immunoglobulins for immunochemical and genetic studies.

myelomatosis: *see* multiple myeloma.

myenteric plexus: *see* nerve plexus, digestive.

Myerhold, Vsevolod Yemilyevich (1874–1942), Russian theatrical producer.
·costume design and expressionistic style **17**:563g

Myers, F(rederic) W(illiam) H(enry) (b. Feb. 6, 1843, Keswick, Cumberland—d. Jan. 17, 1901, Rome), poet, critic, and essayist

F.W.H. Myers, detail of an oil painting by W.C. Wontner, *c.* 1895; in the National Portrait Gallery, London
By courtesy of the National Portrait Gallery, London

whose later life was increasingly devoted to the work of the Psychical Research Society that he helped to found in 1882. Having been a fellow of Trinity College, University of Cambridge, and classical lecturer there from 1865, he gave up teaching in 1872 to become a school inspector. *St. Paul* (1867) is his best known poem, though more mature work is to be found in *The Renewal of Youth* (1882). He was an authority on William Wordsworth's poetry, and his collection of *Essays, Classical and Modern* (2 vol., 1883) also contains a fine critical study of the Latin poet Virgil. Works devoted to psychical studies include *Human Personality and Its Survival of Bodily Death* (1903), *Phantasms of the Living* (1886), and *Science and a Future Life* (1893).

Myers, L(eopold) H(amilton) (b. 1881, Cambridge, Cambridgeshire—d. April 8, 1944, Marlow, Buckinghamshire), philosophical novelist whose most compelling works explore the spiritual turmoil and despair of his characters.

Myers studied at Eton, continued his education in Germany, and then briefly attended Cambridge University. In 1901, when his father died, he turned his attention exclusively to writing, although he also travelled widely, living for some time in Colorado.

Myers worked on his first novel, *The Orissers*, for over 13 years. Published in 1922, it marked him as an author of distinction. His next novel, *The Clio* (1925), reflected the then-fashionable ideas of Aldous Huxley. Myers' major work, an Indian tetralogy set in the late 16th century, the time of Akbar the Great, consists of *The Near and the Far* (1929), *Prince Jali* (1931), *The Root and the Flower* (1935), and *The Pool of Vishnu* (1940). Myers' interests in psychology, philosophy, and Eastern religion are evident in this tetralogy, which was published in 1940 as a single volume entitled *The Near and the Far*. A feeling of embittered despair also emerges from this monumental work. Four years after its publication Myers committed suicide.
·literary theme and influence **10**:1219e

Myerson, Goldie: *see* Meir, Golda.

My Fair Lady (1956), U.S. musical comedy by Alan Jay Lerner and Frederick Loewe.
·first runs and translations **12**:698a

My Heart is Inditing (1685), anthem by Henry Purcell for the coronation of James II.
·Purcell's liturgical music **15**:298c

myiasis, infestation of the body with the larvae (maggots) of certain species of flies. Intestinal myiasis results from ingestion of food contaminated with eggs or larvae and may produce cramps, nausea, vomiting, and diarrhea. Within a short time, however, the organisms are destroyed by gastrointestinal juices and passed in the feces. Superficial myiasis occurs when flies attracted to open or infected wounds or to odoriferous discharges from the eyes, ears, nose, mouth, or vagina lay their eggs on these areas. The larvae hatch and feed on the involved tissues, sometimes causing extensive or even fatal damage. The larvae of some species penetrate the unbroken skin, especially of infants, producing boil-like lesions or creeping eruptions. Treatment of superficial infestation involves removing the larvae by irrigation and by mechanical extraction.

Because larvae feed on dead tissue and foreign matter in open wounds, they were sometimes deliberately introduced to supplement surgical removal of dead or diseased tissue and to prevent infection.
·insect damage factor **9**:610g
·zoonoses, table 9 **5**:878

Myingyan, administrative headquarters of Myingyan District (*kayaing*), Mandalay Division (*taing*), Upper Burma; a port on the Irrawaddy River, it is an important cotton-trading centre, at the head of a branch railway to Thazi and the main Mandalay–Rangoon line. There is a hydroelectric plant nearby and a model village at Pyawbwelay to the northeast. The district (area 3,078 sq mi [7,972 sq km]) is in the heart of Burma's dry zone and mainly comprises low, undulating country. The Irrawaddy forms its northwestern boundary and the Taungtha Hills and Mt. Popa (an extinct volcano, 4,985 ft [1,519 m]) are prominent features. Popa's woody and grassy crater is a habitat of the venomous king cobra (hamadryad) as well as many flowers akin to those of temperate lands. The poorly irrigated land yields cotton for export as well as rice, sesame, beans, and peanuts (groundnuts). The ruins of Pagan (*q.v.*), the famous old capital, stand on a bluff along the Irrawaddy. Part of the Singu-Chauk oil field occupies the extreme southwest corner of the district. Pop. (latest census) town, 36,536; district, 75,548.
·map, Burma **3**:505

Myiodactylidae, family of insects of the order Neuroptera.
·classification and features **12**:1070c

Myiopagis (bird genus): *see* elaenia.

Myitkyina, administrative headquarters of Myitkyina District (*kayaing*) and capital of Kachin State, Upper Burma, on the Irrawaddy River, 25 mi (40 km) below the confluence of its two headstreams, Mali Wang and Nmai Hka, whence it is navigable for more than 1,000 mi to the sea. Its name means Close to the Big River. A trading centre on the Stilwell (Ledo) Road (which links with the Burma Road into China), Myitkyina is also the terminus of the railway north from Rangoon. An old mule track leads to Putao, 150 mi north, and to the Tibetan border. Because of these extensive communication links, Myitkyina is one of the most important river ports in northern Burma. A strategic point in the struggle for Burma during World War II, it fell to the Allies in August 1944. It has an airport and a diesel electric plant. Myitkyina is the site of the great Kachin traditional religious feast of Manao (held each January). Myitkyina College is affiliated to the Arts and Science University, Mandalay. Pidaung game reserve is west of town.

The district (22,317 sq mi [57,800 sq km]) is predominantly hilly and forested and is drained by the headstreams of the Irrawaddy and the Upper Chindwin rivers. Teak and other timbers are extracted. The agricultural villages of Mogaung and Mohnyin are along the railway. Pop. (latest census) town, 12,833; district, 16,381.

·Irrawaddy River ports and navigation **9**:898f
·map, Burma **3**:505

myittaza, epistolary type of Burmese literature originating in the 15th century.
·Burmese literary development **17**:234f

Mykerinos (ancient Egyptian king): *see* Menkaure.

Mylae, ancient city on the north coast of Sicily.
·settlement and importance **8**:330f

Mylae, Battle of (260 BC), in the First Punic War between Rome and Carthage; notable for the Roman naval victory in which the use of boarding bridges and grappling irons enabled Roman soldiers to fight under conditions similar to a land engagement.
·naval history of ancient Rome **12**:886g

Mylagaulidae, family of extinct mammals of the order Rodentia.
·classification and general features **15**:978b

My Lai 4, also called SONG MY, village, South Vietnam.
·war crimes investigation **19**:557e

Mylapore, district, Madras, Tamil Nadu, India.
·Madras' caste linked neighborhoods **11**:285c; map 284

Mylar, trademark name of a versatile plastic used mainly as a film; it consists of a polyester manufactured from xylene, a petroleum-derived aromatic hydrocarbon.

A dielectric (nonconductor of electricity), Mylar plastic film is used in certain capacitors and transducers, as in microphones. In the form of a thin tape, Mylar is a thermoplastic insulation for wire; it has good dielectric strength, resistance to chemicals, impermeability to water, and tensile strength.

Mylar film is used to construct the large balloons used for meteorological explorations. These balloons need no complex ballast systems because Mylar is strong enough to withstand the internal pressure increases that result from solar heating.

Thin Mylar films may be used as a base for applying metallic coatings that are then dyed and cut to produce metallic yarns. Mylar tape is used extensively as the base material for a magnetic coating in tape recording.

My Life in Art (1922–24), autobiography by Stanislavsky.
·Stanislavsky's autobiography **17**:582b

My Life to Live, English title of VIVRE SA VIE (1962), French film by Jean-Luc Godard.
·theme and message **8**:221g

Myliobatidae (fish family): *see* stingray.

Mylius-Erichsen, Ludwig (b. Jan. 15, 1872, Viborg, Den.—d. November 1907, Greenland), journalist and explorer who led two productive expeditions to Greenland. The first (1902–04) yielded much information on the languages and customs of the polar Eskimos of the northwest. The second (1906–08) had the object of charting the western coast of Greenland. Though Mylius-Erichsen and his two companions perished on this venture, his papers were subsequently found by another Danish explorer, Ejnar Mikkelsen.

Mylodon, extinct genus of ground sloth found in South American deposits of Pleistocene age (the Pleistocene Epoch began about 2,500,000 years ago and ended about 10,000 years ago). *Mylodon* was a large animal and attained a length of about 3 metres (10 feet); its skin contained numerous bony parts that probably served as a protective device against attack from predators. *Mylodon* remains found in South American cave deposits in association with human artifacts indicate that men hunted and ate these ground sloths. *Mylodon* and its relatives are distinguished from other ground sloths by the presence of upper canine teeth, triangular cheek teeth, and a reduced first toe on the hind limbs. *Mylodon* probably subsisted on the leaves and foliage of trees and shrubs. Well-developed claws were probably used to dig up tubers or to hold branches while the animal stripped them of leaves. *Mylodon* and its relatives were the dominant group of South American ground sloths. A closely related form, *Paramylodon*, was widely distributed and even spread into many regions of North America. The ground sloths survived until the end of the Pleistocene Epoch.
·evolutionary career. characteristics, and classification **6**:302d

mylonite: *see* cataclastic rocks.

Mymaridae, small family of minute insects called fairyflies of the order Hymenoptera.
·characteristics and classification **9**:132e

Mymensingh, formerly NASIRĀBĀD, administrative headquarters of Mymensingh district, Dacca division, Bangladesh (formerly East Pakistan), just north of an old bed of the Brahmaputra River. Once noted for its glass-bangle manufacture, it now has cotton-textile and sugar mills. It was incorporated as a municipality in 1869 and houses an agricultural university and 11 government colleges affiliated with the University of Dacca.

A fishing boat on a marshy pool in Mymensingh district, Bangladesh
Frederic Ohringer from the Nancy Palmer Agency—EB Inc.

Mymensingh district (area 6,361 sq mi [16,475 sq km]), the largest in Bangladesh, consists chiefly of a level, open area drained by the Jamuna and Old Brahmaputra rivers. The eastern sector is a low-lying area that is submerged during the rainy season and intersected by extensive marshes and *haor*s (depressed pools of stagnant water). The western sector is generally higher and contains part of the Madhupur Jungle. Chief crops are rice, jute (20 percent of Bangladesh's yield), sugarcane, tobacco, oilseeds, and pulses. Trade is conducted by rail and river. The Brahmaputra Project, proposed in the early 1970s, provides for two power stations and the revival of the old riverbed to take off high floods. Pop. (1972 est.) city, 63,400; (1971 est.) district, 5,974,903.
·map, Bangladesh **2**:688

myna, or MYNAH, any of a number of Asian birds of the family Sturnidae (order Passeriformes) of somewhat crowlike appearance. (For pied myna, *see* starling.) Renowned as a "talker" is the hill myna (*Gracula religiosa*) of southern Asia, called grackle in India. It is about 25 centimetres (10 inches) long, glossy black, with white wing patches, yellow wattles, and orangish bill and legs. In the wild

Hill myna (*Gracula religiosa*)
Eric Hosking

it chuckles and shrieks; caged, it learns to imitate human speech far better than its chief rival in mimicry, the gray parrot. Importation of this bird into the U.S. was prohibited in 1972 after one had been found to have Newcastle's disease, a serious fowl disease. The common, or Indian, myna (*Acridotheres tristis*) is about 20 centimetres long, black-and-brown, with white in the wings and tail, orange skin around the eyes, and heavy dark wattles; it has been introduced into Australia, New Zealand, and Hawaii. The crested myna (*A. cristatellus*) is black, with white wing patches and yellow legs and bill; native to China and Indochina, it was introduced into Vancouver Island, B.C., in 1900 but has not spread.
·classification and general features **13**:1062g
·pet ownership **14**:150f

Mynster, Jacob Pier (d. 1854), Danish bishop of the state church.
·Kierkegaard's dual relationship **10**:467c

Myobatrachidae, family of frogs, order Anura, including 18 genera and about 75 species found in Africa, Australia, and New Guinea.

The African myobatrachids (*Heleophryne*) are rare and little-known frogs whose tadpoles develop in swift mountain streams. The ghost frog (*H. rosei*), one of the better known species, is about 6 centimetres (2½ inches) long and is green with reddish markings. Its internal organs show through the thin, white skin of the abdomen.

The Catholic frog (*Notaden bennetti*) is a yellow or greenish Australian myobatrachid about 4 centimetres (1½ inches) long. Named for the dark, crosslike pattern on its back, it frequents dry regions and lives underground, emerging from its burrow after a heavy rain.

The flat-headed frog (*Chiroleptes platycephalus*) is a desert-dwelling Australian myobatrachid. It lives in burrows and is noted for its ability to store enough water in its body to take on a ball-like shape.

The family Myobatrachidae is considered as part of the family Leptodactylidae by some authorities. An African subfamily, Heleophryninae, is sometimes separated as the family Heleophrynidae.
·classification and general features **1**:1008g

Myobia musculinus, species of chiggers of the class Arachnida.
·mite and tick diversity, illus. 1 **1**:19

myoblast, cell that gives rise to muscle tissue.
·human nerve development **12**:996b
·muscle cell origins and development **6**:751h
·muscle development in vertebrates **12**:644g

myocardial infarction, death of a section of heart muscle because of the inability of a coronary artery to supply sufficient oxygen-laden blood to the muscle. The artery may be blocked by formation of a blood clot (a condition called coronary thrombosis) or by an embolism (*q.v.*) or may be narrowed by fatty plaques in its lining (coronary atherosclerosis, the most usual cause). Other possible causes are syphilis, which may block the opening from the aorta into a coronary artery, and polyarteritis nodosa (*q.v.*). Myocardial infarction is what is often meant by the term heart attack.

An affected person experiences chest pain resembling that felt in angina pectoris (*q.v.*) but not precipitated by exertion or relieved by administration of nitroglycerin. The heart may beat rapidly, the blood pressure may be reduced, there may be characteristic sounds at the base of the lungs, and there may be moderate fever. The affected person may experience difficulty in breathing.

In the early 1970s a person with myocardial infarction had the best chance of recovery if he were admitted to a special hospital unit for the care of such patients. There, electronic devices were available for monitoring the heart's action and detecting abnormalities in its rhythm. Other electronic devices were used to correct these abnormalities. Drugs also were used to control abnormalities in heart rhythm and to strengthen the action of the heart muscle. When other measures were ineffective, open-chest surgery was employed to correct the abnormalities.

Persons who had recovered sufficiently so that they no longer needed intensive care remained inactive for a period of convalescence, during which scar tissue formed at the site of the infarction. Then, they gradually returned to an active existence. Some who had suffered minor attacks were able to return to work within four to six weeks.

·arteriosclerosis complications **5**:862d
·causation, symptoms, and treatment **3**:889b
·coronary-care units **3**:889d
·shock onset and symptoms **16**:701c

myocardial revascularization, restoration of blood circulation in the heart tissues after a heart attack.

·atherosclerosis treatment **3**:897c

myocarditis, inflammation of the heart muscle.

·infectious and allergenic causation **3**:892e
·symptoms and treatment **4**:226b

myocardium, muscle that is the middle and principal component of the heart wall. On the inner side of the muscle, and forming the surface of the heart cavities, is endocardium (*q.v.*). Covering the muscle on the outside of the heart is epicardium, the inner of the two layers of synovial (moisture-exuding) membrane in the pericardium (*q.v.*), the sac that encloses the heart. The myocardial fibres are striped, with the appearance of the striped skeletal muscle, which is under voluntary control, but the fibres function like the smooth (involuntary) muscle in the walls of other hollow structures of the body—*e.g.*, in the walls of arteries or of the urinary bladder. The heart muscle fibres are arranged in layers and bundles. Some of the muscle fibres have become specialized and act as elements of the heart's conduction system, which regulates its beat *See* atrioventricular node; atrioventricular bundle; sinoatrial node; Purkinje fibres.

·animal tissue comparisons **18**:448h
·cell structure and function **3**:1061g
·contraction structures and mechanisms **12**:630d
·embryonic origin and development **5**:636g; illus.

human
·anatomy and contractility **3**:878f; illus.
·autonomic regulation of contraction **12**:1025d
·congenital disorders **3**:887d
·hormonal and infectious diseases **3**:892d
·musculature of vertebrate heart **12**:640c; illus. 639
·vertebrate heart embryology **4**:631b

Myocastor coypus (rodent): *see* nutria.

myocyte, a contractile cell or muscle cell. In sponges, myocytes form a sphincter, or contractile ring, around an external pore and thus regulate the flow of water. In certain gregarine protozoans the myocyte is a contractile ectoplasmic layer.

·muscle contraction dynamics **12**:639e
·sponge cell types **14**:852c

Myodocopa, order of ostracods of the arthropod class Crustacea.

·classification and general features **5**:317f

myofilament, elements that, when combined in a bundle, form the myofibril, which is the basic unit of muscle fibres.

·muscle cell contractile organelle **12**:637g

myoglobin, a protein found in both invertebrate and vertebrate animals. In vertebrates it occurs exclusively in red muscle and is the pigment responsible for the red colour. There is a close chemical similarity between myoglobin and hemoglobin (*q.v.*), the red pigment of vertebrate blood. Like hemoglobin, myoglobin combines reversibly with oxygen. It is thought that myoglobin functions by storing molecular oxygen for use by the working muscle. In invertebrates the function is apparently similar to that in vertebrates.

In venous blood, myoglobin combines with oxygen more readily than does hemoglobin; this favours the transfer of oxygen from blood to muscle cells, in which oxygen is consumed during chemical reactions that provide energy for the exercising muscle. The combination of oxygen with myoglobin occurs in such a way that the ratio of the concentration of oxygenated myoglobin, or oxymyoglobin, to unoxygenated myoglobin is equal to a constant times the oxygen pressure. This simple relationship follows from the fact that there is one heme group (*i.e.*, iron-containing chemical group with which oxygen combines) in each molecule of myoglobin, and all the heme groups are alike but act independently. Hemoglobin, on the other hand, has four heme groups per molecule; and the heme groups within a molecule interact and differ in their affinity for oxygen. As a result, the combination of hemoglobin with oxygen is more complex than the combination of myoglobin with oxygen.

Myoglobin has been obtained in pure crystalline form from many sources. It has a molecular weight (based on the weight of hydrogen as 1) of 16,000, about one-fourth that of hemoglobin. Though the heme portion of all myoglobins is the same, the protein portions vary considerably from species to species.

Myoglobin has been of great importance in the elucidation of protein structure. The complete amino acid sequence of sperm whale myoglobin is known. In 1962 the Nobel Prize for Chemistry was awarded jointly to the English biochemist John Cowdery Kendrew and to Max Ferdinand Perutz, an Austrian-born molecular biologist, for their work on the structure of myoglobin and hemoglobin, respectively. Kendrew's work, utilizing the technique of X-ray diffraction, permitted construction of a three-dimensional model of crystalline sperm whale myoglobin.

·bird muscles and pigment variation **2**:1058a
·diving animal oxygen storage **15**:762h
·internal structure resolution **15**:88d
·meat colour change in oxidation **11**:747a
·muscle cell oxygen supply **12**:640c
·muscle contraction metabolism **12**:628f
·oxygen transport within muscles **15**:759e
·properties and occurrence in animals **4**:918g
·transition element biological functions **18**:609a
·variation in muscle types **12**:622e

myoglobinuria, excretion of myoglobin, a protein found in muscle tissue, in the urine. It is a symptom of such diseases as advanced or protracted ischemia of the muscle.

·muscle disease causes and symptoms **12**:635d
·noninfectious diseases of animals, table 3 **5**:872

Myōhō-renge-kyō (Buddhist text): *see* Saddharmapuṇḍarika-sūtra.

myo-inositol, also called INOSITOL, formerly known as MESO-INOSITOL, is a carbohydrate compound. Related to the vitamins in activity, it is an essential factor for the growth of certain yeasts and other fungi. *Myo*-inositol, which occurs in most plant and animal cells, is present in the human body in large amounts, principally as a constituent of one of a complex class of lipids, or fats, called phospholipids. Its chemical structure closely resembles that of the sugar glucose.

Myo-inositol occurs in grains in the form of phytin, an insoluble salt of phytic acid. It also forms this insoluble salt in the intestines of mammals.

Myo-inositol, which has not yet been established as an essential nutrient for man, is probably synthesized in the body.

·nutrient function for some organisms **13**:405g
·storage in body **19**:492a

myometrium, muscular tissue layer in the wall of the uterus.

·human anatomic interrelationships **15**:694h

myoneural junction (biology): *see* neuromuscular junction.

Myō-ō, in the Buddhist mythology of Japan, fierce protective deities, corresponding to the Sanskrit Vidyārāja ("king of knowledge"), worshipped mainly by the Shingon sect. They take on a ferocious appearance in order to frighten away evil spirits and to destroy ignorance and ugly passions. They are depicted with angry expressions, a third eye in the middle of their foreheads, and surrounded by flames.

The five great Myō-ō, popularly called Godaison, are the agents of the five "self-born" Buddhas. Of these Fudo Myō-ō (*q.v.*), the fierce form of the Buddha Vairocana, is the most important and occupies the central position. Go Sansei, the fierce form of Akṣobhya, reigns in the east; Dai Itoku, a form of Amitābha, in the west; Gundari-yasha, a form of Ratnasambhava, in the south; and Kongō-yasha, a form of Amoghasiddhi, in the north. Other prominent Myō-ō are the god of love, Aizen Myō-ō (*q.v.*), and Kujaku Myō-ō, who sits on a peacock.

myopathies, in domestic animals, apparently related disorders marked by muscular degeneration and associated with nutritional, metabolic, or congenital illness. Heritable myopathies are often lumped as "muscular dystrophy" because of a resemblance to the dystrophies of man (*see* muscular dystrophy). Azoturia, or blackwater, a myopathy of horses, causes hindleg paralysis; the disease may disappear in hours with rest or may progress to death within four days. The urine, voided with difficulty, may be red, brown, or blackish with pigment from destroyed muscle cells. Cording up, or myositis of horses, may be a mild form of azoturia. White muscle diseases of calves, lambs, and foals are severe and often fatal myopathies. The above disorders respond variably to vitamin E and selenium supplements, suggesting a deficiency mechanism.

A related disorder, steatitis, or yellow fat disease, occurs in cats. It is marked by fever, inflammation of fatty tissue, and pain on touch. Food rich in fat from marine animals appears to be a contributing factor. Treatment includes vitamin E supplement and change of diet. German shepherd dogs are susceptible to a myositis of unknown cause, in which the jaw muscles and eventually the esophagus are involved, making eating and swallowing difficult. There is no cure; discomfort can be minimized by drugs. Other myopathies of mysterious origin occur in swine, cattle, horses, and rabbits; many are related to metabolic disruptions.

Myophoria, extinct genus of clams found as fossils in Triassic rocks; it is readily identified by its distinctive shell form and ornamenta-

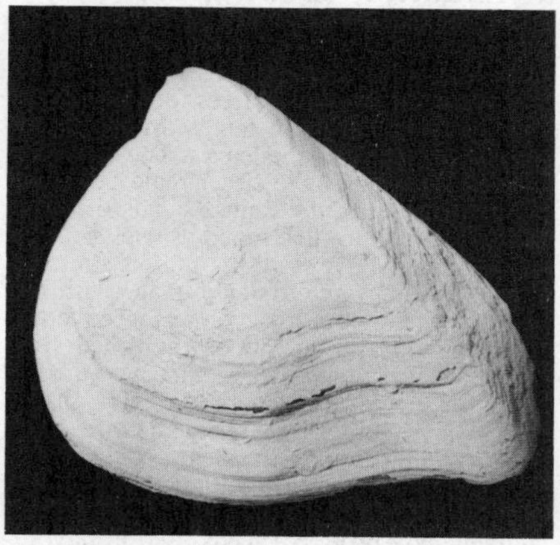

Myophoria, of Triassic age

tion, and thus it is a useful guide or index fossil for the Triassic Period, (between 225,-000,000 and 190,000,000 years ago). The shell in *Myophoria* is angular, with prominent ribs that radiate from its apex. Fine growth lines encircle the shell at right angles to the ribs.

myopia, or NEARSIGHTEDNESS, visual defect in which the resting eye focusses the image of a distant object at a point in front of the retina, the light-sensitive layer of tissue that lines the back and sides of the eye. Myopic eyes, which are longer than normal from front to rear, are somewhat more susceptible to retinal detachment (*q.v.*) than are normal or farsighted eyes. Myopia is corrected by glasses that are concave on both surfaces.
·focal power comparisons 7:100d
·refractive errors 7:124b
·visual disorders due to growth changes 5:653f

Myoporaceae, family of flowering plants of the order Scrophulariales.
·general features and classification 16:417f

Myoprocta (rodent): *see* agouti.

Myopus (rodent): *see* lemming.

myōshu, Japanese feudal landlord of the Tokugawa period.
· Muromachi village structure 10:68a

myosin, the most abundant protein in skeletal muscle. A long thin protein with a complex molecular structure, myosin has enzymatic (catalytic) activity. It acts with actin in the contraction and relaxation of muscle fibres.
·animal tissue comparisons 18:449a
·flow birefringence property 15:86f
·invertebrate smooth muscle 12:632h
·meat muscle tissue 11:747a
·muscle cell composition 3:1061g
·muscle contraction and ATP 14:437e
·muscle contraction mechanisms 12:628h
·physical properties 12:623d; illus. 624a
·structure, composition, and function 15:91e;
   table 90

myositis, inflammation, and frequently infection, of muscle tissue; it may be caused by any of a number of bacteria, viruses, and parasites; in many cases it is of unknown origin. Most inflammatory muscle diseases are destructive to the tissue involved and the surrounding areas. They may occur at any age; children seem to have a higher incidence than adults.
Bacteria may cause damage by direct infection of the muscles or by producing substances—toxins—that poison the tissue. The commonest bacterial infections are strep-

tococcal or staphylococcal. The muscle tissue is generally highly resistant to bacterial invasion, but when physical injuries occur there is a weakening of defense mechanisms that leads to infection. The onset of disease may be manifested by headaches, fever, chills, and sweating. There is local pain and swelling in the tissue, commonly followed by pustulant abscesses. Initially the muscle remains intact; as the infection progresses there is infiltration by white blood cells, lymph cells, and fibrous scar tissue (fibrosis). The tissue affected may be destroyed, and abscesses may become fibrous cysts that may require surgical removal.
Gas gangrene is caused by bacteria, particularly *Clostridium welchii* and *C. oedematiens.* Occurring only in wounded tissue that is not well oxygenated, it leads to rapid decomposition and bubble formation in the tissue. Frequently it develops in deep puncture wounds, lacerations, or fractures. The wound becomes painful, red, and swollen initially, but, as the tissue begins to disintegrate, the blood circulation is hampered and the area becomes greenish-black. Once the organism starts to grow it spreads to the neighbouring healthy tissue; the most common treatment in cases of advanced gas gangrene is surgical removal of the involved tissue as well as the surrounding tissue; antibiotic medications in the early stages of this disease may prevent tissue destruction.
Chronic diseases such as tuberculosis or syphilis are known to involve the muscles. In tuberculosis there may be abscesses and calcification of the muscle. The tissue can degenerate into fatty and fibrous elements. The disease may be totally incapacitating to the sufferer in the advanced stages. Syphilis does not generally affect the muscles until the terminal stages of the disease. It may cause soft tumours in the eyes, chest, extremities, throat, and heart; and muscles may be converted into scar tissue.
Parasites such as tapeworms or protozoa may enter the body in contaminated food, invade the intestines, and enter the bloodstream to lodge in the muscle tissue. The pork tapeworm larva, *Cysticercus,* is one parasite that causes nodules in the muscle tissue and brain. The organism grows, lays its eggs, and then dies. The nodes become calcified and may be seen on X-rays. The parasite *Sarcocystis* encapsulates in the muscle also. These organisms either may cause no symptoms or may produce weakness, aching, and impaired reflexes. The cysts are commonly found in the heart, esophagus, abdomen, diaphragm, and larynx. The protozoan *Toxoplasma* may cause severe brain inflammation as well as muscle-cell deterioration. Among the initial manifestations are fever, pain, delirium, and skin eruptions.
In many instances of severe muscle inflammation the agent is unknown. Sometimes the illnesses are thought to be related to allergic reactions, vitamin deficiencies, or endocrine disorders. The skin, nerves, and muscles may all be affected. The myositis causes swelling, pain, degeneration, and fibrosis (formation of scar tissue).
After prolonged muscle inflammation, calcium deposits may be formed that solidify the muscle and immobilize the affected person (a condition called myositis ossificans). Badly degenerated muscle fibres do not repair themselves in most cases.
·muscle inflammation causes 12:635h

myositis ossificans, also known as STIFFMAN SYNDROME, rare disorder in which muscle tissue is replaced by bone. In the commoner local type (myositis ossificans circumscripta) only one area is affected; ossification is usually observed to follow injury to the part. In the progressive type (myositis ossificans progressiva), group after group of muscles become ossified until the individual is completely rigid. Breathing and swallowing become difficult, and death usually follows respiratory infec-

tion. The cause of the disease is unknown; steroid treatment of muscle injury and the use of drugs to prevent calcification may slow its progress.
·muscle injury effects 12:636b
·symptoms and course 5:19d

Myosotis (plant genus): *see* forget-me-not.

Myospalax: *see* mole rat.

Myosurus (plant): *see* mousetail.

Myotis: *see* brown bat.

myotome, in vertebrate embryos, any of the segmentally arranged blocks of muscle tissue that give rise to the voluntary muscles of the adult body. The segmental arrangement is more or less maintained in fishes, in which the repeating muscle masses of adults are called myomeres.
·embryonic muscle developments 5:635b;
   illus. 632
·vertebrate muscle developments 12:644h

myotonia, prolonged contraction of a muscle with the inability to relax it. The condition is unlike that in myasthenia gravis (*q.v.*), in which muscles become progressively weaker after use and require a rest to regain function. In myotonia, the muscles are unable to function properly after resting but, once warmed up, seem to function better. All of the bodily muscles, or only a few, may be affected. The cause of the disorder is unknown, but it seems to be a difficulty inherent in the muscles themselves and not in the nervous system.
One rather rare form of the disorder, thought to be inherited in most instances, is known as myotonia congenita. The disease is first noticed in early childhood.
The eyelids and eyes can be affected; the eyes appear to be stuck in one position and the lids remain closed after forceful shutting. There may be difficulty in swallowing or in talking because the throat muscles are involved. A quick movement such as running to catch a bus causes muscle stiffening. The muscles do not show weakness when used, and the fibres are usually more developed than in the normal person. It is thought that this hypertrophy is caused by involuntary and repeated isometric exercises during attempts to make the muscle react normally, or that there might be some replacement of the tissue with fat and fibrous scar tissue.
Some cases of muscular dystrophy (*q.v.*), in which there is usually a gradual weakening of the muscles, also show stages of myotonia. This form is also inherited, but it does not become apparent until the third or fourth decade; the muscles do not overdevelop but gradually degenerate. The stiffening effect of the myotonia may precede the degeneration by two to three years. Most instances of myotonia can be distinguished from muscular dystrophy because the myotonia fails to show the dystrophy symptoms of weakness, cataracts, baldness, and gonadal atrophy.
In the early 1970s a cure for the condition was not available. It could be alleviated, however, by administration of analgesics, anesthetics, and anticonvulsant drugs.
·biomedical models, table 1 5:866
·muscular dystrophy symptoms and
   course 12:635e
·myotonia congenita symptoms, causation, and
   treatment 12:1056h

myotonic muscular dystrophy, muscular dystrophy (*q.v.*) in which there is myotonia (*q.v.*), the prolonged contraction of a muscle with inability to relax it.
·symptoms, course, and treatment 12:1057a

My Past and Thoughts: The Memoirs of Aleksandr Herzen (1924–26), English translation by Constance Garnett of BYLOYE I DUMY, the autobiography of Aleksandr Herzen.
·style and themes 8:828f

Myra, modern DEMRE, one of the most important towns of ancient Lycia, located at the mouth of the Andriacus River in Antalya *il* (province), Turkey. Its early history is unknown. St. Paul is known to have visited the city, and in the 4th century St. Nicholas was its bishop. The Eastern Roman emperor Theodosius II made Myra the capital of Byzantine Lycia until the city fell to the caliph Hārūn ar-Rashīd in AD 808. The western scarp of its acropolis, dating from the 5th to the 3rd century BC, was sculptured into a large number of rock-cut sepulchres, imitating wooden houses and shrines, with pillared facades and reliefs. At the foot of the acropolis are the remains of a magnificent theatre, one of the largest and finest in Anatolia.
36°16′ N, 29°58′ E
·map, Turkey **18**:784

Myra's Journal of Dress and Fashion, British magazine, published between 1875 and 1912.
·magazine publishing history **15**:250c

myrcene, sweet-smelling liquid terpene occurring in bay oil and hop oil.
·isoprenoid classification and formulae **9**:1045b

Myrdal, (Karl) Gunnar (1898–), Swedish economist, public official, author of an influential study of U.S. Negroes, *An American Dilemma* (1944).
·Gandhi's sound economic insights **7**:878g

Mýrdalsjökull, glacier, southern Iceland; it is 30 mi (48 km) long, 20 mi wide, and covers an area of 310 sq mi (802 sq km) inclusive of its western extension, Eyjafjallajökull. Only a few miles inland from the shores of the Atlantic Ocean, it reaches its highest elevation, 5,466 ft (1,666 m) above sea level, in Eyjafjallajökou. The southeastern part of the glacier surrounds Katla, an active volcano the 1918 eruption of which caused great floods and a considerable modification of the coastline.

Myres, Sir John Linton (1869–1954), British historian of classical antiquity, founded the anthropological journal *Man* in 1901 and helped to extend the teaching of anthropology at Oxford University, where he was professor of ancient history.

myriapod 12:768, convenient general name for a group (formerly a class) of about 11,000 species of many-legged animals of the phylum Arthropoda, including centipedes, millipedes, pauropods, and symphylids.

The text article is concerned with general features, natural history, form and function, and evolution and paleontology of myriapods, and it includes an annotated classification of the group.

REFERENCES in other text articles:
·arthropod anatomy, movement, and habitats **2**:65c; illus. 66
·characteristics and soil importance **16**:1014g; illus. 1015
·circulatory system anatomy **4**:621f
·fossil remains of problematic type **7**:565f; illus. 564
·insect ancestry candidate **9**:618d
·insect and other hexapod evolution **1**:1025e
·limb movement and synchronization **11**:20a
·poisonous animal, table 8 **14**:617a
·repellant used by millipede family **12**:215a
·reproductive behaviour patterns **15**:685a
·social parental behaviour patterns **16**:938c

RELATED ENTRIES in the *Ready Reference and Index:*
centipede; millipede; pauropod; symphylid

Myricales, an order of dicotyledonous flowering plants, found throughout the world, containing one family (Myricaceae), three genera, and about 40 species of trees and shrubs with aromatic leaves that often bear yellow glandular dots on the surface, from which the characteristic odour of these plants emanates, and with single-seeded fruits often covered with waxy granules, bumps, or layers.

Sweet fern (*Comptonia peregrina*)
Kitty Kohout from Root Resources—EB Inc.

The flowers are small, greenish, inconspicuous, and usually are separately male and female on the same or different plants in clusters called catkins. Male flowers have 2 to 16 (but usually 4) stamens, or pollen-producing structures, attached just above two small scalelike structures (bracteoles). The female flowers consist of a one-chambered ovary composed of two carpels (structural segments) that are extended on top into a two-branched style (pollen-receptive organ), the whole associated with two or four bracteoles.

Useful plants include the sweet gale or bog myrtle (*Gale belgica*, formerly *Myrica gale*), a shrub of bogs and wet areas with resinous leaves useful in medicines; and the wax myrtle, or bayberry, (*M. cerifera*), a tall shrub or small tree to about 11 metres (35 feet), plus others of the same genus, from which myrtle wax, used in candles, is obtained by boiling the fruits. The sweet fern (*Comptonia peregrina*) is a small aromatic shrub of eastern North America, the leaves of which have been used in folk medicines and as a seasoning.

The largest genus of the order is *Myrica*, with 35 species. Relationships are obscure but the order is thought to be near the orders Casuarinales (beefwood), Betulales (birches), and Juglandales (walnuts) (*q.q.v.*).
·angiosperm features and classification **1**:883a

Myriocephalon, Battle of (September 1176), victory of the Seljuq Turks under Qïlïch Arslan II (reigned 1155–92) over the Byzantine army of Manuel I Comnenus (reigned 1143–80) in a mountain pass near the ruined fortress of Myriocephalon (southeast of Ankara, Tur.) in Phrygia; it ended Byzantium's last hope of expelling the Turks from Anatolia.

Manuel determined to reassert his suzerainty over former Byzantine territory by capturing Iconium (now Konya, Tur.), a city of the Seljuq Sultanate of Rūm. Ignoring Qïlïch Arslan's attempts to arrange a peace treaty, Manuel led his army across the plains of Anatolia. Slowed by heavy wagons carrying supplies and siege machinery, the Byzantines failed to prevent the Turks from devastating the countryside through which they marched. Making their way up into the Phrygian mountains, they arrived at the pass of Tzibritze, which permitted access to the fort of Myriocephalon. The Turkish army massed on the hills flanking the pass.

Manuel's experienced generals warned of impending disaster, but he chose instead to follow the advice of the battle-hungry younger princes, sending the vanguard of the army through the pass. The Turks feigned flight, circling around into the hills, then charged down the narrow pass onto the main body of the army. Manuel panicked and fled back through the pass, throwing his army into disarray, and the Turkish victory was complete.

Myristicaceae, the nutmeg family, of the magnolia order (Magnoliales), best known for the fragrant, spicy seeds of nutmeg (*Myristica fragrans*). The family contains 15 other genera and about 380 species of trees found throughout moist tropical lowlands. Most species have fragrant wood and leaves. The evergreen trees, often large, have either male or female petal-less flowers, the united sepals of which form a three- to five-lobed funnel or cup. Male flowers have 2 to 20 united stamens; female flowers have a single ovary with one ovule (potential seed). A fleshy covering, known as an aril, surrounds the fluted seed, which has much endosperm (starchy nutritive tissue for the developing embryo). The simple leaves have smooth margins and are alternately arranged along the stem.

In addition to nutmeg, a 30-metre (100-foot) Central American tree known as *Virola guatemalense* produces seeds used in flavouring and in the manufacture of candles; the whorled young branches are utilized as egg-beaters. Many of the approximately 38 species of the genus *Virola* provide lumber for local use.

Other genera of the family Myristicaceae are sources of oils, waxes, soaps, and timber. *See also* mace, nutmeg.
·economic use and classification **11**:342f

Myrmecobius fasciatus (marsupial family): *see* numbat.

myrmecochory, method of plant seed dispersal using ants as the agents of dispersal.
·dispersal agents and mechanisms **16**:485a; illus.

Myrmecocystus, a genus of honey ant of the order Hymenoptera.
·honeydew storage method **9**:126f

Myrmecophagidae: *see* anteater.

myrmecophilism, in biology, the habitual sharing by an organism of the nest of a species of ant.
·plant and ant symbiosis **7**:129d

myrmekite, irregular, wormy penetration by quartz in plagioclase feldspar; these wartlike, wormlike, or fingerlike bodies may develop during the late stages of crystallization of igneous rocks if the two minerals (quartz and feldspar) grow simultaneously in the presence of a volatile phase. Myrmekite also occurs after the rock crystallizes by replacement of the plagioclase during metasomatism or hydrothermal alteration. In rare cases the plagioclase may be almost completely obliterated by the quartz intergrowths. Although the origin is not always clear, it is evidently a late development in the rock. Acidic rocks, such as granite, most commonly display this feature, especially if the plagioclase feldspar is adjacent to potash feldspar; rocks displaying this feature are said to have a myrmekitic texture.

Myrmeleontidae (insect family): *see* antlion.

Myrmica, a genus of ant of the family Formicidae and of the order Hymenoptera.
·ant guest deceptive secretions **9**:129d

Myrmidons, in Greek legend, the inhabitants of Phthiotis in Thessaly. According to some authorities, they later crossed over from Thessaly to Aegina. Their name is derived from one of two sources: (1) a supposed ancestor, son of Zeus (the king of the gods) and Eurymedusa, the daughter of King Myrmidon of Thessaly, who was seduced by Zeus in the form of an ant (Greek *myrmēx*), or (2) the re-peopling of Aegina (after all its inhabitants had died of a plague) with ants changed into men by Zeus at the prayer of Aeacus, king of the island. As the fierce and devoted followers of the hero Achilles, their name came to be applied in modern times to subordinates who carry out orders implacably.

Myrmonyssus, genus of mites of the order Acarina and of the class Arachnida.
·lepidopteran host relationship **10**:823c

Myrocongridae, family of eels of the order Anguilliformes.
·characteristics and classification **1**:900b

Myron (fl. *c.* 480–440 BC), Greek sculptor, an older contemporary of the sculptors Phidias and Polyclitus, considered by the ancients as one of the most versatile and innovative of all Attic sculptors.

"Discobolus," Roman marble copy of Greek bronze by Myron, *c.* 450 BC; in the Museo Nazionale delle Terme, Rome
Alinari

Born in Eleutherae, he lived most of his life in Athens and is repeatedly called Athenian by the 1st-century-AD traveller Pausanias. The 1st-century writer Pliny cites Myron as the first to achieve lifelike representation in art. Working almost exclusively in bronze, he is most famous for his many studies of athletes in action. Of his many works, only two representations positively survive: the group of Athena and Marsyas, originally standing on the acropolis of Athens, and the "Discobolus" ("Discus Thrower"), both in marble copies made in Roman times.

The group of Athena and Marsyas, described by Pliny, has been recognized on representations of Roman coins from the reign of Hadrian (117–138 AD); on a red-figure vase (now in Berlin); on a marble vase (in Athens); and on several Roman marble copies. The best of the Marsyas is in the Lateran collection, Rome; of the Athena, in a collection in Frankfurt. The bronze group originally stood on the acropolis of Athens. Representations of the "Discobolus" have been found on engraved gems; the finest copy of it, in marble, is in the Museo Nazionale Romano.

Both the "Discobolus" and the Athena and Marsyas are dated *c.* 450 BC. In both works Myron has captured that crucial moment at which a part of the action has just been completed and the next sequence is about to begin.

Many other works attributed to Myron include: "Anadumenus," a youth winding a fillet round his head; a standing Heracles (in Boston and in Oxford); and a head of Perseus with replicas (Palazzo del Conservatori, Rome; Museo Nazionale Romano; and British Museum). The "Hecate" (on Aegina) has been thought to be Myron's only cult statue and his only work in wood.

There are other works by Myron, known to us through extant epigrams from antiquity, which have not, as yet, been rediscovered. The most famous of these are "Ladas," the Argive runner and Olympic victor, and the bronze cow in the marketplace of Athens. A possible copy of the cow may be reproduced in a bronze statuette in the Cabinet des Médailles in Paris.
·sculpture style of Classical period **19**:292d
·style and influence **8**:351g

Myrothamnaceae, family of flowering plants of the order Hamamelidales.
·habitat, drought resistance, and classification **8**:578g *passim* to 580b

myrrh (from Arabic *murr*, "bitter"), bitter-tasting, agreeably aromatic, yellow to reddish-brown oleoresinous gum obtained from various small, thorny, flowering trees of the genus *Commiphora*, or the incense-tree family (Burseraceae), as *C. myrrha* or *C. abyssinica*.

Myrrh was highly esteemed by the ancients; in the Near East and Mediterranean regions, it was an ingredient of costly incenses, perfumes, and cosmetics and was used in medicines for local applications and in embalming. In medieval Europe myrrh was also regarded as rare and precious; but in modern commerce it is of trifling value. Modern uses are chiefly as an ingredient in dentifrices, perfumes, and stimulating tonics and as a protective agent in pharmaceuticals. Myrrh has slight antiseptic, astringent, and carminative properties and has been employed medically as a carminative and in tinctures to relieve sore gums and mouth. An essential oil distilled from myrrh is a constituent of certain heavy perfumes.

Myrrh is exuded as a fluid from resin ducts in the tree bark when the bark splits naturally or is cut in tapping. Upon exposure to air, myrrh hardens slowly into globules and irregular lumps called tears.

Myrrh contains 25 to 45 percent resin, 3 to 8 percent essential oil, and 40 to 60 percent gum.
·spice centre in Arabia **17**:502c

Myrrhis odorata (plant): *see* cicely.

Myrrour for Magistrates, A, 16th-century work including English historical moralistic legends from the time of Richard II to Edward IV.
·literature of the Renaissance **10**:1138g

Myrsinaceae, family of flowering plants of the order Primulales.
·classification and general features **14**:1049c

Myrtaceae, family of shrubs and trees in the order Myrtales, containing about 100 genera and 3,000 species that are widely distributed in the tropics. They have rather leathery evergreen leaves with oil glands. Some members of economic importance are the *Eucalyptus*, guava, rose apple, Surinam cherry, and feijoa. Allspice, clove, and oil of bay rum are spices derived from this family. Other members include Brisbane box, *Callistemon*, *Eugenia*, *Leptospermum*, myrtle, and jaboticaba (*qq.v.*).
·angiosperm diversity, illus. 1 **1**:877
·range, life cycle, uses, and classification **12**:772h

Myrtales 12:772, an order of flowering, primarily woody plants comprising nearly 10,000 species that include *Eucalyptus*, evening primrose, *Fuchsia*, loosestrife, mangrove, monkey pot, myrtle, and water chestnut.

The text article covers general features of the order, natural history, form and function, and evolution, and contains an annotated classification.

REFERENCE in other text article:
·angiosperm features and classification **1**:883f

RELATED ENTRIES in the *Ready Reference and Index: for*
common plants: see anchovy pear; Brisbane box; cannonball tree; enchanter's nightshade; evening primrose; jaboticaba; loosestrife; mangrove; monkey pot; myrtle; water chestnut
family: Onagraceae
plant genera: Callistemon; Cuphea; Epilobium; Eucalyptus; Eugenia; Fuchsia; Leptospermum; Terminalia

Myrtilus (Greek mythology): *see* Pelops.

myrtle, common name for more than 100 species of evergreen shrubs in the genus *Myrtus* (family Myrtaceae, order Myrtales). Most occur in Southern America; some are found in Australia and New Zealand. True myrtles have a central midrib and a major vein just inside and parallel to the leaf margin. Other plants known as myrtles are wax myrtle, bog myrtle or sweet gale, crape myrtle, sand myrtle, gum myrtle, downy myrtle, and Oregon myrtle or California laurel. The creeping, or running, myrtle is the periwinkle (*see* Apocynaceae.

The aromatic common myrtle (*M. communis*) is native to the Mediterranean region and western Asia and is cultivated in Southern England and the warmer regions of North America. It may grow more than 5 metres (about 16.5 feet) high. The opposite leaves are thick and lustrous, with many small, translucent, oil-bearing glands. The solitary white flowers, about 1.8 centimetres (about 0.7 inch) long, are borne on short stalks. The fruit is a purplish-black, many-seeded berry. Myrtol, a volatile oil found in most parts of the plant, was formerly used as an antiseptic and tonic.

Variegated, yellow-fruited, and white-fruited varieties of the common myrtle are cultivated for ornament. The Chilean guava (*M. ugni*), which has hemispherical white flowers and edible red berries, and *M. bullata*, a New Zealand shrub, are also grown for this purpose.
·distribution and abundance **12**:773e

Myrtle Beach, city, Horry County, South Carolina, U.S., on the Atlantic Coast, between the ocean and the Intracoastal Waterway. It is a year-round resort for golfing, fishing, and swimming. Named for the native myrtle bushes that abound there, it is the centre of the 50-mi (80-km) beach area, Grand Strand, which extends from the North Carolina border to Pawleys Island. To the south are Myrtle Beach State Park and Brookgreen Gardens, an outdoor museum of U.S. sculpture. Myrtle Beach Air Force Base, nearby, is an economic asset. Inc. town, 1938; city, 1961. Pop. (1980) 18,758.
33°42′ N, 78°52′ W

myrtlewood (tree): *see* California laurel.

Mysia, ancient district in northwest Anatolia adjoining the Sea of Marmara on the north

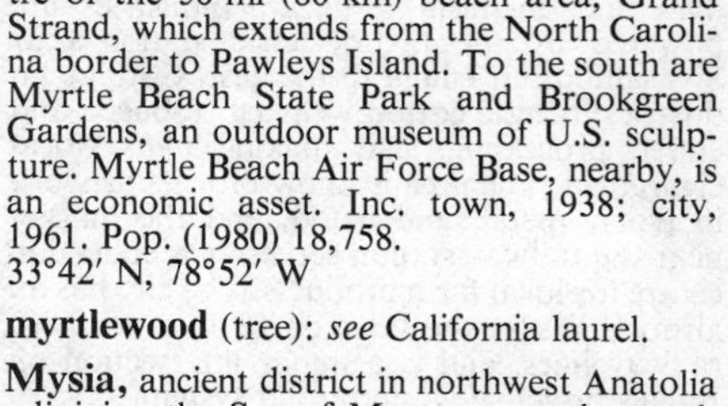

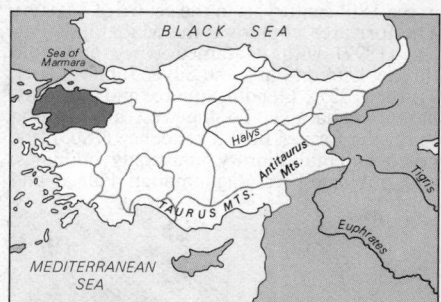

Mysia under the Roman Empire
From W. Shepherd, *Historical Atlas*, Harper & Row, Publishers (Barnes & Noble Books), New York; revision copyright © 1964 by Barnes & Noble, Inc.

and the Aegean on the west. A vague inland perimeter was bounded by Lydia on the south and by Phrygia and Bithynia on the east. Mysia designated a geographical rather than a political territory and encompassed Aeolis, Troas, and the region surrounding Pergamum. The Mysians, after whom the region was named, were mentioned by Homer as primitive allies of the Trojans, but historically there is no record of their action as an independent nation. Mysia passed under the successive rule of Lydia, Persia, and Pergamum, after which it was incorporated into the Roman province of Asia (129 BC).
·Greek record of non-Greek Anatolians **1**:823b

Mysidacea: *see* opossum shrimp.

Mysore 12:776, constituent state of the Republic of India, on the west coast. It has an area of 74,037 sq mi (191,757 sq km) and is bounded by the territory of Goa (north) and by the states of Mahārāshtra (north), Andhra Pradesh (east), Tamil Nadu (southeast), and Kerala (south), and by the Arabian Sea (west). The state was renamed Karnataka in 1973. The administrative capital is Bangalore. Pop. (1971 prelim.) 29,263,334.

The text article covers Mysore's history, physical geography, population, administration, social conditions, economy, transport system, and cultural life.

REFERENCES in other text articles:
·area and population table **9**:288
·Neolithic stone-ax cultures **9**:338a

Mysore, city, administrative headquarters of Mysore district and division, in the south central part of Karnataka (formerly Mysore) state; it lies northwest of Chamundi Hill and midway between the Cauvery and Kabbani rivers on the undulating Deccan Plateau at an altitude of 2,525 ft (770 m). A royal city of wide streets and numerous parks (including zoological gardens), it is surrounded by rain-filled shallow depressions (tanks).

Mentioned in the epic *Mahābhārata* as Mahishmati (Mahiṣmatī), the site was known as Purigere in the Mauryan era (3rd century BC) and later became Mahishapura. It was the administrative capital of Mysore (1799–1831) and remains the second largest city (after Bangalore) of Karnataka.

An important manufacturing and trading centre, Mysore has textile (cotton and silk), rice, and oil mills, sandalwood oil and chemical factories, and tanneries. The suburb of Belagula, to the northwest, produces chrome dyes and chemical fertilizer. Industries are powered by the hydroelectric station near Sivasamudram Island to the east. Cottage industries include cotton weaving, tobacco and coffee processing, and making *bidis* (local cigarettes). The area is known for its artwork in ivory, metal, and wood, and the market near the railway station serves as a collection centre for local farm products. The city has an airport, lies at the junction of two northern railway lines, and is a major intersection on India's principal western road system.

An ancient fort, rebuilt along European lines in the 18th century, is in the centre of Mysore. The fort area comprises the Maharaja's Palace (1897) with its famed ivory and gold throne, Curzon Park, the Silver Jubilee Clock Tower (1927), Gandhi Square, and two statues of maharajas. To the west are Gordon Park, the former British residency (1805), the noted Oriental Library, university buildings, and public offices. Jaganmohan Palace and Lalitha Mahal are other notable buildings. The University of Mysore was founded in 1916; other educational facilities include Maharaja's College, Maharani's College for Women, and affiliated colleges of medicine, law, engineering, and teacher training. There are also several institutions for the advancement of Kanarese (Kannada) culture.

The raja's palace at Chamundi Hill, Mysore, Karnataka state, India
Picturepoint—Publix

Pilgrims frequent Chamundi Hill (about 3,490 ft) with its monolith of Nandi, the sacred bull of Śiva; the summit affords an excellent view of the Nīlgiri Hills to the south. Krishnarāja Sāgara, a 50-sq-mi (130-sq-km) reservoir with a dam, lies 12 mi (19 km) northwest at the Cauvery River. Spreading below the dam are the terraced Brindavan Gardens with their cascades and fountains, floodlit at night.

Somnāthpur, to the east, has a famous temple built (1268) under the Hoysaḷa dynasty. Bandipur Sanctuary, part of the 310-sq-mi Venugopal Wild Life Park (1941), is usually approached from Mysore; it is noted for herds of gaur (wild ox) and spotted deer, has a network of roads for observation, and adjoins Mudumalai Sanctuary in Tamil Nadu state.

Mysore district (area 4,613 sq mi [11,947 sq km]) is drained by the Cauvery and its tributaries. In Nanjangūd and Chāmrājnagar *talukas* (administrative divisions), cotton is grown on large tracts of black soil. The southwest of the district abounds in wild animals, while the open country produces both wet and dry crops. Rice, millet, and oilseed are exported.

Mysore division encompasses seven districts (Mysore, Mandya, Hassan, Chikmagalūr, Shimoga, South Kanara, and Coorg) in the southwestern portion of the state. Pop. (1971) city, 355,685; district, 2,077,238.
·map, India **9**:279
·history and development **12**:777a

Mysore Wars (1767–69; 1780–84; 1790–92; 1799), four wars in India between the British and the rulers of Mysore. In about 1761 a Muslim adventurer, Hyder Ali, already commander in chief, made himself ruler of the Hindu state of Mysore and set about expanding his dominions.

In 1766 the East India Company joined the Niẓām of Hyderābād against Hyder Ali in return for the cession of the Northern Sarkārs. But the Niẓām abandoned the war in 1768, leaving the British to face Hyder Ali alone. In 1769 Hyder Ali appeared before the company's government in Madras and dictated peace on the basis of the status quo.

In the second war, Hyder Ali joined the Marāthās in 1780 and again devastated the Carnatic. The tide was turned by the dispatch of British help from Calcutta and by the death of Hyder Ali in December 1782. French help came too late to affect the issue. Peace was made with Hyder Ali's son Tippu Sultan by the Treaty of Mangalore (1784).

The third war began in 1790, when Governor General Cornwallis dropped Tippu's name from the list of the company's "friends." After two campaigns, Tippu was brought to bay at Seringapatam and forced to cede half his dominions (1792).

The fourth war was undertaken by Governor General Lord Mornington (later Wellesley) on the plea that Tippu was receiving help from France. Seringapatam was stormed in May 1799, and Tippu died in the fighting.

Mystacinidae, a family of New Zealand short-tailed bats of the order Chiroptera.
·classification and general features **4**:436c

Mystacocarida: *see* mustache shrimp.

mystagōgos, a word used in Greco-Roman mystery religions to refer to the leader of the candidates for initiation.
·mystery cult terminology **12**:778g

Mysterium Fidei (1965; "The Mystery of Faith"), encyclical of Pope Paul VI on the Eucharist.
·transubstantiation dogma
reaffirmation **13**:960b

mysterium tremendum (religion): *see* numinous.

mystery, in religion, the absolute incomprehensibility and sublimeness of sacred or divine reality, which remains a mystery even where there has been revelation about or experience of God.

The term has also been applied to God's thoughts and acts, the hidden meaning of Scripture, the Christian sacraments, certain pagan rites (*see* mystery religions), and other religious phenomena.
·Manichaean initiatory rituals **11**:447c
·man's knowledge of God **18**:266h
·mysticism and sacred reality **12**:789d
·non-Pauline terminology in
Ephesians **2**:963h
·Otto's reflections on numinous **13**:770c
·Roman Catholicism and revelation **15**:993g

mystery plays and miracle plays, two kinds of vernacular drama performed by communities in England during the Middle Ages. They were the chief means by which lay people gave public expression to their religious faith.

In France, a play that dramatized some episode in Scripture, from either the Old or the New Testament, was called a *mystère;* one that dramatized the life, or an incident in the life, of a saint was called a *miracle.* In England during the Middle Ages and Renaissance both kinds of play were called "miracles"; the term mystery play was not used in England until the 18th century.

"The Road to Calvary," staging of a medieval mystery play is probably reflected in this illuminated page by the Limburg brothers from the *Très Riches Heures du duc de Berry* (MS 65, fol. 147r.) 1416; in the Musée Condé, Chantilly
By courtesy of the Musee Conde, Chantilly; photograph, Giraudon

Some scholars, wishing to make clear the distinction that the French words conveniently express, have referred to the scriptural play as a "mystery" and to the saint's play as a "miracle." Others, however, preferring to follow the original English terminology, have referred to both kinds as "miracles." Additional problems of ambiguity are posed because the organization of the plays in England (and elsewhere) passed into the hands of fraternities, or trade guilds, of craftsmen. In medieval and Elizabethan England an occupation or craft was called a "mystery," the word deriving from *ministerium*, Latin for "service." Many people have therefore erroneously supposed that mystery plays are so called because they were acted, or organized, by the "mysteries," or guilds.

Several modern scholars have abandoned the traditional terminology altogether and prefer to use the expression "sacred drama" as the general term and "scriptural drama"

and "saint's play" as the particular terms. *See* scriptural drama; saint's play.
·costume design history **17**:560f
·drama and communal belief **5**:985c
·dramatic style and medieval ritual **5**:983g
·Elizabethan tragedy precursor **18**:582h
·medieval dramatic literature **10**:1099h
·origin, performance, and development **18**:242f; illus. 243
·origins, music, and language **12**:701c
·production and Christian themes **18**:222a *passim* to 224e
·secular and miraculous element use **18**:252g
·wind instrument leitmotif utilization **19**:852d

mystery religions **12**:778, secret cults of the Greco-Roman world that offered to individual initiates a way to have religious experiences not provided by the official public religions. The constitutive features of the mystery societies, which reached their peak of popularity in the first three centuries of the Christian Era, were common meals, dances, and ceremonies, especially initiation rites in which death and resurrection were symbolically represented.

The text article covers the history of mystery religions, tracing them from their Hellenic roots (especially Dionysiac, Eleusinian, and Orphic) through the Hellenistic period, when Oriental ideas were absorbed, to Roman imperial times; the beliefs and practices, noting common features (such as priesthood, rites, and festivals), literature, and theology; the religious art and iconography; and, finally, the relationship of the mystery religions and Christianity.

REFERENCES in other text articles:
history
·Anatolian Cybele cult in Roman Empire **2**:192h
·Christian esoteric adoptions **4**:529d
·Christian opposition **4**:539a
·Christian tradition elements **4**:497d
·Egyptian religious cults **6**:506b
·Greek emphasis in Hellenistic era **8**:408b
·Hadrian's initiation **8**:540d
·Hellenistic Age religious activity **8**:749a
·Hellenistic cults in Rome **14**:786h
·Nero's interest and obsession **12**:966b
·religious matrix of Christianity **2**:947d
·Rome's Greek and Oriental syncretism **15**:1121e
·vitality in Empire **15**:615e
practices and beliefs
·celibate practices and influence **3**:1042a
·classification of ritual actions **17**:904b
·Dionysian theme of chaotic fecundity **1**:915d
·dualistic body–soul concepts **5**:1067a
·esoterism in worship **19**:1015d
·Gnostic elitist tradition **8**:214g
·man's dualistic nature and incarnation **5**:534a *passim* to 535a
·monotheistic belief form of Isis cult **12**:382c
·mystical uses of drugs **12**:788b
·Pythagorean mysticism and subjectivism **15**:322h
·sacramental elements and Christian parallelism **16**:115b *passim* to 117b
·salvific concepts surrounding Osiris **16**:203a

RELATED ENTRIES in the *Ready Reference and Index:*
Andania Mysteries; Bacchanalia; Cabeiri; Celeus; Eleusinian Mysteries; Eumolpus; Great Mother of the Gods; hierophantes; Iacchus; Orpheus

mystery story, an ages-old popular genre of tales dealing with the unknown; it may be a narrative of horror and terror, a pseudoscientific fantasy (*see* science fiction), a crime-solving story (*see* detective story), an account of diplomatic intrigue, an affair of codes and ciphers and secret societies, or any situation involving an enigma. By and large, mystery stories may be divided into two sorts: tales of the supernatural and riddle stories.

Supernatural tales are of ancient origin and form a substantial part of the body of folk literature. But the literary cultivation of fear and curiosity for its own sake began to emerge in the 18th century pre-Romantic era with the Gothic novel (*q.v.*). It was invented by a worldly Englishman, Horace Walpole, whose *Castle of Otranto* (published 1765) may be said to have founded the horror story as a permanent form. Mary Shelley, the wife of the poet, introduced the pseudoscientific note in her famous novel *Frankenstein* (1818), about the creation of a monster that ultimately destroys its creator.

In the Romantic era the German storyteller E.T.A. Hoffmann and the American Edgar Allan Poe raised the mystery story to a level far above mere entertainment through their skillful intermingling of reason and madness, eerie atmosphere and everyday reality. They invested their spectres, doubles, and haunted houses with a psychological symbolism that gave their tales a haunting credibility.

The Gothic influence persisted throughout the 19th century in such works as Joseph Sheridan Le Fanu's *House by the Churchyard* and "Green Tea," Wilkie Collins' *Moonstone*, and Bram Stoker's vampire tale *Dracula*. Later masters of the mystery tale were Ambrose Bierce, Arthur Machen, Algernon Blackwood, Edward Dunsany, and H.P. Lovecraft; but isolated masterpieces have been produced by writers not usually associated with the genre, for example, Guy de Maupassant's "Horla," A.E. Coppard's "Adam and Eve and Pinch Me," Saki's "Sredni Vashtar" and "The Open Window," and W.F. Harvey's "August Heat." Some of the best-known mystery stories owe their power to their development of full-bodied characters in a realistic social environment and the very absence of mysterious atmosphere. In this category are Aleksandr Pushkin's "Queen of Spades" and W.W. Jacob's "Monkey's Paw."

Riddle stories, too, have an ancient heritage. The riddle of Samson, propounded in the Bible (Judges 14:12–18), is the most famous early example, but puzzles were also popular among the ancient Egyptians and the Greeks. The distinguishing feature of the riddling mystery story is that the reader be confronted with a number of mysterious facts and situations, explanation of which is reserved until the end of the story.

Poe's short story "The Gold Bug" is a classic example of one perennially popular type of mystery, the story of a search for lost treasure. In the more sinister field of murder are innumerable tales of roguery involving mystery and crime but without the familiar detective interludes. Two notable riddle stories of modern times offered no solution to the riddle posed and gained wide attention by their novelty: "The Lady or the Tiger" by Frank R. Stockton, and "The Mysterious Card" by Cleveland Moffett.

More nearly akin to the detective story than any of these are the spy stories, tales of international intrigue and adventure, entertainingly written by John Buchan, Valentine Williams, Cyril McNeile, William Le Queux, and many others. Two directions taken by the modern spy story were typified by Ian Fleming's enormously popular James Bond thrillers, using technical marvels that approached science-fiction fantasy, and John Le Carré's (pseudonym of David Cornwell) almost sordidly realistic stories (*e.g.*, *The Spy Who Came in from the Cold*, 1963).
·novel type and characteristics **13**:288e

mystēs, a word used in Greco-Roman mystery religions to refer to the candidates for initiation.
·mystery cult terminology **12**:778g

mystical body of Christ, a designation for the Christian church made popular by Pope Pius XII in his encyclical *Mystici Corporis* (1943). It signifies a supernatural (not merely figurative) reality that unites all Christians with Christ, who is their head. The New Testament parable of Christ as the vine and men as the branches is interpreted as an expression of this doctrine. In a wider sense, all persons of the human race are, potentially at least, members of the mystical body of Christ inasmuch as Christ, according to Christian teaching, died for all men and desires their salvation.
·Christian collective ethical doctrines **4**:525b
·Christian Last Judgment concepts **4**:508c
·Christian principles of unity **4**:463b *passim* to 464f
·ecumenical conception of church **6**:293f
·implication for marriage **4**:522h
·Orthodox dogma on intercession for dead **4**:477a
·Roman Catholic definition **15**:988g
·St. Paul's discussion in I Corinthians **2**:960c

Mysticeti, suborder of whale-bone whales of the order Cetacea and of the class Mammalia.
·evolutionary relationships, illus. 6 **11**:414

Mystici Corporis (1943; "The Mystical Body"), encyclical of Pope Pius XII on the nature of the church.
·mystical body as the church **15**:988h

mysticism **12**:786, an approach denoting in general a spiritual quest for hidden truth or wisdom the goal of which is union with the divine or the sacred (the transcendent realm). A form of living in depth, mysticism indicates that man, a meeting ground of various levels of reality, is more than one-dimensional and that he may progress to his spiritual goal by various stages, usually designated as purgation, purification, illumination, and unification.

The text article covers the relation of mystical experience to other kinds of experience, definitions of mysticism and mystical experience, universal types of mystical experience, the goal of mystical experience and mysticism, the mystical relationship between man and the sacred, semantics and symbolism in mystical experience, psychological aspects of mysticism, and the semantic exposition of mystical experience. The article further considers mysticism as a social factor and the influence of mystically oriented persons in the modern world.

REFERENCES in other text articles:
·accounts of Leuba, Otto, and Underhill **15**:621c
·aesthetic fundamentals in Orient **1**:160b
·aesthetic view of religious experience **1**:157d
·asceticism and union with the divine **2**:136b
·Buddhist forms and approaches **3**:414h
·Buddhist meditative stages and states **3**:378b
Christian emphases in method and belief **4**:545e
·Beatific Vision **4**:478c
·Böhme and Renaissance views **2**:1202b
·deification concept **4**:490c
·Eckehart's teaching and influence **6**:187d
·Joachim of Flora's three illuminations **10**:225b
·Palamas' Greek Orthodox Hesychasm **13**:905d
·Pietist awakening in devotional writing **14**:456c
·Pseudo-Dionysius negative theology **16**:354b
·Quaker Inward Light **7**:743b
·Radical Pietist history **14**:458a
·Roman Catholic Church's attitude **15**:1000b
·St. Bernard's letters and sermons **2**:861f
·St. Ignatius as theological guide **11**:166h
·Teilhard de Chardin's evolutionary ethics **12**:876f
·dualistic mystery cults of Greece **5**:1067a
·epistemological considerations **15**:601h
·Gnostic qualified acceptance **8**:217d
Hindu theory and method history **8**:923c
·sainthood of Hindu mystics **16**:164h
·Vaiṣṇavite religious attitude to God **8**:892h
·Idealist reality intuited **9**:191a
·instructional disciplinary techniques **15**:641a
·Isaiah's visionary calling to ministry **2**:917a
·Japanese intuitive form **15**:600a
Judaic reconciliation with monotheism **10**:183d
·philosophical thought **10**:208f
·rabbinic attitudes and concepts **10**:287a
·Spinozistic epistemological system **17**:510f
·man's faith by personal God experience **18**:267c
·Neoplatonic stress of inwardness **2**:365e
·Neo-Taoism transcendental reality **4**:417h
·new tribal cults characteristics **18**:699h

·Oman's theory of revelatory inferiority **15**:625a
pharmacological paths to religious experience **14**:199f
 ·drug ecstasies and characteristics **5**:1048f
 ·experimental comparison with drug state **14**:202f
·Plains Indians' religious experience **18**:699e
·Platonism and humanistic scholarship **8**:1172a
·prayer as vehicle of divine encounter **14**:948f *passim* to 953a
·priestly prerogative and perquisite **14**:1008a
·prophet-like intimacy with godhead **15**:62e
·Pythagorean mystic numbers **15**:322g *passim* to 323h
·reality definition from God concept **18**:265d
·religion's impact on artistic style **2**:116f
·religious experience personalities **15**:651b
·religious experience typing **15**:649h
·sainthood and instructional mission **16**:167c
·shamanic techniques and experiences **16**:638c
·Socrates' belief in divine symbols **16**:1002g
·spiritual orientation of Taoism **15**:136c
Ṣūfī statutes and discipline **9**:945f
 ·Ibn ʿArabī's Islāmic esotericism **9**:143e
 ·Javanese acceptance **9**:483c
 ·Muḥāsibī's principle of reason **12**:611h
 ·mystical intoxication **8**:556a
 ·philosophical syncretism **9**:1023a
 ·Rūmī's ecstatic poetry **10**:15b
·Swedenborg's dreams and visions **17**:856b
·symbolism in mystical practice **17**:903d
·Taoist parallels to Western mystics **17**:1043f
·theories of forms, goals, and attitudes **15**:625g *passim* to 627f
·theosophic direct experience of God **18**:276f
·Weber's divine grace theory **19**:716c
·worship forms for individuals **19**:1016d
·Yinger's alienation theory **15**:607a

RELATED ENTRIES in the *Ready Reference and Index:*
ecstasy; meditation; nature mysticism

myth and mythology 12:793, two terms used in the study of religion and culture the subjects of which are accounts about gods or superhuman beings and extraordinary events or circumstances in a time that is altogether different from ordinary human experience. Myth, a collective term used for one kind of symbolic communication, specifically indicates one basic form of religious symbolism, as distinguished from symbolic behaviour (such as cult and ritual) and symbolic places and objects (such as temples and icons). Mythology is a term that is used for the study of myth and also for the body of myths in a particular religious tradition.

The text article covers definitions, functions, and the study of myth and mythology, myth in human culture (including myth and psychology, society, science, religion, and the arts), and major types of myths (including myths of origin, eschatology and destruction, culture heroes and soteriological figures, time and eternity, Providence and destiny, rebirth and renewal, memory and forgetting, high beings and celestial gods, founders of religions and other religious figures, kings and ascetics, and transformation, and myths and tales illustrating religious doctrine or reaffirming standards of conduct). The article concludes with an assessment of myth in modern society, including the secularization of the myth, demythologization of major religious traditions, survivals in modern consciousness and behaviour, and the political and social uses of myth in modern times.

REFERENCES in other text articles:
·angels and demons in world religions **1**:871g
animal and plant types and themes **1**:911h
 ·elephant charms and graveyards **15**:2b
 ·Eskimo animal-centred mythology **19**:791d
 ·kingfishers in Greek legend **5**:157a
·Arabian spice legends **17**:502c
artistic use **2**:116c
 ·drama's religious origin **17**:530f
 ·epic themes and traditions **6**:906g
 ·Mann's response to modern needs **11**:457a
 ·mask representation and use **11**:579b; illus.
 ·Mesopotamian literary themes and genres **11**:1009b
 ·novel's levels of meaning **13**:280d
 ·Ovid's etiological poetry **13**:798e
 ·South Asian artistic depictions **17**:150f
 ·tragic drama origins **18**:580g
·Baltic forms of Indo-European archetype **2**:664g
·Buddhist mythology development **3**:419a
·Buddhist primary and subsidiary faith **3**:424f
·Bultmann's existentialist theology **3**:478h
·cargo cults among tribal peoples **18**:698d
·Celtic beliefs and Roman influence **3**:1075a
·Chinese legend on birth of music **12**:672b
·Chinese mythical sources **4**:410f
·Christian forms and traditions **4**:550f
creation story types **5**:239a
 ·African creation myth variety **1**:237f
 ·Aztec cosmogony and eschatology **2**:550a
 ·basketry in creation stories **2**:760d
 ·folk literature and importance of myth **7**:456d
 ·folklore studies and cultural theories **7**:461h
 ·Homeric treatment of Greek gods **8**:1021c
 ·Icelandic legendary sagas **16**:146d
 ·Mayan cosmology and creation myths **11**:720d
·cult presuppositions in ancient Judaism **10**:304g
·divine sanction for god's actions **15**:282a
·dualism manifest in gods' conflicts **5**:1066f
·Eleusinian mysteries and the Kore myth **12**:778h
·Epicurean view of gods **14**:256b
·eschatological themes and forms **6**:959b
·ethical function of Lurianic myth **10**:189b
·fear of death and journey to afterworld **5**:534e
·Finno-Ugric common traditions **7**:311c
·flight capability of legendary beings **7**:381f
·Greek gods and heroes **8**:402e
·Greek influences on Roman religion **15**:1060a
·Hellenistic concern with good and evil **8**:751a
·Hindu personal and social significance **8**:927a
·Inca ancestry origins **1**:848a
·Islāmic contributions and Qurʾānic revelation **9**:949a
·Japanese myths and legends **10**:97d
·Jewish types and functions **10**:191d
·Khoisan deity creation and function **10**:449e
·Khoisan pantheon characteristics **10**:449e
·language origin accounts **10**:643d
·Manichaean cosmological system **11**:445e
·map representation of constellations **2**:225e
·Meso-American cosmic view of universe **11**:946b
·Mesopotamian art and Sumerian mythology **19**:259c
·Mesopotamian world view and its expression **11**:1003d
·messianistic allegories and symbols **11**:1021h
·meteorite origin early beliefs **12**:40b
·musical instrument legends **17**:744h
·music's supernatural powers **12**:298c
·mystical theme of dichotomy **12**:790d
·nature worship and myth-making **12**:878c
·Near East religious communality **12**:919h
·philosophical justification **15**:602h
·Polynesian migration legends **14**:778d
·polytheistic forces and objects **14**:785d
·Puruṣa's division into four varṇas **3**:984c
·religion and magic **1**:923b
·religious experience expressive forms **15**:650h
·religious schooling in sacred reality **15**:641b
ritual and myth correlation **15**:626d
 ·Amerindian themes and ceremonial use **1**:659c
 ·Canaanite fertility ritual **2**:908e
 ·Hindu and Vedic ritual functions **8**:890f
 ·Near East relationship **12**:921a
 ·uses and correspondences **15**:863g *passim* to 866d
·sacred experience and renewal **16**:123h
·sacredness of sacred scripture **16**:126d
·saints of mythic times **16**:167g
·semisacred status as religious writing **16**:127g
·shamanistic cosmological system **16**:639a
·Shintō borrowings from continental Asia **16**:672b
·South American forest culture beliefs **17**:124e
·studies of 19th and 20th centuries **15**:623h
·study of Johann von Herder **15**:616f
·symbolic centrality in religion **15**:605f
·symbolism in religious tradition **17**:903c
·Taoist use of Chinese myths **17**:1036f
·theology as identified by Greeks **18**:274b
·transcendent truth articulation **14**:1045a
·trees venerated as deities **18**:690a
·value expression and interpretation **7**:132h
·witch cross-cultural characteristics **19**:896f

RELATED ENTRIES in the *Ready Reference and Index:*
cycle; folktale; hero

My Tho, autonomous municipality (*thi xa*) and capital of Dinh Tuong province, in the flat Mekong Delta region of southern South Vietnam. An inland port on the north bank of the Song (river) My Tho, it is directly linked by highway to Saigon, 45 mi (72 km) to the northeast. Formerly Khmer (Cambodian) and known as Misar, it was annexed by the Annamese toward the end of the 17th century. In 1862 Emperor Tu Duc of Annam ceded My Tho and surrounding provinces to France. With the draining of the marshes by French army engineers, agricultural development began. Between 1881 and 1885 a railway (now dismantled) was completed linking My Tho to Saigon. Subsequently the district became known for coconut production; it functions primarily, however, as a transshipment point from the coastal waterway and as a light manufacturing centre. It has a hospital and a commercial airport. Pop. (1971 est.) 92,891. 10°21′ N, 106°21′ E
·area and population table **19**:142
·map, South Vietnam **19**:140

Myth of Sisyphus, The (1955), translation of LE MYTH DE SISYPHE (1942), long essay by Albert Camus developing themes of the irrational nature of the world and the absurdity of man's position in it, and inquiring about the justification of suicide. Camus later called the essay his most important early exposition of the philosophical doctrine of the Absurd. His terminology in this essay led to the Theatre of the Absurd's being so called.
·nihilism analysis **3**:712f

Myth of the Bagre, The (1972), a book edited by Jack Goody.
·primitive religion's modern tradition **14**:1043b

mythopoeic school, in literature, a group of writers who create their works from an existing body of mythical reference or create their own mythical structure in their works. Frequently, their works have elements of both existent myth and an altered vision and restatement of that myth in contemporary terms. James Joyce, for example, applied the Homeric myth of *Ulysses* to the actions and thoughts of an advertising canvasser in Dublin and, in the course of 20 hours of that man's life, adhered to the structure and situational conflicts of the existing myth of voyage and return. William Butler Yeats created an entire cosmology and cyclical historical pattern in his book *A Vision*, which had been prefigured in his early poetry and was elaborated on in his late works.

The American author William Faulkner, borrowing the motifs of agrarian honor and industrial decline and evoking the stylistic patterns of the Bible, created a mythical county in Mississippi—its land deeds, accounting records, family lines—and chronicled its history in terms of universal American traits. Other writers of this school of literature include: Melville, Hawthorne, Ernest Hemingway, John Barth, Thomas Pynchon, Jorge Luis Borges, Iris Murdoch, William Gass, and Robert Coover.

Mytilene, Modern Greek MITILÍNI, chief town of the island of Lesbos and of Lesbos *nomós* (department), Greece. Mytilene, whose name is pre-Greek, is also the seat of a metropolitan bishop of the Orthodox Church. The ancient city, lying off the east coast, was initially confined to an island that later was joined to Lesbos, creating a north and south harbour. From 1355 to 1462 the Gateluzzi family occupied the island, rebuilding (1373) the Byzantine fortress. In 1462 Lesbos fell to the Turks, who held it until 1912, when it joined the Greek kingdom. In 1958 a Greek

The harbour and town of Mytilene from the citadel, Lesbos, Greece

Tomas Friedmann—Photo Researchers

theatre, overlooking the town from the hillside, was excavated. Pop. (1971) 23,426.
39°06′ N, 26°32′ E
·growth and importance in Archaic period 8:345g; map 326
·map, Greece 8:315
·Peloponnesian War against Athens 14:22a

Mytilus (genus of mussels): *see* mussel.

Mytishchi, city, centre of a *rayon* (district), Moscow *oblast* (administrative region), western Russian Soviet Federated Socialist Republic, situated northeast of the city of Moscow. The importance of Mytishchi in the past derived from its position on the important road between Moscow and the prosperous Trinity-St. Sergius Monastery. It was also the source of Moscow's water supply until the 20th century. In 1908 Mytishchi became the site of the first artificial-fibre factory in Russia. Since its incorporation in 1925, the city has become a centre of machine building. Pop. (1974 est.) 127,000.
55°55′ N, 37°46′ E

My Universities (1952), English translation of MOI UNIVERSITETY (1923), third volume of an autobiographical trilogy by Maksim Gorky.
·content and author's skill 8:256h

Mývatn, shallow lake, northern Iceland, 30 mi (48 km) east of Akureyri, drained by the Laxá (river), which flows northward to the Greenland Sea. Nearly 6 mi long, 4 mi wide, and covering an area of 14 sq mi (37 sq km), it

Lava formations in Mývatn, Iceland

J. Allan Cash—EB Inc.

is the fourth largest lake in Iceland. Mývatn, a tourist attraction, is dotted with many volcanic islands and is surrounded by numerous craters, hot springs, and a variety of lava formations. The lake and the river draining it are noted for salmon, trout, and char fishing. Diatomaceous earth, which has many applications in industry, is mined and processed nearby.
65°37′ N, 16°58′ W
·Iceland's geography and wildlife 9:172a
·map, Iceland 9:171
·volcanic basin origin 10:603b

myxedema (medicine): *see* hypothyroidism.

Myxicola, genus of annelid worms of the family Sabellidae, class Polychaeta, phylum Annelida.
·giant nerve fibre functioning 1:934h

Myxinidae (family of hagfishes): *see* hagfish.

Myxobolus (genus of protozoans): *see* myxosporidian.

Myxogastromycetidae, also called ENDOSPOREAE or MYXOGASTRES, subclass of slime molds (class Myxomycetes), whose spores are within fruiting structures. There are five orders and approximately 500 species.
·plasmodium and spore features 16:884h

myxomatosis cuniculi: *see* infectious myxomatosis.

Myxomycetes, a class of primitive eucaryotic (*i.e.*, having true nuclei), terrestrial organisms within the division Myxomycophyta (Mycota of some authors), commonly known as true slime molds. Like other myxomycophytes, they resemble both Protozoa (one-celled animals) and fungi. Distributed worldwide, they usually occur in decaying plant material. About 500 species have been described.

The vegetative (active, growing, feeding) phase consists of a multinucleate amoeboid mass or sheet (plasmodium). This transforms into fungus-like fruiting structures (sporangia) with one to many spores. In nearly all species (constituting the group Endosporeae), the spores are borne within the sporangium. In three known species (the Exosporeae), the spores are apparently borne externally; each spore, however, is a much reduced sporangium with the true spore within.

Lycogala

Walter Dawn

Upon germination, a spore produces one or more individual cells known as myxamoebas, which may transform into so-called swarm cells with two flagella (long, whiplike structures). The swarm cells often revert to the amoeboid stage. Formerly, it was believed that reproduction was by the nonsexual fusion of swarm cells, but the process is now known to be sexual.

The plasmodium, with cytoplasm streaming through it, changes shape as it crawls slowly over or within damp wood, leaves, or soil, ingesting bacteria, molds, and fungi. Characteristically, the entire mass of the plasmodium is covered by an external layer of slime, which is continually secreted and, as the plasmodium creeps, continually left behind as a network of collapsed tubules. The most frequently occurring colours of plasmodia are yellow and orange, but they may also be colourless, red, white, buff, maroon, or, rarely, blue, black, or green.

Stemonitis is a common genus found on wood. *Physarum cinereum* often appears on lawns, lending a bluish colour to the grass. *Major ref.* 16:884d
·cell reproduction processes 15:677a

Myxophyta (algal division): *see* blue-green algae.

myxosporidian, any parasitic protozoan of the cnidosporidian order Myxosporida; characterized by spores with a two-valved membrane and one or more coiled structures (polar filaments). Mainly parasites of fish, myxosporidians also attack amphibians and reptiles. Infection may be fatal; common infective sites are the hollow organs (gallbladder, urinary bladder), skin, muscles, and gills. After the spores are ingested by an animal, a sporoplasm leaves the spore case and migrates to an organ or tissue to feed and develop. After cytoplasmic growth and nuclear division occur, new spores, produced within cysts of host tissue, are released when the cyst breaks or the host dies. Representatives are *Unicapsula muscularis*, the cause of wormy disease in halibut; *Myxobolus pfeifferi*, the cause of boil disease in barbels; and *Myxosoma cerebralis*, the cause of a nervous system disorder known as twist disease in salmonid fishes.
·protozoan evolution and classification 15:127b

myxovirus, any of a group of viruses including those that cause some common colds, influenzas, mumps, measles, dog distemper, rinderpest of cattle, and Newcastle disease of fowl. The virus particle is enveloped in a fatty membrane; is variable in shape, from cubical to filamentous, and in size, from 60 to 300 nanometres (nm; 1 nm = 10^{-9} metre) in longest dimension; is studded with spikelike protein projections; and contains ribonucleic acid (RNA). These viruses react with mucin (mucoprotein) on the surface of red blood cells (hence the prefix *myxo-*, Greek for "mucin"); many of them cause red cells to clump together (agglutinate). A problematic group of similar viruses suspected of belonging in this family includes fowl-tumour virus, rodent-leukemia virus, and rabies virus.

Myzodendraceae, family of flowering plants of the order Santalales.
·characteristics and classification 16:227c *passim* to 229c

Myzomela (genus of birds): *see* honeyeater.

Myzopodidae, family of Old World sucker-footed bats of the order Chiroptera.
·classification and general features 4:436b

Myzostomida, order of segmented worms of the class Polychaeta and of the phylum Annelida.
·classification and general features 1:936e

Myzus (genus of insects): *see* aphid.

Mzab, also spelled M'ZAB, major Saharan oasis region in Laghouat *wilāyah* (province), Algeria. It was founded about 1010 by Mzabites (*q.v.*), Berber members of a heretical Muslim sect expelled from the Tell Atlas and Ouargla. The Mzab was annexed to France in 1882 and reverted to Algeria in 1962.

Minaret of the mosque at Ghardaïa, Mzab oasis, in Algeria
Bernard P. Wolff—Photo Researchers

The oases stretch along the Oued Mzab and are surrounded by *chebka*, arid country crossed by dry riverbeds. The region comprises the Pentapolis, five towns of varying size and importance. Ghardaïa (*q.v.*) is the chief settlement, while el-Ateuf is the oldest. Beni Isguene is the sacred town of the Mzabites; Arabs and Jews are not permitted within its walls, and no non-Mzabite may spend the night there. Melika, populated by black Africans, contains large cemeteries. Bou Noura, built on a rock overhanging the river bed, is the poorest of the towns. Two other towns, Guerara and Berriane, were added to the Pentapolis in the 17th century.

Date palm groves extend 5 mi (8 km) upstream and are watered from six barrages built across the river. The sound of the pulleys of more than 4,000 wells is called the "Song of Mzab." Fruit, cereals, and legumes are raised beneath the palms. A Saharan trade centre, the oasis is dependent upon its dates and fine handicrafts. An assembly of 12 religious scholars (*ḥalqah*) administers the five towns.

The towns of the Mzab are attractive, with houses rising in brightly coloured cubes along the banks of the *oued*. Many observers have compared the appearance of the towns to Cubist paintings, and they attract tourists. The population of the oasis is about 100,000, two-fifths of whom live in Ghardaïa.
32°29′ N, 3°40′ E
·distinctive features **1**:559e
·map, northern Algeria **1**:561

Mzabites, or MOZABITES, also called MZAB and BENI MZAB, Berber people who inhabit the Mzab oases of southern Algeria, members of the Ibāḍīyah subsect of the Muslim Khārijite sect. They are descendants of the Ibāḍī followers of 'Abd ar-Raḥmān ibn Rustam, who were driven from Tiaret (now Tagdempt) by the persecution of the orthodox and took refuge (probably in the 9th century) in the desert. According to tradition, they arrived at Sedrata, near present-day Ouargla, in 911, and a century later, choosing, for reasons of defense, the most inhospitable region they could find, they settled along the Oued Mzab, their first settlement being el-Ateuf, around 1010. Towns founded subsequently were Melika, Bou Noura, Beni Isguene, and Ghardaïa, in that order. To this Pentapolis were added Guerara and Berriane in the 17th century.

The form of Islām practiced by the Mzabites is extremely strict, egalitarian, and separatist. No non-Ibāḍī is admitted into a Mzabite mosque. The code of morals is rigid, and the standards of religious purity are high. For this reason, Mzabites do not marry outside their sect, and in consequence they are physically quite homogeneous, tending to be short, thickset, and short-headed and having a short, broad face. The women are heavily veiled and never leave the community. The men, however, are found throughout Algeria, running small businesses, often groceries, but returning to the oasis periodically. The Mzabites produce a variety of handicrafts, including pottery, brassware, jewelry, and carpets; there is a carpet festival in the spring.

Tombs in a Mzab cemetery at Melika, Alg.
Klaus D. Francke—Peter Arnold

An immense palm grove, the result of perfected methods of cultivation, provides work for the population between May and December. Scientific approaches to the distribution of water (according to a strict and complicated code) and the construction of dams have been effectively carried out, and the lushness of the Mzab gardens is legendary.

Mzilikazi, also spelled UMSILIGASI and MOZELEKATSE (b. *c.* 1790, near Mkuze, in modern South Africa—d. Sept. 9, 1868, Ingama, Matabeleland, near Bulawayo, now in Rhodesia), South African king who founded the powerful Ndebele (or Matabele) kingdom in what is now Rhodesia. The second greatest Bantu warrior after Shaka, king of the Zulus, Mzilikazi took his small Kumalo tribe on a trek of more than 500 miles from South Africa to Rhodesia, creating en route an immense and ethnically diverse nation called the Ndebele (*q.v.*). Though noted primarily for his military prowess, Mzilikazi was a statesman of great ability, able to weld the conquered tribes into a centralized kingdom.

Originally a lieutenant of Shaka, he revolted from the Zulu king in 1823 and withdrew his tribe northward to safety from their home on the southeast coast of Africa. He travelled to Mozambique and then west into the Transvaal, settling there by 1826. Continued attacks by coalitions of his enemies caused him to move west again to what is now Botswana, and in 1837 northward to present-day Zambia. Unable to conquer the Kololo nation there, Mzilikazi moved his followers, now numbering 15,000 to 20,000, eastward into what is now southwestern Rhodesia, where he settled Matabeleland (*c.* 1840). He organized the country in a system of regimental towns strong enough to repel Boer attacks (1847–51) and to force the Transvaal government to conclude a peace with him in 1852.

Mzilikazi was generally friendly to European travellers, but the discovery of gold in Matabeleland in 1867 brought a flood of Europeans that he was unable to control and that eventually led to the downfall of the kingdom.
·Ndebele leadership and empire creation **17**:282b

Mzimba, administrative headquarters of Mzimba District, northwestern Malawi, overshadowed by Mt. Hora (5,742 ft [1,750 m]) to the north. The district (area 4,018 sq mi [10,407 sq km]) is the nation's largest and includes the Mzimba Plain, the northern extension of the Central Region Plateau, and the Vipya Highlands. Poor soils support subsistence agriculture and a Turkish tobacco cash crop. Pop. (latest census) town, 4,156; district, 229,736.
·district area and population table **11**:362
·map, Malawi **11**:361

Mzora, archaeological site in Algeria.
28°26′ N, 0°07′ W
·North African tomb architecture **13**:146d

N, symbol for the chemical element nitrogen (*q.v.*) and for the number of neutrons in the nucleus of an atomic species element.

Na, chemical symbol for the element sodium (*q.v.*).

NAACP: *see* National Association for the Advancement of Colored People.

Naas, Irish NÁS NA RIOGH, urban district, market and garrison town and county town (seat) of County Kildare, Ireland. Naas was one of the royal seats of the ancient province of Leinster, and St. Patrick, the patron saint of Ireland, is said to have visited it. After the Anglo-Norman invasion (12th century and following) a castle was built there, of which the north moat is a surviving remnant. Naas was an important town in the medieval period, and is now the administrative centre of County Kildare, with a racecourse and cotton mills. Pop. (1971) 5,078.
·map, Ireland **9**:882

Naassenes (Gnostic sect): *see* Ophites.

Naba Bidhan, also called NAVA VIDHANA or NEW DISPENSATION, a Hindu social group formed by Keshab Chandra Sen in 1881.
·Keshab's vision of universal church **8**:918c

Nabadwīp, formerly NADIA, town, Nadia district, Jalpaiguri division, West Bengal state, India, at the confluence of the Bhāgīrathi and Jalangi rivers. The Bhāgīrathi River has so shifted its course that the town is cut off from the rest of the district. Metalware and brass manufacture are major industries. Reputedly founded in 1063, the town served as the ancient capital of the Sena dynasty. Called the Benares of Bengal, it is an important pilgrimage centre, famous for its sanctity. Caitanya (1485–1533), a Hindu mystic who founded a Vaiṣṇava sect, was born there. It is also noted for its traditional Sanskrit schools, or *ṭols*. Constituted a municipality in 1869, it has a college affiliated with the University of Calcutta. Pop. (1971 prelim.) 93,986.
23°25′ N, 88°22′ E
·map, India **9**:278[7]

Nabataean alphabet, writing system used between approximately 150 BC and AD 150 in the Nabataean kingdom of Petra in the Arabian Peninsula. Used by the Nabataeans to write the Aramaic language, this alphabet was

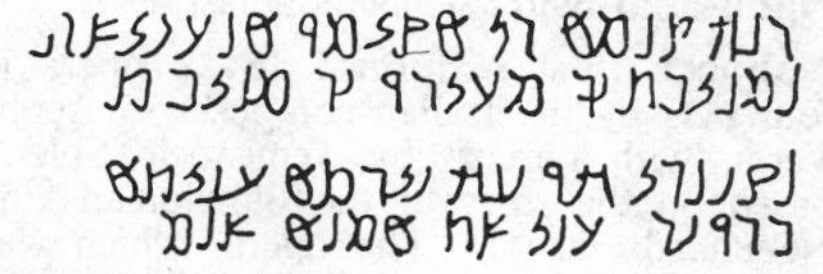

Nabataean inscription

From *The Alphabet* by David Diringer. Copyright 1948 by David Diringer. With permission of Funk & Wagnalls Publishing Company, Inc. and Hutchinson Publishing Group Ltd.

related to the Aramaic alphabet, one of the major Semitic scripts. The Nabataean script gave rise to the neo-Sinaitic alphabet, the ancestor of the Arabic alphabet. Like its Semitic precursors, Nabataean had 22 letters, all representing consonants, and was written from right to left. Nabataean inscriptions have been found in Egypt and Italy and on coins from Petra. A bilingual inscription in Nabataean and Greek scripts was discovered on the Aegean island of Kos.
·Arabic calligraphy styles and use **3**:663e

Nabataeans, a people of ancient Arabia whose settlements lay in the borderlands between Syria and Arabia, from the Euphrates River to the Red Sea. Little is known about them before 312 BC, when they were unsuccessfully attacked by Demetrius I Poliorcetes, king of Macedonia, in their mountain fortress of Petra south of the Dead Sea. The Nabataean monopoly of the rich caravan trade that passed from the interior of Arabia to the coast was the chief source of their prosperity.

As the Seleucid kingdom grew weaker in the 2nd century BC, the Nabataean kingdom in-

Nabataean obelisk tomb in Petra

Julian Huxley

creased in strength and extended its frontiers to the north and east and probably to the south along the eastern coast of the Red Sea. The Nabataeans occupied Ḥawrān, and shortly after 85 BC their king Aretas III ruled Damascus and Coele Syria (Lebanon). Upon the Roman general Pompey's entry into Palestine (63 BC), Aretas became a Roman vassal, retaining Damascus and his other conquests; Damascus, however, was later annexed by the Roman emperor Nero (reigned AD 54–68).

The final period of Nabataean history was one of peaceful prosperity as allies of Rome. Hellenistic influences may be traced in the royal coinage and in the rock-cut architecture at Petra. When the Roman emperor Trajan annexed the kingdom (AD 105–106) and set up the new province of Arabia, Bozrah (Bostra), east of the Jordan River, was chosen in place of Petra as the provincial capital.
·Arabian kingdoms' choice of pantheons **1**:1058c
·Damascus under rule **5**:447e
·Syrian and Palestinian history **17**:948c; map 949

Naberezhnye Chelny, city, Russian Soviet Federated Socialist Republic. It was called Chelny until it became a city in 1930. Pop. (1970) 38,000.
55°42′ N, 52°19′ E
·heavy truck factory construction **16**:95f

Nabeul, Arabic NĀBUL, town and seat of Nābul *wilāyah* (governorate), northeastern Tunisia, on the Gulf of Hammamet. Formerly a Phoenician settlement, it was destroyed by the Romans in 146 BC and later rebuilt as a Roman colony called Neapolis (New City). It is a pottery and ceramics handicraft centre and the eastern terminus of a railroad from Tunis, 40 mi (65 km) northwest. Other industries include stone cutting, quarrying (chalk), citrus fruit and flower growing, and the manufacture of perfume and macaroni. The coastal region, especially to the southwest near Hammamet (al-Ḥammāmāt) is a popular beach-resort area. Latest census 34,134.
36°27′ N, 10°44′ E
·map, Tunisia **18**:746

Nabidae (insect family): *see* damsel bug.

Nābighah, an-, in full AN-NĀBIGHAH ADH-DHUBYĀNĪ (fl. *c.* AD 600), one of the seven pre-Islāmic Arab poets whose works were collected in the *Muʿallaqāt*.

Nābighah, actually Ziyād ibn Muʿāwiyah, belonged to the tribe of Dhubyān. The origin of his name is uncertain, as are details of his early life. He lived in luxury and favour for many years at the court of the Lakhmid kings of al-Ḥīrah, incurring the jealousy of the other courtiers. According to legend, his poem in praise of King Nuʿmān's wife, Mutajarridah, was inspired by an accidental view of her naked; when the poem was recited to the King, the poet had to take refuge at the court of Ghassān until Nuʿmān pardoned him. It is more likely, however, that Nābighah had at some time written in praise of the Ghassanids, enemies of the Lakhmids, for which Nuʿmān banished him. Nābighah, in any case, became a favourite of the court of Ghassān, interceding several times on behalf of his tribesmen during their wars and defeats. He attempted to return to al-Ḥīrah, but arriving after Nuʿmān's death, he returned to his own tribe.

One of the most highly respected of the pre-Islāmic poets, Nābighah possessed a vivid, sensitive style, full of imagination and fine imagery. His verse, mainly eulogies and satires on tribal strife, displays an impressive command of language and its artifices.

Nabis (d. 192 BC), last ruler (207–192) of an independent Sparta. Nabis carried on the revolutionary tradition of Kings Agis IV and Cleomenes III. Since ancient accounts of him are mainly abusive, the details of his laws remain obscure, but it is certain that he confiscated a great deal of property and enfranchised the helots (Spartan serfs). He undoubtedly was not the monster depicted by the Greek historian Polybius.

Overshadowed by the struggle between Rome and Philip V of Macedonia, Nabis adroitly maintained his power. After the Peace of Phoenice (205) between Rome and Macedonia, he went to war with the Achaean League. The league's general, Philopoemen, rescued Messene from him and later defeated him at Scotitas in Laconia. In 197 Nabis acquired Argos from Philip V of Macedonia, who was then at war with Rome, and kept it by coming to terms with the Roman commander Titus Quinctius Flamininus. But Flamininus, having defeated Philip, proclaimed the Greek states autonomous, accused Nabis of tyranny, took Gythium in Laconia, and forced Nabis to surrender Argos. He tried to recover Gythium when the Romans left in 194 but was badly defeated by Philopoemen north of Sparta. Eventually the Aetolians, as part of their scheme to precipitate war between Rome and Antiochus III of Syria, murdered Nabis and temporarily occupied Sparta.
·communism and the Achaean proletariat **15**:1094a

Nabis, the name of a group of artists who, through their widely diverse activities, influenced virtually every facet of art in France during the late 19th century. Preaching that a work of art is the end product and visual expression of an artist's synthesis of nature into

"Interieur," Nabis painting by Pierre Bonnard, oil on canvas, 1897; in the North Carolina Museum of Art, Raleigh

By courtesy of the North Carolina Museum of Art, Raleigh

personal aesthetic metaphors and symbols, they paved the way for the early 20th-century development of abstract and nonrepresentational art.

The Nabis were greatly influenced by Japanese woodcuts, French Symbolist painting, and English Pre-Raphaelite art. Their primary inspiration, however, stemmed from the so-called Pont-Aven school which centred upon the painter Paul Gauguin. Under Gauguin's direct guidance, Paul Sérusier, the group's founder, painted the first Nabi work, "Landscape at the Bois d'Amour at Pont-Aven" (also called the "Talisman," 1888; private collection, France).

Armed with his painting and the authority of Gauguin's teachings, Sérusier returned to Paris from Pont-Aven and converted many of his artist friends, who received his aesthetic doctrines as a mystical revelation. Assuming the name Nabis (from Hebrew *navi*, "prophet," or "seer"), the original members of the group were the French artists Maurice Denis (with Sérusier, the group's main theoretician), Pierre Bonnard, Henri-Gabriel Ibels, Ker-Xavier Roussel, Paul Ranson, Édouard Vuillard, and René Piot. Later, a Dutch painter, Jan Verkade, and the Swiss-born Félix Vallotton joined the group, as did two French sculptors, Georges Lacombe and Aristide Maillol.

In 1891 the Nabis held their first exhibition, attempting in their works to illustrate Denis's dictum: "A picture, before being a war horse, a nude woman, or some anecdote, is essentially a flat surface covered by colours in a certain order." They soon began to apply this idea to such varied works as posters, stained glass, theatre sets, and book illustrations. But dissensions and desertions quickly occurred within the group, which finally disbanded in 1899. Only Vuillard and Bonnard, who came to call themselves Intimists (*see* Intimism), and Maillol continued to produce major works of art.

·Bonnard's works **3**:36d
·Symbolism and modern art history **19**:476g

Nablus (Israeli-occupied Jordan): *see* Nābulus.

nabob, variation of NAWAB, title of a deputy ruler, or viceroy, under the Mughal Empire in India, applied in England to men who made fortunes working for the British East India Company and returned home to purchase seats in Parliament.

·Akbar's governmental reforms **1**:400h

Nabokov, Vladimir **12**:804 (b. April 23, 1899, St. Petersburg, now Leningrad—d. July 2, 1977, Montreux, Switz.), a gifted and erudite writer and critic, best known as author of the novel *Lolita* but a writer of much else of value.

Abstract of text biography. Son of an old aristocratic Russian family, he spent his early years in pre-Revolutionary Russia. He studied at Trinity College, Cambridge, where he took first-class honours in French and Russian literature (1922). He spent a long period in France and Germany and emigrated in 1940 to the United States, of which he became a citizen in 1945. He was professor of Russian and European literature at Cornell University, Ithaca, N.Y., from 1948 till 1959.

While at Cambridge he wrote Russian and English poetry. His first novel, *Mashenka* (1926), was in Russian and is semi-autobiographical. With *The Defense* (1930), he established himself as the outstanding young Russian émigré novelist, though it gained him little financial reward. His first novels in English, *The Real Life of Sebastian Knight* (1941) and *Bend Sinister* (1947), are inferior to his best Russian work, but with *Lolita* (1955)—with its anti-hero Humbert Humbert, who is possessed by overpowering desire for very young girls—he won great fame, though perhaps the book was appreciated for the wrong reasons. *Pale Fire* (1962), a novel comprising a long poem and a commentary on it, completes his mastery of unorthodox structure. *Ada* (1969) is a parody of the family-chronicle type of novel. Nabokov's critical works include a study of Gogol (1944) and a translation of Pushkin's *Eugene Onegin* (1964), with a full commentary. Nabokov also published many scientific papers on entomology.

REFERENCES in other text articles:
·Expressionistic tradition in the novel **13**:285b
·literary works and recognition **10**:1226g

Nabonassar, also spelled NUBU-NASIR (d. 734 BC), king of Babylonia (ruled 747–734 BC).

·Tiglath-pileser's Assyrian empire **18**:401g

Nabonidus, also spelled NABU-NA'ID (meaning Reverer of [the god] Nabu), king of Babylonia from 556 till 539 BC, when Babylon fell to Cyrus, king of Persia. After a popular rising led by the priests of Marduk, chief god of the

Nabonidus, stone stela, 6th century BC; in the British Museum
By courtesy of the trustees of the British Museum

city, Nabonidus, who favoured the moon god Sin, made his son Belshazzar coregent and spent much of his reign in Arabia. Returning to Babylon in 539 BC, he was captured by Cyrus' general Gobryas and exiled. *Major ref.* **11**:988g

·Babylon's vulnerability and fall **2**:555c
·Cyrus' diplomacy and conquest **9**:833e
·Nebuchadrezzar's reputed madness **12**:926d
·Ur's ziggurat architecture **18**:1022d

Nabopolassar, also spelled NABU-APAL-USUR (meaning Nabu Protect the Son), first king of the Chaldean dynasty of Babylonia (reigned 625–605 BC).

·Median alliance and conquest of Assyria **11**:987h

Naboth, in the Old Testament, the owner of a vineyard in Jezreel adjacent to the country palace of King Ahab. On Naboth's refusal to sell the vineyard to Ahab, the King's wife, Jezebel, by treachery had him stoned to death. The crime led the prophet Elijah to curse both Ahab and Jezebel. The story is related in I Kings 21.

·execution at Jezebel's prompting **2**:915c

Naboth's follicle, also called NABOTHIAN OVULE (named for a German anatomist, Martin Naboth), cystlike formations in the mucosa of the uterine cervix, caused by blockage of the openings of certain glands, which then become distended with retained secretions.

·human anatomic location **15**:694g

Nabu, Old Testament NEBO, a major god in the Assyro-Babylonian pantheon. He was patron of the art of writing and a god of vegetation. Nabu's symbols were the clay tablet and the stylus, the instruments held to be proper to him who inscribed the fates assigned to men by the gods.

Samsuditana, the last king of the 1st dynasty of Babylon (reigned 1625–1595 BC), introduced a statue of Nabu into Esagila, the temple of Marduk, who was the city god of Babylon. Not until the 1st millennium BC, however, did the relationship between Marduk and Nabu and their relative positions in theology and popular devotion become clear. Marduk, the father of Nabu, took precedence over him, at least theoretically, in Babylonia. But in popular devotion it was Nabu, the son, who knows all and sees all, who was chief, especially during the centuries immediately

Nabu, statue from the entrance of the Temple of Nabu, Nimrūd, *c.* 780 BC; in the British Museum
By courtesy of the trustees of the British Museum

preceding the fall of Babylon. He had a chapel named Ezida in his father's temple Esagila, where at the New Year feast he was installed alongside Marduk. In his own holy city, Borsippa, he was supreme.

Goddesses associated with Nabu were Nana, a Sumerian deity; the Assyrian Nissaba; and the Akkadian Tashmetum, queen of Borsippa, stepdaughter of Marduk, and, as her abstract Akkadian name indicates, Lady of Hearing and of Favour. She was rarely invoked apart from her husband, Nabu.

·Nineveh's temples and palaces **13**:116d
·writing patronage **19**:1043a

Nabu-apal-iddin, king of Babylonia (reigned *c.* 887–855 BC).

·Aramaean invasion repulsion **11**:983b

Nabu-apal-usur: *see* Nabopolassar.

Nabucco (first performed 1842), opera in four acts by the Italian composer Giuseppe Verdi, with libretto by Temistocle Solera, based on the story of the Babylonian king Nebuchadrezzar II. The opera, which was first performed at La Scala in Milan, established Verdi's reputation in Italy.

·first production at La Scala **19**:82h

Nabuco de Araujo, Joaquim Aurelio Barreto (b. Aug. 19, 1849, Recife, Braz.—d. Jan. 17, 1910, Washington, D.C.), statesman and diplomat, leader of the abolitionist movement in Brazil, and man of letters. He was a member of an old aristocratic family in

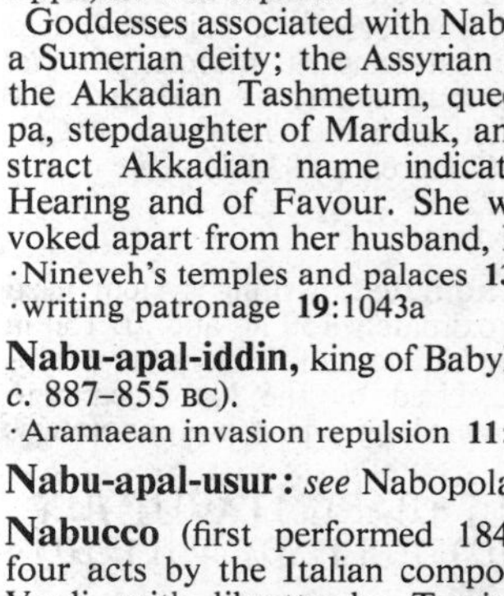

Nabuco de Araujo
By courtesy of the Library of Congress, Washington, D.C.

northeastern Brazil. Both in the national Chamber of Deputies (from 1878) and in the Brazilian Anti-Slavery Society, which he founded, he worked tirelessly for the emancipation of Brazil's slaves, which was proclaimed on May 13, 1888. In the ensuing economic disruption, the emperor Pedro II was overthrown (1889) and a republic was established. Nabuco, a confirmed monarchist, retired from public life until 1900, when he accepted the republic and entered its service. From 1905, as ambassador to the United States, he distinguished himself as an advocate of Pan-Americanism.

Among Nabuco's writings are *Camões e Os Lusíadas* (1872) and *O Abolicionismo* (1883), both in Portuguese, and *Pensées détachées et souvenirs* (1906), in French.
·abolition movement role **3**:146a

Nabu-kudurri-usur: *see* Nebuchadrezzar II.

Nābul, also spelled NABEUL, governorate, northeastern Tunisia.
·area and population table **18**:747

Nābul (city, Tunisia): *see* Nabeul.

Nābulus, also spelled NABLUS, biblical Hebrew SHECHEM, or SICHEM, classical NEAPOLIS, city of central Palestine, the largest community of the West Bank (Judaea and Samaria) territory under Israeli administration since 1967. Under Jordanian rule, it was the capital of Nābulus *muḥāfaẓah* (governorate).

A Canaanite city, Shechem was important in ancient Palestine because of its position in an east–west pass between Mt. Gerizim and Mt. Ebal (Arabic Jabal aṭ-Ṭūr and Jabal ʿAybāl, respectively). Its ruins are under the stratified mound of Tall al-Balāṭah, just east of the present city, which shows evidence of settlement from the Middle Bronze II period (*c.* 1900–*c.* 1750 BC), generally associated with the time of the biblical patriarchs. In the Bible it is first mentioned in Gen. 12:6, where, after coming into Canaan, "Abram passed . . . to the place at Shechem, to the oak [or terebinth] of Moreh." Jacob bought land there, and it was the site of the rape of his daughter Dinah by the son of the local Hivite chieftain, and of her brothers' subsequent revenge (Gen. 34). The town is mentioned in Egyptian documents of the 19th century BC; during the rule of the Hyksos kings of Egypt (17th–16th century BC), Shechem was a walled city with a triple gate, a fortress-temple, and an acropolis.

Later, after King Solomon's death, the 10 northern tribes of Israel revolted in Shechem against his son Rehoboam and installed Jeroboam as king in his place (I Kings 12). After the Assyrian conquest of the northern Kingdom of Israel (722 BC) the city declined. It was resettled by the Samaritans, who established their sanctuary on adjacent Mt. Gerizim, and was important in the Hellenistic period but was destroyed by the Maccabean ruler John Hyrcanus (ruled 135/134–104 BC).

The later city of Nābulus is not identical with the ancient site, but the two have been closely (though erroneously) linked for almost 2,000 years. Both rabbinic and early Christian literature commonly equated Nābulus with ancient Shechem, and Nābulus has been called Shekhem in Hebrew to the present. Founded under the auspices of the Roman emperor Vespasian in AD 72, and originally named Flavia Neapolis, it prospered because of its strategic site and the abundance of nearby springs. Later called Julia Neapolis, or simply Neapolis (Greek: New City), it is portrayed on the 6th-century Ma'dabā map (*see* Ma'dabā). It was conquered by the Arabs in AD 636; the modern name is an Arabic corruption of Neapolis. It was held from 1099 till 1187 by the crusaders, who called it Naples; it was briefly the crusader capital.

Though it is the principal centre of the numerically tiny Samaritan community, Nābulus has been a Muslim Arab city for centuries. In modern times, it was part of the Palestine mandate from 1920 to 1948; taken by Arab forces in the Arab–Israeli war of 1948–49, it was subsequently annexed to Jordan. A principal centre of Arab opposition both to Britain and to the Zionist movement during the mandate, it was the scene of frequent unrest. Much of the city was destroyed in a severe earthquake in 1927. The economy, both under the mandate and under Jordanian rule, was based on agricultural trade, olive-oil and soap manufacture, and handicrafts. A centre of terrorist activities against Israel from 1948 to 1967, it was the southern anchor of "the triangle" of Arab guerrilla centres (Nābulus, Ṭūl Karm, Janīn). Resistance to Israeli occupation continued after the Six-Day War of 1967, but by the early 1970s the situation was returning to normal; in 1972 Nābulus was the site of the first all-West Bank agricultural fair. Notable places include the Jāmiʿ al-Kabīr and Jāmiʿ an-Nasr mosques, built on the remains of Byzantine churches, the old Samaritan quarter, and the traditional site of "Jacob's Well," south of the city. Pop. (1971 est.) 44,200.
32°13′ N, 35°16′ E
·map, Jordan **10**:271
Shechem
·Abraham's life and wanderings **1**:12g
·ancient cultic importance and Abimelech's monarchy **2**:908e
·covenant under Joshua to establish Israel **5**:228e
·David's religious reforms **5**:519b
·Hebrew settlement in Palestine **17**:940c; map 943

Nabu-na'id (king of Babylon): *see* Nabonidus.

Nabu-nasir, also spelled NABONASSAR (d. 734 BC), king of Babylonia (ruled 747–734 BC).
·Tiglath-pileser's Assyrian empire **18**:401g

Nabu-rimanni, also called NABURIANOS, NABURIANNUOS, NABURIANNU, or NABURIMANNU (fl. *c.* 491 BC, Babylonia), the earliest Babylonian astronomer known by name, who devised the so-called System A, a group of tables giving the positions of the Moon, Sun, and planets at any given moment. He also calculated the length of the synodic month (from New Moon to New Moon) to be 29.530614 days (the true value is 29.530596 days).
·Babylonian astronomy **11**:989g
·eclipse and celestial motions **6**:196h

NACA, abbreviation of NATIONAL ADVISORY COMMITTEE FOR AERONAUTICS, U.S. research body established in 1915, the functions of which were transferred to the National Aeronautics and Space Administration (*q.v.*) in 1958.
·aeronautical research in the U.S. **7**:396c

Nacaome, capital, Valle department, southern Honduras, on the Nacaome River. It was founded in the 16th century and given city status in 1845. In addition to its administrative functions, Nacaome is a manufacturing and commercial centre. Beverages and bricks are made in the city, which also contains tanneries. The surrounding agricultural lands yield principally sesame and cotton. Gold and silver are mined at El Tránsito, just west of the city. Nacaome is on the Pan-American Highway, and from nearby Jicaro a highway leads northward to Tegucigalpa, the national capital. Pop. (1974) 29,038.
13°31′ N, 87°30′ W
·map, Honduras **8**:1058

Naccache, Alfred, (1888–1978), first president of postcolonial Lebanon, from 1941 to 1943.
·French power in Lebanon **17**:958g

Nachi-katsuura, town, Wakayama Prefecture (*ken*), Honshu, Japan, facing the Pacific Ocean. Lying within Yoshino-Kumano National Park, the town is a summer resort renowned for its proximity to more than 40 waterfalls. The main fall is one of the highest in Japan, dropping 427 ft (130 m); it is approached through a large gate set in a grove of ancient cedars. The 7th-century temple called Seiganto-ji is an important Shintō pilgrimage centre. Nearby is the highly venerated Kumano-Nachi Shrine, which was founded in the 4th century. Pop. (1975) 23,596.
33°30′ N, 135°55′ E
·map, Japan **10**:36

The main Nachi Waterfall, Wakayama Prefecture, Japan
Kokunai Jigyo Kouku

Nachikufan industry, industry of the African Late Stone Age practiced by hunting-gathering peoples who occupied the wooded plateaus of south-central Africa some 10,000–11,000 years ago. It is characterized by projectiles with several kinds of microlithic heads, heavy stone scrapers that were probably for working wood and its by-products, flattish stones with centre-bored holes that served as parts of a spring trap or for digging-stick weights, edge-ground axes, and grindstones for the preparation of wild foodstuffs.
·southern African development features **17**:274h

Nāchnā-Kutharā, temple site in Madhya Pradesh, India.
·Pārvatī Devī temple construction **17**:174h

Nachtanz: *see* afterdance.

Nachtigal, Gustav (b. Feb. 23, 1834, Eichstedt, Brandenburg, now in East Germany—d. April 19, 1885, at sea, off Cape Palmas, Liberia), explorer of the Sahara who also helped Germany obtain protectorates in western equatorial Africa. After spending several years as a military surgeon, he went to Tunisia as physician to the bey (ruler) and took part in several expeditions to the interior. In 1868 the king of Prussia, William I, sent him on a mis-

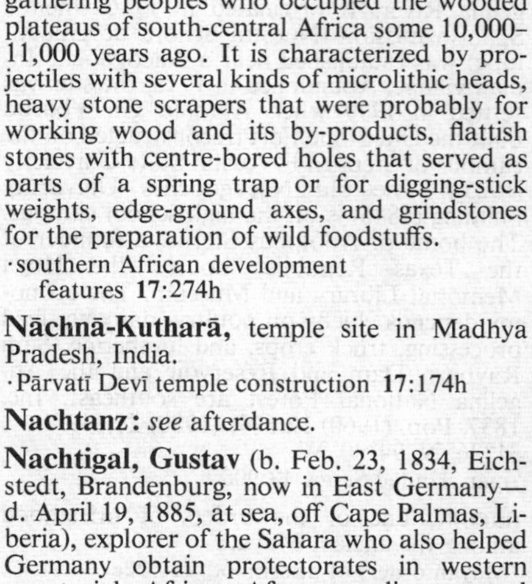

Nachtigal, detail from an engraving by V. Froer (born 1828)
Historia-Photo

sion to the kingdom of Bornu, now in northern Nigeria. He travelled by way of central Sahara regions then unknown to Europeans, including the Tibesti and Borku regions, which today lie within northern Chad. From Bornu he crossed the sultanate of Baguirmi, also in Chad, and, continuing by way of the Kordofan province of the Sudan, reached Cairo in November 1874. *Sahărâ und Sûdân* (1879–81) gives an account of his expedition. While serving as German consul at Tunis (1882–84), he was sent by Bismarck to western Africa ostensibly to make trade agreements, but secretly to help secure German protectorates over regions now in Togo and Cameroon.

Nacional Financiera, Mexican bank whose stock is owned mostly by the government and which serves as the channel for negotiating and administering loans obtained from abroad and as the principal source of funds for industrial development.
·financial and industrial importance **12**:73d
·Mexican governmental business support **12**:87h

Nacka, town, in the *län* (county) of Stockholm, southeastern Sweden, on the Södertörn peninsula of the *landskap* (province) of Södermanland. A southeastern suburb of Stockholm, it developed into a residential and industrial area with the coming of the railroad in 1893, and in 1949 was incorporated as a town. Leading industries include chemical technology, flour milling, and the manufacture of motors. Pop. (1970) 47,738.
59°18′ N, 18°10′ E

NaCl (chemistry): *see* sodium chloride.

Nacogdoches, city, seat of Nacogdoches County, eastern Texas, U.S., near the Angelina River. It originated in 1716 when a Spanish mission (Nuestra Señora de Guadalupe) was established near a Nacogdoche Indian village. Abandoned in 1718, the site was settled in 1779 when Antonio Gil Ybarbo built the Old Stone Fort (reconstructed on the campus of Stephen F. Austin State University [1923]). The old Nacogdoches University building (1845) is on the high school campus. The home of Adolphus Sterne, a founder of the Texas Republic, houses the Hoya Memorial Library and Museum. The economy depends chiefly on poultry, dairying, feed processing, truck crops, and lumbering. Sam Rayburn Dam and Reservoir and the Angelina National Forest are southeast. Inc. 1837. Pop. (1960) 12,674; (1980) 27,149.
31°26′ N, 94°39′ W
·map, United States **18**:908

nacom, one of the orders of priesthood among the ancient Maya.
·Mayan orders of priesthood **11**:722c

nacre (mollusk-formed concretion): *see* pearl.

nacreous cloud, or MOTHER-OF-PEARL CLOUD, nearly motionless cloud that resembles a cirrus or lens-shaped altocumulus cloud and occurs infrequently in winter at high latitudes and heights between about 20,000 and 30,000 metres (70,000 and 100,000 feet). During the daytime these clouds resemble pale cirrus clouds, but at sunset they exhibit bright colorations (irisations) that are ascribed to diffraction by spherical particles, presumably ice because of the low temperatures. As the sky darkens, the clouds increase in brilliance, and as the sun lowers further they become orange, pink, and then gray.
·cloud formations over mountains **4**:758g

nacrite (mineral): *see* kaolinite.

Nadar, pen name of GASPARD-FELIX TOURNACHON (b. April 5, 1820, Paris—d. 1910, Paris), writer, caricaturist, and photographer, remembered primarily for his photographic portraits, considered to be among the best done in the 19th century. As a young man, he reluctantly studied medicine in Lyons, Fr., but, when his father's publishing house went bankrupt in 1838, he was forced to earn his own livelihood. He began to write newspaper articles that he signed "Nadar," the pseudonym he used the rest of his life.

In 1842 Nadar settled in Paris. He taught himself to draw and began to sell caricatures to humour magazines. In 1849 he made a number of unsuccessful attempts to find a secure source of income, including an undistinguished career as the secretary of Ferdinand de Lesseps, the builder of the Suez Canal.

When a friend suggested he take up photography, Nadar at first was horrified, considering photography beneath his dignity as a caricaturist. But, by 1853, he had become an expert photographer and had opened a portrait studio. Nadar's immediate success stemmed partly from his sense of showmanship. He had the entire building that housed his studio painted red and his name printed in gigantic letters across a 50-foot (15-metre) expanse of wall. The building became a local landmark and a favourite meeting place of the intelligentsia of Paris. When, in 1874, the painters later known as Impressionists needed a place to hold their first exhibit, Nadar lent them his gallery. He was greatly pleased by the storm the exhibit raised; the notoriety was good for business.

Nadar, however, continued to consider himself primarily a caricaturist. In 1854 he completed his "Panthéon-Nadar," the first volume of what was to be a four-volume series of lithographic caricatures of all prominent persons in Paris. When he began work on the second volume of "Panthéon-Nadar," he realized the convenience of working from photographs and made photographic portraits of the persons he intended to caricature. Such portraits as those of the French illustrator Gustave Doré (*c.* 1855) and the French poet Charles Baudelaire (1855) are direct and naturally posed. They form a dramatic contrast to the majority of contemporaneous portraits, notable mainly for their artificial settings and stiff poses. In other remarkable character studies, such as those of the French writer and critic Théophile Gautier (*c.* 1855) and the French painter Eugène Delacroix (1855), Nadar's eye for caricature was sharpened by his personal knowledge of the sitters.

Nadar was a tireless innovator. In 1855 he patented the idea of using aerial photographs in map making and surveying. It was not until 1856 or 1858, however, that he was able to make an aerial photograph, the world's first, from a balloon. This led Daumier to issue a satirical lithograph of Nadar photographing Paris from a balloon. It was titled "Nadar Raising Photography to the Height of Art."

Nadar became a passionate aeronaut. He built a balloon, called "Le Géant" ("The Giant"), that was three times larger than any other balloon then built and could carry 49 men in its two-storied gondola. On a flight over Germany, however, it went out of control in a landing attempt; the passengers were dragged 25 miles before the balloon finally came to rest. Both of Nadar's legs were broken and his wife was severely injured. Nadar abandoned ballooning except for a brief period during the Franco-Prussian War in 1870, when he operated a balloon passenger and postal service between Paris and Tours.

In 1858 he began to photograph by electric light, making a series of photographs of Paris sewers. And, in 1886, he made the first "photo interview," a series of 21 photographs of the French scientist Eugène Chevreul in conversation. Each picture was captioned with Chevreul's responses to Nadar's questions, giving a vivid impression of the scientist's personality.

Nadar also wrote extensively throughout his career. He wrote novels, essays, and satires, but he was particularly well known for such autobiographical works as *Mémoires du Géant* ("Memoires of the Giant") and *Quand j'étais photographé* ("When I Was Photographed," *c.* 1900).
·balloon use for aerial photography **7**:383d
·photographic studies **14**:312a

Nadel, S(iegfried) F(rederick) (b. April 24, 1903, Vienna—d. Jan. 14, 1956, Canberra, Australia), anthropologist whose investigations of African ethnology led him to explore theoretical questions. Before turning to anthropology he pursued musical interests. He wrote a biography of the Italian composer Ferruccio Benvenuto Busoni and a work on musical typology, and he toured with his own opera company. In 1932 he entered the London School of Economics, encountering anthropologists C.G. Selignam and Bronisław Malinowski. He made his first expedition to the Nupe and other Nigerian peoples (1934–36) and then examined the Nuba of the Anglo-Egyptian Sudan (1938–40). His first major work, *A Black Byzantium* (1942), dealing with the Nupe, analyzed the theoretical basis of his ethnographic method. In *The Nuba* (1947) he examined structural constants shared by ten tribal groups.

Nadel was a reader in anthropology at the University of Durham in England (1948–50) and professor of anthropology at the University of Canberra (1950–56). Apart from *Nupe Religion* (1954), his other works are theoretical and reveal the influence of, among others, Malinowski, the sociologist Max Weber, the philosopher Alfred North Whitehead, and the psychologist Kurt Koffka. In *The Foundations of Social Anthropology* (1951) he asserts that the main task of the science is to explain as well as to describe aim-controlled, purposive behaviour. Suggesting that sociological facts emerge from psychological facts, he indicates that full explanations are to be derived from psychological exploration of motivation and consciousness. He analyzed a number of anthropological concepts and probed the basic difficulties in concept and method facing anthropologists. In his posthumous *Theory of Social Structure* (1958), sometimes regarded as one of the 20th century's foremost theoretical works in the social sciences, Nadel examines social roles, which he considers to be crucial in the analysis of social structure.
·micropolitical function of witchcraft **19**:899h

Nadelman, Elie (b. Feb. 20, 1882, Warsaw—d. Dec. 28, 1946, New York City), sculptor whose mannered, curvilinear human figures greatly influenced early 20th-century U.S. sculpture. He left home at 19 and, after brief attendance at the Warsaw Art Academy, spent six months in Munich studying the city's art collection. In 1903 he was in Paris where he worked independently but was influenced by Rodin. In 1905 Nadelman began his analysis of the relationship between sculptural

"Man in the Open Air," bronze figure by Elie Nadelman, *c.* 1915; in the Museum of Modern Art, New York

By courtesy of the Museum of Modern Art, New York, gift of William S. Paley (by exchange)

volume and geometry. His research culminated in the series of drawings *Toward a Sculptural Unity* (published 1914). His first one-man show in Paris (1909) was a sensational success, as was his 1915 exhibition at Alfred Steiglitz's gallery. At this time he began making his characteristic humorous mannikins—*e.g.*, "Man in the Open Air" (*c.* 1915; Museum of Modern Art, New York)—which were possibly influenced by the doll collection he had once studied in Munich's Bayerischen Nationalmuseum. In his late work he turned from humour and caricature to a decorative commercial style. A sensitive portraitist and masterful architectural sculptor, Nadelman worked in his last decade on small-scaled sculpture fitted to modern domestic living.
·Stieglitz American art promotion **17**:691b

Na-Dené languages, major grouping (phylum or superstock) of North American Indian languages, consisting of three language families—Athabascan (or Athapascan), Haida, and Tlingit—with a total of 22 languages. Twenty of these languages belong to the Athabascan language family; they are spoken in Canada around the Hudson Bay region west to Cook Inlet in Alaska, in two isolated areas of the Pacific coast (southwestern Oregon and northern California), and in the southwestern United States (mostly in New Mexico and Arizona). Tlingit and Haida are each single languages making up separate families; they are spoken, respectively, in southeastern Alaska and British Columbia. The most important language of the Na-Dené group is Navajo, with more than 80,000 speakers, in Arizona and New Mexico. It is one of the few North American Indian languages whose speakers are increasing in number. Other large languages of the phylum are Western Apache, with about 8,000 speakers in western Arizona; and the Chipewyan dialects of the Northwest Territories in Canada, with about 4,500 speakers.

Characteristic of many American Indian languages is a polysynthetic word structure, in which words are made up of many so-called bound elements (which cannot stand by themselves but only in conjunction with other elements). A single polysynthetic word may incorporate the information it would take an entire sentence to say in English. The Na-Dené languages are somewhat polysynthetic, although not as much so as the Algonkian or Eskimo languages; words are often built up from a number of loosely bound elements, primarily nouns or nounlike forms. More typical of the Na-Dené languages, however, is the use of tones to distinguish otherwise identical words. Navajo uses two pitches in this way—high, represented by an acute accent (´), and low, represented by a grave accent ( ). Thus, in Navajo, *yàzíd* means "you pour it down," and *yàzìd* means "I have poured it down." Other characteristics of the Na-Dené languages are a clear distinction between active and static verbs, a greater emphasis on verb aspect and voice than on tense, and frequent derivation of verbs from nouns.

Athabascan family
·North American language areas **10**:671e
·Sapir's reconstruction of protolanguage **13**:213a
·North American Indian languages classification table **13**:209; map 210

Nader, Ralph (1934–), U.S. lawyer and consumer advocate, organized and led investigations and studies on issues of public interest in various fields after publication of *Unsafe at Any Speed* (1965), a criticism of the safety engineering of U.S. automobile manufacturers.
·investigative methods **5**:103h

Nāder Khān (d. 1933), king of Afghanistan.
·Afghanistan's internal reforms **1**:176e

Nāder Shāh, also known as ṬAHMĀSP QOLĪ KHĀN (b. NĀDER QOLĪ BEG, Oct. 22, 1688, Kobhān, Iran—d. June 1747, Fatḥābād), Iranian ruler and conqueror, known for the severity of his rule, who created an Iranian empire that

Nāder Shāh, painting by an unknown artist, *c.* 1740; in the Victoria and Albert Museum, London

By courtesy of the Victoria and Albert Museum, London

stretched from the Indus River to the Caucasus Mountains.

Nāder Qolī Beg had an obscure beginning in one of the Turkish tribes loyal to the Ṣafavid *shāh*s of Iran. In 1726, as head of a group of bandits, he led 5,000 followers in support of the Ṣafavid *shāh* Ṭahmāsp II, who was seeking to regain the throne his father had lost four years earlier. Nāder Qolī Beg gained success after success in battle and rapidly acquired power. Restored to the throne, Ṭahmāsp II proved ineffective, and in 1732 Nāder Qolī Beg deposed him and put Ṭahmāsp's infant son on the throne. Four years later the young *shāh* died, and Nāder Qolī Beg arranged for his own ascendancy as Nāder Shāh.

In February 1739, after capturing several cities of the Mughal Empire of northern India, Nāder Shāh moved against the main Mughal armies at Karnāl, India. He won the battle and entered Delhi, returning to Iran with vast amounts of loot, including the fabulous Peacock Throne and the Koh-i-noor diamond. He then led successful campaigns against the Russians and the Ottoman Turks.

Nāder Shāh was always harsh and ruthless, but these traits became more pronounced as he grew older. He even ordered the blinding of his own son when he suspected the young man of plotting against him. The economy of Nāder Shāh's empire began to strain under the cost of his continual military campaigns. His attempts to convert his subjects from the Shiʿah sect of Islām to a form of the Sunnī sect that he supported met with resistance. His suspicions continued to grow, and wherever he went he had people tortured and executed. In the end, he was assassinated by his own troops.

War and conquest were Nāder Shāh's sole talents. He is often called the "Napoleon of Iran."
·Afghanistan and Persian conquest **1**:174f
·career and conquests **9**:936c
·Indian conquest and sack of Delhi **9**:385g
·Iranian empire and military emphasis **9**:859e
·Iraq invasion failure **11**:995a
·Teheran bazaar and wallr **18**:57h
·Uzbek political decline **18**:795c
·victory over Mughal Empire **8**:663d

NADH, abbreviation for HYDROGENATED NAD, chemically reduced form of the co-enzyme, nicotinamide-adenine dinucleotide (NAD).
·chemical conversion of alcohol **1**:438g

Nadia, district, Jalpaiguri division, West Bengal state, India. Its area (1,514 sq mi [3,921 sq km]) consists of vast alluvial plains lying at the head of the Gangetic Delta; they are somewhat elevated in the north. It is intersected by numerous rivers, streams, and swamps. The Bhāgīrathi, Jalangi, and Mātabhānga—called the Nadia streams—are slowly dying because of the eastward shift of the Ganges; and the district's arable lands, deprived of fertilizing silt, have lost their fertility. A proposed water-control system across the Ganges at Farakka may help in resuscitation. Autumn and winter rice are grown in loamy soil where water is available; jute, legumes, sugarcane, and oilseeds are other important crops. Sugarcane processing is an important industry. Nadia's cottage industries, notably cotton weaving, once flourished; great quantities of fabrics were purchased by the British East India Company. Robert Clive's victory (1757) over the Nawab of Bengal at Plassey resulted in progressive English annexation of Bengal. In 1947 Nadia's eastern sector was partitioned to form the district of Kushtia in East Pakistan (now Bangladesh). Nadia district headquarters are in Krishnanagar (*q.v.*). Pop. (1971 prelim.) 2,229,022. E

Nadia (town, India): *see* Nabadwīp.

Nadiād, town, Kaira district, Gujarāt state, west central India, in the lowlands between the Vindhya Range and the Gulf of Cambay. It is a major industrial and commercial centre and a road and rail junction. Pop. (1971 prelim.) 108,268.
22°42′ N, 72°52′ E
·map, India **9**:278

nadir (astronomy): *see* zenith.

Nadoja (South Indian poet): *see* Pampa.

Nador, town and province of northeastern Morocco. The town, built by the Spaniards, is a small port on the lagoon of Sebkha Bou Areg and a trading centre for local fruits and livestock. It is linked to the Spanish *plaza* of Melilla, 9 mi (15 km) north, by road and railway. Nador province, with an area of 2,367 sq mi (6,130 sq km), comprises the eastern part of the former Spanish Morocco. It embraces an arid coastal plain of pastureland and a limited amount of irrigated cropland. Southwest of Nador, near Segangane, revitalized iron mines are worked by a Spanish company. Pop. (1971) town, 32,490; province, 480,517.
·area and population table **12**:444; map **12**:448
·map, Morocco **12**:446

Naemorhedus goral (mammal): *see* goral.

Nae-ong (Korean painter): *see* Yi Chŏng.

Naess, Arne (1912–), Norwegian philosopher.
·skepticism as mental health **16**:833h

Næstved, city, Storstrøms *amtskommune* (county), southern Sjælland (Zealand), Denmark, on the Suså (river). It originated around a Benedictine monastery, founded in 1135. The monks moved at the end of the 12th century, and the town developed as a market centre for southern Sjælland. Chief among its medieval landmarks are St. Peder Kirke (church), the only survival of the monastery; the later Gothic St. Morten's Kirke; and the Helligåndshuset, the remains of a medieval hospital, now a museum. North of Næstved is the Herlufsholm school for boys (founded in 1565), resembling an English public (*i.e.*, "private") school, with a 12th-century chapel. Industries include paper, glass, pottery, and textiles. A small harbour, constructed in 1938, supports fishing. Pop. (latest census) city, 31,008; (1971 est.) mun., 42,024.
55°14′ N, 11°46′ E

Naevius, Gnaeus (b. *c.* 270 BC, ancient Capua, Italy—d. *c.* 199, 202, or 204 BC, Utica, modern Utique, Tunisia), second of a triad of early Latin epic poets and dramatists, between Livius Andronicus and Ennius, who was the originator of historical plays (*fabulae praetextae*) based on Roman historical or legendary figures and events. Titles of two *praetextae* are known, *Romulus* and *Clastidium*, the latter celebrating the victory of M. Claudius Marcellus in 222 and probably produced at his funeral games in 208.

During 30 years of competition with Livius, Naevius produced half a dozen tragedies and more than 30 comedies, many known only by their titles. Some were translated from Greek plays, and in adapting them he created the Latin *fabula palliata* (from *pallium*, type of Greek cloak), perhaps being the first to introduce song and recitative, transferring elements from one play into another, and adding variety to the metre. He instilled into the form his own critical remarks on Roman daily life and politics, the latter leading to his imprisonment and perhaps exile. Many of the comedies used the stereotypes of character and plot and the apt and colourful language later characteristic of Plautus. *Tarentilla*, one of his most famous plays, clearly foreshadows the Plautine formula with its vivid portrayal of Roman lowlife, intrigue, and love relationships.

Naevius chronicled the events of the First Punic War (264–261) in his *Bellum Poenicum*, relying for facts upon his own experience in the war and on oral tradition at Rome. It presents the wanderings of Aeneas, including his sojourn with Dido at Carthage, as a cause of the war between Rome and that city. The scope of the tale and the forceful diction qualify it as an epic, showing a marked advance in originality beyond the *Odusia* of Livius and a probable influence upon the *Annales* of Ennius and on Virgil's *Aeneid*.

·Latin epic on Punic Wars **15**:1098g
·Roman comedy development **10**:1096c
·Roman native drama development **18**:220g

Nafana, a Voltaic tribe of West Africa of the Senufo cluster.

·mask form and ritual use **1**:260c

nafcillin, brand name UNIPEN, an antibiotic that is stable in stomach acid, is penicillinase-resistant, and has the same antimicrobial spectrum as penicillin G.

·antibiotic stability, action, and spectrum **1**:988b

Näfels, Battle of (April 9, 1388), a major victory for the Swiss Confederation in the first century of its struggle for self-determination against Habsburg overlordship. Though the catastrophic defeat of the Austrians at Sempach in 1386 was followed by a truce, hostilities against the Habsburgs were subsequently continued by the rebellious men of Glarus, a district that had adhered to the confederacy in 1352 but had been restored to the Habsburgs in 1355. After the expiration of the truce (February 1388), the Habsburg Albert III of Austria advanced with an army against Glarus; but the rebels, reinforced by troops from Schwyz, first checked the invasion by holding the heights above Näfels, at the northern entrance to their valley, and then repelled it by a bloody counterattack. Further Swiss offensives achieved more successes, and in April 1389 a seven-year truce was ratified by Duke Albert, who allowed the Swiss to keep their alliances and their conquests intact.

Nafūd, an-, English GREAT NAFŪD, desert, Saudi Arabia.

·area, features, and dune form **1**:1054a; map 1053

Nafūsah, Jabal, also transliterated GEBEL NEFUSA, hilly limestone massif of western Libya that extends in a west–easterly arc between the Gefara Plain and the Ḥammādah al-Ḥamrā'. With heights ranging from 1,500 to 3,000 ft (460 to 910 m), it runs latitudinally for 119 mi (191 km) from the Tunisian border to the Meshar Hills, where it is cut short by the Kiklah Trough, and then gradually turns northeast for 93 mi, ending in hills near the Mediterranean coast at al-Khums. It is crowned by a plateau from 12 to 16 mi wide, covered by scrub bush and grasses on the north and barren basalt and lava rock on the south. Rainfall varies from 2 to 16 in. (51 to 406 mm). There is scattered cultivation (olives, figs, grains, tobacco, esparto grass [for cordage, shoes, and paper], and legumes) and grazing of nomadic herds. Towns include Nālūt, Jādū, Yafran, and Gharyān.
31°50′ N, 12°00′ E

·size, agriculture, and people **10**:876b *passim* to 879f

nāga (Sanskrit: "serpent"), in Hindu and Buddhist mythology a class of semidivine beings, half-human and half-serpentine. They are considered to be a strong, handsome race who can assume either human or wholly serpentine form, potentially dangerous, but in some ways superior to men. They live in an underground kingdom called Nāga-loka, or Pātāla-loka, which is filled with resplendent palaces, beautifully ornamented with precious gems. Brahmā is said to have relegated the *nāga*s to the nether regions when they became too populous on earth and to have commanded them to bite only the truly evil or those destined to die prematurely. They are also associated with waters—rivers, lakes, seas, and wells—and are generally regarded as guardians of treasure. The *Mahābhārata* ("Great Epic of the Bharata Dynasty") and the *Purāṇas* ("ancient stories"; medieval sacred encyclopaedic works) include many tales of *nāga*s; their traditional enmity with the bird Garuḍa; the origin of their forked tongue, which was split when they licked up the drink of immortality, the *amṛta*, from the sharp-bladed *kuśa* grass; their struggles with Janamejaya, who attempted to destroy them in a sacrificial fire. Three notable *nāga*s are Śeṣa (or Ananta), who in the Hindu myth of creation is said to support Viṣṇu-Nārāyaṇa as he lies on the cosmic ocean and on whom the created world exists; Vāsuki, who was used as a churning rope to churn the cosmic ocean of milk; and Takṣaka, the tribal chief of the snakes.

Nāga couple, stone statue from Bihār Sharīf, Bihār, India, 9th century AD; in the Indian Museum, Calcutta
Pramod Chandra

The *nāgī*s, according to tradition, are serpent princesses of striking beauty, and the dynasties of Manipur in northeastern India, the Pallavas in southern India, and the ruling family of Funan (ancient Indochina) are among those that traced their origin to the union of a human and a *nāgī*.

In modern Hinduism the birth of the serpents is celebrated on Nāga-pañcami in the month of Srāvaṇa (July–August). The snake goddess Manasā is a popular folk divinity in Bengal, and snakes are particularly associated with the god Śiva (Shiva), who wears them round his neck and as a girdle. Stone tablets, called *nāgalkal*s, carved with an entwined serpent pair or a half-snake, half-human mother supporting children are often set up under trees as votive offerings by couples desiring offspring.

In Buddhism, *nāga*s are often represented as door guardians or, as in Tibet, as minor deities. The snake king Mucalinda who sheltered the Buddha from rain for seven days while he was deep in meditation is beautifully depicted in the 9th–13th century Mon-Khmer Buddhas of Siam and Cambodia. In Jainism, the Tirthaṅkara (Jaina Saviour) Pārśvanātha is always shown with a canopy of snake hoods above his head.

In art, *nāga*s are represented in a fully zoomorphic form, as hooded cobras but with from one to seven or more heads; as human beings with a many-hooded snake canopy over their heads; or as half-human, with the lower part of their body below the navel coiled like a snake and a canopy of hoods over their heads. Often they are shown in postures of adoration looking on as one of the major gods or heroes is shown accomplishing some miraculous feat.

·animal worship and polytheism **14**:786a
·Buddhist use of nāga symbols **3**:420g
·Indonesian artistic representations **17**:272b; illus.
·Karkoṭa dynasty name and artistic use **17**:131e
·myths in North and South India **8**:931h
·Southeast Asian diverse representations **17**:233c

Nāga, group of tribes inhabiting the Nāga Hills that separate the Indian state of Assam from Burma. They include 15 or more tribes of mixed origin, varying cultures, and very different physique and appearance. The numerous Nāga languages are tonal and agglutinative, belonging to the Tibeto-Burman group; within each language area almost every village has its own dialect. Different groups of Nāga communicate in Assamese, or sometimes in English and Hindi. The largest tribes are the Ao, Sangtam, Angami, Lhota, Chakhesang, Chang, Konyak, Rengma, Phom, Yimchungr, Khienmungan, Kalyo-Kenyu, Tangkhul, Zeliang, and Old Kuki.

Their small villages are placed on spurs of the hillsides, near water and easily defended. Small patches of hillside are cleared, the chief crop being rice; some of the more advanced tribes practice terracing. Manufactures and the arts among the Nāga include weaving (on simple tension looms), dyeing, pottery, blacksmith's work, and rough wood carving. Nāga fishermen are noted for the use of intoxicants to kill or incapacitate the fish.

Political organization has ranged from autocracy (Konyak) through gerontocracy (Ao) to purest democracy (Angami). Descent is traced through the paternal line.

Since the 1890s a substantial minority of the Nāga has been Christianized. The Nāga Baptist Christian Convention has a large local membership.

In response to nationalist political sentiment among the Nāga tribes, the government of India created the state of Nāgāland in 1961. Its population in 1971 was about 516,000.

·cannibalism and Christianity **9**:284d
·descent and clan group pattern **17**:127a; map 126
·geographic distribution map **2**:194
·Indian Mongoloid groups' distribution **14**:846g
·language, population, and culture **11**:452b
·Nāgārjuna's tie to South Indian peoples **12**:808d
·name associations and tribes **12**:805g

Naga, capital, Camarines Sur province, southeastern Luzon, Philippines, on the Bicol River, south of San Miguel Bay. Founded in 1573 as Nueva Caceres by the Spaniards, who built the church of Nuestra Señora de (Our Lady of) Peñafrancia, the patroness of Bicolandia (the Bicol Peninsula), it remains an important centre of Spanish culture. The city is a regional commercial centre, serving the densely populated agricultural Bicol Plain. It is a major stop on the Manila-South Railroad, a major road junction, and it has an airport. The University of Nueva Caceres (1948) is in Naga, which also has a large cathedral and is the seat of a bishopric. Inc. city, 1948. Pop. (1970) 79,846.
10°12′ N, 123°45′ E
·map, Philippines **14**:233

Nāgabhaṭa II (reigned *c.* 793–833), king of the Rāṣṭrakūṭa dynasty of India.
·conquest and loss of Kannauj **9**:361c

Nāga Hills, form part of the complex mountain barrier on the frontiers of India and Burma. A section of the northern Arakan Yoma system, they reach a height of 9,890 ft (3,014 m) in Mt. Jāpṿo near the border with Manipur state. Until 1961 they constituted the Nāga Hills district of Assam and are now part of Nāgāland. The hills receive a heavy monsoon rainfall and are naturally clothed with dense evergreen forest. The area is sparsely inhabited by Nāgas, former headhunters who were subdued (1865–80) by the British.
26°00′ N, 95°00′ E
·landscape and environment **11**:451h
·Nāgāland's physical geography **12**:806c

Nagai Kafū, real name NAGAI SŌKICHI (b. Dec. 3, 1879, Tokyo—d. April 30, 1959, Tokyo), novelist strongly identified with Tokyo and its immediate premodern past. Rebellious as a youth, he failed to finish his university studies and was sent abroad to the United States from 1903 to 1907 and to France in 1907 and 1908. Before he left, he had produced three novels, which he considered to be derived from the French naturalistic novelist Émile Zola. After he returned to Japan he continued to be a student and translator of French literature, principally the Romantic and Symbolist poets. He also did his most important writing at this time, work which is likely to seem, in its lyricism and delicate eroticism, nearer 19th-century Japanese literature than French. The lyricism is particularly apparent in *Sumidagawa* (1909; *The River Sumida*, 1965), a novelette about the disappearance of the gracious past in the city of Tokyo. For some years after his return, Kafū was a professor at Keiō University and a leader of the literary world. After his resignation in 1916, a stronger note of rancour at what the modern world had done to the old city came into his work. After *Ude Kurabe* (1917; *Geisha in Rivalry*, 1963), a caustic study of the geisha's world, he fell into almost complete silence, broken in the next two decades by dry sketches of graceless modern successors to the classical geisha. Only in 1937, with *Bokutō Kidan* (*A Strange Tale from East of the River*, 1965), did he return to the nostalgic, lyrical vein of his post-French influence days. A book-length study, *Kafū the Scribbler* (1965), by E. Seidensticker, also includes a number of translations.

Nagai Kafū
By courtesy of Nippon Kindai Bungaku-kan, Tokyo

nāgakals (Hindi: "serpent-stones"), in Indian iconography, stone tablets depicting *nāgā*s, or serpents.
·Hindu folk practices **8**:899f

nagal, Punjabi comic sketch.
·prop and performance **17**:170c

Nāgāland 12:805, state of the Republic of India, bordering Burma on the east and bounded by the states of Manipur (south) and Assam (west and northwest). A small section in the north borders on the union territory of Arunachal Pradesh, formerly North East Frontier Agency. Nāgāland has an area of 6,366 sq mi (16,488 sq km). Its capital is Kohīma. Pop. (1971 prelim.) 515,561.
The text article covers Nāgāland's history, physical geography, population, administration, social conditions, economy, communications, and cultural life.
REFERENCES in other text articles:
·area and population table **9**:288
·Assam's internal divisions **2**:207f

nagana, a form of trypanosomiasis (*q.v.*) chiefly of cattle and horses, caused by several species of the protozoan *Trypanosoma*. The disease, which occurs in southern and Central Africa, is carried from animal to animal chiefly by tsetse flies. Signs of infection include fever, muscular wasting, anemia, and swelling of tissues (edema). There is discharge from eyes and nose. First the hindlegs and then other parts of the body become paralyzed. The spleen, lymph nodes, and liver become enlarged, and the spinal cord is affected.
Other forms of trypanosomiasis transmitted by flies include surra (found in Southeast Asia and Africa), a disease of cattle and horses caused by *T. evansi*; and mal de caderas, caused by *T. equinum* and occurring in South America.
·beef and dairy cattle diseases **10**:1281f
·diseases of animals, table 10 **5**:879

Nagano, landlocked prefecture (*ken*), central Honshu, Japan, occupying an area of 5,071 sq mi (13,133 sq km). Most of the prefecture is more than 2,600 ft (790 m) in elevation, and 15 peaks, mostly volcanic, rise to more than 9,800 ft. Such large rivers as the Tenryū-gawa, Kiso-gawa, Chikuma-gawa, and Shinano-gawa have been harnessed for hydroelectricity.

The Buddhist Zenkō Shrine, Nagano, Japan
Photos Pack—EB Inc.

Most of the population occupies small mountain basins (Suwa, Matsumoto, Ina, Hida, Zenkoji), in which sericulture and apple raising are specialities. Forest land, one-third in national forests, is a rich resource. Industry is based on sericulture.
Nagano, the largest city and capital of the prefecture, is located in the Zenkoji Basin. Formerly known as Zenkoji, it dates from the 7th century. It is now an important commercial and education centre, housing two universities. The Zenkō-ji (Zenko Shrine) is said to house the oldest Buddha image of its kind in Japan. Pop. (1970) city, 285,355; prefecture, 1,956,917.
·area and population, table 1 **10**:45
·prefecture map, Japan **10**:36

Nagano Osami (b. 1880, Kōchi, Japan—d. Jan. 5, 1947, Tokyo), admiral who planned and ordered the attack on the U.S. naval base at Pearl Harbor, Dec. 7, 1941, that triggered U.S. involvement in World War II. In 1913, as a language officer in the U.S., Nagano studied law at Harvard University. Returning to Japan, he became known as an expert on the U.S. As naval attaché in Washington between 1920 and 1923, he attended the Washington Conference (1921–22), in which the big powers agreed to a détente in the Pacific and fixed an arithmetic ratio of 5:5:3 for (respectively) the U.S., Britain, and Japan on the number and total tonnage of capital ships that each country could possess. When the big powers resumed their naval disarmament talks at the London Naval Conference of 1930, Nagano attended as a member of the Japanese general staff. He was the chief Japanese delegate at the London Naval Conference of 1935–36. The results of these conferences convinced Nagano and the Japanese military staff that international agreements would not allow Japan sufficient military power to guarantee her national security, and Japan began to build up her army and navy. Nagano became naval minister in 1936 and naval chief of staff in April 1941, in which capacity he planned and executed the Pearl Harbor attack. This attack, which put a large part of the U.S. Pacific fleet out of action, destroyed more than 80 planes on the ground, and inflicted more than 3,300 military casualties (of whom some two-thirds were fatalities), cost the Japanese fewer than 100 men, 29 planes, and 5 midget submarines. Nagano's reputation rose after Pearl Harbor, but later reverses caused his dismissal in February 1944. After the end of the war he assumed responsibility for the Pearl Harbor attack before the international military tribunal but died while on trial.

Nagaoka, city, Niigata Prefecture (*ken*), Honshu, Japan, on the middle reaches of the Shinano-gawa (Shinano River). A castle town in the 1600s, it prospered with the discovery of the Higashiyama oil well in the early 20th century. Despite heavy damage suffered during World War II, the city continued to grow, its industries producing chemicals, machinery, and processed foods. Nagaoka is a hub of rail and road transportation and serves as a base for the popular ski grounds on nearby Yūkyū-zan (Mt. Yūkyū). Pop. (1970) 162,262.
37°27′ N, 138°51′ E

Nagaoka, Hantaro (1865–1950) Japanese physicist who, in 1904, proposed that an atom is a miniature planet, with mutually repellent electrons circling in orbit about a central, positive nucleus.
·atomic model concept **2**:336b

Nāgappattinam, formerly NEGAPATTAM, seaport, Thanjāvūr district, Tamil Nadu state, southern India, on the Bay of Bengal. An ancient port known to have traded with Europe in Greek and Roman times, it became a Portuguese and later a Dutch colony. Its influence declined with the growth of Madras, 250 mi (400 km) north. Now the third largest port in Tamil Nadu, it is expanding rapidly. Industry includes ship repair, fishing, steel rolling, and the manufacture of metal goods. Pop. (1971 prelim.) 68,015.
10°46′ N, 79°50′ E

Nāgarakertāgama, Javanese epic poem written in 1365 by Prapanca. Considered the most important work of the vernacular litera-

ture that developed in the Majapahit era, the poem venerates King Hayam Wuruk (reigned 1350–89) and gives a detailed account of life in his kingdom. It also includes information about King Kertanagara (reigned 1268–92), great-grandfather of Hayam Wuruk.
·history of Kertanagara's reign **10**:435h
·indigenous style and significance **17**:235g
·Javanese poetry as art form and worship **9**:480g *passim* to 482b

Nagar Haveli (India): *see* Dādra and Nagar Haveli.

Nāgarī (Indian script): *see* Devanāgarī.

Nāgārjuna **12**:808 (b. *c*. AD 150—d. *c*. 250), Indian Buddhist monk-philosopher and founder of the Mādhyamika (Middle Path) school whose clarification of the concept of *śūnyatā* ("emptiness") is regarded as an intellectual and spiritual achievement of the highest order. He is recognized as a patriarch by several later Buddhist schools.

Abstract of text biography. Little is known of Nāgārjuna's life, which may have included a childhood as the son of a Brahmin (member of the Hindu priestly caste) in South India. His conversion to the Mahāyāna (Greater Vehicle) form of Buddhism marked a critical stage in his life. Several works attributed to him are extant only in Chinese and Tibetan. The two basic works that are substantially his and that have remained available in Sanskrit are *Mūlamadhyamakakārikā* (more commonly known as *Mādhyamika Kārikā*) and *Vigrahavyāvartanī*, both critical analyses of views about the origin of existence, the means of knowledge, and the nature of reality.

REFERENCES in other text articles:
·Mahāyāna Buddhism origins **1**:861g
·pantheist enlightenment via negation **13**:951b
·philosophical contributions **9**:324a
·salvation technique through philosophy **3**:406g
·skepticism about reality of world **16**:833d
·teachings and school **3**:381f
·writings and philosophic system **3**:436d

Nāgār junakoṇḍa, ruins of an ancient university in Andhra Pradesh, India.
·relief sculpture style **17**:192d

Nagasaki, prefecture (*ken*), northwestern Kyushu, Japan, facing the East China Sea. Its area of 1,582 sq mi (4,098 sq km) includes the islands of Tsushima, Iki, Hirado, and the Gotō-rettō (*q.v.*; Gotō Group). The prefecture has an irregular shape, with rounded Shimabara-hantō (Shimabara Peninsula) in the southeast; Nomo-saki (Cape Nomo) and Nishisonoki-hantō enclose Ōmura-wan (Ōmura Bay) in the southeast. Dominated by mountains, the limited agricultural land is intensively cultivated with rice, sweet potatoes, and mandarin oranges. Thriving fisheries support a seafood processing industry. Coal is mined, but there is little heavy industry except for the shipbuilding of Nagasaki, the prefectural capital, and the naval base of Sasebo. Important towns include Isahaya, at the head of the Shimabara-hantō. Pop. (1970) 1,570,245.
·area and population, table 1 **10**:45

Nagasaki, capital and largest city, Nagasaki Prefecture (*ken*), western Kyushu, Japan, at the mouth of the Urakami-gawa (Urakami River) where it empties into Nagasaki-kō (Nagasaki Harbour). The harbour is comprised of a narrow, deep-cut bay, formed at the meeting point of Nomo-saki (Cape Nomo; south) and Nishisonoki-hantō (Nishisonoki Peninsula; northwest). The city is shaped like an amphitheatre, its crooked streets and tiered houses clinging to the hillsides that enclose the inner bay. Reclaimed land at bayside and the Urakami Basin provide some level land.

Nagasaki's charm derives from its history as Japan's oldest open port. Portuguese traders

Oura Catholic Church, Nagasaki City, Japan
Shiro Shirahata—Bon

first arrived in the mid-16th century, and the port continued to trade with foreign countries throughout the centuries. Roman Catholicism was introduced by the Portuguese, and the city still houses the largest Japanese Christian community. In the 19th century Nagasaki became a leading East Asian coaling station and served as the winter port of the Russian Asiatic fleet until 1903. In the early 20th century the city became a major shipbuilding centre, and on Aug. 9, 1945, it was struck by an atomic bomb dropped by the United States Air Force. Since World War II, the city has been rebuilt. It is now an important tourist centre; its industry is based upon its large shipyards, which are grouped along the western and inner parts of the harbour.

Nagasaki contains numerous historic sites. The Sofuku-ji (Chinese temple; 1629) is a fine example of Chinese Ming dynasty architecture, whose residents include Chinese Buddhist monks. The Oura Catholic Church, built in Gothic style, was erected (1864) to commemorate the execution of 26 Christian saints in 1597. A fine view of Nagasaki-kō is offered by the Glover Mansion, the home of a 19th-century British merchant and reputed to be the site of Puccini's opera, *Madama Butterfly*. Peace Park, on the Urakami-gawa, was established in memory of the destruction caused by the atomic bombing. Pop. (1970) 421,114.
32°48′ N, 129°55′ E
·atomic bomb destruction **13**:326a
·map, Japan **10**:36
·Truman bombing justification **18**:725e
·Western artistic contact exclusiveness **19**:239g
·World War II bomb destruction **19**:1012h

Nāgasena, a possibly legendary Buddhist sage, and one of the main characters in the dialogue *Milindapañha* ("Questions of Milinda").
·Buddhist noncanonical Pāli literature **3**:435c

nāgasuram, Indian double-reed instrument related to the shawm (*q.v.*) and oboe.

Nagata Tokuhon (1513–1630), Japanese physician.
·treatises and theory of therapeutics **11**:826b

Nāgaur, also spelled NAGOR, town and headquarters of Nāgaur district, Rājasthān state, India. Connected by rail and road with Bīkaner and Merta, it is a trade centre for bullocks, wool, hides, and cotton. Industries include handloom weaving and the manufacture of camel fittings, metal utensils, and ivory goods. Nāgaur, a walled town held successively by the 12th-century Hindu ruler of Dillī (Delhi), Pṛthvī Rāj, by the 12th- and 13th-century Muslim conqueror Muḥammad of Ghūr, and by Bīkaner and Jodhpur chieftains, is said to take its name from its traditional founders, the Nāga Rājputs, warrior rulers of the historic region of Rājputāna. The fort contains palaces and a 17th-century mosque built by the Mughal emperor Shāh Jahān (reigned 1628–58). A hospital and two colleges affiliated with the University of Rājasthān are located there.

Nāgaur district (area 6,883 sq mi [17,828 sq km]), formerly part of Jodhpur princely state, comprises a sandy plain bordered east by the Arāvalli Range. Bajra (pearl millet), sorghum (jowar), and pulses are the chief crops, and an excellent breed of oxen is reared. Marble (at Makrāna) and gypsum deposits are worked. Pop. (1971 prelim.) town, 36,433; district, 1,259,447.
·map, India **9**:278

nagauta (Japanese: "long song"), basic lyric musical accompaniment of Japanese Kabuki and classical dances (*buyō*). The genre is found in the Kabuki plays by the mid-17th century, although the term itself is common in much earlier poetic forms.

The standard complete instrumentation of a *nagauta* piece consists of singers; players of the three-stringed, plucked *samisen;* and performers on the three drums and flute found in the *hayashi* ensemble of the earlier Nō theatre. In *nagauta*, the flute player may also use a second bamboo flute (*take-bue*) derived from folk traditions. The drums play both the stereotyped patterns found in the Nō style and more direct imitations of the rhythmic phrases of the *samisen*.

The forms of *nagauta* also reflect interesting combinations of Nō drama structure with Kabuki innovations. In the 19th century, *nagauta* began to be composed and performed in concerts as well as for dance accompaniments. Its repertoire of over 100 standard pieces (usually some 20 minutes in length) and new compositions, together with its several guilds of professional and amateur performers, speaks of its continued viability in the 20th century.
·Kabuki theatre association **12**:687d

na gCopaleen, Myles: *see* O'Brien, Flann.

nageire (Japanese: "thrown in"), in Japanese floral art, the style of arranging that stresses fresh and spontaneous designs adhering only loosely to the classical principles of triangular structure and colour harmony. A single long branch with shorter branches and flowers at the base arranged in a tall upright vase are

Nageire arrangement of iris, camellia, and *Kerria japonica*
By courtesy of the International Society for Educational Information, Tokyo

characteristic of the *nageire* style. *Nageire* was originally a general term meaning all arrangements that differed from the ancient, highly stylized temple art of *rikka*. It was later applied to the lavish large-scale arrangements popular during the 17th century and now refers to flexible designs that reflect the changing patterns of modern life.
·floral decoration style development **7**:418f

Nagel, Ernest (b. Nov. 16, 1901, Nové Město, Bohemia [now in Czechoslovakia]), U.S. philosopher and John Dewey professor of philosophy at Columbia University (1955). Formerly an exponent of logical realism, he later abandoned a realistic ontology for a functional and theoretical philosophy of science. Among his writings are *An Introduction to Logic and Scientific Method* (1934; with Morris R. Cohen); *Logic Without Metaphysics* (1957); and *The Structure of Science: Problems in the Logic of Scientific Explanation* (1961).
·science as propositional system **16**:384g
·vitalism and biophilosophy **12**:873e

Nägeli, Hans Franz (b. *c.* 1497, Aigle, Savoy, now in Switzerland—d. Jan. 9, 1579, Bern), politician and military leader who was the most prominent individual in the public affairs of Bern, Switz., for nearly 40 years.

Captain of the Bernese forces in the campaign against the adventurer-robber baron Giangiacomo Medici, lord of Musso (1531) and also during the occupation of the frontier of the canton of Valais in the second Kappel War (an intercantonial religious struggle), Nägeli subsequently commanded a Bernese contingent of 6,000 men in the liberation of the canton of Vaud from Savoyard control (January 1536) and led an expedition against the bishop of Lausanne (March 1536) that freed the legendary François Bonivard from the castle of Chillon. Between 1540 and 1568 he served as chief magistrate for Bern. He determined much of the canton's foreign policy and served as Bernese representative on numerous diplomatic missions.

Nägeli, Karl Wilhelm von (b. March 27, 1817, Kilchberg, Switz.—d. May 10, 1891, Munich), botanist famous for his work on plant cells.

Nägeli's earliest training was from the German nature-philosopher Lorenz Oken, whom he left to study botany under Augustin Pyrame de Condolle at the University of Geneva. He studied philosophy again at the University of Berlin but then resumed his botanical studies under Matthias Jakob Schleiden at the University of Jena (now in East Germany). Nägeli began his teaching career as a professor at the universities of Zürich, Freiburg, and Munich.

At the age of 25 he wrote a paper on pollen formation of seed and flowering plants and described cell division with great accuracy. He noted what he called transitory cytoblasts, which later were identified as chromosomes. He also witnessed cell division in unicellular algae and investigated the process of osmosis in them. In 1844 he discovered the antheridia (reproductive structures in which male sex cells develop) and the spermatazoids of the fern.

Nägeli introduced into botany the concept of meristem, by which he meant a group of plant cells always capable of division. This led him to the first accurate account of apical cells (the initial point of longitudinal growth), which he erroneously believed to be the main site of meristematic growth in all plants. In 1858 he demonstrated the importance of the sequence of the cell divisions in determining the form of the plant parts. While studying different forms of starch, he formulated the hypothetical micella (unit of structure); this concept became the foundation for understanding the structure of starch grains.

Nägeli and Hugo von Mohl, a German physician and botanist, were the first to distinguish the plant cell wall from the inner contents, which von Mohl named protoplasm in 1846. Nägeli believed that cells received their hereditary characters from a certain part of the protoplasm, which he called idioplasma. He also demonstrated, by chemical analyses, the presence of nitrogenous matter in the protoplasm.

Nägeli, a stubborn man who held tenaciously to such ideas as spontaneous generation, did not accept environmental factors acting on variations in species, believing instead that evolution occurred in jumps. He possibly anticipated the discovery of mutation. According to Nägeli, species variation was caused internally by an inherent force that drove evolutionary changes in a particular nonrandom direction, such as increased size. His beliefs led him to reject a paper sent him by the monk Gregor Mendel, which when rediscovered 40 years later, served as the source of the Mendelian laws of inheritance.
·biological sciences development **2**:1025a
·misjudgment of Mendel's research **11**:899d

Nāgercoil, administrative headquarters of Kanniyākumāri district, Tamil Nadu state, southern India, situated west of the Aramboli Gap in the Western Ghāts. It controls the major routes between Madras and Trivandrum and is a commercial centre for a rich agricultural area. Its name, meaning Snake Temple, indicates the early significance of the town's Śaiva temple.

Although historically a part of the Hindu kingdom of Travancore, Nāgercoil has developed as an important Christian centre. Its expanding industries include cotton and rice milling, motor repairing, and the manufacture of rubber goods using raw material from Kerala state. The town also houses four colleges affiliated with Madurai University. Nine miles west is the tourist centre of Padmanābhapuram palace, former residence of the Travancore raja. Pop. (1971 prelim.) 141,207.
8°11′ N, 77°26′ E
·map, India **9**:278

Naginimārā, town, Nāgāland, India.
26°44′ N, 94°51′ E
·Nāgāland's coal resources **12**:807f

nagoda: *see* Croato-Hungarian compromise of 1868.

Nagor (India): *see* Nāgaur.

Nagorno-Karabakh autonomous oblast, administrative division of the Azerbaijan Soviet Socialist Republic, occupies an area of 1,700 sq mi (4,400 sq km) on the northern flank of the Karabakh Range of the Little Caucasus. The environments vary from steppe on the Kura lowland through dense forest of oak, hornbeam, and beech on the lower slopes and birchwood and alpine meadows higher up, to the peaks, which culminate in Mt. Gyamysh (12,217 ft [3,724 m]). The livelihood of the predominantly Azerbaijani and Armenian population is almost entirely agricultural. Vineyards, orchards, and mulberry groves for silkworms are intensively developed in the valleys, together with grain growing; many cattle, sheep, and pigs are kept. Stepanakert (*q.v.*), the administrative centre, and the other small towns process the farm products. Pop. (1970) 149,000.
·Azerbaijan's administrative links **2**:544b

Nagoya 12:809, capital of Aichi Prefecture (*ken*), Japan, and one of Japan's leading industrial cities. It is located at the head of Ise-wan (Ise Bay) in the Chūbu (midland) area of Honshu. Pop. (1970) city, 2,036,053; metropolitan area, 6,574,847.

The text article covers Nagoya's history, the contemporary city, transportation, population, economic life, government, services, education, cultural life, and the communications media.
35°10′ N, 136°55′ E

REFERENCES in other text articles:
·map, Japan **10**:36
·population and prefecture, table 2 **10**:45

Nāgpur, administrative headquarters, Nāgpur district and division, Mahārāshtra state, western India, on the Nāg River. Almost at the geographical centre of India, the present city was founded in the early 18th century by Bakht Buland, a Gond raja. It became the capital of the Bhonsles of the Marāthā confederacy but in 1817 came under British influence. In 1853 the city lapsed into British control and became the capital of the Central Provinces in 1861. The advent of the Great Indian Peninsula Railway in 1867 spurred its development as a trade centre. After Indian independence, Nāgpur became the capital of Madhya Pradesh state. In 1956 it was designated the district headquarters for Mahārāshtra state, alternating with Bombay as the seat of the Mahārāshtra state legislature.

The growing of cotton in the region about the time of the construction of the railway led to the establishment of a large textile mill and signalled the development of the city as an important industrial centre. Since that time the industrial complex has diversified considerably and in the 1970s was expanding to absorb the nearby town of Kāmptee with its factories producing ferromanganese products, transport equipment, and other metal goods. Situated at the junction of road, rail, and air routes from Bombay to Calcutta and from Madras to Delhi, Nāgpur has developed a flourishing trade.

The town is dominated by the British fort built on the twin hills of Sitabuldī in the centre of the city. An educational and cultural centre, the city has a large museum specializing in local exhibits. It is the site of the University of Nāgpur (1923), with 22 branch colleges in the city.

Nāgpur district (3,842 sq mi [9,952 sq km]), in eastern Mahārāshtra state, is an undulating plateau rising northward to the Sātpura Range, from 889–2,142 ft (271–653 m) high. In the northeast are the Rāmtek Hills, site of a temple at Rāmtek that draws many pilgrims to its sacred annual festivals. Interspersing the hills are two major rivers—the Wardha (west) and the Wainganga (east)—both tributaries of the Godāvari. The district is important agriculturally; jowar (a type of millet) and cotton are major crops. The district is especially known for its oranges, which are shipped all over India. Extensive coal and manganese deposits support growing industry.

Nāgpur division includes the districts of Akola, Amraoti, Bhandāra, Buldāna, Chandrapur, Nāgpur, Wardha, and Yeotmāl (*qq.v.*). Pop. (1971 prelim.) town, 866,144; district, 1,941,097.
·Dalhousie's British annexation strategy **5**:439c
·map, India **9**:278

Nags Head, resort town, Dare County, eastern North Carolina, U.S. Pop. (1980) 1,020.
35°57′ N, 75°37′ W
·location and name tradition **13**:231e

Nāg Tibba, range of mountains, India.
30°20′ N, 78°24′ E
·Lesser Himalayan ranges **8**:883b; map 882

Naguabo, municipality, eastern Puerto Rico.
18°12′ N, 65°47′ W
·area and population table **15**:261; map

nagual, personal guardian spirit believed by some Meso-American Indians to reside in an animal or a bird. The word derives from the Nahuatl word *nahualli* ("disguise"), applied to the animal forms magically assumed by sorcerers. The person who was to receive his nagual traditionally went into the forest and slept there; the animal that appeared in his dreams or that confronted him when he awakened would thereafter be his particular nagual. Among many modern Meso-American Indians, it is believed that the first creature to cross over the ashes spread before a newborn baby becomes that child's nagual.

When a man's nagual animal died, that man supposedly also died, and vice versa. The nagual is similar to the West African bush soul and to the ancient Roman individual *genius*.

nagualism (derived from Aztec *naualli*), a widespread belief among North, Central, and South American Indians that certain individuals have the power to transform themselves into animals in order to perform evil activities.

This belief frequently has been confused with another Indian belief that each individual possesses an animal guardian spirit.
- ·Ankermann's link with totemism **18**:532c
- ·polytheism and animal worship **14**:786b
- ·prehistoric religious forms and beliefs **14**:986f *passim* to 988h
- ·totemism on individual basis **18**:530b

Naguib, Mohammad (b. 1901, Khartoum, Sudan), Egyptian army officer and statesman who played a prominent role in the revolutionary overthrow of King Faruk I in 1952.

A professional soldier, Naguib distinguished himself during the Egyptian defeat at the hands of Israel (1948) and won the respect of the Free Officers, a nationalist military group led by Gamal Abdel Nasser. In 1952 the Free Officers helped Naguib win election as president of the officers club in opposition to a man backed by King Faruk. The Free Officers

Naguib
Camera Press—Pix

engineered a coup that overthrew Faruk that July, and they saw Naguib as the man to represent their new regime to the public. Thus in 1953 he became president of the newly formed republic, although he had a more conservative political outlook than did Nasser and many of the other Free Officers. Naguib wanted a speedy return to constitutional government, and he objected to the summary sentences passed on various politicians by the Revolutionary Tribunal. In February 1954 he resigned the presidency, but strong demands by civilian and military groups impelled him to resume the office. Nasser, however, steadily consolidated his own position and became prime minister. Nasser shrewdly acceded to some of Naguib's wishes by allowing the revival of political parties and calling for a constituent assembly to draft a constitution. An assassination attempt was made on Nasser in 1954, in which Naguib was vaguely implicated. Naguib was placed under house arrest and thereafter ceased to play any role in Egyptian politics.
- ·RCC establishment in Egypt **6**:499f
- ·Revolutionary Command Council of 1952 **12**:844g

Nagy, Ferenc (b. Oct. 8, 1903, Bisse, Hung.), statesman who in his brief post-World War II term as premier tried to bring democracy to Hungary. Nagy helped organize the Smallholders' Party, representing the interests of the farming majority, in the early 1920s. He became the party's first general secretary in 1930, served in Parliament from 1939 to 1942, and was jailed by the German Gestapo in 1944. After the war he became premier (1946) of an anti-Fascist coalition government. His policies, however, were thought by the Soviet-backed Communist Party to be too conservative, and he was indicted in 1947 for crimes against the state. Before his trial he succeeded in escaping to Austria and thence to the U.S. His book *The Struggle Behind the Iron Curtain* (1948) recounts his experiences. In 1961–62 he served as chairman of the Assembly of Captive European Nations.

Nagy, Imre (b. June 7, 1896, Kaposvár, Hung.—d. June 16, 1958, Budapest), statesman, independent Communist, and premier of the 1956 revolutionary government whose attempt to establish Hungarian independence from the Soviet Union cost him his life.

Born to a peasant family, Nagy was apprenticed as a locksmith before being drafted in World War I. Captured by the Russians, he joined the Communists and fought in the Red Army. In 1929 he went to live in Moscow, where, as a member of the Institute for Agrarian Sciences, he remained until late 1944. He returned again to Hungary under Soviet occupation and helped establish the post-war government, holding several ministerial posts between 1944 and 1948. Because of his steadfast support of the peasants' welfare, Nagy was excluded from the Communist government in 1949 but was readmitted after public recantation. He became premier (1953–55) and then again was forced out because of his independent attitude, whereupon he took up a teaching post.

During the October 1956 revolution, the anti-Soviet elements turned to Nagy for leadership, and he became once more premier of Hungary. On the last day of the unsuccessful uprising, he appealed to the West for help against the Soviet troops. Treacherously deported to Romania after leaving sanctuary in the Yugoslav embassy, he was returned to Hungary, tried, and put to death.
- ·Communist rule and Hungarian revolution **4**:1024f
- ·reform and revolutionary governments **9**:42e
- ·Soviet support and revolt role **9**:763b

Nagy Alföld (Europe): *see* Great Alföld.

Nagybánya (Romania): *see* Baia Mare.

Nagybánya, Miklós, Horthy de: *see* Horthy de Nagybánya, Miklós.

Nagykanizsa, town, Zala *megye* (county), southwest Hungary. On the Principális-Csatorna (canal) connecting the Zala and Mura rivers, it is 9 mi (15 km) from the Yugoslav frontier. An old strategic fortified settlement, it was located on a wooden pile road that crossed the surrounding marshy terrain. First built in 1300, the fortress was frequently besieged by the Turks between 1532 and 1600. After its capture, the Turks held it until 1690. The parish church was built in 1760 from the stones of a Muslim temple and minaret. The Thury György Múzeum commemorates the legendary captain of Nagykanizsa's fortress in the battles against the Turks. Post-World War II industrialization has been in brewing, glassworking, and the supply of machines and equipment to the petroleum industry. The town is located on important road and rail routes. Pop. (1970 prelim.) 39,411.
46°27′ N, 17°00′ E
- ·map, Hungary **9**:22

Nagykikinda (Yugoslavia): *see* Kikinda.

Nagy Magyar Alföld (Europe): *see* Great Alföld.

Nagyszeben (Romania): *see* Sibiu.

Nagyszombat (Czechoslovakia): *see* Trnava.

Nagy-várad (Romania): *see* Oradea.

Nagyvárad (VÁRAD), **Peace of** (Feb. 24, 1538), secret treaty that ended the Hungarian Civil War (1526–38) by partitioning the country between two contenders for the throne; the unsatisfactory settlement resulted in renewed hostilities, which ended with the Ottoman Turks seizing a large portion of Hungarian territory.

When King Louis II of Hungary (reigned 1516–26) died after the Battle of Mohács (Aug. 29, 1526), Ferdinand, the Habsburg archduke of Austria, claimed the Hungarian throne on the basis of agreements made between his grandfather Maximilian and King Louis (Treaty of Pressburg, 1491; and the Vienna agreement, 1515). The Hungarian Diet, however, refused to recognize Ferdinand as king and elected (Nov. 10, 1526) instead János (John) Zápolya, *voivode* (governor) of Transylvania, and crowned him king. Another Diet at Pozsony, however, formally elected Ferdinand (Dec. 17, 1526).

At the end of 1526 Zápolya actually controlled most of Hungary. But by the following summer Ferdinand had gathered his forces; he drove Zápolya out of Buda in August and was crowned king on Nov. 3, 1527. Zápolya fled to Poland and formed an alliance with the anti-Habsburg Ottoman Turks. At the end of 1528 he re-entered Hungary and conquered Transylvania and a large section of eastern Hungary. With Turkish aid he entered Buda the following year. But when the Turks retreated, Ferdinand, who had been pushed back to Vienna, returned to Hungary (spring 1530) and gained control of the western third of the country.

The conflict continued for years, but neither opponent was able to gain a substantial advantage over his rival. Finally the two kings concluded the Peace of Nagyvárad. Ferdinand recognized Zápolya as ruler of Transylvania, the central portion of Hungary, and the capital city, Buda. Zápolya recognized Ferdinand's control over western Hungary and Croatia and agreed that when he died (Zápolya was much older than Ferdinand), Ferdinand should be his successor. If Zápolya (who was childless in 1538) produced an heir, the child was to receive a duchy in northern Hungary as compensation.

Both parties honoured the treaty until Zápolya's death in 1540. Then Zápolya's supporters claimed the Hungarian throne for Zápolya's infant son, John Sigismund, and Ferdinand laid siege to Buda. The Turkish sultan Süleyman seized this opportunity to invade Hungary. Claiming to be John Sigismund's protector, he occupied Buda (1541) and incorporated the southern and central two-thirds of Hungary into the Ottoman Empire.

In 1547 Süleyman made a truce with Ferdinand, in which the Habsburgs recognized the Turks' conquests and, in return, gained possession of western Hungary. Transylvania and the eastern Hungarian provinces became an autonomous principality within the Turkish Empire (1564).

Naha, capital, Okinawa Prefecture (*ken*), Japan, on Okinawa-jima (Okinawa Island) of the Ryukyu Islands. Long the chief city of the archipelago, it contains the Sogen-ji (Sogen Temple), burial place of the rulers of the early

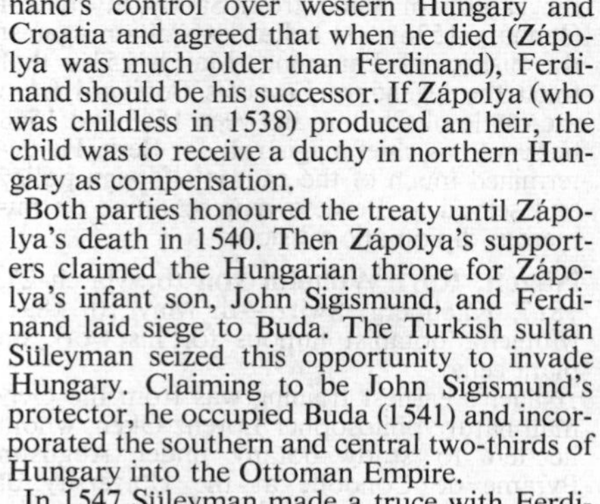

Shureino Gate, destroyed during World War II and rebuilt in 1958, Naha, Japan
Orion Press—FPG

Okinawa kingdom. Shureino Gate is a fine example of Ryukyuan architecture. Naha was the seat of the post-World War II U.S. military and Okinawan governments and became the prefectural capital in 1972. Because of its deepwater port, it is the commercial centre of the Ryukyu Islands chain. Naha is the seat of the University of the Ryukyus. Pop. (1970) 276,380.
26°13′ N, 127°40′ E
- ·map, Japan **10**:36

Nahali language (India): *see* Munda languages.

Nāhan, headquarters town of Sirmūr district, Himachal Pradesh state, northwestern India. It lies south-southeast of Simla, the state capital, at the foot of the Siwālik Range and is a trade centre for agricultural produce and timber. Its industries include handweaving, wood carving, and ironworking. Nāhan was the capital of the Punjab Hill State of Sirmūr during the British rule in India. Pop. (1971) 16,017.
30°33′ N, 77°13′ E
·economy and administration **8**:881e
·map, India **9**:278

Nahariyya, city, northwestern Israel, on the Mediterranean coast halfway between ʿAkko (Acre) and the Lebanese border at Rosh ha-Niqra. The name comes from the Hebrew *nahar* ("river") and is an allusion to the watercourse Naḥal Gaʿaton, which flows through the heart of the city.

Nahariyya was founded in 1934 as an agricultural settlement by German-Jewish refugees. It rapidly developed as a resort, based on a fine sand beach and equable seaside climate. In recent years, industry has developed; principal manufactures are cutting tools and tips, processed foods, and finished textiles. In 1947, during excavation for the foundations of a house, the ruins of a Canaanite temple of the 16th century BC, dedicated to the worship of the goddess Astarte, were found. Inc. 1961. Pop. (1972 prelim.) 24,000.
33°00′ N, 35°05′ E
·map, Israel **9**:1060

Nahāvand, Battle of (642), a military clash in Iran between Arab and Sāsānian forces; a major turning point in Iranian history, the battle ended in disastrous defeat for the Sāsānian armies and paved the way for the Arab conquest, which resulted in the Islāmization of Iran.

At Nahāvand some 30,000 Arab forces, under the command of Nuʿmān, attacked a Sāsānian army alleged to number 150,000 men. The Sāsānian troops, commanded by Fīrūzan, were entrenched in a strong fortified position. After an indecisive skirmish, Nuʿmān pretended to be defeated and withdrew from the battlefield. Fīrūzan then abandoned his position and pursued his foe. The pursuit proved to be a major tactical error because the Sāsānians were forced to fight on unfavourable ground; the Sāsānian army, caught between two mountain defiles, was massacred by the Arabs. Both Nuʿmān and Fīrūzan died in the battle, and Iranian casualties were said to number 100,000.

After the battle the Arabs consolidated their position, and by 651, with the death of Yazdegerd III, the last Sāsānian emperor, their conquest of Iran was completed.
·Irānian Sāsānid collapse **9**:852a

nahcolite, a carbonate mineral, naturally occurring sodium bicarbonate. Its name comes from the letters in its chemical formula, $NaHCO_3$. Notable occurrences are as large concretions in oil shale near Rifle, Colo., and in large quantities in the salt beds at Searles Lake, in California. For detailed physical properties, *see* carbonate minerals.
·composition and evaporites table **6**:1133e

naḥdah al-adabīyah, an-: *see* Arabic literary renaissance.

Nahdatul Ulama, Indonesian political party formed in 1952.
·Indonesian culture-based politics **9**:489e

Naḥḥās Pasha, Muṣṭafā an- (b. June 15, 1876, Samannūd, Egypt—d. Aug. 23, 1965, Alexandria), statesman who, as the leader of the nationalist Wafd party, was a dominant figure in Egyptian politics until the revolution of 1952.

A lawyer by profession, Naḥḥās was appointed a judge in 1904. Soon after World War I he joined the recently formed Wafd, assuming the chairmanship upon Saʿd Zaghlūl's death in 1927. Thus he embarked upon a career during which he was prime minister of Egypt on five occasions. His first term of office as prime minister began in March 1928. His dismissal in June was occasioned by King Fuʾād I's antipathy to constitutional government and the displeasure of the British high commissioner over his introduction of legislation demanded by the extreme nationalist wing of the Wafd. Returned to power in 1929, he resigned in 1930 after differences with the King over limitation of the sovereign's power. Appointed prime minister for the third time in May 1936, he headed the Egyptian delegation to London to negotiate an Anglo-Egyptian treaty of alliance (August 1936) in response to the Italian invasion of Ethiopia.

After Fuʾād's death in April 1936, the young King Farouk I immediately disagreed with Naḥḥās over limiting the king's powers and, significantly, over international policies; he dismissed the Prime Minister in December 1937. At the onset of World War II, Naḥḥās supported the Allied position, while the King vacillated. Naḥḥās' pro-Allied position brought him to power once again in 1942. The British ambassador, armed with an ultimatum and backed by a show of military force, confronted Farouk with the choice of abdicating or appointing Naḥḥās prime minister. Farouk chose the latter, dismissing him in 1944, when the British had withdrawn their support.

Naḥḥās' final term of office began in January 1950, amid signs of collaboration with the King. Once in office he called for the abrogation of the 1936 treaty with Britain and declared Farouk king of Egypt and The Sudan. By this time popular opposition was growing both to the corruption in and policies of the palace and the Wafd, resulting in agitation and disorders in Cairo, on the basis of which Farouk dismissed Naḥḥās in 1952.
·political position and four dismissals **6**:498f

Nahienaena (b. 1815, Keauhou, Hawaii—d. Dec. 30, 1836, Honolulu), princess, the only child of Kamehameha I, conqueror and consolidator of the Hawaiian Islands, and his highest ranking wife, Keopuolani, was sent to a U.S. Protestant missionary school and brought up as a Christian by her mother. Keopuolani's death in 1823 left the child without defense against the influence of both the American missionaries and their opponents, the Hawaiian chiefs, who vied for control over the royal children.

Nahienaena was always close to her brother, Prince Kauikeaouli, later Kamehameha III, and she was more than willing to accede to the chiefs' demands that they marry and produce an heir. The missionaries were vehement in their objections to this incestuous liaison and expelled her from the church when the marriage was consummated in 1834. In 1835 she took Leileiohoku, Chief Kalanimoku's son, as a husband and sought the forgiveness of the missionaries. Her repentance was too late, however, for she was already pregnant with her brother's child. The missionaries ignored her, and her people, now won over to the church, shunned her. She lived in anxious isolation until the child was born, but the infant died shortly after the delivery. Nahienaena never recovered from the shock and, deeply repentant, was at last received into favour by the missionaries shortly before her own death.

Nahj al-balāghah, English THE ROAD OF ELOQUENCE, Arabic work incorporating sayings attributed to the caliph ʿAlī.
·style, contents, and influence **9**:958g

Naḥmanides, real name MOSES BEN NAḤMAN, also called NAHMANIDES RAMBAN (*c.* 1195–1270), Spanish Talmudist, commentator on the Bible, and Jewish religious leader, whose writings reflect Kabbalistic beliefs. After a public disputation held in the presence of King James I, he was exiled from Spain (1263) and settled in Palestine.
·kabbalistic influence on Judaism **10**:186d

Naḥman of Bratslav (1772–1811), teller of Ḥasidic tales.
·folk stories fame and quality **10**:197b

Nahr al-ʿĀṣī (Asia): *see* Orontes River.

Nahr an-Nīl (Africa): *see* Nile River.

Nahua, Middle American Indian population of central Mexico, of which the Aztecs (*see* Aztec) of pre-Conquest Mexico are probably the best known members. The language of the Aztecs, Nahuatl, is spoken by all the Nahua peoples in a variety of dialects (*see* Nahuatl language).

The modern Nahua are an agricultural people; their staple crops are corn (maize), beans, chili peppers, tomatoes, and squash. Also common are maguey (the Mexican century plant), sugarcane, rice, and coffee. The primary farming tools are the wooden plow, hoe, and digging stick. Groups of three or four men may cultivate corn, beans, and squash collectively, using slash-and-burn techniques to clear new land. Chickens and turkeys are also raised, and pigs, goats, and donkeys are often kept. Settlements consist of central villages divided into four sections (barrios) grouped around a central church; each barrio recruits compulsory labour to work village common lands in addition to private farming.

Weaving of cotton and wool is the chief craft among the Nahua, whose skill is great in this respect. Both men and women weave, men usually on the European upright loom and women more often on the native belt loom. Fibres of the maguey plant are also woven to make carrying cloths and sacks. Pottery, rope making, palm-fibre weaving, and adobe brick-making are other crafts practiced.

Nahua houses are usually one-room structures of cane, wood, adobe, or stone, with thatch or tile roofs. Traditional clothing consists of a long wraparound skirt, blouse (*huipil*), sash (*faja*), short triangular cape (*quechquemitl*), and a shawl (*rebozo*) for women; short white cotton pants, cotton shirt, *faja*, woollen overshirt, sandals, and straw hat for men. Ready-made clothes are commonly worn by Nahua men, however, and women may wear dark skirts and white blouses made of commercial cloth.

The social institution of godparenthood (*compadrazgo*) is widely practiced, and parents and godparents are felt to have strong ties. The Nahua are Roman Catholics, oriented toward the patron saints of their villages as well as the Virgin of Guadalupe and various "Cristos" involved in local legend. Witchcraft is commonly believed in, along with a variety

Nahua family threshing near Cholula, Mex.
Shostal Assoc.

of pagan or semipagan supernatural creatures. Pagan religious rituals, except as they relate to witchcraft, are no longer practiced.
·Meso-American Indian distribution map **11**:955
·range and classification **11**:958h

Nahuan languages, subgroup of the Uto-Aztecan languages, including Pochutec, the Nahuatl or Aztec languages, and Pipil; sometimes considered a subfamily co-ordinate with Shoshonean and Sonoran, and sometimes included in the Sonoran subfamily; spoken by over 1,000,000 people throughout southern Mexico and Central America.
·Meso-American languages table **11**:958b; map 957

Nahuatl (AZTEC) **language,** an American Indian language of the Uto-Aztecan family, spoken by about 1,000,000 persons in central and western Mexico. Nahuatl is the most important of the Uto-Aztecan languages; it was the language of the Aztec and Toltec civilizations of Mexico. A large body of literature in Nahuatl, produced by the Aztecs, survives from the 16th century, recorded in an orthography that was introduced by Spanish priests and based on that of Spanish.

The phonology of Classical Nahuatl, the language of the Aztecs, was notable for its use of a *tl* sound produced as a single consonant and for the use of the glottal stop, a sound produced by brief closure of the glottis (the space between the vocal cords). The glottal stop has been lost in some modern dialects—replaced by *h*—and retained in others. The *tl* sound, however, serves to distinguish the three major modern dialects: central and northern Aztec dialects retain the *tl* sound, as can be seen in their name, Nahuatl. Eastern Aztec dialects, around Veracruz, Mex., have replaced the *tl* by *t* and are called Nahuat. Western dialects, spoken primarily in the Mexican states of Michoacán and México, replace the *tl* with *l* and are called Nahual.

Classical Nahuatl used a set of 15 consonants and four long and short vowels. Its grammar was basically agglutinative, making much use of prefixes and suffixes, reduplication (doubling) of syllables, and compound words. Compound words often had syllables such as *ti* and *ka* (called ligatures) to link the compounded forms. Typical of these grammatical processes is *tepē-ti-kpak* "on top of the mountain" from *tepē(tl)* "mountain," *ti* ligature, *(i)kpak* "on top of."
·Aztec religion and history **2**:548b
·Meso-American language groups **11**:935c
·pre- and post-Columbian status and features **11**:961f *passim* to 963d
·pre-Columbian and present use **6**:733g
·subdivisions and dialect status **11**:959d; table 958b

Nahuel Huapí, Lake, largest lake (210 sq mi [544 sq km]) and most popular resort area in Argentina's lake district, lies in the wooded eastern foothills of the Andes at an altitude of 2,516 ft (767 m). Nahuel Huapí (Araucanian Indian for "island of the jaguars") was discovered in 1670 by the Jesuit priest Nicolás Mascardi, who built a chapel on the lake's Huemul Peninsula and established an Indian *reducción* (work mission). The lake is dotted with islands, including Isla Victoria, site of a forestry research station. Its waters are deep (more than 1,400 ft), clear, and cold. It receives small mountain streams and rivers, and the Río Limay, its outlet, joins with the Neuquén and Negro rivers. The lake region, designated in 1934 as a national park (area 3,032 sq mi), was declared a national monument in 1943. Boating, fishing, and mountaineering facilities draw large numbers of tourists.
41°00′ S, 71°32′ W
·map, Argentina **1**:1136

Lake Nahuel Huapí at Puerto Blest, Arg.
Arthur Griffin—EB Inc.

Nahuel Huapi National Park, Spanish PARQUE NACIONAL NAHUEL HUAPÍ, in Río Negro and Neuquén provinces, southwestern Argentina; it encompasses Lago (lake) Nahuel Huapí in the Andes adjacent to the Chilean border. It originated as a reserve in 1903 with a private donation of 37,000 acres (15,000 hectares) and was increased to 106,000 acres in 1907 and to its present 3,057 sq mi (7,918 sq km) in 1922. It became Argentina's first national park in 1934, deriving its name from a Pampa Indian term meaning "Tiger Island." It is a region of dense forests, numerous lakes, rapid rivers, waterfalls, snowclad peaks, and glaciers (including Perito Moreno). Among its peaks are the 11,660-ft (3,554-m) El Tronador (the Thunderer); Cerro Catedral, noted for its skiing; Cerro López; and Cerro Otto. Lago Traful is outstanding for its trout and salmon fishing. Among the wildlife are guanaco, fox, puma, and deer, as well as condor, cormorant, gulls, and numerous other birds. The gateway to the park is San Carlos de Bariloche, the starting point for mountain climbing, hiking, and riding exhibitions and for launch and motoring excursions.
·establishment and features **17**:91a

Nahum (7th century BC), in the Bible, minor Hebrew prophet.
·tirade against Assyria **2**:921c

Nahum, Book of, the seventh of 12 Old Testament books that bear the names of the 12 Minor Prophets. The title identifies the book as an "oracle concerning Nineveh" and attributes it to the "vision of Nahum of Elkosh."

The fall of Nineveh, the capital of the Assyrian Empire, provided the occasion for this prophetic oracle. The mighty Assyrian Empire, which had long been a threat to the smaller nations of the ancient Near East, was a particular menace to the Israelite people. Its decline, therefore, in the face of the Neo-Babylonian power of the Medes and the Chaldeans and its final collapse in the destruction of Nineveh (612 BC) gave the prophet Nahum cause for extolling the turn of events. These events occurred, he announced, because Assyria's policies were not in accord with God's will.

The book contains many types of material, among which are an acrostic hymn, oracles of judgment, satire, a curse, and funeral laments, all of which were brought together and related to the fall of Nineveh. It is possible that the book was used, or parts of it were used, liturgically in the New Year festival celebrated annually in the Temple of Jerusalem.
·Assyria's overthrow prediction **2**:921c

Nāī, or NHĀVĪ (from Sanskrit *snāpitṛ*, "bather"), the barber caste, which is widespread in northern India. Because of the ambulatory nature of his profession, which requires his going to patrons' houses, the barber plays an important part in village life, peddling news (except of death) and matchmaking. Certain castes assign a role to the barber in their domestic rituals. Nevertheless, his social position is low because he also acts as leech and bonesetter and comes in touch with the human body. The caste has a great many endogamous subcastes. Members marry outside their villages; widow remarriage is countenanced. Their marriage and domestic rites generally are regulated by the Brahmins. They dispose of their married dead by means of cremation and of the unmarried by burial or by submersion in the river. The consumption of liquor is permitted, as is the eating of goat flesh, mutton, and venison.

naiad (entomology): *see* nymph.

Naiads (from Greek *naiein*, "to flow"), in Greek mythology, the nymphs of flowing water—springs, rivers, fountains, lakes. The Naiads, appropriately in their relation to freshwater, were represented as beautiful, lighthearted, and beneficent. Like the other classes of nymphs, they were extremely long-lived, although not immortal.
·folk and nature dieties **8**:405b

naidid, any worm of the family Naididae (class Oligochaeta, phylum Annelida), small, aquatic relatives of the earthworm. Naidids occur almost worldwide, chiefly as bottom dwellers in lakes and ponds. Most are microscopic to 2.5 centimetres (about one inch) in length. They usually reproduce by transverse fission; *i.e.*, the body of the adult constricts and separates into two individuals. *Stylaria lacustris*, a cosmopolitan species, occurs in aquatic vegetation; it is 1.8 centimetres (0.7 inch) long. *Paranais* is found in brackish water and in the waters of the Atlantic.

Naidu, Sarojini, *née* CHATTOPADHYAY (b. Feb. 13, 1879, Hyderābād, India—d. March 2, 1949, Lucknow), "the Nightingale of India," a political activist, feminist, poet-writer, and the first Indian woman to be president of the Indian National Congress and to be appointed an Indian state governor.

Sarojini was the eldest daughter of Aghorenath Chattopadhyay, a Bengali Brahmin who was principal of the Nizam's College, Hyderābād. She entered Madras University at the age of 12 and in 1895–98 studied at King's College, London, and later at Girton College, Cambridge. Her marriage in 1898 to M.G. Naidu, a Rājput (warrior caste) who rose to be principal medical officer in the Niẓām's service, was frowned upon by orthodox Hindus as the breaking of Brahminical caste.

After her experience in the suffragist campaign in England, Mrs. Naidu was drawn to India's Congress movement and to Mahatma Gandhi's Non-cooperation campaigns. In 1924 she travelled in East and South Africa in the interest of Indians there, and the following year became the first Indian woman president of the National Congress—having been preceded eight years earlier by the English feminist Annie Besant. She toured North America as a Congress spokesman in 1928–29. Back in India her anti-British activity brought her a number of prison sentences (1930, 1932, and 1942–43). She accompanied Gandhi to London for the inconclusive second session of the Round Table Conference for Indian–British cooperation (1931) and served as a member of the Indian government's delegation to South Africa on the Indian question (1932). On the outbreak of World War II she supported the Congress Party's policies, first of aloofness, then of avowed hindrance to the Allied cause. After the war she took part in the discussions that brought about Indian independence in 1947, when she became governor of the United Provinces (now Uttar Pradesh), a post she retained until her death.

Sarojini Naidu also led an active literary life and attracted Indian intellectuals to her salon in Bombay. Her first volume of poetry, *The Golden Threshold* (1905), was followed by *The Bird of Time* (1912), and in 1914 she was elected a fellow of the Royal Society of Literature. Her collected poems, all of which she wrote in

English, have been published under the titles *The Sceptred Flute* (1928) and *The Feather of the Dawn* (1961).
·poetic works in English **17**:149h

Naigeon, Jean (1757–1832), French painter.
·Monge oil painting illus. **12**:361

Naihāti, town, Twenty-four Parganas district, Jalpaiguri division, West Bengal state, India, just east of the Hooghly River. Connected by road and rail with Calcutta, it has milling plants for jute, rice, paper, and oilseed, as well as paint manufacture. It was constituted a municipality in 1869, but its area was curtailed by the separation of Bhātpāra (*q.v.*) municipality in 1899 and Hālisahar (*q.v.*) municipality in 1903. Naihāti has a college affiliated with the University of Calcutta. Pop. (1971) 82,080.
22°54′ N, 88°25′ E

nail, among primates, horny plate that grows on the back of each finger or toe at its outer end. The nail corresponds to the claw, hoof, or talon of other vertebrates. *Major ref.* **16**:843g
·diagnosis of pathological changes **5**:688c
·embryonic origins and development **6**:749h
·inflammation and malformation **16**:849h
·structure and derivation **9**:668e

nail, metallic fastener of various sizes, pointed at one end and flattened to a head at the other, designed to be hammered into place for fastening wood and wood products.
·cable wire products and production **15**:1149e

nailhead, projecting ornamental molding (*q.v.*) resembling the head of a nail, used in early Gothic architecture. Nailheads were used to fasten nailwork to a door, which was often studded with them decoratively, as well. They show great variety in design and are sometimes very elaborate.

On the few original doors of Norman style that still exist, the nailheads fix the hinges and iron scrollwork on the front; although the nails are usually not large on such doors, the heads sometimes project conspicuously. In the 16th and 17th centuries, the hammer-shaped knockers of doors usually struck upon a large-headed nail.

Locks also, especially on the outsides of doors, are very frequently decorated with ornamental patterns of tracery and studs, formed by the heads of the nails as well as sometimes with small moldings.

A nailhead molding is a type common in Norman architecture, so-called because of the resemblance of the series of projections to the heads of nails.

nail-patella syndrome, rare, heritable disorder characterized by small nails that show a tendency to split, small or absent kneecap (patella) with associated underdevelopment of parts of the knee, elbow joints, and shoulder blade along with bilateral spurs of bone on the inside of the pelvis and signs of kidney insufficiency.

The syndrome is a unique combination of hypoplasia and hyperplasia of bone. Affected persons often experience dislocations, limited joint mobility, and early onset of osteoarthritis. Treatment is mainly orthopedic.
·blood group's genetic linkage **2**:1147e; table

nail polish, lacquer-based paint applied to the fingernails for cosmetic purposes.
·manicure preparations and usage **5**:198g

Nailsea glass, English glass of the late 18th and early 19th centuries traditionally associated with Nailsea, near Bristol, but in fact made elsewhere as well. It was gaily coloured, being spotted, festooned, or striped with opaque glass and white milk glass (*q.v.*), which was first produced in 15th-century Venice.

Naima, Mustafa (b. 1655, Aleppo, Syria—d. 1716, Peloponnese, Greece), Turkish historian who wrote a history, *Tarih*, of the period 1591–1659. He went at an early age to Constantinople, where he entered palace service and held various offices. Protected and encouraged by Hüseyin Paşa, the grand vizier, he was appointed official chronicler (1709). His *Tarih* ("Chronicle"; Eng. trans., *Annals of the Turkish Empire from 1591–1659 of the Christian Era*, 1832) is a compilation from the work of his predecessors (Sharihülmenarzade, whose work is lost; Kâtib Chelebi; Hasanbeyzade; and others), together with his own comments. The *Tarih* was first published in two volumes (1730) and later in six (1884).

Naʿīmah (NUʿAYMAH), **Mikhāʾīl,** also transliterated MIKHAÏL NOUAYME (b. Nov. 22, 1889, Biskintā, Lebanon), literary critic, playwright, essayist, and short-story writer whose works deal primarily with his native Lebanon.

Naʿīmah was educated at the Arabic-speaking Russian school at Biskintā, the Russian seminary at Nazareth (1902–06), and the theological seminary at Poltava in the Ukraine (1906–11). After graduating in law from Washington State University in the United States, he settled in New York City and worked on the Arabic-language paper *al-Funūn* ("The Arts") until it ceased publication during World War I. After brief service with the U.S. Army in Europe (1918–19), Naʿīmah studied at the University of Rennes, Fr. (1919), took a diploma in literary studies, and returned to journalism in New York. There he joined ar-Rābiṭah al-Qalamīyah (the Pen League) and formed a close friendship with another Arab writer, Khalil Gibran. In 1932 he returned to Lebanon a highly celebrated author and settled in his native village.

Naʿīmah depicts the lives and problems of Lebanese emigrants and Lebanese village life with simplicity of language, ease of style, elegance of expression, and great optimism. His two outstanding books are a highly subjective biography of Gibran (1934) and his autobiography, *Sabʿūn* (3 vol., 1959–60; "Seventy"). Also notable are a play, *al-Abā wa al-banūn* (1917; "Fathers and Sons"); the essays *al-Ghirbāl* (1923; "The Sieve"); and the collections of short stories *al-Marāhil* (1933; "The Stages"), *Kana ma kāna* (1937; "Once upon a Time"), and *al-Bayādir* (1945; "The Threshing Floors").

Naiman, Mongol tribe of western Mongolia, conquered by Genghis Khan in 1204.
·Mongol empire territorial expansion **12**:371h

Naini Tāl, administrative headquarters, Naini Tāl district, Uttar Pradesh state, northern India, in the Siwālik Range. Founded in 1841, it is a popular resort, lying at 6,346 ft (1,934 m) above sea level. The town is built around a beautiful lake and is surrounded by forested hills. Naini Tāl is linked by road with the rail terminus at Kāthgodām, to the south. It is the site of St. Joseph's College and the summer seat of the state government. A disastrous landslide occurred there in 1880.

Sailboats on the lake at the town of Naini Tāl, Uttar Pradesh, India
Vidyavrata

Naini Tāl district is 2,622 sq mi (6,792 sq km) in area; it includes part of the Siwālik Range (north) and a strip of the Ganges Plain (south) and touches the Nepal border (east). Much of the mountainous section is forested. The plain, called the Tarai, is humid and unhealthful. Crops include rice, wheat, tea, and fruit; sugar processing is important. The Indian Veterinary Research Institute is located in Mukteswar. Bhowāli houses a tuberculosis sanatorium, and the Uttar Pradesh Agricultural University (1960) is at Pant Nagar. Pop. (1971) town, 23,986; district, 790,080.
29°23′ N, 79°27′ E
·map, India **9**:278

Nāʾīn rugs (20th-century Iranian rugs): *see* Isfahan carpets.

Naipali, or NEPALI (dialect): *see* Pahari language.

Naipaul, V(idiadhar) S(urajprasad) (1932–), Trinidadian novelist.
·West Indian novelists **13**:293b

Nair (Hindu caste): *see* Nāyar.

Nair, Sir Chettur Sankaran (Indian jurist and statesman): *see* Sankaran Nair, Sir Chettur.

Nairi, in ancient times, an ill-defined district around the upper headwaters of the Tigris and Euphrates rivers and around Lake Van (called by the Assyrians the Sea of Nairi) and Lake Urmia. It is known chiefly from Assyrian inscriptions: of Tiglath-pileser I (reigned *c.* 1115–*c.* 1077 BC), who calls himself the conqueror of the lands of Nairi, and Ashurnasirpal II (reigned 883–859 BC), who asserts that he destroyed 250 towns of Nairi. It appears to have been a loose confederation of petty kingdoms, the ruler of one of which, Sarduri I (*c.* 840–830 BC) of Urartu, overcame the others and founded the first Urartian dynasty.
·Assyrian empire 858–627 BC map **11**:985
·Urartian empire territorial expansion **18**:1039c

Nairn, district, Highland (*q.v.*) region, northern Scotland; until the reorganization of 1975, it was the county of Nairn. It has an area of 163 sq mi (422 sq km); the town of Nairn is the seat of the district authority.

The district extends 20 mi (32 km) south from its coastline to the highest point, Carn Glas (2,162 ft [659 m]) in the western Highlands. The nine miles of shore along Moray Firth are fringed by a belt of windblown sand, part of which has been forested. The northern lowlands, drained by the lower course of the River Nairn, have thick, fertile deposits of clay and glacial sands and gravels. Farther south the Highlands, dissected by the River Findhorn, rise in two broad plateau surfaces at 1,000 ft and 1,500–1,700 ft to summits of about 2,000 ft.

The northern lowlands, with fertile soils and an annual rainfall of less than 30 in. (750 mm), constitute a rich farming area supporting a mixed crop–livestock economy. The warmer soils of the postglacial raised beaches along the coast (25–100 ft) produce oats, barley, and potatoes. Dairy farming is important in the lowland and sheep raising in the hills. Salmon fishing in the rivers is productive, but sea fishing from Nairn has seriously declined. There are few industries in the district apart from whisky distilling, granite quarrying, brickmaking, and tourism. The town of Nairn is the only royal burgh (chartered town; since the early 12th century) and small town. It is situated on the Moray Firth and has a harbour, constructed in 1820 by the Scottish engineer Thomas Telford. Since the decline in fishing it has developed as a seaside resort.

The town of Nairn was peopled in prehistoric times by the northern Picts, and several of their stone circles survive. Roman coins are occasionally discovered. By the 10th century the Picts had been subdued by the Danes, and the area soon became an integral part of the kingdom of Scotland. Hardmuir Wood near Nairn is the heath on which Macbeth is reputed to have met the three witches, while Cawdor Castle, 5 mi south of Nairn, is traditionally the scene of King Duncan I's murder by Macbeth.

Although Nairn is not a Highland crofting area, it has close links with the Highlands to the west. Pop. (1974 est.) 8,906.

·map, United Kingdom **18**:866

Nairne, Carolina, Baroness (b. Aug. 16, 1766, Gask, Perth—d. Oct. 26, 1845, Gask), songwriter and laureate of Jacobitism, who wrote "Charlie Is My Darling," "The Hundred Pipers," "The Land o' the Leal," and "Will Ye No' Come Back Again?" The daughter of a Jacobite laird, Laurence Oliphant, who was exiled (1745–63), she followed Burns's example of writing in the folk tradition. Her songs helped to create the myth that the Stuart cause was the cause of the common people. She married Maj. William Nairne, who became 5th Baron Nairne upon the restoration of titles of Jacobite families in 1824. Her songs first appeared in *The Scottish Minstrel* (1821–24) under the pseudonym of Mrs. Bogan of Bogan. Their gentle pathos and occasional wit appealed to all tastes, and the songs soon found their way back into the folk repertory. A collected edition, *Lays from Strathearn* (1846), appeared after her death.

Nairobi **12**:812, capital of Kenya, in East Africa, on the Athi Plains where the Gikuyu Escarpment begins, 300 mi (480 km) northwest of Mombasa, its port on the Indian Ocean. Pop. (1975 est.) 700,000.

The text article covers Nairobi's history, natural setting, and the contemporary city.
1°17′ S, 36°49′ E

REFERENCES in other text articles:
·map, Kenya **10**:424
·population, economic, and cultural roles **10**:426a

Nairobi National Park, in south central Kenya, East Africa, lies just outside the city of Nairobi. The park, established in 1948 with an area of 44 sq mi (114 sq km), lies about 5,000–6,000 ft (1,500–1,800 m) above sea level and consists partly of thick woods near the city outskirts, partly of rolling plains and valleys, and partly of a wooded confluence of several rivers. Acacias and other thorny varieties, *muhuhu*, Cape chestnut, and Kenya olive are the most important trees. Scores of mammals, such as the lion, gazelle, black rhinoceros, giraffe, various species of antelope, and zebra, inhabit the park, as well as reptiles and hundreds of species of birds. Only by establishing migration routes into nearby Ngong Reserve has it been possible to maintain wildlife in the area at its present levels. The park's headquarters are at Nairobi.

·location and attraction **12**:812f
·map, Kenya **10**:424

Naiṣadhacarita, English THE LIFE OF NALA, KING OF NIṢADHA (12th century), a Sanskrit poem by Śrīharṣa.

·theme and style **17**:136g

Naismith, James A. (b. Nov. 6, 1861, Almonte, Ont.—d. Nov. 28, 1939, Lawrence, Kan.), physical education director who, in December 1891, at the International Young Men's Christian Association Training School, afterward Springfield (Mass.) College, invented the game of basketball.

As a young man, Naismith (who had no middle name but adopted the initial "A.") studied theology and excelled in various sports. In the autumn of 1891 he was appointed an instructor by Luther Halsey Gulick, Jr., head of the Physical Education Department at Springfield. Gulick asked Naismith and other instructors to devise indoor games that could

Naismith holding a ball and a peach basket, the first basketball equipment
UPI Compix

replace the boring or dangerous exercises used at the school during the winter. For his new game Naismith selected features of soccer, U.S. football, field hockey, and other outdoor sports but (in theory) eliminated body contact between players. Because his physical education class at that time was composed of 18 men, basketball originally was played by 9 on each side (eventually reduced to 5).

In 1898 Naismith received the M.D. degree from Gross Medical College, Denver, Colo., afterward the University of Colorado School of Medicine. From that year until 1937 he was chairman of the Physical Education Department at the University of Kansas, Lawrence. In addition to basketball, he is credited with inventing the protective helmet for football players. The Naismith Memorial Basketball Hall of Fame, Springfield, Mass., was incorporated in 1959.

·basketball invention and development **2**:750h

Naitasiri, province, Central division, Fiji.
·area and population table **7**:297

Naivasha, Lake, in the eastern arm of the East African Rift System, 35 mi (56 km) southeast of Nakuru, Kenya. It is flanked by the Ilkinopop (Kinangop) Plateau (east) and the Mau Escarpment (west). The lake lies on an alluvium-covered flat in the valley floor and is flanked on the north by an extensive papyrus swamp. It is the highest of the lakes

Pelicans silhouetted at dusk on Lake Naivasha, Kenya
Gerald Cubitt

in the eastern part of the rift system, situated at 6,180 ft (1,884 m) above sea level. Its level and size fluctuate periodically; in the mid-1970s it covered about 81 sq mi (210 sq km). Main tributaries are the Engare Melewa and Gilgil rivers.

Although it has no outlet, the lake's waters are fresh. Several species of *Tilapia* and black bass (introduced) are the basis of commercial and sport fishing. Lake Naivasha serves as a weekend resort for residents of Nairobi, the capital of Kenya, to the southeast.
0°46′ S, 36°21′ E

·map, Kenya **10**:424
·geography, hydrography, and industry **6**:116d; map 119

naïve artists: *see* Primitivism.

Naja (genus of snakes): *see* cobra.

Najadales, sometimes called POTAMOGETONALES, an order of monocotyledonous flowering plants containing 10 families, 19 genera, and 250 species of aquatic and marsh-dwelling herbs. The plants are so diverse in appearance, structure, and technical characters that they are unified as an order by their aquatic habit and lack of endosperm (nutrient tissues in the seed for the developing embryo) rather than by the structure of the flower as in most other flowering plant groups. A further diagnostic character of some value in characterizing this order is the presence in most genera of small scales near the leaf bases; however,

Arrow-grass (*Triglochin maritima*)
Ingmar Holmasen

some members of the order Arales also exhibit this feature. The order is considered to be closely related to the water-plantain order (Alismales) and probably evolved from it.

The families Scheuchzeriaceae and Juncaginaceae are composed of emergent (upright, not submerged) plants of marshes and bogs. The two species of the genus *Scheuchzeria*, which comprise the family, grow in wet sphagnum bogs. The arrow-grass family (Juncaginaceae), with four genera and about 18 species, includes the flowering quillwort (*Lilaea subulata*), *Triglochin* (15 species), and two more single-species genera.

The families Aponogetonaceae (the lattice plant family) and Potamogetonaceae (the pondweed family) are composed mainly of freshwater aquatic plants with submerged or floating leaves but frequently with emergent flowering shoots. *Aponogeton*, the only genus of its family, contains 30 species, mostly from Africa, of which *A. distachys* is often grown ornamentally in aquariums and pools. The lattice plant of Madagascar (*A. fenestralis*) has unusual underwater leaves that consist of veins only. The pondweed family contains two genera (*Potamogeton*, 100 species; and *Groenlandia*, one species) of widely distributed plants important as food for waterfowl and cover for fishes.

The families Ruppiaceae (widgeon grass family, one genus, *Ruppia*, with two species), Zannichelliaceae (three genera, including the horned pondweed, *Zannichellia*), and Najadaceae (the naiad family, one genus, *Najas*, with 50 species) are submerged aquatics of freshwater or brackish water.

The family Zosteraceae (the eelgrass family),

with 2 genera (*Phyllosphadix* and *Zostera*) and 12 species, consists entirely of submerged marine plants in temperate regions of the world. The eelgrass, or wrack, is *Zostera marina*, an important tidewater plant whose leaves are used for packing glass articles and stuffing cushions. The family Cymodoceaceae

Aponogeton distachys
Syndication International—Photo Trends

(4 genera and 21 species) is also a group of plants that grow in shallow saltwater bays and brackish streams, but it is principally found in warmer coastal waters such as Florida. Its largest genera are *Cymodocea* (10 species) and *Helodule* (7 species). The family Posidoniaceae (one genus, *Posidonia*, with two species) is a Mediterranean and Australian group similar to the eelgrass; its stems are also used for packing glass.

·angiosperm features and classification **1**:884c

Najaf (Iraq): *see* an-Najaf.

Najāḥids, a Muslim dynasty of Ethiopian Mamlūks (slaves) that ruled Yemen in the period 1022–1158 from its capital at Zabīd. The Ziyādid kingdom at Zabīd (819–1018) had in its final years been controlled by Mamlūk viziers, the last of whom divided Yemen between two slaves, Nafīs and Najāḥ. Nafīs murdered the last Ziyādid ruler in 1018, and, after several years of bitter fighting and the death of Nafīs, Najāḥ emerged victorious and took control of Zabīd early in 1022. Najāḥ obtained the recognition of the ʿAbbāsid caliph and established his rule over the Tihāmah (coastal lands), though the highlands, a stronghold of tribal chieftains, remained recalcitrant. Najāḥ's murder *c.* 1060 threw the kingdom into chaos, allowing the Ṣulayḥid ruler ʿAlī to take Zabīd, and reduced Najāḥid history to a series of intrigues.

Two of Najāḥ's sons, Saʿīd and Jayyāsh, who had fled the capital, plotted to restore themselves to the Najāḥid throne and in 1081 killed ʿAlī. Saʿīd, supported by the large Ethiopian Mamlūk population, easily secured control of Zabīd. ʿAlī's son al-Mukarram, however, heavily influenced by his mother, took Zabīd *c.* 1083, forcing the Najāḥids to flee again. Saʿīd regained power briefly (1086–88) but was finally murdered by al-Mukarram's wife as-Sayyidah. Jayyāsh, meanwhile, had fled to India. He returned in disguise and assumed power with little difficulty, restoring equilibrium to the Yemeni kingdom during his reign (1089–*c.* 1106). After much family feuding over a successor to Jayyāsh, his grandson al-Manṣūr was installed in Zabīd *c.* 1111 by the Ṣulayḥids as their vassal. Manṣūr was poisoned in 1123 by his Mamlūk vizier Mann Allāh, who proceeded to fight off an attempted invasion by the Fāṭimids of Egypt and to reduce the Najāḥid ruler to a puppet figure. The Yemeni government passed from one Mamlūk vizier to another after Mann Allāh's murder in 1130, as rival factions struggled among themselves for primacy. The threat of ʿAli ibn Mahdī, a Khārijite (member of a puritanical and fanatical Islāmic sect) who had murdered the vizier Surūr in 1156, forced the Ethiopians to seek outside help from the Zaydī *imām* of Ṣanʿāʾ Aḥmad al-Mutawakkil and agree to recognize him as ruler of Zabīd. The Ethiopians were, however, defeated, and ʿAli ibn Mahdī took the Najāḥid capital in 1159.

·Arabia under African and ʿAbbāsid rule **1**:1047h

Najā Plateau, in Yemen (Aden).

·description and drainage basins **1**:1052d; map 1053

Najd, also called NEJD, region, central Saudi Arabia, comprising a mainly rocky plateau sloping eastward from the mountains of Hejaz. On the northern, eastern, and southern sides, it is bounded by the sand deserts of an-Nafūd, ad-Dahnāʾ, and Rubʿ al-Khali. It is sparsely settled, except for the fertile oases strung along the escarpment of Jabal (mountains) Ṭuwayq and the al-ʿArmah plateau. The arid region remained politically divided among rival tribes until the mid-18th century when it became the centre of the Wahhābī, a puritanical Islāmic movement. Led by the Muslim scholar Muḥammad ibn ʿAbd al-Wahhāb and the Āl Saʿūd family, the movement consolidated the Najd and expanded into Mecca in 1803. This expansionist policy antagonized the Turks, who seized the provincial capital of ad-Dirʿīyah. The Āl Saʿūd,

A camel hauling a load of freshly-cut alfafa to market at Najd, Saudi Arabia
Standard Oil Co., N.J.

however, quickly regained control, and, with Riyadh as the new capital from 1824, the dynasty has ruled the Najd continuously, save for a brief period around the turn of the century when the Rashīd dynasty extended its power over the province. Ibn Saʿūd proclaimed the unified Kingdom of Saudi Arabia in 1932, and his provincial capital of Riyadh became the national capital. Oases groups within the Najd region include al-Kharj, al-Maḥmal, as-Sudayr, al-Washm, al-ʿĀriḍ, al-Qaṣīm, and Jabal Shammar. Latest pop. est. 1,200,000.

·map, Saudi Arabia **16**:279
·religion, people, roads, and resources **16**:276h *passim* to 278e

Naj ʿHammadi, a town in Egypt, on or near the site of the ancient town of Chenoboskion.

·Gnostic library **8**:214g *passim* to 218e
·Jung Codex discovery **13**:1079f

Najīb ud-Dawlah, also called NAJĪB KHAN, 18th-century Indian Ruhelā leader.

·military and political career **9**:386b

Najin-dong, port city, Hamgyŏng-pukto (North Hamgyŏng Province), northeastern North Korea. It is on Najin-man (bay), on the Sea of Japan, or East Sea. Protected by Taech'o and Soch'o islands, it has a good natural harbour. Formerly a poor village, it developed rapidly after the construction of the rail line connecting it with the urban centres of Manchuria in 1932. Fisheries are important; the neighbouring waters offer good fishing grounds for codfish, pollack, and herring. Shipbuilding is carried on. It is a station on the rail line passing through Wŏnsan, to the south, through Hamhŭng and Ch'ŏng-jin, and continuing past the city to Unggi, to the north, via the Ungna Tunnel (12,631 ft [3,850 m] long), longest tunnel in the country. Beyond Unggi, the rail line parallels the Chinese border, and then crosses into China. Latest pop. est. 34,388.

42°15′ N, 130°18′ E

·map, North Korea **10**:518

Najrān, town, oasis, and district of southern Asir region, southwestern Saudi Arabia, in the desert along the Yemen (Ṣanʿāʾ) frontier. First visited by the Romans in 24 BC, it was the seat of an important Christian colony in 500–635. In more recent times it has been the subject of controversy between Saudi Arabia and Yemen (Ṣanʿāʾ). By the Treaty of aṭ-Ṭāʾif in 1934, it was given to Saudi Arabia, but the boundary was denounced by Yemen (Ṣanʿāʾ) during the civil war of the 1960s. An extremely fertile agricultural area, the oasis produces dates and grains and is used for stock raising. The town of Najrān is the southern terminus of highways from Mecca and Riyadh. Latest pop. est. 10,000.

·Ethiopian Aksumite military expeditions **6**:1007f
·map, Saudi Arabia **16**:279
·province area and population table **16**:277

Nakae Tōju, original personal name GEN, pen name MOKKEN (b. March 7, 1608, Ōmi, modern Shiga, Japan—d. Aug. 25, 1648, Ōmi), Neo-Confucian scholar who established in Japan the Idealist thought of the Chinese philosopher Wang Yang-ming.

Nakae was originally a follower of the teachings of the Chinese Neo-Confucian Rationalist Chu Hsi, whose doctrines had become a part of the official ideology of the Japanese government. In 1634 he asked to be released from the post he held as retainer to his feudal lord so he could return to his native village and carry out his filial obligations to his widowed mother. He left despite the fact that his lord refused him permission. At home he devoted himself to teaching and study, eventually abandoning his adherence to the Chu Hsi school of thought and becoming a propagator of the philosophy of Wang Yang-ming. His fame spread throughout the land. He attracted many distinguished disciples and became known as the sage of Ōmi Province.

Both Wang and Nakae believed that the unifying principle of the universe exists in the human mind and not in the external world. They taught that the true Way could be discovered through intuition and self-reflection, rejecting Chu Hsi's idea that it could be found through empirical investigation. In his conviction that a concept can be fully understood only when acted upon, Nakae emphasized practice rather than abstract learning. His action in leaving his lord to fulfill obligations to his aged mother is often cited as an outstanding example of Wang Yang-ming's idea of the unity of knowledge and action. This emphasis on individual action made Nakae's philosophy popular among the zealous reformers and patriots of the 19th and 20th centuries. Nakae, however, emphasized the religious aspects of the doctrine more than Wang Yang-ming had intended: he insisted on faith in the trinity of Jōtei (a kind of divinity he created, personifying Heaven, the creator, and the sovereign ruler). *Tōju sensei zenshū* ("The Complete Works of Master Tōju") was published in five volumes in 1940.

Nakae Tokusuke, better known by his pen name NAKAE CHŌMIN (b. 1847, Tosa Province, now Kōchi Prefecture, Japan—d. 1901, Hokkaido), noted writer who popularized the equalitarian doctrines of the French philosopher Jean-Jacques Rousseau in Japan. As a result, Nakae is often considered the spiritual founder of the Japanese democratic movement. Early interested in Western learning, Nakae studied French and Dutch as a boy and served for a while as a translator for the French minister to Japan. In 1871 he was sent abroad as a member of the Ministry of Justice and studied philosophy, history, and literature in France. On his return, he served briefly in the government and then retired and began his own French language school.

In 1881 Nakae started the influential daily newspaper, *Tōyō jiyū shimbun* ("Oriental Free Press"), which he used to propagate Western democratic ideas. He also served as a member of the Diet and engaged in a number of business enterprises. His real fame, however, came from his popularization of Rousseau; he translated *Du contrat social* and then, while he lay dying of a malignancy, wrote two best-selling books in which he explained French democratic ideas to the Japanese.

·Japanese social philosophy **10**:107h

Nakajima, Japanese artisan family of the 18th and 19th centuries.

·Hokusai's early life **8**:989g

Naka Michiyo (1851–1908), Japanese historian.

·chronology of Japanese history **4**:573f

Nakamura Nakazō I (1736–90), Japanese Kabuki actor.

·Kabuki theatre actors account **10**:370a

Nakamura Nakazō III (1809–86), Japanese Kabuki actor.

·Kabuki theatre actors account **10**:370a

Nakano Ōe: *see* Tenchi Tennō.

Nakanuma Shikubu: *see* Shōkadō Shōjō.

Nakanune (1860), English ON THE EVE, novel by Ivan Turgenev.

·theme and style **18**:780c

Nakatomi Kamatari, also called FUJIWARA KAMATARI, or KAMAKO (b. 614, Japan—d. 669, Japan), founder of the great Fujiwara family that dominated Japan from the 9th to the 12th century. Nakatomi's reforms helped strengthen the power of the central government and transform the Japanese political and economic system into a replica of T'ang China (618–907). In the early 7th century, the Soga family totally dominated the Japanese Imperial court. In 645, however, along with an Imperial prince who later reigned as the emperor Tenchi (661–671), Nakatomi murdered the head of the Soga family and carried out a coup d'etat.

As a reward for his services, Nakatomi was given the position of minister of the interior, and in this role he was able to carry out a series of far-reaching measures known as the "Reforms of Taika" (*Taika no kaishin*; *see* Taika). Taika, meaning "Great Change," was the term adopted for this whole era (645–710) in accord with the Chinese custom of counting time by arbitrary "year periods" (*nengō*). Nakatomi's reforms represented, in fact, an attempt to adapt the entire Chinese political and social system to Japan. Laws were codified, arable land was surveyed, and all households were registered. Both the private holdings of land and the private ownership of agricultural workers were abolished; former owners were appointed to supervise the property they had once owned, although theoretically they were considered employees of the central government, whose power was conspicuously enlarged. A new capital metropolitan region was established, the country was divided into provinces ruled by appointees of the central government, a series of new roads and post stations was constructed to improve communications with outlying districts, and a uniform system of taxes was introduced. These measures helped to complete the process of centralization and Sinicization that the government had begun 100 years earlier.

In 669, as a reward for his services, Nakatomi was given the new surname of Fujiwara, and under him the Fujiwara clan became firmly entrenched.

·Imperial defense and name award **7**:771c
·policies and accomplishments **10**:60d

Nakatsu, city, Ōita Prefecture (*ken*), Kyushu, Japan, on the mouth of the Yamakuni-gawa (Yamakuni River), facing the Inland Sea. The city developed around a castle built in 1587 by the Kuroda family. Nakatsu is now a commercial centre for rice and silk produced in the surrounding region. Industrial development began with the introduction of textiles in 1896, and the city now produces steel and china. Pop. (1975) 59,111.
33°34′ N, 131°13′ E

·map, Japan **10**:37

Nakayama Miki (b. 1798, Yamato province, Japan—d. 1887), founder of the Tenrikyō ("Religion of Divine Wisdom"), a sect of the Shintō religion of Japan. The daughter of a local landowner, she married (*c.* 1810) a landowner from Shōyashiki village (now Tenri city), near Nara. She gave birth to one son and five daughters and, according to tradition, experienced great pain in childbirth. Her first spiritual experience occurred *c.* 1839 during an illness of her son. After her husband's death in 1853 she lived in poverty but discovered powers to heal the sick and ease childbirth. By 1867 she had developed the model for her songs, the *Mikagura-uta*, that express her religious teachings, and between 1869 and 1882 she produced her *Ofudesaki*, religious writings in traditional poetic form. By 1881, when the Tenri-kyō headquarters were moved to Tenri, her following had spread throughout Japan. See also Tenri-Kyō.

·Japan's new faiths **10**:77b
·religious dress use **15**:639g
·Shintō sect formation **16**:673c

Nakaz: *see* Instruction of Catherine the Great.

Naked and the Dead, The (1948), novel by Norman Mailer.

·scope and dimension in the novel **13**:279h

Naked Cult (New Hebrides): *see* cargo cults.

Naked Lunch, The (1959), novel by William Burroughs.

·Expressionistic technique **13**:285a

Naked Night (1953), English title SAWDUST AND TINSEL, U.S. title for Swedish film directed by Ingmar Bergman.

·lighting effects **12**:506g

naker, small kettledrum that reached Europe from the Middle East in the 13th century, during the Crusades. Made of wood, metal, or clay and sometimes equipped with snares, nakers were almost always played in pairs, being struck with hard sticks. They were probably tuned to high and low notes of identifiable pitch. Like the similar Arabic *naqqārah*, from which they (and their name) derived, they were used in military and battle music as well as in the softer indoor chamber music and in dance accompaniments. They continued in use through the 16th century.

·introduction to Europe **14**:64c

nakharar, in ancient Parthia, class of clan chiefs, or barons.

·Armenian internal conflicts **18**:1041h

Nakhi (ethnology): *see* Yi.

Nakhichevan, capital of the Nakhichevan Autonomous Soviet Socialist Republic, within the Azerbaijan Soviet Socialist Republic, on the river known as the Nakhichevanchay. Nakhichevan is extremely old, dated by some archaeologists to about 1500 BC. Until 1828 it was capital of the khanate of Nakhichevan, and it became capital of the autonomous republic in 1924. It now has varied industries, in particular food, furniture, leather, and building materials. There is a museum of local culture and an agricultural college. Pop. (1973 est.) 35,000.
39°12′ N, 45°24′ E

Nakhichevan Autonomous Soviet Socialist Republic, administrative division of the Azerbaijan Soviet Socialist Republic, in the southern part of the Transcaucasian plateau bounded by the Armenian S.S.R. (north and east), Iran (south and west), and Turkey (west). Covering an area of 2,124 sq mi (5,500 sq km), the republic, which is mostly mountainous except for a plain in the west and southwest, lies to the east and north of the middle Aras River, which forms the frontier with Iran and Turkey. Kapydzhik in the Zangezur Mountains rises to 12,808 ft (3,904 m). The area is subject to earthquakes, that of 1931 having been particularly severe. Winter temperatures in the dry continental climate average 20° to 24° F (−7° to −4° C); summer temperatures range from 75° to 84° F (24° to 29° C). The scarcity of rainfall on the plain, no more than 20 in. (500 mm), produces a steppe type of vegetation. In the mountains, where rainfall averages 25 to 30 in., the flora is mountainous steppe, with dwarf oak and Iberian maple occurring in the upper valleys. Gray alluvial soils prevail in the plain, giving way above 3,300 ft (1,000 m) to brown and chestnut soils.

The republic, especially Nakhichevan, the capital, has a long history dating back to about 1500 BC. Armenian tradition ascribes the founding of the city to Noah. From the 13th to the 19th century the area was under Persian domination. In 1828, however, the area passed to Russia, and in 1924 it became an autonomous republic. Azerbaijanis make up 94 percent of the population, the balance being mainly Armenians and Russians. Chief cities, besides the capital, are Ordubad and Dzhulfa. Agriculture, the principal economic activity, is carried on with the aid of irrigation. The most important crops are grains (winter wheat, some spring wheat, and barley), cotton, tobacco, mulberries (food for silkworms), and fruits. Sheep raising provides wool for the Azerbaijan carpet industry. Cattle, goats, horses, and donkeys are also raised, and there is some beekeeping in the mountains. Industrial activity is limited to mining (salt, molybdenum, lead), cotton ginning, silk textile production, and food processing. The Yerevan–Baku railway follows the Aras Valley through the republic; motor roads link the capital to Yerevan, to Dzhulfa on the Iranian frontier, and to Yevlakh in Azerbaijan proper; and there is regular air service to Baku. Pop. (1978 est.) 235,000.

·economic aspects and prospects **2**:546d

Nakh languages, spoken in the Caucasus in the Chechen-Ingush Autonomous Soviet Socialist Republic, Dagestan A.S.S.R., and Akhmeta district of the Georgian Soviet Socialist Republic. The group, with the approximate number of speakers of each language, includes Chechen, 613,000; Ingush, 158,000; and Bats (Tsova-Tushian), 3,000. As Bats has no written form, its speakers use Georgian as their literary language. The Nakh group, sometimes called the Central Caucasian languages, is often classified by scholars with the Dagestanian languages (among which are Avar and Lezgian) in a Nakho-Dagestanian, or Northeast Caucasian, language group. Nakh languages are characterized by a number of pharyngeal consonants produced with constriction of the muscles in the throat (as in Arabic) and have relatively simple consonant systems. *See also* Georgian language; Dagestanian languages.

·Caucasian Mountains languages survey **3**:1018c
·comparative phonology and grammar **3**:1013e
·Soviet Union nationalities distribution, table 3 **17**:338

nakhlite, stony meteorite containing about 75 percent diopside and 13 percent olivine, with plagioclase and augite. Nakhlites are similar to no known terrestrial rock. *See* achondrite.

Nakho-Dagestanian languages, group of languages spoken in the northeastern Caucasus. The Nakh division consists of the languages of the Checken, Ingush, and Bats. The Dagestanian division is more multifarious and includes such groups as the Avar-Ando-Dido languages, the Lakk-Dargwa languages, and the Lezgian languages.
·languages, phonology, and grammar **3**:1013e
·Southwest Asian language area survey **10**:667b

Nakhodka, town, Primorsky *kray* (territory), eastern Russian Soviet Federated Socialist Republic, at the head of Nakhodka Bay on the Sea of Japan. Nakhodka developed rapidly as a port after 1945, with the building of a railway link to the Trans-Siberian line. It is the terminus of a passenger ferry to Yokohama, Japan, and the base of a fishing fleet. Pop. (1970) 105,000.
42°48′ N, 132°52′ E
·map, Soviet Union **17**:322

Nakhon Nayok, also spelled NAKHORN-NAYOK, administrative headquarters of Nakhon Nayok province (*changwat*), south central Thailand, on the Mae Nam (river) Nakhon Nayok, a tributary of the Mae Nam Chao Phraya. It is a collection centre for a rice-growing region. The province has an area of 931 sq mi (2,414 sq km). Apart from Nakhon Nayok town, the main population centres are Ban Na, Pak Phli, and Ongkharak. Pop. (latest est.) town, 8,628; (1970 prelim.) province, 161,000.
14°12′ N, 101°13′ E
·map, Thailand **18**:198
·province area and population table **18**:202

Nakhon Pathom, also spelled NAKORN PATHOM, province (*changwat*), south central Thailand, occupying an area of 841 sq mi (2,178 sq km) on the Mae Nam Chao Phraya (Chao Phraya River) Delta plain. Its rich alluvium receives 49 in. (1,240 mm) of rain annually, which is supplemented by irrigation from the Mae Nam Nakhon Chai Si. The main agricultural products (rice, hogs, coconuts, and pomelo) are marketed through nearby Bangkok, making Nakhon Pathom one of Thailand's wealthiest provinces.

A prosperous commercial centre, Nakhon Pathom city lies 29 mi (47 km) west of Bangkok, with major road and rail connections in all directions. It has access to the Chao Phraya Delta waterways through a canal from the Mae Nam Nakhon Chai Si. The city is a religious and military centre.

Nakhon Pathom is sometimes called "the oldest city in Thailand," and it is believed that Buddhism was first introduced to the Tai people there by Indian missionaries in the 2nd century BC. Phra Pathom, the highest *stūpa* in Thailand, towers 380 ft (116 m); and the large orange, bell-shaped pagoda covers nearly a square mile. Rebuilt a number of times, the original Indian *stūpa* dates to AD 500. An annual festival in November attracts many pilgrims. Pop. (1970) town, 34,300; (1970 prelim.) province, 411,000.
·area and population table **18**:202
·Chinese influence on Thai architecture **17**:258g
·map, Thailand **18**:198

Nakhon Phanom, also spelled NAKORN PHANOM, province (*changwat*), northeastern Thailand, occupying an area of 3,764 sq mi (9,749 sq km). It shares a long eastern border with Laos along the Mekong River. The local soil, an infertile sandy loam, retains little moisture, making agriculture difficult. There are, however, strips of fertile land along the Mekong and its tributaries. Rice is the main crop.

The main towns are Nakhon Phanom (the provincial capital), Mukdahan, and Ban Um Mao. That Phanom is a religious centre in the south. Nakhon Phanom town is a commercial centre on the Mekong River opposite Thakhek, Laos; it is linked by road and air west to Udon Thani and east by a road into Laos. Pop. (1970) town, 20,385; (1970 prelim.) province, 561,000.
·area and population table **18**:202
·map, Thailand **18**:198

Nakhon Ratchasima, also spelled NAKONRATCHASIMA, province (*changwat*), northeastern Thailand, occupying an area of 7,564 sq mi (19,590 sq km) in the southwestern portion of the Khorat Plateau. The province was formerly known as Khorat. Nearer to Bangkok than other provinces in the region, it has become the crossroads of the northeast. The population is a mixture of Thai, Lao (Laotian), and Khmer (Cambodian) peoples.

Agriculture (rice, corn, tobacco) is concentrated on the alluvial soils of the Mae Nam Mun (Mun River) and its tributaries. Much of the land is devoted to raising cattle and hogs. Apart from the provincial headquarters of Nakhon Ratchasima, the main towns are Non Thai and Chakkarat.

The 11th-century ruins at Phimai are considered the Angkor Wat (a spectacular Cambodian temple complex) of Thailand. Part of the Khao Yai National Park is in the southwest. Ruins indicate that settlement on the Mun River is ancient. Except for a few short-lived conquests by Cambodia, the area has been part of Thailand since the 14th century.

Nakhon Ratchasima city is the transportation, commercial, financial, and governmental centre of the northeast. The railway from Bangkok branches north to Nong Khai on the Mekong River and east to Ubon Ratchathani. The city also is linked to Bangkok by air and by the American-built "Friendship Highway." A network of roads stretches to every part of the region from the city, which is a collecting centre for rice and livestock, which are shipped to Bangkok. Educational facilities include the Northeastern Technical Institute. Silk is produced and woven in nearby villages. A statue of the Thai heroine Thao (Khunying) Suranari commemorates her leadership during a Laotian invasion (1826). Pop. (1970 prelim.) city, 102,095; province, 1,547,000.
·area and population table **18**:202
·map, Thailand **18**:198

Nakhon Sawan, also spelled NAKORN SAWAN, province (*changwat*), central Thailand, occupying an area of 3,736 sq mi (9,677 sq km) and drained by the Mae Nam Ping (Ping River), Mae Nam Nan, and Mae Nam Yom. Its waterways are crucial to the teak trade of the north. Rice, beans, corn (maize), cotton, jute, and sesame are produced.

Nakhon Sawan (Heavenly City), the provincial capital, is located at the Ping-Nan confluence, where the Mae Nam Chao Phraya is formed. It is the leading up-country river port for rice and teak logs. At a major road junction, the town lies across the Chao Phraya from the Pak Nam Pho station of the Bangkok-Chiengmai rail line. There are mills for processing rice, lumber, and paper. The town of Chum Saeng, at the Yom-Nan confluence to the northeast, is also a timber-collection point. Pop. (latest est.) town, 46,135; (1970 prelim.) province, 758,000.
15°42′ N, 100°06′ E
·area and population table **18**:202
·map, Thailand **18**:198

Nakhon Si Thammarat, also spelled NAKON SRITHAMARAJ, province (*changwat*), southwestern Thailand, occupying an area of 3,926 sq mi (10,169 sq km) on the Malay Peninsula. A rich agricultural region, its chief crops are rice, fruit, coconuts, and rubber. There are substantial deposits of phosphate, iron ore, lead, and tin. The coastline of 140 mi (225 km) is the site of the towns of Si Chon, Tha Sala, and Ban Hua Sai.

The walled provincial capital of Nakhon Si Thammarat, one of Thailand's oldest cities, lies on the east coast of the peninsula near the Gulf of Thailand. Founded more than 1,000 years ago, it was the capital of a powerful state that controlled the middle portion of the peninsula; it was often called Ligor until the 13th century. The city is the province's commercial centre and is the site of Nakorn Sithammarat Agricultural College. The manufacture of Thai nielloware (a type of metalwork) began in the area. The city's outport, Pak Phanang, is the site of the temple complex of Wat Mahathadu. Latest pop. est. city, 41,084; (1970 prelim.) province, 927,000.
8°26′ N, 99°58′ E
·area and population table **18**:202
·map, Thailand **18**:198

Nakīr (angel): *see* Munkar and Nakīr.

Nakorn Pathom (Thailand): *see* Nakhon Pathom.

Nakorn Phanom (Thailand): *see* Nakhon Phanom.

Nakorn Sawan (Thailand): *see* Nakhon Sawan.

Nakota (people): *see* Dakota.

Na-k'ou, mountain pass, near Peking.
·North China communications **14**:2g

nakṣatra system: *see* calendar, Hindu.

Nakskov, city, Storstrøms *amtskommune* (county), Lolland Island, Denmark, on Nakskov Fjord. Founded as a market centre in the early 13th century, it burned down in 1420, was occupied by the forces of Lübeck (a Baltic town of the Hanseatic League) in 1510 and was occupied by the Swedes in 1658. Important commercially since the 17th century, it is now a major sugar-refining centre with shipyard facilities. The Gothic St. Nikolaj Kirke (church) is notable for fine ornamental carving. Pop. (latest census) 16,515; (1971 est.) mun., 17,203.
54°50′ N, 11°09′ E
·map, Denmark **5**:582

Naktong River, Korean NAKTONG-GANG, in the Yŏngnam area of Kyŏngsang-namdo and

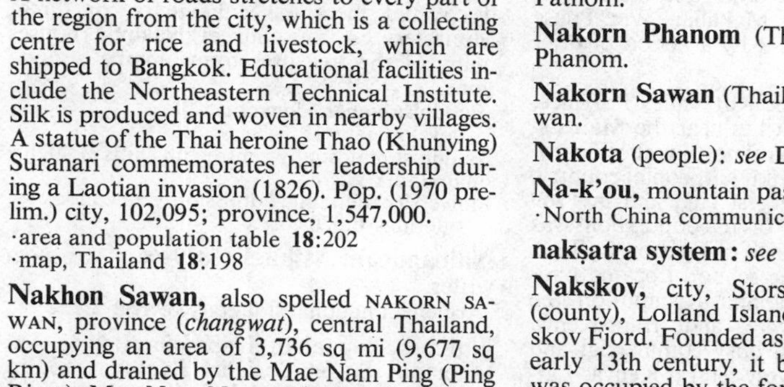

Sammangjin bridge, the longest bridge in South Korea, over the Naktong River
Shostal

Kyŏngsang-pukto (South Kŏngsang and North Kyŏngsang provinces), southeastern South Korea. During the Korean War it was the last defense line of the United Nations forces. Korea's second longest river (325 mi [525 km]), it flows southward from the T'aebaek-san (mountains) and enters the Korean Strait at Tadaepo, a suburb of Pusan. The river, with its principal tributaries, the Naesŏng, Panbyŏn, Wi, Kŭmho, and Nam, has a drainage basin of 9,212 sq mi (23,860 sq km). Flowing slowly over old hilly districts, it has formed the fertile Kimhae delta plain and, including the plain, more than 23 percent of the drainage basin is used for cultivation of crops. The river supplies water for industrial and general use in the big cities. The Nam, which flows in the central part of Kyŏngsang-namdo, has a multipurpose dam near Chinju, constructed in 1968. The Naktong is navigable for 214 mi (344 km) from the mouth up to Andong in Kyŏngsang-pukto.
35°07′ N, 128°57′ E
·Korean physical geography **10**:522g
·map, South Korea **10**:524

Nakulīśa, also known as LAKULĪŚA (1st or 2nd century AD), an Indian teacher and founder of the Pāśupata sect of ascetics.
·Śaivite sect foundation **8**:912f

Nakuran Wet Phase, division of post-Pleistocene time and deposits in Africa (the Pleistocene Epoch began about 2,500,000 years ago and ended about 10,000 years ago). The Nakuran Wet Phase, a time of increased moisture, began about 2,700 years ago and continues to the present. The Nakuran is equivalent in time with the inception of modern climatic conditions in Europe and elsewhere. The Nakuran follows the Makalian Wet Phase and is separated from it by a period of drier climatic conditions.

Nakuru, capital of the Rift Valley Province, Kenya, East Africa. It lies near the Mau Escarpment, 95 mi (153 km) northwest of Nairobi, near the heart of Kikuyu (people) country. It is Kenya's third largest city, and in 1969 more than one-tenth of its population was non-African. It is the site of Egerton College, an agricultural training school. Located midway between Nairobi and Kisumu on the Kenya–Uganda railway and trans-Kenya highway, Nakuru is a busy commercial and transport centre for west central Kenya. Latest census 47,151.
0°17′ S, 36°04′ E
·map, Kenya **10**:424

Nakuru, Lake, in Rift Valley Province, western Kenya, is one of the saline lakes of

Pelicans on the saline Lake Nakuru, near Nakuru, Kenya
M.P. Price—Keystone

the East African lake system lying in the Great Rift Valley. The settlement of Nakuru, capital of the province, lies on its north shore; Lake Nakuru National Park extends around the southern and eastern shores.
0°22′ S, 36°05′ E
·map, Kenya **10**:424
·pH value studies **10**:606c
·rift valley lake hydrography **6**:117e; map 119

Nala, 6th-century Indian dynasty of the Deccan plateau.

Nālandā, a celebrated Buddhist monastic centre, often spoken of as a university, north of Rājgīr (ancient Rājagṛha) in the Patna district of Bihār, India. Nālandā's traditional history goes back to the time of the Buddha (6th–5th centuries BC) and Mahāvīra, the founder of the Jaina religion. According to a later Tibetan source, Nāgārjuna, the 2nd–3rd-century AD Buddhist philosopher, began his studies there. Extensive excavations carried out by the Archaeological Survey of India indicate, however, that the foundation of the monasteries belongs to the Gupta period (5th century AD). The powerful 7th-century ruler of Kanauj, Harṣavardhana, is reported to have contributed to them. During his reign the Chinese pilgrim Hsüan-tsang stayed at Nālandā for some time and left a clear account of the subjects studied there and of the general features of the community. I-ching, another pilgrim a generation later, also provided a minute account of the life of the monks. Nālandā continued to flourish as a centre of learning under the Pāla dynasty (8th–12th centuries). Numerous manuscripts copied at Nālandā exist, and it became a centre of religious sculpture in stone and bronze. Nālandā was probably sacked during Muslim raids in Bihār (*c.* 1200) and never recovered.

According to pilgrims' accounts, from Gupta times the monasteries of Nālandā were surrounded by a high wall. The excavations revealed a row of ten monasteries of the traditional Indian design—oblong brick structures with cells opening onto four sides of a courtyard, with a main entrance on one side and a shrine facing the entrance across the courtyard. In front of the monasteries stood a row of larger shrines, or *stūpa*s, in brick and plaster. The entire complex is referred to on seals discovered there as Mahāvihāra, or Great Monastery. A museum at Nālandā houses many of the treasures found in the excavations.
·Buddhist higher education development **15**:643a
·Buddhist philosophy centre and shifts **3**:407b
·map, India **9**:278
·university founding, admission, and course offerings **6**:320a

Nalbandean, Mikael (1829–66), Armenian writer.
·Armenian nationalist literary revival **2**:23g

Nalchik, capital of Kabardino-Balkar Autonomous Soviet Socialist Republic, southwestern Russian Soviet Federated Socialist Republic, lying on the Nalchik River where it leaves the Caucasian foothills. Founded as a Russian fortress in 1818, the town remained unimportant until after the October Revolution. Now it is a popular holiday, climbing, and health resort, with several sanatoria. There is considerable industry, including engineering, hydro-metallurgy (molybdenum), and artificial leather and foodstuff manufacture. A university and a Kabardino-Balkar research institute are located in the town. Pop. (1970) 146,000.
43°29′ N, 43°37′ E

Nalgonda, administrative headquarters, Nalgonda district, Andhra Pradesh state, southern India. It is a road junction and trade centre specializing in rice and oilseed milling.

Nalgonda district occupies an area of 5,487 sq mi (14,212 sq km) on the Deccan Plateau and is bordered (south) by the Krishna River. Also drained by the Mūsi River, it is composed mainly of sandy red soils and alluvial deposits conducive to the cultivation of millet, oilseeds, and rice. Major towns include Bhongīr, Nalgonda, and Suriapet. Pop. (1971 prelim.) town, 32,879; district, 1,808,602.
·map, India **9**:278

Nałkowska, Zofia (1884–1954), Polish author.
·themes of major works **10**:1253d

Nallamala Range, a series of parallel hills and valleys of the Eastern Ghāts in eastern Andhra Pradesh state, southern India. Located south of the Krishna River, the hills run north to south, parallel to the Coromandel Coast on the Bay of Bengal. Their total length is about 265 mi (430 km); the northern boundary is in the Palnād Basin, and the southern boundary in the Tirupati Hills.

About 19 mi (31 km) wide, the range rises to an average altitude of 2,900–3,600 ft (900–1,100 m). The rugged, sparsely populated hills are composed primarily of jumbled quartzites and slates and exemplify the mountain scenery of the Eastern Ghāts.
15°45′ N, 78°50′ E

nalorphine, or N-ALLYLNORMORPHINE, morphine derivative and the pharmacologic antagonist to morphine, meperidine, and methadone. Like these depressants, nalorphine is considered a narcotic, but it reverses respiratory depression and other symptoms of an overdosage of narcotics. Since nalorphine precipitates acute withdrawal symptoms when administered to morphine addicts, it has been used to diagnose addiction. Nalorphine is ineffective against respiratory depression caused by barbiturates and general anesthetics. Its overdose may cause serious bodily disturbances.

The chemical formula of nalorphine is $C_{19}H_{21}NO_3$.

Nal-Tel, small-eared variety of maize.
·Meso-American agricultural development **11**:936g

Nalu (or NALOU), African tribe in Senegal, Guinea, The Gambia, and Portuguese Guinea.
·visual art forms **1**:262f

Nama, Hottentot people of southern Africa, one of the few groups that have been able to preserve their Hottentot identity, language, and some customs. In their traditional culture subsistence was based on nomadic pastoralism and communities were organized into a loose confederation of clans.
·Hottentot cultural preservation **10**:450a
·pre-German annexation conflict with Herero **17**:289g

nāma (Hindi *nām*), a Sanskrit word referring to a name of God, particularly when repeated as a devotional exercise.
·Sikh path to liberation from saṃsāra **16**:746f

Namakwaland, or NAMALAND (South West Africa): *see* Namaqualand.

Nama language, most important of the Hottentot languages. *See* Hottentot languages.

Namangan, *oblast* (administrative region), eastern Uzbek Soviet Socialist Republic, with an area of 3,010 sq mi (7,800 sq km), in the northern part of the Fergana Valley. It is traversed by the Syrdarya (river) and by the Severny Fergansky irrigation canal. The economy is predominantly agricultural. Because of the dry climate, almost all crops are grown on irrigated land along the Syrdarya and in the river valleys of the Chatkal Mountains. About 70 percent of the sown acreage is under cotton; grain, fruit, vegetables, grapes, and fodder are also cultivated, and sericulture is important. The pasturelands are poor, but a number of sheep, goats, and cattle are raised, primarily in the west. Industry is concentrated in the capital, Namangan. The ancient settlement of Chust is the home of the *tyubeteyka*, the traditional Uzbek square skullcap, and Chartak spa attracts visitors from all over the Soviet Union. Uzbeks made up over 80 percent of the inhabitants, the remainder including Tadzhiks, Russians, Tatars, and Kirgiz. More than two-thirds of the people are rural. Pop. (1970) 847,000.
·Uzbek S.S.R. demography and industry **19**:11g

Namangan, city and administrative centre of Namangan *oblast* (region), Uzbek Soviet Socialist Republic, in the north of the Fergana Valley. The first mention of the settlement dates from the end of the 15th century. By the mid-18th century its many craftsmen made it one of the foremost cities in the Fergana Valley. In the same century it became part of the khanate of Kokand and the centre of a political unit.

Industry processing local agricultural raw materials, particularly cotton, began to develop after the Fergana Valley was annexed by Russia in 1876, and Namangan is now known for its food and other light industries. It is on the Fergana circular railway and has a teacher-training institute, a theatre, and a museum. Pop. (1977 est.) 224,000.
41°00′ N, 71°40′ E

·map, Soviet Union **17**:322
·Uzbek S.S.R. demography and industry **19**:11f

Namaqualand, Afrikaans NAMAKWALAND, also called NAMALAND, region, southwestern Africa, extending from near Windhoek, in South West Africa, southward into Cape of Good Hope province, South Africa, and from the Namib Desert eastward to the Kalahari. The area, roamed over by the Nama Hottentots before the German occupation of South West Africa in the 19th century, is divided by the Orange River into Little Namaqualand in South Africa and Great Namaqualand in South West Africa. It is primarily desert, with annual rainfall between 2 and 8 in. (50 and 200 mm). Most of the eastern part of the area has been marked off as *sperrgebiet*, or restricted area, which cannot be entered without a pass, for it is extremely rich in diamonds, the mining of which is strictly controlled. Mining operations are conducted on a large scale, and production approaches 1,000,000 carats a year, about 80 percent of which is of gem quality.

The South African portion of Namaqualand consists of the administrative district of Little Namaqualand, Cape of Good Hope province. It has an area of 18,518 sq mi (47,961 sq km). Its chief town and administrative centre is Springbok. Pop. (1970 prelim.) South African portion, 55,318.

nāma-rūpa (Sanskrit: "name and form"), a term used in Buddhist philosophy for the principle of individual identity.

·Buddhist law of dependent origination **3**:375h

Namazga-Tepe, also spelled NAMAZGA-DEPE, Bronze Age site in the area of Ashkhabad, southern Turkmen S.S.R.

·area and pottery discoveries **3**:1131f

namāzlik: *see* prayer rug.

Namba, also called LAMBA, a people of northern Togo.

·Togo culture and language **18**:472d

Nambikwara, also spelled NAMBICUARA, South American Indian people of the southern Mato Grosso, Brazil. The aboriginal population, once estimated at more than 20,000, has been almost extinguished by disease; fewer than 2,000 survive today. Their language is apparently unrelated to any other.

Nambikwara subsistence patterns vary according to the season. In the dry season, bands engage in hunting and gathering, spending each night in a different place. In the rainy season, temporary settlements are set up in the gallery forests, and slash-and-burn agriculture is carried on.

Polygyny is practiced by the chief of a village and other important men, usually with several sisters or with a woman and her daughters by a previous husband. Cotton is spun and woven to make bands and belts, although neither men nor women wear clothing.

The Nambikwara believe in spirits connected with natural forces. A leading role is played by the shaman, who has the power to cure sickness and to communicate with spirits.

·cultural and economic patterns **17**:113d *passim* to 115h
·geographic distribution map **17**:113
·language classification and location table **17**:108

Nambour, principal town of the Sunshine Coast resort area, southeast Queensland, Australia. It originated as a coach stop between Brisbane and Gympie and grew in the 1860s by absorbing many of the frustrated miners deserting the nearby Gympie goldfield. Its name is derived from *nambur*, an Aboriginal term meaning "red flowering tea-tree." On the Bruce Highway and the main northern rail line to Brisbane (55 mi [89 km] south), the town serves a district producing sugarcane, tropical fruits, strawberries, ginger, macadamia nuts, and timber (from the Blackall Range, 10 mi west). There are local deposits of asbestos and manganese. Pop. (1976 prelim.) 7,435.
26°38′ S, 152°58′ E

Nambucca Heads, town and promontory, north coastal New South Wales, Australia. The name, derived from an Aboriginal term meaning "entrance of waters," comes from the Nambucca River, which flows 70 mi (113 km) through heavily timbered country to enter the Pacific just south of the promontory. The town, at the river's mouth, was founded (1842) by cedar lumbermen, but by the 1870s dairy farmers were appropriating the deforested river flats. Proclaimed a village (1885), it became a shire in 1915. Connected to Sydney (250 mi southwest) by rail and the Pacific Highway, it serves a region of mixed farming (bananas, dairying, beef, maize [corn], and vegetables) and lumbering. Tourism, based on the nearby New England National Park, fishing and surfing facilities, and the spectacular view of the coast afforded by Yarrahampi Lookout, provides additional income. Pop. (1971) 2,708.
30°39′ S, 153°00′ E

Nambūdiri, also spelled NAMPŪTIRI, the dominant caste of the Indian state of Kerala; orthodox in the extreme, its members regard themselves as the true repositories of the ancient Vedic religion and of the precepts of the traditional Hindu code. The caste follows a distinctive marriage alliance with the important warrior caste of the Nāyars (*q.v.*). Though the eldest son of a Nambūdiri household customarily marries a Nambūdiri woman, thus observing the typical caste practice of endogamy, the younger sons marry Nāyar women and obey the matrilineal descent system of the Nāyars.

In contrast to other Brahmin castes in southern India, the Nambūdiris place great emphasis on their sacerdotal status and do not normally engage in profitable professions. They derive their wealth from their landholdings, and they constitute the chief landowners of Kerala.

There are five subdivisions: Tampurakkal, the highest in status, who with the Adhyas form an endogamous subcaste; the Adhyas, who are temple priests; the Visistas, some of whom are ritualists, while others pursue traditional learning and philosophy; the Samanyas, who study the Veda; and the Jatimatras, who are the leading physicians according to the Ayurvedic school of medicine.

Namcha Barwa, peak at the east end of the Himalayas, southeastern Tibet.
29°38′ N, 95°04′ E

·Great Himalayan range **8**:882b; map

Namchi, also spelled NAMCHE, village and administrative headquarters of Namchi District in the Himalayan Indian state of Sikkim. A regional trading centre, it has a hospital, higher secondary school, and a rest house. Roads lead northeast (19 mi [31 km]) to Gangtok, the capital of Sikkim, and southwest to Darjeeling. There is a small hydroelectric project at Naya Bazar, southwest on the Great Rangit River. Several Buddhist monasteries (notably Tashiding, Sangachelling, and Pemiongchi) are nearby.
27°09′ N, 86°23′ E

·Sikkim administration **16**:748h; map

Nāmdev (b. 1270?, Narasi, India—d. 1350?, Pandharpur), a leading poet-saint of the Indian medieval period who wrote in the Marathi language.

The son of a tailor and thus of low caste, Nāmdev married and had five children. As a youth, he was a member of a murderous gang of thieves but was overcome with remorse one day on hearing the plaintive lamentations of a woman whose husband he had killed. He was about to take his own life when he was saved by a revelation of Lord Viṣṇu (Vishnu).

Nāmdev then turned to a life of devotion and became the foremost exponent of the Vārakarī ("Pilgrim" school, so called because of the emphasis it placed on pilgrimages to Pandharpur to worship a local image of Viṣṇu called Viṭṭhal [Viṭhobā]). The school is known for its expression of *bhakti* (loving devotion to a personal god) and for its freedom from caste restrictions in a religious setting.

Nāmdev wrote a number of *abhaṅga*s (hymns) expressive of his surrender to God. Extremely popular in Mahārāshtra and in the Punjab, some of his verses are included in the *Ādi Granth*, the holy scripture of the Sikhs. His enthusiasm fired members of his household and even his personal servant, Jānabāī, to compose lyrics. Nāmdev inspired a tradition of devotional poetry that continued in Mahārāshtra for four centuries, culminating in the great devotional hymnist Tukārām.

·Marathi bhakti poets **17**:143h

Nāmdhārī, also called KŪKĀ, name of an austere sect within Sikhism, a religion of India. The movement was founded by Balak Singh (1797–1862), who did not believe in any religious ritual other than the repetition of god's name (or *nām*, for which reason members of the sect are called Nāmdhārīs). His successor, Rām Singh (1816–85), introduced the sect's distinctive style of wearing the turban (bound straight across the forehead rather than at an angle), of dressing only in clothing made from white, handwoven cloth, and the practice of frenzied chanting of hymns culminating in shrieks (*kūk*s; hence the name Kūkās). Under Rām Singh's leadership the Nāmdhārīs sought a resurgence of Sikh rule in the Punjab. After a clash with the police in January 1872, 66 of them were apprehended and executed by being tied to the mouths of cannons that were then fired. Rām Singh was exiled to Rangoon, where he died. The Nāmdhārīs continue to maintain their own *gurdwārā*s (houses of worship) and do not marry outside the sect.

Nam Dinh, city, capital of Ha Nam Ninh province, northern Vietnam; it lies on a canal linking the Song (river) Day and the Red River and has road and railway links with Hanoi, 50 mi (80 km) northwest. Manufactures include textiles and distillery and salt products. The city is also an educational centre.
20°25′ N, 106°10′ E

·map, North Vietnam **19**:135
·North Vietnam settlement patterns **19**:132g; illus.

Namen (Belgium): *see* Namur.

names 12:814, words or phrases designating individual persons, places, or things, as opposed to common nouns, which designate classes of items.

The text article covers the distinction between names and common nouns; the science of names, including categories and forms; the processes of conferring names on persons and places; and the development of names, including legal influences and the patterns of naming peculiar to various regions and cultures.

REFERENCES in other text articles:
·Austro-Asiatic vocabulary taboos **2**:483f
·Carolingian practices **12**:144e
·Carthaginian theophoric forms **13**:148h
·Chinese Dialecticians' interpretation **4**:417e
·Meso-American inheritance traditions **11**:955c
·Mesopotamian practices **11**:970f
·referential model of meaning **16**:507g
·Russell's philosophical analysis **1**:803e
·sacred power in words **16**:126d
·taboos and other cultural attitudes **10**:643c
·totemic and theriophoric form **1**:916c
·totemism origin in Lang's view **18**:531e
·Woodlands Indian name ownership **6**:171g

RELATED ENTRIES in the *Ready Reference and Index*:
epithet; Mac; nickname; onomastics; patronymic; place-name; surname; toponymy

Namgyal, the ruling dynasty of Sikkim from 1642 to 1975. In the mid-17th century the chief monks at Yoksam recognized the need for a formal government in Sikkim and established Phuntsog (or Penchoo) Namgyal, a seventh-generation descendant of a Tibetan noble, as the first *chogyal* of the Sikkimese theocratic state. The dynasty continued through the 11th *chogyal*, Palden Thondup Namgyal, during whose reign Sikkim became the 22nd state of India.
·history of Sikkim **16**:749a

Nam Ha, former province of northern Vietnam, situated in the lowland delta region of the Red River (Song Hong). Created in 1965 upon the union of Nam Dinh and Ha Nam provinces, it was bounded by the provinces of Thai Binh, Ha Tay, and Ninh Binh on the north and west, and by the Gulf of Tonkin on the east. In a further reorganization (1975–76), Nam Ha was merged with Ninh Binh to form the province of Ha Nam Ninh. Nam Dinh, the provincial capital, is a commercial and industrial centre.

Namib Desert 12:819, a cool desert, 80 to 100 mi in width, extending for 1,200 mi (1,900 km) along the southwest coast of Africa from Moçâmedes (Angola) in the north, across South West Africa, to the Orange River in South Africa.

The text article surveys the physiography, drainage and soils, climate, vegetation and animal life, inhabitants, and transport facilities of the desert.

REFERENCES in other text articles:
·map, Africa **1**:179
·map, South West Africa **17**:301
·South West African landscape features **17**:300e
·vegetation types **5**:616b
·water balance and topography **5**:607f

Namibia (Africa): *see* South West Africa.

Namier, Sir Lewis (Bernstein) (b. June 27, 1888, near Łuków, Pol.—d. Aug. 19, 1960, London), British historian most noted for his work on the 18th century, immigrated to England in 1906, and went to Balliol College, Oxford. He took British nationality before World War I, in which he served first in the army and then in the Foreign Office, where he remained until 1920. Namier failed to get a teaching post at Oxford, went into business, and later devoted his time to research. The appearance of *The Structure of Politics at the Accession of George III* in 1929 revolutionized 18th-century historiography and remains his most considerable work. By intensive research over a brief period he aimed to show why men entered politics, and he rejected the simple classification of Whig and Tory in favour of personal, family, or regional interests. He was professor of modern history (1931–53) at Manchester and produced various books of essays and two important works: *1848: The Revolution of the Intellectuals* (1946) and *Diplomatic Prelude, 1938–39* (1948). Of an official *History of Parliament*, begun under his editorship, part I, *The House of Commons, 1745–90*, in three volumes, was published in 1964.

Namier was made an honorary fellow of Balliol in 1948 and was knighted in 1952. His approach to history attracted many followers but also created opposition among historians who felt that he ignored irrational elements in history and other aspects of society in favour of a preoccupation with the mechanism of politics.

Namier's wife, Julia Michaelovna, *née* Kazarin (1893–1977), was an author who published a number of books under the pseudonym Iulia de Beausobre. These included *The Woman Who Could Not Die* (1938), an account of her imprisonment in the Soviet Union, and *Flame in the Snow, a Russian Legend* (1945), a biography of St. Seraphim of Sarov. She also wrote a biography of her husband, *Lewis Namier*, published in 1971.

Namikawa Sōsuke (1847–1910), Japanese craftsman who established a factory for the manufacture of cloisonné enamels.
·enamelwork style and manufacture **6**:779e; illus.

Namiki Gohei (1747–1808), Japanese Kabuki playwright.
·contribution to Kabuki theatre **10**:368a

Namiki Shōzō I (1730–73), Japanese Kabuki playwright.
·Kabuki theatre innovations **10**:368c

Namiki Shōzō II, also called NYUGATEI GANYU (d. 1807), Japanese Kabuki playwright.
·contribution to Kabuki theatre **10**:368b

Namirembe Agreement (1955), British compromise in Uganda giving native Ugandans a parliamentary majority.
·East African unrest solution attempts **6**:103a

Nammal River, stream of the Salt Range, Pakistan.
32°40′ N, 72°35′ E
·course nature **16**:199g

Nammālvār (*c.* 9th century), greatest of the Ālvārs (*q.v.*).

Namosi, province, Fiji.
·area and population table **7**:297

Nampa, city, Canyon County, southwestern Idaho, U.S., in the centre of the Boise Valley. Founded in 1886, on the main line of the Union Pacific Railroad at the junction of a branch to Boise (20 mi [32 km] east), it was a hamlet in the sagebrush desert until irrigation transformed the area into farms. It was named for Nampuh (Bigfoot), a Shoshoni Indian chief.

An agricultural processing and shipping centre and freight terminal, the city has developed some light industry. Nampa is the seat of Northwest Nazarene College (1913). Inc. 1890. Pop. (1960) 18,013; (1970) 20,768; (1980) 25,112.
43°34′ N, 116°34′ W
·map, United States **18**:908

Nam Phan (Vietnam): *see* Cochinchina.

Nam Phong, city, Thailand.
16°45′ N, 102°52′ E
·map, Thailand **18**:199
·Mekong River area hydroelectric project **11**:862g

Namp'o, formerly CHINNAMP'O, city, western P'yŏngan-namdo (South P'yŏngan Province), western North Korea. It is 30 mi (50 km) southwest of P'yŏngyang, on the estuary of the Taedong-gang. Formerly a small fishing village, it developed rapidly after it became an open port in 1897. The harbour accommodates ships of 10,000 tons but is frozen during the winter. The chief seaport of the province, it is connected to the interior by rail and by river transport on the Taedong. It is a market centre for marine products, including shellfish, and its industries include copper and gold refining, shipbuilding, glassmaking, and electrode manufacturing. Along the coast are solar-evaporation salt pans. The area is known for the quality of the apples it produces. Latest pop. est. 130,000.
38°45′ N, 125°23′ E
·map, North Korea **10**:519

Nam Pung, English PUNG RIVER, tributary of the Mekong in northeastern Thailand.
16°47′ N, 101°14′ E
·Mekong River area hydroelectric project **11**:862g

Nampūtiri (caste): *see* Nambūdiri.

Namquit Point, also called GASPEE POINT, Narragansett Bay, Rhode Island, U.S.
41°45′ N, 71°28′ W
·Rhode Island Revolution incident **15**:808b

Namua, island, Western Samoa.
14°00′ S, 171°22′ W
·Samoan geography and culture **16**:205f

Namur, Flemish NAMEN, province, southeastern Belgium, extending northward from the French border between the provinces of Hainaut (west) and Luxembourg (east), with an area of 1,413 sq mi (3,660 sq km), drained by the Meuse, Sambre, and Lesse rivers. It is divided into three administrative *arrondissements* (Namur, Dinant, and Philippeville) with the capital at Namur. French is the principal language of the entire province.

Much of the eastern part formerly belonged to the prince-bishops of Liège, while the northern part was the medieval county of Namur. Ceded to Hainaut in 1188 and temporarily raised to a marquisate in 1199, it passed to Flanders in 1263. It was sold to the dukes of Burgundy in 1421, and its history merged with that of the Burgundian Netherlands.

The rich alluvial soils of the Hesbaye Plateau to the north support wheat, sugar beets, fodder crops, and orchards. The mild climate and calcareous loams, clays, and alluvial soils of the Sambre and Meuse valleys (which form a "T" across the centre of the province) are well farmed and support mixed agriculture and dairying. The historic region of Condroz, a rock plateau in the southeast with sandstone ridges and limestone valleys, is similar to Entre-Sambre-et-Meuse in the southwest; the ridges of both are wooded, and the valley clays support wheat, winter barley, rye, potatoes, fodder, flax, dairying, cattle raising, and horse breeding. The Famenne depression, south of these plateaus, has much woodland and pasture; in places limestone has given rise to underground streams, striking rock formations, and grottoes, such as the Han grottoes in the Lesse Valley and the caverns near Rochefort on the Lomme River. Also to the south is a small area of the rocky Ardennes region, with peat moors, bogs, patches of coniferous plantation, and limited pasture for beef cattle; some farming is practiced in the valleys.

The Sambre and Meuse valleys are part of the "industrial crescent" of southern Belgium. Although the small Namur coal basin is now exhausted, steel-related industries, metallurgical and chemical works, and glassworks still thrive. Sugar refining and manufacturing of agricultural machinery prevail in the north, and a growing resort industry in the south, along the Meuse and its tributaries. Limestone, granite, marble, and sandstone are quarried from the Condroz. The province is served by several rail lines, and the Meuse and Sambre are both canalized.

Population centres are Namur and Dinant (*qq.v.*) on the Meuse, Ciney on the Condroz, Philippeville in Entre-Sambre-et-Meuse, and Gembloux on the northern plateau. Unusual rock formations along the rivers and medieval châteaus and abbeys throughout the province attract tourists. The Natural Reserve of Champale and Poilvache (1969) includes some of these formations and the ruins of the feudal château of Poilvache. Pop. (1977 est.) 398,916.

·area and population table **2**:821
·map, Belgium **2**:819

Namur, Flemish NAMEN, capital of Namur province, south central Belgium, at the junction of the Sambre and Meuse rivers. A pre-Roman *oppidum* (fortified town), it was the seat of the counts of Namur from 908 until it passed to Burgundy in 1421. It has been an episcopal see since 1559. Its strategic position at the head of routes into France made Namur the scene of many battles and sieges: it passed from French to Allied domination seven times between 1692 and 1794 and was Dutch from 1815 until Belgian independence (1830). The citadel, high on a rock above the town, was originally the castle of the counts; it was fortified in the 15th, 16th, and 19th centuries before being abandoned (1862). The new outlying fortifications (1893) were destroyed by the Germans in World War I, and the town was severely damaged in World War II.

A rail junction and centre of art and tourism, Namur is also an industrial town, its industries including the manufacture of glass, paper, leather and steel goods, and cement. Landmarks are the Baroque Cathedral of St. Aubain, with notable paintings and metalwork; the Jesuit Church of St. Loup; the Convent of the Sisters of Our Lady, containing 13th-century treasures of silver and gold craftsmanship; and the Meat Hall (1588), housing the archaeological museum. The Diocesan Museum exhibits the Carolingian shrine of Andenne and the golden crown and portable altar of the counts (1217). A restored 11th-century bridge crosses the Meuse. Pop. (1977 est.) 30,845.

50°28′ N, 4°52′ E
·Frisian commercial development **11**:133b
·map, Belgium **2**:819

Namur, Belg., at the confluence of the Meuse and Sambre rivers
Photo Research International

Namur, sieges of, two campaigns during the War of the Grand Alliance (1689–97) against the town of Namur, strategically located at the juncture of the Sambre and Meuse (Maas) rivers, 35 miles (55 kilometres) southeast of Brussels.

From May 25 to June 5, 1692, the Dutch defenders and their Spanish and German allies manned the defenses built by the Dutch engineer Menno, baron van Coehoorn. When they surrendered on June 5, they had suffered about 5,000 killed and wounded, or twice the casualties of the French attackers. The siege was organized by the French engineer Sébastien de Vauban, who improved the defenses after his victory.

Three years later 14,000 French troops, led by Louis-François, duc de Boufflers, held the city from early July until Sept. 1, 1695, against 18,000 Allied attackers, led by William III, king of England and stadholder of the Netherlands. Assisted by van Coehoorn, the besiegers finally took the town; their casualties, however, were double those of the French defenders. The war became deadlocked from this point.

Namurian Series, major division of Upper Carboniferous rocks and time throughout the Eastern Hemisphere (the Upper Carboniferous Period began about 325,000,000 years ago and lasted about 45,000,000 years). It was named for and is characterized by exposures studied in the Namur Basin, Belgium, and is the lowermost series of the Upper Carboniferous; Namurian rocks precede those of the Westphalian Series and overlie the rocks of the Viséan Series, in the Lower Carboniferous Period.

Although continental deposits are also known, Namurian rocks in Europe are predominantly marine; they are characterized by the occurrence of fossil cephalopod genera *Homoceras*, *Reticuloceras*, and *Eumorphoceras*. Because of the occurrence of distinctive fossil faunas, worldwide correlation of Namurian rocks has been possible.

·Upper Carboniferous strata boundaries **3**:859d

Nam Viet, Chinese NAN YÜEH (meaning Southern Kingdom), ancient semi-sinicized kingdom occupying much of what is now northern Vietnam and the southern Chinese provinces of Kwangtung and Kwangsi.

The kingdom was formed in 207 BC during the breakup of the Ch'in dynasty (221–206 BC), when the Ch'in governor of Nan Yüeh (now Kwangtung and Kwangsi provinces) declared his territory independent. His son Chao T'o (Trieu Da) expanded the new kingdom southward, incorporating the Red River Delta and the area as far south as Da Nang.

Nam Viet, or Nan Yüeh, remained independent, though loosely associated with the Han dynasty, until it was conquered by the Han emperor Wu Ti in 111 BC. Following the conquest, the area became a region for Chinese settlement, a policy that eventually resulted in the sinicization of Kwangtung and Kwangsi and introduced Chinese culture to northern Vietnam, The attempt to absorb Vietnam into China also engendered an increasing self-consciousness among the people of the northern and central regions of Vietnam.

In AD 939 the term Nam Viet appeared again as the name of the kingdom centred in the Red River Valley at Co Loa. Ngo Quyen (*q.v.*) drove the Chinese out of the area and founded his own dynasty, which endured only until 954.

The term was revived again in 1802 by the emperor Gia Long but was inverted to Viet Nam.

·Au Lac conquest and incorporation **19**:121b
·history of Kwangsi **10**:550c
·Six Dynasties period maps **4**:316

Nan, administrative headquarters of Nan province, north central Thailand, at the head of the Mae Nam (river) Nan Valley, in the Doi Luang Phra Bang Range, near the Laotian border. It is a commercial centre for teak and agricultural products. A road leads southwest to Den Chai. The province (area 4,516 sq mi [11,696 sq km]) is inhabited mainly by the Lao people, but the primitive Yumbri, or Phi Tong Luang, tribes dwell in its remote parts. Pop. (1972 est.) town, 15,200; (1970) province, 310,734.

18°48′ N, 100°46′ E
·map, Thailand **18**:199
·province area and population table **18**:202

Nan, Mae Nam, river (*mae nam*) in northwestern Thailand, rises in the northern portion of the Doi Luang Phra Bang Range on the Laotian border, and flows south for 390 mi (627 km) receiving the Mae Nam Yom near Chum Saeng. Just above Nakhon Sawan the Ping and the Nan-Yom combine to form the Mae Nam Chao Phraya (*q.v.*). The major towns of Nan, Uttaradit, Phu Miang (head of navigation), Phichai, and Phitsanulok are on its banks.

15°42′ N, 100°11′ E
·map Thailand **18**:199

Nana (Sumerian goddess): *see* Nabu.

Nāna Fadnavis (d. 1800), Marāthā minister in India.

·resistance to British expansion **9**:390e

Nanai, also spelled NANAY, also called GOLD and in China HOCHE, Manchu people of the Soviet Union and China.

·China's population, table 3 **4**:272
·geographic distribution map **2**:194
·Soviet Union nationalities distribution, table 3 **17**:339

Nanai (NANAY) **language,** minor language of the Manchu-Tungus subfamily of the Altaic languages, spoken by about 10,000 Nanais living around the lower reaches of the Amur River in the Soviet Union and by another 1,000 in China. *See also* Manchu-Tungus languages.

·affiliation and distribution, table 3 **1**:636

Nanaimo, city, southwestern British Columbia, Canada, on Vancouver Island and the Georgia Strait. Founded as Colvilletown around a Hudson's Bay Company trading post, it developed after 1849 when coal fields were discovered nearby by the Indians. In 1860 the settlement was renamed Sne-ny-mo (from which Nanaimo is derived) from an Indian word meaning "a big, strong tribe," which was applied to a tribal confederation. An important distributing centre, Nanaimo is connected with Vancouver and the mainland by ferries.

Coal mining was the main industry until the last mine closed in 1953. The economy now depends chiefly on lumbering, pulp processing, commercial fishing, agriculture, shipbuilding, and tourism. The federal government maintains a fisheries and oceanographic research station at the north edge of the city. Historic features are Petroglyph Park, with its ancient rock carvings, and the Bastion, part of

The Bastion, remnant of a Hudson's Bay Company's fort, Nanaimo, B.C.

J. Barras Walker

a fortress built by the Hudson's Bay Company in 1853 to protect the miners and settlers. Inc. city, 1874. Pop. (1971 prelim.) 14,762.
49°10′ N, 123°56′ W
·map, Canada **3**:716

Nānak 12:821 (b. April 15, 1469, Rāi Bhoi dī Talvandī, near Lahore, India—d. 1539, Kartarpur), Indian spiritual teacher who was the first gurū of the Sikhs, a religious group that combines Hindu and Muslim influences in a monotheistic, meditative doctrine of salvation.

Abstract of text biography. Nānak belonged to a mercantile family of relatively high social rank. He undertook an extended pilgrimage to Muslim and Hindu religious centres in India and possibly abroad. By 1520 he had returned to the Punjab and soon attracted a large following to Kartārpur. His teachings, expressed through devotional hymns, many of which still survive, stressed salvation from rebirth through meditation on the divine name.

REFERENCES in other text articles:
·Punjab's spiritual leaders **15**:287c
·Sikhism's relation to Kabīrpanthīs **8**:917e
·Sikh traditions and legends **16**:744d

Nanao, city, Ishikawa Prefecture (*ken*), Honshu, Japan, on the Noto-hantō (Noto Peninsula), facing Nanao-wan (Nanao Bay). It was a small castle town in the 14th century, and its natural harbour served as a base for coastal shipping. The port was opened to trade with Russia, China, and Korea after the arrival of a railway in 1899. In its most prosperous days, the port was visited by an estimated 7,000 ships annually. Nanao's importance declined, however, with the development of land transportation in the 20th century. Imports are now largely restricted to small quantities of wood and manganese ore from the Soviet Union. Pop. (1970) 47,855.
37°03′ N, 136°58′ E
·map, Japan **10**:36

Nana Sahib, real name DHONDU PANT (b. *c.* 1820—d. *c.* 1859), a prominent leader in the Indian Mutiny of 1857. Although he did not plan the outbreak, he assumed leadership of the sepoys (British-employed Indian soldiers).

Adopted in 1827 by Bājī Rāo II, the last Marāthā peshwa (prince), Nana Sahib was educated as a Hindu nobleman. On the death of the exiled Bājī Rāo in 1852, he inherited his home in Bithur (now in Uttar Pradesh), rent-free, and his private property. Although his adoptive father had pleaded that his 80,000-pound-a-year life pension be extended to Nana Sahib, the British governor general of India, Lord Dalhousie, refused. Nana Sahib sent an agent, Azimullah Khan, to London to push his claims—but without success. On his return, Azimullah told Nana Sahib he was unimpressed by supposed British military strength in the Crimea against Russia. This report, the refusal of his claim, and threats of the sepoys led him to join the sepoy battalions at Cawnpore (Kānpur) in rebellion in June 1857. He had sent Sir Hugh Wheeler, commander of British forces at Cawnpore, a letter warning of the attack—a sardonic gesture to his former friends. A safe conduct given to the British under General Wheeler by Nana Sahib was broken on June 27, and British women and children were massacred at his palace. Lacking military knowledge, he could not command the mutinous sepoys though he had the satisfaction of being declared peshwa in July 1857, by Tantia Topi and his followers after the capture of Gwalior. Defeated by Gen. Henry Havelock and in December 1857 by Sir Colin Campbell, he appointed a nephew, Rao Sahib, to give orders to Tantia. Nana Sahib was driven into the Nepal hills in 1859, where he is thought to have died.

Nanay, Manchurian people living in the lower basin of the Amur River in the U.S.S.R. and China. They speak a Manchu-Tungus language.
·China's population, table 3 **4**:272
·geographic distribution map **2**:194
·Soviet Union nationalities distribution, table 3 **17**:339

Nançen Pinco, Chimú emperor, reigning from 1370 AD.
·Chimú culture and conquests **1**:846c

Nan-ch'ang, Pin-yin romanization NANCHANG, city in Kiangsi Province (*sheng*), China. Nan-ch'ang, as the provincial capital, forms an autonomous subprovincial level municipality (*shih*). The city is situated on the right bank of the Kan Chiang (river) below its confluence with the Chin Chiang and some 25 mi (40 km) south of its discharge into the P'o-yang Hu (lake). The city was founded and first walled in 201 BC, when the county (*hsien*) town was given the name Nan-ch'ang. It was also the administrative seat of a commandery (*chün*), Yü-chang. In 589 this commandery was changed into a prefecture named Hung-chou, and after 763 it became the provincial centre of Kiangsi Province, which was then beginning the rapid growth that by the 12th century made it the most populous province in China. In 959, under the Southern T'ang regime, it became Nan-ch'ang Superior Prefecture (*fu*) and also the southern capital. After the conquest by the Sung regime in 981 it reverted to the name Hung-chou. In 1164 it was renamed Lung-hsing Superior Prefecture, which name it retained until 1368. At the end of the Yüan (Mongol) period (1279–1368) it became a battleground between Chu Yüan-chang, the founder of the Ming dynasty (1368–1644), and the rival local warlord, Ch'en Yu-liang. At the beginning of the 16th century it was the power base from which Chu Ch'en-hao, the Prince of Ning, launched a rebellion against the Ming regime. In the 1850s it suffered considerably as a result of the Taiping Rebellion (1850–64), and its importance as a commercial centre declined as the overland routes to Canton were replaced by coastal steamship services in the latter half of the 19th century.

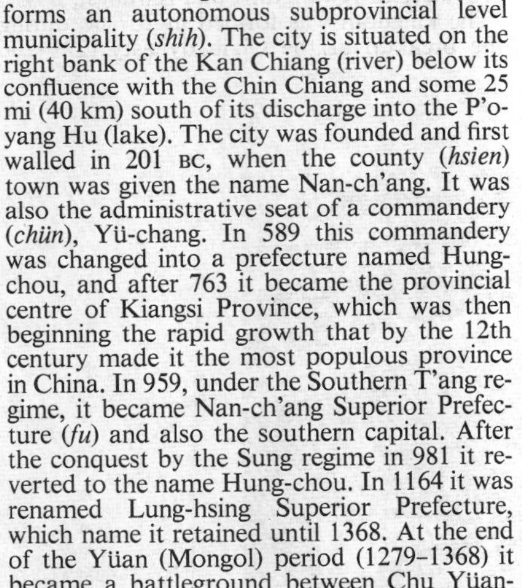

Rice paddy, southwest of Nan-ch'ang, Kiangsi Province, China; rice is shipped to the city for milling

G. Damian Loescher—Pictorial Parade

Nan-ch'ang has, however, remained the undisputed regional metropolis of Kiangsi, although Chiu-chiang, on the Yangtze River (Ch'ang Chiang), which offers direct access to large ships, has tended to rival it as a commercial centre. In 1949 Nan-ch'ang was still essentially an old-style administrative and commercial city, with little industry apart from food processing; it had a population of about 275,000. Nan-ch'ang first acquired a rail connection in 1915, when the line to Chiu-chiang was opened. Several other rail links have since been opened. After World War II a line was completed to Lin-ch'uan and Kung-ch'i in the Ju Shui (river) Valley to the south-southeast. Since 1949 Nan-ch'ang has been extensively industrialized. It is a large-scale producer of cotton textiles and cotton yarn. Paper making is also a large industry, as is food processing (especially rice milling). Heavy industry began to be important in the mid-1950s. A large thermal power plant was installed using coal brought by rail from Feng-ch'eng, to the south. A machinery industry grew up, at first mainly concentrated on the production of agricultural equipment and diesel engines. Nan-ch'ang then became a centre of the automotive industry, producing trucks and tractors and also such equipment as tires. An iron-smelting plant helping to supply local industry was installed in the later 1950s. There is also a large chemical industry, producing agricultural chemicals and insecticides as well as pharmaceuticals. Pop. (1948) 267,000; (1953) 398,000; (latest est.) 520,000.
28°41′ N, 115°53′ E
·map, China **4**:262
·population and industry **10**:459e

Nanchao, a Tai kingdom that arose in the 8th century in western Yunnan Province in southern China, a region to which the Tai peoples trace their origin. Many fragmented Tai kingdoms had occupied this region, centred at Lake Tali between the Mekong, the Yangtze, and the sources of the Red River, under varying degrees of Chinese control, since the 1st century AD.

Nanchao (from Chinese: Southern Princedom) was formed by the unification of six Tai kingdoms in 729. Pi-lo-ko, the leader of one small tribal state, extended his control over the five neighbouring kingdoms while acting in alliance with China, which needed an ally against the aggressive Tibetans. Once unification was complete, Pi-lo-ko established Nanchao's centre of power in the Lake Tali Plain. Geographic factors rendered the capital impregnable, and two Chinese attacks were repulsed in 751 and 754. Nanchao was also able to dominate the East–West trade routes from China and Tongking through Burma to India. By the 9th century, Nanchao became an imperialistic state waging war deep into Burma in 832 and into Tongking in 862.

Nanchao attained a high level of culture. Skilled artisans taught the weaving of cotton and silk gauze. Salt and gold were mined in many parts of the kingdom, and a complex system of government and administration was developed.

The Mongols under the leadership of Kublai Khan conquered a declining Nanchao in 1253. During the preceding two centuries, however, the Tais had been moving southward in large numbers, eventually forming the bulk of the population in what is present-day Thailand.
·foundation of Thai kingdom **16**:718e
·Kwangsi's conflict and Chuang support **10**:550d
·T'ang dynasty's internal instability **4**:328a
·threat to Chinese power **19**:1113d
·Yüan dynasty conquest **6**:123a

Nan-ching (province, China): *see* Nanking.

nan ch'ü, Chinese music drama of Sung dynasty.
·description of style **12**:675b

Nan-ch'ung, Pin-yin romanization NAN-CHONG, city in east central Szechwan Province (*sheng*), China. Nan-ch'ung is a county-(*hsien-*) municipality (*shih*) and the administrative seat of the Nan-ch'ung Area (*ti-ch'ü*), controlling 11 counties in the valley of the Chia-ling Chiang (river), a northern tributary of the Yangtze River. Nan-ch'ung is situated on the west bank of the Chia-ling, which provides easy water transport to Chungking, some 95 mi (150 km) to the south. To the north, highways give access to southern Shensi Province, while Nan-ch'ung is on the important east–west route of the Ch'eng-tu to Wan-hsien highway.

Nan-ch'ung's name goes back to the early Sui (581–618) period. From Sung times (960–1279) it was the seat of the Shun-ch'ing Superior Prefecture (*fu*), by which name it is still commonly known. The original Nan-ch'ung was some 12½ mi (20 km) further upstream; the present town dates from Ming times (1368–1644).

Nan-ch'ung is not only an important communications hub but is also the chief market for an extremely prosperous and productive agricultural plain. It is a major grain market (supplying rice to Chungking) and also markets sweet potatoes, cotton, hemp, tobacco, and other agricultural products.

The city is notable as one of the largest centres of the silk industry in Szechwan, with silk filatures, weaving, dyeing, and printing plants producing silks of high quality. Nan-ch'ung also has a handicraft industry specializing in lacquer goods. There is a small metalworking and light engineering industry. Exploitation of a major oil field in the district, discovered in 1958, began in the 1960s, with production becoming large scale in the 1970s. A refinery has been built at Nan-ch'ung. There are also major coal deposits at Shih-tzu-t'an, some 25 mi (40 km) south of Nan-ch'ung. Pop. (1948) 60,000; (1953) 165,000; (latest est.) 206,000.
30°54′ N, 106°06′ E
·map, China **4**:262

Nancy, capital, Meurthe-et-Moselle *département*, eastern France, in what was formerly the province of Lorraine, west of Strasbourg, near the left bank of the Meurthe River.

Place Stanislas (commemorating Stanisław I, last duke of Lorraine) in front of the town hall, Nancy, Fr.
Shostal

Until the 18th century, Nancy was composed of two distinct fortified towns. To the north stood the medieval city, the Ville-Vieille (Old Town), and to the south the Ville-Neuve (New Town), founded in the late 16th century. In 1750, Stanisław I (Stanisław Leszczyński), king of Poland and father-in-law of Louis XV, king of France (1715–74), pulled down the walls that separated the two towns and built a new, well-planned city centre. The town was further enlarged after the Franco-Prussian War of 1870–71 and during the 20th century.

The central group of buildings erected by Stanisław I constitutes one of the most perfect and homogenous existing examples of 18th-century French architecture. The rectangular Place Stanislas, 400 by 350 ft (120 by 105 m), has four cutoff corners ornamented by wrought-iron railings edged with gilding. On one side is the handsome Hôtel de Ville. On the opposite side, a monumental arch, built in honour of Louis XV, opens onto the oblong Place de la Carrière (16th–18th century). The 18th-century Palais du Gouvernement, standing at the end of the square, has a fine Greek Ionic colonnade. Adjoining the building is the former Palais Ducal (mostly 16th-century), which now houses the Musée Historique Lorrain, with its rich collection of regional art and folklore.

In the 11th century Nancy was a small township dominated by a castle. Fortified in the 12th century, it became the capital of the dukes of Lorraine. In 1477 Charles the Bold, duke of Burgundy (1467–77), was killed while trying to capture the town. During the 16th century it became prosperous; and Charles III, the Great Duke of Lorraine and the Bar (1543–1608), founded a separate new town, the Ville-Neuve, which was captured by the French in 1633 and restored to the dukes of Lorraine after the Treaty of Rijswijk in 1697. Louis XV granted Nancy and the duchy of Lorraine to Stanisław I after he lost the Polish crown in 1735. At his death in 1766, the city passed to France. After the Franco-Prussian War of 1870–71, the population increased considerably, as Nancy became the main refuge of emigrants from Alsace and from the city of Metz, which were under German rule. Nancy suffered damage in World War I but was almost unharmed during World War II.

Nancy, which has been largely supplanted by Metz (30 mi [50 km] to the north) as an industrial centre, has chemical, clothing, and food-processing industries. The town has developed as an administrative and financial capital. The old university (founded 1572) was closed during the French Revolution. A university was re-established during the 19th century. Pop. (1971 est.) 120,900.
48°41′ N, 6°12′ E
·map, France **7**:584

Nanda, dynasty that ruled Magadha, in northern India, between *c.* 343 and 321 BC; it immediately precedes the dynasty of the Mauryas, and, as with all pre-Maurya dynasties, what is known about it is a mixture of fact and legend. Indigenous traditions, both Brahminical and Jaina, suggest that the founder of the dynasty, Mahāpadma (Mahāpadmapati, Ugrasena), had a socially based origin—a fact confirmed by classical scholarship. Mahāpadma took over from the Śaiśunāgas not only the reins of Magadhan power but also the policy of systematic expansion. His probable frontier origin and early career as an adventurer helped him to consolidate the empire with ruthless conquests. The authenticity of the Purāṇic statement that he was the "destroyer of all Kṣatriyas" and that he overthrew such disparately located powers as the Ikṣvākus, Pañcālas, Kāśīs, Haihayas, Kaliṅgas, Aśmakas, Kurus, Maithilas, Śūrasenas, and Vītihotras is borne out by independent evidence, which also associated the Nandas with the distant Godāvari Valley, Kaliṅga, and part of Mysore.

The post-Mahāpadma genealogy is perfunctory in the *Purāṇas*, which mention only Sukalpa (Sahalya, Sumālya), while the Buddhist text *Mahābodhivaṃsa* enumerates eight names. Dhanananda, the last of this list, possibly figures as Agrammes, or Xandrames, in classical sources, a powerful contemporary of Alexander the Great. The Nanda line ended with him around 321 BC when Candragupta laid the foundation for Maurya power.

The brief spell of Nanda rule, along with the lengthy tenure of the Mauryas, represents the political aspect of a great transitional epoch in early Indian history. The changes in material culture in the Ganges Valley beginning in the 6th–5th centuries BC, chiefly characterized by settled agricultural technology and growing use of iron, resulted in production surplus and a tendency toward the growth of commerce and urban centres. It is significant in this context that in many sources, indigenous and foreign, the Nandas are portrayed as extremely rich and as ruthless collectors of various kinds of taxes. In Alexander's period, Nanda military strength is estimated at 20,000 cavalry, 200,000 infantry, 2,000 quadriga (chariots), and 3,000 elephants. In administration, the initiatives of the Nanda state are reflected in references to irrigation projects in Kaliṅga and the organization of a ministerial council.
·origins and governmental policies **9**:350b

Nanda Bayin (reigned 1581–99), king of the Toungoo dynasty of Burma whose reign ended with the dismemberment of the empire established by his father, Bayinnaung.

Upon coming to the throne, Nanda Bayin was faced with a rebellion of his uncle, the viceroy of Ava, whom he defeated three years later. In December 1584 Nanda Bayin marched into Siam, which had been a vassal of his father, to subjugate the Siamese patriot Naresuan (Phra Naret). For the next three years he sent several armies into the Mae Nam Chao Phraya Valley, but Naresuan defeated all of them. The Siamese then went on the offensive, taking Tavoy and Tenasserim in 1593. Nanda Bayin's troubles were compounded when another of his father's subject peoples, the Mon of Lower Burma, revolted and invited the Siamese to occupy Martaban and Moulmein on the Salween River. In 1595 Nanda Bayin was obliged to retreat to Pegu, the Burmese capital, and defend it from a Siamese attack.

In 1599 Nanda Bayin's brothers, the viceroys of Toungoo, Prome, and Ava, revolted and, inviting Minyazagyi, the king of Arakan, to join in the fray, besieged Pegu, took Nanda Bayin prisoner, and dismembered the last remnants of Bayinnaung's empire. Nanda Bayin's reign had been a series of catastrophes, but this was due less to a lack of energy and initiative on his part than to the overreaching ambition of his father, who had built an empire too large to govern.

Nanda Devi, twin peaks in the outer Himalaya Mountains, on the border of Garhwāl district in Uttar Pradesh state, northern India. The highest is 25,646 ft (7,822 m). A U.S.-British team was the first expedition (1936) to successfully ascend them.
30°22′ N, 79°59′ E
·map, India **9**:278
·mountaineering record and data table **12**:585

Nandakumar, 18th-century maharaja of Bengal during the governor generalship of Warren Hastings.
·opposition to Hastings and hanging **8**:666b

Nānder, also spelled NĀNDED, administrative headquarters, Nānder district, Mahārāshtra state, western India, on the banks of the Godāvari River. Its name is derived from *Nānda tat* ("Nānda border"), a term that refers to the boundary of the Magadha kingdom during the 7th century BC. Primarily a commercial centre, it also has cotton spinning and weaving mills. The town is known as a centre of Sanskrit learning and as the location of the Sikh *gurdwārā* ("temple and kitchen") built on the site of Gurū Gobind Singh's assassination in 1708. Nānder was the birthplace of three Marāthā saint-poets—Vishnupant Sesa, Raghunāth Sesa, and Vāman Paṇḍit. It now has four colleges affiliated with Marāthwādā University.

Nānder district occupies 4,056 sq mi (10,504 sq km) in the Marāthwāda section of the Godāvari River Valley. It was an impoverished part of the kingdom of the Niẓām of Hyderābād until 1947, when it was incorporated into the Indian Union. Despite economic progress since then, it remains one of the less developed districts of Mahārāshtra. Most of the population is dependent upon agriculture; jowar (a type of millet) and rice are the major food crops, and cotton is the basic cash crop. Cattle breeding is also important. Major industries are cotton and oilseed processing. Nānder and Dīglūr are the chief towns. Pop. (1971 prelim.) town, 126,400; district, 1,397,277.

·map, India **9**:278

Nandi (d. 1827), Zulu princess and mother of Zulu chief Shaka.

·Shaka's career and character **16**:614c

Nandi, people inhabiting the western part of the Kenya highlands. They speak a language of the Eastern Sudanic branch of the Chari-Nile group. In 1969 they numbered 260,000.

The Nandi are primarily intensive cultivators. Major crops are millet, maize, and sweet potatoes. Cattle remain important, providing food and bride-price payments and holding great ritual importance.

The people are divided among 17 patrilineal clans, dispersed throughout Nandi territory. Members of the same clan do not marry one another. The most important traditional social groups are the age-sets, to one of which every male belongs from birth. The Nandi age-grade system is of the cyclical type, with seven named grades covering approximately 15 years each, a single full cycle being 105 years. Men advance through the warrior grades, and upon entering the grade of elder hold political and juridical authority. No political authority transcends this local council of elders.

General polygyny is the rule, with a substantial bride-price in livestock expected. Nandi society was traditionally egalitarian; no slaves were kept.

·Masai influence on power growth **6**:97g

Nandi, the bull *vāhana* (mount) of the Hindu god Śiva (Shiva). Some scholars suggest that the bull was originally the theriomorphic form of Śiva, but from the Kuṣāṇa (Kushan) age onwards (*c.* 1st century AD), he is identified as the god's vehicle. Every Śiva temple has the figure of a white, humped bull reclining on a raised platform and facing the entrance door of the shrine so that, according to tradition, he may perpetually gaze on the lord in his symbolic form, the *liṅga* (phallus). Nandi is considered as one of Śiva's chief *gaṇa*s (attendants) and occasionally is depicted in sculpture as a bull-faced dwarf figure. He is known also in a wholly anthropomorphic form, called variously Nandikēśvara, or Adhikāranandin. Sculptures of him in human form, found at the entrance door of many Śiva temples in South India, are often confused with images of the deity, as they are alike in such iconographic features as the third eye, crescent moon in the matted locks, four arms, two of which hold the battle axe and an antelope. Usually a distinguishing feature is that Nandi's hands are pressed together in adoration. The respect shown the bull in modern India is due to his association with Śiva. In traditional cities such as Beneras (Vārānasi), certain bulls are given the freedom to roam the streets. They are considered to belong to the lord, and they are branded on the flank with the trident insignia of Śiva.

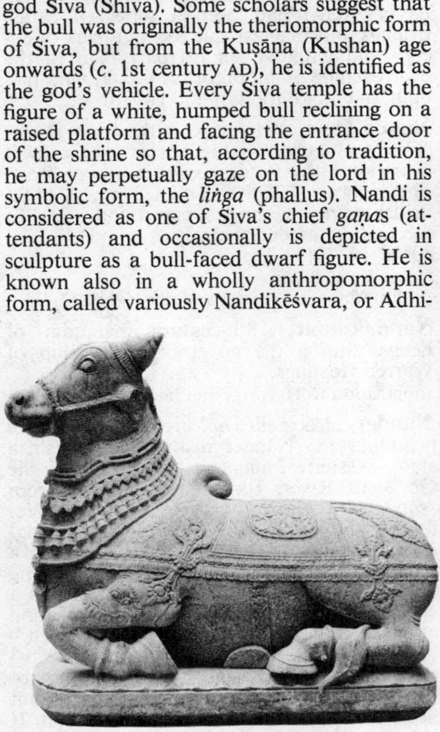

Nandi, granite sculpture from South India, late 15th century AD; in the M.H. de Young Memorial Museum, San Francisco

By courtesy of the Center of Asian Art and Culture, San Francisco, Calif., gift of the Atholl McBean Foundation

Nandidae, small family of freshwater fishes (order Perciformes) native to southern Asia and the Malay Archipelago; sometimes considered to include the members of the family Polycentridae, of fresh waters of Africa and the American tropics. Members of both families are small and often have deep bodies, very large, protrusible mouths, and some transparent fins. Most species are fish eaters. Some are kept in home aquariums.

Several members of the families are known as leaf fishes, from their close resemblance in both appearance and swimming behaviour to dead, drifting leaves. An example is the South American leaf fish (*Monocirrhus polycanthus*), about 7.5 centimetres (3 inches) long, mottled brown, with serrated dorsal and anal fins that resemble the saw edges of leaves and a chin barbel that looks like a broken leaf stem. It lives in quiet waters, drifting about, often head down, and propelling itself with transparent tail and pectoral fins. When feeding, it awaits prey or moves toward it slowly, taking it with a sudden gape of the huge mouth.

·classification and general features **14**:52f

Nandi language: *see* Nilotic languages.

Nandinaceae, family of flowering plants of the order Ranunculales.

·classification and general features **15**:511e

Nandinia (mammal): *see* civet.

Nand Kumar, 18th-century Indian merchant hung by the British for perjury.

·perjury trial consequences **9**:398b

Nandronga-Navosa, province, Fiji.

·area and population table **7**:297

nanduti lace, 19th-century lace made in some of the Hispanic colonies of Central and South America, especially in Paraguay and on the island of Tenerife. It is a kind of needle lace (lace made with a needle), circular motifs being built up from a spider-web-like skeleton of cotton or silk thread. It was admired in Europe for its spidery texture.

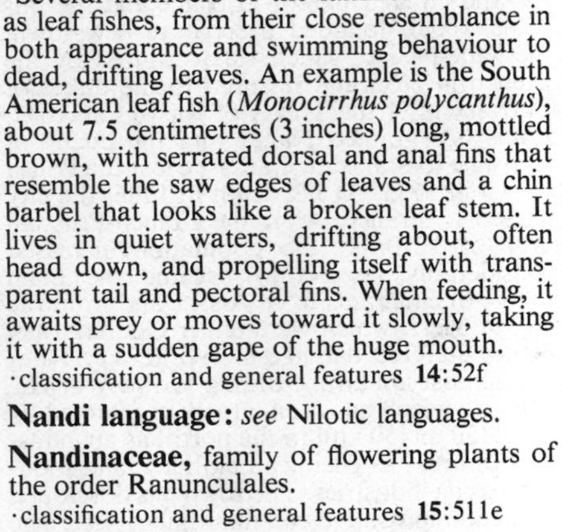

Nanduti lace from Paraguay, late 19th–early 20th century; in the Rijksmuseum, Amsterdam

By courtesy of the Rijksmuseum, Amsterdam

·Paraguayan craft development **13**:989f

Nan-ga, or SOUTHERN PAINTING, also known as BUNJIN-GA or LITERATI PAINTING, a style of painting practiced by numerous Japanese painters of the 18th and 19th centuries.

Some of the most original and creative painters of the middle and late Edo period belonged to the Nan-ga school. The style is based on developments of 17th- and 18th-century individualism in the Ch'ing dynasty painting of China, but is transformed into a new and creative manner, and so it is more than imitation. Nan-ga artists tended to exaggerate elements of Chinese literary men's painting, not only in composition but in brushwork. A decided sense of humour is often evident. Ike Taiga (1723–76), Yosa Buson (1716–83), and Gyokudo (1745–1820) are among the most famous Nan-ga artists.

"Forbidden to the Vulgar," *Nan-ga* or *bunjin-ga* style hanging scroll (*kakemono*) by Uragami Gyokudō (1745–1820), ink on paper, Edo period; in the Cleveland Museum of Art

By courtesy of the Cleveland Museum of Art, Mr. and Mrs. William H. Marlatt Fund

The style was introduced in the early 18th century at a time when Japanese intellectuals were taking an eager interest in the outside world and new Chinese paintings were entering Japan through Nagasaki. The *Chieh-tzu yüan hua chuan* ("Mustard Seed Garden"), a painting manual published in China in 1679 and in Japan in 1748 contributed to the formation of the principles of this school.

Nan-ga painting became trapped by mannerism in the 19th century, when it became exclusively a subjective vehicle of expression, too often lacking form or a sense of solid construction. Self-consciousness of the intellectual superiority of their adopted Chinese culture often had the effect of making literati painters excessively subtle.

·Chinese origin and proponents **19**:239a

Nānga Parbat, or DIAMIR, one of the world's highest mountains (26,660 ft [8,126 m]), in the western Himalayas 17 mi (27 km) west-southwest of Astor, in north Pakistan. The mountain's steep south wall rises nearly 15,000 ft above the valley immediately below, and the north side drops about 23,000 ft to the Indus River. The British Alpine climber Albert F. Mummery led the first attempt to ascend the glacier- and snow-covered mountain in 1895, but he died in the effort. At least 30 more climbers (mostly German-led) also perished because of the severe weather conditions and the frequent avalanches, before the German

climber Herman M. Buhl reached the top in 1953. The Kashmiri name Nānga Parbat is derived from the Sanskrit words *nagna parvata*, meaning "naked mountain." Diamir is a local name meaning King of the Mountains.
35°14′ N, 74°35′ E
·Indus River course features **9**:492d
·map, Pakistan **13**:893
·mountaineering record and data table **12**:585

Nangarhār, also called NANGRAHAR or NINGRAHAR, formerly SANT-E MASHREQI or EASTERN PROVINCE, in eastern Afghanistan, 2,771 sq mi (7,176 sq km) in area, with its capital at Jalālābād (*q.v.*). It is bounded by the provinces of Laghmān and Konarhā (north), by Kāpīsā, Kābul, and Lowgar (west), Paktīā (south), and by Pakistan (east). Nangarhār encompasses part of the Kābul River Valley; on its eastern border is the Khyber Pass, an age-old gateway between Afghanistan and Pakistan.

The history of Nangarhār is that of struggles among the local tribes and between them and various invaders, including the Macedonian Alexander the Great, the Mughal Bābur, and the British. The Khyber Pass (*q.v.*) particularly has been the scene of numerous battles. Extensive agriculture is carried on under irrigation in Nangarhār; crops include wheat, rice, tea, citrus fruit, figs, bananas, and sugarcane. Rural-development programs have been established in many of the province's villages to provide medical, agricultural, and educational assistance. Pop. (1970 est.) 717,905, mainly Shinwārīs, Khūgyānīs, Mohmands, and Pathans.
·area and population table **1**:169
·map, Afghanistan **1**:167

Nangnang, known as LO-LANG in Chinese, one of four colonies (Nangnang, Chinbŏn, Imdun, and Hyŏnto) established in 108 BC by emperor Wu Ti of the Han dynasty (206 BC–AD 220) of China when he conquered the ancient Korean state of Wiman (later named ancient Chosŏn). Nangnang, which occupied the northwestern portion of the peninsula and had its capital at P'yŏngyang, was the only one of the four colonies to achieve success. It lasted until AD 313, when it was finally conquered by the expanding northern Korean state of Koguryŏ. Chinbŏn and Imdun were abandoned in 82 BC and Hyŏnto in 75 BC.

An extremely prosperous state with a population of around 400,000, Nangnang was the centre of Chinese culture and influence in Korea at the time. The Chinese officials assigned to govern Nangnang brought with them all the customs of their motherland and created a miniature Chinese society. The tombs left behind by this Chinese ruling class contain some of the finest examples of Chinese art in existence.

Though the Chinese culture and social institutions appear to have had little impact on the general population of Korea at the time, its technology, especially the metalworking techniques, strengthened the native tribal communities outside of Chinese dominance.
·Chinese lacquerwork evidence **19**:184c
·Chinese visual arts influence **19**:207g

Nangnim Mountains, Korean NANGNIM-SANMAEK, north central North Korea, stretch from north to south, west of the Kaema Highlands (*q.v.*). They form the watershed between Kwanbuk (the northeastern part of the Korean Peninsula) and Kwansŏ (the northwestern part), and generally follow the boundaries of Chagang-do (province), Yanggang-do, and Hamgyŏng-namdo. With average heights of approximately 5,000 ft (1,500 m), the peaks include: Maengbu-san (7,421 ft [2,262 m]), Sobaek-san (9,003 ft), Nangnim-san (7,165 ft), and Paek (6,152 ft). Spurs—the Kangnam, Chŏgyu, and Myohyang mountains—all of which are also over 3,000 ft high, stretch toward the southwest. The Taedong-gang (river) and the Ch'ŏngch'ŏn-gang originate in the mountains and flow with their tributaries between the spurs to the Yellow Sea. Although the mountains are high enough to obstruct natural trade routes between the Kwanbuk and Kwansŏ areas, the regions have been connected by the construction of railways and roads.
40°30′ N, 127°00′ E
·major division and extensions **10**:516h
·map, North Korea **10**:518

nang sbek, shadow puppet theatre of Cambodia.
·Thai and Cambodian coordination of music and dance **17**:237d *passim* to 239f

nang talung, type of puppet shadow play popular in southern Thailand.
·Thai puppet use and Malaysian style **17**:246a

nang yai, type of shadow play using masked mime.
·Thai Brahmanic theme and puppet use **17**:245e

Nan Hai: *see* South China Sea.

Nāñhaithya, an Indo-Iranian god appearing in the Avesta, whose Vedic counterpart is Nāsatya.
·Indo-Iranian three-functional cosmology **9**:871b

nan-hsi, southern Chinese drama in the Hangchow area during the Southern Sung dynasty (1126–1279).
·origin and development **5**:471g

Nan-hu (poet): *see* Hsü Chih-mo.

nan hu, type of Chinese fiddle used as a melodic instrument for opera and puppetry.
·construction and playing technique **12**:676d

Nan Hua chen Ching (Chinese classic): *see* Chuang-tzu.

Nan Huai-jen: *see* Verbiest, Ferdinand.

Naning War (1831–32), disastrous attempt by the British to exact tribute from the Minangkabau people of the Malay state of Naning, near Malacca. Claiming to have inherited a right formerly held by the Dutch, officials at Malacca demanded one-tenth of Naning's annual crop in 1829. Naning's ruler, Abdul Said, refused and defeated a British force sent against him in 1831. A second expedition ended Naning's resistance after a three-month campaign in 1832, but the costly and humiliating war discouraged British expansion in Malaya for the next four decades.

nankeen, durable, firm-textured cotton cloth originally made in China and now imitated in various countries. The name is derived from Nanking, the city in which the cloth is said to have been originally manufactured. The characteristic yellowish colour of nankeen is attributed to the peculiar colour of the cotton from which it was originally made. The cloth is finished without size or bleach.

Nanking 12:822, Western conventional for Chinese NAN-CHING, Pin-yin romanization NAN-JING, capital of Kiangsu Province (*sheng*), central eastern China; it is a port on the Yangtze River and a major industrial centre. Pop. (1970 est.) 1,700,000.

The text article covers Nanking's history, location, size, climate, city plan, transportation system, demography, economic life, political institutions, health and education services, and cultural life.
32°03′ N, 118°47′ E
REFERENCES in other text articles:
·Catholic bishopric establishments map **15**:1019
·Kiangsu geography and industrialization **10**:462c
·map, China **4**:262
·population table 2 **4**:270
·Six Dynasties' rule and artistic center **19**:184f
·Taiping Rebellion establishment **4**:360a

Nanking, Treaty of (1842): *see* unequal treaties.

Nanking porcelain, Chinese blue-and-white porcelain made for export during the Ch'ing dynasty (especially in the reign of K'ang-hsi, 1662–1722) at Ching-te Chen and shipped to Europe in great quantity from the port of Nanking; it came to be known by this term among Western dealers in the 19th century. Although made for export, the shapes and decoration were mostly traditional Chinese. English potters extensively copied and adapted Nanking decoration such as the popular Willow pattern (*q.v.*). Nanking porcelain varied in quality, the glaze becoming increasingly gray and the decoration rudimentary.

Nan Koko Nor Shan, English SOUTH KOKO NOR MOUNTAINS, Tsinghai Province, China.
36°30′ N, 100°00′ E
·Koko Nor depression **10**:499b

Nan-lan Ch'eng-te, also called NARA SINGDE, 17th-century Manchu poet.
·poetry style **10**:1057e

Nan Ling, Pin-yin romanization also NAN LING, mountain range—more exactly a series of ranges—in South China that forms the divide and watershed between Hunan and Kiangsi provinces (*sheng*) and the Yangtze River Basin to the north and Kwangtung and the Kwangsi Chuang Autonomous Region and the Hsi Chiang (river) Valley to the south.

Village in the Nan Ling (mountains), southeastern China
Andrew J. Watson

In traditional times they were referred to simply as the Ling (Ranges), while the area to the south was known as Ling-wai (Beyond the Ranges) or Ling-nan (South of the Ranges). Until the 12th century AD or even later, the far south was still an exotic, semicolonized area not fully assimilated into China, and the Nan Ling formed a major cultural boundary. As a human boundary it played almost as important a role as the Tsinling Shan (mountains) ranges in the north (which run west to east from Kansu to Shensi provinces), though it is a comparatively small-scale mountain range.

Structurally the Nan Ling is complex, the landforms resulting from two distinct periods of folding—the first in the later part of the Mesozoic Era (from 225,000,000 to 65,000,000 years ago), which produced massive folding with a west–east axis, and the second representing a later stage that superimposed the southwest to northeast folding characteristic of Southeast China. The latter forms predominate in the eastern section of the Nan Ling. The entire system is some 870 mi (1,400 km) long and consists of a wide mountain belt rather than a single sharply defined range. The central section, on the borders of southern Hunan and Kiangsi, is the broadest and most complex in structure, with many subordinate chains that are often at right angles to the main axis. The altitude of the ranges is comparatively low and is seldom more than 3,300 ft (1,000 m). The geology of the area, like its topography, is also extremely complex. The main axis of the ranges is formed of granites and very ancient sedimentary rocks, heavily metamorphosed by heat and pressure. The flanks are formed of red sandstone dating from the Cretaceous Period (from 136,000,000 to 65,000,000 years ago) and the Tertiary Period (from 65,500,000 to 2,500,000 years ago). The whole range is much eroded by a complex drainage system, and large limestone areas have a typical karst topography (*i.e.*, with sinks or karst holes as well as tunnels dissolved out of the limestone plateau).

The Nan Ling has long been an important source of mineral wealth. A major source of silver in medieval times, it now yields tin, copper, wolfram, zinc, antimony, tungsten, and iron. There are also small coal deposits to the north of Shao-kuan (Kwangtung) in the central range. Little of the area is cultivated apart from valley bottoms, and much of the ranges suffer badly from soil erosion. Three major passes cross the range: (1) the Kuei-lin, followed by the Ling Ch'ü (canal), which affords an easy passage from southern Hunan to Kuei-lin and eastern Kwangsi, the chief route in early times; (2) the Che-ling, northwest of Shao-kuan, which connects Hunan with central Kwangtung and is followed by the Canton to Wu-han (Hankow) railway; and (3) the Mei-ling (Ta-yu), northeast of Shao-kuan, which led into southern Kiangsi and was the major north–south route until the end of the 19th century.

25°00′ N, 112°00′ E

·China's physical geography **4**:265d
·Hunan's geographic features **9**:12c
·map, China **4**:262

Nan Matol, also known as METALANIM, archaeological site on the island of Ponape, eastern Caroline Islands.

·Micronesian city design and settlement **12**:124c

Nan Mountains (China): *see* Nan Shan.

Nanna, Akkadian SIN, in Mesopotamian religion, Sumero-Akkadian god of the moon, city

The king pouring libations to Nanna, Ur-Nammu stele, *c.* 2050 BC; in the University Museum of the University of Pennsylvania, Philadelphia

By courtesy of the University Museum of the University of Pennsylvania, Philadelphia

god of Ur and of the neighbouring Gaesh in the southern cowherding region. His name Nanna may have designated him particularly as the full moon; another of his names, Ensun, Lord Wild Bull, as the half-moon; a third, Ashimbabbar, as the new light. His original form, the moon, was sometimes visualized as a boat, sometimes as the horned crown of divinity, but most characteristically it was seen through the herdsman's eye as the horns of a great bull leading the herd of stars. In human form the god became a cowherd driving his herd over the sky. Nanna was the son of Enlil and Ninlil; his spouse was Ningal. *See also* Sin.

·Abraham and the religion of Ur **1**:12b
·Ur's ziggurat architecture **18**:1021g

Nannaya Bhaṭṭa (*c.* 11th century), Indian grammarian who translated the Mahābhārata into Telugu.

·Telugu language translations **1**:861h
·version of the Mahābhārata **17**:140d

Nanni di Banco (b. 1385/80?, Florence—d. 1421, Florence), Florentine sculptor whose works exemplify the stylistic transition from the Gothic to the Renaissance that occurred

"Quattro Coronati" ("Four Crowned Saints"), lifesize marble sculpture by Nanni di Banco, *c.* 1411–13; in the church of Or San Michele, Florence

Brogi—Alinari

in Italy during the first decades of the 15th century.

Nanni was trained by his father, Antonio di Banco, a sculptor who worked with Niccolò d'Arezzo on the cathedral of Florence. It is not surprising, therefore, that Nanni's first important work, a life-size marble statue of the prophet Isaiah, was commissioned for the cathedral. Installed on the cathedral's west facade, this figure is more Gothic in feeling than his more classical and Humanistic works for the guilds of the Or San Michele in Florence. Of the latter the "Quattro Coronati" ("Four Crowned Saints"; *c.* 1411–13) is considered his masterpiece. Influenced by antique art, the four saints are dressed in Roman togas and have heads that are modelled after ancient portrait sculpture.

A relief of the Assumption of the Virgin Mary that was placed above the Porta della Mandorla was begun *c.* 1414. This was his last major work and was probably finished posthumously by Luca della Robbia, who is generally thought to have been Nanni's student.

Nan-ning, also known as YUNG-NING, Pin-yin romanization, respectively, NAN-NING and YONG-NING, city in south central Kwangsi Chuang Autonomous Region (*tzu-chih-ch'ü*), China. Nan-ning is the provincial capital and forms an autonomous subprovincial-level municipality (*shih*) while also being the seat of administration of the extensive Nan-ning Area (*ti-ch'ü*), which controls 13 counties (*hsien*) in the southwest of the province. Nan-ning is on the north bank of the Yung Chiang (river), the chief southern tributary of the Hsi Chiang, some 19 mi (30 km) below the confluence of the Yu Chiang and the Tso Chiang. The Yung Chiang (which later becomes the Yü Chiang) affords a good route to Canton, navigable by shallow-draft junks and motor launches even though obstructed by rapids and sandbanks.

A county seat was first established there in AD 318 called Chin-hsing, which also became the administrative seat of a commandery. In 589 the commandery was suppressed, and the county was renamed Hsüan-hua. Under the T'ang dynasty (618–907), the prefecture (*chou*) of Yung was established there; it was garrisoned to control the non-Chinese districts in Kwangsi and on the Yunnan–Kweichow border. In the mid-9th century the T'ang and the Yün-nan state of Nan-chao fought over it, and after 861 it was briefly occupied by Nan-chao. It remained a frontier prefecture throughout the Sung dynasties (960–1279), being the scene of a rebellion led by Nung Chih-kao in 1052, and thereafter a garrison town. Under the Ming (1368–1644) and Ch'ing (1644–1911) dynasties, it was a superior prefecture (*fu*), Nan-ning. Opened to foreign trade by the Chinese in 1907, it grew rapidly. From 1912 to 1936 it was the provincial capital of Kwangsi, replacing Kuei-lin. Early in the 20th century the city spilled over from the old walled city into a southern suburban area. In the 1930s Nan-ning became the centre of a "model provincial government" under the warlord Li Tsung-jen, and a spacious modern city was laid out. During the Sino-Japanese War (1937–45), Nan-ning was temporarily occupied in 1940 by the Japanese. It later became an important U.S. air base, supporting the Chinese armies in Kwangsi, but during 1944–45 was again under Japanese occupation.

In 1949 Nan-ning again became the provincial capital, first of Kwangsi Province and then (1958) of the Kwangsi Chuang Autonomous Region, which replaced it. Until then Nan-ning had essentially been a commercial centre dependent on Canton and on the Hsi Chiang system. In the late 1930s a railway was begun, joining Heng-yang in southern Hunan Province with Kuei-lin, Liu-chou, Nan-ning, and the Northern Vietnam border, while another was begun from Liu-chou to Kuei-yang in Kweichow. The construction of the Nan-ning section of this line was halted in 1940 by the Japanese advances, however, and not completed until 1951, after which Nan-ning was directly linked with central China; completion of a branch line to the port of Chan-chiang in 1957 gave it a direct outlet to the sea. During the French war in Indochina (1946–54), Nan-ning was the chief support base in China for the Vietnamese forces, and in the hostilities in Vietnam in the 1960s and early 1970s it again became a staging post for supplies.

Formerly an essentially commercial and administrative centre, Nan-ning from 1949 experienced industrial growth. The city is surrounded by a fertile agricultural region, producing subtropical fruits and sugarcane; food processing, flour milling, sugar refining, meat-packing, and leather manufacture are important. It is a centre for printing and paper manufacture. Nan-ning is also important in heavy industry.

After the recognition of the Chuang ethnic minority in 1958, Nan-ning became the chief centre for the training of minority-group leaders. Kwangsi University, a large medical school, and a school of agriculture all date from the 1920s. Pop. (1948) 200,000; (1953) 195,000; (latest est.) 260,000.

22°48′ N, 108°20′ E

·map, China **4**:262
·population table 2 **4**:270
·urban location and focus **10**:551f

nannyberry: *see* Viburnum.

Nanook of the North (1922), documentary film by Robert Flaherty.

·documentary film evolution **12**:523a; illus.

Nan-p'an Chiang, English SOUTH PAN RIVER, river, southern China.

24°56′ N, 106°12′ E

·Kweichow forest areas and composition **10**:559b

Nan-p'-in, also called SHEN CH'ÜAN, 18th-century Chinese artist.
·Japanese flower-and-bird painting effect **19**:240a

Nan-p'ing, Pin-yin romanization NAN-PING, city in northwestern Fukien Province (*sheng*), China. Nan-p'ing, which occupies an important position in the communications of northern Fukien, is a county- (*hsien-*) level municipality (*shih*) and also is the administrative centre of the Nan-p'ing Area (*ti-ch'ü*), which is a very extensive one, controlling 13 counties in northwestern Fukien. Nan-p'ing is situated on the northwest bank of the Min Chiang (river) at the place where it is formed by the confluence of three major tributary systems, the Sha Ch'i (river) flowing from the southwest, the Chen Ch'i flowing from the northeast, and the Fu-t'un Ch'i flowing from the west. All of these valleys are natural routes through the rugged and difficult country of the Fukienese interior, leading toward the neighboring provinces. Nan-p'ing County was established at the end of the Later Han period (AD 23–220). The name was later changed to Chien-an and Yen-an but was suppressed. In the early 10th century it was a minor town called Yen-p'ing Chen; but when Wang Yen-cheng established himself as an independent ruler in north Fukien in 944, it was promoted to the status of Lung-chin County and made the seat of an independent prefecture of T'an-chou. When northern Fukien was conquered by the Southern T'ang state in 945, it was renamed Chien-chou; but in 979 the Sung conquerors of the south renamed it Nan-chien-chou. Under the Sung dynasties (960–1279) it prospered as an important producer of copper, lead, and tin. In 1302 its name was changed to Yen-p'ing, and under the Ming (1368–1644) and Ch'ing (1644–1911) dynasties it formed the superior prefecture (*fu*) of Yen-p'ing. Under the Ch'ing its commerce—mostly in forest products, timber, bamboo, and paper—rose considerably. Nan-p'ing had traditionally sent its goods, particularly lumber, to Foochow by river. Since the Communists came to power in 1949, the Min Chiang has been improved for navigation. More important, however, has been the opening in 1956 of the railway from Kiangsi Province to Amoy, which is joined at Nan-p'ing by another line to the port of Foochow. It thus became the most important rail junction in Fukien and subsequently developed some industries, among which the most important are timber working, papermaking, and the manufacture of cement and chemicals. Nan-p'ing became a municipality in 1957. Latest pop. est. 65,000.
26°38′ N, 118°10′ E
·map, China **4**:262

Nansei-Shoto (Japan): *see* Ryukyu Islands.

Nansen, Fridtjof 12:824 (b. Oct. 10, 1861, Store-Frøen, Nor.—d. May 13, 1930, Lysaker), Arctic explorer, oceanographer, statesman, and humanitarian.
Abstract of text biography. After successfully crossing Greenland and studying its Eskimo inhabitants (1888–89), Nansen embarked in his ship "Fram" on an expedition to investigate the drift of polar sea ice and to explore the Arctic (1895–96). He served as a professor of zoology at the Christiania (now Oslo) university from 1896 to 1908, in which year he was appointed professor of oceanography and continued his scientific work, publishing the results of his earlier expedition, going on more oceanographic cruises (1900–14), improving instrument designs, and explaining wind-driven sea currents as well as various features of Arctic water. Becoming engaged in politics around 1905, he was appointed head of the Norwegian delegation to the League of Nations (1920) and took an active part in the repatriation of prisoners after World War I. Later he directed the program to bring relief to famine-stricken Russia. His work culminated in the award of the Nobel Peace Prize to him in 1922.
REFERENCES in other text articles:
·Arctic exploration activity **7**:1045a
·Arctic Ocean exploration **1**:1119c
·Barents Sea currents research **2**:722a
·Greenland Sea scientific studies **8**:414h
·ocean water-sampling bottle invention **18**:848f
·refugees of Russia and Armenia protection **15**:571d
·Vladivostok visit and observations **19**:495f

Nansen Basin, submarine depression, Arctic Ocean.
84°30′ N, 75°00′ E
·location and depth **1**:1120b; map

Nansen bottle, ocean-water sampler devised late in the 19th century by the Norwegian oceanographer Fridtjof Nansen and subsequently modified by various workers. The standard Nansen bottle has a capacity of 1.25 litres and is equipped with plug valves at either end. The bottle is affixed to a winch wire with its valves open, and the winch wire is paid out until the bottle is approximately at its desired sampling depth. A weight, or "messenger," then is allowed to slide down the cable. The upper attachment of the Nansen bottle is disengaged from the cable by the impact of the messenger; and the bottle is reversed end over end, its valves closing in the process to trap the water sample. Thermometers usually are attached to the Nansen bottle to record the temperature and pressure of the sample site. Several Nansen bottles are employed during a single hydrographic cast, each bottle releasing another messenger when tripped, in order to trigger the deeper bottles in turn.
·design and use **18**:848f

Nan Shan, Pin-yin romanization also NAN SHAN, the general term applied to a vast mountain range, actually a complex of ranges, in Northwest China. The ranges lie between the Tsaidam Basin to the southwest and the plateau of northwestern Kansu Province (*sheng*) to the north. The Nan Shan consists of a complex system of ranges with a predominantly northwest to southeast axis, forming a complex of folded blocks separated by syncline troughs (*i.e.,* folds in rocks in which the strata dip inward from both sides toward the troughs), much faulted and grabens (blocks that have been downthrown between faults on either side). The ranges are for the most part about 13,000–16,500 ft (4,000–5,000 m) high; however individual peaks often exceed 20,000 ft and the highest peak reaches 20,820 ft (6,346 m). The ranges are higher and more complex in the west, to the south of Tun-huang and Yü-men (both in Kansu), where, in spite of the aridity of the climate, many peaks are covered with snow and glaciers. The eastern section of the mountains is somewhat lower, and only a few high peaks have a permanent snow cover. Among the ranges are a number of large intermontane depressions and fault basins. The largest of these is the depression in which lies Koko Nor (lake).
The northernmost range, fronting the Kansu Corridor, is the Ch'i-lien Shan-mo (mountains). The ranges to the south are the T'o-lai Shan and the Ta-t'ung Shan. The Ta-t'ung ranges form the northern side of the two major lake depressions, Ha-la Hu in the northwest and Koko Nor to the southeast, both being areas of internal drainage. South of these depressions are the Ch'ing-hai-nan Shan (South Koko Nor Mountains) and the A-te-erh-kan Ling (Adirgan Ula), again enclosing further basins with lakes and saline swamps.
The western part of these mountains is extremely arid. Vegetation is everywhere sparse, and great areas of the Nan Shan are completely barren. Elsewhere the cover largely consists of hardy desert type plants, of sparse grassland on higher ground, and of a sort of mountain tundra (treeless plain) above 12,500 ft. The eastern sections of the mountains are much wetter, and the vegetation cover is more diverse and richer. On the wetter slopes there are spruce forests, and alpine meadows are found up to the snowline. The dry intermontane basins, however, have semidesert or steppe (grassland) vegetation. East of Koko Nor, a widespread coniferous forest cover occurs between 8,000 and 10,000 ft, mostly consisting of spruce, pine, and birch. Above this elevation are alpine shrubs and sub-alpine meadows similar to those of the borderlands of Szechwan Province. Generally speaking, the environment of the western parts of the range is typical of Central Asia, while that of the eastern sections is more typically Chinese.
The Nan Shan area is very sparsely peopled, and vast areas are virtually uninhabited. Most of the inhabitants are semi-nomadic Tibetan or western Mongol (Khoshot or Tu-Mongor) herdsmen.
·iron ore deposit discovery **10**:389c
·Koko Nor climate and drainage **10**:498h
·Kunlun Mountains' systems **10**:544c

Nanshe, or NAZI, in Mesopotamian religion, Sumerian city goddess of Nina (modern Surghul) in the southeastern part of the Lagash region of Mesopotamia. According to tradition, Nanshe's father Enki (Akkadian Ea) organized the universe and placed her in charge of fish and fishing. Her husband was Nindara, the "tax gatherer" of the sea. Although at times overshadowed by her more prominent sister Inanna (Akkadian Ishtar), Nanshe was, nevertheless, important in her own geographical area, and many rulers of Lagash record that they were chosen by her.

Nantahala River, rises in Nantahala Mountains southwest of Asheville, North Carolina, U.S., near the Georgia–North Carolina line and flows 40 mi (64 km) northwest through the Nantahala National Forest, emptying into the Fontana Reservoir in the Little Tennessee River. Nantahala Dam (1942), southwest of Bryson City, impounds Nantahala Reservoir, sometimes called Aquone Lake.
35°30′ N, 83°30′ W

Nanterre, western industrial suburb of Paris, capital of the Hauts-de-Seine *département*. Located on the east bank of a loop of the meandering Seine River, and separated from Paris by the suburbs of Puteaux and Neuilly-sur-Seine, it has an area of 4.7 sq mi (12.2 sq km). Nanterre is a centre for precision foundries and automobile construction and produces electrical equipment, perfumes, hosiery, paints, and toys. The suburb, 3 mi (5 km) west of the city limits of Paris, has grown into an administrative and educational centre. It is the seat of a branch (opened 1971) of the Université de Paris and is an episcopal see. Originally named Nemetodor, a Gallic place of worship, it was called Nemetodorum under the Romans. It is the traditional birthplace of Ste. Geneviève (*c.* AD 422–500), patron saint of Paris. Latest census 90,332.
·University of Paris campus site **13**:1015h

Nantes, capital of Loire-Atlantique *département*, western France. Situated at the head of the Loire Estuary, where it is joined by the Erdre and the Sèvre rivers, 35 mi (56 km) from the sea and southwest of Paris, it is one of the French towns most changed in the 20th century.
Nantes derives its name from the Namnètes, a Gallic tribe who made the town their capital. It became a commercial centre under the Romans. The Normans, after pillaging the town, occupied it from 834 to 936. After a long struggle in the Middle Ages between the counts of Nantes and Rennes for the sovereignty of Brittany, in 1560, Frances II, king of France (1559–60), granted Nantes a communal constitution. During the Wars of Religion (1562–98), Nantes joined the Catholic League and only opened its gates to Henry IV, king of France (1589–1610), in 1598, the same year he signed the Edict of Nantes, a charter assuring religious and civil liberties to the Protestants. During the French Revolution, Nantes suffered the ruthless repression

of an envoy of the revolutionary Committee of Public Safety named Jean-Baptiste Carrier. In 1793 Carrier replaced executions by the guillotine, which he considered too slow, by mass drownings. The city was occupied by the Germans during World War II.

Greatly modified by an urban renewal plan begun in 1920, Nantes was further altered and extended after being partly destroyed in World War II. Arms of the river have been filled up and made into roads; the railway, which used to cut across the town, now runs largely underground; and the port has been extensively rebuilt. Under a national planning scheme, Nantes has been made a major economic development centre. In the early 1970s, road, air, and rail communications were being extended, and vast industrial zones were being built. The well-equipped port has more than 2 mi of quays, and the river has been dredged to allow access to larger vessels.

The shipbuilding yards are important. The chemical (fertilizers, paint) and mechanical (rail and aircraft equipment) industries were in full expansion in the early 1970s. The original university (founded 1460) was abolished during the French Revolution, but a new one was established in 1961.

Although the cathedral of Saint-Pierre was built over a period between the 15th and 20th centuries, it retains a Gothic unity. The imposing facade (1434–1508) has three finely sculptured doorways and two high towers. The cathedral, bombed during World War II, was nearly completely restored in 1972 when a fire largely destroyed the roof. The magnificent Renaissance tomb of Francis II, duke of Brittany (ruled 1458–88), was luckily unharmed. The medieval castle had been rebuilt in 1466 by this same Francis II. Viewed from without, it looks like a fort with crenelated towers, but the inner courtyard is a typical Renaissance palace. The Musée des Beaux-Arts has one of the most important and varied collections of paintings in France. Pop. (1971 est.) 269,400.
47°13′ N, 1°33′ W
·annexation to Brittany by Nomeinoë **7**:614b
·map, France **7**:584

Nantes, Edict of, law promulgated at Nantes in Brittany on April 13, 1598 by Henry IV of France, which granted a large measure of religious liberty to his Protestant subjects, the Huguenots. The edict upheld Protestants in freedom of conscience and permitted them to hold public worship in many parts of the kingdom, though not in Paris. It granted them full civil rights and established a special court, the Chambre de l'Édit, composed of both Protestants and Catholics, to deal with disputes arising from the edict. Protestant pastors were to be paid by the state and released from certain obligations; finally, the Protestants could keep the places they were still holding in August 1597 as strongholds, or *places de sûreté*, for eight years, the expenses of garrisoning them being met by the king.

The edict also restored Catholicism in all areas where Catholic practice had been interrupted; and it made any extension of Protestant worship in France legally impossible. Nevertheless, it was much resented by Pope Clement VIII, by the Roman Catholic clergy in France, and by the *parlements*. Catholics tended to interpret the edict in its most restrictive sense. The cardinal de Richelieu, who regarded its political clauses as a danger to the state, annulled them by the Peace of Alès (1629). On Oct. 18, 1685, Louis XIV revoked the Edict of Nantes and deprived the French Protestants of all religious and civil liberties.
·circumstances of adoption and repeal **4**:593c
·Henry IV's religous toleration **8**:774f
·Huguenot security provisions **7**:631h
·Huguenot toleration in Catholic France **15**:112b
·Louis XIV and the revocation **11**:123b
·Louis XIV's revocation **7**:636b
·provisions and violation **15**:558b
·revocation background under Louvois **11**:130e
·textile industry development **18**:171f
·toleration of Huguenots **15**:554c

Nantes, Université de, English UNIVERSITY OF NANTES, coeducational, autonomous, state-financed institution of higher learning at Nantes, Fr., founded in 1970 under France's 1968 Orientation Act, providing for reform of higher education. It replaced the former University of Nantes, founded in 1962, which traced its history to the original University of Nantes, founded in 1461. Among its faculties are medicine, pharmacy, economics, ancient and modern languages, mathematics, physics, chemistry, and natural sciences. Student enrollment in the early 1970s was about 15,000.

Nanteuil, Robert (b. 1623/30, Reims, Fr.—d. Dec. 9, 1678, Paris), line engraver. He became known by his crayon portraits and was pensioned by Louis XIV and appointed designer and engraver of the cabinet to that monarch. It was mainly because of his influence that the king granted the edict of 1660, which pronounced engraving distinct from the mechanical arts and gave its practitioners the privileges of other artists.

The plates of Nanteuil, several of them almost life-size, number about 300. In his early practice he imitated the technique of his predecessors, working with straight lines, strengthened but not crossed in the shadows, in the style of Claude Mellan, and in other prints crosshatching like Nicolas Regnesson, his teacher and brother-in-law, or stippling in the manner of Jean Boulanger. He then gradually acquired an individual style, modelling the faces of his portraits with the utmost precision and completeness and employing various methods of touch for the draperies and other parts of his plates. Among the finest of his mature works are portraits of Pomponne de Bellièvre, Gilles Ménage, Jean Loret, the duc de la Meilleraye, and the duchesse de Nemours.
·Condé portrait illus. **4**:1079f
·portrait engraving style **14**:1087f; illus. 1088

Nantgarw porcelain, an English granular, soft-paste porcelain, pure white in colour, containing bone ash. It was made at a factory founded in 1813 by William Billingsley at Nantgarw, Glamorgan, Wales. The ware was transparent and restrained in shape. It attracted the London trade, and much of Nantgarw was delivered to London white and decorated

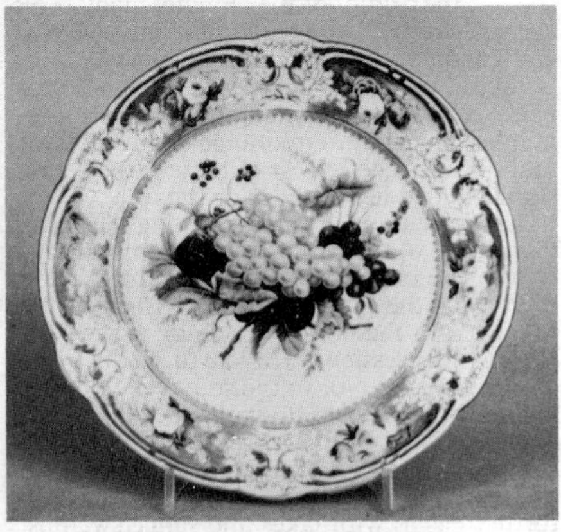

Nantgarw porcelain plate painted in London, *c.* 1815; in the Victoria and Albert Museum, London
By courtesy of the Victoria and Albert Museum, London; photograph, EB Inc.

there, generally with iridescent halos surrounding the paintings. The ware usually is impressed with "Nantgarw" in full. The factory closed in 1822.

Nanticoke, a confederacy of Algonkian-speaking Indians who lived along the eastern shore of what are now Maryland and southern Delaware; their name means Tidewater People. They were related to the Delaware and the Conoy (*qq.v.*). Nanticoke subsistence depended largely on fishing and trapping, and their social organization probably included a head chief, as well as subordinate chiefs of the various tribes. They were at war with the Maryland colonists from 1642 to 1678; in 1698 reservations were set aside for them. Some time after 1722 most of the Nanticoke began moving northward, some settling with the Iroquois in western New York; many emigrated westward about 1784 and were incorporated into the Delaware in Ohio and Indiana. Only a few Nanticoke remain in their original home region.

Nanticoke, city, Luzerne County, northeast central Pennsylvania, U.S., on the Susquehanna River. In the early 18th century white settlers were attracted to the site of a Nanticoke Indian village, and set up a gristmill, iron forge, and sawmill at the Susquehanna Rapids. The Indians migrated to New York in 1793. In 1825 the first anthracite coal mine was opened in the locality and by 1878 Nanticoke was a major coal-mining centre. Coal mining declined with the widespread use of fuel oil, natural gas, and electricity; population decreased and virtually all the mines were closed by the 1970s. Nanticoke is now basically residential with some light manufacturing development. Inc. borough, 1874; city, 1926. Pop. (1930) 31,000; (1980) 13,044.
41°12′ N, 76°00′ W

Nan-tong (China): *see* Nan-t'ung.

Nantosuelta (Celtic: She of the Winding River), a pagan Celtic goddess worshipped

Nantosuelta and Sucellus, relief from Sarrebourg, Fr.; in the Musée Metz, Metz, Fr.
Jean Roubier

primarily in Gaul; she was sometimes portrayed together with the god Sucellus (Good Striker). One of her attributes was the raven, which thus linked her with the Irish goddess Morrígan (*q.v.*) and her two companions. She was sometimes shown holding a small house on the end of a pole, which may have been either a dovecote or a model of a Gallo-Roman temple. In the Gaulish iconography of Sucellus and Nantosuelta there appears to have been a continental parallel with the Irish divine couple, the Dagda (Good God) and Morrígan (Queen of Demons), who, like Nantosuelta, also had clear aquatic associations.

Nan-t'ou Hsien, county, Taiwan.
·area and population table **17**:997

Nantucket, island in the Atlantic, 25 mi (40 km) south of Cape Cod, Massachusetts, U.S., across Nantucket Sound and separated from Martha's Vineyard (15 mi west) by the Muskeget Channel. Coextensive with Nantucket

Upper Main Street, Nantucket, Mass.
Arthur Griffin—EB Inc.

town, it forms (with nearby Tuckernuck and Muskeget islands) Nantucket County, Massachusetts. Nearly 15 mi long and 3 mi wide, it is of glacial origin with wide, sandy beaches, a commodious harbour, and a moderate climate. Discovered in 1602 by Bartholomew Gosnold, the island was purchased from the Plymouth Colony by Thomas Mayhew in 1641 and administered as part of New York. It was settled in 1659 by Quakers, and fishing, boatbuilding, and trading were early activities. It was ceded to Massachusetts in 1692 and given its Indian name, meaning "far away land." The town was incorporated in 1687 and the county formed in 1695. Whaling, begun in the early 18th century, reached its peak just before the Revolutionary War, when the island was home port to more than 125 whaling ships. Commercial activity declined after the War of 1812, and Nantucket was soon bypassed by other ports; it never regained its early maritime prominence. Later, with improved transportation, the island developed a lively summer tourist trade (now the economic mainstay), attracted by its colonial houses, cobblestone roads, museums, art galleries, and yachting facilities. Resort villages include Nantucket (county seat), Siasconset, Wauwinet, and Polpis. Nantucket is connected to the mainland by steamer and air services. Sankaty Head Lighthouse (1850) is on an East Coast bluff. Inc. town, 1687. Pop. (1980) 5,087.
41°16′ N, 70°03′ W
·location and seasonal popularity **11**:591g
·map, United States **18**:909

Nan-t'ung, Pin-yin romanization NAN-TONG, city, eastern Kiangsu Province, China, and a subprovincial-level autonomous municipality and administrative centre of the Nan-t'ung Area. Nan-t'ung is situated on the northern shore of the head of the Yangtze River estuary. Northward, it is connected with the Yün-yen Ho canal system, which serves the coastal zone of Kiangsu north of the Yangtze and connects westward with the Grand Canal (Yün Ho). T'ien-sheng-chiang, about 7.5 mi (12 km) to the west, provides Nan-t'ung with a port on the Yangtze. Since the creation of the autonomous municipality, the seat of Nan-t'ung County has been moved from Nan-t'ung to Chin-sha, some 12½ mi (20 km) to the east.

During the Han dynasty (206 BC–AD 220), and even as late as the Sui (581–618) and T'ang (618–907) periods, the seacoast was much farther west than at present; and the area now called Nan-t'ung was an outlying county, Hai-ling, subordinate to Yang-chou. It grew into a commercial, communications, and strategic centre and became a prefecture (*chou*) under the name of T'ung in 958. After 1368 it lost its prefectural status and again became a county subordinate to its wealthy neighbour, Yang-chou. In 1724, however, it was again created a prefecture and was given the name Nan-t'ung (literally Southern T'ung) to avoid confusion with T'ung-chou, near Peking. After 1912 it became a county, retaining its old name.

The coastal area to the east and northeast has always been famous for salt, and the inland area to the north and northwest is a rich rice- and cotton-growing region. It is above all on cotton that Nan-t'ung's prosperity has depended. Domestic-scale spinning and weaving of cotton had long been established, but the modern industry was almost entirely the creation of a statesman and modernizer named Chang Chien (died 1926), who was a native of the district. After the disasters of the Sino-Japanese War of 1894–95, Chang decided to abandon politics and to devote himself to developing Nan-t'ung into a model district. In 1895 he founded the Dah Sun Cotton Mill at T'ang-chia-chia, some 5½ mi (9 km) west of Nan-t'ung. This mill came into production in 1899 and proved more efficient than any other private textile firm of the same period. Out of its profits, Chang, between 1900 and 1905, built up an industrial complex in Nan-t'ung that included flour and oil mills, a modern factory for reeling silk, a distillery, and a machine shop. He also founded a shipping line and, after 1901, formed the T'ung-hai Land Reclamation Company—the first of a number of such companies that brought much of the saline coastal zone of Chiang-pei under cotton cultivation.

Chang also founded the first teachers' training colleges in China—the Nan-t'ung normal schools—which staffed hundreds of primary schools. Later he founded an agricultural college, a textile school, and a medical college (1910–12), which eventually merged to form Nan-t'ung University. He also founded museums, libraries, and theatres, so that Nan-t'ung became an important cultural centre as well as a prosperous industrial town. In the early republican period (after 1911) Nan-t'ung was commonly called Chang Chien's Kingdom, or the Model County.

Like all centres of cotton manufacture in China, Nan-t'ung suffered seriously during the years of economic depression in the 1930s, after which the area came under Japanese occupation. In the 1970s it remained heavily dependent upon the textile industry and upon cotton. Pop. (1936 est.) 40,000; (1948) 226,000; latest est. 240,000.
32°02′ N, 120°53′ E

Nantwich, market town, Cheshire, England, in the Weaver Valley; it is the centre of a prosperous dairy-farming area. Brine springs were formerly important for the salt industry and still supply brine for an open-air swimming pool. One of the few buildings to survive a fire of 1583 was Churche's Mansion, in "black-and-white" architectural style. There is also a 14th-century church and a modern civic hall. Pop. (1973 est.) 12,160.
53°04′ N, 2°32′ W

Nan-yang, Pin-yin romanization also NAN-YANG, a city in southwestern Honan Province, China. It is an autonomous county-level municipality and is the administrative centre of the Nan-yang Area, which covers the part of Honan lying southwest of the mountain range known as Fu-niu Shan. Nan-yang is situated on the Pai Ho, a tributary of the Han Shui. It was from early times an important centre, commanding a major route between Sian in Shensi Province and Hsiang-fan in Hupeh Province and south to the Yangtze River Valley and also two routes across the Fu-niu Shan into the central plain of Honan, leading to Lo-yang and K'ai-feng. Another route extends southeastward into Anhwei Province.

In the early part of the 1st millennium BC, Nan-yang was the seat of the state of Shen. For most of the period from 600 to 220 BC it was on the borders of the southern state of Ch'u and was known as Wan-i. With the Ch'in conquest in 221 BC, it became Wan County, seat of the commandery of Nan-yang. It became important under the Han (206 BC–AD 220), both as a centre of commerce and as the seat of state iron foundries and of other state manufactories. It was also the point at which converged the major routes leading from the western capital at Ch'ang-an (modern Sian) and the eastern capital at Lo-yang to the Yangtze River at Chiang-ling and the far south. In Later Han times (AD 23–220), its local magnates played a large part in the restoration of Han power. In the 1st and 2nd centuries its name was a byword for refinement and luxury. For a time it was given the designation of the southern capital. Later, however, its importance declined, and it remained a county town, subordinated to Teng-chou, until the last years of the 13th century, when the Mongols established it as the superior prefecture of Nan-yang. It kept this status until 1912, when it became a county town. In the 20th century its importance has somewhat declined, since the route of the Peking–Hankow railway lies east of it. Nan-yang is still a local commercial centre of considerable importance, however, providing a market for the grain, beans, sesame, tobacco, and other crops produced in the surrounding basin and transported by boat on the Pai Ho to the Han Shui or by a rail line to Lo-ho, opened in 1969. From early times the city has had a reputation for handicrafts, including the cutting and polishing of gemstones and jade. The surrounding region has a highly developed sericulture industry, producing raw silk, silk yarn, silk textiles, and embroidery. The city has developed a considerable industrial capacity, mostly based on small units. In the late 1950s an iron and steel industry was founded there. Latest census 50,000.
33°00′ N, 112°32′ E
·map, China **4**:263

Nan Yüeh (ancient kingdom): *see* Nam Viet.

Naod, Ethiopian emperor (reigned 1484–1508) who attempted to initiate contact with the Western world.
·political relations with Europe **6**:1009b

Naoero (island republic): *see* Nauru.

Naoetsu (Japan): *see* Jyoetsu.

Naogaon (India): *see* Nowgong.

Naomi, also spelled NOEMI, a central figure in the Old Testament Book of Ruth. In time of famine, Naomi and her husband, Elimelech, emigrated with their two sons from their home in Bethlehem, in Judah, to Moab, where Elimelech died. The sons married Moabite wives, and later they, too, died. Naomi, determining to go back to her home, urged her daughters-in-law to return to their families, and one of them did so. Ruth, however, refused to desert her mother-in-law, saying (in the beautiful words of the King James Version) "whither thou goest, I will go; and where thou lodgest, I will lodge: thy people shall be my people, and thy God my God." The two women went together to Bethlehem, arriving penniless at the beginning of the barley harvest. Naomi, contrasting the meaning of her name (Pleasant) with the misery of her fate, asked to be called Mara (Bitter). Ruth, however, attracted the attention of Boaz, a relative of Elimelech, who redeemed his relative's property and that of his sons and married Ruth. Their child was said to be the son of Naomi, since in him the line of Elimelech was preserved.

naorai, a Shintō sacramental meal.
·Shinto communion with kami **16**:674h

Naoroji, Dadabhai (b. Sept. 4, 1825, Bombay—d. June 30, 1917, Bombay), nationalist and critic of British economic policy in India. Educated at Elphinstone College, Bombay, he served as professor of mathematics and natural philosophy there before turning to politics and a career in commerce that took him to England, where he spent much of his life. In 1874 the gaekwar (ruler) of Baroda (in the state of Gujarāt, India) appointed him chief minister, but Naoroji resigned two years later when his proposals for administrative reforms proved unacceptable to the gaekwar. He later returned to England and stood unsuccessfully for election to Parliament as Liberal candidate for the Holborn borough, London, in 1886. In 1892, however, he was elected Liberal member of Parliament for Central Finsbury, London. He became widely known for his unfavourable opinion of the economic consequences of British rule in India and was appointed a member of the royal commission on Indian expenditure in 1895. In 1886, 1893, and 1906 he also presided over the annual sessions of the Indian National Congress, which led the nationalist movement in India. In the session of 1906 his conciliatory tactics helped to postpone the impending split between moderates and extremists in the Congress party. In his many writings and speeches and especially in *Poverty and Un-British Rule in India* (1901), Naoroji argued that India was too highly taxed and that its wealth was being drained away to England.

·campaign for Parliament **10**:223g
·economic criticism of British rule **9**:413h

Naosari (India): *see* Navsāri.

Nap (card game): *see* Napoleon.

NAP, abbreviation for NON-ARBOREAL POLLEN, pollen grains produced by non-tree types of vegetation. In the fossil pollen record, nonarboreal pollen indicates the presence of meadows, grasslands of various sorts, or cultivated fields; aquatic plants may also be indicated by NAP.

Napa, city, seat of Napa County, west central California, U.S., on the Napa River. It was founded as the county seat in 1848 by Nathan Coombs partly on the Rancho Napa, an 1838 Spanish grant. As the head of river navigation, it became a port for shipment of cattle, lumber, and quicksilver to San Francisco.

Napa Valley vineyards, California
Fred Lyon—Rapho Guillumette

It developed as an outlet for farm produce and is known for its table wines. Later economic factors include the manufacture of steel pipe and leather goods, Napa State Hospital, Napa Junior College (1942), and Mare Island Naval Shipyard at Vallejo, 20 mi (32 km) south. Lake Berryessa (formed by Monticello Dam [1957]) is 15 mi northeast. Inc. 1872. Pop. (1970) 35,978; (1980) 50,879.
38°18′ N, 122°17′ W

Napaeae (Greek mythology): *see* nymph.

Napaeozapus: *see* jumping mouse.

napalm, the aluminum salt or soap of a mixture of naphthenic and aliphatic carboxylic acids (organic acids of which the molecular structures contain rings and chains, respectively, of carbon atoms), used to thicken gasoline for use as an incendiary in flame throwers and fire bombs. The thickened mixture, now also called napalm, burns more slowly and can be propelled more accurately and to greater distances than gasoline. It was developed by U.S. scientists during World War II.

In a typical formulation of napalm, oleic acid constitutes 25 percent of the carboxylic acids, mixed acids derived from coconut oil make up 50 percent, and mixed naphthenic acids (derived from petroleum) account for the remainder. The most effective gelling agent results from the use of a quantity of aluminum hydroxide 50 percent in excess of that required for exact neutralization of the acids. Addition of 4 to 12 percent of napalm to gasoline converts it into a sticky thixotropic gel (one that is firm when at rest but that flows freely when forced through a nozzle).

Napalm is also employed in formulating a pyrotechnic gel containing gasoline and heavier petroleum oil, powdered magnesium, and sodium nitrate; this composition burns at a temperature of about 1,000° C (1,800° F), compared to 675° C (1,250° F) for thickened gasoline.

·chemical warfare in weapons history **19**:695a
·introduction and potency **19**:1012e
·Vietnam War use **18**:52f

Napata, the capital in *c.* 750–590 BC of the ancient kingdom of Cush (Kush) in Nubia, situated downstream from the Fourth Cataract of the Nile, near Kuraymah in the northern province of what is now the Democratic Republic of The Sudan.

An area rather than a single town, Napata extended to the east and south of Karima, from Nuri to Kurru. Very early it came under Egyptian influence; its main feature, the hill of Barkol, was regarded perhaps from as early as the Egyptian New Kingdom (1567–1320) as a holy mountain, the seat of the god Amon; under it lay the ruins of several temples. A stela of Thutmose III (reigned 1504–1450), on which a fort was mentioned, has been found there, and Amenhotep II (reigned 1450–25) sent an Asian prisoner to be hanged on its walls.

By the beginning of the 1st millennium, Egypt was in decline, with Lower Egypt increasingly prey to Libyan mercenaries. A body of the priests of Amon at Thebes voluntarily exiled themselves to Napata, where they appear to have Egyptianized the native princes of Cush and to have inspired them—from about 750—to conquer a degenerate Egypt. Five of the priests, together with their descendants, are known as the 25th dynasty of Egypt; they are remembered for being largely responsible for restoring to Egypt ancient customs and beliefs that had been abandoned under the New Kingdom. During this period Napata became the capital of the ancient world, and Sudanese kings intrigued with Tyre, Sidon, Israel, and Judah in a vain attempt to repel the Assyrians.

The Egyptian custom of royal burial under pyramids was introduced in Cush, as may be seen at Kurru and at Nuri, where the largest pyramid, that of the king Taharqa (reigned 689–664), is situated. Taharqa, who also built several Egyptian-style temples at Napata and elsewhere, was defeated by the Syrians in Judaea and expelled from Egypt.

Though the rulers of Cush thought of the reconquest of Egypt for some time after Taharqa's defeat, their plans were thwarted by the 26th (Saite) dynasty, which sent an expedition of Greek and Carian mercenaries to sack Napata in 590. The capital of Cush was thereafter transferred to Meroe, on the opposite bank of the Nile. Napata remained the religious capital, however, and royal burials continued to take place at Nuri until 315 BC. Two subsequent and separate royal burials at Barkol have given rise to the hypothesis that Napata may twice have made itself independent of Meroe.

·Egyptian political administration **13**:109d

napatähti (mythology): *see* põhjanael.

Naperville, city, Du Page County, northeastern Illinois, U.S., on the west branch of the Du Page River. The oldest town in the county and the county seat from 1839 until 1867, it was laid out in 1832 by Capt. Joseph Naper, who built a sawmill on the river. The coming of the Chicago, Burlington and Quincy Railroad (1864) stimulated its growth. Primarily residential, Naperville has some manufacturing (furniture and electronic switching equipment). North Central College, founded in Plainfield in 1861, was moved to Naperville in 1870. The Evangelical Theological Seminary was established there in 1873. Inc. village, 1851; city, 1890. Pop. (1970) 23,885; (1980) 42,330.
41°47′ N, 88°09′ W

Naphtali, tribe of, one of the 12 tribes of Israel, an ancient division of the Hebrews. The tribe bears the name of the younger of two sons born to Jacob and Bilhah, a maidservant of Jacob's second wife, Rachel. After Joshua led the Hebrews into the Promised Land, he divided the new territory among the 12 tribes, assigning a region northwest of the Sea of Galilee to the tribe of Naphtali.

After the death of King Solomon (922 BC), the ten northern tribes established an independent Kingdom of Israel. In 734 BC the Naphtalites were conquered by the Assyrian king Tiglath-pileser III, whose armies in 721 BC gained control over the entire northern kingdom. Israelites who were deported into slavery and those who remained behind were gradually assimilated by other peoples. The tribe of Naphtali thus lost its identity and became known in Jewish legend as one of the Ten Lost Tribes of Israel.

naphtha, any of various volatile, often highly flammable liquid hydrocarbon mixtures used chiefly as solvents and diluents and as raw materials for conversion to gasoline. Naphtha was the name originally applied to the more volatile kinds of petroleum issuing from the ground in the Baku district of the Soviet Union and Iran. As early as the 1st century AD, naphtha was mentioned by the Greek writer Dioscorides and the Roman writer Pliny the Elder. Alchemists used the word principally to distinguish various mobile liquids of low boiling point, including certain ethers and esters.

In modern usage the word naphtha is usually accompanied by a distinctive prefix. Coal-tar naphtha is a volatile commercial product obtained by the distillation of coal tar. Shale naphtha is obtained by the distillation of oil produced from bituminous shale by destructive distillation. Petroleum naphtha is a primarily U.S. name for petroleum distillate containing principally aliphatic hydrocarbons and boiling usually higher than gasoline and lower than kerosine.

·uncured rubber tack control **15**:1181e

naphthalene, the simplest of the fused or condensed ring hydrocarbon compounds composed of two benzene rings sharing two adjacent carbon atoms; chemical formula, $C_{10}H_8$. It is an important hydrocarbon raw material that gives rise to a host of substitution products used in the manufacture of dyestuffs and synthetic resins. Naphthalene is the most abundant single constituent of coal tar, a volatile product from the destructive distillation of coal, and is also formed in modern processes for the high-temperature cracking (breaking up of large molecules) of petroleum. It is commercially produced by crystallization from the intermediate fraction of condensed coal tar and from the heavier fraction of cracked petroleum. The substance crystallizes in lustrous white plates, melting at 80.1° C (176.2° F) and boiling at 218° C (424° F). It is almost insoluble in water but is readily soluble in ether and in hot alcohol. Naphthalene is highly volatile and has a characteristic odour; as carbon balls or mothballs, it is commonly used as moth repellent.

In its chemical behaviour, naphthalene shows the aromatic character associated with benzene and its simple derivatives. Its reactions are mainly reactions of substitution by halogen atoms, nitro groups, sulfonic acid groups, and alkyl groups. The alkyl derivatives of naphthalene (*e.g.*, methylnaphthalene, dimethylnaphthalene) have played an important part in the elucidation of the molecular structures of the naturally occurring sesquiterpenes, triterpenes, and related compounds. Large quantities of naphthalene are converted to naphthylamines and naphthols, naphthalene derivatives with an amino or hydroxy group, respectively, for use as dyestuff intermediates. The use of (beta) β-naphthylamine in the dyestuff industry has been prohibited because it was shown to cause bladder cancer. Naphthoquinones are naphthalene derivatives with two oxygen atoms ($C_{10}H_6O_2$). Many derivatives of a form of naphthoquinone have been found to occur in nature. Examples are juglone (5-hydroxy-1,4-naphthoquinone), which occurs in unripe walnut shells; lawsone (2-hydroxy-1,4-naphthoquinone), a yellow pigment extracted from the leaves of henna; and phthiocol (2-hydroxy-3-methyl-1,4-naphthoquinone) isolated from human tubercle bacilli. Vitamins K_1 and K_2, substances that must be supplied to the diet for adequate clotting of blood, have naphthoquinone structures.

·coal tar distillation products **1**:456c
·dye manufacture from distillation of coal tar **5**:1100c
·dyestuff technology and production **5**:1115b
·fluorescence and phosphor use **15**:397d
·hydrocarbon sources and uses **9**:91h
·luminescence activation by cascading **11**:183f
·petroleum composition and properties **14**:167d
·solubility characteristics table 2 **16**:1057
·structural determinants of phase **12**:315d
·tar composition and chemical recovery **4**:787a; table 786

naphthol, either of two colourless, crystalline organic compounds derived from naphthalene and belonging to the phenol family; each has the molecular formula $C_{10}H_7OH$. Both compounds have long been identified with the manufacture of dyes and dye intermediates; they also have important uses in other areas of the chemical industry.

The compound 1-naphthol or α-naphthol, made by heating 1-naphthalenesulfonic acid with caustic alkali or by heating 1-naphthylamine with water under pressure, is used directly in making several dyes, and large amounts of it are converted to compounds ultimately incorporated into other dyes. Reaction of 1-naphthol with salicylic acid gives the ester alphol, used as an antiseptic and antirheumatic; reaction with methylcarbamic acid gives the ester carbaryl (Sevin), used as an insecticide. 1-Naphthol forms as colourless crystals that darken when exposed to light and melt at 96° C (205° F); the liquid boils at 288° C (550° F). It is slightly soluble in water but dissolves freely in common organic solvents.

The compound 2-naphthol, or β-naphthol, is regarded as the most important chemical intermediate based on naphthalene. It is manufactured by fusing 2-naphthalenesulfonic acid with caustic soda and is converted into numerous dyes and dye intermediates, as well as into tanning agents, antioxidants, and antiseptics. Its methyl and ethyl ethers have odours resembling those of orange blossoms and acacia, respectively, and are used in perfumery. 2-Naphthol forms as colourless crystals that darken when exposed to light and melt at about 123°–124° C (253°–255° F); the liquid boils at 295° C (563° F). It is insoluble in water but dissolves freely in common organic solvents.

·agricultural protection measures **1**:353f

naphthoquinone, any of three isomeric yellow to red crystalline compounds with the formula $C_{10}H_6O_2$ derived from naphthalene. *See also* quinone.

·types, occurrence, and commercial use **4**:915h

naphthylamine, either of two isomeric crystalline compounds ($C_{10}H_7NH_2$) derived from naphthalene by replacing a hydrogen atom by an amino group (NH_2); both substances are principally employed in making dyestuffs.

·cancer hazard in industry **3**:764b
·cancer involvement **5**:858h
·chemical industry production and use **4**:135b
·urinary tract tumour incidence **7**:60c

Napier, port, in east North Island, New Zealand, on the southwest shore of Hawke Bay. Laid out in 1856, the town was made a borough in 1874. It was the capital of now defunct Hawke Bay Province until 1876 and was declared a city within Hawke Bay County in 1950.

Napier, on a small headland known as Napier Hill, is linked to Wellington (200 mi [320 km] southwest) by rail. It serves an agricultural and livestock district and is the nation's leading wool trade centre. Industries are woollen mills, tobacco and fertilizer works, wineries, and commercial fishing. Its outlet, Port Ahuriri, ships wool, frozen meat, dairy products, hides, and tallow. The harbour, once a natural bay, was destroyed by an earthquake in 1931 and is now artificial. The city, a winter resort, has an Anglican cathedral. It was named for Sir Charles Napier, a 19th-century British military commander in India. Pop. (1971) 40,186.
39°29′ S, 176°54′ E

·map, New Zealand **13**:44

Napier, Sir Charles (b. March 6, 1786, near Falkirk, Stirling—d. Nov. 6, 1860, near Catherington, Hampshire), admiral in the Portuguese and British navies, controversial commander of the British Baltic Fleet during the Crimean War of 1853–56. Created Conde Napier de São Vicente in the Portuguese peerage, he was less elegantly known in Great Britain as "Black Charley" and "Mad Charley."

Charles Napier, detail of an oil painting by E.W. Gill, 1854; in the National Portrait Gallery, London
By courtesy of the National Portrait Gallery, London

Becoming a midshipman in 1800, Napier served in the Napoleonic Wars and in the War of 1812 against the U.S. In 1831 he was in the Azores to assist supporters of the Portuguese princess Maria da Glória (afterward Queen Maria II). Subsequently, as commander of the Portuguese loyalist navy, he destroyed the fleet of Dom Miguel, pretender to the Portuguese throne, off Cape St. Vincent on July 5, 1833. The next year he directed the loyalist forces in the defense of Lisbon against the Miguelites.

Rejoining the British Navy in 1836, Napier for a time was second in command in the Syrian expedition of 1840–44, taking part in the capture of Beirut and Acre (October–November 1840). From 1847 to 1849 he commanded the Channel Fleet. In February 1854, at the beginning of the Crimean War, he was appointed commander of the Baltic Fleet. The British public's extravagant confidence in him turned to odium when, alleging insufficient firepower, he refused to attack the great Russian naval base of Kronshtadt. After his recall he was never again offered a command.

Napier, Sir Charles James (b. Aug. 10, 1782, London—d. Aug. 29, 1853, Portsmouth, Hampshire), British general, conqueror (1843) and governor (1843–47) of Sind, now in Pakistan.

A relative of the statesman Charles James Fox, Napier was a veteran of the (Iberian) Peninsular War against Napoleonic France and of the War of 1812 against the U.S. In 1839, when the Chartist agitation for political and social reform threatened to lead to violence, Napier was given command in northern England, where, by tempering his sympathy for the industrial workers with insistence on law and order, he kept a dangerous situation under control for two years. In 1841 he went to India, and in August 1842 he was assigned to the Sind command, subordinate to Edward Law, earl of Ellenborough, governor general of India (1841–44). In February 1843, Ellenborough forced the armies of Sind to sign a treaty providing for the permanent annexation of British-occupied bases in Sind and for the transfer of large northern areas to Bahāwalpur in the event that Napier found the Sindhi *amīrs* (rulers) disloyal. Soon convincing himself that some of them were untrustworthy, Napier provoked a war, and, after winning major battles at Miani (February 17) and Dabo (Dubba), near Hyderābād (March 24), he was made governor of Sind. In that office he established a model police force, encouraged trade, and began work on a breakwater and water-supply facilities for Karāchi. He also repulsed marauding hill tribes on the northern Sindhi border.

Having left for England in 1847, Napier returned to India in 1849 as commander in chief in the Second Sikh War (1848–49), but the conflict had ended by the time he arrived. A quarrel with the governor general, James Ramsay, 1st marquess of Dalhousie, caused him to leave India finally in 1851.

A bronze statue of Napier, by the sculptor G.G. Adams, is in Trafalgar Square, London. Accounts of his career include Rosamond Lawrence's *Charles Napier Friend and Fighter, 1782–1853* (1952), and H.T. Lambrick's *Sir Charles Napier and Sind* (1953).

·aggressive policies in Sind **9**:404e
·Burton's early career **3**:526g

Napier (NEPER), **John 12**:826 (b. 1550, Merchiston Castle, near Edinburgh—d. April 4, 1617, Merchiston Castle), mathematician and theological writer who originated the concept of logarithms as a mathematical device to aid in calculations.

Abstract of text biography. Napier studied at the University of St. Andrews. In 1594 he wrote the dedication to his *Plaine Discovery of the Whole Revelation of Saint John.* After publication of that work he occupied himself with the invention of weapons. His work on logarithms is contained in *Mirifici Logarithmorum Canonis Descriptio* (1614; Eng. trans., *Description of the Marvelous Canon of Logarithms,* 1857) and *Mirifici Logarithmorum Canonis Constructio* (1619; Eng. trans., *Construction of the Marvelous Canon of Logarithms,* 1889).

REFERENCES in other text articles:
·computer history and early machines **4**:1046b
·history of calculatory device and table **11**:650d
·mathematical calculation theory and use **11**:682e

Napier, MacVey (1776–1847), Scottish lawyer, first professor of conveyancing at the University of Edinburgh, was an innovative editor of the Supplement to the 4th, 5th, and 6th editions of *Encyclopædia Britannica* and editor of the 7th edition.

Napier, Robert (1791–1876), British ship designer.

·steamship bow design improvement **16**:680b

Napier, Sir William Francis Patrick (b. Dec. 17, 1785, Celbridge, County Kildare—d. Feb. 10, 1860, Clapham Park, Surrey, now in London), British general and historian who fought in the Napoleonic Wars, particularly in the Peninsular War in Spain and Portugal; he wrote the popular *History of the War in the Peninsula . . .* (6 vol., 1828–40), based partly on his own combat experiences and partly on information supplied by two commanders in that conflict, the Duke of Wellington and the French marshal Nicolas-Jean de Dieu Soult.

Sir William Napier, drawing by George Frederic Watts (1817–1904)

During the Peninsular War, Napier fought in the major battles of Fuentes de Oñoro (May 5, 1811), Salamanca (July 22, 1812), and the Nivelle River (Nov. 10, 1813) and was wounded several times. He retired in 1819.

Napier began his *History* in 1823. Widely acclaimed for its vigorous battle scenes and powerful style, his account was attacked for inaccuracy and bias. Nonetheless, it remained the standard work on the subject until the publication of Sir Charles Oman's *History of the Peninsular War* (1902–30). Napier also wrote several books about his brother Sir Charles James Napier, conqueror of Sind (now a region of Pakistan).

Napier grass: *see* Pennisetum.

Napier of Magdala, Robert (Cornelis) Napier, 1st Baron (b. Dec. 6, 1810, Colombo, Ceylon, now Sri Lanka—d. Jan. 14, 1890, London), British field marshal who had a distinguished military and civil engineering career in India and commanded military expeditions to Ethiopia and China.

The son of Major Charles Frederick Napier, a British artillery officer stationed in Ceylon, he attended the military college of the East India Company at Addiscombe, joined the Bengal Engineers in 1826, was stationed at Calcutta in 1828, and began employment on the East Jumna Canal irrigation works in 1831. In Europe he studied engineering and railway works (1836–39). He laid out the settlement of Darjeeling (1839–42) and the cantonment at Ambāla (1842). At the outbreak of the First Sikh War (1845) he joined the army of the Sutlej as commanding officer of engineers and was at the battles of Mudki, Sobrāon, and Fīroz Shāh, where he was wounded. In 1846 he took the hill fort of Kāngra. After the Sikh government surrender he became consulting engineer to the resident at Lahore. In the Second Sikh War (1848–49) he directed the siege of Multan and then commanded the engineers of the right wing of the army of the Punjab at the battle of Gujarāt and in the pursuit to Attock, ending the campaign. As civil engineer to the Punjab Board of Administration (1849–51), he executed public works of roads, canals, bridges, buildings, and frontier defenses. He was recalled to military service for the Hazara expedition (1852) and for the campaign against the Bori clan in Peshawar (1853).

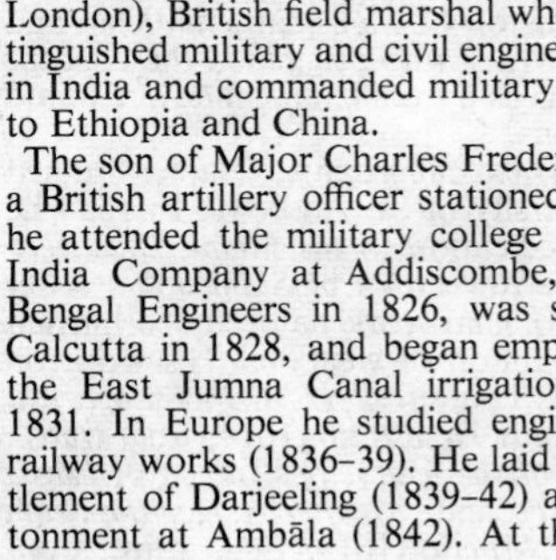

Baron Napier of Magdala, detail of an oil painting by T. Jensen, 1867; in the Prince of Wales Museum of Western India, Bombay

Napier went on leave to England in 1856, returned to India as a lieutenant colonel, and in the Indian Mutiny of 1857 was chief engineer to the Lucknow relief force under Sir James Outram. He directed an active defense against the sepoys and was wounded during the second relief, led by Sir Colin Campbell, but participated in the final attack on the city. A brigadier general under Sir Hugh Rose at the capture of Lucknow in March 1858, he defeated Tantia Topi at Jaora Alipur and routed Fīroz Shāh in December 1858. He was afterward placed in command of the final operations in the area and made a Knight Commander of the Bath.

Napier's troop division in the 1860 expedition to China under Sir Hope Grant crippled forts north of the Pei Ho (river) and advanced to Peking, leading to the Chinese surrender. In 1861 he returned to India, was promoted to major general, and served as military member of the governor general's council (February 1861–March 1865). He acted as viceroy and governor general from Nov. 21 to Dec. 2, 1863. In 1865 he was given command of the Bombay army and in 1867 was promoted to lieutenant general and given command of the expedition to Ethiopia, defeating Emperor Tewodros II (*q.v.*) at Magdela (Magdala) in April 1868. He was rewarded with titles, the thanks of parliament, and an annual pension of £2,000. He was created Baron Napier of Magdala (1868) and in 1870–76 was commander in chief in India. After service as governor of Gibraltar (1876–82) he was appointed field marshal in 1883 and served as constable of the Tower of London from 1887 until his death.

Napier's bones, form of rearrangeable multiplication tables, so-called for its inventor, John Napier (1550–1617) and because they were printed on sticks of bone or ivory.
·computer history and early machines **4**:1046b

Naples 12:827, Italian NAPOLI, ancient NEAPOLIS (New Town), city in Campania region, southern Italy. It lies around a fine bay on the western shore of a peninsula, 120 mi (193 km) southeast of Rome. Naples is a great port, intellectual centre, and financial capital of southern Italy. Pop. (1971 prelim.) 1,258,721.

The text article covers the history of Naples and the character, economy, topography and architectural heritage of the contemporary city.
40°51′ N, 14°17′ E

REFERENCES in other text articles:
·cuisine ingredients and menu **7**:946a
·diplomacy and wars from 1494 **6**:1083b
·Garibaldi's conquest and dictatorship **7**:909e
·Ludovico Sforza's alliance and war **16**:612g
·map, Italy **9**:1088
·opera seria and other historical styles **13**:580h
·procession of St. Januarius **9**:1113a
·province area and population table 1 **9**:1094

Naples, city, seat (1962) of Collier County, southern Florida, U.S., at the edge of the Everglades, on the Gulf of Mexico. Named for the Italian city, it developed as a resort after attracting the attention of Henry Watterson, a Kentucky journalist, in the late 19th century. Tourism and truck gardening are the economic mainstays. Nearby are the Caribbean Gardens (a tropical exhibit) and Collier Seminole State Park. The city's recreation facilities are enhanced by a 7-mi (11-km) mainland beach and the abundance of game fish in the Ten Thousand Islands, about 30 mi southeast. Inc. town, 1923; city, 1949. Pop. (1970) 12,042; (1980) 17,581.
26°08′ N, 81°48′ W

Naples, Bay of, ancient SINUS CUMANUS, Italian GOLFO DI NAPOLI, semicircular inlet of the Tyrrhenian Sea (an arm of the Mediterranean Sea), southwest of the city of Naples, southern Italy. It is 10 mi (16 km) wide and extends southeastward for 20 mi from Capo Miseno to Punta Campanella. The bay is noted for its scenic beauty, enhanced by the steep, mainly volcanic hills surrounding it (including the still-active Mt. Vesuvius). The major port is Naples; other coastal towns along the bay are Pozzuoli, Torre Annunziata, Castellammare di Stabia, and Sorrento. Along the bay shore are the extensive ruins of the ancient cities of Pompeii and Herculaneum. At the bay's entrance are the islands of Ischia and Procida and Capri. The Gulfo di Pozzuoli is a northwest inlet.
40°43′ N, 14°10′ E
·map, Italy **9**:1088

Naples, Kingdom of, state covering the southern portion of the Italian peninsula from the Middle Ages to 1860, often united politically with Sicily.

The Kingdom of the Two Sicilies in the 19th century

By the early 12th century, the Normans had carved out a state in southern Italy and Sicily in areas formerly held by the Byzantines, Lombards, and Muslims. In 1130 Roger II, on uniting all the Norman acquisitions, assumed the title of king of Sicily and Apulia. The existence of this Norman state was at first contested by the popes and Holy Roman emperors, who claimed sovereignty over the south. In the late 12th century, the kingdom passed to the Hohenstaufen emperors (the most notable of whom was Emperor Frederick II, king of Sicily from 1198–1250). Under these early rulers, the kingdom was at the height of its prosperity. Politically, it was one of the most centralized states of Europe; economically it was a major commercial centre and grain producer, and culturally, a point of diffusion of Greek and Arab learning into western Europe.

After the extinction of the legitimate Hohenstaufen line, Charles of Anjou, brother of the French king Louis IX, gained control of the kingdom (1266), responding to an invitation from the pope, who feared the south would pass to a king hostile to him. Charles transferred the capital from Palermo, Sicily, to Naples, a shift that reflected the orientation of his policy toward northern Italy, where he was leader of the Guelf (pro-papal) Party. But his harsh rule and heavy taxation provoked the revolt known as the Sicilian Vespers (*q.v.*; 1282), which resulted in the political separation of Sicily from the mainland and in the acquisition of the island's crown by the Spanish House of Aragon.

The episode had important consequences for both Naples and Sicily. In the struggles between the Angevins and the Aragonese that lasted for more than a century, the real victors were the barons, whose powers were extended by grants from the kings. In the prevailing anarchy, feudalism gained a firm hold on both kingdoms.

Naples enjoyed a brief period of prosperity and importance in Italian affairs under Robert, king of Naples (1309–43), but from the mid-14th to the 15th century, the history of the kingdom was a story of dynastic disputes within the Angevin house. Finally, in 1442, Naples fell to the ruler of Sicily, Alfonso V of Aragon.

At the end of the 15th century, the Kingdom of Naples continued to be involved in the struggles among the foreign powers for domination of Italy. It was claimed by the French king Charles VIII, who held it briefly (1495). Won by the Spanish in 1504, it was ruled for two centuries by their viceroys, as was Sicily. Under Spain, Naples was regarded merely as a source of revenue and experienced a steady economic decline. Provoked by high taxes, the lower and middle classes rebelled in the 1640s (revolt of Masaniello; *q.v.*), but the Spanish and the barons combined to suppress the uprising.

As a result of the War of Spanish Succession (1701–14), the Kingdom of Naples came under the influence of the Austrian Habsburgs. (Sicily, for a brief period, was held by Piedmont.) In 1734 the Spanish prince Don Carlos de Borbón (later King Charles III) conquered Naples and Sicily, which were then governed by the Spanish Bourbons as a separate kingdom. During the 18th century the Bourbon kings, in the spirit of "enlightened despotism," sponsored reforms to modernize the state, but these reforms were limited to ecclesiastical affairs.

When Napoleon gained control of Italy, Naples was formed into the Parthenopean Republic (1799) and in 1806 into a kingdom, first under Napoleon's brother Joseph and from 1808 under his brother-in-law Joachim Murat. Under the French, Naples was modernized by the abolition of feudalism and the introduction of a uniform legal code. The Bourbon king Ferdinand IV (later Ferdinand I of the Two Sicilies) was twice forced to flee to Sicily, which he held with the aid of the English.

With the Restoration of 1815, the kingdom, now officially called the Two Sicilies (*see* Two Sicilies, Kingdom of the), aligned with the conservative states of Europe. Since many in the kingdom adopted liberal ideas while the kings were more and more confirmed in their absolutism, political clashes were inevitable. Serious revolts broke out in 1820, when Ferdinand I was forced to grant a constitution, and again in 1848 under Ferdinand II, when Sicily tried to win its independence. The poor political and economic condition of the kingdom led to its easy collapse in the face of Giuseppe Garibaldi's invasion in 1860, and both Naples and Sicily voted overwhelmingly for unification with northern Italy in the plebiscite of October of the same year.

·Alexander VI French conflict **1**:468b
·Alfonso V's campaigns and conquest **1**:484c
·Austrian administration and reforms **9**:1153g
·Bourbon accession to throne **3**:82d
·Christina of Sweden's aspiration to throne **4**:564h
·diplomacy and wars from 1494 **6**:1082b; map 1103
·dynastic changes and Sicilian union **9**:1139h
·Frederick I's promises and campaigns **7**:697h
·French expulsion and redivision **9**:1148a *passim* to 1150a
·Hohenstaufen dynastic decline **8**:78f
·medieval chancery development influence **5**:813b
·Nelson's diplomatic and military relation **12**:947h *passim* to 949a
·Renaissance history and culture **15**:663d
·Sicilian conflict of Gregory IX and Frederick II **8**:419e
·Spanish acquisition and French rivalry **17**:423h

Naples, University of (Italy): *see* Napoli, Università degli Studi di.

Naples Stage, division of Upper Devonian rocks and Late Devonian time in the northeastern U.S. (the Devonian Period began about 395,000,000 years ago and lasted about 50,000,000 years); the Naples Stage was named for exposures studied near the town of Naples, Ontario County, New York. It precedes the Chemungian Stage, follows the Genesee Stage, and is correlative with the upper portion of the Fingerlakes Stage. The Naples Stage grades from red beds in the east, in the Catskill region, to black shales in the west, in Pennsylvania.

Napo, province, northeast Ecuador, bounded by Colombia along its entire northern frontier. The western part is in the Cordillera Occidental of the Andes, but the much larger eastern section is in El Oriente, at the Amazon headwaters. Created from part of the former Napo-Pastaza province in 1959, it is covered with tropical rain forest. The economy is primarily of a subsistence level.

The provincial capital, Tena (*q.v.*), located just north of the Río Napo, is a small missionary settlement. Pop. (1974) 62,186.

·area and population table **6**:288
·map, Ecuador **6**:286

Napoleon 12:831, in full NAPOLEON BONAPARTE, originally spelled BUONAPARTE (b. Aug. 15, 1769, Ajaccio, Corsica—d. May 5, 1821, St. Helena Island), general and emperor of the French, one of the most celebrated personages in the history of the West, who temporarily extended French domination over a large part of Europe and left a lasting mark on the lands that he ruled.

A Corsican by birth, Napoleon was educated in France, becoming an army officer in 1785. He fought during the French Revolution and was promoted to brigadier general in 1793. The threat of revolt brought him the command of the army of the interior in 1795; he then commanded the army of Italy in several victorious campaigns. His expedition to Egypt and Syria in 1798–99 ended in defeats by the British, however, and he returned to France. A coup in 1799 brought him to supreme power as first consul, and he instituted a military dictatorship.

In the early 1800s, Napoleon made numerous reforms in government and education. He defeated the Austrians in 1800, went to war against Great Britain in 1803, and had himself crowned emperor in 1804. His greatest victory, the Battle of Austerlitz, against Austria and Russia, came in 1805; thereafter, except for temporary setbacks in Spain, he was successful, consolidating most of Europe as his empire about 1810. His downfall began with his disastrous invasion of Russia in 1812. The Allied coalition revived, and in 1814 Napoleon was defeated and exiled to the island of Elba.

The next year Napoleon returned to France and regained power (for the period known as the Hundred Days) until defeated at Waterloo by the British (under the Duke of Wellington) and the Prussians. He was exiled again, to St. Helena in the South Atlantic, where he died.

TEXT BIOGRAPHY covers:
The revolutionary period **12**:832b
The Consulate 833f
The empire 834h
Elba and the Hundred Days 837a
Exile on Saint Helena 837e
The Napoleonic legend 838a

REFERENCES in other text articles:
·Alexander I's diplomatic relation **1**:474c
·Amsterdam and French policies **1**:712e
·army size and mobilization **19**:543g
·Austrian defeats in French wars **2**:461a
·bed construction and material **7**:790f
·Beethoven's symphony dedication **2**:797g
·Bernadotte as friend and rival **4**:59e
·Buenos Aires' rejection of French rule **3**:445e
·career and domestic and war policy **7**:658b
·Carnot's opposition and later support **3**:945b
·Corsican separatism eradication **5**:192a

cultural and social policies
·arrangement of church–state relations **15**:1015e
·civil service organization structure **4**:668c
·European cultural influence **6**:1068a
·higher education system of France **8**:857g
·Jewish homeland restoration plan **8**:829d
·Jewish policies and institutions **10**:298a
·local government reforms **4**:650c
·rabbinic council of 1807 **10**:323e
·Romantic movement in France **19**:456d
·secondary and higher education reform **6**:364b

·David's role as government artist **5**:521e
·Destutt's idéologie's French reception **9**:194c
·diplomatic and military ambitions **6**:1100e; maps
·Duchy of Warsaw **14**:648c
·Dutch Republic strategic importance **11**:151h
·Egyptian expedition scholarship **6**:462f
·Egypt occupation problems **6**:492h
·Fourier's Egyptian expeditions **7**:577e
·Geneva unsuccessful protectorship **7**:1011f
·Haiti's war of independence **18**:536g
·Holy Roman Empire alteration **8**:101e
·Illyrian Provinces and Austria **2**:625a
·Indonesian colonial policy **9**:485a
·Isthmus of Suez survey **17**:767g
·Italian war strategy **9**:1155g
·Kosciuszko's exile in France **10**:535e
·Latin American independence influence **13**:516f
·map of Europe plan **11**:474e
·Metternich's making of second marriage **12**:63a
·military campaigns and theory **7**:718g; maps 720

military tactics and strategy
·artillery battle tactics **19**:684b
·artillery tactics development **8**:490a
·logistics of food supply and transport **19**:588d
·logistics of supply requisition **11**:78f
·war strategy of victory by battle **19**:560d

·military tactics of earlier victories **19**:579b
·Monge involvement in public affairs **12**:361f
·Ney's military service **13**:55h
·Notre-Dame sale annulled **13**:1011c
·Russian policies and invasion **16**:57e *passim* to 60h
·San Marino relations **16**:223d
·Spanish American independence influence **1**:1144a
·Talleyrand's foreign ministry **17**:1004e
·Vienna rearrangement **19**:117d
·Wellington's military career **19**:755c

Napoléon (1926), motion picture directed by Abel Gance.

·innovative film techniques **12**:502b; illus.

Napoleon, known colloquially as NAP, card game, once considered the national game of England. Any number may play. The cards rank as at Whist, and five are dealt to each player. The player to the dealer's left then looks at his hand and declares, or bids, the number of tricks he can win against the rest, the usual rule being that more than one must be declared; in default of declaring he says "I pass." The next player has a similar option of declaring to make more tricks than the previous bid or passing and so on all round. A bid of five is called going nap. The player who bids highest tries to make his bid, and the others, without consultation, try to prevent him. The declaring hand plays first, and the card he leads determines the trump suit. The players, in rotation, must follow suit if able.

If the declarer succeeds in making his bid, he wins whatever stakes are played for; if not, he loses. If the player declaring nap wins, he receives double stakes from all players; if he loses, he only pays single stakes all round. Sometimes, however, a player is allowed to go "Wellington" over "nap" and even "Blücher" over "Wellington." Both are bids of five, but the caller of "Wellington" wins four times the stake and loses twice the stake, and the caller of "Blücher" receives six times and loses three times the stake. Sometimes a player is allowed to declare *misère; i.e.,* no tricks. This ranks, as a declaration, between bids of three and four, but the player pays a double stake if he wins a trick and receives a single if he takes none.

·history, strategy, and bidding **3**:903e

Napoleon II, the title given by Bonapartists in 1815 to FRANÇOIS-CHARLES-JOSEPH BONAPARTE, later DUKE OF REICHSTADT (b. March 20, 1811, Paris—d. July 22, 1832, Schönbrunn, Austria), only son of Emperor Napoleon I and Empress Marie-Louise; at birth styled king of Rome.

Three years after his birth, the French empire to which he was heir collapsed and he was taken by the Empress to Blois (April 1814). Upon Napoleon's abdication in his son's name as well as his own, Marie-Louise rejected appeals by his uncles Jerôme and Joseph Bonaparte to leave her son in France as figurehead for resistance and took him to the court of her father, the Austrian emperor Francis I. Excluded from succession to his mother's Italian dominions by the Treaty of Paris (1817), he received the Austrian title of duke of Reichstadt (1818). Allowed no active political role, he was instead used by Metternich, the Austrian statesman, in bargaining with France; and his name was also used by Bonapartist insurgents. In 1830, when Charles X of France was overthrown, Reichstadt was already ill with tuberculosis and was unable to take advantage of events.

Napoleon III **12**:839, more commonly known as LOUIS-NAPOLÉON (b. CHARLES-LOUIS-NAPOLÉON BONAPARTE, April 20, 1808, Paris—d. Jan. 9, 1873, Chislehurst, Kent), emperor of the French, 1852–70, gave his country two decades of prosperity under a stable, authoritarian government, and revived its prestige in Europe but finally led it to defeat in the Franco-German War (1870–71).

Abstract of text biography. Louis-Napoléon, nephew of Napoleon I, lived in exile (1815–30) in Switzerland and Germany. He was involved in rebellions in central Italy and in Rome (1830–31). Considering himself his family's claimant to the French throne, he attempted a coup in 1836, for which he was exiled to the United States. He settled in England in 1838. A second coup failed in 1840. He was sentenced to confinement but escaped (1846) to Great Britain. He was elected president of France in 1848; in 1852, after another coup and a new constitution was decreed, he proclaimed himself emperor and instituted a dictatorial regime sanctioned by periodic plebiscites. Together with Piedmont-Sardinia, he declared war on Austria in order to expel it from Italy and received Nice and Savoy as a reward. He intensified the extension of French power in Indochina and promoted industrial expansion at home. In the 1860s, his popularity began to decline, and failures in foreign affairs strengthened the anti-imperial opposition. After defeat in the Franco-Prussian War (1871), he was deposed; and the Third Republic was proclaimed.

REFERENCES in other text articles:
·Bagehot's defense of coup d'etat **2**:584e
·Bismarck's power in foreign diplomacy **2**:1078f
·career, policies, and political philosophy **7**:664e
·Cavour and the Plombières Conference **9**:1161c
·diplomatic and military ambitions **6**:1106h
·diplomatic tactics and failures **8**:111g
·Francis Joseph's Italian diplomacy **7**:686f
·French Canadian interest revival **3**:748b
·French policy towards Algeria **13**:164a
·government promotion of artistic freedom **4**:10f
·Hugo's political attitude change **8**:1134b
·Italian independence movement **2**:466f
·Italian unification aid against Austria **3**:1032a
·Juarez' French imperial problem **10**:282e
·Kossuth military pact against Austria **10**:536h
·McCormick honoured for contributions **11**:226b
·Mexican Empire scheme and outcome **12**:82b
·Napoleonic legend and power **12**:838d
·Papal States, Piedmont, and Austria **14**:483g
·Paris' parks inspired by English visit **13**:1018e
·Thiers' exile and political rise **18**:333c
·Vietnam invasion by France **19**:125d

Napoleon III style: *see* Second Empire style.

Napoleon, Prince: *see* Bonaparte, Napoleon-Joseph-Charles-Paul.

Napoleonic Code: *see* Code Napoléon.

Napoleonic Wars: *see* French Revolutionary and Napoleonic Wars.

Napoleon in His Study (1812), painting by Jacques-Louis David.

·propagandistic style **5**:521e

Napoli (Italy): *see* Naples.

Napoli, Golfo di (Mediterranean Sea): *see* Naples, Bay of.

Napoli, Università degli Studi di, English UNIVERSITY OF NAPLES, coeducational state university at Naples, founded in 1224 as a *studium generale* (*see* university) by the Holy Roman emperor Frederick II. Under stringent royal control, its existence was sporadic for two centuries and itinerant until 1777, when it was reconstituted and removed to the Jesuits' convent in the rear of the present building. These premises were enlarged (1887–1908), but the university's 10 faculties (law, economics, humanities, medicine, mathematics and physical and biological sciences, pharmacy, engineering, architecture, agriculture, and veterinary medicine) are not all centred there but are scattered. In the early 1970s enrollment was 42,000.

·foundation and expansion **12**:830h
·Frederick II's civil service **7**:700d
·Vico's academic career **19**:104b

Napo River, Spanish RÍO NAPO, in northeastern Ecuador and northeastern Peru, flows from the eastern slopes of the Andes in Napo province, Ecuador, and descends generally eastward to the Peruvian border. There it turns southeastward and continues through the dense tropical rain forests of Loreto department, joining the Amazon River approximately 50 mi (80 km) downstream from Iquitos. Explored first by the Spanish soldier and Amazon explorer Francisco de Orellana in 1540 and then by the Portuguese Amazon explorer Pedro Teixiera in 1638, the river, 550 mi (885 km) long, is an important transportation artery, for much of it is navigable. Cattle are raised along its banks, and the forests yield rubber, chicle, timber, and furs.
3°20′ S, 72°40′ W

·confluence and course **6**:285g
·map, Ecuador **6**:286
·map, Peru **14**:128

Nappanee, city, Elkhart County, northern Indiana, U.S., 21 mi (34 km) southeast of South Bend. Founded in 1874, it adopted an Algonkian Indian name (probably meaning "flour") and developed along the Baltimore & Ohio Railroad. There is a large concentration of Amish farmers in the vicinity, and their horse-drawn buggies are a familiar sight around the public square. The city's economy centres on the agricultural markets (mint, onions, grain); manufactures include furniture, mobile homes, electronic and steel products. Inc. 1926. Pop. (1980) 4,694.
41°27′ N, 86°00′ W

nappe, large body or sheet of rock that has been moved forward a distance of about two kilometres or more from its original position by faulting or folding. A nappe may be the hanging wall of a low-angle thrust fault (*see* fault) or it may be a recumbent fold (*see* fold) of large dimensions; both processes position older rocks over younger rocks. In places, erosion may cut into the nappe so deeply that a circular or elliptical patch of the younger, underlying rock is exposed and completely surrounded by the older rock; this patch is called a fenster, or window. A fenster generally occurs in a topographic basin or deep, V-shaped valley. Elsewhere, an eroded, isolated remnant of the older rock or nappe may be completely surrounded by the younger, underlying rock; this is known as a klippe or thrust outlier. Mythen Peak in the Alps in a typical example of a klippe.

·analytic geometry fundamentals **7**:1079b
·formation in Alpine-type mountains **12**:589g
·mountain building by folding **12**:579g; illus. 581
·structure and gravity tectonics **15**:918c

napping, the process of raising the nap of a fibre or cloth.

·textile finishing processes **18**:184h

Naqādah, town, Upper Egypt, on the west bank of the Nile, in the great bend of the river, opposite Qūṣ. One of the oldest antiquity sites of Egypt, it is the site of Neolithic burial grounds of the late Predynastic period (before 3100 BC). They were first excavated by the British archaeologist Sir Flinders Petrie (1853–1942), and are referred to by scholars as Naqādah I and Gerzean (Naqādah II), though the latter form developed in Lower Egypt far from Naqādah. It is thought possible that there was a nome (province) type of political organization centred there in Predynastic times, with the god Seth as tutelary deity. Latest census 21,279.
25°54′ N, 32°43′ E

·map, Egypt **6**:447
·Neolithic nome organization in Egypt **6**:464c; map

Naqādah I (Egyptian archaeological period): *see* Amratian.

Naqādah II (Egyptian archaeological period): *see* Gerzean.

naqqārah (drums): *see* nakers.

Naqqāsh, Mārūn an- (1817–55), Lebanese dramatist.

·theatrical productions in Beirut **9**:981d

Naqshbandīyah, orthodox fraternity of Islāmic mystics (Ṣūfīs) found in India, China, the Central Asian Soviet republics, and Malaysia. It claims a lineage extending back to Abū Bakr, the first caliph. Bahā' ad-Dīn (died 1384), founder of the order at Bukhara, Turkistan, was called *an-naqshband,* "the painter," because of the impression of God that his prescribed ritual (*dhikr*) should leave upon the heart, and so his followers became known as Naqshbandīs. The order has no mass support, for its litanies are subdued and emphasize repetition of the *dhikr* (ritual prayer) to oneself. Through the reforming zeal of Aḥmad Sirhindī (1564–1624), the Naqshbandīs were given new life in India in the 16th century.

·Islāmic orthodoxy and mysticism **9**:922h
·Islāmic reform and renewal **9**:936f
·monastic esoteric trend in Islām **12**:342d
·Mughal syncretism and purist reaction **9**:944b

Naqsh-e-Rostam, Achaemenid and Sāsānian Persian archaeological site in Iran near Per

sepolis (*q.v.*). The Achaemenid necropolis consists of four hypogea, or rock tombs, cut into the cliff sides. These date from the 5th and 4th centuries BC: the tombs of Darius I the Great (reigned 552–486 BC), Darius II, Xerxes I, and Artaxerxes I. There are also Sāsānian relief sculptures dating from the 3rd and 4th centuries AD carved on the cliffs.
·Achaemenian rock reliefs **19**:271c
·Iranian iconography **19**:1176a
·Sāsānian art **9**:849f
·Sāsānian sculpture style **19**:273c
·tombs and carvings **14**:106b

Nara, prefecture (*ken*), Japan, occupying 1,425 sq mi (3,692 sq km) on the central Kii-hantō (Kii Peninsula). Its southern and northeastern portions are mountainous, while the northwest is composed of the lowland of the Nara-bonchi (Nara Basin). The basin, separated from Ōsaka (west) by the Ikoma-yama (Ikoma Mountains) and Kongōdōji-yama, contains most of the prefecture's population, main cities, agricultural land, and transport facilities. Though a historic area, the basin is being increasingly drawn into the commercial orbit of Ōsaka, to which it sends a daily stream of commuters, agricultural products, cotton goods, and handicrafts.

Nara, the prefectural capital and largest city, is located in the hilly northeastern edge of the Nara-bonchi, 25 mi (40 km) east of Ōsaka. It served as the national capital of Japan from 710 to 784 and retains the atmosphere of ancient Japan. The city is most noted for the many ancient Japanese Buddhist buildings and artifacts within its confines. The five-storied pagoda of the Kōfuku-ji (Kōfuku Temple) dates from 710. The Tōdai-ji (752) is noted for the Daibutsu, or Great Buddha; the largest bronze statue in the world, it rises to a total height of 72 ft (22 m). Kasuga Taisha (Grand Shrine of Kasuga) is one of Japan's oldest Shintō shrines. Its best known feature is a long path lined with more than 3,000 stone lanterns. Many religious artifacts have been preserved for more than 1,000 years in a log storehouse, the Shōsō-in repository. These

The Tōdai-ji, Nara, Japan
By courtesy of the Consulate General of Japan, New York City

splendid remnants of early Japanese civilization form the basis of Nara's tourism industry. The city is also a leading commercial and educational centre and has some manufacturing. Pop. (1978 est.) city, 282,381; prefecture, 1,158,000.
·area and population table 1 **10**:45
·establishment and palace layout **19**:222c; illus.
·history and development **13**:752a
·map, Japan **10**:37

Nāra Canal, important water channel in Sind Province, Pakistan, now utilized for the eastern Nāra Canal (226 mi [364 km]), the largest of the Sukkur Barrage canals. From its source above Rohri, it runs southward through Khairpur and Thar Pārkar districts, discharging into the Puran River, an old channel of the Indus River, which flows to the sea farther south through the Rann of Kutch. Because of uncertain water supply received through the Nāra, it was connected in 1858–59 with the Indus at Rohri by a 12-mi-long supply channel. A part of the Sukkur Barrage zone since 1932, it irrigates more than 1,500,000 ac (600,000 ha). With its chief canal, the Jāmrao, serving Thar Pārkar and Hyderābād districts, it has a length of 513 mi and provides a perennial water supply to branch canals.
27°40′ N, 68°51′ E
·map, Indus River Basin **9**:493

Naracoorte, town and rail junction, southeastern South Australia, southeast of Adelaide, near the Victoria border. Founded in 1845, it took its name from an Aboriginal word meaning "running water." During the 1850s, Naracoorte was an important stopping place along the route to the Victorian goldfields. Created a municipality in 1924, it now serves as a market for wool, wheat, and dairy products. Limestone quarrying and lumbering are also local occupations. Tourism, based on the nearby Naracoorte Caves (10 large limestone caverns), is an added source of income. Pop. (1976 prelim.) 4,571.
36°58′ S, 140°44′ E
·map, Australia **2**:401

Nāradiśikṣā, auxiliary text of the Sāmaveda.
·Vedic tone derivation from stress **17**:152c

Narai, also known as NARAYANA (d. 1688, Ayutthaya, Siam, now Thailand), king of Siam (1657–88) best known for his efforts in foreign affairs and whose court produced the first "golden age" of Thai literature.

On becoming king, Narai sought to free himself from domination by the Dutch, who had held commercial monopolies since 1622. When he favoured English and French traders, the Dutch blockaded the harbour at Ayutthaya, the Siamese capital, thereby forcing him, in 1664, to grant them trade and extraterritorial privileges. Denied help by the British East India Company, the King the same year allowed two French Catholic missionaries, Bishops Pallu and Lambert de la Motte, to establish their headquarters (Société des Missions Étrangères) at Ayutthaya. The two missionaries promoted the conversion of Siam to Christianity, and through them Narai sought diplomatic relations with the French government (1673). The British then reactivated a trade mission at Ayutthaya, an enterprise that eventually proved unprofitable; when they withdrew in 1684 the Siamese king committed himself wholeheartedly to seeking an alliance with the French.

The alliance was negotiated by Narai's favourite, Constantine Phaulkon (*q.v.*), a Greek adventurer employed by the British before defecting to the French in 1682. Phaulkon induced the King to send a mission to the court of Versailles to conclude a treaty, but in 1687 Narai was forced to accept a French garrison at Bangkok. After his death anti-foreign elements expelled the French.
·poetic themes, style, and significance **17**:235a
·Thai foreign contacts **16**:721c

Narakāsura, legendary king of Kāmarūpa, ancient kingdom of Assam, in northern India.
·Assam's ancient history **2**:207b

Narameikhla, also called MENG SOAMUN, founder (reigned 1404–34) of the Mrohaung dynasty in Arakan, the maritime country west of Lower Burma on the Bay of Bengal, settled by the Burmese in the 10th century.

When Arakan became the scene of a struggle between the Burmese and the Mon people in the 15th century, Narameikhla, the son of King Rajathu (reigned 1397–1401), was forced, in the first year of his reign, to flee to Bengal, where he became a vassal to King Aḥmad Shāh of Gaur. With the aid of Aḥmad Shāh's successor, he regained control of Arakan in 1430. In 1433 he built at Mrohaung a new capital, which remained the capital of Arakan until the 18th century. As a nominal vassal of the Muslim kings of Gaur, Narameikhla employed Muslim titles in his coins and inscriptions, though he and his subjects were Buddhists.

Naram-Sin (*c.* 2254–*c.* 2218 BC), fourth of the five kings of the southern Mesopotamian dynasty of Akkad. *See* Lullubi.
·Akkadian conflicts and institutions **11**:973a
·divinity of kings **12**:919e
·Elamite history **9**:831d
·epic inspiration **11**:1012a
·Nebuchadrezzar's ancestor **12**:925f
·Ninevite bronze sculpture **13**:116g
·relief sculpture of Akkadian period **19**:261f; illus. 262

Naranjito, city and municipality, northeast central Puerto Rico. The town is on the highway 14 mi (23 km) southwest of San Juan in a tobacco growing region. Pop. (1980 prelim.) town, 2,845; mun., 23,613.
18°18′ N, 66°15′ W
·map, Puerto Rico **15**:263
·Puerto Rico area and population table **15**:261

Nara period (AD 710–784), in Japanese history, period in which the imperial government was at Nara and Sinicization and Buddhism were most highly developed. Nara (*q.v.*), the country's first permanent capital, was modelled on the Chinese T'ang dynasty (618–907) capital, Ch'ang-an. Nara artisans produced refined Buddhist sculpture and erected grand Buddhist temples. A network of roads connected the capital with remote provinces.

Chinese language and literature were studied intensively; the Chinese script was adapted to the Japanese language; and numerous Chinese manuscripts, particularly Buddhist scriptures, were copied. Two official histories, the *Koji-ki* and *Nihon shoki*, were compiled. The *Kaifūsō*, a collection of Chinese poems by

Panel on a bronze lantern depicting one of the heavenly musicians, Nara period (710-784); at the Tōdai-ji, Nara, Japan
Asuka-en, Japan

Japanese poets, and the *Manyō-shū*, an anthology of native poetry, were produced. Legal codes based on Chinese models were compiled to replace the native tradition of legal process based on the individual ruler's interpretation of the unwritten Shintō doctrines. *Major ref.* **19**:221d; illus. 222
·administrative units development **10**:42d
·art forms illus. **19**:Visual Arts, East Asian, Plate 13
·Buddhism's nationalization **3**:409g
·Buddhist sect development **10**:110b
·Chinese artistic influence on silverwork **11**:1117d
·codification of court music **12**:681g
·dress style Chinese influence **5**:1037b
·Japanization of Buddhism **10**:111g
·literary history **10**:1066b

·political and cultural developments **10**:61b; map 65
·pottery styles and decoration **14**:926f

Narasa Nāyaka, regent (1490–1503) of the Vijayanagar empire in India who usurped power in all but name and left his own dynasty to rule.
·regency and military expansion **9**:375g

Narashino, city, Chiba Prefecture (*ken*), Honshu, Japan, on the northeastern shore of Tōkyō-wan (Tōkyō Bay). Formed in 1951 by the merger of Minomi, Maka, Tsuda-numa, and Okubo, Narashino has no city centre because the former towns are lined up along two railways to Tokyo. Formerly the site of a military base, the city is now a residential suburb of Tokyo. Pop. (1978 est.) 120,137.
35°41′ N, 140°02′ E

Narasiṃha (Sanskrit: Man-Lion), fourth of the 10 *avatāra*s (incarnations) of the Hindu god Viṣṇu (Vishnu). The demon Hiraṇyakaśipu, twin brother of the demon overthrown by Viṣṇu in his previous incarnation as Varāha, obtained a boon from Brahmā that he could not be killed by man or beast, from inside or outside, by day or by night, and that no weapon could harm him. Thus, feeling secure, he began to trouble heaven and earth. His son, Prahlāda, on the other hand, was a devotee of Viṣṇu, even though his father threatened his life because of it. One day the demon challenged Prahlāda, and, kicking a stone pillar, asked: "If your god is omnipresent, is he in this pillar also?" Viṣṇu emerged from the pillar in the form of a man-lion and slew the demon at dusk on the threshold.

Narasiṃha, stone sculpture from Devangana, Rājasthān, India, 9th century AD
Pramod Chandra

The incident is often depicted in art, with Narasiṃha appearing out of the pillar or engaged in ripping open the belly of the demon, one of his numerous pairs of hands holding up the entrails like a garland. The animal aspect is shown by a curly mane of hair, sharp curved teeth, and leonine facial features. The body, though human, has a thick neck, large shoulders, and slender abdomen and waist. Seated images of Narasiṃha are also found in which the lion face has a pacific expression.
·Vishnu incarnations **8**:930h; illus.

Narasiṃhadeva I, king (reigned 1238–64) of the Gaṅga (*q.v.*) dynasty of Orissa, in India.
·Orissa's Sun Temple construction **13**:739e

Narasiṃha Jayanti, Hindu festival.
·bhagavatha mela performance **17**:162g

Narasiṃha Sāluva, ruler (1485–90) of the Vijayanagar (*q.v.*) Empire in India.
·regency and military expansion **9**:375f

Narasiṃhavarman I Mahāmalla, also called MĀMALLA, king (reigned *c.* 630–668) of the Pallava dynasty of South India.
·naval expeditions to Ceylon **9**:360a

Nara Singde, Chinese name NA-LAN CH'ENG-TE, 17th-century Manchu poet.
·poetry style **10**:1057e

Narathiwat, known locally as BANG NARA, administrative headquarters of Narathiwat province (*changwat*), southern Thailand. It is a minor port on the South China Sea. The province has an area of 1,632 sq mi (4,228 sq km) and is heavily planted in coconuts and rice. Pop. town (1972 est.) 24,069; province (1970) 326,633.
6°25′ N, 101°48′ E
·map, Thailand **18**:199
·province area and population table **18**:202

Narayan, Jaya Prakash, also written JAI PRAKASH NARAIN (b. Oct. 11, 1902, Sitab Diyara, Bihār, India—d. Oct. 8, 1979, Patna), political leader and theorist. In 1932 he was sentenced to a year's imprisonment for participation in the civil disobedience movement against British rule in India. Upon release he took a leading part in the formation of the Congress Socialist Party, a left-wing group within the Indian National Congress, the organization that led the campaign for Indian independence. He was imprisoned again in 1939 for his opposition to the war but made a dramatic escape and tried to organize violent resistance to the government before his recapture in 1943. After his release in 1946 he tried to persuade the Congress leaders to adopt a more militant policy.

In 1948 he, with most of the Socialists, left the Congress Party and in 1952 formed the Praja Socialist Party. Soon becoming dissatisfied with party politics, he announced in 1954 that he would thenceforth devote his life exclusively to the Bhoodan Yajna movement, founded by Vinoba Bhave, which demanded that land be distributed among the landless. His continuing interest in political problems, however, was revealed when in 1959 he argued for a "reconstruction of Indian polity" by means of a four-tier hierarchy of village, district, state, and union councils.

In 1974 he irrupted on the Indian political scene as a severe critic of what he saw as the corrupt and increasingly undemocratic government of Indira Gandhi. Though he gained a following from students and opposition politicians, there was less enthusiasm from the masses. The next year a lower court convicted Gandhi of corrupt election practices, and Narayan called for her resignation. Instead she declared a national emergency and jailed Narayan and other opposition leaders. In prison his health collapsed. He was released after five months but never regained his health. When Gandhi and her party were defeated in 1977, Narayan advised the victorious Janata party in its choice of leaders.
·anarchist influence **1**:812d
·Socialist Party and independence struggle **9**:420b

Narayan, R(asipuram) K(rishnaswamy) (b. Oct. 10, 1906, Madras, India), one of the finest Indian authors of his generation writing in English. After finishing college and marrying (1934), Narayan worked as a teacher in a small village school. After a few months he became discontented with teaching and devoted his time to writing. His first novel, *Swami and Friends* (1935), describes the adventures of a group of schoolboys.

All Narayan's works are set in the large, fictitious South Indian town of Malgudi. Narayan does not delve into the problems of man's relationships to God, politics, good and evil, or issues of social reform but portrays, often masterfully, the peculiarities of human relationships and the ironies of Indian daily life. His writing is marked by genial humour and elegance and simplicity of style.

Among his novels are *The Financial Expert* (1952), *Waiting for Mahatma* (1955), *The Guide* (1958), *The Man-Eater of Malgudi* (1961), *The Vendor of Sweets* (1967), and *The Painter of Signs* (1976). Collections of short stories include *Lawley Road* (1956) and *A Horse and Two Goats* (1970). He published shortened modern prose versions of the Indian epics *The Ramayana* (1972) and *The Mahabharata* (1978) and a "memoir," *My Days* (1974).
·craftsmanship and audience **17**:150a
·Indian novel tradition **13**:292g

Narayana: *see* Narai.

Nārāyanganj, city, Dacca District, Bangladesh, on the Lakhya River at its confluence with the Dhaleswari. The chief river port for Dacca, it has steamer connections with inland ports and Chittagong. Nārāyanganj is the busiest trade market in the country, a collection centre for hides and skins, and a terminal market for jute. Together with Dacca it also forms the largest industrial region of Bangladesh, with the largest number of jute presses and jute and cotton mills. Other industries include ship repair and varied manufactures. Constituted a municipality in 1876, it houses a college, a hospital, and a library. Historic buildings include Kadam Rasul (1801), a shrine built by Ghulām Muḥammad of Tippera; a 16th-century fort of the Bara Bhaiyas; and the 12th-century temple of Lakṣmī-Nārāyaṇa, after which the town is named. Pop. (1974) 176,459.
23°37′ N, 90°30′ E
·map, Bangladesh **2**:689

Narbada River (India): *see* Narmada River.

Narbonensis, or GALLIA NARBONENSIS, one of the four provinces of Gaul formally established by the Roman emperor Augustus. Located in what is now southeastern France, between the Alps, the Mediterranean Sea, and the Cévennes mountains, it had a climate and history markedly different from those of the rest of Gaul. Narbonensis attracted a large number of Roman immigrants, and several prominent Romans were born there. It was outstanding for its numerous cities, impressive public buildings, and high level of culture. The provincial capital was at Narbo (Narbo Martius), on the Aude River.
·Celtic history **3**:1074e
·maps, Ancient Rome **15**:1092, 1128
·Roman conquest and domination **7**:960h; map

Narboni, Moses (philosopher): *see* Moses of Narbonne.

Narbonne, city, Aude *département*, southeastern France, lying on a vine-growing plain 8 mi (13 km) from the Mediterranean and east of Carcassonne.

Narbonne was the site of Narbo Martius (Narbo), the first colony founded by the Romans in Gaul (118 BC), from which the town derived its name. Then on the Mediterranean, it became a flourishing port. In 413 it was seized by the Visigoths, who later made it their capital. In 719 the Saracens captured the town, occupying it until 759. During the Middle Ages, the southern part of the town was ruled by the counts of Toulouse, while the northern part was under episcopal administration. At the beginning of the 16th century, Narbonne was united to the French crown.

The cathedral of Saint-Just, begun in 1272 but never completed, has only a choir and two square towers. Built in the style of the cathedrals of northern France, the choir, which is of exceptional height, has pleasingly harmonious proportions. The basilica of Saint-Paul-Serge (mainly 12th and 13th centuries) is an interesting example of early Gothic architecture in the south of France. The three square towers of the fortified Palais des Archevêques date from the 13th and 14th centuries, but the Gothic-style town hall was added to the palace only in the 19th century. The building now houses two museums with collections of paintings, ceramics, and Roman artifacts.

The Canal de la Robine, a branch of the Canal du Midi, runs through the city, separating the northern part historically known as the Cité from the Bourg to the south. The old town, now surrounded by boulevards, has picturesque, narrow, winding streets. A major road and rail junction, Narbonne specializes in the trade of Aude wines. A uranium processing plant was built just outside the town in 1959. Other industries are mainly connected with wine production (fertilizers and agricultural machinery). Latest census 35,236.
43°11′ N, 3°00′ E
·map, France **7**:584

Narborough Island (Galápagos Islands): *see* Fernandina Island.

narcissism, character disorder originally described by Sigmund Freud as the fixation of libidinal energy upon the self, so-called from the Greek mythological Narcissus. According to this theory, the sexual energy that initially should focus upon the parent and thereafter be transferred to others never attains either of these expressions. Because of a lack of love or response on the part of the parents, the libidinal energy can never be discharged upon another person with satisfaction. Distrust of the other person in relationships persists into adult life, so that the narcissistic character prefers autoeroticism (masturbation, for example) to normal sexual intercourse.

Narcissus, in Greek mythology, the son of the river god Cephissus and the nymph Leiriope; he was distinguished for his beauty. His mother was told that he would have a long life, provided he never looked upon his own features. His rejection, however, of the love of the nymph Echo or of his lover Ameinias drew upon him the vengeance of the gods. He fell in love with his own reflection in the waters of a spring and pined away (or killed himself); the flower that bears his name sprang up where he died. According to another source, Narcissus, to console himself for the death of a favourite twin sister, his exact counterpart, sat gazing into the spring to recall her features by his own.

Narcissus, wall painting from the House of Lucretius Fronto, Pompeii, Italy, 14–62 AD
Alinari—Mansell

The story may have been connected with the ancient Greek superstition that it was unlucky or even fatal to see one's own reflection. Hence is derived the term narcissism, used in psychiatry and especially psychoanalysis for a morbid condition in which the subject is intensely interested in his own body.
·transformation in myth **8**:406b

Narcissus (d. AD 54), freedman who used his position as correspondence secretary (*ab epistulis*) to the Roman emperor Claudius (ruled 41–54) to become, in effect, a minister of state. He exercised great influence over Claudius and accumulated immense wealth. At first Narcissus allied himself with Claudius' third wife, Valeria Messalina, but fear that she and her lover, Gaius Silius, were conspiring to seize power made him join with others to have her executed (48). By failing to support Claudius' subsequent marriage to Agrippina the Younger, Narcissus lost influence in the government. The finance secretary, Pallas, who had favoured the match, became Claudius' favourite. Narcissus' power was further undermined when he backed Britannicus, son of Claudius and Messalina, for the succession even after Agrippina had persuaded Claudius to designate as his successor her own son (by a previous marriage), Lucius Domitius Ahenobarbus. In 54 Claudius died, evidently poisoned by Agrippina. Domitius took power as the emperor Nero and immediately had Narcissus arrested. Shortly afterward the freedman committed suicide.
·Vespassian's military career boast **19**:95f

Narcissus, genus of bulbous, often fragrant, ornamental plants in the family Amaryllidaceae, about 40 species, native primarily to Europe. Daffodil, or narcissus (*N. pseudonarcissus*), jonquil (*N. jonquilla*), and poet's narcissus (*N. poeticus*) are popular garden flowers. The central crown of each yellow, white,

Daffodil (*Narcissus pseudonarcissus*)
Walter Chandoha

or pink flower ranges in shape from the form of a trumpet, as in the daffodil, to a ringlike cup, as in the poet's narcissus. The rushlike or flattened leaves arise from the base of the plant; they may be only 5 to 7.5 centimetres (2 to 3 inches) high or up to 0.6 to 1.2 metres (2 to 4 feet). Some species hybridize in the wild, and many man-made crosses between species have resulted in attractive garden hybrids. The bulbs of *Narcissus* species, which are poisonous, were once used in medicines as an emetic and cathartic. An oil from jonquil flowers is used in perfumes.

narcolepsy, sudden, uncontrollable spells of sleep during the day, with disturbances of sleep at night. Among possible causes are brain tumour, syphilis of the central nervous system, head injury, and hardening of the arteries. After onset the disorder tends to persist for the rest of the affected person's life.
·causation and auxiliary symptoms **16**:881e
·stimulant drug therapy as treatment **17**:694b

narcotic **12**:841, a drug that dulls the senses, relieves pain, causes lethargy or stupor in large doses, and tends to produce addiction. In most countries a governmental agency limits the production, trade, and use of narcotics because of their detrimental effects and the incidence of narcotic drug abuse.

The text article covers the general characteristics of narcotics, relationships between chemical structures and narcotic action, biological dispositions of narcotic drugs, physical dependence, the clinical use of narcotics in the treatment of pain, and narcotic antagonists.

REFERENCES in other text articles:
·analgesic groups and properties **1**:717h
·botany history and applications **3**:70e
·figwort order as medicine source **16**:414g
·industrial medicine requirements **9**:529d
·kava use and effects **14**:468e
·overdose treatment with caffeine **17**:695a
·Papaverales opium derivatives and use **13**:963f
·pharmacological religious practices **14**:199h
·plant organ commercial uses **13**:726d
·smuggling in New York **13**:29d
·suicide victims' use **17**:780e
·tranquillizer use to ease withdrawal **18**:596b
·UN commission to control drug traffic **18**:900b
·use and effect **5**:1045f

RELATED ENTRIES in the *Ready Reference and Index*:
apomorphine; codeine; dextromethorphan; dihydrocodeinone; dihydromorphinone; fentanyl; heroin; laudanum; levallorphan; meperidine; methadone; morphine; nalorphine; opium; paregoric; phenazocine

Nardi, Jacopo (b. July 21, 1476, Florence—d. after 1563, Venice), statesman and historian who wrote a history of Florence that sharply criticized the ruling Medici family.

Nardi was born to a family that was long hostile to the Medici. He followed a military career until the expulsion of the Medici in 1494; he then served in several posts as a magistrate and became one of the principal republican partisans of Girolamo Savonarola, the religious reformer who virtually ruled Florence in 1494–98. When the Medici returned in 1512, Nardi continued to occupy several minor posts. With the final fall of the Florentine Republic in 1530–31, he was exiled and his property confiscated. Nardi spent the rest of his life in Venice, wrote to support his family, and represented the Florentine exiles in 1535, when they made a formal accusation against Alessandro de' Medici before the Holy Roman emperor Charles V.

Nardi is best known for his *Istorie della citta' di Firenze* (1582; "History of the City of Florence"), which covers the period 1494–1538 and is a valuable discussion of Florentine politics during the time of Savonarola and the republic. He also wrote two comedies in verse, *L'amicizia* (1503–12; "Friendship") and *I due felici rivali* (before 1519; "Two Happy Rivals"), and translated several classics.

Nardini, Pietro (b. April 12, 1722, Leghorn, Italy—d. May 7, 1793, Florence), violinist and composer, one of the most eminent violinists of the 18th century. The most famous pupil of the composer and virtuoso violinist Giuseppe Tartini, he was solo violinist at the court at Stuttgart from 1753 to 1767. He then returned to Leghorn and lived with Tartini during Tartini's last illness until his death in 1770. In 1770 he became music director to the duke of Tuscany. He enjoyed great fame as a composer and performer, his playing praised by contemporaries for its beauty and emotional power. His violin compositions, though not numerous, are melodious and highly playable and are valued as technical studies. Several sonatas and quartets were reprinted in modern editions.

Nardò, town, Lecce province, Puglia (Apulia) region, southeastern Italy, southwest of Lecce city. Originally the Roman city of Neretum, Nardò was both Byzantine and Norman; it has a 13th–14th-century cathedral in the Romantic-Gothic style, and an unusual circular chapel called the Osanna, dating from 1603. Examples of Baroque architecture in the town include the church of S. Domenico. Modern Nardò is an agricultural centre, trading in wheat, olive oil, and tobacco. Pop. (1971 prelim.) mun., 28,212.
40°11′ N, 18°02′ E

Nardostachys (plant): *see* spikenard.

Narendranath Datta (Hindu philosopher): *see* Vivekananda.

Naresuan, real name PHRA NARET, popularly known as THE BLACK PRINCE, probably because of his dark complexion (b. *c*. 1555, Ayutthaya, Siam, now Thailand—d. May 16,

1605, on the Salween River, now in Burma), king of Siam in 1590–1605, regarded as a national hero by the Siamese people for having liberated the country from the Burmese. In 1569 the Burmese king Bayinnaung (reigned 1551–81) conquered Siam, placing Naresuan's father, Maha Dhammaraja, on the throne as his vassal. The capital, Ayutthaya, was pillaged, thousands of Siamese were deported to Burma as slaves, and Siam then suffered numerous invasions from Cambodia.

At the age of 16 Naresuan was also made a vassal of Burma and appointed governor of the northern province of Phitsanulok, where he led numerous campaigns against Cambodia. In 1584 he renounced his allegiance to Bayinnaung's son King Nanda Bayin (reigned 1581–99); in a series of brilliant military operations, he defeated three Burmese armies that had invaded Siam, frustrated attempts of the Burmese to capture the capital, and drove out the Cambodians. Becoming king in 1590, Naresuan took the offensive: he captured the Cambodian capital of Lovek, made Cambodia a vassal of Siam, and established suzerainty over the northern kingdom of Chiang Mai. He seized the Burmese peninsular provinces of Tavoy and Tenasserim but refrained from attempting to become overlord of all Burma, though he killed the Burmese heir apparent in battle in 1592. Burma ceased to be a threat to Siam when a civil war broke out between King Nanda Bayin and his brothers, the princes of Prome, Ava, and Toungoo; the Arakanese, whose kingdom lay to the west of Burma, then intervened and sacked the Burmese capital of Pegu in 1599.

Although Naresuan was known primarily as a military commander, he also promoted Siamese commerce, particularly when the annexation of Tavoy and Tenasserim gave him access to the Indian Ocean. He conducted peaceful relations with the Portuguese in Malacca and the Spanish in Manila and laid the foundation that made Siamese commerce a rich prize for European merchants in the 17th century. He died on a military campaign in the Shan states in 1605 and was succeeded by his brother Ekathotsarat.

·Thai revolt against Burma **16**:720g

Nariño, department of southwestern Colombia, bounded by the Pacific Ocean (west) and Ecuador (south). The population of the territory, 11,986 sq mi (31,045 sq km), is concentrated principally in the volcanic Andean highlands above 5,000 ft (1,500 m). The densely settled Altiplano (High Plateau) of

Wheat farming in Nariño department, Colombia
Carl Frank

Túquerres-Ipiales, on the Ecuadorian frontier, is separated by the Río Guáitara from that of the departmental capital of Pasto (*q.v.*). The economy is based almost entirely on agriculture (wheat, barley, beans, and potatoes). Bananas cultivated in the Pacific lowlands are exported from the port of Tumaco, which handles large, oceangoing vessels. A railroad from Tumaco crosses the lowlands and ascends to El Diviso in the Andean foothills. Pop. (1979 est.) 1,018,941.

·area and population table **4**:870
·map, Colombia **4**:869

Nariño, Antonio (1765–1823), Colombian revolutionary writer and leader of the Colombian independence movement.

·French revolutionary influences **10**:702f

naris, in anatomy, opening into the nose (*q.v.*) or into the nasal cavity. An external naris is called a nostril.

Narita, town, Chiba Prefecture (*ken*), central Honshū, Japan. It is a commercial centre for an agricultural area, and is the site of a Buddhist temple, Shinshō-ji, that attracts millions of pilgrims annually.

Nearby is the New Tokyo International Airport, which opened in 1978. Originally planned to open in 1971, it was not completed until 1973. A coalition of farmers, whose land had been expropriated for the airport, and radical students led protests, built towers that prevented the use of runways, and destroyed vital radio equipment, preventing use of the facility for more than five years. Pop. (1975) 50,915.

35°47′ N, 140°19′ E

·map, Japan **10**:36
·Tokyo-Yokohama airport **18**:479g

Närke, *landskap* (province), *län* (county) of Örebro, south central Sweden, between the *landskapen* (provinces) of Västmanland on the north, Södermanland on the east, Östergötland on the southeast, Västergötland on the southwest, and Värmland on the west. With a land area of 1,615 sq mi (4,183 sq km), it is one of Sweden's smallest *landskapen.* Dominating its landscape is the great central plains area, bordered by Kilsbergen (915 ft [279 m]) on the northwest and wooded heights on the south. Two of Sweden's largest lakes—Vättern and Hjälmaren—lie partly within its boundaries. The oldest remains of occupation date from the post-glacial period, *c.* 6500 BC. Based on the many small iron ore deposits, ironworking was prevalent during the Middle Ages. The central plains area is one of the most agriculturally productive of central Sweden. Since the end of the 19th century the acreage of arable land has been greatly increased by the reclamation of swampland and by the lowering of lake levels. Among the leading industries are shoe manufacturing and food processing. Principal towns include Örebro, Kumla, and Askersund. Pop. (1979 est.) 172,219.

Narkidae (fish family): *see* electric ray.

Narmada (NARBADA OR NERBUDDA) **River,** in central India, rises in the Maikala Range of Mandla district, Madhya Pradesh state. Following a tortuous course through the hills of Mandla, it enters the structural trough between the Vindhya and Sātpura ranges at Marble Rocks Gorge and then flows westward across Madhya Pradesh and Gujarāt states, entering the Gulf of Cambay through a 13-mi (21-km) -wide estuary, just below Broach. Along its 801-mi (1,289-km) course, the Narmada drains the northern slopes of the Sātpura Range.

Called the Namades by the 2nd-century-AD Greek geographer Ptolemy, the river has always been an important route between the Arabian Sea and the Ganges Valley. Hindus believe it sprang from the body of the god Śiva, so that the Narmada ranks only after the Ganges in sanctity. The *pradakṣiṇā* pilgrimage takes the devoted 1,600 mi up one bank from Broach to Amarkantak, and down the other.

21°38′ N, 72°36′ E

·map, India **9**:278
·silt deposit in Gulf of Cambay **8**:479b
·tribal inhabitants' moral systems **3**:987c

Narmer, presumed first Egyptian king sometimes identified with Menes (*q.v.*).

Narmer Palette (*c.* 3100 BC), Egyptian votive cosmetic palette of slate dating from the Old Kingdom (*see* Menes).

·artistic style and Egyptian ideology **19**:250a; illus.

Nārnaul, administrative headquarters, Mahendragarh district, Haryana state, India, on the Chhalak River. A trade and communications centre, it has chief industries of handloom weaving and lime and cart manufacturing. The name is probably derived from Narrashtra, a term in an ancient Hindu epic, the *Mahābhārata,* connoting the country south of Delhi. A former Muslim cultural centre, Nārnaul contains the tomb of Ibrāhīm Khān Gārdi (15th century) and was the centre of the Satnāmī religious revolt against Emperor Aurangzeb (1672). Constituted a municipality in 1906, it has a college affiliated with Punjab University. Pop. (1971) 31,875.

28°03′ N, 76°06′ E

·map, India **9**:278

Narni, town, Terni province, Umbria region, central Italy, on a hilltop above the Nera River. It originated as the Roman Nequinum (later Narnia) and was the birthplace of Pope John XIII (10th century), the Roman emperor Nerva (1st century), and the condottiere Erasmo da Narni (15th century). The town's ruined castle dates from the 14th century; the Palazzo Comunale houses paintings by the 15th-century painters Benozzo Gozzoli and Domenico Ghirlandaio. Besides its 12th-century cathedral, medieval churches include those of Sta. Maria in Pensole and S. Francesco. Linoleum, woodwork, and electrical appliances are manufactured. Pop. (1978 est.) mun., 20,775.

42°31′ N, 12°31′ E

Narnia, Chronicles of (1950–56), series of seven children's books by C.S. Lewis.

·sources and critical evaluation **4**:234g

Narodna Odbrana, English NATIONAL DEFENSE, Serbian nationalist organization founded in 1908 that gathered recruits from Bosnia-Hercegovina, Serbia, and Croatia to foment an anti-Habsburg revolution in Bosnia. Although it transformed itself into a cultural society in 1909, it continued its clandestine operations and was mistakenly blamed by Austrian authorities for the assassination of Archduke Francis Ferdinand (1914).

Narodnaya, Mount, Russian GORA NARODNAYA (People's Mountain), peak of the subarctic Urals in the Russian Soviet Federated Socialist Republic, rising to 6,214 ft (1,894 m). The highest mountain in the Urals range, it is composed largely of quartzites. Several small glaciers have been found on the slopes of Narodnaya and nearby mountains. Coniferous forests lie on the lower slopes, whereas tundra occurs higher up. The gentler slopes are used as reindeer pasture in summer.

65°04′ N, 60°09′ E

·map, Soviet Union **17**:322

Narodnaya Volya, English PEOPLE'S WILL, OR PEOPLE'S FREEDOM, 19th-century Russian revolutionary organization that regarded political assassination as the best means of forcing political reform and overthrowing the autocracy. Narodnaya Volya was organized in 1879 by members of the revolutionary Populist party, Zemlya i Volya (Land and Freedom), who were disillusioned by the failure of their efforts to promote social revolution by agitating among peasants. The new group, emphasizing the need for a political struggle against the state structure, used terror to force political reform as well as to undermine the state. Led by Andrey I. Zhelyabov and Sofya L. Perovskaya, it elected an executive committee that planned the assassination of government officials, and even of the emperor Alexander II, who was killed on March 13 (March 1, old style), 1881. The assassins were arrested and hanged. Narodnaya Volya aroused enthusiasm among revolutionaries in Russia and abroad and frightened the government but was unable to alter the character of the tsarist regime.

·Russian pre-Revolutionary communism **4**:1020d
·terrorist political doctrine **16**:62f

Narodniki, or POPULISTS (Russian sing. Narodnik), members of a Socialist movement of 19th-century Russian intellectuals who believed that social transformation in Russia was dependent upon the peasantry (the people, *narod*) and that a modern socialist society could be constructed on the basis of the peasants' traditional communal social institution, the *mir* (*q.v.*). Developing from the revolutionary circles of the 1860s, particularly the Chaykovsky circle (1869–74), the movement was composed of professional people, students, and *raznochintsy* (intellectuals from nongentry classes).

In 1873–74, taking their cue from A.I. Herzen, the Narodniki practiced a "going to the people" (*khozhdenie v narod*). Hundreds of Narodniki, following the idealist philosophies of M.A. Bakunin and P.L. Lavrov, went into the countryside and mingled among the peasants, either directly inciting rebellion or spreading propaganda intended to educate the masses politically and indirectly inspire a revolt. The campaign failed to arouse the peasantry and resulted mainly in the arrest of many Narodniki, who were subsequently tried in two major public trials in 1877–78: the "Trial of the 50" and the "Trial of the 193."

The Narodniki became more organized and secretive, forming Zemlya i Volya (*q.v.*) in 1876. They continued to work in the countryside and now settled among the peasants, providing medical, technical, and educational services and at the same time gradually enlightening and politicizing them. But many Narodniki, hampered by police repression and peasant recalcitrance, became impatient and turned to terrorism as a more immediate and effective way of stimulating revolutionary social change.

In 1879 Zemlya i Volya split into two groups: Narodnaya Volya (*q.v.;* People's Will), a terrorist party that disintegrated after it assassinated Emperor Alexander II (1881), and Chyorny Peredel (Black Repartition), a party that continued to emphasize work among the peasantry until its members converted to Marxism and shifted their attention to the urban proletariat (1880s). The Populist ideology of the Narodniki was revived by the 20th-century Socialist Revolutionary Party (*q.v.*). *Major ref.* **16**:968h

·Gorky's rejection **8**:256a
·Lenin's and Plekhanov's attacks **10**:792h
·peasant revolutionary-potential theory **16**:62e
·peasant role in Socialist revolution **8**:1167c
·Plekhanov's devotion and later criticism **14**:569h
·Russian growth, development, and evolution **4**:1020d

narodnye druzhiny (Russian: "people's patrols"), in the Soviet Union, volunteers who assist the militia in the maintenance of public order.

·public order and organizations in Soviet Union **17**:351b

Naro-Fominsk, centre of a *rayon* (district), Moscow *oblast* (administrative region), western Russian Soviet Federated Socialist Republic, on the Nara River southwest of the capital. It was formed in 1926 from three villages and textile centres. The town Fominsk was totally destroyed in World War II, but has re-emerged with a slightly modified economy, the cotton-based economy of the past having given way to a huge silk-weaving combine. Pop. (1973 est.) 52,000.
55°23′ N, 36°43′ E

Narooma, coastal resort, southeast New South Wales, Australia, at the mouth of the Wagonga River. Settled in the 1860s as a cattle station and surveyed in 1883, it takes its name from *noorooma*, an Aboriginal word meaning "clear, blue water." During the 1930s, Narooma's principal resource, good offshore game fishing, was widely publicized by the U.S. novelist Zane Grey. The sport continues to bring many anglers both to the town and to Montague Island (6 mi [9.6 km] offshore). Accessible from Sydney (174 mi north) via the Prince's Highway, Narooma serves a district of dairying and lumbering and has fish canneries. Pop. (1971 prelim.) 1,551.
36°13′ S, 150°03′ E

Narottama (king of Cambodia): *see* Norodom.

narra, also ASANA, any of several timber trees of the genus *Pterocarpus* of the pea family (Fabaceae or Leguminosae), especially *P. indicus*, or India padauk, or the hard wood, noted for its ability to take a high polish, derived from the trees. Narra wood is used for cabinetwork; it is usually red or rose colour, often variegated with yellow, and is hard and heavy. The trunk of the tree is surrounded (or, occasionally, supported) by huge buttresses extending outward and upward for about 15 feet (5 metres); these are sometimes made into table tops, the pattern of the grain and the colouring being hardly equalled by any other timber. A small chip of the wood placed in water soon gives it an opalescent colour because of a substance in the wood cells. Narra wood is known also as Burmese rosewood, Andaman redwood, and kiabooca wood.

Narrabri, town, north New South Wales, Australia, on Narrabri Creek (tributary of the Namoi River), at the foot of the Nandewar Range, in the Liverpool Plains district. Surveyed in 1859 and declared a municipality in 1883, it derives its name from an Aboriginal word meaning "big creek" and "forked stick." On the Newell Highway, with regular air and rail service to Sydney (264 mi [425 km] southeast) and Brisbane, Narrabri serves an area of dairy, sheep, cereal, and cotton farming (on the Namoi flats) and rutile mining. The town has freezing, engineering, sheet plaster, and joinery works and flour mills and sawmills. Several research establishments, including an experimental irrigation farm, wheat institute, and astronomical observatory, are nearby. Pop. (1971 prelim.) 6,875.
30°19′ S, 149°47′ E
·map, Australia **2**:401

Narraganset, Algonkian-speaking Indian tribe that occupied most of what is now Rhode Island west of Narragansett Bay.

Ninigret, sachem of the Narraganset; painting by an unknown American artist, 18th century
By courtesy of the Museum of Art, Rhode Island School of Design, Providence

They were grouped in eight territorial divisions, each with a chief who was in turn subject to a head chief. Their subsistence depended on the cultivation of maize (corn), hunting, and fishing.

The Narraganset maintained good relations with whites until King Philip's War (*q.v.*) in 1675–76, in which they sided with the hostile tribes. Soon after a battle at Kingston, R.I., in 1675, in which nearly 1,000 Narraganset were killed or captured, they abandoned their territory. Most joined the Mahican or Abnaki or fled to Canada, from which some later received permission to return. The latter were settled among other Algonkian groups that had remained neutral in the war. The combined tribes, known as the Narraganset, decreased in number, and in 1788 many joined Indian settlements in New York, composed of remnants of various Algonkian tribes. Some joined the Mohegan in Connecticut, and a few remained near Charlestown, R.I.

·Rhode Island Great Swamp fight **15**:808a
·tribal independent churches **18**:702f
·Woodlands Indian culture **6**:169b

Narragansett, town (township), southeastern Washington County, southern Rhode Island, U.S., at the entrance to Narragansett Bay. The Pettaquamscutt River forms the western boundary of this resort community, which includes the village of Narragansett Pier and the fishing villages of Galilee and Jerusalem. Near Galilee is Point Judith Lighthouse (1816), an important beacon. Settled in 1657–59 and set off from South Kingstown in 1888, Narragansett was named for the Narraganset Indian tribe, mostly driven out during King Philip's War (1675–76). Inc. 1901. Pop. (1980) 12,088.
41°26′ N, 71°27′ W

Narragansett Bay, inlet of the North Atlantic Ocean, extending northward (from Rhode Island Sound of the Atlantic Ocean) for 28 mi (45 km) into Rhode Island, U.S., almost dividing the state into two parts. The bay is 3 to 12 mi wide and receives the Taunton, Providence, and Sakonnet rivers. It includes Rhode, Prudence, and Conanicut islands and Mt. Hope Bay (a northeastern arm), which is crossed by one of the longest bridges in New England. Since the colonial period, the bay (named for the Narraganset Indians) has been an active shipping centre, the chief ports being Providence (capital of Rhode Island) and Newport.
41°20′ N, 71°15′ W
·description and commercial importance **15**:809b

Mt. Hope Bay, an arm of Narragansett Bay
J.L. Stage—Photo Researchers

Narrandera, town, south central New South Wales, Australia, on the Murrumbidgee River. Settled (1863) as a livestock station, it was proclaimed a town in 1880 and given an

Aboriginal name meaning Place of Lizards. Gazetted a borough (1885), it was merged with Yanco Shire in 1960. Lying within the Murrumbidgee Irrigation Area, it serves, with the nearby towns of Leeton and Griffith, a district producing beef, fodder, merino sheep, wheat, and wool. Industries include flour mills and sawmills and factories for concrete, pipe, and plasterboard. Narrandera is at the junction of the Newell and Sturt highways and has rail and air connections to Sydney, 272 mi (438 km) east-northeast, and to Melbourne. Pop. (1971 prelim.) 4,825.
34°45′ S, 146°33′ E
·map, Australia **2**:400

narrative poetry, sets out to narrate a sequence of events and shape them as a story—for example, Geoffrey Chaucer's *Canterbury Tales*.

Narrenschiff, Das (1494), translated as THE SHIP OF FOOLS (1509), allegorical work by Sebastian Brant.
·religious nonfiction prose
development **10**:1081h

Narrogin, town, southwest Western Australia. It developed in the 1880s, when the Great Southern Railway came through the site and a hotel was erected at the trackside. The settlement, which grew around the hotel, became a town (1895) and municipality (1906). Its name derives from the Aboriginal term *gnargajin*, meaning "water hole." Situated on the Great Southern Highway and near Albany Highway, the town is the junction of rail lines extending east to the Wheat Belt (*q.v.*), west and south to the coast, and northwest to Perth (105 mi [170 km]). It is a market for the grain, wool, beef, and fodder produced in the area. Large mallet-tree plantations yield tannin. The Narrogin Farm School was founded in 1914. Pop. (1971 prelim.) 4,843.
32°56′ S, 117°10′ E
·map, Australia **2**:400

narrow-mouthed toad, collective name for amphibians of the family Microhylidae, which

Eastern narrow-mouthed toad (*Microhyla carolinensis*)
George Porter—National Audubon Society

includes 56 genera and more than 200 species. Narrow-mouthed toads are found in North and South America, Africa, Asia, and the Australian region. Typically, they are small, stocky, and smooth skinned with short legs, small heads, pointed snouts, and narrow mouths. They live on land, underground, or in trees and are generally secretive in nature. Most species are less than five centimetres (two inches) long.

The eastern narrow-mouthed toad, *Microhyla carolinensis* (*Gastrophryne* of some authorities), is a small, terrestrial microhylid of the United States. It is gray, reddish, or brown with darker stripes, spots, or blotches. The Mexican narrow-mouthed toad, or sheep frog (*Hypopachus cuneus*), is similar but has a yellow stripe on its back. It hides in burrows, pack rat nests, or, as does the eastern narrow-mouth, under objects lying on the ground.

A variety of microhylids are found in Asia and Africa. The genus *Breviceps* includes a number of plump, short-faced, African species. These live and breed on land. The rain frog (*B. gibbosus*) is a burrowing South African form that is thought by the natives to control the coming of rain.

Among the Oriental microhylids are *Glyphoglossus molossus*, a pug-nosed native of southeastern Asia, and *Kaloula pulchra*, a frequent visitor to gardens in China and Malaya.

The African genus *Phrynomerus* (sometimes separated as the family Phrynomeridae) includes about six species of arboreal frogs; *P. bifasciatus* is a black and red, striped form whose skin secretions are strong enough to irritate human skin.
·classification and general features **1**:1009d

Narses, also spelled NARSEH (d. *c.* 302), king of the Sāsānian Empire in ancient Persia whose reign (293–302) saw the beginning of 40 years of peace with Rome. Narses was the youngest son of an earlier king, Shāpūr I. On the death of Bahrām II (293), Narses, at that time viceroy of Armenia, successfully contested the succession of Bahrām's son, Bahrām III.

Narses later antagonized Rome by occupying the independent portion of Armenia. In the following year he suffered a severe reverse, losing his war chest and his harem. He then concluded a peace (296), by the terms of which Armenia remained under Roman suzerainty, and the steppes of northern Mesopotamia, with Singara and the hill country on the left bank of the Tigris as far as Gordyene, were also ceded to the victors. In return Narses recovered his household. By this peace, which lasted for 40 years, the Sāsānians withdrew completely from the disputed districts.
·Sāsānian concessions to Rome **9**:850d
·war against Rome in the East **15**:1125c
·Zoroastrian priestly power struggle **19**:1172d

Narses (d. *c.* 503), a Christian writer of Edessa.
·Edessene Nestorian theology **13**:1084d

Narses (b. *c.* 480, Armenia—d. 574, probably Rome or Constantinople), Byzantine general under Emperor Justinian I; his greatest achievement was the conquest of the Ostrogothic kingdom in Italy for Byzantium.

A eunuch, Narses became commander of the imperial bodyguard of eunuchs and eventually rose to be grand chamberlain. When rioting broke out in Constantinople in 532, Narses helped save Justinian's throne both by timely military action and by skillful and lavish political bribes. He was sent to Alexandria (535) to ensure the establishment of the imperial candidate Theodosius as patriarch and to quell disturbances that had arisen from the election. In 538 he became imperial treasurer and was sent to Italy to assist Belisarius, commander of an expedition for the reconquest of Italy, but was also ordered to spy upon him. The rivalry, misunderstanding, and mutual antipathy between the two soon paralyzed all military operations and led to the recapture and devastation of Milan by the Ostrogoths. Consequently, Justinian recalled Narses in 539.

In the summer of 551 Narses was in charge of operations against barbarian raiders, mainly Huns, Gepids, and Lombards, who were devastating the Balkans. Later that year, with the resurgence of Ostrogothic power in Italy under Totila, Narses headed for Italy with 30,000 troops. Moving in from the north in the spring of 552, he defeated the Ostrogothic forces under Totila (who died of his wounds) at the end of June, at Taginae in the Apennines. During the next two years, he crushed scattered Ostrogothic resistance and stopped attempts by the Franks and Alamans to enter northern Italy.

Narses seems to have exercised both military and civil authority in Italy until the death of Justinian I. In 567, however, Justinian's sucessor, Justin II, removed him from his command, and he retired to a villa near Naples. When the Lombards invaded Italy and conquered large parts of it the following year, it was rumoured that Narses had retaliated for his dismissal by inviting the Lombards into Italy, but this report has never been confirmed.
·Byzantine triumph over Ostrogoths **10**:363g
·military campaigns in Italy **3**:553f

Narsimhapur, also called NARSINGHPUR, administrative headquarters, Narsimhapur district, Madhya Pradesh state, central India, on the Singri River. It is a rail junction and is heavily engaged in trade in agricultural produce and timber. Sawmilling is the chief industry. Once called Chhota Gadarwara, the town was renamed Narsinghpur after the Narasiṃha (the man-lion, an incarnation of Viṣṇu) temple, erected *c.* 1800. The Singri River divides the town into two parts, Kandeli (east) and Narsimhapur (west). There is one college affiliated with the University of Saugar.

Narsimhapur district (area 1,979 sq mi [5,126 sq km]) occupies a narrow alluvial strip between the Narmada River (north) and the Sātpura Range (south). Wheat, jowar, gram, and oilseeds are the chief crops. Forest products are important, and coal deposits are worked. Pop. (1971 prelim.) town, 25,558; district, 519,565.
·map, India **9**:278

Narsinghgarh, also called NARSINGARH, town, Rājgarh district, Madhya Pradesh state, central India. A major road and rail junction, it is an agricultural market centre. Cloth weaving is the chief industry. Founded in 1681, it served as capital of the former princely state of Narsinghgarh. The town is adjacent to a lake backed by a hill ridge on which the fort and palace stand. There are a musical academy and one college affiliated with Vikram University. Pop. (1971 prelim.) 13,820.
23°43′ N, 77°06′ E

narthex, a long, narrow enclosed porch, usually colonnaded or arcaded, crossing the entire width of a church at its entrance. The narthex is usually separated from the nave by columns or a pierced wall, and in Byzantine churches the space is divided into two parts. An exonarthex forms the outer entrance to the building and bounds the esonarthex, which opens onto the nave. Occasionally the exonarthex does not form an integral part of

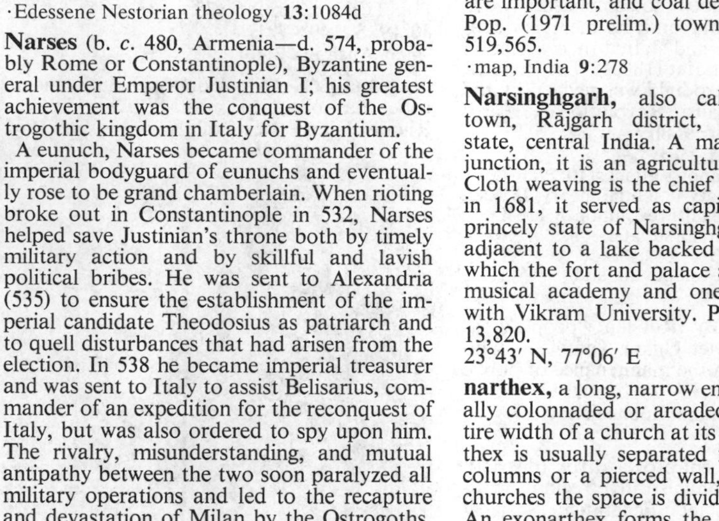

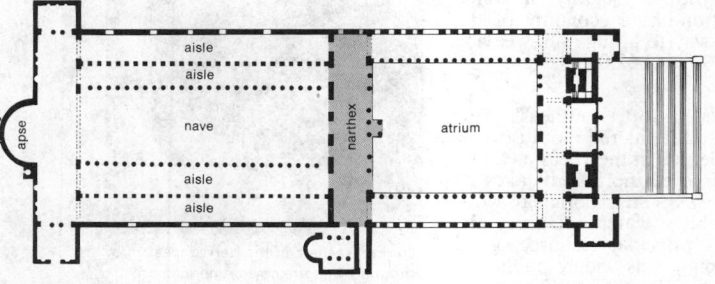

Location of the narthex on a plan of the original basilican church of St. Peter's, Rome, AD 330
From Sir Banister Fletcher, *A History of Architecture on the Comparative Method*, p. 259 (1961)

the main body of the church but consists of a single-storied structure set against it.

In the early days of Christianity, the narthex was the only portion of the church to which catechumens (those preparing for the sacrament of Baptism) and penitents were admitted.

·Istanbul churches converted to mosques **9**:1071h

Narts, heroic beings in Iranian mythology.

·Iranian religious traditions **9**:869h

Naruszewicz, Adam (Stanisław) (b. Oct. 20, 1733, Pinszczyzna, Lithuanian S.S.R.—d. July 6, 1796, Janów, now in Poland), first Polish historian to use modern methods of scholarship and a poet whose work reflects the transition from Baroque to classical styles. As a young man he entered the Roman Catholic Church, eventually becoming bishop of Smolensk.

Naruszewicz' most important work is *Historja narodu polskiego od przyjęcia chrześcijaństwa*, 7 vol. (1780–86; "The History of the Polish Nation from its Conversion to Christianity"), which records events to the end of the 14th century. Aided in this task by King Stanisław August, who obtained many documents from archives abroad, he used as many primary sources as possible and included not only accounts of kings and battles but also descriptions of the economic, social, and cultural life of each period.

Naruto, city, Tokushima Prefecture (*ken*), Shikoku, Japan, facing the Naruto-kaikyō (Naruto Strait), which connects the Inland Sea with the Pacific Ocean. During the

Naruto-kaikyō (Naruto Strait), between Shikoku and Awaji islands, Japan

Kokunai Jigyo Kouku

Tokugawa era (1603–1867) Naruto was a flourishing port and centre of salt manufacture. Since the late 19th century, chemicals and medicines have been produced there. Traditional products include socks and knitwear. Fishing and the gathering of seaweed are still important.

Naruto is perhaps best known as a base for viewing the Naruto-kaikyō, popularly known as the Awa-no Naruto (Roaring Gateway of Awa Province), a strait 1 mi (1.5 km) wide that is filled with rushing water and whirlpools at each ebb and flow of the tide. Pop. (1970) 60,634.

34°11′ N, 134°37′ E

·map, Japan **10**:36

Narutowicz, Gabriel (1865–1922), president of Poland in 1922, was assassinated shortly after taking office.

·Polish democratic government **14**:464h

Narva, city, Estonian Soviet Socialist Republic, on the Narva River 7 mi (11 km) above its outfall into the Gulf of Finland. It is historically important for its two great medieval fortresses, one of Russian and one of Danish origin, and as the scene of Peter I the Great's defeat by the Swedes in 1700. Modern Narva is a major textile centre. Pop. (1970) 58,000.

59°23′ N, 28°12′ E

Battle of Narva

·campaigns of Charles XII against Russia **4**:58a

·Peter I's assessment and participation **14**:158g

Narváez, Ramón María, duque de Valencia (b. Aug. 5, 1800, Loja, Granada, Spain —d. April 23, 1868, Madrid), general and conservative political leader, who supported Queen Isabella II of Spain and was six times prime minister (1844–66). During the First Carlist War (1833–39) he was one of Regent María Cristina de Borbón's most capable military leaders. In 1838 he was elected to the Spanish Cortes (Parliament), led an unsuccessful rising at Seville against the Progresistas (Liberals) of Gen. Baldomero Espartero, and had to go into exile.

After he and the generals Juan Prim and Francisco Serrano staged a successful coup d'état against Espartero in 1843, Narváez was asked to form a government under Isabella II. In his first ministry the constitution of 1845 was promulgated, and the finance minister, Alejandro Mon, reformed the tax system. His government fell early in 1846.

Narváez reached other significant achievements in his third ministry (October 1847–January 1851), among them suppression of a new Carlist revolt and the completion of numerous public works. Although he announced his retirement in 1851, he returned briefly to power three times, always in the service of Isabella II, who was deposed a few months after his death.

·rise to power and domestic programs **17**:438a

Narval, French submarine designed by Maxime Laubeuf and launched in 1899.

·submarine development and modern concepts **17**:748e; illus.

Narvik, city and ice-free seaport, Nordland *fylke* (county), northern Norway, near the head of Ofotfjorden. It is a major trans-shipment point for iron ore from the rich Kiruna-Gällivare mines in northern Sweden, since the Swedish ports on the Gulf of Bothnia are frozen in winter. The site was chosen as an ore port by an Anglo-Swedish consortium in 1883 and was named Victoriahavn (Victoria's Port) in 1887 to honour the Crown Prince of Sweden. The original developers went bankrupt in 1889, but the Norwegian government took over the work in 1892; the name Narvik was adopted in 1898. The city was incorporated in 1902 and grew rapidly after the completion of one of the world's most northerly rail lines. In World War II, Narvik was seized by German forces during their invasion of Norway (April 1940); important naval battles between British and German forces ensued offshore. An Anglo-French expeditionary force succeeded in capturing the port on May 28 but was compelled to evacuate it on June 9, due to the collapse of the front in France. After the war Narvik was rebuilt and resumed its function as an ore port. This export trade, plus some fishing, are its economic mainstays. Pop. (1971 est.) 13,181.

68°26′ N, 17°25′ E

·map, Norway **13**:266

Narwar, historic town, Shivpuri district, Gwalior division, Madhya Pradesh state, India, just east of the Sind River. Traditionally said to have been the capital of Raja Nala of the Sanskrit epic *Mahābhārata*, the town was called Nalapura until the 12th century. Its fort, which stands on a steep scarp of the Vindhya Range, figured significantly in medieval Indian history. From the 12th century onward Narwar was held successively by Kachwāhā, Parihār, and Tonwar Rājputs (warrior caste) until its capture by the Mughals in the 16th century. It fell to the Marāthā chief Sindhia in the early 19th century. Outside the walled town are memorial pillars of the Tonwar chiefs.

25°40′ N, 77°57′ E

narwhal (*Monodon monoceros*), small whale of the family Monodontidae found along coasts and, sometimes, in rivers throughout the Arctic. Mottled gray in colour, the narwhal is usually about 3.5 to 5 metres (11.5 to 16 feet) long. It lacks a dorsal fin and has only two teeth, both at the tip of the upper jaw.

Narwhal (*Monodon monoceros*)

Painting by Richard Ellis

The left tooth develops in the male into a straight tusk protruding forward from the upper lip. This tusk, prized in medieval times as the fabled horn of the unicorn, grows up to 2.7 metres (9 feet) in length and is grooved on the surface in a left-handed spiral. Rare males may develop two tusks; females usually develop none. The function of the tusk is not known; it apparently is not used in spearing or digging food or in combat between males of the species.

The narwhal is a gregarious whale usually found in groups of 15 to 20. It feeds on fish, cephalopods, and crustaceans. It is hunted by the Eskimos, and its tusk is used commercially, although it contains a central cavity and is thus limited to the manufacture of small articles.

·body plan, illus. 1 **19**:805

Naryan-Mar, inland port and capital of the Nenets national *okrug* (area), Arkhangelsk *oblast* (administrative region), northwestern Russian Soviet Federated Socialist Republic, on the Pechora River 68 mi (110 km) from its mouth on the Arctic Ocean. Building commenced in 1933 in connection with the development of the Pechora coalfield in the Soviet First Five-Year Plan; it was incorporated in 1935. The town, whose name means Red Town in the Nenets language, is a centre of the fishing and forestry industries. There is a local museum and teacher-training school. Pop. (1970) 17,000.

67°39′ N, 53°00′ E

·map, Soviet Union **17**:322

Naryn, *oblast* (administrative region), southeastern Kirgiz Soviet Socialist Republic, with an area of 19,500 sq mi (50,400 sq km). The least accessible part of the republic, inhabited mainly by Kirgiz people, it occupies the inner Tien Shan at an altitude of 4,300 ft (1,300 m) or more and is separated from the rest of Kirgiziya by the Terskey-Alatau, Kirgiz, Dzhumgoltau, Susamyrtau, and Fergana ranges. On the frontier with China in the south, the Kokshaal-Tau Range rises to 19,626 ft (5,982 m). The climate is continental, and annual precipitation is only 8 to 12 in. (200 to 300 mm) in the valleys. Sheep, raised on the extensive steppe and alpine pastures, are the mainstay of the economy. There is little industry, but the exploitation of the hydroelectric potential of the Naryn River, which bisects the *oblast* east–west, was begun with the Atbashi power station (1970) near the administrative centre, Naryn. The sparse population, only 28 percent of which is urban, is concentrated in the Kochkor, Dzhumgol, middle Naryn, Atbashi, and Toguz-Tarau valleys. Pop. (1970) 186,400.

Naryn, city and administrative centre of Naryn *oblast* (region), Kirgiz Soviet Socialist Republic, on the Naryn River at an altitude of 6,725 ft (2,050 m). Founded as a fortified point on the trade route from Kashgar in Sinkiang to the Chu Valley, it was made a city in 1927. There are a number of small industrial undertakings and a music and drama theatre. Pop. (1970) 21,098.
41°26′ N, 75°59′ E

Naryn River, in the Kirgiz and Uzbek Soviet Socialist republics, is fed by the glaciers and snows of the central Tien Shan. It becomes the Syrdarya (river) after merging with the Karadarya in the Fergana Valley. It flows westward for 430 mi (700 km), receiving many tributaries and draining an area of 22,540 sq mi (58,370 sq km). High water occurs in May. The annual flow varies between 8,500,000,000 and 24,400,000,000 cu m. The reservoir of the Toktogul hydroelectric station, under construction on the lower reaches in the mid-1970s, was planned to help regulate the flow and to increase irrigation in the area.
40°54′ N, 71°45′ E

·flow and importance **10**:487g
·Tien Shan region geographical features **18**:393f; map

Naryshkina, Natalya Kirillovna (b. 1651, Russia—d. 1694, Moscow), second wife of Tsar Alexis of Russia and mother of Peter I the Great; after Alexis' death she became the centre of a political faction devoted to placing Peter on the Russian throne.

The daughter of the provincial nobleman Kiril Naryshkin, Natalya was raised and educated in a western European manner by Alexis' friend Artamon Matveyev. In 1691, two years after Alexis' first wife, Mariya Miloslavskaya, died, Natalya married the Tsar and subsequently introduced elements of western European culture into the Russian court. After she gave birth to Peter, Natalya and her relatives and associates, including Matveyev, also increased their political influence.

Immediately after Alexis' death, Natalya's adherents, known as the Naryshkin party, tried to obtain the throne for Peter. But Fyodor, the eldest son of Alexis by his first wife, succeeded his father, and the Naryshkin party was displaced from its influential political positions by Fyodor's maternal relatives, the Miloslavsky family. Nevertheless, during Fyodor's reign (1676–82), Natalya, though living in relative obscurity in the village of Preobrazhenskoye and taking no part in government affairs, gained the additional support of the patriarch of Moscow, Ioakim, as well as of many boyar and gentry families.

When Fyodor died, Ioakim bypassed Ivan, the late tsar's brother, and secured the throne for Peter, naming Natalya regent (April 1682). But the Miloslavsky family, claiming the throne for Ivan, encouraged the *streltsy* (sovereign's bodyguard), who were the only organized armed force in Moscow, to revolt. After Matveyev and several members of the Naryshkin family had been killed, the Naryshkin party submitted to the *streltsy* demands and recognized Ivan V (*q.v.*) and Peter as co-rulers, with Ivan as the senior tsar and his sister Sophia as regent for both youths.

During the period of Sophia's regency (1682–89) Natalya and Peter were effectively confined to Preobrazhenskoye, and the Naryshkin family was again excluded from governmental affairs. But in 1689, when Sophia apparently tried to seize the throne in her own name, the Naryshkins rallied their supporters and forced her to yield the throne to Peter (September 1689). Subsequently, until Peter assumed personal control over the government in 1694, Natalya, aided by her brother Lev and Patriarch Ioakim, played the major role in the Muscovite government and restored many of the traditional institutions and customs that had been undermined by the modernizing influences introduced by Fyodor III and Sophia. *See also* Fyodor III; Naryshkin family.

Naryshkin family, relatives of Natalya Kirillovna Naryshkina (*q.v.*), the second wife of the Russian tsar Alexis (ruled 1645–76). After the deaths of both Alexis and his immediate heir, Fyodor III (ruled 1676–82), the Naryshkin family and its supporters promoted the accession of Natalya's son Peter (Peter I the Great) and engaged in factional struggles against the Miloslavskys, the family of Alexis' first wife, who supported Ivan V.

·Peter I's political support **14**:157g
·Romanov succession dispute **16**:48e

NASA (U.S.): *see* National Aeronautics and Space Administration.

nasal cancer (malignant growth in the nose): *see* nasal tumour.

nasal cavity, interior of the nose, from the openings into the nostrils to the nasal portion of the throat (nasopharynx). *See also* nose.

·ectodermal origins of respiratory tract **6**:753f
·human respiratory system anatomy **15**:764a; illus.
·olfactory receptors of mammals **4**:186f
·phonetic study of speech production **14**:276a; illus. 275
·speech sound grouping **17**:484d

nasal conchae, also called TURBINATE, or TURBINAL, BONES, thin, curled, leaflike bones within the nose that serve to enlarge the surface area of the nasal cavity. In some mammals these bones may be extensive; in man, however, they have become reduced. They have three components: the inferior conchae (also called maxilloturbinates) and the middle and superior conchae (also called ethmoturbinates).

·human respiratory system anatomy **15**:764g; illus.
·human skeletal interrelationships **16**:813h; illus.
·reptile skull joint types **15**:733b

nasal consonant: *see* nasal sound.

nasal duct (passage carrying tears to the nasal cavity): *see* nasolacrimal duct.

nasal epithelium, tissue lining the walls of the nasal cavity.

·smell mechanism in nasal cavity **16**:553g; illus.

nasal gland, in birds and reptiles that drink seawater, gland that excretes salt. Its function was unknown until 1957, when K. Schmidt-Nielsen and coworkers solved the long-standing problem of how oceanic birds can live without fresh water. They found that the gland, located above each eye, removes sodium chloride from the blood far more efficiently than does the avian kidney and excretes it as brine through a duct into the nasal cavity. It is discharged from the nostrils (sometimes the mouth) in head-shaking movements characteristic of cormorants, penguins, and other marine species. In marine reptiles a similar gland is located between eye and nostril.

·charadriiform maintenance of blood's ionic balance **4**:40d

Nasalis larvatus (monkey species): *see* proboscis monkey.

nasalization: *see* nasal sound.

nasal pharynx, also called NASOPHARYNX, one of the three divisions of the pharynx, lying behind the nose and above the soft palate. *See* nose; pharynx.

·human digestive system anatomy **5**:792a

nasal polyp, lump of tissue that protrudes into the nasal cavity and sometimes obstructs it. Polyps can form as the result of allergic conditions or of inflammation. Allergic polyps are usually bright red because of their extensive network of blood vessels. These polyps are commonest along the side and upper walls of the nose. Sometimes they arise in the sinus cavities and emerge into the nasal cavity. They may be excised surgically but usually recur until the allergic source is eliminated. Inflammatory polyps result from infections and from injuries to the nose. They do not recur after removal. These polyps contain less fluid than allergic polyps do, but there is an abundance of white blood cells. Polyps can also sometimes arise from closely associated blood vessels that expand as a result of previous injuries to the nose or of high blood pressure. *See also* polyp.

nasal septum, wall of soft and hard tissues that divides the nose and nasal cavity into two compartments.

·human respiratory system anatomy **15**:764f

nasal sound, in phonetics, speech sound in which the airstream passes through the nose, as a result of the lowering of the soft palate (velum) at the back of the mouth. In the case of nasal consonants, such as English *m*, *n*, and *ng* (the final sound in "sing"), the airstream is expelled entirely through the nose. Sounds in which the airstream is expelled partly through the nose and partly through the mouth are classified as nasalized. Nasalized vowels are common in French (*e.g.*, in *vin* "wine," *bon* "good," and *enfant* "child"), Portuguese, and a number of other languages. There are also instances of nasalized consonants in which the feature of nasalization carries over to a typically non-nasal consonant; *e.g.*, the *l* in French *branlant* "shaky."

·acoustic characteristics **14**:279b
·phonetic description and definition **14**:276e
·phonetic study of vowel features **14**:278b
·phonological status in Romance **15**:1038g
·Slavic–Baltic divergence **16**:871b; table
·speech production physiology **10**:649b
·speech sound grouping **17**:484e

nasal tumour, abnormal growth in the nose. Tumours may be malignant or may remain localized and nonrecurrent. The nose is a common site for tumour growth in the upper respiratory tract because it is exposed to external weather conditions, as well as irritants in the air. Some tumours of the nose arise from the mucous membrane that lines the nose; others originate in the brain and spread to the nose.

Epithelial papilloma is one of the commoner benign tumours of the nose. It affects the nasal mucous membrane and is composed of tall column-shaped cells, mucous cells, which have small hairlike structures called cilia. The tumour grows in small nipplelike protrusions. Nasal carcinoma, a malignant growth, also is found in the nasal mucous membrane; it occurs in adults, primarily. Frequently this type of tumour obstructs the nasal and sinus cavities; it can also erode the bone by invasion and rapid growth. Nasopharyngeal carcinoma is a cancer found at the extreme back of the nasal cavity, near the juncture with the throat. It arises commonly in males and spreads rapidly to the lymphatic nodes in the neck. It spreads under the surface mucous membrane without ulceration of the membrane.

Olfactory neuroblastoma is a highly malignant tumour that originates in the olfactory (smell) receptor cells, located in the upper rear portion of the nose. The tumour cells are round or oval and grow in clusters. This tumour is one of the few that can generally be obliterated with radiation treatment.

Nasarawa, also spelled NASSARAWA, town, Benue Province, Benue-Plateau State, central Nigeria, on the Okwa River and at the intersection of roads from Keffi and the Benue River ports of Loko and Umaisha. It was founded *c.* 1838 in the Afo (Afao) tribal territory, known as Kwotto, by Umaru, a dissident official from the nearby town of Keffi, as the capital of the new emirate of Nassarawa (the Victorious Ones). Umaru proclaimed himself *sarkin* ("chief") *Kwotto* (a title used by subsequent emirs), expanded his domain by conquering some of the Basa and Igbira territory northeast of the confluence of the Niger and Benue rivers, and made Nassarawa a vassal state to Zaria (175 mi [282 km] north). One of his successors, Muhammadu, who reigned from 1878 to 1922, enlarged the emirate by various conquests, fought Keffi, and, in 1900, was one of the first emirs to pledge allegiance to Britain.

Farming and mining (for tin and columbite) are the principal activities of the emirate's predominantly Afo population. The town of Nasarawa, which is a market centre for yams, guinea corn, millet, soybeans, shea nuts, and cotton, is served by a hospital, a health office, and a dispensary. Pop. (1972 est.) 17,478.
8°30′ N, 7°40′ E

·map, Nigeria **13**:86

Nāsatyas (Hindu mythology): *see* Aśvins.

Nasby, Petroleum V(esuvius), pen name of DAVID ROSS LOCKE (b. Sept. 20, 1833, Binghamton, N.Y.—d. Feb. 15, 1888, Toledo, Ohio), humorist who had considerable influence on public issues during and after the Civil War.

From an early age Locke worked for newspapers in New York and Ohio. In 1861, as

Petroleum V. Nasby

By courtesy of the Library of Congress, Washington, D.C.

editor of the *Findlay* (Ohio) *Jeffersonian*, he published the first of many satirical letters purporting to be written by one Petroleum V. Nasby. For more than 20 years Locke contributed "Nasby Letters" to the *Toledo Blade*, which under his editorship gained national circulation. Many of the letters appeared also in book form, including *The Nasby Papers* (1864) and *The Diary of an Office Seeker* (1881).

An ardent Unionist and foe of slavery, Locke vigorously supported the Northern cause. His chief weapon was a heavy irony. He let his character Nasby, a "Copperhead," argue in favour of the Southern position; but because Nasby is stupid, illiterate, coarse, and vicious, he damns the cause he favours. His reasoning is absurd; his grammar and spelling are atrocious. Used for a serious end, such verbal fooling delighted Northern readers, including President Lincoln, who occasionally read Nasby letters to his Cabinet. But topical satire and humour date quickly, and among the many humorists who flourished during and immediately after the Civil War, Locke is today one of the least readable.

Nascimento, Edson Arantes do: *see* Pele.

Nascimento, Francisco Manuel do, pseudonym FILINTO ELISIO (b. Dec. 23, 1734, Lisbon—d. Feb. 25, 1819, Paris), the last of the Portuguese Neoclassical poets whose conversion late in life to Romanticism helped prepare the way for that movement's triumph. Of humble birth and probably illegitimate, he was educated by Jesuits and ordained in 1754. In 1768 he became tutor to the daughters of the Marquis of Alorna and fell in love with one of them, the "Maria" of his poems. Disapproving of the low-born poet's affection for his daughter, the Marquis may have been ultimately responsible for Nascimento's being denounced to the Inquisition in June 1778. He succeeded in escaping to France and there, except for some four years in The Hague during the revolutionary Terror, he remained, living by translations and by taking private pupils. When he died, it was recognized that Portugal had lost its foremost poet.

The themes of Nascimento's poetry—which is usually in blank verse, polished, robust, but often overladen with archaisms—range from denunciations of the tyranny of the aristocracy, the Inquisition, and the hierarchy, to homely evocations of the joys of life in his native land and laments on the poverty and loneliness of exile. His demonstration of the flexibility and richness of the Portuguese language, his choice of themes, and his translations of such works as Wieland's *Oberon* and Chateaubriand's *Les Martyrs* influenced the Romantic writers.

·Portuguese literature development **10**:1176a

Naseby, Battle of, fought June 14, 1645, about 20 miles south of Leicester, between the Parliamentary New Model Army under Lieut. Gen. Oliver Cromwell and Sir Thomas Fairfax and the Royalists under Prince Rupert of the Palatinate, largely decided the first phase of the English Civil War. The New Model Army followed in pursuit of the Royalists, who had left Oxford and stormed Leicester on May 30. The two armies met about a mile north of Naseby and deployed along parallel ridges between which lay a valley known as Broad Moor. The Royalists, though outnumbered 14,000 to nearly 10,000, attacked all along the line. Rupert was successful in driving back the left wing of Parliamentary cavalry under Gen. Henry Ireton but made the mistake of engaging in wild pursuit. The successful Parliamentary cavalry on the right under Cromwell was able to regroup and deliver a decisive assault on the centre. The Royalist army was completely routed, and in its captured baggage was found correspondence implicating King Charles I in foreign intrigues.

·Charles I's defeat by Cromwell **4**:54d

Naselli, Alberto, 16th-century Italian commedia dell'arte actor who called himself Zan Ganassa after the character he created.

·commedia influence on European theatre **4**:983e

Nāṣer-e Khosrow, in full ABŪ MOʿĪN NĀṢER-E KHOSROW AL-MARVĀZĪ AL-QUBĀDIYĀNĪ (b. 1004, Qubādiyān, Merv, now in Turkmen S.S.R.—d. *c.* 1072–77, Yumgān, Garm, now in Tajikistan S.S.R.), Persian poet, theologian, and religious propagandist, one of the greatest writers in Persian literature. He came of a family of government officials who belonged to the Shīʿah sect of Islām and attended school for only a short while. In 1045 he went on a pilgrimage to Mecca and continued his journey to Palestine and then to Egypt, ruled at that time by the Fāṭimid dynasty. The Fāṭimids belonged to the Ismāʿīlī sect, an offshoot of Shīʿah Islām, and they were engaged in propagating that doctrine by missionaries throughout the Islāmic world. Nāṣer-e Khosrow became such a missionary, though it is not certain whether he became an Ismāʿīlī before his trip to the Fāṭimid capital or after. His vigorous advocacy of that heresy forced him to flee to Badakhshān (now in Afghanistan), where he spent the rest of his days, lamenting in his poetry that he was unable to be an active missionary.

Nāṣer-e Khosrow's most celebrated prose work is the *Safarnāme* (Eng. trans., *Diary of a Journey Through Syria and Palestine*, 1888), describing his seven-year journey. His philosophical poetry includes the *Rawshanaʾināme* (Eng. trans., *Book of Lights*, 1949). In his *Jāmiʿ al-ḥikmatayn* ("Union of the Two Wisdoms") he attempted to harmonize Ismāʿīlī theology and Greek philosophy. His style was straightforward, vigorous, and of great technical virtuosity.

·Persian prose works **9**:963d

Nāṣer od-Dīn (b. July 17, 1831, Tehrān—d. May 1, 1896, Tehrān), *shāh* of Iran in 1848–96 who began his reign as a reformer but became increasingly conservative, failing to understand the accelerating need for change or for a response to the pressures brought by contact with the Western nations.

Although a younger son of Moḥammad Shāh, Nāṣer od-Dīn was named heir apparent through the influence of his mother. Serious disturbances broke out when he succeeded to the throne on his father's death in 1848, but these were quelled through the efforts of his chief minister, Mīrzā Taqī Khān.

Under Taqī Khān's influence, Naṣer od-Dīn began his rule by instituting a series of needed reforms. Taqī Khān, however, was later pushed from power by his enemies, who included Nāṣer od-Dīn's mother, and was disgraced, imprisoned, and finally murdered. In 1852 an attempt was made on Naṣer od-Dīn's life by two Bābīs (members of a religious sect considered heretical); he responded with a fierce, cruel, and prolonged persecution of the sect.

Unable to regain territory lost to Russia in the early 19th century, Nāṣer od-Dīn sought compensation by seizing Herāt, Afg., in 1856. Great Britain regarded the move as a threat to British India and declared war on Iran. The British forced the return of Herāt as well as Iranian recognition of the kingdom of Afghanistan.

Nāṣer od-Dīn was effective in certain areas. He curbed the secular power of the clergy, introduced telegraph and postal services, built roads, opened the first school offering education along Western lines, and launched Iran's first newspaper. He visited Europe in 1873, 1878, and 1889 and was impressed with the technology he saw there. In the later years of his rule, however, he steadfastly refused to deal with the growing pressures for reforms. He also granted a series of concessionary rights to foreigners in return for large payments that went into his own pockets. In 1872 popular pressure forced him to withdraw one concession involving permission to construct such complexes as railways and irrigation works throughout Iran. In 1890 he made an even greater error in granting a 50-year concession on the purchase, sale, and processing of all tobacco in the country, which led to a national boycott of tobacco and the withdrawal of the concession. This last incident is considered by many authorities to be the origin of modern Iranian nationalism.

Increasingly unpopular among various Iranian factions, Nāṣer od-Dīn was assassinated in Tehrān by a fanatic.

·Afghani's political activities **10**:20f
·economic and religious blunders **9**:860e

Nash, John (b. 1752, London—d. May 13, 1835, Cowes, Isle of Wight), architect and city planner best known for his development of Regent's Park and Regent Street, a royal estate in north London partly converted into a varied residential area and connected with the Westminster district of government buildings by a new street that decisively separated Soho from the more fashionable West End of London. Begun in 1811, this major project was named for Nash's official patron, George, prince of Wales, at that time regent for his father, King George III, and afterward (from 1820) king as George IV.

Trained by the architect Sir Robert Taylor, Nash became a speculative builder and architect in London. After going bankrupt in 1783 he moved to Wales, where, as a country-house architect, he rehabilitated himself professionally. In the late 1790s he returned to London as an informal partner of a landscape gardener named Humphry Repton. From 1798 he was employed by the Prince of Wales, perhaps because he married in that year a young woman who was thought to have had a scandalous relationship with the Prince himself or with some other man or men whom the

Prince wished to protect. Soon acquiring considerable wealth, Nash built for himself East Cowes Castle (from 1798), which, combining a castellated "baronial" exterior, an irregular plan, and a classical interior, had much influence in the early Gothic Revival period.

In 1811 Marylebone Park reverted to the crown, and on that land Nash laid out Regent's Park. This development comprises the Regent's Canal, a lake, a large wooded area, a botantical garden, and, on the periphery, shopping arcades and picturesque groupings of residences (for working class as well as more prosperous families). Nash's East and West Park Villages (completed after his death by James Pennethorne) served as models for "garden suburbs" of separate houses informally arranged. Regent Street, with its colonnades (demolished 1848) and its Quadrant leading into Piccadilly Circus, was finished about 1825.

From 1813 to 1815 Nash held the government post of deputy surveyor general. He rebuilt the Royal Pavilion, Brighton, Sussex (1815–23); redesigned St. James's Park, London (1827–29); and began to reconstruct Buckingham House, London, as a royal palace (from 1821). When George IV died in 1830, Nash was dismissed before he could complete the Buckingham Palace project, and in 1831 he faced an official inquiry into the cost and structural soundness of the building.

Cumberland Terrace, Regent's Park, London, by John Nash, begun 1811; engraving by James Tingle, after a drawing by Thomas H. Shepherd, 1827

By courtesy of the trustees of the British Museum; photograph, J.R. Freeman & Co. Ltd.

·Gothic Revival castellation **19**:447d
·London's architecturaL development **11**:104e

Nash, (Frederic) Ogden (b. Aug. 19, 1902, Rye, N.Y.—d. May 19, 1971, Baltimore), writer of humorous poetry who won a large following in both the U.S. and Britain for his audacious verse. His rhymes are jarringly off or disconcertingly exact, and his ragged stanzas vary from lines of one word to lines that meander the length of a paragraph, often interrupted by inapposite digressions. He said he learned his prosody from the unintentional blunders of the notoriously slipshod poet Julia Moore, the "Sweet Singer of Michigan." He employed his craft in limning the little woes of the urban upper middle classes. Some of his observations—such as "Candy is dandy/But liquor is quicker"—have passed into folklore.

After a year at Harvard (1920–21), Nash held a variety of jobs—advertising, teaching, editing, bond selling—before the success of his poetry enabled him to work full-time at it. He sold his first verse (1930) to *The New Yorker* magazine, on whose editorial staff he was employed for a time, helping to set its sophisticated tone. With the publication of his first collection, *Hard Lines* (1931), he began a 40-year career during which he produced 20 volumes of verse with such titles as *The Bad Parents' Garden of Verse* (1936), *I'm a Stranger Here Myself* (1938), and *Everyone But Thee and Me* (1962). Making his home in Baltimore, he also did considerable lecturing on tours throughout the U.S. He wrote the lyrics for the musicals *One Touch of Venus* (1943) and *Two's Company* (1952) as well as several children's books.

Nash, Paul (b. May 11, 1889, London—d. July 11, 1946, Boscombe), painter, printmaker, illustrator, and photographer, who was appointed (1917 and 1940) an official war artist by the British government in both World Wars I and II. He studied at the Slade School, London. In 1914 he enlisted in the Artists' Rifles and his 1918 exhibition of paintings portrayed, in an abstract, Cubist-influenced style, shattered war landscapes such as "The Menin Road" (1918; Imperial War Museum, London). There followed seascapes ("Wall Against the Sea," 1922; Carnegie Institute, Pittsburgh) and landscapes ("Oxenbridge Pond," 1928; City Museum and Art Gallery, Birmingham, Eng.) of distinguished design and cool, vibrating colours. He also did book illustrations and wood engravings. He was largely responsible in 1933 for organizing Unit One, a group of British artists including Ben Nicholson, Barbara Hepworth, and Henry Moore, who stressed the formal instead of the mimetic aspects of art. In the 1930s his paintings developed freer design and richer colour, together with a symbolic, "fourth-dimensional" vision influenced by Surrealism (*q.v.*). One of his best known paintings of World War II was "Totes Meer" (1940–41; Tate Gallery, London). Later paintings reveal his imaginative poetic symbolism—*e.g.*, "Solstice of the Sunflower" (1945; National Gallery of Canada, Ottawa). A volume of his writings, *Outline: An Autobiography and Other Writings* (1949), and a collection of his photographs, *Fertile Image* (1951), were posthumously published.

"Totes Meer," oil painting by Paul Nash, 1940–41; in the Tate Gallery, London

By courtesy of the trustees of the Tate Gallery, London

·Unit One membership **12**:433f

Nash, Sir Walter (b. Feb. 12, 1882, Worcestershire, Eng.—d. June 4, 1968, Auckland, N.Z.), New Zealand statesman who was prime minister 1957–60 and who earlier, as finance minister during the Depression and through World War II, first guided the Labour Party's economic recovery program and then directed the government's wartime controls.

Sir Walter Nash, 1966

Ronald D. Woolf—Camera Press from Publix

After studying law, Nash worked in the bicycle industry in Birmingham, where he became a wholesale merchant in 1907. He emigrated to New Zealand in 1909, soon joining the Labour Party, and from 1919 to 1960 he was a member of the party's executive. He entered Parliament in 1929 and became the first Labour minister of finance in 1935. In 1938 he was named to head the newly formed social security program, which provided guaranteed medical care and improved pensions.

During World War II he introduced a program to control prices, wages, and costs; raise taxes; impose rationing; and increase family welfare benefits—a program under which New Zealanders experienced a smaller decline in their standard of living than did the peoples of other Allied nations. From 1942 to 1944 Nash also served as New Zealand's minister to the United States and as a member of the Pacific War Council. In addition, he took on the post of deputy prime minister from 1940 to 1949 and was a delegate to the United Nations financial conference at Bretton Woods, N.H. (1944).

After leading the Labour Party opposition in Parliament during 1950–57, Nash served as prime minister and minister of external affairs and Maori affairs (1957–60). He headed the Labour opposition again from 1960 to 1963. In foreign policy, he opposed the U.S. involvement in Vietnam and favoured the seating of the People's Republic of China in the United Nations. Nevertheless, he supported New Zealand's defense treaties with the U.S.

Nashe (NASH), **Thomas** (b. 1567, Lowestoft, Suffolk—d. 1601?, Yarmouth, Norfolk), pamphleteer, poet, dramatist, and author of *The unfortunate traveller, or, the life of Jack Wilton* (1594), the first picaresque novel in English. He was educated at Cambridge, and about 1588 he went to London, where he became associated with Robert Greene and other professional authors. In 1589 he wrote *The anatomie of absurditie* and the preface to Greene's *Menaphon*. Both works reveal the author as a recent university graduate in their traditional espousal of literary standards, hostility to popular literature, conventional misogynic attitude, and style marked by euphuism (self-conscious elegance of language).

In 1589 and 1590 he evidently became a paid hack of the episcopacy in the Marprelate controversy, and matched wits with the unidentified Puritan "Martin." Almost all the Anglican replies to Martin have variously been assigned to Nashe, but only *An Almond for a Parrat* (1590) has been convincingly attributed. He wrote the preface to Thomas Newman's unauthorized edition of Sir Philip Sidney's *Astrophel and Stella* (1591). Though Nashe penned an extravagant dedication to Sidney's sister, the countess of Pembroke, the book was withdrawn and reissued in the same year without Nashe's foreword.

Pierce Penilesse his supplication to the divell

(1592) revealed Nashe's artistic strengths and weaknesses. His prose had become a combination of colloquial diction and idiosyncratic coined compounds, ideal for controversy and for his eccentric discussion of the seven deadly sins. Verbal facility was frequently an end in itself; Nashe rambled and failed to impose a consistent structure upon his material. Having become involved in his friend Greene's feud with the writer Gabriel Harvey, Nashe satirized Harvey and his brothers in *Pierce* and then joined combat in an exchange of pamphlets with Harvey, *Strange newes* (1592) and *Have with you to Saffron-Walden* (1596). If Harvey is to be credited, Nashe was a hack for the printer John Danter in 1593. The controversy was terminated in 1599, when the Archbishop of Canterbury ordered that "all Nasshes bookes and Doctor Harveyes bookes be taken wheresoever they maye be found and that none of theire bookes bee ever printed hereafter."

Apparently Nashe wrote *Strange newes* while he was living at the home of Sir George Carey, who momentarily relieved his oppressive poverty. In *Christs teares over Jerusalem* (1593) Nashe ominously warned his countrymen during one of the worst plagues that unless they reformed, London would suffer the fate of Jerusalem. *The Terrors of the Night* (1594) was a discursive, sometimes bewildering, attack on demonology. Both works were medieval in their attitudes and almost puritanical in the moral indictments.

Nashe, woodcut from *The Trimming of T. Nashe Gentleman* by Gabriel Harvey, 1597

By courtesy of the trustees of the British Museum; photograph, J.R. Freeman & Co. Ltd.

Pierce Penilesse excepted, Nashe's most successful works were his masque *Summers last Will and Testament* (1592, published 1600), his picaresque novel *The unfortunate traveller, or, The life of Jacke Wilton* (1594), and *Nashes lenten stuffe* (1599). *The unfortunate traveller* is a brutal and realistic tale of adventure narrated with speed and economy. *Lenten stuffe*, in praise of herrings, contained a charming description of Yarmouth, Norfolk, which was a herring-fishery.

Nashe was the first of the English prose eccentrics, an extraordinary inventor of verbal hybrids, and, according to C.S. Lewis, "the supreme master of literary *sansculottisme*."

The Works were edited by R.B. McKerrow, five volumes (1904–10; revised edition by F.P. Wilson, 1958).

·early British novel tradition **13**:290b
·literature of the English Renaissance **10**:1139b

nashiji, in Japanese lacquerwork, form of *maki-e*, or lacquer decorated in gold or silver, frequently employed for the background of a pattern. Gold or silver flakes called *nashiji-ko* are sprinkled onto the surface of the object (excluding the design), on which lacquer has

Five-case *inrō* with Samurai design done in *taka-maki-e* against a background sprinkled with red-gold *nashiji-ko*, signed Kajikawa, Edo period (1603–1867)

From Melvin and Betty Janss, *Inro and Other Miniature Forms of Japanese Lacquer Art*; Charles E. Tuttle, Inc.

been applied. *Nashiji* lacquer is then applied and burnished with charcoal, so that the gold or silver can be seen through the lacquer. The name *nashiji* is thought to have originated in the resemblance that the lacquer bears to the skin of a Japanese pear, *nashi*.

The technique flourished in the Muromachi period (1338–1573). During the Azuchi-Momoyama period (1574–1600), variations of the technique were developed, such as *e-nashiji*, in which *nashiji* is applied to parts of the design. Later, in the Edo period (1603–1867), more variations were devised; *muranashi-ji*, for example, in which gold or silver flakes are sprinkled thickly in some parts and lightly in others to depict clouds or to create an irregular effect in the design.

·characteristics and process **10**:576e

Nashim (Hebrew: "women"), the third of the six major divisions, or orders (*sedarim*), of the Mishna (codification of Jewish oral laws), which was given its final form early in the 3rd century AD by Judah ha-Nasi. *Nashim* covers principally aspects of married life. The seven tractates (treatises) of *Nashim* are: *Yevamot* ("Levirates"; *i.e.*, a husband's brothers), *Ketubot* ("Marriage Contracts"), *Nedarim* ("Vows"), *Nazir* (a "Nazirite"; *i.e.*, a vowed ascetic), *Soṭa* ("A Woman Suspected of Adultery"), *Giṭṭin* ("Bills of Divorce"), and *Qiddushin* ("Marriages"). The Palestinian and Babylonian Talmuds both have Gemara (extensive critical notes) on each of the seven tractates.

·tractates and scope **17**:1008d

Nashua, city, seat of Hillsborough County, southern New Hampshire, U.S., on the Merrimack and Nashua rivers. Settled about 1655, it was a part of Massachusetts until a 1741 boundary settlement placed it in New Hampshire. Local resentment caused a five-year delay before it was chartered as Dunstable, N.H. In 1803 the village of Indian Head, across the Nashua River, took the name of Nashua (allegedly derived from a local Indian tribe). The two settlements merged as Nashua in 1837. The northern section withdrew, as Nashville, in 1842 over a dispute in locating the town hall. They were reunited under a city charter in 1853. Since the closing of the textile mills after World War II, the city has developed a diversified industrial base. Manufactures now include shoes, asbestos, electronic components, chemicals, office equipment, and machinery for manufacturing plastics and sophisticated paper for use in industry and science. Rivier, a Roman Catholic college (1933), is in the city. Benson Wild Animal Farm and Silver Lake State Park are nearby. Pop. (1960) city, 39,096; (1980) city, 67,865; metropolitan area (SMSA), 114,221.
42°46′ N, 71°27′ W
·map, United States **18**:908

Nashville, town, seat of Brown County, south central Indiana, U.S. The town is headquarters for tourists, artists, and photographers who are attracted by the rustic setting and beautiful fall and spring scenery in the nearby Brown County State Park. An art gallery and a museum are operated by Brown County artists who are permanent residents. Pop. (1980) 705.
39°12′ N, 86°15′ W
·map, United States **18**:908

Nashville, capital (1843) of Tennessee, U.S., and seat (1784) of Davidson County in the north central part of the state, on the Cumberland River. It is the centre of a metropolitan area that embraces Davidson, Sumner, and Wilson counties. Old Hickory Lake, impounded on the river, is 15 mi (24 km) northeast.

Founded in 1779, it was originally named Fort Nashborough for Revolutionary War general Francis Nash, who was killed in the Battle of Germantown. (A replica of the fort stands on a bluff above the river.) A force behind Nashville's settlement was Richard Henderson, a North Carolina jurist who in 1775 acquired most of middle Tennessee and Kentucky in the Transylvania Purchase from the Cherokee Indians. He is also credited with having written the *Cumberland Compact*, the articles of self-government adopted by the settlers, which contained the first known provision in the U.S. for recall of elected officials.

Renamed Nashville in 1784 and incorporated in 1806, the community developed as a river trade depot for middle Tennessee and became the political centre of the state. Its commercial importance was further enhanced by the advent of the railroads in the 1850s. During the Civil War, Nashville was occupied by Federal troops in February 1862. The last major Civil War battle (Dec. 15–16, 1864) took place outside Nashville, when Federal forces under Gen. George H. Thomas defeated the Confederates under John B. Hood (*see* Nashville, Battle of).

Nashville's industrial development was accelerated in the 1930s by the availability of cheap electric power from the Tennessee Valley Authority and from the Cumberland River dams. The city's modern economy is a diversified mix of commerce, industry, and agriculture. Several large insurance and finance companies have headquarters there. Manufactures include auto glass, clothing, shoes, heating and cooking equipment, and tires.

Nashville has a reputation for country and Western music, the basis of a large recording industry. Regular radio broadcasts of the Grand Ole Opry, a folk music program, began in 1925 and went on national networks in 1939. The Country Music Hall of Fame and Museum is a tourist attraction.

Nashville is widely known as a religious educational centre, and several denominations have publishing headquarters there, including the United Methodist Publishing House, said to be the largest of its kind in the world. The city is the national headquarters of several boards and agencies of the United Methodist Church and the Sunday School Board of the Southern Baptist Convention; it is also the international headquarters of the Disciples of Christ Historical Society. Religious-affiliated educational institutions include Scarritt College for Christian Workers (1892; United Methodist), Belmont College (1951; established by the Tennessee Southern Baptist Convention), David Lipscomb College (1891; Churches of Christ), Fisk University (1867; American Missionary Association), Meharry Medical College (1876; United Methodist), and Trevecca Nazarene College (1901). Nashville is also the seat of Tennessee Agricultural and Industrial State University (1912), Vanderbilt University (1873), and George Peabody College for Teachers (1785; founded as Davidson Academy).

Centennial Park on the state centennial exposition grounds features a full-scale replica of the Parthenon (Athenian temple), built in 1897 to commemorate Tennessee's admission to statehood in 1796. The state capitol (completed 1855) was designed along the lines of a Greek Ionic temple by William Strickland, the Philadelphia architect; U.S. president James Polk is buried in its grounds. The Hermitage, the home of U.S. president Andrew Jackson, is 12 mi east. Other historic buildings include the Belle Meade Mansion, plantation home built in 1835 on one of America's first thoroughbred horse farms, and Travelers' Rest (1792), built by John Overton (law partner of Andrew Jackson) and maintained as a museum.

A metropolitan charter (1963) established one government for Nashville and Davidson county. Pop. (1980) city, 455,651; metropolitan area (SMSA), 850,505.
36°09′ N, 86°48′ W
·city government experiment and cultural importance **18**:129b
·early social and economic aspects **10**:1e

Nashville, U.S. warship that prevented Colombian troops from stopping a revolt in Panama on Nov. 2, 1903; Panama proclaimed its independence from Colombia the next day, and the United States acquired the Panama Canal Zone the following May.

Nashville, Battle of (Dec. 15–16, 1864), in the U.S. Civil War, decisive Union victory over the Confederates, ending organized Southern resistance in Tennessee for the remainder of the war. Hoping to cut supply lines of Union Gen. William T. Sherman and perhaps to threaten Cincinnati, Ohio, and other Northern cities, Confederate Gen. John B. Hood moved back into Tennessee and approached Nashville in early December 1864. Commanding a Union force composed of quickly assembled heterogeneous troops, Gen. George H. Thomas marched out of the city and administered a resounding defeat to the South on December 15–16. The Confederate Army retreated in near disorder to Alabama, and though Hood escaped, his army virtually ceased to exist as a fighting force.
·defense tactics and consequences **4**:679g; map

Nashville Dome, southward extension of the Cincinnati Arch (*q.v.*) that is prominent in Tennessee. Ordovician rocks comprise the oldest strata exposed in the core of the dome; they are surrounded by overlapping Mississippian and Pennsylvanian strata. (The Ordovician Period began about 500,000,000 years ago and lasted about 70,000,000 years.) The dome was submerged at various times, while during others the central portions were elevated above sea level and exposed to erosion.

Two major uplifts affected the Nashville Dome. The first occurred in Late Devonian time; considerable erosion occurred and some 150 metres (500 feet) of deposits were removed. The second major tectonic event occurred in Late Mississippian and Early Pennsylvanian time, when extensive erosion again occurred.

Nasi (ethnic group): *see* Yi.

nasi, in the Talmud, the president ("prince") of the Great Sanhedrin, who shared jurisdiction with the *av bet din* ("presiding justice"); together they were known as the *zugot* ("pairs").
·Ezekiel's oracle on good shepherd **2**:919f
·political and religious functions **10**:297e

Nasi, Joseph (b. 1520, Portugal—d. Aug. 2, 1579, Istanbul), Jewish statesman and financier who rose to a position of power in the Ottoman Empire under the sultans Süleyman the Magnificent and Selim II.

Of Marrano (Spanish Christianized Jew) descent, Nasi was baptized under the Christian name of João Miguez. As a young man he gained a thorough knowledge of commercial and financial affairs in the service of his relatives, the bankers Mendes of Antwerp. In 1554 he settled at Istanbul, declared himself a Jew, and married his cousin Reyna. He soon attained high favour with Sultan Süleyman, who granted him the town of Tiberias and seven adjoining villages in Palestine. There Nasi strove to establish a community of Jewish refugees from Europe.

In 1566 Sultan Selim II made him the duke of Naxos, in Greece. Hostile to Venice, he contributed to the Ottoman decision in 1571 to attack Cyprus. After Selim II's death in 1574, Nasi found himself excluded from an active role in public affairs and spent the last years of his life in virtual retirement at his villa of Belvedere near Galata in Istanbul.

Näsijärvi, Lake, in Hämeen *lääni* (Häme province), southwestern Finland, extending northward from the city of Tampere, northwest of Helsinki. Approximately 20 mi (32 km) long and 2–8 mi wide, it is the largest of the Pyhäjärvi lakes and the central lake of the western branch of the system. Vankavesi, the northern arm of Näsijärvi, is connected by canal (built 1854) to Lakes Palovesi and Ruovesi. This route allows passenger-ferry service to connect the town of Ruovesi with Tampere to the south. The Näsijärvi drains southward into the Pyhäjärvi via the Tammerkoski (rapids). The southern banks of the lake are flat and barren whereas the northern shore is more developed. The village of Teisko is located on the eastern shore. Ferry service has operated on Näsijärvi since 1858.
61°37′ N, 23°42′ E
·map, Finland **7**:304

Nāsik, administrative headquarters, Nāsik district, Mahārāshtra state, western India, on the Godāvari River and major road and rail routes. An important religious centre, it attracts thousands of pilgrims annually. It is the legendary home of Rāma, hero of the Hindu *Rāmāyaṇa* epic, and the site of Buddhist and Jain cave temples dating to the 1st century AD.

Nāsik, Mahārāshtra, India
Foto Features

Of its many Hindu temples, Kāla Rām and Gora Rām are among the holiest. Tryambakeśvar, a Śaivite Jyotirliṅga temple 14 mi (22 km) from Nāsik, is the most important of the pilgrim sites. In the second half of the 20th century the town has industrialized; silk and cotton weaving and sugar and oil processing are important. Ozar is a new suburban township. Nāsik houses four colleges affiliated with the University of Poona.

Nāsik district (6,020 sq mi [15,591 sq km]) borders (west) on the Sahyādri Hills of the Western Ghāts. It is drained by the Girna and Godāvari rivers, which flow through open, fertile valleys. The chief crops are wheat, millet, and peanuts (groundnuts). Sugar is an important irrigated cash crop. Industries consist primarily of sugar and oil processing and cotton spinning and weaving. Mālegaon, Nāsik, and Yeola are the chief towns; Igatpuri and Manmād contain railway workshops. Pop. (1971 prelim.) town, 176,187; district, 2,367,002.
·map, India **9**:278
·rock-cut temple and monastery sculpture **17**:188f

Nāṣin-ud-Dīn Muḥammad: *see* Humāyūn.

Nāṣir, al-Malik an- (1284–1340), Mamlūk sultan of Egypt of the Bahri dynasty.
·Egyptian prosperity **6**:491a

Nāṣir, an- (d. 1225), last major ʿAbbāsid caliph and the longest ruling one, reigning from 1180 to 1225. He tried to restore the caliphate to its former glory, engaging in lavish display and great building programs, subduing domestic feuds, and managing to stave off the advances first of the Persians and then of the Mongols. His dynasty, along with the capital, Baghdad, was destroyed 28 years after his death.
·Almohad decline in Spain **9**:932c
·caliphal politics and eastern invaders **3**:641a
·religio-political policies **11**:993h

Nāṣira, an- (Israel): *see* Nazareth.

Nasirābād (Bangladesh): *see* Mymensingh.

Nāṣir ad-Dawlah (d. 969, Iraq), a prince of the Ḥamdānid family and a participant in the confused events that surrounded the decline in political influence of the caliphate (the caliph was the titular leader of the Muslim community). As a young man he aided his father in the governorship of Mosul, the seat of the Ḥamdānid family. When his father died in 929, Nāṣir al-Dawlah succeeded to leadership of the family, and, in the face of a continued decline in the authority of the ʿAbbāsid caliphs, he pushed to extend his territorial dominions. He extended the already large Ḥamdānid lands in Syria and Iraq and even made two unsuccessful attempts, in 934 and 938, to secure control of Azerbaijan. Nominally he was a subject of the caliph. This condition was expressed both in his obligation to pay an annual tribute and in his possession of official sanction to govern the Ḥamdānid lands. At times each needed the aid of the other, there being occasions when the caliph fled to the Ḥamdānid prince for protection. But when strong enough, each attempted to assert himself at the expense of the other, Nāṣir ad-Dawlah withholding the tribute or demanding authority to govern more land, and the Caliph sending an army against him or appointing a governor to replace him. The Ḥamdānids never suffered any permanent loss of important lands to the Caliph and were more deeply affected by the nature of Nāṣir al-Dawlah's rule: his taxation policies were ruinous, and he tyranically seized land for himself whenever possible. After his son Sayf ad-Dawlah died in 967, he became almost totally oblivious to the interests of the Ḥamdānid family and concentrated his energies on amassing as much wealth as possible. Other Ḥamdānid princes secured his imprisonment and death in 969.

Naṣīr Khān (1750–93), ruler of Baluchistan.
·political and cultural achievement **2**:677d

Nāṣir-ud-Dīn Maḥmūd (reigned 1246–66), ruler of the Delhi sultanate.
·military struggles with Rājputs **9**:367b

Naskapi (people): *see* Montagnais and Naskapi.

naskhī script: *see* Arabic alphabet.

Nasmyth, Alexander (1758–1840), Scottish portrait and landscape painter who also designed theatrical sets and worked as an architect.
·Burns's portrait illus. **3**:516

Nasmyth, James (b. Aug. 19, 1808, Edinburgh—d. May 7, 1890, London), Victorian engineer known primarily for his invention of the steam hammer.

Son of the well-known Edinburgh painter Alexander Nasmyth, he showed an extraordinary mechanical inclination while still a schoolboy in Edinburgh, building successful model steam engines. For two years he worked in Henry Maudslay's machine shop in London and, after returning to Edinburgh for an interval, moved to Manchester, where rapid industrialization was in progress. In 1836 he began to build his own foundry near the junction of the Bridgewater Canal with the newly opened Liverpool and Manchester Railway. There he made machine tools of all kinds, along with a variety of steam-powered machines. Isambard Kingdom Brunel, when designing his steamship, "Great Britain," originally made plans for paddle wheels of exceptional size. Nasmyth solved the challenging problem of forging the drive shaft by designing and fabricating a powerful steam hammer, which he patented in 1842. Though the "Great Britain" was eventually furnished with screw propellers instead of paddle wheels, the steam hammer at once became an important part of the metallurgical arsenal of the Industrial Revolution.

Besides steam hammers, Nasmyth manufactured more than 100 steam locomotives, many small high-pressure steam engines, and a variety of pumps, hydraulic presses, and other machines. At the age of 48 he retired from the foundry to devote himself to his hobby, astronomy. At the Great Exhibition of London in 1851, his steam hammer was given a place of honour, and his lunar cartography was awarded a prize. He wrote *The Moon: Considered as a Planet, a World, and a Satellite* (1874).

·machine tool improvement and development **11**:260c
·steam hammer development **18**:42d

Nás Na Riogh (Ireland): *see* Naas.

Naso, Publius Ovidius: *see* Ovid.

nasociliary nerve, branch of the ophthalmic division of the trigeminal nerve; it supplies the mucous membrane, nasal septum, and certain areas of the skin of the nose.

·anatomic relationships **12**:1019b

nasolacrimal (NASOLACHRYMAL) **duct,** or NASAL DUCT, in anatomy, component of the lacrimal apparatus (*q.v.*). Tears flow along this channel from the tear sac into the nasal cavity.

·structure and function in human eye **7**:93b
·watering eye resulting from blockage **7**:117c

Naṣr I, Sāmānid emir who received license to govern all Transoxania in AD 875.

·Sāmānid influence expansion **9**:854e

Naṣr, Aḥmad Shāh Bahādur Mujāhid-ud-Dīn Abū (Mughal emperor): *see* Aḥmad Shāh.

Naṣr City, subsection, Cairo.

·Cairo's postrevolutionary development **3**:581h

Nasreddin Hoca, in Turkish, JUḤĀ in Arabic, MUSHFIQĪ in Tadzhik, comic Islāmic literary character, characterized as a type of low-class theologian.

·role in popular literature **9**:966h

Naṣr ibn Sayyār (d. 748), governor of Khorāsān and other eastern provinces from 739 to 748, under the last of the Umayyad caliphs. Between 738 and 740 he led the armies that temporarily repelled ʿAbbāsid encroachments, but he died while in flight from a new ʿAbbāsid invasion in 748.

·Mā Warāʾ an-Nahr administration **18**:793a
·Umayyad decline in the provinces **3**:631f

Naṣrids, last of the Muslim dynasties in Spain, rising to power following the defeat of the Almohads at the Battle of Las Navas de Tolosa, in 1212. They ruled Granada from 1238 to 1492. The first Naṣrid ruler, Muḥammad I al-Ghālib (d. 1273), a tributary vassal of Ferdinand III of Castile and later of Alfonso X, began the construction of the Alhambra (from Arabic *al-ḥamrāʾ*, "the red [fortress]") and laid the basis of Granada's prosperity by welcoming Muslim refugees from Seville, Valencia, and Murcia. The dynasty that succeeded Muḥammad, weakened by dynastic and factional strife, wavered between submission to Christian Castile and dependence on their Marīnid kinsmen of Fès (in modern Morocco); but the African alliance finally proved disastrous, leading to the defeat of Yūsuf I (1333–54) at Río Salado (1340) by Alfonso XI. In 1469, Christian Spain united under the marriage of Ferdinand II of Aragon and Isabella I of Castile; then, when Abū al-Ḥasan ʿAlī (1466–85) introduced a succession struggle at home, while externally antagonizing Castile by refusing to pay tribute, Naṣrid rule was finally ended by the Christian conquest of Granada (1492).

·Almoravid political and social history **17**:417h
·Ferdinand II's military campaign **7**:233b
·Muslim attempt to capture Ceuta **8**:777h
·Spanish military campaign and conquest **9**:907e

Nassarawa (Nigeria): *see* Nasarawa.

Nassau, historic region of Germany, located in what is now the western part of the *Land* of Hesse and the Montabaur district of the *Land* of Rheinland-Pfalz, Federal Republic of Germany. The Lahn River divides the region roughly into halves; in the south are the Taunus Mountains; in the north, the Westerwald. By the 12th century the counts of Laurenburg had established themselves near the town of Nassau; Walram (d. 1198) assumed the title count of Nassau. His grandsons divided the inheritance: Walram II took the south; Otto I, the north. The former's son, Adolf of Nassau, was the German king (1292–98). The lands of both lines underwent numerous partitions in succeeding centuries. The Ottonian, William of Nassau (William the Silent, Prince of Orange), had extensive holdings in the Netherlands and founded the dynasty of stadholders prominent in the Dutch Republic in the 16th, 17th, and 18th centuries. In 1801, Napoleonic France acquired Nassau lands west of the Rhine; in 1803 the two Walramian branches, Nassau-Weilburg and Nassau-Usingen, made common cause and received considerable additions of territory. A cession to the grand duchy of Berg in 1806 was balanced by additions, mainly from Ottonian Nassau. Walramian Nassau was made a duchy and joined the Confederation of the Rhine set up by Napoleon I. By supporting the losing Austrian side in the Seven Weeks' War (1866), Duke Adolf lost the duchy to Prussia; thereafter, it formed most of the Wiesbaden district of Prussia's Hesse-Nassau province. Meanwhile, having lost his German possessions to Napoleon in 1806, William VI of Orange was awarded Luxembourg in 1815 and also succeeded to the Kingdom of The Netherlands as King William I. His descendants still reign in The Netherlands today, but Adolf of the Walramian line succeeded to Luxembourg in 1890.

Nassau, capital of the Bahamas, port on the northeastern coast of New Providence Island, and one of the world's chief pleasure resorts. It took its present name in the 1690s from the family name of King William III of England, but it was not laid out until 1729. The climate is temperate, the beaches fine, and the scenery beautiful, and though the city proper is comparatively small, residential districts stretch far along the coast. Notable buildings include Ft. Fincastle (1793), situated on a ridge south of Nassau; Government House, a white building overlooking the city; the Anglican Christ Church Cathedral, on a street leading downhill to the town; and administrative offices in the city centre. Higher education facilities consist of the College of the Bahamas (founded 1974), which is a junior community college. Offshore, at the eastern end of the harbour, are marine gardens, with glass-bottomed boats available for underwater sight-seeing.

Columbus monument at Government House, Nassau, Bahamas

John Phillips—Photo Researchers

Nassau's spectacular natural vegetation includes scarlet poinciana trees, poinsettias, and purple bougainvillea; and the Ardastra Gardens west of the city contain many rare tropical plants. Paradise Island, a developing recreation centre, connects with Nassau by a bridge 1,500 ft (460 m) long and shelters the harbour, which accommodates ships of 24-ft draft. There are no important industries; but sisal, sponges, citrus fruits, tomatoes, and pineapples are exported. Nassau is reached by international sea or air routes and has local service to other islands. Pop. (1970) city, 3,233; metropolitan area, 101,503.
25°05′ N, 77°21′ W

·economic and cultural importance **2**:591h
·map, Bahamas **2**:590

Nassau, coral formation of the Cook Islands, a dependency of New Zealand in the southwest Pacific Ocean. The only island of the northern Cooks that is not an atoll, Nassau is oval in shape and has a total land area of 300 ac (121 ha). Surrounded by a fringing reef, the island has sand dunes 35 ft (11 m) high. Nassau's discovery (1835) is credited to an American whaling captain, who named it after his ship. It was annexed to Britain in 1892 and exports copra. Pop. (1976) 123.
11°33′ S, 165°25′ W

·map, Pacific Islands **2**:433

Nassau, Frederick Henry, count of: *see* Frederick Henry, prince of Orange.

Nassau County, southeastern New York, U.S., on central and western Long Island, just east of the Borough of Queens, New York City. Mainly residential, it comprises 2 cities (Glen Cove and Long Beach), 3 towns or townships (Hempstead, North Hempstead, and Oyster Bay), and more than 70 villages, including Mineola, the county seat. It was formed in 1899 from Queens County, has an area of 300 sq mi (777 sq km), and took its name in honour of William of Nassau, prince of Orange. Pop. (1950) 672,765; (1970) 1,428,838; (1980). 1,321,582.

Nassau Memorandum, reform program prepared by Karl, Freiherr vom Stein, for Prussia in 1807.

·Stein's Prussian reforms **17**:667e

Nassau Range (Indonesia): *see* Sudirman Range.

Nassau-Siegen, Johan Maurits, graaf van: *see* John Maurice of Nassau.

Nasser, Gamal Abdel 12:844 (b. Jan. 15, 1918, Alexandria, Egypt—d. Sept. 28, 1970, Cairo), president of Egypt, one of the most popular and influential Arab leaders of modern times.

Abstract of text biography. Nasser graduated from the Royal Military Academy. He helped form the Free Officers, a secret revolutionary organization aimed at ousting the British and the Egyptian royal family. On July 23, 1952, Nasser and other Free Officers staged a coup d'etat against the monarchy. The country was taken over by a Revolutionary Command Council controlled by Nasser. In 1954 he named himself prime minister. In 1956, under Nasser, Egypt became an Islāmic, Arab, welfare state with a one-party political system; and later that year he was elected president. In 1956, and again in 1967, he fought and lost brief wars with Israel. He was for many years prominent among the leaders of the African and Asian nations.

REFERENCES in other text articles:
·Arabian anti-British nationalism **1**:1051c
·British intervention in 1950s **3**:280h
·Dulles' foreign policy toward Egypt **5**:1081h
·Israel and France against United Arab Front **2**:837d
·nationalist leadership and problems **9**:776b
·RCC power solidification and presidency **6**:499f
·socialist role **16**:972g
·Soviet support dependence **9**:761d
·Suez crisis leadership **9**:762f *passim* to 763g
·Syria and the U.A.R. **17**:961h

Nasser, Lake, important reservoir on the Nile River, in Upper Egypt and northern The Sudan. It was created by the impounding of the Nile's waters by the Aswān High Dam (Arabic: Sadd al-ʿĀlī), built in the 1960s and dedicated 1971. With a gross capacity of 127,392,090,000 cu m, Lake Nasser's waters, when discharged downstream, have brought 800,000 ac (*c.* 324,000 ha) of additional land under irrigation, and have converted 700,000 ac from flood to perennial irrigation. The lake has been stocked with food fish; in 1971, *c.* 20 tons per day were caught. It is named for Gamal Abdel Nasser, president (1956–70) of Egypt.
22°40′ N, 32°00′ E
·map, Egypt **6**:447
·map, Sudan **17**:758
·Nile water resources and river physiography **13**:107e; map 103
·topography and population **6**:449b

Nassonow gland, a gland opening on the dorsal side of the abdomen of bees; produces a substance used to mark the bee hive entrance and food sources away from the hive.
·labelling function in bees **9**:130f

Nast, Thomas (b. Sept. 27, 1840, Landau, Ger.—d. Dec. 7, 1902, Guayaquil, Ecuador), cartoonist, best known for his attack on the political machine of William M. Tweed in New York City in the 1870s. He arrived in New York as a boy of 6. He studied art at the National Academy of Design and at the age of 15 became a draftsman for *Frank Leslie's Illustrated Newspaper* and at 18 for *Harper's Weekly*. In 1860 he went to England for the *New York Illustrated News* and in the same year went to Italy to cover Garibaldi's revolt for *The Illustrated London News* and U.S. publications.

With the outbreak of the U.S. Civil War, Nast vigorously supported the cause of the Union and opposed slavery from his drawing board at *Harper's Weekly*. His cartoons "After the Battle" (1862), attacking Northerners opposed to energetic prosecution of the war, and his "Emancipation" (1863), showing the evils of slavery and the benefits of its abolition, were so effective that President Lincoln called him "our best recruiting sergeant." During Reconstruction, his cartoons portrayed Pres. Andrew Johnson as a repressive autocrat and characterized Southerners as vicious exploiters of helpless blacks, revealing his bitter disappointment in postwar politics.

Many of Nast's most effective cartoons, such as his "Tammany Tiger Loose" and "Group of Vultures Waiting for the Storm to Blow

Thomas Nast, self-portrait etching, 1892

By courtesy of the Library of Congress, Washington, D.C.

Over" (both 1871), were virulent attacks on New York's Tammany Hall political machine led by "Boss" Tweed. His cartoons were probably one of the chief factors in the machine's downfall. Nast's caricature of the fleeing political boss led to Tweed's identification and arrest in Vigo, Spain, in 1876.

By 1885, Nast's disagreements with the editors of *Harper's Weekly* were becoming increasingly frequent; his last *Harper's* cartoon appeared in 1886. His contributions to other journals became infrequent and, having lost nearly all his savings in the failure of the brokerage house of Grant & Ward in 1884, he became destitute. He was appointed consul general at Guayaquil, Ecuador, in 1902.

Nast did some painting in oil and book illustrations, but his fame rests on his caricatures and political cartoons. From his pen came the Democratic Party's donkey, the Republican Party's elephant, Tammany Hall's tiger, and one of the most popular images of Santa Claus.
·satirical style and symbol creation **3**:912g; illus. 913

nastaʿlīq script, predominant style of Persian calligraphy during the 15th and 16th centuries. The inventor was Mir Ali of Tabriz, the most famous calligrapher of the Timurid period (1402–1502). A cursive script, *nastaʿlīq* was a combination of the *naskh* and *taʿlīq* styles, featuring elongated horizontal strokes and exaggerated rounded forms. The diacritical marks were casually placed, and the lines were flowing rather than straight. *Nastaʿlīq* was often incorporated into the paintings of the early Safavid period (16th century) and is traditionally considered to be the most elegant of the Persian scripts.
·Arabic calligraphy styles and use **3**:664f

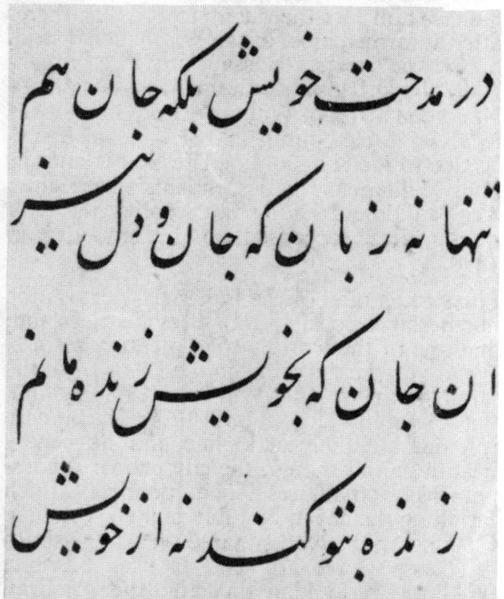

Nastaʿlīq script from "Laylā Majnūn," calligraphy by Sultan ʿAlī Mashhadī, 1506 (London, India Office Library, MS. Ethé 1204, fol. 5r)

By courtesy of the India Office Library, London

nastic movement, movement of a plant organ (*e.g.*, leaf, bud scale) that is oriented with respect to the plant as a whole rather than to an external stimulus; the movement may be initiated, however, by a stimulus such as diffuse light (photonasty) or temperature (thermonasty) that influences the plant equally from all directions.
·plant growth and responses **17**:673f

nāstika (Indian philosophy): *see* āstika.

nasturtium, any of various annual plants of the genus *Tropaeolum* (family Tropaeolaceae) native to Mexico, Central America, and northern South America and introduced into other regions as cultivated garden plants. *Nasturtium* is also a genus of aquatic herbs of the family Cruciferae (*see* watercress).

Common nasturtium (*Tropaeolum majus*)

Derek Fell

The peppery-tasting leaves are sometimes used in salads. The brilliant yellow, orange, or red flowers are funnel-shaped and have a long spur that contains sweet nectar.

Tropaeolum majus, the common nasturtium, is also known as Indian cress. The young flower buds and fruit are sometimes used as seasoning. The plant grows 2.4–3.6 metres (8–12 feet) tall, and the flowers are commonly yellow-orange with red spots or stripes. *T. minus*, the dwarf nasturtium, has flowers 3 centimetres across or less. *T. peltophorum*, the shield nasturtium, is a climbing plant with orange-red flowers about 2.5 centimetres long. *T. peregrinum* is commonly known as the canary creeper (*q.v.*).

Nasua (mammal genus): *see* coati.

nat, generic term for a group of spirits that are the objects of an extensive, probably pre-Buddhist, Burmese folk cult; in Thailand a similar spirit is called *phi*. Most important of the Burmese *nat*s are a group collectively called the "thirty-seven," made up of spirits of human beings who have died violent deaths. They are capable of protecting the believer when kept properly propitiated and of causing harm when offended or ignored.

Other types of *nats* are nature spirits, who inhabit trees, waterfalls, hills, and fields; hereditary *nats*, whose annual tribute is an obligation inherited by the original inhabitants of a particular area; and village *nats*, who protect an entire village or group of villages from wild animals, bandits, and illness and whose shrine is attached to a tree or large pole near the entrance to each of the villages. Most households also hang a coconut from the southeast pillar of the house in honour of Min Mahagir, the house *nat*.

Nats are propitiated by offerings of food or flowers, given on all important occasions. Among the special *nat* festivals are those honouring the Taungbyon brothers—a prominent, rather rowdy, pair of *nats* said to have been executed in the 11th century—and the king of the "thirty-seven," Thagya Min, associated by scholars with the Indian god Indra (known in Burma as Sakka).

·Burmese beliefs and Buddhist influence **17**:253f
·Burmese religious focus on spirits **17**:225b
·Burmese worship and drama development **17**:238h
·Southeast Asian religious aspects **17**:225b

Natal 12:845, province of South Africa, with an area of 33,578 sq mi (86,967 sq km). It is bounded by Lesotho and the Orange Free State and Transvaal provinces (west), by Swaziland and Mozambique (north), by the Province of Cape Hope (south), and by the Indian Ocean (east). Its capital is Pietermaritzburg. Pop. (1970) 2,140,166.

The text article covers Natal's history, physical geography, climate, vegetation, animal life, population, administration, social conditions, economy, and transport and communications systems.

REFERENCES in other text articles:
·Luthuli's racial justice effort **11**:201h
·map, South Africa **17**:62
·19th-century public education provision **6**:394g
·population distribution and density **17**:67f; table
·Shaka's career and empire **16**:614c
·Voortrekker migration and British settlement **17**:284d *passim* to 285g

Natal, capital, Rio Grande do Norte state, northeastern Brazil, near the mouth of the Rio Potengi, or Rio Grande do Norte, on the Atlantic coast. Founded by the Portuguese in 1597 near the site of a fort (Tres Reis Magos, or The Three Magi), Natal was given town status in 1611. The state's principal commercial centre, it produces cotton textiles, sugar, salt, hides, and skins, has a seaport and a large airport, and is the focus of railroads and highways from the interior as well as from other coastal urban centres. Natal is the seat of the Universidade Federal do Rio Grande do Norte (1958). Pop. (1970 prelim.) 250,787.
5°47′ S, 35°13′ W
·historic and geographic features **15**:861c
·map, Brazil **3**:124

Natal Basin, submarine depression, Indian Ocean.
30°00′ S, 40°00′ E
·Indian Ocean floor features map **9**:308

Natal grass, common name for several southern African grasses of the family Poaceae but applied principally to *Rhynchelytrum repens* (formerly *Tricholaena rosea*), also known as Natal red top. A tufted, perennial grass with glossy, purple or pink hairs on the seed heads, Natal grass is found on disturbed soils (*i.e.*, those not in a natural state) in tropical America and Australia and is cultivated as a forage and ornamental grass in parts of southern North America.

Natalidae, a family of funnel-eared bats of the order Chiroptera.
·classification and general features **4**:435h

Natalis, Alexander, French ALEXANDRE NOËL (b. Jan. 19, 1639, Rouen, Fr.—d. Aug. 21, 1724, Paris), controversial theologian and ecclesiastical historian who clashed with Rome for expressing Gallicanism, a French position advocating restriction of papal power, and for defending Jansenism, a religious movement of nonorthodox tendencies that became connected in France with the struggle of the Gallicans against the papacy. He joined the Dominicans at Rouen (1655), received a doctorate in divinity from the Sorbonne (1675), and was regent of studies at Saint-Jacques, Paris. Natalis' chief work, *Selecta historiae ecclesiasticae capita* (24 vol., 1676–86; "Selected Chapters of Ecclesiastical History"), was condemned by Pope Innocent XI in 1684 because of its defense of Gallican claims. Natalis issued a revised edition, *Historia ecclesiastica veteris et novi testamenti* ("Ecclesiastical History of the Old and New Testaments"), in 8 volumes in 1699, but it was not until 1734 that the edition was removed from the Index of Forbidden Books.

In 1701 he signed the *Cas de conscience* ("Case of Conscience"), a document allowing "silent submission" to a Jansenist asking for absolution, but, when it was condemned by Pope Clement XI, Natalis submitted. He appealed against Clement's bull *Unigenitus* (1713), which condemned propositions of one of the leading Jansenists, Pasquier Quesnel, but again submitted. Thereafter, he retired to Saint-Jacques, exhausted and having become blind. A. Hänggi's *Der Kirchenhistoriker Natalis Alexander* ("The Church Historian Natalis Alexander") appeared in 1955.

natality (birthrate): *see* vital rates.

Natalya, the Boyar's Daughter, novel by Nikolay Karamzin.
·Russian novel development **13**:293d

Natanson, Mark Andreyevich, pseudonym BOBROV (1850–1919), Russian revolutionary and leader in the Narodniki (Populists) movement.

Natanya (Israel): *see* Netanya.

Naṭarāja (Lord of Dance), the Hindu god Śiva (Shiva) in his form as the cosmic dancer, represented in metal or stone in most Śaiva temples of South India.

In the most common type of images, which includes the magnificent Cōḷa bronzes of the 10th–11th centuries, Śiva is shown with four arms and flying locks dancing on the figure of a dwarf, the Apasmā-rapuruṣa (a symbol of man's ignorance; *puruṣa* meaning man, and *apasmāra* forgetfulness or heedlessness). The back right hand of Śiva holds the *ḍamaru* (hourglass shaped drum); and the front right hand is in the *abhaya-mudrā* (the "fear-not" gesture, made by holding the palm outward with fingers pointing up); the back left hand carries *agni* (fire) in a vessel or in the palm of the hand; the front left hand is held across the chest in the *gajahasta* (elephant-trunk) pose, with wrist limp and fingers pointed downward toward the uplifted left foot. The locks of Śiva's hair stand out in several strands, and are interspersed with the figures of Gaṅgā (the river Ganges personified as a goddess), flowers, a skull, and the crescent moon. His figure is encircled by a ring of flames, the *prabhāmaṇḍala*. This form of dance, which is the most common representation of Naṭarāja, is called in the classic Sanskrit treatises on dance the *bhujaṅgatrāsa* ("trembling of the snake").

The legend accounting for the portrayal is that Śiva once visited the forest of Tāraka, where a group of heretical ascetics lived. In anger the ascetics first set a tiger against him, but Śiva flayed the beast with his fingernail and wore it as a garment; next they sent a serpent, which he took as a garland and began to dance; finally they sent the Apasmārapuruṣa, the dwarf called Muyalaka. Śiva broke the dwarf's back with the toe of his foot and continued to dance. The serpent Śeṣa was so taken with the dance that he did penance to Śiva and asked to see it once more. Śiva promised that he should, in Chidambaram. The Chidambaram *sabhā* (the hall in South Indian Śaiva temples where the Naṭarāja is kept), was already famous in the 7th century AD, and the sculptures of its *gopura* (temple gateway) show all the 108 different modes of dance listed in the Sanskrit dance treatise, the *bhārata-nāṭya śāstra*.

The significance of the Naṭarāja sculpture is said to be that Śiva is shown as the source of all movement within the cosmos, represented by the arch of flames. The purpose of the dance is to release men from illusion, and the place, Chidambaram, called the centre of the universe, is in reality within the heart. The gestures of the dance represent Śiva's five activities (*pañcakṛtya*): creation (symbolized by the drum), protection (by the "fear-not" pose of the hand), destruction (by the fire), embodiment (by the foot planted on the ground), and release (by the foot held aloft).

Naṭarāja, dancing Śiva, Indian bronze image, 12th–13th century AD; in the Museum van Aziatische Kunst, Amsterdam
By courtesy of the Rijksmuseum, Amsterdam

Other dances of Śiva seen in sculpture and painting are the wild *tāṇḍava*, which he performs on cremation grounds in the company of his consort Devī, and the evening dance performed on Mt. Kailāsa before the assembly of gods, some of whom accompany him on various instruments.
·Hindi symbolic theology **8**:906a

Natchez, Muskogean-speaking North American Indian tribe that inhabited the east side of the Lower Mississippi River. In the early 18th century, at the time of the first French settlement, the tribe numbered about 6,000, living in nine villages between the Yazoo and Pearl rivers, near the site of the present-day city of Natchez, Miss.

Relations between the French settlers and the Natchez were friendly at first; but three French–Natchez wars in 1716, 1723, and 1729 resulted in the French, with the aid of the Choctaw (*q.v.*), driving the Natchez from their villages. Some 400 were captured and sold into the West Indian slave trade; the remainder took refuge with the Chickasaw and later with the Upper Creeks and Cherokee. When the latter tribes were forced to move west into Indian Territory (present Oklahoma), the Natchez went with them. A few Natchez retained their language into the early 20th century, and there were still a few tribe members living in northeastern Oklahoma in the 1960s.

The Natchez, allied in general culture to other Muskogean tribes, were a primarily agricultural people. They made clothes by weaving a fabric from the inner bark of the mulberry; excelled in potterymaking; and built large temples—similar to those of the Creeks—of wattles and mud set upon eight-foot mounds. Their dwellings—built in precise rows around a plaza or common ground—were four-sided and constructed of sun-baked mud and straw with arched cane roofs.

They were sun worshippers, ruled by a monarch called the Great Sun, who had the power of life and death over them. He maintained several wives and a household of volunteers to work and hunt for him; all were killed at his death, along with any others who wished to join him in the afterlife. Integral to their religion was a perpetual fire kept burning in the temple. It was allowed to die once a year on the eve of their midsummer festival, the Busk, or Green Corn, ceremony (similar to that of the Creeks). The fire was remade at dawn of the festival day, and all the village fires were then made anew from the sacred fire. The Natchez were notable for the peculiar caste system, in which the people were classified as suns, nobles, honoured people, and commoners. The chief, or Great Sun, and the heads of the villages claimed descent from the sun. Persons of the sun caste were not allowed to intermarry. Rather, they were required to marry commoners. The offspring of female suns and commoners were suns, while the children of male suns and commoners belonged to the caste of honoured people.

- political and religious origin of castes **3**:991d
- rank system, king's status, and area **17**:219g; map
- solar traditions **12**:880d

Natchez, city, seat of Adams County, southwestern Mississippi, U.S., on the Mississippi River (there bridged to Vidalia, La.). Established in 1716 as Ft. Rosalie by Jean-Baptiste Le Moyne, sieur de Bienville, it survived a massacre (1729) by Natchez Indians on whose land it had been built and for whom it was later renamed. It passed from France to

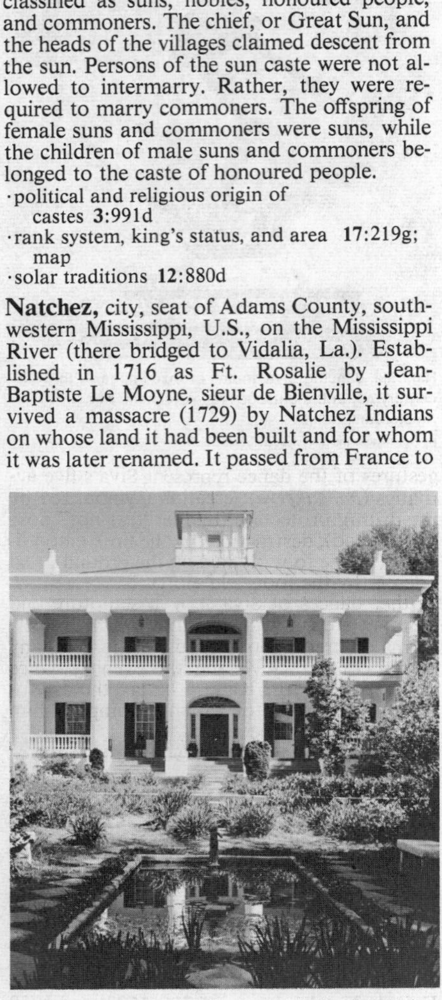

D'Evereux mansion, one of many antebellum homes in Natchez, Miss.

Arthur Griffin—EB Inc.

England (1763) at the conclusion of the French and Indian War, and was a haven for Loyalists expelled from the rebelling colonies during the American Revolution. In 1779 it was captured by a Spanish expedition under Bernardo de Gálvez and remained under Spanish dominion until 1798 when the U.S. took possession and made it the first capital (1798–1802) of the Territory of Mississippi. During the ensuing years it burgeoned as the commercial and cultural centre of a vast and rich cotton-producing area. It was the southern terminus of the Natchez Trace, overland trail from Nashville, Tenn., and an important river port. During the Civil War it was bombarded by Federal gunboats and was taken over in July 1863.

Natchez emerged from its post-Civil War decline as one of the state's leading industrial centres. Timber, petroleum, and natural gas reserves have enticed manufacturers of rubber, wood, paper, and textile products as well as producers of petroleum and natural gas. It has become the stereotype of the antebellum South and is noted for its annual Pilgrimage, during which antebellum homes are open to the public and historical pageants are held. Natchez Junior College was established in 1885. Homochitto National Forest and Emerald Indian Mound (dating from 1300–1600) are nearby. Inc. 1803. Pop. (1980) 22,015.
31°34′ N, 91°23′ W

- map, United States **18**:908

Natchez Trace Parkway, highway in the U.S., about 450 miles (725 km) long, following an Indian trail northeastward from Natchez, Miss., across northwest Alabama, to Nashville, Tenn. From 1800 to 1820, it was the most important highway in the Old Southwest—militarily, economically, and politically. With the advent of the river steamer and of newer and more direct roads after the War of 1812, it began a gradual decline. Among the historical landmarks along its route are the Emerald and Bynum Indian ceremonial mounds and Chickasaw Village in Mississippi and Napier Mine and Metal Ford in Tennessee, harking back to frontier iron mining and smelting. In 1938, the parkway became part of the National Park system and in 1961 Ackia Battleground and Meriwether Lewis National Monuments were added to its area.

- conservation and transportation role **12**:278d

Natchitoches, city, seat (1805) of Natchitoches Parish, northwestern Louisiana, U.S., on Cane River Lake. The oldest permanent settlement in Louisiana, it began in 1714 as Ft. St. Jean Baptiste, founded by the French to forestall Spanish occupation of the area. Many French Colonial homes survive. Renamed for the Natchitoches Indians, it developed as a cotton market, but its commercial importance declined after 1832, when the Red River, then its main artery of transportation, changed course (5 mi [8 km] east). After 1950 it acquired diversified industry. Northwestern State College (founded 1884) is an economic asset. Segments of the Kisatchie National Forest are nearby. Inc. 1872. Pop. (1980) 16,664.
31°46′ N, 93°05′ W

- map, United States **18**:908

Nātha cult, a popular all-India religious movement that strives for immortality by transforming the human body into an imperishable divine body. It combines esoteric traditions drawn from Buddhism, Śaivism (worship of the Hindu deity Śiva), and Haṭha Yoga (stresses physical discipline), with a liking for the occult. The term is derived from the names of the nine traditional masters, all of which end in the word *nātha* ("master, lord"). Texts do not agree on the lists of the nine. All are believed to have successfully transformed their bodies through yogic discipline into indestructible spiritual entities, and, according to popular belief, they reside as demigods in the Himalayas. The nine *nātha*s are in many respects similar to the 84 "great perfect ones," the *mahāsiddha*s, common to both Hinduism and Buddhism, and their names appear on both lists. Ādinātha (the First Master) is identified by Hindus with Lord Śiva and by Buddhists with Buddha, in the form of Vajrasattva. Matsyendranāth is considered the first of the human *guru*s (spiritual guides) and in Nepal is merged with the *bodhisattva* ("Buddha-to-be") Avalokiteśvara.

The Nātha cult is essentially made up of yogis whose aim is to achieve *sahaja*, defined as a state of neutrality transcending the duality of human existence. This is accomplished through the cultivation of *kāya-sādhana* ("culture of the body"), with great emphasis laid on the control of semen, breath, and thought. Guidance of an accomplished *guru* is considered essential. The Nātha yogis share with similar esoteric cults a liking for paradox and enigmatic verse.

- Śaivite sect practices and influence **8**:916e

Nathan, biblical Hebrew prophet in the reign of David, reproved David for causing the death of Uriah, the Hittite general whose wife Bathsheba David seduced and eventually married.

- prophetic stages in Jewish history **15**:64a
- uncovering of David's adultery **2**:913a

Nathan, George Jean (b. Feb. 14, 1882, Fort Wayne, Ind.—d. April 8, 1958, New York City), author, editor, and drama critic, of whom, at the time of his death, *The New York Times* reported, "No other American critic of the period had so greatly raised the

George Nathan

By courtesy of the Library of Congress, Washington, D.C.

standards of play producers or so determinedly elevated the tastes of play goers." He graduated from Cornell University in 1904 and joined the staff of the *New York Herald*. Beginning in 1906, he was at various times drama critic for numerous magazines and newspapers, but his name is particularly associated with *The Smart Set*, of which he was co-editor (1914–23) with H.L. Mencken, and with the *American Mercury*, which, also with Mencken, he helped to found in 1924. As a critic Nathan championed the plays of Ibsen, Strindberg, Shaw, O'Neill, O'Casey, and Saroyan. He published his *Theatre Book of the Year* annually from 1943 through 1951, as well as more than 30 volumes of lively essays on theatrical and other subjects. Nathan married the actress Julie Haydon in 1955.

Nathanael: *see* Bartholomew, Saint.

Nathan of Gaza (*c.* 1644–90), Jewish Kabalist and messianic enthusiast.

- Sabbetaian propagandizing **10**:189d

Nathan the Wise (1781), English translation of NATHAN DER WEISE, play (performed 1779), by the German dramatist Gotthold Ephraim Lessing, advocating religious tolerance; written in iambic blank verse, it was associated with German Neoclassical drama. The figure of Nathan was taken from Lessing's friend, the philosopher Moses Mendelssohn. In the play a symbolic demonstration of the affinity of all religions is afforded when Nathan, brought before the Muslim sultan Saladin for the crime of raising the Christian girl Recha as a Jew, reveals that Recha is actually the sister of the Christian knight who has fallen in love with her, and that both are the children of the Sultan's brother. Asked by the Sultan to name the one true religion, Nathan in effect declines by relating a parable of three rings: The magic ring, traditionally bequeathed to the favourite son, marking him the new family head to whom is assured the love of God and man, came to reside with a father who loved his three sons equally. Having made two exact copies of the ring, he presented a ring to each son. The resulting dispute was mediated by a wise judge who advised each son to live so as

to gain the love of God and man, the determination of true ownership to be made a million years hence.
·parable of Deist view **5**:563c
·style, characters, and ethical concern **10**:840f

Nathdwāra, town, Udaipur district, Rājasthān state, India, just south of the Banās River. Connected by road with Udaipur and close to the Malvi rail junction, Nathdwāra (literally, "Portal of God") is a place of Hindu pilgrimage and contains a 17th-century Vaiṣṇavite shrine that is one of the most famous in India. Within the temple is a celebrated image of the god Kṛṣṇa (Krishna), popularly said to date to the 12th century BC. The town is an agricultural market and has one government college affiliated with the University of Rājasthān. Pop. (1971 prelim.) 18,909.
24°56′ N, 73°51′ E
·map, India **9**:278

nat houses and images, in Burmese art, shrinelike structures and statues created as part of the cult of nature spirits. The *nats* are various deities representing the spirits of trees,

Burmese *nat*, teak, 19th century; in the Ashmolean Museum, Oxford
By courtesy of the Ashmolean Museum, Oxford, England

rivers, mountains, snakes, ancestors, and the like. Their number was fixed at a canonical 36, the Buddha being included as the 37th in the 10th century.

Even in the 20th century, every village has its own *nat* house, conceived as a part of the domain of the spiritual located on Earth. Built in a tree, the house is a fragile, elegant little wood structure with carved panels of undulating pattern and flamelike finials at the roof peaks. Basically it is similar to the Burmese house, a small box on stilts. Statues of *nats* are usually of wood, and for this reason most of the existing examples are of recent date. They are lively little figures with simplified bodies and broad, round faces. Comparison with an earlier *nat* statue in bronze, a rarity, shows little change in style. This indigenous nat tradition influenced the Buddha image in Burma, with its broad face, flattened features, and large ears that turn outward.

Nathusia rugosa, fossil olive (order Oleales).
·Oleales fossil record **13**:558f

Natica, a genus of snail of the class Gastropoda of the phylum Mollusca.
·feeding specificity on mollusks **7**:209b

Natick, town (township), Middlesex County, eastern Massachusetts, U.S., just southwest of Boston. The first settlement was made in 1650, when the missionary John Eliot was granted the land for use as a plantation for his "praying Indians." Eliot published his Indian Bible in 1663, a copy of which the town possesses. After the Indians were crowded out by white settlers, Natick (an Indian tribal name) became a farming community. The modern town is a residential suburban community with a growing industrial development (leather, paper, and food products). Inc. 1781. Pop. (1980) 29,461.
42°17′ N, 71°21′ W

nation, in medieval universities, a group of students from a particular region or country who banded together for mutual protection and cooperation in a strange land. In some universities nations were responsible for educating and examining students; in all of them protection and defense were afforded the member of a nation. Each one was governed by its own proctor, who was elected for terms varying from one month (at the University of Paris) to a year (University of Bologna). Through participation in elections and meetings the students—many of whom in later life were to serve on committees and councils of kings and princes—were exposed to the practical workings of constitutional government.

At Bologna, the original site of the division into nations and the model for this development in other universities, there were four nations—Lombards, Tuscans, Romans, and Ultramontanes. Students who were Bolognese citizens were not admitted to a nation: they did not need the protection afforded foreign students. Also, for a citizen of Bologna there would be the question of divided loyalties, since members owed their first allegiance to their nation.

Nation, U.S. liberal weekly periodical, founded in 1865.
·magazine publishing history **15**:256c

Nation, Carry (Amelia), *née* MOORE (b. Nov. 25, 1846, Garrard County, Ky.—d. June 9, 1911, Leavenworth, Kan.), temperance advocate famous for her demolition of barrooms with a hatchet. The scourge of barkeepers and drinkers in Kansas and elsewhere, she received little support from the national or world temperance movements, but her activities may have helped bring about the ratification of the Prohibition Amendment to the U.S. Constitution in 1919.

Although she held a teaching certificate from a state normal school, her education was intermittent. In 1867 she married a young physician, Charles Gloyd, whom she left after a few months because of his alcoholism. In 1877 she married David Nation, a lawyer, journalist, and minister, who divorced her in 1901 on the ground of desertion.

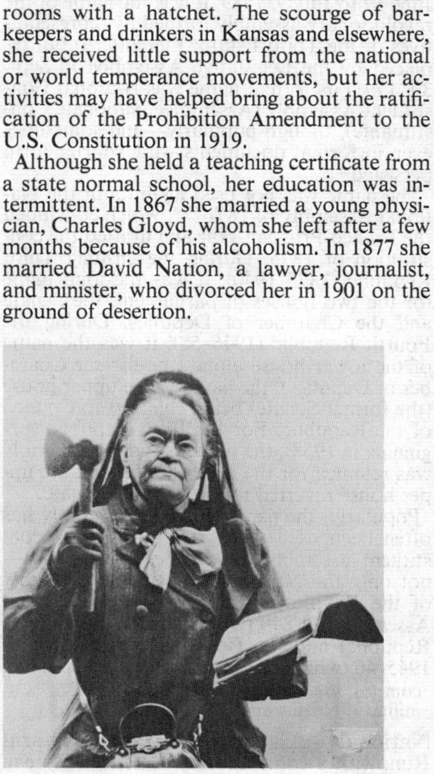

Carry Nation
Brown Brothers

She entered the temperance movement in 1890, when a U.S. Supreme Court decision in favour of the importation and sale of liquor in "original packages" from other states weakened the prohibition laws of Kansas, where she was living. In her view, the illegality of the saloons flourishing in that state meant that anyone could destroy them with impunity. A formidable woman, nearly 6 feet tall and weighing 175 pounds, she dressed in stark black and white clothing of vaguely religious appearance. Alone or accompanied by hymn-singing women, she would march into a saloon and proceed to sing, pray, hurl biblical-sounding vituperations at the "rummies" present, and smash the bar fixtures and stock with a hatchet. At one point, her fervour led her to invade the governor's chambers at Topeka. Jailed many times, she paid her fines from lecture tour fees and souvenir hatchet sales, at times earning as much as $300 per week. She herself survived numerous physical assaults.

Carry Nation's destructive urge was also directed toward fraternal orders, tobacco, foreign foods, corsets, skirts of improper length, and mildly pornographic art of the sort found in some barrooms of the time. She was an advocate of women's suffrage. A dispassionate biography by Herbert Asbury, *Carry Nation* (1929), contrasts with her own disjointed book, *The Use and Need of the Life of Carry A. Nation* (1904). A more recent biography, *Vessel of Wrath* (1966), was written by Robert Lewis Taylor.

National, Le, French opposition newspaper of the 19th century.
·financing, editorship, and orientation **7**:663f

National Academy (China): *see* Hanlin Academy.

National Academy of Engineering (NAE), association of engineering founded in 1964 in Washington, D.C.
·engineering in government decision **6**:862e

National Academy of Sciences, nongovernmental U.S. organization of scientists and engineers, established March 3, 1863, by act of Congress to serve as an official adviser to the government in all matters of science and technology. It is a self-perpetuating body of limited membership; new members are co-opted on the basis of distinguished contributions to research. In 1916 the academy established the National Research Council to coordinate the activities of various scientists and engineers in universities, industry, and government; the council issues many publications and awards a number of postdoctoral fellowships. The academy organized U.S. participation in such international efforts as the International Geophysical Year (1957–58) and the International Biological Programme (1967–72).

national accounts budget, government budget based on concepts of national income accounting. It presents government receipts and expenditures as part of the overall pattern of national economic activity.
·government budgets analysis **3**:443c

National Action Bloc, Arabic KUTLAH AL-'AMAL AL-WAṬANĪ, first Moroccan political party, founded in 1934 to counteract mounting French domination of Morocco and to secure recognition of the equality of Moroccans and Frenchmen under the French protectorate.

The National Action Bloc attracted young, educated Moroccans of many different views. Informally in existence since 1930, under the leadership of such notable figures as Mohammed Allal al-Fassi and Ahmad Balafrej, it maintained a number of publications and launched a vigorous campaign of political instruction among the Muslim population. The bloc became a formal political body in December 1934. While the reform measures it presented to increase the Muslim share of the Moroccan government were rejected by the French, Arabic was finally admitted as a language of the press, alongside French, in 1937. The party, having gained in popular support and influence, was dissolved by the French in the same year, and late in 1937 its leaders either were exiled or fled the country. Ahmad Balafrej returned to Morocco in 1943 and founded the Istiqlāl party, which was to lead in Morocco's struggle for liberation from France.

National Action Party, Spanish PARTIDO ACCIÓN NACIONAL, established 1939, chief minority political party in Mexico with a church-oriented, largely middle-class membership.

·ideology and success **12**:75d

National Advisory Committee for Aeronautics (NACA), U.S. research body established in 1915, the functions of which were transferred to the National Aeronautics and Space Administration in 1958.

·aeronautical engineering history **1**:129f
·aeronautical research in the U.S. **7**:396c

National Aeronautics and Space Administration (NASA), the U.S. agency, established in 1958, charged with responsibility for planning and conducting the country's program of space exploration.

·Braun's Saturn rocket development **3**:123c
·communication satellite projects **16**:262c
·New Orleans plant establishment **13**:8h
·research laboratories of government **15**:740h
·robot device design for scientific use **15**:913b
·space programs **17**:362h
·UFO reports **18**:856d

national anthem, hymn or song expressing patriotic sentiment and either governmentally authorized as an official national hymn or holding that position in popular feeling.

The oldest national anthem is Great Britain's "God Save the Queen [King]," which was described as a national anthem in 1825, although it had been popular as a patriotic song and used on occasions of royal ceremonial since the mid-18th century.

During the 19th and early 20th centuries, most European countries followed Britain's example, some national anthems being written especially for the purpose, others being adapted from existing tunes. The sentiments of the texts vary, from prayers for the monarch to allusions to nationally important battles or uprisings ("The Star-Spangled Banner," U.S.; "La Marseillaise," France) to expressions of patriotic feeling ("O Canada!").

National anthems vary greatly in musical merit; and the verse or text, like the music, has not in every case been written by a national of the country concerned. Changes in politics or international relationships often cause the texts to be altered or a new anthem to be adopted. For example, the present national anthem of the Soviet Union, the "Gimn Sovetskogo Soyuza" ("Hymn of the Soviet Union"), was adopted as the national anthem in 1944, replacing the Communist hymn the "Internationale" (the words and music of which were written in the late 19th century by two French workers), a change reflecting at least in part an increased emphasis on national patriotism during World War II.

Few national anthems have been written by poets or composers of renown, a notable exception being the first Austrian national anthem, "Gott erhalte Franz den Kaiser" ("God Save Emperor Francis"), composed by Haydn in 1797 and later (1929) sung to the text "Sei gesegnet ohne Ende" ("Be Blessed Forever"). Haydn's melody was also used for the German national anthem "Deutschland, Deutschland über alles" ("Germany, Germany Above All"), adopted in 1922; beginning with its second verse, "Einigkeit und Recht und Freiheit" ("Unity and Right and Freedom"), it continues in use as the national anthem of West Germany. The German national anthem before 1922 had been "Heil dir im Siegerkranz" ("Hail to Thee in Victor's Garlands"), sung to the melody of "God Save the Queen."

The text of the U.S. national anthem was written by Francis Scott Key in 1814 as he watched the bombardment of Baltimore, Md., from a British ship on which he was detained. The melody, to which the text was immediately sung, was the song of the Anacreontic Society (a gentlemen's music-making club), "To Anacreon in Heaven," by John Stafford Smith. Other songs have served as unofficial national anthems, however, among them "Hail Columbia," text by Joseph Hopkinson (son of the patriot Francis Hopkinson) in 1798, melody, "The President's March," probably composed earlier by Philip Phile; "America," or "My Country 'Tis of Thee," text by the Rev. Samuel Francis Smith in 1831, sung to "God Save the Queen"; and the poem "America the Beautiful" (1893) by Katharine Lee Bates, sung to various melodies, those by Will C. Macfarland and Samuel A. Ward being most common.

The French national anthem, "La Marseillaise," was written (words and music) by an army engineer officer, Claude-Joseph Rouget de Lisle, on the night of April 24, 1792. It was sung by army volunteers from Marseilles as they joined in the storming of the Tuileries on August 10, and it became known as a song of revolution.

East Asian notation
·Chinese chevé-derived music **12**:677c; illus.
·Japanese gagaku form **12**:689h; illus. 690

National Archives of the United States, branch of the National Archives and Records Service of the General Services Administration, the repository for national and historically valuable regional records dating from about 1774.

·document collection significance **19**:632a; map 624

National Assembly, French ASSEMBLÉE NATIONALE, name of various historical French parliaments or houses of parliament. From June 17 to July 9, 1789, it was the name of the revolutionary assembly formed by representatives of the Third Estate; thereafter (until replaced by the Legislative Assembly on Sept. 30, 1791) its formal name was National Constituent Assembly (Assemblée Nationale Constituante), though popularly—and sometimes even in formal documents—the shorter form persisted.

The name was not used again until the National Assembly of 1871–75, which concluded the Franco-Prussian War and drafted the constitution of 1875. During the ensuing Third Republic (1875–1940), it was the joint name for the two houses of parliament, the Senate and the Chamber of Deputies. During the Fourth Republic (1946–58), it was the name of the lower house alone (the former Chamber of Deputies), the name of the upper house (the former Senate) being changed to Council of the Republic. For the Fifth Republic (beginning in 1958), the name National Assembly was retained for the lower house, and the upper house reverted to the name of Senate.

Popularly, the name National Assembly has often been used when referring to any constituent assembly (*assemblée constituante*)—not only the National Constituent Assembly of the Revolution but also the Constituent Assembly of 1848 (which created the Second Republic) and the Constituent Assembly of 1945–46 (which created the Fourth Republic).

·composition, tenure, and election **7**:603h
·military reforms and conscription **7**:719e

National Association for Pastoral Renewal, a contemporary American Roman Catholic reform group.

·celibacy option for clergy **3**:1043e

National Association for the Advancement of Colored People (NAACP), U.S. voluntary interracial organization created to work for the abolition of segregation and discrimination in housing, education, employment, voting, and transportation; to oppose racism; and to ensure Negroes their constitutional rights. Founded in 1909, the NAACP was created with the merging of the Niagara Movement, a group of young Negroes led by W.E.B. Du Bois, and a group of concerned whites.

Since its founding, the NAACP has been most successful in the areas of legal redress. Other areas of activity have included political action to secure enactment of civil rights laws, programs of education and public information to win popular support, and direct action to achieve specific goals. In 1939 the NAACP Legal Defense and Education Fund was established independently of the NAACP to act as the legal arm of the civil rights movement, and it was the NAACP's legal council that carried to the Supreme Court the case (*Brown* v. *Board of Education*) that resulted in the high court's school desegregation decision in 1954.

By the 1970s the NAACP had become a nationwide association of more than 450,000 members in over 1,700 local units. The organization maintains its headquarters in New York City.

·black church involvements in 20th century **12**:939a
·Du Bois's ambivalent affiliation **5**:1075f

National Association of Evangelicals, a fellowship of evangelical Protestant groups in the U.S., founded in 1942 by 147 evangelical leaders. It comprises more than 40 denominations, many independent religious organizations, local churches, groups of churches, and individual Christians. All members must subscribe to a Statement of Faith that requires belief in the Bible "as the inspired, the only infallible, authoritative word of God" and commitment to a well-defined category of fundamental Christian doctrines.

The association renders services in the major fields of Christian activity with commissions and affiliated agencies for evangelism and church extension, higher education, Christian day schools, Sunday schools, publications, foreign missions, laymen's work, public affairs, radio and television broadcasting, government chaplaincies, world relief, international relations, social action, stewardship, spiritual life, and theological concerns. Among its related agencies are the Evangelical Foreign Missions Association, the National Sunday School Association, the National Religious Broadcasters, and the National Association of Christian Schools. By the later 1970s the association claimed 3,500,000 full members and a service constituency of more than 10,000,000. Besides its national headquarters in Wheaton, Ill., it has offices in Washington, D.C., New York City, and other major U.S. cities. The organization is officially related to the World Evangelical Fellowship, with offices in London.

·Fundamentalist ecumenism **7**:779h

National Association of Free Will Baptists, an association of Baptist churches organized in Nashville, Tenn., in 1935. It traces its history back to two groups of Free Will, or Arminian, Baptists. These Baptists believed in free will, free grace, and free salvation, in contrast to most Baptists, who were Calvinists (*i.e.*, who believed that Christ died only for those predestined to be saved).

One Free Will Baptist group was organized in North Carolina in 1727, and its churches were located primarily in North and South Carolina. The second group originated with the work of Benjamin Randall (died 1808), who became a Baptist in 1776 and began travelling in New England as an evangelist. He preached free-will doctrine, and established many Baptist churches. The movement eventually spread to the Middle West through the work of evangelists and preachers. In 1827 the General Conference of Free Will Baptists was organized. The majority of this group merged with the Northern (later American) Baptist Convention in 1911, but some of the churches did not take part in the merger. In 1935 the free-will congregations reorganized into the National Association of Free Will Baptists.

This group continues to emphasize Arminian

rather than Calvinist doctrine, and they believe that salvation is available to all who accept Christ. Local congregations are independent and belong to state associations. The National Association meets annually; headquarters are in Nashville, Tenn.

National Autonomist Party (Argentina): *see* Partido Autonomista Nacional.

National Autonomous University of Mexico: *see* Mexico, National Autonomous University of.

national bank, in the U.S., commercial bank chartered and supervised by the federal government and operated by private individuals. The national banking system of the U.S. was founded with the National Bank Act of 1863. For earlier central banks, *see* United States, Bank of the.

The National Bank Act of 1863 provided for federal charter and supervision of national banks; they were to circulate a stable, uniform national currency secured by federal bonds deposited by each bank with the comptroller of the currency (often called the national banking administrator). The act regulated the minimum capital requirements of national banks, the kinds of loans they could make, and the reserves that were to be held against notes and deposits; it also provided for the supervision and examination of banks and for the protection of noteholders. While the 1863 act did not prohibit state banks from issuing their own currency, Congress did impose a 10 percent tax on state bank notes that effectively eliminated such a rival currency.

The inflexibility of national bank-note supplies and a lack of reserves led to the formation of the Federal Reserve System (*q.v.*) in 1913. By 1935 the national banks had transferred their note-issuing powers to the Federal Reserve. The national banks have become primarily commercial in nature, although some also maintain savings and trust functions. They are required to be members of the Federal Reserve System. *See also* central bank.

National Baptist Convention, U.S.A., Inc., one of two associations of Negro Baptist churches formed as a result of a schism in 1915 within the National Baptist Convention. The second organization then established was the National Baptist Convention of America (*q.v.*). In 1961, a dispute within the National Baptist Convention, U.S.A., Inc., resulted in the establishment of a third organization, the Progressive Baptist Convention.

The National Baptist Convention, U.S.A., Inc., has a mission program in the Bahamas and carries on home-mission and other programs. It holds an annual convention.

·black Baptist church organization **12**:940b

National Baptist Convention of America, one of two associations of Negro Baptist churches that was formed as a result of a schism in 1915 in the National Baptist Convention. The parent body originated at the end of the Civil War, when many independent Negro Baptist congregations were established. Eventually these congregations joined in various national organizations, including the Foreign Mission Baptist Convention (1880); a merger of several of these groups in Atlanta in 1895 produced the National Baptist Convention. Disagreements over the organization's publishing house and adoption of a charter resulted in a schism in 1915. The larger and continuing group adopted the charter and took the name National Baptist Convention, U.S.A., Inc., and the other group rejected the charter and continued as the National Baptist Convention of America.

The National Baptist Convention of America carries on mission, benevolence, youth, and other work. It has mission programs in Africa, Jamaica, and Panama. An annual conference is held.

·black Baptist church organization **12**:940c

National Baseball Hall of Fame and Museum: *see* Baseball Hall of Fame.

National Basketball Association (NBA), professional basketball league formed in the

Dave Cowens (18) and John Havlicek, Boston Celtics, and Ricky Sobers (40), Phoenix Suns, poised for a rebound during the playoff for the 1975–76 National Basketball Association championship; the Celtics won the title for the 13th time

Dick Raphael

United States in 1949 by the merger of two rival organizations, the National Basketball League (founded 1937) and the Basketball Association of America (founded 1946). In 1976, the NBA was augmented by the absorption of four teams and individual players from the former American Basketball Association (*q.v.*). The top ranking teams at the end of each season engage in a playoff to determine the NBA champion, which claims the title of world champion. Probably the most outstanding team in NBA history was the Boston Celtics, which won 13 titles from 1956–57 to 1975–76. NBA headquarters are in New York City. *See also* sporting record.

·basketball innovations **2**:755d
·expansion during 1960s **17**:515d

National Bison Range, U.S. wilderness area established in 1908 in the mountains of western Montana for the protection of the American bison.

·Montana landscape and animal life **12**:398c

National Bloc, Arabic KUTLAH AL-WAṬANĪYAH, a coalition of Syrian nationalist parties (1925–49) that opposed the French mandate and demanded independence.

The Bloc was a powerful minority in the first Constituent Assembly of 1928 and in the same year was instrumental in drawing up a strongly worded constitution that ignored France's mandatory powers (and was subsequently rejected by the French high commissioner).

Popular support for the Bloc grew after the French dissolved the Assembly in 1930. Its insistent demands for independence forced the French to consider negotiations for a treaty in 1933, but no agreement could be reached. A Franco-Syrian treaty was finally concluded in 1936, assuring Syrian independence and satisfying nationalist demands for the inclusion of the Druze and ʿAlawī (Nuṣayrī) states and the former Ottoman sanjak of Alexandretta within Syria proper. The Syrian government immediately ratified the treaty, and the National Bloc assumed ministerial control. Less than three years later (February 1939), the National Bloc cabinet was forced to resign; it had antagonized the ʿAlawīs and Druzes to rebellion, allowed the French to hand over Alexandretta to Turkey, and was finally unable to persuade the French to ratify the 1936 treaty.

The Free French proclamation of an independent Syria in 1941 brought the National Bloc back to prominence, and, led by Shukri al-Kuwatli, it swept the elections for the new Chamber of Deputies in 1943. Its program pressed for the ouster of all French influence in Syria and the attainment of full independence. When the French left in 1945, however, the internal rivalries of the Bloc were exposed, and new opposition parties began to form. It maintained its majority in the government, however, until March 1949, when the last National Bloc cabinet and subsequently the party itself were overthrown by a military coup.

·Syrian independence **17**:958g

National Board of Medical Examiners (NBME), U.S. organization founded in 1915 to prepare and administer qualifying examinations for the practice of medicine; its examinations are accepted in all but five states.

·medical licensure control **11**:850g

National Botanic Gardens of South Africa, botanical garden in Kirstenbosch, near Cape Town.

·map, Cape Town **3**:796
·size and species variety table **3**:64

National Botanic Garden of Belgium, French JARDIN BOTANIQUE NATIONAL DE BELGIQUE, botanical garden in Meise, Belgium.

·size and species variety table **3**:64

National Botanic Gardens, botanical garden in Dublin.

·size and species variety table **3**:64

National Boxing Association of America: *see* World Boxing Association.

National Campmeeting Association for the Promotion of Holiness, U.S. 19th-century Protestant group.

·Holiness church growth **8**:994e

National Capital Parks, system of national monuments and government-owned parks and recreation areas in and around Washington, D.C. Comprising hundreds of units with a combined area in 1979 of 6,470 ac (2,618 ha), the system was authorized by Congress in 1790 and became part of the National Park Service in 1933. The overwhelming majority of units are located in Washington, D.C.; others are in Virginia and Maryland.

The National Capital Planning Commission (1926) formulates and directs plans for roads, recreation areas, improved transportation facilities, and slum clearance.

·park maintenance and development **19**:632b

National Capital Transportation Agency, founded in the U.S. in 1960 to formulate plans for mass-transportation services in the Washington, D.C., area. Its functions were transferred to the Washington Metropolitan Area Transit Authority in 1967.

·transportation evaluation function **19**:631a

National Central Library (Great Britain): *see* British Library.

National Centre for Scientific Research, French CENTRE NATIONAL DE LA RECHERCHE SCIENTIFIQUE, advisory organization that recommends to the French government the methods and funding for research projects in both the natural and social sciences. It was founded in 1939 in Paris.

·Irène Joliot-Curie's founding role **5**:373c

National Centre of Independents and Peasants (French political party): *see* Centre National des Indépendants et Paysans.

National Centre Party, Estonian political party formed in the 1920s with its base in the city of Tartu.

·Estonian political factions **2**:674e

National Church of Nigeria, an independent African church that, in 1964, united with the Edo National Church.

·tribal adaptation of Christian thought **18**:703c

National City, city, San Diego County, California, U.S., immediately south of the city of San Diego, on San Diego Bay. Founded by Frank Kimball in 1868, the site was part of the Rancho de la Nación and developed with the growth of San Diego and nearby U.S. naval installations. Manufactures include electronic equipment, missile components, and fabricated metals. Inc. city, 1887. Pop. (1980) 48,772.
32°40′ N, 117°06′ W

National Collegiate Athletic Association (NCAA), founded in the United States in 1906 as an advisory body to establish competition and eligibility rules for intercollegiate athletics. In 1921 the NCAA conducted a track-and-field championship and subsequently extended its jurisdiction over other sports and the various college associations, or conferences. Its National Collegiate Sports Services compiles statistics on college football, baseball, basketball, and track, and its College Athletics Publishing Service publishes rule books and guides on these sports as well as on fencing, gymnastics, lacrosse, ice hockey, soccer, skiing, swimming, and wrestling. In the 1960s and early '70s the NCAA was engaged in a struggle with the Amateur Athletic Union (AAU) for control over amateur athletes in the U.S. NCAA membership by the 1970s included more than 700 institutions; its headquarters were at Kansas City, Mo.

·football's early history in America **7**:508d
·track-and-field history and administration **18**:539b
·wrestling styles and rules **19**:1027c

National Committee of Black Churchmen, an organization founded in New York in 1966, formerly National Committee of Negro Churchmen.

·black church response to Black Power **12**:939g

National Communism, policies based on the principle that in each nation the means of attaining ultimate Communist goals must be dictated by national conditions rather than by a pattern set in another nation. The term is particularly identified with assertions by Eastern European Communists of independence from Soviet leadership or example. Two major factors have influenced the Soviet response to National Communism: (1) the traditional Russian desire for a "friendly" zone along the border with Europe as protection against Western aggression (*see* peaceful coexistence) and (2) the Soviet effort to overcome the Chinese challenge to Soviet hegemony in the Communist world.

The Yugoslav Communist leader Tito first brought National Communism into direct confrontation with Soviet aims when he attempted to pursue an independent foreign policy. Soviet–Yugoslav tensions mounted until, in 1948, Tito's party was expelled from the Cominform (Communist Information Bureau), an organ of international Communist solidarity under Soviet domination, which Tito had enthusiastically helped to found the previous year. After this, purges reminiscent of those Stalin had conducted domestically in the 1930s took place throughout eastern Europe with the goal of eradicating "Titoism" in party ranks. In Poland the top-ranking Communist Władisław Gomułka was stripped of his party and state positions and imprisoned from 1951 to 1955 for his deviation from Stalinist norms. Communist leaders in other countries were executed. Tito himself, a popular national leader, however, managed to defy Stalin and remain in power despite a Soviet military and economic blockade of his country.

The slight domestic liberalization of the Soviet regime that followed Stalin's death in 1953 raised hopes for a parallel liberalization in eastern Europe. That year the liberal Communist Imre Nagy took power in Hungary and instituted reforms that constituted a marked retreat from Socialism. His National Communist program returned retail trade and craft industries to private enterprise, made possible the dissolution of collective farms, de-emphasized industrial investments while increasing agricultural investments, and instituted an official policy of religious tolerance. In 1955 the Soviets restored cordial relations with Tito's Yugoslavia. In 1956 unrest in Poland led to the reassumption of power by Gomułka, who thereafter succeeded in liberalizing Communist rule without at the same time arousing Soviet fears. In the mid-1950s the Soviets began to seek eastern European support in their growing struggle with China to maintain a pre-eminent position in the Communist world. Now nations alienated by any Soviet stifling of National Communism could shift their support to China.

Nevertheless, when in 1956 the liberal Nagy, who had lost his party and state posts in 1955 and regained them after a popular uprising, attempted in Hungary to restore his anti-Soviet regime in a coalition with non-Communists, Soviet troops occupied Hungary. The National Communist János Kádár, who was prepared to be less hostile to the Soviets than Nagy had been, assumed party and state control. Soviet–Yugoslav relations cooled once more when Tito openly took exception to Soviet actions in Hungary; no Yugoslav delegation attended an international Communist solidarity conference held in Moscow in 1957. In the years after 1956 the idea of a polycentric Communist world won the support of the Italian Communist Party, led by Palmiro Togliatti.

In 1968 the Soviets imposed a military siege on Czechoslovakia until the liberal Communist party leader Alexander Dubček was replaced by centrists more responsive to the Soviet will. The Yugoslavs and the Romanians condemned the Soviet action, however, and proclaimed their readiness to resist any such incursions into their own countries.

East European Communist parties
·Albanian Party of Labour programs **1**:420h
·Balkan social reform movement **2**:634a
·Balkan World War II resistance **2**:636b
·Baltic states Marxist organizations **2**:673c
·Bulgarian growth as People's Republic **3**:468d *passim* to 475a
·Czech parties and governments **2**:1196b
·East German political repression **6**:176h
·Estonian membership and activities **6**:968c
·Finnish political role since 1948 **16**:336b
·Gomułka's leadership in Poland **8**:253c
·Latvian administrative conditions **10**:707c
·Polish Communists formation, dissolution, and reemergence **14**:651g *passim* to 654a
·Romanian parties rise and organization **15**:1054a
·Soviet bloc ideological and practical disunity **9**:768f *passim* to 773g
·Tito's wartime resistance and party organization **18**:463a
·nationalism's development and effects **12**:852f

National Conference (of National Football League): *see* National Football League.

National Congress of British West Africa (NCBWA), West African political body organized in 1918 to develop native parliaments.

·Ghana origin, purposes, and extent **19**:783g

National Conservatory of Dramatic Art (France): *see* Conservatoire National d'art Dramatique.

National Conservatory of Music (established 1885), school for music located in New York City.

·Dvořák's directorship in 1892 **5**:1098d

National Convention, French CONVENTION NATIONALE, assembly that governed France from Sept. 21, 1792, until Oct. 26, 1795, during the most critical period of the Revolution.

Elected to provide a new constitution for the nation after the overthrow of the monarchy (Aug. 10, 1792), the National Convention numbered 749 deputies, including businessmen, tradesmen, and many professional men. Among its early acts were the formal abolition of the monarchy (September 21) and the establishment of the republic (September 22).

The struggles between two opposing Revolutionary factions, the Montagnards and the Girondins, dominated the first phase of the Convention (September 1792 to May 1793). The Montagnards favoured granting the lower classes more political power, while the Girondins favoured a bourgeois republic and wanted to reduce the power of Paris over the course of the Revolution. Discredited by a series of defeats in the war they promoted against the anti-Revolutionary European coalition, the Girondins were purged from the Convention by the popular insurrection of May 31 to June 2, 1793.

The Montagnards controlled the Convention during its second phase (June 1793 to July 1794). Because of the war and the internal rebellion, a revolutionary government with dictatorial powers (exercised by the Committee of Public Safety) was set up. As a result, the democratic constitution approved by the Convention on June 24, 1793, was not put into effect, and the Convention lost its legislative initiative; its role was reduced to approving the Committee's suggestions.

Reacting against the Committee's radical policies, many members of the Convention participated in the overthrow of the most prominent member of the Committee, Robespierre, on July 27, 1794 (9 Thermidor). The Thermidorian reaction followed, corresponding to the final phase of the Convention (July 1794 to October 1795). The balance of power in the assembly was then held by the moderate deputies of the Plain (la Plaine). The Girondins were recalled to the Convention, and the leading Montagnards were purged. In August 1795 the Convention approved the constitution for the regime that replaced it, the bourgeois-dominated Directory (1795–99).

·military reforms and levée en masse **7**:719g
·Paine's participation and imprisonment **13**:868h
·popular music banned in Convention hall **14**:809b
·Talleyrand's exile from France **17**:1004d

National Council of Churches of Christ in the U.S.A., an interdenominational organization formed in 1950 by merger of 12 national interdenominational agencies, several of which had been organized as early as 1908. Its purpose was to provide an organization through which member churches could express their common faith and cooperate with one another on programs to which the churches themselves consented or which they initiated. The council has no authority over its constituent churches.

The National Council of Churches initiated many interchurch activities. These included ecumenical study of the faith and order of the church; a revision of the English Bible; publication of religious education, evangelism, and family-life materials; promotion of religious and moral values in broadcasting; encouragement of Church Women United, World Day of Prayer, and Christian Unity Week observances. The council also encouraged the collaboration with overseas churches in the modern use of the mass media; it fought against illiteracy and for what it considered to be relevant education; enlisted local churches to fight against hunger through better agriculture, nutrition, and family planning; and it was concerned with meeting emergency relief needs caused by natural disasters and war.

In addition, it carried on a continuing critical ministry addressed to the secular institutions of society, particularly to government and business. This ministry was concerned with such matters as religious and other civil liberties and with human rights; actions on behalf of racial and social justice; the promotion of basic welfare and prison reforms; and with a theological and political critique of certain phases of U.S. foreign policy, particularly with respect to China and Indochina. This area of activity that considered controversial public matters often brought criticism upon the council.

In the 1970s the constituent denominations moved to restructure the council organization with the intent of highlighting certain issues and developing more flexible modes of operation. The four major program divisions of the council in the 1960s—Christian Life and Mission, Overseas Ministries, Christian Education, and Christian Unity—were reshaped. The membership questioned the effectiveness of the council in dealing with five principal areas of concern: inner renewal of the church for evangelization and mission; relief of human need; struggle for changes in society; improvement of the quality of life in the American culture; and advancement of Christian unity.

In the 1970s the possibility of bringing the Roman Catholic Church and several conservative Protestant denominations into membership was being explored. Also under consideration was the holding of occasional "ecumenical congresses" that would seek to bring all the U.S. religious traditions into dialogue on the urgent issues of the time.

In the early 1970s council membership was made up of 33 Protestant and Eastern Orthodox churches as full members, with more than 40 other church bodies, including conservative Protestants and Roman Catholics, involved in one or more of its programs. The full-member churches had a combined membership of about 42,000,000. The annual budget, more than 60 percent of which was devoted to cooperative ministries overseas, has varied between $14,000,000 and $20,000,000 in recent years.

·Disciples of Christ ecumenism **5**:835d
·organization and purpose **6**:296b

National Covenant, a solemn agreement inaugurated by Scottish Presbyterians on Feb. 28, 1638, in the Greyfriars' churchyard, Edinburgh. It rejected the attempt by King Charles I and William Laud (1573–1645), archbishop of Canterbury, to force Scottish Presbyterians to conform to English episcopacy.

Composed of the King's Confession (1581), additional statements by Alexander Henderson (1583–1646), a leader in the Church of Scotland, and an oath, the National Covenant discussed the Presbyterian faith, denounced the attempted changes, but also urged loyalty to the king. It was signed by many Scotsmen throughout the country.

·Edinburgh's religious struggles **6**:305g
·opposition to Charles I's reforms **3**:242h

National Covenant, Turkish pact adopted by the Turkish national congress in 1919.

·Mustafa Kemal's revolution **2**:256d
·Turkish independence policy **13**:790g

National Czech Evangelical Church, a body formed as a result of the Confessio Bohemica of 1575.

·Moravian Church evangelism and dispersion **12**:436b

national debt: *see* public debt.

Nationaldemokratische Partei Deutschlands (NPD), called in English NATIONAL DEMOCRATIC PARTY OF GERMANY, West German nationalist party calling for German unification and expansion, law and order, and an end to German "guilt" for World War II; the NPD's success in elections of the mid-1960s alarmed West German moderate political parties.

In the 1950s, right-wing parties in West Germany failed to attract voters away from the moderate government that had presided over Germany's recovery. In November 1964, however, right-wing splinter groups united to form the NPD. West German discontent with a lagging economy and with the leadership of Chancellor Ludwig Erhard contributed to the NPD's success in the federal republic's 1967 state elections. At the end of 1967 the party appeared to have established an electorate of 6 to 9 percent of West Germany's national vote, in spite of a party split between Adolf von Thadden and Fritz Thielen, a more moderate leader. Its following was not large enough to upset the established political balance in the state parliaments, but the party's existence threatened West Germany's relations with eastern European countries.

Although the NPD showed growth in the state elections of 1969, it failed to gain representatives to the national assembly, the Bundestag, that year, and it failed even to retain its representation in state parliaments in the elections of early 1971.

·national organizational structure **8**:14c
·Nazi sentiment resurgence **8**:63g
·right-wing threat **8**:124c

National Education Association (NEA), U.S. professional teachers' organization, founded in 1857.

·origin and extension **6**:383a

National Endowment for the Humanities, U.S. organization created by Congress in 1965 for assisting education in the humanities.

·curricula definition **8**:1179g

National Environmental Policy Act of 1969, U.S. law providing for policing maintenance of the environment by the federal government.

·conservation problems and legislation **5**:43g

National Fellowship of Brethren Churches: *see* Brethren.

National Film Archive, located in Pune, India, founded in 1954 to preserve the heritage of the national film industry.

·foundation and goals **9**:301h

National Film Board of Canada, organization which directs the Canadian government's production and distribution of national information films both in Canada and internationally. The nine-member federally appointed board advises the government on all matters relating to the motion picture industry, represents the government in dealings with the commercial movie studios, and sponsors experiments in new film techniques. The Board was established in 1939 by the National Film Act (redefined by the National Film Act of 1950) as an outlet for the British Ministry of Information newsreels and military information films. Based on a plan formulated by John Grierson, the pioneer British documentary film maker who was commissioner of the Film Board for the first six years, it released such quality documentaries as the *World in Action*, introduced in 1942, and *Canada Carries On* newsreels. It absorbed the production and distribution facilities of the Government Motion Picture Bureau (established 1921) in 1941 and expanded into rural areas through a system of itinerant projectionists who travelled rural circuits and visited regional libraries and local industries. Later, local film councils handled distribution of the Board's products and, in urban areas throughout the world, theatres, film libraries, and diplomatic posts distributed the films.

The Board maintains a library of negatives and prints for use by government agencies and in schools, is Canada's major producer of audio-visual aids for the classroom, conducts film study seminars, and, since the 1950s, has produced specialized programs for television.

The National Film Board has an international reputation for productions of consistently high quality, rich in content and experimental in technique. In short subjects, and, since 1963, in feature-length productions, aspects of Canada's social, economic, and cultural life are imaginatively examined. Subjects range from travelogues and environmental topics to the study of highway safety and explanations of such scientific phenomena as DNA (deoxyribonucleic acid, one of the basic components of cell nuclei). In the mid 1960s the project Challenge for Change/Société Nouvelle was initiated to consider such contemporary social problems as poverty and racial discrimination. One of the Board's most outstanding achievements was Labyrinthe (1967), the world's first multimedia exhibition developed for Montreal's Expo 67.

·purpose and international acclaim **3**:732a

National Football League (NFL), the major professional football organization in the United States, founded in 1920 at Canton, Ohio, as the American Professional Football Association. Its first president was Jim Thorpe, an outstanding American Indian athlete. The league adopted its present name in 1922.

The NFL became the strongest U.S. professional league and survived several challenges by rival organizations, the most serious being that of the American Football League in the 1960s. The National and American leagues completed a merger in 1970, creating a 26-team circuit under the name of the older NFL, aligned as follows:

National Conference:
Eastern Division: Dallas Cowboys, New York Giants, Philadelphia Eagles, St. Louis Cardinals, Washington Redskins.
Central Division: Chicago Bears, Detroit Lions, Green Bay Packers, Minnesota Vikings.
Western Division: Atlanta Falcons, Los Angeles Rams, New Orleans Saints, San Francisco Forty-Niners.
American Conference:
Eastern Division: Baltimore Colts, Boston (New England) Patriots, Buffalo Bills, Miami Dolphins, New York Jets.
Central Division: Cincinnati Bengals, Cleveland Browns, Houston Oilers, Pittsburg Steelers.
Western Division: Oakland Raiders, Kansas City Chiefs, San Diego Chargers, Denver Broncos.

The league season culminates with an annual playoff among its top teams for the world championship title. The NFL has headquarters in New York City and since 1962 has maintained a professional football hall of fame in Canton, Ohio. *Major ref.* 7:518c

·merger with American Football League **7**:518h

national forests, in the U.S., forest areas set aside under federal supervision for the purposes of conserving water, timber, wildlife, fish, and other renewable resources and providing recreational areas for the public. National forests, administered by the Forest Service in the Department of Agriculture, number 154 and occupy a total area of over 350,000 sq mi (906,000 sq km). They are managed according to the principle of multiple use, whereby various resources are utilized so that they produce the combination of values that best serves the nation's interests without reducing the land's capability to produce more.

Water from the national forests is used for irrigation and for industrial and domestic uses. Timber is cut under government regulation for wood and paper products, and many wild animals are protected. Livestock are allowed to graze on grasslands established within the National Forest System. The forests are visited annually by large numbers of people seeking relaxation and recreation.

The U.S. national forests began in 1891 as a system of forest reserves, the establishment of which had been urged by Secretary of the Interior Carl Schurz. Pres. Theodore Roosevelt created the Forest Service in 1905 and estab-

lished additional forest reserves. In 1907 the forest reserves were renamed national forests.
·conservation history, practice, and multiple-use concept **5**:43c *passim* to 54e

National Front, Spanish FRENTE NACIONAL, dominant political coalition in Colombia from 1957 to 1974.
·Conservative and Liberal alliance **4**:873a
·Liberal–Conservative coalition **4**:876e

National Front for the Liberation of the South (Vietnam): *see* National Liberation Front.

National Front Party, Spanish FRENTE NACIONAL POPULAR, reorganized in 1961 as POPULAR ACTION, Spanish ACCIÓN POPULAR, Peruvian political party organized by Fernando Belaúnde-Terry in 1956.
·Belaúnde's leadership and programs **14**:136a

National Gallery, British museum of European paintings from the 13th to the 19th century. It was founded in 1824 and located in its present building on Trafalgar Square, London, in 1838. It directs the operation of the adjacent National Portrait Gallery (founded 1856) and from 1897 to 1955 operated the Tate Gallery of British and modern art.

National Gallery of Art, U.S. federally operated museum of art, located at the east end of The Mall, Washington, D.C. It was founded in 1937 when the financier and philanthropist Andrew W. Mellon donated to the government a collection of paintings by European masters and a large sum of money to construct the gallery's Classical-style building. The National Gallery, which opened in 1941, now houses European and American paintings, sculpture, decorative arts, and graphic arts from the 12th to the 20th century. Its activities include research in conservation and art history, special exhibits, and educational programs for adults and children.
·Washington's art collections **19**:631f; map 624

National Gazette, Jeffersonian Republican newspaper edited (1791–93) by Philip Freneau in Philadelphia.
·newspaper publishing history **15**:239e

National Geographic (1888–), in the U.S., monthly journal of the National Geographic Society.
·magazine publishing history **15**:251b

National Geographic Society, U.S. scientific society founded (1888) in Washington, D.C., by a small group of eminent explorers and scientists "for the increase and diffusion of geographic knowledge." By the late 1970s it had become the largest scientific and educational society in the world, with an international membership of 9,500,000. Members receive the society's monthly *National Geographic* magazine and many maps issued as supplements. The society's activities, which have included more than 200 major scientific projects and expeditions, are supported by annual membership dues.

The organization has supported Arctic and Antarctic exploration, including the expeditions of Walter Wellman, Robert E. Peary, Richard E. Byrd, and Paul A. Siple. In the early 1930s its giant stratosphere balloons, launched jointly with the U.S. Army Air Corps, pioneered in scientific exploration of the upper air and attained the greatest elevation reached by man up to that time (13.71 mi [22.06 km]). Other expeditions, often cosponsored with the Smithsonian Institution and other organizations, have studied volcanic eruptions and earthquakes, excavated Machu Picchu, and discovered in Mexico the oldest dated work of man in the New World.

The society also helped explore and bring into the U.S. national park system such treasures as the Valley of Ten Thousand Smokes (Alaska), Carlsbad Caverns and Pueblo Bonito (New Mexico), the giant sequoia trees (California), and, in 1958, Russell Cave (Alabama), in which a record of 9,000 years of North American prehistory was uncovered. Later activities included archaeological examination of the long-forgotten capital of Maya civilization, Dzibilchaltún, in Yucatán, and anthropological research in the 1960s of L.S.B. and Mary Leakey in the Olduvai Gorge of East Africa that has produced remarkably complete fossil remains of pre-human hominids. The society was also one of the many sponsors of the U.S. expedition that ascended Mt. Everest in 1965.

In 1949–56 the society and the California Institute of Technology, Pasadena, produced an unprecedented *Sky Atlas*. Other activities include a school service that issues weekly bulletins to educators, librarians, and students; a news service; publication of scientific books and atlases; and educational television.
·Bell's role in journal improvement **2**:827h
·map format and importance **11**:479g

National Guard, U.S.: *see* militia.

National Health Service, in Great Britain, comprehensive public health service under government administration, established by the National Health Service Act of 1946 and subsequent legislation. Its hospital and specialist services cover all types of care. Doctors and dentists are free to contract in or out of the service and may have private patients while within the scheme. Local health authority services cover maternity and child welfare, health visiting, home nursing, and clinical and ambulance services. The greater part of the cost is met by general taxation.
·dental hospital care service **5**:594h
·economics of health and disease **8**:691a
·founding and implemental legislation **3**:279f
·nursing regulation function **13**:399a
·public and private medical practice **11**:842c
·United Kingdom welfare services **18**:888d

National Health Service Act (1946), British measure that established the National Health Service.
·public health services in U.K. **15**:206a
·terms and significance **3**:279f

National Hockey League (NHL), organization of professional ice hockey teams in North America, formed in 1917 by five Canadian teams, to which the first U.S. team was added in 1924. The NHL became the strongest league in North America and in 1926 took permanent possession of the Stanley Cup, representing world supremacy in ice hockey. League membership rose to 10, then dropped, and held steady at six after 1942. In 1961 an NHL Hockey Hall of Fame was established in Toronto to honour outstanding players, coaches, and other contributors to professional hockey. After a period of expansion and reorganization in 1967 and 1970, the NHL consisted of 14 teams in an Eastern and a Western Division. In 1974 membership was increased to 18 (later 17) teams in four divisions. In 1979 the NHL absorbed four teams from the World Hockey Association; of the league's four divisions, one then had six teams and the others five teams each. At the end of the league's regular winter season, the top teams in each division engage in a play-off for possession of the Stanley Cup. NHL headquarters are in Montreal. *See also* sporting record.
·membership, expansion, and influence **9**:162c

national income accounting 12:847, system of measuring the total production of a nation. The basic concept is that of national product, usually defined as the total market value of goods and services produced for final use, not counting intermediate products such as raw materials and semifinished goods used up in production. If flour is baked into bread, for example, only the bread is counted. National product may be measured not only as the value of the final output but also in terms of the incomes arising from production; then it is called national income.

The text article gives definitions of these and other concepts. It also covers the ways in which the statistics are broken down for analytical purposes and gives examples. In addition, the article covers the uses of national income accounting, the sources from which the data are drawn, and some of the problems of measurement involved.

REFERENCES in other text articles:
·budgets and budgeting by government **3**:443c
·capital valuation and inherent problems **3**:800f
·defense-spending measurement **19**:551g
·distribution of income **19**:673f; tables 675
·econometric model development **6**:201b
·economic planning adjustments **6**:260e
·expenditure analysis for sectors of various nations, table 1 **5**:105
·forecasting of GNP components **6**:211c
·income determination theory and models **9**:264c; graph 265
·per capita income as criterion of economic development **6**:202a
·price indexes and economic analysis **14**:998d

RELATED ENTRIES in the *Ready Reference and Index:*
gross national product; income, national; income, personal

National Industrial Relations Court, established in the United Kingdom by the Industrial Relations Act of 1971 (*q.v.*).
·membership and function **18**:881h

National Institute of Agrarian Reform, Spanish INSTITUTO NACIONAL DE REFORMA AGRARIA (INRA), Cuban Cabinet ministry created in 1959.
·reform attempts and results **5**:358c

National Institutes of Health (NIH), in the U.S., agency of the Public Health Service of the Department of Health, Education, and Welfare. With the objective of improving the health of the American people, it conducts and supports biomedical research into the causes, prevention, and cure of disease. Its major components are the National Cancer Institute, National Heart, Lung, and Blood Institute, National Library of Medicine, National Institute of Arthritis, Metabolism, and Digestive Diseases, National Institute of Allergy and Infectious Diseases, National Institute of Child Health and Human Development, National Institute of Dental Research, National Institute of Environmental Health Sciences, National Institute of General Medical Sciences, National Institute of Neurological and Communicative Disorders and Stroke, National Eye Institute, National Institute on Aging, Clinical Center, Fogarty International Center, Division of Computer Research and Technology, Division of Research Resources, Division of Research Services, and Division of Research Grants.
·Kidney Transplant Registry **18**:630b
·medical research service **19**:631f

National Insurance Act (1911), British act of Parliament that established national unemployment insurance.
·hospital insurance coverage **8**:1115b
·Lloyd George's social legislation **3**:274f
·Lloyd George's social reforms **11**:7f

National Intelligence and Security Organization, also called SAVAK, founded in Iran in 1957 to maintain internal security.
·Iranian police services **9**:827e

national interest, that which is believed to be in the best interests of a country as a whole and that may serve as the basis of its foreign policy.
·economic planning consensus **6**:261e
·state and individual in conflict **17**:614d

National Invitational Tournament (NIT), collegiate basketball competition initiated in the United States in 1938 by New York City basketball writers and held annually since then in Madison Square Garden under the auspices of the Metropolitan College Association. It is a single-elimination tournament (a

loss brings elimination) with 16 of the nation's outstanding college teams invited to participate. For winners, see sporting record.
·competition among amongdependent colleges 2:753b

National Iranian Oil Company, founded in 1951 to process and market Iran's oil resources.
·international marketing agreements 9:825c

nationalism 12:851, an ideology and sentiment that involves the commitment of the individual's secular loyalty to the nation-state.
The text article covers the political philosophy and history of nationalism, its emergence as a prime determining force in European politics during the 17th and 18th centuries, and its impact on the course of world politics during the 19th and 20th centuries.

nationalism, in music, stylistic movement in which composers attempted to produce music that reflected a particular national or ethnic spirit, in opposition to the nonregional or international style more typical of the mainstream of Western music. The greatest surge of nationalism in music occurred during the 19th-century awakening of political nationalism that made its influence felt in both literature and art. Various national schools occasionally rose to prominence before 1800 and then declined. Even in the 19th century, it is possible to speak of "northern" and "southern" trends within the framework of an international style. But these were merely regional variations of a basic general movement dominated by Italy, France, and the German-speaking countries, particularly Austria. The reaction of the more peripheral countries of Europe against the artistic dominance of those central nations was to be expected.

The earliest important exponent of nationalist music was the Russian composer Mikhail Glinka, whose operas *A Life for the Tsar* (first performed, 1836) and *Ruslan and Lyudmila* (1842) provided the impetus for the great flourishing of Russian national music. His music, as well as that of his contemporary Aleksandr Dargomyzhsky, set the stage for the famous Russian Five of the following generation: Mily Balakirev, Aleksandr Borodin, César Cui, Modest Mussorgsky, and Nikolay Rimsky-Korsakov. Peter Tchaikovsky, who composed such obviously nationalistic works as *Marche slave* and the *1812 Overture*, was frequently criticized by his compatriots for having been influenced by the German symphonic tradition.

No other national group achieved the prominence of the Russian school, although many small countries produced talented composers with definite nationalistic inclinations. Foremost was Czechoslovakia (Bohemia), whose peasant culture inspired the music of Bedřich Smetana and Antonín Dvořák. The music of

the Scandinavian composers—among them Niels Gade of Denmark, Edvard Grieg of Norway, and Jean Sibelius of Finland—tends to exhibit a less deeply nationalistic colour than that of its Russian and Bohemian counterparts.

Polish music, as represented by the salon piano pieces of Frédéric Chopin and the virtuoso violin works of Henri Wieniawski, only occasionally is tinged with patriotism; most of its works are predominantly international in character. Likewise, the Spanish composers Isaac Albéniz, Enrique Granados, and Manuel de Falla produced music that, although grounded in the Spanish idiom, also showed the influence of French Impressionism. Hungarian music was represented by Ferenc Erkel, who wrote a number of operas on Hungarian literary themes, and Franz Liszt, who created a rather popularized "gypsy" style in his piano music. That style was generally assumed to represent the authentic Hungarian folk idiom, a supposition that was proved incorrect in the 20th century by the folk-music research and nationalistic compositions of Béla Bartók and Zoltán Kodály.

England, always extremely susceptible to foreign influence, spent almost all of the 19th century in the shadow of the international style. A belated surge of nationalism may be observed in the music of Sir Edward Elgar (died 1934) and particularly Ralph Vaughan Williams (died 1958), although both men remained receptive to continental influences. In the United States, the powerful vogue of European music tended to stifle any independent national tendencies. The 19th-century composer-pianist Louis Gottschalk did make occasional use of American Indian and Negro melodies in compositions that were extremely popular in their day; but Charles Ives (died 1954), who worked in almost total obscurity, was the true pioneer of U.S. national music.

The above-mentioned composers employed a variety of techniques in writing music to embody the spirit of their homeland and its people. They often incorporated authentic folk tunes or national hymns into their works or created melodies that resembled folk songs. They adopted the characteristic rhythms and scales of the authentic peasant songs and dances and wrote operas and tone poems based upon folk legends, often depicting the exploits of national heroes.
·folk music as object of pride 7:469h
·Ghana ideology effect on art 8:144g
·music of Romantic era 12:712e passim to 713h
·opera history outside European mainstream 13:592c
·stylistic uniformity within nations 2:130c
·Wagner's music as expression 19:517c

nationalism, economic: see autarky.

Nationalist China: see Taiwan.

Nationalist Party (China): see Kuomintang.

Nationalist Party, Lithuanian right-wing political party which overthrew a left-democratic regime in 1926.
·Smetona's authoritarian government 2:674g

Nationalist Party, political party of Northern Ireland which advocates reunion with the Republic of Ireland.
·Northern Ireland's politico-religious issues 13:241c

Nationalist Party (Philippines): see Partido Nacionalista.

Nationalists, name adopted by the opponents of the Spanish Republic during the Spanish Civil War.
·Civil War foreign intervention 19:979a

Nationalities Law of 1868, in Hungarian history, act that defined the status of national minorities in Hungary by guaranteeing equal rights to all Hungarian citizens. When Hungary attained internal autonomy (Austro-Hungarian Compromise of 1867), it had to confront the problem of organizing a viable state composed of a variety of different nationality groups. In 1868 the Hungarian parliament approved the Nationalities Law, which asserted that Hungary was a single, unified state and that all its citizens were entitled to equal political rights.

Although the law made Magyar the official language of the Hungarian parliament and administration, and of its courts of law, universities, and county councils, minority languages could be used in county assemblies and in correspondence between the local government bodies and the central authorities. Also, in the local law courts citizens could use their native languages, presiding judges were required to know the local languages, and verdicts had to be translated for all the participants in each case.

In counties dominated by non-Magyars, members of the national minorities were to fill the chief administrative positions; bureaucratic officials serving in non-Magyar communities had to use the local language. Furthermore, state schools operating in areas where a national group lived together in "considerable numbers" were to use the language of the national group. Churches that ran their own schools were entitled to choose the language of instruction.

The law, which attempted to reach a compromise between Magyar nationalism and the minority nationality groups, satisfied neither the Magyar chauvinists, who jealously guarded their exclusive privileges (*e.g.*, access to jobs in the government bureaucracy and the professions), nor the minority leaders, who demanded the formation of a federation of autonomous national regions or of a multinational state. Within a few years the law demonstrated its ineffectiveness; the Hungarian government failed actively to enforce it, and later, despite the law, Kálmán Tisza (prime minister 1875–90) introduced a policy of Magyarization throughout Hungary.

·minorities problem legislation **9**:37e

nationality, as a legal relationship, denotes membership in a nation or sovereign state. In general, nationality implies duties of allegiance on the part of the individual and of protection on the part of the state.

Individuals, companies (corporations), ships, and aircraft all have nationality for legal purposes. It is in reference to natural persons, however, that the term finds most frequent use. Nationality is in fact commonly regarded as an inalienable right of every human being. Thus, the UN Universal Declaration of Human Rights (1948) states that "everyone has the right to a nationality" and that "no one shall be arbitrarily deprived of his nationality." Nationality is of cardinal importance to every person because it is mainly through nationality that the individual comes within the scope of international law and his access to the political and economic rights and privileges conferred by modern states on their nationals.

The state, through constitutional and statutory provisions, sets the criteria for determining who shall be its nationals. The right of a state to confer its nationality is, however, not unlimited, for otherwise it might impinge upon other states' rights to determine what persons shall be their nationals. By one rule of international customary law, a person who is born within a state's territory and subject to its jurisdiction acquires that state's nationality by the fact of such birth. By another rule, one has a nationality as an inheritance from one or both of one's parents. States vary in the use of the two principles.

When one state cedes territory to another, inhabitants of the region that is ceded commonly have an opportunity to acquire that state's nationality. Practice, however, supports the idea that the individuals concerned should be allowed a free choice. Another method of acquiring nationality is through the process of naturalization (*q.v.*).

In international law, nationality assumes significance in a variety of circumstances. In extradition treaties, for example, states include clauses making it optional for them to surrender aliens and even their own nationals. If a state desires to expel a person from its territory, only the state of which the person is a national is obligated to receive him.

A state's failure to afford reasonable protection to aliens may lead to claims by other states, the adjudication of which will require the resolving of questions concerning the nationality of claimants.

Differences in national legislation and the absence of universally binding laws or practices have given rise to a number of unsettled questions on nationality; these include the problem of dual or multiple nationality and the problem of stateless persons—that is, persons having no nationality.

·lawsuit participation procedure **15**:7f

nationalization, alteration or termination of control or ownership of private property by the state. It is historically a more recent development than and differs in motive and degree from "expropriation" or "eminent domain," which is the right of government to take property for particular public purposes (such as the construction of roads, reservoirs, or hospitals), normally accompanied by the payment of compensation. Nationalization is often, though by no means exclusively, associated with the implementation of communist or socialist theories of government, as was the case in the transfer of industrial, banking, and insurance enterprises to the state in Russia after 1918 and the nationalization of the coal, electricity, gas, and transport industries in the United Kingdom and France between 1945 and 1950. More recently, the conscious implementation of political and economic doctrine has on occasion become mixed with resentment of foreign control over industries upon which the state may be largely dependent, as in the nationalization of the oil industries in Mexico in 1938 and Iran in 1951, and in the nationalization of foreign businesses in Cuba in 1960. A third motive for recent nationalizations may be the belief in some developing countries that state control of various industrial operations is at least temporarily necessary because of the lack of a developed capital market or supply of entrepreneurial talent in the domestic private sector.

Nationalization may occur through the transfer of the assets of the nationalized companies to the state or through the transfer of the share capital, leaving the company in existence to carry on its business under state control. Questions of international law normally arise only when the property is owned either by aliens or by companies in which aliens have a large shareholding interest. It has become established as a matter of general principle that aliens carrying on activities or owning property in foreign states are entitled to treatment in accordance with a "minimum standard of international law." As a result of a number of diplomatic episodes and international arbitrations, it is acknowledged, at least in relation to isolated takings of private property, that such taking is lawful only if accompanied by the payment of fair compensation. It remains a matter of controversy whether these precedents apply with equal force when the scale of the taking of alien property is expanded from isolated expropriation to large-scale nationalization. No international tribunal has yet been placed in a position to express an authoritative view on the controversy.

States whose nationals tend to be investors are placing increasing reliance upon specific treaty clauses providing for the protection of investments. The United States, in particular, since the end of World War II has entered into treaties of friendship, commerce, and navigation which contain mutual undertakings on this point, coupled with clauses conferring compulsory jurisdiction upon the International Court of Justice. Insurance against nationalization is also offered by the U.S. government.

Nationalization cases with particularly far-reaching consequences are those involving waterways and other transport passes. The nationalization of the Suez Canal Company in 1956 by Egypt is said to have resulted in the invasion of the canal zone by the French and British (coinciding with the invasion of the Sinai Peninsula by the Israelis), whose oil supplies depended in large measure upon access to the canal. The canal was closed in 1956 as a result of the war, and again closed in June 1967 as a result of a new Arab-Israeli conflict.

The Panama Canal has a similar potential for crisis. The canal is essential to U.S. commerce; on the other hand, U.S. control of the Canal Zone is strongly resented by Panamanian nationalists.

·Austrian economic planning **2**:445g
·auto industry in West Germany **2**:531e
·British economic planning results **3**:277f
·Cárdenas' industrial experimentation **3**:875c
·French secularization of church lands **17**:1003h
·Irish state corporations **9**:884f
·public enterprise in England, France, and Italy **15**:199c
·Soviet economic planning origins **6**:256e
·Soviet industrial centralization **16**:71d
·United Kingdom economic structure **18**:880h

National Labor Relations Board, in the United States, an independent federal agency created by the U.S. Congress in 1935 to administer the National Labor Relations Act (the Wagner Act); the act was amended in 1947 (the Taft–Hartley Act) and in 1959 (the Landrum–Griffin Act). The primary functions of the NLRB are (1) to determine by secret-ballot elections conducted by the agency whether employees wish to be represented by labour unions in collective bargaining; and (2) to prevent or correct unfair labour practices by employers or unions. The agency deals with labour disputes by means of investigation and informal settlements or through quasi-judicial proceedings. The general counsel of the board is responsible for issuing formal complaints and for prosecuting complaints and court cases. The NLRB has no independent power to enforce its orders but may seek enforcement through a U.S. court of appeals; parties to the orders may also seek judicial review. The board may not act on its own motion: charges and representation petitions must be initiated by employers, individuals, or unions.

·collective bargaining and labour board **15**:1140a
·provisions, union aid, and significance **18**:990f

National League, the oldest existing major league professional baseball organization in the United States. The league began play in 1876 as the National League of Professional Baseball Clubs, replacing the failed National Association of Professional Baseball Players. The league's supremacy has been challenged by several rival organizations over the years, beginning with the American Association in 1882–91. Of these, only the American League, formed in 1900, has survived. Champions of the National and American leagues have engaged in a year-end World Series since 1903 to decide the world championship of professional baseball.

Early in the 1970s, the National League consisted of 12 teams aligned in two divisions. In the East were the Chicago Cubs, Montreal (Quebec) Expos, New York Mets, Philadelphia Phillies, Pittsburgh Pirates, and St. Louis Cardinals. In the West were the Atlanta Braves, Cincinnati Reds, Houston Astros, Los Angeles Dodgers, San Diego Padres, and San Francisco Giants.

National League for Nursing, U.S. organization founded in 1952 in New York City.
·nursing organizations and programs **13**:399e

National Lending Library for Science and Technology, part of the British Library (*q.v.*).

National Liberal Party, Danish political party formed in 1848.
·Schleswig–Holstein question **16**:324h

National Liberal Party, German NATIONALLIBERALE PARTEI, political party active first in Prussia from 1867, then in the German Empire during the period 1871–1918. With purely middle class support, the National Liberals hoped to make the government under Chancellor Otto von Bismarck less autocratic. Originally a moderate section of the old Prussian Liberals, the nucleus of the National Liberals broke from that party in 1867 in support of Bismarck's drive to unite Germany under Prussia. From 1871 until 1879 the National Liberals, led by Rudolf von Bennigsen and Johannes von Miquel (*qq.v.*), supported Bismarck enthusiastically in the Reichstag (Imperial Diet) and constituted a virtual government party, winning more seats than any other party. Conflict with Bismarck arose in the years 1877–79 because of National Liberal demands for a parliamentary ministry; and this was exacerbated by disagreement over taxes when the National Liberals wanted to give the Reichstag control over revenues. They split over this issue in 1880 after losing many seats in the election of 1879. In 1890 they were in coalition with the Conservatives in support of the government, but thereafter their influence waned.
·Bismarck's domestic political struggles **2**:1080a *passim* to 1082e
·German political development **8**:112e
·Stresemann's political career **17**:732d

National Liberation, Committee of, Italian coalition established Sept. 9, 1943.
·resistance movement growth **9**:1170a

National Liberation Federation, British political organization founded in 1877 that followed the policies of Joseph Chamberlain.
·British 19th-century political growth **3**:271h

National Liberation Front (Algeria): *see* Front de Libération Nationale.

National Liberation Front (Greece): *see* EAM-ELAS.

National Liberation Front (NLF), official name NATIONAL FRONT FOR THE LIBERATION OF THE SOUTH, Vietnamese MAT-TRAN DAN-TOC GIAI-PHONG MIEN-NAM, Vietnamese political organization formed Dec. 20, 1960, to effect the overthrow of the South Vietnamese government and the reunification of North and South Vietnam. An overtly Communist People's Revolutionary Party was established in 1962 as a central component of the NLF, but both the military arm, the Viet Cong (*q.v.*), and the political organization of the NLF included many non-Communists. The NLF was represented by its own diplomatic staffs in all Communist countries and in several neutral countries.

Unlike the Viet Minh (anti-French guerrilla force, many members of which became part of the Viet Cong), it did not establish a provisional government until June 1969, when the Provisional Revolutionary Government (PRG) of South Vietnam was announced. The PRG became an ever-increasing force against the government of Nguyen Van Thieu. As U.S. support for Thieu waned, and his military base weakened, Thieu was finally forced to resign in April 1975. Although two presidents came in rapid succession, the PRG reached its objective, the collapse of the Saigon government, on April 30. On the reunification of Vietnam in 1976, the NLF joined the Vietnamese Communist Party and the other political organizations in forming a National United Front. *See also* Nguyen Huu Tho.
·origin and position in South Vietnam **19**:138c
·South Vietnam's revolutionary politics **19**:143g
·Vietnamese insurrection struggle **19**:130e

National Liberation Front, the sole recognized political party of Yemen (Aden).
·British ouster from Arabia **1**:1051b
·struggle for independence **19**:1082g

national liberation movement, organized group in rebellion against a colonial government, against a national government alleged to be dominated by a foreign imperial power, or against almost any government charged with corruption or inefficiency. Generally arising in underdeveloped countries, such movements aim to establish independent governments and economic and social reforms.

The term has no precise definition. National liberation movements are as varied as the Algerian FLN (Front de Libération Nationale), the Vietnamese NLF (National Liberation Front), the Cuban 26th of July Movement, the "Free India" battalion of Subhas Chandra Bose, and the Hukbalahap movement in the Philippines. They may be wholly indigenous in origin or dependent on a foreign power. Some of them have commanded the support and sympathy of a majority of their countrymen; others have been led by determined minorities seeking power through force and extralegal means.

Most national liberation movements have been hostile to the Western powers, having been organized, in the main, in the former colonies of those powers. The movements often espouse radical Socialist ideologies. Lenin called the rebellions of such groups "wars of national liberation," which he considered to be essential to the overthrow of "capitalist imperialism," and Communist parties often support or participate in them.
·anticolonial movements **4**:902d
·Gandhi's nonviolent activism **13**:850b
·Mao guerrilla warfare guidelines **8**:460f

National Library of Medicine, in Bethesda, Md., the chief source of medical information in the United States. The library, since 1956, is a component of the National Institutes of Health of the Department of Health, Education, and Welfare.
·automated library systems **10**:873e
·medical resource proliferation **11**:812e
·Medlars system **9**:573c

National Lutheran Council: *see* Lutheran Council in the United States of America.

National Meteorological Center, one of the agencies of the U.S. National Weather Service.
·weather prediction and forecast **2**:327f

National Military Organization: *see* Irgun Zvai Leumi.

National Ministries, Board of, missionary division of the American Baptist Churches in the U.S., founded in 1832 as the American Baptist Home Mission Society.
·formation and functions **2**:715c

National Mod, music festival held annually in Scotland to help preserve the Gaelic tradition.
·sponsorship and purpose **16**:411a

national monuments, in the U.S., areas reserved by act of Congress or presidential proclamation for the protection of objects or places of historic, prehistoric, or scientific interest. They include natural physical features, remains of Indian cultures, and places of historic importance.

In 1906 Pres. Theodore Roosevelt established the first national monument, Devils Tower in Wyoming, under the American Antiquities Act passed earlier that year. Many more were added during the next few years. Their jurisdiction was unified in 1933 under the National Park Service in the Department of the Interior.

National Museum of Anthropology (Mexico City): *see* Museo Nacional de Antropología.

National Nonpartisan League (U.S.): *see* Nonpartisan League.

National Oceanic and Atmospheric Administration, exploratory and predictive organization established in 1970 as part of the U.S. Department of Commerce.
·weather prediction and forecast **2**:327f

National Ocean Survey, formerly U.S. COAST AND GEODETIC SURVEY, U.S. agency within the Department of Commerce.
·control point location density **11**:482a
·formation and responsibilities **6**:83e
·seismograph station network **16**:492d

National Organization of Cypriot Struggle: *see* EOKA.

national origins system, U.S. policy of restricted immigration (1924–68).
·basis, effect, and changes **18**:931a
·eugenic immigration restrictions **6**:1024a
·quota system establishment **12**:188h
·U.S. immigration policy **18**:988b

National Pact, Lebanese agreement of 1943 between Christians and Muslims.
·Christian–Muslim political balance **17**:958h

National Palace Museum, collection of the Republic of China, at Taipei, Taiwan, formerly housed at Peking.
·Taipei's cultural features **17**:994f; illus.

national parks, areas set aside by a national government for the preservation of plants, animals, landscapes, or a combination of these in their natural state for the purpose of public recreation. National parks in the U.S. and Canada protect both land and wildlife, those in Britain mainly the land, and those in Africa primarily animals. Other countries with large national parks are Brazil, Japan, India, West Germany, the Soviet Union, and Australia.

The national parks of these various countries vary greatly in their effectiveness in protecting their resources. Most national parks have a built-in paradox: although they often depend for their existence on tourism stimulated by public interest in nature, the preservation of their wildlife depends on its not being molested. This paradox is usually resolved by allowing visitors to travel only within limited areas in the park. *See also* nature reserve; national forests; national monuments. *Major ref.* **5**:53a
·African wildlife management **1**:197g
·history and philosophy **5**:43a
·Rocky Mountain area conservation **15**:968d
·South American conservation **17**:90h
·Zairian sites of distinction **19**:1122c

National Park Service, agency of the U.S. federal government, in the Department of the Interior, established (1916) to administer national parks, national monuments, and historical parks and sites.
·environmental management practices **5**:53a
·governmental support of museum **12**:652b
·history and philosophy **5**:43b

National Party, Spanish PARTIDO NACIONAL, Chilean right-wing coalition formed in 1965.
·formation and right-wing coalition **4**:258f

National Party, Arabic AL-ḤIZB AL-WAṬANĪ, an extremist nationalist organization, founded in Alexandria, Egypt, on Oct. 22, 1907, by Muṣṭafā Kāmil. The party demanded full Egyptian independence, the elimination of all foreign troops from Egyptian soil, and the inclusion of the Sudan in the new Egyptian state. The National Party depended on mass emotion and violent action to achieve its ends. Through its newspaper, *al-Liwāʾ* ("The Standard"), published in Arabic, English, and

French, Kāmil rallied Egyptians to his party and attracted funds to establish several extremist schools.

Kāmil's death early in 1908 and the assumption of leadership by Muḥammad Fāris, a man lacking Kāmil's dynamic appeal, diminished the party's potential force. At the end of World War I in 1918, it was no longer strong enough to represent the Egyptian people aggressively in negotiations with the British, a function assumed by the newly formed Wafd. The National Party survived, however, as a minor party until 1952, when it was dissolved by the military government of the Revolutionary Command Council.

National Party, one of the two major political parties of New Zealand, representing a moderately conservative point of view.
·constituency and ideology **13**:48g
·New Zealand history and politics **13**:55b

National Party, Afrikaans NASIONALE PARTY, in office in South Africa from 1948. Its following includes most of the Dutch-descended Afrikaners and many English-speaking whites. It follows the policy of apartheid ("apartness" in Afrikaans), or separate development of the races, considered by many to be a rationalization for discrimination against nonwhites.
·origin, election success, and philosophy **17**:295d

National Party, Turkish political party founded in 1948 by conservative forces.
·Kemalist government opposition **13**:792e

National Physical Laboratory, English institution established in 1900 at the behest of the Royal Society and now under the Department of Industry, located at Teddington, in the Greater London borough of Richmond upon Thames.
·industrial research history **15**:739h

National Popular Liberation Army (Greece): *see* EAM-ELAS.

National Popular Rally, French RASSEMBLEMENT NATIONAL POPULAIRE, French Fascist political party founded during World War II by Marcel Déat (*q.v.*).
·organization and aims **7**:187g

National Primitive Baptist Convention, Inc., an association of independent Negro Baptist churches in the U.S. that were joined in a national convention in 1907. The convention developed from Negro congregations formed after the Civil War by emancipated slaves who had previously attended Primitive Baptist churches with whites. The white people helped the Negroes set up their own congregations and ordained ministers for them.

Although they have followed much of the doctrine and practice of the white Primitive Baptists, the Negro Primitive Baptists have set up a national convention and have established Sunday schools and aid societies, all of which are rejected by the whites. In 1972 the convention reported 1,645,000 members.

National Radio Astronomy Observatory, at Green Bank, W.Va., the site of a partially steerable parabolic antenna, 300 feet (about 90 metres) in diameter, that was completed in 1962. The antenna depends on the Earth's rotation to bring celestial objects within its narrow east–west range and thus can be aimed at any source for no more than a few minutes.

In 1965 a fully steerable 140-foot (43-metre) radio telescope was completed at Green Bank. In 1970–71 the 300-foot telescope was resurfaced with aluminum mesh to allow operation at shorter wavelengths.
·meridian transit dish installation **18**:102e

National Reclamation Act (1902), U.S. legislation that set aside the proceeds of public land sales to finance construction and maintenance of irrigation projects in arid regions.
·Roosevelt conservation plan and provisions **18**:984f

National Recovery Administration (NRA), U.S. government agency established in the first administration of Pres. Franklin D. Roosevelt to stimulate business recovery through fair practice codes during the Great Depression.

The NRA was an essential element in the National Industrial Recovery Act (June 1933), which authorized the president to institute industry-wide codes intended to eliminate

The NRA Blue Eagle holding Uncle Sam aloft; cover of *Vanity Fair*, September 1934
The Granger Collection

unfair trade practices, reduce unemployment, establish minimum wages and maximum hours, and guarantee the right of labour to bargain collectively.

The agency ultimately established 557 basic codes and 208 supplementary codes that affected some 22,000,000 workers. Companies that subscribed to the NRA codes were allowed to display a Blue Eagle emblem, symbolic of cooperation with the NRA. Although the codes were hastily drawn and overly complicated and reflected the interests of big business at the expense of the consumer and small businessman, they nevertheless did improve labour conditions in some industries and also aided the unionization movement. The NRA ended when it was invalidated by the Supreme Court in 1935, but many of its provisions were included in subsequent legislation.

National Industrial Recovery Act
·administration and provisions **18**:989g
·constitutionality and legislative power **5**:91b
·economic recovery measures **6**:246h
·public works funds and business codes **15**:1139d

National Review, U.S. conservative national newspaper founded in 1955.
·magazine publishing history **15**:256d

National Revolutionary Party, Mexican political party formed in 1929 by Plutarco Elías Calles to stabilize the gains of the revolution, now the Partido Revolucionario Institucional (*q.v.*).
·Mexican factional membership and purpose **12**:86e

National Rifle Association (NRA), governing organization for the sport of shooting with rifles and pistols, formed in Great Britain in 1860. An organization of the same name and purpose was formed in the United States in 1871 and by the mid-1970s claimed a membership of about 1,100,000 target shooters, hunters, gun collectors, gunsmiths, and police. Among its more publicized activities in the 1960s and 1970s was highly effective political lobbying against various legislative proposals for control of firearms. Both the British and American groups sponsor regional and national competitions and select teams for international events. The British NRA has its headquarters at Woking, Surrey, the American in Washington, D.C.
·target shooting history **16**:704b

National Road (U.S.): *see* Cumberland Road.

National Round, in archery, a target shooting event consisting of 48 arrows (eight ends of six arrows each) shot from a distance of 60 yards (55 metres) and 24 arrows (four ends) shot from 50 yards (46 metres).

national seashores, in the U.S., coastal areas reserved by the federal government for recreational use by the public. Cape Hatteras, North Carolina, was established as the first national seashore in 1953. Others have since been added and include Cape Cod (Massachusetts), Padre Island (Texas), Point Reyes (California), Fire Island (New York), Assateague Island (Maryland and Virginia), Cape Lookout (North Carolina), Gulf Islands (Florida and Mississippi), Canaveral (Florida), and Cumberland Island (Georgia). Their attractions include beaches, waterfowl and other wildlife, and fishing.

National Security Act (1947), act passed by the U.S. Congress and amended in 1949, which created a coordinated command of the U.S. armed forces under the Department of Defense (known from 1947 to 1949 as the National Military Establishment). The act also created the National Security Council, within the Executive Office of the President, to advise the president with respect to the integration of domestic, foreign, and military policies relating to national security. Its membership includes the president, vice president, secretary of state, and secretary of defense. The Central Intelligence Agency, under the National Security Council, was also created by the act.
·army control reorganization provisions **18**:993e
·intelligence agencies organization **9**:682c

National Socialism, in Germany, the name of a movement led by the Nationalsozialistische Deutsche Arbeiterpartei (National Socialist German Workers' Party), known as the Nazi Party. Its leader from 1933 to 1945 was Adolf Hitler. *See also* Nazi Party.
·Bauhaus closing and effect **12**:172h
·Christian status and Vatican concordat **4**:510h
·effects on city government **4**:647f
·German resurgence and reparations **8**:63g
·Heidegger's human malady interpretation **8**:740e
·Ludendorff's theory of total war **19**:564f
·Lutheran crisis in Germany **11**:198c
·Mann's early German loyalty **11**:456e
·mass society relationship theories **11**:602e
·state and nationalism **17**:612g

National Socialist German Workers' Party: *see* Nazi Party.

National Socialist Party, Bohemian political party formed in the 1890s by Václav Klofáč.
·Bohemian nationalist factions **2**:1194f

Nationalsozialistische Deutsche Arbeiterpartei: *see* Nazi Party.

National Spiritualist Association of Churches (NSAC), Spiritualist association in the U.S., founded in 1893.
·orientation and functions **17**:512b

National Theatre, first Bengali professional theatre company, founded in 1872.
·founding, tour results, and influence **17**:167a

National Theatre Act (1949), British law establishing a national theatre.
·grant utilization **18**:234c

National Theatre Company, government financed British national theatre company opened in London in 1964 with Sir Laurence Olivier as director.
·location and financing **18**:234c

National Trust for Historic Preservation (NTHP), U.S. society chartered by Congress in 1949 to preserve and administer for the public benefit donated sites, buildings, and objects significant in U.S. history and culture.

National Trust for Places of Historic Interest or Natural Beauty, British society founded in 1895 that was incorporated by the National Trust Act (1907) and empowered to acquire by gift, purchase, or devise sites and buildings in Great Britain to be held in perpetuity for the public. The trust has been given many important town and country houses in addition to places of scenic beauty in the United Kingdom. It carries out its work under several acts of Parliament under which tax concessions can be obtained in respect of houses made over to the trust.
·architecture conservation program **2**:58e
·England's conservation programs **6**:868f

National Union, South African political party formed in 1894 in the Transvaal to agitate for union with Cape Colony.
·Cape Colony struggle with Transvaal **15**:814a

National Union Catalog, catalog replacing the *Library of Congress Catalog*, established 1901, began publication in 1948.
·bibliographic material unification **2**:978e

National Union Convention, also called the ARM-IN-ARM-CONVENTION (Aug. 14–16, 1866), political coalition of Pres. Andrew Johnson's supporters, who met in an effort to gain control of the Republican Party in order to implement a conciliatory national policy toward the South, recently defeated in the Civil War. Meeting in Philadelphia, the convention attracted many war Democrats, moderate Southerners, some Republicans, and a few Whigs, especially from border states. Hoping to abate sectionalism, the convention endorsed presidential Reconstruction policies and declared that the Southern states had a right to be represented in Congress. This platform was in direct opposition to that of the Radical Republicans (*q.v.*), who favoured congressional control of Reconstruction and who resisted the return to power of the white Southern planter aristocracy. The National Union candidates were overwhelmingly defeated in the congressional election of 1866, when the Radicals won a resounding victory.
·Johnson Reconstruction reaction **18**:972c

National Unionist Party (NUP), Sudanese political party formed in 1951.
·anti-colonialist movement **13**:114f

National Union of Popular Forces, Moroccan political party formed in 1958 by Abd er-Rahim Bouabid.
·Moroccan independent party formation **13**:171b

National Union of Tanganyika Workers, founded in 1964, the only group authorized to represent workers in Tanzania.
·labour administration in Tanzania **17**:1032b

National Union of Women's Suffrage Societies, British organization founded in 1867.
·Mill's association with early suffrage **12**:199e

National Unity Committee, Turkish provisional government installed by a military coup in 1960.

National University of Ireland, founded in 1909, composed of four colleges, at Dublin, Cork, Galway, and Maynooth.
·founding and organization **9**:887e

National Urban League, U.S. voluntary service agency of business, labour, civic, and religious leaders established to eliminate all forms of discrimination based on race or colour and to achieve full citizenship for Negroes. Originally known as the National League on Urban Conditions Among Negroes, the League was created in 1910 with the combination of several groups that had been working on the urban problems of housing, employment, family disorganization, and juvenile delinquency. Its early action was aimed at opening new opportunities in industry to Negroes and at assisting newly arrived migrants from the rural South in their adjustment to city life. Current activities include efforts to ensure equal job opportunity, guidance and counselling services, and enlarged housing opportunities.

The Urban League claimed more than 50,000 members in over 90 local groups by the 1970s. It maintains its headquarters in New York City.
·black church contributions in 20th century **12**:939a

National Zoological Park, Washington, D.C., established under the Smithsonian Institution by acts of Congress in 1889 and 1890, when a 71-hectare (176-acre) site in the wooded valley of Rock Creek, a tributary of the Potomac, was purchased. The Smithsonian was authorized to transfer to the zoo a group of living animals kept in small cages at the rear of the Smithsonian Institution. Various government departments, including the foreign consular service, donated specimens, and many exotic specimens have been received as gifts from foreign governments. The zoo developed one of the finest small mammal collections in the world and became famous for breeding pygmy hippopotamuses. Rarities include a white Bengal tiger, received in 1960, and a pair of pandas, gift of mainland China in 1972. A remodelling program in the 1960s resulted in the construction of an outstanding great flight cage and new hoofed-stock areas. The zoo has about 2,400 specimens of 780 species and an annual attendance of more than 5,000,000.
·area and vegetation **19**:632c; map 624

Nation of all the Mongols, Mongol tribal power of the 9th to 12th centuries.
·Mongol tribal league **12**:371b

Nation of Islām: *see* Black Muslims.

Nation Party (Egypt): *see* Ummah Party.

Nations, Battle of the: *see* Leipzig, Battle of.

nation-state: *see* state, the.

Natitingou, town in Dahomey. Latest census 5,519.
10°19′ N, 1°22′ E
·gold and chrome ore deposits **5**:422e; map

Native American Church: *see* peyotism.

Native Brotherhoods, organizations of Indians in southeast Alaska and coastal British Columbia that promote acceptance of white culture, Indian unity, and Indian rights.
·purpose and effect **13**:255d

native cat: *see* dasyure.

native companion (bird): *see* crane.

Native Dancer, popularly known as the GRAY GHOST (1950–67), U.S. Thoroughbred who won 21 of 22 starts and achieved widespread popularity as the first outstanding horse whose major victories were seen on national television. Sired by Polynesian out of Geisha, the gray stallion was undefeated in nine races as a 2-year-old. In the 1953 U.S. Triple Crown competition for 3-year-old Thoroughbreds he met his only defeat, finishing second to Dark Star in the Kentucky Derby, but he won the Preakness Stakes and the Belmont Stakes. In 1954, although he was troubled by a foot injury, he won all four of his starts before being retired to stud.

native elements 12:853, chemical elements that occur in the Earth's crust as minerals, which can be pure or mixed with other elements in solid solution. The native elements are divided into three groups, namely, metals (*e.g.*, gold, copper, lead, zinc), semi-metals (arsenic, antimony, bismuth), and nonmetals (sulfur, carbon, tellurium, selenium). Some native elements, among them gold, copper and sulfur, are widespread and are sufficiently abundant to be important ores. Others, such as mercury, tin, or selenium, occur only rarely in the elemental state; native iron is mainly found in meteorites. Some native elements—gold, silver, platinum, and diamond—are among man's most valued substances.

The text article covers the mineral and crystallographic characteristics of the native elements and their occurrence and distribution in nature. (For Table of native elements, *see* pp. 218–219.)

REFERENCES in other text articles:
·Australian ferroalloy and nonferrous metals **2**:397d; illus. 396
·deposition in hydrothermal veins **9**:225c
·Europe's ferroalloy and nonferrous metals reserves **6**:1050d; illus. 1053
·gold mining and processing **8**:237a
·metallurgical processing development **11**:1061b; table 1062
·meteoritic and native iron comparison **12**:41d
·occurrence and varieties **12**:236e
·ore deposit forms, alloys, and sites **13**:662a; illus. 663
·Precambrian mineral locations **6**:13a
·tool and jewelry use **8**:610h

RELATED ENTRIES in the *Ready Reference and Index: for*
metals and alloys: see amalgam; electrum; kamacite; nickel iron; platiniridium
mixed compounds: cohenite; schreibersite
nonmetals and semi-metals: allemontite; diamond; diamond, industrial; graphite; iridosmine

Native Land Acts (1862, 1865), legislation of the New Zealand Parliament that provided for the private purchase of Maori land and the abolition of tribal ownership of Maori holdings, leading to the destruction of traditional Maori society. The 1862 act, passed after the First Taranaki War between European settlers and the Maoris, reversed the 1840 Treaty of Waitangi, which had provided for the exclusive right of the government to purchase Maori land; now settlers and speculators were free to deal directly with the Maoris. The act also created a Native Land Court that reviewed tribal titles before transactions could be made.

The 1865 act, in an effort to individualize Maori holdings for easier purchase, provided that the court not grant title certificates to more than ten members of a tribe. The ten owners could then sell their block in the name of the entire tribe, or any joint owner could sell his share of the land without consultation with his partners. The many Maori who refused to go before the court to clarify their titles forfeited their right of ownership.

The acts succeeded in opening enormous areas for settlement. The Maori nation achieved little benefit, however. The Maoris who boycotted the court lost their land outright; those who succumbed to the enticements of the speculators usually found that their profits quickly dwindled during protracted court sessions in the towns. By the time private purchase of Maori land was again abolished in 1892, the Maori had generally been reduced to rural labourers; their population fell rapidly, and their traditional society was disorganized.
·New Zealand Maori land losses **13**:52f

Native Land Husbandry Act (1951), Rhodesian legislation providing some economic landholdings to Africans.
·passage and purpose **17**:292c

Native Representation Act (New Zealand): *see* Maori Representation Act.

Natives' Land Act (1913), South African law securing cheap labour by limiting African land ownership and transforming African farmers into wage labourers.
·land division terms and impact **17**:292a

Natives' Trust and Lands Act (1936), South African legislation providing "autonomous areas" to native Africans.
·land division terms and impact **17**:292a

nativism (philosophy): *see* heredity–environment controversy.

nativism, in political science, a policy of favouring local inhabitants over immigrants; or the perpetuation or revival of an indigenous culture as opposed to acculturation; or the modification, for example, of foreign institutions in order to invest them with characteristics more compatible with a native culture.
·anti-Samaritan post-Exile Judaism **10**:309f
·Egyptian resistance to Hellenism **8**:854c
·Gandhi's nonviolent activism **13**:850b
·Negro cults' history and beliefs **12**:942b
·North African Donatism in social context **13**:153e

Native elements

name formula	colour	lustre	Mohs hardness	specific gravity	habit or form	fracture or cleavage	refractive index or polished section data	crystal system space group	remarks
allemontite AsSb	tin-white; reddish gray	metallic	3–4	5.8–6.2	kidney-like masses	one perfect cleavage	fine graphic intergrowth of allemontite with arsenic or antimony	hexagonal $R\bar{3}m$	
amalgam									
gold-amalgam Au_2Hg_3 (?)	yellowish	metallic		15.5	lumps or grains	conchoidal fracture		isometric, in part (?)	
moschellandsbergite Ag_2Hg_3	silver-white	bright metallic	3½	13.5–13.7	dodecahedrons; massive	two distinct cleavages		isometric Im3m (?)	
potarite Pd_3Hg_2 (?)	silver-white	bright metallic	3½	13.5–16.1	grains or nuggets		intergrowth of "potarite groundmass" (white, isotropic, high reflectivity) and "potarite inclusions" (light gray; anisotropic)	isometric	
antimony Sb	tin-white	metallic	3–3½	6.6–6.7	massive	one perfect cleavage; two less so	brilliant white; very strong reflectivity	hexagonal $R\bar{3}m$	
arsenic As	tin-white, tarnishing to dark gray	nearly metallic on fresh surfaces	3½	5.6–5.8	granular massive; concentric nodules	one perfect cleavage	white; strong reflectivity; anisotropic	hexagonal $R\bar{3}m$	
arsenolamprite As	lead-gray	brilliant metallic	2	5.3–5.5	massive	one perfect cleavage			may be either impure native arsenic or a distinct modification
bismuth Bi	silver-white, with reddish hue; tarnishes iridescent	metallic	2–2½	9.7–9.8	network or tree-like crystal groups	one perfect and one good cleavage	brilliant creamy white, tarnishing yellow; anisotropic	hexagonal $R\bar{3}m$	sectile; when heated, somewhat malleable
carbon									
diamond C	pale to deep yellow or brown; white to blue-white; sometimes variable	adamantine to greasy	10	3.5	flattened octahedrons; dodecahedrons	one perfect cleavage; conchoidal fracture	$n = 2.4175$	isometric Fd3m	triboelectric; strong dispersion
graphite C	black to dark steel-gray	metallic	1–2	2.1–2.2	platy or flaky massive	one perfect cleavage	pleochroism and birefringence extreme	hexagonal $C\frac{6}{m}mc$ (?)	electrical conductor; greasy feel; thermo-electrically negative; thin fragments transparent and deep blue
cohenite (Fe, Ni)$_3$C	tin-white, tarnishes to light bronze or gold-yellow		5½–6	7.2–7.7	elongated tabular crystals	three cleavages		orthorhombic Pbnm	strongly magnetic
copper Cu	light rose, tarnishes quickly to copper-red and brown	metallic	2½–3	8.95	plates and scales; wire-like, tree-like crystal groups; twisted bands; malformed crystals	no cleavage; hackly fracture	rose-white; isotropic; strong reflectivity	isometric Fm3m	highly ductile and malleable
gold Au	gold-yellow (when pure); silver-white to orange-red	metallic	2½–3	19.3	elongated or flattened crystals; wire-like, tree-like, or spongy forms	no cleavage; hackly fracture	brilliant gold-yellow; isotropic; high reflectivity	isometric Fm3m	very ductile and malleable
iridosmine (Ir, Os)	tin-white to light steel-gray	metallic	6–7	19.0–21.0	flakes or flattened grains	one perfect cleavage	slightly yellowish white	hexagonal $C\frac{6}{m}mc$ (pure Os) Fm3m (pure Ir)	slightly malleable; forms solid solution with siserskite, (Os, Ir), ranging from 77% Ir to almost 80% Os
iron Fe	steel-gray to iron-black	metallic	4	7.3–7.9	small blisters or large masses (terrestrial); plates and lamellar masses intergrown with nickel-iron (meteoritic)	one cleavage; hackly fracture	white; isotropic	isometric Im3m	magnetic; malleable

· prophetic leaders in various religions **15**:67e
· prophets' role in Yahwist purism **15**:64b
· validity of term's use for tribal religious movements **18**:698a

Nativity, a theme in Christian art depicting the newborn Christ with the Virgin Mary and other figures, following descriptions of Christ's birth in the Gospels and Apocrypha.

A very old and popular subject with a complicated iconography, the Nativity was first represented in the 4th century, carved on Early Christian Roman sarcophagi, and was later included with other scenes from Christ's life in monumental decoration of Early Christian basilicas. It was a very important subject for Early Christian art from the 5th century because it emphasized the reality of the incarnation of Christ and the validity of the Virgin's newly established (431) title of Theotokos, Mother of God. The Early Christian version of the Nativity shows the Virgin seated, to emphasize that the birth was painless, and the Child, in swaddling clothes, lying in a manger. The two, along with an ox and an ass, are under the roof of a barnlike stable. Usually one or two shepherds, who symbolize the revelation of Christ to the Jews, and often also the

Native elements (continued)

name formula	colour	lustre	Mohs hardness	specific gravity	habit or form	fracture or cleavage	refractive index or polished section data	crystal system space group	remarks
lead Pb	lead-gray; gray-white on fresh surfaces	dull; metallic on fresh surfaces	1½	11.4	rounded masses; thin plates	no cleavage	fresh surfaces gray-white, isotropic, high reflectivity; quickly dulled	isometric Fm3m	very malleable; somewhat ductile
mercury Hg	tin-white	very brilliant metallic		13.596	isolated drops; occasionally in larger liquid masses			hexagonal (at −39° C)	liquid at normal temperatures
nickel-iron (Fe, Ni)	silver- to grayish-white	metallic	5	7.8–8.2	pebbles, grains, fine scales (terrestrial); intergrown with or bordering meteoritic iron (meteoritic)	no cleavage		isometric Fm3m	strongly magnetic; malleable; flexible
palladium Pd	whitish steel-gray	metallic	4½–5	11.9	grains	no cleavage	white; high reflectivity; isotropic	isometric Fm3m	ductile; malleable
platiniridium (Ir, Pt)	yellowish silver-white; gray on fresh surfaces	metallic	6–7	22.6–22.8	rounded or angular grains	hackly fracture		isometric Fm3m	somewhat malleable
platinum Pt	whitish steel-gray to dark gray	metallic	4–4½	14–19	grains or scales; sometimes in lumps or nuggets	no cleavage; hackly fracture	white; isotropic	isometric Fm3m	malleable; ductile; sometimes magnetic
schreibersite $(Fe, Ni)_3P$	silver- to tin-white; tarnishes to brass-yellow or brown	highly metallic	6½–7	7.0–7.3	plates; rods or needles	one perfect cleavage		tetragonal $I\bar{4}$	strongly magnetic
selenium Se	gray	metallic	2	4.8	crystals, often hollow or tube-like; glassy drops	one good cleavage	fairly high reflectivity; creamy white; pleochroic; very strongly anisotropic	hexagonal $C3_12$ or $C3_22$	electrical conductor; thin fragments transparent and red
silver Ag	silver-white; tarnishes gray to black	metallic	2½–3	10.1–11.1 (10.5 pure)	crystals, often in elongated, wire-like, or tree-like groups; massive as scales or coating	no cleavage; hackly fracture	brilliant silver-white; greatest reflectivity known; isotropic	isometric Fm3m	ductile and malleable
sulfur S									
rhombic (α-sulfur)	sulfur-, straw- to honey-yellow; yellowish brown or gray, greenish, reddish	resinous to greasy	1½–2½	2.07	transparent to translucent tabular crystals; spherical or kidney-like masses; crusts; powder	three imperfect cleavages; conchoidal to uneven fracture	$n = 1.957$	orthorhombic Fddd	electrical non-conductor; negatively charged by friction
monoclinic (β-sulfur)	light yellow: nearly colourless; brownish due to included organic matter		slightly greater than α-sulfur	1.958, 1.982	thick tabular or elongated crystals	two cleavages	$n = 2.038$	monoclinic	
nacreous (γ-sulfur)	light yellow; nearly colourless	adamantine	low	less than α-sulfur	minute transparent crystals	no observed cleavage		monoclinic	reverts slowly to α-sulfur at room temperature
tantalum Ta	grayish yellow	bright	6–7	11.2	minute crystals; fine grains			isometric Im3m	
tellurium Te	tin-white	metallic	2–2½	6.1–6.3	columnar to fine granular massive; minute crystals	one perfect cleavage	strongly anisotropic; white; very strongly reflective	hexagonal $C3_12$ or $C3_22$	
tin Sn	tin-white	metallic	2	7.3	irregular rounded grains; natural crystals unknown	hackly fracture		tetragonal $I\frac{4}{a}md$	ductile; malleable
zinc Zn	slightly grayish white	metallic	2	6.9–7.2		one perfect cleavage		hexagonal $C\frac{6}{m}mc$	though reported, existence in native form is doubtful

Magi—Wise Men from the East who symbolize his revelation to the Gentiles—appear in the scene. Also included is the motif of the adoring ox and ass, whose presence has an apocryphal source and who symbolize, according to a prophecy of Isaiah, the homage paid by the humblest and least of creation.

By the 6th century another version of the Nativity had appeared in Syria. This became universal in the East throughout the Middle Ages, and in Italy until the late 14th century.

"The Nativity at Night," oil painting by Geertgen tot Sint Jans, late 15th century; in the National Gallery, London

It differs from the earlier version, which was retained with some modifications in northwestern Europe, mainly in that it ignores the concept of the painless birth and thus shows the Virgin lying on a mattress. The Child is again in swaddling clothes in a manger, and the ox and ass are retained, but the stable is not a barn but a cave, as was the custom in Palestine. Angels usually hover above the cave, and Joseph sits outside of it. The Magi and the shepherds are often present. Frequently an angel announcing the miraculous birth to the shepherds and the journey of the Magi are depicted simultaneously in the background. In the foreground is another simultaneous representation that remained standard in Eastern Nativities: the bathing of the Child by two midwives. The presence of the midwives, also apocryphal, alludes to an allegory of Christ's divinity: one of the midwives, who doubted the supernatural Virgin birth, was stricken with a withered arm and then cured by touching the Child. The bathing of the Child has no known literary source but probably derives from classical scenes of the birth of the god Dionysus and is a prefiguration of Christ's Baptism. This version of the Nativity appeared in every sort of religious art. As the emblem of a major feast day, it figured prominently, usually in its most complicated form, in the liturgical iconography of Byzantine church decoration.

In the late 14th century an abrupt transformation of the iconography of the Nativity occurred throughout western Europe, including Italy, and a second major version came into being. This was essentially an adoration; the most important change is that the Virgin is no longer experiencing the aftermath of childbirth but kneels before the Child, who is now nude and luminous and lies not in a manger but on the ground on a pile of straw or a fold of the Virgin's mantle. Often Joseph, too, kneels in adoration. Most of the other details,

except the ox and ass, have been omitted, especially in earlier works. This version, which seems to have spread from Italy, follows in detail—and in fact almost certainly originates with—an account of a vision by St. Bridget of Sweden, an influential 14th-century mystic, in which the Virgin appeared to her and gave a detailed account of the birth, emphasizing especially its painlessness. Universally adopted in western Europe by the 15th century, this version is widely depicted in altarpieces and other devotional works.

In the Renaissance, angels reappeared, and the scene was often combined with the adoration of the shepherds (q.v.), which had recently developed as a separate theme. The midwives were still included occasionally. In the 16th century the Counter-Reformation Council of Trent outlawed the midwives, the ox and ass, and the bathing of Christ as ignoble, apocryphal, and theologically unsound (the bathing of the Child is inconsistent with the doctrine of a pure and supernatural birth).

In the 17th century a more prosaic representation reappeared, with the Virgin again reclining and holding the Child. After the 17th century, Christian religious art in general declined; the Nativity, however, remained an important theme in the popular arts.
·folk art crèches 7:474f
historical event
·Christian traditions historicity 10:148g
·chronology of Christian history 4:580a
·stained glass window, illus. 17:Stained Glass, Plate II
·Tintoretto's significant features and style 18:435g
·Uccello's artistic career 18:825b

Nativity of the Virgin Mary, feast celebrated in the Roman Catholic Church and the Eastern churches on September 8 to honour the Mother of the Son of God. It originated in the Eastern Church and was celebrated in Rome by the time of Sergius I (pope from 687 to 701).

Nativity play, medieval drama dealing with the birth of Jesus Christ.
·dramatic style of children's plays 5:987h

natkadaw, wife of a *nat*, or Burmese spirit.
·Burmese shadow play origins 17:244a

NATO: *see* North Atlantic Treaty Organization.

Natorp, Paul (1854–1924), German Neo-Kantian philosopher, represented the Marburg school in the philosophy of science and inquired particularly into its necessary presuppositions after the fashion of Kantian "transcendental logic." He wrote *Die logischen Grundlagen der exakten Wissenschaft* (1910; "The Logical Bases of Exact Science").
·Idealism of Marburg school 9:191g
·logistic Neo-Kantianism at Marburg 10:396f

Natrix (snake): *see* water snake.

natrolite, a hydrated sodium and calcium aluminosilicate mineral, ($Na_2Al_2Si_3O_{10}$·$2H_2O$), in the zeolite family; its typical occurrences are colourless or white, glassy, slender crystals or fibrous masses filling cavities or fissures in basaltic rocks, as in Trentino, Italy; Brevik, Nor.; Belfast, County Down; the Faeroe Islands; and northeastern New Jersey. One of the first zeolite minerals for which cation-exchange properties (dissolved sodium, potassium, calcium, and magnesium readily replacing one another in the molecular structure) were discovered, natrolite is used in softening water.
Natrolite is the principal member of a group of zeolite minerals whose molecular structure is predominately chains of linked silicate tetrahedra (four oxygen atoms arranged at the points of a triangular pyramid about a central silicon atom); relatively few lateral bonds between chains result in the characteristic fibrous appearance of the group. Other zeolites in the natrolite group are mesolite, scolecite, thomsonite, and gonnardite; all have

similar modes of occurrence, molecular structures, and physical properties, even though they have different crystal symmetries: mesolite and scolecite crystallize in the monoclinic system (three unequal axes with one inclined to the plane of the other two), whereas natrolite, thomsonite, and gonnardite crystallize in the orthorhombic system (three unequal axes at right angles to one another). Mesolite (from Greek, "middle stone") is so named because it is chemically intermediate to natrolite and scolecite. For chemical formulas and detailed physical properties, *see* table under zeolites.
·crystal structure and habit 19:1140a
·structure and bonding 16:763b

natron (salt compound): *see* thermonatrite.

Natron, Lake, in northern Tanzania on the border with Kenya, lying in East Africa's Great Rift Valley, 70 mi (113 km) northwest of Arusha. It is 35 mi long and 15 mi wide and contains salt, soda, and magnesite deposits. The Gelai volcano (9,652 ft [2,942 m]) is situated at the lake's southeast edge.
2°25′ S, 36°00′ E
·geology and climatology 15:843a
·map, Tanzania 17:1026
·rift lake geography and fauna 6:116e; map 119

Natron fossil, nearly complete, well-preserved jawbone, found at Peninj, near Lake Natron, Tanzania, in 1964. The deposits in which the mandible (jawbone) was buried are apparently as old (about 1,000,000 years) as Bed II at Olduvai Gorge, Tanzania. The mandible closely resembles a jawbone (SK 23) from Swartkrans, S.Af., of the more robust of the australopithecines, *Paranthropus* (q.v.); the Natron mandible has not been assigned taxonomically as yet. A modified Natron mandible, made from a cast, has been articulated with the skull of *Zinjanthropus boisei* (q.v.), to produce a good visual impression of the head of this manlike creature.

Natshinnaung, 16th-century king of Toungoo, Burma, who wrote poetry.
·Burmese poetry development 17:234g

Natsume Sōseki, pseudonym of NATSUME KINOSUKE (b. 1867, Tokyo—d. Dec. 9, 1916), outstanding novelist of the Meiji Restoration period and the first to depict articulately and persuasively the plight of the alienated modern Japanese intellectual. Sōseki received a degree in English from the University of Tokyo (1893) and taught in the provinces until 1900,

Natsume Sōseki

when he went to England on a government scholarship. In 1903 he became lecturer in English at the University of Tokyo. His reputation as a novelist was established with two highly successful comic novels, *Wagahai-wa Neko-de aru* (1905–06; *I Am a Cat*, 1961) and *Botchan* (1906; *Master Darling*, 1918). Both works satirize contemporary philistines and intellectual mountebanks. His third book, *Kusamakura* (1906; *The Three-Cornered World*, 1965), which he called "a novel in the manner of a haiku," is a lyrical tour de force describing a painter's sojourn in a remote village.

After 1907, when he gave up teaching to devote himself to writing, he produced his more characteristic works, which were sombre without exception. They deal with man's effort to escape from loneliness. His typical heroes are well-educated middle-class men who have betrayed, or who have been betrayed by, someone close to them and through guilt or disillusionment have cut themselves off from other men. In *Kōjin* (1912–13; *The Wayfarer*, 1967) the hero is driven to near madness by his sense of isolation; in *Kokoro* (1914; Eng. trans. by Edwin McClellan, 1957) the hero kills himself; and in *Mon* (1910; "The Gate") the hero's inability to gain entrance to the gate of a Zen temple to seek religious solace is a frightening symbol of frustration, isolation, and helplessness.

In his awareness of his originality, Sōseki claimed that he owed little to the native literary tradition. Yet, for all their modernity, his novels have a delicate lyricism that is uniquely Japanese. It was through Sōseki that the modern realistic novel, which had essentially been a foreign literary genre, found its most natural expression and took root in Japan.
·famous works **10**:1072e

Natta, Giulio (b. Feb. 26, 1903, Imperia, near Genoa—d. May 2, 1979, Bergama, Italy), chemist who contributed to the development of high polymers useful in the manufacture of films, plastics, fibres, and synthetic rubber. His achievements, along with those of Karl Ziegler of Germany, were honoured with the 1963 Nobel Prize for Chemistry. He took his doctorate in chemical engineering at the Politecnico di Milano (1924) and held chairs in chemistry at the universities of Pavia, Rome, and Turin before returning to the Politecnico as professor and research director of industrial chemistry (1938).

His earlier work formed the basis of modern industrial syntheses of methanol, formaldehyde, butyraldehyde, and succinic acid. In 1953 he began intensive study of macromolecules. Using Ziegler's catalysts, he experimented with the polymerization of propylene and succeeded in obtaining isotactic (same shape) polypropylenes containing uniformly oriented methyl groups. The properties—viz., high strength, high melting points—of these polymers soon proved their considerable commercial importance.

Nattier, Jean-Marc (b. March 17, 1685, Paris—d. Nov. 7, 1766, Paris), painter noted for portraits of the ladies of King Louis XV's court in classical mythological attire.

Nattier received his first instruction from his father, a portraitist, and at the age of 15 took first prize at the French Academy, Paris. In 1715 he went to Amsterdam, where the Russian tsar, Peter the Great, and his wife, Empress Catherine, sat for him. Between 1715 and 1720 he painted the "Battle of Poltava" for Peter and a work on a theme from Greek mythology, which won him election to the academy. Near financial ruin in 1720, he turned to portraiture. Notable examples of his straightforward approach are the "Portrait of Marie Leczinska" (Musée des Beaux-Arts, Dijon, Fr.) and "The Artist Surrounded by His Family" (1730). Among his famous allegorical likenesses are the four portraits of the daughters of Louis XV with attributes of the four elements (1751; Museu de Arte São Paulo, Braz.).

Natufian, Mesolithic culture of Palestine and southern Syria dating from about 9,000 BC. Mainly hunters, the Natufians supplemented their diet by gathering wild grain; they probably did not actually cultivate the grain. They had sickles of flint blades set in straight bone handles for harvesting the grain and stone mortars and pestles for grinding it. Some groups lived in caves, while others occupied incipient villages. They buried their dead along with their personal ornaments in cemeteries. Carved bone and stone artwork have been found.
·Asian modern population distinctions **2**:204g
·cultural patterns and agriculture **17**:927g
·development of agriculture **1**:325a

natural (music): *see* accidental.

Natural Bridge, natural limestone arch, Rockbridge County, western Virginia, U.S., in Jefferson National Forest, near the village of Natural Bridge. The arch, spanning a gorge cut by Cedar Creek, is 215 ft (66 m) high, 90 ft long, and varies in width from 50 to 150 ft. Highways U.S. 11 and Interstate 81 pass over it. The bridge was included in a tract of land purchased by Thomas Jefferson, then a member of the Virginia Legislature, for 20 shillings in 1775. Jefferson built a two-room log cabin near the bridge, reserving one room for guests. A floodlit musical drama is presented in a woodland setting beneath the bridge in the season from May to October.
37°40′ N, 79°40′ W

Natural Bridge, near Lexington, Va.
Bob Glaze—Artstreet

natural bridge, or NATURAL ARCH, naturally created arch formation resembling a bridge. Most natural bridges are erosion features that occur in massive, horizontally bedded sandstone or limestone. Some may be formed by the collapse of a cavern's roof that may leave remnant portions as bridges. Others may be produced by entrenched rivers eroding through meander necks to form cutoffs. Still others are produced by exfoliation and may be enlarged by wind erosion.

Popularly, the term often refers to Natural Bridge (*q.v.*) in western Virginia. Other examples include Natural Bridges National Monument, containing three such arches, and Rainbow Bridge National Monument (*qq.v.*), both in Utah.

Natural tunnels are often quite similar to bridges in origin. A related form is the sea arch, produced where remnant headlands may be cut through by waves. Collapse of the bridge portion of a sea arch commonly produces a sea stack.
·formation association with piping **5**:611a; illus.

Natural Bridges National Monument, in southeastern Utah, U.S., 42 mi (68 km) west of Blanding. Established in 1908 and occupying a 12-sq-mi (31-sq-km) site, it comprises three natural sandstone bridges, carved by two winding streams that formed on the western slopes of Elk Ridge. The largest bridge, Sipapu, rises 220 ft (89 m) above the stream bed and has a 268-ft span with thicknesses varying between 31 and 53 ft. The Kachina and Owachomo bridges are respectively 210 ft and 106 ft high with spans of 206 ft and 180 ft. Kachina, the most massive of the three bridges, is approximately 100 ft thick at its narrowest point, while Owachomo, the oldest and smallest bridge, is only 9 ft thick. There are many Indian ruins in the vicinity, and pictographs were carved on the abutments of Kachina by early cliff dwellers. An 11-mile paved road links the bridges with the camping area and visitors' centre.

Owachomo Bridge, Natural Bridges National Monument, Utah
Bjorn Bolstad—Peter Arnold, Inc.

natural childbirth, synonymous with normal childbirth until the 20th century, when applied to systems of managing parturition in which the need for anesthesia, sedation, or surgery is largely eliminated by psychological conditioning. In 1933, the British obstetrician Grantly Dick-Read wrote in his book *Natural Childbirth* that fear was a cultural and psychological basis for labour pains, and he proposed that expectant women perform relaxation exercises and attend a course about the birth process. (Later Dick-Read conceded that some pain could not be entirely avoided.) Dick-Read's and other similar methods became popular in the mid-1950s.
·development and premises **13**:1040f

Naturales quaestiones (*c.* AD 63), prose work by Seneca.
·Stoic influence on Seneca **16**:530g

natural gas 12:858, mixture of gaseous hydrocarbons, particularly methane and ethane, that occurs beneath the surface of the Earth.

The text article treats the physical and chemical properties, behaviour, origin, accumulation, and entrapment of natural gas. Also covered are its world distribution, production, processing, transportation, and storage.

REFERENCES in other text articles:
·agricultural potentials and progress **1**:366a
·cave system formation from cooling lava **3**:1022e
·composition and helium origin **6**:708d
·cryogenics and automobile fuel **5**:319g
·detection instruments **4**:777a
·extraction, distribution, properties, and processing **7**:923d
·formation from organic matter in shales **16**:634g
·gas and petroleum occurrence **14**:176d
·hydrocarbon sources and composition **9**:83h
·lighting development in the 1800s **10**:958a
·liquid gas tankers **16**:685h

· materials handling and storage **11**:615h
· open-hearth furnace operation **17**:647d
· paleogeography and marine origin of gas **13**:908f
· petroleum composition and properties **14**:167c
· petroleum conservation practices **5**:50e
· pipeline use of gas turbines **18**:776a
regions of occurrence
· African distribution and cubic footage **1**:198f
· Algerian quality and economic effects **1**:563f *passim* to 567b
· Asian reserves **2**:171g
· Australian deposits **2**:396c
· Egypt's deposits **6**:453h
· European reserves **6**:1050c; illus. 1053
· Iran's reserves and planned production **9**:825d
· Louisiana industrial utilization **11**:127g
· Moscow's underground supply system **12**:484c
· Nigeria's reserves **13**:91g
· North American fuel deposits **13**:193b; map 198
· occurrence in Atlantic and exploitation **2**:303c
· Pacific areas of occurrence **13**:844a
· Russian deposits and extraction **16**:91d
· Sahara desert resources **16**:151a
· U.S. resource areas and production comparisons **18**:931f
· Victoria's resource areas **19**:112e
· salt dome beds and gas reservoirs **16**:197g *passim* to 199b
· salt dome traps **6**:1133a
· subsurface accumulation and flow **8**:438f; fig. 439
· Upper Carboniferous coals as source **3**:856f

RELATED ENTRIES in the *Ready Reference and Index: for*
composition and products: see butane; ethane; gas–oil ratio; liquefied petroleum gas; methane; propane
occurrence: dry gas; reservoir, gas; trap, petroleum; wet gas
other: will-o'-the-wisp

natural group, also known as PRIMORDIAL GROUP, PRIMARY GROUP, or COMMUNAL GROUP, special-interest groups based on relationships such as kinship, lineage, neighbourhood, or religious confession.
· interest group structure **17**:445f

Natural History (Leclerc): *see* Histoire Naturelle.

Natural History, Museum of, founded in Paris in 1635.
· science during French Revolution **16**:372g

Natural History and Antiquities of Selbourne (1789), book by Gilbert White.
· literary survival **10**:1042b

Natural History of Religion, The, book by the Scottish philosopher David Hume (1757).
· anthropomorphism in religion **15**:616d
· God idea and personification of nature **18**:267h
· primitive religion origin theory **14**:1041b

natural immunity, genetically innate resistence to a harmful agent, without previous immunization or sensitization to the agent.
· infectious disease defense mechanism **9**:534g

natural increase (in population): *see* vital rates.

Naturalism, late 19th- and early 20th-century aesthetic movement, inspired by adaptation of the principles and methods of natural science, especially the Darwinian view of nature, to literature and art. In literature, it extended the tradition of Realism, aiming at an even more faithful, unselective, representation of reality, a veritable "slice of life," presented without moral judgment. Naturalism differed from Realism in its assumption of scientific determinism, which led naturalistic authors to emphasize man's accidental, physiological nature rather than his moral or rational qualities. Individual characters were seen as helpless products of heredity and environment, motivated by strong instinctual drives from within, and harassed by social and economic pressures from without. As such, they had little will or responsibility for their fates, and the prognosis for their "cases" was pessimistic at the outset.

Naturalism originated in France and had its direct theoretical basis in the critical approach of Hippolyte Taine, who announced in his introduction to *Histoire de la littérature anglaise* (1863–64; Eng. trans., *History of English Literature*, 1871), ". . . there is a cause for ambition, for courage, for truth, as there is for digestion, for muscular movement, for animal heat. Vice and virtue are products, like vitriol and sugar . . ." Though the first "scientific" novel was the Goncourt brothers' case history of a servant girl, *Germinie Lacerteux* (1864), the leading exponent of Naturalism was Émile Zola, whose *Le Roman expérimental* (1880; "The Experimental Novel") became the literary manifesto of the school. According to Zola, the novelist was no longer to be a mere observer, content to record phenomena, but a detached experimenter who subjects his characters and their passions to a series of tests and who works with emotional and social facts as a chemist works with matter. Few naturalistic writers were so conscious or deliberate or so exclusively dedicated to their method as Zola, yet the naturalistic style became widespread and affected to varying degrees most of the major writers of the period. Guy de Maupassant's popular story "The Necklace," beginning, "She was one of those pretty, charming young ladies . . .," heralds, with the phrase "one of those," the introduction of a character who is to be treated like a specimen under a microscope. The early works of Joris-Karl Huysmans, of the German dramatist Gerhart Hauptmann, and of the Portuguese novelist José Maria Eça de Queirós were based on the precepts of Naturalism. In the theatre, the Théâtre Libre was founded in Paris in 1887 by André Antoine and the Freie Bühne of Berlin in 1889 by Otto Brahm to present plays dealing with the new themes of Naturalism in a naturalistic style with naturalistic staging. A parallel development occurred in the visual arts. Painters, following the lead of Gustave Courbet, were choosing themes from contemporary life. They deserted the studio for the open air, finding subjects in the street and capturing them as they found them, unpremeditated and unposed, so that their finished canvases had the freshness and immediacy of sketches. Zola, the spokesman for literary Naturalism, was also the first to champion Édouard Manet and the Impressionists.

Despite their claim to complete objectivity, the literary Naturalists were handicapped by certain biases inherent in their deterministic theories. Though they faithfully reflected nature, it was always a nature "red in tooth and claw." Their views on heredity gave them a predilection for simple characters dominated by strong, elemental passions. Their views on the overpowering effects of environment led them to select for subjects the most oppressive environments—the slums or the underworld—and they documented these milieus, often in dreary and sordid detail. The drab palette of Vincent van Gogh's naturalistic painting "The Potato Eaters" (1885; Rijksmuseum, Amsterdam), was the palette of literary Naturalism. Finally, they were unable to suppress an element of romantic protest against the social conditions they described.

As a historical movement, Naturalism per se was short-lived; but it contributed to art an enrichment of Realism, new areas of subject matter, and a largeness and formlessness that was indeed closer to life than to art. Its multiplicity of impressions conveyed the sense of a world in constant flux, inevitably jungle-like, because it teemed with interdependent lives.

In U.S. literature, Naturalism had a delayed blooming in the work of Hamlin Garland, Stephen Crane, Frank Norris, and Jack London; and it reached its peak in the art of Theodore Dreiser. James T. Farrell's "Studs Lonigan" trilogy (1932–35) is one of the latest expressions of true Naturalism.
· culture pattern relationship theory **14**:1032h
· Daudet and fellow Naturalists **5**:513h
· dramatic theory and stylistic development **5**:986d
· European cultural trends in 1800s **6**:1077e
· Hellenistic influence on Indian art **17**:191e
· Japanese fiction **10**:1072e
· novel's stylistic periods **13**:283h
· Pestalozzi and Rousseau's theories **13**:1100d
· Rousseau's basic expression and effect **6**:410e
· Rousseau's educational philosophy **6**:353g
· staging style of Meiningen troupe **17**:543g
· Stanislavsky method and theatre design **18**:253a *passim* to 254d
· Strindberg's dramatic style and impact **17**:737h
· Taine's theoretical basis **17**:992d
· tragic themes in modern drama **18**:586g
· Zola's and Stanislavsky's impact on drama **18**:228a
· Zola's development and philosophy **19**:1156d
· Zola's theories and artistic impact **2**:45h

naturalism, a philosophical theory that relates scientific method to philosophy by affirming that all beings and events in the universe (whatever their inherent character may be) are natural. Consequently, all knowledge of the universe falls within the pale of scientific investigation. Although naturalism denies the existence of truly supernatural realities, it makes allowance for the supernatural, provided that knowledge of it can be had indirectly—that is, that natural objects be influenced by the so-called supernatural entities in a detectable way. In such a case, the supernatural itself is reduced to a natural status verifiable by science.

Naturalism presumes that nature is in principle completely knowable. There is in nature a regularity, a unity, a wholeness that implies objective laws, without which the pursuit of scientific knowledge would be absurd. Man's endless search for concrete proofs of his beliefs is seen as a confirmation of naturalistic methodology. Naturalists point out that even when one scientific theory is abandoned in favour of another, man does not despair of knowing nature, nor does he repudiate the "natural method" in his search for truth. Theories change; methodology does not.

Because the world is too rich and complex for final certitudes, man's knowledge never stagnates, is never final. Countless avenues lead toward truth; experiences admit of great diversity. But only those approaches that have a scientific basis yield true knowledge.

While naturalism has often been equated with Materialism, it is much broader in scope. Materialism is indeed naturalistic, but the converse is not necessarily true. Strictly speaking, naturalism has no ontological preference: dualism and monism, atheism and theism, Idealism and Materialism are all per se compatible with it. So long as all of reality is natural, no other limitations are imposed. Naturalists have in fact expressed a wide variety of views, even developing a theistic naturalism.

Except rarely, naturalists give scant attention to metaphysics (which they deride) and make no philosophical attempts to establish their position. Naturalists simply assert that nature is reality, the whole of it. There is nothing beyond, nothing "other than," no "other world" of being.

Naturalism's greatest vogue occurred during the 1930s and 1940s, chiefly in the U.S.
· explanation in natural terms **12**:26a
· Husserl's phenomenological critique **14**:211g
· Japanese Confucian philosophy **10**:106d
· Marcel's metapsychically-based challenge **11**:488g
· medieval University of Paris dispute **7**:622e
· meta-ethical cognitivist theory **6**:983c
· meta-ethics and normative ethics **6**:977f
· religious experience issues **15**:647g
· Santayana's philosophical theories **16**:231b

Naturalism and Religion (1907), Eng. trans. of NATURALISTISCHE UND RELIGIÖSE WELTANSICHT (1904) by the German philosopher and theologian Rudolf Otto.
·contrast in naturalistic and religious interpretations of world **13**:769f

naturalistic fallacy, in the ethical philosophy of the 20th-century English philosopher G.E. Moore (*q.v.*), any attempt to define "good" (in the sense of "good in itself"). For Moore, goodness was a simple unanalyzable concept, a nonnatural quality or entity; to attempt to define it, therefore, through ethical or nonethical concepts, is to fall into a naturalistic fallacy.
·aesthetic theory of value **1**:158a
·definition and development **6**:980g

Naturalistic Photography, in full NATURALISTIC PHOTOGRAPHY FOR STUDENTS OF THE ART (1889), handbook by the English photographer and physician Peter Henry Emerson (*q.v.*).
·aesthetic considerations of photography **14**:316f

Naturalist on the River Amazons, The, 2 vol. (1863), scientific and travel journal by Henry Walter Bates (*q.v.*).
·Amazon River animal life study **1**:655a

naturalization, act of investing an alien with the status of a national in a given state. Acquired by a person after birth, it may be accomplished as the result of voluntary application, special legislative direction, marriage to a citizen, or parental action. It may also be accomplished when one's home territory is annexed by a foreign power, to which citizenship is transferred.

The conditions under which the privilege of naturalization is granted vary from nation to nation. (International law, however, does impose some limits on the power of a state to naturalize persons, especially nonresidents.) In normal cases, the usual requirements for naturalization are a certain period of residence, which varies from 2 to 15 years, intention to reside permanently, a minimum age, capacity to act according to the law of the state of the former nationality or of the state applied to or of both, good character, physical and mental health, a sufficient command of the language of the prospective adopting country, ability to earn a livelihood or to support oneself, and evidence that, upon naturalization, the applicant's former nationality will be lost or that steps have been taken to renounce it.

natural kinds, in philosophy, view that groupings of beings correspond to objective reality, implying that such categories are not simply imposed by the mind.
·ontological ground of classification **12**:16g

natural law 12:863, or LAW OF NATURE, system of right or justice thought to be common to all mankind, derived from nature rather than from the rules of society, or positive law.

The text article covers the development of natural law thinking in the Greek and Roman eras; by medieval philosophers, especially Thomas Aquinas; in the Renaissance and the Age of Reason; and the reactions against it at the beginning of the 19th century and its minor revival in the 20th.

REFERENCES in other text articles:
·anarchism as man's natural state **1**:808b
·Burke's defense of British Constitution **5**:63g
·Chinese legal derivatives **4**:408d
·Grotius' international relations theory **6**:888a
·Hobbes's conditions for observance **8**:971d
·international legal theory made flexible **9**:745c
·Jewish political and moral philosophy **10**:214b
·Locke's concept of the state and laws **5**:85e
·LPC extension for axiomatic bases **11**:54b
·pacifist basis of Stoics **13**:847f
·philosophy, history, and analysis **10**:715c *passim* to 720d
·political sovereignty's limitations **17**:310a
·principal–agent relationship conflict **1**:291g
·Pufendorf's nontheological treatment **15**:265d
·role in various political philosophies **14**:687d
·state sovereignty and limitations **17**:610c
·Stoicism and Roman law **17**:700f
·Talmudic concepts and implementation **17**:1012a
·Tolstoy's determinism theory **18**:484f

natural philosophy, once the designation for natural science, including the areas of knowledge that were to become distinct sciences—such as astronomy, physics, chemistry, earth sciences, and biology. *See also* nature, philosophy of.
·philosophy of science **16**:375h

natural religion: *see* Deism.

natural resources: *see* conservation of natural resources.

natural rights, doctrine that individuals enjoy certain claims against others and against the state by virtue of the laws of nature. Such rights or claims include, according to two early formulations of the doctrine, the right of men "to order their actions and dispose of their persons and possessions as they think fit, within the bounds of the law of nature" (John Locke, *Two Treatises of Government* [1690]) and, according to the American Declaration of Independence (1776; *q.v.*), the "unalienable" rights to life, liberty, and the pursuit of happiness, as well as the right to alter or abolish governments that render such objectives unobtainable. The French National Assembly made a similar assertion in the Declaration of the Rights of Man and of the Citizen (1789; *q.v.*), and the doctrine has persisted into the 20th century, finding expression, for example, in the Universal Declaration of Human Rights adopted by the General Assembly of the United Nations in 1948.

For the texts of the Declaration of Independence, the Declaration of the Rights of Man, and the Universal Declaration of Human Rights, *see* Addenda, vol. x; *see also* human rights.
·Burke's defense of British Constitution **5**:63g
·constitutional theories of Hobbes and Locke **5**:95e
·importance in Hobbes's philosophy **8**:971d
·liberal understanding **10**:849a
·limits to state authority **17**:610h *passim* to 612f
·natural law and role of state **12**:865b
·Patrick Henry's advocacy **8**:775g

natural selection (biology): *see* selection.

natural theology, knowledge of God acquired by natural reason unaided by divine revelation, as opposed to revealed theology. Natural theology seeks to establish, for example, the fact that God exists and to derive analogous knowledge of his nature from a study of the visible world that he created.
·concerns and relation to revelation **15**:601h
·importance for Christian philosophy **4**:560b
·Nominalist challenge **15**:1007b
·rational approach to the holy **15**:622c

Nature (1836), book by the U.S. author Ralph Waldo Emerson.
·idealism in Emerson's philosophy **6**:755a

Nature, British international journal of science, founded in 1869 by Sir Joseph Norman Lockyer (*q.v.*).
·magazine publishing history **15**:250h

nature, philosophy of 12:865, investigation of substantive (as contrasted with methodological or epistemological) issues in the philosophies of physics and biology. The most fundamental, broad, and seminal features of natural reality as such are explored; and their implications for mankind's metaphysics (theory of reality), *Weltanschauung* (world view), anthropology, and ethics are assessed on the assumption that mankind's understanding of the natural setting in which life is staged strongly conditions the beliefs and attitudes in many fields.

TEXT ARTICLE covers:
Physics as a field of inquiry **12**:866a
Basic characteristics and parameters of the natural order 867c
Special problems in the philosophy of physics 869e
The range of topics 872e
The nature of biological systems 873c
Philosophy in evolution 874d
Evolution as a world view 875b
Biology and ethics 875c

REFERENCES in other text articles:

folklore
·allegorical explication of cosmology **7**:134g
·medieval to 19th-century literary views **7**:137d
·Polynesian order of precedence **14**:778d
·Southwest American Indian view of life **17**:306a
·Woodlands Indian world view **6**:172a

natural sciences
·biological theories and development **2**:1026a
·Broglie wave theory of matter **3**:323d
·Cartesian mechanistic physics **3**:968d
·changing conceptions of science **14**:384c
·chemical element concept **4**:114c
·Driesch's vitalistic theories **5**:1040f
·electron as key to properties of matter **6**:665a
·evolution of natural sciences **16**:375h
·Galen's teleological beliefs **7**:850a
·Newton's interpretation of mechanism and the Hermetic tradition **13**:17c *passim* to 18g
·physics principles and theory **14**:428f
·religious versus scientific systems **15**:595f
·science as intelligible organization of empirical data **16**:382b
·science history and interpretation **16**:366b
·uniformitarian and catastrophic earth development **18**:857b

philosophy
·Aristotelianism history and development **1**:1155g
·Aristotle's philosophic system **1**:1167g
·Aristotle's Physics and Metaphysics **12**:10f
·Burke's interpretation and the historical process **3**:501h
·Comte's view of intellectual inquiry **14**:877d
·Epicurean Atomistic physics **6**:911b
·Hegel's view of being and becoming **8**:730g
·Idealist conceptions in 18th century **16**:982c
·Indian Sāṃkhya speculation **9**:320d
·Jewish philosophical thought **10**:215g
·knowledge of physical objects **6**:927a
·Lucretius' explication of atomism **11**:174b
·main currents in epistemology **6**:931c
·Marxist philosophy of human activity **11**:554c
·Mullā Ṣadrā's concept of creation **9**:1024f
·natural law in various conceptions **12**:863e
·pantheist and panentheist ontologies **13**:948h
·Renaissance continuing Greek thought **14**:263a
·Renaissance Humanist tradition **15**:669h
·Schelling's rejection of the ego **16**:339c
·Scholasticism culmination in Aquinas **16**:356c
·Socratic hypothetical method and Forms **16**:1003h
·Sophist moral basis in natural law **17**:13c
·Sophist theory of natural law **12**:863f
·Spencer's necessary evolution **17**:492h
·Stoicism and the cosmos **17**:698d

theology and religious worldviews
·African traditional religious views **1**:285b
·animals and plants in creation myths **1**:912d
·astrological conceptions **2**:219h
·Baltic biregional cosmology **2**:664g
·Christian view of man's relationship **4**:520h
·eschatological themes and conceptions **6**:959b
·Hindu macrocosm and microcosm **8**:936h
·Homer's view of nature's indifference **8**:1021f
·Jain matter, beings, and processes **10**:9c
·Japanese Buddhist law of origination **10**:102c
·Jewish doctrinal conceptions **10**:292b
·Jewish mystical cosmology of sefirot **10**:184g
·magic as a phenomenon of cosmology **11**:299e
·mystical principles of Hinduism **8**:923c
·mythic bases of Western science **4**:554f
·nature concept in religious study **12**:877e
·primitive relation to world as personal **14**:1045h
·religious belief influences **15**:594g
·ritual control of the elements **18**:218g

·salvation and the physical universe **16**:202b
·Swedenborg's theory of cosmology **17**:855c
·Taoism conceptual basis **4**:416f
·Taoist microcosm–macrocosm concept **17**:1035c
·Vedic cosmology and concept of time **8**:929b

RELATED ENTRIES in the *Ready Reference and Index: for*
cosmology: see cosmogony; cosmology
natural philosophy: hylozoism; teleology
nature of life: creative evolution; emergence; noösphere; vitalism

Nature and Destiny of Man, The (1941), theological work by Reinhold Niebuhr.
·context, theme, and intent **13**:74g

Nature and the Greeks (1954), work by Erwin Schrödinger.
·Schrödinger's thoughts on ancient works **16**:361c

nature mysticism, form of mysticism in which the divine, or sacred, is perceived in natural forms and phenomena. The visible and sensible world, experienced in this special way, is central in this kind of mysticism. It may be distinguished from other types of mysticism in which the soul and its states, or an utterly transcendent ground or Godhead, is central.
·Böhme's theological development **2**:1202g
·mystical and other forms of experience **12**:786f

nature–nurture controversy: *see* heredity-environment controversy.

nature reserve, an area set aside by a government for the purpose of preserving certain animals, plants, or both. Nature reserves differ from national parks (*q.v.*) in that the latter protect land and wildlife for public enjoyment, while nature reserves protect animals for their own sake.

Endangered species are often kept in reserves, away from the hunters who brought them close to extinction. In the U.S., numerous wildlife refuges have served this purpose, especially with respect to birds. Nature reserves are also numerous in Europe, India, Indonesia, and some African countries.

The origin of modern nature reserves lies in medieval times, when landowners established game preserves for the protection of animals they hunted. The idea of protecting animals simply to keep them from dying out did not arise until the 19th century. *Major ref.* **5**:52e
·zoos of open-space variety **19**:1162g

nature worship 12:877, a working concept limited primarily to those involved in or influenced by the modern, especially Western, study of religion and concerned with the veneration of individual natural phenomena. The concept of nature as an entity in itself is a philosophical or poetic conception that has been developed among advanced civilizations. Nonliterate or primitive peoples comprehend individual natural phenomena as objects or forces that influence them and are thus worthy of being venerated or placated.

The text article covers nature as a sacred totality; heaven and earth as sacred spaces, forces, or processes; celestial phenomena as objects of worship or veneration; the forces of nature; and the worship of animals, animalism, and totemism.

REFERENCES in other text articles:
·African ceremonial dances **1**:253b
·Akhenaton's religious reforms in Egypt **1**:402h
·animal and plant deities and spirits **1**:912f
·Aztec and Toltec deities and beliefs **2**:549c
·Baltic form of Indo-European archetype **2**:665a
·Celtic deities and beliefs **3**:1068h
·Chinese myths and rites **4**:412a
·Chinese visual arts theme basis **19**:175h
·divinized sky in monotheism **15**:626f
·Egyptian religious anthropomorphism **6**:504h
·Egyptian 5th-dynasty Heliopolitan trend **11**:895g
·Finno-Ugric monotheistic elements **7**:311g
·Hindu development to pantheism **13**:950d
·Hindu marginal folk deities **8**:899a
·Inca feline, lunar, and solar deities **9**:259d
·Iranian religious traditions **9**:869h
·Japanese visual art influence **19**:243d
·Meso-American religion **11**:955g
·Mesopotamian forms **11**:1003b
·mythological sources of deities **12**:801c
·Near East divine–earthly correspondence **12**:918f
·Near East fertility motif in antiquity **16**:115g
·polytheistic forces and objects **14**:785d
·prehistoric theriomorphic higher beings **14**:986f *passim* to 988h
·pre-Incan animal deities **1**:842c *passim* to 845a
·rust deity propitiation of Romans **12**:758a
·sacred settings for ritualistic objects **3**:1175f
·seasonal renewal and food supply ritual **7**:198h
·Söderblom's religions classification **15**:632d
·South Asian ritual and symbolism **17**:129g
·South Asian spirits' artistic uses **17**:131d
·Southeast American Indian beliefs **17**:221e
·Syrian and Palestinian antiquity **17**:966b
·totemistic world view **18**:529e
·trees venerated as deities **18**:690a
·water's healing powers **8**:686b

Nāṭya-śāstra, in full, BHĀRATA NĀṬYA-ŚĀSTRA, detailed treatise and handbook on dramatic art that deals with all aspects of the classical Sanskrit theatre. It was probably written between *c.* AD 100 and *c.* AD 200 by the mythic Brahmin sage and priest Bharata. The style of dance drama described in the *Nāṭya-śāstra* owes a great deal to Vedic ritual, as Bharata acknowledged, but it also has a strong element drawn from non-Vedic traditions. The strictly Vedic elements are said to have sprung from Brahmā, the rest from Śiva. With the growing prominence of Śiva (especially in his form of Naṭarāja, the lord of the dance) the importance of the Vedic elements was obscured and can be traced only occasionally in the surviving traditions.

Of the four main schools of South Asian dance drama that have survived in modern times, the closest to the art described in the *Nāṭya-śāstra* is the style generally called *bhārata-nāṭya* (*q.v.*), derived from the dance as performed by the *devadāsī*s in the South Indian temples. It is, however, not *nāṭya* ("drama") but *nṛtya* ("descriptive dance") mixed with *nṛtta* ("pure dance"), mostly to the accompaniment of very intricate drumming. *Major ref.* **5**:986e
·dance gesture stylization **5**:469h
·musical theatrical technique **17**:152e
·staging of Indian dance drama **17**:533e

nauarch, in ancient Greece, an admiral or supreme commander of the navy, used as an official title primarily in Sparta in the late 5th and early 4th centuries BC. The nauarch could hold office only once, for a period of one year, and being subject to the highest magistrates, the ephors, could be deposed if proved incompetent. Acting independently of the kings and hampered by no colleague, however, the nauarch exercised considerable power and influence.

In the period before the increased specialization of function in the Greek states, naval and military operations were combined under the *strategus* (*stratēgos*), who commanded the fleet as well as the army; thus the term nauarch originally was a general designation for a head of any naval unit or the entire navy.

Naucoridae (insect family): *see* creeping water bug.

Naucrates ductor (fish species): *see* pilot fish.

Naucratis (ancient Greek settlement): *see* Naukratis.

Naudé, Gabriel (b. Feb. 2, 1600, Paris—d. July 30, 1653, Abbeville), French physician and librarian, considered the first important theoretician of modern library organization. He was a practicing librarian when he was appointed (1633) honorary physician to the French king Louis XIII. His treatise on library science, *Avis pour dresser une bibliothèque* (1627), was influential. As librarian to Cardinal Jules Mazarin from 1642, he organized the Bibliothèque Mazarine. This 40,000-volume collection, available to researchers from 1643, was dispersed during the revolutionary Fronde period (1648–53), when Naudé was exiled to Sweden.
·library history and function **10**:859d
·library science development **10**:867c

Naugatuck, town and borough, New Haven County, southwestern Connecticut, U.S., on the Naugatuck River just south of Waterbury. First settled *c.* 1704 by Samuel Hickox, it was called Judd's Meadows and South Farms. The town of Naugatuck (Algonkin Indian: One Tree) originated as Salem Parish or Salem Bridge. It was incorporated from parts of Waterbury, Bethany, and Oxford in 1844. The industrial borough of Naugatuck (established 1893) became coextensive with the town in 1895. Naugatuck includes Union City and part of the Naugatuck State Forest. Abundant waterpower led to an early transition from farming to manufacturing, and the town's basic rubber industry was established in 1843 by Henry Goodyear, who perfected the vulcanization process. The economy is now well diversified to include the production of chemicals, plastics, metals, machinery, clocks and watches, and instruments. Pop. (1980) 26,456.
41°30′ N, 73°04′ W

naughts and crosses (game): *see* ticktacktoe.

Nauheim, Bad (West Germany): *see* Bad Nauheim.

Naujan Lake, on the northeastern coastal plain of Mindoro, Philippines, is the Philippines' third largest lake, 8.5 mi (14 km) long and 4 mi wide, and a productive freshwater fishing site. It is the central feature of Naujan Lake National Park (established in 1956), which comprises a 5,377-ac (2,175-ha) area of marshes and forest that serve as breeding grounds for marsh birds, crocodiles, and sailfinned lizards.

Naujan Lake was formerly a popular hunting and sport-fishing area; fishing rights are retained only by neighbouring towns, for whom the lake is a source of livelihood.
13°10′ N, 121°21′ E

Naukratis, also NAUCRATIS, ancient Greek settlement in the Nile Delta, on the Canopic (western) branch of the river. An *emporion* ("trading station") with exclusive trading rights in Egypt, Naukratis was the centre of cultural relations between Greece and Egypt in the pre-Hellenistic period. The station was established by Milesians in the 7th century BC, but Greeks from other cities also settled there. It flourished throughout the classical period but declined after Alexander's conquest of Egypt and the foundation of Alexandria (332).

The site of Naukratis was discovered in 1884 by W.M. Flinders Petrie and excavated by Petrie and Ernest Gardner (1884–86) and by D.G. Hogarth (1899, 1903). They uncovered dedications to deities and Greek pottery that threw light on the early history of the alphabet and the commercial activity of various Greek states, especially in the 6th century BC.
·archaeological study of Greek trade **14**:164c
·establishment and growth **8**:330c; map 335

Naulahka, The (1892), novel by Rudyard Kipling and Wolcott Balestier.
·co-authorship with Wolcott Balestier **10**:486d

naulatähti (mythology): *see* põhjanael.

naumachia, Greek word denoting a naval battle, used by the Romans as a term for a mimic sea battle and for a specially constructed basin in which such a battle sometimes took place. These entertainments also took

place in flooded amphitheatres. The opposing sides were prisoners of war or convicts, who fought until one side was destroyed. The earliest naumachia recorded (46 BC) represented an engagement between the Egyptian and Tyrian fleets and was given by Julius Caesar on a lake constructed by him in the Campus Martius. In 2 BC Augustus staged a naumachia between Athenians and Persians in a basin newly constructed on the right bank of the Tiber at Rome. In the naumachia arranged by Claudius on Lake Fucino in AD 52, 100 ships and 19,000 men participated.
·Augustus' site for mock sea battles **1**:1037b

Naumann, Friedrich (b. March 25, 1860, Störmthal, Prussia, now in East Germany—d. Aug. 24, 1919, Travemünde), political and social theorist, publicist, and reformer who became one of the most influential partisans of German economic and cultural imperialism.

As a young pastor, Naumann had joined the Christian Social movement of the Prussian court chaplain Adolf Stoecker, but he was eventually repelled by Stoecker's social and theological conservatism. Through 1893 he shaped the journal *Die Hilfe* ("Assistance") into a forum for his ideas and shortly, under the influence of the young sociologist Max Weber, founded the National Social Union (1896)—an organization that combined a program of democratic and social reform with a call to national strength. After 1903, however, having failed to establish a political party based on his association, he joined the Freisinnigen Vereinigung (Liberal Union)—later (1910) merged with the Progressive People's Party—and in 1907 was elected to the Reichstag (parliament). Though he strongly opposed a policy of imperial annexation, his *Mitteleuropa* (1915) provided the vision of a postwar German cultural and economic imperium in central Europe. In 1919 he was one of the founders of the Democratic Party and served as the party's leader until his death. He was a man of considerable intelligence and great personal integrity whose ideas exerted a wide-ranging influence over a whole generation of German liberal intellectuals.
·association with Gustav Stresemann **17**:732d
·Weber's ideological influence **19**:715f

Naumburg, city, Halle *Bezirk* (district), southern East Germany, on the Saale River, near the mouth of the Unstrut River, southwest of Halle. Founded by the margraves of Meissen *c.* 1000, it was granted to the Bishop of Zeitz when he transferred his seat to Naumburg in 1028. It received town rights in 1142. A member of the Hanseatic League in the 15th century, it fell to Saxony in 1564 and to Prussia in 1815. Its Romanesque and Gothic 13th–14th-century cathedral of SS. Peter and Paul is notable, and there are remains of four churches from the 16th–18th centuries. Naumburg's industries include the manufacture of foodstuffs, textiles, machinery, and toys. Pop. (1974 est.) 36,900.
51°09′ N, 11°48′ E
·cathedral Gothic sculpture **19**:367d; illus. 368
·map, German Democratic Republic **8**:8

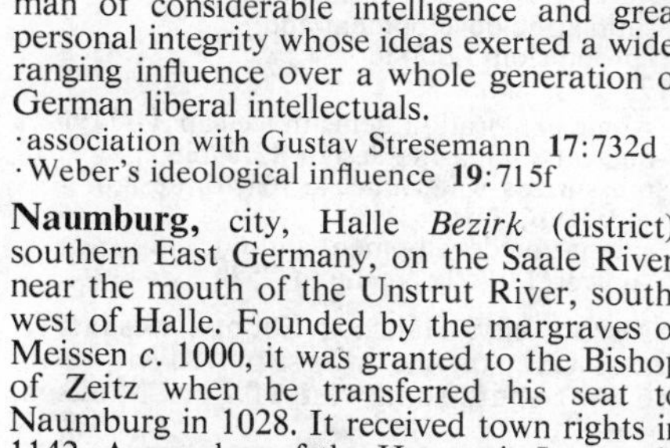

The cathedral at Naumburg, E.Ger.
W. Krammisch—Bruce Coleman Inc.

Ñaupán, Cerro, mountain, Ecuador, located in the Nudo de Azuay, a transverse range of the Cordillera Central.
2°24′ S, 78°52′ W
·Andes location and elevation **1**:858c

Nauplia, Modern Greek NÁVPLION, chief town of Argolís *nomós* (department), in the Peloponnese (Pelopónnisos), Greece, at the head of the Argolikós Kólpos (gulf). The port, southeast of Argos, sits on the north slope of twin crags; Itche Kale (279 ft [85 m]), the western crag, forms a small peninsula in the bay, while the much higher Palamídhion (705 ft [215 m]), with a Venetian castle, dominates the port from the southeast. The tiny island of Boúrtzi off Nauplia has a Venetian fortress, the Castel Pasqualigo (1471), which has been converted into a hotel.

Nauplia fell to Argos about 625 BC and thereafter played little part in classical history. In earlier Mycenaean times, however, it probably had been the maritime outlet for Argos, for the name Nauplia means Naval Station. It revived in Byzantine times but in AD 1210 was captured by the Franks and became, with Argos, a fief of the duchy of Náxos. In 1388 it was bought by the Venetians, who called it Napoli di Romania. It repelled several Turkish sieges but fell in 1540, becoming the capital of the Turkish Morea (Peloponnese). In 1686 Venice recovered it and fortified the Palamídhion rock, but it lost control again in 1715 to the Turks, who held it until the Greeks captured it in 1822 during the War of Greek Independence. From 1829 to 1834 it was the seat of the Greek government. In 1941 the British lost several large ships in the gulf while evacuating their forces through the port.

Venetian fortress on the island of Boúrtzi, off Nauplia, Greece
Farrell Grehan—Photo Researchers

With its Byzantine, Frankish, and Venetian castles and fortifications, Nauplia retains a strong medieval character. On one corner of Síndagma (Constitution) Square is the mosque of Vouleftiko, in which the first assembly of free Greece met. Pop. (1971) 9,281.
37°34′ N, 22°48′ E
·map, Greece **8**:316

nauplius, in biology, free-swimming larval stage found in crustaceans such as the copepods, ostracopods, decapods, and barnacles. These larvae are microscopic and usually have three pairs of appendages, a median eye, and little or no segmentation of the body.
·appendages and locomotion **5**:543e; illus. 546
·barnacle larval development **4**:642b; illus.
·branchiopod life cycle **3**:114d
·crustacean developmental stages **5**:312g; illus. 313
·larval anatomy and life-style **5**:640f

nauratan (Hindi: "nine jewels"), early type of Hindu amulet worn as a necklace.
·Hindu amulet design **10**:179h

Nauru, officially NAOERO, island republic in the southwest Pacific Ocean, about 2,400 mi (3,900 km) southwest of Hawaii. Oval in shape, it has a circumference of 12 mi and an area of 8.2 sq mi (21.3 sq km). It is an uplifted coral formation with a central plateau, 200 ft (60 m) high, covered with beds of phosphate rock and including Buada Lagoon, a depression that fills intermittently with seepage water. Below the plateau a level band of fertile land encircles the island and is the major zone of settlement. Beyond a sandy beach is a fringing reef. Generally hot and humid, Nauru has an annual rainfall of 80 in. (2,000 mm) but occasionally experiences severe droughts. Vegetation includes coconut palms, pandanus, and some scrub hardwood. Bird life is sparse; pigs and poultry have been introduced.

Visited (1798) by a British navigator, John Hunter, the island was named Pleasant because of the friendly welcome extended by its inhabitants. Whalers often called there in the 19th century. Nauru was annexed by Germany in 1888 as part of its Marshall Islands protectorate. In 1906 a British company began to exploit its valuable phosphate deposits. After World War I, the island came under a League of Nations mandate granted to Britain, New Zealand, and Australia. Occupied by Japanese troops from 1942 to 1945, Nauru was made a United Nations trust territory under Australian administration in 1947 and gained complete independence in 1968. It became an associate member of the (British) Commonwealth of Nations in 1969. Its parliamentary government consists of a president, cabinet, and legislature. The capital is Yaren.

The economy of Nauru is based entirely on the export of phosphate rock. Because its fringing reef does not provide good anchorage, ships must anchor offshore and receive their cargo via a complex system of conveyor belts and cantilevers similar to that found on Ocean Island, 190 miles east.

Nauruans are of mixed racial characteristics, dominantly Polynesian, who speak a distinct language. Education is compulsory and provided by government schools; there is a teacher training centre at Aiwo, one of the 14 local districts. A road encircles the island, and there is a rail line to move phosphate rock. The airport has had regularly scheduled flights to Australia and Fiji since 1969. Pop. (1973 est.) 7,000.
·geographical features **13**:827b
·map, Pacific Islands **2**:433
·Micronesian cultural patterns **12**:122b
·Oceanian economic development **13**:471f
·Pacific Ocean floor map **13**:841
·phosphate deposit administration **2**:432e
·politics, area, and population **13**:829f; table 830

naus (Greek: "ship"), Catalan NAVETAS, megalithic graves of the long cairn type, built of closely fitting blocks of stone in the shape of an overturned boat with a rounded stern and a squared or slightly concave front. The tombs, located on the Balearic Isles, were built with a small door in the front that gave access to a slab-roofed passage leading to a long rectangular burial chamber. Constructed during the Neolithic Period, the graves were the equivalent of the long barrow (*q.v.*) of western Europe.

·megalithic architecture of Bronze Age **19**:279c

nausea, named for the Greek word for seasickness, a feeling of discomfort in the pit of the stomach that is associated with a revulsion for food and an expectation that vomiting will follow, as it often does. Nausea is usually attended by secretion of unusual quantities of saliva and may arise from any of the causes of an abnormal lack of appetite—for example, shock, pain, intracranial pressure, badly fitting dentures, disease of the liver or of the kidneys. Nausea may be associated with dizziness (vertigo) as a result of diseases of the inner ear or of the brainstem or in association with epilepsy or migraine. It may arise from an injury to the head or, finally, from motion sickness, as its name implies.

·digestive disorder symptoms **5**:769a

Nausée, La (1938), English translation NAUSEA (1949), early novel of the French Existentialist writer Jean-Paul Sartre. Written in diary form, the work expresses the revulsion the writer Roquentin feels for the "viscous" world of matter, and his yearning in vain for a certain, masculine universe. He finally finds salvation in art, creating imaginary worlds which have the formal perfection that the real world lacks. In 1950 it was one of 12 novels selected for the Grand Prix des Meilleurs Romans du Demi-siècle, a special literary award for the best French novels in the first half of the 20th century.

·analysis of theme **16**:256f
·novel as philosophical vehicle **13**:282d

Nauset, also known as CAPE INDIANS, an Algonkian-speaking tribe that occupied most of what is now Cape Cod, in Massachusetts. They probably came into contact with whites at an early date because of their location, and Samuel de Champlain is known to have encountered them in 1606. Their subsistence was probably based on fishing, but they are also known to have cultivated corn (maize) and beans. They were semi-sedentary, moving between fixed sites with seasonal changes in food resources.

Although hostile to the Plymouth colonists at first, the Nauset later became their friends, supplying food to the starving colonists in 1622. Most Nauset remained loyal to the settlers through King Philip's War (*q.v.*). Many had been converted to Christianity before the war broke out, and by 1710 all were organized into churches. In that year many died of fever, and by 1802 only four Nauset were said to survive. Other Indian tribes, however, driven from their own territories, had joined the Nauset, and a number of mixed descendants survive.

·Woodlands Indian culture **6**:169b

Naushahra (Pakistan): *see* Nowshera.

nautanki, folk theatre of Uttar Pradesh state, India.

·actors' participation in chorus **17**:165g

nautilus, common name for two genera of cephalopod mollusks: the pearly or chambered nautilus (*Nautilus*), to which the name properly applies; and the paper nautilus (*Argonauta*), a cosmopolitan genus related to the octopus (*q.v.*).

The pearly nautilus has a smooth, coiled shell about 25 centimetres (10 inches) in diameter, consisting of about 36 chambers, the last of which it lives in. The chambers are connected by a tube that absorbs gases from the chambers, allowing the shell to act as a float. *Nautilus* swims about the ocean bottom in search of shrimp or other prey. It uses up to 94 small, suckerless, contractile tentacles for capturing prey. *Nautilus*, the last surviving genus of the ancient order Nautiloidea, is important in paleontology for dating the strata in which it appears.

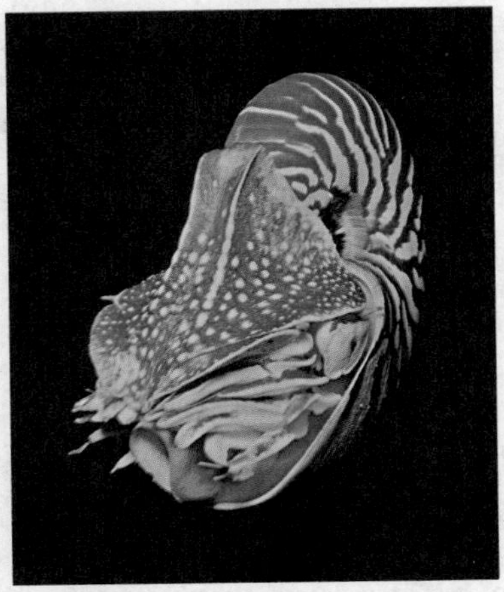

Chambered nautilus (*Nautilus*)
Douglas Faulkner

The paper nautilus is usually found near the surface of tropical and subtropical seas feeding on plankton; the females differ from other members of the order Octopoda in possessing a thin unchambered coiled shell, formed by large flaps, or membranes, on the dorsal arms, in which the eggs are laid and the young hatch. Large shells, which attain a diameter of 30 to 40 centimetres (12 to 16 inches), are very fragile. The male is only about $\frac{1}{20}$ the size of the female, possesses no shell, and was once thought to be parasitic in the shell of the female. The female resembles the genus *Octopus* in other features.

·anatomy, habits, and classification **3**:1149e; illus. 1154a
·buoyancy control in locomotion, traits, and appraised classification **12**:330c; illus. 326
·buoyancy device structure and function **16**:820d

fossil forms
·Cambrian evolution **3**:691a
·characters and phylogenetic relations **7**:561g; illus.
·evolutions, traits, and classifications **12**:330c
·fossil occurrence, illus. 3 **17**:721
·Jurassic forms and shell diversity **10**:358c
·life style, traits, and classification **3**:1152g
·Lower Triassic fossils **18**:695d
·Ordovician evolution **13**:659f
·Permian life **14**:97f
·photoreceptive mechanism comparisons **14**:356a

Nautilus, name of at least three historic submarines, including the world's first nuclear-powered undersea craft, and a fourth famous in science fiction.

The U.S. engineer Robert Fulton built one of the earliest submersible craft in 1800 in France, under a grant from Napoleon. A collapsing mast and sail provided surface propulsion, and a hand-turned propeller drove the craft when submerged. A notable feature was the iron plates over the wooden hull. Despite some experimental successes in diving and even sinking ships, Fulton's "Nautilus" failed to attract development support from either the French or the British.

In 1870 Jules Verne's science-fiction classic *Twenty Thousand Leagues Under the Sea* was published, describing the voyage of Captain Nemo's "Nautilus."

In 1886, Andrew Campbell and James Ash of England built a "Nautilus" driven by electric motors powered by a storage battery; it augured the development of the submarine powered by internal-combustion engines on the surface and by electric-battery power when submerged.

The name "Nautilus" was chosen for the United States Navy vessel launched Jan. 21, 1954 (*see* Figure), as the first true submarine capable of prolonged, instead of temporary, submersion. Powered by propulsion turbines driven by steam produced by a nuclear reactor, the "Nautilus" was capable of submerged speeds in excess of 20 knots (nautical miles per hour) and furthermore could maintain such a speed almost indefinitely. Much larger than the older type of submarine, the "Nautilus" was 319 feet (97 metres) long and displaced 3,180 tons. On Aug. 1–5, 1958, the "Nautilus," under Commander William R. Anderson, made an historic underwater cruise from Point Barrow, Alaska, to the Greenland Sea, passing beneath the North Pole. The "Nautilus" set many standards for future nuclear submarines, including extensive protection against possible radiation contamination and auxiliary diesel-electric power.

1800
·Fulton's design and testing **7**:776d
·submarine inventions and development **17**:747f

1886
·submarine development and propulsion **17**:748d

1954
·Arctic exploration beneath ice cap **1**:1119f
·nuclear submarine design **12**:896h
·pressurized-water nuclear reactor design **13**:319b; illus.
·submarine development and nuclear power **17**:750g *passim* to 752h

Nauvoo, city, Hancock County, western Illinois, U.S., on the Mississippi River, 10 mi (16 km) south-southwest of Fort Madison, Iowa.

Nauvoo's significance in Illinois history is especially related to the Mormon era. When the Mormons arrived in 1839, there were already a few buildings in what was called Commerce; renamed Nauvoo by their leader Joseph Smith, it grew to be a Mormon community of about 20,000. Following the exodus of the Mormons to Utah in 1846 (after the death of Smith and his brother at the hands of a mob at the jail in nearby Carthage), Nauvoo was settled temporarily by the Icarians, a group of Socialists, chiefly of French origin, whose founder was Étienne Cabet. At their peak, the Icarians at Nauvoo numbered be-

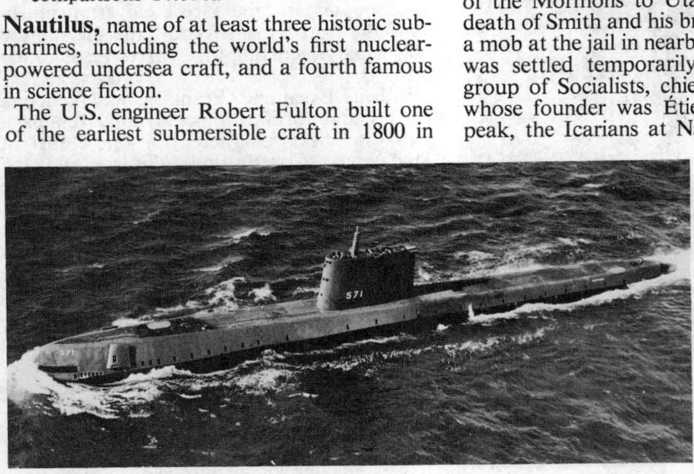

USS "Nautilus"
By courtesy of the U.S. Navy

tween 1,200 and 1,800. The community was open to anyone who would pay the introductory sum of 300 francs and would donate all his possessions to the community. The Icarian communal venture, however, was doomed to early failure. A crisis developed when Cabet was refused dictatorial powers. Voted from office, he left Nauvoo with 180 followers and went to St. Louis, Mo., where he died in 1856.

The Joseph Smith residence, Nauvoo, Ill.

By courtesy of the Illinois Department of Business and Economic Development

The community never recovered from the split; it soon disbanded, and the members were absorbed into the general population. The Icarian School (1853), the last remaining evidence of the Icarian settlement, was demolished in 1972 as part of the project underway to restore the Mormon community as it was 1839–46.

Historic landmarks include the Joseph Smith Homestead (1802), the original log hut of the Smith Family; the Joseph Smith Mansion (1843), built as Smith's permanent home; and the Brigham Young Home, which has been restored.

Wine and blue cheese making, the milling of whole wheat flour, and tourism are the chief sources of income. There are extensive vineyards and apple orchards in the area. St. Mary's Academy, a Roman Catholic boarding school for girls, was established (1874) in the city. Nauvoo State Park is nearby. Inc. 1841. Pop. (1980) 1,133.
40°33′ N, 91°23′ W

·foundation by the Mormons **9**:240c
·Mormon foundation and settlement **12**:442g

Navadvīpa, an ancient Indian philosophical school, in Bengal.

·principal exponents and doctrines **9**:327e

Navaho, U.S. surface-to-surface missile.

·design, operation, and use **15**:930b

Navaʿi, (Mir) Ali Shir (b. 1441, Herāt, now in Afghanistan—d. Jan. 3, 1501, Herāt), Turkish poet and scholar who was the greatest representative of Chagatai Turkish literature (written in an eastern Turkic dialect).

Born into an aristocratic military family, he studied in Herāt and in the city of Mashhad. After his school companion, the sultan Husayn-i Bāyqarā, succeeded to the throne of Herāt, Navaʿi held a number of offices at court. He was also a member of the Naqshbandī dervish order, and under his master, the renowned Persian poet Jāmī, he read and studied the works of the great mystics. As a philanthropist, he was responsible for the construction of many mosques, hospitals, mausoleums, bridges, and caravansaries. His other interests included miniature painting, music, architecture, and the art of calligraphy.

He devoted the latter part of his life to poetry and scholarship, writing first in Persian and then in Chagatai. He left four great *dīvāns* ("collections") belonging to different phases of his life and five romances based on conventional themes in Islāmic literature, such as his famous rendition of the well-known story *Farhād and shīrīn*, in 12,000 lines. Among his main prose works are the *Muhakamat al-lugatayn* (Eng. trans., *The Trial of the Two Languages*, 1966), a comparison of the Turkish and Persian languages; the *Majālis an-nafāis* (1965; "Séances of the Exquisite"), containing much autobiographical information and facts about the lives of Turkish poets; and *Mizan al-awzan* (1965–68; "The Measure of Metres"), a treatise on Turkish prosody. Navaʿi's mastery of the eastern Turkic Chagataī language was such that it came to be known as "the language of Navaʿi."

·Chagatai literary works **9**:965g

Navajo, also spelled NAVAHO, the most populous of all Indian groups in the United States, with about 100,000 individuals in the early 1970s scattered throughout northwestern New Mexico, northeastern Arizona, and southeastern Utah. The Navajo speak an Apachean language and, like their Apache cousins, are classified in the Athabascan language family. It is uncertain when the Navajo and Apache migrated to the Southwest from Canada, where most other Athabascan-speaking Indians still live, but it was probably between AD 900 and 1200. Those early Navajo would have borne more resemblance to contemporary Apache than to contemporary Navajo, for the Navajo came under the strong influence of the Pueblo Indians (*q.v.*). These Pueblo influences included farming as the primary mode of subsistence, with a concomitant trend toward a sedentary existence. In historic times farming has been supplemented—and, in some regions, superseded—by herding of sheep, goats, and cattle.

The Navajo resemble other Apachean peoples in their lack of a centralized tribal or political organization. Formerly the Navajo were organized into small bands of related kinsmen, with local headmen. Similar local groups, based on locality of residence rather than kinship, still exist, and many of these local groups have elected headmen. A Navajo local group is not a village or town, but rather a collection of dwellings scattered over a wide area.

Navajo contacts with Pueblo Indians are recorded at least as early as the 17th century, when refugees from some of the Rio Grande Pueblo came to the Navajo after the Spanish suppression of the Pueblo Revolt. During the 18th century, some Hopi Indians (*see* Hopi) left their mesas because of drought and famine and came to live with the Navajo, particularly in Canyon de Chelly in northeast Arizona. These Pueblo visits influenced the Navajo not only in agriculture but also in the arts. Painted pottery and the famous Navajo rugs, as well as elements of Navajo ceremonialism such as dry-sand painting, are all products of these contacts. Another famous Navajo craft, silversmithing, dates from the middle of the 19th century and was probably first learned from Mexican smiths.

The Navajo religious system was intricate. Some of the many myths related the emergence of the first people from various worlds beneath the surface of the Earth; other stories justified the numerous rites that were performed. Some of these were simple rituals carried out by individuals or families for luck in travel, trade, and gambling and for protection of crops and herds. The more complex rites demanded a specialist, who was paid according to his skill and the length of the ceremonial. Most rites were primarily for curing bodily and psychiatric illness. In other ceremonies there were simply prayers or songs, and dry paintings might be made of pollen and flower petals. In some cases there were public dances and exhibitions at which hundreds or thousands of Navajo gathered. Many of the rites are still performed.

Although the Navajo never raided as extensively as the Apache, their raiding was serious enough to cause the U.S. government in 1863 to order Col. Kit Carson to subdue them. This order resulted in the destruction of large amounts of crops and herds and the incarceration of about 8,000 Navajo, along with 400 Mescalero, at Bosque Redondo, 180 miles south of Santa Fe, N.M. This four-year (1864–68) captivity left a legacy of bitterness and distrust that has still not entirely disappeared. *See* Apache and Navajo Wars.

The Navajo Reservation and government-allotted lands in the states of New Mexico, Arizona, and Utah today total more than 24,000 square miles (64,000 square kilometres). The region, however, is mainly arid and generally will not support enough agriculture and livestock to provide a livelihood for everyone. Thousands earn their living as transient workers away from the Navajo country, and appreciable numbers have settled on irrigated lands along the lower Colorado River and in such places as Los Angeles and Kansas City, Mo.

·American Indian local races **15**:349b
·amulet worship **3**:1175e
·Arizona tribal governing responsibilities **2**:3a
·Earth-centred cosmogony **5**:240e
·habitation and cultural patterns **17**:305h; map
·jewelry design and techniques **10**:181d
·myth, art, and music in ritual **1**:659f
·mythic biological class system **1**:917b
·New Mexico Indian settlement **13**:3a
·origins and cultural borrowings **13**:216b
·pre-Colombian silverwork **11**:1118b
·purification and ritual medicine **15**:303c
·Utah region of inhabitance **18**:1103d
·vertical loom use **18**:177g
·weaving influences and jewelry **1**:678g; illus. 680
·witchcraft beliefs **19**:896g

Navajo Sandstone Formation, division of Upper Triassic (and in part, Lower Jurassic) rocks in the U.S. that occurs over a wide area including parts of Arizona, Nevada, New Mexico, Utah, and Colorado (the Triassic Period, which preceded the Jurassic, began about 225,000,000 years ago and lasted about 35,000,000 years). The Navajo Formation, the uppermost division of the Glen Canyon Group, overlies the Kayenta Sandstone, underlies rocks of the San Rafael Group, and was named for exposures studied on the Navajo Indian Reservation in Arizona. The Navajo Formation primarily consists of wind-blown sandstones representing a widespread dune field of dual age, partly Triassic and partly Jurassic, that gradually spread eastward. Today, excellent exposures of the Navajo Sandstone may be seen in the walls of Zion Canyon, in Zion National Park, Utah. The Navajo weathers in a characteristic pattern and forms striking natural arches and dome-shaped masses.

·varved deposit formation **19**:35b

Navajo war: *see* Apache and Navajo wars.

Navajo weaving, blankets and rugs made by the Navajos and thought to be the most colourful and best made textiles produced by North American Indians.

Formerly a semi-nomadic tribe, the Navajos settled in the southwestern United States toward the late 17th century. With a new life as a sedentary and agricultural people, the tribe

Navajo weaver in Arizona

Richard Erdoes—Alpha

began to practice weaving, which had been virtually unknown to them, learning from the Hopi Indians how to build looms and construct fabrics on a large scale. They also began to raise sheep for wool.

The Hopis had limited their designs to striped patterns, but the Navajos introduced geometric shapes, diamonds, lozenges, and zig-zags. Symbolic representations of such phenomena as the elements, the seasons, and the times of day did not develop until about 1820.

Before 1800, Navajo blankets were largely made of natural coloured wool—black, white, and a mixture of the two that produced grey; a limited amount of dyeing was done, with roots, herbs, and minerals from the rich soil of the area, primarily producing, dark colours, like those of the Hopis. Shortly after the turn of the 19th century, however, red *bayeta* cloth purchased from the Spaniards was unravelled and the thread used to make Navajo textiles. The introduction of aniline dyes in the late 19th century led to a period in Navajo weaving characterized by bright and even gaudy designs. Vividly coloured yarns were used to weave into the rugs and blankets a broad range of decorative motifs based on commonplace modern objects; representations of automobiles, bottles, tomato cans, and airplanes, for example, found their way into the formerly dignified and restrained fabrics. More traditional, geometric designs subsequently regained their popularity and are once again the dominant patterns.

In the Navajo tribe, as in most Indian nations, women are the weavers, and by tradition they are limited to abstract, geometrical designs and representations of nonliving objects. Only the men are allowed to create pictographic art showing man, animals, birds, or fish. The major exceptions in Navajo art are blankets woven on the design of sand paintings (*q.v.*), drawings done with different coloured sands. In this case, women are permitted to weave representations of living things, but only because the original designs, considered to be the real art, have been created by men.

naval academies: *see* military, naval, and air academies.

naval aircraft: *see* aircraft, military.

naval architecture: *see* ship design and construction.

naval base, shore installation that furnishes the principal logistic support to naval ships and craft. Though fortified harbours, natural and artificial, have served as bases for fighting ships since earliest times, the term naval base only acquired a high degree of significance with the introduction in the 19th century of steam propulsion, which made it impossible for fleets to remain at sea for long periods. The major maritime powers soon acquired naval bases in areas remote from home to permit their fleets to refuel regularly in distant waters. In addition to fuel and ammunition supplies, naval bases furnish facilities for maintenance and repair and usually for rest and recreation for crews.

The development of nuclear propulsion, especially in the form of nuclear submarines, has considerably diminished the importance of bases in naval strategy because nuclear vessels can remain at sea for almost indefinite periods.

Naval Laws, German legislation of 1898 to 1900 formulated by Admiral Alfred von Tirpitz to enlarge the German navy.
·Anglo-German arms race **19**:943g

Naval Observatory, Washington D.C., is the official source in the United States for standard time. Positional measurement of celestial objects for purposes of timekeeping and navigation has been the main work of the observatory since its beginning. In 1833 the first small observatory building was constructed near the Capitol. Time signals for the public were first given (1844) by the dropping of a ball from a staff on an observatory building. In 1904 the observatory broadcast the world's first radio time signals.

The observatory has been enlarged and moved several times. A 40-inch (102-centimetre) reflecting telescope acquired in 1934 was moved in 1955 to Flagstaff, Ariz., to obtain better atmospheric conditions, and a 61-inch (155-centimetre) reflector has been in use at Flagstaff since 1964. Other stations are maintained in Florida and in Argentina.

naval ships and craft 12:884, include all types of vessels large (ships) and small (craft), used by navies in combat and support roles.

The text article traces the history of warships from the galleys of the ancient world through the ages of sail and steam to the latest missile-armed, electronically equipped, and nuclear-powered ships.

REFERENCES in other text articles:
·aircraft carrier development **7**:390a
·aircraft carrier steam catapult **17**:633a
·air-cushion machines as troop carriers **1**:394e
·amphibious tank design **17**:1024b
·ancient rowing vessels of war **2**:1157f
·Anglo-German rivalry of World War I **19**:949f
·British air power in World War I **7**:394h
·Curtiss' experiments for U.S. Navy **7**:390a
·enemy warning and detection systems **19**:598h
·European militarism and arms race **4**:895d
·galley hull reinforcement **16**:677d
·gas turbine applications **18**:776b
·gunnery technology and functions **8**:497b
·life-support system in submarines **10**:923e
·logistics of supply and transport **19**:588h
·military transport since World War II **19**:594g
·nuclear reactors in submarines **13**:316d
·sailing ship design development **16**:157d
·tonnage, age, and cost characteristics **19**:549a
·transport vessels of the nuclear age **11**:86b
·weapons carriers of 20th century **19**:691f
·weapons systems of ancient times **19**:682d
·World War II battles and innovations **19**:981d
·World War II landing ships **11**:81c

RELATED ENTRIES in the *Ready Reference and Index: for*
classes of naval vessels: see aircraft carrier; battleship; cruiser; destroyer; frigate; galleon; galley; ironclad; launch; minesweeper; monitor, naval; submarine
specific naval vessels: Bismarck; Constitution; Dreadnought; Enterprise; Fulton; Long Beach; Missouri; Victory

naval stores, products such as tar, pitch, turpentine, pine oil, rosin, and terpenes obtained from the pine and other coniferous trees. Originally, the term designated materials used in building and maintaining wooden sailing ships and included flax, cordage, masts, and timber in addition to the products of the trees. Naval stores are produced chiefly by the United States and France, with large amounts coming also from Greece, Spain, Portugal, and Mexico.

Gum naval stores are derived from the oleoresin, a natural fluid commonly called crude turpentine, that exudes from incisions made in the living trees; wood naval stores are obtained by processing deadwood.

Oleoresin, also called gum or pitch, the raw material of the gum naval stores, is a semifluid substance composed of resins dissolved in turpentine oil, its chief component being pinene. It is extracted from the pine by cutting through the sapwood into the heartwood of the tree, in which the resins accumulate, and collecting the exudate that issues from the wound. From the cleansed and purified gum, turpentine is extracted by steam distillation, and the residual compounds harden into a pure, translucent, pale amber rosin.

Wood naval stores are derived from salvaged pinewood, such as tree stumps, and downwood, or lightwood, pine from which the bark and sapwood have fallen away in decay. Although methods of treating the wood vary, usually it is shredded and subjected to heat under pressure. The volatile components are driven off, condensed, and refined by fractional distillation; they yield wood turpentine and pine oil, the latter product unobtainable from the oleoresin of the living tree. The residual resin retained in the shredded wood is extracted by treatment with a mineral-oil solvent. The resulting resinous solution is purified and the solvent evaporated to obtain wood rosin.
·forestry and sustained yield principles **7**:528c

Navan, Irish AN UAIMH, urban district and county town (seat) of County Meath, Ireland, at the confluence of the Rivers Boyne and Blackwater. The Great Motte, an imposing earthwork 52 ft (16 m) high, is on its western outskirts. The town was walled and fortified by Hugh de Lacy and later became an outpost of the English Pale (territory). At Donaghmore are remains of a 13th-century Celtic church and a round tower. Navan is a shopping and market centre; it manufactures furniture, carpets, and woollen goods. Just northwest of Navan is Teltown Hill, site of an ancient royal residence, one of four built by the Irish king Tuathal. Pop. (1971) 4,605.
53°39′ N, 6°41′ W

Navarātrī (Sanskrit: Nine Nights), in Hinduism, the first 10 lunar days of the bright fortnight of the month of Āśvina (September–October); a major festival period in different parts of India.

Among followers of the goddess Durgā, particularly predominant in Bengal and Assam, the Durgā-pūjā (Worship of Durgā) is celebrated during this period. Special images of Durgā commemorating her victory over the buffalo-headed demon Mahiṣāsura are worshipped daily and on the 10th day (Daśaharā) are taken in large and jubilant processions to nearby rivers or tanks for immersion in water. Durgā-pūjā is traditionally the time for daughters to return to their fathers' homes. In addition to family feasting and visiting, the *pūjā* days are also celebrated with public concerts, recitations, plays, and fairs.

In other parts of India the 10th day, Daśaharā, is associated with the victory of the god Rāma over the demon-king Rāvaṇa. In North India the Rām Līlā (Play of Rāma) is the highlight of the festival. On successive nights different episodes of the epic poem the *Rāmāyaṇa* are dramatized by young actors elaborately costumed and masked; the pageant is always climaxed by the burning of huge effigies of the demons. Athletic tournaments and hunting expeditions are often organized. Tools and implements are worshipped during these holidays, a ceremony particularly popular among Kṣatriyas (members of the warrior class) and soldiers, who worship their arms.

Many other, lesser observances are associated with Navarātrī in varying ways throughout the country. On the first day of Navarātrī, a *pūjā* is celebrated in honour of the goddess of learning, Sarasvatī, in which she is worshipped together with the sacred books of the house; this is a favourite observance among the Bengali population of India. In certain parts of Mahārāshtra, the fifth day is given to the worship of the goddess Lalitā and is thus known as Lalitā-pañcamī (Lalitā's Fifth Day). *Major ref.* **8**:903a
·dance performance in Kṛṣṇa's honour **8**:480e
·enactment of Rāma's life **17**:158h

Navarin, Bay of, Greek ÓRMOS NAVARÍNOU, small, deep, almost landlocked inlet of the Ionian Sea in Messenia *nomós* (department), in the southwestern Peloponnese (Pelopónnisos), Greece. Known also as Pylos (Pílos) bay after Old Pylos, the headland at the north entrance, it was renamed after the town of Navarino, which was built on the south headland by the French in 1829 two years after the combined fleets of Great Britain, France, and Russia destroyed the Turko-Egyptian fleet in the bay during the War of Greek Independence. The historic island of Sfaktiría (Sphac-

teria) functions like a giant breakwater for the inner lagoon or shipping lane, leaving a broad channel on the south and the Stenón (channel) Sikiás on the north. The bay is known as one of the safest anchorages in the Mediterranean. At Palaiókastron (Paleo Kastro) are the ruins of a Frankish castle built in 1278.
36°52′ N, 21°39′ E

Navarin, Cape, tip of the Kamchatka Peninsula, Russian Soviet Federated Socialist Republic.
62°16′ N, 179°10′ E
·Bering Sea map **2**:845

Navarino (Greece): *see* Pylos.

Navarino, Battle of (Oct. 20, 1827), the decisive naval engagement of the Greek War of Independence against Turkey, fought in the harbour of Navarino in the southwestern Peloponnesus, between an Egyptian–Turkish fleet under Tahir Pasha and a combined British–French–Russian fleet under Adm. Sir Edward Codrington. The Egyptian–Turkish fleet (3 ships of the line, 15 frigates, and over 50 smaller ships) was at anchor in the harbour. The British–French–Russian fleet (totalling 11 ships of the line, 9 frigates, and 4 smaller ships), which had been sent to aid the Greek forces by intercepting Turkish supplies, met outside the harbour. Shortly after this fleet entered the harbour on October 20, the battle broke out. The superior European guns sent three-fourths of the Egyptian–Turkish fleet to the bottom and forced others aground. No European ships were sunk. Navarino was the last significant battle between wooden sailing ships. The Turkish defeat was so complete that within ten months they began to evacuate Greece, leading to the creation of the independent Kingdom of Greece in 1832.
·Greek independence inevitability **13**:786d
·Greek rebellion against Turkey **2**:625f

Navarre, Spanish NAVARRA, one of the four Basque provinces of northern Spain, bounded by the French Pyrenees to the north and the provinces of Guipúzcoa (northwest), Alava and Logroño (west), Zaragoza (south and southeast), and by Huesca (east); it has an area of 4,024 sq mi (10,421 sq km). Originally formed as a kingdom in the 9th century by the Basques, a people inhabiting the western Pyrenees on the Bay of Biscay, it was not annexed to Spain until 1512. In the remote districts, Lower and Upper Navarrese (Basque subdialects) and Navarro (Aragonese dialect) are still spoken.

Navarre has a great variety of scenery as it stretches from the western Pyrenees to the Río Ebro steppes. A tripartite division is clear: the Pyrenean sector, the central basin and hills, and the southern plateaus and steppes. The Pyrenean sector consists of a tangled relief of forested mountains and well-watered valleys, drained largely by the Río Bidasoa. Ironworkings have encouraged small metallurgical industries at Vera and Elizondo, linked by a narrow-gauge railway to Irún; but the dense stands of timber and pastoralism are the main sources of income. The central depression has united the diverse Pyrenean valleys and focussed commerce on the provincial capital of Pamplona (*q.v.*). In this climatically transitional zone, cereal cultivation mingles with forest lands and stock rearing, and settlements become more nucleated into villages. The southern half of Navarre consists essentially of foothills and steppes through which the valleys of the Ega, Arga, and Aragón rivers converge on the Río Ebro. Tudela, near the confluence of these valleys, serves as a regional market town. The landscape is more arid and monotonous with cultivation of cereals, and large settlements—*e.g.*, Estella and Tafalla. Las Bárdenas on the southeastern borders is true steppe. Pop. (1970) 464,867.
·area and population table **17**:389
·map, Spain **17**:382

Navarre, Kingdom of, in the Middle Ages, an independent kingdom of northern Spain (known until the last half of the 12th century as the Kingdom of Pamplona, after its capital); it occupied what is now the Spanish province of Navarre (Spanish *Navarra*) and the western part of the French *département* of Basses-Pyrénées.

Pamplona was under Muslim rule after 711, but the Basque magnates of the region early achieved some degree of autonomy and in *c.* 798 one of them, Iñigo Arista, established himself as an independent ruler there and for a time accepted Frankish suzerainty. By the time of Garcia Iniguez (*c.* 860–880), this dynasty was strong enough to assume regal titles and to establish diplomatic and family relations with the neighbouring Christian kingdom of Asturias.

The Navarrese Muslims were allowed to serve in the army and also provided an important source of skilled artisans. Large Jewish *aljamas* (congregations) existed in the chief towns and were protected by the Navarrese kings when persecution became serious elsewhere. Another important element were the *francos*—mostly French and Gascon immigrants—who inhabited separate quarters in Pamplona and other towns, and whose relations with the native Navarrese population were often strained.

Despite its small size in the later Middle Ages, Navarre's part in international politics was important, not only because of its involvement in French affairs but also because it controlled the main pass into Spain in the western Pyrenees and was a buffer state between Gascony, Castile, and Aragon. The chief pilgrim roads from the north to the shrine of Santiago de Compostela thus traversed it. From its earliest days to the 13th century the kingdom's history fell within a wholly Spanish context and was closely associated with that of Aragon. After 1234 it was ruled by a succession of French dynasties, and was affected by French influence.

In 1512 Ferdinand II the Catholic of Aragon occupied the Spanish portion of Navarre. In 1515 the country was formally annexed to the Castilian crown but retained its status, institutions, and law as an independent kingdom until the 19th century. As a province, it still preserves its civil administration and law.

The rest of Navarre continued as a separate kingdom until 1589, when its ruler became king of France as Henry IV. Thereafter it was united with France, whose sovereigns bore the title "king of France and Navarre" until the French Revolution of 1789.
·Ferdinand II's occupation and reign **7**:233d
·Hundred Years' War expansion of kingdom **9**:17h
·marital basis for Capetian acquisition **7**:617g; map 620
·political, economic, and cultural history **17**:408a
·royal marriage into House of Bourbon **3**:80c

Navarro, Pedro (*c.* 1460–1528), Spanish soldier of fortune, won his reputation as the foremost military engineer of his time by his mining operations against French-held Neapolitan castles in 1503.

Navarro Group, division of Upper Cretaceous rocks in the western Gulf region of the U.S. (the Cretaceous Period began about 136,000,000 years ago and lasted about 71,000,000 years). The Navarro Group is the uppermost division of the Gulf Series; it overlies the Taylor Marl and underlies the Midway Group (Tertiary Period). Named for exposures studied in Navarro County, Texas, the Navarro Group consists of about 200 metres (650 feet) of limestones and marls that are overlain by shales and clays. During Late Navarro deposition, extensive coral reefs flourished.

Navas de Tolosa, Battle of Las, major battle, called *al-ʿUqāb* in Arabic, of the Christian reconquest of Spain, in which the Almohads (a Muslim dynasty of North Africa and Spain) were severely defeated (1212) by the combined armies of Leon, Castile, Aragon, and Navarre.

Immobilized for several years by his crushing defeat at Alarcos (1195) at the hands of the Almohads, King Alfonso VIII of Castile and Leon gained the sympathy of the archbishop of Toledo, Rodrigo Jiménez de Rada, who proceeded to stir up religious indignation at the Muslim victory over Christians. A proclamation of a crusade was obtained from Pope Innocent III, which elicited further support from the bishops of Narbonne, Bordeaux, and Nantes (in France); and in the spring of 1212 contingents of French knights and Knights Templars began to converge on Toledo. After some delay, during which time the crusaders began to massacre the Toledan Jewry, the crusade set out on June 21, augmented by the armies of Aragon, Castile, and Leon. Despite their success in taking the Muslim fortresses of Malagón and Calatrava, the non-Spanish forces were soon discouraged by adverse climatic and living conditions and returned home. The armies of Navarre, however, were then recruited for the expedition.

Meanwhile, on June 22 the Almohad caliph Muḥammad an-Nāṣir had moved to Jaén, then the mountainous area around Baeza, intending to cut off the Christians at the plain of Las Navas de Tolosa. Soon after their arrival on July 12 the Christians took Castroferral with hopes of then reaching the Muslim encampment through the pass of La Llosa. The pass was heavily guarded, however, and it was through a local shepherd who directed the Christians to an alternate opening that they were able to reach the Muslim base. Alfonso himself led the Christians into battle and shattered the Almohad forces on July 16, 1212. An-Nāṣir fled, while Alfonso followed up his victory by immediately taking Baeza and Úbeda. The extensive effects of the Muslim defeat did not become apparent until after 1233, when the Almohad Empire was disintegrated by dynastic squabbles, and the Muslim hold on Spain, lacking a central leader, slipped rapidly before the armies of the Christian reconquest.
·Almohad decline in Spain **9**:932c
·Almohad defeat by crusaders **13**:159a

nave, central and principal part of a church, extending from the entrance (the narthex, *q.v.*) to the transepts (transverse aisle crossing the nave in front of the sanctuary in a cruciform church) or, in the absence of transepts, to the chancel (area around the altar). In a basilican church (*see* basilica), which has side aisles, nave refers only to the central aisle. The nave is that part of a church set apart for the laity,

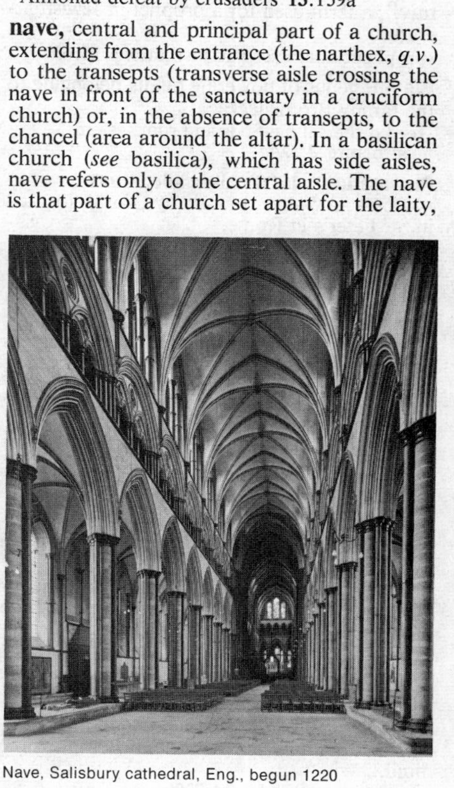

Nave, Salisbury cathedral, Eng., begun 1220
A.F. Kersting

as distinguished from the chancel, which is reserved for the choir and clergy. The term nave derives from the Latin *navis*, meaning "ship," and it has been suggested that it may have been chosen to designate the main body of the building because the ship had been adopted as a symbol of the church.
The form of the nave was adapted by the early Christian builders from the Roman hall of justice, the basilica. The nave of the early Christian basilica was usually lighted by a row of windows near the ceiling, called the clerestory (*q.v.*); and the main, central space was usually flanked on either side by one or two aisles, as in the Basilica of Old St. Peter's (AD 330) and S. Paolo Fuori le Mura (380), both in Rome. A flat timber roof normally covered the nave until the Romanesque and Gothic eras, when stone vaulting became almost universal in the major churches of northern Europe (*see* Romanesque art; Gothic art).
Medieval naves were generally divided into many bays, or compartments, producing the effect of great length by the repetition of forms. The standard medieval division of the nave wall into ground-floor arcade, tribune (a vaulted gallery space over the side aisles), optional triforium arcade (a blind or open arcade between the tribune and clerestory), and clerestory became more flexible during the Renaissance, so that frequently—as in S. Lorenzo (Florence; 1421–29) by Filippo Brunelleschi—the tribune and triforium are eliminated, and the nave wall is divided only into arcade and clerestory. During the Renaissance, the nave also was divided into fewer compartments, giving a feeling of spaciousness and balanced proportion between the height, length, and width. Extreme, dramatic effects, such as the marked verticality of the Gothic in cathedrals such as Reims (begun *c.* 1211), gave way to a more rationally designed nave space in which no single directional emphasis or sensation was stressed; St. Paul's Cathedral in London (1675–1711), rebuilt by Sir Christopher Wren after the Great Fire of 1666, provides a fine example.
·Indian use in various styles **17**:174a

navetas (grave): *see* naus.

navi', a term used for a prophet in Jewish literature.
·prophetic character and institutions **15**:63g

Navia, genus of flowering plants belonging to the family Bromeliaceae.
·seed dispersal methods and root system structure **3**:324g

Navicella (*c.* 1300), also called CHRIST WALKING ON THE WATER, mosaic by Giotto, located in St. Peter's in Rome.
·commission and remaking in 17th century **8**:162h

Navidad, (Villa de) La, Hispaniola settlement established by Columbus in 1492.
·Columbus establishment and abandonment **4**:939g; map

Navier, Claude-Louis-Marie-Henri (1785–1836), French civil engineer who specialized in road and bridge building, was most important as one of the first to develop a theory of elasticity. In 1821 he published a set of general equations for the equilibrium and vibration of an elastic solid. Later (1826) he published the first systematic work on the strength of materials and on structural analysis. In addition, he began to develop a theory of suspension bridges, which before his time had been built according to empirical principles.
·fluid mechanics development **11**:780h
·fluid motion and elastic solids **5**:554f

Navier-Stokes equations, equations of linear momentum for a viscous compressible fluid.
·fluid flow principles **11**:790b

navigation **12**:902, the science of conducting a craft or vehicle by the method of determining its position, course, and distance travelled. The text article covers, in the first section, animal instinct, human art, and the three stages of navigation and, in the second, modern navigation techniques.

REFERENCES in other text articles:
·aircraft design, control, and history **1**:370e
·air traffic control, signals, and routes **18**:576b
·air traffic control methods **18**:639f
animal instinct
·bee flight cues and communication **9**:129g
·biological clock, migration, and orientation **14**:69e
·bird flight orientation **10**:742c
·instinctive use of celestial objects **12**:902c
·migration homing abilities **12**:182e; illus. 183
·path recognition methods **17**:381b
·waterfowl innate and learned behaviour **1**:942b
·antenna and direction finding **1**:968a
·automated use of radio signals **2**:511b
·battle manoeuvring of wooden ships **19**:583c
·celestial object observation **2**:249e
·chronometer marine voyage usefulness **4**:748g
·compass history and development **4**:1039d
·Cook's surveying and charting **5**:131e
·early Chinese direction determinant **19**:181a
·Halley's magnetic sea charts **8**:557c
·Henry the Navigator's contribution **8**:777d
·inertial guidance systems **8**:527f
·instruments used by mariners **6**:75e
·international rules of navigation **11**:503g
·map and geographic knowledge improvement **11**:473c
·mathematical calculation theory and use **11**:675c
·medieval technological developments **18**:34e
·military warning and detection systems **19**:599g
·nautical chart description and use **11**:470b
·ocean charts and charting procedure **9**:98a
·radar and war tactics **15**:370f
·radio navigation systems **15**:431b
·sailing in the 15th century **4**:880g
·sailing ship instrument evolution **16**:157d *passim* to 159g
·satellite navigation systems **17**:373b
·satellite orbit guidance system **16**:263d
·ship navigation development **18**:651h
·sonar development and uses **17**:1b
·spacecraft use of computer system **15**:911b
·submarine design and control **17**:752a
·surveying methods of direction finding **17**:830h
·wind systems and Atlantic sailing routes **19**:868d

RELATED ENTRIES in the *Ready Reference and Index: for*
radio navigation systems and instruments: see compass; consol; direction finder; distance-measuring equipment; gyroscope; loran; radio beacon; radio range; shoran
other related entries: astrolabe; great circle; inertial guidance; latitude and longitude; loxodrome; sextant

Navigation Acts, in English history, a series of laws designed to restrict England's carrying trade to English ships, effective chiefly in the 17th and 18th centuries. The measures, originally framed to encourage the development of English shipping, so that adequate auxiliary vessels would be available in wartime, became a form of trade protectionism. The first such act, passed in 1381, remained virtually a dead letter, because of a shortage of ships. In the 16th century, various Tudor measures had to be repealed because they provoked retaliation from other countries. The system came into its own at the beginning of the colonial era, in the 17th century. The great Navigation Act passed by the Commonwealth government in 1651 was aimed at the Dutch, then England's greatest commercial rivals. It distinguished between goods imported from European countries, which could be brought in either English ships or ships of the country of origin, and goods brought from Asia, Africa, or America, which could travel to England, Ireland, or any English colony only in ships from England or the particular colony. Various fish imports and exports were entirely reserved to English shipping, as was the English coastal trade. The law was re-enacted in 1660, and the practice was introduced of "enumerating" certain colonial products, which could be shipped direct only to England, Ireland, or another English colony. These included sugar (until 1739), indigo, and tobacco; rice and molasses were added during the 18th century. Non-enumerated goods could go in English ships from English colonies direct to foreign ports. From 1664 English colonies could receive European goods only via England. Scotland was treated as a foreign country until the Act of Union (1707) gave it equal privileges with England; Ireland was excluded from the benefits of the laws between 1670 and 1779. Although English tonnage and trade increased steadily from the late 17th century, critics of the navigation system argue that this would have occurred in any case and that the policy forced up freight prices, thus ultimately making English manufactured goods less competitive. At first colonial merchants benefitted from an assured market, but the tightening of the laws in 1764 contributed to the unrest leading to the rebellion of England's American colonies; their achievement of independence made the first serious breach in the navigation system, and from then on exceptions were increasingly made. Enumeration was abandoned in 1822, and the navigation laws were finally repealed in 1849 and 1854.
·American trade controls and importance **18**:950b
·British colonial trade restrictions **3**:302e
·Charles II commercial policy advancement **4**:55f
·Dutch resentment and hostility **18**:716h
·Dutch shipping restrictions **11**:147c
·mercantile economic restrictions **4**:888e
·mercantile marine growth role **6**:227g
·terms and significance **3**:247c

Navigator, The (1925), film directed by Donald Crisp and Buster Keaton.
·Keaton and comedy technique **12**:522d

Năvodari, town in Romania on the Black Sea. Latest census 6,344.
44°19′ N 28°36′ E
·tourist industry development **15**:1046h

Navoi, city in the Uzbek Soviet Socialist Republic. Pop. (1970) 61,000.
40°15′ N 65°15′ E
·Uzbek S.S.R. demography and industry **19**:11f

Navojoa, city, southern Sonora state, northwestern Mexico. On the Gulf of California coastal plain near the Río Mayo, at 125 ft (38 m) above sea level, Navojoa is the commercial and manufacturing centre for a large area in which population and production have grown markedly since the 1950s with the development of irrigation for agriculture. Cotton, corn (maize), dates, and chick-peas are the principal crops; cattle are also raised. Major highways and railroads from Mexicali and Nogales to Mexico City pass through Navojoa, which also has air connections with Mexico City and the largest cities of northwestern Mexico. Pop. (1950) 17,342; latest census 30,560.
27°06′ N, 109°26′ W
·map, Mexico **12**:68

Navotas, town, Rizal province, central Luzon, Philippines, on Manila Bay across Dagatdagatan Lagoon from Caloocan City. It is an important fishing centre for Manila, just to the south; about one-half of the total Philippine commercial fish catch is landed there. Bagoong (prawn paste) and other fish preparations are produced at Navotas and nearby Malabon. Pop. (1970) 83,245.
14°40′ N, 120°57′ E

Návplion (Greece): *see* Nauplia.

Navsāri, also spelled NAOSARI, town, Bulsār district, Gujarāt state, west central India, in the coastal lowland, on the Pūrna River. It is the home of the Parsis, descendants of Zoroastrians who emigrated from Persia, and

contains their most venerated fire temples. The town is a market for cotton, millet, and timber and contains various milling, weaving, metal, and leather industries. Navsāri lies on the Western Railway and major highways. Pop. (1971) 72,979.
20°51′ N, 72°55′ E
·map, India **9**:279

Navy, Royal: *see* Royal Navy.

Navy, United States, major branch of the U.S. military organization, charged with the defense of the nation at sea, the support of all other U.S. military services, and maintenance of freedom of the seas.

The Continental Navy was established by the Second Continental Congress on Oct. 13, 1775, to supply and support the Continental Army during the War of Independence. The navy was disbanded in 1784 and until 1798 U.S. merchant ships sailed unprotected. To counter the harassment of French and Barbary pirates, the U.S. Congress established the Department of the Navy on April 30, 1798. The navy gained valuable experience against the Royal Navy of Great Britain in the War of 1812 and was an important factor in the Union victory in the Civil War (1861–65).

Sea victories during the Spanish–American War (1898) led to a period of steady growth. Naval aviation was inaugurated in 1910 when a civilian pilot, Eugene Ely, flew an airplane of a cruiser at Hampton Roads, Va.; the next year he landed on and took off from a cruiser in San Francisco Bay. The Office of the Chief of Naval Operations was set up in 1915, and a shipbuilding program was begun in 1916.

Although the U.S. Navy did not engage in sea battles during World War I, it grew eightfold. Activities included the transport and supply of ground and air troops and laying an anti-submarine mine field in the North Sea.

During the interwar years, the first U.S. aircraft carrier, the USS "Langley," was launched (1922), a naval patrol was placed in the Atlantic (1939), and the escort of Allied convoys was begun (1941). The U.S. entered World War II after the Japanese attack on the American naval base at Pearl Harbor, Hawaii, on Dec. 7, 1941. In addition to support and transport duties, the U.S. Navy fought an active sea and air war in the Pacific and engaged in submarine warfare in the Atlantic.

Since the 1950s the U.S. Navy has become one of the most mobile sea forces in the world. It has developed nuclear-powered ships such as the "Triton" (launched 1960), the first submarine to circumnavigate the globe while submerged, and the aircraft carrier USS "Enterprise" (1960) and has adapted cruisers and submarines for the firing of guided missiles with nuclear warheads.

The Department of the Navy was placed within the Department of Defense by the 1949 amendments to the National Security Act of 1947. The navy includes the U.S. Marine Corps (*see* Marine Corps, United States) and the U.S. Coast Guard when it is operating as a service of the navy. The department is headed by a civilian secretary of the navy who is appointed by the president acting as commander in chief. The chief of naval operations, the senior military officer of the navy, advises the president and the secretary, is a member of the Joint Chiefs of Staff, is commander of the navy's operating forces (except the Marine Corps), and directs the Naval Reserve.

The four operating forces are the Military Sealift Command, which provides ocean transport on government or commercial vessels for the Department of Defense and other federal agencies, provides at-sea logistic support to the armed forces, and conducts scientific and other projects for federal agencies; the Pacific Fleet, which operates in the Pacific and Indian Oceans; the Atlantic Fleet, which operates in the Atlantic Ocean and the Mediterranean Sea; and Naval Forces, Europe.

There are also 10 functional field commands. They are the Naval Material Command, Bureau of Naval Personnel, Bureau of Medicine and Surgery, Oceanographer of the Navy, Naval Telecommunications Command, Naval Security Group Command, Naval Intelligence Command, Naval Education and Training Command, Naval Reserve Command, and Naval Districts, 12 geographic areas the commandant of each of which is responsible for shore activities and public affairs. The U.S. Naval Academy, established in 1845, is located at Annapolis, Md.

Navya-Nyāya, English NEW NYĀYA, Indian philosophical school founded *c.* 13th century.
·principal exponents and doctrines **9**:327d

nawab, also called ṢŪBADĀR, title of a provincial governor of the Mughal Empire.
·Akbar's governmental reforms **1**:400h

Nawābshāh, town and district, Sind Province, Pakistan. The town, the district headquarters, is an industrial centre (small boats, cotton, and silk textiles). It has a government college affiliated with the University of Sind.

Nawābshāh District (area 2,896 sq mi [7,501 sq km]) is a fertile tract lying just east of the Indus River, bordered (south) by Hyderābād and Sānghar districts and (east and north) Khairpur District. The chief crops are cotton, millet, sugarcane, and fruit. Pop. (1972) town, 80,779; (1972 prelim.) district, 1,345,000.
26°15′ N, 68°25′ E
·map, Pakistan **13**:893

Nawab Sirajudawla, Bengali folk drama.
·historical plot and popularity **17**:171b

Nawaday (1498?–?1588), Burmese soldier and poet.
·Burmese court literary style **17**:234g

nawbah, in Islāmic music, song form which is a suite of four movements. The first movement (*qawl*) and the fourth (*furudasht*) are stated to resemble a *basīṭ* (a setting of Arabic verse in one of three given rhythms with an instrumental prelude); the second (*ghazal*) is a setting of Persian verse; the third (*tarāna*) is a setting of a quatrain (*robāʿī*, or *rubāʿī*) in either Arabic or Persian, and is subject to the same rhythmic limitations as a *basīṭ*. The same melodic and rhythmic modes might be used in all four movements, each of which could be prefaced by an instrumental introduction.
·multisectional arrangement **12**:729a
·origins, structure, and modern use **9**:976f

Nawbakhtī (fl. 10th century), Iraqi Shīʿite family that occupied high state offices under the ʿAbbāsid dynasty.
·use of Muʿtazilite doctrines **9**:1017d

Nawiliwili (Hawaii): *see in* Lihue.

Nawqid Plain, sandy region of Socotra island.
12°20′ N, 53°55′ E
·topography and size **19**:1079h

Nawrūz, 13th-century lieutenant of Maḥmūd Ghāzān.
·Maḥmūd Ghāzān's rise to power **8**:146e

Naxalbari, town and plains region, west of Silīguri, West Bengal, India. Pop. (1971) *tahsil*, 50,799.
30°11′ N, 88°12′ E
·West Bengal's Naxalite violence **19**:786g

Naxos, ancient Greek city of Sicily, destroyed by Dionysius I the Elder of Syracuse in 403 BC; its ruins are south of Taormina.
·settlement, growth, and importance **8**:330f

Náxos, largest of the Greek Cyclades islands in the Aegean Sea, with the highest peak of that group, Oxiá Óros (mount; 3,304 ft [1,007 m]). The 165-sq-mi (428-sq-km) island forms an *eparkhía* (district) with adjacent smaller islands. The capital and chief port, Náxos, on the west coast, is on the site of ancient and medieval capitals.

In the 7th and 6th centuries BC, a white, deep-grained marble was exported for statuary, contributing much to the island's prosperity. During the 6th century the tyrant Lygdamis ruled Náxos in alliance with Peisistratus of Athens. In 490 it was captured by the Persians and treated with severity; Náxos deserted Persia in 480, joining the Greeks at the Battle of Salamis and then the Delian League. After revolting from the league in 471, Náxos was immediately captured by Athens, which controlled it until 404. In AD 1207 a Venetian captured Náxos, initiating the duchy of Náxos, which flourished until captured by the Turks in 1566. In 1770 the island was occupied by the Russians. Regained by the Turks in 1774, it joined the Greek kingdom in 1830.

Fertile and well-watered valleys produce outstanding white wine, citron, and citrus, but the chief export is emery. The inhabitants are mainly Orthodox, though the island has a Roman Catholic archbishop and two convents. Excavations of the Mycenaean settlement have been made at Grotta, north of the capital. Pop. (1971) city, 2,882; island, 14,201.
37°02′ N, 25°35′ E
·Aegean civilizations map **1**:112
·map, Greece **8**:314
·struggle against Athenian supremacy **8**:352b; map 326

Nāyak, 14th-century local landholder of South India.
·revolt against the Delhi sultanate **9**:374b

Nāyaṉār, term denoting the Tamil poet-musicians of the 7th and 8th centuries AD who composed devotional hymns of great beauty in honour of the Hindu god Śiva. The poets Ñānacampantar, Appar, and Cuntaramūrtti were often known as "the three"; their images are worshipped in South Indian temples.

The hymns of the Nāyaṉārs were collected in the 10th century by Nambi Āṇḍar Nambi under the title *Tēvāram* and set to Dravidian music for use in South Indian temples. An inscription of the Cōḷa king Rājarāja the Great (985–1014) records his introduction of the singing of the hymns in the great temple at Thanjāvūr (Tanjore). Often associated with the Nāyaṉārs, though probably slightly later in date, is the superb devotional poet Māṇikkavācakar, whose hymns are collected under the title *Tiruvācakam* ("Sacred Utterance"). *Cf.* Ālvārs. *Major ref.* **17**:139h
·bhakti poetry characteristics **8**:914d
·early bhakti in South India **9**:360b

Nāyar, also spelled NAIR, Hindu caste of the Malabar Coast in Kerala, southwest India. Before the British conquest in 1792, the royal and noble lineages, militia, and most land managers of the area's small kingdoms were drawn from the Nāyars and related castes, who ranked below the Nambūdiri Brahmins, or religious authorities. During British rule, Nāyars became prominent in politics, government service, medicine, education, and law.

Unlike most Hindus, Nāyars traditionally were matrilineal. Their family unit, the members of which owned property jointly, included brothers and sisters, the latter's children, and their daughters' children. The oldest man was legal head of the group. Rules of marriage and residence varied somewhat between kingdoms. In central Kerala, adults of the matrilineal group lived together, and husbands merely visited their wives. In the extreme north and in southern Kerala, by the 18th century, men of the group tended to live with their wives and immature children in the joint-family house.

Between the 16th and 18th centuries, Nāyars in the central kingdoms of Calicut, Walluvanad, Pālghāt, and Cochin had highly unusual marriage customs that have been much studied. Before puberty a girl ritually married a Nāyar or a Nambūdiri Brahmin. The husband could visit her (but was not obliged to); in some cases ritual divorce immediately followed the ceremony. After puberty a woman could receive a number of visiting husbands of her own or higher caste. Nāyar men might visit as many women of appropriate rank as they chose. Women were maintained by their matrilineal groups, and fathers had no rights or obligations in regard to their children.

Early in the British period, Nāyar armies were disbanded. Perhaps partly as a result, plural marital unions gradually died out in the 19th century. Children began to be maintained by their father, to support him in his old age, and to perform the ceremonies at his death. Laws passed in the 1930s enforced monogamy, permitted division of the matrilineal estate among male and female members, and gave children full rights of maintenance and inheritance from the father. By the 1960s it was increasingly common, especially in towns, for nuclear families to form separate residential and economic units.

·Kerala ethnic communities **10**:434e
·kinship and marriage patterns **17**:128b

Nayarit, state, west central Mexico, on the Pacific Ocean. It is bounded northwest by Sinaloa, northeast and east by Durango, and south by Jalisco. The Sierra Madre Occidental rises steeply from the narrow Pacific littoral and, running southeast, cuts the state's 10,664-sq-mi (27,621-sq-km) terrain into deep gorges and narrow valleys. Peaks include the volcanoes Ceboruco and Sangangüey. The coastal lagoons are well-known wild bird refuges. The main river, Grande de Santiago, flowing northwestward into Nayarit from Lake Chapala, is sometimes considered a continuation of the Lerma (*q.v.*). The Santiago moves westward through Nayarit and empties north of San Blas, chief Pacific port of Nayarit. Its valley is extremely fertile. Known until 1917 as the federal territory of Tepic, Nayarit includes the largely undeveloped Marías Islands (*q.v.*). Mining is important in the mountains, but the state is primarily agricultural. Major west-coast highways and railroads traverse Nayarit, linking Tepic (*q.v.*), the state capital, with Mazatlán and the plateau cities. There are small, scattered villages of Cora and Huichol Indians throughout the Sierras. Pop. (1977 est.) 725,395.

·area and population table and map **12**:71

Naya River, stream of southern Colombia. 3°14′ N, 77°30′ W

·location and features **4**:865a; map 867

Nayrab, ancient Near Eastern settlement, near the present city of Aleppo, Syria.

·Abraham and his times **1**:12f

Nazaré, fishing port and resort, Leiria district, western Portugal. It occupies two levels, the lower one extending along the beach. A pilgrimage chapel overlooks the town at 360 ft (110 m) from the upper level. The inhabitants, said to be of Phoenician origin, are among Europe's most distinctive people. The characteristic dress of the community and its religious ceremonies associated with fishing are local attractions. The town is also a watchmaking centre. Pop. (1970 prelim.) town, 8,553; mun., 12,860.
39°36′ N, 9°04′ W

·map, Portugal **14**:857

Nazarene, a title applied to Jesus, who in his early life resided in Nazareth, a town in Judah. The term was used later to describe his followers, the sect of the Nazarenes. It is derived from two Greek words in the New Testament (*Nazarēnos* and *Nazōraios*); *Nazarenos* means "coming from Nazareth," but *Nazōraios* has always presented problems for biblical exegetes. Nazōraios may imply that Jesus was viewed as a Nazirite, a holy man consecrated to God. In adopting vows to maintain an ascetic way of life, Nazirites reacted against Canaanite religious beliefs and practices.

The term Nazarene also was applied to a Judaizing Christian group in the 2nd century that believed that Jesus was the Son of God but maintained a strict observance of the Jewish Law, a practice that had been dropped by the majority of Christians. According to Epiphanius, a 4th-century theologian, there also was an Ebionite (*q.v.*) sect called the Nazarenes. The relationship of these sects to Jewish Christians of the 1st century, however, cannot be determined.

·Jewish–Christian separation **10**:315e

Nazarene, Church of the: *see* Church of the Nazarene.

Nazarenes, German NAZARENERN, members of the Lucas Brotherhood, or Lukasbund (for St. Luke, the patron saint of painting), an association formed by a number of young German painters in 1809 to return to the medieval spirit in art. Reacting particularly against 18th-century Neoclassicism, the brotherhood was the first effective anti-academic movement in European painting. The Nazarenes believed that all art should serve a moral or religious purpose; they admired painters of the late Middle Ages and early Renaissance and rejected most subsequent painting. They also thought that the mechanical routine of the academy system could be avoided by a return to the more intimate teaching and learning situation of the medieval workshop. For this reason, they worked and lived together in a semimonastic existence.

"The Triumph of Religion in the Arts," oil painting by Friedrich Overbeck, one of the Nazarenes, 1840; in the Städelsches Kunstinstitut, Frankfurt am Main

By courtesy of the Stadelsches Kunstinstitut, Frankfurt am Main

The original members of the brotherhood were six students at the Vienna Academy. Four of them, Friedrich Overbeck, Franz Pforr, Ludwig Vogel, and Johann Konrad Hottinger, moved in 1810 to Rome, where they occupied the abandoned monastery of S. Isidoro. There they were joined by Peter von Cornelius, Wilhelm von Schadow, and others who at various times were associated with the movement. They soon acquired the originally derisive nickname Nazarenes because of their affectation of biblical style of hair and dress. The major project of the Nazarenes was to revive the medieval art of fresco painting. They were fortunate in receiving two important commissions, the fresco decoration of the Casa Bartholdy (1816–17) and the Casino Massimo (1817–29) in Rome. By the time of the completion of the Casino Massimo frescoes, all except Overbeck had returned to Germany and the group had dissolved. *See also* Pre-Raphaelite Brotherhood.

·drawing stylistic techniques **5**:1000h
·Romantic painting style **19**:456a

Nazareth, Arabic AN-NĀṢIRA, Hebrew NAẒERAT, historic city of Lower Galilee, northern Israel; the largest Arab city of the country. It is closely associated with the childhood of Jesus and is a centre of Christian pilgrimage. The etymology of the name is uncertain; it is not mentioned in the Old Testament or rabbinic literature; the first reference is in the New Testament (John 1). The contempt in which this then insignificant village was held is expressed in the same chapter ("Can anything good come out of Nazareth?"). From there, Jesus went to perform his first miracle, that of the changing of water to wine at Cana (John 2). Christian holy places in Nazareth are first mentioned after Christianity became the state religion of the Roman Empire (AD 313). The only site that can be definitely identified as dating back to New Testament times is the town well, now called St. Mary's Well.

During the Crusades, Nazareth was fought over bitterly; when the Norman-Sicilian crusader Tancred captured Galilee (1099), he set himself up as prince of Galilee, with his capital at Nazareth. After the victory of Saladin over the crusaders at the Horns of Ḥaṭṭīn (1187) and their final expulsion from Palestine (1291), Christian influence waned; when the Ottoman Turks took Palestine (early 16th century), they expelled all Christians from the city. Only under Fakhr ad-Dīn II, amir of Lebanon (ruled 1590–1635), were Christians permitted to return to Nazareth; they now form the majority of the population.

Nazareth's chief attractions are its many churches. Of these, the Roman Catholic Church of the Annunciation (completed 1966, on the site of a previous church of 1730 and a crusader foundation) is perhaps the best known. In it is the Grotto of the Annunciation, where, according to the New Testament, the archangel Gabriel appeared to the Virgin Mary and announced that she was to be the mother of Jesus (Luke 1:26–31). The grotto has part of a mosaic floor dating back to the 5th–6th century AD. The church is the largest Christian house of worship in the Middle East. Other important churches include Gabriel's Church, held by Greek Catholics to be the site of the Annunciation; the Synagogue Church, on the traditional site of the synagogue where Jesus preached (Luke 4); the Church of Joseph, on the reputed site of Joseph's carpentry shop; the Mensa Christi (Table of Christ) church, where tradition holds that Jesus dined with the Apostles after his resurrection; and the Basilica of Jesus the Adolescent, on a hill overlooking the city.

Nazareth, Israel, with the Church of the Annunciation in the left foreground

Keystone

Modern Nazareth is a regional market and trade centre for the Arabs of Galilee; tourism and light manufacturing are also important. Many workers commute to industrial jobs in the Haifa Bay area and to agricultural and construction work in the Jewish settlements of the ʿEmeq Yizreʿel (Plain of Esdraelon).

Beginning in 1957, the Jewish suburb called Nazerat ʿIllit (Upper Nazareth) was built on the hills to the east of the city. It has auto-assembly, food-processing, and textile plants. It also is the administrative seat of Israel's Northern District. Pop. (1977 est.) 37,700.
32°42′ N, 35°17′ E

Nazas River, Spanish RÍO NAZAS, in Durango and Coahuila states, northern Mexico. Formed in Durango by the confluence of the Oro (or Sestín) and Ramos rivers, which descend inland from the Sierra Madre Occidental and meet at El Palmito, the Nazas flows first southeast and then east-northeast to the Laguna District, where during the rainy season it would reach Mayrán Lagoon. Its total length was approximately 180 mi (290 km). As part of the land redistribution program of the Laguna District (*q.v.*), the Lázaro Cárdenas Dam was built across the Nazas at Palmito, Durango, impounding the river. Since the mid-1960s, lack of rainfall in the headwaters of the Nazas has prevented the planned reservoir from filling to projected capacity. The vast irrigation scheme has thus been a partial failure, although the Nazas is still referred to as the Mexican Nile. Several large cities, including Lerdo, Gómez Palacio, and Torreón, lie on the river's banks.
25°55′N, 103°25′ W

Nazca, the name applied to the culture located on the southern coast of present-day Peru during the Early Intermediate Period (*c.* 200 BC–AD 600), so called from the Nazca Valley but including also the Pisco, Chincha, Ica, Palpa, and Acarí valleys. Nazca pottery is multicoloured, or polychrome. Modelling was sometimes employed, particularly in the later phases; it is, however, rather simply done. In the polychrome painting it is not unusual for four or more colours to have been employed.

Polychrome vessel depicting a seated woman, Nazca culture, *c.* AD 600; in the Textile Museum, Washington, D.C.
Ferdinand Anton

Backgrounds are usually white or red with designs outlined in black and filled in with various shades of red, orange, blue-gray, or purple. The designs are naturalistic (people, animals, birds, fish, plants) but quite stylized and often stiff or angular. Early Nazca pottery tends to be confined to either open bowl forms or double-spouted jars with flat bridge handles, and the painted designs are relatively uncomplicated and bold; the Late Nazca (Ica) style runs to other vessel forms, including some modelled effigies, and the designs incorporate more fine detail.

·architecture and pottery development **1**:843f; map 840
·craft excellence and mass production **1**:690c; illus.
·death cult and feline deity **9**:259e
·jewelry design **10**:181c
·Nazca ceremonial centres **1**:843h
·pottery painting and style variety **14**:929g

Nazca Ridge, oceanic ridge in the Pacific Ocean off the coast of South America.
·geologic feature importance **13**:475b

Nazi (deity): *see* Nanshe.

Nazım Hikmet Ran: *see* Hikmet, Nazım.

Nazimmudin, Khwaja (d. 1964), Pakistani prime minister.
·political career and dismissal **9**:426e

Nazi Party, in full in German NATIONALSOZIALISTISCHE DEUTSCHE ARBEITERPARTEI (NSDAP), English NATIONAL SOCIALIST GERMAN WORKERS' PARTY, dominated Germany from 1933 to 1945.

It was founded as the German Workers' Party by Anton Drexler, a Munich locksmith, in 1919, changed its name in 1920, and was led by Adolf Hitler beginning in 1921. The party achieved power in 1933 and governed Germany by totalitarian methods until 1945. It based its ideology on racialist (especially anti-Semitic) sentiment, the Prussian military tradition, anti-rational political romanticism, extreme nationalism, and widespread German resentment against economic hardship and the harsh post-World War I peace terms. Although Nazism was originally conceived as an ideology that would combine nationalist and Socialist doctrines, the Socialist element, always de-emphasized by Hitler, was virtually ignored in later years. Anti-democratic, anti-liberal, and belligerent, the party won vital support from German military circles and, as a bulwark against Communism, from capitalists. At first Nazi influence operated chiefly in Bavaria, where an abortive coup in 1924 was treated leniently, but mass propaganda exploited the economic collapse of 1929 to give the party 18 seats (the second largest number of any party) in the Reichstag elections of 1930. Still greater successes followed in the next three elections; in 1933 the Nazis won 44 percent of the votes, more than any other party. From March 21, 1933, Hitler's government assumed dictatorial control, and in July the NSDAP was declared Germany's only political party. An over-radical Nazi element, the SA (*q.v.*; Sturmabteilung), was purged in 1934, and thereafter Hitler's word was the supreme and undisputed command. Although the Nazi Party appeared to be centralized and its outward unity seemed impressive, there were dissensions on all levels, particularly after 1938, when Germany's trained civil servants and army leaders were replaced by party members. Nazi policy aimed at territorial expansion and the ultimate rule of the German master race over a hierarchy of subordinate people. World War II effectively prevented this, but before Hitler's downfall millions of Jews and other people were put to death in Nazi concentration camps.

There have been minor Nazi movements in other countries (such as the United States) but after 1945, Nazism was unimportant.

·Austrian anti-democratic movement **2**:477h
·Barth's insights and opposition **2**:726d
·Buber's opposition activity **3**:359f
·economic policies **6**:246a
·education philosophy and control **6**:376a
·education upset by facist ideology **6**:422c
·electorate's gradual acceptance **19**:974b
·Fascism in Germany **7**:186b
·forced labour conditions in Germany **16**:853h
·Göring's rise to power **8**:254c
·Hindenburg's ineffectual opposition **8**:888b
·Hitler's rise to power **8**:966e
·human genetics fallacy **7**:1007a
·Joseph Goebbels' political career **8**:223d
·Leo Baeck's role as leader of German Jewry **2**:581e
·Munich origins and ideology **8**:117d
·Munich's political history **12**:617e
·Pius XII's conduct presented **14**:486f
·propagandistic art's limitations **2**:108f
·Protestant response in Germany **15**:118d
·role in government **14**:683h
·suppression of Webern's atonal music **19**:718a
·war criminals punishment after collapse **19**:555f

Naẓīr Akbarābādī (d. 19th century), Indian-Muslim poet.
·literary style and themes **17**:145h

Nazirite (Hebrew *nazar*, "to dedicate"), among the ancient Hebrews, a sacred person whose separation was most commonly marked by his uncut hair and his abstinence from wine. Originally, the Nazirite was endowed with special charismatic gifts and normally held his status for life. Later, he was a man who had voluntarily vowed to undertake special religious observances for a limited period of time, the completion of which was marked by the presentation of offerings (Num. 6; I Macc. 3:49; Acts 21:24).

The early Nazirite was a holy man whose peculiar endowment, credited to his possession of "the Spirit of the Lord," was displayed in unusual psychic or physical qualities marked by spontaneity, ecstasy, and dynamic enthusiasm. In this respect he had much in common with the early ecstatic prophets and with diviners, such as Balaam (Num. 22–24), both indigenous to the Near East. Both the Nazirite and the prophet were also close to the warrior, who was likewise in a sacred state while on duty. Samson the Nazirite was a holy warrior whose special power was most closely related to his unshorn hair. In Israel, such natural powers as were represented by the growth of hair were treated as signs of the power of the God of Israel, to be used in God's service.

The later Nazirite as described in Num. 6 and in the Mishna was not a charismatic person. He simply retained the old requirements of abstinence from wine and long hair and was forbidden to touch a corpse. These requirements were treated as external signs of a vow.
·Samson's dedication to Yahweh **2**:910c

Nazism: *see* National Socialism.

Nazwā, also spelled NIZWA, town in Oman. Located at the southern, or landward, foot of the rugged range of al-Jabal al-Akhḍar, Nazwā is a trade centre. An experimental agricultural station has also been established. There is some light industry, including handicrafts and copper and brass working. Nazwā was formerly Oman's capital. Latest pop. est. 6,000.
22°56′ N, 57°32′ E
·Ibāḍīs' centre **13**:567e

Naẓẓām, Ibrāhīm an-, in full ABŪ ISḤĀQ IBRĀHĪM IBN SAYYĀR IBN HANĪʾ AN-NAẒẒĀM (b. *c.* 775, Basra, Iraq—d. *c.* 845, Baghdad), brilliant Muslim theologian of classical Islām, a polished man of letters, and a poet, historian, and jurist. He spent his youth in Basra, moving to Baghdad as a young man. There he studied speculative theology under the great Muʿtazilite theologian Abū al-Hudhayl al-Allāf but soon broke away from him to found a school of his own. It seems to have been an-Naẓẓām who began the struggle against the intellectual influences of Asiatic Hellenism, which the Muʿtazilites represented, a struggle that Muslim thinkers were to continue for centuries. In his theological thinking he was the first to formulate several problems that were of major importance to orthodox theologians. He convincingly argued that the material world had been created in time by God and did not exist from all eternity to all eternity. Much more important, though, was the question of human free will. Muslim theology stressed the transcendent power of God, which brought into question the efficacy of human will in determining human actions. To an-Naẓẓām man consisted of two aspects. One was his material self, which was reflected in his actions and movements in the material world and which was under the sway of God's power. Man, however, was equally spirit, not subject to the determinism of the material world but free to make choices and thus become morally responsible.

Nazzari, Francesco, 17th-century Italian scholar, ecclesiastic, and publisher.
·Giornale de letterati **15**:248a

Nb, symbol for the chemical element niobium (*q.v.*).

NBA: *see* National Basketball Association.

NBG, abbreviation of NEUE BACH-GESELLSCHAFT, musical society (1900) that organizes festivals and publishes popular editions of Johann Sebastian Bach's works and a research journal (from 1904).
·activities and major publication **2**:560d

NC-4, seaplane built by Glenn Curtiss for the U.S. Navy, which in 1919 made a transatlantic crossing.
·historic flight record, illus. 4 **7**:390

NCAA: *see* National Collegiate Athletic Association.

Ncheu, administrative headquarters of Ncheu District, southern Malawi. Subsistence agriculture is supplemented by a potato cash crop. Kyanite (an aluminum silicate) and iron deposits are mined locally. Bordering on Mozambique (west), the district (area 1,319 sq mi [3,416 sq km]) is divided between the Dedza Highlands and the Kirk Range to the west and the Shire Rift Valley to the east. Pop. (latest census) town, 1,118; district, 164,685.
14°49′ S, 34°38′ E
·district area and population table **11**:362
·map, Malawi **11**:361

Nchisi (Malawi): *see* Ntchisi.

Nd, symbol for the chemical element neodymium (*q.v.*).

Ndaka, also called BANDAKA, Bantu people of Central Africa.
·Bantu tribe population **9**:1177d

ndako gboya, indigenous ritual of the Nupe tribesmen of Africa.
·mask form and ritual **1**:261a

Ndau (people): *see* Shona.

Ndé, department, Ouest (West) province, Cameroon.
·area and population table **3**:698

Ndebele, formerly called MATABELE, a people of southern Africa that originated early in the 19th century as an offshoot of the Nguni of Natal (*see* Nguni peoples). Mzilikazi, a Nguni military commander under the orders of Shaka, king of another Nguni people, the Zulu, fell foul of his master and in 1823 was forced to flee, migrating with his followers first to Basutoland (now Lesotho) and then north to the Marico Valley. In 1837, after conflict with settlers of the Transvaal Republic, he moved northward across the Limpopo River, ultimately (*c.* 1840) settling in the present Matabeleland (in Rhodesia), where his successor, Lobengula, was able to extend the tribe's power, absorbing Sotho, Shona, and other extraneous tribal elements. The establishment of the British South Africa Company (1890) led to further conflict with colonists, and the Matabele (as they were then known) were defeated in a war of 1893, after which they were administered by the company as a number of separate districts.

Ndebele woman
Paul Almasy

The short-lived Matabele state became stratified into a superior class (Zansi) composed of peoples of Nguni origin; an intermediate class (Enhla), comprising people of Sotho origin; and an inferior class (Lozwi or Holi) derived from the original inhabitants. Men of all classes were organized into age groups that served as fighting units. The men of a regiment, on marriage, continued to live in their fortified regimental village. *See also* Lobengula; Mzilikazi.
·death rite symbolism **7**:201e
·Mzilikazi empire creation and conquest **17**:282c
·numbers, tribal affiliations, and culture **6**:110d
·Rhodesia's African people composition **15**:818c
·Rhodes mining development schemes **17**:288a
·South Africa ethnic composition map **17**:66
·visual art forms **1**:270g; illus.

Ndembu, or NDEMBO, sometimes DEMBA, Bantu people of the Congo region, one of the Lunda peoples (*q.v.*). They are savanna dwellers who cultivate grain crops.
·African ritualistic drama **1**:253b
·sociocultural identity and Lunda ties **4**:1119b; map
·Zambian population and language **19**:1132f; map

n-dimensional space (mathematics): *see* multidimensional space.

n-dimensional sphere (geometry): *see* hypersphere.

N-dimethylaminosuccinamic acid: *see* Alar.

N'Djamena, formerly FORT-LAMY, capital of the Republic of Chad and of Chari-Baguirmi *préfecture*, in west central Africa. It lies on the east bank of the Chari River at its confluence with the Logone in an alluvial plain that is flooded during the rainy season (July-September). N'Djamena is connected by road with Nigeria, The Sudan, and the Central African Republic, as well as with such major towns of Chad as Abéché and Sarh. It is also served by an international airport, through which passes more air traffic than any other in French-speaking Africa. N'Djamena is in the centre of cotton-growing, cattle-raising, and fishing areas and is consequently an important market site. The town is also a nucleus for many specialized educational and research institutes. In 1971 a national university was established there. Pop. (1973 est.) 192,891.
12°07′ N, 15°03′ E
·map, Chad **4**:13
·urbanization and population growth **4**:14h

Ndjili (Zaire): *see* Kinshasa.

Ndlamba, also spelled NDHLAMBE (people): *see* Xhosa.

Ndogo, a people of The Sudan, the Congo region, and the Central African Republic, speaking a language of the Adamawa-Eastern group of the Niger-Congo family.
·The Sudan ethnic composition map **17**:762

Ndola, third largest town in Zambia, south central Africa, located in the north central Copperbelt Province on the Zaire border. It is linked by rail to the capital, Lusaka, and Livingstone, and thus to Rhodesia, as well as to Zaire. Industries include a copper refinery, a sugar refinery, and a tire factory. It is now the terminus of the Tazama fuel pipeline from Dar es Salaam, Tanzania. There are two libraries in the town, and the Northern Technical College provides technical education. Pop. (1974 est.) 222,000.
12°58′ S, 28°38′ E
·ethnic population distribution **19**:1133a
·map, Zambia **19**:1130

Ndolo (Zaire): *see* Kinshasa.

Ndongo, southern African kingdom of the Mbundu people that rose to prominence in the 16th century and was conquered by the Portuguese in 1618.
·structure and Portuguese effect **17**:278g

NDP (West Germany): *see* Nationaldemokratische Partei Deutschlands.

Ndumu Game Reserve, in Natal, South Africa, is on the Mozambique border at the confluence of the Usutu and Pongolo rivers. Much of its 40-sq-mi (100-sq-km) area is occupied by Lake Nyamiti and other small bodies of water. The reserve (established in 1924) is best known for its varied birdlife.
·map, South Africa **17**:62

Ndwandwe, tribal confederation of southern Africa conquered by Shaka *c.* 1820.
·Zwide Zulu rivalry leadership **17**:281g

Ne, symbol for the chemical element neon (*q.v.*).

Neagh, Lough, in Northern Ireland, the largest lake in the British Isles, covering 150 sq mi (388 sq km), with a catchment area of 2,200 sq mi (5,700 sq km). It is bounded by counties Londonderry and Antrim (north), County Tyrone (west), and counties Down and Armagh (south). The chief feeders of the lake are the Upper River Bann, the Blackwater, and the Main, and it is drained northward by the Lower Bann. Lough Neagh averages 15 mi (24 km) wide, is 19 mi long, and is less than 40 ft (12 m) deep. From ancient deposits in Toome Bay, a lake indentation, the oldest recorded artifacts of man in Ireland have been recovered. There are other archaeological remains on Coney Island. In 1959 flood-control works lowered the lake level to 50 ft (15 m) above sea level.
54°38′ N, 6°24′ W
·map, United Kingdom **18**:866

Neagle, John (b. Nov. 4, 1796, Boston—d. Sept. 17, 1865, Philadelphia), painter; he and his father-in-law, Thomas Sully, were the chief portrait painters in Philadelphia prior to the Civil War. Starting as an apprentice coach painter, Neagle developed a style suggestive of Gilbert Stuart and Sully. Technically, however, he was inferior to his two more famous contemporaries, and most of his large output is monotonous. His best known works are "Pat Lyon at the Forge" (1827; Pennsylvania Academy of the Fine Arts) and a portrait of Gilbert Stuart (1825).

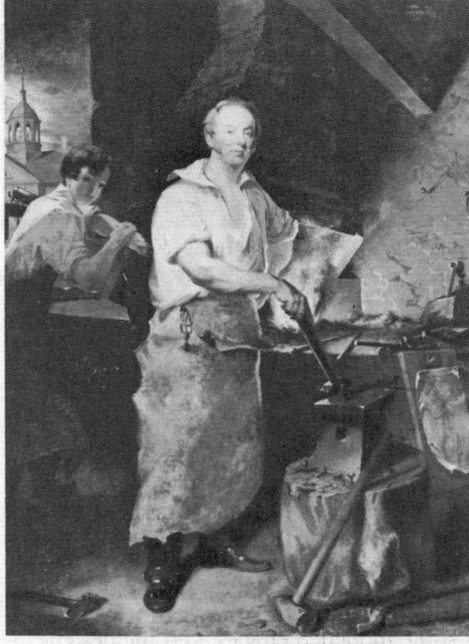

"Pat Lyon at the Forge," oil painting by John Neagle, 1827; in the Pennsylvania Academy of the Fine Arts, Philadelphia
By courtesy of the Pennsylvania Academy of the Fine Arts, Philadelphia, gift of the Pat Lyon Family, 1842

Neal, John (b. Aug. 25, 1793, Portland, Maine—d. June 20, 1876, Portland), novelist, critic, poet, and lawyer. Although he had little formal education, Neal became widely known in the United States and England as a perceptive critic of American writers. In 1823–27 he lived in England and became the first American to introduce native writers to Britain. In the 1830s, back in the United States, he was the first to praise Edgar Allan Poe in print. Neal was better known, however, as a novelist, producing numerous works from 1817 until his death. While in England he had stayed in the house of the Utilitarian philosopher Jeremy Bentham, and he later published Bentham's *Morals and Legislation* (1830), translating the work from French.

Neamț, district (*judet*) of northeastern Romania. Created in 1968 from the three northernmost *raioane* (districts) of the former Bacău Region, it has four major physiographic zones (west to east): a portion of the Outer Eastern Carpathian Mountains, their foothills, the Moldavian sub-Carpathians, and the valleys of the Bistrița, Moldova, and Siretul rivers. The most important cities are Piatra-Neamț, the capital; Bicaz; and the former district centres Roman and Tîrgu-Neamț (*qq.v.*). Pop. (1973 est.) 529,400.
·area and population, table 1 **15**:1051

Neanderthal man 12:910, a type of prehistoric man that inhabited much of Europe and the areas surrounding the Mediterranean during the earlier Late Pleistocene Epoch. The name Neanderthal is derived from the Neander Valley near Düsseldorf, W.Ger., where remains of a human skeleton—a Neanderthal man—were first discovered in 1856.

The text article covers the ancestors of Neanderthal man, Neanderthals of the Third Interglacial Period, and Neanderthals of the Fourth Glacial Period, including their physical characteristics and inferred cultural adjustments. It also treats Neanderthal man in comparison with the later Cro-Magnon man and with broadly contemporaneous Asian and African populations.

REFERENCES in other text articles:
·Asian fossil discoveries **2**:201a
·dating of human burial practices **5**:533b
·evolutionary position and culture **5**:290e
·fossils and evolutionary status **11**:426e
·fossil sites and extinction theories **8**:1046c
·human evolution and ancestry **7**:20d
·Iberian fossil discoveries **17**:401c
·North African cultural antiquity **13**:145h
·Syrian and Palestinian prehistory **17**:927c
·tools and toolmaking technique **8**:608h
·tools for clothing manufacture **5**:1016a

RELATED ENTRIES in the *Ready Reference and Index:*
Homo neanderthalensis; La Chapelle-aux-Saints fossil; paleoanthropology

Neanthes (genus of worms): *see* rag worm.

Neanuridae, an extinct family of insects of the order Collembola of the subclass Apterygota.
·characteristics and classification **1**:1026a

Neapolis (Italy): *see* Naples.

Neapolis (Israeli-occupied Jordan): *see* Nābulus.

Neapolitan opera (style of Italian opera): *see* opera seria.

Néa Psará (Greece): *see* Eretria.

neap tide, tide of minimal range occurring near the time that the Moon and Sun are in quadrature. This condition is geometrically defined as the time that the line from the Earth to the Moon is at right angles to the line from the Earth to the Sun. Thus, the tide-producing effects of the Sun and the Moon cancel each other, and tidal ranges are usually 10 to 30 percent less than the mean tidal range. Quadrature and neap tides occur twice each synodic month. *Cf.* spring tide.
·tidal forces interference **13**:495e

Nearchus (d. probably 312 BC), officer in the Macedonian army under Alexander the Great who, on Alexander's orders, circumnavigated the Arabian Peninsula from the mouth of the Euphrates River to the Isthmus of Heroönpolis (Suez). Earlier, in 333, Alexander had made him satrap of the newly conquered Lycia and Pamphylia in Anatolia. Nearchus embarked on his expedition in 325, when Alexander descended the Indus River to the sea. He chronicled the journey in a detailed narrative, a full abstract of which is included in Arrian's *Indica* (2nd century AD). Following the death of Alexander in 323, Nearchus obtained his former satrapies and supported Antigonus I Monophthalmus in the succession struggles.
·Alexander's Eastern conquests **8**:375f; map 374
·Alexander's retreat from India **1**:471e
·Indian campaign exploration **7**:1038d

Nearctic subregion (biogeography): *see* Holarctic region.

Near East, a term usually referring to the lands around the eastern shores of the Mediterranean Sea, including northeastern Africa, southwestern Asia, and, occasionally, the Balkan Peninsula. Near East was used by the first modern Western geographers to refer to the nearer part of the Orient, a region roughly coextensive with the Ottoman Empire. Since World War II, the name has been largely supplanted by Middle East (*q.v.*), though frequently they are used interchangeably.

Near East, ancient 12:913. The ancient Near East is defined here as the area comprising Egypt, Nubia, Palestine and Syria, Armenia, Asia Minor (Anatolia), and Mesopotamia, with the outlying areas of North Africa, the Aegean, Iran (Persia), and the Indus Valley, during the period *c.* 9000 BC to the 4th century BC.

The text article traces the late prehistory of the Near East, which saw the emergence of sedentary cultures (*c.* 9000–*c.* 3000 BC). During this period, agriculture and irrigation were first practiced. Because of the favourable transportation routes, climate, and water supply of the Near East, the area was subjected to successive waves of immigration and the rise and fall of numerous empires—among others, the Egyptian, Hittite, Assyrian, Babylonian, and Persian. During this long period, the Near East contributed many of the foundations of Western culture—monotheism, the bases of science, technology, law, and logic, and the alphabet. The great age of the ancient Near East ended when the Macedonians under Alexander the Great conquered the area in the 4th century BC, though indigenous kingdoms survived in Iran and Arabia until the Arab conquest in the 7th century AD.

REFERENCES in other text articles:
agriculture
·agricultural crops and techniques **1**:324h *passim* to 327b
·domesticated plant origins **5**:938c
·alphabet origins research **1**:618f; illus. 620
·Anatolian civilization development **1**:814a
·archaeological evidence of hunting role **9**:47d
arts
·calligraphy styles and development **3**:661f
·copper, bronze, and iron artwork **11**:1094e *passim* to 1110f
·dress styles **5**:1016e; illus. 2–9
·epic poetry tradition **6**:908e
·furniture construction history **7**:794a
·interior design styles **9**:702h; illus. 703
·landscape design development **7**:891g; illus.
·literary record beginnings in written form **7**:454g
·literature history and development **10**:1088b
·mosaic art development by Sumerians **12**:465h; illus. 466
·music tradition of common past **16**:793e
·pottery-making development in the West **14**:897d
·visual arts throughout region **19**:248g
·Ashurbanipal's military conquests **2**:144d
·Asian fossil remains **2**:201b
·basketry use and remains **2**:761b
·beer drinking in Mesopotamia **5**:730a
·calendar systems development **3**:604f
·censorship in ancient Israel **3**:1084a
·chronological source materials **4**:576d
·coinage origin and use in 7000 BC **4**:821h
·cultural continuity and economics **12**:167f
·cultural evolution and urbanization **4**:659h
·cuneiform law discoveries **5**:368g
·Cyrus II's territorial expansion **5**:409g
·Darius I's wars and administration **5**:491a
·David's political career **5**:517f
·drums in cult and ceremony **14**:65a
·eating custom elaboration **7**:940b
·eclipses as chronological confirmation **6**:195f *passim* to 197a
·education control and pedagogy **6**:318b
·Egyptian cultural and political development **6**:460a
·epigraphic evidence of Mesopotamian, Hittite, and Iranian history **6**:916a
·Greek civilization expansion **8**:326a
·Greek conquests and Hellenistic kingdoms map **8**:374
·Hammurabi's conquests and legacy **8**:598g
·historiography in antiquity **8**:946d
·Hittite capital historical importance **2**:1181f
·Indus–Mesopotamian cultural contact **9**:338g *passim* to 343h
·Iranian civilization development **9**:829h
·Jeremiah's influence in Judaea **10**:134b
·Jericho's civilization stages **10**:136b
·Jewish educational structure and methods **6**:322c
·library history and function **10**:856g
·Macedonian wars and alliances **1**:990e
·Memphis cultural prominence **11**:895b
·Mesopotamian history and cultures **11**:963h; map 976
·Nebuchadrezzar's life and achievements **12**:925f
·Nineveh's ancient urban culture **13**:116c
·Nubian–Egyptian history **13**:108f
·Old Testament basis in history **2**:895h
religion
·agricultural basis of rites **16**:115g
·astrology origins and development **2**:220f
·Hebrew prophecy compared to other traditions **2**:906f
·Judaic culture and history **10**:303a; map
·mythical context of Judaism **10**:191f
·prophetic forms and institutions **15**:63a
·religious and social communality **12**:916a
·Syro-Palestinian religious developments **17**:967a
·wisdom literature origination **2**:924f
·Sargon II and the Assyrian empire **16**:248d
·Sargon's Mesopotamian empire **16**:247e
science and technology
·biology's early records **2**:1016h
·irrigation and drainage systems **9**:899h; illus. 900
·mathematics history from antiquity **11**:639h
·medicine in Babylonia and Egypt **11**:823f
·petroleum product usage **14**:165c
·tool and toolmaking history **8**:611b *passim* to 613c
·seal designs and official use **16**:741e
·Sennacherib's Assyrian empire **16**:542c
·slave sources, conditions, and laws **16**:855g
·Solomon's empire consolidation **16**:1044d
·spice trade routes **17**:502c
·Syria and Palestine in early times **17**:928d; map
·Thutmose's reign and conquests **18**:366a
·Tiglath-pileser's Assyrian empire **18**:401c
·Tigris and Euphrates Valley aqueducts **1**:1035g
·Ugaritic artifacts and libraries **18**:832e
·Urartian and Armenian empires **18**:1039a
·urban design patterns **18**:1065g
·writing development and systems **19**:1036d
·Xerxes' military and political career **19**:1057b

RELATED ENTRIES in the *Ready Reference and Index: for*
cities and archaeological sites: see Alexandria; Bozrah; Hierapolis; Shahr-e Sokhta; Soli; Tall al-ʿAjjul; Tall al-Farʿah; Tall-e Bakun; tell; Tappeh Ḥeṣār Dāmghān; Tepe Yahya
cultural development: Bronze Age; Iron Age
peoples: Akhlame; Amorites; Aramaeans; Hurrians; Mitanni; Sea Peoples
other: Asia, Roman province of; Fertile Crescent; Ophir

Near Eastern religions, ancient 12:916, the religious beliefs, attitudes, and practices of the peoples of the ancient Near East from *c.* 3000 to 330 BC. These religions, including those of the Egyptians, Hebrews, Moabites, Phoenicians, Ugaritians, Arabians, Aramaeans, Sumerians, Babylonians, Assyrians, Hittites, and Iranians, are the antecedents of the major Western religions (*i.e.*, Judaism, Christianity, and Islām) and have thus had an enduring influence and effect on Western civilization.

The text article covers sources for modern scholarly knowledge of these religions, world views and basic religious thought (including views on the sacrality of nature and natural forces, man and society, basic values and ends of human life, myths, and magical concepts and attitudes), and religious practices and institutions.

REFERENCES in other text articles:

·Arabian and Greek deity parallels **1**:1058d
·Astarte and Resheph in 1400-BC Egypt **6**:473e
·astrology origins and dissemination **2**:220f
·Babylonian Enuma elish creation myth **5**:240g *passim* to 242a
·Canaanite agricultural religion **2**:908e
·Canaanite deities and cults **17**:938g
·Christian and Jewish mythic borrowings **4**:551e
·Christian syncretism in Mariology **4**:482h
·covenant origins and early functions **5**:226g
·Cushitic cultural origins **13**:109g
·deity conception impact on social order **18**:219b
·Egyptian and Mesopotamian educational control and purpose **6**:318a
·Egyptian art's social role **19**:249c
·epic poetry immortality themes **6**:908e
·Hebrew eclecticism **10**:303a
·influence on Greek religion **16**:501h
·Iranian cult and Zoroastrian connection **9**:837a
·Judeo-Christian uniqueness **7**:62f
·Manichaean history and doctrines **11**:442f
·man's nature and burial customs **5**:533e *passim* to 537h
·Mesopotamian archaeological discoveries **11**:970e
·mystery cults and sacred kingship **12**:780d
·mythical context of Judaism **10**:191f
·mythic festival worship of New Year **19**:1017a
·Near East cultural heritage of West **12**:914h
·New Year symbolic festivities **7**:198e *passim* to 200c
·Nineveh and the cult of Ishtar **13**:116h
·pigeons as sacred objects **4**:933a
·polytheism in complex forms **14**:787b
·prayer concepts, hymns, and litanies **14**:949g
·priestly office and power in society **14**:1008f
·prophetic forms and institutions **15**:63a
·research into Judeo–Christian milieu **15**:618a
·ritual and myth correlation **15**:626e
·ritual basis in myth **15**:865d
·sacramental emphasis on fertility **16**:115g
·sacred kingship rites and beliefs **16**:119c
·Sinai name derivation **16**:779b
·spells and other magical practices **11**:298f
·Sumerian–Hebrew contrast on death **16**:202d
·theist triumph over pantheism **13**:951c
·Urartian and Hurrian religious parallels **18**:1039b
·Ur's religion and Judaic history **1**:12b
·Yahweh worship as radical alternative **12**:489g

Near Ipiutak culture, Eskimo culture of northwest Alaska dating from about the 1st century AD.

Near Islands, westernmost group of the Aleutian Islands, southwestern Alaska, U.S., about 1,500 mi (2,400 km) west of the tip of the Alaska Peninsula. The largest islands are Agattu, Attu, and Semichi. The islands, mountainous and barren, were so named by early Russian explorers because they are the closest to Asia of any of the Aleutians. They were strategically important in the Aleutian campaign of World War II. Except for Attu and Semichi, they are uninhabited. Pop. (1970) 1,131.
52°40′ N, 173°03′ W

near-money, highly liquid assets, such as savings deposits, shares in savings and loan associations, and short-term government obligations, that can be quickly converted into money (currency or demand deposits) without risk of loss. Such assets are not classified as money because they are not generally acceptable as a means of payment. Near-money assets provide a good substitute for money in meeting the need to make unexpected payments because, though highly liquid, they also pay some return. Because near-money assets can be converted so quickly into cash, changes in them can have significant effects on the money supply.

nearsightedness: *see* myopia.

Neath, Welsh CASTELL-NEDD, borough (including the adjacent town of Briton Ferry), county of West Glamorgan (until 1974 it was a metropolitan borough of the former Glamorganshire), Wales, on the River Neath (Nedd). The Romans, *c.* AD 75, chose the site for a fort, Nidum, to protect their road from Gloucester to Carmarthen at the lowest practicable crossing of the River Neath. In the 12th century a castle was constructed there, and the adjoining town was granted a charter by Earl William of Gloucester. In 1231, however, the castle was destroyed by the Welsh prince Llywelyn ap Iorwerth, only the gateway remaining. The 12th-century Cistercian foundation, Neath Abbey, is also now a ruin.

The town flourished in the post-medieval period, but its modern character and importance can be said to date from 1584, when a copper-smelting works was built using locally mined coal and Cornish ore, brought cheaply by sea into the river estuary. Other nonferrous metals (*e.g.*, tin, lead, and silver) came to be smelted there, too, and during the 19th and 20th centuries Briton Ferry became a centre for steelmaking, as the older local industries progressively declined. Engineering concerns and others that use steel (*e.g.*, tin-box manufacturing) are still important, while at Baglan, near Briton Ferry, a large petrochemical industry has grown up since World War II. As a shopping and service centre, Neath has now only localized influence, being overshadowed by the port of Swansea, 7 mi (11 km) to the west; but it is still the natural focus for the industrial and mining communities of the Vale of Neath. This valley, running northeast from the town, has steep and lofty sides now largely cloaked in extensive Forestry Commission plantations (Rheola Forest). The town has railway service. Pop. (1971 prelim.) 28,568.
51°40′ N, 3°48′ W
·map, United Kingdom **18**:866

neat's-foot oil, pale yellow, fatty oil made usually by boiling the feet and shinbones of cattle; used chiefly as a high-grade leather dressing and fine lubricant. It is produced principally in the United States, Europe, and South America.

Nebelwerfer, German weapon used in World War II, capable of firing large-calibre (15- and 21-centimetre) rockets up to 8,000 metres from a 6-barrelled launcher. The shell weighed about 80 pounds (36 kilograms).
·design, size, and range **15**:928c

Nebit-Dag, city, western Turkmen Soviet Socialist Republic, at the southern foot of the Bolshoy Balkhan Ridge. Its name means Oil Mountain, and it is the headquarters of the Turkmen oil industry. Nebit-Dag grew up on the Transcaspian Railway after large oil deposits had been discovered in the area in the early 1930s; it became a city in 1946. It has been carefully planned, with much greenery to mitigate the effects of the surrounding desert. Pop. (1970) 56,000.
39°30′ N, 54°22′ E
·map, Soviet Union **17**:322

Neblina Peak, Portuguese PICO DA NEBLINA, in the Serra Tapirapecó, Amazonas state, northern Brazil, near the Venezuelan border. Reaching 9,889 ft (3,014 m) above sea level, it is the highest point in Brazil. Until Neblina was discovered in 1962, the Pico da Bandeira was thought to be Brazil's highest mountain.
1°00′ N, 66°50′ W
·map, Brazil **3**:124

Nebo (deity): *see* Nabu.

Nebraska 12:922, west central state of the U.S., admitted to the Union in 1867 as the 37th state. Occupying an area of 77,227 sq mi (200,017 sq km), it is bounded by South Dakota (north), by Iowa and Missouri (east), by Kansas (south), by Colorado (southwest), and by Wyoming (west). Its capital is Lincoln. Pop. (1980) 1,570,006.

The text article, after a brief survey of the state, covers its history, natural and human landscape, people, economy, administration, social conditions, and cultural life and institutions.

REFERENCES in other text articles:

·area and population, table 1 **18**:927
·map, United States **18**:908
·pre-statehood expansion maps **18**:966

Nebraska City, seat of Otoe County, Nebraska, U.S., on the Missouri River. It originated around Ft. Kearney (1846; moved west to Platte River site in 1848), was incorporated in 1854, and combined in 1857 with the adjacent settlements of Kearney City and South

J. Sterling Morton House in Arbor Lodge State Historical Park, Nebraska City, Nebraska
Milt and Joan Mann from CameraMann

Nebraska City to form one incorporated community. Its growth as an unloading point on the river for westbound freight was sustained by the arrival of the Midland Pacific Railroad (1871). John Brown's Cave was a station for runaway slaves on the Underground Railroad. Markers indicate other historic spots, such as the Overland Trail passing point and the Pony Express headquarters. The Nebraska School for the Visually Handicapped dates from 1876. A prevailing mixed farm economy is supplemented by small manufacturing (chiefly gas meters). The home of J. Sterling Morton (founder of Arbor Day) is in Arbor Lodge State Historical Park at the city's western edge. Pop. (1980) 7,127.
40°41′ N, 95°52′ W.
·map, United States **18**:908

Nebraskan Glacial Stage, major division of Pleistocene time and deposits in North America (the Pleistocene Epoch began about 2,500,000 years ago and ended about 10,000 years ago). The Nebraskan Glacial Stage precedes the Aftonian Interglacial Stage and is the oldest generally recognized Pleistocene episode of widespread glaciation in North America; the Nebraskan was named for deposits studied in the state of Nebraska, although representative exposures in that state are rather poorly developed. The Nebraskan throughout North America is not well-known; although its position as the earliest of the four Pleistocene glaciations of North America is well established, much remains to be done to delineate that position more precisely. The practice of naming glacial deposits below the Kansan as Nebraskan needs to be revised. The Elk Creek Till and the overlying Iowa Point Till, both found in the state of Nebraska, are of Nebraskan age. Nebraskan

deposits are best developed in the midwestern regions of the U.S., including parts of Missouri, Nebraska, Iowa, and Kansas. Nebraskan age deposits found elsewhere are not considered to have been established as fact. Established Nebraskan deposits are rich in clays.
·Iowa geological history **9**:817d
·Pleistocene glacial chronology **14**:559f

Nebraska Sand Hills, sand dune region with thin vegetation cover, covering much of the state of Nebraska.
·area, depth, and Pleistocene relation **14**:567a

Nebrodi, mountain range of northern Sicily, Italy.
37°55′ N 14°35′ E
·location, elevation, and form **16**:727g

Nebuchadrezzar I, Babylonian form NABU-KUDURRI-USUR (reigned *c.* 1124–1103 BC), Babylonian king of the 2nd Isin dynasty, conquered Elam and ruled most of Mesopotamia.
·Babylonian territorial expansion **11**:981h

Nebuchadrezzar II **12**:925, Akkadian NABU-KUDURRI-USUR (b. *c.* 630 BC—d. 562), king of the Chaldean (Neo-Babylonian) Empire, was the greatest member of his dynasty and was known for his military might, the splendour of his capital, Babylon, and his important part in Jewish history.

Abstract of text biography. The oldest son and successor of Nabopolassar, founder of the Chaldean Empire, he is known from cuneiform inscriptions, the Bible and later Jewish sources, and from classical authors. In 606–605 BC, as crown prince, he served as commander in chief of the army. He ascended the throne within three weeks after his father's death, on Aug. 16, 605. Pursuing a policy of expansion, he engaged in campaigns in Syria, Palestine, and other countries. After capturing Jerusalem (August 586), he deported its prominent citizens.

REFERENCES in other text articles:
·Babylon's urban fortification **2**:555b
·conquest of Jerusalem **17**:946d
·Daniel's dream interpreting **2**:929g
·Egyptian conflict over Syria–Palestine **6**:480c
·Jeremiah and Judaean politics **10**:135b
·Judaea's destruction by Babylon **7**:126h
·reign and accomplishments **11**:988c
·visual art of Neo-Babylonian period **19**:264g

Nebuchadrezzar III, 6th-century-BC claimant to the Babylonian throne who usurped power from Darius I and ruled for ten weeks.
·Babylonian revolts against Darius I **11**:989e

nebula **12**:926, in astronomy, a relatively dense but still tenuous mass of gas or dust (or a mixture of both) in the space between the stars, which may glow by its own emission or by starlight reflected from dust surrounding the star. Dark nebulae may be detected by their obscuration of the light from stars, in the line of sight to an observer, that are embedded in it or are behind it.

The text article describes the observations of such clouds of material, their physical characteristics, their chemistry, distribution in the Sun's Galaxy and in others, classification and nomenclature, and probable modes of formation and evolution.

REFERENCES in other text articles:
·astronomical map depiction **2**:224b
·cosmic ray supernova origin **5**:205c
·Eddington's study on stellar systems **6**:297e
·Galaxy distribution of nebulae **7**:839c
·infrared source research **9**:582g
·interstellar medium population **9**:790f
·map and catalogue designations **2**:229g
·meteorite origin **12**:47c
·pulsars and stellar explosions **15**:268d
·radio-wave emissions **15**:473f
·relation to external galaxies **7**:828c
·spectroscopic research methods **2**:242e
·William Herschel's early hypotheses **8**:825c

RELATED ENTRIES in the *Ready Reference and Index: for*
individual nebulae: see Coalsack; Crab Nebula; Great Rift; Gum Nebula; Horsehead Nebula; Orion Nebula; Ring Nebula; Trifid Nebula
types: H I and H II regions; nebula, dark; nebula, diffuse; nebula, globular; nebula, planetary; solar nebula; Strömgren spheres

nebula, dark, interstellar dust or gas concentrated sufficiently to produce conspicuous obscuring of the stars beyond. Dark nebulae vary widely in real and apparent size and in degree of light absorption. Light passing through is scattered, reddened, and partially polarized; *i.e.*, its vibrations tend to be restricted to one plane. Until the early 20th century, it was thought at least possible that dark nebulae were only "holes" or tunnels in space, for some reason empty of stars. The photographic work of the U.S. astronomer Edward Emerson Barnard and the German astronomer Max Wolf proved the reality of dark obscuring clouds. *See also* nebula, diffuse.
·Galaxy idenfification **7**:834h
·Lagoon Nebula properties, illus., **12**:Nebula, Plate II
·structure, properties, and research **12**:931a

nebula, diffuse, cloud of tenuous gas or of dust in interstellar space. A diffuse nebula appears bright if it reflects strong starlight or if radiation from hot stars embedded in it creates enough electrical charge (ionization) in its gas to make it glow; otherwise the nebula is dark, visible only by its obscuring effect on stars, galaxies, and bright nebulae beyond it. The density of matter within diffuse nebulae is on the average far lower than in the best vacuum obtainable in a laboratory on Earth.
·infrared source research **9**:582g
·structure, properties, and research **12**:930e; illus., Nebula, Plate II

nebula, extragalactic: *see* galaxies, external.

nebula, globular, one of a class of small dark nebulae, most often seen against a bright nebular or starry background. Some astronomers think these globules are stars in an early stage of formation.

nebula, planetary, any one of a class of bright nebulae that may somewhat resemble planets when seen by telescope but are in fact expanding clouds of fluorescent gas outside the solar system. In nearly all planetary nebulae a central star is visible, and all are thought to contain hot stars whose radiation causes them to glow. At least 1,000 planetary nebulae have been discovered in the Galaxy, and many thousands more are believed to exist. Their origins and evolution are uncertain; they were formerly thought to be the results of exploding stars (novae), but their relatively high masses and low rates of expansion (tens of kilometres per second instead of hundreds, in the case of novae) do not fit this theory.
·emission spectra features **2**:243c
·Galaxy distribution and characteristics **7**:839c
·infrared source research **9**:582h
·interstellar matter radiation processes **9**:794a
·radio-wave emissions **15**:473h
·Ring Nebula, illus., **12**:Nebula, Plate II
·structure, properties, and research **12**:932f
·velocity dispersion in Galaxy **7**:847a; illus.

nebulium, hypothetical element whose existence was suggested in 1868 by the English astronomer Sir William Huggins as one possible explanation for the presence of unidentified (forbidden) lines (at 3,726, 3,729, 4,959, and 5,007 angstroms wavelength) in the spectra of gaseous nebulae. It is now known that the elements oxygen and nitrogen ionized (*i.e.*, electrically charged) under conditions unobtainable on Earth are responsible for these spectral lines. *See also* forbidden lines.
·astronomical spectroscopy research **2**:242h
·nebular spectra research **12**:929h

nebuly, type of heraldic line characterized by successive short curves made to resemble a cloud.
·heraldic shield divisions, illus. 10 **8**:789

Necati (NEJATİ), **İsa** (d. 1509, Istanbul), considered the first great lyric poet of Ottoman Turkish literature.

Probably born a slave, Necati, while still very young, went to the city of Kastamonu and began to develop his skill in calligraphy and his reputation as a poet. About 1480, he journeyed to the Ottoman capital, Istanbul, and wrote verses for the Ottoman sultan Mehmed II (1451–81). After the accession of Sultan Bayezid II (1481–1512), Necati briefly entered the service of one of his sovereign's sons, Prince Abdullah (died 1483). Upon his return to Istanbul, Necati was once again awarded a government post with another of the Sultan's sons, Prince Mahmud, in whose service the poet enjoyed great favour. Necati was soon left patronless again, however, when Prince Mahmud died in 1507/08. After returning to the capital, Necati refused any further appointments and lived in retirement until his death in 1509.

Apart from a few scattered lines from the many pieces attributed to Necati, the only extant work is his *Dīvān* ("Collected Poems"), in which there are numerous examples of his graceful and refined verse. Considered an original and eloquent poet, he won the praises of his contemporaries and later Turkish writers, securing for himself an important place in Turkish literary history.

Necator: *see* hookworm.

necessity, in law, controlling force so strong that it admits no choice of action.
·criminal responsibility and defenses **5**:278b

Necessity, Fort, scene of an American Revolution battle, located at Great Meadows, Pennsylvania.
·Washington's defeat and French evacuation **19**:611h

necessity and contingency. Philosophical concepts, aspects of which are treated under nature, philosophy of.

Necessity of Atheism, The (1811), pamphlet by Percy Bysshe Shelley.
·content and results of authorship **16**:659f

Nechako River, in central British Columbia, Canada, is a major tributary of the Fraser River. It originates at Kenney Dam and flows eastward for nearly 150 mi (240 km) draining the Nechako Plateau into the Fraser at Prince George, B.C. Stuart River, a 258-mi-long tributary, joins the Nechako midway between Fort Fraser and Prince George, a stretch that is paralleled by the Canadian National Railway. Once a 287-mi-long stream rising in the Coast Mountains of western British Columbia, the Nechako River was bisected in 1952 by Kenney Dam as part of a colossal engineering project of the Aluminum Company of Canada, Ltd. The 340-ft- (104-m-) high dam created an 18,000,000-ac-ft (2,200,000-cu-m) reservoir (Lakes Ootsa, Whitesail, and Tahtsa), the overflow of which is tunnelled westward through the Coast Mountains to Kemano, where it generates electricity for the giant Kitimat aluminum smelter.
53°56′ N, 122°42′ W
·drainage area and hydroelectric use **7**:696f

Nechayev, Sergey Gennadiyevich (1847–82), Russian revolutionary known for his organizational scheme for a professional revolutionary party and for his ruthless murder of a member of his party; Fyodor Dostoyevsky used Nechayev as a model for the character Pyotr Verkhovensky in *The Possessed*.
·friendship with Bakunin **2**:608f

Necho I (fl. *c.* 672–664 BC), governor of Sais, a city of the Egyptian Nile Delta, under the Assyrians and ancestor of the 26th dynasty; he survived the frequent changes of political fortune in Lower Egypt between 670 and 660.

Necho's ancestor was probably a prince of Libyan descent of the 24th Egyptian dynasty. When in 671 Esarhaddon, king of Assyria, wrested Lower Egypt from Taharqa, the

Kushite ruler of the 25th dynasty, Necho was among the local rulers installed by the Assyrians as vassals. He adopted Assyrian names for his son and his city. After the Assyrians departed, Taharqa recaptured Lower Egypt, and according to the Assyrian Annals, the vassals fled. The new Assyrian king, Ashurbanipal, reconquered Egypt in 667 and re-installed the vassals, placing two key cities under Necho, who now appeared in first position in the Assyrian list of Egyptian vassals. The Kushites again captured the Delta in 664 and, according to their own records, encountered resistance, probably from Necho and his fellow vassals. Eventually an understanding was reached by the vassals and the Kushite ruler. Ashurbanipal mounted a new campaign against Egypt in 663 and, after conquering Thebes, deported Necho to Nineveh, the Assyrian capital, perhaps because he had conspired against Assyria while Ashurbanipal was sacking Thebes. His crimes, however, were apparently not serious, for Ashurbanipal restored him as governor of Sais and appointed his son ruler of another city in the Delta. Necho probably died soon after his return, for Psamtik I, his son, soon rebelled against Assyria and proclaimed himself king of Egypt.

Necho II, king of Egypt (610–595 BC), a member of the 26th dynasty, who unsuccessfully attempted to aid Assyria against the Neo-Babylonians and later sponsored an expedition that circumnavigated Africa.

Necho II, bronze statue, 7th century BC
By courtesy of the University Museum, Philadelphia

According to the Greek historian Herodotus, Necho began the construction of a canal from the Nile River to the Red Sea, probably in response to the growth of trade in the Egyptian Delta, but an oracle persuaded him to discontinue the project. A threat developed in Mesopotamia, where the Assyrian Empire was falling to the Babylonians. Necho built fleets on the Mediterranean and Red seas, with which he undertook a Syrian campaign in 608 to assist the battered Assyrian armies. When Josiah, king of Judah and an ally of the Neo-Babylonians, was slain in battle at Megiddo, Necho replaced Josiah's chosen successor with his own nominee and imposed tribute on Judah. In 606 the Egyptians routed the Neo-Babylonians, but at the great Battle of Carchemish (a Syrian city on the middle Euphrates River) in 605 the Neo-Babylonian crown prince, Nebuchadrezzar, soundly defeated Necho's forces. Egypt itself was threatened in 601, but Necho repelled the enemy and continued to promote anti-Babylonian coalitions in Syria–Palestine.

Herodotus also reports that Necho sent an expedition to circumnavigate Africa, a feat his navigators apparently accomplished, for they reported that, after a certain point in their voyage, the sun rose on their right (they had rounded the Cape of Good Hope into the Atlantic).

·Palestinian and Syrian ventures **6**:480c

Nechung oracle, the state oracle-priest of Tibet who, until the conquest of Tibet in 1959 by the People's Republic of China, was consulted on all important occasions. The oracle is the chief medium of Pe-har, a popular folk divinity incorporated into Buddhism, and resides at the Nechung (Gnas-chung-lcog) monastery near 'Bras-spungs (Drepung), the centre of the Pe-har cult. The oracle is said to have first been appointed government adviser during the time of the fifth Dalai Lama (1617–82). He is required to journey to Lhasa once a year, during the New Year festivities, to prophesy the year's coming events, and is consulted whenever a search is conducted for a new Dalai Lama. Ordinary persons are not normally allowed to consult him but may present questions to him when he is in a trance and after state business has been completed.

neck, portion of the body joining the head to the shoulders and chest in land vertebrates. Some important structures contained in or passing through the neck include the seven cervical vertebrae and enclosed spinal cord, the jugular veins and carotid arteries, part of the esophagus, the larynx and vocal cords, and the sternocleidomastoid and hyoid muscles in front and the trapezius and other nuchal muscles behind. Among the primates, man is characterized by having a relatively long neck. The term neck is also applied to any constricted part of the body that resembles the neck of an animal; *e.g.*, the neck of a bone—a constricted part between the head and shaft of the bone, as in the femur or humerus. The surgical neck designates an area that is more often fractured than more robust areas. The cervix uteri is also called the neck of the uterus.

·cranial nerve distribution **12**:1017e; illus.
·embryonic growth during eighth week **6**:748b; illus. 747
·lymph node enlargement **11**:216c
·spinal nerve distributions **12**:1023b

Neck, Jacob van, late-16th-century Dutch explorer of India.

·spice trade routes **17**:503a

Neckam, Alexander (b. Sept. 8, 1157, St. Albans, Hertfordshire—d. early 1217, Kempsey, Worcestershire), schoolman and scientist, theology instructor at Oxford and later (from 1213) Augustinian abbot at Cirencester, Gloucestershire. His textbook *De utensilibus* is the earliest known European writing to mention the magnetic compass as an aid to navigation. His *De naturis rerum*, a two-part introduction to a commentary on the Book of Ecclesiastes, is a miscellany of scientific information at that time novel in Western Europe but already known to Greek and Muslim savants. By securing, in his capacity as abbot, a royal charter (1215) for a fair at Cirencester, he helped to make that town a great medieval market for wool.

·compass early documentation **4**:1039g
·medieval encyclopaedia functions **6**:788f

Neckarland, region of West Germany.

·profusion of vineyards and population density **2**:578d

Neckar River, right-bank tributary of the Rhine River in West Germany; it is 228 mi (367 km) long, rising in the Schwarzwald (Black Forest) near Schwenningen am Neckar, near the headwaters of the Danube River. It flows north, then northeast, along the northwestern edge of the Schwäbische Alb (Swabian Jura Mountains), passing Rottweil, Rottenburg, and Tübingen. At Plochingen it changes to a northwesterly course as far as Bad Cannstatt near Stuttgart. There the valley is very picturesque, and, as the river continues northward, it becomes broader and deeper and passes between vine-clad hills crowned by feudal castles. The river flows by Heilbronn and Bad Wimpfen to Eberbach where it takes a tortuous westerly course, cutting through the wooded hills of the southern Odenwald. Winding by Neckarsteinach and Neckargemünd, it sweeps beneath the Königstuhl (1,857 ft [566 m]), passes Heidelberg, and enters the Rhine from the right at Mannheim. The Neckar is canalized as far as Plochingen and is navigable for 1,000-ton barges. 49°31′ N, 8°26′ E

·food produce and medieval ruins **2**:578d
·map, Federal Republic of Germany **8**:46
·Rhine confluence location **15**:806d; illus.

Necker, Anne-Louise-Germaine: *see* Staël, Madame de.

Necker, Jacques 12:935 (b. Sept. 30, 1732, Geneva—d. April 9, 1804, Coppet, Switz.), banker who served as minister of finance under Louis XVI of France.

Abstract of text biography. Necker began his career as a bank clerk at the age of 16, transferring to the bank's headquarters in Paris (1750) and becoming a wealthy and prominent banker as a result of adroit speculation. In 1768 he was appointed Geneva's resident minister in Paris and became a director of the French East India Company. Transferring his banking responsibilities to his brother, he began to write on financial topics. Necker was appointed director of the French royal treasury in 1776 and director general of finances in 1777. In an attempt to raise funds to finance French participation in the American War of Independence he published *Compte rendu au Roi* (1781), claiming a surplus of funds, despite an actual deficit. Forced to resign, he retired to Saint-Ouen, where he wrote a justification of his policy, *De l'administration des finances de la France* (1784). Recalled as finance minister in 1788, with France near bankruptcy, he proposed a program of social and constitutional reforms in June 1789 before a meeting of the States General, comprised of representatives of the clergy, nobility, and commons: he was dismissed on July 11, 1789. Retiring to Switzerland, he was summoned on July 20 to resume his office. He tendered his final resignation in September 1790.

REFERENCES in other text articles:
·Louis XVI's refusal to support reforms **11**:124d
·Mirabeau's attack on the economy **12**:269a
·policy, dismissal, and recall **7**:647e *passim* to 649c
·public opinion effect on society **15**:210h

Necker, Suzanne Curchod (b. May 1739, Crassier, Vaud, Switzerland—d. May 6, 1794, Beaulieu, near Lausanne), wife of the French finance minister under Louis XVI, Jacques

Suzanne Necker, engraving by Johann Heinrich Lips (1758–1817)
H. Roger-Viollet

Necker; mother of Madame de Staël; and witty mistress of a brilliant Parisian salon. At first she was engaged to the English historian Edward Gibbon, but his father broke off the match. In 1764 she married Necker, then a banker, and encouraged him in his political career. Her salon attracted such figures as the naturalist Georges Buffon and the authors Jean-François de La Harpe and Jean-François Marmontel. Madame Necker also established a hospital in 1776 and was the author of several books.

Necker cube, visual illusion involving ambiguity in interpretation by the observer, who may view a cube alternately as if he were looking up at its base or down on its top; it is named for Swiss physicist and mathematician Louis Necker (1730–1804).
·visual illusions and ambiguous drawings **9**:241h; illus. 242

necklace, string of beads or of other small objects that is worn about the neck.
·jewelry's historical development **10**:167h; illus.

necklace problem, in mathematics, an enumeration problem of determining the number of different necklaces of a specified number of beads that can be made from an infinite supply of beads having a specified number of colours.
·combinatorics theory and method **4**:945d

necklaceweed: *see* baneberry.

necrolysis, epidermal, cellular death and loosening of the epidermal layer of the skin.
·staphylococcal skin diseases **9**:550f

necromancy, communication with the dead, usually in order to obtain insight into the future or to accomplish some otherwise impossible task. Such activity was current in ancient times among the Assyrians, Babylonians, Egyptians, Greeks, Romans, and Etruscans; in medieval Europe it came to be associated with black (*i.e.*, harmful or antisocial) magic and was condemned by the church. Its practitioners were skilled magicians who used a consecrated circle in some desolate spot, often a graveyard, to protect themselves from the anger of the spirits of the dead. In the event of a premature or violent death, the corpse was thought to retain some measure of unused vitality, and so the use of parts of corpses as ingredients of charms came to an important technique of witchcraft. Necromancy was especially popular in the Middle Ages and Renaissance, and its temptations and perils were vividly described in the Faust stories of Marlowe and Goethe.

necrophilia, sexual deviation involving erotic interest in, and stimulation from, corpses. The condition seems extremely rare; and scarcely any study of it has been accomplished, most descriptions being based on speculation.
·behaviour patterns and causes **16**:607h

necropolis ("city of the dead"), archaeological term designating an extensive and elaborate burial place of an ancient city. In the Mediterranean world, they were customarily outside the city proper and often consisted of a number of cemeteries used at different times over a period of several centuries. The locations of these cemeteries were varied. In Egypt many, such as western Thebes, were situated across the Nile River opposite the cities, but in Greece and Rome a necropolis often lined the roads leading out of town. One of the most famous of these was discovered in the 1940s under the central nave of St. Peter's Basilica in Rome.
·foundation and design of Ṣaqqārah **18**:1065h
·Memphis remains and cultural inferences **11**:895b *passim* to 897b

necropsy: *see* autopsy.

necrosis, death of a circumscribed area of plant or animal tissue as a result of an outside agent; natural death of tissue is called necrobiosis. Necrosis may follow a wide variety of injuries, both physical (cuts, burns, bruises) and biological (effects of disease-causing agents). The sign of necrosis—dead tissue—is called a lesion; it is often of diagnostic value. Necrosis is brought about by intracellular enzymes that are activated upon injury and proceed to destroy damaged cells for what appears to be the good of the entire organism.
·agricultural damage causes **1**:360f
·animal cell and tissue changes **5**:871a
·bacterial plant disease symptoms **5**:889a; table 884
·brown recluse spider bite **1**:1071d
·burns and tissue death **3**:519g
·heart attack consequence **3**:889a
·joint disease from bone death **10**:263f
·RES function of liver macrophages **15**:782c

Nectanebo I, also called NEKHTNEBF I or NEKHTNEBEF I, first king (reigned 380–363 BC) of the 30th dynasty of Egypt; he successfully opposed an attempt by the Persians to reimpose their rule on Egypt (373). When Nectanebo came to the throne, a Persian invasion was imminent. A powerful army, gathered by a previous king, Achoris (reigned 393–380 BC), and largely composed of Greek mercenaries, was entrusted by Nectanebo to the Athenian Chabrias. The Persians, however, succeeded in causing Chabrias' recall and marched against Egypt with a force of 220,000. The Egyptians suffered an initial reverse, but, through the indecision of the Persian general Pharnabazus, they were able to collect their forces, outflanking the delaying invaders near Mendes in the Delta and forcing them to retreat. Nectanebo was relieved of further Persian intervention during the rest of his rule because of satrap rebellions throughout the Persian Empire.

Nectanebo also undertook much building activity, especially at Philae, Edfu, and Hermopolis Magna, and the arts in particular flourished during his reign.
·Egyptian–Persian conflict **6**:481d

Nectanebo II, also called NEKHTHARHEB II or NEKHTHAREHBE II, third and last king (reigned 360–343 BC) of the 30th dynasty of Egypt; he was the last of the native Egyptian kings. Nectanebo, with the aid of the Spartan king Agesilaus II, usurped the throne from Tachas. A rival pretender almost succeeded in overthrowing the new king, but Agesilaus defeated him and left Nectanebo firmly established as ruler. His most powerful enemy was the Persian king Artaxerxes III Ochus, who, after an earlier, futile attempt, swept down through Phoenicia and Palestine, entered three mouths of the Nile at once, and easily took control of Egypt. Nectanebo fled first to Memphis and then to Upper Egypt; thereafter nothing more is known of him.
·enthronement and Persian conquest **6**:481e

nectar, sweet, viscous secretion from the nectaries, or glands, in plant blossoms, stems, and leaves. It attracts insects, who aid in effecting pollination by transferring from plant to plant the pollen that clings to their bodies. Nectar is the raw material used by the honeybee to produce honey. Mainly a watery solution of the sugars fructose, glucose, and sucrose, it also contains traces of proteins, salts, acids, and essential oils. Sugar content varies from 3 to 80 percent, depending upon such factors as flower species and soil and air conditions. Honeybees gather nectar mainly from the blossoms and rarely gather nectars having less than 15 percent sugar content.

In Greek mythology, nectar is the drink of the gods.
·beekeeping and honey production **2**:791g
·orchid production and locations **13**:650c
·pollination and angiosperm development **14**:744b
·Ranunculales pollination mechanism **15**:510b

nectarine (*Prunus persica* variety *nectarina*), smooth-skinned peach of the family Rosaceae, known for more than 2,000 years. In tree shape and leaf characteristics the peach and nectarine are indistinguishable, but nectarine fruits look more like plums than peaches because of the smooth skin. The stones and kernels of the two fruits are alike in appearance. Nectarines have red, yellow, or white flesh and are a source of vitamins A and C. They are adapted to the same soil and climatic conditions suitable for peaches and require the same cultural treatments for successful production.

As in peaches, there are clingstone and freestone nectarines. When some peaches are crossed or self-pollinated, the resulting seeds that carry the factor for smooth skin may give

Nectarine (*Prunus persica* var. *nectarina*)
J.C. Allen and Son

rise to nectarines, while those that do not carry this factor will be peaches. Nectarines may sometimes appear on peach trees as a result of the process of bud variation, or bud sporting, a vegetative deviation from the normal, and peaches may occur on nectarine trees in the same manner. Cultivation of nectarines is essentially the same as for peaches.
·fruit farming economics **7**:757b; table 766

Nectariniidae (bird family): *see* sunbird.

nectary, gland or specialized group of cells on a flower, capable of secreting a sweet substance (nectar), which is attractive to many pollinating insects. The cells are located on either the floral parts or external bracts (modified leaves) at the base of the flower.
·Asterales flower structure **2**:215a
·celastrales nectar disk **3**:1038d
·orchid types and locations **13**:650c
·pollination and angiosperm development **14**:744b
·Ranunculales pollination mechanism **15**:510a

Nectonema, a genus of hair worms of the class Nectomorpha of the phylum Aschelminthea.
·nectonematoidea classification and larval growth **2**:138f

Necturus (salamander genus): *see* mud puppy.

Neddermeyer, Seth H(enry) (1907–), U.S. physicist.
·atomic bomb detonator proposal **13**:325f

Nederburgh, Sebastian Cornelius (b. March 7, 1762, The Hague—d. Aug. 3, 1811, 's-Gravenzande, Neth.), conservative statesman who was chiefly responsible for the Charter of 1801, or Nederburgh's Charter, which established Dutch colonial policy after the government's take-over of the Dutch East India Company.

Nederburgh became a lawyer for the company in 1787. He went to Batavia (now Djakarta) and in 1791 was appointed governor general of the company, which was suffering financially. To save it, he proposed further economization and an increase in compulsory labour. He came into conflict with the progressive company official, Dirk van Hogendorp, whose ideas were exciting interest at the time.

In 1701, when the Indies came under direct Dutch control, both men were called on to draw up a new charter for them. Nederburgh's ideas prevailed. The charter asserted that the colonies existed for the good of the mother country, prohibited free trade, and decreed that the colonies would be governed directly by a semi-autonomous native bureaucracy and indirectly by a Dutch bureaucracy. The charter called for the distinct separation of the executive, ruling branch, and the judiciary. The administration in Europe would be presided over by a Council for Asiatic Government. The charter indicated the main conservative trends in Dutch colonial policy that reappeared intermittently during the length of the Dutch stay in Indonesia.

Nederland, city, Jefferson County, southeast Texas, U.S., within the Beaumont–Port Arthur–Orange industrial complex. It was founded and settled by immigrants from The Netherlands in 1897 (whence its name). Its early economy was based on cattle raising, dairying, and rice farming. Construction in 1922 of an oil refinery on nearby Neches River resulted in the present large concentration of refineries and petrochemical plants producing butadiene, organic chemicals, plastics, synthetic rubber, asphalt, and road-surfacing materials. Inc. 1940. Pop. (1980) 16,855.
29°58′ N, 93°60′ W

Nederlandse Antillen (Caribbean Sea): *see* Netherlands Antilles.

Nedim, Ahmed (b. 1681, Istanbul—d. 1730, Istanbul), one of the greatest lyric poets of Ottoman Turkish literature. The son of a judge, Nedim was brought up as a scholar, and, winning the patronage of the prime minister, received an appointment as a librarian. Later, he became İbrahim Paşa's close friend—thus his name Nedim meaning Boon Companion. He lived during the Tulip Age (Lâle Devri) of Ottoman history, in the reign of Sultan Ahmed III (1703–30), so called because a passion for tulip growing had became a fad among the Ottoman elite. It was also a rather peaceful interval, and one in which the imperial household began to take a greater interest in European culture.

Greatly influenced by the relative peace and prosperity, the poems of Nedim present a vivid picture of the wealth and elegance of early 18th-century Istanbul. His *qaṣīdah*s (odes) and *ghazal*s (lyrics) are bright and colourful, and he excelled especially in the writing of charming and lively *şarqıs*, (songs), which are still sung today. Nedim was a poet of the old school who freed himself from its fetters sufficiently to be able to express his personality and charm in an original way. He is known for his divan which exhibits his masterly handling of the language and accounts for his popularity. Nedim was killed during a civil revolt against the Ottoman government.
·reflection of Turkish society **9**:969a
·Tulip Period and environmental awareness **13**:784c

Nédoncelle, Maurice (1905–), French philosopher.
·Christian attitude in philosophy **4**:555f

Nedunjēral Ādan, 1st-century-AD Cēra king in South India.
·caṅkam literary references **9**:355a

need (psychology): *see* drive.

Needham, town (township), Norfolk County, eastern Massachusetts, U.S., on the Charles River; it is a southwestern suburb of Boston. Settled in 1680, it was named for Needham, England. Inc. 1711. Pop. (1980) 27,901.
42°17′ N, 71°14′ W

Needham, John Turberville (b. Sept. 10, 1713, London—d. Dec. 30, 1781, Brussels), English naturalist and Roman Catholic divine, first clergyman of his faith to become a member of the Royal Society of London (1768). He was ordained in 1738 but spent much of his time as a teacher and tutor. His reading about animalcules (microscopic organisms) aroused an interest in natural science, and in 1746–49 he studied in that field in London and Paris. He became a staunch advocate of the theories of spontaneous generation (life from inorganic matter) and vitalism (doctrine holding that life processes cannot be explained by the laws of chemistry and physics). In 1750 he presented a paper (in French) explaining the theory of spontaneous generation, and for several years he was regarded as the first person who attempted to offer scientific evidence supporting the theory. In 1767 he retired to the English seminary at Paris to pursue his scientific experiments. He also served as the director of the Imperial Academy in Brussels until 1780.
·biological sciences development **2**:1022g
·Spallanzani's abiogenesis refutation **17**:444f

Needian Interglacial Stage, major division of Pleistocene time and deposits in The Netherlands (the Pleistocene Epoch began about 2,500,000 years ago and ended about 10,000 years ago). The Needian Interglacial followed the Taxandrian and preceded the Drenthian Glacial Stage. The Needian has been correlated with the Hoxne Interglacial Stage of Great Britain and the Holstein Interglacial Stage of northern Europe. The tendency is to apply the term Holstein rather than Needian to the Dutch deposits; the term Needian is gradually losing favour in The Netherlands.

needle, basic implement used in sewing or embroidering and, in variant forms, for knitting and crocheting. The sewing needle is small, slender, rodlike, with a sharply pointed end to facilitate passing through fabric and with the opposite end slotted to carry a thread. Bone and horn needles have been used for at least 20,000 years. The earliest iron needles, dating to the 14th century, had no eye but had a closed hook to carry the thread. Eyed needles were manufactured in the Low Countries in the 15th century. Modern sewing needles are steel. Crocheting needles are eyeless, with one hooked end, and made in several sizes, commonly of steel or plastic. Knitting needles are long, made of a variety of materials, and bluntly pointed at one or both ends, sometimes with a knob at the end opposite the point. The earliest were hooked, but modern needles are straight.
·clothing industry and construction aids **4**:750f
·knitting machine technology **18**:181g
·Paleolithic bone toolmaking **8**:609d

needle bearing, a roller bearing with very slender rollers varying typically from 0.08 to 0.16 inch in diameter.
·design and application **11**:250e

needlefish, any of the long, slim, primarily marine fish of the family Belonidae (order Atheriniformes), found throughout temperate and tropical waters. Needlefish are adept jumpers, carnivorous in habit, and distinguished by long, slender jaws equipped with sharp teeth. They are silvery fish, with blue or green backs, and are edible, though the bones are characteristically green. The family includes about 60 species, the largest growing about 1.2 metres (4 feet) long. Among the species are the garfish (*Belone belone*) of Europe and the houndfish (*Tylosurus crocodilus*), found everywhere in the tropics.

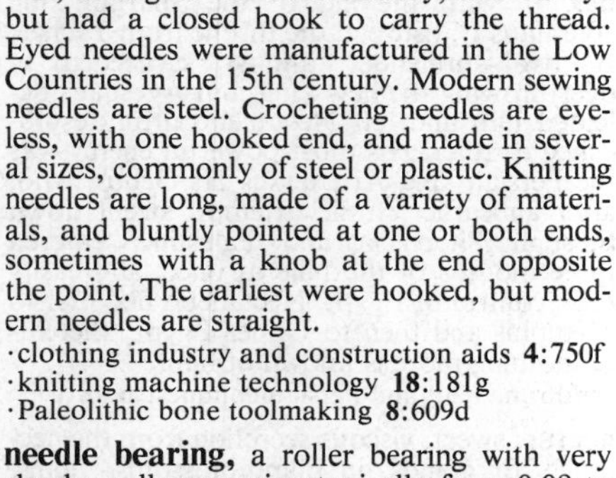

Needlefish (*Strongylura marina*)
Jim Annan—Annan Photo Features

·classification and general features **2**:273f
·coloration pigments' protective uses **4**:919g

needlegrass, common name for grasses of the genus *Stipa* (family Poaceae), about 150 species with a sharply pointed grain and a long, threadlike awn (bristle). In some species,

Needlegrass (*Stipa pennata*)
Syndication International—Photo Trends

such as porcupine grass (*Stipa spartea*), the sharp grain may puncture the faces of grazing animals. Most needlegrasses provide good forage in dry areas before the seed is formed. They grow from 0.3 to one metre (one to 3 feet) tall. Some are highly drought resistant. Esparto grass (*S. tenacissima*, and a species of the genus *Lygeum*), also known as alfa or halfa, is used in the western Mediterranean area to make ropes, cords, and paper.
·chemical inhibition competitive result **2**:1048g
·fibre content and papermaking use **13**:969a
·grassland habitation areas **8**:284e
·grass weeds and habitat **14**:586f

needlepoint, type of embroidery known as canvas work until the early 19th century. In

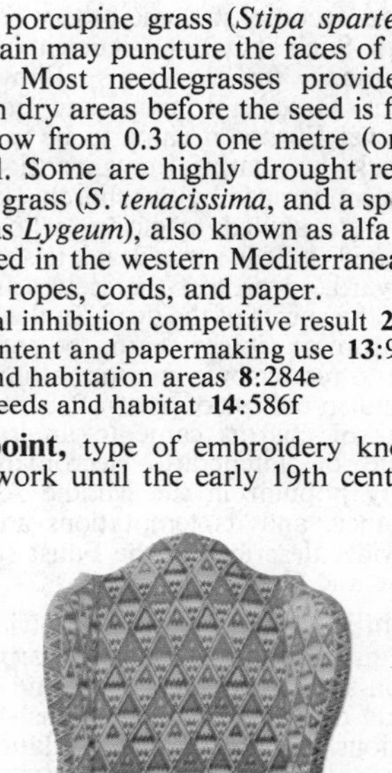

English wing chair upholstered with canvas stitch embroidery (needlepoint) in Florentine, or bargello, stitches, *c.* 1720; in the Governor's Palace, Williamsburg, Va.
The Colonial Williamsburg Foundation

needlepoint the stitches are counted and worked with a needle over the threads, or mesh, of a canvas foundation. Either single or double mesh canvas made of linen or cotton is used. If needlepoint is worked on a canvas that has 16 to 20 or more mesh holes per linear inch, the embroidery is called petit point; if the number of holes ranges from 7 or 8 to 16 squares per inch, it is called gros point; and if the mesh openings are less than 7, it is known as quick point, a technique that has achieved much popularity since the 1960s because it can be worked rapidly. From the 16th to the 18th century most needlepoint was petit point with 20 to 45 squares per linear inch.

There are more than 150 canvas embroidery stitches, most of which are a variation or combination of the long stitch, covering more than one mesh, or thread, and the short stitch, which covers only one square. Since the 16th century the most commonly used stitches have been the slanted tent, or continental stitch, the vertically worked Florentine stitch (also called the flame, bargello, or Hungarian stitch), and the cross-stitch. In the 20th century the basket weave, or diagonal stitch, has achieved widespread popularity.

Wool is generally used for needlepoint, though silk yarn can be employed for embroidering. For petit point, finer crewel yarns are used, while gros point is most frequently worked in two-ply Persian yarn or four-ply tapestry yarn.

Needlepoint as it is known today can be said to have originated in the 17th century, when the fashion for furniture upholstered with embroidered fabrics prompted the development of a more durable material to serve as the foundation for the embroidery. The early single-mesh canvas at its coarsest was not unlike burlap or, at its finest, muslim. Double-mesh, or penelope, canvas was introduced in England either during the Queen Anne period (1702–14) or approximately 100 years later, when two-thread canvas was used for Berlin wool work (*q.v.*) and therefore was often referred to as Berlin canvas.

Originally, needlepoint designs were drawn either by the amateur embroiderer, often from pattern books published in Europe since the 16th century, or by professional embroiderers, who, until the 18th century, were mostly attached to a court or a wealthy family. By the mid-18th century the number of professional embroiderers in Europe was so numerous that many opened shops where embroidery supplies were sold as well as needlepoint and embroidery kits that included a designed canvas and all the materials needed to complete it.

needlepoint lace, in Italian PUNTO IN ARIA, in French POINT À L'AIGUILLE, with bobbin lace (*q.v.*), one of the two main kinds of lace. In needlepoint lace, the design is drawn on a piece of parchment or thick paper, cloth-backed. An outlining thread stitched onto this serves as a supporting framework, and the lace is worked with a needle and a single thread in a succession of buttonhole stitches in varying degrees of tightness and in straight lines that support further stitches. The needle never penetrates the backing. When the work is finished, a knife is passed between the two layers of backing to cut the stitching thread and the lace is lifted off the pattern.

(Top) *Venise reticella* needlepoint lace from Italy, 16th-17th century, (bottom) *Venise gothique* or *point d'ivoire* needlepoint lace from Italy, 16th-17th century; both in the Museum Boymans-van Beuningen, Rotterdam

By courtesy of the Museum Boymans-van Beuningen, Rotterdam

The beginning of needlepoint lace can be dated to the late 15th century. The question of its place of origin—Italy or Flanders—has not been resolved, but most agree that it was developed in Italy.

needlerun net, embroidery on net, the appearance of which approximates lace. It is similar to tamboured net (*q.v.*), in which a form of chain stitch is used sometimes with a hook instead of a needle. In needlerun, however, needlepoint stitches are run in, out, over and under the mesh. Often both techniques are used in Limerick lace (*q.v.*).

Needlerun net lace from Limerick, Ire., first half of the 19th century; in the Victoria and Albert Museum, London

By courtesy of the Victoria and Albert Museum, London

needle trade: *see* clothing and footwear industry.

Neefe, Christian Gottlob (1748–98), German musician.
·Beethoven's early musical training **2**:795f

Néel, Louis-Eugène-Félix (b. Nov. 22, 1904, Lyons), co-recipient, with the Swedish astrophysicist Hannes Alfvén, of the 1970 Nobel Prize for Physics for his pioneering studies of the magnetic properties of solids. His discoveries are major contributions to solid-state physics and have found numerous useful applications, particularly in the development of improved computer memory units.

Néel was professor, successively, at the French universities of Strasbourg (1937) and Grenoble (1946). During the early 1930s he studied forms of magnetism on the molecular level that differ from the most common variety, ferromagnetism, in which the electrons line up (or spin) in the same direction at low temperatures. He discovered that in some substances alternating groups of atoms align their electrons in opposite directions (much like placing together two identical magnets with opposite poles aligned), thus neutralizing the net magnetic effect. This magnetic property is called antiferromagnetism.

Néel proposed the name ferrimagnetic to describe compounds that have oppositely aligned electrons (as in antiferromagnetic substances) but, because of unequal individual magnetic fields, have a net magnetic field (as in ferromagnetic substances). His studies of fine-grain ferromagnetics provided an explanation for the unusual magnetic memory of lava, basalt, and brick deposits that has provided information on changes in the direction and strength of the Earth's magnetic field during the past.

Néel became director of the Institut Polytechnique, Grenoble, in 1954, and also of the Centre d'Études Nucléaires, Grenoble, in 1956. Mainly because of his contributions, ferromagnetic materials can be manufactured to almost any specifications for technical applications, and a flood of new synthetic ferrite materials has revolutionized microwave electronics.
·ferrite properties theory **7**:248d
·magnetism theory development **11**:312c

Neelidae, family of insects of the suborder Symphypleona of the class Collembola.
·characteristics and classification **1**:1026b

Néel temperature (physics): *see* anti-ferromagnetism; Curie point.

Ne'eman, Yuval (1925–), Israeli physicist.
·subatomic particle research **13**:1031d

Ñeembucú, department, southwestern Paraguay. Bounded south and west by Argentina, from which it is separated by a 250-mi (400-km) frontage along the Paraguay and Paraná rivers, the territory has an area of 5,354 sq mi (13,868 sq km) and consists mainly of floodplain. Cattle raising and subsistence agriculture are the principal economic activities. Pilar (*q.v.*), the departmental capital and a river port, is linked to the Asunción–Encarnación highway, but otherwise Ñeembucú lacks the transport routes to exploit more fully the richness of its agricultural potentialities. Pop. (1972 prelim.) 73,001.
·area and population table **13**:987
·map, Paraguay **13**:986

Neemuch (India): *see* Nīmach.

Neenah, city, Winnebago County, east central Wisconsin, U.S., on Lake Winnebago and the south channel of the Fox River. The city, with adjoining Menasha on the north channel, forms one economic-social community. It was first settled in 1835 and called Winnebago Rapids (in 1856 renamed Neenah; Winnebago Indian for water). Flour milling was an early enterprise, but with the decline of wheat growing the city turned to papermaking, still the main industry. Other manufactures include iron castings and wood products. Inc. village, 1850; city, 1873. Pop. (1960) 18,057; (1980) 23,272.
44°11′ N, 88°28′ W

Neepawa, town, southwestern Manitoba, Canada, on the western slope of the Neepawa Creek Valley, west of Lake Manitoba. The site, on the old Fort Ellice Trail, was settled in 1878. Neepawa is a Salteaux Indian word meaning Place of Plenty—that is, fertile lands, woods, game. It is a grain-shipping point and service centre for an extensive agricultural region known as Beautiful Plains. Salt, discovered in 1910, is a major economic factor. Smaller industries include dairy processing, marble and granite working, and the making of canvas and cabinets. The community was incorporated in 1883, when the Manitoba and North Western Railway reached the area. Pop. (1971 prelim.) 3,216.
50°13′ N, 99°29′ W

Neer, Aert (AERNOUT) **van der** (b. 1603/04, Amsterdam—d. Nov. 9, 1677, Amsterdam), painter of the Baroque period, famed for his nocturnal landscapes. He probably did not begin his painting career until after 1630 and then was unable to make a reasonable living from his art. In 1658 he opened a wineshop, but this venture ended in bankruptcy in 1662. Subsequently he probably reverted to painting, for he is described as a painter in the inventory that was made of his few belongings at the time of his death. Apart from a number of accomplished winter scenes, such as "Riverscape in Winter" (Rijksmuseum, Amsterdam) in the manner of H. Avercamp, he specialized in canal and river landscapes seen by the light of late evening or early dawn or (most characteristic of all) by moonlight; *e.g.*, "River Scene by Moonlight" (Rijksmuseum, Amsterdam). Within this limited range he has no rival among his contemporaries; his best pictures are distinguished by sensitive handling of subdued light and its reflections on water and in the windows of riverside houses.

Neerwinden, commune (*gemeente*), Brabant province, east central Belgium. Part of the Duchy of Brabant during Habsburg (Spanish and Austrian) rule of the Netherlands, it was the scene of two battles. In the War of the Grand Alliance, the allies under William III of England were defeated there by the French under the Duke of Luxembourg (1693). In the second battle, during the French Revolutionary Wars, the French under Gen. Charles Dumouriez were defeated by the Austrians under the Prince of Coburg and Graf von Clerfayt (1793). Pop. (1972 est.) 3,201.
50°46′ N, 5°03′ E

nef, European vessel in the form of a medieval ship, often complete with rigging. Al-

Silver gilt nef, probably French, *c.* 1530; in the British Museum
By courtesy of the trustees of the British Museum

though occasionally made of Venetian glass, nefs were usually elaborately constructed of precious metals and sometimes had a hull of rock crystal, hardstone, or nautilus shell. Perhaps first used as a drinking vessel, by the 14th century it had become a table ornament to denote the host's place or a container (usually smaller) for salt and spices or table utensils. More rarely it was used as an alms dish in royal households. Although still being made in the early 17th century in Germany, the nef had by this time declined in artistic importance and had virtually ceased to exist in the rest of Europe.

·automata craftsmanship using spring **2**:495e
·Byzantine ship design **16**:678h

Nef, John Ulric (b. June 14, 1862, Herisau, Switz.—d. Aug. 13, 1915, Carmel, Calif.), chemist whose studies demonstrated conclusively that the element carbon can have a valence (*i.e.*, affinity for electrons) of two as well as a valence of four, thus greatly advancing the understanding of theoretical organic chemistry.

Brought to the United States by his father, a textile mill foreman who settled at Housatonic, Mass., Nef studied at Harvard University in Cambridge (A.B., 1884; Kirkland travelling fellowship, 1884–87) and at the University of Munich (Ph.D. *summa cum laude*, 1886), where he was a student of Alfred von Baeyer. After working a year in Baeyer's laboratory, Nef taught at Purdue University (West Lafayette, Ind.) from 1887 to 1889; at Clark University, a graduate institution, from 1889 (its founding date) to 1892, when he resigned to become professor of chemistry at the University of Chicago at its founding in 1892. In 1896 he became head of the department. Nef was a leader in establishing graduate study in the United States, bringing with him standards and techniques of the university organic chemistry laboratories of Europe.

Nef's major research was in the chemistry of isocyanides, nitroparaffins, and fulminates, from the last of which came his work on carbon valence. He resolved a disagreement between the German chemist Friedrich A. Kekule von Stradonitz, who had proposed the single valence of carbon as four, and the Scottish chemist Archibald S. Couper, who proposed the variable valences of carbon as four and two. Nef's findings also enhanced the value of Couper's system of writing the structural formulas of organic compounds.

NEFA (India): *see* Arunachal Pradesh.

Neferirkare (*c.* 2494–2345 BC), third king of the 5th dynasty of Egypt.

·pyramid papyri on temple foundation **6**:467e

Neferkare, Pepi II: *see* Pepi II Neferkare.

Nefertari, Egyptian queen of the 18th dynasty and favourite wife of Ramses II.

·art styles under the Ramessids **19**:255d

Nefertiti, queen of Egypt and wife of King Akhenaton (ruled 1379–62 BC) who supported her husband's religious revolution and is thought by some to have adhered to the new cult of the sun god Aton even after the King began to compromise with the upholders of the old order.

Nefertiti is best known for her portrait bust of painted limestone found at Tell el-Amarna (ancient Akhetaton), the King's new capital in Middle Egypt, and now in the Berlin Museum. Her parentage is uncertain but some scholars believe she was an Asian princess from Mitanni. She appeared prominently at her husband's side in reliefs found at the new capital, and she was a faithful follower of his new cult. Nefertiti bore six daughters, two of whom later became queens of Egypt.

In the 12th year of Akhenaton's reign, or possibly later, Nefertiti either retired after losing favour with the King or, less probably, died. Her eldest daughter and her husband, as co-regent, replaced Nefertiti in the royal inscriptions. Objects belonging to the Queen

Nefertiti, painted limestone bust, *c.* 1363–43 BC; in the Ägyptisches Museum, East Berlin
By courtesy of the Staatliche Museen zu Berlin

have been found at the northern palace in Amarna, suggesting that the Queen may have retired there. Her tomb has never been located.

·Akhenaton's cultural influence **1**:402c
·family connections **6**:474e
·foundation and layout of Tell el-Amarna **18**:1066d
·visual art style under Akhenaton **19**:255c

nefesh, Hebrew designation for the human soul ("breath"), the function of which was to animate the body.

·biblical and exegetical interpretations **10**:289c
·comparison with ruaḥ **15**:152h

Neff, Casper, 16th-century German calligrapher.

·calligraphic chancery cursive spread **3**:658g

Nef'i, pseudonym of ÖMER, also known as NEF'I OF ERZURUM (b. Hasankale, now Pasinler, Tur.—d. 1635/36, Istanbul), one of the greatest classical Ottoman poets and one of the most famous satirists and panegyrists in Ottoman Turkish literature. Little more is known of his early life than that he served as a minor government official in the reign of the Ottoman sultan Ahmed I (1603–17). It was not until the time of Sultan Murad IV (1623–40), himself a poet of some distinction, that Nef'i succeeded in gaining court favour. He became famous as a court panegyrist and also developed his reputation as a powerful satirist. With the exception of his patron, the Sultan, Nef'i attacked the highest public figures in the land with his vituperative pen. These satirical sketches, expressed in a witty style and often in obscene and vulgar language, reveal the poet's most candid opinions of those in power. He frequently satirized a figure he had eulogized earlier in his career. Nef'i's biting invective caused his downfall, for he created numerous enemies at the Ottoman court. One such, Bayram Paşa, deputy prime minister and brother-in-law of the Sultan, finally succeeded in securing his execution in 1635/36.

Nef'i is considered one of the finest *qaṣīdah* (ode) writers of Ottoman literature. His famous divan contains many examples of his eloquent poetic style and his magnificent language, which is both musical and vividly imaginative. Though his *qaṣīdahs*, mainly eulogies, are considered to be extremely tasteful and proper, his satirical works are held to be calumnous and abusive. Nef'i also left a Persian divan that brought him great praise from his patron, Murad IV, who was a great admirer of Persian letters.

·satiric poetic style **9**:969a

Nefta, Arabic NAFṬAH, oasis town, Qafṣah (Gafsa) *wilāyat* (governorate), southwestern Tunisia, on the west shore of the Chott Djerid, a saline lake and an important source of phosphates. It is a date-growing and trans-Saharan caravan centre. The larger oasis of Tozeur (Tawzar) is 15 mi (24 km) east-northeast. Latest census 10,404.
33°52′ N, 7°33′ E

·map, Tunisia **18**:746
·spring temperature and water quality **17**:517d

Nefusa, Gebel (Libya): *see* Nafūsah, Jabal.

Negapattam (India): *see* Nāgappattinam.

Negaprion brevirostris (lemon shark): *see* Carcharhinidae.

negative acceleration-stress, physiological changes that occur to the body when there is acceleration in the direction from feet to head. Pilots are especially prone to the effects of acceleration because of the high speeds at which they travel. Rapid changes in acceleration are felt more dramatically than gradual ones and the body adjusts and compensates for gradual increases more easily than it does for surges of acceleration. Negative acceleration-stress causes a slight displacement of the internal organs in the abdomen and chest and a rush of blood to the face accompanied by the feeling of congestion. As the acceleration increases in the direction from feet to head, pressure is felt against the restraining belts across the thighs and shoulders; this is usually ignored because of the discomfort around the head and face.

With further increase the congestion increases and throbbing pains are felt throughout the head. When the force is from 3 to 4.5 gs (a g is a unit of gravitational acceleration; a force of 3 gs, for example, is equivalent to an acceleration three times that of a body falling near the Earth), the eyes feel as though they are protruding and there is a gritty feeling under the eyelids because of swelling in the small blood vessels. There may be temporary loss of vision or all objects may appear red; this latter condition is known as "red-out." The mental confusion that develops at higher accelerations may lead to unconsciousnesss.

In acceleration in the direction from feet to head the blood pressure in the skull rises. In order to relieve the pressure in the skull the velocity of the blood flow to the rest of the body must be increased. Temporary cardiac arrest may occur at around 5 gs. Respiration is also impaired because of the pressure upon the lungs from the abdominal contents and the muscular diaphragm (the wall between the chest and the abdomen). Bleeding can occur under the skin of the face; weak arteries or veins in the head region can rupture while under such stress. The average endurable times for negative stress are a few seconds at 5 gs, 15 seconds for 4.5 gs, and around 30 seconds for 3 gs. Stunt fliers and pilots experienced with accelerations in the direction from feet to head seem to tolerate its effects better than new or inexperienced fliers.

negative carving (sculpture): *see* intaglio.

negative electron (physics): *see* electron.

negative income tax: *see* guaranteed minimum income.

negative of a number, compared with a given number, a specific number that when added to the given number equals zero. If n is a number, its negative is written $-n$.

negative theology: *see* apophantic theology.

Neg'ator, also known as CONSTANT-FORCE SPRING, a spring introduced in 1949 that forms a tightly wound spiral in its relaxed or unstressed condition.

·design and application **11**:259c; illus.

negatron (physics): *see* electron.

Negeri Sembilan, formerly NEGRI SEMBILAN, state (*negeri*), southwestern West Malaysia (Malaya), bounded by the states of Selangor (northwest), Pahang (north), Johor (formerly Johore [east]), and Melaka (formerly Malacca [south]). Its area of 2,565 sq mi (6,642 sq km) is drained by the Linggi and Mirar rivers and has a 30-mile (48-km) coastline on the Strait of Malacca.

Its princes, who trace their ancestry from the monarchs of Śrivijaya (a maritime empire based on Sumatra), came from Minangkabau (Sumatra) and Celebes in the 14th century. The Minangkabaus brought a matrilineal society and laws known as Adat Perpateh to the peninsula. Their culture and architecture, while not widespread, are unique to the state.

Nine states (*negeri sembilan*), including parts of present-day Selangor, Melaka, Johor, and Pahang, were loosely confederated in 1773. The British, interested in the key tin-producing state of Sungei Ujong, offered the group protection after 1874, which was accepted. Negri Sembilan became one of the Federated Malay States (1895) and after World War II it joined the Federation of Malaya.

The state is now ruled by a constitutional sultan (Yang di-Pertuan Besar) selected from the territorial chiefs, a system peculiar among Malaysian states.

The inhabitants engage in paddy (rice) farming at the bottoms of the steep-sided valleys; fruit cultivation is also common and rubber is extensively grown. A few declining alluvial tin mines are in the western valleys and along the coast. The towns are dominated by Chinese and Indians. Negeri Sembilan contains part of the west coast "tin and rubber" belt road network, one of the few east–west peninsular routes, and there is a junction of railway lines on either side of the mountains at Gemas. The main towns are Seremban (*q.v.*; the capital), Kuala Pilah, and Port Dickson. Pop. (1970 prelim.) 479,312.

·area and population, table 1 **11**:373
·Malayan agricultural society and democracy **11**:366f
·matrilineal social organization **17**:226f

Negev, also spelled NEGEB, Hebrew HA-NEGEV (meaning "the southland"), southern part of Israel, occupies almost half of Palestine west of the Jordan, and about 60 percent of Israeli territory under the 1949–67 boundaries. The name is derived from the Hebrew verbal root *n-g-b*, "to dry, to wipe dry." Triangular shaped with the apex at the south, it is bounded by the Sinai Peninsula (west) and the Jordan Rift Valley (east). Its northern boundary, where the region blends into the coastal plain in the northwest, Har Yehuda (the Judaean Hills) in the north, and the Wilderness of Judaea (Midbar Yehuda) in the northeast, is indistinct. Many use an arbitrary line at about 30°25′ north latitude for the northern boundary. Within these limits, the Negev has an area of about 4,700 sq mi.

Geologically, the area is one of northeast-southwest folds, with many faults. Limestones and chalks predominate. A unique feature is the large elongate *makhteshim*, or erosion craters, surrounded by high cliffs. These were created by the erosion of upward-folded strata (anticlines), combined with horizontal stresses. The largest of these are Makhtesh Ramon, 23 mi (37 km) long and up to 5 mi wide, and ha-Maktesh ha-Gadol (The Great Crater), about 9 mi long and up to 4 mi wide. The floors of these craters expose chalks, marls, and gypsums, geologically much older than the walls or surrounding plateaus.

Biblical references such as Ps. 126:4 ("Restore our fortunes, O Lord, like the watercourses in the Negeb") point to the semi-arid character of the region from early recorded times. The Negev should not, however, be considered a desert as such; in the Beersheba area (altitude about 800 ft [250 m]), rainfall varies from 8 in. (200 mm) to 12 in. in some years. The latter amount permits unirrigated grain farming. Precipitation decreases to the south; the central Negev plateau (altitude 820–3,395 ft [250–1,035 m]) receives 3–4 in.; rainfall is negligible at Elat at the southern tip. The amount of rainfall varies considerably throughout the region from year to year. Flash flooding is common in the winter rainy season. Most of the rugged region is heavily dissected by wadis, or seasonal watercourses.

Remains of prehistoric and early historic settlements are abundant. Flint arrowheads of the Late Stone Age (*c.* 7000 BC) and implements of the Copper and Bronze ages (*c.* 4000–1400 BC) have been found on the central Negev plateau. The Negev was a pastoral region in biblical times, but the Nabataeans, a Semitic people centred in what is now Jordan, developed techniques of terracing and of conserving winter rains, which made the Negev a thriving agricultural area. It was an important granary of the Roman Empire. After the Arab conquest of Palestine (7th century AD), the Negev was left desolate; for more than 1,200 years it supported only a meagre population of nomadic Bedouin.

Modern agricultural development in the Negev began with three kibbutzim (collective settlements) in 1943; others were founded just after World War II, when the first large-scale irrigation projects were initiated. After the creation of the State of Israel (1948), the importance of development of this large portion of the country was realized. Under the National Water Plan pipelines and conduits bring water from northern and central Israel to the northwestern Negev, which has almost 400,000 ac (more than 160,000 ha) of fertile loess soils. Irrigation, combined with the area's year-round sunlight, produces fine crops of grain, fodder, fruits, and vegetables. Double-cropping is not uncommon.

Exploitation of mineral resources has accompanied agricultural development. Potash, bromine, and magnesium are extracted at Sedom (*q.v.*), at the southern end of the Dead Sea; copper is mined at Timnaʿ (*q.v.*); there are large deposits of ball clay and glass sand for the ceramic and glass industries; phosphate works have been established at Oron and Zefaʿ, and natural gas fields at Rosh Zohar.

Urbanization has come in the wake of modern settlement; Beersheba (*q.v.*), "capital of the Negev," is the largest city in Israel not in the environs of Tel Aviv–Yafo, Jerusalem, or Haifa. Planned cities in the Negev include ʿArad (founded 1961), Dimona (1955), and the port-city of Elat (settled 1949; *qq.v.*), Israel's outlet to the Red Sea.

30°45′ N, 34°50′ E

·Israel's geographical influences **9**:1059f
·map, Israel **9**:1060
·National Water Carrier canal **7**:851c
·Ramses II's military victories **15**:502f

Neghelli, Rodolfo Graziani, marchese di: *see* Graziani, Rodolfo, marchese di Neghelli.

negligee, an informal gown, usually of a soft, sheer fabric, worn at home by women. In the days of tightly corseted and laced clothing, the negligee was a loose-fitting gown worn during the rest period after lunch. Women's

Desert scene in the eastern Negev, near the Israel–Jordan frontier
Josef Muench

Woman wearing a negligee, "Lady Reading," chalk and pastel drawing by François Guérin; in Albertina, Vienna

By courtesy of Graphische Sammlung Albertina, Vienna

dresses were also referred to as negligés after the Restoration of Charles II, when the trend was toward loose fashions characterized by "studied negligence."

negligence, in law, the failure to meet a standard of behaviour established to protect society against unreasonable risk. Negligence is the cornerstone of tort liability and a key factor in most personal injury and property-damage trials.

Roman law used a similar principle, distinguishing intentional damage (*dolus*) from unintentional damage (*culpa*) and determining liability by a behavioral standard. Germanic and French law early maintained very stringent liability for accidents and still do. Negligence became a basis of liability in English law only in 1825.

The doctrine of negligence originally applied to "public" professionals, such as innkeepers, blacksmiths, and surgeons, but it was probably prompted by industrialization and increased occupational accidents. At first liability was harsh, then was softened to encourage industrial growth. The later trend is toward greater liability.

No man must eliminate all risk from his conduct—only all unreasonable risk, which is measured by the seriousness of possible consequences. Thus a higher standard applies to nitroglycerin manufacturers than to those making kitchen matches. In certain critical fields—*e.g.*, the milk industry—the law imposes liability for any mistakes, even when the strictest precautions are taken, a policy known as strict liability.

The standard of behaviour is external. Generally the law examines only conduct, not the excitability, ignorance, or stupidity that may cause it. The courts determine what the hypothetical "reasonable man" would have done in the situation. Such standards also demand a degree of foresight in anticipating the negligence of others—especially of special groups such as children.

The reasonable-man test presumes certain knowledge—*e.g.*, that fire burns, water may cause drowning, and cars may skid on wet pavement. Community custom will influence such presumptions, such as the practice of driving on a certain side of the road even on private roads, a situation in which laws do not apply. Emergencies, however, can soften the application of such standards.

Allowances may be made for physical (but not mental) handicaps, such as blindness, but the law demands that handicapped persons avoid needlessly placing themselves in situations in which their inability may cause harm. Other than distinguishing between children and adults, the doctrine of negligence does not usually consider factors of age or experience.

Ordinarily the plaintiff in a negligence suit must prove defendant's negligence by a preponderance of the evidence, which may be circumstantial so long as it is not too speculative. In some situations, once the plaintiff has established an apparent connection between his injury and the defendant's apparent negligence, the latter must disprove that connection. This is the doctrine of *res ipsa loquitur* (Latin: "the matter speaks for itself"). Generally the damages recoverable for negligence are a monetary compensation for injuries or losses that are deemed to have flowed "naturally and proximately" from the negligent act. *See also* contributory negligence. *Major ref.* **18**:527b

·air laws and airline liability **1**:399a
·carriage of goods and liability law **3**:961e
·common law defenses in negligence cases **9**:656f
·industrial accidents and safety laws **8**:697a
·liability insurance rationale **9**:647f *passim* to 648f
·maritime law and assessing of liability **11**:501e *passim* to 502h
·medical evidence in civil actions **11**:813f
·physician malpractice law **11**:815c

negotiable instruments, instruments such as checks, bills of exchange, promissory notes, and some bonds, that can be assigned or transferred from one person to another in exchange for equivalent value.

·bills of lading and carriage of goods **3**:963c
·checks and history of banking **2**:701b
·commercial law and bills of exchange **4**:991g

Negra, Cordillera, range of the Andes Mountains in west-central Peru. It extends for about 110 mi (176 km) southeast from the Santa River (the valley of which separates it from the Cordillera Blanca), and rises to a height of 14,764 ft (4,430 m).
9°30′ S, 77°30′ W

·Andes source, name, and union **1**:857g
·map, Peru **14**:128

Negreti, Jacopo: *see* Palma, Jacopo.

Negri bodies, oval or round microscopic masses in the cytoplasm of nerve cells (especially those in certain areas of the brain). They are diagnostic of rabies (*q.v.*) whenever present but are not demonstrable in all cases of the disease. Although their precise nature is unknown, they contain lipid material as well as the rabies virus. Negri bodies were discovered in 1903 by the Italian physician Adelchi Negri.

Negrín, Juan (b. Feb. 3, 1894, Las Palmas, Canary Islands, Spain—d. Nov. 14, 1956, Paris), Republican prime minister of Spain who held office during the last two years of the Spanish Civil War (1936–39). He was a courageous and determined wartime leader but was forced to rely heavily on Communist support during his time in power.

Negrín, of a prosperous merchant family, became a physiologist of repute and held a chair at Madrid University (1923–31). In 1929 he turned to politics and as a democratic Socialist was elected to the Cortes in 1931, 1933, and 1936. As wartime minister of finance (September 1936–May 1937) he played an important role in shipping much of Spain's gold reserves to the Soviet Union.

In May 1937 Negrín succeeded Largo Caballero as prime minister and from the outset committed himself to a policy of resolute resistance to the Nationalists. This stance led him to substantial reliance on the Soviet Union, the Republic's only source of arms, and on the powerful Spanish Communist Party. Though he retained a degree of independence and autonomy, Negrín's Communist dependence contributed to the alienation of the non-Communist Left and aroused suspicion among Western nations.

The Negrín government pursued a socially moderate course and attempted with limited success to unify the war effort. Negrín urged resistance even after the collapse of Catalonia (February 1939), but an anti-Communist military rising in Madrid favouring a negotiated peace forced his resignation in March.

Negrín was in exile in Paris until the German occupation, when he fled to Great Britain and then to the United States. He was prime minister of the Republican government in exile but resigned in 1945.

·Communist takeover of the Spanish Civil War **17**:441h

Negri Sembilan (West Malaysia): *see* Negeri Sembilan.

Negrito local race, a population with affinities to the Australoid geographical race, the Micronesian and Melanesian–Papuan geographical races, and perhaps to the Southeast Asian local race of the Mongoloid geographical race as well. The Negritos are found in several rather isolated groups on the islands of Luzon, Mindanao, and Palawan in the Philippines; the Semang people of Malaysia and the Andaman Islanders also belong to the Negrito local race. The group's chief physical characteristics are short stature (under five feet tall), yellowish-brown skin, curly to frizzly hair, and rather Australoid facial features, including large teeth and prognathous (projecting) jaw, long head, and broad nose. The Andamanese women show marked steatopygia (massive fat deposits in the buttocks supported by fibrous tissue). *See also* local race; Southeast Asian local race; Australoid geographical race; Micronesian geographical race; Melanesian geographical race.

·Australoid racial characteristics **14**:844f
·Burmese legendary ages **3**:510f
·New Guinea migration **12**:1089e
·Vietnam and its early inhabitants **19**:120c

Negritude, a literary movement of the 1930s, '40s, and '50s which was born among French-speaking African and Caribbean writers (who were living in Paris at the time) as a protest against French rule and the policy of assimilation. Its leading figure was Léopold Sédar Senghor (elected first president of the Republic of Senegal in 1960), who, along with Aimé Césaire from Martinique and Léon Damas from French Guiana, began to examine Western values critically and to reassess African culture. The group's quarrel with assimilation was that although it was theoretically based on a belief in the equality of man, it still assumed the superiority of European culture and civilization over that of Africa (or rather assumed that Africa had no history or culture). They were also disturbed by wars in which they saw their fellow countrymen not only dying for a cause that was not theirs, but being treated as inferiors on the battlefield. They became increasingly aware, through their study of history, of the suffering and humiliation of the black man first under the bondage of slavery and then under colonial rule. These views inspired many of the basic ideas behind Negritude: that the mystic warmth of African life, gaining strength from its closeness to nature and its constant contact with ancestors, should be continually placed in proper perspective against the soullessness and materialism of Western culture; that Africans must look to the richness of their past and of their cultural heritage in order to choose which values and traditions could be most useful to the modern world; that committed writers should not only use African subject matter and poetic traditions in their writings but should also inspire their readers with a desire for political freedom; that Negritude itself encompasses the whole of African cultural, economic, social, and political values; and that above all, the value and dignity of African traditions and peoples must be asserted.

In Senghor's poetry one finds all of these themes, and he inspired a number of other writers: Birago Diop from Senegal, whose poems explore the mystique of African life; David Diop, writer of revolutionary protest poetry; Jacques Rabemananjara, whose poems and plays glorify the history and culture of the Malagasy Republic; Cameroonians Mongo Beti and Ferdinand Oyono, who wrote anti-colonialist novels; and the Congolese poet Tchicaya U Tam'si, whose very personal poetry does not neglect the sufferings of the African peoples. Since the early 1960s, however, with the political and cultural objectives of the movement achieved in most African countries, there has been much less work produced with Negritude themes, and the focal point of literary activity in West Africa has moved now from Senegal to Nigeria.

- ·Senghor's belief in African heritage **16**:541a *passim* to 542a
- ·philosophy of a black Africa **16**:539e

Negro, American, a person of black African ancestry either born in the U.S., naturalized as a U.S. citizen, or, until emancipation in the 1860s, bonded as a slave. Persons have often been considered Negro if they possess any black African ancestry, regardless of how many white or Indian ancestors they may also possess. Dissatisfaction with the traditionally discriminatory term Negro has led to the advocacy and use of such alternatives as black American and Afro-American. *See also* American Coloured local race.

- ·African music and European tradition **16**:792g
- ·baseball players' league status **2**:732e
- ·Black Caucus official protest **18**:999b
- ·Black Muslim ideology and belief **2**:1094a
- ·Canadian immigration and settlement **12**:414b
- ·Carver's contribution to race relations **3**:972e
- ·civil-rights movement literary counterpart **18**:941f
- ·civil rights protest and legislative advancement **18**:995g *passim* to 997b
- ·colonial slave population increase **18**:952a
- ·dramatic treatment and contributions **18**:235b
- ·Du Bois's statement of black dilemma **5**:1076a
- ·folklore and America's mixed culture **7**:464h
- ·historical and contemporary integration **13**:195g
- ·income distribution analysis **19**:675g; table
- ·integration rate and operative factors **15**:365d
- ·intelligence test performance **9**:676g
- ·living conditions in the 19th century and postwar role **18**:963g *passim* to 967h
- ·Methodist membership and involvement **12**:61d
- ·minority group characteristics and status **12**:261b
- ·Nebraska immigration and ghetto problem **12**:923e
- ·Negro cults' history and characteristics **12**:942d
- ·New Orleans population jazz contribution **13**:6d
- ·sickle-cell anemia affliction **11**:1050c
- ·slavery in the U.S. **16**:861a
- ·South American racial mixing **17**:95c
- ·status and civil rights movement change **18**:928f *passim* to 930h
- ·Western dance influenced by culture **5**:463f

Negro bug (insect): *see* burrower bug.

Negro churches (in the United States) 12:936, the churches of those Americans known variously as Negroes, Afro-Americans, and blacks. These churches have increasingly been called black churches.

The text article covers the nature and significance of the Negro churches, emphasizing the influence of slavery on the liturgical styles and aspirations expressed in black worship; the history of the Negro churches from slavery times to the post-World War II period of black liberation, Black Power, and Black Theology; the major Negro churches and some of the Negro sects; and practices, including worship, the role of the minister, and social, cultural, political, and educational activities.

REFERENCES in other text articles:

- ·Baptist conventions **2**:715d
- ·Black Muslim history and practice **2**:1093b
- ·Church of God in Christ founding **14**:32h
- ·exclusive worship forms **19**:1015f
- ·Methodist union and church history **12**:61d

RELATED ENTRIES in the *Ready Reference and Index:*

African Methodist Episcopal Church; African Methodist Episcopal Zion Church; Christian Methodist Episcopal Church; National Baptist Convention, U.S.A., Inc.; National Baptist Convention of America; National Primitive Baptist Convention, Inc.; Progressive National Baptist Convention, Inc.

Negro cults (in the United States) 12:942, as a subject, covers the religious beliefs and practices of an extremely varied and syncretistic group of religious organizations that have generally been predominant in Negro urban enclaves, especially in the 20th century; they originate among a plethora of peoples from many different African countries, replete with dozens of foreign dialects.

The text article covers the history of the subject, including its formative and expansionist periods and types of cults that developed in urban centres, spiritualist cults, cults centred around individuals, nationalistic cults, and nativistic movements. The article concludes with an assessment of Negro cults as depositories of residual Afro-American cultural elements.

REFERENCES in other text articles:

- ·Caribbean belief patterns **3**:905h
- ·emergence and difference from storefront churches **12**:939c

negrohead, large block of coral limestone that occurs along the margin of a coral reef and is usually covered with black, dead algae or a crust of lichen. These were probably broken off the outer edge of a reef by storm waves and thrown up on the reef flat as jetsam. Negroheads that are flat on top are thought to be erosional remnants of an older platform reef that was dissected.

Negro River near Manaus, Braz.
Luis Villota

Negroid (AFRICAN) **geographical race,** a group of human populations (local races and microraces) occupying sub-Saharan Africa. Characteristic of the Negroid race are medium to heavy skin pigmentation, curly to extreme spiral-tuft hair forms, linear (slim, angular) body build, broad lips, broad nose, minimal body hair and little pattern balding, some incidence of fatty deposits in the buttocks (steatopygia, *q.v.*), high frequency of blood type R_0 (*see* Rh blood group system), presence of the U-negative blood type (*see* MNSs blood group system), rare blood types Fy (*see* Duffy blood group system) and V, haptoglobin variants, abnormal hemoglobins, and G-6-PD deficiency. Some anthropologists divide the Negroid race into two races, the Congoid and the Capoid. The Congoid race is exemplified by the "typical" Negro type: dark skin, kinky hair, medium to tall stature. The Capoid race is composed of the Bushmen and Hottentots of southern Africa: yellowish skin, extreme spiral-tuft hair, short but linear stature. Although the physical differences between the Capoids and Congoids are fairly marked, there is no evidence of distinctions in blood type between the two groups.

- ·African continent settlement patterns **1**:204h
- ·Asian population **2**:174c
- ·Bantus and pygmies of the Ituri Forest **9**:1176h
- ·blood group frequencies in populations **2**:1148e; table
- ·climatic influence on man **4**:729b
- ·Congoid racial characteristics **14**:843e
- ·evolution, appearance, and cultures **1**:281c
- ·sickle-cell anemia characteristics **4**:225c
- ·skin cancer incidence **15**:390f
- ·Spanish colonial slavery development **10**:696b
- ·theoretical Oceanian racial link with Africa **13**:468h
- ·West African kingdoms origin theories **19**:761f

Negroli, Filippo, 16th-century Italian armourer.

- ·embossed steel arms design illus. **2**:32

Negro River, Spanish RÍO NEGRO, southern Argentina, whose major headstreams, the Neuquén and Limay rivers, rise in the Andes near the Chilean border. At Neuquén they meet to form the Negro, which flows generally east-southeastward across northern Patagonia, through Río Negro province, and empties into the Atlantic Ocean southeast of Viedma and Carmen de Patagones. Although the Negro is approximately 400 mi (644 km; 700 mi including the Neuquén) in length, only the lower 250 mi are navigable. Waters of the Negro are used for hydroelectricity and for irrigation of grains, fruit, and wine grapes.
41°02′ S, 62°47′ W

- ·length and irrigation importance **1**:1135f
- ·map, Argentina **1**:1136

Negro River, RÍO NEGRO in Brazil and RÍO NEGRO in Uruguay, rises in the southern highlands of Brazil just east of Bagé. The Negro flows southwestward into Uruguay, where it separates the Cerro Largo and Tacuarembó departments. Turning west-southwestward, the river, dammed near Paso de los Toros to create the large Río Negro reservoir, forms the border between Tacuarembó and Durazno departments. Downstream from another dam at Rincón de Baygorna, it meanders generally westward past Mercedes and between Río Negro and Soriano departments to join the Uruguay River at Soriano. The confluence is marked by several islands, the largest of which are Vizcaíno, Lobos, and Infante. Although the Negro is approximately 500 mi (800 km) long, it is navigable for only 45 mi (70 km) upstream from its mouth. A large hydroelectric plant is located at Embalse (lake) del Río Negro (Rincón del Bonate).
26°01′ S, 50°30′ W

- ·map, Uruguay **18**:1094

Negro River, Portuguese RIO NEGRO, Spanish RÍO NEGRO, major tributary of the Amazon, originates in several headstreams, including the Vaupés (Mapés) and the Guiania, which rise in the rain forest of eastern Colombia. The Guiania flows east and then arches northeast and southeast, forming the Colombia–Venezuela border. Below its junction near San Carlos de Río Negro with the Brazo Casiquiare, a natural waterway that brings water from the Orinoco River in Venezuela, the river acquires the name Negro and enters Brazil. The Negro meanders generally east-southeastward, picking up the Branco River (*q.v.*) and other tributaries, to Manaus. There it joins the Solimões (*q.v.*) to form the Amazon. Its length is about 1,250 mi (2,000 km), of which 850 mi are in Brazil.

Although settlement along its banks is sparse, the river is a major transportation artery. The clear, jet-black water of the Negro, whence comes its name, is caused by the decomposition of organic matter in marginal swamps (*igapós*); its colour contrasts dramatically with the yellowish, silt-laden Branco and with the Amazon.
3°08′ S, 59°55′ W
·map, Brazil **3**:124
·origin and development **13**:737e; map
·Orinoco water diversion to Amazon **19**:59b
·vegetation types **1**:651d

Negros, one of the Visayan islands, central Philippines, separated from the islands of

Sugar refinery and railroad siding on Negros, Philippines
Jules Bucher—Photo Researchers

Panay (northwest) and Cebu (east) by the Guimaras and Tañon straits and washed north and south by the Visayan and Sulu seas.

Shaped like a boot, it has an area of 4,905 sq mi (12,704 sq km). A lofty central mountain range runs nearly its entire 135-mi (217-km) length and is deeply dissected by erosion. The range contains Mt. Silay (5,049 ft [1,539 m]), Mandalagan (6,165 ft), and the active Mt. Canlaon, a volcano that at 8,071 ft is the highest point in the Visayas. The island varies from 22 to 49 miles in width. Its coastal areas are densely populated. The east coast has discontinuous piedmont plains; the western coastal plains, however, are among the broader Philippine lowlands, comprising 5- to 30-mi-wide strips and extending nearly 100 mi along the shoreline. The major rivers are the Binalbagan, Ilog, Tolong, and Tanjay. The southeastern peninsula (the toe of the boot) contains the crater lakes of Danao and Balinsasayan, and eruptions from the volcanic Cuernos de Negros (6,102 ft) have built up a plain around its base. Most of southwestern Negros comprises the Tablas, an undeveloped plateau with a varied landscape.

Nomadic Negritos inhabit the upland interior. Language reflects the settlement patterns of the coastal areas: Panay-Hiligaynon, from Panay, is widely spoken in western Negros, whereas Cebuano, from Cebu, is dominant in the eastern areas.

The island produces more than 50 percent of the nation's sugar; the sugarcane farms and mills are concentrated in the north and west. Rice, coconuts, bananas, papayas, and mangoes are secondary crops. Corn (maize) is the major food crop. Timber extraction and processing is important. Mineral deposits include copper (mined at Sipolay) and gypsum; salt is produced in the east.

Negros' two administrative provinces, Negros Occidental and Negros Oriental, are divided by the central mountain range and reflect the linguistic division of the island. Chartered cities are Bacolod, Dumaguete, Silay, San Carlos, and Bago (*qq.v.*). Pop. (1970) 2,219,022.
10°00′ N, 123°00′ E
·population density map **14**:235

Negros Occidental, province, western and northern Negros, Philippines, facing Panay across Guimaras Strait. Its area of 3,060 sq mi (7,926 sq km) includes a large coastal plain built from sediments eroded from the igneous mountain mass of the interior. It is one of the wealthiest and most politically influential provinces in the nation, with much of its income derived from sugar (more than one-half of the Philippine commercial crop). There are modern centrals (mills producing raw sugar from cane) at Binalbagan, Victorias, La Carlota, Hawaiian-Philippine (near Saravia), Talisay-Silay, Ma-ao, Bacolod-Murcia, San Carlos, Lopez (at Sagay), and Danao (near Escalante). Large numbers of migrant sugar workers annually cross the strait from Iloilo province, Panay. A modern lumber mill is at Fabrica on the Himuga-an River, but local timber stands have been largely exhausted. A minor coal deposit is near Escalante. Volcanic Mt. Canlaon (*see* Canlaon, Mount) at 8,071 ft (2,460 m) is at the province's eastern boundary.

The city of Bacolod (*q.v.*) on the northwest coast is the provincial capital and principal urban settlement. Other population centres are La Carlota, San Carlos, Bago, Silay (*q.v.*), Cadiz, Calatrava, and Kabankalan. Pop. (1970) 1,503,782.
·area and population table **14**:236
·map, Philippines **14**:233

Negros Oriental, province, eastern and southern Negros, Philippines, bordered southwest by the Sulu Sea and separated from Cebu by the narrow Tañon Strait. Its area of 2,218 sq mi (5,746 sq km) is mountainous and sparsely populated, except for the fertile eastern plain, where corn (maize), rice, sugarcane, and coconuts are grown and where the main towns are located. More than 25 percent of the province is forested with small sawmilling operations at Bayawan, La Libertad, and Tanjay. Large quantities of rattans and bamboos are harvested, and lumber is shipped to Japan.

Dumaguete (*q.v.*), the provincial capital, is in the southeast, opposite the subprovince of Siquijor Island (130 sq mi). Bais is the site of the province's only sugar central (mill) and has a subsidiary distillery and paper mill. A coastal highway links the population centres of Canlaon City, Calamba, Guihulñgan, Bayawan, and Zamboanguita. Pop. (1970) 715,240.
·area and population table **14**:236

Negro World, a weekly newspaper published by Marcus Garvey in the 1930s.
·black nationalist beliefs and leadership **12**:943d

Neguib, Muhammad: *see* Naguib, Mohammad.

Neheh (Egyptian religion): *see* Hu, Sia, and Heh.

Nehemiah (fl. 5th century BC), Jewish leader in the rebuilding of Jerusalem after the Persian king Artaxerxes I released Israel (*c.* 444 BC) from Babylonian Exile. After regaining Jerusalem, he also instituted extensive moral and liturgical reforms in rededicating the Jews to Yahweh.
·covenant in ritualistic terms **5**:229c
·governorship of Judah **7**:128a
·Old Testament basis in history **2**:897h
·reforms in Jerusalem **17**:947c

Nehemiah, Book of (Bible): *see* Ezra and Nehemiah, books of.

Nehru, Jawaharlal **12**:944 (b. Nov. 14, 1889, Allahābād, India—d. May 27, 1964, New Delhi), first prime minister of independent India (1947–64), established parliamentary government, and was idolized by his countrymen.

Becoming associated with Gandhi's Congress Party in 1919, Nehru committed himself to Indian independence and was made head of the party in 1929. Nehru, like Gandhi, was imprisoned a number of times by the British for his activities. When India did become independent in 1947, he became its prime minister. In subsequent years he attempted to set the nation on a course of nonalignment in world affairs, a policy that was only partially successful.

TEXT BIOGRAPHY covers:
Early years **12**:944c
Political apprenticeship 944g
Struggle for Indian independence 945c
Imprisonment during World War II 945f
Achievements as prime minister 946a
Assessment 946f

REFERENCES in other text articles:
·Gandhi's influence on policy **7**:878f
·Hinduism's role in secular politics **8**:919e
·Indian modern history **9**:419g
·Meghalaya tribal protection **11**:858d
·Patel's secondary role through Gandhi **13**:1070e

Nehru, (Pandit) Motilal (b. May 6, 1861, Delhi, India—d. Feb. 6, 1931, Lucknow), a leader of the Indian independence movement, co-founder of the Swaraj (self-rule) Party, and the father of India's first prime minister, Jawaharlal Nehru.

Motilal, a member of a prosperous Kashmiri Brahmin family, early established a lucrative law practice and was admitted to the Allāhābād High Court in 1896. He shunned politics until middle age, when, in 1907, at Allāhābād, he presided over a provincial conference of the Indian National Congress, a political organization striving for dominion status for India. He was considered a moderate (one who advocated constitutional reform in contrast to the extremists who employed agitational methods) until 1919, when he made his newly radicalized views known by means of a daily newspaper he founded, *The Independent*.

The massacre of hundreds of Indians by the British at Amritsar in 1919 prompted Motilal to join Gandhi's non-cooperation movement, giving up his career in law and changing to a simpler, non-anglicized style of life. In 1921 both he and Jawaharlal were arrested by the British and jailed for six months.

In 1923 Motilal helped found the Swaraj Party (1923–27), the policy of which was to win election to the Central Legislative Assembly and obstruct its proceedings from within. In 1928 he wrote the Congress Party's Nehru Report, a future constitution for independent India based on the granting of dominion status. After the British rejected these proposals, Motilal participated in the civil disobedience movement of 1930, for which he was imprisoned. He died soon after release.
·Congress party history **9**:419b
·family involvement in nationalism **12**:944e
·Gandhi and the Congress Party split **7**:877b

Nehru, Swarup Kumari: *see* Pandit, Vijaya Lakshmi.

Nehru–Liaqat Pact: *see* Delhi Pact.

Neiba, capital, Baoruco province, southwestern Dominican Republic, in the lowlands between the eastern shore of Lago Enriquillo and the Yaque del Sur River. It was founded around the beginning of the 18th century and made provincial capital in 1943. Sugarcane and fine timber are the principal products of the area; rock salt deposits are located in the vicinity. The city is accessible by secondary highways from Barahona and Jimaní, and it has an airfield. Pop. (1970 prelim.) 10,194.
18°28′ N, 71°25′ W

Nei-chiang, Pin-yin romanization NEI-JIANG, city in central Szechwan Province (*sheng*), China. It is a county- (*hsien-*) level municipality (*shih*) and the administrative centre of the Nei-chiang Area (*ti-ch'ü*). Situated on the T'o Chiang (river), it is also at the junction of the

Ch'eng-tu–Chungking railway and the southern branch line to I-pin. These railways were completed in 1956, making Nei-chiang an important transportation and commercial centre. A southward rail line to K'un-ming in Yunnan was projected in the 1970s.

The county is an ancient one, first set up in the 1st century AD; it received its present name and moved to its present site in 582. In medieval times it was located in an important salt-producing area, but in recent times its name has been associated with sugar; it is commonly called the sugar capital of Szechwan. The city and the nearby towns of Pai-ma-ch'ang and Ho-shih-ssu have large sugar-refining plants and also make sweet preserves and alcohol. This industry, formerly carried on by hand in hundreds of small plants, was centralized after 1949 and modernized; the small local plants now produce molasses. By-products of the sugar mills are used in paper manufacture and are also used to produce fertilizer, animal feed cake, and glucose. Nei-chiang also has an engineering industry, producing sugar-processing equipment and farm implements, as well as a textile industry. Pop. (1948) 32,000; (latest est.) 180,000.
29°35′ N, 105°03′ E
·map, China **4**:262

Neichia-shan Series, division of Ordovician rocks in southern China (the Ordovician Period began about 500,000,000 years ago and lasted about 70,000,000 years). The Neichia-shan Series overlies the Ichang Series and precedes rocks of the Chientang-kiang Series. The Neichia-shan is divisible into two smaller divisions: the lower stage is the Hulo Stage, which is followed by the Yenwashan Stage.
·Ordovician strata correlations, table 2 **13**:919

Neidhart von Reuenthal (b. *c.* 1180, Bavaria—d. *c.* 1250), late medieval knightly poet who, in the period of the decline of the courtly love lyric, introduced a new genre called *höfische Dorfpoesie* ("courtly village poetry"). It celebrated, in summer and winter dancing songs, the poet's love of village maidens rather than noble ladies. The summer songs open with a description of the season, followed by a dance on the village green and a love episode dealing with a knight's (Neidhart's) conquest of a village belle. The winter songs, usually more satirical, describe a dance in a farmhouse and ridicule the boorish peasant youths who are the knight's rivals for the village beauty. A winter song often ends with a brawl. The novelty of Neidhart's settings and his coarse humour inspired many imitators, and mockery of the peasants became a popular theme. In the 15th century many spurious satires of peasants were attributed to him.

Neididae (insect family): *see* stilt bug.

Neighborhood Playhouse School of the Theatre, in New York City, houses a two-year theatrical school and is one of the leading centres in the United States for training in dramatic art. Since its founding in 1927 it has trained many distinguished performers and teachers of theatre. The School of the Theatre grew out of the Neighborhood Playhouse, which until 1915 was a theatrical project of the Henry Street Settlement House on the Lower East Side.

Neighbors (1952), animated film by Norman McLaren.
·animated film and pixilation **1**:921c

neighbourhood, or NEIGHBORHOOD, in mathematics, term for the concept of proximity or vicinity in topological space. A neighbourhood can be the set of all points within a given distance of an initial point, for example. It also may refer to the segment of a curve or portion of a region within which a particular property holds.
·algebraic geometry fundamentals **7**:1074c
·differential topology principles **18**:503d
·Euclidean geometry principles **7**:1110g
·topological group theory **18**:491b

neighbourhood (NEIGHBORHOOD) **houses:** *see* social settlements.

Neihardt, John G(neisenan) (1881–1973), poet laureate of the state of Nebraska, U.S.
·literary theme and national honour **12**:925b

Nei-jiang (China): *see* Nei-chiang.

ne'ila (Hebrew: "closing"), in Judaism, the last of the five Yom Kippur services, the most sacred of the yearly liturgy, expressed in melodies of great solemnity. When the *shofar* (ritual ram's horn) sounds, the synagogue service ends and the day-long fast is over.

In ancient times, 24 groups of laymen attended the Temple sacrifice (in turns of one week each) as representatives of the common people. Each day, when the Temple gates were being closed, these deputations prayed the *ne'ila;* simultaneously, villagers outside Jerusalem joined their representatives in spirit by reciting the *ne'ila* on their own. The *ne'ila* was also recited on public fast days.

Modern Jews view the *ne'ila* as the symbolic closing of the gates of heaven when God's final judgment is passed on man. Though Reform Judaism has modified the *ne'ila* service, the mood of reverence and solemnity is clearly evidenced.

Neilson, James Beaumont (b. June 22, 1792, Shettleston, Lanark—d. Jan. 18, 1865, Queenshill, Kirkcudbright), inventor who introduced the use of a hot-air blast instead of a cold-air blast for the smelting of iron, thus greatly advancing the technology of iron production. In 1817 he was appointed foreman of the Glasgow Gasworks. Soon afterward he became manager and engineer, and he remained with the firm for 30 years.

During the early 19th century, ironworkers in Great Britain believed that a blast of cold air was the most efficient method for smelting iron. Neilson demonstrated that the opposite was true. His idea, first tested at the Clyde Ironworks, Glasgow, was patented in 1828. Use of the hot blast tripled iron output per ton of coal, doubled its yield per unit amount of blast, and permitted profitable recovery of iron from lower grade ores. It also made possible the efficient use of raw coal and lower grades of coal instead of coke and permitted construction of larger smelting furnaces.

Nei-meng-gu (Asia): *see* Inner Mongolia.

Neira, Alvaro de Mendaña de: *see* Mendaña de Neira, Alvaro de.

Neisseria meningitidis (bacterium): *see* meningococcus.

Neisse River, conventional German name for either of two rivers now in southwestern Poland (until 1945, in Germany). The better known Nysa Łużycka, or Lusatian Neisse, is the longer (157 mi [252 km]) and more westerly; it forms part of the East German–Polish frontier (*see* Oder–Neisse Line). The Nysa Kłodzka (Glatzer Neisse), or Neisse of the city of Kłodzko (Glatz), is the shorter (113 mi) and lies entirely within Poland. Both rise in the Sudeten mountains, flow northward, and empty into the Oder River.
Nysa Kłodzka, 50°49′ N, 17°50′ E
Nysa Łużycka, 52°04′ N, 14°46′ E
·map, German Democratic Republic **8**:9
·Oder River watercourse splitting **13**:507b
·Potsdam agreement frontier **8**:6h

nei tan, Chinese Taoist term for internal alchemy, a means of attaining immortality by means of such practices as thought control, regulated breathing, and diet.
·theory and mystical techniques **17**:1040d

Neithardt, Mathis Gothardt: *see* Grünewald, Matthias.

Neiva, capital of Huila department, south central Colombia, on the upper Río Magdalena. After unsuccessful attempts by Juan de Cabrera in 1539 and by Juan Alonso in 1550 to establish a permanent settlement, the city was officially founded in 1612, when Capt. Diego de Ospina claimed it for the Spanish crown; he named it for the Río Neiva in Haiti. Its citizens were active in the independence struggle (1810–20) as well as in the civil war (1899–1902). Primarily an agricultural centre (for cotton, rice, corn [maize], and sesame), Neiva manufactures cotton goods and cement and processes marble. The marketing of products is sustained by excellent air, land, and water routes. The rural atmosphere of the city inspired the works of José Eustasio Rivera (1889–1928), the Colombian poet and novelist. Pop. (1972) 105,400.
2°56′ N, 75°18′ W
·map, Colombia **4**:867

Nei-wu-fu, Manchu DORGI YAMUN, under the Chinese Ch'ing dynasty, the Office of Household.
·Ch'ing Imperial household reform **10**:379h

Nejapa, small crater lake of Nicaragua.
12°07′ N 86°19′ W
·sulfurous waters' importance **13**:59a

Nejati, İsa: *see* Necati, İsa.

Nejd (Saudi Arabia): *see* Najd.

Nekhbet, also spelled NEKHEBET, in Egyptian religion, vulture or serpent goddess, the pro-

Nekhbet hovering over Menkaure, relief, 5th dynasty; in the Louvre, Paris
Alinari

tectress of Upper Egypt and especially its rulers, often portrayed as spreading her wings over the pharaoh, while grasping in her claw the royal ring or other emblems. Her special colour was white, in contrast to the red regalia of her counterpart, Buto, goddess of Lower Egypt. She also appeared as a woman, sometimes with a vulture's head, wearing a white crown. In another aspect, as a goddess of the Nile and consort of the river god, she was associated with Mut, a sky and Nile River goddess. The centre of Nekhbet's cult was the early capital, Elkab (Greek Eileithyiaspolis).

Nekhen (ancient Egyptian city): *see* Hierakonpolis.

Nekhtharheb: *see* Nectanebo II.

Nekhtnebf: *see* Nectanebo I.

Nekrasov, Nikolay Alekseyevich (b. Dec. 10 [Nov. 28, old style], 1821, Yuzvin, now in Ukrainian S.S.R.—d. Jan. 8 [Dec. 27, 1877, O.S.], 1878, St. Petersburg, now Leningrad), Russian poet and journalist whose main theme was compassion for the sufferings of the peasantry, though he also expressed the racy charm and vitality of peasant life in his adaptations of folk songs and poems for children.

He studied at St. Petersburg university, but his father's refusal to help him forced him into literary and theatrical hackwork at an early age. An able businessman, he published and edited literary miscellanies and in 1846

Nekrasov, lithograph by an unknown artist
Novosti Press Agency

bought from Pyotr Pletnev the magazine *Sovremennik* ("The Contemporary"), which had declined after the death of its founder, Aleksandr Pushkin.

Nekrasov managed to transform it into a major literary journal and a paying concern. Both Turgenev and Tolstoy published their early works in it, but after 1856, influenced by its subeditor, Nikolay Chernyshevsky, it began to develop into an organ of militant radicalism. It was suppressed in 1866, after the first attempt to assassinate Alexander II. In 1868 Nekrasov, with Mikhail Y. Saltykov, took over *Otechestvennye zapiski* ("Fatherland Annals"), remaining its editor and publisher until his death.

Nekrasov's work is uneven through its lack of craftsmanship and polish and a tendency to sentimentalize his subjects, but his major poems have lasting power and originality of expression.

Moroz krasny-nos (1863; "Red-Nosed Frost," in *Poems*, 1929) gives a vivid picture of a brave and sympathetic peasant woman, and his long narrative poem, *Komu na Rusi zhit khorosho?* (1879; *Who Can Be Happy and Free in Russia?*, 1917), shows to the full his gift for vigorous realistic satire.

nekton, all aquatic animals that swim freely, independent of water motion or wind. Only three phyla are represented by adult forms. Chordate nekton include numerous species of bony fishes, the cartilaginous fishes such as the sharks, several species of reptiles (turtles, snakes, and saltwater crocodiles), and mammals such as the whales, porpoises, and seals.

Molluscan nekton include the squids and octopods. The only arthropod nekton are decapods, including shrimps, crabs, and lobsters.

Herbivores are uncommon, although a few near-shore and shallow-water species subsist by grazing on plants. Of the nektonic feeding types, zooplankton feeders are the most abundant and include, in addition to many bony fishes, such as the sardines and mackerel, some of the largest nekton, the baleen whales. The molluscans, sharks, and many of the larger bony fishes consume animals bigger than zooplankton. Other fishes and most of the crustaceans are scavengers.

Nektonic species are limited in their areal and vertical distributions by the barriers of temperature, salinity, nutrient supply, and type of bottom. The number of nektonic species and individuals decreases with increasing depth in the ocean.

·lacustrine community characteristics **10**:614c
·ocean biological community organization **1**:1032a

Nelligan, Émile (1879–1941), French-Canadian poet who was a major figure in the Montreal literary school despite the termination of his writing by insanity in 1899. His collected poems were published in 1903; a selection, translated into English, appeared in 1966.

Nellore, Indian breed of large, steel-gray to almost white cattle used chiefly for heavy draft. Nellore cattle have been introduced in many warm regions for crossbreeding with European cattle.

·general features and popularity **10**:1280e

Nelseco engine, diesel engine built by the New London Ship and Engine Company in Groton, Conn.

·diesel engine use in submarines **5**:727a

Nelson, city, southeastern British Columbia, Canada, on the west arm of Kootenay Lake, a few miles south of Kokanee Glacier Provincial Park. The discovery of gold at nearby Fortynine Creek in 1867 led to the development of several mines near Cottonwood Creek Delta, the original townsite. Founded in 1887, the community was first known as Stanley or Salisbury. In 1888 it was renamed in honour of Hugh Nelson, lieutenant governor of British Columbia. The city was the first in the province to undertake municipal hydroelectric development on the Kootenay River in 1907. It is now a service point for an

A sawmill in Nelson, B.C.
John de Visser

extensive farming, lumbering, and mining area and also the chief administrative centre for the West Kootenay District. Industries include railroad repair shops, sawmills, and transportation and communication utilities. The city is the site of Notre Dame University of Nelson (1950) and of the Provincial Vocational School. It has been the scene of the World's Midsummer Curling Bonspiel Championships since 1945, and is a base for fishing, hunting, skiing, and water sports. Inc. city, 1897. Pop. (1976) 9,235.
49°29′ N, 117°17′ W

·map, Canada **3**:716

Nelson, borough and textile manufacturing town, Lancashire, England. Industrial development began in the 18th century with the establishment of a small wool factory. The town now specializes in silk and cotton weaving. Nelson was incorporated in 1890. Pop. (1973 est.) 31,220.
53°51′ N, 2°13′ W

Nelson, port, northern South Island, New Zealand, on an inlet at the head of Tasman Bay, at the mouth of the Matai River. Settled by the New Zealand Company in 1842 and named after Admiral Lord Nelson, it was retarded in its development by a Maori attack two years later. Declared a city in 1858, it prospered during the gold rush of the 1860s. It was made a borough in 1874 and was the capital of Nelson province (abolished in 1876).

Nelson is a resort and retirement centre strongly oriented toward Wellington (121 mi [195 km] east). It serves a productive agricultural and livestock region; industries include food-processing plants, sawmills, and engineering works. The port exports tobacco, fruit, timber, and meat and imports petroleum products.

The city contains an Anglican cathedral and the Cawthorn Institute of Scientific Research. Pop. (1977 est.) 33,100.
41°17′ S, 173°17′ E

·map, New Zealand **13**:45
·regional area and population table **13**:47
·rugby football in New Zealand **16**:5c
·19th-century education system **6**:368e

Nelson, Lord 12:947, in full HORATIO NELSON, VISCOUNT NELSON (b. Sept. 29, 1758, Burnham Thorpe, Norfolk—d. Oct. 21, 1805, off Cape Trafalgar, Spain), British naval commander in the wars with Revolutionary and Napoleonic France, who won crucial victories in the battles of the Nile and Trafalgar, and is still regarded as Britain's most appealing national hero.

Abstract of text biography. Nelson first went to sea in 1771 with his uncle, a navy captain. He became a Royal Navy officer in 1777 and fought during the American Revolutionary War. From 1784 to 1787 he commanded a frigate in the West Indies, but he did not receive another command until 1793, in the Mediterranean. He distinguished himself in 1797 at Cape St. Vincent, then in 1798 in the decisive Battle of the Nile. His scandalous private life with Lady Hamilton was causing controversy by the time he returned to England in 1800. He successfully attacked Copenhagen the following year, and in 1803 he returned to war against Napoleon. He was killed by enemy fire during the Battle of Trafalgar, which established British naval supremacy for more than a century.

REFERENCES in other text articles:
·Battle of the Nile **12**:833d
·naval victories over France **7**:723c

Nelson, Byron (b. Feb. 4, 1912, Fort Worth, Texas), one of a long line of outstanding Texan professional golfers who set several records in a career that he was obliged to shorten for reasons of health.

He won the U.S. Open (1939), the Masters' (1937 and 1942), and the Professional Golfers' Association of America (PGA) championship (1940 and 1945). He finished in the money 113 consecutive times and in 1945 won 11 tournaments. Almost mechanically accurate with his iron shots, he won the 1939 Western Open over the difficult Medinah No. 3 course near Chicago without leaving the fairway once in 72 holes. He kept in close touch with the game after his postwar retirement and was nonplaying captain of the Ryder Cup team in 1965.

Nelson, David (1918–), U.S. mathematician.

·Intuitionistic formal arithmetic **11**:638d

Nelson, Leonard (1882–1927), German philosopher.

·psychological Neo-Kantianism **10**:397b

Nelson, Thomas, the Younger (1822–92), son of the Scottish founder of the publishing firm of Nelson and Sons; he established a branch of the business in London (1844) and invented a rotary press (1850).

Nelson Island, in the Bering Sea, separated by a narrow channel from the southwestern coast of Alaska.
60°35′ N 164°45′ W

·Bering Sea map **2**:845

Nelson River, in northern Manitoba, Canada, drains Lake Winnipeg and discharges into Hudson Bay near Port Nelson. Navigable for the lower 56 mi of its 400-mi (644-km) course, it drains a basin of 444,000 sq mi. Together

with the Bow and Saskatchewan rivers, it forms a 1,600-mi waterway extending as far west as the Canadian Rockies. It was discovered in 1612 by the English explorer Sir Thomas Button, who named it after his sailing master. A Canadian National Railway branch line to Churchill, Man., now follows most of the river's course. Power for the nickel-mining operations at Thompson on the Burntwood River, a major tributary, is generated from Kelsey Dam on the Grand Rapids.
57°04′ N, 92°30′ W
·continental water supply and drainage **13**:188b
·delta, tides, and discharge table **15**:868
·drainage area and discharge table **15**:877
·early exploration of Manitoba **11**:452g
·fluvial processes in icy rivers **7**:446b
·map, Canada **3**:722

Nelson's Column, Trafalgar Square, London, monument to Admiral Lord Nelson, facing Whitehall. Built 1840–43, it is 185 ft (56.4 m) high overall including the 17-ft statue of Nelson by E.H. Baily; at the corners of the plinth are four sculptured lions by Sir Edwin Landseer.
·location and size **11**:102f; illus.

Nelumbonales, order of flowering plants composed of one family (Nelumbonaceae)

Lotus (*Nelumbo nucifera*)
Derek Fell

with two species of attractive aquatic plants resembling water lilies. One of these is the sacred lotus of the Orient (*Nelumbo nucifera*) of tropical and subtropical Asia; the other is the American lotus, or water chinquapin (*N. pentapetala*), found in the eastern United States and south to Colombia. The plants are no longer included in the water-lily order because of important botanical characteristics that suggest a different evolutionary origin from the other water lilies. Differences are found in the structure of pollen grains and embryos, the presence of pores in the seed coat, and lack of latex-bearing tubes, and there are also chromosomal differences. The order is further characterized by circular, centrally stalked, slightly hairy leaves up to about 60 centimetres (2 feet) across, with the margins turned up, forming a funnel- or saucer-shaped depression. The leaves extend, in the Asian species, as much as 2 metres (6½ feet) above the water instead of floating on it. The large, attractive flowers also stand high above the water on strong, leafless stalks. They may be up to 25 centimetres across and have many petals, which close at night. The flowers of the sacred lotus, which stand as much as 1.8 metres above the water, are pink or rose coloured and fragrant. The American lotus has pale yellow flowers that rise about 60 centimetres above the water.

Many varieties of the sacred lotus exist in cultivation, including dwarf forms and colour varieties ranging from white to red. The numerous nutlike fruits are produced in the flat upper surface of a spongy receptacle or expanded, fleshy, capsule-like structure, which is wider at the upper end than at the base. The whole structure dries out at maturity, breaks off, and floats about, releasing the seeds, actually the true fruits, through numerous holes in the flat surface. The seeds sink to the bottom, where they establish new plants.

The whole plant of both species is edible. The seeds of *N. nucifera* are used as food in Kashmir. Its rootstocks (rhizomes), eaten in Asia either boiled or preserved in sugar, are the source of the starch known as lotus meal. Boiled young leaves are eaten as vegetables. Even the stamens (male pollen-producing flower structures) are used in Indochina for flavouring tea. The American lotus is similarly edible, especially the large rhizomes, which were once a major source of starchy food for the American Indians.

The plants are particularly beneficial to wildlife. Beaver, for instance, eat the rootstocks, and fish obtain shade and shelter among the underwater portions of the plants.

The seeds of the Oriental lotus have been ascribed remarkable powers of longevity and, under ideal conditions, may survive many years. Seeds of this species recovered from an ancient peat bog in Manchuria and shown by radioactive carbon dating to be approximately 1,000 years old are capable of producing flowering plants.
·angiosperm features and classification **1**:882f

Nemachilus barbatula (fish): *see* loach.

Nemain (Celtic goddess): *see* Morrígan.

Nemanja dynasty, ruling family descended from Stephen Nemanja (*q.v.*; chieftain of the Serbian region of Raška, *c.* 1167–96) that governed Serbia (late 12th to late 14th century) and developed it into a vast empire; it reached its peak during the reign of Stefan Dušan (1331–55).
·Serbian imperial growth **2**:619e
·Stefan Dušan's reign **17**:664a

Neman River, Lithuanian NEMUNAS, German MEMEL, OR NJEMEN, Polish NIEMEN, in the Belorussian and Lithuanian Soviet Socialist republics, 582 mi (937 km) long and draining about 38,000 sq mi (98,000 sq km). It rises near Minsk in the Minsk Upland and flows west through a broad, swampy basin; it then turns north into Lithuania, cutting through terminal moraines in a narrow, sinuous valley. Near Kaunas, where there is a hydroelectric plant, it turns west and crosses another marshy basin to enter the Kurisches Haff of the Baltic Sea south of Klaipėda (Memel; hence the German name). Navigation is possible for 416 mi to Belitsa; much timber is rafted. Freeze-up lasts from late November to mid-March.
55°18′ N, 21°23′ E
·Lithuanian physical geography **10**:1265b
·map, Soviet Union **17**:322

Nemathelminthes (worms): *see* Aschelminthes.

Nematistiidae, family of roosterfishes of the order Perciformes.
·classification and general features **14**:54f

Neʿmat-nāmeh, 16th-century Persian illuminated manuscript.
·illustration style for Mālwa sultan **17**:198e

nematocide: *see* fumigant.

nematocyst, also called STINGING CELL, in zoology, minute, elongated or spherical capsule found chiefly in members of the phylum Cnidaria (*e.g.*, jellyfish, corals, sea anemones). The capsule, which occurs on the body surface and is produced by a special cell called a cnidoblast, contains a coiled, hollow, usually barbed thread, which quickly turns outward from the capsule upon stimulation. The purpose of the thread, which often contains poison, is to ward off enemies or to capture prey.

When stimulated, a lidlike structure on the top of the capsule pops aside, and the thread is everted with a twisting motion. As eversion and twisting proceed, the barbs act like drills, penetrating into (and pulling the thread into) the foreign object. If a toxin is present, it passes through the hollow thread, penetrating and paralyzing the victim's tissues. After eversion, the thread separates from the nematocyst. The threads of some nematocysts ensnare small prey by wrapping about them. The stinging effect of nematocysts in the Portuguese man-of-war and other jellyfish (*qq.v.*) can be extremely painful to human beings and may cause paralysis, shock, and even death.
·chemoreception and coelenterate feeding **4**:177f
·cnidarian structure and production **4**:770e; illus. 768
·poisonous animal, table 7 **14**:614d

Nematoda: *see* roundworm.

Nematomorpha: *see* gordian worm.

Nembire (African king): *see* Mbire.

nembutsu: *see* Pure Land Buddhism.

Nemea, Battle of (394 BC), one of the series of conflicts (Corinthian War, 395–387 BC) in which a coalition of Greek city-states sought to destroy the ascendency of Sparta after its victory in the Peloponnesian War. The Spartans' defeat of the troops from Thebes, Corinth, Athens, and Argos temporarily broke the force of the coalition.

Nemean Games, in ancient Greece, athletic and musical competitions held in honour of Zeus, in July, at the great Temple of Zeus at Nemea, in Argolis. They occurred biennially, in the same years as the Isthmian Games. Their origin was attributed to such legendary figures as Heracles and Adrastus of Argos. The presidency of the games was held by the city of Cleonae till about 460 BC, thereafter by Argos. Winners in the competitions were awarded a wreath of fresh wild celery. After 573 BC they were open to all Greeks, and the Nemea became one of the great panhellenic festivals. A group of archaeologists from the University of California, Berkeley, which began work at the site in 1973, discovered the remains of a stadium on a hillside near the temple.
·origin legends and Olympic similarity **2**:275a

Nemerov, Howard (b. March 1, 1920, New York City), poet whose verse is often praised for its elegance, satiric power, and, often, elegiac beauty. He is also a novelist and critic.

After receiving his degree from Harvard University in 1941, Nemerov served as a pilot (1941–45) in World War II in a unit of the Royal Canadian Air Force attached to the U.S. Army Air Force. After leaving the service, he held posts at Hamilton College, Clinton, N.Y. (1946–48); Bennington College, Bennington, Vt. (1948–66); and Brandeis University, Waltham, Mass. (1966–69); in 1969 he became professor of English at Washington University, St. Louis, Mo. From 1963 to 1964 he was consultant in poetry to the Library of Congress.

Nemerov's first book of verse, *The Image and the Law*, appeared in 1947, followed by *The Salt Garden* (1955), *Mirrors and Windows* (1958), *New and Selected Poems* (1960), *The Next Room of the Dream: Poems and Two Plays* (1963), *Blue Swallows* (1967), *Gnomes and Occasions* (1973), *The Western Approaches* (1975), and *Collected Poems* (1977). His poetry often involves use of the traditional iambic line and fixed or fairly regular forms. The natural world often appears in his poems, which are written without flourish and are frequently marked by irony and a self-deprecatory wit. He seems obsessed by time, at heart perhaps his chief theme, hence the strong melancholy strain in his work. Frequently a social critic, he has produced poems of strong satiric power. Among his considerable body of critical writing is *Figures of Thought: Speculations on the Meaning of Poetry and Other Essays* (1978).

Nemerov's fiction includes The *Melodramatists* (1949), a novel of the dissolution of a Boston family; *The Homecoming Game* (1957), a witty tale of a college professor who flunks a small college's football hero; and *A Commodity of Dreams and Other Stories* (1960).

Nemertea 12:950, also known as NEMERTINEA and RHYNCHOCOELA, a phylum of about 600 species of invertebrate animals commonly called ribbonworms or proboscis worms. They are the simplest animals to have a digestive system that begins with a mouth and ends with an anus and to have a true vascular system for blood circulation.

The text article covers natural history, form and function, and evolution and contains an annotated classification of the phylum.

REFERENCE in other text article:
·circulatory system anatomy **4**:621a; illus.
·excretory methods and anal development **6**:721a
·optical mechanism properties **14**:360b

Nemesianus, Marcus Aurelius Olympius (fl. *c.* AD 280), Roman poet born in Carthage who wrote pastoral and didactic poetry. There survive four eclogues and an incomplete poem on hunting (*Cynegetica*). Two small fragments on bird catching (*De aucupio*) are generally attributed to him. The four eclogues are in the Virgilian tradition, influenced also by Calpurnius, purely imitative and of conventional form and imagery, and yet attractive because of their smooth diction and melodious movement. The *Cynegetica* gives instruction about dogs, horses, and hunting equipment; it is a gracefully written piece in the literary genre of the *Georgics* and of the *Cynegetica* of Grattius.

Nemesis, in Greek religion, the name of two divine conceptions. The first was a goddess (perhaps of fertility), worshipped at Rhamnus in Attica, who was very similar to Artemis (a goddess of wild animals, vegetation, childbirth, and the hunt). In post-Homeric mythology, she was pursued by Zeus, the chief god, who eventually turned himself into a swan and caught her in the form of a goose. Nemesis then laid an egg from which Helen was hatched. *See also* Leda.

Nemesis, classical sculpture; in the Vatican Museum
H. Roger-Viollet

The second divine entity of this name was an abstraction—*i.e.,* indignant disapproval of wrongdoing, particularly the disapproval of the gods at human presumptions, and, also, the eventual personification of that disapproval. That the abstraction was worshipped, at least in later times, is beyond doubt; her first altar was said to have been erected in Boeotia by Adrastus, leader of the Seven Against Thebes (*q.v.*). In Rome, especially, her cult was very popular, particularly among soldiers, by whom she was worshipped as patroness of the drill ground (Nemesis *campestris*).

Nemesius of Emesa (fl. late 4th century), Christian philosopher, apologist, and bishop of Emesa, now Homs, Syria, author of *Peri physeōs anthrōpou* (Greek: "On the Nature of Man"), the first-known compendium of inductive psychology and theological anthropology with a Christian orientation. The treatise considerably influenced later Byzantine and medieval Latin philosophical theology.

A man of extensive culture, Nemesius integrated elements from various sources of Hellenistic philosophical and medical literature. He used the experimental physiology of the 2nd-century Greek physician Galen and the observations of other men of science, the philosophy of Neoplatonic Idealism (Alexandrian influence), and Aristotelian Realism (Antiochene influence). The result is a Christian synthesis that cannot be characterized as representing any specific philosophical school because of Nemesius' critical correctives and discriminating use of texts. "On the Nature of Man" lacks logical unity in its arrangement of material, and its abrupt ending indicates that the work was unfinished or was intended for revision. The opening chapter criticizes the concepts of man advanced by the Greeks from pre-Christian Plato to 3rd-century Christian sectarians; it then emphasizes the place of man in the plan of creation as delineated in the Mosaic literature of the Old Testament and in the Christian letters of St. Paul. Because man bridges the spiritual and material worlds, Nemesius maintains, he requires a unique intelligent principle of life, or soul, proportionate to his dignity and responsibility. Neither Plato nor Aristotle, he continues, provides an adequate teaching on the soul, one making the soul too independent of the body, the other reducing the soul to little more than a quality of the body. Consequently, Nemesius submits that the soul must be an incorporeal, intellectual entity, subsistent in itself, immortal, and yet designed to be one with the body. He implies that it pre-exists the body but not in the manner of the Platonic myth. Alluding to Antiochene doctrine on Christology, he suggests, in an original manner, that the body–soul relationship parallels Christ's union of the divine Word with his human nature in the incarnation. In subsequent chapters Nemesius examines the function of the brain, the operation of the senses, imagination, memory, reasoning, and speech; this treatment provided medieval philosophers with a wealth of data from Greek Stoic and other classical empirical philosophers. After considering the emotional and irrational (instinctive) functions of the soul, termed involuntary passions, Nemesius concludes with a study of human will. Repudiating Stoic fatalism and astrology and advocating the Christian belief in divine providence, he explains free will as a concomitant of reason: if man is rational, he must operate with a freedom of choice; otherwise his intelligent, deliberative powers are meaningless. Either as a cause or an effect of immortality, volitional powers are given to mutable man so that he might become immutable.

Such teaching became the keystone of medieval and renaissance Christian psychology, mediated by other Greek authors from the 5th to the 8th centuries. Nemesius' work was sometimes attributed to the eminent 4th-century Greek theologian Gregory of Nyssa because of faulty Latin translations. Already contained in the series *Patrologiae Graeca* (vol. 40, 1860; "Greek Patrology") of J.P. Migne, a definitive edition of "On the Nature of Man" was in preparation in the 1970s by F. Lammert, using a 10th-century Greek codex, the oldest manuscript available. An English version was done by William Telfer, *Cyril of Jerusalem and Nemesius of Emesa*, in *The Library of Christian Classics* (1955).

Nemestrinidae, a family of tangle-veined flies of the order Diptera.
·classification and features **5**:824a

Nemi, Lake, Italian LAGO DI NEMI, crater lake in Lazio (Latium) region, central Italy, in the outer ring of the ancient Alban crater, in the Colli Albani (Alban Hills), east of the Lago (lake) di Albano and 15 mi (24 km) southeast of Rome. About 3½ mi in circumference and 110 ft (34 m) deep, it is drained via a tunnel about 2 mi long. In ancient times it was included in the territory of Aricia (modern Ariccia) and was called Lacus Nemorensis and sometimes the Speculum Dianae ("Mirror of Diana") from a temple and grove (*nemus*) sacred to that goddess. Excavations (now filled in) led to the discovery of the temple, a comparatively small building (98 by 52 ft), although it had been one of the richest in Latium. The remains of the temple precinct—a large platform, the back of which is formed by a wall of concrete, with niches, resting against the cliffs—are situated a little above the level of the lake, on the northeast.

It had long been known that two Roman galleys rested on the lake bottom on the west side, but attempts to raise them were unsuccessful; they were raided by divers in 1895 and some of the most valuable objects were removed. Finally, in the 1920s, the water level was lowered and the ships were raised. They were pleasure ships of the period of the emperor Caligula, one measuring 210 by 66 ft, the other 233 by 80 ft. Many of the objects found on the ships are in the museums in Rome, but the ships unfortunately were burned by the retreating German army on May 31, 1944.
41°43′ N, 12°42′ E

Nemichthyidae, a family of snipe eels of the order Anguilliformes.
·characteristics and classification **1**:900c

Nemināthа (Jaina saint): *see* Ariṣṭaneminātha.

Nemipteridae, a family of fish of the order Perciformes.
·classification and general features **14**:53c

Nemirovich-Danchenko, Vladimir Ivanovich (b. Dec. 23, 1858, Makharadze, U.S.S.R. —d. April 25, 1943, Moscow), playwright, novelist, producer, and co-founder of the famous Moscow Art Theatre.

At the age of 13, Nemirovich-Danchenko was directing plays and experimenting with different stage effects. He received his formal education at Moscow State University, where his talents as a writer and critic began to appear. As a young dramatist, his plays, which were presented at the Maly Theatre (Moscow), were highly praised and respected, and he received at least two awards for playwriting, including the distinguished Griboyedov prize. In 1891 he became an instructor of dramatic art at the Moscow Philharmonic Society. Olga Knipper, Vsevolod Meyerhold, and Yevgeny Vakhatangov were only a few of the actors and directors who came under his influ-

Nemirovich-Danchenko
H. Roger-Viollet

ence and who eventually went on to win recognition on the Russian stage. In 1897, discontented with the existing condition of the Russian stage, Nemirovich-Danchenko and his friend Konstantin Stanislavsky (*q.v.*) formulated the aims and policies of a new theatre, an actor's theatre called the Moscow Art Theatre (1898). Although Stanislavsky was given absolute authority over staging the productions, the contributions of Nemirovich-Danchenko were considerable. Both as producer and as literary adviser, he was chiefly responsible for the reading and selection of new plays, and he instructed Stanislavsky on matters of interpretation and staging as well. Nemirovich-Danchenko encouraged both Anton Chekhov and Maksim Gorky to write for the theatre, and he is credited with the successful revival of Chekhov's *Seagull* after it had failed at the Aleksandrinsky Theatre. Nemirovich-Danchenko applied the dramatic reforms of the Moscow Art Theatre to light opera when he founded the Moscow Art Musical Studio in the early 1920s. He achieved outstanding success with his staging of *La Périchole* and *Lysistrata* in New York City (1925). His autobiography was translated as *My Life in the Russian Theater* (1936).
·association with Stanislavsky **17**:581b
·direction of Chekhov plays **5**:827b
·Moscow Art Theatre formation **18**:228f
·naturalistic staging of realistic drama **17**:548b

Nemobius vittatus (insect): *see* cricket.

Nemophila, genus of annual herbs of the family Hydrophyllaceae; the 13 species, most of which bear blue or white, bell-like blooms,

Baby blue-eyes (*Nemophila menziesii*)
G.E. Nicholson

are North American, mostly Pacific Coast in origin. Baby blue-eyes (*N. menziesii*) often blooms along the borders of moist woodlands in California. Its bright five-lobed flowers range in colour from blue to white and may have blue veins; the wheel-shaped flowers measure up to 4 centimetres (1½ inches) across. The leaves are divided into five to nine lobes. The plants, sometimes creeping, can grow to 50 centimetres (20 inches) tall.

Nemopteridae, family of thread-winged lacewings of the insect order Neuroptera.
·classification and features **12**:1070b

Nemours, town, Seine-et-Marne *département*, north central France, south of Fontainebleau and southeast of Paris. In Roman times the locality, pleasantly situated on the Loing River, was called Nemoracum, derived from *nemora* (Latin: "woods"). It was fortified in the Middle Ages by the dukes of Nemours and was in English hands from 1420 to 1437. In 1528 King Francis I of France gave the duchy to the House of Savoy. Philip of Orléans, younger brother of Louis XIV, received it as an appanage (grant) in 1672. The town is the ancestral home of the du Pont de Nemours family, members of which are now chemical manufacturers in Delaware, U.S. Nemours has a medieval castle, rebuilt in the 15th and 17th centuries, which houses a museum. Gothic and Renaissance styles are blended in the 16th-century church of Saint-Jean-Baptiste. Pop. (1975) 11,159.
48°16′ N, 2°42′ E
·map, France **7**:584

Nemours, Louis-Charles-Philippe-Raphaël d'Orléans, duc de (b. Oct. 25, 1814, Paris—d. June 26, 1896, Versailles), second son of King Louis-Philippe (reigned 1830–48); after the abdication of his father in 1848, Nemours tried until 1871 to unite exiled Royalists and restore the Bourbon monarchy.

Louis d'Orléans, duc de Nemours, lithograph by Antoine Maurin
By courtesy of the Bibliotheque Nationale, Paris

Nemours was made a colonel of cavalry in 1826. He was elected king of the Belgians in 1831, but Louis-Philippe refused that crown in his son's name. Nemours was present at the French siege of Antwerp in 1832, and he later accompanied three expeditions to Algeria (1836, 1837, and 1841). His conservatism antagonized the liberal opposition in France, and in 1840 the Chamber of Deputies refused to grant the dowry proposed for his politically valuable marriage to the Princess Victoria of Saxe-Coburg-Gotha. In 1842 the death of his elder brother, Ferdinand, duc d'Orléans, made Nemours the prospective regent of France in the event that their father died before Ferdinand's son, Louis-Philippe-Albert, comte de Paris, came of age. But again Nemours's conservatism and unpopularity worked against him and certain factions desired that, instead of Nemours, Ferdinand's wife, the Duchesse d'Orléans, become regent for her son. On the outbreak of revolution in 1848, Nemours organized the defense of the Tuileries palace to cover the King's escape and then tried to accompany the Duchesse d'Orléans (Helena of Mecklenburg-Schwerin) to the Chamber of Deputies to press her son's claims. He was unsuccessful, and the deputies proclaimed the Second Republic. Nemours, the Duchesse, and her children fled, and Louis-Philippe abdicated.

In exile in England, Nemours sought to effect a reconciliation between the House of Orléans and the Comte de Chambord, the exiled grandson of Charles X and a pretender to the French throne, as the indispensable preliminary to a restoration of the Bourbon monarchy in France. After the Franco-Prussian War and the removal of the legal disabilities of the French princes (1871), Nemours returned to France and was restored to his army rank of divisional general. An attempt by the Comte de Chambord to reunite France under a Bourbon monarchy failed, and Nemours's hopes of a restoration were dashed.

Nemrut Daği, extinct volcano west of Lake Van, Turkey.
38°40′ N 42°12′ E
·Lake Van formation and topography **19**:21b

Nemunas River (Soviet Union): *see* Neman River.

Nemur (Egyptian religion): *see* Mnevis.

Nenagh, Irish AONACH URMHUMHAN, chief town of northern County Tipperary, Ireland, near the River Nenagh. Ancient ruins include a circular keep of Nenagh Round castle, dating from about 1217, and parts of a Franciscan friary. Nenagh is now an agricultural centre, with some industry. Pop. (1979) 5,687.
52°52′ N, 8°12′ W
·map, Ireland **9**:882

Nen Chiang (China): *see* Nen River.

néné, also called HAWAIIAN GOOSE (*Branta sandvicensis*), rare relative of the Canada goose that evolved in the Hawaiian Islands into a nonmigratory, nonaquatic species with shortened wings and half-webbed feet. It belongs to the family Anatidae (order Anseriformes). It measures about 65 centimetres (25 inches) long and has a gray-brown barred body, dark-streaked buffy neck, and black face. It feeds on berries and grasses on high lava slopes. By 1911 its numbers had been reduced by hunters and animal predators to a few small flocks. From that year shooting of the néné was forbidden, but the species declined further. The breeding of captive nénés and restocking of the islands promises continuance of the species. The néné is now rigidly protected as Hawaii's state bird.
·breeding in captivity and extinction prevention **19**:1161g
·conservation efforts **1**:940a
·vulnerability to extinction **1**:939e

Nenets: *see* Samoyedic languages; Samoyeds.

Nenets autonomous okrug, autonomous area and part of Arkhangelsk *oblast* (administrative region), northwestern Russian Soviet Federated Socialist Republic, with an area of 68,200 sq mi (176,700 sq km) extending along the northern coast of European Russia, from Mezen Bay to Baydarata Bay. The surface is a level plain, broken by the northern ends of the Timan Hills and the Urals.

The Nenets people, whose Samoyedic language, also called Nenets, belongs to the Uralic group, live chiefly by reindeer herding. The formerly nomadic tribes now are settled in permanent villages. The area's inhabitants of Russian nationality live mainly in the administrative centre, Naryan-Mar (*q.v.*), and in the urban district of Amderma. Pop. (1980) 48,000.
67°30′ N, 54°00′ E
·Soviet Union nationalities distribution **17**:329f; table 338

nengō (Japanese: "reign-year title"), designation in Japan of a particular year of a particular imperial reign.
·chronology of Japanese history **4**:573h

Nengone Island (New Caledonia): *see* Maré, Île.

Neni-nesu (ancient Egyptian city): *see* Heracleopolis.

Nenna, Pomponio, 16th-century Italian composer known particularly for his madrigals.
·artist's experimental madrigal style **4**:448g

Nenni, Pietro (b. Feb. 9, 1891, Faenza, Italy—d. Jan. 1, 1980, Rome), journalist and Italian Socialist leader who led his party to participation in a coalition government following a 16-year period of exclusion.

Nenni, who was always a passionate Socialist, was incarcerated for protesting the Italo-Turkish War (1911–12). During 1911–14 he edited several journals and urged revolution in the Romagna (now Emilia-Romagna) region to protest the Italian invasion of Libya.

He served in the Italian Army (1915–18) during World War I, after which he carried on his journalistic career, editing several publications, including *Avanti!*, the official organ of the Italian Socialists. When *Avanti!* was suppressed (1926), he fled to Paris. He fought in the International Brigade against Mussolini's troops in Spain (1936–38). During World War II, in 1943, he was imprisoned by the Germans, who sent him to Italy. Nenni was released after the fall of the Fascists and became vice premier in the government of Ferruccio Parri (June 1945). Elected to the

Constitutional Assembly (1946), he was minister of foreign affairs in the government of Alcide de Gasperi.

At the Socialist Party Congress in 1947, Nenni led the group favouring unity with the Communists. The other group, favouring autonomy, split off to form its own party. Because of this split, Nenni stepped down as foreign minister, thus beginning his party's policy of noncooperation with the government.

In 1952 he received the Stalin Peace Prize. Later, however, he changed his mind about the Communists and broke with the Communist leader Palmiro Togliatti when Soviet forces invaded Hungary (1956). Finally winning autonomy from the Communists in 1959, Nenni began working to get his Socialists included in a coalition government.

In 1963 Nenni became vice premier in the Aldo Moro government, a decision that cost him about 40 percent of his parliamentary followers, who broke off and formed the Party of Proletarian Unity. In 1969, while minister of foreign affairs and party president, Nenni was unable to prevent another party split and resigned his cabinet position.

·socialist role and contribution **16**:972c

Nennius (fl. *c.* 800), Welsh antiquary who between 796 and *c.* 830 compiled or revised the *Historia Britonum*, a miscellaneous collection of historical and topographical information including a description of the inhabitants and invaders of Britain and providing the earliest known reference to the British leader Arthur.

Nen River, Wade-Giles romanization NEN CHIANG, Pin-yin romanization NEN JIANG, also known as NONNI RIVER, river in Heilungkiang Province (*sheng*), China. The Nen River is the principal tributary of the Sungari River, itself a tributary of the Amur River. The Nen River proper rises in the area where the Greater and Lesser Khingan ranges come together in northern Heilungkiang. It then flows southward to the northern section of the Manchurian Plain, joining the Sungari near Ta-an. It receives the waters of a great many tributaries that run off the eastern slopes of the Greater Khingan and the western slopes of the Lesser Khingan ranges. Although annually frozen for some four months in winter and subject to serious flooding during the summer months, especially around its confluence with the Sungari, the Nen River is an important water route, navigable by small steamers as far as Ch'i-ch'i-ha-erh (Tsitsihar) and by small craft much farther to the north. The river was even more important in the early period of Chinese settlement in Heilungkiang in the 19th century, when rivers were virtually the only means of communication.

In the plain, which is wide and flat, the gradient of the Nen River is very low, and the river's course meanders. The plain is subject to flooding during the spring thaw, and again during the summer months. The plain itself is wet, and in places waterlogged, having many salt bogs, swamps, and brackish lakes. The total length of the Nen River is 725 mi (1,170 km).

45°26′ N, 124°39′ E

·China's transport system map **4**:284
·Heilungkiang physical geography **8**:741g
·map, China **4**:262

Nen (NENE) **River,** rising in the east Midlands, England, flowing 90 mi (145 km) from limestone uplands in a generally northeastward course to the Wash, a shallow North Sea inlet. It flows past Northampton and Oundle to Peterborough in a broad valley. Thence its course for 30 mi across the Fens (a drained area) past Wisbech into the Wash is an artificially embanked channel with a gradient hardly more than 8 in. per mile. This cut off is 17 mi shorter than the old natural course through March. The river has locks as far as Northampton. Several of its upper tributaries have been dammed to form small reservoirs for urban water supply.

52°48′ N, 0°13′ E

Nentsy (peoples): *see* Samoyeds.

neoblast, undifferentiated cell from which cells of new tissue can develop, especially in regeneration.

·annelid worm regeneration **1**:930g
·biological development types and phases **5**:646a
·planaria regeneration role **14**:547f

Neocathartes, genus of fossil birds of the family Neocathartidae, order Falconiformes.

·bird fossils and stork relationship **2**:1060f

Neoceratodus forsteri: *see* lungfish.

neocerebellum, in anatomy, the phylogenetically youngest part of the cerebellum, associated with the cerebral cortex in the integration of voluntary limb movements and comprising most of the cerebellar hemispheres and the superior vermis.

·brain structure and development **12**:984c

Neochen jubatus: *see* sheldgoose.

Neoclassicism, in music, stylistic approach employed in certain musical compositions by composers writing in every major country in at least western Europe and the Western Hemisphere from *c.* 1920 to the present. These Neoclassical compositions most often have their aesthetic or technical roots in music of the 18th century. The term Neobaroque, however, might be an equally valid designation for Neoclassical music, for the style owes allegiance to both the last half of the 18th century, which falls within the so-called Classical period, and the first half, which falls within the so-called Baroque period. Regardless of terms, it is often difficult to point to specific compositions from the 18th century that are the prototypes of modern Neoclassical works.

Neoclassicism arose partly as a reaction to what many composers considered the distasteful excesses of Romanticism and Postromanticism (*see* Postromantic music). In comparison with Romantic music, Neoclassical music often seems objective and intellectual, more subtle in its emotional appeal, and more aloof from sentiment in its inherently more abstract formal logic. It is perhaps this desired emphasis on order and design, on clarity, and on lack of frills and of useless ornaments that led Neoclassical composers to hold up the 18th century, rightly or wrongly, as a more favourable era for musical models than the 19th century.

Occasionally Neoclassical composers have transformed specific music from several earlier eras: Igor Stravinsky wrote a ballet, *Pulcinella* (first performed 1920), based on themes from the 18th-century Italian composer Giovanni Pergolesi; Paul Hindemith wrote an orchestral work, *Symphonic Metamorphoses* (1943), on themes of the early 19th-century German Carl Maria von Weber. Parody and satire are also involved in some Neoclassicism, as can be seen from the very titles of some of the works of the French composer Erik Satie; *e.g.*, *Embryons desséchés* (*Desiccated Embryos*, 1913) and *Trois Morceaux en forme de poire* (*Three Pieces in the Shape of a Pear*, 1903). Hindemith's opera *Neues vom Tage* (*News of the Day*, 1929) parodies many conventions of 18th-century opera, and the French composer Darius Milhaud has written three full operas, each of which lasts about eight minutes.

Milhaud's "minute operas," as they are called, are but one example of another common characteristic of Neoclassicism: brevity, which for many composers has implied not only short compositions but also vastly reduced numbers of players, more restricted range of surface emotional expression, and more intense and tightly woven musical development. Good examples of all these features are found in the *Symphony No. 1* (1916–17; appropriately subtitled *Classical*) of Sergey Prokofiev and Stravinsky's *Symphonies of Wind Instruments* (1920).

Renewed interest in the music of J.S. Bach has often led Neoclassical composers to experiment with new types of counterpoint; *i.e.*, the combining of distinct melodic lines. Further interest in Baroque music is revealed by the many Neoclassical compositions with forms and titles clearly deriving from Baroque prototypes; *e.g.*, *Concerto Grosso No. 1* (1925) by Ernest Bloch, *Toccata* (1948) for orchestra by Walter Piston, and *Aspen Serenade* (1957) by Milhaud. Many Neoclassical composers have also shown marked interest in new kinds of concerti and symphonies, the two most popular idioms of orchestral music in the 18th century, as well as in chamber music, which also originated as such in the 18th century.

A further characteristic of Neoclassicism includes experimentation with new rhythms and harmonies still within a framework of tonality (the system of harmonic organization that dominated European music from about 1700 to about 1900). Excellent examples of this can be found in almost any music written by Milhaud and Piston, and by Stravinsky between about 1920 and 1950.

Among the many other composers who have shown Neoclassical tendencies in some of their music are the Italian Alfredo Casella and the French Francis Poulenc.

·aesthetic intentions and emphases **12**:714f
·anti-Impressionist orchestration **13**:646h
·contemporary technique and past form **12**:720h
·innovative movement status **12**:668b
·organ development in 20th century **13**:681g
·Stravinsky's neoclassical period **17**:730b
·20th-century concertos on Baroque and Classical patterns **4**:1074b

Neoclassicism, in art and architecture, a taste for classical serenity and archaeologically correct forms that began to be perceptible *c.* 1750 and flourished in all branches of the visual arts from *c.* 1780 until the mid-19th century. In Europe it represented a reaction against the excesses of the last phase of the Baroque and was symptomatic of a new philosophical outlook. As the Baroque had been the style of Absolutism, so Neoclassicism corresponded loosely to the Enlightenment and the Age of Reason, representing an attempt to recreate order and reason through the adoption of classical forms. Coincidental with the rise of Neoclassicism and exerting a formative and profound influence on the movement was a new and more scientific interest in classical antiquity. The discovery, exploration, and archaeological investigation of classical sites in Italy, Greece, and Asia Minor was crucial to the emergence of Neoclassicism.

Outstanding among Neoclassical architects were the Frenchmen Jacques-Germain Soufflot and Jacques-Ange Gabriel, the Adam brothers in England, and the Americans Benjamin Latrobe, Thomas Jefferson, and William Strickland; among painters, the Frenchmen Jacques-Louis David and Jean-Auguste-Dominique Ingres and an American living in England, Benjamin West; among sculptors, the Italian Antonio Canova, the Englishman John Flaxman, and the Dane Bertel Thorvaldsen. *See also* Biedermeier; Empire; Federal; Greek Revival; Regency style; Palladianism.

·Canova's sculptural style **3**:780c
·David's break from Rococo style **5**:519g
·Edinburgh's urban design **6**:307d
·furniture design and decoration **7**:788d
·gold, silver, and ironwork **11**:1106f
·interior design features and influences **9**:713g; illus. 714
·Italian and French theatre impact **18**:222e
·painting styles, illus., **19**:Visual Arts, Western, Plates XIX and XX
·pottery production of Wedgwood **14**:912h; illus. 913
·Robert Adam's redefinition **1**:71h
·visual art forms and styles **19**:432e

neocolonialism, term used to mean the continued domination of the more powerful nations over former colonial areas through economic, cultural, or military influence.
·African 20th-century political climate **1**:209d
·Western control in the Third World **4**:904h

Neocomian Stage, division of Lower Cretaceous rocks and time (the Cretaceous Period began about 136,000,000 years ago and lasted about 71,000,000 years). The Neocomian includes the four lower stages of the Lower Cretaceous Series: from oldest to youngest, these are the Berriasian, Valanginian, Hauterivian, and Barremian stages. In effect, the Neocomian is a superstage, and the name is sometimes used in a time sense only, without any implication of rock sequence, so that lack of precision limits its utility.
·deposit types and rock series **5**:249a; tables 247

Neo-Confucianism: *see* Confucianism; Confucianism, History of.

Neo-Confucianism in Japan, the official guiding philosophy of the Tokugawa feudal regime (1603–1867), which profoundly influenced the thought and behaviour of the educated class. The tradition, introduced into Japan from China by Zen Buddhists in the medieval period, provided a heavenly sanction for the existing social order. In the Neo-Confucian view, harmony was maintained by a reciprocal relationship of justice between a superior, who was urged to be benevolent, and a subordinate, who was urged to be obedient and to observe propriety.

Neo-Confucianism in the Tokugawa period contributed to the development of the Bushido (Code of Warriors). The emphasis of Neo-Confucianism on the study of the Chinese Classics furthered a sense of history among the Japanese and led in turn to a renewed interest in the Japanese classics and a revival of Shintō studies (*see* Fukkō Shintō). Most significantly, Neo-Confucianism encouraged scholars to concern themselves with the practical side of human affairs, with law, economics, and politics.

Three main traditions of Neo-Confucian studies developed in Japan. They were the Shushigaku (*q.v.*), based on the Chinese school of the philosopher Chu Hsi; the Ōyōmeigaku (*q.v.*), an interpretation of the teachings of the Chinese philosopher Wang Yang-ming; and Kogaku (*q.v.*), which considered itself a return to the original thought of the Chinese sages Confucius and Mencius.
·Japanese philosophical developments **10**:105c
·Tokugawa religious policies **10**:110g

Neoconocephalus: *see* cone-headed grasshopper.

Neo-Destour, the political party that, from its creation in 1934, led the Tunisian national struggle for independence from France.

The Neo-Destour was formed by discontented young members of the more conservative Destour (Liberal Constitutional Party). After a bitter struggle with the parent organization, it became the predominant party under the leadership of Habib Bourguiba in 1937. Harassed by French authorities throughout the 1940s, it began an armed rebellion in 1953 that led to Tunisian independence in 1956.

A Neo-Destour government was then formed, and the elections that followed the proclamation of independence (March 20, 1956) gave the party a solid electoral backing. In 1958 Bourguiba was appointed the first premier of Tunisia and on Nov. 8, 1959, was overwhelmingly voted president.

Internally, however, the Neo-Destour had begun to split in the early 1950s, one group supporting Bourguiba, the other aligning itself with Salah Ben Yusuf, who had led the party when Bourguiba had been imprisoned by the French. Ben Yusuf was expelled from the party in 1955, established himself in Cairo, and initiated a guerrilla and propaganda campaign against the Neo-Destour, the French, and Bourguiba. After several years of terrorist activity, Ben Yusuf was found murdered on Aug. 14, 1961, and his followers soon disappeared. The Neo-Destour meanwhile consolidated its hold on all levels of Tunisian society and constituted itself as Tunisia's sole political party.
·Bourguiba and Tunisian independence **3**:85a
·political dominance **18**:748g
·structure and ideology **14**:684a

Neodrepanis: *see* false sunbird.

neodymium (from Greek *neos*, "new"; *didymos*, "twin"), symbol Nd, chemical element, rare-earth metal of transition group IIIb of the periodic table, used for special glasses and alloys. Of silvery-white colour, neodymium tarnishes in air to form an oxide, which chips, exposing the metal to further oxidation. The metal must be sealed in a plastic covering or kept in mineral oil for preservation. It reacts gradually with cold water and rapidly with hot water to liberate hydrogen. Carl Auer von Welsbach discovered neodymium (1885) by separating ammonium didymium nitrate prepared from didymia (a mixture of rare-earth oxides) into a neodymium fraction and a praseodymium fraction by repeated crystallization. Of the rare earths, only cerium and yttrium are more plentiful than neodymium. In the igneous rocks of the Earth's crust it is nearly twice as abundant as lead and about half as plentiful as copper. Neodymium occurs in the minerals monazite and bastnaesite and is a product of nuclear fission. Ion-exchange techniques have supplanted fractional crystallization for separation and purification of neodymium. The metal itself is prepared by electrolysis of the fused halides or by thermoreduction of the fluoride with calcium or lithium.

The metal is used in the electronics industry, in the manufacture of steel, and as a component in a number of alloys, among them misch metal (15 percent neodymium) used for cigarette-lighter flints. Its compounds are used in the ceramics industry for glazes and to colour glass. The crude oxide is used to counteract the green colour of iron(II) in glass; and the more pure compound is used in the production of the only known glass that is bright purple in colour. This neodymium glass can be used instead of ruby as a laser material. A mixture of neodymium and praseodymium absorbs light in the region of the harmful sodium-D (spectral) lines and therefore is used in the glass of welder's and glass blower's goggles.

Natural neodymium is a mixture of seven isotopes: neodymium-142 (27.11%), neodymium-144 (23.85%), neodymium-146 (17.62%), neodymium-143 (12.17%), neodymium-145 (8.30%), neodymium-148 (5.73%), and neodymium-150 (5.62%). All are stable except the weakly radioactive neodymium-144, the lightest natural nuclide that certainly decays by alpha emission. Several allotropes (structural forms) exist; at room temperature the structure is hexagonal close packed. The element forms the usual rare-earth trivalent compounds such as the oxide Nd_2O_3, and the hydroxide $Nd(OH)_3$; the Nd^{3+} ion is stable in water. A few divalent compounds have been prepared such as the di-iodide NdI_2, and the dichloride $NdCl_2$; the Nd^{2+} ion is unstable in aqueous solution.

atomic number	60
atomic weight	144.240
melting point	1,010° C
boiling point	3,127° C
specific gravity	7.003 (25° C)
valence	3
electronic config.	2-8-18-22-8-2 or (Xe)$4f^4 5d^0 6s^2$

·atomic weight and number table **2**:345
·geochemical abundances, table 1 **6**:702
·laser light production **10**:686g
·oxide rare-earth properties and uses **15**:526a
·rare-earth element properties and uses **15**:515a; table 518
·solar abundances, table 2 **17**:803

Neofiber alleni (rodent): *see* muskrat.

Neogaean realm: *see* Neotropical region.

Neogene Period, uppermost of two divisions of the Cenozoic Era; it began about 26,000,000 years ago and follows the Paleogene Periods. It includes the Miocene, Pliocene, Pleistocene, and Holocene (Recent) epochs. The term Neogene has gained wide acceptance in Europe as a geological division but not in North America, where the Cenozoic Era is divided into the Tertiary Period and Quaternary Period. In Europe, however, an added complication has been created because the Quaternary is still recognized. Thus, the Neogene only includes the Miocene and Pliocene epochs, and the Cenozoic Era is divided into three parts.
·nomenclature adoption **18**:151d
·rock types and distribution **3**:1080g

Neoglaziovia, a genus of the pineapple family (Bromeliaceae) containing two species of perennial South American plants. The leaves of *N. variegata*, a reedlike plant, are up to 1.2 metres (4 feet) long. They contain a fibre known as caroa, which is used to make rope, fabric, netting, and packing material.
·cultivation and use **3**:324f

Neogrammarians, German JUNGGRAMMATIKER, a group of German scholars that arose around 1875; their chief tenet concerning language change was that sound laws have no exceptions. This principle was very controversial because there seemed to be several irregularities in language change not accounted for by the sound laws, such as Grimm's law (*q.v.*), that had been discovered by that time. In 1875, however, the Danish linguist Karl Verner explained the apparent exceptions to Grimm's law; his formulation of the principle governing those exceptions is known as Verner's law (*q.v.*). Subsequently, many other important sound laws were discovered and formulated to account for other apparent exceptions, and, by the end of the 19th century, the hypothesis of the regularity of sound change had been generally accepted. The leading exponent of Neogrammarian principles was the German linguist Karl Brugmann, a student of Georg Curtius, an opponent of Neogrammarian beliefs.
·sound change regularity principle **10**:994b

Neogregarinida, protozoan order of the class Telosporea.
·protozoan features and classification **15**:128h

Neo-Hawaiian local race, the population of the state of Hawaii, of highly mixed and extremely variable genetic composition. Three geographical races are measurably represented in this mixture: Caucasoid (European), Mongoloid (Asian; including Chinese, Japa-

Neo-Hawaiian local race
N. Myers—Bruce Coleman Inc.

nese, and Filipino), and Polynesian (the aboriginal Hawaiian population). Very few unmixed Polynesians remain in Hawaii; according to studies of blood groups, persons who consider themselves "Hawaiian" (Polynesian) have an average of over 8 percent Caucasoid and about 14 percent Mongoloid admixture. Physical characteristics of the Neo-Hawaiian local race have not become uniform enough to speak of any typical or representative physical type. *See also* local race; Polynesian geographical race; Caucasoid geographical race; Mongoloid geographical race.

·historical geographic range **15**:349a

Neohermes: *see* fishfly.

Neo-Impressionism, movement in French painting of the late 19th century that reacted against the empirical realism of Impressionism (*q.v.*) by relying on systematic calculation and scientific theory to achieve a determined

"Sailing-boats in the Harbour at St. Tropez," Neo-Impressionist painting by Paul Signac, oil on canvas, 1893; in the Von der Heydt-Museum der Stadt Wuppertal, West Germany

By courtesy of the Von der Heydt-Museum der Stadt Wuppertal, West Germany

effect. While the Impressionists spontaneously recorded nature in terms of the fugitive effects of colour and light, the Neo-Impressionists applied scientific optical principles of light and colour to create strictly formalized compositions. Neo-Impressionism was led by Georges Seurat, its original theorist and most significant artist, and by Paul Signac, also an important artist and the movement's major spokesman. Other Neo-Impressionists were Henri-Edmond Cross, Albert Dubois-Pillet, Maximilien Luce, Théo Van Rysselberghe, and, for a time, the Impressionist painter Camille Pissarro. The group founded a Société des Artistes Indépendants in 1884.

The technical basis of the Neo-Impressionist style was Divisionism, also called Pointillism, a scientific development of the Impressionist technique of achieving luminosity with bits of broken colour. In Divisionism tiny dots of contrasting pigment were scientifically chosen to blend from a distance into a single colour. The entire canvas was covered with these dots, which defined form without the use of lines and bathed all objects in an intense, vibrating light. In each picture the dots were of a uniform size, calculated to harmonize with the overall size of the painting. In place of the hazy forms of Impressionism, those of Neo-Impressionism had solidity and clarity and were simplified to reveal the carefully composed relationships between them. Though the light quality was as brilliant as that of Impressionism, the general effect was of immobile, harmonious monumentality, a crystallization of the fleeting light and atmosphere of Impressionism.

Signac's later work showed an increasingly spontaneous use of the Divisionist technique, which was more consistent with his poetic sensibility. Seurat, however, continued to adopt a theoretical approach to the study of various pictorial and technical problems, including a reduction of the expressive qualities of colour and form to scientific formulas.

By the 1890s the influence of Neo-Impressionism was waning, but it was important in the early development of several artists of the late 19th and early 20th centuries, including van Gogh, Gauguin, Toulouse-Lautrec, and Matisse.

·colour theory principle experiments **13**:872f
·modern visual art history **19**:477a
·Mondrian's interest in colour **12**:344f
·Pissarro's adaptation of Seurat's style **14**:474h
·textural effects in painting **13**:872g

Neókastro (Greece): *see* Pylos.

Neolin, 18th-century North American Indian prophet from the Ohio tribe.

·new tribal religious movements in North America **18**:702a

Neolinognathidae, a family of lice of the order Phthiraptera.

·classification of Phthiraptera **14**:376b

Neolipoptena ferrisi: *see* louse fly.

Neolithic, term introduced in 1865 by the English anthropologist Sir John Lubbock to describe all archaeological inventories that included stone tools shaped by polishing or grinding and that preceded the appearance of metal tools in the Bronze Age (*q.v.*). He believed it followed the Paleolithic Period (*q.v.*), or age of chipped-stone tools. The term Neolithic reflects an outdated trend in archaeological thought characterized by belief in a worldwide unilinear evolutionary scheme; and the term has been used with some confusion to represent either chronological age, developmental level, or typological description of artifacts.

The Neolithic stage of development was attained during the Holocene Epoch (the last 10,000 years of Earth history). As contrasted to the earlier periods of human history, the Neolithic is characterized by a climatic, geographic, and biologic environment essentially similar to the modern one. Men became herdsmen and cultivators, modifiers of their environment to a much greater extent than ever before. Social structure became more complex in response to new problems and ways of dealing with situations. Animal domestication was an important factor in Neolithic life as was agriculture, including the planting, care, and growing of crops. Stone implements and weapons were generally polished and mining was practiced. It appears that religious ideas of the Neolithic were more complex than those previously in existence. Communities tended to be more settled, with dwellings purposely constructed and generally in the open. Archaeological work has greatly complicated concepts of Neolithic life and times. The hunting-gathering cultures that preceded the Neolithic apparently were able to maintain a high level of living standards by the efficient exploitation of the natural environment. They lived in relatively stable, more or less permanent, villages and were able to support complex social structures and organizations—all this without practicing agriculture in the usual sense and without domestication of animals. Natural growing grains, the wild ancestors of domesticated grains, were harvested. Research has shown that the harvesting of wild grains can be virtually as productive as the harvesting of cultivated crops. Wild crops may also prove more varied and nutritious than cultivated counterparts. Similarly, if game, shellfish, and fish are available, there is no shortage of protein.

Numerous sites have been found having characteristics of Neolithic settlements but without domesticated animals (except for the dog, perhaps) or any indication that plant cultivation was practiced. Yet, permanent or at least seasonal villages were present, and the way of life was relatively sedentary. It appears that agriculture developed in several regions independently and that the development of full sedentism (condition of fixed abode) in the classic Neolithic sense was more the process of natural evolution than revolution.

·Aegean early cultures **1**:113c
·Anatolian economic and cultural traits **1**:813h
·Arctic and sub-Arctic sites **1**:1129b
·artifact classification and archaeological time scale **5**:501d; illus. 500
·Asian hunting cultures and tools **2**:199a
·Asian Russian cultural sites and visual arts evidence **3**:1131c
·Athens' prehistoric traces **2**:265d
·Cambodia's prehistoric evidence **3**:681d
·Central African technical advance **3**:1091b
·cereal agricultural development **3**:1157c
·Ceylonese prehistoric cultures **4**:1f
·Chinese pottery culture features **19**:177b; illus.
·Chinese stone tool culture discoveries **4**:298e; map
·clothing manufacture, fibres, and dyes **5**:1016d
·copper history and uses **5**:148b
·Eastern European civilizations **2**:612a; table
·Egyptian culture and implements **6**:463e
·European beginnings of agriculture **6**:1059e
·European cultural evolution **6**:1124g
·European folk and architectural arts **17**:706d; illus.
·garment materials and construction **4**:750f
·Geneva lake-dwelling community growth **7**:1011a
·human expansion and diversification **7**:22f
·Iranian cultural progress **9**:830c
·Ireland's prehistoric peoples **3**:282h
·Japanese pottery decoration and types **19**:216g
·Jericho's human culture development **10**:136f
·Jōmon and Yayoi cultures **10**:57f
·Kashmir prehistoric culture **9**:337h
·Korean pottery production and design **19**:207g
·Korean prehistoric cultures **10**:506h
·Maltese cultures and remains **11**:391d
·Mesopotamian prehistoric cultures **11**:967c
·Nineveh's earliest settlement **13**:116e
·North African cultural transmission **13**:146b
·Oceanian artifacts and technology **13**:444c
·Oceanian primitive technology **13**:470e
·Portuguese prehistoric cultures **14**:865a
·religious practices and beliefs **14**:985d
·Sahara desert relics and man **16**:150a
·Scandinavian peoples and cultures **16**:304h
·Scotland's prehistoric cultures **3**:232g
·Shensi area cultural evidence **16**:664e
·Southeast Asian toolmaking artistry **17**:251f
·Southern African cultures, organization, and habits **17**:274h *passim* to 275c
·Spanish archaeological deposits **17**:401d
·Syrian and Palestinian prehistory **17**:928b
·technology development and importance **18**:26f
·tool and toolmaking history **8**:606h; illus. 610
·urbanization and city evolution **18**:1074g
·wheat agricultural importance **3**:1157c

Neolloydia: *see* barrel cactus.

neolocal residence (sociology): *see* residence.

neologism: *see* vocabulary.

Neo-Lutherans, mid-19th-century German Pietist group.

·Pietism influenced by Romanticism **14**:459b

Neo-Melanesian language: *see* Melanesian Pidgin.

Neomeris phocoenoides: *see* porpoise.

Neomorphus: *see* ground cuckoo.

neomycin, an antibiotic or mixture of antibiotics produced by a soil actinomycete and active against a variety of bacteria.

·synthesis and antimicrobial action **1**:989g

neon, symbol Ne, chemical element, inert gas of group O (noble gases) of the periodic table, used in electric signs and fluorescent lamps. Colourless, odourless, tasteless, and lighter than air, neon (Greek *neos*, "new") gas occurs in minute quantities in the Earth's atmosphere and trapped within the rocks of the Earth's crust. Though neon is about 3½ times as plentiful as helium in the atmosphere, dry air contains only 0.0018 percent neon by volume. This element is more abundant in the cosmos than on Earth. Neon liquefies at −246.048° C (−411° F) and freezes at a temperature only 2½° lower. When under low pressure, it emits a bright orange-red light if an electrical current is passed through it. This property is utilized in neon signs (which first became familiar in the 1920s), in some fluorescent and gaseous conduction lamps, and in high-voltage testers.

Neon was discovered (1898) by the English chemists Sir William Ramsay and Morris W. Travers as a component of the most volatile fraction of liquefied crude argon obtained from air. It was immediately recognized as a new element by its unique glow when electrically stimulated. The gas is produced industrially by the fractional distillation of liquid air; the most volatile fraction is composed of a mixture of helium, neon, and nitrogen. Nitrogen is removed by condensation under increased pressure and reduced temperature, followed by adsorption on highly cooled charcoal. Neon is separated from helium by selective adsorption on activated charcoal at low temperatures. It takes 88,000 pounds of liquid air to produce one pound of neon.

No stable chemical compounds of neon have been observed. Molecules of the element consist of single atoms. Natural neon is a mixture of three stable isotopes: neon-20 (90.92 percent); neon-21 (0.26 percent); and neon-22 (8.82 percent).

atomic number	10
atomic weight	20.183
melting point	−248.67° C (−415.5° F)
boiling point	−246.048° C (−411° F)
density (1 atm, 0° C)	0.89990 g/litre
valence	0
electronic configuration	2-8 or $1s^22s^22p^6$

Major ref. **13**:137e
·atmospheric chemical composition **2**:308d
·atmospheric composition, table 8 **6**:710
·atmospheric deficiency theories **2**:314g
·atomic spectra properties **17**:464d
·atomic weight and number table **2**:345
·chemical bond and electronic stability **4**:85h
·electronic component operation **6**:686b
·isotope discovery and behaviour **2**:335h
·isotope separation by diffusion method **9**:1058f
·life and matter origin connected **10**:900h
·lighting and sign use **10**:959b
·production from liquid air **7**:926f
·radiation detection mediums **15**:394g
·solar abundances, table 2 **17**:803
·stellar nuclear reactions and abundance **17**:602g; table

Neo-orthodoxy, an influential 20th-century Protestant theological movement in Europe and America; it was known in Europe as crisis theology and dialectical theology. The name crisis theology referred to the crisis of Christendom that occurred after World War I. The phrase dialectical theology referred to the apparently contradictory statements made in the interests of "truth" by theologians in order to point out both the majesty of human life and the limits of human thought.

The theologians in the movement were called Neo-orthodox because they spoke the traditional language of the Christian Church as found in the Bible, the creeds, and the main line of orthodox Protestant theology. They wrote of the Trinity, the Creator, the Fall of man and original sin, Jesus Christ the Lord and Saviour, justification, reconciliation, and the Kingdom of God. The language is that of Protestant orthodoxy, but, as the orthodox were quick to see, the meaning of the language had undergone radical changes.

The Neo-orthodox theologians repudiated the literalism of orthodoxy. They were modernists in that they accepted modern critical methods of interpreting the Bible and thus knew that it contained much that is not literally true. The miracle of the Christian faith for them was Jesus Christ and his gospel proclaimed in the church for the salvation of the world. In Europe the outstanding theologian of the movement was Karl Barth, and in the United States it is generally held that the works of Reinhold Niebuhr constituted the most important Neo-orthodox writing. Other important Neo-orthodox theologians include Emil Brunner, Rudolf Bultmann, Nikolay Berdyayev, and Paul Tillich.

According to Neo-orthodox theology God as the sovereign Other is the Person who places man under an inviolable responsibility. God transcends man as Creator and Redeemer and, therefore, as the source of responsibility, which is neither in man nor in his world. God speaks his Word to man, and in this personal act he lays his claim upon man and obligates him to respond and thus to exist as a human being.

Jesus Christ is the Word become flesh for our salvation. God reveals himself in the freedom and love of Jesus and in his forgiveness. But forgiveness reveals man's sin. Therefore, man knows God and knows himself as a sinner; without such knowledge he knows neither God nor himself. Man knows himself as a person only as he knows himself as a sinner under God's forgiveness. Thus, the knowledge of sin is an occasion for acknowledging both man's misery and his grandeur. It is the antidote both to despair and to pride and to the degradation of human culture that follows these twin evils.

Sin for Neo-orthodoxy is the violation of persons as seen in contrast to the love of God in Jesus for sinners. It is man's rebellion against his limited life and powers that comes both before and after his repudiation of responsibility, which in turn is the sign of death both for the individual and for the community. From it come dehumanization and the consequent evils of egotism, stupidity, and guilt, as well as the loneliness, the loss of meaning, anxiety, enmity, and cruelty that plague human life. The Neo-orthodox defend such a view of sin as biblical and in line with a realistic knowledge of the condition of man.

Neo-orthodox criticism of modern culture led its theologians to examine political and economic institutions with a new awareness of their significance for responsible human existence. These theologians argued that religion, ethics, economics, and politics are aspects of a larger whole that is the culture of a society and that these aspects cannot be understood and dealt with separately. Therefore, the theologians concerned themselves with social institutions and problems and attempted to understand the controversial issues of the day, such as Communism, race relations, and nuclear weapons, from a Christian viewpoint. There was no unanimity among them as to the answers to perplexing public problems, but they were one in seeing the Word of God as addressed to the total human situation.
·Barth's impact on Protestantism **2**:726c
·Niebuhr's influence and differences **13**:74g
·Protestant reactions to liberal theology **15**:119c
·revelation and human religious response **15**:624d
·Ritschl reconstructionism criticism **15**:863d

neopallium, the part of the brain developed in the course of mammalian evolution. In man it makes up the greater part of the gray matter covering the cerebral hemispheres.
·evolutionary cerebral differentiation, illus. 8 **12**:991
·mammalian nervous system advances **11**:409f

neopentane, also known as TETRAMETHYL METHANE, gaseous or volatile liquid hydrocarbon found in petroleum and natural gas.
·catalytic reaction path selectivity **3**:1003g

neopentyl alcohol, volatile crystalline alcohol that gives off a peppermint odour.
·carbonium ion and molecular rearrangement **3**:862h

Neophema, genus of grass parrot of the family Psittacidae, order Psittaciformes.
·classification and general features **15**:141d

Neophoca (seal genus): *see* sea lion.

Neophocoena phocoenoides: *see* porpoise.

neophyte (from a Greek word meaning "newly planted"), used by early Christians in the figurative sense of "one recently baptized." The term occurs once in the New Testament (I Tim. 3:6) and is translated in various English Bibles as "neophyte," "novice," "convert," "newly baptized," or "recent convert." According to this passage, a neophyte cannot become a bishop.

The word was also common in epitaphs, notably on the sculptured sarcophagus, dated AD 359, of the Roman prefect Junius Bassus that is preserved in the Vatican grotto. By extension neophyte came to be used to describe a newly ordained priest or a novice in a convent, and eventually, any beginner.

Neophytus, 18th-century Greek Orthodox bishop of Philippolis.
·ecumenical exchange with Anglicans **6**:294h

Neopilina (mollusk genus): *see* Monoplacophora.

neoplasm, in domestic animals, tumorous growth initiated by any number of factors including viruses, parasites, chemicals, irradiation, and injury. Each species has its own peculiar repertoire of neoplasms. All except skin tumours are generally far advanced and beyond help by the time they are diagnosed. Some surface tumours regress automatically in one to three months; severe cases require surgical removal, X-ray therapy, and other developing treatments. Neoplasms of cats, dogs, and other small animals appear in greatest numbers after five years of age. Among larger animals, cattle have the largest number of types of neoplasms; swine have the lowest incidence of tumours among livestock.

human disease
·reticiculoendothelial malignancies **15**:783c
·tumour causation mechanisms **5**:858d

neoplastic disease, any disease condition resulting from abnormal tissue growths.
·disease classification systems **5**:863b

Neoplasticism, aesthetic doctrine advanced in 1920 by the de Stijl painter Piet Mondrian that advocates pure abstraction or totally objective art. *See also* Stijl, de.
·de Stijl movement in architecture **19**:468a
·Mondrian and the de Stijl movement **12**:345e

Neoplatonism: *see* Platonism and Neoplatonism.

neoprene, any of a class of elastomers, or rubberlike synthetic organic compounds of high molecular weight (polymers), made by chemical combination of the simpler compound 2-chloro-1,3-butadiene (chloroprene); it is used in numerous products, such as shoe soles, hoses, and adhesives, that require better resistance than natural rubber to oil, solvents, heat, and weathering.

The neoprenes, discovered in 1931, were the first synthetic rubbers developed in the United States. The starting material, chloroprene, is derived by the reaction of two molecules of acetylene, which yields vinylacetylene; a second reaction, with hydrogen chloride, produces chloroprene, which readily polymerizes (links together into long chains) without the aid of a catalyst. The neoprenes are ordinarily vulcanized by using magnesium oxide or zinc oxide, although sulfur is sometimes employed. The products are too expensive for use in making tires, but their resistance to

chemicals and to oxidation makes them valuable in specialized applications. *See also* rubber, synthetic.
·unsaturated hydrocarbon products **4**:132b; illus. 131

neoprioniodiform, conodonts (small toothlike phosphatic fossils of uncertain affinities) that are characterized by a main terminal cusp, varying numbers of subsidiary cusps or denticles that may be completely fused, and an underside region that is deeply grooved. The neoprioniodiform conodonts are similar in form to the genus *Neoprioniodus*, a genus found in marine rocks of Ordovician to Triassic age (190,000,000 to 500,000,000 years old). Several genera are included in the neoprioniodiforms, including excellent guide fossils for the Ordovician Period.

Neoptera, an order of the class Insecta.
·phylogeny and wing evolution **9**:619a; illus. 618

Neoptolemus, in Greek legend, the son of Achilles, the hero of the Greek army at Troy, and of Deïdameia, daughter of King Lycomedes of Scyros; he was sometimes called Pyrrhus, meaning the Fair. In the last year of the Trojan War, the Greek hero Odysseus brought him to Troy after the Trojan seer Helenus had declared that the city could not be captured without the aid of a descendant of Aeacus, who had helped to build its walls; Neoptolemus was Aeacus' grandson. He fought bravely and took part in the capture of Troy but committed the sacrilege of slaying the aged King Priam at an altar. By Andromache, Priam's daughter-in-law, he was the father of Molossus, ancestor of the Molossian kings. He later married Hermione but shortly thereafter was murdered at Delphi.
·Antigonus' military conflict **1**:991e
·aqueduct of Anio Vetus and its financing **1**:1036g
·attempts of expansion **8**:382f

Neo-Punic (language): *see* Phoenician language.

Neo-Pythagoreanism, philosophical movement that arose at Alexandria in the 1st century AD.
·history and doctrines **15**:325b

Neorealism, Italian, or NEOREALISMO, in literature, a movement that originated late in the 1920s and, suppressed for nearly two decades by Fascist control, emerged in great strength after the regime fell at the end of World War II. *Neorealismo* is similar in general aims to the earlier Italian movement *verismo* (Realism), from which it originated, but differs in that its upsurge was brought about by the intense feelings, experiences, and convictions that Fascist repression, the Resistance, and the war had instilled in its many gifted writers. Added impetus was given the movement by the translation of many socially conscious U.S. and English writers during the 1930s and 1940s.

Among the outstanding Neorealist writers are Nobel Prize winning-poet Salvatore Quasimodo and the fiction writers Alberto Moravia, Ignazio Silone, Carlo Levi, Vasco Partolini, Carlo Bernari, Cesare Pavese, Elio Vittorini, Carlo Cassola, Italo Calvino, Curzio Malaparte (in postwar writings), and Carlo Emilio Gadda.

The emergence of Neorealism during the Fascist years was sporadic. Moravia wrote perhaps the first representative work in *Gli indifferenti* (1929; first Eng. trans., 1932, best trans., *The Time of Indifference*, 1953). Ignazio Silone was internationally known for anti-Fascist works written from Swiss exile, beginning with *Fontamara* (1930; Eng. trans., 1934). and Elio Vittorini wrote veiled criticism of the Fascist regime in a brilliant, Hemingway-like novel, *Conversazione in Sicilia* (1941; Eng. trans., *Conversation in Sicily*, 1948). Many Neorealist writers were driven into hiding (Moravia), put in prison (Pavese, Vittorini), or sent into exile (Silone, Levi); many others joined the Resistance (Vittorini, Calvino, Cassola); some took refuge in introspective movements like Hermeticism (Quasimodo) or in translating the works of others (Pavese, Vittorini).

After the war, the movement exploded in full strength. Vasco Pratolini left his autobiographical work behind and published such vivid and moving accounts of the Florentine poor as *Il quartiere* (1944; Eng. trans., *The Naked Streets*, 1952) and one of the finest novels of the Neorealist movement, *Cronache di poveri amanti* (1947; Eng. trans., *A Tale of Poor Lovers*, 1949). Curzio Malaparte, who had repudiated his earlier Fascist loyalties, produced two powerful novels about the war, *Kaputt* (1944; Eng. trans., 1946) and *La pelle* (1949; Eng. trans., *The Skin*, 1952). Elio Vittorini wrote openly about his Resistance experiences in *Uomini e no* (1945; "Men and Non-men"). And Carlo Levi earned international fame with his compassionate study of the plight of peasants in southern Italy (where he had been exiled), *Cristo si è fermato a Eboli* (1945; Eng. trans., *Christ Stopped at Eboli*, 1947).

Other writers also felt the compulsion to communicate life as it then was or as it had been. Salvatore Quasimodo emerged from Hermeticism and began to publish poetry about the war and social problems, beginning with *Giorno dopo giorno* (1947; "Day After Day"). Moravia resumed his writing and published many outstanding Neorealistic novels. Cesare Pavese contributed two accounts of his life in a Fascist prison and many introspective novels about contemporary despair. Italo Calvino and Carlo Cassola left stirring accounts of the Resistance experience, Calvino in *Il sentiero dei nidi di ragno* (1947; Eng. trans., *The Path to the Nest of Spiders*, 1957) and Cassola in *Il taglio del bosco* (1959; "The Felling of the Forest") and *La ragazza di Bube* (1960; Eng. trans., *Bubo's Girl*, 1962). It may be said that these novels, along with Neorealist films, constituted the most vigorous and stimulating art products of the decade immediately following World War II. *See also* Neorealist films.
·Italian literature development **10**:1238c
·monist theory of cognition **15**:541f

Neorealist films, series of films made in Italy 1945–50, dealing with events of the recently concluded World War II and with postwar social problems. The movement in film paralleled the Italian literary movement, also known as Neorealism. The films' style was a documentary-like objectivity; actors either were or looked like ordinary people involved in commonplace situations. Although Neorealist productions were often hastily made and crude, their radical departure from the escapist idealization of traditional moviemaking and their boldness in handling contemporary themes had an international impact.

The first of such pictures to appear was Roberto Rossellini's *Open City* (1945), an anti-Fascist film showing the brutal decisions imposed on the Italians by the Nazi occupation. Rossellini's *Paisan* (1946), six vignettes of the war in Italy, had a similar harrowing quality. Other important Neorealist films were Vittorio De Sica's *Shoeshine* (1946) and *The Bicycle Thief* (1948), dealing with the everyday life of working class Italians, and Luchino Visconti's *La terra trema* (1948; "The Earth Trembles"), a story of impoverished Sicilian fishermen, which used no professional actors. After 1950 the trend of Italian films turned from realism toward fantasy, symbolism, and literary themes.
·Italian directors and directing **5**:831f
·Italian post-war film artistry **12**:534d
·low-budget films influence on industry **12**:495d

Neoregelia, a genus of about 40 species of epiphytes (plants that grow upon tree branches) of the pineapple family (Bromeliaceae) native to tropical South America. Several species, including *N. carolinae*, are grown as indoor ornamentals for their colourful flowers and leaves. The leaves often are mottled, marbled, or banded. They form a rosette with small white, blue, or purple flowers deep in the centre of the cup. The leaves of some species bear spines or scales, and the central leaves often become coloured during flowering periods.
·house plants and their care **8**:1120b

Neoregelia carolinae
G.E. Hyde—EB Inc.

Neoromanticism, in music, term that most often implies a return to the 19th-century Romantic period approaches and styles; the notion of a continuation of Romanticism leading directly to more advanced "modernism" is more properly Postromanticism (*see* Postromantic music).

In addition to embracing some of the strictly musical characteristics of Romanticism and Postromanticism, Neoromanticism has often shown the effects of intense nationalism. Thus, Neoromanticism can be found in most of the compositions written since the 1930s by composers of the Soviet Union, because that country has placed direct requirements of national appeal on its artists. Good examples of this Soviet Neoromantic nationalism are the later operas of Sergey Prokofiev and the *Fifth Symphony*, *Seventh Symphony*, *Eleventh Symphony*, and *Twelfth Symphony* of Dmitry Shostakovich. In such compositions musical form is rarely obscure, and there is clear emphasis on melody and tonality.

In most Neoromantic music there is a tendency toward the subjective and emotional rather than the objective and intellectual, often brought about through the uses of exotic subject matter, large instrumental forces, expansive forms and styles, and, in general, techniques of composition not far removed from those of the 19th century.

Other Neoromantic composers include the Englishman Josef Holbrooke and the Americans Roy Harris and Aaron Copland, although by no means can all of their works be considered Neoromantic.

Neoscholasticism, philosophical movement of the 19th and 20th centuries.
·historical context of rise and decline **16**:357c

Neoscopelidae, family of fish belonging to the suborder Myctophoidei of the order Salmoniformes.
·classification and general features **16**:191f

Neosho, city, seat (1839) of Newton County, southwest Missouri, U.S., in the Ozark Mountains, southeast of Joplin. Founded in 1839, its name, of Osage Indian derivation, meaning Clear and Abundant Water, probably refers to the nine flowing springs (the largest of which is at Big Spring State Park) within the city limits. During the Civil War, Neosho was the scene of many skirmishes; actual battles were fought at Newtonia 12 mi (19 km) east (April 30, 1861, and Oct. 28, 1864). A marker in the Neosho courthouse yard commemorates the meeting of the Civil War Secession Legislature (October 1861).

The city's economy depends on agriculture (fruit), dairying, light manufactures (including toys, barbecue grills, wire products, and furniture), and rocket-engine testing facilities. There are lead and zinc mines in the vicinity. One of the oldest U.S. fish and wildlife service hatcheries (1887) is at Neosho. Crowder College (1964), on the site of Ft. Crowder, is nearby. Artist Thomas Hart Benton is a native son. Inc. 1855. Pop. (1980) 9,493.
36°52′ N, 94°22′ W

Neosho River, rises north of Council Grove in Morris County, Kansas, U.S., and flows generally southeast into Oklahoma, where it is also known as the Grand, to join the Arkansas River, near Fort Gibson, after a course of about 460 mi (740 km). *Neosho* is a Kaw Indian word meaning "wet bottomland." The crossing at Council Grove was the starting point for the Santa Fe Trail.

With a drainage area of 12,660 sq mi (32,789 sq km), flow at its mouth varies from 133,000 cu ft (3,800 cu m) per second to as little as 35 cu ft. In Kansas, irrigation and flood-control installations along the river include dams and reservoirs at Council Grove and below Neosho Rapids (John Redmond Dam). In Oklahoma, Grand Lake (Lake of the Cherokees) is impounded by Pensacola Dam on the east edge of the Cherokee Plain, Fort Gibson Dam and Reservoir is near the confluence of the Neosho and Arkansas rivers, and Markham Ferry Dam is just southeast of Pryor.
35°48′ N, 95°18′ W

neo-Sinaitic alphabet, writing system used in many short rock inscriptions in the Sinai Peninsula, not to be confused with the Sinaitic inscriptions (*q.v.*), which are of much earlier date and not directly related. Neo-Sinaitic

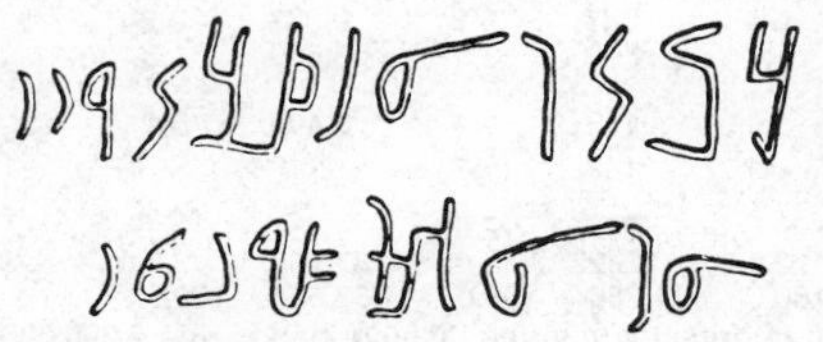

Neo-Sinaitic inscription

From *The Alphabet* by David Diringer. Copyright 1948 by David Diringer. With permission of Funk & Wagnalls Publishing Company, Inc. and Hutchinson Publishing Group Ltd.

evolved out of the Nabataean alphabet in the 1st century AD and was in use perhaps until the 4th century AD; inscriptions date primarily from the 2nd and 3rd centuries. The chief importance of the neo-Sinaitic alphabet is as the probable link between the Nabataean alphabet and the Arabic.

Neositta (bird genus): *see* sitella.

Neos Philopator, Ptolemy VII: *see* Ptolemy VII Neos Philopator.

Neospirifer, genus of extinct brachiopods (lampshells) found as fossils in Pennsylvanian to Permian marine rocks (between 325,000,000 and 225,000,000 years old); many forms or species are known. The shell or valves of *Neospirifer* are robustly developed and frequently well preserved as fossils. A prominent furrow, or sulcus, and a distinctive ridge, or fold, are generally developed in the shell, aiding rapid identification. *Neospirifer* is a useful index fossil for stratigraphic correlations.

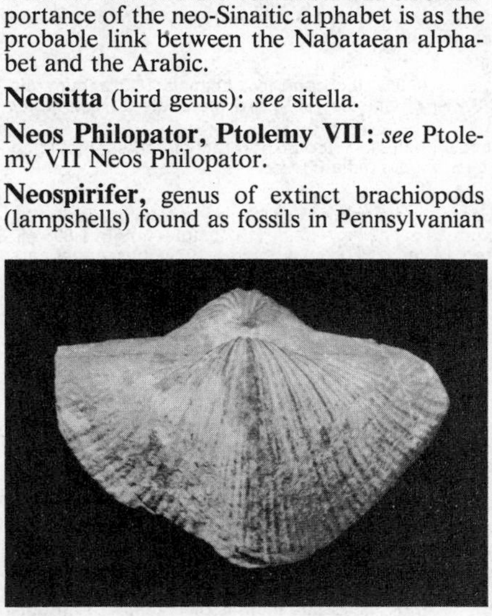

Neospirifer

By courtesy of the trustees of the British Museum (Natural History); photograph, Imitor

neossoptile, one of the downy feathers of a newly hatched bird.
·feather types and arrangement **9**:671a

Neostethidae, a family of fish belonging to the suborder Artherinoidei of the order Atheriniformes.
·classification, range, and features **2**:274a

neostigmine, cholinergic drug used in the diagnosis and treatment of myasthenia gravis and in the relief of postoperative atony of the intestines and urinary bladder.
·anesthetics and muscle activity **1**:868g

neotenin (biology): *see* juvenile hormone.

neoteny, persistence of larval characteristics in the adult organism. Examples of this condition are the retention of gills in some salamanders (*see* axolotl) and the permanently larval form of Larvacea, an order of tunicates. The typical adult stage is never reached by these organisms. *Cf.* paedogenesis.
·angiosperm evolutionary evidence **1**:881b
·biological development and evolution **5**:649g
·Darwin's barnacle evolution theories **4**:641e

neōteroi (Greek: "newer poets"), group of poets who sought to break away from the didactic-patriotic tradition of Latin poetry by consciously emulating the forms and content of Alexandrian Greek models. The *neōteroi* deplored the excesses of alliteration and onomatopoeia and the ponderous metres that characterize the epics and didactic works of the Latin Ennian tradition. They wrote meticulously refined, elegant, and sophisticated epyllia (brief epics), lyrics, epigrams, and elegies. They cultivated a literature of self-expression and a light poetry of entertainment and introduced into Latin literature the aesthetic attitude later known as "art for art's sake."

First arising in the 2nd century BC, the school was essentially non-Roman; it centred on the Milanese poet-teacher Publius Valerius Cato, and most of its adherents came from remote regions of northern Italy. Among them is Catullus, who, during the Ciceronian period (70 to 43 BC) of the Golden Age, wrote finely wrought love lyrics and epyllia in Latin and Greek.

In the Augustan Age (43 BC to AD 18), the influence of the *neōteroi* can be discerned particularly in the pastoral idylls of Virgil and the elegies of Sextus Propertius and Tibullus and in a general refinement of works of the didactic patriotic tradition. Two centuries later a group called the novel poets modelled themselves after the *neōteroi*, writing in Greek and following Greek models.
·membership and literary style **3**:1010d

neo-Thomism (philosophy): *see* Thomism.

Neotoma: *see* wood rat.

Neotragus pygmaeus: *see* royal antelope.

Neotropical region, or SOUTH AMERICAN REGION, one of the six major land areas of the world, biologically defined on the basis of its characteristic animal life. It constitutes the realm Neogaea, and extends south from the Mexican desert into South America as far as the subantarctic zone. The vegetational division roughly corresponding to the region is called the Neotropical kingdom. It includes such animals, as the llama, tapir, deer, pig, jaguar, puma, a variety of oppossums, many rodents and fishes, and extremely rich insect and bird populations. Among the conspicuous plants are ornamental grasses, ancestors of garden flowers, agaves, the rubber tree, and a variety of timber trees.
·characteristic life and conditions **2**:1005f; illus. 1001
·mammalian distribution and evolution **11**:402a
·prehistoric locales of early man **14**:839f
·reptile examples and comparisons in habits and anatomy **15**:726h

Neottia nidus-avis: *see* bird's-nest orchid.

Neottiophilidae, family of flies of the order Diptera.
·classification and features **5**:824f

Neotyrrhenian Stage (geology): *see* Tyrrhenian Stage.

Neo-Utraquists, Lutheran faction that gained control of the Utraquist church prior to 1561.
·Bohemian religiopolitical importance **2**:1191b

NEP (Soviet economic plan): *see* New Economic Policy.

Nepal 12:951, independent kingdom in the Himalayan region of southern Asia, bounded by the Chinese Tibetan Autonomous Region (north), by Sikkim and the Indian state of West Bengal (east), and by the Indian states of Bihār and Uttar Pradesh (south and west).

The text article covers Nepal's relief, drainage and soils, climate, vegetation, animal life, traditional regions, landscape under human settlement, people and population, national economy, transportation system, administration, social conditions, cultural life and institutions, and prospects for the future. (For statistical details, *see* p. 258.)

REFERENCES in other text articles:
·armed forces statistics, table 2 **2**:16
·art of Tibet and Nepal, illus., **3**:Central Asian peoples, Arts of, Plate II
·Christian denominational demography map **4**:459
·Great Himalayan peaks **8**:882b; map
·Himalayan transportation improvements **8**:886c
·Hindu and Buddhist caste systems **3**:986g
·Hindu Pāśupata practices giving offense **8**:895f
·Indic racial characteristics **14**:847a
·Indo-Iranian languages distribution map **9**:442
·map, Asia **2**:148
·Mt. Everest's geographical features **6**:1139g
·newspaper publishing statistics table **15**:237
·Sikkim and territorial wars **16**:749c
·Sino-Tibetan languages distribution map **16**:797
·social organization and religious base **17**:125g; map 126
·Tibetan and Indian music influence **3**:1127b
·urban population ratio table **16**:26

Nepal, history of 12:957. The history of the small Himalayan kingdom of Nepal is marked by a synthesis of Buddhist and Brahmanic Hindu traditions.

The text article covers the emergence of Nepal's history from legendary traditions with the establishment of the Licchavi dynasty (*c.* 4th–*c.* 10th centuries AD). From the Indian plains, the Licchavis set the precedent in Nepal of rule by Hindu kings over a non-Hindu population; during their rule Nepal became the major intellectual and commercial centre between South and Central Asia. Under the Malla dynasty (10th–18th centuries), legal and social codes influenced by Hinduism were introduced; and Nepal was broken into three major and several minor principalities. The modern state was founded in 1769, when the ruler of the Gorkha principality, Prithvi Narayan Shah, conquered Nepal Valley and moved his capital to Kāthmāndu. Until the 1950s, Nepalese politics were dominated by confrontation between the royal family and the nobles. The revolution of 1950 firmly established the royal family's power. The constitution of 1959 introduced the first democratic political system of Nepal's history, but the constitution of 1962 made the crown the true source of authority.

REFERENCES in other text articles:
·Buddhism's Indian foundation **3**:411c
·Ch'ing dynasty's history **4**:355f *passim* to 362d
·chronology of Hindu history **4**:574d
·independence of Tibetan rule **9**:361g
·monastic eremitic organization **12**:338a
·precious metal use in architecture **11**:1116a
·Treaty of Kāthmāndu **9**:401f
·visual arts features and development **3**:1140a

Nepalese, the people of Nepal, including chiefly the Gurung, Limbu, Magar, Newar, Pahari, Sherpa, Tamang, and Tharu (*qq.v.*), along with the Rai, Tarai, and Sunwar.
·Himalayan ethnic distribution **8**:885h

Nepālganj, also spelled NEPALGUNJ, town, southwestern Nepal, in the Tarai, a low, fertile plain, northeast of Nānpāra, India. It is a trading centre for rice, wheat, corn (maize), oilseeds, and hides. The largest town in western Nepal, it is 4 mi from a railway terminus across the border in India. It also has road connections to villages to the west and to a nearby airfield and is the terminus of a trail leading north to Tibet. Nepālganj is also headquarters of the western Nepalese police zone, and it has a hospital built in 1963 with Soviet aid. Pop. (1971) 23,523.
28°03′ N, 81°38′ E
map, Nepal **12**:952

Nepali language, Eastern Pahari dialect spoken in Nepal. *See* Pahari language.

Nepali literature, writings that, until the Gurkha (Gorkha) conquest of 1769, were written in the Sanskrit and Newari languages as well as in Nepali. The works hold more historical than literary interest, except for the memoirs (*c.* 1770) of the Gurkha king Prithvi Narayan Shah. Literary writing in the language began only in the 19th century.

Nepenthales 12:958, order of flowering plants distinguished chiefly by insect-trapping leaves, and consisting of Venus's-flytrap, sundew, and Old World pitcher plants.

The text article covers general features, natural history, form and function, and evolution and includes an annotated classification of the order.

REFERENCES in other text articles:
·angiosperm features and classification **1**:883f
·Sarraceniales classification schema **16**:255g

RELATED ENTRIES in the *Ready Reference and Index:*
Droseraceae; Nepenthes; sundew; Venus's-flytrap

Nepenthes, a genus of flowering plants commonly called pitcher plants belonging to the family Nepenthaceae, order Nepenthales. About 80 species are known, mostly native to Southeast Asia and Australasia. The common North American plants that are more often designated by the name pitcher plant (*q.v.*) are of the family Sarraceniaceae.

Nepenthes species are perennial, shrubby, sometimes herbaceous, stemmed plants, often climbing by their leaves, and anchored in the soil or growing as epiphytes (*i.e.*, obtaining support, but not nourishment, from another plant or some other aerial structure). The leaves are alternate and have a winged or expanded portion followed by a constricted, often coiled tendril. This is terminated by a

Pitcher plant (*Nepenthes*)
Gerald Cubitt

NEPAL

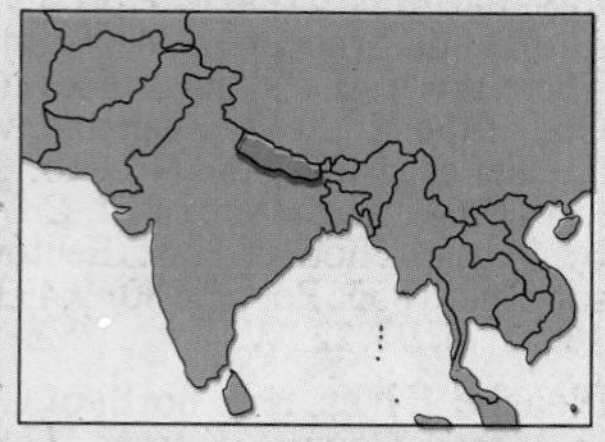

Official name: Nepāl Adhirājya (Kingdom of Nepal).
Location: southern Asia.
Form of government: constitutional monarchy.
Official language: Nepali.
Official religion: none.
Area: 54,362 sq mi, 140,797 sq km.
Population: (1971 census) 11,555,983 (de jure); (1976 estimate) 12,857,243.
Capital: Kāthmāndu.
Monetary unit: 1 Nepalese rupee (NRe.) = 100 pice.

Demography

Population: (1976 estimate) density 236.5 per sq mi, 91.3 per sq km; (1975 estimate) urban 4.8%, rural 95.2%; (1976 estimate) male 50.33%, female 49.67%; (1976 estimate) under 15 40.8%, 15–29 25.4%, 30–44 18.0%, 45–59 10.4%, 60–74 4.8%, 75 and over 0.6%.
Vital statistics: (1970–75) births per 1,000 population 42.9, deaths per 1,000 population 20.3, natural increase per 1,000 population 22.6; (1976) life expectancy at birth—45.0; major causes of death—no data available, though major diseases are malaria, tuberculosis, typhoid, and cholera.
Ethnic composition (1961): Nepalese (Gurkha, Khasi, and others) 51.1%, Tharu 13.8%, Bihari 10.7%, Tamang 6.1%, Newar 4.8%, Magar 3.3%, Kiranti 2.9%, other 7.3%. *Religious affiliation* (1971): Hindu 89.4%, Buddhist 7.5%, Muslim 3.0%, other 0.1%.

National accounts

Budget (1974–75). Revenue: NRs. 959,700,000 (import duties 17.3%, income from property 13.5%, excise duties 12.2%, sales tax 11.3%, income tax 5.7%, export duties 3.3%). Expenditures: NRs. 1,740,900,000 (economic services 54.8%, social services 21.8%, general administration 6.2%, defense 6.2%, interest on public debt 3.1%, economic and administration and planning 2.0%, foreign service 1.2%). *Total national debt* (1974): NRs. 502,100,000. *Tourism* (1974). Receipts from visitors: U.S. $9,080,000.

Domestic economy

Gross national product (GNP; at current market prices, 1974): U.S. $1,310,000,000 (U.S. $110 per capita).

Origin of gross domestic product (at current factor cost):	1961–62		1961		1972–73		1971	
	value in 000,000 NRs.	% of total value	labour force	% of labour force	value in 000,000 NRs.	% of total value	labour force	% of labour force
agriculture, forestry, hunting, fishing	2,393	64.5	4,040,607	93.8	7,704	68.4	4,579,552	94.4
mining, quarrying	17	0.5	154	—	3	nil	36	nil
manufacturing	450	12.1	80,768	1.9	1,082	9.6	51,902	1.1
construction	141	3.8	5,588	0.1	153	1.4	5,016	0.1
electricity, gas, water	1	nil	1,453	—	29	0.3	1,596	nil
transport, storage, communications	37	1.0	16,371	0.4	347	3.1	9,637	0.2
trade	183	4.9	47,185	1.1	390	3.5	63,560	1.3
banking, insurance, real estate	22	0.6	...	...	163	1.4	3,466	0.1
ownership of dwellings	338	9.1	...	...	779	6.9	...	...
public administration, defense	77	2.1	...	...	228	2.0	...	...
services	50	1.3	114,713	2.7	382	3.4	137,759	2.8
total	3,709	100.0*	4,306,839	100.0	11,260	100.0	4,852,524	100.0

Production (metric tons except as noted, 1974). Agriculture, forestry, hunting, fishing: paddy rice 2,200,000, corn (maize) 800,000, wheat 225,000, sugarcane 265,000, millet 104,000, jute 64,600, potatoes 300,000, milk 678,000, cheese 77,300, oilseeds 62,000, tobacco 7,500; livestock (number of live animals): cattle 6,535,000, buffalo 3,831,000, sheep 2,266,000, goats 2,348,000, pigs 324,000; roundwood 9,272,000 cu m†. Manufacturing: meat 61,000†; sawed wood 220,000 cu m†; sugar 13,600‡; jute 9,600‡; beer 406,600 hectolitres‡; cigarettes 1,878,000 units.
Energy (1972): installed electrical capacity 53,000 kW, production 101,000,000 kWhr (8.6 kWhr per capita).
Persons economically active (1971): 4,852,524 (42.0%), unemployed—no data available.
Price and earnings indexes (1970 = 100):

	1971	1972	1973	1974
consumer price index§	101.3	112.7	119.3	142.9

Land use (1971): total area 14,080,000 ha (forested 31.8%; meadows and pastures 14.2%; agricultural and under permanent cultivation 14.1%; built-on, wasteland, and other 40.0%).*

Foreign trade

Imports (1973–74): NRs. 1,551,000,000 (manufactured goods 46.3%, food and live animals 18.3%, minerals and fuels 10.2%, machinery and transport equipment 9.2%, chemicals 7.6%, raw materials 6.1%‖). *Major import source:* India 90.7%.
Exports (1973–74): NRs. 757,000,000 (food and live animals, including rice 60.6%, raw materials, including jute 24.6%, manufactured goods 9.8%‖). *Major export destination:* India 83.1%.

Transport and communications

Transport. Railroads (1973): total length 72 mi, 115 km; passengers carried 556,000; short tons cargo 65,146, metric tons cargo 59,100. Cable railway (1972): total length 26 mi, 42 km. Roads (1972): total length 1,895 mi, 3,050 km (paved 746 mi, 1,200 km; earth roads and others 1,149 mi, 1,850 km). Vehicles (1972): passenger cars 11,130, trucks and buses 1,940. Merchant marine (1975): vessels (100 gross tons and over) none. Air transport: (1974) passenger-mi 34,000,000, passenger-km 55,000,000, short ton-mi cargo 3,400,000, metric ton-km cargo 5,000,000; (1976) airports with scheduled flights 21.
Communications. Daily newspapers (1971): 30, total circulation 39,000, circulation per 1,000 population 3. Radios (1972): 100,000 (1 per 118 persons). Television (1974): none. Telephones (1973): 8,000 (1 per 1,520 persons).

Education and health

Education (1973–74):	schools	teachers	students	student-teacher ratio
primary (age 6–11)	7,585	18,074	392,229	21.7
secondary and vocational (age 11–17)	1,761	7,749	216,309	27.9
higher	80	1,499	19,198	12.8

College graduates (per 100,000 population, 1968): 7.2. *Literacy* (1971): total population literate (age 15 and over) 862,279 (12.5%); males literate 771,745 (22.4%), females literate 90,534 (2.6%).
Health: (1972) doctors 122 (1 per 96,311 persons); (1971) hospital beds 2,006 (1 per 5,628 persons); (1970) daily per capita caloric intake 2,050 calories (FAO recommended minimum requirement 2,200 calories).

*Percentages do not add to 100.0 because of rounding. †1973. ‡Nine months of 1973–74. §Kāthmāndu only; excluding rent. ‖1969–70.

hanging but upright, cylindrical or urn-shaped, often highly coloured, insect-trapping, pitcher-shaped structure with a lid. Water within the pitcher drowns insects that fall inside.

The flowers, which have no petals, are inconspicuous. Cultivated species include *N. dominii*, *N. hookeriana*, *N. mastersiana*, *N. phyllamphora*, and *N. veitchii*.

·angiosperm diversity, illus. 1 **1**:877
·leaf structure and function **13**:730c

Neper, John: *see* Napier, John.

Nephele (Greek mythology): *see* Argonauts; Athamas.

nepheline, or NEPHELITE, sometimes called ELEOLITE when in coloured, greasy, rough crystals or irregular masses; the most common feldspathoid mineral; a sodium and potassium aluminosilicate ($Na_3KAl_4Si_4O_{16}$).

Nepheline from Litchfield, Maine

By courtesy of the Field Museum of Natural History, Chicago; photograph, John H. Gerard—EB Inc.

It is sometimes used as a substitute for feldspars in the manufacture of glass and ceramics. Nepheline is the characteristic mineral of alkaline plutonic rocks, particularly nephelinesyenites and nephelinegneisses. It occurs in beautiful crystal form with mica, garnet, and sanidine feldspar on Monte Somma, Vesuvius, Italy. For detailed physical properties, *see* table under feldspathoids.

Carnegieite is synthetic, high-temperature nepheline. Kaliophilite is the high-temperature form of kalsilite, the potassium-rich variety of nepheline. Kaliophilite is unstable at normal temperatures and rarely occurs in nature. *Major ref.* **7**:218e

·expanded basalt tetrahedron, illus. 4 **13**:562
·feldspathoid assemblage photograph 2 **7**:219
·igneous rock composition, illus. 5 **9**:207
·silica saturation in igneous rocks **9**:220e
·solid solution and occurrence **16**:762f

nephelinebasalt: *see* nephelinite; basalt.

nephelinebasanite: *see* nephelinite; basanite.

nephelinesyenite, medium- to coarse-grained intrusive igneous rock, a member of the alkali-syenite group (*see* syenite) that consists largely of feldspar and nepheline. It is always considerably poorer in silica and richer in alkalies than granite. The extraordinarily varied mineralogy of the nephelinesyenites and their remarkable variation in habit, fabric, appearance, and composition have attracted much attention; more petrographic research has been devoted to them than to any other plutonic rock. Nephelinesyenite from Canada is used to replace feldspar in the manufacture of ceramic and glass products.

The feldspar in nephelinesyenite may be cryptoperthite or, rarely, a mixture of albite and microcline. Nepheline is sometimes wholly or partly replaced by sodalite or cancrinite. The commonest dark silicate is green pyroxene; and alkaline amphibole (green, brown, or blue) is also abundant. In some areas pyroxene is virtually absent, and it is replaced by a mixture of hornblende and biotite. Rocks that contain more than 30 percent (by volume) of either dark silicates or nepheline usually are not called nephelinesyenite. Quartz and calcium-rich plagioclase feldspar are absent, but calcite is almost never absent and may be abundant. Minerals rich in zirconium, titanium, and rare earths occur frequently and sometimes in great abundance.

The amount of nephelinesyenite and related volcanic or plutonic rocks in the lithosphere is very small; the known or reasonably inferred volume of these rocks is probably less, for instance, than the volume of a single large gabbro complex. Yet they occur in great variety on every major landmass, and volcanic representatives are known from a considerable number of oceanic islands. Plutonic nepheline rocks ordinarily occur in small complexes, some quite isolated, but most in close association with effusive rocks of similar composition. The largest known masses include one on the Kola Peninsula, U.S.S.R., which underlies about 1,950 square kilometres (750 square miles); one in Pilansberg, western Transvaal, South Africa, which underlies about 500 square kilometres; and a third near Julianehåb, Greenland, which underlies about 250 square kilometres. No other dominantly plutonic complexes of comparable size are known, and most, including some of the most closely studied, are very much smaller.

The magmas that give rise to nepheline rocks must be derived from other more abundant magmas or from reaction between these magmas and previously solidified rocks. Despite the great interest in the nephelinesyenites and an immense amount of work that has been done upon them, there is little agreement about the manner in which these rare rocks were formed.

·crust formation and composition changes **5**:1091g
·igneous rock classification **9**:206f; table 207
·mineralogical composition, illus. 5 **9**:207

nephelinetephrite: *see* nephelinite; basanite.

nephelinite, silica-poor (basic) lava that contains nepheline and pyroxene and is usually completely crystallized. Despite its wide geographic distribution and occasional extensive local development, it is a very rare rock. Known only from Tertiary strata (about 2,500,000 to 65,000,000 years in age), nephelinites are abundant in the Canary Islands, the Azores, the Cape Verde Islands, and Isla Fernando de Noronha off the coast of Brazil. Specimens from the Eifel and Kaiserstuhl regions, West Germany, are common in petrographic collections, as are those from central Bohemia, Czechoslovakia, and the Odenwald (Katzenbuckel), West Germany. On the whole they are not common in the Mediterranean area, but leucite-bearing representatives are known from Monte Vulture, Italy, and from Tripoli, North Africa. Nepheline-rich basic lavas are perhaps most extensively developed in eastern Africa, especially in Somalia, Kenya, and Nigeria. In the U.S. they are best known from the Big Bend region, Texas; the Bearpaw Mountains, Montana; and Cripple Creek, Colo.

The pyroxene in nephelinites may be either titanium-rich augite or aegirine; plagioclase, if present, is commonly labradorite. Varieties rich in leucite and haüynite are well-known. Biotite is characteristic in some types; amphibole is scarce. Accessory minerals may include sanidine, melilite, sodalite, perovskite, apatite, and chromite.

The nomenclature of nepheline-rich basalts is confusing but firmly established. The plagioclase-free varieties are called nephelinite if they also lack olivine and nephelinebasalt if olivine is an essential constituent. The plagioclase-bearing varieties are called nephelinetephrite if they lack olivine and nephelinebasanite if olivine is an essential constituent. They are otherwise similar in mineralogy, appearance, structure, and occurrence. The relative abundance of the plagioclase-free and plagioclase-bearing members of the group is a matter of conjecture, as is their quantitative importance compared to normal (*e.g.*, nonfeldspathoidal) basalts.

·archaeological use of petrology **1**:1081g
·dating and correlating methods **8**:999b
·tektite similarities and differences **18**:60b
·Teotihuacán uses and trade **11**:941a

Nephelium lappaceum (tree): *see* rambutan.

nephelometry and turbidimetry, methods for determining the amount of cloudiness or turbidity in a solution based upon measurement of the effect of this turbidity upon the transmission of light. Turbidity in a liquid is caused by the presence of finely divided suspended particles. If a beam of light is passed through a turbid sample, its intensity is reduced by scattering, and the quantity of light scattered is dependent upon the concentration and size distribution of the particles. In nephelometry, measurement is made of the intensity of the scattered light, while, in turbidimetry, measurement is made of the intensity of light transmitted through the sample. Nephelometric and turbidimetric measurements are used in the determination of suspended material in natural waters and in processing streams. The technique is also used for determination of sulfur, which is precipitated as barium sulfate, in coal, oil, and other organic materials.

nephrectomy, in surgery, removal of a kidney.

·post-operative existence of REF **6**:817e
·pregnancy affected by kidney removal **14**:979b
·toxic effects of kidney removal **7**:35f

nephric tubule, or SECRETORY TUBULE, that portion of a nephron (*q.v.*) that conducts urine from the Bowman's capsule to a urine-collecting tube. Cells lining the nephric tubule usually reabsorb water and useful nutrients and actively secrete nitrogenous wastes into the urine.

·animal tissue comparisons **18**:445f
·embryonic kidney developments **5**:635h; illus. 632

human

·anatomic relationships of convoluted tubules **6**:816d; illus.
·renal damage caused by poisons **7**:56h
·water and salt balancing function **7**:429h
·urine formation in distal and proximal tubules **7**:38a

nephridiopore, one of the paired external openings of the nephridia (excretory tubes) in some invertebrates.

·excretory system of annelids **7**:47d
·Sipuncula gamete emission into sea **16**:809h

nephridium, unit of the excretory system in many primitive invertebrates and also in the amphioxus; it expels wastes from the body cavity to the exterior (usually aquatic). The evolution of nephridia encouraged tissue specialization by eliminating the need for all cells of an organism to be in contact with seawater for diffusion of metabolic wastes. The primitive protonephridia of flatworms, ribbon worms, and rotifers are usually scattered among the other body cells. More advanced, segmented invertebrates, such as earthworms, possess metanephridia, usually arranged in pairs.

The protonephridium consists of a hollow cell located in the body cavity and a duct leading from it to an exterior opening (nephridiopore). Fluid in the body cavity filters into the hollow cell, called a flame cell if it possesses cilia or a solenocyte if it has a flagellum. The cilia or the flagellum wave filtered urine down the tube to the outside.

The metanephridium tubule lacks a flame cell and opens directly into the body cavity. Cilia lining the tubule draw up cavity fluids and conduct them to the exterior; tubule cells actively reabsorb useful nutrients as they pass.

·animal excretory system comparisons **13**:723d
·annelid anatomy and function **1**:933f
·echiurids and role in reproduction **6**:186d

·entoproct morphology and function **6**:895g; illus.
·excretory organs of annelids **7**:47b
·protonephridia in annelid anatomy and functioning **1**:933g
·protonephridia in aschelminth excretory system **2**:141c
·Sipuncula and role in reproduction **16**:809h
·urine formation function **7**:37g

nephrite, a gem-quality silicate mineral in the tremolite–actinolite–ferrotremolite series of amphiboles; it is one form of jade. The less prized of the two types of jade, nephrite is usually found as translucent to opaque, compact, dense aggregates of finely interfelted tufts of long, thin fibres. It may be distinguished from jadeite (*q.v.*), jade's other form, by its splintery fracture and oily lustre. Most often coloured green, nephrite is usually mottled or is flecked with dark inclusions.

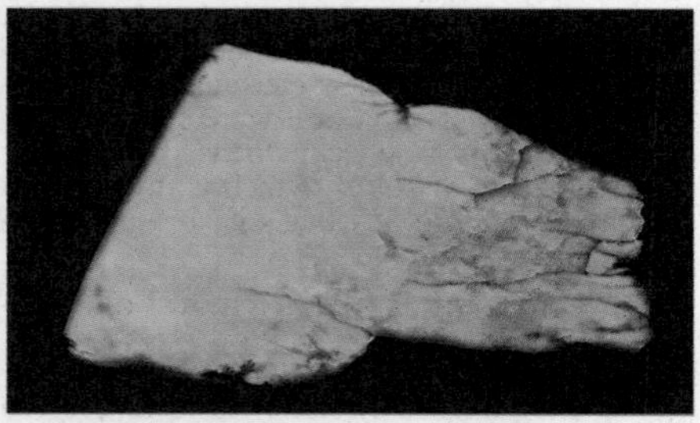

Polished slice of nephrite from South Island, New Zealand

By courtesy of the Field Museum of Natural History, Chicago; photograph, John Gerard—EB Inc.

Nephrite occurs in low-grade, regionally metamorphosed rocks; its occurrences are more numerous than those of jadeite. China's most important source throughout history has been the region of Khotan (Ho-t'ien) and Yarkand in central Asia. Other important sources include the Lake Baikal area, Siberia; South Island, New Zealand; near Kotzebue, Alaska; along the Sweetwater River, Wyoming; and the canton of Graubünden, Switzerland. Great boulders of nephrite have been found near Jordanow Slaski (Jordansmühl) in Silesia, Poland, and in the valleys of the Turnagain and Fraser rivers in British Colombia. Nephrite was found in 1960 at Mashaba, Rhodesia, the first find on the African continent. In 1965 it was found near Hualien. Taiwan (Formosa).

·Chinese source and visual arts **19**:180h
·gem characteristics and economic value **7**:972f
·physical properties and jade use **1**:707e

nephritis (medicine): *see* glomerulonephritis.

nephroblastoma, malignant renal (kidney) tumour of early childhood. The cancer is known by a number of other names including embryoma and Wilms' tumour. In 75 percent of the cases, the tumour grows before the age of five; about two-thirds of the instances are apparent by two years of age. One or both of the kidneys may be affected. The tumour grows and can approach the weight of the rest of the body. It rarely appears in adults. In its early stages the nephroblastoma causes no symptoms. Later, fever, distortion of the kidney mass, evidence of secondary tumours elsewhere in the body, abdominal and flank pain, weight loss, nausea, loss of appetite, and vomiting are possible symptoms.

The tumour begins in the outer (cortical) tissue of the kidney. At first it is surrounded by a dense fibrous capsule. It is usually a grayish-white, soft mass. The tumour tends to destroy the whole kidney and spreads to neighbouring organs. It often causes secondary tumours (metastases) in the lungs, liver, brain, and bones.

The usual treatment, if diagnosis is early enough, is a course of radiation treatments before an operation, removal of the mass by surgery, and postoperative irradiation. Sometimes chemicals are given to slow the cell growth.

·birth defects due to malignant tumours **2**:1074d
·incidence, origin, and prognosis **3**:768b
·renal disease in childhood **7**:58h

Nephrochloris (protozoan): *see* heterochlorid.

nephrogenic diabetes insipidus, passage of excessive amounts of dilute urine, due to failure of the kidneys to reabsorb water and concentrate the urine.

·cause, symptoms, and treatment **6**:820d

nephroid, in geometry, a kidney-shaped algebraic curve of the sixth order.

·analytic geometry fundamentals **7**:1089h

nephron, functional unit of the kidney, responsible for regulating water balance in the body and removing nitrogenous wastes. The most primitive nephrons, found in the pronephros of primitive fish, amphibian larvae, and embryos of more advanced vertebrates, process fluid from two different sources: the body cavity and the bloodstream. Body fluids enter the nephron tubule via a duct called the nephrostome; protein-free blood plasma is filtered from a small knot of capillaries (glomerulus) into an outgrowth of the nephric tubule (the Bowman's capsule) that surrounds the glomerulus. The tubule cells then usually reabsorb water and nutrients and actively secrete wastes into the urine. *See* pronephros.

The nephrons of the mesonephros, found in amphibia, in most fish, and in late embryonic development of more advanced vertebrates, usually lack ducts to the body cavity; in other respects they are like pronephric nephrons. *See* mesonephros.

The most advanced nephrons occur in the adult kidney (metanephros) of land vertebrates—reptiles, birds, and mammals—and are characterized by long nephric tubules where reabsorption and secretion take place; this lengthy process results in a urine that is more concentrated than the blood, an advance that enabled these animals to retain sufficient water for life on land.

The mammalian nephron consists of a Bowman's capsule, which filters plasma from a glomerulus and has a three-part nephric tubule. The portion leaving the Bowman's capsule (proximal convoluted tubule) is tightly coiled and twisted; it leads to the loop of Henle, which is a long, hairpin-shaped section of tubule. The final section, or distal convoluted tubule, again is tightly coiled; it empties into a collecting tubule, each of which serves many nephrons.

·aldosterone effect on sodium metabolism **8**:1082h
·animal tissue comparisons **18**:445e
human
·excretory function and structure **7**:35e
·glomerular filtration in kidney **7**:54h
·kidney and duct system development **6**:752g
·kidney structure and function **7**:51g; illus. 52
·water and salt balancing function **7**:429h
·kidney structure in mammals **7**:48d; illus.
·mammalian excretory mechanism **11**:408b

Nephrops norvegicus: *see* lobster.

nephrosclerosis, hardening of the walls of the small arteries and arterioles (small arteries that convey blood from arteries to the even smaller capillaries) of the kidney. This condition is caused by hypertension (high blood pressure). Hypertension can be present in a person for 20 to 30 years without evidence of kidney involvement; such persons usually die of other effects of hypertension such as congestion of blood in the heart, hardening of the heart tissue, or cerebral (brain) hemorrhage. If these maladies do not occur first, there is usually some eventual renal (kidney) involvement. Nephrosclerosis is classified as benign or malignant.

Benign nephrosclerosis is a gradual and prolonged deterioration of the renal arteries. The kidney may appear either smooth and normal or small, hard, and granular, depending on the length of involvement. The surface often contains small cysts or pale nodules. The arteries and arterioles reveal the nephrosclerosis. First the inner layer of the walls of smaller vessels thickens, and gradually this thickening spreads to the whole wall, sometimes closing the centre channel of the vessel. Fat then becomes deposited in the degenerated wall tissue. The larger arteries gain an excess of elastic tissue, which may block their channels. Both of these conditions cause the blood supply to the vital kidney areas to be blocked, and tissue deterioration ensues.

In malignant nephrosclerosis, a similar process occurs but at a much faster rate. The disease may develop so rapidly that there is little time for gross kidney changes to occur. The surface of the kidney, however, is nearly always covered with large red blotches at points where bleeding has occurred. In the malignant disease the arteriole walls thicken and may be closed off by rapid cell growth. These fast-growing cell layers develop in concentric rings, which usually presents an onionskin appearance. Next the nuclei of these cells die, and the elastic fibres disappear. With the loss of the elastic fibres, the walls of the vessels become much more fragile and easily distended. Massive ruptures and hemorrhages are not infrequent. The arterioles often suffer spasms that can force blood through lesions in the vessel walls; the tissues become swollen as a result.

The symptoms include impaired vision, blood in the urine, loss of weight, and increasing levels of urea in the blood. Urea and other nitrogen waste products accumulate in the blood (*see* uremia). In the early 1970s no cure was known for nephrosclerosis, although persons affected by it may survive for many years. Treatment was directed toward elimination of infection and of any obstruction.

nephrostome, in invertebrate and primitive vertebrate excretory systems, ciliated pore or duct through which body fluids are passed from the body cavity to the nephridium or the nephron.

nephrotic syndrome, group of signs of kidney malfunction, including a low level of albumin (a protein) and a high level of lipids (fats) in the blood, proteins in the urine, and the accumulation of fluid in the tissues. It may result from streptococcal infection, lupus erythematosus (an inflammatory disease of the connective tissues), or heavy metal poisoning.

The nephrotic syndrome occurs usually in young children or young adults. Persons affected may lack appetite and experience irritability, vomiting, and diarrhea. High levels of fluids in the tissues can cause an increase in body weight of up to 50 percent. In children the syndrome shows gross swelling of the face, while in adults the legs are most frequently afflicted. Low blood pressure and low plasma volume from lack of serum proteins occasionally cause severe vascular collapse. Protein malnutrition also leads to muscle wasting and growth retardation, especially in children. The urine often shows lipid particles and crystalline structures known as casts. In treatment, attention is given to the underlying disease and to reduction of the tissue fluids by inducing urination.

·renal disease with proteinuria **7**:56b
·symptoms and treatment **4**:226d

nephrotome, in embryology, a cellular plate in the mesoderm (*q.v.*) that gives rise to much of the urogenital system.

·embryonic kidney developments **5**:635h; illus. 632
·kidney origins and embryogenesis **6**:752f

Nepidae: *see* water scorpion.

Nepos, Cornelius (b. *c.* 100 BC—d. *c.* 25 BC), Roman historian, correspondent and friend of Cicero, biographer of Atticus, and the friend to whom Catullus dedicated his poems. He came, like Catullus, from north Italy.

His principal writings were *De viris illustribus*, brief biographies of distinguished Romans and foreigners; *Chronica*, introducing to the Roman reader a Greek invention, universal comparative chronology; *Exempla*, anecdotes, perhaps a model for the biographer Valerius Maximus; possibly a universal geography to match the *Chronica;* and lives of the elder Cato and Cicero. There survive one complete and one partial book from the *De viris illustribus*. Nepos is not notable as a literary stylist; he writes simply, but without elegance or purity.

·Latin biographical literature **10**:1098f

Nepos, Julius (d. May 9, AD 480), last legitimate Western Roman emperor (ruled 474–480). Born of a distinguished family, he was sent by the Eastern ruler, Leo I, to govern Italy as patrician or supreme magistrate. Nepos at once deposed the Western emperor Glycerius, proclaiming himself emperor in June 474. A year later he was obliged to recognize the independence of the Visigothic kingdom centred near present Toulouse, Fr. Later that year the patrician Orestes rebelled, forcing Nepos to flee to Dalmatia (August 475). He lived at Salona (modern Split, Yugos.) for five years, recognized in Gaul and in the East as emperor, though his position in Italy had been usurped by Orestes' young son, Romulus Augustulus. Nepos was eventually murdered by friends of Glycerius.

nepotism (from Latin *nepos*, "grandson" or "nephew"), favouritism shown to nephews and other relatives, as in the practice of appointing people to positions (*e.g.*, in a government, church, or business organization) on the basis of family relationship.

·Han dynasty royal consort influence **4**:310b
·Innocent IV's use of benefices **9**:607f
·kinship loyalty practices **10**:483a
·Pius IV's effective use **15**:1012e

Nepszabadsag ("People's Freedom"), Hungarian daily newspaper and official organ of the Communist Party. Published in Budapest, its circulation was 750,000 in 1969.

Nepticulidae: *see* midget moth.

Neptune, Latin NEPTUNUS, Etruscan NETHUNS, in Roman religion, god of freshwater and hence not originally a sea god. His female counterpart, Salacia, was perhaps a goddess of leaping springwater. By 399 BC, however, he was identified with the Greek Poseidon and thus became a deity of the sea. Subsequently Salacia was equated with the Greek Amphitrite.

Neptune holding his trident, classical sculpture; in the Lateran Museum, Rome

Alinari

Neptune's festival (Neptunalia) took place in the heat of the summer (July 23) when water was scarcest; thus its purpose was probably the propitiation of the freshwater deity. Neptune had a temple in the Circus Flaminius at Rome; one of its features was a sculptured group of marine deities headed by Poseidon and Thetis. In art Neptune appears as the Greek Poseidon, whose attributes are the trident and the dolphin.

·earthquake causes **6**:74h

Neptune 12:963, in astronomy, the eighth major planet from the Sun.

The text article covers the calculations and events leading to the discovery of the planet in 1846; the results of observation since then; theories of Neptune's constitution; and measurements of its rotation rate and diameter and calculation of its density. The concluding section describes the two known satellites.

REFERENCES in other text articles:
·confirmation of Newtonian mechanics **14**:388g
·life's origin and possible existence **10**:901a
·Pluto's perturbations and discovery **14**:580b; illus.
·prediction and discovery **8**:288e
·radio-wave emissions **15**:470e
·Solar System bodies data table **16**:1029g
·spectroscopic research findings **2**:241h

Neptune satellites include Triton and Nereid. Triton, whose estimated diameter is about 3,700 kilometres (about 2,300 miles), is probably larger than Earth's Moon and may be one of the few satellites in the solar system massive enough to hold some atmosphere. It revolves around Neptune in the retrograde direction—*i.e.*, in a direction opposite to that of Neptune's rotation—in 5.877 days, at about 355,000 kilometres (about 220,000 miles) distance. Its circular orbit is inclined at 159.9° (or 20.1° taking account of Triton's retrograde motion) to the plane of Neptune's equator. Triton was discovered Oct. 10, 1846, by the English astronomer William Lassell.

Neptune satellites Nereid (left of arrow) and Triton (below Neptune on the right); image of Neptune is deliberately overexposed

By courtesy of Hale Observatories; photograph, M. Humason

Nereid, estimated to be about 300 kilometres (190 miles) in diameter, revolves in the same direction Neptune rotates, in 359.881 days. The inclination of Nereid's orbit is only 27.7°, but the orbital eccentricity is so high (0.749) that Nereid approaches as near as 1,330,000 kilometres (826,000 miles) to Neptune and recedes as far as 9,760,000 kilometres (6,100,000 miles). Nereid was discovered in 1949 by the U.S. astronomer Gerard P. Kuiper.

·discovery and orbit changes **12**:965a; table
·Solar System bodies' satellites **16**:1030b

neptunium (after planet Neptune), symbol Np, radioactive chemical element of the actinide series in Group IIIb of the periodic table, first transuranium element to be artificially produced, atomic number 93. Though traces of neptunium have subsequently been found in nature, where it is not primeval but produced by neutron-induced transmutation reactions in uranium ores, Edwin M. McMillan and Philip H. Abelson first found neptunium in 1940 after uranium had been bombarded by neutrons from the cyclotron at Berkeley, Calif. Neptunium has been produced in weighable amounts in breeder reactors as a by-product of plutonium production from the fertile uranium isotope, uranium-238 (about one part neptunium is produced for every 1,000 parts plutonium). All neptunium isotopes are radioactive; the stablest is neptunium-237 (alpha emitter of 2,140,000-year half-life).

Neptunium, a silvery metal, exists in three crystalline modifications; the room-temperature form (alpha) is orthorhombic. Neptunium is chemically reactive and similar to uranium with oxidation states from +3 to +6. Neptunium ions in aqueous solution possess characteristic colours: Np^{3+}, pale purple; Np^{4+}, pale yellow-green; NpO_2^{+}, green-blue; NpO_2^{2+}, varying from colourless to pink or yellow-green, depending on the acid present.

atomic number	93
stablest isotope	237
melting point	640° C (1,184° F)
specific gravity (alpha)	20.45
valence	3,4,5,6
electronic config.	2-8-18-32-22-9-2 or (Rn)$5f^4 6d^1 7s^2$

·atomic weight and number table **2**:345
·compound stability and valency **1**:69c
·transuranium element origins **18**:678e

neptunium series, one of four radioactive series (*q.v.*), is a set of artificially produced and unstable species of atomic nuclei that are genetically related through alpha and beta decay, ending with stable bismuth-209 (atomic number 83) and named for its longest lived member, neptunium-237.

Alpha (α-) decay, symbolized by a larger arrow in the accompanying diagram, involves the ejection from an unstable nucleus of a particle composed of two protons and two neutrons. Thus alpha emission lowers the atomic number (proton number) by two units, the neutron number by two units, and the mass number (total number of protons and neutrons) by four units. Thus neptunium-237 (Np, atomic number 93) decays by alpha emission to protactinium-233 (Pa, atomic number 91).

Negative beta (β^--) decay, symbolized by a smaller arrow, involves the ejection from an unstable nucleus of an electron and an antineutrino that are produced by the decay of a neutron into a proton. Negative beta emission, therefore, lowers the neutron number by one unit, raises the atomic number by one unit, and leaves the mass number unchanged. Thus protactinium-233 decays by negative beta emission to uranium-233 (U, atomic number 92).

Because the two pertinent decay processes result either in no change or a change of four units in the mass number, the mass numbers of all the members of the series are divisible by four with a remainder of one. The mass number of each, therefore, may be expressed as four times an appropriate integer (n) plus one or simply as $4n + 1$. The neptunium series is sometimes called the $4n + 1$ series. After uranium, the series continues on to thorium-229, radium-225, actinium-225, francium-221, astatine-217, bismuth-213, which branches by negative beta decay (97.8 percent) to polonium-213 and by alpha decay (2.2 percent) to thallium-209. Both of these in turn decay to lead-209 (Pb), which disintegrates into the stable end product, bismuth-209. Two antecedents of neptunium, plutonium-241 and americium-241, are also included.

The half-life of each member (time interval for half of a given sample to decay into its daughter product) is enclosed in parentheses.

The longest half-life is that of neptunium-237 (2,200,000 years), a short interval compared with the age of the Earth. No primordial nep-

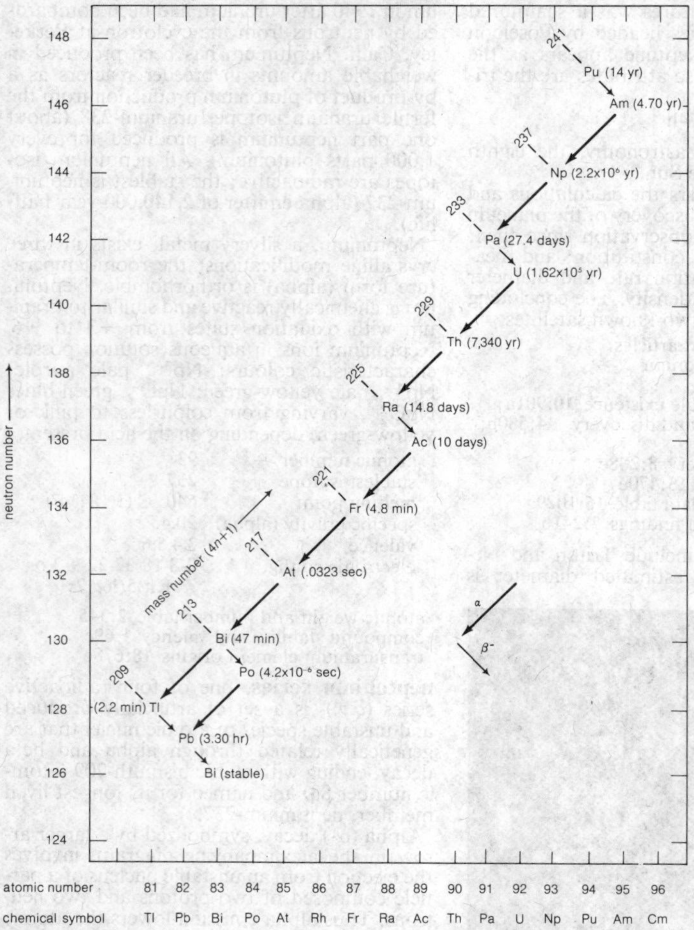

Neptunium series

tunium is left on Earth, so that the members of this series do not occur in nature, but they are produced artificially by nuclear reactions.
·discovery and decay-products **13**:325a
·fissionable material preparation **13**:302e
·uranium chain reaction in atomic bomb **13**:315d

Neptunus (crab): *see* swimming crab.

Nepveu, Pierre (d. 1542), French architect and sculptor.
·Chambord château execution **19**:390g

Nerbudda River (India): *see* Narmada River.

Nerchinsk, town, Chita *oblast* (administrative region), east central Russian Soviet Federated Socialist Republic, on the Nercha River just above its confluence with the Shilka. It was founded as a fort in 1658; in 1689 the Treaty of Nerchinsk between Russia and China gave Transbaikalia to Russia and the Amur Valley to China. Once an important customs post and trading centre on the route to China, Nerchinsk declined into insignificance when bypassed by the Trans-Siberian Railroad in the late 19th century. There are minor electromechanical and food-processing industries. Latest pop. est. 15,000.
51°58′ N, 116°35′ E

Nerchinsk, Treaty of (1689), peace settlement between Russia and the Manchu Chinese Empire, checked Russia's eastward expansion by removing its outposts from the Amur Basin. Russia lost easy access to the Sea of Okhotsk and Far Eastern markets but secured its claim to Transbaikalia and gained the right of passage to Peking for its trade caravans. The border between the two countries was set along the Stanovoy Range and the Argun River. A success for V.V. Golitsyn's foreign policy, the treaty prevented Russia's potential military defeat and gained China's implied recognition of Russia as a state of equal status, an accomplishment not achieved by other European countries. Confirmed and expanded by the Kyakhta treaty (1727), the Nerchinsk treaty remained the basis of Russo-Chinese relations until 1858–60.
·Ch'ing dynasty's Russian relationships **4**:355b
·Heilungkiang Sino-Russian border clash **8**:741e
·K'ang-hsi's precipitation of crisis **10**:380f
·Russian expansion in Manchuria **11**:437b
·Russo-Chinese border settlement **9**:600h

Nereid (astronomy): *see* Neptune satellites.

Nereids, in Greek mythology, the daughters (numbering 50 or 100) of a sea god, Nereus (eldest son of Pontus, a personification of the sea), and of Doris, daughter of Oceanus (the god of the water encircling the Earth). They were imagined as young girls, inhabiting any water, salt or fresh, and as benign toward mankind. The best known of the Nereids were Amphitrite, consort of Poseidon (a sea and earthquake god); Thetis, wife of Peleus (king of the Myrmidons) and mother of the hero Achilles; and Galatea, a Sicilian figure loved by the Cyclops Polyphemus.
·Hesiod's genealogy of the gods **8**:830f

Nereis: *see* rag worm.

Nereocystis luetkeana, species of marine brown kelp of the family Lessoniaceae, order Laminariales.

Neretva River, in the republics of Bosnia and Hercegovina and Croatia, Yugoslavia, rises on Lebršnik Mountain, and flows northwest past Konjic to Jablanica Lake (Jablaničko Jezero), then southwest via Mostar to enter the Adriatic Sea; its total length is 135 mi (218 km). The upper course runs through canyons and gorges in unsettled country. The Jablanica Dam created a manmade lake for a hydroelectric station. The lower valley is an area of inland penetration of the Mediterranean climate of the Dalmatian coast. During World War II, the crossing of the Neretva by partisan forces avoided encirclement by superior German forces.
43°01′ N, 17°27′ E
·map, Yugoslavia **19**:1100

Nereus, in Greek religion, sea god called by Homer "Old Man of the Sea"; noted for his wisdom, gift of prophecy, and ability to change his shape. He was the son of Pontus, a personification of the sea, and Gaea, an Earth goddess. The Nereids (water nymphs) were his daughters by the Oceanid Doris, and he lived with them in the depths of the sea, particularly the Aegean. Aphrodite, the goddess of love, was his pupil. The Greek hero Heracles, in his quest for the golden apples of the Hesperides,

Nereus struggling with Heracles, detail from a Greek water jar found at Vulci, *c.* 490 BC; in the British Museum
By courtesy of the trustees of the British Museum

obtained directions from Nereus by wrestling with him in his many forms. Nereus frequently appears in vase paintings as a dignified spectator.
·Hesiod's genealogy of the gods **8**:830f

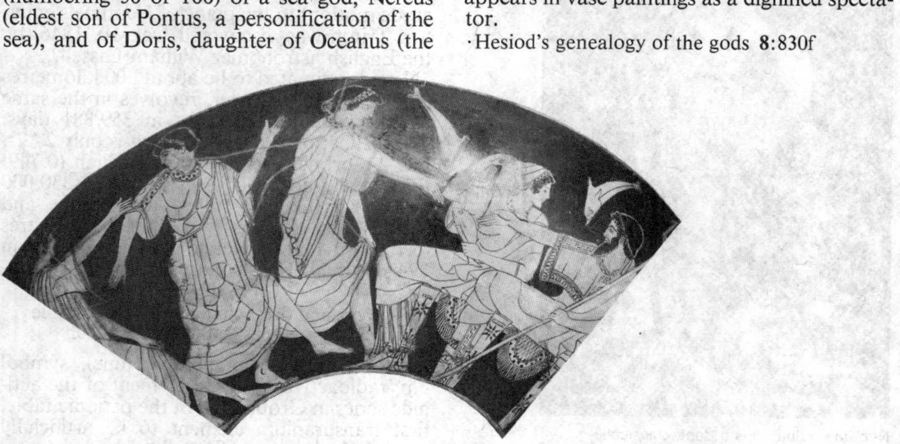
Nereus and the Nereids, detail of a red-figure cup; in the Louvre
Alinari

Nergal, in Mesopotamian religion, secondary god of the Sumero-Akkadian pantheon. He was identified with Irra, the god of scorched

Nergal, holding his lion-headed staffs, terra-cotta relief from Kish, *c.* 2100–*c.* 1500 BC; in the Ashmolean Museum, Oxford, Eng.

By courtesy of the Ashmolean Museum, Oxford, Eng.

earth and war, and with Meslamtaea, He Who Comes Forth from Meslam. Cuthah (modern Tall Ibrāhīm) was the chief centre of his cult. In later thought he was a "destroying flame" and had the epithet *sharrapu* ("burner"). Assyrian documents of the 1st millennium BC describe him as a benefactor of men, who hears prayers, restores the dead to life, and protects agriculture and flocks. Hymns depict him as a god of pestilence, hunger, and devastation.

The other sphere of Nergal's power was the underworld, of which he became king. According to one text, Nergal, escorted by demons, descended to the underworld where the goddess Ereshkigal (or Allatum) was queen. He threatened to cut off her head, but she saved herself by becoming his wife, and Nergal obtained kingship over the underworld.

Nergal did not figure prominently in epics and myths, although he did have a part in the *Epic of Gilgamesh* and the deluge story. The cult of Nergal was widespread beyond the borders of Sumer and Akkad, where it first appeared. He had a sanctuary at Mari (modern Tell al-Ḥarīrī), on the Euphrates. He is named in inscriptions of Assyrian kings, and evidence of his cult is found in Canaan and at Athens.

Nergal-Shar-Usur (reigned c. 559–556 BC), Babylonian king of the Chaldean dynasty and son-in-law of Nebuchadrezzar.
·Babylonian territorial expansion **11**:988g

Neri (d. 1394): *see* Acciaiuoli, Ranieri I.

Neri, Saint Philip, originally FILIPPO NERI (b. July 21, 1515, Florence—d. May 26, 1595, Rome), one of the outstanding mystics during the Counter-Reformation and founder of the Congregation of the Oratory (Oratorians), a congregation of secular priests and clerics. He went to Rome *c.* 1533, where he tutored, studied, and undertook many charitable works. In 1548 he founded a society of laymen dedicated to the care of the poor, convalescents, and pilgrims. After ordination in 1551 he moved to the ecclesiastical community at San Girolamo della Carità, Italy. There he held religious conferences that became so popular that a large room was built over the church nave to accommodate his audiences. This room was called the Oratory, a name that subsequently referred to those who met there and to the devotional, charitable, and recreational activities that Philip instituted, including musical performances (hence "oratorio").

Philip was rector of the church of San Giovanni, Italy, from 1564 to 1575, during which period he ordained his disciples. In 1575 Pope Gregory XIII granted him Sta. Maria Church in Vallicella, Italy, where he established the Institute of the Oratory. A house was built for the priests, and Philip, elected provost of the congregation in 1577, resided there after 1583.

Although Philip helped influence Pope Clement VIII to absolve (1595) King Henry IV of France from excommunication, he had little to do with contemporary political events. Noted for his personal spirituality, he underwent numerous ecstatic religious experiences, and many miracles were attributed to him.

"Madonna and Child Appearing to San Filippo Neri," oil painting by Giovanni Battista Piazzetta (1682-1754); in the National Gallery of Art, Washington, D.C.

By courtesy of the National Gallery of Art, Washington, D.C., Samuel H. Kress Collection, 1961

Pope Gregory XV canonized him in 1622, and his feast day is May 26. Several lives have been translated into English, including those by F.I. Antrobus (1902) and T.A. Pope (1926); V.J. Matthews' *St. Philip Neri* appeared in 1934.

Nerina, Nadia, originally NADINE JUDD (b. October 1927, Cape Town), South African-born prima ballerina renowned for her remarkable versatility of roles. After touring South Africa in 1942, she went to England in 1945, where she studied under Dame Marie Rambert. Nerina became prima ballerina of the Royal Ballet in 1951, excelling in both classical, especially *La Fille mal gardée*, and modern repertoires. Among her greatest performances was the title role in *Elektra* (1963), which was created for her by Sir Robert Murray Helpmann. In the U.S.S.R. she appeared as guest artist with the Bolshoi and Leningrad Kirov ballets.

Nering, Johann Arnold (1659–95), German architect.
·Berlin summer palace Baroque design **2**:849g

Nerio (mythology): *see* Bellona.

neritic zone, the shallow marine environment extending from mean low water down to 200-metre (660-foot) depths, generally corresponding to the continental shelf. Neritic waters are penetrated by varying amounts of sunlight, which permits photosynthesis by both planktonic and bottom-dwelling organisms. The zone is characterized by relatively abundant nutrients and biologic activity because of its proximity to land. Coarse, land-derived materials generally constitute the bottom sediments, except in some low-latitude regions that favour coral-algal reef development.
·Atlantic characteristics **2**:302g
·location with respect to littoral zone, illus. 2 **13**:485

Nerium oleander, species of plant of the family Apocynaceae, order Gentianales.

Nernst, Walther Hermann (b. June 25, 1864, Briesen, Prussia, now in East Germany—d. Nov. 18, 1941, Muskau, now in East Germany), one of the founders of modern physical chemistry. His formulation of the third law of thermodynamics gained him the 1920 Nobel Prize for Chemistry. Simply stated, the law postulates that, at a temperature above absolute zero (0° K or −273° C), all matter tends toward random motion and all energy tends to dissipate. Educated at the universities of Zürich, Graz (Austria), and Würzburg (now in West Germany), in 1887 he became an assistant to Wilhelm Ostwald who, with Jacobus van't Hoff and Svante Arrhenius, was establishing the independence of physical chemistry. He was appointed to the physics department of the University of Göttingen (now in West Germany) in 1890 and in 1905 went to the University of Berlin where he was director of the Institute for Experimental Physics from 1924 to 1933.

Nernst's research concerning the theory of galvanic cells, the thermodynamics of chemical equilibrium, the properties of vapours at high temperature and of solids at low temperature, and the mechanism of photochemistry has had important applications in industry and science.

Nernst was also interested in applied science. He invented an improved electric light and an electronically amplified piano. His influential textbook of theoretical chemistry was first published in 1893. In later years he concerned himself chiefly with astrophysical theories.
·electrochemical diffusion layer **6**:644f
·heat principles and theory **8**:704g
·relaxation process of nitrogen tetroxide **15**:589c
·thermodynamics mathematical theory **14**:407b
·thermodynamic theory development **18**:291g

Nernst equation, mathematical relationship between the potential of an electrolytic cell (*q.v.*) and the equilibrium constant of a reversible oxidation-reduction reaction that can occur within the cell. *See also* chemical equilibrium.
·chemical reactions and equilibrium **7**:1030c
·electrochemical electrode potential **6**:644a
·oxidation-reduction analysis **13**:808c

Nernst heat theorem, also called THIRD LAW OF THERMODYNAMICS (physics): *see* thermodynamics, laws of.

Nero 12:965, original name LUCIUS DOMITIUS AHENOBARBUS (b. Dec. 15, AD 37, Rome—d. 68, Rome), the fifth Roman emperor, remembered for his unstable character and his cruelty.

Abstract of text biography. Emperor from 54, he was a model sovereign until AD 59, when he put his mother to death. He did the same to his wife, Octavia, in 62. Fancying himself an artist and an actor, he also became obsessed with novel religious cults. His court's extravagance necessitated heavy exactions from the provinces, provoking unrest and making enemies for Nero outside the city; and his bizarre private and public actions alienated powerful Romans. Revolts broke out, and the Senate condemned Nero to death. Abandoned by his guards, he fled and probably committed suicide.

REFERENCES in other text articles:
·adoption and political inheritance 4:697d
·canal construction attempt 3:755b
·Christian ridicule through mime 18:221b
·despotism and persecutions 15:1112d
·Domus Aurea construction 15:1077c
·liberation of Greece 8:390d
·millennialist portrayal as Antichrist 12:201e
·Olympics sportsmanship abuses 17:514a
·performance in Theatre of Dionysus 18:237b
·Petronius' role as arbiter of taste 14:190b
·symbolic representation in Revelation to John 2:972g
·urban planning and development 15:1069a
·Vespasian's career advancement 19:95g
·water purification in Rome 1:1037g

Nero, Gaius, Roman general, consul in 207 BC.
·Punic Wars Roman victories 15:279e

Nero Claudius Drusus: *see* Drusus, Nero Claudius.

Nerocystis, genus of kelp (*q.v.*).

Neronov, Ivan (1591–1670), Russian priest.
·Nikon's reform movement influences 13:101e

ner tamid (Hebrew: "eternal light"), lamp that burns perpetually in a Jewish synagogue before or near the holy ark (*aron ha-qodesh*). It reminds the congregation of the holiness of the Torah scrolls that are stored within the ark and calls to mind God's abiding presence

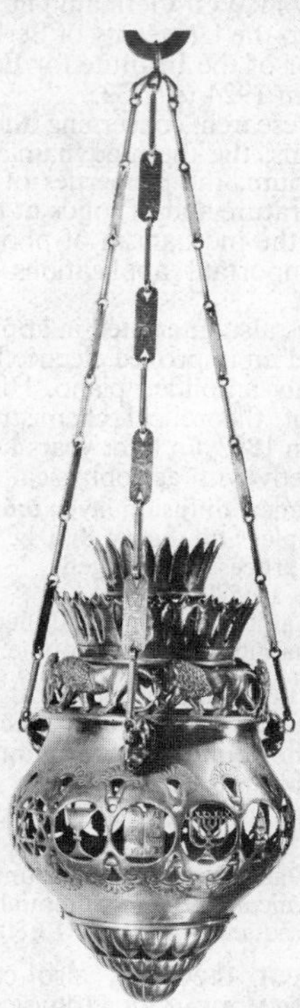

Ner tamid, Russian or Polish, 1884

Picture from the photographic archives of the Jewish Theological Seminary of America, New York; Frank J. Darmstaedter

and his providential care of the Jewish people. The *ner tamid* also represents the light that burned continuously in the western section of the Temple of Jerusalem.

Nerthus, ancient Germanic goddess known from a report of her given by the Roman historian Tacitus, who in his *Germania* (late 1st century AD) refers to her as Terra Mater, or Mother Earth, and says that she was worshipped by seven tribes (among whom were the Angles, who later invaded England). Her worship centred on a temple in a sacred grove on an island in the Baltic Sea. She was said to enjoy coming among her people, riding in a chariot pulled by cows. Her presence was discerned by her priest, and while she was among them her people lived in peace, with no war or fighting and much rejoicing. When she returned to her temple, she and her chariot were washed in a sacred lake by slaves, who were then drowned in the lake.

Her name is to be identified with that of Njörd, who, however, was a god. Thus her sex is questionable, and she may have been hermaphroditic. Many elements of her ritual can be seen in later Germanic religion.
·Germanic religion pantheon 8:38c

Neruda, Pablo 12:967, original name NEFTALÍ RICARDO REYES (b. July 12, 1904, Parral, Chile—d. Sept. 23, 1973, Santiago), diplomat and, as one of the most prolific and original of poets writing in the Spanish language, winner of the Nobel Prize for Literature in 1971.

Abstract of text biography. The son of a railway worker, Neruda started to write poetry at a very early age. When he began to publish it, he adopted his pseudonym so as not to offend his father, and it became his official name in 1946. In October 1921 he won first prize in the Federation of Chilean Students' poetry competition with "La canción de la fiesta." His first book, *Crespusculario* (1923), was published at his own expense, but the next year he found a publisher willing to shoulder the risk for *Veinte poemas de amor y una canción desesperada* (1924; *Twenty Love Poems and a Song of Despair*, 1969). In 1927 he began his career in the Chilean foreign service, serving in a succession of Asian posts until 1933, when he was transferred to the consulate at Buenos Aires, where he met the Spanish poet Federico García Lorca. Assigned next to Barcelona, then Madrid, Neruda began to be recognized in Spain, but the Spanish Civil War interrupted normal cultural exchanges, and Neruda, horrified by the excesses, became an avowed Communist. Recalled in 1938 and sent to Mexico, Neruda wrote much poetry, stimulated by the onset of World War II. The Russian defense of Stalingrad impressed him particularly. Returning to Chile in 1943, Neruda received a great welcome and went into politics, becoming a senator in 1945. From 1948 until 1952, to avoid persecution by the rightist government, Neruda absented himself from Chile, travelling widely. Under less repressive Chilean regimes from 1953, he devoted himself to writing, though he undertook a final diplomatic assignment in 1970 to Paris, residing there until shortly before he died.

REFERENCE in other text article:
·political tone and influence 10:1241b

Nerva, in full MARCUS COCCEIUS NERVA (b. *c.* AD 30—d. end of January, 98), Roman emperor from Sept. 18, 96, to January 98, the first of a succession of rulers known as the "five good emperors." A member of a distinguished senatorial family, he was distantly related by marriage to the Julio-Claudian house, and had been twice consul (AD 71 and 90) when, on the assassination of the emperor Domitian, he became emperor. A number of elder statesmen emerged from retirement to help him govern the empire. The keynote of Nerva's regime was a skillfully propagandized renunciation of the terrorist means by which Domitian had imposed his tyranny. Sound, though uninspired, laws were implemented in Italy, including the last *lex populi* in Roman history and an agrarian reform measure. The one imaginative innovation commonly attributed to Nerva's government, the system of *alimenta*, or trusts for the maintenance of poor children, was probably the work of Trajan. In order to secure the succession, Nerva in 97 adopted and took as his colleague Marcus Ulpius Traianus (Trajan), governor of one of the German provinces. Trajan became emperor on Nerva's death.
·Hadrian's political rivalry origin 8:539c
·liberal policy failure 15:1113f
·Tacitus' political experience 17:983c
·Trajan's succession selection and acceptance 18:593d

Nerva, town, Huelva province, Andalusia, southwestern Spain, a small mining town situated approximately 35 mi (55 km) northwest of Seville. Near Río Tinto, the centre of one of the oldest mining districts in the world, Nerva still relies economically on the mining of copper and pyrites. The mines themselves, probably worked by the Phoenicians and certainly by the Romans (AD 96–400), still yield copper ore of significant economic value. Pop. (1970) 10,915.
37°42′ N, 6°32′ W

Nerval, Gérard de, pseudonym of GÉRARD LABRUNIE (b. May 22, 1808, Paris—d. Jan. 26, 1855, Paris), poet, one of the first of the Symbolists and Surrealists in French literature. Nerval demonstrated an understanding of the dream as a means of communication between the everyday and supernatural worlds. His writings are a reflection and analysis of his own experiences and dreams, the visions and fantasies that constantly threatened his grip on sanity.

His father, a doctor, was sent to serve with Napoleon's Rhine army; his mother died when he was two years old, and he grew up in the care of a great-uncle at Montefontaine in the Valois. The memory of his childhood there was to haunt him as an idyllic vision for the rest of his life. In 1820 he went to live with his father in Paris and attend the Collège de Charlemagne, where he met the poet Théophile Gautier, with whom he formed a lasting friendship. Nerval began to frequent cafes with other artists, painters, romantics, and bohemians. He received a legacy from his grandparents and was able to travel in Italy, but the rest of his inheritance he poured into an ill-fated drama review. Nerval was at this time very much interested in German literature: he adapted Goethe's *Faust* into French, and wrote a collection of stories, *La Main de gloire* (1832; "The Hand of Glory"), in the manner of E.T.W. Hoffmann.

In 1836 Nerval met Jenny Colon, an actress with whom he fell passionately in love; two years later, however, she married another man, and in 1842 she died. She became for Nerval a figure of the dream, the opening up of the flow of the dream into ordinary life.

In the same year, 1842, Nerval travelled to the Levant, the result being some of his best work in *Voyage en Orient* (1843–51; "Voyage to the East"), a travelogue that also examines ancient and folk mythology, symbols, and religion.

During the period of his greatest creativity, Nerval was afflicted with severe mental disorder and was confined at least eight times. He had identified Jenny Colon with the Virgin Mary, who promised him salvation in *Aurélia* (1853–54). *Des Filles du feu* (1854; "Girls of Fire"), which includes the story "Sylvie," evokes his dream of a lost paradise of beauty, fulfillment, innocence, and youth. *Les Chimères* (1854; "The Chimeras") are sonnets that perhaps best convey the musical quality of his writing. Nerval's years of destitution and anguish ended in 1855, when he was found hanging from a lamppost in the rue de la Vieille Lanterne, in Paris.
·French literature of the 19th century 10:1194a

nerve: *see* nerves and nervous system.

nerve cell (biology): *see* neuron.

nerve cord, part of the nervous system of all vertebrates and many invertebrates, leading from clusters of nerve cells called ganglia or from a brain to the posterior of the body. Animals with a single, hollow nerve cord above (or, in bipeds, behind) the digestive system

are called chordates. Invertebrates have solid nerve cords beneath the digestive system. Most of these animals have one or two nerve cords, but invertebrates with radial symmetry have radially arranged nerve cords.
·chordate distinguishing characteristics **4**:450d
·comparative development of nervous system **12**:980a *passim* to 981c

nerve deafness, loss of hearing due to some sort of damage to the auditory nerve.
·cause, symptoms, and treatment **5**:1136d

nerve ending, sensory receptors, which are ends of peripheral nerve fibres located in the skin or subcutaneous tissues. The endings may be free, have expanded tips, or be encapsulated. Their function is the reception and transmission of tactile sensations (*i.e.*, heat, cold, pain, pressure, vibration) to the brain.
·automata theory and mathematical models **2**:497e
·chemoreceptive structures of amphibians **4**:184d
·pain reception and perception **13**:866d
·skin senses and reception process **16**:548h; illus. 549

nerve fibre, a long extension or process extending from a nerve cell body (neuron). The fibre may be an axon, which carries impulses away from the cell body, or a sensory fibre, which relays impulses from a muscle.
·aging effects in spine and sense organs **1**:302c
·autonomic system anatomy and physiology **12**:1024f
·axon growth and function **12**:996a
·brain and spinal cord components **12**:998d
·cranial nerve structures and functions **12**:1017c
·joint nerve supply **10**:258f
·neuron structure and function **12**:978a
·neurosecretory cell structure **6**:847a; illus.
preganglionic fibre
·locations, structure, and function **12**:1024g; illus. 1026
·peripheral nervous system structures **12**:1017d
·spinal nerve components **12**:1022b
·structure, length, and function **12**:969a; illus. 971

nerve gas, chemical warfare gas the principal poisonous effect of which is upon the nervous system. *See also* chemical warfare.
·enzyme inhibition mechanisms **6**:900h
·ocean pollution consequences **1**:1031d
·organic phosphate compounds **13**:703e

nerve impulse 12:968, the electrical unit of information carried by nerve fibres throughout the bodies of multicellular animals. Nerve impulses consist of brief electrical events called action potentials, which occur in response to a stimulus.
The text article deals with the following topics: the structure of nerve cells, the general features of a nerve impulse, the way in which an action potential originates and is conducted as a result of the electric currents it generates, the mechanisms involved in transmitting impulses between cells, and ways by which the nerve impulse is studied.
REFERENCES in other text articles:
·anatomic basis of transmission **12**:996c
·anesthesia's interference with transmission **1**:867f
·animal tissue comparisons **18**:446c
·annelid giant nerve fibre function **1**:934g
·automata theory and mathematical models **2**:497e
·autonomic transmission mechanisms **12**:1033g
·avoidance behaviour and locomotion **2**:543a
·bioelectric mechanism **2**:999a
·bioelectric responses to stimuli **3**:1050b
·biophysical research topic **2**:1036b
·cerebral neuron firing rates in sleep **16**:878g
·conduction speed and intensity **12**:1011a
·drug action on neurotransmitters **17**:692g
·duration and time perception **18**:423a
·eye anatomy and function **7**:102e
·hearing mechanism in man **5**:1127g
·hearing organ direct measurements **17**:42b
·heartbeat regulation mechanism **3**:879f
·Helmholtz' velocity research **8**:752f
·inflammatory reaction control **9**:561g
·information transfer physiology **14**:438f
·learning and neurophysiology **18**:600d
·mathematical analysis **2**:999a
·mechanoreceptive nerve stimulation **11**:801h
·muscle contraction mechanisms **12**:624c; illus.
·muscle innervation and contraction **12**:641b
·nervous system's general features **12**:976a
·photoreceptive physiological responses **14**:364e
·properties and technological imitation **2**:1033e
·sedative-hypnotic drug effects **16**:456h
sensory impulse
·nervous system dynamics **12**:976h
·transmission characteristics **12**:968g; illus.
·sensory-reception theory **16**:545g
·sensory receptor structure and process **16**:547h
·thermoreceptors and nerve activity **18**:328d *passim* to 332d
RELATED ENTRIES in the *Ready Reference and Index: for*
electrical events: see action potential; end-plate potential; excitatory postsynaptic potential; resting potential
other: acetylcholine; synapse

nerve net, primitive nerve arrangement forming the entire nervous system of many cnidarians and a part of more advanced nervous systems. Cytoplasmic processes join the nerve cells (neurons) of nerve nets. In cnidarians the neurons are joined to epithelial receptors and to contractile cells. In vertebrates, nerve nets may be found around blood vessels and the alimentary tract.
·comparative development of nervous system **12**:979d; illus. 981
·muscle control in coelenterates **12**:643d

nerve plexus, digestive, intricate layers of nervous tissue that control movements in the lower esophagus, stomach, and intestines. The mechanics of the nervous system's regulation of digestive functions is not fully known. Two major nerve centres are involved: the myenteric plexus (Auerbach's plexus) and the submucous plexus (or Meissner's plexus). The myenteric plexus is situated between the circular muscle layer and the longitudinal muscle layer in the lower esophagus, stomach, and intestines. The submucous plexus, as its name implies, is located in the submucosal tissue, which connects the surface mucous membrane lining to the deeper muscle layers in the stomach and intestines.
The myenteric plexus receives its messages from the vagus nerve of the parasympathetic nerve system. The plexus responds by transmitting the message to muscle cells, which are thereby activated to contract. Control of nerve impulses is involuntary. The muscles of the stomach and intestines play an active role in digestion, as waves of muscle contractions (peristaltic waves) push food along through the different segments of the digestive tract. It is thought that the myenteric plexus stimulates the muscles to contract in peristaltic waves and that it helps keep muscle tone throughout the intestine walls, promotes secretions of intestinal juices, and allows muscular constrictions (sphincters) to open, thus permitting food to pass from one part of the digestive system to another.
The function of the submucous plexus is not as clearly defined. In the stomach its role may be partly inhibitory, working against the myenteric plexus to control the muscular contractions more finely. In the intestines it is generally believed to work in accord with the myenteric plexus in producing peristaltic waves and increasing digestive secretions. The nerve impulse is again involuntary.
·cardiospasm causes and treatments **5**:798d
·digestive system anatomy **5**:792g
·megacolon causation and treatment **5**:801b

nerve ring, in some invertebrate animals, a rudimentary central nervous system consisting of a ring of nerves around the mouth or esophagus.
·comparative development of nervous system **12**:979f
·nematode nervous system **2**:141e; illus. 140

nerves and nervous systems 12:975, the means by which living organisms react to changes in both their external and internal environments.
TEXT ARTICLE covers:
General features **12**:975f
Nervous coordination 976b
Invertebrate nervous systems 979a
The vertebrate nervous system 982a
Biodynamics of the vertebrate nervous system 991f
REFERENCES in other text articles:
comparative zoology
·adrenaline and noradrenalin release **8**:1081g
·aggressive behaviour brain sites **1**:296b
·aging processes and effects **1**:302b
·animal organ systems comparisons **13**:722e
·animal tissue comparisons **18**:446b
·automata theory and mathematical models **2**:497e
·avoidance behaviour and locomotion **2**:543a
·bioelectric signalling mechanisms **2**:998a
·biological development regulation **5**:648g
·bioluminescence mechanism in organisms **2**:1029d
·cells' oxygen deprivation response **5**:527f
·communication in animals **17**:477h
·digestive system regulation **5**:788a
·embryonic origins, development, and sense organs **5**:632b; illus. 629
·endocrine system interrelationships **6**:839d; illus. 840
·feeding behaviour control mechanisms **7**:210e
·growth rate of nerve fibres **8**:441f
·hearing in vertebrates and invertebrates **17**:40f
·heart and circulation regulation **4**:633h
·Helmholtz' research on fibres and cells **8**:752e
·homeostatic feedback functions **8**:1015d
·impulses and bioelectrical changes **12**:968e
·instinct and reflex activity **9**:628h
·learning ability evolution **10**:738d
·locomotion feedback and control **11**:24a
·Malpighi's microscopic studies **11**:388h
·Müller's study and experimentation **12**:615e
·muscle contraction mechanisms **12**:621g; illus. 624
·Pavlov physiological and psychological discoveries **13**:1096a
·photoreceptor-brain transmission **14**:361g
·physiological changes of hibernation **5**:964g
·physiology of information transfer **14**:438f
·pineal body's innervation **12**:453e
·potassium ion uptake by membranes **11**:882h
·radiation-induced congenital defects **15**:385e
·regeneration dependence on nerve supply **15**:578b
·respiratory system controls **15**:760f
·technology goals seen in natural systems **2**:1033a
·thermoreceptive structures and processes **18**:331b
·hormone and nervous system interaction **8**:1074c
·insect neurosecretory centres **8**:1085f
invertebrate systems
·algae neuromotor apparatus **1**:494a
·annelid worm anatomy, neurosecretion, and coordination **1**:933g; illus. 928
·Araneida sense organ system **1**:1070f
·arrowworm sensory reception **4**:18g
·arthropod characteristics **2**:68e
·arthropod heartbeat regulation **4**:622b
·Aschelminth structure and location **2**:141e
·bivalve structure and function **2**:1090g
·bug ganglion cephalization **8**:849h
·cephalochordate anatomical features **3**:1148d
·chordate nerve cord **4**:450d
·cnidarian sense organ system **4**:770g; illus. 771
·crustacean brain variations **5**:315g
·crustacean neuroendocrine mechanisms **6**:845e; illus. 846
·echinoderm coordination and nerve rings **6**:183e
·ganglionic cephalization in cephalopods **3**:1152h
·hemichordate epidermal features **8**:756a
·insect ganglia and neurons **9**:617d; illus.
·insect neuroendocrine mechanisms **6**:845h; illus. 846

·mollusk evolutionary trends **12**:329a
·oncopod structural variations **13**:569f
·Platyhelminthes neural description **14**:549c
·ribbonworm and simple nerve arrangement **12**:951b; illus. 950
·sponge coordination and contraction **14**:853e
·tick and mite brain **1**:22e; illus.
·tunicate neural gland function **18**:740b
·muscle innervation **12**:643b *passim* to 648d
·pain fibre functions **13**:866e
sensory nerves and nerve fibres
·endocrine system stimulation **6**:839e; illus. 840
·impulse conduction along specific path **12**:968g; illus. 969
·joint innervation and function **10**:258f
·sensory-reception theory and processes **16**:545g
vertebrate systems
·fish level of development **7**:335h
·human structures and functions **12**:994f; illus. 998
·mammalian structures and adaptations **11**:409d
·primate neural adaptations **14**:1024d
·reptile tiny brains **15**:733b
·salamander brain and sense organs **18**:1087e
·salmoniform sense organs **16**:189g
·sedative-hypnotic drug effects **16**:456e

RELATED ENTRIES in the *Ready Reference and Index: for*
brain: see association area; brain; cerebellum; cerebrum; choroid plexus; corpus callosum; cranial nerve; forebrain; hindbrain; hypothalamus; medulla oblongata; mesencephalon; olfactory lobe; paraventricular nucleus; thalamus; ventricle, brain
nerve cell and fibre: axon; dendrite; giant nerve fibre; interneuron; motor neuron; myelin; neuron; neurosecretory cell; Schwann sheath; sensory neuron; vestibular nerve
primitive nervous system: nerve net
spinal cord: spinal cord; spinal nerve; vertebral canal
vertebrate nervous system: autonomic nervous system; ganglion; innervation; meninges; nerve cord; neural tube; neuroglia; reflex arc; spinal ganglion

Nervi, Pier Luigi **12**:993 (b. June 21, 1891, Sondrio, Italy—d. Jan. 9, 1979, Rome), engineer and architect, internationally renowned for his technical ingenuity and dramatic sense of design, especially as applied to large-span structures built of reinforced concrete.

Abstract of text biography. Nervi's first significant work was a cinema in Naples (1926–27), followed by a municipal stadium in Florence (1930–32). In 1935–41 he built a series of concrete hangars for the Italian Air Force; all of these were destroyed in World War II. He invented *ferrocemento*, a heavily reinforced concrete that proved vital to the prefabricated 309-foot-span arch he designed for the Turin Exhibition of 1949–50. In 1947 he became professor at the University of Rome. In 1953–58, in collaboration with Marcel Breuer and Bernard Zehruss, he built the UNESCO headquarters in Paris. Also in collaboration, he designed the first skyscraper in Italy, the Pirelli Building (1955–59) in Milan, and in 1957 and 1958–59 he built two sports palaces for the Rome Olympic Games. His first building in the United States was the George Washington Bridge Bus Terminal in Manhattan (1961–62).

REFERENCES in other text articles:
·Formalist architecture style **19**:472c
·Roman sports complex design **17**:527g
·works and influences **9**:1111g

Nervii, Celtic tribe that, in the 1st century BC, inhabited the region between the Meuse and Scheldt rivers, now part of Belgium. They had no cavalry, but their foot soldiers offered strong opposition to Roman troops led by Julius Caesar in 57 BC. Three years later, during a serious rebellion in northwestern Gaul, the Nervii led a coalition of tribes that attacked and besieged a Roman camp commanded by Quintus Cicero, brother of the orator. The siege was lifted and the Nervii were finally subjugated in a fierce battle in which Caesar himself took part.

Nervo, Amado, original name JUAN CRISÓSTOMO RUIZ DE NERVO (b. Aug. 27, 1870, Tepic, Mex.—d. May 24, 1919, Montevideo, Urug.), poet and diplomat, generally considered the most distinguished Mexican poet of the late 19th- and early 20th-century Modernist movement in Spanish American literature, which attempted to revitalize Spanish poetic language through experiments with rhythm, metre, and imagery. Nervo's introspective poetry, characterized by deep religious feeling and simple forms, reflects his struggle for self-understanding and inner peace in an uncertain world.

Nervo abandoned his studies for the priesthood in 1888 to begin a career as a newspaperman in Mazatlán. In 1894 he moved to Mexico City, where he wrote his first novel, *El bachiller* (1895; "The Baccalaureate"), and his first volume of poetry in the Modernist idiom, *Perlas negras* (1898; "Black Pearls"). In 1898 he was one of the founders of the *Revista moderna* ("Modern Review"), which soon became one of the most influential journals of the Modernist movement.

As a diplomat, Nervo lived in Madrid between 1905 and 1918, serving as secretary to the Mexican legation there and spending much time in Paris literary circles. During that period he wrote most of the poems, essays, and short stories that have been collected in 29 volumes. The titles of his later works, in which appear the poems generally considered his finest—"Serenidad" (1914; "Serenity") and "Plenitud" (1918; "Plenitude")—reflect his achievement of the inner peace for which he had striven throughout his life, attained in some measure through the study of Buddhist philosophy.

After his return to Mexico in 1918, Nervo was appointed Mexican minister to Argentina and Uruguay, serving in Montevideo until his death.
·Latin-American literary developments **11**:1240e

nervous system, human **12**:994, neural structures such as the brain, spinal cord, and nerves that serve to receive stimuli, to process and store their effects, and to generate behaviour.

The text article covers the origin and evolutionary development of the human nervous system; characteristic structures of the nervous system; nerve degeneration and regeneration; the central nervous system, including the brain and the spinal cord; the peripheral nervous system, including the cranial nerves and the spinal nerves; and the autonomic nervous system, including its general organization and function, the levels of structural organization, early development, comparative features, autonomic transmission, general and integrative functions, and pathophysiology.

REFERENCES in other text articles:
·aging and neuron loss **1**:307b
·aging process comparison **1**:302c
·alcohol consumption effects **1**:439d
·animal tissue comparisons **18**:446b
·automata theory and mathematical models **2**:497e
·automated feedback loop analog **2**:506e
·biomedical monitoring instrumentation **9**:640c
·bladder emptying control **7**:56d
·blood circulation regulation **2**:1126d
·cells' oxygen deprivation response **5**:527f
·cerebrospinal fluid function **3**:1172f
·computer and brain comparisons **2**:1033h
·development of cells and tissues from birth through adolescence **5**:651h
·digestive system relationship **5**:789e *passim* to 795h
·disease causation and treatment **12**:1041d
·dreaming and physiological change **5**:1012g
drug effects **5**:1046c
·anesthesia's effect on activity **1**:867e
·hallucinogen effect on nerve function **8**:558b
·narcotic action on central nervous system **12**:842e
·opiate and cocaine effects **5**:1053c
·sedative-hypnotic drug effects **16**:456e
·stimulant and anti-depressant drugs **17**:692e
·tranquillizer types, uses, and effects **18**:595a
·ear anatomy and function **5**:1127e; illus. 1120
·ectodermal origins and histogenesis **6**:750c
·emotional states and visceral correlates **6**:758g
·endocrine system interrelationships **6**:800c
·exercise effects and learning of skill **7**:71a
·eye anatomy and function **7**:97e
·fatigue and neural activity in brain **7**:190h
·hallucinations and neural traces **9**:244c
·heartbeat regulation mechanism **3**:880d
·hominid evolutionary changes **8**:1026b
·hypothalamus' water and salt balancing mediation **7**:430f; illus. 432
·inflammatory reaction mediation **9**:561g
·joint nerve supply **10**:258e
·kidney and bladder innervation **7**:51e
·liver innervation **10**:1268h
·memory storage theories **10**:738d *passim* to 740b
·memory systems, short- and long-term **11**:892e
·muscle and nerve function **12**:634a
·pain reception **13**:866c
·reproductive system relationships **15**:691e
·respiratory system regulation **15**:766e
reticular activating system
·attention to stimuli **2**:356c
·speech control in man **17**:484h
·sensorimotor skill performance and limits **16**:543h
·sensory reception processes **16**:548h *passim* to 552c
·sexual behaviour dynamics **16**:595f
·sinuses and nerve systems **16**:807a
·skeletal protection systems **16**:813d *passim* to 816e
·sleep processes and functions **16**:878a
·urinary bladder function in micturition **7**:42c

RELATED ENTRIES in the *Ready Reference and Index:*
autonomic nervous system; brain; cranial nerve; reflex; spinal cord; spinal nerve

nervous system diseases **12**:1041, disorders resulting from pathology of neural tissue of the brain, spinal cord, or autonomic or peripheral nervous system. The disorders may range from minor personality changes to paralysis, blindness, or violent behaviour.

The text article describes the neurological examination and deals, in some detail, with the various kinds of neurological diseases and disorders, their symptoms, treatment, and prognosis.

REFERENCES in other text articles:
·alcohol-associated brain diseases **1**:440f
·atrophy of brain and nerves **2**:352f
·biomedical models, table 1 **5**:866
·birth defects and related disorders **2**:1074g
·bladder disorders **7**:42h
·bladder emptying disorders **7**:56d
·bone tissue affected by nerve injury **3**:24c
·childhood disorders and treatment **4**:222e *passim* to 225c
·diagnosis by neurological examination **5**:692d
·digestive disorders from tension **5**:768b *passim* to 771b
·drugs affecting nervous system **5**:1046c
·ear disorders and treatments **5**:1134f
·education of neurologically handicapped **6**:431h
·endocrine system disorders **6**:828h
·esophagus spasm and aganglionic megacolon **5**:798d *passim* to 801c
·genetic brain defects **7**:1001c
·industrial environment risks **9**:529f
·infectious disease symptoms and effects **9**:534e
·maternal risks during pregnancy **14**:980d
·meningitic and chronic hydrocephalus **12**:999a
·metabolic disorders and effects **11**:1058g *passim* to 1060e
·muscle disease causes and symptoms **12**:634a *passim* to 635h

·organic psychoses and behaviour change **15**:178c
·psycholinguistic aspects of aphasia **10**:1010g
·radiation dose and tissue injury types **15**:418c; illus.
·radiation effects **15**:385f *passim* to 389f
·regeneration of nerves after injury **18**:629a
·sedative-hypnotic drug treatments **16**:457c
·sensory reception disorders **16**:549f *passim* to 552c
·spinal cord severance effects **12**:1039c
·surgical treatment of impairments **17**:823a
·therapeutic drugs **18**:282g
·toxins' effects on brain **14**:621g
·tranquillizer use in nervous disorders **18**:595a
·visual disorders **7**:123a
·vitamin B_{12} deficiency and spinal cord pathology **2**:1135f
·voice and speech changes **17**:478g
·Wallerian degeneration **12**:978e
·X-ray examination of nervous system **15**:463e

RELATED ENTRIES in the *Ready Reference and Index: for*
convulsive disorders: see chorea; convulsions; epilepsy; focal seizures; grand mal; hystero-epilepsy; jacksonian epilepsy; petit mal; psychomotor seizure
degenerative diseases: amyotrophic lateral sclerosis; kuru; multiple sclerosis; neuritis; Parkinson's disease
inflammatory diseases: encephalitis; meningitis; poliomyelitis
paralysis: cerebral palsy; hemiplegia; paralysis; paraplegia; pseudobulbar palsy
signs and symptoms: aphasia; apraxia; ataxia; athetosis; neuralgia; tic
other: concussion; delirium; lumbago; sciatica; syringomyelia

nervous system malformations, congenital defects of the brain and spinal cord (usually with accompanying defects in the skull or vertebral column) as a result of abnormal development of the neural tube during early embryonic life.

Anencephaly is characterized by a poorly developed or absent cerebrum and lack of a skull vault; most fetuses having this defect are stillborn. Though rare, it occurs three times more often in females than in males and is commoner in Caucasians than in Negroes. In hydranencephaly the forebrain is also missing, but the vault is fully formed; life at a simple level is possible for a few months. Primary macrocephaly is a rare disorder in which brain and skull are abnormally large, but the intelligence is subnormal.

Arhinencephalia, congenital absence of the rhinencephalon of the brain, is characterized by cleft lip and palate, malformed nose (if present at all), tiny eyes, and visceral abnormalities. Related but more severe malformations include cyclopia (single central orbit with normal, reduced, or absent eye; tube-shaped nose set above the orbit; and gross malformation of the cerebrum), and cebocephalia (relatively normal face but fused cerebral hemispheres and other malformations). Most infants born with these defects die soon after birth.

Hydrocephalus ("water on the brain") is an uncommon (one or two out of every 1,000 live births) disorder that slows the flow of cerebrospinal fluid through the ventricles of the brain—usually because of the narrowing or absence of the passages. It is often associated with spina bifida or the Arnold-Chiari malformation (two tonguelike projections of the cerebellum that extend onto and are attached to an elongated medulla oblongata, the lowest part of the brain). If allowed to progress, the accumulation of fluid will severely damage the brain and eventually cause death; treatment by installation of a shunt to carry away excess fluid is frequently successful.

Spina bifida is a limited defect in the development of the vertebral column. In the relatively common spina bifida occulta, the vertebral arches fail to develop or do not fuse in the midline, so that the spinal cord and its coverings are unprotected by bone; this malformation nearly always occurs in the sacral or lumbar vertebrae and is often symptomless, remaining undetected throughout life.

Meningocele (syringomeningocele) is a form of spina bifida in which the coverings of the spinal cord (the meninges) protrude through the vertebral defect, forming a liquid-filled sac; the condition may be treated surgically. Meningomyelocele (syringomyelocele) develops similarly, but the meningeal sac contains some nerve tissue. Associated paraplegia or sphincter malfunction is common, and treatment is more difficult.

Encephalocele occurs when a meningeal sac containing brain material protrudes from the vault; prognosis depends on the amount of brain tissue involved.

Underdevelopment of neurons, lack of certain areas of the brain, and abnormally small or large convolutions on the surface of the brain also occur as malformations of the nervous system. *Major ref.* **12**:1045f

·anencephaly genetic interpretation **7**:1001c
·biological malformation types **11**:379e
·biomedical models, table 1 **5**:866
·birth defects and incidence of death **2**:1074c
·cerebrospinal fluid circulation **3**:1174a
·cerebrospinal fluid obstructions **12**:999a
·neural symptoms of spina bifida **12**:1045f
·symptoms and treatment **4**:224h
·treatment in early life **9**:674d

nervus intermedius: *see* intermediate nerve.

Nesbenebded, also known as SMENDES, king of Egypt *c.* 1085 BC, founder of the 21st dynasty, who permanently established the capital at Tanis, in the northeast Delta, while high priests of Amon ruled Thebes and Upper Egypt.

Nesbenebded, a native of the Delta, probably secured his right to rule through his queen, Tentamon, who was possibly related to the previous dynasty. Though the high priests of Amon held the real power in Upper Egypt, they recognized Nesbenebded as pharaoh and cooperated with him. Nesbenebded was evidently buried at Tanis, as shown by a piece of his funerary equipment found there.

Nesch, Rolf (1893–1975), German-Norwegian printmaker.

·metal graphic printmaking **14**:1080a; illus.

Nesebŭr, historic town, Burgas *okrŭg* (province), Bulgaria, on the Black Sea coast on an island connected to the mainland by a narrow strip of land. The Greek colony of Mesembria was founded on the site late in the 6th century BC and thrived on the trade between Greece and Thrace. It was relatively unimportant during the Roman occupation but regained its former prosperity during Byzantine times. Nesebŭr's gradual decline under the Turks was accelerated by the development of the port of Burgas after 1878. Narrow, cobbled streets, stone and wooden houses, and trim courtyards sheltering fig trees and arbors are characteristic of the town. It also contains more than 40 churches, many now in ruins. The oldest, the now roofless Old Metropolitan Church, dates from the 6th century; the most recent is the late 12th-century New Metropolitan Church. Beach facilities for tourists have been developed on the mainland. Pop. (1974 est.) 4,261.
42°39′ N, 27°44′ E

·map, Bulgaria **3**:471

Nesimi, Seyid İmadeddin (d. *c.* 1418, Aleppo, Syria), poet, considered one of the greatest Turkish mystical poets of the late 14th and early 15th centuries.

Very little about his early life is known. It is certain, however, that he became acquainted with the founder of an extremist religious sect, the Ḥurūfīs, the Iranian mystic Faḍl Allāh of Astarābād, who was flayed to death for his heretical beliefs in 1401/02. Ḥurūfism was based on a kabbalistic philosophy associated with the mystical significance attributed to the letters of the alphabet and their combinations (hence the name, *ḥurūf*, "letters" in Arabic). Nesimi seems to have studied with various mystical teachers before he met Faḍl Allāh, but after their meeting he became a zealous adherent of the sect, acting as missionary. Regarded as a heretic by the *ʿulamāʾ*—*i.e.*, those learned in the Muslim sciences—of Aleppo, he was accused of heresy and suffered the same fate as his master in about 1418.

Nesimi wrote two *dīvān*s (or collections of poetry), one in Persian and one in Turkish, and a number of poems in Arabic. The Turkish *Dīvān*, which is considered his most important work, contains 250–300 *ghazals* ("lyrics") and more than 150 *rubāʿīs* ("quatrains"). He expresses in his poetry both Ṣūfī and Ḥurūfī sentiments. Abounding in allusions to the martyred Faḍl Allāh, the poet's ecstatic verse repeats the basic Ḥurūfī conception that man is the incarnation of God. His lyrical and elegant style makes him one of the most prominent early *dīvān* masters, assuring him an important place in Turkish literary history.

Nesiotes (sculptor): *see* Critius and Nesiotes.

Neskaupstadhur, town, Sudhur-Múlasýsla (county), eastern Iceland, on Nordfjördhur (fjord). The easternmost settlement on the island, it is a local market centre and fishing port with freezing, curing, and canning plants. The town, which is linked to other parts of the island by road and by air service, was severely damaged by an avalanche, and several people were killed, in December 1974. Pop. (1974 est.) 1,653.
65°10′ N, 13°43′ W

·map, Iceland **9**:171

Nesokia indica: *see* bandicoot rat.

nesosilicates, formerly ORTHOSILICATES, compounds with structures that have independent silicate tetrahedrons (a central silicon atom surrounded by four oxygen atoms at the corners of a tetrahedron). Because none of the oxygen atoms is shared by other tetrahedrons, the chemical formula contains a multiple of SiO_4, as in zircon, topaz, or olivine.

Nespelim (North American Indians): *see* Salish.

Neşri, in full HÜSEYIN IBN EYNE BEG (b. Karaman, Tur.—d. *c.* 1520, Bursa), historian who was prominent in early Ottoman historiography. There is a great deal of controversy over the events of his life. It seems that he lived in the city of Bursa and was probably a member of the *ʿulamāʾ* (the learned religious leaders) and a poet of minor distinction. From his chronicle it is learned that he was in the Ottoman army camp near Gebze when the sultan Mehmed II died on May 3, 1481, and that he went to Istanbul, the Ottoman capital, where he observed the riots of the Janissary corps, which took place after the Sultan's death. These events, which are mentioned in his history, appear to be the only ones to which he was an actual witness.

His *Cihannüma* ("The Cosmorama") was, as the title suggests, designed to be a universal history. The sixth part, the longest section of which is devoted to a history of the Ottoman dynasty, was presented to Sultan Bayezid II and is the only part extant. Neşri relied heavily on the work of an earlier Ottoman historian, Aşikpaşazâde's *Tevârih-i Âl-i Osman* ("The Chronicle of the House of Osman"), as a source. He also used the royal calendars, a type of almanac prepared to provide the court with astrological information and containing lists of historical events, as well as a chronicle known as the Oxford Anonymous History. Neşri is considered a true historian in that he appears to have examined his sources carefully and to have tried to establish the correct facts and chronology objectively.

Ness, Loch, district of Inverness, Highland region, Scotland, largest and probably best known mass of freshwater in Great Britain

(Loch Lomond is larger in area). It lies in the Great Glen that bisects the Scottish Highlands, is 754 ft (230 m) deep, and 22½ mi (36 km) long, forming part of a system of waterways across Scotland that were linked by the engineer Thomas Telford in 1824. Like some other very deep lochs in Scotland and Scandinavia, it is said to be inhabited by an aquatic monster, accounts of which have been much publicized.
57°15′ N, 4°30′ W

Loch Ness, Inverness, Scotland, showing the monastery at Fort Augustus at the head of the loch

A.F. Kersting

Nesselrode, Karl Robert (Vasilievich), Count (b. Dec. 13 [Dec. 2, old style], 1780, Lisbon—d. March 23 [March 11, O.S.], 1862, St. Petersburg, now Leningrad), foreign minister of imperial Russia (1822–56) whose policy toward the Ottoman Empire helped precipitate the Crimean War (1853–56).

Son of a German count of the Holy Roman Empire, who served as Russia's ambassador to Portugal, Nesselrode entered the Russian navy at the age of 16 and became a naval aide-de-camp to Emperor Paul I (ruled 1796–1801). When he failed to distinguish himself in the armed forces, he transferred to the diplomatic corps and served in the Russian embassies to Prussia and the Netherlands (1801–06) and as diplomatic secretary to several generals during the war against Napoleonic France (1806–07). After assisting in the conclusion of the Franco-Russian peace of Tilsit (1807), he was attached to the Russian embassy at Paris, where he encouraged his superiors to pursue a pro-Austrian, anti-French policy but also attempted unsuccessfully to avoid a renewal of war between France and Russia.

After France's defeat Nesselrode attended the Congress of Vienna (1814–15), where he urged the Russian emperor Alexander I (ruled 1801–25) to support the restoration of the Bourbons in France. In 1816, despite damage done to his prestige by the discovery of a Franco-Austrian agreement aimed against Russia, Nesselrode was appointed director of the college of foreign affairs and in 1822 assumed full control of the conduct of Russia's foreign affairs.

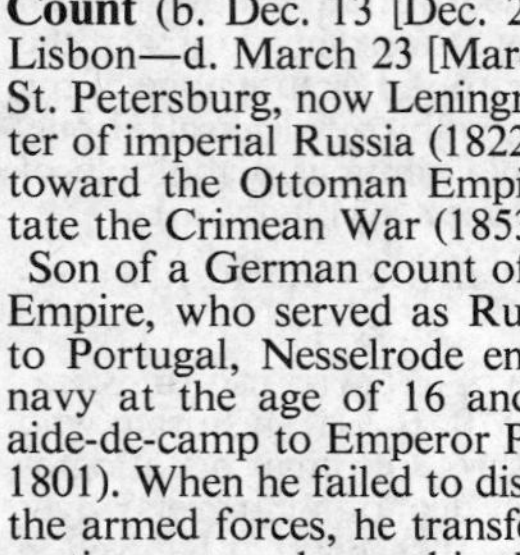

Nesselrode, engraving by Louis Hoffmeister, 19th century

By courtesy of the Bibliotheque Nationale, Paris

Following the accession of Emperor Nicholas I (1825), Nesselrode attempted to maintain the Ottoman Empire as a weak power dependent upon Russia. Toward this end he arranged a defensive alliance with the Turks (Treaty of Unkiar Skelessi; 1833) but abandoned it because of the objections of the British, who feared Russian influence in the Mediterranean. Instead, he concluded an Anglo-Russian alliance that resulted in the Straits Convention of 1841, an international agreement recognizing the Ottoman sultan's right to prevent warships of any nation from passing through the straits leading to the Black Sea. The two powers also agreed to support the continued existence of the Ottoman Empire, while recognizing the necessity of negotiations for territorial distribution, in the event the empire disintegrated (1844).

After the outbreak of the Hungarian Revolution of 1848, Nesselrode, who had restrained Nicholas from intervening in the French revolutions of 1830 and 1848, suggested that Russia aid Austria in suppressing it; this act not only crushed the Hungarian rebels but also contributed to the general misconception that Russia was the most powerful nation in Europe. Encouraged by this success, Russia's leaders assumed a more active role in foreign affairs and, in attempting to curb France's growing influence over the Ottoman Empire, they helped precipitate an international crisis in 1853. Nesselrode, trying to avoid hostilities, prolonged diplomatic negotiations but could not prevent the onset of the Crimean War. At its conclusion he signed the Treaty of Paris (1856), which destroyed the results of his patient efforts to establish Russian preponderance in the Balkan peninsula. Retiring from the foreign office, he retained only his post as imperial chancellor, which he had held since 1845.

Nessorhamphidae, a family of eels of the order Anguilliformes.
·characteristics and classification 1:900c

nest, a structure created by an animal to house its eggs, young, or, in some cases, itself. Nests are built by a few invertebrates, especially the social insects, and by some members of all the major vertebrate groups.

The social insects (termites, ants, bees, and wasps) build the only true nests found among the arthropods. These nests are often elaborate systems of chambers and tunnels, above or below ground. Chambers are often provided for the queen, eggs, larvae, and pupae, as well as passages for ventilation and movement.

The nests of fishes vary from shallow depressions scooped in sand or gravel, used by many groups, to enclosed structures constructed of plant materials.

Among amphibians, only certain frogs build nests, which may be simple mud basins (some *Hyla* species) or floating masses of hardened froth (many diverse groups).

A few reptiles build nests; most do not. The alligator (*Alligator mississipiensis*) builds a mound of mud and vegetation in which the eggs are laid and guarded by the female. Cobras build nests of leaves and forest debris, carried by kinking their necks, and both sexes guard the eggs.

The nests of birds, by far the best known, are highly varied, from no real structure at all (*e.g.*, falcons, owls, many seabirds and shorebirds) to the elaborate retort-shaped nests of weavers (Ploceidae), woven with grass strands tied with knots. Between these extremes lie the majority of bird nests, cup-shaped or domed and constructed of twigs, leaves, mud, feathers, or even spiderwebs. Bird nests vary in diameter from about 2 centimetres (the smaller hummingbirds) to more than 2 metres (6½ feet), in the nests of the larger eagles, and in weight from a few grams to more than a ton.

Many smaller mammals build nests in trees, on the ground, or in burrows. These may function as permanent homes or merely as places to bear and rear young.
·animal behaviour patterns 2:805e
bird
·apodiform egg incubation technique 1:1013h
·birds and methods of construction 2:1054f
·caprimulgiform diverse nesting habits 3:808e
·ciconiiform breeding habitats 4:612f; illus. 613
·colonial habits of Charadriiformes 4:35e
·colonial habits of pelecaniforms 14:16a
·cuckoo brood parasitism 5:360b
·falconiform site and construction 7:147h
·grebe parental behaviour 14:596f
·grouse's concealment of egg 4:924c
·hornbill nest sealing behaviour 5:158a
·megapode egg incubation 7:855d
·owl inquilinism 17:735e
·passerine nest variations 13:1053e
·piciform habitat and parental care 14:448f
·waterfowl site selection and building 1:943d
·crocodilian styles and care 5:288a
·desert arthropod adaptations 5:618c
·fish building types 7:332e
·insectivore methods and uses 9:624e
·instinctive behaviour patterns 9:628d
·Perciformes reproductive behaviour 14:48e
·reproductive behaviour and parental care 15:682c
·reptile patterns and parental care 15:728g
·rodent nest structure and food storage 15:973f
·stickleback mating behaviour 2:808c; illus.
·termite mounds and environment 9:1051e; illus. 1052
·thermal regulation and animal adaptation 12:121b
·wasp, ant, and bee activities 9:127f
·wasp cell informative shapes 4:1013e

Nestegis, genus of New Zealand olive of the family Oleaceae, Oleales.
·Oleales floral features 13:558d

Nesticidae, family of spiders of the order Araneida.
·classification and general features 1:1073d

Nestor, in Greek legend, king of Pylos (Navarino) in Elis. All of his brothers were slain by the Greek hero Heracles, but Nestor alone escaped. In the *Iliad* he is about 70 years old and sage and pious; his role is largely to incite the warriors to battle and to tell stories of his early exploits, which contrast with his listeners' experiences, which are shown to be soft and easy.

Nestor (b. *c.* 1056, Kiev—d. Oct. 27, 1113, Kiev), Russian monk of the Monastery of the Caves in Kiev, author of several works of hagiography and an important historical chronicle. He was received into the monastery about 1074 and is thought to have been still alive in 1113. He wrote the lives of SS. Boris and Gleb, the sons of St. Vladimir of Russia, who were murdered in 1015, and the life of St. Theodosius, abbot of the Monastery of the Caves (died 1074). A tradition first recorded in the 13th century ascribes to him the authorship of the *Povesti vremennykh let* ("The Tale of Bygone Years"; Eng. trans., *The Russian Primary Chronicle*, 1930), the most important historical work of early medieval Russia. Modern scholarship, however, regards the *Chronicle* as a composite work, written and revised in several stages, and inclines to the view that the basic (though not final) version of the document was compiled by Nestor about 1113. The *Chronicle*, extant in several medieval manuscripts, the earliest dated 1377, was compiled in Kiev. It relates in detail the earliest history of the Russian people down to the second decade of the 12th century. Emphasis is laid on the foundation of the Kievan state—ascribed to the advent of Varangians (a tribe of Norsemen) in the second half of the 9th century; the subsequent wars and treaties between the Russians and Byzantium; the conversion of Russia to Christianity *c.* 988; the cultural achievements of the reign of Yaroslav the Wise of Kiev (1019–54); and the wars against the Turkic nomads of the steppe.

Written partly in Old Church Slavonic, partly in the Old Russian language based on the spoken vernacular, the *Chronicle* includes material from translated Byzantine chronicles, west and south Slavonic literary sources, official documents, and oral sagas. This borrowed material is woven with considerable skill into the historical narrative, which is enlivened by vivid description, humour, and a sense of the dramatic.

Nestor (minor planet 659): *see* Trojan planets.

Nestorian alphabet: *see* Syriac alphabet.

Nestorian monument: *see* Hsi-an monument.

Nestorians, historically, those Christians of Asia Minor and Syria who refused to accept the condemnations of Nestorius and his teachings by the councils of Ephesus (AD 431) and Chalcedon (AD 451). Nestorians stressed the independence of the divine and human natures of Christ and in effect thus suggested that they were two persons loosely united by a moral union. In modern times they are represented by the Church of the East or Persian Church, usually referred to in the West as the Assyrian or Nestorian Church. Most of its members—numbering perhaps 100,000—live in Iraq, Syria, and Iran.

The origins of Christianity in Persia are obscure. There is written evidence of a church at Edessa (modern Urfa, Tur.), destroyed in a flood in 201, and Christian communities were probably formed after 260. Christianity faced intermittent persecution, until the Persian Church formally proclaimed its full independence in 424, thereby freeing itself of suspicion as a local church with foreign links. Under the influence of Barsumas, the metropolitan of Nisibis, the Persian Church acknowledged Theodore of Mopsuestia, the chief Nestorian theological authority, as guardian of right faith in February 486. This position was reaffirmed under the patriarch Babai (497–502), and since that time the church has been Nestorian.

Nestorius had been anathematized at Ephesus in 431 for denouncing the use of the title Theotokos ("God-bearer") for the Blessed Virgin, insisting that this compromised the reality of Christ's human nature. Those who refused to accept Nestorius' condemnation formed a centre of resistance at the renowned theological school of Edessa. When the school was closed by imperial order in 489, a small but vigorous Nestorian remnant migrated to Persia.

The Persian Church's intellectual centre then became the new school in Nisibis (*see* Nisibis, School of), which carried on the venerable traditions of Edessa. By the end of the 5th century there were seven metropolitan provinces in Persia proper and several bishoprics abroad—in Arabia, and in India. The church survived a period of schism (*c.* 521–*c.* 537/539) and persecution (540–545) through the leadership of the patriarch Mar Aba I (reigned 540–552), a convert from Zoroastrianism, and also through the renewal of monasticism by Abraham of Kashkar (501–586), the founder of the monastery on Mt. Izala, near Nisibis.

After the Arab conquest of Persia (637), the caliphate (Islāmic political administration) recognized the Church of the East as a separate religious community (millet) and granted it legal protection. Nestorian scholars played a prominent role in the formation of Arab culture, and patriarchs occasionally gained influence with rulers. During the more than three centuries that the church prospered under the caliphate, it became worldly and lost leadership in the cultural sphere; externally, however, it expanded greatly. By the end of the 10th century there were 15 metropolitan provinces in the caliphate itself and 5 beyond the border, including India and China. Nestorians also spread to Egypt, where Christianity was under Monophysite (those who acknowledge only one nature in Christ) control. In China there was a considerable Nestorian Christian community that flourished from the 7th to the 10th century. In Central Asia certain Tatar tribes were almost entirely converted, Christian expansion reaching almost to Lake Baikal (eastern Siberia). Western travellers to the Mongol realm found Christians well established there, even at the court of the Great Khan, though they commented on the ignorance and superstition of the Nestorian clergy. When the Mongols converted to Islām after the collapse of the Crusades late in the 13th century, the Church of the East was seriously threatened and during the 14th century was virtually exterminated by the raids of the Turkic leader Timur. Nestorian communities lingered on in a few towns in Mesopotamia but were concentrated mainly in Kurdistan, between the Tigris River and Lakes Van and Urmia, partly in Turkey and partly in Persia.

In 1551 a number of Nestorians reunited with Rome, hence to be known as Chaldeans, and the original Nestorians have since been denoted Assyrians. The Nestorian Church in India, part of the group known as the Christians of St. Thomas allied itself with Rome (1599), then split, half of its membership transferring allegiance to the Syrian Orthodox (Monophysite) patriarch of Antioch (1653).

The Assyrians lost about one-third of their people during World War I through massacre, disease, and exposure; a considerable group consequently migrated to Mesopotamia and the United States. The Assyrian patriarch was also compelled to relocate in the United States (in San Francisco) for political reasons.

- Assyrian incident of 1933 **11**:996g
- Byzantine religious controversy **3**:550h
- canon law development **3**:774e
- condemnation of teaching by Justinian **10**:365b
- Jordanian Christian communities **10**:272c
- Latin Kingdom religious milieu **5**:303h
- missions to Korea and China **10**:531g
- origins and historical development **6**:138c
- patristic Christological debates **13**:1083f
- Peshitta biblical canon **2**:889b
- Sāsānian Christian heresy **9**:850h
- Syriac studies in 5th and 6th centuries **1**:1157g
- Tatian canon usage **2**:940h
- Yüan dynasty's population and policy **4**:344c

Nestorius 12:1057, (b. late 4th century AD, Germanicia, modern Maraş, Tur. —d. *c.* 451, Panoplis, Egypt), early bishop of Constantinople whose views on the nature and Person of Christ led to the calling of the third ecumenical council to Ephesus in AD 431, and to the creation of separate Nestorian churches that still exist.

Abstract of text biography. Nestorius was consecrated bishop of Constantinople on April 10, 428. He became the centre of theological debate by objecting to the title of Mother of God as applied to Mary, on the grounds that it compromised Jesus' divinity. His views were condemned by Cyril, bishop of Alexandria. Following the convening of the Council of Ephesus (June 22, 431), he was deposed from his see, and was first relegated to his monastery near Antioch (431–435), then exiled (*c.* 436–437) to the Great Oasis in the Libyan Desert. He wrote an apologetic work entitled *Book of Heraclides of Damascus*.

REFERENCES in other text articles:
- Mary as Mother of God debate **11**:562a
- Nestorian Church origins **6**:138c
- patristic Christological controversy **13**:1084c
- theology and later influence **3**:550h

Nestor notabilis: *see* parrot.

Nestor's Cup, example of Mycenaean gold work.
- object representation illus. **11**:1102

Néstos River, Greek NÉSTOS POTAMÓS, Bulgarian MESTA, in southwestern Bulgaria and western Thrace, Greece, rises on Kolarov peak of the Rila mountains of the northwestern Rhodope (Rodopi) massif. Its upper confluents separate the Rila and Pirin mountains from the main Rhodope. Crossing the Bulgarian frontier into Greece, the Néstos divides Greek Macedonia from Greek Thrace. From just west of Stavroúpolis to its mouth on the Aegean Sea, 150 mi (240 km) from its source, it forms the boundary between Kaválla and Xánthi *nomoí* (departments). Above Paranésti, however, the river is confined to inaccessible gorges as it traverses the sparsely populated, mountainous Dráma *nomós* (department), in which the Néstos and the Dhespátis tributary are hemmed in between the Rhodope and the Falakrón Óros (mountain) on the west. West of Xánthi the Néstos reaches the marshy, alluvial coastal plain of Khrisoúpolis (Chrysopolis), known to the Turks as Sari Saban (Yellow Plain). At Parádhisos a dam controls the irrigation of the delta, in which high-quality tobacco is grown. 40°41′ N, 24°44′ E
- map, Greece **8**:314

Nestroy, Johann Nepomuk Eduard Ambrosius (b. Dec. 7, 1801, Vienna—d. May 25, 1862, Graz, Austria), one of Austria's greatest comic dramatists who dominated the mid-19th-century Viennese popular stage. He was also a brilliant character actor. After a career as an opera singer (1822–31) in several European cities, he returned to Vienna and began writing and acting. His 50 plays, virtually all adaptations of stories from earlier plays or novels, usually centre on a brilliant, detached

Nestroy, detail of a lithograph by Adolf Dauthage, 1860

By courtesy of the Bild-Archiv, Osterreichische Nationalbibliothek, Vienna central character (played by Nestroy himself) whose part requires a virtuoso performance in language, diction, and timing to convey its sharp nuances. He aimed at the complaisance of the newly rich bourgeoisie, and many of the leading figures of Viennese life were among his victims. He used satire, irony, and parody to carry his humour. From 1854 until he retired in 1860 he managed the Carl-Theater in Vienna.

Among his best known works are *Der böse Geist Lumpazivagabundus* (1833); *Der Zerrissene* (1844; *A Man Full of Nothing*, 1967); *Das Mädl aus der Vorstadt* (1841); and *Einen Jux will er sich machen* (1842; adapted by Thornton Wilder as *The Matchmaker*, 1954, and later adapted as the musical play and film *Hello, Dolly!*).

·commedia characters' Viennese depiction **4**:986d

net (mesh): *see* netting.

Netanya, also spelled NATANYA, city, west central Israel, on the Mediterranean coast, north of Tel Aviv–Yafo. It was founded in 1928 and named for the American-Jewish merchant and philanthropist Nathan Straus (1848–1931).

Established as a noncollective agricultural settlement (*moshava*), the area was originally devoted to citrus cultivation. Jewish immigration from Nazi-held European countries after 1933, and further immigration after World War II, gave it an increasingly urban character; Netanya is now the focus of a large urban agglomeration.

Diamond cutting and polishing, one of Israel's most important industries, is centred there; although diamond trading is principally conducted on the Diamond Exchange at Ramat Gan, most of the actual workshops are at Netanya. A new industrial area, developed since 1950–52, includes textile mills and factories producing rubber and plastic articles, complex machinery, and raw materials for the pharmaceutical industries. Just south of the city is one of Israel's largest breweries. Netanya has also developed as a resort centre. During the Six-Day War (1967), the city was bombed by a lone Iraqi plane, whose pilot mistook it for Tel Aviv–Yafo. Inc. 1948. Pop. (1975 est.) 79,500.
32°20′ N, 34°51′ E

·map, Israel **9**:1060

netball, a popular game in girls' schools in England and several other countries, similar

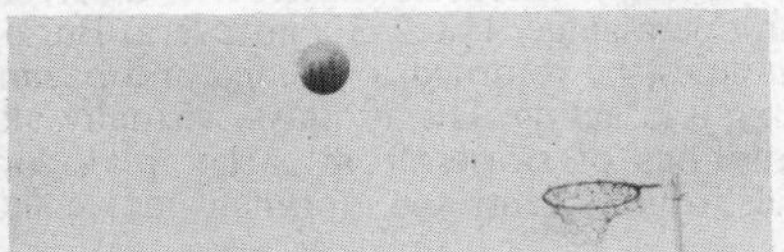

Netball world tournament, 1963 (England versus Jamaica)
Sport and General

to six-player girls' basketball in the United States. It is played on a hard-surfaced rectangular court 100 feet long and 50 feet wide (30 by 15 metres), clearly marked into three zones with half circles 16 feet (5 metres) in radius at either end for shooting. The goal posts stand 10 feet (3 metres) high with rings that are circular and nets at the top through which the ball must pass from above to score a point. The rings are 15 inches (38 centimetres) in diameter, and the ball is almost always of leather or rubber, about 8.5 inches (22 centimetres) in diameter and 14–16 ounces (400–450 grams) in weight.

The game is played between two teams, each consisting of seven players—three centre players, two attackers, and two defenders, with each player restricted in movement to certain areas of the court. The ball must be passed from hand to hand from player to player, and no one may run with it. The centre players try to pass the ball up the court into the circle for the attackers to shoot (the two attackers are the only ones who may shoot). The defenders, by guarding their opponents and by intercepting passes, try to prevent goals from being scored.

A game consists of four 15-minute periods or two 20-minute halves.

net current assets, also called WORKING CAPITAL, in accounting, funds available for uses other than payment of short-term debt, being the excess of current assets over current liabilities.

·accounting, balance sheet, and funds statements **1**:36e; tables 37

Netherlandic (DUTCH-FLEMISH) **language,** national language of The Netherlands and, with French, one of the two official languages of Belgium. Although speakers of English usually call the Netherlandic of The Netherlands "Dutch" and the Netherlandic of Belgium "Flemish" (Vlaams in Netherlandic), they are actually the same language.

Netherlandic, which occurs in both standard and dialectal forms, is the language of most of The Netherlands, of northern Belgium, and of a relatively small part of France along the North Sea, immediately to the west of Belgium. Netherlandic is also used as the language of administration in Surinam and the Netherlands Antilles; Afrikaans, which is a derivative of Netherlandic, is, together with English, one of the two official languages of the Re-

THE NETHERLANDS

Official name: Koninkrijk der Nederlanden (Kingdom of The Netherlands).
Location: western Europe.
Form of government: constitutional monarchy.
Official language: Dutch (Netherlandic).
Official religion: none.
Area: 15,892 sq mi (land area 14,680 sq mi), 41,160 sq km (land area 38,022 sq km).
Population: (1971 census) 13,045,785 (de jure); (1975 estimate) 13,681,000 (de jure).
Capital: Amsterdam (national), The Hague (seat of government).
Monetary unit: 1 guilder = 100 cents.

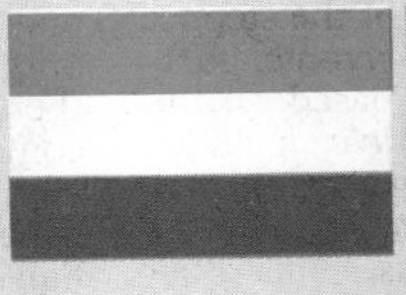

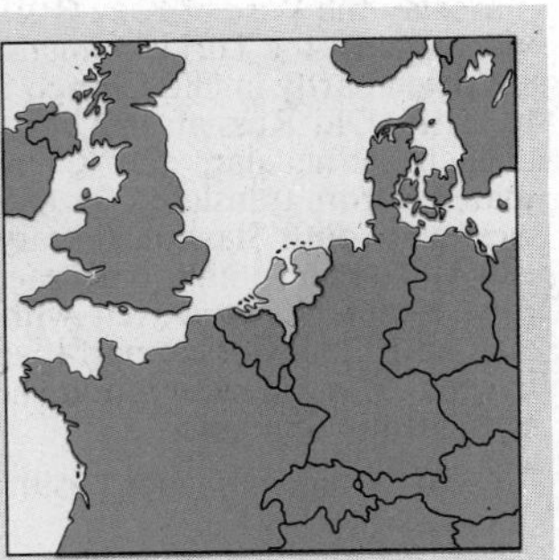

Demography

Population: (1975 estimate) density 860.9* per sq mi, 332.4* per sq km; urban 76.8%, rural 23.2%; male 49.90%, female 50.10%; (1974) under 15 26.1%, 15–29 25.3%, 30–44 18.1%, 45–59 15.7%, 60–74 11.0%, 75 and over 3.9%.†
Vital statistics: (1974) births per 1,000 population 13.8, deaths per 1,000 population 8.0, natural increase per 1,000 population 5.8; (1973) life expectancy at birth—male 71.2, female 77.2; (1972) major causes of death (per 100,000 population)—malignant neoplasms, including neoplasms of lymphatic and hematopoietic tissues 197.5; ischemic heart disease 190.2; cerebrovascular disease 97.9; motor vehicle accidents 23.8.
Ethnic composition (by nationality, 1973): Netherlander 97.8%, Turkish 0.4%, German 0.3%, Spanish 0.2%, Moroccan 0.2%, Belgian 0.2%, Italian 0.1%.† *Religious affiliation* (1971): Roman Catholic 39.5%, Dutch Reformed 23.0%, Reformed Church and other 15.0%, no religion 22.5%.

National accounts

Budget (1976). Revenue: 74,517,000,000 guilders (income tax 38.2%, turnover tax 21.3%, corporation tax 7.8%, excise duties 7.5%, import duties 1.5%). Expenditures: 89,626,000,000 guilders (education and culture 23.2%, social security and public health 22.2%, local authorities shares in taxes 10.2%, defense 8.7%, transport and public works 7.7%, housing and town and country planning 7.1%, public order and security 3.9%, agriculture and fishery 1.7%, European Communities shares in taxes 1.3%). *Total national debt* (1975): 46,735,000,000 guilders. *Tourism* (1974). Receipts from visitors: U.S. $1,033,000,000; expenditures by nationals abroad: U.S. $1,346,000,000.

Domestic economy

Gross national product (GNP; at current market prices, 1974): U.S. $66,060,000,000 (U.S. $4,880 per capita).

Origin of net domestic product (at current factor cost):	1960 value in 000,000 guilders	1960 % of total value	1960 labour force	1960 % of labour force	1974 value in 000,000 guilders	1974 % of total value	1974 labour force	1974 % of labour force
agriculture, forestry, hunting, fishing	3,781	10.9	446,695	10.7	7,250	4.7	304,000	6.7
mining, quarrying	642	1.8	60,696	1.5	46,500	30.5	10,000	0.2
manufacturing	11,171	32.1	1,245,784	29.9			1,118,000	24.6
construction	2,558	7.4	404,365	9.7	11,550	7.6	453,000	10.0
electricity, gas, water	579	1.7	46,905	1.1	3,050	2.0	44,000	1.0
transport, storage, communications	2,709	7.8	288,940	6.9	10,720	7.0	306,000	6.7
trade					22,000	14.4	824,000	18.1
banking, insurance, real estate	6,236	17.9	675,899	16.2	31,750	20.8	293,000	6.4
services	3,201	9.2						
public administration,			980,516	23.5			1,198,000	26.3
defense	3,894	11.2			24,240	15.9		
other	...	...	18,826	0.5	−4,470	−2.9	...	...
total	34,771	100.0	4,168,626	100.0	152,590	100.0	4,550,000	100.0

Production (metric tons except as noted, 1974). Agriculture, forestry, hunting, fishing: wheat 746,000, potatoes 5,595,000, sugar beets 4,911,000, barley 315,000, oats 163,000, rye 78,000, onions 394,000, tomatoes 350,000, cabbages 229,000, carrots 140,000, rapeseed 45,000, green peas 55,000, rippled flax 43,000; livestock (number of live animals): cattle 4,978,000, pigs 6,713,000, sheep 749,000, horses 60,000, goats 20,000, chickens 62,388,000, ducks 765,000; milk 9,900,000, butter 170,000, cheese 370,700, eggs 292,922; roundwood 982,000 cu m‡; fish catch 343,800‡. Mining, quarrying: natural gas 90,852,000,000 cu m§, crude petroleum 1,416,000§, coal 756,000. Manufacturing: steel ingots 5,817,000; crude steel 4,824,000§; pig iron 3,972,000§; sulfuric acid 1,296,000§; beer 11,066,000 hectolitres‡; meat 1,548,000; paper 1,579,000; cement 3,636,000§; tinplate 478,000; iron castings 310,000; seagoing and coasting tankers and cargo and passenger ships 886,000 gross tons; aluminum 260,400§; zinc 123,600§; nitrogenous fertilizers 1,159,000; phosphate fertilizers 346,000; coal tar 105,000; synthetic rubber 244,800; cotton yarn 29,400§; rayon yarn 27,480§; woollen yarn 9,240§; strawboard 113,000; shoes and boots 13,500,000 pairs; building bricks 2,369,000,000 units; sugar 707,000. Construction: dwellings 7,686,000,000 guilders, commercial 2,739,000,000 guilders, schools 668,000,000 guilders, farm buildings 517,000,000 guilders, health care facilities 668,000,000 guilders.

public of South Africa (*see* Afrikaans language).

The spoken language exists in a great many varieties ranging from Standard Netherlandic (Algemeen Beschaafd Nederlands, or "General Cultured Netherlandic")—the language used for public and official purposes, including instruction in schools and universities—to the local dialects that are used among family, friends, and others from the same village (these exist in far more variety than does the English of North America). Standard Netherlandic is characterized grammatically by the loss of case endings in the noun.

In Belgium efforts were made to give Netherlandic equal status with French, which assumed cultural predominance under the French rule of 1795–1814; in 1938 Netherlandic was made the only official language of the northern part of Belgium.

The use of Standard Netherlandic together with the local dialect is much more widespread among the people of The Netherlands than it is in Belgium. The dialects of the area bounded roughly by Amsterdam, The Hague, and Rotterdam are closer to the Standard Netherlandic than are those of the other dialect areas.

Together with English, Frisian, and German, Netherlandic is a West Germanic language. It is descended primarily from the speech of the Salic Franks (which is often called Low Franconian) although it also has some non-Frankish features that were probably borrowed from the pre-Frankish Germanic inhabitants of the North Sea coast. The earliest documents in the Netherlandic language date from approximately the end of the 12th century, although a few glosses, names, and occasional words appeared somewhat earlier. *Major ref.* **8**:21g

·Bible translation history **2**:892f
·English vocabulary borrowings **6**:878d

Netherlands, Revolt of the: *see* Eighty Years' War.

Netherlands, The 12:1058, often called in English HOLLAND, kingdom of western Europe, bounded by the North Sea (north and west), by West Germany (east), and by Belgium (south). Much of the country lies below sea level and is protected by dikes.

The text article covers the natural and human landscape, the people, the national economy, transportation, administration and social conditions, cultural life and institutions, and outlook. *See also* Low countries, history of the.

REFERENCES in other text articles:

agriculture, forestry, and fishing
·arable land per capita **1**:320d
·crops and technology **1**:332f
·estuaries and land reclamation **6**:975d
·land-reclamation and drainage systems **9**:903f
·milk production and utilization, table 1 **5**:426
·tulip crop importance **8**:1112c
·wheat yield yearly averages, table 1 **3**:1158

art, archaeology, and architecture
·Baroque visual art forms and styles **19**:416e
·copper, bronze, gold, and silverwork **11**:1095e *passim* to 1111b
·designers and form **8**:195c
·de Stijl abstract aesthetics **9**:516a
·folk art regions and cultural sources **7**:477h
·furniture styles and decoration **7**:787f
·Nagasaki cultural contact policy **19**:239g
·pottery tradition and development **14**:911a; illus.
·Vermeer's major themes and techniques **19**:86a
·Versailles influence in garden design **7**:895g; illus. 896

commerce, industry, and mining
·Amsterdam's trade and commerce **1**:710h
·apprenticeship and employee training **1**:1020d
·China's trade relationship, table 5 **4**:280
·coal mining methods **4**:774f
·glass imports and exports, table 2 **8**:206
·natural gas production and reserves, table 3 **12**:861
·petroleum and natural gas association **14**:169a
·petroleum production and consumption, tables 1, 2, and 3 **14**:187
·petroleum production statistics, table 1 **14**:176
·pharmaceutical production table **14**:199
·Rotterdam port use by West Germany **8**:60b
·spice import, export, and value, table 3 **17**:506
·wastepaper stock consumption, table 1 **13**:968

constitution and law
·military law rules and procedures **12**:195c
·patent application procedures **13**:1073c

culture and education
·adult education centres **1**:100a
·educational system and administration **6**:380g
·encyclopaedia production **6**:797e
·Frisian dialect areas **8**:20g
·law study requirements for practice **10**:775h

economics, finance, and currency
·Amsterdam stock exchange operations **16**:450c *passim* to 452d
·Benelux Economic Union **5**:380c
·business associations, structure, and investments **3**:530g
·defense expenditures table **19**:552
·foreign aid distribution **7**:523g; table 2, 524
·gross national debt percentage, table 4 **15**:193
·health services expenditure graphs, table 2 **8**:692
·hospital operating costs **8**:1115d
·income tax exemptions and deductions **9**:274b
·inheritance tax rates **5**:530h
·national expenditure analysis, tables 1 and 4 **5**:105
·property taxation practices **15**:60e

government
·armed forces statistics, table 2 **2**:16
·Brussels growth and political role **3**:349g
·socialism's history and evolution **16**:967e
·Surinam administration and politics **17**:827c

natural resources
·coal production and reserves, table 5 **4**:781

Energy: (1973) installed electrical capacity 13,407,000 kW; (1975) production 54,264,000,000 kWhr (3,966 kWhr per capita).

Persons economically active: (1974) 4,550,000 (33.6%); (1975) unemployed 195,300 (4.8%).

Price and earnings indexes (1970 = 100):	1971	1972	1973	1974	1975
consumer price index	107.6	116.0	125.2	137.3	151.3
hourly earnings index	112	126	143	167	190

Land use (1973): total land area 3,685,000 ha (meadows and pastures 34.4%; agricultural and under permanent cultivation 22.6%; forested 8.2%; built-on, wasteland, unused but potentially productive, and other 34.8%).

Foreign trade

Imports (1974): 87,420,000,000 guilders (machinery and transport equipment 20.7%, of which, machinery, other than electrical 7.9%, electrical machinery 6.7%, transport equipment 6.1%; manufactured goods classified by material 19.7%, of which, iron and steel 5.3%, textile yarn and fabrics 4.1%; mineral fuels and lubricants 18.1%, of which, petroleum and products 17.3%; food and live animals 11.1%, of which, cereals and cereal preparations 3.4%; miscellaneous manufactured articles 10.1%, of which, clothing 3.4%; crude materials, inedible 7.9%, of which, wood, lumber, and cork 1.6%, textile fibres and waste 0.7%; organic and inorganic chemicals 4.2%; animal and vegetable oils and fats 1.4%). *Major import sources:* West Germany 26.6%, Belgium–Luxembourg 12.9%, United States 9.1%, France 7.3%, United Kingdom 5.5%, Italy 3.4%, Sweden 2.0%, Switzerland 1.3%, Saudi Arabia 1.2%, Finland 0.6%, Argentina 0.5%, Kuwait 0.4%, Indonesia 0.3%, Libya 0.1%.

Exports (1974): 87,925,000,000 guilders (chemicals 17.5%, of which, organic and inorganic chemicals 7.1%; food and live animals 17.3%, of which, meat and meat products 4.1%, dairy products and eggs 3.8%, fruits and vegetables 3.0%; manufactured goods, classified by material 17.2%, of which, textile yarn and fabrics 4.6%, iron and steel 4.5%; machinery and transport equipment 16.8%, of which, machinery other than electrical 7.0%, electrical machinery 6.8%, transport equipment 4.1%; mineral fuels and lubricants 16.0%, of which, petroleum and products 12.5%; miscellaneous manufactured articles 6.5%; crude materials, inedible 5.6%, of which, animal and vegetable 2.1%; animal and vegetable oils and fats 1.6%; beverages and tobacco 1.1%). *Major export destinations:* West Germany 30.2%, Belgium–Luxembourg 14.0%, France 9.9%, United Kingdom 9.1%, Italy 5.3%, United States 4.0%, Sweden 2.3%, Denmark 1.7%, Switzerland 1.7%, Spain 1.2%, Norway 0.9%, Austria 0.9%, Japan 0.5%, Soviet Union 0.5%.

Transport and communications

Transport. Railroads (1975): length 4,556 mi, 7,332 km; passenger-mi 5,286,600,000, passenger-km 8,508,000,000; short ton-mi cargo 1,865,800,000, metric ton-km cargo 2,724,000,000. Roads (1975): total length 51,497 mi, 82,877 km (primary 31,114 mi, 50,074 km; secondary 20,383 mi, 32,803 km). Vehicles (1975): passenger cars 3,440,000, trucks and buses 347,000. Merchant marine (1975): vessels (100 gross tons and over) 1,348, total deadweight tonnage 8,631,289. Air transport: (1974) passenger-mi 5,823,500,000, passenger-km 9,372,000,000; short ton-mi cargo 435,900,000, metric ton-km cargo 636,372,000; (1976) airports with scheduled flights 5.

Communications. Daily newspapers (1973): total number 93, total circulation 4,175,000, circulation per 1,000 population 311. Radios (1973): total number of receivers 3,811,000 (1 per 3.5 persons). Television (1975): receivers 3,545,000 (1 per 3.9 persons). Telephones (1975): 4,678,945 (1 per 2.9 persons).

Education and health

Education (1972–73):	schools	teachers	students	student/teacher ratio
primary (age 6–12)	9,173	56,745	1,539,676	27.1
secondary (age 12–18)	1,502	41,738	662,145	15.9
vocational	2,005	39,600	438,050	11.1
teacher training	45	1,000	10,685	10.7
higher	336	17,500‖	247,964¶	. . .

College graduates (per 100,000 population, 1971–72): 62.4. *Literacy* (1976): total population literate (age 15 and over) virtually 100%.

Health: (1975) doctors 20,200 (1 per 677 persons); (1972) hospital beds 156,555 (1 per 85 persons); (1974) daily per capita caloric intake 3,290 calories (FAO recommended minimum requirement 2,697 calories).

*Based on land area. †Percentages do not add to 100.0 because of rounding. ‡1973. §1975. ‖1969–70. ¶1971–72.

·Delta Plan for land reclamation **8**:642e
·North Sea fishing and petroleum **13**:251b
·petroleum reserves of the world table **14**:175
physical geography
·Holocene coastal formations **8**:1003f; illus. 2 1002
·map, Europe **6**:1034
·Rhine course and breakup **15**:807c; illus. 806
religion
·Christian denominational demography map **4**:459
·Old Catholic Church membership **13**:555c
science and technology
·automotive industry's supranational operation and production **2**:533f; table 534
·canal system improvements **3**:760h
·general medical practice vitality **11**:843g
social issues
·alcohol consumption patterns table **1**:444
·fire death and property loss table **7**:314
sports and recreation
·ice speed skating development **19**:887c
·kolven popularity and golf comparison **8**:242f
·motor racing and regulation **12**:567c; illus.
transportation and communications
·broadcasting organization and services **3**:319f
·merchant fleet and shipping statistics **18**:673c
·newspaper publishing statistics table **15**:237
·railway systems data table **15**:482

Netherlands Antilles, Dutch NEDERLANDSE ANTILLEN, two widely separated groups of islands (total area 383 sq mi [993 sq km]) of the Lesser Antilles in the Caribbean Sea. They are an integral part of the Kingdom of The Netherlands, and are fully autonomous in internal affairs. The southern group (also called the Leeward Islands), consisting mainly of igneous rocks and fringed with coral reefs, comprises Curaçao, Aruba, and Bonaire (*qq.v.*), which lie less than 60 mi (100 km) off the coast of Venezuela. The northern group, consisting of volcanic rocks, comprises Sint Eustatius, Saba, and the southern part of Saint-Martin (*qq.v.*); these are also called the Windward Islands, although they lie geographically within the Leeward Islands. Executive authority is vested in the governor, appointed by the crown, and in a council of ministers of 11 members. They are responsible to the unicameral legislature (Staten, or States) of 22 members (12 from Curaçao, 8 from Aruba, 1 from Bonaire, and 1 from the northern islands) elected by universal suffrage. The capital is Willemstad on Curaçao. Pop. (1979 est.) 246,500.
·newspaper publishing statistics table **15**:237

Netherlands East India Company: *see* Dutch East India Company.

Netherlands East Indies: *see* Dutch East Indies.

Netherlands Guiana: *see* Suriname.

Netherlands school (music): *see* Franco-Netherlandish school.

Netherlands Trading Society, NEDERLANDSCHE HANDEL-MAATSCHAPPIJ, also translated as NETHERLANDS TRADING COMPANY, organized by William I (*q.v.*) in 1824.
·Indonesian colonial exploitation **9**:485h
·William I economic programs **11**:152f

Nethuns (god): *see* Neptune.

net income, also called NET PROFIT, in accounting, residual earnings after all costs and expenses incurred have been deducted. *Major ref.* **1**:36g; tables 37

Netley, village, Hampshire, England, on Southampton Water, an inlet of the English Channel. There are extensive remains of a 13th-century Cistercian abbey. One of the south coast forts of Henry VIII survives as a convalescent home.
50°53′ N, 1°21′ W

net national product: *see* gross national product.

Neto, (Antônio) Agostinho (b. Sept. 17, 1922, Icolo e Bengo, Angola—d. Sept. 10, 1979, Moscow), poet, physician, and first president of the People's Republic of Angola. Neto first became known in 1948 when he published a volume of poems in Luanda and joined a national cultural movement that was aimed at "rediscovering" indigenous Angolan culture (similar to the Negritude movement of the French-speaking African countries).

His first of many arrests for political activities came shortly thereafter in Lisbon, where he had gone to study medicine. He returned home as a physician in 1959 but was arrested in June 1960 because of his militant opposition to the colonial authorities. When villagers protested his arrest the police opened fire, killing several (the number is disputed) and injuring 200. Neto spent the next two years in detention on the Cape Verde Islands and in Portugal, where he produced a new volume of verse. In 1962 he escaped to Morocco, where he joined the Angolan liberation movement in exile. At the end of 1962 he was elected president of the Movimento Popular de Libertação de Angola (MPLA). When in 1975 Angola became independent, it was divided among its three warring independence movements. The MPLA forces, with Cuban help, held the central part of the country, including the capital, and Neto, a committed Marxist, was proclaimed president.

Neto is widely recognized as a gifted poet writing in Portuguese. His work has been published in a number of Portuguese and Angolan reviews and in Mário de Andrade's *Antologia da Poesia Negra de Expressão Portuguesa* (1958).
·Angolan arts **1**:897c

Netochka Nezvanova (1849), novel by Fyodor Dostoyevsky.
·intent and interruption by imprisonment **5**:966h

Netsch, Walter (Andrew) (U.S. architect): *see* Skidmore, Owings & Merrill.

Netscher, Caspar (b. *c.* 1635, Heidelberg, Palatinate—d. Jan 15, 1684, The Hague), Baroque portrait painter who established a fashionable clientele in The Hague. He was brought up in Arnhem, where his first master was Hendrick Coster, and later studied under Gerard Terborch. In 1658 or 1659 he set out by sea for Rome but went no farther than Bordeaux. By 1662 he had settled in The Hague.

Netscher's earlier genre pieces are closely related to the works of Gabriel Metsu and Terborch, from whom he acquired great skill in rendering textures. "The Lace-Maker," in the Wallace Collection, London, is an example of this style. The later biblical and mythological subjects and the small, glossy portraits tend to be superficial despite their elegance.

Netscher's sons Theodoor (1661–1732) and Constantijn (1668–1723) were among his many pupils and imitators.
·Huygens portrait illus. **9**:75a

Netsilingmiut, Eskimo group of Canada.
·name origin, area, and hunting methods **1**:1126d; map 1124

netsonde, in commercial fishing, fish-finding device that signals the distance of the trawl from the bottom or from the water surface, registers the size of the trawl mouth, and signals if fish are entering the trawl.
·fish-finding techniques **7**:359f

netsuke, ornamental toggle-like piece, usually of carved ivory, used in Japan to attach an *inrō* (*q.v.*; medicine box), pipe, or tobacco pouch to a man's sash. During the Tokugawa period (1603–1868), netsukes were an indispensable item of dress as well as, often, fine works of miniature art. Because the members of the newly risen middle class, ranking below the samurai, were not permitted to wear jewelry, netsukes took the place of other personal adornment. Originally carved from boxwood, netsukes were first made in various kinds of ivory during the first half of the 18th century. In the latter part of that century, netsuke makers devised a method of inlaying, using coral, ivory, pearl shell, horn, and precious metals on lacquer and wood; some of these substances also were used for inlaying ivory.

Netsuke, carved ivory, 19th century; in the Tokyo National Museum
By courtesy of the Tokyo National Museum

With the end of the Tokugawa regime, netsukes became obsolete, though some were still carved to supply the demand of foreign residents and tourists.
·Japanese jewelry design **10**:179b
·Japanese lacquerwork **10**:578e

Nettapus: *see* perching duck.

Netta rufina (duck): *see* pochard.

Nettastomatidae, family of eels of the order Anguilliformes.
·characteristics and classification **1**:900c

netting, in textiles, ancient method of constructing open fabrics by the crossing of cords, threads, yarns, or ropes so that their intersections are knotted or looped, forming a geometrically shaped mesh, or open space.

Modern net fabrics are usually produced by machine by the netting method or by weaving, knitting, and crocheting. The meshes vary greatly in shape and size, and weights range from fine to coarse. Tulle is a very fine, soft net with hexagonal-shaped meshes, and bobbinet also has hexagonal meshes. Apparel and home-furnishing uses of nets include veils, hat shapes, dresses, curtains, and trimmings. Industrial applications include fishing and cargo nets. *Major ref.* **18**:183b
·commercial fishing method and gear **7**:353b; illus.

nettle, stinging (*Urtica dioica*), plant of the nettle family (Urticaceae), native to Europe and Asia, characterized by bristly, stinging hairs on leaves and stems.

nettle tree (plant): for species of the genus *Celtis*, *see* Celtis; for species of *Laportea*, *see* Urticaceae.

net-winged beetle, any of the soft-bodied, brightly coloured 2,800 species of the predominantly tropical family Lycidae (order Coleoptera). The broad, leathery wing covers (elytra), which are wider at the tip than at the base, and the raised network of lines on the elytra give this family its common name. The adults feed either on plant juices or on other insects and can easily be seen as they fly slowly between plants or crawl on flowers.

The bold colouring of orange and black or blue probably warns predators of their acid-burning taste. Other insects that have evolved the same colour patterns share in the same protection. Such association of a given colour pattern with an offensive taste is called aposematic mimicry. Sometimes this mimicry is mutually beneficial, as when both the net-winged beetle and a similarly patterned insect have a bad taste. After a predator has tasted either, it shies away from both (Mullerian mimicry).

·traits and classification **4**:835c; illus. 829

network analysis (operations research): *see* critical path analysis.

network lace: *see* filet lace.

network theory: *see* probability, theory of.

net worth, excess of a business's or individual's assets over its liabilities. It therefore reflects the amount of investment in the business by the owners and the amount of income that has been retained for reinvestment. In considering the firm as a credit risk or analyzing its securities, net worth is defined to exclude intangible assets such as patents and good will (*q.v.*). More popular terms for net worth are total equity and stockholders' or owners' equity.

·tax on net worth **17**:1077a

Netzahualcoyotl, district of Mexico City.

·economic conditions of residents **12**:91e

Neuber, (Friederike) Caroline *née* WEISSENBORN (b. March 9, 1697, Reichenbach, Saxony—d. Nov. 30, 1760, Laubegast, near Dresden), actress-manager, one of the most important influences on the development of modern German theatre. Rebelling against her tyrannical father, she ran away with a young clerk, Johann Neuber, at the age of 20 and married him in 1718. They served their theatrical apprenticeship in the travelling companies of Christian Spiegelberg (1717–22) and Karl Caspar Haack (1722–25). In 1727 they formed their own company and were granted a patent by the elector of Saxony, Frederick Augustus I, to perform at the Leipzig Easter Fair. As early as 1725 Caroline Neuber's acting had attracted the attention of Johann Christoph Gottsched, the critic and drama reformer who modelled his work on classical French tragedy and comedy. "Die Neuberin," as he came to call her, substituted in her company a careful learning of parts and rehearsal for the heavily improvised farces and harlequinades that then dominated the German stage. The collaboration of Gottsched and the Neuberin, which lasted until 1739, is usually regarded as the turning point in the history of German theatre and the start of modern German acting. Returning to Leipzig in 1737 after three years of engagements in other German cities, the Neuber Company found that their patent, after the death of Augustus in 1733, had gone to the company of Johann Ferdinand Müller, a proponent of the old improvisations and harlequinades. The Neuberin reacted with a

Caroline Neuber, lithograph by C. Lödel after E.G. Hausmann

Deutsche Fotothek Dresden

bravura gesture: on stage she enacted the banishment of Harlequin from the theatre. The company never regained its hold, and the addition of musical interludes between the acts proved inadequate to offset the current popularity of the musical shows. In 1740, on the invitation of the Empress Anna, the Neuder company introduced modern theatre to Russia. But the Empress died in 1741, and by the time the company returned to Leipzig, Gottsched had allied himself with another company. His difference with the Neuberin intensified: she replaced the togas he had specified for his play *Der sterbende Cato* with flesh-coloured tights; he attacked her in his reviews; she represented him in a prologue as a bat-eared censor; an obscene pamphlet in reply cast aspersions on the actress' private life.

In 1747 she quit the stage but in the following year returned with a new company, which successfully presented Lessing's first play, *Der junge Gelehrte*. Indifferent success, however, dogged the company as it played at Dresden, Frankfurt, and Warsaw, as well as Leipzig. In 1753–54 the Neuberin attempted to establish herself in Vienna but failed; and the outbreak of the third Silesian War (1756), her husband's death (1759), and the bombardment of Dresden (1760) forced her to leave. She died in a peasant's hut, and although she was refused burial in holy ground, a monument was erected in 1776, commemorating her as "the foundress of good taste in the German theatre." She had already been immortalized as Madame Nelly in Goethe's *Wilhelm Meister*.

·commedia's unpopularity among actors **4**:986e
·Lessing's first play production **10**:838d

Neuberg, Carl (1877–1956), German chemist, discovered carboxylase in yeast and yeast juice (1911)—an important discovery for understanding fermentation. In 1912 he showed that if fermentation occurs in the presence of a salt, such as sodium sulfite, sugar can yield more than 30 percent of its weight in glycerol.

Neubrandenburg, *Bezirk* (district), northeastern East Germany, formed in 1952 from parts of the former states of Mecklenburg and Brandenburg, is mainly agricultural. Its area of 4,167 sq mi (10,793 sq km) mostly comprises the Mecklenburgische Seenplatte (Mecklenburg Lake Plateau), a hilly morainic region supporting wheat, sugar beets, and fruit. The heathlands of the Ückermünder Heide (northeast) and the Uckermark (southeast) support rye, potatoes, and pinewoods. Industries in the principal towns of Neubrandenburg (the capital) and Neustrelitz (*qq.v.*) include engineering, distilling, sugar refining, and woodworking. Pop. (1971 prelim.) 636,930.

·labour force distribution **8**:11b
·map, German Democratic Republic **8**:8

Neubrandenburg, capital of Neubrandenburg *Bezirk* (district), northeastern East Germany, near the northern end of the Tollensesee (Tollense Lake), south of Stralsund. Founded in 1248 by the margraves of Brandenburg as a fortified outpost, it passed to Mecklenburg in 1292 and was the capital of the duchy of Mecklenburg-Stargard from 1352 to 1471. Most of its medieval buildings were destroyed by bombing in World War II. Much rebuilt since it became the *Bezirk* capital (1952), Neubrandenburg has engineering, food-processing, chemical, wood, leather, and paper industries. Pop. (1971 prelim.) 45,601. 53°33′ N, 13°15′ E

·area and population table **8**:10
·map, German Democratic Republic **8**:8

Neuburg Beds, division of Upper Jurassic rocks in western Germany. (The Jurassic Period began about 190,000,000 years ago and lasted about 54,000,000 years.) The beds were named for exposures studied at Neuburg, on the Danube, West Germany. They consist of about 40 metres (130 feet) of limestones noted for their rich and varied fauna of fossil ammonite cephalopod (mollusk) forms; on the basis of these fossils it is considered to be of Late Kimmeridgian age—the Kimmeridgian Stage being a division of Late Jurassic rocks and time. Two ammonite zones (shorter spans of time) are recognized in the Neuburg Beds; the earlier zone is that of the species *Anavirgatites palmatus* and is followed by the zone of *Berriasella ciliata*. Many other ammonite species occur, providing a wealth of information useful for correlation of rocks found elsewhere and for paleontologic purposes.

Neuchâtel, canton, western Switzerland, bordering France to the northwest, Lake Neuchâtel to the southeast, and bounded by the cantons of Bern (northeast) and Vaud (southwest). Occupying an area of 308 sq mi (797 sq km), it lies in the central Jura Mountains and is drained by Lake Neuchâtel (leading to the Rhine) and Le Doubs River (leading to the Rhône). It consists of three regions: a low-lying strip along the lake called Le Vignoble (from its vineyards); an intermediate region, Les Vallées, comprising the two principal valleys of the canton (the Val de Ruz, watered by the Seyon, and the Val de Travers, watered by L'Areuse), which lie at an altitude of 2,300 ft (700 m); and the highest region, Les Montagnes Neuchâteloises (3,000–3,500 ft), mainly composed of a long valley in which stand the industrial centres of La Chaux-de-Fonds, Le Locle, La Sagne, Les Ponts-de-Martel, and La Brévine.

Novum Castellum (Neuchâtel) was first mentioned in the will of Rudolf III, the last king of Burgundy, who died in 1032. About 1034 the town and its territories were granted in fief to Count Ulrich von Fenis, whose dynasty gradually increased its dominion, until by 1373 it held practically all the area of the present canton, with the exception of the lordship of Valangin, which was held by a cadet line of the house until about 1592. In 1406 Neuchâtel entered into union with Bern and later played an important role in shaping Swiss destiny. It passed in the early 15th century to the lords of Freiburg im Breisgau in the German Rhineland and in 1504 to the French ducal house of Orléans-Longueville. The Reformation was introduced there in 1530 by Guillaume Farel, the French preacher, and Neuchâtel became a principality in 1648. With the extinction of the house of Orléans-Longueville in 1707, it passed to Frederick I, the first king of Prussia. The nominal role of the Prussian king lasted until 1848, with a brief interval from 1806 to 1814 when the principality was granted by Napoleon to his marshal, Louis-Alexandre Berthier. It was admitted to the Swiss Confederation in 1815 as the 21st canton and the only nonrepublican member, its hereditary rulers the last to maintain their position in Switzerland. A republican form of government was established by a peaceful revolution in 1848, and after long negotiations and several attempts at counter-revolution, including the so-called Neuchâtel crisis (1856), the King of Prussia renounced his claims to sovereignty in 1857.

The population is mainly French speaking and about two-thirds Protestant and one-third Catholic. The principal towns are Neuchâtel (the capital), La Chaux-de-Fonds, and Le Locle (*qq.v.*). In addition to excellent wineries, some fruit is grown in Le Vignoble and horses are raised. There are pastures for cattle in the valleys and some cheese is made. The most valuable mineral product is asphalt, concentrated in the Val de Travers. The most characteristic industry is watchmaking, which has been prominent since the early 18th century in the highland valleys of La Chaux-de-Fonds, Le Locle, and Fleurier. Road and rail communications are highly developed. Pop. (1970) 169,173.

·area and population table **17**:874
·map, Switzerland **17**:868

Neuchâtel, German NEUENBURG, capital (since 1815) of Neuchâtel canton, western Switzerland, on the northwestern shore of Lake Neuchâtel, at the mouth of the Seyon River, partly on the slopes of the Chaumont (3,870 ft [1,180 m]) and partly on land reclaimed from the lake. A Burgundian town by the 11th century, it was chartered in 1214. It was the centre of the former countship and principality (1648–1707) of Neuchâtel. Historic landmarks include the medieval castle (now the seat of the cantonal administration) and the Collégiale Notre-Dame (12th–13th centuries), now Protestant and containing the monumental tomb of the counts (1372). There are several fine 17th- and 18th-century patrician dwellings, including the Hôtel du Peyrou (*c.* 1765) and the town hall (1784–90), which is in classic style. The town's institutions include the University of Neuchâtel (founded as an academy in 1838), the Institute of Physics, the Swiss Laboratory of Horological Research, the commercial school, the conservatory of music, the museum and public library in the Collège Latin, the cantonal observatory, and the fine Musée des Beaux-Arts. The city has an important wine market and its manufactures include watches, chocolate, tobacco, and paper. Pop. (1970) 38,784.
46°59′ N, 6°56′ E

Neuchâtel, Lake, French LAC DE NEUCHÂTEL, German NEUENBURGERSEE, ancient LACUS EBURODUNENSIS, largest lake wholly in Switzerland; its area of 84 sq mi (218 sq km) is divided among the cantons of Neuchâtel, Vaud, Fribourg, and Bern. Lakes Neuchâtel, Biel (Bienne), and Morat, connected by canals, are survivors of a former glacial lake in the lower Aare Valley, at the base of the Jura Mountains. Lake Neuchâtel is about 23½ mi (38 km) long and from 3¾ to 5 mi wide; it lies at an altitude of 1,407 feet (429 m), and its greatest depth is 502 ft. Thièle River enters at its southwestern end and issues from it at its northeastern end. The lake also receives the Areuse and Broye rivers. The main lakeshore towns are Neuchâtel (Neuenburg), on the northwest shore, and Yverdon (Iferten; the Roman Eburodunum), at the southwest extremity. The northwestern shore (Neuchâtel canton) is the most thickly settled, and the slopes are covered with vineyards. On the north shore is La Tène, famous for prehistoric finds, which gives its name to the late Iron Age culture. There are steamer services between the lakeside towns.
46°52′ N, 6°50′ E

·map, Switzerland **17**:868
·size, altitude, and territory table **1**:632

Neuchâtel crisis (1856–57), a tense episode of Swiss history that had repercussions among the Great Powers of Europe. The Congress of Vienna (1814–15), in its general settlement of territorial questions after the Napoleonic Wars, ordained that Neuchâtel (or Neuenburg) should have a dual status: it was to be a canton of the reorganized Swiss Confederation and, at the same time, a hereditary principality belonging personally to the king of Prussia but separate from the Prussian kingdom. This arrangement caused dissatisfaction among the people of Neuchâtel, and in March 1848, when the Swiss were revising their constitution and when France, Germany, Austria, and Italy were all being shaken by revolutionary movements, a successful insurrection established a republic there. Frederick William IV of Prussia, preoccupied with his kingdom's troubles, could take no effective counteraction at the time. Four years later, in the London Protocol of 1852, the other Great Powers formally acknowledged his rights in Neuchâtel, but with the proviso that Prussia should do nothing to assert them without their concurrence. In September 1856 there was an unsuccessful pro-Prussian coup d'etat in Neuchâtel, conducted by loyalist aristocrats under the leadership of members of the family of Pourtalès. When its leaders were arrested, Frederick William appealed to the Swiss Federal Council for their release and also asked the French emperor Napoleon III to intercede for them. The Swiss at first persisted in declaring that the rebels must be brought to trial. Prussia severed diplomatic relations with Switzerland and began preparations for war—though it remained doubtful whether the south German states, under Austrian influence, would allow Prussian troops to cross their territory and though Great Britain was ready to back France in support of Switzerland. Napoleon III at last, in January 1857, induced the Swiss to release the prisoners into temporary exile, on the understanding that he would then negotiate a final settlement of the main question in Switzerland's favour; and, after a conference of the neutral powers in Paris (March–April), a treaty was signed in May 1857 whereby Frederick William renounced his sovereignty over Neuchâtel, keeping only the princely title.

Neue Bach-Gesellschaft (NBG), musical society that organizes festivals and publishes popular editions of Bach's works and a research journal (from 1904).
·activities and major publication **2**:560d

Neue Gedichte (1844), translated as NEW POEMS (1906), collection of poetry by Heinrich Heine.
·artistry and contemporary relevance **8**:744g

Neue Künstlervereinigung, English NEW ARTISTS' ASSOCIATION, group founded in 1909 by Wassily Kandinsky, Alexey von Jawlensky, Gabriele Münter, and numerous others who were united by opposition to the official art of Munich rather than by similarity of style. Joined by Adolf Erbslöh, Alexander Kanoldt, Alfred Kubin, Marianne von Werefkin, Karl Hofer, and several other artists as well as lay people, the group held its first exhibition in December 1909, at Moderne Galerie Tannhäuser, Munich. The works exhibited, which primarily reflected Jugendstil (*q.v.*) and Fauvist (*see* Fauvism) styles, were not favourably received by the critics or the public. Their second exhibition, held September 1910 at Tannhäuser, was international in scope, including, in addition to their works, those of Pablo Picasso, Georges Braque, Georges Rouault, Kees van Dongen, André Derain, Maurice de Vlaminck, Henri Le Fauconnier, and David and Vladimir Burlyuk. The exhibition was denounced for, among other things, including foreign artists, especially Russians, who were considered dangerous to Bavarian culture.

While preparing for their third exhibition, held December 1911 at Tannhäuser, differences in aesthetic outlook caused a split in the group, partially brought on by the jury's rejection of Kandinsky's large, rather abstract painting, "Last Judgment." Franz Marc (the last painter to join the group) and Kandinsky, favouring freedom of expression, were aligned against the more conservative art historian Otto Fischer (who later became the group's spokesman), Kanoldt, and Erbslöh. Kandinsky and Marc left the association (as did Münter and Kubin) and together formed Der Blaue Reiter (*see* Blaue Reiter, Der), exhibiting their works that same month at Tannhäuser, in rooms adjoining those of the Neue Künstlervereinigung.

Neuenburg (Switzerland): *see* Neuchâtel.

Neuenburgersee (Switzerland): *see* Neuchâtel, Lake.

Neuen Münicher Sezession, association of German artists, founded 1914.
·exhibition of Klee's works **10**:493b

Neue Physiologische Anstalt (1896; PHYSIOLOGICAL INSTITUTE), research centre founded at Leipzig, Germany, by Carl Ludwig.
·physiologic research centres **14**:436f

Neue Pinakothek (art collection, Munich): *see* Bayerische Staatsgemäldesammlungen.

Neuer Frühling (1844; "New Spring"), series of Heinrich Heine's poems published in his *Neue Gedichte*.
·mannered love poems and ballad poetry **8**:744g

Neue Sachlichkeit (German: New Objectivity), name given in 1924 by Gustav F. Hartlaub, director of the Mannheim Kunsthalle, to a group of artists whose works were executed in a realistic style (in contrast to the prevailing styles of Expressionism and Abstraction) and reflected what Hartlaub characterized as the resignation and cynicism of the post-World War I period in Germany. In a 1925 exhibition assembled at the Kunsthalle, Hartlaub displayed the works of the members of this group: George Grosz, Otto Dix, Max Beckmann, Georg Schrimpf, Alexander Kanoldt, Carlo Mense, Georg Scholz, and Heinrich Davringhausen.

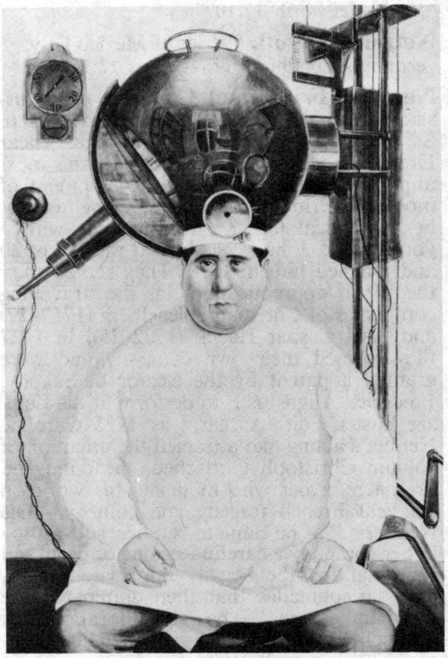

"Dr. Mayer-Hermann," by the Neue Sachlichkeit painter Otto Dix, oil and tempera on wood, 1926; in the collection of the Museum of Modern Art, New York

By courtesy of the Museum of Modern Art, New York, gift of Philip C. Johnson

Various trends and styles have been noted within Neue Sachlichkeit. Three subdivisions are sometimes proposed. The Veristic includes the socially critical (and frequently bitter) works of Grosz, Dix, and the early Beckmann. The Monumental, or classical, is represented by Schrimpf, Kanoldt, Mense, and Davringhausen, whose paintings displayed smooth, cold, and static qualities, partially derived from the Italian *pittura metafisica* (*see* Metaphysical painting); the term Magic Realism, one of the names sometimes applied to the entire Neue Sachlichkeit movement, best describes the style of these particular painters. Finally, the Rousseau school includes works by Walter Spiess and Scholz, for example, which are deliberately naïve, emulating the style of the French painter Henri Rousseau.

Although many Neue Sachlichkeit artists continued working in representational styles after the 1920s, the movement itself ended with the rise of Nazism.

Neues Theater, Berlin, taken over by Max Reinhardt in 1903.
·Reinhardt's acting and producing theory **18**:229g

Neue Vahr, town, Hessen, West Germany.
50°51′ N 9°07′ E
·Bremen's expansion since 1957 **3**:155e

Neue Veste, English NEW FORTRESS, Wittelsbach residence in Munich built in 1385.
·Munich's architectural landmarks **12**:617g

Neue Zeitschrift für Musik (German: "New Journal for Music"), music journal founded by Robert Schumann in 1834.
·music criticism influence by Schumann **12**:724f

Neue Zürcher Zeitung, Swiss newspaper founded in 1780 and noted for its international audience.

Neuf, Pont (bridge, Paris): *see* Pont Neuf.

Neufchâteau, François de (1750–1828), French statesman.
·industrial exhibition under Directory **7**:658g

Neufchâtel, a mild, white, creamy cheese first made in France.
·characteristics and classification **5**:432h

Neu-Guinea Kompagnie (1884–99): *see* German New Guinea Company.

Neuhof (NEUHOFF), **Theodor, Baron** (b. Aug. 24/25, 1694, Cologne, now in West Germany—d. Dec. 11, 1756, London), German adventurer, an indefatigable intriguer in military, political, and financial affairs throughout Europe, who was for a time, as Theodore I, the nominal king of Corsica. After serving in the French and Bavarian armies, he went to England and then to Spain to conduct negotiations on behalf of Sweden. Later he was involved in the speculations of the Scottish financier John Law. In Genoa he convinced some Corsican prisoners that he would free their island from Genoese tyranny if they made him their ruler. With their help and that of merchants in Tunis he landed on Corsica, where he was proclaimed king. At first he fought successfully against Genoa, but after his defeat a civil war broke out on Corsica, and he fled late in 1736. Twice, in 1738 and 1743, he returned to the island but failed to re-establish his authority. Imprisoned in London for debt, he secured his release by mortgaging his "kingdom."

Neuilly, Treaty of (Nov. 27, 1919), peace treaty between Bulgaria and the victorious Allied powers after World War I that became effective Aug. 9, 1920. Bulgaria was forced to cede lands to Yugoslavia and Greece (thus depriving it of an outlet to the Aegean) involving 300,000 people, to reduce its army to 20,000 men, and to pay reparations, 75 percent of which were later remitted.
·Balkan territorial rearrangement **2**:633a; map
·European realignment and reparations **19**:967f

Neuilly-sur-Seine, residential northwestern suburb of Paris, in Hauts-de-Seine *département*, immediately west of the capital and north of the Bois de Boulogne. Its main thoroughfare is the wide avenue de Neuilly, a prolongation of the Champs-Élysées and of the avenue de la Grande Armée. The 18th-century Pont de Neuilly, which bridges the avenue at the western border over the Seine River, regarded as an outstanding piece of engineering, was rebuilt and widened to 115 ft (35 m) in 1935–40. The American Hospital of Paris is located in Neuilly, which is served by the Paris Métro (subway). Pop. (1975) 65,941.

Neu Lauenburg: *see* Duke of York Islands.

Neumann, (Johann) Balthasar (b. 1687, Eger, Bohemia—d. 1753), German architect of diverse talents, a master of the late Baroque style. In 1709 he emigrated to Würzburg, where he learned his profession. Neumann designed palaces, housing, public buildings, bridges, a water system, and more than 100 churches. He ran a glass factory, became a colonel of engineers, and was a professor of architecture. A stolid and conventional man, he produced works brilliant in design and elegant in engineering. Neumann the dreamer would conceive the most intricate and original interiors; Neumann the builder realized them, achieving a maximum of security from a minimum of material. He directed squadrons of painters, sculptors, wood-carvers, iron founders, and

Interior of the church of Vierzehnheiligen, near Lichtenfels, W.Ger., by Balthasar Neumann, 18th century
GEKS

landscape gardeners in creating the sumptuously harmonious decoration of his masterpieces. The Residenz in Würzburg (1719–44), designed by Neumann with the assistance of Germain Boffrand and others, is one of the great palaces of the Baroque period. Neumann's church of Vierzehnheiligen (near Lichtenfels, in Bavaria) is a triumph in Rococo styling. Among his other works are the episcopal palaces of Bruchsal and Werneck and the pilgrimage churches of Neresheim and Käppele near Würzburg.
·Rococo architectural developments **19**:418g

Neumann, Erich (1905–60), German analytical psychologist.
·Gnostics described in Jungian terms **8**:219a

Neumann, Franz Ernst (b. Sept. 11, 1798, Joachimsthal, now in East Germany—d. May 23, 1895, Königsberg, East Prussia, now Kaliningrad, Russian S.F.S.R.), mineralogist, physicist, and mathematician who devised the first mathematical theory of electrical induction, the process of converting mechanical energy to electrical energy. Neumann's early work in crystallography gained him a reputation that led to his appointment as lecturer at the University of Königsberg, where he became in 1828 extraordinary professor and in 1829 ordinary professor of mineralogy and physics. In 1831 he formulated a law of molecular heat by extending the law of the heat of elements and stating that the molecular heat is equal to the sum of the heat of each constituent atom. Neumann published his theory of electrical induction in two papers (1845, 1847). He also made contributions in optics and mathematics.

Neumann, Franz (Leopold) (1900–54), German political scientist.
·Nazism cause theory **11**:602f

Neumann, Saint John Nepomucene (b. March 28, 1811, Prachatice, Bohemia—d. Jan. 5, 1860, Philadelphia), bishop of Philadelphia and a leader in the Roman Catholic parochial school system in the United States. After university study in Prague, he went to New York, where he was ordained in 1836. In 1840 he joined the Redemptorists, a religious congregation dedicated to parish and foreign missions, later becoming superior of all Redemptorists in the U.S. In 1852 Pope Pius IX appointed him bishop of Philadelphia.

He spent the rest of his life building churches, schools, and asylums for his diocese. Devoted to education, he was the first ecclesiastic to organize a diocesan school system in the U.S. He was beatified on Oct. 13, 1963, and canonized, as the first American male saint, on June 19, 1977, by Pope Paul VI; his feast day is January 7. *Venerable John Neumann, C.SS.R.*, by Michael J. Curley, C.SS.R., appeared in 1952.

Neumann, John von 12:1066 (b. Dec. 3, 1903, Budapest—d. Feb. 8, 1957, Washington, D.C.), mathematician who made important contributions in quantum physics, logic, meteorology, and in the development of computers. His theory of games had a significant influence on economics.

Abstract of text biography. In 1926 Neumann received a diploma in chemical engineering from the Technische Hochschule in Zürich and a Ph.D. in mathematics from the University of Budapest. When he was 20 years old, he published a definition of ordinal numbers that has been universally adopted. He was a lecturer at the University of Berlin, 1926–29, and at the University of Hamburg, 1929–30. He became a visiting lecturer in 1930 at Princeton University and was appointed professor there in 1931. In 1932 he gave a precise formulation and proof of the ergodic hypothesis of statistical mathematics and published a work on quantum mechanics. He became a professor at the Institute for Advanced Study in 1933. In the late 1930s he published works dealing with rings of operators (now called Neumann algebras). During World War II he served as a consultant to the armed forces. He stated the mathematical cornerstone of his theory of games, the minimax theorem, in 1928 and published the theorem's elaboration and applications in 1944, jointly with the economist Oskar Morgenstern, in *Theory of Games and Economic Behavior*. He was appointed to the Atomic Energy Commission (AEC) in 1955. In 1956 he received the Enrico Fermi Award.

REFERENCES in other text articles:
·atomic bomb detonator design **13**:325f
·automata theory **2**:497h
·computer development and EDVAC **4**:1047d
·functional analysis fundamentals **1**:758c
·game theory in economic measurement **11**:740d
·logic history from antiquity **11**:71e
·optimization theory and method **13**:622d
·topological group theory **18**:495b
·transfinite induction and ordinals **16**:572f
·weather computation **6**:88e

Neumann, Therese (b. 1898, Konnersreuth, Bavaria—d. Sept. 18, 1962, Konnersreuth), German stigmatic on whose body appeared marks resembling the wounds suffered by Jesus Christ on the hands, feet, and side. At the age of 20 she underwent a severe nervous shock after the outbreak of a fire and later suffered from hysterical paralysis, blindness, and gastric troubles. In 1926 a blood-coloured serum began to ooze from her eyes, and during Lent of the same year the stigmata appeared. Throughout the next 30 years these continued to bleed on many Fridays, especially during the last two weeks of Lent, and were accompanied by trances and other striking phenomena that attracted many visitors. Following her stigmatization, Therese claimed to live without food or drink, being sustained only by Holy Communion. At the request of her bishop she was subjected to a fortnight's investigation in 1927. Later the church authorities recognized this to have been inconclusive, as hysterical subjects are known to be able to sustain a complete fast for more than three weeks; in 1932 and 1937 she was requested to submit to another examination but refused, alleging that her father forbade her to do so. Hence her bishop issued no more permits for visits to her, which nevertheless reached a new peak in the years after World War II, when U.S. soldiers and others came to Konnersreuth in large numbers. After

1950 the Passion ecstasies became much less frequent, though she continued to be visited by thousands each year until her death. The controversy about the supernatural or purely neurotic origin of the phenomena continues.

Neumann-Bernays-Gödel axioms, a version of set theory in which arbitrary collections are called classes and certain rules are prescribed specifying which classes are sets. Not all classes are sets, because indiscriminate set formation leads to paradoxes, such as Cantor's paradox.

Neumann lines, in some iron meteorites (*see* hexahedrite), fine, straight, scratchlike marks that appear when the meteorite is cut open and the exposed surface polished and etched. The lines reveal an internal structure thought to result from some violent strain, such as a collision between astronomical bodies, that the meteorite was subjected to before its fall. They are named for their discoverer, German mineralogist Franz Ernst Neumann (1798–1895). *See also* Widmanstätten pattern.
·meteorite lamellar structure **12**:45c; illus. 46

Neumann problem, in mathematics, a second boundary value problem for an elliptic partial differential equation.
·differential equation principles **5**:762a

Neumark, historical district, Austria.
·Babenberg gains in Lower Austria **2**:450e

neumatic style, melodic style of Gregorian prose chants characterized by more frequent use of groups of two to four or more notes to one syllable.
·approach to text-melody relationship **12**:716g

neume, in musical notation, sign used to show one or more successive musical pitches, predecessor of modern musical notes. Neumes are used in notation of Jewish and Christian (*e.g.*, Gregorian, Byzantine) liturgical chants.

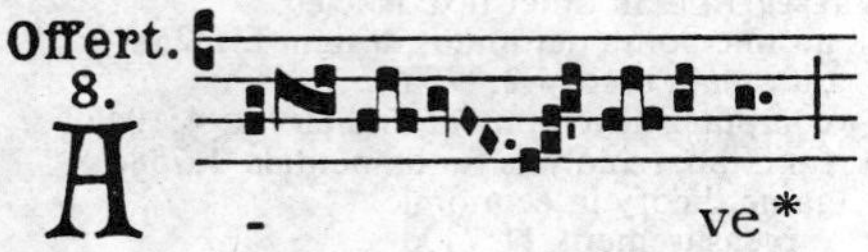

Neumatic notation from the plainsong "Ave Maria"
From *Liber Usualis* (1952); reproduced by permission of Desclee & Co., Belgium

In the Middle Ages they were also used to notate polyphony (music in several voices, or parts) and some secular music consisting of a single melodic line. Early neumes, thin squiggles written without a musical staff, developed from Greek textual accents that were gradually modified into various shapes showing pitch direction and vocal ornament. These staffless, or chironomic, neumes enabled a singer to recall a memorized melody and were capable of indicating subtle nuances. By the 11th century in European music, neumes were "heighted," or arranged to suggest melody line. A musical staff of four lines evolved in Europe in the 10th and 11th centuries. Neumes placed on the staff showed exact pitch, allowing a singer to read an unfamiliar melody. By about 1200 neumes had assumed a characteristic square shape, still used in modern notation of Gregorian chant. Whether and how neumes indicated rhythm is unknown and a subject of controversy. Musical notes with time values evolved from neumes in the last half of the 13th century.

A distinct system of neumes is used for the notation of Japanese Buddhist chant.
·early shōmyō chant notation **12**:683h
·staff notation's root in monophony **12**:734a
·Tibetan Buddhist chant and Japanese psalm illus. **12**:737

Neumünster, city, Schleswig-Holstein *Land* (state), northeastern West Germany, 30 mi (50 km) southwest of Kiel. Its name is derived from *novum monasterium* ("new minster"), the church of the monastery founded in 1127 by the Augustine missionary Vicelin, known as the apostle of the Wends. St. Vicelin's Church (1828–34) is in the town, which was chartered in 1870. The city suffered heavy air-raid damage in World War II and has been rebuilt on modern lines. It has several industrial training schools, including one for textile engineering, and a textile museum, a municipal museum, and a zoological garden for native animals. Neumünster is a busy road and rail junction; manufactures include textiles, leather, machinery, metalware, chemicals, and paper. Pop. (1970) 86,013.
54°04′ N, 9°59′ E
·map, Federal Republic of Germany **8**:46

Neunkirchen, city, in the Saar *Land* (state), southwestern West Germany, on the Blies River, just northeast of Saarbrücken. It was first mentioned in 1281 in historical documents as the town "with the new church" ("*neuen Kirchen*"). There is evidence of early iron founding (1595), but the town remained a rural village until the wealth of local coal deposits stimulated rapid growth in the late 19th century. It gained civic rights in 1922. Although coal and steel dominate the economy, there are also sawmills, breweries, and textile factories. Pop. (1970 est.) 44,326.
49°20′ N, 7°10′ E
·industrial and population concentration **16**:114b
·map, Federal Republic of Germany **8**:46

Neuquén, province, west central Argentina, bordered by Chile (west), the Río Colorado (north), and the Río Limay (south). The greater part of its area (36,324 sq mi [94,078 sq km]) is mountainous, with fertile, well-watered valleys and valuable forests. The eastern part, however, contains large plains with stunted vegetation and numerous saline deposits. Long droughts in this region have deterred agricultural development. The city of Neuquén, the provincial capital, is at the confluence of the Neuquén and Limay rivers, which there form the Río Negro—the chief river of the province, a transportation route, and the source of irrigation and hydroelectric power. The largest of a group of lakes in the higher Andean valleys is the celebrated Nahuel Huapí (*q.v.*), which lies in the southwest and overlaps into Río Negro province; it is the source of the Limay. Neuquén formed part of the Patagonia national territory until 1884, when it was made a separate national territory. It attained provincial status in 1955. Agriculture (mainly fruit) and stock raising provide the main sources of income. Exploitation of oil resources is growing in importance. Pop. (1970 prelim.) 154,570.
·area and population table **1**:1139
·map, Argentina **1**:1136

Neuquén, capital of Neuquén province, west central Argentina, at the confluence of the Neuquén and Limay rivers, opposite Cipolletti. Founded in 1904, the city is an inland river port and a processing and market centre (fruit, wines, and alfalfa) for the irrigated agricultural area served by the nearby Río Negro dam. Pop. (1970 prelim.) 43,001.
39°00′ S, 68°05′ W
·map, Argentina **1**:1136

Neuquenian Stage, uppermost major division of Upper Cretaceous rocks and time in Chile and Argentina (the Cretaceous Period began about 136,000,000 years ago and lasted about 71,000,000 years). Rocks of the Neuquenian Stage overlie those of the Diamantian Stage. The Neuquenian consists of as much as 2,000 metres (6,500 feet) of nonmarine red sandstones, variegated shales, and conglomerates as well as of marine shales and conglomerates. In the Andes the Neuquenian is represented by the thick Quirquina Volcanic Beds.

Neuradaceae, family of plants of the order Rosales.
·classification and general features **15**:1154a

neural arch (anatomy): *see* vertebral column.

neural crest, group of embryonic cells that are pinched off during the formation of the neural tube, precursor of the spinal cord, but do not remain as a part of the central nervous system. The cells of the neural crest migrate to numerous locations in the body and contribute to the formation of diverse structures often associated with the nervous system. The factors determining migration and differentiation are not known.

The most conspicuous of the neural crest derivatives are the melanocytes, cells in the deep layers of the epidermis that contain pigment and are responsible for skin coloration. In the head region the neural crest cells contribute significantly to the formation of the facial skeleton. Odontoblasts, the cells that help form the teeth, have their origin in the neural crest, as do many of the cranial nerve cells. The neural crest also contributes to the formation of the meningeal covering of the brain and is the source of Schwann cells, which surround and insulate nerve fibres in the peripheral nervous system. In addition to Schwann cells and melanocytes, the neural crest of the trunk region gives rise to paired chains of sympathetic nerve ganglia and to certain cells of the adrenal gland.

animal
·nervous system development **12**:989c
·origin and later embryogenesis **5**:632c

human
·autonomic nervous system embryology **12**:1032h
·ganglion cell and neuroblast origins **6**:750g
·origin and derivatives **12**:995c

neural fold, upward growth from the neural plate (*q.v.*) to form a side of the neural groove, a stage in the development of the central nervous system.
·animal nervous system development **12**:989a
·human nervous system embryology **6**:746f; illus. 743

neuralgia, cyclic attacks of acute pain in the distribution of a peripheral sensory nerve; cause is unknown, and pathological changes in nerve tissue cannot be found. Neuralgia is frequently confused with another disorder, neuritis (*q.v.*). The terms are not synonymous. There are two principal types of neuralgia: trigeminal neuralgia (tic douloureux) and glossopharyngeal neuralgia.

Trigeminal neuralgia is a complex of symptoms of unknown cause characterized principally by attacks, of short duration, of severe pain along any of the branches of the trigeminal nerve. There is usually no evidence of change in the nerve tissue itself. The disease may occur at any age after puberty but usually begins somewhat after middle age. It affects women more frequently than men. The intense pain is usually described by patients as "stabbing," "shooting," or "lightning-like" and extremely brief. In early stages of the disease, these pains last for less than a minute or two, with weeks or months between attacks. As the condition progresses, the periods between attacks become shorter. Areas around the nose and mouth become hypersensitive and, when touched, trigger an attack. Attacks are also touched off by talking, eating, drinking, or by exposure to cold. Analgesics offer temporary relief. The condition can be cured permanently by severing the sensory root of the nerve proximal to the ganglion. Simple decompression of the roots and of the posterior part of the ganglion have had some good results.

Glossopharyngeal neuralgia is a relatively rare disorder characterized by recurring severe pain in the pharynx, tonsils, back of the tongue, and middle ear. The cause is unknown, and the disease usually has its onset after age 40, more frequently in males than in females. No pathological changes are noted in the nerve tissue. The pains may be excruciating, beginning in the throat and radiating to the ears or down the side of the neck. They

may occur spontaneously or be triggered by sneezing, coughing, yawning, chewing, or talking. The attacks are usually separated by long intervals and, when they do occur, last only a few seconds to a minute or two. Medical treatment is usually ineffective, for the attack subsides before analgesics exert their action. Surgery is indicated in extreme cases.
·pregnancy complications **14**:980e
·types, symptoms, and treatment **12**:1046d

neural groove, in anatomy, in the early embryo, a longitudinal depression in the region called the neural plate. From it forms the neural tube, the main rudiment of the central nervous system.
·animal nervous system development **12**:989a
·human nervous system embryology **6**:746e

neural nets, in automata theory, mathematical models the components of which are roughly patterned after elements of the human nervous system.
·automata theory and mathematical models **2**:497f

neural plate, in early embryo, thickened portion of the ectoderm (outer cell layer) from which the central nervous system ultimately develops.
·chordate embryonic structures **5**:632b; illus. 629
·human precursors and derivates **12**:995c
·vertebrate nervous system development **12**:989a

neural tube, canal that forms in vertebrate embryos and eventually develops into the brain and spinal cord. It is formed from outer embryonic tissue (ectoderm) that migrates inside to form a groove, which then closes as a tube.
·chordate embryo, illus. 7, 10, and 11 **5**:629
·human histogenesis **6**:750c; illus. 743
·human neural embryology **12**:995c
·vertebrate eye morphology **14**:361h
·vertebrate nervous system development **12**:989d

neurasthenia, a syndrome marked by physical and mental fatigue accompanied by withdrawal and depression.
·fatigue in stress situations **7**:192b
·symptom complex and therapy **15**:170g

Neurath, Otto (1882–1945), German philosopher and sociologist, director of the International Union of Pedagogy, was noted for using neo-Positivist thought as the basis for Behaviourist sociology and economics. Among his writings are *Empirische Soziologie* (1931; "Empirical Sociology") and *Foundations of the Social Sciences* (2nd ed., 1947).
·encyclopaedia's educational function **6**:782d
·Positivism of Vienna and Berlin schools **14**:879a
·protocol sentences and thing-language **14**:880f
·Unity of Science movement **16**:388g

neurilemma (biology): *see* Schwann sheath.

neuritis, general term for degenerative, noninflammatory disease of nerve tissue. (Because the ending "-itis" ordinarily means "inflammation," neuropathy, or "nerve disease," is a better term for the conditions covered by "neuritis.") If confined to a single nerve, the disease is designated mononeuritis; to two or more nerves, but in separate locations, mononeuritis multiplex; or to many nerves simultaneously, polyneuritis. Neuritis implies a complex of motor, vasomotor, sensory, and reflex symptoms, singly or in combination, resulting from neural pathology. The pathology can be produced by a variety of agents, including infectious, metabolic, toxic, vascular, or mechanical.

Sensory symptoms have been described as tingling, prickling, burning, boring, or stabbing pains that are worse at night and are aggravated by touch or temperature change. Motor symptoms start with weakness and may progress to complete paralysis. Muscles lose tone, become tender, and may atrophy. Vasomotor symptoms include hyperemia (congestion of blood), sweating, and the appearance of large blisters when partial and irritative lesions are present. With complete lesions, pallor, skin dryness, and osteoporosis are usually present.

Both single and multiple mononeuritis are characterized by weakness, pain, and paresthesia (prickling, burning, numbness) in the affected part. Bell's palsy, which, because of a lesion in the facial nerve, causes a characteristic distortion of the face, is a form of mononeuritis.

Polyneuritis (multiple peripheral neuritis), as opposed to mononeuritis, which is asymmetrical, occurs as a bilateral, symmetrical, and simultaneous involvement of motor, vasomotor, and sensory nerves. Symptoms are numbness, tingling, and other paresthesias, including burning pain. These start in the digits and progress up the extremities. Muscular weakness is associated with progressive atrophy and reduced reflex ability. Edema (abnormal accumulation of fluid in tissues or serous cavities) and skin discoloration are frequently present.

Treatment is directed toward the causative agent. Analgesics may be required for pain. Under proper therapy, recovery is usually rapid in less severe cases; repetition of the original cause may bring about recurrence. In severe cases, recovery may be incomplete, with some residual motor and sensory disturbances.
·pregnancy complications **14**:980e
·types, symptoms, causation, incidence, and course **12**:1046a

neuroblast, embryonic cell from which a nerve cell (neuron) develops.
·nerve cell development from gray matter **6**:750c
·vertebrate nervous system development **12**:989d

neurochord, a prominent strand of nervous tissue, the primitive central nervous system.
·hemichordate epidermal nervous system **8**:756b

neurocirculatory asthenia, or SOLDIER'S HEART, syndrome caused by anxiety and stress, marked chiefly by difficult breathing, fatigue, racing heart, and pain in the heart–stomach region.
·fatigue in stress situations **7**:192b

neurofibromatosis, or VON RECKLINGHAUSEN'S SYNDROME I, relatively common (1 per 3,000 births) congenital disorder characterized by benign soft tumour formation and destructive changes in the bones. It is a heritable disease (autosomal dominant). Tumours may be locally confined or widespread and may occur in the skin and viscera (fibroma molluscum) and along nerve trunks (neurofibromata). Thinning and cystic degeneration of bones occurs, sometimes associated with enlargement of bone or soft tissues or both in the extremities. Café au lait (pale brown) spots on the skin accompany these changes. Complications include progressive scoliosis (lateral curvature of the spine) in childhood, which must be treated with spinal fusion, disability from intracranial tumour development, and change of a benign tumour into a sarcoma. The disease begins in midchildhood; it may cease at puberty or may be progressive through life.
·human genetic disorders **7**:1005a

neurogenic arthropathy, also known as CHARCOT'S JOINT (after Jean-Martin Charcot, a 19th-century French neurologist), massive destruction of a stress-bearing joint, with development of large flanges and spurs of new bone at the sides of the joint. The condition eventually causes inability to use the joint but is accompanied by little or no sensation of pain or discomfort. The disorder accompanies damage to the nervous system in which sensory knowledge of joint position and strength is lost; the affected individual is not aware of overuse or injury so that destructive changes can develop quickly.

The most common cause of Charcot's joint is tabes dorsalis, a form of nervous system disease that occurs in untreated tertiary venereal syphilis; the knee, hip, ankle, and lower back are most often affected. Neurogenic arthropathy of the foot occurs as a complication of diabetes. Other diseases that destroy the sense of joint position or of pain may also cause Charcot's joint, such as leprosy, spinal cord injury, or pernicious anemia. Treatment involves complete protection of the joint from further stress or injury, commonly by the use of a brace.
·innervation impairments in joints **10**:264a

neurogenic shock, shock caused by the relaxation of the nervous system and dilation of blood vessels.
·causes of increased circulatory capacity **16**:700d *passim* to 701g

neuroglia, in vertebrate nervous systems, cells located around nerve cells (neurons). Neuroglia cells separate and support individual neurons and may also provide nutrition.
·aging effects on tissues **1**:302d
·animal tissue comparisons **18**:446d
·vertebrate central and peripheral nervous systems **12**:987b
·vertebrate nerve specializations **12**:969g

neurogram (neurophysiology): *see* engram.

neurohemal organ, in anatomy, the region at which are released into the bloodstream specialized secretions (neurohormones; *q.v.*) of nerve cells called neurosecretory cells, which translate nervous signals into chemical stimuli.
·hormone role in nerve impulse transmission **8**:1074d; illus.
·neuroendocrine interactions **12**:992f
·structure, function, and innervation **6**:839e

neurohormone, a secretion that converts neural signals into chemical stimuli. After being produced by specialized nerve cells (neurosecretory cells), neurohormones pass along nerve-cell extensions (axons) and are released into the bloodstream at special regions called neurohemal organs. Sometimes, however, the neurosecretory nerve endings are so close to their target sites that vascular transmission is not necessary, as it is for most other hormones.

The neurohormones in most mammals are oxytocin and arginine vasopressin, both of which are produced in the hypothalamic region of the brain. The primary actions of oxytocin are the promotion of uterine contraction (of value in obstetrical medicine) and the release of milk during suckling. Although vasopressin causes an increase in blood pressure in mammals through contraction of the blood vessels, its primary action is on the kidney; it brings about a reduction in the output of urine.
·acetylcholine's role in nerve impulse **14**:438h
·biochemistry of hallucinogens **8**:558b
·bird mating mechanism **18**:447h
·function and release mechanisms **6**:839f
·nerve impulse propagation **8**:1074c; illus.
·neuroendocrine interactions **12**:992f

neurohypophysis: *see* pituitary gland.

neurolemma, or SHEATH OF SCHWANN, membrane of cells covering both myelinated and unmyelinated nerve fibres.
·neural crest differentiation **6**:750h

neurolinguistics, the study of the neurological mechanisms underlying the storage and processing of language. Although it has been fairly satisfactorily determined that the language centre is in the left hemisphere of the brain in right-handed people, controversy remains concerning whether individual aspects of language are correlated with different specialized areas of the brain. One kind of research carried on in this field is the study of

aphasia, a condition of the brain in which language ability is impaired or destroyed. Temporary aphasia has been induced by electrically stimulating the cortex of conscious patients in order to determine the location of the various functions of language. While very general centres of language have been proposed, it seems that there are no highly specialized centres; several cases have been reported of patients who, after having their left hemisphere of the brain removed, adapted in the right hemisphere the language function that the left hemisphere had had. In general, however, very little is known about the neurological aspects of language.
·cerebral lobes and language performance **10**:1010h

neurological model, model of a portion of the nervous system of a living creature used in the study of automata.
·automata theory and mathematical models **2**:497e

neurologic surgery, surgical specialty concerned with treatment of diseases and injuries of the nervous system. Injury to the brain from skull fracture is the condition most commonly requiring the services of the neurologic surgeon. Other conditions with which he is involved include tumours of the brain and diseases and defects of the spinal cord and of the peripheral nerves.
·aphasia experiments **10**:1011a
·contributions of Macewen and Cushing **11**:838a
·lobotomy origin and usage **15**:144e

neurology, the medical specialty that deals with the nervous system and its diseases. Board requirements, examinations for specialization and practice, and residencies vary from country to country.

Neuroloma: *see* granite moss.

neuromuscular blocking agent, any of various drugs that interfere with the transmission of nerve impulses from nerve to muscle. The drugs affect the action of acetylcholine, a compound that is released by nerve endings to initiate muscle contraction.
·acetylcholine antagonism by atropine **17**:693b
·anesthesia and muscle paralysis **1**:868f

neuromuscular junction, site of chemical communication between a nerve cell and a muscle cell, the function of which is to transmit information from the nerve to the muscle so that muscle contraction results. A nerve impulse arriving at the nerve terminal accelerates the secretion of acetylcholine from the nerve ending. Acetylcholine molecules flow across the gap between the nerve cell and muscle cell and act on special receptor sites of the muscle cell. Acetylcholine is then destroyed by acetylcholine esterase, an enzyme (biological catalyst) in the receptor area. This destruction is important, for it terminates the nerve-to-muscle signal, thus permitting the muscle to relax.
·nerve and muscle interactions **12**:968f
·structures and mechanisms in muscle contraction **12**:624d

neuromuscular spindle, the stretch receptors of skeletal muscles, which signal passive stretching of the muscle.
·sensory reception of motion **16**:550f; illus.

neuron, or NERVE CELL, basic cell of the nervous system in vertebrates and most invertebrates from the level of the cnidarians. It transmits nerve impulses. A typical neuron has a cell body containing a nucleus and two or more long fibres. Impulses are carried along one or many of these fibres, the dendrites, to the cell body; in higher nervous systems, only one fibre, the axon, carries the impulse away from the cell body. Bundles of fibres from neurons are held together by connective tissue and form nerves. Some neurons of large vertebrates are several feet long.

comparative anatomy and physiology
·aging processes and effects **1**:302b
·animal tissue comparisons **18**:446c
·automata theory and mathematical models **2**:497e
·cell theory and classification **3**:1061e
·embryonic origins and development **5**:633h
·hormonal influence on nerve impulse **8**:1074c
·impulse propagation and nerve structure **12**:969a; illus.
·insect types, placement, and functions **9**:617e
·invertebrate and vertebrate nervous systems **12**:977b
·learning and behaviour theories **10**:738h
·length in man, elephant, and whale **12**:454e
·muscle contraction mechanisms **12**:624c; illus.
·muscle tissue innervation patterns **12**:641d
·neurosecretory cell structure **6**:847a; illus.
·radioresistance and radiosensitivity **15**:383c
·respiratory system control reflexes **15**:760g
·sensory reception theory and processes **16**:547a
·sponge sense reception **14**:852c
·thermoreceptive functions **18**:331g
·tissue culture illus. **18**:440

human structure and function **12**:996c; illus. 1025
·disease effects on muscle **12**:634a
·drug action on neurotransmitters **17**:692f
·ear anatomy and hearing mechanism **5**:1127f
·endocrine system interrelationships **6**:800d
·evolution and embryology **12**:994h
·eye anatomy and function **7**:95f
·gray matter embryology **6**:750d
·perception's physiological basis **14**:39g
·prenatal and postnatal growth **5**:651h
·psychophysiologic aspects of function **15**:159h
·reduction of total number during aging **1**:307b
·sensory reception structures and processes **16**:547h
·spinal cord structures and functions **12**:1008h
·Nissl body structure, function, and location **12**:996g

neuronal junction (biology): *see* synapse.

neuropharmacological agent, drug affecting the nervous system and resulting in changes in behaviour, perception, thought, and emotion.
·drug action mechanism **12**:992c

neurophysiology, study of the functioning of the nervous system.
·biophysics source discipline **2**:1035c

neuroplasm, the protoplasm, exclusive of special inclusions, of a nerve cell.
·contents and locations in man **12**:996h

neuropteran 12:1067, common name for any weak-flying insect of the alderfly order Megaloptera, the snakefly order Raphidiodea, and the lacewing order Neuroptera (or Planipennia).

The text article includes information on the natural history, form and function, evolution and paleontology, and classification of the neuropterans.

RELATED ENTRIES in the *Ready Reference and Index:*
alderfly; antlion; dobsonfly; dustywing; fishfly; lacewing; mantispid; owlfly; snakefly; spongillafly

Neuropteris, genus of fossil seed ferns from the Devonian to the Triassic.
·fossil plants and eras, illus. 14 **7**:575

neuroradiology, branch of medical science dealing with the use of radiant energy in the diagnosis and treatment of nervous system disorders.
·radiologic methodology and applications **15**:463e

neurosecretion, a substance released from a nerve cell, or neuron.
·annelid worm cells and functions **1**:934e
·autonomic influences of the human hypothalamus **12**:1029e
·endocrine–nervous interrelationship **2**:812h
·human hypothalamic hormones **6**:810d
·invertebrate structures and functions **6**:845g

neurosecretory granule
·hormone production and transport **6**:841a; illus. 847
·neuroendocrine interactions **12**:992f

neurosecretory cell, a neuron, or nerve cell, the function of which is to translate neural signals into chemical stimuli. Such cells produce secretions (neurohormones) that pass along the nerve cell axon and are typically released into the bloodstream at special regions (neurohemal organs) in which the axon endings are in close contact with blood capillaries. They occur in most multicellular animals and are usually distinguished from other neurons by the unusually large size of the cell nucleus, axon endings, and the cell itself.
·arthropod nervous system **12**:981h

vertebrate
·endocrine system interrelationships **6**:839f
·physiologic regulation by hormones **14**:439e
·structure, properties, and functions **6**:846h; illus. 840

neurosis (psychology): *see* psychoneurosis.

Neurospora (fungi): *see* Ascomycetes.

neurosyphilis (disease): *see* paresis.

neurotoxin, any substance that is poisonous to nervous tissue.
·animal and plant poisons **14**:606h; tables 608
·snake venom action **16**:565b

neurotransmitter, a chemical (*e.g.*, acetylcholine, norepinephrine) that diffuses across the gap (synaptic cleft) from the end of one nerve cell to a neighbouring one. Release of the neurotransmitter is stimulated by an electrically excited state.
·nerve impulse transmission **12**:978g
·stimulant and antidepressant drugs **17**:692g

Neurotrichus gibbsii (mammal): *see* mole.

neurula, in embryology, the embryonic stage in which the neural tube develops from the neural plate.
·embryonic growth and differentiation **6**:746f

Neusalz (Poland): *see* Nowa Sól.

Neusatz (Yugoslavia): *see* Novi Sad.

Neus Berg Ridge, feature of the Orange River valley, South Africa.
28°48′ S 20°47′ E
·Orange River shore topography **13**:640g

Neuse River, in northeast central North Carolina, U.S., is formed by the junction of the Flat and Eno rivers in Durham County. It flows about 300 mi (480 km), generally southeast; 35 mi from the Atlantic Ocean, it is joined by the Trent River to form an estuary 5 mi wide and about 40 mi long. It flows past Croatan National Forest before reaching Pamlico Sound on its way to the Atlantic.
35°06′ N, 76°30′ W

Neuserre, sixth king of the 5th dynasty (*c.* 2494–*c.* 2345) of Egypt; he is primarily known for his temple to the sun god Re at Abū Jirāb (Abu Gurab) in Lower Egypt. The temple plan, like that built by Userkaf (the first king of the 5th dynasty), consisted of a valley temple, causeway, gate, and temple court, which contained an obelisk (the symbol of Re) and an alabaster altar. The sun-temple reliefs revealed an exceptionally high development of artistry and technique. Few written records were left from Neuserre's reign, but the pyramid he used as a burial place has been located at Abū Ṣīr near the sun temples of Abū Jirāb. Though impressive in size, Neuserre's pyramid was exceeded both in height and in length by his sun temple, indicating the unusual prominence of the cult of Re during the 5th dynasty.
·royal renewal ceremony celebration **6**:467c
·temple architecture of Old Kingdom **19**:250g

Neusiedler Lake, German NEUSIEDLERSEE, Hungarian FERTŐ, in Burgenland (east Aus-

Neusiedler Lake from Burgenland, Austria

Toni Schneiders—Bruce Coleman

tria) and northwest Hungary, takes its names from the Austrian town of Neusiedl and the Hungarian word for "swamp lake." Formed several million years ago during the Pleistocene (geological) Epoch, probably as a result of tectonic subsidence, it is Austria's lowest point (371 ft [113 m] above sea level). Slightly saline with no natural outflow and very shallow (rarely more than 4–6 ft deep), it fluctuates in level and size (135 sq mi [350 sq km]) with climatic variations. A canal (built 1873–95) connects it to the Rabnitz (Hungarian Répce) River, a tributary of the Danube. A heavy reed growth along its shores provides sanctuary for many species of rare and migratory birds. The lake regulates climate and groundwater, provides raw materials for the cellulose industry, and serves as a recreation area for nearby Vienna. Major lakeside towns are Neusiedl, Podersdorf (the main summer resort), and the wine centre of Rust.
47°50′ N, 16°46′ E

·Europe's nature preservation efforts **6**:1049f
·map, Austria **2**:442

Neusohl (Czechoslovakia): *see* Banská Bystrica.

Neuss, city, Nordrhein-Westfalen (North Rhine-Westphalia) *Land* (state), northwestern West Germany, linked to the Rhine by the Erft-Kanal, opposite Düsseldorf; its harbour is accessible to small oceangoing ships. Founded *c.* 12 BC as a Roman fortress (the Novaesium of Tacitus), it was captured by the Franks and renamed Niusa. It was chartered 1187–90. As a defensive outpost of the Cologne electors, it was unsuccessfully besieged by Charles the Bold (1474–75). It was sacked by Alessandro Farnese in 1586 and passed to Prussia in 1816.

The Quirinus Church (1209), with its Baroque dome (1741), and the town hall (1634–38) were damaged in World War II but have been restored. The 13th-century Obertor (a massive gatehouse), part of the medieval fortifications, houses the Clemens-Sel municipal museum, and the Zeughaus (1639), or arsenal, is now a concert hall. The famous Rhineland rifle marksmanship contest, the "Neusser Kirmes," is held there every August.

Neuss is an important rail junction, port, grain market, and industrial centre. Its manufactures include machinery, screws, rivets, chemicals, concrete, rope, ceramics, and bricks. Pop. (1970 est.) 117,600.
51°12′ N, 6°41′ E

·map, Federal Republic of Germany **8**:46

Neustadt an der Weinstrasse, formerly NEUSTADT AN DER HAARDT, city, Rheinland-Pfalz (Rhineland-Palatinate) *Land* (state), southwestern West Germany, on the eastern slope of the Haardt Mountains, at the mouth of the Speyer-bach, southwest of Ludwigshafen. Founded in 1220 and chartered in 1275, its historic buildings include the Casimirianum (the seat of Heidelberg University, 1578–83, now a popular convention hall), the town hall (formerly a Jesuit college), and the 14th-century Gothic abbey church (Stiftskirche). The centre of the Pfalz wine trade (German *Weinstrasse*, "wine route"), the famous Deutsche Weinlesefest (wine festival) is held annually in the city, which is also the site of a training and research institute of viticulture and horticulture. A rail junction, its convenient location and picturesque setting at the foot of Mt. Kalmit (2,241 ft [683 m]) make it a favourite tourist base. Other economic activities include food processing and the manufacture of metal products, textiles, paper, and concrete. Pop. (1970 est.) 51,058.
49°21′ N, 8°08′ E

·map, Federal Republic of Germany **8**:46

Neustettin (Poland): *see* Szczecinek.

neuston, ecological term for organisms found on top of or attached to the underside of the surface film of water. The neuston includes insects such as whirligig beetles and water striders; some spiders and protozoans; and occasional worms, snails, insect larvae, and hydras. It is distinguished from the plankton, which only incidentally becomes associated with the surface film.

·characteristics and destructiveness **1**:1032h

Neustrelitz, city, Neubrandenburg *Bezirk* (district), northern East Germany, on the Zierker See (lake), north of Berlin. Founded in 1726 by the grand dukes of Mecklenburg-Strelitz, it became their capital after their earlier residence at nearby Strelitz burned down (1712). It remained the capital of Mecklenburg-Strelitz until 1934, when that state and Mecklenburg-Schwerin were combined. It was chartered in 1773. Widespread destruction in World War II included damage to the former grand ducal palace (1726–31). The centre of an extensive agricultural region, Neustrelitz is a junction on the Berlin–Stralsund railway and has foodstuffs, wood, and engineering factories. Pop. (1971 est.) 27,788.
53°21′ N, 13°04′ E

·map, German Democratic Republic **8**:8

Neustria, during the Merovingian period (6th–8th centuries) of early medieval Europe, the western Frankish kingdom as distinct from Austrasia, the eastern kingdom. By derivation, Neustria was the "new" (French *neuf;* German *neu*) land; *i.e.*, the area colonized by the Franks since their settlement in northern Gaul. It corresponded roughly to the area of present France west of the Meuse and north of the Loire rivers. In the 7th century Austrasia and Neustria were rivals, but the victory of Pepin of Herstal, mayor of the palace in Austrasia, over the Neustrians at Tertry (687) assured the ultimate ascendancy of Austrasia. In the later Merovingian period, Neustrian writers used the names Neustria and Francia (France) interchangeably, implying that Neustria formed the heart and core of the Frankish lands. Later, the name Neustria came to denote a much smaller area, and, by the 11th and 12th centuries, it was sometimes used synonymously with Normandy.

·Charles Martel and union of Franks **4**:61g
·Merovingian territorial partitions **11**:928b; maps

Neuth (Egyptian goddess): *see* Nut.

Neutra (Czechoslovakia): *see* Nitra.

Neutra, Richard Joseph (b. April 8, 1892, Vienna—d. April 16, 1970, Wuppertal, W. Ger.), architect particularly known for his role in introducing the International Style into U.S. architecture. Educated at the Technische Hochschule (technical university), Vienna, and the University of Zürich, Neutra, with the German architect Erich Mendelsohn, won an award in 1923 for a city planning project for Haifa, Israel. Neutra moved to the United States the same year, working briefly for the firm of Holabird and Roche in Chicago and at Taliesin, Spring Green, Wis., with Frank Lloyd Wright.

Neutra's most important early work was the Lovell House, Los Angeles (1927–29), which has glass expanses and cable-suspended balconies, stylistically similar to the contemporary work of Le Corbusier and Mies van der Rohe in Europe. Throughout the 1930s he designed houses in the International Style. Other early works were the Corona School, Los Angeles (1935), and the Channel Heights Housing Project, San Pedro, Calif. (1942–44).

Neutra, 1968

By courtesy of Dion Neutra, Richard and Dion Neutra Architects and Associates

Shortly after World War II, Neutra created his most memorable works: the Kauffmann Desert House, Palm Springs, Calif. (1946–47), and the Tremaine House, Santa Barbara, Calif. (1947–48). Elegant and precise, these houses are considered exceptionally fine examples of the International Style. Carefully placed in the landscape, Neutra's houses often have patios or porches that make the outdoors seem part of the house. He believed that architecture should be a means of bringing man back into harmony with nature and with himself, and was particularly concerned that his houses reflect the way of life of the owner.

During the 1950s and 1960s Neutra's works included office buildings, churches, buildings for colleges and universities, housing projects, and cultural centres. After 1966 he was in partnership with his son, the firm name becoming Richard and Dion Neutra, Architects and Associates. He died while on a tour of Europe. Among his voluminous writings are *Survival Through Design* (1954) and *Life and Human Habitat* (1956).

Neutral, a confederacy of Iroquoian-speaking Indians who lived in what are now southern Ontario, western New York, northeastern

Ohio, and southeastern Michigan; they received their name from the French because they were neutral in the known wars between the Iroquois and the Huron before the mid-17th century. Their neutrality did not extend to all other tribes, and during the early 17th century the Neutral were at war with groups to the west, particularly the Potawatomi. Neutral villages of bark-covered houses were situated on high, defensible ground; their economy was based on agriculture, supplemented by game, which was plentiful in this area. Villages were governed by civil chiefs and councils of elders; war chiefs were concerned with military matters.

During the war between the Huron and the Iroquois in 1648–49, the Neutral attempted to gain favour with the Iroquois by seizing those Huron who had sought refuge with them as well as other Huron; the Iroquois nevertheless attacked and destroyed the Neutral in 1650–51. The last mention of them as an independent group was a report of 800 members of the tribe living in the vicinity of Detroit in 1653. The remainder were either killed or absorbed by the Iroquois.

·Woodlands Indian culture **6**:169b

neutral fat: *see* triglyceride.

neutralism, in international politics, the policy of nonalignment with major power blocs as pursued by such countries as India, Burma, Kenya, Yugoslavia, and most of the new states of Asia and Africa in the post-World War II period. These countries refused, for the most part, to align themselves with either the Communist bloc, led by the Soviet Union, or the Western bloc, led by the United States. Though neutralist in this sense, they were, however, not neutral or isolationist, for they not only participated actively in international affairs but also took positions on international issues and controversies.

Neutralism must also be distinguished from neutrality; while neutralism refers to the foreign policy of a state in time of peace, neutrality is a term in international law referring to the rules that states are obliged to follow during a legal state of war in which they are not belligerents. Their neutral status implies strict impartiality and abstention from any assistance to the belligerent parties.

The widespread espousal of neutralism as a distinct policy is a post-World War II phenomenon, but similar policies have been followed, though to a lesser extent, in the past. The so-called isolationist policy and the avoidance of entangling alliances, advocated for the United States by Presidents Washington and Jefferson and pursued during the European wars between France and Great Britain following the French Revolution and for a century after the peace of 1815, are analogous to the modern policy of neutralism.

States that pursue a policy of neutralism in recent times have justified their position on a number of grounds. They have declined to assume that the United States, the Soviet Union, or any other country necessarily intends to embark upon aggressive action designed to violate their territorial integrity and have, therefore, refused to enter into alliances or collective defense arrangements directed against particular states. They have also declined to assume that the ideological or political or economic system by which a nation conducts its domestic affairs dictates its international actions. Neutralist states believe such a policy is necessary to preserve their independence and that it serves their national interests. The new nations of Asia and Africa, which constitute the largest group of neutralist states, are mostly former colonies of the Western powers. The new nations are, on the one hand, wary of permanent and close alignments with these powers in the Western bloc for fear of being drawn into a newer form of dependence; on the other hand, though generally attracted by the rapid economic advances made by the Communist systems, they fear that intimate ties with the Soviet Union may also infringe their independence by throwing them into a satellite-type subjugation. Also, a neutralist policy often enables them to get much-needed economic assistance from both power blocs.

In the 1960s, some neutralist states sought to form a bloc of all neutralist states with a unified policy in international affairs, but these attempts did not succeed because of the divergence of national interests among them on specific issues and policies.

·Nehru's attempts and setbacks **12**:946c
·Wilson's World War I diplomacy **19**:956e

neutrality, the legal status arising from the abstention of a state from all participation in a war between other states, the maintenance of an attitude of impartiality toward the belligerents, and the recognition by the belligerents of this abstention and impartiality. Under international law this legal status gives rise to certain rights and duties between the neutral and the belligerents.

The law concerning the rights and duties of neutrality are contained, for the most part, in the Declaration of Paris of 1856, the Hague Convention V, 1907 (neutrality in land war), and the Hague Convention XIII, 1907 (neutrality in maritime war). One of the first recommendations of the last convention was that, when war breaks out between certain powers, each nation wishing to remain impartial should normally issue either a special or general declaration of neutrality. Such a declaration, however, is by no means absolute. A neutral state may, during the course of the hostilities, repeal, change, or modify its position of neutrality, provided that such alterations are in accordance with international law and are applied without bias to all belligerents.

The most important of the rights that result from a declaration of neutrality is the right of territorial integrity. Belligerents may not use a neutral's territory as a base of operations or engage in hostilities therein. This right applies not only to neutral territory and water, but extends to air space above that territory as well. Thus, under the Hague Rules of Air Warfare, 1923, neutrals have the right to defend their air space from passage of belligerent aircraft. The emergence of ballistic missiles and space satellites as tools of warfare, however, has raised serious (and yet unanswered) questions regarding the extent of a state's upper boundary.

Besides the right of inviolability of territory, a neutral's rights include: the right to maintain diplomatic communications with other neutral states and with the belligerents; the right to demand compliance with its domestic regulations designed to insure its neutrality; and the right to require belligerents not to interfere with the commercial intercourse of its citizens, unless such interference is warranted by international law.

The events of World Wars I and II foreshadowed a breakdown of some of the basic concepts of neutrality. With the German invasion of Belgium, the Italian invasion of Greece, the English occupation of Iceland, and the passage by the United States of the Lend-Lease Act (1941), the traditional rules of neutrality appeared no longer viable. By the middle of the 20th century new developments in the law of neutrality were evident. (1) The total character of modern war, with its use of economic as well as mechanized means of warfare, has sharply reduced the traditional area of freedom of the neutral. (2) Under the provisions of the Charter of the United Nations, neutrality, as a permissive legal status, disappears for those members that the Security Council "calls upon" or requires in specific instances to take military or other measures of coercion against an aggressor (Articles 41, 48); in such cases, however, permissive neutrality continues to exist for those members not so designated. (3) The socialization of national economies may result in a lessening of neutral trade; many business enterprises that could formerly trade with belligerents as private traders may no longer be legally able to do so as state enterprises.

·laws of war pertaining to neutral states **19**:541b
·U.S. early reaction to World War II **15**:1140g
·Wilson's reaction to belligerent moves **19**:837f

neutralization (chemistry): *see* salt.

neutral lipid (biochemistry): *see* triglyceride.

neutral monism, in the philosophy of mind, theories that hold that mind and body are not separate, distinct substances but are composed of the same sort of neutral "stuff."

David Hume, an 18th-century Scottish Skeptic, developed a theory of knowledge that led him to regard both minds and bodies as collections of "impressions" ("perceptions"), the primary data of experience. Bertrand Russell, an eminent 20th-century British logician and philosopher, called the neutral entities "sensibilia" and argued that mind and matter are "logical constructions." William James, a pre-World War I Pragmatist, held that the neutral primary stuff is not a series of atomistic perceptions but is a "booming, buzzing confusion" that he termed "pure experience," with mind or consciousness and body as names of discernible functions within it.

Neutral monist theories have been criticized as inadequate in their account of either mind or body. Hume himself said (*A Treatise of Human Nature*) that his concept of mind as a bundle of perceptions inadequately accounts for the identity and simplicity of the mind. Others have criticized the notion that physical bodies are comprised of some sort of primary experience as implicitly Idealistic. Hence, the central problem for neutral monism is seen as that of specifying clearly the nature of the neutral stuff without qualifying it in an exclusively mental or physical fashion.

neutrino, subatomic particle proposed (1931) by W. Pauli to bring the radioactive beta-decay hypothesis in agreement with the law of conservation of energy and momentum; it has no mass, no electric charge, one-half unit of spin, and always travels at the speed of light. E. Fermi further elaborated (1934) the proposal, giving the particle its name. Neutrinos are the most penetrating of subatomic particles because they react with matter only through the force of weak interaction (like radioactive decay). A neutrino is emitted along with a positron in positive beta decay, while an antineutrino is emitted with an electron in negative beta decay. Causing no ionization, neutrinos have a range in lead equivalent to about 3,500 light-years. Only one in 10,000,000,000, travelling through matter a distance equal to the earth's diameter, reacts with a proton or neutron. Neutrinos were first experimentally observed (1956) when a beam of antineutrinos from a nuclear reactor produced neutrons and positrons after reacting with protons. Compared with the two electron neutrinos associated with the above processes, two other neutrinos, produced when pions (mesons) decay into muons and neutrinos, were conclusively shown (1962) to be a different species, the muon neutrino and its antiparticle. Although they are as unreactive as the other neutrinos, they were found occasionally to produce muons (and not electrons) when they reacted with protons and neutrons. No satisfactory answer can yet be given why two species of neutrinos exist and what part they play in the force of weak interaction.

·absence in solar cosmic rays **5**:205f
·antineutrino in neutron decay process **12**:1070g
·electron and muon peculiar similarities **6**:668g; illus. 669
·fission product energy distribution **13**:304e
·galactic x-ray black-body source refutation **19**:1066e

·nuclear beta decay process **13**:337d
·nuclear fusion in stars **13**:309g
·particle theory and quantum physics **12**:870a
·radiation's particulate nature **15**:399f
·radioactive emissions **15**:435d
·relativity theory applications **15**:588a
·subatomic particle properties **13**:1022h; tables 1024
·Sun's hydrogen-helium conversion **17**:807h
·symmetry and energy conservation **5**:37c; table 34
·theory and discovery **11**:801b
·viscosity and properties of universe **18**:1018c

neutron 12:1070, a constituent particle of every atomic nucleus (except ordinary hydrogen), having no electric charge and a mass slightly less than that of a hydrogen atom.

The text article covers the neutron's various properties, such as absence of charge, mass, spin, wave properties, and structure. Neutrons as components of nuclei are considered. Neutron production is concerned with the energy and yield of neutrons freed in nuclear reactions by artificial means. Other topics covered include moderation (slowing down) and diffusion of neutrons as applied to nuclear reactors, velocity selectors used in experimental physics, and neutron optics (neutrons treated as waves). After reviewing nuclear reactions produced by neutrons (including fission), the text article concludes with a summary of the various techniques used in detecting slow and fast neutrons.

REFERENCES in other text articles:
·antineutron production and reactions **11**:703c
·atomic charge and number **4**:169c
·atomic structure principles **9**:1032e
·biological effects of radiation **15**:379d; table
·chain reaction in nuclear reactor **13**:314d
·chemical element atomic structure **4**:116a
·constants of electron charge and mass **5**:75g
·cosmic ray interactions in atmosphere **5**:208d
·crystal defects and particle interaction **9**:806f
·discovery and implications **11**:800e
·Earth's magnetic field characteristics **6**:27g
·Fermi's work on uranium reactions **8**:545f
·fissionable actinide element production **1**:65f
·geological form relationships **7**:1058d
·isotope structure and nuclear stability **9**:1054f
·Joliot-Curies' role in discovery **5**:372h
·magnetic structure and dipole interaction **7**:252b
·nuclear fission process **13**:301d
·nuclear fusion in stars and H-bomb **13**:307e *passim* to 310e
·nuclear interactions and symmetries **5**:34e; table
·nuclear structure and properties **13**:334b
·nuclear structure and radioactivity **15**:434h *passim* to 440c
·nucleon binding energy **4**:118f
·particle theory and quantum physics **12**:870a
·particulate nature and characteristics **15**:408d
·production by beryllium nuclear reaction **1**:593b
·proton–neutron interconversion **6**:668g
·radiation interactions with atoms **15**:393a
·radiation particle properties **15**:399f
·radioisotope production by fission **15**:453c
·radiologic application development **15**:467b
·rare-earth comparative chemistry **15**:517c
·reaction control with nuclear fuel **11**:1075b
·Rutherford's nucleus experiments **16**:108c
·steel tensile strength and irradiation **11**:630a
·subatomic particle properties **13**:1022g; table 1024
·transuranium element applications **18**:684g
·Van Allen radiation particle source **19**:22b

RELATED ENTRIES in the *Ready Reference and Index*:
neutron, prompt; neutron, thermal; neutron capture; neutron optics; star, neutron

neutron, delayed: *see* neutron, prompt.

neutron, prompt, in nuclear fission reactions, a nuclear particle without charge that is emitted instantaneously by a nucleus undergoing fission—in contrast to a delayed neutron, which is emitted by an excited nucleus among the fission products at an appreciable time interval (seconds or minutes) after fission has occurred. Neutrons released in fission reactions are predominantly prompt; for example, only about one in 140 neutrons emitted in uranium-235 fission is delayed. *Major ref.* **13**:304a
·chain reaction in nuclear reactor **13**:314e
·nuclear repulsive forces and fission **13**:343f

neutron, thermal, any free neutron (one that has been ejected from an atomic nucleus) that has an energy of motion (kinetic energy) corresponding to the average energy of the particles of materials at room temperature. Relatively slow and of low energy, thermal neutrons are essential for certain types of nuclear fission and certain applications of neutron optics. Thermal neutrons are produced by slowing down more energetic neutrons in a substance called a moderator after they have been ejected from atomic nuclei during reactions such as fission.

Quantitatively, the room-temperature, or thermal, energy per particle is about 0.025 electron volts. Thus, thermal neutrons have a kinetic energy near 0.025 electron volts—an amount of energy that corresponds to a neutron speed of about 2,000 metres per second and a neutron wavelength of about 2×10^{-10} metre (or about two angstroms). Because the wavelength of thermal neutrons corresponds to the natural spacings between atoms in crystalline solids, beams of thermal neutrons are ideal for investigating the structure of crystals. Also, thermal neutrons are required for producing nuclear fission in naturally occurring uranium-235 and in artificially produced plutonium-239 and uranium-233.

neutron capture, type of nuclear reaction in which a target nucleus absorbs a neutron (uncharged particle) followed by the emission of a discrete quantity of electromagnetic energy (gamma-ray photon). The target nucleus and the product nucleus, the mass number of which is one unit more than that of the target nucleus because of the addition of a neutron, are isotopes or forms of the same element. Thus phosphorus-31 on undergoing neutron capture becomes phosphorus-32. The heavier isotope that results is generally radioactive, so that neutron capture, which occurs with almost any nucleus, is a common way of producing radioactive isotopes.

Neutron capture is also named neutron-gamma or (n,γ) reaction from the bombarding particle (n for neutron) and the emitted particle (γ for gamma-ray photon) and sometimes called neutron radiative capture because of the prompt emission of only electromagnetic radiation. Among the elements, boron, cadmium, and gadolinium are the best absorbers of neutrons by the capture process.
·cosmic production of radioisotopes **5**:208d
·effective cross-section calculation **15**:443g
·element synthesis and capture processes **4**:121d
·fissionable actinide element production **1**:65f
·neutron interactions with matter **15**:408e
·nuclear reaction and excitation energy **13**:343h
·nuclear reactions with neutrons **12**:1074a
·stellar heavy element generation **17**:602h
·transuranium element production by neutron irradiation **18**:679d; illus. 680
·uranium transmutation reaction **13**:315c

neutron decay, transformation of neutrons in the Earth's magnetosphere into protons and electrons.
·Earth's magnetic field characteristics **6**:27g

neutron optics, branch of physics comprising the wave behaviour of neutrons, the neutral subatomic particles that are one of the constituents of all atomic nuclei except those of ordinary hydrogen. A beam of free neutrons, produced in nuclear reactors by ejecting neutrons from the core of atoms in reactions such as fission, are reflected, scattered, or diffracted by materials on which the beam is directed.

In particular, in contrast to fast neutrons that act more exclusively as particles when they strike materials, slow neutrons have longer wavelengths of about 10^{-10} metre (or about an angstrom unit), which corresponds to the distance between atoms in crystals. Slow neutrons scattered by the atoms in solids undergo mutual interference (similar to the behaviour of X-rays and light) to form diffraction patterns from which details of crystal structure and magnetic properties of solids are deduced.

neutropenia, abnormally low number of neutrophilic leukocytes, a type of white blood cell, in the blood.
·biomedical models, table 1 **5**:866
·infection risks in blood diseases **2**:1140c

neutrophil, also called HETEROPHIL, white blood cell with no particular affinity either for acid or for basic stains; it is the most numerous type of white blood cell in vertebrates, accounting for 65–75 percent of leukocytes. It is classed with the granulocytes because its cytoplasm contains many small granules and with the polymorphonuclear leukocytes because the shape of its nucleus varies widely. The neutrophil nucleus has three to five lobes connected by thin strands of chromatin (readily stainable nuclear material); older cells have a greater number of lobes. The cytoplasm contains many granules but has a clear periphery that forms pseudopods (cytoplasmic extensions like feet) during locomotion. Neutrophils move by ameboid action and are in nearly constant motion. They move in a direction dictated by chemical emanations from bacteria and foreign matter elsewhere in the body, a process called chemotaxis. Pseudopods are stretched ahead of the cell and become filled with active granules; the nucleus is carried along passively near the back of the cell and may become distorted during movement. Neutrophils from different species differ in size, shape, and number of granules, and often in the type of stain they take in the laboratory. The function of neutrophils is to ingest foreign material, including bacteria; they are thus important in the defense of the body against infection and disease. *See also* leukocyte; phagocyte.

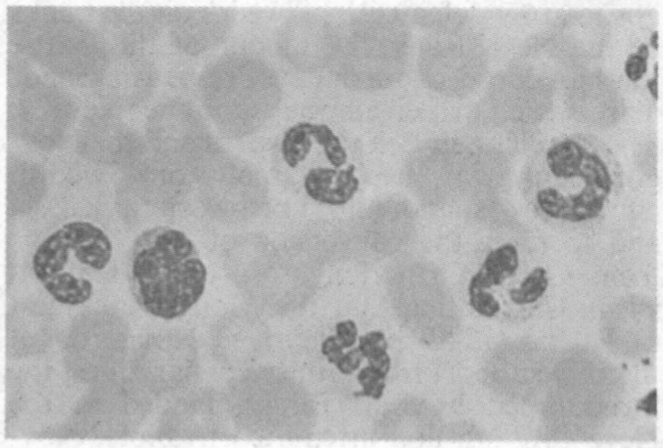

Human neutrophils
Manfred Kage—Peter Arnold

·animal disease inflammation mechanism **5**:871c
human
·blood cell adaptations for defense **2**:1117h
·connective tissue defense reserves **5**:15g
·diseases causing increase **2**:1139f

Neuve-Chapelle, Battle of (March 10, 1915), unsuccessful British offensive on the Western Front during World War I.
·Haig's strategic innovations **19**:952a
·tactics of chemical warfare **19**:580d

Neuville, Lemercier de, 19th-century French puppeteer.
·puppet theatre literary production **15**:294g

Neuwied, town, Rheinland-Pfalz (Rhineland-Palatinate) *Land* (state), western West Germany, on the right bank of the Rhine (there bridged to Weissenthurm) near the Wied stream, just northwest of Koblenz. Founded in 1653 by the Count of Wied for religious refugees, it was chartered in 1662 and became a flourishing commercial and craftsman's town in the 18th century. Seat of the county (principality after 1784) of Wied-Neuwied until 1806, when it was included in the duchy of Nassau, the town passed to Prussia in 1815. In 1904 it absorbed the village of Heddesdorf, where Roman fortifications have been excavated. The former Moravian School (1756–1910), attended by many British boys, was the forerunner of the many specialized schools in modern Neuwied. Historic landmarks include the Baroque château (1707–57) of the princes of Wied and 17th- and 18th-century houses.

Industries include iron and steel production, engineering, and the manufacture of veneer, paper, chemicals, and pumice building materials made from the local volcanic sand. The poetess Carmen Sylva (Princess Elizabeth of Wied, later a queen of Romania) was born there. Pop. (1970 est.) 31,359.
50°25′ N, 7°27′ E
·map, Federal Republic of Germany **8**:46

Neva, Battle of the (July 15, 1240, old style), military engagement in which the Novgorod army defeated the Swedes on the banks of the Neva River; in honour of this battle the Novgorod commander, Prince Aleksandr Yaroslavich, received the surname Nevsky. The conflict between the Swedes and the Novgorodians was based largely on Swedish efforts to expand into northwestern Russia and to force the conversion of the Russians from Greek Orthodoxy to Roman Catholicism. Calculating that the Mongol conquest of Russia (1240) had deprived Novgorod of military support from other Russian cities, the Swedes, led by Earl Birger, landed at the Neva's mouth and attempted to block Novgorod's approach to the Baltic Sea. Nevsky led an army against them and destroyed most of the Swedish force. Birger sailed back to Finland with the few Swedish survivors.

Nevada 12:1076, western state of the U.S., admitted to the Union in 1864 as the 36th state. Occupying an area of 110,540 sq mi (286,297 sq km), it is bounded by Oregon and Idaho (north), by Utah (east), by Arizona (southeast), and by California (southwest and west). Its capital is Carson City. Pop. (1970) 488,738; (1980) 799,184.

The text article, after a brief overview of the state, covers its history, landscape, people, economy, administration, social conditions, and cultural life and institutions.

REFERENCES in other text articles:
·Antler orogeny during Triassic **18**:696g
·area and population, table 1 **18**:927
·basin and range topography **14**:528c
·gambling revenue and legality **7**:869c
·Great Basin Indian cultures **13**:204g; map 205
·ignimbrite field description **9**:231b; table
·inheritance tax and tax havens **5**:531g
·map, United States **18**:908
·Rocky Mountain building and deformation **15**:967h
·territorial expansion 1854–61 map **18**:969

Nevada, Sierra, mountain range in southeastern Spain, near the Mediterranean coast, is the highest division of the Baetic Cordillera (*see* Penibético, Sistema). The Nevada itself is a domed mountain elongated for about 26 mi (41 km) from east to west. It is clearly defined by the faulted troughs of the vega (plain) of Granada to the northwest, the Guadix tableland to the northeast, and the Alpujarras depression to the south. The main peaks of the range are the Cerro de Mulhacén (11,411 ft [3,478 m]), the highest point of the Iberian Peninsula, and the Veleta (11,128 ft). Several other summits rise above the snow line of 10,000 ft and have given significance to the name, which means Snowy Range. The combination of Mediterranean climate and height has produced a sequence of flora from subtropical to alpine species.
37°05′ N, 3°10′ W

Nevada Fall, located on the Merced River in Yosemite National Park, east-central California, U.S., about 5 mi (8 km) above its confluence with Tenaya Creek. One of the park's major falls, it has a drop of 594 ft (181 m).

Nevadan orogeny, name originally applied to a mountain-building event in the Sierra Nevada region of eastern California, believed to have taken place in the latest Jurassic time (about 140,000,000 years ago). The term now is used for numerous orogenic pulses in the western portion of the Cordilleran Geosyncline of western North America that range in age from Late Jurassic to Middle Cretaceous (from about 160,000,000 to 104,000,000 years ago).

Early phases of the Nevadan orogeny are evidenced by Late Jurassic igneous intrusions and folding and thrust faulting on the western slope of the Sierra Nevadas and in the Klamath Mountains of northern California. Medial and late phases of the Nevadan orogeny are represented by the formation of vast batholiths (igneous bodies greater than about 40 square miles in area) of Early and Middle Cretaceous age in southern California, the Sierra Nevadas, in Idaho, and in British Columbia. Folding and faulting of strata in western Nevada also may be attributed to the Nevadan orogeny.

The Nevadan orogeny may be the result of underthrusting of the western portion of the North American Plate by oceanic crust, along a former oceanic trench located in the western portion of the Cordilleran Geosyncline.

Nevada Test Site, U.S. Atomic Energy Commission experiment station in the post-World War II years; included Yucca Flats near Las Vegas and a facility near Fallon.
·establishment and facilities **12**:1078f

Nevado de Toluca National Park, Mexico state, central Mexico, in the municipality of Zinacantepec, on the Mexico–Toluca–Guadalajara highway west of Mexico City. Established in 1936, it has an area of 259 sq mi (671 sq km). The park lies in the Nevado de Toluca (or Zinantecatl) Mountains, which rise above 15,025 ft (4,580 m). Among the chief features are an extinct, snowcapped volcano 10,381 ft high, in the crater of which are picturesque lagoons that reflect glaciers and clouds. The crater's rim is reached by a road, said to be the highest in the country. The lower slopes of the mountains are heavily wooded with pine and oyamel.

Nevāʾī, ʿAlī Shīr (1441–1501), Turkish poet and scholar, the greatest representative of Chagatai Turkish literature.

Neva River, in Leningrad *oblast* (administrative region), northwestern Russian Soviet Federated Socialist Republic, is the outlet for Lake Ladoga, from which it issues via a delta into the Gulf of Finland. Although it is only 46 mi (74 km) long, its drainage basin covers 109,000 sq mi (282,000 sq km) and includes Lakes Ladoga, Onega, and Ilmen and the Svir and Volkhov rivers. Freeze-up lasts from early December to late April. The river derives importance not only from its navigability by large ships—it forms part of the White Sea-Baltic and Volga-Baltic waterways—but also from the presence of Leningrad city at its mouth.
59°55′ N, 30°15′ E
·Leningrad's islands and defenses **10**:797g; illus. 801
·map, Soviet Union **17**:322

névé (snow): *see* firn.

Neve, Felipe de, 18th-century governor of California.
·Los Angeles River basin settlement **11**:107h

Nevelskoy, Gennady Ivanovich (1814–76), Russian naval officer and explorer of far eastern Siberia.
·Amur Basin exploration **1**:717d

Nevelson, Louise (b. 1899, Kiev, Russia), U.S. sculptor and painter known for her often large scale wooden assemblages (*q.v.*) that are usually painted white, black, or gold. She moved to the United States in 1905 and was raised in Maine. She was educated at the Art Students League in New York City and in 1931 she went to Munich to study with the abstract painter Hans Hofmann (*q.v.*). From 1932 to 1933 she was an assistant to the Mexican muralist Diego Rivera (*q.v.*) and painted frescoes. Her first exhibition of sculpture was held in New York City in 1941. Her characteristic wood assemblages such as "Sky Cathedral" (1958; Albright-Knox Art Gallery, Buffalo, N.Y.) were first constructed in the 1950s.
·assemblage sculpture method illus. **16**:430

Nevers, city, central France, capital of Nièvre *département*, south southeast of Paris. Situated on the high right bank of the Loire River at its confluence with the Nièvre River, it is a typical old provincial town that has been modernized after the establishment of new industries in the vicinity. At the end of the Roman era it was known as Nevirnum, a name believed to be a contraction of its earlier Roman name Noviodunum Aeduorum. In the Middle Ages it changed hands among the powerful families of Europe several times. In the 16th century it was acquired by the Gonzaga family of Mantua who introduced the manufacture of ceramics. The cathedral of Saint-Cyr-et-Sainte-Juliette, built between the 11th and 16th centuries, has been restored after being severely damaged by bombing in World War II. The former Palais ducal de Nevers now houses the lawcourts. The chapel of the Saint-Gildard Convent contains the body of St. Bernadette Soubirous, the visionary of Lourdes, who lived at Nevers from 1860 to 1879. Latest census 42,092.
47°00′ N, 3°09′ E
·map, France **7**:584

Nevers faience, French tin-glazed earthenware introduced from Italy to Nevers in 1565, by two brothers named Corrado. As the Conrade family, they and their descendants dominated Nevers faience manufacture for over a century. The earliest authenticated piece of Nevers, dated 1589, is a large oval polychrome dish depicting a mythological subject, the triumph of Galatea.

Nevers faience dish decorated in the *istoriato* style, mid-17th century; in the Victoria and Albert Museum, London

By courtesy of the Victoria and Albert Museum, London

Although inspired by Italian models, this first period of Nevers faience already showed a freedom in interpretation that was to grow more distinctive in the post-Conrade period, after 1674. Nevers became the first French centre to use Chinese decorative motifs, but it did so on vases that were not always Eastern in shape. It added a distinctive manganese purple to the original white and blue of the Chinese ware of the time.

At almost the same period, Nevers produced vases in the "Persian manner"; these too were free interpretations. Besides these costly wares, Nevers produced cheaper ones: the so-called "talking faience," pots and plates illustrated with scenes from everyday life treated in a satirical manner; and the "revolutionary

Nevers faience jar in the "Persian manner," second half of the 17th century; in the Victoria and Albert Museum, London

By courtesy of the Victoria and Albert Museum, London; photograph, EB Inc.

faience," bearing political slogans of the time. Only six factories remained in 1797 out of the 11 in 1743; two of these are still in existence. The decline of Nevers was caused less by the Revolution than by the competition of cheaper English earthenware.

·ceramic faience ware tradition **14**:907d

Nevers glass figures, ornamental glassware made in Nevers, Fr., from the late 16th century through the early 19th. Only a few inches high, they have been mistaken for fine porcelain but were made of glass rods and tubes

Nevers glass figure made in Nevers, Fr., 17th century; in the Victoria and Albert Museum, London

By courtesy of the Victoria and Albert Museum, London

blown or manipulated and were often made on a wire armature. The subjects are religious, mythological, historical, allegorical, or anecdotal. Nevers glass owes its origins, like Nevers faience, to an influx of Italian workers in the 16th century, notably to the Sarode family. The first known French glassworkers in Nevers were Jean Prestereau (1595) and his son Léon. Allegedly, Louis XIII, as a child, played with toy glass animals from Nevers. Similar glass objects were made elsewhere in France; and often it is difficult to distinguish Nevers wares, though the glass figures are, like Nevers faience, generally dull yellow, white, red, or blue.

Never Weaken (1923), film by Harold Lloyd.

·plot and technique **12**:522h

Neves, city, Rio de Janeiro state, Brazil, on the eastern shore of the Baía de Guanabara opposite Rio de Janeiro. Neves, a northeastern suburb of Niterói, the state capital, is an industrial centre and the terminus of a railroad that runs eastward to Cape Frio. It has shipyards and a metallurgical plant. Pop. (1970) 112,912.
22°51′ S, 43°06′ W

Nevi'im, called in English the PROPHETS, the second division of the Hebrew Bible, or Old Testament, the other two being the Torah (the Law) and the Ketuvim (the Writings, or the Hagiographa). In the Hebrew canon the Prophets are divided into (1) the Former Prophets (Joshua, Judges, Samuel, and Kings) and (2) the Latter Prophets (Isaiah, Jeremiah, Ezekiel, and the Twelve [Minor] Prophets, which include Hosea, Joel, Amos, Obadiah, Jonah, Micah, Nahum, Habakkuk, Zephaniah, Haggai, Zechariah, and Malachi).

This canon, though somewhat fluid up to the early 2nd century BC, was finally fixed by a council of rabbis at Jabneh (Jamnia), now in Israel, *c.* AD 100.

The Protestant canon of the Prophets does not include the Hebrew Former Prophets in its division of the Prophets; instead, this section is called the Historical Books. In addition to the first three Hebrew Latter Prophets, the Protestant canon includes the books of Daniel and The Lamentations of Jeremiah from the Writings and the Twelve (Minor) Prophets. Thus, instead of eight prophetic works, the Protestant canon includes 17 books. The Eastern Orthodox and the Roman Catholic churches also accept these 17; in addition, the Roman Catholic Church accepts the book of Baruch, including the Letter of Jeremiah.

The Protestant canon of the Historical Books follows the Septuagint, the Greek version of the Old Testament, separating Samuel and Kings into two sections each (I and II Samuel and I and II Kings). Some Roman Catholic and Eastern Orthodox versions have divided these two works into I, II, III, and IV Kings. I and II Maccabees are also accepted in the Roman Catholic and Orthodox canons of the historical books. *Major ref.* **2**:906d

·canonicity and dating theories **2**:882e
·Near East mythic themes and allusions **10**:191g

Neville, the name of an English baronial family that, by the number of its members in high positions, and particularly through the influence of its most famous scion, Richard Neville, earl of Salisbury and of Warwick (d. 1471), virtually ruled England during the first part of the reign (1461–70, 1471–83) of King Edward IV. Its members held the earldoms of Westmorland (1397–1601) and of Salisbury (1429–71); another branch of the family, the Nevilles of Abergavenny, acquired in 1784 the earldom and in 1876 the marquessate of Abergavenny.

Neville, Richard, earl of Warwick: *see* Warwick, Richard Neville, earl of.

Neville's Cross, Battle of (Oct. 17, 1346), English victory over the Scots—under David II—who, as allies of the French, had invaded England in an attempt to distract Edward III from the Siege of Calais (France). Edward, however, had foreseen the invasion and left a strong force in the northern shires. The battle took place near Durham and resulted in a decisive defeat for the Scots. David was captured, southern Scotland was occupied, and the English were able to pursue the French war.

·Scottish defeat and capture of David II **9**:17g

Nevin, Ethelbert Woodbridge (b. Nov. 25, 1862, Edgeworth, Pa.—d. Feb. 17, 1901, New Haven, Conn.), composer of light songs and piano pieces. He studied in New York City, Boston, and Berlin, first appearing as a pianist in Pittsburgh (1886) and later in Boston, Chicago, New York, and other U.S. cities. His early songs on English and German texts were influenced by Schubert and Schumann. His later pieces, in a lighter style, include the much-loved "Rosary" (1898) and "Mighty lak' a Rose" (1900). His best known piano piece was "Narcissus" (1891), from the *Water Scenes.*

His brother Arthur Finley Nevin (1871–1943), a composer and conductor, did research on the music of the Blackfoot Indian and used this music in his opera *Poia* (Berlin, 1910).

Nevinnomyssk, town, Stavropol *kray* (territory), western Russian Soviet Federated Socialist Republic, on the Kuban River at the mouth of the Bolshoy Zelenchuk River. Until the mid-1950s it was an agricultural market town, but in 1962 a chemical complex utilizing nearby natural gas reserves was constructed. A fertilizer plant was opened in 1962, and enlarged in 1965. Since 1968 plastics and chemical fibres have been manufactured. It is also a rail centre, with freight yards and workshops. Pop. (1970) 85,000.
44°38′ N, 41°56′ E

Nevis (West Indies): *see* Saint Kitts-Nevis-Anguilla.

Nevşehir, town and capital of Nevşehir *il* (province), central Turkey. It lies on the lower slopes of a hill crowned by a ruined citadel dating from the Seljuq period. Other monuments include the mosque Kurşunlu Cami, with its attached *medrese* (theological college), *imaret* (hospice), and *kütüphane* (library) built in the early 18th century by Damad İbrahim Paşa, grand vizier of the Ottoman sultan Ahmed III. A market for the agricultural products of the region, Nevşehir is linked by road with Ankara, Adana, and Kayseri.

Nevşehir *il*, with an area of 2,111 sq mi (5,467 sq km), is drained by Kızıl Irmak; it is a prosperous grain-producing district. Occupying a part of the ancient region of Cappadocia, the *il* is rich in historical sites, notably the rock-carved churches and monasteries at Göreme, east of Nevşehir town. Hacıbektaş, north of Nevşehir, is the traditional birthplace of Ḥājjī Bektāsh Wālī (died before 1295), founder of the influential Bektāshī order of dervishes (mystics); it contains the order's large *tekke* (monastery). Pop. (1970 prelim.) town, 57,556; *il*, 231,873.

·map, Turkey **18**:784
·province area and population table **18**:787

Nevsky, Alexander: *see* Alexander Nevsky.

Nevsky Prospect (Russian publication, 1835, English translation, 1945), short story by Nikolay Gogol.

·romantic–realist contrast theme **8**:234g

Nevsky Prospekt, chief avenue of Leningrad, U.S.S.R.

·location, buildings, and squares **10**:799g; map 798

nevus, general term referring to any congenital lesion or discoloured patch of the skin caused by abnormal pigmentation or by the aggregation or enlargement of blood or lymph vessels; a congenital pigmented area on the skin constituted of an aggregation of melanocytes, the cells of the skin that synthesize the dark brown pigment melanin. The more general meaning of nevus encompasses a wide variety of nevi, each variety being referred to as nevus, qualified by an additional word that usually indicates either the specific colour or shape of the particular lesion, the specific body organ or type of tissue with which it is associated, or the depth of the skin at which it is located. Nevi that are named according to their colour or shape are qualified by the following words in italics: *Amelanotic*, no pigment; *anemicus*, discoloration due to poor blood supply; *arachnoideus*, also called *spider* or *stellar*, represented by red lines radiating from a central red point, caused by capillary dilation; *blue*, formed by pigmented cells in the deeper part of the skin and having a dark bluish cast; *corneum*, characterized by horny elevations; *cavernosus*, involving relatively large blood vessels that form caverns or hollow spaces (*see* hemangioma); *cerebelliformis*, elevated nevus with furrows producing a surface resembling that of the brain; *flammeus*, also called port-wine stain, reddish lesion (*see* hemangioma); *halo*, surrounded by a ring of depigmentation; *linear* or *papillaris*, collection of elevated spots occurring in streaks and due to an overdevelopment of the horny covering of the skin; *papillomatosus*, a fleshy pigmented growth; *pigmented* (*see* mole); *spilus* (Greek *spilos*, "stain"), flat. Those nevi named according to the body organ or type of tissue with which they are predominantly associated are modified by the following words in italics: *Angiomatodes*, diffuse tumour constituted of blood and lymph vessels, located in the connective tissues underlying the skin; *capillary*, involving capillaries of the skin; *epithelial*, skin tumour containing no melanocytes; *fibrosus*, having a fibrous structure; *follicularis*, involving the hair follicles; *hepatic*, in liver tissue; *lipomatosus* or *fatty*, containing large amounts of fat or surrounding a small fatty tumour; *lymphatic*, skin growth containing lymph and blood elements; *nape*, light birthmark on the back of the neck; *pilosus*, covered with hair; *sanguineus*, red elevation composed of aggregated small blood vessels (*see* hemangioma); *sebaceous*, fleshy growth composed of mature sebaceous, or oil-secreting, glands; *spongiosus albus mucosae*, white spongy lesion of the mucous membrane; *unius lateralis*, bandlike nevus occurring on one side of the body only; *vascularis*, reddish patch caused by enlarged blood capillaries; *venosus*, patch of dilated veins; *verrucosus*, having a surface with small fleshy protuberances. In naming nevi according to their position in the skin, the basis of reference are the two major divisions of the skin—the dermis, or deeper vascular layer, and the epidermis, or outermost horny nonvascular layer. *Intradermal nevus* is located inside the dermis; *junction nevus*, between the dermis and the epidermis; and *compound nevus*, partly in the dermis and partly in the epidermis (*see* mole).

·epidermal and dermal diseases **16**:848b
·skin lesion comparisons **4**:225h

New Albany, city, seat of Floyd County, southeastern Indiana, U.S., on the Ohio River (bridged) opposite Louisville, Ky. It was founded in 1813 by Joel, Abner, and Nathaniel Scribner, who bought the land from Col. John Paul of Madison and named the settlement for their hometown, Albany, N.Y. By the 1840s and early 1850s (when it was the largest city in Indiana), New Albany was an important steamboat-building centre. Diversified manufactures now include plywood, veneer, prefabricated houses, furniture, electronic equipment, fertilizer, and clothing. The boyhood home (*c.* 1850) in New Albany of poet-dramatist William Vaughn Moody is preserved, as are the Scribner House (1814) and the Culbertson Mansion (1868). Inc. city, 1839. Pop. (1980) 37,103.
38°18′ N, 85°49′ W

·map, United States **18**:908

New Albany, city, seat of Union County, northern Mississippi, U.S. Settled in 1840 on the site of an Alibano Indian village, it was a stagecoach stop on the Holly Springs–Pontotoc Line before the Civil War. After the war, the Gulf, Mobile, and Northern Railroad was built through the town. An agricultural and dairying trade centre, it also produces clothing, furniture, and electrical and steel products. It is the birthplace of William Faulkner, novelist and Nobel Prize winner. Inc. 1888. Pop. (1980) 7,072.
34°29′ N, 89°00′ W

New American School (1900), photographic exhibit held in London.

·Steichen's increasing fame **14**:317g

New Amsterdam (French Southern Antarctic Territory): *see* Nouvelle Amsterdam.

New Amsterdam, capital, East Berbice district, northeastern Guyana, on the Berbice River near the point at which it empties into the Atlantic Ocean. Built in 1740 by the Dutch and first named Ft. St. Andries, it was made seat of the Dutch colonial government in 1790; in 1803 it was taken over by the British. Although a Dutch air still pervades the town, it has an Anglican cathedral. New Amsterdam vies with the mining camp at Mackenzie as Guyana's second largest city. It is the commercial and manufacturing centre for the agricultural and pastoral coastal lowlands, where sugarcane, rice, and cattle are raised. The city can be reached by railroad and highway from Georgetown, the national capital, and via a ferry across the Berbice to Rosignol. Pop. (1970 prelim.) 18,199.
6°17′ N, 57°36′ W

·map, Guyana **8**:507
·population, location, and appearance **8**:508d

New Apostolic Church, organized in Germany in 1863 as the Universal Catholic Church, by members of the Catholic Apostolic Church who believed that new apostles must be appointed to replace deceased apostles and rule the church until Christ returns. The present name was adopted in 1906. Doctrines are similar to the parent church, but the new church was influenced by continental Protestantism, and its worship services and tendencies became less Catholic and more Protestant.

The church emphasizes the gifts of the Holy Spirit, which include prophecy, speaking in tongues, and miraculous healing. Sacraments are Baptism, Holy Communion, and holy sealing (the "dispensing and reception of the Holy Spirit"). Sealing can only be conferred by the laying on of hands on the head of a member by an apostle, and it assures the member of participation in Christ's rule on earth for 1,000 years after he returns. Like the Latter-day Saints, the New Apostolic Church teaches that the sacraments can be received by a living member for a dead person.

The church is ruled by a hierarchy composed of the chief apostle and the other apostles. The apostles appoint bishops, district elders, pastors, and evangelists. In the 1960s about 4,500 congregations with 700,000 members throughout the world were reported. About 20,000 members were in the U.S. and about 80 percent of the members lived in Germany. Each congregation is a part of the international organization, which has headquarters in Frankfurt am Main, W. Ger.

Newar, people of mixed descent who comprise about half the population of the Kāthmāndu Valley in Nepal. They speak a language belonging to the Tibeto-Burman family, but their culture has been strongly influenced by Indian religious and social institutions. The Newar population of Nepal is estimated to be about 450,000.

Most of the Newar are Hindus, but some practice an Indian form of Buddhism. There are about 70 castes, Buddhist as well as Hindu, covering approximately the same spectrum as the caste system of India; they include the Brahmin, Kṣatriya, Vaiśya, and Śūdra *varṇa*s as well as numerous groups of untouchables.

The Newar have a wide range of occupations. Many are farmers; others are prominent in the retail trades; and some occupy high political and administrative posts. They have traditionally been noted as architects and artisans, the builders of the famous temples and shrines of Kāthmāndu. From the 10th to the 16th centuries painting and sculpture flourished among the Newar, along with crafts such as pottery making, papermaking, wood carving, and metallurgy. Each of the crafts has traditionally been the specialty of a particular caste.

·Himalayan ethnic distribution **8**:885h
·Indian racial types and distribution **14**:846g
·Sikkimese mint and copper mining **16**:749b

Newark, city, Alameda County, western California, U.S., linked to Palo Alto on the west side of San Francisco Bay by the Dumbarton Bridge. Originally called Mayhew's Landing, it was founded in 1875 by James G. Fair and by A.E. Davis (who renamed it for his home town in New Jersey). Earlier salt-extracting operations were followed, after World War II, by planned industrial growth with railroads as major promoters. Fremont-Newark Junior College (1966) is there. Inc. 1955. Pop. (1950) 1,532; (1980) 32,126.
37°32′ N, 122°02′ W

Newark, city, New Castle County, northern Delaware, just west-southwest of Wilmington. Established in the late 1680s as the New Worke Quaker meeting house, it developed as an early crossroads meeting place for travellers. Nearby Cooch's Bridge on Christina Creek was the scene (Sept. 3, 1777) of the only Revolutionary War battle fought in the state. One of Newark's earliest enterprises was a paper mill built on White Clay Creek. Principal industries now include the manufacture of vulcanized fibre, concrete products, processed foods, and the assembly of automobiles. Newark is the seat of the University of Delaware (founded 1743; achieved university status 1921). Inc. town, 1887; city, 1951. Pop. (1950) 6,731; (1980) 25,247.
39°41′ N, 74°45′ W

Newark, city and port of entry, northeastern New Jersey, U.S., on the west bank of the Passaic River and Newark Bay, the seat of Essex County. Puritans migrating from Connecticut founded Newark in 1666 on land purchased from local Indians. The settlement was first named Pesayak Towne and later New Milford after Milford, Conn. It was renamed, according to one interpretation, for the home of the Rev. Abraham Pierson, who went there from Newark-on-Trent, England. Other versions hold that the name was of Biblical significance, New Ark, or derived from New Work, referring to a new project. Newark was chartered as a township in 1693 and incorporated as a city in 1836.

The city grew slowly until after the American Revolutionary War. Its industry started with a shoe factory (*c.* 1790), and it soon became a centre for leather tanning and shoe manufacturing. Inventors attracted to the city included Seth Boyden, who developed the process for making patent leather (1818) and malleable cast iron (1826); the Rev. Hannibal Goodwin, who patented a flexible film for motion pictures (1888); and Edward Weston, who invented electrical measuring instruments (1888).

The city's proximity to New York (it is 8 mi west of lower Manhattan) places it near the heart of the country's largest, most highly industrialized, and most populous area (it is a part of the New York-Northern New Jersey Standard Consolidated Area, which has a population of about 15,000,000). The largest city in the state and one of the country's leading manufacturing centres, its products include electronic equipment, leather goods, celluloid, jewelry, metal goods, nails, wire, springs, needles, hand tools, cutlery, chemicals, paints and varnish, paperboard and industrial machinery, malt liquors, and foodstuffs. A number of insurance companies have their home offices there. Newark is a transportation centre and a major East Coast distributing point. Newark Airport, one of the pioneer U.S. airports, was established in 1928. Starting in the late 1960s it underwent a $200,000,000 expansion. Port Newark, a seaport of 675 ac (273 ha), started by the city in 1914, is now leased and operated by the Port of New York Authority.

Although there has been movement of population to the suburbs, the concentration remaining in the city resulted in overcrowded and substandard housing to a degree that brought Newark proportionately more federal housing aid than any other city in the United States. The movement of whites from the city to the suburbs, although temporarily stemmed in the mid-1950s, continued and raised the proportion of blacks in the population from 17 percent in 1950 to over 50 percent by the 1970s. Racial tensions were high, and in July 1967 the National Guard was called out to help restore order after four days of interracial rioting and looting. In 1970 blacks obtained some political power in Newark when Kenneth A. Gibson was elected as the city's first black mayor.

Located in Newark are the Newark College of Engineering (1881); the Newark campus of Rutgers, the state university; a branch of Seton Hall University (Roman Catholic, 1856); and Essex County College (1968).

Near the centre of town is Military Park, used as a drill ground in colonial times and now the site of a bronze group of figures, "The Wars of America," by Gutzon Borglum. Branch Brook, a county park, is noted for its Japanese cherry trees. In front of the county courthouse, designed by Cass Gilbert, is a seated statue of Abraham Lincoln also by Borglum. Among churches of historic interest are Trinity Cathedral (1743), used as a hospital during the American Revolution; House of Prayer with its two-centuries-old stone rectory, Plume House (1710); and the old First Presbyterian Church (1791).

Notable Newark residents have included Mary Mapes Dodge, author of *Hans Brinker, or the Silver Skates*, and Edmund Clarence Stedman, poet; Stephen Crane, author of *The Red Badge of Courage*, was a native son, as was Aaron Burr. Pop. (1960) city, 405,220; (1980) city, 329,248; New York–Northeastern New Jersey Standard Consolidated Area, 16,120,023.
40°44′ N, 74°10′ W

·map, United States **18**:908

Newark, village in the Town (township) of Arcadia, Wayne County, western New York, U.S., on the New York State Barge Canal. It was created by the merger of Lockville and Miller's Basin when the Erie Canal was opened (1825). The Newark State Hospital (for mental defectives) is there. Nurseries, fruit orchards, and vegetable farms characterize the area, and immediately south of the village are the extensive Jackson and Perkins Rose Gardens. An annual rose festival is held in the summer. At nearby Hydesville, modern spiritualism was begun by the Fox family (1848). Inc. 1853. Pop. (1980) 10,017.
43°03′ N, 77°06′ W

·demographic and ethnic distinctions **12**:1097e

Newark, city, seat (1808) of Licking County, central Ohio, U.S., at the junction of the North and South forks of the Licking River and Raccoon Creek. Indian earthworks in the local Mound Builders, Wright Earthworks, and Octagon state memorials attest to the existence of a pre-Columbian cultural settlement on the site. Platted in 1802, the community was named for the New Jersey home of the first settlers led by Gen. William C. Schenck. It prospered as an agricultural trading centre, and industrial development was spurred by its location near the Ohio and Erie Canal system begun (1825) at Licking Summit, 4 mi (6 km) south, and with the arrival of the first railroad (1852).

The modern economy is well diversified, based on agriculture (dairying, livestock, grain, fruit) and manufacturing (fibre glass and aluminum, truck axles and transmissions, lawn mowers, containers, plastics, and petroleum products). The Newark campus of Ohio State University opened in 1957. Points of interest include Buckingham House (1815), Licking County Museum, and the Sullivan Building (1914), designed by Chicago architect Louis H. Sullivan. Nearby are Buckeye Lake, Dawes Arboretum, Dillon Dam and Reservoir, and the Ohio Canal Lock. Granville, 5 mi west, is the seat of Denison University (1831). Inc. town, 1826; city, 1860. Pop. (1980) 41,200.
40°04′ N, 82°24′ W

·map, United States **18**:908

Newark Basins, chain of depositional troughs in eastern North America from Nova Scotia to North Carolina that received thick deposits of Late Triassic sediments (the Triassic Period began about 225,000,000 years ago and lasted about 35,000,000 years). Late in the Triassic, strains in the crust of the Earth produced a series of block mountains in eastern North America that were bordered by downfaulted troughs. Through time, more than 6,100 metres (20,000 feet) of Triassic sediments were deposited; the mountains were eroded, and only the basins remain.

Newark Group, division of Upper Triassic rocks in the eastern U.S., from Massachusetts to North Carolina (the Triassic Period began about 225,000,000 years ago and lasted about 35,000,000 years). The Newark Group, named for exposures studied near Newark, N.J., consists of about 6,100 metres (20,000 feet) of conglomerates, sandstones, siltstones, shales, and lava flows. Rocks of the Newark Group were deposited in a series of troughs bordering a series of block mountains that paralleled the eastern border of the U.S. in the Late Triassic. The sediments that formed the rocks of the Newark Group were derived from the erosion of the block mountains. The rocks are predominantly reddish and are poorly sorted; the sandstones are arkosic (feldspar rich). Intrusive volcanic rocks and trap rock such as diabase penetrate the sedimentary strata; a prominent feature along the Hudson River, the Palisades Sill, consists of diabase. Fossils found in rocks of the Newark Group include freshwater fish, reptiles such as the crocodile-like phytosaur genus *Rutiodon*, plants, and dinosaur tracks.

·mountain deformation and rock structure **12**:583h

Newark-upon-Trent, borough (1548) and market town in Nottinghamshire, England, on the River Trent, at the crossing of the ancient Roman Fosse Way with the modern British route, the famous Great North Road (A1).

The earliest known occupation of the site, then known as Niweweorce, was in Anglo-Saxon times. In 1055 the town was granted to the bishops of Lincoln, in whose hands it remained until 1549. Bishop Alexander built a castle and bridge over the Trent there (1123–35), the castle being replaced by a stone building about 1173. Much of the structure was destroyed in the English Civil War of the mid-17th century, and only the gatehouse and west tower of the original building remain. In the Middle Ages, Newark had a flourishing cloth industry. It is now a small engineering centre, with many agricultural industries.

The parish church of St. Mary Magdalene, one of England's finest, has architecture dating from the Norman period. It has one of the largest 14th-century brasses in the country and a tower and spire 246 ft (75 m) high. Among old brick buildings are a grammar and song school (founded 1529) and an 18th-century town hall. Pop. (1971 prelim.) 24,631.
53°05′ N, 0°49′ W

·map, United Kingdom **18**:866

New Artists' Association: *see* Neue Künstlervereinigung.

New Aspects of Politics (1925), book by Charles E. Merriam.

·psychological approach to politics **14**:704c

Newaya Krestos, also known as SAIFA ARED, 14th-century Ethiopian empress.

·Coptic text translations **6**:1009b

New Baptists: *see* Brethren.

New Bauhaus, also called INSTITUTE OF DESIGN, art school opened by László Moholy-Nagy in Chicago in 1937.

·graphic design technical development **1**:111a

New Bedford, city, one of the seats of Bristol County (with Fall River and Taunton), southeastern Massachusetts, U.S., at the mouth of the Acushnet River near Buzzards Bay. The site, settled by Plymouth colonists in 1652, was part of Dartmouth. A small fishing community was established there in 1760. By 1765 it had developed into a small whaling port and shipbuilding centre. Its harbour, used by American privateers during the Revolutionary War, was attacked (Sept. 7, 1778) and the village burned by British forces. Following a rapid recovery, it was separately incorporated (1787) as the town of Bedford (later renamed New Bedford, to distinguish it from another Bedford, in Middlesex County). By 1820 it was one of the world's leading whaling ports. Following the decline in whaling, the town turned to the manufacture of cotton fabrics but was affected by the movement to the southeast of the textile industry during the 1920s. A diversified economy now prevails with the manufacture of clothing, electrical equipment and machinery, rubber goods, drills, and metal goods. It is a sailing point for the Cape Cod area and continues to be an important fishing port. The Old Dartmouth Historical Society Whaling Museum, Ft. Rodman (built during the Civil War), and the Seamen's Bethel reflect the city's historic past. Inc. city, 1847. Pop. (1920) city, 121,217; (1980) city, 98,478; metropolitan area (SMSA), 169,425.
41°38′ N, 70°56′ W

The Seamen's Bethel (chapel), New Bedford, Mass., with cenotaphs described in Herman Melville's *Moby Dick* on the walls

Mark Sexton

·map, United States **18**:908

Newberg, city, Yamhill County, northwestern Oregon, U.S., in the Willamette Valley, just southwest of Portland. Founded in 1869 as the first Quaker settlement in the Pacific Northwest, it was named by one of the settlers for his German birthplace. President Herbert Hoover spent part of his boyhood in Newberg living with an uncle.

The city is now the trade, processing, and shipping centre for an area producing lumber, fruit, nuts, and paper and wood products. It is the seat of George Fox College, established in 1885 as Friends Pacific Academy. The Champoeg State Park is nearby. Inc. 1893. Pop. (1980) 10,394.
45°18′ N, 122°58′ W

New Bern, city, seat (1723) of Craven County, eastern North Carolina, on the Neuse River at the mouth of the Trent. Settled in 1710 by Christopher von Graffenried, of Bern, Switz., it was incorporated in 1723 after near destruction by Indians.

North Carolina's first printing press (1749) and first tax-supported school (1764) were located there. Construction (1767–70) by Gov. William Tryon of a governor's house (restored, 1952–59, as Tryon Palace) made it the colonial capital of North Carolina. The first and second provincial congresses in North Carolina that opposed the English met in New Bern in 1774 and 1775.

New Bern had a thriving seaport trade with New England and the West Indies through Pamlico Sound until the city was captured by Federal forces in 1862. Its connection with the Atlantic Intracoastal Waterway and the port at Morehead City has made it the service centre for nearby summer resorts, the U.S. Marine Corps Air Station at Cherry Point, and farmlands producing corn (maize), tobacco, and cotton. It has diversified manufacturing. The New Bern National Cemetery has graves of many Civil War dead. One of the first public schools for Negroes was established in New Bern in 1862. Pop. (1980) 14,557.
35°07′ N, 77°03′ W

·map, United States **18**:909

Newberry, city, seat of Newberry County, northwest central South Carolina, U.S., at the southern entrance to the Enoree Division of the Sumter National Forest. It developed around the county courthouse, which was established in 1799.

The city's economy depends on agricultural activities (livestock raising, dairying, and the production of poultry and eggs) and on light industries (food processing and the manufacture of corrugated boxes, glass fibre products, and hosiery). Newberry College (Lutheran) was founded in 1856. Inc. 1919. Pop. (1980) 9,866.
34°17′ N, 81°37′ W

·map, United States **18**:909

Newberry Library, major research library in Chicago, established by Walter L. Newberry in 1887 as a public reference library in the humanities and social sciences.

Newbery, John (b. 1713, Waltham St. Lawrence, Berkshire—d. Dec. 22, 1767, London), merchant, editor, and first major publisher of children's literature in England. The son of a farmer, Newbery was largely self-taught. In 1730 he moved to Reading, where he worked on a provincial newspaper. In 1737 Newbery inherited part of his employer's estate and later married his widow. After touring England, he founded his publishing house in 1740 and in 1745 moved to London. There he sold patent medicines and books and published newspapers and magazines distributed in London and other cities. His writers included Christopher Smart, who married Newbery's stepdaughter, and Oliver Goldsmith, who used Newbery as the basis for one of the characters in *The Vicar of Wakefield* (1766).

Newbery was one of the first to publish books specifically for children; his company produced *A Little Pretty Pocket-Book* in 1744. The Newbery Medal, awarded annually for distinguished children's literature in the U.S., was named for him.

·promotion of nondidactic children's literature **4**:232e

Newbery Medal, annual award given to the author of the most distinguished U.S. book for children of the previous year. It was established by Frederic G. Melcher, of the R.R. Bowker Publishing Company, and named for John Newbery, the 18th-century English publisher who was among the first to publish books exclusively for children. The first award was given in 1922. It is presented at the annual conference of the American Library Association along with the Caldecott Medal, an award to an artist for the best illustrations for a children's book.

Newbolt, Sir Henry (John) (b. June 6, 1862, Bilston, Staffordshire—d. April 19, 1938, London), poet, best known for his patriotic and nautical verse. He was educated at Clifton Theological College and Corpus Christi College, Oxford, was admitted to the bar at Lincoln's Inn in 1887, and practiced law until 1899. His first book was a novel, but it was the appearance of his ballads *Admirals All* (1897), which included the stirring "Drake's Drum," that created his literary reputation. These were followed by other volumes collected in *Poems: New and Old* (1912; rev. ed. 1919), in which he extended his range to include nostalgic and contemplative poems and affirmed his admiration for traditional English values.

Newbolt edited *The Monthly Review* from 1900 to 1904 and published several novels, including *The Old Country* (1906) and *The New June* (1909). During World War I he was comptroller of wireless and cables and was later commissioned to complete the official naval history of the war. He also edited various anthologies of verse, which reveal his catholic and progressive taste in poetry. He was knighted in 1915 and appointed a Companion of Honour in 1922.

New-Born, The (1915), sculpture by Constantin Brancusi.

·egg-shape motif development **3**:117d

New Braunfels, city, seat of Comal County, on the Balcones Escarpment in south central Texas, where the Comal River (3 mi [5 km] long and within the city limits) flows into the Guadalupe.

The community was established in 1845 by a group of German immigrants led by Prince Carl of Solms-Braunfels and sponsored by the Society for the Protection of German Immigrants in Texas (properly Mainzer Adelsverein, a group of German noblemen). Named for Braunfels, Hesse (now in West Germany), the city was incorporated in 1846.

Although after the 1940s the German influence lessened, the community has retained much of its old culture. Sophienburg, former home of the prince, is a museum, and there is a monument to the German pioneers. Tourism based on nearby Landa Park, Natural Bridge Caverns, and Canyon Lake augments the economy. Industrial activities include cotton (gingham), woollen, and hosiery mills, flour and seed mills, and a limestone-crushing plant. There are also ranching, agriculture, and dairying interests in the surrounding area. Pop (1975 est.) 20,308.
29°42′N, 98°08′ W

New Bremen Glassmanufactory: *see in* Amelung glass.

New Brighton, section of New York City, on the northeast shore of Staten Island (borough of Richmond), at the junction of Kill Van Kull and Upper New York Bay. It was developed in 1834 as a residential and resort area by Thomas E. Davis (who purchased extensive property in the area) and the New Brighton Association. Incorporated as a village in 1866, it was absorbed by Richmond and joined to New York City in 1898. There is light manufacturing, and it is the site of the Sailors' Snug Harbor, a home for retired seamen opened in 1833.

New Britain, city, coextensive with New Britain Town, Hartford County, central Connecticut, U.S. Settled as the Great Swamp in 1686, the name was changed to New Britain in 1754. Metalworking began there in the 18th century. Berlin (*q.v.*), now a suburb, was the home of the brothers Edward and William Pattison, who in 1740 turned out the first tinware made in North America, and of Simeon North, contemporary of Eli Whitney and a pioneer in the use of interchangeable parts in the manufacture of small arms. Hardware and machinery are the principal modern industries. It is the seat of Central Connecticut State College (established as New Britain State Normal School, 1849) and the New Britain Museum of American Art (founded 1901). The city was the birthplace of Elihu Burritt (1810–79), philanthropist and advocate of peace. Inc. town, 1850; city, 1870; town and city consolidated, 1905. Pop. (1980) city, 73,840; metropolitan area (SMSA) 142,241.
41°40′ N, 72°47′ W

New Britain, largest island of the Bismarck Archipelago, southwest Pacific, in the nation of Papua New Guinea, 55 mi (88 km) across Dampier Strait from the southeasternmost extension of New Guinea. Measuring 370 mi long by 50 mi at its widest, the crescent-shaped island has a 1,000-mi coastline bordered by fringing reefs; its total area is 14,100 sq mi (36,500 sq km). From narrow coastal plains, it rises to a rugged central mountain spine of the Whiteman, Nakanai, and Baining ranges, with several peaks exceeding 7,000 ft (2,100 m).

There are three areas of active volcanism: in the extreme west, on the north coast near Open Bay, and in the northeast on the Gazelle Peninsula (*q.v.*) near Rabaul, where the Matupi and Vulcan cones present a constant threat to the town. An eruption in 1937 killed 263 people. The island has an equatorial climate.

New Britain was sighted in 1616 by a Dutch navigator, Jacques Le Maire, who conceived it as being part of a landmass including New Guinea and New Ireland. His theory was disproved (1699–1700) by William Dampier, an Englishman who found Vitiaz Strait (west) and named the island, and Philip Carteret, who found St. George's Channel (east) in 1767. As Neu-Pommern (New Pomerania), the island became part of a German protectorate in 1884. It was mandated to Australia following World War I, taken by the Japanese in 1942, and reoccupied by Australia in 1945, as part of the UN Trust Territory of New Guinea administered by Australia. It became part of Papua New Guinea in 1975 when that nation attained independence.

The most developed and populous area is the Gazelle Peninsula, where, on the rich coastal plains, copra and cocoa are produced on commercial plantations and native plots and marketed through Rabaul, Kokopo, and Keravat. These same crops are raised at other points along the coast and shipped from smaller harbours such as Talasea. A feature of this development was the success of cooperative societies of the aborigines. A variety of other crops is grown in village gardens for local consumption. In the more primitive interior, a system of shifting cultivation is practiced involving rotation of plots used only at long intervals. Other island resources are timber, copper, gold, iron, and coal.

Since July 1966, New Britain has comprised two territorial administrative units (originally called districts, now provinces). The 8,100-sq-mi (21,000-sq-km) west province, which includes the Vitu Islands (*q.v.*), has its headquarters at Kimbe. The east, which with the Duke of York Islands (*q.v.*) has an area of 6,000 sq mi, is administered from Rabaul. Pop. (1976 est.) east, 118,276; west, 80,180.
6°00′ S, 150°00′ E

·geographical features, area, and population **12**:1090d; table 1091
·island arc formation and composition **9**:1027g
·linguistic profile **2**:491e
·map, Trust Territory of New Guinea **12**:1091
·mask design and use by Dukduk society **11**:580e; illus.
·Oceanian peoples and cultures **13**:468e
·tapa cloth mask illus. **13**:464

New Brunswick 12:1080, province of Canada, lies on the country's eastern seaboard. It is bounded by the province of Quebec (north) and by the U.S. state of Maine (west). To the east and south, respectively, lie the Gulf of St. Lawrence and the Bay of Fundy. Between them, the narrow Isthmus of Chignecto forms a link to Nova Scotia. It has an area of 28,354 sq mi (73,437 sq km), and its capital is Fredericton. Pop. (1970) 634,557.

The text article covers the landscape, people, local economy, administration, social conditions, and cultural life.

REFERENCES in other text articles:
- area and population table **3**:721; map 722
- Canadian Confederation question **3**:740b
- geographic features and population composition **3**:714h *passim* to 722e
- loyalist settlement and later immigrant population **3**:738a
- map, Canada **3**:716
- 19th–20th-century expansion map **3**:746
- Nova Scotia division **13**:274e

New Brunswick, city, seat of Middlesex County, eastern New Jersey, U.S., on the Raritan River, at the terminus of the old Delaware and Raritan Canal. The site, first known as Prigmore's Swamp, was settled in 1681 by John Inian, who later operated a ferry across the river. Known as Inian's Ferry (1713), it was renamed for George I, who was also the duke of Brunswick. George II granted it a town charter in 1730. Washington's troops, retreating from New York, occupied the town in 1776, evacuating at the approach of the British under Gen. William Howe, who remained there for about seven months. Washington returned after the Battle of Monmouth (1778) and while in the city issued orders for the march south culminating in the Yorktown victory. During this period the city's port was a base for privateers who preyed upon British ships around Manhattan.

The Camden and Amboy Railroad (later the Pennsylvania) reached New Brunswick in 1838. Since the late 19th century, when Robert W. and James W. Johnson established a firm (Johnson & Johnson) to make adhesive tape and surgical dressings, New Brunswick has been a major producer of hospital supplies and pharmaceuticals. Other manufactures include clothing, chemicals, leather goods, and automobile parts.

Rutgers University, the only state university with a colonial charter, was founded there as Queen's College in 1766 and made the state university in 1945. New Brunswick Theological Seminary, oldest theological school in the United States, founded in 1784, has been in the city since 1810. The birthplace of the poet Joyce Kilmer and the national headquarters of the Boy Scouts of America are in New Brunswick. Inc. city, 1784. Pop. (1980) 41,442.
40°29′ N, 74°27′ W

New Brunswick cedar (tree): *see* American arborvitae.

New Brutalism, term applied in 1954 by the English architects Peter and Alison Smithson to the post-1930 style of the major French architect Le Corbusier. New Brutalism was one aspect of the International Style (*q.v.*) created by Le Corbusier and his leading fellow architects Mies van der Rohe and Frank Lloyd Wright, which demanded a functional approach toward architectural design. Le Corbusier's expressionist interpretation of the International Style involved the use of monumental sculptural shape and of raw, unfinished molded concrete, an approach that, in contrast to Mies van der Rohe's use of glass and steel, represented a New Brutalism to the English architects.

New Brutalism: Hunstanton School, Norfolk, Eng., by Alison and Peter Smithson, 1954
The Architectural Review

Newburgh, small royal burgh (town) in the county of Fife, Scotland, situated on the south bank of the River Tay. Newburgh gradually developed near the now-ruined 12th-century Benedictine Abbey of Lindores and was granted a royal burgh charter in 1266. The town now serves as regional centre for the Tay salmon fisheries. Remains of a Pictish (early British) fort with a triple line of earthworks are found at Clachard Craig, one-half mile to the southeast. Pop. (1971 prelim.) 2,106.
56°20′ N, 3°15′ W

Newburgh, city, Orange County, southeastern New York, U.S., on the west bank of the Hudson River (opposite Beacon). First settled by Germans from the Palatinate in 1709, it became a parish in 1752 and was named for Newburgh, Scot. It served as Washington's headquarters (1782–83) and was a key American command post in the strategic Hudson Valley during the Revolutionary War. It was there that Washington renounced the idea of a kingship and disbanded the Continental Army. Hasbrouck House, Washington's headquarters, is now a state historical site and museum. Newburgh's early growth was influenced by its position as a river port; it shared in the 19th-century whaling boom and was a ferry point for coal shipped from Pennsylvania to New England. Its industries include shipbuilding and the manufacture of textiles, clothing, aluminum products, and machinery. The city serves as the trade–distribution centre for the surrounding dairy and fruit region and nearby oil-tank farms contribute to the city's economy. Mount Saint Mary College was established (1930) in Newburgh. Inc. village, 1800; city, 1865. Pop. (1920) 30,366; (1980) 23,438.
41°30′ N, 74°01′ W

Jonathan Hasbrouck House, Newburgh, N.Y.
Milt and Joan Mann from CameraMann

Newburgh Addresses, two resolutions issued during the American Revolution regarding officers' pay claims.
- Washington's censure order **19**:615g

Newburn, industrial community in the metropolitan county of Tyne and Wear (formerly in Northumberland), England, on the western boundary of the metropolitan complex of Newcastle upon Tyne. A residential and manufacturing district, it has a large industrial estate. The Anglo-Scottish Battle of Newburn was fought there in 1640. The Church of St. Michael and All Angels dates from 1190. Pop. (1971 prelim.) 39,379.
54°59′ N, 1°43′ W

Newbury, market town and borough of Berkshire, England, lying on the River Kennet, on the Kennet and Avon Canal, and at the intersection of important southern English routeways. Much evidence of Roman occupation has been found. In 1152, Newbury's castle was besieged and captured by Stephen, 12th-century Norman sovereign of England. The first charter of incorporation was granted (1596) by Elizabeth I, and revocations and renewals were made by a number of subsequent monarchs. During the English Civil War two important battles occurred at Newbury: in 1643, 6,000 men fell in battle when the day was won by Parliamentary forces; in the following year, Royalists overcame their opponents and were able to relieve Donnington Castle. In 1795, Newbury's suburb of Speenhamland gave its name to a system of parish relief for the unemployed.

The Church of St. Nicholas, early-16th-century Perpendicular in style, was largely built through the munificence of John Winchcombe (Jack of Newbury), an eminent clothier. The Jacobean cloth hall is now the borough museum and adjoining it is an old, two-story galleried granary. The grammar school originated in 1466 and Sandleford Priory, site of an Augustinian priory, *c.* 1200, is now also a school. Shaw House is a notable Elizabethan mansion. Principal industries are marine and light engineering, flour milling, woodworking, and the manufacture of light aircraft. One of the best racecourses in England lies to the east of the town. Pop. (1971 prelim.) 23,696.
51°25′ N, 1°20′ W
- map, United Kingdom **18**:866

Newburyport, city, seat of Essex County (with Salem and Lawrence), northeastern Massachusetts, U.S., at the mouth of the Merrimack River. Settled in 1635 (as part of Newbury), its location attracted early fishing, shipbuilding, and craft industries and led to its incorporation as a separate town in 1764. Its sheltered harbour was home port for a large merchant fleet that brought wealth and fame to the town in the years prior to the Revolutionary War. Stately federal-style houses (built by shipowners and sea captains) line its streets as a reminder of its mercantile heritage. The Jefferson Embargo of 1807–08 (against all foreign trade), a disastrous fire in 1811, and the War of 1812 set a decline in motion that ended the town's importance as a commercial port. A brief economic boom was experienced during the 1840s when local shipyards produced several famous clipper ships under direction of Donald McKay. After 1850 the production of textiles, shoes, silverware,

Newburyport, Mass.
Porterfield-Chickering—Photo Researchers

and rum were significant. Tourism and the manufacture of electrical machinery are now the economic mainstays.

A statue in Brown's Park honours abolitionist William Lloyd Garrison, a native of Newburyport. Inc. city, 1851. Pop. (1860) 13,401; (1980) 15,900.
42°48′ N, 70°52′ W

Newby, P(ercy) H(oward) (b. June 25, 1918, Crowborough, Sussex), writer whose novels and short stories consistently evoke a telling atmosphere and reveal nuances of character. Several of his novels, notably *The Picnic at Sakkara* (1955) and *Revolution and Roses* (1957), are set in Egypt, which he knew as a university lecturer. A sense of religious mystery pervades some of his works, while in others, such as *A Guest and His Going* (1959), about an Egyptian in England, the comic spirit reigns.

He grew up in the Midlands and South Wales and was educated at St. Paul's College, Cheltenham, Gloucester. During World War II he served first in France and then in Egypt, where he was assigned to teach English literature at the Fuad I University, Cairo (1942–46). His first novel, *A Journey to the Interior* (1945), won the Somerset Maugham Award. He went to work for the British Broadcasting Corporation in 1949, rising to director of programs for BBC in 1971.

New Cadre, Korean independence movement organized by intellectuals in the 1920s.
·mass resistance to Japan **10**:511h

New Caledonia, French NOUVELLE-CALÉDONIE, largest island of the French overseas Territory of New Caledonia, in the southwest Pacific Ocean, 750 mi (1,200 km) east of Australia. It is 248 mi long, 31 mi wide, and has an area of 7,374 sq mi (19,099 sq km). From its coast, which is encircled by the world's second longest barrier reef (after the Australian Great Barrier Reef), the island rises to a double chain of central mountains, the highest peak of which is Mt. Panié, 5,413 ft (1,650 m). The geological makeup of the island is quite complex. The climate is basically subtropical, with mean monthly temperatures ranging from about 63° F (17° C) to 90° F (32° C). Rainfall is highest from December to March; on the east coast, which is subject to the trade winds, it is about 80 in. (2,000 mm) annually and on the west coast less than 40 in. Forests occur along the east coast and in some valleys, and the west coast has savannas; the niaouli, or cajeput tree, and *Araucaria* (a type of pine) are characteristic. Natural fauna, except for fish and birds, is sparse.

Discovered (1774) and given the Roman name for Scotland, Caledonia, by the British navigator James Cook, the island was visited by Bruni d'Entrecasteaux, a Frenchman, in 1792. A French Roman Catholic mission was established in 1843, and the island was annexed by France in 1853. From 1864 to 1894 it served as a penal colony, during which time there were several attempted revolts of the indigenous people. When the French overseas territory was formed in 1946, the island became part of it.

The chief town, port, and territorial capital is Nouméa (*q.v.*) on the southwest coast. Industries include processing of nickel ore, the leading export; meat-preserving works, which are supplied by the large herds of cattle grazing on the southwest slopes; and timber mills, receiving local kauri pine. The island has significant ore deposits (nickel, iron, chrome, cobalt, manganese) and exports coffee (to France) and copra. Airlines link the island, also known as Grande Terre (Mainland), to Australia and the U.S., and there are more than 1,700 mi of roads.

While the majority of the population is Melanesian, there are many Europeans and also small communities of Wallis Islanders, New Hebrideans, Indonesians, and Vietnamese, all of whom were brought in as labourers. Latest census including neighbouring islets, 86,802.
21°30′ S, 165°30′ E

New Caledonia, Territory of, French TERRITOIRE DE LA NOUVELLE-CALÉDONIE, French overseas territory in the southwest Pacific Ocean comprising the islands of Bélep, New Caledonia, Pins, Loyalty, Huon, Chesterfield, Walpole, and Hunter (*qq.v.*). New Caledonia is by far the largest and is the site of Nouméa (*q.v.*), the territorial capital.

The group, with a total land area of 7,366 sq mi (19,079 sq km), has a subtropical climate. Rainfall is heaviest from December to March. On the higher islands (up to 5,000 ft [1,500 m]), the east coasts are subject to the trade winds and enjoy more rainfall than do the west coasts; the higher islands are geologically complex in contrast to the lower islands, which are composed chiefly of sedimentary or coral limestone. Coconut palms are found on most islands, and, except for birds, land fauna is generally sparse.

New Caledonia became a French overseas territory in 1946. The government consists of a governor, appointed by France, who is assisted by a government council of five members, and an elected territorial assembly of 35 members. The territory is represented in the French National Assembly and Senate by one deputy and one senator.

The islands are rich in minerals, and nickel (in the form of ore, partly refined matte, and castings) and iron ore are exported. There are also deposits of chrome, cobalt, manganese, and other metals. Large numbers of cattle are grazed for domestic use on the drier western pastoral lands of the largest island. Coffee is exported to France. By the 1970s, tourists, principally from Australia and New Zealand, were visiting the territory in greater numbers. Pop. (1972 est.) 121,073.
·art and sexual attitudes **13**:450c
·biogeographic regional traits **2**:1005a
·cultural and social patterns **11**:865b *passim* to 870b
·map, Australia and Oceania **2**:383
·Melanesian racial characteristics **14**:845a
·newspaper publishing statistics table **15**:237
·nickel production table **13**:71
·Oceania's physical and social contrast **13**:443g
·politics, area, and population **13**:829h; table 830

New Canaan, town (township), Fairfield County, southwestern Connecticut, U.S., just northeast of Stamford. Settled *c.* 1700, it was known as Canaan Parish (for the biblical Canaan) and was part of the Stamford and Norwalk areas. It was separated and incorporated as the town of New Canaan in 1801. Primarily residential, with many large estates, it also has some light industry. The Silvermine College of Art and Guild of Artists exhibits works of leading artists. Pop. (1980) 17,931.
41°09′ N, 73°30′ W

New Castile (Spain): *see* Castilla la Nueva.

New Castile, name given by conquistadores to the Inca empire in Peru.
·Pizarro as captain general **14**:488a

Newcastle, city and port, New South Wales, Australia, at the mouth of the Hunter River.

The harbour with steelworks in the background, Newcastle, New South Wales
David Moore—Black Star

It originated as the small Coal River Penal Settlement in 1801 and developed as an outlet for coal (from the Newcastle–Cessnock field) and for farm produce of the fertile hinterland. Iron and steel industries, established in 1915 by the Broken Hill Proprietary Company, now rival the coal trade. Diversified industrialization followed, including metallurgy, engineering, shipbuilding, and major textiles. Port facilities (based on North Harbour, the Basin, and Port Waratah) include a floating dock. Entrance to the harbour (1,200 ft [366 m] wide) is by a channel (500 ft wide) with a depth of 36 ft at low water. The University of Newcastle (formerly Newcastle University College) was established in 1965. Proclaimed a municipality, 1859; city, 1885. Pop. (1971 prelim.) 145,718.
32°55′ S, 151°45′ E
·map, Australia **2**:400

Newcastle, town, seat of Northumberland County, New Brunswick, Canada, northwest of Moncton. A port of entry opposite Chatham, near the mouth of the Miramichi River, it was founded in 1785 and developed with the lumber and allied trades, especially pulp and creosote. The town hall, Old Manse Library, and The Enclosure (a park and historic site) were gifts from Lord Beaverbrook (William Maxwell Aitken), publisher and financier, who spent his boyhood in the town. During World War I, Newcastle was the site of a British radio receiving station. Inc. 1899. Pop. (1971) 6,460.
47°00′ N, 65°34′ W
·map, Canada **3**:716

Newcastle, town and urban district, County Down, Northern Ireland, on Dundrum Bay, at the foot of Slieve Donard (2,796 ft [852 m]), the highest peak in the Mourne Mountains. It is a popular seaside resort and tourist centre for exploring the mountains. Nearby Tollymore Forest Park (1,200 ac [486 ha]) is a government forestry estate and includes 135 species of trees. Light engineering products are made in the town. The new castle from which the town takes its name, was a Magennis (MacGinnis) stronghold, built in 1588. Pop (1971) 4,619.
·map, United Kingdom **18**:866

Newcastle, town, western Natal province, South Africa, on the Incandu River at the foot of the Drakensberg mountains. It is in an area of coal mining and steel production. Latest census 17,554.
27°49′ S, 29°55′ E
·map, South Africa **17**:62
·Natal's industrial progress **12**:847c

New Castle, city, New Castle County, northern Delaware, on the Delaware River, where it is linked to New Jersey by the Delaware Memorial Bridges. The original settlement, called Santhoeck, was established in 1651 when Peter Stuyvesant, the Dutch administrator, built Ft. Casimir there. Seized by the Swedes in 1654, the settlement was regained by the Dutch in 1655. Then called Niew Amstel (for a suburb of Amsterdam) and made the Dutch capital of the southern Delaware region, it was renamed in 1664 (probably for William Cavendish, earl of New Castle), after the British conquest of the Dutch. William Penn, the English Quaker, took possession in 1682. An early cultural centre, New Castle was seat of the Lower Counties-on-Delaware (1704–76). On Sept. 21, 1776, a convention of counties, meeting there, formed the state of Delaware, and New Castle served briefly as state capital until it was moved to Dover in 1777. Three signers of the Declaration of Independence (George Read, George Ross, and Thomas Mckean) at one time lived in New Castle.

The Immanuel Church (Episcopal; 1703–*c.* 1710) is a historic landmark. George Read, American lawyer and revolutionist, is buried in its churchyard. Other colonial landmarks include Amstel House Museum (*c.* 1730), home of Nicholas Van Dyke, seventh gover-

The Immanuel Church, New Castle, Del.
Milt and Joan Mann—CameraMann

nor of Delaware; Old Dutch House, perhaps the state's oldest dwelling, built in the late 17th century, now maintained as a museum; and the Green (town square), laid out by Peter Stuyvesant in 1655. Local industries include the manufacture of rayon, steel, shoes, paint, and drugs. Inc. 1875. Pop. (1980) 4,907.
39°40′ N, 75°34′ W

New Castle, city, seat of Henry County, eastern Indiana, U.S., on the Blue River. Founded in 1819, it was incorporated in 1839. In 1900 a decade of expansion began when automobile and piano manufacturing, as well as other industries, were started there. During this same period, the large-scale commercial growing of roses was developed. Diversified manufactures include automobile parts and steel products. A farm nearby was the birthplace of Wilbur Wright. Pop. (1980) 20,056.
39°55′ N, 85°22′ W

New Castle, city, seat (1849) of Lawrence County, western Pennsylvania, U.S., at the juncture of the Shenango, Mahoning, and Beaver rivers, and in the foothills of the Allegheny Mountains. Originally the site of a Delaware Indian village, it was settled *c.* 1798 by John Stewart, who built an iron furnace and named the place for the English industrial city of Newcastle upon Tyne. Laid out in 1802, it became the terminus for the Erie Extension Canal in 1833. Local deposits of coal, iron ore, limestone, and fire clay provided a natural base for industry. Manufactures include steel and allied products, pottery, chemicals, and leather goods.

Moraine State Park and the 1,924.5-ac (779-ha) McConnell's Mill recreation area are nearby. Inc. borough, 1825; city, 1869. Pop. (1970) 38,559; (1980) 33,621.
41°00′ N, 80°20′ W
·map, United States **18**:908

Newcastle, city, seat (1890) of Weston County, northeastern Wyoming, U.S., near the Black Hills and the South Dakota border. Founded in 1889 and named for the English coal port, Newcastle upon Tyne, it was originally a coal-mining town. With the discovery of local oil fields, it has developed as an oil refining centre. Inc. 1889. Pop. (1980) 3,596.
43°50′ N, 104°11′ W

New Castle, locomotive built by Richard Trevithick (1771–1833).
·design, use, and difficulties **15**:478g; illus. 479

Newcastle, Thomas Pelham-Holles, 1st duke of (b. July 21, 1693—d. Nov. 17, 1768, London), prime minister of Great Britain from 1754 to 1756 and from 1757 to 1762. Through his control of government patronage, he wielded enormous political influence during the reigns of the kings George I and George II.

By the time he came of age in 1714, Newcastle was one of the wealthiest Whig landowners in England. He helped bring about the succession of King George I (ruled 1714–27) and as a reward was given the title duke of Newcastle-upon-Tyne. In 1724 Robert Walpole, the chief minister, made him secretary of state, a post he held for 30 years.

Newcastle gained even more power when his brother, Henry Pelham, became prime minister in 1743. Upon Pelham's death in March 1754, Newcastle was made prime minister, but the setbacks suffered by the English in the opening months of the Seven Years' War (1756–63) with France led to his resignation in October 1756. He was then created duke of Newcastle-under-Lyme. Eight months later he again became prime minister in an uneasy coalition with his former enemy William Pitt (later 1st earl of Chatham), who became secretary of state. While Newcastle procured parliamentary majorities in support of their ministry, Pitt directed the war and turned initial defeat into a brilliant victory. In May 1762 Newcastle lost his office to John Stuart, 3rd earl of Bute, favourite of young King George III (ruled 1760–1820).
·Britain's 18th-century political growth **3**:252e
·Pitt the Elder's first ministry **14**:476d
·resignation and opposition to Bute **7**:1125h

Newcastle disease, or AVIAN PNEUMOENCEPHALITIS, a serious viral disease of birds, marked by respiratory difficulty and nervousness. Some adult birds recover, although mortality rates are high in tropical and subtropical regions. Young chickens are especially susceptible and rarely survive. Symptoms are variable in turkeys and almost absent in ducks. Man can become infected by handling sick birds but usually develops only a temporary conjunctivitis (inflammation of the mucous membrane lining the inner surface of the eyelid). There is no effective treatment. Vaccines are available and are given repeatedly for best protection.
·zoonoses, table 9 **5**:877

Newcastle-under-Lyme, borough, Staffordshire, England, bounded on three sides by the city of Stoke-on-Trent. It takes its name from the "new castle" erected *c.* 1145 by Ranulf de Gernons, the earl of Chester, for the greater protection of his fief lying "under" (*i.e.*, near) what was the Roman Limes Britannicus (the British frontier). The derivation is also attributed to the proximity of the former Lyme Forest. The castle became obsolete in Tudor times. The town received its first royal charter of incorporation in 1173. In 1932 the borough was enlarged by the inclusion of Wolstanton, Clayton, and part of Keele. Chesterton, Knutton, and Silverdale are also in the borough. Industries include coal mining, brick and tile making, and engineering. The parish Church of St. Giles, rebuilt 1876, is the fourth or fifth on the same site. The University College of North Staffordshire (1949) became the University of Keele in 1962. Pop. (1971 prelim.) 76,970.
53°00′ N, 2°14′ W
·map, United Kingdom **18**:866

Newcastle upon Tyne, city (1882) in the metropolitan county of Tyne and Wear and former county borough (1888) in Northumberland, England, on the north bank of the River Tyne, 8 mi (13 km) from its North Sea mouth.

The community dates from the Roman period, when a fort (Pons Aelius) was built on a site close to the present Tyne Bridge. In 1080 the New Castle was built, but its functions were local and restricted. It was only in the 12th century that the town became of primary importance as a fortress settlement, with a key position in the frontier defenses, guarding the east coast route to Scotland. In 1172 a massive stone keep (still standing) was constructed to guard the bridge across the Tyne, and walls were built to enclose a small site northwest of the castle. Protection afforded by the fortress attracted religious (principally a community of Black Friars) and commercial bodies, and the town rapidly expanded. The inhabitants reaped the benefits of burghal freedom and privileges granted in numerous charters (the most important being given in 1216 and 1400), and the town became a thriving commercial centre. The wool trade was especially important, and in 1353 Newcastle became a staple (wool-manufacturing) town. By the late Middle Ages it had a thriving cloth industry.

In the following centuries growth continued steadily. In the 16th century, coal, destined for the growing London market, succeeded wool as the principal export. By 1800 Newcastle had become an important industrial and financial centre (the first banking houses being established after 1755), with expanding ironworking and glassmaking. The Tyne became a major focus for shipbuilding, and although this activity subsequently declined, the associated marine and heavy engineering industries remain important. The present economy rests on the city's function as a major service centre.

Municipal, commercial, and retail functions are located within the area of the medieval town, between the Tyne and the Town Moor. Post-World War II redevelopment in the north of this area has involved a civic centre, new main shopping precinct, and university campus. Outside the town walls, population increase since 1800 has resulted in the growth of many middle class suburbs—Gosforth and Tesmond in the north, Walker and Heaton in the east, Denton and Kenton in the west. Along the river bank, areas of 19th-century working class terrace housing, such as Scotswood, Elswick, and Byker, were being redeveloped in the early 1970s. The present metropolitan area also embraces several formerly distinct settlements. Five principal road and rail bridges link Newcastle with Gateshead on the south bank of the river—most famous being the Tyne Bridge (1928), part of a major British road link. The rail link between London and Edinburgh also crossed the Tyne at Newcastle (the High Level Bridge, 1844–49). The electrically operated Swing Bridge (1865–76), one of the greatest engineering achievements of its time, is on the site of Roman and medieval bridges.

The cathedral church of St. Nicholas dates from the 14th century, although a church occupied the site in 1123. The 15th-century tower and steeple are early Perpendicular in style. The Guildhall (rebuilt 1655–56) stands on the Sandhill, the old city centre. The best preserved portions of the old town walls lie between Westgate Road and Gallowgate, close to the ruins of the medieval Black Friars' priory.

Newcastle is an important education centre. The University of Newcastle upon Tyne was founded in 1937 as King's College by the merging of Armstrong College and the College of Medicine, both of which were attached to the University of Durham. The links with Durham remained until 1963, when King's College was granted a separate charter and became the present university. Further education is also provided by the Municipal College of Technology, Rutherford College of Technology, and a college of education. The Royal Grammar School, founded in the reign of Henry VIII (1509–47), was incorporated in 1600, and Dame Allan's School was endowed in 1705.

Important Roman and other archaeological finds are housed by the Museum of Antiquities (belonging to the university) and the Society of Antiquities. Industrial history of the

region is displayed in the Museum of Science and Technology. Collections of several natural history societies are preserved in the Hanlock Museum. Both the Laing Art Gallery and Museum and the Hollon Gallery have permanent collections of paintings. Pop. (1971 prelim.) 222,153.
54°59′ N, 1°35′ W
·map, United Kingdom **18**:866

Newcastle Waters, settlement, in north central Northern Territory, Australia, on Newcastle Creek (flowing to Lake Woods). The name refers to the permanent waterholes found there in 1861 by John McDouall Stuart at the northernmost point reached by his party in an unsuccessful attempt to cross the continent; they were named after Henry Pelham Fiennes Pelham, the fifth duke of Newcastle, then secretary of state for the colonies. A cattle staging post was established at the site with an Overland Telegraph Line station. It is now an important centre for the transshipment of cattle from the east–west stock routes, such as the Murranji Track, to the north–south Stuart Highway leading to railheads at Larrimah (130 mi [209 km] north) and Alice Springs (479 mi south).
17°24′ S, 133°24′ E
·map, Australia **2**:400

New China News Agency, Chinese news agency that is the chief provider of English-language news releases; headquarters in Peking.
·Peking publishing industry **14**:13e

New Church, commonly called SWEDENBORGIANS, organized in the General Conference of the New Church, the General Convention of the New Jerusalem in the U.S.A., and the General Church of the New Jerusalem. Its members are followers of the theology of Emanuel Swedenborg, the 18th-century Swedish scientist, philosopher, and theologian. Swedenborg did not himself found a church, but his theology was quite different from the Lutheran Church, which he never left. He believed, however, that his writings would be the basis of a "New Church," which he related to the New Jerusalem mentioned in the book of Revelation.

Shortly after Swedenborg's death, a group in England decided to establish a separate church. In 1788 the first building for New Church worship was opened in Great East Cheap, London, and was rapidly followed by others. In 1789 a conference met in the London church, and, except for 1794–1806 and 1809–14, the General Conference of the New Church has met annually.

Swedenborg's writings on religion were introduced into America in the 1780s. The first society was organized in Baltimore in 1792, and the first American ministers were ordained in 1798. The General Convention of the New Jerusalem in the U.S.A. was founded in 1817 in Philadelphia. Differences of interpretation within the convention led to the formation in 1897 of a separate group, the General Church of the New Jerusalem.

Worship in the Swedenborgian churches is almost always liturgical. Preaching of the Scriptures is based on Swedenborg's teaching that Scripture should be interpreted spiritually. Baptism and the Lord's Supper are the two sacraments of the church. Marriage is most holy and, when true, continues in heaven. To the established Christian festivals is added New Church Day (June 19).

Church government in the three New Church groups varies. The British General Conference and the U.S. General Convention annually appoint a general council, which, with a ministerial council, is the controlling authority. The General Church is episcopal. Candidates for the ministry, apart from those trained in Africa for service there, normally pass through a full-time four-year course in one of the two American colleges (in Cambridge, Mass., and Bryn Athyn, Pa.) or in Woodford Green, Essex, before being ordained.

The three groups all have extensive mission operations; African missions especially are strong. New Church societies, generally allied with one of the three groups in the United States and Britain, are small but are found in many parts of the world. Australia has its own conference, closely allied to that in Britain. The New Church groups in continental Europe are nearly all assisted from the United States.

Membership in the three groups is not large. In the early 1970s the General Conference had some 4,500 members in 57 societies and several groups in Great Britain. In the United States the General Convention had about 5,000 members and the General Church had about 3,000. Membership in the isolated societies in the various mission fields greatly increased these numbers.
·New Thought origins **13**:15c
·Puritan England as covenant nation **15**:304d
·Swedenborg's philosophy and theology **17**:854h

Newchwang (China): *see* Ying-k'ou.

new code of 581, penal code issued in China by the emperor Yang Chien, founder of the Sui dynasty.

Newcomb, Simon 12:1083 (b. March 12, 1835, Wallace, Nova Scotia—d. July 11, 1909, Washington, D.C.), astronomer and mathematician who prepared ephemerides—tables of computed places of celestial bodies over a period of time—and tables of astronomical constants, still useful.

Abstract of text biography. Despite his early lack of formal education, he was appointed to the American Nautical Almanac Office (1857) and received a degree from Harvard (1858). In 1877 he was put in charge of the American Nautical Almanac Office, from which he retired in 1897 with the rank of rear admiral. He was professor of mathematics and astronomy (1884–93) at Johns Hopkins University. His writings on astronomy include popular and technical books.

REFERENCE in other text article:
·Ephemeris Time computation **18**:415c

New Comedy, Greek drama from *c.* 320 BC to mid-3rd century BC that offers a mildly satiric view of contemporary Athenian society especially in its familiar and domestic aspects. Unlike Old Comedy, which parodied public figures and events, New Comedy features fictional average citizens and has no supernatural or heroic overtones. Thus, the chorus, the representative of forces larger than life, recedes in importance and becomes a small band of musicians and dancers who periodically provide light entertainment.

The plays commonly deal with the conventionalized situation of thwarted lovers and contain such stock characters as the cunning slave, the wily merchant, the boastful soldier, and the cruel father. One of the lovers is usually a foundling, the discovery of whose true birth and identity makes marriage possible in the end. Although it does not realistically depict contemporary life, New Comedy accurately reflects the disillusioned spirit and moral ambiguity of the bourgeois class of this period.

Menander introduced New Comedy around 320 BC and became its most famous exponent, writing in a quiet, witty style. Although most of his plays are lost, they are known through the works of the Roman dramatists Plautus and Terence, who translated and adapted them, along with other stock plots and characters of Greek New Comedy, for the Roman stage. Revived during the Renaissance, New Comedy influenced European drama through the 18th century. The *commedia erudita*, plays from printed texts popular in Italy in the 16th century, and the improvisational commedia dell'arte that spread throughout Europe from the 16th to the 18th century used characters and plot conventions that originated in Greek New Comedy. They were also used by Shakespeare and other Elizabethan and Restoration dramatists. The Rogers and Hart musical *The Boys from Syracuse* (1938) can be traced back through Shakespeare's *Comedy of Errors* and Plautus' *Menaechmi* to Greek New Comedy.
·comic style and influence **4**:961f
·costume conventions of Greek drama **17**:560c
·Greek literature development **10**:1092e

Newcomen, Thomas (b. 1663, Dartmouth, Devon—d. Aug. 5, 1729, London), engineer and inventor of the atmospheric steam engine, a precursor of James Watt's engine. As an ironmonger at Dartmouth, he became aware of the high cost of using the power of horses to pump water out of the Cornish tin mines.

With his assistant John Calley (or Cawley), a plumber, he experimented for more than ten years with a steam pump. It was superior to the crude pump of Thomas Savery. In Newcomen's engine the intensity of pressure was not limited by the pressure of the steam. Instead, atmospheric pressure pushed the piston down after condensed steam had created a vacuum in the cylinder.

As Savery had obtained a master patent for his pump in 1698, Newcomen could not patent his engine. Therefore, he entered into partnership with Savery. The first recorded Newcomen engine was erected near Dudley Castle, Staffordshire, in 1712.

Newcomen invented the internal-condensing jet for obtaining a vacuum in the cylinder and an automatic valve gear. By using steam at atmospheric pressure he kept within the working limits of his materials. Watts' later engine used steam to move the pistons. For many years Newcomen's engine was used to drain mines and raise water to power waterwheels.

steam engine
·development role **18**:35h; illus. 36
·early history **17**:624h; illus.
·use in coal mines **6**:230f

Newcomes, The, novel by William Makepeace Thackeray published serially in 1853–55.
·content and style **18**:196h

New Connection General Baptists: *see* Baptist Union of Great Britain and Ireland.

New Course, The, open letter by Leon Trotsky published in 1923 detailing reforms necessary in the Central Committee of the Russian Communist Party.
·Stalin's ascension to power **18**:719f

New Covenanters, also known as DAMASCUS SECT, an ancient Jewish sect whose existence is documented in the Dead Sea Scrolls.
·beliefs and organization **10**:314h

New Criticism, the post-World War I school of critical theory that insisted on the intrinsic value of a work of art and focussed attention on the individual work alone as an independent unit of meaning. It was opposed to the critical practice of bringing historical or biographical data to bear on the interpretation of a work.

The primary technique employed in the new critical approach is close, analytic reading, a technique as old as Aristotle's *Poetics*. The new critics, however, introduced refinements into the method. Early seminal works in the tradition were those of the English critics I.A. Richards (*The Principles of Literary Criticism*, 1924) and William Empson (*Seven Types of Ambiguity*, 1930). The movement did not have a name, however, until the appearance of John Crowe Ransom's *The New Criticism* (1941), a work that loosely organized the principles of this basically linguistic approach to literature.

To the new critics, poetry was a special kind of discourse, a means of communicating feeling and thought that could not be expressed in any other kind of language. It differed qualitatively from the language of science or philosophy, but it conveyed equally valid meanings.

Such critics set out to define and formalize the qualities of poetic thought and language, utilizing the technique of close reading with special emphasis on the connotative and associative values of words and on the multiple functions of figurative language—symbol, metaphor, and image—in the work.
·critical criteria and controversy **2**:42c
·literary criticism development **10**:1040b

New Criticism, The (1941), critical work by John Crowe Ransom.
·theory and prominence **15**:799a

New Culture Movement, in the early 20th century, aimed at displacing Confucianism as China's dominant ideology.
·Confucianism and China's modernization **4**:1103d
·general philosophy and innovations **6**:388c

New Deal, name given the domestic program of the administration of U.S. Pres. Franklin D. Roosevelt between 1933 and 1939, which took action to bring about immediate economic relief as well as reforms in industry, agriculture, finance, waterpower, labour, and housing, vastly increasing the scope of the federal government's activities. The term was first used in Roosevelt's speech accepting the Democratic nomination for the presidency on July 2, 1932. Reacting to the ineffectiveness of the Hoover Administration in meeting the ravages of the Great Depression, U.S. voters the following November overwhelmingly voted in favour of the Democratic promise of a "new deal" for the "forgotten man." Opposed to the traditional U.S. political philosophy of laissez-faire, the New Deal generally embraced the concept of a planned economy aimed at achieving a balance among conflicting economic interests.

Cartoon from *The New York Times* showing Congress kicking up its heels in protest over Roosevelt's "court-packing" plan, 1937
The Granger Collection

The new administration's first objective was to alleviate the suffering of the unemployed. Such agencies as the Works Progress Administration (WPA) and the Civilian Conservation Corps (CCC) were established to dispense emergency and short-term governmental aid and to provide temporary jobs, employment on construction projects, and youth work in the national forests. Before 1935, the New Deal focused on revitalizing the country's stricken business and agricultural communities. To revive industrial activity, the National Recovery Administration (NRA) was granted authority to help shape industrial codes governing wages, hours, child labour, and collective bargaining. The New Deal was aimed at regulating the nation's financial hierarchy to avoid a repetition of the stock market crash of 1929 and the massive bank failures that followed. The Federal Deposit Insurance Corporation (FDIC) granted government insurance for bank deposits in member banks of the Federal Reserve System, and the Securities and Exchange Commission (SEC) was formed to protect the investing public from fraudulent stock market practices. The farm program was centred in the Agricultural Adjustment Administration (AAA), which attempted to raise prices by controlling production of staple crops through cash subsidies to farmers. In addition, the arm of government reached into the area of electric power, establishing in 1933 the Tennessee Valley Authority (TVA), which was to cover a seven-state area and supply cheap electricity, prevent floods, improve navigation, and produce nitrates.

In 1935 the New Deal emphasis shifted to measures designed to assist labour and other urban groups. The Wagner Act of 1935 greatly increased the authority of the federal government in industrial relations and strengthened the organizing power of the unions, establishing the National Labor Relations Board (NLRB) to execute this program. To aid the "forgotten" homeowner, legislation was passed to refinance shaky mortgages and guarantee bank loans for both modernization and mortgage payments. Perhaps the most far-reaching programs of the entire New Deal were the Social Security measures enacted in 1935 and 1939, providing old-age and widows' benefits, unemployment compensation, and disability insurance. Maximum hours and minimum wages were also set in certain industries in 1938.

Certain New Deal laws were declared unconstitutional by the U.S. Supreme Court on the grounds that neither the commerce nor the taxing provisions of the Constitution granted the federal government authority to regulate industry or to undertake social and economic reform. By 1937, however, Roosevelt was able to make enough new appointments to achieve a court majority favouring legislative social change. Despite resistance from the business and other segments of the community to "socialistic" tendencies of the New Deal, many of its reforms gradually achieved national acceptance. Roosevelt's domestic programs were largely followed in the Fair Deal of Pres. Harry S. Truman (1945–1953), and both major U.S. parties came to accept most New Deal reforms as a permanent part of the national life.
·Canadian adoption **3**:744d
·economic recovery programs **6**:246e
·legislation, purposes, and results **18**:989e
·policies, opposition, and court fight **15**:1138f
·trade unionism and labour legislation **18**:566c

New Deal cultural projects, federal projects conceived during the 1930s by the administration of Franklin D. Roosevelt, chiefly as relief measures to help Depression-stricken U.S. artists. In the visual arts both the Department of Treasury and the Work Progress Administration (WPA) established programs. In 1933–34 the Department of Treasury operated the Public Works of Art Project (*q.v.*), or PWAP, which was, in effect, a pilot project for subsequent art-support programs. It was followed by the Treasury Section of Painting and Sculpture (*q.v.*), or Section (1934–43), and the Treasury Relief Art Project (*q.v.*), or TRAP (1935–39). Parallel in time with these two Department of Treasury projects was the WPA's Federal Project No. I, begun in 1935, which supported the visual arts through the Federal Art Project (*see* WPA Federal Art Project) and the literary and performing arts through the Federal Writers', Music, and Theatre projects. Federal Project No. I ended in 1939, and the Theatre Project was liquidated. The other three projects continued within the Federal Works Agency as part of the renamed Work Projects Administration. They, along with the Section, declined with the onset of World War II and were ended early in 1943.

New Delhi (India): *see* Delhi.

New Democratic Party (NDP), Canadian political party with a democratic Socialist position. Founded in 1961, the NDP is in favour of a planned economy, broadened social benefits, and an internationalist foreign policy.
·British Columbian politics **3**:297h
·foundation and represented factions **13**:576g
·postwar prosperity and new politics **3**:297g
·Saskatchewanian political history **16**:258e

New Dunciad, The (1742), by English Neoclassical poet and critic Alexander Pope, reprinted as the fourth book of a revised *Dunciad* (*q.v.*) in which the literary critic Lewis Theobald was replaced as satirical "hero" by the actor-manager and critic Colley Cibber.
·Horatian and contemporary standards comparison **14**:798c

New Economic Method, in Hungary, program of mixed Socialism introduced in 1968.
·profit motive and reform measures **9**:43e

New Economic Policy (NEP), policy introduced by the Communist Party in Soviet Russia in 1921, representing a temporary withdrawal from its previous policy of extreme centralization and doctrinaire socialism. The new policy permitted freedom of trading within the country, sanctioned overtime and piece rates for workers, offered encouragement to foreign capitalists and concessionaires, and by implication recognized the rights of private property that had been previously abolished. The operation of the economy was returned to a money basis in 1927.
·agricultural system changes **6**:1129d
·education concentration adjustment **6**:386a
·ideological basis and implementation **16**:71h
·industrial development programs **6**:247f
·Lenin's program of private enterprise **4**:1021d
·provisions and necessity of adoption **10**:796d
·reversion to private enterprise in 1921 **17**:314f
·Soviet economic planning stages **6**:256e
·Trotsky and trade unionism **18**:719c

new economics: *see* Keynesian economics.

Newe Inne, or The light Heart (1631), play by Ben Jonson.
·dramatic failure **10**:268g

newel, or NEWEL-POST, an upright post rising at the foot of a stairway, at its landings, or at its top. These posts usually serve as anchors for handrails. Often the stringboards, which cover and connect the ends of the steps, are framed into the newels. Made of the same substance as the stairway itself—wood, stone, or metal—the newels may be simple and functional, as in most contemporary examples, or highly ornamental, as in the Elizabethan or Jacobean styles.

Originally, a newel was the central post of a winding or circular stairway. If such a stairway has no central post, it is said to be of hollow-newel construction. In Gothic architecture a post used to support a vaulted-arch roof was sometimes called a newel.
·staircase design and construction **3**:954e

Newell, Norman Denis (b. Jan. 27, 1909, Chicago), paleontologist known for his studies of invertebrate fossils and evolution. Newell was a member of the Kansas Geological Survey from 1929 until 1934, when he joined the faculty at the University of Kansas, Lawrence; in 1937 he moved to the University of Wisconsin, Madison, and from there to Columbia University in 1945. He wrote *Late Paleozoic Pelecypods* (1937), *Geologic Studies on the Great Bahama Bank* (1957), *The Nature of the Fossil Record* (1959), *Paleontological Gaps and Geochronology* (1962), and *Paraconformities* (1967).

Newell, Peter (1862–1924), U.S. cartoonist.
·cartoon style and costume focus **3**:916d

Newell lock, also called PARAUTOPTIC LOCK, created in the 19th century by the firm of Day and Newell in New York; its features were two sets of lever tumblers, a plate that revolved with the key to prevent inspection of the interior, and a key with interchangeable bits so the key could be readily altered.
·design and construction **11**:11b

New England, region in New South Wales, Australia.
·New South Welsh political separatism **13**:12e

New England, region in the northeast U.S., including Maine, New Hampshire, Vermont, Massachusetts, Rhode Island, and Connecticut. Named by Capt. John Smith, who explored its shores in 1614 for some London merchants, colonial New England was settled by religious refugees seeking a more abundant life (*see* Pilgrim Fathers). The Puritan ethic, which discouraged idleness and luxury and glorified saving, served admirably the need of fledgling communities where the work to be done was so prodigious and the hands so few. During the 17th century the high esteem for an educated clergy and enlightened leadership encouraged development of public schools as well as such institutions of higher learning as Harvard (1636) and Yale (1701). Isolated from the mother country, New England colonies evolved representative governments, stressing town meetings, an expanded franchise, and civil liberties. The area was initially distinguished by the self-sufficient farm, but its abundant forests, streams, and harbours soon promoted the growth of a vigorous shipbuilding industry as well as of commerce.

In the 18th century, New England became a hotbed of Revolutionary War agitation for independence from Great Britain (*see* Liberty Poles; Correspondence, Committees of; Boston Tea Party), and its patriots played leading roles in establishing the new nation. In the early decades of the republic, the region strongly supported a national tariff and the policies of the Federalist Party. Resistance to the War of 1812 resulted in an abortive secessionist movement (*see* Hartford Convention).

In the 19th century, New England was characterized culturally by its literary flowering and its deep evangelical dedication frequently manifested in zeal for reform: temperance, abolition of slavery, improvements in prisons and insane asylums, an end to child labour. The antislavery movement finally came to predominate, however, and New England stoutly supported the cause of the Union in the U.S. Civil War (1861–65). As the frontier pushed westward, New England gradually lost its rural character, but meanwhile it spawned whole colonies of migrants who transplanted its patterns of culture and government intact to new frontiers in New York and the Middle West.

Though sea trade had revived after the War of 1812, the Industrial Revolution successfully invaded New England in this period and manufacturing came to dominate the economy. Such products as textiles, shoes, clocks, and hardware were distributed as far west as the Mississippi River by the itinerant Yankee peddler. After the Civil War a new labour force from eastern Europe flooded the urban centres, causing an ethnic revolution and forcing the traditional religions to share their authority with Roman Catholicism.

In the 20th century, New England continued to enhance its reputation as a centre for higher education and, despite the loss of its textile and leather industries to the South, as a manufacturer of quality products of small bulk and high value.
·agricultural expansion in 18th century **1**:335f
·Appalachian physical feature comparison **18**:907f
·architecture styles of the 17th century **19**:419c
·area and population, table 1 **18**:927
·Baptist growth and persecution **2**:714e
·Boston's role and influence **3**:55d
·colonial political structure and economic orientation **18**:950h *passim* to 952b
·colonial school development **6**:357b
·colonial settlement and control changes **18**:948c; maps
·Congregationalist experiment **4**:1129a
·Connecticut River Valley illus. **13**:184
·continental mountain evolution **13**:180h
·cultural development and distinctions **18**:924a
·dialectal regions **5**:700a; map
·early genealogical record sources **7**:993d
·early settlement organization and village description **18**:919c *passim* to 920b
·English Separatist colonists **15**:111d
·health problems and legislation **8**:695e
·housing design in 17th–19th centuries **9**:719f; illus. 720
·hurricane destruction statistics **9**:59b
·Mather family politico-religious legacy **11**:696g
·pre-Revolution problems and Revolution leadership **18**:955a
·property tax roles and practice **15**:57c
·public education development leadership **6**:366b
·religious education stress of Puritans **15**:45e
·town layout and influence **18**:1081g
·varved deposit study inferences **19**:33e
·Webster's political representation **19**:719c
·19th-century sectionalism growth **18**:967g

New England, Council for, in U.S. colonial history, joint stock company organized in 1620 by a charter from the British Crown with authority to colonize and govern the area now known as New England and including trade and fishing rights. Drawing from landed gentry rather than merchants, the company was dominated by its president, Sir Ferdinando Gorges, who intended to distribute the land as manors and fiefs among the Council's 40 members. Success eluded the organization, however, and instead of the Council's plan for a monolithic, artistocratic, Anglican province, New England colonization was dominated by two vigorous, Puritan, middle class enterprises: the Pilgrims (1620) and the Massachusetts Bay Company (1629). In order to untangle confused land titles under the Council and to resolve conflicting lines of political authority, the Massachusetts Company took possession of its charter directly from the King. In this way, the Council for New England was eliminated as an intermediary.

New England, Dominion of (1686–89), a kind of supercolony established in America by the British government to increase control over its colonies there. In an effort to retard the semi-independence of English settlements, especially in New England, Sir Edmund Andros was sent to America to assume administrative control of the New England colonies and later of New York and New Jersey as well. Because colonial charters and representative assemblies were abolished in the process, the establishment of the Dominion of New England was deeply resented in America. When news reached the colonies that James II had been overthrown (1688), Andros was deposed and colonial governments were restored to their former status.
·New York participation and revolt **18**:949d
·organization purpose and overthrow **18**:951a

New England Anti-Slavery Society (1832), antislavery organization founded by William Lloyd Garrison.
·founding and orientation **7**:913d

New-England Courant, a weekly newspaper founded in 1721 by James Franklin, brother of Benjamin Franklin.
·newspaper publishing history **15**:239c

New England Glass Company, American glass company, in East Cambridge, Mass., from around 1818 until 1888, when its then owner Edward D. Libbey met a strike of his workers by moving the factory to Toledo, Ohio, where it is still active under the name of the Libbey Glass Company. The New England Company made a large variety of wares ranging from pocket bottles and tumblers to attractive art glasses by techniques of molding, mechanical pressing, cutting, and engraving. Some of the finest of blown glass was produced by this factory; it was characterized by its high lead content, simplicity of line, and careful finish. New England glass was also famous for its rich colours, especially a ruby red. Another specialty of great public appeal was silvered glass (for which the company acquired a patent in 1855), used to make doorknobs and tableware in imitation of silver. It is from the last decades of its production that some of the company's most successful art glasses date: a Peachblow glass (*q.v.*), called Wild Rose, which is an opaque coloured glass with a glossy finish shading from white to deep rose; the Amberina glass, with pale amber and ruby tones; and the Pomona (*see* Pomona glass), which has a frosted surface and a light yellow colour.
·glass types and decorative techniques **8**:191a

Sugar bowl of clear flint glass molded and threaded, made by the New England Glass Company, Cambridge, Mass., *c.* 1820; in the Toledo Museum of Art, Ohio
The Toledo Museum of Art, Ohio, gift of Edward Drummond Libbey

New England Historic Genealogical Society, located in Boston and concerned with the recording and granting of heraldic arms in the United States.
·committee on heraldry **8**:797h

New England National Park, in northeastern New South Wales, Australia, occupies 89 sq mi (231 sq km) on the eastern slope of the New England Range, 45 mi (72 km) east of Armidale. It was established in 1935 and was named for its climatic and scenic resemblance to England. Point Lookout (5,280 ft [1,609 m]), the park's highest elevation, overlooks the headwaters of the Bellingen and the northern tributaries of the Macleay and Nambucca rivers. The park's eastern slopes are covered mainly with virgin forest, including heavy stands of red cedar, hoop pine, and tallowood. There are few exotic plants or animals in the area.

New England Range, or NORTHERN TABLELAND, section of the Eastern Highlands or Great Dividing Range, northeast New South Wales, Australia. Extending 200 mi (300 km) north from the Moonbi Range (near Tamworth) to the Queensland border and 80 mi from east to west (10–50 mi inland from the coast), it is Australia's largest plateau, having 9,000 sq mi (23,000 sq km) above 3,000-ft (1,000-m) elevation. The loftiest point is at Round Mountain (5,300 ft) on the eastern escarpment. With rainfall varying from 75–90 in. (1,900–2,300 mm), along that escarpment, to 20 in. in the west, the New England Range is generally wooded and is the source of many rivers, including the Richmond, Macleay, Clarence, Gwydir, Namoi, and Macintyre. The numerous river valleys are fertile and intensively cultivated with mixed crops, fruits, and potatoes. Cattle and sheep are grazed, timber is cut, and diamonds, sapphires, emeralds, gold, and tin are mined. Major centres are Inverell, Armidale, Glen Innes, and Tenterfield, which are linked by the New England (north–south) and the Oxley, Gwydir, and Bruxner (east–west) highways.

The district, explored (1818) by John Oxley, received its first settlers in 1832. It was so

named because the new inhabitants saw there some climatic and scenic resemblance to England. Regional identity is strong in New England and there have been repeated calls for separation from New South Wales and the creation of an independent state.
·map, Australia 2:401

New England Renaissance: *see* American Renaissance.

New England Seamount Chain, submarine feature of the Atlantic Ocean.
38°00′ N, 61°00′ W
·Atlantic Ocean floor features map **2**:296

New English Bible (1961–70), translation of the Old and New Testaments and the Apocrypha into British English. *See* Bible, translations of the.
·biblical criticism and translation **7**:61e
·textual editing of biblical literature **18**:189e
·vocabulary style and commercial success **2**:892d

New English Dictionary on Historical Principles, A (1884–1928): *see* Oxford English Dictionary, The.

New Essays Concerning Human Understanding (1898; translation of NOUVEAUX ESSAIS SUR L'ENTENDEMENT HUMAIN, written 1700–05, published 1765), work by Gottfried Wilhelm Leibniz.
·analysis of Locke's Empiricism **6**:770b
·influence on Lutheranism **11**:197g

New Forest, extensive woodland tract, Hampshire, England, between Southampton Water, the Solent (both English Channel inlets), and the River Avon (East Avon). It occupies a belt of infertile sands and gravels where native oak woodland is interspersed with heathland grazed by half-wild ponies and modern plantations of conifers. Encroachment by extension of the surrounding farmland has reduced the New Forest's extent since it was placed outside the common law of England by William I the Conqueror in 1079 as a royal hunting preserve. It still occupies 145 sq mi (376 sq km), of which 100 sq mi are owned by the Forestry Commission, a state body. The region formerly provided oak for the British Royal Navy; many ships were built there at the time of the Napoleonic Wars and launched from Buckler's Hard. Traversed by main roads and easily accessible from populous areas, the New Forest is much used for recreation, including camping, while its natural amenities are carefully safeguarded by British planning bodies.

New Forest, breed of hardy pony originating in the New Forest of southern England, used primarily as saddle ponies. The native stock was improved by introducing Oriental blood. Docile and surefooted, they stand 12 to 14 hands (48 to 56 inches, or 122 to 142 centimetres) tall, have short necks, sturdy shoulders, and deep bodies.

Newfoundland 12:1084, easternmost portion of the North American continent; a province of Canada since 1949. It comprises the roughly triangular island of Newfoundland (area 43,359 sq mi [112,299 sq km]), at the mouth of the Gulf of St. Lawrence, and the much larger—but very scantily peopled—mainland coastal region of Labrador (area about 112,800 sq mi), which lies farther north, across the narrow Strait of Belle Isle. The capital is St. John's. Pop. (1979) 574,000.

The text article covers the history of Newfoundland, its physical environment, regions, and people and their way of life.

REFERENCES in other text articles:
·area and population table **3**:721; map 722
·colonial religious education concern **6**:358f
·continental mountain evolution **13**:180h
·early British discovery **3**:733h
·education system with religious influences **6**:428c
·geographic features and population composition **3**:714g *passim* to 722e
·iceberg and pack ice extent **9**:155g; illus.
·map, Canada **3**:716
·19th-century educational structure **6**:367c
·19th-century immigration impact **3**:738e
·19th–20th-century expansion map **3**:746

Newfoundland, working dog developed in Newfoundland, possibly from crosses between native dogs and the Great Pyrenees dogs taken to North America by Basque fishermen in the 17th century. Noted for rescuing persons

Newfoundland
Sally Anne Thompson—EB Inc.

from the sea, the Newfoundland is a huge, characteristically gentle and patient dog standing 66 to 71 centimetres (26 to 28 inches) and weighing 50 to 68 kilograms (110 to 150 pounds). Powerful hindquarters, a large lung capacity, large webbed feet, and a heavy, oily coat contribute to the dog's ability to swim and to withstand cold waters. In addition to rescue work, the Newfoundland has served as a watchdog and companion and as a draft animal. The typical Newfoundland is solid black; the Landseer Newfoundland, named after Sir Edwin Landseer, the artist who painted it, is usually black and white.

New 4th Army, major Communist force in central and eastern China during World War II, which had great military success against the Japanese, who had invaded China in 1937. The Kuomintang (Nationalist) attack on its headquarters in January 1941 destroyed the alliance between the Communists and the Nationalists. After the Communists came to power in 1949, the egalitarian spirit and energy of the New 4th Army were held up as models for the Chinese people.

Established in 1937, the New 4th Army was composed of the few small Communist guerrilla bands then existing in central China; it originally numbered fewer than 12,000 men. As one of the two Communist forces in existence during the war against the Japanese (the other was the 8th Route Army), the New 4th Army was placed under the nominal leadership of the Nationalist high command. Resorting to both guerrilla and conventional warfare, the army expanded very rapidly; it not only fought the enemy but also propagandized in the territory through which it passed. Decisions were jointly discussed by officers and common soldiers, and morale and discipline were very high. By 1940 the New 4th Army had become the only force in central China fighting the Japanese troops. In spite of severe Japanese counterattacks late in that year, the army managed to grow to some 135,000 men by early 1941.

The Nationalists, however, were displeased by the expansion of Communist forces in the fertile central region of China, near the great industrial centre of Shanghai (previously a Nationalist stronghold). On Jan. 4, 1941, they launched a surprise attack on the New 4th Army headquarters. The assistant chief of staff, Hsiang Ying, was killed, and almost all of the army's leaders (including its commander, Yeh T'ing) were taken prisoner. Many were executed, and the Communists suffered several thousand casualties among their rear guard.

Although weakened by this incident, the New 4th Army continued to gain popular support, and by 1945 it comprised 260,000 men. That same year its name was changed to the East China People's Liberation Army and then to the 3rd Field Army. As such, the army battled the Nationalists for control of East China during the civil war and in 1949 liberated Shanghai. The new head of the army, Ch'en I, one of the greatest revolutionary heroes of the war, became mayor of Shanghai after the war and, in 1958, Chinese foreign minister, a position he continued to hold until his death in 1972.
·Chinese armed forces **4**:293f
·Communist guerrilla warfare **4**:373f

New France, French colony (*c.* 1600–1763), roughly corresponding at its widest extent to the Quebec, Ontario, and Maritime provinces of Canada, together with parts of the northeastern and Great Lakes areas of the U.S.
·Champlain's explorations and colonies **4**:29c
·exploration, settlement, and control **3**:734h
·government under Frontenac **7**:746f
·La Salle's colonies and explorations **10**:684a
·Parkman's history **13**:1020b
·Quebec city history **15**:336d
·Quebec's early history **15**:330d

New France, Company of, also called HUNDRED ASSOCIATES, French joint-stock company chartered by Cardinal Richelieu in 1627 to colonize and trade with New France (Canada).
·establishment and British war effects **3**:734g

New Freedom, in U.S. history, political ideology of Woodrow Wilson, enunciated during his successful 1912 presidential campaign, pledging to restore unfettered opportunity for individual action and to employ the power of government in behalf of social justice for all. Supported by a Democratic majority in Congress, Wilson succeeded during his first term in office (1913–17) in pushing through a number of meaningful measures: tariff reduction, banking regulations, antitrust legislation, beneficial farmer-labour enactments, and highway construction using state grants-in-aid. In actual practice, the Wilsonian program assumed much of the spirit and direction of the New Nationalism (*q.v.*) program of his main 1912 presidential opponent, Progressive candidate Theodore Roosevelt. By the extensive use of federal power to protect the common man, the New Freedom anticipated the centralized paternalism of the New Deal 20 years later.
·major reforms and Roosevelt contrast **18**:985b
·Wilson's program principles **19**:837a

New Frontier, in U.S. history, phrase used by John F. Kennedy, president in 1961–63, to describe his concept of the challenge facing the nation in the 1960s. In his Los Angeles address accepting the Democratic nomination for the presidency (July 1960), Kennedy said that the American people must be prepared to sacrifice in the years ahead and that there were stimulating "new frontiers" of unknown opportunities and perils to be crossed. The term "New Frontier" was never used to delineate specific proposals, although that autumn the Democratic Party successfully campaigned on a platform emphasizing more governmental action to stimulate the economy and to expand national defense and foreign aid programs.
·Kennedy presidency **10**:417f

Newgate Prison, famous prison in the City of London. It was originally called Newgate Gaol and consisted of a few cells over Newgate. The first great structure was built in 1422, and the last, in 1770–78, was a Neoclassic building designed by George Dance the Younger. It was demolished in 1902; the Cen-

tral Criminal Court ("Old Bailey") was erected on its site.
·English Neoclassical architecture **19**:434b

New General Catalogue of Nebulae and Clusters of Stars (NGC), astronomers' basic reference list of star clusters, nebulae, and galaxies. It was compiled in 1888 by Johan Ludvig Emil Dreyer (*q.v.*), who based his work on earlier lists made by the Herschel family of British astronomers. Dreyer included some 8,000 celestial objects, a total raised to about 13,000 by his first and second *Index Catalogues* (IC), published in 1895 and 1908, respectively. With these supplements the NGC covers the entire sky, although many objects visible with modern instruments are not listed.
An object may be known by several designations; *e.g.*, the Crab Nebula is also called NGC 1952 and M1, the latter being its number in the Messier catalog.
·nebula classification and listing **12**:927d
·star catalogue development **17**:604f
·star cluster and nebula designation **2**:229h

New Georgia Group, volcanic island group, Solomon Islands, southwest Pacific, 90 mi (145 km) northwest of Guadalcanal. The main islands (northwest to southeast) are Vella Lavella, Ganongga, Gizo Island, Kolombangara (cone-shaped with an extinct volcano, 5,800 ft [1,768 m]), Vona Vona, New Georgia (the largest, 50 mi long and 20 mi across at its widest point), Rendova, Tetipari, Vangunu, and Gatukai. The islands are picturesque, surrounded by extensive reefs and lagoons; they are rugged, well forested, with a virtual absence of animal life and an abundance of rivers. New Georgia rises to two peaks, Vina Roni (3,300 ft) in the north and Mt. Mangela (2,671 ft) in the centre. Gizo, which has timber operations, is the Western District headquarters. Products include copra, taro, sweet potatoes, and yams. During World War II, Japanese airfields were established at several places on New Georgia. U.S. forces took the islands from the Japanese on Oct. 7, 1943, after an intense struggle that began on June 29. *See also* Solomon Islands. Pop. (1976) 27,879.
8°30′ S, 157°20′ E
·linguistic profile **2**:491f; table 5

New Georgian language: *see* Georgian language.

New Glarus, village, Green County, southern Wisconsin, on a branch of the Sugar River. The settlement was founded in 1845 by immigrants from the canton of Glarus in Switzerland who had been driven from their homes by famine. It was originally organized on a semicommunal basis, with mineral rights and all streams and springs owned in common and the land apportioned by lot. New Glarus was incorporated in 1901. The village is still largely populated by descendants of the original settlers. Located in a rich dairying region, it is noted for its cheese, as well as for the production of Swiss-style embroidery. Tourism is important in the local economy; points of interest include replicas of the Swiss-style buildings originally constructed on the site and a replica of a Swiss château. A Swiss Volksfest honouring the founding of the Swiss nation is held in August, and the Wilhelm Tell Festival in September includes the presentation of Friedrich Schiller's drama *Wilhelm Tell* in German. New Glarus Woods State Park is situated south of the village. Pop. (1980) 1,763.
42°49′ N, 89°38′ W

New Glasgow, town, Pictou county, northern Nova Scotia, Canada, northeast of Truro, on the East River. Founded in 1809, following the discovery of local coal deposits in 1798, it was named by the first settlers, who were mostly Scots. A service centre for a farming and coal-mining region, the town manufactures heavy machinery, boilers, prefabricated houses, pulp and paper, electronic products, mattresses, and knitwear. The first Nova Scotian steamer, "Richard Smith," was built in New Glasgow. "Samson," the first Canadian locomotive built (1839) to operate on steel rails, may be seen at the Canadian National Railway's station. Inc. 1875. Pop. (1976) 10,672.
45°35′ N, 62°39′ W
·map, Canada **3**:717

New Granada, Viceroyalty of, Spanish VIRREINATO DE NUEVA GRANADA, in colonial Latin America, a Spanish viceroyalty, established temporarily between 1717 and 1724 and permanently in 1740, that included present Colombia, Panama (after 1751), Ecuador, and Venezuela and had its capital at Santa Fé (present Bogotá, Colombia). The separation of these territories from the viceroyalty of Peru, one of the principal colonial administrative changes effected by the Bourbon monarchs of Spain, reflected the growing population and increasing commercial importance of the area in the early 18th century. Subsequent commercial and political reforms and rising European demand for colonial products led to a period of prosperity and intellectual and cultural activity, which, however, exacerbated the divisions between peninsular Spaniards and middle and upper class Creoles. The viceroyalty ceased to exist in 1810, when most of the component jurisdictions ejected their Spanish officials. Initially, the new governments swore allegiance to the Spanish monarch, and they did not begin to declare independence until the following year. A series of civil wars facilitated reconquest of the United Provinces of New Granada by Spain between 1814 and 1816, and liberation of the area was not completed until 1823. The name Estado de Nueva Granada (State of New Granada) was adopted by Colombia in the period 1830–58.
·Bogotá political importance **2**:1183e
·Bolívar and the independence movement **2**:1206e
·Bourbon colonial reforms **10**:701a; map

New Granada Treaty (1846): *see* Bidlack Treaty.

Newgrange, County Meath, Ireland, site of a Neolithic passage grave; together with the similar passage graves in the mounds of Dowth and Knowth, it is part of the Brugh na Bóinne cemetery.
The structure is architecturally composite, the first construction having started as early as 3100 BC. The tomb is a narrow passage, 62 ft (19 m) long, lined with vertical slabs and roofed with lintels and corbelled stones. The ground plan at the end of the passages is cruciform, with an end chamber and two side chambers. Excavations in 1967 uncovered stone pendants, beads, and burned bone fragments. The tomb is covered by a cairn of stones and surrounded by a curb of stone slabs. It is believed that the curb was surmounted by a retaining wall of white quartz, 10 ft (3 m) high, which ran for 98 ft (30 m) on each side of the entrance. The cairn is set within a ring of standing stones that may predate the tomb structure.
A unique feature of the Newgrange tomb is a roof box about 3 ft (1 m) wide and 10 in. (25 cm) high over the entrance lintel. This would permit light to penetrate through the oblong window over the door even if the entrance were closed with a large slab. The ground on which the passage was built slopes upward, and the design is such that a line from the distant horizon passes through the roof box to the floor of the burial chamber and the back wall of the end chamber. The passage was built with a slight sinuosity, and the double curve somewhat restricts a beam of light entering the window. Research done in the late 1960s and early '70s indicates that the structure may have been engineered to permit sunlight to enter the tomb momentarily on the morning of the winter solstice. The tolerance in the design was such that the phenomenon still occurs, even though the solar declination has changed by about one degree since the year 3000 BC.
Newgrange is also remarkable for its carvings. Many of the slabs are decorated over almost their entire surface with double spirals and lozenges. There are lozenges, and a cut believed to have been made for rainwater drainage, on the lintel of the roof box. The far wall in the deep recess of the tomb is decorated with three interlocking double spirals that wind clockwise and unwind counterclockwise. The significance of this motif is unknown.
53°40′ N, 6°28′W
·engraved patterned stone **17**:707g; illus.
·Irish passage tombs **3**:283e

New Grub Street (novel): *see* Grub Street.

New Guard, Australian Fascist organization that was active in the commonwealth's political life in 1931–35. Organized along paramilitary lines and centred in the Sydney area, the New Guard espoused support for the British Empire, vigilant anti-Communism, and opposition to the Depression policies of Jack Lang, the Labor Party prime minister of New South Wales (1925–27, 1930–32). Founded by Eric Campbell, who held the rank of commander in chief, the New Guard was governed by a "council of action" under Campbell and had both civilian and military sections. The organization made the probably exaggerated boast of a membership of 100,000 in 1932. After the New South Wales state election of 1932, which put Lang out of office, the New Guard, robbed of its chief target, mellowed in its tone; by 1935 the organization had dissolved.
·New South Wales history **2**:421b

New Guinea 12:1088, island of the eastern Malay Archipelago, in the western Pacific Ocean, north of Australia. Covering an area of about 315,700 sq mi (817,700 sq km), it is administratively divided into Irian Jaya (*q.v.*; formerly Irian Barat, a province of Indonesia) and Papua New Guinea (*q.v.*), an independent parliamentary state from 1975. The second largest island (after Greenland) in the world, New Guinea is about 1,500 mi (2,400 km) long and about 400 mi wide at its widest part. It is a region of great ethnic, cultural, and linguistic diversity.
The text article covers New Guinea's history, geology, physical regions, climate, vegetation and animal life, ethnolinguistic groups, cultural patterns, demography, and economy.
5°00′ S, 140°00′ E
·arts development **13**:450d *passim* to 463h
·Australian World War II military activity **2**:420g
·cargo cults of highland peoples **18**:698d
·ceremonialism and animism **1**:924a
·continental island size and fertility **13**:826g
·headhunters' ritual mutilations **8**:1034e
·hunting and gathering societies **8**:1161a
·inhabitants and culture patterns **11**:864g *passim* to 870b
·Kuma courtship carrying leg custom **10**:479c
·life-forms of Australian region **2**:1004h
·linguistic profile **2**:491b; map 485
·MacArthur World War II Pacific operations **11**:220d
·map, Australian External Territories **2**:433
·map, Indonesia **9**:461
·mask design and cultural significance **11**:581c; illus. 580
·Melanesian physical characteristics illus. **15**:351
·Oceania's geographical and historical development **13**:443g
·pigeon population evolution **4**:933g
·politics, area, and population **13**:829h; table 830
·racial migrations and cultural isolation **13**:468e *passim* to 470h
·rain forest varieties, characteristics, and locations **10**:338d; map 337
·Tasman's voyages and discoveries **17**:1071a

·urban population ratio table **16**:26
·weevils carrying symbiotic organisms **4**:832b
·World War I invasion **19**:950f

New Guinea plateless turtle, common name for living members of the superfamily Carettochelyoidea (order Chelonia).
·classification and features **4**:76c

New Gulliver, The (1935), first important sound feature film made with puppets by Aleksandr Ptushko.
·entertainment cartoons **1**:920f

Newhall, Nancy, *née* WYNNE (1908–74), U.S. photography critic, conservationist, and editor of photography books who was the primary contributor to the development of the photograph book as an art form. Her career began in 1943, when she became acting curator of the photography department at the Museum of Modern Art, New York City, substituting for her husband, Beaumont Newhall, the photography historian and founder of the department, while he was in military service. Among her 22 books are *Time in New England* (1950), with photos by Paul Strand; *This Is the American Earth* (1960), with photos by Ansel Adams; and the biography *Ansel Adams* (1963).
·photographic books **14**:324g

New Hall porcelain, English hard-paste, or true, porcelain and bone china (*qq.v.*) produced by a company of potters at New Hall factory at Shelton, Staffordshire, between

New Hall porcelain teapot decorated with Chinese figures, Shelton, Staffordshire, *c.* 1800; in the Victoria and Albert Museum, London
By courtesy of the Victoria and Albert Museum, London

1782 and *c.* 1825. True porcelain was manufactured until 1810, when it was replaced by a glassy, opaque bone china. In both types of ware, New Hall's production consisted largely of tea ware made in simple shapes derived from silverware and decorated with simple sprig designs or scenes inspired by contemporary Chinese export porcelain.

New Hall wares, which were copied extensively by other Staffordshire factories, are seldom marked.
·English porcelain variations **14**:914f

Newham, one of the 32 London boroughs of Greater London, England, established (April 1, 1965) by the amalgamation of the former county boroughs of East Ham and West Ham and small parts of Woolwich (north of the Thames) and Barking (western part). The River Thames joins the southern boundary of the borough, which includes the districts of North Woolwich, Silvertown, Custom House, Canning Town, Plaistow, Upton Park, East Ham, Manor Park, Little Ilford, Forest Gate, and Stratford.

The Cistercian abbey of Stratford Langthorne was founded in 1135 and flourished for four centuries; its monastic inhabitants were responsible for draining the riverside marshes and for developing agriculture and a wool trade. The area grew extensively with the 19th-century industrial expansion of London, and this resulted in poor social and housing conditions, especially in the southwestern sector. By the 1960s much of the substandard housing had been replaced by modern housing estates.

Newham's northern and eastern parts are mainly residential in character. To the south, the Royal Docks predominate in a large Thames-side industrial area that concentrates on engineering, milling, and manufacturing activities.

Two major routes eastward from the city—Barking Road and Romford Road—cross the borough. In the south, the Silvertown Way and East Ham–Barking by-pass connect the Royal and Tilbury docks. The North Circular Road ends at Woolwich Ferry, which carries traffic across the Thames. Newham is served by London Underground (subway) District and Central lines and the Eastern Region of British Rail.

Wanstead Flats in the north is a detached portion of Epping Forest.

The West Ham College of Technology is the largest educational establishment in the area. Joseph Lister, who introduced antiseptic surgery, and the poet Gerard Manley Hopkins were both born in the borough. Philanthropist Elizabeth Fry lived successively at Plashet and Upton Lane House (both now demolished). Pop. (1978 est.) 227,100.
51°32′ N, 0°03′ E

New Hampshire 12:1092, one of the 13 original states of the U.S. Located in New England, northeastern U.S., it is bounded by the Canadian province of Quebec (north), the state of Maine and an 18-mile-long stretch of the Atlantic Ocean (east), the state of Massachusetts (south), and Vermont (west). Its area is 9,304 sq mi (24,097 sq km). The capital is Concord. Pop. (1980) 920,610.

The text article, following a brief survey of the state, covers its history, natural and human landscape, people, economy, administration and social conditions, and cultural life and recreation.

REFERENCES in other text articles:
·Appalachian geology and ecology **1**:1016a
·area and population, table 1 **18**:927
·map, United States **18**:909
·Massachusetts colonial control **18**:949b; maps

New Hampshire, also called NEW HAMPSHIRE RED, breed of single-combed general-purpose domestic fowls developed from Rhode Island Red stock and noted for rapid maturing and heavy winter egg production.
·general features and breeding **10**:1285h

New Hampshire Grants, term used prior to the American Revolution to refer to the territory that subsequently became the state of Vermont. The area was initially claimed by New Hampshire, and the first land grant there was issued in 1749 by the first governor of New Hampshire, Benning Wentworth. By 1764, 131 townships had been chartered. In 1765 New York, which also claimed the territory, began issuing grants of its own, some of which conflicted with those already made by New Hampshire. Armed conflicts between the rival claimants were common, and the Green Mountain Boys (*q.v.*) were organized to expel the settlers from New York. The dispute was resolved when Vermont (originally New Connecticut) was established as an independent republic in 1777.
·New Hampshire's boundary question **12**:1092c
·territorial grants disputes **19**:88c

New Hampshire versus Louisiana (109 U.S. 76 [1883]), U.S. Supreme Court case (combined with *New York* v. *Louisiana*) concerning an attempt by the states of New Hampshire and New York to force Louisiana to pay interest on state bonds owned by citizens of the plaintiff states and assigned to those states for collection. Laws had been passed by New Hampshire in 1879 and by New York in 1880 under which a citizen of either of those states who held a valid, overdue claim against another state could assign the claim to his state in writing; the state attorney general could then bring suit against the defaulting state, and money that was recovered, less the costs of litigation, was to be given to the original owner. The Supreme Court dismissed the cases on the ground that the laws in question violated the spirit and purpose of the Eleventh Amendment to the United States Constitution, according to which "The judicial power of the United States shall not be construed to extend to any suit" brought against one of the United States by citizens of another state.

New Harbour Group (geology): *see* Moine Schists.

New Harmony, town, Posey County, southwestern Indiana, U.S., on the Wabash River, at the Illinois border.

The site was first occupied by prehistoric Mound Builders and later was a camping ground for Piankashaw and other Indians. The settlement of Harmonie was founded in 1814 by George Rapp (*q.v.*), a German Pietist preacher who originally (before electing to move westward) came in 1803 with his followers to Pennsylvania from Württemberg, Germany. A prosperous Indiana colony evolved, but unrest brought on by hostile neighbours spurred the Rappite leaders to sell their holdings in 1825 to Robert Owen.

Owen, a British reformer, had come to the United States to found a cooperative community based on plans for mankind's salvation through "rational" thinking, cooperation, and free education. Owen renamed the town New Harmony. He was aided by William Maclure, a geologist, businessman, and philanthropist, who agreed to finance the schools and supply teachers, scientific equipment, and a library.

About 1,000 settlers responded to Owen's public appeal, but most were misfits who ate his rations, argued over government, and debated the merits of the "new system." Farms and workshops lay idle while virtual anarchy reigned. By May 1827, Owen's cash had been used in payments for land and supplies, and he returned to Britain in 1828. (*See also* utopianism.) The property was divided among Maclure and Owen's three sons, who, with some of the scientists and teachers, stayed on to develop one of the most notable pre-Civil War cultural centres in the United States.

A laboratory, built by David Dale Owen (first U.S. geologist), was headquarters for what later became the U.S. Geological Survey. It has since been restored.

New Harmony is now the trade centre for a rich agricultural area. The town was made a national historic landmark in 1965, and many of the Harmonist and Rappite buildings have been restored, including the Fauntleroy Home, the Rapp-Maclure Mansion (1814), Workingmen's Institute Library and Museum, Barrett-Gate House (1814), Dormitory Number 2, and the Restored Labyrinth with its baffling pathways. The Roofless Church (1959) has a Jacques Lipchitz sculpture. The ashes of the theologian Paul Tillich are interred in Tillich Park. An arts and crafts festival is an annual event in mid-June. Inc. 1850. Pop. (1980) 945.
38°08′ N, 87°56′ W
·local autonomy pattern in settlements **9**:303f
·Owen's social reform program **13**:801g
·U.S. reform movements **18**:966d
·utopian movements **18**:965h

Newhaven, English Channel port, county of East Sussex, England, at the mouth of the River Ouse. "New" haven developed after the great storm of 1570, when the course of the lower Ouse shifted westward from its former outlet at Seaford. The port is the English terminus of a cross-Channel ferry service to Dieppe, Fr. There is some light industry, boatbuilding, and a considerable tourist trade. Pop. (1973 est.) 9,970.
50°47′ N, 0°03′ E

New Haven, city, coextensive with New Haven Town, seat of New Haven County, south central Connecticut, U.S. It is a port of entry on Long Island Sound at the Quinnipiac River mouth. Originally settled as Quinnipiac in 1638 by a company of English Puritans led by John Davenport and Theophilus Eaton, it was renamed in 1640 for Newhaven, East Sussex, in England. In 1643 it combined with several adjacent towns, including Milford and Guilford, to form the New Haven Colony, of which Eaton was governor until his death in 1658. Reluctantly, in 1664 New Haven Colony accepted absorption into the more liberal and democratic Connecticut Colony, which was based on Hartford and enjoyed a royal charter. From 1701 New Haven was co-capital with Hartford, a position it maintained in both colony and state until 1875. During the Revolution it was sacked (July 5, 1779) by Loyalist forces under Gen. William Tryon. The town was an important centre of Abolitionist sentiment during the Civil War.

The Green, a park in downtown New Haven, Conn.
Ewing Galloway

New Haven's pre-eminence in many industrial fields is illustrated by the number of inventions that first appeared there. These include Eli Whitney's mass-production technique, Charles Goodyear's vulcanized rubber, Samuel Colt's improved repeating revolver, Lee De Forest's Audion (elementary radio tube), and sulfur matches. Diversified manufacturing and shipping are the modern economic mainstays. In 1957 New Haven was one of the first Eastern cities to undertake wholesale urban renewal of its decaying downtown district.

A noted educational and cultural centre, New Haven is the seat of Yale University (founded in 1701 as the Collegiate School of Connecticut and moved to New Haven in 1716), Southern Connecticut State College (1893), Albertus Magnus College (1925), South Central Connecticut Community College (1968), Connecticut College of Pharmacy, and the Winchester Gun Museum. Inc. city, 1784; town and city consolidated, 1895. Pop. (1920) city, 137,707; (1980) city, 126,109; metropolitan area (SMSA), 417,592.
41°18′ N, 72°56′ W

·history and population groups **5**:9h
·map, United States **18**:909

New Hebrides, French NOUVELLES-HÉBRIDES, now called VANUATU, island republic (1980) chain of 12 principal and many smaller islands in the southwest Pacific Ocean, 500 mi (800 km) west of Fiji and 1,100 mi east of Australia, jointly administered by France and Britain. The islands extend (north–south) for 400 mi and have a total area of 5,700 sq mi (14,763 sq km); they include Banks, Espíritu Santo, Oba, Pentecost, Malekula, Ambrim, Efate, and Eromanga. A diverse relief—ranging from rugged mountains and high plateaus to rolling hills and low plateaus, with coastal terraces and offshore coral reefs—characterizes the islands. Sedimentary and coral limestones and volcanic rock predominate; frequent earthquakes indicate structural instability. The highest point is Mt. Tabwemasana, 6,195 ft (1,888 m), on Espíritu Santo, the largest island. All of the islands are well forested, despite the decrease in average rainfall and temperatures from north to south. Abundant bird life contrasts with the sparse land fauna.

The islands were discovered (1606) by the Portuguese navigator Pedro Fernández de Quirós; they were rediscovered by the French explorer Louis de Bougainville (1768) and were chartered and named (for the Scottish Hebrides Islands) by the English navigator James Cook (1774). Conflicting British and French interests were resolved by the creation (1887) of a joint naval commission to administer the islands. In 1906 the two nations agreed to the establishment of a condominium government. Anglo-French high commissioners were delegated to exercise their powers through resident commissioners stationed at Vila, the capital, on Efate. Joint sovereignty is held over the indigenous people, but each nation retains responsibility for its own nationals according to the protocol of 1914 (ratified 1922). The group escaped Japanese invasion during World War II and became a major Allied base.

Sandalwooders came to the islands in the mid-19th century and were followed by cotton planters about 1868. Cotton gave way to bananas and coffee after 1880, only to be replaced by coconuts and maize (corn) after 1900. Unprecedented prosperity, based on copra, cacao, and coffee produced by imported Vietnamese labour, lasted through the 1920s until the worldwide depression of the 1930s. The economy of the New Hebrides is now based primarily on copra, but its production is marginal because of high costs, low productivity, and remoteness from markets. Exports, mostly to France, also include cacao, coffee, and some meat products; these are shipped from Vila and Luganville (on Espíritu Santo). There is some tuna fishing, and the tourist business is growing.

The indigenous population is Melanesian, but there is also a substantial multiracial community of Europeans, Chinese, Vietnamese, Tahitians, Wallis Islanders, and New Caledonians. Malaria is the greatest health hazard, but there are hospitals on most of the major islands. Kawenu Teacher Training College is near Vila. Pop. (1972 est.) 89,000.

·art craftsmanship and specialization **13**:462h
·cultural and social milieu **11**:865b
·island arc formation and composition **9**:1027g
·map, Pacific Islands **2**:433
·politics, area, and population **13**:829g; table 830

New Hebrides Trench, submarine trough in the southwestern Pacific Ocean, southwest of the New Hebrides islands; it reaches a maximum depth of 24,836 ft (7,570 m).
20°00′ S, 168°00′ E

·Pacific Ocean floor features map **13**:841

New Humanism, a critical movement in the U.S. between 1910 and 1930, based on the literary and social theories of the English poet and critic Matthew Arnold.

Reacting against the scientifically oriented philosophies of literary realism and naturalism, New Humanists refused to accept deterministic views of man's nature. They argued that: (1) man is unique among nature's creatures, (2) the essence of experience is fundamentally moral and ethical, and (3) the human will, although subject to genetic laws and shaped by the environment, is essentially free. With these points of contention, the New Humanists—Paul Elmer More, Irving Babbitt, Norman Foerster, and Robert Shafer, to name only a few—outlined an entire program and aesthetic to incorporate their beliefs.

Arnold's redemptive appeal was to recapture the moral quality of past civilizations in an age of industrialization and materialism. In assigning to art a position of moral authority in the modern world, Arnold proposed the values that art would of necessity have to adopt to foster the essentially human character of the Hellenic and Hebraic cultures.

As a social ethic, New Humanism appealed to the possibility of greatness that each civilization strives to fulfill. But as an aesthetic, it became entangled in its own definitions of the ultimate good. In general, the New Humanists came to be regarded as cultural elitists and advocates of social and aesthetic conservatism. Their influence was negligible after the mid-1930s.

New Iberia, city, seat (1868) of Iberia Parish, southern Louisiana, U.S., on the Bayou Teche (connected via canal with the Intracoastal Waterway). First settled in the 18th century by French, Spanish, and Acadians, it was laid out in 1835. It was incorporated in 1839. In 1863 it was occupied (with nearby salt mines) by Federal forces. It developed as a processing and shipping centre for salt, sugarcane, rice, peppers, vegetables, and oil and acquired some light manufacturing. New Iberia has retained strong French characteristics and includes Shadows-on-the-Teche, a restored antebellum mansion. The Louisiana Sugar Cane Festival is held annually in September. Nearby are the Longfellow-Evangeline State Park; a federal livestock experimental station; and Avery and Jefferson islands, noted for their scenic gardens. Pop. (1980) 32,766.
30°00′ N, 91°49′ W

·map, United States **18**:909

Ne Win, U, also known as THAKIN SHU MAUNG (b. May 24, 1911, Paungdale, Burma), Burmese general who served as head of state in a military government from March 1962. After the general election of 1974, when his Burma Socialist Programme Party won 99 percent of the seats in the unicameral legislature, he continued in power as chairman of the State Council, the supreme authority of the state.

Ne Win studied at University College, Rangoon, from 1929 to 1931, joined the nationalist Dobama Asi-ayone ("We-Burmans Association") in 1936 and became involved in the struggle for independence from the British. During World War II, after the Japanese invasion of Burma, he was one of the Thirty Comrades who, in 1941, went with the Burmese independence leader Aung San to Taiwan (Formosa) to receive military training from the Japanese. Ne Win was commander of the Japanese-sponsored Burma National Army from 1943 to 1945, but, becoming disillusioned with the Japanese, he helped organize the underground resistance. After Burma gained independence on Jan. 4, 1948, he served as commander in chief of the Burmese Army.

In 1958 Ne Win became prime minister in a "caretaker government," after former prime minister U Nu's administration proved incapable of dealing with the country's great economic and social problems. On the restoration of parliamentary government in 1960, Ne Win stepped down, but on March 2, 1962, he carried out a coup d'état, imprisoning U Nu and establishing the Revolutionary Council of the Union of Burma, whose members were drawn almost exclusively from the armed forces. On April 30 Ne Win declared the Burmese Way to Socialism, a program of military dictatorship combined with thoroughgoing nationalization of economic enterprises. He was successful in breaking overseas Chinese and Indian control of the economy, forcing some 300,000 foreigners to leave Burma after the coup. His regime drastically curtailed freedom of speech and movement; abolished all political parties, except for Ne Win's own Burma Socialist Programme Party; and took a hard line toward the minority peoples (the Shans, Karens, and Kachins) who were agitating for autonomy.

Ne Win was unable to halt economic stagna-

tion or political corruption. Prices in the nationalized "people's stores" soared, goods became extremely scarce, and the black market flourished. Although Burma had once been the world's greatest exporter of rice, farmers now grew hardly enough to feed themselves. His regime has, moreover, been repeatedly challenged by minority and Communist insurrections, by violent student demonstrations, and by a resistance movement organized by U Nu, who left Burma in 1969.
·influence on Burmese Buddhism **3**:400b
·premiership and Burma's socialism **3**:515g

Newington, town (township), Hartford County, west central Connecticut, U.S., southwestern suburb of Hartford. It was first settled in 1670 as part of Wethersfield. Newington Parish was organized in 1721 and was named either for Newington in Kent or for Stoke Newington, now part of London. It was incorporated as a separate town in 1871. Its public library (1750) was one of the first in the state, and the Church of Christ (Congregational) dates from 1797. The town is mainly residential with some light manufactures. There is some farming and milk processing. Pop. (1980) 28,841.
41°43′ N, 72°45′ W

New Iran Party: *see* Irān Novīn.

New Ireland, island of the Bismarck Archipelago, in the nation of Papua New Guinea, lying just north of New Britain, from which it is separated by St. George's Channel, southwest Pacific. The island stretches for about 220 mi (350 km) from northwest to southeast but is very narrow, with the southeastern portion only 30 mi wide and the 150-mi northwest arm no broader than 15 mi and as narrow as 5 mi. It is generally rugged, especially in the south, where the Rossel Mountains rise to 6,738 ft (1,871 m), and in the north, where the Schleinitz Mountains reach 1,860 ft. Limestone highlands occupy much of the northwest, the Lelet Plateau averaging 2,000 ft in elevation. There is a fringe of coastal plain of raised coral or alluvium. The latter is deposited by numerous streams, the largest being the 25-mi Weitin River. There are few good harbours.

New Ireland was sighted in 1616 by a Dutch navigator, Jacques Le Maire, who conceived it as being part of a landmass including New Britain and New Guinea. This theory was disproved when Philip Carteret found St. George's Channel in 1767 and named the island Nova Hibernia (New Ireland). An unsuccessful settlement attempt was made in 1880. Annexed by Germany in 1884, it was renamed New Mecklenburg. After World War I the island was mandated to Australia. Occupied by the Japanese in 1942, it became part of the UN Trust Territory of New Guinea, administered by Australia, after World War II. When Papua New Guinea achieved independence in 1975, it became part of that nation.

Commercial development is dominated by copra production, particularly on the east coast. Most of the inhabitants live in the north. This section is administered from Kavieng, chief port, which is linked by an east coast road to Samo. The southern portion is administered from Namatanai. New Ireland is the largest island in a 3,700-sq-mi (9,600-sq-km) province that includes Lavongai (New Hanover), the St. Matthias Group, and Tabar, Lihir, Tanga, Feni, and Djaul. Pop. (1976 est.) province, 67,620.
3°20′ S, 152°00′ E
·cultural and social milieu **11**:866d *passim* to 868h
·geographical features, area, and population **12**:1090d; table 1091
·map, Trust Territory of New Guinea **12**:1091
·Oceanian arts development **13**:450a *passim* to 463g
·Oceanian peoples and cultures **13**:468e

New Ironsides, ironclad ship used during the U.S. Civil War.
·Confederate attack by torpedo boats **12**:891c

New Jersey **12**:1095, Middle Atlantic state and one of the 13 original states of the U.S. Occupying an area of 7,836 sq mi (20,295 sq km), it is bounded by New York (north and northeast), by the Atlantic Ocean (east and south), by Delaware (southeast), and by Pennsylvania (west). Its capital is Trenton. Pop. (1980) 7,364,158.

The text article covers the state's history, natural and human landscape, people, economy, administration and social conditions, and cultural life and institutions.

REFERENCES in other text articles:
·area and population, table **18**:927
·colonial settlement and control **18**:949g; maps
·map, United States **18**:909
·War of Independence battle sites and importance **19**:603h; map

New Jersey, College of: *see* Princeton University.

New Jersey Plan: *see in* Constitutional Convention, U.S.

New Jersey tea: *see* Ceanothus.

New Jerusalem: *see* New Church.

New Kensington, city, Westmoreland County, western Pennsylvania, U.S., on the Allegheny River, and near the Pennsylvania Turnpike. Established in 1891 by a group of Pittsburgh merchants interested in the reduction of aluminum, it was laid out on the site of Ft. Crawford (built during the Revolutionary period) and named for Kensington in London. Incorporated as a borough in 1892, it absorbed neighbouring Parnassus in 1931 and became a city in 1934.

Since 1892 it has been one of the world's leading producers of aluminum. Other manufactures include steel, glass, textiles, and metal and petroleum products. Several industrial research and development centres are also located in the area. The New Kensington branch of Pennsylvania State University was opened in 1958. Crooked Creek State Park is nearby. Pop. (1980) 17,660.
40°34′ N, 79°46′ W

New Kingdom, also called NEW EMPIRE, in ancient Egypt, the period of the 18th, 19th, and 20th dynasties (1567–1085 BC). *Major ref.* **6**:471f
·dress styles and Kha tomb **5**:1016h; illus. 1017
·Memphite importance **11**:896c
·Near Eastern ancient dynastic conflicts **12**:914b
·Nubian conquests and administration **13**:109d
·Ramses II's reign and military feats **15**:501g
·religious reforms of Amenhotep IV **6**:508f
·Thutmose's empire expansion **18**:366a
·visual art forms and style **19**:253g

Newlands, John Alexander Reina (b. Nov. 26, 1837, London—d. July 29, 1898, London), chemist whose "law of octaves" noted a pattern in the atomic structure of elements with similar chemical properties and contributed in a significant way to the development of the periodic law. He studied at the Royal College of Chemistry, London, fought as a volunteer under Giuseppe Garibaldi for Italian freedom (1860), and later worked as an industrial chemist. In 1864 he published his concept of the periodicity of the chemical elements then known, which he had arranged in order of atomic weight. He pointed out that every eighth element in this grouping shared a resemblance, by analogy, with the intervals of the musical scale. The "law of octaves" thus enunciated, at first ignored and ridiculed, later took its place as an important generalization in modern chemical theory. Newlands collected his various papers in *On the Discovery of the Periodic Law* (1884).
·periodic law and law of octaves **14**:75f

New Laws of the Indies: *see in* Indies, Laws of the.

New Leader, U.S. Socialist periodical founded in 1927.
·magazine publishing history **15**:256d

New Life Lodge: *see* sun dance.

New Life Movement, an attempt at the moral regeneration of China, carried out by Chiang Kai-shek between 1934 and 1937 in an attempt to oppose Communism and achieve national unity. Through a network of 1,300 branches, Chiang exhorted the Chinese people with a mixed Christian and Confucian message; he urged the public to be clean, prompt, truthful, and courteous and to practice the four traditional virtues of politeness (*li*), integrity (*lien*), self-respect (*ch'ih*), and righteousness (*i*). To understand these principles, Chiang encouraged the reading of the works of the great 19th-century Confucian scholar-official Tseng Kuo-fan, who primarily stressed loyalty and public service.

Offering no answer to China's grave social problems, the New Life Movement only increased the growing disenchantment of Chinese intellectuals with the Nationalist regime. *Major ref.* **4**:383h
·Chiang Kai-shek's unification measures **4**:206h

New Liskeard, town, Timiskaming District, eastern Ontario, Canada, on the north end of Lake Timiskaming (an expansion of the Ottawa River), near the Quebec border. Originally known as Thornloe, the town developed on land that the provincial government opened for settlement in 1822. Its present name is derived from Liskeard, Cornwall, the birthplace of the town's founder, John Armstrong. A market and distributing town for the surrounding farming, lumbering, and cobalt- and silver-mining region, New Liskeard, 90 mi (145 km) northeast of Sudbury, also serves as a hunting and fishing resort. Industries include ironworks, dairies, canneries, pulp and lumber mills, and a printshop. Pop. (1976) 5,601.
47°30′ N, 79°40′ W

New London, city, coextensive with New London Town, New London County, southeastern Connecticut, U.S., port of entry on Long Island Sound at the mouth of the

Hempsted House, New London, Conn., built in 1678
By courtesy of the Antiquarian & Landmarks Society Inc. of Connecticut

Thames River. Founded by John Winthrop the Younger in 1646, it was called Pequid until 1658. In 1709 Connecticut's first printing press was established there. A rendezvous of privateers during the Revolution, it was attacked (Sept. 6, 1781) by a large British force under Benedict Arnold that burned the wharves and stores. It has one of the deepest harbours on the Atlantic Coast. The whaling industry began there in 1784, flourishing in the early 19th century but declining after 1846.

New London is the seat of the U.S. Coast Guard Academy (1932) and site of a U.S. naval submarine base (1916) and the U.S. Navy

Underwater Sound Laboratory. These greatly influence its economy, which includes the building of nuclear submarines. The city is the seat of Connecticut College (1911; until 1969 for women only) and Mitchell (junior) College (1938). The annual Yale–Harvard boat races on the Thames finish at New London. Inc. 1784. Pop. (1980) city, 28,842; metropolitan area (SMSA), 248,554.
41°21′ N, 72°07′ W
·map, United States **18**:909

New Look, style for women's clothing introduced by Christian Dior in 1947.
·style features and period of popularity **5**:1034c; illus. 1033

New Machiavelli, The (1911), novel by H. G. Wells.
·autobiographical theme **19**:758d

New Madrid, city, seat (1821) of New Madrid County, southeast Missouri, U.S., on the right bank of the Mississippi River. It originated as an Indian trading post about 1783. In 1789 Col. George Morgan of New Jersey received a large land grant from Spanish authorities as part of a plan to attract U.S. settlers to the Spanish province of Louisiana. Morgan laid out a straggling townsite but then left the area because of a disagreement with the Spanish governor. New Madrid, however, grew rapidly in farming and trade after the purchase of the Territory of Louisiana by the U.S. in 1803. Its growth was retarded by violent earthquakes in 1811–12, as well as by floods and the shifting of the river's course, which caused several removals of the city to other sites. The town was the site of a Civil War battle in 1862.

New Madrid's economic mainstay is diversified agriculture (cotton, soybeans, corn [maize], grain sorghum, and livestock). Aluminum ingots, electrical conductors, and clothing are manufactured, and there is some lumbering.

The Old Dawson Home (restored) served as a Federal hospital during the Civil War. The Lilbourn site, a fortified prehistoric Indian ceremonial centre, is 6 mi west. Inc. 1808. Pop. (1980) 3,204.
36°36′ N, 89°32′ W

New Madrid, Battle of (March 13, 1862), fought during the U.S. Civil War around the small town of New Madrid, Mo., on the right bank of the Mississippi. When the loss of Ft. Henry and Ft. Donelson made their base at Columbus, Ky., untenable, the Confederates withdrew downriver 60 miles to Island No. 10, a heavily fortified position of great natural strength at a sharp bend in the river. New Madrid, seven miles farther downriver, was also occupied. The Federals immediately pushed downriver in pursuit, employing the amphibious tactics that were proving so effective on western waters. After considerable manoeuvring, the Confederates, who were trapped between Federal forces and unable to escape into Tennessee because of high water in the swamps, were forced to surrender on Island No. 10 on April 8.
·Civil War strategic repercussions **4**:677a; map 679

Newman, Arnold (1918–), U.S. photographer specializing in portraits characterized by posing the sitter with objects associated with his work or personality.
·Chagall portrait illus. **4**:19
·Saarinen photograph illus. **16**:112

Newman, Barnett (b. Jan. 29, 1905, New York City—d. July 3, 1970, New York City), painter, one of the Abstract Expressionists, who took an emotional approach to the conception and execution of their works. He developed a simplified style based on colour, maintaining the integrity of the canvas with a

Barnett Newman, 1961, with his painting "Onement VI"
Alexander Liberman

single image that entirely filled it. He studied at the Art Students League and at the City College of New York (1927) and taught at the University of Saskatchewan (1959) and the University of Pennsylvania (1962–64). He presented his first one-man show in New York City in 1950. His series of 14 paintings called "Stations of the Cross" was exhibited at the Solomon R. Guggenheim Museum, New York City, in 1966. With the painters William Baziotes, Robert Motherwell, and Mark Rothko, he was a founder of the school called "Subject of the Artist" (1948), which held open sessions and lectures for other artists.

Newman, Ernest (1868–1959), British music critic and author.
·music criticism made scientific **12**:722b

Newman, Hugh George de Willmott, later called MAR GEORGIUS (1905–), British clergyman.
·episcopal succession in Old Catholic Church **13**:554d

Newman, John Henry **13**:1 (b. Feb. 21, 1801, London—d. Aug. 11, 1890, Birmingham), one of the most remarkable churchmen and men of letters of the 19th century, led the Oxford Movement in the Church of England and later became a cardinal-deacon in the Roman Catholic Church.

Abstract of text biography. Newman was educated at Trinity College, Oxford, and began his career as a teacher and churchman. He became the leading figure in the Oxford Movement (begun in 1833), which tried to revive High Church ideals and practices in the Church of England. His books, often characterized by sensitive and lyrical prose, played a leading role in the movement, especially his *Parochial and Plain Sermons* (1834–42), *Lectures on the Prophetical Office of the Church* (1837), and *University Sermons* (1843). A great spiritual crisis occurred in Newman's life when he began to question the true catholicity of the Church of England. Resigning as vicar of St. Mary's, Oxford, on Sept. 18, 1843, he preached his last Anglican sermon at Littlemore one week later. On Oct. 9, 1845, he was received into the Roman Catholic Church. While serving as first rector of the Catholic university in Dublin he published *The Idea of a University* (1852). His *Apologia pro Vita Sua* (1864), giving a history of his religious opinions, restored Newman to national prominence. He was made cardinal-deacon of St. George in Velabro in 1879 by Pope Leo XIII.

REFERENCES in other text articles:
·Coleridge's theological influence **4**:841a
·doctrine dissemination theory **5**:928b
·English literature of the 19th century **10**:1185f
·Mary's devotional status impetus **11**:562a
·Matthew Arnold's symbol of classicism **2**:36g
·opinion of infallibility doctrine **13**:552h
·Protestant independence within state church **15**:117a
·university education purpose **6**:363h

Newmarket, town, seat of York County, southeastern Ontario, Canada, on the Holland River, south of Lake Simcoe, 27 mi (43 km) north of Toronto. Originating as a Quaker settlement founded about 1800 by Timothy Rogers, it became the county seat in 1954 when Toronto, the former seat, and its suburban municipalities formed the urban district of metropolitan Toronto. Manufactures include pencils, furniture, candy, clothing, plastics, and dairy products. Newmarket is the site of Pickering College, a school for boys. Pop. (1976) 24,795.
44°03′ N, 79°28′ W

Newmarket, market town in the county of Suffolk, England, on chalk downland, on the main London–Norwich road. The community is the home of the Jockey Club and has been celebrated for its horse races from the time of James I; it is also known for the training of racehorses on its heath. Charles I instituted the first cup race there in 1634. Newmarket is the site of an annual sale of more than 3,000 head of bloodstock and possesses a unique Equine Research Centre. In 1967 the National Stud was opened by Queen Elizabeth II. Some light engineering industries have been established. Just outside the town and in Cambridgeshire county lies the Devil's Ditch, or Devil's Dyke, an earthwork extending 7½ mi (12 km) and thought to have been built by the East Anglians as a defense against the Mercians about the 6th century AD. The district is covered by chalk downland, with its unique flora and fauna, and Wicken Fen (in Cambridgeshire northwest of Newmarket), a nature reserve belonging to the National Trust, is a surviving part of the now largely drained Fens. Pop. (1973 est.) 13,370.
52°15′ N, 0°25′ E
·horse racing history **8**:1093e
·map, United Kingdom **18**:867
·racing course layout **8**:1099h

New Martinsville, city, seat (1846) of Wetzel County, northwestern West Virginia, U.S., on the Ohio River south of Wheeling. Settled by Edward Doolin in 1780, it was called Martin's Fort to honour Presley Martin, who bought the land and organized defense measures after Doolin died in an Indian massacre. The name was changed to Martinsville in 1838; "New" was added in 1846 to avoid confusion with Martinsville, Va. The city is an agricultural-trade centre with some industrial development, including the manufacture of glassware and chemicals. The New Martinsville Regatta is an annual river event. Inc. town, 1838; city, 1950. Pop. (1980) 7,109.
39°39′ N, 80°52′ W

New Masses, U.S. periodical published from 1926 to 1948.
·magazine publishing history **15**:256d

new math, curricular improvements in the teaching of elementary and high school mathematics, not actually new subject matter. The new math was designed to increase understanding of technological and scientific advances of the space age. Concepts encountered in set theory, number theory, algebraic structures, combinatorics, various types of analysis, and various types of topology that are generally taught beyond high school are introduced in the new math, developing ideally from example, discovery, and exploration. The success of the improvements has been acclaimed by some and questioned by other educators.

New Mexico **13**:2, southwestern state of the U.S., bounded on the north by Colorado, on the east by Oklahoma and Texas, on the south by Texas and the Mexican state of

Chihuahua, and on the west by Arizona. It has an area of 121,666 square miles (315,115 square kilometres). New Mexico was admitted to the Union in 1912 as the 47th state. Its capital is Santa Fe. Pop. (1980) 1,299,968.

The text article, after a brief overview of the state, covers its history, physical environment and human settlement, ethnic composition and demography, economy, administration and social conditions, and cultural life and institutions.

REFERENCES in other text articles:
·area and population, table 1 **18**:927
·Civil War battle activity **4**:676e
·common village features **18**:920d
·Indian animal and agricultural dances **1**:671b *passim* to 675a
·map, United States **18**:908
·Rocky Mountain ranges and faults **15**:967d
·Spanish colonial mission activity **10**:698a
·territorial expansion 1812–61 maps **18**:962 *passim* to 969

New Milford, borough, Bergen County, northeastern New Jersey, U.S., immediately north of Hackensack on the east bank of the Hackensack River. Early Dutch settlers established a plantation-type farm called Vriesendael, which was pillaged by Indians in 1643. In 1675 David des Marest, a French Huguenot, and his sons established a permanent settlement. Their mill, known as Demarest Landing, became a shipping point for iron ore. The home of des Marest's son Samuel is preserved in replica near the Steuben House Museum; the house of another son, David, stands on River Road. The New Bridge Inn (1739) is still in operation. Originally included in Palisades Township (organized in the 1800s), the borough was established in 1922 when three small settlements, Peetzburg, New Milford Manor, and New Bridge, amalgamated and incorporated as New Milford. An agricultural community until the early 1900s, it is now basically a commuting town. Pop. (1980) 16,876.
40°56′ N, 74°01′ W

New Model Army, army formed in February 1645 that won the English Civil War for Parliament and itself came to exercise important political power. When war broke out in 1642, Parliament had at its command the local militia, or trainbands, of those districts supporting its cause, notably London, the eastern counties, and southeast England. But militia were always unwilling to fight far from their homes, so in addition Parliament authorized (as did King Charles I) its prominent supporters to raise troops of horse and infantry companies from among their own tenants and associates. These private parliamentary armies were perhaps in better condition than those raised for the King, because Parliament provided for their pay; but strategically they were not effective because of the lack of unified command. Toward the end of 1644 a dispute about the conduct of the war developed between Henry Montagu, earl of Manchester, one of the main parliamentary generals, and his lieutenant general, Oliver Cromwell. In December Cromwell argued in a major speech that the war would never be brought to a conclusion unless Parliament's military resources were improved. There was already some general feeling that members of Parliament holding military command might be tempted to prolong the war in order to continue their personal power. As a result, the New Model Army was brought into existence; it was planned to comprise 11 regiments of horse of 600 men each, 12 regiments of foot of 1,200 men each, and 1,000 dragoons (mounted infantrymen). The cavalry, always easier to raise, were mainly veterans drawn from the original armies of Manchester, the earl of Essex, and Sir William Waller; the infantry included some veterans from the armies, with a majority of pressed men drawn from London, the east, and southeast. In April 1645, by the Self-Denying Ordinance, members of Parliament resigned all military and civil office and command acquired since November 1640. Sir Thomas Fairfax (afterward 3rd Baron Fairfax —the "younger" Fairfax) was appointed captain general of the New Model Army, with authority to appoint his senior officers. The army's organization and the thorough training of its men were accomplished by Fairfax, not Cromwell, who, despite the Self-Denying Ordinance, became his leader of horse just before the great parliamentary victory at Naseby (June 14, 1645). After Naseby the army was mainly occupied in sieges, but it obtained such political power that eventually its authority eclipsed that of Parliament. Under Cromwell it won Dunbar and Worcester, the great battles of the Commonwealth period, against Charles II and the Scots.
·Cromwell's defeat of Charles I **4**:54c
·political disputes and views **3**:245a
·Puritan control of Parliament **15**:306b

New Monthly Belle Assemblée, The, British women's magazine published from 1847 to 1870.
·magazine publishing history **15**:250b

New Moon, occurs every 29.53 days (or once every synodic month) when the Moon passes between the Sun and Earth. Its illuminated crescent, as seen from Earth, has dwindled to the vanishing point. Eclipses of the Sun occur at this time, on the rare occasions when the three bodies involved are exactly in line. *Cf.* Full Moon.
·Moon–Earth orbits and synodic period **12**:415g
·solar eclipse cycles **6**:190f

Newnan, city, seat of Coweta County, northwestern Georgia, U.S. Founded in 1827, it was named for Gen. Daniel Newnan, a veteran of the War of 1812. During the Civil War, it served as a hospital centre for wounded from both armies. Agriculture (cotton, fruit, and livestock), once the economic mainstay, has given way to manufacturing, chiefly textiles and metal products. The Dunaway Gardens, a multiterraced natural rock garden containing many spring-fed pools, is 5 mi (8 km) north. Inc. 1828. Pop. (1980) 11,449.
33°23′ N, 84°48′ W

New Nantucket Island (Pacific Ocean): *see* Baker Island.

New Nationalism, in U.S. history, political philosophy of Theodore Roosevelt, an espousal of active federal intervention to promote social justice and the economic welfare of the underprivileged. Roosevelt used the phrase "New Nationalism" in a 1910 speech in which he attempted to reconcile the liberal and conservative wings of the Republican Party. Unsuccessful, he became a Progressive and went on to promulgate his ideas as that party's presidential candidate in the election of November 1912. His program called for a great increase of federal power to regulate interstate industry and a sweeping program of social reform designed to put human rights above property rights. With the Republican vote split, Roosevelt and his New Nationalism went down to defeat before Democratic candidate Woodrow Wilson and his New Freedom.
·major reforms and Wilson contrast **18**:985b
·Wilson's program comparison **19**:837a

New Negro Movement (literature): *see* Harlem Renaissance.

Newnes, George, 19th-century British publisher who founded the magazine *Tit-Bits* in 1881.
·magazine publishing history **15**:249c

New Netherland, Dutch North American colony in present New York, New Jersey, and Connecticut (1624–64).
·Dutch colonization and economic failure **4**:886c
·Dutch founding and British conquest **18**:949c
·pre-British colonial education attempts **6**:358b

New Norfolk, town, southeast Tasmania, Australia, on the Derwent River. Originating in 1807–08 when the inhabitants of Norfolk Island (in the South Pacific Ocean) were resettled in the district then known as the hills, the town site was chosen by Gov. Lachlan Macquarie and named Elizabeth Town after his wife. It was renamed (1827) by the settlers for their earlier island home. New Norfolk was gazetted a shire in 1863. Linked to Hobart (14 mi [23 km] southeast) by rail and the Lyell Highway, the town serves a locale yielding 80 percent of the hops used for brewing in Australia, apples, oats, and sheep. Since 1941, the principal local industry has been the production of the nation's only domestic newsprint. Australia's first fish hatchery (1864), Salmon Ponds, on the Plenty River, is there. Historic buildings include Bush Inn (Australia's oldest licensed hotel, 1815) and St. Matthew's Church (1825). Pop. (1971 prelim.) 6,839.
42°47′ S, 147°03′ E
·map, Australia **2**:400

New Norwegian language, in Norwegian NYNORSK, formerly called LANDSMÅL (Country-wide Language), less widespread of Norway's two official languages, created during the middle of the 19th century by the language scholar Ivar Aasen (*q.v.*) on the basis of the rural dialects of Norway's western districts to carry on the tradition of Old Norse that had been interrupted in the 15th century. The language was recognized by the government in 1885 and has been used in schools since 1892. Although New Norwegian is now used in literature, theatre, broadcasting, churches, education, and government, its use is much less widespread than that of Dano-Norwegian, the other of Norway's two official languages. New Norwegian is somewhat more puristic than Dano-Norwegian, with fewer German and Danish elements in its vocabulary. Parliamentary acts and the spelling reforms of 1907, 1917, and 1938 have decreased the differences between the two Norwegian languages in the 20th century. In 1952 a permanent advisory language commission was appointed with an equal number of representatives for both New Norwegian and Dano-Norwegian to work toward amalgamation of the two standards in a single common Norwegian language, Samnorsk, but opposition has been vigorous. *See also* Dano-Norwegian language; Old Norse; Norwegian language.
·creation and current status **13**:265b
·Norwegian traditions and development **8**:28c
·Scandinavian comparative features **8**:28d

new novel: *see* nouveau roman.

New Nyāya, Sanskrit NAVYA-NYĀYA, Indian philosophical school founded *c.* 13th century.
·principal exponents and doctrines **9**:327d

New Objectivity (artists' group): *see* Neue Sachlichkeit.

New Orleans 13:6, largest city of Louisiana, U.S., on the east bank of the Mississippi River, about 110 mi (180 km) from its mouth. Coextensive with Orleans Parish (county), it is a major port and tourist centre as well as a commercial and industrial metropolis of the South. It was founded *c.* 1718, and its location along a bend in the river accounts for its popular name of "Crescent City." New Orleans is the core of an expanding metropolitan area defined by the parishes of Jefferson, Orleans, St. Bernard, and St. Tammany. Pop. (1980) city, 557,482 (55% black); metropolitan area (SMSA), 1,186,725 (33% black).

The text article covers the character of New Orleans, its history, peoples, economy, politics and government, and educational, cultural, and recreational life.
29°58′ N, 90°07′ W

REFERENCES in other text articles:
·cultural importance and tourist trade **11**:129e
·Eads's channel deepening contribution **5**:1118a
·French exploration and settlement **4**:887c
·ironwork structures and ornamentation **11**:1114a; illus.
·Louisiana Purchase map **18**:960
·map, United States **18**:908
·metropolitan population density map **18**:930

New Orleans, steamboat made in 1811 by Robert Fulton in Pittsburgh and sailed on the Mississippi River.
·Fulton's construction and operation **7**:776h

New Orleans, battles of, brilliant U.S. victory against Great Britain (Jan. 8, 1815) in the War of 1812, and capture of the city by Union naval forces (April 25, 1862) during the U.S. Civil War.

In the autumn of 1814, a British fleet of more than 50 ships commanded by Gen. Edward Packenham sailed into the Gulf of Mexico, preparing to attack New Orleans, strategically located at the mouth of the Mississippi River. On December 1 Gen. Andrew Jackson, commander of the U.S. Army of the Southwest, hastened to the defense of the city. Jackson's army of between 6,000 and 7,000 troops consisted chiefly of militiamen and volunteers from southern states. Because of slow communications, news of the peace treaty at Ghent (Dec. 24, 1814) did not reach America in time to avert the battle, which Jackson fought against 7,500 British regulars who stormed his position on Jan. 8, 1815. So effective were the barricades of cotton bales that fighting lasted only half an hour, ending in a decisive U.S. victory and a British withdrawal. British casualties numbered more than 2,000 (289 killed); U.S., only 71 (31 killed). News of the victory reached Washington, D.C., at the same time as that of the Treaty of Ghent and did much to raise the low morale of the capital. The Battle of New Orleans greatly enhanced the reputation of Jackson as a national hero.

Early in the U.S. Civil War (spring 1862), a Union naval squadron of 43 ships under Adm. David G. Farragut entered the lower Missisippi near New Orleans and soon breached the heavy chain cables that were stretched across the river as a prime defense. Realizing that resistance was useless, Confederate gen. Mansfield Lovell withdrew his 3,000 troops northward, and the city fell on April 25. On May 1 Gen. B.F. Butler led 15,000 Union troops into the city to take command for the remainder of the war. The permanent loss of New Orleans was considered one of the worst disasters suffered by the Confederacy in the western theatre.
·Jackson's defeat of British army **10**:2c

New Orleans Race Riot (July 1866), after U.S. Civil War, incident of white violence directed against Negro urban dwellers in Louisiana; influential in focussing public opinion in the North on the necessity of taking firmer measures to govern the South during Reconstruction. With the compliance of local civilian authorities and police, whites in late July killed 35 New Orleans black citizens and wounded more than 100. This race riot was similar to many others throughout the South and, together with the establishment of the highly restrictive Black Codes (*see* Black Codes, U.S.), helped win a commanding majority for the Radical Republicans and their vigorous Reconstruction policies in the November 1866 national elections.

New Orleans style, in jazz, manner of collective improvisation that characterized the emergent days of jazz; so called because in the 20 or so years before the closing of Storyville (the New Orleans red light district) in 1917, jazz music was so strictly confined to that city and the area around it that it might almost be called a local musical dialect.

The conventional front-line instrumentation of the New Orleans group was clarinet, trumpet, and trombone. Because the music was performed out-of-doors, the trumpet, being the loudest instrument, predominated; and the city's leading trumpeters and cornettists—*e.g.*, Buddy Bolden, Freddie Keppard, King Oliver, Louis Armstrong—became its most famous musicians. The music was drawn mostly from blues, with strong infusions of ragtime and march tunes. Usually the trumpet stated and embellished the melody, while the clarinet, above, and the trombone, below, wove contrapuntal patterns based on the harmonies of that melody. Whereas the clarinet voice was usually quite fluid, the trombone often confined itself to a fairly basic and unadorned statement of the root notes of each chord. The art of the New Orleans musician was thus to amplify his fellow without duplicating him. It was advantageous for a group to maintain a consistent personnel, allowing the members to learn each other's stylistic idiosyncrasies and develop a corporate awareness that kept them from trespassing on each other's musical areas.

Because it evolved in the earliest days of jazz, New Orleans style is often romanticized, and some purists believe that the music lost its innocence forever when the simplistic methods of its ensemble improvisation were forsaken for more complex approaches. It may also be, however, that functional as well as aesthetic forces influenced the concentration on the ensemble to the virtual obliteration of the individual voice: there may have at first been no individual voices coherent enough to stand out. Significantly, the first great New Orleans virtuosos, Louis Armstrong and Sidney Bechet, instinctively forsook the strict ensemble rules of their youth the moment they found themselves in a position to dictate musical terms. In this sense, the classical New Orleans style held the seeds of its own destruction.

Dixieland (*q.v.*) and other attempts to revive the New Orleans style or re-create the working conditions that nurtured it are essentially retrogressive and often are sentimental. One such movement culminated in the early 1940s with the rediscovery of the New Orleans cornettist Bunk Johnson; but it faded fairly quickly, as did its exaggerated claims to Johnson's historical importance.
·communal function and instrumental style **10**:121g
·jazz museum establishment and festival **13**:10g

New Paltz, town (township), Ulster County, southeastern New York, U.S., on the Wallkill River; it includes the village of New Paltz. The site was settled by French Huguenots in 1677 who named it for an earlier European refuge, the Rhenish Palatinate (German *Pfalz*). Three stone houses, all built in the 1690s and part of the original settlement, are maintained by the Huguenot Historical Society. The village (incorporated 1887) is now a resort in a fertile agricultural area producing fruit, dairy products, and poultry. The State University College at New Paltz was established in 1828. Of interest is the Narrow Gauge Wallkill Valley Railroad. Pop. (1980) town, 10,183; village, 4,941.
41°45′ N, 74°05′ W

New Peoples Associations, student and intellectual organizations established by Yoshino Sakuzō in Japan in the 1920s.
·Marxism and the educated class **10**:82h

New Philadelphia, city, seat (1808) of Tuscarawas County, northeastern Ohio, U.S., on the Tuscarawas River, south of Canton. It was founded in 1803 by John Knisely, a tavern keeper from York, Pa., on federal lands set aside for distribution to Revolutionary War veterans. Named for Philadelphia, Pa., the community developed after the Civil War, when utilization of large local coal and clay deposits created an industrial climate. Manufactures now include textile machinery, construction equipment, machine tools, ceramics, plastics, industrial fans, spark plugs, and batteries.

The nearby Zoar Village (now a state memorial) was a commercial settlement (1817–98) founded by German Separatists. Ohio's first village, Schoenbrunn (1772–98; now restored), a few miles southeast, was built by Christian Indians, sponsored by Moravian missionaries; Fort Laurens State Memorial (1778; 14 mi north) is the site of the state's only American fort in the American Revolution. Ohio's major flood-control and recreation project, the Muskingum Watershed Conservancy District, is headquartered in New Philadelphia. Inc. town, 1833; city, 1883. Pop. (1980) 16,883.
40°30′ N, 81°27′ W

New Physical Hypothesis, Latin HYPOTHESIS PHYSICA NOVA . . . (1671), work by the German philosopher Gottfried Wilhelm Leibniz.
·problems of motion and space **10**:786b

New Pien Canal, Anhwei Province, China.
·Anhwei waterway construction **1**:901a

New Plymouth, city and port, west North Island, New Zealand, on North Taranaki Bight. The settlement, founded in 1841 by the New Plymouth Company under the auspices of the New Zealand Company, drew many of its first immigrants from Cornwall and Devonshire, England. In time, land disputes between these people and the native Maoris built up to the open hostilities of the 1860 Taranaki War. The town was the capital of the former Taranaki province, was designated a borough in 1877, and was constituted a city within Taranaki County in 1949.

Linked to Wellington (251 mi [404 km] southeast) and Auckland (286 mi north) by rail and road, New Plymouth is New Zealand's chief dairy centre. With its artificial harbour, it is the area's chief port, importing cement, petroleum products, and fertilizer and exporting dairy products and meats, which are chiefly produced in the vicinity and processed within the town. Natural gas is piped north to Auckland from an oilfield at nearby Moturoa. New Plymouth, noted for its parks and called the "Garden of New Zealand," lies close to Egmont National Park and is a resort centre, especially for winter sports at Mt. Egmont. One of the city's oldest buildings is St. Mary's Church (1846). Pop. (1971) 34,314.
39°04′ S, 174°04′ E
·map, New Zealand **13**:44

New Poems (1964), original German NEUE GEDICHTE (1907–08), collection of lyric poetry by Rainer Maria Rilke.

Newport, a market town and borough, the Isle of Wight, England. It lies toward the centre of the diamond-shaped island at the head of the River Medina's wide estuary, 5 mi (8 km) from its English Channel mouth at Cowes. Newport was probably the Roman settlement of Medina, but there is no trace of subsequent Saxon inhabitation. The first charter was granted between 1177 and 1184, the Saturday market dating from 1184; the borough was incorporated in 1608. The Church of St. Thomas of Canterbury was rebuilt in the Decorated Gothic style (1854), and the Town Hall (1816) was designed by a noted British architect John Nash. Newport early superseded nearby Carisbrooke (now a suburb) as the island's capital because of its facilities for trade. It remains the island's agricultural centre, and the harbour is used for trading with the mainland. Other industries include plastics, woodwork, milling, and brewing. Parkhurst, a major British maximum-security prison, stands on the outskirts. Pop. (1971) 22,309.
50°42′ N, 1°18′ W
·map, United Kingdom **18**:866

Newport, city, seat of Jackson County, northeastern Arkansas, U.S., on the White River. It was founded in 1870 by the Cairo and Fulton Railroad (now part of the Missouri Pacific Railroad) after townspeople of Jacksonport, to the north, refused to grant the railroad right-of-way and permission to bridge the river. As a "new port" on the river, it was incorporated in 1875 and replaced Jacksonport as county seat in 1892. It developed as a processing and shipping centre for White River Valley farm produce. Mussels from the river were gathered for pearls, and button blanks were cut from their shells. The former military airport (to the northeast), deeded to Newport after World War II, is now the site of an industrial park. Pop. (1980) 8,339.
35°37′ N, 91°17′ W

Newport, city, one of the seats (1796) of Campbell County (the other is Alexandria), Kentucky, U.S., opposite Cincinnati, Ohio, on the Ohio River near the mouth of the Licking River. The first settlement, planned in 1790 by a young soldier, Hubbard Taylor, was named in honour of Christopher Newport, commander of the first ship to reach Jamestown, Va., in 1607. The only anti-slavery newspaper (*The Free South*), published in Kentucky during the 1850s, was edited in Newport by William Shreve Bailey, who, after a pro-slavery mob threw his presses and type into the street (Oct. 28, 1859), moved to Cincinnati. The city experienced its greatest growth in the 1880s and 1890s with an influx of German settlers and the completion of bridges to Cincinnati. Newport was the scene of a seven-year (1921–28) strike by steelworkers.

Local industries include steel, clothing, and brewing. Inc. village, 1795; city, 1835. Pop. (1890) 24,918; (1950) 31,044; (1980) 21,587.
39°06′ N, 84°29′ W

Newport, city, seat (1893) of Lincoln County, Oregon, U.S., on the north shore of Yaquina Bay and the Pacific. Settled in 1855 as a fishing village, it was platted in 1866 and developed as a seaside resort with steamer connections to San Francisco. The city serves the lumber industries at nearby Toledo and maintains fish canneries and tourist facilities. The Oregon State University Marine Science Center is there and the Yaquina Head Light Station (established in 1873 and automated in 1966) stands at the north entrance to the bay. Old Yaquina Bay Lighthouse (1871) is a museum in Yaquina Bay State Park. Inc. 1882. Pop. (1980) 7,519.
44°38′ N, 124°03′ W

Newport, city, occupying the southern end of the island of Rhode Island (also known as Aquidneck Island), Narragansett Bay (there bridged to Jamestown), U.S.; it is a port of

The dining room in Marble House, one of many elaborate homes in Newport, R.I.
By courtesy of the Preservation Society of Newport County

entry and the seat of Newport County. From the harbour on the west, the city rises up a gentle hillside to a plateau at about a 250-ft (76-m) elevation.

Newport was founded in 1639 by a group of refugees from the Antinomian controversy (theological dispute begun by Anne Hutchinson in Massachusetts, 1636), who had settled at the north end of the island in the present town of Portsmouth. Following a schism in that settlement, a group led by William Coddington moved to the south end of the island and established Newport, which, because of its excellent harbour and strategic position for waterborne commerce, soon became one of the most flourishing cities in colonial North America. Printing in Rhode Island was begun at Newport in 1727 by James Franklin, an older brother of Benjamin. In 1758 James Franklin, Jr., established the *Newport Mercury*, still published as a weekly newspaper.

The British occupation of Newport (1776–79) during the American Revolution resulted in the flight of almost all of the leading merchants to the mainland. Immediately after the Civil War, probably because of its climate and its colonial seaport atmosphere, the city developed as an opulent summer resort.

The area's largest industry is a vast complex of naval installations located at Newport, Middletown, and Portsmouth and comprising the Naval War College and the components of the Newport Naval Base, including the Naval Station, the Naval Underwater Weapons Research and Engineering Station, the Officer Candidate School, the Naval Supply Center, and the Naval Hospital. Industries include the manufacture of electrical instruments and appliances and electronic devices.

Until 1900, Newport was one of Rhode Island's two capital cities, the other being Providence. The Old Colony House (1739) still stands at Washington Square. Nearby are Trinity Church (1726); Touro Synagogue (1763), the oldest in America (designated a national historic site in 1946); the Redwood Library and Athenaeum (1747); and the Newport Artillery Company Military Museum (chartered 1741), with a large collection of military uniforms.

The old section, known as The Point, on the harbour front has homes of colonial merchants, some of them restored as museums by the Preservation Society of Newport County. In Touro Park at the top of the hill is the Old Stone Mill, thought to be the remains of the 17th-century windmill built by Benedict Arnold, an early settler and namesake ancestor to the "traitor." Other points of interest and attractions include the Newport Casino, scene of an annual grass-court tennis tournament; the National Lawn Tennis Hall of Fame and Tennis Museum (founded 1954); the jazz festival (first in the U.S. held in 1954); The Breakers, former summer mansion built in 1895 for Cornelius Vanderbilt, the capitalist, and The Breakers Stable, which contains an outstanding collection of horse-drawn carriages. Salve Regina College was established in Newport in 1947, and Vernon Court Junior College in 1963.

Newport was incorporated as a city in 1784, resumed the town form of government in 1787 but in 1853 was reincorporated as a city. Pop. (1960) 47,049; (1980) 29,259.
41°13′ N, 71°18′ W

·colonial settlement and consolidation **18**:949b
·map, United States **18**:908
·tourism, capital, commercial importance, and cultural life **15**:807f *passim* to 810g

Newport, city, seat of Orleans County, northern Vermont, U.S., at the south end of Lake Memphremagog, near the Canadian border. The first house in the settlement (originally called Duncansboro) was built in 1793 by Deacon Martin Adams. The name Newport was adopted in 1816. Newport Town, including Newport Center, is adjacent to the west. The city is a port of entry and a railroad junction of the Canadian Pacific Railway. It has developed as a trade centre and a resort (skiing and water sports) and lies in an extensive dairy region; the handling and processing of milk is important. Light manufactures include clothing, wood products, and plastics. Inc. 1918. Pop. (1980) 4,756.
44°57′ N, 72°12′ W

Newport, Welsh CASNEWYDD-AR-WYSG, industrial seaport and borough, county of Gwent (until 1974 it was a county borough of the former Monmouthshire), Wales, at the Bristol Channel mouth of the Usk (Wysg). A medieval borough with a castle (now in ruins) dating from *c.* 1126, Newport enjoyed commercial privileges conferred by various charters, such as that of 1385. Its present importance, however, dates from the 19th-century industrialization of the west Monmouthshire coalfield, and its docks are still significant in relation to the varied industrial activities of that region, notably in steel, aluminum, and engineering; but the coal trade that brought considerable prosperity to the port up to 1913 was diverted to the port of Barry (now in East Glamorgan) in 1964. Newport itself acquired a range of industries, including steel processing, papermaking, and chemicals; but since 1959 it has become one of the most important steel-making centres in Britain, with the construction at Llanwern, east of the town, of the Spencer Works, including a strip mill and integrated, modern, and highly efficient operations. The inadequacy of the docks to accommodate large ore carriers has led to suggestions that an ore terminal be constructed east of the mouth of the Usk.

The town has few historic buildings. There is a Tudor house near the castle ruins; and St. Woolos' Church, since 1921 the procathedral for the Monmouth diocese of the Church in Wales, dates from Norman times and has a late-15th-century tower. In 1839 Newport was the scene of the popular uprisings known as the Chartist riots, bullet marks from which are still visible in the pillars of the Westgate Hotel. A Transporter bridge 245 ft (75 m) high spans the river near the docks, and a road bridge built in 1964 was the first cable cantilever bridge in Britain. Newport is the chief shopping and service centre for west and central Gwent. Newport has rail service and the M4 motorway to London skirts the town. Pop. (1971 prelim.) 112,048.
51°35′ N, 3°00′ W

·map, United Kingdom **18**:866

Newport, a class of U.S. tank landing ships.

·naval craft design **12**:900f

Newport, Treaty of (1647), concluded between English King Charles I and Oliver Cromwell.

·Charles I's acceptance of terms **3**:245d

Newport Beach, city, Orange County, southern California, U.S., on Newport Bay (Pacific inlet, former mouth of the Santa Ana River), south of Long Beach. Capt. S.S. Dunnels sailed into the bay in 1865 looking for "new port" facilities; he developed Newport Landing, which in 1873 became a lumber terminal. Known as McFaddens Landing and Port Orange, it was laid out in 1892 as Newport. It developed around yachting, sport fishing, and beach activities, and as a residential community for commuters to Los Angeles and Long Beach. There has been light industrial development, mainly aerospace electronics. Encompassing Lido Isle, Balboa Island and Peninsula, and Corona Del Mar, it has extensive marina facilities. Inc. 1906. Pop. (1950) 12,120; (1980) 63,475.
33°37′ N, 117°56′ W

Newport News, independent city and port of entry, southeastern Virginia, U.S., on the north side of Hampton Roads (harbour) and the James River, a focus of the Newport News–Hampton metropolitan area. The site was settled by Daniel Gookin (1621), who brought 50 colonists from Ireland. Known as Newportes Newes as early as 1619, the origin of the place-name is obscure but is traditionally associated with Christopher Newport, commander of five expeditions to Jamestown during 1606–12.

The city's development began after 1880, when it was chosen as a coal-shipping port for the Chesapeake and Ohio Railway. It was laid out in 1882 and by 1886 its prosperity was assured when the Newport News Shipbuilding and Dry Dock Company was founded. One of the largest and most complete shipyards in the world, it has produced the luxury liners "America" and "United States," the aircraft carriers "Forrestal" and "Enterprise," and many nuclear-powered submarines designed for firing Polaris guided missiles. Newport News was an important supply and embarkation port in both world wars.

In 1952 the city was made independent of Warwick County, in which it was located. That same year Warwick County was incorporated as the city of Warwick, the county ceasing to exist. In 1958 Newport News and Warwick merged as the city of Newport News. In addition to its port facilities, which can handle more than 11,000,000 tons annually of coal, bulk liquids, and general cargo, it has diversified manufactures (textiles, paper, electronic equipment, and petroleum products). The Mariners Museum (1930) has interesting collections and a library. Inc. 1896. Pop. (1980) city, 144,903; Newport News–Hampton metropolitan area (SMSA), 364,449.
37°04′ N, 76°28′ W

·map, United States **18**:908

New Prophecy (religious movement): *see* Montanism.

New Providence, borough, Union County, northeastern New Jersey, U.S., on the Passaic River and on the slopes of the Watchung Mountains. Mainly residential, it is the home of the Murray Hill Laboratories, headquarters of Bell Telephone Laboratories, Inc., of the American Telephone and Telegraph and Western Electric companies. The borough has many greenhouses and nurseries and a trade in cut flowers. The community, originally named Turkie, or Turkey for the local wild turkeys, was settled about 1720. In 1778, after a gallery in the Presbyterian Church collapsed and the congregation escaped injury, the settlement's name was changed in gratitude to Divine Providence. Originally part of Elizabethtown, New Providence Township was separated in 1793 and joined Springfield Township. It withdrew in 1809 from Springfield but again amalgamated in 1869 to form Summit Township. In 1899 New Providence was incorporated as a separate borough. Pop. (1980) 12,426.
40°42′ N, 74°24′ W

New Providence Island, principal island of the Bahamas, between Andros Island (west) and Eleuthera Island (east). With a length of 21 mi (34 km), and a width of 7 mi, the island is mostly flat, with swamps and several shallow lakes. Nassau (*q.v.*), the island's chief town, is also the capital of the Bahamas. New Providence's name supposedly derives from a 16th-century governor's thanks to Divine Providence for surviving a shipwreck: the "New" was added later to avoid confusion with a pirate stronghold off British Honduras. The island was settled in the late 17th century with the establishment of several British forts. Agriculture and fishing are important economic factors. A world-famous tourist area has developed around the city of Nassau. Pop. (1978 est.) 133,288.
25°25′ N, 78°35′ W

·area and population table **2**:592
·map, Bahamas **2**:590

New Provinces Act (1858), legislation of the New Zealand General Assembly that made possible the creation of new, weak provinces from outlying districts of the six existing provinces, thus weakening provincial authority in favour of the central government. With the passage of the act began a process that led to the abolition of provincial government by 1876.

According to the constitution of 1852 and the "Compact of 1856," New Zealand's provincial councils had many prerogatives independent of the central government. Among these were the right to dispose of revenues derived from land sales, as well as responsibility for education, immigration, and public works. The act of 1858 enabled any district with at least 1,000 European residents and from 500,000 to 3,000,000 acres (200,000 to 1,200,000 hectares) of land to secede from its parent province upon presentation to the central ministry of a petition signed by 150 registered voters. Neither the consent of the parent province nor of the central legislature was necessary. In short order four new provinces, all dependent on the central government, came into being. (One later returned to its parent province.)

In the course of the next 18 years the provinces declined, losing control of public works and immigration to the central government. In 1876 the Abolition of the Provinces Act ended the provincial system in New Zealand in favour of a clearly unitary state. This enabled the colony to develop along modern Western lines.

Newquay, seaside town on the Bristol Channel and Atlantic coast of the county of Cornwall, England. The town, on the tidal River Gannel, is almost entirely a modern seaside resort, having grown since the mid-19th century from a small fishing village. It stands on cliffs overlooking sandy beaches and is sheltered on the west from the Atlantic by Towan Head. The climate is equable, and

Beach at Newquay in Cornwall, England
Eric Carle—Shostal

tropical plants grow in the Trenance (valley). The small harbour, in the shelter of Towan Head, is now used only by local fishing and pleasure boats. Pop. (1973 est.) 13,890.
50°25′ N, 5°05′ W

·map, United Kingdom **18**:867

New Quebec (Canada): *see* Nouveau-Québec.

new religions, Japanese SHINKŌ SHŪKYŌ or SHIN SHŪKYŌ, popular religious movements in Japan that have had a phenomenal growth in the post-World War II period. Although they exhibit a wide variety of often highly eclectic doctrines, they share certain characteristics, such as preoccupation with a material and spiritual salvation realizable in this world, charismatic leadership, simple and appealing forms of worship, direct line of access from the individual to the sacred, and membership cutting across former hereditary and geographical lines. Faith healing is a dominant feature of many of the groups. They are usually well organized and above all possess a vitality that has made for rapid growth.

Despite the term new, the movements draw upon one or more of the pre-existing traditions—Shintō, Buddhism, Confucianism, Taoism, Christianity, and folk religion—and some, considered as prototypes for subsequent movements, actually originated in the 19th century. These include Ōmoto-kyō (Religion of Great Fundamentals), Tenri-kyō (Religion of Divine Wisdom), Konkō-kyō (Religion of Konkō), and Kurozumi-kyō (Religion of Kurozumi). The lifting in 1945 of government control over religious bodies allowed many subsects and splinter groups that had earlier been forced to incorporate with one of the major denominations to assert their independence. Three of the most important new religions to emerge from a background of Nichiren Buddhism are Sōka-gakkai (Value Creation Society), Reiyū-kai (Association of the Friends of the Spirit), and Risshō-Kōsei-kai (Society for the Establishment of Righteousness and Friendly Intercourse). Other prominent new religions are PL Kyōdan (Order of Perfect Liberty), a postwar revitalization of an earlier popular cult; Hito-no-michi (the Way of Man); and Tenshō-kōtai-jingū-kyō (more commonly known as Odoru Shūkyō, the Dancing Religion).

·laity roles in modern Buddhism **3**:413f
·political and social roles **10**:114g
·Sōka-gakkai and other modern movements **3**:401e
·vestments and secular dress **15**:639g

RELATED ENTRIES in the *Ready Reference and Index:*
Hito-no-michi; Konkō-kyō; Kurozumi-kyō; Ōmoto-kyō; PL Kyōdan; Reiyū-kai; Risshō-Kosei-kai; Sōka-gakkai; Tenri-kyō; Tenshō-kōtai-jingū-kyō

New Republic, Zulu territory in South Africa appropriated by Transvaal Boers in 1884 in return for their support of the Zulu royal family in the civil wars following the Zulu War (1879), despite Zulu appeals for British intervention. Annexed by the Transvaal in 1887, it was taken over by Natal in 1903 after the South African War, as the districts of Vryheid, Utrecht, and Paulpietersburg. Its large African population remained as rightless "squatters" on white farms. The Zulu Territorial Authority continues to agitate for the return of these lands, which also contain a number of Zulu royal grave sites. *See also* Pretoria Convention.

New Republic, The, U.S. weekly founded 1914 by Herbert Croly.

·Dewey's contribution **5**:681h
·magazine publishing history **15**:256c

New River, in southwest Virginia and southern West Virginia, U.S., formed by the junction of North and South forks in Ashe County, northwest North Carolina. It flows north across the state of Virginia into West Virginia and joins the Gauley River after a course of 320 mi (515 km) to form the Kanawha River in south central West Virginia.
38°10′ N, 81°21′ W

·Appalachian geography and erosion **1**:1016g
·West Virginia explorations **19**:800e

New Rochelle, city, Westchester County, southeastern New York, U.S., on Long Island Sound. Founded in 1688 by a group of Huguenot refugees, it was named for La Rochelle in France. Its modern suburban-residential character is emphasized by parks, golf courses, and shoreline recreation facilities. There are a few local light industries producing electrical equipment, surgical instruments, and plumbing supplies. The Thomas Paine Monument (dedicated in 1899), the Paine Cottage (now a museum), and the Paine Memorial House (erected in 1925) honour the revolutionary author, who lived there from 1804 to 1806. Ft. Slocum, used as a military base from 1862 to 1966, on offshore David's Island, is now privately owned. The College of New Rochelle was founded in 1904 and Iona College in 1940. Inc. village, 1857; city, 1899. Pop. (1980) 70,794.
40°55′ N, 73°47′ W

New Rome, name given to Constantinople (modern Istanbul) after the emperor Constantine the Great made it capital of the Roman Empire in 324–330; it remained the centre of the Byzantine Empire for more than 1,000 years. The title "New Rome" rapidly replaced "second Rome," indicating the new capital

was to supplant the "old" Rome as the residence of the emperor, even if the empire was to remain "Roman." In 381 the second ecumenical council extended the political role of Constantinople to the ecclesiastical sphere. It stated that "the bishop of Constantinople shall have privileges of honor after the bishop of Rome, because Constantinople is New Rome" (canon 3). During the medieval period, the bishop of the capital was further titled archbishop of Constantinople, New Rome, and ecumenical patriarch. The title survived the fall of Constantinople to the Turks (1453) and even today continues to point to the Byzantine imperial origin of the patriarchate of Constantinople.
·Istanbul enlargement by Constantine **9**:1068f *passim* to 1069g

New Romney, ancient borough of the county of Kent, England, one of the medieval Cinque Ports (*q.v.*) of the English Channel, now more than a mile from the sea. It is surrounded by Romney Marsh, a level tract built up largely in historic times by silting of a former inlet of the sea. The marsh has been reclaimed to form very rich grazing for the summer fattening of a distinctive local breed of sheep. The River Rother once entered the sea at New Romney but changed its course in 1287, and the gradual accretion of land behind the shingle spit of Dungeness brought about the decline, as ports, of New Romney, Winchelsea, and Rye. Before 1563 the Brodhull, or annual assembly of the Cinque Ports, was held there. King John recognized the liberties of the town in 1205, and the liberties of the Cinque Ports were confirmed in a general charter of 1278. After the Elizabethan charter of 1563, the town, hitherto known as Romney, was officially called New Romney, but, with the port dead, urban functions lapsed. Its old buildings still provide evidence of its former dignity and wealth, and many records of the Cinque Ports are kept in the court room of the town hall. The community of Littlestone-on-Sea has developed (since 1886) between the old town and the sea. Pop. (1971 prelim.) 3,414.
50°59′ N, 0°57′ E

New Ross, Irish ROS MHIC TREOIN, town, County Wexford, Ireland, on the River Barrow, just below its junction with the Nore. St. Abban founded the abbey of Rossmactreoin in the 6th century, which gave rise to the ancient city Rossglas, or Rossponte. By 1269 the town, which stands on a steep hill overlooking the river, was walled.

Inland water communications reach Dublin by means of the Barrow and the Grand Canal. New Ross has breweries and tanneries, a salmon fishery, and a fertilizer factory; it exports agricultural produce. The nearby village of Dunganstown is the ancestral home of John F. Kennedy, president of the United States (1961–63), whose great-grandfather sailed for the U.S. from New Ross in the 1840s. Pop. (1971) 4,775.
52°24′ N, 6°56′ W
·map, Ireland **9**:882

Newry, seaport, urban district, and market town, County Down, Northern Ireland, on the River Clanrye and Newry Canal, near Carlingford Lough and the Mourne Mountains. The town developed around a Cistercian abbey founded on the Clanrye by St. Malachy *c.* 1144 and was granted a charter in 1157. The Irish name of the town (Iubhar Cinn Trágha) means The Yew Tree at the head of the Strand and it is said that the original yew, the symbol of immortality, was planted by St. Patrick. Because of its position in a gap of the hills, Newry has often been attacked. It was burned by James II's forces in 1689. St. Patrick's Church, founded in 1578, was the first Protestant church to be built in Ireland. Newry is the seat of the Roman Catholic bishop of Dromore, and the Cathedral of SS. Patrick and Colman was completed in 1825.

Industries include spinning and weaving of linen and cotton, the manufacture of waterproof clothing, food processing, and granite quarrying. Pop. (1971) 11,371.
54°11′ N, 6°20′ W
·map, United Kingdom **18**:866

news agency, a commercial organization that collects and supplies news to subscribing newspapers, periodicals, and news broadcasters.
·newspaper publishing history **15**:240g

newscast, radio or television summary of news events read by a newscaster or produced with a combination of reading and audio tape for radio or a combination of reading and film or video tape for television. It ranges from the one-minute dateline radio summary (usually a reading of five or six brief news items, each preceded by the city, state, or country in which it occurred) to the 15-minute newscast (usually divided into three groups: international, national, and local) to the 30-minute or one-hour newscast (generally longer items, integrating international, national, and local news and grouped according to related events).

The newscast had a slow and difficult start in the U.S. in the 1920s in the form of infrequent readings of headlines and front-page stories from the late editions of newspapers. That start eventually led to a series of battles, beginning in 1933, between the radio stations on the one hand and, on the other, the major American newspapers and the three news-service agencies that sustained them—the Associated Press, the United Press, and the International News Service. The most significant outgrowth of the conflict, after two years, was the formation by the networks of their own news-gathering organizations. Public interest in news increased significantly with the events that led to World War II, and the networks' news organizations gave the first proof of their potential during that period.

The voices of Adolf Hitler, Neville Chamberlain, and Benito Mussolini were broadcast to American listeners. Columbia Broadcasting System made 151 shortwave pickups during the eighteen-day Munich Crisis of 1938, and National Broadcasting Company made 147. Newscasts during that period also brought fame to such newscasters as Edward R. Murrow, who broadcast minute-by-minute reports from Vienna on Hitler's move into Austria; William L. Shirer, who reported from London on Britain's defense against Nazi forces; and H.V. Kaltenborn, who during the Munich crisis made 85 broadcasts from CBS studios in New York City, giving instant translations of German and French shortwave pickups and providing immediate analysis.

The television newscast began in 1953 as a televised version of the radio form, with elements adopted from the theatre newsreel. In fact, the staffs of television's newscasts were drawn largely from newsreel organizations. The increasing frequency and popularity of newscasts led to controversies by the end of the 1960s involving their objectivity. The Federal Communications Commission code (1941) governing broadcasters reads, ". . . the broadcaster cannot be an advocate," and the code (1939) of the National Association of Broadcasters says, "Since the number of broadcasting channels is limited, news broadcasts shall not be editorial . . . ." Broadcasters were said by some to have violated these regulations, especially in newscasts. One of the most important of such accusations was made on Nov. 13, 1969, by U.S. Vice President Spiro T. Agnew. The significance of such an accusation by a high government official lay in its implied threat of government censorship.
·impersonal nature of commentary **18**:126c; table 124
·radio and television developments **3**:315f

New Scientist, British quarterly founded in 1956.
·magazine publishing history **15**:256a

New Scotland Limestone Formation (geology): *see* Helderbergian Stage.

News from Nowhere, romance by William Morris first serialized in *Commonweal* in 1890.
·publication and content **12**:457f

New Shoreham (Rhode Island): *see* Block Island.

New Siberian Islands, Russian NOVOSIBIRSKYE OSTROVA, archipelago, Russian Soviet Federated Socialist Republic, lies north of Eastern Siberia in the Arctic Ocean, and divides the Laptev Sea to the west from the East Siberian Sea to the east. It is separated from the Siberian mainland by Dmitry Laptev Strait. The archipelago is a part of the Yakut Autonomous Soviet Socialist Republic. The area of the islands approximates 14,500 sq mi (38,000 sq km). The New Siberian Islands consist of three groups: to the south the Lyakhovskye Islands, separated by Sannikova Strait from the New Siberian Islands proper, and to the northeast the small De Long Islands. The New Siberian Islands proper consist of the large islands of Novaya Sibir, Belkovsky, Kotelny, and Faddeyevsky. Between the last two lies Zemlya Bunge (Bunge Land), a low sandy plain occasionally inundated by the sea.

The islands do not rise above 1,227 ft (374 m). The climate is severe and typically Arctic, with snow covering the ground for over nine months of the year. The vegetation is poor tundra, even bushes being absent, and there is much swamp and barren sand. Fauna include the Arctic fox, northern deer, and lemming, with an abundant bird life in summer.
75°00′ N, 142°00′ E
·map, Soviet Union **17**:322
·preglacial ice and mammoths **10**:681g

newsletter, a printed sheet, pamphlet, or small newspaper reporting news or information of current interest to the interests of a special group.
·information distribution methods **9**:569b

New Smyrna Beach, city, Volusia County, northeast Florida, U.S., south of Daytona Beach, on the Atlantic coast, bisected by the Hillsborough River (lagoon). The site, once occupied by the Indian village of Caparaco and the Spanish Mission of Atocuimi (1696), was colonized in 1767 by a mixed immigrant group of Greeks, Minorcans, and Italians led by Andrew Turnbull, a Scottish physician, who named the place New Smyrna for his wife's Asia Minor birthplace. Because of Revolutionary strife, the colony was abandoned in 1777 but not before sugar and indigo were planted and a system of irrigation–drainage canals were built. In 1803 settlement was renewed with land grants. Under the stimulus of the Florida East Coast Railway and the Atlantic Intracoastal Waterway, it developed as a processing–distribution point for citrus, farm produce, and seafood (especially shrimp). Tourism, boating, and sport fishing became economic assets, and in 1937, reflecting the white, sandy shore, "Beach" was added to the city's name. Industrial parks were subsequently established. Inc. town, 1887; city, 1903. Pop. (1980) 13,557.
29°02′ N, 80°56′ W

New Society, British periodical founded in 1962.
·magazine publishing history **15**:256a

News of the World, British weekly (Sunday) newspaper published in London and founded in 1843.
·newspaper publishing history **15**:241f

New South Wales 13:11, state of the Commonwealth of Australia, bounded by the Pacific Ocean (east) and by the states of Victoria (south), South Australia (west), and Queensland (north). It covers an area of 309,433 sq mi (801,428 sq km). Its capital is Sydney. Pop. (1971 prelim.) 4,589,600.

The text article covers the state's relief, drainage, soils, climate, vegetation, and animal life, as well as its traditional regions, landscape under human settlement, population, economy, transportation, administration, social conditions, cultural life and institutions, and prospects for the future.

REFERENCES in other text articles:
·aboriginal cultures distribution map **2**:425
·Australian colonization origins **3**:303c
·Australian district political history **2**:417b
·Australian physical and economic form **17**:209b
·church–state education compromise **6**:367h
·coal mining methods **4**:774d
·gemstone discoveries and mines **7**:969h
·map, Australia **2**:400
·physical and social aspects **2**:399e *passim* to 410d
·population groups and government centre **17**:889d
·Rugby competition and championships **16**:8c
·Silurian rocks and paleogeography **16**:775e
·Upper Paleozoic formations, table 2 **13**:928

New South Wales, University of, coeducational institution of higher education located at Kensington, Australia. It was founded in 1949 as the New South Wales University of Technology. In 1958, courses in the liberal arts and medicine were added, and it became a general university. Included in the university are faculties of physical and biological sciences, architecture, engineering, humanities, medicine, and law. In the early 1970s there were over 15,000 full-time and part-time students.

Associated with the University of New South Wales is Wollongong University College at Wollongong. Graduates of Wollongong (bachelor of arts and science and higher degrees in some fields of study) are awarded degrees of the University of New South Wales.

New South Wales Corps (1789–1809), a British military force formed for service in the convict colony of New South Wales; it figured prominently in the early history of Australia. With the arrival of the corps in 1791–92, the colony gained a new dynamic force: officers and soldiers received land grants, becoming soldier-settlers; many officers became involved in business ventures, most notably the rum trade; and the ranks of the corps also provided the colony with explorers, surveyors, and scholars. From the time of the departure of the colony's first governor, Arthur Phillip, in December 1792 until the arrival of Gov. John Hunter in September 1795, the corps, under the command of Francis Grose, administered the settlement. During this period its military prowess enabled it to extend the border of the colony to the Hawkesbury River, despite the presence there of "unfriendly" Aborigines. The corps also distinguished itself by putting down the 1804 rebellion of Irish convicts (the Castle Hill Rising). The officer in charge of this operation, Maj. George Johnston, was later among the leaders of the corps' 1808 Rum Rebellion against the administration of Gov. William Bligh, the celebrated victim of the earlier "Bounty" mutiny. Relations had long been strained with Bligh, who had accused the corps of corruption and ineptitude. After deposing him on Jan. 26, 1808, the corps controlled the colony until the arrival of Gov. Lachlan Macquarie at the end of 1809. In the course of 1809, the name of the corps was changed to the 102nd Regiment of the Line as a preliminary to its recall to England. In May 1810, half of the regiment accepted reassignment, while the rest chose to remain in Australia and joined either the 73rd Regiment or the Veteran Corps.
·Australian colonial political activity **2**:414e

New Spain, Viceroyalty of (1535–1821), Spanish colonial territory comprising, at its greatest extent, Mexico, the Caribbean islands, Central America north of Panama, the coast of Venezuela, Florida, and the present southwestern United States.
·Meso-America's Spanish heritage **11**:954h
·Mexico City political importance **12**:90d
·Spanish viceroyalty boundaries **10**:694b; map 701
·territorial expanse and administration **12**:79b

newspaper, publication devoted to the dissemination of news and general affairs of interest. Newspapers are a relatively modern development, and publication on a regular basis did not occur until the 17th century. Newspapers appeared in Germany, Austria, the Netherlands, and Italy at that time (*see also* Japanese newspapers). Previously, the functions of a newspaper had been performed by various means; these include newsletters, which had been supplied by individual writers since Roman times, town criers, posted proclamations, troubadours, and news pamphlets and broadsides. The latter usually dealt with a battle, disaster, coronation, or marvel and were sold at fairs and in shops during the 16th century in Germany and other European countries.

The German compilations of events on a six-month basis were particularly noteworthy in this regard. Called *Messrelationen*, they served as the basis for similar compilations in England from 1590 onward; the *Mercurius Gallobelgicus* (1594–1635) was especially popular. The first publication with regular periodicity in England, however, was the single-sheet *Corante, or, newes from Italy, Germany, Hungarie, Spaine and France*, which appeared in London in September 1621. The first newspaper in the U.S. was *Publick Occurances Both Forreign and Domestick*, which appeared in Boston in September 1690. This three-page paper was, however, suppressed by the authorities after its first number.
·publishing history **15**:235g

newsreel, short motion picture of current events introduced in England about 1897 by the Frenchman Charles Pathé. Newsreels were shown regularly, first in music halls between entertainment acts and later between the featured films in motion picture theatres. Because spot news was expensive to shoot, newsreels covered expected events, such as parades, inaugurations, sport contests, and bathing beauty contests, and residual news, such as floods. Among the best known newsreel series were the *Pathé-Journal* (1908), shown first in England and France, and the *Pathé Weekly* (1912) produced for U.S. audiences. *The March of Time* (1935), produced in the United States by Time, Inc., illustrated the influence of the documentary film by combining filmed news with interpretive interviews and dramatizations. With the rising popularity of television news reports and specials, the number of newsreels declined markedly.
·early silent films **12**:541c
·origins and innovations **12**:527a

News Review, British periodical founded in 1936.
·magazine publishing history **15**:253e

New State, Portuguese ESTADO NÔVO, Brazilian government established on Nov. 10, 1937, by Getúlio Vargas.
·Vargas' establishment and reforms **19**:27c

New State, Portuguese ESTADO NÔVO, government created in Portugal by Antonio de Oliveira Salazar under the Constitution of 1933.
·Portuguese Constitution of 1933 **14**:873d

New Statesman, British periodical founded in 1913.
·magazine publishing history **15**:256a

new style calendar: *see* calendar, Gregorian.

New Sweden, only Swedish colony in America, established by the New Sweden Company in March 1638, captured by the Dutch in 1655. The first expedition, including both Swedes and Dutchmen, was commanded by Peter Minuit, who purchased land from the Indians and named the settlement Ft. Christina (later Wilmington, Del.), in honour of Sweden's queen. Johan Printz, who became governor in 1643, established additional settlements during his ten-year rule and attempted to deal with the Dutch, who considered the Swedes competitors and interlopers. He was succeeded in 1654 by Johan Claesson Rising, who arrived with more colonists and forced the Dutch to surrender Ft. Casimir. The next year a Dutch force under Peter Stuyvesant laid siege to Ft. Christina and compelled New Sweden's surrender. The Swedish colonists were allowed, however, to keep their lands and possessions and continue their customs.
·Delaware early colonization **5**:567d

New System, in French SYSTÈME NOUVEAU DE LA NATURE ET DE LA COMMUNICATION DES SUBSTANCES, AUSSI BIEN QUE DE L'UNION QU'IL Y A ENTRE L'ÂME ET LE CORPS (1695), work by the German philosopher Gottfried Wilhelm Leibniz.
·dynamic theory of motion **10**:787g

newt, or EFT, common name for about 42 species of salamanders constituting the widely distributed family Salamandridae of the order Urodela. Certain species are more commonly termed newts, while other species are efts. The name newt is derived from the expression "an eft," which became "a neft" and the letter "f" was transformed by popular usage to a "w."

Newt (*Triturus cristatus*)
Toni Angermayer

The body is long and slender and commonly rough-skinned. The tail is flattened laterally (higher than wide). In Great Britain the newt is represented by three species of the genus *Triturus*, members of which are sometimes called tritons. The most common British newt is the smooth newt, *T. vulgaris*, a spotted form that also occurs widely throughout Europe. The largest European newt is the warty newt, *T. cristatus*, which grows to about 17 centimetres (7 inches). The giant California newt, *Taricha torosa*, found in humid regions of western North America, grows to about 15 centimetres (6 inches) in length. A common species of eastern North America is the red eft, *Diemictylus viridescens*. The red eft lives on land for two or three years before becoming permanently aquatic. As it does so it turns from bright red to dull green with a row of red spots on the sides. The Japanese newt, *Cynops pyrrhogaster*, is often kept as a pet, surviving for several years in captivity.
·classification and general features **18**:1088c
·heart rudiment in embryo **5**:636h
·regenerative capacity, illus. 1 **15**:577
·respiration and habitat **15**:757e
·Triturus reproductive behaviour pattern **15**:687d

New Territories, part of the British Crown Colony of Hong Kong, comprises an area of

366 sq mi (948 sq km) north of Kowloon Peninsula from Mirs Bay on the east to Deep Bay, an inlet of the Pearl River, on the west. It includes Lan Tao and other islands. The New Territories were leased to Great Britain from China in 1898 for 99 years.
·Hong Kong's geography and history **8**:1061b
·map, Hong Kong **8**:1063

New Testament: *see* biblical literature.

New Thought 13:14, a mind-healing movement based on religious and metaphysical presuppositions that originated in the United States in the 19th century. The movement's views and styles of life are extremely diverse, making it difficult to determine either membership or adherents. New Thought groups are found not only in the United States, but also in the United Kingdom, continental Europe, Asia, Africa, and Australia.

The text article covers the history of the New Thought movement, teachings and practices, and New Thought groups, including Unity, Psychiana, and the I Am movement. The article concludes with an assessment of the influence of New Thought within the larger Christian denominations.

REFERENCES in other text articles:
·Christian Science comparison **4**:562f
·theosophy as religious revival catalyst **18**:278c

RELATED ENTRIES in the *Ready Reference and Index:*
Divine Science; I Am movement; International New Thought Alliance; Psychiana; Unity School of Christianity

New Tōkaidō Line, high-speed passenger railway line between Tokyo and Ōsaka, built in the first half of the 1960s by the Japanese National Railways as the first segment of a new high-speed, standard-gauge rail network. The New Tōkaidō was given a wholly new roadbed, designed for speed, including 320 miles (515 kilometres) of track, of which 40 miles (64 kilometres) are in tunnel, 27 miles (43 kilometres) on bridges, and 60 miles (96 kilometres) on trestles. The largest bridge, the Fujigawa, a seven-span truss, is nearly 4,000 feet (1,200 metres) long. Of the 66 tunnels, 12 are more than a mile in length, the longest, the New Tanna, nearly 5 miles (8 kilometres). Ties are of prestressed concrete, track is made up of mile-long welded sections, and many other innovations were introduced to facilitate fast, reliable operation. The electric-powered trains were the most highly automated in the world at the time of their introduction. The engineer normally acts only to start and stop the train and to open and close the doors. The trains travel up to 130 miles (210 kilometres) per hour, and are operated about 18 hours per day; the remaining hours are used for track and equipment maintenance. Regular service was inaugurated in time for the Olympic Games in Tokyo in 1964.
·construction, service, and success **15**:481h; illus. 493
·establishment, speed, and operation **10**:51e
·speed and efficiency **18**:575h
·suitability of conventional technology **18**:663d
·track construction advantage **18**:657g

Newton, town, seat (1831) of Baker County, southwest Georgia, U.S., on the Flint River. It was named for Sgt. John Newton, a Revolutionary War soldier who captured 10 British soldiers as they were taking prisoners to Savannah to be hanged; he was taken prisoner at the surrender of Charleston, S.C., and died of smallpox. Situated on a coastal agricultural plain, 22 mi (35 km) south-southwest of Albany, Newton is a trading centre for an area producing corn (maize), peanuts (groundnuts), sugarcane, pecans, livestock, and lumber. Inc. 1872. Pop. (1980) 711.
31°19′ N, 84°20′ W

Newton, city, seat of Jasper County, central Iowa, U.S. Settled in 1846, it was named for a Revolutionary War soldier. The railroad arrived in the 1860s, and in 1898 the manufacture of washing machines began. Frederick L. Maytag introduced a "hand power" washer there in 1907.

Newton is a rail junction and agricultural trading centre. The manufacture of washing machines remains the economic mainstay. The Maytag Historical Museum and the boyhood home (1857) of Emerson Hough, author of *The Covered Wagon*, are in the city. Rock Creek State Park is nearby. Inc. 1857. Pop. (1980) 15,292.
41°42′ N, 93°03′ W
·map, United States **18**:909

Newton, city, seat (1872) of Harvey County, central Kansas, U.S. Founded in 1871 and named for Newton, Mass., it was a railhead for the Chisholm Trail cattle drives from 1871 to 1873. In the 1870s Russian Mennonite settlers began raising Turkey Red wheat brought from their homeland, and this variety became Kansas' principal agricultural product.

Newton is now a trade and shipping centre for the surrounding wheat-growing area. There are railroad maintenance shops, food-processing and grain-milling plants, and factories making mobile homes. Coeducational Bethel College (1887) is the largest and oldest Mennonite college in the nation. The Kauffman Museum features collections of antique automobiles and pioneer relics. Inc. 1872. Pop. (1980) 16,332.
38°03′ N, 97°21′ W
·map, United States **18**:909

Newton, city, Middlesex County, eastern Massachusetts, U.S., on the Charles River. Settled in 1639, it was part of Cambridge until separately incorporated as New Towne in 1688. Adopting its present name in 1691, it developed early milling and forge industries at the upper and lower falls of the Charles. Suburban growth was stimulated by completion of the Boston and Worcester (now ConRail) Railroad in 1834. A hilly setting has helped to sustain a semi-rural atmosphere (14 individual "villages") despite population increases. Industry is limited by zoning laws.

The city is noted for its educational institutions, being the home of Andover Newton Theological School (1808), three junior colleges (Lasell [1851], Mount Ida [1899], and Newton [1946]), and Newton College of the Sacred Heart (1946). Chestnut Hill is the site of Boston College (1863) and the Mary Baker Eddy home. Inc. city, 1873. Pop. (1970) 91,263; (1980) 83,622.
42°21′ N, 71°11′ W

Newton, city, seat of Catawba County, west central North Carolina, U.S., at an altitude of 996 ft (304 m) above sea level. The first land was granted in the area in 1748, and the region was settled largely by Pennsylvania Dutch. Authorized to be laid out in 1845, Newton was named for Isaac Newton Wilson, a member of the state General Assembly who in 1842 introduced the bill to create Catawba County.

The economy is based on the textile industry, including the manufacture of hosiery and apparel; other industries include the manufacture of furniture and paper boxes. Newton is also an agricultural trading centre for the surrounding region (cotton, corn [maize], wheat, hay, livestock, dairy products, poultry, and pine and oak timber). There is a memorial to the men killed in the Johns River massacre, which took place during a forced march against the Cherokee Indians in 1776. Inc. 1855. Pop. (1980) 7,624.
35°40′ N, 81°13′ W

newton, unit of force in the metre–kilogram–second system of physical units. Named in honour of Isaac Newton, it is defined as the force that gives to a mass of one kilogram an acceleration of one metre per second per second and is equal to 100,000 dynes, or about 0.2248 pound. The abbreviation is N.

Newton, Alfred (b. June 11, 1829, Geneva—d. June 7, 1907, Cambridge, Cambridgeshire), zoologist, one of the foremost ornithologists of his day. He studied at Magdalene College, Cambridge, and from 1854 to 1863, as a holder of the Drury Travelling Fellowship, visited Lapland, Iceland, the West Indies, North America, and Spitsbergen on ornithological expeditions. Later he made several summer voyages around the British Isles, studying sea birds and their nesting places. In 1866 he became the first professor of zoology and comparative anatomy at the University of Cambridge, where few of the faculty or students were acquainted with zoology. Newton held the position for the remainder of his life, continually stimulating the growth of zoology as a distinct discipline. He was instrumental in securing passage of the first acts of Parliament for the protection of birds. He edited the ornithological journal *Ibis* (1865–70) and *The Zoological Record* (1870–72). Of his books, probably the most important is *A Dictionary of Birds* (1893–96), which grew from numerous articles on birds that he contributed to the 9th edition of *Encyclopædia Britannica*. His article "Ornithology" as amended in the 11th edition is still considered a valuable source of information on the history of ornithology and bird classification.
·parrot classification opinion **15**:141f

Newton, Sir Charles Thomas (b. Sept. 16, 1816, Bredwardine, Herefordshire—d. Nov. 28, 1894, Margate, Kent), archaeologist who excavated sites in southwestern Turkey and disinterred the remains of one of the seven wonders of the ancient world, the Mausoleum of Halicarnassus (present-day Bodrum). He also helped to establish systematic methods for archaeology and, as the first keeper of Greek and Roman antiquities at the British Museum, London, greatly enriched its collection by making outstanding acquisitions.

An assistant in the museum's Department of Antiquities (1840–52), he was sent to the Aegean as vice consul at Mytilene, on Lesbos, with the charge of looking after the museum's interests in Anatolia. In 1852 and 1855 he secured a series of inscriptions from the island of Calymnos. In 1856–57 he excavated the remains of the mausoleum and later unearthed the ground plan of Cnidus. Along with the chief remains from Halicarnassus, he brought to the museum the bronze Delphian serpent from Istanbul, a sculpture of the Greek goddess Demeter, the colossal lion from Cnidus, and statues from the road to Didyma (Branchidae). While serving as curator, he was also professor of archaeology at University College, London (1880–88), and did much to promote Hellenic studies in Britain. Knighted in 1887, he published, jointly with R.P. Pullan, his assistant at Cnidus, *A History of Discoveries at Halicarnassus, Cnidus, and Branchidae* (2 vol., 1862–63).

Newton, Sir Isaac 13:16 (b. Jan. 4, 1643 [Dec. 25, 1642, old style], Woolsthorpe, Lincolnshire—d. March 31 [March 20, O.S.], 1727, London), physicist and mathematician, the culminating figure of the 17th-century scientific revolution and author of one of the most important single works in the history of modern science.

Abstract of text biography. Newton received a bachelor's degree at Trinity College, Cambridge, in 1665. During the next two years while the university was closed because of plague, Newton laid the foundation of calculus and extended his ideas on colour. He also examined the mechanics of planetary motion and derived the inverse square law, later crucial to his theory of universal gravitation. He returned in 1667 as a fellow to Trinity College, where he became Lucasian professor of mathematics in 1669.

Newton had a long career: as a scientist he discovered the composition of white light and formulated the three fundamental laws of mechanics, leading to the law of gravitation; as a mathematician he invented the infinitesimal calculus; and as a civil servant he was warden of the mint. His lifelong bitter controversies with Robert Hooke, the English natural philosopher, and Gottfried Wilhelm Leibniz, the German philosopher, are delineated. Two of Newton's great works are *Opticks* (1704) and the *Principia* (1687; Eng. trans., 1729).

REFERENCES in other text articles:
·atomic theory contributions **2**:333b
·biological development philosophies **5**:643b
·biological sciences development **2**:1021h
·celestial mechanics foundation **11**:756h
·centrifugation principles **3**:1143h
·chromatic aberration in refractors **18**:98d
·classical mechanics development **11**:762h
·colour's physical origin theory **4**:913f
·cometary orbit study **4**:970a
·corpuscular theory and wave motion **19**:665e
·Deist's theological use of theory **5**:562e
·differential equation principles **5**:738b
·Earth's figure deductions **6**:2e
·Earth shape theory **6**:59b
·electromagnetic radiation theory **6**:646h
·Enlightenment philosophy of nature **14**:266d *passim* to 269a
·fluid mechanics development **11**:780f
·galaxy formation theory **18**:1008h
·geophysics history **6**:75h
·gravitational theory development **8**:287b
·gravitation law and Rationalism **6**:888d
·Halley's theoretical and practical aid **8**:556f
·Hume's use of scientific method **8**:1192a
·Huygens' association and disagreement **9**:75d
·Laplace and theory of gravitation **10**:680f
·light properties theory **10**:929c
·lunar observations and gravitation **12**:416h
·mathematics history from antiquity **11**:643e
·metaphysical aspects of system **12**:20f
·Mill's system of inductive logic **12**:198d
·nerve impulse speculation **2**:1034g
·optical experimentation and theory **15**:401c
·orbit theory development **2**:250d
·philosophical basis of science **16**:378c *passim* to 380g
·philosophy of physics **12**:866d
·physical constant measurement methods **5**:77c
·physics influence on Kant **10**:390f
·physics principles and development **14**:424f
·Positivist rejection of Newtonianism **14**:878g
·real analysis principles **1**:784b
·reflecting telescope with speculum **18**:98g
·relativity theory development **15**:581h
·science history and philosophy **16**:371a
·scientific revolution culmination **14**:387b *passim* to 391e
·solar spectrum experiments **2**:234h
·sound velocity determination **17**:20a
·theoretical reworking of empirical data **16**:384e
·time as absolute metaphysical entity **18**:413c
·universality of physical laws **18**:1013c
·Wallis' Arithmetica Infinitorum impact **19**:533d

Newton, John (1725–1807), a leader of the Evangelical revival, to which his main contribution came through his devotional letter writing, especially his *Cardiphonia; or, the Utterance of the Heart* (1781). He was a friend of the poet William Cowper, with whom he published the *Olney Hymns* (1779).

Newton, Richard, late-18th-century British caricaturist.
·cartoonists' influence on style **3**:918f

Newton, Sir William (1785–1869), British miniature painter.
·views on aesthetics of photography **14**:312d

Newton Abbot, market town in the county of Devon, England, near the head of the Teign Estuary. The churches of St. Mary's, Wolborough, and All Saints', Highweek, are in Perpendicular style. Bradley Manor (15th century) is now a National Trust (conservation group) property, while the Jacobean Forde House (1610) was visited by William, prince of Orange, the 17th-century contender for the English throne, who first read his famous declaration to the people of England at Newton Abbot market cross. The town now has a cattle and a general market; it is a shopping centre and railway junction with various light industries. Pop. (1971 prelim.) 30,459.
50°32′ N, 3°36′ W
·map, United Kingdom **18**:866

Newtonian fluid (physics): *see* fluid.

Newtonian mechanics: *see* mechanics, classical.

Newtonian transformations (physics): *see* Galilean transformations.

Newton's interpolation formula, in numerical analysis, formula expressed by Newton for the remainder which results when a function is expressed in terms of divided differences.
·numerical analysis fundamentals **13**:383b

Newton's laws of motion, the relations between the forces acting on a body and the motion of the body, which, although formulated for the first time in usable form by Isaac Newton, had been discovered experimentally by Galileo about four years before Newton was born. The laws cover only the overall motion of a body; *i.e.,* the motion of its centre of mass. This concept is equivalent to assuming that the body is a particle with a definite mass but no size.

Strictly speaking, the laws are valid only for motions relative to a reference frame (coordinate system) attached to the fixed stars. Such a reference frame is known as a Newtonian, Galilean, or an inertial frame. Because the Earth rotates, a reference frame attached to the Earth is not inertial, and in some cases this rotation must be considered when applying Newton's laws. In most applications, however, the Earth's rotation can be neglected.

Newton's first law states that, if a body is at rest or moving at a constant speed in a straight line, it will remain at rest or keep moving in a straight line at constant speed unless it is acted upon by a force. This postulate is known as the law of inertia, and it is basically a description of one of the properties of a force: its ability to change rest into motion or motion into rest or one kind of motion into another kind. Before Galileo's time it was thought that bodies could move only as long as a force acted on them and that in the absence of forces they would remain at rest. Those who sought to find the forces that kept the planets moving failed to realize that no force was necessary to keep them moving at a practically uniform rate in their orbits; gravitational force, of which they had no conception, only changes the direction of motion.

Newton's second law is a quantitative description of the changes that a force can produce in the motion of a body. It states that the time rate of change of the velocity (directed speed), or acceleration, a, is directly proportional to the force F and inversely proportional to the mass m of the body; *i.e.,* $a \propto F/m$ or $F = ma$: the larger the force, the larger the acceleration (rate of change of velocity); the larger the mass, the smaller the acceleration. Both force and acceleration have direction as well as magnitude and are represented in calculations by vectors (arrows) having lengths proportional to their magnitudes. The acceleration produced by a force is in the same direction as the force; if several forces act on a body, it is their resultant (sum), obtained by adding the vectors tail-to-tip, that produces the acceleration.

The second law is the most important, and from it all of the basic equations of dynamics can be derived by procedures developed in the calculus. A simple case is a freely falling body. Neglecting air resistance, the only force acting on the body is its weight acting down, and it produces a downward acceleration equal to the acceleration of gravity, symbolized as g, which has an average value of 32.2 feet per second per second near the surface of the Earth.

Newton's third law states that the actions of two bodies upon each other are always equal and directly opposite; *i.e.,* reaction is always equal and opposite to action. The proposition seems obvious for two bodies in direct contact; the downward force of a book on a table is equal to the upward force of the table on the book. It is also true for gravitational forces; a flying airplane pulls up on the Earth with the same force that the Earth pulls down on the airplane. The third law is important in statics (bodies at rest) because it permits the separation of complex structures and machines into simple units that can be analyzed individually with the least number of unknown forces. At the connections between the units, the force in one member is equal and opposite to the force in the other member. The third law may not hold for electromagnetic forces when the bodies are far apart.
·derivation of gravitation law **14**:387c
·energy laws and principles **6**:849g
·kinetics theory and principles **11**:769h
·mathematical concepts and formulations **14**:392f
·mechanics principles and development **14**:424g
·Newtonian system development **13**:19d
·relativity theory principles **15**:582a
·third law rocket propulsion application **15**:936f

Newton's rings, in optics, a series of concentric light- and dark-coloured bands observed between two pieces of glass when one is convex and rests on its convex side on another piece having a flat surface. Thus, a layer of air exists between them. The phenomenon is caused by the interference of light waves; *i.e.,* the superimposing of trains of waves so that when their crests coincide, the light brightens; but when trough and crest meet, the light is destroyed. Light waves reflected from both top and bottom surfaces of the air film between the two pieces of glass interfere. The rings are named after the English 17th-century physicist Sir Isaac Newton, who first investigated them quantitatively.

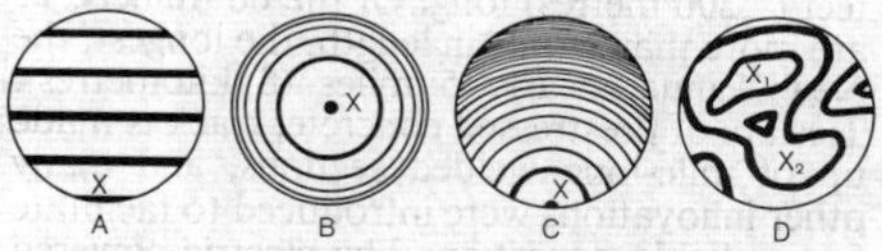

Interference patterns formed with test surfaces

From A.C. Hardy and F.H. Perrin, *The Principles of Optics.* Copyright (1932). Used with permission of McGraw-Hill Book Co.

The principle is often used in testing the uniformity of a polished surface by studying the interference pattern the surface makes when placed in contact with a perfectly flat glass surface. The Figure shows contour patterns formed by various surfaces under test. In the Figure, A is produced by a flat surface with point of contact at X. In B and C the test surface is slightly convex, the points of contact indicated by X in each case. An irregular surface may give an interference pattern shown in D, with two points of contact X_1 and X_2.
·explanation by Newton **14**:387f
·lens-design testing procedures **13**:607h
·light interference properties **10**:937c
·light patterns, illus., **10**: Light, Plate II
·phenomena investigation and properties **13**:18e

new town, a form of urban planning designed to relocate populations away from large cities by grouping homes, hospitals, industry and cultural, recreational, and shopping centres to form entirely new, relatively autonomous communities. The first new towns were proposed in Great Britain in the New Towns Act of 1946; between 1947 and 1950, 12 were designated in England and Wales and 2 in Scotland, each with its own development corporation financed by the government. The new towns were located in relatively undeveloped sites. Each was to have an admixture of population so as to give it a balanced social life. Proposed ultimate population figures of this first group of new towns ranged from 29,000 to 140,000. After 1961, target population figures for proposed new towns rose to 70,000 to 250,000.

The idea of new towns found favour in many other countries, notably in the United States, various countries of western Europe, and Soviet Siberia.

The chief criticism of new towns has been that they may be too static in conception. In Sweden, for example, a master plan prepared in 1952 envisaged establishing around the periphery of Stockholm some 18 communities, each with its own residences, places of employment, and shopping and cultural facilities. What was not satisfactorily anticipated in the plans, however, was the dramatic increase in commuting and other forms of personal mobility that obviated the need for the new towns to be so self-contained. Of the 27,000 wage earners in the suburb of Vallingby, for instance, 25,000 were found to be commuting out, half of them to the centre of Stockholm; in fact, Vallingby's own industries were drawing in commuters from outside. **18**:1083e
·Birmingham's population loss **2**:1064d
·Hungary's new industrial areas **9**:24d
·problems and prospects **18**:1061g; illus.

Newtownabbey, urban district, County Antrim, Northern Ireland, on the shores of Belfast Lough (lake), adjoining the northern boundary of Belfast. The second largest town in Northern Ireland, it was formed in 1958 by the amalgamation of seven village communities.

Newtownabbey includes a civic centre and public parks. Its basic textile industries have been supplemented by the establishment of several central government factory estates. Pop. (1971) city, 58,114; metropolitan area, 60,140.
·map, United Kingdom **18**:866

Newtownards, town and municipal borough, County Down, Northern Ireland, at the northern end of Strangford Lough (lake), just east of Belfast. It was founded by Sir Hugh Montgomery in 1608, at the site of a ruined Dominican friary (established 1244 by Walter de Burgh, earl of Ulster).

Newtownards is now a manufacturing centre, with linen, hosiery, and engineering industries. At nearby Movilla (Magh Bhile) are the remains of a 6th-century abbey church. Pop. (1971) 15,356.
54°36′ N, 5°41′ W
·map, United Kingdom **18**:867

Newtown St. Boswells, village, district of Roxburgh, Borders region, Scotland, lying in the Tweed Basin southeast of Edinburgh on the Edinburgh–Newcastle road and the Edinburgh–Carlisle railway. Before 1929 its population consisted mainly of railway employees; since then its main function has changed to administrative services, and it has importance as an agricultural centre with important livestock sales and a regional agricultural college. Dryburgh Abbey, located 1¼ mi east, was founded in 1150 for the Premonstratensian order. It contains the tombs of Sir Walter Scott and Field Marshal Earl Haig. Pop. (1971) 1,253.
55°34′ N, 2°40′ W
·map, United Kingdom **18**:866

New-Uighur language: *see* Uighur language.

New Ulm, city, seat of Brown County, southern Minnesota, U.S., on the Minnesota River, near the mouth of the Cottonwood. Founded in 1854 by German immigrants, it was named for Ulm in Württemberg. The town was almost destroyed in the Sioux uprising of 1862; the Defenders' Monument commemorates the event. Overlooking the city on a bluff is a 102-ft (31-m) bronze statue (*c.* 1898) honouring Hermann (Arminius), a German tribal leader who inflicted a major defeat on the Romans at the Teutoburg Forest in AD 9. Dr. Martin Luther College dates from 1884. New Ulm's economy is based on agriculture (food processing), augmented by light manufacturing (chiefly electronics equipment and plastics). Nearby is Flandrau State Park. Inc. village, 1857; city, 1876. Pop. (1980) 13,755.
44°19′ N, 94°28′ W
·map, United States **18**:909

Building in traditional Germanic style, New Ulm, Minn.
Milt and Joan Mann from CameraMann

New Valley (Egypt): *see* al-Wādī al-Jadīd.

New Vienna School, term used in reference to the Viennese 12-tone composers Arnold Schoenberg, Alban Berg, and Anton von Webern in the period 1924–51.
·Nazi opposition **19**:718b

New View of Society; or, Essays on the Principle of the Formation of the Human Character, A (1813), by Robert Owen, an exposition of Owen's system of educational philanthropy.
·Owen's social philosophy **13**:801d
·Utopian alternatives to competition **14**:692g

New Waterford, town, Cape Breton Island and county, Nova Scotia, Canada, immediately northeast of Sydney, at the entrance to Sydney Harbour. Offshore is the picturesque Flat Point Lighthouse. New Waterford is chiefly a coal-mining community, its collieries being linked by rail to shipping piers at Sydney. Founded in 1908, the settlement was named for Waterford, Ire. Inc. 1913. Pop. (1976) 9,223.
46°15′ N, 60°05′ W
·map, Canada **3**:717

New Waterway, Dutch NIEUWE WATERWEG, canal built (1866–72) to link the Rhine River port of Rotterdam directly with the North Sea. One of the major Dutch navigation routes, it is located in Zuid-Holland province, southwestern Netherlands. It is 5 mi (8 km) long and does not require locks because of low tidal change and the large volume of river discharge. Its depth has been increased gradually to 38 ft (12 m).

Since World War II three large industrial areas in Rotterdam—Botlek, Europoort, and Maasvlakte—have been built along the south bank of the New Waterway to accommodate the expanding petroleum industry. The New Waterway itself is too shallow for deep-draft oil tankers. These are accommodated by the Caland Canal, named for Pieter Caland, designer of the New Waterway. The Caland Canal runs parallel to the south bank of the New Waterway and directly serves the Europoort harbour complex.
·construction and use **12**:1164b *passim* to 1166b
·harbour navigation improvement **8**:643c

New Wave, French NOUVELLE VAGUE, the term commonly used to describe the style of a number of highly individualistic French film directors of the late 1950s. Pre-eminent among New Wave directors were Louis Malle, Claude Chabrol, François Truffaut, Alain Resnais, and Jean-Luc Godard, most of whom were associated with the film magazine *Cahiers du Cinéma*, the publication that popularized the *auteur* theory (*q.v.*) in the 1950s. The theory held that certain directors so dominated their films that they were virtually the authors of the film. Films by New Wave directors were often characterized by a fresh brilliance of technique that was thought to have overshadowed their subject matter. An example occurs in Godard's *Breathless* (1960), in which scenes change in rapid sequence ("jump cuts") to create a jerky and disconnected effect. Although it was never clearly defined as a movement, the New Wave stimulated discussion about the cinema and helped demonstrate that films could achieve commercial along with artistic success. *Major ref.* **12**:536a
·aesthetic theory of French cinema **18**:723f
·French directing innovations **5**:831d
·Resnais status and background **15**:744c

New Way To Pay Old Debts, A (performed 1621; published 1633), play by Philip Massinger.
·literature of the Renaissance **10**:1142e

New Westminster, city, southwestern British Columbia, Canada, on the Fraser River estuary, immediately southeast of Vancouver. Founded in 1859 on a site chosen by Col. Richard C. Moody, it was originally called Queensborough, until renamed by Queen Victoria.

New Westminster was the capital of colonial British Columbia (1859–66) and the province's first (1860) incorporated city. Recovering from a disastrous fire in 1898, it has become one of western Canada's busiest ports, a major rail junction, and one of the province's largest industrial and marketing centres. Known for the manufacture of forest products, New Westminster also has other industries, including food processing (salmon, fruit, vegetables), distilling, brewing, shipbuilding, and oil refining. The city is the site of Columbian and St. Louis colleges and St. Ann's Academy. Pop. (1976) 38,393.
49°12′ N, 122°55′ W
·map, Canada **3**:716

New Windsor (England): *see* Windsor.

New Windsor, town, Orange County, southeastern New York, U.S., on the Hudson River, immediately south of Newburgh. The old village was laid out in 1749 and the town was established in 1763. George Clinton, first governor of New York, and his nephew De Witt Clinton were born there, at Little Britain.

The New Windsor Cantonment, great winter camp of the Continental Army, has been partially restored. There, at Temple Hill, Washington ended a conspiracy among his officers and also established the Badge of Military Merit (forerunner of the Purple Heart). Stewart Air Force Base (1942) is within the town's boundary. Pop. (1980) 19,534.
41°29′ N, 74°02′ W

New World monkey: *see* Platyrrhini.

New World Symphony (1893), composition by Antonín Dvořák.
·Largo movement's three-part form **12**:725f

New Writing, British periodical published from 1936 to 1946.
·magazine publishing history **15**:256b

New Year festival, or AKITU FESTIVAL, one of the major religious celebrations of ancient Mesopotamia. The festival was held in a special temple in the fields, and thus it probably originated as an agricultural celebration connected with sowing and harvest; later, however, it became the occasion for the crowning and investiture of a new king. Though the New Year Festival was celebrated in various places, such as Ashur, Nineveh, Haran, and Uruk, the ceremonies at Babylon during the 1st millennium BC are the best known.

At the Babylonian festival two currents of religious thought, the myth of Creation and the Sacred Marriage, were carefully blended together, with the god Marduk playing the dual role of a fertility god and the champion and king of the deities.

The festival began on the first day of Nisan (March–April) and lasted 11 days. The statues of numerous gods were brought to Babylon. On the eighth day a great procession made its way through Babylon and out of the city to a temple in the fields, where the gods remained for three days. During that time Marduk's triumph over evil was celebrated, and, some scholars believe, the Sacred Marriage was consummated. On the 11th day the gods returned to Babylon, and a great banquet closed the festival.

·kingly role in religious rites **16**:121h
·Mesopotamian myth and kingship celebration **11**:1005d
·mythic worship ceremonies **19**:1017a
·New Year symbolic festivities **7**:198e *passim* to 200c
·purpose and ceremony **3**:394a
·Sumerian and Babylonian practices **18**:219d

New Year festival, Japanese, the most popular annual festival, celebrated January 1–3. In some rural districts it continues to be observed according to the lunar–solar calendar on dates varying between January 20 and February 19, and the traditions connected with the festival confirm its original connection with the coming of spring and a time of rebirth. The festival is called in Japanese Ganjitsu (Original Day), signifying the beginning of the new year, and also Shōgatsu (Standard Month), referring to the belief that the good or bad fortune met with during the first few days of the new year may be taken as representative of the fortune for the entire coming year. Together with the midsummer festival of Bon, it is one of the two main occasions for honouring the spirits of the family ancestors and of the dead generally, who are believed to return to their homes on those two days.

The festival is customarily celebrated with ceremonial house cleaning, feasting, and exchanging visits and gifts. The house gateway or entrance is often hung with a *shimenawa* (a sacred rope made of rice straw) to keep out evil spirits and decorated with fern, bitter orange, and lobster, signifying good fortune, prosperity, and longevity. Foods special to the holidays are *mochi* (cakes of rice paste) and *zoni* (a soup of vegetables and *mochi*). Traditional amusements are shuttlecock and *utagaruta*, a card game that involves matching lines of 100 poems.

Other observances—once widespread but now diminished—included, early on the first day, visits to Shintō shrines of the tutelary deities or to Buddhist temples. On the second day arts and crafts were ritually recommenced. On the seventh day a rice gruel containing seven purifying herbs was traditionally served and the decorations removed.

·shrine and temple pilgrimages **10**:56a

New Year festivals, primitive, religious, social, and cultural celebrations linked to the cycles of nature that mark seasonal renewal among agricultural and hunting and gathering peoples. Every culture has a notion of time and distinguishes particularly important times, such as the cycle of an individual's life (*e.g.*, birth, puberty, marriage, and death). There also may be times in the rhythms of community life, such as the Eskimo's summer migration inland to catch caribou and salmon and their winter journey to the coast to catch seals on the sea ice. In addition to such "natural" times, there are a series of extraordinary times. The most widespread and most important group of these are first times, which are always celebrated and remembered. Within any culture there are many first times. Among the Iatmul people of New Guinea, for example, a ceremony is held the first time a boy performs various acts; *e.g.*, killing a bird, fish, eel, tortoise, flying fox, or man or planting yams, tobacco, taro, coconut, areca, betal, sago, or sugarcane.

There also are mythical first times for a society: the time when the ancestors of the tribe were created or first settled in the present area; the time when the god first revealed himself to his people; the time when a custom was first ordained; the time when a tool was invented or given to man. Each of these first times will be celebrated on its anniversary.

For most cultures, there is an absolute first time, the time of the creation of the cosmos, which is the object of complex celebration and which serves as the model for all of these other first times. First times are important because the acts performed are fresh and unexhausted, because the power that is present in a given deed is present in a pristine, highly potent state. Successive performances of the deed will deplete this energy, and it becomes necessary to renew this power by remembering or re-enacting this first time. This renewal is the essence of the New Year. It is a remembrance or repetition of the creation of the cosmos on the anniversary of its creation in order that the gods, the cosmos, and the community may be strengthened.

There have been many attempts by scholars to discern a common pattern to New Year scenarios. In broad outline, the New Year festival consists of (1) a deliberate disruption of the order of the created cosmos in order to return symbolically to primordial chaos through the breaking of social norms, the orgy, the extinguishing of fires, the closing of religious shrines, and the tradition of the dead mingling with the living; (2) acts of purgation and purification to cleanse the society of its past and prepare it for new birth through sacrifice, confession, and ritual combat between the powers of good and evil; (3) repetition of the creation by recitation of the creation myth or by performing actions symbolic of the creation that reinvigorates the cosmos; and (4) celebration of new birth with communal feasts and the restoration of the order that was broken at the beginning of the festival.

New Year Letter (1941), U.S. title THE DOUBLE MAN, book of prose and poetry by W.H. Auden.

·religious–autobiographical theme **2**:364a

New Year's Day, the first day of the year. One of the oldest and most universally observed festivals, the New Year has often been welcomed with rites and ceremonies that express mortification, purgation, invigoration, and jubilation over life's renewal. According to recorded history, New Year's festivals have been celebrated for more than 5,000 years. For the Egyptians, Phoenicians, and Persians, the year began with the autumnal equinox, and for the Greeks, until the 5th century BC, with the winter solstice. By the Roman republican calendar, the year began on March 1; after 153 BC the official date was January 1, which was continued by the Julian calendar (46 BC).

The Jewish religious year begins with *Rosh Hashana*, the first day of the month of Tishri (Sept.–early Oct.). In early medieval times most of Christian Europe regarded March 25 (Annunciation, or Lady Day) as the beginning of the year, though for Anglo-Saxon England, New Year's Day was December 25. William the Conqueror decreed in the 11th century that the year start on January 1, but later England began its year with the rest of Christendom on March 25. The Gregorian calendar (1582) restored January 1 as New Year's Day and was immediately adopted by Roman Catholic countries. Other countries slowly followed suit: Scotland, 1660; Germany and Denmark, about 1700; England, 1752; Sweden, 1753; and Russia, 1918.

In modern times, New Year's Day is a holiday in many countries, and various customs and traditions are still observed. New Year's Eve is often the occasion for parties, and at midnight the New Year is welcomed with much noise and merrymaking. In Christian countries the New Year has traditionally been observed with church services and the ringing of church bells.

·Hindu celebration in Lakṣmī's honour **8**:902h
·ritual enactment of creation myths **15**:865c
·symbolic importance and festivities **7**:198e *passim* to 200d
·worship in mythic constructs **19**:1017a

new-year's gift (plant): *see* winter aconite.

New Year's Mail Service, system introduced in Japan in 1900 which handles New Year's cards posted between December 15 and 31, retaining them at post offices so that they can all be delivered on January 1.

·postal system special services **14**:889h

New York (State) **13**:21, northeastern U.S., in the Middle Atlantic region, one of the 13 original states. Occupying an area of 49,576 sq mi (128,401 sq km), it is bordered from west to north by Lake Erie, the Canadian province of Ontario, Lake Ontario, and Quebec province; on the east by Vermont, Massachusetts, and Connecticut; on the southeast by the Atlantic Ocean; and on the south by New Jersey and Pennsylvania. Its capital is Albany. Pop. (1980) 17,557,288.

The text article, after a brief survey of the state, covers its history, natural and human landscape, people, economy, administration and social conditions, and cultural life and institutions.

REFERENCES in other text articles:
·Appalachian geology, history, and ecology **1**:1016a
·area and population, table 1 **18**:927
·colonial settlement and control **18**:949c; maps
·colonial socio-political structure **18**:951e
·cultural origin and regional overlap **18**:925d
·early U.S. agricultural specialties **18**:963a
·education system centralization **6**:421g
·Estates, Powers, and Trust Law of 1966 **9**:591h
·F.D. Roosevelt's offices and policies **15**:1137f
·Hamilton's influence in state politics **8**:585d
·infectious jaundice annual incidence **9**:536c
·map, United States **18**:908
·pre-Revolution political rivalry **18**:954g
·War of Independence battle sites and importance **19**:603e; map
·Washington's military forces and Howe clash **19**:614e

New York (City) **13**:27, city and port at the mouth of the Hudson River, southeastern New York state, occupying Manhattan and Staten islands, the western end of Long Island, a portion of the mainland, and various islands in New York Harbor and Long Island Sound. It comprises five counties of New York state (New York, Kings, Queens, Bronx, and Richmond) constituting the boroughs of Manhattan, Brooklyn, Queens, the Bronx, and Richmond (Staten Island). It is the largest city in the Western Hemisphere. Pop. (1980) city, 7,071,030; urbanized area, 16,120,023; Standard Metropolitan Statistical Area (including parts of New York and New Jersey), 9,119,737.
40°43′ N, 74°01′ W

TEXT ARTICLE covers:
The proliferation of crisis 28e
The history of New York 29h
The boroughs and their people 31d
Demographic change 34f

Economic life 35h
Politics and government 37c
Public services 38g
Cultural life and institutions 40g
Problems and prospects 42d

REFERENCES in other text articles:
·administrative problems **4**:646g
·aqueduct construction and history **1**:1041g
·Bronx River Parkway system **15**:899h
·building design temperature, tables 1 and 3 **8**:713
·commodity trading operations **4**:995a
·economic, social, and political influence **13**:21c
·financial and commercial leadership **14**:216f
·fur auctions and fur processing **7**:815b
·horse racing and off-track betting **8**:1104g
·interior design in colonial period **9**:719h
·map, United States **18**:909
·money market and banking activity **12**:358b
·New Jersey economic association **12**:1096g
·newspaper publishing history **15**:239c
·r-less dialect and social status **5**:701b
·steel construction in skyscrapers **17**:635a
·urban transportation development **18**:658f
·Verrazano-Narrows Bridge construction **3**:184a

New York, State University of, established 1948, a coeducational, state-supported system of higher education located throughout the state of New York. The system comprises university centres at Albany, Binghamton, Buffalo, and Stony Brook; 13 colleges of arts and sciences; 9 specialized colleges within private universities (*e.g.*, School of Industrial and Labor Relations at Cornell University, Ithaca); 6 agricultural and technical colleges; and 38 locally sponsored two-year colleges. Also under the state system are Downstate Medical Center at Brooklyn and Upstate Medical Center at Syracuse.

In 1971 the state university initiated a program of learning centres, known collectively as the Empire State College, in which students may pursue their studies without having to enroll in traditional courses or be attached to a specific campus.
·establishment and influence **13**:26f

New York Botanical Garden, 230-acre garden (incorporated 1891) around the gorge of the Bronx River in the Bronx; it was patterned after the Royal Botanic Gardens at Kew, England. Its museum houses an herbarium with more than 3,000,000 plants, and Lorillard Snuff Mill (1840) on the grounds now serves as a restaurant.
·size and species variety table **3**:64

New York City Ballet, resident ballet company of the New York City Center of Music and Drama. The company, first named Ballet Society, was founded in 1946 by the choreographer George Balanchine (artistic director) and Lincoln Kirstein (general director) as a private subscription organization to promote lyric theatre. It is a descendant of the American Ballet company. In 1948 Ballet Society gave its first public performance in the City Center Theater and changed its name to the New York City Ballet. From 1950 the company increased its prestige with foreign tours. Its performing home became the New York State Theater at the Lincoln Center for the Performing Arts in 1964.

In addition to ballets choreographed by Balanchine, the company performed works by Jerome Robbins (associate artistic director, 1950–59; ballet master from 1969), William Dollar, Todd Bolender, Francisco Moncion, Lew Christensen, and Sir Frederick Ashton. Its principal dancers have included Maria Tallchief, Tanaquil LeClercq, Melissa Hayden, Patricia Wilde, Violette Verdy, Suzanne Farrell, Gelsey Kirkland, Patricia McBride, André Eglevsky, Jacques d'Amboise, Edward Villella, and Peter Martins.
·Balanchine's choreographic contributions **2**:609e
·international recognition **2**:652c
·modern dance **12**:294g
·theatrical music **12**:696f

New York City Center, in full, NEW YORK CITY CENTER OF MUSIC AND DRAMA, also called CITY CENTER, first U.S. cultural centre, founded in 1943. Its original home was the City Center Theater (formerly the Mecca Temple) on 55th Street, but it added the New York State Theater at the Lincoln Center for the Performing Arts to its operation in 1966. Its best known and longest lived performing organizations are the New York City Opera Company (from 1944) and the New York City Ballet (from 1948).
·Balanchine's ballet company **2**:609e

New York City Opera, resident opera company of the New York City Center of Music and Drama. Opening in 1944 under its music director (until 1951) László Halász, its original purpose was to present good opera at popular prices. Under the musical and artistic directorship (1957–79) of Julius Rudel, it became a major company, staging much contemporary repertory and many premieres of U.S. operas. Its performances were in the City Center Theater until 1966, when it moved to the New York State Theater at the Lincoln Center for the Performing Arts. Soprano Beverly Sills became director of the company in 1979.

New York County, southeastern New York, U.S., coextensive with the borough of Manhattan (*q.v.*), New York City. It was formed in 1683, has an area of 22 sq mi (57 sq km), and was named in honour of the Duke of York. Pop. (1980) 1,427,533.

New York Craps (dice game): *see* Bank Craps.

New York Daily News, first U.S. tabloid newspaper, founded in 1919 by Joseph Medill Patterson.
·newspaper publishing history **15**:244a

New Yorker, The, U.S. weekly magazine founded in 1925 by Harold Ross. Noted for its fiction, essays, cartoons, and verse, it has celebrated urbanity and an appreciation of fine style.
·biographical profile tradition **2**:1008e
·cartoonists' style and class view **3**:916e
·influence of advertising **15**:252b
·magazine publishing history **15**:256d

New York Evening Post, The, newspaper founded by Alexander Hamilton in 1801 as a Federalist journal.
·Hamilton founding and political stand **8**:587h

New York from Its Pinnacles, series of five photographs exhibited by Alvin Langdon Coburn (*q.v.*) in 1913.
·photographic emphasis on form **14**:318d

New York Hat, The (1912), film directed by D.W. Griffith.
·pastoral simplicity and goodness **12**:516g

New York Herald, U.S. newspaper founded in 1835 by James Gordon Bennett (*q.v.*). It is often cited as the beginning of modern U.S. journalism. It merged with the *New York Sun* in 1920 to form the *Sun and New York Herald* and with the *New York Tribune* in 1924, becoming the *New York Herald Tribune* (1926–66).
·history of publishing **15**:240d *passim* to 243g
·Sir Henry Morton Stanley **17**:583c

New York Island (Northern Line Islands): *see* Washington Island.

New York Philharmonic Orchestra, major symphony orchestra in New York City, which traces its roots back to the Philharmonic Society of New York (founded 1842), making it America's oldest. The New York Symphony Society was founded in 1878 by Leopold Damrosch, maintaining a competitive orchestra until the two merged in 1928, forming the New York Philharmonic-Symphony Society.

New York Review of Books, The, periodical of literary criticism established in New York City in 1963.
·literary criticism function **10**:1037f

New York school, collective designation for those painters who participated in the development of contemporary art from the early 1940s in or around New York City. During and after World War II, leadership in avant-garde art shifted from war-torn Europe to New York, and the New York school has maintained a dominant position in world art into the 1970s. Abstract Expressionism, the most important art movement to emerge after World War II, Minimal art, Pop art, and new realist styles of the late 1960s, among others, all had their beginnings in New York. *See also* Abstract Expressionism; Action painting; Minimal art; Pop art.

New York State Barge Canal System, commonly called BARGE CANAL, 520 mi (837 km) of waterways linking the Hudson with Lake Erie, with extensions to Lakes Ontario, Champlain, Cayuga, and Seneca. It incorporates the Erie Canal (*q.v.*). It can accommodate barges 300 ft (91 m) long, 42 ft wide, with a draft of 10 ft and a cargo capacity of 2,200 tons (2,000 metric tons). Authorized in 1903, it was completed in 1918.

Section of the Barge Canal near Rochester, N.Y.
Milt and Joan Mann from CameraMann

·New York state canal system **3**:755c *passim* to 761h
·Niagara River navigation significance **13**:57f

New York State College of Ceramics, at Alfred University, established in 1900 as the State School of Clay Modeling and Ceramics.
·Charles Binns' founding and support **14**:917b

New York State Theater, part of the Lincoln Center for the Performing Arts, administered by the New York City Center of Music and Drama, and the permanent home of the New York City Ballet (from 1964) and the New York City Opera (from 1966).
·Balanchine's ballet company **2**:609e

New York Stock Exchange, also called BIG BOARD, world's largest marketplace for securities. From a group of 24 men meeting in 1792 under a buttonwood tree, on what is presently Wall Street in New York City, evolved the New York Stock and Exchange Board, formally constituted in 1817. The present name was adopted in 1863. Membership, limited to 1,366 since 1953, is obtained by purchasing (since 1868) a seat from an existing member, subject to approval by the exchange.
·New York City economic activity **13**:37b
·securities trading history **16**:449h *passim* to 452e
·United States financial services **18**:934b

New York Times, The, daily newspaper founded in 1851. Owned by several publishers during its history, *The Times* was purchased in 1896 by Adolph Simon Ochs (*q.v.*), who made it into one of the great newspapers of the world. In 1913 he began publishing the *New York Times Index*, the only complete U.S. newspaper index.
·history of publishing **15**:240e *passim* to 245e

New York Tribune, U.S. newspaper established in 1841 under owner-editor Horace Greeley.
·newspaper publishing history **15**:240e

New York Zoological Park: *see* Bronx Zoo.

New Youth, translated from HSIN CH'ING NIEN, Chinese magazine founded in 1915 to agitate for reform.
·New Culture Movement role **4**:368e

New Zealand 13:43, constituent member of the Commonwealth of Nations, comprising two main islands (North and South islands) and smaller associated islands in the South Pacific Ocean about 1,000 mi (1,600 km) southeast of Australia.

The text article covers the land and people of New Zealand, the economy, administrative and social conditions, and cultural life.

REFERENCES in other text articles:

agriculture, forestry, and fishing
·animal grazing, soils, and diseases **6**:708h
·dairy cattle feed ration and milk production **5**:425h; table 426
·dairy farming methods **7**:175e
·meat production and consumption **11**:746b
·sheep breeding for meat production **1**:343a
·armed forces statistics, table 2 **2**:16
commerce, industry, and mining
·coal production and reserves, table 5 **4**:781
·electric power production **6**:636e
·jade use in tools and ornaments **7**:972f
constitution and law
·bankruptcy laws **2**:696b
·inheritance and disinheritance laws **9**:588c
culture and education
·English dialect features **6**:885f
·novel and literary tradition **13**:292f
·sculpture materials and characteristics **13**:465b
·20th-century educational development **6**:385a
economics, finance, and currency
·economic productivity and level of output **15**:31h; table 32
·gross national debt percentage, table 4 **15**:193
government
·Samoan administration goals **13**:447f
·socialism's evolution **16**:973d
·two-party system aspects **14**:682h
labour and management
·apprenticeship program regulation **1**:1021b
·arbitration of wage disputes **10**:567d
·trade union membership and history **18**:569d
·petroleum reserves of the world table **14**:175
physical geography
·Cook's discovery and charting **5**:131e; map
·Cretaceous rock types and sequence, table 2 **5**:248
·geyser action considerations **8**:134c
·map, Australia and Oceania **2**:383
·origin and environmental range **14**:777g
·rain forest varieties, characteristics, and locations **10**:338d; map 1337
·Triassic sedimentary facies **18**:694h
population and demography
·Christian denominational demography map **4**:459
·fire death and property loss table **7**:314
·Polynesian blood types **14**:845c
·urban population ratio table **16**:26
religion
·Catholic population distribution map **15**:1019
·new tribal religious movements **18**:704g
social issues
·alcohol consumption patterns **1**:444c; table
·dental care aid to developing countries **5**:592e
·meat consumption per capita **10**:1279d
·railway systems data table **15**:482
sports and recreation
·big game importations **9**:48f
·cricket popularity and Test matches **5**:262c *passim* to 264e
·Rugby history and playing styles **16**:5d
transportation and communications
·broadcasting organization and services **3**:320a
·newspaper publishing statistics table **15**:237
vegetation and animal life
·biogeographic subregional traits **2**:1005a
·moa importance to early settlers **14**:777g
·tuatara traits and relict status **15**:824b

New Zealand, Church of the Province of, an independent Anglican church that developed from missionary work begun in the 19th century. The first missionaries arrived in New Zealand from Australia in 1814. The work flourished, and in 1841 George Augustus Selwyn (1809–78) was appointed the first bishop of New Zealand, where he served until 1867. The church grew as white settlers moved to the country, and it also gained converts among the native Maori population. In 1857 it adopted its own constitution and became an independent church.

NEW ZEALAND

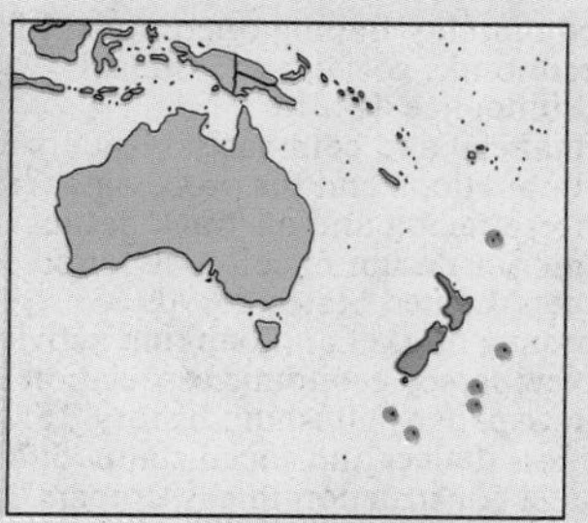

Official name: New Zealand.
Location: southwestern Pacific.
Form of government: parliamentary state.
Official language: English.
Official religion: none.
Area: 103,736 sq mi, 268,676 sq km.
Population: (1966 census) 2,676,919; (1971 census) 2,862,631.
Capital: Wellington.
Monetary unit: 1 New Zealand dollar (NZ$) = 100 cents.

Demography

Population (1971 census): density 27.6 per sq mi, 10.7 per sq km; urban 81.4%, rural 18.6%; male 49.98%, female 50.02%; under 15 31.6%, 15–29 23.9%, 30–44 16.7%, 45–59 15.0%, 60–74 9.4%, 75 and over 3.0%, unknown 0.4%.

Vital statistics: (1970) births per 1,000 population 22.1, deaths per 1,000 population 8.8, natural increase per 1,000 population 13.3; (1965–67) life expectancy at birth—(non-Maori) male 68.7, female 74.8, (Maori) male 61.4, female 64.8; (1969) major causes of death (per 100,000 population)—ischemic heart disease 241.3; malignant neoplasms, including neoplasms of lymphatic and hematopoietic tissue 150.8; cerebrovascular disease 110.6; pneumonia 49.6.

Ethnic composition (1966): European 90.6%, Maori 7.5%, other 1.8%.* *Religious affiliation* (1966): Church of England 33.7%, Presbyterian 21.8%, Roman Catholic 15.9%, Methodist 7.0%, Baptist 1.7%, none 1.2%, not stated 8.6%, other 10.1%.

National accounts

Budget (1970–71). Revenue: NZ$1,649,028,000 (income and social security taxes 58.0%, customs duties 8.4%, sales tax 7.6%, highways tax 5.0%). Expenditures: NZ$1,560,852,000 (social security benefits 19.6%, education 16.1%, health 15.5%, interest on debt 9.8%, development of industry 7.6%, defense 7.0%). *Total national debt* (1970): NZ$2,877,113,000. *Tourism* (1969–70). Receipts from visitors: NZ$26,400,000. Expenditures by nationals abroad: NZ$50,100,000.

Domestic economy

Gross national product (GNP; at current market prices, 1970): U.S. $7,610,000,000 (U.S. $2,700 per capita).
Origin of gross domestic product: no data available.

Production. Agriculture, forestry, hunting, fishing (metric tons except as noted, 1970): beef cattle 5,048,048 head, dairy cattle 3,729,284 head, sheep 60,276,000 head, pigs 577,925 head, milk 5,708,000, wheat 324,000, oats 49,000, barley 227,000, maize (corn) 58,690, potatoes 249,204,000, roundwood 7,800,000 cu m, fish catch 49,400.† Mining, quarrying (gross value in 000 NZ$, 1969): coal 13,673; sand, rock, gravel for roads, and ballast 18,486. Manufacturing (gross value in 000 NZ$, 1969): frozen and preserved meat 457,319; butter, cheese, and other milk products 243,141; assembled motor vehicles 86,389; petroleum and coal products 77,895; pulp, paper, and paperboard 75,829; sheet metal products 61,410. Construction (gross value in 000 NZ$, 1970): new residential 192,590, commercial buildings 61,950, school buildings 32,714.

Energy (1970): installed electrical capacity 3,682,700 kW, production 12,926,000 kW-hr (4,582 kW-hr per capita).

Persons economically active (1971): 1,112,000 (38.8%) (agriculture, forestry, hunting, fishing 12.3%; mining, quarrying 0.4%; manufacturing 24.7%; construction 7.8%; electricity, gas, water 1.2%; transport, storage, communication 9.2%; trade 16.8%; banking, insurance, real estate 6.0%; defense 1.0%; services 20.1%; other 0.1%), unemployed 1,400 (0.1%).

Price and earnings indexes (1963 = 100):	1964	1965	1966	1967	1968	1969	1970	1971
consumer price index	103.5	107.0	109.9	116.6	121.6	127.6	135.0	150.1
weekly earnings index	103	109	112	118	123	130	150	179

Land use (1970): meadows and pastures 47.3%, forested 24.0%, built-on and wasteland 22.0%, agricultural and under permanent cultivation 3.5%, other 3.2%.

Foreign trade

Imports (1970): NZ$1,006,022,000 (transport equipment 13.5%; machinery other than electric 13.1%; textile yarn, fabrics, made-up articles, and related products 9.3%; iron and steel 7.9%; petroleum and petroleum products 7.5%; electrical machinery, apparatus, and appliances 5.5%; nonferrous metals 4.2%; crude fertilizers and crude minerals excluding coal, petroleum, and precious stones 3.4%; chemical elements and compounds 3.3%; manufactures of metals 3.2%). *Major import sources:* United Kingdom 29.6%; Australia 20.9%, United States 13.1%, Japan 8.3%, Canada 4.0%, West Germany 3.9%.

Exports (1970): NZ$1,087,026,000 (meat and meat preparations 34.0%; textile fibres, not manufactured into yarn, thread, or fabrics, and waste 18.8%; dairy products and eggs 17.3%; hides, skins, and fur skins, undressed 4.5%; wood and cork 3.1%; paper, paperboard, and manufactures thereof 2.0%; fruit and vegetables 2.0%). *Major export destinations:* United Kingdom 35.5%, United States 15.2%, Japan 9.8%, Australia 8.0%, Canada 4.2%, West Germany 2.7%.

Transport and communication

Transport. Railroads (1970): length 3,063 mi, 4,929 km; passenger mi 315,000,000, passenger km 507,000,000; short ton-mi cargo 2,200,000,000, metric ton-km cargo 3,212,000,000. Roads (1971): total length 58,309 mi, 93,837 km (paved 25,985 mi, 41,818 km; gravel and crushed stone 32,324 mi, 52,019 km). Vehicles (1970): passenger cars 891,200, trucks and buses 181,700. Merchant marine (1970): vessels (over 1,000 gross tons) 48, total deadweight tonnage 174,000. Air transport (1970): passenger mi 1,045,708,000, passenger km 1,682,908,000; short ton-mi cargo 25,245,000, metric ton-km cargo 36,857,000; airports with scheduled flights 37.

Communication. Daily newspapers (1970): total number 41, circulation per 1,000 population 375, total circulation 1,045,000. Radios (1971): total number of receivers 696,734 (1 per 4.1 persons). Television (1971): receivers 675,413 (1 per 4.2 persons); broadcasting stations 4. Telephones (1971): 1,262,427 (1 per 2.2 persons).

Education and health

Education (1971):	schools	teachers	students	student–teacher ratio
primary (age 5 to 12)	2,593	18,791	517,537	27.5
secondary (age 13 to 18)	386	9,932	186,743	18.8
vocational	8	859	45,850‡	53.4
higher§	20	2,642	31,231	11.8

College graduates (per 100,000 population, 1969): 184. *Literacy* (1969): total population literate (over 15) virtually 100%.

Health: (1969) doctors 4,435 (1 per 633 persons); (1970) hospital beds 28,723 (1 per 98 persons); (1969) daily per capita caloric intake 3,324 calories (FAO recommended minimum requirement 2,610 calories).

*Percentages do not add to 100.0 because of rounding. †1969. ‡Includes 43,968 part-time students. §Includes teacher training.

Although other denominations also established missions in New Zealand, the Anglican Church remained the largest church. It consists of one province divided into several dioceses. The seat of the primate is in Christchurch. In 1968 it reported an inclusive membership of 835,434.

New Zealand, history of 13:50. The island nation of New Zealand developed in one century from a British colony into a stable, independent dominion within the Commonwealth of Nations.

The text article covers the European discovery of the Pacific islands constituting New Zealand (1642) and the exploration of them by the British naval officer James Cook, 1769–70. Although the native Polynesians, the Maori, resisted early foreign settlement, European colonies flourished; and in 1841 Great Britain annexed the islands. By 1847 the Maori had been pacified and in the early 1850s a representative, constitutional government was established to rule the six provinces of New Zealand. Despite a decade of renewed hostilities between the Maori and the European settlers (1860s) and a long period of economic instability (marked by depressions in the late 1860s and 1880s), New Zealand by the early 20th century had developed a firm central government and a sound economy based on agricultural exports. After supporting Great Britain during World War I, New Zealand exercised an increasing degree of autonomy in both domestic and foreign affairs. It did not adopt the Statute of Westminster that made it a fully autonomous dominion until 1947. After World War II New Zealand became a pioneer in social legislation and also participated more actively in international politics, particularly in affairs relating to the South Pacific and Southeast Asia.

REFERENCES in other text articles:
·Antarctic territorial claims table 1:963
·British Empire and Commonwealth growth 3:303h
·British Empire extension map 3:305
·cricket introduction and popularity 5:262c *passim* to 264f
·Maori fortified villages and kin groups 14:779d
·Tasman's discovery and exploration 17:1070h
·19th-century educational development 6:368d

RELATED ENTRIES in the *Ready Reference and Index: for*
Maori: see Bay of Islands War; Hauhau Movement; Mana Maori Motuhake; Maori King Movement; Maori Representation Act; Maori Wars; Native Land Acts; Wairau Affray; Waitangi, Treaty of; Young Maori Party
political development: Kororareka Association; New Provinces Act; New Zealand Legion; New Zealand Political Reform League; Young New Zealand Party
other: Advances to Settlers Act; New Zealand Company; Waihi Strike

New Zealand Association, British crown company founded by Edward Gibbon Wakefield in 1837 to promote the colonization of South Australia.
·colonization and corrupt land purchases 13:51e

New Zealand Company (1838–58), British joint-stock company responsible for much of the early settlement of New Zealand. Formed in the summer of 1838 after a parent New Zealand Association failed to receive a royal charter to proceed with the settlement of the still independent islands, the company sent a land purchase expedition to New Zealand in 1839. In 1840 it founded the settlements of Wellington and Nelson and, in 1841, through a subsidiary organization (the Plymouth Company), the settlement of New Plymouth.

While the advance group was buying land, Britain annexed New Zealand (May 1840) on terms that necessitated a review of the company's land purchases from the Maori (*see* Waitangi, Treaty of). From 1840 to 1845 many of its transactions were ruled invalid. Immigrants who had heeded the company's propaganda found that there was little land to be had when they arrived. While the company had finally received a royal charter to continue its work (1841), it found itself in serious financial difficulty. The massacre in 1843 of its officials (*see* Wairau Affray) and the 1844–47 Bay of Islands War exacerbated the company's plight. By 1858 it was dissolved.

The New Zealand Company had sought to settle New Zealand in accordance with the colonizing theories of Edward Gibbon Wakefield, its unofficial leader. While it did not achieve this goal—the transplanting of stable English social classes to virgin soil—its effort had brought many capable settlers to the colony.

New Zealand Legion (1933–35), a Fascistic organization that challenged New Zealand's parliamentary democracy at the height of the world Depression. Spawned by economic crisis and attendant waves of rioting and repression in New Zealand, the legion was founded early in 1933 by Dr. Robert Campbell Begg. It had no clear program but stressed the evil of party politics and called for a new form of government sufficiently well-organized and authoritarian to cope with New Zealand's chaotic conditions. The legion never attained a large following and dissolved with the first signs of the lifting of the Depression early in 1935.

New Zealand Political Reform League, commonly called the REFORM PARTY after 1908, a conservative political party formed from various local and sectional organizations that took power in the national elections of 1912 and held control of the government until 1928. The NZPRL first acted as a united group in 1905, but it was not formally constituted and organized along party lines until after the 1912 election.

Based primarily on urban business interests and the small farmers of the North Island dairy industry, the NZPRL won the 1912 election by a promise to transform agricultural leasehold property into freehold on terms that would enable farmers to reap a significant profit from the sale of their land. It also benefitted from its opposition to growing labour union defiance of New Zealand's anti-strike Industrial Conciliation and Arbitration Act (1894).

Led by W.F. Massey, the party's leader and New Zealand's premier from 1912 until his death in 1925, the NZPRL dealt violently with the strikes of 1912–13 (*see* Waihi Strike). But it was mortally weakened during a depression of the late 1920s, when its business and agrarian wings turned against one another. The NZPRL returned to power in coalition with the United Party (1931–35) but was dissolved in 1936. Its remnant entered the new National Party.
·New Zealand political history 13:53g

New Zealand red pine: *see* rimu.

New Zealand short-tailed bat, common name for members of the mammalian family Mystacinidae (order Chiroptera).
·classification and general features 4:436c

Nexø, Martin Andersen (b. June 26, 1869, Copenhagen—d. June 1, 1954, Dresden, East Germany), writer who was the first in Danish literature to make the lot of the proletariat his cause and to champion social revolution, thus doing much to raise social consciousness in Denmark and throughout Europe. He came from an extremely poor family in the Christianhavn slums of Copenhagen but spent most of his childhood in Bornholm, where he worked as a shepherd, then as a shoemaker's apprentice, and came to know the extreme deprivation suffered by the proletariat. With the help of a patron, he was later able to go to school, after which he worked as a teacher until 1901, when he was able to support himself by his writing.

Nexø's two major works became known all over the world. The first, *Pelle erobreren*, 4 vol. (1906–10; Eng. trans., *Pelle the Conqueror*, 1913–16), tells of Pelle's development from a humble position as the son of a farm labourer, through the awakening of his class consciousness as a worker in Copenhagen, to becoming a militant labour leader. The second is the five-volume *Ditte mennskebarn* (1917–21; Eng. trans., *Ditte, Daughter of Man*, 3 vol., 1920–22) depicting the hard life of a poor, courageous, and loving girl and woman for whom there is no escape from oppression. A third novel, not quite as well known, *Midt i en Jaerntid* (1929; Eng. trans., *In God's Land*, 1933), is critical of wealthy farmers during the period of agricultural inflation brought about by World War I. Nexø was a great admirer of the Soviet revolutionary experiment; he became a Communist after World War I and travelled to Russia a number of times. A book of his first impressions of the Soviet Union is entitled *Mod dagningen* (1923; "Toward the Dawn"). In the 1930s he started writing his memoirs, which were collected in two volumes as *Erindringer* (1932–39; first part: Eng. trans., *Under the Open Sky*, 1938). In 1945 Nexø published a sequel to *Pelle*, *Morten hin Røde* (1945; "Morten the Red"), in which Morten is the revolutionary and Pelle is shown as having turned bourgeois, like many of the labour leaders in the West. Nexø left Denmark in 1949, after the signing of the North Atlantic Pact, and settled in the German Democratic Republic, where he remained for the rest of his life.
·themes and major works 10:1248d

nexum, in very early Roman law, a type of formal contract involving the loan of money under such oppressive conditions that it might result in the debtor's complete subjection to the creditor. The transaction was accomplished by means of a ritual employing scales and copper, the traditional symbols of transfer of property. The procedure was discontinued in the late 4th century BC, when the so-called Lex Poetelia released all those who were *nexi* (*i.e.,* insolvent debtors held in bondage by their creditors).

Ney, Michel 13:55, titled as DUC D'ELCHINGEN and PRINCE DE LA MOSKOWA (b. Jan. 10, 1769, Sarrelouis [Saarlouis], Fr.—d. Dec. 7, 1815, Paris), the most famous of Napoleon's marshals, a courageous though sometimes insubordinate military hero whose execution by a firing squad made him a symbol of resistance to the Bourbon restoration in France.

Abstract of text biography. A soldier from the age of 19, Ney took part in the French Revolutionary Wars and became general of a division. In 1804 the newly proclaimed emperor Napoleon I made Ney a marshal. Thereafter he fought for Napoleon in Switzerland, Austria, Germany, Spain, and Russia; but he then helped to induce the Emperor to abdicate. After Napoleon's return in 1815, Ney repudiated his brief allegiance to the Bourbon dynasty and, along with the Emperor, was defeated at Waterloo. Failing to escape from France after the second Bourbon restoration, he was arrested and condemned to death.

REFERENCE in other text article:
·Austrian campaign strategy 7:726a

Neyagawa, city, Ōsaka Urban Prefecture (*fu*), Honshu, Japan, in the northern part of the Kōchi-gawa Plain. Many ancient relics attest to prehistoric settlement in the area. With the construction of a railway line to Ōsaka in 1910, Neyagawa grew as a residential suburb. The few large-scale factories produce metal products, transportation equipment, and textiles. Pop. (1970) 206,961.
34°46′ N, 135°38′ E

Neyman, Jerzy (b. April 16, 1894, Bendery, Romania), U.S. mathematician and statistician who helped to establish the statistical theory of hypothesis testing.

After serving as a lecturer at the Institute of Technology, Kharkov, in the Ukraine, from 1917 to 1921, Neyman was appointed statistician of the Institute of Agriculture at Bydgoszcz, Pol. In 1923 he became a lecturer at the College of Agriculture, Warsaw, and joined the faculty of the University of Warsaw in 1928. He served on the staff of University College, London, from 1934 to 1938, and then emigrated to the U.S., where he joined the faculty of the University of California, at Berkeley. There he built, with the help of a growing number of statisticians and mathematicians who studied under him, what became known as a leading world centre for mathematical statistics. A highly successful series of symposia on probability and statistics were carried out under his guidance.

Neyman's work in mathematical statistics, which includes theories of estimation and of testing hypotheses, has found wide application in genetics, medical diagnosis, astronomy, meteorology, and agricultural experimentation. He was noted especially for combining both theory and its applications in his thinking.

Neyshābūr, also transliterated NĪSHĀPŪR, town, Khorāsān *ostān* (province), Iran, at an altitude of 3,980 ft (1,213 m) in a wide, fertile plain at the southern foot of the mountain Kūh-e Bīnālūd. Cereals and cotton are grown in the area, and industries include agricultural marketing and the manufacture of carpets and pottery. Neyshābūr is linked by road and railway with Tehrān and Meshed.

Nīshāpūr, named after its alleged founder, the Sāsānian king Shāpūr I (died 272), was important in the 5th century as a royal residence but was insignificant by the 7th century. Under the Ṭāhirid dynasty (821–873) it flourished again, and it rose to importance under the Sāmānid dynasty (ended 999). Toghrïl Beg, the first Seljuq ruler, made Nīshāpūr his residence in 1037, but it declined in the 12th century and in the 13th twice suffered earthquakes as well as the Mongol invasion. Nearby are the Qadamgāh (1643), a fine domed mausoleum, and rich medieval and pre-medieval remains, and the mosque of the Emāmzādeh Maḥroq, near which is the tomb of the 12th-century astronomer-poet Omar Khayyam. Pop. (1972 est.) 40,000.
36°12′ N, 58°50′ E

·excavation pottery findings **9**:992c
·Sāmānid pottery styles **14**:902a

Nezahualcóyotl, Aztec king of Texcoco (reigned 1431–72).

·Aztec temple for unknown god **2**:552b

Neẓāmī, more complete name ELYĀS YŪSOF NEẒĀMĪ GANJAVĪ (b. *c.* 1141, Ganja, now Kirovabad, Azerbaijan S.S.R.—d. 1203/17, Ganja), greatest romantic poet in Persian literature, who brought a colloquial and realistic style to the Persian epic.

Neẓāmī spent his entire life in Ganja, leaving only once to meet the ruling prince. Although he enjoyed the patronage of a number of rulers and princes, he was distinguished by his simple life and straightforward character.

His poetry, full of reflections on life and people, reveals broad sympathies and deep insight. His wide learning is seen in his frequent references to historical, literary, and scientific topics (he was especially interested in astronomy and music), and a love of nature is evident from his apt descriptions and his charming characterizations of animals.

Only a handful of his *qaṣīdah*s ("odes") and *ghazal*s ("lyrics") have survived; his reputation rests on his great *Khamseh* ("The Quintuplet"), a pentology of poems written in *maṡnavī* verse form (rhymed couplets) totalling 30,000 couplets. Drawing inspiration from the Persian epic poets Ferdowsī and Sanā'ī, he proved himself the first great dramatic poet of Persian literature. The first poem in the pentology is the didactic poem *Makhzan ol-asrār* (Eng. trans., *The Treasury of Mysteries*, 1945), the second the romantic epic *Khosrow o-Shīrīn* ("Khosrow and Shīrīn"). The third is his rendition of a well-known story in Islāmic folklore, *Leyli o-Mejnūn* (Eng. trans., *The Story of Leyla and Majnun*, 1966). The fourth poem, *Haft paykar* (Eng. trans., *The Seven Beauties*, 1924), is considered his masterwork. The final poem in the pentology is the *Sikandar* or *Eskandar-nāmeh* ("Book of Alexander the Great"; Eng. trans. of part I, *The Sikander Nama*, 1881). This philosophical portrait of Alexander is divided into two sections, the *Sharaf-nāmeh* ("Book of Honour") and the *Iqbāl-nāmeh* ("Book of Fortune").

Neẓāmī is admired in Persian-speaking lands for his originality and clarity of style, though his love of language for its own sake and of philosophical and scientific learning makes his work difficult for the average reader.

Nezara viridula (insect): *see* stinkbug.

Nezhin, centre of a *rayon* (district), Chernigov *oblast* (administrative region), Ukrainian Soviet Socialist Republic. Nezhin dates from the 11th century and was incorporated in 1781. It contains several buildings from the 17th and 18th centuries, including the cathedrals of St. Nicholas and of the Annunciation. A minor industrial centre before the October Revolution, it now has engineering and food industries. The teacher-training institute is named after the novelist Nikolay Gogol, who studied in a Nezhin lyceum. Pop. (1974 est.) 63,000.
51°03′ N, 31°54′ E

Nezib, Battle of (1839): *see* Nizip, Battle of.

Neziqin (Hebrew: "Damages"), the fourth of the six major divisions, or orders (*sedarim*), of the Mishna (codification of Jewish oral laws), which was given its final form early in the 3rd century AD by Judah ha-Nasi. *Neziqin* deals principally with legally adjudicated damages and financial questions. The 10 tractates (treatises) of *Neziqin* are: *Bava qamma* ("First Gate"), *Bava metziʿa* ("Middle Gate"), *Bava batra* ("Last Gate"), *Sanhedrin* (the supreme executive and legislative body), *Makkot* ("Stripes"), *Shevuʿot* ("Oaths"), *ʿEduyyot* ("Testimonies"), *ʿAvoda zara* ("Idolatry"), *Avot* ("Fathers"), and *Horayot* ("Decisions"). Both the Palestinian and the Babylonian Talmud have commentaries on all the tractates, with the exception of *Avot* and *ʿEduyyot*.

·tractates and scope **17**:1008d

Nez Percé, Sahaptian-speaking North American Indian people centring on the lower Snake River and such tributaries as the Salmon and Clearwater rivers in what is now central Idaho and adjacent areas of Oregon and Washington. They were the largest, most powerful, and best known of the Sahaptin (*q.v.*) and were called by various names by other peoples; the French name, Nez Percé (Pierced Nose), referred to the wearing of nose pendants, though the fashion does not seem to have been widespread among them.

Their culture was primarily that of the Plateau culture area and more specifically that of the Sahaptin tribes. As one of the easternmost groups, however, they were influenced by the Plains Indians living just east of the Rockies. Typical of the Plateau, their domestic life traditionally centred on small villages located on streams having abundant salmon, which, dried, formed their main source of food. They also sought a variety of game, berries, and roots. Their dwellings were communal lodges, A-framed and mat-covered, varying in size but sometimes housing as many as 30 families.

After acquiring horses early in the 18th century, however, Nez Percé life began to change dramatically, at least among some groups. They were able to mount expeditions for bison hunts and to trade with peoples beyond the Rockies. Always somewhat warlike, they now became more so, adopting many war honours, war dances, and horse tactics imitative of the custom of the Plains; the Plains tepee was also used. The Nez Percé built up one of the largest horse herds on the continent and were almost unique among American Indians in learning selective breeding. As this enrichment and expansionism led to more tribal or intervillage consultation, they tended to dominate negotiations with other tribes.

The arrival of whites gradually changed their life. Just six years after the explorers Meriwether Lewis and William Clark visited the Nez Percé in 1805, fur traders and trappers began penetrating the area, followed later by missionaries. By the 1840s, white settlers were moving through on the Oregon Trail, leading in 1855 to a treaty with the U.S. that created a large Nez Percé reservation, encompassing most of their traditional land. The discovery of gold on the Salmon and Clearwater in 1860, however, and the influx of thousands of miners and then settlers, led U.S. commissioners in 1863 to force renegotiation of the treaty, fraudulently reducing the size of the reservation by three-fourths; subsequent invasions of homesteaders reduced the area even more. Many Nez Percé, perhaps a majority, had never accepted either the old treaty or the new, and hostile actions and raids by both whites and Indians finally evolved into the Nez Percé War of 1877. For five months a small band of 250 Nez Percé warriors, under the leadership of Chief Joseph, held off a U.S. force of 5,000 troops led by Gen. O.O. Howard, who tracked them through Idaho, Yellowstone Park, and Montana before they surrendered to Gen. Nelson A. Miles on October 5. In the campaign, Chief Joseph lost 239 persons, including women and children, and the U.S. lost 266. The tribe was then assigned to malarial country in Oklahoma rather than being returned to the Northwest as promised (*see also* Joseph, Chief).

In 1972, some 1,485 Nez Percé still remained on the Nez Percé Reservation in Idaho, but most had left to join the general U.S. population, largely as small landowners or labourers.

·habitation area and culture **13**:228a *passim* to 230b
·Idaho settlement patterns **9**:187e

NFL: *see* National Football League.

Ngag-dbang-rgya-mtsho (1617–82), fifth Dalai Lama of Tibet, reigned 1640–82.

·consolidation and Manchu relations **18**:380h

Ngaju (people): *see* Dayak.

Ngambo, district of Zanzibar city, Tanzania.

·economic and social growth **17**:1029d

Ngami, Lake, shallow depression at the southeast corner of the 4,000-sq-mi (10,400-sq-km) Okavango Swamps in northwestern Botswana, southern Africa. The swamps and the lake are fed by the Okavango River, which loses most of its flow through evaporation in the marshes. Lake Ngami is 3,057 ft (932 m) above sea level. When the explorer David Livingstone first sighted it in 1849, he estimated it to be more than 170 mi (275 km) in circumference, but by 1950 it had become a sea of grass, and during a severe drought in 1965–66 it dried up completely. As thousands of cattle belonging to the local inhabitants were dependent on the lake for water, the drought caused much hardship. Abundant rains since then have again filled the lake, although it is much smaller than it was when Livingstone first saw it. It is rich in birdlife and contains barbel fish, which are able to survive in mud for months while the lake is dry. Lake Ngami has no natural outlet; if it became filled, the Kunyere and Nghabe valleys would be submerged, and any excess water would be deflected into the Boteti (Botletle) River.
20°37′ S, 22°40′ E

·discovery by David Livingstone **11**:1e; map
·Kalahari Desert relief features **10**:373b
·map, Botswana **3**:72
·Okavango River drainage **3**:71f

Ngamiland, political district in northwestern Botswana. It contains Lake Ngami and the extensive Okavango Swamp. Maun is the district headquarters.
·area and population table **3**:74
·map, Botswana **3**:72

Nganasan language: *see* Samoyedic languages.

Nganasans (peoples): *see* Samoyeds.

Ngandong deposits (geology): *see* Trinil Faunal Zone.

Ngaoundéré, also spelled N'GAOUNDÉRÉ or N'GAUNDÉRÉ, headquarters of Adamaoua department, East Cameroon state, Cameroon, on the Adamaoua (Adamawa) Plateau. The major north–south road from Garoua to Bertoua and Yaoundé passes through this agricultural centre and carries its exports of livestock and peanuts (groundnuts) to southern Cameroon. Industries include dairying, slaughtering, hides and skins, perfume manufacture, and cotton ginning.

Major bauxite deposits to the south are scheduled to be exploited upon completion of the Trans-Cameroon Railway in the mid-1970s. Linking Ngaoundéré with Yaoundé and Douala to the southwest, the railway was planned to provide a direct shipping route to the Atlantic.

Historically, Ngaoundéré is important as a traditional capital of the rulers of the Fulani (Fulbe) people, nomadic pastoralists who politically dominate the Adamaoua region. The town was founded in the first half of the 19th century as a part of the kingdom of Adamawa by the Fulani emir Modibbo (The Learned One) Adama.

Ngaoundéré is a centre for big-game hunting, with large game reserves to the northeast and northwest; tourist encampments in the area offer facilities for shooting and photography. A hospital, an airfield, a hydroelectric plant, and customs and meteorological stations serve the town. Pop. (1970 est.) 20,000.
7°19′ N, 13°35′ E
·map, Cameroon **3**:696

ngarong, a protector spirit of the Iban, a Southeast Asian people.
·Iban methods of acquisition **18**:530h

Ngasaunggyan, Battle of (1277), Mongol defeat of Burmese troops that led to the demise of the Pagan dynasty of Burma. After unifying China, the Mongol ruler Kublai Khan sent envoys to neighbouring kingdoms, obliging them to accept Mongol vassalage. The Pagan king Narathihapate (reigned 1254–87) shunned the first Mongol embassy and massacred the members of the second. Confident of victory because of recent Burmese conquests of the territory up to Nanchao, Narathihapate advanced boldly into Yunnan in 1277, accompanied by scores of elephants and soldiers. He met the Mongol troops at Ngasaunggyan, where he was decisively defeated. Thereafter Burmese opposition disintegrated. The border fortresses near Bhamo fell in 1283, thus opening the Irrawaddy Valley to invasion. Narathihapate fled southward to Bassein, where he decided to submit to Mongol vassalage, but he was assassinated by his son in 1287. The Mongols, in full control as far south as Pagan, installed a puppet in Burma in 1289, thus extinguishing the power of the Pagan dynasty.

Ngata, Sir Apirana Turupa (b. July 3, 1874, Kawaka, N.Z.—d. July 14, 1950, Waiomatatini), political and cultural leader of the Maori community in New Zealand who, as minister of native affairs (1928–34), improved Maori agriculture and consolidated their land holdings.

Earning his law degree in 1897, Ngata became the first Maori graduate of a New Zealand university and worked briefly as a lawyer before becoming active in the nationalist Young Maori Party. In 1905 he began his 39-year term of office in Parliament, representing the eastern Maori consituency. His advocacy of Maori interests under Prime Minister Sir Joseph Ward (1909–12) and as minister of native affairs (1928–34) was a major factor behind the improvement of government policy concerning the Maoris during that period.

In 1931 Ngata inaugurated his Maori land development plan, which improved the quality of his people's agriculture and expanded the amount of Maori land under cultivation. His efforts to improve educational opportunities for Maoris included the founding of the Maori Purposes Fund to finance school construction.

Deeply committed to the preservation of the Maori culture, Ngata helped to found the Maori Board of Ethnological Research and served as its chairman from 1928 to 1934. His contributions to Polynesian anthropology included a nine-year term as president of the Polynesian society and his *Nga Moteatea* (1929), largely a collection of songs and chants of the various Maori tribes.

Ngaterian Stage (geology): *see* Clarence Series.

Ngatik, atoll, Ponape district, East Caroline Islands, Trust Territory of the Pacific. Pop. (1970) 449.
5°51′ N, 157°16′ E
·Micronesian Ponapean cultural link **12**:122d

Ngawen Chandi, a Javanese Buddhist temple consisting of five shrines, each facing East.
·architectural plan and Buddha symbology **17**:266d

Ngbaka, also called BWAKA, native tribe of northwestern Zaire.
·mask and figure carving **1**:276c

Ngbandi, Niger-Congo-speaking people of the Eastern Sudan. Their subsistence is based on agriculture, fishing, and river trading. They occupy compact villages, each of which is under the authority of a headman. Descent, inheritance, and succession follow the male line.
·mask and figure carving **1**:276c
·peoples of the eastern Sudan map **6**:165

Ngbanye (chiefdom): *see* Gonja.

NGC (astronomical list): *see* New General Catalogue of Nebulae and Clusters of Stars.

NGC 224: *see* Andromeda Nebula.

NGC 1952: *see* Crab Nebula.

NGC 1976: *see* Orion Nebula.

NGC 2070: *see* 30 Doradus.

NGC 2261: *see* R Monocerotis.

NGC 3372: *see* Eta Carinae.

NGC 4486 (galaxy): *see* M 87.

NGC 5139: *see* Omega Centauri.

NGC 6514: *see* Trifid Nebula.

NGC 6523: *see* Lagoon Nebula.

NGC 6720: *see* Ring Nebula.

NGC 6853: *see* Dumbbell Nebula.

NGC 7000: *see* North America Nebula.

Ngelengwa (African ruler): *see* Msiri.

Ng-gokha River, part of Okavango drainage system, Botswana.
19°05′ S, 22°45′ W
·Chief's Island drainage **13**:540e

Nghe An, province (*tinh*) of North Vietnam, situated south of the Red River (Song Hong) Delta. Bounded on the north by Thanh Hoa province, on the west by Laos, on the south by Ha Tinh province, and on the east by the Gulf of Tonkin, it includes the hills bordering Laos and the coastal lowlands of the Song (river) Lo, which flows through the province. The Song Lo Delta is the most densely populated agricultural area, particularly near the city of Vinh. Nghe An was the home province of Ho Chi Minh (*c.* 1890–1969), founder and first president of North Vietnam. Latest census province, 1,221,800.
·provincial population table **19**:133

Ngo Dinh Diem (b. Jan. 3, 1901, Quang Binh province, Vietnam—d. Nov. 2, 1963, Cho Lon), Vietnamese political leader who served as president, with dictatorial powers, of the Republic of Vietnam (South Vietnam) from 1954 until his assassination in 1963.

Diem was born into one of Vietnam's royal families; his ancestors in the 17th century had been among the first Vietnamese converts to Roman Catholicism; he was on friendly terms with the Vietnamese imperial family in his youth and served as the emperor Bao Dai's minister of the interior in the 1930s. In 1945 he was captured by the forces of the Communist leader Ho Chi Minh, who invited him to join his independent government in the North, hoping that Diem's presence would win Catholic support. But Diem rejected the proposal and fled the country, living abroad for most of the next decade.

In 1954 Diem returned to head a U.S.-backed government in South Vietnam. With the south torn by dissident groups and political factions, he established an autocratic regime, staffed at the highest levels by members of his own family. His own Catholicism and his preference for fellow Catholics made him unacceptable to Buddhists, who were an overwhelming majority in South Vietnam. Diem never fulfilled his promise of land reforms, and, during his rule, Communist influence and the power of the Communist-inspired National Liberation Front, or Viet Cong, grew in numbers and in political appeal.

Diem's imprisonment and killing of hundreds of Buddhists, whom he alleged were abetting Communist insurgents, finally persuaded the United States to withdraw its support of him. Diem's generals assassinated him during a coup d'etat.
·Buddhist persecution and politics **3**:413e
·South Vietnam government establishment **9**:760b
·Vietnamese nationalists and France **19**:129f

Ngo Dinh Nhu (1910–63), Vietnamese political leader, brother and chief adviser of Ngo Dinh Diem, president of South Vietnam; both were assassinated in the coup of 1963.
·Vietnamese internal problems **19**:130c

Ngombe, also called NGALA or BANGALA, Bantu-speaking people of the forest region of the middle Congo River. Their subsistence is based on fishing, river trade, and the cultivation of root crops. Ngombe social organization is based on patrilineages, groups of kin related through the male line.

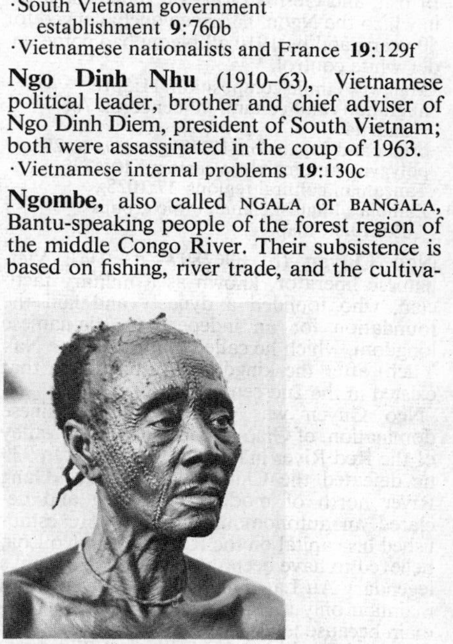
Ngombe woman with facial cicatrization
E. Lebied

·Congo sociocultural groupings **4**:1119a; map
·fish poisoning method **4**:1126f

Ngonde, also called NKONDE, Central African people of Malawi.
·Malawi's ethnic composition **11**:361h

Ngoni, approximately 12 groups of people of the Nguni (*q.v.*) branch of the Bantu, scattered throughout eastern Africa and numbering some 600,000 in the 1970s. Their dispersal was a consequence of the rise of the Zulu Empire early in the 19th century, during which numerous refugee bands moved away from Zululand. One Ngoni chief, Zwangendaba, led his party to Lake Tanganyika; the descendants of his group, the Ngoni cluster proper, now number about 400,000 and are located in northern Malawi, in Zambia, and in southern Tanzania. Another group found its way to Gaza district, Mozambique.

Each Ngoni group formed a small independent state with a central administration based on patrilineal succession. It raided its weaker neighbours for some of its food supply, and, when the fertility of its own cultivated area was exhausted, the group moved elsewhere.

The superior military organization of the Nguni, based, like that of the Zulu, on universal conscription into age-set regiments, enabled them to capture many of the people whose lands they seized or pillaged. Some captives were sold as slaves to Arabs, but many were assimilated into the tribe, some achieving high rank in the army and administration. Despite losses from warfare, the population increased greatly, leading eventually to splits in the state and the dispersal of rival segments.

Internally, each state, at least among Zwangendaba's people, was divided into several such segments, many of which were under the nominal leadership of queens. Selected captives were appointed lieutenants to their lord and might succeed him if he had no son. The settlement pattern was characterized by large, compact villages surrounding a cattle pen. Villages were built quite close to one another and might contain 2,000 or 3,000 inhabitants. A belt of empty no-man's-land surrounded the settled area, separating it from the territories of the tribes raided by the Ngoni.

At the end of the 19th century Portuguese, British, and German forces invaded the areas in which the Ngoni had been unchallenged for 50 years, and by 1910 all Ngoni had come under white control.
·Malawi's ethnic composition **11**:361h
·migrations and cultural influence **6**:97b; map 94
·origin and expansion **17**:281g *passim* to 283a
·polygyny and marriage customs **10**:479f
·Tanzanian cultural regions **17**:1028g
·Zambia's linguistic and ethnic groups **19**:1132h; map

Ngo Quyen (b. 896/897—d. 944), Vietnamese liberator, known as a military tactician, who founded a dynasty and laid the foundation for an independent Vietnamese kingdom, which he called Nam Viet (*see* Nan Yüeh) after the kingdom by that name that existed in the 2nd century BC.

Ngo Quyen was prefect, under Chinese domination, of Giao-chi province in the valley of the Red River in northern Vietnam. In 939 he defeated the Chinese at the Bach Dang River north of modern Haiphong and declared an autonomous kingdom. He established his capital on the Red River at Co Loa, believed to have been the capital of Vietnam's legendary Au Lac dynasty. Ngo Quyen could maintain only a tenuous control over his domain because feudal lords, known as *su quan*, refused to cooperate with his centralized authority. They tried to wrest power from Ngo Quyen, who barely managed to save the throne for his successors.

Ngo Quyen's military tactics, used to expel the Chinese in 939, were imitated by later generals in the course of Vietnamese history. His reign marked a turning point for Vietnam. Although China attacked repeatedly for centuries, the kingdom of Nam Viet remained autonomous until the French seized control in the 19th century. Ngo Quyen's heirs, however, proved unable to maintain a unified state. After his death, Duong-Binh Vuong Tam-Kha usurped the throne for a time before Ngo Quyen's two sons, Ngo Nam-Tan Vuong Xuong-Van and Ngo Thien-Sach Vuong Xuong-Ngap, established a joint rule that lasted until the collapse of the Ngo dynasty in 954.
·Vietnam independence from China **19**:122g

Ngorongoro Crater, extinct volcanic crater in the Great Rift Valley, northern Tanzania, 115 mi (185 km) west of the town of Arusha. The crater rim rises to 7,800 ft (2,400 m), while its floor (126 sq mi [326 sq km]) is 5,577 ft below the rim. The game-filled crater is the focus of one of Africa's major parks, Ngorongoro Conservation Area (established 1956), and has an overwhelming "crater-of-the-Moon" appearance.
3°10′ S, 35°35′ E
·map, Tanzania **17**:1027
·Tanzania's physical features **17**:1025g

Ngouabi, Marien (1938–77), president (1969–77) of the Congo.
·Congo (Brazzaville) political trends **3**:1100h
·Congo political system **4**:1118c

N'Gounié, administrative *région*, Gabon. Pop. (1975 est.) 124,830.
·area and population table **7**:819
·map, Gabon **7**:821

Ngo Van Chieu, also called LE VAN TRUNG (b. 1878, Binh Tay, Vietnam—d. 1926, Tay Ninh), founder of the Vietnamese religious sect Cao Dai (*q.v.*), or Third Amnesty of God.

Ngo Van Chieu was graduated from a provincial college in My Tho and entered the colonial immigration service, where he served until 1902. During a séance he received a revelation that called him to perform a religious mission. After a period of study and meditation, he announced the formation of Cao Dai (Taoist term for supreme being).

The sect, formally established in 1926, contains elements of Confucianism, Taoism, Buddhism, and Roman Catholicism. Its hierarchy is headed by a pope, an office held by Ngo Van Chieu until his death.

Ngoy, Kingdom of, Central African Bantu state founded about the 16th century.
·Congo political structures **3**:1094d; map 1092

Ngozi, town and province, northern Burundi. Pop. (1970 est.) town, 5,000.
2°54′ S, 29°50′ E
·map, Burundi **3**:528
·province population growth 1965–70 table **3**:529

Ngugi wa Thiong'o, formerly called JAMES NGUGI (b. 1938, Limuru, Kenya), one of East Africa's leading writers, whose popular *Weep Not, Child* (1964) was the first published novel in English by an East African author. The work, awarded prizes at the Festival of Negro Arts in Dakar, Senegal, in 1965, and by the East African Literature Bureau, exemplifies Ngugi's thesis that it is the duty of the artist to give moral direction and vision to the struggles of an exploited people.

Weep Not, Child tells the story of a Kikuyu family drawn further and further into the struggle for Kenyan independence during the state of emergency and the Mau Mau rebellion. A different aspect of the same period is explored in *A Grain of Wheat* (1967), generally held to be artistically more mature, which focusses on the many social, moral, and racial issues of the struggle for independence. Ngugi's novel *The River Between* (1965), actually written before the others, tells of lovers kept apart by the conflict between Christianity and traditional ways and beliefs and seems to advocate a return to older values. All three novels have a noteworthy sincerity, and the characters are sympathetically sketched.

In addition to novels, Ngugi has written several plays, of which *The Black Hermit* (published 1968) is considered by some to be his best. His short stories have appeared in many journals and anthologies, and he has edited two literary magazines, *Penpoint* (during his student days at Makerere University College, Kampala, Uganda, from which he graduated with honours in English) and *Zuka: A Journal of East African Creative Writing*.

After doing graduate work at the University of Leeds, in England, he served as lecturer in English at University College, Nairobi, Kenya, and on the staff of Northwestern University, Evanston, Ill., later becoming head of the Department of Literature at the University of Nairobi. On Dec. 31, 1977, he was arrested and on Jan. 12, 1978, detained under public security regulations, no reason being given for the action.
·East African literature development **1**:241a

Ngum River, Laotian NAM NGUM, stream in Vientiane province, central Laos.
18°09′ N, 103°06′ E
·map, Laos **10**:675
·Mekong River area hydroelectric project **11**:862g; map 861

Nguni, a group of Bantu-speaking peoples of southern Africa, numbering some 12,250,000 in the late 1970s; they comprise the largest ethnic division of the Bantu peoples. Before the early 19th century the Nguni are thought to have been confined largely to the present South African provinces of Natal, Cape of Good Hope, and Transvaal. Later, however, they expanded north in a series of migrations. Three main groups may presently be distinguished: (1) the southern Nguni, occupying approximately the original homeland, including the Zulu, Swazi, and Xhosa (*qq.v.*); (2) the Ndebele (*q.v.*) of Matabeleland, southern Rhodesia; (3) the Ngoni (*q.v.*) of northern Malawi, Zambia, southern Tanzania, and Gaza district, Mozambique. The latter two groups moved out of the Natal area early in the 19th century to escape Zulu domination.

Nguni economy relies both on cultivation and animal husbandry. Corn (maize) is a staple, and millet, beans, sweet potatoes, groundnuts (peanuts), bananas, and other crops are of varying importance in different localities. Cattle are kept for their milk, as a store of value, and for bride-price payments; they are usually taboo for women, so that only men are allowed to do the herding and milking.

Polygyny is common, the choice of spouse being circumscribed by strict rules of exogamy; first cousin marriages are prohibited, as are marriages with a member of the patrilineal kin group of either parent. Descent, succession, and inheritance follow the male line. Wives rank in status according to the order in which they married the male family head, and only the first two (three, among the Ndebele and Zulu) occupy separate huts. Each senior wife is allocated land and livestock, which her eldest son inherits. On the death of her husband, a widow goes to live with, but does not marry, her husband's younger brother, any children she subsequently bears being regarded as offspring of the dead husband.

All of the Nguni groups manifest a considerable degree of political development. Important officeholders were originally (and among some groups continue to be) patrilineal kinsmen of the senior lineage. The great Zulu chief Shaka, however, established his power on a personal and military basis, imposing himself as the supreme religious and political authority in the early 19th century. His army was composed of regiments consisting of men of a particular age group; these were stationed in barracks, their members being forbidden to marry until the King gave collective permission. The Ndebele and Swazi later adopted a similar pattern of state and military organization.
·numbers, tribal affiliations, and culture **6**:110d; map

·South Africa ethnic composition map **17**:66
·South African geographic distribution **17**:66h
·Swaziland ethnic populations **17**:843d

Nguru, town, Bornu Province, North-Eastern State, northern Nigeria, near the Hadejia River, a seasonal tributary of the Komadugu Yobe, which flows into Lake Chad. It lies at the end of the railway that runs from Lagos through Kano, and it has road connections to Gashua, Hadejia town, Gumel, Matsena, and Yamia (Niger).

Precisely when the town was founded is unknown, but by the early 16th century it had been incorporated into the Bornu kingdom (*see* Kanem-Bornu) of the Kanuri people and was the seat of the *galadima*, the Bornu governor of the western provinces. Its location in the disputed area between the Hausa states and Bornu led it to be temporarily occupied by the forces of Muḥammad Kisoki, the Hausa king (1509–65) of Kano, 149 mi (240 km) west-southwest. It was also the site *c.* 1561 of the major victory by Kebbi, a Hausa state to the west, over Bornu; but Bornu regained the town shortly thereafter. Nguru was once again the seat of the *galadima c.* 1808, when Fulani warriors almost destroyed the town in their victorious *jihād* ("holy war").

Nguru, now in Bornu emirate, has prospered since the arrival of the railroad in 1929. Probably Nigeria's major collecting point for gum arabic, it also ships peanuts (groundnuts), cotton, hides, and skins by rail to Lagos. A modern abattoir and refrigeration plant was built there in the 1960s. The town also serves as the chief trade centre (guinea corn, millet, peanuts, cowpeas, cotton) for the environs' predominantly Muslim Kanuri, Bede (Bedde), and Manga peoples. It has a government hospital and a dispensary. Pop. (1972 est.) 53,999.
12°52′ N, 10°27′ E
·map, Nigeria **13**:87

Nguyen Ai Quoc (Vietnamese political leader): *see* Ho Chi Minh.

Nguyen Anh (Vietnamese emperor): *see* Gia Long.

Nguyen Bun Dao (Vietnamese emperor): *see* Khai Dinh.

Nguyen Cao Ky (b. Sept. 8, 1930, Son Tay, northern Vietnam), controversial South Vietnamese military and political leader known for his flamboyant manner and overbearing policies.

A member of the French forces that opposed the Vietnamese liberation movement, Ky joined the South Vietnamese air force after the nation was partitioned in 1954. He attracted much attention because of his vehement anti-Communism, as well as his bravado, and was highly favoured by U.S. advisers in Vietnam. As a result he was named commander of South Vietnam's air force after the 1963 overthrow of the Ngo Dinh Diem government. With U.S. aid, Ky soon built up a fighting force of 10,000 men.

In June 1965 Ky, together with Maj. Gen. Nguyen van Thieu and Gen. Duong van Minh, led a military coup in unseating the government of Premier Phan Huy Quat. As the head of that triumvirate, Ky's authoritarian policies provoked widespread opposition. In 1967 the top military leaders reached an agreement by which Thieu would run for president and Ky for vice president of a new regime. Unhappy with his new position, Ky became an outspoken critic of Thieu's administration. In 1971 he attempted to oppose Thieu for the presidency but was forced to step out of the race and returned to the air force.

His book *Twenty Years and Twenty Days* was published in 1976.
·Vietnamese military regime **19**:130d

Nguyen Du, in full NGUYEN-DU THANH-HIEN, pen name TO NHU (b. 1765, Tien Dien, Vietnam—d. Aug. 10, 1820, Hue), best loved poet of the Vietnamese and creator of the poem *Kim Van Kieu*, written in *chu-nom* (southern characters), an epic that is admired as literature by Vietnamese of all political persuasions.

Considered by some to be the father of Vietnamese literature, Nguyen Du passed the mandarin examinations at the age of 19 and succeeded to a modest military post under the Le dynasty. He served the Le rulers, as his family had done for generations, until their dynasty (1428–1787) fell before the rebellion led by the Tay Son brothers (*q.v.*) that destroyed the power of the northern-based Trinh and nearly destroyed the Nguyen lords in the south of the country. Nguyen Du was for a period linked with efforts to restore the Le to power, but, unable to achieve this goal, he withdrew to the mountains of Hong Linh near his native village. When in 1802 the new Nguyen ruler Gia Long succeeded in uniting the country and called Nguyen Du to court, he reluctantly obeyed and later held many official posts.

While serving in Quang Binh in northern Vietnam in 1813, he attained the rank of Column of the Empire and was subsequently appointed head of a delegation to Peking. During this mission he translated a Chinese novel, dating from the Ming period, into Vietnamese poetry as *Kim Van Kieu* (English translation by Huynh Sanh Thong, *The Tale of Kieu: The Classic Vietnamese Verse Novel*; 1973). As an exploration of the Buddhist doctrine of karmic retribution for individual sins, his poem expresses his personal suffering and deep humanism. He also wrote "Words of a Young Hat Seller," a shorter poem in a lighter vein; *Chieu Hon* ("Address to the Dead"); and many others written in Chinese rather than Vietnamese.

Nguyen Du was assigned to two other ambassadorial missions to Peking; before he could depart on the last one, he died of a long illness for which he stoically refused treatment.
·popular style and Chinese influence **17**:235f
·Vietnamese modern cultural development **19**:144b

Nguyen dynasty (1802–1945), the last Vietnamese dynasty.

Although Vietnam was nominally under the rule of the Later Le dynasty (*q.v.*) from 1428 to 1788, it had actually been divided between the Trinh family in the north and the Nguyen family in the south by the middle of the 16th century. A peasant revolt, begun in 1771 and led by the Tay Son brothers (*q.v.*), overthrew the power of the two great feudal clans. But Nguyen Anh, the surviving heir of the Nguyen family, managed to retain a piece of territory in the south and, with French aid, finally suppressed the rebellion and established the Nguyen dynasty. He ruled Vietnam as emperor under the name Gia Long (*q.v.*).

Modelling their administration after that of the Chinese Ch'ing dynasty (1644–1911), the Nguyen, particularly after Gia Long's death in 1820, followed a conservative policy that opposed foreign missionary activity in Vietnam. The French, partly as a result of this anti-missionary policy, invaded Vietnam in 1858, initially landing at Tourane (Da Nang), and then established a base at Saigon. They forced the emperor Tu Duc (*q.v.*), then facing revolts elsewhere, to cede the three eastern provinces of southern Vietnam, called Cochinchina (*q.v.*) by the French, to France in 1862. Five years later the French gained control of all Cochinchina. French control over the whole of Vietnam was established following invasions in 1883–85, and Vietnam's ancient vassalage relationship with China was ended. The Nguyen dynasty was, however, retained in Hue with nominal control over central Vietnam, called Annam (*q.v.*) by the French, and over northern Vietnam, called Tonkin (*q.v.*) by the French. Cochinchina, in contrast, had the status of a colony. The French continued to dominate the throne until 1945, when the last emperor, Bao Dai (*q.v.*), abdicated, following the Vietnamese Nationalist forces' proclamation of independence. Bao Dai served as chief of state from 1949 until he was deposed by Ngo Dinh Diem in a national referendum in 1955.
·Ch'ing dynasty's support of Le dynasty **4**:355g
·Vietnamese political division **19**:124a

Nguyen family, powerful Vietnamese family that emerged into prominence in the 16th century, when Vietnam was under the Le dynasty (*see* Later Le dynasty). The family is the predecessor of the Nguyen dynasty (*q.v.*).

After Mac Dang Dung usurped the Vietnamese throne in 1527 (*see* Mac family), Nguyen Kim fought to restore a Le emperor in 1533, leaving the Mac in power in the northern section of the country. Members of the Nguyen family acted as mayors of the palace to the weak Le rulers, but by the mid-16th century this role passed to the Trinh family (*q.v.*), and Nguyen power became associated with the southernmost sections of the Vietnamese state. Long-standing rivalry between the Nguyen and the Trinh became open warfare in 1620, with hostilities continuing intermittently until 1673. By that date both families accepted a de facto division of the Vietnamese state.

Although never accorded royal status by the Chinese, the Nguyen ruled over southern Vietnam in an essentially independent fashion. During the 17th and 18th centuries the Nguyen encouraged Vietnamese settlement into lands formerly occupied by the Chams and the Cambodians. Champa ceased to exist as a state, and Cambodian control over the Mekong River Delta region was eroded. Among the more outstanding of the Nguyen lords during this period was Nguyen Phuoc Tan (Hien Vuong; *q.v.*).

Nguyen power in southern Vietnam was challenged and nearly eclipsed by the revolt of the Tay Son brothers (*q.v.*) that broke out in 1771. A young prince, Nguyen Anh, survived to lead an eventual recovery of Nguyen territory and finally to become the emperor Gia Long (*q.v.*), who ruled over the whole of Vietnam from 1802 and was the founder of the Nguyen dynasty.

Nguyen Hue (Vietnamese revolutionary leader and emperor): *see* Tay Son brothers.

Nguyen Huu Tho (b. Aug. 10, 1910, Cho Lon, southern Vietnam), president of the National Liberation Front (NLF), the South Vietnamese guerrilla organization formed in 1960 in opposition to the U.S.-backed Saigon government.

The son of a rubber plantation manager killed during the First Indochina War (1946–54), Nguyen Huu Tho studied law in Paris in the 1930s. Returning to Saigon, he set up practice, remaining politically inactive until 1949, when he led student demonstrations against the French; he also organized protests in 1950 against the patrolling of the South Vietnamese coast by U.S. warships. Imprisoned, he won popular acclaim for his prolonged hunger strike in protest of the war.

After the Geneva Agreements had divided Vietnam into northern and southern zones in 1954, Tho cooperated with the southern regime of Ngo Dinh Diem until he was arrested for advocating nationwide elections on reunification. Except for a short interval in 1958, Tho remained in prison from 1954 to 1961, when he escaped with the aid of some of his anti-Diem followers. These men formed the National Liberation Front that same year, making Tho, a non-Communist, provisional and then full-time chairman.

Tho's guerrilla forces began to register massive gains against the South Vietnamese government. But after 1964, when increased U.S. military intervention caused the Hanoi regime to commit its own forces to the battle in the South, Tho's control over the NLF grew weaker. In June 1969 the NLF established a Provisional Revolutionary Government (PRG) with Huynh Tan Phat as president and Nguyen Huu Tho as chairman of its advisory council. The PRG, in effect, became the government of South Vietnam in April 1975, when the Saigon government's troops surrendered to the North Vietnamese and PRG forces.

Nguyen Khanh (b. 1927), military and political leader who participated in a successful coup d'etat against the South Vietnamese dictator, Pres. Ngo Dinh Diem, in 1963 and served briefly as president of South Vietnam in 1964.

Khanh served in the French colonial army until 1954 and rose through the ranks of the Vietnamese Army to become chief of staff to Gen. Duong van Minh. He joined Duong van Minh and other high military officials in deposing Diem by assassination on Nov. 1, 1963, and led a counter-coup against Minh in 1964. Khanh administered the government of the Republic of Vietnam in January–October 1964. His regime was undermined by several coups; he himself resigned once. After Gen. Nguyen Cao Ky took control of the government in February 1965, Khanh was named roving ambassador but was, in effect, exiled to France.

Nguyen Lu (Vietnamese revolutionary leader): *see* Tay Son brothers.

Nguyen Nhac (Vietnamese revolutionary leader): *see* Tay Son brothers.

Nguyen Phuoc Chi Dam (Vietnamese emperor): *see* Minh Mang.

Nguyen Phuoc Hoang Nham (Vietnamese emperor): *see* Tu Duc.

Nguyen Phuoc Tan (Vietnamese ruler): *see* Hien Vuong.

Nguyen Thai Hoc (1904–1930), leader of the Viet Nam Quoc Dan Dang (*q.v.*; Vietnamese Nationalist Party), a revolutionary organization that ordered a general Vietnamese uprising against the French on the night of Feb. 9, 1930. Its failure resulted in the beheading of Nguyen Thai Hoc and 12 of his collaborators on June 17.
·Vietnamese resistance to France **19**:128b

Nguyen That Thanh (Vietnamese political leader): *see* Ho Chi Minh.

Nguyen Tri Phuong (b. 1806, near Saigon —d. Nov. 20, 1873, Hanoi), general dedicated to protecting Vietnam from European influence and military conquest by France; he was a conservative and a close adviser to the emperor Tu Duc (reigned 1847–83).

The son of a provincial administrator, Nguyen Tri Phuong entered the military service and distinguished himself by repelling the Siamese invasion of Chau Doc, on the Cambodian border, and recapturing nearby Ha Tien. At the death of Gen. Truong Minh Giang in 1841, Nguyen Tri Phuong was named as successor and became viceroy of lower Cochinchina (modern southern South Vietnam).

Nguyen Tri Phuong linked himself to the monarchy by arranging the marriage of one of his daughters to Tu Duc, becoming one of the most powerful ministers at the court of Hue. Together, he and Tu Duc kept Vietnam closed to the West but, in refusing to adopt Western technology, left the country backward and vulnerable to conquest by the French.

Nguyen Tri Phuong delayed French conquest by his stubborn defense against Adm. Charles Rigault de Genouilly at Tourane (now Da Nang) in 1859, but he was decisively beaten in 1861 by Adm. Léonard Charner at Chi Hoa, near Saigon, and France was ceded several southern provinces. His final defeat in 1873 occurred in the defense of the Hanoi citadel. Taken prisoner, he availed himself of a traditional Vietnamese means of political and moral protest by tearing at his bandages and starving himself to death.

Nguyen Truong To (b. 1828, Nghe An province, Vietnam—d. 1871), an early advocate of modernization and political reform in Vietnam who was among the first Vietnamese to travel abroad and to realize the adjustments his country needed in order to survive.

A convert to Roman Catholicism, Nguyen Truong To travelled with French priests to Italy and France; upon his return to Vietnam in the 1860s, he was received by Emperor Tu Duc, to whom he advocated modernization. In 1866 Tu Duc sent him back to Europe as an official emissary to purchase equipment and to engage Western specialists for the introduction of modern technology into Vietnam. The project, however, was never realized because the French conquest of southern Vietnam in 1867 persuaded the Emperor, on the advice of his mandarins, to pursue a policy of isolation from the West.

Nguyen Truong To advocated stringent political and economic reforms, fighting the conservative elements at court. He urged a reduction in the number of officials and an increase in their responsibilities and salaries in order to fight corruption. He also advocated political cooperation with all foreign powers on the basis of equality to prevent any single power from gaining ascendancy. His other suggestions included the governmental, social, and educational reforms and the use of Western technological knowledge and scientific equipment in order to exploit the natural resources of the country.

Nguyen Truong To's repeated demands brought severe reprisals from the court. Vietnam's leaders refused to listen to his reasoning; they closed their minds to the problems facing them and tried in vain to keep the modern world out of the country.

Nguyen Van Hieu, pen name KHAI MINH (b. 1922, Ca Mau Peninsula, southern Vietnam), roving minister for the National Liberation Front (NLF), political wing of the Viet Cong guerrilla forces in South Vietnam during the Indochina War, who became well-known through his goodwill tours abroad and through his writings. Nguyen Van Hieu began his career as a journalist and participated in the uprisings in 1945 against the French in his native region. During Pres. Ngo Dinh Diem's purges in 1958, he was forced to go underground, and he joined the NLF. In the early 1970s Nguyen Van Hieu, with his wife, Ma Thi Chu, shared a number of positions in the Communist-dominated NLF.

Nguyen Van Thieu (b. April 5, 1923, Ninh Thuan, Vietnam), president of the Republic of Vietnam (South Vietnam) from 1967 until the government of the republic fell to the Viet Cong (*q.v.*) in 1975.

The son of a small landowner, Thieu joined the Communist-oriented Viet Minh in 1945 but later fought for the French colonial regime against the Viet Minh. In 1954 he was put in charge of the Vietnamese National Military Academy and, after 1956, continued to serve under the regime of Ngo Dinh Diem.

Thieu played an important part in a successful coup against Diem in 1963. In 1965 he became chief of state in a military government headed by Premier Nguyen Cao Ky. In 1967 he was elected president under a new constitution promulgated in that year. He was reelected without opposition in 1971.

Thieu's emergence coincided with the beginning of major U.S. intervention in the war against the Viet Cong insurgents and North Vietnam. Despite criticism of the authoritarian nature of his regime, he retained the support of the United States throughout the administrations of the U.S. presidents Lyndon B. Johnson and Richard M. Nixon. He continued to consolidate his power after the peace agreements of 1973 (in which his government was a somewhat reluctant participant) and the withdrawal of U.S. troops.

Communist gains in the northern provinces early in 1975 prompted him to recall troops to defend the capital city, Saigon. Badly managed, the retreat turned to a rout, allowing Communist forces to surround the capital. After resisting for several days, Thieu was persuaded that his resignation might permit a negotiated settlement of the war. On April 21, 1975, in a speech denouncing the United States, he resigned in favour of his vice president, Tran Van Huong, and shortly afterward left the country.
·political arrest of religious leaders **15**:611d
·Vietnamese governmental opponents **19**:130e

Nguyen Van Thinh (d. Nov. 10, 1946, Saigon), Vietnamese statesman who in 1946 served briefly as president of a French-controlled government of Cochinchina (southern Vietnam).

Thinh was a French citizen—a privilege granted to select Vietnamese nationals during the French rule of Vietnam. After World War II he helped plan an allegedly free Vietnamese republic created by the French in early 1946. Thinh's official title was president of the provisional government of the Republic of Cochinchina, but the republic was actually controlled by the French. Feeling dishonoured by his ineffectual role, Thinh committed suicide.

Nguyen Vinh Thuy (Vietnamese emperor): *see* Bao Dai.

Ngwenya, peak rising to 6,001 ft (1,829 m) in the Highveld of western Swaziland.
26°11′ S, 31°02′ S
·Highveld physical geography **17**:842e

nha nhac, Vietnamese court music of the 15th to the 18th century, performed by two orchestras, one in the upper hall of the court and the other in the lower hall.
·Vietnamese adoption of Chinese music **17**:239h

Nha Trang, meaning WHITE HOUSE, autonomous municipality (*thi xa*), port city, and provincial seat, Khanh Hoa province, southeastern Vietnam. The city lies at the mouth of the Song (river) Cai, 256 mi (412 km) northeast of Saigon.

Its history is known back to the 3rd century AD when, as part of the independent land of Kauthara, a Champa kingdom, it acknowledged the suzerainty of Funan. In 1653 it was incorporated into the territory of the lords of Vietnam and after 1802 into the kingdom of Vietnam. After 1862 Nha Trang was acquired by the French, who in 1895 established there the Pasteur Institute for research in tropical diseases. In 1912 the Saigon–Hanoi railway reached the town.

As a port, Nha Trang has only limited facilities. It has, however, a fine, sandy beach, and under the French it became a seaside resort. On the north bank of the Song Cai, opposite Nha Trang, is the village of Thon Cu Lao, behind which, on a granite knoll, sits Po Nagar (Lady of the City), a well-preserved cluster of four Cham shrines dedicated to Śiva and erected or rebuilt between the 7th and 12th century. Pop. (1973 est.) 216,200.
12°15′ N, 109°11′ E
·area and population table **19**:142
·map, South Vietnam **19**:141

Nhāvī (caste): *see* Nāī.

Nhill, town, Wimmera District, Victoria, Australia, founded in 1877. Its name is derived from the Aboriginal *nyell*, meaning "a place of spirits" or "white mist on the water." Situated midway between Melbourne and Adelaide, it is connected to both cities by road and rail. Nhill has a large grain storage facility, a flour mill, and a plastics factory. Pop. (1971) 2,109.
36°20′ S, 141°39′ E

NHL: *see* National Hockey League.

NHM: *see* Netherlands Trading Society.

Nhue Giang, Song, canal flowing north–south for about 70 mi (113 km) through the Ha Dong-Phu Ly district of North Vietnam. It was built just before World War II by the French colonial government to regulate the flow of water in the wet-farming area south of Hanoi, which covers 272,000 ac (110,000 ha) between the Red River (Song Hong in Vietnamese) and the Song Day. The creation of the canal and of the large Song Day barrage, 853 ft (260 m) wide, ensured what was known to the Vietnamese as a "tenth-month" harvest by draining the water. Irrigation water for "fifth-month" crops is supplied by a catch basin and distributed via the canal.

Ni, symbol for the chemical element nickel (*q.v.*).

niacin: *see* nicotinic acid.

niacinamide: *see* nicotinamide.

Niagara, also called NIAGARA-ON-THE-LAKE, town, Lincoln County, southeastern Ontario, Canada, on the southern shore of Lake Ontario, at the mouth of the Niagara River, about 22 mi (35 km) below the falls. The town was established in 1792, when it was chosen as the first capital of Upper Canada and named Newark by Lieutenant Governor John Simcoe. Because of its location opposite a U.S. arsenal, the capital was moved to Toronto in 1796, and its name was changed to Niagara-on-the-Lake. Now most commonly known as Niagara, the town is a summer resort and a centre of a fruit-growing region. Industries include canning, boatbuilding, basket weaving, and the manufacture of jam and marmalade. Ft. George, built in the late 1790s and playing an important role in the War of 1812, and Navy Hall are popular tourist attractions. Pop. (1971) 12,552.
43°15′ N, 79°04′ W

Niagara, Fort, stone fortification built by the French at the mouth of the Niagara River (on the site of the earlier Fort-Conti, built in 1679 but later destroyed), north of present Youngstown, N.Y., in 1726 to guard the fur-trade route to the west. Captured by the British in 1759, it was ceded to the U.S. in 1796 and briefly reoccupied by the British during the War of 1812. It is now a National Historic Landmark and has been restored to its original condition.
·park creation and historic features **13**:58c
·U.S. territory to 1803 map **18**:958

Niagara Bible Conference, an annual summer meeting of U.S. Fundamentalist groups between 1876 and 1899.
·Fundamentalist unification 7:777h *passim* to 780d

Niagara Escarpment, also known as LAKE RIDGE, in North America, extends with breaks for more than 650 mi (1,050 km) from the Door Peninsula (*q.v.*), in eastern Wisconsin, through the Manitoulin Islands in northern Lake Huron, southward across the Bruce Peninsula and then eastward around the southwestern end of Lake Ontario, crossing the Canadian–U.S. boundary at Niagara Falls, and terminating east of Rochester, N.Y., near the town of Sodus. Its forested crest, sloping steeply toward the north, stands from 250 ft (75 m) to 1,000 ft above the surrounding lowlands. Several rivers, notably the Niagara, have cut gorges through the scarp, leaving recessed cataracts, including the famous Niagara Falls. Such cities as Rochester have grown up adjacent to the falls, taking advantage of the cheap power supply. The escarpment also shelters the intensive Niagara fruit belt along the southern shore of Lake Ontario.
·location and landscape significance **13**:574d

Niagara Falls, city, Welland County, in the regional municipality of Niagara, southeastern Ontario, Canada, on the left (west) bank of the Niagara River, opposite Niagara Falls, N.Y. Development of the city, named Elgin in 1853, began with the completion in 1855 of the first suspension bridge across the Niagara Gorge. The city was renamed Clifton in 1856 and received its present name in 1881. In 1963 it merged with Stamford Township, increasing its area 12-fold. Niagara Falls' importance is due largely to the cataract, a major source of electrical power for Ontario, and one of the nation's most popular tourist attractions. Now connected to Niagara Falls, U.S., by three bridges, including the Rainbow and Whirlpool Rapids bridges, the city is also a customs port and industrial centre. Manufactures include chemicals, fertilizers, abrasives and refractories, silverware, cereals, machinery, sporting equipment, paper goods, and food products. Niagara Falls is the site of Mount Carmel College. Queen Victoria Park stretches along the bank of the river above and below the falls and includes the Oakes Garden Theatre. Inc. 1904. Pop. (1971) city, 67,163; St. Catherines–Niagara metropolitan area, 303,429.
43°06′ N, 79°04′ W

Niagara Falls, city and port of entry, Niagara County, western New York, U.S., at the great falls of the Niagara River, opposite the city of Niagara Falls, Ont. The site, visited by Fr. Louis Hennepin in 1678, was of strategic importance to the French and British in their struggle for control of the Great Lakes. The British built Ft. Schlosser there in 1761, and in 1805 Augustus Porter established a grist mill and a settlement called Manchester. Both the settlement and the fort were burned during the War of 1812, but development of the surrounding farmlands continued; the villages of Manchester, Suspension Bridge, and Clarksville (later to merge into Niagara Falls) grew up along the river. Hydropower was developed in 1881, and with the formation of the Niagara Falls Power Company in 1886 the industrial future of the city was assured. Its hydroelectric plants (among the world's largest) now supply power to much of the state and to the city's electrochemical, electrometallurgical, and aerospace industries. Other manufactures include paper, abrasives, flour, machinery, and electrical equipment.

The New York State Niagara Reservation (established 1885) includes Prospect Park and areas along the river, including Luna, Goat, and other smaller islands. Tourism is a major economic factor, with millions of visitors a year. Rainbow Bridge, completed in 1941 to replace the Falls View Bridge that collapsed in 1938, is one of several that cross the river downstream from the falls. Niagara County Community College was founded there in 1963, and Niagara University (1856) is just outside the city limits. Tuscarora Indian Reservation is 5 mi (8 km) northeast. Inc. city, 1892. Pop. (1980) 71,384.
43°06′ N, 79°02′ W
·map, United States **18**:908

Niagara Falls (U.S.–Canada): *see* Niagara River and Falls; Horseshoe Falls.

Niagara Frontier, recreation area in western New York, U.S., extends mainly along the Niagara River between Lakes Ontario and Erie and lies in the counties of Erie and Niagara and part of Cattaraugus. The centre of the region is the Niagara Reservation (435 ac [176 ha]) established in 1885 at Niagara Falls. New York's oldest state park, it includes an observation tower, elevators that descend into the gorge at the base of the American Falls, and boat trips into the turbulent waters at the base of the Horseshoe Falls.

Fort Niagara State Park (284 ac), at the mouth of the Niagara River on Lake Ontario, includes old Ft. Niagara (also known as the Castle) built by the French (1725–27); a few miles to the east lies the Four Mile Creek Annex to the park (248 ac) devoted largely to camping. Whirlpool State Park (109 ac) is located at the Lower Rapids 3 mi (5 km) north of the falls; and Devil's Hole State Park (42 ac) at the Lower Gorge overlooks the end of the Lower Rapids. Buckhorn Island State Park (896 ac) is a wildlife sanctuary at the north end of Grand Island, south of the falls. Big Six Mile Creek Boat Basin (19 ac) is on the west side of the island, and Beaver Island State Park (918 ac) is a recreational area at its southern tip. Evangola State Park (733 ac), near Farnham on the south shore of Lake Erie, includes a broad sandy beach 4,000 ft (1,220 m) long.

Robert Moses State Parkway, formerly Niagara Parkway (1,266 ac), links the Grand Island parks with Niagara Falls, Ft. Niagara, and Lake Ontario. The Grand Island South Parkway (88 ac) and West River Parkway (633 ac) combine to form a scenic route around the island and provide a connection with the New York State Thruway, Robert Moses State Parkway, Beaver Island and Buckhorn Island state parks, and Buffalo.
43°02′ N, 78°58′ W

Niagara Gorge, on the Niagara River below Niagara Falls, between Ontario, Canada, and New York state, U.S.
·hydrologic and geologic features **13**:57d

Niagara Movement (1905–10), forerunner of the National Association for the Advancement of Colored People (NAACP); organization of black intellectuals led by W.E.B. Du Bois calling for full political, civil, and social rights for black Americans in contrast to the accommodation philosophy proposed in the "Atlanta Compromise" (*q.v.*) of 1895. In the summer of 1905, 29 prominent Negroes, including Du Bois, met secretly at Niagara Falls, Ont., and drew up a manifesto calling for full civil liberties, abolition of racial discrimination, and recognition of human brotherhood. Subsequent annual meetings were held in such symbolic locations as Harpers Ferry and Boston's Faneuil Hall.

Despite the establishment of 30 branches and the achievement of a few scattered civil rights victories at the local level, the group suffered from organizational weakness and lack of funds as well as a permanent headquarters or staff, and it never was able to attract mass support. After the Springfield (Ill.) Race Riot (*q.v.*) of 1908, however, white liberals joined with the nucleus of Niagara "militants" and founded the NAACP the following year. The Niagara Movement disbanded in 1910, with the leadership of Du Bois forming the main continuity between the two organizations.
·Du Bois's agitation for civil rights **5**:1075d

Niagaran Series, second of the three major divisions of Silurian rocks and time in North America (the Silurian Period began about 430,000,000 years ago and lasted about 35,000,000 years). It was named by James Hall in 1842 for exposures studied in Niagara County, New York. The characteristic exposures for the series are found in the gorge of the Niagara River below Niagara Falls; the gorge is rimmed by a resistant dolomite formation, the Lockport Dolomite, below which fossiliferous shales and thin limestones comprise the remainder of Niagaran rocks in the area. West of the Cincinnati Arch, Niagaran strata are largely calcareous, very widespread, and often attain a considerable thickness. In the Niagaran dolomites of Indiana, Illinois, and Wisconsin, fossil coral reefs are frequently encountered, some of which are about 10 kilometres (6 miles) in diameter and attain a thickness of about 300 metres (1,000 feet).
·Silurian strata correlations, table 3 **13**:920

Niagara River and Falls 13:57, form part of the boundary between the U.S. and Canada. The river, flowing in a northerly direction for 35 mi (56 km) from Lake Erie to Lake Ontario, acts as the drainage outlet for the four Upper Great Lakes, whose aggregate basin area is about 260,000 sq mi (673,000 sq km). The falls, an important source of hydroelectric power and one of North America's most famous spectacles, lie between the cities of Niagara Falls, N.Y., and Niagara Falls, Ont. They are divided into the Horseshoe Falls, adjoining the left, or Canadian, bank (height 162 ft [49 m]; length of crest 2,600 ft), and the smaller American Falls, adjoining the right bank (height 167 ft; crest length 1,000 ft).

The text article covers the physical evolution and contemporary environment of the Niagara River and Falls and their human exploitation.

43°15′ N, 79°04′ W

REFERENCES in other text articles:
- dating by erosion rate estimate **5**:511d
- falls recession and plunge pools **19**:642f
- Grand Trunk Bridge construction **3**:178f *passim* to 179h
- hydrologic features and uses **13**:57c
- power production impact on Ontario **13**:574a
- recession due to rockfalls **6**:64c
- significance and site distinctions **13**:23b
- Steinmetz' plan for electric power **17**:669a
- uniformitarian gorge development **18**:858d

Niah Cave, site of significant archaeological evidence concerning prehistoric man's existence in Southeast Asia, located in Sarawak, Malaysia, 10 miles inland from the South China Sea. The Niah Cave provides examples of early Pleistocene man's habitat in Sarawak and was the site of almost continuous human dwelling until the 19th century. The cave was first described to Westerners in 1864 by Alfred Russell Wallace, the originator, along with Charles Darwin, of the theory of natural selection. Although a Sarawak civil servant visited the cave seven years later, only in the 20th century, following its purchase by the Sarawak Museum, was the importance of the site revealed.

The Niah Cave itself is massive, with five openings, or mouths. The main cave is called the painted cave because of red hematite wall and ceiling paintings. Its mouth is about 100 yards high by 200 yards wide. While other sections of the cave are dark, moist, and inhabited by millions of bats and swiftlets, the painted cave is dry, well lit, and favourable for human dwelling. The first archaeological digging, by Tom Harrisson in 1954, uncovered considerable evidence of past human habitations. The earliest flakes and chopper tools date from *c.* 40,000 BC. The most important discovery at Niah was the remains of a skeleton of an adolescent male, *c.* 38,000 BC, the earliest *Homo sapiens* remains found in the Far East; these bones are of particular interest because this individual lived at the same time as Solo man of Java, the Rhodesioids of Africa, and the classic Neanderthals of Europe—all *Homo sapiens*, but of far less modern looking and gracile (slender) type. Other discoveries include the burial place "boats of the dead."

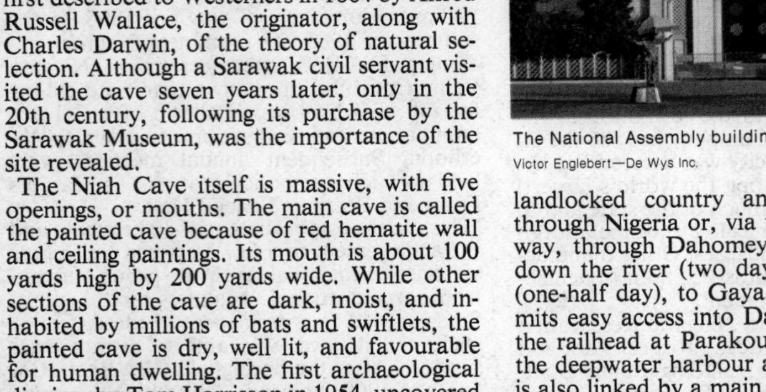

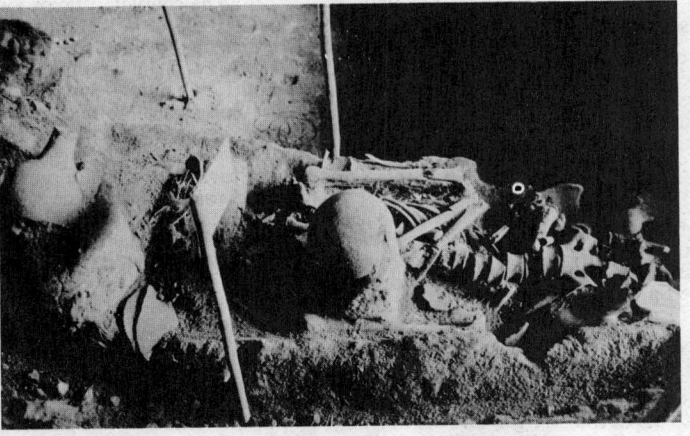

Pot and human skeleton dating from Neolithic Period found in Niah Cave

Nigel Cameron—Rapho Guillumette

nialamide, synthetic drug of the monoamine-oxidase inhibitor type, used to treat mental depression. Like other monoamine-oxidase inhibitor drugs, nialamide prevents the enzymatic breakdown of norepinephrine, the brain-neurotransmitter substance concerned with emotional stimulation. It does so by inhibiting the enzyme monoamine oxidase (MAO), which normally breaks down norepinephrine at nerve endings. Nialamide is administered orally. The onset of action is delayed, the effects of the drug developing slowly over the first two weeks of therapy. As with other monoamine-oxidase inhibitor drugs, liver damage is a possible side effect.
- MAO inhibitor characteristics **17**:693g

Niall of the Nine Hostages (d. 405), Irish king; founder of O'Neill family, a major power in Ulster in the 5th to 7th centuries.
- Irish political development **3**:284e

Niamey, capital of Niger, West Africa. On the Niger River in the southwest corner of the republic, it is important as a commercial and transport centre because the river gives the landlocked country an outlet to the sea through Nigeria or, via the Benin-Niger Railway, through Dahomey. Goods are shipped down the river (two days), or taken by road (one-half day), to Gaya, where a bridge permits easy access into Dahomey and down to the railhead at Parakou, and then by rail to the deepwater harbour at Cotounou. Niamey is also linked by a main east–west highway to Ouagadougou, Upper Volta, and thence to the Ivory Coast, and to Maradi and other main towns in western Niger. It has an international airport.

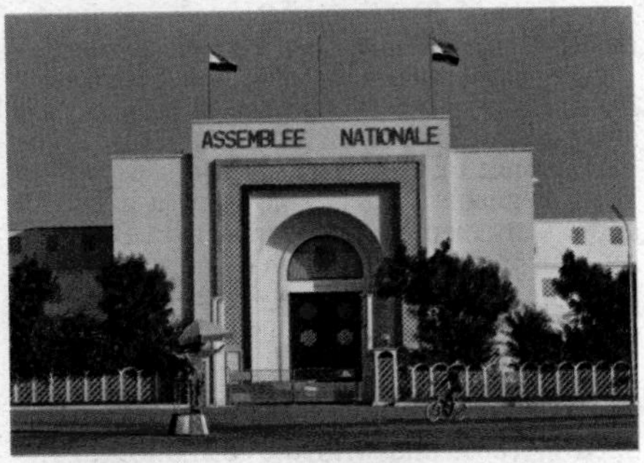

The National Assembly building in Niamey, Niger

Victor Englebert—De Wys Inc.

Niamey was established as a capital in 1926, before which it was a collection of villages of Zerma (Djerma) cultivators. Today it is occupied by Yoruba and Hausa traders, merchants, officials, and craftsmen from Nigeria, Dahomey, and Togo, as well as from other parts of Niger. The city supports some industry and is the site of a training school for civil servants, agricultural and scientific research centres, and a national museum. Pop. (1972 est.) 102,000.

13°31′ N, 2°07′ E
- area and population table **13**:83
- growth and cultural character **13**:82d
- map, Niger **13**:80

Niam-Niam (African peoples): *see* Azande.

Nian-ching-tang-gu-la Shan (China): *see* Nien-ch'ing-t'ang-ku-la Mountains.

Niandan River, tributary of the Niger River, Guinea.
- Niger River's upper tributaries **13**:97a; map 98

Niani, village, Siguiri Region, northeastern Guinea, on the left bank of the Sankarani River (a tributary of the Niger). A former administrative centre of Kangaba (a small state subservient to the old Ghana empire), it was named the capital of the new empire of Mali by its Mandingo (Malinke) founder, King Sundiata Keita (Mari Djata; reigned *c.* 1230–55). Niani remained the capital of the Muslim Mandingo empire for 300 years; it reached its zenith as Mali's political, commercial, and caravan centre (gold, salt, kola nuts, slaves) in the reign of Mansa Mūsā (1307–32). Raids by Songhai cavalrymen in the early 15th century marked the beginning of Niani's gradual decline. The site of the medieval Malian capital was not confirmed until excavations were made by a Guinean–Polish archaeological team in the mid-1960s around present-day Niani, which lies in a valley irrigated for rice and occasionally mined for alluvial gold.

11°23′ N, 8°24′ W

Niantic, North American Indian tribe of the eastern woodland region.
- Woodlands Indian culture **6**:169b

Niari, *région* (first-order administrative subdivision) in eastern Congo (Brazzaville), bordered by Gabon (north) and Zaire (south). The capital is at Dolisie. Main products include gold, maize (corn), sugar cane, palm oil and kernels, peanuts (groundnuts), and bananas.
- area and population table **4**:1116
- map, Congo (Brazzaville) **4**:1114

Niari River, in southern Congo (Brazzaville), rises in the Monts de Cristal (Crystal Mountains) northwest of Brazzaville city. Its 370-mi (600-km) course runs south to Galobondo, west to Loudima, northwest to Makabana, and southwest to the Atlantic Ocean near Kayes, north of Pointe-Noire. Below Makabana its lower course is known as the Kouilou (Kwilu) River. The river is frequently broken by rapids but is navigable for about 40 mi below Kakamoéka. The Niari Basin is rich in copper, lead, and zinc deposits. A large hydroelectric complex on its lower course was planned in the early 1970s.

3°56′ S, 12°12′ E
- coastal drainage basin **4**:1115b
- map, Congo (Brazzaville) **4**:1114

Nias, Indonesian PULAU NIAS, island, Sumatera Utara (North Sumatra) province, Indonesia; it is the largest of a chain paralleling the west coast of Sumatra. With an area of 1,842 sq mi (4,772 sq km), it has a geography much like that of western Sumatra but without volcanoes. The highest elevation is 2,907 ft (886 m). Coasts are rocky or sandy and without any ports, and ships must anchor offshore of Guningsitoli and Telukdalem.

Most of the people are animists, belong to the early (Proto-) Malay stock, and speak dialects of a distinct branch of the Austronesian (Malayo-Polynesian) language family. Some are Christian and Muslim converts. Megalithic mounuments and wooden sculptures honouring the dead or representing fertility symbols are common throughout the island. In north Nias, villages are small and located on hilltops, each enclosing a stone-paved rectangle. Larger villages in south Nias may include a bathing pool. Houses are built on piles, the

chief's house being particularly large with a high roof and massive carved pillars and beams. Latest census 314,829.
1°05′ N, 97°30′ E
·map, Indonesia **9**:460
·musical emphasis on gongs **17**:237h

Niassa, administrative district, northwestern Mozambique (Portuguese East Africa). From 1894 to 1929, it was administered by the Companhia do Niassa and was united administratively with Cabo Delgado 1930–41. It is the least populated district in Mozambique. Vila Cabral is the headquarters.
·Mozambique population distribution **12**:595g
·population and land area table **12**:597

Niaux, archaeological site at Ariège, France, containing black-outlined cave paintings of bison and wild horses.
·cave painting style **17**:704h

Nibbāna (religious goal): *see* Nirvāṇa.

Nibelungen, Die (1924), German Expressionist film directed by Fritz Lang.
·Expressionist elements **12**:506e; illus.

Nibelungenlied, modern accepted title of a Middle High German epic poem written about 1200 by an unknown Austrian from the Danube region. It is preserved in three main 13th-century manuscripts, A (now in Munich), B (St. Gall), and C (Donaueschingen); modern scholarship regards B as the most trustworthy. An early Middle High German title is *Der Nibelunge Nôt* (from the last line of the poem) but does not seem an entirely satisfactory indication of the content of the poem—a dissatisfaction that was evident in the superscription on one of the manuscripts from the early 14th century: "The Book of Kriemhild."

The story has a long history and, as a result, contains a number of disparate elements. For example, the word Nibelung itself presents difficulties. In the first part of the poem, it appears as the name of Siegfried's lands and peoples and his treasure, but, throughout the second, it is an alternate name for the Burgundians.

The poem's content falls into two parts. It begins with two cantos (*aventiuren*) that introduce, respectively, Kriemhild, a Burgundian princess of Worms, and Siegfried, a prince from the Lower Rhine. Siegfried is determined to woo Kriemhild despite his parents' warning. When he arrives in Worms, he is identified by Hagen, a henchman of Kriemhild's brother King Gunther. Hagen then recounts Siegfried's former heroic deeds, including the acquisition of a treasure. When war is declared by the Danes and Saxons, Siegfried offers to lead the Burgundians and distinguishes himself in battle. Upon his return, he meets Kriemhild for the first time, and their affections develop during his residence at court.

At this point a new element is introduced. News reaches the court of a queen of outstanding strength and beauty who may be won only by a man capable of matching her athletic prowess. Gunther decides to woo Brunhild with the aid of Siegfried, to whom he promises the hand of Kriemhild if successful. Siegfried leads the expedition to Brunhild's abode, where he presents himself as Gunther's vassal. In the ensuing contests, Gunther goes through the motions of deeds actually performed by Siegfried in a cloak of invisibility. When Brunhild is defeated, she accepts Gunther as her husband. Siegfried and Kriemhild are then married as promised, but Brunhild remains suspicious and dissatisfied. Soon the two queens quarrel; Brunhild twits Kriemhild for marrying a vassal, and Kriemhild reveals the deception of Brunhild by Siegfried and Gunther.

Now Hagen becomes a prominent figure as he sides with Brunhild and takes the initiative in plotting vengeance. He wins Kriemhild's confidence and learns Siegfried's one vulnerable spot and then strikes the fatal blow.

During these events, Brunhild drops almost unnoticed out of the story, and the death of Siegfried does not appear to be so much vengeance on her part as an execution by Hagen, who is suspicious of Siegfried's growing power. Siegfried's funeral is conducted with great ceremony, and the grief-stricken Kriemhild remains at Worms, though for a long time estranged from Gunther and Hagen. Later they are reconciled in order to make use of Siegfried's treasure, which is brought to Worms. Kriemhild begins to distribute it, but Hagen, fearing her influence will grow, sinks the treasure in the Rhine.

The second part of the poem is much simpler in structure and deals basically with the conflict between Kriemhild and Hagen and her vengeance against the Burgundians. Etzel (Attila), king of the Huns, asks the hand of Kriemhild, who accepts, seeing the possibilities of vengeance in such a union. After many years, she persuades Etzel to invite her brothers and Hagen to his court. Though Hagen is wary, they all go to Etzel's court, where general carnage ensues. With Siegfried's sword Kriemhild slays the bound and defenseless Hagen, who to the last has refused to reveal where Siegfried's treasure is hidden. She in turn is slain by Hildebrand, who is at Etzel's court with his master, Dietrich von Bern.

In the *Nibelungenlied* some elements of great antiquity are discernible. The story of Brunhild appears in Old Norse literature. The brief references to the heroic deeds of Siegfried allude to several ancient stories, many of which are preserved in the Scandinavian *Poetic Edda*, *Völsunga saga*, and *Thidriks saga*, in which Siegfried is called Sigurd. The entire second part of the story, the fall of the Burgundians, appears in an older Eddaic poem, *Atlakvida* ("Lay of Atli"). Yet the *Nibelungenlied* does not appear to be a mere joining of individual stories but, rather, an integration of component elements into a meaningful whole.

It is the second part of the poem that suggests the title "The Book of Kriemhild." The destruction of the Burgundians (Nibelungen) is her deliberate purpose. The climax of the first part, the death of her husband, Siegfried, prepares the ground for the story of her vengeance. Furthermore, Kriemhild is the first person introduced in the story, which ends with her death; and all through the story predominating attention is paid to Hagen. This concentration on Kriemhild and on the enmity between her and Hagen would seem to suggest that it was the poet's intention to stress the theme of Kriemhild's vengeance.

Probably no literary work has given more to Germanic arts than the *Nibelungenlied*. Many variations and adaptations have appeared in recent centuries; a worthy example is Friedrich Hebbel's drama *Die Nibelungen* (1862). The most significant modern adaptation, of course, is Richard Wagner's famous opera *Der Ring des Nibelungen* (1853–74).
·Burgundian conflict with Huns **3**:497b
·Middle High German literary traditions **10**:1116a

Nibelunge Not mit der Klage, Der (1826), collection of German poems edited by Karl Lachmann.
·textual editing of Lachmann **18**:194d

nibhatkhin, Burmese miracle plays based on local folk feasts.
·Burmese musical foundation **17**:238h

niblick (golf): *see* golf club.

Nicaea, Greek name for the modern Turkish city of İznik in eastern Anatolia. Founded in the 4th century BC by the Macedonian king Antigonus I Monophthalmus, it was an important centre in late Roman and Byzantine times.
·Byzantine governments in exile **3**:566f; map 567

Nicaea, councils of, the first and seventh ecumenical councils of the Christian Church. The first Council of Nicaea (325) was called by the emperor Constantine I, an unbaptized catechumen, or neophyte, who presided over the opening session and took part in the discussions. He hoped a general council of the church would solve the problem created in the Eastern Church by Arianism, a heresy first proposed by Arius of Alexandria that affirmed that Christ is not divine but a created being. Pope Sylvester I did not attend the council but was represented by legates.

The council condemned Arius and, with reluctance on the part of some participants, incorporated the nonscriptural word *homoousios* ("of one substance") into a creed (the Nicene Creed) to signify the absolute equality of the Son with the Father. The Emperor then exiled Arius, an act that, while manifesting a solidarity of church and state, underscored the importance of secular patronage in ecclesiastical affairs.

The council also attempted but failed to establish a uniform date for Easter. But it issued decrees on many other matters, including the proper method of consecrating bishops, the condemning of lending money at interest by clerics, and the refusal to allow bishops, priests, and deacons to move from one church to another. Socrates Scholasticus, a 5th-century Byzantine historian, said that the council intended to make a canon enforcing celibacy of the clergy, but it failed to do so when some objected. It also confirmed the primacy of Alexandria and Jerusalem over other sees in their respective areas.

The second Council of Nicaea (787) attempted to resolve the Iconoclastic Controversy initiated in 726, when Emperor Leo III issued a decree against the worship of icons. The council declared that icons deserved reverence and veneration, but not adoration. Convoked by the patriarch Tarasius, the council was attended by delegates of Pope Adrian I, and the Pope confirmed the decrees of the council. Its authority was challenged in France as late as the 11th century, however, partly because certain doctrinal phrases had been incorrectly translated from the Latin documents. But Rome's original verdict was eventually accepted, and the second Council of Nicaea was accepted as the seventh ecumenical council.

Nicaea I (325)
·Basil the Great's orthodox stand **2**:747a
·Christian doctrine and censorship **3**:1085c
·Church character and unity pronounced **6**:294c
·Constantine's condemnation of Arius **15**:1126g
·Constantine's participation and effect **5**:72f
·creedal standard of orthodoxy **5**:244g
·Eastern Orthodox synod concept roots **6**:146f
·Eusebius of Caesaria in disagreement **6**:1130b
·Gregory of Nazianzus' formulations **8**:420c
·issues and ecumenical status **15**:990d
·Mary's devotional status impetus **11**:562a
·Monarchian and Arian heresies **4**:541b
·patristic struggle with Arianism **13**:1082b
·priestly marriages condemned **3**:1043b

Nicaea, empire of, founded in 1204 by Theodore I Lascaris (1208–22) as an independent principality of the fragmented Byzantine Empire; it served as a political and cultural centre from which a restored Byzantium arose in the mid-13th century under Michael Palaeologus.

Theodore fled to Anatolia with other Byzantine leaders after the Latin conquest of Constantinople in 1204, establishing himself at Nicaea, 40 miles to the southeast. Crowned emperor in 1208, Theodore gradually acquired control over much of western Anatolia. He and his successors sponsored a revival of Greek studies at their capital.

The next Nicaean emperor was John Vatatzes, who sought to retake Constantinople before his rivals Theodore Angelus, despot of Epirus, or John Asen II of Bulgaria (1218–41). He defeated Theodore at Klokotnitsa (in Bulgaria) in 1230. Between 1240 and 1250 he negotiated with the Western emperor Frederick II (1220–50) for help in reconquering Constantinople, but nothing came of the pact.

Theodore II Lascaris (1254–58) and John IV Lascaris (1258–61) maintained Nicaean strength against the invading Mongols during their brief reigns. In 1261 a Nicaean general, Michael Palaeologus, retook Constantinople and, as Michael VIII, founded the last dynasty of the Byzantine emperors.

·Byzantine Empire history **3**:566f; maps 563

Nicaragua **13**:58, largest republic of Central America, bounded by Honduras (north), the Caribbean Sea (east), Costa Rica (south), and the Pacific Ocean (west).

The text article covers Nicaragua's relief, drainage and soils, climate, vegetation and animal life, traditional regions, and patterns of settlement, as well as its people and population, national economy, administration and social conditions, cultural life, and prospects for the future. *See also* Central American states, history of; Latin America and the Caribbean, colonial.

REFERENCES in other text articles:
- ·armed forces statistics, table 2 **2**:16
- ·Christian denominational demography map **4**:459
- ·gold production table **8**:239
- ·gross national debt percentage, table 4 **15**:193
- ·Lake Nicaragua and related features **13**:63f
- ·map, North America **13**:177
- ·Meso-American Indian languages **11**:956g; map
- ·newspaper publishing statistics table **15**:237

Nicaragua, Lake **13**:63, Spanish LAGO DE NICARAGUA, the largest freshwater lake of Central America. With an area of 3,190 sq mi (8,262 sq km), it is 110 mi (177 km) long and has an average width of 36 mi.

The text article covers the lake's formation, hydrography, islands, navigation, history, and resources.

11°35′ N, 85°25′ W

REFERENCE in other text article:
- ·map, Nicaragua **13**:61

Nicarao, a Middle American Indian people who inhabited the Pacific coast of Central America in the 16th and 17th centuries.

·Central American cultures **3**:1107f; map

Nicaro, city, Oriente province, eastern Cuba. It is situated on the Bahía de Levisa, a nearly landlocked arm of the Atlantic Ocean, at the base of the Lengua de Pájara peninsula. Nicaro is Cuba's major centre for the refining of nickel and cobalt from nickel oxide, which is mined nearby in the foothills of the Sierra del Cristal. Other economic activities include motor repairing and the processing of dairy products; the city is also the home port of a small fishing fleet. Nicaro is connected by road with other coastal cities, and there is an airport on the peninsula southeast of the city. The area was the scene of major fighting in 1958 during Fidel Castro's revolt against the regime of Fulgencio Batista. Pop. (1970 prelim.) 9,506.

20°42′ N, 75°33′ W

Niccoli, Niccolò (*c.* 1364–1437), wealthy Renaissance Humanist from Florence whose collections of ancient art objects and library of manuscripts of classical works were instrumental in shaping a taste for the antique in 15th-century Italy. He was also an accomplished calligrapher whose slightly inclined *antica corsiva* script influenced the development of italic type. Written with a fairly narrow, rounded nib, Niccoli's script was characterized by a narrowing of the bodies of the letters resulting from a rapid up-and-down movement of the pen.

- ·Humanist calligraphic script type **3**:657c; illus.
- ·libraries history and function **10**:858b

niccolite, an ore mineral of nickel, nickel arsenide (NiAs). Typical occurrences are

NICARAGUA

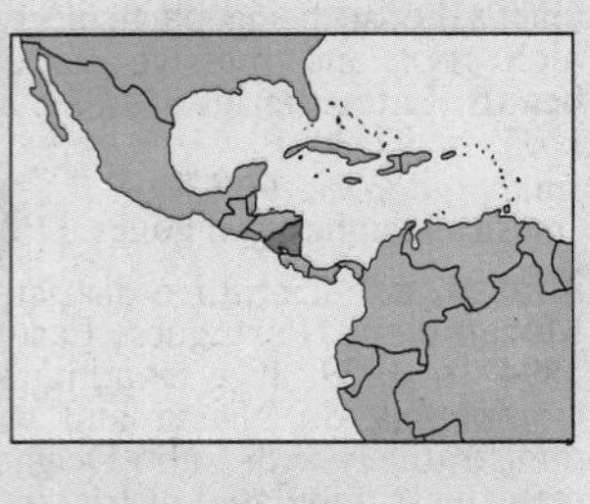

Official name: República de Nicaragua (Republic of Nicaragua).
Location: Central America.
Form of government: republic.
Official language: Spanish.
Official religion: none.
Area: 49,759 sq mi (land area 45,698 sq mi), 128,875 sq km (land area 118,358 sq km).
Population: (1971 census) 1,877,972; (1974 estimate) 2,084,000.
Capital: Managua.
Monetary unit: 1 córdoba = 100 centavos.

Demography

Population: (1974 estimate) density 45.5* per sq mi, 17.6* per sq km; (1975 estimate) urban 47.9%, rural 52.1%; male 49.53%, female 50.47%; (1971) under 15 48.1%, 15–29 25.6%, 30–44 14.1%, 45–59 7.4%, 60–74 3.6%, 75 and over 1.1%.

Vital statistics: (1970–75) births per 1,000 population 48.3, deaths per 1,000 population 13.9, natural increase per 1,000 population 34.4; life expectancy at birth—male 51.2, female 54.6; (1967) major causes of death (per 100,000 population)—senility without mention of psychosis, ill-defined and unknown causes 108.9; gastritis, duodenitis, enteritis, and colitis, except diarrhea of the newborn 49.9; malaria 34.0; homicide and operations of war 29.4.

Ethnic composition (mid-1970s): mestizo, zambo, mulatto 70%, white 17%, black 9%, Amerindian 4%. *Religious affiliation* (1973): Roman Catholic 92%, other 8%.

National accounts

Budget (1975). Revenue: 2,009,800,000 córdobas (indirect taxes 44.1%, of which, sales tax 26.6%, customs 17.5%; direct taxes 13.2%, of which, income tax 8.7%, property tax 2.2%; nontax revenue 6.9%). Expenditures: 2,093,800,000 córdobas (current expenditure 54.0%, of which, purchases and remunerations 33.5%, current transfers 12.1%; capital expenditures 46.0%, of which, direct investment 30.0%, indirect investment 10.0%).

Total national debt (1975): 571,100,000 córdobas. *Tourism* (1973): Receipts from visitors U.S. $10,978,000; expenditures by nationals abroad U.S. $16,768,000.

Domestic economy

Gross national product (GNP; at current market prices, 1974): U.S. $1,310,000,000 (U.S. $650 per capita).

Origin of gross domestic product (at constant prices of 1958):	1963				1973		1974	
	value in 000,000 córdobas	% of total value	labour force	% of labour force	value in 000,000 córdobas	% of total value	labour force	% of labour force
agriculture, forestry, hunting, fishing	806	25.5	283,106	59.7	1,325	24.7	307,417	49.2
mining, quarrying	44	1.4	4,013	0.8	36	0.7	4,144	0.7
manufacturing	578	18.3	55,631	11.7	1,218	22.7	61,849	9.9
construction	80	2.5	15,852	3.3	190	3.5	24,243	3.9
electricity, gas, water, sanitary services	43	1.4	1,264	0.3	95	1.8	3,896	0.6
trade	708	22.4			1,218	22.7	60,745	9.7
finance, insurance, real estate	322	10.2	34,553	7.7	394	7.3	10,973	1.8
transport, storage, communications	180	5.7	12,009	2.5	310	5.8	21,248	3.4
services, including government and defense	399	12.6	67,546	14.2	582	10.8	130,108	20.8
other, not adequately described	...	...	986	0.2	...	...	...	...
total	3,162†	100.0	474,960	100.0†	5,367†	100.0	624,623	100.0

Production (metric tons except as noted, 1974). Agriculture, forestry, hunting, fishing: sugarcane 2,054,000, seed cotton 363,000, bananas 250,000, corn (maize) 193,000, lint cotton 138,000, rice 82,000, sorghum 60,000, dry beans 52,000, coffee 41,600, cassava 18,000; livestock (number of live animals): cattle 2,600,000, pigs 600,000, chickens 3,400,000; roundwood 2,471,000 cu m‡; fish catch 13,900‡. Mining, quarrying: copper concentrate 1,775, gold 2,570 kg, silver 8,397 kg. Manufacturing: sugar 172,000‡; meat 65,000; beer 200,000 hectolitres‡; cigarettes 1,460,000,000 units‡; cement 205,000‡.

Energy: (1970) installed electrical capacity 170,200 kW; (1971) production 649,000,000 kWhr (343 kWhr per capita).

Persons economically active (1974): 624,623 (29.8%), unemployed—no data available.

Price and earnings indexes (1963 = 100):	1964	1965	1966	1967	1968	1969
consumer price index§	104.6	107.6	111.2	113.5	116.6	117.0
hourly earnings index‖	95.0	104.0	166.3	177.0	189.5	...

Land use (1963): total area 13,000,000 ha (forested 49.6%; meadows and pastures 7.1%; agricultural and under permanent cultivation 6.7%; built-on, wasteland, and other 36.6%.

Foreign trade

Imports (1974): U.S. $562,700,000 (chemical and pharmaceutical products 12.5%, machinery and apparatus 11.8%, motor vehicles and spare parts 10.1%, gasoline 9.1%, iron and steel manufactures 7.2%, foodstuffs 6.1%). *Major import sources:* United States 31.7%, Japan 7.4%, West Germany 6.9%, El Salvador 6.5%, United Kingdom 2.7%, The Netherlands 2.2%, Belgium 1.7%, Panama 1.1%.

Exports (1974): U.S. $381,600,000 (raw cotton 35.6%, coffee 11.7%, meat 5.7%, sugar 3.2%, timber 1.6%, bananas 1.4%, seed cotton 1.4%, gold 1.0%). *Major export destinations:* United States 18.9%, West Germany 11.3%, Japan 9.5%, El Salvador 6.3%, The Netherlands 4.6%, Belgium 3.8%, Canada 1.3%.

Transport and communications

Transport. Railroads: (1975) length 235 mi, 378 km; (1974) passenger-mi 13,563,300, passenger-km 21,828,000; short ton-mi cargo 7,576,500, metric ton-km cargo 11,061,500. Roads (1974): total length 8,017 mi, 12,902 km (paved 830 mi, 1,336 km; gravel and crushed stone 697 mi, 1,121 km; earth 2,519 mi, 4,054 km; unimproved 3,971 mi, 6,391 km). Vehicles (1975): passenger cars 29,970, trucks and buses 15,443. Merchant marine (1975): vessels (100 gross tons and over) 26, total deadweight tonnage 45,156. Air transport: (1974) passenger-mi 48,500,000, passenger-km 78,000,000; short ton-mi cargo 1,400,000, metric ton-km cargo 2,000,000; (1976) airports with scheduled flights 7.

Communications. Daily newspapers (1973): total number 6, total circulation 53,000¶, circulation per 1,000 population—no data available. Radios (1973): total number of receivers 125,000 (1 per 16 persons). Television (1973): receivers 63,000 (1 per 32 persons). Telephones (1975): 20,447 (1 per 102 persons).

Education and health

Education (1972–73):	schools	teachers	students	student/teacher ratio
primary (age 7–12)	2,115	8,154	314,425	38.6
secondary (age 13–18)	185	1,578	54,139	34.3
vocational	39	336	5,613	16.7
teacher training	5	93	1,332	14.3
higher	6	694	11,618	16.7

College graduates (per 100,000 population, 1970): 19. *Literacy* (1971): total population literate 57.6%.

Health: (1972) doctors 1,357 (1 per 1,437 persons); (1972) hospital beds 5,017 (1 per 396 persons); (1974) daily per capita caloric intake 2,380 calories (FAO recommended minimum requirement 2,245 calories).

*Density based on land area only. †Detail may not add to total given because of rounding. ‡1973. §Managua only. ‖Manufacturing only. ¶Refers to three dailies only.

with other nickel arsenides and sulfides, as in the Natsume nickel deposits, Japan; Andreas-Berg, E.Ger.; Sudbury, Ont.; and Silver Cliff, Colo. Niccolite is classified in a sulfide mineral group of the AX type, the members of which exhibit a characteristic hexagonal structure. The name, a derivative of the German word *Kupfernickel*, is a reference to subterranean imps (*Nickel*) who teased miners. For detailed physical properties, *see* table under sulfide minerals.

·sulfide mineral physical properties **17**:787f

Niccolò dell'Arca, also known as NICCOLÒ DA BARI (fl. *c.* 1460–94), early Renaissance Italian sculptor famed for his expressionistic use of northern Gothic realism in combination with true compositional principles of Renaissance art. Niccolò takes his name from the tomb (*arca* in Italian) of St. Dominic in the church of S. Domenico, Bologna, where he made the canopy and most of the freestanding figures (1469–94). His masterpiece is the passionately dramatic lamentation over the dead Christ (six figures; 1463, S. Maria della Vita, Bologna). Another terra-cotta sculpture group of the Madonna and saints (1478) is above the main entrance of the Palazzo Comunale in Bologna.

Niccolo di Giovanni di Massio: *see* Gentile da Fabriano.

Nice, Mediterranean tourist centre, capital of Alpes-Maritimes *département*, southeastern France, on the Baie (bay) des Anges, 20 mi (32 km) from the Italian border. Sheltered by beautiful hills, Nice has a pleasant climate and is the leading resort city of the Côte d'Azur, or French Riviera. The Paillon River, now partly built over, separates the new town to the west from the old town, the harbour, and the commercial district to the east. The old town, with narrow winding streets, stands at the western base of a granite hill known as Le Château, although the castle that used to crown it was destroyed in 1706. The harbour, begun in 1750 and extended after 1870, is used by commercial vessels (imports include cereals and vegetable oils), fishing craft, and pleasure boats. There is also a regular passenger service to Corsica. The most striking part of the new town is the famous Promenade des Anglais, which originated in 1822 as a path along the shore built by the English colony. It stretches 2.5 mi (4 km) along the waterfront, and consists of two wide carriageways separated by flower beds and palm trees. Nice has excellent road, rail, and sea communications; the airport is one of the most important in France.

Tourism is the leading commercial activity of the town, both in summer and winter. Numerous festivities are organized every year, the most important being the Carnival of Nice, which was first held in 1873. Industries include food processing, olive oil works, distilleries, and manufacture of perfumes. A flower and fresh-fruit market was established in 1963. Nice is also a growing cultural centre. A university with faculties of law, science, and letters was established in 1965; the Centre Universitaire Méditerranéen (founded 1933; first director, the French poet Paul Valéry) holds conferences on contemporary problems and language studies; and an international art school was established in 1970.

The Musée Jules Chéret des Beaux-Arts and the Musée Masséna have collections of early Italian paintings, and works by 19th-century and contemporary artists. A memorial to the painter Marc Chagall has been built to house a collection of biblical paintings donated by the artist in 1966. A mile northeast of the city centre is the ancient episcopal town of Cimiez, which contains the majestic ruins of a Roman amphitheatre. Nearby stands a 17th-century villa housing an archaeological museum and a collection of more than 40 paintings and drawings by the French artist Henri Matisse.

Founded by the Phocaeans of Marseilles (a colony of Greek mariners) around 350 BC, the city was probably named in honour of a victory (*nikē* in Greek) over a neighbouring colony. Conquered by the Romans during the 1st century AD, it became a busy trading station. The town was held by the counts of Provence during the 10th century, and in 1388 passed under the protection of the counts of Savoy, who held it until 1860, although it was captured and occupied several times by the French during the 17th and 18th centuries. Nice was ceded to France by the Treaty of Turin (1860), after which a referendum ratified the decision. Pop. (1971 est.) 338,300.
43°42′ N, 7°15′ E

·Cavour's cession to France **3**:1032f
·French annexation and its consequences **12**:840g
·map, France **7**:584

Nice, Truce of (1538), agreement between France and Spain.

·Paul III and the Reformation wars **8**:89g

Niceforo, Alfredo (b. Jan. 23, 1876, Castiglione di Sicilia, Catania, Italy—d. March 2, 1960, Rome), sociologist, criminologist, and statistician who posited the theory that every man has a "deep ego" of antisocial, subconscious impulses that represent a throwback to precivilized existence. Accompanying this ego, and attempting to keep its latent delinquency in check, according to his concept, is a "superior ego" formed by man's social interaction. This theory, which he published in 1902, bears some resemblance to the discoveries of psychoanalysis that were being made about the same time.

Niceforo taught criminology in Lausanne (Switzerland), Brussels, and elsewhere and statistics at the universities of Naples and Rome (from 1931). Initially he was influenced by the Italian criminologist Cesare Lombroso (1836–1909), who had theorized the existence of a criminal type, identifiable by certain physical features. Niceforo came to believe, however, that crime could be understood only through a thorough investigation—biological, psychological, and sociological—of the normal human being.

One of the first empirical social scientists in Italy, he applied statistics to the problem of finding regularities in social behaviour. Out of these studies came his theory that persons in all societies exhibit certain constant features, which he called residues, one of which was diversity among individuals. He also discerned in every society the stratification of men into social hierarchies and their collection into a mass, observable especially in religious and national ideological systems.

In elaborating his theory of man's dual ego, he maintained that the deep ego often successfully evades the attempts of the superior ego to control it. This view is detailed in his *L' "io" profondo e le sue maschere* (1949; "The Deep Ego and Its Masks").

Nicene Creed, more correctly called NICENO-CONSTANTINOPOLITAN CREED, a Christian statement of faith that is the only ecumenical creed because it is accepted as authoritative by the Roman Catholic, Eastern Orthodox, Anglican, and major Protestant churches. The Apostles and Athanasian creeds are accepted by some but not all of these churches. The Nicene Creed has been accepted as an indispensable standard of belief in any merger of Christian churches.

Until the early 20th century, it was universally assumed that the Niceno-Constantinopolitan Creed was an enlarged version of the Creed of Nicaea, which was promulgated at the Council of Nicaea (325). It was further assumed that this enlargement had been carried out at the Council of Constantinople (381) with the object of bringing the Creed of Nicaea up to date in regard to heresies about the incarnation and the Holy Spirit that had risen since the Council of Nicaea.

Additional discoveries of documents in the 20th century, however, indicated that the situation was more complex, and the actual development of the Niceno-Constantinopolitan Creed has been the subject of scholarly dispute. Most likely it was issued by the Council of Constantinople even though this fact was first explicitly stated at the Council of Chalcedon in 451. It was probably based on a baptismal creed already in existence, but it was an independent document and not an enlargement of the Creed of Nicaea.

The so-called *Filioque* clause (Latin *filioque*, "and from the son"), inserted after the words "the Holy Spirit . . . who proceedeth from the Father," was gradually introduced as part of the creed in the Western Church, beginning in the 6th century. It was probably finally accepted by the papacy in the 11th century. It has been retained by the Roman Catholic, Anglican, and Protestant churches. The Eastern churches have always rejected it because they consider it theological error and an unauthorized addition to a venerable document.

The Nicene Creed was originally written in Greek. Its principal liturgical use is in the Eucharist in the West and in both Baptism and the Eucharist in the East. The text is as follows, with Western additions in brackets:

I believe in one God the Father Almighty; Maker of heaven and earth, and of all things visible and invisible.

And in one Lord Jesus Christ, the only-begotten Son of God, begotten of the Father before all worlds [God of God], Light of Light, very God of very God, begotten, not made, being of one substance [essence] with the Father; by whom all things were made; who, for us men and for our salvation, came down from heaven, and was incarnate by the Holy Ghost of the Virgin Mary, and was made man; and was crucified also for us under Pontius Pilate; he suffered and was buried; and the third day he rose again, according to the Scriptures; and ascended into heaven, and sitteth on the right hand of the Father; and he shall come again, with glory, to judge both the quick and the dead; whose kingdom shall have no end.

And [I believe] in the Holy Ghost, the Lord and Giver of Life; who proceedeth from the Father [and the Son]; who with the Father and the Son together is worshipped and glorified; who spake by the Prophets. And [I believe] in one Holy Catholic and Apostolic Church. I acknowledge one Baptism for the remission of sins; and I look for the resurrection of the dead, and the life of the world to come. Amen.

·acceptance by various churches **5**:244g
·Christian creedal tradition **4**:492f
·Church as communion of saints **16**:165e
·Filioque dispute and Photian Schism **6**:153h
·Gregory of Nazianzus' teachings **8**:420g
·Holy Spirit formula **4**:484a
·patristic struggle with Arianism **13**:1082b
·Photian position on Filioque insertion **14**:291c
·Theodosius support and edict **18**:272f
·West Christian Filioque insertion **6**:143c

Nicephorus (NIKEPHOROS) **I, Saint** (b. *c.* 758, Constantinople, modern Istanbul—d. June 2, 829, near Chalcedon, modern Kadiköy, Tur.), Greek Orthodox theologian, historian, and patriarch of Constantinople (806–815) whose chronicles of Byzantine history and writings in defense of Byzantine veneration of icons provide data otherwise unavailable on early Christian thought and practice.

Although his conservatively Orthodox family had suffered at the hands of iconoclast (image-destroying) regimes during the Isaurian dynasty (717–820), Nicephorus succeeded to the imperial secretariat and represented the emperor Constantine VI as imperial commissioner to the second Council of Nicaea (787), which approved the use of liturgical icons. After having retired for a number of years into monastic seclusion, he was called to be director of Constantinople's refuge centre for the poor soon after the accession of the empress Irene (ruled 797–802).

Though still a layman, he was nominated patriarch of Constantinople in 806. That move stirred the opposition of zealous monks led by Theodore Studites of the Studius monastery. They attacked his unconventional succession to the patriarchate, his compromising stand on an adulterous marriage at court, and his generally conciliatory position on theology. Later, however, his repudiation of the iconoclastic policies of the Isaurian emperor Leo V the Armenian won the monks' respect.

Subsequently, in 815, an iconoclastic synod at Constantinople deposed and exiled Nicephorus to a monastic retreat near Chalcedon; thenceforth, he produced a series of influential anti-iconoclastic tracts and Byzantine chronicles. His theological arguments achieved a measure of toleration from the emperor Michael II (ruled 820–829). Chief among his theological works was his *Major Apology* (817), an exhaustive treatise on the legitimacy of icon veneration. He modelled his arguments on the 8th-century theologian St. John of Damascus and responded minutely to the contrary opinions in Greek patristic sources. Nicephorus succeeded in neutralizing his theological adversaries and contributed to the eventual vindication of the use of icons by the mid-9th century.

Two of his historical works became universally popular: *Breviarium Nicephori* ("Nicephorus' Short History"), which narrated events during Byzantine reigns from 602 to 769 and is significant for material on the founding of Bulgarian settlements; and his *Chronological Tables*, which listed civil and ecclesiastical offices from the time of Adam to the year 829. Both works circulated in the West through the Roman Anastasius the Librarian's late 9th-century Latin compilation of the *Chronologia tripartita* ("Tripartite Chronicle").

Nicephorus I (b. Seleucia, Pisidia, now in Turkey—d. July 26, 811, Bulgaria), Byzantine

Nicephorus I, coin, 9th century; in the British Museum
Peter Clayton

emperor from 802 who late in his reign alienated his subjects with his extremely heavy taxation and frequent confiscations of property.

Nicephorus became a high financial official under the empress Irene, and, when a revolution deposed Irene in 802, he was proclaimed emperor. In the following year he crushed a rebellion by Bardanes Turcus, a rival candidate for the throne, and in 808 he put down a similar revolt led by Arsaber.

When Nicephorus withheld the tribute that Irene had agreed to pay the Baghdad caliph Hārūn ar-Rashīd, war followed, and Arab forces defeated the Byzantine emperor at Crasus in Phrygia (805). In 806 Hārūn invaded Asia Minor with more than 135,000 men and captured Heraclea, Tyana, and other places. Nicephorus was forced to agree to pay a yearly tribute of 30,000 gold pieces.

Although Nicephorus' religious policy was Orthodox rather than Iconoclast (*e.g.*, he permitted the veneration of images), he exercised strong control over the church, even going so far as to sponsor the convocation of a synod (809) that decreed that the emperor was exempt from ecclesiastical laws.

During Nicephorus' reign Venice, Istria, and the Dalmatian coast were in dispute between Byzantium and the empire of Charlemagne until 810. Then a tentative agreement was reached, under which the disputed areas were to be returned to Byzantium in exchange for Byzantine recognition of Charlemagne's title of emperor. The details were worked out two years later during the reign of Nicephorus' successor, his son-in-law Michael I.

In 807–809 Nicephorus I conducted campaigns against the Bulgars, who were harassing Byzantium's northern frontiers. In 811 he invaded Bulgaria, rejecting the Bulgar khan Krum's repeated offers for peace. The Bulgars, however, managed to trap the Byzantines in a mountain defile, where they killed Nicephorus together with most of his army. Krum had Nicephorus' skull lined with silver and used it as a drinking cup.

·military and financial policies **3**:558h

Nicephorus II Phocas 13:64 (b. 912, Cappadocia—d. Dec. 10/11, 969, Constantinople), Byzantine emperor from 963 to 969 whose military achievements contributed to the resurgence of Byzantine power in the 10th century.

Abstract of text biography. Born into a great aristocratic landowning family, Nicephorus became commander in chief of the Byzantine armies of the East (955) and directed a successful military campaign against the Arabs in Crete (960–961) that brought imperial mastery of the eastern Mediterranean and reconsolidated the Christian world. After the death of Romanus II (963), Nicephorus was crowned emperor and married the widowed empress Theophano. He continued his campaigns against the Arabs and extended the imperial boundaries. His domestic policies aroused discontent, and he was assassinated by former friends.

REFERENCE in other text article:
·victories against the Arabs **3**:561a *passim* to 563c

Nicephorus III Botaneiates (fl. late 11th century), Byzantine emperor (1078–81) whose use of Turkish support in acquiring and holding the throne tightened the grip of the Seljuq Turks on Anatolia.

Nicephorus, who belonged to the military aristocracy of Asia Minor and who was related to the powerful Phocas family, became commander of the Anatolian theme (administrative district). When discontent against the government of Michael VII Ducas led to rioting in Constantinople, Nicephorus was proclaimed emperor (Jan. 7, 1078) by his supporters there. With some support from Suleiman, the Seljuq ruler in Anatolia, Nicephorus was acclaimed emperor by his troops at Nicaea (in northwestern Anatolia) and entered

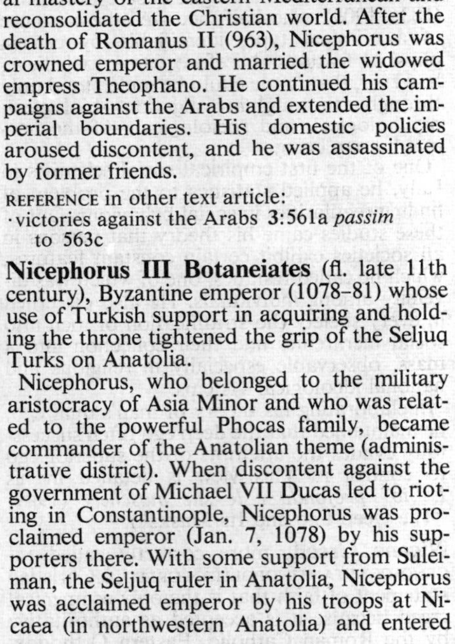

Nicephorus III, detail of a manuscript; in the Bibliothèque Nationale, Paris (Ms. Coislin 79)
By courtesy of the Bibliotheque Nationale, Paris

Constantinople three months later. His imperial claim was ratified by the aristocracy and clergy, who had already deposed Michael VII. Nicephorus III defeated a rival claimant to the throne, Nicephorus Bryennius, the empire's commander in Albania; he also defeated a later pretender, Nicephorus Basilacius, who succeeded Bryennius in Albania.

After the death of Nicephorus' wife, he married Mary, the wife of the deposed but still living Michael VII, and named Michael's son Constantine as his successor but then later decided on one of his own nephews instead. He relegated Constantine's fiancee, a daughter of the Norman leader Robert Guiscard, to a convent. Nicephorus' action provided an excuse for Guiscard's later successful attacks against the empire.

In 1080 another usurper, Nicephorus Melissenus, appeared in Asia Minor and also sought Turkish assistance. As a result of such constant internal strife, with one faction or another requesting aid from the Turks, most of Asia Minor was lost to Byzantium and became incorporated in the Seljuq Sultanate of Rūm (modern Konya, Tur.).

Unable either to save the empire from disintegration or to maintain his own position as ruler, Nicephorus abdicated on April 4, 1081, and entered the Peribleptos monastery in Constantinople.

Nicephorus Bryennius: *see* Bryennius, Nicephorus.

Nicephorus Callistus Xanthopoulos (b. *c.* 1256—d. *c.* 1335), Byzantine historian and litterateur whose stylistic prose and poetry exemplify the developing Byzantine Humanism of the 13th and 14th centuries, and whose 23-volume *Ecclesiasticae historiae* ("Church History") constitutes a significant documentary source for material on primitive Christianity, its doctrinal controversies and Christological heresies, and for hagiographical, liturgical, and legendary texts from Byzantine culture.

One of the clerics attached to Constantinople's basilica of Hagia Sophia (Greek: Holy Wisdom), Nicephorus was trained in the florid, rhetorical style of Renaissance Byzantine historiography; he taught rhetoric and theology and in his later years became a monk. Using the basilica's manuscript library, he compiled his major work, an 18-volume "Church History," from the origins of Christianity to the execution of the emperor-tyrant Phocas in 610; an appendix of 5 volumes continued the chronicle, summarizing events until the death of Emperor Leo VI the Wise (912). Taking as a point of departure several celebrated ecclesiastical histories, including those of the 6th-century Byzantine Evagrius Scholasticus and the 4th-century Eusebius of Caesarea (modern Turkey), integrated with accounts of an anonymous 10th-century text, Nicephorus paraphrased a chronicle the value of which must be determined by the quality of the individual sources used. In the manner of Byzantine Humanism, the "History," written in an affected style that often impedes textual clarity, was dedicated to the emperor Andronicus II Palaeologus (1282–1328) and contributed to that monarch's nationalist movement exalting Greek culture and Orthodoxy above Latin Christianity. The 16th-century Latin translation, however, served to support the argument for the use of religious images in controversies involving certain Protestant iconoclasts.

Among Nicephorus' other works are commentaries on the writings of the chief patristic Greek theologian, Gregory of Nazianzus (*c.* 329–*c.* 389); treatises on the annual cycle of Byzantine worship, with annotations on Lenten and Easter hymnody; original liturgical orations in prose and poetry; rigid Byzantine verse forms cataloging emperors, patriarchs, and other dignitaries; and, as an exception, secular themes in verse and rhetorical forms.

Nicetas of Remesiana (fl. early 5th century AD), Greek bishop, theologian, and composer of liturgical verse, whose missionary activity and writings effected the Christianization of the Serbian Slavic regions and cultivated a Latin culture among the simple barbarians in the lower Danube Valley.

After becoming bishop of Remesiana (modern Niš, Serbian Yugoslavia) *c.* 366, Nicetas twice visited Paulinus, bishop of Nola, in Campania (near modern Naples), a fellow missioner, the foremost Latin literary figure of his age, and the primary source for knowledge of Nicetas' life and pastoral activity. Scholarship, having laboriously reconstructed substantial portions of Nicetas' theological tracts, has furnished sufficient evidence to identify his principal doctrinal work, the "Six Books of Instructions for Baptismal Candidates." The lengthy excerpts from this catechetical series, particularly "On the Meaning of Faith," "On the Power of the Holy Spirit," and the "Commentary on the Apostolic-Nicene Creed," indicate that Nicetas stressed the orthodox position in Trinitarian doctrine consonant with the leading 4th-century theologian, Cyril of Jerusalem. Accordingly, Nicetas opposed any attribution of a created nature—either to the Son, contrary to the Arians, or to the Holy Spirit, as against the Macedonians. Moreover, these documents contain, apparently for the first time in early Christian literature, the term communion of saints, in reference to the belief in a mystical bond uniting both the living and the dead in a confirmed hope and love. This expression henceforth played a central role in formulations of the Christian creed.

Other patristic writers, including the 5th-century church historian Gennadius of Marseilles, credit Nicetas with promoting Latin sacred music among his newly converted primitive Serbians for use during their eucharistic worship with its vigil from Saturday evening to Sunday morning. He wrote a rationale for such practice and reputedly composed a number of liturgical hymns, among which some 20th-century scholars identify the major Latin Christian acclamation chant of thanksgiving, the "Te Deum Laudamus" (Latin: "God, We Praise Thee").

Nicetas Stethatos (b. *c.* 1000—d. *c.* 1080), Byzantine mystic, theologian, and outspoken polemist who played the principal theorist role in the 11th-century Greek Orthodox–Latin church controversy concluding in the definitive schism of 1054. A monk of the Studius monastery in Constantinople, Nicetas allied himself *c.* 1020 with his spiritual tutor, Symeon the New Theologian, whose biographer and apologist he became when Symeon was attacked for his system of contemplative prayer. In his "Life of Symeon the New Theologian" Nicetas integrated his own views on the inner experience of beatifying illumination that derived from a monastic prayer discipline involving both body and spirit, known as Hesychasm (Greek: "prayer of quiet"). Furthering this tradition he wrote a treatise, the "Spiritual Paradise," and several commentaries on ascetical practices.

In the 11th-century conflict between the Greek and Latin churches, Nicetas served as theologian-polemist to Constantinople's patriarch Michael Cerularius, who, during 1053–54, disputed sharply with the papal legate Cardinal Humbert of Silva Candida. Nicetas' "Précis Against the Latins" criticized Western doctrine on the manner of relating the Holy Spirit to the divinity, on the claims of papal supremacy, on mandatory clerical celibacy, and on the use of unleavened bread in Roman eucharistic worship. Excerpts from this and other theological tracts against the Armenian Church and against the Jews were included in a 13th-century Byzantine *Thesaurus of Orthodoxy*.

niche, in ecology, the smallest unit of a habitat that is occupied by an organism. Habitat niche refers to the physical space occupied by the organism; ecological niche refers to the role it plays in the community of organisms found in the habitat. The activities of an organism and its relationships to other organisms are determined by its particular structure, physiology, and behaviour. Two organisms that occupy similar niches but that are native to different geographical areas are termed ecological equivalents.

·African wildlife adaptation **1**:197c
·animal social behaviour patterns **16**:933h
·arachnid adoption of cryptozoic habitat **1**:1063b
·canids in various habitats **3**:928h
·cephalopod aquatic life styles **3**:1152g
·coraciiform feeding patterns **5**:159b
·dormancy as survival mechanism **5**:959b
·ecosystem dynamics and classification **18**:147c
·genetic and environmental compatibility **8**:814c
·interspecific competition hypotheses **2**:1047h
·larva–adult ecological differentiations **5**:640c
·Lepidoptera adaptations to food plants **10**:820c
·living organism's wide adaptability **10**:898b
·psammon community **10**:614d
·rain forest species evolution **10**:342f
·rodent territory system **15**:971e
·roles of civet group in various areas **3**:935a
·scavenger importance of hyena **3**:935h
·species adaptations for survival **7**:10g
·species diversity and competition **4**:1029b
·temperature-range separation of lizards **15**:735g
·temporal activity cycles and biological clocking cues **14**:69f
·woodpecker habitat adaptations **14**:448f

niche, decorative recess set into a wall for the purpose of displaying a statue, vase, font, or other object. Niches were used extensively in both interior and exterior walls by the architects of ancient Rome. A fine extant example of such use is found at the Roman Temple

Niche with statue of Apollo, by Jacopo Sansovino, in the Loggetta, Venice, 1540
Alinari

of Diana at Nîmes, Fr. Gothic examples are ubiquitous, including niches in such medieval structures as the English cathedrals of Wells and Peterborough. Later architects, especially those of the Italian Renaissance and the classic revival of 17th- and 18th-century Europe, all made use of the niche. Semicircular niches are often featured, many having shell-like fluting at the apex.

Nichinan, city, Miyazaki Prefecture (*ken*), Kyushu, Japan, facing the Pacific Ocean. Japanese (Obi) cedar has been cultivated in the area since the early 19th century and forms the basis of the city's timber, paper, and pulp industries. Nichinan's two ports—Aburatsu and Oodotsu—are the main centres for coastal fishing (bonito, yellowtail, tuna) in southern Kyushu. The city is bordered (north) by low, rounded hills, and its picturesque sea-

Tropical vegetation in Nichinan-kaigan Quasi-national Park, Japan
Tokyo Photo—FPG

coast is part of Nichinan-kaigan Quasi-national Park. Pop. (1970) 53,288.
31°36′ N, 131°23′ E
·map, Japan **10**:36

Nichiren 13:65, as a child called ZEN-NICHI, as a priest called himself ZENSHŌBŌ RENCHŌ (b. 1222, Kominato, Japan—d. Nov. 4, 1282, Ikegami District, in what is now Tokyo), militant Japanese Buddhist prophet who contributed significantly to the adaptation of Buddhism to the Japanese mentality and who remains one of the most controversial and influential figures in Japanese Buddhist history.

Abstract of text biography. Nichiren entered Kiyosumi monastery at the age of 11 and was ordained a monk four years later. In 1233 he went to Kamakura and embarked on a study of each of the major schools, concluding (in 1253) that the *Lotus Sutra* teaching was the only true doctrine suitable for his age and that all others were false and misleading. He was expelled from his monastery and began to preach at the crossroads in Kamakura. In 1260 he warned (in his tract, *Risshō ankokuron*) that the deplorable condition of the country could be corrected only by banishing the other Buddhist sects—a prophecy he regarded as fulfilled by the Mongol demand for tribute in 1268. He was exiled to Izu-hantō from June 1261 to 1263 and in 1271 was condemned to death. The penalty was commuted at the last minute, and he was exiled to Sado island. There (in 1272) he wrote his systematic work, *Kaimokushō*. Following his pardon in the spring of 1274, he retired to a hermitage in Minobu-san, where he remained until shortly before his death.

REFERENCES in other text articles:
·Buddhist reform on basis of Lotus Sūtra **10**:112f
·philosophy and school **3**:385e
·religious and social ideology **10**:110e
·sainthood and veneration **16**:164g
·salvation theology and consequences **10**:103a
·salvation theory and national influence **3**:410e
·writings and literary style **3**:440e

Nichiren Buddhism, a school of Japanese Buddhism named after its founder, the 13th-century militant prophet and saint, Nichiren. It is one of the largest schools of Japanese Buddhism; in the late 1960s the total membership of its numerous subsects was reported to be approximately 30,000,000.

Nichiren believed that the quintessence of the Buddha's teachings was contained in the *Lotus Sūtra* (Sanskrit *Saddharmapuṇḍarīka-sūtra;* "The Scripture of the Lotus of the

Good Law"). According to him, the other sects then existing in Japan misunderstood the truth, and he vehemently denounced them and the government that supported them. He blamed the social unrest of the period on the erroneous religious beliefs of the nation, and proclaimed that the salvation of the Japanese nation depended on devotion to the truth contained in the *Lotus Sūtra*. He came to conceive of himself as the *bodhisattva* (Buddha-to-be) Jōgyō, who was destined to suffer for proclaiming the truth in an era of darkness, an identification apparently verified by the severe persecution he suffered.

Nichiren believed that the historical Buddha Śākyamuni was identical with the original, eternal Buddha, and inasmuch as all men partake of the Buddha-nature, all men are manifestations of the eternal. He devised three ways of expressing this concept, known as the *sandai-hihō* ("three great secret laws," or "mysteries"). The first, the *honzon*, is the chief object of worship in Nichiren temples and is a ritual drawing showing the name of the *Lotus Sūtra* surrounded by the names of divinities mentioned in the *sūtra* (words of the Buddha). The second "great mystery" is the *daimoku*, the "title" of the *sūtra;* and Nichiren instituted the devotional practice of chanting the phrase *namu Myōhō renge-kyō* ("salutation to the *Lotus Sūtra*"). The third mystery relates to the *kaidan*, or place of ordination, which is sacred and belongs to the "Lotus of the Good Law."

After Nichiren's death the school split into various subsects, most notably Nichiren-shū, which still controls the main temple, the Kuon-ji, founded by him at Mt. Minobu (Yamanashi Prefecture), and the rapidly growing Nichiren-shō-shū, an offshoot of which is the politically active lay religious group the Sōka-gakkai.

·derivation and philosophy **3**:385d; table 377
·religious impact of Sōka-gakkai **10**:114h
·ritual dress and symbolism **15**:639g
·social and political effects in Japan **10**:110e *passim* to 112g
·Tokugawa period religious movements **10**:76h

Nichiren-shō-shū, a sect of the Nichiren school of Japanese Buddhism that has had phenomenal growth since 1950, mainly because of intensive conversion efforts of its associated lay religious group, the Sōka-gakkai.

Nichiren-shō-shū (True Nichiren sect) traces its line of succession back to one of Nichiren's six disciples, Nikkō, who established his own temple, Daiseki-ji, in 1290 at the foot of Mt. Fuji, still the headquarters of the sect. It bases its claim to orthodoxy on copies the sect holds of two documents (the originals having been lost) by Nichiren naming the disciple Nikkō as his successor and on Nichiren-shō-shū's possession of a wooden tablet (the *daigohonzon*, "great object of worship") on which the holy phrase *namu Myōhō renge-kyō* ("salutation to the *Lotus Sūtra*") is said to have been written by Nichiren himself. Nichiren-shō-shū differs from the other Nichiren sects in its elevation of the founder, Nichiren, to a rank higher even than that of the historical Buddha, as the only true Buddha to preach in the present degenerate age.

Among its rival Nichiren sects Nichiren-shō-shū had only minor influence until the emergence of the Sōka-gakkai lay organization brought it into its present dominant position in Japanese politics. The sect claimed a membership of more than 6,000,000 families in the mid-1960s and has established branches outside Japan. In the United States the lay organization equivalent to the Sōka-gakkai is called Nichiren-shō-shū of America. The U.S. group listed its membership in 1970 as 60,000 families.

·origin and doctrines **3**:386a

Nichiren-shū, a sect of the Nichiren school of Japanese Buddhism that still has its headquarters at the Kuon-ji at Mt. Minobu (in Yamanashi Prefecture), the chief temple of the school's 13th-century founder, Nichiren. The Nichiren-shū (Nichiren sect) maintained a dominant position among Nichiren Buddhists until the years following World War II, when it was eclipsed by the Nichiren-shō-shū, whose phenomenal growth stemmed from its lay organization, the Sōko-gakkai.

·origin and following **3**:385h

Nicholas, Saint, also known as NICHOLAS OF MYRA, corrupted in English-speaking countries into SANTA CLAUS, after the Dutch "Sinter Claes" (fl. 4th century, Myra, Lycia, near modern Finike, Tur.), one of the most popular saints commemorated in the Eastern and Western churches, multifariously honoured as a patron; now traditionally associated with the festival of Christmas, particularly in England and the United States. His existence, however, is not attested by any historical document, so nothing certain is known of his life except that he was probably bishop of Myra in the 4th century.

Traditionally, he was born in the ancient Lycian seaport city of Patara (near modern Kalamaki, Tur.), and, when young, he travelled to Palestine and Egypt. He became bishop of Myra soon after returning to Lycia. Imprisoned during the Roman emperor Diocletian's persecution of Christians, he was released under the rule of Emperor Constantine the Great and attended the first Council (325) of Nicaea (modern Iznik, Tur.). In the 6th century his shrine was well-known at Myra, from where, in 1087, Italian sailors or merchants brought his body to Bari, Italy; this removal, commemorated on May 9, greatly increased his popularity, and Bari became one of the most crowded pilgrimage centres. His relics are enshrined in the 11th-century basilica of S. Nicola, Bari.

Legends about Nicholas multiplied rapidly. The earliest account (from a Greek text, which may be from the 6th century) is the famous miracle of the three officers condemned to death but saved by Nicholas' appearance in a dream of Constantine's. The 6th-century abbot Nicholas of Sion, near Myra, is believed to have written his biography and accounts of numerous miracles, of which the best known deal with saving children from tragedy. Devotion to Nicholas extended to all parts of the world; his name has been given to places in many countries; numerous surnames of persons are derived from Nicholas (*e.g.*, Nichols, Nicholson, Colson, Collins). He was chosen patron saint of countries such as Russia and Greece, of charitable fraternities and guilds, of children and sailors (whom he reputedly saved off the coast of Lycia), and of cities such as Fribourg, Switz., and Moscow. Thousands of European churches are dedicated to him, one as early as the 6th century, built by the Roman emperor Justinian I, at Constantinople, now Istanbul. His miracles were a favourite subject for medieval artists and liturgical plays, and his traditional feast day, December 6, was the occasion for the ceremonies of the Boy Bishop, a widespread European custom in which a boy was elected bishop and reigned until Holy Innocents' Day (December 28).

The transformation of Nicholas into Father Christmas or Father January occurred first in Germany, then in countries where the Reformed churches were in the majority, and finally in France, the feast day being celebrated on Christmas or New Year's Day. Dutch Protestant settlers in New Amsterdam (now the city of New York) replaced Nicholas ("Sinter Claes") with the benevolent magician who became known as Santa Claus, thus contributing further to his spreading folklore. In the United States and England, Nicholas is patron of Christmas, traditionally regarded as a festival of the family and of children, when presents are exchanged. In 1969 he was among a group of saints whose feast days were dropped but are now commemorated jointly on January 1. *Hagios Nikolaos* (2 vol.; Greek texts ed. by G. Anrich) appeared in 1913–17, followed in 1931 by K. Meisen's *Nikolauskult und Nikolausbrauch in Abendland* ("Cult and Customs of Nicholas in the West").

·Christmas tradition **4**:604a

Nicholas, Russian NIKOLAY NIKOLAYEVICH (b. Nov. 18 [Nov. 6, old style], 1856, St. Petersburg, now Leningrad—d. Jan. 6, 1929, Antibes, Fr.), Russian grand duke and army officer, commander in chief against the Germans and Austro-Hungarians in the first year of World War I, and subsequently (until March 1917) Emperor Nicholas II's viceroy in the Caucasus and commander in chief against the Turks.

The son of the emperor Alexander II's brother, the grand duke Nikolay Nikolayevich "the Elder," Nicholas was educated at the general staff college and commissioned in 1872. He served in the Russo-Turkish War of 1877–78 and as inspector general of cavalry (1895–1905), introducing major reforms in training and equipment. He was made commander of the St. Petersburg military district in 1905 and also was appointed first president of the short-lived imperial committee of national defense; it was abolished in 1908.

When World War I began, Emperor Nicholas II abandoned his intention to lead the Russian armies himself and appointed the grand duke Nicholas commander in chief. Despite their early successes, the Russians were outgeneraled by the German chief of staff Erich Ludendorff and eventually were immobilized by munitions shortages. The Grand Duke is considered to have done as well as possible with the general staff's plans he was obliged to follow.

On Sept. 5 (Aug. 23, O.S.), 1915, however, the Emperor assumed the supreme command. He sent the Grand Duke to the Caucasus, where he remained till the overthrow of the monarchy in 1917. The Emperor's last official act was to appoint the Grand Duke commander in chief once more; but his appointment was cancelled almost immediately by Prince Georgy Y. Lvov, head of the provisional government. Two years later Grand Duke Nicholas sailed from Russia in a British warship. He lived in France until his death.

Nicholas I the Great, Saint (b. *c.* 819–822, Rome—d. Nov. 13, 867, Rome), pope from 858 to 867, master theorist of papal power, considered to have been the most forceful of the early medieval pontiffs, whose pontificate was the most important of the Carolingian period and prepared the way for the 11th-century reform popes. He had served in the Curia for almost 15 years before his election in April 858 as Pope Benedict III's successor. His reign was marked by three historically significant contests.

Nicholas supported the patriarch St. Ignatius of Constantinople, who was uncanonically replaced by the scholar Photius after the Byzantine emperor Michael III had unjustly humiliated and deposed him. To investigate this state of affairs, Nicholas dispatched legates to Constantinople, but when they confirmed judgment against Ignatius in 861, he disavowed them. After receiving word from the exiled Ignatius in 862, Nicholas, having studied the case, favoured Ignatius and excommunicated Photius (863), who counter-deposed the Pope in 867. Nicholas did not live to learn of this act or of its extreme culmination: the Photian Schism, a split between the Eastern and Western churches.

Nicholas' second great struggle was with King Lothair of Lorraine, who wanted to divorce his wife, Theutberga, on false charges of incest. Theutberga appealed to Nicholas, while a synod at Aachen, Ger., in April 862 gave Lothair permission to remarry. At a synod at Metz, Fr., in 863, Lothair obtained confirmation of the Aachen decision, probably through bribery, from Nicholas' legates, Archbishops Günther of Cologne and Theutgaud of Trier (Trèves). When these legates arrived in Rome with the libellous decree of Metz, Nicholas, treating Lothair as his ecclesiastical subject, quashed the whole proceedings against Theutberga and, creating a precedent, deposed the Archbishops.

The third great ecclesiastical affair of Nicholas' pontificate involved the deposition in 862 of Bishop Rothad II of Soissons by Archbishop Hincmar of Reims, a classic example of the right of bishops to appeal to Rome against their metropolitans. Nicholas, a strict upholder of Rome's primacy of jurisdiction, ordered an examination that led to Rothad's restoration in 865 by using, probably for the first time, the False Decretals, a 9th-century collection of revolutionary but partially forged documents that, in part, maintained bishops' independence against the encroachments of archbishops who were attempting to extend their power.

For Nicholas, the Roman see, having power by divine commission, was the head and the epitome of the Catholic Church. Consistently urging the supremacy of Rome, he fully endorsed the papal inheritance of sacerdotal and royal functions as conferred by Christ on St. Peter and the delegation of temporal power to the emperor for the protection of the church. He reacted against Carolingian domination in ecclesiastical matters and claimed the right to legislate for the whole of Christendom. Thus, his teaching contained the rudiments of papal theocracy and helped to found Roman supremacy over the Western sees by declaring that what the pope decides, all must observe. Nicholas' feast day is November 13. M. Maitland's English translation of J. Roy's *St. Nicholas I* appeared in 1901, followed by E. Perels' *Papst Nikolaus I und Anastasius Bibliothekarius* in 1920.

·conflict with Photius **3**:560c
·faction and schism **4**:544d
·jurisdictional controversy with Photius **14**:290h

Nicholas I of Russia **13**:67, Russian NIKOLAY PAVLOVICH (b. July 6 [June 25, old style], 1796, Tsarskoye Selo, now Pushkin, Russian S.F.S.R.—d. March 2 [Feb. 18, O.S.], 1855, St. Petersburg, now Leningrad), Russian emperor, a reactionary ruler considered the personification of classic autocracy.

Abstract of text biography. Nicholas had an extensive education from which he profited little, being interested primarily in the army. He married Princess Charlotte of Prussia (afterward called Empress Alexandra) in 1817, in a political match. He held several military posts before he acceded to the throne in 1825. As emperor, Nicholas ruled autocratically; his regime was one of militarism and bureaucracy, and he prevented reform or change of almost any kind. His reign ended with Russia's defeat in the Crimean War.

REFERENCES in other text articles:
·educational class establishment **6**:365d
·November Insurrection in Poland **14**:648f
·Prussian–Austrian power struggle **2**:465b
·Pushkin's association with the tsar **15**:310e
·reputation, reign, and policies **16**:57f; map 55
·Slavophile opposition to rule **10**:452h

Nicholas I (b. Oct. 7 [Sept. 25, old style], 1841, Njegoš, Montenegro, now in Yugoslavia—d. March 2, 1921, Antibes, Fr.), prince of Montenegro from 1860, who transformed his small principality into a sovereign European nation.

Heir presumptive to his uncle Danilo Ii, who was childless, Nicholas came to the throne in August 1860 after Danilo's assassination. Educated abroad in Paris and Trieste, he was throughout his reign faced with the difficult task of popularizing Western ways. A strong prince and an outstanding leader, he fought the Turks in 1862 and again in 1876, when he conducted a brilliant campaign. At the Congress of Berlin (1878), Montenegro was doubled in size, with an outlet to the Adriatic, and recognized as a sovereign state. Alexander II of Russia, whose friendship with Nicholas dated back to a state visit to St. Petersburg (now Leningrad) in 1868, supplied him regularly with money and arms and at one point favoured his candidacy for the Serbian throne. A clever diplomat, Nicholas strengthened his dynastic connections through the marriages of his daughters: Elena married (1896) the future king of Italy, Victor Emmanuel III; Zorka married Peter Karađorđević (1883) but died before he became king of Serbia; two other daughters married Russian grand dukes. In Balkan politics Nicholas conspired, sometimes with, and sometimes against, Serbian rulers, to create a South Slav state.

Styling himself "Royal Highness" (December 1900), Nicholas became more despotic until he was forced to grant a constitution in 1905. Political dissension, nevertheless, continued, culminating in the Cetinje bomb plot against him (1907). On Aug. 28, 1910, Nicholas declared himself king. Hoping to gain prestige through the addition of new territories, he joined in the Balkan War of 1912–13 against Turkey; but his territorial acquisitions were disappointing. In World War I he supported Serbia against Austria-Hungary. Defeated, he concluded a separate peace in January 1916 and then went into exile in Italy. When the victorious Serbs occupied Montenegro after the defeat of Austria-Hungary, Nicholas and his dynasty were formally deposed by a national assembly (Nov. 26, 1918), and Montenegro was joined to Serbia, later to become part of the Kingdom of the Serbs, Croats, and Slovenes (Yugoslavia).

Nicholas I the Mystic (b. 852, Constantinople, now Istanbul—d. May 15, 925), Byzantine patriarch of Constantinople (901–907; 912–925), who contributed measurably to the attempted reunion of the Greek and Roman churches and who fomented the tetragamy controversy, or the question of a fourth marriage for the Eastern Orthodox.

A close associate of the controversial patriarch Photius of Constantinople, Nicholas began his career in the Byzantine civil service but became a monk when his patron Photius was deposed in 886 on theological and political grounds. Named a secretary counsellor (Mysticus) by the emperor Leo VI (886–912), Nicholas was appointed patriarch of Constantinople in 901. Having refused on grounds of religious legality and propriety to grant the Emperor's request for a dispensation to contract a fourth marriage after the death of his third wife, and declining to consult Pope Sergius III in the matter, Nicholas was banished to a monastery outside Constantinople. Recalled either by Leo in the last year of his reign, or by Emperor Alexander (912–913), Nicholas was invited to act as regent for Prince Constantine VII during his minority.

Because of his harsh retaliation against patriarch Euthymius, his successor during exile, Nicholas alienated many of the clergy and people, among them Leo's family, creating a rivalry between their respective supporters. During the rule of the emperor Romanus I Lecapenus (920–944), Nicholas was reconciled with Patriarch Euthymius, thus ending the bitter internal struggle within the Eastern Orthodox Church. His negotiations with Pope John X (914–928) concerning cooperative union between Eastern and Western Christendom and an agreement over the ecclesiastical law of marriage for the Eastern Church inaugurated a rare period of harmony. In a synod (920) Nicholas issued a decree of union settling the tetragamy question by ordinarily limiting Greek Christians to three marriages but validating the fourth marriage of Leo VI for the good of the state in order to settle the imperial line of succession by a legitimate heir.

Nicholas also engaged in various diplomatic affairs, as is evidenced by his letters on Byzantine–Bulgarian relations and concerning questions of Greek estates in Italy. He is revered as a saint by the Eastern Orthodox Church.

·role as Constantine VII Porphyrogenitus' regent **5**:74f

Nicholas II, originally GERARD (b. Lorraine, now in France—d. Aug. 27, 1061, Florence), pope from 1058 to 1061, a major figure in the Gregorian reform. He was bishop of Florence when he was elected, *c.* December 1058 at Siena, Italy, to succeed Pope Stephen X (IX), in opposition to Antipope Benedict X, who had been chosen by the anti-reformist Roman aristocracy. In January 1059 Benedict was expelled from the papacy.

At the Lateran Council of April 1059, a milestone in papal history, Nicholas promulgated his famous bull on papal elections (April 13); he did so in reaction to the disorders that interrupted his own election. He assigned the leading part in elections to the seven cardinal bishops (*i.e.*, those who had the predominant position among the higher clergy), who were to choose a suitable candidate and then summon the other cardinals. The remaining clergy and the people were to acclaim the choice, and the imperial role was dismissed. Nicholas' legate, sent to notify the German court of the election decree, was refused an audience, and an imperialist version of the decree was circulated. At a synod of 1061, the German bishops declared Nicholas' decree void and quashed all his acts, signifying the ruptured alliance between Germany and Rome and launching the contest between empire and papacy.

Nicholas' relations with the Normans, firmly entrenched in southern Italy, were friendly, however. By the treaty of Melfi (Aug. 23, 1059) he invested Robert Guiscard as duke of Apulia, Calabria, and Sicily (with papal suzerainty over these lands) and Richard of Aversa as prince of Capua, in return for allegiance. A. Clavel's *Pape Nicholas II: son oeuvre disciplinaire* ("Pope Nicholas II: His Disciplinarian Work") appeared in 1906.

·Lateran Council decisions **9**:1129e
·papal election reforms **13**:957d
·papal elections regulatory decree **15**:1003d

Nicholas II of Russia **13**:70, Russian NIKOLAY ALEKSANDROVICH (b. May 18 [May 6, old style], 1868, Tsarskoye Selo, now Pushkin, Russian S.F.S.R.—d. July 29/30 [July 16/17, O.S.], 1918, Yekaterinburg, now Sverdlovsk, Russian S.F.S.R.), the last Russian emperor, generally judged as an inept and autocratic ruler, was executed by the Bolsheviks after they had seized power.

Abstract of text biography. Nicholas received a conventional, largely military upbringing; contracted a marriage in 1894 to a woman of stronger character than his own, the German princess Alexandra; and acceded to the throne in 1895, viewing himself as a ruler by divine right. After his country's thorough defeat in the Russo-Japanese War of 1904–05, he was forced by a massive uprising to agree to a constitution. The influence exerted on him and (especially) on the Empress by Rasputin, a dubious "holy man," further eroded public confidence in his ability. In 1917, when a German victory over Russia in World War I seemed inevitable, Nicholas was deposed by revolutionaries, and the next year he and his family were murdered in captivity.

REFERENCES in other text articles:
·Armenian repression policy **18**:1043h
·Austrian agreement on Turkey **2**:472h
·church renewal before 1917 revolution **6**:159f
·reign, revolution, and dethronement **16**:63a

Nicholas III (b. GIOVANNI GAETANO ORSINI, *c.* 1225, Rome—d. Aug. 22, 1280, Soriano nel Cimino, Italy), pope from 1277 to 1280. Of noble birth, he was made cardinal in 1244 by Pope Innocent IV and protector of the Franciscans in 1261 by Pope Urban IV. After a colourful and celebrated service in the Curia, he was elected pope on Nov. 25, 1277, and initiated an administrative reform of the Papal States.

In matters of the church, Nicholas issued the important bull of 1279, temporarily settling the Franciscan struggle over the interpretation of perfect poverty that had split the order into two factions, the Conventuals and the Spirituals. His bull revoked the concessions concerning the use of money made by Pope Innocent IV and clarified Innocent's ruling that all possessions of the order, except those reserved by the donors, belonged to the papacy.

Nicholas successfully continued Pope Gregory X's policy of restraining the ambitious Sicilian king Charles I of Anjou and did not renew Charles's positions as imperial vicar of Tuscany and senator of Rome, an office Nicholas prevented from ever again being filled by a foreign ruler. He induced the German king Rudolf I to acknowledge that the Italian province of the Romagna (though it was not incorporated until much later) belonged to the church. Anxious to maintain a balance of power between Rudolf and Charles, who had invaded Italy and who was supported by the ruling Florentine party, Nicholas sent his nephew Cardinal Malebranca to Florence in 1279 on a mission that resulted in a reorganization of that government.

In May 1280 he arranged a treaty to terminate the claims of the sovereign dynasties—the Habsburgs and the Angevins—for the possession of Sicily. His early death ruined his plans to reorganize the Holy Roman Empire and led to a renewal of Angevin-French influence on the papacy under his successor, Pope Martin IV. Nicholas was a political realist; he accepted the idea that every cardinal was the agent of a political interest, and he exalted his own family, the Orsini, who acquired increasing influence in church policy and administration.

Nicholas III (fl. late 11th century), Eastern Orthodox patriarch of Constantinople (1084–1111), theologian and liturgical scholar noted for combatting doctrinal heresy and composing sacramental prayer texts for the Byzantine liturgy. He also initiated the temporary restoration of harmonious relations with the Roman Church. A monk of Constantinople's Prodromos monastery, Nicholas succeeded the deposed Eustratius Garridos as patriarch. He functioned as mediator between ecclesiastics and the emperor Alexius I Comnenus on various disciplinary and doctrinal questions, particularly in the controversy over the donation of the church's sacred jewelled art and vessels to ease the urgent needs of the imperial treasury; some Orthodox churchmen denounced this secularization of religious objects as a form of iconoclasm.

Among Nicholas' liturgical compositions are prayers and responses in the service rituals for baptism, marriage, confession, fasting, and communion. At first inimical to union with the Roman Church, he later convened a synod in September 1089 and sent a letter to Pope Urban II favouring the resumption of intercommunion. In specific matters, however, he rejected any departure from Greek Orthodox doctrine and practice, including opposition to universal papal authority, the distinctive Byzantine concept of the Holy Spirit (*Filioque* question), and the Eastern Church's use of leavened bread in the Communion service. Frequently intervening in monastic affairs, Nicholas strengthened discipline in the community of Mt. Athos (Greece) and probably wrote a monastic Rule (*Typikon*) adapted from the original text of the early Palestinian monastic founder St. Sabas.

In a final theological judgment, Nicholas condemned as heretical the Bogomil leader Basil the Physician and his adherents, an exclusive sect originating in Bulgaria and teaching a form of religious dualism that attributed two sons to the Creator, Christ and Satan. In 1118 the emperor Alexius had Basil burned at the stake.

Nicholas IV (b. GIROLAMO MASCI, Sept. 30, 1227, near Ascoli Piceno, Italy—d. April 4, 1292, Rome), pope from 1288 to 1292, the first Franciscan pontiff. He joined the Franciscans when young and became their minister for Dalmatia, now the Yugoslav coast. In 1272 Pope Gregory X sent him to Constantinople, now Istanbul, where he took part in effecting a brief reunion with the Greeks. From 1274 to 1279 he was minister general of the Franciscans, and in 1281 Pope Martin IV made him cardinal bishop of Palestrina, Italy. He was elected on Feb. 22, 1288, to succeed Pope Honorius IV, after the papacy had been vacant for almost 11 months.

Nicholas IV relied heavily on a powerful Italian family, the Colonna, and increased the number of Colonna cardinals. In a bull of 1289 he granted half of the church's revenues and a share in its administration to the College of Cardinals, thereby increasing their importance in church and Papal States affairs. In 1290 he issued a new bull against the Apostolici, various Christian sects that sought to re-establish the life and discipline of the primitive church by a literal observance of continence and poverty.

Like his predecessors Popes Nicholas III, Martin IV, and Honorius IV, Nicholas IV strove to keep the balance between the sovereign dynasties of the Habsburgs (the German king Rudolf I) and the Anjous (the Sicilian king Charles I). As feudal overlord of Sicily, Nicholas tried vainly to force the royal house of Aragon to restore Sicily to the Anjous, and in 1291 he ended the conflict between France and the Kingdom of Aragon.

Nicholas was unable to revive the crusade, and in 1291 the last Christian crusader state, the Palestinian fortress of Acre, fell to the Mamlūk sultan of Egypt. Nicholas' wish to ally the Western powers with the Mongols against the Muslims was given hope through the Il-Khan Arghun of Persia, who sent urgent requests for joint action to Nicholas and Kings Philip IV of France and Edward I of England. Although the plan did not materialize, Nicholas sent the celebrated Franciscan missionary Giovanni da Montecorvino to Kublai Khan's court, which led to establishment of the first Roman Catholic Church in China. He also sent missionaries, mostly Franciscans, to the Balkans and the Near East. He did much for Roman architecture and art, especially in restoring the basilicas of S. Giovanni in Laterano and Sta. Maria Maggiore.

·Boniface VIII's clerical advancement **3**:32g
·crusading spirit decline **5**:309f

Nicholas V, Pope 13:66, originally TOMMASO PARENTUCELLI (b. Nov. 15, 1397, Sarzana, Italy—d. 1455, Rome), influential Renaissance pope and founder of the Vatican Library.

Abstract of text biography. Parentucelli spent 20 years in the diplomatic service serving the cardinal-archbishop of Bologna, Italy. Made bishop of Bologna (1444), he was not able to enter the city because of rebellious citizens. He took part in the Council of Ferrara-Florence (1438–45) and later served on papal diplomatic missions. On March 6, 1447, he was elected pope; soon afterward he brought the schism caused by rivalries between popes and councils to an end and restored peace to the papal states and to Italy by 1455. He furthered reform, to some extent, in the church and proclaimed 1450 a jubilee year. Nicholas began a program for the rebuilding of many of Rome's architectural wonders, including St. Peter's Church, and became the patron of many artists, artisans, Humanists, and literary scholars. His failure to promote real religious reform, however, helped to bring about the Reformation of the 16th century.

REFERENCES in other text articles:
·Alberti's patronage in architecture **1**:428h
·Peace of Lodi negotiations **9**:1144e
·Renaissance reconstruction of Rome **15**:1070e
·Valla's career as papal secretary **19**:19h

Nicholas V (b. PIETRO RAINALDUCCI, Rieti, Italy—d. Oct. 16, 1333, Avignon, Fr.), last imperial antipope, whose reign in Rome rivalled the pontificate of Pope John XXII at Avignon. An assembly of priests and laymen in Rome under the influence of the Holy Roman emperor Louis IV the Bavarian, whom John had excommunicated, elected the Franciscan monk Pietro Rainalducci as the antipope Nicholas V. Having little support, Nicholas' cause proved fruitless. After John excommunicated him in April 1329, Nicholas, having been assured a pardon, renounced at Avignon his illegal claim to the papacy on Aug. 25, 1330. He remained in honourable imprisonment in the papal palace until his death.

·John XXII authority conflict and submission **10**:233h

Nicholas Nickleby (serialized 1838–39; published as a book 1839), novel by Charles Dickens, its melodramatic and complicated story recounting the fortunes of Nicholas after his father dies, leaving the son penniless. In an episode set in a school, Dotheboys Hall, where Nicholas was for a time employed as a schoolmaster, Dickens so effectively attacked the appalling conditions that existed in many schools of the time that reformative measures were prompted. The novel is full of vividly drawn characterizations, none more so than Mr. Vincent Crummles, leader of a troupe of strolling actors.

Nicholas of Autrecourt (b. *c.* 1300, Autrecourt, near Verdun—d. after 1350, Metz, Lorrain), philosopher and theologian known principally for developing the medieval school of Skepticism to its extreme logical conclusions, which were condemned as heretical.

An advanced student in liberal arts and philosophy at the Sorbonne faculty of the University of Paris (1320–27), Nicholas became one of the most notable adherents to the thought of William of Ockham, a 14th-century advocate of Nominalism, a school of thought holding that only individual objects are real and that universal concepts simply express things as names. Nicholas' chief writings are commentaries on the 12th-century *Sentences* of Peter Lombard, the basic medieval compendium of philosophical theology, and on the *Politics* of Aristotle; nine letters to the Franciscan monk-philosopher Bernard of Arezzo; and an important treatise usually designated by the opening words *Exigit ordo executionis* ("The order of completion requires"), which has been preserved only in a single manuscript. This tract contains the 60 theses controverted at Nicholas' heresy trial, convened by Pope Benedict XII at Avignon, Fr., in 1340.

Termed by later historians "the medieval Hume," after the 18th-century English radical Empiricist, Nicholas rejected the traditional Aristotelian objectivism, with its allusions to a single intellect for all men, and proposed that there are only two bases for intellectual certitude: the logical principle of identity, with its correlative principle of contradiction, which states that a thing cannot simultaneously be itself and another; and the immediate evidence of sense data in experimental observation. Consistent with his Nominalist doctrine, he denied that any causal relation could be known experientially and taught that the very principle of causality could be reduced to the empirical declaration of the succession of two facts. The consequence of such a concept of causality, he averred, was to reject the possibility of any rational proof for the existence of God and to deny any divine cause in creation. Indeed, he held as more probable that the world had existed from eternity.

Philosophically, Nicholas' extreme Nominalism precluded the possibility of knowing anything as a permanent concept, allowing only the conscious experience of an object's sensible qualities. Replacing Scholastic–Aristotelian philosophy and physics with an atomism that was reminiscent of the 3rd-century-BC Greek philosopher Epicurus, Nicholas concurred with the teaching that the physical and mental universe is ultimately composed of simple, indivisible particles or atoms. He maintained, moreover, that his innovative thought did not affect his fidelity to Christian religious tradition, including the moral commandments and belief in a future life. Faith and reason, he taught, operate independently from each other, and one could assent to a religious doctrine that reason might contradict. Because of the fallibility of the senses and the human inclination—even in Aristotle—toward erroneous judgment, evidence and truth are not always identical, and philosophy at best is simply the prevalence of the more probable over the less probable.

The ecclesiastical judges at Nicholas' heresy trial, however, labelled his avowals of Christian belief as mere subterfuge and denounced him. Generally, he exhorted his readers and students to examine critically all classical Greek philosophical teachings, with their Arabic interpretations, and to accept nothing on the basis of prestige or authority alone.

Condemned in 1346 by Pope Clement VI, Nicholas finally was ordered in 1347 to resign his professorship, recant his error, and publicly burn his writings. That he took refuge with Emperor Louis IV the Bavarian is a legend created to form a parallel with the life of William of Ockham. Nicholas became dean of the cathedral at Metz in 1350, after which nothing more is heard of him. His *Exigit* manuscript was discovered by A. Birkenmayer at the Bodleian Library, Oxford, and was published in 1939 by J.R. O'Donnell in *Medieval Studies*.

·skeptical aspect of Ockhamism **14**:261a

Nicholas of Clémanges, originally NICOLAS POILLEVILAIN (b. *c.* 1363, Clémanges, Fr.—d. 1437, Paris), theologian, Humanist, and educator who denounced the corruption of institutional Christianity, advocated general ecclesiastical reform (anticipating the 16th-century Protestant Reformation), and attempted to mediate the Western Schism (rival claimants to the papacy) during the establishment of the papal residence in Avignon, Fr.

Named rector of the University of Paris in 1393 after acquiring repute as a liberal Humanist, Nicholas attempted to resolve the papal schism at the suggestion of his colleagues. In 1397 on the strength of his fame as a Latinist, he became secretary to the antipope Benedict XIII at Avignon, while Pope Urban VI resided in Rome. Narrowly escaping the plague in 1398 and frustrated by the continuation of the schism, Nicholas withdrew his allegiance to Benedict in 1408, when the Antipope lost the support of the French. After retiring to a Carthusian monastery at Fontaine-au-Bois, near Avignon, he addressed a communication to the Council of Constance in 1414, supporting the theory of the subordination of the pope to a general council. At the Council of Chartres in 1421, he defended the freedom of the Gallican church, and in 1432 he returned to his teaching career at the College of Navarre.

Reflecting an attitude of sober Humanism, transcending the partisan church politics of his day, Nicholas preferred the equanimity of intellectual and moral suasion rather than combative means to influence the contending factions dividing Christendom. He aimed at expressing disputed philosophical and religious questions in pre-Christian classical literary form. His works *De fructu rerum adversarum* ("On the Fruit of Adversities") and *De fructu eremi* ("On the Fruit of Seclusion"), written at the height of the papal crisis in 1408, proposed criteria for settling the schism. In addition to several biblical commentaries he composed the tract *De studio theologico* ("On Theological Study"), in which he criticized the abstractions of medieval scholastic philosophy and urged theologians to a more direct exposition of biblical doctrine to guarantee continued inspiration for the scholar and the general populace.

In his treatise *De lapsu et reparatione justitiae* ("On the Failure and Renewal of Justice") and in companion works (*c.* 1415) discussing the decline of the church and the ravages of simoniacal practices (the selling of religious offices) by ecclesiastical authorities, Nicholas deplored clerical avarice and the abuse of power. The essay *De corrupto ecclesiae statu* ("On the Corrupt State of the Church"), formerly attributed to him, is of dubious authenticity, according to more recent scholarship. His works, including the collection of stylistic letters on controversial issues and several pieces of poetry, were edited by J.M. Lydius (2 vol., 1613) and by A. Coville (1936).

Nicholas of Cusa, German NIKOLAUS VON CUSA, Latin NICOLAUS CUSANUS (b. 1401, Kues, now in West Germany—d. Aug. 11, 1464, Todi, Italy), cardinal, mathematician, scholar, experimental scientist, and influential philosopher who stressed the incomplete nature of man's knowledge of God and of the universe. At the Council of Basel in 1432, he gained recognition for his opposition to the candidate put forward by Pope Eugenius IV for the archbishopric of Trier. To his colleagues at the council he dedicated *De concordantia catholica* (1433; "On Catholic Concordance"), in which he expressed support for the supremacy of the general councils of the church over the authority of the papacy. In the same work he discussed the harmony of the church, drawing a pattern for priestly concord from his knowledge of the order of the heavens. By 1437, however, Cusa's respect for the council had declined, finding it unsuccessful in preserving church unity and enacting needed reforms. He therefore reversed his former position and became one of Eugenius' most ardent followers until the Pope's death in 1447. Ordained a priest about 1440, Cusa was made a cardinal in Brixen (Bressanone), Italy, by Nicholas V, pope from 1447 to 1455, and in 1450 was elevated to bishop there. For two years Cusa served as Nicholas' legate to Germany, where he preached frequently and helped reform the clergy, after which he began to serve full-time as bishop of Brixen.

A model of the "Renaissance man" because of his disciplined and varied learning, Cusa was skilled in theology, mathematics, philosophy, science, and the arts. In *De docta ignorantia* (1440; "On Learned Ignorance") he described the learned man as one who is aware of his own ignorance. In this and other works he typically borrowed symbols from geometry to demonstrate his points, as in his comparison of man's search for truth to the task of converting a square into a circle. Just as one can never derive a circle from a square by continuing to double equilateral sides from square to an octogon and so on (because even though the resulting polygon approaches a perfect circle, it never becomes one), says Cusa, so one can never approach truth completely.

Among Cusa's other interests were diagnostic medicine and applied science. He emphasized knowledge through experimentation and anticipated the work of the astronomer Copernicus by discerning a movement in the universe that did not centre in the earth, although the earth contributed to that movement. Cusa's study of plant growth, from which he concluded that plants absorb nourishment from the air, was the first modern formal experiment in biology and the first proof that air has weight. Numerous other developments, including a map of Europe, can also be traced to Cusa. A manuscript collector who discovered a dozen lost comedies by the Roman writer Plautus, he left an extensive library that remains a centre of scholarly activity in the hospital he founded and completed at his birthplace in 1458.

BIBLIOGRAPHY. H. Bett, *Nicholas of Cusa* (1932); K.H. Volkmann-Schluck, *Nicolaus Cusanus* (1957); P.E. Sigmund, *Nicholas of Cusa and Medieval Political Thought* (1963).

·Christian tolerance of Islām **4**:492c
·pacifism through religious toleration **13**:848h
·pantheism and transcendentalism **13**:952f
·Platonism of Florentine Academy **14**:544h
·Pseudo-Dionysius epistemology influence **16**:354d
·religious toleration appeal **4**:528f
·revival of Neoplatonism **14**:261c
·skeptical advocacy of learned ignorance **16**:831d
·Valla's study of Scripture **19**:19h

Nicholas of Damascus (fl. 1st century BC), Greek historian and philosopher whose works included a universal history from the time of the Assyrian empire to his own days. He instructed Herod the Great in rhetoric and philosophy, and attracted the notice of Augustus when he accompanied his patron on a visit to Rome. Later, when Herod's conduct aroused the suspicions of Augustus, Nicholas was sent on a mission to bring about a reconciliation. He survived Herod and it was through his influence that the succession was secured for Herod Archelaus. Fragments of his universal history, his autobiography, and his life of Augustus have been preserved, chiefly in the extracts of Constantine Porphyrogenitus.

Nicholas of Hereford (fl. early 15th century—d. after 1417, Coventry, Warwickshire), theological scholar and advocate of the English reform movement within the Roman Church who later recanted his unorthodox doctrine and aided in repressing innovators. With John Wycliffe he collaborated in the first complete English translation of the Bible.

Fellow of Queen's College, Oxford, *c.* 1374, Nicholas was influenced by the Reform theology of Wycliffe, founder of an evangelical Christian group called Lollards. Developing Wycliffe's teaching principally through preaching, he denounced the papal hierarchy and clerical luxury and insisted on the right of each Christian to establish his personal belief by meditating on the Scriptures. Throughout early 1382 Nicholas publicly contended with Peter Stokes, his chief opponent from the Oxford monastic community. Having preached a sermon in English in Oxford on May 15, 1382, the feast of Christ's Ascension, criticizing the church's wealth and its prohibition of the use of English in worship and theology, he was condemned with Wycliffe and his supporters at a council in London convened June 12 by William Courtenay, archbishop of Canterbury. Refusing to appear before the Archbishop's court, the Lollards were excommunicated on July 1 and, according to a witness, escaped death only through the protection of John, duke of Lancaster. Nicholas immediately appealed his case to Pope Urban VI at Rome but was again convicted and sentenced to confinement for life, having avoided execution, it is said, because of the Pope's friendship for the English scholars. He escaped from prison during a popular uprising against the Pope in June 1385 but was jailed by the Archbishop of Canterbury on his return to England. Subjected to harsh treatment at Saltwood Castle, Kent, during 1388–89, his writings were seized by order of King Richard II. By 1391 Nicholas abjured Lollard doctrine and was appointed theological inquisitor of suspected heretics. Chroniclers state that he vigorously disputed his former Lollard colleagues. In 1391 he was appointed chancellor of Hereford Cathedral and in 1395 chancellor of St. Paul's, London. It is probable that shortly before his death he became a Carthusian monk in Coventry.

Nicholas apparently was entrusted by Wycliffe with the translation of the Old Testament, his most significant literary work, and completed the major part of it by 1382, the beginning of his difficulties with church authorities. The English version was described as scholarly but literal, awkward, and obscure, requiring a later revision by Wycliffe and an associate, John Purvey, which was published in 1388.

Among the documents preserving Nicholas' addresses are the proceedings of his trial, including his *Confession of 1382*, declaring the Lollard theological position, and a conservative interpretation of the sacrament of the Lord's Supper. Guarded in what he published as a Lollard, only a collection of his sermons was recorded from that period; these sermons and his later orthodox tracts, *The Censure of Wycliffe's Doctrine* and *On the Apostasy of the Brethren from Christ*, are lost. Nicholas' extant works have been republished in *Fasciculi Zizaniorum Magistri Johannis Wyclif*, ed. Walter Waddington Shirley (1858) 289–329; and *Chronicon Henrici Knighton*, ed. Joseph Rawson (1889–95) 170–174. His reply to the charges of heresy is given in D. Wilkins' *Concilia Magnae Britanniae et Hiberniae*, 4 vol. (1737) 3:157–168. Nicholas' original English version of the Old Testament, in a manuscript at Oxford's Bodleian Library, is contained in *The Bible in Its Ancient and English Versions*, ed. Henry Wheeler Robinson (1954).

·Wycliffite Bible translation issues **2**:890a

Nicholas of Lyra, Latin NICOLAUS LYRANUS (b. *c.* 1270, Vieille-Lyre, Fr.—d. 1349, Paris), author of the first printed commentary on the Bible and one of the foremost Franciscan theologians and influential exegetes (biblical interpreters) of the Middle Ages. Becoming a Franciscan *c.* 1300, by 1309 he was a professor at the Sorbonne, where he taught for many years. From 1319 he headed the Franciscans in France and in 1325 founded the College of Burgundy, Paris.

Nicholas' chief work is his monumental 50-volume *Postillae perpetuae in universam S. Scripturam* ("Commentary Notes to the Universal Holy Scripture"), a commentary on the whole Bible that became a leading manual of exegesis. The importance of the *Postillae* lies in its emphasis on a literal, rather than a mystical or an allegorical, interpretation of Scriptures. Some scholars claim that the work had an important influence on Martin Luther.

·Christian exegetical contributions **7**:67c

Nicholas of Verdun (fl. *c.* 1150–1210, Flanders), the greatest enamellist and goldsmith of his day and an important figure in the transition from late Romanesque to early Gothic style. He was an itinerant craftsman who travelled to the site of his commission; therefore most of what is known of his life is inferred from his works.

"Moses on Mt. Sinai," champlevé enamel plaque by Nicholas of Verdun, completed 1181; from the Klosterneuburg Altar in the Abbey Church of Klosterneuburg, near Vienna

Erwin Meyer

The altarpiece (1181) of the Abbey Church of Klosterneuburg, Austria, is his best known work and reveals his absolute mastery of metalworking and the technique of champlevé enamelling, in which compartments hollowed out from a metal base are filled with vitreous enamel. The program of scenes on the altar is the most ambitious of its kind in the 12th century and is often considered the most important surviving medieval enamel work. The earlier scenes are done in a mature Romanesque style, but later scenes become progressively more bold and classical.

The reliquary (1205) of SS. Piatus and Nicasius in the Cathedral of Tournai, Belgium, subordinates enamel work to beaten metalwork. Though much damaged by restoration, it remains a masterful work of early Gothic sculpture, with its slender figures and supple drapery.

The Shrine of the Three Kings in the treasury of Cologne Cathedral is the most important of the Cologne reliquaries attributed to Nicholas. Much of the reliquary is the work of assistants, but the general design and the figures of the prophets are by Nicholas. Powerful and expressive, the prophets have been called the most important metal sculptures of the late 12th century. Two reliquaries attributed to Nicholas, the shrines of St. Anne in Siegburg and of St. Albanus in Saint-Pantaleon, Cologne, have suffered so much by restoration that they no longer reveal the hand of Nicholas except in the overall design.

·enamelwork tradition of the Middle Ages **6**:776e
·Gothic sculpture developments **19**:366f
·Three Kings shrine sculpture **11**:1104e

Nicholas Oresme: *see* Oresme, Nicoled.

Nicholasville, city, seat of Jessamine County, central Kentucky, U.S., in the Bluegrass region. It was settled in 1798 near the site of a gristmill and named to honour Col. George Nicholas, a member of the state constitutional convention in 1792. The city is the trading centre for an agricultural area producing tobacco, dairy products, livestock, corn (maize), and wheat. The town is only 13 mi (21 km) south-southwest of Lexington, and there are several noted Thoroughbred horse breeding farms in the area. The Kentucky Palisades are spectacular rock cliffs bordering the nearby Kentucky River. Pop. (1980) 10,400.
38°54′ N, 84°33′ W

Nichols, Ernest Fox (1869–1924), U.S. physicist, particularly known for measuring planetary heat and determining light pressure by means of the extremely sensitive radiometer he devised.

Nichols, John (b. Feb. 2, 1745, London—d. Nov. 26, 1826, London), writer, printer, and antiquary who, through numerous volumes of literary anecdotes, made an invaluable contribution to posterity's knowledge of the lives and works of 18th-century men of letters in England. Apprenticed in 1757 to William Bowyer the younger, known as "the learned printer," who took him into partnership in 1766, he undertook his first literary work as editor of the works of Jonathan Swift (1775–79). In 1778, Nichols became part manager of the *Gentleman's Magazine* and in 1792 sole managing editor. Of his original work, *Bibliotheca Topographica Britannica* (1780–90) and *The History and Antiquities of the County of Leicester* (1795–1815) are especially valuable. They are the fruit of his own meticulous observation and research. A friend of most of the leading literary figures of his age, he published Samuel Johnson's *Lives of the English Poets*, exercising much editorial influence and supplying a good deal of basic information.

John Nichols, engraving by Charles Heath after a portrait by J. Jackson

Radio Times Hulton Picture Library

His own work as a biographer of the age began with his memoir of Bowyer, expanded into *Biographical and Literary Anecdotes of William Bowyer* (1782). This formed the basis of *Literary Anecdotes of the Eighteenth Century* (begun 1812, completed by his son, John Bowyer Nichols).

Nicholson, Ben (b. 1894), leading English abstract painter, studied at the Slade School of Art and held his first one-man show in 1922. From 1920 onward, under the influence of Cubism and the de Stijl movement, he began his severe, geometrical designs, notable for an icy brilliance of colour.

·Unit One membership **12**:433f

Nicholson, John (b. Dec. 11, 1821, Dublin—d. Sept. 23, 1857, Delhi, India), British soldier and administrator who brought relief to Delhi during the Indian Mutiny of 1857. Nicholson became a cadet in the Bengal Army at the age of 17 and fought at Ghaznī during the First Afghan War of 1841–42. Subsequently, he held political posts in Kashmir and the Punjab and took part in the Second Sikh War of 1848.

John Nicholson, detail of a chalk drawing by William Carpenter, 1854; in the National Portrait Gallery, London

By courtesy of the National Portrait Gallery, London

During the rebellion of 1857 Nicholson was promoted to brigadier general after pacifying the Punjab and led a swift advance on Delhi, which was under siege by rebel forces. His arrival in Delhi early in August and his victory at Najafgarh inspired the besieged British troops; on September 14 he led an attacking column against the Kashmir Gate. The gate was taken, but he was wounded in battle and died shortly thereafter.

Nicholson, Reynold Alleyne (b. Aug. 18, 1868, Keighley, Yorkshire—d. Aug. 27, 1945, Chester), English orientalist, lecturer in Persian (1902–26) and Sir Thomas Adams professor of Arabic (1926–33) at Cambridge University, was a foremost scholar in the fields of Islāmic literature and mysticism. His *Literary History of the Arabs* (1907) remains the standard work on that subject in English; while his many text editions and translations of Ṣūfī writings, culminating in his eight-volume *Mathnawi of Jalalu'ddin Rumi* (1925–40), eminently advanced the study of Muslim mystics.

He combined exact scholarship with notable literary gifts; some of his versions of Arabic and Persian poetry entitle him to be considered a poet in his own right. His deep understanding of Islām and of the Muslim peoples was the more remarkable in that he never traveled outside Europe. A shy and retiring man, he proved himself an inspiring teacher and an original thinker; he exercised a lasting influence on Islāmic studies.

Nicholson, Seth Barnes (b. Nov. 12, 1891, Springfield, Ill.—d. July 2, 1963, Los Angeles), astronomer best known for discovering four satellites of Jupiter: the 9th in 1914 (at Lick Observatory, Mt. Hamilton, Calif.), the 10th and 11th in 1938, and the 12th in 1951 (all at Mt. Wilson Observatory). Educated at Drake University, Des Moines, Iowa, and at the University of California (Ph.D., 1915), he was on the Mt. Wilson Observatory staff from 1915 to 1957. Of greater astrophysical significance than his satellite discoveries was his investigation of sunspots, especially their magnetic properties and terrestrial effects. With U.S. astronomer Edison Pettit he made many thermocouple measurements of stellar and planetary radiation.

·infrared astronomy development **9**:581c
·Venus clouds water content **19**:77g

Nicholson, William (b. 1753, London—d. May 21, 1815, Bloomsbury, London), chemist, discoverer of the electrolysis of water, which has become a basic process in both chemical research and industry.

Nicholson invented a hydrometer (an instrument for measuring the density of water) in 1790. In 1800, after he heard of the invention of the electric battery by the Italian physicist Alessandro Volta, he built one of his own. He then discovered that when leads from the battery are placed in water, the water breaks up into hydrogen and oxygen, which collect separately to form bubbles at the submerged ends of the wires, thus for the first time producing a chemical reaction by electricity.

In 1797 Nicholson founded the *Journal of Natural Philosophy, Chemistry and the Arts*, the first independent scientific journal. *Introduction to Natural Philosophy* (1781) was the most successful of his published works.

·rotary-movement printing press **14**:1054g

Nichrome, an alloy of nickel, iron, chromium, and carbon.

·diesel engine design **5**:727e

Nicias (d. 413 BC, Sicily), Athenian politician and general during the Peloponnesian War (431–404 BC) between Sparta and Athens; he was in charge of the Athenian forces engaged in the siege of Syracuse, Sicily, the failure of which contributed greatly to the ultimate defeat of Athens. In the first ten years of the conflict, he proved his ability as a leader of offensive expeditions and in 421 negotiated the Peace of Nicias and an alliance with Sparta. The hostility of Sparta's allies and the opposition of the Athenian general Alcibiades, however, foiled Nicias' efforts to uphold the peace. Warfare was renewed, and in 415 Nicias reluctantly allowed himself to be appointed, with Alcibiades and Lamachus, leader of the Sicilian expedition.

The recall of Alcibiades and death of Lamachus left him, although ill, in sole charge of the siege. The wall he attempted to build around Syracuse was not completed, and Nicias asked to be relieved of his command, but instead, reinforcements under Demosthenes arrived early in 413. When these failed to reverse the situation, Demosthenes favoured departure, but an eclipse of the moon occurred on Aug. 27, 413, and the superstitious Nicias accepted his soothsayers' advice to delay setting out. The Syracusans forced the surrender of the Athenian forces, including Nicias, whom they executed.

·Alcibiades opposing Sparta policy **1**:436h
·Peace of Nicias terms and effects **8**:358a
·Peloponnesian conflict and politics **14**:22g
·role in Peloponnesian Wars **8**:358c

Nicias (fl. 4th century BC), Athenian painter, a younger contemporary of Praxiteles, painted some of the latter's statues and was noted for his skill in the use of light and shade.

Nicias is described in some detail by Pliny the Elder, who relates that when Praxiteles was asked which of his works in marble he admired most, he replied, "those which had been touched by the hands of Nicias." He also reports that Ptolemy I of Egypt once offered Nicias a large sum of money for his painting of "Odysseus Questioning the Dead in the Underworld," but that Nicias chose instead to make the painting a present to his native Athens.

None of Nicias' original paintings still exist. Among those listed by Pliny are "Evocation of the Dead After the Odyssey," "Portrait of Alexander," "Io," and "Perseus and Andromeda."

nickel (from German *Kupfernickel*, "Old Nick's copper"), symbol Ni, chemical element, ferromagnetic metal of transition Group VIII of the periodic table, markedly resistant to oxidation and corrosion. Silvery-white, tough, and harder than iron, nickel is widely familiar because of its use in coinage, but is more important either as the pure metal or in the form of alloys for its many domestic and industrial applications. Elemental nickel very sparingly occurs together with iron (*q.v.*) in terrestrial and meteoric deposits. The metal was isolated (1751) by a Swedish chemist and mineralogist, Baron Axel Fredrik Cronstedt, who prepared an impure sample from an ore containing niccolite (nickel arsenide). Earlier, an ore of this same type was called *Kupfernickel* after "Old Nick" and his mischievous gnomes because, though it resembled copper ore, it yielded a brittle, unfamiliar product. Twice as abundant as copper, nickel constitutes about 0.016 percent of the Earth's crust; it is a fairly common constituent of igneous rocks, though singularly few deposits qualify in concentration, size, and accessibility for commercial interest. The most important sources are pentlandite, found with nickel-bearing pyrrhotite and chalcopyrite, and nickel-bearing laterites, such as garnierite.

Nickel (atomic number 28) resembles iron (atomic number 26) in strength and toughness but is more like copper (atomic number 29) in resistance to oxidation and corrosion, a combination accounting for many of its applications. About half the nickel produced is used in alloys with iron, about a quarter in high-nickel alloys, such as the corrosion-resistant ones with copper and the heat-resistant alloys with chromium. Nickel is also used in electrically resistive, magnetic, and many other kinds of alloys, such as nickel silver (with copper and zinc but no silver). The unalloyed metal is utilized to form protective coatings on other metals, especially by electroplating. Finely divided nickel is employed to catalyze (speed up without changing the products of) the hydrogenation of unsaturated organic compounds (*e.g.*, fats and oils, in the process called fat hardening).

Natural nickel consists of five stable isotopes: nickel-58 (67.76 percent), nickel-60 (26.16 percent), nickel-62 (3.66 percent), nickel-61 (1.25 percent), and nickel-64 (1.16 percent). The two allotropic forms (forms with different structural arrangement) are close-packed hexagonal (alpha) and face-centred cubic (beta). Nickel is ferromagnetic up to 358° C, or 676° F (its Curie point). The metal is uniquely resistant to the action of alkalies and is frequently used for containers for concentrated solutions of sodium hydroxide. Nickel reacts slowly with strong acids under ordinary conditions to liberate hydrogen and form Ni^{2+} ions. Nickel compounds have been prepared in oxidation states from −1 to +4, though nickel(II) is by far the commonest. It forms complex ions, most often with a coordination number of 6. Nickel compounds have been used mainly in electroplating, in the production of nickel catalysts, in ground-coat enamels, in storage batteries of the Edison type, and in the production of special nickel powders. Nickel carbonyl, $Ni(CO)_4$, was the first simple metal carbonyl isolated (1890). Nickel ferrites are used as magnetic cores for antennas, transformers, and other electrical and electronic equipment. Nickel and its compounds are relatively nontoxic, and any quantities that might be ingested incidentally through the use of nickel or nickel-alloy cooking utensils or in fats hydrogenated over nickel catalysts are considered harmless.

atomic number	28
atomic weight	58.71
melting point	1,453° C (2,647° F)
boiling point	2,732° C (4,950° F)
specific gravity	8.90 (20° C)
valence	2
electronic config.	2-8-16-2 or (Ar)$3d^84s^2$

Major ref. **18**:617f
·abundance in geochemical materials, tables 1, 4, and 6 **6**:702
·atomic weight and number table **2**:345
·battery cell construction and reaction **2**:767b
·cobalt occurrence and recovery **4**:808c
·concentration by magmas **9**:220a
·concentration factor in marine organisms, table 1 **6**:714
·Earth's core characteristics **6**:55a
·electrorefining cell and electrolyte **11**:1071e
·element abundance, table 6 **17**:602
·element synthesis at high temperature **4**:121c
·ferromagnetic dipole alignment **7**:251d *passim* to 253e
·jet engine alloy research **10**:159f
·luminescence electron capture **11**:183e
·magnet composition and properties **11**:336g; table
·North American mineral deposits **13**:192e; map 198
·oil hydrogenation and catalyst actions **13**:530b
·ore exploration and processing **13**:71d
·organometallic compound preparation **13**:718g
·petroleum product composition **14**:167f
·physical properties of nickel–iron **12**:855c
·radioisotope medical use, table 6 **15**:447
·solar abundances, table 2 **17**:803
·steel alloys properties and uses **17**:657b
·tin alloy production and use **18**:431h; table
·transition element general properties **18**:601c; tables
·U.S. consumption and world reserves, table 7 **13**:504
·welding compatibility and extensive use **19**:741d
·world mineral production table **12**:247

nickel carbonyl, or TETRACARBONYLNICKEL, a colourless volatile liquid formed by the action of carbon monoxide on finely divided nickel. It is used as a carrier of carbon monoxide in the synthesis of acrylates (compounds used in the manufacture of plastics) from acetylene and alcohols. The pure compound has a specific gravity of 1.32 (17° C), boils at 43° C (109° F), and solidifies at −25° C (−13° F). It is poisonous and highly flammable. Its chemical formula is $Ni(CO)_4$.

Nickel carbonyl was the first of a class of compounds, called metal carbonyls, to be discovered. It is characterized by an electronic configuration in which the nickel atom, like that of the noble gas krypton, is surrounded by 36 electrons. Many of the simple metal carbonyls have electronic configurations that are comparable, on a formal basis, to the noble gas atoms.

·metal carbonyl reactions and uses **18**:607a
·platinum and nickel production **14**:530d
·preparation and nickel extraction **11**:1066c

nickel-chromium steel, developed by the French in 1891 by adding chromium to nickel steels; used for all types of forgings and machine parts.

·alloy types, composition, and uses **17**:642a

nickel–iron, alloy of native nickel and native iron that contains between 24 and 77 percent nickel. It occurs in the gold washings of the Gorge River, N.Z.; in the platinum sands of the Bobrovka River, Urals; and in the gold dredgings of the Fraser River, B.C. It also occurs in large ellipsoidal masses (some over 37 kilograms [100 pounds]) in Oregon.

Nickel–iron also can be of meteoritic origin. Called taenite, it is found in some ataxites and in all octahedrites. Plessite, an intergrowth of taenite and kamacite (meteoritic iron), is also a constituent of all octahedrites. For detailed physical properties, *see* the Table in the entry native elements.

·physical properties and occurrence **12**:855c
·taenite physical properties **12**:855d

Nickelodeon, early motion picture theatre with an admission price of five cents.

·bright screen picture development **12**:541d

nickel products and production 13:71. Although first identified as an element in the 18th century, nickel had, nevertheless, been used as an alloying agent with other metals for 2,000 years before it was identified; its strength, corrosion resistance, and ductility make it one of the most important industrial metals.

The text article covers its history and contains sections on the ores and their locations, the recovery and refining processes, and the most important applications of nickel and its various alloys and compounds.

REFERENCES in other text articles:
·austenitic steel composition and uses **4**:571a
·auto materials consumption, table 4 **2**:534
·battery cell construction and reaction **2**:767b
·cobalt extraction and processing **4**:808e
·electroplating techniques **6**:692e
·electrorefining cell and electrolyte **11**:1071e
·iron magnetic alloy uses **9**:897f
·jet engine heat-resistant alloy research **10**:159f
·metal carbonyl reactions and uses **18**:607a
·platinum simultaneous production **14**:530b
·sulfide mineral ore association **17**:790b

RELATED ENTRIES in the *Ready Reference and Index:*
Monel; nickel; stainless steel

nickel–silver, also known as PAI-T'UNG, ancient Chinese alloy containing 10–30 percent nickel with the balance of zinc and copper used as a base for silver-plated ware.

·nickel production development **13**:71e

nicking, for organ flue pipes, the practice of cutting notches in the edge of the languet so as to produce a short sluggish attack.

·organ pipe construction and voicing **13**:677h

Nicklaus, Jack (William) (b. Jan. 21, 1940, Columbus, Ohio), professional golfer who came nearest to dominating world golf from the middle 1960s, and who in 1972 became the greatest winner of prize money in the history of the game, with earnings in excess of $1,500,000.

Nicklaus, 1963
Wide World Photos

While a student at Ohio State University, Columbus, Nicklaus won the U.S. Amateur championship in 1959 and 1961. He turned professional in December 1961 and was immediately successful on the U.S. Professional Golfers' Association (PGA) circuit of tournaments. By 1966 he had become the fourth golfer to win the four tournaments composing the modern "Grand Slam"— so called when a player wins all four in a single year. Nicklaus won the U.S. Open (1962, 1967, 1972), the Masters (1963, 1965, 1966, 1972), the U.S. PGA (1963, 1971), and the British Open (1966, 1970). In 1965 he set a record for the Masters with a score of 271, 17 under par. In the World Series of Golf, contested by the winners of each year's "Grand Slam" events, he won on four occasions (1962, 1963, 1967, 1970).

·championship career record **8**:247g

nickname, an informal name given to an individual in place of, or in addition to, his given name. Nicknames are usually descriptive of the individual (*e.g.*, Slim, Curly, Big John) or are familiar variations on his given name (Rich, Dick, Ricky as nicknames for Richard). Historical figures are often known to us by their nicknames (*e.g.*, Scipio Africanus, Caligula ["Little Boot"], Eric the Red, Good Queen Bess), and the use of nicknames in Western culture long predates the use of family names; nicknames were in fact often the source of family names. In English, surnames such as White, Young, Scott, Fox, and Reed (red) were originally nicknames applied to particular individuals that came to refer to the descendants of the individuals regardless of whether the terms were any longer fitting.

Nicobarese languages, Austro-Asiatic languages spoken on the Nicobar Islands by about 10,000 people. The Nicobarese languages are sometimes classified into four groups: North Nicobar, including the Car, Chowra, Teressa, and Bompaka languages; Central Nicobar, including the Camorta, Nancowry, Trinkat, and Katchall languages; South Nicobar, including the Coastal Great Nicobar and the Little Nicobar languages; and Inland Great Nicobar, including the Shompe language. (Some specialists divide the languages into six groups.) Some scholars believe that the Nicobarese languages constitute a branch of the Mon-Khmer group of Austro-Asiatic languages, while others consider them to constitute a separate Austro-Asiatic branch.

·Austro-Asiatic language distribution map **2**:484
·distribution and development **9**:286f
·Southeast Asian insular language areas **10**:668f

Nicobar Islands, group of 19 islands in the Bay of Bengal, southeast of India. With the nearby Andaman Islands, they comprise a union territory of India. They are 740 sq mi (1,624 sq km) in area; the largest island is Great Nicobar. *See also* Andaman and Nicobar Islands. Latest census 14,563.
8°00′ N, 93°50′ E

·Austro-Asiatic language distribution map **2**:484
·map, India **9**:278
·Marco Polo voyage map **14**:758

Nicodemus the Hagiorite (b. 1748, Naxos Island, Greece—d. July 14, 1809, Mt. Athos, Greece), Greek Orthodox monk and author of ascetical prayer literature influential in reviving the practice of Hesychasm, a Byzantine method of contemplative prayer and mysticism.

Forced to flee Turkish persecution in the midst of his studies at Smyrna, Nicodemus entered the monastery of Mt. Athos. He was inspired to theological scholarship by a contemporary, Macarius of Corinth, whose *Philocalia*, or collection of Eastern prayer texts, Nicodemus edited. After this edition had occasioned a renewed interest in Hesychasm, with its litanies (the "Jesus Prayer") and intense meditation, he then edited Macarius' essays on liturgical prayer, emphasizing the Eucharist, or the Lord's Supper. Although this work was at first criticized for erroneous doctrine, its orthodoxy was later vindicated by the Synod of Constantinople in 1819.

Nicodemus' outstanding work, the *Pedalion*, or *Rudder of the Ship of Knowledge*, is a commentary on Greek Church law. Its bias against the Latin Church, although partly attributable to interpolations by another editor, reflects the author's negative feelings toward the institutions of Western Christianity. Nicodemus did not hesitate, however, to use the treatises of Latin theologians on asceticism and contemplative prayer. Thus, he wrote Greek versions of the *Spiritual Combat* by Lorenzo Scupoli, and the *Spiritual Exercises* of Ignatius of Loyola, 16th-century founder of the Jesuit order. In 1782 he wrote his own *Philocalia* (3rd ed. 1958), his *Enchiridion of Counsels* (1801), a handbook on the religious life, continues to guide modern Greek spirituality. He was proclaimed a saint by the Greek Orthodox Church on May 31, 1955.

·Orthodox translations of Western texts **6**:156d

Nicol, Abioseh (b. DAVIDSON NICOL, 1924, Freetown, Sierra Leone), diplomat, physician, and medical researcher whose short stories and poems are among the best to have come out of West Africa. Nicol was educated in medicine and natural sciences in Sierra Leone, Nigeria, and England and served as researcher and resident physician at London Hospital, on the medical faculty of the University of Ibadan, and in varying capacities as medical officer and pathologist for the Nigerian and Sierra Leonean governments. Known for his research into the structure of insulin, he has lectured (at Yale University and Mayo Clinic and elsewhere) and written widely on medical topics. He was principal of Fourah Bay College, Freetown (1960), vice chancellor of the University of Sierra Leone, and ambassador to the United Nations, beginning in 1968.

Critical appraisal of Nicol's writing has been continually favourable. His short stories, simple and realistic presentations of everyday events, are sensitively written with astute insight into what he sees as life's mixture of the tragic and the absurd. *Two African Tales* (1965) and *The Truly Married Woman, and Other Stories* (1965) centre upon life in the government service, upon the interaction of Africans with colonial administrators, and upon the skein of human understanding in pre-independent Sierra Leone. Besides appearing in anthologies and journals, his short stories and poems have been broadcast by the British Broadcasting Corporation. He has written a number of articles on the history of West African literature and edited a collection of writings by the 19th-century nationalist Africanus Horton.

Nicolai, Christoph Friedrich (b. March 18, 1733, Berlin—d. Jan. 8, 1811, Berlin), writer, bookseller, and a leader of the German Enlightenment (Aufklärung) who, as editor of the reformist journal *Allgemeine Deutsche Bibliothek* ("German General Library"), was critical of such new-movement writers as Goethe, Friedrich Schiller, and Kant.

The son of a well-known bookseller, Nicolai went to Frankfurt an der Oder, where he learned his father's bookselling business and became acquainted with English literature. On his return to Berlin (1752), he took part in a literary controversy over Milton by defending the English poet against the grammarian

Johann Christoph Gottsched. Nicolai's *Briefe über den jetzigen Zustand der schönen Wissenschaften in Deutschland* (1755; "Letters on the Current State of the Fine Arts in Germany"), published anonymously, was directed against both Gottsched and Gottsched's Swiss opponents, the critics Johann Jakob Bodmer and Johann Breitinger. His enthusiasm for English literature gained him the friendship of Gotthold Ephraim Lessing and the philosopher Moses Mendelssohn. He cofounded, with Mendelssohn, the periodical *Bibliothek der schönen Wissenschaften* (1757–60; "Library of Fine Arts") and, with both Lessing and Mendelssohn, *Briefe die neuste Literatur betreffend* (1761–66; "Letters on the Modern Literary Question"). He also edited the *Allgemeine Deutsche Bibliothek* (1765–92), the organ of the "popular philosophers" who fought against authority in religion and what they conceived to be extravagance in literature.

Christoph Nicolai, oil painting by A. Graff (1736–1813)

Historia-Photo

Nicolai wrote many independent works. His *Charakteristischen Anekdoten von Friedrich II* (1788–92) is an account of events in the court of Frederick II the Great and has some historical value. His romances are forgotten, although *Das Leben und die Meinungen des Magisters Sebaldus Nothanker* (1773–76; "The Life and Opinions of Master Sebaldus Nothanker") and his satire on Goethe's Werther, *Die Freuden des Jungen Werthers* (1775; "The Joys of Young Werther"), were well known in their time. *Die Beschreibung einer Reise durch Deutschland und die Schweiz* (12 vol., 1788–96; "The Description of a Journey Through Germany and Switzerland"), a record of Nicolai's reflections on man and the state of science, religion, industry, and morals, had become widely read by 1796 and reflects the conservativism of his views in later life.

Nicolai, Friedrich Bernhard Gottfried (1793–1846), German astronomer.
·Uranus study and discovery of Neptune **12**:963c

Nicolai, (Carl) Otto Ehrenfried (b. June 9, 1810, Känigsberg, East Prussia, now Kaliningrad, in the Russian S.F.S.R.—d. May 11, 1849, Berlin), composer known for his comic opera *Die lustigen Weiber von Windsor* (*The Merry Wives of Windsor*), based on Shakespeare's comedy. In his youth he was exploited as a prodigy by his father. He studied in Berlin in 1827 and later under Giuseppe Baini in Rome. From 1838 onward he produced successful operas in Italy and Vienna. In 1841 he became court conductor in Vienna and founded the Philharmonic Society there in 1842. In 1847 he became conductor of the Berlin Opera, where he produced *Die lustigen Weiber von Windsor* in 1849. It remains one of the most popular comic operas of the 19th century.

Nicolas Poillevilain: *see* Nicholas of Clémanges.

Nicolaus of Damascus, 1st-century-BC Greek historian and philosopher.
·Aristotle's doctrinal writings **1**:1156e

Nicola Valley, region of British Columbia, Canada.
·agricultural market changes **7**:697b

Nicolay, John (1832–1901), Bavarian-born U.S. biographer.
·biographies from primary sources **2**:1008f

Nicole, Pierre (b. Oct. 19, 1625, Chartres, Fr.—d. Nov. 16, 1695, Paris), theologian, author, moralist, and controversialist whose writings, chiefly polemic, supported Jansenism, a movement within Roman Catholicism emphasizing original sin and God's sovereignty. Educated in Paris, Nicole taught literature and philosophy at Port-Royal des Champs, Fr. From this community, a stronghold of Jansenism, Nicole's textbook *The Port-Royal Logic* (1662, with Antoine Arnauld) and the epithet for the movement's advocates—"Port Royalists"—take their names. He was an influential spokesman from 1655 to 1668 through his writing or editing of most of the Jansenist pamphlets. He was probably the source of the celebrated distinction between the "questions of fact," an adroit device allowing him to separate into two parts the charge of heresy often made against the Jansenists. The two questions were: Are Jansenist doctrines rightly called heretical? And did Jansen in fact teach these doctrines? By answering the first question affirmatively and the second negatively, Nicole enabled the Jansenists to pursue their program of criticism and reform without openly breaking with the Roman Catholic Church.

Nicole, detail of an engraving by Cornelius Vermeulen after a painting by Élisabeth Chéron (1648–1711)

J.E. Bulloz

From 1669 Nicole used his talents to defend Catholic dogma against Protestant criticism. A friend of the French philosopher Blaise Pascal, he used one of his numerous pseudonyms to translate into Latin Pascal's *Provinciales* ("Provincial Letters"). Nicole's best known work is the *Essais de morale* (4 vol., 1671; "Essays on Morality"), eventually enlarged to 14 volumes, in which he discussed the problems raised for ethics by human nature, which he found seldom capable of virtue.

Nicoleño (people): *see* Gabrielino.

Nicolet, Jean (1598–1642), French explorer, the first known European to discover Lake Michigan and the present state of Wisconsin (1634).
·Great Lakes and European explorations **8**:301c

Nicoletti, Paolo, also called PAULUS VENETUS, 14th–15th-century Italian philosopher.
·Aristotelianism and the Renaissance **1**:1160a

Nicolle, Charles-Jules-Henri (b. Sept. 21, 1866, Rouen, Fr.—d. Feb. 28, 1936, Tunis, Tunisia), bacteriologist who received the 1928 Nobel Prize for Physiology or Medicine for his discovery (1909) that typhus is transmitted by the body louse. After practicing and engaging in bacteriological research in Rouen, Nicolle became director of the Pasteur Institute in Tunis (1902–32). There he founded the Archives de l'Institut Pasteur de Tunis, and during his tenure the Institute became a distinguished centre for bacteriological research and for production of serums and vaccines to combat infectious diseases. He extended his work on typhus to distinguish between the classical louse-borne form and murine typhus, conveyed to man by the rat flea; he also made valuable contributions to the knowledge of rinderpest, brucellosis, measles, diphtheria, and tuberculosis.

Nicolls, Richard (1624–72), first English governor of the colony of New York.
·horse racing's origins in America **8**:1093e

Nicolò II (1338–88), Este ruler of Ferrara.
·Este Castle construction **6**:965f

Nicolò III, also known as NICHOLAS III (1384–1441), duke of Ferrara, Modena, Palermo, and Reggio.
·Este family political expansion **6**:965g

Nicol prism, type of optical device used for the production or analysis of polarized light.
·light polarization properties **10**:941f; illus.

Nicolson, Sir Harold (George) (b. Nov. 21, 1886, Tehrān—d. May 1, 1968, Sissinghurst Castle, Kent), British diplomat and man of letters. His works include *Peacemaking 1919* (1933), an account of the Parish Peace Conference; *Curzon: The Last Phase* (1934); *The Congress of Vienna* (1946); and *Sainte-Beuve* (1957).

Nicolson was in the diplomatic service (1909–29) and was a member of Parliament (1935–45). He was married to the novelist and poet Victoria Sackville-West.
·biographical literature development **2**:1012h

Nicomachean Ethics, exposition of basic ethical doctrines by Aristotle; his son, Nicomachus, has been credited with editing the work.
·ethics as a practical science **1**:1169h
·Luther's conflict with justice concept **11**:189e
·rejection of Platonic epistemology **6**:932a

Nicomachus (fl. 4th century BC, Thebes, now Thívai, Greece), Greek painter little-known because his work was overshadowed by that of his great contemporaries; but the Roman connoisseur Vitruvius said that if his fame was less than that of others, it was the fault of fortune rather than of demerit. Pliny the Elder gave a list of his works, including "Rape of Persephone," "Victory in a Quadriga," a group of Apollo and Artemis, and the "Mother of the Gods Seated on a Lion." Pliny also said that he was a rapid worker and used only four colours.
·Aristotle's early education **1**:1162d

Nicomachus of Gerasa (fl. *c.* AD 100, Gerasa, now Jarash, Jordan), Neo-Pythagorean philosopher and mathematician who wrote *Arithmētikē eisagōgē* (Eng. trans., *Introduction to Arithmetic*, 1926), the first work to treat arithmetic as a discipline independent of geometry. Considered a standard authority for 1,000 years, it sets out the elementary theory and properties of numbers and contains the earliest known Greek multiplication table. In his *Arithmētikē* numbers are no longer denoted by lines, as in Euclid, but are written in the Arabic numerals. General principles are stated with particular numbers taken as illustrations. A Latin translation by Apuleius of Madaurus (*c.* AD 125) is lost, but Boethius' version survived and was used as a school book up to the Renaissance. Nicomachus' *Encheiridion Harmonikēs* ("Handbook of Harmony") is on the Pythagorean theory of music. He also wrote *Theologoumena arithmetikēs* (2 vol., "The Theology of Numbers"), on the mystic properties of numbers, but only fragments of the work have survived.

Housing units in Nicosia, Cyprus

Georg Gerster—Rapho Guillumette

Nicomedes I, king of Bithynia (reigned *c.* 279–*c.* 255 BC).
·Celtic invasion of Anatolia **1**:824g
·establishment of Hellenistic Kingdom **8**:381a

Nicomedes III Euergetes, king of Bithynia (reigned *c.* 127–*c.* 94 BC).
·Mithradates VI's military career **12**:288b

Nicomedes IV Philopator, king of Bithynia (reigned 94–75/74 BC), Roman ally who bequeathed his kingdom to Rome.
·First Mithradatic War **12**:288b
·Roman war over Bithynia **15**:1104a

Nicopolis, Battle of (Sept. 25, 1396), Turkish victory over an army of European crusaders that ended massive international efforts to halt Turkish expansion into the Balkans and central Europe.

When Sultan Bayezid I (*q.v.;* ruled 1389–1402) laid siege to Constantinople (1395), the Byzantine emperor Manuel II Palaeologus appealed to the Christian rulers of Europe for aid. King Sigismund (*q.v.*) of Hungary responded by organizing a crusade. In July 1396 knights from France, Burgundy, England, Germany, and the Netherlands joined Sigismund at Buda and set out first to evict the Turks from the Balkans and then to march through Anatolia and Syria to Jerusalem.

Having entered Turkish territory (August) and conquered the garrisons at Vidin and Rahova, the crusaders laid siege to Nicopolis, the main Turkish stronghold on the Danube. While they waited for the well-stocked, well-fortified town to submit, Bayezid marched from Constantinople and established his army on a hill several miles from Nicopolis. Although Sigismund urged his allies to maintain a defensive position, the knights charged up the hill, scattering the first lines of the Turkish cavalry and infantry. Bayezid awaited them, however, with another cavalry contingent reinforced by a Serb army, and the Western forces were too exhausted to fight effectively. Sigismund, whose army had not participated in the initial attack, tried to rescue them, but his Walachian and Transylvanian contingents deserted and his Hungarian force was insufficient. The Turks slaughtered most of the crusaders and pushed the remainder back to the Danube. Although a small portion of the allied army, including Sigismund, escaped, most survivors were captured and executed by Bayezid, who held only a few of the prisoners for ransom.

By their victory at Nicopolis, the Turks discouraged the formation of future European coalitions against them. They maintained their pressure on Constantinople, tightened their control over the Balkans, and became a greater menace to central Europe.

Nicopolis Actia, modern NIKÓPOLIS, previously PALAIOPRÉVEZA, about four miles (six kilometres) north of Préveza, northwest Greece, ancient city founded in 31 BC by Octavian, who in 27 BC was to become the Roman emperor Augustus, in commemoration of his victory over Antony and Cleopatra at Actium. Nicopolis Actia became the capital of the coastal region encompassing Acarnania and southern Epirus (modern Ípiros).

Nicosia, Greek LEVKOSIA, Turkish LEFKOŞA, capital of the Republic of Cyprus, Nicosia District, on the Pedieas River, about 500 ft (150 m) above sea level in the centre of the Mesaöria Plain between the Kyrenia Mountains (north) and the Troödos range (south). It is also the archiepiscopal seat of the autocephalous Church of Cyprus.

Under the control of the Byzantines (330–1191), the Lusignan kings (1192–1489), the Venetians (1489–1571), the Turks (1571–1878), and the British (1878–1960), Nicosia reflects the vicissitudes of Cypriot history and both Oriental and Western influences. Nicosia, known in antiquity as Ledra, is a medieval corruption of the Byzantine Lefkosia. It was a kingdom in the 7th century BC and has been a bishopric from the 4th century AD and the seat of government since the 10th century. Walled fortifications, originally erected by the Lusignan kings and later rebuilt by the Venetians to encompass a smaller area (3 mi [5 km] round), did not prevent invasion by the Genoese in 1373, the Mamlūks in 1426, and the Turks in 1570. Standing in mute testimony to the religious and political changes of the city is the Cathedral of St. Sophia. Begun in 1209, completed in 1325, and pillaged by invaders, it was converted into the chief mosque of Cyprus in 1571; in 1954 its name was changed to the Selimiye Mosque in honour of the sultan Selim under whose reign Cyprus was conquered.

In the 20th century the city boundaries have been extended beyond the existing circular Venetian walls, and the old town within them has been rebuilt. Light industries, mainly serving the local market, include the manufacture and processing of cotton yarns and textiles, cigarettes, flour, confectionery, soft drinks, footwear, and clothing. Nicosia is connected by good roads with the port of Famagusta and the other major towns of the island and by air with London, New York, and numerous airports of Europe and the Middle East. The Cyprus Museum in the city houses many archaeological treasures. Pop. (1970 est.) city, 115,000; (1978 est.) inc. suburbs, 160,000. 35°11′ N, 33°21′ E
·Cyprus' government and transport centre **5**:402d *passim* to 404c
·district area and population table **5**:403
·map, Cyprus **5**:402

Nicotiana, plant genus of the family Solanaceae (*q.v.*) within the order Scrophulariales. Many of its more than 100 species, native mostly to North, Central, and South America, are grown as ornamentals, and from one, *N. tabacum*, comes tobacco (*q.v.*). *Major ref.* **16**:414c
·nicotine synthesis experiments **1**:606b
·tobacco cultivation, production, and use **18**:464c

nicotinamide, also called NIACINAMIDE or NICOTINIC ACID AMIDE, the amide of nicotinic acid; it is an active form of the pellagra-preventive vitamin, nicotinic acid (vitamin B complex). *See* nicotinic acid.

nicotine, organic compound, the principal alkaloid of tobacco, occurring throughout the plant, especially in the leaves. The term alkaloid refers to the group of nitrogenous organic compounds with marked physiological properties. The plant (*Nicotiana tabacum*) and the compound are named for Jean Nicot, a French ambassador to Portugal, who sent tobacco seeds to Paris in 1550.

Crude nicotine was known by 1571, and the compound was obtained in purified form in 1828; the correct molecular formula ($C_{10}H_{14}N_2$) was established in 1843, and the first laboratory synthesis was reported in 1904. It is one of the few liquid alkaloids, colourless and extremely toxic.

In the nicotine molecule, one of the nitrogen atoms is present in a six-membered ring, the pyridine ring, the other in a five-membered ring, the pyrrolidine ring. In the tobacco plant, the pyrrolidine portion is apparently synthesized from the amino acids ornithine and methionine, but the origin of the pyridine ring has not been established with certainty.

Nicotine is commercially obtained from tobacco scraps; it is used as an insecticide and as a veterinary vermifuge. Nitric acid or other oxidizing agents convert it to nicotinic acid, which is used as a food supplement.
·alkaloids as respiratory stimulants **1**:596b
·autonomic system effects **12**:1035b
·derivation from amino acids **1**:606b
·insecticidal characteristics **14**:140h
·lobeline drug action **3**:704g
·pyridine alkaloid classification **1**:602d
·tobacco scrap extraction and use **18**:466h
·toxicity rating for drugs, table 2 **14**:619

nicotinic acid, also called NIACIN, water-soluble vitamin of the vitamin B group (vitamin B complex); it is also called the pellagra-preventive vitamin, or vitamin PP, because an adequate amount in the diet prevents pellagra (*q.v.*), a chronic disease characterized by skin lesions, gastrointestinal disturbance, and nervous symptoms.

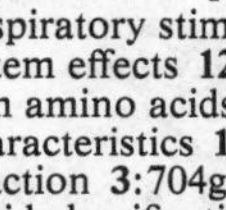

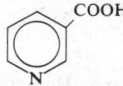

Nicotinic acid is active in either of two forms, the acid itself and its amide, nicotinamide, both of which contain nitrogen.

Nicotinic acid, which was identified in 1937, is widely distributed among plants and animals. Lean meat is generally a good source. Approximately 10 to 20 milligrams per day (1 milligram = 0.001 gram) of nicotinic acid is required by man. In the intestines of some mammals, the amino acid tryptophan can be converted to nicotinic acid by bacterial action and thus can serve as a source for part of the nicotinic acid required by the animal. With diets high in good-quality protein, the amount of tryptophan present may be sufficient to reduce the dietary requirement for nicotinic acid to zero. This explains the early observations that the protein in such foods as eggs and milk, both of which are poor sources of nicotinic acid, can prevent or cure pellagra in man.

Nicotinic acid is one of the most stable vitamins, resisting most cooking and preserving processes.

Like vitamin B_1 (thiamine) and vitamin B_2 (riboflavin), nicotinic acid is involved in enzyme systems concerned with the metabolism of carbohydrates. It acts in these systems to catalyze the oxidation of sugar derivatives and other substances.

Nicotinic acid is prepared commercially from β-picoline, a solvent, or from quinoline, a coal-tar distillate. Its chemical formula is $C_6H_5NO_2$. The chemical formula for nicotinic acid amide is $C_6H_6N_2O$.

·coenzyme biosynthesis, table 3 **6**:898
·deficiency's effect on children **4**:224a
·hallucinogen effects counteracted **8**:559a
·meat as human nutrition source **11**:746e
·milk product content, table 5 **5**:428
·nicotine derivation **1**:606b
·nutrient of varied organisms, table 5 **13**:406
·pellagra and vitamin deficiency **13**:411a
·vegetable chemical composition, table 1 **19**:44
·vitamin activation and coenzymes **19**:489e; table

Nicoya, Gulf of, Spanish GOLFO DE NICOYA, inlet of the Pacific Ocean, bounded on the north by Guanacaste province and on the east and west by Puntarenas province. It extends northward and northwestward from Cape Blanco and Judas Point for about 50 mi (80 km). Cape Blanco, on the Nicoya Peninsula, and Judas Point, on the mainland, are about 25 mi apart, but the gulf narrows to a width of approximately 15 mi farther northward. The Tempisque, Abangares, and Tárcoles rivers empty into it; and it has several islands, most notably Chira, the largest, and San Lucas. The largest town and port of the many settlements on the shores of the gulf is Puntarenas, on the east.
9°47′ N, 84°48′ W
·map, Costa Rica **5**:210

Nicoya Peninsula, Spanish PENÍNSULA DE NICOYA, Guanacaste and Puntarenas provinces, western Costa Rica, bounded on the west and south by the Pacific Ocean, on the northeast by the Cordillera de Guanacaste, and on the southeast by the Gulf of Nicoya. Costa Rica's largest peninsula, Nicoya measures about 85 mi (140 km) northwest–southeast and 40 to 60 mi (65 to 100 km) southwest–northeast. The base of the peninsula lies in the arid Guanacaste lowlands, but in the central and southern parts a range of mountains rises abruptly to over 3,000 ft (900 m). Descendants of the pre-Columbian Chorotega-Mangues Indians are still found in villages on the peninsula. There is some mining of gold in the north. Nicoya, the principal town—as well as the other main villages on the peninsula—is linked by highway to Liberia, capital of Guanacaste province.
10°00′ N, 85°25′ W
·map, Costa Rica **5**:210

Nictheroy (Brazil): *see* Niterói.

nictitating membrane, present in many vertebrates, fold of transparent or semitransparent mucous membrane that can be drawn over the eye like a third eyelid.
·crocodilian type and use **5**:288d
·functioning and possessors **15**:734g

nidāna (Sanskrit: "introduction"), in Buddhist texts, an introductory section outlining the purpose of the text.
·Buddhist sacred text variations **3**:432h

Nidānakathā (Pāli: "Narration of the Beginnings"), a narrative of the life of the Buddha.
·Buddha's Pāli biography description **3**:435f

Nidaros (Norway): *see* Trondheim.

Niddesa, one of the 15 sections of the *Khuddhaka Nikāya*, which is itself the fifth of five sections of the *Sutta Pitaka*, a Buddhist scripture.
·Buddhist commentary classification **3**:434e

Niderviller ware, French faience (tin-glazed earthenware) and porcelain produced in the 18th and 19th centuries by a factory at Niderviller, in Lorraine. Production of the faience falls into three periods. In 1755–70, under the ownership of Baron de Beyerlé and the artistic directorship of his wife, the decoration was polychrome and made up of naturalistically rendered flowers, birds, and landscapes. In 1770–90, under Count de Custine, the decoration was inspired by the painter Nicolas Lancret. The Lanfrey period, 1790–1827, was the most original, producing strange *trompe l'oeil* wares.

Niderville faience figures, *c.* 1775; in the Victoria and Albert Museum, London
By courtesy of the Victoria and Albert Museum, London

The secret of the porcelain was introduced by a workman from Saxony, but when the town became part of France in 1766, its manufacture was forbidden because of the monopoly held by the town of Sèvres on the making of hard-paste porcelain. The Count de Custine ignored the interdiction and resumed production in 1770.

The decor of Niderviller porcelain is, on the whole, the same as that of its faience.

Nidhogg, Old Norse NÎDHÖGGR, in Norse mythology, the evil serpent (or dragon) who lived by the spring Hvergelmir in Niflheim (the dark world of the dead) and gnawed perpetually at the roots of the world tree, Yggdrasill. In an old Icelandic manuscript, the *Völuspá* ("Sibyl's Prophecy"), it is foretold that Nidhogg will suck the blood of the dead at the end of the world.

Nidulariales (fungi): *see* Basidiomycetes.

Nidularium, a genus of 20 to 30 South American plants of the pineapple family (Bromeliaceae) that grow upon the branches of trees. Several species are cultivated indoors as decorative plants for their handsome foliage and colourful red, purplish, or white flowers.
·house plants and their care **8**:1120b

Nidwalden, half canton, central Switzerland, forms with Obwalden half canton the canton of Unterwalden (*q.v.*). Drained by the Engelberger Aa (river), its area of 106 sq mi (274 sq km) occupies the eastern part of Unterwalden. Nidwalden means Below the Forest, referring to the great forest of Kerns that divided the two half cantons in the Middle Ages. Nidwalden was the first of the two half cantons to ally with Uri and Schwyz in the Everlasting League in 1291, the nucleus of the Swiss Confederation. It acted independently of Obwalden in its revolt against the Helvetic Republic in 1798 and in its refusal to accept the federal constitution of 1815. The latter action resulted in its loss of the abbey lands of Engelberg to Obwalden. A sovereign half canton with its capital at Stans (*q.v.*), it is administratively independent of Obwalden. Nidwalden offers winter sports and tourist facilities along Lake Lucerne (Vierwaldstätter See). The population (25,634 in 1970) is German-speaking and Catholic.
·area and population table **17**:874
·map, Switzerland **17**:868
·Swiss history and conflicts **17**:879e

Niebuhr, Barthold Georg (b. Aug. 27, 1776, Copenhagen—d. Jan. 31, 1831, Bonn, Ger., now W.Ger.), German historian who started a new era in historical studies by his method of source criticism; all subsequent historians are in some sense indebted to him. Niebuhr was the only son of the Danish explorer Carsten Niebuhr. Up to his matriculation at the University of Kiel he had a solitary education that perhaps intensified his leaning toward a life of scholarship. But on his father's advice he spent over a year in England and Scotland and then embarked on a career in state service, becoming private secretary to Count Schimmelmann, the Danish minister of finance, and in 1804 director of the national bank. In 1806, at the request of Baron von Stein, the Prussian chief minister, he took up a similar post in Prussia. Two years after Stein's fall (1808), however, disapproving of Prince von Hardenberg's policy, he resigned and became state historiographer. At the same time he became a member of the Berlin Akademie der Wissenschaften and was thereby empowered to lecture at the newly founded university of Berlin. In 1810 he began the series of lectures on Roman history that were the basis of his great book and made a sensation in Berlin. In 1816 he went as Prussian ambassador to the Vatican, retiring to Bonn in 1823.

Niebuhr's chief work was done while he was employed in public service. His interests were academic (to the fine arts he was wholly indifferent; it has been said that to him Rome was only a collection of unsolved problems) and he never wholly reconciled himself to his official career; yet he held that no one could understand the history of Rome without knowing the state as it is seen by the statesman; and his work, above all his gift for analogy, benefited greatly from his practical life.

Niebuhr's *Römische Geschichte* (3 vol., 1811–32; Eng. trans., *History of Rome*, 1828–42) marked an era in the study of its special subject and had a momentous influence on the general conception of history. Niebuhr made particular contributions of value to learning, *e.g.*, his study of social and agrarian problems; on the other hand some of his theories were extravagant and his conclusions mistaken. But his permanent contribution to scholarship was his method. The failings of classical sources were already recognized, but it was Niebuhr who evolved what Goethe called "tätige Skepsis"—the constructive skepticism which is the root of a scientific method of criticism. It was Niebuhr who showed how to analyze the strata in a source, particularly poetical and mythical tradition, and how to discard the worthless and thereby lay bare the material from which the historical facts could be reconstructed. He thus laid the foundation for the great period of German historical scholarship.

Niebuhr, Carsten (b. March 17, 1733, Lüdingworth, Hanover, now in West Germany—d. April 26, 1815, Meldorf, Holstein), traveller who was the sole survivor of the first scientific expedition to Arabia and the compiler of its results. He learned surveying in his early years and in 1760 was invited to join the Arabian expedition being sent out by Frederick V of Denmark. The party visited the Nile, Mt. Sinai, Suez, and Jidda, the port of Mecca, and then went overland to Mocha (al-Mukhā) in southwestern Arabia. The death of the expedition's philologist (May 1763) was followed by that of the naturalist in July. The remaining party members visited Sana, the capital of Yemen, and returned to Mocha. The group then sailed for Bombay, where the artist and the surgeon of the expedition died, leaving Niebuhr alone. He stayed 14 months in India and then turned homeward by way of Muscat (in southeastern Arabia), Persia,

Niebuhr, detail from an engraving by an unknown artist
Bavaria-Verlag

Mesopotamia, Cyprus, and Asia Minor, reaching Copenhagen in November 1767. He wrote *Beschreibung von Arabien* (1772; "Description of Arabia") and *Reisebeschreibung nach Arabien und andern umliegenden Ländern* (1774; *Travels Through Arabia*).
·Arabian Desert scientific exploration **1**:1056c
·cuneiform alphabets identification **11**:966a

Niebuhr, H(elmut) Richard (1894–1962), U.S. theologian.
·social status and religious outlook **15**:607b

Niebuhr, Reinhold 13:74 (b. June 21, 1892, Wright City, Mo.—d. June 1, 1971, Stockbridge, Mass.), one of the most important American theologians of the 20th century who had extensive influence on political thought. His criticism of the prevailing theological liberalism of the 1920s significantly affected the intellectual climate within American Protestantism.

Abstract of text biography. Niebuhr studied at Elmhurst College in Illinois, Eden Theological Seminary, St. Louis, Mo., and Yale Divinity School (B.D., 1914; M.A., 1915). He was ordained to the ministry of the Evangelical Synod in 1915 and was a pastor in Detroit from 1915 to 1928, where his exposure to the problems of American industrialism, before labour was protected by unions and legislation, caused him to advocate Socialism. He broke with the Socialist Party in the 1930s and became a Democrat. From 1928 to 1960 he was a professor at Union Theological Seminary, New York City. A former pacifist, he actively persuaded Christians to support the war against Hitler and after World War II had considerable influence in the U.S. State Department.

Niebuhr wrote many books and numerous essays and articles. His most prominent theological work was *The Nature and Destiny of Man* which was planned as a synthesis of the theology of the Reformation, with its emphasis on sin and grace, with the insights of the Renaissance, with its hopefulness about cultural achievements.

REFERENCES in other text articles:
·anthropomorphism in faith **15**:605c
·Martin Luther King's ideas influenced **10**:472b
·nonviolence, conscience, and coercion **13**:851g
·Protestant reaction to liberal theology **15**:119c

Niederdeutsch (language): *see* Low German.

Niedere Tauern, also known as LOWER TAUERN, range of the Eastern Alps in central Austria; lying between the Enns and Mur rivers, it extends 75 mi (121 km) westward to the headstreams of the two rivers. The scenic, well-forested mountains rise to Hochgolling (9,393 ft [2,863 m]), and a road crosses the range at the Radstädter Tauern (pass; 5,705 ft). The range is divided into the Radstädter Tauern, Schladminger Tauern, and Rottenmanner Tauern. Summer resorts and winter sports centres lie in the mountains, which are also noted for their cattle-grazing meadows on the south slopes and their chamois (small, goatlike antelope) hunting on the north slopes.
47°18′ N, 14°00′ E
·map, Austria **2**:442

Niederösterreich, English LOWER AUSTRIA, *Bundesland* (federal state), northeastern Austria, bordering Czechoslovakia (north and east) and bounded by the states of Burgenland on the southeast, Steiermark (Styria) on the south, and Oberösterreich (Upper Austria) on the west. Lying astride the Danube from the mouths of the rivers Enns (west) and March (east), it has an area of 7,402 sq mi (19,170 sq km). The Waldviertel (forest quarter) in the northwest, with deeply incised rivers, is part of the granite plateau, called the Mühlviertel (Mühl District), and extends to the Manhartsberg Mountain and across the Danube (south). The Weinviertel (Wine District) in the northeast is low, hilly country with extensive loess soil cover and a favourable climate. The southern Vienna Basin south of the Danube, bordered by the Leithagebirge (mountains, in the east) and by the fault scarp of the limestone mountains (west), belongs structurally to the Alps. Its landscape resembles the lowlands of the northern Vienna Basin, though its gravels support only pine woods and heaths. The southern part of the *Bundesland* includes parts of the Central Alps with heights exceeding 6,500 ft (1,980 m). Woodland predominates at lower altitudes and in the Flysch (sandstone) Alps, which reach their greatest extent and terminate in the Wiener Wald (Vienna Woods). Along the Danube and to the south in the eastern part of the state is a small but economically important Alpine foreland, a hilly, well-watered region, widely covered by loess.

There were prehistoric settlements in the Wachau (Danube Gorge), around Horn, in the Alpine foreland, and in the Vienna Basin. Later, the area was part of the Roman province of Noricum and of Charlemagne's empire. It was granted to the Bavarian Babenberg margraves in 976; the name Ostarichi (Eastern Region) dates from that period. Permanent division between Upper and Lower Austria was made *c.* 1450. Although the official name until 1918 was Österreich unter der Enns, it was popularly called Niederösterreich. An area near Gmünd was ceded to Czechoslovakia after World War I. Niederösterreich became a *Bundesland* in 1918, and in 1920 it lost Vienna, except as the seat of its administration. It was part of the Reichsgau Niederdonau (Lower Danube Reich District) during the *Anschluss*, or "union," with Germany (1938–45). In 1938 Niederösterreich yielded land to Vienna; it regained *Bundesland* status in 1945 and recovered most of the lost area (309 sq mi) in 1954 under a district reorganization law.

Ethnically, the population is German. Most of the people are Roman Catholic, but there are small Protestant communities. About half of all Austrian towns are in Niederösterreich, the principal ones being Sankt Pölten, Wiener Neustadt, Klosterneuburg, Baden, Krems, Mödling, Schwechat, Amstetten, and Stockerau (*qq.v.*). Rural settlement is characterized mainly by villages and small farms of less than 12 ac (5 ha).

Agriculture and forestry support nearly half of the working population; more than half of the land surface is used for farming, and more than one-third is forested. Grain (wheat, rye, maize [corn], barley) and root crops (potatoes, sugar beets, fodder beets) are grown in the eastern lowland and in the Alpine foreland. There is extensive viticulture in the Weinviertel and the Wachau, along the southern bank of the Danube east of Vienna, and on the slopes of the Vienna Basin; and fruit is grown in these areas and in the Alpine foreland. Livestock raising is widespread, with market gardening around Vienna.

Oil and natural gas are found in the northern Vienna Basin, and there are hydroelectric power stations at Ybbs-Persenbeug on the Danube and Sankt Pantaleon on the Enns. Gypsum is mined near Grünbach, graphite in the Wachau, and limestone is quarried for a cement plant near Mannersdorf. Metal and textile industries, food processing, sugar refining, brewing, sawmilling, and paper, cellulose, and chemical factories are important. The Semperit rubber plants at Traiskirchen and Wimpassing are owned by the *Bundesland*'s largest industrial firm. The tourist trade is significant in the Alps and at the thermal spas along the limestone fault scarp. River (Danube), rail, and road transport make the state a commercial throughway, and Vienna's airport at Schwechat is the largest in Austria. Pop. (1971 prelim.) 1,411,771.
·geography, population, and resources **2**:441g; table 444
·map, Austria **2**:442

Niedersachsen 13:75, English LOWER SAXONY, a *Land* (state) of West Germany. Its area of 18,304 sq mi (47,407 sq km) extends westward from The Netherlands border across the North German Plain to the boundary with East Germany. To the north, the *Länder* of Hamburg and Schleswig-Holstein separate it from the Denmark peninsula, while an extensive low coastline fronts on the North Sea. Niedersachsen also surrounds the *Land* of Bremen. To the south are the *Länder* of Nordrhein-Westfalen and Hessen. The capital is Hannover. Pop. (1970) 7,082,000.

The text article covers the landscape, people, economy, transportation, administration, social conditions, and cultural life.

REFERENCES in other text articles:
·local government functions **4**:648a
·map, Federal Republic of Germany **8**:46
·regions, resources, area, and population **8**:52e; table 53

Niel, Adolphe (b. Oct. 4, 1802, Muret, Fr.—d. Aug. 13, 1869, Paris), army officer, aide to Napoleon III, and marshal of France who, as minister of war, made an unsuccessful attempt to reorganize the French Army in 1868.

Trained as an engineer, Niel spent most of his life in military service after receiving his commission in 1825. In 1849 he distinguished himself in the defeat of the Roman republicans. General of division in 1853, he twice commanded the engineers during the Crimean War. The next year he became aide to Napoleon III and, in 1857, senator. He was present in Turin in January 1859 at the conclusion of an alliance between France and Sardinia-Piedmont; in the ensuing war against Austria, he played a decisive role in the Battle of Solferino, for which he was made marshal the next day (June 25, 1859). Appointed minister of war on Jan. 18, 1867, he planned a radical reorganization of the army but met with obstruction and did not live long enough to put his program into effect.

Niel, Cornelis B(ernardus) van (1897–), Dutch biologist.
·photosynthetic hydrogen transfer studies **14**:368a

niello, black metallic alloy of sulfur with silver, copper, or lead used to fill designs incised on the surface of a metal (usually silver) object. The black niello contrasts with the bright silver to produce an attractive decorative effect.

Niello was used by the Romans, and the ring of King Aethelwulf (839–58) in the British Museum demonstrates that the technique was well established in England at an early date. The art of using niello reached its peak in 15th-century Italy in the workshop of the Florentine goldsmith Maso Finiguerra. Russian goldsmiths working in Tula in the late 18th century revived the craft. Niello was extensively employed in the East, and fine qual-

"Coronation of the Virgin," sulfur cast of the engraved silver niello by Maso Finiguerra, *c.* 1459-64; in the British Museum

By courtesy of the trustees of the British Museum; photograph, J.R. Freeman & Co. Ltd.

ity work is still being produced in India and the Balkans.

- ·jewelry-making techniques **10**:166a
- ·linear effects **5**:998g
- ·metalwork art techniques and objects **11**:1093f *passim* to 1104b
- ·Tassilo Chalice illus. **11**:1094

Niels (1063–1134), king of Denmark.

- ·Danish political consolidation **16**:308b

Nielsen, Carl (August) (1865–1931), Danish composer at first influenced by the Romantics, later evolving to polytonality, produced six symphonies, three concerti, two operas, and some chamber and piano music.

- ·sonata form using progressive tonality **17**:10b

Nielsen, Morten (b. Jan. 3, 1922, Aalborg, Den.—d. Aug. 29, 1944, Copenhagen), poet who became the symbol of his generation's desire for freedom and who was killed as a result of his participation in the organized Danish resistance to the German occupation. Nielsen was only 22 when he was killed, but the role he played in Denmark was not that of a martyr or agitator, but of a poet. He had been able to express, in well-formed verse, matters that were engaging the minds of his generation and his fellow countrymen. In contrast to most of the poetry of the occupation, Nielsen's verse is still read in Denmark. A large edition of the collected poems was published 10 years after his death.

Niemann-Pick disease: *see* lipid storage diseases.

Niemcewicz, Julian Ursyn (b. Feb. 6, 1757/58, Skoki, Pol.—d. May 21, 1841, Paris), Polish playwright, poet, novelist, and translator whose writings, inspired by patriotism and concern for social and governmental reform, reflect the turbulent political events of his day and, thus, have a more historical than intrinsic interest. He was the first Polish writer to know English literature thoroughly; he translated works of such authors as John Dryden, John Milton, Alexander Pope, and Samuel Johnson during a period of imprisonment in 1794–96 and introduced the historical novel to Poland, his *Jan z Tęczyna* (3 vols, 1825; "Jan of Tęczyn") being influenced by the Scottish novelist Sir Walter Scott.

Educated in the Warsaw cadet corps between 1770 and 1777, he spent most of the period 1783–88 in western Europe and in 1788 was elected deputy to the Sejm (parliament) of Poland. In 1790, he wrote *Powrót Posła* ("The Deputy's Return"), a political comedy very popular in its day. After participating in the unsuccessful insurrection of 1794, he was captured at Maciejowice and imprisoned in St. Petersburg for two years. Upon his release, he travelled to England and then to the U.S., where he married and remained until 1807, when he returned to Poland once more. Until 1831 he held no public position, devoting himself instead to literary work. Two important works that appeared during this period were *Śpiewy historyczne* (1816; "Historical Songs"), a series of simple song poems aimed at a wide audience that became very popular, and *Lebje i Siora* (1821; "Leybe and Syora"), the first Polish novel to discuss the Jewish problem. In 1831 Niemcewicz journeyed to

Niemcewicz, lithograph by Francols le Villain (19th century) after a portrait by Fabian Sarnecki (1800–94)

By courtesy of the Muzeum Narodowe, Krakow, Pol.

England to attempt to persuade the western European powers to intervene on behalf of the Polish insurrection against the Russians. He failed to do so, however, and spent the last years of his life in Paris, campaigning for Polish freedom. His memoirs appeared in 1848.

Niemeyer (Soares Filho), Oscar (b. Dec. 15, 1907, Rio de Janeiro), architect and early exponent of modern architecture in Latin America, particularly noted for his work on Brasília, the new capital of Brazil.

He studied architecture at the National School of Fine Arts, Rio de Janeiro. Shortly before his graduation in 1934, he entered the office of Lúcio Costa, a leader of the modern movement in Brazilian architecture. He worked with Costa in 1936 on the design for the Ministry of Education and Health building, considered by many to be the first modern architectural masterpiece in Brazil. Le Corbusier, the Swiss-born French architect, was a consultant on the building, which shows his influence. Niemeyer also worked with Costa on the designs for the Brazilian Pavilion for the New York World's Fair of 1939–40.

The plan for Pampulha, a new suburb of Belo Horizonte, was Niemeyer's first major project on his own. The project, commissioned in 1941 by Juscelino Kubitschek de Oliveira, then mayor of Belo Horizonte, is notable for the free-flowing forms used in many of its buildings. Many other commissions followed, and in 1947 Niemeyer represented Brazil in the planning of the United Nations buildings in New York City.

Oscar Niemeyer, 1972

Claus C. Meyer—Black Star

Following his election to the presidency of Brazil in 1956, Kubitschek asked Niemeyer to design the new capital city of Brasília. Niemeyer agreed to design the government buildings but suggested a national competition for the master plan, a competition subsequently won by his mentor, Lúcio Costa. Among the Brasília buildings designed by Niemeyer are the President's Palace, the Brasília Palace Hotel, the presidential chapel, and the cathedral. Since 1961 Niemeyer has lived in Paris and Israel. In 1966 he designed an urban area in Grasse, near Nice, Fr., and a building for the French Communist Party in Paris.

- ·Brasília's architectural design **3**:120e

Niemöller, (Friedrich Gustav Emil) Martin (b. Jan. 1, 1892, Lippstadt, now in West Germany), prominent anti-Nazi theologian and pastor, founder of the Bekennende Kirche ("Confessing Church") and a president of the World Council of Churches. The son of a pastor, Niemöller served Germany as a naval officer in World War I before beginning theological studies at Münster (in modern West Germany).

In 1931 Niemöller became a pastor in Dahlem, a fashionable suburb of Berlin. Two years later, as a protest against interference in church affairs by the National Socialists (Nazi Party), Niemöller founded the Pfarrernotbund (Pastors' Emergency League). Among other activities, the group helped combat rising discrimination against Christians of Jewish background. As founder and a leading member of the "Confessing Church," within the larger Evangelical Church (Lutheran and Reformed)

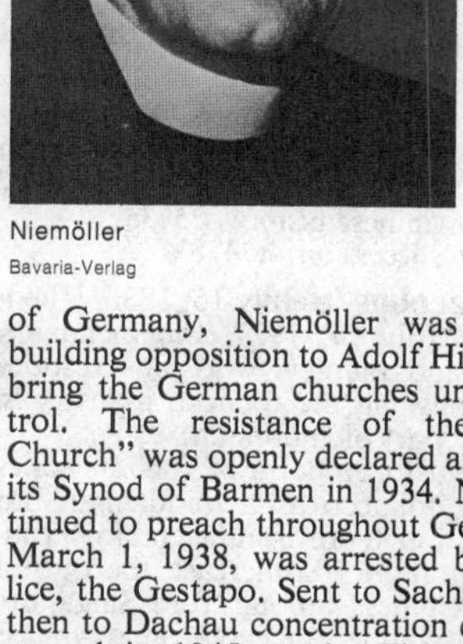

Niemöller

Bavaria-Verlag

of Germany, Niemöller was influential in building opposition to Adolf Hitler's efforts to bring the German churches under Nazi control. The resistance of the "Confessing Church" was openly declared and solidified at its Synod of Barmen in 1934. Niemöller continued to preach throughout Germany and on March 1, 1938, was arrested by Hitler's police, the Gestapo. Sent to Sachsenhausen and then to Dachau concentration camps, he was moved in 1945 to the Tirol, where Allied forces freed him at the end of World War II. He helped rebuild the Evangelical Church, in 1945 becoming head of its foreign-relations office and in 1947 president of the Hesse-Nassau regional church.

Increasingly disillusioned with the prospects for demilitarization, both in his own country and in the world, Niemöller became a controversial pacifist. Lecturing widely, he spoke freely in favour of international reconciliation and against armaments. In 1961 he was elected one of the six presidents of the World Council of Churches. His writings include several volumes of sermons and an autobiogra-

phy, *Vom U-Boot zur Kanzel* (1934; Eng. trans., *From U-Boat to Concentration Camp*, 1939). His life is recorded in D. Schmidt's *Pastor Niemöller* (Eng. trans., 1959), and in C. Start-Davidson's *God's Man* (1959).
·Protestant resistance to Hitler **15**:118d
·Synod of Barmen **2**:726d

Nien-ch'ing-t'ang-ku-la Shan, Pinyin romanization NIAN-CHING-TANG-GU-LA SHAN, also called NYENCHEN TANGLA RANGE, mountain range forming the eastern section of a mountain system in the southern part of the Tibetan Autonomous Region, China, often called the Trans-Himalaya. In the west, the system comprises a northern range, the A-ling Shan (mountains), and a southern range, the Kailas Range (*q.v.*), which is much more rugged and heavily glaciated, though its highest peak, at 22,031 ft (6,715 m), is lower than those of the A-ling Shan. East of about longitude 86° E the two chains unite in the Nien-ch'ing-t'ang-ku-la Shan proper, which form a high watershed between the Ya-lu-tsang-pu Chiang (river) valley of southern Tibet and the area of inland drainage and salt lakes on the high plateau. Southern slopes of the range are very rugged; many sections are above 20,000 ft, with some individual peaks well above 23,000 ft in the area northwest of Lhasa, the capital of the Tibetan Autonomous Region. The southern slopes also are comparatively well watered, and the natural environment is clearly divided into vertical zones, rich in grasses and shrubs affording good mountain pastures. These slopes drain into the Ya-lu-tsang-pu Chiang (Tsangpo), the Chinese name for the Brahmaputra. In the west, the northern slopes of the range form part of the interior drainage of the southeast area of the Ch'iang-t'ang basin and are generally dry and covered with hardy grasses; at the eastern end of the range the northern slopes drain into the upper headwaters of the Salween River and have a much richer cover of alpine grasses. The main route across the range crosses the Shang-shung Shan-k'ou, a pass between Yang-pa-ching and Hei-ho. This carries the main road from Lhasa north to the Tsaidam Basin and to the Sinkiang Uighur Autonomous Region.
30°10′ N, 90°00′ E
·Brahmaputra River, map **3**:105
·Himalayan drainage pattern **8**:884b; map 882

nien-fo, Japanese NEMBUTSU: *see* Pure Land Buddhism.

nien-hao (Chinese: "year name"), term for the era names taken by Chinese monarchs on ascending the throne, a system begun 163 BC.
·chronology of Chinese history **4**:573c
·Ming dynastic succession **4**:347b

Nienhuys, Jacobus (b. July 15, 1836, Rhenen, Neth.—d. July 27, 1927, Bloemendaal), businessman and planter, who was responsible for establishing the tobacco industry in Sumatra (now part of Indonesia).

Nienhuys went to Sumatra in 1863 in hopes of purchasing tobacco as a middleman but found production there insufficient for commercial exploitation. To increase the output he imported Chinese labour from Singapore and began cultivating tobacco around what is now the Medan area. The leaves produced there were of exceptionally high quality and were normally used as wrappers for cigars.

Nienhuys in 1869 established the Deli Company, dealing in tropical produce, and returned to The Netherlands the following year for reasons of health. From 1880 until his death he was commissioner for the company.

Nien Rebellion, major revolt in the North China provinces of Shantung, Honan, Kiangsu, and Anhwei; it occurred when the Ch'ing dynasty (1644–1911) was preoccupied with the great Taiping Rebellion (1850–64) in South and central China. An offshoot of the Buddhist-inspired White Lotus secret societies, the Nien were motley bands of peasants, army deserters, and salt smugglers who had fomented sporadic outbreaks since the first decade of the 19th century. Oppressed by famine resulting from flooding during the 1850s and stimulated by government preoccupation with the Taipings, several Nien bands formed a coalition under Chang Lo-hsing in 1852–53 and began to expand rapidly.

Numbering from 30,000 to 50,000 soldiers and organized into five armies, they conducted raids into adjacent regions. In 1863 they received a setback when their citadel, Chih-ho, was captured and their leader, Chang Lo-hsing, was killed. But they soon reorganized, and in 1864 they were joined by those Taiping soldiers not defeated in the fall of the Taiping capital at Nanking that same year. They adopted guerrilla hit-and-run tactics, using mobile mounted units to strike at the weak points of the Ch'ing armies and retreating into strategic hamlets where they were protected by the local populace. But, with the government free from problems with the Taipings, it concentrated on the Nien and adopted a strategy of blockade. The rebels were gradually trapped and defeated.
·strategy and popular support **4**:360d
·Tseng Kuo-fan's military command **18**:730f

Niepce, (Joseph-) Nicéphore (b. March 7, 1765, Chalon-sur-Saône, Fr.—d. July 5, 1833, Chalon-sur-Saône), inventor, the first to make a permanent photographic image. The son of a wealthy family suspected of royalist sympathies, Niepce fled the French Revolution but returned to serve in the Army under Napoleon Bonaparte. Dismissed because of ill health, he settled in his native town of Chalon-sur-Saône.

In 1807 he and his brother invented an internal combustion engine, which they called the Pyréolophore. Working on a piston and cylinder system similar to 20th-century gasoline-powered engines, it used lampblack and finely ground resin for fuel, and Niepce claimed to have used it to power a boat.

When lithography became a fashionable hobby in France in 1813, Niepce began to experiment with the then novel printing technique. Unskilled in drawing, and unable to obtain proper lithographic stone locally, he sought a way to provide images automatically. He coated pewter with various light-sensitive substances in an effort to copy superimposed engravings in sunlight. From this he progressed in April 1816 to attempts at photography, which he called heliography (sun-drawing), with a camera. He recorded a view from his workroom window on paper sensitized with silver chloride but was only partially able to fix the image. Next he tried various types of supports for the light-sensitive material bitumen of Judea, a kind of asphalt, which hardens on exposure to light. Using this material he succeeded in 1822 in obtaining a photographic copy of an engraving superimposed on glass. Four years later, in 1826, using a camera, he made a view from his workroom on a pewter plate. Metal had the advantage of being unbreakable and was better suited to the subsequent etching process to produce a printing plate, which was Niepce's final aim. While the first camera photograph (now in the Gernsheim Collection, University of Texas, Austin) was not suitable for the purpose, the same year, 1826, he produced another heliograph, a reproduction of an engraved portrait, which was etched by the Parisian engraver Augustin-François Lemaître, who pulled two prints. Thus Niepce not only solved the problem of reproducing nature by light, but he invented the first photomechanical reproduction process.

In 1827, while on a visit to England, he addressed a memorandum on his invention to the Royal Society, London, but his insistence on keeping the method secret prevented the matter from being investigated.

Unable to reduce the long exposure times by either chemical or optical means, Niepce in 1829 finally gave in to the repeated overtures of Louis-Jacques-Mandé Daguerre (*q.v.*), a Parisian painter, for a partnership to perfect and exploit heliography. He died without seeing any advance, but, building on Niepce's knowledge and working with his materials, Daguerre eventually succeeded in reducing the exposure time through his discovery of a chemical process for development of (making visible) the latent (invisible) image formed upon brief exposure.
·discovering basis for photogravure **14**:1056g
·photographic printing plate beginnings **14**:301a
·photography development role **18**:44f
·photography's historical development **14**:309b; illus. 310

Nier, Alfred O(tto Carl) (1911–), U.S. physicist.
·mass spectrometer development **11**:607h

Nieszawa Privilege, also called PRIVILEGIUM OF NIESZAWA (1454), agreement by Casimir IV of Poland not to impose new taxes without the consent of the nobility.
·Polish aristocracy domination **14**:642b
·Polish nobility's political growth **3**:980b

Nietzsche, Friedrich 13:76 (b. Oct. 15, 1844, Röcken, near Leipzig—d. Aug. 25, 1900, Weimar, Thuringian States), classical scholar, philosopher, and critic of culture who had a powerful influence on continental philosophy and literature.

Abstract of text biography. He studied classical philology at Bonn and Leipzig (1864–68) and became professor of classics at Basel (1869), where he wrote *The Birth of Tragedy* (1872), which contains his well-known Apollonian-Dionysian dichotomy. During the 10 years that followed his retirement in 1879, he turned out such important works as *Thus Spake Zarathustra* (first three parts published 1883–84), *Beyond Good and Evil* (1886), and *On the Genealogy of Morals* (1887). When living in Switzerland, Nietzsche had been a friend and admirer of the composer Richard Wagner. With the passing of time, however, their philosophies diverged, the formal break coming in 1878. Nietzsche published *The Case of Wagner* in 1888, the same year Georg Brandes began lecturing on Nietzsche at the University of Copenhagen, the first significant public notice of his works and thought. In 1889 Nietzsche suffered a breakdown and spent about a year in an asylum; he was thereafter attended by his mother and later his sister.

REFERENCES in other text articles:
·aesthetic theory fulfilled in drug use **5**:1048f
·atheism and the will to power **2**:259h
·Buber's Zionist response to influence **3**:359c
·Christian joy as mark of redemption **4**:489f
·exclusivist ethical criteria **6**:995a
·Existentialist development of ideas **7**:73d
·Fascist origins in elitist ideology **7**:183g
·German literature of the 19th century **10**:1198a
·Greek tragedy deterioration theory **18**:582e
·music as symbolic and dynamic **12**:664d
·philosophy's destructive task **14**:271f
·psychology of power **15**:154a
·recording the historical process **10**:1079g
·religion and class resentment **15**:607c
·skepticism circumvented through action **16**:833a
·Thomas Mann's philosophic directions **11**:455h
·tragedy, aesthetic effects, and reality **18**:592b

Nieuwe Gids, De ("The New Guide"), periodical in The Netherlands founded in 1885 by Willem Kloos and Albert Verwey (*qq.v.*).
·Dutch literature of the 19th century **10**:1199c

Nieuwe Rotterdamse Courant, Dutch newspaper of high reputation, founded in Rotterdam in 1844, now merged with *Algemeen Handelsblad.*

Nieuwland, Julius Arthur (b. Feb. 14, 1878, Hansbeke, Belg.—d. June 11, 1936,

Washington, D.C.), chemist whose pioneering studies of acetylene culminated in the discovery of neoprene, the first commercially successful synthetic rubber.

Ordained a Roman Catholic priest in 1903, Nieuwland was professor of botany from 1904 to 1918 and professor of organic chemistry from 1918 to 1936 at the University of Notre Dame, South Bend, Ind. His doctoral research concerned the chemistry of acetylene, a lifelong interest. Early in his studies he discovered divinylchloroarsine; but because of its highly poisonous properties, he suspended all research on it. Later known as lewisite, this compound was one of the deadliest gases used in World War I.

In 1920 Nieuwland discovered that acetylene molecules could be polymerized (combined to form giant molecules) to produce a substance similar to rubber. Nine years later, in collaboration with chemists of E.I. du Pont de Nemours & Company, he succeeded in producing neoprene by adding chlorine at an early stage of acetylene polymerization.

Nieuw Nickerie, port and chief town of Nickerie district, in northwestern Surinam. It lies on the Nickerie River, near the mouth of the Courantyne (Dutch Corantijn) River, 3 mi (5 km) from the Atlantic coast. Rice is the principal crop grown in the area, but cocoa, rice, lumber, and balata are the chief exports. Vessels of moderate draft can reach the port, and there is regular service to Paramaribo, the capital of Surinam, about 150 mi (240 km) to the east, to which Nieuw Nickerie is also linked by road. Pop. (1971 prelim.) 35,178.
5°57′ N, 56°59′ W

·geography, population, and commerce **17**:825e
·map, Surinam **17**:824
·port facilities, area, and population **17**:825e; table 826

Nieuwpoort, French NIEUPORT, municipality, West Flanders, western Belgium, on the Yser (IJzer) River. Established in the 12th century as a new port for Ypres (replacing Lombardsijde), it was besieged 10 times after it was first fortified in 1163. The scene of a Dutch victory over the Spanish in 1600, it was the key to the defense of the Ypres salient in World War I. Its six sluices flooded the entire area, halting the German advance and completely destroying the town, which was rebuilt after 1918. An important port for fishing and oyster culture, it is in a coastal resort region. The North Sea resort of Nieuwpoort-Bad is 2 mi (3 km) northwest. Pop. (1973 est.) 8,270.
51°08′ N, 2°45′ E

Nièvre, *département*, central France, created from the historic province of Nivernais (*q.v.*) and a small part of Orléanais. Its area of 2,640 sq mi (6,837 sq km) includes the mountainous, forested Morvan in the east; the hilly, wooded Nivernais plateau in the centre; and the valley of the Loire River (*q.v.*) in the west. The terrain attains elevations of more than 2,600 ft (800 m) in the Morvan and 1,400 ft in the centre. The lowest parts, 460 ft (140 m), are in the Sologne region in the northwest between the Loire and Vrille, which form the western boundary. The Loire River enters in the south, passes through the ancient town of Decize, where it is joined by the Aron, and through Nevers (*q.v.*), the capital, where it receives the Nièvre, a small tributary after which the *département* is named. Southwest of Nevers, the Loire is joined by the Allier and flows north before entering Loiret *département*.

In the Morvan the climate is variable, with early winters and hot summers, while on the Nivernais plateau it is continental and in the Loire Valley mild. The *département* is predominantly agricultural—cattle, sheep, cereals, and forestry. Some industry, including metallurgical and chemical works, is found in the Nevers region and in Clamecy and Decize. The white wines of Pouilly-sur-Loire have good standing in France.

The view across the Loire of the town of La Charité, with its Romanesque abbey church, its 16th-century stone bridge, and its ramparts, is one of the most delightful in central France. The old towns of Château-Chinon and Clamecy, in the Morvan mountains on the Yonne River (*q.v.*), are popular tourist attractions. The *département* is divided into the *arrondissements* of Nevers, Château-Chinon, Clamecy, and Cosne-sur-Loire. It is in the educational division of Dijon. Pop. (1974 est.) 249,000.

·area and population table **7**:594

Niffer (ancient Mesopotamian city): *see* Nippur.

Niflheim, Old Norse NIFLHEIMR, in Norse mythology, the cold, dark, misty world of the dead, ruled by the goddess Hel (*q.v.*). In some accounts it was the last of nine worlds, a place into which evil men passed after reaching the region of death (Hel). Situated below one of the roots of the world tree, Yggdrasill, Niflheim contained a well, Hvergelmir, from which many rivers flowed. In the Norse creation story, Niflheim was the misty region north of the void (Ginnungagap) in which the world was created.

Nifo, Agostino, Latin AUGUSTINUS NIPHUS, or NIPHUS SUESSANUS (b. *c.* 1473, Sessa, Italy—d. after 1538, possibly Salerno), Renaissance philosopher noted for his development from an anti-Christian interpreter of Aristotelian philosophy into an influential Christian apologist for the immortality of the individual soul.

At the University of Padua around 1490, Nifo studied the Averroist Aristotelianism of Nicoletto Vernia and Siger of Brabant, a philosophical school that interpreted Aristotle according to the Neoplatonic principles of the 12th-century Arab philosopher and physician Averroës and that emphasized the eternity of the world and an immortal, universal intellect subsuming the souls of all individuals at death. Nifo expressed such teaching in his *De intellectu et daemonibus* (1492; "On the Intellect and Demons"). Later, however, he made a critical edition of Averroës' commentaries on Aristotle with conclusions more open to Christian doctrine, in the manner of Siger (*see* Siger of Brabant).

After succeeding the strict Averroist Pietro Pomponazzi (*q.v.*) in the chair of philosophy at Padua in 1496, Nifo resigned when Pomponazzi returned. He then assumed teaching posts successively at Naples, Rome, and Salerno. Through the Neoplatonic influence of the Florentine school, he adapted his Aristotelianism to the 13th-century Christian synthesis of St. Thomas Aquinas. Consequently, at the request of Pope Leo X, he wrote *Tractatus de immortalitate animae contra Pomponatium* (1518; "Treatise on the Immortality of the Soul Against Pomponazzi") as a refutation of Pomponazzi's view that the human soul is essentially a material organism dissolving at death. Nifo argued, in a polemic that amounted to a personal attack, that Pomponazzi had neglected to consider the intrinsic relation between the nonmaterial idea and the intellectual power able to communicate it, thus making the soul something more than a bodily organism. He further charged that Pomponazzi had failed to note this fact in both Platonic and Aristotelian teaching. The success of this work earned Nifo in 1520 the title of count.

Named as professor at the University of Pisa, Nifo by 1523 had published a plagiarized version of Niccolò Machiavelli's treatise on the ethics of ruling, *Il principe* (1513), under the title *De regnandi peritia* ("On Skill in Governing"). This action has prompted some commentators to judge that by this time Nifo had exchanged his intellectual interests for those of a timeserving courtier. Among his other writings are commentaries on the works of Aristotle (14 vol., 1654; reprinted in 1967); treatises on politics and morality; and a romantic essay, *De Pulchro et Amore* ("On Beauty and Love").

·Atomism of minima naturalia **2**:349g

Nigantha Nātaputta, an ancient Indian philosopher identified in Jaina tradition with Mahāvīra, the 6th-century-BC founder of Jainism.

·ascetic philosophical views **9**:317b

Niğde, capital of Niğde *il* (province), south central Turkey; it lies at an altitude of 4,100 ft (1,250 m) below a hill crowned by a ruined 11th-century Seljuq fortress on the road between Kayseri and the Cilician Gates, north-northwest of Adana. The town is thought

Niğde, Tur.
Farrell Grehan—Photo Researchers

by some historians to be on the site of Nakida, mentioned in Hittite texts. After the decline of ancient Tyana (10th century), Niğde and nearby Bor emerged as the towns controlling the mountain pass, a vital link on the northern trade route from Cilicia to inner Anatolia and Sinope (modern Sinop) on the Black Sea coast. A prosperous and important city of the Seljuq Sultanate of Rūm, Niğde by 1333 was, nevertheless, in ruins (probably because of the wars between the Mongols and Karaman, a Turkmen principality that succeeded the Sultanate of Rūm) when the North African traveller Ibn Baṭṭūṭah visited there. Thereafter it changed hands among the Turkmen principalities of Eretna, Karaman, and Burhanettin before its absorption into the Ottoman Empire in the second half of the 15th century.

Niğde has many notable medieval buildings, some of which date from Seljuq as well as Ottoman times. These include the mosques Alâeddin Cami (13th century); Sungur Bey Cami (14th century), built by the Mongol chief; and Diş Cami (16th century). The octagonal Hudavend Türbesi (mausoleum) dates from 1312. The Ak Medrese (1409), a former theological college, now houses the regional museum of antiquities.

Industries include flour milling and wine making and the manufacture of cement, textiles, and tools. The town is linked by rail with the principal centres of Turkey.

Niğde *il* (area 5,519 sq mi [14,294 sq km]), part of the central Anatolian Plateau, is semiarid steppe country bounded on the south by the high ranges of the Taurus Mountains (Toros Dağları) and northwest by the massive volcanic Melendiz Dağları. Soils are fertile when irrigated, producing potatoes, onions, rye, fruits, and raisins. Stock raising is important. Mohair goats are raised for their wool. The *il*'s mineral deposits include lignite (chiefly at Aksaray) and antimony. Pop. (1970) town, 26,936; *il*, 408,441.

·map, Turkey **18**:785
·province area and population, table 2 **18**:787

Nigel (d. 1169), bishop of Ely (1133–69) and finance minister of Henry I of England. In the reign of Stephen, Nigel was harassed first by the King as an adherent of the Angevins, then by the King's brother Henry, bishop of Winchester, for misspending the funds of Ely. Nigel was recalled as head of the exchequer at the accession of Henry II.

·Stephen's turbulent reign **3**:207b

Nigella damascena (plant): *see* love-in-a-mist.

Niger 13:79, a republic of West Africa, traversed by the Niger River. Landlocked, it is bounded on the northwest by Algeria, on the northeast by Libya, on the east by Chad, on the south by Nigeria and Benin, and on the west by Upper Volta and Mali.

The text article covers Niger's landscape, people and population, national economy, transportation, administration and social conditions, cultural life and institutions, and prospects for the future. *See also* West Africa, history of.

REFERENCES in other text articles:

·African languages distribution map **1**:226
·African political divisions map and population table **1**:208
·armed forces statistics, table 2 **2**:16
·Christian denominational demography map **4**:459
·Hamito-Semitic languages map **8**:590
·indigenous peoples and Fulani groups **1**:279g
·map, Africa **1**:179
·newspaper publishing statistics table **15**:237
·Niger River navigation and course **13**:97c; map 98

Niger, Pescennius, in full GAIUS PESCENNIUS NIGER JUSTUS (d. AD 194), rival Roman emperor from 193 to 194. An equestrian army officer from Italy, he was promoted to senatorial rank *c.* 180. Most of his earlier service had been in the eastern provinces, but in 185–186 he commanded an expeditionary force against deserters who had seized control of a number of cities in southern Gaul. After serving a term as consul (*c.* 189), he was appointed legate of Syria. By the end of the emperor Commodus' reign in 192, Niger had won great popularity, both in the East and among the urban populace of Rome. When Commodus' successor, Pertinax, was murdered in the spring of 193, Niger was proclaimed emperor by his legions and accepted as ruler in all the Asiatic provinces. Septimius Severus, proclaimed emperor by the troops of Upper Pannonia, marched east and decisively defeated Niger in the Battle of Issus (in southeast Anatolia) in the autumn of 194. Niger fled but was overtaken and killed.

·Istanbul destruction and massacre **9**:1069g
·Syrian revolt and defeat **15**:1119f

Niger-Congo languages, large family of about 900 African languages spoken in an area extending from northern Senegal and Kenya in the north to South West Africa and eastern Cape Province (South Africa) in the south. Linguists usually divide the Niger-Congo languages into six groups: West Atlantic, Mande, Voltaic (or Gur), Kwa, Benue-Congo (including the Bantu subgroup), and Adamawa-Eastern.

Ten languages of the family have more than 3,000,000 speakers each. These are Fulani, spoken in Senegal, Guinea, and other countries of West Africa and belonging to the West Atlantic group; Malinke and its related dialects, spoken in an area centred on western Mali and belonging to the Mande group; Mossi (or Mosi), spoken primarily in Upper Volta and belonging to the Voltaic (or Gur) group; Yoruba, Igbo, and the Akan dialects, spoken primarily in Nigeria, Ghana, and Ivory Coast and belonging to the Kwa group; and Rwanda (also called Banyaruanda and

NIGER

Official name: République du Niger (Republic of the Niger).
Location: western Africa.
Form of government: republic.
Official language: French.
Official religion: none.
Area: 489,000 sq mi, 1,267,000 sq km.
Population: (1959–60 census) 2,700,060; (1974 estimate) 4,476,000.
Capital: Niamey.
Monetary unit: 1 CFA franc (CFA Fr.) = 100 centimes.

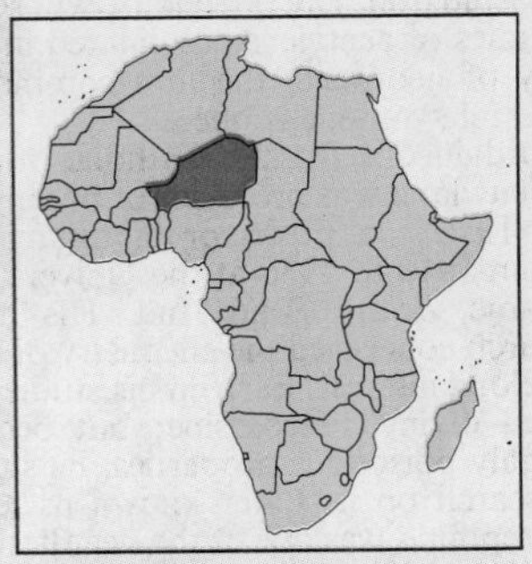

Demography

Population: (1974 estimate) density 9.1 per sq mi, 3.5 per sq km; (1975 estimate) urban 9.8%, rural 90.2%; (1973 estimate) male 49.83%, female 50.17%; (1973 estimate) under 15 44.5%, 15–29 23.3%, 30–44 17.4%, 45–59 10.1%, 60–69 3.1%, 70 and over 1.6%.
Vital statistics: (1970–75) births per 1,000 population 52.2, deaths per 1,000 population 25.5, natural increase per 1,000 population 26.8; (1970–75) life expectancy at birth—male 37.0, female 40.1; (1970) major causes of death—main diseases are sleeping sickness, malaria, leprosy, tuberculosis, and trachoma.
Ethnic composition (1972 estimate): Hausa 53.7%, Zerma Songhai 23.6%, Fulani 10.6%, Beriberi and Manga 9.1%, Tuareg and other 3.0%. *Religious affiliation* (1972 estimate): Muslim 95.0%; traditional beliefs, Christians, and other 5.0%.

National accounts

Budget (1976). Revenue: CFA Fr. 24,310,000,000 (customs duties 41.3%; direct taxes 30.4%, of which, income tax 22.7%; indirect taxes 18.5%; registrations and fees 4.7%). Expenditures: CFA Fr. 24,310,000,000 (education 14.0%, interior 7.4%, health 7.0%, defense 6.2%, rural economy 4.1%). *Total national debt* (1973): U.S. $116,700,000.* *Tourism:* no data available.

Domestic economy

Gross national product (GNP; at current market prices, 1974): U.S. $470,000,000 (U.S. $100 per capita).

Origin of gross domestic product (at constant prices of 1970):	1960				1970			
	value in 000,000 U.S. $	% of total value	labour force	% of labour force	value in 000,000 U.S. $	% of total value	labour force	% of labour force
agriculture, forestry, hunting, fishing	143.0	65.4	743,850	96.9	189.5	55.7	1,112,000	91.4
mining, quarrying	...	...	...	...	3.0	0.9	§	...
manufacturing, including public utilities	11.4	5.2	990‡	0.1	24.8	7.3	§	...
construction	13.9	6.4	‡	...	12.6	3.7	§	...
services (trade, public administration, etc.)	50.2	23.0	23,150	3.0	113.2	33.3	105,000§	8.6
total	218.5	100.0	767,990	100.0	340.4‖	100.0‖	1,217,000	100.0

Production (metric tons except as noted, 1974). Agriculture, forestry, hunting, fishing: millet 550,000, sorghum 250,000, paddy rice 43,000, unshelled peanuts (groundnuts) 180,000, cassava 180,000, dry beans 100,000, sugarcane 75,000, dry onions 30,000, cotton lint 2,500; livestock (number of live animals): cattle 2,800,000, sheep 1,800,000, goats 4,800,000, camels 340,000; roundwood 2,490,000 cu m♀; fish catch 12,500♀. Mining, quarrying: uranium 1,000♀; tin concentrates 93♀. Manufacturing: meat 43,000; cattle hides 3,800; goatskins 2,600; sheepskins 750.
Energy (1973): installed electrical capacity 18,000 kW, production 57,000,000 kWhr (13.3 kWhr per capita).
Persons economically active (1970): 1,217,000¶ (31.6%); (1973) unemployed 660♂.

Price and earnings indexes (1970 = 100):	1971	1972	1973	1974
consumer price index□	104.3	114.4	127.8	132.2

Land use (1973): total area 126,700,000 ha (agricultural and under permanent cultivation 11.8%; forested 9.5%; permanent meadows and pastures 2.4%; built-on, wasteland, and other 76.3%).

Foreign trade

Imports (1973): CFA Fr. 15,281,000,000 (trucks 8.8%; petroleum products 7.9%; cotton fabrics, woven 7.3%; sugar and honey 3.6%; other road vehicles 2.8%; rubber tires and tubes 2.4%; wheat meal and flour 1.5%; medicinal and pharmaceutical products 1.4%; telecommunication apparatus 1.2%). *Major import sources:* France 43.1%, United States 7.8%, West Germany 6.9%, Nigeria 5.7%, Italy 3.8%, Ivory Coast 3.8%, The Netherlands 3.5%, United Kingdom 3.0%, Venezuela 2.6%, China 2.2%.
Exports (1973): CFA Fr. 12,698,000,000 (live animals, including cattle, sheep, lambs, and goats 18.1%; peanuts (groundnuts), green 14.5%; peanut (groundnut) oil 6.6%; peanut (groundnut) cake 2.1%; cotton, raw 0.7%). *Major export destinations:* France 52.2%, Nigeria 22.6%, Italy 5.6%, West Germany 5.5%, United Kingdom 2.6%, Dahomey 2.1%, Ghana 1.1%.

Transport and communications

Transport. Railroads (1974): none. Roads (1974): total length 4,315 mi, 6,944 km (paved 816 mi, 1,313 km; gravel and crushed stone or stabilized soil surface 1,585 mi, 2,550 km; unimproved 1,914 mi, 3,081 km). Vehicles (1975): passenger cars 8,600, trucks and buses 9,116. Merchant marine—none. Air transport: (1973) passenger-mi 62,000,000, passenger-km 100,000,000; short ton-mi cargo 6,000,000, metric ton-km cargo 8,800,000; (1976) airports with scheduled flights 6.
Communications. Daily newspapers (1971): total number 1, total circulation 2,000, circulation per 1,000 population 0.5. Radios (1971): total number of receivers 150,000 (1 per 28 persons). Television (1971): receivers 100 (1 per 40,160 persons). Telephones (1971): 4,000 (1 per 1,030 persons).

Education and health

Education (1973–74):	schools	teachers	students	student-teacher ratio
primary (age 7–13)	932	2,736	110,437	40.4
secondary (age 12–19)	40	474	10,494	22.1
vocational	1	25	237	9.5
higher	1	47	280	6.0

College graduates: no data available. *Literacy* (early 1970s): total population literate 5.8%.
Health: (1973) doctors 100 (1 per 43,000 persons); (1972) hospital beds 2,545 (1 per 1,654 persons); (1970) daily per capita caloric intake 2,180 calories (FAO recommended minimum requirement 2,350 calories).

*External debt only. †Detail does not add to total given because of rounding. ‡Manufacturing includes construction. §Services includes all nonagricultural sectors. ‖Total includes statistical discrepancy. ¶Unofficial estimate. ♀1973. ♂Registered applicants for work in Niamey. □Niamey only.

Ruanda), Makua, Xhosa, and Zulu (Rwanda is spoken in Rwanda, Zaire, Uganda, Tanzania, and Burundi; Makua in Mozambique; and Xhosa and Zulu in South Africa), all belonging to the Bantu subgroup of the Benue-Congo group.

Some scholars place the Niger-Congo family of languages together with the small Kordofanian group (spoken in The Sudan) in a Niger-Kordofanian language family. *Major ref.* **1**:221g

·African language classification **10**:670e
·Congo ethnolinguistic relationships **4**:1118g
·Western Sudan groups **19**:796f

RELATED ENTRIES in the *Ready Reference and Index:*
Adamawa-Eastern languages; Bantu languages; Benue-Congo languages; Fulani language; Igbo language; Kwa language; Makua language; Mande languages; Swahili language; Voltaic languages; West Atlantic languages; Xhosa language; Yoruba language; Zulu language

Nigeria 13:85, largest of the West African coastal nations and, in population, the largest country in Africa. A federation of 19 states, it is bounded by Niger (north), by Chad and Cameroon (east), by the Gulf of Guinea (south), and by Benin (west).

The text article covers the landscape, people and population, national economy, transportation, administration and social conditions, cultural life and institutions, and prospects for the future. (For statistical details, *see* pages 340–341.) *See also* West Africa, history of.

REFERENCES in other text articles:
·African languages distribution map **1**:226
·African political divisions map and table **1**:208
·armed forces statistics, table 2 **2**:16
·Christian denominational demography map **4**:459
·coal production and reserves, table 5 **4**:781
·folklore as essential part of culture **7**:464f
·foreign aid from OECD countries **7**:522e; table
·health service expenditures, table 2 **15**:207
·horse armour material and use **2**:28h
·Ibadan's location and history **9**:140f
·Ife and Benin lost-wax sculpture **11**:1118e
·indigenous peoples and Fulani groups **1**:279g
·Lagos' central position **10**:594f; illus. 595
·map, Africa **1**:179
·mission school development **6**:396h
·newspaper publishing **15**:247a; table 237
·petroleum production statistics, table 1 **14**:176
·petroleum reserves of the world table **14**:175
·physician, nurse, and hospital bed ratios to population, table 1 **15**:207
·railway systems data table **15**:482
·rain forest characteristics **10**:337c; map
·spice import, export, and value, table 3 **17**:506
·tin production, table 1 **18**:427
·Tiv kinship residence structure **10**:482a
·20th-century literary dominance and contributions **1**:236g *passim* to 240f

Nigerian theatre, variety of folk opera of the Yoruba people of southwestern Nigeria, which emerged in the early 1940s. It combines a brilliant sense of mime, colourful costume, and traditional drumming, music, and folklore. Directed toward a local audience, it uses Nigerian themes, ranging from modern-day satire to historical tragedy. Although the plays are performed entirely in the Yoruba language, they may be understood and appreciated by members of other ethnolinguistic groups with the aid of a translated synopsis.

Nigerian theatre deals with three types of themes: the fantastic folktale, the farcical social satire, and the historical or mythological account derived from oral tradition. Generally speaking, both text and music evolved from a synthesis of liturgies from different religious sects.

Although there are more than a dozen travelling theatre companies, three professional troupes stand in the foreground: those of Hubert Ogunde (*Yoruba Ronu* ["Yorubas, Think!"], *Journey to Heaven*); E.K. Ogunmola (*The Palmwine Drinkard*, *Love of Money*); and Duro Ladipo (*Oba Kò So* ["The King Did Not Hang"], *Eda* ["Everyman"]). Each of these troupes has created a distinctive style shaped by the tastes of its founder, who generally writes or adapts and produces the plays, arranges the music, and performs the leading roles.

This contemporary dramatic form grew out of biblical episodes in Christmas and Passion plays presented by separatist African churches in the 1930s and '40s. Some of these plays have been performed abroad, notably, *Oba Kò So*, *Eda*, and *The Palmwine Drinkard*.

In 1945 Ogunde was the first to establish a professional touring company. Some of his plays are satires on Yoruba types: the jealous husband, the stingy father, the reckless son; others are more aggressive and deal with topical events in Nigerian politics.

In 1947 Ogunmola organized some of his pupils into an acting troupe, forming his own Theatre Party. Ogunmola opera reveals a Christian influence in the use of biblical material for the basic plots. Ogunmola employs folklore by incorporating praise poetry, proverbs, and incantations into the dialogue, as evidenced in his celebrated production of Amos Tutuola's novel *The Palmwine Drinkard.*

In the early 1960s, Duro Ladipo, a composer of church music who wished to preserve the traditional arts, wrote cultural plays based on historical material. While he was no doubt influenced by his predecessors, Ladipo employs ritual drumming, chanting, and singing as well as traditional costume appropriate to specific historical or religious groups represented in his productions. Some of Ladipo's actors have performed in religious rituals before joining the theatre company; thus, their ceremonial material has been incorporated within a contemporary mold. *Major ref.* **1**:242b

Niger-Kordofanian languages: *see* Niger-Congo languages.

Niger River 13:97, principal stream of West Africa, about 2,600 mi (4,200 km) in length. Rising in the Fouta Djallon highlands of Guinea, it flows through Mali, Niger, and Nigeria before emptying via Africa's largest delta into the Atlantic Ocean. Its main tributary, the Benue, rises in Cameroon and unites with the Niger at Lokoja in Nigeria.

The text article covers the physiography of both the river and the Niger Basin and deals also with climate and hydrology, vegetation and fauna, human ecology, history of the mapping of the river, and irrigation and navigation.
5°33′ N, 6°33′ E

REFERENCES in other text articles:
·African continent drainage pattern **1**:190g
·Atlantic Ocean floor features map **2**:296
·British exploration and discovery **7**:1043g
·British slave trade development **19**:763b *passim* to 775d
·delta environment and political development **8**:474g
·delta plains and river data **15**:869d; table 868
·drainage area and discharge table **15**:877
·Gulf of Guinea and delta deposits **8**:471h
·Ivory Coast northeastern culture **9**:1183c
·Mali's physical geography **11**:381d
·map, Guinea **8**:467
·map, Mali **11**:385
·map, Nigeria **13**:87
·rainfall's influence on flow **13**:81a
·relief and importance **13**:85e
·West Africa history map **19**:762

Niger State, west central Nigeria, created in 1976 from the former Niger Province, with which the state is coterminous. Its wooded savanna area of 28,666 sq mi (74,245 sq km) is bounded on the south and west by the Niger River and includes the floodplains of the Kaduna River. It is Nigeria's least populated state, largely because of slave raiding by the Fulani armies of Kontagora and Nupe emirates in the 19th century. Created by the British in 1908 and known as Nupe province from 1918 to 1926, it now includes the Abuja, Agaie, Bida, Kontagora, and Lapai (*qq.v.*) emirates, the Gwari (Gbari), Kamuku, and Wushishi chiefdoms, and the Zuru federation. It is populated mainly by Nupe tribesmen in the south, Gbari in the east, and Kamberi (Kambari), Hausa, Fulani, Kamuku, and Dakarki (Dakarawa) in the north. Islām is the predominant religion.

Most of the inhabitants are engaged in farming. Cotton, shea nuts, yams, and peanuts (groundnuts) are cultivated both for export and for domestic consumption. Guinea corn, millet, cowpeas, maize (corn), tobacco, palm oil and kernels, kola nuts, sugarcane, and fish are also important in local trade. Paddy rice is widely grown as a cash crop in the floodplains of the Niger and Kaduna rivers, especially in Bida emirate. Cattle (mainly owned by the Fulani), goats, sheep, chickens, and guinea fowl are raised for meat. Gold, tin, iron, and quartz (used by the glass artisans in Bida) are mined only for local craftsmen. Pottery, brasswork, glass manufactures, raffia articles, and locally dyed cloth are significant exports.

Minna (*q.v.*), the state capital, and Bida, the political and commercial centre of the Nupe people, are by far the largest towns; but the various emirate headquarters, Baro, Zungeru (*qq.v.*), Badeggi, Mokwa, and Zuru are also sizable market centres. Pop. (latest census) 1,399,000.

Nigger, The (1909), play by Edward Sheldon.
·black American dramatic treatment **18**:235b

Nigger of the "Narcissus," The (1897), novel by Joseph Conrad.
·basis in Narcissus voyage **5**:29g

Niggli, Paul (b. June 26, 1888, Zofingen, Switz.—d. Jan. 13, 1953, Zürich), mineralogist who originated the idea of a systematic deduction of the space group (one of 230 possible three-dimensional patterns) of crystals by means of X-ray data and supplied a complete outline of methods that have since been used for the determination of the space groups.

Niggli studied at the Federal Polytechnic School in Zürich and the University of Zürich, where his thesis research, a field study of schistose rocks, was a pioneering application of physicochemical principles to the study of stress metamorphism. After postgraduate work, he moved in 1915 to a chair at the University of Leipzig, and in 1918 to Tübingen. He succeeded to the chair of mineralogy and petrology at the University of Zürich in 1920.

Niggli's synthesis of mathematical crystallography and experimental X-ray techniques forms the foundation of crystal-structure analysis. His *Lehrbuch der Mineralogie und Kristallchemie* (1920; "Textbook of Mineralogy and Crystal Chemistry") set a new standard of achievement and provided a new vista of the content of modern mineralogy.
·ore deposit divisions and categories **13**:667c

Night and Fog, French NUIT ET BROUILLARD (1955), documentary film directed by Alain Resnais.
·theme and collaboration **15**:744g

Night and Fog Decree, German NACHT-UND-NEBEL-ERLASS, secret order issued by Adolf Hitler on Dec. 7, 1941, under which "persons endangering German security" in the territories occupied by Nazi Germany were to be spirited away under cover of "night and fog." The exact number of persons captured is uncertain, although about 7,000 are known to have been placed in concentration camps.

night blindness: *see* vitamin A deficiency.

night-blooming cereus (genus of plants): *see* moon cactus.

Nightcaps, also called CAPS, nickname of an 18th-century Swedish mercantilist political party.
·foreign and economic policies **16**:322a

nightclub: *see* cabaret.

nightglow (atmosphere): *see* airglow.

nighthawk, name applied to birds (several species) comprising the subfamily Chordeilinae of the family Caprimulgidae (*q.v.*). Unrelated to true hawks, they belong to the order Caprimulgiformes. They are buffy, rufous, or grayish brown, usually with light spots or patches, and range in length from about 15 to 35 centimetres. They fly about at night, especially at evening and dawn, catching flying insects in their mouths.

Common nighthawk (*Chordeiles minor*)
Kenneth W. Fink—Root Resources

The common nighthawk (*Chordeiles minor*), or bullbat, inhabits most of North America, migrating to South America in winter. It is about 20 to 30 centimetres long, grayish brown, with a white throat and wing patches. It has a sharp nasal call. During courtship it dives swiftly, creating audible whirring sounds.

Related species are found in the Southwestern U.S. and Central and South America. *See also* nightjar. *Major ref.* **3**:806f

nightingale, any of several small Old World thrushes (family Turdidae, order Passeriformes), renowned for their song; in particular, the Eurasian nightingale (*Erithacus*, or *Luscinia*, *megarhynchos*), a brown bird, 16 centimetres (6½ inches) long, with a rufous tail. Its strong and varied song, in which crescendo effects are prominent, is uttered by day or night from perches in shrubbery.

Eurasian nightingale (*Erithacus megarhynchos*)
H. Reinhard—Bruce Coleman Inc.

The thrush nightingale, or sprosser (*E. luscinia*), is a closely related, somewhat more northerly species with slightly darker plumage. Its song lacks the crescendo.

The term nightingale is also applied to other birds with rich songs, such as the neotropical nightingale-thrushes (*q.v.*; *Catharus*), the Chinese nightingale (*see* Leiothrix), and, in the West Indies, the mockingbird (*q.v.*; *Mimus*).
·birdsong imprinting sensitivity **2**:811g
·classification and general features **13**:1061f
·longevity comparison, table 1 **10**:913

Nightingale, Florence 13:99 (b. May 12, 1820, Florence—d. Aug. 13, 1910, London), English nurse and the founder of trained nursing as a profession for women.

Abstract of text biography. The daughter of well-to-do parents, she was educated largely by her father. On Feb. 7, 1837, she believed she heard the voice of God telling her that she had a mission. She entered the Institution of Protestant Deaconesses at Kaiserswerth, Ger., in 1850 to be trained as a nurse, and in 1853 she was appointed superintendent of the Institution for the Care of Sick Gentlewomen in London. In 1854, during the Crimean War, she was put in charge of nursing in the military hospitals at Scutari, in Turkey, where she coped with conditions that were appalling in terms of crowding, insanitation, and inadequacy of basic necessities, as well as with the hostility of the doctors. In March 1856 she was made general superintendent of the Female Nursing Establishment of the Military Hospitals of the Army, with expanded duties. When she returned to England, she took actions that led to the appointment of the Royal Commission on the Health of the Army (1857). In 1860 she established at St. Thomas's Hospital in London the Nightingale School for Nurses, the first such in the world. In 1907 she became the first woman to receive the Order of Merit.

REFERENCES in other text articles:
·hospital dietary innovation **7**:496h
·nursing profession **13**:396c

Nightingale Island (Atlantic Ocean): *see* Tristan da Cunha.

nightingale-thrush, collective name for 11 species of thrushes of the New World genus *Catharus* (family Turdidae, order Passeriformes), of slender build, rather drab plumage, and rich songs—qualities reminiscent of the European nightingale. In tropical species, the eye rims, bill, and legs are yellowish and the underparts are unspotted; an example is the orange-billed nightingale-thrush (*C. aurantiirostris*), 16 centimetres (6½ inches) long, of mountain forests from Mexico to Venezuela. In more northerly species, sometimes placed in the genus *Hylocichla*, the eye rims are whitish, the bill is dark, and the underparts are spotted. An example is the hermit thrush (*C. guttatus*), 18 centimetres (7 inches) long, a famous singer of Canadian and U.S. coniferous woodlands. Common in eastern broadleaf forests of the U.S. is a spotted,

Orange-billed nightingale-thrush (*Catharus aurantiirostris*)
Peter L. Ames—EB Inc.

NIGERIA

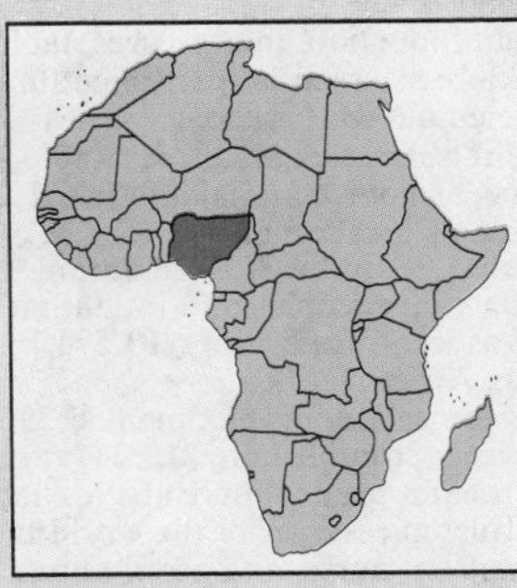

Official name: Republic of Nigeria.
Location: western Africa.
Form of government: republic.
Official language: English.
Official religion: none.
Area: 356,669 sq mi, 923,768 sq km.
Population: (1963 census*) 55,670,055; (1973 census*) 79,760,000.
Capital: Lagos.
Monetary unit: 1 naira = 100 kobo.†

Demography
Population: (1973) density 223.6 per sq mi, 86.3 per sq km; (1970) urban 22.8%, rural 77.2%; (1963) male 50.50%, female 49.50%; (1963) under 15 43.0%, 15–29 31.9%, 30–44 16.6%, 45–59 5.1%, 60–74 2.5%, 75 and over 1.0%.‡
Vital statistics: (1965–70) births per 1,000 population 49.6, deaths per 1,000 population 24.9, natural increase per 1,000 population 24.7; (1965–66) life expectancy at birth—male 37.2, female 36.7; (1969) major causes of death§—pneumonia 921; senility without mention of psychosis, ill-defined and unknown causes 672; gastritis, duodenitis, enteritis, and colitis, except diarrhea of the newborn 609; malaria 338.
Ethnic composition (1961): Hausa 21.4%, Ibo 17.9%, Yoruba 17.8%, Fulani 10.3%, Tiv 5.6%, Kanuri 4.9%, Ibibio 4.7%, Edo 3.6%, other and unknown 13.9%.‡ *Religious affiliation* (1963): Muslim 47.0%, Protestant 4.5%, Roman Catholic 4.5%, other Christian 25.5%, traditional beliefs 18.1%.‡

National accounts
Budget (1974–75). Revenue: 2,496,000,000 naira (excludes 626,000,000 naira statutory appropriation to state governments; 80% of revenue from petroleum). Expenditures: 2,634,000,000 naira (capital expenditure 62.2%, of which, land transport 8.6%, education 8.1%, urban and rural planning 7.6%, electricity and fuel 7.4%; recurrent expenditure 37.8%, of which, defense 12.8%, education 3.5%). *Total national debt* (1973): 1,158,600,000 naira.
Tourism (1972). Receipts from visitors: U.S. $10,000,000. Expenditures by nationals abroad: no data available.

Domestic economy
Gross national product (GNP; at current market prices, 1972): U.S. $9,350,000,000 (U.S. $130 per capita).‖

Origin of gross domestic product (at current producers value):	1963–64¶		1973–74	
	value in 000,000 naira	% of total value	value in 000,000 naira	% of total value
agriculture, forestry, hunting, fishing	1,673.8	61.0	2,311.3	40.0
mining, quarrying	54.8	2.0	898.1	15.5
manufacturing	163.0	5.9	451.1	7.8
construction	117.8	4.3	477.4	8.3
electricity, gas, water	14.6	0.5	34.6	0.6
transport, storage, communication	132.6	4.8	159.7	2.8
trade	346.6	12.6	642.2	11.1
public administration, defense	79.6	2.9	417.9	7.2
education	82.6	3.0	148.4	2.6
health	18.2	0.7	62.8	1.1
services	62.2	2.3	176.6	3.1
total	2,745.8	100.0	5,780.1	100.0‡

Production (metric tons except as noted). Agriculture, forestry, hunting, fishing (1972): yams 14,300,000; cassava 9,570,000; sorghum 3,988,000; millet 3,414,000; peanuts (groundnuts), unshelled 1,233,000; corn (maize) 1,188,000; cowpeas, dry 990,000; palm oil 650,000; sugarcane 650,000; rice, paddy 600,000; green peppers 510,000; palm kernels 423,000; cocoa beans 244,000; cottonseed 214,000; sesame seed 213,000;

rusty-headed form, the wood thrush (*Hylocichla mustelina*), 20 centimetres (8 inches) long.
·gray-cheeked thrush migration routes **12**:184f
·wood thrush seasonal responses to stimuli **2**:806g

nightjar, general name for about 60 to 70 species of birds that make up the subfamily

Common nightjar (*Caprimulgus europaeus*)
Eric Hosking

Caprimulginae of the family Caprimulgidae (*q.v.*) and sometimes extended to include the nighthawks (*q.v.*; subfamily Chordeilinae) or applied to the entire order Caprimulgiformes.

True nightjars occur almost worldwide in temperate to tropical regions, except for New Zealand and some islands of Oceania. They have protective colouring of gray, brown, or reddish brown. They feed on insects.

The common nightjar (*Caprimulgus europaeus*) is representative of some 35 similar species making up the largest genus in the order Caprimulgiformes. About 30 centimetres long, it breeds throughout Europe and in western Asia, wintering in Africa.

The lyre-tailed nightjar (*Uropsalis lyra*) inhabits northwestern South America. Its outermost tail feathers may measure 60 centimetres or more, accounting for 80 to 90 percent of the bird's total length.

The pennant-winged nightjar (*Semeiophorus vexillarius*) of Africa gets its name from its boldly patterned black and white wing, which has greatly lengthened innermost primary flight feathers (50 to 70 centimetres); the remaining primaries also are longer than normal.

North American relatives are chuck-will's-widow, pauraque, poorwill, and whippoorwill (*qq.v.*). *Major ref.* **3**:806f
·seasonal migration patterns **12**:180h

night lizard, common name for any of the 12 species of the lizard family Xantusiidae.
·classification and features **16**:288b

nightmare, a frightening dream, accompanied by a sense of oppression and sometimes of suffocation, that usually awakens the sleeper.
·behavioral disturbances during sleep **5**:1013h
·types and associated sleep stages **16**:882b

night monkey (*Aotus*, or *Aotes, trivirgatus*): *see* durukuli.

nightshade, plants of the genus *Solanum* (family Solanaceae; *q.v.*), which has about 1,700 species, and certain other plants of the same family and other families. The species usually called nightshade in North America and England is *Solanum dulcamara*, also called bittersweet and woody nightshade. Its foliage and egg-shaped red berries are poisonous, the active principle being solanine, which can cause convulsions and death if taken in large doses. The black nightshade (*S. nigrum*), with black berries, is also poisonous.

The deadly nightshade, or dwale, is the belladonna (*q.v.*; *Atropa belladonna*), a tall, bushy herb of the same family and the source of several alkaloid drugs. Enchanter's nightshade is a name applied to plants of the genus

Nightshade (*Solanum dulcamara*)
Roche

Circaea (family Onagraceae). Malabar nightshade refers to twining herbaceous vines of the genus *Basella* (family Basellaceae).
·alkaloid protection of plants **1**:597e

Nights of Cabiria, The, Italian LE NOTTI DI CABIRIA (1956), motion picture directed by Federico Fellini.
·theme and plot **12**:535a

nightstick (club used by police): *see* baton.

night terror, or PAVOR NOCTURNUS, in children, a sudden awakening from sleep, sometimes preceded by a scream, and sitting up with wide-open eyes, expression indicating fear, and rigid posture. The child returns to sleep in a few minutes and generally does not remember the experience. *Major ref.* **5**:1013h
·symptoms and associated sleep stage **16**:882b

night vision, also called SCOTOPIC VISION, or SCOTOPIA, ability to see in dim light. This ability is at its highest when the subject has been in darkness for a considerable length of time and when the object viewed is looked at from the corner of the eye, rather than directly.
·retina structure and function **7**:101b

Nightwatch, formal title THE COMPANY OF CAPTAIN FRANS BANNING COCQ AND LIEUTENANT WILLEM VAN RUYTENBURCH (1642), painting by Rembrandt.
·dramatic style, history, and criticism **15**:656c

Nightwood (1936), novel by Djuna Barnes.
·cult novel tradition **13**:288b

nigodas, according to the Jaina philosophy of India, minute clusters of invisible souls distributed throughout the four elements of earth, air, fire, and water. They belong to the lowest class of *jīva* (*q.v.*), or "living matter," possess only the sense of touch, share common functions such as respiration and nutrition, and experience intense pain. The whole space of the world is said to be packed with *nigodas*. They are the source of souls to take the place of the infinitesimally small number that have up till now been able to attain *mokṣa*, or release from the cycle of rebirths.

nigre, in the manufacture of soap, a dark-coloured water solution of soap and impurities formed by settling from the neat soap.
·soap production processes **16**:917d

milk 205,000; sweet potatoes 204,000; eggs 105,000; coconuts 90,000; soybeans 63,000; natural rubber 62,000; cotton, lint 38,000; roundwood, nonconiferous 59,800,000 cu m; livestock (no. of live animals): cattle 11,405,000 head, sheep 8,000,000 head, goats 23,500,000 head, chickens 83,500,000 head. Mining, quarrying (1973): crude petroleum 101,760,000, natural gas 19,778,000,000 cu m, coal 324,000, tin ore 5,828. Manufacturing (1973): woven cotton fabrics 262,400,000 sq m; petroleum products 1,968,000; cement 1,240,500; cigarettes 10,635,000,000 pieces♀; beer 1,841,394 hectolitres; soft drinks and aerated waters 1,033,782 hectolitres; paint 143,049 hectolitres; sawnwood 566,000 cu m; beef and veal 175,000♀; mutton and goat meat 100,000♀; footwear 17,631,000 pairs; wheat flour 274,000.

Energy: (1971) installed electrical capacity 805,000 kW, (1973) production 2,628,000,000 kWhr (44.1 kWhr per capita).

Persons economically active: (1970) 22,534,000, (1963) unemployed 344,925.

Price and earnings indexes (1970 = 100):	1971	1972	1973
consumer price index§	113.5	116.8	121.0♁

Land use (1961): total land area 92,377,000 hectares (forested 34.2%; meadows and pastures 27.9%; agricultural and under permanent cultivation 23.6%; built-on, wasteland, and other 14.3%).

Foreign trade

Imports (1973): 1,224,800,000 naira (machinery and transport equipment 40.1%, of which, general machinery 10.8%, passenger cars 6.3%, commercial road motor vehicles 4.9%; chemicals 10.9%, of which, medicinal and pharmaceutical products 3.2%; iron and steel 8.0%, of which, tubes, pipes, and fittings of iron or steel 2.7%; textile yarns and fabrics 7.0%, of which, cotton yarn and thread 3.4%; petroleum products 6.9%; cereals 3.8%; paper and paper products 2.8%; sugar 2.5%). *Major import sources:* United Kingdom 27.1%, West Germany 14.8%, United States 10.3%, Japan 9.2%, France 7.1%, Italy 4.1%, The Netherlands 4.0%.

Exports (1973): 2,278,400,000 naira (petroleum, crude 83.4%; cocoa beans 5.0%; peanuts (groundnuts) 2.0%; peanut (groundnut) oil 1.0%; rubber 0.9%; palm kernels 0.8%; peanut (groundnut) cake 0.8%; tin 0.7%; cocoa butter 0.7%). *Major export destinations:* United States 24.2%, United Kingdom 18.7%, The Netherlands 13.2%, France 12.6%, Japan 4.6%, West Germany 3.6%, Italy 2.7%, Belgium–Luxembourg 1.0%.

Transport and communication

Transport. Railroads (1973): length 2,680 mi, 4,313 km; passenger-mi 611,600,000, passenger-km 984,300,000; short ton-mi cargo 936,000,000, metric ton-km cargo 1,366,600,000. Roads (1971): total length 57,006 mi, 91,738 km (paved 10,076 mi, 16,215 km; gravel or earth 46,930 mi, 75,523 km). Vehicles (1973): passenger cars 115,000, trucks and buses 60,000. Merchant marine (1974): vessels (100 gross tons and over) 78, total deadweight tonnage 157,772. Air transport: (1972) passenger-mi 190,000,000, passenger-km 305,000,000; short ton-mi cargo 5,500,000, metric ton-km cargo 8,100,000; (1974) airports with scheduled flights 10.

Communication. Daily newspapers (1972): total number 17; total circulation 238,000,□ circulation per 1,000 population 3.□ Radios (1972): total number of receivers 1,550,000 (1 per 37 persons). Television (1972): receivers 75,000 (1 per 774 persons). Telephones (1974): 106,326 (1 per 750 persons).◇

Education and health

Education (1971–72):	schools	teachers	students	student–teacher ratio
primary (age 5 to 12)	14,536	130,355	4,391,197	33.7
secondary (age 12 to 17)	1,209	16,720	399,732	23.9
vocational	66	1,178	15,953	13.5
teacher training	148	1,907	37,904	19.9
higher	18	2,341	22,927	9.8

College graduates (per 100,000 population, 1967): 2. *Literacy* (early 1960s): total population literate (15 and over) 25.0%.

Health: (1970) doctors 2,683 (1 per 20,526 persons); (1971) hospital beds 35,716 (1 per 1,582 persons); (1970) daily per capita caloric intake 2,290 calories (FAO recommended minimum requirement 2,300 calories).

*Census populations may be substantially overstated; UN 1973 estimate: 59,607,000. Per capita figures based on UN estimates unless otherwise indicated. †The naira replaced the Nigerian pound on Jan. 1, 1973, at a rate of 2 naira per Nigerian pound. ‡Percentages do not add to 100.0 because of rounding. §Lagos only. ‖Based on World Bank population estimate of 69,524,000. ¶Value in Nigerian pounds for 1963–64 converted to naira for comparison with 1973–74. ♀1972. ♁Average of less than 12 months. □Refers o 8 dailies only. ◇Based on 1973 census.

Nigrinus, 2nd-century-AD work by the Greek satirist Lucian.
·Greek mythology satire **11**:173b

Nigronia (insect genus): *see* fishfly.

nigun, wordless song sung by Ḥasidic Jews (members of a pietistic movement that began in the 18th century) as a means of elevating the soul to God. Because they lacked words, the *nigunim* were felt to move the singer beyond the sensual and rational toward the mystic. Such songs were spontaneously extemporized by a rabbi or one of his disciples, the entire group of men then repeating the song in unison. Melodically, the songs are strongly influenced by Slavic folk song, but they are freer in rhythm. In the 18th century, when persecutions caused many eastern European Jews to migrate to western Europe, the *nigunim* were often appropriated by cantors who sought to make them more florid or to combine them with western European musical styles; only rarely were such combinations truly successful. A number of *nigunim* have been preserved in musical notation.

Nihaṅg Sāhibs, in the Sikh religion of India, a semi-monastic and militaristic order.
·monastic militarism in Sikhism **12**:339c

nihilism, in contemporary usage, philosophy of negation involving a rejection of traditional morality, order, and authority, together with the feeling that no basis exists on which a new order can be erected.

The term was applied to certain heretics during the Middle Ages; it has since taken on varying meanings in different historical and intellectual contexts. Appearing in philosophical discussions by the late 18th century, it denotes an extreme skepticism in which the skeptic denies that there is any objective basis of truth and obligation. Its modern currency stems from its use by 19th-century Russian literary and political groups after being popularized by the novelist Ivan Turgenev in his characterization of Bazarov in *Fathers and Sons* (1862). There was a positive side to the Russian nihilism of this period: nihilists such as Bazarov advocated utilitarianism and scientific rationalism. The popular conception of a nihilist, however, was that of a dishevelled, unruly terrorist. In contemporary usage the term denotes only an attitude.
·Camus's attempt to overcome **3**:712f
·Turgenev's treatment of social change **18**:780d

Nihonbashi, historical district in Tokyo.
·early Tokyo city trade activity **18**:478d

Nihon Keizai shimbun: *see* Japanese newspapers.

Nihon ryōi-ki (1822), collection of Japanese stories, written in Chinese and containing Buddhist narratives of the Nara period, compiled by the Buddhist priest Kyōkai.
·contents and intent **10**:1067f

Nihon Shakaitō (Japanese political party): *see* Nippon Shakaitō.

Nihon shoki, also known as NIHON-GI (both titles meaning literally in Japanese "Chronicles of Japan"), comprising, together with the *Koji-ki* (*q.v.*), the first written records in Japan and sacred texts of the Shintō religion.

The *Nihon shoki*, compiled by court order in 720, consists of 30 chapters covering the entire history of Japan from the origin of the world down to 697, just before the Nara period. The first part deals with many myths and legends of ancient Japan and is an important source for Shintō thought. The later chapters, for the period from about the 5th century on, are historically more accurate and contain records of several of the politically powerful clans as well as of the Imperial family. The *Nihon shoki* was written in Chinese and reflects the influence of early Chinese civilization on Japan. Among the events described are the introduction of Buddhism and the Taika reforms of the 7th century.

The *Nihon shoki* is the first of six officially compiled chronicles that were continued to 887 by Imperial command, and it was read ceremonially before the emperor at the Imperial court during the Heian period. The first printing of the part entitled "Divine Age" appeared in 1599; the most complete commentary, *Nihon shoki tsūshaku*, was published in 1899 by Iida Takesato.
·chronology of Japanese history **4**:573e
·Japanese literary history **10**:1066a
·mythological origin of music **12**:680g
·Nara period cultural developments **10**:61g
·origin, compilation, and heroic themes **6**:910d
·Shintō tradition and Neo-Confucian thought **16**:672h
·sources and Chinese influence **10**:97d

Niigata, prefecture (*ken*), central Honshu, Japan, on the Sea of Japan. Its area of 4,856 sq mi (12,577 sq km) includes the offshore islands of Sado and Awa-shima. Combined deposition of the Shinano-gawa (Shinano River) and Ara-kawa in the central part of the long coastline has created the lowland called the Echigo-heiya (Echigo Plain). The rest of the prefecture is mostly mountainous.

Mouth of the Shinano River at Niigata, Japan
Kokunai Jigyo Kouku

Niigata Prefecture is one of Japan's largest rice producers, its surpluses being shipped to city markets. Coastal fishing is practiced. Plentiful hydroelectric power generated in the interior mountains has stimulated industrial growth (chemicals, metals, machinery) in such cities as Niigata, Kashiwazaki, Naoetsu, Sanjō, and Takada. The prefecture also produces large amounts of petroleum (Nagaoka, Kashiwazaki) and natural gas.

Niigata, the prefectural capital and largest city, is located on the edge of the Echigo-heiya at the mouth of the Shinano-gawa. An important rice port in feudal times, it has continued as the leading port on the Sea of Japan. The city is also a major commercial and industrial centre. A severe earthquake hit the city in 1964. Pop. (1970) city, 383,919; (1973 est.) prefecture, 2,359,000.
·area and population, table 1 **10**:45
·map, Japan **10**:36

Niihama, city, Ehime Prefecture (*ken*), Shikoku, Japan, on the Inland Sea coast. Originally a small fishing village, it grew after 1691 as a transit port for copper from the inland Besshi Copper Mine to Ōsaka. The foundation of modern smelting works (1883) and a hydroelectric company (1913) laid the basis of present industrialization. The port was enlarged for the importation of foreign copper ores, and in the early 1970s Niihama was the core of the East Ehime New Industrial City Program. Pop. (1970) 126,033.
33°58′ N, 133°16′ E
·map, Japan **10**:36

Niihau, volcanic island, Kauai County, Hawaii, U.S., 17 mi (27 km) southwest of Kauai Island. It was sold in 1863 by King Kamehameha IV (with a large area of land on Kauai at Makaweli) to Elizabeth Sinclair of Scotland. Her descendants, the Kamaaina (meaning "old-timer") Robinson family, continue to live at Makaweli and have attempted to preserve Hawaiian culture on Niihau. Residency is restricted to Hawaiians, and tourism is prohibited; in 1959 it was the only island to vote against statehood. Although English is taught, residents prefer to speak the old Hawaiian language.

Mostly arid lowland except for the rocky east coast, the island (area 72 sq mi [186 sq km]) cannot support crops; ranching is the main occupation. The chief village, Puuwai, is on the west coast. Pop. (1980) 226.
21°55′ N, 160°10′ W
·map, United States **18**:908

Niijima, Joseph Hardy, originally NIISHIMA JŌ (1843–90), Japanese Christian educator.
·Christian mission work **10**:113e

niiname-sai, a Japanese harvest festival.
·Japanese religious festivals **10**:114d

Niislel Khureheh (Mongolia): *see* Ulaanbaatar.

Niitsu, city, Niigata Prefecture (*ken*), Honshu, Japan, on the Uetsu Main Line (railway), northeast of Tokyo. Oil was discovered southeast of Niitsu in the 17th century, and exploitation began in 1898. Three railway lines were subsequently opened through the city. Al-

Tulip plantation, Niitsu, Japan
Shiro Shirahata—Bon

though the output of the oil fields has decreased significantly, Niitsu continues to be an important transport and commercial centre, producing tulip and hyacinth bulbs for export to the United States. In the late 1960s it began to develop as a residential suburb of Niigata city. Pop. (1970) 57,089.
37°48′ N, 139°07′ E
·map, Japan **10**:36

Nijhoff, Martinus (b. April 20, 1894, The Hague—d. Jan. 26, 1953, The Hague), greatest Dutch poet of his generation, who achieved not only an intensely original imagery but also an astounding command of poetic technique.

In his first volume, *De wandelaar* (1916; "The Wanderer"), his negative feelings of isolation and noninvolvement are symbolized in wildly grotesque figures, and the image of the dance of death is prevalent. The only solution to this spiritual frustration is suicide, as enacted in the short verse drama *Pierrot aan de lantaarn* (1918; "Pierrot at the Lamppost"). The demonic element is again apparent in his second volume, *Vormen* (1924; "Forms"), which also reveals Nijhoff's realistic, direct approach to Christianity in, for example, "De soldaat die Jezus kruisigde" ("The Soldier Whom Jesus Crucified").

Nijhoff's best volume, *Nieuwe gedichten* (1934; "New Poems"), shows a spiritual rebirth, an affirmation of the richness of earthly existence, which is most apparent in the optimism of the magnificent "Awater." This tale of a mythical, biblical character set in a sober modern townscape combines a sensitive use of colloquialism with extreme virtuosity of form.

"Awater" and *Het uur U* (1942; "U-Hour"), the story of a stranger's shattering effect on a self-satisfied community, firmly establish Nijhoff as one of Europe's foremost 20th-century poets.

Nijinska, Bronisława (1891–1972), Polish-born choreographer famous for her massive ensemble groupings and talent for depicting follies of contemporary society; she was the sister of the great dancer Vaslav Nijinsky.
·contribution to ballet **5**:466f

Nijinsky, Vaslav 13:100 (b. March 12 [Feb. 28, old style], 1890, Kiev, now in Ukrainian S.S.R.—d. April 8, 1950, London), ballet dancer of almost legendary fame, celebrated for his spectacular leaps and sensitive interpretations.

Abstract of text biography. The son of notable dancers, Nijinsky entered the Imperial School of Dancing at the age of nine and became a soloist at the Mariinsky Theatre, St. Petersburg, in 1907. He was instantly acclaimed and, until 1911, danced all the leading parts in classical ballets there. Meanwhile he had been invited in 1909 by the impresario Sergey Diaghilev to join his touring company of members of the Mariinsky and Bolshoi theatres: Nijinsky's superb dancing, in Paris and then in other European capitals, caused a sensation. He appeared in such classical ballets as *Giselle*, *Swan Lake*, and *The Sleeping Beauty*, and for him the choreographer Michel Fokine created *Le Spectre de la rose*, *Petrushka*, *Schéhérazade*, and other ballets. Nijinsky also became a choreographer and created such works as *L'Après-midi d'un faune* and *Le Sacre du printemps*. In 1913 he married Romola, countess de Pulszky-Lubocy-Cselfalva. In 1919 he fell a victim of schizophrenia and was forced to retire.

REFERENCES in other text articles:
·choreographic innovations **4**:454c
·contribution to ballet **5**:466e
·male role re-establishment **2**:651d

Nijlen, Jan van (1884–1965), one of the most distinguished Flemish poets of his generation. Of a retiring nature, van Nijlen usually published his verse in limited editions. He became more famous when in 1938 he at last published a one-volume selection from his works, *Gedichten, 1904–1938*. Van Nijlen's characteristic tone is melancholic and elegiac, which reflects the disillusionment of the modern world. His verse is marked, however, by its classical clarity and finish. Van Nijlen also wrote studies of the French authors Charles Péguy and Francis Jammes.

Nijmegen, German NIMWEGEN, municipality (*gemeente*), Gelderland province, eastern Netherlands, on the Waal River (southern arm of the Rhine). It originated as the Roman settlement of Noviomagus and is the oldest town in The Netherlands and the largest in Gelderland. Often an imperial residence in the Carolingian period, it became a free city and later joined the Hanseatic League. In 1579 it subscribed to the Union of Utrecht against Spain. It was taken by the French (1672) in the third of the Dutch Wars, and the treaties—between Louis XIV, the Netherlands, Spain, and the Holy Roman Empire—that ended the hostilities were signed there in 1678–79. Nijmegen was the capital of Gelderland until its capture in 1794 by the French, who moved the capital to Arnhem. It served as a frontier fortress until its defenses were dismantled in 1878. Occupied by the Germans during World War II, the town was badly damaged and was the scene of a U.S. airborne landing in 1944. Rebuilt, it is now an important industrial centre, a rail junction, and an inland shipping centre.

A scenic park, the Valkhof (Falcon's Court), contains ruins of Charlemagne's castle, which was destroyed by the Norsemen but rebuilt by Frederick Barbarossa in 1155 before being demolished by French Revolutionary troops in 1796; the choir of its 12th-century church and a 16-sided baptistry, consecrated in 799, survive. The fine Renaissance Grote Kerk (Great Church) of St. Stephen and the town hall (1554) both suffered war damage but have been restored. Other notable buildings include the Latin School (1544–45), the Weighhouse (1612), and the modern Church of St. Peter Canisius (1960). Nijmegen has a Roman Catholic university, the Katholieke Universiteit Nijmegen (1923), with an important medical faculty and hospital; a municipal museum; the Rijksmuseum G.M. Kam te Nijmegen (1922), with a notable collection of Roman antiquities; and a theatre and a concert hall. Pop. (1973 est.) 149,205.
51°50′ N, 5°50′ E
·map, The Netherlands **12**:1061
·Roman stool example **7**:795f

Nijmegen, Arnoult of (*c.* 1470–1540), Flemish stained-glass maker.
·stained-glass painting in 16th century **17**:575a

Nijmegen (NIMWEGEN), **Treaties of** (1678–79), the treaties of peace ending the Dutch War (*q.v.*) of 1672–78 in which France opposed Spain and the Dutch republic. France gained advantages by arranging terms with each of its enemies separately. Although negotiations had begun in 1676, the first treaty, between France and the United Provinces, was not concluded until Aug. 10, 1678. France agreed to return Maastricht and to suspend Jean-Baptiste Colbert's anti-Dutch tariff of 1667; these concessions represented a major victory for Dutch naval power and commerce. In the second treaty, concluded between France and Spain on Sept. 17, 1678, Spain was forced to make major concessions, indicating that its power had declined since the Peace of Westphalia in 1648. Spain gave up Franche-Comté, Artois, and 16 fortified towns in Flanders to France. France returned some of its enclaves in the Spanish Netherlands to Spain to round out the formerly arbitrary frontier line. On the whole, France gained substantially by the possession of a more rational border and of border fortresses that secured the safety of Paris. Furthermore, with Franche-Comté finally in French possession, Spain had lost its "corridor" between Milan and the Spanish Netherlands. The Holy Roman emperor Leopold I finally accepted French terms on Feb. 5, 1679, keeping Philippsburg but giving up Freiburg im Breisgau to France and granting free access through his territory to it from Breisach (French since 1648). France also continued to occupy Lorraine, since its duke, Charles V, refused the conditions imposed for his restoration. Two further treaties in 1679 terminated hostilities between France and Brandenburg (Peace of Saint-Germain-en-Laye) and between France and Denmark (Peace of Fontainebleau). Brandenburg and Denmark restored to France's ally, Sweden, territories taken by them.
·Austrian losses to Louis XIV **2**:456b
·background and significance **6**:1093e
·French annexation of Franche-Comté **3**:499c
·French territorial acquisitions **7**:637c
·Leopold I and Louis XIV **8**:95c
·Spain's wars with France **17**:432d

Nijō Castle, in Kyōto, built in 1603 by Tokugawa Ieyasu.
·construction and current status **10**:562g

Nika (African people): *see* Nyika.

Nika insurrection, also known as NIKA RIOTS, or NIKA REVOLT (532), revolt against the Byzantine emperor Justinian I in Constantinople. *Major ref.* **3**:552a
·Belisarius' strategy and acclaim **2**:826d
·Istanbul fire and rebuilding **9**:1070c
·Justinian's retention of throne **10**:364f

Nikan Wailan, 16th-century Juchen leader.
·Nurhachi's Juchen power consolidation **13**:392h

Nikāyas (Buddhist texts): *see* Sutta Piṭaka.

Nike, in Greek religion, the goddess of victory, daughter of the giant Pallas and of the infernal river Styx. Nike probably did not originally have a separate cult at Athens. As an attribute of both Athena, the goddess of wisdom, and the chief god, Zeus, Nike was represented in art as a small figure carried in the hand by those divinities. Athena Nike was always wingless; Nike alone was winged. She also appears carrying a palm branch or a wreath (sometimes a Hermes staff as the messenger of victory), erecting a trophy, or, frequently, hovering with outspread wings over the victor in a competition; for her functions referred to success not only in war but in all other undertakings.

Nike, sculpture from a bronze vessel, probably made in a Greek city of southern Italy, *c.* 490 BC; in the British Museum
By courtesy of the trustees of the British Museum

At Rome, where Nike was called Victoria, she was worshipped from the earliest times. She came to be regarded as the protecting goddess of the Senate, and her statue in the Curia Julia was the cause of the final combat between Christianity and paganism toward the end of the 4th century.

Among artistic representations of Nike are the sculpture by Paeonius (*c.* 424 BC) and the "Nike of Samothrace." The latter, discovered

on Samothrace in 1863 and now in the Louvre, Paris, was probably erected by Rhodians *c.* 203 BC to commemorate a sea battle. Excavations have shown that the sculpture was placed alighting on a flagship, which was set in the ground in such a way that it appeared to float.
·sculpture style of Classical Greece **19**:294h

Nike missile, any of a group of U.S. guided missiles designed primarily for defense against air attack. First developed was Nike Ajax, test-fired in 1951, a 21-foot- (6.4-metre-) long, 12-inch- (30-centimetre-) diameter, 2,455-pound (1,114-kilogram) missile, having a range of 25 miles (40 kilometres), capable of speeds up to 1,500 miles per hour on liquid propellant, and guided by radar. Nike Ajax missiles were installed throughout the United States for defense of vital areas.

Nike Hercules missile in firing position
By courtesy of the U.S. Army

In 1958, Nike Hercules was introduced. Larger than Nike Ajax, it had a solid propellant engine, could carry either a nuclear or a high-explosive warhead, and ranged 75 miles. Capable of flying at supersonic speeds to altitudes above 150,000 feet, the Nike Hercules was 27 feet long and 31.5 inches in diameter and weighed 5,000 pounds. Nike Zeus, first anti-missile missile, was about 50 feet long and weighed 10,000 pounds. A further development was Nike X, which had a fixed radar antenna that could be electronically scanned. Nike Cajun, a sounding rocket, was capable of lifting a 50-pound payload of scientific instruments to a height of 90 miles.
·anti-aircraft artillery **8**:496c
·design, development, and range **15**:932d
·payload and altitude, table 5 **15**:941
·sounding rocket development **17**:363a
·systems applications **17**:974h

Nikephoros I, Saint: *see* Nicephorus I, Saint.

nikethamide, central nervous system stimulant affecting heart and respiratory action.
·respiratory disease treatment **18**:283h

Nikisch, Arthur (b. Oct. 12, 1855, Lébényi Szentmiklós, Hung.—d. Jan. 23, 1922, Leipzig), one of the finest conductors of the late 19th century. After study in Vienna, in 1878 he was appointed choral coach at the Leipzig Opera, becoming principal conductor in 1879. From 1889 to 1893 he was conductor of the Boston Symphony Orchestra, then conducted the Gewandhaus Orchestra at Leipzig from 1895 until his death. From 1897 he also led the Berlin Philharmonic Orchestra, with which he toured widely. He succeeded Hans von Bülow as conductor of the Philharmonic Concerts at Hamburg in 1897, toured the U.S. with the London Symphony Orchestra in 1912, and conducted Wagner's *Ring* cycle of operas at Covent Garden in 1913. Although he excelled in performances of Wagner, he was a conductor of broad musical tastes. His style was marked by intensity of Romantic expression, and his technique by precision and economy of gesture. As an accompanist at the piano, he appeared in recitals with his pupil Elena Gerhardt, the lieder singer.

Nikita Minion (Russian patriarch): *see* Nikon.

Nikitin, Afanasy, 15th-century Russian author, merchant, and explorer.
·medieval regional literature **10**:1129c

Nikkal (goddess): *see* Yarikh.

Nikkatsu Motion Picture Company, Japan's oldest film company. Established as an independent company in 1912 with the title Nippon Katsudo Shashin (Japan Cinematograph Company), it had previously been a part of the Greater Japan Film Machinery Manufacturing Company, Ltd., an attempted monopoly of the industry modelled after the Motion Picture Patents Company in the U.S. By 1915 Nikkatsu had captured two-thirds of the viewing market. It employed the first Japanese star, Matsunosuke Onoe (1875–1926), and the first prominent Japanese director, Shōzō Makino (1878–1929). It was the first to successfully experiment with night photography in *Ningenku* (1923; *Human Suffering*), and, in the early 1930s, it had the best perfected sound system in Japan, the Western Electric sound process.

Poor business management eventually caused financial difficulty, and, in 1942, its production facilities were incorporated into the newly formed Daiei Company. Nikkatsu remained as a theatre-holding chain only until 1954, when it resumed production. Two years later the tremendous popularity of *Taiyo no Kisetsu* (*Season of the Sun*) and *Kurutta Kajitsu* (*Crazed Fruit*), based on novels by Shintaro Ishihara and dealing with revolt against tradition, gave Nikkatsu a place among the leading studios. The work of Mizoguchi Kenji (*q.v.*; 1898–1956), famous as a director of women and a pioneer in the use of the camera, gave the company added prestige. Nikkatsu attracts a widely diversified audience and has expanded into television broadcasting.

Nikkō (13th century), Japanese Buddhist monk and disciple of Nichiren. *See also* Nichiren-shō-shū.
·Nichiren-shō-shū founding **3**:386a

Nikkō, city, Tochigi Prefecture (*ken*), Honshu, Japan, on the Daiya-gawa (Daiya River), north of Tokyo. One of the major pilgrimage and tourist centres in Japan, it is situated at the edge of Nikkō National Park. A Shintō shrine may have existed at Nikkō as early as the 4th century AD, and in 767 a Buddhist temple was founded there. Since the 17th century, however, the town has been dominated by the great Tōshō-gū (shrine), dedicated to Tokugawa Ieyasu, the first Tokugawa shogun, who was buried there in 1617. Also important is the Daiyuin mausoleum, dedicated to Iemitsu, the third Tokugawa shogun, who died in 1651. The shrines and associated buildings are notable for their red colour, gilt ornamentation, and detail.

Torii (portal entrance) to the Futaarasan Shrine in Nikkō, Japan
Bob and Ira Spring—EB Inc.

There are scores of hot mineral springs in the Nasu-dake (Mt. Nasu) area of Nikkō National Park. The park also contains mountains such as Nantai-zan, which is crowned by the Futaarasan Shrine; waterfalls such as the 325-ft (99-m) Kegon-no-taki (Kegon Falls); and lakes, including the recreation centre of Chūzenji-ko (Lake Chūzenji). Pop. (1975) 26,279. 36°45′ N, 139°37′ E
·map, Japan **10**:36
·Tosho-gu shrine illus. **19**:Visual Arts, East Asian, Plate 19

Nikolais, Alwin (b. Nov. 25, 1912, Southington, Conn.), choreographer, composer, and designer whose abstract dances relate movement to sound, property, and lighting effects. Initially a pianist, Nikolais began his study of dance around 1935 with Truda Kaschmann, a student of modern dancer Mary Wigman, to understand Wigman's use of percussion accompaniment. In 1937 he founded a dance school and company in Hartford, Conn., and was director of the dance department of Hartt College of Music (now part of the University of Hartford) from 1940 to 1942 and from 1946 to 1949. After serving in World War II, Nikolais resumed dance studies with Hanya Holm and became her assistant. In 1948 he joined the Henry Street Settlement in New York City and founded its school of modern dance; the following year he became artistic director of its playhouse.

Nikolais
Martha Swope

The Alwin Nikolais Dance Company (originally called the Playhouse Dance Company) was formed in 1951. In 1953 the company presented Nikolais' first major work, *Masks, Props, and Mobiles*, in which the dancers were wrapped in stretch fabric to create unusual, fanciful shapes. In later works, such as *Kaleidoscope* (1956), *Allegory* (1959), *Totem* (1960), and *Imago* (1963), he continued experiments in what he has called the basic art of the theatre—an integration of motion, sound, shape, and colour, each given relatively equal emphasis. Nikolais frequently composed electronic scores for these productions. His later works include: *Sanctum* (1964), *Somniloquy* (1967), *Tent* (1968), *Scenario* (1971), *Cross-Fade* (1974), and *The Tribe* (1975).

Nikolais received grants from the Guggenheim Foundation and the National Endowment for the Arts and served on committees for Fulbright scholarships and the U.S. Office of Education's arts program. In 1967 he was elected president of the Association of American Dance Companies, an organization of both modern dance and ballet troupes.

·choreographic principles **4**:455c
·costume design and dance style **17**:563h
·movement quality analysis **12**:294c
·stage lighting and projection use **17**:556f

Nikolay Aleksandrovich: *see* Nicholas II of Russia.

Nikolayev, *oblast* (administrative region), Ukrainian Soviet Socialist Republic, with an area of 9,550 sq mi (24,700 sq km) on the Black Sea Plain, sloping down gently from the Dnepr Upland in the north to the sea coast. The north is greatly dissected by gullies, and soil erosion generally is severe. There is little surface water other than the Yuzhny Bug River, and even the larger rivers nearly dry out in summer. The coast has many lagoons and long estuaries, often sealed off by sandbars. The whole area is steppe, with fertile soils, and a high proportion is ploughed up for winter wheat, corn (maize), sunflowers, and sugar beets. Vineyards and orchards are widespread, especially on the Bug, and cattle and sheep are kept in large numbers. Apart from the capital, Nikolayev, cities are small and concerned chiefly with processing agricultural products. In the north considerable granite is quarried. Pop. (1970) 1,148,000.

Nikolayev, city and administrative centre of Nikolayev *oblast* (region), Ukrainian Soviet Socialist Republic, on the estuary of the Yuzhny Bug River, about 40 mi (65 km) from the Black Sea. It was founded in 1788 as a naval base after the Russian annexation of the Black Sea coast, near the site of the ancient Greek Olbia. In 1862 a commercial harbour was opened, and in 1873 a railway was built to the port. It is now one of the most important Soviet Black Sea ports, serving the Krivoy Rog area and extensive steppe grain lands; it is one of the biggest shipbuilding centres of the U.S.S.R. The city also has a wide range of other engineering and consumer-goods industries. Nikolayev is a modern city in appearance, laid out on a gridiron pattern of broad streets. The city has shipbuilding and teacher-training institutes. Pop. (1970 prelim.) 331,000.
46°58′ N, 32°00′ E
·commercial rise and social hierarchy **16**:54e
·map, Soviet Union **17**:322

Nikolayev, Andriyan Grigoryevich (b. Sept. 5, 1929, Shorshely, Chuvash A.S.S.R.), cosmonaut who piloted the Vostok 3 spacecraft, launched Aug. 11, 1962. When Vostok 4, piloted by Pavel R. Popovich, was launched a day later, there were, for the first time, two manned craft in space simultaneously. The two made radio and visual contact, but there was no attempt at docking. Both landed on August 15.

The son of a worker on a collective farm, Nikolayev studied and worked in forestry until drafted into the Soviet Army in 1950. An early interest in flying persisted, and he soon transferred to the air force; in 1954 he became a pilot. In 1957 he joined the Communist Party and in March 1960 entered cosmonaut training.

On Nov. 3, 1963, Nikolayev married Valentina Tereshkova, who in June 1963 had become the first woman to travel in space. Nikolayev and Vitaly I. Sevastyanov manned the Soyuz 9 flight on June 1, 1970, and set a space endurance record of almost 18 days in orbit. The mission, primarily one of determining the effects of prolonged spaceflight, ended on June 19.
·manned space flight, table 3 **17**:368

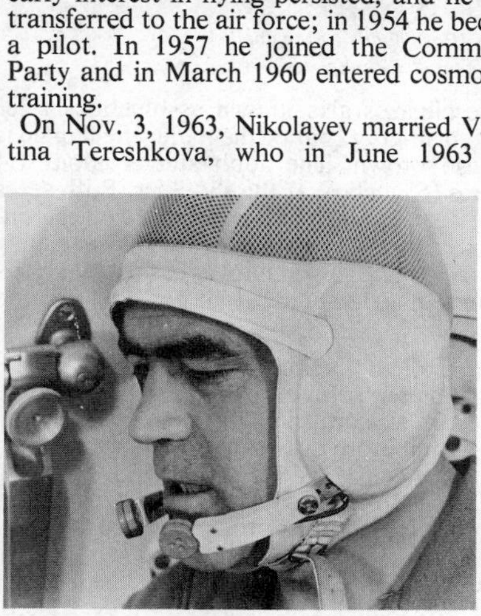
Nikolayev in a Soyuz 9 spaceship, 1970
Novosti Press Agency

Nikolayeva, Galina Yevgenyevna, pen name of GALINA YEVGENYEVNA VOLYANSKAYA (1914–), Soviet author.
·Soviet Union cultural history **17**:354a

Nikolayevsk-na-Amure, city, Khabarovsk *kray* (territory), far eastern Russian Soviet Federated Socialist Republic, at the head of the Amur River Estuary. It was founded in 1850, but its importance as a Pacific port and naval base was overshadowed by the later development of Vladivostok and Sovetskaya Gavan, both with rail communications to the interior. It has ship repair yards and industries of local significance only, and a fishing fleet is based there. Pop. (1970) 30,000.
53°08′ N, 140°44′ E
·map, Soviet Union **17**:322

Nikolay Pavlovich: *see* Nicholas I of Russia.

Nikolev, Nikolay Petrovich (1758–1815), Russian poet and dramatist.
·Russian literature development **10**:1178b

Nikolsburg, Peace of (July 26, 1866), preliminary peace leading to an end of the Seven Weeks' War between Austria and Prussia. The victorious Prussians annexed Schleswig-Holstein, Hanover, Hesse-Kassel, Nassau and Frankfurt, while assuming leadership of the new North German Confederation. Austria was excluded from Germany but lost none of its own territory. The South German states were allowed to form their own independent confederation. On August 23 these terms were incorporated into the final Treaty of Prague.
·Austrian and Prussian manipulation by Bismarck **2**:1079h
·Bismarck's reasonable peace terms **2**:467e
·Prussian diplomacy under Bismarck **8**:111b

Nikolsburg, Treaty of (Dec. 31, 1621), peace settlement concluded during the Thirty Years' War between Transylvania, in Eastern Europe, and the Habsburgs of Austria that enlarged Transylvania's territory and guaranteed the political and religious rights of Hungarian Protestants. When the Protestants of Bohemia rebelled (1618) against the Holy Roman emperor Matthias (reigned 1612–19), Gábor Bethlen, prince of Transylvania (1613–29), supported the Bohemians in order to prevent the Austrian king from oppressing the Protestants in the portion of Hungary controlled by the Roman Catholic Habsburgs. Forming an alliance with the Bohemians (1619), Bethlen marched into Habsburg Hungary in September; he captured Kashau (Sept. 5, 1619), entered Pressburg (modern Bratislava, Czech.), where he acquired the Hungarian crown (October), and, accompanied by a Bohemian force, proceeded to Vienna (November). He withdrew, however, on Dec. 5, 1619, when he received news that another section of his army had been defeated (Nov. 21, 1619) by the Cossack troops of an ally of Matthias' successor, Emperor Ferdinand II (reigned 1619–37). Bethlen concluded an armistice with the Emperor in January 1620, but further negotiations failed to result in a peace settlement. Hostilities were resumed and continued even after the Emperor's forces defeated the Bohemians at the Battle of the White Mountain (Nov. 8, 1620). But Transylvania could not maintain the struggle indefinitely without allies. Peace negotiations were reopened in late 1621, and the Treaty of Nikolsburg was concluded on December 31. Bethlen returned the Hungarian crown to Ferdinand (he had refused to be crowned king of Hungary in August 1620) but received the titles prince of Transylvania and Hungary and duke of the German Empire. Western Hungary reverted to Ferdinand's control; but the Habsburg emperor promised to uphold the rights of the Protestants in that region, reaffirmed the Habsburg promise to rule according to the traditional laws and customs of Hungary (as pledged in the Peace of Vienna; June 23, 1606), and granted amnesty to his opponents. Transylvania received possession of seven counties from Habsburg Hungary as well as the Silesian duchies of Oppeln and Ratibor. The treaty, however, was not conclusive; Transylvania, having demonstrated its power in eastern Europe, continued to participate in anti-Habsburg coalitions through most of the Thirty Years' War.

Nikon 13:101, original name NIKITA MININ (b. 1605, Veldemanovo, now in Russian S.F.S.R.—d. Aug. 27 [Aug. 16, old style], 1681, en route to Moscow), religious leader who unsuccessfully attempted to establish the primacy of the Orthodox Church over the state in Russia and whose reforms led to a schism in the church.

Abstract of text biography. Representing an influential reform group, Nikon was made patriarch of Moscow by Tsar Alexis in 1652. He then broke with his former backers and persecuted them, introducing changes in church ritual that provoked the schism of the Raskolniki (Old Believers). His attempts to increase the power of the church alienated the Tsar and led to his downfall, but the reforms he introduced were retained.

REFERENCES in other text articles:
·liturgical and bureaucratic reforms **16**:48b
·liturgical issue of Church Slavonic **16**:869g
·political and liturgical reforms **6**:157e

Nikopol, town, Pleven *okrŭg* (province), northern Bulgaria, on the Danube River near the mouth of the Osŭm (Ossăm) and opposite Turnu Măgurele, Romania. In the past it was confused with Nicopolis and Istrum, founded by the Roman emperor Trajan, but in 1871 the site of the latter was established at the village of Nikyup on the Rositsa River, about 45 mi (70 km) southeast. Nikopol was an important Danubian stronghold—ruined fortresses still dominate the town—founded by the Byzantine emperor Heraclius in AD 629. In 1396 Sultan Bayezid I defeated a crusader army led by King Sigismund of Hungary, an event that contributed significantly to the fate of the Balkans for five centuries. Occupied by the Turks in 1393–1877, it was again fortified and became an important town. Its population grew to approximately 40,000 before it was destroyed by the Russians in 1810; thereupon the Turks re-established in Vidin and Nikopol declined. The Russians liberated Nikopol in 1877. Farming, viticulture, and fishing are the main means of livelihood; as a port, it has been superseded by Somovit. Pop. (1970 est.) 5,715.
43°42′ N, 24°54′ E
·map, Bulgaria **3**:470

Nikopol, city, Dnepropetrovsk *oblast* (administrative region), Ukrainian Soviet Socialist Republic, on the northern shore of the Kakhovka Reservoir on the Dnepr River and on the Zaporozhye–Krivoy Rog railway. Founded as Nikitin Rog in the 1630s at a strategic crossing of the river, it was renamed Nikopol in 1782. It is important as the centre of the world's largest deposit of manganese, first mined there in 1886. Reserves are estimated at more than 500,000,000 tons, with a 20–35 percent metal content. The city's metallurgical industry produces ferroalloys, steel tubes, cranes, and agricultural machinery; food processing and brewing are also significant. A dam protects the lower part of the city from inundation by the reservoir. Pop. (1970 prelim.) 125,000.
47°35′ N, 34°25′ E
·map, Soviet Union **17**:322

Nikópolis (Greece): *see* Nicopolis Actia.

nikṣa, a gold ornament used in Indian Vedic rituals.
·ornaments worn in sacrificial rites **3**:1181h

Nikšić, second-largest town in Montenegro, Yugoslavia, in the valley of the Zeta River. The Romans built a castrum (camp) called Anagostum there, probably on an old tribal settlement site. By the 12th century, the name had been transliterated to Onogošt, and the name Nikšić was used by the Montenegrins *c.* 1355. It was held by the Turks from 1455 to 1877.

Nikšić is an important industrial centre, with a major steelworks, a brewery, a malt factory, sawmills, woodworking factories, and a hydroelectric station. Bauxite is obtained from one of the largest mines in Europe. The planned development of backward Montenegro after World War II brought new buildings, parks, and service projects to Nikšić. An ancient Roman bridge crosses the Zeta, and traces of Anagostum and another settlement at nearby Zavrh remain. Around the old Church of St. Peter is a graveyard of the heretical Bogomil sect that died out in the late Middle Ages. Pop. (1971) 28,500.
42°46′ N, 18°56′ E
·map, Yugoslavia **19**:1100

Nikuradse experiment (hydrology): *see* roughness.

Nildarpan, in English MIRROR OF THE INDIGO (1860), drama by Indian playwright Dina Bandhu Mitra.
·theme, North Indian tour, and banning **17**:167a

Nile, Battle of the (August 1, 1798), with Trafalgar, one of the two greatest victories of the British admiral Lord Nelson. Nelson, with 14 ships of the line, caught a French squadron of 13 ships of the line under Adm. François-Paul Brueys d'Aigailliers at anchor in Abu Qir Bay, near Alexandria, Egypt. In a daring attack that lasted far into the night, he destroyed or captured all but two of Bruey's ships, isolating Napoleon in Egypt and securing British control of the Mediterranean.
·British Mediterranean naval supremacy **7**:723d
·Nelson's naval campaigns **12**:948f
·Nelson's surprise attack **12**:833d

Nile, West, northern district, Uganda.
·area and population table **18**:828

Nile crocodile: *see* crocodile.

Nile perch (*Lates niloticus*), large food and game fish of the family Latidae (order Perciformes), found in the Nile and other rivers and lakes of Africa. A large-mouthed fish, the Nile perch is greenish or brownish above, silvery below, and attains a length and weight of about 1.8 metres (6 feet) and 140 kilograms (300 pounds). It has an elongated body, a protruding lower jaw, a rounded tail, and two dorsal fins.

The family Latidae includes several other species, some found in the river systems of Africa, the others in estuaries and along the coasts of Asia and Australia. The members of the family are sometimes classified with snooks and glassfishes in the family Centropomidae.
·classification and general features **14**:52a

Nile River 13:102, longest river of Africa and of the world (4,132 mi [6,648 km]), rises in highlands south of the Equator (where the principal section is known as the White Nile) and flows northward through the East African lake region to unite with the Blue Nile (at Khartoum) and the Atbara before entering the Mediterranean Sea in a broad delta north of Cairo.

The text article covers the Nile Basin, the river's physiography, climate, plant and animal life, human ecology, exploration and mapping, damming (including the Aswān High Dam), water resources and their use, and prospects for the future.
30°10′ N, 31°06′ E

REFERENCES in other text articles:
·African continent drainage pattern **1**:190c
·ancient irrigation systems **9**:899g
·basin topography and population **6**:449a
·British source search and success **7**:1044d
·Burton's explorations **3**:527a
·delta marsh distribution and importance **17**:838e
·delta plains and river data **15**:869d; table 868
·delta region evolution **17**:766d
·deposition of sediment theories **6**:77b *passim* to 78c
·desert evaporation and water flow **5**:608a
·drainage area and sediment load, table 1 **16**:474
·Egyptian ancient religious concern **12**:920c
·Egyptian dependence on flooding **6**:460e
·Egypt's dominant landscape features **6**:445e
·Ethiopian Aksumite imperial power **6**:1008c
·European source search and achievement **6**:98d
·fluvial rate of sedimentation **7**:444g
·Holocene flood levels **4**:735g; table 736
·Holocene rains and sedimentation **8**:1004g
·irrigation, drainage, and discharge **15**:875c; table
·man's effect on basin physiographic features **14**:430d
·map, Africa **1**:179
·Mediterranean sediment deposition **11**:855d
·Mosaic plague legend and historicity **12**:488h
·mystery cult seasonal rites **12**:782f
·Near Eastern irrigation agriculture **12**:913h
·Pleistocene climate correlation **14**:566c
·Pleistocene form and racial settlement **14**:840g
·rift lake geography and hydrography **6**:116e; map 119
·silt yield comparison with major rivers **8**:1130c
·sources in Rwanda **16**:109a
·Sudan drainage system and flow **17**:756f
·Sudanese historical development **13**:108h *passim* to 113h
·Ugandan physical geography **18**:827a

Niles, village, Cook County, Illinois, U.S., just northwest of Chicago. Settled about 1832 by German immigrants and originally known as Dutchman's Point, it was probably renamed after an early settler. It is mainly residential but has some light manufactures including teletype and electronic parts, business machines, and beverages. Inc. 1902. Pop. (1980) 30,363.

Niles, city, Berrien County, southwestern Michigan, U.S., on the St. Joseph River. The site of a Jesuit mission (1690), it is the only locality in the state to have been under four flags. The French built a blockhouse-fort (1691), which was captured in 1761 by the British. The Spanish flag was raised there on Feb. 12, 1781, and the Americans gained the territory through a 1783 peace treaty with the British. It became a stagecoach stop between Chicago and Detroit, was permanently settled in 1827, and developed as a centre for the farm produce of the river valley. It later acquired diversified industries. Ring Lardner, Montgomery Ward, and the Dodge brothers of automotive fame were natives of Niles. Inc. village, 1829; city, 1838. Pop. (1980) 13,115.
41°50′ N, 86°15′ W

Niles, city, Trumbull County, northeastern Ohio, U.S., in the Mahoning Valley Industrial Area, just northwest of Youngstown. Ruben Harmon, the first white settler (1797), discovered with others deposits of coal, iron ore, and limestone. James Heaton built a foundry and founded the Township of Heaton's Furnace (1806), which was renamed Nilestown in 1834 (shortened in 1843) to honour Hezekiah Niles, editor of the *Niles' National Register* (1811–49). Industrialization was fostered by the railroads (the first arrived in 1856, and by 1874 there were three). Manufactures include prefabricated houses, steel, lathes, tools and dies, sheet metal, and truck and trailer chassis.

The McKinley Memorial, Niles, Ohio
Milt and Joan Mann from CameraMann

Pres. William McKinley, whose father was a founder at Heaton's plant, was born in Niles and is commemorated by the McKinley Memorial, a familiar landmark in the centre of the city. Inc. village, 1865; city, 1895. Pop. (1980) 23,088.
41°11′ N, 80°45′ W

Niles, John Jacob (b. April 28, 1892, Louisville, Ky.), U.S. folksinger, ballad collector, and composer of solo and choral songs. Educated at the music conservatories in Cincinnati, Ohio, and Lyons, France, and at the Schola Cantorum of Paris, he toured widely in the United States and Europe as a folksinger. He made his own lutes and Appalachian dulcimers and specialized in the songs of the Appalachian Mountain region. His ballad collections frequently include material he composed or arranged as well as ballads transcribed directly from oral sources. His published works include *Songs My Mother Never Taught Me* (1929; with Douglas Moore), *Songs of the Hill Folk* (1934), *Ballads and Tragic Legends* (1937), *The Anglo-American Ballad Study Book* (1945), and *The Shape Note Study Book* (1950).

nilgai (*Boselaphus tragocamelus*), Indian antelope, family Bovidae (order Artiodactyla), ranging alone or in small groups in open plains or light forests.

Nilgai (*Boselaphus tragocamelus*)
Kenneth W. Fink from Root Resources—EB Inc.

The nilgai is also known as bluebuck after the bluish-gray coat of the male; the female is reddish brown. The adult stands about 1.4 metres (55 inches) at the shoulder. Both sexes have a short mane and have white on the underparts, ears, face, throat, and immediately above the hooves. The male has short, slightly curved horns and a tuft of black hair on the throat.

Nīlgiri (Hindi: Blue Hills), district, Tamil Nadu state, southern India, bordering the states of Mysore (north) and Kerala (west), and Coimbatore district (east and south). It is named after the Nīlgiri Hills, which form the major part of its territory. The hills consist of a compact plateau approximately 1,000 sq mi (2,590 sq km) in area, with peaks rising abruptly from the surrounding plains to 6,000–8,000 ft (1,800–2,400 m) in altitude. One of the peaks, Doda Betta (8,648 ft [2,636 m]), is the highest point in Tamil Nadu. Part of the

Western Ghāts, the hills are separated from the Mysore plateau (north) by the Noyar River, and from the Anaimalai and Palni hills (south) by the Pālghāt Gap.

The district was developed in the 19th century with the founding of Ootacamund (the district administrative headquarters), Kotagiri, Coonoor, and Wellington. It is considerably cooler and wetter than the surrounding plains, the upper hills forming undulating grassy downs. Tea, cinchona (trees and shrubs whose bark yields quinine), coffee, and vegetables are grown extensively. Chief industries, apart from tourism, are tea and quinine processing and textile manufacturing. Pop. (1971 prelim.) 491,330.

Nillatun, Araucanian shamanistic harvest ceremony combining Christian ritual and an indigenous mass dance.

·dramatic interludes and influences 1:676b

Nilo-Hamites (African peoples): *see* Nilotes.

Nilo-Hamitic languages: *see* Nilotic languages.

Nilópolis, city and a northwestern suburb of the city of Rio de Janeiro, in Rio de Janeiro state, Brazil, lies in the Guandu–Mirim River Valley, at 92 ft (28 m) above sea level. Nilópolis has metallurgical plants, and there are orange groves nearby. Pop. (1970) 86,720.

Nilo-Saharan languages, large group of African languages thought by some scholars to compose a language family. This hypothetical language family includes Songhai, Fur, the Koma languages, the Maba languages, the Saharan languages, and the Chari-Nile languages. Nilo-Saharan languages are spoken in an area extending from Mali in the west to Ethiopia in the east and from Egypt in the north to Tanzania in the south. *See also* Chari-Nile languages; Saharan languages.

·African language areas and statistics 10:670d
·distribution and subgroups 1:281e
·Greenberg's classification system 1:220d
·members, range, and features 1:225e; maps
·Zaire ethnic and linguistic diversity 19:1123c

Nilotes, various east central African tribes living in southern Sudan and northern Uganda and extending into neighbouring territories. The name refers to their habitat, mostly the region of the upper Nile and its tributaries, and to a linguistic unity that distinguishes them from their neighbours with similar physique and culture. Nilotic languages are closely related to the Nilo-Hamitic languages, particularly in vocabulary; but their affinities in a wider classification of African languages are obscure, and there is considerable disagreement in the literature. *See* Nilotic languages.

The genetic origins of the Nilotes are likewise uncertain and disputed. A mixture of Hamitic and Negro ethnotypes in their ancestry is a basic assumption. Blood-group studies suggest that a very high frequency of the Rh chromosome, cDe, may be a special Nilotic character. There is considerable genetic divergence between the northern and southern groups both in ABO blood-group frequency and the presence of the sickle-cell trait. Nilotes tend to be dolichocephalic with frizzy hair and dark complexion; northern Nilotes are tallest (average 1.78 metres, or 5 feet 10 inches), with slender build. Although a distinctive ethnic group, Nilotic tribes vary in culture, and exceptions to any generalization can be found among one or more tribes. The southern Luo tribes in particular are divergent because of admixture with Nilo-Hamitic and Bantu neighbours. Material culture is poor, although the Jo Luo were noted ironworkers.

Most Nilotes occupy savanna country alternately subject to flooding and drought. They pursue a mixed economy of pastoralism and hoe cultivation, supplemented by fishing, hunting, and a little food gathering. Although Nilotes may cultivate out of necessity, all except the Anuak are pastoralists with a great love of cattle, which enter into every aspect of society. Milk, milk products, and grain are staple foods. Cattle are not slaughtered indiscriminately for meat; they are paid in compensation and bridewealth, and their ownership determines status and wealth. Nilotic peoples have a rich cattle vocabulary; they spend much time caring for the herds and erecting large stables, or kraals, for their protection. A man commonly trains and decorates the horns of his favourite ox, and in many cases he is addressed by the animal's name. Cattle assume ritual importance, being dedicated and sacrificed to ancestors or spirits.

Nomadic or transhumant movements are especially pronounced among the Nuer and Dinka. In the wet season they live in permanent village settlements above flood level and cultivate and herd in the vicinity of well-built circular houses. In the dry season they occupy temporary cattle camps near permanent water supplies and pasture, living in windbreaks. Other Nilotic tribes are more sedentary.

The Shilluk are the most highly organized, having a divine king who symbolizes the whole realm. Organized chieftainships, associated with rainmaking, court ceremonial, and royal emblems, are found also among the Anuak, Acholi and others. In contrast, the Nuer, Dinka, and Luo of Kenya are classified as tribes without rulers, their egalitarian society being based on a relationship between lineage segments coordinated with territorial segments. A dominant clan is associated with a tribal territory; dominant lineages of this clan are found in subdivisions of the tribe. The principle opposition between segments and their fusion in relation to larger segments is marked; descent is patrilineal.

Ritual experts are often rainmakers; among the Dinka and Nuer they act also as mediators and peacemakers in feuds between lineages and between territorial subdivisions. There are strong ancestor cults and belief in a supreme being. Totemism exists in some tribes but is important only among the Dinka.

·anthropometry in racial typing 15:351g
·culturolinguistic and racial identity 1:221e
·migration pattern and influence 6:96d
·Nile River population patterns 13:105e
·numbers, tribal affiliations, and culture 6:109g; map 110
·Sudan tribal groups and distinction 17:762b
·Ugandan linguistic and ethnic groups 18:828b
·Zaire ethnic and linguistic diversity 19:1123b; map

Nilotic languages, group of related languages spoken in Uganda, Kenya, southern Sudan, and northern Tanzania. These languages are usually classified as belonging to the Eastern Sudanic branch of the Chari-Nile language family. The languages of this group were formerly divided, primarily on the basis of racial and cultural considerations, into two groups named Nilotic (which includes Shilluk, Dinka, and Nuer in southern Sudan; Acholi in northern Uganda; and Luo in western Kenya and in Tanzania) and Nilo-Hamitic (which includes Bari and Lotuho in southern Sudan; Karamojong, Nandi, and Suk in Uganda; Turkana in Kenya; and Masai, extending from southern Kenya into northern Tanzania). Recently, however, a number of scholars have produced a considerable amount of evidence showing that the two groups of languages are closely related and should be considered as one group; these linguists often divide the Nilotic languages into a western group, including Shilluk, Nuer, and Luo; an eastern group, including Masai and Turkana; and a southern group, including Nandi and Suk.

In Nilotic sentences, the subject of a principal clause usually precedes the verb. The languages are tone languages, often using tones to distinguish the singular of a noun from its plural or to indicate the syntactic role of a word in a particular sentence. Some of the languages also indicate plurals by means of suffixes. *Major ref.* 1:225g; map

·classification and characteristics 1:226g *passim* to 228c
·Ethiopian endemicity 6:1000d
·Kenya tribal members and location 10:426c
·Nilo-Hamitic controversy 1:226g
·Tanzanian social backgrounds 17:1029e
·Ugandan linguistic and ethnic groups 18:828a

Nilotic Sudan, history of the 13:108. The Sudan is a zone that extends across the African continent south of the Sahara and north of the equatorial rain forest. The Nilotic Sudan, as defined in the text article, is the area along the Nile River south of Egypt, corresponding approximately to ancient Nubia and to the northern and central parts of the present Democratic Republic of Sudan. The earliest known inhabitants of this area were Mesolithic hunters and gatherers. The development of Nubian culture was profoundly influenced by contact with ancient Egypt, and following the decline of Egypt (11th century BC), the Nubian Kingdom of Cush controlled all of Egypt for a brief period. It ruled the Middle Nile for another 1,000 years, preserving its distinctive Egyptian-Nubian culture. In the 6th century AD, Nubia was converted to Christianity; and the powerful Christian kingdoms that developed there held off encroachments from Muslim Egypt until the 15th century. The Funj state that arose in the 16th century adopted Islāmic religion. In 1821 Egypt conquered the Nilotic Sudan, and European influence in the area increased. In 1881 Islāmic reformers (the Mahdists) seized control of the area, only to lose it to an Anglo-Egyptian force in 1898. An Anglo-Egyptian condominium governed the Sudan from 1899 to 1955; in 1956 it became an independent republic. From 1958 to 1964 a military regime ruled, and the army seized control again in 1969.

TEXT ARTICLE covers:

Ancient Nubia to the 4th century AD 13:108f
Christian and Islāmic influence to 1821 109h
Egyptian-Ottoman rule 111d
The Mahdīyah 112g
The Anglo-Egyptian Condominium 113h
The Republic of The Sudan 114h

REFERENCES in other text articles:

·British intervention in 1880s 3:272b
·Egyptian Arab invasions from 600s 6:488e
·Egyptian invasions from 16th century 6:492e *passim* to 500a
·Egyptian military, commercial, and cultural connections 6:467b *passim* to 473h
·Egyptian military action from 18th to 20th dynasty 6:475b *passim* to 478a
·Ethiopian–Sudanese rivalry 6:1008d
·exploration and settlement from 200 AD 1:206d
·independence of Egypt and acquisition of kingship 6:479c *passim* to 481f
·jewelry depicting Egyptian conquests 10:167g; illus. 168
·Kushite culture and defeat by Aksum 1:282c
·Memphis siege and conquest of Egypt 11:896g
·Middle Eastern cultural continuity 12:167f
·Muḥammad ʿAlī Pasha's invasion and rule 12:610f
·Nubian visual art forms and style 19:249d
·Ramses II's temple-building 15:502g
·states' rise and decline 19:797a

RELATED ENTRIES in the *Ready Reference and Index:*

Anglo-Egyptian Condominium; Darfur; Fashoda Incident; Meroë; Napata; Nubia

Nils Holgerssons underbara resa genom Sverige (1906–07), translated as THE WONDERFUL ADVENTURES OF NILS (1907), a novel by Selma Ottiliana Lovisa Lagerlöf.

·artistic instructional materials 4:238g

Nilson, Johann Esaias (1721–88), German ceramist and engraver.

·German Rococo ceramic ware 14:910a

Nilson, Lars Fredrik (1840–99), Swedish chemist.

Nilus of Ancyra, Saint, also called NILUS THE ASCETIC (d. *c.* 430, Ancyra, now Ankara, Tur.), Greek Byzantine abbot and author of extensive ascetical literature that influenced both Eastern and Western monasticism. He also participated in the prevalent theological controversies concerning the Trinity and the person and work of Christ.

A protégé of the staunchly orthodox and reform patriarch of Constantinople, St. John Chrysostom, Nilus consistently supported him during his conflicts with ecclesiastical rivals and the imperial court. Thus influenced, Nilus composed several letters to leaders of the Goths in which he strongly refutes Arianism, the heretical doctrine that teaches the created nature of the Son and Holy Spirit in the Christian Trinity. In them he contends that Christ is God and man in one individual person; his mother is therefore Theotokos ("God-bearer"). Leaving Constantinople, Nilus became a monk and eventually abbot of a monastery near Ancyra and soon won a reputation as a wonder-worker and spiritual counsellor. He wrote tracts on moral and monastic subjects, including *De monastica exercitatione* ("On Monastic Practice") and *De voluntaria paupertate* ("On Voluntary Poverty"), which stress the essence of monastic obedience as the renunciation of the will and all resistance to the religious superior, whose duty is to guide the prayer life of the monk and put him on guard against the wiles of Satan. The greatest poverty, Nilus states, is the exclusive dedication to the service of God; consequently, the ascetical life is led more effectively in the wilderness than in the city because, among other reasons, it avoids vainglory.

Supplementing these longer studies, Nilus wrote approximately 1,000 letters, which survive in a mutilated collection, to varied recipients. His letters are written in a blunt, sometimes coarse style, which established his reputation as an early master of Christian spirituality, balancing religious insight with worldly astuteness. He seems to have coined the term spiritual philosophy to indicate his central theme of casting Christ as man's effective exemplar for controlling his impulses. The object of this discipline, initiated by a divine gift or grace, is union with God. Moreover, Nilus criticized exaggerated asceticism, particularly that of the Stylite monks, contemplative solitaries who sat atop rocks or pillars, whence they sometimes dispensed advice. Throughout his writings are frequent interpretations of biblical texts, commentaries following the literal or historical sense, as is characteristic of the Antiochian school, although he occasionally uses allegory. In another essay he discusses the expression of religious art in mosaics.

Certain works attributed to Nilus in the standard collection of early Greek Christian authors edited by J.P. Migne, *Patrologiae Graeca* (vol. 79, 1861; "Greek Patrology"), including treatises *De oratione* ("On Discourse"), a standard work on the subject, and *De malignis cogitationibus* ("On Evil Thoughts") are probably the work of the Greek theologian Evagrius Ponticus (346–399). Many authors suspected of heresy have hidden behind Nilus' reputation in the history of monasticism by affixing his name to their works. The sifting of the spurious from the genuine is still in process. The account, under Nilus' name, "Concerning the Capture of the Monks on Mount Sinai," depicting an invasion of the monastery by Saracens in 410, and the ransom of a certain Nilus of Sinai and his son Theodulus, refers to a legendary figure. This story has given rise to the "Nilus Question" in historical scholarship. The account, surprisingly for a Christian author, describes the cultic practice of animal sacrifice.

Nilus of Rossano, Saint, also called NILUS THE YOUNGER (*c.* 905–1005), abbot, promoter of Greek monasticism in Italy, founded several communities of monks in the region of Calabria following the Greek rule of St. Basil of Caesarea. A supporter of the regular successors to the papal crown in their controversies with antipopes, he also helped establish (1004) the noted abbey of Grottaferrata, near Rome, that remains today the centre of Greek monasticism and liturgy in Italy.

·calligraphy provincial style **3**:650d
·monastic reform movement **9**:1129b

Nima, district of Accra, Ghana.

·Accra's living conditions and slum areas **1**:44b

Nīmach, or NEEMUCH, town, Mandasor district, Indore division, Madhya Pradesh state, India. Located on a barren ridge, it is a road junction and distribution centre for agricultural products and building stone. Handloom weaving is the major industry. Formerly a large British cantonment of Gwalior princely state, the town in 1822 became the headquarters of the combined Rājputāna–Mālwa political agency and of the Mālwa Agency in 1895. There are two colleges affiliated with Vikram University. The surrounding country was once famous as a tiger-hunting area. Pop. (1971 prelim.) 49,773.
24°28′ N, 74°52′ E

Nimāvats (sect): *see* Nimbārka.

nimba, a large mask carved by the Baga tribesmen of Africa.

·form and ritual use **1**:263c; illus.

Nimba County, administrative division (since 1964) of northeastern Liberia. A forested region of 4,650 sq mi (12,045 sq km), it is mainly inhabited by the Mano, Gio (Dan), and Mandingo peoples. In the Nimba Range (*q.v.*) and around Kitoma (*q.v.*) are large reserves of iron ore. Besides the ore, which is sent by rail to the Atlantic port of Buchanan, the region exports diamonds, rubber, coffee, and cocoa. Sanniquellie, the county seat, and Ganta (*qq.v.*) are its chief agricultural trade centres. Latest pop. est. 173,829.

·area and population table **10**:853
·map, Liberia **10**:852

Nimba Range, mountain chain extending in a southwest–northeast direction along the Guinea–Ivory Coast–Liberia border, reaches

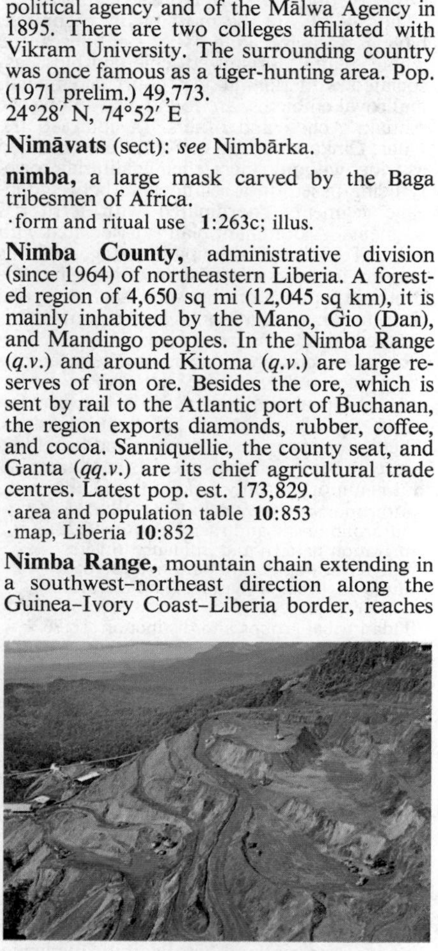

Iron ore mine in the Nimba Range of West Africa
Jacques Jangoux

its highest elevation at Mont Nimba (5,747 ft [1,752 m]) in Guinea. Surrounded by lowland rain forest to the south and savanna to the north, the mountains are the source of the Nuon (Nipoué, Cestos) and Cavalla rivers, which join to form the Liberia–Ivory Coast boundary. All three countries have set aside nature and forest reserves on the mountain slopes.

The range's extensive iron ore deposits were first mined by the Liberian American–Swedish Minerals Company (Lamco) in 1963 and exported via its 168-mi (270-km) railroad to the Liberian port of Buchanan. A mining concession was granted to Consafrique, a European consortium, to mine the Guinean section of the range after an agreement had been reached with Liberia to use the Lamco railway.
7°35′ N, 8°28′ W

·Ivory Coast physical geography **9**:1181e
·map, Guinea **8**:467

Nimbārka, also called NIMBĀDITYA or NIYAMĀNANDA (fl. 12th or 13th century?, South India), Telugu-speaking Brahmin, yogi, minor philosopher, and prominent astronomer who founded the *bhakti*s (devotional sect called Nimbārkas or Nimāvats) that worshipped the deity Kṛṣṇa and his consort, Rādhā.

Nimbārka has been identified with Bhāskara, a 9th- or 10th-century philosopher and celebrated commentator on the *Brahma-sūtra* (*Vedānta-sūtra*). Most historians of Hindu mysticism, however, hold that Nimbārka probably lived in the 12th or 13th century because of the similarities between his philosophical and devotional attitudes and those of Rāmānuja (traditionally dated 1017–1137). Both adhered to *dvaitādvaita*, the belief that the creator-god and the souls he created were distinct but shared in the same substance, and both stressed devotion to Kṛṣṇa as a means of liberation from the cycle of rebirth. The Nimanda sect flourished in the 13th and 14th centuries in eastern India. Its philosophy held that men were trapped in physical bodies constricted by *prakṛti* (matter) and that only by surrender to Rādhā-Kṛṣṇa (not through their own efforts) could they attain the grace necessary for liberation from rebirth; then at death the physical body would drop away. Thus Nimbārka stressed *bhakti* yoga, the yoga of devotion. Many books were written about this once-popular cult, but most sources were destroyed by Muslim fanatics during the reign of the Mughal emperor Aurangzeb (1659–1707), and thus little information has survived about Nimbārka and the Nimandas.

·metaphysical system and school **9**:331f
·Vaiṣṇava sect foundation and impact **8**:916c

nimbostratus, principal cloud genus that appears as a gray, often dark, layer that often looks diffuse because of the more or less continuous fall of precipitation—rain, snow, or sleet—which usually reaches the ground and is not accompanied by lightning or thunder. Nimbostratus, thick enough (usually many thousands of metres) and dense enough to obscure the sun, is composed of water droplets (sometimes supercooled), ice crystals, raindrops, snowflakes, or a mixture of these particles. Nimbostratus usually forms from the thickening of altostratus. As precipitation falls from its base, which may be difficult to locate because of falling rain or snow, low, ragged clouds may occur under the main cloud.

·clouds and rain precipitation **4**:759d

nimbus: *see* halo.

Nimbus, series of U.S. meteorological satellites, launched from 1964.

·atmospheric water vapour research **17**:372c
·weather observation methods **12**:58g

Nîmes, capital of Gard *département*, southern France, in the traditional region of Languedoc, south-southwest of Lyon. Situated at the foot of some barren hills called the Monts Garrigues to the north and west of the city, Nîmes stands in a vine-planted plain extending

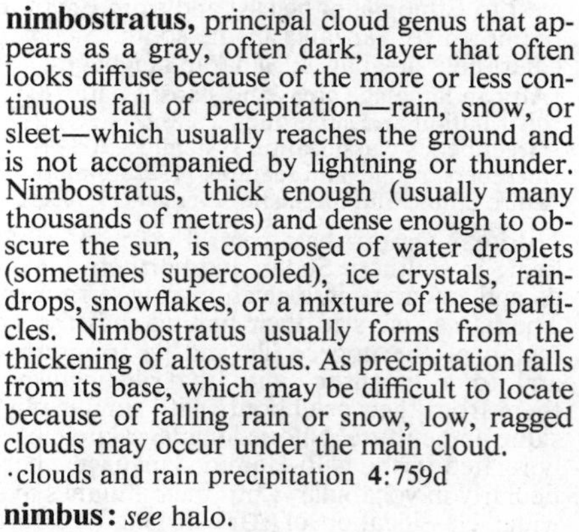

Tour Magne, a ruined Roman tower, Nîmes, Fr.
E.P.A. Inc.—EB Inc.

south and east. Once one of the richest towns of Roman Gaul, the city is famous for its many Roman remains, which are mostly in an excellent state of preservation. The vast amphitheatre, probably built in the 1st century AD to seat 24,000 at gladiatorial shows, chariot races, and naval spectacles, is an ellipse (440 by 330 ft, or 135 by 100 m), standing 69 ft (21 m) high. From outside it presents the aspect of a double row of 60 arches surmounted by an attic. It was built of large stones from a nearby quarry, which were put together without mortar. It was used as a fortress in the 5th century by the Visigoths, and in the Middle Ages houses, and even a church, were built inside it. Cleared of buildings in 1809, it is now used for bullfights. Despite this checkered history, it is one of the best preserved Roman amphitheatres in existence.

The Maison-Carrée (1st century AD), a temple 82 ft (25 m) long by 40 ft (12 m) wide, dedicated to Gaius and Lucius Caesar, adopted sons of the first Roman emperor, Augustus, is one of the most beautiful monuments built by the Romans in Gaul, and certainly the best preserved. Strongly influenced by Greek architecture, it has fine sculptured capitals, and its pillars are irregularly spaced to avoid monotony. Like the amphitheatre, the building has had varied uses (town hall, private house, stable, and church) through the ages. It now houses a collection of Roman sculptures.

The Tour Magne, atop a hill just outside the city, is the oldest Roman building, 92 ft high, but probably originally higher. Its original function is not known, but it was incorporated into the Roman wall in 16 BC. Near the top of the tower is a platform from which may be seen a fine panoramic view of the city and beyond. Nearby is a reservoir from which the water carried by the great Roman aqueduct, the Pont du Gard, was distributed throughout the town. Other Roman remains include the partly ruined city gate known as the Porte d'Auguste, and the Temple of Diana, which was probably connected with the baths. The pleasant Jardin de la Fontaine, on the edge of the city, was designed in 1745. The fountain and the canals that flow through it are partly Roman. The Archaeological Museum (Musée Archéologique), housed in a former Jesuit college, has a fine collection of Roman objects and some Iron Age artifacts.

The traditional manufacture of textiles and clothing still flourishes. New industries include shoe manufacturing, food processing (canned fruit, brandy), and the manufacturing of electrical and agricultural equipment. Nîmes is also an important market town.

Named after Nemausus, the genie of a sacred fountain, Nîmes was the capital of a Gallic tribe that submitted to Rome in 121 BC. The emperor Augustus founded a new city there and gave it privileges that rapidly brought it prosperity. In the 5th century, Nîmes was plundered by the Vandals and the Visigoths. It was subsequently occupied by the Saracens, who were driven out in 737. In the 10th century, the city passed to the jurisdiction of the counts of Toulouse, and it was joined to the French crown in 1229.

At the time of the Reformation, Nîmes became largely Protestant and suffered from persecution after the revocation in 1685 of the Edict of Nantes, which had accorded a measure of religious liberty to Protestants. Damaged in 1815 during the fighting between Royalists and Bonapartists, Nîmes became prosperous once more with the coming of the railways later in the 19th century. Pop. (1975) 123,914.

43°50′ N, 4°21′ E

·map, France 7:585
·Roman architectural influence **19**:306h; illus. 307

Nimitz, Chester W(illiam) (b. Feb. 24, 1885, Fredericksburg, Texas—d. Feb. 20, 1966, near San Francisco), commander of the U.S. Pacific Fleet during World War II; one of the navy's foremost administrators and strategists, he exercised authority over all land and sea forces in the Pacific area.

A graduate (1905) of the U.S. Naval Academy at Annapolis, Nimitz served in World War I as chief of staff to the commander of the U.S. Atlantic submarine force, a tour of duty that convinced him of the effectiveness of submarine warfare. He held a variety of posts at sea and on shore until 1939, when he was appointed chief of the Bureau of Navigation of the U.S. Navy.

Nimitz, 1941

By courtesy of the U.S. Navy

After the Japanese attack on Pearl Harbor (December 1941), Nimitz was elevated to commander in chief of the Pacific Fleet with headquarters in Hawaii; he complemented the Southwest Pacific command under Gen. Douglas MacArthur. His orders were to maintain island positions between the U.S. mainland and the southwest Pacific, to protect air and sea communications, and to "prepare for the execution of major amphibious offenses" in the Pacific area. By June 1942 he had announced the victory at the battles of Midway and the Coral Sea, where enemy losses were 10 times greater than those of the U.S. at Pearl Harbor. In succeeding years, the historic battles of the Solomon Islands (1942–43), the Gilbert Islands (1943), the Marshalls, Marianas, Palaus, and Philippines (1944), and Iwo Jima and Okinawa (1945) were fought under his direction.

The Japanese capitulation was signed aboard his flagship, the USS "Missouri," in Tokyo Bay on Sept. 2, 1945. In December 1944 Nimitz had been promoted to the navy's newest and highest rank, that of fleet admiral.

After the war, Nimitz served for two years as chief of naval operations (1945–47). In 1947, in answer to interrogatories by the German Adm. Karl Dönitz, on trial for war crimes, Nimitz gave his justification for the unrestricted nature of U.S. submarine warfare in the Pacific during World War II. He collaborated with E.B. Potter in editing *Sea Power, a Naval History* (1960).

·island hopping strategy **19**:991b

Nimravinae, taxonomic classification of the extinct false sabre-toothed cat (*see* sabre-toothed cat).

Nimrod, legendary biblical figure, described in Gen. 10:8–12 as "the first on earth to be a mighty man. He was a mighty hunter before the Lord." The only other references to Nimrod in the Old Testament are Mic. 5:6, where Assyria is called the land of Nimrod; and I Chron. 1:10. The beginning of his kingdom is said in Genesis to be Babel, Erech, and Akkad in the land of Shinar. Nimrod is said to have built Nineveh, Calah (modern Nimrūd), Rehoboth-Ir, and Resen.

The description of Nimrod as a "mighty hunter before the Lord" is an intrusion in this context, but probably, like the historical notices, derived from some old Babylonian saga; however, no equivalent of the name has yet been found in the cuneiform records. In character there is a certain resemblance between Nimrod and the Mesopotamian epic hero Gilgamesh.

Nimrūd, modern name of the site of the ancient Assyrian city of CALAH, also spelled KALHU, or KALAKH, situated south of Mosul in Nīnawā (Nineveh) *muḥāfaẓah* (governorate), Iraq. The city was first excavated by A. H. Layard during 1845–51 and afterward principally by M.E.L. (later Sir Max) Mallowan (1949–58).

Founded in the 13th century BC by Shalmaneser I, Calah remained unimportant until King Ashurnasirpal II (reigned 883–859 BC) chose it as his royal seat and the military capital of Assyria. His extensive work on the Acropolis—which covered about 65 acres (26 hectares)—and the outer walled town was completed by his son Shalmaneser III and other monarchs. The most important religious building, founded in 798 by Queen Sammuramat (Semiramis of Greek legend), was Ezida, which included the temple of Nabu (Nebo), god of writing, and his consort Tashmetum (Tashmit). The temple library and an annex contained many religious and magical texts and several "treaties," including the last will and testament of Esarhaddon (reigned

Winged bull of alabaster, guardian of a gate of the palace of Ashurnasirpal II at Nimrūd; in the Metropolitan Museum of Art, New York

By courtesy of the Metropolitan Museum of Art, New York, gift of John D. Rockefeller, Jr., 1932

680–669). In the outer town the most important building is Ft. Shalmaneser, an arsenal that occupied at least 12 acres (4.9 hectares). This and other buildings have yielded thousands of carved ivories, mostly made in the 9th and 8th centuries BC, now one of the richest collections of ivory in the world.

In the 7th century BC, Calah declined in importance because the Sargonids tended to use Nineveh as their residence; nonetheless it continued to be extensively occupied till the fall of Nineveh in 612 BC.

·art forms and styles of Assyria **19**:263c
·founding by Shalmaneser I **11**:981e; map 976
·tile brick and glazed ceramics use **14**:897e

Nīmrūz, formerly CHAKHĀNSŪR, *velāyat* (province) in southwestern Afghanistan, 20,979 sq mi (54,336 sq km) in area, with its capital at Zaranj. It is bounded by Pakistan (south), by Iran (west), and by the Afghan provinces of Farāh (north) and Helmand (east). Nīmrūz essentially comprises the flat Khāsh Desert, crossed by the Helmand, Farāh, Khāsh, and Hārūt Rūd rivers, which empty into the Seistan (Helmand) swamps. Sparsely inhabited, it has the nation's lowest population density. Disputes between

Afghanistan and Iran have revolved around the Nīmrūz–Iran border and each nation's share of the Helmand River waters, vitally important to both for irrigation. Pop. (1975 est.) 101,000.
·area and population table 1:169
·map, Afghanistan 1:167

Nimule, town, al-Istiwā'īyah *mudīrīyah* (Equatoria province), southern Sudan, on the Bahr el-Jebel (there also called the Albert Nile) at the Uganda border. It is a transportation centre and has a customs station. Nimule is the northern terminus for river navigation from Lake Albert.
3°36′ N, 32°03′ E
·map, Sudan 17:759
·Nile River system physiography 13:103f; map

Nimwegen (The Netherlands): *see* Nijmegen.

Nimwegen, Treaties of: *see* Nijmegen, Treaties of.

Nimzowitsch, Aron (1886–1935), Russian Chess master.
·hypermodern Chess theory 4:199e

Nin, Anaïs (b. Feb. 21, 1903, Paris—d. Jan. 14, 1977, Los Angeles), U.S. novelist, short-story writer, and, above all, diarist. Living in Paris in the 1920s and '30s and in New York City in the '40s, she was a friend of many leading literary figures, among them Edmund Wilson, James Agee, Henry Miller, and Lawrence Durrell, and was much influenced in her writing by the Surrealists and by psychoanalysis. Unable at first to find a publisher for her novels and short stories, she herself printed and published *Winter of Artifice* (1939) and *Under a Glass Bell* (1944). Though she had received a great deal of praise from critics and had a small but faithful following of readers, it was not until the publication of the first volume of *The Journals of Anaïs Nin* (U.S. title, *The Diary . . .*) in 1966 that she was generally recognized as an important writer. Combining observations and impressions of her friends with an analysis of her own thoughts and emotions, the diary has been compared with the writings of Proust.

Niña, one of the three ships in Columbus' first expedition to the New World.
·Columbus' voyages 4:938f

Nīnawā, *muḥāfaẓah* (governorate) in northwestern Iraq. Created in 1969 from the greater part of former al-Mawṣil *liwā'* (province), it is 14,701 sq mi (38,076 sq km) in area. Nīnawā consists mostly of arid land with intermittent streams and salt pans, except in the east, where the Tigris River crosses from north to south. In some reaches the Tigris flows in a deeply incised channel, but elsewhere it lies in flat, open terrain. Cultivation is concentrated along the river, with wheat, barley, and fruit the principal crops. Many of the people of the *muḥāfaẓah* are nomads, migrating seasonally with their herds. Petroleum production from important fields has become the most important facet of the economy. Nīnawā contains several significant archaeological sites, including the ancient city of Nineveh, just north of Mosul (*q.v.*), capital of the *muḥāfaẓah*. Pop. (1975 est.) 909,402.
·area and population table 9:877
·map, Iraq 9:875

Ninazimua: *see* Ningishzida.

Ninazu, in Mesopotamian religion, Sumerian deity, god of Enegir, a city located on the Euphrates River between Larsa and Ur. He was also the city god of Eshnunna (modern Tall al-Asmar, Iraq) in the Diyālā region. Ninazu, whose name means Water Knower, was primarily an underworld deity, although the exact nature of his character or functions is not clear. In Enegir he was considered the son of Ereshkigal, goddess of the netherworld; according to another tradition, however, he was the son of Enlil and Ninlil. His spouse was Ningirda, a daughter of Enki.

Ninčić, Momčilo (1876–1949), Yugoslav statesman.
·collective security program 19:972g

nine-banded armadillo (*Dasypus novemcinctus*): *see* armadillo.

Nine Classics: *see* Confucian texts, classical.

Nine Men's Morris, variously called also MORRIS, MORELLES, MERELLES, MERELS, and MILL, OF THE MILL, board game of great antiquity, most popular in Europe during the 14th century, played throughout the world in various forms.

The board is made up of three concentric squares and several transversals, making 24 points of intersection. In modern play the diagonal lines of the board are usually omitted. Two players, each provided with nine counters, lay pieces alternately upon the points, the object being to get three in a row (a "mill") upon any line. On doing so, the player is entitled to capture one adverse counter, but not one that is in a mill. Having placed all their counters, the players continue moving alternately, with the same object. A mill may be opened by moving one piece off the line; returning the same piece to its original position counts as a new mill. The player who captures all but two of the adverse pieces wins. A move is normally from one point to the next in either direction along a line, but the rule is sometimes made that when a player has only three pieces left he may move them from any point to any point regardless of the lines.

The Mill game was played by shepherds with stones upon a diagram cut into the turf. Shakespeare alludes to this practice in *A Midsummer Night's Dream* (Act II, scene 1):

> The nine men's morris is fill'd up with mud,
> And the quaint mazes in the wanton green
> For lack of tread are indistinguishable.

Morris (*i.e.*, Moorish) is the name of a square dance to which the game bears a fanciful resemblance.
·rules of play and board design 2:1152h; illus. 1153

Nine Officers' Plot (1959), in Turkey, abortive attempt to overthrow the government of the Democrat Party.
·Democrat Party political opposition 13:793a

ninepins, bowling game that probably originated in continental Europe during the Middle Ages. Many regional variations of the game developed. Early German ninepins lanes were made of clay or cinders; later a single plank about one foot wide was added, on which the ball was rolled. The pins were set up in a square formation with one corner toward the bowler. These features are retained in the modern games asphalt, bohle, and schere, recognized for international competition by the Fédération Internationale des Quilleurs (International Federation of Bowlers). Skittles (*q.v.*), a British variation of ninepins, is also still played. The game of ninepins was brought to America by early Dutch colonists, but it was supplanted there in the mid-19th century by the tenpin game.
·history and development 3:88b

Nine States (Malaya): *see* Negeri Sembilan.

Nineteen Day Feast, in the Bahā'ī religion, a gathering held on the first day of each month of the Bahā'ī calendar, which is based on 19 months of 19 days each; attendance is a spiritual obligation for Bahā'īs.
·Bahā'ī practices and purposes 2:589d

Nineteen Eighty-four (1949), novel by the English author George Orwell that describes a totalitarian anti-Utopia in which the authority of the state extends to the inmost thoughts and feelings of each individual. The book is a general political satire that attacks uncritical faith in progress and warns that centralized economies carry within themselves the seeds of ruthless regimentation.

Winston Smith, a minor Party functionary who falsifies archives for the Ministry of Truth, establishes a liaison with Julia, a member of the Anti-Sex League who secretly chafes at the Party's puritanism. Discovered by the omnipresent agents of Big Brother, the supreme authority, they are arrested and tortured until their spirits are extinguished. It is the unrelieved negativity of Orwell's vision that imparts to the novel its distinctive tone.
·literary theme and significance 10:1219f
·novel as philosophical vehicle 13:282d
·warning against totalitarianism 13:751e

Nineteen Propositions (1642), Parliament's terms for the surrender of Charles I of England; the King rejected them, and the English Civil War followed.
·Charles I's rejection of terms 3:243g
·Parliamentarians' ultimatum to Charles I 4:53h

Ninetyeast Ridge, oceanic ridge in the northeastern part of the Indian Ocean.
4°00′ S, 90°00′ E
·Indian Ocean floor features 9:310b; map 308
·size and geologic features 13:475f

Ninety-five Theses, propositions for debate concerned with the question of indulgences, written (in Latin) and posted by Martin Luther on the door of the Schlosskirche (Castle Church), Wittenberg (now in East Germany), on Oct. 31, 1517; the event was eventually considered to represent the beginning of the Protestant Reformation.

Luther was simply following current practice when he nailed the theses to the church door, since this was the way scholars brought subjects and problems to the attention of others for debate and discussion. Ordinarily, Luther's theses would have been of interest only to professional theologians, but various political and religious situations of the time, and the fact that printing had been invented, combined to make the theses known throughout Germany within a few weeks. Luther did not give them to the people, although he did send copies to the Archbishop of Mainz and to the Bishop of Brandenburg. Others, however, translated them into German and had them printed and circulated. Thus, they became a manifesto that turned a protest about an indulgence scandal into the greatest crisis in the history of the Western Christian Church.

The doctrine concerning indulgences (*q.v.*) in the Roman Catholic Church was uncertain prior to the Council of Trent (1545–63), which defined the doctrine and eliminated abuses. Indulgences were the commutation for money of part of the temporal penalty due for sin—*i.e.*, the practical satisfaction that was a part of the sacrament of penance. They were granted on papal authority and made available through accredited agents. Not at any time did they imply that divine forgiveness could be bought or sold or that they availed for those who were impenitent or unconfessed. But during the Middle Ages, as papal financial difficulties grew more complicated, they were resorted to very often, and abuses grew common. Further misunderstanding developed after Pope Sixtus IV extended indulgences to souls in purgatory. The often outrageous statements of indulgence sellers were a matter of protest among theologians.

The immediate cause of scandal in Germany in 1517 was the issue of an indulgence that was to pay for the rebuilding of St. Peter's in Rome. But by secret agreement of which most Germans, probably including Luther, were unaware, half the proceeds of the German sales were to be diverted to meet the huge debt owed to the financial house of Fugger by the archbishop and elector Albert of Mainz, who had incurred the debt in order to pay the Pope for appointing him to high offices. Such a prince could not afford to be squeamish about the methods and language used by his agents, and the agent in Germany, the Dominican Johann Tetzel, made extravagant and scandalous claims for the indulgence he was selling. The sale of this indulgence was forbidden in Wittenberg by the elector Frederick III the Wise, who preferred that the faithful make their offerings at his own great collection of relics, exposed on feast days in the Church of All Saints. But Wittenberg church members went to Tetzel, who was preaching nearby, and they showed the pardons for their sins received from him to Luther. Outraged at what he considered grave theological error, Luther wrote the Ninety-five Theses.

The theses were tentative opinions, about some of which Luther had not decided. They did not deny the papal prerogative in this matter, though by implication they criticized papal policy; neither did they attack the doctrine of purgatory. But they did stress the spiritual, inward character of the Christian faith. They also attacked the fact that money was being collected from poor people and sent to the papacy, a point popular with the Germans, who had long resented the money they were forced to contribute to Rome.

Subsequently, the Archbishop of Mainz, alarmed and annoyed, forwarded the documents to Rome in December 1517, with the request that Luther be inhibited. A counterthesis was prepared by a Dominican theologian and defended before a Dominican audience at Frankfurt in January 1518. When Luther realized the extensive interest his tentative theses had aroused, he prepared a long Latin manuscript with explanations of his Ninety-five Theses, published in the autumn of 1518. The document showed that Luther's original protest had been based on an important theological problem.

The practice of dating the beginning of the Reformation from the date that the Ninety-five Theses were posted did not develop until after the mid-17th century.

·Luther and reform demands **8**:88a
·Luther's denunciation of Catholic abuses **15**:549h
·Luther's first strike at papal church **11**:197a
·Luther's protest against Church error **11**:190h
·Protestant history **15**:109b

Ninety Mile Beach, comprising the west coast of Aupori Peninsula, the northernmost extension of North Auckland Peninsula, North Island, New Zealand. It stretches for 55 mi (88 km) from Scott Point (northwest) to Ahipara Bay (southwest) and is bordered by scrubland and sand dunes.

In 1643, the Dutch navigator Abel Tasman referred to the beach as "a desert coast." Now a resort area, it offers fishing (especially for toheroa, a shellfish delicacy) and automobile racing on the hard-packed strand.
34°48′ S, 173°00′ E

Nineveh 13:116, ancient Assyrian city, the ruins of which are on the east bank of the Tigris River, opposite modern Mosul, Iraq.

The text article covers the excavations conducted there intermittently since 1820. Settlement at Nineveh dates from the 7th millennium BC to the 16th century AD. The city achieved magnificence as the capital of the Assyrian Empire (*c.* 700 BC–612 BC). The remains of this period include parts of Sennacherib's palace, the city wall with its 15 gates, a complex canal system, and Ashurbanipal's library with its 20,000 tablets of the "K" collection.

REFERENCES in other text articles:
·art forms and styles of Assyria **19**:263d
·Ashurbanipal's collection of library **2**:145d
·Assyrian history and culture **11**:977e; map 985
·glassmaking in 8th–6th centuries BC **8**:181g
·map, Iraq **9**:874
·Median conquest of Assyrian focus **9**:833a; map 834
·Mesopotamian archaeological excavations **1**:1079a
·Mesopotamian library specimens **11**:1008d
·Sennacherib's construction program **16**:542c

Nineveh and Its Remains (2 vol., 1849), book by Austen Henry Layard.
·Mesopotamian archaeological excavations **1**:1079a

ninfale d'Ameto, Il, English AMETO'S STORY OF THE NYMPHS, often shortened to AMETO, also called COMMEDIA DELLE NINFE FIORENTINE (written 1341–42), narrative in prose and terza rima by Giovanni Boccaccio.
·Boccaccio's writings **10**:1121f
·style and content **2**:1174g

ninfale fiesolano, Il (written 1344–45), poetic narrative by Giovanni Boccaccio.
·style and content **2**:1174g

Ningal (goddess): *see* Nanna.

Ningirda (goddess): *see* Ninazu.

Ningirsu (god): *see* Ninurta.

Ningishzida, in Mesopotamian religion, Sumerian deity, city god of Gishbanda, near Ur in the southern orchard region. Although Ningishzida was a power of the netherworld, where he held the office of throne bearer, he seems to have originally been a tree god, for his name apparently means Lord Productive Tree. He probably was god of the winding tree roots, since he originally was represented in serpent shape. When pictured in human form, two serpent heads grow from his shoulders in addition to the human head, and he rides on a dragon. He was a son of Ninazu and Ningirda and was the husband of Ninazimua, Lady Flawlessly Grown Branch.

Ning-kuo (China): *see* Hsüan-ch'eng.

Ning-po, also known as YIN-HSIEN, Pinyin romanization, respectively, NING-BO and YIN-XIAN, city in the coastal plain of northeastern Chekiang Province (*sheng*), China. It is an autonomous subprovincial-level municipality (*shih*) and also the administrative centre of Ning-po Area (*ti-ch'ü*).

Ning-po is situated on the Yung Chiang (river), some 16 mi (25 km) upstream from its mouth, at the junction with its chief western tributary, the Yu-yao. Ning-po was from an early period itself a port, although the mouth of the river was masked by a mud bar. It also has an outport on the western bank of the estuary, called Chen-hai, a fishing port. Ning-po was the commercial centre of the coastal plain to the east of Shao-hsing and an outport for the Yangtze River (Ch'ang Chiang) Delta area, to which it was linked by the Che-tung Canal leading to Shao-hsing and the Ch'ien-t'ang Chiang.

After Kou-chang County (*hsien*), a few miles to the east, was transferred to what is now Ning-po in 625, it became the seat of an independent prefecture (*chou*), Ming, in 738. In 908 the county seat's name, Mao-hsien since 625, was changed to Yin-hsien, which it has since retained. Under the Southern Sung (1126–1279), Ming Prefecture was promoted in 1198 to a superior prefecture (*fu*), Ch'ing-yuan. It kept this name through the Yüan (Mongol) period (1279–1368). In 1368 it became Ning-po Superior Prefecture, which name it kept until 1912, when it was demoted to county status, taking the formal name of Yin-hsien.

Ning-po first rose to importance during the latter part of the 5th century, when Korean shipping found it the most convenient port for contacts with the southern capital at Nanking, then called Chien-k'ang. Under the T'ang (618–907) this traffic continued. Although official relations lapsed after 838, private trade continued on a large scale. In the 11th century Ning-po became a centre of the coastal trade. Its importance grew with the establishment of the Southern Sung capital at Hangchow in 1127, when overseas trade to and from the capital flowed through Ning-po. Ning-po grew rapidly during the Sung (960–1279) and Yüan periods.

The early period of the Ming dynasty (1368–1644) brought a setback to Ning-po's development. Overseas trade was deliberately curtailed by the government, the building of oceangoing ships prohibited, and even coastal trade severely restricted. Ning-po was attacked by Japanese pirates, and it became a defensive base of some importance. Its growth seems to have stagnated, however, until the last quarter of the 15th century, when the prosperity of its hinterland began to recover.

This recovery was assisted when the Portuguese began trading in Ning-po in 1545, at first illicitly, but later (after 1567) legally. Still later, Dutch and British merchants arrived, and the Ning-po merchants began to trade with the China coast from Manchuria to Canton, as well as with the Philippines and Taiwan (Formosa). As a result, in the 17th and 18th centuries, the Ning-po merchants became important in China's internal commerce and began to play a national role as bankers by the early 19th century. In 1843 Ning-po was opened to foreign trade as a treaty port, but trade declined, and its place was taken by Shanghai.

In the early 1970s, Ning-po was a local commercial centre and a busy port for northeastern Chekiang. Steamships of 3,000 tons can use the port, and there are regular steamer services to Shanghai. There is a rail link with Hangchow and Shanghai, and Ning-po is also the centre of a transportation network of coastal junk traffic, canals, and roads. It is a collection centre for cotton and other agricultural produce of the plain, for the marine products of the local fishing industry, for timber from the mountains in the hinterland, and a major distribution centre for coal, oil, textiles, and consumer goods.

Cotton-spinning mills, flour mills, textile plants, and tobacco factories were established before World War II, and from 1949 industrialization continued. The textile industry expanded, and food processing—flour milling, rice polishing, oil extraction, wine making, and particularly the canning of foodstuffs—became a large-scale industry. A large shipbuilding industry constructs fishing vessels. Factories at Ning-po produce diesel engines, agricultural and other machinery, generators, and machine tools. Pop. (latest est.) 280,000.
29°52′ N, 121°31′ E
·map, China **4**:263
·Ming dynasty's reception of tribute **4**:350a

Ningrahar (Afghanistan): *see* Nangarhār.

Ningre-Tongo (creole language): *see* Sranantonga.

Ningsia carpets, rugs and carpets woven in Ningsia Hui Autonomous Region, China, characterized by their stylized pictorial designs and subtle use of blue, red, and beige. Geometrical patterns are sometimes used, and the heavy wool pile is cut so that the design is in relief. The foundation weave is cotton.

Ningsia Hui 13:117, in full NINGSIA HUI AUTONOMOUS REGION, Chinese NING-HSIA-HUI-TSU TZU-CHIH-CH'Ü, Pinyin romanization NINGXIA HUIZU ZIZHIQU, autonomous region (*tzu-chih-ch'ü*) of the People's Republic of China, bounded on the north by the Inner Mongolian Autonomous Region, on the east in part by Shensi Province, and on the east, south, and west by Kansu Province. Its area is 65,600 sq mi (170,000 sq km). The capital is Yin-ch'uan. Pop. (1970 est.) 2,200,000.

The text article covers the history, physical geography, population, administration, social conditions, economy, transportation, and cultural life of the autonomous region.

REFERENCES in other text articles:
·area and population, table 4 **4**:274
·Kansu region jurisdictional changes **10**:387c
·map, China **4**:263
·Marco Polo voyage map **14**:758

Ningsia plain, area of northwestern China.
·topography and delimitation **13**:118a

Ning Tsung (b. 1168, Hangchow, China—d. 1224, Hangchow), 13th emperor of the Sung dynasty whose reign (1195–1224) is noted as a period of intellectual and cultural achievement; Chu Hsi, the great Neo-Confucian philosopher, wrote some of his most famous works during this time. The government, however, was plagued by rising inflation, and the Emperor came under the domination of the minister Han T'o-chou, who attempted to recover the Sung territory in North China that had been lost to the Juchen several generations earlier. The war was disastrous, and more territory was lost to the Juchen, who now demanded a huge annual indemnity. During the negotiations with the Juchen, Han was assassinated, and a peace treaty was finally signed in 1208.
·patronage of Ma Yüan **11**:724a
·Sung dynasty's wars with Juchen **4**:336c

Ning-xia Hui (China): *see* Ningsia Hui.

Ning-yüan (China): *see* Kuldja.

Ninhar, also called NINGUBLA, in Mesopotamian religion, a Sumerian deity, the city god of Kiabrig near Ur in the southern herding region. Ninhar was god of the thunder and rainstorms that made the desert green with pasturage in the spring; as such he was represented in the form of a roaring bull. He was the son of Nanna and Ningal and the husband of Ninigara, the Lady of Butter and Cream, goddess of the dairy.

Ninh Thuan, province, on the South China Sea, southeastern Vietnam. Hills of the Chaîne Annamitique in the north open into a broad valley in the south drained by the Cong Sa and its tributaries. The area of 1,325 sq mi (3,431 sq km) produces rice in the canalized Cong Sa valley, and tobacco and castor beans; salt is extracted from the sea. Phan Rang, the provincial seat, is 3 mi (5 km) upstream from its port, Thon Ninh Chu, on the left bank of the Cong Sa. It lies 201 mi northeast of Ho Chi Minh City (Saigon) and 54 mi southeast of Da Lat, to which it is linked by highway and by cog railway from the Ho Chi Minh City–Hue main line. There is a major hydroelectric plant on the Da Nhim in the western highlands.

On the first foothills of the Chaîne Annamitique north of Phan Rang are found the Hoilai, a group of towers constructed by the Cham people, who still constitute a large minority of the provincial population.Pop. (1972 est.) 216,007.
·area and population table **19**:142

Ninhursag, also spelled NINHURSAGA, Akkadian BELIT-ILI, in Mesopotamian religion, a Sumero-Akkadian deity, city goddess of Adab and of Kish in the northern herding regions; she was the goddess of the stony, rocky ground, the *hursag*. In particular, she had the power in the foothills and desert to produce wildlife. Especially prominent among her offspring were the wild onagers of the western desert.

As the sorrowing mother animal Ninhursag appears in a lament for her son, a young colt, but as goddess of birth she is not only the goddess of animal birth but the Mother of All Children, a mother-goddess figure. Her other names include Dingirmakh, the Exalted Deity; Ninmakh, the Exalted Lady; Aruru, the Dropper (*i.e.*, the one who "loosens" the scion in birth); and Nintur, Lady Birth Giver. Her husband is the god Shulpae, and among their children were the sons Mululil and Ashshirgi and the daughter Egime. Mululil seems to have been a dying god, like Dumuzi, whose death was lamented in yearly rites.
·Mesopotamian pantheon position and worship **11**:1004c
·Sumerian myths of creation and mankind **11**:1009e

ninhydrin, pale yellow crystalline compound used for the detection of free amino acids of proteins and peptides.
·chromatography and solute detection **4**:567g

Ninian, Saint, also called NINIAS, RIGNA, TRIGNAN, NINNIDH, RINGAN, NINUS, and DINAN (traditionally b. *c.* 360, Britain,—d. *c.* 432, Britain), bishop, church founder, first Christian missionary to what is now Scotland, where he began the conversion of the southern Picts.

According to the essentially untrustworthy life by the 12th-century Cistercian abbot Aelred of Rievaulx, Ninian was the son of a chieftain and was educated at Rome, where he was consecrated bishop. He returned, travelling through Gaul, where he befriended St. Martin of Tours.

More certainly, Ninian, then the first bishop of Galloway, established his see at what subsequently became known as Whithorn, Wigtown. There he built *c.* 397 a whitewashed stone church called Candida Casa (Latin: White House; Anglo-Saxon Huit-aern, or Whithorn), which by the 6th century was a leading Anglo-Saxon monastic centre.

The conversion of Scotland was difficult. In Bede's 8th-century *Ecclesiastical History of the English People*, it is implied that Ninian had already converted some of the Picts before St. Columba of Iona began his celebrated Christianization of Scotland, and church dedications to Ninian are widespread, suggesting that his apostolate was not confined to Galloway and to the neighbouring kingdom of Strathclyde. Although disputed, Ninian's apostolate seems to have been more effective among the Celts than the Picts. It is generally agreed that he prepared the missionary foundation for SS. Columba and Kentigern. St. Ninian's shrine at Whithorn drew many pilgrims, among them King James IV of Scotland, who was a regular visitor. The Roman Catholic diocese of Galloway retains Candida Casa as its official name. Ninian's feast day is September 16.

BIBLIOGRAPHY. A.B. Scott, *St. Ninian, Apostle of the Britons and the Picts* (1916); W.D. Simpson, *Saint Ninian and the Origins of the Christian Church in Scotland* (1940); J. MacQueen, *St. Nynia* (1961); M. Anderson, *St. Ninian* (1964).
·Scotland's conversion **3**:233f

Ninigara, Sumerian deity, wife of Ninhar (*q.v.*).

Ninigi, Japanese deity; grandson of the sun goddess Amaterasu, whose descent to earth established the divine origin of the Yamato clan, the Imperial house of Japan. He is said to have been the great-grandfather of the first emperor, Jimmu Tennō.

Amaterasu delegated Ninigi to assume ownership and rule of the central land of the reed plains (Japan) and gave him three signs of his charge: a jewel (symbolizing benevolence), a mirror (purity), and Kusanagi, the "herb quelling" sword (courage). A jewel, mirror, and sword are still the Japanese Imperial symbols. On his descent to earth Ninigi landed on Kyushu, the southernmost of the main islands. Ōkuni-nushi, who was already sovereign there, was reluctant to give up his own right to rule but submitted when he was permitted to retain control of "secret" (religious) affairs, Ninigi supervising "public" (political) affairs.
·marriage and its effect on man **10**:99f

Ninigo Islands, archipelago, Manus province, Papua New Guinea, about 160 mi (260 km) northwest of Manus Island, in the Pacific Ocean, just south of the Equator. The archipelago is made up of large islets scattered over seven atolls. Six of the atolls are connected by coral lagoons; the seventh is encircled by a reef.

The islands were sighted by the French explorer Louis-Antoine de Bougainville in 1768. The Micronesian population declined in the early 20th century upon contact with Europeans, who established coconut plantations on the islands. The current population, however, is of Micronesian descent.
1°15′ S, 143°30′ E
·map, Trust Territory of New Guinea **12**:1091

Nininsina, also called NINKARRAK (goddess): *see* Bau.

Ninlil, in Mesopotamian religion, member of the Sumero-Akkadian pantheon, spouse of Enlil and city goddess of Tummal near Nippur, where she was known as Egitummal, and of Shuruppak, where she was known as Sud. Both of her cult centres were located in the farming regions.

Ninlil was the Varicoloured Ear (of barley), goddess of the grain and particularly, perhaps, of the seed corn. She was regarded as the daughter of Haia, god of the stores, and Ninshebargunu, Lady Varicoloured Barley, the goddess of ripening barley, a form of the goddess Nissaba. *See also* Belit.
·Sumerian myth of creation **11**:1009d

Ninmakh (goddess): *see* Ninhursag.

Ninmar, in Mesopotamian religion, a Sumerian deity, the city goddess of Guabba, a port located on the shore of a lake or lagoon near Lagash in the southeastern marshland region. She was apparently a bird goddess, and her emblem, a bird, probably represents her original nonhuman form. Ninmar was the daughter of Nanshe and therefore the granddaughter of Enki.

Ninnescah River, river of southwestern Kansas, U.S. It is formed by two branches, the North fork, which flows 87 mi (140 km) east and is dammed at the Cheney; and the South fork, which flows 92 mi east past Pratt and Kingman. The branches join 6 mi southeast of Cheney; the river then flows 49 mi southeast to meet the Arkansas River 19 mi north of Arkansas City.
37°37′ N, 98°31′ W

Ninnidh: *see* Ninian, Saint.

Ninomiya Sontoku (b. 1787, Sagami, now Kanagawa Prefecture, Japan—d. 1856, Japan), agrarian reformer who helped improve Japanese agricultural techniques and whose writings exalting rural life earned him the affectionate appellation of "Peasant Sage of Japan."

Born into a poor family, Ninomiya was completely self-educated. Through diligence and careful planning he developed and increased his family's landholdings. His success came to the attention of local officials, and he was soon invited to join the government. There was nothing revolutionary in his system. He taught peasant families how to budget their expenses and plan their work, and he advocated mutual aid and cooperation in farm communities. Nevertheless, his methods achieved remarkable success in improving agriculture; his fame became widespread when the regions he had developed suffered very little during the great national famine of 1836.

Ninomiya was also a moral leader who believed in the value of hard work and the dignity of manual labour and was able to instill in the peasants pride in their own occupations and the urge to follow his example of working to improve the general welfare.
·Tokugawa period religious naturalism **10**:113d

Ninsei, pseudonym of NONOMURA NINSEI, SEIBEI, or SEISUKE (*c.* 1574–1660/66), Japanese potter active in Kyōto. He learned his art by working at the Awata-guchi kiln in Kyōto and at the Seto kiln in Mino. His patron, the prince of the Ninna-ji at Omuro Katama-

Enamelled jar decorated with wisteria flower by Ninsei, late 17th century; in the Atami Art Museum, Japan

By courtesy of the Atami Art Museum, Japan

chi, allowed him to build his kiln in front of the temple complex. He specialized in tea ceremony wares, notable for their delicate shapes and fine glaze, although the decorative motifs were traditional. Some of his finest works are his tea urns, or *cha-tsubo*.

·earthenware pottery decoration **14**:928b
·tea pottery design and production **19**:240f

Ninsun, in Mesopotamian religion, Sumerian deity, city goddess of Kullab in the southern herding region. As Ninsun's name, Lady Wild Cow, indicates, she was originally represented in cow form and was considered the divine power behind, and the embodiment of, all the qualities the herdsman wished for in his cows—she was the "flawless cow," and a "mother of good offspring that loves the offspring." She was, however, also represented in human form and could give birth to human offspring. The Wild Bull Dumuzi (as distinct from Dumuzi the Shepherd) was traditionally her son, whom she lamented in the yearly ritual marking his death. In her role as a mother figure, her other Sumerian counterparts include Ninhursaga and Ninlil. Ninsun's husband was Lugalbanda.

ninth cranial nerve, or GLOSSOPHARYNGEAL NERVE, a major nerve of the head, originating in the medulla.

·disease symptoms and causes **12**:1049b

Nintoku, 5th-century Japanese emperor.

·tomb location and dimensions **19**:218b

Nintur (Mesopotamian goddess): *see* Ninhursag.

Ninurta, in Mesopotamian religion, city god of Girsu (Ṭal'ah or Telloh) in the Lagash region, where he was known as Ningirsu, Lord of Girsu. Ninurta was the farmer's version of the god of the thunder and rainstorms of the spring. He was also the power in the floods of spring and was god of the plow and of plowing. Ninurta's earliest name was Imdugud (now also read as Anzu), which means Rain Cloud, and his earliest form was that of the thundercloud envisaged as an enormous black bird floating on outstretched wings roaring its thunder cry from a lion's head. With the growing tendency toward anthropomorphism, the old form and name were gradually disassociated from the god as merely his emblems; enmity toward the older inacceptable shape eventually made it evil, an ancient enemy of the god.

Ninurta was the son of Enlil and Ninlil and was married to Bau, in Nippur called Ninnibru, Queen of Nippur. A major festival of his, the Gudsisu Festival, marked in Nippur the beginning of the plowing season.

·Sumerian myth of contests with other gods **11**:1009h

Ninus (saint): *see* Ninian, Saint.

Ninus, in Greek mythology, king of Assyria and the eponymous founder of the city of Nineveh; also the name of the city itself. He was said to have been the son of Belos, or Bel, and to have conquered in 17 years all of western Asia with the help of Ariaeus, king of Arabia. During the siege of Bactra he met Semiramis, the wife of one of his officers, Onnes; he then took her from Onnes and married her. The fruit of the marriage was Ninyas—*i.e.*, the Ninevite.

Another Ninus is described by some authorities as the last king of Nineveh, successor of Sardanapalus.

Ni-ō (Japanese: "two kings"), in Japanese Buddhist mythology, protector of the Buddhist faith, who makes a dual appearance as the guardian on either side of temple gateways. The guardian on the right side is called Kongō ("thunderbolt") or Kongō-rikishi; he holds a thunderbolt, with which he destroys evil, and is associated with the *bodhisattva* ("Buddha-to-be") Vajrapāṇi. The guardian on the left side of the gateway is called Misshaku or Misshaku-rikishi.

Ni-ō at the south gate of the Tōdai-ji, Nara, wood sculpture by Unkei, 1203

Asuka-en

The two are depicted as gigantic figures, either heavily armoured or with naked chests and flowing scarves, as seen in the superbly spirited 13th-century guardians of the Tōdai-ji (temple) at Nara.

Niobe, in Greek mythology, the daughter of Tantalus (king of Sipylos in Lydia) and wife of King Amphion of Thebes; she was the typical sorrowful woman, weeping for the loss of all her children. Traditionally, she had six sons and six daughters and boasted of her progenitive superiority to the Titaness Leto (*q.v.*), who had only two children, the twin deities Apollo and Artemis. As punishment for her pride, Apollo killed all Niobe's sons, and Artemis killed all her daughters. After ten days the bodies were finally buried by the gods, and Niobe went back to her Phrygian home, where she was turned into a rock on Mt. Siphylus (Yamanlar Dağı, northeast of Izmir, Tur.), which continues to weep when the snow melts above it.

The story of Niobe illustrates the favourite Greek theme that the gods are quick to take vengeance (*nemisis*) on human pride and arrogance (*hubris*). The name Niobe may have been of non-Greek origin and perhaps derived from Asia Minor, which seems also to have been the source of her story.

·divine jealousy in myth **8**:406a

Niobid Painter (active *c.* 475–450 BC), painter of flower-shaped Greek vases, distinguished for a calyx krater (mixing bowl) with a repre-

"Herakles and the Argonauts," calyx krater by the Niobid Painter, *c.* 455–450 BC; in the Louvre, Paris

Cliche Musees Nationaux, Paris

sentation of the death of the children of Niobe, now at the Louvre, Paris. It is from this work that the Niobid Painter has received his "name." The vessel is thought to reflect the now lost mural paintings of Polygnotus, another Greek painter.

In the scene of the death of the children of Niobe and in the scene of Athena and Heracles on the other side of the krater, the Niobid Painter has arranged his figures so that they are set on different levels, suggesting different ground lines by means of a fine, painted white line. Landscape setting, too, is suggested: Athena and Heracles appear to be standing on a hilly terrain. Apparently, the Niobid Painter attempted to express space and depth.

·early Classical painting style **19**:293d; illus.

niobium (from Niobe, daughter of Tantalus), symbol Nb, chemical element, metal of transition Group Vb of the periodic table, used in alloys, tools and dies, and superconductive magnets. Closely associated with tantalum (atomic number 73) in ores and in properties, rediscovered and named (1844) by the German chemist Heinrich Rose, niobium was first discovered (1801) in a New England mineral by the English chemist Charles Hatchett, who called the element columbium. International agreement among chemists (about 1950) finally established the name niobium, though columbium persisted in the U.S. metallurgical industry.

The pure metal is soft and ductile; it looks like steel or, when polished, like platinum. Although it has excellent corrosion resistance, niobium needs protection against oxidation above about 400° C (750° F). Completely miscible with iron, it is added in the form of ferroniobium to some stainless steels to give stability on welding or heating. Niobium is used as a major alloying element in nickel-base high-temperature alloys and as a minor but important additive to high-strength structural steels. Because of its compatibility with uranium, resistance to corrosion by molten alkali-metal coolants, and low thermal-neutron cross section (1.1 barns), it has been used in nuclear reactor cores. Cemented carbides to be used as hot-pressing dies and cutting tools are made harder and more resistant to shock and erosion by the presence of niobium. Niobium is useful in constructing cryogenic (low temperature) electronic devices of low power consumption. Wire of a niobium–zirconium alloy (critical temperature, 11.6° K [−261.5° C, −440.7° F]) has been used to wind superconductive electromagnets. Niobium–aluminum (Nb_3Al) is a superconductor below 17.1° K; niobium–tin (Nb_3Sn), below 18.45° K; and niobium metal itself, below 9.15° K.

Niobium, more plentiful than lead and less abundant than copper in the Earth's crust, occurs dispersed except for a relatively few minerals, of which columbite and pyrochlore are the principal commercial sources. Natural niobium is entirely the stable isotope niobium-93. Separation from tantalum, when necessary, is effected by solvent extraction; other methods such as fractional crystallization and distillation also have been used. Among methods for reducing the purified compounds to metal are reduction of the oxide by carbon or niobium carbide in vacuum, hydrogen or magnesium reduction of the chloride, sodium reduction of double fluorides, and fusion electrolysis. Niobium is consolidated and purified further by electron-beam or vacuum-arc melting. Vacuum sintering (making coherent by heating without melting) of powder is also used for consolidation.

Compounds of niobium are of relatively minor importance. Those found in nature are pentavalent, but compounds of lower valences (2–4) have been prepared. Tetravalent niobium, for example, in the form of the carbide, NbC, is used for making cemented carbides.

atomic number	41
atomic weight	92.906
melting point	2,468° C (4,474° F)
boiling point	4,927° C (8,901° F)
specific gravity	8.57 (20° C)
valence	2, 3, 4, 5
electronic config.	2-8-18-12-1 or (Kr)$4d^45s^1$

Major ref. **18**:621b
·abundance and physical properties, tables 1 and 2 **18**:601
·African distribution and tonnage **1**:200c
·atomic weight and number table **2**:345
·geochemical abundances, table 1 **6**:702
·solar abundances, table 2 **17**:803
·superconductor transition temperature **17**:812h
·tin alloy production and use **18**:431g; table

Niobrara Limestone Formation, division of Upper Cretaceous rocks in the U.S. (the Cretaceous Period began about 136,000,000 years ago and lasted about 71,000,000 years). Named for exposures studied along the Missouri River near the mouth of the Niobrara River, Knox County, Nebraska, the Niobrara occurs over a wide area of midwestern and western America including Nebraska, Kansas, North and South Dakota, Minnesota, Montana, Wyoming, Colorado, and New Mexico. The Niobrara Formation varies in thickness from about 60 metres (200 feet) to over 270 metres (900 feet) and consists of chalks, shales, limestones, and many thin layers of bentonite (altered volcanic-ash deposits that appear like soapy clays). In South Dakota the Niobrara overlies the Carlile Shale and underlies the Pierre Shale Formation.

The Niobrara is an important key formation and marks the withdrawal of the Cretaceous seas from the region of the Rocky Mountain geosyncline. Aquatic reptiles such as the mossasaur *Clidastes*, which was about 4.5 metres (15 feet) long, and flying reptiles such as *Pteranodon*, possessing a 7.5-metre (25-foot) wingspread, have been found in the Niobrara.

Niobrara River, rises near Lusk, Wyo., U.S., and flows east across the High Plains, the northern edge of the sandhills, and the low eastern plains of Nebraska to join the Missouri at the village of Niobrara, Neb., at the South Dakota line. The name is of Indian origin and means "running or spreading water." Both are apt designations because the Niobrara has a more uniform flow than do most plains streams, due to steady groundwater contributions from tributaries in the sandhills, while in its lower course it is wide and shallow. The river is 447 mi (720 km) long and drains 12,000 sq mi (31,080 sq km). Box Butte Dam (1946), part of the Mirage Flats irrigation project, is near Marsland, Neb.
42°45′ N, 98°00′ W
·map, United States **18**:908

Niochmia ruficauda (bird): *see* grass finch.

Niort, capital of Deux-Sèvres *département*, western France, situated between the productive Marais Poitevin (Poitevin Marshes) and the farmlands of the Poitou region. A market town for agricultural products and a commercial centre, it is built on the slopes of two hills facing one another on the left bank of the Sèvre Niortaise River. The keep of the 12th- and 13th-century castle, erected by Henry II of England and his son Richard the Lion-Heart (Coeur-de-Lion), dominates the river; it houses a museum. The 15th- and 16th-century church of Notre-Dame stands south of the keep; and the 16th-century former Hôtel de Ville is on the opposite hill. Françoise d'Aubigné, marquise de Maintenon (1635–1719), second wife of Louis XIV of France, was born at Niort.

Beside its traditional leather industry, Niort specializes in the plywood industry and has electrical and chemical factories. Latest census 46,749.
46°19′ N, 0°27′ W
·map, France **7**:584

Nipawin, town, east central Saskatchewan, Canada, on the North Saskatchewan River, at the head of Tobin Rapids. Its name was derived from a Cree Indian word meaning "standing place." Although a fur-trading post was built on its site in 1768, the area was not permanently settled until after 1900, and the town did not develop until after the arrival of the railroad in 1924. Nipawin serves as a marketing centre for a mixed-farming and lumbering region, especially noted for alfalfa. Economic activities also include dairying, flour milling, and the production of honey, sugar beets, and rapeseed. Squaw Rapids Dam (1959), the province's first hydroelectric plant, is on the Saskatchewan River, 42 mi northeast of town, and Nipawin Provincial Park is 40 mi (60 km) northwest. Inc. village, 1924; town, 1939. Pop. (1971) 4,057.
53°22′ N, 104°00′ W
·map, Canada **3**:716

Niphus, Augustinus: *see* Nifo, Agostino.

Nipigon Lake, Thunder Bay District, west central Ontario, Canada, 80 mi (130 km) northeast of Thunder Bay. It is about 70 mi long, 50 mi wide, and has an area of 1,870 sq mi (4,843 sq km) and an elevation of 852 ft (260 m). Its Indian name means deep, clear water and it reaches depths of 540 ft. It is studded with numerous islands. Promontories and large bays characterize its shoreline. The lake is drained southward into Lake Superior by the Nipigon River, which drops 250 ft in its 30-mi course to Nipigon Bay. A hydroelectric development provides power for mining and for the entire lakehead region.
49°50′ N, 89°30′ W
·map, Canada **3**:716

Nipissing, Lake, southeastern Ontario, Canada, midway between the Ottawa River and Georgian Bay. It is 330 sq mi (855 sq km) in area and has a maximum length of 50 mi (80 km) and width of 30 mi. A remnant of glacial Lake Algonquin, which emptied eastward via the Ottawa River, Lake Nipissing (Lake Little Water) is now drained by the French River westward to Georgian Bay. It was discovered by a French explorer, Étienne Brulé, about 1610 and later served as a fur-trapping route linking the Ottawa River with the upper Great Lakes. The Trans-Canada Highway and two transcontinental railways skirt the north shore of the lake and connect Sturgeon Falls and North Bay, the largest riparian communities.
46°17′ N, 80°00′ W
·Great Lakes formation and drainage **8**:301h

Nipkow, Paul Gottlieb (b. Aug. 22, 1860, Lauenburg, Pommern, now Lębork, Pol.—d. Aug. 24, 1940, Berlin), German discoverer of television's scanning principle, in which the light intensities of small portions of an image are successively analyzed and transmitted. Nipkow's invention in 1884 of a flat, rotating disk (Nipkow disk), with one or more spirals of holes around the outer edge, made a mechanical television system possible. The Nipkow disk was supplanted in 1934 by electronic scanning devices.
·television system design and operation **18**:105h; illus. 109

Nipmuc, Algonkian-speaking tribes who occupied the central plateau of what is now Massachusetts, especially the southern part of Worcester County, and extended into what are now northern Rhode Island and Connecticut. Their subsistence was based on the cultivation of maize (corn), hunting, and fishing; they moved seasonally between fixed sites to exploit their food resources. They were divided into territorial bands, which were groups of related families living in one or more villages, each ruled by a sachem (chief). Their villages were not united politically, and different areas were attached to their more powerful neighbours, such as the Massachuset, Wampanoag, Narraganset, and Mohegan.

By 1674 New England missionaries had established seven villages of Christian converts, but in the following year most of the Nipmuc joined the hostile Indians on the side of King Philip against the colonists (*see* King Philip's War). At the close of the war they fled to Canada or to the Mahican and other tribes on the Hudson River.
·Woodlands Indian culture **6**:169b

nippapañca (Buddhist philosophy): *see* niṣprapañca.

Nippon (country, Asia): *see* Japan.

Nippon Shakaitō, English JAPANESE SOCIALIST PARTY, leftist reform party supporting a socialized economy and a neutralist foreign policy; it is the second party in Japan's two-party system, which, however, is dominated by the Japanese Liberal-Democratic Party (Jiyū-Minshutō, *q.v.*).

Japan's first Socialist parties appeared in the mid-1920s; moderate factions of this labour movement combined to form the Shakai Taishūtō (Social Mass Party) in 1932. The left failed to elect many candidates before World War II, and all traditional parties "voluntarily" dissolved themselves on the eve of war in 1940.

In November 1945, Japanese political parties began to re-form under the U.S. occupation. The Japanese Socialist Party combined three or four pre-war proletarian parties to win around 18 percent of the vote in the 1946 election. In 1947 the Socialists won 26 percent of the vote and formed a coalition government with the centrist Minshutō (Democratic Party).

This period in power broke the coalition and weakened the Socialists; in 1952 they split into left and right Socialist parties, and each won roughly 13 percent of the vote until the two wings rejoined in October 1955. The union lasted until autumn of 1959, when the Socialists again split into the left-wing Japanese Socialist Party and the right-wing Minshu Shakaitō (Democratic Socialist Party).

In the 1960s the Japanese Socialists clearly dominated Japanese reform politics, holding, in late 1965, 144 lower chamber seats to the Democratic Socialists' 23, and 73 upper chamber seats to their former comrades' 7. The growth of the Japanese left, which began in 1952 and narrowed the conservatives' margin of victory from three-to-one to two-to-one by 1963, ended in the early 1960s. This levelling off, combined with the Socialist split and the continued left- and right-wing factionalism within the Japanese Socialist Party, kept the Japanese Socialists out of power through the 1960s.

Nippotaeniidea, order of small tapeworms in the phylum Platyhelminthes.
·classification and general features **14**:551a

Nippur, modern NIFFER or NUFFAR, ancient city of Mesopotamia, now in ad-Dīwānīyah *muḥafāẓah* (governorate), Iraq. Although never a political capital, Nippur played a dominant role in the religious life of Mesopotamia.

In Sumerian mythology Nippur was the home of Enlil, the storm god and representation of force and the god who carried out the decrees of the assembly of gods that met at Nippur. Enlil, according to one account, created man at Nippur. Although a king's armies might subjugate the country, the transference to that king of Enlil's divine power to rule had to be sought and sanctioned. The necessity of this confirmation made the city and Enlil's sanctuary there especially sacred, regardless of which dynasty ruled Mesopotamia.

The first U.S. archaeological expedition to Mesopotamia excavated at Nippur from 1889 to 1900; the work was resumed in 1948. The eastern section of the city has been called the scribal quarter because of the great number of Sumerian tablets found there; in fact, the excavations at Nippur have been the primary source of the literary writing of Sumer.

Female figure of gypsum with a gold mask which stood at a temple altar in Nippur, *c.* 2700 BC; in the Iraq Museum, Baghdad

By courtesy of the Iraq Museum, Baghdad; photograph, David Lees

Little is known about the prehistoric town, but by 2500 BC the city probably reached the extent of the present ruins and was fortified. Later, Ur-Nammu (reigned 2112–2095), first king of the 3rd dynasty of Ur, laid out Enlil's sanctuary, the E-kur, in its present form. A ziggurat, probably three stories high, and a temple were built in an open courtyard surrounded by walls.

Parthian construction later buried Enlil's sanctuary and its enclosure walls, and in the 3rd century AD the city fell into decay. It was finally abandoned in the 12th or 13th century.
·library history and function **10**:856g
·Mesopotamian archaeology and history **11**:969c; map 976
·political and religious status **11**:1003a
·religious myth epigraphic evidence **6**:920h
·temple library collection significance **11**:1008e

NIRA (U.S.): *see* National Industrial Recovery Act.

Nirala, pen name of SURYA KANT TRIPATHI (1898–), Hindu poet of Uttar Pradesh state, India.
·literary development **17**:148b

Niraṅkārīs, a reform movement within Sikhism, a religion of India. It was founded by Dayāl Dās (died 1855), who belonged to a half-Sikh, half-Hindu community in Peshāwar. He believed that god is formless, or *niraṅkār* (hence the name Niraṅkārīs).

The chief contribution of the Niraṅkārīs is their standardization of rituals connected with birth, marriage, and death based on the Sikh scriptures. They differ from the orthodox Sikhs in their disapproval of the militant brotherhood, the Khālsā, and in the homage they accord Dayāl Dās and his successors, whom they hold to be living Gurūs (*see* Gurū, Sikh). The present headquarters of the sect is at Chandīgarh, in the Punjab state.

Nirenberg, Marshall Warren (b. April 10, 1927–), U.S. biochemist who played a major role in deciphering the genetic code by showing that, with the exception of triplets called "nonsense codons," each possible combination of three (called a codon) of four different kinds of nitrogen-containing bases found in deoxyribonucleic acid (DNA) and, in some viruses, in ribonucleic acid (RNA) ultimately causes the incorporation of a specific amino acid into cell proteins.

Nirgranthas ("those who have cast off their bonds"), the name by which the early Jaina religious community of India was referred to by their Buddhist and Hindu contemporaries. Mahāvīra, most recent of the Jaina saints, was identified in early Buddhist literature as head of a religious order called the Nirgranthas. Later, the term was used to include not only the Jaina clergy but the entire brotherhood, and still later, the term went out of use.

nirguṇa (Sanskrit: "distinctionless"), a concept of primary importance in the orthodox Hindu philosophy of Vedānta, raising the question of whether the supreme being, Brahman, is to be characterized as without qualities or as possessing qualities (*saguṇa*).

The Monist (Advaita) school of Vedānta assumes on the basis of selected passages of the *Upaniṣads* that Brahman is beyond all polarity and therefore cannot be characterized in the normal terms of human discursive thought (*vyavahāra*). This being the case, Brahman cannot possess qualities that distinguish it from all other magnitudes, as Brahman is not a magnitude but all.

The fundamental text of this apophantic tenet is the *Bṛhadāraṇyaka Upaniṣad* definition of Brahman as *neti-neti* ("not this! not that!" 2.3.6). The scriptural texts that ascribe qualities to Brahman, leading to the conception of a qualified Brahman (*saguṇa*) are, according to the Advaita school, merely preparatory assists to man's meditations.

Others, notably the theistic schools of Vedānta (as, for example, Viśiṣṭādvaita), argue that God (Brahman) is possessed of all perfections (*saguṇa*) and that the passages denying qualities only deny imperfect ones.

nirjarā, in Jaina religious belief of India, the destruction of *karman* (merit and demerit). Getting rid of existing *karman* and preventing the accumulation of new *karman* are necessary for the soul to achieve *mokṣa*, or liberation from rebirths. *Nirjarā* is accomplished by such physical and spiritual austerities as fasting, mortification of the body, confession and penance, reverence to superiors, service to others, meditation and study, and indifference to the body and its needs, the last practice in its extreme form leading to self-starvation. The prevention of new *karman* is called *saṃvara* and is accomplished by the observation of moral vows (*vratas*); control of the activities of body, speech, and mind; care in walking and handling things; and the development of moral virtues and the patient endurance of troubles.

Nirmal-akhādā, a Sikh monastic order founded in the late 17th century.
·monastic influence on Sikhism **12**:339b

Nirmalas, an ascetic order of the Sikhs, a religious group of India. Nirmalas ("those without blemish") at first wore only white garments but later adopted the ochre robes worn by Hindu ascetics and shared some other practices such as birth and death rites with Hindus. Like the Udāsīs (another order of Sikh ascetics) the Nirmalas carried on missionary activities for the Sikhs and served as *mahants* (priests) of their temples.

nirmāṇa-kāya (Buddhism): *see* tri-kāya.

Nirvāṇa (Sanskrit: Extinction or Blowing Out), in Pāli NIBBĀNA, in Indian religious thought, the supreme goal of the meditation disciplines. It is most characteristically used in Buddhism, in which it describes the transcendent state of freedom achieved by the extinction of desire and of individual consciousness. According to the Buddhist analysis of the human situation, delusions of egocentricity and their resultant desires bind man to a continuous round of rebirths and its consequent suffering (*dukkha*). It is release from these bonds that is synonymous with enlightenment, or the experience of Nirvāṇa. Liberation from rebirth does not imply immediate physical death, and with an *arhat* (a perfected person) or a Buddha the subsequent death is usually called the *parinirvāṇa*, or "complete Nirvāṇa." In the Mahāyāna tradition of Buddhism, the realization of Nirvāṇa is deferred by the *bodhisattva* (Buddha-to-be) while he continues to work for the salvation of others.

Nirvāṇa is conceived somewhat differently within various schools of Buddhism. In the Theravāda (Way of the Elders) tradition, it is tranquility and peace. In the schools of the Mahāyāna (Great Vehicle) tradition, Nirvāṇa is equated with *śūnyatā* (emptiness), with *dharma-kāya* (the real and unchanging essence of the Buddha), and with *dharma-dhātu* (ultimate reality).
·Buddhist arhat myths **3**:419f
·Buddhist modes of attainment **3**:406d
·Buddhist mystical function **3**:415b
·Buddhist teachings summary **3**:376c
·emancipation from rebirth cycle **3**:427g
·eschatology of Buddhist thought **6**:960g
·Hindu scriptural discussions **15**:600f
·Idealist nature of Theravāda conception **15**:599e
·monastic meditation goal as negation **12**:341f
·Nāgārjuna's theme of reality as relative **12**:809a
·Otto's theory of human response to Holy **15**:625g
·philosophical description **9**:317f
·sainthood in Theravāda Buddhism **16**:164d
·salvific meaning and implications **16**:203d

Niš, or NISH, town in Serbia, Yugoslavia, on the Nišava River. The town is important for its command of the Morava–Vardar and the Nišava River corridors, the two principal routes from central Europe to the Aegean. The main rail line from Belgrade and the north divides at Niš for Thessaloníki (Salonika), in Greece, and Sofia. Niš is also the meeting point for several roads.

The ancient Roman city, Naissus, which probably succeeded a Celtic settlement, was mentioned as an important place in the 2nd century by Ptolemy, in his *Guide to Geography*. The old fortress on the right bank of the river is believed to have been built on this site. Under its walls, in AD 269, the emperor Claudius II defeated an army of the Goths. Niš is the birthplace of Constantine the Great (*c.* 280). During barbarian migrations of the 5th century, the town was destroyed, and, in the 9th century, the Bulgarians conquered it but ceded it in the 11th century to the Hungarians, from whom the Byzantine emperor took it in 1173. Toward the end of the 12th century, the town came under the Serbian

Nemanja dynasty, but in 1375 the Turks captured it from the Serbians.

Niš was recovered briefly several times, but Turkish domination lasted for 500 years, and the town became an important station on the route from Istanbul to Hungary. In the first Serbian uprising (1809), the Serbs fired their powder magazine and destroyed themselves and a large number of the enemy; in the ruins of the Turkish-built Ćele Kula (Tower of Skulls) are embedded the skulls of more than 900 of these Serbians. The Serbs' army liberated Niš in 1877, and the town was ceded to them by the Treaty of Berlin (1878). In World War I, Niš was for a period the capital of Serbia.

Heavy bomb damage from World War II and consequent postwar construction erased much of the town's Turko-Byzantine style. Historical buildings include a 5th-century Byzantine crypt.

Industries include textiles, beer, tobacco products, locomotives, household appliances, and electronic materials. A university was opened in 1965. Pop. (1971 prelim.) 127,178. 43°19′ N, 21°54′ E

·map, Yugoslavia **19**:1100

Nisa, also called PARTHAUNISA, first capital of the Parthians, located near modern Ashkhabad in Soviet Turkistan. Nisa was traditionally founded by Arsaces I (reigned *c.* 250–*c.* 248 BC), and it was reputedly the royal necropolis of the Parthian kings. Excavations at Nisa have revealed substantial buildings,

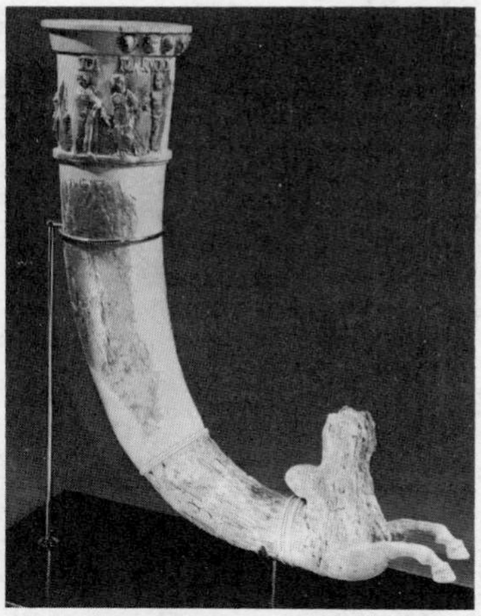

Ivory rhyton from Nisa, 2nd–1st century BC; in the Hermitage, Leningrad

By courtesy of the State Hermitage Museum, Leningrad

many inscribed documents, and a looted treasury. Also many Hellenistic art works have been uncovered, as well as a large number of ivory rhytons, the outer rims decorated with Iranian subjects or classical mythological scenes. In fact, almost all the art and architecture at Nisa exhibits a great intermingling of Western and Iranian styles. Nisa was later renamed Mithradatkirt by Mithradates I (reigned 171–138 BC).

Niscemi, town, Caltanissetta province, southern Sicily, Italy, in a cork-growing district; it has wine and sugar industries. Pop. (1971 prelim.) mun., 22,673. 37°08′ N, 14°24′ E

nise-e ("lifelike painting" or "realistic portraiture"), sketchy portraits that became fashionable in the court circles of 12th- and 13th-century Japan.

Realistic art was originally outside the tradition of Japanese portraiture, which, until the 12th century, was purely religious in character. Alongside the rise of scroll painting, which depicted incidents of real life, a parallel trend in the field of portraiture arose in the second half of the 12th century. The skill of

Nise-e of Minamoto Kintada, one of the 36 poets, from a handscroll by Fujiwara Nobuzane, Kamakura period (1192–1333); in the Freer Gallery of Art, Washington, D.C.

By courtesy of the Smithsonian Institution, Freer Gallery of Art, Washington, D.C.

nise-e consisted in catching a man's character in a few simple lines, although portraits expressed not so much a feeling for the individual and his characteristics as veneration for his accomplishments. The angular, geometric, almost abstract, treatment of robes contrasts strikingly with the realistic treatment of the face.

Fujiwara Takanobu (1142–1205) initiated the trend, and his son, Fujiwara Nobuzane, a courtier and poet like his father, won a great reputation as a painter.

·popularity and examples **19**:230h

Nisei, second-generation Japanese in the United States; the focus of national attention during World War II when all persons of Japanese ancestry on the West Coast were forcibly evacuated from their homes and relocated in inland detention centres as a result of mass hysteria following the Japanese attack on Pearl Harbor (Dec. 7, 1941). The government claimed it was forced by public hysteria, agitation of press and radio, and military pressure to establish the War Relocation Authority by executive order (March 18, 1942) to administer the mass evacuation.

Under jurisdiction of the Western Defense Command, 110,000 Japanese-Americans (including a number who were still aliens) during the spring and summer of 1942 were placed in ten war relocation centres located from the Sierra Nevada to the Mississippi River. The sparsely furnished military barracks afforded meagre "work opportunities" for adults and a minimal education for children. By the time the evacuation was complete, the U.S. was largely in command of the Pacific and all danger of a possible Japanese invasion past. After individual screening at the centres to prove their loyalty, 17,600 Nisei were accepted for service in the U.S. armed forces, with many of their units later cited for bravery. The wartime detention centres provided a precedent for the later establishment (by Title II of the 1950 Internal Security Act, repealed in 1970) of six "emergency centres" to be used for possible peacetime dissenters.

·California's World War II isolation **3**:616d
·San Francisco forced inprisonment **16**:220c
·social position after World War II **11**:110g
·World War II relocation and contribution **18**:992h

Nish (Yugoslavia): *see* Nīs.

Nīshāpūr (Iran): *see* Neyshābūr.

Nishapur pottery, Islāmic ceramics produced at Nishapur (modern Neyshābūr, Iran) that were of bold style and showed links with Sāssānian and Central Asian work. The style originated in Transoxania, an ancient district of Iran, during the 9th century AD and showed such specific characteristics as black and ochre birds with dashes of white and green. A rougher type portraying human and animal figures against an ornamental background also existed.

Nishi Armane (b. 1829, Tsuwano, Shimane Prefecture, Japan—d. 1897, Tokyo), thinker who helped introduce Western philosophy, especially British Empiricism, to Japan.

After study at the University of Leiden, The Netherlands, he became a professor at Kaiei-sho College in Tokyo. Together with Mori Yurei (1847–89), later minister of education, Nishi founded the famous Meirokusha publishing house. Its journal featured articles on such people as the 18th-century French philosophers Jean-Jacques Rousseau and Montesquieu and the 19th-century philosopher and biologist Ernst Haeckel, as well as the British 19th-century philosopher John Stuart Mill, the 19th-century British social philosopher Herbert Spencer, and the 19th-century British historian Henry Buckle. The publishing house also introduced Western civilization to Japan.

Nishi not only translated Mill's *Utilitarianism* but wrote many commentaries on Western philosophy. He is regarded as the first philosopher to create modern philosophical terminology in Japanese, which permitted Japanese philosophers to compare oriental and Western thought.

·Japanese interest in Western philosophy **10**:107f

Nishida Kitarō 13:118 (b. April 19, 1870, near Kanazawa, Ishikawa Prefecture, Japan—d. June 7, 1945, Kamakura), an outstanding philosopher who exemplified Japan's attempt to assimilate Western philosophy into its Oriental spiritual tradition.

Abstract of text biography. Nishida's early education included study of the Confucian Classics in Chinese. His lifelong friendship with D.T. Suzuki, a renowned Buddhologist, greatly influenced his thinking. He attended the University of Tokyo (1891–94) as a non-regular student of philosophy. While teaching in secondary schools (1895–1909), he practiced Zen Buddhism. He taught for one year at Gakushūin University, Tokyo, and at Kyōto University from 1910 until his retirement in 1928. In his *Tetsugakulon bunshū* ("Philosophical Essays"), written after his retirement, he explained his mature "philosophy of the *topos* [place] of Nothingness," an attempt to overcome the dichotomy of the mind and its object. The progressive development of Nishida's thought is apparent in his writings: *Zen-no-kenkyū* (1911; Eng. trans., *A Study of Good*, 1960), which first drew attention to him as an original thinker, *Jikaku-ni okeru chokkan to hansei* (1917; "Intuitions and Reflection in Self-Consciousness"), and *Hataraku-mono kara miru-mono e* (1927; "From the Acting to the Seeing Self").

REFERENCES in other text articles:
·Hegel-influenced Idealism **9**:192e
·philosophy of unifying transcendence **10**:108e

Nishijima, Kazuhiko (1926–), Japanese physicist.
·subatomic particle research **13**:1031b

Nishikawa Sukenobu, first name also MAGOUEMON (b. 1671, Kyōto—d. 1751), painter of the Ukiyo-e school of popular, colourful paintings and prints, who also was a book designer of the Kyōto–Ōsaka area.

"Kesho suru onna" ("Woman Making-up"), painting by Nishikawa Sukenobu; in the Atami Art Museum, Japan
By courtesy of the Atami Art Museum, Japan

Nishikawa studied painting with masters of two schools, the Kanō (stressing Chinese subjects and techniques) and the Japanese-oriented Tosa school. Eventually, however, he was influenced by Ukiyo-e painters, especially Hishikawa Moronobu (died 1694). In his time Edo, now Tokyo, was already considered the centre of Ukiyo-e, and that school's prints were often referred to as Edo-e or Edo paintings and prints.

Nishikawa established his own school of Ukiyo-e and gathered numerous pupils in the Kyōto area, where the classical tradition predominated. His style was graceful and sensuous, and it influenced many Edo artists, such as the famous late-18th-century painters Suzuki Harunobu and Ishikawa Toyonobu. He was a prolific artist and particularly known for his diverse kimono designs. The two-volume illustrated book *Hyakunin jorō shinasadame* ("One Hundred Types of Women") is one of his masterpieces.

nishiki-e, Japanese polychrome woodblock prints of the Ukiyo-e (*q.v.*) school that were first made in 1765. The invention of the technique is attributed to Kinroku, and its greatest early master was Suzuki Harunobu.
·18th-century Japanese printmaking **14**:1092b
·Japanese print, illus., **19**:Visual Arts, East Asian, Plate XIX
·technique development and popularity **19**:239f

Nishinomiya, city, Hyōgo Prefecture (*ken*), Honshu, Japan, at the mouth of the Muko-gawa (Muko River) on the Inland Sea. It is part of the continuous urban-industrial belt between Kōbe (west) and Ōsaka (east). The city occupies a narrow lowland between Ōsaka-wan (Ōsaka Bay) and interior Rokkō-zan (Mt. Rokkō). Nishinomiya is famed for its fine *sake* (rice wine). Its coastal areas are assigned to industry (metals, machinery, chemicals, rubber goods, soap, cosmetics, beer) and to bathing resorts. The city houses a professional baseball stadium and has excellent railway and road connections with adjacent urban areas. Pop. (1970) 377,043.
34°43′ N, 135°20′ E

Nishio, city, Aichi Prefecture (*ken*), Honshu, Japan, on the lower reaches of the Yahagi-gawa (Yahagi River). Nishio was a castle town and commercial centre during the Tokugawa era (1603–1867). The opening of two railways through the city in 1911 and 1928 resulted in the establishment of industry (textiles, metal castings). Tea is cultivated on Inari-yama (Mt. Inari) in the western part of the city. Pop. (1970) 75,193.
34°52′ N, 137°03′ E
·map, Japan **10**:36

Nishiyama Sōin (1605–82), Japanese haiku poet.
·poetry ideal **10**:1070a

Nisibin, or NISIBIS (Turkey): *see* Nusaybin.

Nisibis, Peace of (298 AD), agreement between Diocletian and Persia.
·Roman victory to hold the East **15**:1125d

Nisibis, School of, the intellectual centre of East Syrian Christianity (the Church of the East, or Nestorian Church) from the 5th to the 7th century. The School of Nisibis originated soon after AD 471, when Narsai, a renowned teacher and administrator at the School of Edessa, and his companions were forced to leave Edessa (modern Urfa, Tur.) because of theological controversies. Under Narsai's directorship (471–496), a number of former teachers and students from the School of Edessa were enlisted in the new institution and gave shape to Christianity according to the Nestorian creed, which so stressed the independence of the divine and human natures of Christ that it appeared as though the natures were in effect two persons loosely joined in a moral union.

The school experienced tremendous growth during Abraham de Bet Rabban's tenure (ended *c.* 569). Its teachers wrote in the fields of literature, history, philology, and theology, as well as translating from Greek into Syriac. The school gained renown in the West and became a major centre of education for members of the clergy and hierarchy.

The Nestorian theology of the school, however, was undermined by Ḥenānā (*c.* 570–*c.* 609), who preferred Origen (a Christian theologian who flourished in the early 3rd century) to Theodore of Mopsuestia, the recognized Nestorian authority; and it required royal power to support him in position in the face of a student revolt.

The only outstanding figure after Ḥenānā was Surin, who held office for some time in the second quarter of the 7th century. His literary work must have created considerable attention; and its vitality sustained the school in its subsequent history of decline, especially in the areas of historiography and monastico-historical inquiry. The school was unable to retain its pre-eminence among other schools and was superseded by the school of Seleucia-Ctesiphon.

Two sets of statutes—the first established by Narsai in 496 and the second by Ḥenānā in 590—provide insights into the operation of the school in matters of administration, teaching staff, personnel duties, curriculum, student body, discipline, and daily life. Nisibis was at once a school and a community under rigid control. Its program was restricted to the study of theology, primarily of the Bible. Theodore of Mopsuestia was regarded as the chief authority, and his exegetical writings were closely followed. Greek learning was disavowed, though Aristotelian logic was admitted; indeed the main logical treatises of Aristotle, together with Porphyry's famous introduction, had been translated into Syriac at Edessa by Bishop Ibas. It was primarily through Syriac translations that the Arabs became acquainted with Greek thought.
·Japanese popular philosophical tenets **10**:107d
·Nestorian philosophical activity **6**:138h
·Syriac school of theology **13**:1084e

Niska (dialect): *see* Tsimshian.

Nísoi Aiyaíou (Greece): *see* Aegean Islands.

niṣprapañca (Sanskrit: "what is devoid of verbal manifoldness"), in Pāli NIPPAPAÑCA, in the Mādhyamika (Middle View) and Vijñānavāda (Consciousness Affirming) schools of Buddhist philosophy, ultimate reality, which is not possible to express verbally. *Prapañca* (manifoldness, plurality) is usually used to describe the manifoldness of worldly phenomena. According to Buddhist philosophers of the Mādhyamika and Vijñānavāda schools, illusions are produced by conceptual constructions of the mind, which associates a thing with a name of a conception. Such a conceptual construction is a superimposition of what is unreal upon an object. In everyday language, the judgment usually takes the form of "This is that," consisting of analysis into subject and object or subject and predicate. This expression presupposes the existence of names of conceptions. Also in everyday life, people apply a name to a thing by convention in order to communicate information regarding knowledge of the thing. By using words, they share a common understanding about something, and this understanding may be admitted as empirically true. Words, however, denote no real entity at all, since they are produced by the conceptual construction and are superimposed upon the real entity. The conventional reality based upon common understanding or logic is illusion in the final analysis. Man's thought, being based on words and fictitious in itself, has no touch with ultimate reality. This verbal and fictitious plurality of appearances is destroyed by understanding of the ultimate truth that everything has no permanent substance. Thus, a word differentiation always accompanies conventional reality, while ultimate reality is nondifferential, cannot be expressed in words, and is devoid of verbal manifoldness (*niṣprapañca*). The *yogin*'s intuition of reality is not associated with any conceptual construction.

Nissaba, in Mesopotamian religion, Sumerian deity, city goddess of Eresh on the ancient Euphrates River near Erech in the farming regions; she was goddess of the grasses in general, including the reeds and the cereals. As goddess of the reeds and provider of the scribe's reed stylus, she became the patroness of writing and the scribal arts, particularly of accounting.

Nissen, Rudolf (1896–), German surgeon.
·thoracic surgery advances **11**:839e

Nissim ben Jacob ben Nissim, sometimes called NISSIM BEN JACOB IBN SHAHIN (d. *c.* 1050), Talmudic exegete of al-Qayrawān (in modern Tunisia).
·Jewish mythology collections **10**:194e

Nistri periscope, periscope used by the Nerici Foundation of Milan and Rome for cave excavations.
·archaeological site location **1**:1080b

Nistrul River (Soviet Union): *see* Dnestr River.

Nisus, the name of two figures in classical mythology and literature.

Nisus, in Greek mythology, was a son of King Pandion of Megara. His name was given to the Megarian port of Nisaea. Nisus had a purple lock of hair with magic power: if preserved, it would guarantee him life and continued possession of his kingdom. When King Minos of Crete besieged Megara, Nisus' daughter Scylla fell in love with Minos or was bribed; she betrayed her city by cutting off her father's purple lock. Nisus was killed or killed himself and became transformed into a sea eagle. Scylla later drowned, possibly at the hand of Minos, and was changed into a sea bird (Greek *keiris*, Latin *ciris*), possibly a heron, constantly pursued by the sea eagle.

Nisus in Virgil's *Aeneid* was the second figure. He was a Trojan, the son of Hyrtacus, and a friend of Euryalus the Argonaut. In the funeral games after the fall of Troy, he slipped and fell but helped Euryalus win the footrace by tripping the leader. Later, fighting the Italians, he sacrificed himself in vain to rescue Euryalus.

NIT (basketball): *see* National Invitational Tournament.

Niten (Japanese artist): *see* Miyamoto Musashi.

niter (potassium nitrate): *see* nitre.

Niterói, city, Rio de Janeiro state, Brazil, on the eastern side of the entrance to Guanabara Bay. The city of Rio de Janeiro on the opposite side is connected to Niterói by ferry, railroad, and, since 1974, the Presidente Costa e Silva Bridge, spanning Guanabara Bay. Both cities are located on low ground at heads of the numerous inlets that indent the shores, with various sections separated by steep rocky ridges extending into the bay.

Icarai Beach on Guanabara Bay, Niterói, Braz.

Walter Aguiar—EB Inc.

Founded in 1671, the settlement became a village in 1819, with the name of Villa Real da Praia Grande. It was made the capital of Rio de Janeiro state in 1835, one year after the city of Rio de Janeiro and the Federal District were separated from Rio de Janeiro state. In 1836 it became a city and was renamed Niterói (or Nictheroy, from an Indian term meaning "hidden water"). It lost its capital status temporarily in 1894–1903 to Petrópolis and permanently from 1975 to the city of Rio de Janeiro.

Niterói also serves as a residential suburb of the city of Rio de Janeiro and is well developed industrially. It is the site of Brazil's chief shipbuilding and ship-repair yards; it also has metal industries, food-processing plants, textile mills, and a wide variety of manufacturing establishments. It is the seat of the Fluminense University (1961; Universidade Federal Fluminense). Pop. (1970) 291,970.
22°53′ S, 43°07′ W

·map, Brazil **3**:125
·Rio de Janeiro linkage **15**:853e

Nithard (b. 790?—d. June 14, 844), Frankish count and historian whose works, utilizing important sources and official documents, provide an invaluable firsthand account of contemporary events during the reign of the West Frankish king Charles II.

The son of Charlemagne's daughter Bertha and the renowned poet and imperial chancellor Angilbert, Nithard was reared at court. On the death of the emperor Louis I the Pious (840), he became counsellor to the youngest of Louis's sons, Charles II (Charles the Bald). Failing to prevent a civil war, Nithard fought for Charles in the Battle of Fontenoy (841) against Lothair I, Charles's elder half brother. In the same year Charles requested that Nithard write an account of recent events. The resulting *Historiarum libri IV* ("History of the Sons of Louis the Pious") deals with the discord between the sons of Louis during the years 840–843.

In 843 Charles made Nithard lay abbot of Saint-Riquier, a position he held for only a few months before he died in a battle against the forces of Pepin II of Aquitaine.

Nithsdale, district, Dumfries and Galloway (*q.v.*) region, southwestern Scotland; created by the reorganization of 1975, it comprises the western part of the former county of Dumfries (*q.v.*) and a small portion of eastern Kirkcudbright. The district, area 553 sq mi (1,432 sq km), reaches 2,000 ft (610 m) in the north, from which the River Nith issues into Nithsdale and flows southeastward through broadening lowland into the Solway Firth. The district is agricultural, sheep being bred in the hills and pastured in the lowland, where the principal crops are barley, oats, and potatoes. Dumfries, on the Nith, is the seat of the district authority and a manufacturing town, with tweed, hosiery, and other industries. Coal is mined in upper Nithsdale. Pop. (1974 est.) 55,924.

Nithsdale, William Maxwell, 5th earl of (b. 1676—d. March 20, 1744, Rome), Scottish Jacobite adherent of the Stuarts, remembered chiefly for being rescued by his wife from the Tower of London. During the Jacobite rising of 1715 he was captured at Preston, Lancashire, and early in 1716 he was tried and condemned to death.

His wife, Winifred, daughter of William Herbert, 1st marquess of Powys, travelled to London to secure his release. King George I, however, refused to receive her petition. Giving up hope of a pardon, the Countess planned her husband's rescue. With two other women she gained access to the Tower and disguised the Earl as a woman, enabling him to leave the prison with them on the night before the day fixed for his execution (Feb. 24, 1716).

Nithsdale fled to France and eventually was joined there by his wife. Later they went to Rome, where they lived in poverty. The Countess died in 1749, five years after her husband.

Nitidulidae (insect family): *see* sap beetle.

Nitinat (people): *see* Nootka.

Nitra, German NEUTRA, Hungarian NYITRA, town, Západoslovenský *kraj* (Western Slovakia Region), Czechoslovakia, on the Nitra River.

The centre of the Nitra principality in the beginning of the 9th century, it was later a stronghold and religious centre. The first Christian church in what is now Slovakia was established there in AD 830 and consecrated by SS. Cyril and Methodius. Town privileges were acquired in 1248. Modern Nitra is an important road junction and a food-processing centre for the farming area to the south. Nitra Agricultural College was founded in 1946. Dominant features are the old fortification gate, above which the Zobor (a hill 1,929 ft high) rises to the north, and the medieval castle enclosure, which includes the cathedral. Pop. (1975 est.) 50,041.
48°20′ N, 18°05′ E

·map, Czechoslovakia **5**:413

Nitrariaceae, family of flowering plants of the order Geraniales.

·characteristics and classification **8**:5d

nitrate, any member of either of two classes of compounds derived from nitric acid (*q.v.*). The salts of nitric acid are ionic compounds containing the nitrate ion, NO_3^-, and a positive ion, such as NH_4^+ in ammonium nitrate (*q.v.*). Esters of nitric acid are covalent compounds having the structure $R{-}O{-}NO_2$, in which R represents an organic combining group, such as ethyl (C_2H_5) in ethyl nitrate.

·active transport in plant roots **11**:883e
·agricultural pollutants **1**:361f
·aquarium water accumulation **1**:1028b
·meat curing colour fixation **11**:750f
·nitrogen fixation–denitrification cycle **2**:1040f
·occurrence in freshwater **7**:734h
·solubility in water and decomposition **13**:128b
·uranium compound production **18**:1036a

nitrate and iodate minerals, small group of naturally occurring inorganic compounds that are practically confined to the Atacama Desert of northern Chile; the principal locality is Antofagasta. The minerals occur under the loose soil as beds of grayish caliche (a hard cemented mixture of nitrates, sulfates, halides, and sand) 2–3 metres (7–10 feet) thick. The much rarer iodate minerals occur sporadically, intermixed with the nitrates, and are distinguished from the former by their yellow colour. The caliche has accumulated as a result of drainage; because most of these compounds are soluble and unstable, they are practically confined to arid regions and soils, which possess a paucity of micro-organisms.

Before World War I, Chile possessed a near monopoly on nitrates, with as many as 100 plants in operation. Introduction of practical methods for the fixation of nitrogen early in the 20th century resulted in a decline of the marketing of natural nitrates.

The nitrate and iodate minerals are structurally related to the carbonate minerals. The most important nitrate species are soda nitre, nitre (saltpetre), darapskite, and humberstonite. Among the iodates are lautarite and dietzeite.

·Atacama Desert deposits **2**:255a
·evaporite origins and mineralogy **6**:1133c; table

nitration, any chemical reaction that results in the formation of a nitrate, such as nitroglycerin (glyceryl trinitrate), or of a nitro compound, such as trinitrotoluene.

·drug production by organic synthesis **14**:196b
·dye manufacturing processes for intermediates **5**:1100e
·electron density effects on reaction path **6**:670c

nitre, also spelled NITER, or called SALTPETRE, also SALTPETER, naturally occurring potassium nitrate, KNO_3; soda nitre, also known as cubic nitre or Chile saltpetre, is sodium nitrate (*q.v.*), $NaNO_3$. Nitre was employed in the 13th century in the preparation of nitric acid and the manufacture of gunpowder and fireworks. It occurs as crusts on the surface of the Earth, on walls and rocks, and in caves. It forms in certain soils in Spain, Italy, Egypt, Iran, and India and occurs with soda nitre in Chile and in caves in the Mississippi Valley.

Nitre is white in colour and soluble in water; it has a vitreous lustre and a cool and salty taste.

·composition and evaporites table **6**:1133f

nitric acid, colourless, fuming, and highly corrosive liquid (freezing point −42° C [−44° F], boiling point 83° C [181° F]), a common laboratory reagent and important industrial chemical for the manufacture of fertilizers and explosives. It is toxic and can cause severe burns.

The preparation and use of nitric acid were known to the early alchemists. A common laboratory process used for many years, ascribed to a German chemist, Johann Rudolf Glauber (1648), consisted of heating potassium nitrate with concentrated sulfuric acid. Three French chemists advanced the knowledge of nitric acid: Antoine-Laurent Lavoisier showed that it contained oxygen, and Joseph-Louis Gay-Lussac and Claude-Louis Berthollet established its chemical composition in 1816. Nitric acid (HNO_3) has been called *eau forte, aqua dissolutiva, aqua prima, spiritus acidus nitri, spiritus nitri fumans Glauberi*, and *aqua fortis*.

The principal method of manufacture of nitric acid is the catalytic oxidation of ammonia. In the method developed by a German physical chemist, Wilhelm Ostwald, in 1901, ammonia gas is successively oxidized to nitric oxide and nitrogen dioxide by air or oxygen in the presence of a platinum gauze catalyst. The nitrogen dioxide is absorbed in water to form nitric acid. The resulting acid in water solution (about 50–70 percent by weight acid) is usually dehydrated by distillation with sulfuric acid.

Nitric acid decomposes into water, nitrogen dioxide, and oxygen, forming a brownish-yellow solution. It is a strong acid, completely ionized into hydrogen and nitrate ions in aqueous solution and a powerful oxidizing agent (one that acts as electron acceptor in oxidation–reduction reactions). Among the many important reactions of nitric acid are: neutralization with ammonia to form ammonium nitrate, a major component of fertilizers; nitration of glycerol and toluene, forming the explosives nitroglycerin and trinitrotoluene, respectively; preparation of nitrocellulose; and oxidation of metals to the corresponding oxides or nitrates.

nitric oxide, colourless, toxic gas, the most stable oxide of nitrogen, formed from nitrogen and oxygen by the action of electric sparks or high temperatures or, more conveniently, by the action of dilute nitric acid upon copper or mercury. It was first prepared about 1620, and it was first studied, in 1772, by the English chemist Joseph Priestley, who called it "nitrous air."

Nitric oxide, which has the formula NO, liquefies at −151.8° C (−241.2° F) and solidifies at −163.6° C (−262.5° F); both the liquid and the solid are blue in colour. The gas is almost insoluble in water, but it dissolves rapidly in a slightly alkaline solution of sodium sulfite, forming the compound sodium dinitrososulfite, $Na_2(NO)_2SO_3$. It reacts rapidly with oxygen to form nitrogen dioxide, NO_2. Nitric oxide is one of the few stable compounds containing an odd number of electrons; it can gain or lose one electron to form the ions NO^- or NO^+, which are present in the nitrosyls, compounds somewhat similar to the carbonyls formed from carbon monoxide and transition metals.

An industrial procedure for the manufacture of hydroxylamine (*q.v.*) is based on the reaction of nitric oxide with hydrogen in the presence of a catalyst. The formation of nitric oxide from nitric acid is applied in a volumetric method of analysis for nitric acid or its salts.

nitride, any of a class of inorganic compounds in which nitrogen is combined with one or more metals. Certain nitrides are unstable and most react with water to form ammonia and the oxide or hydroxide of the metal; but the nitrides of boron, vanadium, silicon, titanium, and tantalum are extremely refractory, resistant to chemical attack, and hard—useful as abrasives and in making crucibles. Nitrides are formed during the nitriding (surface hardening) of certain steel alloys.

nitriding, in steel production, method of surface hardening. It consists of heating the steel with ammonia at temperatures usually between 950° and 1,050° F (500° and 550° C) for periods of from 5 to 100 hours, depending upon the thickness of hardened case desired. The steels so treated must be special alloy steels having nitride-forming elements, such as aluminum, chromium, or molybdenum, dissolved in the iron. During the nitriding cycle, nitrogen from the ammonia diffuses into the steel and forms alloy nitrides, which precipitate along the crystal planes of the iron and cause an increase in hardness. The reaction is dependent upon temperature and the amount and nature of the nitride-forming elements in the steel. Aluminum is the most effective hardening element.

Nitriding produces a harder and more wear-resistant case than do other methods of surface hardening, and distortion is slow. Nitriding results in surface compressive stresses, which impart resistance to crack formation.

nitrification (biology): *see* nitrogen cycle.

nitrile, also called CYANO COMPOUND, any of a class of organic compounds having molecular structures in which a cyano group (−C≡N) is attached to a carbon atom (C). Nitriles are neutral substances derived from carboxylic acids by replacement of the oxygen atoms with nitrogen.

Acrylonitrile, produced in large quantities from hydrogen cyanide and either acetylene or ethylene oxide, is an important component of several polymeric (large-molecule) substances, including the acrylic textile fibres and synthetic rubbers and thermoplastic resins.

Some nitriles are manufactured by heating carboxylic acids with ammonia in the presence of catalysts (substances that speed up chemical reactions without changing their composition and amount). This process is used to make nitriles from natural fats and oils, and its products are used as softening agents in synthetic rubbers, plastics, and textiles and for making amines.

Phthalonitrile is the starting material for the phthalocyanine pigments and dyes, which possess excellent fastness and brilliance.

nitrile rubber, also called BUNA N or NBR, type of synthetic rubber that is known for its high resistance to oil. It is used for seals, gaskets, or other items subject to contact with hot oils.

nitrite, any member of either of two classes of compounds derived from nitrous acid. Salts of nitrous acid are ionic compounds containing the nitrite ion, NO_2^-, and a positive ion such as Na^+ in sodium nitrite ($NaNO_2$). Esters of nitrous acid are covalent compounds having the structure R−O−N−O, in which R represents a carbon-containing combining group such as ethyl (C_2H_5) in ethyl nitrite. The covalent nitrites are isomers of the nitro compounds—*e.g.*, nitrobenzene (*q.v.*)—which are considered to be derivatives of nitric acid rather than of nitrous acid.

Nitro, city, Putnam and Kanawha counties, western West Virginia, U.S., on the Kanawha River, just northwest of Charleston. The city sprang up with the construction of a large government explosives plant in 1918, its population reaching 35,000. Production ceased in 1919 and factories were scrapped; many houses were shipped downriver on barges to coal-mining towns. Nitro survived, however, as a Charleston suburb. Chemicals and textiles are manufactured there. Inc. 1932. Pop. (1980) 8,074.
38°25′ N, 81°50′ W

Nitrobacter, genus of rod-shaped bacteria (order Pseudomonadales), one of a group of the so-called nitrifying bacteria that are important in the nitrogen cycle (the process by which ammonia in the soil is converted into nitrates, which are used by plants). *Nitrobacter winogradskyi* oxidizes nitrites, formed from ammonia by *Nitrosomonas* and *Nitrosococcus* species, to nitrates.

nitrobenzene, aromatic nitro compound that is used in the manufacture of aniline, benzidine, and other organic chemicals and, as oil of mirbane, in perfumery.

Nitrobenzene was prepared in 1834 by Eilhardt Mitscherlich, who treated benzene with fuming nitric acid. Commercially, both batch and continuous processes employing mixed nitric and sulfuric acids are used to make nitrobenzene.

Nitrobenzene, with molecular formula $C_6H_5NO_2$, has chemical properties that reflect the mutual influence of the phenyl ($-C_6H_5$) and the nitro (NO_2) groups. Thus, it undergoes nitration, halogenation, and sulfonation much more slowly than does benzene. Nitrobenzene may be reduced to a variety of compounds, depending on the reaction conditions. Most nitrobenzene produced is reduced to aniline; smaller amounts are converted to azobenzene, hydrazobenzene (the intermediate for benzidine), and phenylhydroxylamine. Reduction of both the nitro group and the benzene ring affords cyclohexylamine. Nitrobenzene is used as a mild oxidizing agent in the syntheses of quinoline and of fuchsin.

Nitrobenzene is a pale yellow, oily, highly toxic liquid with the odour of bitter almonds. It freezes at 5.7° C (42.3° F) and boils at 210.9° C (411.6° F).

nitrocellulose, common name for the highly flammable compound cellulose nitrate, the nitric ester of cellulosic materials, usually cotton linters and wood pulp. It is a fluffy white substance that retains some of the fibrous structure of untreated cellulose. Nitrocellulose is not stable to heat, and even carefully prepared samples will ignite on brief heating to temperatures over about 150° C (300° F).

In 1838 T.-J. Pelouze discovered that cotton could be made explosive by dipping it in concentrated nitric acid. In 1845 C.F. Schönbein made nitrocotton by dipping cotton in a mixture of nitric and sulfuric acids and then washing the substance to remove the excess acid. In about 1860 Maj. E. Schultze of the Prussian army produced a gunpowder using a nitrocellulosic propellant. Gelatinized nitrocellulose propellants were introduced in the 1880s, after it was discovered that dry or moist nitrocellulose could be exploded by a detonator, thus starting the use of the substance as a high explosive.

Nitrocellulose is unstable, and when it decomposes it forms products that catalyze further decomposition. If not stopped, this reaction results in explosion. In 1868 Sir Frederick Augustus Abel showed that the methods then used for washing nitrocellulose after nitration were inadequate, and that a large amount of acid remained. Changes in washing methods improved the product, but powder magazines continued to explode. The

French chemist Paul Vieille added special stabilizers to nitrocellulose to neutralize the catalytically active decomposition products; the first stable and reliable propellant, smokeless powder, resulted from his work.

Guncotton is nitrocellulose having more than 13 percent nitrogen. It is soluble in acetone but has very low solubility in ether–alcohol solution. It is used for propellants, either alone or combined with lower grades of nitrocellulose. Moist guncotton was once widely used as a high explosive but has been replaced by safer materials.

Less completely nitrated celluloses are called collodion cotton, pyroxylin, or soluble nitrocellulose because they dissolve in ether–alcohol solvent. They are inferior to guncotton in explosive properties. Collodion with a nitrogen content not over 12 percent is used chiefly for lacquers and celluloid plastics. Materials with a nitrogen content of about 11.5 percent were once used as artificial silk but have been replaced by other materials such as viscose rayon. This same material was used for manufacture of photographic film until safety film, made of cellulose acetate plastics, became popular. Collodion with 12 percent nitrogen is used in the manufacture of propellants and gelatin dynamites.

Pyrocellulose, discovered by the Russian chemist Dmitry Mendeleyev, has the highest degree of nitration (12 percent) that will still yield a product soluble in alcohol–ether solvent; it is used extensively in the manufacture of propellants.

·adhesive limitation **1**:89g
·ammunition design and development **1**:700a
·cotton fibre esterification **7**:276c
·ether's industrial applications **1**:459a
·explosive development **7**:84h
·gunnery technology development **8**:490b
·motion picture film improvements **12**:546b
·nitric acid production and use **4**:135b
·rocket propellant composition **15**:938a
·small arms cartridges of late 1900s **16**:897g
·synthetic fibre development **7**:257h
·thermoplastic resin production **14**:513c
·weaponry improvements of 1800s **19**:688c
·wet-collodion process **14**:301c

nitro compound, organic compound containing the nitro (nitrogen and oxygen) radical $-NO_2$.

·properties, preparation, and reactions **13**:700a

nitrogen, symbol N, a nonmetallic element of Group Va of the periodic table; a colourless, odourless, tasteless gas, the most plentiful element in the Earth's atmosphere, and a constituent of all living matter. Daniel Rutherford, a medical student in Edinburgh, is usually credited with the discovery of nitrogen (1772) because he was first to publish his findings; but in England the chemists Joseph Priestley and Henry Cavendish and in Sweden the chemist Carl Wilhelm Scheele also discovered it about the same time. The French chemist Antoine Lavoisier first recognized the gas as an element and named it azote because of its inability to support life (Greek *zōē*, "life"). The present name (from 'nitre' plus the suffix "-gen," thus "nitre-forming") was coined in 1790 to indicate the presence of the element in nitre (potassium nitrate, KNO_3).

Among the elements, nitrogen ranks sixth in cosmic abundance. It occurs in the Earth's atmosphere to the extent of 78 percent by volume or about 75 percent by weight. Free nitrogen also is found in many meteorites, in gases of volcanoes, mines, and some mineral springs, in the Sun, and in some stars and nebulae. In combination it is found in the minerals nitre (saltpetre) and Chile saltpetre (sodium nitrate, $NaNO_3$); in the atmosphere, rain, soil, and guano as ammonia and ammonium salts; in seawater as ammonium (NH_4^+), nitrite (NO_2^-), and nitrate (NO_3^-) ions; and in living organisms as complex organic compounds such as proteins. Animals obtain the nitrogen of their tissue proteins from vegetable or other animal proteins of food; plants synthesize their proteins from inorganic nitrogen compounds from soil and to some extent from uncombined nitrogen in the air. A bacterium living in the roots of leguminous plants, such as peas, beans, clover, alfalfa, and peanuts, assimilates atmospheric nitrogen. Certain free-living anaerobic bacteria and some algae also can extract nitrogen from the air. Other micro-organisms in soils convert ammonium salts to nitrates. Lightning and sunlight cause a limited amount of nitrogen to combine with atmospheric oxygen, forming several oxides that are conveyed by rain in the form of nitric and nitrous acids to the soil, where they are neutralized, becoming nitrates and nitrites. The nitrogen content of cultivated soil is generally enriched and renewed artificially by fertilizers containing nitrates and ammonium salts. Excretion and decay of animals and plants return nitrogen compounds to the soil and air, and some bacteria in soil decompose nitrogen compounds and return the element to the air.

Inhaled nitrogen dissolves slightly in the blood and in other body fluids; under increased pressure, the amount dissolved is greater. The bends, or decompression sickness, is caused mainly by bubbles of nitrogen coming out of solution in the bloodstreams of persons such as divers, aviators, and those who work in deep caissons on whom the air pressure has been reduced too quickly.

Commercially, nitrogen is prepared almost entirely by fractional distillation of liquid air. Nitrogen, which has a lower boiling point (−195.8° C, or −320.4° F) than oxygen (−183° C, or −297° F), tends to evaporate first. On a small scale, pure nitrogen is made from its compounds, for example, by heating ammonium nitrite, NH_4NO_2, or barium azide, $Ba(N_3)_2$. Large quantities of nitrogen are used together with hydrogen in the Haber process for making ammonia, NH_3, from which nitric acid, HNO_3, and other nitrogen compounds are produced that are eventually converted into a wide variety of dyes, drugs, explosives, and fertilizers. Liquid nitrogen is used as a coolant. Because of its inertness, nitrogen gas is utilized in the chemical industry as a diluent or as a blanket to exclude oxygen and moisture.

Chemically, nitrogen gas is quite inert, especially at ordinary temperatures, because a relatively large amount of energy is required to disturb the electrons of the normal nitrogen molecule, N_2, so that they can interact with other atoms. A form called active nitrogen is produced by passing a high-voltage electric discharge through the gas at reduced pressure. The resultant gas has a yellow afterglow, is very reactive, and consists mostly of nitrogen atoms, N. The oxides of nitrogen are: nitrous oxide, N_2O, also called laughing gas, a colourless anesthetic gas with a pleasant, sweetish odour and taste; nitric oxide, NO, which is toxic, as are the higher oxides of nitrogen; dinitrogen trioxide, N_2O_3; the reddish-brown gas, nitrogen dioxide, NO_2, and its colourless dimer, dinitrogen tetroxide, N_2O_4; dinitrogen pentoxide, N_2O_5; and the unstable trioxide, NO_3.

Natural nitrogen on Earth consists of a mixture of two stable isotopes, nitrogen-14 (99.63 percent) and nitrogen-15 (0.37 percent). The first artificially induced nuclear transmutation was reported (1919) by a British physicist, Ernest Rutherford, who bombarded nitrogen-14 with alpha particles to form oxygen-17 nuclei and protons. Nitrogen in the upper atmosphere absorbs cosmic-ray neutrons, which convert the nitrogen to carbon atoms.

atomic number	7
atomic weight	14.0067
melting point	−210° C (−346° F)
boiling point	−195.8°C (−320.4°F)
density (1 atm, 0° C)	1.2506 g/1
usual oxidation states	−3, +3, +5
electron configuration	2-5 or $1s^2 2s^2 2p^3$

·abundance in geochemical materials, tables 1, 5, and 8 **6**:702
·agricultural operations and effects **1**:350a
·air-liquefaction production process **7**:925c; illus.
·alkaloid molecular structure **1**:597e
·atmospheric physics and chemistry **2**:308a *passim* to 311h
·atomic weight and number table **2**:345
·aurora causes and spectral features **2**:375d
·bends causation and symptoms **5**:853f
·caisson disease from diving **4**:1045b
·carbon-14 production in atmosphere **5**:507d
·catalytic reaction mechanism **3**:1003a
·clay mineral adsorption properties **4**:704f
·cosmic ray interactions in atmosphere **5**:207c
·cryogenic properties **5**:319e *passim* to 322a
·cryosurgery techniques **17**:819d
·dehydration and rate of excretion **5**:561d
·Earth geological composition **6**:60g
·element abundance, table 6 **17**:602
·excretion of by-products in animal types **7**:45a
·fertilizer industry and soil nutrition **4**:133c; illus. 131
·Haber ammonia process development **8**:529e
·helium synthesis catalysis **4**:121a
·heterocycle structure and chemistry **8**:832e
·industrial environment potential hazards **9**:530e
·interstellar gas and nebulae **9**:793d
·ionosphere formation process **9**:811a; illus. 813
·isolation through combustion **8**:703e
·juvenile source and atmospheric development **2**:315b; table 318
·lake water sources and losses **10**:606d
·laser production from hot gases **10**:687b
·Lavoisier combustion theory and air analysis **10**:714d
·life and matter origin connected **10**:900h
·luminescent reaction of adhesives **11**:180a
·Martian atmosphere analysis **11**:527h; table
·metal hardening by cyaniding **11**:622f
·nitrogen group comparative chemistry **13**:120h; table 121
·nuclear components and statistics **13**:337g
·nutrient metabolisms of organisms, tables 1 and 2 **13**:402
·organic compounds and biosphere cycling **2**:1040f
·organic nitrogen compound chemistry **13**:693g
·organic qualitative and quantitative analysis methods **4**:80f
·petroleum product composition **14**:167e
·pigment classes in plants and animals **4**:914f
·pressure change and breathing disorders **14**:995g
·production, properties, and reactions **13**:124f; table 122
·protein requirement during pregnancy **14**:975f
·radioisotope medical use, table 7 **15**:447
·respiratory disorders and depth breathing **15**:747c
·respiratory system concentrations and pressures **15**:749b; table
·soil organisms and protein breakdown **16**:1015g
·solar abundances, table 2 **17**:803
·steel compositions and properties **17**:644a
·sulfide products manufacture and use **17**:793a
·transmutation reaction **13**:343g
·urine composition derived from diet **7**:41d

nitrogen, fixation of, process of taking free nitrogen from the air and converting it into some compound that can be made useful. This process occurs both in nature and in modern chemical factories.

Ordinarily, nitrogen is inert—that is, it does not react readily with other elements—but it is found in combined form in coal and certain naturally occurring chemicals as saltpetre and ammonia and in all fertile soil, which is a source utilized by plants. Fixed nitrogen is in the nucleus of living cells of plants and animals.

In nature, nitrogen from the atmosphere is fixed by conversion to ammonia by certain soil bacteria, *Azotobacter;* then other soil bacteria convert the ammonia to nitrates, which are utilized by plants. In industry, nitrogen from the atmosphere is fixed by conversion to ammonia in the Haber–Bosch process (*q.v.*);

the ammonia is used as a raw material in many manufacturing operations, such as production of other chemicals, fertilizers, plastics, resins, dyes, and explosives.

Another form of fixed nitrogen, nitric acid, occurs naturally in the atmosphere when lightning discharges. Nitric acid is produced industrially by oxidation in an electric arc.

·agricultural green manuring practice **1**:351e
·alder root nodules **17**:841g
·algae fixation of free nitrogen **1**:494c
·bacteria role in soils **2**:572b
·ecosystem structure and dynamics **6**:283g
·Fabales symbiotic cycle **7**:130e
·fixation by aquatic micro-organisms **14**:495g
·germfree life study in plants **8**:127c
·legume-bacteria symbiosis **2**:1050h
·lightning and bacterial processes **13**:125b
·natural and industrial synthesis **4**:135c
·plant requirements and gaseous cycles **2**:1040f
·plant suppression advantages **2**:1048g
·soil organism effects on free nitrogen **16**:1016a

nitrogen, oxides of: *see* nitric oxide; nitrogen dioxide.

nitrogen compounds, organic: *see* organic nitrogen compounds.

nitrogen cycle, in biology, the process by which inorganic nitrogen is converted to nitrates, consumed and metabolized by living organisms, and finally returned to an inorganic state. Inorganic nitrogen exists as a free element in the atmosphere and as ammonia compounds in the soil. Nitrogen-fixing bacteria and some blue-green algae convert atmospheric nitrogen to nitrates; nitrifying bacteria convert soil ammonia into nitrites and then to nitrates. Plants introduce these nitrates into a food chain in which they are converted into amino acids and proteins. Ammonia is released to the environment by the decomposition of organisms and their wastes. Atmospheric nitrogen is regenerated from nitrates by denitrifying bacteria; fixed by lightning, cosmic radiation, and meteor trails; and supplied by volcanic eruption.

Man's cultivation of crops associated with nitrogen-fixing bacteria and his use of fertilizers is increasing the amount of nitrogen fixed in nature.

·algae fixation of free nitrogen **1**:494c
·aquatic micro-organism nitrogen fixation **14**:495g
·bacterial role in soil **2**:572b
·biosphere conservation of matter **2**:1040f; illus. 1041
·ecosystem structure and dynamics **6**:283g
·environment and soil interaction **5**:46g
·Fabales symbiotic fixation **7**:130e
·nitrogen for plant utilization **2**:1040b
·soil organism and inorganic compounds **16**:1015g
·soil organism nitrogen cycle **16**:1015h

nitrogen dioxide, reddish gas that exists in equilibrium with its dimer, dinitrogen tetroxide (N_2O_4), the mixture sometimes called nitrogen peroxide, an irritant and poison present in smog and automobile exhausts. Nitrogen dioxide (NO_2) is an intermediate in the manufacture of nitric acid and is used as an oxidizing agent (one that serves as electron acceptor in oxidation–reduction reactions) in chemical processes and in rocket fuels. It is produced by the direct union of nitric oxide (NO) and oxygen, by the thermal decomposition of lead nitrate, $Pb(NO_3)_2$, or by the action of nitrosylsulfuric acid ($HOSO_2ONO$) on potassium nitrate (KNO_3).

·air pollution sources and control **14**:750h *passim* to 752e
·atmospheric oxidation reactions **2**:309b
·industrial environment hazards **9**:529c
·production and chemical properties **13**:127g
·radiation and pollutant formation **14**:296g
·relaxation process and pressure changes **15**:589f
·toxin reaction site and effect, table 4 **14**:622
·urban pollutants and effects **18**:1050e

nitrogen-fixing bacteria: *see* eubacteria.

nitrogen group elements and their compounds **13**:120, the fifth main group of elements in the periodic table and the compounds formed by them. This group of elements consists of nitrogen (N), phosphorus (P), arsenic (As), antimony (Sb), and bismuth (Bi). The elemental substances vary widely in their physical and chemical properties, ranging from the relatively inert, colourless gas nitrogen to the silvery-white metal bismuth. Whereas nitrogen and phosphorus are nonmetals, arsenic and antimony are metalloids, and bismuth is typically metallic.

The text article covers the discoveries of the elements; the family of compounds for each element; and the occurrence and distribution, properties and reactions, analytical chemistry, biological and physiological significance, and principal isotopes of each element.

REFERENCES in other text articles:
·alkaloid molecular structure **1**:597e
·aquarium water purification **1**:1028a
·atmospheric nitrogen compounds **2**:309b
·chalcogen compound properties **13**:820d
·chemical industry production and use **4**:134b
·Chilean nitrate deposits **2**:255a
·heterocyclic compound structure **8**:844e
·meat curing colour fixation **11**:750f
·nitrate production in Chile **4**:251g
·organic phosphorus compound classes **13**:701a
·periodicity in properties of elements **14**:78d
·semimetal theory and properties **12**:855f; table
·soil organisms' role in plant nutrition **16**:1015g *passim* to 1018a
·stereoisomeric tetrahedral structures **9**:1041d

RELATED ENTRIES in the *Ready Reference and Index: for*
elements: see antimony; arsenic; bismuth; nitrogen; phosphorus
arsenic compounds: arsenic acid; arsenious oxide; arsine
nitrogen compounds: ammonia; ammonium chloride; ammonium hydroxide; ammonium nitrate; calcium cyanamide; hydrazine; hydrogen cyanide; hydroxylamine; lead azide; nitric acid; nitric oxide; nitrogen dioxide; nitrous acid; nitrous oxide; sodium azide
phosphorus compounds: phosphine; phosphoric acid; phosphorous acid; phosphorus pentoxide; superphosphate

nitrogen narcosis, the anesthetic or intoxicating effects produced by the gas nitrogen (*q.v.*) when it is breathed under increased pressure. Nitrogen, a major constituent of air, is a relatively inert gas and, therefore, is passed into the fluids and tissues of the body without being utilized. Even though it is not used to sustain the bodily functions, it nevertheless has certain effects upon the tissues when it is in excess of the normal amounts breathed at atmospheric pressures.

Underwater divers and people living in pressurized environments are those most readily afflicted by nitrogen narcosis. Divers breathe compressed air. As they descend in the water, the pressure upon their bodies increases proportionally to the water depth; in order for them to breathe normally, the compressed air must be equal in pressure to that of the water. A diver situated at 100 feet (30 metres) under water is breathing air that is four times more dense than at sea level; the quantity of nitrogen is, likewise, four times greater.

Certain tissues in the body seem most susceptible to nitrogen absorption. Nitrogen is absorbed by the fatty tissue (lipids) much faster than by other tissues; the brain and the rest of the nervous system have a high lipid content. Consequently, when a high concentration of nitrogen is breathed, the nervous system becomes saturated with the inert gas molecules, and normal functions are impaired. The concentration of nitrogen depends primarily upon the diver's depth. Each individual has his own threshold of susceptibility; some divers experience narcosis at 50 feet, while others can go to 200 feet without any apparent effects. Most often, nitrogen narcosis begins to be apparent at about 100 feet of depth. As a diver goes deeper, the symptoms increase in severity. When the diver ascends, the symptoms terminate with essentially no aftereffects or permanent harm done.

The symptoms of nitrogen narcosis vary greatly according to the amount of nitrogen breathed, the individual's tolerance to nitrogen, and the environmental conditions. Mild cases begin as an intoxicating feeling of lightheadedness, euphoria, numbness, and carefreeness. The reasoning ability and manual dexterity may next be slowed down. Emotional instability and irrationality may then ensue. Persons severely affected lapse into convulsions and unconsciousness. Divers swimming in clear, warm water seem to experience pleasant sensations, while those in dark, cold water seem to encounter panic, fear, anxiety, and depression. Unless the narcosis is severe, the victim is capable of functioning physically and may not fully realize that his rationality is being impaired. Divers have been known to take off their equipment at 200 feet of depth in order to "feel more freedom like the fish" while under the effects of narcosis; those experiencing panic and fear may hallucinate nonexistent dangers and attempt to escape them. Irrationality itself can cause the diver to inflict bodily harm upon himself by rising too fast or by failing to realize that his air supply has been depleted.

In order to avoid the effects of nitrogen narcosis, certain other breathing mixtures have been experimentally tried. In the early 1970s the gas mixture that was most often used for deep diving and that gave the most favourable results was a mixture of helium and oxygen. Helium is inert, but it is not as readily absorbed by the fatty tissue as is nitrogen. While breathing helium, divers have gone to depths of 600 feet with only relatively mild cases of narcosis. The best way to avoid narcosis is to limit one's depth; the U.S. Navy encourages sport divers to remain at depths above 125 feet (38 metres) while breathing compressed air.

·pressure effects on nitrogen in lungs **14**:995g

nitrogen peroxide: *see* nitrogen dioxide.

nitrogen tetroxide, an alternate name for the compound dinitrogen tetroxide, N_2O_4; *see* nitrogen dioxide.

·relaxation process and pressure changes **15**:589e
·rocket propellant systems **15**:939f

nitroglycerin, or GLYCERYL TRINITRATE, a powerful explosive and an important ingredient of most dynamites. It is also used with nitrocellulose in some propellants, especially for rockets and missiles, and it is employed as a vasodilator in the easing of cardiac pain, such as occurs in angina pectoris.

Nitroglycerin was first prepared in 1846 by the Italian chemist Ascanio Sobrero by adding glycerol to a mixture of concentrated nitric and sulfuric acids. The hazards involved in preparing large quantities of nitroglycerin have been greatly reduced by widespread adoption of continuous nitration processes. Nitroglycerin, with molecular formula $C_3H_5(ONO_2)_3$, has a high nitrogen content (18.5 percent) and contains more than enough oxygen atoms to oxidize the carbon and hydrogen atoms while nitrogen is being liberated so that it is one of the most powerful explosives known. Its decomposition to gaseous products is represented by the following equation: $4C_3H_5(ONO_2)_3 \rightarrow 6N_2 + 12CO_2 + 10H_2O + O_2$.

Detonation of nitroglycerin generates gases that would occupy more than 1,200 times the original volume at ordinary room temperature and pressure; moreover, the heat liberated raises the temperature to about 5,000° C (9,000° F). The overall effect is the instantaneous development of a pressure of 20,000 atmospheres; the resulting detonation wave moves at approximately 7,700 metres per second (more than 17,000 miles per hour). Nitroglycerin is extremely sensitive to shock and to rapid heating; it begins to decompose at 50–60° C (122–140° F) and explodes at 218° C (424° F).

Dynamite, developed by the Swedish scientist Alfred Bernhard Nobel in the 1860s, provided safer explosives (much less sensitive to shock) than nitroglycerin. Nobel introduced several dynamites, in which the liquid nitroglycerin was mixed with such inert absorbents as diatomaceous earth, with active substances (nonexplosive, but capable of sustaining explosion; *e.g.*, sodium nitrate), or with other explosives (as nitrocellulose). Nitroglycerin converts nitrocellulose to blasting gelatin, a very powerful explosive. Nobel's discovery of this gelatinizing action led to the development of ballistite, the first double-base propellant and a precursor of cordite.

A serious problem in the use of nitroglycerin results from its relatively high freezing point (13° C or 55° F) and the fact that the solid is even more shock-sensitive than the liquid. This disadvantage is overcome by using mixtures of nitroglycerin with other polynitrates; for example, the mixture of nitroglycerin and ethylene glycol dinitrate freezes at −29° C (−20° F).

Pure nitroglycerin is a colourless, oily, somewhat toxic liquid having a sweet, burning taste. Its specific gravity is 1.59 (20° C); it is slightly soluble in water or in glycerol, more soluble in ethyl alcohol, and miscible with ether, acetone, or benzene.

·drug effect on heart diseases **5**:1045a
·explosive detonation development **7**:84e
·organic nitrogen compound chemistry **13**:696e
·propellants in ammunition design **1**:700b
·rocket propellant composition **15**:938b

nitromersol, disinfectant for application to the skin and mucous membranes and for sterilizing surgical instruments, is sometimes marketed under the trade name Metaphen. An organic compound containing mercury, related to merbromin (Mercurochrome) and thimerosal (Merthiolate), nitromersol disinfects by the action of the mercury in the molecule, precipitating the protein of micro-organisms and disrupting their metabolism. Nitromersol occurs as a yellowish powder or granules, soluble in alkaline solutions. It is used as a 0.5- percent alcoholic tincture and as a 0.2-percent aqueous solution. Its chemical formula is $C_7H_5HgNO_3$.

nitroso compound, any of a class of organic compounds having molecular structures in which the nitroso group (−N=O) is attached to a carbon or nitrogen atom. Substances in which this group is attached to an oxygen atom are called nitrites, that is, esters of nitrous acid; those in which the −N=O group is attached to a metal ion are called nitrosyls.

Nitroso compounds are usually prepared by the action of nitrous acid or a derivative of it upon a substance containing an easily replaced hydrogen atom. Certain members of the class are obtainable by oxidation (addition of oxygen) of amines or by reduction (removal of oxygen) of nitro compounds.

Examples of nitroso compounds are the nitrosodimethylanilines and the nitrosophenols, used in the manufacture of dyes. Nitroso derivatives of amides decompose upon heating with formation of nitrogen and can be used as foam-producing agents; if they are heated in the presence of alkalies, the decomposition takes a different course, yielding diazoalkanes, toxic, reactive compounds used in organic syntheses.

Many nitroso compounds can be converted into more stable compounds, the oximes. The reaction is commercially applied in the manufacture of cyclohexanone oxime from nitrosocyclohexane; the oxime is used for making nylon-6.

·nitrosamine toxin reaction site and effect, table 4 **14**:622
·properties, preparation, and reactions **13**:700a
·transition metal coordination compounds **18**:606f

Nitrosomonas, a genus of rod-shaped bacteria (order Pseudomonadales), one of a group of so-called nitrifying bacteria. Nitrifying bacteria are important in the nitrogen cycle (*q.v.*), the process by which ammonia in the soil is converted into nitrates, which are used by plants. *Nitrosomonas* oxidizes ammonia to nitrites. (Nitrites are oxidized to nitrates by *Nitrobacter*.) One of the few species known to be able to carry out this transformation is *Nitrosomonas europaea*.

·nitrogen-fixation cycle **2**:1041b
·soil organisms and nitrate reduction **16**:1015h

nitrostarch, also known as STARCH NITRATE, a high explosive similar to cellulose nitrate, that is obtained as a white powder by nitrating starch, and is used chiefly in blasting and demolition explosives.

·explosive composition and advantages **7**:86c

nitrous acid, an unstable, weakly acidic compound that has been prepared only in the form of cold, dilute solutions, useful in chemistry in converting amines into diazo compounds (*q.v.*), which are used in making azo dyes. It is usually prepared by acidifying a solution of one of its salts, the nitrites, which are more stable.

Nitrous acid, HNO_2, decomposes into nitric oxide, NO, and either nitrogen dioxide, NO_2, or nitric acid, HNO_3. It may react as either an oxidizing or a reducing agent; that is, its nitrogen atom may either gain or lose electrons in reactions with other substances. Nitrous acid, for example, oxidizes iodide ion to elemental iodine but reduces bromine to bromide ion.

Potassium nitrite was discovered in 1772 by a Swedish chemist, Carl Wilhelm Scheele, as a product of heating nitre (potassium nitrate). Nitrites usually are prepared by absorption of nitric oxide and nitrogen dioxide in an alkaline solution; in an older method, sodium nitrate was fused with lead, and the resulting sodium nitrite was dissolved in water and separated from the by-product, lead oxide, by filtration.

·organic ester properties and reactions **13**:700b
·salt decomposition **13**:127g

nitrous oxide, also called DINITROGEN MONOXIDE OR LAUGHING GAS, one of several oxides of nitrogen, a colourless gas with pleasant, sweetish odour and taste, which when inhaled produces insensibility to pain preceded by mild hysteria, sometimes laughter. Nitrous oxide (N_2O) was discovered by the English chemist Joseph Priestley in 1772; another English chemist, Humphry Davy, later called it nitrous oxide and showed its physiological effect. The principal use of nitrous oxide is as an anesthetic in surgical operations of short duration; prolonged inhalation causes death. The gas is also used as a propellant in food aerosols. It is prepared by the action of zinc on dilute nitric acid, the action of hydroxylamine hydrochloride ($NH_2OH \cdot HCl$) on sodium nitrite ($NaNO_2$), and, most commonly, by the decomposition of ammonium nitrate (NH_4NO_3).

·anesthetic improvement role **18**:43c
·anesthetic uses and disadvantages **1**:868a
·atmospheric chemical composition **2**:308d
·childbirth drug therapy complications **13**:1038d
·Davy's studies of therapeutic gases **5**:523d
·infrared analyzer measurement table **9**:635
·narcotic usage with general anesthetics **12**:843g
·production, makeup, and decomposition **13**:127e

Ni Tsan (b. NI YÜN-LIN, 1301, Wu-hsi, Kiangsu—d. 1374), one of the group of painters later known as the Four Great Masters of the Yüan dynasty (1279–1368). Although Ni Tsan was born to wealth, he declined to serve the foreign Mongol dynasty of the Yüan, and instead lived a life of retirement and cultivated

Landscape after Ni Tsan, hanging scroll in ink and colour by Wang Yüan-ch'i (1642–1715) in the Cleveland Museum of Art

By courtesy of the Cleveland Museum of Art, John L. Severance Fund

the scholarly arts (of poetry, painting and calligraphy), collected artistic works of the past, and associated with those of a similar temperament. He was characterized by his contemporaries as particularly quiet and fastidious; and many of those qualities are found in his paintings. He was much imitated by later painters, and therefore originals are difficult to authenticate. Generally it may be said that his paintings, usually landscapes, are spare in elements, are in ink monochrome only, and that great areas of the paper are left untouched. There is often a rustic hut, without any further suggestion of human presence, a few trees and other scant indications of plant life, and elemental land forms with a sombre quiet throughout. The art of Ni Tsan and his peers in the Yüan dynasty was almost diametrically opposed to the preceding standards of the Southern Sung academy that so immediately appealed to the eyes through obvious displays of ink virtuosity and a convincing pictorial reality. The new direction demanded concentrated viewing before the larger and, in fact, more complex plays of ink may be seen behind the apparent blandness of surface; thus, the viewer acquires a closer understanding of the painter than of his subject. Toward the end of his life Ni Tsan is said to have distributed all of his possessions among his friends and adopted the life of a Taoist recluse, wandering and painting in his mature style. After the restoration of Chinese rule under the Ming dynasty in 1368, he returned to urban life.

·landscape style and technique **19**:199c
·Ma Yüan's painting's ownership **11**:724f

Nitta Yoshisada (b. 1301, Japan—d. 1338), warrior whose support of the Imperial restoration of the emperor Daigo II (1287–1339) was crucial in destroying the Kamakura shogunate, the military dictatorship that governed Japan from 1192–1333. The ultimate defeat of Nitta resulted in the end of the Imperial restoration and the rise to power of the Ashikaga family, which dominated Japan from 1338 to 1573.

When Daigo II first rebelled against the Kamakura shogunate in 1331, Nitta, as a Kamakura retainer, helped defeat the Emperor's armies. The following year, however, Nitta switched allegiance and led the army that attacked and destroyed the Kamakura shogunate. He was one of the strongest men in the new court government, but he soon had a falling out with Ashikaga Takauji, another former Kamakura retainer who had also switched sides. Daigo II supported Nitta in the ensuing struggle, and in 1335 Takauji was driven from the capital, only to return a year later at the head of a large army and navy recruited from provincial warriors. The Emperor's forces were crushed, and Nitta fled the capital, taking Daigo II with him.

Takauji established a new puppet emperor at Kyōto, while Nitta set up Daigo II at Yoshinoyama, in south central Japan, thus dividing the country between a northern court at Kyōto and a southern court at Yoshino. Nitta temporarily regained power in 1338, but died a few months later when he was hit by a stray arrow in a surprise enemy attack.

·revolt against Hōjō family **8**:989d

Nitti, Francesco Saverio (b. July 19, 1868, Melfi, Italy—d. Feb. 20, 1953, Rome), Italian statesman who was prime minister for a critical year after World War I. After a career as a journalist and professor of economics, he was elected deputy in 1904. A Left Liberal, he became minister of agriculture, industry, and commerce (1911–14) and minister of the treasury (1917–19). He succeeded Vittorio Emanuele Orlando, the wartime prime minister, in June 1919, in the midst of foreign and domestic crises involving Italian territorial claims disputed by other Allied countries and the economic and fiscal problems created by the war and demobilization. Nitti's adoption of the system of proportional representation (Aug. 15, 1919) resulted in large increases in the number of deputies elected by the Socialists (156) and the Christian Democrats, or Popolari (100), but he did not succeed in conciliating these parties, and an epidemic of strikes by the industrial workers and disorders on the part of the new Fascist Party of Mussolini undermined not only Nitti's government but the democratic regime itself. Nitti resigned on June 9, 1920. Re-elected to parliament in 1921, he served until 1924, not entering his name in the election of that year held by the new Fascist regime. For several years he remained in exile in France, devoting himself to writing. During World War II Nitti was arrested by the Germans (August 1943) and interned in Austria but was freed by the Allied victory in 1945; he became a senator of Italy in June 1948.

Nitti

B. Pellegrini

·domestic and foreign policies **9**:1167d

Ni Tuan (fl. 1426–35), Chinese landscape painter employed at the Ming court in Peking.

·landscape style and technique **19**:201b

Niuafoo, most northerly island of Tonga, in the southwest Pacific Ocean. The generally wooded land area of 19 sq mi (49 sq km) includes a volcanic peak 853 ft (260 m) high, a crater lake, and numerous hot springs. During a particularly violent eruption in 1946, the island's inhabitants were evacuated to Eua, several hundred miles to the south. They have been returning to Niuafoo since 1958. Because of an unusual method of exchanging letters in cans with passing ships, Niuafoo has gained the nickname "Tin Can Island." Pop. (latest census) 599.

15°34′ S, 175°40′ W

Niuatoputapu (NIUATOBUTABU, or KEPPEL) **Island,** one of the northernmost islands of Tonga, in the southwest Pacific Ocean. Of volcanic origin, it has an area of 7 sq mi (19 sq km) and rises to 350 ft (110 m). It is a regular port of call for inter-island shipping between Tonga and Samoa. Copra and breadfruit are produced. Pop. (latest census) 1,294.

15°57′ S, 173°45′ W

Niue, island in the southwest Pacific Ocean, 1,340 mi (2,156 km) northeast of Auckland, N.Z.; in October 1974 it became an internally self-governing country in free association with New Zealand, of which it formerly was a territory. It is a coral formation with a circumference of 40 mi and an area of 102 sq mi (263 sq km). Its surface has two distinct levels: one 90 ft (30 m) and the other 220 ft above sea level, probably caused by two periods of tectonic uplift. The interior of the island is wooded, but its coral terrain precludes the existence of surface streams (freshwater is obtained from subterranean caves). All settlement is concentrated along the coast, the east side of which receives more rainfall.

The European discoverer of Niue, Capt. James Cook, arrived in 1774, and after a hostile reception from the indigenous people, he named the place Savage Island. Hostility was still evident when envoys of the London Missionary Society were expelled in 1830. Christianity was not widely accepted until a Polynesian missionary settled in 1861. Niue became a British protectorate in 1900. Annexed (1901) to New Zealand as part of the Cook Islands, Niue came under separate administration in 1903.

The present government consists of an elected assembly, which elects the premier, who in turn nominates three other members as his cabinet. A representative of the government of New Zealand is stationed in Niue. The seat of government is at Alofi, a port on the west coast with the island's only open anchorage, at which lighters are used to transport cargo between ship and shore. Copra, woven ware, passion fruit pulp, honey, and limes are exported mainly to New Zealand.

There are 14 settlements, each with a village council. The inhabitants, who speak a distinctive Polynesian dialect, grow taro, cassava, and yams for subsistence. They are served by seven elementary schools and one high school, a teacher training college, and a hospital. Many Niueans also live in New Zealand. Pop. (1975 est.) 4,048.

19°02′ S, 169°52′ W

·map, Pacific Islands **2**:433

·politics, area, and population **13**:829f; table 830

Nivelle, Robert-Georges (b. Oct. 15, 1856, Tulle, Fr.—d. March 23, 1924, Paris), commander in chief of the French armies on the western front for five months in World War I, whose career was wrecked by the failure of his offensive in the spring of 1917. Nivelle commanded a brigade (1914) and an army corps (1915) and in May 1916 succeeded Gen. Philippe Pétain as commander of the 2nd Army at Verdun. After two dazzlingly successful French counterattacks, Nivelle was promoted over the heads of many seniors to succeed Gen. Joseph-Jacques Joffre as commander in chief of the French armies. He then proclaimed that his methods at Verdun could win the war. David Lloyd George, the British prime minister, enthusiastically subscribed to Nivelle's theory of great violence allied with great mass and placed the British armies in France under Nivelle's command for his great offensive. Nivelle, however, steadily lost the confidence of his own chief subordinates, and in the final offensive (April 1917) he failed to break through the German lines. The next month there were widespread mutinies in the French armies. On May 15, 1917, Nivelle was replaced by Pétain as commander in chief, and in December 1917 he was transferred to North Africa.

·Battle of Arras strategy **19**:957c

·Pétain's assumption of command **14**:152g

Nivelles, town, Belgium. Pop. (1976 est.) 18,061.

50°36′ N, 4°20′ E

·Low Countries medieval urbanization **11**:138a

·map, Belgium **2**:819

Niven, Frederick John (b. March 31, 1878, Valparaiso, Chile—d. Jan. 30, 1944, Vancouver, B.C.), author of more than 30 novels, many of them historical romances set in Scotland and Canada. Three of his best known novels—*The Flying Years* (1935), *Mine Inheritance* (1940), and *The Transplanted* (1944)—form a trilogy dealing with the settlement of the Canadian west.

Niven was educated in Scotland and worked in libraries in Glasgow and Edinburgh. He went to Canada about 1900 and worked in construction camps in the west. Returning to the British Isles, he was a writer and journalist in England until after World War I, when he settled in Canada. Niven also published two volumes of verse and an autobiography, *Coloured Spectacles* (1938), a collection of essays based on personal experiences.

Nivernais, in France, the area administered from Nevers during the *ancien régime* and until the French Revolution the last great fief still not reunited to the French crown. Bounded southwest by Bourbonnais, west by Berry, north by Orléanais, and northeast, east, and southeast by Burgundy, Nivernais was detached from Burgundy by the end of the 10th century. The countship passed through various houses until 1539, when it was made a duchy of France, and came in 1601 to a branch of the House of Gonzaga, which sold it to Cardinal Jules Mazarin in 1659. Mazarin's nephew Philippe-Julien Mancini and his descendants held the duchy until 1790, when Nivernais became the *département* of Nièvre.

The *gouvernement* of Nivernais in 1789

·généralités in 1789 map **7**:639

Nivkhs (people): *see* Gilyaks.

nivṛtti (Sanskrit: "cessation"), in Hinduism, renunciation of worldly activities and interests.

·Hindu dichotomy of lay and ascetic lives **8**:904g

nix, also known as NIXIE, or NIXY, in Germanic mythology, half-human, half-fish priestess who lives in a beautiful underwater palace and assumes various physical forms—young, old, beautiful, ugly, or even invisible—in order to mingle with human beings.

One of three features may betray the nix's disguise: she loves music, dances well, and tells prophecy. Though usually malevolent,

"The Miller Sees the Nixy of the Mill Pond," illustration by H.J. Ford from the *Yellow Fairy Book*, edited by Andrew Lang, 1894

Dover Publications, Inc.

a nix can be easily propitiated with gifts. Nixes have been known in legends to abduct human children and to lure human beings into deep water to drown. Nixes are also said to have married human beings and to have borne human children.

Nix Olympica: *see* Olympus Mons.

Nixon, Richard M(ilhous) (b. Jan. 9, 1913, Yorba Linda, Calif.), lawyer, Republican politician, and 37th president of the United States (1969–74), the only president who resigned that office. He also was vice president

Nixon, 1970

UPI Compix

for eight years (1953–61) under Pres. Dwight D. Eisenhower.

Nixon graduated from Whittier (Calif.) College in 1934 and from the law school of Duke University, Durham, N.C., in 1937. He entered law practice in Whittier in 1937 and served briefly in the Office of Price Administration in Washington, D.C., soon after the outbreak of World War II. In August 1942 he joined the navy and served as an aviation ground officer in the Pacific theatre of war. Following his return to civilian life, he was twice elected to the U.S. House of Representatives (1947, 1949) and served two years in the U.S. Senate. His reputation for anti-Communism made him a desirable running mate for Eisenhower in the 1952 campaign, which emphasized that issue. After his defeat (by the Democrat John F. Kennedy) in the 1960 presidential election and in the California gubernatorial election in 1962, Nixon announced his retirement from politics and moved to New York City.

As a Wall Street lawyer, Nixon travelled widely abroad and worked for Republican candidates (1964, 1966). He re-entered politics as a candidate for president and defeated Hubert H. Humphrey in 1968. After his inauguration (January 1969), he announced what is known as the Nixon Doctrine of reducing U.S. military forces abroad by assisting smaller nations to defend themselves through military and economic aid. During his first administration he withdrew progressively larger numbers of U.S. ground troops to terminate U.S. participation in the Vietnamese war.

In domestic affairs, inflation was President Nixon's most persistent economic problem. Initially, he tried to cut federal expenditures; but the annual budget deficits of his administration grew to become the largest in history up to that time. In 1971 and 1973 the administration devalued the dollar in an attempt to achieve a balance of trade. Despite his well-known aversion to government controls, Nixon initiated (Aug. 15, 1971) his New Economic Policy, which included unprecedented peacetime controls on wages and prices. Most mandatory controls were lifted in January 1973, although the President's authority to impose them did not expire until May 1974, and administration attempts to stabilize wages and prices continued. With the opportunity to appoint four Supreme Court justices, the President was able to redirect the court toward the "strict constructionism" he espoused.

In foreign affairs, Nixon's most significant action may have been the reopening of direct communications with the People's Republic of China after a 21-year estrangement. In February 1972 he paid a state visit to China. This rapprochement in East Asia gave Nixon a stronger position during his visit to Moscow in May—the first by a U.S. president. At its conclusion the U.S. and the Soviet Union announced a major advance in nuclear arms limitation as well as a bilateral trade accord and plans for joint scientific and space ventures.

At the Republican National Convention in August 1972, Nixon was nominated for a second term. In November he defeated his Democratic challenger, Sen. George S. McGovern, in one of the largest landslide victories in U.S. presidential history.

U.S. participation in the war in Vietnam effectively came to an end in January 1973, when agreement was reached with the involved Vietnamese parties on a cease-fire, withdrawal of U.S. troops and advisers in South Vietnam, return of prisoners of war, and creation of an International Commission of Control and Supervision. U.S. bombing raids on Cambodia continued, however, until August 15, and the administration came under attack when it was revealed in July that the U.S. Air Force had secretly bombed Cambodia in 1969 and early 1970 and that the Air Force and the Department of Defense had falsified reports to hide the fact.

The President's second term, however, was dominated by the so-called Watergate (*q.v.*) scandal, which stemmed initially from actions by the Committee for the Re-election of the President and by the Finance Committee to Re-elect the President. The scandal broadened as investigations of an incident of burglary and wiretapping at the Democratic Party's national headquarters were pursued; by July 1974, several of the President's closest aides, including two former Cabinet officers, had been indicted on criminal charges, and several had been convicted. In that month the Committee on the Judiciary of the House of Representatives voted three articles of impeachment against Nixon.

On August 4 Nixon revealed what he and his aides had previously steadfastly denied: that he had in fact participated in efforts to conceal the facts about the Watergate break-in and within a few days after the event had directed the Federal Bureau of Investigation away from inquiries that were leading it toward the White House. The revelation resulted in a dissolving of support from his own party, both in Congress and throughout the country. He announced his resignation on the evening of August 8, effective August 9, and was succeeded by Vice Pres. Gerald R. Ford.

BIBLIOGRAPHY. Earl Mazo and Stephen Hess, *Nixon: A Political Portrait* (1968); Theodore H. White, *The Making of the President 1968* and *1972* (1969; 1973); Rowland Evans, Jr., and Robert D. Novak, *Nixon in the White House: The Frustration of Power* (1971); Richard M. Nixon, *RN: The Memoirs of Richard Nixon* (1978).

·Chinese diplomatic relations **4**:399d
·economic policies and effects **18**:935a
·Japanese relations with China **10**:89f
·Nixon Doctrine basic statement and reiteration **18**:998c
·nomination and administration **18**:998b
·Vietnam War policies **19**:131a
·Washington, D.C., development **19**:622c

nixy (Germanic mythology): *see* nix.

niyama (in Indian philosophy): *see* yama.

Niyamānanda (Indian philosopher): *see* Nimbārka.

Niyazi, Ahmed (1873–1912), Ottoman military leader who led an uprising in July 1908 against the sultan Abdülhamid II.

·Young Turk Revolution precipitation **13**:789a

Niza, Marcos de, also called FRAY MARCOS (b. *c.* 1495, Nizza, Savoy, now Nice, Fr.—d. March 25, 1558, Mexico), Franciscan friar who claimed to have sighted the legendary "Seven Golden Cities of Cibola" in what is now western New Mexico, U.S. He went to the Americas in 1531 and served in Peru, Guatemala, and Mexico. At Culiacán, Mex., he freed Indian slaves from regions to the north. Under orders from the viceroy Antonio de Mendoza, Niza and a Moor, Esteban, led an expedition across the desert to the cities of Cibola (1539). Esteban was killed; Marcos claimed to have come within sight of large towns rich in precious stones, gold, and silver. The following year Francisco de Coronado found the "seven cities" to be small and poor Indian pueblos. Marcos became provincial of his order for Mexico in 1541.

Nizāmābād, also called INDUR, town and district, northwestern Andhra Pradesh state, southern India. The town is the district's headquarters; it is located on the Hyderābād–Godāvari Valley line of the Central Railway, north-northwest of Hyderābād. Historical points of interest include a temple that now houses a water supply tank, the fort of Indur, and a college of arts and science. Nizāmābād is situated in an area that grows sugarcane and is a focus for the local road system.

The district, on the Deccan Plateau, has an area of 3,077 sq mi (7,969 sq km). A reservoir dams the Mānjra River and irrigates the district's fields of sugarcane and rice. The district also provides valuable timber. Industrial centres include Bodhan and Kāmāreddi, which have sugar and alcohol factories. Pop. (1971) town, 115,640; district, 1,313,268.
18°40′ N, 76°06′ E

·map, India **9**:278

Niẓām al-Mulk **13**:135 (b. 1018 or 1019, near Ṭūs, Iran—d. Oct. 14, 1092, near Nehāvand), vizier (minister) of Iran for the Seljuq sultans in 1063–92. Niẓām al-Mulk (Persian: Regulator of the Kingdom) was his title; his personal name was Abū ʿAlī Ḥasan ibn ʿAlī. Niẓām al-Mulk was known for his unusual capabilities as statesman and for his influence in shaping the administration of the Seljuq dynasty.

Abstract of text biography. The son of a Persian administrative official, Niẓām al-Mulk rose to power following the Seljuq invasion. In spite of his position, he was unable to transform the government to suit his ideals completely. In his *Seyāsat-nāmeh* (*The Book of Government; or, Rules for Kings*, 1960) he criticized the Sultan for disregarding protocol and for his neglect of the intelligence service; he also criticized the Shīʿah branch of Islām, particularly the Ismāʿīlīyah sect. He was assassinated, probably by a member of a dissident sect.

REFERENCES in other text articles:
·ʿAbbāsid culture and the Seljuqs **3**:640g
·educational centres and the state **9**:922e
·Isfahan architectural development **9**:911b
·Islām under the sultans **9**:931c
·Seljuq counseling relationship **9**:856d
·Seljuq empire and Assassins **16**:504c
·writings on government **9**:965h

nizam-ı cedid (Turkish: "new order"), term originally applied to a program of westernizing reforms undertaken by the Ottoman sultan Selim III (*q.v.*; reigned 1789–1807); later it came to denote exclusively the new, regular troops established under this program.

In 1792–93 Selim III, assisted by a committee, promulgated a series of reforms that included new regulations on provincial governorships and taxation, on land tenure, and on the control of grain trade. More significant, however, were military reforms: a new corps of regular infantry trained and drilled on Western lines was founded; an attempt was made to introduce discipline into the decadent Janissary Corps (elite troops); new regulations were introduced into the artillery, bombardier, and miners corps; the fleet was reorganized; new military and naval schools provided training in gunnery, fortification, and navigation; technical and scientific books were translated into Turkish from Western languages. To finance these projects a special treasury was established.

The reforms were inspired by Western models, and in their application Selim had to rely heavily on French assistance. The growing French influence and the reforms evoked a strong reaction from a conservative coalition of the Janissaries and the *ʿulamāʾ* (men of religious learning). In 1805 that coalition was joined by *ayan* (local notables) of the Balkan provinces to stop an attempt to organize *nizam-ı cedid* troops in Edirne. In 1807 a mutiny of the *yamak*s (auxiliary levies) compelled Selim to abolish the reforms and brought about his deposition.
·organization, training, and financing **13**:784e

Niẓāmīyah, *madrasah*s (colleges of higher learning) founded by the Iranian vizier to the Seljuq sultans, Niẓām al-Mulk, to combat Shīʿī propaganda and to provide competent administrators throughout the empire. The first and best known was founded in Baghdad in 1065–67.
·al-Ghazālī's teaching **9**:931d
·history of education **6**:333a
·Nizām al-Mulk **13**:135h
·Seljuq educational system **11**:993f

Niẓām Shāhī dynasty, succession of rulers of the kingdom of Ahmadnagar in the Deccan of India from 1490 to 1637. The first ruler was Malik Aḥmad Niẓām-ul-Mulk, who in 1490 fixed his capital on a new site called Ahmadnagar after himself. The kingdom lay in the northwestern Deccan, between the states of Gujarāt and Bijāpur. It secured the great fortress of Daulatābād in 1499 and added Berār in 1574. The dynasty was engaged in constant warfare. Burhān Shāh (reigned 1509–53) allied with the Hindu state of Vijayanagar, but his successor Husain (reigned 1553–65) joined the alliance that overthrew it (1565). An attack by the Mughals from the north was gallantly resisted by Chānd Bībī, queen dowager of Bijāpur, but Berār was ceded (1596) and Ahmadnagar fell after her death (1600). A part of the state remained, and the dynasty survived until the fall of Daulatābād, in 1632.
·founding of Ahmadnagar kingdom **9**:372g

Niẓām-ul-Mulk (Governor of the Kingdom), title borne by various Indian Muslim princes. In 1713 it was conferred on Chīn Qilich Khān (Āṣaf Jāh from 1725) by the Mughal emperor and was held by his descendants, the rulers of the princely state of Hyderābād (*q.v.*), until the mid-20th century.
·Hyderābād under the Niẓāms **9**:76c
·independence of imperial rule **9**:385f
·Marāthā military rivalry **9**:389b

Nizār, an- (*c.* 11th–12th century), elder son of the Fāṭimid caliph al-Mustanṣir.
·Shīʿī internal conflicts **9**:932e

Nizārīs (Islāmic sect): *see* Ismāʿīlīyah.

Nizhnyaya Tunguska River, English LOWER TUNGUSKA, in Western Siberia, right-bank tributary of the Yenisey that flows through Krasnoyarsk *kray* (territory) and Irkutsk *oblast* (administrative region) of the Russian Soviet Federated Socialist Republic. Its length is 1,857 mi (2,989 km); the area of its basin is 187,900 sq mi (471,300 sq km). The river rises near the watershed between the Yenisey Basin and that of the Lena-Angara and flows in a generally westerly direction across the Central Siberian Plateau. Above its confluence with the Ilimpeya, it has a broad valley with numerous sandbanks, but below this point the valley narrows, and there are numerous gorges and rapids. In the river basin lies the extensive Tunguska coalfield.
65°48′ N, 88°04′ E
·map, Soviet Union **17**:323

Nizhny Novgorod (Russian S.F.S.R.): *see* Gorky.

Nizhny Tagil, city, Sverdlovsk *oblast* (administrative region), western Russian Soviet Federated Socialist Republic, on the Tagil River. One of the oldest smelting centres of the Urals, it was founded in 1725 in connection with the construction of a metallurgical factory that used iron ore of Vysokaya Gora. It became a city in 1917 and is now an important iron and steel centre. Manufactures include machine tools, railway cars, and building materials. Teachers and mining colleges are located in the city as well as an applied-art college. Pop. (1979 prelim.) 398,000.
57°55′ N, 59°57′ E
·map, Soviet Union **17**:322

Nizip (NEZIB), **Battle of** (June 24, 1839), military clash between forces of the Ottoman Empire and those of Muḥammad ʿAlī Pasha, viceroy of Egypt, at Nizip (now in southeastern Turkey), in which the Ottomans were defeated. Their empire was spared only by the intervention of Great Britain, Austria, Russia, and Prussia.

The Convention of Kütahya (1833) that awarded the Ottomans' Syrian provinces and Adana to Muḥammad ʿAlī was not satisfactory to either party, and a new war developed. The Ottoman Army was decisively defeated at Nizip by Egyptian forces under Muḥammad ʿAlī's son Ibrāhīm, and the Ottoman fleet surrendered at Alexandria. The great powers, except France, intervened on behalf of the Ottomans, forcing the Egyptians to evacuate Syria in 1840. On Feb. 3, 1841, Sultan Abdülmecid I (*q.v.*) signed a *firman* (official edict) appointing Muḥammad ʿAlī as hereditary governor of Egypt.
·Muhammad ʿAlī Pasha **12**:610f

Nízké Tatry (mountains, Czechoslovakia): *see* Tatras.

Nizwa (Oman): *see* Nazwā.

Njala, town, Southern Province, south central Sierra Leone, on the Jong (Taia) River. The town, headquarters of the Department of Agriculture until independence in 1961, is the site of an experimental farm and oil-palm nursery. Its agricultural and teacher-training schools, incorporated as Njala University College in 1963, became a constituent part of the University of Sierra Leone in 1967. Local Mende farmers are engaged in the cultivation of rice, ginger, and palm oil and kernels. Pop. (latest census) 561.
8°07′ N, 12°05′ W

Njáls saga, called NJÁLA for short, one of the longest and generally considered the finest of the 13th-century Icelandic family sagas. It presents the most comprehensive picture of Icelandic life in the heroic age and has a wide range of complex characters. Its two heroes—Gunnar and Njáll—are men of peace, but, in a society in which the ties of blood impose inescapable obligations and the memories of past injuries may always be rekindled, neither Gunnar's good will nor Njáll's wisdom can save them from their fate.

Gunnar meets death at the hands of his enemies when his wife, the beautiful but capricious Hallgerd, in retaliation for a blow he once gave her in anger, refuses him a strand of her hair to string his bow.

Njáll is drawn into a feud through the headstrong actions of his sons. He accepts the consequences stoically in a powerful scene in which he and his family are burned to death in their home by a reluctant "enemy," whose honour demands this vengeance. A third part deals with the vengeance for Njáll by his son-in-law Kári, the sole survivor of the family.

The characters of the *Njála* are vividly drawn and range from comic to sinister. The high tide of Icelandic life is revealed in the meetings of the heroes at the Althing (parliament) in times of peace and good fortune; but the overriding mood is one of pessimism.
·folk literature of Iceland **16**:146h
·major Icelanders' sagas **10**:1119b

Njarasa, Lake (Tanzania): *see* Eyasi, Lake.

Njemen River (U.S.S.R.): *see* Neman River.

Njörd, Old Norse NJÖRDR, in Norse mythology, god of the sea and its riches. He was the father of Freyr and Freyja (*qq.v.*) by his own sister. Traditionally, Njörd's native tribe, the Vanir, gave him as a hostage to the rival tribe of Aesir, the giantess Skadi (*q.v.*) choosing him to be her husband. The marriage failed because Njörd preferred to live in Nóatún, his home by the sea, while Skadi was happier in her father's mountain dwelling place. Several traditions hold that Njörd was a divine ruler of the Swedes, and his name appears in numerous Scandinavian place-names.
·Germanic Aesir and Vanir myths **8**:36f

Njuli cults, religious movements in southeast Borneo after World War I.
·Islāmic-influenced tribal cults **18**:704c

Nkambe, town and district in Northwest province, Donga-Mantung department, Cameroon. Pop. (1970) town, 5,000; (1976) district, 133,921.
·map, Cameroon **3**:697

Nketia, J.H. Kwabena (b. June 22, 1921, Mampong, Ashanti, Gold Coast, now Ghana), musicologist and author of numerous articles on African music and culture whose *Funeral Dirges of the Akan People* (1955) and *Folk Songs of Ghana* (1963) are among the best and most authentic collections of oral traditions produced by African writers and scholars. In addition to his folk collections, Nketia has published numerous books in the Twi language. He served as director of the Institute of African Studies at the University of Ghana and in 1969 became a professor of music at the University of California at Los Angeles.

Nkhata Bay, administrative headquarters of Nkhata Bay District, northern Malawi. Its port has a sheltered anchorage on the western shore of Lake Nyasa near the mouth of the Luweya River and is equipped with modern floating and piled jetties. It exports the

Jetty at Nkhata Bay on Lake Nyasa, Malawi
D. Rawson—Photo Researchers

agricultural produce of the hinterland. It is also a noted scenic spot where the Vipya Mountains descend to the lake and has tourist rest houses. The district (area 1,576 sq mi [4,082 sq km] extends about 90 mi (145 km) along the lakeshore from Ruarwe south to Bandawe. Tea is grown on an experimental basis, and there is subsistence fishing along the rapids of the Luweya River. Pop. (latest census) town, 1,188; district, 83,911.
·area and population table **11**:362
·map, Malawi **11**:361

Nkhotakota, formerly NKOTA KOTA or KOTA KOTA, administrative headquarters of Nkhotakota District, central Malawi, on Lake Nyasa. It originated as a group of villages in the 19th century, served as a depot for Arab slave traders, and is now the largest traditional African town in the country. It is situated on the slope of a rocky ridge overlooking a natural harbour, formed by a north–south sand spit. A trading centre for the produce of the district (rice, maize [corn], cotton, fish), it also has a tourist industry depending upon natural hot springs and a rest house. The district (area 1,641 sq mi [4,250 sq km]) occupies a narrow strip along the lake's western shore and includes the isolated 435,200-ac (176,100-ha) Nkhotakota Game Reserve (established 1954). Pop. (latest census) town, 1,117; district, 62,918.
12°55′ S, 34°17′ E
·area and population table **11**:362

Nkole, also called ANKOLE, BANYANKOLE, or NYANKOLE, people of the Interlacustrine Bantu group who occupy the area between Lakes Edward and George and the Tanzania border in southwestern Uganda. A 1971 estimate places their numbers in excess of 500,000.

Though they speak a common Bantu language, the Nkole are divided into two quite distinct social groups: the pastoral Hima (10 percent) and the agricultural Iru (90 percent). Though marriage between Hima and Iru was traditionally prohibited, each borrowed extensively from the culture of the other. Both groups are divided into patrilineal clans and groups. Both marry with the payment of a substantial bride-price in livestock. Polygyny is general.

The differing economic pursuits of Hima and Iru give rise to different modes of life. The Hima live in scattered kraals (fenced homesteads) about a mile apart, each containing a number of different families. They subsist almost entirely on the products of their herds. The Iru are sedentary hoe cultivators, for whom the staple crop is eleusine. They live in settlements consisting of from 40 to 100 homesteads. Much Nkole traditional history is concerned with explaining how the two groups came to found a single society.

The Nkole maintained a despotic state, headed by the *mugabe* (king). Hima were bound to the *mugabe* by an oath of fealty. Iru headmen were appointed over communities of their fellows, and through them Hima chiefs collected tribute. When the British took up the Uganda Protectorate, the Nkole were recognized as a separate kingdom.
·numbers, tribal affiliations, and culture **6**:109h
·sacrificial customs **16**:132f

Nkonde, also called NGONDE, central African tribe of Malawi.
·Malawi's ethnic composition **11**:361h

nkongi, a Congolese group of fetishes consisting mainly of human figures.
·human and animal forms and use of metal **1**:273d

Nkongsamba, also spelled N'KONGSAMBA, or NKONGSOMBA, headquarters of Mungo department, East Cameroon state, Cameroon, near the border of West Cameroon state. It is the terminus of the railway from Douala and has road connections to Bamenda (north), Bafoussam (northeast), and Buea (southwest). Its pleasant climate makes it a popular tourist resort, and its teacher-training school attracts students from nearby towns. Large palm-oil, banana, and coffee plantations in the area make Nkongsamba a commercial centre. Coffee and tobacco from the north are shipped via rail to Douala for export. The town has a sawmill and a food-processing plant. Nkongsamba is served by an airfield, hospital, Roman Catholic and Protestant missions. Pop. (1970 est.) 71,000.
4°57′ N, 9°56′ E
·map, Cameroon **3**:696

Nkosi, Lewis (b. 1938, Natal, S.Af.), author, critic, journalist, and broadcaster. A trenchant critic, he has held that most South African writers produce journalism rather than art. He was exiled from South Africa from 1960, when he accepted a Nieman Fellowship to study journalism at Harvard.

After attending the M.L. Sultan College for Advanced Technical Education in Durban for a year, he worked as a journalist first in 1955 for *Ilanga lase Natal* ("Natal Sun") and then as chief reporter for the *Drum* magazine and its Sunday newspaper, the *Post*. Living in a Johannesburg ghetto gave him a greater understanding of his criticism that most black South African writers produce journalistic rather than meditative novels: he found life there too transient, too harried, too degraded by the laws of apartheid to be conducive to reflective writing.

From 1961 Nkosi wrote for U.S., British, and African periodicals. Many of his critical essays were published in *Home and Exile* (1965; awarded a prize at the Dakar World Festival of Negro Arts).

The Rhythm of Violence, a drama set in Johannesburg in the early 1960s, handles the theme of race relations, both ideologically and practically. Nkosi worked in the 1960s and 1970s as literary editor of *The New African*, as host-moderator for a National Educational Television (New York City) series on modern African writers, and as a free-lance writer in London.

Nkota Kota (Malawi): *see* Nkhotakota.

Nkoya, central African people of Zambia.
·Zambia ethnic composition map **19**:1132

Nkrumah, Kwame 13:136 (b. September 1909, Nkroful, Gold Coast, now Ghana—d. April 27, 1972, Bucharest, Romania), first prime minister of Ghana and president of the republic, headed the country from independence in 1957 to 1966.

Abstract of text biography. Nkrumah graduated from Achimota College in 1930, taught at Catholic junior schools in Elmina and Axim, and later studied in the United States and at the London School of Economics. Opposed to British rule in his country, he published *Towards Colonial Freedom* in 1947; and in 1948 he began publishing the *Accra Evening News* as a vehicle for his views. In 1949 he formed the Convention People's Party and in 1950 initiated a campaign of non-cooperation with the British authorities. In the first general elections in 1951 Nkrumah's party won, and he became the first prime minister in 1952. After independence in 1957 Nkrumah forced the regional opposition parties to merge and secured legalization of imprisonment without trial for security risks with the Preventive Detention Act of 1958. When Ghana became a republic in 1960, he became its president. Failure of the Second Development Plan in 1961 and an attempt on his life in 1962 resulted in tightened internal security measures, and in 1964 he declared Ghana a one-party state. The army seized power from Nkrumah while he was on a trip to China in 1966; he was granted asylum in Guinea, where he was named co-head of state. His published works include *Handbook of Revolutionary Warfare* (1968) and *Class Struggle in Africa* (1970).

REFERENCES in other text articles:
·Ghana national economy mismanagement **8**:141f
·Gold coast independence role and Ghana political leadership **19**:784a *passim* to 785c
·socialist role **16**:972f

NKVD, in full NARODNY KOMISSARIAT VNUTRENNIKH DEL, in English PEOPLE'S COMMISSARIAT OF INTERNAL AFFAIRS, Soviet police agency (1934–43) responsible for internal security and corrective labour camps. The NKGB (the agency in charge of state security within the NKVD) became an independent commissariat in 1943 and remained in charge of state security until 1946. Concerned mainly with political offenders, the NKVD used its broad investigative and judicial powers to carry out Stalin's massive purges of the 1930s. Ultimately, the purges extended to the NKVD itself, involving even its leaders Genrikh Yagoda (1934–36) and Nikolay Yezhov (1936–38). After Yezhov's removal, Lavrenty Beria headed the NKVD until March 1946, when it was dissolved and all the people's commissariats were renamed ministries. At that time, the NKVD became the MVD.
·forced labour conditions in Russia **16**:864d
·Soviet economic planning system **6**:256h
·Soviet intelligence preceding KGB **9**:684a

NLF: *see* National Liberation Front.

NLRB: *see* National Labor Relations Board.

Nmai Hka, English NMAI RIVER, in northern Burma, rises in the Languela glacier and flows generally south, joining the Mali Hka to form the Irrawaddy River. The Nmai, virtually unnavigable because of the strong current, is about 300 mi (480 km) long.
25°42′ N, 97°30′ E
·Irrawaddy River at source **9**:898e
·map, Burma **3**:505
·Yunnan's drainage pattern **19**:1114a

N-manifold (mathematics): *see* manifold.

NMC, in full NATIONAL METEOROLOGICAL CENTER, Washington, D.C., U.S., meteorological centre housing the National Weather Service.
·weather prediction and forecast **2**:327f

NMR: *see* nuclear magnetic resonance.

No, chemical symbol for the element nobelium (*q.v.*).

NOAA, in full NATIONAL OCEANIC AND ATMOSPHERIC ADMINISTRATION (1970), U.S. government agency.
·weather prediction and forecast **2**:327f

Noachian Laws (Judaism): *see* Noahide Laws.

Noah, also spelled NOE, the hero of the biblical Flood story in the Old Testament book of Genesis, the originator of vineyard cultivation, and, as the father of Shem, Ham, and Japheth, the representative head of a Semitic genealogical line. A synthesis of at least three biblical source traditions, Noah, whose name in Semitic means Rest or Comfort, is the image of the righteous man made party to a covenant with Yahweh, the God of Israel, in which nature's stability against catastrophe is assured.

The oldest Hebrew tradition recorded in the Old Testament (Gen. 9:20–27) presents Noah as a farmer and the first to plant a vineyard. Noah reflects the diversity of the biblical sources and the mixed attitude toward wine drinking. Often commended, wine is sometimes disapproved, a feeling probably reflecting a nomadic culture that does not drink wine. Noah's drunkenness and the disrespect it provokes in his son Ham (or Canaan) suggests, moreover, that the Flood did not cure man's sinful nature. Noah's curse on Ham and his descendants may symbolize the ethnic and social division of Palestine: the Israelites (from the line of Shem) will separate from the pre-Israelite population (Canaan and, by extension, Egypt, depicted as licentious), who will live in subjection to the Hebrews.

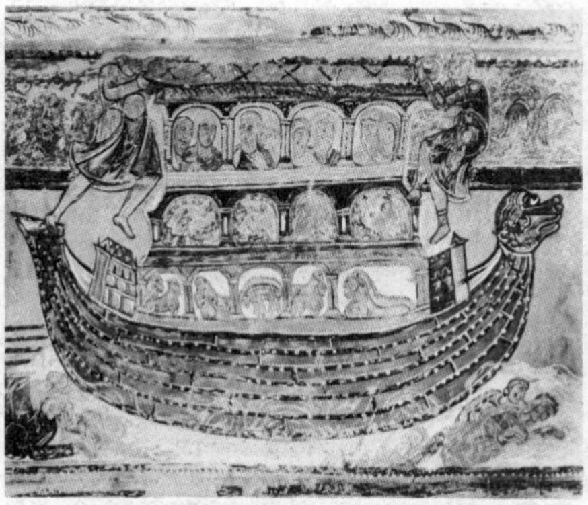

Noah's ark, 12th-century fresco in the nave of the church at Saint-Savin-sur-Gartempe, Fr.

Jean Roubier

According to another tradition given in Genesis, Noah is a good, quiet man identified with the hero of the Mesopotamian story of the Flood (Gen. 6:11-9:19). The last of the pre-Flood sheikhs, he and his family, in a test of obedience to God's command, alone were saved in an ark of gopherwood, when the rest of mankind were destroyed. In the ark he took with him specimens of all kinds of living creatures, whereby the species were providentially preserved. Consequently, according to this narrative, the entire surviving human race descended from Noah's three sons. Such a genealogy set a universal frame within which the subsequent role of Abraham, as the father of Israel's faith, assumed its proper dimensions. The Genesis story appears to have been at least materially influenced by similar ancient Middle Eastern traditions, such as the stone-tablet record of the Sumerian and Mesopotamian Gilgamesh epic.

The religious meaning of the Flood is conveyed after Noah's heroic survival. He then built an altar on which he offered burnt sacrifices to God, who then bound himself to a pact never again to curse the earth on man's account. For this covenant the rainbow is the stipulated token; *i.e.*, visible guarantee (Gen. 8:20–9:17). God also renews his commands given at creation with two changes: man can now kill animals and eat meat, and the murder of a man will be punished by men.

In the New Testament Noah is mentioned in the genealogy of the Gospel According to Luke (3:36) that delineates Jesus' descent from Adam. Jesus also uses the story of the Flood that came on a worldly generation of men "in the days of Noah" as an example of Baptism, and Noah is depicted as a preacher of repentance to the men of his time, a predominant theme in Jewish apocryphal and rabbinical writings.

The story of Noah was a popular theme in Christian art during the Middle Ages.

·ark legendary location **18**:782g
·Islām and prophetic messengers **9**:914a
·Jewish–Babylonian flood epic parallels **10**:191g
·Mesopotamian correspondences **11**:1008b
·Near East common thought on sacrifice **12**:919c
·Near East covenantal prototype **12**:921b
·Old Testament account of the Flood **2**:899g

Noah covenant: *see* covenants, biblical.

Noahide (NOACHIAN) **Laws,** a Jewish Talmudic designation for seven biblical laws given to Adam and to Noah before the revelation on Mt. Sinai and consequently binding on all mankind.

Using Gen. 2:16 as a starting point of exegesis, the Babylonian Talmud listed the first six commandments as prohibitions against idol worship, blasphemy, murder, adultery, and robbery and the positive command to establish courts of justice (with all that this implies). After the Flood a seventh commandment, given to Noah, forbade the eating of flesh cut from a living animal (Gen. 9:4).

Though the number of laws was later increased to 30 with the addition of prohibitions against castration, sorcery, and other practices, the "seven laws," with minor variations, retained their original status as authoritative and as the source of other laws.

As basic statutes safeguarding monotheism and guaranteeing proper ethical conduct in society, these laws provided a legal framework for alien residents in Jewish territory. Maimonides thus regarded anyone who observed these laws as one "assured of a portion in the world to come." Throughout the ages scholars have viewed the Noahide Laws as a link between Judaism and Christianity, as universal norms of ethical conduct, as a basic concept in international law, or as a guarantee of fundamental human rights for all.

In addition to the Noahide Laws, Jews are further obliged to observe the laws proper to their own religion.

·Jewish political and moral philosophy **10**:214c

Noailles, French noble family, named for its medieval lordship of Noailles in Limousin. Notable in public affairs since the 16th century when Antoine (1504–62) became admiral of France (1547) and was ambassador to England (1553–56); his brother François (1519–85) was bishop of Dax from 1555, ambassador to England (1556–57), to Venice (1557–69), and to the Ottoman Empire (1572); and a third brother, Gilles (1524–97), preceded Francois as ambassador to England, was ambassador to Poland and the Ottoman Empire, and succeeded him as bishop of Dax. The family accumulated hereditary honours in both France and Spain.

Noailles, Louis-Marie, vicomte de (1756–1804), served with Lafayette in the U.S. War of Independence; was a deputy in the French States General of 1789, where he proposed the abolition of "feudal" (seigniorial) privileges. He emigrated to the U.S. in 1792 and took part in French operations in Haiti in 1803.

Noailles, Louis-Antoine, cardinal de (1651–1729), archbishop of Paris from 1695 and cardinal from 1700, is famous for his obstruction (sustained despite embarrassments until 1728) of the French government's efforts to have Jansenism condemned by the French episcopacy as well as by Rome.

Noailles, Anna (-Élisabeth, princess Brancovan, comtesse Mathieu) de (b. Nov. 15, 1876, Paris—d. April 30, 1933, Paris), poet, a leading literary light in France in the pre-World War I period.

The daughter of a Romanian prince and granddaughter of a Turkish pasha, she adopted France and its language for her life and writings even before her marriage to a French count. Every gift was lavished on her: wealth, beauty, love, motherhood. Her friends included the novelists Marcel Proust and Colette and the poets Paul Valéry and Jean Cocteau. In her literary salon she kept most of the writers of her time under the spell of her inexhaustible verbal magic. Her volumes of poems, *Le Coeur innombrable* (1901; "The Numberless Heart"), *Les Éblouissements* (1907; "Resplendence"), and *L'Honneur de souffrir* (1927; "The Honour of Suffering"), are vibrant with a sensual love of nature. Her lyricism draws from the great Romantic themes of the 19th-century poets Alfred de Vigny and Alphonse de Lamartine. Her later works reflect her terror at the thought of the inevitable collapse of her physical powers. She was made a commander of the Légion d'Honneur and elected to the Académie Royale de Langue et de Littérature Française de Belgique.

Noākhāli, administrative headquarters, Noākhāli District, Chittagong Division, Bangladesh (formerly East Pakistan), on the Noākhāli Khal (New Cut Watercourse) near the Meghna Estuary. The port is connected by road and rail with Comilla and by steamer with Barisāl. Industries include handloom cotton weaving and brassware manufacture. Formerly called Sudhārām, the city was constituted a municipality in 1876 and contains three government colleges affiliated with the University of Dacca.

Noākhāli District (area 1,855 sq mi [4,804 sq km]), formerly called Bhulua, was constituted in 1822. It comprises a mainland tract and numerous islands in the Meghna River mouth, the largest of which are Sandwīp and Hātia. The mainland alluvial plain is annually inundated and fertilized by silt deposits from the Meghna Estuary; it is broken only by a hilly tract in the northeast known as Bāraiyādhāla. Rice, jute, oilseeds, pulses, betel nuts, chillies, and sugarcane are the chief crops. Latest census city, 19,874; district, 2,383,145.

·map, Bangladesh **2**:688

Nōami, also called SHINNŌ (b. 1397, Japan—d. 1494), poet, painter, and art critic, the first nonpriest who painted in the *suiboku* ("water-ink"), or Chinese, style. He was in charge of the art collection of Ashikaga Yoshimitsu, the military dictator who ruled Japan from 1368 to 1394, and was perhaps the first great art expert in Japan. His catalog of Yoshimitsu's collection, *Kundaikan sayū chōki* (1476; "A Treatise on the Scrolls in the Lord's Watchtower"), is invaluable as an early Japanese appraisal of Chinese artists.

Many of Nōami's paintings have been preserved. Among the best known are "The Pines of Miho," a landscape executed on a screen in the soft ink-wash technique associated with Mu-ch'i Fa-ch'ang, the 13th-century Chinese priest-painter whose work Nōami admired, and "The White-robed Kannon," a portrait in ink of the Buddhist goddess of mercy painted for his child's memorial service. Nōami's son, Geiami (died 1485), and grandson, Sōami, also served the Ashikaga court as painters and art advisers; together they are known as the San Ami (Three Amis).

nobat, Malaysian instrumental ensemble dating back to the 16th century.

·Malaysian historical tradition **17**:241a

Nobatae, also called X-GROUP, Nubian tribe that settled in The Sudan in the 6th through 8th centuries.

·Medieval Meroitic culture **13**:109h

Nobatia, 6th-century Christian kingdom of the Nilotic Sudan.

·Christianity in medieval Sudan **13**:109h
·visual art forms and style **19**:257g

Nobel, Alfred Bernhard (b. Oct. 21, 1833, Stockholm—d. Dec. 10, 1896, San Remo, Italy), chemist, engineer, and industrialist who invented dynamite and other, more powerful, explosives and founded the Nobel prizes. Through his mother he was descended from the Swedish naturalist Olof Rudbeck, noted for his discovery of the lymphatic vessels (*c.* 1653). From his father, Immanuel Nobel, he learned the fundamentals of engineering, and, like his father, he had a talent for invention.

The Nobel family left Stockholm in 1842 to join the father in St. Petersburg (Leningrad). Educated mainly by tutors, young Nobel was a competent chemist at 16 and was fluent in English, French, German, Russian, and Swedish. He left Russia in 1850 to spend a year studying chemistry in Paris and four years in the U.S. working under the direction of John Ericsson, builder of the ironclad warship "Monitor." Upon his return to St. Petersburg, Nobel worked in his father's factory until the firm went bankrupt in 1859.

Alfred Nobel, portrait (from a photograph) by Emil Österman, 1915; in the Nobel Foundation, Stockholm

By courtesy of the Svenska Portrattarkivet

Returning to Sweden, Nobel began the manufacture of the liquid explosive nitroglycerin. Shortly after production got under way in 1864, the factory blew up, causing the death of his youngest brother, Emil, and four other persons. Forbidden by the Swedish government to rebuild the factory, Nobel, who had become stereotyped as a "mad scientist," began experimenting on a barge in a lake to find a way to reduce the danger of handling nitroglycerin. A chance discovery that the substance was absorbed to dryness by an organic packing material and could thus be handled safely led him to perfect dynamite and the necessary detonating cap. Granted patents for dynamite in Britain (1867) and the U.S. (1868), he further experimented and developed a more powerful form of dynamite, blasting gelatin, patented in 1876. About a decade later, he produced ballistite, one of the first nitroglycerin smokeless powders. His claim that the ballistite patent also covered cordite was rejected by the courts.

Nobel's worldwide interests in explosives, as well as large holdings in the Baku oil fields of Russia, brought him an immense fortune but required him to travel almost constantly. He had the inclinations of a recluse, however. Though he was essentially a pacifist and hoped that the destructive powers of his inventions would help bring an end to wars, his view of mankind and nations was pessimistic. He had an abiding interest in literature, and in his youth he had written poetry in English. After his death, the beginnings of a novel were found among his papers.

Generous in humanitarian and scientific philanthropies, he left the bulk of his fortune in trust to establish what came to be the most highly regarded of international awards, the Nobel prizes for peace, literature, physics, chemistry, and physiology or medicine. The Nobel Prize for Economics was established (and funded) by the National Bank of Sweden in 1968.

·nitroglycerin and dynamite development **7**:84e

Nobel, Immanuel (1801–72), Swedish architect, engineer, and inventor, manufacturer of steamships and underwater explosives for the Russian government; the father of Alfred Nobel.

·nitroglycerin detonation development **7**:84e

nobelium, symbol No, synthetic chemical element of the actinide series in Group IIIb of the periodic table, 10th transuranium element, atomic number 102. Not occurring in nature, nobelium (as the isotope nobelium-254) was unambiguously discovered (April 1958) by Albert Ghiorso, T. Sikkeland, J.R. Walton, and Glenn T. Seaborg at the University of California, Berkeley, by the bombardment of curium (atomic number 96) with carbon ions (atomic number 6) accelerated in a heavy-ion linear accelerator. An international team of scientists working at the Nobel Institute of Physics in Stockholm claimed less than a year before that they had synthesized the same element, which they named nobelium (for Alfred Nobel); but experiments performed in the Soviet Union (at the I.V. Kurchatov Institute of Atomic Energy, Moscow, and at Dubna) and in the United States (Berkeley) failed to confirm the discovery. The Berkeley and Dubna teams have subsequently produced more than a half dozen isotopes of nobelium; nobelium-255 (three-minute half-life) is the stablest. Using traces of this isotope, radiochemists have shown nobelium to exist in aqueous solution in both the +2 and +3 oxidation states. The +2 state is very stable, an effect more pronounced than was anticipated in comparison with the homologous lanthanide element ytterbium (atomic number 70).

atomic number	102
stablest isotope	255
valence	2,3
electronic config.	2-8-18-32-32-8-2 or (Rn)$5f^{14}7s^2$

Major ref. **1**:70g

·transuranium elements, tables 1 and 2 **18**:679

Nobel prizes, awarded annually in physics, chemistry, physiology or medicine, literature, and peace since 1901, under the terms of the will of Alfred Nobel, Swedish chemist and engineer, who died in 1896. A sixth prize, for economics, was instituted in 1968 by the National Bank of Sweden and was first awarded in 1969. The prizes in physics, chemistry, and economics are awarded by the Royal Swedish Academy of Sciences; in physiology or medicine by the Royal Caroline Medico-Chirurgical Institute; in literature by the Swedish Academy; and in peace by the Nobel Committee, appointed by the Norwegian Storting (Parliament). (For lists of Nobel prize winners by year, *see* pages 369–372.)

·artistic stimulus of awards **2**:102a

·Swedish origin and administration **17**:854c

Nobeoka, city, Miyazaki Prefecture (*ken*), Kyushu, Japan, on the delta of the Gokasegawa (*gawa*, "river"). It developed as a castle town in the 12th century and has been a fishing port since the mid-18th century. Nobeoka is now the largest industrial city of the prefecture, housing several large chemical plants. Pearls are cultivated along the coast, and rice and wheat are grown in the surrounding area. Pop. (1977 est.) 136,543.

32°35′ N, 131°40′ E

·map, Japan **10**:37

Nobile, Umberto (b. Jan. 21, 1885, Lauro, near Salerno, Italy—d. July 30, 1978, Rome), aeronautical engineer and pioneer in Arctic aviation who in 1926, with the Norwegian explorer Roald Amundsen and Lincoln Ellsworth of the U.S., flew over the North Pole in the dirigible "Norge," from Spitsbergen, north of Norway, to Alaska. As a general in the Italian Air Force and a professor of aeronautical engineering at the University of Naples in 1928, Nobile began a new series of flights over unexplored Arctic regions with a craft similar to the "Norge." On the third flight the airship crashed on the ice north-northeast of Spitsbergen. Though Nobile and 7 companions were rescued, 17 lives were lost. When an Italian commission of inquiry found him responsible for the disaster, he resigned his commission. In 1931 he took part in a Soviet voyage to the Arctic. After World War II the commission's report was discredited, and he was reinstated in the air force. He resumed teaching at Naples and was a deputy in the Italian Constituent Assembly (1946). Nobile's own account of his Arctic adventures is given in *Gli italiani al Polo Nord* (1959; *My Polar Flights*, 1961).

nobility, the body of persons forming the noble class; *i.e.*, the class in a community having pre-eminence over others. *See* baron; count; duke; earl; margrave; marquess; viscount. *See also* related articles baronet; chivalry; knight; knighthood, orders of; page.

·aristocracy in Middle Ages **12**:143h

Noble, Sir Andrew, 1st Baronet (b. Sept. 13, 1831, Greenock, Renfrew—d. Oct. 22, 1915, Argyll), physicist and gunnery expert, considered a founder of the science of ballistics. His pioneering research on fired gunpowder, often in conjunction with the British chemist Frederick Abel, contributed greatly to the progress of gunnery.

Educated at Edinburgh Academy and the Royal Military Academy, Woolwich, London, he entered the Royal Artillery in 1849. As secretary of the Select Committee on the Relative Merits of Smoothbore and Rifled Cannon, he devised a method of comparing the accuracy of fire of each gun. He became assistant inspector of artillery in 1859 but later left the service to join the engineering and ordnance firm of Sir William (later Lord) Armstrong, of which he became chairman in 1900.

About 1862 he applied his invention, the chronoscope, a device for measuring very small time intervals, to determine the velocity of shot in gun barrels. His experiments helped establish the science of ballistics and also led to new types of gunpowder, the redesigning of guns, and new methods of loading. Noble was elected a fellow of the Royal Society (1870) and was created a baronet (1902).

noble gases and their compounds 13:137, a family of six chemical elements (known as Group 0 of the periodic table) and the compounds formed by those elements. The noble gases are helium (symbol He, atomic number 2), neon (Ne, 10), argon (Ar, 18), krypton (Kr, 36), xenon (Xe, 54), and radon (Rn, 86). The term noble alludes to the extreme lack of chemical reactivity of these gases.

The text article covers the occurrence, uses, and discovery of the individual members of the group; the relationship of their stability to their electronic structures; their physical properties; and the structures, properties, and reactions of the compounds of the noble gas elements.

REFERENCES in other text articles:

·atmospheric deficiency theories **2**:314g

·atmospheric sources of argon and helium **6**:711g

·chemical bond electronic stability **4**:85f

·electric lamp development **10**:959a

·electron distribution and reactivity **4**:169g

·gas production process and uses **7**:925h

·helium and argon in natural gas **12**:860e

·periodic law development and gas discovery **14**:75h

·platinum–xenon reaction **18**:625g

RELATED ENTRIES in the *Ready Reference and Index: for*

noble gases: see argon; helium; krypton; neon; radon; xenon

compounds: xenon compounds

noble metal, any of several metallic chemical elements that have outstanding resistance to oxidation, even at high temperatures; the grouping is not strictly defined but usually is considered to include rhenium, ruthenium,

Nobel prize winners*

	physics			chemistry		
1901	Wilhelm Röntgen	(Ger.)	discovery of X-rays	Jacobus Van't Hoff	(Neth.)	laws of chemical dynamics and osmotic pressure
1902	Hendrik Antoon Lorentz	(Neth.)	investigation of the influence of magnetism on radiation	Emil Fischer	(Ger.)	work on sugar and purine syntheses
	Pieter Zeeman	(Neth.)				
1903	Antoine-Henri Becquerel	(Fr.)	discovery of spontaneous radioactivity	Svante Arrhenius	(Swed.)	theory of electrolytic dissociation
	Pierre Curie	(Fr.)	investigations of radiation phenomena discovered by A.-H. Becquerel			
	Marie Curie†	(Fr.)‡				
1904	Lord Rayleigh	(Brit.)	discovery of argon	Sir William Ramsay	(Brit.)	discovery of inert gas elements and their places in the periodic system
1905	Philipp Lenard	(Ger.)	research on cathode rays	Adolf von Baeyer	(Ger.)	work on organic dyes, hydroaromatic compounds
1906	Sir J.J. Thomson	(Brit.)	researches into electrical conductivity of gases	Henri Moissan	(Fr.)	isolation of fluorine; introduction of Moissan furnace
1907	A.A. Michelson	(U.S.)‡	spectroscopic and metrological investigations	Eduard Buchner	(Ger.)	discovery of noncellular fermentation
1908	Gabriel Lippmann	(Fr.)	photographic reproduction of colours	Lord Rutherford	(Brit.)	investigations into the disintegration of elements and the chemistry of radioactive substances
1909	Guglielmo Marconi	(Italy)	development of wireless telegraphy	Wilhelm Ostwald	(Ger.)	pioneer work on catalysis, chemical equilibrium and reaction velocities
	Karl Braun	(Ger.)				
1910	J. van der Waals	(Neth.)	research concerning the equation of state of gases and liquids	Otto Wallach	(Ger.)	pioneer work in alicyclic combinations
1911	Wilhelm Wien	(Ger.)	discoveries regarding laws governing heat radiation	Marie Curie†	(Fr.)‡	discovery of radium and polonium; isolation of radium
1912	Nils Gustaf Dalén	(Swed.)	invention of automatic regulators for lighting coastal beacons and light buoys	Victor Grignard	(Fr.)	discovery of the Grignard reagents
				Paul Sabatier	(Fr.)	method of hydrogenating organic compounds
1913	H. Kamerlingh Onnes	(Neth.)	investigation into the properties of matter at low temperatures; production of liquid helium	Alfred Werner	(Switz.)‡	work on the linkage of atoms in molecules
1914	Max von Laue	(Ger.)	discovery of diffraction of X-rays by crystals	Theodore Richards	(U.S.)	accurate determination of the atomic weights of numerous elements
1915	Sir William Bragg	(Brit.)	analysis of crystal structure by means of X-rays	Richard Willstätter	(Ger.)	pioneer researches on plant pigments, especially chlorophyll
	Sir Lawrence Bragg	(Brit.)				
1916	(no award)	—	—	(no award)	—	—
1917	Charles Barkla	(Brit.)	discovery of characteristic X-radiation of elements	(no award)	—	—
1918	Max Planck	(Ger.)	discovery of the elemental quanta	Fritz Haber	(Ger.)	synthesis of ammonia
1919	Johannes Stark	(Ger.)	discovery of Doppler effect in positive ion rays and division of spectral lines in electric field	(no award)	—	—
1920	Charles Guillaume	(Switz.)	discovery of anomalies in alloys	Walther Nernst	(Ger.)	work in thermochemistry
1921	Albert Einstein	(Switz.)‡	services to theoretical physics	Frederick Soddy	(Brit.)	chemistry of radioactive substances; occurrence and nature of isotopes
1922	Niels Bohr	(Den.)	investigation of atomic structure and radiation	Francis Aston	(Brit.)	work with mass spectrograph; whole-number rule
1923	Robert Millikan	(U.S.)	work on elementary electric charge and the photoelectric effect	Fritz Pregl	(Austria)	method of microanalysis of organic substances
1924	Karl Siegbahn	(Swed.)	work in X-ray spectroscopy	(no award)	—	—
1925	James Franck	(Ger.)	discovery of the laws governing the impact of an electron upon an atom	Richard Zsigmondy	(Austria)	elucidation of the heterogeneous nature of colloidal solutions
	Gustav Hertz	(Ger.)				
1926	Jean-Baptiste Perrin	(Fr.)	work on discontinuous structure of matter	Theodor Svedberg	(Swed.)	work on disperse systems
1927	Arthur Holly Compton	(U.S.)	discovery of wave-length change in diffused X-rays	Heinrich Wieland	(Ger.)	researches into the constitution of bile acids
	Charles Wilson	(Brit.)	method of making visible the paths of electrically charged particles			
1928	Sir Owen Richardson	(Brit.)	discovery of Richardson's law	Adolf Windaus	(Ger.)	constitution of sterols and their connection with vitamins
1929	Louis de Broglie	(Fr.)	discovery of the wave nature of electrons	Sir Arthur Harden	(Brit.)	investigations on the fermentation of sugars and the enzymes acting in this connection
				H. von Euler-Chelpin	(Swed.)‡	
1930	Sir C. Raman	(India)	work on light diffusion; discovery of Raman effect	Hans Fischer	(Ger.)	hemin, chlorophyll research; synthesis of hemin
1931	(no award)	—	—	Karl Bosch	(Ger.)	invention and development of chemical high-pressure methods
				Friedrich Bergius	(Ger.)	
1932	Werner Heisenberg	(Ger.)	formulation of indeterminacy principle of quantum mechanics	Irving Langmuir	(U.S.)	discoveries and investigations in surface chemistry
1933	P.A.M. Dirac	(Brit.)	introduction of wave-equations in quantum mechanics	(no award)	—	—
	Erwin Schrödinger	(Austria)				
1934	(no award)	—	—	Harold Urey	(U.S.)	discovery of heavy hydrogen
1935	Sir James Chadwick	(Brit.)	discovery of the neutron	Frédéric Joliot-Curie	(Fr.)	synthesis of new radioactive elements
				Irène Joliot-Curie	(Fr.)	
1936	Victor Hess	(Austria)	discovery of cosmic radiation	Peter Debye	(Neth.)	work on dipole moments and diffraction of X-rays and electrons in gases
	Carl Anderson	(U.S.)	discovery of the positron			
1937	Clinton Davisson	(U.S.)	experimental demonstration of the interference phenomenon in crystals irradiated by electrons	Sir Walter Haworth	(Brit.)	research on carbohydrates and vitamin C
	Sir George Paget Thomson	(Brit.)		Paul Karrer	(Switz.)	research on carotenoids, flavins, and vitamins
1938	Enrico Fermi	(Italy)	disclosure of artificial radioactive elements produced by neutron irradiation	Richard Kuhn	(Ger.)	carotenoid and vitamin research (declined)§
1939	Ernest Lawrence	(U.S.)	invention of the cyclotron	Adolf Butenandt	(Ger.)	work on sexual hormones (declined)§
				Leopold Ruzicka	(Switz.)‡	work on polymethylenes and higher terpenes
1943‖	Otto Stern	(U.S.)‡	discovery of the magnetic moment of the proton	George de Hevesy	(Hung.)	use of isotopes as tracers in chemical research
1944	Isidor Rabi	(U.S.)‡	resonance method for registration of magnetic properties of atomic nuclei	Otto Hahn	(Ger.)	discovery of the fission of heavy nuclei
1945	Wolfgang Pauli	(Austria)	discovery of the exclusion principle	Artturi Virtanen	(Fin.)	invention of fodder preservation method
1946	Percy Bridgman	(U.S.)	discoveries in the domain of high-pressure physics	James Sumner	(U.S.)	discovery of enzyme crystallization
				John Northrop	(U.S.)	preparation of enzymes and virus proteins in pure form
				Wendell Stanley	(U.S.)	
1947	Sir Edward Appleton	(Brit.)	discovery of Appleton layer in upper atmosphere	Sir Robert Robinson	(Brit.)	investigations on alkaloids and other plant products

Nobel prize winners* (continued)

	physics			chemistry		
1948	Patrick Blackett	(Brit.)	discoveries in the domain of nuclear physics and cosmic radiation	Arne Tiselius	(Swed.)	researches on electrophoresis and adsorption analysis; serum proteins
1949	Yukawa Hideki	(Japan)	prediction of the existence of mesons	William Giauque	(U.S.)	behaviour of substances at extremely low temperatures
1950	Cecil Powell	(Brit.)	photographic method of studying nuclear processes; discoveries about mesons	Otto Diels Kurt Alder	(Ger.) (Ger.)	discovery and development of diene synthesis
1951	Sir John Cockcroft Ernest Walton	(Brit.) (Ire.)	work on transmutation of atomic nuclei by accelerated particles	Edwin McMillan Glenn Seaborg	(U.S.) (U.S.)	discovery of and research on transuranium elements
1952	Felix Bloch Edward Purcell	(U.S.)‡ (U.S.)	discovery of nuclear magnetic resonance in solids	Archer Martin Richard Synge	(Brit.) (Brit.)	development of partition chromatography
1953	Frits Zernike	(Neth.)	method of phase-contrast microscopy	Hermann Staudinger	(Ger.)	work on macromolecules
1954	Max Born Walther Bothe	(Brit.)‡ (Ger.)	statistical studies on wave functions invention of coincidence method	Linus Pauling¶	(U.S.)	study of the nature of the chemical bond
1955	Willis Lamb, Jr. Polykarp Kusch	(U.S.) (U.S.)‡	discoveries in the hydrogen spectrum measurement of magnetic moment of electron	Vincent Du Vigneaud	(U.S.)	first synthesis of a polypeptide hormone
1956	William Shockley John Bardeen♀ Walter Brattain	(U.S.) (U.S.) (U.S.)	investigations on semiconductors and discovery of the transistor effect	Nikolay Semyonov Sir Cyril Hinshelwood	(U.S.S.R.) (Brit.)	work on the kinetics of chemical reactions
1957	Tsung-Dao Lee Chen Ning Yang	(China) (China)	discovery of violations of the principle of parity	Sir Alexander Todd	(Brit.)	work on nucleotides and nucleotide coenzymes
1958	Pavel A. Cherenkov Ilya M. Frank Igor Y. Tamm	(U.S.S.R.) (U.S.S.R.) (U.S.S.R.)	discovery and interpretation of the Cherenkov effect	Frederick Sanger♂	(Brit.)	determination of the structure of the insulin molecule
1959	Emilio Segrè Owen Chamberlain	(U.S.)‡ (U.S.)	confirmation of the existence of the antiproton	Jaroslav Heyrovsky	(Czech.)	discovery and development of polarography
1960	Donald Glaser	(U.S.)	development of the bubble chamber	Willard Libby	(U.S.)	development of radiocarbon dating
1961	Robert Hofstadter Rudolf Mössbauer	(U.S.) (Ger.)	determination of shape and size of atomic nucleons discovery of the Mössbauer effect	Melvin Calvin	(U.S.)	study of chemical steps that take place during photosynthesis
1962	Lev D. Landau	(U.S.S.R.)	contributions to the understanding of condensed states of matter	John C. Kendrew Max F. Perutz	(Brit.) (Brit.)‡	determination of the structure of hemoproteins
1963	J.H.D. Jensen Maria Goeppert Mayer Eugene Paul Wigner	(Ger.) (U.S.)‡ (U.S.)‡	development of shell model theory of the structure of atomic nuclei principles governing interaction of protons and neutrons in the nucleus	Giulio Natta Karl Ziegler	(Italy) (Ger.)	structure and synthesis of polymers in the field of plastics
1964	Charles H. Townes Nikolay G. Basov Aleksandr M. Prokhorov	(U.S.) (U.S.S.R.) (U.S.S.R.)	work in quantum electronics leading to construction of instruments based on maser-laser principles	Dorothy M.C. Hodgkin	(Brit.)	determining the structure of biochemical compounds essential in combating pernicious anemia
1965	Julian S. Schwinger Richard P. Feynman Tomonaga Shin'ichirō	(U.S.) (U.S.) (Japan)	basic principles of quantum electrodynamics	Robert B. Woodward	(U.S.)	synthesis of sterols, chlorophyll, and other substances once thought to be produced only by living things
1966	Alfred Kastler	(Fr.)	discovery of optical methods for studying Hertzian resonances in atoms	Robert S. Mulliken	(U.S.)	work concerning chemical bonds and the electronic structure of molecules
1967	Hans A. Bethe	(U.S.)‡	discoveries concerning the energy production of stars	Manfred Eigen Ronald G.W. Norrish George Porter	(Ger.) (Brit.) (Brit.)	studies of extremely fast chemical reactions
1968	Luis W. Alvarez	(U.S.)	work with elementary particles, discovery of resonance states	Lars Onsager	(U.S.)‡	work on theory of thermodynamics of irreversible processes
1969	Murray Gell-Mann	(U.S.)	discoveries concerning classification of elementary particles and their interactions	Derek H.R. Barton Odd Hassel	(Brit.) (Nor.)	work in determining actual three-dimensional shape of certain organic compounds
1970	Hannes Alfvén Louis Néel	(Swed.) (Fr.)	work in magnetohydrodynamics and in antiferromagnetism and ferrimagnetism	Luis F. Leloir	(Arg.)‡	discovery of sugar nucleotides and their role in the biosynthesis of carbohydrates
1971	Dennis Gabor	(Brit.)‡	invention of holography	Gerhard Herzberg	(Can.)‡	research in the structure of molecules
1972	John Bardeen♀ Leon N. Cooper John R. Schrieffer	(U.S.) (U.S.) (U.S.)	development of the theory of superconductivity	Christian B. Anfinsen Stanford Moore William H. Stein	(U.S.) (U.S.) (U.S.)	fundamental contributions to enzyme chemistry
1973	Leo Esaki Ivar Giaever Brian Josephson	(Japan) (U.S.)‡ (Brit.)	tunnelling in semiconductors and superconductors	Ernst Fischer Geoffrey Wilkinson	(Ger.) (Brit.)	organometallic chemistry
1974	Sir Martin Ryle Antony Hewish	(Brit.) (Brit.)	work in radio astronomy	Paul J. Flory	(U.S.)	studies of long-chain molecules
1975	Aage Bohr Ben R. Mottelson L. James Rainwater	(Den.) (Den.)‡ (U.S.)	work toward understanding of the atomic nucleus that paved the way for nuclear fusion	J.W. Cornforth Vladimir Prelog	(Brit.) (Switz.)	work in stereochemistry
1976	Burton Richter Samuel C.C. Ting	(U.S.) (U.S.)	discovery of new class of elementary particles (psi, or J)	William N. Lipscomb	(U.S.)	structure of boranes
1977	Philip W. Anderson Sir Nevill Mott John H. Van Vleck	(U.S.) (Brit.) (U.S.)	contributions to understanding of the behaviour of electrons in magnetic, noncrystalline solids	Ilya Prigogine	(Belg.)	widening the scope of thermodynamics
1978	Pyotr L. Kapitsa Arno A. Penzias Robert W. Wilson	(U.S.S.R.) (U.S.)‡ (U.S.)	invention and application of helium liquefier discovery of cosmic microwave background radiation, providing support for the big-bang theory	Peter D. Mitchell	(Brit.)	energy transfer processes in biological systems
1979	Sheldon Glashow Abdus Salam Steven Weinberg	(U.S.) (Pakistan) (U.S.)	establishment of analogy between electromagnetism and the "weak" interactions of subatomic particles	Herbert C. Brown Georg Wittig	(U.S.)‡ (W.Ger.)	introduction of compounds of boron and phosphorus in the synthesis of organic substances
1980	James W. Cronin Val L. Fitch	(U.S.) (U.S.)	demonstration of simultaneous violation of both charge-conjugation and parity-inversion symmetries	Paul Berg Walter Gilbert Frederick Sanger♂	(U.S.) (U.S.) (Brit.)	first preparation of a hybrid DNA development of chemical and biological analyses of DNA structure

*Nationality given is the citizenship of recipient at the time award was made.
†Awarded two Nobel prizes: physics (1903); chemistry (1911).
‡Naturalized citizen.
§Hitler forbade Germans to accept Nobel prizes (January 1937).
‖No awards made, 1940–42.
¶Awarded two Nobel prizes: chemistry (1954); peace (1962).
♀Shared two Nobel prizes for physics (1956 and 1972).
♂Awarded two Nobel prizes for chemistry (1958 and 1980).

Nobel prize winners* (continued)

	physiology or medicine			literature		peace	
1901	Emil von Behring	(Ger.)	work on serum therapy	Sully Prudhomme; poet	(Fr.)	Jean Henri Dunant	(Switz.)
						Frédéric Passy	(Fr.)
1902	Sir Ronald Ross	(Brit.)	discovery of how malaria enters an organism	Theodor Mommsen; historian	(Ger.)	Élie Ducommun	(Switz.)
						Charles Albert Gobat	(Switz.)
1903	Niels R. Finsen	(Den.)	treatment of skin diseases with light radiation	B. Bjornson; novelist, poet, dramatist	(Nor.)	Sir William Cremer	(Brit.)
1904	Ivan Pavlov	(Russ.)	work on the physiology of digestion	Frédéric Mistral; poet	(Fr.)	Institute of International Law	(founded 1873)
				J. Echegaray y Eizaguirre; dramatist	(Spain)		
1905	Robert Koch	(Ger.)	tuberculosis research	H. Sienkiewicz; novelist	(Pol.)	Bertha von Suttner	(Austria)
1906	Camillo Golgi	(Italy)	work on the structure of the nervous system	Giosue Carducci; poet	(Italy)	Theodore Roosevelt	(U.S.)
	S. Ramón y Cajal	(Spain)					
1907	Alphonse Laveran	(Fr.)	discovery of the role of protozoa in diseases	Rudyard Kipling; poet, novelist	(Brit.)	Ernesto Teodoro Moneta	(Italy)
						Louis Renault	(Fr.)
1908	Paul Ehrlich	(Ger.)	work on immunity	Rudolf Eucken; philosopher	(Ger.)	Klas Pontus Arnoldson	(Swed.)
	Ilya Mechnikov	(Russ.)				Fredrik Bajer	(Den.)
1909	Emil Kocher	(Switz.)	physiology, pathology and surgery of thyroid gland	Selma Lagerlöf; novelist	(Swed.)	Baron d'Estournelles de Constant	(Fr.)
						Auguste Beernaert	(Belg.)
1910	Albrecht Kossel	(Ger.)	researches in cellular chemistry	Paul von Heyse; poet, novelist, dramatist	(Ger.)	International Peace bureau	(founded 1891)
1911	Allvar Gullstrand	(Swed.)	work on dioptrics of the eye	Maurice Maeterlinck; dramatist	(Belg.)	Tobias Asser	(Neth.)
						Alfred Fried	(Austria)
1912	Alexis Carrel	(Fr.)	work on vascular suture; transplantation of organs	Gerhart Hauptmann; dramatist	(Ger.)	Elihu Root	(U.S.)
1913	Charles Richet	(Fr.)	work on anaphylaxis	Sir R. Tagore; poet	(India)	Henri Lafontaine	(Belg.)
1914	Robert Bárány	(Austria)	work on vestibular apparatus	(no award)	—	(no award)	—
1915	(no award)	—	—	Romain Rolland; novelist	(Fr.)	(no award)	—
1916	(no award)	—	—	V. von Heidenstam; poet	(Swed.)	(no award)	—
1917	(no award)	—	—	Karl Gjellerup; novelist	(Den.)	International Red Cross Committee	(founded 1863)
				H. Pontoppidan; novelist	(Den.)		
1919†	Jules Bordet	(Belg.)	discoveries in regard to immunity	Carl Spitteler; poet, novelist	(Switz.)	Woodrow Wilson	(U.S.)
1920	August Krogh	(Den.)	discovery of capillary motor regulating mechanism	Knut Hamsun; novelist	(Nor.)	Léon Bourgeois	(Fr.)
1921	(no award)	—	—	Anatole France; novelist	(Fr.)	Karl Branting	(Swed.)
						Christian Lous Lange	(Nor.)
1922	Archibald Hill	(Brit.)	discovery relating to heat production in muscles	J. Benavente y Martínez; dramatist	(Spain)	Fridtjof Nansen	(Nor.)
	Otto Meyerhof	(Ger.)	work on metabolism of lactic acid in muscles				
1923	Sir F.G. Banting	(Can.)	discovery of insulin	William Butler Yeats; poet	(Ire.)	(no award)	—
	J.J.R. Macleod	(Brit.)					
1924	Willem Einthoven	(Neth.)	discovery of electrocardiogram mechanism	Władysław Reymont; novelist	(Pol.)	(no award)	—
1925	(no award)	—	—	George Bernard Shaw; dramatist	(Ire.)	Sir Austen Chamberlain	(Brit.)
						Charles G. Dawes	(U.S.)
1926	Johannes Fibiger	(Den.)	contributions to cancer research	Grazia Deledda; novelist	(Italy)	Aristide Briand	(Fr.)
						Gustav Stresemann	(Ger.)
1927	J. Wagner von Jauregg	(Austria)	work on malaria inoculation in dementia paralytica	Henri Bergson; philosopher	(Fr.)‡	Ferdinand Buisson	(Fr.)
						Ludwig Quidde	(Ger.)
1928	Charles Nicolle	(Fr.)	work on typhus	Sigrid Undset; novelist	(Nor.)	(no award)	—
1929	Christiaan Eijkman	(Neth.)	discovery of antineuritic vitamin	Thomas Mann; novelist	(Ger.)	Frank B. Kellogg	(U.S.)
	Sir F. Hopkins	(Brit.)	discovery of growth-stimulating vitamins				
1930	Karl Landsteiner	(U.S.)‡	grouping of human blood	Sinclair Lewis; novelist	(U.S.)	Nathan Söderblom	(Swed.)
1931	Otto Warburg	(Ger.)	discovery of nature and action of respiratory enzyme	Erik Axel Karlfeldt; poet	(Swed.)	Jane Addams	(U.S.)
						Nicholas Murray Butler	(U.S.)
1932	Edgar D. Adrian	(Brit.)	discoveries regarding function of the neurons	John Galsworthy; novelist	(Brit.)	(no award)	—
	Sir C. Sherrington	(Brit.)					
1933	Thomas Hunt Morgan	(U.S.)	heredity transmission functions of chromosomes	Ivan Bunin; novelist	(U.S.S.R.)	Sir Norman Angell	(Brit.)
1934	George R. Minot	(U.S.)	discoveries concerning liver therapy against anemia	Luigi Pirandello; dramatist	(Italy)	Arthur Henderson	(Brit.)
	William P. Murphy	(U.S.)					
	George H. Whipple	(U.S.)					
1935	Hans Spemann	(Ger.)	organizer effect in embryo	(no award)	—	Carl von Ossietzky	(Ger.)
1936	Sir H.H. Dale	(Brit.)	work on chemical transmission of nerve impulses	Eugene O'Neill; dramatist	(U.S.)	Carlos Saavedra Lamas	(Arg.)
	Otto Loewi	(Ger.)					
1937	Albert Szent-Györgyi	(Hung.)	work on biological combustion	Roger Martin du Gard; novelist	(Fr.)	Viscount Cecil of Chelwood	(Brit.)
1938	Corneille Heymans	(Belg.)	discovery of role of sinus and aortic mechanisms in respiration regulation	Pearl Buck; novelist	(U.S.)	Nansen International Office for Refugees	(founded 1931)
1939	Gerhard Domagk	(Ger.)	antibacterial effect of prontosil (declined)§	Frans Eemil Sillanpää; novelist	(Fin.)	(no award)	—
1943†	Henrik Dam	(Den.)	discovery of vitamin K	(no award)	—	(no award)	—
	Edward A. Doisy	(U.S.)	discovery of chemical nature of vitamin K				
1944	Joseph Erlanger	(U.S.)	researches on differentiated functions of nerve fibres	J.V. Jensen; novelist	(Den.)	International Red Cross Committee	(founded 1863)
	Herbert S. Gasser	(U.S.)					
1945	Sir A. Fleming	(Brit.)	discovery of penicillin and its curative value	Gabriela Mistral; poet	(Chile)	Cordell Hull	(U.S.)
	Ernst Boris Chain	(Brit.)‡					
	Lord Florey	(Austr.)					
1946	Hermann J. Muller	(U.S.)	production of mutations by X-ray irradiation	Hermann Hesse; novelist	(Switz.)‡	Emily Greene Balch	(U.S.)
						John R. Mott	(U.S.)
1947	Carl F. Cori	(U.S.)‡	discovery of how glycogen is catalytically converted	André Gide; novelist, essayist	(Fr.)	American Friends Service Committee	(U.S.)
	Gerty T. Cori	(U.S.)‡				Friends Service Council	(London)
	Bernardo Houssay	(Arg.)	pituitary hormone function in sugar metabolism				
1948	Paul Müller	(Switz.)	properties of DDT	T.S. Eliot; poet, critic	(Brit.)‡	(no award)	—
1949	Walter Rudolf Hess	(Switz.)	discovery of function of middle brain	William Faulkner; novelist	(U.S.)	Lord Boyd-Orr	(Brit.)
	António Egas Moniz	(Port.)	therapeutic value of leucotomy in psychoses				
1950	Philip S. Hench	(U.S.)	research on adrenal cortex hormones, their structure and biological effects	Bertrand Russell; philosopher	(Brit.)	Ralph Bunche	(U.S.)
	Edward C. Kendall	(U.S.)					
	Tadeusz Reichstein	(Switz.)‡					

Nobel prize winners* (continued)

	physiology or medicine			literature		peace	
1951	Max Theiler	(S.Af.)	yellow fever discoveries	Pär Lagerkvist; novelist	(Swed.)	Léon Jouhaux	(Fr.)
1952	Selman A. Waksman	(U.S.)‡	discovery of streptomycin	François Mauriac; poet, novelist, dramatist	(Fr.)	Albert Schweitzer	(Alsatian)
1953	Fritz A. Lipmann Sir H.A. Krebs	(U.S.)‡ (Brit.)‡	discovery of coenzyme A citric acid cycle in metabolism of carbohydrates	Sir Winston Churchill; historian, orator	(Brit.)	George C. Marshall	(U.S.)
1954	John F. Enders Thomas H. Weller Frederick Robbins	(U.S.) (U.S.) (U.S.)	cultivation of the poliomyelitis viruses in tissue culture	Ernest Hemingway; novelist	(U.S.)	Office of the United Nations High Commissioner for Refugees	(founded 1951)
1955	Axel Hugo Theorell	(Swed.)	nature and mode of action of oxidation enzymes	Halldór Laxness; novelist	(Ice.)	(no award)	—
1956	Werner Forssmann Dickinson Richards André F. Cournand	(Ger.) (U.S.) (U.S.)‡	discoveries concerning heart catheterization and circulatory changes	Juan Ramón Jiménez; poet	(Spain)	(no award)	—
1957	Daniel Bovet	(Italy)‡	production of synthetic curare	Albert Camus; novelist, dramatist	(Fr.)	Lester B. Pearson	(Can.)
1958	George W. Beadle Edward L. Tatum Joshua Lederberg	(U.S.) (U.S.) (U.S.)	genetic regulation of chemical processes genetic recombination	Boris Pasternak; novelist, poet (declined award)	(U.S.S.R.)	Dominique Georges Pire	(Belg.)
1959	Severo Ochoa Arthur Kornberg	(U.S.)‡ (U.S.)	work on producing nucleic acids artificially	Salvatore Quasimodo; poet	(Italy)	Philip Noel-Baker	(Brit.)
1960	Sir Macfarlane Burnet Peter B. Medawar	(Austr.) (Brit.)	acquired immunity to tissue transplants	Saint-John Perse; poet	(Fr.)	Albert Lutuli	(S.Af.)
1961	Georg von Békésy	(U.S.)‡	functions of the inner ear	Ivo Andrić; novelist	(Yugos.)	Dag Hammarskjöld	(Swed.)
1962	Francis H.C. Crick James D. Watson Maurice Wilkins	(Brit.) (U.S.) (Brit.)	discoveries concerning the molecular structure of deoxyribonucleic acid	John Steinbeck; novelist	(U.S.)	Linus Pauling‖	(U.S.)
1963	Sir John Eccles Alan Lloyd Hodgkin Andrew Huxley	(Austr.) (Brit.) (Brit.)	study of the transmission of nerve impulses along a nerve fibre	George Seferis; poet	(Gr.)	International Red Cross Committee League of Red Cross Societies	(headquarters of both in Geneva)
1964	Konrad Bloch Feodor Lynen	(U.S.)‡ (Ger.)	discoveries concerning cholesterol and fatty-acid metabolism	Jean-Paul Sartre; philosopher, dramatist (declined award)	(Fr.)	Martin Luther King, Jr.	(U.S.)
1965	François Jacob André Lwoff Jacques Monod	(Fr.) (Fr.) (Fr.)	discoveries concerning regulatory activities of the body cells	Mikhail Sholokhov; novelist	(U.S.S.R.)	United Nations Children's Fund (UNICEF)	(founded 1946)
1966	Charles B. Huggins Francis Peyton Rous	(U.S.)‡ (U.S.)	research on causes and treatment of cancer	Shmuel Yosef Agnon; novelist Nelly Sachs; poet	(Isr.)‡ (Swed.)‡	(no award)	—
1967	Haldan Keffer Hartline George Wald Ragnar A. Granit	(U.S.) (U.S.) (Swed.)	discoveries about chemical and physiological visual processes in the eye	Miguel Angel Asturias; novelist	(Guat.)	(no award)	—
1968	Robert W. Holley H. Gobind Khorana Marshall W. Nirenberg	(U.S.) (U.S.)‡ (U.S.)	deciphering of the genetic code	Kawabata Yasunari; novelist	(Japan)	René Cassin	(Fr.)
1969	Max Delbrück Alfred D. Hershey Salvador E. Luria	(U.S.)‡ (U.S.) (U.S.)‡	research and discoveries concerning viruses and viral diseases	Samuel Beckett; novelist, dramatist	(Ire.)	International Labour Organisation	(founded 1919)
1970	Julius Axelrod Sir Bernard Katz Ulf von Euler	(U.S.) (Brit.)‡ (Swed.)	discoveries concerning the chemistry of nerve transmission	Aleksandr Solzhenitsyn; novelist	(U.S.S.R.)	Norman E. Borlaug	(U.S.)
1971	Earl W. Sutherland, Jr.	(U.S.)	action of hormones	Pablo Neruda; poet	(Chile)	Willy Brandt	(Ger.)
1972	Gerald M. Edelman Rodney Porter	(U.S.) (Brit.)	research on the chemical structure of antibodies	Heinrich Böll; novelist	(Ger.)	(no award)	—
1973	Karl von Frisch Konrad Lorenz Nikolaas Tinbergen	(Austria) (Austria) (Neth.)	discoveries in animal behaviour patterns	Patrick White; novelist	(Austr.)	Henry Kissinger Le Duc Tho (declined award)	(U.S.) (N.Viet.)
1974	Albert Claude Christian R. de Duve George E. Palade	(U.S.)‡ (Belg.) (U.S.)‡	research on structural and functional organization of cells	Eyvind Johnson; novelist Harry Martinson; novelist, poet	(Swed.) (Swed.)	Satō Eisaku Sean MacBride	(Japan) (Ire.)
1975	Renato Dulbecco Howard M. Temin David Baltimore	(U.S.)‡ (U.S.) (U.S.)	interaction between tumour viruses and the genetic material of the cell	Eugenio Montale; poet	(Italy)	Andrey D. Sakharov	(U.S.S.R.)
1976	Baruch S. Blumberg D. Carleton Gajdusek	(U.S.) (U.S.)	studies of origin and spread of infectious diseases	Saul Bellow; novelist	(U.S.)‡	Mairead Corrigan¶ Betty Williams¶	(N.Ire.) (N.Ire.)
1977	Rosalyn S. Yalow Roger Guillemin Andrew Schally	(U.S.) (U.S.) (U.S.)	development of radioimmunoassay; research on pituitary hormones	Vicente Aleixandre; poet	(Spain)	Amnesty International	(founded 1961)
1978	Werner Arber Daniel Nathans Hamilton O. Smith	(Switz.) (U.S.) (U.S.)	discovery and application of enzymes that fragment deoxyribonucleic acids	Isaac Bashevis Singer; novelist	(U.S.)‡	Menachem Begin Anwar as-Sadat	(Isr.) (Egypt)
1979	Allan M. Cormack Godfrey N. Hounsfield	(U.S.)‡ (Brit.)	development of the CAT (computed axial tomography) scan, a radiographic diagnostic technique	Ődysseùs Elýtis; poet	(Greece)	Mother Teresa of Calcutta	(India)‡
1980	Baruj Benacerraf George D. Snell Jean Dausset	(U.S.)‡ (U.S.) (Fr.)	investigations of genetic control of the response of the immunological system to foreign substances	Czesław Miłosz; poet	(U.S.)‡	Adolfo Pérez Esquivel	(Arg.)

Winners of the Nobel Memorial Prize in Economic Science

1969	Ragnar Frisch Jan Tinbergen	(Nor.) (Neth.)	work in econometrics
1970	Paul A. Samuelson	(U.S.)	work in scientific analysis of economic theory
1971	Simon Kuznets	(U.S.)‡	extensive research on the economic growth of nations
1972	Sir John Hicks Kenneth J. Arrow	(Brit.) (U.S.)	contributions to general economic equilibrium theory and welfare theory
1973	Wassily Leontief	(U.S.)‡	input analysis
1974	Gunnar Myrdal Friedrich von Hayek	(Swed.) (Brit.)‡	pioneering analysis of the interdependence of economic, social, and institutional phenomena
1975	Leonid V. Kantorovich Tjalling C. Koopmans	(U.S.S.R.) (U.S.)‡	contributions to the theory of optimum allocation of resources
1976	Milton Friedman	(U.S.)	consumption analysis, monetary theory, and economic stabilization
1977	Bertil Ohlin James Meade	(Swed.) (Brit.)	contributions to theory of international trade
1978	Herbert A. Simon	(U.S.)	decision-making processes in economic organizations
1979	W. Arthur Lewis Theodore W. Schultz	(Brit.) (U.S.)	analyses of economic processes in developing nations
1980	Lawrence R. Klein	(U.S.)	development and analysis of empirical models of business fluctuations

*Nationality given is the citizenship of recipient at the time award was made.
†No awards given in these categories in 1918, 1940–42.
‡Naturalized citizen.
§Hitler forbade Germans to accept Nobel prizes (Jan. 1937).
‖Awarded two Nobel prizes: chemistry (1954); peace (1962).
¶Award not given until 1977.

rhodium, palladium, silver, osmium, iridium, platinum, and gold; *i.e.*, the metals of Groups VIIb, VIII, and Ib of the second and third transition series of the periodic table.

Silver and gold, which with copper are often called the coinage metals, and platinum, iridium, and palladium comprise the so-called precious metals, used in jewelry.

·electronic structure and properties **11**:1091a
·silver occurrence and extraction **16**:776d
·transition element chemistry **18**:618g

Nobles, Battle of the (North African history): *see* Barghawāṭah.

noble savage, in literature, an idealized concept of uncivilized man who symbolizes the innate goodness of natural man uncorrupted by civilization.

The glorification of the noble savage is a dominant theme in the Romantic writings of the 18th and 19th centuries, especially in the works of Jean-Jacques Rousseau. For example, *Émile* (1762) is a long treatise pointing up the corrupting influence of traditional education; *Confessions* (written 1765–70), Rousseau's autobiography, reaffirms the basic tenet of man's innate goodness; and *Dreams of a Solitary Walker* (1776–78) contains descriptions of nature and man's natural response to it. The concept of the noble savage, however, can be traced to ancient Greece, where Homer, Pliny, and Xenophon idealized the Arcadians and other primitive groups, both real and imagined. Later Roman writers such as Horace, Virgil, and Ovid gave comparable treatment to the Scythians. From the 15th to the 19th century, the noble savage figured prominently in popular travel accounts and appeared occasionally in English plays such as Dryden's *Conquest of Granada* (published 1672), where the term noble savage was first used, and in *Oroonoko* (1696) by Thomas Southerne, based on Aphra Behn's novel about a dignified African prince enslaved in the British colony of Surinam.

Chateaubriand sentimentalized the North American Indian in *Atala* (1801), *René* (1802), and *Les Natchez* (1826), as did James Fenimore Cooper in the "Leatherstocking" tales (1823–41), which feature the noble chief Chingachgook and his son Uncas. The three harpooners of the ship "Pequod" in Melville's *Moby Dick* (1851), Queequeg, Daggoo, and Tashtego, are other examples.

·Rousseau's philosophical anthropology **15**:1172a

Nobles' Land Bank, Russian governmental financial institution founded in 1885 to provide low-interest loans to large landowners.

·agrarian reforms obstacles **16**:63c

noblesse de robe, English NOBILITY OF THE ROBE, in 17th- and 18th-century France, a class of hereditary nobles who acquired their rank through holding a high state office. Their name was derived from the robes worn by officials. The class was already in existence by the end of the 16th century, but it was only in the 17th century that its members acquired the right to transmit noble status to their heirs. The period of 1640s and 1650s was pivotal in the development of the *noblesse de robe*. In an attempt to bargain for political support during the troubled minority of Louis XIV, the crown granted detailed charters of nobility to judicial officials. At the summit of this newly created privileged class were the officers of such sovereign courts as the Parlement of Paris.

Because of their bourgeois background, the families of the *noblesse de robe* were at first disdained by nobles who derived their rank from military service (*noblesse d'épée*) and from long-standing possession (*noblesse de race*). The distinction between the old and the new aristocracies, between the sword and robe, gradually blurred during the 18th century as both groups worked to defend privilege against attempts at reform by the king. In fact, it was the *noblesse de robe* that, because of its wealth, its rising social status, and its control of official positions, took the lead in opposition to reform.

·prerevolutionary aristocratic fusion **7**:640g

Nobre, António (b. Aug. 16, 1867, Porto, Port.—d. March 18, 1900, Foz do Douro), poet whose verse marked a departure in Portuguese poetry from objective realism and social commitment to subjective lyricism and an art-for-art's sake point of view. Of a well-to-do family, he studied law unsuccessfully at Coimbra and, from 1890 to 1895, studied political science in Paris, where he absorbed the influence of the French Symbolist poets. There he wrote the greater part of the only book he published in his lifetime, *Só* (1892; "Alone"). Inspired by nostalgic memories of a childhood spent in the company of peasants and sailors in northern Portugal, *Só* combines the simple lyricism of Portuguese traditional poetry with the more refined perceptiveness of Symbolism.

At first *Só* met with a mixed reception, but it became one of the most popular and most imitated works of poetry in Portugal. A final version appeared in 1898. Nobre's assimilation of folkloric elements imparts a childlike freshness to his vision of Portugal, but an aura of defeat and narcissism is never absent from his work.

A consumptive, Nobre spent his remaining years in travel, seeking a favourable climate. Two more volumes of poetry were published after his death: *Despedidas* (1902; "Farewells") and *Primeiros versos* (1921; "First Poems").

Nóbrega, Manuel da (b. Oct. 18, 1517, Portugal—d. Oct. 18, 1570, Rio de Janeiro), founder of the Jesuit mission of Brazil and leader of the order's activities there from 1549 to 1570. Father Nóbrega with five other Jesuit missionaries sailed from Lisbon to Bahia (modern Salvador, Braz.) in 1549. His first concern there was the protection and conversion of the Indians. He established a school near São Paulo in 1553 and resisted the hostility of planters seeking Indians for slaves. He also condemned African slavery, though Jesuits finally accepted the institution and even owned black slaves themselves. He was named the first provincial of the Society of Jesus in Brazil (1553–59), and, although he was again named provincial in 1570, he died before news of the appointment reached him.

When the French under Nicolas Durand de Villegaignon, including many Huguenots, settled in Rio de Janeiro (1555), Nóbrega worked earnestly for their expulsion. The Protestants were in fact forced out (1563), in part because the Jesuit won the Tamóio Indians over to the Portuguese side. In this and in other ways Nóbrega shaped the destiny of southern Brazil into remaining both Catholic and Portuguese.

·São Paulo foundation role **16**:238b

nocardiosis, chronic systemic fungal disease of many animals and man originating in the respiratory tract and disseminated by way of the blood to other organs, especially the brain. It is caused either by introduction into the skin or by inhalation of *Nocardia asteroides*, a normal inhabitant of soil and compost heaps. The disease usually begins with malaise, loss of weight, fever, and night sweats. Most often it causes a cough productive of purulent and blood-tinged sputum (pseudotuberculosis). The disease may be treated, at least in the earlier stages, by sulfonamide drugs, streptomycin, and the tetracyclines.

Noce i dnie (1932–34; "Nights and Days"), book by Maria Dabrowska.

·theme and style **10**:1253f

Nocera Inferiore, ancient NUCERIA ALFATERNA, or NOCERA DEI PAGANI, town and episcopal see, Salerno province, Campania region, southern Italy, in the Sarno River Valley, northwest of Salerno. It originated as the Oscan and Roman town of Nuceria Alfaterna, which was sacked by the Carthaginian general Hannibal in 216 BC but was rebuilt by the emperor Augustus. In the old castle, ruins of which are extant, Helen, widow of King Manfred of Sicily, died in captivity (1271) five years after Manfred's death in the battle of Benevento. The origin of the epithet *dei Pagani* (of the Pagans) is not historically established and is sometimes attributed to a nearby medieval settlement of Saracen colonists or to Pagano, the name of an important local medieval family. Although there are several old churches and convents, the town is primarily modern in appearance. In the nearby village of Nocera Superiore is the 5th-century circular domed church of Sta. Maria Maggiore.

Nocera Inferiore is economically one of the most important centres in the province because of its agricultural exports, lumber mills, and canning, macaroni, and textile plants. Pop. (1971 prelim.) commune, 50,596.
40°44′ N, 14°38′ E

·Samnite League in Campania **14**:789g

Nocomis bigguttata (fish): *see* chub.

Noctilionidae: *see* bulldog bat.

Noctiluca, genus of one-celled marine organisms having characteristics of both plants and animals (*see* dinoflagellate). It is one of several organisms that cause luminescence in the seas.

·bioluminescence mechanism **2**:1028h; illus. 1029

noctilucent cloud, rare cloud, probably composed of ice crystals and meteoric dust, that occurs at a higher altitude than any other cloud form (about 82 kilometres, or 50 miles). It is silvery or bluish white and is visible only on summer nights in high latitudes. Despite the thinness of the air and the consequent scarcity of water vapour, the ice crystals form because this level is the coldest in the entire upper atmosphere; and thus even minute amounts of water vapour freeze. The cloud often exhibits a tenuous, wavy pattern that indicates the existence of strong winds at that altitude.

·formation and characteristics **9**:788c

Noctis Lacus, a Martian feature so named by the French astronomer E.-M. Antoniadi, although the name is no longer included among the names officially recognized by the International Astronomical Union.

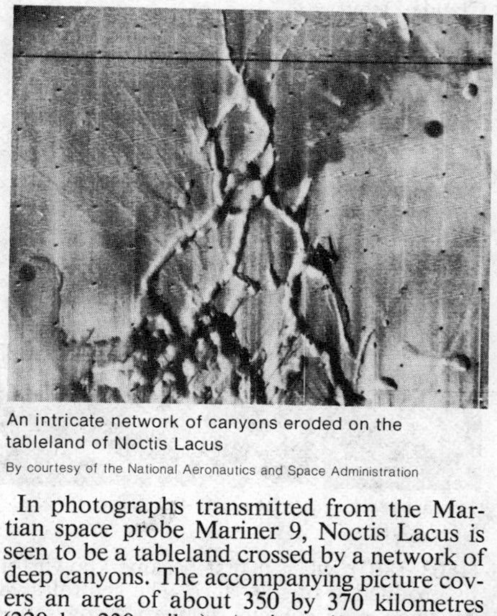

An intricate network of canyons eroded on the tableland of Noctis Lacus

By courtesy of the National Aeronautics and Space Administration

In photographs transmitted from the Martian space probe Mariner 9, Noctis Lacus is seen to be a tableland crossed by a network of deep canyons. The accompanying picture covers an area of about 350 by 370 kilometres (220 by 230 miles). An inversion effect that may cause the canyons to appear as raised ridges is due to the direction of lighting and can usually be dispelled by turning the picture around.

Noctuidae: *see* owlet moth.

noctule (*Nyctalus*), any of about nine species of bats, family Vespertilionidae, found in Europe and Asia. Noctules are yellowish to dark brown and 5–10 centimetres (2–4 inches) long without the 3.5–6.5-centimetre tail. They are swift, erratic fliers and commonly leave their roosts (caves, buildings, etc.) at or before sunset. They eat insects and apparently are fond of beetles. The best-known and most widely distributed species is the Eurasian *N. noctula*, a reddish-brown, migratory inhabitant of wooded regions.

nocturia, frequent urination during the nighttime. *See* enuresis.

nocturnal emission, popularly called WET DREAM, an involuntary discharge of semen while asleep, usually prompted by an erotic dream.
·behavioral manifestations during sleep **5**:1014a

nocturne (French: "night piece"), musical composition of sombre mood, inspired by or evocative of night. In the 19th century the nocturne became widely cultivated as a character piece for piano. The genre was created by the Irish composer John Field, who published the first set of nocturnes in 1814. He was succeeded by Frédéric Chopin, whose 19 nocturnes are considered the most nearly perfect examples of the form. The German counterpart of the nocturne, the *Nachtstück*, was cultivated by Robert Schumann and, in the 20th century, by Paul Hindemith (*1922 Suite* for piano). The three *Nocturnes* for orchestra by the 19th-century composer Claude Debussy present brilliant contrasts of mood. In the 20th century the most profound cultivator of the nocturne genre is Béla Bartók, whose very personal night-music style—found, for example, in *Out of Doors*, fourth movement, and in the *String Quartet No. 4*, third movement—is characterized by a distinctly macabre quality.

The late 18th-century notturno (Italian), a collection of light pieces for chamber ensemble, appears to have absolutely no connection with the 19th-century nocturne. Similar to such light, several-movement forms as the serenade, cassation, and divertimento, the notturno is a compromise between the Baroque suite and the Classical symphony. It was cultivated by Mozart and Haydn.

Nocturnes (1899), orchestral work by Claude Debussy.
·Impressionist orchestration **13**:646g

Noda, city, Chiba Prefecture (*ken*), Honshu, Japan, between the Edo-gawa (Edo River) and the Tone-gawa. The city was an important river port during the Tokugawa era

Soy sauce factory in Noda (Ōsaka-Kōbe), Japan
Design-Uni—FPG

(1603–1867), when it first became known for its production of soy sauce. The central area of Noda now contains numerous soy sauce factories and others related to its production. Since World War II, Noda has gradually developed as a residential suburb of Tokyo, to which it is connected by rail. Pop. (1970) 68,641.
35°56′ N, 139°52′ E

nodal tachycardia, over-rapid heartbeat originating in the atrioventricular node of the heartbeat impulse conduction system.
·heartbeat impulse changes **3**:893e

noddy (bird): *see* tern.

node (Latin *nodus*, "loop"), in astronomy, the intersection of the orbit plane of some celestial body, such as the Moon, a planet, or comet, with the plane of the ecliptic (the apparent path of the Sun among the stars) as projected on the celestial sphere. The ascending node is the one where the body crosses from the south to the north side of the ecliptic, the opposite one being the descending node. An eclipse of the Sun or Moon can occur only when the Moon is at or near a node; similarly, only when one of the inner planets is at or near a node can it appear in transit across the Sun. *See also* orbit.
·eclipse cycles and prediction **6**:190g
·Moon's orbit, eclipses, and saros **12**:415h
·satellite orbits and perturbations **11**:759h

node (physics): *see* wave, standing.

node, in mathematics, point at which two parts of a curve cross. A double point on a curve is also called a node.
·algebraic structure theory **1**:520a

node, in botany, region of a plant stem at which one or more leaves are attached. A leaf scar remains when a leaf is shed.
·Laurales structural features **10**:710g
·orchid evolutionary trends **13**:651c
·stem growth and development **13**:727c; illus.

node of Ranvier, constriction in a peripheral nerve fibre, in which the fatty substance surrounding the fibre (myelin sheath) is interrupted.
·anatomic site and impulse influence **12**:997c
·nerve impulses in myelinated fibres **12**:969g; illus. 971
·neuron structure and function **12**:978c

Nodier, Charles (b. April 29, 1780, Besançon, Fr.—d. Jan. 27, 1844, Paris), a writer

Nodier, detail of an oil painting by P. Guerin, 1824; in the Musée National de Versailles et des Trianons
Cliche Musees Nationaux, Paris

more important for the influence he had on the French Romantic movement than for his own writings. He had an eventful early life, in the course of which he fell foul of the authorities for a skit on Napoleon. In 1824 he settled down in Paris after his appointment as director of the Bibliothèque de l'Arsenal ("Arsenal Library") and soon became one of the leaders of the literary life of the capital. In his drawing room at the Arsenal, Nodier drew together all the young men who were to be the leading lights of the Romantic movement: Victor Hugo, Alfred de Musset, and Charles-Augustin Sainte-Beuve.

Nodier's tastes were catholic, and he had ample opportunity for wide reading. An ardent admirer of Goethe and Shakespeare, he did much to encourage the French Romantics to look abroad for inspiration. Nodier wrote a great deal, and in his day he was respected as an authority on the French language and on the picturesque antiquities of France. His only works that are still read are his fantastic short stories, rather in the style of the German Romantic E.T.A. Hoffmann. By his revelation of the creative power of the dream and by his equation of a state of innocence with certain conditions normally called mad, Nodier was rebelling against the tyranny of "common sense" and opening up a new literary territory for later generations. His election to the Académie Française in 1833 virtually constituted official recognition that Romanticism had become a significant and respectable literary movement.
·Hugo's early literary association **8**:1132h

Nodosaridcea, suborder of Mesozoic foraminifera.
·fossil shells and era of appearance **7**:558a; illus. 557

Nodosaurus, extinct genus of Late Cretaceous armoured dinosaurs of North America (the Cretaceous Period began 136,000,000 years ago and lasted 71,000,000 years).

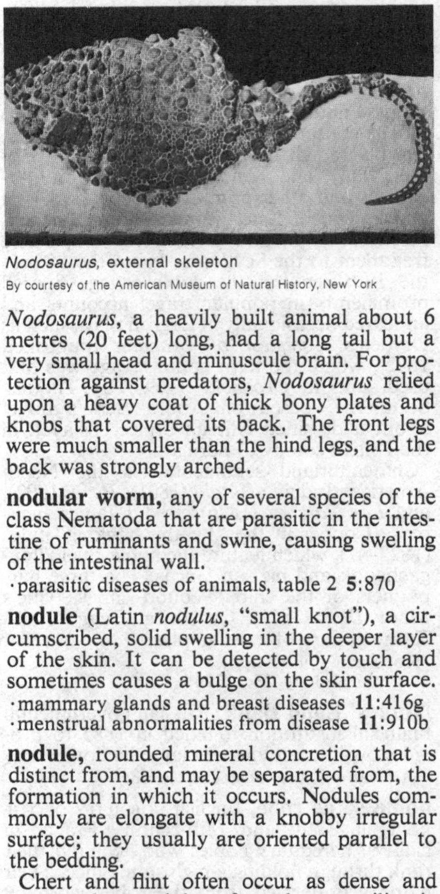

Nodosaurus, external skeleton
By courtesy of the American Museum of Natural History, New York

Nodosaurus, a heavily built animal about 6 metres (20 feet) long, had a long tail but a very small head and minuscule brain. For protection against predators, *Nodosaurus* relied upon a heavy coat of thick bony plates and knobs that covered its back. The front legs were much smaller than the hind legs, and the back was strongly arched.

nodular worm, any of several species of the class Nematoda that are parasitic in the intestine of ruminants and swine, causing swelling of the intestinal wall.
·parasitic diseases of animals, table 2 **5**:870

nodule (Latin *nodulus*, "small knot"), a circumscribed, solid swelling in the deeper layer of the skin. It can be detected by touch and sometimes causes a bulge on the skin surface.
·mammary glands and breast diseases **11**:416g
·menstrual abnormalities from disease **11**:910b

nodule, rounded mineral concretion that is distinct from, and may be separated from, the formation in which it occurs. Nodules commonly are elongate with a knobby irregular surface; they usually are oriented parallel to the bedding.

Chert and flint often occur as dense and structureless nodules of nearly pure silica in limestone or chalk, where they seem to be replacements of the carbonate rock by silica. Clay ironstone, a mixture of clay and siderite (iron carbonate), sometimes occurs as layers of dark gray to brown, fine-grained nodules overlying coal seams. Phosphorites, massive phosphate rocks, often occur in phosphate deposits, in some limestones and chalks, and on the present sea bottom as black, fine-grained, and dense nodules with an elliptical shape and no structure.
·formation in shales **16**:636b
·iron concentration in soils **16**:1021f

nodule bacteria: *see* eubacteria.

nodus lymphaticus (biology): *see* lymph nodule.

Noe (biblical hero): *see* Noah.

Noël, Alexandre: *see* Natalis, Alexander.

Noel-Baker, Philip John (b. Nov. 1, 1889, London), statesman and advocate of international disarmament, received the Nobel Prize for Peace in 1959. Fluent in seven languages, he campaigned widely for 40 years for peace through multilateral disarmament.

The son of Canadian-born Quakers, Baker added his wife's surname, Noel, to his own about 1926. A noted athlete, he ran in the 1912 and 1920 Olympic Games and was captain of the British team in the 1924 Olympics. During World War I he served with ambulance units in France, Belgium, and Italy and was decorated for distinguished service.

A member of the British delegation to the Paris Peace Conference in 1919, Baker (as he then was) subsequently joined the League of Nations secretariat. He assisted Fridtjof Nan-

Noel-Baker
Camera Press—Publix

sen, the Norwegian explorer and humanitarian who received the Nobel Prize for Peace in 1922 for his work with wartime refugees. At the League of Nations assembly in 1923–24, Baker served as personal assistant to Lord Robert Cecil (later Viscount Cecil of Chelwood), promoter of the League and recipient of the Nobel Prize for Peace in 1937. He also was principal assistant to Arthur Henderson, president of the disarmament conference at Geneva, in 1932–33.

Noel-Baker sat in the House of Commons as a Labour member from 1929 to 1931 and from 1936 to 1970. Between 1945 and 1961 he was successively minister of state, secretary of state for air and for Commonwealth relations, and minister of fuel and power. He helped to draft the UN charter and was a member of the British delegation to the General Assembly in 1946–47. In 1960 he became president of the International Council on Sport and Physical Recreation of UNESCO. His survey of the disarmament problem was published as *The Arms Race: A Programme for World Disarmament* (1958).

Noether, (Amalie) Emmy (b. March 23, 1882, Erlangen, now in West Germany—d. April 14, 1935, Bryn Mawr, Pa.), mathematician whose innovations in higher algebra gained her recognition as the most creative abstract algebraist of modern times. She received the Ph.D. degree *summa cum laude* from the University of Erlangen in 1907, with a dissertation on algebraic invariants. From 1913 she lectured occasionally at Erlangen, substituting for her father, Max Noether (1844–1921). In 1915 she went to the University of Göttingen and was persuaded by the eminent mathematicians David Hilbert and Felix Klein to remain there in spite of the objections of some faculty members who wished to exclude women lecturers. She finally won formal admission as an academic lecturer in 1919.

The appearance of "Moduln in nichtkommutativen Bereichen, insbesondere aus Differential- und Differenzen-Ausdrücken" (1920; "Concerning Moduli in Noncommutative Fields, Particularly in Differential and Difference Terms"), written in collaboration with a Göttingen colleague, Werner Schmeidler, and published in *Mathematische Zeitschrift*, marked the first notice of Noether as an extraordinary mathematician. For the next six years her investigations centred on the general theory of ideals (special subsets of rings), for which her residual theorem is an important part. On an axiomatic basis she developed a general theory of ideals for all cases. Her abstract theory helped draw together many important mathematical developments.

From 1927 Noether concentrated on noncommutative algebras, their linear transformations, and their application to commutative number fields. She built up the theory of noncommutative algebras in a new unified and purely conceptual way. In collaboration with Helmut Hasse and Richard Brauer, she investigated the structure of noncommutative algebras and their application to commutative fields by means of cross product. Important papers from this period are "Hyperkomplexe Grössen und Darstellungstheorie" (1929; "Hypercomplex Number Systems and Their Representation") and "Nichtkommutative Algebren" (1933; "Noncommutative Algebras"), both in *Mathematische Zeitschrift*.

In addition to research and teaching, Noether helped edit the *Mathematische Annalen*. From 1930 to 1933 she was the centre of the strongest mathematical activity at Göttingen. The extent and significance of her work cannot be accurately judged from her papers, because much of her work appeared in the publications of students and colleagues; many times a suggestion or even a casual remark by her stimulated another to complete and perfect some idea.

When the Nazis came to power in Germany in 1933, Noether and other Jewish professors at Göttingen were dismissed. In October she left for the United States to become visiting professor of mathematics at Bryn Mawr College and to lecture and conduct research at the Institute for Advanced Study, Princeton, N.J.

no-fault insurance, automobile insurance plan, existing in various forms in some Canadian provinces, Puerto Rico, and several U.S. states, under which a person injured in an accident receives compensation directly from his or her own insurance company without the necessity of proving that another person was at fault. Under the traditional system, derived from a basic premise in Anglo-Saxon tort law, the person whose negligent actions caused the damage is held financially responsible.

Most existing no-fault plans are limited in that they usually permit the insured person to sue the person at fault for damages in excess of those covered by the plan and that they permit insuring companies to recover costs from each other according to decisions on liability. Total no-fault insurance would not permit the insured to enter tort liability actions or the insurer to recover costs from another insurer.

Nō flute, Japanese NŌ-KAN, flute used in music for the Japanese Nō theatre.
·dramatic role in Nō theatre **12**:685f

Nogai (people and language): *see* Nogay; Nogay language.

Nogales (Mexico): *see* Heroica Nogales.

Nogales, city, seat (1899) of Santa Cruz County, southern Arizona, U.S. A port of entry on the Mexican border, it adjoins Heroica Nogales, Sonora. Divided by International Avenue, the two communities are known as Ambos Nogales. Originally called Issaactown (for Jacob Issaacson, who built an inn at Nogales Pass before the arrival of the Southern Pacific Railroad in 1882), it was renamed Nogales for its walnut (*nogal*) trees. It was the scene of fighting between Pancho Villa's forces and U.S. national guardsmen (1916) and between town militia of the two communities (1918).

Nearby are the Tumacacori Mission (since 1908 a national monument) and the ruins of the Guevavi Mission and Tubac, the first white settlement in Arizona. The Coronado National Forest is nearby. Cattle raising, mining, and international trade are the economic mainstays. Pop. (1980) 15,683.
31°20′ N, 110°56′ W

Nogal (NUGAL) **Valley,** geographical depression, northern Somalia, extending about 150 mi (240 km) northwest of the mouth of the intermittent Nogal River.
8°35′ N, 48°35′ E
·geological and climatic characteristics **16**:1057g
·map, Somalia **16**:1059

Nogaret, Guillaume de (b. 1260/70, Saint-Félix-de-Caraman, Toulouse—d. April 1313), magistrate under King Philip IV the Fair of France, who became one of the most vigorous of the *légistes*, or expositors, of the royal power, especially in ecclesiastical affairs; in the conflict between Philip and Pope Boniface VIII he played a direct role in carrying out the King's retribution against the Pope.

Son of a bourgeois, Nogaret began his career as a teacher of jurisprudence at Montpellier in 1291, entered the royal service as *jugemage* at Nîmes about 1294, and seems to have been with Philip in Normandy in 1295. A member of the King's council, he was entrusted in 1296 with missions to Bigorre and to Champagne to establish the King's rights there. In 1299 he began to style himself *miles*, or knight.

On March 7, 1303, Philip authorized Nogaret to go to Italy to take measures against the Pope; and five days later, on March 12, at a meeting in Paris, it was Nogaret who, after denouncing the Pope as irregularly installed, as a heretic, as a simonist, and as a notorious sinner, demanded the summoning of a general council of the church to try him. Proceeding to Italy, he established himself at Staggia in Tuscany, whence he made contact with the Pope's enemies, including some cardinals. The Pope, meanwhile, was spending the summer at Anagni, and intended to issue a bull excommunicating Philip. On Sept. 7, 1303, Nogaret and Sciarra Colonna, whose family was pursuing its own vendetta against Boniface, entered Anagni with a band of mercenaries and arrested the Pope. Nogaret saved the Pope from death at the hands of the Colonna, but the violence of the Colonna faction not only frustrated his carefully prepared show of legality but also provoked the people of Anagni, who had at first connived at the coup, to rise on September 9 and release the Pope. Forced to abandon his enterprise and to flee to Ferentino, Nogaret returned to France early in 1304.

Nogaret had acted as a sincere Christian desirous of freeing the church from a pope whom he thought unworthy; but Boniface's successor, Benedict XI, though he exculpated Philip, issued the bull *Flagitiosum scelus* (June 7, 1304), excommunicating Nogaret and 15 other participants in the outrage. Philip, however, raised Nogaret's pension from 300 to 800 livres and, on Sept. 22, 1307, appointed him keeper of the great seal.

Nogaret was from 1307 much occupied with the conduct of Philip's proceedings against the Templars. After long appealing against his excommunication, he obtained absolution from Pope Clement V on April 27, 1311, with the proviso that he go as a pilgrim to the Holy Land at the first opportunity and stay there until the Pope should recall him. He died, however, before executing this proviso.
·Boniface VIII's opposition to Philip IV **3**:33e
·invasion of Italy **9**:1134a
·Philip IV's conflict with Boniface VIII **14**:224d

Nogaret de la Valette, Jean-Louis de, duc d'Épernon: *see* Épernon, Jean-Louis de Nogaret de la Valette, duc d'.

Nōgata, city, Fukuoka Prefecture (*ken*), Kyushu, Japan, at the confluence of the Onga-gawa (*gawa*, "river") and the Hikosan-gawa. Formed as a castle town in 1626, it de-

clined about 100 years later, barely maintaining its importance as a trade and distribution centre of agricultural products. With the exploitation of the nearby Chikuhō coalfield in the late 19th century, Nōgata revived. After World War II, however, the mines were gradually closed, and the city is now a commercial centre producing machinery and other industrial goods. Nōgata is gradually becoming a suburb of Kita-Kyūshū, to which it is connected by rail. Pop. (1975) 58,551.
33°44′ N, 130°44′ E
·map, Japan **10**:37

Nogay, also spelled NOGAI, Turkic ethnic group of the Soviet Union.
·Soviet Union nationalities distribution, table 3 **17**:339

Nogay (NOGAI) **language,** member of the Turkic language group (a subfamily of the Altaic languages) spoken by some 52,000 persons in the northeastern Caucasus region of the Soviet Union. Nogay belongs to the northwestern, or Kipchak, division of the Turkic languages, along with such languages as Kazakh and Tatar. It has three major dialects: White Nogay, spoken in the Karachay-Cherkess Autonomous Oblast, and Black Nogay and Central Nogay, both spoken in the Dagestan Autonomous Soviet Socialist Republic. Many Central Asian Turkic peoples, such as the Kirgiz and the Kara-Kalpaks, trace their descent from the nomadic Nogay peoples of the Golden Horde. For linguistic characteristics, *see* Turkic languages.
·affiliation and distribution, table 1 **1**:636

Nogent-sur-Marne, town, an eastern suburb of Paris, in Val-de-Marne *département*, north central France, on the right bank of the Marne River and on the eastern edge of the Bois de Vincennes. Nogent is an old residential area. The painter Antoine Watteau died there in 1721. Manufactures include chemicals and hardware. Pop. (1975) 25,469.
48°50′ N, 2°29′ E

nogging, also called NOGGING PIECE, in frame construction, short, horizontal timber fastened between a pair of studs in a partition to stiffen the wall and to support fixtures.
·partition design and construction **3**:955f

Noginsk, city, Moscow *oblast* (administrative region), western Russian Soviet Federated Socialist Republic, on the Klyazma River east of Moscow. Originating as a village called Yamskaya, it became the town of Bogorodsk in 1781 and was renamed Noginsk in 1930. It is one of the largest Soviet textile centres, cotton constituting more than three-quarters of its production. Pop. (1976 est.) 111,000.
55°51′ N, 38°27′ E

Nógrád, *megye* (county), Hungary, occupies an upland area of 982 sq mi (2,544 sq km) dominated by the Cserhát Hills, a continuation of the Transdanubian Mountains. A few monadnocks (*i.e.*, hills of resistant rock) and isolated volcanic intrusions stand out from a sandy, clayey terrain. To the north the Cserhát region is drained into the Nógrád Basin by the Ipoly River. Original forest cover has been cleared where possible for plowland, though agriculture is not so prominent as elsewhere in Hungary, poppy seeds and lentils being the chief crops. There are several clay pits in the vicinity of Romhány. Around the town of Hollókő is the Palóc country, noted for traditional crafts. The industrial centre of Salgótarján (*q.v.*), the *megye* seat, lies in the Tárján River Valley. The town of Balassagyarmat, the former *megye* seat, founded in AD 900, has a notable museum of folk art. Pop. (1976 est.) 234,900.
·area and population table **9**:25
·map, Hungary **9**:22

Noguchi, Hideyo, original name NOGUCHI SEISAKU (b. Nov. 24, 1876, Inawashiro, Japan—d. May 21, 1928, Accra, now in Ghana), bacteriologist who first discovered *Treponema*

Hideyo Noguchi
Boyer—H. Roger-Viollet

pallidum, the causative agent of syphilis, in the brains of persons suffering from paresis. He also proved that both Oroya fever and verruga peruana could be produced by *Bartonella bacilliformis*; they are now known to be different phases of Carrión's disease, or bartonellosis.

Noguchi graduated (1897) from a proprietary medical school in Tokyo and then went in 1900 to the University of Pennsylvania, in Philadelphia, where he worked on snake venoms under Simon Flexner. In 1904 he went to the Rockefeller Institute for Medical Research, New York City, which sponsored his work for almost a quarter of a century. Noguchi devised means of cultivating microorganisms that had never before been grown in the test tube. He studied poliomyelitis and trachoma and worked on a vaccine and serum for yellow fever. He died of yellow fever, contracted during research on the disease in Africa.

Noguchi, Isamu (b. Nov. 17, 1904, Los Angeles), sculptor and designer, one of the strongest advocates of the expressive power of

Isamu Noguchi, photograph by Arnold Newman, 1947
© Arnold Newman

organic abstract shapes in 20th-century American sculpture. He spent his early years in Japan and, after studying in New York City, he worked in Paris for two years as assistant to Constantin Brancusi. There he met Alberto Giacometti and Alexander Calder and became an enthusiast of abstract sculpture. He was also influenced by the Surrealist works of Picasso and Joan Miró.

Much of his work, such as his "Bird C(MU)" (1952–58; Museum of Modern Art, New York City), consists of elegantly abstracted, rounded forms in highly polished stone, which reflect his admiration of Brancusi's work. Such works as "Euripides" (1966; collection of the artist), however, employ massive blocks of stone, brutally gouged and hammered. To his terra-cotta and stone sculptures Noguchi brought some of the spirit and mystery of early art, principally Japanese earthenware, studied during periodic residences in Japan.

Noguchi, who had premedical training at Columbia University, sensed the interrelatedness of bone and rock forms, the comparative anatomy of existence, as seen in his "Kouros" (1945; Metropolitan Museum of Art, New York City). Recognizing the appropriateness of sculptural shapes for architecture, he created a work in low relief (1938) for the Associated Press Building in New York City and designed a fountain for the Ford Pavilion at the New York World's Fair of 1939. His garden for the United Nations Educational, Scientific, and Cultural Organization (UNESCO) in Paris (1958), his playground in Hawaii, and his furniture designs have won international praise. He also designed a monument to the dead and a bridge for Hiroshima, but only the latter was actually produced.
·modern sculpture influence **19**:242h

Noguès, Charles-Auguste (1876–1971), French army officer.
·Allied North African invasion **19**:996e

No hay cosa como callar (1639), English SILENCE IS GOLDEN, play by Calderón.
·Calderón's works and style **3**:594b

noiade, the Lapp shaman, a religious specialist who mediated between the people he served and supernatural beings.

The shamanic practices of the Finno-Ugric peoples have been best preserved among the Voguls (or Mansis) and Ostyaks (or Khants) as well as the Lapps. Basically they consist of the manipulation of the supernatural by a specially trained, usually naturally gifted, sensitive person in order to aid people in various serious troubles, of which illness is probably the commonest. Upon being asked to help, the *noiade* performs a dramatic séance with a traditionally structured sequence of steps, including divinatory procedures, falling into trance, confronting supernatural beings either to fight them or receive aid from them, and the actual ritual treatment of the patient, in the case of illness. The *noiade*s can perform both good and evil and formerly were much feared on account of their powers, which they also used to political and economic advantage. In Finland the term *noita* has been preserved mainly in the sense of an evil-working sorcerer, with another term, *tietäjä*, applied to the specialist in beneficial mediation with the supernatural.

The word *noiade* is genetically related to several other terms used by the Finno-Ugric peoples for their religious specialists. Finnish *noita*, Vogul *nait*, and Estonian *noit* belong together linguistically, and their origin may be traced back to the common Finno-Ugric period before 2500 BC.

Noir, Victor, originally YVES SALMON (b. July 27, 1848, Attigny, Fr.—d. Jan. 10, 1870, Paris), journalist whose death at the hands of Prince Pierre-Napoléon Bonaparte, a first

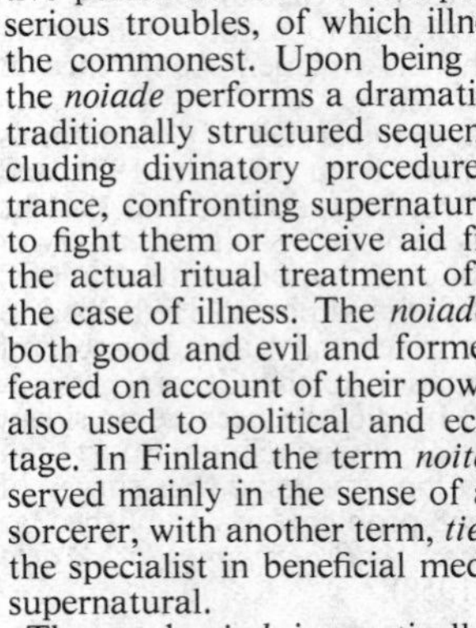

Noir, lithograph by Caleb (19th century)
By courtesy of the Bibliotheque Nationale, Paris

cousin of Emperor Napoleon III, led to an increase in the already mounting revival of republican and radical agitation that plagued the Second Empire in its final months.

Accompanied by a colleague, Ulric de Fonvielle, Noir visited the Prince on Jan. 10, 1870, to deliver a challenge to a duel from another journalist, Paschal Grousset; an altercation ensued in which the Prince killed Noir. Noir's funeral at Neuilly (January 12) was the scene of a mob demonstration against the empire. Tried by a special high court at Tours, the Prince argued that Noir had provoked the shooting by slapping him in the face; Fonvielle denied this allegation, but the prince was acquitted March 25, 1870.

noise, in acoustics, any undesired sound, either one that is intrinsically objectionable or one that interferes with other sounds being listened to. In electronics and information theory, noise means random, unpredictable, and undesirable signals, or changes in signals, that mask desired information content. Noise in radio transmission is called static, and in television it is called snow. White noise is a complex signal or sound having numerous component frequencies, or tones, all of which have equal intensity.

·aircraft cause and physical reactions **1**:144a
·antenna noise source and elimination **1**:967h
·characteristics of measurement systems **11**:732h
·digital system in high frequency telecommunications **18**:87g; illus. 88
·ear's vulnerability to damage **5**:1126c
·environmental factors influencing safety **16**:141g; tables 140
·hearing disorder involvement **5**:1136g
·industrial environment risks **9**:530b
·information transmission, error measurement, and parity check **9**:575b *passim* to 577h
·language and tone symbolism **2**:44b
·lead sheet for noise control **10**:729h
·musical sound's physical characteristics **17**:34h
·music elements and definition **12**:662f
·radar noise sources and reduction **15**:375g
·radio noise causes and preventive measures **15**:426a
·satellite communication interferences **16**:266b
·seismometer explosion detection systems **19**:601d
·sonar disturbance and water acoustics **17**:2e
·telegraph transmission disturbances **18**:73h
·X-ray pulse discrimination in detectors **19**:1068e

noise control, equipment and techniques for maintaining the level of objectionable noise in an area within acceptable limits.

·acoustical engineering principles **1**:54a
·acoustic theory application **17**:33h

Noisy-le-Sec, town, a northeastern suburb of Paris, in Seine-Saint-Denis *département*, north central France. It has metallurgical and chemical industries; manufactures include trucks, steel tubes, and brushes. Latest census 34,058.

Nō-kan, music of the Japanese Nō flute, the main function of which is to signal sections of the Nō drama.

·dramatic function **12**:685f

Nok culture, ancient Iron Age culture that existed on the Benue Plateau of Nigeria between about 500 BC and AD 200. The most characteristic artifacts are clay figurines of animals and stylized human beings, usually heads; thus, the culture is often called the Nok figurine culture. Other artifacts include iron tools, stone axes and other stone tools, and stone ornaments.

·Nigeria's Stone Age examples **13**:96b
·sculptural form and style **1**:257d; illus.

Nokhai, 13th-century Mongol leader.

·rebellion and western Tatar ascendency **16**:43f

Nokrashy (NUGRĀSHĪ) **Pasha, Maḥmūd Fahmī an-** (1888–1948), Egyptian prime minister from 1945 to 1948.

·Wafd, Muslim Brethren, and assassination **6**:498h

Nola, town and episcopal see, Napoli province, Campania region, southern Italy, in the fertile and highly cultivated Campanian plain, just east-northeast of Naples. It originated as a city of the Aurunci, Oscans, Etruscans, and Samnites (ancient Italic peoples) and was known as Novla (New Town), before it passed to the Romans in 313 BC. The emperor Augustus died there in AD 14. It was the birthplace of St. Felix, its first bishop, who was buried with other Christian martyrs at nearby Cimitile. Sacked by Gaiseric, king of the Vandals, in 455 and later by the Saracens, Nola was captured by King Manfred of Sicily in the 13th century and later belonged to the Orsini family, before passing to the kingdom of Naples in 1528. There are traces of an amphitheatre and a necropolis with frescoed tombs and of later basilicas and other constructions of the 4th and 5th centuries. In the seminary at Nola, the Cippus Abellanus, an Oscan inscription named after the ancient Abella (now Avella), was discovered (1750). The Gothic cathedral (1395–1402) is believed to occupy the site of a church erected by the town's patron St. Paulinus (elected bishop of Nola 410) in honour of St. Felix of Nola, whose relics are kept in the crypt. Other notable landmarks are the Palazzo Orsini (1461) and a monument to the philosopher Giordano Bruno, who was born at Nola in 1548.

An agricultural and commercial centre on the Naples–Foggia–Avellino railway, Nola's products include vegetables, fruit, maize (corn), and hemp. Pop. (1971 prelim.) mun., 26,460.
40°55′ N, 14°33′ E

·map, Italy **9**:1088

Nolan, Sidney (b. April 22, 1917, Melbourne, Australia), artist internationally known for his paintings based on Australian folklore. With little formal art training Nolan turned professionally to painting at 21 after varied experiences as a racing cyclist, cook, and gold miner. His early works show the influences of Klee and Moholy-Nagy and include the controversial "Boy and the Moon" (1940)—a splash of yellow against a raw blue background. In 1941 he designed the scenery and costumes for the Serge Lifar ballet *Icarus*, returning to themes from classical mythology in 1960 when he exhibited "Leda and the

"Kelly," oil painting by Sidney Nolan, 1954; in the Collection of Lord and Lady Snow
By courtesy of Lord and Lady Snow, London

Swan," his first series of paintings not based on Australian themes. Apart from his landscapes, most of his works deal with Australian historical or legendary characters and events—notably, the bushranger Ned Kelly, the Eureka Stockade affair, Mrs. Fraser and the convict Bracefell, and the explorers Robert O'Hara Burke and W.J. Wills. His style is highly individual, as are many of the mediums he has employed, such as ripolin and polyvinyl acetate on masonite, glass, paper, or canvas.

·painting series of Ned Kelly **13**:883g

Nolan, Thomas Brennan (b. March 21, 1901, Greenfield, Mass.), geologist known for his regional study of the geology of the Basin and Range Province of the U.S. He became a member of the U.S. Geological Survey in 1925 and served as its director from 1956 to 1965. His work includes determination of the structure and ore deposits of the Basin and Range area.

Nolanaceae, family of flowering plants in the order Scrophulariales.

·evolution and classification **16**:416e

Noland, Kenneth (b. April 10, 1924, Asheville, N.C.), painter of the Abstract Expressionist school of artists, who took an emotional approach to the conception and execution of their works. He was one of the first to use

Noland, photograph by Arnold Newman, 1967
© Arnold Newman

the technique of staining the canvas with thinned paints and of deploying his colours in concentric rings and parallels, shaped and proportioned in relation to the shape of the canvas. He attended Black Mountain College in North Carolina and studied under the French sculptor Ossip Zadkine in Paris (1948–49). He presented his first one-man show there in 1949.

Noland collaborated with the American painter Morris Louis in Washington, D.C., on the technique of staining with thinned paints. This method presented pure, saturated colour as an integral part of the canvas. Noland arrived at his characteristic style in the late 1950s. Typical of his work is "Par Transit" (1966), in which Noland's brilliant, stained paints focus the eye on the interaction of juxtaposed colours to create an optical sensation.

Nolasco, Saint Peter: *see* Peter Nolasco, Saint.

Nolde, Emil (b. EMIL HANSEN, Aug. 7, 1867, Nolde, Ger.—d. April 15, 1956, Seebüll), Expressionist painter, printmaker, and watercolourist known for his violent religious works and his foreboding landscapes. Born of a peasant family, the youthful Nolde made his living as a wood-carver. He was able to study art formally only when some of his early works were reproduced and sold as postcards, providing him with an independent income.

In Paris, Nolde was struck with the Impressionists' colour and brushwork, and he began to paint works that bear a superficial affinity to Impressionistic painting (*see* Impressionism). Nolde, however, applied vibrant colours in rapid, nervous strokes, infusing his compositions with a turbulence alien to the work of the French Impressionists. In 1906 he was invited to join Die Brücke (*see* Brücke, Die), an association of Dresden-based Expressionist artists who admired his "storm of colour." But Nolde, a solitary and intuitive painter, dissociated himself from that tightly-knit group of painter-theorists after a year and a half.

A fervently religious man, Nolde was racked by a deep sense of sin. In such works as "Dance Around the Golden Calf" (1910; Bayerische Staatsgemäldesammlungen, Munich) and "In the Port of Alexandria" from the series depicting "The Legend of St. Maria Aegyptica" (1912; Kunsthalle, Hamburg), the erotic frenzy of the figures and the demonic, masklike faces are rendered with deliberately crude draftsmanship and dissonant colours, revealing Nolde's obsession with the bestiality of man's sinful nature. By contrast, compositions such as "Christ Among the Children" (1910; Museum of Modern Art, New York) illustrate the joyful beatitude of the spiritual life.

"Dance Around the Golden Calf," oil painting by Emil Nolde, 1910; in the Bayerische Staatsgemäldesammlungen, Munich

By courtesy of the Nolde-Foundation; photograph, Bayerische Staatsgemaldesammlungen, Munich

Nolde was, nevertheless, plagued by religious doubts, with which he often struggled in his works. Such compositions as "The Last Supper" (1909; Statens Museum for Kunst, Copenhagen) reflect the artist's despair and display notable psychological insight into the Passion of Jesus, especially in dramatizing the emotional and spiritual isolation of Christ. But in the "Doubting Thomas" from the nine-part polyptych "The Life of Christ" (1911–12; Stiftung Seebüll Ada und Emil Nolde, Seebüll, Ger.), the relief of Nolde's own doubts may be seen in the quiet awe of Thomas as he is confronted with Jesus' wounds.

During 1913 and 1914, Nolde was a member of an ethnological expedition that reached the East Indies. There he was impressed with the power of unsophisticated belief, as is evident in his lithograph "Dancer" (1913).

Back in Europe, Nolde led an increasingly reclusive life on the Baltic coast of Germany. His almost mystical affinity for the brooding terrain led to such works as his "Marsh Landscape" (1916; Kunstmuseum, Basel, Switz.), in which the low horizon, dominated by dark clouds, creates a majestic sense of space. Landscapes done after 1916, such as his watercolour "Windmills on the Marsh" (1926; Stiftung Seebüll Ada und Emil Nolde, Seebüll, Ger.), were generally of a cooler tonality than his early works. But his masterful realizations of flowers—*e.g.*, his watercolour "Red and White Amaryllis" (Kunsthalle, Hamburg)—retain the brilliant colours of his earlier works while avoiding harshness.

Nolde was a prolific graphic artist. He was especially fond of the stark black and white effect that he employed in such crudely incised woodcuts as "Prophet" (1912), "Girls in Fantastic Setting" (1906), and the "Servant" (1912). Yet the same medium also yielded some of his most intimate statements in "Ada Nolde" (1906) and "Young Mother" (1917).

Nolde was an early advocate of Germany's National Socialist Party. But when the Nazis came to power, they declared his work "decadent" and forbade him to paint. After World War II he resumed painting but often merely reworked older themes. His last "Self-Portrait" (1947; Stiftung Seebüll Ada und Emil Nolde, Seebüll, Ger.) retains his vigorous brushwork but reveals the disillusioned withdrawal of the artist in his 80th year.

·drawing and painting combination **5**:1006d
·20th-century German printmaking **14**:1095e

Nöldeke, Theodor (b. March 2, 1836, Harburg, now in West Germany—d. Dec. 25, 1930, Karlsruhe), Semitic language scholar and Islāmic historian noted especially for his history of the Qur'ān (1859). After holding several academic posts, he became professor of Oriental languages at the University of Strasbourg (1872–1906). His large contribution to the history of Semitic languages included the publication of several grammars. His many scholarly works included *Geschichte der Perser und Araber zur Zeit Sassaniden* (1879; "History of the Persians and Arabs to the Sāsānid Period"). Among his works intended for a general readership were *Orientalische Skizzen* (1892; *Sketches from Eastern History*, 1892) and a life of Muḥammad (1863).

·Sāsānian chronology system **9**:846f

Noli, António de (1419–66), Portuguese navigator.

·Cape Verde Islands discovery **3**:798g

Nolichucky River, rises in the Blue Ridge Mountains in western North Carolina, U.S., and flows northwest into Tennessee, then west to empty into the French Broad River after a course of 150 mi (241 km). A dam on the Nolichucky just south of Greeneville, Tenn., impounds Davy Crockett Lake, named for the frontiersman, who was born (1786) on the river near Limestone. John Sevier, first governor of Tennessee, lived on the riverbank (1783–90) and was nicknamed "Nolichucky Jack." The river was named for a Cherokee village, and the word probably means "spruce tree place."
36°07′ N, 83°14′ W

Noli me tangere (1886; "Touch Me Not"), political novel by José Rizal.

·Philippine literary nationalism **17**:236h

Nolina (plant genus): *see* Agavaceae.

Nollekens, Joseph (b. Aug. 11, 1737, London—d. April 23, 1823, London), neoclassical sculptor whose busts made him the most fashionable English portrait sculptor of his day. At 13 he entered the studio of the noted sculptor of tombs and busts Peter Scheemakers, from whom Nollekens learned to appreciate the sculpture of antiquity. In 1760 he went to Rome, where David Garrick and Laurence Sterne were among the English visitors who sat for him. After his return to England in 1770 he became a member of the Royal Academy (1772) and was patronized by George III. Among his famous likenesses are those of George III, William Pitt, Charles Fox, and Benjamin West. Many of his works were influenced by ancient Roman busts of the late Republic style. He personally preferred sculpturing mythological works based on ancient prototypes, especially genteel but erotic Venuses delicately modelled in an almost Rococo manner.

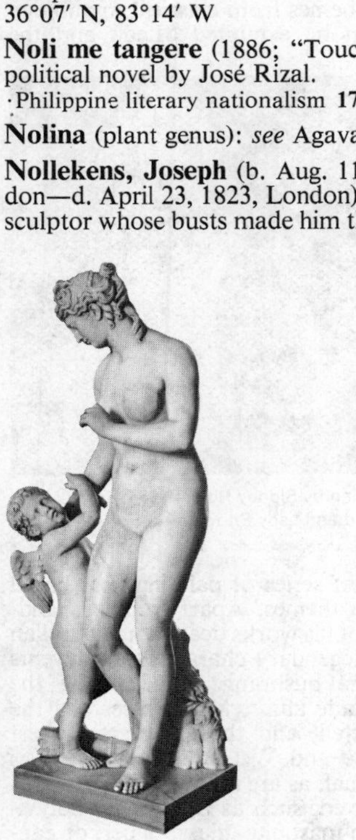

"Venus Chiding Cupid," marble sculpture by Joseph Nollekens, 1778; in the Usher Gallery, Lincoln, Eng.

By courtesy of the Libraries, Museum and Art Gallery, Lincoln, Eng.

nolle prosequi, in Anglo-American law, request by a plaintiff in a civil suit, or by a prosecutor in a criminal action, that the prosecution of the case should cease, either on some or all of the counts or with respect to some or all of the defendants. It is usually used when there is insufficient evidence to insure successful prosecution or when there has been a settlement between the parties out of court.

In English criminal law, the power to enter a nolle prosequi is vested in the attorney general and is rarely used. In the United States, the power is generally exercised at the discretion of the prosecuting officer, typically the district attorney, and is an important adjunct to the administration of criminal justice. Particularly in large cities, many more criminal prosecutions are initiated than it is feasible to try. The nolle prosequi thus serves as a screening device by which the district attorney is enabled to exercise a measure of control over the criminal docket. It is also used to effect an informal settlement, as where a thief agrees to make restitution to his victim. In some states, the common law rule that the entry of a nolle prosequi is within the sole discretion of the district attorney still exists; in others, his discretion is subject to the will of the court. When entered before trial, the nolle prosequi does not bar a subsequent prosecution on the basis of a new indictment or new information.

Nollet, l'Abbé Jean-Antoine (1700–70), French physicist.

·description of osmotic pressure **2**:1035c

nomad cultures, South American: *see* South American nomad cultures.

nomadism, way of life of peoples who do not live continually in the same place but move cyclically or periodically. It is distinguished from migration, which is noncyclic and involves a total change of habitat. Nomadism does not imply unrestricted and undirected wandering but focusses on temporary centres whose stability depends on the availability of food supply and the technology for exploiting it. The term nomad covers three general types: nomadic hunters and gatherers, pastoral nomads, and tinker or trader nomads.

Although hunting and gathering generally imposes a degree of nomadism on a people, it may range from daily movements, as among some Kalahari Bushmen, to monthly, quarterly, or semi-annual shifts of habitat. In areas where resources are abundant or where there are storage facilities, populations may be more or less stable. Nomadic hunters and gatherers are usually organized into small, isolated bands that move through a delimited territory where they know the water holes, the location of plants, and the habits of game.

Pastoral nomads, who depend on domesticated livestock, migrate in an established territory to find pasturage for their animals. Most groups have focal sites that they occupy for considerable periods of the year. Pastoralists may depend entirely on their herds or may also hunt or gather, practice some agriculture, or trade with agricultural peoples for grain and other goods. Some seminomadic groups in Southwest Asia and North Africa cultivate crops between seasonal moves. The patterns of pastoral nomadism are many, often depending on the type of livestock, the topography, and the climate.

Some nomadic groups are associated with a larger society but maintain their mobile way of life. These include tinker or trader nomads, who may make and sell simple products, hunt, or hire out as labourers at each stop along their route. The diverse group loosely termed gypsies is the best known example of this type of nomadism.

Some agricultural peoples may be considered nomads because they periodically change their habitats in order to find new areas in which to raise their crops. They often combine agriculture with hunting and gathering.

Nomadism has declined in the 20th century for economic and political reasons, including the spread of systematic agriculture, the growth of industry, and the policies of governments that view nomadism as incompatible with modern life. *See also* transhumance.

·animistic religion and ceremonialism **1**:923e
·food salting and cultural evolution **16**:192g
·migration as population's norm **12**:185c
regional cultural patterns
·Afghanistan's tribal empires **1**:173d
·ancient Israelite cultural attitudes **2**:908d
·Apache cultural patterns **17**:307g
·Arctic collectivization difficulties **6**:135b
·Arctic herding cultures **1**:1125h
·Asian livelihood and roving patterns **2**:195e
·Central Asian pastoral culture **3**:1119f
·East African aggressive social values **6**:1013e
·European Atlantic coast occurrence **6**:1064g
·Inner Asian socio-economic fragility **9**:600d
·Inner Mongolian modernization effects **9**:602b
·Iranian Scythian block to Alexander **9**:840a
·Iranian tribal patterns **9**:864a
·Iraq's population mobility **9**:876b
·Jordanian increasingly sedentary style **10**:271a
·Maghrib tribal migrations **11**:295a
·Mauritania's human settlement patterns **11**:712c
·Middle East system of urban association **12**:168c
·Mongol tribal structure and migrations **12**:370c
·Moroccan peoples' life styles **12**:446e
·Near East socioreligious setting **12**:916h
·North African economic decay **13**:159e
·Plains Indian social organization **13**:224e
·Shawia agricultural migration **2**:306a
·Siberian peoples' life style **16**:724g
·Somalian life style and feud causes **16**:1060a
·South American culture patterns **17**:112e; map 113
·Tibetan mobile life style **18**:374e
·Turk migration and settlement patterns **18**:786e
·seasonal migration and social structure **1**:168c
·social and cultural aspects of nomadism **8**:1159c
·Thar Desert's population associations **18**:207a

Noma Hiroshi (b. Feb. 23, 1915, Kōbe, Japan), novelist who wrote *Shinkū chitai* (1952; *Zone of Emptiness*, 1956), which is considered to be one of the finest war novels produced after World War II.

Noma was brought up to succeed his father, a head priest of a Buddhist sect, but as a youth he was increasingly drawn to Marxist ideology. He graduated from Kyōto Imperial University in 1938 with a specialty in French literature. During World War II he was drafted and sent to the Philippines and northern China but later was imprisoned (1943–44), on charges of subversive thought, in Osaka Military Prison. He attracted attention after the war with the novels *Kurai e* (1946; "A Dark Picture") and *Kao no naka no akai tsuki* (1947; "The Red Moon in the Face"), both of which present a protagonist's conflict between ideal self-image and carnal desire. *Shinkū chitai* conveys a broad view of the Japanese wartime army by tracing the parallel fate of two soldiers—a cultured middle class idealist and a bewildered peasant youth.

nomarch (ancient Egyptian administration): *see* nome.

Noma Seiji (1877–1938), Japanese magazine publisher.

·magazine publishing history **15**:253a

Nome, city, western Alaska, that serves as a port on the south Seward Peninsula shore of the Bering Sea. The discovery in September 1898 of gulch gold at nearby Anvil Creek resulted in a remarkable mining stampede. The miners' camp, known as Anvil City, had an estimated population of 20,000 in 1900; by 1903 the figure had greatly decreased and the population was 852 at the 1920 census. The settlement was renamed for Cape Nome, socalled on a chart dated 1849 and said to be an Admiralty draftsman's misinterpretation of the query "?Name." Gold mining remained the chief occupation until the dredge fields were closed in 1962. Transportation, tourism, construction, fishing, and Eskimo handicrafts are now the economic mainstays. Nome is served by a network of roads, by several airlines, and, in summer, by steamers. Inc. 1901. Pop. (1980) 2,301, principally Eskimo.
64°30′ N, 165°24′ W

·map, United States **18**:908

nome, administrative division of ancient Egypt. The system of dividing the country into nomes was in force definitely by the Early Dynastic Period (*c.* 3100–*c.* 2686 BC). The system persisted with modifications until the Muslim conquest (AD 640). In the Graeco-Roman Period there were 42 nomes, or provinces, 22 in Upper Egypt and 20 in Lower Egypt. During the dynasty of the Ptolemies (323–30 BC), a *heptanomis* (unit of seven nomes) was formed in Middle Egypt.

Each nome was administered by a nomarch, or district governor, who levied taxes, administered justice, and during some periods maintained an army.

·Egyptian administrative principles **6**:461b
·Egyptian political power dynamics **6**:465c *passim* to 471d
·Near East ancient way of life **12**:916d
·Ptolemaic bureaucratic structure **6**:484c
·Roman retentions and reorganization **6**:486b *passim* to 487a

nomen, also called NOMEN GENTILE, in Roman names, the name carried by all members of the *gens*, or related group of families, to which the bearer belonged.

·Latin system of personal names **12**:817f

nomenclator, in cryptography, term for early Italian code vocabularies.

·Italian cryptography history **5**:332g

nomenclature, in biological classification, system of names used to indicate the taxonomic position of an individual organism. The species to which the organism belongs is indicated by two words, the genus and species names, which are Latinized words derived from various sources. This is the Linnaean system of binomial nomenclature, established in the 1750s by Carolus Linnaeus. Subsequent to the work of Linnaeus, a proliferation of binomial names took place as new species were established and higher taxonomic categories were formed, with the result that by the late 19th century there was much confusion in the nomenclature of many groups of organisms. In the 20th century, the establishment of rules by international committees in the fields of zoology, botany, bacteriology, and virology has done much to improve the situation.

Contrary to the widely held view that scientific names, once assigned, are fixed and universal in their use, continuing research on the relationships of organisms and probing into the history of names, coupled with disagreements among scientists on the validity of certain names, results in multiple names being applied to some well-known species. The international rules, however, are gradually bringing stability to the taxonomy of many groups through the minimizing of name changes, the use of standard methods of establishing new names, and the functioning of respected committees to arbitrate controversies.

·botany history and Linnean system **3**:66g
·hominid fossil classification **8**:1030d
·plant classification and binomial nomenclature **2**:1019f
·species binomial nomenclature **17**:449g
·taxonomy objectives and processes **4**:685a

Nomenoë (d. March 7, 851, Vendôme, Fr.), duke of Brittany who fought successfully against the Frankish king Charles II the Bald.

Nomenoë was appointed duke of Brittany in 826 by the emperor Louis I the Pious; his service to the emperor was distinguished by his success in quelling a serious revolt in 837. When Louis died and war broke out between his sons in 840, Nomenoë was at first a vassal to Charles the Bald, the youngest son. Nomenoë challenged Charles, however, by occupying the Breton town of Rennes. Charles besieged Rennes in 843; Nomenoë defeated Charles in 844 and again in 845, and proclaimed himself an independent ruler.

Nomenoë removed from Breton sees four pro-Frankish bishops, separated the Breton church from the authority of the archbishop of Tours, and so promoted the claim of the Bishops of Dol to be metropolitans of Brittany. In 849–850, still defying Charles the Bald, he ravaged Anjou, seized Nantes, and retook Rennes.

·annexation of Nantes and Rennes **7**:614b

Nomeus gronovii: *see* man-of-war fish.

Nomia, genus of alkali bee of the insect order Hymenoptera.

·pollen expulsion in alfalfa flowers **14**:746b

Nominalism, in philosophy, position taken in the dispute over universals—words that can be applied to individual things having something in common—that flourished especially in late medieval times. Nominalism denied the real being of universals on the ground that the use of a general word (*e.g.*, "humanity") does not imply the existence of a general thing named by it. The Nominalist position did not necessarily deny, however, that there must be some similarity between the particular things to which the general word is applied. Thoroughgoing Nominalists would withhold this concession, as Roscelin, a medieval Nominalist, is said to have done. But unless such similarity is granted, the application of general words to particulars is made to appear entirely arbitrary. Such stricter forms of Nominalism as existed in the Middle Ages can perhaps be viewed as reactions against Platonic Realism, on which some enthusiasts, such as Guillaume de Champeaux, based the opinion that universals had real being. The Realist position invited a defensive alliance between Empiricism and Nominalism; the most notable medieval example of such a synthesis was the work of William of Ockham.

In the Middle Ages, when Platonic and Aristotelian realisms were associated with orthodox religious belief, Nominalism could be interpreted as heresy. But prescinding from its religious implications, Nominalism does indeed reject Platonic Realism as a requirement for thinking and speaking in general terms; and though it seems to deny also Aristotelian Realism, such moderate Nominalists as Thomas Hobbes affirm that some similarity exists between particulars and the general word applied to them—otherwise thought and speech would be impossible. By explaining thought and speech through the use of symbols (such as mental images or linguistic terms) Nominalism seems to imply some form of conceptualism that involves more than the mere correct use of symbols and thus is not clearly distinguishable from conceptualism.

In modern logic a Nominalistic concern is reflected in the form that is given to the "universal quantifier." Instead of saying "man is mortal," or even "all men are mortal," the modern logician circumvents the universal by saying "for any *x*, if *x* is a man it is mortal." Neopositivism, in repudiating metaphysics, has often been explicitly Nominalistic, insisting that there exist only "the facts" of observation and experiment. In the mid-20th century, Nelson Goodman, a philosopher of science and of language, and Willard Van Orman Quine, a logician, have championed a modern Nominalism that specifically rejects classes—Goodman for their being "nonindividuals" and Quine for their being "abstract entities."

·Abelard and Roscelin **14**:258c
·Boethius' thought and influence **2**:1181d
·Hobbes and British Empiricism **14**:264e
·Roman Catholic theology **15**:1007b

nominative case, in grammar, form of nominals (nouns and adjectives) used in Indo-European languages, as well as the languages of some other groups, to indicate the subject of a sentence or clause.

·Etruscan morphology and syntax **6**:1019e
·Hurrian and Urartian singularities **1**:833h

Nomios (god): *see* Apollo.

Nommo, the primal being in the mythology of the Dogon tribe of Mali.

·fire origin myth **12**:882h

nomocanon, Byzantine collection of ecclesiastical legislation (canons) and civil laws (Greek *nomoi*) related to the Christian Church. The nomocanon in its various redactions served as legal text in the Eastern Church until the 18th century. In form and content, it reflected a tight alliance between church and state and met the requirements of judges and lawyers obliged to use simultaneously the ecclesiastical canons and the imperial laws. In the 6th century, two main forms of the nomocanon were accepted simultaneously: the *Nomocanon 50 titulorum* and the *Nomocanon 14 titulorum*. The latter, compiled by the patriarch Johannes Scholasticus (565–577), was later updated by the patriarch Photius (*c.* 820–91) and published anew in 883. A Slavic adaptation of the Byzantine nomocanons was compiled by Sava, the first archbishop of Serbia (1219), under the title of *Kormchaya kniga* ("Book of the Helmsman"), which was adopted by all the Slavic Orthodox churches. In the 18th century, the need for collections of imperial laws having disappeared, new compilations, including only the ecclesiastical canons, replaced both the nomocanons and the *Kormchaya kniga*. The most important of these new compilations, excerpts from the nomocanon, were the *Pēdalion*, or "Rudder," for the Greeks, and the *Kniga pravil* ("Book of Rules"), for the Russians.

·canon law sources of Middle Ages **3**:774c
·Eastern Orthodox dogmatic stance **6**:146b

nomograph, also called ALIGNMENT CHART, calculating chart with scales that contain values of three or more mathematical variables, widely used in engineering, industry, and the natural and physical sciences.

In the most common form, a nomograph consists of three parallel graduated lines, known values on any two scales determining a straight index line (transversal) that passes through the solution value on the third. Some chart forms employ one or more curved graduated lines; or if straight, they may be arranged in the shape of the letter N. *See* variable.

·construction and use in drafting **5**:977b

Nomoi Islands, also known as MORTLOCK ISLANDS, Truk District, East Caroline Islands Trust Territory of the Pacific. Pop. (1970) 1,683.
5°27′ N, 153°40′ E

·Micronesian Trukese cultural affinity **12**:122d

nomos, the conception of law in ancient Greek philosophy. A basic opposition developed between proponents of the view that law is natural and everywhere has the same force, and the view that law is conventional and depends only on human artifice. Each view fostered profoundly different notions of the state.

·Averroës' criticism of Platonism **2**:539c *passim* to 540b
·divine law and the city-state **10**:716a
·Greek mode classification **12**:296d
·Plato's typology of governments **14**:713e
·Sophist theory of natural law **12**:863f

nomos, class of traditional melodies used by ancient Greek epic singers, often with lyre accompaniment. The *nomos* was an important art form both for the professional soloist and in musical competitions. No musical structure, other than division into three, five, or seven movements, was common to every *nomos*, but it is likely that fundamental rhythmic and melodic patterns were used as the bases for the composition of *nomoi*. *Nomoi* were also performed on the kithara (lyre) and the aulos (double-piped oboe). Best known is the *nomos* depicting the god Apollo's victory over the dragon, played on an aulos at Delphi in 586 BC.

Nonae Caprotinae (Latin: "Nones of the Wild Fig"), in Roman religion, festival honouring the goddess Juno, celebrated principally by female slaves on July 7. Possibly an ancient fertility rite relating fig juice to milk, the festival took place under a wild fig tree in the Campus Martius. There the worshippers had a sham fight and abused each other.

nonalignment (international relations): *see* neutralism.

non-arboreal pollen: *see* NAP.

non-associative algebra, in linear and multilinear algebra, vector space with a multiplication satisfying all the postulates for an algebra except the associative law of multiplication; in such an algebra the result of a multiplication is dependent on the grouping of the elements.

·vector and tensor analysis principles **1**:794b

nonbeing, Chinese PEN-WU, in Chinese philosophy, a concept in Taoism, Neo-Taoism, and Neo-Confucianism.

·Chou Tun-i's diagram **4**:418h; illus. 419

noncapsular ligament, ligament between two bones that is not attached to the joint capsule.

·types, components, and locations **10**:258c

non causa pro causa, logical fallacy in which a proposition *a* is rejected because of the falsity of another proposition *b* that appears to be the consequence of *a* but is not.

·definition and various instances **11**:29a

noncognitivism, in ethics, the view that moral utterances are basically directives for action rather than statements of fact.

·definition and theory development **6**:986c

Nonconformists, English Protestants who do not conform to the doctrines or practices of the established Church of England. The word Nonconformist was first used in the penal acts following the Restoration of the monarchy (1660) and the Act of Uniformity (1662) to describe the "conventicles" (places of worship) of the congregations that had separated from the Church of England (Separatists). Nonconformists are also called "dissenters" (a word first used of the five "Dissenting Brethren" at the Westminster Assembly of Divines in 1643–47). As a result of the movement begun in the late 19th century by which Nonconformists of different denominations joined together in the Free Church Federal Council, they are also called "Free Churchmen."

The term Nonconformist is generally applied in England and Wales to all Protestants who have dissented from Anglicanism—Baptists, Congregationalists, Presbyterians, Methodists, and Unitarians—and also to independent groups such as the Quakers, Plymouth Brethren, English Moravians, Churches of Christ, and the Salvation Army. In Scotland, where the established church is Presbyterian, members of other churches, including Anglicans, are considered Nonconformists.

·Baptist Separatism and non-Separatism **2**:713e
·Congregationalist role in English dissent **4**:1128a
·Defoe's political Nonconformism **5**:550h
·educational institution establishment **14**:1012h
·Free Churches evolution in Britain **7**:710c
·Industrial Revolution's impact **3**:262d
·Irish Test Act terms **3**:290e
·Lloyd George's battle for burial rights **11**:6g
·Restoration religious legislation **3**:246h
·Shaftesbury's tolerant legislation **16**:613g
·Unitarian movement in 18th century **18**:860f
·United Kingdom religious denominations **18**:874c
·Wesley brothers' religious background **19**:759f

nonconformity (geology): *see* unconformity.

nonconservative force (physics): *see* conservative force.

Non-cooperation Movement (September 1920–February 1922), an unsuccessful attempt, organized by Mahatma Gandhi, to induce the British government of India to grant self-government, or *swarāj*, to India. It arose from the Amritsar massacre of April 1919, when the British killed about 400 Indians, and from later indignation at the government's alleged failure to take adequate action against those responsible. Gandhi strengthened the movement by supporting (on nonviolent terms) the contemporaneous Muslim campaign against the dismemberment of Turkey after World War I.

The movement was to be nonviolent and to consist of the resignations of titles; the boycott of government educational institutions, the lawcourts, government service, foreign goods, and elections; and the eventual refusal to pay taxes. Non-cooperation was agreed to by the Indian National Congress at Calcutta in September 1920 and launched that December. In 1921 the government, confronted with a united Indian front for the first time, was visibly shaken, but a revolt by the Muslim Moplahs of Kerala (southwestern India) in August 1921 and a number of violent outbreaks alarmed moderate opinion. After an angry mob murdered police officers at Chauri Chaura (February 1922), Gandhi himself called off the movement; the next month he was arrested without incident. The movement marks the transition of Indian nationalism from a middle class to a mass basis.

·Indian independence movement history **9**:418b
·Jinnah's political opposition **10**:224c
·national school development and duration **6**:393f

non-deposition (geology): *see* unconformity.

nondirectional beacon (NDB), a beacon sending its rays equally well in all directions and used as a navigational device.

·aircraft navigation importance **18**:641c

nondirective psychotherapy, also known as CLIENT-CENTRED PSYCHOTHERAPY, an approach to the treatment of mental disorders that aims primarily to foster the patient's general personality growth by helping him gain insight into his feelings and behaviour. The approach is based on the assumption that symptoms of emotional illness are expressions of flaws in the patient's overall approach to life, a discrepancy between perceived self and actual experience. The function of the therapist is to extend consistent, warm "unconditional positive regard" toward the "client" (avoiding the negative connotations of "patient") and, by repeating and restating the client's own verbalized concerns, to enable the client to see himself more clearly and react more openly with the therapist and others. As the client's ability to interpret objectively his own behaviour increases, he realizes the need for change and abandons maladaptive behaviour patterns. Pace and direction of this development are controlled by the client; the therapist merely acts as a facilitator. The decision to terminate therapy, as well as all other decisions, is made by the client.

The nondirective approach was originated by U.S. clinical psychologist Carl Rogers in the 1940s and has strongly influenced later individual and group psychotherapeutic methods.

·psychodynamic treatment methods **15**:145g *passim* to 147b

nondisjunction, in genetics, the failure of paired chromosomes to separate during mitosis (*q.v.*), resulting in one daughter cell having both chromosomes and the other having none. *See also* chromosomal aberration.

·chromosomal abnormalities in meiosis **8**:807g; illus.

·disease causation mechanisms **5**:849a; illus.

non-dualism (Vedanta philosophy): *see* Advaita.

Nonell y Monturiol, Isidro (b. Nov. 30, 1873, Barcelona—d. Feb. 21, 1911, Barcelona), painter who was instrumental in the Catalan artistic revival of the early 20th century and is considered a pioneer of modern painting in Spain. An immensely gifted artist who died at an early age, he is unjustly remembered only as an associate of the young Pablo Picasso.

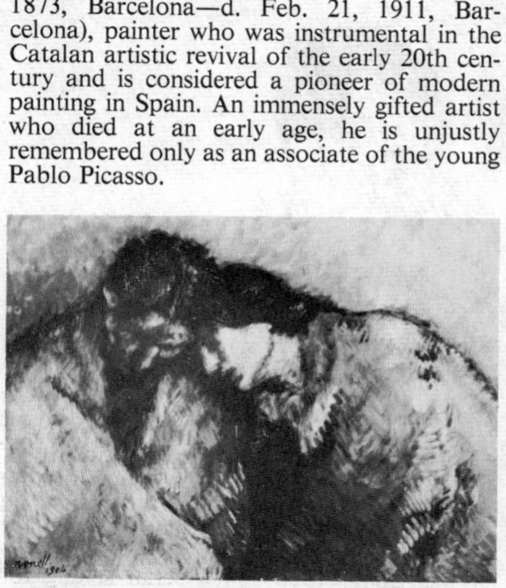

"Miseria," oil painting by Isidro Nonell y Monturiol, 1904; in the Museo de Arte Moderno, Barcelona

SCALA, New York

Beginning as a landscape painter in the Impressionist manner, Nonell turned in 1890 to realistic portraits of Gypsies and poor people. These works were exhibited with success in Barcelona and by the dealer Ambroise Vollard in Paris in 1899. In Barcelona he was the leader of a group of young artists, the Quatre Gats group, which included Picasso, who was a careful student of Nonell's realistic works. After studying the work of the French artists Honoré Daumier and Henri de Toulouse-Lautrec in Paris, he began experimenting with more simplified and abstract forms, notably in a series of expressive still lifes. Very much an avant-garde artist, he did not achieve European fame until a highly successful show in 1910. In the forefront of modern Spanish painting and tending more and more toward abstraction, he died at the peak of his powers.

Nones of the Wild Fig (Roman festival): *see* Nonae Caprotinae.

nonesuch chest, furniture piece decorated with perspective architectural scenes.

·German design and inlay decoration **7**:798h

Nonesuch Press, an influential printing establishment set up in England in 1923 by Francis (later Sir Francis) Meynell in part as a response to a strong political conviction that everyone—even those of limited means—should have the right to be able to acquire finely printed books about important subjects. At the opposite extreme from the individual handcraft approach and fine-printing-for-its-own-sake school of the private press movement of the first years of the 20th century, the Nonesuch represented a deliberate attempt to exploit the lower cost possible in largely mechanized operations and at the same time to achieve the ultimate goal of genuinely fine printing. Nonesuch relied exclusively on machine cut types; rigorously limited the amount of illustration that could be worked into its cost-conscious production schedules; and paid great attention to the selection of binding, paper, and type. It achieved volumes that, at their best, were straightforward, classical, unpretentious, and almost as much a pleasure to hold and to handle as they were to read.

A five-volume Bible that appeared between 1925 and 1927 and a seven-volume Shakespeare that took a decade—between 1923 and 1933—to complete, were among the outstanding achievements of the Nonesuch approach.

·publishing quality and utility **18**:822h

non-Euclidean geometry: *see* geometry, non-Euclidean.

non expedit (Latin: "it is not expedient"), name given to a late-19th- and early-20th-century policy of the Roman Catholic Church prohibiting its Italian members from participating in politics. The *non expedit* dramatically emphasized the pope's refusal to recognize the newly formed Italian state, which had deprived him of his lands in central Italy.

In the early 1860s a Turin journalist, Giacomo Margotti, had coined the phrase *nè eletti nè elettori* (neither elected nor electors) in launching a campaign urging devout Catholics to protest the seizure of papal land by not voting. This policy of nonparticipation, the *non expedit*, was officially adopted by the Holy See in 1868 and was confirmed on successive occasions through the 19th century (notably by Pius IX in 1874).

Enough Catholics observed the *non expedit* to cause a significant political absenteeism and preclude the formation of a strong conservative party in Italian national politics. Local government was exempted from the ban out of fear for the growing power of the Left. Seeking better relations with the Italian government, Pope Pius X virtually ended the *non expedit* in 1904–05. Benedict XV formally ended it in 1919, giving his approval to the Italian Popular Party (PPI). This marked the entrance of Italian Catholics into political life as an organized force.

nonfiction novel, story of actual people and actual events told with the dramatic techniques of a novel. The U.S. writer Truman Capote claimed to have invented this genre with his book *In Cold Blood* (1966). A true story of the brutal murder of a Kansas farm family, the book was based on six years of exacting research during which Capote interviewed in depth neighbours and friends of the victims and established a close relationship with the two captured murderers up to their execution five years after their arrest. The story is told from the point of view of different "characters," and the author attempts not to intrude his own comments or distort fact. Critics have pointed out earlier precedents for this type of journalistic novel, such as John Hersey's *Hiroshima* (1946), an account of the World War II bombing of the Japanese city told through the histories of six survivors.

·contemporary American novel development **13**:281h

nong-ak, Korean agricultural festival dating back to at least the 3rd century BC.

·ancient Korean musical tradition **12**:678b

Nong Khai, also spelled NONGKHAI, province (*changwat*), northeastern Thailand, bordered by the Mekong River and Laos. It occupies an

Temple at Nong Khai town, Thailand

Shostal

area of 2,789 sq mi (7,223 sq km) and is drained by the Huai Luang (Luang River) and the Mae Nam Songkhram (Songkhram River). The major population centres, located along the Mekong, include Nong Khai (the provincial capital and road and rail terminus), Tha Bo, Phon Phisai, and Bung Kan. Pop. (1970) town, 21,150; province, 443,984.

·area and population table **18**:202

nongraded school, in education, schools in which grade levels are abolished and pupils are placed individually according to their progress.

·theory and practice **13**:1101h

Nong Sa Rai, Battle of (1592), the final encounter in the Thai war of independence, which had been waged intermittently against the Burmese since 1584.

In 1569 the Burmese conquered the Thai kingdom of Ayutthaya and reduced it to a vassal state. After the great Burmese conqueror King Bayinnaung was succeeded by his son Nanda Bayin (reigned 1581–99), it soon became apparent that the Burmese empire was in less able hands. Although Prince Naresuen, the actual ruler of Ayutthaya, performed vassal military service to Nanda Bayin against the rebel king of Ava in late 1583, he realized that the time was ripe to pursue Thai independence. His renunciation of vassalage to Burma in 1584 was followed in the next two years by four Burmese invasions of Ayutthaya, all of which Prince Naresuen was able to withstand.

Despite the bloodshed, misery, and resources exhausted by continual warfare, King Nanda Bayin continued to attempt to crush Thai independence. A fifth Burmese expedition led by Crown Prince Minkyi-zwa in 1586 returned to Burma after a stalemated battle with Prince Naresuen's forces. The Burmese king launched a sixth invasion against Ayutthaya in early 1587. He reached the walls of the city, but disease, lack of supplies, and flooding from early rains forced a retreat.

From 1587 to 1590, the kingdom of Ayutthaya experienced three years of relative peace. War had devastated the countryside, however, and earthquakes created additional hardships.

In 1592, the last Burmese invasion was launched by King Nanda Bayin in a final effort to subjugate Ayutthaya. A huge army commanded by the inept Crown Prince Minkyi-zwa invaded the Thai kingdom. Prince Naresuen had previously prepared to invade Cambodia when news of the Burmese invasion was received. The battle took place at Nong Sa Rai, where Prince Naresuen commanded the superior field position. After Naresuen slew the Burmese Crown Prince in a man to man combat, the Burmese forces, confused and demoralized, abandoned the expedition. The Battle of Nong Sa Rai marked the end of years of warfare and misery for both kingdoms. The Burmese did not pose a threat to Thai independence for the next 150 years.

nonhemolytic jaundice: *see* Crigler-Najjar syndrome; Gilbert's disease.

Nonimportation Agreements (1765–75), in U.S. colonial history, attempts to force British recognition of political rights through application of economic pressure. In reaction to the Stamp Act (1765) and the Townshend Acts (*q.v.*; 1767), nonimportation associations were organized by Sons of Liberty and Whig merchants to boycott English goods. In each case, British merchants and manufacturers suffered curtailed trade with the colonies and exerted the anticipated pressure on Parliament. When the acts were subsequently repealed, the boycotts collapsed. After the Intolerable Acts of 1774, the First Continental Congress immediately provided for both nonimport and nonexport committees. Britain had developed new markets in Europe, however, and the expected influence on Parliament did not materialize. For 10 years nonimportation was the main weapon employed by the colonists in an attempt to win their demands from the mother country by peaceful means. When it failed, they resorted to armed resistance.

·Hamilton's pamphlets in defense of colonists' actions **8**:585c

noninertial reference frame (physics): *see* reference frame.

Non-intercourse Act, U.S. (1809): *see* Embargo Act.

Nonintervention Committee (1936), international organization of 27 nations, including all major European powers, established in London to isolate the Spanish Civil War from foreign intervention.

·Axis aggression and Soviet response **19**:976h

Nonius, Petrus (Portuguese mathematician and geographer): *see* Nunes, Pedro.

Nonius Marcellus (b. before the 6th century AD, Thubursicum Numidarum, now Algeria), Latin grammarian and lexicographer, author of the *De compendiosa doctrina*, a lexicon in which are preserved extracts from the works of many earlier writers. It consists of 20 chapters—the 16th is lost. The first 12 deal with language and grammar, and in the brief remaining chapters words are grouped according to the nature of what they refer to. Nonius was a man of little understanding or accuracy, but posterity is indebted to him for preserving fragments of Latin tragedies and the satires of Gaius Lucilius and Marcus Terentius Varro.

Nonjurors, name given to the beneficed clergy of the Church of England and the Episcopal Church in Scotland who refused to take the oaths of allegiance to William III and Mary II after the deposition of James II in the Glorious Revolution (1688). They numbered about 400 in England, including eight bishops and some of the most devout and learned men in the Anglican Church. Among the most prominent Nonjurors were: the archbishop of Canterbury William Sancroft; the saintly-hymn writer Thomas Ken; the ecclesiastical polemicist Jeremy Collier; the historian Henry Dodwell; and Henry Hyde, second earl of Clarendon. They considered William and Mary usurpers, adhered to their oaths to James II, but adopted a policy of nonresistance to the established authorities. From 1694 they maintained a separate ecclesiastical succession, but they were divided over liturgical usages, and their numbers dwindled in the 18th century; the last Nonjuror bishop died in 1805.

In Scotland, the disestablishment of the Episcopal Church in 1690 resulted in the defection of the greater part of the clergy. Unlike their Church of England counterparts, the Scottish Nonjurors actively supported the Stewart cause, participated in the Jacobite uprisings of 1715 and 1745, and suffered severe reprisals. In 1788, with the death of Charles Edward, the Young Pretender, the bishops agreed to recognize George III.

A large number of Presbyterians in Scotland, principally among the Cameronians, also refused to take the oaths of allegiance to William and Mary, but, as their refusal was on different grounds, they are not usually referred to as Nonjurors.

·sacrament of penance **16**:117g

nonlinear programming: *see* programming, mathematical.

nonliterate society, term referring to people without a written language. (It is distinguished from "illiterate," which applies to members of a society who are expected to be able to read and write but who cannot do so.) Such societies are usually characterized by their relative isolation, small number, relatively simpler social institutions and technology, and a generally slow rate of change.

Although the term is not entirely satisfactory because it distinguishes along the sole criterion of written language, it has several advantages over terms such as primitive, preliterate, pre-urban, savage, and others. These terms usually imply that the cultures so characterized are at an earlier stage of cultural development than "higher," or literate, civilizations. Contemporary anthropologists generally prefer to avoid this assumption, which they regard as simplistic. In addition, early writers frequently used these terms with the implication that such peoples were mentally and morally inferior. "Nonliterate" attempts to avoid those negative value connotations.

nonmetal, in chemistry, substance that does not exhibit any of the characteristic properties of metals such as hardness, mechanical adaptability, and the ability to conduct electricity. This classification is generally applied to the chemical elements carbon, nitrogen, phosphorus, oxygen, sulfur, selenium, fluorine, chlorine, bromine, iodine, and the noble-gas elements. These elements have few physical properties in common; most are gases, one (bromine) is liquid, others are solids.

The atoms of nonmetals generally are small and contain relatively large numbers of electrons in their outermost shells. In the noble-gas atoms, the electron shells are completely filled; thus, the elements are almost completely inert. The other nonmetals have nearly filled electron shells, requiring only a few additional electrons to assume the stable, noble-gas electron configuration. Therefore, in the presence of other atoms, these nonmetallic atoms have pronounced tendencies to attract electrons to themselves (high electronegativity). They form chemical compounds by attracting electrons completely away from other atoms of lower electronegativities or by sharing electrons with atoms of comparable electronegativities.

Although there are only a few nonmetallic elements, they constitute a large portion of the earth's crust and are essential for the growth and existence of living things.

·alkali metal reactions **1**:582d
·alkaline-earth compound structure **1**:592b
·chemical element classification **4**:116h
·native sulfur and carbon properties **12**:855h
·oxygen bonding characteristics **13**:815g
·periodicity in properties of elements **14**:78h

non-Newtonian viscosity, also called SHEAR THINNING, viscosity that varies with the rate of shear or varies with time when shear remains constant. *See also* fluid.

·polymer solutions behaviour **18**:676a

Nonni River (China): *see* Nen River.

Nonnula: *see* puffbird.

Nonnus (fl. 5th century AD), most notable Greek epic poet of the Roman period, who was born at Panopolis (Akhmīm) in Egypt. His chief work is the *Dionysiaca*, a hexameter poem in 48 books; its main subject, submerged in a chaos of by-episodes, is the expedition of the god Dionysus to India. Nonnus' fertile inventiveness and felicitous descriptive fantasy, which are well served by a unique command of the language and his vast literary knowledge, made him the often-imitated leader of the last Greek epic school. His style, with its ever-recurring, often daring metaphors and unremittingly bombastic tone, appealed to the taste of the time. Later in life he was converted to Christianity and composed a hexameter paraphrase of St. John's Gospel (*Metabole*), which shows all his earlier stylistic faults without his compensatory descriptive ability.

Nono, Luigi (b. Jan. 29, 1924, Venice, Italy), leading composer of electronic, aleatoric (chance), and serial music. Nono studied with the avant-garde composer Bruno Maderna and the conductor Hermann Scherchen, known for his performances of 20th-century works. Nono came to public attention in 1950 with his orchestral variations on a 12-tone theme of Arnold Schoenberg. Since then he has continued to explore avant-garde techniques and has lectured widely in Europe and the U.S. He is married to Schoenberg's daughter.

Nono
Cameraphoto, Venice

Nono's music is distinguished by its clarity of form. Polyphony, monophony, and rhythm are explored in a straightforward manner in his *Polifonica-Monodia-Ritmica* (1951) for seven instruments. *Il canto sospeso* (*The Suspended Song;* 1955–56), a serial setting for voices, chorus, and orchestra of letters written by victims of Nazism, passes its melody among the instruments and voices with each performer rarely playing more than a single note at a time. Nono also adopted this technique of fragmentation in several works involving voices and percussion. *Per Bastiana Tai-yang Cheng* (*For Bastiana the Sun Rises;* 1967), based on a Chinese folk song and celebrating the birth of Nono's daughter, is somewhat aleatoric and calls for three instrumental groups playing in quarter tones and for magnetic tape. Other works utilizing electronic tapes include *Contrappunto dialettico alla mente* (on stereo tape; 1968), *Musica-Manifesto No. 1* (voices and tape; 1969), and *Y entonces comprendió* (for women's voices, chorus, tape, and electronic equipment, with text by Carlos Franqui; 1969–70).

Among Nono's works incorporating texts of social concern and protest are *Intolleranza* (1961; updated 1970), an opera attacking prejudice and reaction, and *Canti di vita e d'amore* (*Three Songs of Life and Love*; 1962), protests of the bombing of Hiroshima, the torturing of an Algerian girl by the French, and war in general. Later operas were *Non consumiamo Marx* (1969) and *Al gran sale carico d'amore* (1975). His *Epitaffo per Federico García Lorca* (1952) is a set of three pieces in memory of the Spanish poet.

Nonomura Seisuke (Japanese potter): *see* Ninsei.

nonparametric inference, in statistics, part of the theory of statistical inference in which estimators of information about the distribution function are devised. These estimators do not depend on the functional form of the distribution function; hence they are called nonparametric in contrast to parametric estimators, which are used to estimate parameter values of an unknown distribution having an unknown functional form.
·hypothesis testing methods **17**:623a

Nonpartisan League, also called FARMERS' NONPARTISAN LEAGUE and, after 1917, NATIONAL NONPARTISAN LEAGUE, in U.S. history, alliance of farmers to obtain state control of marketing facilities by endorsing a pledged supporter from either major party. It was founded in North Dakota by a Socialist, Arthur C. Townley, in 1915, at the height of the Progressive movement in the Northwest. To protect the farmer from alleged wheat trade monopolies by speculators and officials, the league demanded state-owned mills, grain elevators, banks, and hail insurance companies.
In 1916 the league candidate, Lynn J. Frazier, won the North Dakota gubernatorial election, and in 1919 the state legislature enacted the entire league program. The league gradually declined in the 1920s and after 1932 became a rigid political machine. It affiliated with the Democrats in 1956.
·North Dakota socialistic reforms **13**:234e

Non-proliferation of Nuclear Weapons, Treaty on the, also known as the NUCLEAR NON-PROLIFERATION TREATY, an agreement of July 1, 1968, signed by the United Kingdom, the United States, the Soviet Union, and 59 other states, under which the three major signatories agreed not to assist states not possessing nuclear explosives to obtain or produce them. The treaty became effective in March 1970.
·arms limitation methods **19**:571g
·signing and control agreements **13**:327e

nonreferentialist theory, also called FORMALIST THEORY, or ABSOLUTIST THEORY, in music, the theory that musical art is autonomous and has no meaning outside itself.
·music as extrinsically meaningless **12**:664g

non-REM sleep, or NREM SLEEP, sleep lacking the jerky scanning movements of the eyes associated with dreaming. *Cf.* rapid eye movement sleep.
·sleep processes and functions **16**:878d

nonrepresentational art: *see* abstract art.

nonscheduled airlines, also known as CHARTER AIRLINES, airlines licensed to carry passengers or freight by air between authorized points as frequently as demand requires and not on a regular schedule.
·tourism's influence on growth **18**:636b

nonsense verse, humorous or whimsical verse that differs from other comic verse in its resistance to any rational or allegorical interpretation. Though it often makes use of coined, meaningless words, it is unlike the ritualistic gibberish of children's counting-out rhymes in that it makes these words sound purposeful.
Skilled literary nonsense verse is rare, most of it has been written for children, and it is modern, dating from the beginning of the 19th century. The cardinal date could be considered 1846, when *The Book of Nonsense* was published; this was a collection of limericks composed and illustrated by the artist Edward Lear, who first created them in the 1830s for the children of the Earl of Derby. This was followed by the inspired fantasy of Lewis Carroll, whose *Alice's Adventures in Wonderland* (1865) and *Through the Looking-Glass* (1872) both contain brilliant nonsense rhymes. "Jabberwocky," from *Through the Looking-Glass*, may be the best known example of nonsense verse. It begins thus:

'Twas brillig, and the slithy toves
 Did gyre and gimble in the wabe;
All mimsy were the borogoves,
 And the mome raths outgrabe.

Another of Carroll's poems, *The Hunting of the Snark* (1876), is the longest and best sustained nonsense poem in the English language.
Hilaire Belloc's volume *The Bad Child's Book of Beasts* (1896) holds an honoured place among the classics of English nonsense verse, while, in the U.S., Laura E. Richards, a prolific writer of children's books, published verses in *Tirra Lirra* (1932) that have been compared to those of Edward Lear.
·humour in children's literature **4**:233b

nonspecific immunity, generalized natural resistance against a variety of microbes and parasites that invade the body. The defensive agents include chemical substances in blood and scavenging cells that consume micro-organisms. *See* phagocytosis.
·chemical and cellular mechanisms **9**:248b
·defects and disease causation **9**:258e

nonstoichiometric compound, any solid chemical compound in which the numbers of atoms of the elements present cannot be expressed as a ratio of small whole numbers; sometimes called berthollide compounds in distinction from daltonides (in which the atomic ratios are those of small integers), nonstoichiometric compounds are best known among the transition elements: several of them are important as components of solid-state electronic devices, such as rectifiers, thermoelectric generators, photodetectors, thermistors, and magnets useful in high-frequency circuits.
The existence of nonstoichiometric compounds is related to the presence of defects in the lattice structures of crystalline substances, such as the absence of ions from sites that would normally be occupied. For example, a sodium chloride crystal that lacks a sodium ion and a chloride ion is defective, but still stoichiometric because the numbers of sodium ions and chloride ions are the same; if the sodium ion site, however, is filled by a neutral sodium atom, which then gives up its valence electron to fill the chloride ion site, the crystal defect is remedied, but the crystal is now nonstoichiometric because it contains more sodium ions than chloride ions.
Most nonstoichiometric compounds have compositions that are close to those of stoichiometric compounds and can be expressed by such formulas as WO_{3-x}, $Co_{1-x}O$, or $Zn_{1+x}O$, in which x is a positive quantity much smaller than one. In certain cases apparent nonstoichiometry has been shown to result from the existence of homologous series of stoichiometric compounds, such as the series of molybdenum oxides having the formulas Mo_nO_{3n-1}, in which the compounds corresponding to $n = 8, 9, 10, 11, 12$, and 14 are known; a true nonstoichiometric compound MoO_{3-x} would show a continuous variation of x within some range of values, and no discrete species would be detectable.
·rare-earth crystallization and chemistry **15**:519b
·transition element ionic ratio **18**:604g

Nonthaburi, or NONDHABURI, administrative headquarters of Nonthaburi province (*changwat*), south central Thailand. A northern suburb of Bangkok, the town lies on the east bank of the Mae Nam (river) Chao Phraya and is linked to the metropolis by major roads. The Nonthaburi Institute of Telecommunication is there. The province has an area of 240 sq mi (623 sq km) in the nation's most productive rice-growing area. Fruit cultivation is also important. Pop. (1970) town, 27,465; province, 269,067.
13°51′ N, 100°34′ E
·area and population table **18**:202
·map, Thailand **18**:198

nontronite (mineral): *see* smectite.

nontropical sprue (disease): *see* celiac disease.

nonviolence, the abstention, on principle, from the use of force to attain one's goals, with moral persuasion often seen as an effective substitute.
·Gandhi's conviction and strategy **7**:876b
·Jaina principles of ahiṃsā **10**:10e
·modern examples and theory **13**:849f

nonviolent movements: *see* pacifism and nonviolent movements.

noodle (food): *see* pasta.

Noon, Sir Firoz Khan (1893–1970), Pakistani statesman, United Kingdom high commissioner for India (1936–41), prime minister of Pakistan (1957–58).
·Republican Party leadership **9**:427b

Noonan, Fred J. (1893–1937), U.S. aviator. He was navigator on the trail-blazing flight of a Pan American Clipper from San Francisco to Honolulu in 1935 and on later survey flights in preparation for commercial air service between Honolulu and the Far East. He was acting as navigator for Amelia Earhart (*q.v.*) when their plane disappeared in the South Pacific in July 1937.
·world flight attempt by Earhart **7**:400g

Noone, Jimmie (1895–1944), New Orleans clarinetist.
·stylistic influence on Benny Goodman **10**:123d

Noord-Brabant, English NORTH BRABANT, second largest province of The Netherlands, extending northward from the Belgium border, between the provinces of Zeeland (west) and Limburg (east), to the Maas (Meuse) and Merwede rivers. It occupies an area of 1,971 sq mi (5,105 sq km) and is drained by the Mark (Merk) and Dommel rivers and the Zuidwillemsvaart and Wilhelmina canals. Its capital is 's-Hertogenbosch (*q.v.*). Neolithic, Bronze, and Iron Age remains attest to early occupation of the area; and there were ancient Roman camps along the Maas. After the Dark Ages, the division between east and west (discernible in two different Iron Age groups) was continued in political divisions: the barony of Breda to the west and the Meierij van 's-Hertogenbosch (Bois-le-Duc) to the east, both subject to the duchy of Brabant (*q.v.*). The affinities of the west still lie with Belgium and France and those of the east with the Rhineland. Nearly all of the inhabitants are Roman Catholic.
The province's fertile coastal lands, flooded in 1953, support wheat and sugar beets; the more acid, poorly drained riverine lands are mostly pasture. The southern heaths contain woods, many recently planted conifers, small lakes, and peat bogs. The poor soils support restricted mixed farming. Extensive heathlands were reclaimed in the 19th century, and several new settlements were established in the raised bogs of De Peel (southeast of Deurne), where the sale of peat was combined with horticulture and cattle raising. Reclamation slackened after 1900; emigration from rural areas has been heavy, and more than one-half of the population now is urban. Formerly, Bergen op Zoom (*q.v.*) was the centre of the marshlands, Breda (*q.v.*) of the riverlands, and 's-Hertogenbosch of the inner sandy areas, but the largest provincial communities are now the industrial centres at Tilburg and Eindhoven (*qq.v.*). Pop. (1973 est.) 1,879,800.
·government, area, and population **12**:1062g; table
·Low Countries historical development **11**:133a
·map, The Netherlands **12**:1060

Noord-Holland, English NORTH HOLLAND, coastal province (*provincie*), northwestern Netherlands, comprises a peninsula (area 1,124 sq mi [2,912 sq km]) between the North

Sea (west), the Waddenzee (north), and the IJsselmeer or Zuiderzee (east). It includes the west Frisian island of Texel, off its northern tip. The island of Marken in the IJsselmeer has been connected by embankment with the mainland since 1957; the former island of Wieringen, now united after drainage with the mainland, is the starting point of the Afsluitdijk, the 19-mi (31-km) dike that encloses the IJsselmeer and links Noord-Holland and Friesland. The province, drained by the Zaan, Amstel, and Vecht rivers, mainly comprises low fenland, with dunes, and sea and river clays. Formed by the division (1840) of Holland into North and South, its capital is Haarlem (*q.v.*).

Around the foreshore, sand dunes form a smooth, unbroken protection for the inland regions. Coastal resorts include Zaandvoort, Bergen aan Zee, Egmond aan Zee, and Wijk aan Zee. Of the fishing ports, IJmuiden (*q.v.*), the foreport of Amsterdam at the west end of the North Sea Canal, is most important. This canal area has developed into an important industrial district (IJmond) centred around IJmuiden, Velsen (*q.v.*), and Beverwijk, manufacturing steel products, paper, fertilizer, and chemicals. Haarlem is an industrial town and flower-bulb trading centre.

Sandy geest grounds, behind the inner dunes, support the famous Dutch bulb fields of hyacinths, tulips, narcissus, and crocuses that continue southward from Haarlem into Zuid-Holland, with a large flower auction hall at Aalsmeer (*q.v.*). North of the North Sea Canal, market gardening dominates on the geest. Notable landmarks are the red-brick ruins of Brederode Castle near Haarlem and, to the north, the remains of the castle of the counts of Egmond and the rebuilt church of its famous abbey.

Most of the province lies at or below sea level, consisting of peat in the older parts and clay in the considerable reclaimed areas (polders). To the north of the North Sea Canal (cut 1865–76, after the drainage of the IJ inlet of the IJsselmeer), the Wormer, Schermer, Purmer, and Beemster lakes were drained in the 17th century; several sea polders farther north were added to the mainland in the early 19th century. Wieringermeer was reclaimed by 1930. This part of the province is traversed by the 46-mile North Holland Canal (1819–25) between Amsterdam and Den Helder (*q.v.*). South of the North Sea Canal, the Haarlemmermeer (*q.v.*) polder was reclaimed between 1840 and 1852. This region is typically Dutch, with canals and windmills. There is some market gardening, and the northern polders, especially the Wieringermeer, support grains and sugar beets, but the main occupations are cattle rearing and dairy farming. There are cattle and cheese markets at Purmerend and Alkmaar (*q.v.*). The coastal towns of Enkhuizen, Hoorn (*q.v.*), and Edam (*q.v.*), now small regional centres, were thriving commercial centres on the Zuiderzee in the 16th and 17th centuries. Prosperity later centred around Amsterdam, the chief commercial centre, and the Zaanstreek industrial area, particularly at Zaandam (*q.v.*).

Once heath-covered, with small rural villages, the Gooi region of lakes and woods to the southeast has grown into a considerable resort, residential, and industrial area, centred on Bussum and Hilversum (*qq.v.*). Pop. (1971 est.) 2,259,955.

·government, area, and population **12**:1059e; table 1062
·map, The Netherlands **12**:1060

Noordzeekanaal (The Netherlands): *see* North Sea Canal.

noösphere (from Greek *noös*, "mind"), in theoretical biology, that part of the world of life that is strongly affected by man's conceptual thought; regarded by some as coextensive with the anthroposphere (*q.v.*). The noösphere, as proposed by scientific theorists Pierre Teilhard de Chardin, Vladimir Ivanovich Vernadsky, and Édouard Le Roy, is the level of the intellect, as opposed to the geosphere, or nonliving world, and the biosphere, or living world.

·biosphere organization and components **2**:1037f
·conservation history and philosophy **5**:42b
·Verdansky and Teilhard de Chardin **12**:873c

Noot, Henri van der (b. Jan. 7, 1731, Brussels—d. Jan. 12, 1827, Strombeek, Neth.), Belgian lawyer and political activist who, along with Jean-François Vonck, led the Belgian revolt of 1789 against the regime of the Austrian Habsburg Holy Roman emperor Joseph II. He failed to maintain national support, however, and yielded to an Austrian invasion the following year.

Van der Noot served as an advocate in Brabant and in 1787 began to organize against the sweeping religious and political reforms of Joseph II, which violated traditional local privileges. After influencing the guilds of Brabant to form a militia, he escaped arrest in August 1788 by fleeing to Breda in the United Provinces (Dutch republic). There and in London he offered sovereignty over Belgium to the Dutch House of Orange and won a promise of support from Prussia. In 1789 he joined forces with Jean Vonck's army led by Jean-André van der Meersch at Breda. After the rebels' victory over the Austrians, he returned triumphantly to Brussels in December 1789.

Van der Noot and his supporters, the "statist party," who sought a return to oligarchic rule, were able to force Vonck's democratic faction out of the government. He was unable to unify the country, however, and went into exile (where he remained until 1792) after the Austrians took Belgium in December 1790, defeating a Belgian army weakened by the statists' arrest of van der Meersch. Van der Noot was imprisoned in 1796 by the Directory (the French government of 1795–99) and was never again prominent in public life except for a brief emergence in 1814, when he argued for the return of Belgium to Austrian rule.

·Brabant Revolution leadership **11**:157a

Noot, Jonker Jan van der (b. *c.* 1540, Brecht, Neth.—d. after 1595), first Dutch Renaissance poet to realize fully the new French poetic style in Holland and who influenced English and German poets of the time. He because political exile in 1567, and his first work was published in England—*Het bosken* (1570 or 1571; "The Little Wood"), a collection of his earliest poetry in the style and form of the Italian poet Petrarch and the French poet Ronsard. In 1568 one of his main works had appeared, *Het theatre oft toon-neel* ("Theatre for Voluptuous Worldlings"), a prose defense of the virtues of Calvinism and condemnation of the worldliness of Dutch society. It is prefaced by sonnets and epigrams that were translated by Spenser for the English version.

In van der Noot's unique Renaissance production and main poetical work, the *Olympiados* epic, he described in clear, unadorned language his dream of an allegorical journey toward his divine love, Olympia. Van der Noot interpolated numerous sonnets in the work, and their German translations are the earliest known instances of the pure sonnet in that language.

·literature of the Renaissance **10**:1144d

Nooth, John Mervin, 18th-century British scientist who developed apparatus for preparing small quantities of effervescent waters.

·carbonated water preparation **16**:1010c

Nootka, Indians of the Northwest Pacific Coast of North America, located on the southwest coast of Vancouver Island and Cape Flattery, the northwest tip of the state of Washington. The groups on the southeast end of the island were the Nitinat, those on Cape Flattery, the Makah. Nootka was a Wakashan language (*see* Wakashan). They were culturally related to the Kwakiutl (*q.v.*).

In the central and southern Nootka regions, local groups were socially and politically independent; in northern areas they usually formed larger tribes with common winter villages. There were also several confederacies of tribes, dating to prehistoric times, that shared summer villages near the coast and the fishing and hunting grounds. The Nootka moved seasonally to areas of economic importance, returning to their principal homesites during the winter when subsistence activity slowed.

The Nootka were specialized whale hunters, employing special equipment such as large dugout canoes and harpoons with long lines and sealskin floats. The whale harpooner was a person of high rank, and families passed down the magical and practical secrets that made for successful hunting. There was also a whale ritualist who, by appropriate ceremonial procedures, caused whales that had died of natural causes to drift ashore. Many features of this whaling complex suggest ancient ties with Eskimo and Aleut cultures.

The most important Nootkan ceremony was the shamans' dance, a reenactment of the kidnapping of an ancestor by supernatural beings who gave him supernatural gifts and released him. The ceremony served to define each individual's place in the social order. The public performance ended with a potlatch (*q.v.*), a ceremonial distribution of property.

·basketry latticework technique **2**:759d
·economy and social life in British Columbia **3**:296h
·geographic distribution map **13**:251
·technology and crafts **13**:253f

Nootka Sound controversy, a dispute over the seizure of vessels at Nootka Sound, an inlet on the west coast of Vancouver Island, that nearly caused a war between Great Britain and Spain in 1790. Its settlement ended the Spanish claim to a monopoly of trade and settlement on the western coast of North America and made possible the eventual expansion of the Canadian provinces to the Pacific.

The dispute arose as a result of the seizure by the Spaniards in 1789 of four British trading vessels owned by Capt. John Meares and his associates. In April 1790, Meares appealed to the British government for redress, and a major dispute quickly developed with Spain. The Spaniards claimed possession of the whole northwest coast of America on the basis of a papal grant of 1493, confirmed when their explorers had formally taken possession of the area. Great Britain, on the other hand, contended that rights of sovereignty could be established only by actual occupation of the land.

The British threatened war over the Nootka Sound incident, but because of Spain's military weakness and because of Prussian diplomatic support on behalf of Great Britain, Spain yielded to the British demands in the Nootka Sound Convention signed on Oct. 28, 1790. The convention acknowledged that each nation was free to navigate and fish in the Pacific, and to trade and establish settlements on unoccupied land.

·Spanish trade monopoly claims **14**:479b

Nora, ancient Sardinian site about 22 miles (35 kilometres) southwest of Cagliari (Caralis). Although tradition ascribes its foundation to Iberians from Tartessus, the site, a triangular promontory ending in a steep cliff, is characteristically Phoenician. Apart from remains of a Sardinian *nuraghe*, or towerlike monument, the earliest antiquities discovered at Nora are Phoenician, dating from the 7th century BC. After the Roman annexation of Sardinia, Nora was its capital in the republican period and later became a *municipium* (Romanized community) under the empire (after 27 BC).

Excavations in 1952–54 revealed a wealthy imperial city overlying a typical Phoenician port. The violence during the time of the First Punic War (264–241 BC) is evidenced by a *tofet*, where the bodies of cremated children were buried in great jars under stelae carved with a temple facade and an image of the goddess Tanit.

noradrenaline (hormone): *see* adrenaline and noradrenaline.

Noranda, city, seat of Rouyn-Noranda subregion, Nord-Ouest (Northwest) region, western Quebec province, Canada, immediately north of Rouyn on the western shore of Lac Osisko. Primarily residential, its only important industry is the big Noranda Mines copper smelter. Its twin city, Rouyn (*q.v.*), a copper- and gold-mining community, is the commercial and industrial section for both cities, which are officially called the Metropole of North-Western Quebec. There are two Roman Catholic cathedrals—Notre Dame de Protection and Blessed Sacrament. The population is largely French-Canadian. Founded by Noranda Mines, Ltd., in 1922, Noranda became a town in 1926. Inc. city, 1948. Pop. (1971) 10,741.
48°15′ N, 79°01′ W

norbergite (mineral): *see* humite.

Norbert, Saint (b. *c.* 1080, Xanten, Ger.—d. June 6, 1134, Magdeburg), archbishop of Magdeburg and founder of the Premonstratensians (Norbertines or White Canons), a congregation of priests. He was ordained in 1115. Failing to reform his peers at the collegiate church of Xanten, he travelled throughout France and Belgium, preaching moral reform. In 1119 Pope Calixtus II asked him to found a religious institute at Prémontré, Fr. With such notable disciples as Hugh of Fosses and St. Evermod, he established his community, the Premonstratensians, in 1120. The congregation was dedicated to preaching, pastoral work, and education. Norbert adopted the rule of Bishop St. Augustine of Hippo for his new order, and he modelled its constitutions after the Cistercians, an austere group of cloistered, vegetarian monks practicing perpetual silence. His monastery at Prémontré became the motherhouse of the Premonstratensians.

Norbert was chosen archbishop of Magdeburg in 1126. He became an important church figure four years later when he defended Pope Innocent II, whose claim to the papacy was threatened by Antipope Anacletus II. Norbert won the German Church for Innocent's cause and influenced the German king Lothair II/III to defend Innocent. Norbert was canonized in 1582 by Pope Gregory XIII. His feast day is June 6, but it is celebrated on July 11 by the Premonstratensians. C.J. Kirkfleet's *History of St. Norbert* appeared in 1916, followed by L.T. Anderson's *St. Norbert of Xanten* (1955).

Norbertines (religious order): *see* Premonstratensians.

Nor-bu-gling-ka, monastic palace in Lhasa, Tibet.
·Tibetan and Chinese use **10**:842a

Nord, the most northerly *département* of France, extending for 200 mi (320 km) along the Belgian frontier and bordering the Strait of Dover for 20 mi. With an area of 2,216 sq mi (5,738 sq km), it is the most populous *département* of France after Paris and one of the most productive in agriculture and industry. Created mainly from French portions of the historic provinces of Flanders and Hainaut (*q.v.*), it occupies a low-lying land over which many battles, including those of World Wars I and II, have been fought throughout the history of Europe. From northwest to southeast it comprises the coastal plain reclaimed from the sea and including Dunkirk (*q.v.*); the Flanders plain extending to Armentières (*q.v.*), where the *département* is at its narrowest; the densely populated industrial area of Lille, Roubaix, and Tourcoing (*qq.v.*); the coal basin around Douai, Denain, and Valenciennes (*qq.v.*) through which the Scheldt River (*q.v.*) flows; the territory around Cambrai (*q.v.*); the valley of the Sambre River flowing through Maubeuge; and the area of Avesnes-sur-Helpe on the western approaches of the Ardennes plateau. The entire *département* is laced with an intricate network of canalized rivers, canals, and roads, including the highway linking Lille, the departmental capital, with Paris.

The climate is mild and humid. Cereals, potatoes, beets, flax, and hops are cultivated intensively. Dairy farming and market gardening have been highly developed. The traditional textile industry of Roubaix–Tourcoing remains among the most important of the *département*, which, besides coal mining, coking, and distilling, has a concentration of iron and steel works, particularly in the Valenciennes area. Other activities include engineering, chemical works, food processing, glassworks, and marble cutting. Oil refineries and mineral works have been developed in the area of Dunkirk, one of the main French seaports, which also has an important shipbuilding yard. The colonial administrator Joseph François Dupleix (1697–1763) was born in Landrecies; the artist Henri Matisse (1869–1954) in Cateau; and Charles de Gaulle (1890–1970) in Lille. The *département* has six *arrondissements*—Lille, Cambrai, Douai, Dunkirk, Valenciennes, and Avesnes-sur-Helpe. It is in the educational division of Lille. Pop. (1972 est.) 2,483,700.
·area and population table **7**:594

Nord, Plaine du, region of Haiti.
19°40′ N 72°10′ W
·Haiti's geographical patterns **8**:546d; map

Nordau, Max (b. MAX SIMON SÜDFELD, July 29, 1849, Budapest—d. Jan. 23, 1923, Paris), physician, controversial writer, and early Jewish nationalist who was instrumental in establishing Zionist recognition of Palestine as a potential Jewish homeland to be gained by colonization.

In 1880, after serving as Viennese correspondent for a Budapest newspaper and travelling extensively in Europe, he settled permanently in Paris, where he established a medical practice. A prolific writer of travel books, plays, poems, and essays, he achieved his greatest and most noted success in 1883 with the publication of *Die conventionellen Lügen der Kulturmenschheit* (Eng. trans., *The Conventional Lies of Our Civilization*, 1884), a vitriolic attack on the inadequacy of 19th-century institutions to meet human needs; he took a particularly harsh look at organized religion. Banned in Russia and Austria, the book nevertheless was translated into numerous languages and went into some 73 editions.

After he met the charismatic Jewish nationalist Theodor Herzl in Paris in 1892, Nordau became deeply interested in Zionism and served as vice president of the Zionist congresses under Herzl, delivering a number of brilliant addresses on the condition of world Jewry. Following Herzl's death in 1904, Nordau broke with the "practical Zionists" (younger men advocating colonization of Palestine without guarantees of political sovereignty), who gained control of the Zionist congresses; Nordau refused to participate in these meetings after 1911.
·Herzl's Zionist movement support **8**:829h

Nordenfelt, Torsten Vilhelm (1842–1920), Swedish engineer and inventor.
·submarine construction and development **17**:748d

Nordenflycht, Hedvig Charlotta (b. Nov. 28, 1718, Stockholm—d. June 29, 1763, Stockholm), poet, remembered for her sensitive love poems. She fought all her life to keep her Christian faith, although disturbed by the ideas of the Enlightenment, and this conflict is expressed in her reflective poetry. The deaths of her fiancé in 1737 and of her husband soon after their marriage in 1741 inspired her finest poems, some of them published in *Den Sörgande turtur-dufvan* (1743). During the 1750s she enjoyed a literary collaboration with Gustav Philip Creutz and Gustaf Fredrik Gyllenborg. In 1761 she fell tragically in love with a man much younger than herself, and her poems about him are her highest achievement. Her collected works were edited by H. Borelius and T. Hjelmqvist (4 vol., 1924–38).
·Swedish literature development **10**:1176c

Hedvig Nordenflycht, detail of an oil painting by Johan Henrik Scheffel, 1754; in the Svenska Porträttarkivet, Stockholm
By courtesy of the Svenska Porträttarkivet, Stockholm

Nordenskiöld, (Nils) Adolf Erik, Baron (b. Nov. 18, 1832, Helsinki—d. Aug. 12, 1901, Dalbyö, Swed.), geologist, mineralogist, geographer, and explorer who sailed from Norway to the Pacific across the Asiatic Arctic and thereby completed the first successful navigation of the Northeast Passage. In 1858 he settled in Stockholm, joined an expedition to the Arctic island of Spitsbergen (now Svalbard), off Norway, and became professor and curator of mineralogy at the Swedish State Museum. He returned to Spitsbergen again in 1861 and led his own expeditions there in 1864, 1868, and 1872–73, adding to geological knowledge of the area. In 1870 he also led an expedition to western Greenland to study the inland ice.

Before attempting to cross the Northeast Passage, he made preliminary voyages in 1875 and 1876, on which he penetrated the Kara Sea, north of Siberia, to the mouth of the Yenisei River. Sailing from Tromsø, Nor., aboard the steam vessel "Vega" on July 21, 1878, he reached Cape Chelyushkin, Siberia, roughly the mid-point of his journey, on August 19. From the end of September until July 18, 1879, the ship was frozen in near the Bering Strait. Resuming her course, the "Vega" reached Port Clarence, Alaska, on July 22 and returned to Europe by way of Canton (China), Ceylon, and the Suez Canal. When Nordenskiöld reached Stockholm on April 24, 1880, he was created a baron by King Oscar. In 1883, while returning from west Greenland,

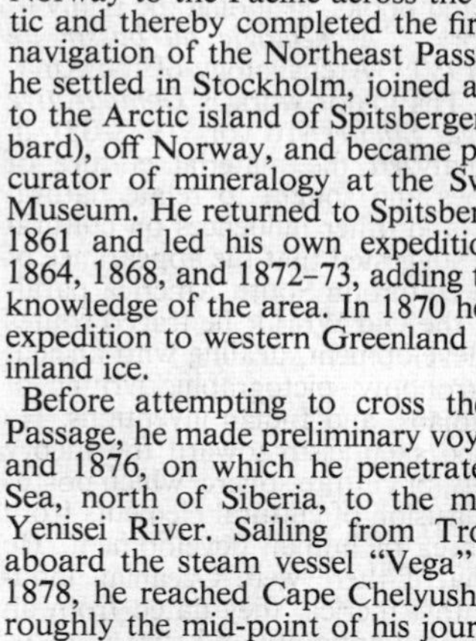

Adolf Erik Nordenskiöld, detail of an oil painting by Georg von Rosen, 1886; in the Nationalmuseum, Stockholm
By courtesy of the Nationalmuseum, Stockholm

where he penetrated far into the inland ice, he became the first to break through the great sea ice barrier of the southeast Greenland coast. Nordenskiöld also made notable contributions to the history of cartography.
·Northeast Passage exploration success **7**:1042e

Nordenskiöld, (Nils) Erland (Herbert) (b. July 19, 1877, Strömm, Swed.—d. July 5, 1932, Stockholm), ethnologist, archaeologist, and a foremost student of South American Indian culture. As professor of American and comparative ethnology at the University of Göteborg, Sweden (1924–32), he had a marked influence on anthropology in Sweden and Denmark.

Son of the scientist-explorer Adolf Erik Nordenskiöld and brother of explorer-geographer Otto Nordenskiöld, he made zoological expeditions to Patagonia (1899) and Argentina and Bolivia (1901–02) but turned to archaeological research in the mountains of Peru and Bolivia (1904–05). He made two subsequent expeditions to the forest lands bordering Bolivia and Brazil, one noteworthy result being his paper (1912) dealing with mounds and urn burials in Bolivia. In 1913 he became principal curator of ethnology at the Göteborg Museum. His final expedition took him to the Chocó and Cuna Indians of Colombia and Panama (1927). Pioneering in methods of mapping the distribution of many elements of South American culture, he succeeded in developing a remarkably clear reconstruction of cultural history in an area of considerable complexity.

In addition to accounts of his travels written in a semi-popular vein, he wrote many scientific articles and books, including the richly illustrated work *L'Archéologie du bassin de l'Amazone* (1930; "Archaeology of the Amazon Basin"). His major work is *Comparative Ethnographical Studies* (10 vol., 1918–38), in which he analyzed the material culture of Bolivian tribes and sought to relate natural environment and other influences on cultural patterns. He suggested that the appearance of Copper Age culture in South America paralleled that of the Old World; he traced routes of cultural development, dealing with ancient Peruvian astronomy, pictographic writing of the Cuna Indians, and Indian inventions. He also expressed skepticism toward the theory of *Kulturkreis*, or culture sphere, which postulates early diffusion of cultural elements from a primeval area of human development. He suggested that if there were Oceanian influences in South America, they dated from an extremely remote antiquity and that impetus to high civilization of America was Indian.

Nordenskjöld, (Nils) Otto (Gustaf) (b. Dec. 6, 1869, Smaland, Swed.—d. June 2, 1928, Göteborg), geographer and explorer whose expedition to the Antarctic was distinguished by the volume of its scientific findings. A nephew of the scientist-explorer Adolf Erik Nordenskiöld, in 1894 he became a lecturer in mineralogy and geology at the University of Uppsala, Sweden, and led a geological expedition to southern South America (1895–97). His findings in Patagonia and Tierra del Fuego formed an important contribution to world glacial geology.

On Oct. 16, 1901, Nordenskjöld sailed aboard the "Antarctic" from Göteborg and the following February established an Antarctic station on Snow Hill Island off Graham Coast, where he wintered with five companions. Their ship, which had wintered at the island of South Georgia, 54° S and due east of Tierra del Fuego, was crushed in the pack ice when it returned to relieve them in February 1903. Nordenskjöld's party was again forced to winter in the Antarctic until rescued by the Argentine vessel "Uruguay" in November 1903.

He published his extensive findings in *Wissenschaftliche Ergebnisse der schwedischen Südpolar-expedition 1901–1903* (1905–20; "Scientific Results of the Swedish South Polar Expedition 1901–1903"). He subsequently became professor of geography (1905) and first rector of advanced commercial studies (1923) at the University of Göteborg.

Norderney, one of the East Frisian Islands off the North Sea coast of West Germany. A part of Niedersachsen (Lower Saxony) *Land* (state), the island is 8 mi (13 km) long and up to 1¼ mi wide, with dunes rising to 68 ft (21 m). The northern coast is exposed to the sea, but the more sheltered water of the *Wattenmeer* (tidal water flooding wide mud flats) lies to the south between the island and the mainland. Most of the population lives in Norderney, a small fishing port and the oldest German seaside resort (1797), which was formerly frequented by fashionable international society and is noted for its fine beach and mild climate. There are ferry connections to Norden on the mainland. Pop. (1970 est.) 9,317.
53°42′ N, 7°10′ E
·map, Federal Republic of Germany **8**:46

Nordfriesische Inseln (Europe): *see* North Frisian Islands.

Nordhausen, city, Erfurt *Bezirk* (district), southwestern East Germany, northwest of Erfurt city. It lies on the Zorge River, at the southern slopes of the Harz mountains, in the fertile lowland known as the Goldene Aue (Golden Meadow). First mentioned in 927 as the site of a royal castle near the older Frankish settlement of Northusen (Nordhusa), it was made a free imperial city in 1220 and accepted the Reformation in 1522. It lost its independence in 1802, when it was annexed by Prussia, forming part of Prussian Saxony, except for a period 1807–13 when it was Westphalian, until 1945. It incorporated the neighbouring villages of Salza and Krimderode in 1950. Historic buildings that survived heavy air attacks in World War II include the 17th-century town hall with the oaken statue of Roland (1717), a symbol of civic liberty; the late Gothic Roman Catholic cathedral with a Romanesque crypt; and the 13th-century Protestant Church of St. Blasius. The city has a civic museum, a theatre, a teachers' training college, an institute of agricultural technology, and a sports school.

Industries include brewing, distilling, the manufacture of tobacco, machinery, clothing, chemicals, and wood products and shaft-sinking processes. Pop. (1971 prelim.) 44,600.
51°30′ N, 10°47′ E
·map, German Democratic Republic **8**:8

Nordhorn, town, Niedersachsen (Lower Saxony) *Land* (state), northwestern West Germany, on the Vechte River at the junction of the Almelo–Nordhorn, Ems–Vechte, and Süd-Nord canals, 4 mi (6 km) from the Dutch border. First mentioned *c.* 1000 and chartered in 1379, it suffered heavily from plague, fire, and war in the 15th and 16th centuries. Part of the Augustinian Frenswegen Abbey (founded 1394) and the 15th-century Protestant church survive. Nordhorn is a textile centre, with petroleum wells nearby. Its area was expanded in the 1920s by the addition of neighbouring communities. Pop. (1970 est.) 42,900.
52°27′ N, 7°05′ E
·map, Federal Republic of Germany **8**:46

Nordic, a traditional racial typing by physical appearance, denoting the characteristics of tall, fair, long-headed persons, such as Scandinavians and Scots.
·Denmark racial composition **5**:582a
·Norway population composition **13**:265a
·racial typing by physical appearance **15**:348b
·Ripley's European population analysis **14**:842b

Nordic, or CLASSIC, in skiing, techniques and events that evolved in the hilly terrain of Norway and the other Scandinavian countries. The modern Nordic events are the cross-country races and ski jumping events. The Nordic combined is a separate test consisting of a 15-kilometre cross-country race and special ski jumping contest, with the winner determined on the basis of points awarded for performance in both. Cross-country racing is sometimes called Nordic racing. Nordic events were included in the first winter Olympic program in 1924; the Alpine events (downhill and slalom) were not added until 1936.

Nordic Council, organization of the Nordic states of Denmark, Finland, Iceland, Norway, and Sweden for the purpose of consultation and cooperation on matters of common interest. The Council was established in March 1952 by statutes drawn up among the governments of the member states. Its main executive organ is the annual Council, composed of representatives from the five national legislatures. The Nordic Council has acted to provide for uniform arrangements among its members on legal, economic, and social matters.
·diplomatic accomplishments since 1953 **16**:333a

Nord i Tåkeheimen (1911), translated as IN NORTHERN MISTS, two-volume historical review of the exploration of the northern regions by Fridtjof Nansen.
·literary criticism **12**:825e

Nordjyllands, *amtskommune* (county), northern Jutland, Denmark, created in 1970 from the former counties of Ålborg and Hjørring, has an area of 2,383 sq mi (6,171 sq km). It comprises most of the Himmerland region between Mariager Fjord and the Limfjorden and extends to the northernmost tip of the Jutland peninsula at Skagen. It has soil of generally poor quality with large areas of moorland in the south and extensive dunes in the north. Its economy depends largely on dairying and agriculture; there are also coastal resorts and some fishing in the north. The port of Ålborg (*q.v.*) serves as the administrative seat; other important centres include Hjørring, Frederikshavn, and Skagen (*qq.v.*). Pop. (1971 est.) 457,165.
·area and population table **5**:584

Nordland, *fylke* (county), northern Norway, bordering the Norwegian Sea. Its many offshore islands include most of the Lofoten–Vesterålen archipelago (*qq.v.*). With an area of 14,798 sq mi (38,327 sq km), including the northern islands, Nordland extends for about 300 mi (500 km) along the coast; about two-thirds of the *fylke* is north of the Arctic Circle. The coastline is rugged and fjord indented. Most residents live on the coastal lowlands and in narrow inland valleys. Narvik and Bodø (the county seat) are the only cities; other larger towns are Svolvær and Mo. The economy is based on fishing (especially cod), stock raising (cattle and goats), some farming (rye and potatoes), and mining. The port of Narvik (*q.v.*) has a direct rail connection to the rich Kiruna-Gällivare iron-ore fields in Sweden. The chief pyrite deposits are near Mo and Sulitjelma, while iron ore is mined in Dunderlandsdalen (Dunderlands Valley). Hydroelectric power has been extensively developed, providing a base for metal-processing industries (steel at Mo, aluminum at Mosjøen). Pop. (1971 est.) 240,951.
·area and population table **13**:265
·map, Norway **13**:266

Nördlicher, Landrüche, land rise in East Germany.
52°00′ N 12°45′ E
·location and altitude **8**:7b

Nördlingen, city, Bavaria (Bayern) *Land* (state), southern West Germany, on the Eger River, east of Aalen. A seat of the bishop of Regensburg in 898, it became a free imperial city in 1215. Several battles in the Thirty Years' War (17th century) and the French Revolutionary Wars (18th century) were fought outside the medieval walls that still surround the old city. Notable buildings include the late-Gothic town hall, the Church

of St. George (1427–1505), and the Church of St. Salvator (1381–1422). The oldest horse race in Germany is held annually in Nördlingen. Industries include the manufacture of textiles, shoes, precision instruments, and paper. Pop. (1970 est.) 14,200.
48°51′ N, 10°30′ E

·map, Federal Republic of Germany **8**:46

Nördlingen, battles of, two military engagements of the Thirty Years' War, fought near Nördlingen in southwestern Germany. The first, Sept. 5–6, 1634, a decisive victory for the forces of the Holy Roman Empire and Spain over the Swedes, led to the dissolution of the Heilbronn alliance (1633), ended Swedish domination in southern Germany, and forced Cardinal de Richelieu to bring France into active participation in the war. Led by Matthias Gallas, the combined imperial and Spanish forces fought the Swedish army, which, under the dual command of Gustav Karlsson Horn and Bernhard of Saxe-Weimar, was weakened by the absence of large contingents that had been sent to fight the Poles. Although the Swedes gained an advantage on the first day of the battle, they could not overcome the incompatibility of their two leaders; Horn was captured and the Swedish army was completely routed.

The second battle, Aug. 3, 1645, was a victory for the French under Turenne and the Duc d'Enghien over an imperial and Bavarian army under Franz von Mercy and Johan von Werth.

·French victory and consequences **18**:777e

Nordmarka, recreation area of Oslo, Norway.

·nature conservation in urban area **13**:756b

Nord-Norge, English NORTHERN NORWAY, unofficial traditional region of Norway, reaching from the Trondheim area about 700 mi (1,100 km) northward to the North Cape (Nordkapp), the northernmost point in Europe. Its 59,580 sq mi (154,310 sq km) include the *fylker* (counties) of Sør-Trøndelag, Nord-Trøndelag, Nordland, Troms, and Finnmark (*qq.v.*). An arm of the Gulf Stream, which flows past its coast, provides a relatively mild maritime climate. Commonly known as "the Land of the Midnight Sun," it has a five-month summer, from May through September; in the far north the Sun does not set from mid-May to late July. The northeastern section, in which herds of reindeer range across the tundra, is part of Lapland. The remainder of the region is extremely mountainous, with dense forests and many rivers. The entire region is dotted with thousands of lakes, while the coastline is indented by numerous fjords. Adjacent to the coast are hundreds of islands, the most important group being the Lofoten–Vesterålen near Narvik.

Nord-Norge is connected to southern Norway via coastal shipping and passenger ferries and by highways and a railroad that runs as far north as Bodø in the middle of the region. Principal economic activities include fishing, farming (as far north as 70° N), shipping (especially Swedish iron ore through Narvik), and tourism. Trondheim (second largest city in Norway), Namsos, Bodø, Narvik, Tromsø, Hammerfest (*qq.v.*), and Namsos are the main towns and ports. Pop. (1971 est.) 806,087.

·physical features and economic activity **13**:264h

Nord-Ostsee-Kanal (Baltic Sea): *see* Kiel Canal.

Nordrhein-Westfalen 13:142, English NORTH RHINE-WESTPHALIA, *Land* (state), West Germany. Occupying an area of 13,145 sq mi (34,044 sq km), it is bordered by The Netherlands and Belgium on the west and by the *Länder* (states) of Niedersachsen (north), Hessen (east), and Rheinland-Pfalz (south). Bonn, the federal capital, is in Nordrhein-Westfalen. Düsseldorf is the state capital. Pop. (1970) 16,914,000.

The text article covers the state's relief, drainage, climate, vegetation and animal life, and settlement patterns, as well as its population, economy, transportation, administration, social conditions, cultural life and institutions, and prospects for the future.

REFERENCES in other text articles:
·area and population table **8**:53
·local government functions **4**:648a
·map, Federal Republic of Germany **8**:46

Nordström, Ludvig Anselm (b. Feb. 25, 1882, Härnösand, Swed.—d. April 15, 1942, Stockholm), writer who enlisted his literary talents in the cause of the new industrial society and whose descriptions of his native province were realistic and socially conscious rather than romantic in keeping with the popular trend. He most delighted his readers with his short stories, such as "Fiskare" (1907; "Fishermen"), "Borgare" (1909; "Burghers"), "Herrar" (1910; "Gentlemen"), and "Lumpsamlaren" (1910; "The Junk Collector"). The four-volume work *Petter Svensks historia* (1923–27; "The Story of Peter Svensk") deals with his vision of an anti-individualistic society, which he called "totalism," in which group and communal values are stressed. He achieved his greatest political influence, however, with two essays: *Bonde-Nöden* (1933; "The Distress of the Peasantry") and *Lort-Sverige* (1938; "Dirt-Sweden"), dealing with the filth of the supposedly "clean" Swedish countryside. They aroused widespread discussion and subsequent reforms.

Nordström, detail of an oil portrait by Leander Engström, 1919; in a private collection, Stockholm
By courtesy of the Svenska Portrattarkivet, Stockholm

·development of the novel in Sweden **10**:1247b

Nord–Süd Canal, West Germany, canal linking Hamburg with the Mittelland Canal and so to the Ruhr region.

·Elbe waterway link **6**:522g

Nord-Trøndelag, *fylke* (county), central Norway, extends from the Norwegian Sea (west) to the Swedish border (east); the southern boundary runs in a general northwest–southeast direction south of Trondheimsfjorden. The *fylke* has an area of 8,673 sq mi (22,463 sq km); the county seat is at Steinkjer (*q.v.*). The major road and rail links between Trondheim and northern Norway pass through narrow Namdalen (Nam Valley) in the north central section. The low, hilly areas in the south are one of the best agricultural areas of Norway (grains, hay, and potatoes). Fishing and fish processing are extensively carried on from the many small coastal ports and offshore islands. Pyrite is mined in the Namdalen and near the Swedish border, and iron ore is extracted west of Trondheimsfjorden. The cities of Steinkjer and Namsos and the towns of Grong and Levanger are manufacturing centres. Pop. (1971 est.) 117,998.

·area and population table **13**:265
·map, Norway **13**:266

Nordweststadt, suburb of Frankfurt am Main, West Germany.
50°15′ N, 8°35′ E

·plan and facilities **7**:692b

Nore, The, sandbank in the Thames Estuary, extends between Shoeburyness (north) and Sheerness (south), in Kent, southeastern England. The Nore Lightship lies 4 mi (6 km) southeast of Shoeburyness and was the first to be established in English waters (1732). The Nore anchorage was much used by the English fleet in the wars of the 17th and 18th centuries. In 1797 sailors at The Nore mutinied against their conditions, and their leader, Richard Parker, was hanged from the yardarm of his ship. Until 1961 The Nore gave its name to a naval command for the eastern area of England. The name is used also for the estuarine area that roughly coincides with the naval port of Sheerness.
51°29′ N, 0°51′ E

No Regrets for Our Youth (1946), film directed by Akira Kurosawa.

·theme and artistic success **10**:546e

norephinephrine (hormone): *see* adrenaline and noradrenaline.

Norfolk, English county bounded by Suffolk (south), Cambridgeshire and Lincolnshire (west), and the North Sea (north and east). Its area is 1,067 sq mi (5,353 sq km).

Norfolk is low-lying; and a large part is drained by the Rivers Wensum, Yare, Bure, and their tributaries into the North Sea. The northwest corner of the county is drained by the Ouse into the Wash, a shallow North Sea inlet. Chalk outcrops in western Norfolk, and, in the eastern half of the county, chalk is overlain by later deposits. Along the northwest edge of the county, clays and sandstones older than the chalk are exposed. Norfolk is a rich farming county, but nevertheless regions of natural or seminatural vegetation survive. Around parts of the 90-mi (145-km) coastline there are sand dunes, as at Blakeney Beach on the northern coast. There are also salt marshes, as at Scolthead Island. Along the valleys of the Yare and Bure are a number of shallow expanses of water and reed swamp—the famous Broads that resulted from medieval peat cutting and a subsequent change in sea level. In the southwest of the county and extending into Suffolk, are the sandy heathlands of Breckland, which have been planted with conifers in many places. Paleolithic, Mesolithic, and Neolithic artifacts have been found in the county; and the most impressive Stone Age monuments are the flint mines, such as Grimes Graves, in Breckland. Long barrows (mounds) and Bronze Age round barrows are also found. In the 3rd century BC the early British Iceni people, of whom later the famous Boudicca (sometimes called Boadicea) was a queen, entered the area from the Continent. During the Roman period, there were two towns in Norfolk, Caister St. Edmund and Caister next Yarmouth. After the ensuing Anglo-Saxon invasions, Norfolk became part of the kingdom of East Anglia. Town life in Norwich and Thetford started at this time, the former town having a mint from 920. Subsequently the area was subjected to Danish raids, and it eventually became part of the administrative entity known as the Danelaw. By the time of Domesday Book (1086), the record of the land survey ordered by William I the Conqueror, Norfolk was one of the most thickly populated and wealthiest regions in England and it remained so throughout the medieval period. The region's prosperity depended largely on wool. Little Walsingham, in the north of the county, was a famous shrine in the Middle Ages attracting pilgrims from far and wide. During the English Civil War of the mid-17th century, Norfolk saw little action because the county was strongly behind Cromwell and the Parliamentary cause. There are several surviving castles in the area, as at Norwich, Caister next Yarmouth, and Oxborough, there are also large private mansions, as at Sandringham (the Norfolk home of the royal family).

Norfolk economy is predominantly agricultural, with barley, wheat, sugar beet, oats, and vegetables, as the major crops. Barley is grown for the distilling industry and for animal feed. Large areas of peas and beans are grown for canning and freezing at such centres as Great Yarmouth. Most types of livestock are raised, but the county is especially famous for its turkeys. Fishing is important at many points around the coast. Norwich has developed an important boot and shoe industry and, together with most other major towns in the county, has attracted some light industry. Catering for holiday makers is also an important industry, especially at points around the coast (Cromer and Great Yarmouth) and on the Broads. Pop. (1971 est.) 624,000.

·United Kingdom political geography **18**:873a

Norfolk, city, Madison County, northeastern Nebraska, U.S., on the north fork of the Elkhorn River. Settled in 1866 by German farmers from Xonia and Watertown, Wis., its name, originally proposed as North Fork, was abbreviated to Norfork and then changed by the post office to Norfolk. The economy depends primarily on agriculture (grain and livestock) and food processing, augmented by manufacturing (medical equipment and fabricated metals). Norfolk Junior College was founded in 1932. Gavins Point Dam and Nebraska Sand Hills Recreation Area are nearby. Inc. village, 1881; city, 1886. Pop. (1980) 19,449.
42°02′ N, 97°25′ W

·map, United States **18**:908

Norfolk, independent city and port of entry, in the Tidewater region of southeastern Virginia, U.S., at the mouth of Chesapeake Bay. It is part of an urban complex that includes the cities of Portsmouth (west), Chesapeake (south), Virginia Beach (east), and Newport News and Hampton (north). Its harbour, Hampton Roads (*q.v.*), is formed chiefly by the tidal estuary of the James River, protected by the Virginia Peninsula. The Albemarle and Chesapeake Canal (1860) and the Dismal Swamp Canal (1828), on the Atlantic Intracoastal Waterway, connect the city with Currituck and Albemarle sounds in North Carolina.

Norfolk was laid out as a town in 1682 following an act of the Virginia General Assembly (1680) that each county should establish a trade centre. The land was bought from Nicholas Wise, a carpenter, for 10,000 lb (4,500 kg) of tobacco. For many years Norfolk was a trade centre for eastern North Carolina (tar, lumber, hides, and tobacco). Later, shipbuilding and ship repairing became important industries. A brisk trade developed with Barbados and the West Indies. In recognition of its importance, the city was presented a silver mace by Gov. Robert Dinwiddie in 1753.

The town was completely destroyed in the American Revolution. In December 1775, the royal governor, Lord Dunmore, made it his headquarters, declared martial law, and defeated the Virginia militiamen at Kempsville, southeast of the city. Later in the month Col. William Woodford and his Virginia riflemen routed the British at Great Bridge and occupied Norfolk, which on Jan. 1, 1776, was bombarded by Dunmore's fleet anchored in the Elizabeth River. The Virginians later burned the town except for St. Paul's Church (which still has a cannonball in its wall) to prevent its use by the British.

Norfolk's recovery was hampered by the stifling of West India trade by Britain, restriction on shipping and privateering by the European powers during the Napoleonic Wars, a disastrous fire in 1799, and intercity rivalry. During the War of 1812 it was twice saved from the British—when a local militia beat off a land attack on Portsmouth and when Gen. Robert B. Taylor's defense of Craney Island prevented a barge invasion.

With subsequent canal and railroad construction, prosperity returned until a yellow fever epidemic struck in 1855 (killing 10 percent of the population). Soon thereafter came the Civil War. In May 1862, Norfolk fell to Federal forces under Gen. John E. Wool and was occupied for the rest of the war. Its prosperity resumed after 1870 with the converging of railways on the port and was stimulated during World Wars I and II with installation of important naval bases. Norfolk is headquarters of the U.S. Atlantic Fleet and the Supreme Allied Command, Atlantic (Saclant), of the North Atlantic Treaty Organization (NATO).

Shipping, shipbuilding, and light industry are the major economic activities. Old Dominion University (1930), Norfolk State College (1968), and Virginia Wesleyan College (1966; partly in Virginia Beach) are located there. A botanical garden, the burial site and memorial for U.S. general Douglas MacArthur, and the Cultural and Convention Center are notable landmarks. Nearby are excellent fishing and bathing facilities. Norfolk's annual International Azalea Festival is dedicated to NATO. Inc. borough, 1736; city, 1845. Pop. (1960) city, 304,869; (1980) city, 266,979 (35% black); Norfolk–Virginia Beach–Portsmouth metropolitan area (SMSA), 806,691.
38°40′ N, 76°14′ W

·map, United States **18**:908
·naval activities economic importance **19**:156b

Norfolk, earls and dukes of, an English title held since 1483 by members of the Howard family. Norfolk is the premier English earldom and dukedom.

Norfolk, Thomas Mowbray, 1st duke of (b. *c.* 1366—d. Sept. 22, 1399, Venice), English lord whose quarrel with Henry of Bolingbroke, duke of Hereford (later King Henry IV, ruled 1399–1413), was a critical episode in the events leading to the overthrow of King Richard II (ruled 1377–99) by Bolingbroke. The quarrel dominates the first act of Shakespeare's play *Richard II*.

The son of John, 4th Lord Mowbray, Thomas was made earl of Nottingham in 1383. Several years later he joined the group of powerful nobles—known as the lords appellant—who from 1387 to 1389 forced Richard II to submit to their authority. Nevertheless, after Richard regained power, he employed Mowbray on military and diplomatic missions. In 1397 Richard arrested three leading appellants, including Thomas of Woodstock, duke of Gloucester. Committed to Mowbray's charge, Gloucester was mysteriously murdered, possibly on orders from Richard.

Although Mowbray was then created duke of Norfolk, he feared that the King would have him arrested for his earlier disloyalty. He confided these fears to Bolingbroke, who immediately denounced him to Richard as a traitor. Mowbray denied the charges and, as the two men were about to decide the dispute by duel, Richard intervened and banished them both (Sept. 16, 1398). Norfolk died in Italy shortly before Bolingbroke forced Richard to abdicate.

Norfolk, Thomas Howard, 3rd duke of (b. 1473—d. Aug. 25, 1554, Kenninghall, Norfolk), powerful English noble who held a variety of high offices under King Henry VIII (ruled 1509–47). Although he was valuable to the King as a military commander, he failed in his aspiration to become the chief minister of the realm. Howard was the brother-in-law of King Henry VII (ruled 1485–1509) and the son of Thomas Howard, 2nd duke of Norfolk. In May 1513 he became lord high admiral, and on September 9 he helped rout the Scots at Flodden Field near Branxton, Northumberland. He became lord deputy of Ireland in 1520 but soon left this post to command a fleet against the French.

Succeeding his father as duke of Norfolk in 1524, he headed the party opposed to Henry's chief minister, Thomas Wolsey. Upon Wolsey's fall in 1529, Norfolk became president of the royal council. He supported the marriage of his niece Anne Boleyn to Henry in 1533, but his relationship with the King was jeopardized when Anne fell in 1536. As lord high steward, Norfolk was assigned to preside at her trial and execution. Nevertheless, he soon regained royal favour by skillfully suppressing the rebellion of Roman Catholics in northern England known as the Pilgrimage of Grace (1536). A conservative in religion, Norfolk became a leading opponent of two influential church reformers: the King's chief adviser, Thomas Cromwell, and the archbishop of Canterbury, Thomas Cranmer. Upon Cromwell's execution (1540) Norfolk emerged as the second most powerful man in England, but his position was again weakened when Henry's fifth wife, Catherine Howard—another of Norfolk's nieces—was put to death in 1542.

3rd duke of Norfolk, detail of a painting by Hans Holbein the Younger (1497?–1543); at Castle Howard, Yorkshire

By courtesy of Castle Howard; photograph, Courtauld Institute of Art

In December 1546 Norfolk was accused of being an accessory to the alleged treasonable activities of his son, Henry Howard, earl of Surrey. Surrey was executed and Norfolk condemned, but before the sentence could be carried out Henry VIII died (January 1547). Norfolk remained in prison during the reign of the Protestant King Edward VI (ruled 1547–53); in August 1553, following the accession of Queen Mary (ruled 1553–58), a Roman Catholic, he was released and restored to his dukedom. He died in 1554 after failing to suppress the general uprising protesting the marriage of Mary I to Philip of Spain.

Norfolk, Thomas Howard, 4th duke of (b. March 10, 1538—d. June 2, 1572, London), English nobleman executed for his intrigues against Queen Elizabeth I on behalf of Mary Stuart, queen of Scots, a Roman Catholic claimant to the English throne. He was the son of Henry Howard, earl of Surrey, who

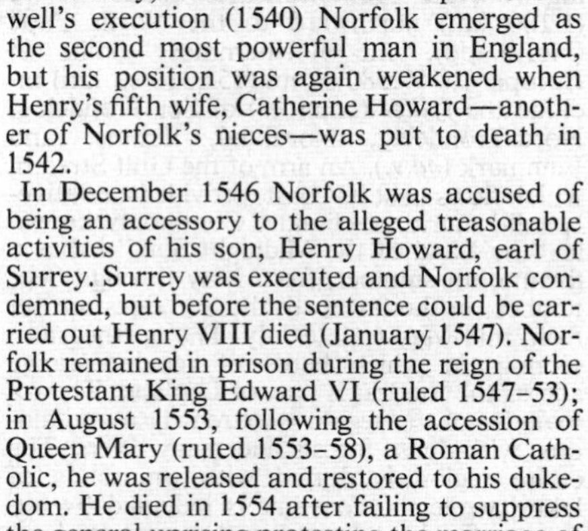

4th duke of Norfolk, detail of a portrait by Sir Anthony More (*c.* 1512–*c.* 1575); in a private collection

Courtauld Institute of Art, London

was put to death for alleged treasonable activities in 1547. Restored to his father's title on the accession of Queen Mary Tudor in 1553, he succeeded his grandfather as duke of Norfolk in 1554. Norfolk was in favour with both Queen Mary and her successor, Elizabeth I. He commanded the English forces that invaded Scotland in 1559–60 and presided over the commission that inquired in 1568 into the quarrel between Mary Stuart and Scotland's Protestant nobility. Mary had just fled to England, where she became Elizabeth's prisoner. Norfolk listened readily to suggestions from the Scottish statesman William Maitland and others that the difficulties between England and Scotland could be resolved if Norfolk would wed Mary and have her declared Elizabeth's successor. Norfolk, however, was neither bold enough to ask Elizabeth's consent for the match nor disloyal enough to raise an insurrection against her. Instead, several Catholic nobles in northern England revolted in an attempt to free the Queen of Scots, marry her to Norfolk, and restore Catholicism to England. The uprising was suppressed, and in October 1569 Elizabeth had Norfolk arrested. He was released the following August, but he soon allowed himself to be drawn into the plot of Roberto Ridolfi, Italian merchant living in London, for a Spanish invasion of England and installation of Mary on the English throne. Discovery of the plot led to Norfolk's imprisonment and execution.

·Catholic intrigue and execution **3**:1035e

Norfolk four-course system, agricultural system in western Europe during the period 1600–1800, characterized by the disappearance of the fallow year and new emphasis on fodder crops.

·agricultural land use developments **1**:333g

Norfolk Island, external territory of Australia, in the southwest Pacific Ocean, 1,035 mi (1,665 km) northeast of Sydney. Volcanic in origin and occupying 14 sq mi (34 sq km), its generally rugged terrain rises to Mt. Bates (1,043 ft [318 m]). The soil, although fertile, is easily eroded if stripped of its vegetation cover. Temperatures average 60° F (15° C) and rainfall exceeds 50 in. (1,270 mm) annually. Phillip (a volcanic pinnacle rising to 900 ft) and Nepean islands (the latter a limestone formation) lie off the south shore.

Discovered (1774) and named after the Duke of Norfolk by the English navigator Capt. James Cook, the island became the second British possession in the Pacific when it was claimed by the Australian colony of New South Wales (1788). It served as a penal colony from 1788 to 1813 and again from 1825 to 1855. The following year the population of

Ruined officers' quarters of the former penal settlement at Kingston on Norfolk Island

Photographic Library of Australia

Pitcairn Island, descendants of the mutineers from the HMS "Bounty," was resettled on Norfolk. Some returned to Pitcairn, but others remained to become the ancestors of many of Norfolk's present inhabitants. An Australian territory since 1913, it is governed by an appointed administrator and a locally elected council.

Kingston, the main settlement and port, is an open anchorage at one of the few points where the coast is not bound by cliffs. The island's income depends mainly on tourists who come by air from Australia and New Zealand. There is also some light industrial assembling and palm and bean seeds are cultivated for export. Impressive *Araucaria excelsa* (Norfolk Island pine) trees, which were once thought to be valuable as timber, have not proven so. Pop. (1971) 1,683.

29°02′ S, 167°57′ E

·Australia establishment and purpose **2**:414a
·penology and mark system development **14**:1099d
·population, climate, and government **2**:435b

Norfolk Island pine (*Araucaria heterophylla*), evergreen timber and ornamental conifer

Norfolk Island pine (*Araucaria heterophylla*)

Robert C. Hermes—National Audubon Society

of the family Araucariaceae, native to Norfolk Island, between New Caledonia and New Zealand. In nature this pine grows to a height of 60 metres (200 feet), with a trunk sometimes reaching 3 metres (10 feet) in diameter.

The wood of large trees is used in carpentry and shipbuilding. The sapling stage is grown throughout the world as a houseplant and as an outdoor ornamental in regions with a Mediterranean climate.

·fruit and nut farming, table 1 **7**:754
·gymnosperm representative form, illus. 1 **8**:519
·house plants and their care **8**:1120e
·needles and cones, illus. 1 **5**:2

Norge, Italian-built semi-rigid airship that carried Nobile and others over the North Pole May 11, 1926.

·airship construction history **1**:371d

Norges konuga sogür (Norwegian saga): *see* Heimskringla.

nori (alga): *see* laver.

noria, undershot waterwheel used to raise water in primitive irrigation systems. It was described by Vitruvius (*c.* 1st century BC). As the noria turns, pots or hollow chambers on the rim fill when submerged and empty automatically into a trough when they reach or exceed the level of the centre of the wheel. In antiquity the wheels may have been as much as 40 feet (12 metres) in diameter. The wheel-turning force of the stream was sometimes augmented by slaves or animals on a connected treadmill.

·Roman use in irrigation systems **18**:31b; illus.

Norian Stage, worldwide standard division of Triassic rocks and time (the Triassic Period began about 225,000,000 years ago and lasted about 35,000,000 years). Rocks of the Norian Stage underlie those of the Rhaetian Series and overlie those of the Karnian Stage; the Norian is included within the Upper Triassic. The Norian Stage, first studied in the Alpine region of Europe, consists of marine rocks characterized by a distinctive ammonoid cephalopod fossil fauna. In some regions, coral limestones or dolomites predominate.

·Upper Triassic correlation table **18**:693; map 694

Noric Alps, German NORISCHE ALPEN, segment of the Eastern Alps extending across southern Austria between the Hohe Tauern range and Katschberg Pass (west) and the city of Graz on the Mur River (east). With the Drava River to the south and the upper Mur River to the north, the mountains rise to Eisenhut (8,008 ft [2,441 m]) and consist of several subranges, the highest of which are the Gurkthaler Alpen in the west. Summer resorts and some skiing centres are within the range.

47°10′ N, 13°00′ E

Noricum, originally a kingdom controlled by a Celtic confederacy, annexed by Rome about 15 BC. It was a region south of the Danube, comprising modern central Austria and parts of Bavaria. Noricum received Roman protection in the late 2nd century BC and, on a foundation of wealth derived from its mineral resources, was able to develop a markedly Romanized culture. Five of its communities were

Noricum in the time of Augustus

Adapted from R. Treharne and H. Fullard (eds.), *Muir's Historical Atlas: Ancient, Medieval and Modern*, 9th ed. (1965); George Philip & Son Ltd., London

made into Roman *municipia* by the emperor Claudius I (ruled AD 41–54), and the province supplied many soldiers for legions and the Praetorian Guard. Franks and Goths settled Noricum before the end of the 5th century AD.

·Celtic tribes in ancient Austria **2**:449f
·Germanic people and Roman citizenship **4**:697a

Norilsk, city, Krasnoyarsk *kray* (territory), central Russian Soviet Federated Socialist Republic, in the Rybnaya Valley amid the Putoran Mountains. Founded in 1935, Norilsk is a mining centre for copper, nickel, cobalt, platinum, and some coal. Power is supplied by a hydroelectric plant on the Khantayka River, and natural gas is piped from northern Tyumen *oblast*. A railway links Norilsk to the port of Dudinka on the Yenisey. Pop. (1970 prelim.) 136,000.

69°20′ N, 88°06′ E

·copper and nickel plant expansion **16**:95d
·map, Soviet Union **17**:322
·population and resources **17**:336e

norito, in the Shintō religious practices of Japan, words addressed by men to a deity; prayer. The efficacy of prayer is founded on the concept of *koto-dama*, the spiritual power that resides in words. According to ancient belief, beautiful, correct words bring about good, whereas ugly, coarse language can cause evil. Accordingly, *norito* are expressed in elegant, classical language, typified by that found in the *Engi-shiki* ("Institutes of the Engi Period"), a 50-volume work compiled in the 10th century. Prayers usually include words of praise for the deities, lists of offerings, and petitions. During the period when State Shintō was under the control of political authorities, the wording of prayers recited at public shrines was determined by the government. At present, the chief priest of a shrine pronounces the *norito* on behalf of the worshippers, and the contents and wordings vary.

norm, rule or standard of behaviour shared by members of a social group. Norms may be internalized—*i.e.*, incorporated within the individual so that there is conformity without external rewards or punishments, or they may be enforced by positive or negative sanctions from without. The social unit sharing particular norms may be small (*e.g.*, a clique of friends) or may include all adult members of a society. Norms are more specific than values or ideals: honesty is a general value, but the rules defining what is honest behaviour in a particular situation are norms. There may be norms relating to any aspect of human activity: perceiving, feeling, thinking, and acting. Norms of social interaction are sometimes called social norms.

There are two schools of thought regarding why people conform to norms. The functionalist school of sociology maintains that norms reflect a consensus, a common value system developed through socialization, the process by which an individual learns the culture of his group. Norms contribute to the functioning of the social system and are said to develop to meet certain assumed "needs" of the system. They are maintained through the rewards of conformity. The conflict school holds that norms are a mechanism for dealing with recurring social problems. The Marxian variety of conflict theory states that norms reflect the power of one section of a society over the other sections and that coercion and sanctions maintain these rules. Norms are thought to originate as a means by which one class or caste dominates or exploits others. Neither school adequately explains differences between and within societies.

Norm is also used to mean a statistically determined standard or the average behaviour, attitude, or opinion of a social group. In this sense it means actual, rather than expected, behaviour.

·collective behaviour and absence of rules **4**:842d
·Norse sacrifice to disir **8**:38f
·social group maintenance function **16**:963g
·social movement concepts and theories **16**:974c

norm, in mathematics, on a real or complex vector space V, is any non-negative real-valued function $\|\cdot\|$ on V such that $\|v\| = 0$ if and only if $v = 0$, $\|v_1 + v_2\| \leq \|v_1\| + \|v_2\|$, and $\|\alpha v\| = |\alpha| \cdot \|v\|$ for every elements v, v_1, v_2 in V and scalar α.

Norma (Latin: "ruler, set square"), a constellation of the southern sky.

·constellation table **2**:226

Normal, town, McLean County, central Illinois, U.S. It adjoins Bloomington and was called North Bloomington until 1857, when the Illinois State Normal (now State) University was established. The town grew up around the school. In addition to the university, economic factors include agriculture and industry. Normal is in one of the world's richest corn-producing areas. Its manufactures include tires and electric machines and controls. Normal is the site of the Illinois Soldier's and Sailor's Children's Home and School and the Baby Fold (a unique child care agency occupying a full city block). Inc. 1865. Pop. (1970) 26,396; (1980) 35,672.
40°31′ N, 89°59′ W

normal, in mathematics, in two dimensions, the line perpendicular to the tangent to a plane curve passing through the point; in three dimensions, a normal (line) to a surface is the line perpendicular to the tangent plane passing through the point. The principal normal at a point on a skew curve is the direction in the osculating (three-point contact) tangent plane that is perpendicular to the direction of the tangent line, the direction of rotation being right. The binormal defines the third axis of the orthogonal right-handed set at the point.

normal distribution, the distribution function that is the indefinite integral of the normal density function, the graph of which is the typical bell-shaped normal curve. The specific form of the normal density function is a constant, k, times the exponential of the negative quadratic $-(x - x_0)/2\,\sigma^2$. The quantity x_0 is the mean, or average, of the distribution and also corresponds to the point at which the distribution function is a maximum. The quantity sigma (σ) is the standard deviation and characterizes the width of the distribution; the probability is about 68 percent that a given value will be found within the interval $x_0 - \sigma$ to $x_0 + \sigma$. The constant,

$$k = 1 \big/ \sigma\sqrt{2\pi},$$

is called the normalizing coefficient and has the effect that the sum or integral of the distribution over all possible values of x will give a total probability of unity.

The normal distribution is also called the Gaussian distribution, named after the German mathematician Carl Friedrich Gauss, and is typical of many types of random fluctuations.

·derivation and measurement application **11**:744b
·Gaussian error curve **7**:967b
·information theory and measurement **9**:575f
·measurement of personality traits **11**:739d
·number theory principles **13**:377g
·probability theory and method **14**:1111d
·statistical theory and method **17**:617a

normal fault (geology): *see* fault.

normal school, or TEACHERS' COLLEGE, institution for the training of teachers. The first school so named, the École Normale Supérieure (1794), was intended to serve as a model for other teacher-training schools; it later became affiliated with the University of Paris. The first public normal school in the United States was established at Lexington, Mass., in 1839.

Normal schools were founded chiefly to train elementary-school teachers. They were commonly state supported and offered a two-year course beyond the secondary level. In the 20th century the tendency has been to extend teacher-training requirements to at least four years and, especially after World War II, for the schools to broaden their programs, so that by the 1960s many former normal schools had become colleges or universities.

·foundation and distinction **6**:401f
·German formation and qualifications **18**:4f
·Japanese founding and growth **6**:390g
·teacher educational training **18**:14g
·U.S. 19th-century status **6**:367a

normal vector, at a point p of an embedded manifold N of a Riemannian manifold M is an assignment of a vector in the tangent space to M at p, which is perpendicular to the subspace consisting of vectors tangent to N and p. A normal vector field on N is an assignment of a normal vector to each point of N.

·differential geometry principles **7**:1094a

Norman, city, seat of Cleveland County, central Oklahoma, U.S., on the South Canadian River. Beginning as a tent city in April 1889, when Oklahoma was opened to white settlement, it was named to honour a Santa Fe Railway engineer. Its development was assured when the University of Oklahoma was established there in 1892 on land donated by

The Bizzell Memorial Library, University of Oklahoma, Norman
Bob Taylor—EB Inc.

its citizens. The marketing and distribution centre of an extensive agricultural area, the city also has some light industry; there are oil and gas wells in the vicinity. The Central State Hospital and the nearby Tinker Air Force Base are additional economic assets. Inc. 1902. Pop. (1970) 52,117; (1980) 68,020.
35°13′ N, 97°26′ W

·commuter importance **13**:543f
·map, United States **18**:908

Normanby Island, member of the D'Entrecasteaux Islands, 10 mi (16 km) across Goschen Strait from the eastern tip of New Guinea, in the Solomon Sea, southwest Pacific, a part of Milne Bay province of Papua New Guinea. It lies southwest across Goschen Strait from Fergusson Island. Volcanic Normanby, measuring 45 mi by 12–15 mi, has a total land area of 400 sq mi (1,050 sq km) and rises to 3,600 ft (1,100 m) in the Prevost Range. Sewa Bay deeply creases the west coast and Sewataitai Bay the east. The island was visited in 1873 by British Capt. John Moresby, who named it after the Marquess of Normanby, governor of Queensland (1871–74). It may have been a secret British military base during World War II. Having once produced gold, Normanby exports copra and some timber.

Midway between Normanby and Fergusson Island to the north is Dobu Island, whose inhabitants have been the subject of several anthropological studies. Pop. (1971 est.) Normanby and Dobu 10,400.
10°00′ S, 151°00′ E

Norman Conquest (1066), invasion of England and seizure of the English throne by William of Normandy.

·heraldic arms development **8**:793f
·linguistic and cultural effects **6**:880h
·motivations and socio-political results **3**:204d
·Wales occupation and cultural impact **3**:230g
·William I's motivation and campaign **19**:829f

Normandes, Îles (England): *see* Channel Islands.

Normandie, 20th-century ocean liner.

·tonnage and propulsion system **16**:682g

Normandy, French NORMANDIE, a former province of northern France, corresponding to the modern *départements* of Manche, Calvados, Seine-Maritime, Eure, and Orne. Famous for the military exploits of its dukes and lords and for its model political institutions, Normandy had a major role in medieval European history. For the origins of Normandy, *see* Normans.

By the mid-11th century, Normandy was the most centralized state in Europe. Its dukes extended feudal principles to increase their power. They had the right to declare law and levy taxes throughout the duchy. Their position was further enhanced by their control over the administration of the church and by their association with the flourishing monasteries. Among the novel offices of the well-organized province was that of viscount, a ducal official with military, financial, and judicial powers in local areas.

His strength in the duchy enabled Duke William II, known to history as William I the Conqueror, to undertake the conquest of England in 1066. On William's death, control of Normandy and England was disputed among his sons until the two areas were reunited under Henry I of England in 1106. After Henry's death in 1135, Normandy was won by Geoffrey Plantagenet, count of Anjou and husband of Henry's daughter Matilda, and from him passed into the Angevin Empire inherited by Henry II of England in the mid-12th century. The political development of Normandy continued under the Angevins: the jury system was introduced; collection of taxes was centralized; and *baillis* were appointed to oversee the viscounts.

As the centre of Angevin power on the Continent, Normandy became a primary objective of the rival Capetian kings of France. It was conquered by the Capetians from John of England (1202–04). The wealth of Normandy was considerable, and its bureaucratic methods influenced Capetian government. French rule brought little change in the political customs of the Normans, whose privileges (consent to taxes) were affirmed by the Charte aux Normands of 1315.

The *gouvernement* of Normandy in 1789

During the Hundred Years' War (1337 to 1453), Normandy was twice invaded by the English and was under their control from 1420 until French reconquest in 1450.

In the 16th century Protestantism made substantial gains in Normandy, and the province was torn by wars between the Catholics and Huguenots (1562–63 and 1574–76). The 17th century witnessed the growth of royal power in Normandy: the Charte was allowed to lapse, and the provincial assembly was abolished in 1666. The province was divided into the *généralités* of Rouen, Caen, and Alençon.

After its division into *départements* in 1790, Normandy was the centre of a major political event of the French Revolution: the federalist revolt against Parisian domination in the summer of 1793.

Its name occurs in the history of World War II as the site of the Allied invasion of German-occupied France in June of 1944.

·consolidation and expansion **19**:828h
·English medieval territorial claims **3**:206a
·French claim and seizure from English **7**:616a; map 620
·John's acquisition and loss **10**:236h
·map, France **7**:584
·population loss from Black Death **7**:627b
·Romanesque religious architecture **19**:357e
·Viking establishment and English union **7**:613c
·Viking settlements in France **16**:306e; map 305

Normandy, the most prevalent breed of cattle in France developed for both milk and meat production.

·breeding and general features **10**:1280g

Normandy Invasion, also known as OPERATION OVERLORD, name given to the Allied invasion of Europe on June 6, 1944. As the trend of World War II began to swing in favour of the Allies, Gen. Dwight D. Eisenhower was charged with the task of forming the largest invasion fleet in history. While plans were being formed in England, Field Marshal Erwin Rommel was building his "Atlantic Wall" on the coastline of France.

After being delayed 24 hours by the worst channel weather in 25 years, the invasion began on D-Day with units of the U.S. 82nd and 101st Airborne divisions landing near the town of Saint-Mère-Église, while British commando units captured key bridges and knocked out Nazi communications. In the morning, the assault troops of the combined Allied armies, including the French, Canadian, British, and the United States landed at five beaches along the Normandy coast code named Utah, Omaha, Gold, Juno, and Sword. While four beaches were taken early, Omaha turned out to be the stiffest test, being nicknamed "Bloody Omaha." By nightfall, sizable beacheads were in control on all five landing areas and the final campaign to defeat Germany was under way.

·Eisenhower's leadership and force size **6**:515a
·logistics of World War II **11**:83b
·strategy of World War II **19**:593c
·World War II history **19**:1001d; map

Norman Empire: *see* Angevin Empire.

Norman French, the divergent dialect of the French language spoken by the Normans of early medieval times—especially that dialect as spoken by the Normans who invaded England in 1066.

·influences on English **6**:881c

Normanichthyidae, family of mail-cheeked fish of the order Scorpaeniformes.

·classification and general features **16**:400h

Normans, originally NORTMANNI, also NORTHMEN, a term used generally in medieval western Europe to denote the barbarian heathen pirates (Vikings) from Scandinavia, who between about 800 and 1050 pillaged or occupied many coastal areas. More particularly, and in modern usage, it refers to those Vikings who settled in what later became the duchy of Normandy in northern France. Late in the 9th century a number of Scandinavians, probably Danes, had secured a foothold on the lower Seine River. In about 911 this group, under a leader, Hrólfr (Rollo), himself probably a Norwegian, gained from the Frankish king Charles III the Simple, formal recognition of their occupation of a north coast area bounded to the east, south, and west by the rivers Bresle, Epte, and Dives (the so-called Treaty of Saint-Clair-sur-Epte). By 933 they had extended their control westward over the Bessin, Avranchin, and Cotentin.

Adopting Christianity and the French language, the Normans nevertheless retained many typically Viking traits, remaining savage and unbridled and never contributing substantially to the arts. Bands from Normandy achieved the conquest (early 11th century) of southern Italy and Sicily; in the mid-11th century William, duke of Normandy, conquered England, and the Normans spread thence to Wales, Scotland, and Ireland.

With a genius for adaptation, and usually producing strong rulers, they systematized feudalism, employing it to the benefit of central authority. They developed cavalry warfare and excelled in castle building. They contributed notably to the growth of medieval governmental institutions and by their alliances with the papacy furthered the 11th-century reform of the Western Church. In a climate of political anarchy they provided good and firm government, both in church and state.

·Alexius I Comnenus' defense against penetration **1**:483c
·Byzantine military rivalry **3**:564e
·Carolingian territorial incursion **11**:929h
·common law development in England **4**:998b
·defeat in Seville **16**:581a
·English Bible translation interruption **2**:889h
·English invasion and repercussions **3**:204d
·Gregory VII's efforts to restrain **8**:417g
·Henry IV's reaction to papal alliance **8**:761b
·hunting purpose and organization **9**:47g
·interior design in medieval castles **9**:706e
·Islāmic decline in Sicily **9**:932a
·Italian and Middle Eastern conquests **2**:1201d
·Italian and Sicilian settlements **9**:1130e
·Italian state and Byzantine alienation **5**:299b
·Italy's conquest and consolidation **15**:906g
·Leo IX's papal defense and effect **10**:805c
·Malta influenced by rule **11**:391g
·medieval kingdoms maps **12**:144
·military engineering at Hastings **6**:863e
·Palermo's growth under rule **13**:930d
·Roger II's Sicilian rule **15**:984e
·Wales occupation and cultural impact **3**:230g
·Welsh urbanizing influence **19**:526e

Normanskill Shale Formation, Middle Ordovician (Champlainian) dark shale unit found in eastern New York, Vermont, and Massachusetts (the Ordovician Period began about 500,000,000 years ago and lasted about 70,000,000 years). The Normanskill Shale Formation was named by R. Ruedemann in 1901 for exposures that he studied in the region of the Normans Kill, a tributary of the Hudson River, near Albany, N.Y. The formation consists of about 300 metres (1,000 feet) of blue to gray, sandy shales with many bands of black, pyrite-bearing shales that contain a rich graptolite (class of extinct colonial marine animals) fauna. The Normanskill Formation is a northward extension of a dark-shale depositional environment that existed during Champlainian time all the way from Alabama to New York. The dark shales represent the fine muds that were eroded from an Appalachian landmass during Champlainian time and deposited near the shore; limestones were simultaneously deposited farther to the west.

Norman style, Romanesque architectural style developed in Normandy and England between the 11th and 12th centuries and the time of the general adoption of Gothic (*see* Gothic art) architecture in both countries. Since it was only shortly before the Norman

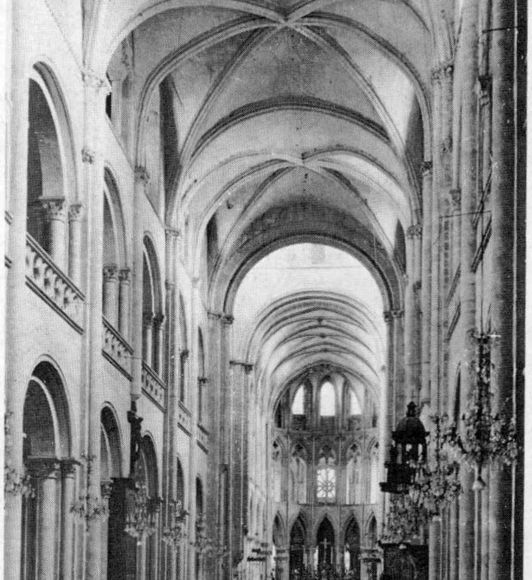

Nave of Saint-Étienne, Caen, Fr., Norman style, begun 1067

Jean Roubier

conquest of England (1066) that Normandy became settled and sophisticated enough to produce an architecture, the style developed almost simultaneously in the two countries; early buildings, erected during the first generation after the Conquest, are extremely similar. Eventually, however, the styles of the two countries diverged, and the architecture of Normandy drew closer in form to typical French Romanesque (*see* Romanesque art), while that of England (called Anglo-Norman architecture) became a much more distinctive national tradition.

The common early Norman style followed the general Romanesque features of massive construction based on the rounded arch and on additive spatial compartmentalization; the building type was a Romanesque elaboration of the Early Christian basilica plan (longitudinal with side aisles and an apse, or semicircular projection of the eastern, or sanctuary, end of the centre aisle)—a raised nave (centre aisle) with windows piercing the upper walls (clerestory), a tripartite interior articulation of the nave into a lower arcade (separating nave from side aisles), a triforium arcade (separating the upper nave from galleries above the side aisles), and the clerestory, transepts (forming a transverse aisle crossing the nave in front of the sanctuary), and a western facade completed by two towers. The definitive example of the early Norman style is the church of Saint-Étienne at Caen (begun in 1067), which provided a close model for the later English cathedrals of Ely (*c.* 1090), Norwich (*c.* 1096), and Peterborough (*c.* 1118), all of which, however, show the peculiarly English characteristic of increased scale.

Later Norman architecture in Normandy was characterized by careful structural articulation and elaboration of tower and spire.

Later Anglo-Norman architecture, though basically an extension of the earlier Norman style, was also affected by influences from other areas and by an increasingly distinct indigenous approach to construction. The chief characteristics of this English architecture are enormously long church plans, massive, dignified appearance (particularly in the frequent use of great round columns sometimes as wide as the spaces between them in the lower nave arcade), and a relative indifference to structural logic. This indifference was expressed in a wide variation of nonessential structural detail (as in the varying proportions of the three storys of the nave and the occasional addition of a fourth story) and in a tendency to encrust masonry surfaces with shallow geometrical and interlaced ornamentation that obscured rather than elucidated basic structure.

With the exception of smaller, parish churches, which preserved the Saxon decorative tradition, figural sculpture was rare. Most Anglo-Norman churches had timber roofs instead of the usual Romanesque rounded stone vaults; the notable exception is Durham cathedral, the nave and choir of which (*c.* 1104) are supported by the first known examples of pointed ribbed vaults (which cross at the top and carry the weight of building to a skeletal structure of vertical shafts), anticipating by nearly a century the general adoption of what was to become the characteristic feature of Gothic construction. A squared-off eastern end instead of a rounded apse is standard in English Gothic architecture. In addition to the cathedrals of Ely, Norwich, Peterborough, and Durham, the major churches begun in the Anglo-Norman style are Canterbury (*c.* 1070), Lincoln (*c.* 1072), Rochester (*c.* 1077), St. Albans (*c.* 1077), Winchester (*c.* 1079), Gloucester (*c.* 1089), and Hereford (*c.* 1107) cathedrals, Southwell Minster (11th century) and the abbey church at Tewkesbury (*c.* 1088).

Less closely related to the main Anglo-Norman tradition but important in their own right are the many Cistercian abbeys built during the Romanesque period in England (*see* Cistercian style); among them, Rievaulx (*c.* 1132), Fountains Abbey (*c.* 1135), Kirkstall (*c.* 1152), Buildwas (*c.* 1155), Byland Abbey (*c.* 1175), Furness (*c.* 1175), and Jervaulx (*c.* 1175).

·stylistic labeling development **2**:124e

Normanton, town, northwest Queensland, Australia, in the Gulf Country (lowlands around the Gulf of Carpentaria), 56 mi (90 km) from the mouth of the Norman River. During the 1860s, it was a port for Gulf Country trade. Normanton, on a rail line to Croydon (southeast), is now the terminus of a cattle-trucking route leading to the railhead at Julia Creek (200 mi south). There are meatworks in the town.

The river, rising in the Gregory Range of the Eastern Highlands, flows for 260 mi northwest through level country to the gulf at Karumba. It is fed by the Carron, Yappar, and Clara rivers and may be perennial only in its lowest reaches. Pop. (1971 prelim.) 739.
17°40′ S, 141°05′ E

·map, Australia **2**:400

Norman Wells, village, Mackenzie District, Northwest Territories, Canada, on the Mackenzie River 70 mi (115 km) west of Great Bear Lake and 90 mi (145 km) south of the Arctic Circle. Oil seepage was discovered in 1911, and the community, which extends for a mile along the river, developed after commercial production began in the early 1920s. An oil refinery was built in 1939, and during World War II the Canol Pipeline served Whitehorse (Yukon) and the Alaska Highway, 600 mi (965 km) west. Norman Wells has an airfield, weather station, hospital, and sewage and water system. Latest census 199.
65°17′ N, 126°51′ W

·Mackenzie River width and oil fields **11**:266d
·map, Canada **3**:716

normative ethics, the branch of ethics that evaluates the normative moral element in man's actions by presenting and appraising criteria for justifying rules and judgments of what is morally right and wrong, good and bad.

·ethics types and relations **6**:984f
·history and theory development **6**:990b

normed vector space, any real or complex vector space V supplied with a nonnegative, real-valued function $\|\cdot\|$ (for symbol, *see* norm) defined on V such that $\|v\| = 0$ if, and only if $v = 0$, $\|v_1 + v_2\| \leqq \|v_1\| + \|v_2\|$, and $\|\alpha v\| = |\alpha| \cdot \|v\|$ (*see* valuation) for all elements v, v_1, v_2 in V and all scalars α.

normetanephrine, a product of the metabolism of the adrenal gland hormone norepinephrine.

·biochemical precursor and metabolite **6**:808g

normoblast, nucleated normal cell occurring in red marrow as a stage or stages in the development of the red blood cell (erythrocyte). Some authorities call the normoblast a late-stage erythroblast, the immediate precursor of the red blood cell; others distinguish the normal immature red cell—normoblast—from an abnormal, overlarge, immature red cell—the megaloblast. *See also* erythrocyte.

·function in erythropoiesis **15**:782d

normochromic anemia, any anemia in which the haemoglobin content of the individual red blood cells is normal.

·diagnosis of hematopoietic disease **5**:687g

normocytic anemia, anemia (*q.v.*) in which the red cells and the hemoglobin (the oxygen-transporting substance in the red cells) are both normal, but loss of blood has left too few red cells and too little hemoglobin to transport sufficient oxygen to the tissues.

·diagnosis of hematopoietic diseases **5**:687g
·iron deficiency blood diseases **2**:1135d

Normzahlen (mathematics and technology): *see* preferred numbers.

Norn (Viking Norse language): *see* Old Norse.

Norns, in Germanic mythology, supernatural beings who corresponded to the Greek Moirai; they were usually represented as three maidens who spun or wove the fate of men. Some sources name them Urd, Verdandi, and Skuld, perhaps meaning Past, Present, and Future. They were depicted as living by Yggdrasill, the world tree, under Urd's well and were linked with both good and evil. In consequence of their presence at births, midwifery was sometimes associated with them. The name Norn appears only in Scandinavian sources, but the cult of Nornlike beings occurs in several European folklores. In Norse literature the Norns are sometimes called *dísir*.

Norodom, also called NAROTTAMA (b. Ang Vody, 1834, Cambodia—d. April 24, 1904, Phnom Penh), Cambodian king (1860–1904) who virtually placed his country under the control of the French in 1864. He became little more than a deputy of France, and his 40-year reign ended the possibility of Cambodian independence.

Ang Vody was the eldest son of King Ang Duong. He was raised and educated in Bangkok, capital of the Siamese kingdom, where he studied Pāli and Sanskrit Buddhist scriptures and the sacred canons of Theravāda Buddhism. The purpose of his early training was to strengthen ties between Siam and Cambodia.

Cambodia had been under the joint vassalage of Annam (now part of Vietnam) and Siam (now Thailand) since 1802. According to established protocol, Cambodian kings were crowned jointly, with representatives of the two suzerains attending. When Ang Duong died in 1859, Ang Vody returned to Cambodia and was chosen the successor, but he remained uncrowned. The Siamese, who held the symbols of Cambodian royalty—the crown, the sacred sword, and the royal seal—refused to release them, insisting that the newly elected king was their deputy and denying the Vietnamese the right to crown Ang Vody; thus the Siamese sought to undermine Vietnamese claims to Cambodia and to assert their own private domination of the vassal state.

An attempted coup d'etat led by Ang Vody's brother, Si Votha, in 1861 was put down only with the aid of Siamese troops. At this point the French, who had been ceded much of Cochinchina (southern Vietnam), sought to assert Annamese claims to Cambodian tribute, seeing the adjacent Cambodian provinces as future colonial possessions. The French tried to convince Ang Vody of the benefits of French protection.

Under conflicting pressures, Ang Vody signed a clandestine treaty with Siam on Aug. 11, 1863, which was ratified on Jan. 22, 1864. It made Ang Vody the viceroy of Siam and governor of Cambodia; Siam acquired the Cambodian provinces of Battambang and Angkor. In April 1864, however, the French consul Doudart de Lagrée forced Ang Vody at gun point to sign another secret treaty that gave France control over Cambodian foreign relations and trading concessions. The plans for Ang Vody's investiture as the deputy of Siam were abandoned, and he was finally crowned at Oudong, Cambodia, in June 1864, with both French and the Siamese officials in attendance. He was installed as king in Phnom Penh in 1866, and the following year Siam officially acknowledged the French protectorate over Cambodia. Ang Vody assumed the title Norodom.

During his reign Norodom initiated land reforms, reorganized Cambodian military forces, and abolished slavery. His reign saw insurrections in 1885–87 and the ever-increasing influence of the French in Cambodian affairs.

·Cambodia under the protectorate **3**:687e

Norodom Sihanouk (b. Oct. 31, 1922, Phnom Penh, Cambodia), successively Cambodia's king, prime minister, and head of state, who attempted to steer a neutralist course in the Indochina War of the 1960s.

Norodom Sihanouk
Wide World Photos

Sihanouk was born the son of Prince Norodom Suramarit and Princess Kossamak Nearirath, the daughter of Sisowath, king of Cambodia from 1904 to 1927. He acceded to the throne at age 18 on the death of Sisowath's son, King Monivong, in 1941. During World War II the young king, encouraged by the Japanese, first attempted to declare Cambodia's independence from France, but when the French military forces moved back into the region he decided to wait until France's retreat from Indochina, which occurred in 1954. He founded the Sangkum Reastre Niyum (People's Socialist Community) in January 1955, won a referendum in February approving its program, and on March 2 abdicated in favour of his father, becoming the new monarch's prime minister.When Suramarit died, on April 3, 1960, Sihanouk became head of state as well. He managed to keep his country neutral and unscathed by the growing war in Vietnam, despite pressure from the People's Republic of China and the presence of U.S. military forces in nearby Vietnam. But as U.S. military pressure on North Vietnamese supply lines within Cambodia grew in the late 1960s, the fighting spread to his country. In early 1970 he began a trip overseas to bring pressure on the United States and North Vietnam to cease their activities in Cambodia. He was in conversation with Soviet leaders when, on March 18, the right-wing general Lon Nol, commander of the Cambodian armed forces, overthrew Sihanouk's government at home, and U.S. and South Vietnamese forces launched an attack on North Vietnamese sanctuaries in Cambodia.

Sihanouk went to Peking in May and announced the formation of a royal government in exile, proclaiming his solidarity with North Vietnam, China, and other anti-U.S. forces in Asia. Cambodian guerrilla forces loyal to Sihanouk, called the Khmer Rouge, joined the North Vietnamese regular forces in Cambodia in fighting Lon Nol's government, and in April 1975 they brought it down. Sihanouk returned to his country in September and soon announced that, while he would remain as head of state, his role in the government would be like that of a roving ambassador and that the people would govern Cambodia. In April 1976, however, he resigned.

·Cambodia's overthrow of monarchy **3**:675b
·Cambodia under his rule **3**:688b
·China's support of Indochina coalition **4**:402b

Nor-Papua, a people of northern New Guinea.

·totem selection and other practices **18**:530f

Norra Karelen (Finland): *see* Pohjois-Karjala.

Norrbotten, *län* (county) of northern Sweden, touching upon the Gulf of Bothnia, Finland, and Norway. With an area of 38,188 sq mi (98,906 sq km), it is Sweden's largest *län*, as well as the northernmost, extending into Lapland and above the Arctic Circle. From the coast the land rises to the barren, mountainous frontier with Norway; this district contains the highest land in Sweden, Kebnekaise (6,926 ft [2,111 m]), which was unexplored until 1880.

Few crops can mature in the short summer, and timber grows only slowly, but the region has achieved considerable significance through its mineral wealth. Vast iron deposits are worked at Kiruna, Gällivare, and Malmberget. The Lilla Luleälv (Little Lule River) has been harnessed at Porjus, where, as at Luleå (*q.v.*), the capital, there is also electrical smelting of iron. Railways extend in the coastal zone through Boden to the frontier town of Haparanda (connecting there with the different rail gauge of Finland), and inland through the Lapp centre of Jokkmokk. Pop. (1975 est.) 261,548.

·area and population table **17**:846
·map, Sweden **17**:848

Nørresundby, city and port, Ålborg municipality, Nordjyllands *amtskommune* (county), northern Jutland, Denmark, on the Limfjorden opposite the city of Ålborg. Formerly the centre of communication and commerce between Ålborg and the Vendsyssel region of northern Jutland, it is now an industrial city, manufacturing cement, chemicals, and textiles. To the north are the remains of redoubts built during the Thirty Years' War and a cemetery of more than 80 Viking "ship monuments," graves enclosed by standing stones in the form of ships. Pop. (1970) 23,150.
57°04′ N, 9°55′ E

·map, Denmark **5**:583

Norris, Frank, pen name of BENJAMIN FRANKLIN NORRIS (b. March 5, 1870, Chicago—d. Oct. 25, 1902, San Francisco), novelist whose work helped shape the Naturalist school in the U.S. He studied art in Paris and attended the University of California and Harvard. He was news correspondent in South Africa, 1895; editorial assistant on the *San Francisco Wave*, 1896–97; and war correspondent in Cuba for *McClure's Magazine*, 1898.

Norris' *McTeague* (1899) is a Naturalist novel set in San Francisco. *The Octopus* (1901), first of a projected trilogy, *The Epic of the Wheat*, pictures with bold symbolism the growth of wheat in California and the struggle of ranchers with the railway corporation. *The Pit* (posthumous, 1903) deals with wheat speculation on the Chicago Board of Trade, and *Wolf*, unwritten at Norris' death, would have shown the wheat relieving an old-world famine. *Vandover and the Brute* (posthumous, 1914) is a study of degeneration.

After the example of Zola and the Naturalists, Norris emphasized the determinism of heredity and environment in human life. Early influenced by Kipling and by popular notions of evolution, he exalted primitivism, but he finally adopted a more humanitarian ideal and began to view the novel as a proper agent for social betterment. He thus gave an impulse to the "muckraking" movement, though he disavowed overt propaganda in the novel. He strove to return American fiction, then dominated by historical romance, to more serious themes. Despite philosophic inconsistencies and romantic intrusions in his work, Norris was a writer of great original force.

His writings were collected (10 vol.) in 1928, and *The Letters of Frank Norris* were edited by Franklin D. Walker in 1956.

·American literature development **10**:1190g
·California literature growth **3**:619d

Norris, George W(illiam) (b. July 11, 1861, Sandusky, Ohio—d. Sept. 2, 1944, McCook, Neb.), U.S. senator noted for his advocacy of political reform and of public ownership of hydroelectric power plants. Largely self-educated, he taught school and studied law at Northern Indiana Normal School (now Valparaiso University). He was admitted to the bar in 1883 and two years later moved to Nebraska to begin practice. In 1902 he was elected to Congress as a Republican and was reelected four times in succession, becoming leader of an insurgent group that in 1910 forced reforms in the House rules to reduce the autocratic control of the speaker.

Elected in 1912 to the Senate, where he served until 1943, Norris became known as an independent, saying he "would rather be right than regular." His strong antiwar convictions led him to vote against U.S. entry into World War I, and he denounced the Treaty of Versailles that followed it. He was the author of

George Norris, 1908
By courtesy of the Library of Congress, Washington, D.C.

the 20th Amendment to the Constitution, which abolished the so-called lame duck sessions of Congress. He fought for the introduction of presidential primaries and for direct election of U.S. senators. One of his most significant contributions was his introduction of the bill establishing the Tennessee Valley Authority. He was co-author of the Norris–La-Guardia Act, which restricted the use of injunctions in labour disputes.

Though always a Republican, Norris felt his party ties lightly; he endorsed Progressives Theodore Roosevelt in 1912 and Robert M. La Follette in 1924 and Democrats Alfred E. Smith in 1928 and Franklin D. Roosevelt in each of his campaigns for the presidency. In 1945 his book *Fighting Liberal* was published. Books written about him include Richard Lowitt's *George W. Norris: The Making of a Progressive, 1861–1912* (1963) and Norman L. Zucker's *George W. Norris: Gentle Knight of American Democracy* (1966).

·Muscle Shoals development controversy **18**:988d

Norris, John (b. 1657, Collingbourne-Kingston, Wiltshire—d. 1711, Bemerton), Anglican priest and philosopher remembered as an exponent of Cambridge Platonism, a 17th-century revival of Plato's ideas centred at the English university, and as the sole English Malebranchist, after the French Cartesian philosopher Nicolas Malebranche (1638–1715). Elected a fellow of All Soul's College, Oxford, in 1680, he was named vicar of Newton St. Loe in Somerset in 1689. Two years later he was transferred to the rectory of Bemerton.

John Norris, bronze sculpture by Sir Henry Cheers, 1756
Thomas Photos, Oxford

Norris' numerous works include poems and translations, theological and philosophical works, and a political tract, *A Murnival of Knaves, or Whiggism Planely Displayed and Laughed out of Countenance* (1683). It is in his moral and mystical writings that the influence of Cambridge Platonism is clearest. In *An Idea of Happiness* (1683), following Plato, he placed the soul's highest happiness in the contemplative love of God. *The Theory and Regulation of Love* (1688) was followed by *Reflections on the Conduct of Human Life* (1690); *Christian Blessedness, or Discourses upon the Beatitudes* (1690); and *Practical Discourses on Several Divine Subjects*, 3 vol. (1691–93).

Norris' first major philosophical work was *Reflections upon a Late Essay Concerning the Human Understanding*, appended to the first edition of *Christian Blessedness*. In this work he anticipated many later criticisms of the essay referred to in the title, *An Essay Concerning Human Understanding* (1690), the major philosophical work of the English Empiricist John Locke. He did agree, however, with Locke's dismissal of the doctrine of innate ideas, which asserts that men hold their mental ideas at birth. Norris' adoption of Malebranche's theory of divine illumination also involved him in controversy with the Quakers, against whose notion of "the Light within" he wrote *Two Treatises Concerning the Divine Light* (1692). His *Account of Reason and Faith* (1697) has been considered one of the better responses to *Christianity Not Mysterious* by the English deist John Toland. According to Norris, divine reason differs from human reason only in degree, not in nature. Thus, the conflict between faith and reason is illusory. Norris' most significant work, *An Essay Towards the Theory of the Ideal or Intelligible World* (1701–04), treats the intelligible world in two parts, first in itself and, second, in relation to human understanding. This work is a complete exposition of the views of Malebranche and refutes the assertions of Locke and others who emphasized the importance of sense experience in arriving at knowledge.

Norris–LaGuardia Act (1932), U.S. legislation that made yellow-dog contracts (under which workers agree not to join a union during the duration of employment) unenforceable in the federal courts.
·trade unionism use of court injunctions **18**:566c

Norristown, borough, seat of Montgomery County, southeastern Pennsylvania, U.S., on the north bank of the Schuylkill River, near Philadelphia and the eastern terminus of the Pennsylvania Turnpike. The site, purchased in 1704 by Isaac Norris and William Trent from William Penn, Jr. (son of the state's founder), was then known as the Manor of William Stadt. It was organized as a township in 1730. In 1712 Norris bought Trent's interest and built a gristmill. The land was acquired in 1776 by the College and Academy of Philadelphia. During the American Revolution, the school was suspected of disloyalty, and the state assembly revoked its charter and transferred its assets to the newly created University of Pennsylvania. When Montgomery County was created in 1784, Norristown (then The Town of Norris) became the county seat. The university holdings were sold (1791) and developed as part of Norristown. Canalization of the Schuylkill and Delaware rivers and completion of a railroad link (1834) to Philadelphia spurred economic development as an industrial centre. Manufactures include carpets, chemicals, machinery, metal products, plastics, steel, rubber, and textiles. Valley Forge State Park, encampment site for George Washington's army during the winter of 1777–78, is nearby. Mill Grove, early home of the naturalist-artist John James Audubon, has been developed as a wildlife sanctuary. Inc. borough, 1812. Pop. (1980) 34,684.
40°07′ N, 75°21′ W
·Philadelphia map insert **14**:218

Norrköping, town and port, *län* (county) of Östergötland, Sweden, on the Motala Ström (river), southwest of Stockholm. *Hällristningar*, or rock carvings, from the Late Bronze Age are found in the area, but the town was not founded till about 1350 and received its charter in 1384. Frequent fires, notably in 1719 during the Northern War, brought about rebuilding on modern lines. Notable structures include medieval churches at Östra Eneby and Tingstad. Industry, first introduced in the 17th century, depended on the falls in the river; they provided power for the textile industry, which dominated the town from the 1660s to the 1950s, and for other manufacturing plants. The Lindö Kanal, completed in 1961, permits the harbour to take vessels of up to 30 ft (9 m) draft. Norrköping is a focus for both rail and road transport between Stockholm and the south and west of Sweden, and there is an airport on the outskirts. Pop. (1974 est.) mun., 120,300.
58°36′ N, 16°11′ E
·map, Sweden **17**:848

Norrland, region, northern Sweden, encompassing the *landskapen* (provinces) of Gästrikland, Hälsingland, Medelpad, Ångermanland, Västerbotten, Norrbotten, Härjedalen, Jämtland, and Lappland. With a land area of 93,927 sq mi (243,262 sq km), it includes about 60 percent of Sweden's total territory. Its most striking features are extensive forests; mountains, notably Kebnekaise Sydtopp and Sarjektjåkko, the highest in Sweden; and great rivers—Ångermanälven, Ljusnan, Ljungan, Indalsälven, Faxälven, the Umeälv, Vindelälven, the Skellefteälv, the Piteälv, the Luleälv, and the Kalixälv—used for transporting timber down to the sawmills near the coast, as well as for hydroelectric power. Beginning in about the mid-19th century, the region was torn by the so-called Norrlandsfrågan (Norrland Question) over the acquisition of land by the lumber companies at the expense of the small landholders and farmers, which was not resolved until 1901–04. There is some agriculture, but the region's vast resources of timber, iron ore, and waterpower have made forestry, mining, and the production of hydroelectric power of prime importance. The region is accessible by road, rail, or air. Pop. (1973 est.) 1,184,055.
·map, Sweden **17**:848
·physical and traditional regions **17**:845d *passim* to 846d

Norseman, town, south central Western Australia, at the south end of intermittent Lake Cowan. Founded with the opening of the Dundas goldfield (1892–93), it became a municipality in 1896. Situated on the Kalgoorlie–Esperance Railroad and near the Great Eastern Highway to Perth (460 road mi [740 km] west), the town is also the western terminus of the Eyre Highway from Port Augusta, South Australia, and is thus an important stop for motor traffic crossing the continent. Norseman (the origin of the name is not known) serves a region of pastoralism and wheat farming. Some gold mines remain in operation, primarily for the purpose of gathering pyrites, a source of sulfur for the production of superphosphates. The town has been served since 1936 by the Goldfields Water Scheme, which brings water from the Mundaring Weir near Perth. Pop. (1971 prelim.) 1,757.
32°12′ S, 121°46′ E
·map, Australia **2**:400

Norsemen (Northmen): *see* Vikings; Normans.

Norske folkeeventyr (1841–44; "Norwegian Folktales"), by Peter Christen Asbjørnsen and Jørgen Engebretsen Moe, collection of folktales and legends that had survived and developed from Old Norse pagan mythology in the mountain and fjord dialects of Norway. Stimulated by a revival of interest in Norway's past, Asbjørnsen and Moe gathered the tales of ghosts, fairies, gods, and mountain trolls and compiled them into a brilliant narration that preserved the oral feeling and distinctively Norwegian characteristics of the tales while rendering them in standard modern Norse. Asbjørnsen's vivid prose sketches of folk life and Moe's poems recaptured the folk heritage of Norway for the modern age. The *Norske folkeeventyr* stimulated further research into folktales and ballads and reawakened a sense of national identity.
·mid-19th century literature **10**:1206e

Norskehavet (Europe): *see* Norwegian Sea.

Norske Intelligenssedler, first newspaper to appear in Norway, founded in Christiania (now Oslo) in 1763.

Norske Selskab, English NORWEGIAN SOCIETY, organization founded in 1772 by Norwegian students at the University of Copenhagen to free Norwegian literature from excessive German influence and from the dominance of Danish Romanticism. The Norske Selskab, which lasted until 1812, not only was a forum for literary discussion and the presentation of new works but also was a nationalistic affirmation of Norway's cultural, if not political, independence of Denmark. In addition to acting as the focus for a number of minor literary talents—Claus Fasting, Claus Frimann, and Jens Zetlitz—and the more important talent of Johan Nordahl Brun, it provided the stimulus for the one deathless work associated with it: *Kaerlighed uden strømper* (1772; "Love Without Stockings") by Johan Herman Wessel (*q.v.*), a parody directed against the Danish imitations of Italian operas and French tragedies that had superseded the comedies of the great Norwegian-born playwright Ludvig Holberg on the Danish stage.
·18th century Norwegian literature **10**:1177b

Nortanhymbre (Anglo-Saxon kingdom): *see* Northumbria.

Norte Channel, dredged navigational channel in the estuaries of the Uruguay River and Río de la Plata, South America.
33°55′ S, 59°00′ W
·location and flow **14**:526d

Norte Chico, traditional region, north central Chile, comprising the southern borderlands of the Atacama Desert and populated mostly in irrigated river valleys and Andean mining communities.
28°30′ S, 70°30′ W
·physical features and economic activity **4**:250a

Norte de Santander, department of northeastern Colombia, bounded east by Venezuela and located where the Andean Cordillera (mountains) Oriental bifurcates, one arm continuing northward as the Sierra de Ocaña and Serranía de los Motilones, the other bending eastward to form the Venezuelan Andes. Created in 1910, it occupies an area of 8,037 sq mi (20,815 sq km).

The Río Catatumbo region, near the Venezuelan border, is an important oil-producing area. In the cooler uplands, grains, potatoes, and horsebeans are the principal crops. Coffee and sugarcane are cultivated on the middle slopes and lower valleys, as in the vicinity of Cúcuta (*q.v.*), the departmental capital. A railroad traverses the department from east to west, and the highway network is well developed. Pop. (1974 est.) 679,500.
·area and population table **4**:870
·map, Colombia **4**:866

Norte Grande, traditional region, northern Chile, comprising the arid and semi-arid core areas of the Atacama Desert and populated mostly in coastal mineral-exporting cities.
22°30′ S, 69°00′ W
·physical features and economic activity **4**:249g

North, Christopher, pen name of JOHN WILSON (1785–1854), Scottish writer and literary critic.
·Tennyson's critical interchange **18**:141e

North, Frederick North, Lord, later 2ND EARL OF GUILFORD (b. April 13, 1732, London—d. Aug. 5, 1792, London), prime minister from 1770 to 1782, whose vacillating leadership contributed to the loss of Great Britain's American colonies in the American Revolution (1775–83).

North was the son of a Tory nobleman. He served as a lord of the treasury from 1759 to 1765 and became chancellor of the exchequer in 1767. In 1770 he succeeded Augustus Henry Fitzroy, 3rd duke of Grafton, as prime minister.

Lord North, detail of a portrait by Sir Nathaniel Dance-Holland; in the National Portrait Gallery, London
By courtesy of the National Portrait Gallery, London

North's easygoing temper and parliamentary skill enabled him to form the first stable ministry of the reign of King George III (1760–1820). At the same time, he subordinated himself totally to the King, who was determined to maintain Great Britain's hold on the American colonies. Thus North was unable to take advantage of opportunities to compromise with the colonists. In 1774 he responded with harsh measures after a group of Boston colonists destroyed a shipment of tea in protest against the tea tax. Nevertheless, when rebellion broke out in the colonies in 1775, North faced the war halfheartedly and was easily depressed by loyalist defeats. After 1777 the King repeatedly had to dissuade him from leaving office.

North finally resigned in March 1782, upon hearing of the surrender of the British commander Lord Charles Cornwallis at Yorktown, Va. In 1783 North enraged King George by allying with a prominent Whig, Charles James Fox. Fox and North served as secretaries of state from April to December 1783 in a ministry that was nominally headed by William, 3rd duke of Portland. Increasing blindness, however, caused North to retire from politics in 1787. Three years later he succeeded to his father's earldom of Guilford.
·Britain's 18th-century political growth **3**:257d
·Fox's opposition and later coalition **7**:578e
·Fox's surprising political alliance **14**:478d
·ministry under George III **7**:1126d

North, Roger (1653–1734), British lawyer and biographer.
·biographical writings **2**:1012b

North, Simeon (b. July 13, 1765, Berlin, Conn.—d. Aug. 25, 1852, Middletown), pistol and rifle manufacturer who, about the same time the U.S. inventor Eli Whitney was doing so, developed the use of interchangeable parts in manufacturing.

After spending his early youth as a farmer, at age 16 North tried but failed to enlist in the Continental Army. In 1795 he opened a small scythe-making business in an old mill next to his farm and four years later was awarded his first government contract to deliver 500 horse pistols within a year. His excellent craftsmanship brought more contracts, including one dated April 16, 1813, for 20,000 pistols. To fulfill the contract he suggested that the specifications call for identical construction of each firearm, so that the pistols could be mass assembled. On Dec. 10, 1823, he received his first rifle contract, for 6,000 rifles to be manufactured and delivered in five years; he continued to supply rifles and carbines to the U.S. government until 1850. In 1825 he devised a repeating rifle that could fire 10 rounds without reloading.

North, Sir Thomas (b. May 28, 1535, London—d. ?1603), English translator whose version of Plutarch's *Parallel Lives* was the source for many of Shakespeare's plays.

North may have been a student at Peterhouse, Cambridge, and he was entered as a student at Lincoln's Inn, London, in 1557, where he joined a group of young lawyers interested in translating. In 1574 he accompanied his brother on a diplomatic mission to France. Thomas North had an extensive military career: he fought twice in Ireland as captain (1582 and 1596–97), served in the Low Countries in defense of the Dutch against the Spanish (1585–87), and trained militia against the threatened invasion of England by the Spanish Armada in 1588. He was knighted about 1596–97; he later served as justice of the peace for Cambridge, and he was pensioned by the Queen in 1601.

In 1557 North translated, under the title *Diall of Princes*, a French copy of the *Libro del emperador Marco Aurelio cō relox de principes* (1529), by the Spanish author Antonio de Guevara. Although North retained Guevara's elaborate mannered style, he was also capable of quite a different kind of work. His translation of Oriental beast fables from the Italian, *The Morall Philosophie of Doni* (1601), for example, was a rapid and colloquial narrative. His *Lives of the noble Grecians and Romanes*, translated in 1579 from Jacques Amyot's French version of Plutarch's *Parallel Lives*, has been described as one of the earliest great masterpieces of English prose. Shakespeare paid North the compliment of putting some of his prose directly into blank verse, with only minor changes.
·Plutarch translation stylistic value **14**:579e

North, the, term for the northern regions of the United States. The North is characterized historically by a common system of free labour, commercial vigour, and agricultural diversity. As early as 1796 Pres. George Washington used the terms North and South, warning against the danger of basing political differences upon geographic lines. The most critical sectional distinction, however, had already been recognized in 1787, when slavery was banned in the Northwest Territory. Soon after the American Revolution, slavery disappeared in all states north of the Mason and Dixon Line, the boundary between Pennsylvania and Maryland.

In the 19th century transportation developed markedly along east–west lines; *e.g.*, the Erie Canal opened up the Great Lakes in 1825, and New York City was connected to Chicago by rail in 1852. Thus, both immigration and trade bound northern sections together, creating a remarkable homogeneity of ideology, political and educational institutions, cultural ties, and economic patterns.

By the 1850s the question of the extension of slavery into the western territories was the most prominent issue uniting the North and bringing it into conflict with the South. On the eve of the Civil War (1861), there were 19 free and 15 slave states, with the boundary between them following the Mason and Dixon Line, the Ohio River, and latitude 36°30′ (except for Missouri, which was a slave state). The North attained its highest self-consciousness as a region during the war, when its name became synonymous with the Union. Including the four border states that fought with the Union, the North at this time had a population of 22,000,000, produced 75 percent of the nation's wealth, and possessed 81 percent of its factories.

After Reconstruction ended (1877), North–South differences tended to be subordinated to such movements as Populism. During the late 1950s, the South was the initial locus of the civil rights movement, but by the late 1960s and '70s, the inclusion of minorities in the political and economic mainstream of the nation was as much a challenge in the North as in the South.
·Civil War causes and strength **18**:968d

North Adams, city, Berkshire County, northwestern Massachusetts, U.S., on the Hoosic River, at the western end of the Hoosac Tunnel (extending 5 mi [8 km] under the Hoosac Range) and the Mohawk Trail. It was the site of Ft. Massachusetts, built by the Massachusetts Bay Colony in 1745 and later burned during the French and Indian Wars; its permanent settlement dates from the 1770s when a Quaker group arrived from Rhode Island. It was set off from the original town of Adams and incorporated as the town of North Adams in 1878. Waterpower from the Hoosic and the completion (1873) of the tunnel led to early industrialization. Manufactures now include leather products, textiles, paper, and electrical machinery.

North Adams State College was opened as a normal school in 1894. A natural rock bridge crosses Hudson Creek within the city limits, and Mt. Greylock (3,491 ft [1,064 m]), the highest peak in the state, is 5 mi southwest. Inc. city, 1895. Pop. (1900) 24,200; (1980) 18,063.
42°42′ N, 73°07′ W

North Africa, in geographical usage, that part of the African continent lying between the Mediterranean coast and the Sahara (desert), encompassing Morocco, Algeria, Tunisia, and Libya; Egypt, which is also part of the North African geographical region, may be alternatively classified as part of the Middle East.

North Africa's total area is 3,664,000 sq mi (5,897,000 sq km), but its 89,110,000 (1979 est.) inhabitants, mainly Muslims, are confined chiefly in a narrow coastal belt and along the lower Nile Valley. Most of North Africa has a marked dry season, and cultivation depends on frequent intensive irrigation. Europeans settled in Morocco, Algeria, Tunisia, and Libya, but their numbers decreased considerably when independent sovereign states were created from the former French and Italian territories after World War II. There are important mineral deposits, including iron ore, phosphates, and petroleum. Manufacturing industries are well developed in many of the rapidly expanding towns.
·African wildlife distribution and types **1**:196c
·jewelry tradition of Berbers and Arabs **10**:171g
·petroleum reserves of the world table **14**:175

North Africa, history of 13:145. North Africa here denotes the area of modern Mauretania, Morocco, Algeria, Tunisia, and Libya. This area has had something of a common history, arising from its geographical isolation by the Mediterranean to the north, the Sahara (desert) to the south, and the Libyan desert to the east.

The earliest known evidence of hominids in North Africa is estimated to be at least 200,000 years old. Lithic industries flourished in the region until the introduction of ironworking. In the 1st millennium BC, contact with Phoenician traders brought North Africa into the mainstream of Mediterranean history. The trading settlement of Carthage (founded in about the 8th century BC) developed as an independent power and in the 5th century BC created an empire centred on the North African coast. The city was destroyed by Rome in 146 BC at the end of the Punic Wars. After a brief flourishing of native kingdoms, Rome established effective control over the Maghrib; the Roman period of North African history was marked by the growth of urban life and of Christianity. In the 5th century AD the Germanic Vandals invaded North Africa, but in the 6th century the area became part of the Byzantine Empire. Following the Arab conquest of all of North Africa in the 7th century, and the establishment of the Islāmic faith, there was considerable political and religious fragmentation. In the 11th and 12th centuries, the Almoravid and Almohad empires arose; in the period of the 13th to the 15th century, North Africa was divided into three kingdoms. Most of the area (except for Morocco) became part of the Ottoman Empire in the 16th century.

In the 19th century, European powers gained control. In 1830 France began the conquest of Algeria; the Algerian War that began in 1954 led to independence in 1962. In 1881 France occupied Tunisia and established a protectorate that ended with Tunisian independence in 1956. Most of Morocco was a French protectorate from 1912 to 1956; a small area was a Spanish protectorate until 1956. Libya achieved independence from Italian rule in 1951, and in 1960 the independent state of Mauritania was created from French territory to the south of Morocco. Spain continued to control the Spanish Sahara until 1976, when Morocco and Mauritania divided the area between them.

REFERENCES in other text articles:
·ʿAbd al-Muʾmin's leadership of Almohads **1**:6b
·ʿAbd ar-Raḥmān III's policy **1**:7e
·Abdelkader and Algerian nationalism **1**:7h
·Algerian, Egyptian, and Moroccan colonial educational development **6**:399d
·Algerian independence movement **7**:604a
·Algerian socio-economic aspects and prospects **1**:558f
·Algiers' rulers and independence **1**:571h
·archaic Greek colonizing expeditions **8**:332f; map 335
·Averroës' philosophy and writings **2**:538c
·Ben Bella's dedication and removal **2**:833e
·Berber law and farming methods **2**:305d
·Bourguiba and Tunisian independence **3**:84d
·Byzantine military campaigns **3**:552e; map 554
·Carthage role in Punic Wars **15**:277d
·Carthaginian Atlantic exploration **7**:1037d
·Cyprian's stand on heresies and papacy **5**:400h
·de Gaulle in World War II and Algiers **7**:963d
·Egyptian Arab raids in 7th century AD **6**:488e
·Egyptian control and Kushite competition **6**:479g *passim* to 481c
·European colonial rivalry **4**:900a; map 901
·European imperialism in 19th century **6**:1111b
·exploration and settlement **1**:206d
·Fāṭimid dynasty and Ismāʿīlī missionaries **7**:193b; map
·Fāṭimid expansion into Egypt **6**:489d
·Hannibal's Second Punic War campaigns **8**:625g
·Ibn Khaldūn's life and writings **9**:148a
·Islāmic and rural–urban continuity **12**:167f
·Islāmic law as basis for legal system **9**:939d
·Italian colonialism under Rudini and Giolitti **9**:1166e
·Justinian expansion of Roman Empire **10**:363b
·Maghrib cultural history **11**:293g
·Mauritania's history, conditions, and role **11**:710d
·monastic Ṣūfīs political power in Libya **12**:339a
·Muʿāwiyah I's expansion of caliphate **12**:605e
·Muslim expansion and conquest **3**:629b
·Near Eastern civilization emergence **12**:913b
·Ottoman Empire historical relation **13**:779f; maps 772
·Portuguese conquest of Ceuta by John I **8**:777e
·Portuguese crusades and conquests **14**:865e
·postwar French opposition **9**:760f
·Ramessid Egyptian subjugation of Libyans **6**:475h *passim* to 478a
·refugee influx in 1960s **15**:569g
·Rommel and Battle of el-Alamein **15**:1135c
·Sahara exploration and occupation **16**:150e
·Scipio military campaign and victory **16**:397a
·Shīʿite political activities **9**:930e
·socialism's growth and influence **16**:972d
·Spain's wars in Morocco **17**:440a
·Sudan's political and cultural history **13**:108e
·Timbuktu conquest by Morocco **18**:409h
·Tunis in ancient times **18**:743h
·Umayyad conquest under ʿAbd al-Malik **1**:5f
·uncongeniality to Roman Catholicism **15**:1018g
·West African conquest **19**:772b
·World War II invasions **19**:986a
·World War I origins and settlement **19**:944b

RELATED ENTRIES in the *Ready Reference and Index: for*
ancient cities and sites: see Carthage; Hadrumetum; Hippo; Iol; Lambessa; Leptis; Lixus; Ptolemais; Sabratha; Tébessa; Thugga; Thysdrus; Tipasa; Utica; Volubilis
historical regions: Africa, Roman province of; Gaetulia; Numidia
peoples and cultures: Barghawāṭah; Capsian culture; Ḥarāṭīn; Ibero-Maurusian stone tool industry; Moors
dynasties: ʿAbd al-Wādids; bled makhzen; Ḥafṣids; Ḥusaynids; Marīnids; Zīrids
political development: Destour; Istiqlāl; National Action Bloc; Neo-Destour; Parti du Peuple Algérien; Union Démocratique du Manifeste Algérien; Young Tunisians
European intervention: Bardo, Treaty of; Organisation de l'Armée Secrète; Three Kings, Battle of the
other: Algerian Ulama, Association of; Barbary pirates; dey; Sanūsīyah

North African peoples and cultures: *see* Maghrib, cultures of the; Middle Eastern and North African peoples and cultures.

Northallerton, market town, county of North Yorkshire (established 1974), England, in the northward extension of the Vale of York, a lowland gateway, here constricted to about 10 mi (16 km) in width, between the highland blocks of the Pennines and the North Yorkshire Moors. The area was still recorded as waste by Domesday Book (1086), after being ravaged by the Norman invaders of 1066.

Northallerton was granted by the Norman king William II Rufus (1087–1100) to the Bishop of Durham. In 1174 its Norman castle was destroyed, and in 1317 the Scots, under Robert I the Bruce, swept down from the north and burned the town, which was to suffer heavily during the long period of Anglo-Scottish warfare. The modern town has livestock markets and is the service centre for an extensive farming area. Its modern administrative functions make it important regionally. Pop. (1971) 10,514.
54°20′ N, 1°26′ W
·map, United Kingdom **18**:867

Northam, town, southeast Western Australia, at the confluence of the Avon and Mortlock rivers. One of the state's oldest settlements, it was founded in 1830 and named by Gov. Sir James Stirling after Northam in Devon, Eng.; it was made a municipality in 1879.

During the 1890s, Northam was a major stop for miners bound eastward for the Yilgarn, Eastern, and Dundas goldfields. It now serves part of the eastern Wheat Belt (*q.v.*), which also produces fodder, sheep, beef cattle, and pigs. The town's industries include flour mills, metal fabrication and cold-storage works, a plasterboard factory, and brick and charcoal kilns.

At the junction of rail lines to Kalgoorlie, Geraldton, Albany, and Perth, it is also at the intersection of the Great Eastern and Southern highways. Northam is the site of the Nuresk Agricultural College, the Holden Immigration Centre, and a military base. Pop. (1971) 7,117.
31°39′ S, 116°40′ E
·map, Australia **2**:400

North America **13**:174, third largest of the continents, lies in the Western Hemisphere and covers an area of about 9,420,000 sq mi (24,400,000 sq km). It is inhabited by more than 350,000,000 people, roughly 9 percent of the world's total. It is bounded by the Pacific Ocean (west), the Arctic Ocean (north), and the Atlantic Ocean (east) and is connected to South America by the Isthmus of Panama.

North America thus includes the whole of what is sometimes referred to as Central America, or Meso-America, and the northernmost part of the culturally defined entity known as Latin America, as well as the islands of the Caribbean Sea. The island of Greenland on the North American continental shelf has firm structural connections with the continent.

TEXT ARTICLE covers:
Geological history **13**:176h
Physical geography 183h
The living environment 188h
The material-resource base 192d
Human resources 194b
Resource development 196c

REFERENCES in other text articles:

agriculture, forestry, and fishing
·agricultural productivity, tables 1, 3, and 4 **1**:316
·English and American fishing techniques **7**:366b
·forestry and world timber use **7**:533h; tables 534
·honey production statistics **2**:793f
·meat production and consumption **11**:746b
·vegetable production, tables 6 and 7 **19**:52
·wood products consumption, graph 8 **19**:924
·wood product world production, table 2 **19**:924

commerce, industry, and mining
·electric power production **6**:634d
·petroleum production and demand statistics, tables 1 and 2 **14**:176
·textile production, tables 1 and 2 **18**:188

history
·Arctic ancient cultures and migrations **1**:1129f
·Cabot's exploration achievements **7**:1041d
·de Soto's southeastern U.S. exploration **17**:18c
·fur trading and exploration **7**:811f
·Indian cultures ancient to modern **13**:213e
·Plateau Indian culture **13**:227e
·Indian populations table **13**:215
·nurse to population ratio, table 2 **13**:400a
·petroleum reserves of the world table **14**:175

physical geography
·Alaskan mountain geological features **1**:414a
·atmospheric moisture statistics, table 4 **19**:645
·Canada geographic features **3**:713b
·Cenozoic rocks and plant and animal life **3**:1081e *passim* to 1082h
·Columbia River features and development **4**:930g
·continental drift evidence **13**:929a
·cordillera geology features **12**:590d
·Cretaceous seas and rock series **5**:249d; tables 1 and 2
·cyclothem strata, theories, and significance **5**:396b
·Devonian system and paleogeography **5**:671h; illus. 672
·geological history and formations **6**:11d
·Great Plains landscape **8**:304c
·Holocene climate, table 2 **4**:736
·Holocene coastal and tectonic features **8**:1001g
·hurricane destruction statistics **9**:59a
·loess distribution and characteristics **11**:25f
·Lower Carboniferous rocks and fossils **3**:853e
·Lower Paleozoic rocks, paleogeography, and correlations **13**:918d; tables
·monsoon tendencies and occurrences **12**:394a
·Niagara River and Falls features **13**:57b
·Ordovician rocks and paleogeography **13**:657d; table 660
·Pacific Coast Range geological history **13**:824d
·permafrost formation and extent **14**:90a; illus. 89

·Permian rocks and paleogeography **14**:96c
·physiographic features and development **6**:46c; tables and graph 43
·plateau and basin distribution **14**:527c
·Pleistocene glacial chronology **14**:559b; table
·Precambrian formations and events **14**:953f; table 954
·pre-Holocene and Holocene climates **4**:732e
·Rocky Mountain ranges and formations **15**:964g; illus. 2966
·Silurian paleogeography **16**:769c
·Silurian sediment types and deposits **16**:775g
·Tertiary rocks, volcanics, and orogeny **18**:151f
·Triassic sediments and volcanism **18**:693h; map 694
·tundra latitude and borders **18**:733c; map 734
·U.S. landscape and settlement patterns **18**:905b
·vegetation zones and distribution **18**:145h

religion
·Catholic missions in colonial America **15**:1018b
·Catholic population distribution map **15**:1019
·Roman Catholic population table **15**:986

transportation and communications
·newspaper publishing statistics table **15**:237
·television system operation **18**:101f; table 109

vegetation and animal life
·animal dispersal across Bering Sea **5**:915a
·characteristic life of Holarctic region **2**:1002d
·forest community characteristics **7**:539g
·furbearing animals **7**:812d
·grassland flora and distribution **8**:284d
·hunting impact on big game resources **9**:49a
·migratory routes of birds **12**:180e
·primitive and European cultural impact and conservation development **5**:42b
·scrublands distribution characteristics **16**:418h

North American Baptist Association: *see* Baptist Missionary Association of America.

North American Baptist General Conference, an association of Baptist churches that developed from churches established by German Baptist immigrants in the United States in the mid-19th century. In 1851, eight German Baptist churches formed an eastern conference, and, as other German Baptist churches were organized in various parts of the country, other local conferences were formed. In 1865, nine conferences of German Baptist churches held their first general conference, and, subsequently, the general conference became the primary administrative unit for these churches.

Each local conference meets annually and conducts the business and activities of the conference. The general conference meets every three years. A general council carries out the work of the general conference between meetings in the areas of education, missions, publications, and social welfare activities. Headquarters and the Roger Williams Press are in Forest Park, Ill. In 1970 a membership of 55,080 was reported.

North American Basin, submarine depression, Atlantic Ocean.
30°00′ N, 60°00′ W
·Atlantic Ocean floor features map **2**:296

North American beaver: *see* beaver.

North American Christian Convention, a religious meeting held in Indianapolis in 1927 under the auspices of the Churches of Christ.
·Disciples of Christ and centralization **5**:835c

North American Desert **13**:203, ecological complex in western North America, extending nearly 2,000 mi (3,200 km) from northern Mexico to southern Canada, over an area of about 1,000,000 sq mi (2,600,000 sq km).

The text article covers location, regional subdivisions, exploration and scientific study, physical geography, vegetation, animal life, and human settlement.
40°50′ N, 120°00′ W
REFERENCE in other text article:
·aridity causation **5**:604g

North America Nebula (NGC 7000, IC 5067, 5068), bright diffuse nebula in the constellation Cygnus, appearing near the star Deneb and lying several thousand light-years from the Earth. Its name, derived from its shape, was given by the German astronomer Max Wolf.

North American Great Basin Indians **13**:204, numerous Indian groups who occupied an arid and semi-arid region of interior western North America centred on the Nevada Great Basin but extending into Oregon, Idaho, Wyoming, Utah, Colorado, Arizona, and eastern California.

The text article covers the main aboriginal groups and languages, social and cultural patterns, religious concepts, and developments since white settlement of the area.
REFERENCES in other text articles:
·dance forms and religious use **1**:674b
·habitation area and culture **13**:216a
·New Mexico tribal settlements **13**:4c
RELATED ENTRIES in the *Ready Reference and Index:*
Bannock; Mono; Paiute; Shoshoni; Ute; Washo

North American Indian languages **13**:208, languages indigenous to the United States and Canada; some of the North American genetic language groupings extend southward into Mexico and Central America. There were originally an estimated 300 Indian languages in North America, which have been classified into 57 language families (groups of genetically related languages). In the mid-20th century the number of living languages was estimated at around 200; these languages are currently spoken by approximately 1,500,000 people.

The text article contains the various classification systems of the Indian languages and a chart of the languages with their locations and numbers of speakers; it covers the effects of contact between Indian and European languages, grammatical and phonological characteristics, vocabulary, the interrelationship of language and culture, and writing and texts.
REFERENCES in other text articles:
·diversity and isolation from Old World **13**:215e
·language areas and affiliations **10**:670h
·linguistic and physical variety of races **15**:349b; illus. 350
·Plains Indian language groups **13**:223g
·Southeast region families **17**:218e
·U.S. linguistic research principles **10**:995c
·Uto-Aztecan groups and speakers **13**:245d
·Uto-Aztecan links and Hokan hypothesis **11**:958h
RELATED ENTRIES in the *Ready Reference and Index:*
Azteco-Tanoan languages; Hokan languages; Macro-Algonkian languages; Macro-Siouan languages; Na-Dené languages; Penutian languages

North American Indian local races, populations of the American Indian geographical race that make up a group of related breeding isolates. Most of the individual local races in this group are equivalent to tribes or language groups. These races are distinguished by tall stature, aquiline noses, and faces with prominent cheekbones, moderate skin pigmentation, coarse, black head hair and sparse facial and body hair, a low incidence of epicanthic (Mongoloid) eyefolds, and a high incidence of shovel-shaped incisors (*q.v.*). They lack blood types B and A_2 in the ABO system, N in the MNS-U system, and Rh-negative in the Rhesus system. *See also* local race; American Indian geographical race.
·racial characteristics and distribution **14**:847c

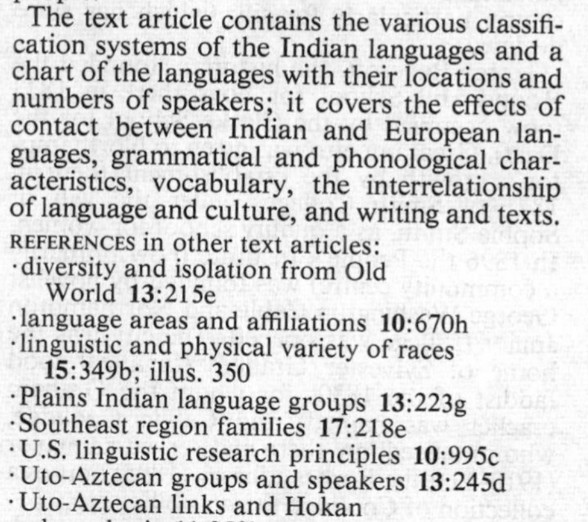
Indian chief, Zuni tribe, New Mexico
Paolo Koch—Rapho Guillumette

North American pack rat: *see* wood rat.

North American peoples and cultures **13**:213, the Indians of North America north of Mexico and their cultural patterns. Not included in this designation are the Eskimo and Aleut.

The text article covers the people (physical types, populations and languages, and culture areas), Indian prehistory, and the history of the Indians since the arrival of Europeans in North America.
REFERENCES in other text articles:
·Abanaki corn myth **12**:795a
·American Indian races and types **14**:847c
·anthropological distinction **16**:991d

arts
·art characteristics and criticism **14**:1032a
·basketry's social value **2**:761h
·folk song in European ballad style **16**:793c
·individual and communal songs **10**:1046f
·jewelry design and techniques **10**:181h; illus. 182
·performing and visual art features **1**:659a
·pottery styles and development **14**:928e

·blood group frequencies in populations **2**:1148f
·calendar and chronology systems **3**:611h
·Canadian tribal structure and adaptation **13**:261f
·design of cities **18**:1069a
·early French Canadian relations **3**:734d
·fasting among Northeastern tribes **5**:729g
·Indian evocation of spiritual contact **14**:1043a *passim* to 1046h
·language areas and relationships **10**:670h
·language features and distribution **13**:208a; map 210
·mana-like religious concepts **12**:878a
·migration, settlement, and exploitation **13**:194c
·naming patterns **12**:818h
·Northwest Coast Indian culture **13**:251c
·Plains Indian culture **13**:223e
·Plateau Indian culture **13**:227e
·stick games and lacrosse origins **7**:870g
·Wissler's Indian culture division **8**:1156c
RELATED ENTRIES in the *Ready Reference and Index:*
Adena culture; Anasazi culture; Clovis complex; Cochise culture; Folsom complex; Hohokam culture; Hopewell culture; Mississippian culture; Mogollon culture

North American Plains Indians **13**:223, aboriginal peoples living in the area between the Mississippi River and the Rocky Mountains, including adjacent areas of Canada. They included tribes speaking Algonkian, Siouan, Caddo, Uto-Aztecan, Athabascan, and Kiowa.

The text article contains a survey of the cultural patterns of the Plains Indians, including their social structures, economic systems, and religious beliefs.
REFERENCES in other text articles:
·artistic development in leatherwork **10**:181a
·arts and myth in ritual **1**:661e
·Colorado exploration and cultural contribution **4**:906c
·cultural impact on Plateau Indians **13**:228b
·culture and land title withdrawal **2**:5h
·early east Texan civilization **18**:164f *passim* to 166c
·Ghost Dance messianic movements **18**:699d

·horse impact on cultures **13**:216c
·Macro-Siouan language distribution **10**:671f
·Mandan and Hidatsa dances illus. **1**:672
·Mississippi River influence **12**:282b
·monotheistic polytheism in Great Spirit **12**:382g
·mythological theme of the culture hero **12**:800b
·naming patterns **12**:818h
·nomadic characteristics of hunting societies **8**:1160d
·racial characteristics **14**:847e

RELATED ENTRIES in the *Ready Reference and Index: for*
Algonkian-speaking peoples: see Arapaho; Atsina; Blackfoot; Cheyenne
Caddoan-speaking peoples: Arikara; Wichita
Siouan-speaking peoples: Assiniboin; Crow; Dakota; Hidatsa; Mandan; Omaha; Osage; Oto; Ponca; Quapaw
other: Comanche; Gros Ventres; Kansa; Kiowa; Sarcee; Tonkawa

North American Plateau Indians **13**:227, the Indian groups who originally inhabited a region bounded on the west by the Canadian Coast Mountains and the Cascade Range of Oregon, on the south by the Blue Mountains and the Salmon River, on the east by the Rocky Mountains and the Lewis Range, and on the north by such low extensions of the Rocky Mountains as the Cariboo Mountains.

The text article covers the peoples and languages of the area, social structures, economic life, belief and aesthetic systems, and description of developments since the coming of Europeans.

REFERENCES in other text articles:
·Flathead music features and influences **1**:666h
·habitation area, economy, and culture **13**:215h
·naming patterns **12**:818h

RELATED ENTRIES in the *Ready Reference and Index:*
Flathead; Kutenai; Modoc and Klamath; Nez Percé; Sahaptin; Salish; Yakima

North American porcupine: *see* porcupine.

North American Review, monthly U.S. literary magazine from 1815 to 1940, revived as a quarterly in 1964.
·magazine publishing history **15**:251a

Northampton, a borough and county town (seat), Northamptonshire, England, situated in the valley of the River Nene. All Saints Church, the focal point of the business centre, was rebuilt in the late 17th century. Other noteworthy churches are St. Sepulchre's, retaining a rotunda (*c.* 1110); St. Peter's, late Norman in style; and St. Matthew's, late 19th century and containing works by 20th-century British artists, among them the sculptor Henry Moore and the painter Graham Sutherland. A Roman Catholic bishopric was founded in 1850; and the cathedral, begun in 1864, was completed in 1960. The Guildhall (1864, with later additions) is an example of Victorian Gothic. The town has a theatre, two museums, an art gallery, grammar (secondary) schools, a school of art, and a college of technology.

The town walls and a castle were built *c.* 1100. A place of importance in the early Middle Ages, Northampton was granted its first charter in 1189 but suffered an economic decline after about 1300. The town walls were demolished after the royalist Restoration of the 17th century as Northampton had been a supporter of the opposing parliamentary forces during the preceding English Civil War. Much of the town was destroyed by fire in 1675. During the late 19th century, the townspeople acquired a national reputation for radical opinions; and Charles Bradlaugh, the free-thinker and social reformer, was elected a member of Parliament in 1880. Shoe manufacturing developed in the 18th and 19th centuries, although Northampton's position meant the town was bypassed by the Grand Union Canal and the main railway line. A branch canal was finished in 1815 and a branch railway in 1845. The present station, opened in 1881 and rebuilt in 1966, is on the site of the medieval castle. The London-Yorkshire motorway, opened in 1959 as an important English routeway, passes nearby.

Northampton is best known for its shoe and leather industry, although this is declining with the growth of, among others, engineering, brewing, and electronics industries. The town, an important retail and market centre, serves both Northamptonshire and North Buckinghamshire. In 1965 it was selected for expansion, and a 1981 population of 230,000 was projected. New residential and industrial sites were also being developed in the early 1970s. Great Brington Church, 6 mi (10 km) to the northwest, contains the tombstone of an ancestor of George Washington, the first president of the United States. Pop. (1971 prelim.) 126,608.
52°14′ N, 0°54′ W
·map, United Kingdom **18**:866

Northampton, city, seat (1662) of Hampshire County, west central Massachusetts, U.S., on the Connecticut River. The site, known as Nonotuck (Indian: "middle of the river"), was settled in 1654 and named for Northampton, in England. It became a self-sufficient farming community where Jonathan Edwards held a pastorate (1729–49). The town was the scene of several debtors' demonstrations during Shays's Rebellion (1786–87). A woollen mill was established there in 1809, and, connected to the Connecticut communities by canal (1834) and by railroad (1845), Northampton developed as a manufacturing centre, particularly for silk (which has since declined).

George Bancroft, the historian, founded the Round Hill School for boys there in 1823 (now occupied by the Clarke School for the Deaf). Great impetus was given to Northampton's growth by the establishment there in 1871 of Smith College, under the will of Sophia Smith, as a quality school for women. In 1896 the People's Institute (now primarily a community centre) was founded by novelist George Washington Cable and Northampton Junior College was opened. The city was the home of Sylvester Graham (fanatical food faddist of the 1830s for whom the Graham cracker was named) and Calvin Coolidge, who practiced law there and served as mayor (1910–11); the Forbes Library (1895) houses a collection of Coolidge memorabilia.

A wide variety of goods is manufactured, including stainless-steel cutlery, hosiery, brushes, plastics, silverware, wood and paper products, optical and precision instruments, and electronic equipment. Inc. town, 1655; city, 1883. Pop. (1980) 29,286.
42°19′ N, 72°38′ W
·Edwards' ministry and contributions **6**:441c

Northampton, earls and marquesses of, an English title, united at times during the 12th century with the earldom of Huntingdon. It was held (1337–73) by William de Bohun and his son Humphrey, eventually passing (1384) with Humphrey's younger daughter to Henry Bolingbroke, earl of Derby, who became King Henry IV in 1399. A marquessate of Northampton held (1547–71) by William Parr, and an earldom (1604–14) by Henry Howard. In 1618 William Compton, 2nd Lord Compton, was created earl of Northampton. His descendant Charles (died 1828) was created marquess (1812). The Compton family has continued to hold the title.
·prosodic development in English poetry **15**:72a

Northampton, Assize of, a text preserved under the year 1176 in two works of the English chronicler Roger of Hoveden and entitled "The Assizes of King Henry, first ordained at Clarendon, and re-enacted at Northampton." It provides the only direct record of business concluded at Henry II's council held at Northampton in 1176. The clauses deal with three main topics: administration of the criminal law; the land law; and instructions for itinerant justices, who were to visit the entire country, working in six circuits. The paragraphs on crime seem to repeat, with certain amendments, provisions of the Assize of Clarendon (1166). The clauses on land law are especially important for their reference to the assize of novel disseisin (of which the original text is lost)—*i.e.*, a procedure introduced in 1166 to provide a remedy for arbitrary ejectment from a free tenement—and the recitation of the new assize of morte d'ancestor, which gave similar protection to an heir. Other paragraphs appear to be instructions for the justices in eyre, perhaps based on some of 1166, but clearly relevant to the political situation 10 years later. The facts—for instance, that the justices were required to exact oaths of fealty to the King from "all" and were to see that castles the demolition of which had been ordered were indeed razed—clearly have reference to the rebellion of 1173–74. The text of the Assize of Northampton is important in reconstructing the enactments of the Assize of Clarendon, surviving texts of which are to some extent apocryphal.

Northampton, Treaty of (1328), agreement between England and Scotland.
·Edward III reluctant power concession **6**:437b

Northamptonshire, abbreviated NORTHANTS, county in the East Midlands region, England. A Jurassic escarpment (ridgelike outcrop) crosses the county from southwest to northeast and is known locally as the Northamptonshire Uplands. The rock strata outcrop to the northwest in clifflike exposures, while the gentler "dip" slope curves away under younger rocks to the southeast. These include Lias formations (worked for bricks at Raunds and Rothwell) and the Northampton sands, important for their iron-ore workings centred at Corby. Boulder clay, plastered over the topography by former Ice Age glaciers, is widely distributed over the uplands and in the east.

The southwest portion of the county forms the principal watershed of the Midlands region. The landscape is unspectacular and mainly farmland.

Pre-Celtic peoples were present in the region, and pre-Christian Celtic objects have been found at Hunsbury Hill and Desborough. Traces of Roman settlements and roads also survive. In the 7th century the area became part of the Saxon kingdom of Mercia. At the time of Domesday Book (1086), the record of the land survey of England ordered by William I the Conqueror, the boundaries approximated those of the modern county, together with the entity known as the Soke of Peterborough (now part of Cambridgeshire). Northampton was a favourite meeting place of Norman and Plantagenet parliaments. The county revolted in 1607 against enclosures of arable land for sheep farming and was on the side of Parliament in the mid-17th-century English Civil War: Charles I (leader of the opposing Royalist forces of England) was defeated at Naseby (1645) and imprisoned at Holdenby (1647). From this time Northamptonshire was noted as a centre of the movement of religious dissenters which became known as Nonconformity.

There are Eleanor Crosses (erected by King Edward I of England, who reigned from 1272 to 1307, to mark the places where the body of his queen, Eleanor of Castile, rested on its way from Harby, Nottinghamshire, to burial in London) at Geddington and Hardingstone. The county has many beautiful churches. The church towers at Earls Barton and Brigstock are Saxon, as is Brixworth's All Saints Church (*c.* 675). The Church of St. Peter and Holy Sepulchre, Northampton, are fine Norman works; the Early English architectural style is represented by the Church of St. Mary, at Higham Ferrers, and by Warmington. Family chapels, places of worship associated with prominent landowners, are to be found at Brington and Warkton. Rockingham Castle is mainly Elizabethan or Jacobean in style. Barnwell Castle is 13th century, while Castle Ashby is Elizabethan and Althorp Park dates from the 16th century. Other noteworthy buildings include the Triangular Lodge (1593–95) at Rushton, Lamport Hall (1654–57), Easton Neston (1700–02), and Sulgrave Manor, the ancestral home of George Washington, the first president of the United States.

The area of the county is 915 sq mi (2,370 sq km) and the population (1971 prelim.) 467,843, of which 126,608 is accounted for by Northampton, a borough and seat of the judicial proceedings known as quarter sessions. Brackley (4,615), Daventry (11,813), Higham Ferrers (4,700), and Kettering (42,628) are also boroughs. Corby, a new town of the 1930s, has a population of 47,716. Some 84 percent of the county remains farmland, despite the encroachment of towns and presence of derelict land (now mostly restored) from opencast mining. The arable acreage, especially cereals, potatoes, and sugar beet, has increased greatly. Livestock rearing is, however, more important, mainly on the uplands. The best known industry is the manufacture of boots and shoes and tanning, but box making, printing, toy making (Wellingborough), and food processing are also of significance. Multiproduct engineering industry is also present, mainly at Northampton, where there is also a large brewery. Clothing is made at Northampton, Kettering, and Desborough. There is a large iron and steel works at Corby. Smaller industry centres include Brackley, Higham Ferrers, Towcester, Rushden, and Daventry. Northamptonshire, lying between London and the North of England, is well served by both road and rail routes.

North Andover, town (township), Essex County, northeastern Massachusetts, U.S., on the Merrimack River. It was originally settled in 1646 as the North Parish of Andover and was separately incorporated in 1855. Lake Cochichewick (560 ac [227 ha]), within its boundaries, recalls its early Indian name meaning Place of the Great Cascade. Textile manufacturing has been an economic factor since the early 19th century. Diversified manufactures now include textile machinery, communications equipment, paper boxes, chemicals, and plastics. Although known as a residential area (adjoining the city of Lawrence), its outlying portions are devoted to agriculture and include the Harold Parker State Forest.

The town's Stevens Memorial Library contains a collection of works by poet Anne Bradstreet, an early resident and wife of the governor of the Massachusetts Bay Colony. The town is the site of Merrimack College (1947) and the Merrimack Valley Textile Museum. Pop. (1980) 20,129.
42°42′ N, 71°08′ W

Northanger Abbey (1817), novel by Jane Austen about the romance between Catherine Morland and Henry Tilney, poking fun at the Gothic novel convention.

·Gothic novel parody **2**:378e

North Anna River, Battle of (1864), in U.S. Civil War, skirmish during Grant's pursuit of Lee across northern Virginia.

·Civil War eastern campaign
map **4**:676

North Arcot, district, Tamil Nadu state, southern India, framed by the edge of the Mysore plateau (north) and occupying the Javādi Hills (south). Between the hills, the Pālār River Valley extends eastward into the Coromandel Coast. Infertile red soils cover much of the 4,736-sq-mi (12,267-sq-km) district, except in the river valleys. The district is hot and dry, and major towns, such as Āmbūr, Arcot, Vellore (the district headquarters), Jalārpet, Kātpādi, Rānipet and Vāniyambādi, have developed along the irrigated Pālār Valley. Industries include cotton handloom weaving and the manufacture of textiles, cigars, and bamboo articles. Pop. (1971 prelim.) 3,738,273.

North Arlington, borough, Bergen County, northeastern New Jersey, U.S., immediately north of Newark, on the Passaic River. William Kingsland built the first house in 1677. One of the first steam engines used in America, built by Josiah Hornblower (1755), was installed there to pump water from a local copper mine. The mine (the ruins are in the face of a cliff) was discovered in 1713 by a Negro slave. In the mid-1880s the Astor family of New York owned a local farm, the produce of which supplied the Astor Hotel in New York City. Manufactures include machinery, concrete forms, and metal goods. Inc. 1896. Pop. (1980) 16,587.
40°47′ N, 74°08′ W

North Atlantic Current, also called NORTH ATLANTIC DRIFT, part of a clockwise-setting ocean-current system in the North Atlantic Ocean, extending from southeast of the Grand Bank, off Newfoundland, Canada, to the Norwegian Sea, off northwestern Europe. It is distinguished from the Gulf Stream (issuing from the Gulf of Mexico) in that it is composed of several broad currents with speeds of about 0.2 knots (nautical miles per hour), as compared to the Gulf Stream's rather concentrated flow at velocities of 1 to 6 knots. Characterized by warm temperature and high salinity, the current is sometimes concealed at the surface by shallow and variable wind-drift movements. The North Atlantic Current often mixes with northern cold polar water to produce excellent fishing grounds near the islands and along the coast of northwestern Europe. The combination of the warm current and prevailing westerly winds helps maintain a mild climate in northwestern Europe. Major branches of the current include the Irminger, Norway, and Canary currents (*qq.v.*). *See also* West Wind Drift.

·Gulf Stream's relationship **8**:486h; illus. 487
·North Sea currents and salinity content **13**:249g
·temperature and course **2**:301c

North Atlantic Treaty Organization (NATO), an organization developed to implement the North Atlantic Treaty of 1949, which sought to establish a military counterweight to a Soviet military presence in Europe. NATO has continued in the postwar period as a primary collective defense agreement of the Western powers in opposition to Communist forces in Europe. Its members include Belgium, Canada, Denmark, France, West Germany, Greece, Iceland, Italy, Luxembourg, The Netherlands, Norway, Portugal, Turkey, the United Kingdom, and the United States.

The primary purpose of NATO is elaborated in Article V of the treaty: "The Parties agree that an armed attack against one or more of them in Europe shall be considered an attack against them all and consequently they agree that, if such an armed attack occurs, each of them . . . will assist the Party or Parties so attacked . . . to restore and maintain the security of the North Atlantic area." The geographical scope of the treaty covers Europe and North America, the North Atlantic area north of the Tropic of Cancer, and the Mediterranean.

Three main periods characterized NATO's first two decades:

1. initial organization (1949–55), with the U.S. providing massive economic and military aid and West Germany joining the organization in 1955;

2. the building up of NATO's military strength (1955–67), re-establishing the balance of power in Europe and reorganizing military strength on the basis of nuclear power;

3. the abating of the earlier fears of Soviet expansionism (1967 and after), resulting in efforts to develop a detente, but without sacrificing the military effectiveness of NATO.

In the early 1970s NATO continued as a viable defense organization but was beset with political problems that were bound to affect its future status. The role of the U.S., the dominant partner of NATO from the beginning of NATO's existence, required redefinition with provision for a more equitable sharing of costs. Some of the member states, particularly France, became critical of U.S. domination of NATO. The question of West Germany's future in NATO also remained. The problem centred around efforts to reunify Germany without jeopardizing its security base in NATO. Finally, some of the NATO allies were concerned about the possibility of the U.S. reaching agreements with the other superpower, the U.S.S.R., "over the heads of Europe."

·Canadian modification and commitment **3**:745f
·Cyprus internal struggles **5**:408f
·de Gaulle's withdrawal of France **7**:964g
·Eisenhower's supreme commandership **6**:515b
·formation, members, and agreement **9**:756a; map 752
·French withdrawal reasons **9**:775a
·German diplomatic reintegration **8**:122h
·Greek military regime **2**:638h
·international agreements and open treaties **9**:731c
·Mackinder's prophetic theory and result **11**:268c
·map improvement and standardization **11**:474h
·Norway defense function **13**:269d
·nuclear defense strategy of Europe **19**:570d
·organizational structure and aims **14**:709b
·postwar colonial power support **9**:774a
·postwar negotiation and purpose **18**:993h
·rearmament as initial rationale **19**:570d
·satellite communication project **16**:267a
·Scandinavian postwar alignments **16**:330h
·U.S. protection theory **9**:765d

North Attleboro, also spelled NORTH ATTLEBOROUGH, town (urbanized township), Bristol County, southeastern Massachusetts, U.S., near the Rhode Island border. Settled in 1669 as part of Attleboro, it served as a fortification point during the Indian wars and the American Revolution. Along with Attleboro, the town shares a thriving jewelry industry, which began in 1780. Other manufactures include optical goods, textiles, paper, and machinery. Separately incorporated (from Attleboro) in 1887, it serves as a residential area for nearby Providence, R.I. Pop. (1980) 21,095.
41°59′ N, 71°20′ W

North Auckland Peninsula, alternate name NORTHLAND, North Island, New Zealand, extending 200 mi (320 km) northwest to Cape Reinga and North Cape, and bounded by the Tasman Sea (west) and the Pacific Ocean (east). The peninsula, no more than 50 mi wide, is generally lower than the rest of the island, rising to about 2,500 ft (760 m) in the volcanic Tutamoe and Maungataniwha ranges. The western shore is sandy and indented by the large but shallow Hokianga, Kaipara, and Manukau harbours; Ninety Mile Beach forms the coast of Aupori Peninsula, the island's northernmost extension. On the east, the shoreline is rocky, with good anchorages in Parengarenga and Rangaunu harbours, Doubtless Bay, Bay of Islands, Bream Bay, Hauraki Gulf, and Waitemata Harbour.

Despite early European settlement and post-World War II agricultural advancement, the peninsula is relatively underdeveloped. Livestock is raised, and towns, with the exception of Whangarei, are small. Maoris constitute a large proportion of the peninsula's population.
35°30′ S, 174°00′ E

·area and population table **13**:47

North Battleford, city, west central Saskatchewan, Canada, on the North Saskatchewan River, opposite Battleford and the mouth of the Battle River. Originating as a station on the Canadian National Railway, when the line bypassed the older settlement of Battleford (*q.v.*), the city grew to become an important railroad divisional point overshadowing its neighbour in size and commercial importance. North Battleford is now the distributing centre of northwestern Saskatchewan and the heart of a grain-growing and ranching area. Economic activities include grain storage, lumbering, tanning, and the manufacture of animal feed, cement blocks, and processed wood. Outside the city is the Western Development Museum. Indian reservations are nearby. Inc. village, 1905; town, 1906; city, 1913. Pop. (1971) 12,698.
52°47′ N, 108°17′ W
·map, Canada **3**:716

North Bay, city, seat of Nipissing District, southeastern Ontario, Canada. Named for its location on the north bay of Lake Nipissing, the city originated as a rail yard on the Canadian Pacific Railway in 1882. Now the southern terminus and head office of the Ontario Northland Railway and a major station on two transcontinental lines, North Bay has become an important wholesale- and retail-distributing centre and a popular summer resort 180 mi (290 km) north of Toronto. Industries include lumbering, dairying, fur processing, publishing, and the manufacture of mining machinery. It is the site of a large jet air base, Canada's first missile base, and several small collegiate institutions. Inc. 1925. Pop. (1971) 49,187.
46°19′ N, 79°28′ W
·map, Canada **3**:717

North Bend, city, Coos County, Oregon, U.S., on a peninsula jutting into Coos Bay a few miles inland from the Pacific, in the shadow of the Coast Ranges and adjacent to the city of Coos Bay (a major lumber-shipping port). Settled in 1853 by the Lockhart family and known as Yarrow, it was renamed for the bend in the bay. Its economy is oriented toward timber (paper, paperboard, plywood), augmented by fishing and tourism. It is the site of the Pony Slough Bird Sanctuary and the Coos-Curry Historical Museum. Inc. 1903. Pop. (1980) 9,779.
43°24′ N, 124°14′ W

North Berwick, ancient royal burgh (chartered town) and popular holiday resort, county of East Lothian, Scotland, at the south entrance to the North Sea inlet known as the Firth of Forth. North Berwick Law, a conical volcanic hill (613 ft [187 m]), rises steeply behind the town 1 mi to the south. The community is well known in Scotland as a golfing and holiday resort and now serves to some extent as a commuter suburb for Edinburgh, the Scottish capital (23 mi southwest). There are ruins of a 12th-century church and monastery. Pop. (1973 est.) 4,317.
56°04′ N, 2°44′ W
·map, United Kingdom **18**:866

North Bohemia, Czech SEVEROČESKÝ, region, Czechoslovakia.
·area and population table **5**:415
·map, Czechoslovakia **5**:413

North Borneo (Malaysia): *see* Sabah.

North Brabant (The Netherlands): *see* Noord-Brabant.

Northbrook, Thomas George Baring, 1st earl of (b. Jan. 22, 1826, London—d. Nov. 15, 1904, Stratton Park, Hampshire), statesman and viceroy of India, who entered political life as an aristocratic Whig and became a proponent of free trade and a liberal of the school of Gladstone.

The son of Sir Francis Baring, afterward 1st Lord Northbrook, who was chancellor of the Exchequer and first lord of the Admiralty, Thomas Baring, after education at Christ Church, Oxford, served as private secretary to several officials and became Liberal member of Parliament for Falmouth and Penryn (1857–66). He was a junior lord of the Admiralty (1857–58) and undersecretary for India (1859–61; 1868–72) and for war (1861–66).

After the assassination of Lord Mayo, viceroy of India, in 1872, Prime Minister Gladstone appointed Baring to succeed him. Baring's general policy was to take off taxes, reduce legislation, and give the land rest. A believer in free trade, he abolished most export duties and reduced import duties. In the Bengal famine of 1874 he refused to stop exporting grain but increased the importation of rice; the Sone Canal and North Bengal railway were sanctioned as relief works. He had the Gaekwar of Baroda tried for an attempt on the life of a resident and deposed for misgovernment; Baroda was given to a kinsman and feudatories saw that fears of annexation were groundless. Finding himself repeatedly in disagreement with the secretary of state for India, Lord Salisbury, over matters of policy, Baring resigned in 1876. A monument placed by him at Lucknow honours Indian defenders of the residency there, and his general rapport with Indians is represented by their erection of a statue of him in Calcutta and his founding of the Northbrook Indian Club in London.

He was made earl of Northbrook in 1876 and served as first lord of the Admiralty (1880–85), during which time he was sent on a special mission to Egypt (August–November 1884) to inquire into financial problems. He parted decisively from Gladstone on the Irish question in 1886 and thereafter defended the union against Home Rule.
·Indian colonial history **9**:410c

North Cāchār Hills, district, southeastern Assam state, northeastern India. It occupies an area of 1,888 sq mi (4,890 sq km) and is coextensive with the North Cāchār Hills region. The district headquarters is at Haflong. The growing of rice, cotton, sugarcane, tobacco, and silk is important. Pop. (1971) 76,047.
·Assam, physiography and economy **2**:207g

North Canadian River, main tributary of the Canadian River (*q.v.*), rises in a high plateau in Union County, New Mexico, U.S., and flows east through the Texas and Oklahoma Panhandle past Oklahoma City, joining the Canadian River in Eufaula Reservoir, below Eufaula, Okla. The river is 843 mi (1,357 km) long and drains 14,290 sq mi (37,011 sq km). Above the mouth of Wolf Creek, one of its tributaries, the North Canadian is sometimes known as Beaver River. Irrigation lakes are impounded by Canton Dam (1948) on the main stream in Oklahoma and by Fort Supply Dam (1942) on Wolf Creek.
35°17′ N, 95°31′ W
·map, United States **18**:908

North Canton, city, Stark County, immediately north of Canton, east central Ohio, U.S. It was laid out in 1831 as the first village in Plain Township. As most of its residents were of predominantly German ancestry, it was called New Berlin. The Hoover tannery (forerunner of the electrical appliance company, now the city's largest industry) was established there in 1873. William H. Hoover became the first mayor when the village was incorporated in 1905. In 1918, because of anti-German sentiment, it was renamed North Canton. In 1961 the community achieved city status. Pop. (1980) 14,228.
40°53′ N, 81°24′ W

North Cape, New Zealand, the northernmost point of North Island.
34°25′ S, 173°03′ E
·map, New Zealand **13**:45

North Cape Current, warm oceanic surface current, a branch of the Norway Current (*q.v.*) that flows eastward from the Norwegian Sea of the North Atlantic Ocean into the Barents Sea of the Arctic Ocean.
·discovery, currents, and nutrients **2**:721h
·ocean current systems diagram **13**:438

North Carolina 13:230, southeastern state of the U.S. and one of the original 13 states. Occupying an area of 52,586 sq mi (136,198 sq km), it is bounded by Virginia (north), by Tennessee (west), by South Carolina and Georgia (south), and by the Atlantic Ocean (east). Its capital is Raleigh. Pop. (1980) 5,874,429.

The text article covers the state's history, natural and human landscape, people, economy, administration and social conditions, cultural life, and prospects.

REFERENCES in other text articles:
·Appalachian geology, history, and ecology **1**:1016a
·area and population, table 1 **18**:927
·colonial political control and economic orientation **18**:949h; maps
·Jackson's native state controversy **10**:1c
·map, United States **18**:909
·nursing legislation **13**:398h
·pre-Revolution political demands **18**:954h
·soil hygroscopic properties **2**:1042d
·Southern cultural origin **18**:924e

North Central Hills, hilly upland region of east central and northern Mississippi, U.S. Its poor red clay and sandy soils support some forestry but prevent commercial agriculture.
32°45′ N, 89°10′ W
·soils and economy **12**:277b

North Central Province, Sri Lanka, lies inland and comprises a rolling, jungle-covered terrain of 4,140 sq mi (10,723 sq km), with isolated hills and peaks. The capital is Anuradhapura. Wholly in Sri Lanka's lowland zone, the province has a climate characterized by the seasonal alternation of rains and drought brought on by shifting monsoon winds.

North Central Province's boundaries approximate those of the Rajarata (King's Country) of the ancient Sinhalese, whose capitals, Anuradhapura and Polonnaruwa (*qq.v.*), are the province's two largest towns. The Sinhalese built extensive irrigation works, many of which have been restored to working order to help improve the province's economy; other archaeological sites are scattered over the province. Many of the people practice shifting cultivation in the forests, while others grow rice under irrigation. The province is served by road and rail networks. Pop. (1972 est.) 513,000, mainly Sinhalese.

North-Central State, administrative division of Nigeria (since 1967) comprising Zaria and Katsina provinces (*qq.v.*). Its savanna area of 27,108 sq mi (70,210 sq km) includes the emirates of Zaria, Katsina, and Daura (*qq.v.*) and Jemaa (*q.v.*) division. Much of its southern part suffered greatly from Hausa and Fulani slave raids, and many walled settlements remain in the vicinity of Zaria. Almost all of the state's present Hausa and Fulani inhabitants are Muslims; in the south, however, there are about 30 different pagan tribal groups, of which the largest is the Gbari.

North-Central State is Nigeria's leading producer of cotton for export and a major exporter of peanuts (groundnuts). Other cash export crops include shea nuts, ginger, and peppers; vegetables grown in the riverine *fadamas* (swampy floodplains), brown sugar processed locally from sugarcane, onions, and soybeans are trucked to other parts of the country. Tobacco is a major cash crop around Zaria (where cigarettes are manufactured), and guinea corn is utilized by a brewery in Kaduna. Guinea corn and millet are the staple foods. Cattle, goats, chickens, guinea fowl, and sheep are raised, and hides and skins are tanned for export.

Modern industry is concentrated in Kaduna (*q.v.*), the state capital and Nigeria's leading textile manufacturer, and in Zaria, the state's largest city. Besides cloth and cigarettes, the

state is noted for cosmetics, furniture, and aluminum products. Traditional crafts, especially cotton weaving and dyeing (with locally grown indigo), leather processing, raffia weaving, and pottery designing (notably among the Gbari), also retain considerable economic importance. The ancient practice of tin mining continues in the southern part of Zaria Province near Kafanchan (*q.v.*) on the western edge of the Jos Plateau. The Mairuwa Dam (completed in 1970) on the Sokoto River regulates water supply in the west central part of the state. Pop. (1971 est.) 4,964,119.
·area and population table **13**:91
·map, Nigeria **13**:86

North Channel, northern arm of Lake Huron in south central Ontario, Canada, lying between the Ontario mainland (north) and the islands of Manitoulin, Cockburn, and Drummond (south). It is 120 mi (193 km) long and 1 to 20 mi wide. The channel is connected on the west with St. Marys River (via St. Joseph Channel) and on the east with Georgian Bay. Many small islands lie within the channel. A road and rail bridge extends from the mainland to Great Cloche Island before crossing to Manitoulin Island at the town of Little Current.
46°02′ N, 82°50′ W
·map, United States **18**:908

North Channel, strait linking the Irish Sea with the North Atlantic Ocean and reaching a minimum width of 13 mi (21 km) between the

Along the North Channel coast, County Antrim, Ire.
George Brown—Shostal

Mull of Kintyre (Scotland) and Torr Head (Ireland). The channel includes Arran and Gigha islands; and the Scottish coast is deeply indented by the Sound of Jura, Kibrannan Sound, and the Firth of Forth.
55°10′ N, 5°40′ W
·location and width **9**:893c
·map, United Kingdom **18**:866
·Northern Ireland's link with Europe **13**:237f

North China Plain, also called YELLOW PLAIN, large alluvial, deltaic plain of eastern Asia, built into the sea by deposits of the Huang Ho (Yellow River) and a few other minor rivers. Covering an area of about 158,000 sq mi (409,500 sq km), it is one of the most densely populated areas on earth, and since earliest history has been a major focus of Chinese culture. To the south, it merges into the Yangtze plain.
36°30′ N, 115°50′ E
·drainage, navigation, and flood control **18**:397c
·Honan soils and drainage **8**:1053c
·Hopeh physical and vegetation features **8**:1068c
·Huang Ho basin features and flooding **8**:1128f; map 1129
·Kiangsu geography and drainage **10**:462e
·map, China **4**:262
·Peking's communications importance **14**:2e
·Shantung geology and geography **16**:650d
·soil and water table conditions **4**:261d
·Yangtze floods and flood waves **19**:1075a

North Chŏlla Province (South Korea): *see* Chŏlla-pukto.

North Ch'ungch'ŏng Province (South Korea): *see* Ch'ungch'ŏng-pukto.

Northcliffe, Alfred Charles William Harmsworth, 1st Viscount (b. July 15, 1865, Chapelizod, Dublin—d. Aug. 14, 1922, London), the most successful newspaper publisher in the history of the British press and a founder of popular modern journalism.

Northcliffe, 1918
Associated Newspapers Ltd.

After an impoverished childhood and a few attempts at making a quick fortune, young Harmsworth embarked on free-lance journalism as a contributor to popular papers, rose to editorial positions and, inspired by the success of *Tit-Bits*, a popular weekly of informative scraps, decided to start a similar paper of his own called *Answers to Correspondents*. After some difficulty in securing financial backing, he began publication, soon shortening the name to *Answers*. As the paper gained public favour he was joined by his brother Harold, whose financial ability and capacity for attracting advertising, combined with Alfred's genius for sensing the public taste, made it a success. *Answers* was followed by many other cheap popular periodicals, chief among them *Comic Cuts* ("Amusing Without Being Vulgar") and *Forget-Me-Not*, for the new reading public of women. These formed the basis for what became the Amalgamated Press (from 1959 Fleetway Press), the largest periodical publishing empire in the world.

In 1894 Harmsworth entered the newspaper field, purchasing the nearly bankrupt *London Evening News* and transforming it into a popular newspaper with brief news reports, a daily story, and a column for women. Within a year, circulation had grown to 160,000 copies, and profits were substantial. Conceiving the idea of a chain of halfpenny morning papers in the provinces, he bought two papers in Glasgow, merging them into the *Glasgow Daily Record*. He then decided to experiment with a popular national daily in London. The *Daily Mail*, first published on May 4, 1896, was a sensational success. Announced as "The penny newspaper for one halfpenny" and "The busy man's daily journal," it was exactly suited to the new reading public. All news stories and feature articles were kept short, and articles of interest to women, political and social gossip, and a serial story were made regular features. Although news headlines remained, at first, modest in size, far more were used than in any previous paper. With its first issue, the *Mail* established a world record in daily newspaper circulation, a lead it never lost while its founder lived.

Next he bought the *Weekly Dispatch* when it was nearly bankrupt and turned it (as the *Sunday Dispatch*) into the biggest selling Sunday paper in the country; founded the *Daily Mirror* (1903), which successfully exploited a new market as a picture paper, with a circulation rivalling that of the *Mail;* saved the *Observer* from extinction in 1905, the year in which he was made Baron Northcliffe; and in 1906 reached what he believed to be the pinnacle of his career by securing control of *The Times*.

Though Northcliffe wanted political power, the influence of his newspapers upon public affairs is generally said to have been smaller than he believed. Instead, he became a big businessman who changed the direction of much of the press away from its traditional informative and interpretative role to that of the commercial exploiter and entertainer of mass publics. In his later years, he became a victim of a megalomania that damaged his judgment and ultimately led to the breakdown that preceded his death.
·magazine publishing history **15**:249c
·newspaper publishing history **15**:241g

North College Hill, city, Hamilton County, extreme southwest Ohio, U.S., residential northern suburb of Cincinnati. The first settler, probably Gershom Gard, arrived in 1795. In 1916 three subdivisions in the "Clovernook" area east of Hamilton (Meyersville, Sunshine, and Clovernook) combined to become the village of North College Hill, so named for the now closed Farmers' College, founded there in 1846 by Freeman Grant Cary. It achieved city status in 1940. The Clovernook Home for the Blind (1903) is in the northern part of the city. Pop. (1980) 10,990.
39°12′ N, 84°32′ W

Northcote, James (b. Oct. 22, 1746, Plymouth, Eng.—d. July 13, 1831, London), English portraitist and historical painter, was a pupil and assistant (1771–75) of the eminent painter Sir Joshua Reynolds and studied in Rome (1777–80) before embarking on a career that made him wealthy. Perhaps his best painting is "The Emperor of Russia Rescuing a Boy from Drowning" (1820; London, Royal Society of Medicine). Northcote also fancied himself a writer, producing lives of Reynolds (1813) and of Titian (1830), and two series of fables illustrated from his own designs. The publication in 1826 of his pungent and cynical "conversations" by the essayist William Hazlitt, who assisted Northcote in literary matters, aroused a furore among his friends.
·Hogarth's style modification **3**:918b
·Jenner portrait illus. **10**:133

North Crimea Canal, part of the Dnepr River system, Ukrainian Soviet Socialist Republic.
·irrigation and water transportation **5**:925a

North Dakota **13**:234, west north central state of the U.S. Admitted to the Union in 1889 as the 39th state, it occupies an area of 70,665 sq mi (183,022 sq km). It is bounded by the Canadian provinces of Manitoba and Saskatchewan (north), by Minnesota (east), by South Dakota (south), and by Montana (west). Its capital is Bismarck. Pop. (1980) 652,695.

The text article, after a brief survey of North Dakota, covers its history, landscape, people, economy, administration, social conditions, and cultural life and institutions.

REFERENCES in other text articles:
·area and population, table 1 **18**:927
·county reorganization plans **8**:305c
·map, United States **18**:908
·Tertiary embayment and sediments **18**:153a

Northeast Administrative Commission, Manchurian administration established in 1953 to replace the Northeast People's Government. The Commission was abolished in 1954.
·Chinese administration in Manchuria **11**:439b

Northeast Administrative Region (China): *see* Manchuria.

Northeast Caucasian languages: *see* Nakho-Dagestanian languages.

Northeaster (1895; Metropolitan Museum of Art, N.Y.), painting by Winslow Homer.
·theme and technique **8**:1022d

northeaster, wind that blows from the northeast, especially a strong one. One example is the northeast storm that occurs along the New England and Canadian Atlantic

coast, mainly in winter, and is called nor'easter. Another is the black northeaster, which brings heavy rain to New Zealand and southeast Australia in summer.
·climatic element pathways **4**:719d

North-Eastern Province, Kenya, a semi-arid area of 48,997 sq mi (126,902 sq km) along the Somali frontier. The province supports a sparse, predominantly Somali, population whose main activity is the raising of cattle, hair sheep (for meat), and goats. The area was claimed as part of Greater Somalia by the government of Somalia in the early 1960s, and there were sporadic border clashes and internal Somali resistance until 1968, when the Somali government withdrew its claim. The provincial capital, Garissa, is on the southwestern boundary and is a way station along the main cattle route from the interior to the coast. Pop. (1976 est.) 266,000.
·area and population table **10**:426
·map, Kenya **10**:424

Northeastern school, group of Brazilian regional writers, emerging after 1930, whose fiction dealt primarily with the culture and social problems of Brazil's hinterland Northeast. Stimulated by the revival of nationalism led by the Modernists of the 1920s, the regionalists looked to the diverse ethnic and racial cultures of Brazil for inspiration. The remarkably gifted and dedicated group of prose writers of the Northeastern school included Gilberto Freyre, leader of the movement and author of the monumental *Casa Grande e Senzala* (1933; *The Masters and the Slaves*, 1946); José Lins do Rego (*q.v.*), who depicted the clash of the old and new ways of life in his classic "Sugarcane Cycle" (1932–36); and Jorge Amado, who gave Brazil some of America's best "proletarian" literature in such novels as *Cacau* (1933), *Jubiaba* (1935), and *Terras do Sem-Fim* (1944; *The Violent Land*, 1945). Also associated with the school were Graciliano Ramos, who explored the inner struggle of the individual; and Rachel de Queiroz (*q.v.*), who wrote of the bandits, religious mystics, and forgotten men who inhabit the hinterland.
·regional themes of major writers **10**:1241f

North-Eastern State, administrative division of Nigeria (since 1967) comprising Adamawa, Bauchi, Bornu, and Sardauna provinces (*qq.v.*). Nigeria's largest state (105,025 sq mi [272,015 sq km]), it occupies nearly one-third of the country but has only about 14 percent of its population. Vegetation ranges from wooded savanna in the south to thorn scrub and near desert in the north. Prominent relief features include the Bauchi and Bornu plains, the Gongola Basin, the upper Benue River Valley, the *firki* ("black cotton soil") swamps south and southwest of Lake Chad, the Biu and Mambila plateaus and the eastern part of the Jos Plateau, the Shebshi Mountains (which contain Mt. Dimlang [6,700 ft; 2,042 m], the highest point in Nigeria), and the western extensions of the Mandara and Alantika ranges. The Benue is the principal river, but the Gongola, 330 mi (531 km) long, the Komadugu Yobe (290 mi), and the Yedseram (220 mi) also drain considerable areas.

Most of the region was administered in the 19th century by either the Fulani empire of Sokoto or the Bornu kingdom of the Kanuri people, but there were scattered pockets of successful resistance to these Muslim states. Although all but Dikwa emirate, eastern and southern Adamawa, and eastern and northern Bornu had been incorporated into British Northern Nigeria by 1903, many of the Muslim emirs retained (with the aid of the British policy of indirect rule) considerable power throughout British colonial jurisdiction and after independence (1960). North-Eastern State now includes the emirates of Bornu, Bauchi, Adamawa, Dikwa, Gombe, Katagum, Misau, Jama'are, Muri, Fika, Biu, and Bedde (*qq.v.*).

Most of the state's diverse tribal population is engaged in farming and herding, but fishing is important both in the rivers and in Lake Chad. In addition to millet and guinea corn, the staples in the north, yams, maize (corn), and cassava are cultivated in the south. Peanuts (groundnuts) and cotton are universal cash crops and, with cattle, cow hides, goats and goatskins, sheep and sheepskins, finished leather products, crocodile skins, and gum arabic, constitute the state's main exports. The chief collecting points are the railroad centres of Bauchi, Gombe, Maiduguri, and Nguru (*qq.v.*) and the Benue ports of Jimeta and Numan (*qq.v.*). The national government has sponsored a fish research station since 1969 at Malamfatori near Lake Chad, and the state has established important wheat, rice, sugar, and tobacco cultivation projects. Tin and columbite mining are significant activities in Bauchi Province, and salt extraction is commercially important both along Lake Chad and near the town of Muri.

Maiduguri (called Yerwa in Bornu) is the state's capital and by far its largest city; but Kumo, Deba Habe (*qq.v.*), Gombe, Nguru, Bauchi, Jimeta, and Pindiga are also sizable market towns. Pop. (1971 est.) 9,439,896.
·area and population table **13**:91
·map, Nigeria **13**:86

northeast European local race, a subgroup, roughly corresponding to a breeding isolate in genetics, of the Caucasoid (European) geographical race. It comprises the populations of the northwestern Russian S.F.S.R., the Lithuanian S.S.R., the Estonian S.S.R., and Poland. The chief physical characteristics of the northeastern Europeans are pale skin, a high incidence of ash-blond hair and gray eyes, and a tendency toward brachycephaly, in which the head is relatively short from back to front. There is also a relatively high incidence of blood type B in the ABO system, which has been suggested as evidence of Mongoloid (Asiatic) genetic influences, although occurrence of other Mongoloid physical characteristics is not common enough to sustain the theory. *See also* local race; Caucasoid geographical race; Mongoloid geographical race.

North East Fife, district, Fife (*q.v.*) region, Scotland; created by the reorganization of 1975, it is part of the former county of Fife (*q.v.*). The district, area 291 sq mi (754 sq km), is bounded on the north by the Firth of Tay and faces the North Sea on the east. The fertile northern lowland and Eden valley are mainly arable; in the west the low mass of the Lomond Hills intrudes. Beef and dairy cattle are raised and cereal crops, potatoes, and sugar beets produced. The climate is cool and dry. Textiles are woven, and there is engineering and the refining of sugar beets at Cupar, which is the seat of the district authority. Pop. (1974 est.) 64,769.

North East Frontier Agency (India): *see* Arunachal Pradesh.

Northeast Passage, Russian SEVERNY MORSKOY PUT, or NORTHERN SEA ROUTE, the maritime route along the northern coast of the Eurasian landmass, lying principally off northern Soviet Siberia. Outstanding explorers of the area included Willem Barents and Henry Hudson. Under the auspices of the emperor Peter I the Great, Semyon Dezhnyov probably (1648) and Vitus Bering certainly (1728) sailed through the Bering Strait. Capt. James Cook, however, was the first to see both sides of the strait, and to demonstrate that Asia and North America are two separate continents (1778). After many attempts, the passage was first traversed by the Swedish explorer Baron Adolf Erik Nordenskiöld (*q.v.*) in 1878–79. Since the late 1960s the passage has been kept open in the summer months by Soviet icebreakers, aided by aerial observations and radar and sonar.
·European exploration and discovery **7**:1042c
·Hudson's early exploration purpose **8**:1130h

Northeast People's Government, Manchurian administration established by Kao Kang in 1949.
·Communist victory in Manchuria **11**:438h

Northeast Plain (Manchuria): *see* Manchurian Plain.

norther, strong and cold winter wind that blows from the north in Texas, the western Caribbean Sea, and Central America. It occurs when cold air moves southward from a high-pressure centre over the southern U.S. The name also is applied to a dry, dusty wind in California, a trade wind in Portugal, and a hot, dry desert wind in southeastern Australia.

Northern Andean cultures: *see* Central American and Northern Andean cultures.

Northern Baptist Convention: *see* American Baptist Convention.

Northern Chou (AD 557–581), Chinese kingdom centred at Ch'ang-an during the Six Dynasties (*q.v.*) period.
·unification of Sinicized states **4**:317e
·Wen Ti's power usurpation **17**:782e

Northern District, administrative subdivision, southeastern Papua New Guinea, southwest Pacific. The 8,600-sq-mi (22,300-sq-km) district rises from sea level to the 13,000-ft (4,000-m) peaks of the central Owen Stanley Range in as little as 60–70 mi (100–115 km). The swift Gira, Mambare, Kumusi, and Musa rivers drain the highlands and enter the Solomon Sea at the broad Holnicote, Dyke Ackland, and Collingwood bays. Popondetta is the administrative headquarters of the entire district and its central subdistrict. Other subdistrict centres are Tufi (southeast) and Kokoda (interior). The latter is linked to Popondetta and the coast by a road. Development and settlement of the district are relatively advanced, and rubber, cocoa, and coffee are exported. They replace the gold that was mined in the Yodda and Gira fields early in the 20th century. Occupied by the Japanese in 1942–43, the area was recaptured by Allied forces in a successful drive to halt Japanese occupation of Port Moresby. An eruption of Mt. Lamington (15 mi south of Popondetta) in 1951 destroyed the former headquarters, Higaturu, and killed 3,000 persons. Pop. (1973 est.) 63,037.

Northern Dvina River (Soviet Union): *see* Dvina River, Northern.

Northern Expedition, military campaign undertaken by the Kuomintang (KMT; Nationalist) government of Chiang Kai-shek in 1926 for the purpose of unifying the various warlord regimes into which China was then divided and expanding Kuomintang influence. Originally planned in 1922 by Sun Yat-sen, the founder of the Kuomintang, the expedition was delayed by shifting warlord alliances in the North and then by Sun's death in 1925. Finally, in 1926 Chiang Kai-shek, who had been appointed commander in chief of the KMT armies, began the expedition.

Although Chiang purged the Communists from the high leadership positions they had obtained under Sun, Communists continued to be members of the KMT and helped to mobilize the peasants and workers in the areas through which the KMT armies were to pass. The expedition advanced very rapidly. Within nine months the southern half of China was under KMT control. As a result the KMT leadership insisted that the KMT capital be moved from Canton in South China to the more centrally located city of Wu-han, where leftist influence was predominant.

The right wing of the KMT, supported by Shanghai financial interests, refused to make the move. On April 10, 1927, Chiang Kai-shek began to destroy all Communists in the areas under his control. But the left wing of the KMT maintained a government at Wu-han and continued its alliance with the Communists. The group began its own Northern Expedition, advancing into the north central province of Hunan, where it met with the warlord armies of the left-leaning Feng Yü-hsiang. Meanwhile, Chiang continued his Northern Expedition through the northeastern provinces of Anhwei and Shantung. Feng suddenly abandoned the left and allied with Chiang, leaving the Wu-han government forces surrounded.

Early in 1928 the left wing purged the Communists and reunited with Chiang. Meanwhile, the Northern Expedition continued north and in June 1928 captured Peking, thus unifying the country. Though the goals of the Northern Expedition were thus achieved, Chiang never fully secured the loyalties of local militarists and continually had to contend with uprisings from warlord factions. *Major ref.* **4**:371c
·Lin's first commands **10**:1014c

northern fur seal (*Callorhinus ursinus*): *see* fur seal.

Northern Hemisphere, the half of the Earth that lies north of the Equator.
·cyclone movement and ensuing weather **5**:392b
·Earth's magnetic field trends **6**:30f
·regional climatic variations **4**:717g
·wind pattern and seasonal climate change **19**:867g; illus.

Northern Ireland 13:237, one of the component countries of the United Kingdom, created a self-governing state by the Government of Ireland Act of 1920. Because of continuing civil strife, Northern Ireland's government and Parliament were suspended, and direct rule by the United Kingdom was imposed (1972). Often referred to as Ulster, although it includes only six of the nine counties that made up that historic province, it lies in the northeast part of the island of Ireland, on the extreme western fringe of the European continent. Its area, 5,452 sq mi (14,121 sq km), is about one-sixth of the whole island. The capital is Belfast. Pop. (1974 est.) 1,546,100.

The text article covers the land, people, economy, transportation, administration and social conditions, cultural life, and prospects of Northern Ireland. *See also* Britain and Ireland, history of.
54°40′ N, 6°45′ W

REFERENCES in other text articles:
·Christian denominational demography map **4**:459
·English dialect features **6**:884b
·federalism and political integration **7**:205c
·hereditary diseases and statistics **8**:809d
·map, United Kingdom **18**:866
·political relations with Ireland **9**:888h
·recent educational development **6**:378d
·rugby game, history, and playing styles **16**:5b
·United Kingdom physical and political geography **18**:864a; table 876

Northern Kiangsu Main Irrigation Canal (China): *see* Sü-pei Canal.

northern lights: *see* Aurora Borealis.

Northern Line Islands (Pacific Ocean): *see* Line Islands.

northern Mongoloid local race, a subgroup, roughly corresponding to a breeding isolate in genetics, of the Mongoloid (Asiatic) geographical race, comprising the populations of northern China, Mongolia, northeastern Siberia, Korea, and Japan. Characteristics of these peoples include: lightly pigmented, yellowish skin; coarse, thick, black head hair and little beard or body hair; short to medium skull length from back to front; high incidence of epicanthic eyefolds; long body compared to limb length; flat face with rather small nose; shovel-shaped incisors (*q.v.*); and a high incidence of blood type B in the ABO system. There is apparent adaptation to moderate to severe cold. *See also* local race; Mongoloid geographical race.
·physical traits illus. **15**:350
·racial characteristics and distribution **14**:845c

Korean man

By courtesy of the American Museum of Natural History, New York

Northern Norway (region): *see* Nord-Norge.

Northern Penner River (India): *see* Penner River.

Northern Plain (Haiti): *see* Nord, Plaine du.

Northern Province, administrative division, Sierra Leone. Pop. (1970 est.) 1,040,000.
·area and population table **16**:735

Northern Province, Sri Lanka, on the northern tip of the island-state, comprising low-lying, largely jungle-covered land on the main island, Ceylon, and the Jaffna Peninsula and nearby islands, on which most of the population lives. Its 3,429-sq-mi (8,881-sq-km) area is bounded on the east by the Bay of Bengal, and on the west by Palk Bay and the Gulf of Mannar. It is composed of the administrative districts of Jaffna, Mannar, and Vavuniya. The capital is Jaffna (*q.v.*).

The peninsula consists of coral limestone and has numerous lagoons; this part of the main island is underlain by crystalline rocks, with sandbars and lagoons along the eastern coast. The entire province lies within Sri Lanka's dry zone, with seasonal alternation between heavy rains and extreme drought.

The main island was settled in ancient times by people who left behind many irrigation works and inscriptions. The peninsula's original inhabitants were Sinhalese, but, beginning in the 2nd century BC, Indian Tamils settled there and along the coast of Ceylon. Ceylon Tamils now compose most of the population, with a few Sinhalese and Muslims. The economy is predominantly agricultural; rice, coconuts, tobacco, and other crops are grown. Fishing is carried on in Jaffna Lagoon and off Mannar Island, and there are pearl banks in the Gulf of Mannar. Pop. (1974 est.) 885,000.

Northern Province, Arabic ASH-SHAMĀLĪYAH MUDĪRĪYAH, The Sudan, is bordered by Egypt (north) and Libya (northwest). Formed in 1935 from Halfa, Dongola, and Berber provinces, its area of 184,000 sq mi (477,000 sq km) lies within historic Nubia (*q.v.*) and is traversed by the Nile River, which within it makes a giant S curve. Most of the province, containing ancient remains of Meroe and Napata (*qq.v.*), is uninhabited desert plateau, with sand dunes, sand sheets, and scattered hills.

The agricultural and settled area (only about 500 sq mi [1,300 sq km]) is restricted to the narrow strip of alluvial, riverine soil. Because of granitic rock formations, parts of the Nile are contained within narrow beds with cataracts and rapids, greatly limiting river transport. The climate is extremely hot in summer and unexpectedly cold in winter. Sandstorms are common from April to July. Annual rainfall ranges from 6 in. (150 mm) south of ʿAṭbarah to less than 1 in. in the extreme north. Vegetation reflects the desert conditions, although areas of acacia desert scrub occur in the south; along the Nile, growth is more plentiful.

The economy of the province is primarily agricultural, utilizing some irrigation. Main commercial crops are fruits (chiefly dates) and pulses; vegetables and cereals are grown as staples. Principal towns are ad-Dāmir (the capital), ʿAṭbarah, Barbar, and Shandī. Pop. (1972 est.) 1,220,000.
·extent, area, and population **17**:757c; table
·map, Sudan **17**:758

Northern Province, administrative division of Zambia, adjoins Tanzania and Lake Tanganyika to the north. Soils are generally poor; the chief crop is millet. Kasama is the capital. Pop. (1974 est.) 577,000.
·cultural description and current demographic information **19**:1132g; table 1133
·map, Zambia **19**:1131

Northern Range, hills, Trinidad and Tobago.
10°40′ N, 61°20′ W
·relief and notable features **18**:711h

Northern Region, administrative unit of Ghana between Upper Region (north) and Brong-Ahafo and Volta regions (south). Formed in 1960, it was formerly part of the Northern Territories protectorate. The region (area 27,175 sq mi [70,383 sq km]) belongs chiefly to the Volta Basin and its main affluents, the Black and White Voltas and the Oti. The Gambaga and Konkori scarps mark respectively the northern and western edges of the basin, which otherwise has a gently undulating surface with an average elevation of 1,000 ft (300 m). The climate is harsh, with seven months of rain (40–50 in. [1,000–1,270 mm]) and five months of severe drought. Vegetation is Guinea savanna woodland.

Savanna woodland near Tamale, Northern Region, Ghana

Eric Kohhman—Shostal

The main occupation is agriculture (grains, cassava, yams); shea butter is an important staple and export item. Regional development is based on potential raising of beef cattle and involves improved farming techniques, resettlement schemes, and the introduction of tobacco as a cash crop. Population density is low, and large settlements are few; most concentrations are found in the compound villages north of Tamale (*q.v.*), the regional capital and largest town. Yendi and Savelugu are also significant centres. Communications are generally poor. Pop. (1970 prelim.) 728,572.
·area and population table and map **8**:140
·map, Ghana **8**:138

Northern Region (Tanzania): *see* Arusha Region.

Northern Rhodesia (Africa): *see* Zambia.

Northern Sarkārs (India): *see* Sarkārs, Northern.

Northern Securities Co. v. United States (1904), case in which the Supreme Court upheld (5 to 4) the government's contention that the Sherman Anti-Trust Act (1890) regulated stock transactions as possible violations in restraint of interstate trade. The suit had been brought against a railroad cartel formed by J.P. Morgan, John D. Rockefeller, E.H. Harriman, and James Hill.
·Theodore Roosevelt suit and popular appeal **15**:1142h

Northern Tableland (Australia): *see* New England Range.

Northern Territory 13:242, sparsely populated region (area 520,280 sq mi [1,347,519 sq km]) of north central Australia, bounded by the Timor and Arafura seas (north), Western Australia (west), South Australia (south), and Queensland (east). It is inferior in political status to the states of the Commonwealth of Australia and is administered largely from the federal capital, Canberra. Pop. (1973 est.) 95,600.
The text article covers the territory's physical geography, vegetation and animal life, climate, patterns of settlement, people, economy, administration and social conditions, and cultural life and institutions.
REFERENCES in other text articles:
·aboriginal cultures distribution map **2**:425
·Australian regional administration change **2**:417d
·map, Australia **2**:400

Northern Virginia, Army of, a Confederate army during the U.S. Civil War.
·Lee and eastern Civil War tactics **4**:675f
·Lee's organization and leadership **10**:770h

Northern War, First (1655–60), the final stage of the struggle over the Polish–Swedish succession. Denmark, Brandenburg, and Austria sided with Poland against Sweden, but the Swedes successfully invaded both Poland and Denmark, forcing the Polish sovereigns to renounce their claim to the Swedish throne and acquiring Skåne from Denmark. For the Second Northern War, *see* Great Northern War.
·Frederick William's strategy **7**:709b
·John II Casimir of Poland **14**:645c
·Thirty Years' War military events **18**:341h
·Treaty of Oliva **6**:1091h

Northern Wei sculpture, Chinese sculpture dating from the Northern Wei period (386–534) of the Six Dynasties (220–589) and representing the first major influence of Buddhism upon China. Northern Wei sculpture, produced in northern territory that was occupied and ruled by foreign invaders and that was quick to respond to Buddhism, is distinct from the more traditional indigenous art produced in the south, which was still ruled by native Chinese dynasties. Little Northern Wei sculpture survives from the period prior to 446–452, during which a major persecution of Buddhism was carried out. With surprising suddenness Buddhism was restored to favour and there followed a major period of Buddhist art. The art—consisting primarily of sculpture but also some wall painting and reflecting various iconographic types, with simple images of the Buddha predominating—may be divided into two major periods: the first from immediately following the persecution to 494, when the capital of the Northern Wei was moved from the northern city of P'ing-ch'eng (the present Ta-t'ung, Shansi Province) to the ancient centre of Chinese civilization, Lo-yang (Honan Province); and the second from 494 to the end of the Northern Wei period. The style of the first period is a curious amalgam of foreign influences that are ultimately traceable to the Buddhist art of India, which emphasizes the heavy stylization of blocky volumes, giving a certain naïve and archaic quality to the figures (*see* Yün-kang caves). While that style is found later, it ultimately lost out to an entirely different, Chinese, or Lung-men, style, which clothes the

Stone sculpture of the *bodhisattva* Maitreya, *c.* AD 530, Northern Wei dynasty; in the Museum of Fine Arts, Boston

By courtesy of the Museum of Fine Arts, Boston, gift of Denman W. Ross in memory of Okakura Kakuzo

Buddha in the costume of the Chinese scholar and stylistically emphasizes a svelte and sinuous cascade of drapery falling over an increasingly flattened figure (*see* Lung-men caves).
·art of the Six Dynasties **19**:184e

north-facing slope, hillside surface or plane that slopes down toward the north. In middle latitudes of the Northern Hemisphere, north-facing slopes receive less solar radiation than all other slopes except in midsummer. Thus, they are characterized by a relatively cool climate, with vegetation zones shifted downward; for example, pines found at elevations of 2,000 metres (7,000 feet) on south-facing slopes may cease to occur as low as 1,500 metres (5,000 feet) on north-facing slopes. During the winter half-year (September 23 to March 20) the Sun will not shine at all on north slopes inclined at an angle greater than the elevation angle of the Sun above the horizon at noon. In summer these same slopes will be shaded at noon but exposed to the Sun for a few hours in the morning and afternoon.

Northfield, city, Rice County, southeastern Minnesota, U.S., on the Cannon River, in a mixed-farming area, specializing in Holstein cattle. Founded by John W. North in 1855, it soon became the home of Carleton (1866) and St. Olaf (1874) colleges and the Laura Baker School for Backward Children (1897). Flour milling was the basic industry until the 1880s. Diversified manufactures now include components for Echo satellites. An annual festival, "The Defeat of Jesse James Days," recalls how local citizens foiled a bank robbery attempt by the James–Younger brothers' gang (1876). Inc. village, 1871; city, 1875. Pop. (1980) 12,562.
44°27′ N, 93°09′ W
·map, United States **18**:909

North Frisian Islands, German NORDFRIESISCHE INSELN, Danish NORDFRISISKE ØER, part of the Frisian Islands (*q.v.*), which lie in the North Sea just off the coast of northern Europe. They are divided between West Germany and Denmark.
54°50′ N, 8°12′ E
·map, Federal Republic of Germany **8**:47

North German Confederation, German NORDDEUTSCHER BUND, union of the German states north of the Main River formed in 1867 under Prussian hegemony after Prussia's victory over Austria in the Seven Weeks' War (1866). Berlin was its capital, the king of Prussia was its president, and the Prussian chancellor was also its chancellor. Its constitution served as a model for that of the German Empire, with which it merged in 1871.
·Bismarck and political unification **8**:111e

North Germanic languages: *see* Scandinavian languages.

North German Romantics, writers of the early 19th century, heirs to the Romantic tradition as it had developed at Heidelberg (*c.* 1804–*c.* 1809), preparing the way for a rising against Napoleon. Among them was Prussia's greatest dramatist, Heinrich von Kleist.
·German literature of the 19th century **10**:1196b

North Hamgyŏng Province (North Korea): *see* Hamgyŏng-pukto.

North Haven, urban town (township), just northeast of New Haven, New Haven County, southern Connecticut, U.S., on the Quinnipiac River. First settled *c.* 1650 by William Bradley, it became a parish in 1716 and in 1786 was separated from New Haven and incorporated as a town. Several 18th-century houses, including the parsonage of Benjamin Trumbull (pastor 1760–1820), remain. Brickmaking and shipbuilding were early industries. Manufactures are now well diversified and include aircraft engine parts, chemicals, machinery, and tools. The Cedar Hill classification yard of the New York, New Haven, and Hartford Railroad (now Penn Central) is located almost entirely in the town. Pop. (1980) 22,080.
41°23′ N, 72°52′ W

North Hempstead, town (township), Nassau County, New York, U.S., occupies 56 sq mi (145 sq km) on western Long Island and includes 30 incorporated villages and several large unincorporated communities.
During the American Revolution numerous British units were stationed in the area. Hessian officers were quartered in the Roslyn home of Hendrick Onderdonck (later called the Washington Tavern, to commemorate George Washington's visit, April 24, 1790). North Hempstead separated from Hempstead (*q.v.*) in 1784 and held its first town meeting at Searingtown. It remained agrarian during the 18th century, and an active shipping trade was conducted through its harbours and bays. Sands Point Lighthouse (1806) on Cow Neck remains a conspicuous landmark. Fine examples of colonial mills survive at Plandome, Roslyn, and Saddle Rock. The pre-Revolutionary house of Samuel Latham Mitchill (1764–1831) is at Manhasset.
Urban development was fostered by the Long Island Rail Road, which reached Mineola (1837), Roslyn (1864), and Port Washington (1898). Millionaires built large estates such as the Mackay estate at Roslyn and the Phipps and C.V. Whitney estates at Old Westbury. Many men of letters became residents of the town. Cedarmere, home of the nature poet William Cullen Bryant, is preserved at Roslyn. Other notable residents included Frances Hodgson Burnett (at Plandome), F. Scott Fitzgerald (Great Neck), George M. Cohan (Kings Point), and John Philip Sousa (Port Washington).
The U.S. Merchant Marine Academy was established on the former estate of Walter Chrysler at Kings Point in 1942. During World War II many new industries were brought into the town, notably aircraft engineering at Port Washington.
The county charter of 1936 preserved the rights of existing incorporated villages but denied unincorporated communities the right to

incorporate. The larger villages are Great Neck (incorporated 1921), Mineola (1906), Westbury (1932; *qq.v.*), and East Hills (1931). Unincorporated communities include Manhasset, North New Hyde Park, and Port Washington (*q.v.*). Pop. (1950) 142,613; (1980) 218,624.
40°48′ N, 73°44′ W

North Holland (The Netherlands): *see* Noord-Holland.

North Hwanghae Province (North Korea): *see* Hwanghae-pukto.

North Indian temple architecture, the style spread throughout the northern part of the country and as far south as Bijāpur district, characterized by its distinctive *śikhara*, or tower, with a curvilinear outline. The style is sometimes referred to as Nāgara, a type of temple mentioned in the *Śilpa-śāstras* (traditional canons of architecture), but exact correlation of the *Śilpa-śāstra* terms with extant architecture has not yet been established.

Galaganātha temple at Pattadakal, Mysore, India, North Indian style, early 8th century AD
P. Chandra

The typical Hindu temple in north India, on plan, consists of a small square-shaped sanctuary (called the *garbhagṛha*, or "womb-room") housing the main image, preceded by one or more adjoining *maṇḍapa*s (porches or halls), which are connected to the sanctum by an open or closed vestibule (*antarāla*). The entrance doorway of the sanctum is usually richly decorated with figures of river goddesses and bands of floral, figural, and geometric ornamentation. An ambulatory is sometimes provided around the sanctum. Above the main sanctuary rises a tower (the *śikhara*), which is curvilinear in outline, and smaller rectilinear *śikharas* of the *phāmsanā* type frequently top the *maṇḍapa*s as well. The whole may be raised on a terrace (*jagati*) with attendant shrines at the corners. If a temple is dedicated to the god Śiva, the figure of the bull Nandi, the god's mount, invariably faces the sanctum, and, if dedicated to the god Viṣṇu, standards (*dhvaja-stambha*) may be set up in front of the temple.

The centre of each side of the square sanctum is subjected to a gradated series of projections, creating a characteristic cruciform plan. The exterior walls are usually decorated with sculptures of mythological and semidivine figures, with the main images of the deities placed in niches carved on the main projections. The interior is also frequently richly carved, particularly the coffered ceilings, which are supported by pillars of varying design.

That the prototype of the North Indian temple already existed in the 6th century can be seen in surviving temples such as the Viṣṇu temple at Deogarh in Madhya Pradesh, which has a small stunted *śikhara* over the sanctuary. The style fully emerged in the 8th century and developed distinct regional variations in Orissa, central India, Rājasthān, and Gujarāt. A classification of North Indian temples is generally made on the basis of *śikhara* types, such as the rectilinear *phāmsanā*, the curvilinear *latina*, and its two variations, the *śekharī* and the *bhūmija* (*see* śikhara).

One typical form of the North Indian style is seen in the early temples at Orissa, such as the graceful 8th-century Paraśurāmeśvara temple at Bhuvaneśvara, a city that was a great centre of temple building activity. From the 10th century a characteristic Oriya style developed which exhibited a greater elevation of the wall and a more elaborate spire. The Liṅgarāja temple at Bhuvaneśvara, of the 11th century, is an example of the Oriya style in its fullest development. The Sun Temple at Konārak, the sanctum of which is badly damaged, is the largest and perhaps the most famous Oriya temple.

A development from the simpler to a more elevated and elaborate style is evident in central India, except that the *śekharī* type of superstructure, with multiple tenets, is more favoured from the 10th century onward. Interiors and pillars are more richly carved than in Orissa. The central Indian style in its most developed form makes its appearance at Khajurāho, as seen in the Kaṇḍārya Mahādeva temple, *c.* 11th century. Here an overall effect of harmony and majesty is maintained despite the exuberance of sculpture on the outer walls; the rich profusion of miniature shrines on the *śekharī* spire reinforces the ascending movement considerably.

Large numbers of temples are preserved in Gujarāt, but most of them have been badly damaged. The early-11th-century Sun Temple at Modhera is one of the finest.

·Buddhist influence on Hindu style **8**:913b
·regional styles' development **17**:175c
·style characteristics, illus., **17**:South Asian Peoples, Arts of, Plates IV and V

North Island, smaller (44,281 sq mi) of the two principal islands of New Zealand in the South Pacific Ocean, separated from South Island by Cook Strait. It rises to a central mountain range (a continuation of the South Island range), which reaches its highest at volcanic Mt. Ruapehu (9,175 ft [2,797 m]). As the mountains lie toward the east coast (thus with increasing westerly exposure to rain-bearing winds), rainfall, with a winter maximum, tends to be more evenly distributed than it is on South Island. North Island is gaining an increasingly larger proportion of the national population, concentrated in the vicinity of the major urban areas, Auckland (north) and Wellington (south), the capital.
39°00′ S, 176°00′ E

·geography and culture **13**:43d
·kuari gum tapping and government protection **5**:3b
·map, New Zealand **13**:44

North Island, island and administrative division, Seychelles.

·Seychelles area and population table **16**:611

North Kanara, district, western Mysore state, southern India, paralleled by the Western Ghāts (east) and a coastal strip on the Arabian Sea (west). Formerly called Kanara, it was part of Bombay Presidency until 1956. Its area (3,965 sq mi [10,269 sq km]) is drained by the Kālīnada, Gangavāli, Tadri, and Sharavati rivers, the latter forming Jog Falls (*q.v.*) on the southern border. Rice milling and betel and pepper farming are the main occupations. Coir fibre is processed from coconut from the numerous plantations. There are saltworks and deposits of manganese. Teak, bamboo, and blackwood are obtained from the northern forests. The Dandeli Sanctuary (1949) is a refuge for the tiger, panther, sloth bear, and elephant. Fishing ports include Kārwār (the district headquarters), Honāvar, Belekere, Tadri, and Kumta. Sirsi and Haliyāl are the inland population centres. Pop. (1971 prelim.) 848,604.

North Kansas City, in Clay County, Missouri, U.S., lies across the Missouri River north of Kansas City. Founded in 1912 by the North Kansas City Development Company, it occupies a 4-sq-mi (10-sq-km) area and is highly industrialized, with a moderate resident population (5,183 in 1970) and a working population of more than 50,000. Manufactures include paints and varnishes, cans and containers, paper, plastic products, chemicals, and textiles. There also are printing companies, flour mills, and factories for corn (maize) products. Inc. village, 1912; city, 1924. Pop. (1980) 4,507.
39°08′ N, 94°34′ W

North Karelia (Finland): *see* Pohjois-Karjala.

North Kazakhstan (Kasakh S.S.R.): *see* Severo-Kazakhstan.

North Kingstown, town (township), south central Rhode Island, U.S., on Narragansett Bay on the Hunt and Potowomut rivers. The area, settled in 1641 and originally called Kings Towne, was incorporated in 1674. In 1723 it was divided into North and South Kingstown. North Kingstown includes the villages of Allenton, Davisville, Hamilton, Lafayette, Quonset Point, Saunderstown, Slocum, and Wickford (the administrative centre) and has developed as a resort area.

Quonset Point is the site of one of the world's largest naval air stations, and Davisville has the naval construction battalion centre, home of the Atlantic Seabees. Wickford is the site of the Old Narragansett Church (1707) and of Smith's Castle at Cocumscussoc (*c.* 1678), used as a rendezvous for troops that fought in the Great Swamp Fight (1675; a battle in King Philip's [Indian] War). At Saunderstown the birthplace of Gilbert Stuart, portraitist and creator of the most popular image of George Washington, has been restored; and near the same village the Silas Casey Farm (*c.* 1750) is maintained as a typical New England farmhouse. Lafayette has state fish hatcheries. Pop. (1980) 21,938.
41°34′ N, 71°27′ W

North Korea: *see* Korea, North.

North Kyŏngsang Province (South Korea): *see* Kyŏngsang-pukto.

Northland (New Zealand): *see* North Auckland Peninsula.

North Las Vegas, city and suburb of Las Vegas, Clark County, southeastern Nevada, U.S. Settled in the early 1920s by pioneers attracted by the water supply and originally named Vegas Verde, it was renamed North Las Vegas in 1932. Its first period of expansion began with the construction of Hoover Dam (completed 1936). The next period of growth came with World War II and the establishment nearby of Nellis Air Force Base and the Army Gunnery School (1941). Tourism (attracted by the legalized gambling) is important to the economy. Light industries include the manufacture of metals and electrical products, fertilizer, pumps, and slot machines. Inc. 1946. Pop. (1980) 42,739.
36°12′ N, 115°07′ W

North Little Rock, city, Pulaski County, central Arkansas, U.S., on the Arkansas River opposite Little Rock. It was settled in 1812 as DeCantillon, became Huntersville in 1853, and was renamed Argenta for the Hotel Argenta, built in the late 1850s. The community developed after the arrival of the Memphis and Little Rock Railroad in 1853 and now contains the Missouri Pacific's freight classification yards and maintenance shops. Annexed by the city of Little Rock in 1891, Argenta was separately incorporated as a town in 1901 and renamed North Little Rock. It became a city in 1904 and absorbed the town of Levy (north) in 1946.

It is the home of Shorter College (1886; African Methodist Episcopal affiliated). Camp Joseph T. Robinson military reservation (1917; formerly Camp Pike) and Conway Lake are to the north. Pop. (1980) 64,419.
34°46′ N, 92°14′ W

North Magnetic Pole, the point at which the northern end of the axis of the Earth's magnetic field intersects the Earth's surface. Located on Prince of Wales Island, Canada, in the Arctic Ocean, it lies at a considerable distance from the geographic North Pole. Its precise location gradually changes; in 1971 its coordinates were 76°12′ N, 101°00′ W. *See* magnetic pole.

North Manchester, town, Wabash County, north central Indiana, U.S., on the Eel River. The town was founded in 1834 after the Treaty of Paradise Springs (1826) opened the area to settlement. It is now an agricultural (livestock, grain) and light manufacturing (book bindings, iron castings) centre and the seat of Manchester College (1889), operated by the Church of the Brethren. Thomas R. Marshall, U.S. vice president under Woodrow Wilson, was born there. Inc. 1874. Pop. (1980) 5,998.
41°00′ N, 85°46′ W

North Mashonaland, province, northern Rhodesia, bordered by Zambia (northwest) and Mozambique (northeast). The capital is Sinoia, on the Beira-Lusaka road, which crosses the province (northwest to southeast). Railroads connect the province with Salisbury, other parts of Rhodesia, and surrounding countries. Agricultural products include maize (corn), wheat, tobacco, groundnuts (peanuts), cotton, and cattle. Gold and nickel are found.
·area and population table **15**:819
·map, Rhodesia **15**:816

North Matabeleland, province, western Rhodesia, bordered by Botswana (west and southwest); the Zambezi River and Lake Kariba mark the border with Zambia to the north. The capital is Bulawayo, a road and rail centre. Wankie and Victoria Falls National Park are in the western part of the province. Agricultural products include cattle and tobacco; gold, coal, and tin are found.
·area and population table **15**:819
·map, Rhodesia **15**:816

Northmen (Norsemen): *see* Vikings; Normans.

North Mexican Indian cultures **13**:245, the cultures of the surviving Indians in the area of Mexico north of central Mexico and reaching to the U.S. border. Today in the north only the northern and western states of Baja California, Sonora, Sinaloa, Nayarit, Jalisco, Chihuahua, and Durango retain Indian populations.

The text article gives a listing of the main extant Indian peoples of the area, describes the traditional culture patterns as influenced by European contact, and covers the evolution of the cultures today.

REFERENCES in other text articles:
·cultural development by area **12**:164f
·Yaqui deer dance illus. **1**:671

North Miami, city, Dade County, southern Florida, U.S., northern suburb of Miami. The original settlement on Arch Creek was incorporated in 1926 as the Town of Miami Shores, which was renamed North Miami in 1931. In the early 1930s its boundaries were greatly reduced when large portions of land such as Biscayne Gardens, North Miami Beach, and Graves tract seceded. Miami Shores, adjacent to the south, was separately incorporated in 1932. North Miami grew rapidly after its incorporation as a city in 1952 with the development of Keystone Point (1,500 ft of bay frontage). Economic activities focus on tourism, Studio City (a motion-picture complex), and light manufacturing. Pop. (1980) 42,566.
25°53′ N, 80°10′ W

North Miami Beach, city, Dade County, south Florida, U.S., on the Atlantic coast, just north of Miami Beach. A part of greater Miami, it is primarily residential with resort facilities. It originated as the Town of Fulford, founded by Capt. William H. Fulford, which was incorporated in 1926. In order to survive the Depression, Fulford in 1931 merged with Fulford-by-the-Sea, and the united community was incorporated as the City of North Miami Beach. After World War II the city experienced a building boom and rapid growth. On its western edge is an industrial park, and on its eastern boundary overlooking Biscayne Bay is the Interama (Interamerican Trade and Cultural Center), a permanent exposition divided into four main areas—cultural, festival, industrial, and international. Pop. (1940) 1,973; (1980) 36,481.
25°56′ N, 80°09′ W

North Minch (Scotland): *see* Minch, The.

North Moravia, Czech SEVEROMORAVSKÝ, administrative division, Czechoslovakia.
·area and population table **5**:415

North Okkalapa, town, Rangoon, Burma.
101°00′ E, 13°50′ N
·founding, location, and layout **15**:503g

North Olmsted, city, southwestern suburb of Cleveland, Cuyahoga County, northeastern Ohio, U.S. The land, part of the Connecticut Western Reserve, was originally deeded in 1807 to the heirs of Aaron Olmstead, Revolutionary War soldier and sea captain. The site was first settled (1815) as Kingston (later Lennox) by Capt. David Elijah Stearns and his family. A township was formed in 1826 and the community was renamed Olmsted in 1829 (through usage the "a" was dropped). Prechtel House in the Rocky River Reservation has pioneer relics. North Olmsted was separately incorporated as a village in 1908. After it achieved city status in 1950, its population grew rapidly. Though it is mainly residential, some light industries (printing, machine-tool manufacture) have been developed. Pop. (1950) 6,604; (1980) 36,486.
41°25′ N, 81°56′ W

North Pacific Current: *see* West Wind Drift.

North Pan River (China): *see* Pei-P'an Chiang.

North Platte, city, seat (1867) of Lincoln County, west central Nebraska, U.S., at the confluence of the North and South Platte rivers. Founded in 1866 on the Union Pacific Railroad (of which it became a division headquarters), it developed as a centre for the Nebraska Sandhills cattle industry and for the produce of the irrigated Platte Valley. A University of Nebraska agricultural experiment station and a state walleyed-pike fish hatchery

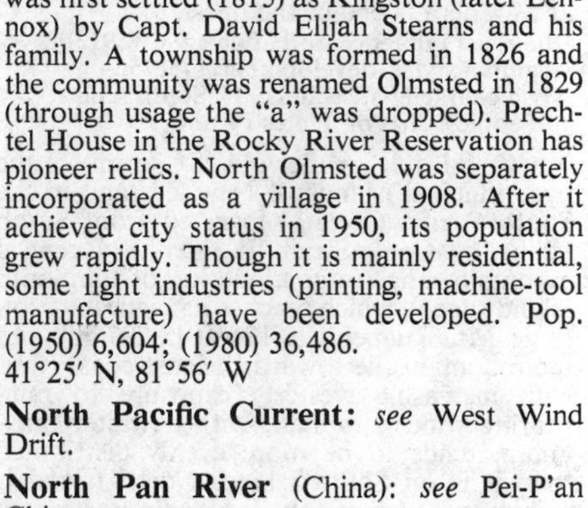

Scouts Rest Ranch home of Col. William F. Cody ("Buffalo Bill") in North Platte, Neb.
Porterfield-Chickering—Photo Researchers

are nearby. Scouts Rest Ranch, home for more than 30 years of Col. William F. ("Buffalo Bill") Cody, where he assembled his Wild West Show in 1884, is 4 mi (6 km) northwest. An annual rodeo is held each June. The Sioux Lookout (overlooking the old Oregon Trail), Fort McPherson National Cemetery, and a museum (with mementos of the West) are in the area. Local hydroelectric and irrigation projects provide several artificial lakes with recreational facilities, notably Lake Maloney. Inc. 1873. Pop. (1980) 24,479.
41°08′ N, 100°46′ W
·map, United States **18**:908

North Platte River, rises in several headstreams in the Medicine Bow and Park ranges and the Rabbit Ears Range of north central Colorado, U.S. It flows north into Wyoming, bends east-southeast at Casper, and flows into western Nebraska past Scottsbluff to North Platte city. There, after a 680-mi (1,094-km) course, it joins the South Platte River to form the Platte River (*q.v.*). In eastern Wyoming the North Platte Valley is 1–10 mi wide and 100–300 ft below the surrounding uplands. On the Wyoming–Nebraska boundary the river flows through Goshen Hole, where the valley has widened to 50 mi in places, and bordering bluffs are 400-ft high. The North Platte is part of a comprehensive, multipurpose (irrigation, power, flood-control) project of the Missouri River Basin. It has large reservoirs and dams (including Pathfinder, 1909; Guernsey, 1927; Seminoe, 1939; Alcova, 1938; Kingsley, 1941; Kortes, 1951; and Glendo, 1958). Its chief tributaries are the Sweetwater and Laramie rivers and Medicine Bow River.
41°15′ N, 100°45′ W
·map, United States **18**:908

North Polar Basin, vast, deep submarine trough on the floor of the Arctic Ocean. It is surrounded by the continental shelves of Eurasia, North America, and Greenland.
89°00′ N, 10°00′ E
·Atlantic ocean features **2**:295a
·Nansen's deep soundings **1**:1119d

north polar sequence, of 96 stars near the north celestial pole, used as standards of magnitude and colour by which other stars are measured. First proposed by the U.S. astronomer Edward Charles Pickering and in use from *c.* 1900, the system based on the north polar sequence has been largely superseded by the UBV (ultraviolet-blue-visual) system.
·astronomical photometry methods **14**:349b

North Pole, the northern end of the Earth's axis, lies in the Arctic Ocean, about 450 mi (725 km) north of Greenland. This geographic north pole does not coincide with the magnetic north pole, to which magnetic compasses point and which lies north-northwest of Boothia Peninsula (at about 76°20′ N, 101°00′ W in 1970); or with the geomagnetic north pole, the northern end of the earth's geomagnetic field (about 78°30′ N, 69°00′ W). The geographic pole, located at a point where the ocean is 13,410 ft (4,087 m) deep and covered with drifting pack-ice, experiences six months of complete sunlight and six months of total darkness each year. First reached by the U.S. explorers Robert E. Peary and Matthew Henson on sledge dog in 1909, it was reached (1929) by another U.S. explorer Richard E. Byrd (by airplane) and by the international team of Roald Amundsen, Lincoln Ellsworth, and Umberto Nobile (by dirigible) in 1926. Since then the north pole has been reached several times, including visits by the U.S. nuclear submarines "Nautilus" (1958) and "Skate" (1959).
·climate variation causes **4**:714h
·location in Upper Carboniferous **3**:857c
·magnetic field differences **6**:26h
·rock magnetism and polarity reversals **15**:945c; illus.
·world climates and their distribution **4**:727d

North Providence, urban town (urbanized township), Providence County, Rhode Island,

U.S., on Woonasquatucket River. It is primarily a residential suburb of Providence, from which it was separated in 1765. Centerdale village is its administrative centre. Inc. 1765. Pop. (1980) 29,188.
41°50′ N, 71°25′ W

North P'yŏngan Province (North Korea): *see* P'yŏngan-pukto.

North Rhine-Westphalia (West Germany): *see* Nordrhein-Westfalen.

North Ridgeville, city, Lorain County, northern Ohio, U.S. The site was first settled as Rootstown in 1810 by a group of farmers from Waterbury, Conn. Ridgeville Township, named for five local ridges (Butternut, Chestnut, Sugar, Center, and Stoney), was organized in 1813, and the first post office was opened in 1820. Gristmilling and sawmilling, butter manufacture, and cider and cheese making were early industries that lapsed by the turn of the century. The city is mainly residential, but some light manufactures developed after World War II. The township was incorporated as a village in 1958 and became a city in 1960. Growth was stimulated by the opening of the Ohio Turnpike (1955). Pop. (1980) 21,522.
41°23′ N, 82°01′ W

North River (China): *see* Pei Chiang.

Northrop, John Howard (b. July 5, 1891, Yonkers, N.Y.), biochemist who received (with James B. Sumner and Wendell M. Stanley) the Nobel Prize for Chemistry in 1946 for successfully crystallizing certain enzymes, proteins that speed the rate of specific chemical reactions occurring in living organisms. He was professor of bacteriology at the University of California, Berkeley (1949–59), and member of the Rockefeller Institute for Medical Research, New York City, from 1925 until his retirement in 1962. He conducted research during World War I on fermentation processes suitable for the industrial production of acetone and ethyl alcohol. This work led to a study of enzymes essential for digestion, respiration, and general life processes.

Demonstrating that enzymes obey chemical laws, he crystallized pepsin, a digestive enzyme present in gastric juice, in 1930 and found that it is a protein, ending a dispute concerning the chemical nature of enzymes. In 1938 he isolated the first bacterial virus.

Northrop also helped prepare in crystalline form pepsin's inactive precursor pepsinogen (converted to the active enzyme through a reaction with hydrochloric acid in the stomach), the pancreatic digestive enzymes trypsin and chymotrypsin, and their inactive precursors trypsinogen and chymotrypsinogen. His major work is *Crystalline Enzymes* (2nd ed., 1948), with M. Kunitz and R.M. Herriot.

Northrop, John Knudsen (b. Nov. 10, 1895, Newark, N.J.—d. Feb. 19, 1981, Glendale, Calif.), aircraft designer and an early advocate of all-metal airplane construction and the flying-wing airplane design. In 1927 he cofounded and became chief engineer of the Lockheed Aircraft Corporation, Los Angeles. While with Lockheed, he designed and built the Lockheed Vega monoplane, an advanced design that set many speed and endurance records. Northrop left Lockheed in 1928 to form the Avion Corporation, which developed a flying-wing design for an all-metal and a multicellular plane. Avion was bought by United Aircraft and Transport Corporation in 1930, the year Northrop built the Northrop Alpha. The Alpha pioneered in multicellular construction in commercial planes and was one of the first low-wing monoplanes.

Northrop left United in 1931 and formed the Northrop Corporation at El Segundo, Calif., the following year. This company supplied the Northrop Gamma and Delta commercial planes, the A-17 and A-17A attack planes, the Navy BT-1 dive bomber (forerunner of the

John Knudsen Northrop, 1949
By courtesy of the Northrop Corporation

Douglas Dauntless), and military craft for other countries. In 1937 Northrop Corporation became the El Segundo division of Douglas Aircraft Company.

Northrop founded Northrop Aircraft, Inc., in Hawthorne, Calif., in 1939, and was director until his retirement in 1952. Northrop Aircraft became Northrop Corporation in 1959. Among the company's military planes were the N3-PB seaplane, the P-61 Black Widow night fighter, the F-89 Scorpion jet and fighter, the XB-35 flying-wing bomber, and the YB-49, a jet-powered version of the XB-35. In 1942, Northrop founded the Northrop Institute of Technology, Inglewood, Calif.

North Saskatchewan River (Canada): *see* Saskatchewan River.

North Sea 13:249, northeastern arm of the Atlantic Ocean, extending between the British Isles (west) and the European continent (south and east). It is about 600 mi (1,000 km) long and 400 mi wide, and it covers an area of 220,000 sq mi (570,000 sq km).

The text article covers the North Sea's geologic history, physical environment, and resources and exploitation.

REFERENCES in other text articles:
·aquatic ecosystem classification **1**:1030c
·area, volume, and depth, table 1 **13**:484
·coastal destruction and flooding in Holland **4**:795f
maps
·Denmark **5**:583
·Europe **6**:1034
·The Netherlands **12**:1061
·United Kingdom **18**:866
·Netherlands land reclamation plan **8**:643a
·ocean–atmosphere interaction **19**:656d
·oscillation wave period and causes **13**:495a
·salt structure types, sizes, and origins **16**:198c
·tidal forces, predictions, and currents **18**:384h; illus. 385

North Sea Canal, waterway in The Netherlands that runs in an east-west direction between Amsterdam and IJmuiden on the North Sea. The canal, which is navigable by oceangoing vessels, is 14 mi (23 km) long, 49 ft (15 m) deep, and 771 ft (235 m) wide. Its construction between 1865 and 1876 made Amsterdam a major seaport. The sea-locks at IJmuiden were destroyed during World War II and were later rebuilt.
52°26′ N, 4°45′ E
·map, The Netherlands **12**:1061

North Sea Germanic languages, languages spoken by Germanic peoples along the coast of the North Sea before the 4th century AD; they are ancestral to the modern English and Frisian languages. The North Sea Germanic languages are often included with German and other Germanic languages in a West Germanic language subfamily.
·distinctive developments and influences on Netherlandic **8**:19e *passim* to 22a
·intra-Germanic relationships **8**:20e; illus. 24

North Siberian Lowland, Russian SEVERO-SIBIRSKAYA NIZMENNOST, east central Russian Soviet Federated Socialist Republic, low-lying region between the lower Yenisey River in the west and the lower Kolyma River in the east. To the south lies the Central Siberian Plateau, to the north the Byrranga Mountains of the Taymyr Peninsula, and, farther east, the Laptev Sea. The western part of the plain is sometimes known as the Taymyr Plain, and the portion east of the Lena River as the Yana-Indigirka and Kolyma plains. The lowland, which has an east–west extent of 1,850 mi (3,000 km) and a width of up to 375 mi (600 km), lies at 165–230 ft (50–70 m) above sea level and is composed of marine deposits, glacial drift, and marine sediments. There are frequent low ridges and hills. The plain is extremely swampy, and the vegetation is tundra or forest-tundra in character.
·location and features **17**:326a
·map, Soviet Union **17**:323

North Star: *see* Pole Star.

North Sydney, town, Cape Breton Island, eastern Nova Scotia, Canada, on Sydney Harbour, between Sydney and Sydney Mines. It is the eastern terminus of the Trans-Canada Highway and the Canadian National Railway and serves as a fishing, refuelling, and ship-repair port. It has ferry connections to Port aux Basques, Newfoundland, and is a base for shore and bank fishing fleets. Industries include coal mining, machine and foundry working, fish packing, and fish-oil refining. Inc. 1885. Pop. (1971) 8,604.
46°13′ N, 60°15′ W

North Tonawanda (New York, U.S.): *see* Tonawanda-North Tonawanda.

North Uist (Scotland): *see* Uist, North and South.

Northumberland, northernmost county of England, bounded north by Scotland, east by the North Sea, and west and south by Cumbria (until 1974 Cumberland), Tyne and Wear (until 1974 parts of Northumberland and Durham), and Durham. It consists of the six districts of Alnwick, Berwick-upon-Tweed, Blyth Valley, Castle Morpeth, Tynedale, and Wansbeck, with an area of 2,019 sq mi (5,229 sq km). It is a county of strongly contrasting landscapes from the eastern coastal plain to the sparsely populated, rugged hills and moors of the west and the densely populated urban and industrial areas of the coalfield and the Tyne Valley to the south.

The Cheviots, rounded hills that stand from 1,000 to about 2,500 ft (300–760 m) high, form the Scottish and Cumberland borders. The western fells, composed of grits and impure limestone, are deeply dissected by the Rivers Rede and North Tyne. Carboniferous rocks dip east and south from the Cheviot Hills to the coast and the Tyne Valley. A notable landscape feature is Whin Sill, a doleritic (lava) intrusion that forms the Farne Islands and Bamburgh Castle Rock and carries sections of a Roman wall. The coastal plain, underlain by limestone in the north and coal measures in the south, is covered by glacial deposits varying in character from light sands and gravels to heavy clays and loams. Upland soils are thin, acid, and peaty. The climate is cool because of its latitude, altitude, and exposure to easterly winds. Winters are severe, springs late, and summers cool, temperatures rarely exceeding 60° F (16° C); the coast suffers from cool sea fogs. Rainfall is generally low, ranging from 25 in. (635 mm) on the coast to 50 in. in the Cheviot Hills. The county is famed for its wild, exposed scenery: half the area is mountain and moorland with large areas, notably Kielder, Wark, and Redesdale forests, taken over by the British Forestry Commission, a state body.

Entrance gateway, Alnwick Castle, Northumberland, England

A.F. Kersting

There is evidence of settlement in prehistoric times before the Roman domination of Northumberland, dating from AD 122, when Hadrian's Wall from the Tyne to the Solway Firth was constructed. Roman finds include an important collection of antiquities and the remains of a fort at Chester (Cilurnum). In 547 the British king Ida built the fortress at Bamburgh (subsequently the seat of Saxon kings) and founded the kingdom of Bernicia. In 603 the combined forces of Strathclyde Britons and Scots were defeated, and the area between the Forth and Humber became known as Northumbria, the most powerful of the 7th-century Saxon states. Lindisfarne Island was the centre for the spread of Christianity throughout the kingdom.

The Normans ruthlessly harried the north and built castles against invasions from Scotland and across the North Sea. Subsequent history until union with Scotland (1603) is a continuous record of border warfare. The Catholic north rose in support of Mary, Queen of Scots, in 1569, and in 1644 Newcastle was captured by the Scots in the English Civil War.

Medieval Northumberland prospered from the production and export of wool and hides. Coal was mined in Roman times, and the coal trade between London and the Tyne developed rapidly from the 13th century. Shipbuilding consequently developed, and in the early 19th century new investment and inventions (including the steam turbine) created the great shipbuilding and repairing works, which now dominate the economy. Local iron foundries were encouraged in the 1830s by the building of iron ships. Industries dependent on coal developed—salt panning at the river mouths and glassmaking, introduced in the early 17th century from Lorraine, in France. For about a century the Tyneside (now Tyne and Wear) chemical industries were among the most important in the country, but, like the glassworks, they failed to survive. Lead, silver, and iron were mined in Allendale from the 12th to the 19th century. Modern industrial complexes on the Rivers Tyne and Blyth produce heavy electrical machinery, pottery, and soap. Approximately 50 percent of Northumberland is mountain and rough hill pasture, 45 percent medium quality farmland, and 5 percent good. The county was not brought into settled agricultural use until late in the 18th century: even in the 1770s at least half of Northumberland was still wasteland, and parts of the moors are still among the most sparsely populated areas of England. Much of the coastal plain is sheep-cattle-barley country with large, highly mechanized mixed farms that include some of the richest fattening pastures in England. Sheep (mainly Cheviots) greatly outnumber cattle. Traditional salmon fishing in the Tyne and Tweed still flourishes, but inshore fishing is virtually confined to North Shields. The larger towns and industrial and mining villages are found in the south and east of the county, while the sparsely populated fells are served by the small market towns of Wooler, Rothbury, and Bellingham. Pop. (1971 est.) 280,000.
54°59′ N, 1°35′ W

·coal mining historical evidence **4**:773b
·United Kingdom political geography **18**:872g
·Western Christian manuscript painting **19**:348b

Northumberland, John Dudley, duke of (b. 1502—d. Aug. 22, 1553, London), politician and soldier who was virtual ruler of England from 1549 to 1553, during the minority of King Edward VI (ruled 1547–53). Almost all historical sources regard him as an unscrupulous schemer whose policies undermined England's political stability. His father, Edmund, was executed by King Henry VIII in 1510. Dudley became deputy governor of the English-occupied port of Calais, Fr., in 1538, and in 1542 he was made Viscount Lisle and appointed lord high admiral. He served under Edward Seymour, earl of Hertford, in the invasion of Scotland in 1544. In September of the same year he captured the French city of Boulogne. The title earl of Warwick was conferred upon him in 1546.

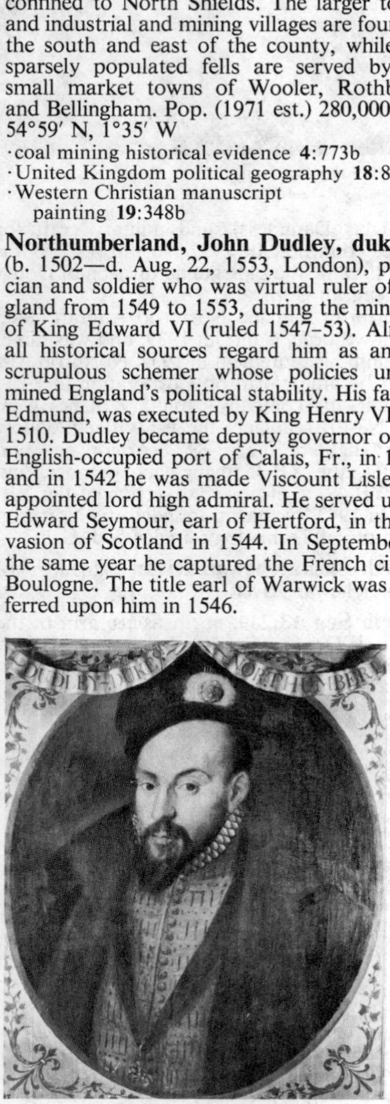

John Dudley, duke of Northumberland, painting by J.V. Belkamp, 1551; in the collection of Lord Sackville

By courtesy of Lord Sackville; photograph, Courtauld Institute of Art, London

Upon Henry VIII's death (Jan. 28, 1547), Warwick became a member of the regency council set up to govern the country during the minority of Edward VI. He acquiesced while Hertford assumed almost supreme power as protector with the title of duke of Somerset. At first the two men continued to work together. Warwick's military ability was chiefly responsible for Somerset's victory over the Scots at Pinkie in September 1547. But in 1549 Warwick took advantage of popular unrest generated by Somerset's policies to join with the propertied classes and the Catholics in a coalition that deposed and imprisoned the protector. When the coalition collapsed, Somerset was released (February 1550), and the two rivals were ostensibly reconciled. But Warwick was now in complete control of the government.

Warwick's foreign policy included the abandonment of English efforts to obtain control of Scotland. At home he reversed Somerset's liberal agrarian policies by suppressing peasants who resisted enclosure—the taking by propertied classes for pasturage of arable land held in common by the peasants. In continuing the consolidation of the Protestant Reformation in England, he seized for himself and his henchmen much of the remaining wealth of the Roman Catholic Church. The general unpopularity of his rule caused him to strengthen his position by making himself duke of Northumberland and by having the potentially dangerous Somerset arrested and (on Jan. 22, 1552) executed. Thereafter he imposed strict conformity to Protestant ceremony and doctrine. The only aspects of his policies that historians have applauded were his attempts to deal with England's economic ills by fighting inflation and expanding trade.

When it became evident in 1553 that the 15-year-old Edward VI would die of tuberculosis, Northumberland caused his son, Guildford Dudley, to marry Lady Jane Grey and persuaded the King to will the crown to Jane and her male heirs—thereby excluding from the succession Henry VIII's daughters, Elizabeth and Mary Tudor. Edward died on July 6, 1553, and on July 10 Northumberland proclaimed Jane queen of England. But the councilors in London and the populace backed the rightful heir, Mary Tudor. Northumberland's supporters melted away, and on July 20 he surrendered to Mary's forces. A month later he was executed for treason.

·Cecil's knighthood and later opposition **3**:1035a
·Cranmer resistance to succession scheme **5**:237h
·John Knox's distrust of government **10**:495e
·regency policies and rebellion failure **3**:225e

Northumberland, earls and dukes of, an English title deriving its origin from the kings of Northumbria, who became known as earls of Northumbria in the later Anglo-Saxon period. In the 12th century the earldom was alienated to the kings of Scotland. The Percy family held the earldom from 1377; Lancastrians, they suffered considerably during the War of the Roses, and after the death of the 3rd Earl in battle (1461), the earldom was given (1464) to John Neville, a brother of Richard Neville, earl of Warwick ("the kingmaker"). Restored (1470) to the Percies when Edward IV quarrelled with Warwick, it remained in their family until the death (1537) of the 6th Earl. John Dudley, earl of Warwick, who wielded supreme power in the later part of Edward VI's reign (1547–53), had himself created duke of Northumberland in 1551. His abortive attempt to make his daughter-in-law, Lady Jane Grey, queen after Edward's death instead of the legal heir, Mary I, led to his execution for treason. Restored to the Percies in 1557, the title continued in their male line until 1670. Passing then twice by marriage, it was inherited (1750) by Sir Hugh Smithson, who took the Percy name and arms; he was created 1st duke of Northumberland and Earl Percy in 1766. His descendants retain the title.

Northumberland Strait, channel at the southern end of the Gulf of St. Lawrence separating Prince Edward Island from Nova Scotia and New Brunswick, Canada. About 200 mi (322 km) long and 9 to 30 mi wide, it was named for HMS "Northumberland" (flagship of Admiral Lord Colville of Culross) by Joseph Frederick Wallet Desbarres, who surveyed the Nova Scotian and Cape Breton coasts, 1763–73. Ferry service is operated across the strait.
46°00′ N, 63°30′ W

Northumbria, Old English NORTANHYMBRE, those living north of the Humber, one of the most important kingdoms of Anglo-Saxon England. During its most flourishing period, it extended from the Irish Sea to the North Sea, between two west–east lines formed in the north by the Ayrshire coast and the Firth of Forth and in the south by the rivers Ribble, or Mersey, and the Humber. Its military strength was greatest in the 7th century, when the supremacy of three of its rulers, Edwin (616–632), Oswald (633–641), and Oswiu (641–670), was recognized by the southern English kingdoms. But Northumbria's most significant contribution to Anglo-Saxon history was made in the late 7th and in the 8th century, in the religious, artistic, and intellectual achievements of what has often been called a golden age. The twin monasteries of Wearmouth and Jarrow achieved pre-eminence in the intellectual life not only of England but of western Europe. Bede (died 735), a theologian and historian who won international fame, was a monk of Jarrow; but the excellent library there, which made his scholarship possible, was probably equalled in the monasteries of Hexham, Whitby, and Lindisfarne. The Gospel book from Lindisfarne (now in the British Museum) epitomizes Northumbrian attainment in writing and illumination, and the skill of Northumbrian sculptors survives in the stone crosses at Bewcastle and Ruthwell.

Northumbria was formed from the coalition of two originally independent states, Bernicia (*q.v.*), a pirate settlement at Bamburgh on the Northumberland coast, and Deira (*q.v.*), lying to the south of it. Aethelfrith, ruler of Bernicia (593–616), won control of Deira, thereby creating the kingdom of Northumbria. He was killed in battle by supporters of Edwin, a representative of the Deiran royal house, who then ruled both kingdoms; but thereafter, apart from a few very short intervals, Bernician royalty controlled a united Northumbria. The kingdom probably reached the west coast by the mid-7th century, and it also rapidly expanded northward, at one time extending as far as the River Tay.

The cultural life and the political unity of Northumbria were destroyed by the arrival of the Danes. The Danish "great army" captured York in 866, and many of its members settled in that area. Early in the 10th century, other Scandinavians entered and settled western Northumbria from the Irish Sea. Meanwhile, in the north, the newly formed kingdom of Scotland drove the Northumbrian boundary back to the River Tweed. Eventually, the rulers of the southern kingdom of Wessex imposed their authority throughout England. After the last Scandinavian ruler of York was expelled in 944, there ceased to be independent kings of Northumbria, which then became an earldom within the kingdom of England.

·cultural prestige in 8th century **6**:879h; map 880
·English history and culture **3**:200b; map 199
·Scottish historical relation **3**:233f; map 199

Northumbrian dialect, Old English dialect that was the language of culture and learning throughout England from the 7th century until the Viking invasions of Northumbria in the early 9th century and the subsequent shift of the centres of learning south, to Wessex, under King Alfred (ruled 871–899).
·cultural prestige in 8th century **6**:879h; map 880
·geographic extent **6**:884e; map

North Vancouver, city, southwestern British Columbia, Canada, on Burrard Inlet of the Strait of Georgia, linked to Vancouver by the Lions Gate and Second Narrows bridges. The community, founded shortly after a sawmill was built on the site in 1863, was for years the largest settlement on the inlet. In 1872 it was named Moodyville (after Sewell Moody, who owned the sawmill). In 1907 it was renamed North Vancouver and was incorporated as a city. Its economy depends chiefly on the shipping of grain, lumber, and ore, and on shipbuilding and sawmilling. There is also some light manufacturing. Fishing, mountain climbing, and skiing attract tourists and sportsmen. Pop. (1971 prelim.) 31,863.
49°19′ N, 123°04′ W
·map, Canada **3**:716

North Vancouver, district municipality forming a northern suburb of Vancouver, southwestern British Columbia, Canada, on Burrard and Indian Arm inlets. Mainly residential, it adjoins the city of North Vancouver and is connected to Vancouver by the Lions Gate and Second Narrows bridges. Mountains up to nearly 5,000 ft (1,500 m) and coniferous forests within the district make it an important recreation and lumbering area. Inc. 1891. Pop. (1971 prelim.) 57,123.
49°19′ N, 123°04′ W

North Venezuelan Trough, submarine feature, Caribbean Sea.
12°00′ N, 76°00′ W
·Caribbean Sea map **3**:907

North Vietnam: *see* Vietnam, North.

North Warm Springs, Chinese PEI-WEN-CH'ÜAN, Pei-p'ei, Szechwan, China.
·Chungking recreational facilities **4**:588f

North Wazīristān (Pakistan): *see* Wazīristān.

North West Cape, on the west coast of Western Australia state, it occupies the tip of a peninsula jutting into the Indian Ocean.
21°45′ S, 114°10′ E
·map, Australia **2**:400

Northwest Caucasian languages: *see* Abkhazo-Adyghian languages.

Northwest Coast Indians 13:251, the native peoples of the Pacific coast of North America from Yakutat Bay in southeastern Alaska to Cape Mendocino in northern California. None of these peoples engaged in agriculture or animal husbandry; all were fishers, hunters, and gatherers of wild vegetable foods. They nonetheless had highly complex, sophisticated societies.

The text article covers the general characteristics of the area and people, the traditional culture patterns, and modern cultural developments under the influence of Western ideas and technology.

REFERENCES in other text articles:
arts
·arms design tradition illus. **2**:34
·art style, social aspects, and economy **1**:683c
·basketry style uniqueness **2**:762a
·jewelry forms and design **10**:182g
·cultural impact on Plateau group **13**:228a
·economy, population, and culture **13**:215f
·myth importance to family and ceremony **1**:660a
·naming patterns **12**:818h
·phonological richness and language distribution **13**:211d; map 210
·potlatch and impact on Plateau culture **13**:229f
·racial characteristics **14**:847d
·semi-heraldic nature of totemism **8**:783e
·winter initiation ceremony **1**:673h

RELATED ENTRIES in the *Ready Reference and Index:*
Bella Coola; Chinook; Coast Salish; Haida; Hupa; Kwakiutl; Nootka; Tlingit; Tsimshian; Wakashan; Wiyot; Yurok and Karok

North West Company, a fur-trading company formed in Canada in the late 18th century; the chief rival of the powerful Hudson's Bay Company.

Founded in 1783, it enjoyed a rapid growth. The company originally confined its operations to the Lake Superior region and the valleys of the Red, Assiniboine, and Saskatchewan rivers but later spread north and west to the shores of the Arctic and Pacific oceans. It even penetrated the area then known as the Oregon Country, where it constructed posts in what are now the U.S. states of Washington and Idaho. Its wilderness headquarters was located first at Grand Portage on Lake Superior and after 1805 at Ft. William (also on Lake Superior, at the site of the present city of Thunder Bay, Ont.).

Competition with the Hudson's Bay Company became especially intense when that company established the colony of Assiniboia on the Red River (in present-day Manitoba) in 1811–12, interrupting the North West Company's line of communications. Several years later, open conflict broke out, during which North West Company men destroyed the Red River colony (*see* Seven Oaks Massacre), and Hudson's Bay Company men destroyed the North West Company post of Ft. Gibraltar (located on the site of modern Winnipeg, Manitoba) and captured Ft. William.

Under pressure from the British government, the old North West Company and the Hudson's Bay Company were merged in 1821 under the name and charter of the latter company.

The New North West Company, or XY Company, had a brief existence (1798–1804) as a competitor of the old North West Company before being absorbed by the latter.
·Columbia River exploration role **4**:930h
·Mackenzie River posts and supply system **11**:265f
·Montrealer organization and rivalry **3**:738h
·trade rivalry and consolidation **3**:739h
·trading post importance in Manitoba **11**:452h

North West District, administrative division, Guyana.
·population table **8**:508; map

North Western Province, Sri Lanka (Ceylon), faces the Gulf of Mannar on the western coast and has an area of 3,016 sq mi (7,811 sq km). The capital is Kurunegala (*q.v.*). The terrain is generally low and fairly flat, except for the southeastern margin, into which the foothills of the Sri Lanka hill country intrude. The climate varies, with the north considerably drier than the south. Two rivers, the Deduru Oya and the Mi Oya, drain the province.

The interior of what is now North Western Province was part of an ancient civilization centred in Anuradhapura, and numerous irrigation works and ruins remain. The port of Puttalam was used by the later Sinhalese kingdom. Agriculture is the province's chief occupation, with rice the biggest crop; in the north it is grown under irrigation. Some graphite mining is carried on. The province has a good road network and some railway lines. Pop. (1971) 1,407,894, mainly Sinhalese and Tamil.

North-Western Province, Zambia, adjoins the Angolan and Zaire border. Its economy is based on cultivation of cassava and millet and on hunting. Solwezi is the capital.
·cultural description and current demographic information **19**:1132f; table 1133
·map, Zambia **19**:1130

northwestern sagebrush lizard (*Sceloporus graciosus gracilis*), subspecies of lizard (suborder Sauria) occurring in sandy habitats in southeastern New Mexico and western Texas.
·habitat and maturation **15**:729f

North-Western State, administrative division of Nigeria (since 1967) comprising Niger and Sokoto provinces (*qq.v.*). It occupies an area of 65,143 sq mi (168,720 sq km), and its vegetation ranges from wooded savanna in the south to thorn scrub and near desert in the north. The Niger River forms most of its southern boundary with West Central State; but it is also drained by the Sokoto (Kebbi), Kaduna, Rima, Zamfara, and Gulbin Ka rivers. Peanuts (groundnuts), cotton, and tobacco are generally grown both for domestic consumption and for export; swamp rice is important in the riverine *fadamas* ("floodplains"), especially in Bida and Sokoto emirates; and shea nuts and yams are significant exports to other parts of Nigeria from the southern part of the state. There is also considerable local trade in kola nuts, sugarcane, rice, onions, beans, cassava, and fish as well as in the staples of guinea corn, millet, cowpeas, and maize (corn). Cattle, goats, sheep, chickens, and guinea fowl are mainly raised for local use but are also sent to the urban centres to the south; goatskins and sheepskins and cattle hides and camel hides are exported.

Leather crafts, especially those using the skins of the Sokoto Red Goat, from the northern part of the province are famous as are the brass wares and glass products from Bida (*q.v.*) and the pottery from Abuja (*q.v.*). Cotton weaving and dyeing (with locally grown indigo) are widespread traditional arts. Modern industries are limited but include cement manufacture, tanning, and meat processing at Sokoto town (*q.v.*) and textile manufacture, peanut crushing, and cotton processing in Gusau (*q.v.*). Except for the limestone deposits around Sokoto, mining (gold, tin, iron, quartz) supplies only local needs.

Most of the state's inhabitants are Muslims belonging to the Hausa, Fulani, Nupe, Gbari (Gwari), Kamberi, Dakarki (Dakarawa), Kamuku, or Reshe (Gungawa, Gungunci) tribes. Almost all of the region was conquered in the *jihād* ("holy war") conducted by the Fulani people in the early 19th century; and the state presently contains Sokoto and Gwandu (*qq.v.*), the two most senior emirates of the former Fulani empire, and Abuja, Agaie, Argungu, Bida, Kontagora, Lapai, and Yauri (*qq.v.*) emirates. Sokoto (the state capital), Gusau, Minna (*q.v.*), and Bida are by far the largest towns. Pop. (1971 est.) 6,944,518.

·area and population table **13**:91
·map, Nigeria **13**:86

northwest European local race, a subgroup, roughly corresponding to a breeding isolate in genetics, of the Caucasoid (European) geographical race. It comprises the populations of the British Isles, northern Germany, The Netherlands, Iceland, Scandinavia, and related populations in North America, South Africa, Australia, and New Zealand. The chief physical characteristics of the northwest Europeans are relative depigmentation (in which the skin is not only pale but also burns rather than tans under exposure to sunlight), with associated high incidence of blue eyes and blond hair; and the greatest average height in Europe, particularly evident among the Scots and Scandinavians. Dolichocephaly (in which the skull is relatively long from back to front) is frequent, and there is evidence of adaptation to moderate cold. *See also* local race; Caucasoid geographical race.

·Caucasoid populations analysis **14**:842c
·European breeding populations **15**:349c; illus.

Northwest Frontier Province 13:255, northernmost province of Pakistan; with an area (including centrally-administered tribal areas) of 39,283 sq mi (101,742 sq km), it is bordered by Afghanistan (west and north), Jammu and Kashmir (northeast), Punjab province (southeast), and Baluchistan province (southwest). Its capital is Peshāwar. Pop. (1972 prelim.) 10,909,000.

The text article covers the province's history, physical geography, population, administration, social conditions, economy, transport and communications, and cultural life.

REFERENCES in other text articles:
·physical and social features, area, and population **13**:894f; table 898
·political and diplomatic background **9**:412c
·tribal incursions' effect on caste **3**:987f

North West Mounted Police: *see* Royal Canadian Mounted Police.

Northwest Ordinances (1785, 1787), in U.S. history, the major accomplishment of the Congress under the Articles of Confederation, establishing the prototype for development of all subsequently acquired territory. The ordinances outlined the method for survey and sale of the vast territory north of the Ohio River and set aside land for public schooling in each township. Further provision was made for the franchise, self-government, a bill of rights, and the prohibition of slavery, thereby establishing an important precedent in a sensitive area of sectional differences.

The 1787 ordinance also embodied the first full declaration of U.S. Indian policy, stating that "the utmost good faith shall always be observed towards the Indians, their lands and properties shall never be taken away without their consent. . . . " This doctrine was embodied in an act of Congress (Aug. 7, 1789), one of its first official declarations.

·education supported by land grant **6**:421c
·Indian property rights **13**:221d
·Jefferson's anti-slavery provision **10**:129a
·Nebraska settlement pattern **12**:923c
·Ordinance of 1787 educational provision **6**:365g

Northwest Passage 13:257, historical sea passage of the North American continent, representing centuries of effort to find a route from the Atlantic to the Pacific through the Arctic archipelago of what became Canada.

The text article, after a historical introduction, covers the environment of the region, the voyage of the ship "Manhattan" in 1969, the economic significance of the Northwest Passage, and prospects for the future.
74°40′ N, 100°00′ W

REFERENCES in other text articles:
·Atlantic Ocean floor features map **2**:296
·Canadian route exploration **13**:260f
·Cook's attempt to locate passage **5**:131h
·European exploration and discovery **7**:1042e
·Hakluyt's exploration espousal **8**:553h
·Hudson's later exploration objective **8**:1131a
·pack ice and navigational difficulties **9**:159b
·Washington historical importance **19**:618a

North West River, village, southeast central Labrador, Newfoundland, Canada, at the head of Lake Melville on the mouth of Grand Lake (an extension of Naskaupi River). Originally established as a fur-trading post by Louis Fornel about 1743, the site was later settled as a Hudson's Bay Company post (1836) named Ft. Smith; in 1840 it was renamed North West River House. The post has been in continuous operation since its founding, although lumbering, sawmilling, and the nearby Goose Bay air base have replaced trapping in the local economy. Incorporated in 1969 as a local improvement district, it is the site of a small hospital run by the International Grenfell Association, organized by Sir Wilfred Grenfell, the British medical missionary. Latest census 835.
53°32′ N, 60°09′ W

Northwest Territories 13:260, a region (area 1,304,903 sq mi [3,379,683 sq km]) comprising more than one-third of Canada. Lying to the north of the Canadian provinces, it extends from the Yukon Territory in the west, straddling the northernmost portion of the North American continent as far east as Baffin Island in the Atlantic Ocean, and reaches far above the Arctic Circle. The territorial capital is Yellowknife, and the region is administratively divided into the districts of Mackenzie, Keewatin, and Franklin. Pop. (1971) 34,807.

The text article covers the history of the territories, the physical environment and natural life, and the people and conditions of life, including population, economy, transportation, administrative and social conditions, and cultural life.

REFERENCES in other text articles:
·Alberta's political delineations **1**:423f
·area and population table **3**:721; map 722
·Baffin Bay characteristics **2**:583a
·Canadian Arctic Island geography **1**:1115g; illus. 1116
·creation and federal control **3**:728a *passim* to 729f
·Hudson Bay physical geography **8**:1131f
·Laurentian Shield frozen inlet illus. **13**:180
·map, Canada **3**:716
·provincial creation problems **3**:741g
·trade competition, land sale, and political consequences **3**:739h *passim* to 740h
·Yukon's economic growth **19**:1109b

Northwest Territory, U.S. territory created by Congress in 1787 encompassing that region lying west of Pennsylvania, north of the Ohio River, east of the Mississippi, and south of the Great Lakes. Virginia, New York, Connecticut, and Massachusetts had claims to this area, which they ceded to the central government between 1780 and 1800. Land policy and territorial government were established by the Northwest Ordinances of 1785 and 1787. Ultimately five states—Ohio, Indiana, Illinois, Michigan, and Wisconsin—were organized from the territory, and a small part, the land lying between the St. Croix and Mississippi rivers, was incorporated into Minnesota.

·Indiana's territorial origin **9**:303d
·Jefferson's Virginia cession support **10**:129a
·Michigan's growth and Detroit's role **12**:105a
·Tecumseh's settlement activities **18**:55b
·territorial expansion map **18**:962

Northwich, market town, Cheshire, England. Local brine springs, used to produce salt since Roman times, have caused severe subsidence of buildings in the town. The present large-scale chemical industry has developed from the ancient salt trade. Other manufactures include iron and steel, leather goods, carpets, and clothing. Pop. (1971 prelim.) 18,109.
53°16′ N, 2°32′ W

·map, United Kingdom **18**:866

Northwood, John (1837–1902), British glassmaker.

·cameo glass technique **8**:192d; illus.

North Yemen: *see* Yemen (Ṣan'ā').

North York, one of the five boroughs that with the City of Toronto constitute the Municipality of Metropolitan Toronto, southern Ontario, Canada. It has an area of 69.4 sq mi (180 sq km) and is bounded by the townships of Vaughan and Markham (north), by Scarborough (east), by East York, the City, and York (south), and by Etobicoke, York, and the Humber River (west). North York Township (created in 1922 from York Township) was reconstituted as a borough on Jan. 1, 1967. Since World War II there has been planned industrial and residential development. The borough has more than 4,000 ac (2,000 ha) of parks and open space and the 475-ac campus of York University (1959) forms part of its northern boundary. The Black Creek Pioneer Village depicts the early settlers' way of life. Pop. (1970) 504,150.

North Yorkshire, county in the north of England, formed in 1974 from the North Riding and parts of the West and East Ridings of Yorkshire. Its area is 3,213 sq mi (8,321 sq km).

The county has two distinctive upland areas. In the west are the Pennines, the major upland region of northern England. This upland (reaching its highest levels of over 2,200 ft [670 m] in the northwest at Pen-y-Ghent, Whernside, Ingleborough, and Mickle Fell) is deeply dissected by deep valleys (dales) of the rivers Swale, Ure, Nidd, and Wharfe. In the east, limestones and sandstones form the upland mass of the Cleveland Hills, North York Moors, and Tabular Hills, whose major rivers drain southward into the lowlands of the Vale of Pickering. Separating these two regions is the Vale of York, a glacial drift-covered lowland sloping southward from about 100 ft above sea level to less than 20 ft.

Evidence of prehistoric man dates from the Mesolithic Period, and there is an 8th-millennium winter hunting camp at Star Carr near Seamer. Dry, upland sites were most favoured in the Neolithic Period and Bronze Age and provided suitable defensive positions for Iron Age hill forts (*e.g.*, Stanwick). Roman occupation was principally military in character, since the region acted as a frontier base for operations against northern invaders. Eboracum (York), established as a fortress, was linked with London by Ermine Street. Evidence suggests the survival of a Romano-British kingdom, Elmet, in the south of the county until the 7th century. York became the centre of a thriving Anglian civilization in the 8th century, but this was destroyed by subsequent invasions of Danes in the east and Norsemen in the northwest, the importance of these peoples being reflected by place-name evidence. In 1069–70, many settlements of the county were laid waste by William I, following rebellions against his rule.

In the Middle Ages, North Yorkshire was very much a peripheral region. Numerous castles (*e.g.*, Richmond, Helmsley, Pickering, Scarborough, Bolton) signify the former power of great landowning families. The remote, empty wastes attracted society-shunning religious bodies, and the county became one of the most important centres of English monasticism. The Cistercian foundations at Jervaulx, Fountains, Rievaulx, and Byland grew wealthy from the products of sheep farming. The area, frequently the scene of rebellion and anarchy, played a significant part in the 15th-century Wars of the Roses and the English Civil War of the mid-17th century.

The modern economy of the county is primarily agricultural. The large holdings of the Vale of York are major grain producers, while dairy farming is especially important in the wetter, western areas of the Pennine dales and lower slopes. Hill sheep farming is characteristic of the moorlands of the Pennines and North York Moors. Manufacturing industry, which has close links with agriculture, does not have an important place in the economy and is restricted to the larger towns. York, the principal centre, has a variety of light engineering and food-processing activities. The towns of Harrogate and Scarborough (frequent settings for English political conferences and conventions) are also centres of a growing tourist industry associated with the Yorkshire Dales and the North York Moors national parks. The major rail and road links connecting London and Edinburgh traverse the county. Pop. (1971 est.) 629,000.

Norton, town, South Mashonaland Province, north central Rhodesia. Developed in the 1960s as a planned industrial township, it is located west of Salisbury on the road and rail line to Bulawayo, and 5 mi (8 km) from Lake McIlwaine. The European residential section is designed to provide all community needs, and the African area, adjacent to the industrial zone, contains its own Chibero College of Agriculture (1961). Latest census 3,380.
17°53′ S, 30°42′ E

Norton, Caroline Elizabeth Sarah, *née* SHERIDAN (b. March 22, 1808, London—d. June 15, 1877, London), poet and novelist whose matrimonial difficulties and her resultant efforts to secure legal protection for married women made her a notorious figure in mid-Victorian society. One of three beautiful granddaughters of Richard Brinsley Sheridan, she began to write before she was out of her teens. In 1827 she made an unfortunate marriage to the Hon. George Norton, whom she left after three years. In retaliation, Norton brought action against her friend Lord Melbourne for seducing his wife. The suit may have been a political move to discredit Melbourne. When the case came to trial, the evidence was so flimsy that the jury decided against Norton without leaving the courtroom. Norton then refused his wife access to their children, and her outcries against this injustice were instrumental in introducing the Infant Custody bill, which was finally carried in 1839. In 1855 she was again involved in a lawsuit because her husband not only refused to pay her allowance but demanded the proceeds of her books. Her eloquent letter of pro-

Caroline Norton, detail of an oil painting by John Hayter (*c.* 1800–91)

By courtesy of the trustees of the Chatsworth Settlement, Derbyshire

test to Queen Victoria had great influence on the Marriage and Divorce Act of 1857, abolishing some of the inequities to which married women were subject.

Among her contemporaries, Mrs. Norton held a high literary reputation. *The Dream, and Other Poems* appeared in 1840 to critical enthusiasm, and *Aunt Carry's Ballads* (1847), dedicated to her nephews and nieces, was written with tenderness and grace. Her novels —*Stuart of Dunleath* (1851), *Lost and Saved* (1863), and *Old Sir Douglas* (1867)—were based on her own unhappy experiences. She edited various literary annuals and wrote many popular songs. Mrs. Norton is said to have been the model for Diana Warwick, the engaging but indiscreet heroine of George Meredith's *Diana of the Crossways* (1885). After her husband's death in 1875, she had a brief period of happiness as the wife of Sir William Stirling-Maxwell.

Norton, Charles Eliot (b. Nov. 16, 1827, Cambridge, Mass.—d. Oct. 21, 1908, Cambridge), scholar and man of letters, an idealist and reformer by temperament who exhibited remarkable energy in a wide range of activity. Graduated from Harvard in 1846, he opened a night school in Cambridge, was director of a housing experiment in Boston, worked zealously as an editor for the Union cause, was co-editor (1864–68) of the *North American Review* and one of the founders of *The Nation* (1865). From 1874 to 1898 he lectured on the history of art at Harvard, where he was one of the most popular teachers of the day and an "oracle of the humanities." A friend of many literary greats, including Carlyle, Emerson,

Charles Eliot Norton, 1903

By courtesy of the Library of Congress, Washington, D.C.

Ruskin, Longfellow, and Lowell, he contributed valuable editions of their letters and other biographical material. Norton also wrote on art and edited collections of poetry, notably the poetry of John Donne (1895–1905). Probably his best literary work was his prose translation of *The Divine Comedy* (1891–92). His *Letters . . . with Bibliographical Comment* were edited by Sara Norton and M.A. De Wolfe Howe (1913).

Norton, Thomas (1532–84), poet and playwright, author, with Thomas Sackville, of *Gorboduc*, the earliest English tragedy (1st performed 1561; printed 1565).
·literature of the Renaissance **10**:1140g

Norton culture, Eskimo hunting and fishing culture of northwestern Alaska dating from about 500 BC.

Norton Sound, arm of the Bering Sea, indents for 125 mi (200 km) the west coast of Alaska, U.S., and is 70 mi wide between the Seward Peninsula (north) and the Yukon River Delta (south). The sound is navigable from May to October. The city of Nome, on the northern shore, is the commercial centre of northwest Alaska. Capt. James Cook, the navigator, discovered the sound in 1778 and named it for the speaker of the English House of Commons, Sir Fletcher Norton.
63°50′ N, 164°00′ W
·Bering Sea map **2**:845

nortriptyline, drug used as an antidepressant, with the possible side effects of drowsiness, dizziness, blurred vision, and dry mouth.
·use, action, and effects **17**:694a

Nōrūz, in Zoroastrianism and Parsiism, the New Year festival. Among the Parsis, the Nōrūz is a Yashan holiday, that is, a celebration that warrants the performance of five prescribed liturgies: the Āfringān, prayers of love or praise, obligatory for the Yashan; the Bāj, prayers honouring *yazata*s (angels) or *fravashi*s (guardian spirits); the Yasna, a rite which includes the sacrifice of the sacred liquor, *haoma;* the Fravartigan or Farokhshi, prayers commemorating the dead; and the Satum, prayers recited at funeral feasts. Throughout the day, Parsis greet one another with the rite of *hamāzor*, in which the right hand of one person is passed between the palms of the one greeting him. Words of greeting and good wishes are then exchanged.

The Nōrūz at one time fell on the vernal equinox, March 21. The Persian use of an intercalary month once every 120 years eventually moved the New Year from spring to autumn. A discrepancy then arose between the Zoroastrians and their Parsi coreligionists in India. The Persians had abandoned the intercalary month first, while the Parsis continued it for one cycle and hence celebrated the New Year one month later than the Zoroastrians. An attempt to reconcile the two celebrations in the mid-18th century only split the Parsi community, the majority retaining the Parsi reckoning.
·renewal significance **7**:199c
·Zoroastrian yearly worship of summer **19**:1175d

Norwalk, city, Los Angeles County, southwestern California, U.S. Once a part of the Rancho Los Coyotes, a 1784 Spanish land grant, it was founded as Corvallis in 1868 by Gilbert and Atwood Sproul. Renamed for Norwalk, Conn., after the arrival of the Southern Pacific Railroad in 1875, it became a service point for lumbering, dairying, and ranching. Located at the intersection of major freeways, it experienced rapid industrial development after World War II. Since 1964 it has held an annual Space, Science and Technology Show. Cerritos (junior) College was founded there in 1955. Inc. 1957. Pop. (1950) 35,350; (1980) 85,232.
33°54′ N, 118°05′ W

Norwalk, city, coextensive with Norwalk Town, Fairfield County, southwest Connecticut, U.S., on Long Island Sound at the mouth of the Norwalk River. Roger Ludlow purchased the land from the Norwalk Indians in 1640. In 1779, during the Revolution, the settlement was burned by Loyalist forces under Gen. William Tryon. It was from Norwalk that Nathan Hale crossed Long Island Sound to Long Island, where he was captured by the

British and executed as a spy. The manufacture of hats, long the principal industry, is now part of a diversified industrial economy including textiles, machinery, and hardware. Although known for its oysters in earlier years, over-exploitation and pollution of the waters have virtually ended the oyster fishery. It is a summer resort and has two colleges—Norwalk Community and Norwalk State Technical—which were opened in 1961.

The town of Norwalk, organized in 1651, contained the cities of Norwalk (incorporated borough, 1836; city, 1893) and South Norwalk (incorporated 1870), as well as some small villages. In 1913 all these divisions were consolidated and incorporated as the city of Norwalk. Pop. (1980) city, 77,767; metropolitan area (SMSA), 126,692.
41°07′ N, 73°27′ W

Norwalk, city, seat (1818) of Huron County, northern Ohio, U.S. It was originally part of the Western Reserve known as Sufferer's Lands, or Fire Lands, set aside in 1792 for Connecticut residents whose homes were burned during the American Revolution. The settlement was founded by Platt Benedict in 1817 and named for Norwalk, Conn. The Firelands Historical Museum, formerly Preston Wickham House (1836), contains Indian and pioneer relics. Pres. Rutherford B. Hayes attended the old Norwalk Academy, a widely known institution in the 1830s. Since World War II there has been steady growth of both population and industry. Inc. village, 1828; city, 1881. Pop. (1980) 14,358.
41°15′ N, 82°37′ W

Norway 13:263, kingdom of northern Europe, occupying the western part of the Scandinavian Peninsula. It is bounded on the north by the Arctic Ocean; on the east by Sweden, except in the extreme northeast, where it adjoins parts of both Finland and the Soviet Union; on the south and southeast by the North Sea; and on the west by the Atlantic Ocean and North Sea.

The text article covers the natural environment, national regions, the Norwegian people, the national economy, the Norwegian government, and social conditions. *See also* Scandinavia, history of.

REFERENCES in other text articles:

agriculture, forestry, and fishing
·farm-building value and farm size, table 2 **7**:177
·mink production **7**:812d
·whaling innovations and industry decline **19**:812a

commerce, industry, and mining
·coal production and reserves, table 5 **4**:781
·electric power production **6**:636d
·glass imports and exports, table 2 **8**:206
·magnesium production **11**:304h
·paper production, table 1 **13**:974
·titanium production, table 1 **18**:456

constitution and law
·business associations, structure, and investments **3**:530g
·military law rules and procedures **12**:195c
·widowhood and inheritance system **10**:484d

culture and education
·adult education programs **1**:98g
·cuisine regional specialties **7**:946f
·development of children's literature **4**:239b
·education systems of Scandinavia **6**:419h
·encyclopaedia production **6**:797f
·Lapp minority's national integration **6**:135d
·Lapp-speaking areas **18**:1026e; map 1023
·theatre financial difficulties **18**:234d

economics, finance, and currency
·foreign aid distribution **7**:523g; table 524
·gross national debt percentage, table 4 **15**:193
·spice import, export, and value, table 3 **17**:506

government
·Antarctic territorial claims **1**:963f; table 962
·armed forces statistics, table 2 **2**:16
·Nansen as statesman and humanitarian **12**:825f
·police control and training **14**:665c
·map, Europe **6**:1034

population and demography
·fire death and property loss table **7**:314
·suicide rate trends, table 1 **17**:779

religion
·Christian denominational demography map **4**:459
·Norse religion's historical persistence **8**:40a

social issues
·alcohol consumption patterns **1**:443h; table 444
·folk cultures **6**:1064h *passim* to 1065b

transportation and communications
·merchant fleet and shipping statistics **18**:673d
·newspaper publishing statistics table **15**:237
·railway systems data table **15**:482

Norway, Church of, Norwegian NORSKE KIRKE, the established (state-supported) Lutheran Church in Norway, which changed from the Roman Catholic faith during the 16th-century Protestant Reformation. Unsuccessful attempts were made to win converts to Christianity in Norway during the 10th century, but in the 11th century the kings Olaf I Tryggvason and Olaf II Haraldsson, both of whom had been baptized outside Norway before becoming king, forced many of their subjects to accept Christianity. Olaf II brought clergy from England to organize the church. After he was killed in battle, he became a national hero and was eventually canonized as Norway's patron saint (1164). The country was primarily Christian by the end of the 11th century. In 1152 the church was organized nationally, with the seat of the archbishop in Nidaros (now Trondheim).

The Reformation was brought to Norway by Christian III, king (1534–59) of Denmark and Norway, who was converted to Lutheranism as a young man. Norwegians officially accepted the new faith in 1539. Catholic bishops and clergy who would not accept Lutheranism were forced out of the church, and the church's property was taken over by the government. By the end of the 16th century the church had been reorganized, and Lutheranism was accepted by most of the people and clergy.

During the 17th century, Lutheran orthodoxy prevailed, but in the 18th century the church was influenced by Pietism, a movement that began among German Lutherans and emphasized personal religious experience and reform. A work with a Pietistic emphasis, *Truth Unto Godliness*, an explanation of Lu-

NORWAY

Official name: Kongeriket Norge (Kingdom of Norway).
Location: northern Europe.
Form of government: constitutional monarchy.
Official language: Norwegian.
Official religion: Evangelical Lutheran.
Area: 125,066 sq mi (land area 118,736 sq mi), 323,920 sq km (land area 307,525 sq km).
Population: (1970 census) 3,874,133 (de jure); (1977 estimate) 4,035,365.
Capital: Oslo.
Monetary unit: 1 krone = 100 oere.

For the Norway flag, *see* Addenda, Volume X, page 1057. For comparative statistics, *see* Volume X, page 910 ff.

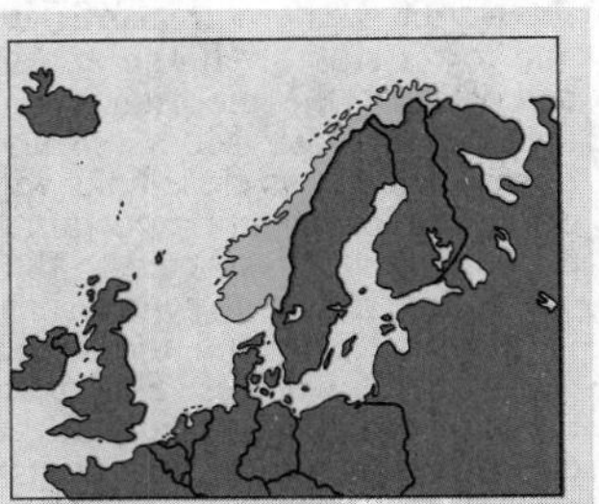

Demography

Population: (1977 estimate) density 34.0 per sq mi,* 13.1 per sq km*; (1976) urban 44.5%, rural 55.5%; (1977) male 49.64%, female 50.36%; (1977) under 15 years 23.4%, 15–29 22.8%, 30–44 17.1%, 45–59 17.2%, 60–74 14.0%, 75 and over 5.4%.†
Vital statistics: (1976) births per 1,000 population 13.3, deaths per 1,000 population 9.9, natural increase per 1,000 population 3.4; (1974–75) life expectancy at birth—male 71.7, female 78.0; (1976) major causes of death (per 100,000 population)—ischemic heart disease 255.3; malignant neoplasms, including neoplasms of lymphatic and hematopoietic tissue, 202.2; cerebrovascular disease 142.0; pneumonia 71.2.
Ethnic composition (by country of citizenship, 1977): Norway 98.2%, Denmark 0.4%, United States 0.3%, Sweden 0.2%, United Kingdom 0.2%, Pakistan 0.1%, other 0.6%. *Religious affiliation* (1976): Evangelical Lutheran 97.0%, Pentecostal 1.0%, Lutheran Free Church 0.5%, Methodist 0.4%, Baptist 0.3%, Roman Catholic 0.3%, Seventh-day Adventist 0.2%, other 0.3%.

National accounts

Budget (1978 estimate): Revenue: 54,878,000,000 kroner (indirect taxes 70.5%, direct taxes 19.6%). Expenditures: 59,903,000,000 kroner (public health and other social services 16.8%, education 13.5%, national defense 11.7%). *Total national debt* (1977): 50,290,300,000 kroner. *Tourism* (1975): receipts from visitors, U.S. $356,500,000; expenditures by nationals abroad, U.S. $520,000,000.

Domestic economy

Gross national product (GNP; at current market prices, 1976): U.S. $29,920,000,000 (U.S. $7,420 per capita).

Origin of gross domestic product (at current market prices):	1966				1976			
	value in 000,000 kroner	% of total value	labour force‡	% of labour force	value in 000,000 kroner	% of total value	labour force‡	% of labour force
agriculture, forestry, hunting, fishing	4,120	8.4	31,100	2.8	10,342	5.9	168,000	9.4
mining, quarrying	544	1.1	7,300	0.6	1,047	0.6	11,000	0.6
manufacturing	13,108	26.7	359,800	32.2	35,361	20.1	415,000	23.2
construction	3,881	7.9	102,400	9.2	12,742	7.2	148,000	8.3
electricity, gas, water	1,389	2.8	14,100	1.3	5,795	3.3	19,000	1.1
transport, storage, communications	8,591	17.5	136,100	12.2	19,002	10.8	161,000	9.0
trade	6,080	12.4	156,600	14.0	35,678	20.3	296,000	16.5
banking, insurance, real estate	1,211	2.5	29,900	2.7	16,731	9.5	82,000	4.6
ownership of dwellings	1,509	3.1	...	...	...	...	...	...
public admin., defense	2,342	4.8	68,900	6.2	...	...	} 487,000	27.2
services	6,317	12.9	211,800	18.9	32,607	18.6		
other	...	...	...	...	6,356	3.6	2,000	0.1
total	49,092	100.0†	1,118,000	100.0†	175,661	100.0†	1,789,000	100.0

Production (metric tons except as noted, 1976). Agriculture, forestry, hunting, fishing: barley 486,200, oats 286,900, potatoes 483,900, grains and dry peas 846,200, wheat 65,300; roundwood 9,756,000 cu m (1975); livestock (number of live animals): cattle 921,000, sheep 1,667,000, pigs 698,000, goats 68,000, chickens 6,594,000; fisheries 3,183,200. Mining, quarrying: crude petroleum 13,692,000, iron ore 3,924,000, coal 540,000. Manufacturing: cement 2,676,000, pig iron and ferroalloys 1,476,000, crude steel 900,000, aluminum 604,800, newsprint 434,400 (1975), sulfuric acid 402,000, plastics and resins 120,480 (1975), caustic soda 74,040, zinc 62,880, smelted and refined copper 40,500. Construction (square metres): residential 3,684,000; nonresidential 2,340,000, of which mining and manufacturing 639,000, commercial 578,000, educational services 310,000.

ther's Small Catechism published in 1737 by Erik Pontoppidan (1698–1764), a Danish-Norwegian Lutheran professor and bishop, extensively influenced Norwegian religious life for about 200 years. A Pietistic revival was led by Hans Hauge (1771–1824), a peasant's son who experienced a religious conversion when he was 25. Although laymen were legally forbidden to preach, Hauge did so throughout the country and established brotherhoods that met for religious study and prayer. Despite opposition from some of the clergy and being imprisoned several times for his activities, he and his followers remained within the Church of Norway and influenced it greatly. The work of Gisle Johnson (1822–94), a theological professor who combined Lutheran orthodoxy and Pietism, also influenced the clergy and people and led to the establishment of mission programs.

In the 20th century the church experienced theological disagreements between liberals and conservatives. During World War II the bishops and clergy led the resistance movement against the Nazis, who attempted to control the church after defeating Norway. The bishops gave up their state offices and almost all the clergy resigned from their parishes, but they continued to work with and were supported by the people. After Germany's defeat, pastors returned to their churches and the state church again resumed functioning.

Norway is divided into dioceses, each headed by a bishop, with the bishop of Oslo as the primate of the bishops. The king and Parliament retain power to determine church organization, practices, doctrine, and education in the church. The king has complete freedom in appointing bishops and pastors, and the government has refused to authorize changes in church organization requested by the bishops that would allow more autonomy for the church. Since 1845 a Norwegian could legally withdraw from the state church and join another or no church, but more than 90 percent retain official membership in the state church. In the late 1960s, 3,500,000 members were reported.

Norway, history of: *see* Scandinavia, history of.

Norway, Nevil Shute: *see* Shute, Nevil.

Norway Current, branch of the North Atlantic Current (*q.v.*) and sometimes considered a continuation of the Gulf Stream (issuing from the Gulf of Mexico), enters the Norwegian Sea north of Scotland and flows northeastward along the coast of Norway before flowing into the Barents Sea. With subsurface temperatures ranging from 46° F (8° C) in the south to about 39° F (4° C) in the north, the current exerts a moderating influence on the climate of Norway and northern Europe. The main flow of water reaches a velocity of about ½ knot, or ½ nautical mi per hour, and is dispersed westward in eddies that meet those of the southwest-flowing East Greenland Current. This thermal mixing of the water creates excellent fishing grounds, especially around coastal regions of the Faeroe and Shetland islands and Norway.

·composition and effect on Barents Sea **2**:722c
·Greenland Sea hydrology **8**:415b

Norway Deep, also called NORWEGIAN TRENCH, in the North Sea, trench extending from Ålesund, running parallel to the coast of Norway, into the Skagerrak as far as Oslo; depths of 2,400 ft (730 m) have been recorded in the Skagerrak.
59°00′ N, 4°30′ E

·bottom water flow and submarine ridge **2**:301f

Norwegian Antarctic Expedition (1910–12), expedition led by Roald Amundsen, the first to reach the South Pole.

·route and transport method **1**:962f

Norwegian Basin, submarine depression in the North Atlantic Ocean.
68°00′ N, 2°00′ W

·Atlantic ocean features **2**:295a; map 296

Norwegian–British–Swedish Expedition (1949–52), international Antarctic expedition that carried out extensive explorations in Queen Maud Land.

·area explored and territorial claims **1**:963h

Norwegian elkhound, breed of dog that originated thousands of years ago in western Norway, where it was used as an all-purpose hunter, shepherd, guard, and companion. It generally excels in tracking European elk and has also been used for hunting bear, lynx, and lion. A medium-sized dog with erect, pointed ears, the Norwegian elkhound has a short, compact body and a thick, smooth coat of black-tipped gray hairs; it carries its tail curled high over its back. It stands 46 to 52 centimetres (18 to 20 inches), weighs 18 to 23 kilograms (40 to 50 pounds), and is characterized as a bold, energetic dog.

Norwegian elkhound
Sally Anne Thompson—EB Inc.

Norwegian Gyral, cyclonic ocean current flow centred at 68° N, 13° W in the Norwegian Sea. The Norwegian Gyral separates the Norway Current from a southeastward-flowing branch of the East Greenland Current.

Norwegian language, North Germanic language of the West Scandinavian branch, existing in two distinct and rival norms (Dano-Norwegian, or Bokmål, and New Norwegian, or Nynorsk) in Norway since 1917. Dano-Norwegian (Bokmål, the name adopted in 1917), formerly called Riksmål (National Language), stems from the written Danish introduced during the union of Denmark and Norway (1380–1814). New Norwegian, formerly known as Landsmål (Country-wide Language), was created by the language scholar Ivar Aasen (*q.v.*) during the middle of the 19th century, primarily from the dialects of the western rural districts, to carry on the tradition of Old Norse. The use of Dano-Norwegian is more widespread than that of

Energy (1970): installed electrical capacity 12,961,000 kW, production 57,605,000,000 kW-hr (14,847 kW-hr per capita).

Persons economically active (1970): 1,228,351 (31.8%), unemployed 19,451 (1.6%).

Price and earnings indexes (1963 = 100):	1964	1965	1966	1967	1968	1969	1970
consumer price index	105.7	110.2	113.8	118.8	123.0	126.8	140.2
hourly earnings index	106	116	124	134	144	158	177

Land use (1968): forested 25.7%, agricultural and under permanent cultivation 2.5%, meadows and pastures 0.4%, other 71.3%.†

Foreign trade

Imports (1970): 26,442,545,000 kroner (transport equipment 18.0%, of which, ships exceeding 100 gross tons 11.3%, passenger cars 2.3%; machinery other than electric 11.6%; petroleum and petroleum products 6.7%, of which, fuel oil 1.5%; iron and steel 6.3%, of which, plates and sheets, uncoated 2.6%; electrical machinery, apparatus, and appliances 5.9%; nickel matte 4.0%; textile yarn, fabrics, made-up articles, and related products 4.0%; chemical elements and compounds 3.8%, of which, aluminum oxide 2.1%; clothing 3.4%; nonferrous metals 2.7%). *Major import sources:* Sweden 20.1%, West Germany 14.4%, United Kingdom 12.3%, United States 7.3%, Denmark 6.2%, Canada 4.7%, Japan 4.4%, Netherlands 3.3%.

Exports (1970): 17,549,369,000 kroner (nonferrous metals 18.9%, of which, aluminum 10.6%, nickel 4.3%, copper 2.1%; ships exceeding 100 gross tons 12.4%; fish and fish preparations 7.7%, of which, frozen fillets of fish excluding herring 2.6%; paper and paperboard and manufactures thereof 7.6%, of which, newsprint paper 2.4%, writing and printing paper 1.8%; iron and steel 7.3%; machinery other than electric 5.4%; pulp and waste paper 4.3%; electrical machinery, apparatus, and appliances 3.4%). *Major export destinations:* West Germany 17.9%, United Kingdom 17.9%, Sweden 16.2%, Denmark 7.2%, United States 5.7%, France 3.6%, Netherlands 3.3%, Italy 2.8%.

Transport and communication

Transport. Railroads: (1969) length 3,373 mi, 5,429 km; (1970) passenger mi 977,500,000, passenger km 1,573,100,000; short ton-mi cargo 1,949,000,000, metric ton-km cargo 2,845,000,000. Roads (1970): total length 44,901 mi, 72,261 km (paved 7,603 mi, 12,236 km; oil, gravel, and crushed stone 5,897 mi, 9,490 km; other 31,401 mi, 50,535 km). Vehicles (1970): passenger cars 747,237, trucks and buses 156,027. Merchant marine (1970): vessels (over 1,000 gross tons) 1,164, total deadweight tonnage 29,941,000. Air transport (1970): passenger mi 1,214,000,000, passenger km 1,954,000,000; short ton-mi cargo 44,000,000, metric ton-km cargo 64,000,000; airports with scheduled flights 21.

Communication. Daily newspapers (1970): total number 81, circulation per 1,000 population 383, total circulation 1,487,000. Radios (1970): total number of receivers 1,191,000 (1 per 3.3 persons). Television: (1970) receivers 854,000 (1 per 4.6 persons); (1971) broadcasting stations 37. Telephones (1971): 1,144,795 (1 per 3.4 persons).

Education and health

Education (1970–71):	schools	teachers	students	student–teacher ratio
primary (age 7 to 14)	3,869	28,635	545,477	19.0
secondary (age 14 to 20)	339	4,907	83,865	17.1
vocational	683	5,233	74,969	14.3
teacher training	48	1,360	14,930	11.0
higher‖	10	2,422	27,483	11.3

College graduates (per 100,000 population, 1970): 92. *Literacy* (1969): total population literate (over 6) 3,410,700 (99.3%), males literate 1,689,200 (99.3%), females literate 1,721,500 (99.3%).

Health: (1969) doctors 5,412 (1 per 714 persons); (1969) hospital beds 35,450 (1 per 109 persons); (1968–69) daily per capita caloric intake 2,910 calories (FAO recommended minimum requirement 2,580 calories).

*Based on land area. †Percentages do not add to 100.0 because of rounding. ‡Salaried employees and wage earners only. §1970. ‖1969–70.

New Norwegian. Both of these mutually intelligible languages are used in government and education, and plans have been made to bring them closer together gradually into a common Norwegian language, Samnorsk, though resistance to these plans has been vigorous.

Old Norwegian diverged from the other Scandinavian languages at the end of the Common Scandinavian period (600–1050) but failed to develop as a national language because of the cultural decline after the Black Plague in the mid-14th century and the political unions, first with Sweden (1319) and then with Denmark (1380). The last documents in pure Norwegian (without Danish influence) date from the period 1450–1500. *See also* Dano-Norwegian language; New Norwegian language; Danish language; Old Norse.

·Bible translation history **2**:894a
·development and modern changes **13**:265a
·English vocabulary borrowings **6**:879b
·Germanic language evolution, illus. 2 **8**:24
·juvenile literature development **4**:239b
·literary handicap in 16th century **8**:27f
·Nynorsk and Bokmål developments **8**:28c
·Scandinavian comparative features **8**:28g
·Scandinavian language–dialect classes **10**:646a

Norwegian literature, body of writings of the Norwegian peoples that, among the literatures of modern Europe, is remarkable for being so late flowering and yet so impressively deep rooted. Only after the separation of Norway from Denmark in 1814 is it possible to point to a literature that is unambiguously Norwegian; its roots, of course, reach back more than 1,000 years into the pagan Norse past. In its evolution Norwegian literature became intertwined with Icelandic and then with Danish literatures. By the end of the 19th century, however, Norwegian literature—particularly by virtue of the massive achievements in drama of Henrik Ibsen—occupied an influential position in Western literature. Its achievements in the first half of the 20th century lie mainly in the novel and in lyric poetry. *Major ref.* **10**:1161e

·development of children's literature **4**:239b
·Ibsen's works and social themes **9**:151g
·medieval differentiation from Icelandic **10**:1118d

Norwegian Sea, Norwegian NORSKEHAVET, section of the North Atlantic Ocean, bordered by the Greenland and Barents seas (northwest through northeast); Norway (east); the North Sea, the Shetland and Faeroe islands, and the Atlantic Ocean (south); and Iceland and Jan Mayen Island (west). The sea reaches a maximum depth of about 13,020 ft (3,970 m); and it maintains a salinity of about 35‰ (35 per mille, or 3.5 percent). A submarine ridge linking Greenland, Iceland, the Faeroe Islands, and north Scotland separates the Norwegian Sea from the open Atlantic, and thus, cut by the Arctic Circle, it is often associated with the Arctic Ocean to the north. The warm Norway Current flows northeastward off the Norway coast and produces generally ice-free conditions. Colder currents mixing with this warm water create excellent fishing grounds (mainly for cod, herring, and whitefish), especially around coastal regions of Iceland and Norway and the Shetland and Faeroe islands.
70°00′ N, 2°00′ E

·climatic elements and cooling effect **4**:720e
·map, Norway **13**:266

Norwich, cathedral and university city, county of Norfolk, England, on the navigable River Wensum a short distance north of its confluence with the River Yare. Chalk is exposed in the valley of the Wensum, but the city has also spread onto the later deposits that lie above it.

Although prehistoric man was active in East Anglia, a traditional division of England of which Norwich is the regional capital, the present site does not seem to have been occupied until Saxon times, when the village of Northwic was founded on a gravel terrace above the Wensum. By 1004, when the town was sacked by the Danes, it had become an important market centre. Shortly after the Norman Conquest (1066), the cathedral church and a Benedictine monastery were founded on low ground near the river. Remains of the monastery are extant, and the cathedral still has a Norman apse and nave, besides a 15th-century stone spire (315 ft [96 m] high) and well-preserved 14th- and 15th-century cloisters, the largest in England. The precincts are entered from the ancient fairground of Tombland through the richly sculptured Erpingham Gate (1420) and St. Aethelberht's Gate (1316). A Norman castle, constructed (12th century) in a prominent position to the east of the town's principal market, has been since 1894 the city's main museum and art gallery, with an archaelogical collection and paintings of the Norwich School, which flourished in the first half of the 19th century.

Until the late 18th century Norwich was one of the most prosperous of English provincial towns, challenged only by Bristol and York. The first charter dates from 1158 and a second was given by Richard I in 1194. The prosperity of the medieval town is reflected in the number of churches dating from this period, 30 of which still exist, including St. Julian's, St. Andrew's, and St. John Maddermarket. Prosperity was based upon the woollen industry, which was aided by Edward III (ruled 1327–77), who induced Flemish weavers to settle in Norwich in 1336, and also by the influx of strangers (mainly from the Low Countries) during the reign of Elizabeth I (1558–1603). In 1579 nearly a third of the town's population of 16,000 were immigrants. During the 15th century, the flint Guildhall was built overlooking the market square. At the time of the English Civil War (1642–51), the population was predominantly behind Cromwell and the Parliamentary cause. Except for the sacking of churches and the cathedral, the town saw little of the strife that many parts of the country witnessed. From the 18th century and the coming of the Industrial Revolution, Norwich declined in relation to the new industrial centres of the north; in the 1970s little weaving, except in silk, was practiced. This industry has been replaced in importance by the manufacture of boots and shoes, of which Norwich now is one of the largest centres in the country, especially in the production of ladies' fashion shoes and children's shoes. Engineering, printing, and the processing of mustard, are also important industries.

The city's grammar school was founded by Edward VI (ruled 1547–53), and the British naval hero Horatio Nelson was one of its most eminent pupils. Establishments of higher education in the city include the Norwich School of Art, founded in 1846, the Keswick Hall College of Education, and the University of East Anglia, founded in 1961 but not admitting its first students until 1963. The university, which includes the Centre of East Anglian Studies, is situated at Earlham Hall, long associated with the Gurney family (of which the reformer Elizabeth Fry was a member). The city also has a central library and the little Maddermarket Theatre. Pop. (1971 prelim.) 121,688.
52°38′ N, 1°18′ E

Norwich, city, coextensive with Norwich Town, New London County, southeastern Connecticut, U.S., at the confluence of the Yantic and Shetucket rivers, which there form the Thames. Norwich Town was founded in 1659 by settlers from Saybrook led by Capt. John Mason and the Rev. James Fitch. The shipbuilding industry and shipping were important in the 18th century, and from the Revolution to the Civil War firearms were made there. Textiles then dominated the economy until after 1912, when there was a trend toward diversification. Norwich is the birthplace of the Revolutionary War traitor Benedict Arnold and the prominent 19th-century educator Daniel Coit Gilman, and is the home of the Huntington family, many members of which were leaders in early American civil and military affairs. It is the seat of Thames Valley State Technical Institute (1963). Inc. 1784; town and city consolidated, 1952. Pop. (1980) 38,074.
41°32′ N, 72°05′ W

Norwich school, term designating a group of glass painters that flourished in England during the Middle Ages and a more significant group of regional landscape painters that was established in February 1803 as the Norwich Society of Artists and flourished in Norwich, Norfolk, in the first half of the 19th century. The work of the leaders of the latter group, John Crome (died 1821) and John Sell Cotman (died 1842), was inspired by the Dutch landscapists and by the English painter Thomas Gainsborough. Other members of the Norwich school were Miles Edmund and John Joseph Cotman (sons of John Sell), John Bernay Crome (the son of John), George Vincent, James Stark, John Thirtle, Joseph Stannard, John Middleton, Robert Dixon, and Henry Bright.

Norwich terrier, short-legged terrier bred around 1880 in England, where it soon became a fad with Cambridge students. It was later used by various American hunt clubs and has also drawn notice as a rabbit hunter. It is stockily built, with either erect or hanging ears, and it has a dense, wiry, weather-resistant coat, usually reddish brown. A small, characteristically rugged and loyal dog, the Norwich terrier stands about 23 to 28 centimetres (9 to 11 inches) and weighs 4.5 to 6.5 kilograms (10 to 14 pounds).

Norwich ware, delft (tin-glazed) earthenware produced in Norwich, Norfolk, and about which little is known. Around 1567, two Flemish potters, Jasper Andries and Jacob Janson, who had moved to Norwich from Antwerp, made paving tiles and vessels for apothecaries and others. So far nothing made by them in Norwich has been identified. Potting was still active in the town in 1696, but although posset pots and other white ware, as well as a type of puzzle jug often decorated with a tulip on the front, are known to have come from Norfolk, it is not known whether they were imported from the Continent (Holland?) or were of English manufacture. In view of their number it is possible that they were indigenous. They are probably from the latter half of the 17th century.

Norwid, Cyprian Kamil (b. Sept. 24, 1821, Laskowo-Gluchy, near Warsaw—d. May 23, 1883, Paris), the most original and innovative Polish poet of the 19th century, whose genius was not appreciated until his rediscovery in the 20th century. He is one of the most tragic figures among the generation of Polish poets who lived in exile after the suppression of the insurrection against Russia of 1830–31. From 1842 Norwid lived for some time in Italy, where he studied painting and sculpture. In 1849 he went to Paris and in 1852 to the U.S. but in 1854 returned via England to Paris, where he led a life of penury and obscurity until his death.

His lack of literary success in his own day was a result of the idiosyncratic and difficult style of his many writings in prose and verse—poems (*Poezye*, 1863), plays (*Krakus*, published 1863; *Wanda*, 1901; *Kleopatra*, 1904), and treatises (*e.g.*, "Promethidion," a treatise on aesthetics, in prose and verse, included in *Poezye*). It was also a result of his intellectual reservations about the ideas of Romanticism; he distinguished between false and genuine ideological coinage too acutely for his contemporaries' comfort. His poetry is essentially philosophical. It shows profound understanding of history, respect for the individual, a fine sense of irony, intellectual integrity, and a self-effacing subordination to his subject, which results in the utmost verbal economy. Norwid's work was restored to posterity by Zenon Przesmycki (pseudonym Miriam), who began publishing his works in 1901.

·Polish literature of the 19th century **10**:1210a
·Young Poland movement participation **10**:1252f

Norwood, town (urbanized township), Norfolk County, eastern Massachusetts, U.S., on the Neponset River, southwest of Boston. Settled in 1678, it was incorporated (from parts of Dedham and Walpole) in 1872. Although primarily residential, it has some industry, chiefly printing and publishing, and the manufacture of electrical machinery and fabricated metal products. The Norwood Memorial Municipal Building has a lofty 170-ft (52-m) tower containing a 52-bell carillon. Pop. (1980) 29,711.
42°11′ N, 71°12′ W

Norwood, city, Hamilton County, southeastern Ohio, U.S., completely surrounded by Cincinnati. Settled in 1804, it became a crossroads coach stop (1809) known as Sharpsburg, after John Sharp, an early settler. The present name was adopted upon its incorporation as a village (1888). Its location on the upland between the Great and Little Miami rivers away from the major travel routes resulted in very slow economic growth until *c.* 1900, when it became a minor railway centre and residential suburb. Manufactures now include office equipment, automobiles, chemicals, playing cards, machine tools, containers, printing, airplane parts, and rubber goods. Norwood is the seat of the Athenaeum of Ohio, a Roman Catholic college for men, founded (1829) as the Seminary of St. Francis Xavier. Mt. St. Mary's Seminary is nearby. Inc. city, 1903. Pop. (1980) 26,342.
39°10′ N, 84°28′ W

nose, the prominent structure between the eyes that serves as the entrance to the respiratory tract and contains the olfactory organ. It provides air for respiration, serves the sense of smell, conditions the air by filtering, warming, and moistening it, and cleans itself of foreign debris extracted from inhalations.

The nose has two cavities, separated from one another by a wall of cartilage. The external openings are known as nares or nostrils. The external portion of the nose is firm but pliable. The skin and tissue contains thick collagen and muscle fibres; close to the skull there is bone and cartilage lining the walls. The function of these structures is to provide a semirigid organ that can resist collapse during inhalation.

The nose is a series of tunnels leading from the outside of the body to the nasal portion of the throat (nasopharynx) together with a small portion at the top that is taken up by the olfactory organ. Behind the mouth there is an expansion into the throat known as the oropharynx that corresponds to the nasopharynx. These two cavernous areas are continuous with each other. The roof of the mouth and the floor of the nose are formed by the palatine bone, the mouth part of which is commonly called the hard palate; a flap of tissue, the soft palate, extends back into the nasopharynx and oropharynx. During swallowing, the soft palate is pressed upward, thus closing off the nasopharynx so that food is not lodged in the back of the nose.

The nasal cavity is of complex shape. The forward section, within and above each nostril, is called the vestibule. Behind the vestibule and along each outer wall are three elevations, running generally from front to rear. Each elevation, called a concha, hangs over an air passage. Beside and above the uppermost concha is the olfactory region of the nasal cavity. The rest of the cavity is the respiratory portion. The tissue lining the vestibule is an extension of the facial skin. It contains many hair follicles, sweat glands, and sebaceous (oil-producing) glands. The respiratory area is lined with a moist mucous membrane that contains tall column-shaped cells. On the surface of these cells are fine hairlike projections known as cilia, which serve to collect and move debris toward the oropharynx. Mucus from cells in the membrane wall also helps to trap particles of dust, carbon, soot, and bacteria. Sinus cavities are located in the bony skull on both sides of the nose.

In the olfactory (smelling) portion of the nose, most of the lining is mucous membrane. A small segment of the lining is given over to the olfactory apparatus. In this segment, there are three types of cells: the nerve cells that are the actual sensory organs, supporting cells, and other cells, called basal cells, which are thought to develop into supporting cells. Fibres, called dendrites, which project from the nerve cells into the nasal cavity, are covered only by a thin layer of moisture. The moisture dissolves microscopic particles that the air has carried into the nose from odour-emitting substances, and the particles dissolved in the fluid stimulate the olfactory nerve cells chemically.

·cranial nerve distribution **12**:1019a
·facial appearance in embryo **6**:748b; illus. 747
·Homo sapiens skull evolution **8**:1045b; illus.
·infectious local diseases **9**:543c
·plastic surgery in ancient India **11**:824g
·primate olfactory sense diminution **14**:1023h
·racial typing by physical traits **15**:352a
·respiratory system anatomy **15**:764c
·sinuses and direct brain infection **16**:806h
·smell mechanism and nerve supply **16**:553g; illus.

Nose, The (1927–28), opera by Dmitri Shostakovich.

·satiric style basis **16**:717d

nosebleed, or EPISTAXIS, a common and usually unimportant disorder in childhood. It may also result from local conditions of inflammation, small ulcers or polypoid growths, or severe injuries to the skull. Vascular disease, such as high blood pressure, may provoke it, and such diseases as scurvy and hemophilia also may be responsible. Usually it is easily controlled by rest and application of cold and pressure. On occasion it may require expert care.

No se emendera jamas, also called CANTATA SPAGNUOLA, early cantata of George Frideric Handel.

·composition and inspiration **8**:603c

no-see-ums (fly): *see* biting midge.

nose fly: *see* bot fly.

nosegay, also called TUSSIE-MUSSIE or POSEY, a small, hand-held bouquet popular in mid-19th-century Victorian England as an accessory carried by fashionable ladies at social affairs. Composed of mixed flowers and herbs and edged with a paper frill or greens, the arrangement was sometimes inserted into a silver filigree holder. When supplied by an admirer, a nosegay became a vehicle for the floral "language of love"; *e.g.*, a red tulip was a declaration of love; a sprig of dogwood returned by the young lady was a sign of indifference; a variegated pink meant that she rejected her suitor's affection. This variety of bouquet has enjoyed periodic revivals.

·floral decoration forms and variety **7**:413d

Young girl holding a nosegay, "The Children of Israel and Sarah Griffith," oil on canvas by Oliver Tarbell Eddy, 1844; in the Maryland Historical Society, Baltimore

By courtesy of the Maryland Historical Society, Baltimore

Nosek, Václav (1892–*c.* 1955), Czech Communist party leader and minister of the interior.

·Czech party solidarity **2**:1198c

noselite, or NOSEAN (mineral): *see* sodalite.

Nosema, a genus of parasitic spore-forming Protozoa, of the order Microsporida, found in host cells where it undergoes repeated asexual divisions followed by spore formation.

The species *N. bombycis*, which causes the epidemic disease pébrine in silkworms, attacks all tissues and all developmental stages from embryo to adult. In advanced infections, small brown spots cover the body of the silkworm. Diseased larvae, which either are unable to spin cocoons or else spin them loosely, die without pupating. Louis Pasteur identified the spores ("corpuscles") of *Nosema* as the disease agent in 1865 and suggested control by destruction of infected silkworm colonies and improved sanitation.

Another species, *N. apis*, attacks the gut epithelium of honeybees (especially workers) and causes a serious form of dysentery in animals, nosema disease.

·bee diseases and pest control **2**:794d
·N. cuniculi in diseases of laboratory animals, table 8 **5**:876

nose ring, ornaments inserted through different parts of the nose for personal adornment and used sometimes to signify social rank. Nose ornaments are found especially among people in India, New Guinea, Polynesia, the pre-Columbian Americas, Australia, and parts of Africa. Sometimes the ala, or wing of the nose, and the septum are perforated. Often, only a small hole is made through the septum; but the hole can also be big enough for a finger to be passed through. Not only gold and jewels are worn in the nose: in New Guinea, especially among the Tuburi and the Solomon Islanders, the men wear great pointed sticks or the tusks of wild pig through holes in the nose.

noshi, Japanese garment formalized in the 12th century, consisting of a hiplength jacket worn with baggy trousers tied at the ankles.

·style and period of origin **5**:1037g

No siempre lo peor es cierto (*c.* 1640), play by Calderón de la Barca.

·Calderón's works and style **3**:594b

Noske, Gustav (b. July 9, 1868, Brandenburg, now in East Germany—d. Nov. 30, 1946, Hannover, now in West Germany), right-wing Social Democratic German politician, notorious for his ruthless suppression of a Communist uprising in Berlin, who was defense minister of the Weimar Republic from 1919 to 1920.

A member of the Reichstag (parliament), he became controversial within his own party for his support of imperial military and colonial programs. Noske joined other conservative Socialists after 1914 in supporting Germany's participation in World War I. Regarded as his party's military expert, he was commissioned by the last imperial government to restore order at Kiel following the sailors' mutiny of October 1918. In December he was elected to the six-member ruling council, which, until the accession of the Weimar National Assembly (February 1919), provided an interim republican government for Germany. In January 1919 he was called upon to suppress the Communist insurrection in Berlin, a task he accomplished brutally but with dispatch. He served as minister of defense in the first Weimar Cabinet from February 1919 until he resigned in March 1920 under growing Socialist criticism in the wake of an abortive right-wing attempt to overthrow the government (the Kapp Putsch). Subsequently, he served as governor of the province of Hannover (1920–33) and in July 1944 took part in the unsuccessful coup against Adolf Hitler.

·German suppression of Communism **6**:177d

Nosopsyllus: *see* flea.

Nossi-Bé (Madagascar): *see* Nosy Be.

Nossob (NOSSOP) **River,** rises in central South West Africa and flows about 500 mi (800 km) southeast into the Auob River shortly before it empties into the Molopo River. It forms part of the border between Botswana and Cape of Good Hope Province (South Africa).
26°55′ S, 20°37′ E

·Kalahari Desert landscape and drainage **10**:373a
·map, South Africa **17**:62

Nostoc, a genus of blue-green algae with cells arranged in beadlike chains that are grouped together in a gelatinous mass. Ranging from microscopic size to walnut size, masses of *Nostoc* may be found on soil and floating in stagnant water. Reproduction is by fragmentation. A special thick-walled cell (akinete) has the ability to withstand desiccation for long periods of time. After 70 years of dry storage, the akinete of one species germinated into a filament when moistened. Like all blue-green algae, *Nostoc* contains two pigments, blue phycocyanin and red phycoerythrin, and has the ability to fix nitrogen. A terrestrial species is a food source in the Orient.

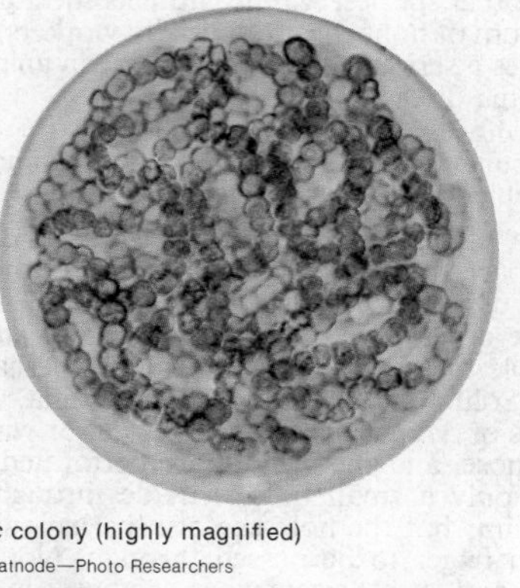

Nostoc colony (highly magnified)
Winton Patnode—Photo Researchers

·lichened relationships and exchanges **10**:883c
·Nostocales classification **1**:496b

Nostradamus, also known as MICHEL DE NOTREDAME OR NOSTREDAME (b. Dec. 14, 1503, Saint-Rémy, Fr.—d. July 2, 1566, Salon), astrologer and physician, the most widely read seer of the Renaissance. Nostradamus began his medical practice in Agen in 1529 and moved to Salon in 1544, where he became well-known for his innovative medicine and treatment during outbreaks of the plague at Aix and Lyons in 1546–47. He began making prophecies about 1547, which he published in 1555 in a book entitled *Centuries*. The work consisted of rhymed quatrains grouped in hundreds, each set of 100 called a century. Astrology was at a peak at this time, and an enlarged second edition, dedicated to the King, was published in 1558.

Some of his prophecies appeared to be fulfilled, and his fame became so widespread that he was invited to the court of Catherine de Médicis, queen consort of Henry II of France, where he cast the horoscopes of her children. He was appointed physician-in-ordinary by Charles IX when Charles became king in 1560. The subject of many commentaries, Nostradamus' prophecies were condemned in 1781 by the Congregation of the Index, the body set up by the Roman Catholic Church for the examination of books and manuscripts. Because of their cryptic style and content, the prophecies have continued to create much controversy. Some of them are thought to have prefigured historical events that have occurred since Nostradamus' time. Others, having no apparent meaning, are said to foretell events that have not yet occurred.

nostril, also called EXTERNAL NARIS, external opening into the nose.

·evolution of function in vertebrates **5**:787e

Nostromo (1904), novel, considered to be Joseph Conrad's masterpiece, a pessimistic vision of history and politics. The San Tomé silver mine, located in an imaginary South American republic, is seen by its idealistic owner, Charles Gould, as an instrument of national prosperity and, therefore, of near-automatic political and social progress. When a military revolution breaks out, Gould decides the silver must be removed by sea. The mission is entrusted to a proud, capable Italian stevedore boss, called "Nostromo" ("Our Man") among Europeans who imagine that his self-esteem renders him incorruptible. The vessel on which Nostromo carries the silver is hit by a rebel ship, but it manages to limp to Great Isabel Island, where he buries the treasure. He then sinks the ship in the bay and swims to the mainland, where his courageous role in one of the battles of the revolution makes him a local hero. When he returns to Great Isabel, Nostromo realizes that since all assume the treasure has been lost, he can keep it without damaging his honour. He enriches himself gradually. One night, visiting the island in secret, he is mistakenly shot by his friend the lighthouse keeper. Before he dies, he confesses the secret of the silver to Mrs. Gould, who never reveals her knowledge.

·factual basis in Saint-Antoine voyage **5**:29c
·social disillusionment theme **10**:1216g

Nosy Be, also called NOSSI-BÉ (*Be*, Great, *Nosy*, Island), volcanic island with forests and numerous craters and crater lakes, lying about 5 mi (8 km) off the northwestern shore of Madagascar (Malagasy Republic). It is 19 mi long, and 12 mi wide and has an area of 120 sq mi (300 sq km). Its highest point is Mt. Passot (1,079 ft [329 m]). Its climate is hot and damp, with temperatures ranging from 95° to 64° F (35° to 18° C) and annual rainfall of 78 to 118 in. (1,975 to 3,000 mm). Products, chiefly sugar and oils for perfumery, also include rum, vanilla, black pepper, and bitter oranges. The capital, in the south, is Hellville, a resort and port for foreign shipping and trade along the west coast of Madagascar. There is an airfield at Fascène, 7 mi away.

Beach on Nosy Be, Madagascar
Gerald Cubitt

The arrival of a Captain Passot's warship "Colibri" in 1840 initiated the cession of the island to the French, and the town Hellville was named after Passot's commander in chief, Admiral de Hell. The island is part of Majunga province and has been administered from Madagascar since 1896. Latest census 25,787.
13°20′ S, 48°15′ E

·map, Madagascar **11**:270

Notabile (Malta): *see* Mdina.

Notacanthidae (fish family): see spiny eel.

Notacanthiformes, order of deep-sea fishes commonly called spiny eels. They have long tapering bodies about 50 cm (20 in.) long and a protruding snout.

·characteristics and classification **7**:343c

Notaden (frog): *see* Myobatrachidae.

notarial will, in law, a will that is executed so that the testator either dictates his provisions to a notary or hands him an instrument declaring that it contains his will.

·inheritance and testate succession **9**:593a

noṭariqon (biblical exegesis): *see* middot.

notary, or NOTARY PUBLIC, a public official whose chief function in common-law countries is to authenticate contracts, deeds, and other documents by an appropriate certificate with a notarial seal. In Roman law the *notarius* was originally a slave or freedman who took notes of judicial proceedings. The work of the modern notary, however, corresponds more to that of the Roman *tabularius*, who took and preserved evidence. In medieval times the notary was an ecclesiastical officer who preserved evidence, but his duties were mainly secular.

The modern notary is appointed, after making application, by a secular official; the appointment usually becomes effective on payment of a fee, on the taking of an oath of office, and, in many parts of the United States, on the deposit of a bond to assure the proper performance of duties.

In the United States, qualifications for the position vary little from state to state, and, in general, a notary must be a citizen of legal age and a resident of the area in which he desires appointment. The jurisdiction of the notary's office is limited to the state or, in some states, only the county in which he resides. In countries such as France and Italy, however, and in the province of Quebec, which follow the civil-law tradition, there are educational requirements similar to those for lawyers.

In the civil-law countries of western Europe, and in Latin American and French areas of North America, the office of notary is a much more important position than in the United States and England. The civil-law notary may be roughly described as a lawyer who specializes in the law relating to real estate, sales, mortgages, and the settlement of estates but who is not allowed to appear in court. Documents prepared by him or authenticated in the proper manner are, in these countries, admissible in court without further proof of their authenticity; the notary guarantees the identity of the parties.

In the Anglo-American-law countries, on the other hand, courts will not accept as true the facts certified by a notary except in the case of a bill of exchange protested abroad. Nor may a notary draw up legal documents such as wills, contracts, mortgages, and deeds for a fee, for such work constitutes the practice of law. Nevertheless, many statutes require that the authenticity of specified documents be certified by a notary; the most common of these in the United States are deeds conveying land. In these cases the notary must not take the acknowledgment of a person who does not appear before him or who is not known to him unless evidence of identification is presented.

Certain other officials may be given notarial functions by statute, such as justices of the peace, consular officials, certain military officers, and various court officials.
·legal role since the Middle Ages **10**:780d

Notation, Kraton (music): *see* Kraton notation.

notation, microtone, a system of musical notation indicating scale degrees of less than a half step.
·modern extension to Western system **12**:735e

Not-Being, denial of, in Eleatic philosophy, the assertion of the monistic philosopher Parmenides of Elea that only Being exists and that Not-Being is not, and can never be. Being is necessarily described as one, unique, unborn and indestructible, and immovable.

The opposite of Being is Not-Being (*to mē eon*), which for the Eleatics meant absolute nothingness, the total negation of Being; hence Not-Being can never be. Parmenides knew that the assertion that Not-Being also exists must be wrong, although no Greek vocabulary for a formal logic existed that would enable him to say precisely what was wrong with it. But he was nonetheless certain about his position: "For you cannot know Not-Being (*to mē eon*), nor even say it."

The problem of the existence of total nothingness or "the void" (Greek *kenon*) was important in the theoretical foundations of Greek Atomism, which asserted, despite the seemingly rigorous logic of the Eleatics, that nothingness must in fact exist. Only atoms and the void are real, they held, and everything that exists must be composed of them. The Atomists' position, as Aristotle explained it, was that "unless there is a void with a separate reality of its own 'what is' could not be moved; nor again could there be a many [as opposed to the Eleatic One] since there is nothing to hold them [as separate pieces of Being] apart."

The void, or absolute Not-Being, thus exists as a necessary condition for the atoms to be many (for without the void separating atoms all would be the Eleatic One) and for the atoms to move (for there must be that into which they move, or void). Aristotle claimed that it was to defend the sensory conviction that motion and change are real physical facts that the Atomic theory, with its declaration that there is a void, was first proposed.

The Eleatic denial of the void is sometimes seen as a direct refutation of an earlier Pythagorean view, a pre-Parmenidian Atomism asserting that a kind of Not-Being, understood as a cosmic air, exists. But no documentary evidence for such a view has survived.
·Eleatic philosophical theory **6**:526c

note, in notation of Western music, sign indicating pitch by its position on the staff and duration by its shape. Notes evolved in the 13th century from neumes (*q.v.*), signs indicating relative or absolute pitch and nuance but not necessarily rhythm. The earliest notes were the longa ▀▌, and brevis ▀, and their derivatives, the maxima ■, and semibrevis ◆. In modern notation the brevis and semibrevis correspond to the double whole note, ||o||, and the whole note, o. Other modern notes, in diminishing time value, are the half note, 𝅗𝅥; quarter note, ♩; eighth note, ♪; sixteenth note, 𝅘𝅥𝅯; thirty-second note, 𝅘𝅥𝅰; and sixty-fourth note, 𝅘𝅥𝅱.

"Note" may also refer to a tone, the sound either produced by a singer or musical instrument or represented by a pitch name (as G, or sol), a neume, or a written note.
·function and types **12**:733b

Notebooks of Malte Laurids Brigge, The (1930), translation of DIE AUFZEICHNUNGEN DES MALTE LAURIDS BRIGGE (1910), prose work by the German poet Rainer Maria Rilke, begun at Rome in 1904, continued mainly in Paris, and published in 1910. This study of the dark side of existence and the night side of the mind reveals the mental and spiritual terrors that the young Danish hero undergoes in Paris and the agonies of fear he lived through in his childhood.
·stylistic variations in prose-writing **10**:1076d
·themes and critical acclaim **15**:847f

Nöteborg, Treaty of (1323), agreement between Sweden and Russia.
·Swedish territorial expansion **16**:310h

Notechis scutatus (snake): *see* tiger snake.

Notemigonus (fish genus): *see* minnow.

Noteridae, family of burrowing water beetles in the insect order Coleoptera.
·traits and classification **4**:834c

Notes d'un peintre (1908), article by Henri Matisse, published in *La Grande Revue*.
·colour and artistic meaning theories **11**:700e

Notes from the Underground, translation of ZAPISKI IZ PODPOLYA (1864), novel by Russian writer Fyodor Dostoyevsky, on the one hand a portrait of the "underground" narrator, mocking his own philosophizing, and on the other an attack on the positivist philosophy of those who believed that material advancement would bring social progress. The work's bitterness and tragic cynicism reflect Dostoyevsky's life at that period.
·dualism, alienation, and radicalism **5**:967g

Notes of a Madman (1884), unfinished short story by Leo Tolstoy.
·audience and theme of despair **18**:485e

Notes Towards the Definition of Culture (1948), essay by T.S. Eliot.
·essay use in societal redefinition **10**:1078e

Noth, Martin (b. Aug. 3, 1902, Dresden, now in East Germany—d. May 30, 1968, Horvot Shivta, Israel), German biblical scholar, professor of theology at Bonn from 1945 to 1965. He postulated that the tribes of Israel that descended from Leah were an original amphictyony (union of communities about a central shrine) around which the 12 tribe amphictyony was formed. He also held the view that the unity called Israel did not exist before the covenant assembly at Shechem related in the Book of Joshua, chapter 24, where, in his view, the tribes accepted the worship and the covenant of Yahweh imposed by Joshua.
·Book of Joshua authorship **2**:907b
·Mosaic tradition analysis and theory **12**:487d

Notharchus macrorhynchos: *see* puffbird.

Notharctus, extinct genus of primitive primates of the fossil family Notharctidae, known from Eocene deposits in Europe and North America (the Eocene Epoch began 54,000,000 years ago and lasted 16,000,000 years). *Notharctus* was small and resembled the modern lemurs on the island of Madagascar. Its dentition was rather primitive; four premolars were retained instead of three, the canine teeth were still primitive, but the upper incisors were relatively modern.
·family classification and fossil record **14**:1028h
·primate ancestry and evolution **14**:1026b; illus.

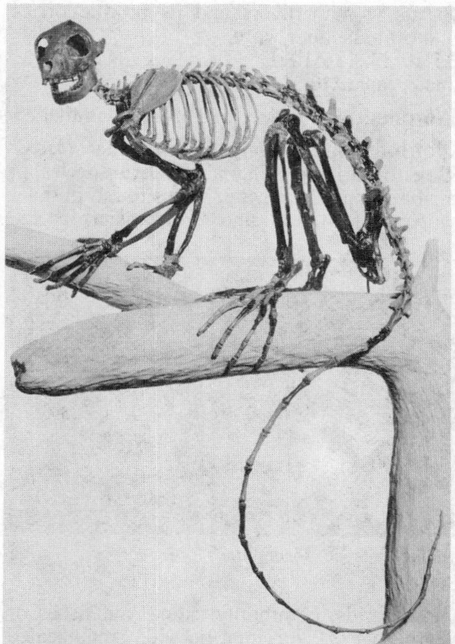

Notharctus osborni

By courtesy of the American Museum of Natural History, New York

Nō theatre 13:270, traditional Japanese theatrical expression in which the performers are storytellers who use their visual appearances and their movements to suggest the essence of the tale rather than its action.

The text article covers the nature and objectives of Nō, its forms and traditions (including repertoire, structural elements, and staging and design conventions), and its historical continuity.

REFERENCES in other text articles:
·actor's status and staging **18**:252h *passim* to 256b
·aesthetic value concept **1**:161b
·directing superfluity **5**:829g
·dramas of the 15th century **10**:1069c
·dramatic style and audience appeal **5**:985b
·dramatic theory of Zeami Motokiyo **5**:986f
·East Asian performing aesthetics **5**:469b *passim* to 470h
·funding, production, and social function **18**:259d
·Kabuki influenced by ancient forms **10**:367c
·Kamakura period origins **10**:69h
·mask design and types **11**:586c
·musical instruments and melodic rules **12**:700g
·mythological basis of performing arts **12**:799a
·origin, acting, scenery, and audience **18**:239a
·pageant drama origins in Far East **13**:862a
·sources, stage design, and costumes **17**:534d
·sources and beginnings **5**:476e; illus. 477
·text setting methods, illus. 8 **12**:685
·tragedy absence in drama **18**:587h
·vocal and instrumental music **12**:684a
·Yeats' adaptation for Irish theatre **19**:1077b

nothingness (mysticism and religion): *see* emptiness.

Nothofagus (tree): *see* beech.

Nothosaurus, genus of primitive marine reptiles found as fossils in Triassic rocks of southwestern and eastern Asia, North Africa, and especially of Europe (the Triassic Period began 225,000,000 years ago and lasted 35,000,000 years). *Nothosaurus* is characterized by a slender body, long neck and tail, and relatively long limbs. Although an aquatic form, the limbs were not particularly specialized for life in the water, even though webbing probably was present between the digits. In many ways, *Nothosaurus* and related forms, known as the nothosaurs, much resembled the more successful plesiosaurs but were not ancestral to them. The palate in the nothosaurs was closed, and the air passages were separated from the food passages, an adaptation to aid feeding while in the water. Numerous pointed teeth were present along the margins of the jaws. *Nothosaurus* probably swam through the water and could whip its long, slender neck about in pursuit of fleeing fish. It is probable that *Nothosaurus* and related forms evolved from terrestrial reptiles.
·Nothosauria fossils, eras, and aquatic traits **7**:570d
·Nothosauria Triassic Tetrapod sea invasion **18**:695h

Nothura, bird genus of the order Tinamiformes.
·feeding behaviour **18**:426a

Nótios Evvoïkós Kólpos (Greece): *see* Euboea, Gulf of.

Notitia Dignitatum, official list of all ancient Roman civil and military posts; a major source of information on the administration of the late empire, of the late 4th or early 5th century. The surviving text includes drawings of the insignia of each magistrate.

Notium, Battle of (407 BC), victory of the Peloponnesian League over the Athenian fleet, costing Athens the supremacy of the Aegean Sea.
·events and effects **8**:360b

Notker, bishop of Liège, Belgium, 972 to 1008.
·prince-bishopric authority expansion **11**:135g

Noto, town and episcopal see, Siracusa province, southeastern Sicily, Italy, on the southern slopes of the Monti (mountains) Iblei (Hyblaei Hills) southwest of Syracuse. It was founded in 1703 about 4 mi (7 km) southeast of the Siculan and Roman city of Netum, which was destroyed in the earthquake of 1693. Between 1837 and 1865 Noto replaced Syracuse as the provincial capital. The cathedral and the Palazzo Ducazio are notable among many fine Baroque churches and palaces. The communal library houses a small local museum.

SS. Mira e Corrado church, Noto, Sicily
E.P.A. Inc—EB Inc.

An agricultural centre, Noto has light industries including food processing and cement and soap manufacture. To the southeast is the small bathing resort of Noto Marina. Pop. (1971 prelim.) mun., 23,551.
36°53′ N, 15°05′ E

Notocactus: *see* ball cactus.

notochord, flexible rodlike structure of cells, principal longitudinal structural element of chordates and of the early embryo of vertebrates, in which it is later replaced by the vertebral column. It derives during gastrulation (infolding of the blastula, or early embryo) from cells that migrate anteriorly in the midline between the hypoblast and the epiblast (inner and outer layers of the blastula). These cells coalesce immediately beneath the developing central nervous system. With the formation of the vertebral column, the notochord becomes vestigial. It is incorporated into the column as the centres of the intervertebral discs, called the nuclei pulposi, and serves to cushion the vertebrae.
·chordate distinguishing features **4**:450c
·embryonic organization and anatomical function **5**:631d; illus. 629
·embryonic origins of human nervous system **6**:746f; illus. 743
·fish vertebral evolution **7**:333c
·flexible endoskeletal systems **16**:819h
·intervertebral disk contributions **10**:253g
·nervous system development **12**:989a
·skeletal development in vertebrates **16**:823c

Notodontidae: *see* prominent moth.

Notograptidae, family of eel-shaped fishes in the order Perciformes.
·classification and general features **14**:56c

Noto-hantō, English NOTO PENINSULA, in Ishikawa Prefecture (*ken*), Honshu, Japan,

Terraced rice paddies on Noto Peninsula, Honshu Island, Japan
Photos Pack—EB Inc.

juts into the Sea of Japan and encloses Toyama-wan (Toyama Bay). The largest peninsula on the northern Honshu coast, it extends northward for 50 mi (80 km) and has a width of about 19 mi. The peninsula is separated from mainland Honshu by the Ōchi-gata (Lake Ōchi) graben (a depression of the Earth's crust bounded by faults). Its mountainous interior is similar to that of Sado (*q.v.*), an island to the northeast.

Noto-hantō has been settled since ancient times, and there is evidence of early contact with the island of Tsu-shima and with northern Korea and Manchuria. The town of Wajima, at the peninsula's northern tip, is known for its woman divers and its production of elaborate lacquer ware.
35°10′ N, 136°10′ E
·map, Japan **10**:36

Notonectidae (insect): *see* back swimmer.

Notopteridae, family of the order Osteoglossiformes including about five species of air-breathing, freshwater fishes found in quiet waters of Africa and southeastern Asia.

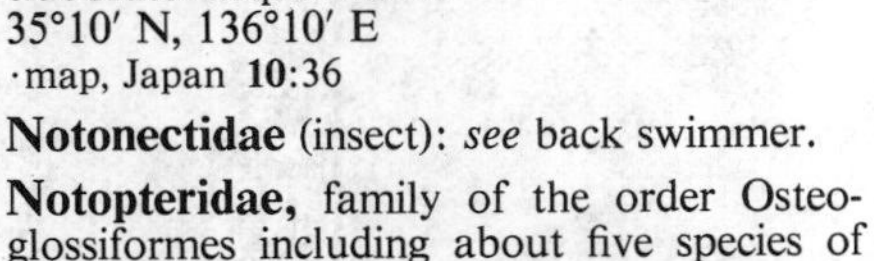

African knifefish (*Xenomystus nigri*)
Jane Burton—Bruce Coleman Ltd.

Notopterids, commonly called knifefishes or featherbacks, are long-bodied, small-scaled fishes with a small dorsal fin (if present) and a long, narrow anal fin that runs along most of the undersurface and continues into the tail fin. Undulations along the anal fin enable the fishes to swim both forward and backward. Notopterids are predacious and nocturnal and in some areas are sought as food. The largest notopterids (*Notopterus chitala*) may grow to a length of about 80 centimetres (32 inches). The notopterids of the species *Xenomystus nigri* are sometimes kept in aquariums.
·classification and general features **13**:765d
·sound production and classification **13**:764f

Notopterus chitala, species of featherback fish in the order Osteoglossiformes.
·reproduction and classification **13**:763h

Notornis mantelli (bird): *see* takahe.

Notoryctes: *see* marsupial mole.

Notostraca: *see* tadpole shrimp.

Nototheniidae, family of Antarctic cod in the fish order Perciformes.
·classification and general features **14**:55f; illus. 50

Notothylas: *see* horned liverwort.

Notoungulata, extinct group of primitive and specialized mammals found mostly in South America late in the Paleocene Epoch (the Paleocene ended 54,000,000 years ago); the oldest known forms seem to have an East Asian origin. The peak of notoungulate evolution was during the Oligocene Epoch (between 38,000,000 and 26,000,000 years ago), and by the Pliocene Epoch (between 7,000,000 and 2,500,000 years ago) they had been reduced in numbers and diversity; the reason may well be a climatic one. In South America the notoungulates were able to evolve and diversify free from competition from more advanced forms that were evolving elsewhere. When North America and South America were again rejoined late in the Pliocene Epoch, the notoungulates were unable to compete with the more efficient forms from North America and became extinct.

In their time the notoungulates included a variety of hoofed animals that in many respects paralleled the evolution of more advanced forms elsewhere. One group, the toxodonts, was clumsily built and rather massive; the toxodonts grew as large as sheep or rhinoceroses, depending upon the form involved. *Toxodon* itself stood about two metres (six feet) high at the shoulder with a bulky, cavernous body. Other notoungulates developed along lines similar to the rabbits and rodents.
·evolution and mammalian relationships **11**:415c; illus. 414
·evolutionary career and extinction **2**:1006a

Notre Dame, University of, Roman Catholic university in Notre Dame, just north of South Bend, Indiana, founded in 1842.
·football highlights and history **7**:509a *passim* to 513g
·quality education of national rating **9**:306d

Notre Dame Bay, inlet (55 mi [90 km] wide) of the Atlantic Ocean, indenting the north coast of Newfoundland, Canada, for 50 mi. It has an irregular shoreline and contains many islands. Fishing villages are scattered along the coast of the inlet.
49°45′ N, 55°15′ W
·map, Canada **3**:716
·physical geography and resources **12**:1085g

Notre-Dame de Paris, most famous of the Gothic cathedrals of the Middle Ages, distinguished for its size, antiquity, and archaeological as well as architectural interest. Maurice de Sully, bishop of Paris, conceived the idea of converting into a single building, on a larger scale, two earlier basilicas. The foundation stone was laid by Pope Alexander III in 1163, and the high altar was consecrated in 1189. The choir, the west front, and the nave were all completed by 1240 and porches, chapels, and other embellishments added over the next hundred years. The interior is 427 by 157 feet (130 by 48 metres) in plan and the roof 115

Notre-Dame de Paris
Ewing Galloway

feet (35 metres) high. The towers are 223 feet (68 metres) high; the spires with which they were to be crowned were never added. The cathedral suffered damage and deterioration through the centuries and was restored in the 19th century. The three great rose windows alone retain their 13th-century glass. The flying buttresses of the apse are especially notable for their boldness and grace.

·Gothic interior design, illus. 1 **9**:688
·Gothic Revival restoration **19**:450g
·Gothic sculptural developments **19**:366g; illus. 364
·Gothic style, structure, and history **13**:1011b; map 1005
·ironwork ornamentation significance **11**:1111f
·melismatic organum **12**:716g
·restoration by Viollet-le-Duc **2**:57a
·University of Paris origin and teaching **6**:337g

Notre-Dame de Paris (1831), novel by Victor Hugo.

·philosophical purpose **19**:450f

Notre-Dame-des-Ermites (Switzerland): *see* Einsiedeln.

Notre-Dame-du-Haut, Chapel of, pilgrimage chapel in the French village of Ronchamp (*département* of Haute-Saône) designed by Le Corbusier and built between 1950 and 1955.

·Le Corbusier principles departure **5**:170e
·Le Corbusier window, illus., **17**:Stained Glass, Plate IV
·modern architectural developments **19**:472c; illus. 471
·stained glass used in concrete setting **17**:576a

Notre Dame Mountains, in eastern Quebec, Canada, are a continuation of the Green Mountains of Vermont, U.S., and an outcrop of the northern Appalachians. Named by Samuel de Champlain, the French explorer, they extend for about 500 mi (800 km) in a northeasterly direction through the Gaspé Peninsula. Elevations average 3,500 ft (1,100 m). An extension, the Shickshock Mountains, forms the backbone of the Gaspé and follows the south shore of the St. Lawrence River for 100 mi, reaching a maximum height of 4,160 ft at Mt. Jacques Cartier, or Tabletop, in the Gaspesian Provincial Park.
48°00′ N, 67°00′ W

·Appalachian geology and ecology **1**:1015h

Notre-Dame school, during the late 12th and early 13th centuries, an important group of composers and singers working under the patronage of the great Parisian Cathedral of Notre-Dame. The Notre-Dame school is important to the history of music because it produced the earliest repertory of polyphonic (multipart) music to gain international prestige and circulation. Its four major forms are organum (*q.v.*), a setting (for two to four voice parts) of a chant melody in which the chant is sung in sustained notes beneath the florid counterpart of the upper voice(s); clausula (*q.v.*), actually a section within an organum composition corresponding to a melismatic (many notes per syllable) section of the chant and characterized by a decisive acceleration of pace in the voice having the chant; conductus (*q.v.*), a processional composition in chordal style and not derived from any pre-existent chant; and motet (*q.v.*), similar to the clausula, from which it evidently evolved, but with the addition of new texts, often secular, in the upper parts.

The composers of the Notre-Dame school are all anonymous except for two, Léonin (*q.v.*), or Leoninus (late 12th century), and Pérotin (*q.v.*), or Perotinus (flourished *c.* 1200), both of whom are mentioned in a 13th-century treatise by an anonymous Englishman studying in Paris. According to the treatise, Léonin excelled in the composition of organa and, in fact, composed the *Magnus liber organi* ("Great Book of Organa"), which contains a series of two-part organa for the entire liturgical year. Pérotin, the apparent successor to Léonin, is cited for his three- and four-voice organa, as well as his "substitute clausulae," newly composed clausulae intended for insertion within the older organa.

·polyphonic church music evolution **12**:705d

Notropis (fish genus): *see* minnow.

Nottawasaga Bay, large inlet of Georgian Bay (and Lake Huron) indenting Grey and Simcoe counties in southeastern Ontario, Canada, and fed by the Nottawasaga, Bighead, Beaver, and Pretty rivers. The bay's entrance lies between Cape Rich (west) and Christian Island (east). Many apple orchards are located near the shores, which form a popular summer-resort area, most notably near the village of Wasaga Beach. Important settlements around the bay include Meaford, Thornbury, and Collingwood. The name is from Huron Indian words meaning "outlet of the river of the Iroquois" (whose war parties used the Nottawasago River to attack the Hurons).
44°40′ N, 80°30′ W

Nottaway River, in western Quebec province, Canada, drains Lake Mattagami at 765 ft (233 m) above sea level and flows northwestward 140 mi (225 km) into Ruperts Bay at the south end of James Bay. Its chief headstreams, the Bell, Chibougamau, and Waswanipi, all flow into Lake Mattagami; each adds over 150 mi to the length of the main stream. The swift-flowing Nottaway, with its great hydroelectric potential, was explored by Robert Bell, a Canadian government geologist, in the 1870s.
51°25′ N, 79°50′ W

·map, Canada **3**:716

Notte, La (1960), film directed by Michelangelo Antonioni.

·Antonioni's direction of Jeanne Moreau **1**:999c

Nottely River, rises in the Blue Ridge Mountains in Union County, northern Georgia, U.S., and flows 40 mi (64 km) north, emptying into the Hiwassee Reservoir near Murphy, in Cherokee County, North Carolina. Nottely Dam (completed 1942), a Tennessee Valley Authority installation impounding Nottely Reservoir for flood control, is 9 mi northwest of Blairsville, Ga. The river's name is probably derived from "Naduhli," a Cherokee village.
34°90′ N, 84°00′ W

Nottingham, borough, county borough from 1888 to 1974, and the county town (seat) of Nottinghamshire, England, on the River Trent.

The original site, on a sandstone hill commanding an ancient crossing of the Trent, was occupied by the Anglo-Saxons in the 6th century. Colonizing the area by river, these peoples gave their settlement the name of Snotingaham, the "ham," or village, of Snot's people. Peaceably occupied by the Danes in the 9th century, the community became one of the five towns of the administrative entity known as the Danelaw. After the Norman Conquest (1066), new rulers founded a borough that existed side by side with the older Saxon town, both communities in fact possessing separate administrations until about 1300. In 1449, Henry VI confirmed all previous privileges, including the right to hold a market and the grant of a guild merchant; instituted the office of sheriff; and granted that the town (excepting the castle and jail) should function as a county in itself.

A marketplace, mentioned in the charter of 1155, was established in the small valley between the Norman and Saxon settlements. The old market square, 5½ ac (2 ha) in area, is now one of the major features of the townscape in the central area of Nottingham. Dominated on the eastern side by the Council House (opened 1928), the square is flanked with shops, but the central area is reserved for pedestrians. The Saxon borough is now marked by Nottingham Castle on Standard Hill, so named because there, in 1642, Charles I raised his standard to mark the outbreak of the English Civil War. The present castle replaces several earlier versions; following renovation by the corporation (1875–78), it now houses a museum and art gallery. The link between Nottingham and the legendary outlaw Robin Hood is commemorated by James Woodford's statue on Castle Green. The grammar school, now known as the High School, was founded in 1513 by the benefaction of Dame Agnes Mellors while the Nottingham High School for Girls (1875) is one of the Girls Public Day School Trust foundations. University College was opened in 1881 and moved to its present site of 260 ac (105 ha) on Highfields, to the west of the city, in 1928. The land was given by Lord Trent, otherwise Jesse Boot, founder of Boots Company, Ltd., who subsequently financed much development at the site. The university was incorporated in 1948. The old college buildings in the city centre now house a public library and part of the Trent Polytechnic. The city has two important theatres—Theatre Royal (1865) and the Playhouse (opened 1963)—and literary figures associated with Nottingham include the 19th-century poet Lord Byron and the 20th-century novelist, D.H. Lawrence.

Nottingham lies at the heart of the East Midlands coalfield and is a centre of rail, road, and river communications. It is also traditionally associated with the hosiery trade and the lace industry; a distinctive lace quarter still survives in the southeast corner of the central area of the city. The city has important pharmaceutical and tobacco industries and a major bicycle manufacturing plant. The service sector of the economy provides the major proportion of employment; but the city's diversified economic structure has resulted in considerable prosperity, although localized pockets of severe poverty persist. The city is now the centre of a metropolitan region consisting of (1971 preliminary figure) 674,882 people. Pop. city (1971 prelim.) 299,758.
52°58′ N, 1°10′ W

·map, United Kingdom **18**:866

Nottingham, Charles Howard, 1st earl of, and 2nd Baron Howard of Effingham (b. 1536—d. Dec. 14, 1624, near Croydon, Surrey), lord high admiral who commanded England's fleet against the Spanish Armada. Although he was not as talented a seaman as his subordinates, Sir Francis Drake and John Hawkins, Howard's able leadership contributed greatly to this important English victory. He was a cousin of Queen Elizabeth I and the son of William, 1st Baron Howard of

Effingham. In 1569 he helped suppress a rebellion of the Roman Catholic lords of northern England. He succeeded to his father's title of Lord Howard of Effingham in 1573 and in 1585 became lord high admiral.

Nottingham, detail of an oil painting by an unknown artist, 1602; in the National Portrait Gallery, London

By courtesy of the National Portrait Gallery, London

In mobilizing his forces against the Armada, Howard, on the flagship "Ark," led the main body of the fleet to join Sir Francis Drake's advance force off the southwest coast of England (May 1588). As the Spanish fleet approached, Howard harassed it from a distance with long-range cannon and slowly shepherded it up the English Channel. His cautious tactics proved successful, but he was open to criticism for stopping to capture a crippled vessel at the moment when the rest of the Armada, its close formation broken by English fireships, was being mauled by Drake off the coast of France (Aug. 7–8, 1588).

In 1596 Howard and Robert Devereux, 2nd earl of Essex, commanded the expedition that sacked Cádiz, Spain. The Queen made Howard earl of Nottingham in 1597, and in the summer of 1599 he was given the exceptional office of lord lieutenant general of England, which he held until 1619. He helped put down Essex's uprising against Elizabeth (1601) and served as a commissioner at Essex's trial. It was to Howard that Elizabeth, on her deathbed, named James I as her successor (ruled 1601–25). The venerable earl served on ambassadorial missions and investigatory commissions throughout most of James's reign.

Nottingham lace, any of the various flat laces and nets machine-made originally at Nottingham, England, and used for curtains, dresses, and tablecloths.
·machine production methods **18**:183d

Nottinghamshire, one of the counties forming the East Midlands region of England, bounded by Lincolnshire, Leicestershire, Derbyshire, South Yorkshire, and Humberside. Its area is 835 sq mi (2,164 sq km).

The county has two main physical divisions. In the west, the eastern edge of the Pennines dips gently eastward. Coal measures, exposed along the western border, become concealed under a narrow belt of limestone forming an area of higher ground (over 600 ft [180 m] near Kirkby-in-Ashfield), with a marked western scarp. An outcrop of sandstone extends southward from Bawtry to Nottingham. Most of the east of the county is lowland, bisected by the vale of the River Trent, covered with alluvium and gravel deposits. Mean annual rainfall varies from 22 in. to just over 30 in. Sherwood Forest, occupying most of the sandstone outcrop, includes large tracts of semicultivated oak and birch woods.

Much of the county was occupied in prehistoric times. Mesolithic settlement occurred in the north, but Neolithic and Bronze and Iron Age remains predominate in the east and south. The most important Roman sites (East Stoke, East Bridgford [Margidunum], and Willoughby) follow the line of the Fosse Way (a major Roman–British route) from Leicester to Lincoln. Anglian settlers, penetrating either from Lincolnshire or Leicestershire, settled in the fertile areas of the east and south, and the county was included in the kingdom of Mercia. After the Treaty of Wedmore (878), Nottingham became one of the five Danish boroughs.

In the Middle Ages, there were many important secular and religious estates in the county. The minster at Southwell (founded in the 12th century by the archbishop of York) was a principal landowner. Monastic houses at Welbeck, Rufford, and Newstead (in an area now known as the Dukeries) became homes of powerful landlords after the Dissolution of the Monasteries (1536–39), while royal grants in Sherwood Forest created estates at Clumber Park, Thoresby Park, and Wollaton Hall.

Nottinghamshire is an important agricultural region, principal crops being barley, wheat, oats, and sugar beet, with dairy farming on heavier soils. Orchards and market gardens are also important.

The principal extractive industry is coal mining. Open seams in the west were exploited from the 16th century, but improved techniques have resulted in the sinking of shafts to the deeper, richer seams in the east. Early gypsum mining produced famous Nottinghamshire alabasters. Gravel quarrying is important, especially in the Trent Valley.

Wollaton Hall, Nottingham, Nottinghamshire, designed by Robert Smythson, 1580–88

A.F. Kersting

The county has traditional links with the textile industry, woollen manufacture flourishing in the Norman period. This declined in the 16th century, but invention of the stocking frame (1589) established Nottingham as the principal centre of the hosiery industry, a position it still retains. Lace-making, introduced in the 18th century, is a major manufacture, and Nottingham is a centre of the garment industry. Modern industries include bicycles, tobacco, pharmaceuticals, and heavy engineering. Pop. (1978 est.) 973,700.
·cricket popularity and championships **5**:261c

notturno (music): *see* nocturne.

Noturus (fish genus): *see* madtom.

Nouadhibou, formerly PORT-ÉTIENNE, town, northwestern Mauritania, on a protective bay on the West African Atlantic coast. It has traditionally been a fishing centre, but, since 1964, with the completion of a special pier and a 419-mi (674-km) railway to the "Iron Mountains" near Fdérik, the port's economic importance has rested primarily on exports of high-grade iron ore to Europe and the U.S. Pop. (1977) 21,961.
20°54′ N, 17°04′ W
·map, Mauritania **11**:711
·Mauritania's new town development **11**:712g

Nouakchott, capital of Mauritania, on a plateau near the West African Atlantic coast, about 270 mi (435 km) north-northeast of Dakar, Senegal. It was developed after independence (1960) as the nation's capital, replacing the port of Saint-Louis, which became part of Senegal. The new city focusses on a square, the Place de l'Indépendance, and includes an airport and industrial area. It is centrally located on the main north–south highway, connecting the more populated agricultural south with the sparsely populated, but mineral-rich, north. A port facility has been built about 5 mi east for the export of petroleum and copper. The copper is mined near Akjoujt (120 mi northeast). While there has been a steady increase in the port's activity, the level of traffic remains below that of the more northern port of Nouadhibou. Pop. (1977) 134,986.
18°06′ N, 15°57′ W
·map, Mauritania **11**:711
·Mauritania's new town development **11**:712g

Place de l'Indépendance in Nouakchott, Mauritania

Picturepoint Ltd.—Publix

Nouayme, Mikhaïl: *see* Naʿīmah, Mikhāʾīl.

nougat, confection of nuts or fruit pieces in a sugar paste.
·candy production methods and ingredients **4**:1082g

Nouméa, also spelled NUMEA, capital, French Overseas Territory of New Caledonia, southwest Pacific; it is a port in the southwestern corner of the island with an excellent deepwater, landlocked harbour protected by Île Nou (Nou Island) and a reef and encircled inland by low hills. The Grand Quai has a 1,450-ft- (442-m-) long frontage. The town has modern buildings, a large public market, and St. Joseph's Cathedral, an old stone structure. Also located there are the Collège La Pérouse, a coral aquarium, a hydroelectric plant at Yaté Falls, and a nickel-refining plant at nearby Pointe Duiambo. Pop. (1976) 56,078.
22°16′ S, 166°27′ E
·map, Pacific Islands **2**:433

noumenon, philosophical term put into currency in the 18th century by Immanuel Kant to designate the thing-in-itself as opposed to what he called the phenomenon—the thing as it appears to an observer. Though the noumenal holds the contents of the intelligible world, Kant claimed that man's speculative reason can only know phenomena and can never penetrate to the noumenon. Man, however, is not altogether excluded from the noumenal because practical reason—*i.e.*, the capacity for acting as a moral agent—makes no sense unless a noumenal world is postulated in which freedom, God, and immortality abide.

The relationship of noumenon to phenomenon in Kant's philosophy has engaged the most acute intellects for nearly two centuries, and some have judged his passages on these topics to be irreconcilable. Kant's immediate successors in German Idealism in fact rejected the noumenal as having no existence for our intelligence. Kant, however, felt that he had precluded this rejection by his "refutation of idealism," and he persisted in defending the absolute reality of the noumenal, arguing that

the phenomenal world is an expression of power and that the source from which this power comes can only be the noumenal world beyond.
·Buddhist thought in China **4**:418e
·Kantian critique of metaphysics **10**:395f
·Mach's operationalist philosophy of science **16**:390b
·Plato's identification with Form **12**:11a
·Positivist criticism of Mach **14**:878a
·Realist view as object of knowledge **15**:539g
·relation to phenomena **6**:935g
·Skeptical knowledge limits set by Kant **16**:832f

nous, in Greek philosophy, mind, or reason. It is the faculty of intellectual apprehension and of intuitive thought. Used in a narrower sense, it is distinguished from discursive thought, and applies to the apprehension of eternal intelligible substances and first principles. It is sometimes identified with the highest or divine intellect.
·Anaxagoras' Materialist view **12**:229e
·Christian theological adoption **4**:485f
·cosmology of Anaxagoras **14**:251g
·intermediary role in cosmos **13**:950c
·knowledge's rational basis **6**:931d *passim* to 932g
·Manichaean theological system **11**:445d
·Neoplatonist levels of being **14**:541b
·Pantheism of Anaxagoras **13**:951h
·Plotinian transcendence **6**:937a

Nouveau-Québec, English NEW QUEBEC, an administrative region constituting the northern half of Quebec province, Canada. The name once was used synonymously with Ungava for that part of the Labrador-Ungava peninsula between Hudson Bay and the Labrador Sea, north of the Eastmain and Churchill (Hamilton) rivers, which was, at the time, a part of the Northwest Territories. In 1912, however, when the territory was annexed by Quebec, the term Nouveau-Québec generally replaced Ungava. Following the establishment of the Quebec-Newfoundland boundary in 1927, usage of the name was limited to a territory in northern Quebec province, which in 1967 became a political subdivision of the province. Governed from the city of Quebec, it is the largest but least populous of Quebec province's 10 regions. The development of immense iron-ore deposits along the Newfoundland border, beginning in the 1950s, led to the founding of Schefferville, now the region's largest settlement and the northern terminus of the only railway serving Nouveau-Québec. Pop. (1971 est.) 10,975.

nouveau roman ("new novel"), revolutionary 20th-century French novel, or anti-novel, as it is sometimes called, that dispenses with the traditional novelistic elements of character, plot, incident, entertainment, moral insight, significance, or depth. Its recognition as a distinct kind came in 1953 with the publication of *Les Gommes* (*The Erasers*, 1964) by Alain Robbe-Grillet, who became one of the leading spokesmen for the "new novelists." The term embraces works by Samuel Beckett (1906–), Michel Butor (1926–), Marguerite Duras (1914–), Jean Lagrolet (1918–), Claude Ollier (1922–), Robbe-Grillet (1922–), Nathalie Sarraute (1902–), Claude Simon (1913–), and others. Though they differ widely in their approach to creating a new novel form, they are all agreed in finding the conventions of the traditional novel hampering and obsolete. They object to the character who gives the illusion of a "real person" and therefore has a job, an address, furniture, clothing, pictures, social position, and a personality. They believe that no one is a miser, a hero, a saint, or an idiot but that everyone is all these things at different times, and they seek to capture an individual consciousness at a particular moment. Their characters, shapeless and often nameless, are reflected by interior monologue, by dialogue (often banal), and by the impressions from the outside world that pass before the characters' eyes. Things and the passing scene are described with great fidelity but with no attempt to give them significance. For this reason they are also called *l'école du regard* ("school of the glance").

The new novelists have been more explicit in their statements about what they are against than about what they are for. Most of them identify their works as experiments or "searches." In determinedly avoiding taking sides with their characters, distinguishing between good and bad or between important and trivial, they make severe demands on their readers. In spite of this, they stimulated new interest in the novel.
·French innovation in novel development **13**:278b
·French novel development **10**:1235a

Nouvelle Amsterdam, an island in the southern Indian Ocean, is administratively a part of Terres Australes et Antarctiques Françaises (*q.v.*). An extinct volcano rising to 2,989 ft (911 m) above sea level with an area of 18 sq mi (47 sq km), it was discovered in 1522 by companions of Ferdinand Magellan and named in 1633 by a Dutch explorer, Anthony van Diemen. With Saint Paul Island, it was annexed by France in 1843. In 1949 a permanent research and administrative station, Camp Heurtin, was established on the island. 37°52′ S, 77°32′ E

Nouvelle-Calédonie (island, Pacific Ocean): *see* New Caledonia.

Nouvelle-Calédonie, Territoire de la (Pacific Ocean): *see* New Caledonia, Territory of.

Nouvelle Continuation des amours (1556), work by Pierre de Ronsard.
·dedication and Anacreon's influence **15**:1136d

Nouvelle Héloïse, La, full title JULIE, OU LA NOUVELLE HÉLOÏSE (1761), epistolary novel by the French writer and philosopher Jean-Jacques Rousseau. The story is that of the impossible love of Julie and Saint-Preux, her tutor. The interest lies in the feelings of the characters, the joys and torments of love, rather than in plot. Sentimental and edifying, the work marked a turning point in the French novel and greatly influenced manners and mores.
·literary style and influence **10**:1170b
·narrative method in novel development **13**:279c

Nouvelle Revue Française, La ("The New French Revue"), French periodical founded in 1909.
·magazine publishing history **15**:256e

Nouvelles de la République des Lettres, monthly literary journal founded by Pierre Bayle in the late 17th century.
·magazine publishing history **15**:248a

Nouvelles-Hébrides (southwest Pacific Ocean): *see* New Hebrides.

Nouvelles libertés de penser (1743), volume of five treatises attributed to several authors.
·content and significance **10**:1170g

Nouvelles Littéraires, Les, French literary periodical founded in 1922.
·magazine publishing history **15**:256e

Nouvelles Méditations poétiques (1823), French poetry by Alphonse de Lamartine.
·publication and metaphysical theme **10**:618e

nouvelle vague (cinema): *see* New Wave.

nova (Latin: "new"), star that in a few days increases in luminosity 100 to 1,000,000 times. Why a star becomes a nova is unknown. A supernova (*q.v.*) may be more than 100 times brighter than an ordinary nova. For the stars sometimes called dwarf novae, *see* star, U Geminorum.

There are several methods for estimating the distances of novae and so finding their absolute magnitudes. The most reliable though only rarely applicable way involves comparing the observed increase in diameter of the ejected gas clouds with the radial velocity of the clouds as determined spectroscopically. Common novae reach absolute visual luminosities 10,000 to 1,000,000 times that of the Sun. The total energy emitted during a large nova outburst is of the order of 10^{45} ergs, equal to the radiation from the Sun in 10,000 years. Should the Sun become a nova, the Earth would be destroyed in a few hours or days; however, stars of the Sun's type seem unlikely to do so.

The brightness of an ordinary nova after maximum may decline at various rates, and it often fluctuates. After a few years the brightness of the nova remnant usually becomes steady again, but the star is estimated to have lost perhaps $\frac{1}{10\,000}$ of its mass. A gas cloud may sometimes be observed around it, expanding at hundreds of kilometres per second.

The spectra of novae may show emission lines of atomic hydrogen, ionized oxygen, and the "nebulium" lines. Spectral changes from the outburst to the final stages of a nova are complex. During the first hours, Nova Persei (1901), Nova Herculis (1934), and Nova Lacertae (1936) had continuous spectra with absorption lines, similar to A- and B-type stars. Later, normal and forbidden emission lines of many elements appear. These lines are widened and sometimes doubled about their normal places because the light comes from shells of gas expanding about the star, part of each shell approaching the Earth, part receding. But dark absorption lines that are also often present in the spectrum can originate only in that portion of the shell between the Earth and the disk of the remnant star that furnishes the background light. Since this part of the shell moves toward the Earth, a shift toward the violet results. Spectra of post-nova stars are mainly continuous, with no pronounced absorption or emission lines. Even 100 years after an outburst, however, faint emission lines are present whose broadenings indicate that gases steam off the remnant star at about 200 kilometres (100 miles) per second.

Novae in the Earth's Galaxy and in the great galaxy in Andromeda (M31) have appeared most often in the densely populated parts, at the rate of 20–50 per year in each galaxy. Novae in other galaxies are also observed. The distinction between novae and irregular variable stars is sometimes vague, and some bodies (*e.g.*, Eta Carinae) are hard to classify. The first nova named as such, Tycho's Nova of 1572, was really a supernova. Nomenclature was somewhat irregular until 1925, from which year all novae found in the Earth's Galaxy have been assigned letter and constellation designations according to the system for variable stars. About five recurrent novae are known to exist in the Galaxy. Repeated outbursts occur in these stars at irregular intervals averaging several decades.
·ancient and medieval views **18**:1012h
·chemical elements origin in stars **2**:314b
·evolution and origin theories **17**:603e
·external galaxies' nature and distance **7**:828e
·Galaxy distribution and magnitudes **7**:839d
·nucleosynthesis in first generation star **18**:1017h
·stellar spectra characteristics **2**:240h
·types and characteristics **17**:593h

Nova, British periodical founded in 1955.
·magazine publishing history **15**:257c

Nova, João (JUAN) **da** (b. 15th century, Galicia, Spain—d. 1509), Spanish navigator in the service of Portugal, who discovered the islands of Ascension and Saint Helena (in the South Atlantic Ocean off Africa) and also established Portugal's first commercial concessions in the East Indies. In 1501 da Nova left Portugal in command of an expedition to the East Indies with a crew that included Amerigo Vespucci (later to be the first European to reach the American continent). On the outward voyage da Nova discovered Ascension, rounded the Cape of Good Hope to land at Mozambique, and sailed across the Indian Ocean to Cannanore and Cochin (on the southwestern coast of India). In return for military services to the Rajah of Cannanore, he acquired trading rights for Portugal. On his return trip to Portugal he discovered St. Helena.

Nova Cassiopeiae 1572, supernova also known as Tycho's Nova (*q.v.*).

novaculite, very dense, light-coloured, even-textured sedimentary rock, a bedded chert in which microcrystalline silica (silicon dioxide, SiO_2) in the form of quartz predominates over silica in the form of chalcedony. Deposits of novaculite exhibit stratification. The name is applied chiefly to formations in Arkansas, Oklahoma, and Texas. *See also* chert and flint.
·siliceous rock formations **16**:765b

Nova Delphini, nova of the constellation Delphinus; it was first visible in 1967.

Nova Express (1964), novel by William Burroughs.
·Expressionistic technique in the novel **13**:285a

Nova Friburgo, city, east central Rio de Janeiro state, in eastern Brazil, on the Rio Grande in the Serra de Nova Friburgo, 2,776 ft (846 m) above sea level. The city has textile mills but is best known as a summer mountain resort built in Swiss Alpine style. It can be reached by railroad and highway from Niterói, southwest, and from Rio de Janeiro. Pop. (1975 est.) mun. 104,980.
22°16′ S, 42°32′ W
·map, Brazil **3**:125

Nova Herculis, also called DQ HERCULIS, one of the brightest novae of the 20th century, discovered Dec. 13, 1934, by the British amateur astronomer J.P.M. Prentice, in the northern constellation Hercules. It reached an apparent visual magnitude of 1.4 and remained visible to the naked eye for months. At its centre was found an eclipsing binary pair of small stars, revolving around each other with a period of 4 hours 39 minutes.

Nova Iguaçu, formerly MAXAMBAMBA, city and a northwestern suburb of the city of Rio de Janeiro, in Rio de Janeiro state, Brazil. It lies in the Sarapuí River Valley, at 85 ft (26 m) above sea level. Its varied industries include marmalade factories, vegetable canneries, and plants manufacturing chemicals, pharmaceutical products, and soft drinks. Extensive orange groves are in the agricultural hinterland. The main railroad and highway linking Rio de Janeiro with São Paulo pass nearby. Pop. (1970) 331,468.

Novák, Vítězslav (b. Dec. 5, 1870, Kamentiz, Bohemia—d. July 18, 1949, Skutec, Slovakia), one of the principal proponents of nationalism in Czech music and teacher of many Czech composers of the 20th century. He studied under Dvořák at the Prague Conservatory and in 1909 began teaching there. His early works were influenced by German Romantic music. A visit to Moldavia impressed him deeply, and he began to write music that reflected the spirit of Czechoslovakia and that made use of folk music. He was also influenced by Debussy and Richard Strauss. His works include four operas, two ballets, and the orchestral works *V Tatrach* ("In the Tatra") and the *Slovakian Suite*. The *De Profundis* for orchestra and the *May Symphony* were written during World War II. He also composed chamber works, songs, and choral works, including the *Autumn Symphony*.

Novakivsky, Oleksandr (1872–1935), Ukrainian artist.

Nova Lima, city in east central Minas Gerais state, Brazil, on the Ribeirão Cristais, at 2,444 ft (745 m) above sea level. It was made a seat of a municipality in 1891 and became a city in 1936. It is known as the site of the Morro Velho (Old Mountain) gold mine, British-owned from 1834 until 1959, when it was sold to a Brazilian concern. The air-cooled shaft, which penetrates 8,501 ft (2,591 m), is one of the deepest in the Americas. Ore crushed at the site and other products are shipped by rail and road to nearby Belo Horizonte, the state capital, and to other neighbouring communities. Pop. (1975 est.) mun., 40,564.
19°59′ S, 43°51′ W

Novalis, pseudonym of FRIEDRICH LEOPOLD, FREIHERR VON HARDENBERG (b. May 2, 1772, Oberwiederstedt, Prussian Saxony—d. March 25, 1801, Weissenfels, Thuringia), early Romantic poet whose works and theories influenced later Romantics in Germany, France, and England. He took his pen name from de Novali, that of his family, which belonged to the Protestant Lower Saxon nobility.

Novalis, detail of an engraving by Eduard Eichens, 1845
By courtesy of the Staatliche Museen zu Berlin; photograph, Walter Steinkopf

Novalis studied law at Jena (1790) and then at Leipzig, where he formed a friendship with the future philosopher and Romantic Friedrich von Schlegel. Novalis was appointed auditor to the government saltworks at Weissenfels after completing his studies at Wittenberg in 1793. His grief at the death in 1797 of his fiancée, Sophie von Kühn, was expressed in the beautiful *Hymnen an die Nacht* (1800; *Hymns to the Night*, 1949), six prose poems interspersed with verse that celebrate death as an entry into a higher life in the presence of God. In the same year he went to study geology at the Freiberg School of Mining under Abraham Gottlob Werner, whom he immortalized as the *Meister* in the fragment *Die Lehrlinge zu Sais* (written 1798; *The Novices of Sais*, 1949), a novel of nature philosophy.

The next two years were very productive for Novalis. He produced encyclopaedic studies, a draft of an Idealist philosophical system, and poetic works. He read at Jena (1799), before a circle of young Romantic poets, his *Geistliche Lieder* (1799; *Sacred Songs*, 1956), the principal work by which his influence was extended. In 1800 he was appointed local magistrate in Thuringia, where he contracted the tuberculosis of which he died.

The two collections of his works, *Blütenstaub* (1798; "Pollen") and *Glauben und Leibe* (1798; "Faith and Life"), are, for the most part, fragments; they attempt to combine poetry, philosophy, and science in an allegorical interpretation of the world. His celebrated mythical romance *Heinrich von Ofterdingen* (1802; *Henry of Ofterdingen*, 1842) reflects the ideas and tendencies of the older Romantic school and, using the symbol of the blue flower for which the hero searches, describes the mission of the poet to transform the world into the poetry of fairy tale through the power of imagination. Novalis' essays, *Die Christenheit oder Europa* (1799; "Christendom or Europe"), depicting the history of Christianity as a threefold process of unity, disintegration, and new unity, established the trend of the Romantic generation toward the Roman Catholic Church.
·German Romantic literature development **10**:1174d

Nova Lisboa (Angola): *see* Huambo.

Nova Methodus Discendae Docendaeque Jurisprudentiae (1667), English NEW METHOD OF TEACHING AND LEARNING JURISPRUDENCE, work by the German philosopher Gottfried Wilhelm Leibniz.

Novanglus, pseudonym used by John Adams in 1775 in letters to the *Boston Gazette*. The letters were rebuttals to the Loyalist arguments of Daniel Leonard, published by the *Gazette* under the pseudonym Massachusettensis. In the letters Novanglus claimed that the colonies were not properly subject to the control of the British Parliament.

Nova Ophiuchi 1604: *see* Kepler's Nova.

Nova Persei, bright nova appearing in the constellation Perseus in 1901, attained an absolute magnitude of −9.2. Spectroscopic observations of Nova Persei provided important information about interstellar gas. The shell thrown off by the exploding star was unusually asymmetrical, and a bright nebulosity near the star appeared to be expanding incredibly fast, at practically the speed of light. This apparent speed is thought to have been an effect of reflection within a pre-existing dark nebula around the star. From this phenomenon, sometimes called a light echo, it was possible to calculate the distance of the nova from Earth, about 650 light-years.

Novara, capital of Novara province, Piedmont region, northwestern Italy, on the Agogna River, west of Milan. It originated as a Gallic town, became the Roman colony of Novaria, and was mentioned by Tacitus as a municipality in AD 69; a new commune, established in the 6th century, was burned by the emperor Henry V in 1110. It recovered to become a member of the Lombard League, an alliance of north Italian towns, in 1167. Novara was dominated by Milan until it passed to Austria in 1714; it was incorporated into Savoy in 1738. It was the scene of Austrian victories in 1821 and 1849; in the second battle, the Austrians, under the aged Joseph Radetzky, defeated Piedmontese forces led by Charles Albert, king of Sardinia-Piedmont, leading to the latter's abdication.

Notable buildings include the cathedral (rebuilt 1863–69) with an ancient baptistery, the church of S. Gaudenzio (rebuilt 1577–1659), the ruins of a castle of the Sforza family, a civic museum, and a picture gallery.

An important agricultural market, particularly for rice, Novara is also growing as an industrial centre, with cotton and silk mills, chemical and printing plants, and cheese and biscuit (cookie) factories. Pop. (1976 est.) mun., 102,011.
45°28′ N, 8°38′ E
·map, Italy **9**:1088
·province area and population, table 1 **9**:1094

Novara, Battle of (March 23, 1849), an engagement of the first Italian War of Independence in which 70,000 Austrian troops under Field Marshal Joseph Radetzky thoroughly defeated 100,000 poorly trained Italian troops (not all of whom were actually employed in the battle) under Charles Albert, king of Sardinia-Piedmont. It was fought at Novara, 28 miles (45 kilometres) west of Milan, 11 days after Charles Albert had denounced the armistice that he had signed the previous August after his defeat at the first Battle of Custoza. This new defeat, a result of Radetzky's military superiority and Piedmont's lack of support from smaller Italian states, led to a treaty on Aug. 9, 1849, which included an indemnity of 65,000,000 francs to be paid to Austria. The defeat also led to the abdication of Charles Albert in favour of his son Victor Emmanuel II.

Novarupta, volcano, Alaska, U.S.
58°16′ N, 155°10′ W
·volcanic destruction of valley **19**:20e

Nova Scotia **13**:274, one of the four Maritime (or Atlantic) Provinces of Canada and one of the four original members of the Dominion of Canada (1867). Comprising the peninsula of Nova Scotia, Cape Breton Island (northeast), and a few small islands, its area is 21,425 sq mi (55,490 sq km). It has a 17-mi (27-km) land boundary with New Brunswick on the west but is otherwise surrounded by the Gulf of St. Lawrence on the north, the Atlantic Ocean on the east and south, and the Bay of Fundy on the southwest. Its capital is Halifax. Pop. (1979 est.) 848,500.

The text article, after a brief overview of the province, covers its history, natural and human landscape, people, economy, administration and social conditions, cultural life and institutions, and prospects.

REFERENCES in other text articles:
·area and population table **3**:721; map 722
·Canadian Confederation question **3**:740b
·Champlain and Scottish settlements **3**:734c
·colonizing efforts from Edinburgh **6**:305c
·loyalist and other immigrant influences **3**:737g
·map, Canada **3**:717
·New Brunswick historic political ties **12**:1080f
·19th–20th-century expansion map **3**:746

Nova Scotia, baronetage of, branch of the "new dignitie between barons and knights" created by King James I of England and VI of Scotland. The English baronetage had been instituted in 1611 and that of Ireland in 1619; in 1624 James devised the baronetage of Nova Scotia for promoting the plantation of that province, which had been granted to Sir William Alexander (later earl of Stirling) in 1621. James announced that he would create 100 baronets, each to support six colonists for two years (or pay 2,000 marks in lieu thereof), and to pay 1,000 marks to Alexander. Each was to receive a "barony," stretching 3 miles along the coast and 10 miles inland.

Sixteen of the land grants were in mainland Nova Scotia, 37 in New Brunswick and Gaspé, 32 on Anticosti Island, and 25 on Cape Breton Island. The number of baronets never reached the limit later set by Charles I of 150, and, when travel became expensive and dangerous because of a war that broke out with France in 1627, the number of applications declined.

When Nova Scotia was ceded to France in 1632, the Nova Scotia baronetage ceased to be a factor in its colonization. The titles were retained, however, and in 1633 Charles I announced that English and Irish gentlemen might receive the honour. The creation ceased to carry with it grants of land in Nova Scotia after 1638, and on the union with England (1707) the Scottish creation ceased. At least 50 of the peers of the United Kingdom still trace their ancestry to the first knights baronets of Nova Scotia. *See also* baronet.

Novatian, probably NOVATIANUS, called NOVATUS by the Greeks (b. *c.* AD 200, Rome—d. *c.* 258), first Roman theologian to write in Latin, who, in leading the Novatian Schism—a break from the Christian Church by rigorists who condemned apostasy—became the second antipope in papal history. He was ordained at Rome and *c.* 250 became a leader of the Roman clergy, in whose name he wrote two letters to Bishop St. Cyprian of Carthage concerning the *lapsi*—*i.e.*, those early Christians who renounced their faith during the persecutions. He had shared with Cyprian a moderate attitude toward apostates, but, when St. Cornelius (*q.v.*) was elected pope in 251, Novatian became the champion of rigorism. By then he had a high reputation as a learned theologian. While a majority favoured Cornelius as pope, a minority declared itself for Novatian, and he set himself up as antipope. His rigorist doctrine was uncompromising, and, by denying the administration of penance, he refused to admit the *lapsi* into the church. Novatian and his followers were excommunicated in 251.

Although Cyprian and Cornelius joined forces against the Novatianists, the schism developed into a sect that spread across the empire and lasted for several centuries. During the persecution of Christians from 251 to 253, Novatian fled Rome. The assertion of the church historian Socrates (died *c.* AD 445) that he was martyred *c.* 258 under the Roman emperor Valerian appears confirmed by the inscription "novatiano . . . martyri" found in a cemetery near San Lorenzo, Rome, in 1932.

Novatian's apologetic *De trinitate* ("On the Trinity"), considered to be his most important work, summarizes and defends the orthodox doctrine of the Trinity against contemporary heresies. In *De cibis Judaicis* ("Concerning Jewish Foods"), he points out that food laws and other practical prohibitions of the Old Testament must be understood spiritually rather than literally. In *De spectaculis* ("On Spectacles"), he condemns Christians who attend public games, and, in *De bono pudicitiae* ("Concerning the Value of Chastity"), he praises chastity. W. Yorke Fausset's edition of *De trinitate* appeared in 1909.
·church authority **4**:537b
·Cyprian's rejection of heretic baptism **5**:401d
·trinitarian speculation and apologetics **13**:1081d

Novato, city, Marin County, western California, U.S., on Novato Creek, between San Pablo Bay (east) and Point Reyes National Seashore (west). The original site was partly on the Rancho de Novato, an 1839 Mexican land grant that occupied most of the Canada de Novato (a valley probably named for a Christianized Indian chief). Francis C. DeLong acquired the land and founded the community in 1888. It remained a small village until 1935, when Hamilton Field was established there. Postwar development has been mainly residential, the chief industry being the large McGraw-Hill Book Distribution Center. Inc. 1960. Pop. (1950) 3,496; (1970) 31,006; (1980) 43,916.
38°06′ N, 122°34′ W

Novatus, Lucius Annaeus (Roman official): *see* Gallio, Junius.

Novaya Zemlya (Russian: NEW LAND), group of islands in European Russia, Russian Soviet Federated Socialist Republic, lying in the Arctic Ocean and separating the Barents and Kara seas. Novaya Zemlya consists of two large islands, Severny (northern) and Yuzhny (southern), aligned for 600 mi (1,000 km) in a south-southwest–north-northeast direction, plus several smaller islands. The two major islands are separated by Matochkin Shar, only 1 to 1.5 mi wide for the most part. The most southerly point, the island of Kusova Zemlya, is separated from Vaygach Island and the mainland by the Kara Strait. The island group has an area of 31,900 sq mi (82,600 sq km).

Novaya Zemlya, a continuation of the Ural Mountains system, is for the most part mountainous, though the southern portion of Yuzhny Island is merely hilly. The mountains, which rise at most to 5,220 ft (1,590 m), consist of igneous and sedimentary materials, including limestones and slates. Over one-quarter of the islands' area, especially in the north, is permanently covered by ice. The climate is severe, and temperature varies from 3° to −8° F (−16° to −22° C) in winter to 36° to 44° F (2.2° to 6.4° C) in summer. There are frequent fogs and strong winds known as *Novozemelskaya bora.* The vegetation in those portions of the islands free from ice is predominantly low-lying tundra. Lemming, Arctic fox, and occasionally polar bear are found on Novaya Zemlya; a rich bird life abounds in summer.

Novaya Zemlya has been known since at least medieval times, though it was not properly explored until the 18th and 19th centuries. Pop. (latest est.) 400.
74°00′ N, 57°00′ E
·landscape and plant and animal life **16**:91b
·map, Soviet Union **17**:322

novecentismo, English NEW CENTURYISM, literary creed expounded by the Italian literary critic Massimo Bontempelli (*q.v.*) that served as a middle ground between 19th-century materialism and its violent modernist reaction.
·Spanish literature development **10**:1239d

Novecento movement, group of Italian artists, formed in 1922 in Milan, that advocated a return to the great Italian representational art of the past. The nationalism of the Novecento (20th-century) movement led to a commitment to Fascism. Members included the sculptors Marino Marini and Arturo Martini and the painters Ottone Rosai, Massimo Campigli, Carlo Carrà, and Felice Casorati.

novel **13**:276, genre of fiction (*i.e.*, prose works created by the imagination), of considerable length and some complexity, in which characters (usually but not always human beings) interact with one another in a specific setting.

TEXT ARTICLE covers:
Elements of the novel **13**:277f
Uses of the novel 280g
Style 283a
Types of novel 285d
The novel in English 290b
Europe 293d
Asia, Africa, Latin America 295e
Social and economic aspects of the novel 296c
Evaluation and study 297h
The future of the novel 298e

REFERENCES in other text articles:
·African colonial and national contributions **1**:239d *passim* to 242g
·Austen's realistic novel of manners **2**:377h
·Balzac characterization contribution **2**:681g
·Cervantes' impact on English novel **3**:1182g
·characterization criteria **2**:52g
·Chinese literary history **10**:1057b
·Cooper's theme innovation and development **5**:132g
·Defoe's contribution to the genre **5**:552b
·D.H. Lawrence's contribution and themes **10**:722f
·Dickens' characters and social criticism **5**:706c
·East Asian development **6**:127f
·Fielding's contribution to the genre **7**:291c
·Fielding's use of satire and parody **4**:964b
·Greek and Roman literature development **10**:1094f
·H.G. Wells' science fiction development **19**:757g
·Hugo's themes and contributions **8**:1132h
·James's contributions in form and style **10**:24e
·Japanese literary history **10**:1067g
·Jewish authors, works, and themes **10**:197c
·Korean literary history **10**:1060c
·medieval Chinese distinctions **6**:341e
·Meredith's psychological style **11**:925g
·origin, characteristics, and popularity **10**:1048e
·plot structure and descriptive technique **10**:1044b
·popular romantic origin **14**:804c
·Proust's style, subject, and influence **15**:131f
·Richardson's development of form **15**:829b
·romance's impact on theme and structure **15**:1024b
·Smollett contribution evaluation **16**:908b
·Thackeray's style and techniques **18**:195f
·Thomas Mann's German classicism **11**:455g
·tragedy embodiment in collateral form **18**:585g
·20th-century view of human nature **4**:965c
·U.S. new form development and emphasis **18**:941g
·Zola's naturalistic theories **2**:45h
·Zola's style and techniques **19**:1156b

RELATED ENTRIES in the *Ready Reference and Index: for*
avant-garde forms: see anti-novel; nouveau roman
traditional forms: apprenticeship novel; Bildungsroman; epistolary novel; Gothic novel; historical novel; international novel; Künstler-

roman; nonfiction novel; novella; novel of manners; picaresque novel; problem novel; psychological novel; robinsonade; roman à clef; roman fleuve; sentimental novel
other: epiphany

Novel Disseisin, law promulgated in England during the reign of Henry II that established procedure for dealing with property right cases.
·Henry II's legal reform **8**:766b

novella, short and well-structured narrative, realistic and satiric in tone, that influenced the development of the short story and the novel throughout Europe. Originating in Italy during the Middle Ages, the novella was based on local events, humorous, political, or amorous in nature; the individual tales often were gathered into collections along with anecdotes, legends, and romantic tales. Writers such as Boccaccio, Franco Sacchetti, and Matteo Bandello later developed the novella into a psychologically subtle and highly structured short tale, often using a frame story to unify the tales around a common theme.

Chaucer introduced the novella to England with the *Canterbury Tales*. During the Elizabethan period Shakespeare and other playwrights extracted dramatic plots from the Italian novella. The realistic content and form of these tales influenced the development of English novel in the 18th century and the short story in the 19th century.

In Germany, where it is known as the *Novelle*, the novella flourished in the 18th, 19th, and early 20th century in the works of writers such as Heinrich von Kleist, Gerhart Hauptmann, Goethe, Thomas Mann, and Franz Kafka. As in Boccaccio's *Decameron*, the prototype of the form, German *Novellen* are often encompassed within a frame story based on a striking news item (plague, war, or flood), either real or imaginary. The individual tales are related by various reporter-narrators to divert the audience from the misfortune they are experiencing. Characterized by brevity, self-contained plots that end on a note of irony, a literate and facile style, restraint of emotion, and objective rather than subjective presentation, these tales were a major stimulant to the development of the modern short story in Germany. The *Novelle* also survived as a unique form, although unity of mood and style often replaced the traditional unity of action; the importance of the frame was diminished as was the necessity for maintaining absolute objectivity.

Sometimes "novella" is used interchangeably with "short novel" or "novelette," to describe a prose form longer than a short story but shorter than a full-length novel.
·novel development and types **13**:277a

Novellae Constitutiones post Codicem, English NOVELS, ordinances of the Roman emperor Justinian I, issued between AD 534 and 565. They formed an important part of the body of Roman law collected by Justinian and known as the Justinian Code (*q.v.*) or Corpus Juris Civilis.
·canon law sources of Justinian **3**:774c
·ordinance dates and legal effect **15**:1056e

Novelle, 15th-century collection of 300 short stories written by Franco Sacchetti.
·short story Italian tales **16**:713g

Novello, Ivor (b. DAVID IVOR DAVIES, Jan. 15, 1893, Cardiff, Wales—d. March 6, 1951, London), composer and playwright, best known for his lush, sentimental, romantic musicals.

Novello, the son of the celebrated Welsh singing teacher, Dame Clara Novello, was educated at Magdalen College, Oxford, and became famous with a phenomenally successful patriotic wartime song, "Keep the Home Fires Burning" (1915). Thereafter he was acclaimed as a composer, playwright, producer, and actor on stage and screen, rivalling the reputation of Noel Coward as a versatile man of the theatre. His greatest musical successes included *Glamorous Night* (performed 1935), *Careless Rapture* (performed 1936), *The Dancing Years* (performed 1939), *Perchance to Dream* (performed 1945), *King's Rhapsody* (performed 1949)—all with lyrics by Christopher Hassall.

Novello also wrote straight plays; and *The Rat* (performed 1924), which he co-authored with Constance Collier, was a notable hit. He also wrote *The Truth Game* (performed 1928), *A Symphony in Two Flats* (performed 1929), and *Fresh Fields* (performed 1934).

Novello, Vincent (b. Sept. 6, 1781, London —d. Aug. 9, 1861, Nice, Fr.), composer, conductor, and founder of the Novello music publishing house. From 1797 to 1822 he was organist at the Portuguese embassy chapel, where he directed the first English performances of masses by Haydn and Mozart. In 1812 he became pianist and conductor at the Italian Opera, London. From 1840 to 1843 he was organist at the Roman Catholic chapel at Moorfields, London. An original member of the Philharmonic Society, he had a distinguished circle of friends, including the Lambs, Leigh Hunt, Shelley, and Keats. Although Novello was a prolific composer, his work as an editor and publisher was more significant. His *Collection of Sacred Music* (1811) marks the founding of the publishing house of Novello. He moved to Nice in 1849.

His daughter Clara Anastasia Novello (1818–1908) was one of the most famous sopranos of her time. His son Joseph Alfred Novello (1810–96) began a career as a bass singer but in 1829 became active in the publishing house, developing the business greatly and introducing inexpensive editions of large-scale choral works to England. In 1857 he retired to Italy. Management of the firm passed to his assistant Henry Littleton, who subsequently bought and expanded it.

novel of manners, one that re-creates a social world conveying with finely detailed observation the customs, values, and mores of a highly developed and complex society. The conventions of the society dominate the story, and characters are differentiated by the degree to which they measure up to the uniform standard, or ideal, of behaviour or fall below it. The range of a novel of manners may be limited, as in the works of Jane Austen, which deal with the domestic affairs of country gentry families and ignore elemental human passions and larger social and political determinations. It may also be sweeping, as in the novels of Balzac, which mirror his age in all its complexity in stories dealing with Parisian life, provincial life, private life, public life, and military life. Whether the novelist's vision is narrow or broad, the novel of manners derives its authority from the assumption that the society is closed and inescapable and that the fate of individuals is necessarily decided within its confines. In the U.S., where writers have traditionally escaped from society to the woods, to the sea, to the open road, or to exile, the novel of manners has never reached high development.
·Austen's theme **2**:378a
·social behaviour and the novel **13**:286f

novel of sensibility: *see* sentimental novel.

November, 11th month of the Gregorian calendar now in general use, has 30 days. It was the ninth month in the early Roman republican calendar; the name comes from the Latin *novem*, "nine."

November, class of submarines in the U.S.S.R.
·nuclear submarine development in U.S.S.R. **17**:751b

November Boughs (1888), poems by Walt Whitman.
·publication and preface **19**:821c

Novembergruppe, English NOVEMBER GROUP, group of artists formed in Berlin in November 1918 by Max Pechstein and César Klein. Taking its name from the month of the Weimar Revolution, this group of Expressionist artists hoped to bring about a new unity in painting, sculpture, architecture, crafts, and city planning, and to bring the artist into close contact with the worker. In an attempt to reach the working masses, the Novembergruppe established Workers' Councils for Art in 1919; support, however, came from the middle classes who, with greater education and leisure, more readily accepted this radical, intellectual group and their new (and often, abstract) art forms. Among the leading artists associated with the Novembergruppe were the architects Walter Gropius, Erich Mendelsohn, Mies van der Rohe, Hans Poelzig, and Bruno Taut; the painters Lyonel Feininger, Otto Müller, and Heinrich Campendonck; the sculptors Gerhard Marcks, László Moholy-Nagy, and El Lissitzky; the film makers Hans Richter and Viking Eggeling; the composers Alban Berg, Paul Hindemith, and Kurt Weill; and the dramatist Bertolt Brecht.

The most important activity of the Novembergruppe consisted of public exhibitions (held through the 1920s); but it also sponsored lectures and avant-garde concerts and film presentations. The group's support of Socialism and its ideal of unification of the arts were common concerns of this period and the goals of other organizations as well, notably of the Weimar Bauhaus, established in 1919 by Walter Gropius (*see* Bauhaus).

November Insurrection (1830–31), Polish rebellion that unsuccessfully tried to overthrow Russian rule in the Congress Kingdom of Poland as well as in the Polish provinces of western Russia. After the Congress of Vienna created the Congress Kingdom and made the Russian emperor its king (1815), various secret patriotic groups formed, some hoping to convince the Russian rulers to abide strictly by the constitution granted in 1815, others aiming toward the attainment of full Polish independence.

When a revolution broke out in Paris (July 1830) and the Russian emperor Nicholas I indicated his intention of using the Polish Army to suppress it, one such secret society of infantry cadets staged an uprising in Warsaw (Nov. 29, 1830). Although the cadets and their civilian supporters failed to assassinate the Emperor's brother Grand Duke Constantine (who was commander in chief of the armed forces in Poland) or to capture the barracks of the Russian cavalry, they did manage to seize weapons from the arsenal, arm the city's civilian population, and gain control of the northern section of Warsaw.

The insurgents' partial success was aided by the Grand Duke's reluctance to take action against them and his eagerness to retreat to safety. But lacking definite plans, unity of purpose, and decisive leadership, the rebels lost control of the situation to moderate political figures, who restored order in the city and futilely hoped to negotiate with Nicholas for political concessions. Although the rebellion gained widespread support and its new leaders formally deposed Nicholas as king of Poland (Jan. 25, 1831), the conservative military commanders were unprepared when Nicholas' army of 115,000 troops moved in (Feb. 5–6, 1831). The Polish Army of 40,000 offered strong resistance at several battles, but it was unable to stop the Russian advance toward Warsaw until February 25, when it fought a major but indecisive battle at Grochow.

The Russians then settled into winter camps, and sympathetic uprisings broke out in Russian-controlled Lithuania, Belorussia, and the Ukraine (spring 1831). Nevertheless the Polish commanders hesitated to strike, preferring to rely on the possibility of foreign assistance and doubting the Polish chances for success. They quickly retreated even after a series of successful attacks on the Russian right wing (March and April). Furthermore, the divided political leaders not only refused to pass reforms to win the support of the peasantry but also failed to gain the foreign aid that the generals were depending on.

As a consequence, the rebellion lost its impetus, particularly after a major Russian victory at Ostrołęka on May 26. Although the Poles finally made several changes in the military command (August) and reorganized their government, they failed to act to halt the advance of the Russians, and their strength declined as they continued to avoid decisive engagements. In the meantime, the uprisings in the western Russian provinces were crushed, and people in the cities were losing confidence in the revolution's leaders. When the Russians finally attacked Warsaw on September 6, the Polish Army withdrew to the north two days later. Leaving the territory of Congress Poland, which subsequently fell under stricter and more repressive Russian control, the Poles crossed the border into Prussia (October 5) and surrendered, thus ending the November Insurrection.

·leadership and defeat **14**:648g

November Revolution (Russian history): *see* October Revolution.

November Treaty, also NOVEMBER PACT OR PACT OF GUARANTEE (Nov. 21, 1855), a defense pact between the Swedish-Norwegian kingdom on the one hand and England and France on the other for joint action against any Russian threat to the territorial integrity of the dual kingdom. The pact was negotiated in the atmosphere of Norwegian–Russian border disputes over certain northern Norwegian grazing areas and in response to English fears that Russia was contemplating seizing an ice-free northern Norwegian port. It offered Anglo-French assistance in checking any Russian aggression that might enhance Russia's strategic position in regard to the Western naval powers. Sweden's desire to regain Finland, lost to Russia in 1809, also played a part in the signing of the pact. The effect of the treaty was to intensify the diplomatic isolation and strategic vulnerability of Russia and to force it to accept defeat in the Crimean War in February 1856.

·Oscar I's foreign policy **16**:326f

Novempopulana, historical region, southwestern France.

·Frankish kingdom boundary fluctuations **11**:927b; map 926

Noverre, Jean-Georges (b. April 29, 1727, Paris—d. Oct. 19, 1810, Saint-Germain-en-Laye), distinguished French choreographer whose revolutionary treatise, *Lettres sur la danse et sur les ballets* (1760), still valid, brought about major reforms in ballet production, stressing the importance of dramatic motivation and decrying overemphasis on technical virtuosity. His first choreographic success, *Les Fêtes Chinoises* (1754), attracted the attention of David Garrick, who presented it in London in 1755. After producing such masterpieces as *Medée et Jason* and *Psyche et l'Amour* (at Stuttgart, 1760–67), he was appointed ballet master at the Paris Opéra in 1776.

·ballet reforms influencing Gluck **13**:582f
·choreographic principles **4**:453b
·contribution to Western dance **5**:464g
·costume design reform in ballet **17**:563c
·technical and theoretical reforms **2**:646a *passim* to 649f

Nove ware, primarily maiolica, or tin-glazed earthenware, made in Nove, Italy, in the 18th century. The factory was founded by Giovanni Battista Antonibon in 1728, and in the latter part of the century it had connections with a factory in nearby Bassano, where maiolica had been made two centuries earlier. Most Nove ware was in the prevalent Rococo style. From 1752 the factory also produced a porcelain with deep reds and yellowish greens. Nove also produced a fine-quality cream-coloured earthenware.

Nove maiolica plate, *c.* 1750; in the Victoria and Albert Museum, London

By courtesy of the Victoria and Albert Museum, London; photograph, EB Inc.

Novgorod, *oblast* (administrative region), northwestern Russian Soviet Federated Socialist Republic, occupies an area of 21,300 sq mi (55,300 sq km) and extends across the morainic Valdai Hills, which rise to 971 ft (296 m); the lowland basins of Lake Ilmen lie to the west and of the upper Volga River to the east. Much of its terrain is in swamp of peat bog or reed and grass marsh, with innumerable small lakes. The remainder is mostly in mixed forest of spruce, oak, pine, and birch, and soils are usually infertile. Agriculture is poorly developed, with under one-tenth of the area plowed. Dairying, especially to supply the Leningrad market, is the principal activity, with some cultivation of flax, rye, oats, and potatoes. Since 1870, much swamp has been drained for pasture and improved forest. Much peat is cut for fuel. Aside from the *oblast* headquarters, Novgorod city, settlements are small and engaged in processing timber and flax. Pop. (1970 prelim.) 722,000.

·geographic and demographic features **17**:330b
·map, Soviet Union **17**:322

Novgorod, city and administrative centre of Novgorod *oblast* (region), northwestern Russian Soviet Federated Socialist Republic, on the Volkhov River just below its outflow from Lake Ilmen. Novgorod is one of the oldest Russian cities, first mentioned in chronicles of 859. In 882 Oleg, prince of Novgorod, captured Kiev and moved his capital there. In 989, under Vladimir, Novgorod's inhabitants were forcibly baptized. In 1019 Prince Yaroslav I the Wise of Kiev granted the town a charter of self-government; the town assembly, or *veche*, elected their prince, chiefly as a military commander. After 1270 the *veche* elected only a burgomaster, and sovereignty resided in the town itself, which was styled Lord Novgorod the Great. The town was divided into five ends, each with its own assembly and each responsible for one-fifth of Novgorod's extensive territorial possessions. It flourished as one of the greatest trading centres of eastern Europe, with links by river routes to the Baltic, Byzantium, Central Asia, and all parts of European Russia. Trade with the Hanseatic League was considerable since Novgorod was the limit of Hanseatic trade into Russia. Prosperity was based upon furs obtained in the forests of northern Russia, much of which came under Novgorod's control. "Daughter" towns were founded by Novgorod in the 12th century at Vologda and Vyatka.

Monument in the Kremlin at Novgorod city, Russian S.F.S.R., commemorating the 1,000th anniversary of Russia (1862) designed by M.O. Mikeshin

Shostal

During the 12th century Novgorod was engaged in prolonged struggles with the princes of Suzdal and gained victories in 1169 and 1216. Although the town avoided destruction in the great Tatar invasion of 1238–40, Tatar suzerainty was acknowledged. Under Alexander Nevsky, prince of Vladimir, Novgorod's defenders repulsed attacks by the Swedes on the Neva River in 1240 and by the Teutonic Knights on the ice of Lake Peipus in 1242. During the 14th and 15th centuries, Novgorod was involved in a long, bitter struggle for supremacy with Moscow and frequently sought help from Lithuania. Although the city survived Muscovite onslaughts in 1332 and again in 1386 by Dmitry Donskoy, it was defeated by Vasily II in 1456. It continued to oppose Moscow and again sought Lithuanian assistance, but in 1471 Ivan III the Great defeated Novgorod and annexed much of its northern territories, finally forcing the city to recognize Moscow's sovereignty in 1478. Opposition by its citizens to Moscow continued until Ivan IV the Terrible in 1570 massacred many of them and deported the survivors. In 1611 Novgorod was captured by the Swedes, who held it for eight years. From the reign (1682–1725) of Peter I the Great, the city declined in importance, although it was made a provincial seat in 1727.

During World War II, the city suffered heavy damage, but the many historic buildings were subsequently restored. These include the kremlin on the Volkhov left bank (the Sofiyskaya Storona). It was first built of wood in 1044, and its first stone walls date from the 14th century. Within the kremlin, the St. Sofia Cathedral, built in 1045–50 on the site of an earlier wooden church, is one of the finest examples of early Russian architecture, with magnificent bronze doors from the 12th century. From the 15th century date the Granite Palace (1433), the bell tower (1443), and the St. Sergey Chapel. The Chapel of St. Andrew Stratilata was built in the 17th century. Across the Volkhov (the Torgovaya Storona) stands the Cathedral of St. Nicholas, dating from 1113. In and around Novgorod are many other surviving churches, including the 12th-century cathedrals of the Nativity of Our Lady and of St. George, the 14th-century churches of the Transfiguration and of St. Theodore Stratilata, and the 17th-century Znamensky Cathedral.

Modern Novgorod is important as a tourist centre and as a major producer of chemical fertilizers. Pop. (1970 prelim.) 128,000.
58°31′ N, 31°17′ E

·Alexander Nevsky's historical relation **1**:478g
·Byzantine and Russian architecture **19**:336a
·chemical complex construction **16**:96a
·history, culture, and institutions **16**:41a
·Leningrad's historical development **10**:799a
·Lithuanian attempts to subjugate **1**:572f
·medieval kingdoms maps **12**:141
·medieval literary tradition **10**:1129c

Novgorod, Treaty of (June 3, 1326), peace treaty ending decades of Russo-Norwegian hostilities in the extreme north of present-day Norway and the Kola Peninsula of Russia, then generally known as Finnmark (including the present Norwegian province of Finnmark). The treaty created a buffer zone between Norway and the principality of Novgorod. Under Norwegian sovereignty, the treaty offered Norwegians, Swedes, Finns, and Russians taxing rights over the indigenous Lapps and freedom to exploit the fish and fur of the region. This arrangement remained in effect until the present Norwegian–Russian frontier was established in 1826.

Novgorod school, important school of Russian medieval icon and mural painting that flourished around the northwestern city of Novgorod from the 12th through the 16th century. A thriving commercial city, Novgorod was the cultural centre of Russia during the Mongol occupation of most of the rest of the country in the 13th and 14th centuries. During that period it preserved the Byzantine traditions that formed the basis of Russian art and at the same time fostered the development of a distinct and vital local style, a style that, though provincial, contained most of the elements of the national Russian art eventually developed in Moscow in the 16th century.

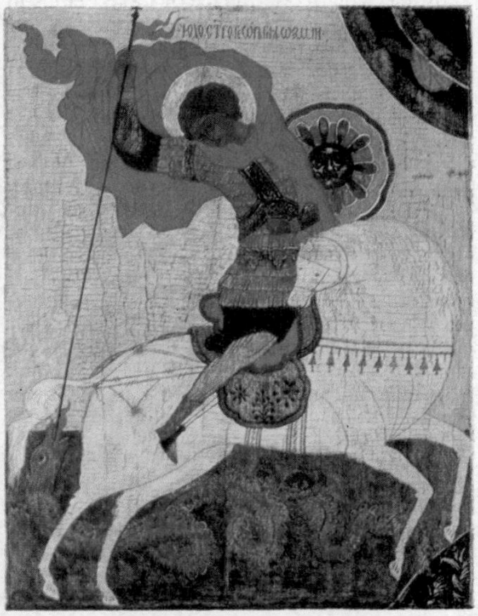

"Miracle of St. George over the Dragon," icon by an anonymous artist of the Novgorod school, egg tempera on panel, beginning of the 15th century; in the State Tretyakov Gallery, Moscow, I.A. Ostroukhov Collection

Novosti Press Agency

The first important phase of the Novgorod school lasted through the 12th and the first half of the 13th century, a period during which the Byzantine tradition spread from Kiev, the first capital and cultural centre of Russia, to the northern centres of Novgorod and Vladimir-Suzdal. In this period fresco painting was the dominant art form. In the second half of the 12th century the hieratic, aristocratic artistic tradition of Kiev was abandoned in favour of a more informal approach that combined Byzantine severity of style with a tenderness of gesture and an anecdotal picturesqueness. This spirit, which remained characteristic of Novgorod painting and was particularly suited to the portrayal of the patron saints favoured by the city, was matched in the beginning of the 13th century by distinct stylistic developments: a shift toward lighter, brighter colours and flatter forms, a softening of facial types, and an increasing definition of form by means of a graceful, rhythmic line. The progressive importance of line over modelled form in Novgorod painting brought about a gradual change in the Byzantine image. Strongly modelled Byzantine figures were characterized by a direct and penetrating gaze that engaged that of the viewer; as the predominance of line flattened forms and the faces of figures in Novgorod painting, the direct gaze receded into a dreamy, abstracted, introspective look. In addition, the line invited a contemplation of its abstract patterns as much as an observation of the forms it described; much of the emotional power of Novgorod painting is transmitted through the lyricism of these patterns.

In the latter part of the 13th century the city's preoccupation with the Mongol threat brought artistic development to a halt. As that threat lessened in the early 14th century, a new artistic inspiration was provided by the introduction of the iconostasis, a screen standing before the sanctuary on which icons, formerly scattered over the walls of the church, could be hung in a prescribed arrangement. The stylistic tendencies that had emerged during the previous period of artistic activity were brought to bear on the visual problems created by the iconostasis and coalesced into a definitive Novgorod style. Although each individual icon was of the greatest importance, and each detail was treated with the intense emotional expression characteristic of Russian art, the complex of paintings on the iconostasis demanded a coherent overall impression as well; this impression was achieved through the use of strong, rhythmic lines and colour harmonies in each icon. The acute colour sensibilities of the Novgorod painters found powerful expression in the juxtaposition of brilliant yet delicately balanced, jewel-like colours, dominated by yellow, emerald green, and fiery vermilion. The silhouette became all-important, as did the line, which assumed unprecedented grace with an elongation of the figure that became standard in Russian art.

A number of Greek artists who arrived from Constantinople at the end of the 14th century brought a more varied subject matter to the Novgorod school and introduced the use of more complex architectural backgrounds. The most influential of these Byzantine immigrants was a mural painter, Theophanes the Greek, who completely assimilated the Russian style and spirit and at the same time contributed a greater understanding of the human form and a subtler use of colour and design to later Novgorod painting.

At the end of the 15th century Novgorod painting became somewhat repetitive, and, although works of outstanding quality continued to be produced, they lacked the freshness of the earlier paintings. The leadership in Russian painting passed in the 16th century to the more cosmopolitan art of the Moscow school, and the final dissolution of the Novgorod school came with the forcible transfer of Novgorod artists to Moscow after a fire in the capital in 1547.

·Russian visual art history **19**:338h *passim* to 341a

Novgorod-Seversky, centre of a *rayon* (district), Chernigov *oblast* (administrative region), Ukrainian Soviet Socialist Republic. The town is believed to date from the early 11th century; from 1098 it was the capital of the principality of Novgorod-Seversky, defending the Russian nation from incursions by nomadic tribes from the steppe. There are many ancient buildings, including the 17th-century Cathedral of the Assumption and the Monastery of the Transfiguration. The town is now a tourist centre, with some light industry. Pop. (1974 est.) 13,500.
51°59′ N, 33°16′ E

Novial, artificial language constructed in 1928 by the Danish philologist Otto Jespersen, intended for use as an international auxiliary language, but little used except experimentally. Its grammar is similar in type and extent to that of Esperanto or Ido; Novial has one definite article, no gender for nouns except those denoting persons, noun plurals in *-s*, forms for a possessive (genitive) and an objective (accusative) case (although these need not be used), adjectives with uninflected form, and verbs that are not inflected for person or number. The chief difference between Novial and Esperanto or Ido is its much larger use of Germanic word roots and grammatical structures (such as auxiliary verbs *sal* "shall, will," *vud* "would," *ha*, *had* "have, had," and *tu* "to" to mark the infinitive of the verb: *tu perda* "to lose"). *Major ref.* **9**:743b

Novikov, Nikolay Ivanovich (1744–1818), Russian writer, philanthropist, and Freemason whose activities, which were intended to raise the educational and cultural level of the Russian people and included the production of social satires as well as the founding of schools and libraries, antagonized the empress Catherine II. She suspended publication of his journals and had him arrested in 1792; he was released by the emperor Paul in 1796.

·Enlightenment doctrine dissemination **16**:56h
·Russian political literature **10**:1177h

Novi Ligure, town, Alessandria province, Piedmont region, northwestern Italy, north of Genoa. A free commune until 1192, it fell successively to Tortona and Milan before passing to Genoa in 1447. It was the scene of the Austro-Russian army's defeat of the French in 1799. Novi Ligure is now an important rail and road junction with iron and steel, food, and textile industries. Pop. (1975 est.) mun., 32,332.
44°46′ N, 8°47′ E
·map, Italy **9**:1088

Novi Pazar, formerly NOVIBAZAR, town of Serbia, Yugoslavia, in the Raška River Valley, built by the Turks in the mid-15th century about 4 mi (7 km) from the site of the ancient Serbian city of Ras; Ras, later called Pazar ("Bazaar"), was the capital in the Middle Ages of a region called Rascia. In the vicinity are Roman baths, and the 9th-century Church of St. Peter, one of the oldest in Yugoslavia, is an interesting example of early Slav architecture. A few miles west is the Monastery of Sopoćani, built in 1260, with vast frescoes portraying the Gospels that are considered by many to be the finest in Europe from this period. The region was captured by the Turks in the 15th century, but the Treaty of Bucharest (1913) after the Balkan Wars made the town a part of Serbia. Agriculture is now the main economic activity; industrial development has centred on textiles. Pop. (1971) 29,100.
43°08′ N, 20°31′ E
·Bucharest treaty realignment **2**:631a
·map, Yugoslavia **19**:1101

Novi Sad, German NEUSATZ, Hungarian UJVIDEK, administrative capital of the ethnically mixed autonomous region of Vojvodina, Serbia, Yugoslavia. A transit port on the heavily trafficked Danube River northwest of

Novi Sad, Yugos.

Salmer—Plessner International

Belgrade, it is on the Belgrade–Budapest rail line. The Bačka canal system connects with the Danube at Novi Sad, which is the economic and cultural focus for north Vojvodina and its large Hungarian minority, comprising about 20 percent of the population. The ethnic diversity of the region is exemplified by Radio Novi Sad, which broadcasts in Serbo-Croatian, Hungarian, Slovakian, Romanian, and Ruthenian.

Before the 18th century Novi Sad was a small fishing village called Petrovaradinski Šanac (Petrovaradin Ditch). In the south bend of the Danube is the Serb Petrovaradin Fortress, rebuilt by the Austrians into the present huge structure after 1699, on the military frontier with the Turkish Empire. Novi Sad became the centre of Serbian culture: the Serbian culture association (Matica Srpska), founded there in 1826, continues to publish texts in minority (*i.e.*, non-Serbo-Croatian) languages.

Novi Sad is the nucleus for the productive Vojvodina agricultural region, and the city hosts an annual international agricultural fair. Industrial development includes food processing, milling, textiles, chinaware, soap, oils, electrical apparatus, and dental equipment. Cultural centres include a university, an art academy, a Serbian National Theatre (1861), and museums. Pop. (1971 prelim.) 141,712.
45°15′ N, 19°50′ E
·map, Yugoslavia **19**:1100

novobiocin, an antibiotic produced by an actinomycete fungus and active against bacteria such as the Stapholococci.
·synthesis and bactericidal action **1**:989c

Novocaine: *see* procaine hydrochloride.

Novocheboksarsk (Russian S.F.S.R.): *see* Cheboksary.

Novocherkassk, city, Rostov *oblast* (administrative region), southwestern Russian Soviet Federated Socialist Republic, at the confluence of the Tuzlov and the Aksay rivers. The original 16th-century town of Starocherkasskaya, the capital of the Don Cossacks, stood on the Don, but it was frequently inundated and was moved to its present site in 1805. Modern Novocherkassk is an industrial centre, producing electric locomotives, mining machinery, machine tools, and chemicals for plastics and synthetic fibres. There are five institutions of higher education and three for research. Pop. (1970 prelim.) 162,000.
47°25′ N, 40°06′ E

Novoevksinsky, Lake, ancient glacial lake, Black Sea area, Soviet Union.
·Ice Age formation **2**:1097g

Novograd-Volynsky, city and centre of a *rayon* (district), Zhitomir *oblast* (administrative region), Ukrainian Soviet Socialist Republic, at the confluence of the Sluch and Smolka rivers. Documents first record the existence of the town in 1257. It was incorporated in 1795, before which it was known as Zvyagel. It contains the ruins of a 14th-century castle. Today the city has machine-building, woodworking, and diverse light industries. Pop. (1970) 41,000.
50°36′ N, 27°36′ E

Novo Hamburgo, city, eastern Rio Grande do Sul state, southern Brazil. Founded by Germans in 1927 and named for Hamburg, Germany, it lies at 115 ft (35 m) above sea level. An industrial city, its manufactures include shoes, hides, leather, and similar products from the cattle and hogs raised in the surrounding area. It is linked by rail and road to Pôrto Alegre, the state capital, to the south. Pop. (1970 prelim.) 81,248.
29°41′ S, 51°08′ W

Novokuybyshevsk, city, Kuybyshev *oblast* (administrative region), western Russian Soviet Federated Socialist Republic, near the Volga River. Founded in 1948 in connection with the development of the oil industry, it received city status in 1952. Situated amid the Volga–Urals oilfield, its industries include oil refining, petrochemicals, and associated industries. Synthetic-alcohol, synthetic-rubber, and plastics are also manufactured. Pop. (1970 prelim.) 104,000.
53°07′ N, 49°58′ E

Novokuznetsk, formerly STALINSK, city, Kemerovo *oblast* (administrative region), west central Russian Soviet Federated Socialist Republic, on the Tom River just below its confluence with the Kondoma. Originally the small village of Kuznetsk, founded in 1617, stood on the right bank; it had about 4,000 inhabitants in 1926. In 1929, under the Soviet First Five-Year Plan, an iron works was founded on the opposite bank; around the works a new town grew up, renamed Stalinsk in 1932. Development was extremely rapid, and the fully integrated iron plant became one of the largest in the U.S.S.R. A second such plant was built in 1960–68. In 1961 the city was renamed Novokuznetsk. In addition to iron and steel, it produces ferroalloys and aluminum. There is also a chemical industry, using by-products, while slag is utilized in making cement. The principal heavy-engineering products are mining machinery and bridge girders. Large-scale coal mining is carried on near the city. Novokuznetsk has metallurgical and teacher-training institutes. Pop. (1970 prelim.) 499,000.
53°45′ N, 87°06′ E
·map, Soviet Union **17**:322
·population and resources **17**:333d

Novomaklakovo, city, Russian Soviet Federated Socialist Republic.
58°27′ N, 92°10′ E
·woodworking complex expansion **16**:96d

Novomoskovsk, formerly STALINOGORSK, city, Tula *oblast* (administrative region), western Russian Soviet Federated Socialist Republic, on the upper Don River. Founded in 1930 as Bobriki, the town developed as a major chemical centre, making fertilizers and plastics and mining lignite. From 1934 to 1961 it was known as Stalinogorsk. Pop. (1970 prelim.) 134,000.
54°05′ N, 38°13′ E
·map, Soviet Union **17**:322

Novomoskovsk, city in Dnepropetrovsk *oblast* (administrative region), Ukrainian Soviet Socialist Republic, on the Samara River, a few miles above its confluence with the Dnepr, and on the Kharkov–Dnepropetrovsk railway and the Moscow–Crimea highway. The settlement of Samarchik, or Novoselitsa, dating from 1650, was resited there in 1784 and renamed Novomoskovsk. The modern city produces metal pipes, railroad ties, and furniture. The major historic landmark is an 18th-century cathedral. Pop. (1970) 61,000.
48°37′ N, 35°12′ E

Novo Redondo, port, capital of Cuanza Sul district, western Angola, on the Atlantic at the mouth of the short Rio Gunza. The harbour has a good anchorage, but port facilities are undeveloped; exports (chiefly coffee and cotton) are transferred to ocean-going vessels by lighter. Pop. (1970) 7,911.
11°13′ S, 13°50′ E

Novorossiysk, city, Krasnodar *kray* (territory), southwestern Russian Soviet Federated Socialist Republic, at the head of Tsemes Bay of the Black Sea. Founded as a fortress in 1838, it developed as a seaport, especially after the coming of the railway in 1888. It is still a major port, with a naval base, shipbuilding yards, refrigeration plant, grain elevators, and an oil-pipeline terminal. Novorossiysk is the largest producer of cement in the U.S.S.R. Pop. (1970 prelim.) 133,000.
44°45′ N, 37°45′ E
·map, Soviet Union **17**:322

Novoshakhtinsk, city, Rostov *oblast* (administrative region), southwestern Russian Soviet Federated Socialist Republic, on the Maly Nesvetay River. It developed as a major coal-mining centre, achieving city status in 1939. Dependence on the coal industry, which suffered as oil and gas increased in importance as fuels in the 1960s, led to a slight decline in its population between the 1959 and 1970 censuses after it had doubled in size between 1939 and 1959. Pop. (1970 prelim.) 102,000.
47°47′ N, 39°56′ E

Novosibirsk, *oblast* (administrative region), west central Russian Soviet Federated Socialist Republic, covers an area of 68,800 sq mi (178,200 sq km) in Western Siberia. It lies across an extremely level plain known as the Baraba Steppe in the north and Kulunda Steppe in the south, most of which is exceptionally swampy, with many lakes. It is drained by the Ob River and by tributaries of the Irtysh and Lake Chany, which has no outlet, is a basin of inland drainage. The swampy forest, or taiga, of the north gives way southward to forest-steppe of birch groves and finally to true steppe on fertile soils.

Apart from the city of Novosibirsk, which is the economic and cultural capital of an area of Siberia that is vastly wider than the limits of the *oblast*, the towns are small, and the economy is almost wholly agricultural. In the north wheat, rye, and flax are grown, while in the more fertile south, which is largely under the plow, spring wheat, oats, barley, and sunflowers predominate. Dairying is dominant in the swampy Baraba Steppe, which has been partly reclaimed. Fishing is important in the Lake Chany region. Pop. (1970 prelim.) 2,505,000.

Akademgorodok, a science centre, near Novosibirsk city in Novosibirsk *oblast*, Russian S.F.S.R.
Novosti Press Agency

Novosibirsk 13:299, until 1925 NOVONIKOLAYEVSK, city, administrative centre of Novosibirsk *oblast* (administrative region) and the heart of Siberia, Russian S.F.S.R., on the Ob River where it is crossed by the Trans-Siberian Railroad. It was founded in 1893 and grew spectacularly in the 20th century. Its academic and scientific community has aroused international interest. Pop. (1973 est.) 1,221,000.
The text article covers the history of the city and its contemporary setting, people, administration, economy, education and culture, and transportation and services.
55°02′ N, 82°55′ E
REFERENCE in other text article:
·map, Soviet Union **17**:322

Novosibirskye Ostrova (Russian S.F.S.R.): *see* New Siberian Islands.

Novosiltsev, Nikolay Nikolayevich, Count (1761–1836), Russian statesman and a confidant of the tsar Alexander I, who made him a member of the Secret Committee (1801–03) for the planning of reforms. Under Alexander and his successor Nicholas I, Novosiltsev served in the administration of Russian Poland.
·Alexander I's domestic reforms **1**:474a
·reform constitution drafting **16**:58c

Novotný, Antonín (b. Dec. 10, 1904, Letňany, now in Czechoslovakia—d. Jan. 28, 1975), Czech Communist leader of a Stalinist faction deposed in a reform movement of 1968.
Trained as a locksmith, Novotný became a member of the Communist Party in 1921 and was imprisoned during the German occupation (1941–45). In 1946 he was elected to the party's Central Committee and in February 1948 he took a leading role in the Stalinist Communist takeover of the Czech government. He was admitted to the Politburo in 1951 and became first secretary of the Communist Party in 1953. After the death of Antonín Zápotocký (Nov. 13, 1957), he assumed the presidency and in 1964 was re-elected to a five-year term.
Continuing his close cooperation with Moscow, Novotný had to face increasing criticism from the party's more nationalistic and less dogmatic reform factions. In January 1968 he was forced to resign the party leadership to Alexander Dubček, and in late March Gen. Ludvík Svoboda replaced him as president. His party offices and membership were withdrawn later in the year. At the party congress of May 1971, with the Stalinists back in power, a compromise was worked out whereby Novotný was reinstated in the party in exchange for leniency toward the ousted Dubček.
·Communist policies and conservatism **2**:1199a

Novotroitsk, city, Orenburg *oblast* (administrative region), Russian Soviet Federated Socialist Republic, on the Ural River, in the Orsk-Khalilovo industrial district of the southern Urals. The centre of ferrous metallurgy in the area, it has an integrated iron and steel plant that was developed in the 1950s on the basis of nearby iron-ore deposits. Chemical production is also of importance. Pop. (1973 est.) 88,000.
51°12′ N, 58°20′ E

Novozemelskaya Trough, Russian NOVOZEMELSKAYA VPADINA, oceanic trench east of, and paralleling the coast of, Novaya Zemlya in the Kara Sea; maximum depth 1,378 ft (420 m).
74°00′ N, 60°00′ E
·location and depth **10**:404f

Novum Organum (1620), by Francis Bacon, a broad investigation of knowledge and an analysis of the causes of error.
·method of new science **6**:939e
·new method of logic, forms, natural history, and idola **2**:563b *passim* to 565g
·new method of reasoning **14**:264a

Novykh, Grigory Yefimovich (Russian mystic): *see* Rasputin, Grigory Yefimovich.

Novy Mir ("New World"), Soviet literary journal founded in 1925.
·magazine publishing history **15**:256f

Nowa Huta, industrial section of Kraków (Cracow) city, southern Poland, on the Vistula River. The original medieval village settlements of Mogiła and Pleszów grew up around a 13th-century Cistercian monastery. After 1949, a large modern iron and steel complex was developed on the site. Nowa Huta, originally a city, was incorporated (1951) into Kraków. Pop. (1970) 160,702.
·map, Poland **14**:626

Nowa Sól, German NEUSALZ, town, Zielona Góra *województwo* (province), west central Poland, on the Oder River. A railroad junction and port on the Oder, Nowa Sól has metalworks, paper and textile mills, chemical and glue plants, and an oil refinery. A museum houses ethnographic and historical displays of the region. Pop. (1973 est.) 35,200.
51°48′ N, 15°44′ E
·map, Poland **14**:626

Nowell, Alexander (b. *c.* 1507, Whalley, Lancashire—d. Feb. 13, 1602, London), scholar, Anglican priest, and dean of St. Paul's Cathedral in London whose tactless preaching brought him into disfavour with Queen Elizabeth I. He was the author of the catechism still used by the Church of England.
Made master of Westminster School, London, in 1543, Nowell became prebendary at Westminster Abbey in 1551. On the accession of the Catholic queen Mary I in 1553, he was deprived of his position and fled to Europe, where at Strassburg and Frankfurt he developed Puritan views. When Mary was succeeded in 1558 by Elizabeth I, who promised religious toleration, he returned to England and received the deanery of St. Paul's, a post he held until his death. His sermons frequently antagonized Elizabeth; on one occasion in 1564 she interpreted his remarks against veneration of the crucifix as alluding to one she kept in the royal chapel.
Nowell's "Small Catechism," inserted before the order of confirmation in the Prayer Book of 1549 and supplemented in 1604, remains the official Anglican catechism. He was also the author of a "Larger Catechism" and a "Middle Catechism," designed for school use, both printed in 1570.

Nowell-Smith, Patrick Horace (1914–), British philosopher.
·noncognitivist ethical theory **6**:988d
·Utilitarianism's ethical rule theory **19**:2f

Nowgong, district of central Assam state, India, encompassing 2,147 sq mi (5,561 sq km) of the Brahmaputra Valley. Crossed by the Kalang River, a tributary of the Brahmaputra, it contains many marshes and lakes, some of which are important fisheries. The encircling forests provide teak, sal, and lac timber. Agricultural products include rice, jute, tea, and silk. The Mīkīr and Kachārī tribes practice shifting cultivation in the hills.
Nowgong town, headquarters of the district, lies on the Kalang. It is an agricultural trade centre and has two colleges affiliated with Gauhāti University, a technical school, and a nursing school. There is a rail junction at Senchoa, 3 mi to the southwest. Other important towns are Silghāt, a river port and rail terminus; Lumding, a railway junction; and Bordowa, a place sacred to Vaiṣṇavites. Pop. (1971) 1,680,895.

Nowgong, or NAOGAON, town, Chhatarpur district, Rewa division, Madhya Pradesh state, India. Nowgong is connected by road with other centres and is a major agricultural distribution centre. Chemical and pharmaceutical works and a distillery are the major industries. An important civil centre and military cantonment, Nowgong served as the British headquarters of the Bundelkhand Agency. The town has a hospital, a government polytechnic institute, a college affiliated with Awadesh Pratap Singh University, and a college for officer training. Pop. (1971) 11,459.
25°04′ N, 79°27′ E

Nowicki, Matthew (1910–49), U.S. architect.
·modern architectural design **19**:472e

Nowra, town, Illawarra district, southeast New South Wales, Australia, in the Shoalhaven River Delta, opposite Bomaderry. It was proclaimed a town in 1857 and given as a name the Aboriginal word for "black cockatoo." Made a municipality (1871), it was incorporated into the shire of Shoalhaven (1948). On the Prince's Highway and terminus of the South Coast rail line from Sydney (75 mi [121 km] northeast), it serves a locality supporting dairy products, pigs, vegetables, maize (corn), and hardwoods. Manufactures include paper and rubber goods. A growing tourist industry is based on scenic river, coastal, and forest surroundings. A lyrebird festival is celebrated each October. Pop. (1971 prelim.) 9,641.
34°53′ S, 150°36′ E

Nowshera, sometimes spelled NAUSHAHRA, town, Peshāwar Division, Northwest Frontier Province, Pakistan. Lying on a sandy plain surrounded by hills, which open north on the Kābul River, Nowshera is a growing commercial and industrial centre, connected by rail and road with Dargai (Malakand Pass), Mardān, Peshāwar, and Rāwalpindi. Industries include cotton, wool, and paperboard mills and chemical and newsprint factories, powered by the Malakand–Dargai and Warsak hydroelectric projects. Nowshera has a government college affiliated with the University of Peshāwar. Pop. (latest census) 21,516.
34°01′ N, 71°59′ E
·map, Pakistan **13**:893

Nowy Sącz, town, southeastern Kraków *województwo* (province), southern Poland, on the Dunajec River, a tributary of the Vistula. It is situated in the fertile Kotlina Sądecka (Sącz Dale), a plain of the Carpathian Mountains noted for its apples. Its scenic surroundings and historic buildings make it a tourist centre as well. The regional museum is located there. The valley, which has been inhabited since prehistoric times, was chosen as the site for Nowy Sącz by King Wenceslas (Wacław) II in 1292. The town became an administrative, economic, and cultural centre for the region. Pop. (1973 est.) 45,600.
49°38′ N, 20°42′ E
·map, Poland **14**:626

Noyan Hutuqtu (1803–56), Mongolian lama responsible for the spread of Buddhist morality plays from Tibet into Mongolia.
·a-che-lha-mo study and introduction **3**:1130d

Noyes, Alfred (1880–1958), English poet, a traditionalist in his literary tastes and remembered chiefly for his lyrical verse. His first volume of poems, *The Loom of Years* (1902), published while he was still at Oxford University, was followed by others that showed patriotic fervour and a love for the sea. Of Noyes's later works, the most notable is the epic trilogy *The Torch-Bearers* (1922–30), which took as its theme the progress of science through the ages.

Noyes, William Albert (1857–1941), U.S. chemist.
·atomic weight determination **2**:344d

Noyon, town, Oise *département,* northern France, north-northeast of Paris. The town, on the lower slopes and at the foot of a hill, occupies both banks of the Verse River, a tributary of the Oise. Noyon formerly was an important ecclesiastical centre. Its cathedral of Notre-Dame is a fine transitional late 12th-century Romanesque-Gothic edifice. The fifth church to be built on the site, it was restored after heavy damage in World War I; the Hôtel de Ville and old ecclesiastical buildings (also ruined in the war) have been rebuilt.

The house in which the Geneva theologian John Calvin was born in 1509 has been rebuilt and contains a museum devoted to him. Charlemagne (later Holy Roman emperor) was crowned king of the western Frankish kingdom of Neustria at Noyon in 768; and Hugh Capet, king of France and founder of the Capetian dynasty (which ruled directly until 1328), was also crowned at Noyon, in 987. The modern town has metal-working and food-processing plants. Latest census 11,567.
49°35′ N, 3°00′ E
·map, France **7**:584

Noyon, Treaty of (1516), agreement between France and Spain.
·background and significance **6**:1084b

Noyon Uul, a rich excavated burial site to the north of Ulaanbaatar, on the Selenge River, Mongolia.
·princely tomb and furnishings **3**:1132g; illus. 1133

Nozaka Sanzō (b. 1892, Hagi, Yamaguchi Prefecture, Japan), leading figure in the Japanese Communist Party throughout the late 1950s and 1960s, responsible for the party's pursuit of its revolutionary goals through peaceful participation in parliamentary politics.

Nozaka first became interested in Communism following the 1917 Bolshevik Revolution in Russia. After studying in England he joined the English Communist Party in 1920 and was deported a few months later. He returned to Japan in 1922 and played a major role in establishing the Japanese Communist Party. Arrested in 1923, he was released at the end of the year and became active in the Japanese labour movement. Arrested again in 1928, he was released because of ill health and went to the Soviet Union in 1931, where he became a member of the executive committee of the Comintern, the Soviet organization in charge of the international activities of the Communist Party. He remained in the Soviet Union until 1943 and then went to the Chinese Communist liberated area in Yenan, where he engaged in propagandist activities against the Japanese Army, which was then attempting to occupy China.

In 1946, Nozaka returned to Japan, where he was elected to the lower house of the Diet, the Japanese parliament. As one of the major Japanese Communist theoreticians, he was blamed by the Cominform, the postwar equivalent of the Comintern, for his doctrine of peaceful evolution into Communism. Nevertheless, U.S. occupation authorities considered Nozaka a dangerous subversive and purged him from politics in 1950. To avoid arrest, Nozaka went underground until 1955, when he was pardoned and emerged as first secretary and leading figure of the Japanese Communist Party.

Nozhat ol-qolūb ("Pleasure of the Hearts"), 14th-century cosmography by Hamdollāh Mastowfī.
·anecdotal approach to cosmography **9**:966c

nozzle, short tube or duct having an inside configuration designed to produce an exiting stream of fluid (liquid or gas) with desirable characteristics. Some nozzles (*e.g.* fire hose nozzles) are adjustable so that the characteristics of the emitted stream can be altered at will. The nozzles of rocket motors are designed to eject the burned fuel in such a manner as to provide maximum thrust.
·ballistic design principles **2**:658c
·fire hose types and utilization **7**:319g
·fluid flow principles **11**:791e
·rocket motor design and operation **15**:938h
·steam turbine operation **17**:628h

Np, chemical symbol for the element neptunium (*q.v.*).

NPD (political party): *see* Nationaldemokratische Partei Deutschlands.

n–p–n-type transistor, semiconductor device in which the base is formed of a so-called *p*-type semiconducting material and the emitter and collector are formed of *n*-type material. It is the reverse of the *p-n-p-* transistor (*q.v.*). *See also* transistor.
·construction and operation **16**:513g
·integrated circuit operation and design **9**:659d; illus.
·radio construction and operation **15**:427h

NRA (U.S. government agency): *see* National Recovery Administration.

NRA (sport organization): *see* National Rifle Association.

Nsanje, formerly PORT HERALD, administrative headquarters of Nsanje District, southern Malawi, on the west bank of the Shire River and north of the Ndindi Marsh. The nation's southernmost town, it serves as a customs post on the Mozambique border and is a trade and transportation centre on the north–south Blantyre-Beira railway (completed 1935). Most of the district (area 751 sq mi [1,945 sq km]) occupies the fertile western Shire Valley. Cotton, tobacco, rice, and maize (corn) are the chief products. Latest census town, 1,373; district, 101,234.
16°55′ S, 35°16′ E
·area and population table **11**:362
·map, Malawi **11**:361

Nsenga, people of the Zambezi River area in central Africa.
·Zambian population and language **19**:1132h; map

Nsiä, a corn festival of the Bamessing tribe in Cameroon.
·water in fertility rites **12**:882e

Nsukka, town, Enugu Province, Central-Eastern State, southern Nigeria, on the Udi Hills at an altitude of 1,300 ft (396 m). It is an agricultural trade centre (yams, cassava, maize [corn], eddoes [cocoyams], pigeon peas, palm oil and kernels) for the Ibo people. Weaving is a traditional local craft. Coal deposits have been discovered east of Nsukka around Obolo, a town on the main Onitsha-Makurdi road.

The University of Nigeria (1960) at Nsukka, the nation's first independent university, and its branch campus (1962) at Enugu (the state capital, 30 mi [48 km] south) were reopened in 1970 after the end of the Nigerian Civil War (1967–70). Nsukka is also the site of an Anglican teacher-training college and several secondary schools sponsored by Christian missions. The town has a hospital, a maternity clinic, and an agrometeorological station. Pop. (1971 est.) 31,676.
6°52′ N, 7°24′ E
·map, Nigeria **13**:86

Ntchisi, formerly NCHISI, administrative headquarters of Ntchisi District, central Malawi. The district (area 638 sq mi [1,652 sq km]) encompasses the heavily forested Ntchisi Mountains (Ntchisi Mountain, 5,430 ft [1,655 m]). The sparse population is dependent upon subsistence agriculture. Latest census town, 1,218; district, 66,762.
·area and population table **11**:362
·map, Malawi **11**:361

Ntem, department, Cameroon.
·area and population table **3**:698

Ntlakyapamuk (people): *see* Salish.

ntomo, cult of Bambara tribesmen to which young boys belong before circumcision.
·mask forms of the Bambara **1**:259c

N-Town plays, an English cycle of 42 scriptural (or "mystery") plays dating from the second half of the 15th century and so called because an opening proclamation refers to performance "in N. town." Since evidence suggests that the cycle was not peculiar to one city or community but travelled from town to town, the abbreviation "N." would indicate that the appropriate name of the town at which the cycle was being presented would have been inserted by the speaker.

The cycle is preserved in the Hegge Manuscript, so called after its 17th-century owner, Sir Robert Hegge, and it is therefore sometimes referred to as the "Hegge cycle." On the flyleaf of the Hegge Manuscript is written "Ludus Conventriae" ("Play of Coventry"), and until the 19th century it was believed that the plays represented the "Coventry cycle," until individual plays from Coventry were discovered and found to be totally different from equivalent plays in the "N-Town cycle." Some scholars have attempted to show that the "N-Town cycle" is closely related to that (lost) cycle, which was performed at Lincoln.

The cycle begins with the creation of the angels and the Fall of Lucifer and ends with the Assumption of the Virgin and the Last Judgment. Among the plays with no equivalent in other cycles are one on the death of Cain and five whose central figure is that of the Virgin, with whom the cycle is generally much preoccupied. The characteristic note of the "N-Town plays" is one of gravity and dignity; the comic relief that distinguishes other surviving cycles (from Chester, York, Wakefield) is markedly absent. A basic difference between the "N-Town plays" and those of the other cycles is that this cycle, because it was a travelling one, was apparently presented by professional actors. It did not employ pageant wagons, a system whereby plays were presented as a procession, but was given in a single open space, with "mansions" (indicating general scenes) set up about a single acting space. The performances may have taken place over two successive days.

n-type semiconductor, a type of solid material in which a small quantity of impurity provides freely moving electrons. The impurity atoms are called donors of electrons, and the name *n*-type indicates the negative charge of the electrons; their free motion constitutes an electrical current.

Pure semiconductor materials, such as silicon, are poor conductors of current because they contain no freely moving electrons. In silicon, the inner electrons of each atom are tightly bound to that atom, while the four outermost electrons bind each atom to its neighbouring atoms. No free negative and no free positive charges are present.

Silicon of *n*-type can be produced by the addition of phosphorous atoms having five outermost electrons. Four of these electrons are used to link the phosphorous atom to its silicon neighbours, but the one extra electron is free to move through the solid. Addition of as few as 10 phosphorous atoms per 1,000,000 silicon atoms yields an *n*-type semiconductor with 1,000 times the conductivity of pure silicon. Addition of more donor atoms increases the conductivity.
·electronic structure and conductivity **6**:671e
·junction transistor construction **6**:680c
·properties and applications **16**:513a
·properties and electron arrangement **16**:525a
·solid state electrical properties **16**:1039f
·thermoelectric semiconductor properties **18**:317a
·transistor composition and properties **15**:427g

Nu, Chinese ethnolinguistic group.
·Yunnan minority population table **19**:1117

Nu, U, also called THAKIN NU (b. May 25, 1907, Wakema, Burma), Burmese independence leader and prime minister of the Union of Burma from 1948 to 1958 and from 1960 to 1962.

U Nu was educated at the University of Rangoon, where he received his B.A. degree in 1929. He returned to the university in 1934 to study law and became involved in student political movements. His expulsion and that of the young independence leader Aung San from the university in 1936 resulted in a student strike. One of the first confrontations between young Burmese nationalists and the British colonial authorities, it gained Nu national prominence. The following year he joined the Dobama Asi-ayone ("We-Burmans Association") and played an important part in the struggle for independence. Jailed by the British in 1940 for sedition, he was released only after the Japanese invaded Burma.

In 1943 U Nu served as foreign minister in Ba Maw's pro-Japanese government. He soon became disillusioned with the Japanese, however, and cooperated actively with the Anti-Fascist Organization led by Aung San.

After the assassination in 1947 of Aung San, the principal nationalist leader, at the war's end, U Nu was asked to become head of the government and leader of Burma's leading political party, the Anti-Fascist People's Freedom League (AFPFL). When independence was declared in January 1948, U Nu became the first prime minister and served for 10 years, with only a brief interlude out of office in 1956–57. Although U Nu was an able and highly respected statesman, his government was plagued by Communist and minority insurrections, economic stagnation, and administrative inefficiency. His 1948 Pyidawtha (welfare) program included a radical Land Nationalization Act, but his efforts to raise the living standard of the people were frustrated by the wide extent of war damage and the drop in rice exports, which had been one of Burma's principal sources of foreign exchange. In 1958 U Nu resigned and a "caretaker" government took over, headed by General Ne Win. In 1960 parliamentary government was restored, and U Nu again became prime minister; but in March 1962 Ne Win staged a coup d'état, establishing a military dictatorship and putting U Nu in prison.

Following his release from prison U Nu left Burma (1969) and began organizing a resistance movement against the Ne Win government.

·Burmese nationalism and ouster **3**:515a

Nuʿaymah, Mikhāʾīl: *see* Naʿīmah, Mikhāʾīl.

Nuba, name commonly used to describe the Negroid inhabitants of the Nuba hills in the southern half of Kordofan province, Republic of The Sudan. This region is studded with rugged granite hills that rise sharply from a wide clay plain and vary considerably in size and content.

The Nuba peoples, numbering more than 500,000 in the 1970s, live on or near the hills (the plains being mainly occupied by Baggara Arabs) in many tribal groups that differ in physical type, language, and culture.

Kinship descent is, broadly speaking, matrilineal in the south and patrilineal elsewhere. The Nuba are agriculturalists (using spade-type hoes), with hill terraces and, now, larger cultivations on the plains. The main crops are millet, sesame, maize (corn), peanuts (groundnuts), beans, onions, cotton, and tobacco. They also keep cattle, sheep, goats, donkeys, fowl, and (except in Islāmized areas) pigs. Religious practices are linked with agricultural rituals; animal sacrifices are made to ancestral spirits; and priestly experts and rainmakers have an important position.

Tribal units are under government-appointed *meks*, or chiefs. Marriage payments are made in livestock, weapons, and other objects and by agricultural service. In the remoter hills men still go naked, and women wear beads and lip slugs; but clothes are increasingly worn. In some parts the lower incisors are removed in both sexes; male circumcision is now more widely practiced. Wrestling and stick fighting are the principal sports. Varying degrees of Islāmization may be observed, and Arabic is used as the lingua franca.

Nuba wrestlers
George Roger—Magnum

·Eastern Sudan primary cultures **6**:165h
·peoples of the eastern Sudan map **6**:165
·Sudan ethnic composition map **17**:762
·wrestling matches in annual festival **19**:1025b

Nubar Pasha, also NUBAR PASHA NUBARIAN (b. January 1825, Smyrna, now İzmir, Tur.—d. Jan. 14, 1899, Paris), Egyptian statesman who was instrumental in negotiating important treaties with the European powers and in dividing authority between Egyptian and British administrators.

Nubar's first important work involved the Suez Canal. The Ottoman khedive of Egypt, Ismāʿīl Pasha (reigned 1863–79), wanted to speed construction of the canal, which was impeded by disputes with the canal company. Nubar represented the Egyptian government in negotiations to annul the disputed provisions. He was also engaged in an attempt to revise the capitulations—treaties that gave important legal rights to European nationals in Egypt. He wanted to establish a system of mixed courts, which would try civil and criminal cases involving Egyptians and Europeans. He proposed that the courts be staffed with Egyptian and foreign judges, who would administer a body of law based on French law and compiled by an international commission. Negotiations were begun in 1867; although France at first rejected the proposals, the new courts were begun in 1875.

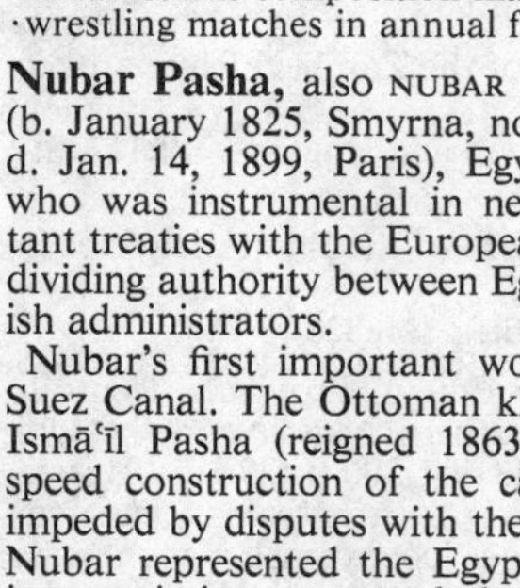
Nubar Pasha, engraving by an unknown artist
By courtesy of the Bibliotheque Nationale, Paris

Nubar was caught up in the events that led to Ismāʿīl's deposition in 1879: under pressure by Britain and France in 1878, Ismāʿīl named Nubar prime minister in a government that was to institute financial and political reforms; these reforms, however, infringed upon Ismāʿīl's authority, and he soon dismissed Nubar. After the British occupation of Egypt (1882), Nubar again became prime minister, in 1884; under the British, khedival authority was considerably curtailed while that of the prime minister was increased. Nubar successfully asserted Egyptian control of the ministries of justice and interior, thus helping to establish a dividing line between British and Egyptian authority in Egypt. His administrative talents provided an element of stability that was important for the peaceful continuance of British rule, but when, in 1888, he became too independent and tried to assert his authority over the provincial police, Britain secured his dismissal. In 1894 Nubar again became prime minister, but ill health and impatience with British domination led to his resignation the following year.

·political ups and downs under Ottomans and British **6**:495h *passim* to 497b

Nubia, ancient region in northeastern Africa, extending approximately from the Nile Valley (near the First Cataract in Upper Egypt) eastward to the Red Sea, southward to about Khartoum (in the present-day Democratic Republic of The Sudan), and westward to the Libyan Desert. It was called Kush (Cush) under the pharaohs of ancient Egypt and called Ethiopia by the ancient Greeks.

The earliest historic mention of Nubia is a reference to a raid by the Egyptian king Snefru (*c.* 2613 BC). Under the 5th and 6th Egyptian dynasties (*c.* 2494–2181), Egypt's contacts with the south were rather more peaceful: although some military forays continued, trading expeditions also took place. Under the 11th dynasty (*c.* 2133–*c.* 1991), Egypt again turned its attention to the south, and the pharaohs of the 12th dynasty (1991–1786) occupied Nubia as far as Semna—about 50 miles (80 kilometres) south of the Second Cataract—where they recorded the level of the Nile flood. Ahmose I, founder of the 18th dynasty, began a reoccupation of Nubia, and his successor, Thutmose I, occupied Kush at least as far as 50 miles south of Abū Ḥamad. Kush was then incorporated into Egypt, under a viceroy whose first duty was to dispatch Nubian tribute to Egypt.

Nothing is known of Nubia between 1100 and 750. But Napata (*q.v.*), the capital, seems still to have been Egyptianized when, in 750, Kashta set himself up there as king, and, conquering Upper Egypt, founded the 25th, or Kushite (Ethiopian) Egyptian dynasty. Piankhi (ruled *c.* 730) included the rest of Egypt in his empire, and his successor Shabaka transferred the capital to Thebes and was known as king of Kush and of Egypt. A disastrous clash with the Assyrians forced Shabaka's successor, Taharqa, to evacuate Egypt. His successor Tanutamon reoccupied Egypt briefly, but in 661 he was forced to evacuate. The Kushite dynasty continued to reign, first at Napata and then at Meroe (*q.v.*), for about 1,000 years.

An Egyptian expedition sacked Napata in *c.* 590 to forestall a Kushite threat to re-establish dominion in Egypt. The kingdom's capital was then transferred to Meroe. The Persians are also believed to have invaded Nubia (522).

Cut off from Egypt, the Egyptian culture of Nubia naturally degenerated until the accession in 45 of Queen Amanishakhete; she and her immediate successors temporarily arrested the degeneration of Egyptian culture, but thereafter it continued unchecked. Meanwhile, in 23, a Roman army under Gaius Petronius destroyed Napata.

By the 3rd century AD the Blemmyes of the eastern, or Arabian, Desert (Beja) had destroyed the Meroitic culture of Lower Nubia, and Meroe itself was destroyed between 320 and 350 by an expedition dispatched by Aeizanes, king of Axum (Aksum). The Meroitic culture was followed in Nubia by what may have been that of the Nobatae, who replaced the northern kingdom of Napata. In *c.* 540 the Nobatae were converted to Christianity, and shortly thereafter their king Silko defeated the Blemmyes and the people of Upper Nobatae. The capital of the Nobatae seems then to have been moved to Pachoras (Faras), until they were amalgamated later in the 6th century, with Makurra (Muqarra) into the single kingdom of Dunqulah. South of Dunqulah was the kingdom of Alwa, or Alodia (Aloa), which became Christian in 580. In 652 a Muslim army from Egypt captured Dunqulah and compelled the kingdom to pay tribute to Egypt; Dunqulah remained Christian until the 14th century, when it was overrun by Mamlūk armies from Egypt. Soba, the Alva capital, survived to the 16th century and then gave way to the Muslim Funj dynasty of Sennar.

- Amenhotep III's suppression of rebels **6**:473h
- ascendancy, metalwork, and defeat **1**:282c
- Egyptian military, commercial, and cultural connections **6**:467b *passim* to 473h
- Ethiopian cultural history **6**:1006f
- historical and cultural development **13**:108f
- Memphis siege and conquest of Egypt **11**:896g
- Ramses II's temple-building **15**:502g
- visual art forms and styles **19**:249d

Nubian, African goat, chiefly Egyptian, large, short-haired with lop ears and Roman nose, of solid colour, parti-coloured or spotted.

- breeding and general features **10**:1283f

Nubian Desert, Arabic AS-ṢAḤRĀ' AN-NŪBĪYA, in northeastern Sudan, northeast Africa, separated from the Libyan Desert by the Nile Valley to the west, while to the north is Egypt; eastward, the Red Sea; and southward, the Nile again. Unlike the Libyan Desert the Nubian Desert is rocky and rugged, though there are some dunes, and toward the Red Sea the desert culminates in precipitous uplands. It is essentially a sandstone plateau interspersed with many wadis (streams) that die out before reaching the Nile. The rainfall is under 5 in. (125 mm) a year.

- map, Africa **1**:179
- map, Sudan **17**:758

Nubian languages, group of languages spoken by about 200,000 people in Egypt and The Sudan, chiefly along the banks of the Nile River between the first and fourth cataracts (Nile Nubian), but also spoken in enclaves in the Nuba Hills of western Sudan (Hill Nubian). Hill Nubian is composed of Midobi and Birked, which are not closely related. Some scholars divide Nile Nubian into three groups, each containing one language (Northern or Kenuzi, Central or Mahas, and Southern or Dongola), while others group Northern and Southern Nubian together. Although many scholars formerly classified the Nubian languages as Hamitic or as Sudanese-Guinean, most now place the Nubian languages in the Eastern Sudanic group of the Chari-Nile language family.

The Nubian languages make much more use of suffixes than of prefixes or infixes, especially in noun inflection. Nouns have forms for the nominative, vocative, objective, genitive, locative, instrumental, and ablative cases in some of the languages. A collective noun used as the subject of a sentence may be followed by either a singular or a plural verb.

Documents in Old Nubian, which appears to be the ancestor of modern Central Nubian, date from the end of the 8th century to the beginning of the 14th century. These are usually translations of Christian writings originally in Greek and are written, as is modern Nubian, in an adaptation of the Coptic alphabet. Speakers of Nubian languages in modern times are Muslims, and the languages contain a number of Arabic borrowings.

- members and range **1**:225h; map 226

Nubians, the occupants of a historical region of the Nile Valley stretching from Aswan in the north to Khartoum in the south. They include the Barabra, Birked, Dilling, Midobi, and Nyima, all of whom speak Chari-Nile languages of the Nilo-Saharan family.

The Nubians reveal an admixture of Negroid and Caucasoid blood, the latter deriving from ancient Egyptian influences and a series of Arab migrations. From the 7th century on, the area was subject to increasing Muslim influence, culminating in 1315 with the accession of a Muslim to the throne of the formerly Christian kingdom of Dongola, which had dominated the area since the middle of the 6th century.

Most Nubian groups rely on cultivation in the Nile Valley and the adjoining arid uplands, although the Birked and Midobi are largely pastoral. Sorghum and millet are staples; barley, dates, peas, figs, and other crops are also grown.

The settlement pattern is characterized by scattered villages of circular huts with walls of stone, wood, wattle, or mud, and conical, thatched, roofs. Barabra houses are of a north-African type—rectangular, flat-roofed structures surrounding an interior courtyard.

Kinship patterns and social organization reflect Islamic influence and are markedly patrilineal. Marriage may be polygynous and involves a bride price.

In the 20th century population pressure has resulted in considerable emigration, particularly to Egypt and the Levant.

- alphabetic tradition **1**:228d
- cultural and social origins **13**:109g
- East African migration influence **6**:95d
- Kenya tribal members and location **10**:426c
- language, culture, and race in Africa **1**:221d
- Nile River population patterns **13**:105e
- Nyima and African languages distribution map **1**:226
- racial and social characteristics **6**:451a
- Somali physical and cultural features **16**:1060e
- Sudan ethnic composition map **17**:762

Nubian Sandstone, principal subsurface strata over much of the eastern Sahara, consisting of a series of sandstone beds of Tertiary age (from 2,500,000 to 65,000,000 years old) with minor occurrences of shale and conglomerate layers. The Nubian Sandstone is the principal groundwater aquifer in this area.

- African water sources and availability **1**:202c
- composition and water storage **16**:780c
- groundwater quantity and quality **8**:434e

Nubian Valley, the former name of the Nile Valley above Aswān, now being submerged in the waters behind the Aswān High Dam and called Lake Nasser. *See* Nasser, Lake.

- topography and population **6**:449b

Ñuble, province, middle Chile, bordering Argentina (east) and fronting the Pacific Ocean (west). Created in 1848, Ñuble has an area of 5,387 sq mi (13,951 sq km), spanning the coastal mountain range, the cool, fertile Central Valley, and the Andean cordillera; it is drained by the northwestward-flowing Río Itata and its main tributary, the Río Nuble. Most of the inhabitants are rural with an economy based upon diversified crops and timber trees, including wheat, wine grapes, sugar beets, and pines. Industries, such as paper mills, have been slow in developing, for Ñuble is overshadowed by its industrialized western neighbouring province and city of Concepción. The Pan-American Highway and the main north–south railroad run the length of the Central Valley, passing through Chillán (*q.v.*), the provincial capital. Pop. (1970 prelim.) 314,738.

- area and population table **4**:251

nucellus, a megasporangium (female spore-producing structure) consisting of a nutritive tissue surrounding a developing seed plant embryo. *See* megaspore.

- angiosperm ovule morphology **1**:880g
- conifer reproductive system **5**:3h
- seed and fruit development **16**:480d

Nuceria Alfaterna (Italy): *see* Nocera Inferiore.

nuchal crest, in anatomy, a region at the back of the neck (nucha).

- human fossil remains analysis **14**:840d
- pongid skull **8**:1028d; illus. 1025

nuchal organ, one of two glandular pits in some polychaetes (phylum Annelida) found on the upper surface of the first segment. The function of the organ is unknown.

- annelid nervous system **12**:980e
- chemoreception in marine annelids **4**:178e

Nu Chiang River (China): *see* Salween River.

Nucifraga (bird): *see* nutcracker.

nuclear clock, a frequency standard (not useful for ordinary timekeeping) based on the extremely sharp frequency of the gamma emission (electromagnetic radiation arising from radioactive decay) and absorption in certain atomic nuclei, such as iron-57, that exhibit the Mössbauer effect. The aggregate of atoms that emit the gamma radiation of precise frequency may be called the emitter clock; the group of atoms that absorb this radiation is the absorber clock. The two clocks remain tuned, or synchronous, only as long as the intrinsic frequency of the individual pulses of gamma radiation (photons) emitted remains the same as that which can be absorbed. A slight motion of the emitter clock relative to the absorber clock produces enough frequency shift to destroy resonance or detune the pair, so absorption cannot occur. This allows for a thorough study at very low velocities of the Doppler effect (the change in the observed frequency of a vibration because of relative motion between the observer and the source of the vibration). Gamma photons from an emitter placed several stories above an absorber show a slight increase in energy, the gravitational shift toward shorter wavelength and higher frequency predicted by general relativity theory. Some pairs of these nuclear clocks can detect energy changes of one part in 10^{14}, being about 1,000 times more sensitive than the best atomic clock.

- time dilation principle **8**:290d

nuclear emulsion (radiation detector): *see* photographic emulsion, nuclear.

nuclear engineering, design, construction, and operation of nuclear reactors. Its methods are derived from physics and the older engineering fields, with special techniques developed to deal with nuclear fission. Broadly, nuclear engineering includes the design of particle accelerators and equipment that makes use of the radiation given off by radioactive materials.

nuclear explosion, extremely rapid chain reaction that occurs when the mass of a fissionable material, such as uranium-235, exceeds its critical mass (*q.v.*), or when the temperature of a light element such as hydrogen reaches a value sufficiently high to cause fusion to take place. *See also* nuclear fission; nuclear fusion.

- fallout problem and control agreements **13**:327c
- fission chain reaction **13**:304h
- meteorite impact simulation **12**:50c
- seismograph detection of detonations **16**:491g
- transuranium element production **18**:680b
- Van Allen radiation belt production **19**:22c

nuclear family, a group of persons united by ties of marriage and parenthood or adoption and consisting of a man, a woman, and their socially recognized children. Also called an elementary family, this unit was widely held, until recently, to be the most basic and universal form of social organization. Anthropological research in the last 20 years, however, has illuminated so much variability of this form that it is safer to assume that what is universal is a nuclear family "complex" in which the roles of husband, wife, mother, father, son, daughter, brother, and sister are embodied by people whose biological relationships do not necessarily conform to the Western definitions of these terms. In matrilineal societies, for example, a child may not be the responsibility of his biological genitor at all but of his mother's brother, whom he calls father.

Closely related in form to the predominant nuclear-family unit are the conjugal family and the consanguineal family. As its name implies, the conjugal family is knit together primarily by the marriage tie and consists of mother, father, their children, and some close relatives. The consanguineal family, on the other hand, groups itself around a descent group or lineage whose members are said to be blood relatives (*see* descent; lineage) and consists of parents, their children, their children's children, and the children's spouses, who may belong consanguineally to another family.

The stability of the conjugal family depends on the quality of the marriage of the husband and wife, and this relationship is more emphasized in industrialized, highly mobile societies in which people frequently must leave the residences of their blood relatives. In peasant and primitive societies, the perpetuation of the line has priority, and the consanguineal family derives its stability from its corporate nature and its permanence.

·family law and parent-child relationship **7**:166f
·household forms and functions **7**:155d
·industrial society advantages **16**:29c
·kinship organizational structures **10**:477f
·marriage union social importance **13**:1048e
·medieval recognition and encouragement **7**:619h

nuclear fission 13:301, the subdivision of a heavy atomic nucleus into two fragments of almost equal mass. The process is accompanied by the release of an enormous amount of energy that can be made self-propagating so as to produce radioactive materials, explosives, and electrical power.

The text article outlines the history of the discovery and application of nuclear fission. A discussion of types of fission and why it occurs follows. Fission chain reaction and its control and the subject of sustained chain reaction are covered, as are the concepts of multiplication factor and criticality. In the final section, treating the theoretical aspects of nuclear fission, various nuclear models are presented to explain the fission mechanism. The text article concludes with a discussion of fission isomers and a conjecture about the existence of superheavy nuclei.

REFERENCES in other text articles:
·atom bomb design **19**:693g
·chain reaction in nuclear reactor **13**:314a
·Einstein's initial reaction **6**:513d
·energy–mass changes in nuclear reactions **4**:119a
·Fermi's experimental development **7**:236g
·fissionable actinide as power source **1**:65e
·gas dissociation relaxation phenomena **7**:922c
·Hahn's experiments and discovery of fission **8**:545g
·Joliot-Curies' research importance **5**:373d
·metallurgical production of nuclear fuel **11**:1075a
·neutron production and reactions **12**:1073g
·nuclear fusion initiation in H-bomb **13**:310e
·nuclear power generation **6**:857b
·nuclear repulsive forces and fission **13**:343e
·nuclear weapon operation principles **13**:324b
·power source possibilities **18**:50e
·radioisotope production by fission **15**:53c
·Seaborg plutonium research and testing **16**:442e
·star formation and collapse **18**:1010a
·thermionic device as energy source **18**:288d
·uranium-235 enrichment by diffusion **18**:1036g
·xenon poisoning effects **13**:140f

RELATED ENTRIES in the *Ready Reference and Index: for*
fissionable materials: see critical mass; fissile material
fission processes: chain reaction; liquid-drop model; photofission; spontaneous fission
fission products: fission product; neutron, prompt; poison

nuclear force (physics): *see* interaction, fundamental.

nuclear fusion 13:307, the formation of an atomic nucleus by the union of two other nuclei of lighter mass. Nuclear fusion yields tremendous energies according to Einstein's law that equates mass and energy; its nuclear fuel is inexhaustible, and it does not produce residual radioactivity.

The text article explains fusion, or thermonuclear, reactions; it describes experiments to produce and control fusion energy as a possible source of industrial power. Stars like the Sun derive most of their energy from thermonuclear reactions. The first practical demonstration of the reaction was the detonation of the hydrogen bomb.

Nuclear fusion is treated on the basis of thermonuclear reactions in plasma, the state of matter when it is a homogeneous mixture of electrons and bare atomic nuclei, produced by an extremely high temperature. Research is concentrated on the production of high-temperature plasmas and the containment of plasmas by magnetic mirrors and traps. The history of research for plasma control is reviewed. Experiments in the impulse compression of plasma focussing are described, and the use of laser beams for plasma heating is suggested.

REFERENCES in other text articles:
·chemical elements' origin **18**:1008f
·electric power generation potential **6**:623b
·energy–mass change in nuclear reactions **4**:119a
·neutron interactions with matter **15**:408f
·nuclear power generation **6**:857a
·plasma properties and characteristics **15**:400a
·power source possibilities **18**:50f
·stars' source of energy production **18**:1010a
·stellar energy generation processes **17**:598f
·Sun's hydrogen-helium conversion **17**:807h
·thermonuclear weapons development **13**:326h

RELATED ENTRIES in the *Ready Reference and Index:*
carbon cycle; proton–proton reaction; thermonuclear reaction

nuclear geology: *see* isotope geology.

nuclear magnetic resonance (NMR), absorption of radio-frequency electromagnetic energy (very high frequency radio waves) by certain atomic nuclei when subjected to an appropriately strong stationary magnetic field, a phenomenon first observed in 1946. Nuclei are the exceedingly dense, positively charged cores of atoms, consisting of protons and neutrons. Protons and neutrons, in turn, are generally paired off within atomic nuclei. In approximately two-thirds of the stable nuclear species and in almost all the unstable nuclear species, at least one proton or one neutron is unpaired. These nuclei have the property of nonzero spin (nonzero angular momentum), act like tiny magnets (have magnetic dipole moments), and are susceptible to nuclear magnetic resonance. For example, nuclear magnetic resonance cannot occur in the common forms of carbon (carbon-12, six protons and six neutrons) and oxygen (oxygen-16, eight protons and eight neutrons) but can occur in common hydrogen (hydrogen-1, one proton) and a rarer form of carbon (carbon-13, six protons and seven neutrons).

Atomic nuclei that contain a circulating unpaired proton or neutron are nuclear magnets. A strong stationary magnetic field exerts a force or, more specifically, a torque on these spinning nuclear magnets, causing them to precess in somewhat the same way as the axes of spinning tops trace out cone-shaped surfaces while they precess in the Earth's gravitational field. The frequency of precession can be tuned (that is, increased or decreased) by increasing or decreasing the strength of the external stationary field. When the natural frequency of the internal precessing nuclear magnets corresponds to the frequency of a weak external radio wave striking the material, energy is absorbed from the radio wave. Resonance may be produced either by tuning the natural frequency of the internal nuclear magnets to that of the weak radio wave of fixed frequency or by tuning the frequency of the weak radio wave to that of the internal nuclear magnets that is maintained by the strong constant external magnetic field. Typical frequencies of the absorbed radio waves are in the range 10 to 100,000,000 hertz (cycles per second). Nuclei of ordinary hydrogen, for example, show a resonance at 42,600,000 hertz when placed in a strong stationary magnetic field of one tesla (10,000 gauss).

Nuclear magnetic resonance may be viewed more simply and more accurately from the perspective of quantum theory. In a strong constant magnetic field, nuclear magnets are oriented in only certain discrete directions corresponding to specific energy values. If a quantum of electromagnetic energy passing through the material is equal to the energy difference between two orientations of the nuclear magnets, resonance can occur. A discrete amount of energy is absorbed by flipping a nuclear magnet from the low-energy orientation to that of high energy.

Nuclear magnetic resonance is used to measure nuclear magnetic moments, the characteristic magnetic behaviour of specific nuclei. Because these values are significantly modified by the immediate chemical environment, however, nuclear magnetic resonance measurements provide information about the nature of various solids and liquids. For this reason, chemists use nuclear magnetic resonance to identify compounds containing hydrogen, especially organic compounds containing ordinary carbon and oxygen. In industry, moisture content in products has been determined by nuclear magnetic resonance.

·alkaloid structure determination **1**:599a
·chemical analysis principles **4**:82d
·electron magnetic field measurement **4**:173b
·heterocycle spectroscopic analysis **8**:836b; table
·hydrogen rotation and spin interactions **12**:305f
·hydrogen structure and analysis **9**:97e
·magnetism research applications **11**:310f
·molecular structure analysis **12**:317h
·organic halogen compound analysis **13**:693d
·theory, development, and applications **11**:306a

nuclear magneton (physics): *see* Bohr magneton.

nuclear membrane, porous structure that separates the nuclear material from the cytoplasm of a cell. *See* nucleus.

·cell junction function and cell division breakdown **3**:1051b
·cytoplasmic barrier function and active transport **11**:878g

nuclear model, description of atomic nuclei (the positively charged, dense, central cores of atoms) that consists of assumptions, experimental data, and inferences usually expressed mathematically. It provides a more or less satisfactory account of the structure and function of atomic nuclei. To explain why nuclei behave as they do, plausible analogies are created to correlate a large amount of information and enable conclusions to be drawn that hopefully reflect properties of the real nuclei.

Nuclear models can be classified into two main groups. The first group, called independent-particle models, includes those in which the main assumption is that little or no interaction exists between the individual particles that constitute nuclei, protons and neutrons, each of which moves in its own orbit and behaves as if the other nuclear particles were passive participants. The shell model (*q.v.*) and its variations fall into this group.

A second group comprises the strong-interaction models or statistical models in which the main assumption is that the protons and neutrons are mutually coupled to each other and behave cooperatively in a way that reflects the strong short-ranged force between them. The liquid-drop model and compound-nucleus model (*qq.v.*) are examples of this group.

Other nuclear models have been developed that incorporate aspects of both groups, such as the collective model (*q.v.*), which is a combination of the shell model and the liquid-drop model.

·chemistry's theoretical postulates **4**:168f
·fission models and theories **13**:305f
·liquid drop, shell, and unified types **15**:441h

nuclear physics, scientific discipline that is concerned with structure of the atomic nucleus. *Major ref.* **14**:426a

·Rutherford's pioneering work **16**:106g

nuclear power: *see* atomic energy.

nuclear reaction, change in the identity or characteristics of an atomic nucleus induced by bombarding it with an energetic particle. The bombarding particle may be one naturally ejected from another nucleus by radioactive decay (such as an alpha particle, equivalent to a helium nucleus, or a gamma-ray photon) or one (such as a proton, deuteron, or heavy ion) that is supplied with sufficient energy in a particle accelerator to react with a nucleus. In either case, the bombarding particle must have enough energy to penetrate the negative electron cloud of an atom and approach the positively charged nucleus to within range of the powerful nuclear force.

A typical nuclear reaction has two reacting particles—a heavy target nucleus and a light bombarding particle—and usually two resulting particles—a heavier product nucleus and a lighter ejected particle. In the first observed nuclear reaction (1919), Ernest Rutherford bombarded nitrogen with alpha particles (helium nuclei, $^{4}_{2}$He or α) from naturally radioactive polonium and identified the ejected lighter particles as hydrogen nuclei or protons ($^{1}_{1}$H or p) and the product nuclei as a rare oxygen isotope. This reaction may be written as the equation $^{14}_{7}\mathrm{N} + ^{4}_{2}\mathrm{He} \rightarrow ^{1}_{1}\mathrm{H} + ^{17}_{8}\mathrm{O}$, in which the sum of the superscript mass numbers on one side of the equation equals the sum of those on the other side because of the conservation of nucleons (protons and neutrons) and the sum of the subscript atomic numbers (number of protons) on one side equals the sum of those on the other because of the conservation of electric charge. The same reaction is commonly abbreviated as $^{14}_{7}\mathrm{N}\,(\alpha, p)\,^{17}_{8}\mathrm{O}$, in which the symbols for the projectile and lighter ejected particle are enclosed in parentheses between those of the target and product nuclei. Nuclear reactions are frequently named after the bombarding particle and emitted particle. Thus, the first observed nuclear reaction is an alpha–proton reaction, or simply an (α, p) reaction. Some nuclear reactions result in more than two particles; for example, nuclear fission produces two nuclei of nearly equal mass and several neutrons.

In the first nuclear reaction produced by artificially accelerated particles (1932), the English physicists J.D. Cockcroft and E.T.S. Walton bombarded lithium with accelerated protons and thereby produced two helium nuclei or alpha particles. As it became possible to accelerate charged particles to increasingly greater energy, many high-energy nuclear reactions have been observed that produce a variety of subatomic particles called mesons, baryons, and resonance particles.

Endothermic reactions consume or absorb nuclear energy, whereas exothermic reactions release nuclear energy. The reactions in the core of the Sun and the stars are exothermic nuclear reactions.

·astatine production from bismuth **8**:575c
·chain reaction in nuclear reactor **13**:314d
·cosmic ray interaction in atmosphere **5**:207b
·energy and mass equivalency **6**:853f
·fissionable isotope production **1**:65f
·fusion reaction types and requirements **13**:307b
·gamma ray resonance absorption **12**:491a
·Hahn experiments and fission discovery **8**:545g
·ionization process in mass spectrometer **11**:605h
·mass changes in fission and fusion **4**:118h
·neutron production and reactions **12**:1072h
·nuclear fission process **13**:301d; illus.
·nuclear properties from reaction data **13**:343g
·nuclear stability towards reaction **9**:1055e
·particle accelerator development **1**:23h
·photonuclear effects **14**:299g
·physics principles and research **14**:426b
·rare-earth industrial use **15**:526e
·stellar energy generation processes **17**:598f
·transuranium element formation **18**:678e

nuclear reactor 13:314, device capable of maintaining a self-sustaining, controlled nuclear fission reaction.

The text article covers nuclear reactor principles and developments; thermal and fast reactors; pressurized-water reactors; boiling-water reactors; high-temperature gas-cooled reactors; aircraft nuclear propulsion; navy nuclear propulsion; research, training, and test reactors; international reactor developments; nuclear fuels; problems of nuclear power and safety.

REFERENCES in other text articles:
·air pollution sources and control **14**:751g
·control of nuclear fusion plasma **13**:310g; illus. 311
·heat exchange process **8**:707b
·heat source and steam power **8**:706a
·industrial ceramics applications **3**:1154h
·irradiated crystal expansion **15**:414e
·metal cladding and cooling system **11**:1075b
·neutron production **12**:1073f
·nuclear fission as power source **13**:302b
·nuclear ship propulsion **16**:684h
·plutonium manufacturing development **13**:325d
·power reactors' discharge of radioactive gas **15**:388b; table 383
·rocket propulsion systems **15**:939h
·ship propulsion operation **16**:697b
·steam power generation of electricity **17**:632a
·submarine power plant and propulsion **17**:752f
·thermal pollutant ice-jam prevention **9**:169h
·thermionic device as energy source **18**:288d
·thermoelectric power generation **18**:319d
·tin alloy production and use **18**:431g; table
·types and power generation **6**:622e
·uranium fuel pellet composition **18**:1036e
·xenon poisoning effect **13**:140f
·zirconium properties and use **18**:620c

Nuclear Test-Ban Treaty, in full, TREATY BANNING NUCLEAR WEAPONS TESTS IN THE ATMOSPHERE, IN OUTER SPACE AND UNDER WATER, was signed in Moscow on Aug. 5, 1963, by the United States, the U.S.S.R., and the United Kingdom as the original parties. The treaty banned nuclear weapon tests in the atmosphere, in outer space, and underwater but permitted underground testing, required no control posts, no on-site inspection, and no international supervisory body. It did not reduce nuclear stockpiles, halt the production of nuclear weapons, or restrict their use in time of war.

The treaty was intended (1) to deter the spread of nuclear weapons to many additional countries, (2) to reduce or end the hazards of radioactive fallout, (3) to slow the pace of the arms race, and (4) to be a step toward reducing international tensions and broadening areas of agreement on the control of nuclear weapons. It was signed within a few months by more than 100 governments, notable exceptions being France and the People's Republic of China.

The three original parties to the treaty, the U.S., the U.K., and the U.S.S.R., have the power to veto treaty amendments. Any amendment must be approved by a majority of all the signatory nations, including all three of the original parties.

·Chinese rejection and alternative **4**:294d
·Khrushchev's role **10**:457c
·nuclear detection devices development **19**:601c
·signatories and agreements **18**:996f
·Sino–Soviet split declaration **9**:771a

nuclear warfare, the use of atomic and thermonuclear weapons in war.

·air defense strategy and warning and detection systems **19**:599b *passim* to 600f
·economics of defense and mobilization **19**:551e
·logistics of nuclear threat **11**:86g
·logistics systems of warfare **19**:597b
·Manhattan Project utilization **19**:1012h
·multipower conflict development **9**:764f
·strategy of war in the nuclear age **19**:566f
·strategy since World War II **19**:694c

nuclear weapons 13:324, bombs and other warheads which derive their force from either the fission or the fusion of atomic nuclei.

The text article briefly covers first the principles of nuclear weapons. It is divided into two major sections: fission weapons; and thermonuclear weapons and their deployment. *See also* atomic bomb; thermonuclear bomb.

REFERENCES in other text articles:
·aerospace products and systems equipment **1**:134d
·ammunition design history **1**:701d
·background radiation source **15**:382f; table
·ballistic missile detection systems **19**:601a
·Bethe's involvement with atomic bomb **2**:871h
·Bikini U.S. testing and research **2**:988b
·cancer relationships of atomic bomb **3**:764h
·China's emergence as nuclear power **4**:396e
·Chinese development and policy **4**:294d
·damage projection for one-megaton bomb **19**:544a
·development and political significance **18**:50c
·Dulles' policy toward Soviet aggression **5**:1081h
·Einstein's U.S. research persuasion **6**:513e
·fission bombs and energy **13**:302a
·fortifications redesign and new uses **7**:554h
·gunnery developments since 1945 **8**:492e
·laws of war concerning use of weapons **19**:539d
·missile nuclear warheads **15**:936d
·outer space legal prohibition **17**:377c
·satellite detection systems **17**:373a
·tank design and use after World War II **17**:1021h
·uranium chain reaction in atomic bomb **13**:315b
·war strategy in the nuclear age **19**:566f
·weapons and delivery systems **19**:693e

nuclease, enzyme that digests nucleic acids, belongs to the class of enzymes called hydrolases. Nucleases are usually specific in action, ribonucleases acting upon ribonucleic acids and deoxyribonucleases acting upon deoxyribonucleic acids. The digestive enzyme, pancreatic ribonuclease, one of the first proteins to undergo sequential amino acid analysis (1959), consists of a single chain of 124 amino acids. In mammals it is secreted into the intestine by the pancreas. Other nucleases occur elsewhere in lower animals and in plants. Some enzymes having a general action (as phosphoesterases, which hydrolyze phosphoric acid esters) can be called nucleases because nucleic acids are susceptible to their action.

nucleation, the initial process that occurs in the formation of a crystal from a solution, a liquid, or a vapour, in which a small number of ions, atoms, or molecules become arranged in a pattern characteristic of a crystalline solid, forming a site upon which additional particles are deposited as the crystal grows.

Nucleation processes are classed as heterogeneous or homogeneous. In the former, the surface of some different substance, such as a dust particle or the wall of the container, acts as the centre upon which the first atoms, ions, or molecules of the crystal become properly oriented; in the latter, a few particles come into correct juxtaposition in the course of their random movement through the bulk of the fluid. Heterogeneous nucleation is more common, but the homogeneous mechanism becomes more likely as the degree of supersaturation (*see* saturation) or supercooling (*q.v.*) increases. Substances differ widely in their susceptibility to nucleation and, hence, in the likelihood that they will crystallize under conditions in which the crystalline state is the inherently stable one; glycerol is a well-known example of a compound resistant to nucleation and therefore prone to supercooling.

·colloid aggregation processes **4**:855g
·crystal growth mechanism **5**:335f
·crystallization separation principles **4**:159e
·electrocrystallization mechanisms **6**:642c; illus.
·glass devitrification process **8**:210a
·ice crystal and snowflake formation **16**:911d *passim* to 913c

nucleic acid 13:328, naturally occurring complex phosphorus-containing compounds forming the genetic material of the cell and directing protein synthesis within the cell. Nucleic acids, composed of phosphoric acid, sugars, and organic bases, are divided into two groups: ribonucleic acids (RNA) and deoxyribonucleic acids (DNA).

The text article covers the general features of nucleic acids and the physical properties and structure of both DNA and RNA.

REFERENCES in other text articles:
·antibiotic alteration of cell metabolism **1**:990b
·antigenic activity after alteration **9**:253g
·bacterial need of precursors **13**:405e; table
·biochemical studies of function **2**:995b
·biosynthesis from building blocks **11**:1044h
·cell properties and structure **10**:895b
·cellular chemical organization **3**:1044c
·chloroquine affinity for parasite cells **4**:190c
·choriocarcinoma treatment by methotrexate **14**:983h
·chromosome composition and heredity **5**:31e
·DNA molecular characteristics **9**:1039c
·DNA mutation types **12**:754c
·DNA reproduction properties **15**:676d
·drug action on cancer cells **5**:1047g
·encoding of biological development **5**:643h
·gene duplication and translation **7**:985d
·heredity and chromosomal composition **8**:808b
·heterocyclic structural components **8**:843a
·hydrophilic colloidal properties **4**:859d
·living system's origins and evolution **14**:377d
·nucleotide substructure and derivatives **13**:330e
·pre-biological synthesis and evolution **7**:17h
·RNA component of biological membranes **11**:876h
·virulence studies in protozoans **15**:122c
·virus morphology and chemistry **19**:164d

RELATED ENTRIES in the *Ready Reference and Index: for*
compounds or chemicals: see deoxyribonucleic acid; nucleoprotein; nucleoside; ribonucleic acid
enzymes: nuclease
proteins: histone; protamine
sugars: deoxyribose; ribose

Núcleo Central, region, Chile.
·physical features and economic activity **4**:250a

nucleolus (cellular biology): *see* nucleus.

nucleon, proton or neutron, subatomic particle constituting atomic nuclei. Protons (positively charged) and neutrons (uncharged) behave identically under the influence of the short-range nuclear force both in the way they are bound in nuclei and in the way they are scattered by each other. This strong interaction is independent of electric charge. Unstable subatomic particles heavier than nucleons (hyperons and baryon resonances) have a nucleon in their final decay products; the nucleon is thus the baryon ground state. The antinucleon includes the antiproton and the antineutron. *Major ref.* **13**:334b

·chemical element atomic structure **4**:116a
·cosmic ray interactions in atmosphere **5**:207b
·fission, fusion, and binding energy **4**:118f
·neutron–proton binding forces **12**:1072f
·nuclear fission and bond breaking **13**:302h
·nuclear fusion reaction types **13**:307e
·spontaneous fission and nucleon ratio **18**:681d
·strong interaction theory **11**:800f
·subatomic particle theory **13**:1022h

nucleophile, in chemistry, an atom or molecule that in chemical reaction seeks a positive centre, such as the nucleus of an atom, because the nucleophile contains an electron pair available for bonding. Nucleophilic substances are usually Lewis bases (compounds that donate electron pairs) and Brønsted bases (compounds that accept protons). Examples of nucleophiles are the halogen anions (I^-, Cl^-, Br^-), the hydroxide ion (OH^-), the cyanide ion (CN^-), ammonia (NH_3), water, and alcohols (ROH, where R is an alkyl group). *See also* electrophile.

·aldehyde and ketone as nucleophilic reagent **1**:460h
·carbanion in substitution reaction **3**:820b
·carbonium ion and reaction mechanisms **3**:862c
·carboxylic acid reaction mechanisms **3**:866d
·heterocycle formation mechanisms **8**:836d
·organic halogen compound reactions **13**:683f
·organic phosphorus compound preparation **13**:702g
·reactant classification and mechanisms **4**:151b

nucleoprotein, conjugated protein consisting of a protein linked to a nucleic acid, either DNA (deoxyribonucleic acid) or RNA (ribonucleic acid). DNA usually occurs in conjunction with either histone or protamine (*qq.v.*); the resulting nucleoproteins are found in chromosomes. Many viruses are little more than organized collections of deoxyribonucleoproteins. Little is known about the proteins linked with RNA; unlike protamine and histone, they appear to contain the amino acid tryptophan.

·DNA complexes in animal tissue **13**:328g
·formation and characteristics **15**:94e
·function performed by nucleic acids **10**:895c

nucleosidase (enzyme): *see* intestinal juice.

nucleoside, a structural subunit of nucleic acids, the heredity-controlling components of all living cells, consisting of a molecule of sugar linked to a nitrogen-containing organic ring compound. In the most important nucleosides, the sugar is either ribose or deoxyribose, and the nitrogen-containing compound is either a pyrimidine (cytosine, thymine, or uracil) or a purine (adenine or guanine).

Nucleosides are usually obtained by chemical or enzymatic decomposition of nucleic acids. Details of the structures of several natural nucleosides determined in the period 1891–1911 include the identities of the sugars and the nitrogenous compounds, the size of the ring of atoms in the sugar molecules, and the point of attachment between the two components. Chemical syntheses of adenosine and guanosine were described in 1948. Puromycin and certain other antibiotics are nucleosides produced by molds or fungi.

·nucleotide structure and derivatives **13**:331g

nucleosynthesis, production on a cosmic scale of all the species of chemical elements from perhaps one or two simple types of atomic nuclei, a process that entails large-scale nuclear reactions including those in progress in the Sun and stars. Chemical elements differ from one another on the basis of the number of protons (fundamental particles that bear a positive charge) in the atomic nuclei of each. Species of the same element, or isotopes, in addition, differ from each other in mass or on the basis of the number of neutrons (neutral fundamental particles) in their nuclei. Nuclear species can be transformed into other nuclear species by reactions that add or remove protons or neutrons or both.

Many of the chemical elements up to iron (atomic number 26) and their present cosmic abundances may be accounted for by successive nuclear fusion reactions beginning with hydrogen and perhaps some primeval helium. By repeated nuclear fusion, four hydrogen nuclei amalgamate into a helium nucleus. Helium nuclei, in turn, can be built up into carbon (three helium nuclei), oxygen (four helium nuclei), and other heavier elements.

Elements heavier than iron and some isotopes of lighter elements may be accounted for by successive neutron capture reactions. The repeated capture of free neutrons by nuclei increases their mass. The accompanying radioactive beta decay converts some neutrons into protons (plus ejected beta particles, or electrons, and antineutrinos). The increase in protons builds up the nuclei to higher atomic numbers.

nucleotidase (enzyme): *see* intestinal juice.

nucleotides 13:330, organic chemical compounds composed of nitrogen-containing units joined to sugar and phosphate units, of importance in biology as the structural groups composing nucleic acids, which make up the fundamental genetic material responsible for storage and replication of hereditary information in living cells. Adenosine triphosphate, the energy-rich compound involved in energy-requiring processess in living cells, is a nucleotide. Many hydrogen acceptors important in metabolism are complex nucleotides, as are some vitamin intermediates.

The text article covers the chemistry of nucleotides, including their composition, relationships to nucleosides, the structure of nucleotides, and oligonucleotides; and the behaviour of nucleotides in biological systems, including their formation and breakdown and their functions as coenzymes and as starting materials for the formation of other classes of compounds.

REFERENCES in other text articles:
·biosynthesis and function **11**:1041h
·cell molecular organization **3**:1044h

nicotinamide adenine dinucleotide (NAD)

·carbohydrate catabolism reactions **11**:1027h
·function and vitamin relationship **6**:898b; tables 2 and 3

RELATED ENTRIES in the *Ready Reference and Index: for*
nitrogen bases: see adenine; cytosine; guanine; thymine; uracil
other: nucleoside; purine; pyrimidine

nucleus, a specialized structure occurring in most cells (except bacteria and blue-green algae) and separated from the rest of the cell by a double layer, the nuclear membrane. This membrane seems to be continuous with the endoplasmic reticulum (a membranous network) of the cell and has pores, which probably permit the entrance of large molecules. The nucleus controls and regulates the activities of the cell (*e.g.*, growth and metabolism) and carries the genes, structures that contain the hereditary information, on long threads called chromatin. When the cell is ready to divide (*see* mitosis; meiosis), the chromatin contracts to form rod-shaped bodies called chromosomes (*q.v.*). Nucleoli are small bodies often seen within the nucleus; they play an important part in the synthesis of ribonucleic acid (RNA) and protein. The gel-like matrix in which the nuclear components are suspended is the nucleoplasm.

A cell normally contains only one nucleus; under some conditions, however, the nucleus divides but the cytoplasm does not (amitosis). This produces a multinucleate cell (syncytium) such as occurs in skeletal muscle fibres. Some cells—*e.g.*, the human red blood cell—lose their nuclei upon maturation. *Major ref.* **3**:1050c

·absence in erythrocytes **2**:1123d
·algae organization and arrangement **1**:487d
·bacterial structures **2**:573e; illus.
·Brown's observations in 1833 **3**:1058g
·cell form and structure **3**:1046f; illus. 1047

·cell reproduction process and theories **15**:677a
·cell theory inadequacies **3**:1060c
·fertilization and karyogamy **7**:257b
·heredity and cell division **8**:805d
·intersexuality's cellular influences **15**:698b
·lymphocytes and cellular composition **11**:210b
·membrane function in cell organelles **11**:878g
·morphological characteristics **12**:454h
·muscle cell patterns **12**:622d
·mutation types and effects **12**:754c
·neuron structures and varieties **12**:977e
·nucleic acid distribution and function **13**:328g
·procaryote and eucaryote cell types **14**:378c
·protozoan variations in number, morphology, and function **15**:124f
·red blood cells of vertebrates **2**:1112a *passim* to 1118a
·regeneration and morphogenetic influences **15**:578e
·tissue culture illus. **18**:441
·transplantation goal in human genetics **7**:1007g
·viruses and reproductive adaptations **5**:838e

nucleus, in the brain, a group of nerve cell bodies; it corresponds to a ganglion (*q.v.*) outside the central nervous system.
·medulla oblongata components **12**:1000e

nucleus, atomic **13**:334, the tiny, positively charged particle at the centre of an atom. The nucleus, in which nearly all the mass of the atom is concentrated, comprises neutrons and protons, the elementary particles called nucleons.

The text article covers the general properties of nuclei, such as mass and electric charge, size, angular momentum, magnetic moments, shapes, and electric quadrupole moments; treats nuclear structure and forces, including components, mass defect and binding energy, energy levels, the coupling-shell and collectively deformed models, and nuclear binding forces; and concludes with a review of nuclear phenomena and reactions.

REFERENCES in other text articles:
·atomic spectra principles **17**:462b
·atomic structure and quantum theory **4**:169a
·Bohr's theory of atomic emission of light **2**:1203d
·Broglie electron orbit theory **3**:323e
·chemical bonding analysis methods **4**:93g
·chemical element atomic structure **4**:116a
·electron as part of nuclei particles **6**:668g; illus. 669
·element abundance and nuclear stability **6**:701h
·energy theory research **6**:854a
·fission and bond breaking **13**:302g
·hydrogen molecules and nuclear spin **9**:94a
·isotope structure and nuclear stability **9**:1054f
·Joliot-Curies' research importance **5**:372g
·magnetic moment and angular momentum **11**:305d
·magnetic moment principles **11**:320c
·mass–energy change in nuclear reactions **4**:118f
·molecular rotation and nuclear spin **12**:305f
·Mössbauer measurement of nuclear energy **12**:491b
·neutron–proton binding forces **12**:1072e
·nuclear model concept development **2**:336c
·physical constant measurement theory **5**:75g
·physics principles and research **14**:426a
·radiation interactions with atoms **15**:392c
·radiation subatomic particles **15**:399d
·relaxation process of excited nucleus **15**:590d
·Rutherford's atomic structure work **16**:108a
·structure and particle physics **11**:799h
·structure and radioactive decay **15**:434h
·subatomic particle properties **13**:1022e
·subatomic particles, symmetry, and conservation laws **5**:34d
·transuranium nuclear structure and decay **18**:680f

RELATED ENTRIES in the *Ready Reference and Index: for*
nuclear models: see collective model; compound-nucleus model; liquid-drop model; nuclear model; optical model; shell model
nuclear reactions: nuclear reaction
structure and properties: atomic number; binding energy; excitation energy; isobar, nuclear; isomer, nuclear; isotone; magic numbers; metastable state; mirror nucleus; nuclide; spin

nucleus, polar (botany): *see* polar nuclei.

nucleus, tube (botany): *see* tube nucleus.

nucleus ambiguus, the set of nerve cells in the medulla oblongata that gives rise to the motor fibres of the vagus, glossopharyngeal, and accessory nerves that supply the striated muscles of the larynx and pharynx.
·anatomic relationships and functions **12**:1020g

nuclide, particular kind of atomic nucleus or atom characterized by the number of protons, the number of neutrons, and the energy state of the nucleus. Thus chlorine-37, the nucleus of which consists of 17 protons and 20 neutrons, is a different nuclide from sodium-23 (nucleus of 11 protons and 12 neutrons) or chlorine-35 (nucleus of 17 protons and 18 neutrons). Nuclear isomers, which have the same number of protons and neutrons but differ in energy content and radioactivity, are also distinct nuclides.

A common method of symbolizing nuclides is by using the chemical symbol with left superscript to designate the total number of protons and neutrons (mass number) and optional left subscript to indicate the number of protons (atomic number); ^{37}Cl or $^{37}_{17}Cl$ signifies an atom or a nucleus of chlorine-37.

The term nuclide is not synonymous with isotope, which designates any member of a set of nuclides having the same proton number and each of which is, therefore, a form of the same chemical element. About 1,700 nuclides are known, of which about 300 are stable and the rest radioactive. *Major ref.* **9**:1054g
·atomic weight variations **2**:343d

Nucula, genus of bivalves of the family Nuculidae, order Nuculacea, commonly called nut shell. The hinge of these small, brownish clams has many sawlike teeth. They are abundant and widely distributed.
·bivalve structural features **2**:1088d; illus. 1089

Nuculana, very long-lived genus of mollusks (clams) that first appeared during the Silurian Period (began about 430,000,000 years ago) and may still be found along beaches today. *Nuculana*, which belongs to the family Nuculanidae, is typical of the Nuculacea order, a group of clams characterized by a small, teardrop-shaped shell that is globous anteriorly and pointed in the back. The interior or hinge region, the dorsal area upon which the shells open and close, is characterized by the presence of many small pits and ridges, sockets and teeth. *Nuculana* has an interior

Nuculana lirata, Devonian in age, collected from the Hamilton Group, Marilla, N.Y.
By courtesy of the Buffalo Museum of Science, Buffalo, N.Y.

shell with two roughened areas at both ends where the muscles for closing the shell are located. *Nuculana* is active and moves about on the substrate.

Nuculopsis, extinct genus of clams whose fossils are restricted to rocks of the Pennsylvanian Period (between 325,500,000 and 280,000,000 years ago). *Nuculopsis* was small, almost spherical in outline, and ornamented with fine growth lines. Because *Nuculopsis* is similar in some respects to the longer lived and commoner genus *Nuculana*, it has been

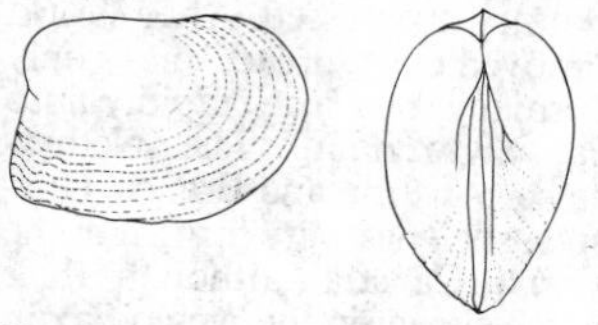

Nuculopsis ventricosa
From C. Dunbar and K. Waage, *Historical Geology* (copyright 1969); by permission of John Wiley & Sons, Inc.

considered a subgenus of *Nuculana*. *Nuculopsis* inhabited the broad, shallow Pennsylvanian seas that covered much of midcontinental North America.

Nuda, in an alternative classification of the sponges that places them in the subkingdom of the Parazoa (rather than in the phylum Porifera), one of the two phyla into which the subkingdom is divided.
·sponge classifications and phylogeny **14**:855b

Nude Descending a Staircase, No. 2 (1912), oil painting in the Cubist manner by Marcel Duchamp that created a sensation when it was exhibited at the Armory Show (*q.v.*) in New York City in 1913; it had previously been refused for the Salon des Indépendants exhibition of 1912 in Paris. The painting now hangs in the Philadelphia Museum of Art. Duchamp painted three other versions between 1911 and 1918.
·notoriety at New York exhibition **5**:1078f

nudibranch, or SEA SLUG, any marine gastropod comprising the order Nudibranchia (subclass Opisthobranchia of the class Gas-

Doridacean nudibranch (*Glossodoris*)
Douglas Faulkner

tropoda). They lack a shell, gills, and mantle cavity. The delicately coloured body has bizarre outgrowths, called cerata, which may be respiratory organs. Antenna-like organs (rhinophores) arise from the head. Nudibranchs occur in all shallow waters, where they feed chiefly on sea anemones. Those of the family Tethyidae can swim. Among bottom creepers in cold northern seas is the bushy-backed sea slug (*Dendronotus frondosus*), a brown and yellow species named for its stalked, lacy cerata. Occurring worldwide in warm seas are the blue sea slug (*Glaucus marina*, or *G. atlanticus*) and the doridacean nudibranchs such as *Doris* and *Glossodoris*.
·characteristics and classification **7**:956d
·evolution, traits, and classification **12**:330a
·nutritional value for human beings **7**:348g
·orientation to light source **17**:676a
·protective coloration mechanisms **4**:924d

RELATED ENTRIES in the *Ready Reference and Index:*
opisthobranch; pteropod; sea hare

Nudimmud (god): *see* Enki.

nudism, practice of nudity without separation of the sexes, commenced at the beginning of the 20th century in the German *Nacktkultur* ("nude culture") movement, one of the results of the permissiveness that was to increase as the century progressed. After World War I, the movement spread, not only throughout Germany but also rapidly into Czechoslovakia, Switzerland, The Netherlands, Scandinavia, Austria, and France. During the 1930s such societies were formed in the United States and Canada, although their progress was much slower in the Anglo-Saxon world and the legal restrictions more numerous.

Nudist practices vary. In Germany they have had a traditionally athletic character, whereas in North America they have been more quietly social. Everywhere, however, the standards for proper, polite, and discreet social behaviour are high, and most nudist camps bar the use of alcohol.

The nudist movement is partly a reaction against dress conventions on the grounds that clothing cuts off the human body from air and sunlight. It is also contended that the practice of nudity is beneficial for health by inducing participants to respect and improve the condition of their bodies, thereby enhancing human beauty.

The criticism of nudism that the genitalia are indecent and arouse shame or guilt in normal people has been refuted by every observer of nudist practices. Shame or a painful consciousness of guilt at the sight of the body usually soon disappears.

Nudists claim, therefore, that nudism creates a healthier attitude toward the body and promotes a fuller psychological acceptance of the self. By removing the last artificial barrier, nudism not only creates a higher standard of sincerity and frankness between the sexes but also weakens sex segregation and promotes human solidarity by removing the false mystique of the body.

nuée ardente (French: "fiery cloud," "glowing cloud"), highly destructive, incandescent mass of gas-enveloped volcanic particles that moves very quickly down even slight inclines. In some volcanic eruptions, violent expansion of gas (vesiculation) shreds the escaping magma into small, discrete particles, each of which, both in the mass itself and in the spectacular convoluting clouds of dust that rise above it, actively liberates more gas. This expanding gas envelope is pushing against similar envelopes surrounding neighbouring particles, accounting for the rapid expansion and nearly frictionless character of the flow and, thus, its great mobility. These glowing avalanches, as they are sometimes called, may attain speeds as great as 160 kilometres (100 miles) per hour and are exceedingly destructive, killing all living things in their paths. In 1902 the cloud of incandescent ash accompanying a glowing avalanche swept down on Saint-Pierre, at the foot of Mt. Pelée in the West Indies, killing about 30,000 persons.

·glowing avalanche characteristics **9**:230h
·size and duration scale, illus. 13 **15**:923

Nuel, space of, gap between the outer rods and the hair cells in the organ of Corti of the inner ear.

·structure and function in human ear **5**:1124b; illus. 1123

Nuer, Nilotic-speaking people who live in the marshy and savanna country on both banks of the Nile in the southern Sudan. Their language is classified in the Eastern Sudanic branch of the Chari-Nile group. They are a cattle-raising people, devoted to their herds, although milk and meat must be supplemented by the cultivation of millet and the spearing of fish. Because the land is flooded for part of the year and parched for the rest of it, they spend the rainy season in permanent villages built on the higher ground and the dry season in riverside camps. In the 1970s their population was estimated at 450,000.

Politically, the Nuer form a group of tribes. There is little unity and much feuding within a tribe; the frequent homicides are settled, if at all, by payments of cattle effected through the mediation of a priest of the leopard skin. Such unity as they display is partly because each tribal territory is owned by one or another patrilineal clan. The members of a clan have in their territory a slightly privileged status, although they form a minority of its population. The majority belong to other clans or are descendants of the neighbouring Dinka (*q.v.*), large numbers of whom have been subdued by the Nuer and incorporated into their society.

In each tribal area the men are divided into age sets. A boy is initiated into his set at puberty with various rites, including the cutting of six deep scars across his forehead. All boys initiated during a period of about six years belong to the same set.

Marriage, which is polygynous, is marked by the giving of cattle by the bridegroom's people to the bride's kin, both paternal and maternal, and by betrothal and wedding ceremonies. Because it is held that every man must have at least one male heir, it is the custom for a man's kin, should he die unmarried, to marry a wife to his name and beget children by her.

The Nuer clans involve segmentary lineages to which the Nuer attach great importance, and everyone knows his exact genealogical relationship to every member of his lineage and clan. Apart from these relationships on the father's side, they also attach importance to kinship ties through their mothers and through marriage; a Nuer can establish kinship of one sort or another with most of the people he meets.

The Nuer are a religious people. They pray and sacrifice to a spirit conceived of as a single creative spirit in relation to mankind as a whole; this spirit is also figured in different representations in relation to different social groups, such as clans, lineages, and age sets, and it may then be symbolized by material forms, often animals or plants. *See also* Nilotes.

·Evans-Pritchard's study of sacrifice **16**:130b
·herding societies and planting taboos **8**:1163a
·kinship widow inheritance custom **10**:480f
·monotheism in polytheistic form **12**:382e
·numbers, tribal affiliations, and culture **6**:109g
·peoples of the eastern Sudan map **6**:165
·religion emphasis on spiritual forces **14**:1042e
·Sudan ethnic composition map **17**:762
·youth social status and behaviour **19**:1092h

Nuer language: *see* Nilotic languages.

Nueva Caracas, land development area, Caracas, Venezuela.

·real estate development construction **3**:813e

Nueva Casas Grandes (Mexico): *see* Casas Grandes.

Nueva Ecija, landlocked province, central Luzon, Philippines. Its area of 2,040 sq mi (5,284 sq km), occupying the eastern part of the Central Plain and drained by the Pampanga River, forms part of the nation's "rice granary." Palayan is the provincial capital; other towns are Cabanatuan, San Jose, Gapan, and Cuyapo. After World War II the region became a focus of the Communist-inspired Hukbalahap activities until the rebellion died out in the mid-1950s. Pop. (1975) 947,995.

·area and population table **14**:236

Nueva Esparta, island state, northeastern Venezuela, off the Península de Araya. Totalling 444 sq mi (1,150 sq km), Nueva Esparta consists of Margarita (*q.v.*), largest of the islands, and two small neighbours, Cubagua and Coche. Margarita dominates the economic life of the state and contains most of the population. Porlamar, in southeastern Margarita, is the largest town; La Asunción (*q.v.*), the state capital, boasts a colourful history and distinguished architecture. Puerto Fermín is an important fishing port, and there are many small fishing villages. Fishing, pearl fishing, a tuna- and sardine-canning industry, and tourism are the principal economic activities. Pearling has been important almost since the time of Columbus, but many of the oyster beds are in danger of depletion. Fresh water is supplied by underwater pipeline from the mainland to Margarita. Pop. (1977 est.) 138,272.

·map, Venezuela **19**:60
·population density map **19**:64

Nueva Granada, Virreinato de: *see* New Granada, Viceroyalty of.

Nueva Isabela, historic site of Santo Domingo, capital city of the Dominican Republic.

·Santo Domingo history **16**:234b

Nueva Ocotepeque, from late 1970s OCOTEPEQUE, capital, Ocotepeque department, western Honduras, on the Lempa River at 2,641 ft (805 m) above sea level. The town was originally situated just to the northeast, at the site of Ocotepeque, but it was relocated after the Marchala River, a tributary of the Lempa, overflowed in 1935. Nueva Ocotepeque is a trading centre in a fertile agricultural region that produces mainly coffee, sugarcane, wheat, tobacco, and livestock. The town is linked by highway to urban centres in Honduras, El Salvador, and Guatemala. Pop. (1974) 8,712.
14°24′ N, 89°13′ W

·map, Honduras **8**:1058

Nueva Planta, Decree of (1716), Spanish proclamation unifying Spain and Catalonia.

·unitary state formation **17**:433e

Nueva Rosita, city, north central Coahuila state, northeastern Mexico. It is situated 1,410 ft (430 m) above sea level, on the Río Sabinas, southwest of Piedras Negras, on the Mexico–United States border. The city's location in the Sabinas coal district led to its development, and since the 1930s it has become a prominent industrial centre, with a zinc smelter producing zinc sulfate and sulfuric acid, as well as coke. Nueva Rosita is on the main Piedras Negras–Mexico City highway and has connections with the Piedras Negras–Escalón (Chihuahua state) railway. Pop. (1970) 34,706.
27°57′ N, 101°13′ W

·map, Mexico **12**:69

Nueva San Salvador, also called SANTA TECLA, capital (since 1865) of La Libertad department, west central El Salvador. Founded in 1854 as Nueva Ciudad de San Salvador at the southern base of San Salvador Volcano, it briefly replaced the national capital, San Salvador (7 mi [11 km] east), devastated by an earthquake. In 1859 the government was moved back to a rebuilt San Salvador. On the Inter-American Highway (a section of the Pan-American Highway) from San Salvador, it is in a densely settled area important for coffee, livestock, corn (maize), vegetables, and fruit. It is the site of the Salvadorean Coffee Grower's Association Research Centre. Nearby is a beach resort, Los Chorros. Pop. (1971) 36,440.
13°41′ N, 89°17′ W

·map, El Salvador **6**:732

Nueva Segovia, department, northwestern Nicaragua, bounded by Honduras (north) and by the Coco River (south and east). Most of the population of the 1,290-sq-mi (3,341-sq-km) department live in the highland basins and valleys in the central portion; the remainder of Nueva Segovia is very sparsely settled because of rugged relief, poor soils, and lack

of transportation. The settled basins and valleys, some with fertile volcanic soils, produce coffee, livestock, corn (maize), vegetables, and subtropical fruits. Ocotal (*q.v.*), the departmental capital, is linked by a poor road to the Pan-American Highway. Pop. (1971 prelim.) 65,719.
·area and population table **13**:59
·map, Nicaragua **13**:61

Nueva Vizcaya, landlocked province, north central Luzon, Philippines. It is mountainous around the junction of the Sierra Madre and the Cordillera Central and has an area of 2,688 sq mi (6,961 sq km). Drained by the headwaters of the Cagayán River and its tributary, the Magat, it has fertile valleys. Much of its area, which contains major timber resources, remains unexplored. The economy is agricultural (rice, corn [maize], sugarcane); industry is limited to logging and related activities. The provincial capital is Bayombong; other towns include Solano, Bambang, and Bagabag. Pop. (1970) 221,965.
·area and population table **14**:236
·Luzon mountain systems **14**:232b

Nuevitas, city, northeastern Camagüey province, east central Cuba. It lies on a peninsula jutting out into sheltered Bahía (bay) de Nuevitas, into which Christopher Columbus sailed to land in the area in 1492. Despite frequent pirate raids in the colonial era, the settlement prospered. Its economic base is now varied: sugarcane, molasses, coffee, sisal, and fruits from the agricultural hinterland are shipped to Nuevitas by railroad and highway. Chief among the city's industrial products are lumber, rope, coffee, textiles, soap, and furniture. Sugar refineries are located nearby, and fishing and lumbering are also widespread. Pop. (1970 prelim.) 20,734.
21°33′ N, 77°16′ W
·map, Cuba **5**:351

Nuevo Laredo, city and port of entry, northern Tamaulipas state, northeastern Mexico, on the Rio Grande (Río Bravo del Norte), across from Laredo, Texas. The city is a cattle and natural gas production centre; irrigation of its hinterland has brought some growth and wealth since the 1950s. A bullring attracts tourists. A highway and a railroad linking San Antonio, Texas, with Mexico City, to the south, pass through Nuevo Laredo. Pop. (1973 est.) 175,750.
27°30′ N, 99°31′ W
·map, Mexico **12**:69

Nuevo León, state, northeastern Mexico, bounded north by the United States, east and southeast by Tamaulipas, south and southwest by San Luis Potosí, and west by Coahuila. Crossed by the southeastward-running Sierra Madre Oriental (average elevation 5,000 ft [1,500 m]), Nuevo León's 24,925-sq-mi (64,555-sq-km) territory contains a variety of climatic and vegetation types. The state produces few minerals, but quantities of cotton, citrus, sugarcane, cereals (especially corn [maize] and wheat), and vegetables are grown, in part with the aid of irrigation water provided by the international Falcón Dam on the Rio Grande (Río Bravo del Norte). Nuevo León's principal importance lies in its industries. Its ironworks and steelworks and smelting plants were the first heavy industrial establishments in Latin America, and the state also supports numerous textile enterprises, a large beer factory, and other industrial activities. The region was made a state in 1824 and was occupied by United States forces during the Mexican War (1846–48). A major railroad and highway linking Laredo, Texas, with the Gulf port of Tampico and Mexico City pass through Monterrey (*q.v.*), the state capital, which also possesses an airport. Pop. (1970) 1,694,689.
·area and population table **12**:71
·population density map **12**:71

Nuffar (ancient Mesopotamian city): *see* Nippur.

Nuffield, William Richard Morris, 1st Viscount (b. Oct. 10, 1877, Worcestershire—d. Aug. 22, 1963, near Huntercombe, Henley-on-Thames, Oxfordshire), industrialist and philanthropist whose automobile manufacturing firm introduced the Morris cars. The son of a farm labourer, he was obliged by his father's illness to abandon plans to study medicine and go to work at age 15. Behind his home he set up a bicycle repair shop, built bicycles to order, and raced them with success. Later he sold and maintained motorcycles, an interest he easily extended to automobiles. In 1903 he took in a partner, but their garage went bankrupt. In 1904, with only his tools

Lord Nuffield, 1962
By courtesy of British Leyland Motor Corporation Ltd.

left and a £50 debt, he started again. He set up works in Cowley, and the first Morris-Oxford, an 8.9-horsepower two-seater, appeared in 1913. The sales of this machine having made him prosperous, he soon brought out the equally famous Morris-Cowley (11.9-horsepower), after he had visited the U.S. with a designer and had contracted to buy an engine to fit his English chassis. With the aim of emphasizing the production of small, reliable cars at the low prices made possible by mass production, Morris revolutionized the automobile industry in England, much as Henry Ford had done in the United States. Morris Motors Ltd., founded in 1919, survived the difficulties of 1920–21 by slashing prices. From then on the business expanded, and in 1923 the Morris Garages built the first MG. In the same year Morris founded Morris Commercial Cars Ltd., and in 1927 he acquired Wolseley Motors Ltd. Morris Motors Ltd. was reorganized in 1935–36 to include these three companies and also Riley (Coventry) Ltd. in 1938. After a merger with the Austin Motor Company in 1952, the resulting firm, the British Motor Corporation, became the third largest automobile company in the world. Morris, who was made a baronet in 1929 and a baron in 1934, was created Viscount Nuffield in 1938. His philanthropic activities began in the early 1930s, beneficiaries including the Nuffield Institute for Medical Research, Oxford University; the Nuffield Trust; Nuffield College, Oxford; and the Nuffield Foundation, established in 1943 to further "health . . . social wellbeing . . . care of the poor . . . and education."
·history of automotive industry **2**:528b

Nuffield Radio Astronomy Laboratories (Cheshire, England): *see* Jodrell Bank Experimental Station.

Nugal Valley (region, Somalia): *see* Nogal Valley.

nugget, in mining, water-worn, fair-sized lump of metal; the word is most commonly used in reference to gold, but copper, silver, platinum, and other metals in this form are also designated as nuggets. Fragments and pieces of vein metal whose history does not include fluvial (water) transport are not called nuggets. Gold nuggets commonly range from the size of a pea to that of a nut; exceptionally large ones include the 64.75-kilogram (2,284-ounce) "Welcome Stranger" from Ballarat, Australia, and the 49.41-kilogram (1,743-ounce) "Blanche Barkley" from Kingower, Australia.

Nugget Sandstone Formation, division of Lower Jurassic (or perhaps Upper Triassic) rocks in North America. (The Jurassic Period began about 190,000,000 years ago and lasted some 54,000,000 years.) The Nugget, named for exposures at Nugget Station, Lincoln County, Wyoming, consists of up to about 300 metres (1,000 feet) of nonfossiliferous sandstones; it varies greatly in thickness. The Nugget Sandstone overlies rocks of the Triassic Chugwater Group and underlies the Twin Creek Limestone.

Nûgssuaq, also spelled NÛGSSUAK, the name of two peninsulas in western Greenland. The larger (70°20′ N, 52°30′ W), separated from Disko Island (southwest) by Vaigat Sound, extends northwest from the inland icecap into Nordost Bay. About 110 mi (180 km) long and 18–30 mi (30–48 km) wide, it has a maximum elevation of 7,339 ft (2,237 m) near Umanak. The peninsula has lignite deposits and petrified flora. At its centre lies Tasersuaq Lake (26 mi [42 km] long, 1–2 mi [1½–3 km] wide) at an elevation of 2,000 ft (610 m).
The smaller peninsula (74°12′ N, 56°35′ W), 30 mi (48 km) long and 1–4 mi (1½–6½ km) wide, extends southwest from Cornell Glacier into Baffin Bay. Kraulshavn, on the south coast, is a fishing outpost.
·map, Greenland **8**:412

nuisance, in law, a human activity or a physical condition that is harmful or offensive to others and gives rise to a cause of action. A public nuisance created in a public place or on public land, or affecting the morals, safety, or health of the community is considered an offense against the state. Such activities as obstructing a public road, polluting air and water, operating a house of prostitution, and keeping explosives are public nuisances. A private nuisance is an activity or condition that interferes with the use and enjoyment of neighbouring privately owned lands, without, however, constituting an actual invasion of the property. Thus, excessive noise, noxious vapours, and disagreeable odours and vibrations may constitute a private nuisance to the neighbouring landowners, although there has been no physical trespass on their lands.
While a public nuisance, as such, is actionable only by the state, by way of either criminal proceedings, injunction, or physical abatement, the same activity or conduct may also create a private nuisance to neighbouring landowners and thus result in a civil suit. The conduct of a business in violation of a zoning ordinance creates a public nuisance, but it may also be actionable as a private nuisance by neighbours who can prove a decrease in the market value of their homes as a result.
Because a private nuisance is based upon interference with the use and enjoyment of land, it is actionable only by persons who have a property interest in such land. If the interference merely makes the use and enjoyment less comfortable, without inflicting physical damage to the land, the courts consider the character of the neighbourhood to determine whether the activity or condition is an unreasonable interference. An activity that causes physical damage to neighbouring land, however, will be held to be an actionable nuisance irrespective of the character of the neighbourhood. Such cases usually involve vibrations that cause walls to crack or noxious vapours that destroy vegetation.
The legal remedies available in the case of a private nuisance are actions to enjoin the operation or continuance of the activity or condition or to collect money damages. If the

abatement of a nuisance by injunction would impose an excessive hardship on the community (the closing of factories that would deprive community workers of their livelihood), the usual practice of the courts is to deny an injunction and award money damages for the injury suffered.
·tort law concerning property rights **18**:526g

Nuit (Egyptian goddess): *see* Nut.

Nuits d'été, Les, or SUMMER NIGHTS, a cycle of six songs (for voice and piano, 1834–41; for voice and orchestra, 1843 and 1856) by Berlioz.
·art song development in France **19**:500h

Nü Kua, in Chinese mythology, the patroness of matchmakers; as wife or sister of the legendary Emperor Fu Hsi, she helped establish norms for marriage (that included go-betweens) and regulated conduct between the sexes. She is described as having a human head but the body of a snake (or fish).

One legend credits Nü Kua with having repaired the pillars of Heaven and the broken corners of earth, which the rebel Kung Kung had destroyed in a fit of anger. To accomplish her task Nü Kua used the feet of a tortoise and melted-down stones that turned into a five-coloured mixture.

Nü Kua is also said to have built a lovely palace that became a prototype for the later walled cities of China. The material of which it was made was prepared overnight by mountain spirits.

By slipping a miraculous rope through the nose of the King of Oxen, she also put a stop to the terror this monster visited on his enemies by means of his enormous horns and ears.

Quite a different legend names Nü and Kua as the first human beings who found themselves at the moment of creation among the Kunlun Mountains. While offering sacrifice, they prayed to know if they, as brother and sister, were meant to be man and wife. The union was sanctioned when the smoke of the sacrifice remained stationary.
·mythical and religious role **4**:411h *passim* to 413c

Nukualofa, capital and chief port of the Tonga islands, on the northern shore of Tongatapu, southern Pacific. Its harbour is protected by reefs. Commercial activities centre on the export of copra, bananas, and vanilla, and the sale of traditional handicrafts from the Malae (Park) Market. Landmarks include

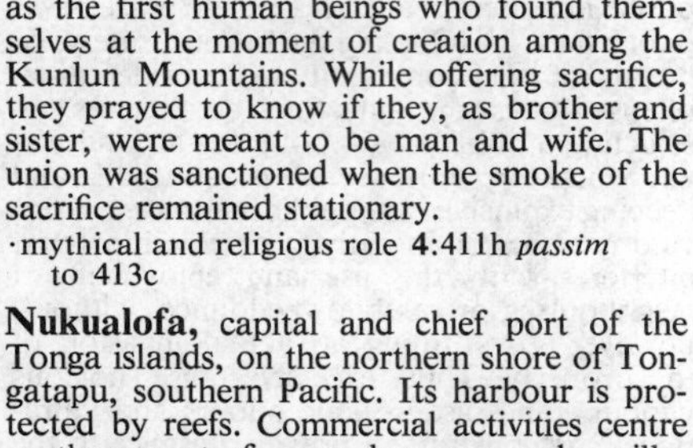

Royal Palace at Nukualofa, capital of the Tonga Islands
Bjorn Klingwall—Ostman Agency

the Royal Palace (1865–67) and Chapel (1862) on the seafront at the end of the old wharf and the Royal Tombs. The town has several colleges (high schools), a teachers' training college, Vaiola Hospital, government offices, and the large Wesleyan Church. Modern buildings include the broadcasting studio and a development outside the town comprising housing, joinery works, and Copra Board enterprises. Pop. (1972 est.) 20,000.
21°08′ S, 175°12′ W

Nuku Hiva, also spelled NUKAHIVA, volcanic island (62 sq mi [161 sq km]) of the Marquesas Islands, French Polynesia, in the central South Pacific. Its rugged terrain rises to Mt. Ketu (3,888 ft [1,185 m]) and is drained by small streams. There is no coastal plain or fringing coral reef. It was claimed (1813) for the U.S. by a naval officer, David Porter, who named it Madison Island, but it was annexed by France (1842). The island had a small sandalwood trade in the 19th century.

While the hills are wooded, the narrow valleys are fertile and, under a warm and humid climate, yield copra and fruit for export. Taiohae (Haka Pehi), the main harbour and port on the south coast, is the administrative seat for the northern Marquesas. Another harbour (Baie d'Anaho) is on the north coast.

Nuku Hiva was the setting for Herman Melville's novel *Typee*. Latest census 1,216.
8°54′ S, 140°06′ W

Nukunono, coral atoll of the Tokelau Islands, a dependency of New Zealand in the southwest Pacific Ocean. It comprises 30 islets, with a total area of 2 sq mi (5 sq km), encircling a lagoon 8 mi (13 km) by 7 mi. Discovered (1791) and named Duke of Clarence Island by the captain of the British ship "Pandora," which was searching for mutineers from the HMS "Bounty," Nukunono's inhabitants were converted to Roman Catholicism (before 1858) by a Samoan missionary. The islanders depend upon coconuts, pandanus, and marine life for subsistence; freshwater is scarce. Shipping is hampered by the lack of an adequate anchorage. The atoll has a local administration (headed by a magistrate) and is considered the unofficial capital of the Tokelau group. Pop. (1970) 408.

Nukus, capital of the Kara-Kalpak Autonomous Soviet Socialist Republic in the Uzbek Soviet Socialist Republic, at the head of the Amu Darya Delta. The tiny Nukus settlement, amid the desert sands, was made the site of the new Kara-Kalpak capital in 1932, when the former one, at Turtkul, to the south, was being eroded by the Amu Darya. The present city has a number of food-processing and other light industries, the Kara-Kalpak branch of the Uzbek Academy of Sciences, a teacher-training institute, a museum, and a theatre. Pop. (1970) 74,000.
42°50′ N, 59°23′ E
·hydrology and climate **1**:715h
·map, Soviet Union **17**:322

Nullagine, shire, northwest Western Australia, on Nullagine Creek, a tributary of the De Grey River. It was founded during a gold rush of 1888. While some gold is still mined, the iron, manganese, asbestos, antimony, beryl, copper, and wolfram deposits found in the locality and in sections of the surrounding 200,000-sq-mi (520,000-sq-km) geological "province" known as the Nullagine Platform, or Series, are far more important. Linked to Port Hedland (140 mi [225 km] northwest) and Perth (869 mi southwest) by road, Nullagine also serves a district producing wool and beef. Pop. (1971 prelim.) 4,687.
·Australian geological history **2**:384g
·map, Australia **2**:400
·physiographic features **19**:793a

Nullarbor Plain, vast plateau, extending westward for 400 mi (650 km) from Ooldea in South Australia into Western Australia and northward from the Great Australian Bight (a wide bay) for 250 mi to the Great Victorian Desert. It occupies 100,000 sq mi (260,000 sq km) of generally flat surface in bedrock (with an average elevation of 600 ft [180 m]), but in places it rises to 1,000 ft. Along the bight in Western Australia, it is bordered by a narrow coastal plain, which in South Australia gives way to cliffs rising 200–400 ft from the sea. A former sea bed with surface deposits of limestone, the plateau lacks surface streams. It is, however, underlain by large systems of caverns, some of which contain percolated water. Its name is derived from the Latin *nullus arbor* ("no tree"), and vegetation consists chiefly of saltbush and blue bush, with some grasses and flowers appearing after rare winter rains (annual average precipitation 10 in. [250 mm] or less).

Discovered and crossed (1841) by the British explorer Edward John Eyre, the plain is traversed 100 miles inland by the world's longest stretch of straight railroad track (330 mi) and by the Eyre Highway, near the coast. There are scattered sheep stations along the margins, supplied by artesian water. Maralinga, just north of the plateau, was established (1956) as an atomic-weapons-testing site.
·formation and composition **2**:389b
·map, Australia **2**:400
·vegetation and soil conditions **5**:616c

null hypothesis, the assumption that any observed difference between two samples of a statistical population is purely accidental and not due to a systematic cause.
·statistical theory and method **17**:621f

nullification, in U.S. history, doctrine upholding the right of a state to declare void within its boundaries federal government actions judged unconstitutional by the state; prominent in the pre-Civil War tariff conflict between South Carolina and the federal government. Thomas Jefferson's resolutions to the Kentucky legislature (1798) and James Madison's resolutions to the Virginia legislature (1798), declared that a state had the right to oppose decisions of the federal judiciary. The doctrine of nullification was fully formulated by John C. Calhoun in his *Exposition and Protest* (1829), which held that the states were sovereign entities. After Calhoun's paper was circulated in the South Carolina legislature, that body adopted an ordinance (1832) nullifying the 1828 and 1832 U.S. tariffs. Congress passed a Force Bill authorizing Pres. Andrew Jackson, who had denounced nullification in a presidential proclamation, to collect the tariff duties by coercion. Under the threat of civil war, a compromise was negotiated in Congress between Henry Clay and Calhoun. Congress approved a Compromise Tariff (1833), and South Carolina rescinded its nullification ordinance.
·Calhoun statement and defense **3**:613f
·Jackson's South Carolina controversy **10**:3f
·Webster–Hayne tariff debate **19**:719g

nullity of marriage (law): *see* annulment.

null set, any set of measure zero. *See* measure.
·algebraic structure theory **1**:519g
·class identity as membership function **11**:53c
·definition and logical necessity **16**:569e

Numan, port on the Benue River, Adamawa Province, North-Eastern State, eastern Nigeria, opposite the mouth of the Gongola River, the principal tributary of the Benue; it has ferry service across the Benue and is connected by road to Gombe, Shellen, Yola, Jalingo, and Ganye. Probably founded by the Njei (Jenjo, Jenge) people, it was occupied in the early 19th century by Bata tribesmen fleeing the advance of the Fulani *jihād* ("holy war") and became the centre of a small Bata kingdom in the 1850s. The town was selected in 1885 as a trading post by the National African (later Royal Niger) Company, which burned it in 1891 after an attack on a company ship by the Bachama tribesmen. Numan was gradually rebuilt, and the British established a garrison there in 1903. In 1912 the town became the headquarters of Numan division, a region that became the Numan federation in 1951. In 1921, Chief Hamma Mbi moved the Bachama tribal headquarters from Lamurde (20 mi [32 km] west-northwest) and constructed his palace in the town.

Modern Numan is a collecting point for peanuts (groundnuts) and cotton and the chief trade centre (guinea corn, millet, cowpeas, fish, cattle, goats, sheep, poultry) for the federation area of 2,214 sq mi (5,734 sq km), which is mainly inhabited by the Longuda (Nunguda), Bachama, Mbula, Fulani, Bata,

Lala, and Dera (Kanakuru) peoples. Its Sudan United Mission sponsors a secondary school and a teacher-training college; but the town is also served by a Roman Catholic secondary school, a government craft institute, a hospital, and a health office. Outside the town along the Benue are the state government's sugarcane estate and sugar-processing plant (1971).

Besides Numan, whose Bachama inhabitants are noted for their tribal dances, the federation's chief settlements are Shellen, the political capital of the Dera; Mbula town; Demsa; and Dukul, the Longuda spiritual headquarters. An annual festival honouring Nzeanzo, the most important god of the Nzeanzo cult, practiced by the Bachama, the Bata, and the Mbula, is held at Farei, 6 mi southeast. Pop. (1972 est.) 24,498.
9°28′ N, 12°02′ E
·map, Nigeria **13**:86

Numan Pasha (d. 1719), Ottoman grand vizier.
·Köprülü historical role and genealogy **10**:506d; table

Numantia, a Celtiberian town located near modern Soria in Spain on the upper Douro (Duero) River. Founded on the site of earlier settlements by Iberians who penetrated the Celtic highlands about 300 BC, it later formed the centre of Celtiberian resistance to Rome, withstanding repeated attacks. Finally, Scipio Aemilianus (Numantinus) blockaded it (133 BC) by establishing six miles of continuous ramparts around it. After an eight-month siege, Numantia was reduced by hunger, and the survivors capitulated, its destruction ending all serious resistance to Rome in Celtiberia. Numantia was later rebuilt by the emperor Augustus, but it had little importance.
·Roman siege and victory **17**:404b
·Roman war of attrition **15**:1099d

Numa Pompilius (fl. *c.* 700 BC), second of the seven kings who, according to Roman tradition, ruled Rome before the founding of the Republic (*c.* 509 BC). He is said to have reigned from 715 to 673. Numa is credited with the formulation of the religious calendar and with the founding of nearly all the earliest religious institutions, including the Vestal Virgins; the cults of Mars, Jupiter, and Romulus deified (Quirinus); and the office of *pontifex maximus*. These developments were, however, undoubtedly the result of centuries of religious accretion, going back to prehistoric times and continuing down to the republican era, and thus are not to be assigned to any single man.

But Numa can be accepted as a historical personage. His name indicates an origin among the central Italic Sabini tribe from the area east of the Tiber in the vicinity of modern Rieti. He is said to have come from the town of Cures and to have been the son-in-law of the Sabine king Titus Tatius.

According to legend, Numa is the peaceful counterpart of the more bellicose Romulus (the mythical founder of Rome), whom he succeeded after an interregnum of one year. His supposed relationship with Pythagoras was chronologically impossible, and the 14 books relating to philosophy and religious (pontifical) law that were uncovered in 181 BC are clearly forgeries.
·Roman law and religion **15**:1085h

Numazu, city, Shizuoka Prefecture (*ken*), Honshu, Japan, at the mouth of the Kano-gawa (Kano River), facing Suruga-wan (Suruga Bay). It developed as a castle town in the early 16th century and later served as a post town on the Tōkaidō Highway. Because of the city's location at the junction of land and sea routes, it became a regional commercial and administrative centre. Industrialization was rapid; products include machinery, metal, and textiles. Fishing and tourism are also important. Numazu Park contains a municipal aquarium and Sembon-matsubara (Thousand-Pines Beach), noted for its ancient, gnarled trees. Pop. (1970) 189,038.
35°06′ N, 138°52′ E
·map, Japan **10**:36

numbat, or BANDED ANTEATER (*Myrmecobius fasciatus*), marsupial mammal of the family

Numbat (*Myrmecobius fasciatus*)
Painting by Richard Ellis

Dasyuridae (*q.v.;* some authorities raise it to a family in its own right, Myrmecobiidae). It forages by day for termites in forests of southern and western Australia. It has a squat body and small, pointed head, together about 20 centimetres (8 inches) long, and a 15-centimetre bushy tail. The pelage is gray-brown to reddish-brown, with about eight transverse white stripes on the rump. The teeth are small, and there are extra molars—52 teeth in all. The tongue is extensible and sticky, and the forefeet are strong-clawed, for digging. The numbat is pouchless; it has two to four young a year.
·traits, behaviour, and classification **11**:540d; illus. 539

number, one of the positive integers, or one of the set of all real or complex numbers, the latter containing the product *bi* which is termed imaginary (*see* number, imaginary). The real numbers consist of rational and irrational numbers. The former are numbers that can be expressed as integers or as the quotient of integers, whereas the irrational numbers are either algebraic irrational numbers—those which cannot be expressed as simple integers or their quotients—or the so-called transcendental numbers—those expressions involving e and π (pi), and certain trigonometric and hyperbolic functions.

Other kinds of numbers include: square numbers, those which are squares of integers; perfect numbers, those which are equal to the sum of their factors; random numbers, those which are representative of random selection procedures; and prime numbers, those which are divisible only by themselves and ± 1, and which are not equal to 0 or ± 1.
·arithmetic laws and principles **1**:1174b
·Cantor's set theory development **3**:784f
·Dedekind real number development **5**:549h
·Gauss's number theory concepts **7**:966f
·Plato's equation with Forms **14**:538e
·Pythagorean mathematical reality **15**:322g *passim* to 324d
·real analysis principles **1**:776g

number, imaginary, a product of any real number and the square root of minus 1 (represented by i), as in the general form of any complex number $a + bi$, in which bi is said to be the imaginary part.
·mathematics history from antiquity **11**:645a
·real analysis principles **1**:775c

number factorization, process of finding numbers the product of which is equal in value to a given number. A standard procedure used in deriving information about collectoons of natural numbers is finding the prime factors; *i.e.,* those that are not divisible by any integer greater than one except themselves.
·number theory principles **13**:358b

number field, a set of real or complex numbers, the nature of which is such that operations of addition, subtraction, division, or multiplication on any two members or elements of the set is in the set.

number games and other mathematical recreations 13:345, any of a wide range of puzzles and games that involve aspects of mathematics.

The text article covers the history and major types of number games and mathematical recreations and the principles on which they are based. Included are sections of arithmetic and algebraic recreations (examples are number patterns, cryptograms, perfect numbers, magic squares), geometric and topological recreations (geometric fallacies, tangrams and mazes, map-colouring problems), manipulative recreations (puzzles involving configurations, chessboard problems, polyominoes), and problems of logical inference (logical puzzles involving overlapping groups, truths and lies, or paradoxes).

REFERENCES in other text articles:
·combinatorics theory and method **4**:945c
·cryptological codes and ciphers **5**:322c

number line, in arithmetic, line with whole numbers marked on it and extending as far as

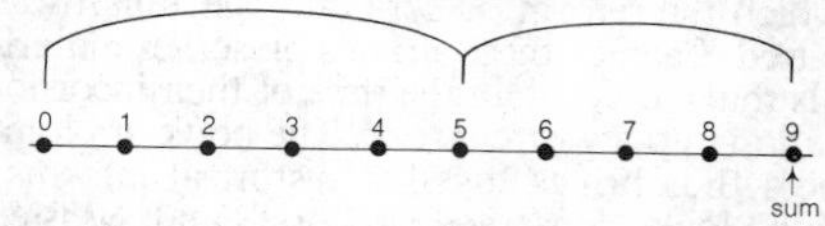

one wants to illustrate a problem in arithmetic. A marker is made to jump from number to number on the line indicating an addition or subtraction. Example: $5 + 4 = 9$ as in the Figure.

number metaphysic, Pythagorean, the philosophic view of the early followers of the ancient Greek sage Pythagoras that the deepest features of reality lie, in some sense, in numbers. The exact nature of the relationship of all things to numbers as viewed by the Pythagoreans is obscure. Both Pythagoras and his early followers avoided, on principle, the commitment of their teachings to writing, and scholars have found that, in general, one cannot recover with assurance the thought of Pre-Socratic philosophers for whom no body of actual words is extant.

As reported by Aristotle, the Pythagoreans were the first to advance the study of mathematics and thought that its principles (Greek *archai*) were the principles of all things. According to Aristotle, they also supposed the elements (*stoicheia*) of numbers to be the elements of all things and asserted that things exist by imitating numbers.

Though it is clear that in some way mathematics governed their metaphysical position, scholars have not yet succeeded in reconstructing the basic theories underlying these assertions.
·influence and importance **14**:252c
·polygonal numbers and Pythagorean triples **13**:348g
·Pythagoras and Plato **12**:15e

Numbers, Hebrew BEMIDBAR (In the Wilderness), the fourth book of the Bible. The Hebrew title is more descriptive of the book's contents than Numbers, which is a translation of the Septuagint (Greek Bible) title and refers to the numbering of the tribes of Israel (chapters 1–4).

The book is basically a presentation of the sacred history of the Israelites as they wandered in the wilderness after the departure from Sinai and before their occupation of Canaan, the Promised Land. The book narrates the sufferings of the Israelites and their numerous complaints against God. Although the people are depicted as faithless and rebellious, God is portrayed as one who provides for and sustains his people.

These accounts continue the sacred story of God's promise that Israel will inhabit the land of Canaan. The story, begun in Genesis and continued in Exodus and Leviticus, does not reach its conclusion until Israel successfully occupies the Promised Land. As the books now stand, that moment occurs in the Book of Joshua. Many scholars have thus maintained that the first six books of the Old Testament form a literary unit, of which Numbers is an integral part. At one time, Numbers possibly contained an account of the occupation of Canaan that was dropped when the Tetrateuch (Genesis, Exodus, Leviticus, and Numbers) was joined to other historical books of the Old Testament. In any case, the first five books of the Bible were the first to be recognized as sacred Scripture, probably in the late 5th or 4th century BC.

Scholars have identified at least three literary traditions in Numbers, designated by the letters J, E, and P. The J strand is a Judaean rendition of the sacred history, perhaps written as early as 950 BC. The E strand gives another version of the same sacred story from the northern kingdom of Israel, about 900–750 BC. The P strand is usually dated in the 5th century BC and is regarded as the law upon which the reform of Ezra and Nehemiah was based. Each of these strands preserves materials much older than the time of their incorporation into a written work. The book of Numbers thus brings together historical information long conserved in oral and written sources. *Major ref.* **2**:902c
·Moses' love for rebellious Hebrews **12**:490a
·Near East religious mobility shown **12**:916h

numbers, complex, graphical representation of, the interpretation of complex numbers as points of a two-dimensional coordinate plane, the real numbers lying on the horizontal axis and the purely imaginary numbers lying on the vertical axis.
·algebraic structure theory **1**:534a
·complex analysis fundamentals **1**:720b

numbers, irrational, numbers (containing nonrepeating decimals) that cannot be expressed as quotients of integers a/b ($b \neq 0$). Examples include $\sqrt{2}$ $(= 1.41423 \cdots)$ and π (pi) $(= 3.14159 \cdots)$.
·Eudoxus' incommensurable quantities **6**:1021e
·metrology and cosmology theory **12**:867c
·Pythagorean square root calculation **15**:324d

numbers, natural, also called COUNTING NUMBERS, the numbers that can be placed into one-to-one correspondence with elements of a set. Such numbers are 1, 2, 3, 4, · · · · Included in the natural members are even numbers, those divisible by two, 2, 4, 6, 8, · · · ; odd numbers, those not divisible by two, 1, 3, 5, 7, · · · ; and other subsets. *See* numbers, square; polygonal numbers; prime number.
·arithmetic laws and principles **1**:1171g
·elementary algebra principles **1**:499d
·genetic method description **11**:631g
·logic history from antiquity **11**:69f
·number theory principles **13**:358a
·real analysis principles **1**:772b
·set theory proof Peano axioms **16**:572d

numbers, square, in mathematics, squares of the natural numbers 1, 2, 3, 4, · · · , n; hence 1, 4, 9, 16, · · · , n^2. The term square number is derived from the fact that each square number indicated by a natural number (greater than 1) can be depicted as a square array of points (●), every edge of which contains the natural number of points:

●= 1   ●●= 2   ●●●= 3   ●●●●= 4, etc.

●= 1   ●●●●= 4   ●●●●●●●●●= 9   ●●●●●●●●●●●●●●●●= 16, etc.

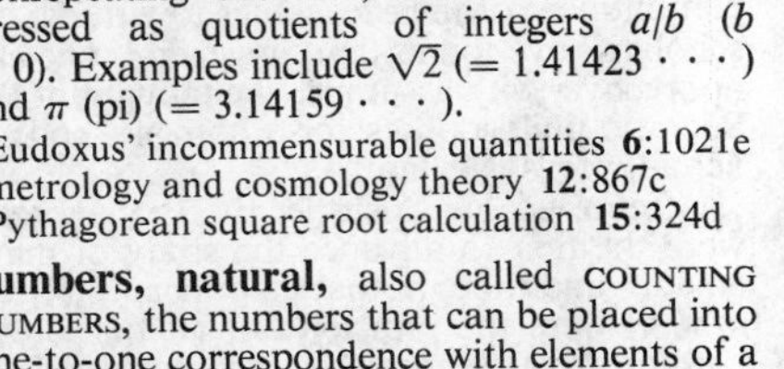

The squares form an arithmetic sequence of

second order, as do the triangular, pentagonal, and other polygonal numbers. If the differences of consecutive terms of this second-order sequence are taken, a first-difference sequence is formed the consecutive terms of which differ by a constant, so that the consecutive terms of the second-difference sequence differ by 0. For square numbers, these sequences are:

$$n^2: 1, 4, \ 9, 16, 25, 36, 49, 64, \cdots$$
$$\text{1st-dif.}: \quad 3, \ 5, \ 7, \ 9, 11, 13, 15, \cdots$$
$$\text{2nd-dif.}: \qquad 2, \ 2, \ 2, \ 2, \ 2, \ 2, \cdots.$$

See also numbers, natural; polygonal numbers; triangular numbers.
·Pythagorean number theory **15**:324b

number sequence, $\{a_n\}$, of complex numbers, any function that assigns to each integer $n = 1, 2, 3, \cdots$ a complex number a_n. The symbol $\{a_n\}$ is thus identified with $a_1, a_2, a_3, \cdots$.

numbers game, the most widespread lottery game in the United States, though illegal wherever it is played. Patrons of the numbers game are drawn chiefly from the low-income classes, with the number of black players disproportionately high. The player may bet 10 cents or less. He selects his own number, any three-digit number from 001 to 999. The winning number is taken each day from a source that the promoters of the game cannot control, *e.g.*, bank financial balances or pari-mutuel totals at racetracks. The odds against winning are 998 to 1; as the game is usually played, the person who selects the winning number is paid 540 to 1, the "runner" who accepted his bet receives 60 units, and the gross profit of the promoters is nearly 40 percent of the amount wagered. The inducement to the bettor is that a 10-cent risk may yield $54. Promoters may pay large sums to politicians and police to protect against arrest. The amounts bet on numbers annually in the U.S. have been estimated as high as several million dollars, although such figures are unverifiable. Legal alternatives have been proposed; and several states initiated state-wide lotteries in the 1960s and 1970s, but the numbers game has continued. *See also* bolita; policy.
·lottery betting procedures **11**:114h

number theory **13**:358, concerns the properties of integers, positive and negative whole numbers and zero, and of certain extended sets of numbers.

TEXT ARTICLE COVERS:
Elementary theory of numbers **13**:358b
Divisibility and prime numbers 358b
The sieve of Eratosthenes 358d
Bernoulli numbers 358h
Fermat's last theorem 359b
Residue classes and congruences 359d
Continued fractions 360b
Algebraic number theory 360e
The Zahlbericht and Hilbert's problems 362f
Hensel's p-adic numbers 362g
Analytic number theory 364b
The distribution of prime numbers 366c
Geometric number theory 373c
Probabilistic number theory 377a
The number of prime divisors 377a

REFERENCES in other text articles:
·algebraic structure theory **1**:533b
·arithmetic laws and principles **1**:1171g
·combinatorics theory and method **4**:946e
·complex analysis fundamentals **1**:720b
·consistency proof for system N **11**:1081g
·elementary algebra principles **1**:503g
·Euclidean geometry principles **7**:1109f
·Eudoxus' irrational numbers **6**:1021e
·Euler law of quadratic reciprocity **6**:1027e
·Fermat prime number studies **7**:234g
·Gauss's methods and concepts **7**:966c
·Leonardo's Diophantine equations proof **10**:817g
·logic history from antiquity **11**:68c
·metrology and cosmology theory **12**:867c
·Pythagorean, Mersenne, and Fibonacci numbers generation **13**:348g
·Pythagoreanism cosmology principles **15**:323g
·real analysis principles **1**:772h

RELATED ENTRIES in the *Ready Reference and Index: for*
algebraic number theory: see algebraic number; complex number; discriminant; field; group; ideal; prime ideal; quadratic form
analytic number theory: arithmetic progression; Diophantine equation; Diophantine problem; Dirichlet series; elliptic functions; Fermat's last theorem; Goldbach problem; meromorphic function; Riemann zeta function; Waring's problem
continued fractions: continued fraction; convergence
divisibility and primality: composite numbers; congruence; divisibility; divisor; Fermat primes; Mersenne, Marin; number factorization; quadratic reciprocity law; quadratic residue; residue class
geometric number theory: covering; Euclidean algorithm
prime numbers: Chinese remainder theorem; Dirichlet's theorem; distribution of primes; Eratosthenes, sieve of; prime; prime number theorem; Wilson's theorem
probabilistic number theory: central limit theorem; Euler phi function; normal distribution
special numbers: Bernoulli number; Fibonacci numbers; perfect number

numbfish: *see* electric ray.

Numea (New Caledonia): *see* Nouméa.

Numedals-lågen (river, Norway): *see* Lågen.

numen, a term used in Roman religion to express a sense of spiritual power or awe.
·Roman religious concept **15**:1060e

Numenius (bird): *see* curlew.

Numenius of Apamea (fl. late 2nd century AD), Greek philosopher chiefly responsible for the transition from Platonist Idealism to a Neoplatonic synthesis of Hellenistic, Persian, and Jewish intellectual systems, with particular attention to the concept of ultimate being, or deity, and its relation to the material world.

Beyond his origins in Apamea (near modern Homs, Syria), nothing is known of Numenius' life. His name may have been a Greek translation of a Semitic original. His contemporaries and later chroniclers described him as fusing Platonism with Pythagoreanism (*i.e.*, the philosophical tenets of the 6th-century-BC Greek Pythagoras, which include a number mysticism and a spirit–matter dualism based on a process of emanation from some absolute being). Such a categorization of Numenius' thought is controverted by scholars who view him more as a syncretistic interpreter of Plato with a dualist emphasis derived more from Eastern, occult religious philosophies than from Greek sources of monism. He showed extensive knowledge of Judaism, and he may have been acquainted with Christianity. Apparently he intended to seek the origin of Platonic ideas in the teachings of the ancient East: the spirit transmigration of Hinduism; the absolute, monotheistic deity and the trinity of divine functions in Judaism; and the esoteric dualism of Gnostic and Hermetic cults. Observing an influence of the older Semitic religions upon Greek thought, he called Plato "an Atticizing Moses." His search for primitive forms of theology was later to interest the Renaissance Humanists.

Central to Numenius' thought is the dualism of an eternal divinity contrasting with eternal matter ("monad" opposed to "dyad"). As supreme deity in absolutely changeless perfection, God can have no contact with inferior being—hence the need for a second god, the Demiurge, of a dual nature, the "soul of the world" related to both God and matter and completing the Trinitarian hierarchy. Accentuating this dualism, Numenius identified matter with evil, relating it also to the evil world soul. Man, moreover, not only comprises the dualism of a body antithetical to his soul but also possesses a twofold soul, rational and irrational. Life is thus a process of escape from this dualism by the deliverance of the spirit from its material confinement.

Numenius' anthropology includes an attempt to rationalize astrology and mystical number theories. His thought has been alleged to have influenced the 3rd-century development of Neoplatonism by Plotinus, the foremost representative of that school; Plotinus' denial of Numenius' tendency towards dualistic mystery cults, however, specifically distinguishes the later evolution of Neoplatonism. The surviving fragments from Numenius' treatises *Peri tēs tōn Akadēmaikōn pros Platōna diastaseōs* ("On the Differences Between Plato and the Academicians"), *Peri tōn para Platōni aporrhētōn* ("On Plato's Secret Doctrines"), *Peri tagathou* ("On the Good"), and *Peri aphtharsias psychēs* ("On the Indestructibility of the Soul") have been collected by F. Thedinga (1875). Analyses of this thought have been made by K.S. Guthrie (1917) and E.A. Leemans (1937).

numerals and numeral systems, symbols and rules for using them to represent numbers, which are used in expressing how many objects are in a given set. Thus the idea of "oneness" can be represented by the Roman numeral I, by the Greek letter alpha α (the first letter) used as a numeral, and the Hebrew letter aleph (the first letter) used as a numeral, or by the modern numeral 1, which is Hindu-Arabic in origin.

Modern numeral or number systems are place-value systems—that is, the value of the symbol depends upon the position or place of the symbol in the representation; for example, the 2 in 20 and 200 represent two tens and two hundreds, respectively. Such ancient systems as the Egyptian, Roman, Hebrew, and Greek number systems did not have this positional characteristic, thus making arithmetical calculations difficult. The most commonly used number system is the decimal-positional number system, the decimal referring to the use of ten symbols 0, 1, 2, 3, 4, 5, 6, 7, 8, 9 to construct all numbers. *Major ref.* **11**:646f

- ·Arabic and Hebrew signs, tables 2 and 3 **8**:593
- ·arithmetic principles and methods **1**:1174h
- ·Babylonian number system **11**:640b
- ·binary arithmetic operation **4**:1049g
- ·Leonardo of Pisa's Hindu–Arabic numerals **10**:817g
- ·mathematical calculation theory and use **11**:671h
- ·Meso-American vigesimal counting **11**:963d
- ·Sumerian dual system significance **11**:969a

numerator, in arithmetic and algebra, quantity above the line in a fraction (*q.v.*). It is the dividend, or expression that is divided by the denominator (*q.v.*) of the fraction. *See* rational number.

- ·arithmetic laws and principles **1**:1173g

Numerian, in full MARCUS AURELIUS NUMERIUS NUMERIANUS (d. AD 284), Roman emperor 283–284. He succeeded his father, Carus, in the summer of 283, in the midst of a war being waged east of the Tigris against the Sāsānians. Numerian was emperor in the East, his brother, Carinus, heading the empire in the West. Numerian led the army home, but contracted an eye disease that confined him to a litter while his father-in-law, the praetorian prefect Aper, commanded the army. Late in 284, after the army had reached the Bosporus, Numerian was found dead. Aper was accused of his murder and executed, and the throne passed to Diocletian, commander of the household guards.

- ·Diocletian's usurpation of power **5**:805d
- ·Persian campaign and death **15**:1124e

numerical analysis 13:381, branch of mathematics that concerns methods of finding numerical solutions to problems.

The text article covers basic concepts, including function, algorithm, iteration, truncation and rounding errors; fundamental operations involving finite differences, interpolation, operational methods in the solution of difference and differential–difference equations; approximation, numerical differentiation and integration; direct and iterative computational methods involving linear equations and nonlinear equations; and numerical solutions of ordinary differential equations, partial differential equations, and integral equations.

REFERENCES in other text articles:

- ·algebraic method development **11**:665b
- ·automata theory and method **2**:500a
- ·differential equation principles **5**:742c
- ·mathematical calculation theory and use **11**:685a

RELATED ENTRIES in the *Ready Reference and Index:*

algorithm; boundary values; continued fraction; difference equation; eigenvalue; error, rounding; error, truncation; integral equation; ordinary differential equation; partial differential equation; relaxation methods; Runge–Kutta method

numerical differentiation, in numerical analysis, a process by which successive derivatives of a function are approximated.

- ·numerical analysis fundamentals **13**:384c

numerical integration, in numerical analysis, process by which the approximate value of an integral is expressed as a linear function of a certain number of values of the function to be integrated.

- ·numerical analysis fundamentals **13**:384c

numerical notation (music): *see* musical notation.

numerical taxonomy (biology): *see* taximetrics.

numerology, use of numbers to interpret a person's character or to divine the future, based on the Pythagorean idea that all things can be expressed in numerical terms because they are ultimately reducible to numbers. Using a method analogous to that of the Greek and Hebrew alphabets (in which each letter also represented a number), modern numerology attaches a series of digits to an inquirer's name and date of birth and from these purports to divine the person's true nature and prospects.

- ·Islāmic number and letter myths **9**:951c
- ·Near East ancient number symbolism **12**:917d
- ·Old and New Testament millennialism **12**:201c
- ·purification rites and sacred numbers **15**:302e
- ·symbolic numbers and mythology **17**:908e
- ·triune symbolism in Christianity **7**:134f

Numic languages, formerly called PLATEAU SHOSHONEAN, North American Indian language group spoken in Nevada, Utah, and portions of California, Oregon, Idaho, Wyoming, Arizona, Colorado, and Oklahoma. These languages are presently divided into three groups: Western Numic, including Mono and Northern Paiute; Central Numic, including Panamint and Shoshoni; and Southern Numic, including Kawaiisu and Ute. Numic represents the northernmost extension of the Uto-Aztecan language family, but the precise groupings within Uto-Aztecan are not yet clear.

- ·Basin Indian language groups and distribution **13**:204h; map 205

Numida meleagris (bird): *see* guinea fowl.

Numidia, Roman name of a part of Africa north of the Sahara, the boundaries of which at times corresponded roughly with those of modern Algeria. From the 6th century BC points along the coast were occupied by the Carthaginians, and Numidians were frequently found in the Carthaginian armies.

The inhabitants remained semi-nomadic, however, until the reign of Masinissa, the chief of the Massyli tribe living near Cirta (Constantine). At first an ally of Carthage, he went over to the Roman side in 206 BC and was given further territory extending as far as the Mulucha (Moulouya) River. He also seized much Carthaginian territory and probably hoped to rule all of North Africa.

On his death in 148 BC the Romans divided his kingdom among several chieftains; but in 118 Jugurtha, an illegitimate prince, usurped the throne and ruled over a reunified Numidia until the Romans again took control in 105. Rome continued to dominate Numidia through client kings, though Numidian territory was considerably reduced. The third and final attempt by a Numidian to found a powerful state was that of Juba I, between 49 and 46 BC, ending with his defeat by Julius Caesar at Thapsus.

Caesar formed a new province, Africa Nova, from Numidian territory, and Augustus united Africa Nova (New Africa) with Africa Vetus (the province surrounding Carthage); but a separate province of Numidia was formally created by Septimius Severus.

The third legion took up its permanent station at Lambaesis (Lambessa), and as a result of the increased security Numidian population and prosperity increased substantially during the first two centuries AD. A few native communities achieved municipal status, but the majority of the population was little touched by Roman civilization.

Christianity spread rapidly in the 3rd century AD, and, in the 4th, Numidia became the centre of the Donatist controversy over the spiritual state of ministers. After the Vandal conquest (AD 429), Roman civilization declined rapidly, and the native elements revived to outlive in some places even the Arabic conquest in the 8th century and to persist until modern times.

- ·Jugurtha's revolt against Rome **15**:1101d
- ·native kingdoms and Roman occupation **13**:150b; maps

Numidicus, Quintus Caecilius Metellus (Roman general): *see* Metellus Numidicus, Quintus Caecilius.

Numididae, family of guinea fowls of the bird order Galliformes.

- ·classification and general features **7**:857a

numinous, the special, nonrational aspect of sacred or holy reality in religious experience. The term was coined from the Latin word *numen* (manifestation of divine might, will, or majesty) by Rudolf Otto in his seminal work, *Das Heilige* (1917; *The Idea of the Holy*, 1923). "Numinous" in his usage refers both to a special category of value and state of mind and to what is apprehended by them—"the numinous" or "the numen." He saw the numinous as an awe-inspiring mystery, the *mysterium tremendum*, which evokes special, very intense feelings of religious dread. In the face of what is experienced as "absolute overpoweringness," "aweful majesty," and powerful energy, the response is not only awe but also "creature-feeling"—the sense of being worthless and null before the numinous reality. He further characterized this reality as the "wholly other," something utterly beyond the world of ordinary experience and understanding, to which the characteristic response is "blank wonder" or "absolute astonishment." Yet at the same time the awe-evoking numinous is in this view a superlatively fascinating object, leading the religious man to rapturous self-surrender.

Otto's analysis has been criticized as overemphasizing mere subjective feelings, to the neglect of the objective factor in religious experience. It has been defended as actually centring on the objective reality of the numinous, to which the feelings described are responses, indicative of its nature and the unique human relation to it. For many students of man's religions and religiousness, including theologians, historians of religion, and anthropologists, the numinous has proved a richly suggestive and useful concept.

- ·Christian concepts of God **4**:477f
- ·Otto's reflections on numinous **13**:770c
- ·religious man's experience of the sacred **16**:122h

numismatics: *see* coin collecting.

Numitor (mythology): *see* Romulus and Remus.

nummulite, any of the thousands of extinct species of relatively large, lens-shaped foraminifers (single-celled marine organisms) that were abundant in Tertiary (from 65,000,000 to 2,500,000 years ago) seas. Nummulites were particularly prominent during the Eocene Epoch (from 54,000,000 to 38,000,000 years ago), and limestone of this age that occurs in the Sahara is called nummulite limestone in reference to the great abundance of its contained nummulites.

·African Tertiary fossils **1**:183d
·Cenozoic evolutionary forms **3**:1082b
·fossil shells and eras of appearance **7**:558b; illus. 557
·Tertiary evolution and dispersion **18**:153g

nun, a term commonly used to designate a woman who is a member of a religious order or group.

Within Roman Catholicism, vows of poverty, chastity, and obedience are taken by women entering the religious life. According to Roman Catholic canon law, only women living under solemn vows are nuns; those living under simple vows are more properly called sisters. The distinction between the types of vows is complex, but simple vows can be dispensed more easily than solemn vows. Nuns, in the strict sense, normally live a strictly enclosed, or cloistered, life, while sisters normally are engaged in non-cloistered, active work. The names nun and sister, however, frequently are used interchangeably, without regard for precise distinction. Religious orders of women date back to the 4th century, when groups of women began forming societies. In the early Middle Ages, all the communities of women lived a life of prayer, reading, and work, such as spinning and weaving, and were retired from the world and living under vow. Beginning in the 16th century, sisterhoods devoted to active work in the community (such as nursing, teaching, and mission work) developed.

In Eastern Orthodoxy, nuns are almost entirely of the contemplative type and do not participate actively in the life of the secular world.

Religious communities for women in the Church of England were abolished during the Reformation in the 16th century but were revived in the 19th century under the influence of the Oxford Movement, which emphasized the Catholic heritage of Anglicanism. Most sisterhoods within Anglicanism combine an active life (such as teaching, nursing, or social work) with a life of prayer and worship. In the 20th century some communities of contemplative nuns were established.

In other Protestant groups, primarily Lutheran and Reformed, religious communities of women were formed in the 19th and 20th centuries. Members of such communities, however, are usually called deaconesses rather than nuns and do not take vows for life.

In Buddhism the number of nuns has never been large. It is said that the Buddha was very reluctant to allow women to form communities, though he finally gave his consent. The women lived apart from the monks and were always considered inferior to them.

In Hinduism women living in organized communities are not common. Certain saintly women, however, who have lived the lives of ascetics, have had an influence in Hinduism.

·Christian monastic dress **15**:636g

nun, any of several birds named for the likeness of its plumage pattern to a nun's habit. For tricolour nun, *see* munia.

nunatak, isolated mountain peak that once projected through a continental ice sheet or an Alpine-type icecap. Because they usually occur near the margin of an ice sheet, nunataks were thought to be glacial refuges for vegetation and centres for subsequent reoccupation of the land. Later studies revealed the existence of more likely areas of refuge and the fact that postglacial weathering may destroy glacial evidence on peaks. Thus, identification of a true nunatak is difficult, and such peaks often cannot be used to determine former ice thicknesses.

Nunc Dimittis, also known as the SONG OF SIMEON, a brief hymn of praise sung by the aged Simeon—a man (possibly a rabbi) who anticipated the coming of the Messiah—on the occasion of the presentation of the infant Jesus by his parents Mary and Joseph at the Temple in Jerusalem for the rite of purification according to Jewish custom and law. Found in Luke 2:29–32, the canticle is so named because of its first words in Latin (*Nunc dimittis servum tuum, domine*, "Lord, now lettest thou thy servant depart").

Because it is a hymn praying for peace and rest, the early church viewed it as appropriate for the ending of the day. Mentioned in the *Apostolic Constitutions* (a 4th-century collection of ecclesiastical law), the Nunc Dimittis probably was a hymn of the ancient service known as the Lucernarium (Office of Lights). Since the 4th century it has been used in evening worship services (*e.g.*, Compline in the Roman Catholic breviary, Vespers in the Eastern Orthodox *Euchologion* and Lutheran service books, and Evensong in the Anglican prayerbook). In the Eastern Orthodox liturgy of St. John Chrysostom, the Nunc Dimittis is repeated by the priest as he takes off his stole, or *epitrakhíli*, the symbol of his priesthood.

nuncio, a Vatican representative accredited as an ambassador to a civil government that maintains official diplomatic relations with the Holy See. He promotes good relations between the government and the Holy See and observes and reports to the pope on the conditions of the church in the region. A full nuncio is named only to those countries that adhere to a decision of the Congress of Vienna (1815) that the papal representative automatically becomes dean of the diplomatic corps. In 1965 the name pro-nuncio was given to those ambassadors whose rank in the diplomatic corps depends solely on seniority. An internuncio is a Vatican diplomat with the rank of minister plenipotentiary; he is accredited to a civil government and performs duties corresponding to those of a nuncio.

Nuneaton, borough (1907) in Warwickshire, England. From the 12th century the town was the site of a Benedictine nunnery, and coal has been worked locally for centuries. There are also clay pits, for brick and tile manufacture, and granite quarries from which road metal is obtained. Pop. (1971 prelim.) 66,979.
52°32′ N, 1°28′ W

·map, United Kingdom **18**:866

Nunes, Pedro, in Latin PETRUS NONIUS (b. 1502, Alcácer do Sal, Port.—d. Aug. 11, 1578, Coimbra), mathematician, geographer, and the chief figure in Portuguese nautical science, noted for his studies of the Earth, including the oceans. Professor of mathematics at Lisbon and Coimbra, he became royal cosmographer in 1529, when Spain was disputing the position of the Spice Islands and maps did not agree in their longitude. He devoted himself to such problems as well as to maps and map projections. He went to Spain in 1538 but returned to Portugal in 1544 to become a leading authority on the new discoveries of Spain and Portugal.

Núñez, Rafael (b. Sept. 28, 1825, Cartagena, New Granada, now Colombia—d. Sept. 12, 1894, El Cabrero), three times president of Colombia, political theorist, and poet who dominated Colombian politics from 1880 and ruled dictatorially until his death. Entering politics in the Liberal Party while in law school, Núñez aided in the drafting of Colombia's first Liberal constitution (1853) while a member of Congress. He later served in the cabinets of several presidents during the long period of Liberal control of Colombia.

In 1863 Núñez left Colombia for Europe, where he studied other forms of governments and came into contact with political thinkers; as a result, he abandoned many of his radical ideas.

Returning to Colombia in 1875, Núñez failed in the following year to win the presidency because the Radicals refused to support him. In 1880, with the support of moderates from both the Liberal and the Conservative parties, he won his first term (1880–82) as president. A rebellion of Radicals and Liberals in 1884 forced him further into an alliance with the Conservatives to win election to his second term (1884–86). The constitution of 1886 solidified his regime and inaugurated 50 years of Conservative dominance. Núñez then instituted a series of reforms called the Regeneration, which replaced the supremacy of the various states with a centralized government and restored the power of the Catholic Church.

Regarded as the leading intellect in Colombia, Núñez wrote on politics and economic policy and composed volumes of poetry. His regime was often administered by deputies in Bogotá while he ruled from his plantation, where he died.

·re-establishment of relations with Vatican **4**:875g

Núñez Cabeza de Vaca, Álvar (b. *c.* 1490, Extremadura, Spain—d. *c.* 1560, Seville), explorer who spent eight years in the Gulf region of present-day Texas and whose accounts of the legendary Seven Golden Cities of Cibola probably inspired the extensive southern and southwestern North American explorations by Hernando de Soto and Francisco Coronado. He was treasurer to the Spanish expedition of 400 under Pánfilo de Narváez that reached Tampa Bay, Fla. in 1528. By September all but his party of 60 had perished; it reached the Texas shore near present-day Galveston. Of this group only 15 were alive the following spring, and eventually only Núñez and three others remained. In the following years he and his companions spent much time among nomadic Indians. Though he found only gravest hardship and poverty during his wanderings, by the time he encountered a party of Spanish raiders in northern Mexico in 1536, he was full of stories of the fabulous riches of a new El Dorado, the Seven Golden Cities of Cibola, lying somewhere beyond the regions he had passed through. He recounted his adventures in *Naufragios* . . . (1542; "Shipwrecks . . ."). He was later appointed governor of the central South American province of Río de la Plata. From November 1541 to March 1542 he blazed a route from Santos, Brazil, to Asunción, Paraguay. His power was usurped by a rebel governor, Domingo Martinez de Irala, who imprisoned him and had him deported to Spain (1545), where he was convicted of malfeasance in office and banished to service in Africa. His *La Relación y Comentarios* . . . (1555), describing his journey from Santos to Asunción, is a valuable geographic work.

·Florida settlement failure **7**:424e
·Iguaçu Falls discovery **9**:234c

Núñez de Arce, Gaspar (b. Aug. 4, 1832, Valladolid, Spain—d. June 9, 1903, Madrid), Spanish poet and statesman, once regarded as the great poet of doubt and disillusionment, though his rhetoric is no longer found moving. He became a journalist and Liberal deputy, took part in the 1868 revolution, and was colonial minister for a time after the Restoration. As a dramatist he had some success, his best play being the historical *El haz de leña* (1872), but he attained celebrity with *Gritos del combate* (1875)—a volume of verse that tried to give poetic utterance to religious questionings and the current political problems of freedom and order.

Nung, Asian people who live in North Vietnam and in Kwangsi Province, China. Their language, Nung, belongs to the Tai language family.
·China's population, table 3 **4**:272
·Vietnam's Chinese influence **19**:133a

Nunivak Island, in the Bering Sea off the southwestern coast of Alaska, U.S. It is 56 mi (89.5 km) long, 40 mi wide, and rises to 830 ft (251 m). Separated from the mainland by Etolin Strait, the island is the site of Nunivak National Wildlife Refuge, notable for its reindeer, musk ox, and shore birds. Latest pop. est. 225.
60°00′ N, 166°30′ W
·Bering Sea map **2**:845
·map, United States **18**:908

Nun River, Portuguese RIO NUN, in southern Nigeria, considered the direct continuation of the Niger River. After the Niger bifurcates into the Nun and Forcados rivers about 20 mi (32 km) downstream from Aboh, the Nun flows through sparsely settled zones of freshwater and mangrove swamps and coastal sand ridges before completing its 100-mi south-southwesterly course to the Gulf of Guinea, a wide inlet of the Atlantic, at Akassa. Precisely when Africans discovered that the Nun was the chief mouth of the Niger is unknown, but a German geographer, Christian G. Reichard, made the conjecture in 1802, and two English explorers, Richard and John Lander, proved the point in an 1830 expedition from Bussa (650 mi up the Niger) to Brass (at a mouth in the Niger Delta).

The river was most extensively used for trade in the 19th century, when the Ibo kingdom centred at Aboh controlled commerce, and Ijaw (Ijo) tribesmen in the Niger Delta dealt directly with Europeans. Most of the trade in the early part of the century was in slaves; Brass (*q.v.*) and Nembe, two slave-collecting centres on the Brass River (which lies just to the east and is connected to the Nun by several small streams), often sent war canoes into the interior to capture slaves to exchange for Western cloth, tools, spirits, and firearms. Later the Nun was a major passageway for palm oil, which was imported from Ibo country to the north and exported from Brass, Nembe, and, especially during the rule (1886–1900) of the Royal Niger Company, from the company port at Akassa. By 1900, however, the accumulation of silt in the bar at the mouth of the river impeded access to the Nun, which was eclipsed in commercial importance by the Forcados River (*q.v.*).

In 1963 petroleum was discovered along the Nun (about 35 mi upstream). With the completion in 1965 of the Trans-Niger Pipeline (which crosses the Nun near its origin and connects the Ughelli field in Mid-Western State to the Bonny oil terminal in the eastern part of the Niger Delta), oil from the Nun River fields has been piped to Rumuekpe, where there is a link with the Trans-Niger line.
4°20′ N, 6°00′ E
·map, Nigeria **13**:86
·Niger River and channel network **13**:97e

Nuori Suomi ("Young Finland"), group of liberal writers founded in the 1880s.
·Finnish literature of the 19th century **10**:1215b

Nuoro, town, capital of Nuoro province, east central Sardinia, Italy, at the foot of Monte Ortobene. Although the site has been inhabited since prehistoric times, the town was first recorded, as Nugorus, in the 12th century. The centre of a province under Piedmontese rule from 1848 to 1860, it became the provincial capital when Nuoro province was created in 1927 out of parts of Cagliari and Sassari provinces. The province (area 2,808 sq mi [7,272 sq km]), consisting essentially of the highland backbone of Sardinia, is the poorest region of the island, occupied mainly by pastoralists; but after 1950, developments included 30 mi (50 km) of new roads, extensive improvement of mountain pastures, and the grafting of 2,000,000 wild olive trees. Nuoro is a market centre and a summer resort for mountain excursions. Pop. (1971 prelim.) mun., 30,944.
40°19′ N, 09°20′ E
·map, Italy **9**:1088
·province area and population, table 1 **9**:1094

nuove musiche, term used by some music historians for music of the whole period around 1600, a landmark in music history since it marks the origin of the opera, oratorio, cantata, and baroque period in general.
·dominating melody in Italian tradition **12**:717e

nuove musiche, Le, innovative collection of madrigals and arias by Giulio Caccini (*q.v.*) published in 1602.
·bel canto style summarization **16**:789h
·dissemination of Camerata ideas **12**:709b
·monodic texture of Florentine opera **13**:580a
·vocal music's performance liberation **12**:718b

Nupe, people of an Islāmicized kingdom at the confluence of the Niger and Kaduna rivers in Nigeria; they speak five dialects of Nupe, a Kwa language of the Niger-Congo family. They are organized into a number of closely related territorial subtribes, of which the Beni, Zam, Batache (Bataci), and Kede (Kyedye) are the most important. The Kede and Batache are river people, subsisting primarily by fishing and trading; the other Nupe are primarily farmers, the staple crops being millet, sorghum, yams, and rice. Commercial crops include rice, groundnuts (peanuts), cotton, and shea nuts. They practice shifting cultivation, using the hoe as their basic tool. Men do most of the farm work, while women prepare and market the crops. There is a highly developed guild organization for blacksmiths, brass smiths, weavers, tailors, and other craft specialists. The Nupe are noted throughout Nigeria for glass beads, fine leather and matwork, and for brass trays and fine cloth. Either men or women may be specialist traders. They numbered about 1,000,000 at the latest estimate.

They live in grass-thatched huts of mud brick built in villages or towns varying in size from a few families to several thousand people. Each village is governed by a chief, with the advice and cooperation of a council of elders composed of family heads. The chief controls community land resources, settles disputes, and organizes all large-scale cooperative actions. The indigenous Nupe kingdom was divided into four zones for purposes of government, with a series of ranked officials who owed a feudalistic allegiance to the king, the *etsu Nupe*. The Beni and the Kede both are organized as kingdoms within the greater Nupe kingdom, their kings owing fealty to the *etsu Nupe*. The office of *etsu Nupe* rotates among three noble families. There are several titled classes above the commoners, who constitute the majority of the population. Through a system of patronage a client may attach himself to a patron's household for political protection, to escape poverty, or to gain position or influence.

The majority of Nupe are now Muslims, but many older rituals are still performed. The indigenous religion includes belief in a sky god who created the world and who made certain mystical forces available to men; in ancestral spirits; and in spirits associated with natural objects. A cult concerned with fertility and general prosperity is found everywhere; other cults and rituals are common to a single subtribe or even a few villages. Witchcraft and divination are practiced.
·Islāmic intervention in 19th century **19**:773b; map 765
·Nigerian peoples composition and cultures **13**:90f; illus.
·trade routes and political development **8**:474g; map 472
·visual art forms and style **1**:260g

Nupercaine: *see* dibucaine hydrochloride.

Nuphar: *see* water lily.

Nuptse, Himalayan mountain in Nepal, just southwest of Mount Everest.
·mountaineering record and data table **12**:585

Nuqrāshī (NOKRASHY) **Pasha, Maḥmūd Fahmī an-** (d. 1948), Egyptian statesman, prime minister 1945 to 1948.
·Wafd, Muslim Brethren, and assassination **6**:498h

nuqṭah (Bābism): *see* point.

Nūr ad-Dīn (Muslim ruler): *see* Nureddin.

Nuraghi, ancient Sardinian culture of the 2nd and 1st millennia BC that was characterized by fortified settlements of round towers, or *nuraghi*, built from blocks of basalt taken from extinct volcanoes. This culture disappeared in the 7th century BC because of tribal warfare and the conquests of the Phoenicians.
·architecture of Bronze Age Sardinia **19**:279d
·origins and remains **16**:244h
·visual art of Metal Age cultures **19**:279f; illus.

Nürburgring, West German automobile road course in the Eifel Mountains in the Rhineland.
·Grand Prix, motorcycle, and formula car racing **12**:566h *passim* to 571b
·map, Federal Republic of Germany **8**:46

Nureddin, in full NŪR AD-DĪN ABŪ AL-QĀSIM MAḤMŪD IBN ʿIMĀD AD-DĪN ZANGĪ, also called AL-MALIK AL-ʿĀDIL (meaning the Just Ruler; b. February 1118—d. May 15, 1174, Damascus), Muslim ruler who reorganized the armies of Syria and laid the foundations for the success of Saladin.

Nureddin succeeded his father as the *atabeg* (ruler) of Halab in 1146, owing nominal allegiance to the ʿAbbāsid caliph of Baghdad. Before his rule, a major reason for the success of the Crusaders was the division among the Muslim rulers of the region, for they were unable to present a unified military front against the invaders. Nureddin waged military campaigns against the Crusaders in an attempt to expel them from Syria and Palestine. Edessa was recaptured from them by his forces shortly after his accession; the important military district of Antakiya was invaded in 1149; Damascus was taken in 1154, and Egypt was annexed by stages in 1169–71.

An able general and just ruler, Nureddin was also noted for piety and personal bravery. He was austere and ascetic, disclaiming the financial rewards of his conquests: instead, he used the booty to build numerous mosques, schools, hospitals, and caravanseries. At the time of death, his rule was recognized in Syria, in Egypt, and in parts of Iraq and Asia Minor. The major beneficiary of Nureddin's heritage was Saladin, who recaptured Jerusalem in 1187 and substantially reduced crusader power in the middle east.
·Crusades military opposition **5**:301h *passim* to 302g
·Damascus' growth under rule **5**:447h
·Islāmic unity and the Crusades **9**:932f
·relations with Saladin **16**:177d
·victories in Syria and Egypt **17**:953c

Nurek Dam, in the early 1970s the world's highest dam, on the Vakhsh River near the Soviet–Afghanistan border. An earth-fill dam, it rises 1,017 feet (310 metres) over an impervious core of concrete reaching 52 feet (15½ metres) to bedrock under the river. The nine-unit power plant associated with the dam has a design capacity of 2,700,000 kilowatts of electricity, and the water impounded will be used to irrigate 1,600,000 acres of farmland.
·highest dams statistics table **5**:443

Nuremberg trials, a series of trials held in Nuremberg (Nürnberg), now in West Germany, in 1945–46 in which former Nazi leaders were indicted and tried by the International Military Tribunal as war criminals. The indictment lodged against them contained four counts: (1) crimes against peace—*i.e.*, the planning, initiating, and waging of wars of aggression in violation of international treaties and agreements; (2) crimes against humanity—*i.e.*, exterminations, deportations, and genocide; (3) war crimes—*i.e.*, violations of the laws of war; and (4) "a common plan or conspiracy to commit" the criminal acts listed in the first three counts.

The authority of the International Military Tribunal to conduct these trials stemmed from the London Agreement of Aug. 8, 1945. On that date, representatives from the United States, Great Britain, the U.S.S.R., and the provisional government of France signed an agreement that included a charter for an international military tribunal to conduct trials of major Axis war criminals whose offences had no particular geographic location. Later, 19 other nations accepted the provisions of this agreement. The tribunal was given the authority to find any individual guilty of the commission of war crimes (counts 1–3 listed above) and to declare any group or organization to be criminal in character. If an organization was found to be criminal, the prosecution could bring individuals to trial for having been members, and the criminal nature of the group or organization could no longer be questioned. In order to insure fair trials, a defendant was entitled to receive a copy of the indictment, to offer any relevant explanation to the charges brought against him, and to be represented by counsel and confront and cross-examine the witnesses.

The tribunal consisted of a member plus an alternate selected by each of the four signatory countries. The first session, under the presidency of Gen. I.T. Nikitchenko, the Soviet member, took place on Oct. 18, 1945, in Berlin. At this time, 24 of the former Nazi leaders were charged with the perpetration of war crimes; and various groups (such as the Gestapo, the Nazi secret police) were charged with being criminal in character. Beginning on Nov. 20, 1945, all sessions of the tribunal were held in Nuremberg under the presidency of Lord Justice Geoffrey Lawrence, the British member.

The trial itself lasted more than ten months (216 actual court sessions). On Oct. 1, 1946, the verdict on 22 of the original 24 defendants was handed down. (Robert Ley committed suicide while in prison, and Gustav Krupp von Bohlen und Halbuch's mental and physical condition prevented his being tried.) Three of the defendants were acquitted; 12 (including Martin Bormann, who was tried in absentia) were sentenced to death by hanging; 3 (including Rudolf Hess) were sentenced to life imprisonment; and 4 (including Albert Speer) were sentenced to imprisonment for terms ranging from 10 to 20 years.

In rendering these decisions, the tribunal rejected the major defenses offered by the defendants. First, it rejected the contention that only a state, and not individuals, could be found guilty of war crimes; the tribunal held that crimes of international law are committed by men and that only by punishing individuals who commit such crimes can the provisions of international law be enforced. Second, it rejected the argument that the trial and adjudication were ex post facto. The tribunal responded that such acts have been regarded as criminal prior to World War II. Despite these rulings, the novelty of the trial and the lack of supporting precedents militated against the universal acceptance of the proceedings.

·Alfred Krupp indictment and outcome **10**:541b
·Göring's defense and death **8**:255d
·human rights and Nazi war crimes **8**:1185f
·laws of war pertaining to criminal offenders **19**:539g
·procedures and verdict **19**:555f

Nūrestān, formerly KĀFIRISTĀN, region in eastern Afghanistan, about 5,000 sq mi (13,000 sq km) in area and comprising the upper valleys of the Alīngār, Pīech, and Landay Sind rivers and the intervening mountain ranges; its northern boundary is the main range of the Hindu Kush, its eastern the Pakistani border, its southeastern the Konar Valley, and its western the mountain ranges above the Panjshēr and Nejrāb valleys. The region is rainy and forested.

Nūrestān's regional unity and distinction from the rest of Afghanistan spring from its isolation and the common cultural characteristics shared by its people, who strongly cherish independence, have a clan organization with village governments, and are now settled agriculturalists (cereals, fruits, livestock) living in the valleys. They speak various Kafir languages (*see* Dardic languages). The region did not become part of Afghanistan until the 1890s, when ʿAbdor Raḥmān Khān, the Afghan *amīr*, conquered it and forcibly converted the inhabitants to Islām. He subsequently changed its name from Kafiristan (Land of the Kāfirs; *i.e.*, infidels) to Nūrestān (Land of the Enlightened). The forested mountain slopes of Nūrestān provide most of Afghanistan's timber.

·Hindu Kush physical and social features **8**:921g

Nureyev, Rudolf (Hametovich) (b. March 17, 1938, Irkutsk, Russian S.F.S.R.), ballet dancer whose suspended leaps and fast turns have often been compared to Nijinsky's legendary feats. After his defection from the Soviet Union, he became well known as Margot Fonteyn's favourite partner and as a popular, unpredictable personality in artistic and social circles. Of Tatar descent, Nureyev began his ballet studies at 11, left school at 15, and supported himself by dancing. At 17 he entered the Leningrad Ballet School, where he was an outstanding but rebellious student, refusing to join the Komsomol (Communist youth organization), disobeying curfew regulations, and learning English privately.

After graduating in 1958, he became soloist with the Leningrad Kirov Ballet and danced leading roles with its touring company. While in Paris with the Kirov Ballet in June 1961, Nureyev eluded Soviet security men at the airport and requested asylum in France. He said later that the rigidly organized Soviet ballet had limited his opportunities to dance frequently and to perform in a variety of roles.

After his defection he danced with the Grand Ballet du Marquis de Cuevas and made his American debut in 1962, appearing on U.S. television and with Ruth Page's Chicago Opera Ballet. Later that year he joined the Royal Ballet (London) as "permanent" guest artist.

Nureyev partnering Margot Fonteyn
Keystone

As Margot Fonteyn's partner, he has interpreted such roles as Albrecht in *Giselle*, Armand in *Marguerite and Armand*, and Prince Siegfried in *Swan Lake*. Also a choreographer, Nureyev reworked *Swan Lake* (Vienna, 1964), giving the dominant role to the male dancer; he has also staged several other ballets for the Vienna State Opera and the Royal Ballet. His autobiography, *Nureyev*, was published in 1962.

·technical and historical contributions **2**:653g

Nurhachi **13**:392, formal title KUNDULUN KHAN, reign title T'IEN-MING, full Juchen title GEREN GURUN BE UJIRE GENGGIYEN (Brilliant Emperor Who Benefits All Nations), temple name T'AI-TSU, posthumous name WU HUANG-TI, later altered to KAO HUANG-TI (b. 1559, Manchuria—d. Sept. 30, 1626), chieftain of a Manchurian tribe and one of the founders of the Manchu, or Ch'ing, dynasty, which ruled China from 1644 to 1911.

Abstract of text biography. As hereditary leader of one of the five Juchen tribes of Manchuria, Nurhachi first had to crush a dissident faction supported by the Chinese Ming dynasty. Next he defeated the other four Juchen peoples, all of whom were likewise backed by China. The triumphs led to his establishment of the Manchu state, incorporating Chinese settlements in Manchuria. He fostered the development of Manchu national consciousness by directing the creation (1599) of a Manchu system of writing. His first attack on China (1618) presaged his son Dorgon's conquest of the Chinese empire.

REFERENCES in other text articles:
·Chien-chou conquest of Manchuria **11**:436e
·Ch'ing victory over Ming dynasty **4**:354a
·Dorgon's rise to power **5**:958c
·Ming territory loss to Manchus **4**:348a
·Mukden Chinese conquest and prestige **12**:612e

Nuri as-Said (b. 1888, Baghdad, Iraq—d. July 14, 1958, Baghdad), Iraqi army officer, statesman, and political leader who maintained close ties with Great Britain and worked for Arab unity.

Nuri as-Said
Keystone

Nuri was commissioned in the Turkish Army in 1909, when Iraq was a province of the Ottoman Empire. During World War I (1914–18) he participated in Ottoman military operations against the British. He was soon captured by the British, however, and in 1916 he joined the Sharīfian Arab army led by Amīr Fayṣal I, which Great Britain was supporting in a revolt against Ottoman rule in the Arab provinces; Nuri distinguished himself in battle. At the war's end Fayṣal established a short-lived Arab state, centred in Damascus, and Nuri served actively in its administration. After the French destroyed this state in 1920, Fayṣal became the first king of Iraq (1921). Nuri returned to occupy a number of influential positions, becoming prime minister in 1930. In this capacity Nuri negotiated a 20-year treaty with Great Britain, which, although maintaining substantial British influence, granted independence to Iraq.

During his political career, Nuri served as prime minister on 14 different occasions. He remained faithful to two dominant policies: the first was his support of the Hashemite dynasty, which King Fayṣal represented until his death in 1933; the second was Nuri's pro-British feeling. Neither of these beliefs was shared by the rising generation of younger army officers, and at the beginning of World War II (1939–45) open conflicts developed. Nuri wished to support the British by declaring war against Germany and breaking off diplomatic relations with Italy. He was opposed by influential army officers, who in April 1941 supported a coup under the leadership of Rashid Ali. Nuri and the King fled into exile. The British defeated the government of Rashid Ali in open warfare; Nuri then returned to Iraq and served as prime minister under British sponsorship in 1941–44.

Nuri advocated a union of Syria, Lebanon, Palestine, and Jordan into a single state, which would join with Iraq. He wanted to strengthen the popular base of his authority by giving the ideals of Arab unity an effective representation. The Arab League, an organization of separate Arab states, was formed in 1945.

Meanwhile Nuri maintained political order in Iraq. He was instrumental in repressing left-wing political groups and other elements that criticized the social and economic policies of the crown. He made tough and effective use of the police and the press. This eliminated opportunities for army intervention, and the army remained under restraint.

But powerful emotional currents swept the Arab Middle East after World War II. Violent nationalist feeling in Iraq precluded renewal of the Anglo-Iraqi treaty, despite Nuri's ardent support. In 1955 the United States sponsored the Baghdad Pact, a mutual security agreement among Middle Eastern states, and Nuri saw Iraqi membership as a solution to the troublesome problem of the Anglo-Iraqi treaty. He thought membership would also provide arms to placate the army. Nuri hoped to induce other Arab states to join the pact and then assert leadership of the Arab unity movement and reap the attendant benefits in popular support in Iraq. Popular resentment against the West, however, had become too widespread for the Baghdad Pact to serve these ends. When Nuri sponsored an Arab union with Jordan in February 1958 (Jordan was closely allied with the West), Iraqi army units, under the leadership of Abdul Karim Kassem, overthrew the monarchy; Nuri died trying to escape.

·Iraqi political development **11**:996e

Nūr Jahān, also known as MIHR-UN-NISĀ' (d. 1645), empress and councillor of Jahangir.

·political career and favouritism **9**:382h

Nurmi, Paavo (Johannes) (b. June 13, 1897, Turku, Fin.—d. Oct. 2, 1973, Helsinki), track athlete who dominated long-distance running in the 1920s, capturing six gold medals in three Olympic Games (1920, 1924, 1928). For eight years (1923–31) he held the world record for the mile run: 4 min 10.4 sec.

Along with numerous other Finns who gained Olympic honours from 1920, Nurmi was inspired by his countryman Hannes Kolehmainen, who won three long-distance races in the 1912 Olympic Games. In training and in races, Nurmi carried a stopwatch so that he could precisely regulate his pace. In the 1920 Olympics in Antwerp, he won the 10,000-m run and the 10,000-m cross-country race; in 1928, in Amsterdam, he took another gold medal in the 10,000-m run. Most spectacular were his feats in the 1924 games in Paris. In little more than one hour on July 10, an extremely hot day, he set Olympic records in the 1,500-m (metric mile) and 5,000-m runs. Two days later, again in oppressive heat, he repeated his 1920 triumph in the 10,000-m cross-country race (an event discontinued after 1924), and the following day he finished first in an unofficial 3,000-m team race that was won by Finland (no medals were awarded). To Nurmi's dismay, he was withheld by Finnish Olympic officials from the 10,000-m run in 1924.

On Aug. 23, 1923, in Stockholm, Nurmi, consulting his stopwatch as he set his mile record, ran each of the first three quarters

Nurmi, 1931
UPI Compix

(440 yd) in exactly 63 seconds and then the final quarter in 61.4 seconds. Despite his success, his method of evenly paced quarters was not widely imitated. In 1928 he set a world record for the one-hour run: 11 mi 1,648 yd (19,210 m).

·running records and pacing style **18**:544e

Nürnberg 13:393, English conventional NUREMBERG, second city (after Munich) of the *Land* (state) of Bayern (Bavaria), West Germany, on the Pegnitz River, where it emerges from the uplands of Franken (Franconia). An ancient route focus and trading centre of central Europe, it is one of the Continent's great historical cities and is now the hub of the important industrial region of northern Bayern. Pop. (1970) 473,600.

The text article covers the historical development of Nürnberg and the topography, institutions, and services of the contemporary city. 49°27′ N, 11°04′ E

REFERENCES in other text articles:
·bombing damage reconstruction illus. **2**:57
·book publishing history **15**:224g
·bronze, gold, pewter, iron, and lead work **11**:1100b *passim* to 1115a
·ceramic faience ware production **14**:909g
·glass form and decorative styles **8**:186d
·map, Federal Republic of Germany **8**:46
·medieval population growth **8**:86d

Nürnberg, Diet of, formal assembly in 1522 of German secular leaders that refused to suppress preachers supporting the Reformation, and that called for a national reforming council.

·secular sympathy to reform movement **11**:193f

Nürnberg, Religious Peace of (July 23, 1532), also called the NÜRNBERG STANDSTILL, truce between the Catholic Holy Roman emperor Charles V and the Protestant Schmalkaldic League that temporarily halted internal fighting over religious matters and allowed Charles to concentrate his attention and troops against the Turks.

·Catholic disunity and weakness **8**:89f
·Protestant toleration **11**:197c
·truce with Reform for Empire's safety **11**:195b

Nürnberg faience, German tin-glazed earthenware made at the Nürnberg factory between 1712 and 1840. It is among the earliest German faience produced, since Nürnberg was a centre of pottery manufacture as early as the 16th century. The few extant specimens from that early period are in the manner of contemporary Italian maiolica ware.

Nürnberg Kleinmeister (artists' group): *see* Kleinmeister.

Nürnberg Laws, two measures approved by a Nazi Party convention in Nürnberg, Germany (Sept. 15, 1935). One deprived Jews of German citizenship, designating them as "subjects of the state." The second forbade marriage or sexual relations between Jews and "citizens of German or cognate blood."

·Hitler and the Jews **8**:119h

Nürnberg trials: *see* Nuremberg trials.

Nūr ol-ʿEyn (diamond): *see* Daryā-e Nūr.

nurse cell, cell that provides nourishment to other cells, especially the germ cells (*e.g.,* ovum).

·gamete production without gonads **1**:928g

nursery, in horticulture, land on which plants are grown under intensive care until they are moved into their permanent locations. Commercial nurseries grow vast areas of garden flowers, shrubs, and trees for later sale to distributors or to the public. A home nursery can be used as a repository for tender, fragile, or sick plants until they can be set out in the garden or used elsewhere.

·gardening as economic venture **7**:901h
·plant types and maintenance **8**:1111h

nurseryfish, common name for members of the fish family Kurtidae (order Perciformes).

·classification and general features **14**:57d; illus. 50

nursery rhymes, verses customarily said or sung to small children. Because most adults, when entertaining children, fall back on the songs and rhymes they heard in their own childhood, the nursery rhyme repertoire remains moderately stable; but a rhyme new when the adult was a child may come to mind and thus enter the stream of tradition. Thus, the ages of nursery rhymes vary considerably. A French poem numbering the days of the month, similar to "Thirty days hath September," was recorded in the 13th century; but such latecomers as "Twinkle, Twinkle, Little Star" (by Ann and Jane Taylor; pub. 1806) and "Mary Had a Little Lamb" (by Sarah Josepha Hale, pub. 1830) seem to be just as firmly established in the repertoire.

Some of the oldest rhymes are probably those accompanying babies' games as "Handy, dandy, prickly, pandy, which hand will you have?" (recorded 1598) and its German equivalent, "Windle, wandle, in welchem Handle, oben oder unt?" The existence of numerous European parallels for "Ladybird, ladybird (or, in the U.S., "Ladybug, ladybug"), fly away home" and for the singing game "London Bridge is falling down" and for the riddle-rhyme "Humpty-Dumpty" suggests the possibility that these rhymes come down from very ancient sources, since direct translation is unlikely.

Such relics of the past are exceptional. Most nursery rhymes date from the 16th, 17th, and, most frequently, the 18th centuries. Apparently most were originally composed for adult entertainment. Many were popular ballads and songs. "The frog who would a-wooing go" first appeared in 1580 as *A Moste Strange weddinge of the ffrogge and the mowse.* "Oh where, oh where, ish mine little dog gone?" was a popular song written in 1864 by the Philadelphia composer Septimus Winner.

Although many ingenious theories have been advanced attributing hidden significance, especially political allusions, to nursery rhymes, there is no reason to suppose they are any more arcane than the popular songs of the day. Some were inspired by personalities of the time, and occasionally these can be identified. Elsie Marley who "is grown so fine,/ She won't get up to feed the swine" was almost certainly an attractive alewife living in county Durham in the 18th century. Somerset tradition associates "Little Jack Horner" (recorded 1725) with a Thomas Horner of Mells who did well for himself during the dissolution of the monasteries.

The earliest known published collection of nursery rhymes was *Tommy Thumb's (Pretty) Song Book* (2 vols; London, 1744). It included "Little Tom Tucker," "Sing a Song of Sixpence," and "Who Killed Cock Robin?" The most influential was *Mother Goose's Melody: or Sonnets for the Cradle*, published by the firm of John Newbery, 1781. Among its 51 rhymes were "Jack and Jill," "Ding Dong Bell," and "Hush-a-bye baby on the tree top." An edition was reprinted in the U.S. in 1785 by Isaiah Thomas. Its popularity is attested by the fact that these verses are still commonly called "Mother Goose rhymes" in the United States. *See also* alphabet rhymes; counting-out rhymes; Mother Goose.

·Danish children's literature **4**:239f
·development of children's literature **4**:230g
passim to 233a
·riddle elements prominent **19**:926g

nursery school, school for children, usually under five years old, combining instruction with entertainment.

·U.S. development and program **6**:381g

nursery-web spider, any member of the family Pisauridae (order Araneida), noted for the female spider's habit of making webs for the young and standing guard near the "nursery" web. Most species are medium to large in size; many are found near the water. Members of the genus *Dolomedes*, the most common North American genus, sometimes have a leg spread of 7.5 centimetres (3 inches).

Nursery-web spider (*Dolomedes triton*) feeding on a minnow
John H. Gerard

The female spider carries her egg sac, which contains a few hundred eggs, until the young spiders are almost ready to emerge. She then attaches the sac to a plant, wraps leaves about it, and remains to guard the young from predators.

·classification and general features **1**:1073e

Nurses Act of 1919, English bill establishing registration of nurses.

·nurse registration provision **13**:399a

nurse shark (*Ginglymostoma cirratum*), Atlantic shark of the family Orectolobidae. The nurse shark is yellow brown or gray brown, sometimes with dark spots, and may grow to over 4 metres (13 feet) in length. It may attack swimmers, especially when provoked. It is not

Nurse shark (*Ginglymostoma cirratum*)
Tom Myers

related to the more dangerous gray nurse (*see* sand shark) of Australia.

·classification and general features **16**:498g

nursing (breast feeding): *see* lactation, human; suckling.

nursing 13:395, profession concerned with caring for and waiting on the infirm, the injured, or the sick; nurses often coordinate their services with those of members of other health and medical professions.

The text article surveys the history of nursing; describes nursing practice, education, and organization; and considers the roles of the International Red Cross and the World Health Organization.

REFERENCE in other text article:
·Christian institutions and contribution **4**:517d

Nusaybin, formerly NISIBIN, ancient NISIBIS, administrative headquarters of Nusaybin *ilçe* (district) in Mardin *il* (province), southeastern Turkey. The town is situated on Görgarbonizra Çayı (where it passes through a narrow canyon and enters the plain), facing the Syrian town of al-Qāmishlī and 32 mi (51 km) south-southeast of Mardin. Strategically commanding the entrance to the upper Syrian plains from the mountain passes of Asia Minor, Nisibis was a frontier outpost of the Assyrian Empire. Captured from the Armenian king Tigranes I the Great by the Roman Lucius Lininius Lucullus in 68 BC, it changed hands intermittently in the Roman-Parthian struggles, was conquered by the Persians in the 5th century, and was then taken by the Arabs *c.* 640. It continued to prosper under the caliphs until the Mongol invasions of the 13th century. It finally declined as a result of invasions and internal troubles. A North African traveller, Ibn Baṭṭūṭah, who passed through in the 14th century, saw it in a state of decline because of the compulsory substitution of wheat for fruit crops.

Nusaybin was also an important centre of trade in antiquity and still retains some significance because of its position on the upper trade routes from Mosul, Iraq, 120 mi southeast, and its location on the Istanbul–Baghdad railway. Pop. (1970 prelim.) town, 13,941; *ilçe*, 43,309.
37°03′ N, 41°13′ E

Nuṣayrīs, also known as ʿALAWITES, sect of Shīʿah Islām.

·Syrian population concentration **17**:922f

Nusku, in Mesopotamian religion, Sumero-Akkadian god of light and fire. His father was Sin, the moon god. Semitic texts describe Nusku as the king of the night, who illuminates the darkness and repels the demons of the dark. On Babylonian boundary stones he is identified by a lamp. He is visible at the new moon and thus is called its son. The last day of the month is sacred to him, so that he is a lunar deity. He figures much in incantations and rituals as the fire.

Nut, also known as NEUTH or NUIT, in Egyptian religion, goddess of the sky, vault of the heavens, usually depicted as a woman arched over Shu, who upheld her elongated body with his upraised arms. She also was represented as wearing a waterpot or pear-shaped vessel on her head, this being the hieroglyph of her name. Nut was sometimes portrayed as a cow, for this was the form she took in order to carry the sun-creator god Re on her back to the sky. On five special days preceding the New Year, Nut gave birth successively to the deities Osiris, Horus, Seth, Isis (*qq.v.*), and Nephthys.

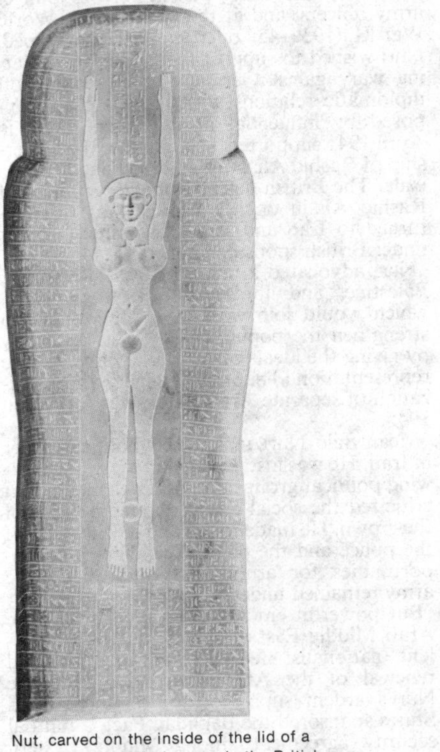

Nut, carved on the inside of the lid of a sarcophagus, 26th dynasty; in the British Museum
By courtesy of the trustees of the British Museum

nut, machine component or fastening device consisting of a square or hexagonal block, usually of metal, with a hole in the centre having internal, or female, threads that fit on the male threads of an associated bolt or screw. A bolt or screw with a nut is widely used for fastening machine and structural components.

In addition to the standard square and hexagonal nuts, there are many special types. Several are illustrated, including the slotted or castellated nut; when the nut is tightened on the bolt, the slots are aligned with a hole in the bolt and locked in place by a cotter pin or wire lacing to prevent loosening or unscrewing. Locking can also be accomplished by tightening a thin nut called a jam nut against a standard nut. Another locknut contains a fibre or plastic insert near the top of the nut; locking occurs when this insert interferes with the bolt threads as the nut is tightened. The wing nut is used in applications in which frequent adjustment is necessary and hand tightening is sufficient.

Self-retained nuts provide a strong, permanent fastener for many types of thin materials; they are threaded blocks held in special enclosures that are attached to the part by welding, riveting, screwing, or snap-on attachments. Single-thread nuts are formed by stamping a thread-engaging impression in a piece of flat metal.

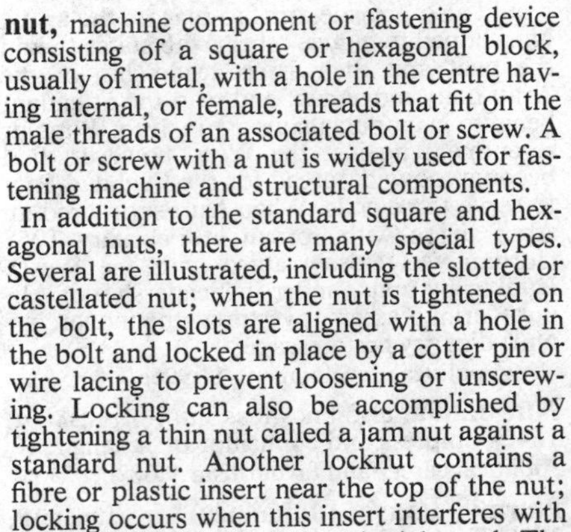

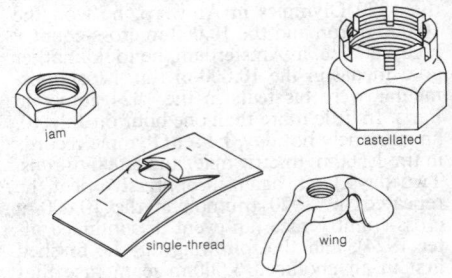

Several types of nuts

nut, a dry, hard fruit that does not split open at maturity to release its single seed. A nut resembles an achene but develops from more than one carpel (female reproductive structure), often is larger, and has a tough, woody wall. Examples are chestnut, hazelnut, and acorn. Although popularly called "nuts," the peanut is a legume, the coconut a drupe, and the Brazil nut a seed. Apart from their importance as food for man and animals, many nuts are processed to obtain a very fine charcoal used for absorption of gases, as in gas masks and industrial filters.
·development of agriculture **1**:328c
·fruit characteristics and types **16**:481g; table 482
·fruit farming economics and crops **7**:751f; tables 754
·hazel nut and filbert importance **2**:873c
·Juglandales economic importance **10**:329c
·rodent food source and storage **15**:972h

nutation, the irregular, spiralling movement of a plant organ (*e.g.*, stem, tendril, root, flower stalk) that results from an inequality of growth rates in tissues at the periphery of the growing tip. It occurs most strikingly in twining plants.
·plant patterns and tropisms **17**:673h

nutation, in astronomy, a small irregularity in the precession of the equinoxes (*q.v.*). Precession is the slow, toplike wobbling of the spinning Earth, with a period of about 26,000 years. Nutation (Latin *nutare*, "to nod") superimposes a small oscillation, with a period of 18.6 years and an amplitude of 9.2 seconds of arc, upon this great slow movement. The cause of nutation lies chiefly in the fact that the plane of the Moon's orbit around the Earth is tilted by about 5° from the plane of Earth's orbit around the Sun. The Moon's orbital plane precesses around the Earth's in 18.6 years, and the effect of the Moon on the precession of the equinoxes varies with this same period. The British astronomer James Bradley announced his discovery of nutation in 1748.
·astronomical observation limitations **2**:246a
·damping and Earth's anelasticity **6**:40f
·Earth oscillation period and amplitude **6**:59e
·gyroscopic motion of Earth **8**:529b
·light aberration in Bradley's observations **10**:950f
·sidereal time variation **18**:414e

nut-bearing torreya (tree): *see* Japanese torreya.

nutcracker (*Nucifraga*), either of two sharp-billed, short-tailed birds of the family Corvidae (*q.v.*; order Passeriformes), found in coniferous forests. The Eurasian nutcracker (*N.*

Clark's nutcracker (*Nucifraga columbiana*)
E.R. Degginger—EB Inc.

caryocatactes) ranges from Scandinavia to Japan and has isolated populations in mountains farther south. It is 32 centimetres (12½ inches) long and brownish, with white streaking and white tail-tip. Clark's nutcracker (*N. columbiana*) of western North America is pale gray, with black wings and tail, showing white patches in flight. Both species live chiefly on seeds and nuts, which they often store for winter use under deep snow.
·classification and general features **13**:1060d

Nutcracker, The, suite and ballet by Peter Ilich Tchaikovsky. The *Nutcracker Suite*, in eight movements, is an arrangement for orchestra by the composer of some of the music from his ballet *The Nutcracker*. Its first performance was in St. Petersburg, 1892. The ballet, which is based on *The Nutcracker and the Mouse King* by E.T.A. Hoffmann, was choreographed by Lev Ivanov and premiered under the title *Casse-Noisette* the same year.
·compositional acclaim **18**:3d

nut gall, a nutlike gall, especially on oak.
·writing ink development **19**:1046b

nuthatch, any of the 15 to 18 species of the genus *Sitta*, of the bird family Sittidae (order Passeriformes). They are bob-tailed, short-necked little birds, tame and fussy, that search tree trunks and rocks for food, often descending headfirst. They are primarily insectivorous but also eat seeds, which they may store for winter use. Nuthatches have persistent metallic or nasal calls and tend to be sociable. The usual nest is a cavity lined with grass or hair.

White-breasted nuthatch (*Sitta carolinensis*)
John H. Gerard

Nuthatches are commonest in Eurasia, eastward to Japan, the Philippines, and Sumatra; four species occur in North America. Most are bluish above and white or reddish below, and there may be a black eye stripe or a cap.
The coral-billed nuthatch (*Hypositta corallirostris*), of Madagascar, is considered an aberrant member of the vanga shrike family (Vangidae).
·classification and general features **13**:1060h; illus. 1053
·climbing method and ability **11**:22a

Nutley, town, Essex County, northeastern New Jersey, U.S., on the Passaic River, adjoining Bloomfield, Belleville, and Clifton. Founded in 1680 by the Dutch as part of Newark, it was detached in 1812 to become part of Bloomfield. In 1874 it became the independent township of Franklin, named in honour of William, son of Benjamin Franklin, last royal governor of New Jersey. In 1902 it was incorporated as a town and renamed after the local Nutley estate of the Satterthwaite family. In the late 19th century it was an authors' and artists' settlement. Manufactures include chemicals, drugs, and metal products. Pop. (1980) 28,998.
40°49′ N, 74°10′ W

nutmeg, spice consisting of the seed of the *Myristica fragrans*, a tropical, dioecious evergreen tree native to the Moluccas or Spice Islands of Indonesia. Nutmeg has a characteristic, pleasant fragrance and slightly warm taste; it is used to flavour many kinds of baked goods, confections, puddings, meats, sausages, sauces, vegetables, and such beverages as eggnog. Grated nutmeg has been used as a sachet; the Romans used it as incense. Around 1600 it became important as an expensive commercial spice of the Western world and was the subject of Dutch plots to keep prices high and of English and French counterplots to obtain fertile seeds for transplantation. The nutmegs sold whole were dipped in lime to prevent their growth.
The tree is cultivated in the Moluccas and the West Indies principally, and elsewhere

Nutmeg (*Myristica fragrans*)
G.R. Roberts

with varying success. The trees may reach about 65 feet (20 metres) tall. They yield fruit 8 years after sowing, reach their prime in 25 years, and bear fruit for 60 years or longer. The stands on the Moluccas thrive in the shade under groves of lofty trees. The nutmeg fruit is a pendulous drupe, similar in appearance to an apricot. When fully mature it splits in two, exposing a crimson-coloured aril, the mace, surrounding a single shiny, brown seed, the nutmeg. The pulp of the fruit may be eaten locally. After collection, the aril-enveloped nutmegs are conveyed to curing areas where the mace is removed, flattened out, and dried. The nutmegs are dried gradually in the sun and turned twice daily over a period of six to eight weeks. During this time the nutmeg shrinks away from its hard seed coat until the kernels rattle in their shells when shaken. The shell is then broken with a wooden truncheon and the nutmegs are picked out. Dried nutmegs are grayish-brown ovals with furrowed surfaces. Large ones may be about 1.2 inches long and 0.8 inch in diameter.
Nutmeg and mace contain 7 to 14 percent essential oil, the principal components of which are pinene, camphene, and dipentene, all having the empirical formula $C_{10}H_{16}$. Nutmeg on expression yields about 24 to 30 percent fixed oil called nutmeg butter, or oil of mace, the principal component of which is trimyristin, $C_{45}H_{86}O_6$. The oils are used as condiments and carminatives and to scent soaps and perfumes. An ointment of nutmeg butter has been used as a counterirritant and in treatment of rheumatism.
The name nutmeg is also applied in different countries to other fruits or seeds: the Jamaica, or calabash, nutmeg derived from *Monodora myristica;* the Brazilian nutmeg from *Cryptocarya moschata;* the Peruvian nutmeg from *Laurelia aromatica;* the Madagascar, or clove, nutmeg from *Ravensara aromatica;* and the California, or stinking, nutmeg from *Torreya californica*.
·fruit and nut farming, table 1 **7**:755
·Magnoliales economic use **11**:342e
·spice history, use, production, and region of origin **17**:503a; tables 504

nutria, or COYPU (*Myocastor coypus*), semiaquatic South American rodent usually placed in the family Capromyidae (order Rodentia). The nutria is a robust, muskrat-like

Nutria (*Myocastor coypus*) feeding
Douglas Fisher

animal with small eyes and ears, a rounded, scaly tail, partially webbed hind feet, and broad, orange incisors. It is about 1 metre (39 inches) long, including the long tail, and may weigh about 8 kilograms (17½ pounds). Its fur is reddish brown and consists of coarse guard hairs overlying a soft undercoat. The nutria lives in a shallow burrow along a pond or river and feeds mainly on aquatic plants. It produces up to three litters of two to eight young a year; gestation takes about 135 days.

Nutria fur is of some value in the fur trade. Persistent hunting in the 19th and early 20th centuries, however, led to a decline in populations. The animal was subsequently introduced into North America and Europe for breeding purposes. Some nutrias escaped or were turned loose, and in many countries have become pests that damage crops and compete with other wildlife.

·Amazon habitation and economic uses **1**:654f
·classification and general features **15**:979c
·distribution, fur source, habitat, and reproductive rate **15**:969h
·fur origin and characteristics table **7**:814

nutrient, substance required by an organism for growth and the sustainment of life. So-called nonessential nutrients are those that can be synthesized by the cell if they are absent from the food. Essential nutrients cannot be synthesized within the cell and must be present in the food. In most living organisms nutrients serve three functions: they provide the energy and electrons necessary for certain vital processes and various materials from which all structural components and enzymes (biological catalysts) can be assembled.

nutrients, oceanic, in the broad sense, all the elements necessary for marine life, presented to the organisms in dissolved or gaseous form. Seawater concentrations of many of these elements including hydrogen, sodium, calcium, and carbon normally are more than adequate to support the organisms. Marine ecologists generally designate as nutrients only those physiologically important substances presented in critically short supply to photosynthesizing organisms, the base of a marine food chain. These nutrients are the inorganic phosphate, nitrate, nitrite, ammonium, and hydrated silicate ions. The phosphatic and nitrogen salts are needed to produce living tissue, and the silicates are used for building shells by the abundant and important diatoms and siliceous algae.

Nutrients are very abundant in waters deeper than about 1 kilometre (3,300 feet) as a result of the decomposition by bacteria of organic debris and the dissolution of siliceous diatom and zooplankton shells; nutrients can be converted by photosynthesis, however, only in the sunlit surface waters, which are critically depleted of their nutrients as a result. The nutrients in deep water must be returned to the surface by the processes of upwelling, turbulence, eddy diffusion, and convection before they can be consumed again.

·Antarctic productivity **1**:959e
·Antarctic upwelling and euphotic zone **2**:302a
·coral locale optima **5**:164c
·Mediterranean nutrient scarcity **11**:856f
·vertical distribution **13**:500g

nutrition 13:401, the study of all the processes by which micro-organisms, plants, and animals absorb and utilize food substances.

The text article covers functions of food, nutritional evolution of organisms, methods of ingestion or penetration of nutrients, determination of essential nutrient requirements, essential inorganic and organic nutrients, comparative magnitudes of the requirements for different types of nutrients, and syntrophism.

REFERENCES in other text articles:

animal
·animal feed requirements and evaluation **1**:908c
·animal food requirements **7**:208a
·animal migration and environment **12**:184b
·blood transport of food substances **2**:1113d
·bone growth and dietary calcium **3**:22f
·cat dietary requirements **3**:998d
·diet deficiency adjustment capacities **1**:34h
·dog food needs and capabilities **5**:933c
·echinoderm variations in feeding habits **6**:180c
·evolution of feeding habits **7**:17h
·fat composition and animal food **13**:524c
·feces-eating by rabbits **10**:589d
·horse's dietary needs **8**:1089g
·ingestion and digestion mechanisms **5**:780h
·insect restricted diets and needs **9**:615e
·larval function in Lepidoptera **10**:822c
·lizards' food preferences **16**:284h
·mammalian reingestion mechanism **11**:408a
·nourishment balance in larval and adult flies **5**:822e
·pigeon provisions for feeding of young **4**:934g
·protozoan food intake and utilization **15**:126b
·protozoan survival and limiting factors **15**:121e
·selective feeding in rats **16**:553d
·sponge feeding habits and absorption **14**:853c
·turtle diet preference **4**:72c

comparative biology
·Aristotle's biological treatises **1**:1168e
·biochemical study of food requirements **2**:995c
·community feeding behaviour **4**:1028e
·gene experiments in minimal media **7**:984c
·gene mutations in microorganisms **8**:811d
·germfree life study problems **8**:129f
·growth regulation factors **8**:442h
·living system's origins and evolution **14**:377d
·Oparin's theory of first organisms **13**:578b
·rain forest reproduction theories **10**:345a
·soil management practices **5**:47d
·spring community size reduction **17**:518d
·stream communities' food supply **15**:890g
·tissue culture requirements **18**:440b

plant
·angiosperm diversity **1**:876f
·bacteria growth requirements **2**:575a
·conifer nutrient deficiency signs **5**:5g
·deficiency's effect on plant colour **4**:917b
·fertilizer materials and production **4**:133c
·fungal food digestion process **12**:762h
·Iridales mycotrophy and saprophytism **9**:891b
·lichen symbiotic exchanges and needs **10**:884c
·moss growth on decay matter **3**:353a
·plant disease control programs **5**:894h
·plant disease development factors **5**:882a
·plant embryo development **5**:662d
·plant internal transport system **14**:500e
·saprophytic and fungus-symbiote orchids **13**:650g
·slime mold growth on laboratory media **16**:888g
·soil organisms as plant food source **16**:1014b
·vegetable farming soil requirements **19**:47h *passim* to 49d
·yolk and placentas in embryo developments **5**:625h; illus. 626
·zoo study and provision of animal diet **19**:1163a

RELATED ENTRIES in the *Ready Reference and Index:*
nutrient; nutritional type; syntrophism

nutritional diseases and disorders 13:408, adverse effects of a deficiency or excess of certain nutrients in body tissues. These effects are most often caused by a faulty diet that is either lacking or excessive in one or more of the essential nutrients or food groups. Less commonly, they may result from constitutional metabolic defects that prevent optimum digestion, absorption, or utilization of the ingested food.

The text article reviews the relationship of nutrition to health from the following standpoints : (1) deficiency diseases; (2) effects of overconsumption; (3) disease as a cause of malnutrition; (4) habitual dietary pattern and disease; (5) sophisticated diets; (6) healthy diets; and (7) therapeutic diets.

REFERENCES in other text articles:
·alcohol related diseases **1**:440f
·anemia from B_{12} deficiency **2**:1135f
·anemia therapy with vitamin B_{12} and liver **2**:1135f
·bone consequences of nutritional disorders **3**:24h
·causes, symptoms, and remedies **13**:418b
·childhood disorders and consequences **4**:223g
·fatigue from nutritional deficiencies **7**:191g
·fetal nutrient shortage effects **4**:220b
·goitre causes and symptoms **6**:826e
·health problems of developing countries **15**:207d
·metabolic disorders **11**:1049a
·mouth lesions in nutritional disorders **5**:797a
·muscle weakness disorders **12**:635b
·pigmentation decrease in skin **16**:848a
·population growth factors in history **14**:816b
·predisposition and resistance to disease **5**:856a
·pregnancy-associated polyneuritis **14**:980e
·protein and vitamin deficiencies **11**:1049a
·replacement of dietary constituents **18**:285h
·salt loss symptoms and causes **7**:44g
·short stature in children **5**:658d
·skin effects of vitamin and protein shortages **16**:845h

starvation
·atrophy from unavailable protein **2**:352b
·glucose synthesis in liver **11**:1048c
·therapeutic effects of drugs and diet **18**:284e
·therapy for beriberi and anemia **11**:835h
·types, causes, and symptoms **5**:860e
·vitamin deficiency symptoms **19**:488h; illus. 489
·vitamin therapies **11**:835g

RELATED ENTRIES in the *Ready Reference and Index: for*
anion deficiencies: see chlorine deficiency; fluorine deficiency; iodine deficiency
avitaminoses: beriberi; pellagra; vitamin A deficiency; vitamin B_2 deficiency; vitamin B_{12} deficiency; vitamin C deficiency; vitamin D deficiency; vitamin E deficiency; vitamin K deficiency
bone involvements: osteomalacia; osteoporosis
hypervitaminoses: vitamin A excess; vitamin D excess
mineral deficiencies: calcium deficiency; cobalt deficiency; copper deficiency; iron-deficiency-anemia; magnesium deficiency; manganese deficiency; mineral deficiency; phosphorus deficiency; potassium deficiency; sodium deficiency; zinc deficiency
protein deficiencies: kwashiorkor; sprue
other: anorexia nervosa; malnutrition; obesity; undernutrition

nutritional marasmus (medicine): *see* kwashiorkor.

nutritional type, general term used to describe organisms classified according to the chemical nature of the nutrients they require. Three separate classification schemes are commonly employed. One scheme is based on the way the functions of food are carried out. Thus, organisms such as green plants and some bacteria that require only inorganic compounds are called autotrophic organisms, or autotrophs; heterotrophs, such as all animals and fungi and most bacteria, require organic as well as inorganic compounds.

A second scheme is based on the nature of the energy source utilized by the organism. Those that trap radiant energy (light) and convert it to chemical energy in the form of adenosine triphosphate (ATP) are phototrophs, or photosynthetic organisms. Chemotrophs, or chemosynthetic organisms, utilize organic or inorganic compounds to satisfy their ATP requirements.

A third scheme is based on the type of electron-donor material utilized to synthesize certain cell constituents. A lithotroph obtains its electron-donor material from inorganic compounds; an organotroph obtains it from organic ones.

An organism may simultaneously be classified under more than one scheme. Thus, a green plant is photolithotrophic, certain bacteria are photoorganotrophic, and other bacteria are chemolithotrophic. Animals, most bacteria, and yeasts are chemoorganotrophic.

autotroph
- agricultural chemicals and applications **1**:350d
- light-accessible surface adaptations **13**:731a
- mineral spring biotic life **17**:518c
- origins of independent food synthesis **7**:18a
- protozoan primary production **15**:120e
- vegetable farming soil requirements **19**:48g

- bacteria nutritional requirements **2**:575a
- community nutrition and food chains **4**:1028f
- ecosystem structure and components **6**:282a; illus.

heterotroph
- evolution of life and feeding habits **7**:18c
- Oparin's theory of first organisms **13**:578b
- soft water spring biotic life **17**:518c

- life energy and metabolism **10**:896b
- living system's origins and evolution **14**:377e
- nutrient intake mechanisms **5**:781a
- nutrient metabolism types and evolution **13**:401f
- phototrophic nutrition and chemical needs of protozoa **15**:126b
- soil organisms, carbon cycle, and nitrogen fixation **16**:1015c

nutrition and diet, human **13**:417, are concerned with the process of assimilating food and with the food and drink people regularly consume.

The text article covers the functions of food (including supplying energy and body-building and body-maintaining materials); basic nutrients essential to normal growth and to good health; the nine basic classes of foods; recommended intakes of nutrients; hunger, satiety, and the regulation of body weight; therapeutic diets of both the restorative and restrictive types; and the role of public health services in nutrition and diet.

REFERENCES in other text articles:
- aging and nutritional requirements **1**:307a
- agricultural advances and applications **1**:364c
- algae food value **1**:489b
- American Subarctic Indian diet **1**:696g
- ancient Indian therapeutics **11**:824d
- aquatic protein value **7**:346a
- bakery product chemical enrichment **2**:607b
- Bantu and Bushman Kalahari diets **10**:374e
- biochemical study of food requirements **2**:995c
- breast and bottle feeding **10**:584a; table
- burn injury management **3**:524f
- calcium importance **3**:586a
- carbohydrate consumption by man **3**:824b
- cereal and cereal-product values **3**:1158c
- consumption patterns of countries **5**:105g; tables 106
- diabetes mellitus therapy **6**:837f
- digestive disorders and food malabsorption **5**:770a
- exercise energy requirements **7**:69f
- Fabale's vitamin and protein value **7**:130g
- fatigue relation to blood-sugar level **7**:190e
- food additives and quality control **7**:487c
- grain and meat consumption efficiency **2**:1043h
- hominid tooth specialization for feeding **8**:1025h; illus. 1026
- Homo erectus feeding behaviour **8**:1034b
- hospital nutritional therapy programs **7**:496g
- joint nutrition and exercise **10**:259b
- life-span and poverty relationships **1**:304e
- lipid occurrence and importance **10**:1015h
- Mashriq cultures low standard **11**:574c
- meat's high nutritive value **11**:746d
- metabolic assimilation of foods **13**:408a
- milk vitamin, protein, and mineral content and value **5**:435d; tables
- North American Plateau Indian food **13**:229d
- oily food consumption **13**:530h
- physical and mental development of children **14**:992d
- Polynesian dependence on sea protein **14**:779e
- prehistoric Bushman diet evidence **1**:288d
- prenatal growth and mother's health **5**:651g
- protein importance and functions **15**:81c
- psychosocial evolution and child-care **7**:20g
- racial body type influence **15**:351h
- salt uses and food-salting development **16**:192d
- seafood proteins, minerals, and vitamins **7**:345d
- urine composition variation **7**:40g
- vegetable's composition and consumption **19**:44c; tables 53
- vitamin intake and physical condition **19**:488g
- vitamins discovery and importance **18**:48b
- world food supply and consumer education programs **7**:501d

Nuttall, George Henry Falkiner (b. July 5, 1862, San Francisco—d. Dec. 16, 1937, London), biologist and physician who contributed substantially to many branches of biology and founded the Molteno Institute of Biology and Parasitology (1921) at Cambridge. He was educated in the United States, France, Germany, and Switzerland. He was appointed lecturer in bacteriology and preventive medicine at Cambridge in 1900, when he acquired British nationality. In 1906 he was elected the first Quick Professor of biology at Cambridge. He made innovative and significant discoveries in studies in immunology, on life under aseptic conditions, blood chemistry, and on diseases transmitted by arthropods, especially ticks. His publications include several books and numerous papers on bacteriology, serology, hygiene, tropical medicine, and parasitology. He founded the *Journal of Hygiene* (1901) and *Journal of Parasitology* (1908), and edited the former until 1937 and the latter until 1933; both became models for other scientific publications.

Nuttall, Thomas (b. Jan. 5, 1786, Long Preston, Settle, Yorkshire—d. Sept. 10, 1859, Nut Grove, Lancashire), British–U.S. naturalist and botanist known for his discoveries of North American plants.

Nuttall worked as a journeyman printer for his uncle before he left England for the United States at the age of 22. He settled in Philadelphia, where he became a good friend of the botanist Benjamin S. Barton, who instructed him in general principles of botany. Nuttall supplemented this help with his own studies, and, thus prepared, made numerous trips to North Carolina, Virginia, Missouri, and Arkansas, collecting and identifying species of plants. These trips provided the information for his principle work, *The Genera of North American Plants* (1818).

Thomas Nuttall, engraving by Thomson, 1825, after a drawing by W. Derby

The Mansell Collection

In 1822 Nuttall became professor of natural history at Harvard University, where he began a study of ornithology. The first volume of his *Manual of the Ornithology of the United States and of Canada* appeared in 1832. He resigned from Harvard to accompany an expedition to the Columbia River and Hawaii, where he also collected plants. In 1841 he returned to England. He spent the rest of his life there as a farmer and horticulturist.

nut weevil: *see* acorn and nut weevil.

Nuuanu Pali (Hawaii, U.S.): *see* Koolau Range.

Nuulua, Nuusafee, and Nuutele, islands, Western Samoa.
- Samoan geography and culture **16**:205f

Nuvolari, Tazio Giorgio (b. Nov. 16, 1892, Castel d'Ario, near Mantua, Italy—d. Aug. 10, 1953, Mantua), considered the greatest driver in the history of automobile racing. He began racing motorcycles in 1920 and won the Italian championship in 1924 and 1926 before turning to automobile competition. His first major victory in an auto race was in the 1930 Mille Miglia. Nuvolari raced as an independent driver in cars constructed by Bugatti, Maserati, and the MG firm. For most of his career, however, he drove for the Italian Alfa Romeo (until 1937) and the German Auto Union teams. He won numerous European Grands Prix, the Le Mans race (1933), the Tourist Trophy (1933), the U.S. Vanderbilt Cup (1936), and various titles, including champion of Italy (1932, 1935–36). His last great race was the Mille Miglia in 1947, when he finished second.

Nuwairi, an- (1272–1332), Egyptian historian and civil servant.
- Egyptian encyclopaedia development **6**:798f

Nuwara Eliya, town, south central Sri Lanka (Ceylon); the headquarters of Nuwara Eliya district of the Central Province. It lies at an altitude of 6,199 ft (1,889 m) above sea level, immediately south of the island's highest summit, Pidurutalagala (8,281 ft [2,524 m]), and 25 mi (40 km) southeast of Kandy. Although part of a major tea-growing region, the town is also a market centre for rubber, vegetables, rice, and fish. A salubrious climate has led to its development as a hill resort and health spa as well. It is the site of a meteorological observatory. Pop. (1971) 16,347.
06°58′ N, 80°46′ E
- district area and population table **17**:522
- map, Sri Lanka **17**:520

Tea picker, Nuwara Eliya, Sri Lanka (Ceylon)

Richard Abeles

Nuwe (Egypt): *see* Thebes.

Nuytsia floribunda: *see* Australian Christmas tree.

Nuzu, modern YORGHAN TEPE, ancient Mesopotamian city, located southwest of Kirkūk, in Kirkūk *muḥāfaẓah* (governorate), Iraq. Excavations undertaken there by U.S. archaeologists in 1925–31 revealed material extending from the prehistoric period to Roman, Parthian, and Sāsānian periods. In Akkadian times (2334–2154 BC) the site was

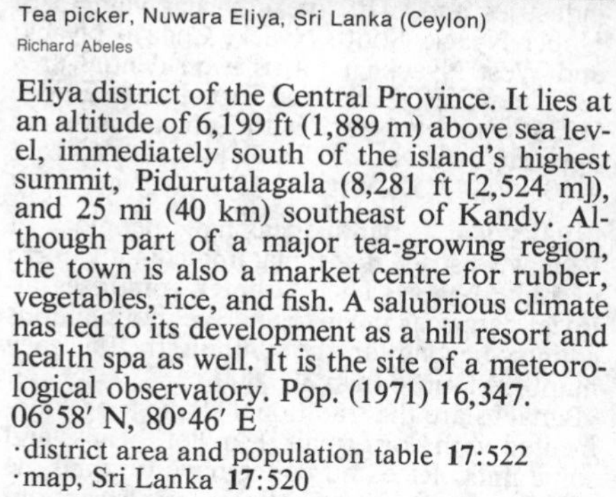

Offering table of Nuzu ware, green glazed terracotta; in the Fogg Art Museum, Cambridge, Mass.

By courtesy of the Fogg Art Museum, Harvard University

called Gasur; but early in the 2nd millennium BC the Hurrians, of northern Mesopotamia, occupied the city, changed its name to Nuzu, and during the 16th and 15th centuries built there a prosperous community and an important administrative centre.

Excavations uncovered excellent material for a study of Hurrian ceramics and glyptic art. An especially outstanding type of pottery, called "Nuzu ware" (or "Mitanni ware") because of its original discovery there, was characterized by one primary shape—a tall, slender, small-footed goblet—and an intricate black and white painted decoration. In addition, more than 4,000 cuneiform tablets were discovered. Although written mostly in Akkadian, the majority of the personal names are Hurrian, and the Akkadian used often shows strong Hurrian influence. The Nuzu material has also made possible an insight into specific Hurrian family law and societal institutions and has clarified many difficult passages in the contemporary patriarchal narratives of the Book of Genesis.

·archaeological discoveries **11**:966f

Nyabingi, the spirit of a woman, important in the religion of many tribes in northern Rwanda.

·Rwanda's population beliefs **16**:109h

Nyack, village, Rockland County, New York, U.S., on the west bank of the Hudson River (there known as the Tappan Zee). Settled in 1684, it was named for an Algonquin Indian tribe and depended on agriculture, fishing, and stone quarrying. After being connected by a railroad in 1874, it developed light industries and, with the adjacent villages of Upper Nyack, South Nyack, Central Nyack, and West Nyack, it forms a residential area for New York City. The Tappan Zee Bridge (1956) connects Nyack with Tarrytown on the opposite bank. Inc. 1883. Pop. (1980) 6,428.
41°05′ N, 73°55′ W

Nyakyusa, Bantu-speaking people of Rungwe district, Tanzania, immediately north of Lake Nyasa. Their country comprises alluvial flats near the lake and the mountainous country beyond for about 40 mi. In 1967 they numbered more than 300,000.

Bananas are the traditional staple food, augmented with corn (maize), millet, beans, and some milk. Rice and coffee have become the principal cash crops. Cattle assume exceptional importance in the local economies. Men and women share equally in the field labour; men alone, however, tend to the herding.

Traditionally the Nyakyusa lived in unique age villages: between the ages of 11 and 13 all the boys of a district left their paternal homes and established a new hamlet of their own, eventually marrying and bringing their wives there. Each hamlet had a headman, or "great commoner," selected by the paramount chief of the district. A village died as its founders died in old age. A number of villages comprised an independent chiefdom of a few thousand people. A district chief was succeeded by two sons, the firstborn of his two "great wives." Succession occurred when the sons were about 35 years old; the chief retired in a great ceremony, dividing his territory between the two sons and assigning definite tracts of land to each recently established village. Old villages might even shift off their land to make room for the villages of their sons. With the modern land shortage the older men are no longer willing to shift, and new age villages seldom become established.

Polygyny is prevalent, with a substantial bride-price expected. Slavery was formerly an accepted institution. Ancestor cults were the main feature of traditional religion.

·dietary customs in social life **5**:729e
·economic and social conditions **17**:1028g
·numbers, tribal affiliations, and culture **6**:110c

Nyala, city, Dārfūr *muḥāfaẓah* (governorate), in the western part of The Sudan. It is a road terminus and trading centre for gum arabic. Latest pop. est. 26,160.
12°03′ N, 24°53′ E

·Chad potential rail transportation link **4**:16c
·map, Sudan **17**:758

nyala (*Tragelaphus angasi*), slender antelope, family Bovidae (order Artiodactyla), found alone or in small groups in southeast African forests. The nyala stands as high as 107 centimetres (3½ feet) at the shoulder and has a distinguishing crest of hair along the back from head to tail. The male, which has loosely spiraled horns and a long fringe on the throat and underparts, is dark brown with reddish brown on the lower legs, white on the face and neck, and vertical white stripes on the body. The female is reddish brown with more conspicuous white striping.

Nyalas (*Tragelaphus angasi*)
Russ Kinne—Photo Researchers

The mountain nyala (*Tragelaphus buxtoni*), a rare antelope found in the mountains of southern Ethiopia, is grayish brown with white on the head, neck, and body. The male has long, divergent, loosely spiraled horns.

Nyama, among the peoples of the Western Sudan, a spiritual power residing in certain human beings and animals.

·similarity to mana **12**:878b

Nyamulagira (NYAMLAGIRI), **Mount,** in the Virunga Range of east central Africa, lies 15 mi (24 km) northeast of Sake, in the Park of the Volcanoes, Zaire. It is a volcano, about 10,023 ft (3,055 m) high, with a central crater that last erupted in 1938, when the southwest slope opened, and lava reached Lake Kivu to the south.
1°25′ S, 29°12′ E

·formation, location, and activity **19**:162f

Nyamwezi, Bantu-speaking inhabitants of a wide area of the western region of Tanzania. In 1967 their population was slightly in excess of 400,000. Their language is closely related to that of the Sukuma (*q.v.*). The Nyamwezi and Sukuma are also very similar culturally. Several other peoples of the area have a good deal in common with them: the Sumbwa, the Kimbu, and the Bende.

The Nyamwezi subsist primarily by cereal agriculture, their major crops being sorghum, millet, and corn (maize). Rice is a significant cash crop. The Nyamwezi have long been famous as travellers and workers outside their own country; as porters they became known throughout East Africa.

Though they once lived in compact villages, the Nyamwezi have dispersed since the 19th century, living now in relatively scattered homesteads. Marriage entails both a bride-price and bride service; polygyny is permitted but limited in practice. Descent is through the female line. There are many secret societies that have initiation ceremonies.

Chiefdoms were formerly highly developed. Each had a hierarchy of territorial officers culminating in that of the *ntemi* ("chief"). There was a large aristocracy and an even larger slave population.

Ancestor worship is the most important facet of religious activity. High gods and spirits are also recognized. A *mfumi* ("diviner") can interpret a situation for an individual or a group, telling them what forces are impinging on their lives. Christianity and Islām have made only limited inroads.

·economic and social changes **17**:1028g
·Ngoni influence on political system **6**:97c
·numbers, tribal affiliations, and culture **6**:109h

Nyanga, administrative region, southwest Gabon, drained by the Nyanga River. The capital, Tchibanga, is the centre of a rice-growing area. The Réserve de la Nyanga is in the eastern part of the region.

·area and population table **7**:819
·map, Gabon **7**:820

Nyanja (people): *see* Maravi.

Nyankole (African people): *see* Nkole.

Nyanza, Province of southwestern Kenya, East Africa, occupies 6,240 sq mi (16,162 sq km), including 1,403 sq mi (3,636 sq km) of Lake Victoria, and has a population density of nearly 440 per sq mi. The principal cash crop is cotton, with coffee and tea production in the northeast. The western districts are populated primarily by the Luo, with the Gusii dominating the eastern districts. Kisumu (*q.v.*), the provincial capital, is the major urban centre in western Kenya. Small amounts of copper and gold are mined at Macalder in the southwest. The province supports some light industry and agricultural processing plants. Latest census 2,122,045.

·area and population table **10**:426
·map, Kenya **10**:424

Nyasa, Lake, also called LAKE MALAWI, southernmost of the Great Rift Valley lakes of East Africa, lying in a deep trough mainly within Malawi; the lake's middle line and its northern and eastern shores form much of Malawi's boundary with Tanzania and Mozambique. Its north–south length is 363 mi (584 km), its width varies from 10 to 50 mi, and its area is 11,430 sq mi (29,604 sq km). The surface is 1,550 ft (472 m) above sea level, and the depth increases to 2,310 ft (704 m) toward the northern end, where the forested Livingstone Mountains to the east and the Nyika Plateau and Vipya Mountains to the west fall steeply down to the lakeshore.

Cormorants on Lake Nyasa
Gerald Cubitt

A fresh southeasterly wind (the *mwera*) prevails from May to August, causing steep, short seas; the coastline offers little shelter. Halfway up the lake is Likoma Island, a mission headquarters and site of an imposing Anglican cathedral (completed 1911). On the heavily populated Malawi shore there are government stations at Fort Johnston, Nkota Kota, Nkhata Bay, and Karonga.

Lake Nyasa (Mass of Water) is fed by 14 perennial rivers, the largest being the Ruhuhu; the sole outlet is the Shire River, a tributary of the Zambezi. Of about 200 recorded species of fish about 80 percent are endemic, being isolated from the Zambezi fauna by the Murchison Falls. Commercial fisheries exist at the southern end of the lake, based chiefly on

Tilapia; the lake fly hatches in clouds large enough to obscure the horizon.

Passenger and cargo vessels are operated by the Malawi Railways company. Cotton, rubber, rice, tung oil, and peanuts (groundnuts) are shipped to the railhead at Chipoka in the south, whence the railway connects through Limbe with Beira, Mozambique.

The existence of the lake was reported by a Portuguese, Caspar Boccaro, in 1616. British explorer-missionary David Livingstone reached it from the south in 1859. *Major ref.* **6**:116h

12°08′ S, 34°30′ E

·age and fauna peculiarities **1**:1032g
·climatic change indications illus. 1 **4**:734
·East African rift system **1**:187c
·lake level variations **10**:612c
·location and formation **17**:1025g
maps
·Malawi **11**:361
·Mozambique **12**:594
·Tanzania **17**:1026
·site and use **11**:360c *passim* to 364b
·Zambezi River distribution and flow **19**:1128e; map

Nyasaland, former territory in present Malawi (*q.v.*), on the western shores of Lake Nyasa, bordering Mozambique, Zambia, and Rhodesia. The area, described as "the casual residuum of geography and treaties," was defined by European agreements in 1890–1901. It was known as the British Central Africa Protectorate until 1907, when it became the Protectorate of Nyasaland. Part of the Federation of Rhodesia and Nyasaland (1953–63), with the achievement of independence it took the name of Malawi.

·British control established **17**:288d

Nyasa Rift, part of the East African Rift System located in Malawi.

·heat flow and gravity values **15**:842c

Nyassa, extinct genus of clams, the shells of which occur as fossils, especially in Devonian marine rocks (the Devonian Period began 395,000,000 years ago and lasted 50,000,000 years).

Nyassa, Pleistocene in age, collected at Brookline, Mass.

By courtesy of the Buffalo Museum of Science, Buffalo, New York

Nyāya (Sanskrit: Rule), one of the orthodox systems (*darśana*) traditionally distinguished in Hindu philosophy, which has given Indian thought a very finely honed instrument of reasoning. The great contribution of the Nyāya system is its working out in profound detail the reasoning method of inference, involving five steps (*see* anumāna). Its fundamental text is the *Nyāya-sūtras*, which is ascribed to Gautama.

The Nyāya system—from Gautama through his important early commentator Vātsyāyana (*c.* AD 450) till Udayana (10th century), who attempted to give proofs of the existence of God—became qualified as the Old Nyāya (Prācīna-Nyāya) in the 11th century, when a new school of Nyāya (Navya-Nyāya; New Nyāya) arose in Bengal. This school is particularly interested in the study of the objective foundations of the relation between the item to be proved (*sādhya*) and the ground submitted (*hetu*) to render the proof. This relationship is broadened and a more precise terminology developed, to the point that modern scholars resort to the symbols of mathematical logic to transcribe the language. The great figure in this Navya-Nyāya is Gaṅgeśa (12th century).

As the Nyāya accepts the authority of language as a means of knowledge, it gave much attention to the question of the denotative power of the word and to linguistic speculation generally. As an example, the question is raised: how do the transitory phonemes, or units of sound, relate to the permanent denotative force (*abhidhāna-śakti*) of an aggregate of such phonemes? The answer is that the mental impression evoked by the phenomenal word is preserved in human memory, so that, when men later hear this word again, it triggers human memory, which then presents the object of the earlier impression to consciousness. This, of course, applies only if one already knows the relation between the series of phonemes and the object denoted; others simply have to learn the language. This inquiry then leads to consideration of levels of meaning, sequence, syntax, and other linguistic matters.

Nyāya-bindu (*c.* 7th century), a work of Buddhist logic by Dharmakīrti.

·theory of perception **9**:324f

Nyāyapraveśa, a Buddhist logic text by Śaṅkarasvāmin.

·Chinese and Japanese Buddhist use **3**:431b

Nyāyārusariṇo Vijñānavādinaḥ (Sanskrit: Vijñānavāda School of the Logical Tradition), one of the principal subdivisions of the Yogācāra or Vijñānavāda (Consciousness Affirming) school of Mahāyāna Buddhism. This branch was founded by Dignāga (*c.* AD 480–540) and is distinguished from the older school of the scriptural tradition (Āgamānusariṇo Vijñānavādinaḥ; *q.v.*). Dignāga maintained that perception and inference are the only means of valid cognition and did not accept any other means of cognition such as the verbal testimony admitted by Buddhist philosophers who preceded him and by orthodox systems of Hindu philosophy. Even the words of the Buddha himself should not be accepted as unconditionally valid until they are critically examined. Dignāga did not consider this radically critical attitude to be a contradiction of the Buddha, as the Buddha himself told his disciples not to follow his words blindly but to examine them carefully. This school is characterized by its exclusive concentration on the theory of knowledge; it does not deal with the question of how to transcend beyond empirical reality. The function of the *ālaya-vijñāna* ("storage consciousness") is divided among the six cognitive consciousnesses. From the epistemological point of view, this school is also described as the *sākāra-vijñānavādins* ("school of Vijñānavādins maintaining that cognition takes the form [*ākāra*] of the object within itself"). Representation in the cognition as the apprehension of the object is constituted by the form of the object and the conceptualization of it, the former being the essence of undefiled cognition, while the latter is the cause of defiled imagination. Illusion arises when one interprets the representation in the mind by the conceptual construction.

Dharmakīrti (*c.* AD 600–660) was the most distinguished successor of Dignāga. He elaborated upon Dignāga's theories and became even more popular than his predecessor. Dignāga and Dharmakīrti influenced profoundly the trend of later Indian Buddhism, especially in the sphere of logic and epistemology.

Nyāya-sūtras, a fundamental philosophical text of the Nyāya school of Hinduism.

·logic history from antiquity **11**:62h
·philosophic categories and doctrines **9**:321h

Nyāya-Vaiśeṣika, the combined school of two Hindu philosophical systems.

·syncretistic philosophical doctrines **9**:326c

Nyborg, city and port, Fyns *amtskommune* (county), eastern Fyn (Funen) Island, Denmark, on the Store Bælt (strait) and Nyborg Fjord. Named for the castle (*borg*) built in 1170 to protect the Store Bælt, it was the favourite meeting place of the Danehof (assembly of nobles and clergy) from 1282 to 1413. The Great Charter, Denmark's first constitution, was issued there in the former year. A large Swedish army surrendered outside the city in 1659. The castle, birthplace (1481) of King Christian II, was restored in 1923 as a museum. Nyborg is the terminus for the ferry to Sjælland (Zealand). It has a large oil storage plant and shipbuilding and textile industries. Pop. (latest census) city, 13,688; (1971 est.) mun., 17,852.

55°19′ N, 10°48′ E

·map, Denmark **5**:582

nyckelharpa (stringed instrument): *see* hurdy-gurdy.

Nyctaginaceae, the four-o'clock family of the flowering plant order Caryophyllales, about 25 to 30 genera with 200 to 300 species of herbs, shrubs, and trees, native to tropical and warm temperate areas of the world. Members of the family have untoothed leaves and petalless flowers; the flowers have coloured bracts (leaflike structures) that fuse together and resemble petals. The small dry fruit bears grooves or is winged. Four-o'clocks (*Mirabilis jalapa*), sand verbena (*Abronia umbellata*), and a showy vine of the South American genus *Bougainvillea* are widely cultivated as ornamentals. Small yellow *Bougainvillea* flowers have reddish or red-dish-purple bracts and hang from long, drooping branchlets. The stem of *B. glabra* may be 18 to 30 metres (about 60 to 100 feet) long in hot climates, and the plant is in flower throughout most of the year. The stem of *B. spectabilis* is covered with many short hairs, and the flowers are relatively short-lived.

Bougainvillea glabra

F.K. Anderson—EB Inc.

·classification and general features **3**:975e

Nyctalus (bat): *see* noctule.

Nyctanthes (plant): *see* Oleaceae.

Nyctea scandiaca: *see* snowy owl.

Nyctereutes procyonoides: *see* raccoon dog.

Nycteribiidae: *see* bat fly.

Nycteridae: *see* slit-faced bat.

Nyctibiidae (bird family): *see* potoo.

Nycticebus (primate): *see* loris.

Nyctidromus albicollis (bird): *see* pauraque.

Nydam boat, or NYDAM BOOT, found in Nydam, archaeological site in Schleswig-Holstein, West Germany; now in a museum in Schleswig.

·sailing ship history and design **16**:157f

Nye, Bill, pen name of EDGAR WILSON NYE (b. Aug. 25, 1850, Shirley, Maine—d. Feb. 22, 1896, Arden, N.C.), journalist and humorist who, with "Artemus Ward," "Petroleum V. Nasby," "Josh Billings," and others, made humorous, often satirical, writing a major element in American literature in the last half of the 19th century. In 1852 the family moved to Wisconsin, where Nye taught school and read law. Settling in Laramie, Wyo., in 1876, he served as postmaster and justice of the peace and contributed to the *Denver Tribune* and *Cheyenne Sun*. His humorous squibs and tales in the *Laramie Boomerang*, which he helped found in 1881, were widely read and reprinted.

Nye, 1889
By courtesy of the Library of Congress, Washington, D.C.

Collected, they form the substance of numerous published volumes, from *Bill Nye and Boomerang* (1881) to *Bill Nye's History of the U.S.* (1894). Later Nye returned to Wisconsin and for several years wrote for the *New York World*. In 1886 he lectured with James Whitcomb Riley, the combination of Nye's wit and Riley's sentiment proving extremely popular. Nye did not employ the political satire or the faulty spelling, grammar, and diction typical of so many humorists of the time. Writing in his own person, rather than in the guise of a foolish character, Nye reveals his own kindly but droll nature. Possibly for these reasons he has worn better than some of his humorous contemporaries.

Nye, John Frederick (b. Feb. 26, 1923, England), glaciologist known for his investigations of the mechanics of glacier flow. A faculty member at the University of Bristol, county of Avon, since 1953, he has studied the surfaces of the polar ice caps and the responses of glaciers to seasonal and climatic changes. He wrote *Physical Properties of Crystals: Their Representation by Tensors and Matrices* (1957).

Nyenchen Tanglha Range (China): *see* Nien-ch'ing-t'ang-ku-la Mountains.

Nyerere, Julius (Kambarage) 13:427 (b. March 1922, Butiama, Tanganyika, now Tanzania), first prime minister of independent Tanganyika (1961), became the first president of the new state of Tanzania and was the major force behind the Organization of African Unity.

Abstract of text biography. Nyerere attended Makere College, Uganda, and Edinburgh University, Scotland, before entering politics. In 1954, as president of the Tanganyika African Association, he converted the organization into the politically oriented Tanganyika African National Union (TANU). When Tanganyika gained responsible self-government in 1960, Nyerere became chief minister; and in December 1961, he became the first prime minister of independent Tanganyika. When Tanganyika became a republic (1962), he was elected president. In 1964 he became president of the United Republic of Tanzania (Tanganyika and Zanzibar).

REFERENCES in other text articles:
·East African federation support and Tanzanian leadership **6**:104h *passim* to 107a
·Socialist policies for economic growth **17**:1025e

Nygaardsvold, Johan (1879–1952), Norwegian statesman and Labour Party leader, served as prime minister in exile during German occupation.
·Norwegian 20th-century political growth **16**:333g

Nyiha, African people living in East Africa.
·Zambia ethnic composition map **19**:1132

Nyika, also called MIJIKENDA or NIKA, Northeast Coastal Bantu tribes including the Digo, who live along the Kenya and Tanzania coast south from Mombasa to Pangani; the Giryama, who live north of Mombasa; and the Duruma, Jibana, Rabai, Ribe, Chonyi, Kaura, and Kambe, who live in the arid bush steppe (Swahili *hyika*) west of the Digo and Giryama. At the end of the 1960s they numbered more than 600,000. All Nyika speak a Bantu language; some have taken over Swahili, once their second language, as a first language. Nyika society shows evidence of significant Arab influence.

The Nyika subsist primarily by agriculture, growing a variety of crops. Animal husbandry is of considerable importance, especially among the Duruma. Fishing holds a prominent place in the economy of the Digo. All Nyika engage extensively in trade.

Polygyny is general, and a substantial bride-price is expected. Most of these peoples trace their descent through the male line, although the Digo, the Duruma, and the Rabai trace descent through both the male and the female lines. They are organized into a number of clans, and the men in the clans into a system of age-grades. Position in this system—a cycling type, borrowed from the adjacent Galla —determines a man's responsibilities. Traditionally the Nyika were ruled by elders deriving authority from their age-grade and their rank in secret societies.

Many Nyika are Muslims, some are Christian, and perhaps a quarter retain the traditional beliefs. There is widespread belief in ancestral spirits who are thought to require ritual pacification.
·numbers, tribal affiliations, and culture **6**:109h

Nyika, thorn-scrub plain in eastern Kenya, lies between the coastal lowlands and central highlands and is watered by the upper reaches of the Tana River. Its name derives from the Nyika, a Bantu tribe.
·landform and climate distinctions **10**:423e
·map, Kenya **10**:424

Nyika Plateau, high grassy tableland (6,500–8,550 ft [1,981–2,606 m]) in Rumphi District, northern Malawi. It is a tilted block extending over an area of 900 sq mi (2,330 sq km) from the Mzimba Plain northeast to the edge of the Great Rift Valley and Lake Nyasa. Its undulating surface is covered with montane grassland and patches of evergreen forest (including the southernmost occurrence of the Mulanje tree [*Juniperus procera*]) and is marked by occasional peaks and ridges (Nganda, 8,851 ft; Chejara, 8,200 ft). A bevelled surface at 5,500 ft rings the plateau. High rainfall generates the formation of perennial rivers in *madambo*, broad grass-covered depressions, and their flow through deep erosional valleys. The main streams include the North Rumphi, Rumphi, Runyina, and North Rukuru rivers. The higher soils are too poor for cultivation and the plateau is virtually uninhabited. Nyika Plateau National Park (founded 1965) covers 360 sq mi of the plateau surface and supports big game and trout fishing.
·map, Malawi **11**:361

Nyima (people): *see* Nubians.

Nyingmapa (Buddhist sect): *see* Rnying-ma-pa.

Nyiragongo, Mount, in the Virunga Mountains of east central Africa, lies in the Park of the Volcanoes, Zaire, near the border with Rwanda, 12 mi (19 km) north of Goma. It is an active volcano, 11,385 ft (3,470 m) high, with a main crater 1.3 mi (2 km) wide and 820 ft deep containing a liquid lava pool. Some older craters on the mountain are noted for their plant life.
1°31′ S, 29°15′ E
·formation, location, and activity **19**:162f

Nyíregyháza, town and county seat of Szabolcs-Szatmár *megye* (county), northeastern Hungary. It is a principal settlement of the upper Tisza River region coinciding approximately with the traditional Nyírség, an area for centuries a wilderness of dunes and swamps from which the land was gradually reclaimed. More recently, the discovery of natural gas and the possibilities of irrigation have improved the region's economic prospects. The original settlement was virtually destroyed during the Turkish occupation. The history of the modern town really begins with the colonization of the Nyírség in the mid-18th century when Count Ferenc Károlyi, the prime mover behind the program, brought in many Slovak immigrants. The region is thickly settled with scores of *tanya* (small, isolated farms or groups of farmsteads). The sandy soils are well suited to potatoes and tobacco. In addition, sunflowers, poppy seeds, melons, apricots, apples, and grapes are produced. There are large numbers of pigs and cattle. Nyíregyháza is still chiefly a market centre for the area's agricultural products. Light industry, including the manufacture of hosiery and other consumer goods, has developed since World War II, and it has become an important road and rail junction leading to the town of Záhony in the extreme north of the county. Nyíregyháza is also a health resort (Sóstó Spa is a medicinal salt lake) and recreation centre. Pop. (1970 prelim.) 70,640.
47°59′ N, 21°43′ E
·map, Hungary **9**:22

Nyitra (Czechoslovakia): *see* Nitra.

Nykøbing Falster, city, seat of Storstrøms *amtskommune* (county), western Falster Island, Denmark, on Guldborg Sund (sound). Founded around a 12th-century castle where Christopher II died (1332) and where Christian V was married (1667), it is now a commercial and industrial centre with sugar refineries, tobacco factories, shipbuilding yards, and fisheries. Medieval remains include ruins of the castle (destroyed 1757) and a 15th-century Gothic church that was part of a monastery until 1532. The house where Peter the Great lived in 1716 is now a local museum. Pop. (latest census) city, 20,775; (1971 est.) mun., 25,907.
54°46′ N, 11°53′ E
·map, Denmark **5**:582

Nyköping, town and port, seat of the *län* (county) of Södermanland, southeastern Sweden, on the Baltic Sea, at the mouth of Nyköpingsån (river). The town is first mentioned in 1250, but it originated earlier as a marketplace near the heights where Nyköpingshus (castle) was built *c.* 1260. With time this became one of Sweden's principal strongholds, notably during the time of Gustav I Vasa and Charles IX; the latter lived there as duke from 1568. The town's industrial beginnings go back to ironworks and brass works powered by falls within the town; flour and textile mills and furniture factories appeared later. As a shipping centre Nyköping has been supplanted by Oxelösund. Historic buildings include the 12th-century St. Nicolai Church and the restored ruins of Nyköpingshus, now housing the Södermanland Museum. Pop. (1970) 46,686.
58°45′ N, 17°00′ E
·map, Sweden **17**:848

nylon, synthetic plastic material usually, but not always, manufactured as a fibre from long-chain polyamides; developed in the 1930s by a research team headed by a U.S. chemist, Wallace H. Carothers, working for E.I. du Pont de Nemours & Company. The successful achievement of a useful fibre by chemical synthesis using carbon, hydrogen, nitrogen, and oxygen—that is, chemical elements readily available from air, water, and coal or petroleum—stimulated expansion of research on polymers, leading to a rapidly proliferating family of synthetics.

Nylon can be drawn, cast, or extruded through spinnerets from a melt or solution to form fibres, filaments, bristles, or sheets to be manufactured into yarn, fabric, and cordage; and it can be formed into molded products. It has high resistance to wear, heat, and chemicals.

When cold-drawn, it is tough, elastic, and strong. Most generally known in the form of fine and coarse filaments in such articles as hosiery, parachutes, and bristles, nylon is also used in the molding trade, particularly in injection molding, where its toughness and ability to flow around complicated inserts are prime advantages.

Polyamides such as nylon may be made from a dibasic acid and a diamine or from an amino acid that is able to undergo self-condensation, or its lactam, characterized by the functional group −CONH− in a ring, such as ϵ-caprolactam. By varying the acid and the amine, it is possible to make products that are hard and tough or soft and rubbery. Whether made as filaments or as moldings, polyamides are characterized by a high degree of crystallinity, particularly those derived from primary amines. Under stress, orientation of molecules begins to occur, which continues until the specimen is drawn to about four times its initial length, a property of particular importance in filaments.

Two of the commonest ingredients used to synthesize nylon, adipic acid and hexamethylenediamine, each contain six carbon atoms, and the product has been named nylon-6,6. When caprolactam is the starting material, nylon-6 is obtained, so-named because it has six carbon atoms in the basic unit.

·bearing design and construction **11**:252d
·chemical composition and qualities **18**:47f
·colloidal polymer synthesis **4**:859b
·formation, structure, and properties **14**:767c
·photoengraving application **14**:303a
·plastics production and uses **14**:516a
·plate preparation in printing **14**:1069d
·production, types, and nomenclature **7**:264a
·rope and cable manufacturing **15**:1145g
·sail and rigging development **16**:163b
·synthetic fibre chemical development **4**:130d; illus. 129
·textile industry thread production **18**:175f
·thermoplastic adhesive polymers **1**:89h

nymph, in Greek mythology, the generic name of a large class of inferior female divinities. The nymphs were usually associated with fertile, growing things, such as trees, or with water. They were not immortal but were extremely long-lived and were on the whole kindly disposed toward men. They were distinguished according to what sphere of nature they were connected with. The Oceanids, for example, were sea nymphs; the Nereids inhabited both saltwater and freshwater; the Naiads presided over springs, rivers, and lakes. The Oreads (*oros*, "mountain") were nymphs of mountains and grottoes; the Napaeae (*nape*, "dell") and the Alseids (*alsos*, "grove") were nymphs of glens and groves; the Dryads or Hamadryads presided over forests and trees.

Italy had native divinities of springs and streams and water goddesses (called Lymphae) with whom the Greek nymphs tended to become identified.

·folklore and mythology **8**:405b

nymph, in entomology, a sexually immature form usually similar to the adult and found in such insects as grasshoppers and cockroaches, which have incomplete, or hemimetabolic, metamorphosis (*see* metamorphosis). Wings, if present, develop from external wing buds after the first few molts. The body proportions of the first nymphal stages are quite different from those of the adult. During each successive growing stage (instar) the nymph begins to resemble the adult more closely.

In contrast to nymphs that develop on land, the aquatic young of dragonflies, stoneflies, and mayflies are sometimes called naiads. Their metamorphosis is more complicated, involving a change to a different environment. The naiad, with gills and other modifications for an aquatic existence, crawls out of the water and becomes a winged adult after its last molt.

·bug hatching, behaviour, and development **8**:846d; illus.
·cicada infestation of tree roots **8**:1037f
·dragonfly larva structure and behaviour **13**:507h
·Ephemeroptera food chain role **6**:903d; illus. 904
·exopterygote insects' immature stage **2**:67h
·louse life cycle **14**:373h; illus. 374
·orthopteran nymph and adult comparison **13**:743g
·respiration of mayflies and dragonflies **15**:753f; illus.
·river habitat adaptations **15**:890b
·segment increase in proturan hexapods **1**:1024d
·tick and mite life cycle stages **1**:19e; illus. 20

Nymphaeaceae (aquatic plant family): *see* water lily.

Nymphaeales 13:428, the water-lily order, containing 4 families with 8 genera and about 70 species of tropical and temperate freshwater flowering plants. Most water lilies are species of the genera *Nuphar*, *Nymphaea*, and *Victoria*. Fanwort (*Cabomba*), hornwort (*Ceratophyllum*), and water shield (*Brasenia*) are other members of the order. Water lilies provide food for wildlife but have little importance for man except as aquatic weeds or cultivated ornamentals.

The text article covers distribution, life cycle, ecology, characteristics, flowering, biochemistry, and evolution of the Nymphaeales. It also includes an annotated classification of the order.

REFERENCES in other text articles:
·angiosperm features and classification **1**:881h
·orchid phylogenic status comparisons **13**:655b

RELATED ENTRIES in the *Ready Reference and Index:*
fanwort; hornwort; water lily; water shield

nymphaeum, ancient Greek and Roman sanctuary consecrated to water nymphs. Originally denoting a natural grotto with springs and streams, traditionally considered the habitat of nymphs, the term later referred to an artificial grotto or a building filled with plants and flowers, sculpture, fountains, and paintings. The nymphaeum served as a sanctuary, a reservoir, and an assembly chamber where weddings were held. The rotunda nymphaeum, common in the Roman period, was borrowed from such Hellenistic structures as the Great Nymphaeum of Ephesus. Nymphaea existed at Corinth, Antioch, and Constantinople; the remains of nearly 20 have been found in Rome; and others exist as ruins in Asia Minor, Syria, and North Africa. The term nymphaeum was also used in ancient Rome to refer to a bordello and also to the fountain in the atrium of the Christian basilica.

In the 16th century, the nymphaeum became a feature of Italian gardens. Different classes of nymphs were appropriate to different kinds of locality. The characteristic garden nymphaeum was associated with fresh water and usually with springs. The site of a spring was usually enclosed in a formal building, as at the Villa Giulia at Rome, but sometimes in a natural or semi-natural cave. The line of demarcation between a nymphaeum and a grotto (*q.v.*) is not always clear, but the nymphaeum puts greater emphasis on the presence of a supposed semi-deity.

Nymphalidae, butterfly family including the anglewing, fritillary, mourning cloak, thistle butterfly, and viceroy (*See* brush-footed butterfly). Sometimes separated into another family is the milkweed butterfly (*q.v.*) group, which includes the monarch butterfly (*q.v.*).

·classification and general features **10**:830f
·mimicry in patterns of warning colours **12**:216a

Nymphenburg, palace, formerly the summer residence outside Munich of the Wittelsbachs, the former ruling family of Bavaria. Begun in 1664 by the Prince Elector Maximilian II Emanuel, the late Baroque palace was enlarged and annexes were built through the reign of Maximilian III Joseph (1745–77). The renowned gardens were designed in 1701 by Carbonet, a pupil of Le Nôtre, who had laid out the gardens of Versailles for Louis XIV. Distributed throughout the garden are many late Baroque garden pavilions of note, including the Pagodenburg (1716–19), the Badenburg (1718–21), and the Amalienburg (1734–39), whose interior by François de Cuvilliés is one of the masterpieces of Rococo decoration.

·Munich's museums and landmarks **12**:617h
·Rococo interior design **9**:715e; illus. 716

Nymphenburg, Alliance of (1741), secret agreement by France, Bavaria, and Spain, later joined by Saxony and Prussia, to oppose Maria Theresa's expansionist policy.

·Austrian Succession diplomacy **2**:458f

Nymphenburg porcelain, German hard-paste, or true, porcelain produced in Bavaria from around the middle of the 18th century until the present day. The first factory was established in 1747 at the castle of Neudeck, outside Munich, by Maximilian III Joseph, elector of Bavaria. The wares produced here are sometimes called "Neudeck–Nymphenburg." In 1761 the factory was moved to Nymphenburg, where it still operates. The tableware and vases produced by Nymphenburg are mainly reminiscent of Meissen (*see* Meissen porcelain), even to their use of the ozier, or basketwork, pattern borders. Nymphenburg's only truly original contribution in this kind of ware was a *réchaud*, or food warmer.

The fame of Nymphenburg rests on its figures, particularly those in the Rococo style modelled between 1754 and 1763 by Franz Anton Bustelli. Bustelli is perhaps best known for his stock figures from the commedia dell'arte, although he also made singers and instrumentalists and cavaliers and ladies, the latter sometimes on a common base. Characteristic of Bustelli's figures are their attenuated bodies and delicate faces; their heightened, theatrical gestures, often emphasized by the dramatic modelling of drapery; and their movement and rhythm, which are accentuated by Bustelli's treatment of Rococo scrollwork.

Bustelli was succeeded as *Modellmeister* by Dominikus Auliczek, who introduced the Empire, Neoclassical style at Nymphenburg; his most interesting works are models of animals and birds. In 1797, Auliczek was succeeded by Johann Peter Melchior, another exponent of Neoclassicism, who had worked at the Höchst and Frankenthal factories before joining Nymphenburg; he is known for the excellent figures he modelled there between 1800 and 1810.

The Nymphenburg factory mark, adopted in 1754, is the Bavarian shield of arms.

·ceramic factory Rococo figure tradition **14**:910h

nymphomania, the behaviour pattern reflecting the need on the part of a woman for incessantly repeating sexual intercourse with

an indefinite succession of men, wherein the need is not due to unrequited genital sexual excitement. The woman may or may not experience orgasm; but even with orgasm the sexual need remains unsatisfied. In psychological usage, the definition does not depend on numbers of partners (that is, promiscuity) but on the motivation that drives the woman to those numbers.
·behaviour patterns and causes **16**:609e

Nymphs, Hill of the, at Athens, where in ancient times the nymphs were worshipped.
·Athens' topography **2**:265a

Nymphus (Latinized Greek: "Bridegroom"), in Mithraism, one of the seven degrees of initiation.
·mystery cult initiation **12**:782a

Nymph with Bittern, sculpture by William Rush.
·Thomas Eakins' portrayal of Rush's work **5**:1119c

Nymylan (Arctic people): *see* Chukchi.

Nyngan, town, central New South Wales, Australia, in the Western Plains region, on the Bogan River. The town, the name of which is derived from an Aboriginal word variously meaning "mussel," "crayfish," and "many streams," developed after the arrival (1882) of a rail line from Dubbo (100 mi [160 km] southeast) and was proclaimed a municipality in 1891. At the junction of the Barrier and Mitchell highways, with air and rail links to Sydney (290 mi southeast), Nyngan serves a pastoral region (wool sheep) and produces wheat in years of adequate rainfall. The Macquarie Marshes, breeding ground for fowl, lie 40 mi north. Pop. (1971 prelim.) 2,478.
31°34′ N, 147°11′ E
·map, Australia **2**:400

Nynorsk language: *see* New Norwegian language.

Nyo, 16th-century Burmese courtier who wrote in the verse form known as *yadu.*
·Burmese court literary style **17**:234g

Nyong-et-Kélé, department, Cameroon.
·area and population table **3**:698

Nyong-et-Mfoumou, department, Cameroon.
·area and population table **3**:698

Nyong-et-Soo, department, Cameroon.
·area and population table **3**:698

Nyong River, in southwestern Cameroon, rises 25 mi (40 km) east of Abong Mbang, in the northern rain forest. Its 400-mi (640- km) course, which roughly parallels that of the lower Sanaga River, follows a westerly direction, emptying into the Gulf of Guinea of the Atlantic Ocean at Petit Batanga, 40 mi south-southwest of Edéa.

Rapids break the flow of the river at Mbalmayo and Déhané. Navigation is possible for about 155 mi for small steamboats from April to November between Abong Mbang and Mbalmayo.
3°17′ N, 9°54′ E
·map, Cameroon **3**:696

Nyoro, people of the Western Lacustrine Bantu group inhabiting the area east of Lake Albert in Uganda between the Victoria Nile and the Kafu River. They speak a Bantu language.

The Nyoro once consisted of two main ethnic groups: the light-skinned, aristocratic, slender Hima, nomadic pastoralists who composed a small minority of the population; and the dark-skinned Negroid, more heavily built Iru, who traditionally were hoe cultivators. A third group, the Bito, were of Nilotic origin; in the period preceding British rule, the Bito provided the head of the state, or *mukama.* Today, however, most Nyoro are alike in physical type, though members of the Bito group still control the government and many Nyoro claim to be of Hima descent.

The Nyoro are predominately agriculturalists, growing sorghum, millet, plantain, sweet potatoes, and beans for food crops. The main economic crops are cotton and tobacco. Fish exports are also a significant source of revenue. Animal husbandry is important.

The Nyoro live in scattered villages that may contain up to 50 or 60 homesteads. Polygyny is practiced. There are about 150 patrilineal clans. Members of the same clan do not marry one another.

The state was traditionally a feudal system of chiefs and lords owing allegiance to and deriving their power from the hereditary *mukama.* Nyoro religion centred upon communication through mediums with the spirits of ancestors and of natural phenomena. There was a pantheon of god-kings (*bacwezi*) who were believed to have formed a dynasty that ruled prior to the Bito.
·numbers, tribal affiliations, and culture **6**:109h

Nyphus, Augustinus: *see* Nifo, Agostino.

Nyquist interval, after Harry Nyquist, U.S. communications engineer; in communications, the maximum time separation that can be given to regularly spaced instantaneous samples of a wave of given bandwidth in order to completely determine the wave form of the signal; its numerical value is half that of the band width.
·communications bandwidth theory **18**:88f; illus.

Nysius, insect genus of the family Lygaeidae (order Heteroptera). For *N. ericae, see* chinch bug; for *N. vinitor, see* lygaeid bug.

Nyssa (plant): *see* tupelo.

Nyssaceae, family of flowering plants in the order Cornales.
·classification and general features **5**:177h

Nystad, Treaty of (Sept. 10 [Aug. 30, old style], 1721), the treaty of peace between Sweden and Russia, signed at Nystad (modern Uusikaupunki, on the southwest coast of Finland); it ended the Great Northern War (1700–21) and also the period of Sweden's military greatness. Sweden was forced to cede to Russia the territories of Livonia, Estonia, Ingria, part of Karelia, and several islands in the Baltic Sea, giving Peter I the Great the "window" on the Baltic that he had sought. Russia retained Vyborg but returned the rest of Finland to Sweden and paid Sweden an indemnity. The overall result of the war, which this treaty confirmed, was that Russia replaced Sweden as the predominant power in the Baltic.
·background and significance **6**:1095c; map 1097
·Peter I's expansion achievements **14**:158h
·Russian gains diplomatic implications **16**:51f
·Russian territorial gains **8**:96b
·Swedish territorial concessions **16**:319c

nystagmus, involuntary back and forth, up and down, or circular movement of the eyes. There are two types of nystagmus with respect to movement. In one type, called pendular nystagmus, the movements are even and rhythmical; in the other, called jerk nystagmus, the movements are jerky and quicker in one direction than in the other. Pendular nystagmus may result from loss of central vision early in life. A subtype of pendular nystagmus, called spasmus nutans, occurs in infants. It is associated with nodding of the head and with holding the neck in a twisted position. Affected infants usually recover in a few months. Jerk nystagmus, the more common type, may occur normally when one is dizzy from being rotated or when one is watching from the window of a moving vehicle: the slow phase of the nystagmus occurs while one's gaze is fixed on a particular object; the quick phase, when his eyes return to their original position. Jerk nystagmus may also result from intoxication with barbiturate drugs or from disease of those portions of the inner ear the function of which is concerned with balance. Disease of the brainstem may also result in jerk nystagmus.
·brainstem structures and functions **12**:1004c
·ear tests for equilibrium function **5**:1131a
·equilibrium sense and rotation **16**:551e
·eye movement comparisons **7**:99b
·mechanoreception of rotatory movements **11**:808b

nystatin, a pale yellow antibiotic obtained from an actinomycete fungus that is active against other fungi.
·synthesis and fungicidal action **1**:990a

Nyugat circle, group of Hungarian writers who came to prominence with a left-wing literary periodical, *Nyugat* ("The West"; founded 1908), which helped lift Hungarian letters to a new and remarkable level. Its editor (until 1929) was Mihály Babits, poet and brilliant translator.
·political orientation of major authors **10**:1258e

Nyx, sometimes known as NIGHT, in Greek mythology, female personification of night but also a great cosmogonical figure, feared even by Zeus, the king of the gods. According to one tradition, she was the daughter of Chaos and mother of numerous primordial powers, including Sleep and Death. Another tradition made her the daughter and successor of Phanes, a creator god; she continued to advise her own successors (Uranus, her son by Phanes; Cronus, youngest son of Uranus; and Zeus) by means of her oracular gifts. Throughout antiquity she caught the imagination of poets and artists but was seldom worshipped.

Nzakara, people of central Africa.
·Central African Republic population **3**:1104d

Nzekwu, Onuora (b. 1928, Kafanchan, Nigeria), teacher, writer, and editor who, in successfully exploring the relationship of the educated Ibo to his traditional culture, exposes the internal conflict of old and new values in the young African.

His first novel, *Wand of Noble Wood* (1961), portrays in moving terms the futility of a Western pragmatic approach to the problems created by an African's traditional religious beliefs. In the hero of *Blade Among the Boys* (1962) traditional practices and beliefs ultimately take precedence over half-absorbed European and Christian values.

Nzekwu has written a third novel, *Highlife for Lizards* (1965), and a children's book, *Eze Goes to School* (with Michael Crowder, 1963). He taught for nine years before becoming editorial assistant and then editor of *Nigeria Magazine.* Foundation grants have enabled him to travel in Europe and America.
·African novel tradition **13**:293a
·contributions and theme **1**:240b

Nzérékoré, headquarters of Guinée Forestière supraregion and capital of Nzérékoré Region, in southeastern Guinea; it lies at the intersection of roads from Ganta (Liberia), Danané (Ivory Coast), Kankan, and Macenta. The chief trade centre (rice, cassava, pepper, tobacco, kola nuts, and palm oil and kernels) for the Guerze (Kpelle), Mano (Manon), and Kono (Konon) peoples of the forested Guinea Highlands, it ships wood, palm products, and coffee to the Liberian port of Monrovia (165 mi [265 km] southwest) for export. Nzérékoré has a sawmill and plywood factory and is the site of a hospital, secondary school, museum, and a Roman Catholic mission. The iron-rich Nimba Range in the southern part of the region contains Mt. Nimba (5,748 ft [1,752 m]), the highest point in the country. Pop. (latest est.) region, 210,000.
7°45′ N, 8°49′ W
·map, Guinea **8**:467

Nzinga, Queen, 15th-century Angolan ruler.
·Portuguese contact and migration leadership **17**:279b

O, symbol for the chemical element oxygen (*q.v.*).

O Abolicionismo, political tract by Joaquim Nabuco de Araújo published in 1883.
·slavery's effects on society **3**:146b

Oahu, island, Honolulu County, Hawaii, U.S., separated from the islands of Kauai and Molokai by the Kauai and Kaiwi channels. Of volcanic origin with an area of 604 sq mi (1,564 sq km), Oahu ("gathering place") is third in size and the most populated of the Hawaiian Islands. Two parallel mountain ranges, the Koolau and Waianae, are connected by a central plateau. Oahu is the site of Honolulu (the state capital), Pearl Harbor, and Waikiki. Other important cities are Aiea, Kailua, Kaneohe, and Wahiawa. Pop. (1970) 630,528; (1980) 762,874.
21°30′ N, 158°00′ W
·groundwater pressure and well discharge **17**:516g
·map, Hawaii **8**:675
·urbanization, population, and transportation **8**:674f

OAIS (old age, invalidity, and survivor insurance programs): *see* social security.

oak, common name for 300 or more species of ornamental and timber trees and shrubs constituting the genus *Quercus* of the beech family (Fagaceae), distributed throughout the North Temperate Zone and at high altitudes in the tropics.

Black oak (*Quercus velutina*)
Walter Dawn

Many trees commonly called "oak" are not *Quercus* species—*e.g.*, African oak, Australian oak, bull oak, Jerusalem oak, poison oak, river oak, she-oak, silky oak, tanbark oak, Tasmanian oak, and tulip oak.

An oak has alternate, simple, deciduous or evergreen leaves with lobed, toothed, or entire margins. The male flowers are borne in pendent yellow catkins, appearing with or after the leaves. Female flowers occur on the same tree, singly or in two- to many-flowered spikes; each flower has a husk of overlapping scales that enlarges to hold the fruit, or acorn, which matures in one to two seasons.

Oaks can be separated into three groups, sometimes considered subgenera: white oaks (*Leucobalanus*) and red or black oaks (*Erythrobalanus*) have the scales of the acorn cups spirally arranged; in the third group (*Cyclobalanus*) the scales are fused into concentric rings. A white oak has smooth, non-bristle-tipped leaves, occasionally with glandular margins. The acorns mature in one season, have sweet-tasting seeds, and germinate within a few days after their fall.

A red or black oak has bristle-tipped leaves, the lining of the acorn shell is hairy, and the bitter fruits mature at the end of the second growing season. Both groups can also be distinguished by the size, shape, and structure of the summerwood pores. Live oaks, with evergreen foliage, belong to the red or black oak group.

Many oaks native to the Mediterranean area have economic value: galls produced on the twigs of the Aleppo oak (*Q. infectoria*) are a source of Aleppo tannin, used in ink manufacture; commercial cork is obtained from the bark of the cork oak; and the tannin-rich kermes oak (*Q. coccifera*) is the host of the kermes insect, once harvested for a dye contained in its body fluids

Two eastern Asian oaks also are economically valuable: the Mongolian oak (*Q. mongolica*) provides useful timber, and the Oriental oak (*Q. variabilis*) is the source of a black dye as well as a popular ornamental. Other cultivated ornamentals are the Armenian, or pontic, oak (*Q. pontica*), chestnut-leaved oak (*Q. castaneaefolia*), golden oak (*Q. alnifolia*), Holm, or holly, oak (*Q. ilex*), Italian oak (*Q. frainetto*), Lebanon oak (*Q. libani*), Macedonian oak (*Q. trojana*), and Portuguese oak (*Q. lusitanica*).

Popular Asian ornamentals include the blue Japanese oak (*Q. glauca*), daimyo oak (*Q. dentata*), Japanese evergreen oak (*Q. acuta*), and sawtooth oak (*Q. acutissima*). The English oak, a timber tree native to Eurasia and northern Africa, also is cultivated in other areas of the world as an ornamental.

Acorns provide food for small game animals and are used to fatten swine and poultry. Red- and white-oak lumber is used in construction, flooring, furniture, millwork, cooperage, and the production of crossties, structural timbers, and mine props.

Oaks can be propagated easily from acorns and grow well in rich, moderately moist soil or dry, sandy soil. They are hardy and long-lived (up to 700 years or more) but are not shade-tolerant and may be injured by leaf-eating organisms or oak wilt fungus.

The taxonomy of the genus *Quercus* is confusing because of the occurrence of many natural hybrids.
·climatic influence on vegetation **4**:728e
·domesticated plant centres of origin **5**:938c
·Fagales genus description **7**:140b; illus.
·forestry and broadleaf characteristics **7**:529c
·furniture use as carcass wood **7**:782e
·geographical distribution in forests **7**:539h
·Peking region oaks in forest zones **14**:3e
·plant disease symptoms illus. **5**:883
·Q. coccifera dye source **7**:140d

RELATED ENTRIES in the *Ready Reference and Index:*
black oak; bur oak; chestnut oak; cork oak; English oak; live oak; pin oak; red oak; scrub oak; white oak; willow oak

oak apple (gall): *see* gall wasp.

Oak Bay, district municipality, southwestern British Columbia, Canada, on southeastern Vancouver Island, facing Haro Strait. It is an eastern residential suburb of Victoria, the provincial capital, and is a popular retirement community, with one of the highest percentages of persons over 65 in Canada. Inc. 1906. Pop. (1971 prelim.) 18,364.
48°27′ N, 123°18′ W

Oakham, town in Leicestershire, England, and former county town (seat) of Rutland, until that county was absorbed by Leicestershire in 1974. A market town, it lies in the Vale of Catmose and is headquarters of the Cottesmore Hunt (a fox-hunting body). By the market place, with its octagonal Butter Cross, stands the Norman castle, originally a fortified manor house. All Saints Church, dating from *c.* 1190, is mainly Perpendicular in style. The grammar school was founded in 1584. Light industries include hosiery and shoe manufacture. Pop. (1971 prelim.) 6,411.
52°40′ N, 0°43′ W
·map, United Kingdom **18**:866

Oak Harbor, town, Island County, northwest Washington, U.S., on Whidbey Island in Puget Sound. It was settled in 1849 by seafaring men, and its first industry was shipbuilding. Dutch immigrants arrived in 1890 and began developing the rich farmland. The chief agricultural products are dairy foods, wheat, poultry, and truck-garden vegetables. The town has become a major trade and recreation centre on the island. The Whidbey Island Naval Air Station is 5 mi (8 km) north. Deception Pass State Park is midway between Oak Harbor and Anacortes. The town is surrounded by giant oak trees, whence its name. Inc. 1915. Pop. (1980) 12,271.
48°18′ N, 122°39′ W

Oakland, city, seat (1873) of Alameda County, California, U.S., on the eastern shore of the San Francisco Bay. Its site was once part of Rancho San Antonio, where Moses Chase leased farmland and laid out the town of Clinton (later named Brooklyn). In 1851 Horace W. Carpentier started a transbay ferry service to San Francisco and acquired a town site (1852) to the west of Brooklyn, naming it Oakland for the oak trees on the grassy coastal plain. In 1854 Carpentier and his associates extended the area and incorporated it as a city. Oakland and Brooklyn—separated by a slough that had been bridged in 1853—became amalgamated in 1872.

Chosen as the terminus of the first transcontinental railroad (1869), Oakland developed its harbour. After the 1906 San Francisco earthquake it received an influx of refugees. The 8¼-mi-long San Francisco–Oakland Bay Bridge to San Francisco (opened 1936) and military and naval installations (built in the 1940s) stimulated expansion; industrial growth has been heavy and diversified. The city is headquarters for Kaiser Industries. Its deepwater port (on an estuary between Alameda Island and the bay shore) covers 19 mi of waterfront in the outer, middle, and inner harbours.

Metropolitan Oakland International Airport fronts the bay to the southwest. Lake Merritt, a saltwater lagoon near the central business district, is a wild fowl refuge surrounded by parkland. Jack London Square honours the

Downtown Oakland, Calif., from a corner of Lake Merritt
Ewing Galloway

author who spent his boyhood years there. Oakland is the site of Mills College (1852), the College of the Holy Name (1868), and the California College of Arts and Crafts (1907). Pop. (1950) city, 384,575; (1980) city, 339,288; San Francisco–Oakland metropolitan area (SMSA), 3,252,721.
37°47′ N, 122°13′ W
·map, United States **18**:908
·metropolitan population density map **18**:930

Oakland, town, seat (1872) of Garrett County, extreme western Maryland, U.S., in the Allegheny Mountains, near the West Virginia line. Established in 1851, Oakland serves a resort and agricultural area. Inc. 1861. Pop. (1980) 1,994.
39°25′ N, 79°24′ W

Oakley, Annie, originally PHOEBE ANNE OAKLEY MOSES (b. Aug. 13, 1860, Darke County, Ohio—d. Nov. 3, 1926, Greenville), noted markswoman who starred in "Buffalo Bill's Wild West" show, where she was often called "Little Sure Shot."

As a youngster Annie Moses (she changed the spelling to Mozee) won acclaim for marksmanship and, after winning a shooting match in Cincinnati with ranking marksman Frank E. Butler, she became a nationally known figure. Later Butler and Annie were married and together they successfully toured the vaudeville circuits and circuses until 1885, when the "Butler and Oakley" team joined the Buffalo Bill (William F. Cody) show and remained with it for 17 years. So startling were "Little Missy's" performances and so enthusiastic her audience response that she was given top billing as "Miss Annie Oakley (a name she selected for herself), the Peerless Lady Wing-Shot," while her husband served as manager and attendant. At 30 paces, she could hit the thin edge of a playing card, a dime tossed in the air, and the end of a cigarette held in Butler's lips. Once, when performing in Berlin, she obliged Crown Prince William (later Emperor William II) by performing the cigarette act while the prince held the cigarette. In 1901 she was severely injured in a train wreck but recovered and continued her performances.

One of many reminders of this remarkable woman was the use of her name to denote a complimentary ticket. The hole customarily punched in such a free pass recalled the bullet holes that she fired into small cards during her theatrical performances. A free ticket thus was long known as an "Annie Oakley." After 1901 Butler and Oakley continued to tour and give lessons and demonstrations in trapshooting. A reliable biography is Walter Havighurst's *Annie Oakley of the Wild West* (1954).

Oakley, Kenneth Page (b. 1911), British anthropologist noted for his studies of fossil man.
·archaeological dating technique **1**:1082b
·hominid classification by behaviour **8**:1044a

oak moss (*Evernia prunastri*), a fructose lichen valued in perfumery for its heavy, oriental fragrance and as a fixative base. It grows on mountain areas throughout much of the Northern Hemisphere. The pale greenish-gray thallus, three to eight centimetres long, is palmately branched, ending in pointed tips. The upper surface is green and warty with pale-gray reproductive bodies (soredia). Disc-shaped sexual bodies (apothecia) are rare. The under surface is whitish with a faint net-like pattern. A less common species (*E. furfuracea*), having similar properties, is often included under the same common name, which is a translation of the French *mousse de chêne*.

Oak moss was used in perfumery as early as the 16th century. Baskets filled with it have been found in the ancient royal tombs of Egypt, but whether it was intended for per-

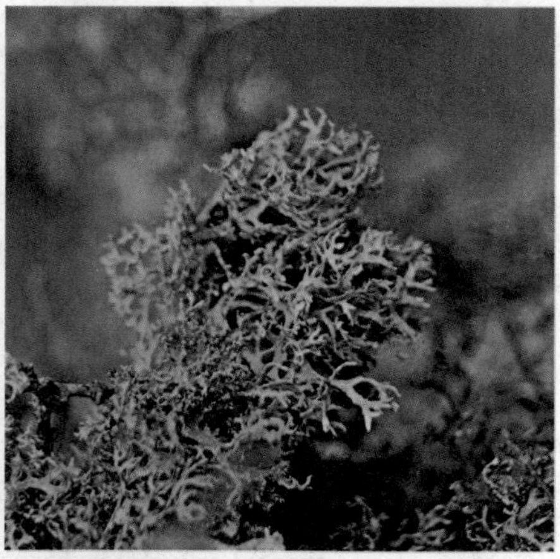

Oak moss (*Evernia prunastri*)
Vernon Ahmadjian

fume or for making bread is not known. Oak moss contains a starchy edible substance. A mixture of usnic and evernic acids extracted from it are used in drugs for treating external wounds and infections.

Oak Park, village, Cook County, Illinois, U.S., western suburb of Chicago. Settled in 1833 by Joseph Kettlestrings, who operated a sawmill on the east bank of the Des Plaines River, it was originally called Oak Ridge and served as a stopping place for farmers taking their produce into Chicago. In 1871, after the Chicago fire, the population grew rapidly. The village, primarily residential with some light industry, has many buildings designed by architect Frank Lloyd Wright, who once lived and maintained his studio there. Ernest Hemingway, Nobel and Pulitzer prize-winning novelist, was born and grew up there. Inc. 1901. Pop. (1980) 54,887.
41°53′ N, 87°48′ W
·Frank Lloyd Wright buildings **9**:240c

Oak Ridge, city on the Anderson–Roane county line, east central Tennessee, U.S., in a high valley along the southern slope of Black Oak Ridge, between the Cumberland and the Great Smoky mountains; it is officially a part of the Knoxville Standard Metropolitan Statistical Area. The site, at the eastern end of a remote 58,000-ac (23,000-ha) tract, was selected in 1942 as the headquarters for the U.S. wartime atomic-energy program, known as the Manhattan Project. Originally called Clinton Engineer Works, it was chosen because it was reasonably isolated, yet accessible to power, water, transportation, and manpower. The town, built by the U.S. Army Corps of Engineers behind security fences, reached a peak population of 75,000 in 1945, which later declined to about 30,000.

Oak Ridge now bears only slight resemblance to the wartime boomtown. In 1949 the fences were removed; in 1953 roads through the plant areas were opened and for the first time land was leased for private construction. In 1955 Congress provided for the sale of property in Oak Ridge, and in September 1956 the first government-owned house was sold. The community voted to incorporate as a city in 1959.

The present economy depends mainly on production and research in the nuclear-energy field. A number of nuclear-related and electronic industries specialize in radioactive pharmaceuticals, electronic instrumentation, and machine making and toolmaking. The Oak Ridge Associated Universities comprise a nonprofit educational and research corporation of 41 southern universities.

The city is the site of the American Museum of Atomic Energy and the Oak Ridge National Laboratory's Graphite Reactor, which is a national historic landmark. Melton Hill Dam, a Tennessee Valley Authority river-control project, is at the southwest edge of Oak Ridge, and Norris Dam on the Clinch River is 17 mi (27 km) north. Pop. (1980) 27,662.
36°01′ N, 84°16′ W
·map, United States **18**:908

Oak Ridge National Laboratory, atomic energy research facility located in Oak Ridge, Tenn.
·rare-earth separation research **15**:522b

Oaks, one of the English classic horse races, an event for three-year-old fillies, established 1779, and run over a 1½-mile (about 2,400-metre) course at Epsom Downs, Surrey. Epsom is also the site of the Derby, another classic race. The Oaks was named for the nearby residence of the 12th earl of Derby, whose horse Bridget won the first running. For winners since 1946, *see* sporting record.

Oakville, town, Halton County, Ontario, Canada, southwest of Toronto, on Lake Ontario at the mouth of Oakville Creek. It was founded in 1830 by Col. William K. Chisholm, who established shipbuilding yards there. It was originally incorporated in 1857, and in 1962 it amalgamated with Trafalgar Township to form the new town of Oakville, which, occupying 69,000 ac (28,000 ha) and spreading northward for 14 mi (23 km) from Lake Ontario, claims to be Canada's largest town in area. An industrial community, it is the site of one of Canada's largest automobile plants. Pop. (1971) 61,483.
43°27′ N, 79°41′ W

Oamaru, borough and port of Waitaki County, southeast South Island, New Zealand. Established (1853) as a grazing run, the town, whose name means "place of Maru," was made a borough in 1866. Situated on a small bay that was being used by whalers and sealers at the close of the 18th century, the town began to improve its harbour in 1872. It has become the chief port for the north Otago district and the Waitaki River Valley of Canterbury—areas of sheep, cattle, grain, and fruit farming. Oamaru lies on the highway between Christchurch (152 mi [245 km] north) and Dunedin (78 mi south) and on the South Island Main Trunk Railway. Industries include dairy factories, freezing works, woollen and flour mills, and plants manufacturing concrete products, motor bodies, coal tar and gas, appliances, and furniture. Oamaru is a commercial fishing port and the place of origin of the Corriedale sheep, and was the site where, in 1852, Walter B.D. Mantell discovered the remains of the moa, an extinct giant flightless bird. Pop. (1971) 13,078.
45°06′ S, 170°58′ E
·map, New Zealand **13**:44

Oannes, in Mesopotamian mythology, an amphibious being who taught mankind wisdom. Oannes, described by the Babylonian priest Berosus (flourished 3rd century BC), had the form of a fish but with the head of a man under his fish's head and under his fish's tail the feet of a man. In the daytime he came up to the seashore of the Persian Gulf and instructed mankind in writing, the arts, and the sciences. Oannes was probably the emissary of Ea, god of the freshwater deep and of wisdom.
·Berosus' account of creation **11**:965e

OAO 2 (Orbiting Astronomical Observatory), U.S. satellite launched Dec. 7, 1968.
·space exploration, table 2 **17**:364

oar, device for propelling or steering a boat, consisting essentially of a long pole with a broad blade at one end, usually supported near the centre. A similar device, but usually shorter and lighter, is used without supports for propelling canoes; it is called a paddle.
·naval ship design history **12**:885e
·rowing and sculling techniques **2**:1157c
·sailing ship design development **16**:157b
·ship propulsion development **16**:677c

oarfish (*Regalecus glesne*), large, long, sinuous fish of the family Regalecidae (order

Lampridiformes), found throughout the tropics in rather deep water. A ribbon-shaped fish, very thin from side to side, the oarfish may grow to a length of about 9 metres (30½ feet) and a weight of 300 kilograms (660 pounds). It is shining silvery, with long, red, oarlike pel-

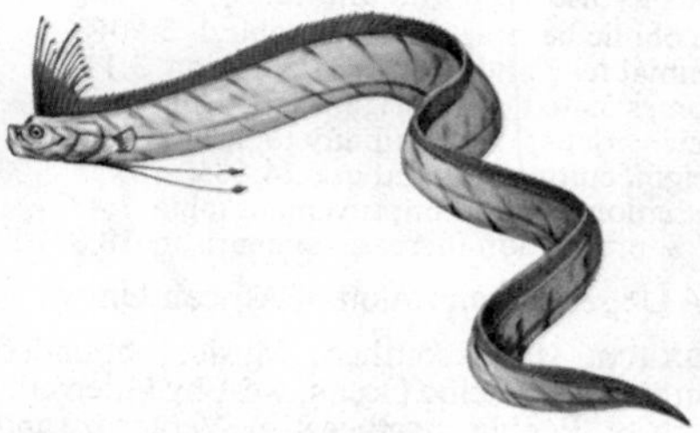

Oarfish (*Regalecus glesne*)

Painting by Richard Ellis

vic fins and a long, red dorsal fin that rises as a manelike crest on top of the head. Seldom seen at the surface, it is credited as the "sea serpent" of some reported sightings. Another name, ribbonfish, is often applied to it and to the related, also band-shaped, dealfish (Trachipteridae) and Lophotidae.

·classification and general features **2**:273d

OAS (America): *see* Organization of American States.

OAS (Algeria): *see* Organisation de l'Armée secrète.

Oasis, southeastern Algeria, largest *wilāyah* (province) of Algeria, entirely within the Sahara. Its area, combined with that of Saoura *wilāyah*, is 780,617 sq mi (2,021,800 sq km). Main centres of population are the oasis towns of Laghouat, Ghardaïa, Touggourt, and Ouargla (*qq.v.*), the *wilāyah* capital. Pop. (1970 est.) 573,000.

·area and population table **1**:563
·map, Northern Algeria **1**:560

oasis, fertile tract of land that occurs in a desert wherever a perennial supply of fresh water is available. Oases vary in size from a hectare or so around small springs to vast areas of naturally watered or irrigated land. Underground water sources account for most oases; their springs and wells, some of them artesian, are supplied from sandstone aquifers whose intake areas may be more than 800 kilometres (500 miles) away, as at al-Khārijah Oasis (Kharga) and ad-Dākhilah Oasis (Dakhla) in the Libyan Desert. Two-thirds of the total population of the Sahara are sedentary peoples living in oases and depending on irrigation; these areas have temperatures conducive to rapid vegetative growth. In all Saharan oases the date palm is the chief tree and the main source of food, while in its shade are grown citrus fruits, figs, peaches, apricots, vegetables, and cereals such as wheat, barley, and millet.

·Arabian Desert agricultural importance **1**:1055c
·Egypt's topography and population **6**:449d
·microclimatic advection and evaporation **12**:117d
·Moroccan Sahara, illus., **18**:Terrestrial Ecosystem, Plate IV
·wind action role in formation **19**:843f

Oaş Mountains, central Romania. 46°50′ N, 25°20′ E

·Romanian physical geography **15**:1045f

oasthouse urine disease: *see* iminoglycinuria.

Oastler, Richard (b. Dec. 20, 1789, Leeds, Eng.—d. Aug. 22, 1861, Harrogate, Yorkshire), industrial reformer known in the north of England as the "Factory King," who from 1831 conducted a campaign for shorter working hours that was in part responsible for the Ten Hours Act of 1847. He was prominent during the period of the political and social reform movement called Chartism, although he had no direct connection with it.

In 1830 Oastler, who was managing a large Yorkshire agricultural estate, learned of the evils of child labour in factories and immediately began a journalistic attack on the employment of young children. The next year he started his agitation for the ten-hour day. Although he was essentially conservative on other issues and never opposed industrialism as such, he considered the existing factory system inimical to what he called the "natural right to live well." He found allies in the House of Commons, especially Lord Ashley and Michael Thomas Sadler. After many rejections, a ten-hour law (sometimes known as Lord Ashley's Act) was passed in 1847.

For his opposition to the Poor Law of 1834 (under which indigent farm labourers could be compelled to work in factories for substandard wages), his employer fired him (May 1838) and had him imprisoned for debt (December 1840–February 1844). While in jail,

Oastler, detail of an engraving by J. Posselwhite (1798–1884) after a painting by B. Garside

By courtesy of the trustees of the British Museum; photograph, J.R. Freeman & Co. Ltd.

Oastler elaborated his social theories in the *Fleet Papers* (3 vol., 1841–43; named for the prison). Afterward, he edited a weekly newspaper. *Tory Radical: The Life of Richard Oastler*, by Cecil Herbert Driver, appeared in 1946.

Oates, Titus (b. Sept. 15 1649, Oakham, Rutland—d. July 12/13, 1705, London), renegade Anglican priest who fabricated the "Popish Plot" of 1678. Oates's allegations that Roman Catholics were plotting to seize power caused a reign of terror in London and strengthened the anti-Catholic Whig Party. The son of an Anabaptist preacher, Oates was expelled from the Merchant Taylors School, London, in 1665. Although he managed to be ordained into the Church of England, he was imprisoned for perjury while serving as a curate in Hastings in 1674. He escaped and joined the navy as a chaplain but was soon dismissed for misconduct.

Oates, engraving by R. White, 1679; in the National Portrait Gallery, London

By courtesy of the National Portrait Gallery, London

Nevertheless, early in 1677 Oates became chaplain to the Protestants in the household of the Roman Catholic Henry Howard, 6th duke of Norfolk. There he had his first extensive contacts with Catholic circles. At the same time, his new acquaintance, the fanatical anti-Jesuit Israel Tonge, urged him to profit by betraying Catholics to the government. Oates, therefore, set out to gather information about them and their activities. He joined the Roman Catholic Church in March 1677, but before long he was expelled from seminaries at Valladolid in Spain and at St. Omer in the Netherlands. Returning to London in 1678 he rejoined Tonge, and the pair invented an account of a vast Jesuit conspiracy to assassinate King Charles II and place his Roman Catholic brother James, duke of York, on the throne. They publicized the tale through a prominent justice of the peace, Sir Edmund Berry Godfrey, and their revelations seemed even more plausible after Godfrey was found murdered in October 1678.

In the wave of terror that swept London, Oates was hailed as the saviour of his country. His testimony was responsible for the execution of some 35 persons, but as the frenzy subsided, inconsistencies were discovered in his story. In June 1684 the Duke of York was awarded damages of £100,000 in a libel suit against Oates. After the Duke of York came to the throne as King James II in 1685, Oates was convicted of perjury, pilloried, flogged, and imprisoned. But when James was deposed in 1688, Oates was released and granted a pension. He became a Baptist in 1693 but was expelled from that church eight years later. He died in obscurity.

·Charles II assassination rumour hysteria **4**:56a
·Dryden's verses on the Popish Plot **5**:1064c
·Pepys's implication in Godfrey's murder **14**:37c
·Popish Plot and Shaftesbury's strategy **16**:613h
·Popish Plot charges **3**:247f

oat grass, common name for perennial plants in two genera of grasses, *Arrhenatherum* and

Oat grass (*Arrhenatherum elatius*)

Syndication International—Photo Trends

Danthonia (family Poaceae). About six species of tall grasses, native to temperate Europe and Asia, comprise the genus *Arrhenatherum*. Tall oat grass (*A. elatius*), introduced into many countries as a pasture grass, grows wild in many areas and is considered a weed, especially *A. elatius* variety *bulbosum*, commonly called onion couch for its bulblike basal stems. Most of the more than 100 species of the genus *Danthonia* are native to temperate regions of the Southern Hemisphere. They are important forage grasses in Australia, New Zealand, and South America. Australian species are commonly called wallaby grasses. Poverty oat grass (*D. spicata*), a grayish-

green, mat-forming species, grows on dry, poor soil in many parts of North America.
·habitation and dominance areas **8**:285a

oath, a statement, assertion, or solemn affirmation usually involving the penalty of divine retribution for intentional falsity, often used in legal procedures. It is not certain that the oath was always considered a religious act; such ancient peoples as the Germanic tribes, Greeks, Romans, and Scythians swore by their swords or other weapons. These peoples, however, were actually invoking a symbol of the power of a war god as a guarantee of their trustworthiness, thus indicating the religious intent behind such acts.

The oath, which thus has its origins in religious customs, has become an accepted practice in modern nonreligious areas, such as in secular legal procedures. A person serving as a witness in court proceedings, such as in Anglo-American legal systems, often has to swear by the following oath: "I do solemnly swear that the testimony I am about to give will be the truth, the whole truth, and nothing but the truth. So help me God."

The swearing of an oath before divine symbols reaches back at least to the Sumerian civilization (4th–3rd millennia BC) of the ancient Near East and to ancient Egypt, where one often swore by his life, or *ankh* ("oath"), which literally means "an utterance of life." In the Hittite Empire of the 14th–13th centuries BC various oath gods (e.g., Indra and Mithra) were appealed to in agreements between states. Mithra, an Iranian god who became the main deity of a Hellenistic mystery (salvatory) religion, was viewed as the god of the contract (*i.e.*, the guardian of oaths and truth). Members of various mystery religions often bound themselves together in a sacred society set apart from the profane world by swearing a holy oath (*sacramentum*).

In Eastern religions (*e.g.*, Hinduism), an Indian, for example, might swear an oath with water from the holy river Ganges, which is a positive symbol of the divine, in his hand.

Among the Western religions (*e.g.*, Judaism, Christianity, and Islām) oaths have been used widely. The Hebrew term *shevuʿah* ("oath") comes from the same root as the number seven, which refers back to a vow (*q.v.*), in which seven ewe lambs were used as witnesses, that the patriarch Abraham made with the Philistine king Abimelech in Genesis, chapter 21. In Judaism, two kinds of oaths are forbidden: (1) a vain oath, in which one attempts to do something that is impossible to accomplish, denies self-evident facts, or attempts to negate the fulfillment of a religious precept, and (2) a false oath, in which one uses the name of God to swear falsely, thus committing a sacrilege. Because oaths are not to be taken lightly, though they may be undertaken to strengthen one's spiritual and moral character and resolve, Judaism generally discourages the taking of oaths. At the time of Jesus in the 1st century, oaths were often misused; and for that reason were often rebuked in early Christianity. In Islām, a Muslim may make a *qasam* ("oath"), in which he swears, for example, upon his life, soul, honour, or faith. Because the *qasam* is primarily a pledge to God, a false oath is considered a danger to one's soul.

At the present time, the most frequent use of the oath occurs when a witness in an authorized legal inquiry states his intention to give all pertinent information and to tell only the truth in relating it. The precise formula varies, usually being prescribed by statute. In Anglo-American legal practice, testimony will not be received unless the witness is subject to some sanction for falsity, either by taking an oath or giving affirmation (*q.v.*). Although it gives little assurance against false testimony, the law nevertheless provides that false testimony under oath constitutes the crime of perjury. Civil-law nations use it more sparingly; they generally do not permit parties to the case to testify under oath, and they make the oath voluntary with many others. In these countries the oath is often administered after testimony.
·covenant and law in ancient world **5**:226f
·evidence proof and law **7**:1d *passim* to 4f
·Mithraic connection with friendship **12**:288h

Oath of the Horatii, oil painting executed in 1784 in Rome by the French artist Jacques-Louis David. The theme depicted is a Roman legend that was also the subject of Pierre Corneille's 17th-century tragedy *Horace*. David's painting, now in the Louvre, is one of the masterpieces of Neoclassical art.
·Neoclassical style beginnings **5**:520d

Oatlands, town, east central Tasmania, Australia, northwest shore of Lake Dulverton, lower Midlands (region). A military-convict settlement, established near the site in 1826, became a staging point between Hobart (40 mi [64 km] south) and Launceston and was made a municipality in 1861. Pop. (1971 prelim.) 548.
42°18′ S, 147°21′ E

oats, cereal plants belonging to the genus *Avena* and their edible starchy grains. The flowering and fruiting structure, or inflorescence, of the plant is made up of numerous branches bearing florets that produce the caryopsis, or one-seeded fruit.

Oats (*Avena sativa*)
Grant Heilman

Wild oats were first found growing in western Europe, apparently as a weed mixed with barley, and spread from there to other parts of the world. Common oats are grown in cool, temperate regions; red oats, more heat tolerant, are grown mainly in warmer climates. Among cereals, oats are second only to rye in ability to survive in poor soils. With sufficient moisture, oats will grow on soils that are sandy, low in fertility, or highly acidic.

Although oats are used chiefly as livestock feed, some are processed for human consumption, especially as breakfast foods. Rolled oats, flattened kernels with the hulls removed, are used mostly for oatmeal; other breakfast foods are made from the groats, kernels with husks removed, but unflattened. Oat flour is not suitable for bread but is used to make cookies and puddings. Oat grains are high in carbohydrates and contain about 13 percent protein and 7.5 percent fat. They are a source of calcium, iron, vitamin B_1, and nicotinic acid. The grain is used as livestock feed in both pure form and in mixtures. The straw is used for animal feed and bedding. Oat plants provide good hay and, under proper conditions, furnish excellent grazing and make good silage (stalk feed preserved by fermentation). In industry oat hulls are a source of furfural, a chemical used in various types of solvents.

In the early 1970s estimated annual world production was nearly 56,600,000 metric tons, produced on about 80,000,000 acres (32,000,000 hectares). Improved varieties, permitting increased yields, have resulted in production remaining steady while the required acreage declined. Leading producing countries included the U.S., the U.S.S.R., Canada, France, Poland, the U.K., West Germany, Australia, and New Zealand. The demand for oats was somewhat reduced by competition from hybrid corn and alfalfa.
·alcoholic beverages source, table 1 **5**:901
·animal feed and oatmeal production **3**:1165d
·domesticated plant origins **5**:939d
·new varieties' susceptibility to disease **5**:881b
·origin, cultivation, and use **14**:585f
·radiation induced improvement table **7**:482
·U.S. production increase comparison **18**:932d

OAU: *see* Organization of African Unity.

Oaxaca, state, southern Mexico, bounded south by the Pacific Ocean, west by Guerrero, north by Puebla, northeast by Veracruz, and east by Chiapas. The state's 36,820-sq-mi (95,364-sq-km) territory includes most of the Isthmus of Tehuantepec (*see* Tehuantepec, Isthmus of) on its Pacific side. The Sierra Madre del Sur ends at the isthmus, which is low, hot, and arid. The Atlantic lowlands near Veracruz are hot and humid, but most of the state enjoys mild, healthful conditions.

Remains of pre-Columbian Zapotec and Mixtec edifices are found at Mitla and Monte Albán. Descendants of these Indians, divided into more than 15 major tribes, form the majority of the population. Oaxaca is an agricultural and mining area, the varied products of which include corn (maize), wheat, coffee, sugarcane, tobacco, fibres, and tropical fruits. Cigarettes, soap, and Indian blankets are manufactured for local consumption. Its mountains are veined with gold, silver, uranium, diamonds, onyx, and other deposits. Although the rail network is incomplete in Oaxaca, air connections are good, there are several Pacific ports, and the Pan-American Highway traverses the state, passing through Oaxaca (*q.v.*), the state capital. Pop. (1970) 2,172,000.
·area and population table **12**:71
·Aztec and Mixtec visual art features **1**:685e
·Monte Albán II culture **11**:939c
·population density map **12**:71

Oaxaca, in full OAXACA DE JUÁREZ, capital of Oaxaca state, southern Mexico, lies in the fertile Oaxaca valley, 5,436 ft (1,657 m) above sea level. Founded in 1486 as an Aztec garrison and conquered by the Spaniards in 1521, Oaxaca has played an important role in Mexican history, being also the home of Benito Juárez and Porfirio Díaz, two of Mexico's most famous presidents. Oaxaca is noted for its 16th-century art and architecture, for the nearby Mixtec ruins of Mitla and the Zapotec ruins of Monte Albán, and for its colourful handicraft market. The Benito Juárez University of Oaxaca was founded there in 1955. Oaxaca is accessible by highway, railroad, and air. Pop. (1970) 99,509.
17°03′ N, 96°43′ W
·map, Mexico **12**:68

Pottery display in the market at Oaxaca city, Mexico
Plessner International

Ob, Gulf of, Russian OBSKAYA GUBA, large inlet of the Kara Sea indenting northwestern Siberia, between the peninsulas of Yamal and Gyda, in the Russian Soviet Federated Socialist Republic. The gulf forms the outlet for the Ob River, the delta of which is choked by a huge sandbar.

The gulf is about 500 miles (800 kilometres) in length and has a breadth varying between 20 and 60 miles. The depth of the sea at this point is 33–40 feet (10–12 metres). Its eastern coastline is steep and rugged; the west is low-lying and marshy. Novy Port (New Port) is the main port of the gulf.
69°00′ N, 73°00′ E
·map, Soviet Union **17**:322

Oba, also called AOBA, volcanic island of Vanuatu (formerly the New Hebrides) in the southwest Pacific Ocean, 30 mi (50 km) east of Espíritu Santo. Its 154-sq-mi (399-sq-km) area is dominated by a 4,000-ft (1,200-m) peak with a lake in its crater. The headquarters of the Melanesian Mission is located at Lolowai, a good harbour on the east coast. The island has a hospital and exports copra. Pop. (1979) 7,772.
15°25′ S, 167°50′ E

Obadiah, Book of, fourth of the Old Testament books that bear the names of the Twelve (Minor) Prophets. The book, which consists of 21 verses forming only one chapter, is the shortest of all biblical books. It purports to be a record of "the vision of Obadiah." Nothing is known of the prophet except for his name, which means "servant of Yahweh."

In the book, Edom, a longtime enemy of Israel, is castigated for its refusal to help Israel repel foreigners who invaded and conquered Jerusalem. To many scholars this reference suggests a date of composition after the Babylonian conquest of 586 BC. Other scholars, noting the anti-Edomite sentiments in II Kings 8:20–22, consider a date as early as the 9th century BC also probable.

In addition to pronouncing a judgment against Edom (1–14), the book announces the approach of the day of judgment for all nations (15–16), when God's power will be manifest, all evil will be punished, and the righteous will be renewed. The final verses prophesy the restoration of the Jews to their native land (17–21).
·judgment of God theme **2**:920h
·prophet's anonymity **2**:920h

Obadya ha-Ger, also called ABDIAS THE PROSELYTE (fl. *c.* 1102), Italian monk who converted to Judaism. He is known for his documents of musical notation, which show a symbiosis of Western and Near Eastern styles of religious music.
·work style and modernity **10**:206h

Ōbaku, one of the three Zen sects in Japan, founded in 1664 by the Chinese priest Yin-yüan (Japanese Ingen); it continues to preserve elements of the Chinese tradition in its architecture, religious ceremonies, and teachings.

Although the sudden, abrupt means of achieving insight as developed by the Rinzai sect are practiced by Ōbaku monks, invocation of the name of the Buddha Amida (*nembutsu*) is also used.

In the early 1980s the number of Ōbaku temples was reported at more than 460 and its membership at nearly 321,000. The head temple of the sect is the Mampuku-ji in Kyōto.

Oban, holiday resort and fishing port, Argyll and Bute district, Strathclyde region, Scotland. It was originally established as a fishing station (1786) and was created a burgh (town) in 1811; it became a local commercial and tourist centre for the western Scottish Highlands by the late 19th century. Regular sea links are maintained with the island groups of the Inner and Outer Hebrides. Economic activities include cattle markets, fishing, whis-

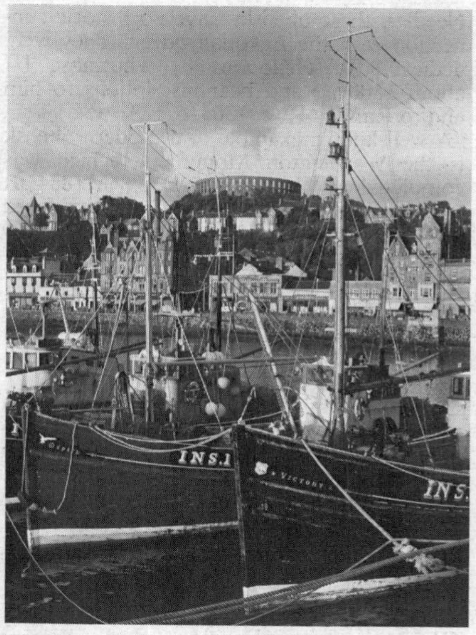
Oban harbour with MacCaig's Tower in the background
A.F. Kersting

ky distilling, tweed and decorative glass manufacture, and tourism. Pop. (1974 est.) 6,410.
56°25′ N, 5°29′ W
·map, United Kingdom **18**:866

Obando, José Maria (b. 1795, Cauca, New Granada, now Colombia—d. 1861), Colombian president (1853–54), whose violent character and career were representative of the political and military leaders of 19th-century Colombia.

Obando fought for the Spanish crown during most of the Latin-American war for independence. He finally joined Simón Bolívar's revolutionary forces but opposed Bolívar's centralist government (Gran Colombia) after independence was achieved. Many historians believe that Obando was responsible for the assassination of Bolívar's lieutenant, Marshal Antonio de Sucre, whose death helped clear the way for Obando's rise in the 1830s to the vice presidency and ministry of war in the State of New Granada.

After attempting an unsuccessful revolution against the Conservative Party government (1838–40), Obando fled to Peru. Following his return to New Granada after the election victory of the Liberal Party (1849), he was elected president in 1853. The high point of his one-year regime was the adoption of the Liberal constitution (1853). Opposition from radicals and conservatives led to his overthrow the following year. After another period of exile, Obando returned to New Granada in 1860, where he was killed fighting in a civil war.

Obbenites, followers of Obbe Philips, who in 1534 organized an independent Anabaptist sect in the Netherlands on a pattern established by Konrad Grebel in Zürich. As part of the left-wing Zwinglian Reformation, they demanded complete independence from the state, espoused pacifism, restricted Baptism to believers, rejected oath taking, and viewed faith as a deliberate exercise of free will. Philips eventually abandoned the group. Menno Simons, a converted Roman Catholic priest, joined the group in 1536 and was ordained an elder; he later broke away and established his own group, the Mennonites. Persecution forced the Dutch Anabaptists into the Rhineland and Danzig areas, where their numbers multiplied.

obbligato (Italian: "obligatory"), in music, essential but subordinate instrumental part. In, for example, an 18th-century aria with trumpet obbligato, the trumpet part, although serving as accompaniment to the voice, may be as brilliant in its writing as that of the voice itself. The term obbligato accompaniment has a more specialized meaning in some 18th-century music (*see* accompaniment).
·evolution of style in Classical era **12**:718h

obedience, religious, voluntary submission of one person to the authority of another for religious motives. In monastic orders it is a requirement for admission and a test of a person's qualifications. In a broader sense, religious obedience is adherence to God's precepts.
·Jewish Torah and human response **10**:287f
·monastic rule requirements **12**:338b
·Ṣūfī masters in Islām **9**:922g
·Ṣūfī monastic discipline **9**:947c

Obelia, genus of invertebrate marine animals of the class Hydrozoa (phylum Cnidaria).

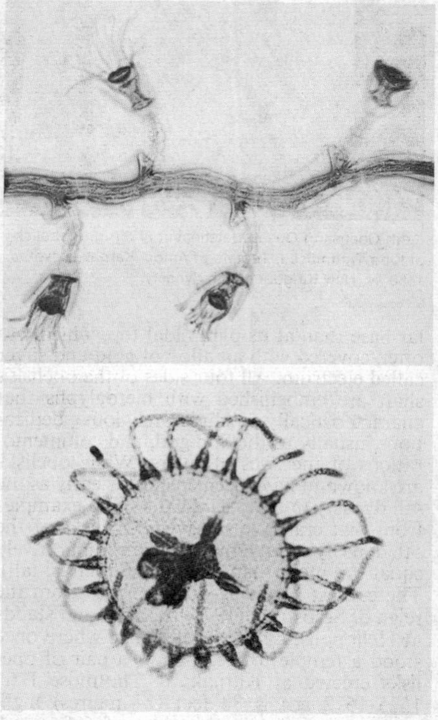
(Top) Polyp (magnified 40 ×) and (bottom) medusoid stages of *Obelia*
Grant Heilman—EB Inc.

The genus, widely distributed in all the oceans, is represented by many species. The animal begins life as a polyp—a stalklike form attached to the ocean bottom or some other solid surface.

The polyp produces medusae, or jellyfish, which in turn produce polyps. Rootlike filaments sent out by the polyp serve as organs of attachment. The stalk lengthens and develops a mouth encircled by tentacles. Buds arise from the stalk, developing into additional polyps, until a treelike colony forms. Polyp modifications (blastostyles) without mouth or tentacles develop buds that separate as medusae and swim away. Eggs and sperm produced by the medusae fertilize and give rise to ciliated larvae (planulae) that swim freely for a time, then settle permanently onto a surface and develop into new polyps.
·life cycle, illus. 1 **15**:703
·life cycle stages and development **15**:678e
·skeleton and polyp, illus. 1 **16**:820

obelisk, tapered monolithic pillar, originally erected in pairs at the entrances of ancient Egyptian temples. The Egyptian obelisk was carved from a single piece of stone, usually red granite from the quarries at Aswān. It was designed to be wider at its square or rectangu-

(Left) Obelisk of Queen Hatshepsut and (right) obelisk of King Thutmose I, Temple of Amon, Karnak, Egypt, *c.* 1550 BC, New Kingdom, 18th dynasty

H. Roger-Viollet

lar base than at its pyramidal top, which was often covered with an alloy of gold and silver called electrum. All four sides of the obelisk's shaft are embellished with hieroglyphs that characteristically include religious dedications, usually to the Sun god, and commemorations of the lives of rulers. While obelisks are known to have been erected as early as the 4th dynasty (*c.* 2613–*c.* 2494 BC), no examples from that era have survived. Obelisks of the 5th dynasty's Sun temples were comparatively squat (no more than 10 feet [3.3 metres] tall). The earliest surviving obelisk dates from the reign of Sesostris I (1971–1928 BC) and stands at Heliopolis, a suburb of Cairo, where once stood a temple to Re. One of a pair of obelisks erected at Karnak by Thutmose I (*c.* 1525–1512 BC) is 80 feet (24 metres) high, square at the base with sides of 6 feet (1.8 metres), and 143 tons in weight.

An inscription on the base of Hatshepsut's obelisk at Karnak indicates that the work of cutting that particular monolith out of the quarry took seven months. In the Temple of Hatshepsut at Thebes are scenes of the transport of the obelisk down the Nile by barge. At its destination workmen put the shaft into place upon its detached base by hauling it up a ramp made of earth and tilting it.

Other peoples, including the Phoenicians and the Canaanites, produced obelisks after Egyptian models. During the time of the Roman emperors, many obelisks were transported from Egypt to present-day Italy. At least 12 went to the city of Rome itself, including one now standing in the Piazza San Giovanni in Laterano that was originally erected by Thutmose III (reigned 1504–1450 BC) at Karnak. With a height of 105 feet (32 metres) and a square base with sides of 9 feet (2.7 metres) that tapers to a square top with sides of 6 feet, 2 inches (1.88 metres), it weighs approximately 230 tons and is the largest ancient obelisk extant.

Late in the 19th century the government of Egypt divided a pair of obelisks between the United States and Great Britain. One now stands in Central Park, New York City, and the other on the Thames embankment in London. Although they are known as Cleopatra's Needles, these obelisks have no historic connection with the Egyptian queen. They were dedicated at Heliopolis by Thutmose III about 1500 BC and bear inscriptions to him and to Ramses II (*c.* 1304–*c.* 1237 BC).

A well-known example of a modern obelisk is the Washington Monument, which was completed in Washington, D.C., in 1884. It was constructed of blocks of granite and faced with Maryland marble; it towers 555 feet (169 metres) and contains an observatory and interior elevator and stairs.

·branchless tree cultic symbolism **3**:1175h
·Egyptian monumental architecture **19**:250g
·Thutmose's dedication and present site of Cleopatra's Needles **18**:367a

Obelisks (16th century), appellation of a manuscript, by the German theologian Johann Eck, that contained observations on Martin Luther's Ninety-five Theses.

·observation and criticism of Ninety-five Theses **11**:191d

Obera, 16th-century Paraguayan Guaraní chief who led a messianic movement.

·new tribal religious movements **18**:701d

Oberammergau Passion play, pageant that is performed, during a brief season, once every 10 years in the Upper Bavarian village of Oberammergau. The tradition of this passion play (German *Passionsspiel*), begun in 1634, is maintained to fulfill a vow made by villagers during an outbreak of the plague (1633).

·pageant origins and customs **13**:865d

oberek (dance): *see* mazurka.

Oberfrohna (East Germany): *see* Limbach-Oberfrohna.

Oberharz (mountains): *see* Harz.

Oberhausen, city, Nordrhein-Westfalen *Land* (North Rhine-Westphalia state), northwestern West Germany, on the Rhein-Herne-Kanal, within the Ruhr industrial belt, adjoining Essen (east), Mülheim (south), and Duisberg (southwest). The city developed around a railway station (named for the Oberhaus Castle on the Emscher River) after the discovery in 1846 of coal and limonite iron ore deposits on the uninhabited Lipperheide (heath). It was chartered in 1874 and it absorbed the older neighbouring towns of Sterkrade and Osterfeld in 1929. Historic landmarks include Sterkrade Abbey (1150), Holten Fortress (1307), and the 16th-century moated castle of Vondern. The Stadthalle (city hall) is a notable example of the city's modern structures. Oberhausen has a workers' high school and a teacher-training academy, several art galleries, and a civic theatre.

Heavy industry is based on steel and coal, along with zinc refineries, dye works, railway workshops, and a large thermoelectric plant. Steam boilers, wire rope, glass, chemicals, sugar, porcelain, and cigars are manufactured. The St. Anthony Iron Works (1758–1876) was the first in the Ruhr. Pop. (1980 est.) 229,613.
51°28′ N, 6°50′ E

·map, Federal Republic of Germany **8**:47

Oberland, Bernese (Switzerland): *see* Bernese Alps.

Oberlin, city, Lorain County, north central Ohio, U.S., southwest of Cleveland. In 1833 the Rev. John L. Shipherd, a Presbyterian minister, and Philo P. Steward, a former missionary to the Choctaw Indians, founded the community and established the Oberlin Collegiate Institute (1834; designated a college after 1850) to train ministers and teachers for work in the West. The name was chosen to honour Johann Friedrich Oberlin, an Alsatian pastor and philanthropist. Charles Martin Hall, an Oberlin alumnus, developed the electrolytic process for the mass production of commercial aluminum there in 1886. Oberlin

The Seeley G. Mudd Learning Center (rear), Oberlin College, Ohio

Joan Anderson—Oberlin College

was a centre for various reform movements, including coeducation and nonsegregation; it was also a station on the Underground Railroad. The Anti-Saloon League was founded there in 1893.

The city is nestled amidst fertile farmlands; its economic and cultural life centres on the college. Inc. village, 1846; city, 1950. Pop. (1980) 8,660.
41°18′ N, 82°13′ W

·map, **18**:United States of America, Plate 14
·Oberlin College founding and development **13**:520g

Oberlin, Johann Friedrich (b. Aug. 31, 1740, Strasbourg, Fr.—d. June 1, 1826, Walderbach, now in West Germany), Lutheran pastor and philanthropist for whom Oberlin (Ohio) College (1833) is named. He spent his life transforming poor parishes in the Vosges region of France into vital spiritual communities.

Oberlin was graduated from the University of Strasbourg in 1758. He was a teacher until he became a pastor in 1767 at Walderbach, the centre of his life's activity.

Johann Friedrich Oberlin, engraving by Henri Charles Müller

By courtesy of the Bibliotheque Nationale, Paris; photograph, J.P. Ziolo

In an effort to raise his parishioners' living standards, Oberlin provided village schools and thus began one of the first systems for supervising and instructing children of working parents. His advanced methods in education, which foreshadowed the work of the German educator Friedrich Froebel (1782–1852), originator of the kindergarten, won the respect of adults, who also came to him for instruction. To encourage better crop production, he held seminars for the exchange of agricultural information based on local experiments, and he made possible the purchase of modern farm implements, bought in bulk and sold at cost, and financed through a bank that he founded. After subsidizing young men to learn crafts in Strasbourg, he established factories for local industries.

Interdenominational in outlook, Oberlin welcomed Calvinists and Roman Catholics to his communion services. His admiration of the French philosopher Jean-Jacques Rousseau and the Swedish mystic Emanuel Swedenborg was reflected in his sermons. His humanism was expressed in his enthusiastic welcome of the French Revolution, and he was honoured by both revolutionary and imperial governments of France for his work.

Oberlin's name was given to the town and college in Ohio as well as to the Oberlinhaus, a German centre for treatment of the deaf, mute, and blind.

·modern preschool program and influence **14**:990b

Oberon, the "king of faërie" in the French medieval poem *Huon de Bordeaux* (*q.v.*). He was introduced into English literature by a prose translation (*c.* 1534) of the French ro-

Oberon (lower right) with Puck and Titania, illustration by J. Moyer Smith to a 1906 edition of *A Midsummer Night's Dream*

By courtesy of the trustees of the British Museum; photograph, J.R. Freeman & Co. Ltd.

mance made by Lord Berners, famed as the translator of Froissart's *Chronicles*. The Oberon of Shakespeare's *Midsummer Night's Dream* owes much to the Berners translation. Shakespeare's Oberon inspired the romantic epic *Oberon* (1780) by the German poet Christoph Wieland (*q.v.*), used, in turn, for Carl Maria von Weber's opera (1826) with the same title.

·German Romantic opera **13**:587a
·Weber's operas **19**:714d

Oberon, one of the five satellites of Uranus.

·Uranus' satellites **18**:1038f; table

Oberösterreich, English UPPER AUSTRIA, *Bundesland* (federal state), northern Austria, bordering West Germany and Czechoslovakia on the west and north and bounded by the states of Niederösterreich (Lower Austria) on the east and Steiermark (Styria) and Salzburg on the south. Lying between the Inn and the Enns rivers and traversed by the Danube River, Oberösterreich has an area of 4,625 sq mi (11,979 sq km). Part of the Austrian granite plateau, called the Mühlviertel (Mühl district, after its main river), lies north of the Danube and toward the east. Sloping gently from northwest to southeast, its undulating surface has poor soil and is extensively wooded, with grassland at lower altitudes. The southern part of the state is Alpine, comprising limestone mountains and the Flysch (sandstone) foothills and including most of the Salzkammergut (*q.v.*) resort region with its many lakes and high peaks. The upland surfaces are barren, with extensive forests on the lower slopes and meadows and some arable land in the valleys. Although the Salzkammergut has long been settled because of its salt resources, Bad Ischl, Gmunden, and Ebensee are the only towns of any size. The most economically important part of the state lies between the Danube and the Alps. The forested hills of the Hausruck and Kobernausser Wald in the centre have deposits of brown coal (lignite).

The region's salt deposits attracted settlement in prehistoric times, especially the civilization at Hallstatt (*q.v.*), and later in the Roman period. In 1192, the Traungau (the nucleus of modern Oberösterreich) became an appendage of the duchy of Austria, and the 10th-century name Ostarichi (eastern region) was extended to areas west of the Enns. Oberösterreich was divided from Niederösterreich *c.* 1450, and Linz became its capital in 1490 (following Enns, Steyr, and Wels). Although the official name until 1918 was Österreich ober der Enns, it was popularly called Oberösterreich. During the *Anschluss*, or "union," with Germany (1938–45), Oberösterreich became the larger Reichsgau Oberdonau (Upper Danube Reich District), afterward reverting to a *Bundesland*.

After World War II, the population was increased by more than 100,000 refugees, and the density is now the highest for all *Bundesländer* except Vienna and Vorarlberg. Ethnically the people are German, and more than 90 percent are Roman Catholic. The principal towns are Linz, Wels, Steyr, Traun, Braunau, Bad Ischl, Gmunden, Leonding, Ebensee, Ried, Vöcklabruck, and Enns (*qq.v.*).

Farming uses over half of the land surface and forestry about one-third. More than half of the agricultural land is grass, mainly in the highest regions. The most intensive stock farming is done in the Alpine foreland, where grain (wheat, rye), sugar beets, potatoes, and fruit are raised. Large tracts of forest, especially in the Alps, are state owned.

Salt is mined in the Salzkammergut and brown coal in the Hausruck; farther west, granite and limestone are quarried. The state leads the nation in major electric power stations. After 1959, oil wells near Ried were in production. There was massive industrial development during the *Anschluss* and after World War II. The important Linz chemical industry and ironworks and steelworks, the Lenzing staple-fibre plant, and the aluminum plant at Ranshofen all date from that period. Other activities include dairying, food processing, beet-sugar refining, brewing, the manufacture of agricultural machinery and textiles, tanning, and sawmilling. The Danube has retained its medieval role in commerce, and Oberösterreich is well served by rail and road. Air traffic at Linz is of minor importance. Pop. (1979 est.) 1,223,444.

·geography, population, and economy **2**:441f; table 444
·map, Austria **2**:443

Oberprokuror, English CHIEF PROCURATOR, secular official appointed by Peter I the Great in 1721 to supervise the Holy Synod of the Russian Orthodox Church.

·Peter's church policy **14**:160e
·Peter the Great's church control **6**:157g

Oberrealschule (education): *see* Realschule.

Oberstdorf, village, Bavaria (Bayern) *Land* (state), southern West Germany, south of Kempten. It is one of the best known summer and winter sports resorts in the Allgäuer Alpen (Allgau mountains). A cable railway serving the Nebelhorn (7,297 ft [2,224 m]) is one of the world's longest (15,912 ft). Chartered in 1495, most of the village was rebuilt after a fire in 1865. Dairying is a local occupation, and there is some spinning and weaving. Pop. (1979 est.) 11,557.
47°24′ N, 10°16′ E

Oberstein (West Germany): *see* Idar-Oberstein.

Oberth, Hermann (Julius) (b. June 25, 1894, Hermannstadt, Transylvania, now in Romania), a founder of modern astronautics.

Oberth

By courtesy of the National Air & Space Museum, Smithsonian Institution, Washington, D.C.

The son of a prosperous physician, he studied medicine in Munich, but his education was interrupted by service in the Austro-Hungarian Army during World War I. Wounded in the war, he found time to pursue his studies in astronautics. He performed experiments to simulate weightlessness and worked out a design for a long-range, liquid-propellant rocket that his commanding officer sent to the War Ministry. The design was rejected as a fantasy. After the war Oberth sought a Ph.D. degree at Heidelberg with a dissertation based on his rocket design. It was rejected by the university in 1922, but Oberth partially underwrote publication expenses, and it appeared as *Die Rakete zu den Planetenräumen* (1923; "The Rocket into Interplanetary Space"). The book, which explained mathematically how rockets could achieve a speed that would allow them to escape earth's gravitational pull, gained Oberth widespread recognition.

Until 1922, he was unfamiliar with the work of Robert Goddard in the U.S. and, until 1925, with that of Konstantin Tsiolkovsky in the Soviet Union. After corresponding with both men, he acknowledged their precedence in deriving the equations associated with space flight. Oberth's *Wege zur Raumschiffahrt* (1929; "Way to Space Travel") won the first annual Robert Esnault-Pelterie–André Hirsch Prize of 10,000 francs, enabling him to finance his research on liquid-propellant rocket motors. The book anticipated by 30 years the development of electric propulsion and of the ion rocket.

In 1938 Oberth joined the faculty of the Technical University of Vienna. He became a German citizen in 1940 and in 1941 transferred to the German rocket development centre at Peenemünde, where he worked for Wernher von Braun, his former assistant.

In 1943 he was sent to another location to work on solid-propellant anti-aircraft rockets. He spent a year in Switzerland after the war as a rocket consultant, and in 1950 he moved to Italy, where he worked on solid-propellant anti-aircraft rockets for the Italian Navy. In the U.S. from 1955, he did advanced space research for the army until he retired to Germany in 1958.

·rocket research contributions **15**:927e
·space pioneers **8**:223a

Obertinghi, medieval Italian family that held power in Genoa and Milan in the 10th century; ancestors of the House of Este.
·Este family historical origins **6**:965d
·territorial possessions and status **9**:1127e

Oberto I (d. 975), marquis of eastern Liguria and count of Luni, powerful feudal lord of 10th-century Italy under King Berengar II and the Holy Roman emperor Otto I whose descendants, the Obertinghi, were the founders of several famous Italian feudal clans.

Member of a family that apparently arrived in Italy in the 9th century with Charlemagne, perhaps from Bavaria, Oberto acquired Genoa and Luni (east of Genoa) in 951, when Berengar seized Liguria and gave the eastern section to Oberto. Nine years later Oberto, dissatisfied with Berengar's rule, travelled to Germany with the Bishop of Como and the Archbishop of Milan to ask Otto to intervene in Italy. After Otto's conquest and coronation as Holy Roman emperor (962), he made Oberto count palatine, second only to his own high office in Italy. Four great families, the Este, the Malaspina, the Pallavicini, and the Massa Parodi, are believed to have descended from his sons.

obesity, excessive accumulation of body fat, usually caused by the consumption of more calories than the body can utilize. The excess calories are then stored as fat, or adipose tissue. Overweight, if moderate, is not necessarily obesity, particularly if the individual is muscular or large boned. In general, however, a body weight 20 percent or more over the optimum tends to be associated with obesity.

The body's ability to adjust food intake to body needs can be disturbed by numerous factors. Of these, hormone imbalances and glandular defects are believed to be of least importance, being demonstrable in only about 5 percent of all obese individuals. Although obesity may be familial, suggestive of a genetic predisposition to fat accumulation, there is also evidence that early feeding patterns imposed by the obese mother upon her offspring may play a major role in a cultural, rather than genetic, transmission of obesity from one generation to the next. More generally, the distinctive way of life of a nation and the individual's behavioral and emotional reaction to it may contribute significantly to widespread obesity. Among the affluent populations, an abundant supply of readily available high-calorie foods and beverages, coupled with increasingly more sedentary living habits that markedly reduce caloric needs, can easily lead to overeating. The stresses and tensions of modern living also cause some individuals to turn to foods and alcoholic drinks for "relief."

Although obesity may be undesirable from an aesthetic sense, especially in parts of the world where slimness is the popular preference, it is also a serious medical problem. Generally, obese persons have a shorter life expectancy; they suffer earlier, more often, and more severely from a large number of diseases than do their normal-weight counterparts. They are also more likely to die prematurely of degenerative diseases of the heart, arteries, and kidneys. More die of accidents and diabetes, and more constitute poor surgical risks than individuals with normal weight. Mental health is also affected; behavioral consequences of an obese appearance, ranging from shyness and withdrawal to overly bold self-assertion, may be rooted in neuroses and psychoses.

The treatment of obesity has two main objectives: removal of the causative factors, which may be difficult if the causes are of emotional or psychological origin; and removal of surplus fat by reducing food intake. Return to normal body weight by reducing calorie intake is best done under medical supervision. Dietary fads and reducing diets that produce quick results without effort are of doubtful effectiveness in reducing body weight and keeping it down, and most are actually deleterious to health.

It is important that obesity not be confused with overweight caused by edema (excess retention of fluids) stemming from various diseases.
·biomedical models, table 1 **5**:866
·causation and complications **5**:860e
·dietary excesses **13**:424c
·drug therapy dangers **17**:694b
·exercise effect on body food reserve **7**:69f
·harmful effects and treatment **13**:413h

ʿObeyd-e Zākānī, also known as ʿUBAYD-I ZĀKĀNĪ (d. 1371), Persian poet and satirist.
·obscene and satirical poetry **9**:965d

Obey River, in northern Tennessee, U.S., is formed by East and West forks in southern Pickett County and flows northwest and north to join the Cumberland River at Celina after a course of 58 mi (93 km). Dale Hollow Dam, impounding the 51-mi-long Dale Hollow Reservoir, is in the Obey River, 7 mi above its confluence with the Cumberland River in the Cumberland Mountains foothills.
36°34′ N, 85°31′ W

obi, wide sash or belt made of a stiff silk material, worn since ancient times by Japanese women. It is about three yards (270 centimetres) long and 10 inches (25 centimetres)

Women wearing obis, woodblock from the series, "The Ten Views of Tea Houses," by Torii Kiyonaga, 1789; in the Museum of Fine Arts, Boston

By courtesy of the Museum of Fine Arts, Boston, Bigelow, Ross Collections and Francis Gardner Curtis Fund

wide and is wound around the waist over a loose gown (kimono) and tied at the back. The contemporary, wide obi evolved in the early 18th century.
·style origin and present use **5**:1037h

Óbidos, town, west central Pará state, northern Brazil. Founded in 1697 as a fortified town, Óbidos overlooks the left (north) bank of the Amazon River 70 mi (110 km) upstream from Santarém at the confluence of the Rio Tapajós, where it narrows to a width of 1¼ mi. River steamers and hydroplanes utilize the facilities at the town, which ships tobacco, cacao, coffee, sugar, lumber, and cattle. It also has plants that manufacture preserved fruits and jute products. Pop. (1970 prelim.) 8,657.
1°55′ S, 55°31′ W

Obihiro, city, southern Hokkaido, Japan, on the Tokachi-gawa (Tokachi River). Founded in 1883, it became the administrative capital of Tokachi sub-prefecture in 1897. The arrival of two railway lines in the early 1900s made Obihiro a trade centre of agricultural products grown in the surrounding Tokachi-heiya (Tokachi Plain). Industry is based on food processing; the city contains one of the largest beet sugar factories in Japan, and the Obihiro College of Stock Raising is the only one of its kind in the country. Pop. (1970) 131,568.
42°55′ N, 143°12′ E
·map, Japan **10**:36

Obi (OMBI) **Islands,** group of the north Moluccas, Maluku province (*daerah tingkat* I), Indonesia, south of the island of Halmahera, north of the island of Ceram, and east of the Kepulauan (islands) Sula. The principal island is Pulau (island) Obi, 52 mi (84 km) long and 28 mi (47 km) wide, which contains the only major village, Laiwui, located on the north coast opposite Pulau Bisa. The island is mountainous, with a peak of 5,285 ft (1,611 m) and a coastal plain around most of the island. Other major islands are Bisa, Obilatu, and Tobalai. Claimed by the Dutch in 1682, the islands produce some sago and forest products. There is no airfield. Latest pop. est. 3,391.
1°23′ S, 127°45′ E

obiter dictum (Latin: "that which is said by the way"), in law, a passage in a judicial opinion that is not necessary for the decision of the case before the court. Such statements lack the force of precedent but may nevertheless be significant. Dicta frequently include statements that go beyond the issues of the case.

Obizzo I (d. 1193), Este marquis in Italy.
·Este family political rise **6**:965e

Obizzo II, 13th-century Este ruler of Ferrara, regined 1264–93.
·Este family political rise **6**:965f

object, physical, that which exists independently of human thought and perception. The principal philosophical problem concerning physical objects is whether man can know them as they are in themselves.
·Berkeley's immaterialist metaphysics **2**:847c
·classification of sense experience **4**:691e
·empirically-oriented theories **6**:937h *passim* to 947d
·Kant's appearance–reality dichotomy **6**:935f
·knowledge and perception **6**:927b
·Lucretius' view of sense perception **11**:174d
·Nishida's transcendence of dichotomy **13**:120a
·perception of sensory stimulus **14**:38h *passim* to 39g
·Phenomenology's concepts and methods **14**:210g
·Rationalist–Empiricist conflict **6**:946d

object constancy (psychology): *see* constancy phenomenon.

objective correlative, as defined by T.S. Eliot, something, such as a situation or chain of events, that symbolizes or renders objective an emotion and that may be employed to evoke a desired emotional response in the reader.
·Eliot's theory of emotion expression **6**:724h

objective test, test designed to minimize scorer unreliability by the use of true-false or multiple choice questions.
·test administration and scoring **11**:736h

objectivism, the ethical theory that there are objective criteria for determining the rightness or wrongness of actions. Objective criteria in this sense are independent of any given mind and thus have a reality based on more than just inward feeling.
·Existentialist opposition **7**:73b
·naturalistic meta-ethics and value **6**:984e

object language, in semantics and logic, the ordinary language used to talk about things or objects in the world—as contrasted with metalanguage, an artificial language used by linguists and others to analyze or describe the sentences or elements of object language itself. The concept was developed by such 20th-century logical positivists as Polish-American Al-

fred Tarski and German-American Rudolf Carnap.
·analysis of artificial language **14**:882c
·Tarski's semantic truth formula **16**:508d

object reading (parapsychology): *see* psychometry.

objets trouvés, term used in the Surrealist theory of art to describe those natural or manufactured "found or ready-made objects" which are said to take on an extraordinary aesthetic significance when displayed away from their customary purpose and environment. *See also* assemblage.

oblast, the term for an administrative region or province in the Soviet Union.
·Soviet Union political structure **17**:349h

oblate (from the Latin *oblatus*, meaning "one offered up"), a term used in the Roman Catholic Church to designate: (1) a lay person connected with a religious order or institution and living according to its regulations; (2) a minor dedicated by its parents to become a monk according to the Benedictine Rule; or (3) a member (in the U.S.) of either the Oblates of Mary Immaculate (O.M.I.) or the Oblates of St. Francis de Sales (O.S.F.S.).
·celibate lay commitment **3**:1041g
·medieval studies program **6**:336b

Oblates of Mary Immaculate (O.M.I.), one of the largest missionary congregations of the Roman Catholic Church, was inaugurated at Aix-en-Provence, Fr., on Jan. 25, 1816, as the Missionary Society of Provence by Charles-Joseph-Eugène de Mazenod. By preaching to the poor, especially in rural areas, Mazenod hoped to renew the life of the church after the French Revolution. On Feb. 17, 1826, Pope Leo XII gave approval to the congregation, henceforth known as the Oblates of Mary Immaculate. In 1831 a general chapter (legislative meeting) voted to begin work in the foreign missions. The first mission foundations were made in Canada in 1841 and a year later in the U.S.

In addition to the three vows of poverty, chastity, and obedience, the Oblates take a vow of perseverance by which they promise to remain in the congregation until death. A superior general in Rome directs the activities of the members, who are located on every continent; their principal apostolate (religious activity) is still to the poor. Where the church has been long established, the task of the congregation is to strengthen the faith, especially by preaching parish missions and retreats, teaching, and directing shrines dedicated to Mary. In Africa, South America, the Orient, and the Arctic it is engaged in pioneering missionary efforts. For current membership, *see* table under religious orders of men, Roman Catholic.

obliquity of the ecliptic, the angle between the ecliptic (the plane of Earth's orbit) and the plane of Earth's Equator. In 1971 the angle was about 23°26′35″ of arc. It is decreasing by about 47″ of arc per century because of gravitational effects of other planets on the Earth; in about 1,500 years the obliquity will begin to increase again. The total amount of its variation is about 1°30′.

Oblivion (Greek mythology): *see* Lethe.

Obo, festival held in Inner Mongolia in the fifth month of every year.
·Inner Mongolian celebrational style **9**:604f

Obodrites, also BODRYCI, a people of the Polab group, the northwesternmost of the Slavs in medieval Europe, who inhabited the country between the lower Elbe River and the Baltic Sea, the area north and northeast of Hamburg in what is now the Federal Republic of Germany. The Obodrites' independent principality, which had been developed by the early 9th century, was conquered in the middle of the 12th century by Henry the Lion, duke of Saxony, after a long resistance directed by its last pagan prince, Niklot (died 1160). Niklot's son Przbyslaw (Pribislav; died 1178) accepted Christianity, acknowledged German suzerainty, and was recognized in 1170 as a prince of the Holy Roman Empire. Both his descendants, who became the dukes of Mecklenburg, and the Obodrite people eventually became Germanized.

oboe, treble woodwind instrument with a conical bore and double reed. Used chiefly as an orchestral instrument, it also has a considerable solo repertory.

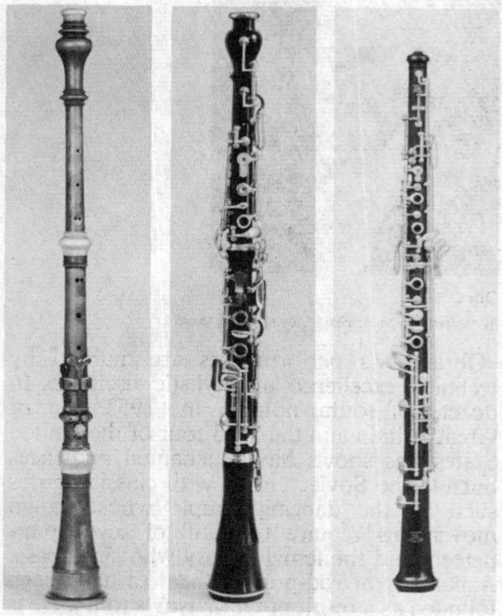

(Left to right) Oboe, *c.* 1775, in the Macgillivray Collection, London; modern Austrian oboe; and Gillet model oboe (all shown without reeds)

By courtesy of (right) T.W. Howarth & Co., Ltd.; photographs (left and centre), L.G. Aubin—EB Inc.

Hautbois (French: "high [*i.e.*, loud] wood"), or oboe, was originally one of the names of the shawm, the violently powerful instrument of outdoor ceremonial. The oboe proper (*i.e.*, the orchestral instrument), however, was the mid-17th-century invention of two French court musicians, Jean Hotteterre and Michel Philidor. Intended to be played indoors with stringed instruments, it was softer and less brilliant in tone quality than the modern oboe. By the end of the century it was the principal wind instrument of the orchestra and military band and, after the violin, the leading solo instrument of the time.

The early oboe had only two keys. Its compass, at first two octaves upward from middle C, was soon extended as high as the next F. In the early 19th century, changing musical styles coincided with several improvements in the manufacture of wind-instrument keywork, particularly the introduction of metal pillars in place of the wooden ridges on which the keys had been mounted. This change greatly reduced the threat to the instrument's airtightness formerly associated with additional keys. In France by 1839 the number of keys had gradually increased to ten.

Before 1800 French players had also adopted the narrow modern type of reed. By the 1860s Guillaume Triébert and his son Frédéric had developed an instrument almost identical with the expressive, flexible, and specifically French oboe of the 20th century. The instrument in which the finger holes are covered by perforated plates, now widely used in the U.S. and France, was produced by François Lorée and Georges Gillet in 1906.

Outside France, the decay of patronage and public enthusiasm for military bands resulted in radically different traditions of playing and manufacture. In Germany and Austria the many-keyed instrument appeared earlier, and the bore and reed developed so as to produce an increased loudness. In these countries this change brought about a period of neglect for the oboe until it was revived in the late 19th century, largely through the efforts of the composer Richard Strauss. After experimentation with an extremely small reed, ill-suited to the large German bore, the French oboe was generally adopted by about 1925.

The history of the oboe in Italy is comparable. The German instrument (with a very small reed) survives in the U.S.S.R.; capable of a certain refinement of tone, it lacks the piquancy and sparkle of the French oboe. In Vienna an oboe resembling the German instrument but more antique in character is played by the Philharmonic Orchestra and the Akademie. Its rather reticent and blending quality is caused perhaps more by the highly specialized reed than by the instrument's inherent qualities.

The chief factor in playing the oboe is the making of the reed and its control by the lips and the mouth. Most serious players make their own reeds, although ready-made reeds can be purchased. The raw material is the plant *Arundo donax*, which resembles bamboo in appearance. It grows in warm temperate or subtropical regions, but only the crops of the southern French *départements* of Var and Vaucluse are satisfactory for reed making.

There are several large varieties of oboe. The English horn (*q.v.*), or cor anglais, is pitched in F, a fifth below the oboe, and is believed to resemble closely J.S. Bach's *oboe da caccia*. The *oboe d'amore*, in A, a minor third below the oboe, is made with a globular bell like that of the cor anglais. Much employed by Bach, it is also used in several 20th-century works. Instruments pitched an octave below the oboe are rarer. The *hautbois baryton*, or baritone oboe, resembles a larger, lower voiced cor anglais in tone quality and proportions. The heckelphone (*q.v.*), with a larger reed and bore than the *baryton*, has a distinctive tone that is rather heavy in the low register. Instruments in other sizes and pitches occur occasionally.

Any folk or non-European double-reed woodwind may also be generically termed an oboe.
·characteristic tone in bore design **12**:729d
·classification, design, and development **19**:848b; illus. 851
·orchestras and ensembles **13**:644a *passim* to 647d

Oboe, British radar beacon bombing system, used in World War II.
·radar and bombing tactics **15**:371c

Oboi, 17th-century Manchu minister, de facto ruler from 1667 to 1669.
·regency for K'ang-hsi **10**:379h

Obolus, extinct genus of brachiopod, or lamp shell, of the Cambrian Age (between 570,000,000 to 500,000,000 years ago). *Obolus* was a small animal with a spherical shape; one valve, or shell, was larger than the other. Unlike the shells of its relatives, the lingulids,

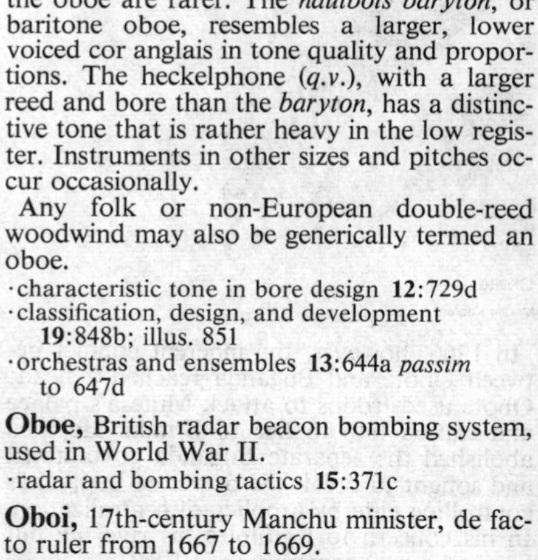

Obolus ella, Middle Cambrian in age, found in Logan, Mont.

By courtesy of the Buffalo Museum of Science, Buffalo, N.Y.

the obolus shells were composed of calcium carbonate. *Obolus* inhabited shallow marine waters.

Öbör Hangay, also spelled ÖVÖRHANGAY, province, Mongolia.
·area and population table **12**:366

Obote, (Apollo) Milton (b. 1925, Lango, Uganda), prime minister and president of the East African republic of Uganda from 1962 to 1971; he led his country to independence in 1962 but was overthrown by a military coup within 10 years.

Obote joined the Uganda National Congress Party when it was founded in 1952 and was elected to the Legislative Council in 1958, where, despite the small number of African delegates, he did not hesitate to criticize the British government. When the old Congress Party split, he formed the Uganda People's Congress (UPC), consisting of his own dissident group and the Uganda People's Union (UPU), the main focus of which was opposition to the continued existence within Uganda of the powerful state of Buganda under King Mutesa II. In 1961 Obote compromised, accepting Buganda's desire for federal status within Uganda; he therefore formed an alliance between his UPC and Buganda's Kabaka Yekka (King Only) Party.

Obote
Marion Kaplan

In 1966, however, the inherent conflict between Obote and Buganda reached a head; Obote used troops to attack Mutesa's palace and caused him to flee to Britain. He then abolished the separate Buganda government and sought to break the power of Buganda's controlling elite by a policy of centralization. In his concern to legitimize his rule, he put forward a new constitution in 1967.

In 1969–70 Obote attempted to develop a new political culture in Uganda, announcing a "move to the left" in the Common Man's Charter. This stance led to opposition by military leaders, who joined forces with the Buganda royalists against him. Early in 1971 Obote was overthrown in a coup led by Maj. Gen. Idi Amin. Amin, in turn, was toppled in 1979 by Ugandan nationalist forces and Tanzanian forces under the leadership of Pres. Julius Nyerere. It was expected that Obote would return to his former office, but the newly formed Uganda National Liberation Front established a provisional government with Yusufu K. Lule as president.
·political problems and removal **6**:104Ba

Obradović, Dositej (1742?–1811), Serbian writer and translator.
·Serbian literary development **10**:1211g
·Serbian nationalistic development **2**:624g

Obraztsov, Sergey (Vladimirovich) (b. July 5 [June 22, old style], 1901, Moscow), puppet master who established puppetry as an art form in the Soviet Union and who is a major figure in his field. The son of a schoolteacher and a railroad engineer, Obraztsov studied painting at the Higher Art and Technical Studios. He became an actor at the Moscow Nemirovich-Danchenko Music Theatre (1922–30) and then at the Moscow Art Theatre (1930–31). He simultaneously gave independent vaudeville-style puppet shows and in 1931 was chosen by the Soviet government as the first director of the State Central Puppet Theatre, Moscow, a position he has continued to hold.

Obraztsov
By courtesy of the Puppentheatersammlung, Munich

Obraztsov's performances are marked by technical excellence and stylistic discipline. In dozens of tours, notably the 1953 tour of Great Britain and the 1963 tour of the United States, his shows have enchanted audiences outside the Soviet Union with classic figures such as the dancing couple whose tango movements require the skill of seven puppeteers and the female gypsy who sings bass. A number of rod-puppet theatres have been founded as a result of Obraztsov's tours. He is also known for his work with a kind of finger puppet called a ball puppet.
·rod puppet development role **15**:291f

Obre II, Butmir archaeological site in west-central Yugoslavia.
·cultural and agricultural artifacts **2**:613e

Obrecht (HOBRECHT), **Jakob** (b. Nov. 22, 1452, Bergen-op-Zoom, Holland—d. 1505, Ferrara, Italy), composer who, with Jean d'Okeghem and Josquin des Prez, was one of the leading composers in the Franco-Flemish, or Franco-Netherlandish, style that dominated Renaissance music. He was the son of Willem Obrecht, a trumpeter. His first certain appointment was in 1484 as instructor of choirboys at Cambrai cathedral, where he was criticized for negligence in caring for the boys. In 1485 he became assistant choirmaster of the cathedral at Bruges. According to Henricus Glareanus, Erasmus was among the choirboys at one of Obrecht's positions. In 1487 he visited Italy, where he met Ercole I, duke of Ferrara, an admirer of Obrecht's music. The duke installed Obrecht in Ferrara and sought a papal appointment for him there. This was not forthcoming, and Obrecht returned to Bergen-op-Zoom in 1488. He travelled to Ferrara again in 1504, where he died of plague.

Obrecht's style is notable for its warm, graceful melodies and its clear harmonies that approach a modern feeling for tonality. His surviving works include 27 masses, 19 motets, and 31 secular pieces.

His masses are largely for four voices; one, however, begins with three voices and builds to seven by the final movement. Most use a cantus firmus taken from plainchant or from a secular song; one mass is built on the folk song "L'Homme armé," used by several contemporary composers. His use of the cantus firmus varies from the customary statement of it in the tenor to fragments of it in each movement and in voices other than the tenor. Some of his late masses use parody technique—using all voices of a pre-existent chanson or motet, rather than a single borrowed melody, as a unifying device.

His motets are largely to texts in honour of the Virgin Mary (*e.g., Salve Regina; Alma Redemptoris Mater*). They characteristically have the cantus firmus melody placed in the tenor in long notes. Some of the motets are polytextual, a rather outdated practice. More progressive is his use of melodic imitation and his frequent consecutive tenths.

Of his secular pieces, four are possibly for instruments. Seventeen of his 27 chansons are to Dutch texts, which is unusual; most chansons of the period are in French. He also wrote eight French and two Italian chansons.
·influence on musical mainstream **12**:706g

Obregón, Álvaro (b. Feb. 19, 1880, Alamos, Mex.—d. July 17, 1928, Mexico City), soldier, statesman, and reformer who as president restored order to Mexico after a decade of political upheavals and civil war that followed the revolution of 1910.

Though Obregón had little formal education, he early learned a great deal about the needs and desires of poor Mexicans from his work as a farmer and labourer. He did not take part in the revolution (1910–11) that overthrew the dictator Porfirio Díaz, but in 1912 he led a group of volunteers in support of Pres. Francisco Madero against the rebellion led by Pascual Orozco. When Madero was overthrown and assassinated by Victoriano Huerta in February 1913, Obregón joined Venustiano Carranza (*q.v.*) against Huerta. Obregón's military skill was in constant display as he defeated Huerta's forces; he occupied Mexico City on Aug. 15, 1914.

Obregón, *c.* 1910
Archivo Casasola

Obregón continued to support Carranza against the challenges of the rebel leaders Pancho Villa and Emiliano Zapata. During the campaign against Villa, Obregón issued decrees instituting anticlerical policies and labour regulations in the areas he conquered. In addition, his was the dominant voice at the constitutional convention of 1917, and it was he who was largely responsible for the radical emphasis of the resulting document. After serving for a short time in Carranza's cabinet (1917), he retired to his farm in Sonora and for two years was politically inactive. In April 1920, however, in response to Carranza's increasingly reactionary policies and his attempt to impose a puppet successor, Obregón took a leading role in the uprising that overthrew the President. On Dec. 1, 1920, Obregón was elected as Mexico's new president.

Obregón managed to impose relative peace and prosperity on his nation, which had gone through 10 years of savage civil war. He gave official sanction to organizations of labourers and peasants. Moreover, his appointment of José Vasconcelos as minister of education heralded an era of significant reform in Mexican schooling. Because he appeared too radical, however, the United States refused to recognize his government until the Bucareli Conference (1923), in which Obregón promised not to expropriate U.S. oil companies.

After suppressing a barracks revolt, Obregón retired on Dec. 1, 1924, and was succeeded by Plutarco Elías Calles. During retirement he increased his vast landholdings in northern Mexico and established a monopoly in the production of *garbanzos* (chick-peas). Again a candidate for the presidency in 1928, Obregón was elected despite another armed revolt,

which was quickly suppressed. Shortly after his re-election he returned from Sonora to Mexico City, where he attended a small victory celebration. While dining with his friends, he was shot and killed by José de León Toral, a Roman Catholic who held Obregón responsible for religious persecutions.
·Mexican political leadership **12**:85g

Obrenovich, Serbian OBRENOVIĆ, dynastic family that provided Serbia with five rulers between 1815 and 1903. Their succession was broken by a rival dynasty, the Karađorđević. Thus, instead of being numbered by their Christian names like other European princes, the Obrenović rulers are numbered according to their place in the dynastic succession. Miloš (*see* Milosh) Obrenović I, who founded the dynasty, was prince of Serbia from 1815 to 1839 and again from 1858 to 1860; his elder son, Milan Obrenović II, reigned for only 25 days before his death in 1839; Miloš's second son, Michael (*q.v.*) Obrenović III, was prince from 1839 to 1842 and again from 1860 to 1868; his successor was a first cousin once removed, Milan (*q.v.*) Obrenović IV, who became prince in 1868 and served as king of Serbia from 1882 until his abdication in 1889; his son Alexander (*q.v.*) Obrenović V followed him to the throne and reigned as king from 1889 until his assassination in 1903, when the dynasty became extinct.
·Michael and Balkan confederation policy **2**:626f
·political and cultural nationalism **2**:624g
·Serbian revolution of 1903 **19**:944a

Obri (people): *see* Avars.

O'Brien, a common Irish surname derived from the famous medieval king Brian Boru; O' (*Ua*) means "grandson" or "descendant." In the two centuries following Brian's death (1014) the great O'Brien sept spread throughout Munster, different groups settling in what are now Counties Tipperary, Waterford, and Clare. Brian's successors remained virtually independent of the English until Murrough O'Brien (died 1551), 57th prince of Thomond, surrendered his Gaelic titles and was created earl of Thomond and Baron Inchiquin. The earldom became extinct but the barony survives. Members of a younger branch, viscounts of Clare (1662–1774), served in the Irish brigade on the continent.

O'Brien, Edna (b. Dec. 15, 1930, County Clare), Irish novelist and screenwriter whose work has been hailed for its energy and bite. Her first novel, *The Country Girls*, was published in 1960. Her second novel, *The Lonely Girl* (1962), was filmed as *Girl with Green Eyes* (1965), for which Miss O'Brien wrote the script. *Casualties of Peace* (1966) is considered her most mature novel, though it has sometimes been criticized for over-emphasizing style at the expense of structural content and character development. In 1969 she wrote the screenplay for *Three Into Two Won't Go*. In 1971 her novel, *A Pagan Place*, appeared, and a stage version was performed in 1972. A short novel, *Night*, appeared in 1972.

O'Brien, Fitz-James (b. *c.* 1828, County Limerick, Ire.—d. April 6, 1862, Cumberland, Md.), U.S. writer whose psychologically penetrating tales of pseudoscience and the uncanny make him one of the forerunners of modern science fiction and an heir of Edgar Allan Poe. He also was a journalist, a poet of no enduring merit, and an author of popular one-act plays.

The son of a lawyer, he ran through his inheritance in two years in London, where he began to work in journalism. In 1852 he moved to New York City to earn his living by writing and soon became an important figure in that city's Bohemia. But his work, though published in the leading periodicals of the day, won him neither the reputation he thought he merited nor the financial ease he desired. At the outbreak of the Civil War he volunteered with the Union forces and died from wounds received during the first year of the fighting.

His best known stories include "The Diamond Lens," about a man who falls in love with a being he sees through a microscope in a drop of water; "What Was It?" in which a man is attacked by a thing he apprehends with every sense but sight; and "The Wondersmith," in which robots are fashioned only to turn upon their creators. These three all appeared in periodicals in 1859. Most of his plays were written for James W. Wallack, a well-known actor-manager. O'Brien's best known stage work was *A Gentleman from Ireland* (1854), performed often after the mid-19th century.

O'Brien, Flann, pseudonym of BRIAN Ó NUALLAIN, also known as MYLES NA GCOPALEEN (b. 1911, Strabane, County Tyrone—d. April 1, 1966, Dublin), Irish novelist, dramatist, and, as Myles na gCopaleen, a columnist for the *Irish Times* newspaper for 26 years. He is most celebrated for his unusual novel *At Swim-Two-Birds*, which, though first published in 1939, achieved fame only after republication in 1960. *At Swim-Two-Birds* has been considered a rich literary experiment, combining folklore, heroic legend, humour, and poetry.

O'Brien was educated in Dublin and later became a civil servant. His novels *The Hard Life* (1961), *The Dalkey Archive* (1964; adapted as a play, *When the Saints Go Cycling In*, performed 1965), and the fantastic *The Third Policeman* (1967), though written on a smaller scale than his masterpiece, are thought equally amusing.
·Irish novel tradition **13**:291c
·literary influence and work **10**:1223g

O'Brien, James Bronterre (b. 1805, Granard, County Longford, Ire.—d. Dec. 23, 1864, London), Irish-born British radical, a leader of the Chartist working class movement, sometimes known as the "Chartist schoolmaster." O'Brien moved to London in 1829, intending to practice at the English bar, but was quickly drawn into radical activities and later into working class journalism, being editor of the radical "*Poor Man's Guardian*" (1831–35) and working on the "Northern Star" (1838–40). In 1850 he was joint founder of the National Reform League, which advocated socialist objectives. In his later years he wrote political poetry.

O'Brien, William (b. Oct. 2, 1852, Mallow, County Cork—d. Feb. 25, 1928, London), journalist and politician, for several years second only to Charles Stewart Parnell (1846–91) among Irish nationalist leaders. He was perhaps most important for his "plan of campaign" (1886), by which Irish tenant farmers would withhold all rent payments from landlords who refused to lower their rents and would pay the money instead into a mutual defense fund on which evicted tenants could draw.

A journalist from 1869, O'Brien was appointed editor of the Irish Land League's weekly *United Ireland* by Parnell in 1881. In October of that year the British authorities suppressed the paper and put O'Brien in Kilmainham jail, Dublin, along with Parnell and others. There he drew up a "No Rent Manifesto," which, when read at a Land League meeting, resulted in the outlawing of the League. Released in 1882, he resumed the editorship of *United Ireland*, and in 1883 he was elected to the British House of Commons. His "plan of campaign" was disavowed by Parnell but nonetheless stirred up fierce agitation. To suppress the movement, the British government passed the Coercion Act of 1887, under which O'Brien was jailed again.

For some time after the O'Shea divorce case (1889–90), in which Parnell was corespondent, O'Brien tried to mediate between the Parnellites and their opponents, although he sided with the majority in rejecting Parnell's continued leadership of the Irish Home Rule struggle. In 1898 he founded the United Irish League, and in 1910, after control of that group had passed to the Parnellite John Redmond, he established the All-for-Ireland League in opposition to the older organization. Most of his personal following, however, had joined Arthur Griffith's Sinn Féin Party by the end of World War I.

O'Brien, William Smith (b. Oct. 17, 1803, Dromoland, County Clare—d. June 18, 1864, Bangor, Caernarvonshire), Irish patriot, originally a moderate and later a revolutionary, a leader of the literary-political Young Ireland movement along with Thomas Osborne Davis, Charles Gavan Duffy, and John Dillon.

William Smith O'Brien, lithograph by H. O'Neill after a daguerreotype by Glukman, 1848

By courtesy of the trustees of the British Museum; photograph, J.R. Freeman & Co. Ltd.

O'Brien sat in the British House of Commons from 1828 to 1848. Although he was a Protestant, he actively favoured Catholic emancipation but at first wished to maintain the Anglo-Irish legislative union (in force from Aug. 1, 1800). In 1828, therefore, he opposed the parliamentary candidacy (in County Clare) of Daniel O'Connell, leading advocate of Catholic political rights and Irish self-government. He continued to support the union until 1843, when he was angered by the British imprisonment of O'Connell. In October of that year O'Brien joined the anti-union Repeal Association, serving as deputy leader while O'Connell was in jail.

On July 27, 1846, after O'Connell had advised against the use of force, O'Brien led the Young Irelanders in withdrawing from the association. In January 1847 they formed the Irish Confederation to press for more effective famine relief. In May 1848, after travelling to Paris to congratulate the leaders of the new French republic, O'Brien was tried for sedition, but the proceedings ended in a hung jury. He then joined his political colleague Thomas Francis Meagher in advocating a violent revolution. On July 29, 1848, he led a futile rising of peasants against police at Ballingarry, County Tipperary. Arrested for high treason, he received a death sentence, which was commuted to life exile to Tasmania. Released in February 1854, he lived in Brussels until he was granted a full pardon in May 1856.

Ob River 13:431, one of the greatest rivers of the Soviet Union; its basin embraces the greater part of Western Siberia, which the Ob traverses on a winding course northwestward from the Altai Mountains to the Kara Sea of the Arctic Ocean. Its length may be calculated as 2,266 mi (3,647 km), from the source of the Ob proper (the confluence of the Biya and Katun rivers) to the head of its gulf on the Kara Sea; or as 3,896 mi, from the source of its great tributary, the Irtysh, to the end of the gulf.

The text article surveys the Ob Basin geographically; describes the course of the

mainstream and its tributaries, vegetation and animal life, and the human imprint.
66°45′ N, 69°30′ E

REFERENCES in other text articles:
·delta, tides, and discharge table **15**:868
·drainage basin and tributaries **18**:1033c
·map, Soviet Union **17**:322
·Novosibirsk's economic growth **13**:299e
·Soviet Union physical geography **17**:327a

O'Bryan, William (b. Feb. 6, 1778, Gunwen, Cornwall—d. Jan. 8, 1868, New York), Methodist churchman who founded the Bible Christian Church (1815), a dissident group of Wesleyan Methodists desiring effective biblical education, a Presbyterian form of church government, and the participation of women in the ministry. The group originated in Devonshire and spread to Canada (1831), the U.S. (1846), and Australia (1850), although O'Bryan left the society over administrative differences and began an itinerant evangelism in the U.S. (1831). The Bible Christians joined with other dissident Methodist groups in 1907 to form the United Methodist Church.

obscene telephoning: *see* coprolalia.

obscenity, in general, that which offends the public sense of decency. Its social importance lies in the history of censorship and legislation for the suppression of obscene acts, especially the publication of indecent matter. That obscenity, like beauty, is in the eye of the beholder is evidenced by the elusiveness of a satisfactory definition.

In most modern nations, the criminality of producing or disseminating obscene materials of a sexual nature is a relatively late phenomenon. In England, for example, except for the Puritan suppression of theatres in the first half of the 17th century, restrictions were applied only to antireligious or seditious acts or publications. In 1727, however, there was a successful prosecution in a temporal court for the publication of indecent matter, and thereafter it became recognized as an indictable misdemeanour by common law. Prohibition of purely sexual material became statutory for the first time with the Obscene Publications Act of 1857. This act, however, did not contain a definition of obscenity. Such a definition was forthcoming in 1868, in *Regina* v. *Hicklin*, in which the test of what was obscene was its tendency "to deprave and corrupt those whose minds are open to such immoral influences," and it was understood that this test need apply only to isolated passages of a work. This view was a precedent for U.S. antiobscenity legislation, beginning with the celebrated Comstock Law of 1873, which broadened the 1865 Mail Act essentially to its present form by providing fine and imprisonment of any person mailing or receiving "obscene," "lewd," or "lascivious" publications.

In the half century that followed, many nations enacted their own forms of legislation banning obscene materials. Thus, the basic legal control has been through the criminal law, but most countries also provide for administrative regulation by the customs, postal service, and national or local boards for the licensing of motion picture or stage performances. Also, more than 50 nations are parties to the UN Convention for the Suppression of the Circulation of and Traffic in Obscene Publications. Interestingly, this convention operates without any definition of obscenity because it was agreed that this would vary from country to country. (Denmark withdrew from the Convention in 1969 after it removed all restrictions within its borders on pictorial and written pornography.)

The variability of definitions is well illustrated by cases in the United States. Until the middle of the 20th century, the British *Regina* v. *Hicklin* definition of obscenity was used. In 1934 in *U.S.* v. *One Book Entitled "Ulysses,"* 72 N.Y. 705 (1934), a New York superior court held that the criterion for obscenity was not the content of isolated obscene passages but rather "whether a publication taken as a whole has a libidinous effect." In 1957, in *Roth* v. *U.S.*, the U.S. Supreme Court tendered a basic redefinition of obscenity: "whether, to the average person, applying community standards, the dominant theme of the material taken as a whole appeals to prurient interests." In 1966, however, the Supreme Court, in a ruling on the book *Fanny Hill*, declared a work pornographic only if it was "utterly without redeeming social value." In June 1973, in decisions on five obscenity cases, the court abandoned the 1966 ruling and declared that the states might prohibit the printing or sale of works "which appeal to prurient interest in sex, which portray sexual conduct in a patently offensive way, and which, taken as a whole, do not have serious literary, artistic, political or scientific value." It held that the definition of "prurient" should be that of "the average person, applying contemporary community standards," and that it would be no defense for a work to have some "redeeming social value."

·censorship history and problems **3**:1086e *passim* to 1089h
·D.H. Lawrence in legal difficulties **10**:722h
·folk literature studies **7**:458f
·perceptual studies using obscene words **14**:44g

Ob Sea, reservoir formed by a dam on the Ob River, Altay *kray* (territory), Russian S.F.S.R.
54°00′ N, 83°00′ E
·location and dam **13**:431h

observable (physics): *see* operator.

Observants (religious order): *see* Franciscans.

observation, in the methodology of science, exercise of sense and experimentation, in which an appeal is made to the knowledge acquired in a laboratory. It is a careful noting of the results of experiment in order to elicit a hitherto unnoticed causal relationship. *See also* scientific method.

·Carnap's use in empirical verification **3**:925h
·empirical data manipulation **16**:382d

Observations on the Faerie Queene of Spenser (1754; 2nd enlarged edition, 1762), book by Thomas Warton (*q.v.*) regarded as a pioneer in literary history.
·18th century literary interests **10**:1165f

Observations on the present State of Affairs (1756), article by Samuel Johnson.
·power politics criticism **10**:247f

observatory, astronomical, structure built primarily for astronomical observation. The date and place of the earliest such structure are unknown. Some scientists consider Stonehenge, England, and similar constructions to have been erected as prehistoric computers to help predict eclipses. The earliest extant records from an observatory are those kept by Hipparchus (*c.* 140 BC), who made star observations on the island of Rhodes. Perhaps the most productive observatory of the Middle Ages was that of the Persian prince Ulūgh Beg, who worked in the early 15th century at Samarkand. Uraniborg, established in 1576 by the Danish astronomer Tycho Brahe, was the finest of the pretelescopic observatories.

Following the invention of the telescope, the number and complexity of observatories steadily increased. In the 20th century, emphasis began to be placed on location in good observing conditions rather than on proximity to universities. Cities with their bright lights and pollution of the atmosphere hinder observations. Many stars and galaxies are never visible from the northern hemisphere, and in the 1960s much construction began in Australia, Africa, and South America. The largest optical telescope in the world, a 236-inch (6-metre) reflector in the Caucasus Mountains of the Soviet Union, began operation in 1976.

Radio observatories are less hampered than optical ones by clouds and the proximity of cities, but they are sensitive to interference from certain kinds of electronic activity. The first crude radio observatories were built in the 1930s; by late in the century, they rivalled optical observatories in expense, complexity, and numbers, the most powerful being the 25-antenna contingent forming the Very Large Array near Socorro, New Mexico.

After World War II, rockets were used to carry telescopes above Earth's blanketing atmosphere, developing into orbiting space satellites that carry a variety of sophisticated equipment to measure and observe natural phenomena in space. The U.S. launched its first Orbiting Solar Observatory in 1962; by 1978 the Soviet Union had placed two men on its space station Salyut 6 for nearly 140 days. Unmanned spacecraft launched into fly-by trajectories for studying outer space are called space probes. The U.S. Pioneer 11, launched in April 1973, reached to within 13,300 mi (21,400 km) of Saturn in September 1979. *Major ref.* **2**:246g

·Brahe's establishment and support **3**:103g
·space exploration **17**:358e
·telescope history and types **18**:97a

RELATED ENTRIES in the *Ready Reference and Index:*
Arecibo Ionospheric Observatory; Cerro Tololo Interamerican Observatory; Crimean Astrophysical Observatory; European Southern Observatory; Hale Observatories; Jodrell Bank Experimental Station; Kitt Peak National Observatory; National Radio Astronomy Observatory; Naval Observatory; Paris, Observatoire de; Pulkovo Observatory; Royal Greenwich Observatory; satellite observatories; Uraniborg

Observer, The, London Sunday newspaper, founded 1791.
·newspaper publishing history **15**:238h

obsessive-compulsive reaction, form of psychological disturbance in which anxiety is associated with recurring unpleasant and morbid thoughts or with repetitive impulses to perform apparently meaningless and ritualistic acts, traditionally classed as one of the psychoneuroses (neuroses). Although the obsessional person may regard these ideas and behaviour as unreasonable, the ability to control them is lacking. Either the obsessive thought or the compulsive ceremonial may arise singly, or both may appear in sequence. The neurotic person regularly repudiates the distressing thoughts, which are often highly repugnant and concerned with violently aggressive or sexually perverse impulses. The greater the struggle to dispel them, however, the more insistently do they intrude. Though fearing the possibility of acting out the disturbing impulses, an obsessional neurotic almost never carries out the thought against which the conscience rebels so strongly.

Occasionally the preoccupations may be with absurd trivialities or circular speculations on abstruse religious or philosophical issues. This concern with abstract thoughts defends against feelings that are prohibited.

The personality of the obsessive-compulsive is characterized by inflexibility, constant doubt, vacillation, and adherence to excessive standards of morality. The individual tends to be overconscientious and inhibited in the expression of pleasure and in the capacity for relaxation. A tendency toward massive attention to unimportant detail contributes toward lack of productivity and the consumption of much energy in unprofitable and wasteful labour. Most compulsive rituals are rather simple—such as persistent hand washing, counting, touching, or the repetition of stereotyped words or phrases. Occasionally, however, the ceremonials are elaborately formalized and time-consuming. The compulsive acts are similar to the magical expiatory rituals of nonliterate societies and similarly attempt to

deal with potentially threatening situations. Should the act be obstructed in some manner, anxiety will be experienced.
·symptom complex and theories of origin **15**:169e

obshchina, Russian village commune responsible for land distribution, crop planning, and tax collection.
·Alexander II administrative reform **16**:62a

Obshchy Syrt, area of high land in the Trans-Volga region of European Russian Soviet Federated Socialist Republic, forming the watershed between the Volga and the Ural rivers. In the Novouzensk region it reaches a height of 330 to 625 ft (100–190 m), while farther to the east it rises to 920 ft (280 m). Obshchy Syrt runs from the Urals foothills in a southwesterly direction toward the area of Caspian salt domes. The western portion consists of a system of dome-shaped eminences, while the east has numerous ridges and steep slopes. Steppe vegetation is typical.

obsidian, natural glass of volcanic origin. It was used by American Indians and many other primitive peoples for weapons, implements, tools, and ornaments and by the ancient Mayas for mirrors. Because of its conchoidal fracture (smooth curved surfaces and sharp edges), the sharpest stone artifacts were fashioned from obsidian; some of these, primarily arrowheads, have been dated by means of the hydration rinds that form on their exposed surfaces through time. Obsidian is usually jet black and is sometimes used as a semiprecious stone.

Most obsidian is associated with volcanic rocks and forms the upper portion of rhyolitic lava flows. Less abundantly it occurs as thin edges of dikes and sills. Well-known are the obsidians of Mt. Hekla in Iceland; Isola Lipari off Italy; and Obsidian Cliff in Yellowstone National Park, Wyoming.

Obsidian has a vitreous lustre and is slightly harder than window glass, or about 5½ on the Mohs scale. Its average refractive index is 1.495, and its average specific gravity is 2.4. The jet black colour is due to abundant closely spaced crystallites (microscopic embryonic crystal growths); so numerous are these tiny inclusions that the glass is opaque except on thin edges. Red and brown obsidian receives its colour from included iron oxide dust, whereas light-gray shades may be due to abundant tiny gas bubbles or finely crystallized patches. Variegated types with banding or mottling in black and red, or black and gray, are common.

In addition to the crystallites, which are too small to show polarizing effects under the microscope, obsidian may carry abundant microlites (tiny polarizing crystals), many of which are large enough to be identified as feldspar. Some obsidians carry numerous large, well-formed crystals (phenocrysts) of quartz, alkali feldspar, and plagioclase; many of these contain abundant inclusions of glass. Less common are phenocrysts of biotite, hornblende, or augite. As the number of phenocrysts increases, these porphyritic glasses pass into a glassy rock called vitrophyre. Many obsidians contain spherical aggregates (spherulites) up to several centimetres across, but generally these are only a millimetre or so in diameter and are composed of radially arranged, needlelike crystals. Some of these spherulites consist of concentric shells separated by ring-shaped interspaces; such structures are known as stone bubbles or lithophysae.

Most obsidians are extremely rich in silica and have compositions roughly equivalent to granite and rhyolite; others correspond to trachyte, dacite, andesite, and latite. Glassy rocks equivalent to basalt are rare and are called tachylyte instead of obsidian (*cf.* tachylyte). Obsidian generally contains less than 1 percent water by weight. This water represents only part of that contained in the original melt, most having escaped as steam when the lava poured out on the surface. A small chip of obsidian heated under a blowpipe will fuse readily and lose its water by volatilization, whereas a second heating will show the material to be highly infusible; this experiment demonstrates the fluxing action of water in rock melts. Under high pressure at depth rhyolitic lavas may contain up to 10 percent water, which helps to keep them fluid even at a low temperature. Eruption to the surface, where pressure is low, permits rapid escape of this volatile water and increases the viscosity of the melt. Increased viscosity impedes crystallization and the lava solidifies as a glass.

Closely related to obsidian are perlite, pitchstone, and pumice. It is believed that under favourable conditions obsidian may be converted to perlite by adding water. Often in such cases the only remnants of the original obsidian are found in the cores of the glassy perlite beads.
·dating by weathering rim measurement **5**:511b
·igneous rock classification **9**:208a; table 207
·mineralogical composition table **9**:221
·physical properties **15**:953b; tables
·prehistoric use in the Near East **17**:929e

obsidian-hydration-rind dating, method of age determination of obsidian (black volcanic glass) that makes use of the fact that obsidian freshly exposed to the atmosphere will take up water to form a hydrated surface layer with a density and refractive index different from that of the remainder of the obsidian. The thickness of the layer can be determined by microscopic examination of a thin section of the sample cut at right angles to the surface. Because diffusion is the mechanism by which water penetrates into the glass, it is reasonable to expect that temperature, composition, and relative humidity would be factors affecting the rate of hydration. The rate of hydration was investigated using samples of known age, and it was found that temperature and chemical composition are the main factors controlling the rate of hydration; relative humidity had a negligible effect. The hydration–rind dating technique also has been used to date glassy rhyolitic flows that have erupted prior to 200 years ago and less than 200,000 years ago.
·theory and limitations **5**:511b

Obskaya Guba (Russian S.F.S.R.): *see* Ob, Gulf of.

obstetrics and gynecology, the medical specialties that deal respectively with management of pregnancy, labour, and the puerperium and with the treatment of the genital tract in women. Board requirements, examinations for specialization and practice, and residencies vary from country to country.
·childbirth stages and complications **13**:1036a
·diagnosis problems **5**:688a
·fetal disease detection **4**:218c
·gynecology techniques and fields of treatment **17**:822a
·history of medicine in Europe **11**:830g
·Semmelweis' study of puerperal fever **16**:529e

Obstfelder, Sigbjørn (b. Nov. 21, 1866, Stavanger, Nor.—d. July 29, 1900, Copenhagen), poet, idiosyncratic Symbolist and visionary who, in contrast to the typical young poets of his period, feared, rather than exploited, his mystic strain; engagement, not detachment, was what he asked from life.

He led a restless youth, travelling a great deal, once even to the U.S. Obstfelder's works all appeared in the 1890s: his first volume of *Digte* (1893; Eng. trans., *Poems*, 1920); a play, *De røde draaber* (1897; "The Red Drops"); two one-act plays, *Om vaaren* (1898; "In Spring") and *Esther* (1899); several short prose works, sketches, articles, drafts, reminiscences; some works he called "poems in prose"; and the posthumously published fragment, *En praests dagbog* (1900; "A Pastor's Diary"). His view is that of a solitary outsider, and his place in his native literature is unique. Obstfelder was the model for the diarist hero in the German poet Rilke's famous *Notebook of Malte Laurids Brigge*.

obstructive jaundice, or CHOLESTATIC JAUNDICE, a noticeable yellowish pigmentation caused by bile pigments' buildup due to obstruction of the bile duct.
·symptoms and causation **10**:1271b

obstructive nephropathy, an obstruction-caused disease of the kidney.
·kidney effects of urine blockage **7**:59c

obstruent, consonant sound produced by partly or completely obstructing the flow of air in the vocal tract; *e.g.*, *p*, *b*, *t*, *d*, *f*, *v*, *s*, and the *j* sound in "jam."
·Proto-Dravidian six articulation points **5**:990h

Ob Trench, submarine trough, Indian Ocean.
33°00′ S, 98°00′ E
·Indian Ocean floor features map **9**:308

obturator nerve, nerve supplying the adductor muscles of the thigh.
·anatomic relationships and functions **12**:1023g

Obuasi, town, Ashanti Region, Ghana. Its growth was stimulated by the discovery of a large gold mine (1897) and the building of the railway from Sekondi (1902). The Obuasi mine (since 1965, the only one in Ghana operated by a private company) has continued as the country's major producer while others have become depleted. Although mining is dominant, the economy has become diversified through commerce and cocoa production. Food must be imported. Migrant labour from Northern Region and the former French Union territories has swelled the population. A mosque serves the Muslim population. A transitory atmosphere is manifest in the suburb of Wawasi, where poor housing and insanitary conditions prevail. Pop. (1970 prelim.) 31,018.
6°12′ N, 1°40′ W
·map, Ghana **8**:138

Ob Ugrians, a Finno-Ugric people of Central Asia and Siberia.
·gods, temples, and ceremonies **7**:312d *passim* to 313f

Ob-Ugric languages, division of the Finno-Ugric branch of the Uralic language family, comprising the Mansi (Vogul) and Khanty (Ostyak) languages; they are most closely related to Hungarian, with which they make up the Ugric branch of Finno-Ugric. The Ob-Ugric languages are spoken by about 20,000 persons in the region of the Ob and Irtysh rivers in the U.S.S.R. They had no written tradition or literary language until 1930; since 1937 they have been written in a modified Cyrillic alphabet but have developed no important literature and are little used in government or education. *See also* Finno-Ugric languages; Mansi language; Khanty language.
·members, distribution, and history **18**:1025c; map 1023

obversion, in traditional logic, transformation of a categorical proposition (*q.v.*), or statement, into a new proposition in which (1) the subject term is unchanged, (2) the predicate is replaced by its contradictory, and (3) the quality of the proposition is changed from affirmative to negative or vice versa. Thus the obverse of "All men are mortal" is "No men are immortal." Because the obverse of any categorical proposition is logically equivalent to it, obversion is a form of immediate inference. *Cf.* conversion.
·definition and examples **11**:51b
·equivalence relations and transformation **17**:892c

Obwalden, half canton, central Switzerland, forms with Nidwalden half canton the canton of Unterwalden (*q.v.*). Drained by the Sarner Aa (river), its area of 190 sq mi (492 sq m) oc-

upies the western part of Unterwalden. Obwalden means Above the Forest, referring to the great forest of Kerns that divided the two half cantons in the Middle Ages. Obwalden acted independently of Nidwalden in its acquisition, with Uri canton, of the Valle Leventina in 1403 and of Bellinzona in 1419 (losing both in 1422). After Nidwalden refused to accept the federal constitution of 1815, Obwalden received the abbey lands of Engelberg that now form a completely detached commune. A sovereign half canton, Obwalden is administratively independent of Nidwalden. Its capital is Sarnen (*q.v.*). A dairying region with Alpine pastures, it has several resorts, notably Engelberg. The population (24,509 in 1970) is German-speaking and Catholic.
·area and population table **17**:874
·map, Switzerland **17**:868
·Swiss Confederation history **17**:879g

Ocagne, (Philibert-) Maurice d' (1862–1938), French mathematician.
·mathematical calculation theory and use **11**:686d

Ocala, city, seat (1846) of Marion County, north central Florida, U.S. It developed around Ft. King, established in 1827. The place-name was derived from Ocali, an obscure Indian word possibly referring to an ancient Timucuan province or the middle part of Florida. After the Seminole Wars, it evolved as a mixed farming centre. Reconstructed after the Civil War, it was incorporated as a city probably in 1885.

Thoroughbred-horse farm, Ocala, Fla.
Eric Carle—Shostal

Local deposits of pure limestone contribute to pastoral activities, which, apart from citrus cultivation, include the growing of vegetables, cattle raising, and the breeding of thoroughbred horses and greyhounds. Other economic factors are food processing, tourism, and light industrial development.

Ocala, just west of the Ocala National Forest, is a regional headquarters of the U.S. and Florida forest services. It is the home of Central Florida Junior College (1957). At nearby Silver Springs (east) and Rainbow Springs (west), marine life can be viewed through glass-bottomed boats. Other local attractions include Six Gun Territory (a re-enactment of the Wild West) and the Early American Museum, which exhibits horse-drawn vehicles and vintage cars. Pop. (1980) 37,170.
29°11′ N, 82°07′ W
·map, United States **18**:908

Ocala National Forest, central Florida, U.S.
·soil and vegetation characteristics **7**:425c

Ocaña, city, Norte de Santander department, northern Colombia, in the Hacari Valley. Founded (*c.* 1570) as New Madrid by Francisco Fernández, it was renamed for Ocaña in New Castile, Spain. An independence convention held there in 1828 is commemorated by a triumphal arch. Barium mining and onion growing are basic economic activities. Ocaña is the superior court of a judicial district and is seat of a diocese. The Palacio de Bellas Artes is associated with the National University of Colombia. Pop. (1972 est.) city, 39,400; mun., 48,700.
8°15′ N, 73°20′ W
·map, Colombia **4**:866

Ocaña, Cordillera de, Andean range, northern Colombia.
8°00′ N, 73°00′ W
·Columbian Andes extension features **1**:858f

ocarina (Italian: "little goose"), globular flute, a late-19th-century musical development of traditional Italian carnival whistles of earthenware, often bird-shaped and sounding

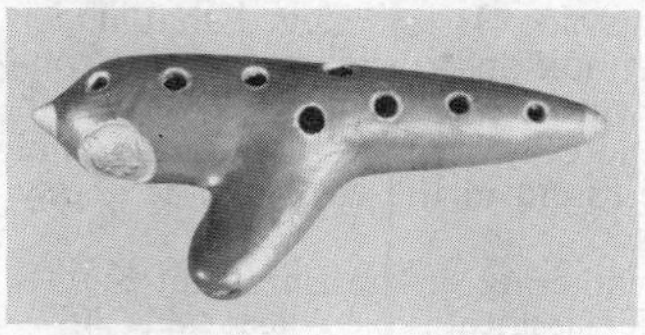

Painted clay ocarina from Italy, 20th century; in the Horniman Museum, London
By courtesy of the Horniman Museum, London

only one or two notes. It is an egg-shaped vessel of clay or metal or, as a toy, of plastic, and is sounded on the flageolet, or whistle flute, principle. It usually has eight finger holes and two thumbholes and may have a tuning plunger. In the 1930s it won professional popularity when ocarinas, or "sweet potatoes," of different sizes were played in harmony in U.S. popular music. The ocarina is a well-known European example of the globular flute, a form that occurs in many ancient and modern cultures.

O'Carolan (CAROLAN), **Turlough,** first name also TERENCE (b. 1670, near Nobber, County Meath—d. March 25, 1738, Alderford, County Roscommon), one of the last Irish harpist-composers and the only one whose songs survive in both words and music in significant number (about 220 are extant). The son of an iron founder, O'Carolan became blind from smallpox at the age of 18. He was befriended by Mrs. MacDermott Roe, the wife of his father's employer, who apprenticed him to a harper and supported him for the three years of his training, then gave him money, a guide, and a horse. As an itinerant harper, he travelled widely in Ireland. Although never considered a master performer, he was highly regarded as a composer of songs and improvised verse. His tunes appeared widely in 18th-century collections; one was used by Thomas Moore for his song "Oh! the sight entrancing."

O'Casey, Sean (b. March 30, 1880, Dublin—d. Sept. 18, 1964, Torquay, Devon), playwright renowned for realistic dramas of the Dublin slums in war and revolution, in which tragedy and comedy are juxtaposed in a way new to the theatre of his time, and for later plays that use the techniques of Expressionism and Symbolism.

Born an Irish Protestant, O'Casey was the youngest of 13 children, only five of whom survived childhood. He knew hunger, poverty, and ill health and saw fear, disease, and

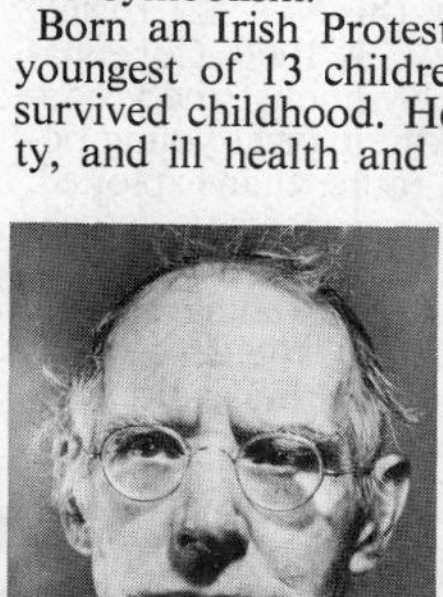

O'Casey, photograph by J. Bown
Camera Press—Pix

drunkenness all about him. With only three years of formal schooling, he educated himself by reading. He started work at 14, mostly at manual labour, including 10 years with the Irish railways. He had great love and respect for his widowed mother, a constant source of encouragement.

Caught up in the Irish national cause, he changed his name from the English form John to the Irish form Sean and learned Irish Gaelic. He was also active in the labour movement and wrote for the *Irish Worker*. He joined the Irish Citizen Army, a paramilitary arm of the unions, and drew up its constitution during a reorganization in 1914. Later that year he left it, however, because he considered it anti-labour. He became increasingly disillusioned with the middle class leadership of the national movement and did not take part in the 1916 Easter Rising against the British authorities.

Disgusted with the existing political parties, he turned his energies to drama. His tragicomedies reflect in part his mixed feelings about his fellow slumdwellers, seeing them as incapable of giving a Socialist direction to the Irish cause but at the same time, admirable for their unconquerable spirit—particularly the women who work, suffer, and sacrifice to try to keep their homes together, in contrast to the men, who tend to be mock heroic, likeable parasites.

After several of his plays had been rejected, the Abbey Theatre, Dublin, produced *The Shadow of a Gunman* (1923), set during the guerrilla strife between the Irish Republican Army and British forces. In 1924 the Abbey staged *Juno and the Paycock*, his most popular play, set during the period of civil war over the terms of Irish independence. *The Plough and the Stars* (1926), with the 1916 Easter Rising as its background, caused riots at the Abbey by patriots who thought the play denigrated Irish heroes. In these plays he created superbly articulate characters; and though portraying the tragic worlds of war and want, he wrote some of the funniest scenes in modern drama.

O'Casey went to England in 1926, met the Irish actress Eileen Carey Reynolds, married her, and henceforth made England his home. His decision to live outside Ireland was motivated in part by the Abbey's rejection of *The Silver Tassie*, an Expressionist anti-war drama produced in England in 1929. Another Expressionist play, *Within the Gates* (1934), followed, in which the modern world is symbolized by the happenings in a public park. *The Star Turns Red* (1940) is an anti-Fascist play, and the semi-autobiographical *Red Roses for Me* (1946) is set in Dublin at the time of the Irish railways strike of 1911.

His later plays, given to fantasy and ritual and directed against the life-denying puritanism he thought had beset Ireland, include *Cock-a-Doodle Dandy* (1949), *The Bishop's Bonfire* (1955), and *The Drums of Father Ned* (1958). His last full-length play was a satire on Dublin intellectuals, *Behind the Green Curtains* (published 1961).

Six volumes of autobiography appeared from 1939 to 1956; they were later collected in two volumes as *Mirror in My House* (1956) in the U.S. and as *Autobiographies* (1963) in Great Britain.

When first produced in the 1920s, O'Casey's plays had an explosive effect on the audiences at the Abbey and helped to enlarge its reputation. His later plays, in which he increasingly made use of Expressionist and Symbolist techniques, did not win the same wide acceptance as those he wrote for the Abbey, partly because they lacked the vigorous characterization and language of earlier works and partly because their purpose was more didactic. The merits of these plays were disputed by critics even after his death. They were produced in Europe with some success, particularly in eastern Europe, where O'Casey's working-class origins and support for Communism—albeit of a personal and undogmatic variety—attracted interest.

occasionalism, a version of Cartesian metaphysics, so named after the Rationalist René Descartes, that flourished in the last half of the 17th century, in which all interaction between mind and body is mediated by God. It is posited that unextended mind and extended body do not interact directly. The appearance of direct interaction is maintained by God, who moves the body on the occasion of the mind's willing and who puts ideas in the mind on the occasion of the body's encountering other material objects. For example, when a person actualizes his desire to pick up an apple, his mind does not act on his body directly, but his willing of the action is the occasion for God to make his arm reach out; and when his hand grasps the apple, the apple does not act on his mind directly, but the contact is the occasion for God to give him ideas of the apple's coolness and softness.

Occasionalism was developed primarily by Arnold Geulincx and Nicolas Malebranche, 17th-century Dutch and 17th–18th-century French philosophers, respectively, to solve a specific problem in Cartesian metaphysics. For Descartes, mind is active, unextended thinking, whereas body is passive, unthinking extension. But these two created substances, the bases of Cartesian dualism, are combined as a third, compound substance—living man. The problem is that the essential unlikeness of mind and body in the Cartesian view makes it difficult to conceive how they can interact—*i.e.*, how unextended mental ideas can push the body around and how bodily bumpings can yield ideas. Descartes's opinion that direct interaction takes place in the pineal gland that dangles from the centre of the brain does not answer the question of how. The orthodox view of the French Cartesians Pierre-Sylvain Régis and Jacques Rohault was simply that God has made mind and body so that they interact directly even if scientists do not know how. The occasionalist's answer to the question is to show how interaction appears to be direct when in fact it is mediated by the fourth, uncreated Cartesian substance, God.

Occasionalism was criticized by Simon Foucher, a 17th-century French Platonist, and others who pointed out that the problem remains of how God—a mental substance—can himself interact with the material substance, body. One answer is that he created it. Foucher believed that Gottfried Wilhelm Leibniz, the famous 17th–18th-century German philosopher and mathematician, took this way out in saying that monads, the units of reality, do not interact but only appear to do so, because God has created them in pre-established harmony. The apparent interaction of mind and body would also be pre-established. This reduction of the occasions of God's mediation to the single occasion of creation was then seen to be both a logical outcome of occasionalism and a *reductio ad absurdum* argument against it.

·Malebranche and Cartesian dualism **3**:968g
·problems in Cartesian interaction **12**:19b

Occidental, Cordillera, or WESTERN CORDILLERA, name applied to a number of mountain ranges in Spanish-speaking countries, notably the Andean ranges in Bolivia, Colombia, Peru, and Ecuador.

·Andes course and geographical features **1**:856c
·geographic, demographic, and economic features **4**:864c *passim* to 865h
·map, Bolivia **3**:2

Occidental Mindoro, province occupying the western half of Mindoro, Philippines. It has an area of 2,270 sq mi (5,880 sq km) and includes several offshore islands, of which the Lubang group (northwest) is the largest. Mamburao (the provincial capital), Paluan, Santa Cruz, and San Jose are the main population centres. Pop. (1970) 144,032.

·area and population table **14**:236

occipital bone, bone forming the back and back part of the base of the cranium, the part of the skull that encloses the brain. It has a large oval opening, the foramen magnum, through which the medulla oblongata passes, linking the spinal cord and brain. The occipital bone adjoins five of the other seven bones forming the cranium: at the back of the head, the two parietal bones; at the side, the temporal bones; and in front, the sphenoid bone, which also forms part of the base of the cranium. The occipital is concave internally to hold the back of the brain and is marked externally by nuchal (neck) lines where the neck musculature attaches. The occipital forms both in membrane and in cartilage; these parts fuse in early childhood. The seam, or suture, between the occipital and the sphenoid closes between ages 18 and 25, that with the parietals between ages 26 and 40.

In four-footed animals the head hangs from the end of the vertebral column, and the foramen magnum is placed posteriorly. The nuchal musculature is strongly developed to support the head, and the occipital markings are heavy.

In apes, with the assumption of semi-erect posture, the foramen has moved partially downward and forward. The nuchal muscles are powerful and attached high up on the occipital near the suture with the parietals, where a crest (lambdoidal crest) sometimes forms. In the evolution of man, the foramen magnum has continued to move forward as an aspect of adaptation to walking on two legs, until the head is now balanced vertically on top of the vertebral column. Concurrently, the line of attachment of the nuchal musculature has moved downward from the lambdoidal suture to a point low on the back of the head. In such ancestors of man as *Australopithecus* and *Homo erectus*, the nuchal markings, often heavy enough to form a protuberance, or torus, fell midway between the high of apes and the low of modern man.

·Asian fossil analysis and classification **2**:202e
·hominid fossils comparison **8**:1044h
·human skeletal interrelationships **16**:813g; illus.
·joint and bone relationships **10**:254d
·occipital condyles **8**:1028d; illus. 1025
·skeletal adaptation to upright posture **12**:637b

occipital cortex, the cerebral cortex of the occipital lobes of the cerebral hemispheres of the brain.

·human eye involvement **7**:99a

Occitan language, also called LANGUEDOC or PROVENÇAL, a Romance language spoken by more than 12,000,000 persons in southern France. All Occitan speakers use French as their official and cultural language, but Occitan dialects are used for everyday purposes and show no signs of extinction. The name Occitan is derived from the geographical name Occitania, which is itself patterned after Aquitania and includes the regions of Limousin, Languedoc, the old Aquitaine, and the southern part of the French Alps, all of the populations of which are Occitan speaking.

The name Languedoc comes from the term *langue d'oc*, a language using *oc* for "yes" (from Latin *hoc*), in contrast to the French language, the *langue d'oïl*, using *oïl* (modern *oui*) for "yes" (from Latin *hoc ille*). Languedoc refers to a linguistic and political–geographical region of the southern Massif Central in France. The name Provençal originally referred to a dialect of the Provence region and is used also to refer to the standardized medieval literary language based on the dialect of Provence.

Literature in Occitan is plentiful, for Provençal was a standard and literary language in France and northern Spain in the 12th to 14th century and was widely used as a vehicle for poetry; it was the primary language of the medieval troubadours. The earliest written material in Occitan is a refrain attached to a Latin poem said to date from the 10th century.

The modern dialects of Occitan are little changed from the speech of the Middle Ages, although they are being affected by their constant exposure to French. The major dialects are those of Limousin, Auvergnat, Provence, and Languedoc. Gascon, a Romance dialect of southwestern France, is usually classified as a dialect of Occitan, although it is sometimes considered a distinct language because it differs a great deal from the other more or less uniform Occitan dialects. Modern Gascon is probably less intelligible to Occitan speakers than is Catalan. Occitan is closely related to Catalan, and, although strongly influenced in the recent past by French, its phonology and grammar are more closely related to Spanish than to French.

·diphthongization, intervocalic p and t, and palatalization tables 1,2, and 3 **15**:1038
·history, dialects, and distinctive features **15**:1028b; map 1026
·medieval literary languages **10**:1101f
·typology, phonology, grammar, and vocabulary **15**:1037c *passim* to 1044b

Occleve, Thomas: *see* Hoccleve, Thomas.

occluded front, weather front (*q.v.*) that is formed when a cold front overtakes a warm front and lifts the warm air; it is characterized by low temperatures, much cloudiness, and widespread precipitation, often in the form of snow. When a cyclonic storm develops in middle latitudes, it often starts out as an undulation, or wave, on a pre-existing frontal boundary between warm and cold air masses. As the wave moves (generally eastward or northeastward in the Northern Hemisphere) and intensifies, its amplitude increases in much the same way that the amplitude of an ocean wave, starting out as a ripple, increases as it moves shoreward. Eventually, the advancing cold air behind the cold front catches up with the slower moving cold air under the warm front. The intervening tongue of warm air is pushed aloft, and the wave breaks or becomes occluded. At this point the kinetic energy of the storm, derived from the sinking of cold air and the rising of warm air, usually reaches its maximum. Classically, there are two types of occluded fronts, warm-front occlusions and cold-front occlusions, depending on whether the cold air behind the cold front is, respectively, warmer or colder than the cold air under the warm front.

·cyclone life cycle and front movement **5**:394e

occultation, in astronomy, the blocking by one celestial body of an observer's view of another body. *See* eclipse, occultation, and transit.

occultism, a general designation for various theories, practices, and rituals based on esoteric knowledge, especially alleged knowledge about the world of spirits and unknown forces of the universe. Devotees of occultism strive to understand and explore these worlds, often by developing the higher powers of the mind. To this end they frequently study very early writings in the belief that such secrets were known to ancient civilizations and can be repossessed. A favourite text is the Chinese *I Ching* ("Classic of Changes").

Occultism covers such diverse subjects as Satanism, astrology, Kabbala, Gnosticism, theosophy, divination, witchcraft, and certain forms of magic.

·mystical function and ambiguous utility **12**:786f
·Odin as Norse patron **8**:36g
·Taoist and Confucian views **17**:1034e
·theosophic affirmation of supernatural **18**:276f

occupancy, in law, acquisition of unowned property by taking possession with intent of ownership.

·original acquisition of property rights **15**:48b

occupational diseases, illnesses associated with certain occupations or industries.

·cancer causation and incidence **5**:858g
·cancer's industrial prevalence **3**:763h

·industrial environment risks **9**:528a
·infectious diseases of man **9**:537c
·safety as environmental control **16**:139a

occupational psychology: *see* industrial psychology.

occupational therapy, the use of selected activity to promote and maintain health, prevent disability, evaluate behaviour, and treat or train patients with physical or psychosocial dysfunction. This form of therapy evolved from the recognition that work helps to restore the mentally and physically ill, particularly after the acute phase of illness has passed. Because any form of therapy must be dependent on others, any treatment program designed by an occupational therapist is coordinated with the work of doctors, nurses, and other related professional personnel in setting up a specific program for a patient.

History. Patients have long been employed in the utility services of mental hospitals. In the late 19th and early 20th centuries, experiments were made in the use of craft activities to occupy mental patients. This practice gave rise to the first occupational therapy workshops and later to schools for the training of occupational therapists. In the 1920s treatment of psychiatric patients was directed toward developing a more satisfying relationship to the world around them and toward assisting patients to release or sublimate their emotional frustration.

Later developments included problem-solving techniques, crafts, and work procedures for young people; and industrial programs and activity programs of jobs for patients within the hospital. In 1952 a World Federation of Occupational Therapists was formed, and in 1954 the first international congress of occupational therapists was held at Edinburgh. The world body serves as liaison between more than 20 national organizations, which themselves examine and register therapists.

Modern activities. Occupational therapy is designed as specific treatment to restore physical function and to establish self-help methods in such simple functions as eating, dressing, and writing, as far as permanent limitations of the patient permit. The occupational therapist, in order to carry out the treatment prescribed by the physician, must have adequate knowledge of anatomy, physiology, medicine, surgery, psychiatry, and psychology, as well as knowledge of the skills used in treatment. A period of supervised clinical experience is usually required.

To rehabilitate and resettle the disabled, either for return to work or for home employment, it is essential to assess their ability to work. Methods vary from simple activity tests to full-scale work tests and psychiatric assessment. After assessment some prevocational training or practice may be necessary, and many occupational therapy departments have units in which the patient may be taught, or gain experience in, the use of tools for trades (*e.g.*, woodwork), light industrial work (*e.g.*, light assembly work), and clerical duties (typing). After initial training many patients are transferred to further training centres or direct to industry, others to employment in sheltered workshops maintained by government or voluntary agencies, and some to work at home. Occupational therapy is vital for reorienting patients hospitalized or unemployed for long periods.

An equally important phase of therapy is rehabilitation for daily living. An equipped kitchen unit is a standard part of most modern occupational therapy departments, and many centres have model living quarters so that practice in home care can be provided for the housewife before she resumes her duties after a serious accident or long illness. The difficulty of caring for the chronically sick is also minimized when the patient is made able to care for himself. Occupational therapy provides not only training in daily living activities but also aids that make eating, dressing, and toilet less fatiguing for the sick or elderly. *See also* physical therapy.

BIBLIOGRAPHY. W.R. Dunton, Jr., and S. Licht, *Occupational Therapy*, 2nd ed. (1957); H. Willard and C. Spackman (ed.), *Principles of Occupational Therapy*, 3rd ed. (1963); M.S. Jones, *An Approach to Occupational Therapy*, 2nd ed. (1964); Journals of the English and American Associations of Occupational Therapists.

·function in treatment of disorders **18**:286g
·industrial medicine concept development **9**:528a

O Ceallaigh, Sean Thomas: *see* O'Kelly, Sean Thomas.

oceanarium, an institution specializing in the display of seagoing creatures, especially oceanic fishes, for purposes of public enlightenment and scientific study. It is a particular type of aquarium, with modifications for the maintenance of saltwater organisms, often associated with a marine biological station or a university.

·first installation and educational role **1**:1027a

ocean–atmosphere interaction, processes that give rise to the transfer of momentum, water vapour, heat, gases, and salt particles across the boundary between the ocean and the overlying atmosphere.

The general circulation of the Earth's atmosphere plays an important role in driving the surface ocean currents around the globe. The ocean currents, in turn, are important in the exchange of heat and water vapour between ocean and atmosphere. This transfer helps maintain an overall heat balance, the result being that polar regions, with an annual radiative heat loss, do not progressively cool off; and tropical regions, with an annual radiative heat gain, do not progressively get warmer. Variations in sea surface temperatures may come about from variations in the atmospheric wind systems. These temperature changes may, in turn, influence the atmospheric circulation because of the heating or cooling effect on the air overlying the affected ocean.

·Atlantic ice, atmosphere, and currents **2**:295d
·carbon dioxide and climatic change **18**:1052e
·climate element movement **4**:719h
·climatic variation causes **4**:739h
·future weather influence of oceans **19**:701e
·heat and water balance relationships **19**:643f
·heat balance, turbulence, and water transport **13**:491g *passim* to 493b
·heat transfer and circulation **9**:124d
·ocean currents and winds **13**:438g
·Pre-Cambrian developments **13**:477d
·research project on energy exchange **18**:845e
·seawater concentrations of gases **13**:486b
·wave formation and dispersal velocity **19**:656d; illus. 659

ocean basins 13:433, large expanses of the deep-sea floor that are separated from one another by oceanic ridges and from the continents by the continental shelf and slope. Ocean basins cover three-fifths of the Earth and with the continents are Earth relief features of the highest order.

The text article treats methods for studying the ocean floor, the origin of ocean basins, and the several principal features, including the oceanic crust, the midocean ridges, trenches and fracture zones, and seamounts, guyots, and abyssal hills and plains.

REFERENCES in other text articles:

·Adriatic shore depth relation to coast **1**:97b
·Andaman Basin formation and topography **1**:839d
·Arabian Sea submarine topography **1**:1060b
·Arctic basin physiography **1**:1119g
·Atlantic basins depth and profile **2**:294g
·Carboniferous sediments and tectonism **3**:853f
·Caribbean Sea's submarine basins **3**:907b; map
·continental drift theory **13**:910d
·continental shelf origins and forms **5**:115b
·definition and types **13**:484b
·Drake Passage's floor composition **5**:980b
·ecosystem consequences of sea-floor spreading **1**:1030f
·estuary cutting and earth movement **6**:969e
·expansion theories and research **9**:125a
·exploration findings **6**:83g
·formation by sea-floor spreading **16**:442h
·freestanding wave origins **13**:494g
·graywacke and marine sediment deposits **8**:298f
·Indian Ocean basin structure **9**:307f
·island arcs, trenches, and sea floor **9**:1026a
·mountain and ocean development theories **12**:581b
·Pacific basin and oceanic islands **13**:826f
·Pacific basins and physiography **13**:836g
·physiography of the ocean floor **6**:47a
·ridge origin, growth, and distribution **13**:472c
·Scotia Sea tectonism **16**:403g
·sea-floor spreading **5**:119g
·temperature inversions **13**:489b
·tidal predictions and sea geometries **18**:385d
·Upper Paleozoic formation **13**:922c
·volcanism and rock formation **9**:215c

RELATED ENTRIES in the *Ready Reference and Index:*

abyssal hills; abyssal plains; fracture zone, submarine; guyot; oceanic deep; oceanic swell; oceanic trench; oceanic trough; sea floor; seaknoll seamount; Sigsbee deep; sill, submarine

ocean currents 13:437, circulation systems that keep the oceans' water in motion from surface to bottom; these currents flow because of the friction of the wind on the ocean surface and the differences in seawater density in various areas.

The text article treats the nature, observation and charting, and causes of ocean currents, and it covers the general oceanic circulation near the surface and in the deep sea. The article also treats the mutual influence of ocean currents and climate and weather.

REFERENCES in other text articles:

·Adriatic surface and wind action **1**:97c
·Aegean currents and wind action **1**:123f
·Alaskan islands climatic effect **1**:410e
·Andaman winds reversing currents **1**:839f
·Antarctic sea circulation **1**:955g
·Arabian Sea circulation system **1**:1060e
·Atlantic types and occurrence **2**:301b
·Beaufort Sea flow and velocity **2**:781g
·Black Sea wind and vertical currents **2**:1098b
·canyon cutting and sediment transport **3**:788e
·Caribbean Sea surface currents **3**:908a
·causes and patterns **13**:495g
·circulation theories **6**:87e
·climate generating factors **4**:719h
·continental shelf forms and features **5**:116c
·cyclothem build-up in ancient seas **5**:399e
·density currents due to saline gradient **5**:590d
·Ekman and hydrodynamic theories **6**:517h
·estuary circulation and tidal influence **6**:970h
·global precipitation regulation **2**:1042b
·graywacke sediment transport and deposits **8**:295e *passim* to 299b
·Gulf of Mexico characteristics **12**:77h
·Gulf Stream's characteristics **8**:486f
·Humboldt Pacific scientific study **8**:1190e
·hydrodynamic research methods **9**:123g
·iceberg drift factor **9**:157c
·Indian Ocean flow and seasonal changes **9**:312a
·Japan Sea hydrography **10**:92g
·marine sediment subsurface movement **11**:498g
·marine surface water nutrient supply **7**:346h
·measurement technology **18**:844d
·Mediterranean density currents **11**:855h
·navigational errors of dead reckoning **12**:903d
·North Sea counterclockwise circulation **13**:249h
·nutrient distribution **13**:500g
·Ordovician animal distribution **13**:659d
·Pacific circulation **13**:842g
·plankton productivity based on nutrient supply **14**:495g
·South Africa rainfall distribution role **17**:61d
·St. Lawrence Gulf and Gaspé Current **16**:172d
·tide complication factors **18**:389g; illus.
·Yellow Sea circulation **19**:1078f

RELATED ENTRIES in the *Ready Reference and Index:*

convergence and divergence; Ekman spiral; El Niño effect; equatorial currents; upwelling, oceanic

Oceania, collective name for the islands scattered throughout most of the Pacific Ocean. The term, in its widest sense, embraces the entire insular region between Asia and the Americas. A more common definition excludes the Ryukyu, Kuril, and Aleutian islands and the Japan archipelago. The most popular usage delimits Oceania further by eliminating Indonesia, Taiwan, and the Philippines, because the peoples and cultures of those islands are more closely related historically to the Asian mainland. Oceania then, in its most restricted meaning, includes more than 10,000 islands, with a total land area (excluding Australia) of approximately 325,000 sq mi (840,000 sq km).

Oceania has traditionally been divided into four parts: Australasia (Australia and New Zealand), Melanesia, Micronesia, and Polynesia (*qq.v.*). As recently as 20,000 years ago no human beings lived in the region. Although disagreeing on details, scientists generally support a theory that calls for a Southeast Asian origin of island peoples. By 1980 about 8,350,000 islanders lived in Oceania (excluding Australia), and many indigenous cultures were being revolutionized by intensive contact with non-Oceanic groups who had intruded from various parts of the Western world.

- armed forces statistics table 2 **2**:16
- Catholic population distribution map **15**:1019
- Cenozoic rock types and distribution **3**:1081d
- farm productivity and arable land **1**:320d; tables 316
- meat production and consumption **11**:746b
- New Guinea settlement and occupation **12**:1090f
- newspaper publishing statistics table **15**:237
- New Zealand's geography and society **13**:43a
- Pacific formation and locations **13**:826f
- Papuan geography and government administration **2**:431f *passim* to 432f
- petroleum production and demand statistics tables 1 and 2 **14**:176
- petroleum reserves of the world table **14**:175
- spice import, export, and value table 3 **17**:506
- Tasman's voyages and discoveries **17**:1070h
- textile production tables 1 and 2 **18**:188

Oceania, history of 13:443. Although the prehistoric development of Oceania can be reconstructed from archaeological evidence and legends, its history in the more conventional sense begins with the first contacts by European explorers in the 16th century.

The text article covers the history of Oceania except for Australia and New Zealand, which are treated in separate text articles. The earliest human settlement in New Guinea dates from about 20,000 years ago; a later settlement of horticulturalists spread over the Pacific Islands from the 2nd millennium BC into the Christian Era. Discovered by Europeans beginning in the 16th century, the islands of Oceania had early contacts with the West through explorers, castaways, missionaries, and traders. European settlement grew during the 19th century, and virtually all of Oceania passed under control of European powers and the United States between 1842 and 1900. Colonial governments were adapted to local circumstances, and after World War II the indigenous peoples began to gain more autonomy. By the late 1970s, most Pacific islands (apart from the French and U.S. territories) had become independent.

REFERENCES in other text articles:
- Australian Aboriginal social patterns **2**:424b
- British Empire and Commonwealth growth **3**:303h
- exploration, colonialism, and war **13**:844d
- Hawaiian race, religion, and domination **8**:673b *passim* to 676b
- island heritage and development **13**:828e
- Japanese repatriation in Micronesia **13**:834d
- Micronesian ancient and modern culture **12**:122g
- Polynesia since European contact **14**:783e
- racial types and modernized culture **13**:468g
- World War I campaigns **19**:950f
- World War II campaigns **19**:990h

Oceanian peoples, arts of 13:448, diverse mediums of expression of the many peoples living in the region generally known as Oceania.

The text article covers the social milieu, demographic influences, historical perspectives, contemporary features, general characteristics of literature, Melanesian literatures, Polynesian and Micronesian literatures, the role of music and dance, musical instruments, regional styles and traditions, study and evaluation of music and dance, general characteristics of the visual arts, Melanesian visual arts, Micronesian visual arts, Polynesian visual arts, and Australian visual arts.

REFERENCES in other text articles:
- arms materials limitation and style description **2**:34g; illus.
- Australian Aboriginal music and art **13**:243h
- Australian Aboriginal religious basis **2**:428b
- basketry construction and use **2**:758f *passim* to 762d
- characteristics and criticism **14**:1032a
- Dong Son cultural commonality **17**:259e
- drums used by Pacific islanders **14**:66e
- Easter Island monumental statues **6**:131f
- idiophones in various cultures **14**:63d
- level of literary development **4**:230e
- mask design, types, and use **11**:580d; illus.
- materials and aesthetic functionality **13**:470e
- Melanesian wood carving, illus. **16**:Sculpture, Art of, Plate 2
- Micronesian decorative and vocal arts **12**:125h
- Polynesian art motifs and sculpture **14**:783c
- visual arts stylistic syncretism **19**:248c

RELATED ENTRIES in the *Ready Reference and Index: for*
carving: see beak style; curvilinear style; hei tiki; korwar style; malanggan style; Massim style; moai figures; rei-miro; Tami style; telum figures; uli figures
fabric: tapa
painting: bark painting; wondjina style; X-ray style

Oceanian peoples and cultures 13:468, indigenous peoples and cultures of the large area of the Pacific stretching from the Mariana and Hawaiian Islands in the north to New Zealand in the south and from Australia in the west to Easter Island in the east. The area may be subdivided into four regions exhibiting distinctive cultural traits: Polynesia, Micronesia, Melanesia, and Australia.

The text article gives a broad survey of the people, culture patterns, and modern developments.

REFERENCES in other text articles:
- animism as religion reduced to magic **1**:923c
- Australian Aboriginal society **2**:424c
- Australoid racial characteristics **14**:844b
- blood group frequencies in populations **2**:1149a
- culturo-linguistic affinities **2**:485b; map
- Easter Island temples and stone statues **6**:131f
- language distribution by family **10**:668g
- linguistic groups and typology **2**:489g
- Melanesian cultural patterns **11**:864g
- Micronesian fragmentation and cohesion **12**:122b
- New Guinea population characteristics **12**:1090h
- New Guinea's genetic semi-isolation **7**:1009g
- Pacific islands' European exploitation **13**:844h
- Papua territory racial types **2**:431g
- Polynesian society and civilization **14**:777d
- polyphony of gardening people **16**:792b
- social contrasts and origin theory **13**:443h
- sorcery beliefs **19**:895d *passim* to 896h
- traditional practices and institutions **13**:827h

RELATED ENTRIES in the *Ready Reference and Index:*
Maori; Moriori; Papuan; Tasmanians

Oceanic, name of two ocean liners built by the White Star Line of Great Britain to ply the North Atlantic. The first "Oceanic," built in 1871, combined sails and a compound engine with a new hull design to permit increased length and speed. Passenger facilities were also enlarged and greatly improved. The ship sailed until 1899, the year in which the second "Oceanic" was launched. This transatlantic ocean liner, 704 feet (215 metres) long, was the first ship to exceed the "Great Eastern" in length. It sailed until 1914.

oceanic atoll: *see* coral islands, coral reefs, and atolls.

oceanic deep, well-defined portion of a depression in the sea floor that exceeds the arbitrarily chosen water depth of 6,000 metres (about 20,000 feet). Thus, the major part of an oceanic trench or marine basin may constitute an oceanic deep and may contain one or more deeps.

oceanic fracture: *see* fracture zones, submarine.

Oceanic (or EASTERN AUSTRONESIAN) **languages,** widespread, highly varied, and controversial language group of the Austronesian language family. Spoken on the islands of Oceania from New Guinea to Hawaii to Easter Island, these languages share so little basic vocabulary that some scholars prefer to classify them in smaller, more cohesive groups. The features shared include a tendency toward use of separate words rather than affixes to express grammatical relationships, a basic five-vowel system, and several common phonetic developments.

- Austronesian languages **10**:668g
- classification and characteristics **2**:489g

oceanic plateau, also called SUBMARINE PLATEAU, large submarine elevation rising sharply at least 200 metres (660 feet) above the surrounding deep-sea floor, and characterized principally by an extensive, relatively flat or gently tilted summit. Most oceanic plateaus were named early in the 20th century prior to the invention of sonic sounding, and many of these features have been shown by modern bathymetric data to be portions of the mid-ocean rises. Thus, the Albatross Plateau of the eastern equatorial Pacific now is recognized as belonging to the East Pacific Rise and has been shown to possess a much more irregular summit than early data indicated.

Most plateaus are steplike interruptions of the continental slopes and appear to be downwarped or downfaulted blocks of former continental shelves. These marginal plateaus are exemplified by the Blake Plateau off the southeastern United States. This plateau's flat surface lies between 700 and 1,000 metres (2,300 and 3,300 feet) below sea level, is more than 300 kilometres wide, and covers approximately 130,000 square kilometres (50,000 square miles) of sea floor. The crust underlying the plateau, although relatively thin and veneered by flat-lying marine sediments, is otherwise continental in character.

Other plateaus, such as the coral-capped plateaus of the South China Sea, occur in the ocean well beyond the continental margins. They stand above the surrounding deep-sea floor as isolated topographic highs and are believed to be composed of continental rock cores overlain by flat-lying marine sediments. Presumably, these midocean plateaus are minor fragments of continent that have been isolated during continental drift and sea-floor spreading.

oceanic ridges 13:472, long, prominent, submarine mountain ridges that divide the ocean floors into separate basins and serve as loci of sea-floor spreading.

The text article treats the historical development of man's knowledge of oceanic ridges and deals with their classification, origin and growth, and occurrence and distribution.

REFERENCES in other text articles:
- Andaman's topography of rift valleys **1**:839e
- Arabian Sea submarine topography **1**:1060b

RELATED ENTRIES in the *Ready Reference and Index:*
archipelagic apron; aseismic ridge; ridge crest, oceanic; ridge flank, oceanic; submarine gap; transcurrent fault

oceanic swell, broad elongate elevation that rises gently from the sea floor. The term is becoming less used, possibly because of the confusion that may arise from the more common usage of the word in reference to oceanic water waves that are propagated by storms. The term merely describes submarine topography and has no genetic significance.

oceanic trench, long, narrow, steep-sided depression in the ocean bottom in which maximum oceanic depths (7,300 to 9,000 metres [24,000 to 30,000 feet]) occur. Typical trench widths are 40 to 120 kilometres (25 to 75 miles), and lengths range from 500 to 4,500 kilometres (300 to 2,800 miles).

Trenches generally lie seaward of and parallel to adjacent volcanic island arcs or mountain ranges of the continental coasts. Only 3 of the Earth's 20 major trenches are not Pacific features. The only Atlantic trenches are the Puerto Rico Trench north of the Caribbean islands and the South Sandwich Trench east of Drake Passage between South America and Antarctica. The locations of these trenches—where the Pacific and Atlantic sea floors are either uninterrupted or are separated only by a narrow span of continental crust—probably is not happenstance. The only major Indian Ocean trench is the Java Trench south of Indonesia.

The cross sections of trenches generally are V-shaped with steeper landward sides. Typical slopes range between 4° and 16°, although slopes as steep as 45° have been measured in the Tonga Trench of the equatorial South Pacific. Narrow, flat abyssal plains of ponded sediment generally occupy trench axes.

Geophysical data provide important clues concerning the origin of trenches. No abnormalities in the flow of internal Earth heat or variations in the Earth's magnetic field occur at trenches. Precision measurements reveal that the force of gravity generally is lower than normal, however. These negative gravity anomalies are interpreted to mean that the lithosphere (crustal and upper mantle rock) underlying trenches is being forced down against buoyant isostatic forces.

This interpretation of gravity data is substantiated by seismological studies. All trenches are associated with zones of earthquake foci. Along the periphery of the Pacific Ocean, earthquakes occur close to and landward of the trenches, at depths within the Earth of 55 kilometres (35 miles) or less. With increased landward distance away from the trenches, earthquakes occur at greater and greater depths—as deep as 700 kilometres (430 miles)—400 kilometres (250 miles) away from trench axes. Seismic foci thus define tabular zones approximately 20 kilometres thick that dip landward at about 45° beneath the continents. Analyses of these seismic zones and of individual earthquakes indicate that the seismicity results from the movement of oceanic lithosphere downward into the earth's interior; oceanic trenches are topographic expressions of this movement.

The downward motion of oceanic lithosphere helps to explain the relative scarcity of sediment that has accumulated within the trenches. Small quantities of brown or red clay, siliceous organic remains, volcanic ash and lapilli, and coarse, graded layers that result from turbidity (sediment-laden) currents and from the slumping of the trench walls occur at trench axes. Sediments on trench walls shallower than 4,500 metres are predominantly calcareous foraminiferal oozes. Large quantities of sediment cannot accumulate because they either are dragged into the Earth's interior by the diving lithosphere or are distorted into folded masses and molded into new material of the continental periphery.

oceanic trough, elongate depression in the sea floor, characteristically shoaler, shorter, narrower, and topographically gentler than oceanic trenches. Maximal depths range between 2,300 metres (7,500 feet) in the Papuan Trough and 7,440 metres (24,400 feet) in the Banda Trough. More typical maximum depths lie between four and five kilometres below sea level. Lengths of the 25 best known troughs range between 270 and 2,300 kilometres (170 and 1,400 miles) and average about 700 kilometres; their widths are from 20 to 100 kilometres and average about 50 kilometres. Unlike trenches, oceanic troughs probably owe their origins to a wide variety of geologic mechanisms.

Oceanids (Greek mythology): *see* nymph.

Ocean Island, or BANABA, coral and phosphate formation in the Gilbert and Ellice Islands, a British crown colony in the west central Pacific Ocean. With a circumference of 6 mi (10 km) and an area of 2 sq mi (5 sq km), the island rises to a central phosphate mass 265 ft (81 m) high. Discovered (1804) by the British ship "Ocean," the island was annexed by Britain in 1900. In that same year the mining and shipping of phosphate began. By the 1970s, annual production was more than 550,000 tons. Part of the crown colony since 1915, the island was occupied by Japanese forces from 1942 to 1945. Tapiwa, on the island, was formerly the administrative headquarters of the crown colony. The original Banaban populace has been resettled on Rambi, an island near Viti Levu, Fiji. As compensation for the disruption of their island, they receive a percentage of the value of phosphate mined. Latest census 2,192.
0°52′ S, 169°35′ E

Oceanitidae (bird family): *see* storm petrel.

oceanodromous fish, a fish migratory in salt water.

Ocean of Rivers of Stories, The, Sanskrit KATHĀ-SARITSĀGARA (written 1063–81), collection of Indian tales by Samadeva.

oceanography, study of all aspects of the world's oceans and seas, including their physical and chemical properties, their contained plants and animals, and their origins and geological framework. Usage varies with both custom and authority, but physical oceanography is commonly considered to embrace the study of such water properties as temperature, salinity, density and pressure, and the transmission of electrical, optical, and acoustical stimuli in the oceans. Dynamic oceanography is concerned with the energy interchange at the air–sea surface and the general motion of seawater, including the tides and the several forms of surface and subsurface waves and currents. Chemical oceanography focuses upon the chemistry of seawater, including identification of all dissolved constituents, the several chemical and biochemical cycles that exist in the oceans, and the geochemical models that provide insight to the origin and development of the world's oceans and seas. Biological oceanography is the name applied to the study of all flora and fauna and their ecological adjustment and life cycles in the sea, and geological oceanography is concerned with the geological character of the ocean basins, their constituent rocks and contained marine sediments. The latter is also the discipline chiefly involved in study of oceanic ridges, rock magnetism and heat flow from the ocean bottoms, and the concepts of sea-floor spreading and continental drift that have emerged since the 1960s.

Oceanography today is the sum total of these several branches, each of which is based on the acquisition of data that are gathered in the course of oceanographic expeditions. In conjunction with formal courses, often of a theoretical nature, students of oceanography commonly participate in such expeditions to facilitate their understanding of how the data are gathered and the nature of their limitations. Modern research in any of the branches of oceanography is dependent upon a variety of underwater sampling and mapping equipment but conclusions, as in other branches of science, are ultimately dependent upon a variety of mathematical models and analytical methods, each of which has been facilitated by the advent of high-speed computers.

ocean perch: *see* redfish.

oceans, development of **13**:476, the origin and evolution of seawater.

The text article deals with the chemical history of the oceans, beginning with the early oceans, which were produced by the reducing reactions between the cooling crust of the Earth and volatile, highly reactive, acidic gases, followed by a transition stage between early and modern conditions, and ending with a detailed discussion of modern oceans. Included are sections on mineral–seawater equilibria, mass balance of the oceans, and the experimental evidence dealing with these problems. The article also covers generally the sedimentary rock mass, the periodic fluctuations in seawater composition, and the present hydrosphere.

REFERENCES in other text articles:
- Atlantic origin and continental drift **2**:295g
- canyon formation forces and locations **3**:786e *passim* to 790c
- Cenozoic sediments and sea level change **3**:1080h
- chemical evolution and sediments **13**:486g
- continental drift and lunar forces **5**:109a
- Darwin's first coral observation theories **5**:493c
- Europe's emergence **6**:1036d
- glaciation and sea level changes **4**:733b
- life origin and photochemical reactions **13**:497d
- Mesozoic sea-floor spreading **11**:1013h
- ocean basin structure formation **13**:436f
- Ordovician sea limits and changes **13**:660g
- Permian paleogeography **14**:99b
- sea-floor spreading hypothesis **16**:443c; illus. 445
- Upper Paleozoic sea floor uplift **13**:922b

RELATED ENTRIES in the *Ready Reference and Index:*
connate water; degassing of Earth's interior; juvenile water

oceans and seas 13:482, the saline waters that cover 71 percent of the Earth's surface.

The text article deals with the chemical evolution, composition, and physical and chemical properties of seawater; the ocean–atmosphere interaction that produces oceanic circulation; ocean currents and sea waves; life in the open sea; and the economic value of oceans and seas for transportation, communication, food, water, waste disposal, and energy resources.

REFERENCES in other text articles:
- Antarctic climate **1**:954h
- biosphere
  - biosphere cycling of matter **2**:1040a *passim* to 1042f
  - marine ecosystem properties **1**:1029a *passim* to 1030f
  - marine life in photic zone **7**:346g
  - migratory patterns of marine animals **12**:177e *passim* to 179f
  - pressure effect and limitation on life **14**:994c
  - respiratory gases in aqueous solution **15**:752b
- composition and element distribution **6**:709d; table 710
- Cook's voyages of discovery **5**:130h; map
- cyclone and anticyclone movement **5**:392g
- cyclothems and ancient inland seas **5**:396d
- density currents due to saline gradient **5**:590d
- earthquake submarine sources **6**:69c
- elements in seawater and biological concentration **6**:715b; table 714
- estuary formation and river water mixing **6**:969c
- floor exploration **6**:83g
- floor geological characteristics **6**:62f
- geological forms and feature development **7**:1064b
- global water distribution and flux **19**:644c
- gold source of six parts per trillion **8**:237c
- hydrologic element roles and analysis **9**:104e
- Jurassic paleogeography illus. **10**:358
- lagoon occurrence and formation **10**:592c
- magnesium sources and processing **11**:302g
- magnetic rock sampling from ocean floor **15**:944f; illus.
- marine sediment types and origins **11**:495h
- mineral resource potential **5**:46d; illus.
- natural gas origins **12**:860c
- ocean currents and deepwater studies **13**:437d; illus. 438
- oceanographic research methods **9**:123e
- oceanothermic and tidal power uses **6**:858a
- oil pollution and dumping restrictions **18**:578g
- Ordovician paleogeography and fauna **13**:658a; figure 660
- origins and evolution **13**:476a
- physiography of the ocean floor **6**:47a
- Pleistocene water mass changes **13**:908c
- pollution sources and control **14**:756d
- refuse disposal problems **15**:574e
- research projects and equipment **18**:843e
- ridge origin, growth, and distribution **13**:472a
- rift discovery and formation processes **15**:841c
- salt composition and production **16**:193b; table
- sea-floor spreading and sea level change **16**:444a
- sedimentary facies and marine environment **16**:459e
- siliceous rocks' biogeochemical origin **16**:766e
- Silurian paleogeography **16**:769d
- soundings, drilling, and ocean study **7**:82d
- tectonic movement evidence **14**:435d
- thermal changes and light penetration **12**:120e
- tidal forces and predictions **18**:383a
- Upper Paleozoic uplift and deposits **13**:922b
- volcanic structures and activity **19**:507a
- volcanism and rock formation **9**:215c
- water distribution and elevation **6**:42f; tables and graph 43
- water distribution percentages **15**:875b
- water sources of the world **19**:649g; table
- wave transmission over varying depths **19**:655h
- weather variations from land **19**:700a
- world's oceans and seas
  - Arabian Sea features and composition **1**:1059h
  - Arctic physiography and exploration **1**:1118h
  - Asian paleogeography **2**:153d; map 150
  - Atlantic physiography and resources **2**:294a
  - Caribbean physiography and climate **3**:906h
  - Caspian Sea geology and hydrology **3**:980c
  - English Channel area and features **6**:873d
  - Gulf of Mexico physical features **12**:77e
  - Indian Ocean physiography and exploration **9**:307b
  - Mediterranean geology and hydrography **11**:854e
  - Pacific physiography and exploration **13**:836c

RELATED ENTRIES in the *Ready Reference and Index:*
abyssal zone; air–sea interface; alkalinity of seawater; bathyal zone; bathypelagic zone; benthos, marine; bloom, marine; bottom water, oceanic; cables, undersea; Challenger Expedition; chlorinity of seawater; deep-scattering layer; density of seawater; desalination; hadal zone; halocline; heavy water; hypolimnion; intermediate water; littoral zone; nekton; neritic zone; nutrients, oceanic; pelagic zone; phosphorescence, marine; photic zone, salinity of seawater; temperature–salinity diagram; thermocline; trace elements, oceanic; transparency of seawater; water mass

Oceanside, city, San Diego County, southern California, U.S., on the Pacific coast, at the mouth of the San Luis Rey River. Bounded south by Carlsbad and east by Vista, it developed as a beach resort and agricultural-trade centre after the arrival of the Southern California Railway in 1883. Its growth was boosted after the establishment in 1942 of Camp Pendleton (U.S. Marine Corps base). The nearby Mission San Luis Rey (founded in 1798) has been restored. Mira Costa (junior) College was established in 1934. Inc. city, 1888. Pop. (1970) 40,494; (1980) 76,698.
33°12′ N, 117°23′ W
- map, United States **18**:908

Ocean Springs, resort town, Jackson County, southeastern Mississippi, U.S., on Biloxi Bay across from Biloxi. It developed around the site of Old Biloxi, where Pierre Le Moyne, sieur d'Iberville, established, in 1699 for France, Ft. Maurepas, the first permanent white settlement in the Lower Mississippi Valley. Its name was changed to Lynchburg (1853), and in 1854 its present name was coined by Dr. George W. Austin, who established a sanitarium to utilize its spring waters. Manufactures include pottery, precision optical equipment, and lumber products. The huge Ruskin Oak on the Many Oaks Estate was named after John Ruskin, the English writer and artist, who visited the spot in 1885. Inc. town, 1892; city, 1947. Pop. (1980) 14,504.
30°25′ N, 88°50′ W

ocean sunfish, common name for three species of oceanic fishes of the family Molidae, also known as molas or headfishes. Ocean sunfishes are distinctive in appearance, with short bodies that end abruptly just behind the tall, triangular dorsal and anal fins. The fishes are also flattened from side to side and have tough skins, small mouths, and fused, beak-like teeth. The ocean sunfish (*Mola mola*) is an enormous, gray or brownish species reaching a maximum length and weight of about 3.3 metres (11 feet) and 1,900 kilograms (4,000 pounds). More or less oval or circular in

Ocean sunfish (*Mola mola*)
Carl Roessler

shape, it takes its name from the millstone, or mola, to which it was likened by Linnaeus. An inhabitant of temperate and tropical regions throughout the world, it is usually found in the open sea, often at the surface. The other ocean sunfishes are longer in the body but similarly cut short behind the dorsal and anal fins. The sharptail mola, *Mola lanceolata* (or *Masturus lanceolatus*), is also very large, but the slender mola (*Ranzania laevis*) is smaller, being about 70 centimetres (30 inches) long.
- classification and general features **18**:163h

Oceanus, in Greek mythology, the river that flowed around the earth (conceived as flat). Beyond it, to the west, were the land of the Cimmerii, where the sun never shone, the country of dreams, and the entrance of the underworld. In Hesiod's *Theogony* Oceanus was the son of Uranus (Heaven) and Ge (Earth), the husband of the Titaness Tethys, and father of 3,000 stream spirits and 4,000 ocean nymphs. In Homer's works he was the origin of the gods. As a common noun the word received almost the modern sense of ocean.

Oceanus Britannicus (Europe): *see* English Channel.

Oceanus Hibernicus (Europe): *see* Irish Sea.

ocelot (*Felis pardalis*), American cat, family Felidae, found from Texas southward to Paraguay. The adult ocelot is from 90 to 130 cm (36–52 in.) long, excluding the 30–40-cm (12–16-in.) tail; stands about 45 cm (18 in.) at the shoulder; and weighs 10–16 kg (22–35 lb). Females are generally smaller than males. The colour of the upper parts varies from pale gray to deep brown. There are small black spots on the head, two black stripes on the cheeks, and four or five longitudinal black stripes on the neck. The body is patterned with elongate, black-edged spots arranged in chainlike bands. The underparts are whitish, spotted with black, and the tail is marked above with dark bars or blotches.

The ocelot climbs well and inhabits forests or brush-covered regions. It hunts chiefly at night, feeding upon small- to medium-sized mammals, birds, and reptiles. Breeding is believed to occur at any season. A litter usually contains two or three young, which, although darker, resemble the adult in coat pattern. The ocelot is frequently maintained in captivity. Some individuals are readily tamed but may become unreliable in temperament as adults.

Ocelot (*Felis pardalis*)
Warren Garst—Tom Stack and Associates

The margay (*q.v.*) closely resembles the ocelot in general appearance and range but differs in coloration.
·fur origin and characteristics table **7**:814

Oc Eo, historic port and archaeological site, located in the Iransbassac area of modern South Vietnam.
·Funan's important remains **3**:682c

ochetus (music): *see* hocket.

Ochikubo monogatari (10th century AD), Japan's earliest novel.
·Heian period musical life of Japan **12**:682c

O-chi-na River, Wade-Giles romanization O-CHI-NA HO, Pin-yin romanization O-JI-NA HE, Mongolian EDZIN GOL, rises in western Kansu Province (*sheng*), China, and flows into the western Ala Shan Desert, northern Kansu. The river is formed by a whole series of small rivers flowing north from the Nan Shan and Ch'i-lien ranges in Kansu, between Chang-yeh and Chiu-ch'üan. The main rivers are the Lin Shui and Jo Shui, which flow together into the O-chi-na Ho. The river then flows northward across the desert into a depression filled with salt marshes and swamps that vary greatly in size from one season to another. The valley is virtually the only part of the Ala Shan plateau that has any permanent agriculture or permanent population. It was colonized on a small scale as long ago as the 1st century BC; its permanent settlement is comparatively recent. In the early 1950s a branch railway was built from the main Kansu–Central Asia line to Shuang-ch'eng-tzu, the principal settlement in the valley. Even with irrigation, however, which is imperative in the arid climate of the area, the intense salinity of the soil is a major problem for agriculture.

The lower course of the O-chi-na Ho from about 102 BC formed a forward defense line for the armies of the Han dynasty (206 BC–AD 220) defending the region against the nomadic Hsiung-nu and was the site of a county (*hsien*) called Chü-yen. In 1930–31, a Sino-Swedish expedition discovered great numbers of documents written on wooden strips and dating from the period before the Later Han (AD 23–220). Most of them date from 73–48 BC and are the earliest surviving Chinese official documents.
42°05′ N, 101°15′ E
·map, China **4**:262

Ochino, Bernardino (b. 1487, Siena, Italy—d. 1564, Austerlitz, Moravia, now Slavkov, Czech.), Protestant convert from Roman Catholicism who became an itinerant Reformer and influenced other radical Reformers by his controversial anti-Catholic views. Taking his surname from the Sienese district dell' Oca, Ochino joined the Franciscan Order in the Roman Catholic Church about 1504, but in 1534 he left for the stricter Capuchin Order, of which he became vicar general (1538–42). His renown as a preacher soon prompted papal regulations of his appearances.

After being commissioned to read and refute works by Protestant Reformers, and after meeting the Spanish religious writer Juan de Valdés in Naples in 1536, Ochino was converted to Protestantism. At first he withheld his open support because he hoped that Italy would embrace the Protestant cause for reform, but in 1542, when the Roman Inquisition summoned him, he fled over the Alps to the community of John Calvin at Geneva. There he demonstrated his Protestantism by marrying a refugee from Lucca, Italy, and in 1545 was made a pastor in the German community of youthful bankers at Augsburg. Fleeing Augsburg after its fall in the Schmalkaldic War (1546–47), Ochino went to England. There he played a prominent part in the Reformation under King Edward VI, praising the reforms of Edward and Henry VIII in his *Tragoedie or Dialoge of the Unjuste Usurped Primacie of the Bishop of Rome* (1549). When the Catholic Queen Mary I ascended the English throne in 1553, Ochino returned to Europe to become a pastor to Italian refugees at Zürich. He antagonized city officials, however, by strident tracts against the Roman Catholic doctrine of purgatory and by minimizing the differences between Calvinist and Lutheran views concerning the Lord's Supper. Attempting to avoid local censorship, he issued at Basel his *Dialogi XXX* (1563), in one of which he appeared to advocate polygamy. For this and for alleged anti-Trinitarian attitudes he was banished from Zürich, and in December 1563 he left for Poland, where his *Tragoedie* was published in Polish in an edition adapted to the local situation. Polish Catholics managed to have him banished, and he died from the plague while travelling in Moravia.

Ochlandra, genus of grass in the order Poales.
·stamen number **14**:590e

Ochna atropurpurea, species of flowering plant in the order Theales.
·plant structures, illus. 1 **18**:209

Ochnaceae, the most primitive family of the order Theales, contains 27 genera and 400 species of tropical trees and shrubs and two genera of herbs (*Sauvagesia* and *Vausagesia*). The largest genus is *Ouratea*, with 210 species. The tropical African and Asian genus *Ochna* has 95 species. All genera bear alternate, simple leaves, except *Godoya*, which has divided leaves. They have clustered flowers, usually with five petals and sepals. Fun shrub, or carnival bush (*Ochna multiflora*), reaches 1.5 metres (5 feet) and has evergreen leaves. Its yellow, buttercup-like flowers have sepals that turn scarlet and remain after the petals fall. There are 3 to 15 projecting, jet-black seeds.
·classification and general features **18**:210b

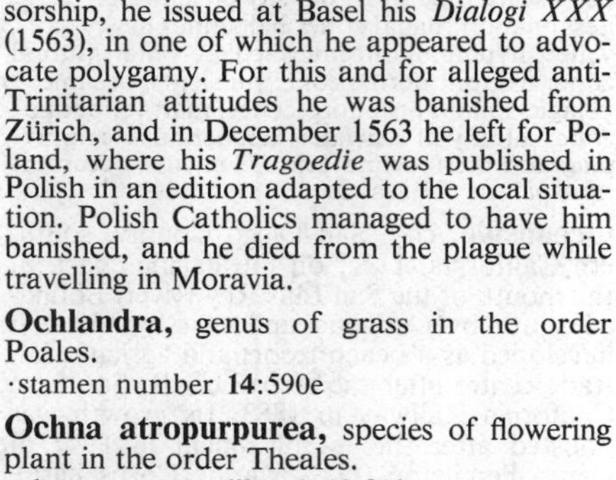

Ochna atropurpurea
G.R. Roberts

Ochoa, Severo (b. Sept. 24, 1905, Luarca, Spain), biochemist, received (with the U.S. biochemist Arthur Kornberg) the 1959 Nobel Prize for Medicine or Physiology for discovery of an enzyme in bacteria that enabled him to synthesize, in the test tube, ribonucleic acid (RNA), a substance of central importance to the construction of proteins by the cell. The enzyme, which he named polynucleotide phosphorylase, has been singularly valuable in enabling scientists to understand and re-create the process whereby the hereditary information contained in genes is translated, through RNA intermediaries, into enzymes that determine the functions and character of each cell.

Ochoa studied the biochemistry and physiology of muscle under the German biochemist Otto Meyerhoff at the University of Heidelberg (1930–31) and served as head of the physiology division, Institute for Medical Research, at the University of Madrid (1935). He investigated the function in the body of thiamine (vitamin B_1) at Oxford (1938–41) and became a research associate in medicine (1942) and professor of pharmacology (1946) at New York University, New York City, where he has served as professor of biochemistry and chairman of the department since 1954.

Ochoa was one of the first to show that energy created by the breakdown of foodstuffs in the cell is stored and utilized by means of energy-rich phosphate compounds; he discovered polynucleotide phosphorylase accidentally in 1955 while studying oxidative phosphorylation, the means by which the cell forms nucleoside triphosphates—energy-rich compounds such as adenosine triphosphate (ATP) and guanosine triphosphate (GTP)—from the diphosphate forms of the compounds, inorganic phosphate, and electrons liberated during the breakdown of foodstuffs.

Using extracts of the bacterium *Azotobacter vinelandii*, Ochoa found an enzyme that, instead of catalyzing the addition of a phosphate to the diphosphate compound, eliminates a phosphate from each compound and links the nucleotides together to form polynucleotide chains very similar to RNA (an organic base, such as adenine or guanine, linked to the 5-carbon sugar ribose, linked to a single phosphate, which in turn is linked to the ribose of the next nucleotide, and so on). Although polynucleotide phosphorylase is not the enzyme that catalyzes the routine construction of RNA in the cell, it has been used to build strands of artificial RNA of known composition, which are invaluable in elucidating the details of cellular heredity on the molecular level.

Ochoan Stage, post-Guadalupian time of deposition of the Upper Permian Series of rock strata in the U.S., characterized by the development of extensive evaporite deposits (the Permian Period began about 280,000,000 years ago and lasted about 55,000,000 years). During Ochoan time, tectonism (deformation of the Earth's crust) in Mexico closed off the Midland, Marfa, and Delaware basins in the southwest from access to the Permian sea. High evaporation rates in the area resulted in a drop of the water levels in the basins, and Capitan Reef and platform areas emerged. Continued aridity caused the precipitation of anhydrite and salt in great quantities. In the Delaware Basin of southwestern Texas, the Castile Formation, consisting of laminated anhydrite, reaches a thickness of as much as 600 metres (2,000 feet), whereas in the eastern portions of the basin, the Salado Formation consists of about 720 metres (2,400 feet) of salt and interbedded anhydrite.

Ocho Rios, town and Caribbean port, Parish of St. Ann, Jamaica, on the north coast,

northwest of Kingston. The Spanish name means "eight rivers," in reference to the number of rivers in the area. The 600-ft (180-m) cataracts of Dunns River Falls make Ocho Rios a popular tourist resort. As a trade centre, it serves an area producing citrus fruits, corn (maize), pimientos, and cattle. Bauxite is mined nearby and transported to Ocho Rios for shipping. Pop. (1970 prelim.) 6,900.
18°25′ N, 77°07′ W
·map, Jamaica **10**:16

Ochotonidae (mammal family): *see* pika.

ochre, also spelled OCHER, an earthy, usually red or yellow and often impure iron ore that is extensively used as a pigment; also any of various ferruginous clays. Ochre is also any of various chiefly yellow to orange pigments prepared from the natural ochres (as by washing, grinding, and sometimes calcining).
·composition and use **13**:888g

Ochroma pyramidale, common name BALSA, species of plant in the order Malvales.
·economic importance **11**:396b

ochronosis, pigmentation of cartilage and other tissues in some metabolic diseases.
·alkaptonuria's clinical symptoms **11**:1054b

ochronotic arthritis, or OCHRONOTIC ARTHROPATHY, in medicine, a joint disease complication of the metabolic disorder ochronosis.
·joint disease and innate metabolic disorders **10**:263a

Ochs, Adolph Simon (b. March 12, 1858, Cincinnati, Ohio—d. April 8, 1935, Chattanooga, Tenn.), newspaper publisher under whose ownership (from 1896) *The New York Times* became one of the world's outstanding newspapers. Despising "yellow (sensational) journalism," he emphasized comprehensive and trustworthy news gathering. Gerald White Johnson's biography, *An Honorable Titan* (1946), indicates both the beneficence and the pervasiveness of Ochs's impact on U.S. newspaper publishing.

Ochs
The New York Times

A son of cultured Jewish immigrants, Ochs delivered newspapers while a schoolboy in Knoxville, Tenn. He became a printer's devil on the Knoxville *Chronicle* in 1872 and later a compositor on the Louisville (Kentucky) *Courier-Journal*. In 1877 he helped to establish the Chattanooga *Dispatch* and in July 1878, only 20, he borrowed $250 to buy a controlling interest in the moribund *Chattanooga Times*, which he developed into one of the leading newspapers in the South. He was a founder of the Southern Associated Press and its chairman from 1891 to 1894; from 1900 until his death he was a director of the Associated Press.

On Aug. 18, 1896, Ochs acquired control of the financially faltering *New York Times*, again with borrowed money ($75,000). In competition with the most powerful representatives of the "yellow press," he adopted the slogan "All the News That's Fit to Print" (first used Oct. 25, 1896) and insisted on reportage that lived up to that promise. Despite an early shortage of capital, he refused advertisements that he considered dishonest or in poor taste. In 1898, when sales were low and expenses unusually high, he probably saved the *Times* by cutting its price from three cents to one cent. He thereby attracted many readers who previously had bought the more sensational penny papers, especially the *World* and the *Journal*. By 1900 Ochs was able to purchase controlling interest in the *Times*. In the next two years he took over and merged two Philadelphia papers, the *Times* and the *Public Ledger*, but in 1912 he sold this enterprise to Cyrus H.K. Curtis.

Ochs was responsible for such innovations as a book review supplement and rotogravure printing of pictures. To make accurate source material available to the public, he began in 1913 to publish *The New York Times Index*, the only complete U.S. newspaper index. He advanced $50,000 annually for ten years from 1925 to support the editorial preparation of the *Dictionary of American Biography*, repayment to be made from royalties.

Ochs, Peter (b. 1752, Nantes, Fr.—d. 1821, Basel?, Switz.), Swiss revolutionary who wrote most of the constitution of the unitary Helvetian Republic (1798).

Though born in France of a family that claimed roots in the Basel aristocracy, Ochs in 1769 settled in Basel, where, after becoming doctor of jurisprudence (1776), he entered into political affairs. Won to the ideas of the Enlightenment, he became an opponent of the "decayed Confederation" and, with the outbreak of the French Revolution, joined the partisans of revolutionary reform in Switzerland. He championed French intervention in the old confederation and urged acceptance of the French Directory's demands for curtailing traditional rights of asylum and expelling émigrés. In Paris (1797) Ochs plotted with Bonaparte the establishment of a Swiss revolutionary government and produced a constitutional draft for the proposed state modelled closely upon the French constitution of 1795. With few emendations, his document was accepted as the charter of the Helvetian Republic (April 12, 1798). In the new regime, Ochs served as first president of the Helvetian Senate and, later, as president of the state executive organ, the Directory. Deposed by the party of Frédéric-César La Harpe (June 25, 1799), he assumed a diminishing role in national politics. In Basel, however, he achieved local prominence for his part in devising new governmental and penal codes (1813, 1821) and reorganizing the city university.

Ochsenbein, (Johann) Ulrich (b. Nov. 24, 1811, Schwarzenegg, Switz.—d. Nov. 3, 1890, Bellevue), Swiss politician and military leader who headed the Confederation government during the Sonderbund War (1847) and presided over the constitutional reform committee of 1848.

An ardent Bernese radical, Ochsenbein organized and directed an abortive military coup against the clerical government of Luzern (March 1845), precipitating the formation by Catholic cantons of a conservative defense league, the Sonderbund. At Berne, he championed the revision of the cantonal constitution (1846) and headed the department of the military. As president of the Bernese government (1847), he simultaneously presided over the Confederation Diet during the proscription of the Sonderbund (July 1847) and the initial phase of the subsequent civil war.

Through February–April 1848 Ochsenbein headed the committee of constitutional revision that directed the reorganization of the federal system, and later that year, in the new bicameral Diet, he presided over the Nationalrat (national assembly). Failing subsequent re-election to the Diet (1851, 1854), he retired briefly to France (1855), to which he was to return again in 1870 to command French troops in the Franco-Prussian War.

Ochteridae (insect family): *see* velvety shore bug.

Ochus: *see* Artaxerxes III; Darius II Ochus.

Ochyroceratidae, family of spiders in the arachnid order Araneida.
·classification and general features **1**:1073a

Ocimum basilicum (plant): *see* basil.

ock, a unit of weight in Turkey. Legal ock (1881) = 100 drachmas; new batman = 10 ocks, and kantar = 10 batmans; ock = 1 kilogram.
·weights and measures, table 5 **19**:734

Ockham, William of 13:504 (b. *c.* 1285, probably Surrey, Eng.—d. probably 1349, Munich, Ger.), most influential 14th-century Scholastic philosopher and founder of Nominalism.

Abstract of text biography. As a young Franciscan he was trained particularly in logic, which became the focus of his later theology. His lectures aroused hostility by their radicalism and he left university without taking his master's degree in theology. While in Avignon, he was denounced for error to Pope John XXII but was not formally condemned.

At that time ecclesiastical politics were dominated by the dispute with the papacy over the strictness of Franciscan poverty. Ockham and the Franciscan general contended that Christ and his Apostles possessed nothing, but John XXII's contrary ruling forced them to flee (1328). Ockham and his colleagues (now excommunicated) sought the protection of the excommunicated emperor Louis IV the Bavarian, in Munich (1330). Ockham continued his polemics, attacking the supremacy of papal power. In 1339 Ockham defended the English king's right to tax church property.

REFERENCES in other text articles:
·Aristotelianism and Scholasticism **1**:1159f
·Christian view of Greek philosophy **4**:558g
·empirical knowledge and existence **6**:768g
·freedom of God and universals **14**:260e
·Jewish philosophy relationship **10**:213e
·logic history **11**:60h
·Luther's Wittenberg faculty **11**:189a
·Nominalist philosophy **15**:1007b
·Scholasticism negation in double truth **16**:356h
·sensory foundation of knowledge **6**:939c
·skepticism about reason **6**:933d
·voluntaristic approach to ethics **6**:978g

Ockham's razor, also called the LAW OF ECONOMY or the LAW OF PARSIMONY (Latin *parsimonia*, "frugality"), the name given to the principle of William of Ockham, a late medieval Scholastic, that "non sunt multiplicanda entia praeter necessitatem"; *i.e.*, entities are not to be multiplied beyond necessity.

The principle was, in fact, invoked before Ockham by Durand de Saint-Pourçain (*c.* 1270–1334), a French Dominican theologian and philosopher of dubious orthodoxy, who used it to explain that abstraction is the apprehension of some real entity, such as an Aristotelian cognitive species, an active intellect, or a disposition, all of which he spurned as unnecessary. Likewise, in science, Nicole d'Oresme, a 14th-century French physicist, invoked the law of economy, as did Galileo in modern times, in defending the simplest hypothesis of the heavens.

Ockham, however, mentioned the principle so frequently and employed it so sharply that it was called "Ockham's razor." He used it, for instance, to dispense with relations, which he held to be nothing distinct from their foundation in things; with efficient causality, which he tended to view merely as regular succession; with motion, which is merely the reappearance of a thing in a different place; with psychological powers distinct for each mode of sense; and with the presence of ideas in the mind of the Creator, which are merely the creatures themselves.

In modern times, Pierre de Maupertuis (1698–1759), a French astronomer, exalted the law of parsimony to a lofty principle of nature, in which action, defined by $\int mv\, ds$—*i.e.*, the integral ($\int$) of inertia (*mv*) over the space-time (*ds*)—is minimized (principle of least action). More recently Ernst Mach (1838–1916), an Austrian physicist and philosopher, held that it is the aim of science to present the facts of nature in the simplest and most economical conceptual formulations. In psychology the law of parsimony appears as Morgan's canon, named after C. Lloyd Morgan (1852–1936), an English biologist and philosopher, who said that no action should be interpreted in terms of a higher psychical faculty when a lower faculty suffices.

·formulation by Ockham **13**:505c

O'Clery, Michael (b. 1575, Kilbarron, County Donegal, Ireland—d. 1643, Louvain, now in Belgium), chronicler who directed the compilation of the *Annála Ríoghachta Éireann* (*The Annals of the Four Masters*, 1636), a chronicle of Irish history from antiquity to 1616 that is a work of incalculable importance to Irish scholarship. He was baptized Tadhg but took the name Michael when he entered the Franciscan convent at Louvain. As he was learned in Irish history and literature, Hugh Macanward, the warden of the college, sent him back to Ireland in 1620 to collect manuscripts. Assisted by other Irish scholars, he began to collect and to transcribe everything of importance he could find. The results were the *Réim Rioghroidhe* (1630; *The Royal List*), a list of kings, their successions, and their pedigrees, with lives and genealogies of saints; the *Leabhar Gabhála* (1631; *Book of Invasions*), an account of the successive settlements of Ireland; and the famous *Annals*. At first a mere record of names, dates, and battles, with occasional quotations from ancient sources, the *Annals* begin to take on the character of modern literary history as they approach the author's own time. O'Clery also produced a martyrology of Irish saints, an Irish glossary, and other works.

·Irish historical literature **10**:1154c

Ocoee River, rises in the Blue Ridge Mountains, 9 mi southeast of Blue Ridge city, Ga., U.S., and flows northwest through Fannin County into Tennessee, past Copperhill, through Polk County, and north to the Hiwassee River, 2 mi north of Benton. Along its 90-mi (145-km) course are four dams—all part of the Tennessee Valley Authority. In northern Georgia (where the river is called the Toccoa) is the Blue Ridge Dam, forming Lake Toccoa; in Tennessee are Ocoee Dam No. 1 (completed 1912), forming Lake Ocoee just south of Benton, Ocoee Dam No. 2 (1913), upstream just north of Copperhill, and Ocoee Dam No. 3 (1943), at Copperhill near the Georgia line. The river's name is probably derived from a Cherokee word meaning "apricot vine place."

35°12′ N, 84°40′ W

O'Connell, Daniel, known in Ireland as THE LIBERATOR (b. Aug. 6, 1775, near Cahirciveen, County Kerry, Ireland—d. May 15, 1847, Genoa, Italy), first of the great 19th-century Irish leaders in the British House of Commons. By his overwhelming victory in an election in 1828, he forced the British government to accept the Emancipation Act of 1829, by which Roman Catholics were permitted to sit in Parliament and to hold public office.

Compelled to leave the Catholic college at Douai, Fr., when the French Revolution broke out, O'Connell went to London to study law, and in 1798 he was called to the Irish bar. His forensic skill enabled him to use the courts as nationalist forums. Although he had joined the United Irishmen, a revolutionary society, as early as 1797, he refused to participate in the Irish rebellion of the following year. When the Act of Union (Aug. 1, 1800) abolished the Irish Parliament, he insisted that the British Parliament repeal the anti-Catholic laws in order to justify its claim to represent the people of Ireland. From 1813, however, he opposed various Catholic relief proposals because the government, with the acquiescence of the papacy, would have had the right to veto nominations to Catholic bishoprics in Great Britain and Ireland. Although permanent political organizations of Catholics were illegal, O'Connell set up a nationwide series of "aggregate meetings" to petition for strictly legal purposes.

O'Connell, portrait miniature by B. Mulrenin, 1836; in the National Portrait Gallery, London

By courtesy of the National Portrait Gallery, London

On May 12, 1823, O'Connell and Richard Lalor Sheil (1791–1851) founded the Catholic Association, which quickly attracted the support of the Irish priesthood and of lawyers and other educated Catholic laymen and which eventually comprised so many members that the government could not suppress it. In 1826, when it was reorganized as the New Catholic Association, it caused the defeat of several parliamentary candidates sponsored by large landowners. In County Clare in July 1828, O'Connell himself, although (as a Catholic) ineligible to sit in the House of Commons, defeated a man who tried to support both the British government and Catholic emancipation. This result impressed on the British prime minister, Arthur Wellesley, 1st duke of Wellington, the need for making a major concession to the Irish Catholics. Following the passage of the 1829 emancipation statute, O'Connell, after going through the formality of an uncontested re-election, took his seat at Westminster. In April 1835 he helped to overthrow Sir Robert Peel's Conservative ministry, and in the same year he entered into the "Lichfield House compact," whereby he promised the Whig Party leaders a period of "perfect calm" in Ireland while the government enacted reform measures. O'Connell and his Irish adherents (known as "O'Connell's tail") then aided in keeping the weak Whig administration of William Lamb, 2nd Viscount Melbourne, in office from 1835 to 1841. By 1839, however, O'Connell realized that the Whigs would do little more than the Conservatives for Ireland, and he founded the Repeal Association to dissolve the Anglo-Irish legislative union. A series of mass meetings in all parts of Ireland led to O'Connell's arrest for seditious conspiracy, but he was released on appeal after three months' imprisonment (June–September 1844). Afterward, his health failed rapidly, and the nationalist leadership was assumed by the radical Young Ireland group.

Among the lives of O'Connell are those by his son John O'Connell, *The Life and Speeches of Daniel O'Connell, M.P.* (1846), and Denis Rolleston Gwynn, *Daniel O'Connell, The Irish Liberator* (1930).

·British reaction to emancipation **3**:264g
·Catholic crisis of 1828–1829 **13**:1107c
·Catholic Dubliners' emancipation **5**:1072g
·emancipation movement leadership **3**:290f

O'Conner, William (1832–89), American journalist.

·Whitman's friendship and vindication **19**:820e

O'Connor, Feargus Edward (b. *c.* July 18, 1796, Connorville, County Cork—d. Aug. 30, 1855, London), prominent Chartist leader who succeeded in making Chartism (the first specifically working class national movement in Great Britain) a mass protest movement. O'Connor, who claimed royal descent from the ancient kings of Ireland, practiced law but exchanged law for politics when he entered the British Parliament in 1832 as a member for County Cork. Unseated in 1835, O'Connor turned to radical agitation in England, although he continued to press Irish grievances and to seek Irish support. As a result of his humour, invective, and energy, O'Connor became the best known Chartist leader and the movement's most popular speaker. His journal, the *Northern Star* (founded in 1837), gained a wide circulation.

O'Connor's methods and views alienated other Chartist leaders, particularly William Lovett, but in 1841, after spending a year in prison for seditious libel, O'Connor acquired undisputed leadership of the Chartists. Failing to lead the movement to victory and vacillating in his attitude toward the middle class and toward the Charter (a six-point bill drafted and published in May 1838), O'Connor began to lose power, although he was elected to Parliament for Nottingham (1847). The failure of the Charter in 1848 marked the beginning of the end for O'Connor, whose egocentricity was already bordering on madness. Declared insane in 1852, he died three years later.

Feargus O'Connor, detail of an engraving by an unknown artist

By courtesy of the trustees of the British Museum; photograph, J.R. Freeman & Co. Ltd.

O'Connor, (Mary) Flannery (b. March 25, 1925, Savannah, Ga.—d. Aug. 3, 1964, Milledgeville), novelist and short-story writer whose works, usually set in the rural South and often treating of human alienation, are concerned with the relationship between the individual and God.

After graduating from Georgia State College for Women, Milledgeville, she studied creative writing at the University of Iowa. Her first published work, a short story, appeared in *Accent* in 1946. Other works include two novels, *Wise Blood* (1952) and *The Violent Bear it Away* (1960), and two collections of short stories, *A Good Man Is Hard to Find, and Other Stories* (1955) and *Everything That Rises Must Converge* (1965).

·American novel development **10**:1227d

O'Connor, Frank (b. MICHAEL O'DONOVAN, 1903, Cork, Ire.—d. March 10, 1966, Dublin), playwright, novelist, and short-story writer who, as a critic and as a translator of Gaelic works from the 9th to the 20th century, has served as an interpreter of Irish life and literature to the English-speaking world. Raised in poverty, a childhood he recounted in *An Only Child* (1961), O'Connor received little formal education before going to work as a librarian in Cork and later in Dublin. As a young man he was briefly imprisoned for his activities with the Irish Republican Army. O'Connor served as a director of the Abbey Theatre, Dublin, in the 1930s, collaborating on many of its productions. During World War II he was a broadcaster for the British Ministry of Information in London. Popular in the United States for his short stories, which appeared in *The New Yorker* magazine from 1945 to 1961, he was a visiting professor at several U.S. universities in the 1950s.

Notable among his numerous volumes of short stories, in which he effectively makes use of apparently trivial incidents to illuminate Irish life, are *Guests of the Nation* (1931) and *Crab Apple Jelly* (1944). Other collections of tales were published in 1953, 1954, and 1956. He also wrote critical studies of Turgenev and of Michael Collins and his role in the Irish Revolution. O'Connor's Gaelic translations include the 17th-century satire by Brian Merriman, *The Midnight Court* (1945), which has been considered by many to be the finest single poem written in Irish. It was included in O'Connor's later collection of translations, *Kings, Lords, and Commons* (1959).

O'Connor, Sir Richard Nugent (1889–), British army officer. He served in World War I and was military governor of Jerusalem in 1938–39. Commanding the Western Desert Corps in Libya (1940–41), during World War II, he was taken prisoner in 1941, escaping in 1943. He served as corps commander in France during 1944 and was promoted general in 1945.
·Cyrenaican frontier campaign **19**:986b

O'Connor, Rory (last high king of Ireland): *see* Roderic.

Ocós (c. 1500–1200 BC), early village culture phase, named for a site on the Pacific coast of present-day Guatemala, of the Formative Period of Meso-American civilization.
·Meso-American early village cultures **11**:936g; map 935

Ocotal, capital, Nueva Segovia department, northwestern Nicaragua, on a sandy plain near the Cordillera Entre Ríos and the Coco River, at an elevation of 2,000 ft (600 m). It serves as a manufacturing and commercial centre: the coffee, sugarcane, tobacco, and other crops cultivated in the agricultural hinterland are processed in the city; shoes, furniture, and beverages are among its manufactures. Ocotal is accessible by highways leading south to the Pan-American Highway and north to the Honduras border. Pop. (1971 prelim.) 8,746.
13°37′ N, 86°31′ W
·map, Nicaragua **13**:61

Ocotepeque, department, western Honduras, bounded on the west by Guatemala and on the south by El Salvador. The department is small (649 sq mi [1,680 sq km]); the population, consisting mainly of highland Indians, is exceedingly isolated and depends entirely on pack and cart transportation. Ocotepeque has no all-weather roads, and all settlements are in small highland valleys. Although only 15 percent of the land in farms is cultivated, Ocotepeque ranks first in Honduras in the production of wheat, third in tobacco, and seventh in potatoes. Several handicraft industries are locally significant. Nueva Ocotepeque (*q.v.*) is the departmental capital and largest town. Pop. (1974 est.) 64,000.
·area and population table **8**:1057
·map, Honduras **8**:1058

ocotillo, also called COACHWHIP, JACOB'S STAFF, and VINE CACTUS, characteristic shrub (*Fouquieria splendens*, family Fouquieriaceae) of rocky deserts from western Texas to southern California and southward into Mexico. Near its base, the stem divides into several slender, erect, furrowed, intensely spiny branches, usually about 2½ to 6 metres (8 to 20 feet) long. The branches bear small, rounded leaves, which fall soon after the end

Ocotillo (*Fouquieria splendens*)
Alan Pitcairn from Grant Heilman—EB Inc.

of the winter rainy season, leaving behind the petioles (leaf stalks), which harden and develop into stout spines. The flowers are showy and bright scarlet in branched terminal clusters 15 to 25 centimetres (6 to 10 inches) long. Ocotillo is grown as a hedge plant and occasional ornamental in its native range. *See also* Tamaricales.

Ocotlán, city, east central Jalisco state, west central Mexico. Situated near the northeastern shore of Lake Chapala (*see* Chapala, Lake), at the confluence of the Zula (or Atotonilco) and Santiago rivers, Ocotlán is most important as a transportation hub. As the gateway to the Chapala resort district, it has considerable tourist traffic. A railroad and a highway from Mexico City to Guadalajara, the state capital, to the northwest, pass through Ocotlán, which is also the terminus of a branch rail line to the town of Atotonilco el Alto (northeast). The city has an airfield. The economy is based on industries, agriculture, fishing, and aviculture, making Ocotlán the major settlement on the lake. Pop. (1970) 35,367.
20°21′ N, 102°46′ W
·map, Mexico **12**:69

octachlor (insecticide): *see* chlordane.

octadecanol (alcohol): *see* stearyl alcohol.

Octagon Conference, also called SECOND QUEBEC CONFERENCE (September 1944), code name for World War II conference at which Pres. Franklin D. Roosevelt and Prime Minister Winston Churchill discussed military strategy for Europe and Asia and the Morgenthau Plan for postwar Germany.
·Pacific Theatre tactical discussions **19**:1008e

octahedrite, iron meteorite (*q.v.*) containing between 6 and 11 percent nickel and having an eight-sided crystal structure. Etching a polished surface brings out an unusual design called the Widmanstätten pattern (*q.v.*), a system of lamellae parallel to the faces of an octahedron. The classification of the octahedrites is based on the width of the lamellae. Besides nickel–iron, major minerals in octahedrites are troilite and schreibersite.
·classification and composition **12**:44a; table 42

octane, a liquid hydrocarbon, more specifically designated *n*-octane (*n* for normal) to differentiate it from its 17 isomers, the best known of which is 2,2,4-trimethylpentane, often called iso-octane.
·Wurtz synthesis **1**:585b

octane number, measure of the ability of a gasoline to resist knocking when ignited in a mixture with air in the cylinder of an internal-combustion engine. The octane number is determined by comparing, under standard conditions, the knock intensity of the gasoline with that of blends of two reference fuels: iso-octane and heptane. The octane number of a gasoline expresses the percentage by volume of iso-octane in the iso-octane–heptane mixture that corresponds in its knock intensity with that of the gasoline.
·automobile fuelling requirements **2**:521b
·gasoline engine performance testing **14**:185f

Octans, constellation of the southern sky.
·constellation table **2**:226

octant (mathematics): *see* quadrant.

octave, in music, an interval the higher note of which has a sound-wave frequency of vibration equal to twice that of its lower note (as, a = 220 hertz [cycles per second]: a′ = 440 hertz). Because of the close acoustical relation between the two notes, the second is perceived by the listener almost as a repetition of the first at a higher pitch. The octave encompasses eight notes of a scale in Western music. It is the only interval to appear as a constant in the musical scales of nearly every culture.
·African tuning modifications and composition structure **1**:244c *passim* to 246c
·consonance of simple frequency ratios **18**:741b
·harmony's basis in intervalic size **8**:647d
·musical sound's pitch organization **17**:37a
·organ pipe configurations and tuning **13**:677g
·South Asian classical music development **17**:152c
·vocal register in normal individual **17**:482c

octaves, law of, in chemistry, the generalization made by the English chemist J.A.R. Newlands in 1865 that, if the chemical elements are arranged according to increasing atomic weight, those with similar physical and chemical properties occur after each interval of seven elements. Newlands was one of the first to detect a periodic pattern in the properties of the elements and anticipated later developments of the periodic table.
·periodic law development **14**:75g

octave species, in early Greek music theory, the various arrangements of tones (T) and semitones (S) within an octave (series of eight consecutive notes) in the scale system. The basic Greek scale ranged two octaves and was called the Greater Perfect System. Central to the scale system was the octave e′–e (E above middle C to the E below), the interval arrangement (descending, T–T–S–T–T–T–S) of which made up the Dorian octave species. The series of notes from d′–d, with the arrangement T–S–T–T–T–S–T, was the Phrygian octave species. Other species and the descending octaves in the Greater Perfect System that produced their characteristic interval arrangements were: a′–a, Hypodorian; g′–g, Hypophrygian; f′–f, Hypolydian; c′–c, Lydian; b–B, Mixolydian.

It is also possible, with the use of sharps and flats, to place each of these different arrangements of tones and semitones within the octave e′–e, which was central to the performance of Greek music.

The term mode has been applied by some modern writers to the octave species but by others to other concepts in Greek music, such as *harmonia* and *tonos* (*qq.v.*).

Octavia, called OCTAVIA MINOR (b. 69 BC—d. 11 BC), full sister of Octavian (later the emperor Augustus) and wife of Mark Antony. She was the daughter of Gaius Octavius and his second wife, Atia. In 54 BC Octavia was married to Gaius Marcellus, by whom she had two daughters and a son. On the death of Marcellus in 40 she was married to Marcus Antonius (Mark Antony), who at the time was ruling the Roman state with Octavian and Marcus Aemilius Lepidus. At first this marriage helped to reduce tensions between Antony and Octavian, and, when the two rul-

ers quarrelled in 37, Octavia brought about peace between them, which resulted in the Treaty of Tarentum. But in 36 Antony left Italy to command troops in Parthia and while in the East resumed his liaison with the Egyptian queen Cleopatra. Although Octavia brought troops and money to him (35), he refused to see her, and in 32 he obtained a divorce. Octavia was a faithful wife and mother who raised Antony's children by Cleopatra along with her own children.
·Antonius' marriage and political effect **1**:1000c

Octavia (1st century AD), Latin tragedy in 983 lines dramatizing the fate of Octavia, the wife of the emperor Nero. It is often printed with the tragedies of Seneca, but it was not written by him.

Octavian (pope): *see* John XII.

Octavian (Roman emperor): *see* Augustus.

Octavian of Monticelli (antipope): *see* Victor IV.

octavillo, a unit of volume in Spain, equal to 0.29 litre, or 0.6 pint.
·weights and measures, table 5 **19**:734

Octavius, Marcus (fl. 2nd century BC), Roman tribune in 133, opposed the agrarian reform measures of his colleague, the tribune Tiberius Gracchus. By having Octavius illegally removed from office, Gracchus provoked increased opposition, and he was killed in the ensuing civil strife.
·opposition to Tiberius Gracchus **8**:262a
·veto of land reform bill **15**:1100e

octet, in chemistry, the eight-electron arrangement in the outer electron shell of the noble-gas atoms used to explain their relative inertness and the chemical behaviour of certain other elements. The chemical elements with atomic numbers close to those of the noble-gas elements tend to combine with other similar elements by losing or gaining electrons, completely or partly, in order that their atoms can have the eight-outer-electron configuration of the noble-gas atoms. This observation, published in separate papers (1916) by German chemist Walther Kossel and U.S. chemist Gilbert Newton Lewis, is known as the rule of eight, or octet rule, and is used to determine the valence, or combining capacity, of several chemical elements.
·chemical bond and electronic stability **4**:85h
·inorganic compound bonding patterns **4**:97e
·nitrogen electron structure **13**:694b
·noble gas electronic structure **13**:138d

October, 10th month of the Gregorian calendar now in general use, has 31 days. It was the eighth month of the early Roman republican calendar, hence its name, from the Latin *octo*, "eight."

October, U.S. title TEN DAYS THAT SHOOK THE WORLD (1928), Russian motion picture by Sergey Eisenstein dealing with the 1917 Revolution and the events that followed.
·Eisenstein's theory and technique **6**:517d

October Diploma, Austrian constitution proclaimed in October 1860 and replaced by the February Patent in February 1861.
·Francis Joseph and liberal reform **8**:109d
·terms and significance **2**:468a

October Horse (ancient festival): *see* Mars.

October Manifesto (Oct. 30 [Oct. 17, old style], 1905), in Russian history, document issued by the emperor Nicholas II that in effect converted the Russian autocracy into a constitutional monarchy. Threatened by the events of the Russian Revolution of 1905 (*q.v.*), Nicholas faced the choice of establishing a military dictatorship or granting a constitution. On the advice of Sergey Yulevich Witte, he issued the October Manifesto, which promised to guarantee civil liberties (*e.g.*, freedom of speech, press, and assembly), to establish a broad franchise, and to create a legislative body (the Duma [*q.v.*]) whose members would be popularly elected and whose approval would be necessary before the enactment of any legislation.

The manifesto satisfied enough of the moderate participants in the revolution to weaken the forces against the government and allow the revolution to be crushed. Only then did the government formally fulfill the promises of the manifesto. On April 23, 1906, the Fundamental Laws, which were to serve as a constitution, were promulgated. Contrary to the provisions of the October Manifesto, the Duma that was created had two houses rather than one, and members of only one of them were to be popularly elected. Further, the Duma had control only over some types of legislation and none at all over the executive branch of the government. In addition, the civil rights and suffrage rights granted by the Fundamental Laws were far more limited than those promised by the manifesto.
·Duma government establishment **16**:66g
·Nicholas II's reluctant concession **13**:70g
·Witte's liberalizing influence **19**:901c

October Revolution, also known as NOVEMBER REVOLUTION (Oct. 24–25 [Nov. 6–7, new style], 1917), uprising by which the Bolshevik Party seized power in Russia, inaugurating the Soviet regime. *See also* Russian Revolution of 1917. *Major ref.* **16**:69a
·Lenin's role **10**:795e

Octobrists, Russian OKTYABRISTY, also called UNION OF OCTOBER 17, conservative Russian political party whose program of moderate constitutionalism called for the fulfillment of the emperor Nicholas II's October Manifesto (*q.v.*). Founded in November 1905, the party was led by the industrialist Aleksandr Ivanovich Guchkov and drew support from liberal gentry, businessmen, and some bureaucrats. As the majority party in the third and fourth Dumas (1907–17), the Octobrists favoured a legislature with real power but insisted that the executive be responsible to the emperor only. The Octobrists, increasingly alienated from the government, finally joined the Kadets (Constitutional Democrats) in the Progressive Bloc (*q.v.*) of 1915, which called for more representative leadership and new reforms. The party did not survive the revolutions of 1917.
·Duma government participation **16**:67a

Octocoralla (coelenterate subclass): *see* Alcyonaria.

Octodontidae, family of ratlike South American rodents (order Rodentia), including five living genera and eight species, the best known of which is the degu (*Octodon degus*). Octodonts are small, stout, and about 13 to 20 centimetres (5 to 8 inches) long without the tail, which may be short or long, depending on the species. The fur, usually long and soft, is grayish, blackish, or some shade of brown. Octodonts are found in various habitats, including cultivated land and rocky mountainsides. Agile animals, they live in burrows and eat plants, occasionally damaging crops or garden plants. Except for the degu, they are apparently all nocturnal.
·classification and general features **15**:979a

Octoknemaceae, family of flowering plants of the order Santalales.
·characteristics and classification **16**:229c

octopus, in popular terms, any eight-armed cephalopod of the order Octopoda; technically, a member of the genus *Octopus*, a large group of widely distributed, shallow-water mollusks.

Octopods vary in size from 5 centimetres to 5.4 metres (2 inches to 18 feet) and may have an armspan of almost 9 metres (30 feet). They crawl about the bottom, or, when alarmed, shoot swiftly backward by means of a jet of

Octopus granulatus, a South African species
Anthony Bannister from the Natural History Photographic Agency—EB Inc.

water. When endangered, they eject an inky substance, which is used as a screen; the substance produced by some species paralyzes the sensory organs of the attacker. The common octopus (*Octopus vulgaris*) can change its colours to an astonishing degree with great rapidity.

O. vulgaris is widely distributed in tropical and temperate seas. It lives in holes or crevices along the rocky bottom, is secretive and retiring, and has been credited with considerable intelligence. *O. vulgaris* has a saccular body: the head has large, complex eyes and eight contractile arms, each bearing two rows of strong, fleshy suckers. The mouth has a pair of sharp, horny beaks and a filelike organ, the radula, for drilling shells and rasping away flesh. In American waters *O. vulgaris* mates during the winter, and the eggs, about 0.3 centimetre (⅛ inch) long, are laid under rocks. During the four to eight weeks required for the larvae to hatch, the female guards the eggs, cleaning them with her suckers and agitating them with water. The young octopus spends several weeks in the drifting plankton or immediately takes refuge on the bottom, depending on the species.

Little is known of the life history of bottom-dwelling, deepwater octopods.

Octopods feed mainly upon crabs and lobsters, although some are plankton feeders, and they are fed upon by a number of marine fishes. They have long been considered a culinary delicacy by peoples of the Mediterranean, the Orient, and other parts of the world. *Major ref.* **3**:1149d
·adaptive colour change, illus., **4**:Coloration, Biological, Plate 6
·coloration pigments' protective uses **4**:912d
·commercial importance **7**:348g
·copper concentration in tissues **6**:715g
·gill chamber and ventilation rates **15**:754b
·habitat, anatomy, and reproduction **12**:326f; illus.
·learning ability studies **10**:738g *passim* to 740b
·O. vulgaris reproductive behaviour and brooding **15**:684f
·poisonous animals, table 7 **14**:614b
·Polynesian lure fishing method **14**:779g
·sensory information and learning **11**:806b

octroi, tax levied by a local political unit, normally the commune or municipal authority, on certain categories of goods as they enter the area. The tax was first instituted in Italy in Roman times, when it bore the title of *vectigal* or *portorium*. Octrois were still in existence in France, Italy, Spain, Portugal, and Austria after World War II, but there has been a marked tendency toward reduction of their area of operation, and in some cases they have been completely suppressed. The cost of tax collection is unduly high in relation to the yield, the levy process sometimes absorbing 50 percent of tax revenues.

ocular dominance, in vision, the tendency to use one eye, though the other is not blind.
·perceptual processes in retina **7**:115f

ocular hypertelorism, developmental defect in which there is an abnormally large distance between the eyes.
·neural symptoms of birth defects **12**:1045g

ocular proptosis: *see* exophthalmos.

oculocerebralrenal syndrome, or LOWE'S SYNDROME, condition marked by mental retardation, glaucoma and other eye troubles, and defective kidney function.
·neurological symptoms of protein metabolism diseases table **12**:1044

oculomotor nucleus, two-part set of nerve cells in the midbrain that sends impulses to the eye muscles.
·anatomic relationships and functions **12**:1018f; illus. 1003

oculus (Latin: "eye"), any of several architectural elements resembling an eye. A small window that is circular or oval in shape, such as an *oeil-de-boeuf* window (*q.v.*), is an oculus. The round opening at the top of some domes, or cupolas, is also an oculus; one example of this kind is found in the Pantheon, in Rome. The capital of every Ionic column (*see* Ionic order) features a characteristic pair of volutes, or spiral scrolls, at the centre of each of which is an eye, or disk, also known as an oculus.

Oculus in the ceiling of the Pantheon, Rome
Ross—Photo Researchers

O'Curry, Eugene (b. 1796, Dunaha, County Clare—d. July 30, 1862, Dublin), Gaelic scholar and industrious copyist and translator of Old Irish manuscripts whose works had an important influence on the revival of the Gaelic language and literature and contributed to the late 19th-century Irish literary renascence. He examined and arranged many of the Irish manuscripts in the Royal Irish Academy and Trinity College library and compiled the catalog of those in the British Museum. In 1854 he was appointed professor of Irish history and archaeology in the new Catholic University of Ireland. His lectures, which give a full account of the medieval chronicles, historical romances, tales, and poems, were published in 1861. Subsequent volumes entitled *On the Manners and Customs of the Ancient Irish* appeared in 1873.

Ocypode: *see* ghost crab.

Odacidae, family of rock whitings in the fish order Perciformes.
·classification and general features **14**:53a

Odaenathus (ODENATHUS), **Septimius,** latinized form of Aramaic ODAINATH (d. AD 267/268), prince of the Roman colony of Palmyra (*q.v.*), in what is now Syria, who prevented the Sāsānian Persians from permanently conquering the eastern provinces of the Roman Empire. A Roman citizen and a member of Palmyra's ruling family, Odaenathus had by 258 attained consular rank and become chief of Palmyra.

When the Roman emperor Valerian was captured by the Sāsānian king Shāpūr I (260), Odaenathus remained loyal to the Romans in order to prevent his city from falling under Sāsānian control. In 260 he defeated Shāpūr's army as it was returning home after sacking Antioch. When he then defeated the usurping emperor Quietus at Emesa (Homs), Valerian's son and successor, Gallienus, rewarded the Palmyrene ruler with the title *corrector totius Orientis* ("governor of all the East"); in addition, Odaenathus styled himself king of Palmyra and, eventually, king of kings. Beginning in 262 he drove the Persians from the Roman provinces of Mesopotamia and Osroëne, and he probably also brought Armenia back into the empire. Although he failed to seize the Sāsānian capital of Ctesiphon, he managed to restore Roman rule in the East. Odaenathus was preparing to drive Gothic invaders from the Roman province of Cappadocia in eastern Asia Minor when he and his eldest son, Herodes, were assassinated. The murders were probably instigated by his wife, Zenobia (*q.v.*), who made Palmyra an independent kingdom before she was subjugated by the Romans in 272.
·defeat of Sāsānians **17**:951d
·Shāpūr I's retreat into Iran **15**:1123e

o-daiko, very large Japanese *taiko* (*q.v.*; barrel drum).
·Kabuki theatre percussion signals **12**:688h

odalisque, in painting, type of female figure, nude or clothed, distinguished by a Middle Eastern setting and dress and a markedly voluptuous characterization; the word odalisque is a French corruption of the Turkish word for a concubine in a sultan's harem. The subject first became popular in Western painting in France in the early 19th century and was particularly favoured by the French painters J.-A.-D. Ingres, Eugène Delacroix, Pierre-Auguste Renoir, and Henri Matisse.

O'Daniel, W. Lee, called PAPPY O'DANIEL (1890–1969), governor of Texas (1939–41) and U.S. senator (1941–49).
·Texas political campaign styles **18**:168c

Oda Nobunaga **13**:505 (b. 1534, Owari Province, Japan—d. June 1582), general who ended a long period of feudal wars by unifying Japan under his rule.

Abstract of text biography. With impressive military strategy, Oda gained control of Owari Province (1560) and the same year defeated Imagawa Yoshimoto of the neighbouring provinces, his first step toward unification. In 1568 he supported Ashikaga Yoshiaki, and when he marched on the capital city, Kyōto, he made Yoshiaki shogun. Their relations soon deteriorated, and in 1573 he deposed the shogun, effectively ending the Ashikaga shogunate. Opposed by the powerful Ikkō Buddhist sect for more than 10 years, he finally received the surrender of their fortress-monastery at Ōsaka in 1580. Established in Kyōto, he aided the Christian missionaries (Jesuit) as a political tactic to restrain Buddhist influence. After subjugating central Japan (1582), he was about to complete the unification of the country by conquering the western sector; but he was wounded while quelling a rebellion and committed suicide.

REFERENCES in other text articles:
·feudal unification policy **10**:70e
·history of Kyōto **10**:561d
·Momoyama period initiation **19**:234h
·Ōsaka victory **13**:752b
·Tokugawa's early alliances **18**:474h
·unification and succession dispute **18**:537b

Odantapurī, also spelled UḌḌANDAPURA, in ancient times, celebrated Buddhist centre of learning (*vihāra*) in India, identified with modern Bihār (town) in the Patna district of Bihār (state). It was founded in the 7th century AD by Gopāla, the first ruler of the Pāla dynasty, no doubt in emulation of its neighbour Nālandā, another distinguished centre of Buddhist learning. It fell into decline during the 11th century, and it was probably destroyed, along with Nālandā, in 1198, by Muslims under Ikhtiyār-ud-Dīn Muḥammad Bakhtiyār Khaljī. *See also* Bihār (town).

Ōdate, city, Akita Prefecture (*ken*), Honshū, Japan, on the Yoneshiro-gawa (Yoneshiro River). As a castle town during the Tokugawa era (1603–1867), it served as a market for the surrounding agricultural region. The city is now a lumbering centre and is known for the production of woodenware. Iron ore was discovered in the vicinity in 1962, and the city serves as a trade centre for the copper and zinc mined along the upper Yoneshiro-gawa. Ōdate is the home of a breed of domestic dog known as Akita. Pop. (1970) 72,958.
40°16′ N, 140°34′ E
·map, Japan **10**:36

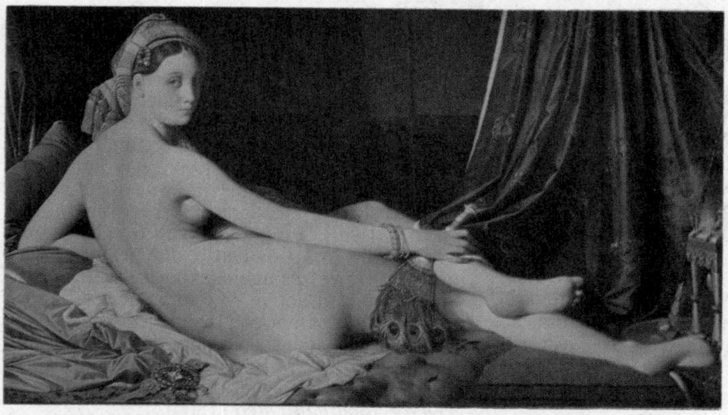

"La Grande Odalisque," oil painting by Jean-Auguste-Dominique Ingres, 1814; in the Louvre
Giraudon

Odawara, city, Kanagawa Prefecture (*ken*), Honshū, Japan, on the coast of Sagami Bay, between the Sakawa and Haya rivers. The city was a local political centre during the Kamakura era (1192–1333), and in the early 15th century a castle was built there; as a consequence, Odawara grew to be an economic and cultural hub of the southern Kantō region. It served as a post town on the Tōkaidō Highway during the Tokugawa era (1603–1867). Since the late 19th century the traditional manufacture of foods and textiles has been industrialized, and the city has become a residential suburb of the Tokyo–Yokohama area. Odawara is a gateway to the Hakone resort area. Its castle, restored in 1960, lies in a public park famous for its apricot and cherry trees. At the entrance to the park is the Hōtoku Ninomiya Shrine, dedicated to the agronomist Ninomiya Sontoku, who was born in the area. Pop. (1978 est.) 176,791.
35°15′ N, 139°10′ E
·map, Japan **10**:36

Odawara Castle, Japan
FPG

Odaw River, seasonal river originating north of, and flowing through, the city of Accra, Ghana.
5°20′ N, 1°20′ W
·Accra's town boundaries and lagoons **1**:43f

Oḍḍakās (ancient people): *see* Oretes.

Oddar Meanchey (Cambodia): *see* Ŏtdâr Méanchey.

Oddi's sphincter, or SPHINCTER OF ODDI, ring of muscle fibres surrounding the common bile duct and the main pancreatic duct at the point where, jointly, they empty into the duodenum. *See also* gallbladder.
·human digestive system relationship **5**:796c
·liver structure and function **10**:1269h

odd-lot dealer, stock-exchange member who acts as a principal in buying and selling shares in quantities of less than the trading unit (round lot, usually 100 shares) for his own account. Trade is only with commission brokers; the major source of income is the odd-lot commission differential added to the round-lot price of the shares. The odd-lot firm maintains an inventory of the various stocks by buying and selling round lots on the market.

Accounting for 10 to 15 percent of all trading on stock exchanges in the United States, the odd-lot system furnishes a continuous market for small lots and allows the small investor to diversify investments.

odd number, in arithmetic, natural (whole) number representing the size of a set that cannot be divided into two equal groups; also the negative of such a number. *Cf.* even number.

Oddr Snorrason (fl. late 12th century), Icelandic monk and historical writer.
·kings' saga perfection **16**:146c

odds, in betting, ratio between the amount to be paid off for a winning bet and the amount of the bet placed. It is usually related to the estimated probability of winning.
·bookmaking in horse racing **8**:1103c
·definition and gambling fallacy sources **7**:868d
·probability theory and method **14**:1104c
·roulette betting and house odds **15**:1168a

ode, ceremonious poem on an occasion of public or private dignity in which personal emotion and general meditation are united. The Greek word *ōdē*, which has been accepted in most modern European languages, meant a choric song, usually accompanied by a dance. Alcman (7th century BC) originated the strophic arrangement of the ode, which is a rhythmic system composed of two or more lines repeated as a unit; and Stesichorus (7th–6th centuries BC) invented the triadic, or three-part, structure (strophic lines followed by antistrophic lines in the same metre, concluding with a summary line, called an epode, in a different metre) that characterizes the odes of Pindar and Bacchylides (*q.v.*). Choral odes were also an integral part of the Greek drama. In Latin the word was not used until about the time of Horace, in the 1st century BC. His *carmina* ("songs"), written in stanzas of two or four lines of polished Greek metres, are now universally called odes, although the implication that they were to be sung to the accompaniment of a lyre is probably only a literary convention. Both Pindaric and Horatian ode forms were revived during the Renaissance and continued to influence lyric poetry through the end of the 19th century.

In pre-Islāmic Arabic poetry, the ode flourished in the form of the *qaṣīdah*. Two great collections date from the 8th and 9th centuries. The *qaṣīdah* was also used in Persian poetry for panegyrics and elegies in the 10th century, gradually being replaced by the shorter *ghazal* for bacchic odes and love poetry. In the hands of Indian poets from the 14th century onward, Persian forms became increasingly obscure and artificial.
·Chinese literature development **10**:1052e
·evaluation of Pindar's works **14**:465d
·Horatian ode form and themes **8**:1072d
·lyric poetry **10**:1091g

RELATED ENTRIES in the *Ready Reference and Index:*
Epinician ode; ghazal; Horatian ode; Pindaric ode; qaṣīdah

Ode: Intimations of Immortality from Recollections of Early Childhood (written 1805–06), poem by William Wordsworth rooted in the Platonic notion that man comes into the terrestrial world with knowledge and perception, but that this lessens with age; nevertheless, according to Wordsworth, some recollection of this earlier state can be regained through memories of childhood.
·decline in poet's creative powers **19**:931h
·English Romantic poetry **10**:1182h

Odeca: *see* Central American States, Organization of.

Odell, Jonathan (b. Sept. 25, 1737, Newark, N.J.—d. Nov. 25, 1818, Fredericton, N.B.), Canadian writer whose works are among the few extant expressions of American Tory sentiment during the Revolutionary War.

Educated in New Jersey, he was a surgeon in the British army, resigning to become an Anglican priest. During the Revolution he served as chaplain to a Loyalist regiment, wrote bitterly satiric verses against the Revolutionists, and played an active role in the negotiations between the American traitor Benedict Arnold and the British. His political satires and patriotic poems were collected and published in *The Loyal Verses of Joseph Stansbury and Doctor Jonathan Odell* (1860).

Odenathus (3rd-century ruler of Palmyra): *see* Odaenathus, Septimius.

Ödenburg (Hungary): *see* Sopron.

Odendaalsrus, town, Orange Free State, Republic of South Africa, southwest of Kroonstad at 4,411 ft (1,344 m) above sea level. Although it obtained municipal status in 1912, Odendaalsrus remained little more than a village until 1946, when one of the world's richest goldfields was discovered near its boundaries. It grew rapidly in size and now contains schools, a hospital, a park, and sports facilities. It is linked by rail to Johannesburg and Cape Town. Pop. (1979 est.) mun., 21,249.
27°48′ S, 26°45′ E
·map, South Africa **17**:63

Oden Forest (Germany): *see* Odenwald.

Odense, city, seat of Fyns *amtskommune* (county), northern Fyn (Funen) Island, Denmark, on the Odense Å (river). It was sacred in pagan times as Odin's *vi*, or the sanctuary of Odin, the Norse god of war, but was first recorded in history *c.* AD 1000. A bishop's seat from the 10th century, it became a centre for religious pilgrimages in the Middle Ages after the canonization of Canute (Knud) II, who was murdered before the high altar in St. Alban's Church in 1086. Odense was burned (1247) during a royal rivalry but recovered to thrive as a commercial centre in the 16th and 17th centuries. Growth and trade were stimulated when it became a port with the construction of the harbour and the opening of the Odense Canal (1804). Industries include manufacturing (tobacco, textiles, sugar), iron foundries, shipbuilding yards, and meat and fish canneries.

Hans Christian Andersen's house (centre), Odense, Den.
Harrison Forman

The Gothic St. Canute's (Knud's) Cathedral (*c.* 1300), originally founded by Canute in the 11th century, houses his shrine and traditional tomb in the crypt. Odense Castle, now the county administrative offices, was rebuilt by Frederick IV in 1720, partly on the foundations of St. Hans's Monastery (13th century), which was built together with St. Hans's Church by the Knights Hospitallers. Other remains include a Franciscan monastery (founded 1279, now an almshouse) and a 12th-century Benedictine monastery.

The home of the writer Hans Christian Andersen (born in Odense in 1805), famous for his fairy tales, is now a museum. There are also an open-air museum (Funen Village) and museums of art, archaeology, and history. The University of Odense, Denmark's third, opened in 1966. Pop. (1976 est.) city, 138,348; (1978 est.) mun., 167,768.
55°24′ N, 10°23′ E
·map, Denmark **5**:583

Odenwald, English ODEN FOREST, wooded upland in West Germany, 50 mi (80 km) long and 25 mi wide, situated mainly in the *Land* (state) of Hessen with small portions in Bayern and Baden-Württemberg. A popular tourist area, Odenwald extends between the Neckar and Main rivers and overlooks the Rhine Valley. The highest points are Katzenbuckel (2,054 ft [626 m]) and Neunkircher Höhe (1,985 ft). The range is bounded against the

Rhine by a rich and densely settled strip called the Bergstrasse (literally Mountain Street), along which Michelstadt is the main town. The wooded heights overlooking the Bergstrasse are studded with castles and medieval ruins. Orchards and vineyards lie along the west slope, and much of the range is within the Bergstrasse-Odenwald National Park.

The Odenwald, hunting ground of the Nibelungs (Burgundians), was the background for the epic poem *Nibelungenlied* (*q.v.*), and the Nibelungenstrasse, a road from west to east between Worms and Würzburg, is marked for tourists according to the events of the poem, though they probably occurred elsewhere in the Odenwald. Another legendary figure, popularized by the German writer and poet Josef Victor von Scheffel, is the "Wild Huntsman of Rodenstein" who supposedly galloped with fearful din to Schnellerts castle, now lying in ruins northwest of the village of Reichelsheim.
49°40′ N, 9°00′ E

·geographic-transportational seclusion **2**:578e
·location and legendary importance **8**:50a
·map, Federal Republic of Germany **8**:46

Ode on a Grecian Urn (1819), poem by John Keats, inspired by the figures caught in a moment of time on a Greek urn, about the eternal quality of art.

·Keats's period of poetic intensity **10**:413g

Ode on the Death of the Duke of Wellington (published 1852), poem by Alfred Lord Tennyson.

·modern and 19th-century critical views **18**:142a

ODEPLAN, Chilean institution created during the administration of Eduardo Frei (served 1964–70) to study problems related to social and economic planning.

·establishment and function **4**:259d

Oderic of Pordenone (*c.* 1274–1331), 14th-century Italian Franciscan monk, missionary to China.

·Asian travel route and account impact **7**:1039c

Oder Mountains, range of Czechoslovakia.
49°45′ N, 17°30′ E

·Oder River watercourse origin **13**:507a

Oder–Neisse Line, Polish–German border determined by the Allied powers at the end of World War II that transferred a large section of German territory to Poland and provided a basis for severe postwar tension between the two countries and in Europe generally.

At the Yalta Conference (February 1945) the three major Allied powers—Great Britain, the Soviet Union, and the United States—moved back Poland's eastern boundary with the Soviet Union to the west, placing it approximately along the Curzon Line. As this settlement involved a substantial loss of territory for Poland, the Allies also agreed to compensate the re-established Polish state by moving its western frontier farther west at the expense of Germany.

But the western Allies and the Soviet Union sharply disagreed over the exact location of the new border. The Soviets pressed for the adoption of the Oder–Neisse Line—*i.e.*, a line extending southward from Świnoujście on the Baltic Sea, passing west of Szczecin, then following the Oder River to the point south of Frankfurt where it is joined by the Neisse River (Lusatian Neisse), and proceeding along the Neisse to the Czechoslovak border, near Zittau. The United States and Great Britain warned that such a territorial settlement would not only involve the displacement of too many Germans but also would turn Germany into a dissatisfied state anxious to recover its losses, thereby endangering possibilities of a long-lasting peace. Consequently, the western Allies proposed an alternate border, which extended along the Oder River and then followed another Neisse River (Glatzer Neisse), which joined the Oder at a point between Wrocław (Breslau) and Opole.

The Oder-Neisse Line, 1945

No decision on the German–Polish border was reached at Yalta.

By the time the Allies assembled again at the Potsdam Conference in July–August 1945 the Soviet Army had occupied all the lands east of the Oder–Neisse Line and the Soviet authorities had transferred the administration of them to a pro-Soviet Polish provisional government. Although the United States and Great Britain strenuously protested that unilateral action, they accepted it and agreed to the placement of all the territory east of the Oder–Neisse line under Polish administrative control (except the northern part of East Prussia, which was incorporated into the Soviet Union). The Potsdam conferees also allowed the Poles to deport the German inhabitants of the area to Germany. But they left the designation of the final Polish–German border to be determined by a future peace conference.

Subsequently, the question of the Polish–German frontier became a major issue of contention in European affairs. The German Democratic Republic (East Germany) signed a treaty with Poland at Zgorzelec (German Görlitz) on July 6, 1950, that recognized the Oder–Neisse Line as its permanent eastern boundary. The West Germans insisted, however, that the line was only a temporary administrative border subject to revision by a final peace treaty. Closely associating that issue with the issue of reunification of the two German states, the West Germans continued to refuse to recognize the line as Poland's frontier until 1970. At that time, the West German government, which for several years had been improving its relations with the eastern European states, signed treaties with the Soviet Union (Dec. 7, 1970) and Poland (Aug. 12, 1970) acknowledging the Oder–Neisse Line as Poland's legitimate and inviolable border.

·Stalin's demands at Yalta **19**:1011a

Oder River 13:506, Polish and Czech ODRA, vital waterway in eastern Europe and second only to the Vistula among the rivers draining to the Baltic. Rising in the Oder Mountains of Czechoslovakia, it flows north and west, forming, in part, the boundary between East Germany and Poland (in the territory of which 90 percent of its watershed area lies). Navigable for 473 mi (761 km) of its 551-mi (886-km) length for 220 to 230 days of the year, it is linked by a network of canals to both eastern and western Europe and is of considerable economic importance.

The text article covers the overall significance of the Oder, its setting and course, hydrology, and historical importance.
53°33′ N, 14°38′ N

REFERENCES in other text articles:
·Baltic Sea's low salinity **2**:668f; map
·Carpathian Mountains' drainage **3**:948c
·Czechoslovakian drainage patterns **5**:411g
·map, German Democratic Republic **8**:8
·Polish political and physical geography **14**:625c
·Potsdam agreement frontier **8**:6h

Odes, Latin CARMINA, poetry by Horace, collected in four books, the first three of which appeared in 23 BC, the last, short book in *c.* 13 BC. The themes of the odes are mainly friendship, love, and the practice of poetry.

·content and style **8**:1071g *passim* to 1073g

Odes, Classic of (Chinese anthology): *see* Shih Ching.

Odescalchi, Benedetto: *see* Innocent XI.

Odessa, *oblast* (administrative region) in the Ukrainian Soviet Socialist Republic, with an area of 12,850 sq mi (33,300 sq km) in the southern Ukraine athwart the estuary of the Dnestr River. The southwest, which until 1954 formed Izmail *oblast*, is a gently sloping coastal plain. In the northeast the *oblast* extends inland to the southern hills of the Volyn-Podolsk Upland. The coast is low, with rapidly silting lagoons and estuaries enclosed by long sandbars. The entire *oblast* lies in the steppe on fertile soils, but little remains unplowed. The climate is dry, and there is little surface water, all but the largest rivers being liable to dry out in summer. Agriculture is intensive and dominated by grains—winter wheat, corn (maize), and barley; sunflowers and sugar beets are the main industrial crops. There is intensive market gardening around Odessa and many orchards and vineyards in the southwest. Livestock husbandry is well developed. Towns are small centres of food processing, with the exception of the great industrial port of Odessa, the administrative centre, in which nearly two-thirds of the urban population live. Pop. (1970 prelim.) 2,390,000.

Odessa, seaport and administrative centre of Odessa *oblast* (region), Ukrainian Soviet Socialist Republic, on a shallow indentation of the Black Sea coast. Although a settlement existed on the site in ancient times, the history of the modern city begins in the 14th century when the Tatar fortress of Khadzhibey was established there; it later passed to Lithuania-Poland and in 1764 to Turkey. It was stormed by the Russians in 1789 and ceded to Russia in 1791. A new fortress was built in 1792–93, and in 1794 a naval base and commercial quay. In 1795 the new port was named Odessa, after the ancient Greek colony of Odessos, the site of which was believed to be in the vicinity. During the 19th century, growth was rapid, especially after the coming of railways in 1866. Odessa became the third city of Russia and the second port, after St. Petersburg; grain formed a major export. The city was one of the chief centres of the 1905 uprising and the scene of the mutiny on the warship "Potemkin"; Sergey Eisenstein's classic film

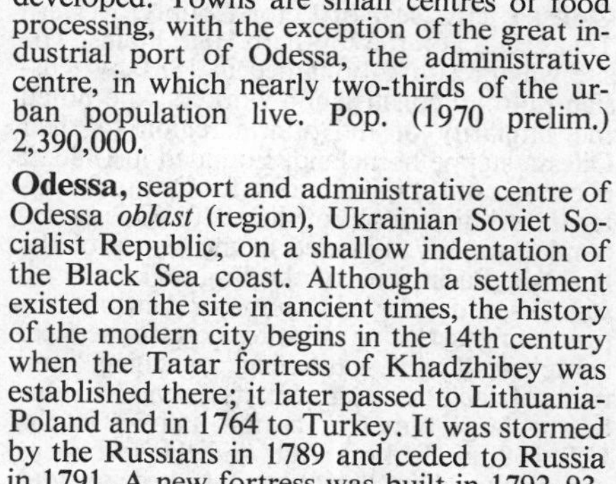
The State Academic Theatre of Opera and Ballet, Odessa city, Ukrainian S.S.R.
Shostal

Potemkin was made there in 1925. Odessa suffered heavy damage in World War II, especially in its prolonged defense against the Germans.

The city remains a major port, one of the largest in the U.S.S.R., with well-equipped docks and ship-repair yards. After 1857 a new outport was built at Ilichevsk, 12 mi (20 km) to the south. Odessa is the base of a fishing fleet and of the Soviet Antarctic whaling fleet. Rail communications are good to all parts of the Ukraine, Moldavia, and Romania. Odessa is also a large industrial centre, with a wide range of engineering industries, including the production of machine tools, cranes, and plows. The chemical industry makes fertilizers, paints, dyes, and other materials. Odessa has an oil refinery, a large jute mill, and a number of consumer goods and food-processing factories. Most factories lie north of the port along the waterfront, with newer plants on the western outskirts.

Odessa is also an important cultural and educational centre. It has a university, founded in 1865, and 16 other institutions of higher education. Its many research establishments are headed by the Filatov Institute of Eye Diseases. There are a number of museums and theatres, including the opera house and ballet theatre, dating from 1809. The seashore south of the harbour is a popular resort area, with numerous sanatoriums and holiday camps. Pop. (1970 prelim.) 892,000.
46°28′ N, 30°44′ E

·commerical rise and social hierarchy **16**:54e
·map, Soviet Union **17**:322
·population and geography **17**:331g

Odessa, city, seat of Ector County, western Texas, U.S., on the southern High Plains. The site was presumably named in 1881 by Russian railroad-construction workers who noted the similarity of the prairie region to their Odessa steppe homeland. Founded in 1886, it became a rail shipping point for livestock. After the oil discoveries of the 1920s, Odessa expanded rapidly. Located in the centre of the Permian Basin, one of the largest known oil reserves, it developed as a major distribution–processing–servicing point for a petrochemical complex. Truck gardening, ranching, and medical facilities augment its economy. One of the largest meteor craters known in the U.S. is 9 mi (14 km) west, and the specimens are displayed in the Odessa Meteorite Museum. Odessa (junior) College was founded in 1946. Inc. 1927. Pop. (1940) city, 9,573; (1960) city, 80,338; (1980) city, 90,027; metropolitan area (SMSA), 115,374.
31°51′ N, 102°22′ W

·map, United States **18**:908

Odessa Crater, a shallow, bowl-shaped pit in the high plains just south of Odessa, Texas, produced by a meteorite. It is about 17 feet (5 metres) deep and 560 feet (168 metres) in diameter; its rim rises only 2–3 feet (0.6–1 metres) above the surrounding area. In 1939 nearly 1,500 iron meteorite fragments were collected from the ground around the crater and on its rim. The original crater bottom was determined to have been 90 feet (27 metres) below the level of the surrounding land. The crater was discovered in 1921 and, because its rim has almost been eroded away, it is considered quite ancient. Three smaller impact crater sites were found nearby in 1939.

Ode to a Nightingale (1819), poem by English Romantic poet John Keats, inspired by the "immortal" song of a nightingale to melancholy reflection on his own mortality. It first appeared in *Annals of the Fine Arts*, then in the collection *Lamia, Isabella, The Eve of St. Agnes, and Other Poems* (1820).

·Keats's period of poetic intensity **10**:413g

Ode to Himself, 17th-century poem by Ben Jonson.

·inspirational occasion **10**:268g

Ode to Psyche (1819), poem by English Romantic poet John Keats.

·Keats's period of poetic intensity **10**:413g

Ode to Zion, also called ZIONIDE, a poem by the 12th-century Jewish poet Judah ha-Levi.

·theme, translation, and author's death **10**:283f

Odets, Clifford (b. July 18, 1906, Philadelphia—d. Aug. 14, 1963, Hollywood), leading dramatist of the theatre of social protest in the U.S. during the Depression era of the 1930s; his important affiliation with the celebrated Group Theatre, New York City, contributed to that company's considerable influence on the American stage. From 1923 to 1928 Odets learned his profession as an actor in repertory companies; in 1931 he joined the newly founded Group Theatre as one of its original troupe members. The company's outstanding productions included Odets' plays: *Waiting for Lefty* (1935), his first great success, which, used both auditorium and stage for action, was an effective plea for labor unionism; *Awake and Sing* (1935), a naturalistic family situation drama that foreshadowed Arthur Miller and related Odets with Tennessee Williams; and *Golden Boy* (1937), tracing the agitated life of an Italian youth who became a professional prizefighter.

Odets
EB Inc.

Odets' masterful *Paradise Lost* (1935) deals intimately with the tragic life of a middle-class family that, ruptured by bankruptcy, faces a remarkable sequence of epiphanies. In 1936 he married the Austrian actress Luise Rainer. After 1937 his fame faded. *Rocket to the Moon* (1938), a social parable, was not, despite its craft, a box-office winner. *Night Music* (1940), a social extravaganza, and *Clash by Night* (1941), a political allegory, failed to focus, splintering turbulently.

Odets moved to Hollywood in the late '30s to write for motion pictures and became a successful director. His later plays include *The Big Knife* (1949), *The Country Girl* (1950; British title *Winter Journey*), and *The Flowering Peach* (1954). A musical based on *Golden Boy* was made in 1964. Odets was one of the first important U.S. writers to break away from the Ibsen tradition of the "well-made play."

·literary style and works **10**:1225b

odeum (Greek: "singing place"), comparatively small theatre of ancient Greece and Rome, in which musicians and orators performed and competed. It has been suggested that these theatres were originated because early Greek musical instruments could not be heard in the vast open amphitheatres in which dramatic performances were held.

According to the Greek biographer Plutarch, of the 1st and 2nd century AD, the first odeum was built at Athens by the statesman Pericles around 435 BC. Adjacent to the Theatre of Dionysus, it was used for rehearsals. It differed from later odeums in its square shape

Odeum of Herodes Atticus, Athens, *c.* AD 161
H. Roger-Viollet

and pointed roof. The Roman architectural historian Vitruvius, of the 1st century AD, states that it was burned during the Mithradatic wars of the 1st century BC. In AD 161, Herodes Atticus, a Grecian scholar and philanthropist, built a new odeum at the base of the Acropolis, in memory of his wife, Regilla. In plan it was much like the semicircular Theatre of Dionysus, to which it was connected by an arcade. With 33 rows of seats, it accommodated approximately 6,000 spectators. It probably had a roof over the playing area. Largely rebuilt, it is still in use. Another odeum was built at Corinth, also by Herodes Atticus. Odeums were also constructed in most cities of the Roman Empire for use as assembly halls as well as for performances and contests.

·Roman use and Palladio's reconstruction **18**:237b; illus. 239

Odi (published 1795, "Odes"), Italian work by Giuseppe Parini.

·Italian literature development **10**:1175b

Odienné, town, administrative headquarters (since 1969) of Odienné *département*, northwestern Ivory Coast, at the intersection of roads from Mali, Guinea, and the Ivorian towns of Korhogo and Man. A traditional trading centre (yams, manioc, cattle, sheep) among the Muslim Malinké people, it was part of the greater Mali (Malinké) Empire in the 14th century. The town is still the chief agricultural market centre for a hilly savanna region that produces manganese and dah (a jute substitute used for making sacks) for export. Pop. (latest est.) town, 8,162; *département*, 118,500.

·area and population table **9**:1184
·map, Ivory Coast **9**:1181

Odin, Old Icelandic ÓÐINN, one of the principal gods in Norse mythology. His exact nature and role, however, are difficult to determine because of the complex picture of him given by the wealth of archaeological and literary sources. The Roman historian Tacitus stated that the Teutons worshipped Mercury; because *dies Mercurii* (Mercury's day) was identified with Wednesday (Woden's day),

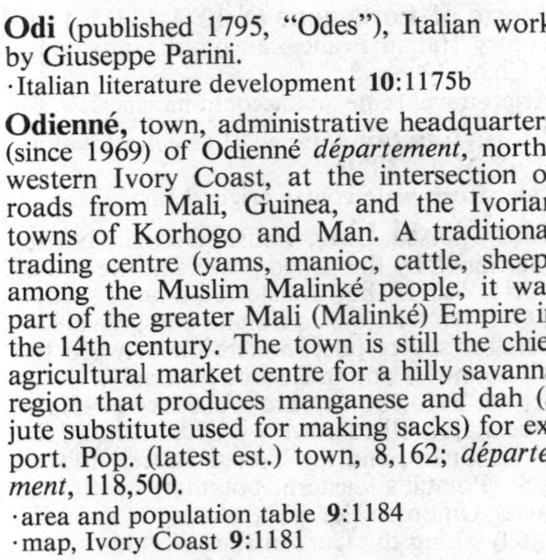
Odin riding his eight-legged horse Sleipnir, detail of a funerary stone from Gotland, Sweden, *c.* 800
By courtesy of the Riksantikvarieambetets Bildarkiv, Stockholm

there is little doubt that the god Woden (Wodan; the earlier form of Odin) was meant. Though Woden was worshipped pre-eminently, there is not sufficient evidence of his cult to show whether it was practised by all the Teutonic tribes or to enable conclusions to be drawn about the nature of the god. Later literary sources, however, indicate that at the end of the pre-Christian period Odin was the principal god in Scandinavia.

From earliest times Odin was a war god, and he appeared in heroic literature as the protector of heroes; fallen warriors joined him in Valhalla. The spear that he normally carried was probably as much a symbol of authority as a weapon; he rode an eight-legged horse, Sleipnir, and the wolf and the raven were dedicated to him. He was also the god of poets, and a story exists telling how he stole the poets' mead; it has been suggested that this mead should be equated with the fluid represented in cosmological speculations as the source of life. Odin was the great magician among the gods and was associated with runes. In outward appearance he was a tall, old man, with flowing beard and only one eye (the other he gave in exchange for wisdom). A wide-brimmed hat covered part of his face, and he wore a cloak.

·Germanic worship of occult and poetry **8**:34d *passim* to 37g
·mythological poetic power **12**:795f
·Norse invention of runes **19**:1043a

Odinga, (Ajuma) Oginga (b. 1912, Sakwa, Kenya), nationalist leader who broke a long association with Jomo Kenyatta, the father of Kenya's independence movement, to form a radical opposition party.

Like many other prominent East Africans, Odinga was educated at Makerere University College and was originally a teacher. He was chosen chairman of the African Elected Members Organization in the legislative council in 1957, and two years later he became president of the Kenya independence movement in the council. With Tom Mboya, he was of the few African members to completely reject the British policy of multiracial political representation put forward in the late 1950s. In 1960 he was a member of the committee to draft a constitution for the Kenya African National Union (KANU), a new party of which he became vice president. Meanwhile, he continued to put Jomo Kenyatta's name forward as a nationalist leader when Kenyatta was still imprisoned in the aftermath of the Mau Mau rebellion of the early 1950s. Odinga was elected a member of the House of Representatives in 1963, and when Kenya became independent in December of that year he became minister for home affairs (1963–64) and then vice president and minister without portfolio. In 1965/66, however, he broke away from KANU and Kenyatta to form a left-wing opposition party, the Kenya People's Union.

·party leadership and election contest **6**:108f

odissi, ancient classical dance form of Orissa state of India.

·origin and classical tradition claim **17**:160c

Odling, William (1829–1921), English chemist.

·chemical classification attempt **11**:900d

Odo (king of France): *see* Eudes.

Odo (duke of Aquitaine): *see* Eudes.

Odoacer, also known as ODOVACAR (b. *c.* 433 —d. March 15, 493, Ravenna, Italy), first barbarian king of Italy. The date on which he assumed power, 476, is traditionally considered the end of the Western Roman Empire.

Odoacer was a German warrior, the son of Idico (Edeco) and a member of either the Sciri or Rugian tribes. About 470 he entered Italy with the Sciri and joined the Roman army. After the overthrow of the Western emperor Julius Nepos by the Roman general Orestes (475), Odoacer led his tribesmen in a revolt against Orestes, who had reneged on his promise to give the tribal leaders land in Italy. On Aug. 23, 476, Odoacer was proclaimed king by his troops, and five days later Orestes was captured and executed in Placentia (now Piacenza), Italy. Odoacer then deposed Orestes' young son, the emperor Romulus Augustulus.

Odoacer's aim was to keep the administration of Italy in his own hands while recognizing the overlordship of the Eastern emperor Zeno. Zeno granted him the rank of patrician, but Odoacer refused to acknowledge Julius Nepos, Zeno's candidate, as Western emperor.

Odoacer introduced few important changes into the administrative system of Italy. He had the support of the Senate at Rome and, apparently without serious opposition from the Romans, was able to distribute land to his followers. Unrest among the German tribesmen led to violence in 477–478, but evidently no such disturbances occurred during the later period of his reign. Although Odoacer was an Arian Christian (one disputing the divinity of Christ) he rarely intervened in the affairs of the Roman Catholic Church.

In 480 Odoacer invaded Dalmatia (in present western Yugoslavia) and within two years conquered the region. When Illus, master of soldiers of the Eastern Empire, begged Odoacer's help (484) in his struggle to depose Zeno, Odoacer attacked Zeno's westernmost provinces. The Emperor responded by inciting the Rugi (of present Austria) to attack Italy. During the winter of 487–488 Odoacer crossed the Danube and defeated the Rugi in their own territory. Although he lost some land to the Visigothic king Euric, who overran northwest Italy, Odoacer recovered Sicily (apart from Lilybaeum) from the Vandals. Nevertheless, he proved to be no match for the Ostrogothic king Theodoric, who was appointed king of Italy by Zeno in 488 in order to prevent the Ostrogoths from raiding in the Eastern Empire. Theodoric invaded Italy in 489 and by August 490 had captured almost the entire peninsula, forcing Odoacer to take refuge in Ravenna. The city surrendered on March 5, 493; Theodoric invited Odoacer to a banquet and there killed him.

·barbarian triumph over Rome **9**:1115e
·deposition of the last Roman emperor **15**:1132b
·Theodoric's capture of Italy **18**:271c

Odobenidae, family in the order Carnivora (suborder Pinnipedia) that contains only one living species, the walrus (*q.v.*; *O. rosmarus*).

·evolutionary lines in pinnipeds **3**:940h; illus. 941

Odobenus rosmarus: *see* walrus.

Odocoileus: *see* mule deer; white-tailed deer.

odometer: *see* speedometer.

Odonata 13:507, order of insects commonly called dragonflies and damselflies, characterized by large compound eyes, two pairs of similar veined wings, beautiful colours, and unusual mating behaviour.

The text article covers the natural history, anatomy, physiology, evolution, and paleontology, and includes an annotated classification of the order.

REFERENCES in other text articles:
·aggressive and defensive behaviour **1**:298h
·Bromeliales ecological relationships **3**:325e
·evolutionary origin and classification **9**:619a; illus. 618
·reproductive behaviour patterns **15**:686a

O'Donnell, a prominent name in Irish history, derived from a 10th-century member, Domhnall (Donnell) of the clan Dalaigh; O' (*Ua*) means "grandson" or "descendant." There were O'Donnell septs in West Clare and Leinster, but by far the largest and most notable was that of Tir Conaill (Tyrconnell), which from the early 13th century held Donegal, later acquiring Inishowen, Fermanagh, and parts of Cavan and Connaught. They resisted English domination until Rory O'Donnell (died 1608) submitted and was created earl of Tyrconnell. He soon escaped to Spain, however, and branches of the clan became established there and also in Austria.

O'Donnell, Leopoldo (b. Jan. 12, 1809, Santa Cruz de Tenerife, Canary Islands, Spain —d. Nov. 6, 1867, Biarritz, Fr.), soldier-politician who played a prominent role in the successful Spanish military insurrections of 1843 and 1854 and headed the Spanish government three times between 1856 and 1866. Though he lacked a coherent political program, he was a staunch supporter of Queen Isabella II (reigned 1833–68) and pursued conservative policies while in office.

O'Donnell gained fame and high rank during the First Carlist War (1833–39). He went into exile in France in 1840 but returned three years later to help overthrow the government of Gen. Baldomero Espartero. He was rewarded with the captain generalship of Cuba (1844–48). In 1854, espousing liberal sentiments, he headed a successful military revolt that brought him to power as minister of war. In this post he shared control of affairs with Espartero, whom he displaced as premier in July 1856. His first administration lasted only until October, but, as head of the moderately conservative Liberal Union, he again held power from 1858 to 1863.

This politically stable period, during which O'Donnell governed under a conservative constitution of 1845, witnessed economic expansion, a compromise solution to the problem of church property, and O'Donnell's opportunistic interventions in Morocco, Santo Domingo, and Mexico. In the Moroccan War (1859–60) he himself commanded the victorious expeditionary force and greatly increased his popularity. O'Donnell resumed office as premier briefly in 1865–66. He at first attempted a conciliatory policy but had to suppress two insurrections in 1866 and was replaced by Queen Isabella with the more repressive Gen. Ramón Narváez. His death not long after his dismissal deprived the Queen of one of her strongest allies, and a year later Isabella was deposed.

·causes of 1854 revolution **17**:438b

O'Donojú, Juan (1762–1821), Mexican military leader.

·Mexican independence acceptance **12**:80b

O'Donovan, Michael: *see* O'Connor, Frank.

Odontaspis: *see* sand shark.

odontoblast: *see* tooth germ.

Odontoceridae, family of caddisflies in the insect order Trichoptera.

·classification criteria **18**:710g

Odontoceti: *see* toothed whale.

Odontoglossum, a genus embracing 200 to 300 species (depending on the authority con-

Odontoglossum
G. Tomsich—Photo Researchers

sulted) of orchids, family Orchidaceae, that are primarily native to mountainous areas of tropical America. Many orchids of other genera have been crossed with species of *Odontoglossum* to obtain beautiful hybrid flowers. Hundred of hybrids also have been obtained by crossing species within the genus. Each large pseudobulb (swollen stem base) of an *Odontoglossum* bears one or more leaves. The flowers are borne on a spike that arises from the base of the pseudobulbs and vary greatly in colour and marking. The sepals of the tiger, or baby, orchid (*O. grande*) have yellow- and brown-striped markings.

·diversity of orchids illus. **13**:648

odontolite, also called BONE TURQUOISE or FOSSIL TURQUOISE, fossil bone or tooth that consists of the phosphate mineral apatite (*q.v.*) coloured blue by vivianite. It resembles turquoise but may be distinguished chemically.

·turquoise structure and occurrence **14**:287d

odontology, a science that treats of the teeth, their structure and development, and their diseases.

·forensic medicine fields of study **11**:814c

odontophore, a cartilagelike mass underlying and supporting the radula (a chewing organ) in many mollusks, especially gastropods.

·snail and slug feeding mechanisms **7**:949b

Odontophorus (bird): *see* quail.

Odontopterygidae, fossil family of the order Pelecaniformes.

·pelecaniform classification **14**:19h

odontostome, any member of the order Odontostomatida; small, wedge-shaped, ciliated protozoans. These protozoans were called Ctenostomatida until the name was found also to designate a bryozoan order. Odontostomes are usually found in fresh or salt water with a high rate of organic decomposition. The semicircular, or arc-shaped, back and the sides are covered with firm plates that form a carapace. These organisms are sparsely ciliated and have eight membranelles (cilia fused into flat plates) in the pouchlike buccal (oral) cavity. The genus *Epalxella*, with the pointed anterior end typical of odontostomes, is a freshwater and marine representative.

Odontosyllis, genus of bioluminescent marine polychaetes of the order Phyllodocemorpha (phylum Annelida) whose sexes are brought together for mating by light signals.

·bioluminescence and courtship behaviour **2**:1029g
·bioluminescence and reproductive cycle **1**:931h

Odo of Bayeux (b. *c.* 1036—d. February 1097, Palermo, Sicily), halfbrother of William the Conqueror and bishop of Bayeux, Normandy. He probably commissioned the famed Bayeux tapestry, which pictures the Norman Conquest of England, for the dedication of his cathedral (1077). Odo was the son of Herluin of Conteville by Arlette, who had previously been the mistress of Duke Robert I of Normandy, William's father. Although scandalously immoral, he was made bishop of Bayeux in 1049 by his halfbrother. Odo typified Norman churchmen before the Cluniac reform. They were essentially scions of great families placed in possession of the church's wealth. Odo took part in the Norman invasion of England (1066) and fought in the Battle of Hastings. The following year he was made earl of Kent and assigned to guard southeast England. With two other men he ruled England during William's frequent absences from the country. In 1082 he was imprisoned by William on a charge of raising troops without royal permission, probably to defend the Pope against the Holy Roman emperor Henry IV. He was released on the accession of William II, in 1087, against whom he rebelled in support of William's brother, Robert Curthose, duke of Normandy. Though the revolt was quelled, Odo was allowed to become Robert's aide. He was active in organizing the First Crusade and was on his way to the Holy Land when he died.

·English ecclesiastical history **3**:205d *passim* to 206a

Odo of Cluny, Saint (b. *c.* 879, Aquitaine, Fr.—d. Nov. 18, 942, Tours), second abbot of Cluny, Fr., who gained for Cluniac monasteries exemption from all but papal authority and whom Pope John XI authorized to reform monasteries in Gaul and Italy, thereby contributing to the great influence of Cluny during the 10th and 11th centuries. Educated in Paris and Tours, he was elected abbot of Cluny in 927. He travelled widely, frequently participating in secular diplomatic negotiations, as exemplified in his arbitration for Pope Leo VII to end the struggle in Italy between King Hugo of Italy and the Roman aristocrat Alberic II. Although probably spurious, several music-theory writings are traditionally attributed to him, most notably the standard medieval method of designating pitches by letters. His feast day is November 18.

Odo of Lagery: *see* Urban II, Pope.

Odoric of Pordenone (b. *c.* 1286, Villanova, near Pordenone, Friuli, now in Italy—d. Jan. 14, 1331, Udine), Franciscan friar and traveller whose account of his journey to China enjoyed wide popularity and appears to have been plagiarized in the 14th-century English work *The Voyage and Travels of Sir John Mandeville, Knight*, generally known as *Mandeville's Travels*. After taking his vows at Udine, Odoric was sent to Asia (*c.* 1316–18), where he remained until 1329. Passing through Asia Minor, he visited Franciscan houses at Trabzon and Erzurum, now in Turkey. He circled through Persia, stopping at the Franciscan house at Tabriz and continuing on to Kashan, Yazd, Persepolis, and Shīrāz before touring the Baghdad region of Mesopotamia. He then went to Hormuz (now in Iran) at the southern end of the Persian Gulf and eventually embarked for India.

After landing at Thāna, near Bombay, about 1332, Odoric visited many parts of India and possibly Ceylon. He sailed in a junk for the north coast of Sumatra, touching on Java and perhaps Borneo before reaching the southeast Asian peninsula. He travelled extensively in China and visited Hangchow, renowned as the greatest city in the world, whose splendour he described in detail. After three years at Peking, he set out for home, probably by way of Tibet, including Lhasa, Central Asia, and northern Persia. By the time he reached Italy, he had baptized more than 20,000 persons. At Padua the story of his travels was taken down in simple Latin by another friar. Several months later Odoric died while on the way to the papal court at the town of Avignon (now in France).

The story of his journeys seems to have made a greater impression on the laity of Udine than on Odoric's Franciscan brethren. The latter were about to bury him when the chief magistrate (*gastaldi*) of the city interfered and ordered a public funeral. Popular acclamation made Odoric an object of devotion, and the municipality erected a shrine for his body. Although his fame was widespread before the middle of the 14th century, he was not formally beatified until 1755.

·Yüan dynasty's contacts with Europe **4**:345g

Odori ji, main dance section of a Kabuki play.

·Nō form parallels **12**:688f

Odoru Shūkyō: *see* Tenshō-kōtai-jingū-kyō.

odour, the property of certain substances, in very small concentrations, to stimulate chemical-sense receptors that sample the environmental air or water surrounding an animal. In insects and other invertebrates and in aquatic animals, the perception of small chemical concentrations often merges with perception via contact of heavy concentrations (taste), and with other chemoreceptive specializations.

·agricultural share toward pollution **1**:361d
·fecal composition **5**:780f
·life-support system and air purification **10**:917f
·oil oxidation and rancidity **13**:527d
·packaging and odour resistant bag **13**:857e
·smell reception research **4**:184h
·smell testing and classification **16**:554c

O'Dowd, Bernard Patrick (b. April 1866, Beaufort, Australia—d. September 1953, Melbourne), poet who gave Australian poetry a more philosophical tone; his work supplanted the old bush ballads that had dominated for many years.

Educated in the arts and law at the University of Melbourne, he taught for a while, worked as a librarian, then made a successful career as a parliamentary draftsman, writing laws for the Australian Parliament. In *Dawnward?* (1903), his first book of verse, he expressed strong political convictions. *The Silent Land* followed in 1905, and the philosophical *Dominion of the Boundary* in 1907. In an important prose pamphlet "Poetry Militant" (1909), O'Dowd, a political and philosophic radical, argued that the poet should educate, propagandize, and indoctrinate. The poet, he believed, should have a strong social conscience and not be afraid to let his views be known. Later work included *The Bush* (1912), a long poem about the Australian nation; *Alma Venus! and Other Verses* (1921), social satire in verse; and *The Poems: Collected Edition* (1941).

Oḍra (India): *see* Oretes.

Oḍra Deśa (India): *see* Orissa.

Odra River (Europe): *see* Oder River.

O'Duffy, Eoin (b. Oct. 30, 1892, Castleblayney, now in the Republic of Ireland—d. Nov. 30, 1944, Dublin), nationalist military leader and popular conservative head of the United Ireland Party who played a significant role in the development of the Irish armed forces and police. His support of Fascism in the 1930s, however, cost him much of his public support.

Joining the Irish rebels against England in 1917, O'Duffy became commander of the Irish Army (1924–25) after the formation of the Irish Free State (1921) and served as chief commissioner of the Civic Guard (police) from 1922 to 1933. After his removal in 1933 he joined the opposition to Pres. Eamon De Valera and helped found the anti-Communist United Ireland Party, serving as its president from 1933 until his forced resignation the next year. Head of the Fascist Blue Shirts from 1933, he lost most of his remaining prestige in an abortive effort to aid Franco during the Spanish Civil War (1936–39) and died disgraced.

Odul language: *see* Yukaghir language.

Odum, Howard Thomas (b. Sept. 1, 1924, Durham, N.C.), ecologist noted for his research involving the measurement of energy flow in both aquatic and terrestrial environments. He has studied a variety of ecosystems, including tropical rain forest and river communities. He has also dealt with the ecological problems involved with polluted marine waters and endangered life on coral reefs.

A graduate of Yale University (Ph.D. 1951), Odum is the author of *Environment, Power, and Society* (1971).

Odum, Howard Washington (b. May 24, 1884, near Bethlehem, Ga.—d. Nov. 8, 1954, Chapel Hill, N.C.), sociologist, a specialist in the social problems of the southern U.S., and a pioneer of sociological education in the South. He worked to replace the sectionalism of that area with a sophisticated regionalism in social planning, race relations, and the arts, especially literature. A student of folk sociology, particularly that of the American Negro, he was ahead of his time in urging equal opportunity for the black American.

Odum studied under the noted psychologist G. Stanley Hall at Clark University, Worcester, Mass., and the sociologist Franklin H. Giddings at Columbia University. After joining the University of North Carolina faculty in 1920, he established departments of sociology and public welfare, a social science research institute, and the journal *Social Forces*.

One of Odum's books on the Negro, *Rainbow Round My Shoulder: The Blue Trail of Black Ulysses* (1928), was praised for its literary quality. Among his other works are *Southern Regions of the United States* (1936) and *Understanding Society* (1947). At Pres. Herbert Hoover's request, Odum and William Fielding Ogburn edited the report *Recent Social Trends in the United States* (2 vol., 1933) for the President's Research Committee on Social Trends.

O'Dwyer, Sir Michael (1864–1940), British administrator in India.
·Amritsar massacre history **9**:417e

O'Dwyer, William (1890–1964), Irish-American mayor of New York City (1946–50), and U.S. ambassador to Mexico (1950–52).

Odysseus, Latin ULIXES, English ULYSSES, the hero of Homer's epic poem the *Odyssey* and one of the most frequently portrayed figures in Western literature. According to Homer, Odysseus was king of Ithaca, son of Laërtes and Anticleia (the daughter of the cunning Autolycus of Parnassus) and, father, by his wife, Penelope, of Telemachus. (In later tradition, Odysseus was the son of Sisyphus and fathered sons by Circe, Calypso, and others.)

Homer portrayed Odysseus as a man of outstanding wisdom, eloquence, resourcefulness, courage, and endurance. In the *Iliad*, Odysseus appeared as the man best fitted to cope with crises in personal relations among the Greeks, and his bravery and skill in fighting were demonstrated repeatedly.

Odysseus' wanderings and the recovery of his house and kingdom are the central theme of the *Odyssey*, which also relates how he accomplished the capture of Troy by means of the wooden horse. Books VI–XIII describe his wanderings between Troy and Ithaca: he first came to the land of the Lotus-Eaters (*q.v.*) and only with difficulty rescued some of his companions from their *lōtos*-induced lethargy; he encountered and blinded Polyphemus the Cyclops, a son of Poseidon, escaping from his cave by clinging to the belly of a ram; he lost 11 of his 12 ships to the cannibalistic Laistrygones and reached the island of the enchantress Circe (*q.v.*), where he had to rescue some of his companions whom she had

turned into swine. Next he visited the Land of Departed Spirits, where he learned from the Theban seer Tiresias how he could expiate Poseidon's wrath. He then encountered the Sirens, Scylla and Charybdis (*q.v.*), and the Cattle of the Sun, which his companions, despite warnings, plundered for food. He alone survived the ensuing storm and reached the idyllic island of the nymph Calypso.

After almost nine years, Odysseus finally left Calypso and at last arrived in Ithaca, where his wife, Penelope, and son, Telemachus had been struggling to maintain their authority during his prolonged absence (*see* Penelope). With the aid of Athena, Odysseus accomplished Penelope's test of stringing and shooting with his old bow, slayed her suitors, and was accepted as Penelope's long-lost husband.

In the *Odyssey*, Odysseus had many opportunities of displaying his talent for ruses and deceptions; but at the same time, his courage, loyalty, and magnanimity were constantly attested. Classical Greek writers presented him sometimes as an unscrupulous politician, sometimes as a wise and honourable statesman. Philosophers usually admired his intelligence and wisdom. Some Roman writers (such as Virgil and Statius) tended to disparage him as the destroyer of Rome's mother city, Troy; others (such as Horace and Ovid) admired him. The early Christian writers praised him as an example of the wise pilgrim. Dramatists have explored his potentialities as a man of policies; and romanticists have seen him as a Byronic adventurer. In fact, each era has reinterpreted "the man of many turns" in its own way, without destroying the archetypal figure.
·apologetic use by Clement of Alexandria **4**:552h; illus. 553
·Homeric treatment of return from Troy **8**:1021b
·Lisbon's foundation legend **10**:1029h
·moira, hubris, and Gilgamesh parallel **6**:908g
·Odyssey and epic tradition **10**:1090h

Odysseus (minor planet 1143): *see* Trojan planets.

Odyssey, epic poem in 24 books traditionally attributed to the ancient Greek poet Homer. This epic and the *Iliad* are said to have provided the basis of Greek education and culture throughout the classical age. The poem is the story of Odysseus, king of Ithaca, who after 10 years of wanderings (although the action of the poem is in fact the final six weeks) returns home from the Trojan War. He finds himself recognized only by his faithful dog and a nurse. With the help of his son Telemachus he destroys the importunate suitors of his wife Penelope and reestablishes himself in his kingdom.
·apologetic reinterpretation of Clement **4**:552h; illus. 553
·circumpolar constellation reference **2**:225f
·eclipse reference possibility **6**:195g
·Homeric scholarship in epic development **8**:1017g
·humanistic scholarship's beginnings **8**:1170h

·immortality theme, moira, and hubris **6**:908g
·literary development and epic tradition **10**:1090h
·Menelaus' Protean encounter **14**:602b
·mythology and popular legend **8**:402h
·Odysseus' bed construction and materials **7**:790a
·Pope's translation critical appraisal **14**:797a
·subject matter and character **2**:46b
·T.E. Lawrence's translation **10**:726h

Oebalus pugneax (insect): *see* stinkbug.

Oeben, Jean-François (b. *c.* 1715, Germany—d. Jan. 21, 1763, Paris), influential French cabinetmaker noted for his outstanding marquetry and for his ingenious mechanical

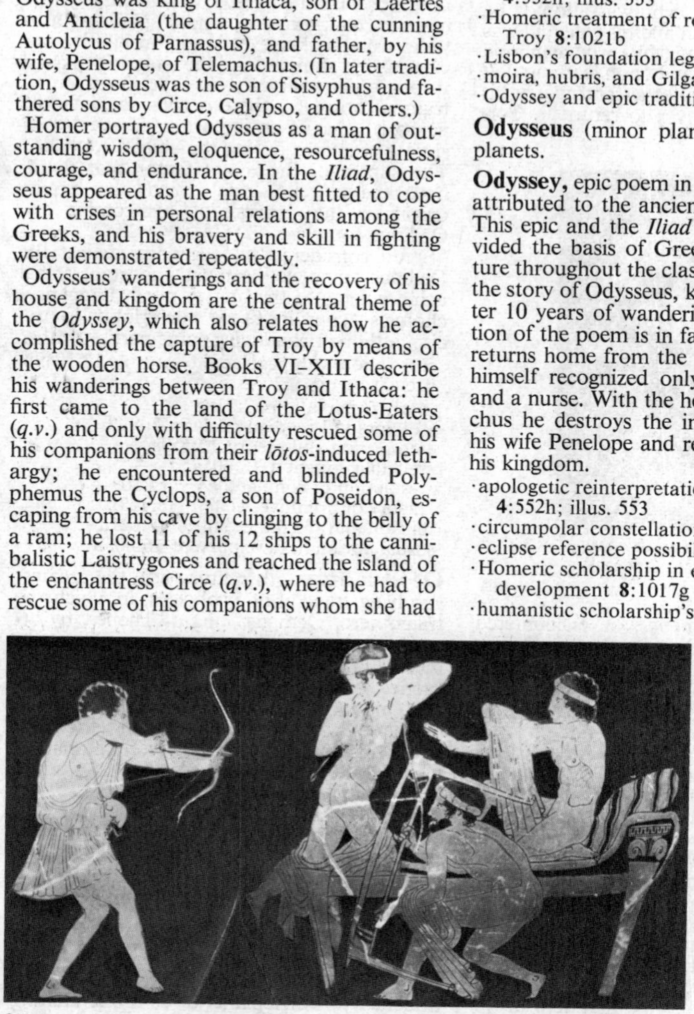

Veneered wood corner cupboard (encoignure) by Oeben, *c.* 1760–62; in the Victoria and Albert Museum, London
By courtesy of the Victoria and Albert Museum, London

devices. He came to France at an unknown date and in 1751 entered the workshop of André-Charles Boulle in the Louvre. He was soon patronized by the King's mistress Mme de Pompadour and in 1754 was appointed *ébéniste du Roi* ("royal cabinetmaker"). Much of his work was done for the royal household. His royal warrant gave him the privilege of a workshop in the Gobelins factory, although he later moved to the Arsenal. His masterpiece, now in the Louvre, is the *bureau du roi*, a desk for the King that he began in 1760 and was working on at the time of his death; it was finished by his younger associate, Jean-Henri Riesener, who also married his widow.
·Rococo writing desk illus. **7**:801

Oecanthus fultoni (insect): *see* cricket.

OECD: *see* Organization for Economic Cooperation and Development.

Oeciacus (insect): *see* bedbug.

Oecobiidae, family of spiders of the order Araneida.
·classification and general features **1**:1074b

Oecolampadius, John, Latinized form of German JOHANNES HUSZGEN (b. 1482, Weinsberg, now in West Germany—d. Nov. 23, 1531, Basel, Switz.), Humanist, preacher, and patristic scholar who, as a close friend of the Swiss Reformer Huldrych Zwingli, led the Reformation in Basel. A student at Heidelberg, he left in 1506 to become tutor to the sons of the Palatinate's elector and in 1510 became preacher at Weinsberg. Three years later he went to Tübingen for further study;

Odysseus slaying the suitors, detail of a red-figure skyphos from Tarquinii, *c.* 450 BC; in the Staatliche Museen zu Berlin
By courtesy of the Staatliche Museen zu Berlin

he became versatile in Greek, Latin, and Hebrew and came into contact with Humanism.

In 1515 Oecolampadius moved to Basel, where he assisted the Humanist scholar Desiderius Erasmus (*c.* 1466–1536) in preparing his edition of the Greek New Testament.

Oecolampadius, a contemporary copy of an original portrait attributed to Hans Holbein the Younger (1497–1543); in the collection of Carl J. Burckhardt, Switzerland

By courtesy of Carl J. Burckhardt, Switzerland

Over the next several years, Oecolampadius produced translations of works by various Greek Fathers of the church, including Gregory of Nazianzus, Basil, John of Damascus, Chrysostom, and Theophylact. In 1518 he became cathedral preacher at Augsburg. His mystical leanings and scholarly temperament led him to enter the Brigittine monastery at Altomünster in 1520, but his growing disillusionment with the Roman Catholic view that the bread and wine of the Eucharist are transubstantiated into the body and blood of Christ and his increasing admiration for Martin Luther caused him to leave in 1522. After serving briefly as chaplain at Ebernburg castle at the invitation of the German nobleman Franz von Sickingen, he returned to Basel, and in 1523 he became lecturer and professor at the university, where he had earned a doctorate in 1518.

Lecturing in three languages to large audiences and preaching at Saint-Martin's church, Oecolampadius soon became the dominant figure in the city. At Baden in 1526, he debated for the Reformation against Roman Catholicism, and again in 1528 he supported the Reformers at the disputation at Bern. During this period Oecolampadius became renowned as a preacher. In a series of writings, particularly in *De genuina verborum domini* (1526; "On the Authenticity of the Words of the Lord"), he supported Zwingli's view that the Eucharist was only a remembrance and not a re-enactment of Christ's sacrifice on the cross. After helping to shape the local ordinances promulgated at Easter in 1529 to establish the Reformation in Basel, Oecolampadius defended Zwingli's position again at the Colloquy of Marburg (October 1529), where he debated Luther. Returning to Basel, in 1530 he opposed the dominant role of local authorities in church affairs and preached in favour of a church discipline in which pastors and lay elders shared in church government. When, in 1531, Zwingli was slain in the Battle of Kappel, the result of political divisiveness over efforts to expand the Reformation, Oecolampadius was overwhelmed by shock and died soon afterward.

·Basel Reformation acceptance **17**:882h
·controversy on Christological doctrine **11**:194f
·Eucharist and church organization views **15**:557e

Oeconomia Regni Animalis (1740–41), in English THE ECONOMY OF THE ANIMAL KINGDOM (1846), a book by Emanuel Swedenborg.
·Swedenborg's psychological studies **17**:855e

Oeconomus: *see* Hofmeister, Sebastián.

Oecophoridae, family of moths, order Lepidoptera.
·classification and general features **10**:829a

OED: *see* Oxford English Dictionary, The.

Oedemagena tarandi: *see* warble fly.

oedemerid beetle, also called FALSE TIGER BEETLE or FALSE BLISTER BEETLE, any of the approximately 1,500 widely distributed species of the family Oedemeridae (order Coleoptera). Slender and soft bodied, the oedemerid beetles are usually pale, although some species have blue, yellow, orange, or red markings. They range from 5 to 20 millimetres (up to 4/5 inch) in length and have long antennae. The adults are usually found around flowers, the larvae in decaying wood.
·characteristics and classification **4**:836d

Oedipe (1718), tragedy by Voltaire.
·success and consequent pseudonym **19**:512f

Oedipus, in Greek mythology, the king of Thebes who unwittingly killed his father and married his mother. Homer related that Oedipus' mother hanged herself when the truth of their relationship became known, though Oedipus apparently continued to rule at Thebes until his death. In the post-Homeric tradition, most familiar from Sophocles' *Oedipus Rex* and *Oedipus Coloneus*, there are notable differences in emphasis and detail.

Traditionally, Laius, king of Thebes, was warned by an oracle that his son would slay him. Accordingly, when his wife, Iocaste (Jocasta; in Homer, Epicaste), bore a son, he exposed the baby on Mt. Cithaeron, first pinning his ankles together (hence the name Oedipus, meaning "swell-foot"). A shepherd took pity on the infant, who was adopted by King Polybus of Corinth and his wife and was brought up as their son. In early manhood Oedipus visited Delphi and upon learning that he was fated to kill his father and marry his mother, he resolved never to return to Corinth.

Oedipus and the Sphinx, interior of an Attic cup, *c.* 430–470 BC; in the Vatican Museum

Alinari-Mansell

Travelling toward Thebes, he encountered Laius, who provoked a quarrel in which Oedipus killed him. Continuing on his way, Oedipus found Thebes plagued by the Sphinx (*q.v.*), who put a riddle to all passersby and destroyed those who could not answer. Oedipus solved the riddle, and the Sphinx killed herself. In reward, he received the throne of Thebes and the hand of the widowed queen, his mother, Iocaste. They had four children: Eteocles, Polyneices, Antigone, and Ismene. Later, when the truth became known, Iocaste committed suicide, and Oedipus (according to another version), after blinding himself, went into exile, accompanied by Antigone and Ismene, leaving his brother-in-law Creon as regent. Oedipus died at Colonus near Athens, where he was swallowed into the earth and became a guardian hero of the land.

Although the Oedipus legend may have originally been based on a core of historical truth, it is impossible to isolate it from its folktale elements. Oedipus appears in the folk traditions of Albania, Finland, Cyprus, and Greece. The ancient story has intense dramatic appeal; through Seneca the theme was transmitted to a long succession of playwrights, including Pierre Corneille, John Dryden, and Voltaire. It has had a special attraction in the 20th century, motivating Igor Stravinsky's secular oratorio *Oedipus Rex*, André Gide's *Oedipe*, and Jean Cocteau's *La Machine infernale*. Sigmund Freud chose the term Oedipus complex to designate a son's feeling of love toward his mother and jealousy and hate toward his father, although these were not emotions that motivated Oedipus' actions or determined his character in any ancient version of the story.

Oedipus at Colonus, Latin OEDIPUS COLONEUS, 5th-century-BC play by Sophocles.
·ego struggle and rebirth **17**:16c

Oedipus complex, in psychoanalytic theory, a desire for sexual involvement with the parent of the opposite sex and a concomitant sense of rivalry with the parent of the same sex; a crucial stage in the normal developmental process. Sigmund Freud introduced the concept in his *Interpretation of Dreams* (1899). The term derives from the Theban hero Oedipus of Greek legend, who unknowingly slew his father and married his mother; its female analogue, the Electra complex, is named for another mythological figure, who helped slay her mother.

Freud attributed the Oedipus complex to children of about the ages three to five. He said the stage usually ended when the child identified with the parent of the same sex and repressed its sexual instincts. If previous relationships with the parents were relatively loving and nontraumatic, and if parental attitudes were neither excessively prohibitive nor excessively stimulating, the stage is passed through harmoniously. In the presence of trauma, however, there occurs an "infantile neurosis" that is an important forerunner of similar reactions during the child's adult life. The superego, the moral factor that dominates the conscious adult mind, also has its origin in the process of overcoming the Oedipus complex.

Freud considered the reactions against the Oedipus complex the most important social achievements of the human mind. Later psychologists consider Freud's description imprecise, although containing some partial truths.
·correlation with passage rite severity **13**:1049b

Freud's theory
·early formulations **7**:739g
·folklore in Freudian analysis **7**:462b
·motivation and theory **12**:559a
·religious function **15**:605a
·resolution of conflict theory **19**:1091g
·theory of primitive religion **16**:129h
·religion and the father image **15**:621d
·sexual deviation development **16**:603b

Oedipus Rex (5th century BC), the greatest surviving tragedy of Sophocles, in which the tragic hero, Oedipus, king of Thebes, by attempting to flee his fate, rushes headlong to meet it. Aristotle, in the *Poetics*, praises it as a model of the tragic form. Its tight construction, mounting tension, and perfect use of the dramatic devices of recognition and discovery make this play the most powerful and haunting of Greek tragedies.
·heroic humanism in tragedy **18**:581f
·myth and reality **17**:16a
·peripeteia and anagnōrisis **18**:588g
·symbolic ritual sacrifice **18**:213c

Oedogoniales, order of algae, class Chlorophyceae, phylum Chlorophyta.
·algae classification **1**:496e

Oedogonium, a genus of filamentous green algae, commonly found in quiet waters, either attached to other plants or as a free-floating mass. Each cylindrical cell, with the exception of the basal cell that serves as a holdfast, contains a netlike chloroplast and a large central

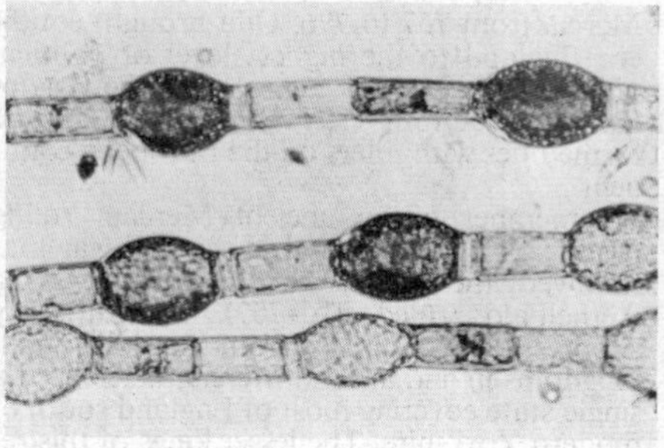

Oedogonium
Hugh Spencer

vacuole. The motile reproductive bodies are characterized by a ring of cilia at the anterior end. Vegetative reproduction results in a ring-like scar at the top of the cylindrical cell (apical cap). Asexual reproduction is by motile and nonmotile spores, formed only in cells with an apical cap. Sexual reproduction is oogamous; the male filament, producing sperm that resemble small spores with long flagella, is either the same size as the female filament or a few cells long, in which case it is attached to the female filament. After fertilization and a resting stage occur, the zygote divides into four motile spores (zoospores) that germinate into new filaments.

OEEC: *see* Organization for European Economic Cooperation.

Oehlenschläger, Adam Gottlob (b. Nov. 14, 1779, Vesterbo, near Copenhagen—d. Jan. 20, 1850, Copenhagen), poet and dramatist who was a leader of the Romantic movement in Denmark and is considered the great Danish national poet. Oehlenschläger wrote his famous poem *Guldhornene* (1802; Eng. trans., *The Golden Horns*, 1913), after his meeting with the Norwegian scientist and philosopher Henrik Steffens, who was eager to spread the doctrine of German Romanticism in Denmark. The ideals of Steffens gave Oehlenschläger the courage to break with 18th-century literary traditions, and *Guldhornene* marks this turning point in Danish literature. His first volume of poetry, which appeared that year, included, among many works, a lyrical drama, *St. Hansaften-spil* (1802; "Midsummer Night's Play"). After the publication of the *Poetiske skrifter* (1805; "Poetic Writings"), which contained two long lyrical cycles, and his *Aladdin* (Eng. trans., 1857), he received a government grant for travel abroad and visited Goethe and the leaders of the German Romantic movement. In his historical plays, *Nordiske Digte* (1807, "Nordic Poems"), he broke somewhat with the Romantic school and hailed Goethe, Schiller, and Shakespeare as his masters. This collection contains the historical tragedy *Hakon Jarl hin Rige* (Eng. trans., 1840), based on a national Danish hero, and *Baldur hin Gode* ("Baldur the Good"), based on Norse mythology. Not only did Oehlenschläger employ Old Norse material in dramas, but he also wrote in *Nordens guder* (1819; Eng. trans., *The Gods of the North*, 1845), a sort of modern Edda. Oehlenschläger's lyrical poetry has outlived his dramatic verse.

·Danish literature of the 19th century **10**:1207a

Oehlenschläger, oil painting by F.C. Gröger, 1815; in the Nationalhistoriske Museum, Frederiksborg, Denmark

By courtesy of the Nationalhistoriske Museum, Frederiksborg, Denmark

oeil-de-boeuf window, in architecture, a small circular or oval window, usually resembling a wheel, with glazing bars (bars framing the panes of glass) as spokes radiating outward from an empty hub, or circular centre. In French, *oeil-de-boeuf* means "eye of the steer," and in the French Renaissance palace of Versailles, erected for Louis XIV between 1661 and 1708, there is a small antechamber called the *oeil-de-boeuf* room, which is lighted by such a small, round window. This type of window, frequently featured in the Jacobean manor houses of 17th-century England, is also called a bull's-eye window.

Ōe Kenzaburō (b. Jan. 31, 1935, Ōse, Japan), novelist whose rough prose style, at times nearly violating the natural rhythms of the Japanese language, epitomizes the rebellion of the post-World War II generation of which he writes. He came of a family of wealthy landowners, who lost most of their property with the occupation-imposed land reform following the war. Ōe entered Tokyo University in 1954, and the brilliance of his writing while he was still a student in the department of French literature caused him to be hailed as the most promising young writer since Mishima Yukio. His literary output has been uneven; although he won a major literary award, the Akutagawa Prize, for *Shiiku* (1958; Eng. trans., *The Catch*, 1966), his next novel, *Warera no jidai* (1959; "Our Generation"), was poorly received. He has been deeply involved in the politics of the New Left. *Kojinteki-na taiken* (1964; *A Personal Matter*, 1968) uses a bizarre situation, the birth of an abnormal baby, to investigate the problem of culturally disinherited postwar youth.

Ōe Kenzaburō

By courtesy of the International Society for Educational Information, Tokyo

Oeland Series, time division of the Ordovician Period in the Baltic–Scandinavian region of northern Europe (the Ordovician Period began about 500,000,000 years ago and lasted about 70,000,000 years). The Oeland Series precedes the Virju Series and is the oldest series of the Ordovician in the region. Lower Oelandian rocks consist mostly of shales and are distinguished by a trilobite (extinct marine arthropod) fauna characterized by the genus *Ceratopyge*. Graptolite (class of extinct colonial marine animals) zones are also recognized and the forms *Dictyonema* and *Bryograptus* are characteristic. The upper portions of the Oeland Series consist of glauconitic limestones, limestones, and shales. The fauna is dominated by the trilobite genus *Asaphus*. Division by graptolite zonation is based upon the genera *Phyllograptus* and *Tetragraptus*.

·Ordovician strata correlations, table 2 **13**:919

Oelwein, city, Fayette County, northeastern Iowa, U.S. Originally settled in 1852, Oelwein was laid out in 1872 and named for a German family who had donated land for construction of a railroad station and right-of-way. It developed as a rail centre; manufactures include air filters, feed supplements, corn cribs, and poultry products. Inc. town, 1888; city, 1897. Pop. (1980) 7,564.
42°41′ N, 91°55′ W

Oenanthe (bird): *see* wheatear.

Oeneus, in Greek legend, king of Calydon, husband of Althaea, and father of Meleager—the leader of the Calydonian boar hunt. He was also independently connected with the Greek hero Heracles as the father of Heracles' bride Deianeira, whom he won from the river god Achelous. Oeneus may have been originally a wine god; his name is derived from the Greek word for wine. According to one story, Dionysus, the great god of wine, was the real father of Deianeira.

Oengus (AENGUS, OENGUS MAC OENGOBANN), **Saint**, also called OENGUS THE CULDEE or GOD'S VASSAL (b. Ireland; fl. 8th/9th century), monk who was the author of the *Félire*, a famous religious verse calendar of the early Irish Church, and was associated with a movement that aimed at the reform of Irish monasticism. The reformed monks called themselves Culdees—*i.e.*, Companions of God. What little is known about Oengus is mainly derived from a poem in a manuscript of *Félire*, which he composed *c.* 800. He was a monk at Clonenagh, County Leix, then became a pupil of the prominent monastic reformer Máelrúain of Tallaght, near Dublin. Later, Oengus founded his own church, Dísert-Oengusa, in County Leix. His feast day is March 11.

The *Félire*, or "Calendar" (W. Stokes [ed.], Eng. trans., 1905), contains a quatrain for each day of the year, a prologue, and an epilogue. Under each day are listed names of saints, each with an epithet or some historical or legendary detail. The recitation of this and similar verse calendars was probably a form of devotion to all the saints, which seems to have held an important place in the liturgy of the early Irish Church.

Oenone, in Greek mythology, a fountain nymph of Mt. Ida, the daughter of the River Oeneus, and the beloved of Paris, a son of King Priam of Troy. Although Oenone and Paris had a son, Corythus, Paris soon deserted her in favour of Helen (*q.v.*). Bitterly jealous, Oenone refused to aid the wounded Paris during the Trojan War, even though she was the only one who could cure him. She at last relented but arrived at Troy too late to save him. Overcome with grief, she committed suicide.

O-er-do-su (China): *see* Ordos Desert.

O-erh-ku-na Ho (Asia): *see* Argun River.

oersted, unit of magnetic field strength, in the centimetre–gram–second system of physical units. Named for the 19th-century Danish physicist Hans Christian Ørsted, it is defined as the intensity of a magnetic field in a vacuum in which a unit magnetic pole (one that repels a similar pole at a distance of one centimetre with a force of one dyne) experiences a mechanical force of one dyne in the direction of the field. Before 1932, the oersted was known as the gauss, a name sometimes still applied, though now more properly used for the unit of magnetic induction. *See* magnetic field strength.

Oêr-t'ai (d. 1745), Manchu statesman.
·Ch'ien-lung's reign and empire **4**:216h

Oertel, Hanns (1868–1952), German linguist who wrote principally on the Vedas, the oldest Hindu religious literature, and made a notable contribution to the study of Sanskrit with his *Syntax of Cases in the Narrative and Descriptive Prose of the Brahmanas* (1926). He taught successively at Yale University and the universities of Basel, Switz., Marburg, Ger., and Munich.

Oerter, Al (1936–), U.S. discus thrower.
·discus throw records and Olympic titles **18**:550g

Oescus (ancient Europe): *see* Iskŭr River.

Oeser, Adam Friedrich (b. Feb. 17, 1717, Pressburg, now Bratislava, Czech.—d. March 18, 1799, Leipzig), painter, sculptor, and engraver who opposed Mannerism in art and allied himself with the classical archaeologist Johann Winckelmann for art reform through the study of ancient masterpieces, although his own work shows little Greek influence.

Trained in the art of modelling by a sculptor, Raphael Donner, Oeser attended the Vienna Academy (1730–39) as a pupil of the German portrait painter Anton Mengs. He then went to Dresden, where he did decorations for the court theatre and, later, mural painting in the Hubertusburg (1749). Named successively professor at the academy at Dresden and the newly founded art school at Leipzig (1764), he painted many works for public buildings and private collections both in oil and frescoes; he remained in Leipzig for the rest of his life.

Among Oeser's most important works are frescoes in the Church of St. Nicholas, a monument of the elector Friedrich August, and small sculptures of the poet Christian Gellert and the Danish queen Mathilde, all in Leipzig. He also left many original engravings modelled after Rembrandt.

Oesling, geographic region, forms part of the Ardennes Mountains in Luxembourg.
·land topography and castle ruins **11**:202h
·map, Luxembourg **11**:203

Oestridae (family of bot flies): *see* bot fly.

Oeta, Mount, Modern Greek OÍTI ÓROS, triangular mountain knot, southern Ethiótis *nomós* (department), central Greece, an outlier of the Pindus Mountains. Its highest point is 7,060 ft (2,152 m) above sea level. In mythology it is the place where Hercules died.
38°49′ N, 22°17′ E
·map, Greece **8**:314

Of a Fire on the Moon (1970), book by Norman Mailer about the U.S. Moon exploration.
·novel as journalistic literature **13**:281h

Ofanto River, southernmost major river (length 83 mi [134 km]) of the east coast of Italy.
41°22′ N, 16°13′ E
·length table of rivers in Apennines **1**:1011
·map, Italy **9**:1089

O'Faolain, Sean (b. SEAN WHELAN, Feb. 22, 1900, Cork, County Cork), fiction writer and biographer who wrote about Ireland's lower and middle classes, often using as themes the decline of the nationalist struggle or the failings of Irish Catholicism. His work reflects the reawakening of interest in Irish culture stimulated by the Irish literary renascence of the early 20th century. O'Faolain fought in the Irish insurrection (1918–21), an experience that influenced the subject matter of his stories. He received M.A. degrees from the National University of Ireland in Dublin and Harvard University in Cambridge, Mass., and from 1926 to 1933 taught Gaelic, Anglo-Irish literature, and English in universities and high schools in Great Britain and the United States. Returning to Ireland, he taught briefly until the success of *Midsummer Night Madness and Other Stories* (1932), his first collection of stories, and *A Nest of Simple Folk* (1933), a novel set in the period between the Easter Rising (1916) and the establishment of the Irish Free State (1921), allowed him to write full time. These first two books evidence O'Faolain's ability to create atmosphere and to delineate sharply drawn characters in the quiet and assured style that characterized all his writings. He later concentrated on writing short stories, essays, biography, and travel works that gave unflattering yet sympathetic and realistic portraits of modern Irish life. His criticisms of church-inspired censorship, the narrowness of the Irish clergy, and restrictive family traditions aroused considerable discussion. His well-known works include *A Life of Daniel O'Connell* (1938) and *Vive moi!* (1964), his autobiography. Historical views of the Irish people are contained in *The Irish, a Character Study* (1949) and *An Irish Journey* (1940).
·literary theme and works **10**:1223f

Of Being, essay by the 18th-century American theologian Jonathan Edwards.
·theme and religious philosophy **6**:441a

Of Cleaving to God, translation (1947) of DE ADHAERENDO DEO, a 14th-century mystical treatise.
·mysticism, introversion, and thought **4**:548d *passim* to 549c

Of Dramatick Poesie, an Essay (1668), essay by the English poet and author John Dryden. Taking the form of a dialogue with four speakers, the essay is a defense of English drama against the champions of both the classical and the modern French theatre.
·comic drama and forms of laughter **4**:960c
·drama and Neoclassical criticism **5**:986b
·Dryden's criticism of drama **5**:1063g
·unities of time and place **18**:590c

Of Drunkenness (1574–75), essay by the French philosopher Michel de Montaigne.
·Montaigne's lessons from life **12**:395b

Of Education (1644), pamphlet by John Milton that is considered to be the last European exposition of Renaissance Humanism. In the work Milton proposed the establishment of an academy based on the study of the ancient classics in subordination to the Bible and Christian teachings.
·curriculum basis and goals **12**:206g
·educational philosophy and pedagogy **6**:351f

Ofen, Treaty of (1254), concluded between Otakar II of Bohemia and Béla IV of Hungary.
·Austrian–Hungarian settlement **2**:451g

Offa (d. 796), one of the most powerful kings in early Anglo-Saxon England. As ruler of Mercia from 757 to 796, Offa brought southern England to the highest level of political unification it had yet achieved in the Anglo-Saxon period (5th–11th centuries AD), and he formed ties with rulers on the European continent.

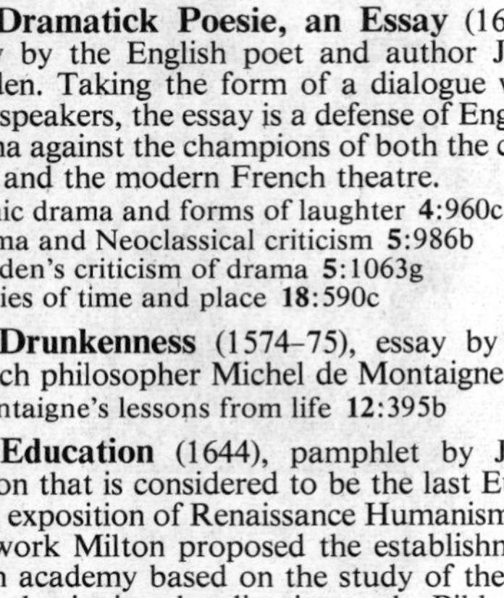

Offa, silver penny, *c.* 787; in the National Portrait Gallery, London

By courtesy of the National Portrait Gallery, London; photograph, Royal Academy of Arts, London

A member of an ancient Mercian ruling family, Offa seized power in the civil war that followed the murder of his cousin, King Aethelbald (ruled 716–757). By ruthlessly suppressing resistance from several small kingdoms in and around Mercia, he created a single state covering most of England south of modern Yorkshire. The lesser kings of this region paid him homage, and he married his daughters to the rulers of Wessex and Northumbria.

Although no 8th-century account of Offa's career has survived, fragmentary sources indicate that he aspired to be accepted as an equal by continental monarchs. Charlemagne, king of the Franks, quarrelled with Offa, but the two rulers concluded a commercial treaty in 796. In addition, Offa maintained a friendly relationship with Pope Adrian I (pope 772–795). He allowed the Pope to increase his control over the English church, and Adrian reciprocated by acceding to Offa's request for the creation of an archbishopric of Lichfield. This remarkable, if temporary, change in church organization freed the Mercian church from the authority of the Archbishop of Canterbury, who was seated among Offa's enemies in the kingdom of Kent.

An impressive memorial to Offa's power still survives in the great earthwork, known as Offa's Dyke, which he constructed between Mercia and the Welsh settlements to the west. Perhaps the most enduring achievement of his reign, however, was the establishment of a new form of coinage bearing the king's name and title and the name of the moneyer responsible for the quality of the coins. Many of them had delicately executed portraits of Offa or his queen, Cynethryth. The principles governing his coinage were employed in England for centuries afterward.
·Mercian political and cultural hegemony **3**:201e

Offa, town, Ilorin Province, Kwara State, southwestern Nigeria, on the railroad from Lagos and at the intersection of roads from Ilorin town, Lafiagi, and Ikirun. A traditional settlement of the Yoruba people in a wooded savanna area, it now serves as a collecting point for yams, cassava, maize (corn), guinea corn, and shea nuts. Cotton weaving and dyeing (with locally grown indigo) are important activities in the town. Offa is served by a hospital and by community-directed and Anglican secondary schools. Pop. (1972 est.) 107,131.
8°09′ N, 4°44′ E
·map, Nigeria **13**:87

Offaly, Irish UABH FÁILGHE, county in the province of Leinster, Ireland. With an area of 771 sq mi (1,998 sq km), it is bounded by counties Westmeath and Meath (north), Kildare (east), Leix and Tipperary (south), and Galway and Roscommon (west). The River Shannon forms its western boundary. Offaly consists mainly of a large section of the central lowland, though its southwestern boundary runs along the crest of the Slieve Bloom mountains. It is mainly a mixture of peat bogs and cultivable land composed of glacial drifts. A notable geologic feature is the fine series of eskers (long ridges of postglacial gravel), notably at Clonmacnois, an ancient monastic site near the Shannon. Seven-tenths of the county is improved agricultural land. Peat bogs supply fuel for electric power stations. Offaly has many raths (prehistoric hill forts) and a chain of mottes, commanding passes of the bogs.

Offaly formed part of the ancient kingdom of Offaly, and was inhabited by O'Connors. It was annexed to the English crown upon title claimed by descent from Roger Mortimer, a lord from Herefordshire, who held sway there and in the adjacent kingdom of Ossory, or Leix, in the 13th century. Offaly was shired as King's County in 1556. A plan for colonizing Leix and Offaly was adopted by the government under Mary I, but the inhabitants resisted for the rest of the century, being subdued only at the beginning of the reign of James I (1603).

Offaly is united with Leix under a county manager but has its own county council. Birr and Tullamore are urban districts; more than two-fifths of the population live in villages and towns, the largest of which is Tullamore (*q.v.*), the assize and county town (seat), which has a worsted mill, malting plant, distillery, and a bacon and sausage factory. Birr and Edenderry (*q.v.*) have footwear factories, Clara a jute mill, and Edenderry a furniture factory. Other smaller places serve as market towns with monthly livestock fairs. Two-thirds of the county's improved farmland is permanent pasture, one-fifth is under crops, and the rest is used as meadow. Wheat is prominent, and barley is sold to maltsters. Tullamore and Clara are on a branch railway line from Athlone to Portarlington, and a canal still carries cargo. Pop. (1971) 51,829.
53°20′ N, 7°30′ W

·area and population table **9**:884
·Catholic land ownership map **3**:288
·map, Ireland **9**:882

Offa of Angel (fl. 4th century AD), powerful continental Anglian ruler from whom the royal house of Anglo-Saxon Mercia claimed descent. According to the Old English poem "Widsith," Offa saved his aged father, King Wermund, from falling under Saxon domination by defeating a Saxon king's son in single combat. Later Offa became ruler of the large kingdom of Angel, and he is said to have established Fifldor (probably the Eider River in the northernmost part of modern West Germany) as the boundary between his domains and those of the neighbouring Myrgings. This legend inspired his namesake, the great 8th-century Mercian ruler Offa, to build a long earthwork, called Offa's Dyke—parts of which still exist—separating the Mercian and Welsh kingdoms. Offa of Angel is probably the same Offa mentioned in the Old English poem *Beowulf*.

Offa's Dyke, boundary dyke along the border of Wales.

·Mercian political hegemony **3**:201g; map 199

Off-Broadway, small professional productions that have served for years as New York City's alternative to the commercially oriented theatres of Broadway. The plays, usually produced on low budgets in small theatres, were freer in style and more imaginative than those on Broadway, where high production costs obliged producers to rely on commercially safe attractions to the neglect of the more serious or experimental drama. The lower costs are permitted in part by more lenient union regulations governing minimum wages and number of personnel. (The terms Broadway and Off-Broadway refer not so much to the location of the theatre as to its size and the scale of production; Broadway theatres are located not on Broadway itself but on the side streets adjacent to it, while some Off-Broadway theatres also are located there, though most are remote from midtown Manhattan.) The Off-Broadway theatres enjoyed a surge of growth in quality and importance after 1952, with the success of the director José Quintero's productions at the Circle in the Square theatre in Greenwich Village. In two decades of remarkable vitality, Off-Broadway introduced many important theatrical talents, such as the director Joseph Papp, whose productions included free performances of Shakespeare in Central Park and who formed the Public Theatre, a multi-theatre complex dedicated to experimental works, such as the phenomenally successful rock musical *Hair*. The works of prizewinning U.S. playwrights such as Edward Albee, Charles Gordone, and Paul Zindel were first produced off Broadway, along with the unconventional works of European avant-garde dramatists such as Ionesco, Betti, Genet, Beckett, and Pinter and revivals of Brecht and O'Neill. The small theatres also trained many noted performers and experts in lighting, costume, and set design.

Like Broadway, Off-Broadway theatres began to suffer from soaring costs; this stimulated the emergence of cheaper and more daring productions, labelled off Off-Broadway. The most successful of these have been such groups as The Negro Ensemble Company, La Mama Experimental Theatre Company, and the Open Theatre.

·directorial competence problems **5**:828c
·income and economic recession **13**:41b
·objectives and production mode **18**:259f
·production styles and popularity **18**:234h

Offenbach, in full OFFENBACH AM MAIN, city, Hessen *Land* (state), south central West Germany, and a river port (coal and oil) on the left bank of the canalized Main, near the Rhine-Main Airport. First mentioned in 977, it was part of the imperial forest of Dreieich, and a mint was established there in 1407. Acquired by Count (later prince) von Isenburg-Birstein in 1486, it began its prosperity with an influx of Huguenot craftsmen in 1698–1703. Annexed to Hesse in 1816, it grew steadily until the proximity (downstream to the west) of metropolitan Frankfurt am Main checked further development after World War I. It has been rebuilt after heavy damage in World War II. New buildings include the town hall, the offices of the federal board for distilled liquors, the directorate of the German meteorological service, the federal customs board, and the chamber of trade and industry. Notable landmarks are the Isenburg Castle (1564–78), the alkaline Kaiser-Friedrich-Spring, feeding a well of 787 ft (240 m), and the Klingspor Museum of modern calligraphy and book printing.

The largest industrial town of old Hesse, Offenbach has a noted tanning and leather goods industry, with a unique leather museum and biennial leather-trade exhibitions. Other industries include steelwork construction and the manufacture of machinery and electrical products, chemicals, soft drinks, and textiles. Pop. (1970) 117,306.
50°08′ N, 8°47′ E

·map, Federal Republic of Germany **8**:46

Offenbach, Jacques, first name originally JACOB (b. June 20, 1819, Cologne—d. Oct. 5, 1880, Paris), composer who created a type of light burlesque French comic opera known as the *opérette*, which became one of the most characteristic artistic products of the period. He was the son of a cantor at the Cologne Synagogue, Isaac Juda Eberst, who had been born at Offenbach am Main. The father was known as "Der Offenbacher" (*i.e.*, the man from Offenbach), and the composer was known only by his assumed name, Offenbach. Attracted by the more tolerant attitude in Paris to the Jews, Offenbach's father took him there in his youth, and in 1833 he was enrolled as a cello student at the Paris Conservatoire. In 1844, having been converted to Catholicism, he married Herminie d'Alcain, the daughter of a Spanish Carlist. In 1849, after playing the cello in the orchestra of the Opéra-Comique, he became conductor at the Théâtre Français. In 1855 he opened a theatre of his own, the Bouffes-Parisiens, which he directed until 1866 and where he gave many of his celebrated operettas, among them *Orphée aux enfers* (1859; *Orpheus in the Underworld*). He then produced operettas at Ems in Germany and an opera-ballet in Vienna (*Die Rheinnixen* [1864; *Rhine Spirits*]), returning in 1864 to Paris, where at the Variétés he produced his successful operetta *La Belle Hélène* (1864). Other successes followed, including *La Vie Parisienne* (1866), *La Grande-Duchesse de Gérolstein* (1867), and *La Périchole* (1868). From 1872 to 1876 he directed the Théâtre de la Gaîté, and in 1874 he produced there a revised version of *Orphée aux enfers*, described then as an *opéra-féerique* ("a fairy-like opera"). This venture was a financial failure, and in 1876 he made a tour of the U.S. The remaining years of his life were devoted to composition.

His only grand opera, *Les Contes d'Hoffmann* (*The Tales of Hoffmann*), remained unfinished at his death. It was orchestrated and provided with recitatives by Ernest Guiraud, who also introduced the famous barcarole taken from *Die Rheinnixen*. Described as an *opéra-fantastique*, it was first produced at the Opéra-Comique on Feb. 10, 1881. *Gaîté Parisienne*, a suite of Offenbach's music arranged by Manuel Rosenthal, remains a popular orchestral work as well as ballet score.

Offenbach is credited with writing in a fluent, elegant style and with a highly developed sense of both characterization and satire (particularly in his irreverent treatment of mythological subjects); he was called by Rossini "our little Mozart of the Champs-Elysées." Indeed, he was almost as prolific as Mozart. He wrote over 100 stage works, many of which, transcending topical associations, were maintained in the repertory of the 20th century.

·operetta composition and influence **12**:700a
·popularity of light operas **13**:586g

Offenburg, town, Baden-Württemberg *Land* (state), southwestern West Germany, in the Kinzig River valley, at the western edge of the Schwarzwald (Black Forest). First mentioned in 1101, it was founded by the Zähringen margraves on the site of a Roman settlement and was an imperial free city from 1289 to 1802. In 1846–49 it was a centre of the revolutionary movement in Baden. There are Gothic and Baroque buildings and remains of the old fortifications. From the nearby Staufenberg Castle, atop the Durbach (1,257 ft [383 m]), the cathedral at Strasbourg, Fr., 10 mi (16 km) northwest, can be seen. The principal town of the Ortenau wine- and fruit-growing district, it is also a road and rail junction with printing, structural steel, machinery, electrical, and textile industries. Tourism is important. Pop. (1970 est.) 32,600.
48°28′ N, 7°57′ E

·map, Federal Republic of Germany **8**:46

Offending the Audience, English title of PUBLIKUMSBESCHIMPFUNG, by the Austrian writer Peter Handke (1942–).

·audience confrontation purpose **18**:253d

Offentliche Kunstsammlung, museum of art in Basel, Switz., established in 1662 by the city and its university. The founding collection, the first publicly owned art collection in Europe, was purchased from extensive holdings of the Amerbach family. Later acquisitions have usually been the gifts of Basel citizens. The museum is noted for its collections of European painting (especially from the Renaissance and modern periods) and of modern sculpture. The decorative arts are also well represented.

offer (law): *see* contracts, law of.

offerings of the five senses, in Tibetan Buddhist ceremonies, pleasurable sense perceptions presented to honour tranquil deities. They are a mirror (to please the sense of form, or sight); a bell or stringed musical instrument (hearing); incense, nutmeg, or scented flower (smell); sugar, a conch filled with curds, or the sacrificial cake *gtor ma* (taste); a piece of silk cloth (touch). The texts refer also to a sixth sense, that of mind, which does not usually figure in a ceremony but which may be honoured by offering a page of scripture.

The offerings of the five senses made to wrathful Tantric deities consist of a skull cup (*kapāla*) containing a heart, tongue, nose, pair of eyes, and pair of ears. The texts refer to these offerings as human organs, but the offerings presented in actual ceremonies are molded of barley flour and butter, realistically coloured and shaped.

The offerings of the five senses are considered internal worship (*nang-mchod*), as distinct from the seven offerings for external worship (*phyi-mchod*).

office landscape, German BÜROLANDSCHAFT, in interior office design, arrangement of open spaces in terms of the relationships of the people to the department, usually without interior walls.

·system origins, solutions, and use **9**:701d

office machines 13:509, various devices used to perform the work of business offices.

The text article covers machines for writing and reproducing including typewriters and those for dictating and transcribing, duplicating and copying; and for computing and accounting and other applications.

REFERENCES in other text articles:

·computers and programming language uses **4**:1046c
·electrophotographic processes **14**:342b
·mathematical calculation theory and use **11**:692a
·printing and copying machines **14**:1059a
·shorthand and sound recording devices **16**:710f
·stock ticker design and development **18**:71f
·telegraphic data transmission **18**:76b
·typewriter history and development **18**:809a; illus.

RELATED ENTRIES in the *Ready Reference and Index*:
blueprint; calculator; cash register; dictating machine; duplicating machine; photocopying machine; tabulating machine

office management, in offices, the functions of planning, organizing, initiating, and controlling the work to be done within the office.

The planning function is concerned primarily with defining the jobs that need to be done; defining and organizing the relations within and among the various units or departments of the enterprise; setting in motion those processes designed to get the job started and completed according to the plans established and the organizational pattern adopted; and having clerical work done satisfactorily at reasonable cost. These functions, in terms of specific management activities, involve the provision of personnel, equipment, and space; analyzing and improving working methods; providing budgets and reports; and handling and storing data.

As office activities have grown in importance and scope, they have been placed more and more under the direction of professionally trained experts in office management.

Office of Economic Opportunity, U.S. government agency established to administer the Economic Opportunity Act of 1964, which provided funds for vocational training, establishment of work-training camps and centres for underprivileged youths, aid to "community action programs" to combat poverty, loans to small businessmen and small farmers, and other antipoverty projects.

·civil rights movement support **11**:128h
·program variety sponsorship **18**:939f

Office of Household, also known as NEI-WU-FU, or DORGI YA MEN, Manchu administrative body that replaced the Thirteen Offices.

·Ch'ing Imperial household reform **10**:379h

Officer Basin, land depression, South Australia.
27°30′ S, 132°30′ E
·formation, relief, and composition **2**:387a

Officer of Arms, one of the 13 officers under the Earl Marshal in the College of Arms in England.

·heraldic officer duties and function **8**:796a

Official Board of Ballroom Dancing, English organization (formed 1929) to determine form and to establish competition rules.

·establishment and purpose **14**:802d

Official Nationality, doctrine promoted by Nicholas I of Russia.

·Nicholas I's three principles **13**:69b

offroad racing, a form of motor racing conducted over rough trails, secondary roads, and generally rugged terrain. Contestants race from checkpoint to checkpoint, and intervening routes are largely decided by the individual. A wide variety of four-wheeled vehicles

Off-road racer (modified Volkswagen sedan)
Toby Palmieri

and motorcycles may compete together, although they are grouped in different classes according to such characteristics as vehicle type and purpose, engine displacement, and degree of modification. Two of the world's foremost offroad races are the Baja 500 and Mexican 1000 events staged in Baja California, Mexico.

·auto and motorcycle events and classes **12**:573d

offset printing, widely used printing technique in which the inked image is printed on a rubber cylinder and then transferred to paper or other material. The rubber cylinder gives great flexibility, permitting printing on wood, cloth, metal, leather, and rough paper.

In offset printing the matter to be printed is neither raised above the surface of the plate, as in letterpress, nor sunk below it, as in intaglio, but remains on the surface; it is based on the principle that water and grease do not mix, so that a greasy ink can be deposited on grease-treated printing areas while nonprinting areas, which hold water, reject the ink. The method was discovered in 1798 by Alois Senefelder of Munich, who used a variety of Bavarian limestone that absorbs grease and water as his plate, giving the process its original name (Greek *lithos*, "stone"); although metal has replaced stone for most offset printing, stone is still preferred by artists for hand-printed lithographs (*see* lithography).

Modern offset printing is done on a press composed basically of three rotating cylinders: a plate cylinder, to which the metal plate is fastened; a blanket cylinder covered by a sheet of rubber; and an impression cylinder that presses the paper into contact with the blanket cylinder. The plate cylinder first comes in contact with a series of moistening rollers that deposit moisture in the granulations of the metal. A series of inking rollers then pass over the plate, and the ink is rejected by the water-holding areas and accepted by the greasy image. The linked image is transferred to the rubber blanket and is then offset to the paper travelling around the impression cylinder. *Major ref.* **14**:1070e

·duplicating machine operation **13**:510h
·printmaking technique and history **14**:1084a; illus.
·refinement of lithography principle **14**:1057b *passim* to 1059b

offshore, zone of shore extending seaward from the mean low tide level. This zone includes the area of greatest wave-break turbulence and provides much of the material from which beaches are constructed. This entry discusses the public-ownership rights of the offshore zone; for additional information concerning offshore as a natural phenomenon, *see* littoral zone.

In recent years the offshore zone has become important in many areas for petroleum producing. In the United States this zone was considered to belong to the coastal states rather than to the federal government. In 1947, however, the Supreme Court decided against California in a federal-state controversy over rights to tideland oil, holding that the federal government had paramount rights and power over the resources of the soil under the water area up to three miles from shore. Similar suits were decided against Louisiana and Texas in 1950.

Congress overrode these Supreme Court decisions in 1953 by passing the Submerged Lands Act, which restored to the coastal states full rights of ownership to the lands under territorial waters, subject only to the federal powers of regulation and control of those lands, for purposes of commerce, navigation, national defense, and international affairs.

offshore bar (geography): *see* sandbar.

offshore drilling, technique used in the search for petroleum in deposits of the continental shelves. The drilling is conducted from large, fixed platforms of special design that can withstand all but the most violent of storms. Areas of offshore drilling in the 1970s included the Gulf of Mexico, North Sea, Persian Gulf, and shelf areas off West Africa and Indonesia.

·petroleum occurrence and distribution **14**:173g
·platform use and well placement **14**:178d
·present and predicted oil yields **13**:502g

offspring of God (Hindu caste): *see* untouchables.

off-track betting, wagering on horse races outside of the racetrack. It may be carried on through bookmakers or in conjunction with the racetrack totalizator. In some countries it is an important source of revenue for horse racing. In most states of the U.S. it is illegal, although New York City legalized it in 1971.

·horse racing and pari-mutuel betting **8**:1104f

Of Human Bondage (1915), naturalistic novel by W. Somerset Maugham set in England in the early 20th century. It is a semi-autobiographical account of a young medical student's painful progress toward maturity.

·French naturalism in British novel **13**:290f

O'Flaherty, Liam (b. 1896, Aran Islands, County Galway), novelist and short-story writer whose works combine brutal naturalism, psychological analysis, poetry, and biting satire with an abiding respect for the courage and persistence of the Irish people. O'Flaherty rejected his training for the priesthood and embarked on a varied career as a soldier in World War I and an international wanderer in South America, Canada, the United States, and the Near East. He laboured in occupations such as lumberjack, hotel porter, miner, factory worker, dishwasher, bank clerk and deckhand. After taking part in a revolutionary bombing plot in Ireland, O'Flaherty settled in England in 1922. There he wrote books that include *Thy Neighbor's Wife* (1923), his successful first novel; *The Black Soul* (1924), the story of a tormented former soldier who seeks tranquillity on a remote western isle; *The Informer* (1925), about a dull-witted revolutionary who betrays his friend during the Irish "troubles" (in 1935, the Hollywood director John Ford transformed it into an Academy Award-winning film); *Famine* (1937), a recreation of the effect of the Irish famine of the 1840s on the individuals of a small community; *Short Stories* (1937) and *Insurrection*

(1950), a novel dealing with the Easter Rising (1916).

Of Mice and Men, phrase from Robert Burns's poem "To a Mouse" ("The best laid schemes of mice and men/Gang aft a-gley") used by John Steinbeck (*q.v.*) as the title of a novelette and a play (both 1937; the play won the Drama Critics' Circle Award). The story was the basis of a motion picture with the same title (1939), produced by Hal Roach and supplemented with a musical score composed by Aaron Copland.
·Copland's musical score for film **12**:699a

Ofonius Tigellinus: *see* Tigellinus, Ofonius.

Of Practice (1574–75), essay by the French philosopher Michel de Montaigne.
·Montaigne's lessons from life **12**:395b

Of Reformation Touching Church Discipline in England (1641), prose work by John Milton.
·Milton's attack on Anglican service **12**:206d

Of the Education of Children (1578), essay by the French philosopher Michel de Montaigne.
·Montaigne's lessons from life **12**:395f

Of the lawes of ecclesiasticall politie, an exposition of the Tudor constitution by Richard Hooker in which he defended the Anglican church against Roman Catholics and Puritans. The work, regarded as a masterpiece of Elizabethan literature, comprised eight books; the first four were published in 1593, the fifth in 1597. Books 6, 7, and 8, possibly tampered with after Hooker's death by enemies of Puritanism, appeared in 1648, 1662, and 1648, respectively.
·content and significance **10**:1149a
·defense of Anglican doctrine and rites **8**:1066d
·natural and transcendent law **14**:689h

Ofu, one of the Manua Islands (*q.v.*) of American Samoa.

Ogadai: *see* Ögödei.

Ōgaki, city, Gifu Prefecture, Honshu, Japan, on the Ibi-gawa (*gawa*, "river"). The site was settled in prehistoric times, but the present city developed around the castle built in 1535. Since the end of the Meiji era (1868–1912), Ōgaki has become a centre of the textile and chemical industries. Machinery is also produced, and rice is grown in the rural parts of the city. Ōgaki Park contains the reconstructed castle, the Tokiwa Shrine, a museum, and a gymnasium. Pop. (1975) 140,424.
35°21′ N, 136°37′ E
·map, Japan **10**:37

Ogam writing: *see* Ogham writing.

Ogaryov, Nikolay Platonovich (1813–77), Russian writer.
·association with Herzen **8**:827g

Ogasawara-guntō (Pacific Ocean): *see* Bonin Islands.

Ogata Kenzan, also called KENZAN (b. 1663, Kyōto—d. June 3, 1743, Edo, now Tokyo), potter and painter of the middle Edo period. He signed his works Kenzan, Shisui, Tōin, Shōkosai, Shuseidō, or Shinshō.

Kenzan was educated in both Chinese and Japanese cultural traditions, pursuing Zen Buddhism. When he was 27 he began studying with the potter Nonomura Ninsei and in 1699 established his own kiln in Narutaki. Encountering financial difficulties, he moved in 1712 to Nijō, near Kyōto, where he established another kiln. But difficulties pursued him there, and in 1731 he moved to Edo and built still another kiln.

In the 40 years of his working life, Kenzan produced *raku* ware (pottery covered with a lead glaze and fired at a comparatively low temperature), *toki* ("ceramics"), and *jiki* ("porcelain"). He used various techniques in ornamentation, his *iro-e* ("colour painting")

Square dish, pottery by Ogata Kenzan, painting by Ogata Kōrin, late 17th–early 18th century; in the Tokyo National Museum
By courtesy of the Tokyo National Museum

being especially good. Many of his designs reflect his classical Chinese and Japanese education. He also produced many paintings, especially in the last five years of his life. His calligraphy, as seen in his wares and his paintings, was distinctive in style. His best known works include a hexagonal plate depicting Jurōjin, the god of longevity, a joint work with his brother Kōrin; a plate bearing a picture of a cedar grove; the "Hana-kago" ("Flower Baskets," a watercolour hanging scroll); and the "Yatsu-hashi" ("Eight Bridges," a painting of a scenic attraction in Mikawa province [modern Aichi prefecture]).
·Kyōto pottery decoration **14**:928b
·pottery design specialization **19**:238f

Ogata Kōrin **13**:515, original name OGATA I-CHINOJO (b. 1658, Kyōto—d. 1716), artist of the Tokugawa, or Edo, era regarded as one of the two masters of the school of decorative painting known as the Sotatsu-Korin school. He is particularly famous for his screen paintings, lacquerwork, and textile designs.

Abstract of text biography. Coming from an old Kyōto family, Ogata grew up in an environment of luxury. When he lost his fortune, he turned to art for a living, and by 1697 he had established himself as a professional painter. In 1701 he was given the rank of Hokkyo, and after that most of his work bears the signature of Hokkyo Kōrin. Among his masterpieces are two sixfold screens depicting the waves at Matsushima and a two-fold screen entitled "God of Thunder and God of Wind." He sometimes collaborated with his brother Ogata Kenzan who was noted as a potter.

REFERENCES in other text articles:
·chōnin class style development **19**:238f
·lacquerwork style and tradition **10**:578e; illus.
·Yatsu-hashi Bridge and Irises, illus., **19**:Visual Arts, East Asian, Plate 19

ogbom headdress, tall headpieces worn by the southern Ibo of Africa.
·visual art of the Ibo **1**:267g

Ogbomosho, town, Oyo (until 1976, Western) State, southwestern Nigeria, on the Plateau of Yorubaland (altitude 1,200 ft [366 m]) in an area of savanna and farmland and at the intersection of roads from Oyo, Ilorin, Oshogbo, and Ikoyi. Founded in the mid-17th century, it remained a minor outpost of the Yoruba Oyo Empire until the beginning of the Muslim Fulani conquests of Oyo in the early 19th century. By surviving the Fulani onslaught, the walled town attracted many Oyo refugees and became one of the largest Yoruba settlements. Ogbomosho's traditional rulers retained control (the refugee population, which was the new majority, was not given political power); and, following Ibadan's victory in 1840 over the Fulani at Oshogbo, 32 mi (51 km) southeast, the town shifted its allegiance from Oyo to Ibadan.

Now the nation's third-largest urban centre, after Lagos and Ibadan, Ogbomosho is inhabited mainly by Yoruba farmers, traders, and artisans. Yams, cassava, maize (corn), and guinea corn are grown for export to the cocoa-producing areas of Yorubaland to the south; teak is also exported, and tobacco is cultivated for the cigarette factory at Ibadan, 58 mi south-southeast. Locally grown cotton is used for weaving *aso oke*, the traditional Yoruba cloth; Ogbomosho weavers also make *sanyan*, a cloth woven from silk brought from Ilorin (32 mi northeast). The indigo dyeing of the cloth is performed exclusively by women. Although the craft of wood carving has declined, the town is known for its early wood artifacts and for its unique *koso* drums. Ogbomosho serves as a staging point and market for cattle, and it has a government livestock station. A shoe and rubber factory was opened in the late 1960s. Local trade is primarily in staple crops, palm oil, kola nuts, beans, fruits, and cotton.

The Oyo–Ilorin road is the main street of the town. A prominent landmark is the great square tower of the central mosque, which rises above the traditional walled compounds of private houses and the parts of the old wall that remain. Ogbomosho has other mosques and several churches and is the headquarters of the American Baptist Church of Nigeria and its theological seminary. It also has Baptist and government hospitals, a tuberculosis clinic, a leper settlement, several maternity centres, and an orphanage. The local government sponsors secondary schools, a teacher-training college, and a technical institute. Pop. (1973 est.) 970,262.
8°08′ N, 4°15′ E
·map, Nigeria **13**:87

Ogboni, among the Yoruba people of Africa, a ritual men's cult that holds ultimate political power in Yoruba society.
·visual art and ritual **1**:265c

Ogburn, William Fielding (b. June 29, 1886, Butler, Ga.—d. April 27, 1959, Tallahassee, Fla.), sociologist known for his application of statistical methods to the problems of the social sciences and for his idea of "cultural lag." A professor at Columbia University (1919–27) and the University of Chicago (1927–51), he frequently served as a labour mediator and was research director of Pres. Herbert Hoover's committee on U.S. social trends (1930–33).

Ogburn's insistence on the verification of social theories by quantitative methods helped to shift the emphasis in sociology from social philosophy and reform programs toward the development of a more nearly exact science of social phenomena. Ogburn considered what he termed invention—a new combination of existing cultural elements—to be the fundamental cause of cultural evolution. He noted that an invention directly affecting one aspect of culture may require adjustments in other cultural areas; he introduced the term cultural lag to describe delays in adjustment. Although lags are usually imperceptible when long periods of history are considered, they may be so acute at a given moment as to threaten complete disintegration of a society. For example, a major innovation in industrial processes may disrupt economics, government, and the social philosophy of a nation. From these disturbances a new equilibrium will be realized.

Among Ogburn's writings are *Social Change* (1922) and *Sociology* (with Meyer F. Nimkoff, 1940).

og clock: *see* ogee clock.

Ogcocephalidae (fish family): *see* batfish.

Ogdai: *see* Ögödei.

Ogden, city, seat of Weber County, at the confluence of the Weber and Ogden rivers, north central Utah, U.S., just west of the Wasatch Range and near Great Salt Lake. Settlement developed around Ft. Buenaventura, a log stockade with an irrigated garden built (1846) by Miles M. Goodyear and purchased by the Mormons in 1847; Goodyear's cabin is preserved. First known as Brownsville, it was laid out in 1850 by the Mormon leader Brigham Young and renamed for Peter Skene Ogden, the fur trader.

After the arrival of the Union Pacific Railroad (1869), Ogden became a distribution point for the agricultural produce of the intermountain region. Transportation, food processing, light manufacturing, and aircraft industries (located at nearby Hill Air Force Base) are the economic mainstays. Golden Spike Day, celebrating completion of the transcontinental railway (1869) at nearby Promontory Point, is observed annually. Weber State College was founded in 1889 as a Mormon academy. The John M. Browning Armory has a collection of the inventor's firearms. The Snow Basin Winter Sports Area, on the east slope of Mt. Ogden, is 18 mi (29 km) east. Inc. 1851. Pop. (1980) city, 64,407; Salt Lake City–Ogden metropolitan area (SMSA), 936,255.
41°14′ N, 111°58′ W
·map, United States **18**:908

Ogden, C(harles) K(ay) (b. 1889, London—d. March 22, 1957, London), writer and linguist who originated Basic English (*q.v.*), a simplified system of the English language intended as a uniform, standardized means of international communication. In 1912 he founded an intellectual weekly, *The Cambridge Magazine*, to which Thomas Hardy, George Bernard Shaw, H.G. Wells, and other noted literary figures contributed. In 1919 he turned it into a quarterly and, with I.A. Richards, began publishing preliminary sketches for a book on the theory of language, *The Meaning of Meaning* (1923). In this work he attempted to draw insights from modern psychological research to bear on the linguistic problem of word meaning. The chapter on definition contained the germ of Basic English, which took its final form in 1928. His *Basic Vocabulary* (1930) and *Basic English* (1930) were followed by *The System of Basic English* (1934). It was not until 1943, however, when Winston Churchill, with the support of Franklin D. Roosevelt, appointed a committee to study the extension of its use, that general interest in Basic English began to develop. Ogden's efforts resulted in conceptions of language learning that are still productive.
·Basic English language invention **9**:743e

Ogden, Peter Skene (b. 1794, Quebec—d. Sept. 27, 1854, Oregon City, Ore.), Canadian fur trader and a giant among the explorers of the American West—the Great Basin, Oregon and northern California, and the Snake River country. He was the first to traverse the intermountain West from north to south.

In his youth Ogden left his home in eastern Canada to embark on the adventurous life of a fur trader with the North West Company during the period of its intense rivalry with the Hudson's Bay Company. During this period he acquired his reputation as a tough, ruthless trader. The two companies merged in 1821, and Ogden was admitted as a chief trader two years later; he continued working for the company in the area beyond the Rockies.

As a fur trader Ogden automatically became an explorer of new territory. For many years he led annual trading expeditions to deal with the Indians in competition with U.S. traders operating out of St. Louis, Mo. In 1825 he reached the river in Utah that now bears his name, in 1826–27 he explored southern Oregon and northeastern California, in 1828 he discovered the Humboldt River in north-

Peter Skene Ogden
By courtesy of the Oregon Historical Society

ern Nevada, and in 1829 he made the first reconnaissance of the eastern face of the Sierra Nevada, discovering Carson and Owens lakes.

From 1831 to 1844 Ogden superintended trade in the British Columbia area, becoming a chief factor (agent) in 1835 and principal officer in the Columbia Department of the Hudson's Bay Company from 1845 on. He was warmly remembered for having rescued the survivors of the Whitman Massacre, in which the missionary Marcus Whitman, his wife, and 12 others were slain in 1847 by Cayuse Indians.

Ogden knew a number of Indian languages and was twice married to Indian women, by each of whom he had children. His *Traits of American-Indian Life and Character* (1853) was published anonymously in London.

Ogden, Schubert Miles (1928–), U.S. philosopher.
·finite God in process idea **18**:268d

Ogden, William B(utler) (1805–77), railway executive and first mayor of Chicago, 1837–41.
·McCormick business partnership **11**:226f

Ogdensburg, city and port, St. Lawrence County, northern New York, U.S., on the St. Lawrence River, linked to Johnstown and Prescott, Ont., by the Seaway Skyway Bridge (1960). The site was settled in 1749 when Abbé François Picquet established Fort-La Présentation as an Indian mission, which was destroyed (1760) by the French in the face of a British advance. The British then built Ft. Oswegatchie, occupying it until 1796; the ensuing settlement was named for Col. Samuel Ogden, a landowner. Ogdensburg was captured by the British during the War of 1812, and the Battle of the Windmill (Nov. 12–16, 1838) took place across the river during the Patriot War, an abortive attempt by Canadian-American groups to free Canada from the "English yoke." A plaque commemorates the Ogdensburg Declaration of 1940. The Remington Art Memorial houses a collection of Frederic Remington's works. St. Lawrence State Hospital for the mentally ill was opened in 1890. The Custom House (1809–10) was officially designated (1964) as the oldest U.S. federal government building. Inc. village, 1817; city, 1868. Pop. (1980) 12,375.
44°42′ N, 75°29′ W
·map, United States **18**:909

Ogdensburg Declaration (Aug. 17, 1940), joint announcement by the U.S. president, Franklin D. Roosevelt, and the Canadian prime minister, W.L. Mackenzie King, made at Ogdensburg, N.Y., of the creation of the Permanent Joint Board on Defense—United States and Canada. Its duties are to carry out studies relating to sea, land, and air problems and to consider in the broad sense the defense of the northern half of the Western Hemisphere.
·purpose and cooperation philosophy **3**:745a *passim* to 746b

Ogdoad of Hermopolis: *see in* Egyptian cosmogony.

ogee (OG) **clock,** clock design that originated in the United States in the 1830s, distinguished by a case the outer edges of which are curved into an S-shape (ogee) formed by the union of a convex and a concave line. A mass-produced variant of the shelf clock, the ogee clock stood about 30 inches (75 centimetres) high, was weight-driven, operated by gears that in the earlier versions were cut from wood, and ran for 30 hours. In the later versions, brass gears were used, and the running time was extended to eight days.

Oggi (Italian: "Today"), Italian periodical, founded 1945.
·magazine publishing history **15**:254b

ogham (OGAM, OGUM) **writing,** alphabetic script dating from the 4th century AD, used for writing the Irish and Pictish languages on stone monuments; according to Irish tradition, it was also used for writing on pieces of wood, but there is no material evidence for this. In its simplest form, ogham consists of four sets of strokes, or notches, each set containing five letters composed of from one to five strokes, thus giving 20 letters. These were incised along the edge of a stone, often vertically or from right to left. A fifth set of five symbols, called in Irish tradition *forfeda* ("extra letters"), is seemingly a later development. The origin of ogham is in dispute; some scholars see a connection with the runic and, ultimately, Etruscan alphabets, while others maintain that it is simply a transformation of the Latin alphabet. The fact that it has signs for *h* and *z*, which are not used in Irish, speaks against a purely Irish origin. (*See also* Ogmios.)

The inscriptions in ogham are very short, usually consisting of a name and patronymic in the genitive case; they are of linguistic interest because they show an earlier state of the Irish language than can be attested by any other source and probably date from the 4th century AD. Of the more than 500 ogham inscriptions known, nearly all are accompanied by Latin transliterations or equivalents. *Major ref.* **1**:625g; illus.
·Gaulish epigraphic remains **1**:838h
·inscription remains **3**:1065d

Oghuz (OGUZ) **languages,** a group of the Turkic languages (*q.v.*).

Oghuz Turks: *see* Oğuz Turks.

Ogier the Dane, French OGIER DE DANEMARCHE, Danish HOLGER DANSKE, an important character in the French medieval epic poems called chansons de geste (*q.v.*). His story is told in a cycle of these poems known as *Geste de Doon de Mayence*, which deals with the wars of the feudal barons against the emperor Charlemagne. The character of Ogier has a historical prototype in Autcharius, a follower of Carloman, Charlemagne's younger brother, whose kingdom Charlemagne invaded in 771 after Carloman's death. Although Ogier is referred to in the chansons as son of the Danish king Gaufrey and later became a national hero celebrated in Danish folk song, the surname "of Danemarche" probably originally signified the marches of the Ardennes and not Denmark.

Ogier was the hero of another chanson of the early 12th century, called *La Chevalerie Ogier de Danemarche*, which told of his military exploits in Italy and of incidents leading up to a reconciliation with Charlemagne. Later in the century *Les Enfances Ogier* placed him at Charlemagne's court, highly esteemed for his military prowess. After he quarrels with the Emperor, over the killing by the latter's son Charlot of Ogier's son, he is imprisoned and word is passed that he is dead. This encourages the Saracens to invade Charlemagne's realm. It is then revealed that Ogier is alive and willing to lead the Frankish troops, provided that Charlot is given up to him. The demand is complied with, and Ogier contents himself with humiliating Charlot by slapping his face. He then leads the Franks to victory over the Saracens and is suitably rewarded by Charlemagne.

Stories about Ogier appeared in Icelandic, Castilian, Catalan, and Italian.

Ogilby, John (b. November 1600, in or near Edinburgh—d. Sept. 4, 1676, London), printer who was a pioneer in the making of road atlases; as a poet and translator he is chiefly remembered for being ridiculed by Dryden in *MacFlecknoe* and by Pope in the *Dunciad*. His early career as a dancing master and theatre owner in Ireland ended with his finances ruined by the outbreak of the English Civil War. Returning destitute to England, he learned Greek and Latin and published translations of Virgil and Homer. At the Restoration, Charles II entrusted him with "the poetical part" of the coronation. Back in Ireland, Ogilby opened another theatre but subsequently settled in London.

After the Great Fire of 1666, he surveyed

Ogilby, engraving by William Camden Edwards, 1820, after a drawing by J. Thurston

The Mansell Collection

disputed London property. He set up as a printer with the title of "king's cosmographer and geographical printer" and produced many volumes notable for their typography and illustrations. His *Britannia . . . a Geographical and Historical Description of the Principal Roads thereof . . .*, published in 1675, was part of a projected world atlas and a landmark in accurate road description.

ogive, in glaciology, band of thick or of debris-laden ice (called, respectively, a wave ogive or a dirt-band ogive) in a glacier, convex, when viewed from above, in the direction of flow.

·types and formation processes **9**:183d

Oglala Sioux, a branch of the Teton division of the Dakota (*q.v.*) Indians.

Oglasa (Italy): *see* Montecristo Island.

Oglethorpe, James Edward (b. Dec. 22, 1696, London—d. June 30/July 1, 1785, Cranham Hall, Essex), army officer, philanthropist, and founder of the British colony of Georgia in America. Educated at Eton College and Corpus Christi College, Oxford, he entered the army in 1712 and joined the Austrian army fighting the Turks in 1717. On his return to England in 1722, he entered Parliament. In 1729 he presided over a committee that brought about prison reforms. This experience gave him the idea of founding a new colony in North America as a place where the poor and destitute could start afresh and where persecuted Protestant sects could find refuge.

In 1732 Oglethorpe secured a charter for his colony in what became Georgia. In 1733 he accompanied the first settlers and founded Savannah. On the outbreak of the war between England and Spain in 1739, he led a vigorous defense of the territory. He was foiled in an attempt to capture the Spanish town of St. Augustine, Fla., but was able to repel an attack on Ft. Frederica, Georgia (1742). Ogle-

Oglethorpe, panel by A.E. Dyer after a portrait by W. Verelst; in the National Portrait Gallery, London

By courtesy of the National Portrait Gallery, London

thorpe's popularity, not only with his hurriedly raised and imperfectly trained troops but also with all classes of the population, helped to assure the safety of the colony.

Oglethorpe returned to England in 1743, where he resumed his parliamentary career. A biography by A.S. Ettinger was published in 1936.

·Georgia settlement plan and control **18**:950b
·settlement of Georgia **7**:1128c

Ogmios, one of the Celtic gods of Gaul, identified with the Roman Hercules. He was portrayed as an old man with swarthy skin and armed with a bow and club. He was also a god of eloquence, and in that aspect he was represented as drawing along a company of men whose ears were chained to his tongue. His Irish equivalent was Ogma, whose Herculean, warlike aspect was also stressed. In Irish tradition he was portrayed as a swarthy man, whose battle ardour was so great that he had to be controlled by chains held by other warriors until the right moment. His name seems to have been connected with ogham writing, which would be a fitting invention for

Ogmios, carved relief; in the Musée Granet, Aix-en-Provence, Fr.

Jean Roubier

a god of eloquence. Ogmios may also have been identified with the Roman god Sol Invictus, as his Irish epithet, Grianainech (of the Sunlike Face), seems to indicate.

·Gallo-Roman gods **3**:1070c
·writing invention legend **19**:1043a

OGO 1 (satellite): *see* Orbiting Geophysical Observatories.

Ögödei, also spelled OGADAI, OGDAI, UGEDEI, etc. (b. 1185, Mongolia—d. 1241, Karakorum, Mongolia), son and successor of the Mongol ruler Genghis Khan. The third son of Genghis, Ögödei succeeded his father in 1229 and greatly expanded the Mongol Empire. He was the first ruler of the Mongols to call himself *khagan* ("great khan"); his father used only the title khan. He made his headquarters on the Orhon River in central Mongolia, where he built the capital city of Karakorum on the site laid out by his father. Like his father, he carried out several simultaneous campaigns, using generals in the field who acted independently but who were subject to orders sent by Ögödei. The orders were transmitted by a messenger system that covered almost all of Asia.

In the East, Ögödei launched an attack on the Chin (Juchen) dynasty of North China. The Sung dynasty in South China wished to regain territory lost to the Chin and therefore allied itself with the Mongols, helping Ögödei take the Chin capital at K'ai-feng in 1234.

Ögödei's Chinese adviser, Yeh-lü Ch'u-ts'ai, persuaded Ögödei to reverse previous Mongol policy. Instead of levelling North China and all its inhabitants in the usual Mongol manner, he preserved the country in order to utilize the wealth and skills of its inhabitants. That decision not only saved Chinese culture in North China but also gave the Mongols access to the Chinese weapons that later enabled them to conquer the technologically superior Sung. Knowledge of governmental techniques gained from the people of North China made it possible for the Mongols to be rulers as well as conquerors of China.

In the western part of his empire, Ögödei sent Mongol armies into Iran, Iraq, and Russia. With the sacking of Kiev in 1240, the Mongols finally crushed Russian resistance. In the next year Mongol forces defeated a joint army of German and Polish troops and then marched through Hungary and reached the Adriatic Sea. Thereafter for more than 200 years Russia remained tributary to the Mongols of the Golden Horde.

Ögödei died during a drinking bout, and his troops called off their intended invasion of western Europe. His widow, Töregene, ruled as regent until 1246 when she handed over the throne to Güyük, her eldest son by Ögödei. Ögödei is described in contemporary sources as a stern, energetic man given to drinking and lasciviousness.

·Chinese bureaucracy reform and relapse **4**:342c
·khanate election and Mongol expansion **12**:372d
·territorial expansion policies **9**:599d

Ogo Highlands, highlands in Somalia that rise steeply to 7,900 ft (2,400 m) from the Gulf of Aden.

10°00′ N, 46°00′ E

·map, Somalia **16**:1059
·maritime range location **16**:1057f

Ogoja, town, administrative headquarters of Ogoja Division, Cross River (until 1976, South-Eastern) State, southeastern Nigeria, on the road from Abakaliki. The chief trade centre (yams, cassava, maize [corn], rice, palm oil and kernels, kola nuts) of a province mainly inhabited by the Ekoi people, the town is the site of a teacher-training college, a Roman Catholic secondary school, and several hospitals and clinics.

Occupying an area of 4,865 sq mi (12,600 sq km), Ogoja Province has wooded savanna in the north, stretches of tropical rain forest in the centre and in the Cross River Valley in the south, and large, scattered belts of "oil palm bush." Cocoa, the chief export crop, is grown

around Ikom, the head of high-water navigation on the Cross River. Circles of sacred stone carvings are found in the vicinity of Ikom. Pop. (1971 est.) town, 38,310; (latest census) province, 357,099.
6°40′ N, 8°48′ E
·map, Nigeria **13**:86

Ogoni, a people of East Africa.
·visual art forms **1**:267h

Ogooué-Ivindo, administrative *région*, Gabon, western Africa. Makokou is the capital.
·area and population table **7**:819
·map, Gabon **7**:820

Ogooué-Lolo, administrative *région*, Gabon, western Africa. Koula-Moutou is the capital.
·area and population table **7**:819
·map, Gabon **7**:820

Ogooué-Maritime, administrative *région*, Gabon, western Africa. Port-Gentil is the capital.
·area and population table **7**:819
·map, Gabon **7**:820

Ogooué (OGOWE) **River,** stream of west central Africa, flowing for almost its entire course in the Gabon Republic and draining an area of almost 86,000 sq mi (222,700 sq km). It rises in the Congo (Brazzaville) on the eastern slopes of the Massif du Chaillu and flows through Gabon in a northwesterly direction past Franceville and Lastoursville; it then turns west and southwest past Booué, Ndjolé, and Lambaréné, collecting water from numerous lakes above Lambaréné before forming a delta and emptying into the Atlantic Ocean south of Cap Lopez near Port-Gentil after a course of 750 mi (1,200 km). Although interrupted by rapids and waterfalls along its upper course, the Ogooué is navigable as far as Lambaréné (114 mi upstream) throughout the year, and to Ndjolé (155 mi upstream) from October to May. Shallow-draft boats can ply the river from Booué to Lastoursville between mid-November and mid-June; and its two major tributaries, the Ngounié and the Ivindo, have seasonal navigable stretches. Other tributaries are the Mpassa, the Sébé, the Djadié, the Okano, the Abanga, the Lolo, and the Offoué. Between the Ngounié and the Ogooué rivers, the Massif du Chaillu, the country's main watershed, rises to more than 3,000 ft.

The first white man to explore its valley was a French-born U.S. explorer, Paul B. du Chaillu. European explorers followed, including Pierre Savorgnan de Brazza, who navigated the entire course of the upper Ogooué (1875–83), locating its source in 1877. The navigable parts of the river are now heavily used for shipping goods, especially lumber, to the coast.
0°49′ S, 9°00′ E
·geological and topographic features **7**:819b
·map, Gabon **7**:820

O'Gorman, Juan (b. July 6, 1905, Coyoacán, Mex.), architect and muralist, particularly notable for his imaginative mosaics used as architectural decoration. He graduated in 1927 from the school of architecture of the National University of Mexico, Mexico City. From 1928 to the mid-1930s he built private houses in Mexico City. These houses, designed while he was under the influence of the functionalist ideas of the Swiss-born, French architect Le Corbusier, are among the first buildings in Mexico in the International Style. Later he was active as an easel and mural painter. His large complex mural in the public library of Patzcuaro, Michoacan (1941–42), presents a history of the Tarascon Indian tribes.

Ciudad Universitaria library building, Mexico City, by Juan O'Gorman, 1951–53
Guillermo Ortiz Maldonado

In 1950 O'Gorman planned and built the Library of the National Autonomous University of Mexico, Mexico City. The tower containing the book stacks was covered with mosaics constructed of natural minerals. This rich, complex decoration symbolically presents a history of Mexican culture. Other important mosaics are "Homage to Cuauhtemoc," at the Hotel de la Mision, Taxco (1957), and "Fraternity of Indo-American Peoples," at the Tupahue swimming pools of the Parque San Cristobal, Santiago, Chile (1963–64).

Perhaps O'Gorman's best known work was his own house outside Mexico City (1953–56, demolished 1969). A fantastic dream structure, it was in part a natural cave in rocks and was designed to harmonize with the lava formations of the landscape. Mosaics covered the interior and exterior.
·mosaic designs in architecture **12**:473d
·University of Mexico mosaic,
illus., **12**:Mosaic, Plate VI

Ogot, Grace (b. 1930, central Nyanza Region, Kenya), widely anthologized short-story writer and novelist and one of the few well-known woman writers in East Africa. Her stories, which have appeared in European and African journals and in a collection, *Land Without Thunder* (1968), give an inside view of traditional Luo life and society and the conflict of traditional with colonial and modern cultures. Her novel *The Promised Land* (1966) tells of Luo pioneers in Tanzania and western Kenya. A nurse by profession, she has also worked as a scriptwriter and an announcer for the British Broadcasting Corporation's East African Service, as a headmistress, as a community development officer in Kisumu, and as an Air India public relations officer.

OGPU, in full OBYEDINYONNOYE GOSUDARSTVENNOYE POLITICHESKOYE UPRAVLENIYE, in English UNIFIED STATE POLITICAL ADMINISTRATION, Soviet security police agency. It was established in 1922 as the GPU and retitled OGPU after the formation of the U.S.S.R. in 1923. Founded to suppress counterrevolution, it was used by the leadership of the Communist Party during the 1920s to uncover political dissidents and after 1928 in the collectivization of agriculture. The OGPU also staged the first "show trials" of alleged saboteurs (1928–31). Made into an all-union agency (Nov. 15, 1923), it assumed more duties, including the administration of corrective labour camps, acquired broad investigative and judicial powers, and, after 1930, had a monopoly on police functions. By that time, OGPU had its own army, with aviation and tank units, and a vast network of spies and informers in factories, government offices, and army units. Its leaders were Feliks Dzerzhinsky (1922–26), former head of Cheka (*q.v.*), Vyacheslav Menzhinsky (1926–34), and Genrikh Yagoda (1934). In 1934 the OGPU was absorbed by the NKVD (*q.v.*).
·forced labour in the Soviet Union **16**:864c
·Soviet intelligence preceding KGB **9**:684a

O'Grady, Standish James (b. Sept. 18, 1846, Castletown, County Cork—d. May 18, 1928, Shanklin, Isle of Wight), historical novelist and literary historian whose popular English versions of the Irish heroic sagas earned him the title of "father of the Irish literary revival." He graduated from Trinity College, Dublin, in 1868. Introduced to the ancient heroic and romantic literature of Ireland through the translations of the Gaelic scholar Eugene O'Curry, O'Grady devoted his career to the study of Irish antiquities. In 1878 he published *History of Ireland: The Heroic Period;* this work was followed in 1880 by *History of Ireland: Cuculain and His Contemporaries.*

The enthusiasm of William Butler Yeats and other young Irish writers eventually brought O'Grady a wider audience and a London publisher, and in 1892 he published *Finn and His Companions*, following it two years later with *The Coming of Cuculain.* He also wrote several works of historical fiction, of which *The Bog of Stars* (1893) and *The Flight of the Eagle* (1897) are probably the best. O'Grady's versions of Irish epic have great narrative vigour and imaginative power and had a profound influence on Yeats and other writers of the Irish literary renaissance at the turn of the 19th century.

ogre-faced spider, any member of the family Dinopidae (order Araneida). One pair of eyes is unusually large, lending an ogrelike appearance. The spiders occur throughout the tropics. One genus, *Dinopis*, which occurs in the United States, carries a web that is thrown over prey.

Ogre-faced spider (*Dinopis stauntoni*)
Anthony Bannister from the Natural History Photographic Agency—EB Inc.

·web-building and predation
techniques **1**:1069g

Ogrinya, dance society of the Idoma people of Africa for men who had killed an elephant, lion, or man.
·function and mask form **1**:261f

Ogun, a god of the Yoruba people of southwestern Nigeria and eastern Dahomey.
·Yoruba peoples beliefs and deities **13**:90d

Ogunde, Hubert (b. 1916), pioneer in the field of Nigerian folk opera (drama in which music and dancing play a significant role) and founder of the Theatre Party (1944), the first professional theatrical company in Nigeria. The popularity of his group was established throughout Nigeria by his timely play *The Strike*, which was produced during the general strike of 1945. After extensive travels overseas to study playacting and stagecraft, the quality of his plays steadily improved. Yoruba theatre became secularized through his careful blending of astute political or social satire with elements of music hall and slapstick. His most famous play, *Yoruba Ronu* (performed 1964; "Yorubas, Think!"), was such a biting attack on the Premier of western Nigeria that the Theatre Party was banned from the region—the first instance in Nigeria of literary censorship. *O Tito Koro* (performed 1965; "Truth is Bitter") also refers to political events in western Nigeria in 1963, and a third play includes a mock election, which is held on the stage.

Ogunde's technique is to write down and re-

hearse only the songs of his plays. The dialogue is improvised, thus allowing the actors to adjust to their audience. Many of his tunes are based on hymn tunes. His Theatre Party performs with equal ease in remote villages and in metropolitan centres of Nigeria (as well as throughout West Africa). His company has set an example for a successful commercial theatre and has accustomed audiences throughout Nigeria to this art form. Of his plays only *Yoruba Ronu* (1964) is available in printed form.
·style and censorship **1**:242b

Ogunmola, E.K. (b. 1925), Nigerian actor, mime, director, and playwright who developed Yoruba folk opera into a serious theatre form through his work with his Ogunmola Traveling Theatre. He studied stagecraft at the University of Ibadan (Nigeria) School of Drama. In his own work he refined the techniques of his colleague Hubert Ogunde by writing much more tightly constructed plays, usually gentle social satires. A typical play is *Love of Money* (performed *c.* 1950), which depicts the downfall of a happy man through foolish ambition. His greatest renown as a director, however, came from *The Palmwine Drinkard* (performed 1963), a production adapted from the novel of the same name by his fellow Nigerian, Amos Tutuola.
·Ogunde technique variation **1**:242b

Oğuz (OGHUZ) **languages:** *see* Turkic languages; Turkmen language.

Oğuz (OGHUZ, GHUZZ) **Turks,** also called GHUZZ, group of nomadic Turkic people who conquered much territory during the 11th century. By the end of that century, the Seljuqs, one branch of the Oğuz, controlled an empire stretching from the Amu Darya to the Persian Gulf and from the Indus River to the Mediterranean Sea. The term Oğuz Turks is sometimes used to refer to speakers of the southwestern branch of the Turkic language subfamily.
·Islāmic cultural history **9**:931a
·Ottoman Empire historical origins **13**:771d
·Seljuq tribal origins **9**:855h

Ogyū Sorai (1666–1728), one of the foremost Japanese scholars of Chinese culture and a leading Confucianist. He stressed the pragmatic application of Confucianism to promote social and political reforms by means of uniform, rational laws. He is also noted for his appreciative commentary on the revered shogunate ruler and administrative reformer Tokugawa Ieyasu (1543–1616).
·Chu Hsi studies decline **10**:75h
·Confucian emphasis on history **10**:106b

Ohain, Hans Pabst von (b. Dec. 14, 1911, Dessau, now in East Germany), designer of the first operational jet engine. After obtaining his doctorate at the University of Göttingen, he became a junior assistant to Hugo von Pohl, director of the Physical Institute there. When the pioneer German aircraft builder Ernst Heinkel asked the university for assistance in design, Pohl recommended Ohain, who joined Heinkel's manufacturing firm in 1936. Ohain's experiments resulted in a bench test by 1937 and a fully operational jet aircraft, the He178, by 1939. The first jet aircraft flight took place in the early morning hours of Aug. 27, 1939; Ohain's centrifugal flow turbojet engine, the HeS3b, performed perfectly, though the failure of the plane's landing gear to retract prevented the test pilot from accelerating to planned speed.

Ohain continued his work, developing an improved engine, the HeS8-A, which was first flown on April 2, 1941. Although the German High Command was kept informed of these developments, it was more interested in rocketry; as a result, Ohain's engines saw little use in World War II.

Ohara, Japanese school of floral art founded by Ohara Unshin in the early 20th century; it introduced the *moribana* style of naturalistic landscapes in shallow dish-like vases. The *moribana* style, while retaining a basic triangular structure, is in the *nageire* (fresh and spontaneous) mood. The Ohara school's use of narrow-mouthed vases is of the *shōka* (free and informal) style, but is known as *heika*. The styles of this school have grown in popularity throughout the 20th century, superseding the traditional and formalistic *rikka* style. *See also* moribana.
·Japanese flower arrangement styles **7**:418g

O-harae (Shintō religion): *see* harai.

O'Higgins, inland region, central Chile, bounded to the east by Argentina, and facing the Pacific Ocean to the west. The province was named, at its formation in 1883, for the nation's first head of state, Bernardo O'Higgins; it was dissolved in 1927 and re-created in 1934. Since 1974 it has comprised the provinces of Cachapoal and Colchagua. It has an area of 6,920 sq mi (17,924 sq km). Most of its western half lies on the alluvial plains of the Central Valley, where irrigation is required because of the long, dry summer season. Water is supplied by streams that rise in the Andes Mountains. The highlands and nonirrigated lowlands support cattle and some sheep. Irrigated pastures are used for dairy herds and to prepare beef cattle for market. Grapes, wheat, barley, legumes, and corn (maize) are the principal crops. The provincial capital, Rancagua (*q.v.*), and Santiago are the major marketing centres. Mining is also important to the economy, which is centred on El Teniente (*q.v.*), Chile's second largest copper mine. The Pan-American Highway and the main north–south railroad cross the province, and the local road network is good. Pop. (1980 est.) 567,511.
·area and population table **4**:251

O'Higgins, Bernardo **13**:516 (b. probably Aug. 20, 1778, Chillán, Chile—d. Oct. 1842, Peru), revolutionary leader and first Chilean head of state, who commanded the military forces that won independence from Spain.

Abstract of text biography. O'Higgins was the son of a Spanish officer of Irish origin. While he completed his education in London, his nationalist ideas were fostered under the influence of the Venezuelan activist Francisco Miranda. O'Higgins was chosen a member of the first national Chilean congress (1811) that convened while Spain was preoccupied with Napoleon I. As chief of Chilean forces, O'Higgins, with the Argentine general José de San Martín, led the army of the Andes, consisting of Argentine troops and Chilean exiles, to triumph over royalist forces at the Battle of Chacabuco (Feb. 12, 1817). O'Higgins, as supreme director of Chile, alienated the conservative aristocracy and the church by his attempt to develop constitutional reform and continental unity. He lived in exile in Peru from 1823 until his death.

REFERENCES in other text articles:
·Chilean independence movement role **4**:255e
·San Martín independence cooperation **16**:225f

O'Higgins, Kevin Christopher (b. June 7, 1892, Stradbally, County Leix—d. July 10, 1927, Booterstown, County Dublin), statesman who attempted severe repression of the Irish Republican Army (IRA) in the years of the Irish "Troubles" following the Anglo-Irish treaty of 1921.

Upon completing his education at University College, Dublin, O'Higgins was apprenticed to his uncle, a lawyer. After the Easter Rising in 1916 he joined the Sinn Féin (Irish: We Ourselves) nationalist movement and was imprisoned. In 1918, while still in jail, he was elected to Parliament from County Leix (Queen's County), and in the next year he became assistant to the minister of local government, William T. Cosgrave.

O'Higgins supported the treaty (Dec. 6, 1921) with Great Britain that created the Irish Free State. In 1922 he was appointed minister of the interior and vice president of the State Executive Council, and in 1923 he was named minister for home affairs and justice. He

Kevin O'Higgins
Radio Times Hulton Picture Library

helped to draft the Irish Free State constitution and secured its passage through the Dáil Éireann (lower house of the legislature). Working for a united Ireland within the British Commonwealth, he played an important part in the Imperial Conference of 1926. He also prominently represented the Free State in the League of Nations.

As minister for justice, O'Higgins organized an unarmed police force known as the Civic Guards and took summary measures to restore order following the conflict between the Free State forces and the IRA. His part in the execution of 77 republicans in 1922–23 made him many enemies, as did his sardonic wit, his inflammatory speeches during the civil war, and his curtailment of the liquor trade. He was assassinated by political enemies.
·administrative reform measures **3**:292g

O'Higgins, Tierra de (Antarctica): *see* Antarctic Peninsula.

Ohio **13**:517, eastern north central state of the U.S., admitted to the Union in 1803 as the 17th state. It occupies an area of 41,222 sq mi (106,764 sq km), excluding 3,457 sq mi of Lake Erie, and is bounded by Michigan (north), Pennsylvania and West Virginia (east), Kentucky (south), and Indiana (west). Its capital is Columbus. Pop. (1980) 10,797,419.

The text article, after a brief survey of the state, covers its history, natural landscape, people, economy, administration and social conditions, and cultural life and institutions.

REFERENCES in other text articles:
·Appalachian geology, history, and ecology **1**:1016a
·area and population, table 1 **18**:927
·Great Serpent Mound illus. **1**:681
·map, United States **18**:909
·territorial expansion 1812–61 maps **18**:962
·U.S. territory to 1803 map **18**:958

Ohio Company, in U.S. colonial history, organization of Englishmen and Virginians, chartered in 1749, to promote trade with groups of American Indians and to secure English control of the Ohio Valley.
·French–British contest over Fort Duquesne **19**:611f

Ohio River, river in east central U.S. that is formed by the confluence at Pittsburgh of the Allegheny and Monongahela rivers. The Ohio flows west and southwest to join the Mississippi River at Cairo, Ill., after a course of 981 mi (1,579 km). It forms several state boundaries: the Ohio–West Virginia, Ohio–Kentucky, Indiana–Kentucky, and Illinois–Kentucky. The Ohio River contributes more water to the Mississippi than does any other tributary and drains an area of 203,900 sq mi (528,100 sq km). Its valley is narrow, with an average width of less than ½ mi between Pittsburgh and Wheeling (W.Va.), a little over 1 mi from Cincinnati (Ohio) to Louisville (Ky.), and somewhat greater below Louisville.

The Ohio is navigable, and despite seasonal fluctuations that occasionally reach flood proportions, its fairly uniform flow has supported important commerce since first settlement began. Following especially destructive floods at Johnstown, Pa. (1889), Dayton, Ohio (1913), and other floods in 1936–37, the federal government built a series of flood-control dams. While not developed for hydropower in Ohio, the river, kept at a navigable depth of 9 ft (3 m), carries cargoes of coal, oil, steel, and manufactured articles. It has a total fall of only 429 ft, the one major hazard to navigation being the Falls of the Ohio at Louisville, where locks control a descent of about 24 ft within a distance of 2½ mi.

The Ohio's tributaries include the Tennessee, Cumberland, Kanawha, Big Sandy, Licking, Kentucky, and Green rivers (*qq.v.*) from the south and the Muskingum, Miami, Wabash, and Scioto rivers (*qq.v.*) from the north. Chief cities along the river, in addition to Pittsburgh, Cairo, Wheeling, and Louisville, are Steubenville, Marietta, Gallipolis, Portsmouth, and Cincinnati in Ohio; Madison, New Albany, Evansville, and Mt. Vernon in Indiana; Parkersburg and Huntington in West Virginia; and Ashland, Covington, Owensboro, and Paducah in Kentucky.

Robert Cavelier, sieur de La Salle, is said to have discovered the Ohio River in 1669 and descended it until his course was obstructed by a fall (said to be the Falls at Louisville). In the 1750s the river's strategic importance (especially the fork at Pittsburgh) in the struggle of the French and the English for possession of the interior of the continent became fully recognized. By the treaty of 1763 ending the French and Indian War, the English finally gained undisputed control of the territory along its banks. When (by an ordinance of 1787) the area was opened to settlement, most of the settlers entered the region down the headwaters of the Ohio.

36°59′ N, 89°08′ W

·discharge effects on Mississippi River **12**:281d
·French claims and French and Indian War **3**:736f
·Indiana's tribal and settlement history **9**:303c *passim* to 305d
·map, United States **18**:908
·Ohio's physiographic provinces **13**:517h
·West Virginia physiographic features **19**:801b

ohm, unit of electrical resistance in the metre–kilogram–second system, named in honour of the 19th-century German physicist Georg Simon Ohm, equal to the resistance (*q.v.*) of a circuit in which a potential difference of one volt produces a current of one ampere; or, the resistance in which one watt of power is dissipated when one ampere flows through it. Ohm's law (*q.v.*) states that resistance equals the ratio of the potential difference to current and the ohm, volt, and ampere are the respective fundamental units used universally for expressing quantities. Impedance, the apparent resistance to an alternating current, and reactance, the part of impedance resulting from capacitance or inductance, are circuit characteristics related to resistance and are also measured in ohms. The acoustic ohm and the mechanical ohm are analogous units sometimes used in the study of acoustic and mechanical systems respectively.

·electronic device resistance **6**:680g
·physical constant measurement standards **5**:79e

Ohm, Georg Simon (b. March 16, 1787, Erlangen, Bavaria, now in West Germany—d. July 7, 1854, Munich), physicist who discovered the law, named after him, which states that the current flow through a conductor is directly proportional to the potential difference (voltage) and inversely proportional to the resistance. Ohm became professor of mathematics at the Jesuits' College at Cologne in 1817. The most important aspect of Ohm's law is summarized in his pamphlet *Die galvanische Kette, mathematisch bearbeitet* (1827; *The Galvanic Circuit Investigated Mathematically*). While his work greatly influenced the theory and applications of current electricity, it was so coldly received that Ohm's feelings were hurt, and he resigned his post at Cologne. He accepted a position at the Polytechnic School of Nürnberg in 1833. Finally his work began to be recognized; in 1841 he was awarded the Copley Medal of the Royal Society of London and was made a foreign member a year later. The physical unit measuring electrical resistance was given his name.

Ohm, detail of a lithograph by an unknown artist
Historia-Photo

·sound reception research **17**:20d

ohmmeter, electrical instrument for measuring resistance on a scale graduated in ohms, megohms (1,000,000 ohms), or both. For high resistances, the scale may be graduated in megohms, and the instrument is called a megohmmeter or "megger."

Ohm's law, in electricity, experimentally discovered relationship that the amount of steady current through a large number of materials is directly proportional to the potential difference, or voltage, across the materials. Thus, if the potential difference V (in units of volts) between two ends of a wire made from one of these materials is tripled, the current I (amperes) also triples; and the quotient V/I remains constant. The quotient V/I for a given piece of material is called its resistance, R, measured in units named ohms. The resistance of materials for which Ohm's law is valid does not change over enormous ranges of voltage and current. Ohm's law may be expressed mathematically as $V/I = R$. That the resistance, or the ratio of voltage to current, for all or part of an electric circuit at a fixed temperature is generally constant had been established by 1827 as a result of the investigations of the German physicist Georg Simon Ohm.

Alternate statements of Ohm's law are that the current I in a conductor equals the potential difference V across the conductor divided by the resistance of the conductor, or simply $I = V/R$, and that the potential difference across a conductor equals the product of the current in the conductor and its resistance, $V = IR$. In a circuit in which the potential difference, or voltage, is constant, the current may be decreased by adding more resistance or increased by removing some resistance. Ohm's law may also be expressed in terms of the electromotive force, or voltage, E, of the source of electric energy, such as a battery. For example, $I = E/R$.

With modifications, Ohm's law also applies to alternating-current circuits, in which the relation between the voltage and the current is more complicated than for direct currents. Precisely because the current is varying, besides resistance, other forms of opposition to the current arise, called reactance. The combination of resistance and reactance is called impedance, Z. When the impedance, equivalent to the ratio of voltage to current, in an alternating current circuit is constant, a common occurrence, Ohm's law is applicable. For example, $V/I = Z$.

With further modifications Ohm's law has been extended to the constant ratio of the magnetomotive force to the magnetic flux in a magnetic circuit (*q.v.*).

·Cavendish's anticipatory researches **3**:1019f
·differential equation principles **5**:763e
·electricity principles and theory **6**:563c
·groundwater study applications **8**:440b

Ohře (German EGER) **River,** tributary of the Elbe River, rises in the Fichtelgebirge (Fichtel Mountains) of West Germany and flows generally east and northeastward into Czechoslovakia past Cheb, Sokolov, Karlovy Vary, Klášterec nad Ohří, Žatec, Louny, and Terezín until reaching the Elbe (Labe) River opposite Litoměřice. The river is 196 mi (316 km) long, and it receives the Teplá and Blšanka rivers from the south and the Chomutovka River from the north.

50°32′ N, 14°08′ W

·map, Czechoslovakia **5**:412

Ohrid, picturesque town in Macedonia, Yugoslavia, on the northeastern shore of Lake Ohrid (Ohridsko Jezero). The chief resort of Macedonia and the site of a summer music festival, Ohrid is linked by rail, road, and air to Skopje. Agriculture, fishing, and tourism provide a livelihood for the population.

In antiquity called Lychnidus, Ohrid was by the 2nd century a post on the Via Egnatia to Bitola and Greece. It was rebuilt by the Romans after a devastating earthquake in 518. Ohrid derives its name from the crag (*hrid*) on which the old town stands. At the summit is the ruined fortress dating chiefly from the late 10th and early 11th centuries, when Ohrid was the capital of a Bulgarian tsar.

Among the churches in the town are St. Sophia's, with 11th–14th century frescoes, and St. Clement's (1295), also with medieval frescoes. In the nearby village of Imaret is the Church of St. Panteleimon, built in 893 by St. Clement (Sveti Kliment), the first Slav bishop of Ohrid. He opened the first Slavic school of higher learning, wrote the earliest works of Slavic literature, and, with St. Naum, translated the Scriptures from Greek into Slav. The 10th-century monastery of Sveti Naum, about 19 mi (31 km) south, crowns a prominent crag on the Yugoslav–Albanian frontier and overlooks Lake Ohrid. Pop. (1971) 26,400.

41°07′ N, 20°47′ E

·map, Yugoslavia **19**:1100

Medieval monastery of Sveti Naum overlooking Lake Ohrid, near Ohrid, Yugo.
Harrison Forman

Ohrid, Lake, on the Yugoslav–Albanian border, the deepest lake in the Balkans.
41°2′ N, 20°43′ E
·age and fauna peculiarities **1**:1032g

Ohthere, also spelled OTHERE (fl. *c.* AD 880), Norwegian sea explorer.
·Atlantic coast exploration extent **7**:1037h

Ohuda (Hungary): *see* Budapest.

Oiapoque, Rio (South America): *see* Oyapock River.

oidium, in fungi (division Mycota), name for a single-celled asexual spore (arthrospore) produced by fragmentation of fungal filaments (hyphae) in lower fungi; the asexual stage of Erysiphaceae (powdery mildew fungi); or, in Basidiomycetes, both an asexual spore (microconidium) and a male cell (spermatium).

oidores, members of an audiencia (governing body) in Spanish colonial America.
·Spanish colonial restrictions and reviews **10**:694e

oikos, Greek concept of house or family.
·Greek religious, legal, and social meaning **8**:400a

oikoumenē, an Eastern orthodox ideology that holds that there is one universal Christian society, ruled jointly by the empire and the church.
·Byzantine background of Schism **6**:152f *passim* to 154f

oil: *see* oils, fats, and waxes.

oil beetle: *see* blister beetle.

oilbird (*Steatornis caripensis*), nocturnal bird that lives in caves in the coastal highlands of South America and feeds on fruit, mainly the nuts of oil palms. The oilbird is an aberrant member of the order Caprimulgiformes; it comprises the family Steatornithidae. About 30 centimetres long, with fanlike tail and long broad wings, it is dark reddish brown, barred with black and spotted with white. It has a strong hook-tipped bill, long bristles around the wide gape, and large dark eyes.

The oilbird uses echolocation, like a bat, to find its way within the caves where it roosts and nests from Trinidad and Guyana to Peru. The sounds the bird emits are within the range of human hearing: bursts of astonishingly rapid clicks (as many as 250 per second). It also utters hair-raising squawks and shrieks that suggested its Spanish name, *guácharo* ("wailer"). At night it flies out to feed, hovering while it plucks fruit from trees.

Two to four white eggs are laid on a pad of organic matter on a ledge high up in the cave. The young, which may remain in the nest for 120 days, are fed by regurgitation until they are 70 to 100 percent heavier than adults. Indians render the squabs for an odourless oil for cooking and light; hence the bird's popular and scientific names.
·echolocation mechanism **1**:1013f
·habitat and activity **3**:806f
·head plan illus. **3**:807
·occurrence and economic importance **19**:63e

Oilbird or *guácharo* (*Steatornis caripensis*)
Russ Kinne—Photo Researchers

oil burner, domestic heating device in which fuel oil is mixed with air under controlled conditions. In most burners oil is supplied under pressure to an atomizing nozzle to produce a fine spray, to which air is added by a motor-driven fan. As the cone-shaped spray emerges from the nozzle, ignition is usually supplied by an electric spark to start the burner. Starting and shut-off are normally controlled by thermostat. In commercial-industrial types of burners, heavier fuel oil is used, requiring mechanical atomization.
·boiler design and use **17**:626c
·direct heating systems **8**:719h

oil cake, residue after oil is removed from various oilseeds, high in protein and valuable as animal feed and fertilizer. It may be broken up and sold as oil cake or be ground into oil meal. *See also* cottonseed; linseed; copra.

oil cell, in botany, a type of cell located in various tissues of some plants. It secretes a droplet of oil, which may be aromatic, as in many plants of the family Laurales.
·Aristolochiales-Magnoliales linkage **1**:1153d
·Laurales structural features **10**:710g
·Valerianaceae anatomical structure **5**:817a

Oil City, city, Venango County, northwestern Pennsylvania, U.S., on a bend of the Allegheny River at the mouth of Oil Creek. Founded in 1860 on the site of a Seneca Indian village, it burgeoned as an oil centre after the drilling of the world's first oil well (Aug. 27, 1859) at Titusville, 16 mi (26 km) up Oil Creek. Incorporated as a borough in 1862, it became a city in 1871 after merging with Venango City. Oil City was the shipping point for crude oil from Oil Creek fields and reached a high point between 1860 and 1870 with river boats transporting millions of barrels to Pittsburgh. The production, refining, and distribution of oil and its products remains the leading industry. Manufactures include steel, glass, and metal products, gas engines, and drilling supplies. The Venango campus of Clarion State College was opened

Oil City (Pa.) near the confluence of the Allegheny River and Oil Creek
Milt and Joan Mann from CameraMann

in 1962. Cook Forest State Park, Kinzua Dam, Drake Well Park, and Pithole (a ghost oil town) are nearby. Inc. borough, 1862; city, 1871. Pop. (1980) 13,881.
41°26′ N, 79°42′ W
·map, United States **18**:908

oil-depletion allowance, income tax write-off for the reduction in capital value of oil resources (assets) of a company due to their consumption or diminution.
·subsidization and its rationale **17**:755e

oil diesel engine: *see* diesel engine.

oil-drop experiment (physics): *see* Millikan oil-drop experiment.

oil (PREEN OR UROPYGIAL) **gland,** an organ in birds, located on the back near the base of the tail. Paired or in two united halves, it is found in most birds. Absent in ostrich, emu, cassowary, bustard, frogmouth, and a few other birds, the oil gland is best developed in aquatic species, notably petrels and pelicans, and in the osprey and oilbird. The secretion it exudes is used by many birds in preening feathers, but other functions have been suggested as well. Its utility may differ among various birds.
·bird skin and plumage protection **2**:1056d
·parrot structure and function **15**:140g

oil grass, any of the 40 species of the genus *Cymbopogon* (family Poaceae), aromatic, oil-

Citronella grass (*Cymbopogon nardus*)
Douglas David Dawn

containing grasses cultivated in the tropics of Asia and Africa and introduced into tropical America. Most species are densely tufted, with long, narrow, flexible leaves. Lemon-oil grass or sweet rush (*Cymbopogon citratus*) contains citral, obtained by steam distillation of the leaves and used in scented cosmetics, food flavouring, and medicine. Citronella grass (*C. nardus*) contains geraniol (citronella oil), used in cosmetics and insect repellents.
·oil importance and use **14**:586c

oil-immersion lens, an objective of short focal distance designed to work with a drop of liquid (as oil or water) between front lens and cover glass.
·microscope-objective characteristics table **12**:131

oil lamp, any device for the production of light or heat by combustion of oil or other flammable liquid. *See* lamp.
·design development in 1700s and 1800s **10**:957h
·stage lighting's early history **17**:554a

oil meal: *see* oil cake.

oil nut: *see* Santalaceae.

oil of bitter almonds: *see* benzaldehyde.

oil of rose: *see* attar of roses.

oil of turpentine: *see* turpentine oil.

oil or gas field, several closely related underground deposits of petroleum or natural gas. A single deposit of commercial value is called an oil or gas pool, a group of pools located on the same geological (either stratigraphic or structural) feature make a field, and several pools or fields occurring in an area and having similar or related geological environments make a petroleum province. All of these features grade into one another.

An oil or gas pool occurs in a separate reservoir and has its own pressure system. Its areal extent may vary from several hectares to many square miles. The individual pools comprising a field may occur at varying depths or may be separated laterally at the same depth. Fields occur in salt plugs, folded rock structures, and complex structures in which folding, faulting, and stratigraphic variation play a part. The amount of oil or gas derived is not a distinguishing characteristic; some pools, such as the east Texas pool, will produce more oil than many fields or even provinces. "Petroleum provinces" loosely refers to larger areas of petroleum production; they often have indistinct boundaries.

·natural gas extraction sites **12**:862d
·petroleum reservoir formation **14**:170e; illus. 171

oil painting, history of, history of Western easel painting (*q.v.*) in oil colours, a medium consisting of pigments ground in drying oils. Oil as a painting medium is recorded as early as the 11th century. The practice of easel painting with oil colours, however, stems directly from 15th-century tempera painting techniques. Basic improvements in the refinement of linseed oil and the availability of volatile solvents or thinners for varnishes and oil paints after 1400 coincided with a need for some other medium than pure egg-yolk tempera to meet the changing requirements of the Renaissance (*see* tempera painting). The new materials allowed new techniques of handling colour, tonal masses, and depth of colour. At first oil paints and varnishes were used to glaze tempera panels, painted with their traditional linear draftsmanship. The technically brilliant, jewel-like portraits of 15th-century Flemish painters, for example, were done this way. Among the earliest of these oil-glazed tempera paintings were the works of Jan van Eyck of Bruges and his brother Hubert. In 1550 the art historian Giorgio Vasari credited "Giovanni da Bruggia" with the "invention" of oil painting. Scholars since 1781 have shown that, although Jan van Eyck, a great master, was important in the history of painting, oil painting was neither his invention nor that of any individual but the result of a long, gradual development.

In the 16th century, oil colour emerged as the basic painting material in Venice. Before exploring the technical possibilities of oil painting, artists learned gradually how to assure themselves of permanent results and how to develop fluent control. By the end of the century, they had become proficient in the exploitation of the basic characteristics of oil painting. Linen canvas, after a long period of development, replaced wooden panels as the most logical and popular support.

One of the 17th-century masters of the oil technique was Velázquez, a Spanish painter in the Venetian tradition, whose direct, uncomplicated use of colour and bold, bravura brushstrokes have frequently been emulated, especially in portraiture. The technical significance of the Flemish painter Peter Paul Rubens as an influence on later painters is the manner in which he loaded, or piled up, his whites and pale colours, opaquely, in juxtaposition to thin, transparent darks and shadows. A third great 17th-century master of oil-painting was the Dutch painter Rembrandt. His technical effects had perhaps the most profound influence of all on later painters, particularly his brushwork, his handling of paint textures and surfaces, and his paint quality and visual effects. A single brushstroke sometimes reveals an effective depiction of rotundity of form and a textural depth combining the rough and the smooth and the thick and the thin. The system of loaded whites and transparent darks, so pronounced in Rubens, is enriched by further touches of broken opaque strokes, which do not obscure the underlying colours, in addition to glazed effects and blendings.

Other basic influences on the techniques of later easel painting are the smooth, thinly painted, deliberately planned, tight styles of painting, in contrast to styles that use bold, crisp brushstrokes and impasto (*q.v.*), areas or spots raised considerably above the level of surrounding colour. A great many admired works (*e.g.*, those of Jan Vermeer) were executed with smooth gradations and blends of tones to achieve rotund forms and subtle colour variation.

An interesting effect seen in some old paintings (*e.g.*, Dutch panels of the 17th-century) is called *pentimento* (*q.v.*), meaning repentance. Because of changes in the refractive index of linseed-oil films after aging, it is possible for thinly painted layers to become transparent, revealing, in a ghostly manner, forms that the artist wished to obliterate. Painters have learned to avoid *pentimenti* by scraping away dark markings before overpainting with paler colours or by making the overpainting sufficiently opaque to preclude this occurrence.

The technical requirements of some schools of modern painting cannot be realized by the use of paints that were developed specifically for the craftsmanship and painterly qualities associated with traditional techniques. Some abstract painters, and to some extent contemporary painters in traditional styles, have expressed a need for an entirely different plastic flow or viscosity than cannot be had with oil paint and its conventional additives. Some require a greater range of thick and thin application and a more rapid speed of dry. Some artists have used the traditional materials in unorthodox ways, such as mixing coarsely grained materials with their colours to create new textures; some have used oil paints in enormously heavier thickness than has been considered safe. Abandoned techniques have been revived and experimental paints based on synthetic resins have been tried.

·Bellini's use of medium **2**:829a
·deterioration and restoration **2**:61g
·development and uses **13**:878d; illus. 871
·Japanese modern style **19**:241c
·Korean introduction attempt **19**:215c
·Monet's outdoor work and effect **12**:347d
·representative international works, illus., **13**:Painting, Art of, Plate IV
·Reynolds' portrait distortion **15**:792g
·style change from technical development **2**:133a
·Western styles, illus., **19**:Visual Arts, Western, Plates VIII–XXVI

oil painting, technique of, technique of painting in oil colours, a medium consisting of pigments ground in drying oils. Among several accepted, standard methods developed to meet the various requirements for easel painting, oil painting has occupied a pre-eminent position for five centuries. The outstanding facility with which fusion of tones or colour is achieved makes it unique among fluid mediums; at the same time, satisfactory linear treatment and crisp effects are easily obtained. Opaque, transparent, and translucent painting all lie within its range. It is unsurpassed for textural variation, the manipulation of smooth and rugged, thick and thin, uniform or varied surfaces. In painting with the water mediums there is a definite (and frequently erratic) colour change when the paint dries; but with oil paints, the colour the artist puts down on the canvas is the colour of the finished painting. The widest range of styles is possible, from the most simple to the most complex visual effects.

When painted with inferior materials, oil paintings on aging will suffer defects and blemishes, such as embrittlement, cracking, darkening, or yellowing. Artists' materials thus must be of superlative quality, prepared with the utmost striving toward perfection.

Artists' oil colours are made by mixing dry powder pigments with selected refined linseed oil to a stiff paste consistency and grinding it by strong friction in steel roller mills. The consistency of the colour is important; the universal use of tube colours demands that they be uniform within well-established limits. The standard is a smooth, buttery paste, not stringy or long or tacky. When a more flowing or mobile quality is required by the artist, a fluid painting medium must be mixed with it. It is important that this be a time-tested, reliable material (such as pure gum turpentine), for many 18th- and 19th-century paintings have deteriorated because of the use of facile but improper additives. In order to accelerate drying, a siccative, or liquid drier, is sometimes used.

Top-grade brushes are made in two types: red sable, made from the tail hairs of the kolinsky or red Tartar marten; and bristle, made from a superlative grade of bleached white hog's bristles. Red sable hair has a minute bulge in the middle and tapers to a very sharp point. The hog's bristle is forked or branched at the tip. Both come in numbered sizes in each of four regular shapes: round (pointed), flat, bright (flat shape but shorter and less supple), and oval (flat but bluntly pointed). Red sable brushes are widely used for the smoother, less robust type of brush stroking. The painting knife, a finely tempered, thin, limber version of the artist's palette knife, is a convenient tool for applying oil colours in a robust manner. It did not come into wide use until the 19th century but had a forerunner in the *cestrum* used in encaustic painting (*q.v.*).

The survival of the work, the ease of its execution, and the final visual effect are all profoundly involved in the selection of the surface on which the artist paints and the support or backing for it. The standard ground for oil painting is a canvas made of pure European linen, of strong, close weave. It is coated with a white oil priming and stretched on a wooden stretcher frame, or chassis. The inner corners of modern, machine-made stretchers have slots for wooden wedges, which, when tapped with a hammer, tighten the canvas.

If rigidity and smoothness are preferred to springiness and texture, a wooden panel may be used with an oil priming or a sized gesso (mixture of chalk and glue) ground. Many other supports, textile and metal, have been tried; but few are in general use or have wide approval.

A coat of picture varnish is usually given to a finished oil painting (which has been allowed to dry thoroughly) to protect it from atmospheric attacks, minor abrasions, and an injurious accumulation of dirt. If the painting is protected by a coating of picture varnish, cleaning by the removal of part or all of the varnish film is a relatively safe and easy procedure. Varnishing also brings the surface to a uniform lustre, and brings the tonal depth and colour intensity to those originally created by the artist with wet paint. Some 20th-century painters, especially those who do not favour the deep, intense type of colouring, have wanted a mat, or lustreless, finish in oil paintings; but this seems unobtainable by any means if the longevity of the painting is to be considered.

·Giovanni Bellini's treatment of light **19**:399g

oil palm, African tree, *Elaeis guineensis*, cultivated as a source of oil in West and Central

Africa, where it originated, and in the United States, Indonesia, Central and South America, and as an ornamental tree in many subtropical areas; or, the American oil palm, *Corozo oleifera*, originating in Central and South America and sometimes cultivated under the erroneous name *Elaeis melanococca*, the oil of which was probably used for making candles by the early American colonizers.

Oil palm (*Elaeis guineensis*)
W.H. Hodge

The African tree is the more important commercially. It has many tiny flowers crowded on short branches that develop into a large cluster of oval fruits 1½ inches (4 centimetres) long, black when ripe, and red at the base. The outer fleshy portion of the fruit is subjected to a fermentation process that yields commercial palm oil.

Palm oil is used chiefly in making soaps, candles, and lubricating greases and in processing tinplate and coating iron plates. Palm-kernel oil, differently constituted chemically, is obtained from the seed kernels by crushing or by a solvent extraction process; it is used primarily in manufacturing such edible products as margarine, chocolate confections, and pharmaceuticals. The cake residue after kernel oil is extracted is a good cattle feed and fertilizer.

The American oil palm resembles the African in flowers and fruit, causing certain botanists to place it in the same genus, although the *Corozo* has a quite different appearance. The trunk of the *Corozo* creeps along the ground, and its leaves are flat, while the African tree has a straight trunk and leaflets attached at various angles.

·Dahomey production and exportation **5**:422e
·domesticated plant centres of origin **5**:938d
·Guinea Coast 19th-century trade **8**:474c
·rendering extraction process **13**:527g

oil pan, the lower section of the crankcase used as a lubricating-oil reservoir on an internal-combustion engine.

·gasoline engine construction **7**:933f; illus.

oil plants, trees such as palm, herbaceous plants such as flax, and even fungi (*Fusarium* species), either under cultivation or growing wild, used as a source of oil.

Vegetable oils are used principally for food (large amounts are contained in shortening, margarines, and salad and cooking oils) and in the manufacture of soap and detergents, in paints and varnishes, and for a variety of other industrial items.

Oil is found in large amounts usually in the seeds of the plants and occasionally in the fleshy part of the fruit, as in the olive and the oil palm. Seeds may contain from 1 to over 60 percent oil. The oil is a reserve of high-energy food for use by the germinating seed, and large amounts of oil are associated with large amounts of protein. After the oil is extracted from the oilseeds, the residual meal, or cake, remaining is so important a by-product that it frequently determines the value of an oil crop. Usually this meal is used as a protein concentrate to feed livestock and poultry; where it is poisonous, as with castor beans and tung nuts, it is used as fertilizer.

Most of the important oil crops, including the oil palm, the castor bean, and the coconut palm, are found in tropical and semitropical areas, particularly the tropical areas of West and Central Africa, Indonesia, the Philippines, and Malaysia. In cool, temperate regions, the oil crops are flax, sunflower, and plants of the mustard family. Most oil plants, with the exception of herbs such as mint, are not readily adaptable to mechanical cultivation. The oil palm produces the highest oil yields of any crop.

Several oils, such as cottonseed, corn, and soybean oil, are by-products of other industries. Even weed seeds removed from cereal grain in large terminal elevators may be processed for their oil, particularly wild radish and wild mustard.

Oil has been obtained from plants since the beginning of recorded history for oil-burning lamps and for anointing and cooking. Castor oil was used as a lubricant for wheels of carts and wagons before the petroleum era. In the 19th century margarine was developed in France as a substitute for butter. During the 20th century, the production of vegetable oils has grown into billions of pounds annually. Edible oils that are high in polyunsaturated fatty acids such as linoleic acid have become popular, particularly in the United States, since the 1950s, and this stimulated interest in safflower oil and corn oil.

RELATED ENTRIES in the *Ready Reference and Index:*
cashew; castor oil; coconut palm; cottonseed; croton oil; linseed; oil palm; olive oil; peanut; poppy seed; safflower; soybean; tall oil; tung oil

Oil Reserves Scandal (U.S., 1921–22): *see* Teapot Dome Scandal.

Oil Rivers, area comprising the delta of the Niger River in West Africa. The Oil Rivers Protectorate was established by the British in 1885. It was renamed the Niger Coast Protectorate in 1893, and in 1900 was joined to the Nigerian territories administered by the British government. Its name derives from the palm oil that was the chief product of the area.

oils, fats, and waxes **13**:522, widely distributed natural substances of animal, mineral, or plant origin, or synthetic compounds. Oils are usually liquid, and fats usually solid or semisolid at ordinary temperatures; both are greasy to the touch and form one of the principal foods. Waxes are also solid, but slick rather than greasy, and harder and more brittle than fats. Essential oils are odoriferous volatile materials from various plant species. *See also* essential oil; oil plants.

TEXT ARTICLE covers:
History of use of fats and oils 13:523b
Functions in plants and animals 523e
Synthesis and metabolism in living organisms 523g
Chemical composition of fats 524h
General methods of extraction 527f
Processing of extracted oil 529c
Edible fat and oil products 530h
Industrial uses of fats and oils 531f
World production of fats and oils 532a
Waxes 532e
Essential oils 532h

REFERENCES in other text articles:
·alcohol's occurrence in nature **1**:452g
·arteriosclerosis and diet relationships **13**:425b
·Capparales economic importance **3**:804d
·carboxylic acid natural occurrence **3**:865f
·commercial uses of Geraniales **8**:1h
·conifer chemical composition **5**:6f
·dietary energy sources **13**:421g
·digestion and absorption **5**:778b
·drug extraction from plants **14**:192f
·emulsion principles and properties **4**:856c
·Eucalyptus commercial uses **12**:773f
·Euphorbiales economic importance **6**:1028c

fats
·animal feed requirements and digestion **1**:908h
·animal tissues and fluids comparisons **18**:444f
·arteriosclerosis and diet relationships **13**:425b
·arteriosclerosis' dietary correlative **3**:888c
·biochemical studies of function **2**:995a
·blood circulation and lymphatic's role **2**:1133e
·butter manufacture stages **5**:431f
·candy production utilization and effect **4**:1082c
·chemical properties and structure **10**:1015h
·coloration mechanisms in animals **4**:923a
·conifer chemical composition **5**:6f
·cultural variations in cooking fat use **7**:940b
·digestive mechanisms in vertebrates **5**:782c
·food value and nutritional disorders **13**:412e
·lichen food storage in algae **10**:887a
·lipid catabolism reactions **11**:1030c
·liver metabolic functions **10**:1270d
·lymph composition and lipid absorption **11**:212b
·meat structure and chemistry **11**:746f
·neural symptoms of metabolic diseases **12**:1044h
·pregnancy's effect on blood lipid **14**:975g
·vitamins, Krebs cycle, and metabolism **19**:489h; illus. 490
·whale blubber processing **7**:356b

·food preservation technology **7**:491b
·food value and nutritional disorders **13**:412g
·homopteran wax production **8**:1041a
·lighting device development role **10**:957h
·Magnoliales economic importance **11**:342h
·new food extraction from oilseeds **7**:481d

oils
·birch oil production **2**:873b
·Dipsacales biochemical substances **5**:817c
·drying oil and varnish production **14**:517b
·dyes and dyeing methods **5**:1104d
·Ebanales seed importance **6**:174h
·fish oil extraction **7**:350d
·gasoline engine lubrication **7**:936f
·gymnosperm economic importance **8**:518f
·hydraulic fluid advantages **9**:79e
·Lamiales commercial value **10**:620a
·lubrication development **11**:169c *passim* to 170h
·lubrication types, uses, and limitations **18**:708h
·machine tool lubrication **11**:261d
·petroleum and energy source demands **14**:165h; illus. 166
·rose petal importance and use **15**:1150g
·Rutales varieties and importance **16**:103e
·sandal oil derivation and use **16**:227d
·seed and fruit importance **16**:480c
·shark liver oil uses **16**:493e
·soybean oil extraction and composition **3**:1167b

·oils and fats in baked goods **2**:598f
·Poales unusual products **14**:586c
·seed and fruit importance **16**:480c
·soap composition and production **16**:915d
·soybean commercial uses **1**:339b
·spice flavourings and seasonings **17**:503g
·sunflower seed importance **2**:213g
·tree's economic importance **18**:689a
·vegetable products and processing **19**:46g

waxes
·African drum sound production **1**:250c
·beeswax production and usage **2**:793g
·bees with wax glands **9**:130g
·earwax production and function **5**:1132e
·encaustic painting techniques **13**:879f
·homopteran production and commercial use **8**:1041a
·leather manufacturing and tanning **10**:760f
·metal sintering and paraffin binders **11**:1074h
·phonograph record production **17**:53h
·plant production importance **18**:452f
·rubber additive function **15**:1181c
·sculptural uses and handling **16**:426g
·sugar by-product use in polishes and cosmetics **17**:776a
·wool processing by-products **7**:284c

·whale products and oil production **19**:811e; table 813
·wood extract elements **19**:918g

oilseed, any of various seeds grown largely for oil, as soybean, cottonseed, peanut, coconut, rapeseed, and sunflower.
·new food sources and extraction process **7**:481d

oil shales 13:535, also called KEROGENITES, dark, layered, cleavable rocks rich in hydrocarbons and fossil organic substances.

The text article covers the organic content of oil shales, properties of oil shales and related coals, origin of oil shales, and their occurrence and distribution.

REFERENCES in other text articles:
·Asian reserves **2**:171g
·beneficiation as conservation practice **5**:50f
·organic matter in shales and kerogen **16**:634h
·salt structure bedding with sandstone **16**:197g *passim* to 199b
·torbanite similarity to coal **4**:794h

RELATED ENTRIES in the *Ready Reference and Index:*
asphaltite; dysodile; gilsonite; kerogen; ozokerite; pyrobitumen; shale oil; torbanite

oil spill, dumping (usually accidentally) of petroleum onto the surface of a body of water from a ship or an oil well. Oil spills as major sources of environmental pollution began to receive widespread public attention in the 1960s, as the use of very large "supertankers" for transporting oil and intensified exploitation of the petroleum resources of the continental shelf increased the danger that oil in large quantities would be released into the oceans.
·conservation need and practice **5**:50e
·ocean pollution consequences **1**:1031c

oil stove, in heating, stove that burns petroleum fuel, such as kerosene.
·direct heating systems **8**:719h

oil–water contact, in a petroleum reservoir, interface above which the pore spaces are filled mainly with oil and below which they are filled with water. This contact may provide information about the reservoir, its geological history, and its role in the accumulation of the trapped gas and oil. Although the contact appears to be a well-defined plane surface, either level or tilted, it is a transition zone a few metres thick in which the pore spaces are filled with both water and oil. Above the contact the water content initially falls off abruptly and afterward more slowly, whereas below it the oil content falls off abruptly.

As a petroleum trap (reservoir) fills with oil, the oil–water contact is lowered. Capillary pressure, however, resists the invasion of oil into pores formerly occupied by water, and consequently the grain size affects the oil–water contact; finer grains oppose the invasion more than coarse ones do, and therefore the contact is higher in fine-grained than in coarse-grained sands and rocks. In some traps the oil–gas contact is tipped, usually no more than a few metres per kilometre but occasionally as much as 150 metres (500 feet) per kilometre; this tilt displaces the oil pool down one flank of the trap. Where there is no water flow, the contact is level, but, where water flowing through the reservoir rock creates hydrodynamic pressure, the contact slopes in the direction of flow. Where the slope is high, the pool's displacement may be great enough to leave the highest part of the structure barren of oil. In some cases the tipping is only apparent, however, and is attributable to local conditions, including changes in the lithology or minor faulting.
·petroleum movement and accumulation **14**:170h

oinochoe, or OENOCHOE, ancient Greek pottery wine jug with delicately curved handle and trefoil-shaped mouth.

Athenian red-figure oinochoe attributed to the Mannheim Painter, depicting three Amazons leaving for battle, *c.* 450 BC; in the Metropolitan Museum of Art, New York

By courtesy of the Metropolitan Museum of Art, New York, Rogers Fund, 1906

ointment, in pharmacology, salve or unguent for application to the skin; specifically a semisolid medicinal preparation usually having a base of fatty or oily material, often balanced with a paraffin base.
·pharmaceutical preparation methods **14**:197b

Oirat (people): *see* Oyrat.

Oirat language: *see* Oyrat language.

Oireachtas, name of the parliament of the Republic of Ireland.
·powers and organization **9**:886e

Oirot language: *see* Altai language.

Oise, *département* of France north of the Paris region, created from part of the historic province of Île-de-France (*q.v.*) and a small part of Picardy. It has an area of 2,261 sq mi (5,857 sq km), the eastern half of which is bisected by the Oise River (*q.v.*), a tributary of the Seine River that flows slowly northeast-southwest through Noyon, Compiègne (*qq.v.*), and Creil along a forested valley. It receives the Aisne River from the east above Compiègne. The cathedral city of Beauvais (*q.v.*), the departmental capital, in the centre of western Oise, is situated on the Thérain River, which joins the Oise at Creil on the border of a forested region northeast of Senlis (*q.v.*). Chantilly (*q.v.*), with its château and racecourse, lies in the forest west of Senlis.

The *département*, consisting of undulating plateaus and gentle valleys, enjoys a mild climate. Cattle are raised, cereals and sugar beets are grown, and market gardening is prevalent in the valleys. Clay and sandstone are quarried. Metallurgical, cement, glass, and chemical industries, which employ most of the active population, are concentrated in the Oise Valley around Creil and Compiègne. Light industries and housing developments are expanding as a result of improved communications with Paris. The Autoroute du Nord, the motorway linking Paris and Lille, passes through Oise.

Two of the finest Romanesque churches in northern France are in Saint-Leu-d'Esserent and Morienval. Other places of interest include the ruins of the 13th-century Chaalis abbey church, next to the "Sea of Sand," a small sand desert; the Gallo-Roman ruins at Champlieu; the reconstructed feudal castle of Pierrefonds; and Royaumont abbey. The *département* has four *arrondissements:* Beauvais, Clermont, Compiègne, and Senlis. Pop. (1979 est.) 634,300.
·area and population table **7**:594

Oise River, rises in Belgium in the Ardennes mountains southeast of Chimay, enters France northeast of Hirson, 9 mi (15 km) from its source, and flows generally southwestward, watering the Paris Basin, to join the Seine at Conflans, after a course of 188 mi. It traverses the Collines de la Thiérache (Thiérache Hills), where it collects its important left-bank tributary, the Serre, and flows through a flat alluvial valley below Guise. It then cuts through the northern part of the limestone platform of the Île-de-France and on through a valley flanked by the forests of Saint-Gobain, Compiègne, Hallatte, and Chantilly. Near Compiègne it receives its main tributary, the Aisne; and below the industrial town of Creil, it is joined by the Thérain. Other towns along the river include La Fère and Pontoise. The Oise is a link in the canal system between the navigable waterways of the Seine system.

Several battles of World War I were fought along the riverbanks.
49°00′ N, 2°04′ E
·map, France **7**:584
·Seine River course to sea **16**:488d

Oisín (legendary warrior): *see* Ossian.

Oistrakh, David (Fyodorovich) (b. Sept. 30, 1908, Odessa, now in Ukrainian S.S.R.—d. Oct. 24, 1974, Amsterdam), world-renowned violin virtuoso acclaimed for his exceptional technique and tone production. A violin student from the age of five, he graduated from the Odessa Conservatory in 1926 and made his Moscow debut in 1933. He gave recitals throughout the Soviet Union and eastern Europe and in 1937 won first prize in the Eugène Ysaÿe violin competition. From 1934 he taught violin at the Moscow Conservatory, and in 1942 he received the Stalin Prize.

Oistrakh was first heard in western Europe and the U.S. through his recordings of 20th-century Russian works as well as the classical violin repertory. From 1951 he toured extensively in Europe and from 1955 in the U.S.

Oistrakh's son, Igor Oistrakh (1931–), also a concert violinist, is considered by many the equal of his father. First-prize winner of the 1952 Wieniawski Competition in Poznań, Pol., he toured Europe and the U.S., occasionally performing in joint recitals with his father.

Ōita, prefecture (*ken*), northeastern Kyushu, Japan, facing the Suō-nada (Suō Sea) and Bungo-suidō (Bungo Strait) of the Pacific Ocean. It occupies an area of 2,337 sq mi (6,053 sq km). Its interior is dominated by a complex mountain system, and most human activity centres on small coastal plains. The long, irregular coastline is marked by deep-cut Beppu-wan (Beppu Bay) and the rounded Kuni-zaki (Cape Kuni). Most of the population is made up of farmers who raise subsistence and some cash crops (tobacco, reeds, citrus fruit) and cattle. Forestry flourishes in the mountains, and some industry (textiles, metals, cement, chemicals) is found in the main coastal cities. Beppu, on Beppu-wan, is one of Japan's best known hot spring resorts.

Ōita, the prefectural capital, is located on the southern coast of Beppu-wan. It achieved its greatest fame in the 16th century but declined during the Tokugawa period. Now a port for the Inland Sea trade, it is a major centre of heavy industry on Kyushu. Pop. (1978 est.) city, 344,847; prefecture, 1,215,000.
·area and population, table 1 **10**:45
·map, Japan **10**:37

oitavo, Portuguese unit of volume, equal to 1.730 litres, or 3.6 pints.
·weights and measures, table 5 **19**:734

Óiti Óros (Greece): *see* Oeta, Mount.

Oja (South Indian poet): *see* Pampa.

Oje, in Ibadan, Nigeria, site of an eight-day periodic market.
·Ibadan's economic life **9**:142e; map 141

Ojeda, Alonso de (1465–1515), Spanish adventurer who served under, and later clashed with, Columbus.
·Surinam discovery and settlement **17**:825f

Ojibwa, or CHIPPEWA, Algonkian-speaking Indians who formerly lived along the northern shore of Lake Huron and both shores of Lake Superior from what are now Minnesota to the Turtle Mountains of North Dakota. In Canada those Ojibwa who lived west of Lake Winnipeg are called the Saulteaux.

Ojibwa (Chippewa) Indians gathering wild rice in Wisconsin; model in the American Museum of Natural History, New York City
By courtesy of the American Museum of Natural History, New York

Each Ojibwa tribe was divided into migratory bands. In the autumn bands separated into family units, which dispersed to individual hunting areas; in summer families gathered together, usually at fishing sites. A few bands also cultivated maize (corn), and the Ojibwa also relied on the collection of wild rice for a major part of their diet. Birch bark was used extensively for canoes, dome-shaped wigwams, and utensils. Exogamous clans, distributed among the bands, served to offset the lack of overall tribal or national chiefs. Chieftainship of the band was originally not a powerful office, but dealings with European fur traders strengthened the position, which became hereditary through the paternal line. The Midewiwin, the annual celebration of the Grand Medicine Society, a secret religious organization open to men and women, was the major Ojibwa ceremonial. Membership was believed to provide supernatural assistance and conferred prestige on its members.

The Ojibwa were not prominent in history because of their remoteness from the frontier during the colonial wars. In the U.S. they constitute one of the largest remnants of the aboriginal population. During the 1970s there were about 30,000 members of the tribe (most of mixed ancestry) on reservations in the states of Michigan, Minnesota, Montana, North Dakota, and Wisconsin; there were also approximately 50,000 Ojibwa in Canadian reservations in the provinces of Ontario, Manitoba, and Saskatchewan.
·animism and fetishism **1**:923f
·dances and Plains tribe influences **1**:673d
·folklore and creation myths **7**:464b
·kin term similarities to Iroquois **10**:477c
·Minnesota habitation and population **12**:257c
·moiety ceremonial dance illus. **1**:670
·musical instrument use **1**:665e
·North Dakota cultural contribution **13**:236g
·totemistic practices and beliefs **18**:529c
·winter lodge construction **1**:696e
·Woodlands Indian culture **6**:169e

O-ji-na He (China): *see* O-chi-na River.

Ōjin Tennō (b. AD 200?, Japan—d. AD 310?, Japan), semi-legendary 15th emperor of Japan who was deified as Hachiman, god of war. During his reign, many Chinese and Koreans were brought to Japan, where they introduced Confucianism and helped to develop the still-primitive Japanese culture.

Ōjō-yōshū ("Essentials of Salvation"), book on Pure Land Buddhism written by Genshin in 985.
·theme and influence **3**:440e

Ojukwu, Chukwuemeka Odumegwu (b. Nov. 4, 1933, Zungeru, Nigeria), military governor of the Eastern Region of Nigeria (1966–67) and head of the secessionist state of Biafra (1967–70) during the civil war. Son of a successful Ibo businessman, Ojukwu was graduated from Oxford University in 1955. He returned to Nigeria to serve in the administration but after two years joined the army and was rapidly promoted. He first entered the Nigerian political scene in 1964 (after the Northern People's Congress had won a disputed election). As a lieutenant colonel, he apparently offered army support to Pres. Nnamdi Azikiwe if he would assume emergency powers in order to save the country from Northern domination. His offer was not taken. He took no part, however, in the coup of January 1966, after which Major General Johnson Aguiyi-Ironsi took over the national government. Subsequently, Aguiyi-Ironsi appointed Ojukwu military governor of the East, and he retained that post when Aguiyi-Ironsi was killed in the Northern "revenge" coup of July 1966.

The rising tide of feeling against Ibos, especially in the Northern Region, increasingly isolated and embittered the Eastern Region, and by the fall of 1966 Ojukwu was seriously out of touch with the federal military government in Lagos, Western Region, under Yakubu Gowon. At a conference of Nigerian leaders in Ghana in January 1967 Ojukwu's main concern—the command of the army, which he wanted decentralized on a regional basis—was one on which a tentative agreement was reached. It was later rejected, however, by the federal government, leaving the East feeling more threatened than ever. Gowon's May 27, 1967, decree that created 12 states out of the four regions cut the Ibos off from the sea, and, on May 30, 1967, Biafra declared itself an independent state, under Ojukwu. The ensuing civil war lasted until January 1970. On the eve of surrender Ojukwu fled to the Ivory Coast, where he was granted asylum.
·Biafra rebellion leadership **19**:785e

Oka-Akoko, also called OKA, town, Ondo Province, Western State, southwestern Nigeria, in the Kukuruku Hills, on roads from Owo and Ikare. An agricultural market centre (yams, cassava, maize [corn], rice, palm oil and kernels, okra, pumpkins) for the local Yoruba people (Owo-Ifon and Akoko branches), it is also a collecting point for cocoa, palm produce, tobacco, and cotton, which is sent to the textile mill at Ado-Ekiti, 41 mi (66 km) west-northwest. It was probably founded in the late 19th century, when the Akoko belonged to the Ekiti–Parapo, a confederation of Yoruba peoples that fought against Ibadan, 128 mi west, for control of the trade routes to the coast. Modern Oka has a Roman Catholic-sponsored secondary school and a government maternity clinic. Pop. (1971 est.) 75,862.
7°29′ N, 5°49′ E
·map, Nigeria **13**:86

Oka Asajirō (b. 1866, modern Shizuoka Prefecture, Japan—d. 1944, Tokyo), biologist who introduced the theory of evolution to the Japanese public and whose researches into the taxonomical and morphological (relating to form) structures of the leech and tunicate (coated with layers) and freshwater jellyfish contributed to understanding of the subject.

After studying in Germany, he taught at Tokyo Higher Teacher's College, specializing in the comparative study of morphology and anatomy. He was known as a scientific essayist and wrote many educational textbooks and critical essays on modern civilization. In his *Lectures on Evolutional Theory* (1904), which was especially popular, being widely read even among the high school students, he explained Charles Darwin's theory of evolution in plain simple language. He dealt with human problems from the point of view of an evolutionist; in his famous work *From the Group of Monkies to the Republic*, he compared the modern political system with ape society. He also criticized the absolutism and one-sided ethical education of Japanese society at that time and emphasized the necessity of an objective education oriented to scientific study.

Okada Beisanjin, also known as HIKOBĒ (b. 1744, Ōsaka, Japan—d. 1820), painter who worked in the *bunjin-ga*, or literati style that originated in China and appealed to intellectuals. The son of a prosperous rice merchant, he enjoyed reading and was fond of the books of paintings that had been collected by his family for generations. He came under the influence of the painter-musician Uragami Gyokudō and other artists who were family friends. Later he became a retainer of a lord, and was his official Confucian teacher. He excelled in painting landscapes in the *bunjin-ga* style that

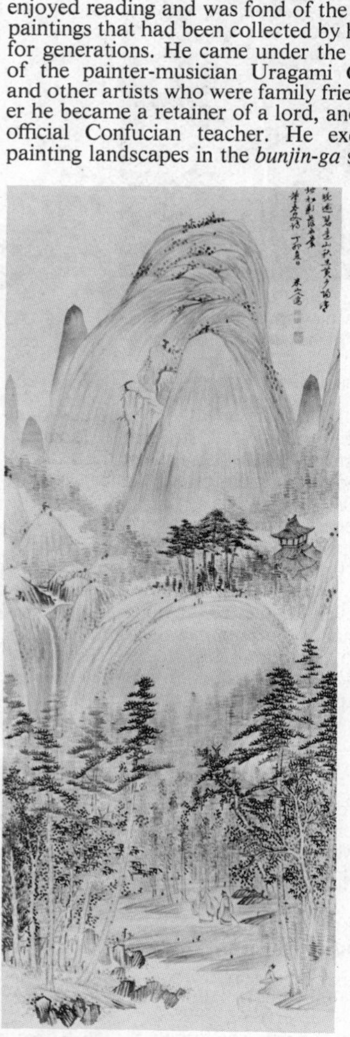

"Landscape with Pine Groves," hanging scroll painting by Okada Beisanjin, 1807, ink and light color on silk; in the collection of Matsushita Ichiyo, Takarazuka, Japan
By courtesy of Matsushita Ichiyo; photograph, the Asia House Gallery, New York

he mastered by studying illustrated books of Chinese paintings. His technique was rather crude, but he drew with an impressive economy of strokes. His works were original and serene, a good example being "Picture Album of Landscape."

Okada Tamechika, name at birth SHINZŌ, later called REIZEI SABURŌ (b. 1823, Japan—d. 1864), painter of the late Edo period (1603–1867) whose talent and efforts contributed a great deal to the revival of the traditional *Yamato-e* (paintings stressing Japanese themes and techniques as against the *Kara-e*, a style under strong Chinese influence). He improved his artistry by copying old *Yamato-e* masterpieces and became a courtier of the Imperial court in Kyōto in order to study at firsthand the traditional practices of the court, which he considered important subject matters. He even frequented the house of a prominent official of the Tokugawa shogunate in order to look at a famous three-scroll *yamato-e* in the official's possession, although he was an ardent supporter of the Imperial cause. These visits, however, caused the pro-Emperor faction to suspect him of disloyalty, and he had to flee Kyōto and hide himself by becoming a monk. He was finally tracked down, lured out of his hideaway, and murdered. The mural and screen paintings at Daiju temple are representative works and show his mastery of the Buddhistic art as well as *Yamato-e*. He was also good at calligraphy and well read in Japanese classics.

"Tadanori shutsujin-zu" (Japanese: "Going to Battle"), painting by Okada Tamechika; in the Tokyo National Museum

By courtesy of the Tokyo National Museum

Okahandja, magisterial district, South West Africa.
·district population and area table **17**:303; map

Oka Kiyoshi (1901–), Japanese mathematician.
·complex analysis fundamentals **1**:727g

Okakura Kakuzō, pseudonym TENSHIN (b. 1862, Yokohama, Japan—d. 1913, Akakura, Niigata Prefecture), art critic with great influence upon modern Japanese art. He graduated (1890) from Tokyo Imperial University, where he had studied government and economics. Soon thereafter he met Ernest Fenollosa, an American art critic and amateur painter who had been invited by the Japanese government to teach art history; at a time when everything Japanese tended to be looked down upon in comparison with things Western, Fenollosa recaptured the value of traditional Japanese art. Under his influence Okakura worked toward re-educating the Japanese people to appreciate their own cultural heritage. He was one of the principal founders of the Tokyo Fine Arts School, opened in 1887, and a year later became its head. He and Fenollosa, also teaching there, intentionally omitted Western painting and sculpture from the new school's curriculum. In 1898 Okakura was ousted from the school in an administrative struggle. He next established the Nippon Bijutsu-in (Japan Academy of Fine Arts) with the help of such followers as Hishida Shunsō and Yokoyama Taikan. A frequent traveller abroad, at the turn of the century he became curator of the Oriental art division of the Boston Museum of Fine Arts. His enthusiasm for traditional Japanese art often led him to assert the superiority of Oriental over Western art. Many of his works, such as *The Ideals of the East* (1903), *The Awakening of Japan* (1904), and *The Book of Tea* (1906), were written in English in order to spread abroad his ideas.
·Japanese native art encouragement **19**:241f

Okamoto Kidō (1872–1939), Japanese dramatist for the Kabuki theatre.
·Kabuki theatre playwright **10**:370b

Okanagon (North American Indians): *see* Salish.

Okanogan Highlands, region in Northern Washington state.
·geographic features **19**:618g

okapi (*Okapia johnstoni*), cud-chewing hoofed mammal placed along with the giraffe (*q.v.*) in the family Giraffidae (order Artiodactyla). Found in the rain forests of the Congo, the okapi was unknown to science until about 1900. The neck and legs are shorter than those of the giraffe and the shoulder height of females, which are larger than males, is about 1.5 metres (5 feet). The coat is sleek and deep brown, almost purple, with the sides of the face dull reddish; the buttocks, thighs, and tops of the forelegs are horizontally striped with black and white, and the lower parts of the legs are white with black rings above the hooves. The eyes and ears are large, and the tongue is long and prehensile. The male has short horns covered with skin except at the tips.

Okapi (*Okapia johnstoni*)

Kenneth W. Fink—Root Resources

The okapi is a shy, elusive animal that lives among dense cover and browses on leaves and fruit. It appears to be solitary. It has been exhibited in many zoological gardens and has been successfully bred in captivity. Gestation is about 14–15 months.
·social behaviour and classification **2**:72d

Okāra, city, Sāhiwāl District, Multān Division, Punjab Province, Pakistan. Connected by road and rail with Lahore and Multān, it is a developing industrial centre, with cotton textile and flour mills and government dairy and sheep farms. Its government college is affiliated with the University of the Punjab. Pop. (1972 est.) 142,100.
30°49′ N, 73°27′ E
·map, Pakistan **13**:893

Okara, Gabriel (Imomotimi Gbaingbain) (b. 1921, Ijaw Country, Nigeria), poet and novelist with an acute perception of Africa's basic problems, whose verse was sufficiently popular in his own country to be translated into several languages by the early 1960s. His novel *The Voice* (1964) is a remarkable linguistic experiment, forcing English into the straightjacket of Ijaw syntax and producing an extraordinary and archaic effect, often as beautiful as it is bizarre.

A largely self-educated man, Okara became a bookbinder after leaving school and soon began writing plays and features for radio. In 1953 his poem "The Call of the River Nun" won an award at the Nigerian Festival of Arts, and by 1960 he was recognized as an accomplished craftsman.

Okara uses a collective lyrical voice and tends to develop his poems through a series of contrasts in which symbols are neatly balanced against each other. The need to reconcile the extremes of experience (life and death are common themes) preoccupies his verse, and a typical poem has a circular movement from everyday reality to a moment of joy and back to reality again.

Okara incorporates African thought, religion, folklore, and imagery into his verse as well as his prose. His method of composition is to translate what he wants to say as literally as possible from his native Ijaw into English. Thus in *The Voice* the physical quality of his prose reflects the idiom, cadence, and word-order of his native tongue.

The Voice is also unusual in other ways. In its exploration of contemporary issues it combines both prose and verse to create a symbolic landscape in which the forces of light and darkness, idealism and materialism, contend. The hero Okolo is both an individual and a universal figure, and the ephemeral "it" that he is searching for could represent any number of moral values or the ideal state toward which all men should strive. Though the book ends tragically, one feels salvation is attainable and that a new order is evolving that will make it unnecessary to choose absolutely between traditional and Western ways. Okara's skilled portrayal of the inner tensions of his hero places him above many of his fellow Nigerian novelists who too often resort to stereotyped characters.

During much of the 1960s Okara served as information officer for the Eastern Nigeria Government Service in Enugu and in 1969 toured the United States with novelists Chinua Achebe and Cyprian Ekwensi, lecturing at various universities.
·experimental linguistic contribution **1**:240e

Oka River, in the Russian Soviet Federated Socialist Republic, is the largest right-bank tributary of the Volga. It is 920 mi (1,480 km) long and drains a basin of 94,600 sq mi (245,000 sq km). It rises in the Central Russian Upland and flows north in a rather narrow, winding valley to Kaluga, where it swings sharply eastward across a broad and often swampy lowland to join the Volga at Gorky. Freeze-up lasts from early December to late March or early April. Navigation extends as far as Belev.
56°20′ N, 43°59′ E
·map, Soviet Union **17**:322
·Volga River system physiography **19**:508d; map 509

Okavango, also called KAVANGO, South West African tribal magisterial district.
·district area and population table **17**:303
·map, South West Africa **17**:301

Okavango River 13:539, fourth longest river of southern Africa; rising in Angola as the Cubango, it flows southeastward to South West Africa and then crosses the Caprivi Strip to empty into the Okavango Swamps in Botswana, after a course of 1,000 mi (1,600 km).

The text article covers the course of the Okavango, its riverine peoples, hydrology, vegetation and animal life, and economic development.
18°50′ S, 22°25′ E

REFERENCES in other text articles:
·Angolan drainage area **1**:891a
·Botswana seasonal drainage pattern **3**:71f
maps
·Angola **1**:893
·Botswana **3**:72
·South West Africa **17**:301
·wetland distribution and ecology **17**:838h

Ōkawa, city, Fukuoka Prefecture (*ken*), Kyushu, Japan, on the mouth of the Chikugo-gawa (Chikugo River). It was a fishing port known as Wakatsu during the Tokugawa era (1603–1867), when it also served as a market for agricultural produce and lumber. In the mid-19th century Dutch techniques of woodworking and cabinetmaking were introduced, and woodworking had become the city's major industry by 1949. Since then, modernization and mechanization of the industry have progressed, using wood imported from the Philippines and Alaska. Pop. (1975) 50,395.
33°12′ N, 130°23′ E

Ōkawa Shūmei (b. 1886, Yamaguchi Prefecture, Japan—d. 1957, Tokyo), ultra-nationalistic political theorist whose writings inspired many of the right-wing extremist groups that dominated Japanese politics during the 1930s. Ōkawa personally organized and participated in many of the major rightist attempts at direct action, and during World War II he helped shape much of the government's domestic propaganda.

Ōkawa was graduated in philosophy from the University of Tokyo in 1911 and became an early associate of the other famous right-wing advocate of the period, Kita Ikki. Together they founded the influential nationalistic Yūzonsha (Society for the Preservation of the National Essence) in 1919. Through its magazine, *Otakebi* ("War Cry"), the Yūzonsha advocated the return of Japan to the simpler military values of its feudal past as well as the institution of a national socialist government. Yūzonsha gained a tremendous following, especially among the military forces. Ōkawa soon fell out with Kita, however, and in 1924 he began to publish his own magazine, *Nippon*, which advocated the creation of a Japanese military government at home and the extension of Japanese rule to Manchuria (Northeast Provinces). His popularity continued to grow, as did his identification with the Japanese economic penetration of Manchuria; in 1929 he was appointed chairman of the government's new East Asian Economic Investigation Bureau as well as special lecturer to the army and navy academy.

In early 1931 Ōkawa, together with a group of young army officers, organized a plan for a military takeover of the government. Although the coup was aborted, it was the first direct attempt against the government by a right-wing group. A second attempted coup in the following October also failed. In 1932, however, Ōkawa was arrested and sentenced to nine years' imprisonment for his involvement in the assassination (May 15) of Premier Inukai Tsuyoshi.

Paroled in 1937, Ōkawa rejoined the East Asian Economic Investigation Bureau two years later, serving simultaneously as head of a special program created at Hosei University in Tokyo to foster ultra-nationalist sentiments among the Japanese people. So famous did his broadcasts and announcements become that he was popularly known as *Toyo-no-ron-kaku* ("Voice of the Orient").

In 1945 Ōkawa was arrested as a Class A category war criminal suspect, but charges against him were dropped on the grounds of insanity. After two years of confinement he devoted the rest of his life to writing, completing a Japanese translation of the Qurʾān.

Okaya, city, Nagano Prefecture (*ken*), Honshu, Japan, on the western shore of Suwa-ko (*ko*, "lake"). Okaya was a small village until the establishment of its first large silk-reeling factory in 1875. After World War II many of the war-damaged silk mills were converted to factories producing precision machinery and processed foods. Pop. (1975) 61,776.
36°03′ N, 138°03′ E
·map, Japan **10**:36

Okayama, prefecture (*ken*), western Honshu, Japan, bordering the Inland Sea. Its area of 2,733 sq mi (7,078 sq km) includes numerous offshore islands. Okayama Prefecture has a predominantly agricultural economy. Rice, grapes, peaches, rush (for matting), and other cash crops are grown in the south, where farm techniques and mechanization are among the most advanced in Japan. Life in the interior mountains, however, is poor and largely dependent upon forestry and small-scale cattle raising. Manufacturing is concentrated in such southern cities as Okayama, Kurashiki, and Tamanoi.

Okayama Castle
Camera Tokyo Service

Okayama city, the prefectural capital, lies in the central Okayama plain, astride the Asahi-gawa (*gawa*, "river"). An old castle town of the Ikeda clan, it dominates prefectural life. It is a major marketing centre with excellent rail connections with cities on the Inland Sea and the Sea of Japan and on Shikoku. Because its river port is shallow, Tamanoi serves as its outport. Industry includes the manufacture of machinery, textiles, and rubber goods. Okayama University is noted for its medical college. Kōraku-en, laid out in 1786, is one of Japan's most celebrated public gardens. The town of Bizen, to the northeast, has been a centre of pottery making since the 8th century. Pop. (1975) city, 513,471; (1976 est.) prefecture, 1,829,000.
·map, Japan **10**:37
·prefecture area and population, table 1 **10**:45

Okazaki, city, Aichi Prefecture (*ken*), central Honshu, Japan, in the Mikawa plain, on the Yahagi-gawa (*gawa*, "river"). It developed around Okazaki Castle after its construction in 1455. During the Tokugawa period (1603–1867) it prospered as one of the stage towns on the Tōkaidō Highway connecting Edo (Tokyo) and Kyōto.

In 1888 Okazaki refused to allow the Tōkaidō Main Line railway to be built through the city. It thereafter declined until it was connected with Nagoya and Toyohashi by rapid-transit lines. Now an industrial centre, it produces textiles, foods, machinery, chemicals, and fabricated metals. Pop. (1975) 234,510.
34°57′ N, 137°10′ E
·map, Japan **10**:37

Okazaki Genshichi (painter): *see* Kaigetsudō Ando.

oke, a unit of dry weight measure having various values as it is used in Bulgaria, Cyprus, Egypt, Greece, and Turkey; also a unit of liquid measure in Bulgaria.
·weights and measures, table 5 **19**:734

Okeechobee, Lake, third largest freshwater lake wholly within the U.S. (after Lake Michigan and Iliamna Lake, Alaska), located 40 mi (65 km) north-northwest of West Palm Beach, Fla., at the northern edge of the Everglades. Bearing the Seminole Indian name for "Big Water," it is 35 mi long with a shoreline of 135 mi and, including three small islands, covers an area of 700 sq mi (1,813 sq km). The surface is 12.5 to 15.5 ft (4 to 5 m) above mean sea level depending upon the water level in the lake; the mean depth is 7 ft, the maximum 15 ft. The chief source is the Kissimmee Valley watershed, immediately to the north, via the Kissimmee River, which flows 100 mi south to Lake Okeechobee. Before the construction of adequate levees and a regulatory outlet system, the overflow produced by the rainy season flooded surrounding areas and spilled over southward into the Everglades. Private and state drainage attempts, all unsuccessful, date from 1881. The last effort failed when hurricane winds flooded the area in 1928. State and federal flood control and reclamation projects were subsequently begun.

In 1937 a 155-mi cross-state waterway, from Stuart on the Atlantic Ocean via the St. Lucie Canal across Lake Okeechobee and down the Caloosahatchee River to the Gulf of Mexico, was completed. Lake communities include Pahokee, Belle Glade, Lake Harbor, Clewiston, Okeechobee, and Canal Point. Seminole Indians still live on the northwest shore of the lake.
26°55′ N, 80°45′ W
·Everglades drainage and water control **6**:1141h
·Florida's vegetation and landscape **7**:425b
·hurricane disaster and protective steps **9**:63g
·map, United States **18**:909

O'Keeffe, Georgia (b. Nov. 15, 1887, near Sun Prairie, Wis.), painter best known for her semi-abstractions derived from nature, an important source of inspiration being the desert of New Mexico. After a childhood spent on her family's Wisconsin farm, she studied at the Art Institute of Chicago (1904–05) and the Art Students League of New York (1907–08).

The photographer Alfred Stieglitz, noted for his role in introducing modern art into the U.S., put a group of her drawings on display in 1916. The next year he presented a one-woman show of her drawings and watercolours. She and Stieglitz were married in 1924, the year in which she began painting large flowers, one of the subjects with which she is particularly associated. The flower forms often suggested human shapes, and sexual associations are common. One of the best known is "Black Iris" (1926; Metropolitan Museum of Art, New York City). Another favourite subject, animal bones, is represented by "Cow's Skull: Red, White, and Blue" (1931; Metropolitan Museum of Art). In 1931 she went to the Gaspé Peninsula, in Quebec, and from that period date paintings such as "White Barn, No. 1" (1932; Wright Ludington

Collection, Santa Barbara, Calif.). Whether flowers, bones, or architecture, she rendered her subjects with emphasis on abstract form.

On a visit to New Mexico in 1929, she was strongly impressed by the beauty of the desert and has never tired of painting it. After the first visit she usually spent the summer there and the winter in New York City or Lake George, N.Y. During the 1950s, she began to travel widely for the first time, and in 1959 she flew around the world. Out of that trip and other flights came a series of works based on the view of the earth from an airplane and later a series on the sky and clouds observed in flight, such as the immense 24-foot-wide painting "Sky Above Clouds IV" (1965; collection of the artist).

"Near Abiquiu, New Mexico," oil on canvas by Georgia O'Keeffe, 1930; in the Metropolitan Museum of Art, New York City

By courtesy of the Metropolitan Museum of Art, New York City, gift of Georgia O'Keeffe, 1963

·Stieglitz' American art promotion **17**:691b

Okefenokee (OKEFINOKEE) **Swamp,** a primitive swamp and wildlife refuge in southeastern Georgia and northern Florida, U.S. A shallow, saucer-shaped depression approximately 25 mi (40 km) wide and 40 mi (65 km) long, it covers an area of more than 600 sq mi (1,550 sq km). About 50 mi inland from the Atlantic Coast, the swamp is bounded on the east by low, sandy Trail Ridge, which prevents direct drainage into the Atlantic. Partially drained southward into the Atlantic by the Suwannee and St. Mary's rivers, the swamp includes low, sandy ridges, wet grassy savannas, small islands (called hummocks) surrounded by marshes, and extensive "prairies," or dark water areas covered by thick undergrowth and trees (including giant tupelo and bald cypress trees festooned with Spanish moss and, where sandy soil is above the water, pine trees). Meandering channels of open water form an intricate maze. Exotic flowers, among them floating hearts, lilies, and rare orchids, abound. The swamp is populated with a variety of wildlife including at least 200 different species of birds. In 1937 371,445 ac (150,319 ha), including most of the swamp in Georgia, were set aside as the Okefenokee National Wildlife Refugee, with headquarters at Waycross, Ga. The swamp's name probably is derived from the Muskogean (Indian) word for "watershaking."
30°42′ N, 82°20′ W

·Georgia vegetation, illus., **18**:Terrestrial Ecosystem, Plate III
·map, United States **18**:908
·wetland distribution and ecology **17**:838g

Okeghem, Jean d', Latin JOHANNES OCKEGHEM (b. *c.* 1430, Flanders—d. *c.* 1495, Tours, Fr.), composer of sacred and secular music, one of the great masters of the Franco-Flemish style that dominated European music of the Renaissance. His earliest recorded appointment is as a singer at Antwerp cathedral (1443–44). He served similarly in the chapel of Charles, duc de Bourbon (1446–48), and later in the royal chapel. He was chaplain and composer to three successive French kings, Charles VII, Louis XI, and Charles VIII, and received the title of *maître de la chapelle de-chant du roy* in 1465. As treasurer of the wealthy Abbey of Saint-Martin at Tours he received a handsome salary. Like many of his Flemish contemporaries he travelled widely and used his visits to distant cities to extend his musical knowledge. As a teacher he had great influence on the following generation of composers. His death was mourned in writing by Erasmus, whose text was set to music by Johannes Lupi; a *Déploration* by Molinet was set by Josquin des Prez.

Okeghem's surviving works include 14 masses (two of which consist of Kyrie, Gloria, and Credo only), 10 motets, and 20 chansons. His work sounds richer than that of his predecessors Guillaume Dufay and John Dunstable; during Okeghem's era the instrumentally supported vocal lines of earlier music were gradually modified to make way for sonorous choral harmony. The bass range in Okeghem's compositions extends lower than in his predecessors' music, and the tenor and countertenor voices cross in and out of each other, creating a heavier texture. The long melodic lines of the different voices cadence in different places so that a continuous flow of music results. Melodic imitation occurs here and there but is not prominent. The austere *Missa pro defunctis* contains hardly any imitation and only the slightest traces of canon, a device of which he was a master. His *Missa prolationum* and *Missa cuiusvis toni* are examples of his highly developed contrapuntal and canonic technique, but the strict device of canon is subtly used and is rarely apparent to the listener. Okeghem frequently used pre-existent material as a device for musical unity and like several other Renaissance composers used the folk song *L'Homme armé* as a *cantus firmus* (simple Gregorian melody) for one of his masses. His ten motets include Marian texts, such as *Ave Maria*, *Salve regina*, and *Alma redemptoris mater*, and a complete setting of the responsory *Gaude Maria*. Unlike other composers of the early 15th century, Okeghem wrote his masses in a style more solemn than that of his secular music. They are normally in four parts (two are in five parts), in contrast to the three parts commonly used in chansons. The melodic lines in the masses are longer than those of the chansons. Melodic imitation is more frequent in the chansons, and the rhythms of the chansons are more straightforward than those of the masses.

Okeghem (with glasses), detail of a manuscript miniature by an unknown artist, late 15th century; in the Bibliothèque Nationale, Paris (MS. Fr. 1537)

By courtesy of the Bibliotheque Nationale, Paris

·influence of musical mainstream **12**:706g
·melodic counterpoint **5**:214e

Okehampton, market town in the county of Devon, England, on the two Okement rivers (tributaries of the Torridge) on the northern edge of the wild heathland known as Dartmoor. There was a Saxon settlement on the site, but this was abandoned shortly after the Norman Conquest in 1066, when a castle was built, the keep of which remains. The town received its first charter of incorporation in the reign of Edward I (1272–1307). Pop. (1971 prelim.) 3,908.
50°44′ N, 4°00′ W

O'Kelly (O CEALLAIGH), **Sean Thomas** (b. Aug. 25, 1882, Dublin—d. Nov. 23, 1966, Dublin), one of the early leaders of the Irish nationalist Sinn Féin (We Ourselves) Party; he served two terms as president of Ireland, June 1945–June 1959.

For some years O'Kelly worked in the National Library, Dublin. In 1905 he became a journalistic associate of Arthur Griffith, principal founder of Sinn Féin. O'Kelly served as honorary secretary of Sinn Féin (1908–10) and general secretary of the Gaelic League (1915–20). From 1913 he helped to raise the Irish Volunteers, and he was imprisoned for a year for fighting against the British in the Easter Rising of 1916 in Dublin.

Intermittently from 1918 to 1945 O'Kelly sat in Dáil Éireann (the Irish assembly), and for a time he was its speaker. In 1919 he represented the Irish Republic at the World War I peace conference, Paris, and later he was envoy to Italy and the U.S. In the government formed by Eamon de Valera in 1932, O'Kelly became vice president of the executive council and minister of local government. Succeeding Douglas Hyde as president in 1945 and reelected in 1952 without opposition, he retired from public life after his second term.

Oken, Lorenz (1779–1851), German naturalist, the most important of the early-19th-century German "nature philosophers," who speculated about the significance of life, which they believed to be derived from a vital force that could not be understood totally through scientific means. He elaborated Wolfgang von Goethe's theory that the vertebrate skull formed gradually from the fusion of vertebrae. Although the theory was later disproved, it helped prepare a receptive atmosphere for Charles Darwin's theory of evolution.

Okene, town, Kabba Province, Kwara State, south central Nigeria, at the intersection of roads from Lokoja, Kabba, Ikare, and Agenebode. Originally founded on a hill near the present site, it now lies in the valley of the Ubo River, a minor tributary of the Niger. It is the chief trade centre (yams, cassava, maize [corn], guinea corn, beans, peanuts, palm oil and kernels, cotton, woven cloth) of the Igbira people and the site of the Igbira *ata*'s ("king") palace. Cotton weaving is a traditional craft, and Okene women are known for their weaving of imported silk.

Okene is the seat of the court offices for Igbira Division (1,146 sq mi [2,968 sq km]) and is also the site of an Igbira secondary school, a government teacher training college, a central mosque, a hospital, and a maternity clinic and dispensary. Although many of the nearby

towns in the division suffered greatly from the Fulani, Yoruba, and Nupe conquests and slave raids in the 19th century, the area around Okene remains fairly densely populated. Islām is the predominant religion in the division. Pop. (1972 est.) 8,298.
7°33′ N, 6°15′ E
·map, Nigeria **13**:87

Okha, port, Jāmnagar district, Gujarāt state, west central India, at the western tip of the Kāthiāwār Peninsula, between the Gulf of Kutch and the Arabian Sea. Formerly part of Amreli district, it was transferred to Jāmnagar district in 1959. The town contains an automobile assembly plant, and a large chemical plant is located at Mithāpur, 5 mi (8 km) southwest. Fishing and salt manufacture are important. Okha is a railway terminus and is served by a highway. Pop. (1971) 10,687.
22°27′ N, 69°04′ E

Okhlopkov, Nikolay Pavlovich (b. May 15 [May 2, old style], 1900, Irkutsk, Siberia—d. Jan. 8, 1967, Moscow), experimental theatrical director and producer, one of the first modern directors to introduce productions in the round on an arena stage in an effort to restore intimacy between the actors and the audience. As director (1931–37) of the Realistic Theatre in Moscow (formerly the Moscow Art Theatre Studio), he drew on the principles of Greek, Chinese, Japanese, and Shakespearean theatre, designing an elaborate stage in the centre of the house and often placing the seated spectators inside the field of action. Although he produced chiefly political and

Okhlopkov
Sovfoto

proletarian dramas tailored to Soviet ideology, his experimentalism eventually led the government to close the Realistic Theatre (1938). From 1938 to 1943, Okhlopkov was a producer at the Vakhtangov Theatre and from 1943 to 1966 at the Moscow Drama (after 1954 called the Mayakovsky) Theatre. He also produced and acted in a number of Soviet films.
·staging experimentation **18**:232h

Okhotsk, Sea of 13:541, Russian OKHOTSKOYE MORE, northwestern arm of the Pacific Ocean enclosed by the northeastern Siberian (Soviet Union) coast of Asia from Cape Lazarev to the mouth of the Penzhina River, by the Kamchatka Peninsula and the Kuril Islands to the east, and by the Japanese island of Hokkaido to the south, and by the Soviet island of Sakhalin to the southwest. It has an area of 611,000 sq mi (1,583,000 sq km) and is connected to the Pacific via passages between the Kuril Islands.

The text article covers the physical characteristics of the sea and its climate, hydrology, marine life, and navigation.

REFERENCES in other text articles:
·area, volume, and depth, table 1 **13**:484
·fishing grounds importance **13**:843h
·geological formation **2**:147e
maps
·Asia **2**:148
·Japan **10**:36
·Soviet Union **17**:323
·pack ice formation and drift **9**:159f; illus. 155

Okhotsk Basin, depression in the northwestern Pacific Ocean.
53°00′ N, 150°00′ E
·geological history **13**:541f

Okhrana, abbreviation of Russian OTDELENIYE PO OKHRANENIYU OBSHCHESTVENNOY BEZOPASNOSTI I PORYADKA, English DEPARTMENT FOR DEFENSE OF PUBLIC SECURITY AND ORDER (1881–1917), pre-revolutionary Russian secret-police organization founded to combat political terrorism and revolutionary activity. Its principal mode of operation was infiltration of labour unions, political parties, and, in at least two cases, newspapers: police agents were editors of the Marxist journals *Nachalo* ("The Beginning") and, in 1912–13, *Pravda*. The Okhrana was particularly active following the unsuccessful Revolution of 1905. After the Revolution of February 1917, it was abolished by the Provisional Government.

Okhwang sangje, deity of the Korean religion known as Poch'ŏngyo (*q.v.*).

Okigbo, Christopher (b. 1932, Ojoto, Nigeria—d. 1967, Nigeria), Nigerian poet whose strong literary and classical background tended to make him shun specifically African literary traditions for the freedom to write as he wished. His musical, intensely evocative, and often obscure verse, and his esoteric style and careful craftsmanship show the influence of Greek and Latin writers as well as of Ezra Pound, T.S. Eliot, the Bible, and his native Ibo mythology and landscape.

After completing his degree in classics at the University of Ibadan in 1956, Okigbo held positions as a teacher, librarian at the University of Nigeria campuses, private secretary to Nigeria's federal minister of research and information, and West African editor of *Transition*, an international literary magazine. When awarded first prize for poetry in the Festival of the Negro Arts in Dakar (1966), he declined the prize because he felt that writing must be judged as good or bad, not as a product of a specific ethnic group or race. Yet, like his fellow writers John Pepper Clark, Wole Soyinka, and Lenrie Peters, he was greatly concerned about the poet's role in society.

In an introduction to *Labyrinths with Path of Thunder* (his collected works, published posthumously in 1971), Okigbo states that all his poems were organically related to one another. One critic explains this relationship by suggesting that each poem is a step in the evolution of a personal religion. Okigbo, in fact, believed that he was a reincarnation of his maternal grandfather, a priest of the river goddess Idoto, and when he began writing poetry seriously he suddenly felt a strong urge to take over his inherited role as priest. His haunting lines in *Heavensgate* (1962), *Limits* and *Distances* (1964), and *Silences* and *Path of Thunder* (1965) are strongly reminiscent both of the broken melody of T.S. Eliot's verse and of Eliot's search for religious meaning in *The Waste Land* and other poems.

In 1967 Okigbo's efforts to launch a publishing company in Enugu with the novelist Chinua Achebe came to an abrupt end by his death while fighting for Biafran independence from Nigeria.
·style and contributions **1**:240d

Oki-guntō, archipelago, Shimane Prefecture (*ken*), Japan, lying in the Sea of Japan off the coast of Honshu. The one large island, Dōgo, and three smaller isles (Chiburi-, Nishino-, and Nakano-shima), are collectively known as Dōzen. The four islands have a combined coastline of 223 mi (359 km) and an area of 134 sq mi (348 sq km). The chief town is Saigō, on the island of Dōgo, about 40 mi from the Honshu port of Sakai.

The archipelago is celebrated in Japanese history because its possession was much disputed during the feudal period and because a former emperor and an emperor were banished there by the Hōjō regents in the 13th century. The islands now form part of Daisen-Oki National Park. Pop. (1975) 29,765.
36°15′ N, 133°15′ E
·map, Japan **10**:37

okina, in Japanese Nō drama, an invocation of peace and prosperity containing dance, song, and dialogue with special masks and costuming; used since the 17th century as the opening piece for a Nō work.
·function in Nō theatre **13**:271h

Okinawa, prefecture (*ken*), Japan, in the East China Sea. Its area of 922 sq mi (2,389 sq km) is composed of the Ryukyu Islands (*q.v.*).

Naha, capital of Okinawa Prefecture, Japan
Kyodo Photo Service

During World War II the islands were the scene of large-scale U.S. amphibious operations (April–June 1945). Pop. (1976 est.) 1,059,000.
·Japanese–American relations **10**:89a
·Japanese ethnic and cultural comparison **10**:55a
·map, Japan **10**:36
World War II
·Allied advance on Japan **19**:1012e; map 990
·Allied logistics problems **11**:81b
·U.S. amphibious operations **12**:896d

Okinawa Trough, oceanic deep in the China Sea.
25°30′ N, 125°00′ E
·China Sea physiography **4**:406a; map 405

Ökin tengri (Buddhist deity): *see* Lha-mo.

Oklahoma 13:542, west central state of the U.S., admitted to the Union in 1907 as the 46th state. Occupying an area of 69,919 sq mi (181,089 sq km), it is bounded on the north by Colorado and Kansas, on the east by Missouri and Arkansas, on the south by Texas, and on the west by Texas and New Mexico. Its capital is Oklahoma City. Pop. (1980) 3,025,266.

The text article, after a brief overview of the state, covers its history, natural and human landscape, people, economy, administration and social conditions, and cultural life and institutions.
35°30′ N, 98°00′ W

REFERENCES in other text articles:
·area and population, table 1 **18**:927
·land rush of 1889 **18**:980f
·map, United States **18**:908
·statehood and Indian displacement **17**:222c

Oklahoma! (1943), American musical comedy, music by Richard Rodgers and lyrics by Oscar Hammerstein II.
·musical theatre development **12**:697f
·popular theatre and musical drama **14**:813h

Oklahoma, card game, member of the Rummy games family with basically similar rules and play. Two 52-card decks and a joker are used. Each player is dealt 13 cards. As in Rummy, players attempt to form melds—sequences of three or more cards in one suit or sets of three or four cards of the same rank. In Oklahoma, however, the joker and all deuces are wild—they may represent any other cards designated by the holder in forming melds. The joker can later be taken back by its player and replaced with the card it represented. Also, to take the top card of the discard pile, a player must take the whole pile and meld the top card at once. The queen of spades may not be discarded unless the player has no other card.

A deal ends when one player has melded all cards in his hand and goes out. Each player's melds count for him and cards left in his hand count against him as follows: aces, 20; queen of spades, melded, 50, left in hand, 100; cards of rank king through 8, 10; cards of rank 7 to 3, 5; joker, melded, 100, left in hand, 200; deuces, melded, value of the card represented, left in hand, 20. The player who went out wins a 100-point bonus. Game score is 1,000 and the winner receives a bonus of 200.

Oklahoma City, capital of Oklahoma, U.S., and seat of Oklahoma County, on the North Canadian River near the centre of the state. Through annexations it has become one of the nation's largest cities in area (more than 650 sq mi [1,680 sq km]). Born of the "Run of '89," it came into being on April 22, 1889, when approximately 10,000 homesteaders congregated at Oklahoma Station (a stop established in 1887 on the Santa Fe Railway) to stake out land claims in central Oklahoma. A provisional town government was organized in a mass meeting in May 1889, but it was not until May 2, 1890, with the organization of Oklahoma Territory, that official incorporation came. While the name Oklahoma City was in popular use from the city's beginning, the U.S. Post Office did not adopt the name until 1923. The city developed as a distribution point for crops and cattle; its designation as state capital in 1910 stimulated its growth. Meat-packing plants were established, and with the arrival of more railroads, wholesale trade increased. Now a major transportation centre, it is the chief market processing point for the state's vast livestock industry and a shipping point for cotton, wheat, and cattle. The first oil well in the Oklahoma City pool came in on Dec. 4, 1928; characteristics of the field were high productivity, enormous gas pressure, and the then unprecedented depths (4,000–7,000 ft [1200–2100 m]) of the wells. Because of fire hazard, ordinances were passed limiting the drilling zone; about 1,400 wells produce oil within the city limits, including some on the state capital grounds.

The city has become one of the nation's foremost aviation centres with Tinker Air Force Base (a large air-matériel depot) and the Federal Aviation Agency Aeronautical Center on the west side of Will Rogers World Airport for training in air safety and airport administration. Highly diversified manufactures include petroleum products, executive aircraft, oil-field machinery, electronic equipment, computers, and fabricated steel. Oklahoma City University was founded in 1904, Oklahoma Christian College in 1950, and a branch of the State University was opened in 1961 in the city. Oklahoma medical facilities focus on the University of Oklahoma Medical Center (1900) and the privately owned Oklahoma Medical Research Institute.

State capitol building, Oklahoma City, Okla.

By courtesy of the Oklahoma Tourism and Information Division

The city is the home of the National Cowboy Hall of Fame and Western Heritage Center (1965). The Oklahoma State Historical Society Building has an outstanding collection of Indian archives. The Oklahoma State Fair and Exposition is held each September and the All Sports Stadium is in the State Fair Arena; the State Fair Park contains the Oklahoma Science and Arts Foundation and the Art Center. Many skyscrapers cap the downtown area and because of the flat terrain can be seen for miles around. Frontier City, a replica of an old Western Town, is 13 mi (20 km) northeast. Pop. (1970) city, 366,481; metropolitan area (SMSA), 640,889; (1980) city, 403,213; SMSA, 834,088.
35°28′ N, 97°32′ W

·location and economic activity **13**:543e
·map, United States **18**:908

Okovango River (Africa): *see* Okavango River.

okra, herbaceous, hairy, annual plant (*Hibiscus esculentus*) of the mallow family (Malvaceae), of the tropics of the Eastern Hemisphere, widely cultivated or naturalized in the tropics and subtropics of the Western Hemisphere. The leaves are heart-shaped and three- to five-lobed; the flowers are yellow with a crimson centre. The fruit or pod, hairy at the base, is a tapering, ten-angled capsule, 10–25 centimetres (4–10 inches) in length (except in the dwarf varieties), containing numerous oval, dark-coloured seeds. Only the tender, unripe fruit, called gumbo, is eaten. It may be cooked and served as a pickled vegetable or prepared like asparagus, and it is also an ingredient in various stews and in the gumbos of the southern United States; the large amount of mucilage (gelatinous substance) it contains makes it useful as a thickener for broths and soups. The fruit is grown on a large scale in the vicinity of Istanbul. In some countries the seeds are used as a substitute for coffee. The leaves and immature fruit long have been popular in the East for use in poultices to relieve pain.

Okra (*Hibiscus esculentus*)

Derek Fell

The musk mallow or abelmosk (*Hibiscus abelmoschus*), a related plant indigenous to India and cultivated in most warm regions of the globe, is a low, slightly woody plant, bearing a conical five-ridged pod about 75 millimetres (3 inches) in length, within which are numerous brown reniform seeds, smaller than those of *H. esculentus*. The seeds possess a musky odour and are known to perfumers under the name of ambrette. The plant yields an excellent fibre and, being rich in mucilage, is employed in upper India for clarifying sugar. The best-perfumed seeds are reported to come from Martinique.

Okrika, port, Degema Province, Rivers State, southern Nigeria, on the north bank of the Bonny River and on Okrika Island. Upstream 35 mi (56 km) from the Bight of Biafra, it can be reached by vessels of a draft of 29 ft (9 m). Formerly a small fishing village of the Ijaw (Ijo) people in the mangrove swamps of the eastern Niger Delta, it became the capital of the Okrika kingdom in the early 17th century and actively dealt in slaves. Although it served as a palm-oil port after the abolition of the slave trade in the 1830s, it was not so great a port as either Bonny (18 mi south) or Opobo (32 mi east-southeast). Completely eclipsed in 1912 by Port Harcourt, Okrika was not revived as a commercial port until 1965, when the nearby Alesa-Eleme oil refinery was completed and pipelines were built to a jetty on Okrika Island. Refined petroleum products were Okrika's only significant exports in the early 1970s.

The town has considerable local trade in fish, oil-palm produce, locally processed salt, cassava, eddoes (coco yams), plantains, and yams. Its hospital and dispensary are located on the mainland. Pop. (1972 est.) 30,148.
4°47′ N, 7°04′ E

·map, Nigeria **13**:86

okrug, term in the U.S.S.R. given to a national district.

·Soviet Union political structure **17**:349h

Oktoberfest, annual festival held in Munich.

·Munich's cultural atmosphere **12**:617b

oktōēchos (music): *see* ēchos.

Oktyabrsky, city, Bashkir Autonomous Soviet Socialist Republic, western Russian Soviet Federated Socialist Republic, on the Ik River. Founded as a settlement in 1937, when extraction of oil began nearby, it was incorporated in 1946. A decline in production since the 1950s has resulted in a switch in the local economy to the manufacture of consumer goods. Pop. (1970) 77,054.
54°28′ N, 53°28′ E

Ōkubo Toshimichi (b. 1831, Kagoshima, Japan—d. May 14, 1878, Tokyo), one of the Samurai leaders who in 1868 overthrew the Tokugawa family, which had ruled Japan for 264 years, and re-established the government of the emperor. After the Meiji Restoration he spent much of his career helping to establish Japan as a progressive nation. Ōkubo early showed great political acumen and became one of the leading figures in the government of Satsuma, one of the largest and most powerful Japanese feudal domains and a hotbed of anti-Tokugawa sentiment. Although Chōshū, another powerful domain, shared the anti-Tokugawa stand of Satsuma, they were on unfriendly terms with each other. This situation was remedied in 1866, when Ōkubo and Saigō Takamori, another leading figure in the Satsuma government, agreed to an alliance with Chōshū in which both domains determined to cooperate in the emperor's behalf.

Shortly thereafter the Tokugawa family was overthrown and Ōkubo became a dominant member of the new Imperial government. After a brief tour of the West he returned, convinced of Japan's need for rapid economic development. To this end he supported the establishment of technical schools, the granting of government loans and subsidies to private business, and the building and managing of factories by the government.

In 1873 he broke with Saigō Takamori over policy toward Korea. Saigō supported a plan of conquest; Ōkubo argued that priority be given to internal reform and development. Ōkubo's views prevailed and were adhered to until 1894, long after his death. Saigō left the government and returned to his native Satsuma, where he led a short-lived rebellion of dissatisfied Samurai. The rebellion was suppressed, but in 1878 Ōkubo was assassinated by Saigō's sympathizers.

·Ito political opportunity and succession **9**:1175e

Ōkuma Shigenobu, Marquess (b. Feb. 16, 1838, Saga, Japan—d. Jan. 10, 1922, Tokyo), prime minister of Japan during the first part of World War I, organized the Rikken Kaishintō (Progressive Party), and founded Waseda University. After receiving a conventional education, Ōkuma turned to Western studies and took the then-unusual step of learning English. Unable to persuade his clansmen to support the restoration of power to the Meiji emperor (1868), Ōkuma at first had to settle for secondary positions in the Meiji government. But his ability and courage soon brought him an important role in government, at first specializing in finance. From 1869 to 1881 he was chiefly responsible for the modernization and reorganization of Japan's fiscal system.

In 1879, when members of the government were asked to propose provisions of a new Japanese constitution to the emperor, Ōkuma waited two years before responding. Then he astounded his colleagues by the radical nature of his proposals. He suggested that elections be held the next year, that a parliament be convened, and that the British system of a cabinet responsible to parliament be established. Later that year he exposed corruption in proposed sales of government property in Hokkaido, one of the northern most Japanese islands.

As a result of his opinions and actions he was dismissed from the government. But he had aroused popular sentiment against the government, and a movement for a constitution, which had been slowly developing, gained great impetus after his dismissal. In response to popular pressure, the Emperor promised that a constitution would be readied by 1890. The document was completed and promulgated a year earlier, on Feb. 1, 1889. Ōkuma formed a political party, the Kaishintō (Progressive Party), oriented toward English parliamentary concepts.

He had rejoined the government the year before as foreign minister but resigned after an attack by a nationalist fanatic nearly cost him his life. In 1896 he served again as foreign minister, and two years later he and Itagaki Taisuke, the founder, in 1881, of Japan's first political party, the Jiyūtō (Liberal Party), joined forces and formed the Kenseitō (Constitutional Party). They formed a government in 1898 with Ōkuma as prime minister, but it foundered over patronage disputes.

Earlier, in 1882, Ōkuma had founded in Tokyo what soon after became known as Waseda University, one of the two leading private univiersities in Japan. He retired from politics in 1907 to devote all his time to Waseda, only to be recalled as prime minister in 1914. During this, his last premiership, Japan experienced a great economic boom, partly as a result of the increased trade brought by World War I. Efforts by the Ōkuma government to force China to give Japan long-term territorial grants caused Japan to become the object of rising nationalist indignation in China. Ōkuma resigned in 1916 and retired from politics because of ill health.

·constitutional movement split **10**:80b
·Ito political battle and results **9**:1175e

Okumura Masanobu, also known as GENPACHI (b. SHINMYŌ, 1686, Edo, now Tokyo—d. 1764), painter and publisher of illustrated books who introduced innovations in woodblock printing and print-design technique in Japan.

Masanobu taught himself painting and print designs by studying the works of Torii Kiyonobu (died 1729), thus starting his career as Torii's imitator. About 1724 Masanobu became a publisher of illustrated books and brought out his own works. He was one of the first to adopt Western perspective through the Chinese prints available in Edo at that time. He produced large-scale prints depicting such scenes as the inside of theatres, stores, and sumptuous living quarters. Such prints were called *uki-e* ("looming picture") prints for the foreshortening effect produced. He is also said to have founded the format of *habahiro hashira-e*, or wide, vertical prints. His style was noted for its vividness with gentle and graceful lines, which also showed restraint and dignity.

"Honuri" (bookseller), woodblock print by Okumura Masanobu; in the Sakai Collection, Tokyo
By courtesy of the Sakai Collection, Tokyo

Among Masanobu's numerous works dealing with diverse subject matters are the print "Shibai jōnaizu" ("Inside the Theatre") and the paintings "Koto-no-ne" ("Sound of the Koto") and "Oshichi Kichisaburō" (*i.e.*, lovers by these names).

·embossing and colour printing **14**:1092b

Ōkuni-nushi, hero of the Izumo cycle of Japanese myths and son-in-law of the storm god, Susanowo. Before becoming "Master of the Great Land," he underwent a series of ordeals, mainly at the hands of his many mischievous brothers. His compassionate advice to the suffering white hare of Inaba (who had been stripped of his fur by a crocodile) was rewarded by the hare, who helped to arrange his marriage with Yakami-hime, the princess of Inaba. His chief consort was Suseri-hime (Forward Princess), the daughter of Susanowo. They made their escape from Susanowo's palace in the nether world when Ōkuni-nushi tied the storm god's hair to the rafters while he slept. Ōkuni-nushi took with him the storm god's most precious possessions: his sword, lute, and bow and arrows. The lute brushed against a tree as it was being carried away and woke Susanowo, who followed in pursuit as far as the pass between the land of light and the land of darkness, then relented and forgave the couple.

Ōkuni-nushi then commenced to build the world with the help of the dwarf deity Sukuna-bikona. The two together formulated the arts of medicine and means of controlling disasters caused by birds and insects. He continued to rule Izumo until the appearance of the divine grandchild, Ninigi, when he turned over political rule to him while retaining control of "secret," or religious, affairs. In modern Japanese folk belief he is venerated as a god who heals and who makes marriages happy.

·adventures and establishment of healing arts **10**:99e

Ōkura Kihachirō (b. 1837, Shibata, Niigata Prefecture, Japan—d. 1928, Tokyo), founder of one of the largest *zaibatsu*, or gigantic industrial-financial combines, that dominated the Japanese economy throughout the late 19th and early 20th centuries.

Abandoning his traditional family business, Ōkura became a weapons dealer in the turbulent period preceding the 1868 coup d'etat that overthrew the feudal Tokugawa regime in Japan. He then formed the Ōkura-Gumi Company, which became one of the first businesses to engage in foreign trade. Under Ōkura's leadership the company later branched out into mining and industrial enterprises. In his later years Ōkura became a philanthropist and a promoter of Sino-Japanese friendship.

Okutama Mountains, mountains west of the Tokyo-Yokohama metropolitan area.

·location and geographic features **18**:476h

Okvik culture, Eskimo culture dating from the pre-Christian era; Okvik remains have been found on the St. Lawrence and Diomede islands, the Siberian coast, and the northwest Alaskan mainland.

·artistic themes and models **3**:1139d; illus.

Okwanuchu: *see* Shastan Indians.

Okwa River, intermittent stream in the Kalahari Desert, Botswana.
22°30′ S, 23°00′ E

·Kalahari Desert landscape and drainage **10**:373g

Ōkyo, full name MARUYAMA ŌKYO, also called MARUYAMA MASATAKA (1733–95), Japanese, founder of a school of painters that incorporated Occidental principles of realism with traditional Japanese style.

·painting style development **19**:238h

Olacaceae, flowering plant family of the order Santalales.

·characteristics and classification **16**:227e

Olaf, Saint: *see* Olaf II Haraldsson.

Olaf I Tryggvason (b. *c.* 964—d. *c.* 1000), Viking king of Norway (995–*c.* 1000), much celebrated in Scandinavian literature, who made the first effective effort to Christianize Norway.

Olaf, the great-grandson of the Norwegian king Harald I Fairhair and the son of Tryggvi Olafsson, a chieftain in southeastern Norway, was born soon after his father was killed by the Norwegian ruler Harald II Graycloak. According to legend, Olaf fled with his mother, Astrid, to the court of St. Vladimir, grand prince of Kiev and of all Russia, and was trained as a Viking warrior. In 991 he joined in the Viking attacks on England, which were resumed with the accession of Ethelred II the Unready to the English throne in 978. Ethelred sued for peace in 991, agreeing to pay large sums in tribute, and again when Olaf invaded with the Danish king Sweyn I Forkbeard in 994.

Already a Christian, Olaf was confirmed at Andover (now in Hampshire) in 994, with Ethelred, with whom he had been reconciled, as his godfather. Learning of the growing revolt against the Norwegian king Haakon the Great, Olaf returned to Norway and was accepted as king on Haakon's death in 995. He forcefully imposed Christianity on the areas under his control, the coast and the western islands, but had little influence in the interior. By commissioning missionaries and baptizing visiting dignitaries, he was able to introduce Christianity to the Shetland, Faroe, and Orkney islands and to Iceland and Greenland. (Christianity was adopted by the Icelandic parliament [Althing] *c.* 1000). Despite his religious zeal, however, he failed to establish lasting religious (or administrative) institutions in Norway.

Olaf met his death in the Battle of Svolder (*c.* 1000) at the hands of the Danish king

Sweyn I (*q.v.*), the Swedish king Olof Skötkonung, and Erik the Norwegian, earl of Lade. The battle is often retold in medieval Scandinavian poems. After his death large regions of the country reverted to foreign rule.
·Icelandic kings' sagas **16**:146c
·Norwegian political development **16**:307d
·Pope Sylvester II's demands **17**:899g
·Thangbrand and conversion of Iceland **8**:39h

Olaf (OLAV) **II Haraldsson,** commonly known as ST. OLAF (b. *c.* 995—d. July 29, 1030), first effective king of all Norway and the country's patron saint, who achieved a 12-year respite from Danish domination and greatly increased the acceptance of Christianity. His religious code of 1024 is considered Norway's first national legislation. The son of the lord Harald Grenske and a descendant of the Norwegian ruler Harald I Fairhair, Olaf was reared as a pagan. He fought against the English in 1009–11 but assisted the English ruler Ethelred II the Unready against the Danes in 1013. When the Danish king Sweyn (Svein) I gained the advantage in England, Olaf went to Spain and also to France, where he was baptized (1013).

Returning to Norway in 1015, Olaf conquered territory previously held by Denmark, Sweden, and the Norwegian earl Haakon of Lade; by 1016 he had consolidated his rule in all Norway. In the next 12 years he built his base of support among the aristocracy in the interior and pressed relentlessly for the acceptance of Christianity, using missionaries he brought from England. The Church of Norway (*q.v.*) may be dated from 1024, when Olaf and his ecclesiastical adviser, Bishop Grimkell, presented a religious code at Moster.

Olaf resolved his conflict with the Swedish king Olof Skötkonung by 1019 and joined forces with the King's son Anund Jakob when Canute, king of England and Denmark, threatened to conquer Norway. Canute's control of the trade routes to the west of Norway, and the prospect of his ruling more indirectly than Olaf had done, won the support of leading Norwegian chieftains. Canute forced Olaf to flee to Russia (1028), where the Norwegian ruler took refuge with his Swedish wife's relatives at Kiev.

Olaf attempted to reconquer Norway in 1030 with help from Anund Jakob but was defeated by a superior Norwegian peasant and Danish army in the Battle of Stiklestad (1030), one of the most celebrated battles in ancient Norse history. Olaf's popularity, his church work, and the aura of legend that surrounded his death, which was accompanied by miracles, led to his canonization the following year. His popularity spread rapidly; churches and shrines were constructed in his honour in England, Sweden, and Rome. He was the last Western saint accepted by the Eastern church.
·Canute's rebellion **3**:786b
·Icelandic kings' sagas **16**:146c
·missionary zeal and tyranny **8**:40a
·Norwegian political centralization **16**:307d

Olaf (OLAV) **III Haraldsson the Quiet,** Norwegian KYRRI (d. 1093, Norway), king of Norway (1066–93) who guided the nation through one of its most prosperous periods, maintaining an extended peace rare in medieval Norwegian history. He also strengthened the organization of the Norwegian church.

A son of King Harald III Hardraade, Olaf fought in the unsuccessful Norwegian invasion of England (1066) in which his father was killed. He subsequently sued for peace with the English king Harold II and returned to Norway to rule jointly with his brother, Magnus II; he became sole monarch on Magnus' death in 1069. In 1068 he concluded a peace treaty with the Danish king Sweyn (Svein) II, by which the Danish king gave up his plan to conquer Norway, and initiated a 25-year period of peace.

Olaf worked to give the Norwegian church a more stable organization, making peace with Pope Gregory VII and Adalbert (Adelbert), archbishop of Bremen and vicar for the Scandinavian countries, who had been an enemy of Olaf's father. Although he attempted to follow the organizational model of the continental churches, the Norwegian church was less influenced by Rome, and Olaf maintained personal control over the nation's clergy.

Olaf's granting of permanent areas to the four dioceses of the country encouraged urban growth. He built a number of churches and founded several towns, including the city of Bergen (*c.* 1070–75). His reign also saw the introduction to Norway of the manners and culture of the continental aristocracy.
·Scandinavian political development **16**:309d

Olaf IV, also spelled OLAV IV, king of Norway, reigned 1103–15. Because he ruled as a child and with two brothers, he is sometimes not counted as a king.
·Norwegian political development **16**:309d

Olaf (OLAV) **V (Håkonsson),** often counted as OLAF IV (1370–87), king of Denmark (1376–87) and Norway (1380–87).
·Margaret of Denmark, Norway, and Sweden **11**:493h
·Scandinavian political development **16**:309c

Olaf V, also spelled OLAV V (b. July 2, 1903, near Sandringham, Eng.), king of Norway from 1957, succeeding his father, King Haakon VII. Olaf was educated at the Norwegian military academy and at Oxford University in England. As crown prince he was a celebrated athlete and sportsman; he competed as a yachtsman in the 1928 Olympic Games. In 1929 Olaf was married to Princess Martha of Sweden, who died in 1954.

Olaf fled to England with the King and the government during the German invasion of Norway in 1940, and he was named head of the Norwegian armed forces in 1944. Olaf returned to Norway a few months before the King in 1945, serving briefly as regent. He again became regent in 1955 when his father suffered an accident, serving in that capacity until Haakon's death in 1957. As king, Olaf V visited many foreign countries.

Olaf (OLAV) **Guthfrithson** (d. 941), king of Dublin and Northumbria, whose invasion of England in 937 is commemorated in the Old English poem "The Battle of Brunanburh" (*q.v.*).
·English invasion failure **3**:203b

Ólafsfjördhur, town, northern Iceland, on a small inlet of Eyjafjördhur (fjord). A fishing port and herring-canning centre, it is linked to other parts of the island by road. Pop. (1977 est.) 1,158.
66°06′ N, 18°38′ W
·map, Iceland **9**:171

Ólafs saga helga ("St. Olaf's Saga"), saga of the life of St. Olaf in the *Heimskringla* (*q.v.; c.* 1220) by the Icelandic poet Snorri Sturluson.
·Icelandic saga tradition **10**:1118h
·kings' sagas **16**:146c

Ólafsson, Eggert (b. 1726, Snaefellsnes, Ice. —d. May 1768, at sea in Breidafjörder), poet and antiquarian, an outstanding figure in the history of Iceland's fight to preserve and revivify its language and culture. Ólafsson's major interests lay in natural history. His great work *Reise igiennem Island* (1772; "Journey through Iceland") recorded a scientific and cultural survey he made in 1752–57.

His poetry voices his zeal for a cultural and political renaissance of Iceland. It is of historical rather than of literary interest. In spite of its heavy and sometimes archaic style, his poetry had a strong emotional appeal to his countrymen, an appeal that was heightened when he and his bride were drowned on their honeymoon journey home. He became an idealized father figure for later generations of young Icelandic patriots.
·literary themes and works **10**:1177b

Ólafsson, Stefán (1620–88), Icelandic poet.
·Icelandic literature development **10**:1161f

ʿolam ha-ba (Hebrew: "the world to come"), Jewish theological term that historically has been interpreted either as "the world after death" or "the messianic millennium," when righteousness and justice will prevail in a reconstructed world. The latter interpretation stemmed from the teachings and exhortations of the prophets, especially during the period of the Second Temple of Jerusalem (516 BC–AD 70). Whatever the interpretation of *ʿolam ha-ba*, it meant for Jews the end of uncertainty, misery, and strife.

Jewish literature contrasts *ʿolam ha-ba* with *ʿolam ha-ze* ("this world"), a time to prove oneself worthy of participating in "the world to come."

ʿolam ha-ze (Hebrew: "this world"), Jewish theological term signifying man's present life on earth, as opposed to *ʿolam ha-ba* ("the world to come"). Historically, *ʿolam ha-ba* has been interpreted either as life after death or as the messianic millennium.

Olancho, department, eastern Honduras, bounded on the southeast by Nicaragua. The largest of Honduras' departments (9,402 sq mi [24,351 sq km]), Olancho comprises more than one-fifth of the national territory. The mountainous western third has most of the population; the rest of the area consists mostly of rainy, forested lowlands with no roads and few people. Agricultural production is largely in the mountain valleys. The department ranks first in Honduras in the production of cattle and swine and third in output of coffee, cotton, and beans. Other significant products are corn (maize), rice, potatoes, gold, and handicraft articles. Juticalpa (*q.v.*), the departmental capital and largest town, is linked with Tegucigalpa by an all-weather road. Pop. (1980 est.) 206,775.
·area and population table **8**:1057
·map, Honduras **8**:1058

Öland, island in the Baltic Sea, separated from the mainland of Sweden by Kalmarsund (Kalmar Sound). With an area of 518 sq mi (1,342 sq km), it is the largest Swedish island after Gotland. Administratively, Öland is included in the *län* (county) of Kalmar, and, together with the surrounding islets, it forms the *landskap* (province) of Öland. Its periphery of limestone and sand ridges encloses a desolate, almost barren tract. The southern portion, Alvaret, presents a surface of bare, characteristically weathered limestone. There are a few streams and one lake, Hornsjön.

On the narrow, alluvial coastland, sugar beets, rye, and potatoes are grown, and there is some cattle raising. Industries include quarrying, cement making, and sugar refining.

Beginning in 775, Öland is frequently mentioned in Scandinavian history, especially as a battleground in the wars between Denmark and Sweden. The only large town, Borgholm, contains the ruins of one of the finest castles and strongest fortresses in Sweden, dating from the 13th century or before. Pop. (1979 est.) *landskap*, 23,241.
56°45′ N, 16°38′ E
·map, Sweden **17**:849
·soil type and Baltic Sea's geography **2**:669b; map 668

Olathe, city, seat of Johnson County, northeastern Kansas, U.S., southwest of Kansas City. Founded in 1857 on the old Santa Fe Trail, it got its name through a misunderstanding of the Shawnee term for "beautiful." The town was raided by the guerrilla leader William C. Quantrill in 1862. Cowboy boots and farm machinery are the chief manufactures. The Kansas School for the Deaf was established there (1866). Nearby is a U.S. naval air station. Inc. 1868. Pop. (1980) 37,258.
38°53′ N, 94°49′ W
·map **18**:United States of America, Plate 9

Olaya Herrera, Enrique (1880–1937), Colombian diplomat and president from 1930 to 1934.
·Depression and ousting of Conservatives **4**:876a

Olbernhau, city, Karl-Marx-Stadt *Bezirk* (district), East Germany, on the upper Flöha River in the eastern Erzgebirge (Ore Mountains). First mentioned in 1346 as Kolonistendorf, the town has been noted since the 16th century for its handicrafts. Other industries include papermaking and matches. A regional centre for the eastern Erzgebirge, Olbernhau became a city in 1902. Pop. (1974) 13,658. 50°39′ N, 13°20′ E

Olbers, (Heinrich) Wilhelm (Matthäus) (b. Oct. 11, 1758, Arbergen, now in West Germany—d. March 2, 1840, Bremen), astronomer and physician who discovered the asteroids (minor planets) Pallas and Vesta as well as five comets. In 1779 Olbers devised a new method of calculating the orbits of comets. Two years later he opened his medical practice in Bremen, where he equipped the upper portion of his house for use as an observatory and devoted the greater part of each night to astronomy.

Olbers, detail from an engraving by an unknown artist
By courtesy of the trustees of the British Museum; photograph, J.R. Freeman & Co. Ltd.

He took a leading role in the search for a planet between Mars and Jupiter. After the Italian astronomer Giuseppe Piazzi had discovered the asteroid Ceres in 1801, only to lose track of it during an illness, Olbers rediscovered it one year later. In March 1802 he also discovered Pallas and became convinced that asteroids are the broken-up remnants of a medium-sized planet that once orbited in the asteroid belt region. This idea gained credence with the discovery of the asteroid Juno in 1804 by Karl Ludwig Harding of Germany and of Vesta in 1807 by Olbers; there was a steady stream of new discoveries later in the 19th century.

In 1811 Olbers formed the theory that the tail of a comet always points away from the Sun because of pressure from the Sun's radiation. (In the 20th century, radiation pressure from light was demonstrated in the laboratory.) Four years later he discovered the object now known as Olbers' Comet. In 1832 he predicted from observations of Biela's Comet that the Earth would pass through its tail. The prediction caused much tumult in Europe, but no catastrophic effects were noticed during the passage.

Olbers also proposed what is known as Olbers' paradox (*q.v.*).
·recognition of Bessel's genius **2**:870a

Olbers' paradox, in cosmology, was proposed in 1826 by the German astronomer Wilhelm Olbers: If stars are infinite in number and evenly distributed in space, the sky should be solidly bright with starlight in every direction; there should be no night or darkness on the surface of the Earth.

Olbers explained his own paradox by the obscuring effect of interstellar dust, which blotted out countless stars, letting the light of only a few reach Earth. By the 1970s, however, most astronomers considered that the night sky is dark because of the expansion of the universe, which reddens and dims the light from extremely distant objects and may carry some of them forever beyond man's sight. Other possible explanations exist.

Olbia, Greek colonial city founded in the 7th century BC at the mouth of the Bug River, near present-day Nikolayev, Ukrainian S.S.R.
·settlement, growth, and importance **8**:332c; map 335

Olbia, town, Sassari province, northeastern Sardinia, Italy, on the Golfo di Olbia, an inlet of the Tyrrhenian Sea. Originating as the Greek colony of Olbia, it later passed to the Romans and was the scene in 259 BC of a Roman victory over the Carthaginian general Hanno. Largely rebuilt in 1198 by Pisan colonists, who called it Terranova Pausania (a name it retained until 1939), it was an important centre of the medieval *giudicato* (judiciary circuit, a territorial division) of Gallura, the capital of which, Tempio Pausania, lies inland. There are traces of Phoenician and Roman tombs, and the Pisan Romanesque church of S. Simplicio is notable. Olbia is the principal Sardinian passenger port for connections with the Italian mainland at Civitavecchia, and trade, fishing, and corkworking are important. Pop. (1973 est.) mun., 26,400. 40°55′ N, 09°29′ E
·map, Italy **9**:1089
·map, Sardinia **16**:244

Olbracht, Ivan, pseudonym of KAMIL ZEMAN (1882–1952), Czech prose writer.
·Czech narrative prose **10**:1255e

Olbrich, Joseph (Maria) (b. Nov. 22, 1867, Troppau, Silesia, now Opava, Czech.—d. Aug. 8, 1908, Düsseldorf, now in West Germany), architect who was a cofounder of the Wiener Sezession, the Austrian manifestation of the Art Nouveau movement. Olbrich was a student of Otto Wagner, one of the founders of the modern architecture movement in Europe.

Olbrich designed the building in Vienna to house the exhibitions of the Sezession (1898–99). It has a blocklike simplicity, but floral Art Nouveau decoration was used on the metal cupola. In 1899 Olbrich was invited to join the artists' colony at Darmstadt established

Olbrich, 1901
By courtesy of the Bild-Archiv, Osterreichische Nationalbibliothek, Vienna

by the Grand Duke Ernest Louis. He designed six of the houses there, as well as a central hall for meetings and studios, which shows the influence of the Scottish Art Nouveau architect Charles Rennie Mackintosh. He also designed the Hochzeitsturm (1907; "Marriage Tower") at Darmstadt, which had rounded, finger-like projections on its roof suggestive of Art Nouveau but also had bands of windows denoting a distinctly modern trend.

Among Olbrich's last works were a house at Cologne-Marienburg (1908–09) and a department store in Düsseldorf (designed in 1906 and completed after his death).

Olcott, Henry Steel (b. Aug. 2, 1832, Orange, N.J.—d. Feb. 17, 1907, Adyar, Madras, India), author, attorney, and philosopher-proponent of a brotherhood of religions, was co-founder of the Theosophical Society, a religious sect incorporating aspects of Buddhism and Brahmanism.

Olcott was agricultural editor of the *New York Tribune* (1858–60), and with the rank of colonel he was special commissioner in the U.S. War and Navy departments (1863–66). He was admitted to the bar in 1866. With Helena Petrovna Blavatsky, William Q. Judge, and others he founded the Theosophical Society in 1875 and became its president. In 1878 he visited India when commissioned by Pres. Rutherford B. Hayes to report on trade relations. He settled in India in 1879 and with Madame Blavatsky established the permanent headquarters of the Theosophical Society of Adyar, Madras, in 1883. He assisted Annie Besant in establishing the Central Hindu College at Vārānasi (Benares). With her, he expounded their Theosophist ideas in appearances in India and Ceylon. Urging educational advancement upon Ceylon Buddhists, he saw three colleges and 250 schools established as a result of his efforts. Identified with Eastern philosophical thought, he helped revive Hindu philosophy; a pandit conferred on him the sacred thread of the Brahmin caste and adopted him as his *putra*.

Olcott edited the *Theosophist* (1888–1907). His *Buddhist Catechism* (1881) was translated into many languages.
·Theosophical Society foundation **18**:277e

old age (geology): *see* geomorphic cycle.

old age, invalidity, and survivor insurance programs: *see* social security.

old age, social aspects of **13**:546, the status and role of older people in modern society. Definitions of old age are not consistent with reference to biology, demography (conditions of mortality and morbidity), employment and retirement, and sociology. For statistical and public administrative purposes, however, old age is frequently defined as 60 or 65 years of age or older.

The text article covers the general demographic, economic, educational, residential, and familial characteristics of the aged; the social and psychological effects of aging; the public programs and policies for the aged; and the future status of the aged.

REFERENCES in other text articles:
·aged population statistics **1**:305h
·euthanasia legalization attempts **17**:779b
·social and welfare programs and services **16**:927a
social position in various societies
·African traditional social authority **1**:284c
·Anatolian age deference **1**:828f
·ancient Chinese respect emphasis **6**:320f
·Australian Aboriginal elder roles **2**:427a
·California Indians social patterns **3**:621c
·Congo elder's political power **4**:1121g
·Florida retirement leisure culture **7**:428d
·Galla age groups as tribal polity **6**:1014a
·Mexican Indian position of elder **13**:246d
·Taoist veneration of longevity **17**:1036d
·welfare programs' historical development **19**:743e

Old Age and Survivors' Insurance, in the U.S., program directed by the Social Security Administration.
·security program coverage and rationale **19**:744f

Old Age Assistance (OAA), in the U.S., program directed by the Social Security Administration.
·welfare and public assistance programs **19**:754c

Old and New (1929), film by Sergey Eisenstein, known as THE GENERAL LINE during production.
·Eisenstein's theory and technique **6**:517d

Old and the Young, The (1928), original Italian I VECCHI E I GIOVANI (1913), novel by Luigi Pirandello.
·theme and style **14**:469f

Old Bachelour, The (1693), first comedy of William Congreve.
·success and reasons for audience appeal **4**:1131e

Old Believers, Russian religious dissenters who refused to accept the liturgical reforms imposed upon the Russian Orthodox Church by the patriarch of Moscow Nikon (1652–58). Numbering millions of faithful in the 17th century, the Old Believers (Starovery), also called Staroobryadtsy (Old Ritualists) or Raskolniki (Schismatics), split into a number of different sects, of which several survived into modern times.

Patriarch Nikon faced the difficult problem of deciding on an authoritative source for the correction of the liturgical books in use in Russia. These books, used since the conversion of Rus' to Christianity in 988, were literal translations from the Greek into Old Slavic. In the course of centuries, manuscript copies of the translations, which were sometimes inaccurate and obscure at the start, were further mutilated by the mistakes of the scribes. Reform was difficult, for there was no agreement as to where the "ideal" or "original" text was to be found. The option taken by Patriarch Nikon was to follow exactly the texts and practices of the Greek Church as they existed in 1652, the beginning of his reign, and to this effect he ordered the printing of new liturgical books following the Greek pattern. This implied the adoption in Russia of Greek usages, Greek forms of clerical dress, and a change in the manner of crossing oneself: three fingers were to be used instead of two. The reform, obligatory for all, was considered "necessary for salvation" and was supported by Tsar Alexis Romanov.

Opposition to Nikon's reforms was led by a group of Muscovite priests, notably the archpriest Avvakum Petrovich. Even after the deposition of Nikon (1658), who broached too strong a challenge to the Tsar's authority, a series of church councils culminating in that of 1666–67 officially endorsed the liturgical reforms and anathematized the dissenters. Several of them, including Avvakum, were executed.

The dissenters were most numerous in the inaccessible regions of north and east Russia (but later also in Moscow itself) and were important in the colonization of these remote areas. Opposed to all change, they strongly resisted the Western innovations introduced by Peter I, whom they regarded as Antichrist. Having no episcopal hierarchy, they split into two groups. One group, the Popovtsy (priestly sects), sought to attract ordained priests and were able to set up an episcopate in the 19th century. The other, the Bezpopovtsy (priestless sects), renounced priests and all sacraments, except Baptism. Many other sects developed out of these groups, some with practices considered extravagant.

The Old Believers benefitted from the edict of toleration (April 17, 1905), and most groups survived the Russian Revolution of 1917; the branches of the Popovtsy that had established their own hierarchies succeeded in becoming registered and thus officially recognized by the Soviet state. Known to be still in existence in the early 1970s were the convention of Belaya Krinitsa, with its centre in the Rogozhski Cemetery community, Moscow (estimated membership 800,000); the Old Believer Church of the Ancient Orthodox Christians (derived from the so-called Beglopopovtsy, Fugitive Priests), with its centre at Kuybyshev; and the Yedinovertsy (Those United in Faith), a group dating from the early 19th century that is under the jurisdiction of the Moscow patriarchate and has a church in Moscow.

Two large communities of Bezpopovtsy in Moscow, the Preobrazheniye (Transfiguration) cemetery group and the so-called Pomortsy, together with those in Lithuania (centred in Vilnius) and in Latvia (centred in Riga), as well as numerous small groups elsewhere, are officially recognized. Little is known, however, of the Old Believer settlements supposed to exist in Siberia, the Urals, Kazakhstan, and the Altai. Some Old Believers outside Russia have been resettled: 11,250 from China to Brazil (1958–61) and from Turkey. In the latter group 1,000 returned to the Soviet Union, and 250 went to the United States. These latter groups have remained especially faithful to their 17th-century way of life and like all Old Believers maintain a remarkably efficient economic management.

In 1971 the Council of the Russian Orthodox Church completely rescinded all the anathemas of the 17th century and recognized the full validity of the old rites.
·liturgical issue of Church Slavonic **16**:869g
·Nikon reform opposition **16**:49f
·reform opposition and anathematization **13**:102b
·Russian 17th-century idea of orthodoxy **6**:157e

Old Bering Sea culture, Eskimo culture of northwest Alaska, St. Lawrence Island, and northeastern Siberia, dating from the first half of the 1st millennium AD. These Eskimo were maritime people who lived in permanent, semi-subterranean houses and who depended for their livelihood mainly on seals, walrus, birds, and fish.

Old Bulgarian language: *see* Old Church Slavonic.

Oldbury, borough (1935) in the metropolitan county of West Midlands (until 1974 it was in the former Worcestershire), England. The *burh* (Anglo-Saxon: stronghold) dates from before the Norman Conquest (1066), and "Ye Big House" is an example of Queen Anne (1665–1714) architecture. Blast furnaces have been important in the modern development of the town, and the principal contemporary industries produce steel tubes, chemicals, and plastics. Latest census 53,948.
52°30′ N, 2°00′ W

Old Castile (Spain): *see* Castilla la Vieja.

Oldcastle, Sir John (b. *c.* 1378, Herefordshire—d. Dec. 14, 1417, London), distinguished soldier and martyred leader of the Lollards, a late medieval English sect that opposed Roman Catholicism. He was an approximate model for 16th-century English dramatic characters, including Shakespeare's Falstaff.

The son of Sir Richard Oldcastle, he fought for England in the Scottish campaign of 1400 and during the Welsh wars gained the friendship of King Henry IV's son Henry, prince of Wales. In 1404 Oldcastle represented Herefordshire in Parliament and served (1406–07) as his county's sheriff. By his marriage in 1408 to Joan, heiress of John, 3rd Lord Cobham, Oldcastle entered nobility and in 1409 was summoned to the House of Lords as a baron. His tendencies toward Lollardy have been traced to the following year. In 1413 he was

Oldcastle, imaginary portrait from the frontispiece of John Balle's *Chronicle*, 1584

By courtesy of the trustees of the British Museum; photograph, J.R. Freeman & Co. Ltd.

indicted by a convocation, presided over by Archbishop Thomas Arundel of Canterbury, for maintaining both Lollard preachers and their opinions. His amicable relationship with the prince of Wales, now Henry V, earned him special consideration, but he failed to honour the King's appeals to submit and was brought to trial the same year. Unyielding in his views, Oldcastle denied the necessity of penance and confession, declaring that popes, cardinals, and bishops could not dictate belief in such matters. He also rejected transubstantiation, the Catholic doctrine of the Eucharist by which the elements of bread and wine assume the substance of Christ's body and blood. Convicted as a heretic, Oldcastle was granted a stay of execution by the King for 40 days and was imprisoned in the Tower of London. Within a month he escaped to refuge with the Lollard bookseller William Fisher at Smithfield, where he conspired to kidnap the King at Kent while Lollards answered a summons to assemble at St. Giles's Fields, near London, the night of Jan. 9, 1414. The King was warned by his agents, and the small group of Lollards in assembly were captured or dispersed. Oldcastle again escaped, evading capture until November 1417. Parliament then reiterated his condemnation and penalty, and on December 14 he was hanged over a fire that consumed the gallows. He was celebrated by John Foxe in his *Book of Martyrs* (1563). In *The Famous Victories of Henry the fifth*, the anonymous source play for Shakespeare's *Henry IV*, Sir John appears briefly as a friend of Prince Hal (or Henry). Shakespeare kept the name for the first version of his play, but changed it to Falstaff before registering it in 1598, though he rendered the character more boisterous than Oldcastle was. Sir John was also the central figure in the anonymous play *The First Part of the True and Honorable Historie, of the Life of Sir John Old-castle, the Good Lord Cobham*, registered in 1600.
·Henry V rebellion plot **3**:216g

Old Catholic churches 13:552, a term used most correctly to describe well-organized local churches that claim to have maintained the essentials of Christian doctrine and the historic succession of the episcopate, but not in communion with the bishop (pope) of Rome. Less correctly, the term is used to describe certain churches that have come into existence as a result of nationalistic movements and are sometimes outside the main stream of Christianity. The term is used incorrectly in conjunction with a large number of small church bodies, usually ephemeral, that have been led by individuals who in one way or another have secured for themselves episcopal consecration and have often named their own church bodies Old Catholic.

The text article covers the history of these churches, the nationalistic church movements, other movements headed by *episcopi vagantes* (wandering bishops), and the doctrines, practices, and organization of the Old Catholic churches. It summarizes the role of the Old Catholic churches in the modern ecumenical movement.

REFERENCES in other text articles:
·ecumenical exchange with Constantinople **6**:295b
·Ultramontanism victorious at Vatican I **14**:485c

RELATED ENTRIES in the *Ready Reference and Index:*
apostolic succession; bishop; episcopi vagantes; Jansenist Church of Holland; Philippine Independent Church; Polish National Catholic Church of America; Vatican Council, first

Old Church Slavonic, also called OLD BULGARIAN or OLD SLAVONIC, Slavic language based primarily on the Macedonian (South Slavic) dialects around Thessalonica (Thessaloníki). It was used in the 9th century by the missionaries SS. Cyril (Constantine) and Methodius, who were natives of Thessalonica, for preaching to the Moravian Slavs and for translating the Bible into Slavic. This first Slavic literary language, written in two alphabets known as Glagolitic and Cyrillic (the invention of Glagolitic has been traditionally ascribed to St. Cyril), was readily adopted in other Slavic regions, where, with local modifications, it remained the religious and literary language of Orthodox Slavs throughout the Middle Ages.

The language as it appeared after the 12th century in its various local forms is known as Church Slavonic; this language has continued as a liturgical language into modern times. It continued to be written by the Serbs and Bulgarians until the 19th century and had significant influence on the modern Slavic languages, especially on the Russian literary language that grew out of a compromise style incorporating many Church Slavonic elements into the native Russian vernacular.
·Bible translation manuscripts **2**:894e
·literary usage in Balkan countries **10**:1127e
·modern Slavic literary influence **16**:869b
·religious and secular literature **10**:1074f

Old City Wall, or WALL OF SULEIMAN, in Jerusalem, surrounds the Old City, which is a small irregular quadrilateral on the east side of the main city.
·reconstruction and religious importance **10**:143a

Old Comedy, initial phase of Greek comedy (*c.* 5th century BC), known through the works of Aristophanes, that is characterized by an exuberant and high-spirited satire of public persons and affairs. Composed of song, dance, personal invective, and buffoonery, the plays also include outspoken political criticism and comment on literary and philosophical topics. The plays, consisting of loosely related episodes, were first performed in Athens for the religious festival of Dionysus. They gradually took on a six-part structure: an introduction, in which the basic fantasy is explained and developed; the *parodos*, entry of the chorus; the *parabasis*, in which the chorus addresses the audience on the topics of the day and hurls scurrilous criticism at prominent citizens; the contest, or *agon*, a ritualized debate between opposing principles or stock characters; a series of farcical scenes; and a final banquet or wedding. The chorus often were dressed as animals while the characters wore street dress and masks with grotesquely exaggerated features.

Old Comedy sometimes is called Aristophanic comedy, after its most famous exponent, whose 11 surviving plays include *The Clouds* (423 BC), a satire on the misuse of philosophical argument directed chiefly against Socrates, and *The Frogs* (405 BC), a satire on Greek drama directed chiefly against Euripides. Other Old Comedy writers include Cratinus, Crates, Pherecrates, and Eupolis.

Athens' defeat in the Peloponnesian War marked the end of Old Comedy, because free speech was curtailed and a sense of disillusionment with the heroes and gods who had played a prominent role in Old Comedy became marked.
·actor–audience relationship **18**:253b
·Aristophanic comic style **4**:962b
·costume conventions of Greek drama **17**:560b
·Greek literature development **10**:1092d

Old Copper, North American cultural and archaeological period specific to the Upper Great Lakes region, named from the presence of copper implements.
·dating and artifacts **13**:217h

Old Cordilleran culture, ancient North American culture of the Pacific Northwest that appeared about 9000 or 10,000 BC and persisted until about 5000 BC in some areas. Subsistence was based on hunting, fishing, and gathering. Simple willow-leaf-shaped, bipointed projectile points are characteristic artifacts.

Old Curiosity Shop, The (1841), novel by Charles Dickens about the misfortunes of Nell Trent (Little Nell) and her grandfather, who loses his curiosity shop through obsessive gambling.
·oppression of child and sentimentality **5**:707d

Old Czechs, moderate group in late-19th-century Czech politics.
·Masaryk's political career **11**:572e

Old Delhi (India): *see* Delhi.

Oldenbarnevelt, Johan van 13:555 (b. Sept. 14, 1547, Amersfoort, Neth.—d. May 13, 1619, The Hague), lawyer, statesman, and, after William I the Silent, the second founding father of an independent Netherlands.

Abstract of text biography. During his eventful career, Oldenbarnevelt participated in the revolt of the Netherlands against Spain (1568), worked to consolidate a Dutch commonwealth, and engaged in a fateful controversy with doctrinaire Calvinists. With William the Silent, prince of Orange, he helped negotiate the Union of Utrecht (1579), the constitutional basis of the Dutch Republic. Named the union's attorney general after William's assassination, he mobilized Dutch forces under William's son, Maurice of Nassau, and devised the anti-Spanish triple alliance with France and England (1596). In the Twelve Years' Truce (1609) he reaffirmed Holland's dominant role in the republic. In later years, he engaged in a bitter quarrel with the strict Calvinist Counter-Remonstrants and was executed on a charge of subverting religion.

REFERENCES in other text articles:
·Dutch religious disputes **8**:431d
·Maurice of Nassau's ruling triumvirate **11**:709d
·Orange military alliance and political opposition **11**:144f *passim* to 146b

Oldenburg, former state of northwestern Germany, now located in the Niedersachsen *Land* of the Federal Republic of Germany. From the early 12th century, a line of counts established themselves at Oldenburg, which developed into a city. Count Christian of Oldenburg was elected to the Danish throne in 1448; he also became king of Norway and, for some years, of Sweden, in 1450 and 1457, respectively, and acquired the duchy of Schleswig and the county of Holstein in 1460. In 1454 he ceded Oldenburg to his brother Gerhard, whose descendants acquired nearby lordships; for his neutrality in the Thirty Years' War, Count Anton Günther received from Emperor Ferdinand II the right to collect tolls from ships passing Elsfleth on the Weser. When Gerhard's line died out in 1667, the territory passed to the Danish crown. Emperor Paul I of Russia acquired it in 1773 but ceded it to his cousin Frederick Augustus, who held the bishopric of Lübeck and was then created duke of Oldenburg by the Holy Roman emperor Joseph II. Oldenburg became a grand duchy in the 19th century; it joined the Zollverein (German Customs Union) in 1853, favoured Prussia in the Seven Weeks' War (1866), and joined the North German Confederation in 1867 and the German *Reich* in 1871. With the adoption of the Weimar Constitution in 1919, the grand ducal regime was replaced by an elected *Land* government. In 1933 Hitler made Oldenburg the centre of a large *Gau* (administrative district).
·annexation by Napoleon **1**:474g

Oldenburg, city, Niedersachsen (Lower Saxony) *Land* (state), northwestern West Germany, at the junction of the Hunte River and the Hunte–Ems Canal. It is at the eastern approach to the North Sea coastal district of Ostfriesland (East Frisia). First mentioned in 1108 and chartered in 1345, it was the seat of the counts and dukes of Oldenburg and then the capital of the former *Land* of Oldenburg, from 1918 to 1946. Notable landmarks include the grand-ducal palace (1607–15), which now houses the provincial museum of art and culture, and the Lamberti Church (1270; rebuilt 1790–97). It has a state theatre, museums, art galleries, botanical gardens, and academies of engineering, administration, and economy. As an agricultural market centre for Ostfriesland, it has important cattle and horse auctions and one of Europe's largest meat-processing factories. Other industries include shipbuilding, glassmaking, and textile manufacture. It has shipping communications with Bremerhaven at the Weser estuary and with the Ruhr. Pop. (1970 est.) 131,400.
53°08′ N, 8°13′ E
·map, Federal Republic of Germany **8**:46
·transference of bishopric to Lübeck **8**:776g

Oldenburg, Christian, count of: *see* Christian I.

Oldenburg, Claes (Thure) (b. Jan. 28, 1929, Stockholm), sculptor associated with the Pop art movement in the United States, best known for his giant, soft sculptures of everyday objects.

Much of his early life was spent in the U.S., Sweden, and Norway, a result of moves his fa-

Oldenburg, photograph by Arnold Newman, 1967

ther made as a Swedish consular official. In his unsettled childhood, fantasy played a large part, exerting an important influence on his later work. He was educated at Yale University (1946–50), where writing was his main interest. In 1952–54 he attended the school of the Art Institute of Chicago. In 1956 he moved to New York City, where he became fascinated with the elements of street life: store windows, graffiti, advertisements, and trash. An awareness of the sculptural possibilities of these objects led to a shift in interest from painting to sculpture. In 1960–61 he created "The Store," a collection of painted plaster copies of food, clothing, jewelry, and other items. Renting an actual store, he stocked it with his constructions. In 1962 he began creating a series of happenings; *i.e.*, experimental presentations involving sound, movement, objects, and people. For some of his happenings Oldenburg created giant objects made of cloth stuffed with paper or rags. In 1962 he exhibited a version of his store in which there were huge canvas-covered, foam-rubber sculptures of an ice-cream cone, a hamburger, and a slice of cake.

These interests led to the work for which Oldenburg is best known: soft sculptures. Like other artists of the Pop art (*q.v.*) movement, he chose as his subjects the banal products of consumer life. He was careful, however, to choose objects with close human associations, and his use of soft, yielding vinyl gave the objects human, often sexual, overtones.

An exhibition of Oldenburg's work in 1966 in New York City included, in addition to his soft sculptures, a series of drawings and watercolours that he called "Colossal Monuments." His early monumental proposals remained unbuilt (such as the giant vacuum cleaner for the Battery in New York City, 1965; "Bat Spinning at the Speed of Light" for his alma mater, the Latin School of Chicago, 1967; and a colossal "Windshield Wiper" for Chicago's Grant Park, 1967); but in 1969 his "Lipstick (Ascending) on Caterpillar Tracks" was placed surreptitiously on the Yale University campus, remaining there until 1970, when it was removed to be rebuilt for its permanent home at Morse College, elsewhere on the campus. This began a series of successes, such as "Clothespin" (1976) in Philadelphia, "Colossal Ashtray with Fagends" at Pompidou Centre in Paris, and "Batcolumn" (1977), provided by the art-in-architecture program of the federal government for its Social Security Administration office building in Chicago.

·Pop art idiom **19**:483g
·sculpture materials and techniques **16**:426h; illus. 427
·United States cultural milieu **18**:942b
·use of Casein colours **13**:879h

Oldenburg, Lutheran Church of, independent Lutheran church in Oldenburg, now a district in the *Land* (state) of Niedersachsen, W.Ger. Pastors who had accepted the Lutheran faith were established in Oldenburg during the Protestant Reformation in Germany, and in 1573 an order for church government and the Lutheran confessions were accepted for the church. Until the German Republic was established after the end of World War I (1918), the church was governed by the secular head of state. After 1918 it became independent of the state, and the system of church government was reorganized. During the Nazi period (1933–45), the church attempted to resist the efforts of the secular government to control it, and after the end of World War II it experienced a period of renewal.

The head of the church is the bishop. Congregations belong to districts, each of which is headed by a superintendent. The church is a member of the Lutheran World Federation and of the Evangelical Church in Germany (EKD), a federation of Lutheran, Reformed, and United (Lutheran and Reformed) territorial churches; but it did not become part of the United Evangelical Lutheran Church of Germany, a union of Lutheran territorial churches (1948).

Old English (ANGLO-SAXON) **language,** spoken and written in England before 1100, the ancestor of Middle English (*see* Middle English language) and Modern English. Scholars place Old English in the Anglo-Frisian group of West Germanic languages. Four dialects of the Old English language are known: Northumbrian in northern England and southeastern Scotland; Mercian in central England; Kentish in southeastern England; and West Saxon in southern and southwestern England. Mercian and Northumbrian are often classed together as the Anglian dialects. Most extant Old English writings are in the West Saxon dialect; the first great period of literary activity occurred during the reign of King Alfred the Great in the 9th century.

In contrast to Modern English, Old English had three genders (masculine, feminine, neuter) in the noun and adjective and inflected nouns, pronouns, and adjectives for case. Noun and adjective paradigms contained four cases—nominative, genitive, dative, and accusative—while pronouns also had forms for the instrumental case. A greater proportion of Old English verbs were strong verbs (sometimes called irregular verbs in grammars of present-day English), such as Modern English "sing, sang, sung," than is the case in Modern English.

·Bible translation developments **2**:889f
·characteristics and history **6**:879g; map 880
·Germanic, Romance, and Celtic elements **6**:869c
·Germanic comparative features **8**:16e
·Scotland's linguistic development **3**:234d

Old English (ANGLO-SAXON) **poetry,** earliest surviving extensive body of verse in a European vernacular, composed from the mid-6th to the end of the 10th century, during the period when the Anglo-Saxons (settlers of Germanic descent) were dominant in England. Remarkable for its high quality and variety, it is the product of two disparate cultural traditions, the ancient heroic oral tradition of the Germanic tribes and the Latin and Biblical tradition of the early medieval church.

In addition to heroic poems and lives of saints, the corpus of Old English verse, of which about 30,000 lines are extant, includes some vivid and poignant lyrics and a number of religious allegories and scriptural paraphrases. There are also "gnomic verses," which embody folk wisdom in the form of proverbs, and the numerous "riddles," which commonly describe familiar utensils or the birds, animals, and other natural features of the English countryside.

Old English verse is patterned on the Germanic four-stress alliterative line. Rhyme is infrequent, although it occurs in a few instances; "The Rhyming Poem" of 87 lines is extant. Except for the fragmentary "Hymn" of the illiterate herdsman Caedmon, celebrated as the first poem of the English language, and four poems signed by Cynewulf, authorship is unknown. The highest achievement of the period is *Beowulf.* Almost all Old English poetry is preserved in four manuscripts: the Beowulf manuscript, the Caedmon (or Junius) manuscript, the Exeter Book, and the Vercelli Book (*qq.v.*). *See also* Beowulf; Battle of Brunanburh, The; Battle of Maldon, The; Caedmon; Cynewulf; Deor; Dream of the Rood, The; Husband's Message, The; Widsith. *Major ref.* **10**:1107c

·prosody tradition and development **15**:70g

Old English (ANGLO-SAXON) **prose,** earliest surviving English prose, written in the period *c.* 600–*c.* 1100. *Major ref.* **10**:1107g

Old English sheep dog, shaggy working dog developed in early-18th-century England and used primarily in driving sheep and cattle

Old English sheep dog

Sally Anne Thompson—EB Inc.

to market. A compact dog with a shuffling, bearlike gait, the Old English sheep dog stands 56 to 66 centimetres (22 to 26 inches) and weighs 25 to 30 kilograms (55 to 66 pounds). Its dense coat is weather resistant and long enough to cover the eyes, though not to obscure totally the dog's vision, which is no worse than that of any other breed. The coat may be gray or blue gray, with or without white markings, and it yields combings that can be made into a type of wool. The dog is often called "bobtail" because its tail is removed soon after birth.

old face type, also called OLD STYLE TYPE, 18th-century type style.

·type classification and development **18**:813b; illus.

Old Faithful, geyser, Yellowstone National Park (*q.v.*).

·eruption time considerations **8**:134f; illus.

Oldfield, Barney, full name BERNA ELI OLDFIELD (b. Jan. 29, 1878, Wauseon, Ohio—d. Oct. 4, 1946, Beverly Hills, Calif.), automobile racing driver, the apotheosis of speed in the first two decades of the 20th century. A bicycle racer from 1894, and briefly a professional boxer, he was hired in 1902 as chief mechanic for Henry Ford's racing team. He soon became the team's driver and achieved fame by guiding the Ford-Cooper "999" to two victories over Alexander Winton's supposedly invincible "Bullet." On June 15, 1903, at Indianapolis, he accomplished the first mile-a-minute performance in an automobile (59.6 sec); in August 1903 he drove five miles in 4 min 55 sec. At Daytona Beach, Fla., March 16, 1910, with a "Blitzen" Benz, he set a world speed record of 131.724 mph. Despite his success he came to dislike auto racing, calling the sport a "Roman circus." After his retirement in 1918 he remained prominent as a driving-safety advocate.

Old Finns, in late-19th- and early-20th-century Finland, then under Imperial Russian rule, the moderate remnant of the Finnish Party (*see* Fennoman movement and party), which chose compliance with Russia's measures to set aside Finland's constitutional rights within the empire.

The Old Finns' compliance led to the breaking away of the "constitutionalist" Young Finns (*q.v.*) from the Finnish Party, but it also led to a 1902 Russian decree granting the Finnish language equality with Swedish as Finland's official language, thus accomplishing the primary aim of the Finnish Party. The Old Finns dominated the Finnish Senate until 1909, when Russification measures finally indicated the bankruptcy of the strategy of compliance. With Finland's achievement of independence in 1918, the Old Finns disbanded, many joining the newly formed National Union Party.

Old Frisian language: *see* Frisian language.

Old Fritz (king of Prussia): *see* Frederick II the Great, of Prussia.

Old German Baptist Brethren, conservative Brethren church that continues traditional Brethren practices. It was established in 1881 by former members of the German Baptist Brethren (now the Church of the Brethren) who left that church when it began adopting what were viewed as more modern practices. The Old German Baptist Brethren do not support missions or educational institutions, do not have Sunday schools, and do not require that their clergy be educated. Members are encouraged to dress plainly, abstain from alcoholic liquors, and live simply. In church government, the Annual Conference is the highest authority, and its decisions are strictly followed. The church allows only its own members to take part in Holy Communion.

In the mid-1960s the church had about 4,200 members.

Old Glory (U.S. flag): *see* Stars and Stripes.

Oldham, borough (1849) and former county borough (1888–1974) of the metropolitan county of Greater Manchester (until 1974 in Lancashire), England, on the northeast periphery of the metropolitan complex centred on Manchester. It lies on the western edge of the Pennines, the upland "spine" of the North of England, near the source of the River Medlock, and was named after the Oldham family who lived in Werneth Hall during the Middle Ages. Linen manufacture was introduced to Oldham in 1630, at which time it was an agricultural town producing wool, but its real growth came with the adoption of Richard Arkwright's inventions for cotton spinning; in the 19th century it became a major British cotton-spinning town. Its contemporary industries are more diversified, especially in the sphere of engineering, and it retains important market functions. Notable buildings within the town are the parish church, rebuilt in 1833 in Early English style, and the town hall. Hulme Grammar School was founded in 1606, and Henshaw's Bluecoat School opened in 1834. Within the urban area are several large parks: the largest, Alexandra Park, covers 60 ac (24 ha). Pop. (1971 prelim.) 105,705.
53°33′ N, 2°7′ W

·map, United Kingdom **18**:866

Oldham, John (*c.* 1600–36), English colonist in North America, explored the Connecticut River and wrote a report of his discoveries that induced colonists from Massachusetts to found the first English settlements in Connecticut.

Oldham, John (b. Aug. 9, 1653, Shipton Moyne, Gloucestershire—d. Dec. 9, 1683, Holm Pierrepont, near Nottingham), pioneer of the imitation of classical satire in English. He took the B.A. degree at Oxford in 1674 and returned home, probably to teach at his father's school. In 1676 he became an usher at Croydon School under the headmastership of John Shepheard.

His poems attracted the attention of the Earl of Rochester, who visited him at Croydon and is said to have "much delighted" in his poetry. Oldham's imitation of Moschus' elegy on Bion at Rochester's death contains a touching expression of his gratitude to him. In 1677 he attempted, apparently unsuccessfully, to win recognition at court by writing a poem on the marriage of the Princess Mary to William of Orange. The remainder of his brief life was divided between tutoring noblemen's children and residence in London, where he was on the fringe of the "court wits" and where he met John Dryden, who lamented that Oldham was "too little, and too lately known" by him and who mourned him in a noble elegy.

Oldham has a notable place in the development of Augustan poetry. The four *Satyrs Upon the Jesuits* (1681), including "Garnet's Ghost," previously published as a broadsheet in 1679, constitute his most widely known work. They are forceful but melodramatic, crowded with coarse images and uneven versification, an attempt to imitate the invective of Juvenal. Like Rochester, Oldham appreciated and utilized Nicolas Boileau's anachronistic devices in his "imitations" of Horace and Juvenal. His satires have the novelty of being directed toward general subjects rather than being personal lampoons. His classical rhetoric sometimes makes his pieces heavy and cumbersome, but there are occasional flashes of brilliant poetry. There is vigour and a fine note of independence in almost everything he wrote.

Oldham, Richard Dixon (b. July 31, 1858, England—d. July 15, 1936), geologist and seismologist who identified the Earth's core from seismic data in 1906. He was a member of the Geological Survey of India from 1879 until 1903, when he became director of the Indian Museum in Calcutta. Oldham also made important contributions to early thought on earthquake and seismic phenomena.

·earthquake record studies **6**:86a

Oldham's coupling, a coupling for parallel shafts slightly out of line consisting of a disk on the end of each shaft and an intermediate disk having two mutually perpendicular feathers on opposite sides that engage slots in the respective shaft disks.

·design and application **11**:246f; illus.

Old Harbour, town and Caribbean port, Parish of St. Catherine, south Jamaica, west of Kingston. Originally called Esquivel after its Spanish founder, it was once Spanish Town's second port, when the latter was capital of Jamaica, and was famous for shipbuilding. After a period of decline it is now important for shipping bauxite as well as sugarcane, tropical fruit, and coffee. There is a U.S. naval base, leased in 1940, nearby. Latest census 4,192.
17°56′ N, 77°07′ W

·map, Jamaica **10**:16

Old High German, collective term for the West Germanic dialects spoken in the highlands of southern Germany, Switzerland, and Austria until the end of the 11th century. The feature by which High German differs most noticeably from the other West Germanic languages is its shift of the *p*, *t*, and *k* sounds to *ff*, *ss*, and *hh*, respectively, after vowels and to *pf*, *tz*, and, in Upper German, *kh* under most other conditions.

In addition to Alemannic and Bavarian, the Upper German dialects of Old High German, a number of Franconian (Frankish) dialects also existed, among which were East Franconian and Rhenish Franconian, spoken just north of the Upper German area, and the Central Franconian dialects spoken along the Moselle and Rhine rivers to the northern borders of the High German speech area.

Important literary works in Old High German include Otfrid's 9th-century poem *Evangelienbuch* ("Book of the Gospels") in the South Rhenish Franconian dialect, the 9th-century religious poem *Muspilli* in the Bavarian dialect, the translations by Notker Labeo from the 10th and 11th centuries in the Alemannic dialect, and the Old High German translation of Tatian's Gospel harmony from the 9th century in the East Franconian dialect. The *Hildebrandslied* ("Song of Hildebrand") fragment from the 8th century is written in an Upper German dialect but also includes Old Saxon elements. The language of Middle High German literature was descended mostly from the Upper German dialects, while modern standard High German is descended mostly from the East Franconian dialect. *See also* Old Saxon; Middle High German; High German; Swiss German; German language; Yiddish language.

·Franconian dialect distribution **8**:55a
·Germanic comparative features **8**:16e
·history and developments **8**:24e

Old Icelandic language: *see* Old Norse.

Old-Katholieke Kerk van Nederland: *see* Jansenist Church of Holland.

Old Kingdom, or PYRAMID AGE (3rd to 8th dynasties, *c.* 2686–*c.* 2160 BC) of Egypt. During this period the Pyramids, which served as the royal burial places, symbolized at first the absolute sovereignty of the king, and later, as their size and expense decreased, the gradual lessening of the king's power. Texts from this period recorded royal expeditions to Sinai, Libya, and Nubia, as well as trading relations with Lebanon. Evidence of the growth of a powerful provincial nobility during the 5th and 6th dynasties suggests that the Old Kingdom probably ended in civil war. *Major ref.* **6**:465b

·diadem design from 4th dynasty tomb **10**:167h
·dress styles of men and women **5**:1016g; illus. 1017
·Egyptian religious system development **6**:504c
·floral decorations evidence **7**:414g
·government administration by pharaoh **6**:502a
·Memphis as capital and cultural centre **11**:895d
·politics, conquests, and architecture **6**:465g
·sunken relief sculpture illus. **16**:433
·visual art forms and social role **19**:249h

Old Kingdom, period of Hittite history, *c.* 1700–*c.* 1500 BC.

·Anatolian Hittite historical records **1**:816h

Old Low German language: *see* Old Saxon.

Old Maid, a simple card game popular with young children. Two or more persons may play. One queen is discarded from a regular 52-card pack. The cards are then dealt one at a time or divided into approximately equal packets for each player; it does not matter if this rough method of "dealing" results in some inequality in the number of cards each receives. Each player examines his hand, pairing up as many cards as possible and discarding the matched pairs face up on the table. There is no need to conceal one's cards while sorting; in fact, players may help one another pick out their pairs.

After all pairs have been discarded, each player mixes his remaining unpaired cards (behind his back or in any other manner that will conceal them from the player at his left). To begin play, one player presents his cards face down to the player at his left, who draws one card and adds it to his own hand. If it matches a card he already has, he discards the new pair, shuffles his remaining cards, and presents them in turn, face down, to the player at his left. Play continues in this way, each person in turn drawing a card from the player at his right, until only the odd queen remains. The player left with the queen is "old maid" and loses the game.

Old Man and the Medal, The (1967), English title of LE VIEUX NÈGRE ET LA MEDAILLE (1956), novel by Ferdinand Oyona.

·purpose and theme **1**:239d

Old Man and the Sea, The (1952), short novel by Ernest Hemingway, the heroic story of an aged Cuban fisherman's long struggle to gaff a giant marlin, only to have it eaten by voracious sharks on the long voyage home. The novel was awarded the Pulitzer Prize in fiction (1953) and was instrumental in winning for Hemingway the Nobel Prize (1954).

·story line and critical acclaim **8**:758b

old man cactus, usually *Cephalocereus senilis*, a columnar species of the family Cactaceae. *Cephalocereus*, one of the most widespread cactus genera, contains about 50 species native to subtropical and tropical America including the West Indies. (Related genera such as *Pilocereus* and *Neobuxbaumia* are sometimes included.)

C. senilis, with wisps of whitish hair along its stem, is a most popular potted plant and grows outdoors well in Mediterranean climates. It must be 6 metres (about 20 feet) tall to flower and can grow to twice that height. Other attractive forms such as woolly torch (*C. palmeri*) flower at about 60 centimetres (2 feet). The flat-faced flowers are produced from a mass of long wool and bristles capping the stem or bearding one side of it, depending on the species. Flowers are night blooming in *C. senilis*, pink outside and white within.

Old man cactus (*Cephalocereus senilis*); a constriction about the middle has been applied by the grower to each of these specimens to accentuate their "human" appearance
Annan Photo Features

Other hairy cacti in cultivation include: golden old man (*C. chrysacanthus*), old man of the Andes (*Espostoa lanata* or *Borzicactus celsianus*), old woman (*Mammillaria hahniana*), Chilean old lady (*Neoporteria senilis*), old man of the mountain (*Borzicactus trollii*).

Old Man of the Mountain (Syrian chief): *see* Assassins; Sinan, as-; Rashīd ad-Dīn.

Oldman River, in southern Alberta, Canada, one of the major headstreams of the South Saskatchewan River. Rising in the Canadian Rockies west of Lethbridge from several sources, it flows eastward through the city and joins the Bow River to form the South Saskatchewan River, 37 mi (60 km) west of Medicine Hat. The Oldman, 250 mi long from the head of the Crowsnest River (its chief headstream), was an important coal transport route in the 19th century. The valley of the river and its three main feeder streams —the St. Mary, Belly, and Little Bow—now form a major irrigation district of over 1,000,000 ac (400,000 ha).
49°56′ N, 111°42′ W

old man's beard: *see* beard lichen.

Old Man's Letters to a Young Prince, An (1751–53), collection of short writings by Count Carl Tessin of Sweden.
·Swedish juvenile literature's origins **4**:238f

Old Men, The (1885), story by Leo Tolstoy.
·moralism and literary merit **18**:485e

Old Mortality (1816), novel by Sir Walter Scott.
·plot device and significance **16**:411g

Old Norse, also called OLD ICELANDIC, classical North Germanic language of Iceland from *c.* 1150 to 1350 in which are written the Norse sagas, skaldic poems, and *Eddas*. The language was almost identical to that of Norway during the same period. (Some scholars use the term Old Norse to refer to all the dialects or languages of the Old Scandinavian period, dividing Old Norse into West Norse—Icelandic and Norwegian—and East Norse—Danish and Swedish.) Old Norse (Icelandic) records are more plentiful and of more value than those written in any other old North Germanic dialect.

The history of early North Germanic until the end of Old Norse times is divided by some scholars into three periods corresponding to the stages in its development:

1. Proto-Scandinavian (sometimes called Primitive Norse) lasted until AD 500 to 700, when the Germanic endings and vowels were still in use. About 150 inscriptions in the Germanic alphabet known as the older runic futhark are extant. A great number of phonetic changes began to take place at the end of this period and continued to occur throughout the Common Scandinavian period. Among these changes are vowel mutations, the loss of unaccented vowels, and a great deal of consonant assimilation.

2. Common Scandinavian (Viking Norse) extended from the end of the Proto-Scandinavian period until 1050. During this time the changes begun at the end of the Proto-Scandinavian period were completed, and the language was carried by Viking expansion to Normandy; the English Danelaw (northern, central, and eastern parts of England colonized in the late 9th century); the Orkneys, Shetland, and Hebrides islands; to Ireland and the Isle of Man; to Greenland; and to the Swedish kingdoms in Russia; but the Scandinavian settlers were all absorbed or died out in these areas in later centuries. Modern evidence for Common Scandinavian consists of about 4,000 inscriptions in the younger 16-character runic alphabet.

3. The Old Scandinavian period dates from the end of the Common Scandinavian period until 1450, during which time North Germanic divided into Old Norse (Icelandic), Old Norwegian, Old Swedish, and Old Danish. From these dialects the modern Scandinavian languages developed. *See also* Icelandic language.
·development and differentiation **8**:27c
·Germanic comparative features **8**:18f
·Germanic language evolution, illus. 2 **8**:24
·Scandinavian comparative features **8**:28g *passim* to 30b
·Scottish assimilation of Norse culture **3**:234a

Old Norwegian language: *see* Norwegian language.

Ol Doinyo Lengai, active volcano in Tanzania, eastern Africa, west of Kilimanjaro and south of Lake Natron.
2°45′ S, 35°54′ E
·lava composition **15**:844b
·lava mineral content distinction **9**:219d
·location and activity **17**:1025g
·map, Tanzania **17**:1026

Old Order Amish Mennonite Church: *see* Amish Mennonites.

Old Order Brethren: *see* Brethren in Christ.

Oldowan stone tool industry, crudely worked pebble (chopping) tools from the early Pleistocene, dating to at least 2,000,000 years ago and not formed after a standardized pattern. The tools are made of pebbles of quartz, quartzite, or basalt and are chipped in two directions to form simple, rough, all-purpose tools capable of chopping, scraping, or cutting. Flakes remaining from such work were also employed as tools. Such implements were made by early man (*Homo habilis* at Olduvai Gorge, Tanzania; *Homo erectus* at Swartkrans, S.Af.) and/or by the more advanced man-ape *Australopithecus africanus* (a form believed ancestral to man; tools are known from sites such as Starkfontein, S.Af.). Oldowan tools found in the same deposits with the robust australopithecine *Paranthropus* (Swartkrans) or *Zinjanthropus* (Olduvai Gorge) are attributed by some scholars to these creatures. Others believe the tools were made by more advanced forms living nearby; they base this argument on the observations that the robust australopithecines were apparently vegetarians for whom tool using would not have been of great advantage and that more advanced forms have several times been found sharing the site with the robust man-ape. Oldowan tools appear to have spread outside of Africa, perhaps carried by *Homo erectus*. Tools of similar type have been found at sites including Vértesszőllős, Hung., and Chou-k'ou-tien, China. Tools of other materials, such as wood or bone, probably were also used by the makers of the Oldowan implements; wood has not been preserved, but bone tools have been recognized from at least two sites: Olduvai Gorge (a "lissoir" in Bed I) and Makapansgat, S.Af.; these form part of the osteodontokeratic tool industry (*q.v.*). Stones arranged in a circle found in Bed I at Olduvai Gorge may have served as weights to hold down the edges of a windbreak used by man-apes. Oldowan tools were made for some 1,500,000 years before gradual improvement in technique resulted in a standardized industry known as the Acheulean, the earlier stages of which are variously called Chellean, Chelles-Acheul, or Abbevillian.
·associated fossil finds **11**:423b *passim* to 424h

Old Pact, Icelandic GAMLI SÁTTMÁLI, in Scandinavian history, 1262 treaty uniting Norway and Iceland in personal union under the Norwegian crown.

According to the treaty, which ended a generation of magnate feuds that had disrupted the commonwealth, Iceland retained a large degree of autonomy. In 1380 sovereignty over Iceland passed to the united Denmark–Norway crown, and many of Iceland's prerogatives were lost.

Old Persian language: *see* Persian language.

Old Persian writing: *see* cuneiform writing.

Old Point Comfort, historic spit and point, part of the City of Hampton, southeastern Virginia, U.S., at the southeast end of the peninsula between the James and York rivers. It is at the entrance to Hampton Roads harbour, opposite Norfolk. Named Poynt Comfort by the colonists of Jamestown (1607) in thanks for the sheltered anchorage it furnished, it has been the site of fortifications since 1608, when Ft. Algernourne was built. Ft. George (built 1727–30) was destroyed by hurricane in 1749. Ft. Monroe (completed 1834), a moated stone-walled structure, served during the Civil War as a Federal base of operations for Gen. George B. McClellan's Peninsular Campaign (1862) and for expeditions against Confederate ports. Following the war, Jefferson Davis, former president of the Confederate States, was imprisoned there for two years. During and after World War II it became headquarters for (successively) the Army Ground Forces and the Army Field Forces. In the early 1970s, it was headquarters of the Continental Army Command and the U.S. Army Forces Strike Command.

Old Point Comfort was a popular seaside resort in the 19th and early 20th centuries.
37°00′ N, 76°19′ W

Old Pretender (English history): *see* James the Old Pretender.

Old Prussian language, West Baltic language extinct since the 17th century; it was spoken in the former German areas of East Prussia and Pomerania (now in Poland and the U.S.S.R.). The poorly attested Yotvingian dialect was closely related to Old Prussian.

Old Prussian preserves many archaic Baltic features that do not occur in the related

East Baltic languages (Latvian, Lithuanian), among them the preservation of the consonants of the Proto-Baltic language (the ancestor of Old Prussian, Latvian, Lithuanian, and the other Baltic languages), the Proto-Baltic diphthong *ei*, and the use of neuter gender in nouns (East Baltic languages have only masculine and feminine gender). Old Prussian also contains many inflectional forms and vocabulary items unknown in East Baltic. As a result of prehistoric contact between Old Prussian and the languages ancestral to the Germanic and Slavic groups, Old Prussian shows closer ties to these groups than do the East Baltic languages.

Modern knowledge of Old Prussian is based primarily on a German–Prussian vocabulary, known as the Elbing vocabulary, compiled *c.* 1300, and the three Old Prussian catechisms dating from the 16th century. *Major ref.* **2**:661f *passim* to 663f

Old Red Sandstone, thick sequence of Devonian rocks (the Devonian Period began about 395,000,000 years ago and lasted about 50,000,000 years), continental rather than marine in origin, that occur in northwestern Europe and have been extensively studied in Great Britain. The rocks were deposited in structural basins between the ranges of the Caledonian Mountains, also of the Devonian Period; extraordinary thicknesses, 11,000 metres (37,000 feet) of sands and muds, slowly accumulated in these sinking basins. The sediments are poorly sorted and quite variable. The sandstones are red, green, and gray, and the shales are gray. Plant fossils occur, and the fossil fauna is characterized by primitive, fishlike vertebrates, which are thought to have inhabited freshwater streams and rivers. *See also* Breconian Stage; Dittonian Stage; Farlovian Stage.

·conglomerate with associated volcanism **4**:1113a; illus.
·Devonian rock correlation **5**:671g; illus. 672
·Elburz Mountains' geology **6**:523c
·Europe's geological structure **6**:1038a
·stratigraphic study and age **17**:723d

Old Régime and the French Revolution, The: *see* Ancien Régime et la Révolution, L'.

Old Régime in Canada, The (1874), work by Francis Parkman.

·theme and literary difference **13**:1020c

Oldřich of Rožmberk, 15th-century Bohemian religious leader.

·Bohemian religio-political conflicts **2**:1189f

Old Ritualists (Russian religious sect): *see* Old Believers.

Olds, town, Alberta, Canada, in the southern part of the province. Situated 57 mi (92 km) north of Calgary on the Canadian Pacific Railway line between Calgary and Edmonton, it is named for J.C. Olds, an official of the Canadian Pacific. The site was sparsely populated before the railway was built in 1891, and its real growth dates from the arrival of a large party of settlers from Nebraska two years later. Olds is a trading centre for a prosperous agricultural region specializing in grain, dairy products, and livestock; logging and natural gas are also important. A provincial school of agriculture and home economics was established at Olds in 1913. Inc. village, 1900; town, 1905. Pop. (1971) 3,376.
51°47′ N, 114°06′ W

·map, Canada **3**:716

Olds, Ransom Eli (b. June 3, 1864, Geneva, Ohio—d. Aug. 26, 1950, Lansing, Mich.), U.S. inventor and automobile manufacturer, designer of the three-horsepower, curved-dash Oldsmobile, the first commercially successful American-made automobile and the first to use a progressive assembly system that foreshadowed modern mass-production methods. In 1899 Olds formed the Olds Motor Works with financial backing from Samuel L. Smith, a wealthy lumberman, in Lansing, Mich. The first Oldsmobiles were marketed in 1901, and the 1904 model, 5,000 of which were sold, remains a collector's item. In 1904 Olds left the company and formed the Reo Motor Car Company. By 1907 he had built Reo into one of the industry's leaders, but after 1908 the company steadily lost ground. After 1915 Olds turned most of his attention to other activities, including the marketing of a lawn mower he had invented and land speculation in Florida.

·history of automotive industry **2**:528c

Old Saxon, also called OLD LOW GERMAN, earliest recorded Low German language, spoken by the Saxon tribes between the Rhine and Elbe rivers and between the North Sea and the Harz Mountains from the 9th until the 12th century. A distinctive characteristic of Old Saxon, shared with Old Frisian and Old English, is its preservation of the voiceless stops (*p*, *t*, *k*) common to all Germanic languages rather than changing them to affricates (*pf*, *tz*, *kch*) or long fricatives (*ff*, *ss*, *ch*) as in High German.

The *Heliand*, a life of Christ in alliterative verse written *c.* 830, and a fragment of a translation of Genesis are the most significant extant Old Saxon literary works. The modern Low German dialects have developed from Old Saxon. *See also* Low German; German language.

·Germanic comparative features **8**:16e *passim* to 19a

Old Saybrook, town, Middlesex County, southern Connecticut, U.S., on Long Island Sound, at the mouth of the Connecticut River. The town includes the resort borough of Fenwick, Old Saybrook Center, and Saybrook Point. It was first settled (1623) by the Dutch, but in 1635 a Puritan settlement, named Saybrook, was established there. The town was the site of Yale University until its removal to New Haven in 1716. In 1776 Old Saybrook was the site of construction of David Bushnell's "Turtle," a submarine used briefly during the Revolution. Old Saybrook is the trading centre for resort colonies on Long Island Sound. There is some light manufacturing. Inc. 1854. Pop. (1980) 9,287.
41°18′ N, 72°23′ W

Old Silla style, Korean visual arts style characteristic of the earlier years (57 BC–AD 668) of the Silla kingdom of the Three Kingdoms period. The art is marked by a sober conservatism, which perhaps explains the preference during this period for granite as a medium for architecture and sculpture. Old Silla sculpture is characterized by puritanical, often stiff, melancholic expression, compared with the more mellow, happy type of Paekche representation. There is also a tendency toward abstraction in sculpture, as in the decorative arts. Old Silla pottery is unglazed, grayish stoneware, with a texture that is almost that of slate. The vessel forms have clean-cut, functional lines, and surface decoration is limited to incised geometric patterns around the shoulder. Old Silla art began to lose its stiffness and develop a more natural, versatile approach toward the turn of the 7th century, apparently under the influence of Chinese Sui and T'ang art.

·Korean art, illus., **19**:Visual Arts, East Asian, Plate 9
·Korean visual arts features **19**:208e

Old Slavonic language: *see* Old Church Slavonic.

Old Stone Age: *see* Paleolithic.

old style type, also called OLD FACE TYPE, type fonts developed between *c.* 1722 and *c.* 1763.

·type classification and development **18**:813b

Old Testament, the Hebrew Bible section of biblical literature (*q.v.*), canonical to Jews and Christians.

Old Town, city, Penobscot County, south central Maine, U.S., on the Penobscot River. In the 1600s the Indian village of Panawambske occupied the site that became part of a tract known as Colburntown (1790). This was later organized as Stillwater and Orono, from which Old Town was set off and incorporated in 1840. Indian Island (Penobscot Indian Reservation) is owned by the Abnaki tribe. Henry David Thoreau wrote of the island and town in *The Maine Woods*. Economic activities are based on lumbering and the manufacture of canoes and moccasins. Inc. city, 1891. Pop. (1980) 8,422.
44°56′ N, 68°39′ W

Old Traitor: *see* Adalbero.

Olduvai (OLDUWAI) **Gorge,** archaeological site in the eastern Serengeti Plains, northern Tanzania, is a steep-sided ravine about 30 miles (48 kilometres) long and 295 feet (90 metres) deep, with subsidiary valleys. Deposits exposed in the sides of the gorge cover a time span from about 2,100,000 to 15,000 years ago. The deposits have yielded a rich fossil fauna, including remains of more than 50 hominids, as well as the longest known archaeological record of stone tool industries.

The Olduvai Beds accumulated in a lake basin about 16 miles (25 kilometres) in diameter, which is underlain by Pliocene volcanic rocks and by metamorphic deposits of Precambrian age. They contain evidence of relatively continuous rift valley fault movements and of a semi-arid climate. Seven major stratigraphic units or formations have been distinguished. From the oldest to the youngest they are: Bed I, Bed II, Bed III, Bed IV, the Masek Beds, the Ndutu Beds, and the Naisiusiu Beds. Bed I is at most 197 feet (60 metres) thick and from about 1,700,000–2,100,000 years old. It consists largely of lava flows, volcanic ash deposits and detrital sediments. The upper part of Bed I (1,700,000–1,850,000 years old) contains a rich and varied fauna and archaeological sites of the Oldowan industry (*q.v.*). Skeletal remains of hominids have been assigned to *Homo habilis* (also classified as *Australopithecus africanus*) and *Australopithecus robustus* (formerly *Zinjanthropus boisei*). Camp sites and a butchery site have also been excavated in Bed I.

Hominid living sites of Bed I times are found principally where streams from the volcanic highlands brought freshwater to the southeastern margin of the alkaline Olduvai lake. Conditions for preservation were unusually favourable at these sites because ash falls from nearby volcanoes and fluctuations of the lake led to rapid burial of the hominid and associated remains. Debris consists of Oldowan tools and the bones and teeth of various animals, notably medium-size antelopes. Long bones and others containing marrow have generally been split and broken.

A loosely built circle of lava blocks found at a lakeside site low in Bed I suggests that crude shelters were constructed by means of branches stuck into the ground, in a circle, and supported by stones piled around the bases. In similar structures built today, the branches are interlaced and grass is piled on top of them to form roofs.

Living sites in Beds II, III, and IV are generally found in former river or stream channels, where the occupational remains have been displaced by water action.

Bed II (1,150,000–1,700,000 years old) is 66–98 feet (20–30 metres) thick and comprises upper and lower divisions of different rock formations separated by a disconformity, or erosional break. The lower part of Bed II was deposited in a lake basin similar to that of Bed I; the upper part was deposited after faulting had reduced the size of the lake and enlarged the area of grassland. Only the Oldowan industry occurs below the disconformity; the Developed Oldowan and Acheulian (*q.v.*) industries occur above. Remains of *Homo habilis* are found in the lower one-third of Bed II, and a cranium of *Homo erectus* was collected near the top of Bed II. *Australopithecus robustus* occurs both high and low in Bed II.

The basin was further modified by faulting about 1,150,000 years ago; Bed III (800,000–1,150,000 years old) and Bed IV (600,000–800,000 years old) were deposited on an alluvial plain. These two units are separable only in the eastern part of the gorge and are combined elsewhere into a single unit. Beds III and IV have a maximum aggregate thickness of about 98 feet (30 metres) and consist almost entirely of stream-laid detrital sediment. Archaeological sites in Beds III and IV represent the Developed Oldowan and Acheulian industries, and hominid remains are assigned to *Homo erectus* and other *Homo* species.

The Masek Beds (400,000–600,000 years old) accumulated during a period of major faulting and explosive volcanism. They have a maximum thickness of about 82 feet (25 metres) and consist of about equal amounts of stream-laid detrital sediment and aeolian (wind-worked) tuff. The climate was drier than during the preceding deposits and was probably much like the present. Only one archaeological site, of the Acheulian industry, is known in the Masek Beds.

The Ndutu Beds (50,000–400,000 years old) were deposited during intermittent faulting, erosion, and partial filling of the gorge. They consist largely of aeolian tuffs but include detritus from older units exposed in the sides of the gorge. The maximum thickness is 79 feet (24 metres). Two archaeologic sites with nondescript material of Middle Stone Age affinity have been found.

The Naisiusiu Beds (15,000–20,000 years old) were deposited on the sides and in the bottom of the gorge after it had been eroded to very near its present level. These deposits

Rock formation at Olduvai Gorge, Tanzania

Cyril Toker—Photo Trends

are as much as 33 feet (10 metres) thick and consist largely of aeolian tuff. The Naisiusiu Beds contain one archaeological site consisting of a microlithic tool assemblage and a skeleton of *Homo sapiens*, both of which have an age of about 17,000 years.

·archaeological studies of Stone Age **1**:1079f
·australopithecine bone findings **8**:1024g
·australopithecine stone tool evidence **2**:439b
·Homo erectus distribution **8**:1031c
·human evolutionary evidence **11**:422h *passim* to 424h
·map, Tanzania **17**:1027
·Paleolithic tool discovery **8**:608c
·prehistoric human settlement **17**:1033g

Olduvai hominid 9: *see* Chellean man.

Old World anthropoid primates: *see* Catarrhini.

Old World grape: *see* grape.

Old-World Landowners (1922), Russian STAROSVETSKIYE POMESHCHIKI (1835), short story by Gogol.

·Gogol's Romanticism and pessimism **8**:234f

Olea capensis, species of black ironwood tree of the family Oleaceae, order Oleales.

·Oleales wood importance **13**:558c

Oleaceae, the olive family of the plant order Oleales, named for the economically important olive tree, *Olea europaea*, also contains many valuable timber and ornamental trees, shrubs, and vines. Most of its 29 genera and 600 species are woody plants native to forest-

Lilac (*Syringa*)

By courtesy of the State of New Hampshire; photograph, Ernest Gould

ed regions. One species of the genus *Menodora* has an unusual distribution pattern; it is found only in South America and southern Africa.

The flowers in most members of the family have two stamens and a single pistil of two united carpels. The petals, usually four, are fused at the base to form a tube. The leaves are opposite each other on the branch except in a few species of jasmine. The fruit may be fleshy, as in the olive; winged, as in the ash (*Fraxinus*); a woody capsule, as in the genus *Schrebera;* or a two-lobed berry, as in jasmine (*Jasminum*).

Both olive and ash trees have close-grained hardwood that is used for ornamental carvings and tool handles.

Many members of the olive family are cultivated for their beautiful and fragrant flowers, such as fringe tree (*Chionanthus*), golden bell (*Forsythia*), jasmine, lilac (*Syringa*), and tea olive (*Osmanthus*). *Abeliophyllum distichum*, from Korea, produces bell-like flowers in early spring. The masses of yellow-centred white flowers cause the shrubs, 90 centimetres (3 feet) tall, to resemble white mounds. A large African shrub, *Schrebera alata*, produces clusters of small, purple-centred white flowers. It has winged, five-parted leaves. The tree of sadness (*Nyctanthes arbor-trista*), of India, also known as night jasmine, is a large, somewhat straggly shrub. Its small, white flowers bloom at night and have a honeylike fragrance. They are used in Hindu religious ceremonies and to make a yellow dye for colouring the robes of Buddhist priests.

Species of mock privet (*Phillyrea*) and privet (*Ligustrum*) are used for hedges and ornamental plantings. *Major ref.* **13**:556h

RELATED ENTRIES in the *Ready Reference and Index:*
ash; Forsythia; fringe tree; jasmine; lilac; mock privet; olive; privet; tea olive

Oleaecarpium germanicum, fossil species of the family Oleaceae, order Oleales.

·Oleales fossil record **13**:558f

Olea europaea (tree): *see* olive.

Oleales 13:556, the olive order of flowering plants, containing only the family Oleaceae, which comprises many plants of major importance to man. Among these are the edible and ornamental olive species, the timber-producing ash trees, the fragrant ornamental lilacs and jasmines, the hedge privets, and the early-spring-flowering forsythia.

The text article covers the diversity and distribution, economic importance, natural history, form and function, and evolution of the Oleales and concludes with an annotated classification.

REFERENCE in other text article:
·angiosperm features and classification **1**:883h

RELATED ENTRIES in the *Ready Reference and Index: for*
common plants: see ash; fringe tree; jasmine; lilac; mock privet; olive; privet; tea olive
other: Forsythia; Oleaceae

Olean, city, Cattaraugus County, western New York, U.S., on the Allegheny River at the mouth of Olean Creek. First settled in 1804 as a lumber camp, it became an embarkation point for settlers bound for the Ohio Valley in flatboats. A town (township) was organized in 1808. Because of its proximity to the Pennsylvania oil fields, an oil-based economy developed. There are also railroad shops and engineering industries. St. Bonaventure University and St. Elizabeth's Academy are 2 mi (3 km) west. A major flood caused by Hurricane "Agnes" occurred in June 1972. Inc. village, 1854; city, 1893. Pop. (1980) 18,207.
42°05′ N, 78°26′ W
·map, United States **18**:909

oleander, ornamental flowering plant species of the family Apocynaceae (*q.v.*).

oleaster, also called RUSSIAN OLIVE and TREBIZOND DATE (*Elaeagnus angustifolia*, family Elaeagnaceae), a small deciduous tree of Eurasia about 4.5 to 6 metres (15 to 20 feet) high. It has brown, smooth branches that

Oleaster (*Elaeagnus angustifolia*)

R.H. Runde

bear spines and narrow, light green leaves that are silvery on the undersides from a hairy covering. The flowers are small, fragrant, and silvery scaled on the outside, as are the edible, olive-shaped, yellowish fruits, which are sweet but mealy. It is commonly cultivated as an ornamental hedge and windbreak plant.

olecranon, the bony prominence of the ulna that forms the tip of the elbow.

·human elbow components **16**:817h; illus.

olefin, also called ALKENE, the generic name given to an unsaturated hydrocarbon containing one or more pairs of carbon atoms linked by a double bond. The olefins are classified in either one or both of the following ways: (1) cyclic or acyclic (aliphatic) olefins, in which the double bond is located between carbon atoms forming part of a cyclic (closed-ring) or of an open-chain grouping, respectively, and (2) a monoolefin, diolefin, triolefin, or polyolefin, in which the number of double bonds per molecule is respectively one, two, three, or an unspecified number greater than two.

Monoolefins have the general formula C_nH_{2n}, C being a carbon atom, H a hydrogen atom, and *n* an integer. They are not found in nature but are formed in large quantities during the cracking (breaking down of large molecules) of petroleum oils to gasoline. The lower monoolefins—*i.e.*, ethylene, propylene, and butylene—have become the basis for the extensive petrochemicals industry. Most uses of these compounds involve reactions of the double bond with other chemical agents. Diolefins, also known as dienes, or alkadienes, with the general formula C_nH_{2n-2}, contain conjugated double bonds; they undergo reactions similar to the monolefins. The best known dienes are butadiene and isoprene, used as building units in the manufacture of synthetic rubber.

Olefins containing two to four carbon atoms per molecule are gaseous at ordinary temperature and pressure; those containing five or more carbon atoms are usually liquid at ordinary temperatures. Olefins are only slightly soluble in water. *Major ref.* **9**:84f

·acid-catalyzed isomerization **1**:49b
·alcohol production reaction principles **1**:453f
·carbene dimerization products **3**:822e
·catalytic oxidation **3**:1002a
·conformation of cyclic compounds **4**:1091a
·coordination compound characteristics **5**:140b
·heterocycle comparative chemistry **8**:833c
·nucleophilic substitution mechanism **4**:152f
·organic halide preparation and reactions **13**:685b
·organic halogen compound classification **13**:683d
·organometal synthesis and polymerization **13**:716b *passim* to 717b
·petroleum cracking and products **14**:186h
·polyethylene and polypropylene fibre production **7**:267b
·synthesis gas and olefin reaction **7**:927h
·transition organometallic compound structure **18**:607f

Oleg (d. *c.* 912), semi-legendary Viking (Varangian) leader who became prince of Kiev and is considered to be the founder of the Kievan Rus state. According to *The Russian Primary Chronicle* of the 12th century, Oleg, after succeeding his kinsman Rurik as ruler of Novgorod (*c.* 879), went down the Dnieper (Dnepr) River with his Varangian retinue and seized control of Smolensk and Kiev (882), which he subsequently made his capital. Extending his authority east and west of the Volkhov–Dnieper waterway, he united the local Slavic and Finnish tribes under his rule and became the undisputed ruler of the Kievan–Novgorodian state.

Described in the chronicle as a skilled warrior, Oleg defeated the Khazars, delivering several Slavic tribes from dependence upon them, and also undertook a successful expedition against Constantinople (907), forcing the Byzantine government to sue for peace and pay a large indemnity. In 911 Oleg also concluded an advantageous trade agreement with Constantinople, which regulated commercial relations between the two states, provided for the legal protection of foreign merchants engaged in trade between the two states, and laid the basis for the development of permanent and lucrative trade activities between Constantinople and Kievan Rus.

oleic acid (unsaturated fatty acid): *see* fatty acid.

Olenellus, extinct genus of fossil trilobites common in but restricted to Lower Cambrian rocks (the Cambrian Period began about 570,000,000 years ago and lasted about 70,000,000 years) and thus a useful guide fossil for the Lower Cambrian. *Olenellus*, a primitive or generalized type of trilobite, had a well-developed head, large and crescentic eyes, and a poorly developed, small tail.
·fossil characteristics and era **7**:564g

Olenellus of Cambrian age, from Vermont
By courtesy of the trustees of the British Museum (Natural History); photograph, Imitor

Olenida, group of Early Paleozoic trilobites.
·fossil era and environment **7**:564g

Olenin, Boris (pseudonym): *see* Chernov, Viktor Mikhaylovich.

Olenus Series, Upper Cambrian rocks that occur in Europe (the Cambrian Period began about 570,000,000 years ago and lasted about 70,000,000 years); the term Olenus Series is sometimes applied to rocks in eastern North America, although the term Croixian Series is more commonly used. Rocks of the Olenus Series are characterized by the presence of trilobites of the family Olenidae, of which the genus *Olenus* is especially prominent. The type area of the Olenus Series is in Wales, where the Lingula Flags are representative.
·Cambrian stratigraphic correlations **13**:918c; table

Olenyok River, rises on the southern slopes of the Bukochan Ridge on the Central Siberian Plateau and flows mainly through the Yakut Autonomous Soviet Socialist Republic, within the Russian Soviet Federated Socialist Republic. The total length of the river is 1,411 mi (2,270 km), and it has a drainage basin of 84,500 sq mi (219,000 sq km). The upper course is characterized by falls and rapids. Below the confluence with the Arga-Sala, its valley widens. Eventually the Olenyok passes onto the North Siberian Lowland, whence it enters the Laptev Sea through a delta. It is navigable as far as Sukhana, about 600 mi (1,000 km) from the sea.
73°00′ N, 119°55′ E
·map, Soviet Union **17**:323

oleograph, also called CHROMOLITHOGRAPH, or CHROMO, colour lithograph produced by preparing a separate stone by hand for each colour to be used and printing one colour in register over another. Sometimes as many as 30 stones were used for a single print. The technique was pioneered in the 1830s but came into wide commercial use only in the 1860s. It then became the most popular method of colour reproduction until the end of the 19th century, when more efficient techniques rendered it obsolete. *See also* lithography.

oleoresin, natural plant product consisting of a resin dispersed in an essential oil. *See also* balsam; plastics and resins; turpentine oleoresin.

olericulture, a branch of horticulture that deals with the production, storage, processing, and marketing of vegetables.
·horticulture scope and practices **8**:1105d

Oléron Island, French ÎLE D'OLÉRON, French island in the Bay of Biscay, forming part of the Charente-Maritime *département*, located off the coast of France south of La Rochelle and north of the Gironde Estuary. Oléron is the second largest French island (after Corsica), with an area of 68 sq mi (175 sq km). More or less bean-shaped, with an average breadth of about 4 mi (6 km) and extending northwest–southeast, it is connected with the mainland by a toll bridge about 1¾ mi long. Most of the island is flat, and one-third of it is wooded. It is bordered by dunes and has extensive marshes. Oysters are cultivated, and vegetables are grown. The small town of Saint-Trojan in the southwest is a seaside resort. A number of small harbour towns and coastal villages accommodate holidaymakers. Pop. (latest census) about 14,800.
45°56′ N, 1°15′ W
·map, France **7**:584
·maritime law development in France **11**:500g

Olesha, Yury (Karlovich) (b. March 3, 1899—d. May 10, 1960, Moscow), writer who dealt with the conflict between the old mentality and the new in the Soviet Union.

Olesha was brought up in Odessa, served in the Red Army, and afterward became a journalist. He published some humorous verse and several sharp, critical articles in the early 1920s. In 1927 he produced the novel for which he is remembered, *Zavist* (Eng. trans., *Envy*, 1936). It is concerned with two main characters who are both rebels against Soviet society and who in different ways question the accepted values of that society. Olesha also wrote other novels, short stories, and a play, but they all deal with variations of the theme presented in *Zavist*.

When in the early 1930s a demand arose for a literature of Socialist Realism (positive portrayal of Communist heroes in real life), Olesha found that he could not write, in his words, "in accordance with the times." He spoke openly of his doubts and misgivings at a meeting of the Union of Soviet Writers in 1934. Presumably because of this admission, Olesha was arrested and imprisoned in the late 1930s. He survived his imprisonment and was released in 1956.

Oleśnicki, Zbigniew (b. 1389, Sienno, Pol. —d. April 1, 1455, Sandomierz), Polish statesman and cardinal who was chief councillor to King Władysław II and regent of Poland (1434–47). A member of the Polish noble house of Dębno of Oleśnica, he became the leading member of the royal Privy Council after he saved the King's life at the Battle of Grunwald in 1410. Ordained a priest in 1412, he was made bishop of Kraków in 1423. Representing the interests of the church and the nobility, Oleśnicki secured a limitation of royal power (March 1430) in exchange for the nobles' recognition of the King's young son Władysław as the heir to the throne, thereby beginning the Polish tradition of an elective monarchy. As regent after Władysław II's death, Oleśnicki opposed the spread of the dissident Hussite religious movement in Poland, defeating the Hussite nobles in 1439. His appointment as the first Polish cardinal by Pope Eugenius IV in 1439 further strengthened his position. When Władysław III died (1444) while on a crusade, the Cardinal ruled the country until the King's death could be proved and his younger brother, Grand Prince Casimir of Lithuania, ascended the throne as Casimir IV (1447).
·Hunyadi's crusade to Byzantium **14**:641f

olethreutid moth, any member of the cosmopolitan family Olethreutidae (order Lepidoptera), containing several species with economically destructive larvae. The pale larvae roll or tie leaves and feed on foliage, fruits, or nuts; *e.g.*, the codling moth (*Carpocapsa*, or *Laspeyresia*, *pomonella*) and the Oriental fruit moth (*Laspeyresia*, or *Grapholitha*, *molesta*). Originally from Europe, the codling moth exists wherever apples are grown. The larvae burrow in the apples and, when fully grown, emerge and pupate under debris or bark or in loose soil.

Often called fruit or bud moths, olethreutids have somewhat square-tipped forewings and fringed hindwings. Wingspan averages 18 millimetres (¾ inch).

The larvae of the Mexican jumping bean moth (*Laspeyresia saltitans*) live inside the seeds of certain shrubs (*Sebastiania*), feeding on the kernels; their movements make the seed jump.
·classification and general features **10**:829c
codling moth
·intraspecific competition effects **2**:1045a
·nonchemical controls **1**:353g

oleum (fuming sulfuric acid): *see* sulfuric acid.

olfaction: *see* smell.

olfactory bulb, in anatomy, one of two rounded structures on the lower frontal surfaces of the cerebral hemispheres, the terminal points of the olfactory nerves from the nose.
·anatomic interrelationships **12**:1018c
·nervous system evolution **12**:991d; illus. 990
·smell mechanism structures **16**:554a

olfactory lobe, one of a paired section of the vertebrate brain that mediates the sense of smell. The olfactory lobes form a large part of primitive brains but become smaller in proportion to the cerebrum, in particular, in more advanced brains. *See* brain.
·mammalian nervous system advances **11**:409f

olfactory nerve, or FIRST CRANIAL NERVE, one of a pair of sensory nerves for smell.
·anatomy and function **12**:1018b; illus. 1017
·cranial bone anatomy **16**:814f
·cranial nerve origins and development **6**:750h
·disease symptoms and causes **12**:1048c
·tests for functional disorders **12**:1042a

Olga, Saint (b. *c.* 890—d. 969, Kiev, now in Ukranian S.S.R.), princess who was canonized as the first Russian saint of the Orthodox Church. She was the widow of Prince Igor I, who was assassinated (945) by his subjects while attempting to extort excessive tribute for his expeditions against Byzantium. Because Igor's son Svyatoslav was still a minor, Olga became regent of the grand principality of Kiev from 945 to 964. She soon had Igor's murderers scalded to death and hundreds of their followers killed. Olga became the first of the royal Kievans to adopt Orthodox Christianity. She was probably baptized (*c.* 957), at Constantinople, then the most powerful patriarchate. Her efforts to bring Christianity to Russia were carried out by her grandson, the grand prince St. Vladimir (died 1015); together they mark the transition between pagan and Christian Russia. Olga's feast day is July 11.
·visit to Constantinople **3**:561f

Olga Rocks, in southwest Northern Territory, central Australia, comprise a circular grouping of more than 30 red conglomerate domes rising from the desert plains north of the Musgrave Ranges. They occupy an area of 11 sq mi (28 sq km) within Ayers Rock-Mt. Olga National Park (established 1958), and culminate at Mt. Olga, 1,500 ft (460 m) above the plain and 3,507 ft (1,069 m) above sea level. Mt. Olga is the most westerly of three giant tors (isolated weathered rocks); the others are Ayers Rock (*q.v.*) and Mt. Conner (*see* Conner, Mount). Visited and named (1872) after Queen Olga of Spain by explorer Ernest Giles, their Aboriginal name Katajuta means Many Heads. The rocks offer visitors a constantly changing array of colour as the sun moves overhead and illuminates the luxurious vegetation in deep clefts between the domes.
25°19′ S, 130°46′ E
·Mt. Olga elevation and formation **13**:243a
·Mt. Olga formation and relief **2**:387a; illus.

Olgierd (grand duke of Lithuania): *see* Algirdas.

Olhão, town and municipality, Faro district, Algarve province, southern Portugal, at the head of the Barra Nova (a shipping channel landward of sandbars fringing the coast), just east of Faro town. Olhão was one of the first Portuguese towns to enter the Peninsular War (1808–14). Now primarily a fishing port, with canning factories, it is also a popular resort frequented by painters. Olhão is often called the "Cubist Town" because of its cube-shaped, flat-roofed houses of Moorish style. Joaquim Lopes (1798–1890), ship's captain and humanitarian decorated by England, Spain, and Portugal for saving lives at sea, was born there. Pop. (1970 prelim.) town, 10,827; mun., 24,923.
37°02′ N, 8°50′ W
·map, Portugal **14**:856

Oli, also called BULI, an African people of the Luba cultural area of the Congo.
·figure carving style **1**:274g

oḷī, a twice yearly ceremony celebrated among the Jainas, a religious group of India.

The ceremony is observed for nine days from the 7th to the 15th of the bright half of the month of Caitra (April–May) and of Āśvina (September–October). The main ritual of worship, or *pūjā*, is the eightfold offering made to the *siddha-cakra* (*see* siddha), or saint-wheel, kept in every Śvetāmbara temple. This consists of *jaḷa-pūjā* (the washing of the image); *candana-pūjā* (marking it with sandalwood paste); *puṣpa-pūjā* (the offering of flowers); *dhūpa-pūjā* (the waving of incense); *dīpa-pūjā* (the waving of a lighted lamp in front of the image); *akṣata-pūjā* (the offering of rice); *naivedya-pūjā* (the offering of sweetmeats); and *phala-pūjā* (the offering of fruit). The ritual carried out by the Digambara has some slight differences; only dried fruit is offered because they believe the giving of fresh fruit involves the taking of life.

Observers of *oḷī* keep a special fast that involves the taking of only one kind of grain each day during the festival period.

olibanum (gum resin): *see* frankincense.

Olier, Jean-Jacques (b. Sept. 20, 1608, Paris—d. April 2, 1657, Paris), founder of the Sulpicians, a group of secular priests dedicated to training candidates for the priesthood.

Olier, engraving by Nicolas Pitau (1632–71)
Harlingue—H. Roger-Viollet

Ordained a priest in 1633, he soon came under the influence of St. Vincent de Paul, founder of a congregation of missionaries known as Lazarists. In 1641 Olier established at Vaugirard, Fr., a seminary for the training of priests, which he moved to Paris the following year when he was made pastor of Saint-Sulpice. The school became known as Saint-Sulpice Seminary, and the Society of Saint-Sulpice (Sulpicians) was approved by the French government in 1645. Olier's writings, edited in 1856 by J.P. Migne, concentrate on the spiritual direction of priests. E.M. Faillon's *Life* (3 vol., 1873) is considered the standard biography of Olier.

oligarchy. A form of political order, aspects of which are treated under political systems.

oligarchy, iron law of: *see* iron law of oligarchy.

Oligocene Epoch, major worldwide division of Tertiary rocks and time that began about 38,000,000 years ago and lasted about 12,000,000 years; it follows the Eocene Epoch and precedes the Miocene Epoch. The term Oligocene is derived from the Greek and means the Epoch of Few Recent Forms, referring to modern animals that originated during the Oligocene.

In western Europe the beginning of the Oligocene was marked by an invasion of the sea that brought with it new molluscan forms characteristic of the epoch. Marine conditions did not exist for long, however, and brackish and freshwater conditions soon prevailed. This cycle of marine transgression, followed by the establishment of brackish and then freshwater environments, was repeated once again during the Oligocene. Three standard divisions of Oligocene rocks and time are recognized; from oldest to youngest, these divisions are the Lattorfian, Rupelian, and Chattian stages. Various other stage names assume local or regional importance; these include the Sannoisian, roughly equivalent to the Lattorfian Stage in France; the Tongrian, the equivalent of the Lattorfian in Belgium, where important lower Oligocene deposits occur; the Stampian from France and Belgium, equivalent to the Rupelian Stage; and the Casselian, a term sometimes used instead of the Chattian and approximately synonymous with it.

During the Oligocene, sediments on the floor of the ancient Tethyan Sea, which covered much of Eurasia, were deformed early in the formation of the European Alps. Oligocene climates appear to have been temperate, and many regions enjoyed subtropical climatic conditions. Grasslands expanded during the Oligocene, and forested regions were less widespread than previously. Tropical vegetation flourished along the borders of the Tethyan Sea. Warm, swampy conditions prevailed over much of what is now Germany, and extensive deposits of lignite, a rock or deposit transitional between peat and soft coal, were formed.

A prominent group of Oligocene marine animals were the Foraminifera, protozoans similar to amoebas but bearing a complex, often calcareous test, or shell. Among the especially prominent foraminiferans were the nummulites, typified by the genus *Lepidocyclina*, which grew to as much as eight centimetres (three inches) across. Other marine forms were essentially modern in aspect. Terrestrial invertebrate life was abundant and diverse. Stream and lake deposits on the Isle of Wight contain the remains, often well preserved, of termites and other forms. In the Baltic, many forms of Oligocene insects, including butterflies, bees, ants, and spiders, are preserved in amber.

Oligocene terrestrial vertebrate faunas are diverse and abundant. Important deposits are known from North America, Europe, Africa, and Asia. The vertebrate faunas of the northern continents have an essentially modern aspect, caused less by the appearance of new forms than by extinction of archaic vertebrates during the Eocene Epoch or at its close. Early Oligocene vertebrate faunas are very similar over the northern continents, a similarity suggesting a relatively free interchange of animals, but later Oligocene faunas evidence a greater degree of provincialism. Bats became more widespread in the Oligocene and at least locally abundant; their droppings in caves contributed to the formation of extensive phosphate deposits that are currently economically significant in many areas. Primitive beavers appeared late in the Oligocene. Throughout the epoch, modern groups of carnivores became diverse and abundant. The largest land mammal of all time, *Baluchitherium*, is known from Asia. *Baluchitherium* stood 5 metres (18 feet) high at the shoulders and was able to browse on leaves high up in trees. The first mastodons are known from the Oligocene of Egypt and occur in the Fayum Beds. In North America, primitive horses were evolving, including three-toed forms such as *Mesohippus* and *Miohippus*. Pigs and peccaries first appeared in the early Oligocene of Europe and reached North America late in the epoch. The earliest apelike form, *Parapithecus*, is known from Oligocene deposits in Egypt, which also have yielded remains of several kinds of Old World monkeys. The earliest New World monkeys are known from late Oligocene deposits in South America. During the Oligocene, South America was isolated from Central and North America, and a unique mammalian fauna developed there. Remarkably, many South American mammals of the Oligocene exhibit extreme paral-

lelism in adaptation to forms that are found elsewhere in the world and are not even closely related.
·African fossils and tectonic movement **1**:183e
·bird fossil record and evolution **2**:1060f
·climatic change indications **4**:732e; illus. 735
·European features **6**:1039e
·evolution of apes and monkeys **11**:421c
·geological time scale, illus. 2 **5**:499
·nomenclature adoption from Mainz Basin **18**:151c
·pollen stratigraphy and evolution **14**:741e
·primate ancestry and evolution **14**:1026c; illus. 1021
·Red Sea formation and continental drift **15**:545d

oligochaete, any worm of the class Oligochaeta (phylum Annelida). About 3,200 living species are known, the most familiar of which is the earthworm (*q.v.*) *Lumbricus terrestris.* Oligochaetes are common all over the world. They live in the sea, in freshwater, and in moist soil.

Oligochaetes, which range in length from a few millimetres (a fraction of an inch) to more than three metres (ten feet), are notable for the absence of a head and parapodia, the flat, lobelike outgrowths used by many other annelids for locomotion. They have few setae, or bristles, on the body. Many species have a clitellum, a thickened region that secretes cocoons for enclosing eggs.

All forms are hermaphroditic; *i.e.*, the functional reproductive organs of both sexes occur in the same individual. Development and growth are direct, with no larval stages.

Oligochaetes, in particular the earthworm, are ecologically important in their roles of turning over and aerating the soil; the earthworm is secondarily important as fish bait.
·anatomy, habits, and classification **1**:928a; illus.
·circulatory system anatomy **4**:621c
·phylogenetic basis of taxonomy **4**:685f
·reproductive behaviour patterns **15**:684a
·reproductive system anatomy **15**:703e

oligoclase (mineral): *see* plagioclase.

oligodendroglia, or OLIGOGLIA, in biology, non-neural cells of the central nervous system, belonging to the neuroglia, or supportive tissue, of the brain and spinal cord; they differ from other neuroglia in having fewer dendrites, projections that transmit nerve impulses toward a nerve cell body.
·anatomic locations and functions **12**:997d
·animal tissue comparisons **18**:446e
·neuron structure and function **12**:978b
·oligodendrocyte form and function **12**:987c

Oligodon: *see* kukri snake.

oligohydramnios, or OLIGOAMNIOS, deficiency of amniotic fluid at the end of pregnancy.
·anomalies related to amniotic fluid **14**:983b

oligomenorrhea, or OLIGOMENORRHOEA, prolonged intervals between menstrual cycles. Menstruation is the normal cyclic bleeding from the female reproductive tract. Most women menstruate every 25 to 30 days if they are not pregnant, nursing a child, or experiencing reproductive disorders. In oligomenorrhea, menstruation may occur only three or four times yearly. The cause of the disorder may be psychological, hormonal, or structural in nature. If there is no acute illness or disease involved, the irregularity becomes important only because it interferes with conception. Absence of menstruation may be a symptom of some other disorder. *See also* amenorrhea.

Oligonicella (insect): *see* mantid.

oligonucleotide, compound containing a small number of nucleotides (*q.v.*).
·structure and synthesis **13**:332g

oligopoly, a market situation characterized by a few firms producing identical or slightly differentiated products. Each producer must consider the effect of a price change on the actions of the other producers. A cut in price by one may lead to an equal reduction by the others, with the result that each firm will retain approximately the same share of the market as before but at a lower profit margin. Competition in oligopolistic industries tends, therefore, to manifest itself in nonprice forms such as advertising and product differentiation. Characteristic oligopolies in the U.S. are the steel, aluminum, and automobile industries.
·competitiveness of market **12**:376d
·consumer protection obstacle **5**:101b
·economic study of industrial organization **6**:271g

oligosaccharide, general term for a carbohydrate of from three to six units of simple sugar (monosaccharide, *q.v.*). A large number have been prepared by partially breaking down more complex carbohydrates (polysaccharides). Most of the few naturally occurring oligosaccharides are found in plants. Raffinose, a trisaccharide found in many plants, consists of melibiose (galactose and glucose) and fructose. Another plant trisaccharide is gentianose.
·carbohydrate structures and properties **3**:829b; table
·composition and occurrence **15**:93f

oligotrich, any spherical to pear-shaped protozoan of the ciliate order Oligotrichida, found in fresh, salt, and brackish water. Body cilia (minute, hairlike projections), when present, are often fused into groups of bristles, or cirri. The oligotrichs have conspicuous adoral (on margin of groove leading to the mouth) ciliature. For many species an anterior spiralling band of membranelles (cilia fused into a flat plate) serves as an efficient, and in some cases the only, means of locomotion. The species *Halteria grandinella* is a common freshwater representative of the order. Small and

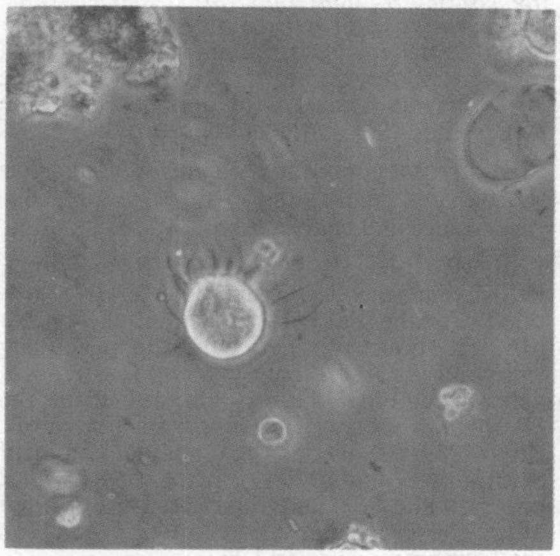

Oligotrich (*Halteria grandinella*)
J.M. Langham

spherical, it has seven groups of three cirri set in small grooves along the middle of the cell, which bounces through the water by the action of the cirri.
·protozoan features and classification **15**:129f

oligotrophic lake, lake with abundant dissolved oxygen and deficient in plant nutrients.
·varved deposit formation **19**:32d

oligouria, in medicine, the production of a small amount of urine in relation to the fluid taken in.
·acute renal failure symptoms **7**:57a

Ólimbos, Óros (Greece): *see* Olympus, Mount.

Olimpo, department, northern Paraguay, bounded on the north by Bolivia and on the east by Brazil. The territory, 7,882 sq mi (20,415 sq km) in area, lies in the Chaco Boreal, a region of scrub forest and grassland on a sandy and often swampy plain sloping eastward to the Paraguay River, which forms the department's eastern border. Its 125-mi (200-km) border with Bolivia has no natural demarcation. Olimpo is the least densely populated of Paraguay's 17 departments. Most of the inhabitants are Indians, cattle herders, or lumberers producing the quebracho hardwood. Large areas are virtually uninhabited, for the population is clustered around the departmental capital, Fuerte Olimpo (*q.v.*), a port on the Paraguay River, which is the sole trading centre serving the department. Pop. (1972 prelim.) 5,528.
·area and population table **13**:987
·map, Paraguay **13**:986

Olinda, city, eastern Pernambuco state, northeastern Brazil; atop a low hill on the At-

Church of São Bento, Olinda, Braz.
Dilson Martins—EB Inc.

lantic coast, just north of Recife, the state capital. Founded by the Portuguese Duarte Coelho Pereira as the colonial capital of Pernambuco captaincy in 1537, by 1600 its economy was based on sugar, and Negro slave labour had made it a feudal and ecclesiastical stronghold. In 1630 the Dutch captured the city, occupying it until 1654. By that time it had declined, its place of leadership being passed to Recife, which became capital. Olinda is noted principally for its 16th- and 17th-century ornate churches and monasteries and for other colonial buildings. Pop. (1970 prelim.) 187,553.
8°01′ S, 34°51′ W
·map, Brazil **3**:124
·Recife historic relationship **15**:543b
·Recife rivalry in 1700s **14**:100c

olingo, or CUATAQUIL (*Bassaricyon*), small arboreal carnivore of the raccoon family, Procyonidae, found in the jungles of Central and northern South America. Olingos, of which there are about four named species, are slender, grayish-brown animals 35–50 centimetres (14–20 inches) long, excluding the bushy, faintly ringed tail, which accounts for an additional 40–50 centimetres (16–20 inches). They have soft fur, pointed muzzles, and rounded ears. They resemble kinkajous but are less stocky and have narrower snouts and longer-haired, nonprehensile tails. Olingos are nocturnal, often travel in small groups, and feed primarily on fruit. Little else is known of their habits.

Oliniaceae, family of flowering plants of the order Myrtales.
·range, life cycle, uses, and classification **12**:773d

olio, second part of a minstrel show that consisted of a series of individual acts (music, dance, parodies, skits) and was concluded by a "hoedown" or "walk-around" in which every member of the company did a specialty number while the others sang and clapped.

Originated *c.* 1846 by Edwin P. Christy, the minstrel show olio encouraged excellence in freedom of experimentation. The olio format was later adopted by vaudeville, also a series of unrelated variety acts.

oliphant, medieval horn (*see also* horn) of ivory or bone associated with the nobility and often richly ornamented.

Oliphant, Laurence (b. 1829, Cape Town—d. Dec. 23, 1888, Twickenham, Middlesex), author, traveller, and mystic, a controversial figure whose quest to establish a Jewish state in Palestine—"fulfilling prophecy and bringing on the end of the world"—won wide support among both Jewish and Christian officials but was thought by some to be motivated either by commercial interests or by a desire to strengthen Britain's position in the Near East. The son of a British official who travelled widely throughout the empire, he received a desultory education; he was called to the bar but soon gave up the law for a life of adventure. Before the age of 24 his travels had provided material for two books, a *Journey to Khatmandu* (1852) and *The Russian Shores of the Black Sea in the Autumn of 1852, with a Voyage Down the Volga, and a Tour Through the Country of the Don Cossacks* (1853). Later experiences in various parts of the world, as

Laurence Oliphant, engraving by an unknown artist after a photograph

Radio Times Hulton Picture Library

secretary to the diplomat James Bruce, earl of Elgin, as war correspondent of *The Times*, and as unofficial British observer and (briefly) first secretary of the British legation in Japan, are recorded with verve in *Episodes in a Life of Adventure* (1887) and other books. The *Narrative of the Earl of Elgin's Mission to China and Japan* (1859) gives a fascinating account of 19th-century gunboat diplomacy. In 1865 appeared his satirical novel of London society, *Piccadilly: A Fragment of Contemporary Biography*, and in the same year he became a Conservative member of Parliament.

In 1867 Oliphant went to the U.S. and joined the Brotherhood of the New Life, first at Amenia and then at Brocton, N.Y., founded by the spiritualist "prophet" T.L. Harris, to whom he signed over his fortune and to whose rule he submitted until 1881. In 1878 he proposed to Disraeli and Robert Cecil, 3rd marquess of Salisbury, a plan for the Jewish colonization of Palestine (he was not Jewish himself). The plan was well received by Salisbury and by eastern European Jews but was refused by the sultan of Turkey, ruler of Palestine. In 1882 Oliphant and his wife settled in Haifa, where they formed a small community and wrote together the esoteric *Sympneumata; or, Evolutionary Forces Now Active in Man* (1885)—apparently a plea for purified sex life. Oliphant also wrote *Altiora Peto* (1883), which has been compared to the novels of Aldous Huxley.

Oliphant, Margaret Oliphant (b. April 4, 1828, Wallyford, Midlothian—d. June 25, 1897, Windsor, near London), prolific Scottish novelist, historical writer, and biographer best known for her portraits of small-town life. In 1852 she married her cousin, Francis Wilson Oliphant, an artist in stained glass, and settled in London. Widowed in 1859, her life became a wearisome struggle to provide, by writing, for her children and later for her brother's children. Between 1849 and her death she published more than 100 separate

Margaret Oliphant, detail of a drawing by J.M. Oliphant, 1895

Radio Times Hulton Picture Library

books of which the best known are the *Chronicles of Carlingford*, published anonymously 1863–66. These four novels of contemporary life in a small town include *Miss Marjoribanks* (1866), a young lady's attempts at social climbing, and *Salem Chapel* (1863), a young intelligent nonconformist minister's trials with his narrow-minded congregation. The best of her Scottish novels are *Passages in the Life of Mrs. Margaret Maitland* (1849), *Merkland* (1851), and *Kirsteen* (1890). Other works include *A Beleaguered City* (1880) and *A Little Pilgrim in the Unseen* (1882), excursions into the realm of the supernatural. She also published historical studies, children's books, biographies, and *Annals of a Publishing House: William Blackwood and his Sons* (1897), a work of importance to literary historians. She wrote with sympathy, insight, and humour about domestic life. Although she was often compared with George Eliot, she lacked the latter's intellectual fibre.

olistostrome, mudflow breccia which has slid far on a gentle slope.

·occurrence and characteristics **4**:1113d

Olitski, Jules (b. March 27, 1922, Gomel, Belorussian S.S.R.), painter generally identified with the Color Field school, and one of the first to use thinned paints in a staining technique to create colour compositions of a delicate, ethereal quality. He studied at the National Academy of Design in New York City (1939–42) and at the Zadkine School of Sculpture in Paris (1949), presenting his first one-man show in Paris in 1951. He exhibited at the Carnegie International in 1961 and won the Corcoran award in 1967.

"High A Yellow," synthetic polymer on canvas by Jules Olitski, 1967; in the Whitney Museum of American Art, New York

By courtesy of the Whitney Museum of American Art, New York

"Prince Patutsky Command" (1965) typifies the opulent results Olitski achieved with his technique of dyeing and spraying. Large areas saturated with brilliant colour alternate with bare canvas to create an effect of light, airy mist, giving an optical impression of atmospheric movement.

Oliva (snail): *see* olive shell.

Oliva, Treaty of (May 3, 1660), peace settlement that finally concluded the Polish–Swedish War of Succession, which had been pursued intermittently from 1600 to 1660. After the Truce of Altmark (1629) expired in 1635, the Poles and Swedes accepted the Truce of Stuhmsdorf, which was to last 26 years; but they failed to resolve their conflicts, and the war was renewed in 1655. In 1660, Poland and its allies forced Sweden to accept French mediation and to negotiate a peace settlement.

The negotiations, held at the monastery of Oliva near Danzig (modern Gdańsk, Pol.), produced an agreement that received the approval of Poland, Sweden, Brandenburg, and Austria. Sweden acquired no new territory but remained in control of the Livonian (Latvian and Estonian) lands it had obtained by the truces of Altmark and Stuhmsdorf. John Casimir of Poland, who claimed the Swedish throne, was permitted to retain the title of king of Sweden for his lifetime, but he was obliged to renounce his claim for himself and his heirs. In addition, the Treaty of Oliva confirmed Poland's 1657 agreement with Frederick William of Brandenburg (Treaty of Wehlau), by which John Casimir transferred sovereignty over Ducal Prussia from the Polish crown to the electors of Brandenburg.

·Brandenburg's annexation of Prussia **7**:709c
·concessions and reservations **14**:645d
·diplomatic significance **6**:1091h; map
·Polish concessions to Prussia **8**:94c
·Polish–Swedish war **2**:455h
·Thirty Years' War states affected **18**:342a

Olivares, Conde-Duque de **13**:559 (b. GASPAR DE GUZMÁN Y PIMENTAL, Jan. 16, 1587, Rome—d. July 22, 1645, Toro, Spain), prime minister and court favourite (*valido*) of King Philip IV of Spain, governed the country for over 20 years in a regime marked by artistic splendour and political decadence.

Abstract of text biography. An aristocrat, Olivares had been Philip's constant companion for eight years before being named prime minister (1623). He embarked on a policy of uniting what he considered Spain's anachronistic division of kingdoms, which ultimately led to revolts in the 1640s. He involved Spain in the Thirty Years' War to establish Spanish–Austrian Habsburg domination of Europe but saw the Protestant forces win important concessions in Germany, while France eclipsed Spain's hegemony in Europe. Emotionally erratic and driven to despair by Spain's reversals at the hands of its foes, Olivares, discredited by court intrigue, was forced to resign (January 1643).

REFERENCES in other text articles:
·diplomacy and reform efforts **17**:430b
·papal election rigging **17**:427f

olive (*Olea europaea;* family Oleaceae), subtropical, broad-leaved, evergreen tree and its fruit. The edible fruit is also pressed to obtain olive oil. The tree, ranging in height from 3–12 metres (10–40 feet) or more, has numerous branches; its leaves, leathery and lance-shaped, are dark green above and silvery on the underside and are paired opposite each other on the twig. The wood is resistant to decay; if the top dies back, a new trunk will often arise from the roots. The tree's beauty has been extolled for thousands of years. In ancient times it dotted the landscapes of Palestine and parts of western Asia.

The trees bloom in late spring; small, whitish flowers are borne in loose clusters in the axils of the leaves. Flowers are of two types: perfect, containing both male and female parts, which are capable of developing into the olive fruits; and male, which contain only the pollen-producing parts. The olive is wind-pollinated.

Fruit setting in the olive is often erratic; in some areas, especially where irrigation and fertilization are not practiced, bearing in alternate years is the rule. The trees may set a heavy crop one year and not even bloom the next.

The olive fruit is classed botanically as a drupe, similar to the peach or plum. Within the stone are one or two seeds. Olives tend to have maximum oil content (about 20–30 percent of fresh weight) and greatest weight six to eight months after the blossoms appear. At that stage they are black and will continue to cling to the tree for several weeks. Fruits for oil extraction are allowed to mature, but, for processing as food, immature fruits are picked or shaken off the tree.

Hundreds of named varieties of both types of olives, table and oil, are grown in warm climates. In California, olives such as the Mission variety are grown almost exclusively for table use. In Europe, olives such as the Picual, Nevadillo, and Morcal are grown mostly for oil.

The edible olive was grown on the island of Crete about 3500 BC; the Semitic peoples apparently cultivated it as early as 3000 BC. According to the Bible, it was an olive leaf that Noah's dove brought back to the ark. Olive oil was prized for anointing the body in Greece during the time of Homer; and it was an important crop of the Romans *c.* 600 BC. Later, olive growing spread to all the countries bordering the Mediterranean.

Olive (*Olea europaea*)
W.H. Hodge

Commercial olive production generally occurs in two belts around the world, between 30° and 45° N latitude and between 30° and 45° S, where the climatic requirements for growth and fruitfulness can be found. Olive varieties do not come true from seed. Seedlings generally produce inferior fruit and must be budded or grafted to one of the named varieties. Olives can be propagated by cuttings, either by hardwood cuttings set in the nursery row in the spring or by small, leafy cuttings rooted under mist sprays in a propagating frame. The nursery trees are planted 8–12 metres (26–40 feet) apart in irrigated orchards or 12–22 metres (40–72 feet) apart in unirrigated groves. They start bearing in 4 to 8 years, but full production is not reached for 15 or 20 years.

In the 20th century, Spain became easily the leader in commercial olive production, with about 26.3 percent of the world's total followed closely by Italy, with 26.0 percent, and Greece, with about 11 percent. Other important olive-producing countries are Portugal, Turkey, Tunisia, France, Morocco, Algeria, Syria, Yugoslavia, Jordan, U.S., Cyprus, Israel, and Argentina. Europe, with nearly 500,000,000 olive trees, has more than three-quarters of the world's cultivated olives, followed by Asia (about 13 percent), Africa (8 percent), and America (3 percent).

Olives are grown mainly for the production of olive oil. In Spain more than 90 percent of the crop is crushed annually for oil extraction.

Fresh, unprocessed olives are inedible because of their extreme bitterness resulting from a glucoside that can be neutralized by treatments with a dilute alkali such as lye. Salt applications also dispel some of the bitterness.

·development of agriculture **1**:330h
·domesticated plant centres of origin **5**:938c
·food preservation technology **7**:494a
·fruit farming economics **7**:756e; tables 755
·origin theories and cultivation **13**:557d

olive, or OLIVA, in anatomy, an oval swelling on each side of the medulla oblongata at the base of the brain.

·anatomic interrelationships **12**:1000e
·hearing mechanism in man **5**:1128a
·inferior olive anatomic interrelationships **12**:1000e; illus.

olive fly: *see* fruit fly.

Olive Glass Works, built 1781 by the Stranger brothers in Gloucester County, New Jersey.

·history and glass type **8**:190f

Oliveira, Juscelino Kubitschek de: *see* Kubitschek de Oliveira, Juscelino.

Oliveira Martins, Joaquim Pedro de (1845–94), Portuguese writer and biographer, was one of the first Portuguese exponents of Socialism.

olive oil, oil extracted from the fleshy part of the ripened fruit of the olive tree, *Olea europaea.* Olive oil varies in colour from clear yellow to golden; some varieties obtained from unripe fruit have a greenish tinge. Oils of varying characteristics and qualities are produced by almost every country that grows olives, the variances depending on the district and the ripeness of the fruit.

Pure olive oil is used largely for culinary purposes and in the preservation of foods, particularly canned fish. It is also used in the textile industry for wool combing, in the manufacture of toilet preparations and cosmetics, in the pharmaceutical industry for medicinal purposes, in the manufacture of high-quality castile soap, and as a lubricant.

Most of the world supply of olive oil is produced in the countries of the Mediterranean Basin, but some is produced in California, South America, and Australia. Leading producers are Spain, Italy, Tunisia, Greece, Portugal, Turkey, the Middle East, Algeria, and Morocco. Most oil produced in the Mediterranean Basin is consumed there.

The ripe olive fruit with the pit removed contains 20 to 30 percent oil, depending on the climate and care in cultivation. Olive oils obtained from the first mechanical pressing without further treatment are called virgin, and their quality depends on the state of the fruit. Only oils from the best fruit are fit for consumption without further treatment. They are rarely exported without treatment, but they may be used as the basis for export oil or may be consumed locally. The crushing apparatus used to express the oil varies from simple Roman presses, consisting of conical stones operated by mule or by hand, to modern hydraulic presses. To prevent rancidity from the formation of free fatty acids, the best quality edible oil must be removed from the pulp, which is putrescible, as soon as possible. After an initial pressing, the residual pulp is pressed again with hot water, and from this second pressing, oil is obtained that has a higher acid content. This oil, together with inferior virgin oils, constitutes the oil called *lampante*, because of its primitive use as fuel in lamps. *Lampante* is further refined to remove acid, colour, and odour and is sold as refined olive oil, which is used largely for mixing with first-extraction oils to produce edible varieties. Another inferior oil, called sulfur oil in commerce, is obtained by extraction with a volatile solvent, usually carbon disulfide; it is used both for food and for industry. Edible olive oil is practically devoid of free fatty acids; most export oils do not exceed 1 percent.

Olive oil is classified into four international grades: (1) virgin, from first pressings that meet defined standards; (2) pure, or edible, a mixture of refined and virgin; (3) refined, or commercial, refined *lampante;* (4) sulfide, extracted with solvents and refined repeatedly. Olive oil is sometimes mixed with other vegetable oils, but this is not legal in all countries; in some countries, it constitutes fraud. Adulteration can be detected by chemical analysis.

·Guadalquivir Basin groves and export **8**:451b
·Italian production and imports **9**:1099c
·North African export to ancient Rome **13**:151h

Oliver (legendary hero): *see* chansons de geste.

Oliver (OLIVIER), **Isaac** (b. 1556?, Rouen, Fr.—d. Oct. 2, 1617, London), miniature painter. His French Huguenot parents took him to England about 1568, where he studied painting and married the daughter of a then well-known portrait painter, Marcus Gheeraerts, the Elder. He soon won renown and royal patronage for his miniatures, including portraits and religious and classical scenes.

"Self-portrait," miniature by Isaac Oliver; in the National Portrait Gallery, London
By courtesy of Christie's, London

His son Peter was his pupil and carried on his father's later style.

·miniature painting tradition **13**:881g

Oliver, King, real name JOSEPH OLIVER (b. May 11, 1885, Abend, La.—d. April 8, 1938, Savannah, Ga.), cornettist who was a vital link between the semi-mythical prehistory of jazz and the firmly documented history of jazz proper; he will always be remembered for choosing as his protégé the man generally considered the greatest of all New Orleans musicians, Louis Armstrong.

Born on a plantation, Oliver went to New Orleans as a boy and began playing the cornet in 1907. By 1915 he was an established leader and two years later was being billed as "King." In the following year, after the closing down of the city's Red Light district, he moved to Chicago. Four years later he sent for Armstrong to join him as second cornettist, thus indirectly ensuring the spread of jazz across the continent and eventually the world. In 1928 he went to New York City, and from then on his fortunes declined. Plagued by dental trouble and outflanked by rapidly evolving jazz styles, he died in obscurity while working as a pool-room marker. His fame is assured, however, through the testimony of Armstrong, who always insisted that Oliver was his dominant influence and sole inspiration.

·early Chicago jazz **10**:122e

Oliver, Roland (1923–), British historian and scholar of African studies.

·Central African Bantu movement map plotting and archaeological evidence **3**:1091e

Oliver Twist (1838), novel of social criticism by the 19th-century English author Charles Dickens.
·critical editing process of Tillotson **18**:189e
·novel and propagandistic function **13**:281e
·theme of social and moral evil **5**:707c

Olives, Mount of (Jerusalem): *see* Mount of Olives.

olive shell, any marine snail comprising the family Olividae (subclass Prosobranchia of the class Gastropoda). Fossils of *Oliva* are common from the Eocene Epoch, about

Olive shell (*Oliva*)
Lynwood M. Chace—National Audubon Society

54,000,000 years ago, to the present. The shell, distinctive and easily recognizable, has a pointed apex and rapidly expands outward to the main body whorl. It is oval in shape, with a long and narrow aperture, and has an agate-like sheen and fine markings. Folds are developed on the end of the body whorl in a characteristic pattern.

Olives burrow in sandy bottoms. Common in southeastern U.S. waters is the lettered olive (*Oliva sayana*), about 6 centimetres (2.5 inches) long. Abundant in the Indo-Pacific region is the 8-cm (3-in.) orange-mouthed olive (*O. sericea*).
·coastal life on Atlantic sandy shores
illus. **4**:803

Olivétan, Latin OLIVETANUS, original name PIERRE ROBERT (*c.* 1506–1538), French Protestant translator of the Bible into the French language.
·translation precedents **2**:892h

Olivette, city, St. Louis County, Missouri, U.S., western suburb of St. Louis. The settlement, established in the early 1800s about halfway between the Mississippi and Missouri rivers, was a stopping point for migrants moving westward. Known successively as Central, Center Town, and Centerton, the community probably took its present name from its Olive Street Road post office. Industries, most of which are zoned in the city's northeast section, include the manufacture of rubber products, carburetors, air filters, mining equipment, and insulated glass. After 1950 Olivette experienced rapid urban development. Inc. village, 1930; city, 1956. Pop. (1950) 1,761; (1980) 8,039.
38°40′ N, 90°24′ W

Olivier, Laurence (Kerr) Olivier, Baron (b. May 22, 1907, Dorking, Surrey), stage and motion picture actor, director, and producer who helped rebuild the Old Vic Theatre Company in London after World War II. He was the first member of his profession to be elevated to a life peerage.

After many stage appearances as a child, Olivier enrolled at the Central School of Dramatic Art in 1924, then began his professional career with the Birmingham Repertory Theatre Company (1926-28). Later Olivier played a supporting role in the original production of Noël Coward's *Private Lives*; and he alternated the parts of Romeo and Mercutio with John Gielgud in *Romeo and Juliet* in London.

In 1937 Olivier joined the Old Vic, where he played many Shakespearean roles and on one memorable occasion played Hamlet to the Ophelia of Vivien Leigh (who was to become his second wife) in a production staged at Elsinore Castle in Denmark (in fact, the Kronborg Slot in the city of Helsingør). After a series of successful films in the U.S., including *Wuthering Heights* (1939), *Rebecca* (1939), and *Pride and Prejudice* (1940), he returned to England to serve in the Fleet Air Arm during World War II.

In 1944 he became co-director of the Old Vic with Ralph Richardson, and together, during six years, they directed the company in some of its greatest productions. Olivier's notable successes in Shakespearean roles during that time included the title role in *Richard III;* Hotspur in *Henry IV, Part I;* and Justice Shallow in *Henry IV, Part II.* He also played Oedipus in Sophocles' *Oedipus Rex.* In 1946 he took the Old Vic to the United States and a year later was knighted for his services to the theatre. During the postwar years he produced, directed, and played in film versions of *Henry V* and *Hamlet*, for which he received an Academy Award.

From 1950 Olivier directed and acted under his own management, notably in Shakespeare's *Antony and Cleopatra* and George Bernard Shaw's *Caesar and Cleopatra*, with Vivien Leigh, and as Archie Rice in *The Entertainer*, by John Osborne (1957). In 1962 he became the director of the new, London-based National Theatre Company, also appearing in many productions there, notably in the title role of *Othello*, in August Strindberg's *Dance of Death*, and in Eugene O'Neill's *Long Day's Journey into Night*. In 1970 he was created a baron.

Laurence Olivier as Edgar in the production (1967) by the National Theatre Company of August Strindberg's *Dance of Death*
Zoe Dominic

His many films of the 1950s and '60s include *The Beggar's Opera* (1953), *Richard III* (1956; British Film Academy Award), and *Othello* (1966). He received the New York Film Critics award in 1973 for his performance in *Sleuth*.
·acting–directing flexibility **5**:828a
·screen adaptations of Shakespeare **18**:217e

Olivier, Émile: *see* Ollivier, Émile.

Olivier, Isaac: *see* Oliver, Isaac.

olivines 13:560, group of common silicate minerals that may be the main constituent of the Earth's mantle. They occur in many igneous rocks (basalt; gabbro; peridotite; and dunite, which is almost entirely olivine), including the oldest rocks known. They also occur in dolomitic marbles and schists, in stony meteorites, and in slag and are a minor constituent of some (type A) lunar rocks.

Olivines are readily weathered and seldom occur as prominent constituents of sediments. Exceptions include the beach sands at Hawaii and other localities that are derived from olivine-rich basalts.

Olivines are silicates of magnesium, iron, calcium, and manganese. Their structure consists of silicate tetrahedra (four oxygen atoms in tetrahedral arrangement about a central silicon atom) linked by metal atoms. Common olivine is relatively infusible, withstanding temperatures of more than 1,500° C (2,700° F), and is sometimes used in refractory brick. Transparent green olivine (the name alludes to this colour) is called peridot and is used as a gemstone. The mineral name olivine is applied to any member of the forsterite–fayalite series.

The text article covers the properties, crystal structure, and occurrence and distribution of the olivines in nature. For characteristics of olivines, *see* Table, p. 523.

REFERENCES in other text articles:
·basalt chemical composition **9**:217b
·Earth's mantle mineralogy **16**:764b
·gabbro texture and Bowen's series, illus. 2 and 5 **9**:221
·heat capacity, illus. 4 **15**:960
·igneous rock composition and Bowen's reaction series **9**:202c; illus. 207
·intrusive igneous rock classification **9**:220f; table 221
·metamorphic process in Earth's mantle **6**:703f
·occurrence in pyroclastic rocks **9**:229f
·pallasite meteorite structure **12**:45g
·peridot characteristics and gem value **7**:973c
·shield volcano structure and form **19**:505d
·structure, chemistry, and occurrence **16**:757h
·upper mantle composition and phase transformations **6**:53f; illus.

RELATED ENTRIES in the *Ready Reference and Index:*
chrysolite; forsterite–fayalite series; humite; monticellite; peridot; tephroite

olivine–spinel transition (geology): *see* mantle transition zone.

olivopontocerebellar atrophy, in medicine, syndrome characterized by the wasting away of certain parts of the brain.
·symptoms, causation, and course **12**:1050f

Öljeitü, Muslim name MOḤAMMAD KHODĀBANAH (b. 1280—d. Dec. 16, 1316, Solṭānīyeh, near Kazvin, Iran), eighth Il-Khan ruler of Iran, during whose reign the Shīʿī branch of Islām became (and still remains) the state religion of Iran.

A great-grandson of Hülegü, founder of the Il-Khan dynasty, Öljeitü was baptized a Christian and given the name Nicholas by his mother. As a youth he converted to Buddhism and later to the Sunnah, the major branch of Islām. After the death (1304) of his brother Maḥmūd Ghāzān, the seventh Il-Khan, he disposed of his rivals easily and began a relatively peaceful reign. In 1307 the Caspian province of Gilan was conquered, strengthening Il-Khan rule, and a potentially dangerous rebellion was crushed in Herāt (now in Afghanistan). The traditional hostility between the Il-Khans and the Mamlūks of Syria and Egypt persisted, however, and a badly organized invasion of Mamlūk territory took place in 1312. The expedition had to be abandoned after expected help from European princes failed to materialize.

Öljeitü changed his religious affiliations several times. His conversion to Sunnī Islām is attributed to one of his wives. During the winter of 1307–08 there was a bitter religious feud between the adherents of the Ḥanafī and Shāfiʿī schools of Sunnī Islāmic law, so disgusting Öljeitü that he considered converting back to Buddhism, a course that proved politically impossible. Greatly influenced by the Shīʿī theologian Ibn al-Muṭahhar al-Ḥillī, he came to embrace the religion; and on his return from a visit to the tomb of ʿAlī in Iraq (1309–10), he proclaimed Shīʿism the state religion of Iran.

An active patron of the arts, Öljeitü built a new capital at Solṭānīyeh that required the efforts of many artists, who made it a masterpiece of Il-Khanid architecture. He lent vital encouragement and support to Rashīd ad-Dīn's monumental world history and to the endeavours of Iranian poets.

·Mongol pacification interpretation **9**:599f

Olkhon Island, in Lake Baikal, is administered as part of Irkutsk *oblast* (administrative region), east central Russian Soviet Federated Socialist Republic. It is separated from the western shore by the straits of Olkhon and the Maloye Sea. Its area is 280 sq mi (730 sq km), and its highest point, Mt. Zhima, rises to 4,186 ft (1,276 m). The island is composed largely of granites and gneisses. The northern part is forested, while the southern has steppe-grasslands. The island has frequent northwesterly winds known as *sarma*.
53°09′ N, 107°24′ E

Ölkofra tháttr, Icelandic humorous saga, possibly 12th century.

·folk literature of Iceland **16**:147c

Ollier, Claude (b. Dec. 17, 1922, Paris), novelist associated with the *nouveau roman*, an avant-garde movement of the 1950s and '60s comprised of French writers opposed to the traditional framework of the novel. Ollier's distinction is to have pursued the art of description to new frontiers: his minute and fanatically precise descriptions of reality often grade into unreality. Although the description is bound to the "object" it describes, it can create a world of fiction and adventure. Things serve as a counterpoint to ideas.

Ollier uses the device of *inquest* in all his books: the hero, a derisive desperado, arrives in a new country (in Africa) to accomplish a mission; he ends forgetting about his mission as he discovers his new surroundings. Eventually, he gets lost, and the interest shifts to secondary characters. His four novels form a cycle beginning with *La Mise en scène*, 1958, Prix Medicis; *Le Maintien de l'ordre*, 1961; and *L'Été indien*, 1963. The last one (*L'Échec de Nolan*, 1967) is a synthesis of the first three and continually refers back to them. It crowns the story with the disappearance of the hero. Ollier is also the author of radio scripts.

Ollier's disease: *see* enchondromatosis.

Ollivier (OLIVIER), **Émile** (b. July 2, 1825, Marseille, Fr.—d. Aug. 20, 1913, Saint-Gervais-les-Bains), French statesman, writer, and orator, who was responsible, as minister of justice under Napoleon III, for moving France and its emperor toward a compromise between Napoleonic autocracy and parliamentary government. He worked to strengthen the bonds between the Emperor and the masses. His historical importance lies more in his aims than his achievements because of his short stay in power.

Ollivier, photograph by P. Petit; in the Bibliothèque Nationale, Paris

By courtesy of the Bibliotheque Nationale, Paris

Trained in the law, and in his early life an adherent of the Socialist and Romantic movements, Ollivier was appointed commissary general of the Bouches-du-Rhône *département* at the outbreak of the Revolution of 1848. When Louis-Napoleon became president of the Republic (December 1948), Ollivier was dismissed from office, and from 1849 to 1857 held no public office. During this time he abandoned his Socialistic activities because of the pressures of the authoritarian Second Empire.

Elected to the legislative assembly in 1857, Ollivier became one of the republican minority known as "the Five," which viewed Napoleon's despotism with hostility. During this time Ollivier evolved his own special brand of republicanism. He believed that the forms of government do not matter so much as civic freedom. He also thought that revolutions impede social progress as often as they advance it, so that liberal reforms should be made by persuasion rather than violence. When the Emperor made liberal concessions in November 1860, Ollivier broke with the republicans and offered his support to Napoleon.

On Jan. 2, 1870, Napoleon appointed Ollivier minister of justice. Ollivier drafted a constitution and set up numerous commissions to prepare the complete reform of such areas as labour, education, and law. He seemed to have transformed the empire from despotism to constitutional monarchy without bloodshed or violence.

A little more than six months after Ollivier came to power he declared (July 19, 1870) war on Prussia, and because of the repercussions from France's defeat in this war all progress toward his envisioned liberal empire was halted. Formerly a pacifist who wished that Napoleon would curtail his foreign entanglements, Ollivier now believed that war was necessary because France's honour had been slighted. He resigned on Aug. 9, 1870, and never returned to politics.

During the remaining 43 years of his life, Ol-

Olivines

name formula	colour	lustre	Mohs hardness	specific gravity	habit or form	fracture or cleavage	refractive indices	crystal system space group	remarks
forsterite-fayalite series									
forsterite Mg_2SiO_4	green to lemon-yellow	vitreous	7	3.2	flattened crystals; compact or granular massive; embedded grains	one distinct, one imperfect cleavage;	$\alpha = 1.631$ $\beta = 1.651$ $\gamma = 1.670$	orthorhombic Pbnm	a continuous solid solution series exists between forsterite and fayalite with iron replacing magnesium in the molecular structure; the intermediate members have properties between these two
fayalite Fe_2SiO_4	greenish yellow to yellow-amber	vitreous	6½	4.4		two imperfect cleavages;	$\alpha = 1.827$ $\beta = 1.869$ $\gamma = 1.879$	orthorhombic Pbnm	
tephroite-fayalite series									
knebelite $(Mn, Fe)_2SiO_4$	brown-black; gray-black	vitreous	6½	4.0–4.2	crystals; grains	one moderate, two imperfect cleavages;	$\alpha = 1.775–1.815$ $\beta = 1.810–1.853$ $\gamma = 1.826–1.867$	orthorhombic Pbnm	a continuous solid solution series exists between fayalite and tephroite with iron replacing manganese in the molecular structure
tephroite Mn_2SiO_4	olive- or bluish-green; ash gray	vitreous	6	3.8		one moderate, one imperfect cleavage;	$\alpha = 1.770–1.788$ $\beta = 1.803–1.810$ $\gamma = 1.817–1.825$	orthorhombic Pbnm	
monticellite $CaMgSiO_4$	gray or colourless	vitreous	5½–6	3.1	small prismatic crystals; grains; twinned crystals	poor cleavage	$\alpha = 1.641$ $\beta = 1.646$ $\gamma = 1.653$	orthorhombic Pnma	forms limited solid solution series with glaucochroite and with kirschsteinite with manganese and iron respectively, replacing magnesium in the molecular structure
humite group									
norbergite $Mg(OH, F)_2 \cdot Mg_2SiO_4$	tawny to chamois	vitreous to resinous	6½	3.2	twinned crystals; grains; intergrown with the other members of the group	poor cleavage; subconchoidal to uneven fracture;	$\alpha = 1.563–1.567$ $\beta = 1.567–1.579$ $\gamma = 1.590–1.593$	orthorhombic Pmcn	minerals in the humite group are regular intergrowths of brucite and forsterite; they are thus related to the olivines
chondrodite $Mg(OH, F)_2 \cdot 2Mg_2SiO_4$	yellow, brown, hyacinth-red	vitreous to resinous	6½	3.2–3.3			$\alpha = 1.592–1.615$ $\beta = 1.602–1.627$ $\gamma = 1.621–1.646$	monoclinic $P\frac{2_1}{c}$	
humite $Mg(OH, F)_2 \cdot 3Mg_2SiO_4$	yellow, dark orange	vitreous to resinous	6	3.2–3.3			$\alpha = 1.607–1.643$ $\beta = 1.619–1.653$ $\gamma = 1.639–1.675$	orthorhombic Pmcn	
clinohumite $Mg(Oh, F)_2 \cdot 4Mg_2SiO_4$	yellow-brown	vitreous to resinous	6	3.2–3.4			$\alpha = 1.629–1.638$ $\beta = 1.641–1.643$ $\gamma = 1.662–1.674$	monoclinic $P\frac{2_1}{c}$	

livier cultivated his wide interests and varied talents. At 65 he wrote *L'Empire libéral* ("The Liberal Empire"), partly a history of the Second Empire and partly memoirs. This monumental work of 17 volumes is historically valuable as a contemporary defense of Napoleon III. His other writings include a study of Michelangelo, a novel, and volumes on ecclesiastical affairs. From 1870 he was a member of the Académie Française.

·attempt to prevent Franco-Prussian War **12**:841d
·Second Empire constitution draft **7**:667e

olm (*Proteus anguinus*), a blind salamander (family Proteidae, order Urodela) found in caves of the Carpathian Mountains in southeastern Europe. It grows to about 30 centimetres (12 inches) long and has a normally white (unpigmented) body, tiny limbs, red gill plumes, narrow head, and a blunt snout. Its vestigial but light-sensitive eyes are covered with skin. The olm usually lays eggs but sometimes bears its young alive.

·classification and general features **18**:1088b

Olm (*Proteus anguinus*), darkened by exposure to light
Jacques Six

Olmec, the name given to the first elaborate pre-Columbian culture of Meso-America; its most important centres were in what is now the southern Veracruz and adjacent Tabasco region of the Mexican Gulf Coast. These centres include La Venta, San Lorenzo, and Tres Zapotes. The first evidences of the remarkable Olmec art style appear at about 1150 BC. Between 1100 and 800 BC this Olmec stylistic influence flourished, from the Valley of Mexico (the Tlatilco culture) to the Republic of San Salvador (the Chalchuapa rock carvings). It has been speculated that these influences were the symbols of political empire, of a trading network, or of a religious cult. While no firm conclusions have been reached as to how the functional nature of the Olmec influences spread, it is clear that later Meso-American native religions and iconography, from all parts of the area, can be traced back to Olmec beginnings. Olmec art is expressed in monumental sculpture, small jade carvings, pottery, and other media. Its dominant motif is that of a jaguar face or a stylized anthropomorphic jaguar. The Olmec ceremonial centres of La Venta and San Lorenzo are marked by great mounds, carved steles, altars, and statues. From these constructions and monuments, as well as from the sophistication and power of the art style, it is evident that ancient Olmec society was complex and nonegalitarian. Olmec stylistic influence disappeared after about 800 BC. Not all of the Olmec sites were abandoned, but Olmec culture gradually changed, and the region ceased to be the cultural leader of Meso-America.

·archaeological studies in Mexico **1**:1079g
·artistic use of jaguar **12**:166c
·civilization and religion **2**:549a
·design of cities **18**:1070b
·language speculation **11**:961e
·Meso-American civilization development **11**:937a
·sculpture and culture distribution **1**:685a; illus.

Olmecan languages, also called POPOLOCAN or MAZATECAN, group of languages of the Otomanguean phylum scattered throughout the region of Mexico south of Mexico City and north of the Isthmus of Tehuantepec, including Popoloca, Chocho, Mazatec, Ixcatec, and Guantinikamam.

·member languages **11**:960d; table and map

Olmedo, José Joaquín (b. March 20, 1780, Guayaquil, Ecuador—d. Feb. 19, 1847, Guayaquil), poet and statesman, whose odes commemorating South American achievement of independence from Spain captured the revolutionary spirit of his time, inspired a generation of romantic poets and patriots, and have remained monuments to the heroic figures of the liberation movement in South America.

After receiving his degree in law in 1805 from the National University of San Marcos in Lima, Olmedo was sent to Spain in 1811 to represent Guayaquil in the Cortes de Cádiz, the revolutionary parliament that promulgated the liberal constitution of 1812, based on the egalitarian ideals of the French Revolution, which was soon to have an influence on the revolutions for independence throughout Spanish America.

Olmedo returned to Guayaquil in 1816, continuing to be active in political life while writing poetry. His forceful themes of battle and liberation, inspired by contemporary events and the Classical poetry of Homer, Horace, and Virgil, soon brought him recognition as an outstanding spokesman of the liberation movement. The ode for which he is best remembered, *La victoria de Junín: Canto a Bolívar* (1825; "The Victory at Junín: Song to Bolívar"), commemorates the decisive battle won there by the forces of the liberator Simón Bolívar against the Spanish armies, a turning point in the South American struggle for independence. Neoclassical in form, yet Romantic in inspiration and imagery, the *Canto a Bolívar* is considered by many critics the finest example of heroic poetry written in Spanish America.

When Ecuador became a republic in 1830, Olmedo was elected its first vice president, but he declined this honour, preferring to remain active in local politics. His later poetry foresaw and deplored the trend toward the militarism and civil wars that were beginning to undermine the unity of South America after its independence from Spain had been achieved.

·Latin-American 19th-century literature **10**:1204d

Olmi, Ermanno (1931–), Italian film director.

·cinematic plots and themes **12**:535e

Olmsted, Frederick Law (b. April 26, 1822, Hartford, Conn.—d. Aug. 28, 1903, Brookline, Mass.), landscape architect whose humanitarian and environmental interests led him to design a succession of outstanding public parks, beginning with Central Park, New York City.

At the age of 14, sumac poisoning seriously affected Olmsted's eyesight and limited his education. As an apprentice topographic engineer for a brief period, he received the basic skills needed for his later career. In 1842 and 1847, his sight having improved, he attended lectures in science and engineering at Yale University. For a time he was interested in scientific farming, which he studied under George Geddes, who had a well-known model farm at Owego, N.Y. During an extensive holiday in Europe, Olmsted was deeply impressed with English landscaping and wrote about his observations in *Walks and Talks of an American Farmer in England* (1852).

Olmsted's open opposition to slavery led the editor of the *New York Times* to send him to the American South from 1852 to 1855 to report weekly on how slavery affected the region's economy. His report, published as *The Cotton Kingdom* (1861) is regarded as a reliable account of the antebellum South. When Central Park in New York City was projected in 1857, Olmsted was superintendent. In competition with more than 30 others the plan proposed by Olmsted and Calvert Vaux, a young British architect, won first prize. Olmsted was made architect in chief in one of the first attempts in the U.S. to apply art to the improvement of nature in a public park. The work attracted widespread attention, with the result that he was engaged thereafter in most of the important works of a similar nature in the U.S.: Prospect Park, Brooklyn; Fairmont Park, Philadelphia; Riverside and Morningside parks, New York City; Belle Isle Park, Detroit; the grounds surrounding the Capitol at Washington, D.C., between 1874 and 1895; Stanford University at Palo Alto, Calif.; and many others. He also designed Mount Royal Park, Montreal.

From 1864 to 1890 Olmstead was chairman of the first Yosemite commission, taking charge of the property for California and succeeding in preserving the area as a permanent public park. Plans for the Niagara Falls park project, among the last in which Olmsted and Vaux collaborated, did much to influence the state of New York to preserve the Niagara reservation.

After 1886, Olmsted was largely occupied in laying out an extensive system of parks and parkways for the city of Boston and the town of Brookline and in working on a landscape improvement scheme for Boston Harbor. In the late 1880s, when the Chicago World's Columbian Exposition was being planned for 1893, Olmsted was chosen to head the land-

Gallaudet College, Washington, D.C., designed by Olmsted and Vaux, 1886
Olmsted Sesquicentennial Committee; photo, Circlescan, Red Bank, New Jersey

scape project, which he later redesigned as Jackson Park. He spent his last years mainly at his home in Brookline. A biography by Laura Wood Roper, *Flo*, was published in 1974.

·Boston's landscaping **3**:58e
·landscape design in United States **7**:898c

Olmütz (Czechoslovakia): *see* Olomouc.

Olmütz, Punctation of, agreement signed at Olmütz (Olomouc, Moravia, in modern Czechoslovakia) between Prussia and Austria in November 1850. By its terms Prussia accepted Austria's reconstitution of the German Confederation, a loose grouping of German states that it had been hoped might replace the Holy Roman Empire (dissolved by Napoleon in 1806). Prussia also promised to assist Denmark in reconquering the insurgent duchies of Schleswig and Holstein, over which Prussia had disputed with Denmark. Prussian ambition elsewhere was one of the causes of the punctation, for Prussia had been working toward supremacy in the German Confederation and had clashed with Austria over the confederation's composition. Consequently, when in autumn 1850 the elector of Hesse appealed for help against rebellious subjects, both Austria and Prussia sent troops and these threatened to clash. The Russian emperor threatened Prussia with invasion, and the Punctation of Olmütz therefore represented a diplomatic reverse for that state. Though the question of Germany's future organization was subsequently settled in April 1851 on terms unfavourable to Austria, Prussia's resentment of the punctation remained.

·Frederick William IV's compromise **7**:708c
·German Confederation restoration **8**:108h
·Schwarzenberg and Habsburg diplomacy **7**:686a

Olney, market town, Buckinghamshire, England, on the River Ouse. The town has agricultural associations, a tannery, and handcrafted furniture industries. The poet William Cowper lived there from 1767 to 1786 and assisted the curate John Newton in the production of *Olney Hymns* (1779). A traditional pancake race is run there on Shrove Tuesday. Pop. (1971) 2,750.
52°09′ N, 0°43′ W

Olney, Richard (b. Sept. 15, 1835, Oxford, Mass.—d. April 8, 1917, Boston), Democratic secretary of state (1895–97) known for his formulation of the Olney Corollary to the Monroe Doctrine, which maintained the right of the United States to intervene in any international disputes within the Western Hemisphere.

Olney, 1895
By courtesy of the National Archives, Washington, D.C.

A Boston attorney who had served only one term in the Massachusetts legislature (1873–74), Olney was suddenly thrust into national prominence when Pres. Grover Cleveland appointed him U.S. attorney general in 1893. In this position, during the strike of railway employees against the Pullman Company in Chicago (1894), he instructed federal attorneys to obtain injunctions to restrain the strikers from acts of violence, thus setting a precedent for what came to be called "government by injunction" (*see* Pullman Strike). He also advised the President to use federal troops to quell disturbances within the city on the ground that the national government must prevent interference with the mails under the interstate commerce clause of the Constitution.

Becoming secretary of state in June 1895, Olney found himself almost immediately involved with the problem of a dispute between Great Britain and Venezuela over the Venezuela–British Guiana boundary. With Cleveland's support Olney issued (July 20) an aggressive note demanding that Britain, in conformity with the Monroe Doctrine, arbitrate the controversy in order to avoid war and asserting the sovereignty of the United States in the Western Hemisphere. The matter was in fact arbitrated in 1899, after Olney's retirement in 1897 to the private practice of law.

Olof Skötkonung, called THE TAX KING (d. 1022, Sweden), king of Sweden whose efforts to impose Christianity were frustrated by the leading non-Christian Swedish chieftains.

The son of King Erik the Victorious, Olof, opposing the development of a strong Norwegian state, joined Sweyn I Forkbeard, king of Denmark, and his allies in a victorious war against Norway in 1000. Olof subsequently married his illegitimate daughter Holmfrith to the earl Sweyn, one of the Danish viceroys in Norway. Initially opposed to Olaf II Haraldsson, king of Norway, he later made peace with him and married his other illegitimate daughter, Astri, to the Norwegian ruler. His legitimate daughter, Ingigerth, married Yaroslav I the Wise, grand prince of Kiev.

A committed Christian, Olof was prevented by advocates of the native Norse religion, based at the temple at Uppsala, from personally enforcing conversion. Missionaries from many European countries, however, carried out the work of conversion. Olof's life is described extensively in Icelandic sagas of the 13th century.

·Sweden in the Viking Age **16**:307d

Olofson, Georg (Swedish poet): *see* Stiernhielm, Georg Olofson.

Olokun (1967–), literary magazine in the Yoruba language, published semi-annually at Ibadan, Nigeria.

·origin and contributors **1**:242d

ololiuqui (plant): *see* Rivea.

Olomouc, German OLMÜTZ, city, Severomoravský *kraj* (Northern Moravia Region), Czechoslovakia, on the Morava River at its confluence with the Bystřice. To the south stretches the fertile Haná farming region.

Olomouc possibly originated as a Roman fort (Mons Iulii) and by the 9th century was an important stronghold. A bishopric, established there in 1063, was raised to an archbishopric in 1777. At the Peace of Olomouc (1478), Moravia was ceded to Hungary. Olomouc was considered the Moravian capital during the Thirty Years' War (1618–48), when it was occupied and plundered by the Swedes. Badly damaged, after 1640 it was displaced by Brno (Brünn) as the first city of Moravia. Until 1886 the main importance of Olomouc was that of a strongpoint. It played a significant role in the mid-18th century during the struggle over Silesia between the Prussians and Austrians. The emperor Ferdinand I of Austria abdicated there in 1848 in favour of the young Francis Joseph I, and the Punctation of Olmütz of 1850 restored the German Confederation. The fortifications were demolished in the late 19th century.

Historic buildings include the 14th-century Gothic St. Wenceslas' Cathedral with a 328-ft (100-m) tower, and the town hall, which is adorned by a 230-ft tower and a 15th-century astronomical clock (restored after damage in World War II). In the Great Square is an 18th-century Trinity column. Olomouc is known for its fountains, notably Triton (1707)

Astronomical clock on the town hall tower, in Olomouc, Czech.
Flip Schulke—Black Star

and Caesar's (1720). The city's university was founded in 1569; it was suppressed in 1858 but was revived after World War II and named after František Palacký, the Czech patriot-scholar.

Manufactures include steel, machine tools, gas appliances, salt, sugar, chocolate, and beer. Olomouc has the largest food-refrigerating plant in Moravia. Pop. (1970) 79,931.
49°36′ N, 17°16′ E

·map, Czechoslovakia **5**:413

Olonets language (dialect of Karelian): *see* Karelian language.

Olorgesailie Beds, Pleistocene deposits in eastern Africa (the Pleistocene Epoch began about 2,500,000 years ago and ended about 10,000 years ago). The Olorgesailie Beds are generally associated with Bed IV of Olduvai Gorge and are correlated with the Kanjeran Pluvial Stage, thought to occupy the time span between 65,000 and 45,000 years ago.

Olosega (American Samoa): *see* Manua Islands.

Olowe of Ise, 20th-century African Yoruba sculptor.

·African sculpture techniques, illus. 10 **1**:255

Olson, Charles (John) (b. Dec. 27, 1910, Worcester, Mass.—d. Jan. 10, 1970, New York City), avant-garde poet whose practice and theory of writing influenced a number of U.S. poets who became prominent in the decade following World War II. He proposed the need for new measures to judge the appropriateness of the structure of a poem, the choice of language, and the physical arrangement on the page. Underlying his proposals is a sometimes esoteric account of how breathing and the phrasing of words should be joined to obtain the most forceful version of a poem. Implied is a rejection of traditional poetic forms. He also believed that the poet should choose the cosmos itself as his ordering source of vision.

Olson's influence on other poets began in the early 1950s, while he served as an instructor and then as rector at Black Mountain College, a short-lived experimental school in North Carolina, attended and staffed by a number of artists and writers, including Robert Creeley, who taught there and edited the *Black Moun-*

tain Review. The designation Black Mountain school of poetry refers to Olson's theories and the poets whose work this magazine published.

Olson's two major works both appeared in 1960: *The Maximus Poems*, a sequence of 38 poems, and *The Distances*, a collection of many of his shorter poems. His concepts of poetry are contained in his *Projective Verse* (1959), from which the term Projectivists was derived to describe those who accepted his ideas. He also wrote on other subjects, including the Mayan Indians, Herman Melville, and U.S. history.

Olsztyn, *województwo* (province), northeastern Poland bordered by the U.S.S.R. to the north and the provinces of Białystok on the east, Warszawa (Warsaw) on the south, Bydgoszcz on the southwest, and Gdańsk on the west. It has an area of 8,133 sq mi (21,064 sq km). There is little industry in the sparsely populated province except for lumber milling and food processing. Its forests and more than

Olsztyn castle, Poland, founded in 1334
CAF, Warsaw

2,000 well-stocked lakes make it a major tourist region. Poland's largest lake, Śniardwy, is located in the southeastern part of Olsztyn. The main towns are Olsztyn, the provincial capital, and Ostróda. Pop. (1970 prelim.) 978,000.

Olsztyn, German ALLENSTEIN, capital, Olsztyn *województwo* (province), northeastern Poland, on the Łyna River in the Masurian lake district. The town serves as a trade centre, with major rail and road connections for the lake district. The Masurian Regional Museum and an agricultural school are located here. The Teutonic Knights built an imposing castle there in 1334, and the settlement that grew around it received municipal rights in 1353. The area became part of Poland in 1945. Parts of the Gothic castle and surrounding walls remain. Pop. (1970 prelim.) 94,100.
53°48′ N, 20°29′ E
·map, Poland **14**:626

Olt, *judet* (district) in Romania.
·area and population, table 1 **15**:1051

Olten, city, Solothurn canton, northern Switzerland, on the Aare River, southeast of Basel. The parish church dates from 1806 and the covered bridge over the Aare was restored in 1805. There is an 11th-century castle at nearby Aarburg. An important rail junction with the main workshops of the Swiss Federal Railways, Olten is a modern industrial centre manufacturing aluminum ware, machinery, electrical apparatus, auto parts and other metal products, shoes, and textiles. It is the centre of Switzerland's Old Catholics. Pop. (1970) 21,209.
47°21′ N, 7°54′ E
·map, Switzerland **17**:868

Olt River, in central and southern Romania, rises close to the headwaters of the Mureş River, in the Ciuc depression, at an altitude of

Olt River flowing between the Făgăraş mountains and the Carpathians in central Romania
William Gelman—Artstreet

5,900 ft (1,800 m) and flows east-southeast, then south for 420 mi (670 km) finally entering the Danube opposite Nikopol, Bulg. It exits from the Ciuc depression through the mountains at Tuşnad, carving out a valley where several resorts and spas are located (Tuşnad, Bicaz, Malnaş); then it flows successively through the Bîsei and Făgăraş valleys before cutting a gorge through the Carpathians after which it flows south through the Danube Plain. Its watercourse across the Carpathians at Pasul (pass) Turnu Roşu is the most important breach of those mountains in Romania. There is some logging along its upper and middle courses, and its lower course below Slatina is navigable for small boats. Its principal tributaries are the Negru, the Lotru, the Olteţul, and the Teslui.
43°43′ N, 24°51′ E
·Carpathian Mountains' gap valleys **3**:948c
·Romanian physical geography **15**:1047c

Oluf I (1052–95), king of Denmark.
·Danish political consolidation **16**:308b

O-lun-chun, ethnic minority of northeast China.
·Heilungkiang population patterns **8**:743a

Olvera Street, brick walkway in Los Angeles, California, lined with shops and a private museum.
·attractions and incorporation into state park **11**:112d

Olvidados, Los (1950; "The Young and the Damned"), film by Luis Buñuel.
·theme and style **3**:480d

Olybrius (d. Nov. 2, AD 472), Western Roman emperor from April to November 472. Before he became head of state, Olybrius was a wealthy senator; he married Placidia, the daughter of Valentinian III (Western emperor 425–455). Gaiseric, king of the Vandals, a Germanic people who maintained a kingdom in North Africa, hoped that Olybrius would be made Western Emperor but his support made Olybrius suspect to the Eastern Roman emperor Leo I. Leo sent Olybrius from Constantinople to Rome, hoping he would be killed by the reigning Western emperor, Anthemius; but the Roman general Flavius Ricimer, known as a kingmaker, elevated him to the throne soon after his arrival (April 472). Anthemius was overthrown and put to death in July 472. Ricimer died in August and his puppet king Olybrius lived only until November. Leo never recognized Olybrius as a legitimate ruler.

Olympia 13:564, a place in Greece's western Peloponnese that was for the ancient Greeks a famous religious sanctuary and site of the Olympic Games.

The text article covers Olympia's history and describes its remains, among them the workshop of the celebrated sculptor Phidias, the Temple of Zeus, (*c.* 460 BC) and that of Hera (*c.* 600? BC), one of ancient Greece's most venerable buildings.

REFERENCE in other text article:
·Classical architecture and sculpture **19**:292b; illus.

Olympia, capital of Washington, U.S., seat of Thurston County, on Budd Inlet and Capitol Lake (at the south end of Puget Sound), at the mouth of the Deschutes River. Laid out in 1851 as Smithfield, it became the site of a U.S. customs house and was renamed for the nearby Olympic Mountains. Chosen territorial capital in 1853 and incorporated in 1859, it developed port facilities and a lumber-based economy, augmented by oyster farming, dairying, berry growing, and poultry raising. Its harbour is the base for a large merchant reserve fleet. The Old Capitol (built 1893) is used as a state office building. The new Capitol Group of buildings in white sandstone, of classic design (completed 1935), stands on a promontory in a 35-ac (14-ha) park. Located at the base of the Olympic Peninsula, the city

New capitol building, Olympia, Wash.
Bond—Publix

is a tourist service centre, gateway to Olympic National Park, and headquarters for the Olympic National Forest. It is the home of St. Martins College (1895). Pop. (1980) 27,447.
47°03′ N, 122°53′ W
·map, United States **18**:908

Olympia (1863; Louvre, Paris), oil painting by Édouard Manet that caused a scandal at the 1865 Salon because the picture, a blatantly realistic portrayal of a contemporary nude woman in her boudoir, was considered indecent by the Parisian public.
·scandal at Louvre first showing **11**:440f

Olympias (b. *c.* 375—d. 316 BC), wife of Philip II of Macedonia and mother of Alexander the Great. She played important roles in the power struggles that followed the deaths of both rulers. The daughter of Neoptolemus, king of Epirus, she apparently was originally named Myrtale. Later she may have been called Olympias as a recognition of Philip's victory in the Olympic Games of 356. Philip's polygamy did not threaten her position until 337, when he married a high-born Macedonian, Cleopatra. Olympias withdrew to Epirus, returning after Philip's assassination (336). She then had Cleopatra and her infant daughter killed. She quarrelled repeatedly with Antipater, regent of Macedonia during the early years of Alexander's invasion of Asia, and eventually retired again, *c.* 331, to Epirus.

Upon the death of Antipater in 319 (Alexander had died in 323), his successor, Polyperchon, invited Olympias to act as regent for her young grandson, Alexander IV. She declined his request until 317, when Antipater's son Cassander established Philip II's half-witted son Philip III (Arrhidaeus) as king of Macedonia. The Macedonian soldiers supported her return. She put to death Philip and his wife, Cassander's brother, and a hundred of his partisans. Cassander entered Macedonia and blockaded Olympias in Pydna, where she surrendered in the spring of 316. She was condemned to death, but Cassander's soldiers refused to carry out the sentence. She finally

was killed by relatives of those she had executed.
·Alexander's youth and early reign **1**:468h

Olympic cubit, ancient Greek unit of measure equivalent to 24 fingers (finger = 19.3 mm).
·Greek linear measurement system **19**:728g

Olympic Cup, award given to an institution or association for outstanding service to amateur sports or to the Olympic Movement.
·qualifications and initial recipient **2**:277e

Olympic Diploma of Merit, award given to an individual for dedication to amateur sports or to the Olympic Movement.
·origin and initial recipient **2**:277e

Olympic Games, the world's foremost amateur sports competition, traditionally first celebrated in 776 BC at Olympia, Greece. Thereafter, the games were held at intervals until *c.* AD 393, when they were abolished by the Roman emperor Theodosius I after Greece lost its independence.

At first the program was confined to one day and consisted only of a single event, a foot-race the length of the stadium. Afterward, additional races, the discus throw, the javelin throw, the broad (long) jump, boxing, wrestling, the pentathlon, chariot racing, and other events were added; and the duration, including religious ceremonies, was extended to seven days. Winners became national heroes: musicians sang their praise, and sculptors preserved their strength and beauty in marble. Their feats of skill and courage were recorded by the poets and writers of the time.

Modern Olympiads. Through the efforts of Baron Pierre de Coubertin of France, a brilliant educator and scholar but not an athlete, the Olympic Games were revived. The games of the first Olympiad of the modern cycle were held under the royal patronage of the King of Greece in 1896 in a new stadium constructed in Athens for the purpose. Subsequent games were held in various cities of the world at four-year intervals, except for lapses during World Wars I and II. A separate cycle of winter games was initiated in 1924 at Chamonix, Fr. The direction of the modern Olympic movement and the regulation of the games is vested in the Comité International Olympique (International Olympic Committee), with headquarters at Lausanne, Switz.

After 1896, interest in the Olympics centred in the sport of track and field (athletics), although at times the program ranged from archery through yachting. Recent Olympic programs have generally included competition in the following sports: archery, basketball, boxing, canoeing, cycling, equestrian sports, fencing, football (soccer), gymnastics, handball, field hockey, judo, modern pentathlon, rowing, shooting, swimming, diving, water polo, track and field, volleyball, weight lifting, wrestling, and yachting. In addition, the program may include two demonstration sports and exhibitions or demonstrations in the fine arts.

The program for the Winter Olympics may include the biathlon (skiing and shooting), bobsled, ice hockey, luge (tobogganing), ice skating, and skiing events. Two demonstration sports may also be included. *See* sporting record. *Major ref.* **2**:276a
·amateurism ideal difficulties in practice **17**:513h
·Australian participation **2**:422d
·boxing history and champions **3**:91h
·canoe classes and events **2**:1161g
·cycling events **5**:391d
·equestrian events **8**:1092c
·field hockey inclusion and competition **8**:984d
·Greek military ideal and expansion **6**:323a
·Greek religious festivals **8**:409g
·history of events and records **18**:538e
·horsemanship and show competition **15**:839f
·horse racing history and origins **8**:1092g
·Mexican sponsorship and variety **12**:88h
·Olympiad and chronology of Greek history **4**:578e
·origin, events, and professionalism **2**:274d
·rowing events and records **2**:1158g
·shooting events and regulations **16**:705h
·soccer history and acceptance **2**:211c
·stadium design and construction role **17**:526f
·volleyball acceptance in 1964 **19**:510h
·winter sports events and champions **19**:887a
·wrestling championships and control **19**:1027d
·yacht classes, regattas, and scoring **2**:1169e

Olympic Mountains, segment of the Pacific Coast Ranges, extend across the Olympic Peninsula south of the Strait of Juan de Fuca and west of Puget Sound in northwestern Washington, U.S. Several peaks exceed 7,000

Olympic Mountains in Olympic National Park, Washington
Ray Atkeson—EB Inc.

ft (2,100 m), including Mts. Anderson (7,648 ft), Deception (7,788 ft), and Olympus (7,965 ft; the highest). The range holds about 60 glaciers. The prevailing westerly wind off the Pacific Ocean produces heavy annual precipitation (more than 140 in. [3,550 mm] in places), resulting in the formation of picturesque rain forests dominated by Douglas fir, Sitka spruce, western red cedar, and hemlock. Some trees reach heights of nearly 300 ft and diameters of 8 ft.

The Spanish navigator Juan Pérez sighted the mountains in 1774. John Meares, an English voyager, named the highest peak in 1788 because it appeared, like the Greek Mt. Olympus, to be a fit home for the gods. The mountains lie within the Olympic National Park (*q.v.*; created 1938) and Forest and are set aside for recreation and for conservation of wildlife and timber resources.
47°50′ N, 123°45′ W
·elevation and unexplored territory **19**:618e
·location and distinction **18**:914d
·relief and geological history **13**:825b

Olympic National Park, in northwestern Washington, U.S., established in 1938 to pre-

Hall of Mosses in the Hoh River section of the Olympic Rain Forest, Olympic National Park, Washington
David Muench—EB Inc.

serve the Olympic Mountains (*q.v.*) and their magnificent forests and wildlife. The park, which is 896,599 ac (362,854 ha) in area, includes a strip of Pacific Northwest shoreline geographically separated from the rest of the park. There are active glaciers on the highest peak, Mt. Olympus (7,965 ft [2,428 m]), and others, more than 60 glaciers in all. On the mountains' western slopes, where rainfall is very heavy, grows a lush rain forest in which conifers reach tremendous size. The forest floor is carpeted with dense mosses and huge fungi. The eastern slopes are less thickly forested and feature lakes and meadows. The ocean-shore section contains scenic beaches, islets, and points; three Indian reservations lie within it.

Wildlife in Olympic National Park includes deer, bears, cougars, and rare Roosevelt elks, as well as numerous varieties of birds.
47°46′ N, 123°35′ W
·undergrowth vegetation types, illus., **18**:Terrestrial Ecosystem, Plate IV

Olympic Peninsula, headland of northwestern Washington state, U.S.
47°40′ N, 123°40′ W
·geographic features **19**:618e

Olympio, Sylvanus (b. September 1902, Lomé, Togo—d. Jan. 13, 1963, Lomé), nationalist politician and first president of Togo as well as the first presidential victim of a wave of African military coups in the 1960s. A leader of the Comité de l'Unité Togolaise after World War II, he was elected president of the first territorial assembly in 1946 and by 1947 was in open (though nonviolent) conflict with the French colonial administration. One of his main early concerns was to unite the Ewe people, who were divided by the boundaries of British and French Togoland. His hopes were dashed in 1956, however, when British Togoland voted by plebiscite to join the Gold Coast (which became independent Ghana in 1957).

Between 1952 and 1958 Olympio was out of office. When Togo received limited self-government in 1956, his rival Nicholas Grunitzky became prime minister. In UN-supervised elections in 1958, however, Olympio's party won an overwhelming victory, and he became prime minister, leading Togo to complete independence in 1960. He was elected president in 1961, under a constitution granting extensive presidential powers. Togo became a one-party state, but its seeming stability was deceptive. Many Togolese, especially those with Western education, resented the regime's authoritarianism; northern leaders felt left out of the predominately southern government, and the more radical members of Juvento (once the party's youth wing) wanted Olympio to be less dependent on French aid. By early 1963 some Juvento leaders were in detention and other opposition figures had left the country. In January 1963 Olympio was assassinated in the first successful army coup in postwar sub-Saharan Africa.

Olympiodorus, the name of several ancient Greek writers, of whom the following are particularly noteworthy:

Olympiodorus of Thebes (fl. 5th century AD), Greek historian famous for a work on the history of the West from 407 to 425 in 22 books. Though the work is lost, an abstract of it has been preserved.

Olympiodorus the Elder, of Alexandria (fl. 5th century AD), Greek Peripatetic philosopher (follower of Aristotle) remembered chiefly as one of the teachers of Proclus.

Olympiodorus the Younger, of Alexandria (fl. 6th century AD), Greek Neoplatonist philosopher famous for having maintained the Platonic tradition in Alexandria after the emperor Justinian had suppressed the Athenian school in AD 529. His works include lucid and valuable commentaries on Plato's *Phaedo*, *Gorgias*, *Philebus*, and *Alcibiades*; a life of Plato; an introduction to Aristotle's philosophy; and commentaries on Aristotle's *Categories* and *Meteora*.

Olympiodorus the Alchemist, author of "On the Sacred Art of the Philosopher's Stone," which can be read in M. Berthelot's *Collection des alchimistes grecs* (1887–88; "Collection of the Greek Alchemists"). He has been variously identified with Olympiodorus of Thebes and with Olympiodorus the Neoplatonist.

Olympische Hymne, musical composition by Richard Strauss written for the opening of the Olympic Games in Berlin, 1936.
·official conducting permission **17**:728c

Olympische Spiele, also called OLYMPIAD, English OLYMPIC GAMES, or OLYMPIA, German film directed in 1936–38 by Leni Riefenstahl. The film's two parts, *Fest der Völker* (*Festival of the Nations*) and *Fest der Schönheit* (*Festival of Beauty*), documented the Olympic Games of 1936 in Berlin, presided over by Adolf Hitler. *Olympische Spiele*, like other films made by Riefenstahl before World War II, had the support of the Nazi Party; it was considered by some viewers to be a propaganda piece for the Nazi movement.

From a technical standpoint, the film won critical praise, particularly for successful use of post-synchronized music and sound effects. It was chosen by the International Olympic Committee as the official film record of the events of 1936. English and French versions were made in addition to the German, and the film was first shown in the U.S. in 1940.
·motion pictures' sound effects **12**:528b

Olympus, Mount, Modern Greek ÓROS ÓLIMBOS, highest peak (9,570 ft [2,917 m]) in Greece, part of the Olympus massif near the Thermaïkós Kólpos (Gulf of Thérmai) of the Aegean Sea. It is also designated as Upper Olympus (Greek Áno Ólimbos) and stands to the north of Lower Olympus (Káto Ólimbos), an adjacent peak rising to 5,210 ft (1,588 m).

Mount Olympus is snowcapped and often has cloud cover. According to Homer's *Odyssey*, however, the peak never has storms and it basks in cloudless *aithēr* (Greek: "pure upper air"). Later writers elaborated upon this description, which may have originated from the observation that the peak is often visible above a belt of relatively low clouds. Mount Olympus is the legendary abode of the gods

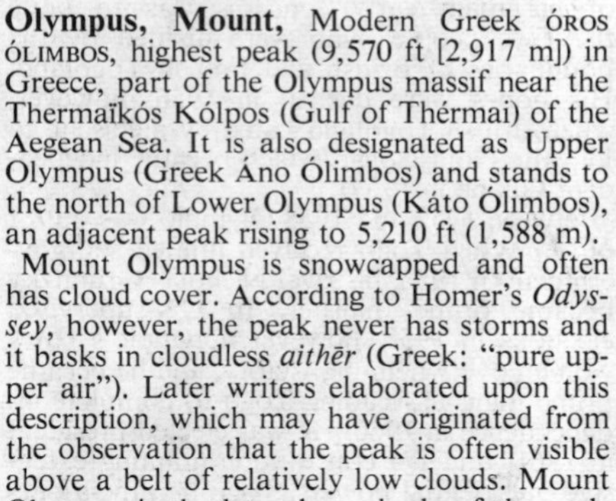

Mt. Olympus on the border of Macedonia and Thessaly, Greece

V-DIA—SCALA, New York

and site of the throne of Zeus. The name Olympus was used for several other mountains as well as hills, villages, and mythical personages in Greece and Asia Minor.
40°05′ N, 22°21′ E
·Aegean Bronze Age map **1**:112
·map, Greece **8**:314

Olympus Mons, on the planet Mars, the largest volcanic mountain known in the solar system. Its base is some 550 km (340 mi) in diameter and its peaks rise to an altitude of 27 km above the surrounding terrain.

The feature was first observed in 1879 by Giovanni Schiaparelli. It was later named Nix Olympica and was believed to be a very large crater. Photographs taken by the U.S. Viking orbiter spacecraft in the late 1970s, however, show that the feature is in fact a volcanic mountain crowned with a complex caldera that indicates several eruptions. Olympus Mons is believed to be about 200 million years old.
·Martian surface character **11**:523c

Olynthiacs, series of three orations by Demosthenes in 349 BC.
·content and effect **8**:367h

Olynthus, modern ÓLINTHOS, in Greece, ancient city north of Potidaea on the mainland of the Chalcidic peninsula. The Bottiaeans, a Thracian people, held Olynthus until 479 BC, when Persian forces killed its inhabitants and handed the city over to Greeks from Chalcidice. The city became the centre of Greek Chalcidice against attacks from Athens, Macedonia, and Sparta. In the 5th century BC it was the chief Greek city west of the Strymon River and by the 4th century was head of the Chalcidic League. By 382 the league had aroused the hostility of Sparta, which, after three years of fighting, defeated Olynthus and disbanded the league. After the demise of Sparta, Olynthus reformed the league and allied with Philip II of Macedon against Athens. When war broke out between Philip and Athens (357), Olynthus, fearing Philip's increasing power, shifted its allegiance to Athens. Philip subsequently razed the city in 348.

Excavations by the American School of Classical Studies at Athens revealed the grid plan of the ancient town and provided material for study of the relations between classical and Hellenic Greek art.
·fate under Macedonians **8**:367h
·Philip of Macedonia's conquest **14**:226b

Olyridae, family of siluriform fishes of the order Siluriformes, class Actinopterygii, phylum Chordata.
·classification and general features **13**:762h

Olyroideae, subfamily of flowering grasses of the family Poaceae, order Poales (flowering grasses and sedges).
·flower structure and lodicule number **14**:590e

Om, in Hinduism and other religions chiefly of India, a sacred syllable that is considered to

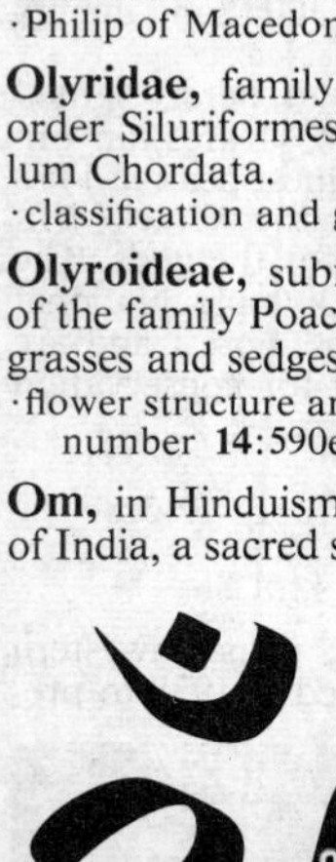

Om

be the greatest of all the *mantras* (sacred utterances of mystical or spiritual efficacy). The syllable *Om* is composed of the three sounds *a-u-m* (in Sanskrit, the vowels *a* and *u* coalescing to become *o*), which represent several important triads: the three worlds of earth, atmosphere, and heaven; the three major Hindu gods, Brahmā, Viṣṇu, and Śiva; and the three sacred Vedic scriptures, Ṛg, Yajur, and Sāma. Thus *Om* mystically embodies the essence of the entire universe. It is uttered at the beginning and end of Hindu prayers, chants, and meditation and is freely used in Buddhist and Jaina ritual also. From the 6th century, the written symbol designating the sound is used to mark the beginning of a text in a manuscript or an inscription.

The syllable is discussed in a number of the *Upaniṣads* (texts of philosophical speculation), and it forms the entire subject matter of one, the *Māndūkya*. It is used in the practice of Yoga and is related to techniques of auditory meditation. In the *Purāṇas* (collections of Hindu myth, legend, and genealogy), the syllable is put to sectarian use; thus the Śaiva mark the *liṅga* (sign of Śiva) with its symbol, whereas the Vaiṣṇava identify the three sounds as referring to a trinity composed of Viṣṇu, his wife Śrī, and the worshipper.
·Sikh symbolism of godhead **16**:746c
·written significance **3**:1174h

Omagh, urban district and town (seat) of County Tyrone, Northern Ireland, on the River Strule. It lies in the ancient O'Neill family territory of Tir Eoghain (Tyrone) and is now the market, shopping, and transport centre for a wide countryside. Local industries include processing of dairy products and shirt manufacture. The regimental headquarters of the Royal Inniskilling Fusiliers, a British army regiment, are in Omagh. Pop. (1980 est.) 41,700.
54°36′ N, 7°18′ W
·map, United Kingdom **18**:866

Omagua, indigenous Indian ethnolinguistic group of the low-forest region of Peru.
·language and economy **14**:130c

Omaha, North American Plains Indian people of the Dhegiha branch of the Siouan language stock. With the other members of this subgroup (the Osage, Ponca, Kansa, and Quapaw [*qq.v.*]), the Omaha migrated westward from the Atlantic Coast. An early settlement was in Virginia and the Carolinas. After a time they moved to the Ozark Plateau and the prairies of what is now western Missouri. At this point the five tribes separated, the Omaha and the Ponca moving north to present-day Minnesota, where they lived until the late 17th century. At that time the two tribes were driven farther west by the migrating Dakota people. They separated in present-day South Dakota, the Omaha moving on to Bow Creek in present-day Nebraska. In 1854, under the pressure of encroaching white settlement, the Omaha sold most of their land to the U.S. government. In 1882 the government allotted land to them to prevent the removal of the tribe to Oklahoma; somewhat later they received U.S. citizenship. The population of the Omaha in 1780 is estimated to have been 2,800. In the early 1980s about 1,500 were reported to be living on the reservation in Nebraska.

Like other prairie tribes, the Omaha combined agriculture with hunting. In spring and autumn they lived in permanent villages of dome-shaped earth lodges, moving into portable tepees for the hunting seasons. Omaha social organization was elaborate, with a class system of chiefs, priests, physicians, and commoners. Rank was inherited in the male line, although an individual could raise his status by distributing horses and blankets or providing feasts.

The tribe was divided into 10 clans organized in 2 groups representing earth and sky. Earth clans were held responsible for ceremonies concerning war and food supply, while the ceremonies overseen by the sky clans were designed to secure supernatural aid. When the entire tribe camped during the summer bison hunt or on migrations, tepees were arranged in a large circle symbolizing the tribal organization. The Omaha, like many other Plains Indians, awarded special insignia for such daring war exploits as touching an enemy in battle, touching a dead enemy surrounded by his tribesmen, and removing a trained horse from the enemy's camp. Killing and scalping the enemy were considered lesser exploits.
·Plains Indian culture **13**:223g

Omaha, city, Nebraska, U.S., port of entry and seat of Douglas County, in the eastern part of the state on the west bank of the Missouri River, opposite Council Bluffs, Iowa. It was founded in 1854 in an area that had been visited by Meriwether Lewis and William Clark (1804) on their exploratory journey to the Pacific Coast and where the pioneer fur trader Manuel Lisa established a trading post during the War of 1812. A Utah-bound group of Mormons spent the winter of 1846–47 there at an encampment that they named Winter Quarters, later called Florence, and subsequently annexed by Omaha.

Omaha, named for the Omaha Indians, was established by Council Bluffs promoters who wanted the capital of the newly created Nebraska Territory to be located directly across the river, in part at least to influence the builders of the then-projected transcontinental railroad to lay their tracks through or near their own city. Omaha was made the capital, and a few years later Pres. Abraham Lincoln designated Council Bluffs as the eastern terminus of the first transcontinental railroad. By the second half of the 20th century, Omaha was one of the largest railroad centres in the United States. As the actual starting point for the railroad (Union Pacific), Omaha soon became a focal point for trade and industry and grew rapidly during the early years, although the capital was moved to Lincoln soon after Nebraska became a state (1867). A succession of drought years following the great blizzard of 1888 and the panic of 1893 halted the population growth, but by 1914 the city had started to grow again. Several suburban communities, including South Omaha, site of the Union Stockyards, were annexed. Offutt Air Force Base, headquarters of the Strategic Air Command, is at nearby Bellevue (*q.v.*).

Omaha's basic economy depends on activities connected with agriculture. The city is the largest livestock market and meat-packing centre in the world, and it buys and sells a large part of the grain produced in the U.S. It also has a large number of insurance companies. Other industries include oil refining, lead smelting, and the manufacture of feed and railroad and farm equipment.

Educational institutions include the University of Nebraska at Omaha (1908; formerly Municipal University of Omaha), Creighton University (Roman Catholic; 1878), the University of Nebraska College of Medicine (1883–87; re-established 1902), and the Roman Catholic women's College of St. Mary (1923). The Joslyn Art Museum houses a collection ranging from ancient times to the present. Fontelle Forest, the largest unbroken native forest in the state, is to the south. Boys Town (*q.v.*) is 11 mi (18 km) west. Pop. (1980) city, 311,681; metropolitan area (SMSA), 570,399. 41°16′ N, 95°57′ W

·capital conflict, population, and institutions **12**:923c *passim* to 925d
·map, United States **18**:909

Omaha (1932–59), U.S. Thoroughbred horse who in 1935 emulated his sire, Gallant Fox, by winning the U.S. Triple Crown for three-year-old Thoroughbreds: the Kentucky Derby, the Preakness Stakes, and the Belmont Stakes. In 1935 the chestnut stallion, whose dam was Flambino, won six of nine races in the U.S. and two of four in England. After his return to the U.S., a recurring ailment forced his retirement to stud.

Omaha Beach, also known as BLOODY OMAHA, in World War II, code name of one of the five Normandy beachheads, landing places for the Allied invasion of northern France on June 6, 1944 (*see* Normandy Invasion).

·Allied landings map **19**:1001

Omaha World Herald (established 1885), newspaper of Omaha, Neb.

·circulation area and persuasion **12**:925d

O'Mahony, John (1816–77), Irish-American founder of the U.S. branch of the Irish nationalist organization known as the Fenians (*see* Fenian Movement).

Omalius d'Halloy, Jean-Baptiste-Julien (b. Feb. 16, 1783, Liège, Belg.—d. Jan. 15, 1875, Brussels), geologist known for his systematic subdivisions of geologic formations in the Earth's crust, proposed in 1830. An authority on the geology of The Netherlands and Belgium, he did work on metamorphism and on ethnography.

Oman 13:566, formerly MUSCAT AND OMAN, independent sultanate on the southeastern coast of the Arabian Peninsula, bounded by the Gulf of Oman (north), the Arabian Sea (east and south), Yemen (Aden; southwest), Saudi Arabia (west), and the United Arab Emirates (northwest).

The text article covers Oman's landscape, people and population, national economy, administration and social conditions, cultural life and institutions, and prospects for the future. History is covered in the article Arabia, history of.

REFERENCES in other text articles:
·map, Asia **2**:149
·petroleum production statistics, table 1 **14**:176
·petroleum reserves of the world table **14**:175

Oman, Gulf of, northwest arm of the Arabian Sea, between the eastern portion (Oman) of the Arabian Peninsula (southwest) and Iran (north). The gulf is 200 mi (320 km) wide between Ra's (cape) al-Ḥadd in Oman and Gwātar Bay on the Pakistan–Iran border. It is 350 mi long and connects with the Persian Gulf (northwest) through the Strait of Hormuz. The small ports along the gulf include Ṣuḥār, al-Khābūrah, Muscat, and Ṣūr, in Oman, and Jāsk and Chāh Bahār, in Iran. Some fishing is carried on, but the gulf's main importance is as a shipping route for the oil-producing area around the Persian Gulf. 24°30′ N, 58°30′ E

·gulf development and physiography **8**:484g; table 482
·map, Iran **9**:822
·United Arab Emirates area and people **18**:862b

Oman, John Wood (b. July 23, 1860, Orkney, Scot.—d. May 17, 1939, Cambridge, Eng.), British Presbyterian theologian. After graduating at Edinburgh University and at the theological college of the United Presbyterian Church, he studied in Germany and subsequently entered the ministry of the Presbyterian Church of England. In 1907 he was appointed professor of systematic theology at its theological college in Cambridge (Westminster College), of which he was later principal (1922–35). Oman taught the uniqueness and independence of the religious consciousness: the sense of "the sacred" establishes man as a personal being in the midst of natural process. In his main work, *The Natural and the Supernatural* (1931), Oman developed this view in a wide-ranging treatment of knowledge and perception, of necessity and freedom, of the history and classification of religions. Doctrinally Oman's theology was built on the essentially personal nature of the divine–human relationship and on the concepts of reverence, sincerity, and freedom. In *Grace and Personality* (1917) these basic themes were wrought out in relation to grace and reconciliation; in *Vision and Authority* (1902), in relation to authority; in *The Church and the Divine Order* (1911), in relation to the church.

·prophetic and mystical religion **15**:624h

Omani dynasties, collective name given to several East African ruling families (*e.g.*, the

OMAN

Official name: Sulṭanat 'Umān (Sultanate of Oman).
Location: southwestern Asia.
Form of government: monarchy (sultanate).
Official language: Arabic.
Official religion: Islām.
Area: 82,000 sq mi, 212,400 sq km.
Population: (1973 estimate) 700,000 to 800,000.
Capital: Muscat.
Monetary unit: 1 rial Omani (R.O.) = 1,000 baizas.

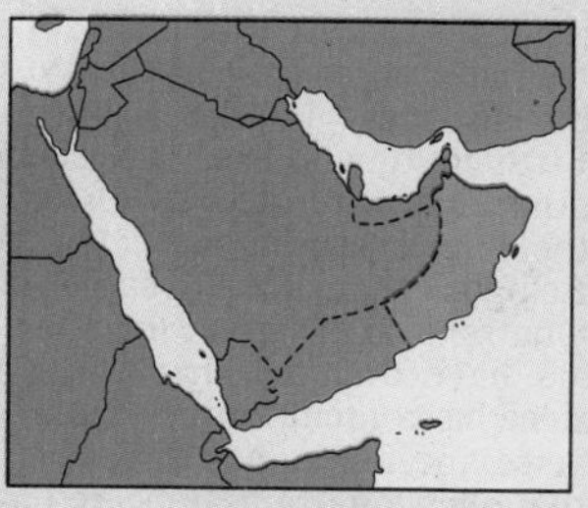

Demography

Population: (1973) density 8.5 to 9.8 per sq mi, 3.3 to 3.8 per sq km; (1970) urban 4.9%, rural 95.1%.
Ethnic composition (1961): Arab 88%, Baluchi 4%, Persian 3%, Indian 2%, African 2%, other 1%. *Religious affiliation* (1970): Ibāḍī Muslim, about 75%; Sunnī Muslim, about 25%.

National accounts

Budget (1972). Revenue: R.O. 49,300,000 (petroleum revenues only, of which, taxes 75.3%, royalties 24.5%). Expenditures: R.O. 29,900,000 (harbours and ports 25.4%, Dhofar development 17.7%, roads 14.4%, airport 9.4%, public buildings 9.4%, health 7.7%, housing 7.0%, education 5.4%).

Domestic economy

Gross national product (GNP; at current market prices, 1972): U.S. $320,000,000 (U.S. $530 per capita*).
Origin of gross domestic product (1971): total GDP R.O. 143,400,000 (agriculture 11.7%, petroleum 65.5%, manufacturing 0.1%, other 22.7%).
Production (metric tons except as noted). Agriculture, forestry, hunting, fishing (1972): alfalfa 115,000; dates 50,000; onions 6,000; limes 1,500; bananas 660,000 bunches; livestock (no. of live animals): cattle 68,000 head, goats 111,000 head,† sheep 29,500 head,† camels 5,100 head†; fish, landed 100,000. Mining, quarrying (1973): petroleum, crude 14,620,000. Manufacturing (1972): cement 626,000.
Energy (1972): installed electrical capacity 52,000 kW, production 130,000,000 kWhr (185.7 kWhr per capita).
Land use (1971): meadows and pastures 4.7%; agricultural 0.2%; built-on, wasteland, and other 95.1%.

Foreign trade

Imports (1972): R.O. 51,400,000, of which, R.O. 18,713,181 private sector or "dutiable goods" (food and live animals 30.2%§; machinery and transport equipment 27.9%§; manufactured material 20.7%§). *Major import sources*§: Persian Gulf countries 21.3%, United Kingdom 20.7%, Japan 10.4%, India 6.0%, Australia 5.7%.
Exports (1972): R.O. 394,100‖; government oil receipts R.O. 49,300,000 (major export is oil, 99.2% of export income). *Major export destinations* (petroleum only, based on quantity): Japan 42.3%, France 15.4%, Norway 10.7%, Singapore 8.4%, Sweden 7.5%, The Netherlands 4.7%, United Kingdom 3.6%.

Transport and communication

Transport. Roads (1972): total length 2,121 mi, 3,414 km (paved 140 mi, 226 km). Vehicles (1972): passenger cars 4,461, trucks and buses 5,310. Merchant marine (1974): vessels (100 gross tons and over) 4, total dead-weight tonnage 2,125. Air transport (1974): airports with scheduled flights 2. *Communication*. Daily newspapers (1972): none. Radios (late 1960s): total receivers 1,000. Telephones (1973): 2,215 (1 per 326 persons).

Education and health

Education (1973–74):	schools	teachers	students	student–teacher ratio
primary (age 6 to 11)	104	1,230	34,572	28.1
secondary (age 12 to 17)	7	¶	341	¶
vocational	1	12	79	6.6

Literacy (1974 estimate): total population literate 20–25%.
Health: (1972) doctors 62 (1 per 11,290 persons); (1970) hospital beds 508 (1 per 1,388 persons).

*For a population of 600,000. †Excluding Dhofar. ‡Males only. §Private only. ‖Excluding petroleum. ¶Same teachers in primary and secondary.

Mazrui at Mombasa and Pemba and the Āl Bū Saʿīdīs at Zanzibar) in the 18th and 19th centuries; they were so called because they originally came from Oman in southern Arabia.

Omar Khayyam, conventional English for GHEYĀS OD-DĪN ABŪ OL-FATḤ ʿOMAR EBN EBRAHĪM OL-KHAYYĀMĪ (b. May 1048?, Neyshābūr, Iran—d. 1122, Neyshābūr), mathematician, physicist, astronomer, physician, and philosopher, renowned in his own country and time for his scientific achievements but known in the West for his *Robāʿīyāt* ("quatrains") in freely translated version, *The Rubáiyát of Omar Khayyám*, by Edward FitzGerald (1859), which in its turn has been translated into many other languages.

His name Khayyam (Tentmaker) may have been derived from his father's trade. He received a good education in the sciences and philosophy in his native Neyshābūr (Nīshāpūr) and in Balkh and then went to Samarkand, where he completed an important treatise in Arabic on algebra. He made such a name for himself that he was invited by the Seljuq sultan Malik-Shāh to undertake the astronomical observations necessary for the reform of the calendar. He was also commissioned to build an observatory in the city of Isfahan in collaboration with other astronomers. After the death of his patron in 1092, Omar went on a pilgrimage to Mecca. Returning to Neyshābūr, he taught and served the court from time to time by predicting events to come. Philosophy, jurisprudence, history, mathematics, medicine, and astronomy are among the subjects mastered by this brilliant man, but only a few brief tracts on metaphysics and a treatise on Euclid survive.

Omar's popularity in the West is based on his discovery by the English poet Edward FitzGerald, who freely translated many of the quatrains attributed to Omar and arranged them in a continuous elegy, or "tessellated Eclogue" as he liked to call it, in which "many Quatrains are mashed together." Some scholars have doubted that Omar wrote poetry, since his contemporaries took no notice of his verse and it was not until two centuries later that a few quatrains appeared under his name. A.J. Arberry, however, using 13th-century manuscripts, has identified at least 250 authentic *robāʿīyāt*. A close reading of the authentic verses reveals him as a man of deep thought, troubled by the eternal questions of the nature of the universe, the passage of time, and man's relationship to God. *See also* FitzGerald, Edward.

·literary evaluation of robāʿīyāt **9**:963d

Omaruru, town and administrative district in west central South West Africa. The town, on the Omaruru River, is a railroad outlet for an area of tin mines and dairy industries. Pop. (1970) 2,783.
21°28′ S, 15°56′ E

·district population and area table **17**:303
·map, South West Africa **17**:301

omasum, also called MANYPLIES and PSALTERIUM, third chamber of the stomach (*q.v.*) of ruminants.

·digestive mechanism in ruminants **2**:77h

Omayyads (dynasty): *see* Umayyads.

OMB, abbreviation of OFFICE OF MANAGEMENT AND BUDGET, U.S. agency, in the Executive Office of the President, established in 1970.

·budget appropriation procedure **3**:443h

Ombella-Mpoko, prefecture in the Central African Empire.

·area and population table **3**:1104
·map, Central African Republic **3**:1103

Ombi Islands (Indonesia): *see* Obi Islands.

Ombos, ancient city of Upper Egypt known primarily for its unique double temple of the Ptolemaic period, now restored. Its site is near the present Kawm Umbū, north of Aswān. The temple was dedicated to the gods Sebek and Haroeris ("Horus the Elder"). Ombos probably owed its foundation to the site's strategic location, commanding both the Nile and the routes from Nubia to the Nile Valley, and was especially prosperous under the Hellenistic Ptolemaic dynasty (323–30 BC) when it was the capital of the nome (province) of Ombites.

Ombre, card game for three players, fashionable in Europe for many years but now practically obsolete. It was similar to Whist, involving concepts of bidding, trump suit, and taking tricks. Originally played with the Spanish packs of 40 or 48 cards, it was adapted to the French pack of 52. In the course of time it acquired terms from Spanish, French, Italian, and English, as well as a great complexity of rules. It has been traced as far back as the 14th century. A variant for four players, called Quadrille, gained great popularity and was one of the five games described by Edmond Hoyle in his *Short Treatise on the Game of Whist* (1742). A simplification of Quadrille, usually called Solo, is still played.

·card game historic development **3**:903e

ombres chinoises (French: "Chinese shadows"), European version of the Chinese shadow puppet show, introduced in Europe in the mid-18th century by returning travellers. Soon adopted by French and English showmen, the

Cardboard and wire shadow puppets from *Don Quichotte et le moulin*, from the Théâtre Séraphin, Paris, *c.* 1800

By courtesy of the Cooper-Hewitt Museum of Decorative Arts and Design, New York

form gained prominence in the shows of the French puppeteer Dominique Séraphin, who presented the first popular *ombres chinoises* show in Paris in 1776. In 1781 he moved his show to Versailles, where he entertained the French court, and three years later he established a highly successful puppet theatre in Paris.

Using silhouettes cast by solid cardboard figures instead of the coloured transparencies popular in China, the *ombres chinoises* usually featured short, amusing fables such as *The Broken Bridge*, a dialogue in song between a farmer and a gentleman. Although most shadow theatres had closed by the 1860s, *ombres chinoises* were played in London until the end of the 19th century.

The technique was revived between 1887 and 1897 at Le Chat-Noir, a Montmartre cafe, by painters, writers, and musicians who presented satirical pieces. *See also* shadow play.

·figure construction and use **15**:292f

Ombrone River, river in Tuscany, central Italy, rises in the Monti Chianti and flows generally southwest to enter the Tyrrhenian Sea after a course of 100 mi (160 km).
42°39′ N, 11°00′ E

·length table of rivers in Apennines **1**:1011
·map, Italy **9**:1088

ombudsman, legislative commissioner for investigating citizens' complaints of bureaucratic abuse. The office originated in Sweden in 1809–10 and has been copied in various forms in Scandinavia, New Zealand, the United Kingdom, West Germany, Israel, and certain states in the U.S. and Australia and provinces in Canada.

The legislature appoints the ombudsman but may not interfere with his handling of particular cases. His authority covers all agencies and boards but sometimes excludes municipal government (New Zealand and Norway), Cabinet decisions (Sweden, Norway, New Zealand, and the U.K.), and the courts. Specialized ombudsmen may exercise jurisdiction only over the police (Israel), the National Health Service (the U.K.), or the medical treatment of prisoners (Minnesota, Connecticut, Michigan, and Kansas). At the municipal level there are sometimes separate ombudsmen for particular cities (Dayton, Ohio, and Seattle, Wash., and Jerusalem, Tel Aviv–Yafo and Haifa, Israel) and a Commission for Local Administration in England. The ombudsman's power is solely recommendatory.

Functions similar to those of an ombudsman are undertaken by procurators general in eastern Europe and by the Administrative Management Agency in Japan. *Major ref.* **1**:96a

·British variant of the office **4**:673b
·constitutional safeguard against bureaucracy **5**:95f
·military ombudsmen in various nations **12**:196f
·Norwegian judicial system **13**:269d
·Sweden's controls on government **17**:852c

Omdurman, one of the Three Towns of The Sudan (with Khartoum and Khartoum North) in Khartoum province, at the confluence of the Blue and White Niles. On the left bank of the main Nile just below the confluence, Omdurman, which is now the largest town in The Sudan, was an insignificant riverine village until the victory of Muḥammad Aḥmad, known as al-Mahdī, over the British in 1885. The Mahdī and his successor, the caliph ʿAbd Allāh, made it their capital, and it grew rapidly as an unplanned town of mud houses. Omdurman was captured by Gen. Sir Herbert (later Lord) Kitchener on Sept. 2, 1898, but continued to develop into the cultural, religious, and commercial centre of The Sudan. ʿAbd Allāh's house is now a museum, and the tomb of al-Mahdī has been restored. The Islāmic University of Omdurman (founded 1961), connected with the principal mosque, teaches Islāmic law and theology. There is a large bazaar trading in hides, gum arabic, textiles, agricultural products, livestock, and handicrafts (in metal, wood, leather, and ivory). Furniture and pottery factories and a tannery are also important to the local economy. Trucking has largely replaced the

The tomb of al-Mahdī, Omdurman, The Sudan

Charles Beery—Shostal

river in the movement of goods. Pop. (1972 est.) 289,000.
15°38′ N, 32°30′ E
·al-Mahdī's empire administration **11**:349a
·map, Sudan **17**:758
·population and Khartoum comparison **17**:757f

Omdurman, Battle of (1898), a decisive military engagement whereby Anglo-Egyptian forces, under Maj. Gen. Sir Herbert Kitchener (later Lord Kitchener), defeated the forces of the Mahdist leader ʿAbd Allāh and so won Sudanese territory that the Mahdists had dominated since 1881.

Preparations for an advance against ʿAbd Allāh's forces at Omdurman began at the end of July 1898, with the dispatch to Kitchener at Wad Ḥamad (above Metemina on the west bank of the Sixth Cataract) of reinforcements from Cairo. There, on August 24, a combined Anglo-Egyptian force of 26,000 men was amassed. It comprised a British division of two brigades under the supreme command of Major General Gatacre, an Egyptian division of four brigades under Major General Hunter, mounted troops, artillery, engineers, and a flotilla. The Mahdist forces numbered some 40,000 but their simple weapons were no match for Kitchener's modern armaments.

While a force of Arab irregulars—friendly to the Anglo-Egyptian forces and under British command—proceeded up river to clear the east bank of all opposition as far as the Blue Nile, the Anglo-Egyptian army under Kitchener proceeded along the west bank unopposed. On September 1, while the flotilla shelled the forts on both sides of the river and breached the wall of Omdurman, Kitchener bivouacked four miles above it at Egeiga on the west bank. He repulsed an attack on his camp by Mahdist forces on September 2 and then marched on Omdurman, whence he drove the Mahdist forces with relatively little loss to his own troops.

The results of the battle were the destruction of ʿAbd Allāh's army, the extinction of Mahdism in The Sudan, and the establishment of British dominance there.
·Kitchener's victory over the Mahdists **13**:113g

Ōme, city, Tokyo Metropolis (*to*), Honshū, Japan, on the Tama-gawa (Tama River). An early trade centre and post town (rest stop), it was known as a weaving centre for cotton textiles. Other traditional industries included the production of lumber and woodwork.

Ōme became a municipality in 1951, with the amalgamation of Ōme and two neighbouring villages, covering an administrative area of 125 sq mi (323 sq km). Industrial plants have been constructed on the outskirts of the city area; electrical machinery and textiles (mainly bedclothes) are major products. Ōme is the gateway to Chichibu-Tama National Park; a shrine crowns Mitake-yama (Mt. Mitake), which rises within the city area. Pop. (1970) 70,954.
35°47′ N, 139°15′ E
·map, Japan **10**:36

Omega, long-range hyperbolic navigation system that transmits interrupted continuous wave signals; phase differences are extracted from these signals.
·radio-navigation position-finding systems **12**:909a

Omega Centauri (NGC 5139), group of stars, nearest (at about 17,000 light-years) and apparently brightest, of the globular type of cluster, lies in the southern constellation Centaurus. Visible to the unaided eye as a faint luminous patch, it is estimated to contain hundreds of thousands of stars; several hundred variables have been observed in it. Sir John Herschel in the 1830s was the first to recognize it as a star cluster and not a true nebula.
·star cluster shape and discovery **17**:604d *passim* to 606d; illus.

omens, name given by the ancients to observed phenomena that were interpreted as signifying good or bad fortune. The signs were numerous and varied and included, for instance, lightning, cloud movement, the flight of birds, and the path of certain sacred animals. Within each type of sign were minor subdivisions, such as the different kinds of bird in flight or the direction of flight in relation to the observer, each of which had a special meaning.
·Anatolian divination methods **2**:191g
·distinction from astrology **2**:220d
·Mesopotamian augury **5**:918f

omental bursa, in human anatomy, the smaller section, or sac, of the double membrane (peritoneum) lining the abdomen and covering the viscera.
·digestive system origins and fusions **6**:753d

omentum (anatomy): *see* peritoneum.

Omeo, town, east central Victoria, Australia, on the Mitta Mitta River in the Eastern Highlands. Founded in 1835, it took its name from an Aboriginal term meaning "mountains." It was the site of a gold discovery in 1851 and was gazetted a shire in 1872. Omeo now serves a region of pastoralism, lumbering, and tin mining. At the junction of the Omeo and Alpine highways, 150 mi (240 km) northeast of Melbourne, the town is a stop on the route to the winter resort of Mt. Hotham in the Australian Alps and the summer resort area of the Bogang High Plains. It has survived several natural disasters, including earthquakes in 1885 and 1892 and a bush fire in 1939. Pop. (1971 prelim.) 296.
37°06′ S, 147°36′ E

Ömer (Ottoman poet): *see* Nef'i.

Ometecuhtli, remote Aztec creator deity; his name means Lord of Duality. With his wife, Omecihuatl (Lady of Duality), he resided in the 13th and the highest of the Aztec heavens. They were alternately known as Tonacatecuhtli and Tonacacíhuatl (Lord and Lady of Our Sustenance). The dual creative principle was sometimes expressed by a supreme deity called Ometéotl (God of Duality) or Tloque Nahuaque (Unique God).

Ometepe Island, Spanish ISLA DE OMETEPE OR ALTA GRACIA, in southwestern Nicaragua, is the largest island in Lake Nicaragua. Ometepe actually consists of two islands joined by a narrow isthmus 2 mi (3 km) in length. The larger, northern one is 12 mi (19 km) from east to west and 10 mi (16 km) from north to south; from it the cone of Concepción volcano rises to 5,282 ft (1,610 m). The smaller, southern island is almost circular, with a 7-mi (11-km) diameter. The combined area is about 150 sq mi (400 sq km); the perfect cone of Madera volcano attains an elevation of 4,015 ft (1,224 m). Ometepe lies 5 mi (8 km) offshore and approximately 8 mi (13 km) east-northeast of the town of Rivas; the land is fertile and largely forested; coffee and tobacco are the principal products. Alta Gracia and Moyogalpa are the island's main towns. Pop. (1971 prelim.) 13,458.
11°30′ N, 85°33′ W
·formation, history, and economy **13**:64a
·map, Nicaragua **13**:60

Ometepe Volcano (Nicaragua): *see* Concepción Volcano.

Ometo, a Sidamo people of southern Ethiopia.
·visual art forms **1**:268f

Omicron Ceti (star): *see* Mira Ceti.

O-mi-t'o Ching (Buddhist text): *see* Sukhāvatī-vyūha-sūtra.

Ōmiya, city, Saitama Prefecture (*ken*), Honshu, Japan, north of Tokyo. It is the site of the Shintō Hikawa Shrine, said to have been established in the 5th century BC. During the Tokugawa era (1603–1867) Ōmiya was a post town. Its growth since 1891 has been as a major railway junction. The city contains the largest workshop of the Japan National Railway and a vast switchyard. Pop. (1970) 268,777.
35°54′ N, 139°38′ E
·map, Japan **10**:36

Omkarji (India): *see* Godarpura.

oṃ maṇi padme hūṃ, the Sanskrit *mantra* or prayer formula, widely encountered in Tibet, that is used to invoke the compassionate *bodhisattva* (Buddha-to-be) Avalokiteśvara. The words are inscribed on ritual objects, on wayside stones (called *maṇi* stones), and on prayer flags, are written on paper that revolves in prayer wheels, and are constantly uttered by the devout. When the words are pronounced with the proper reverence and concentration, the speaker acquires merit and the protection of Avalokiteśvara.

"Mani stone" engraved with the mystical formula *om mani padme hūm;* in the Newark (New Jersey) Museum
By courtesy of the Newark Museum, New Jersey

The phrase is commonly understood to mean "the jewel in the lotus" or "Oh! thou of the jewelled lotus." (*Maṇi* means "jewel" and *padme* means "lotus," while *oṃ* and *hūṃ* are mystical sounds that cannot be translated.) The *mantra* is interpreted in various ways: as an invocation of the *bodhisattva;* as a symbol of the fundamental unity of male (jewel) and female (lotus) principles; and as six mystical syllables each correlated with a colour, part of the human body, one of the six realms of being, and a position of the *maṇḍala* (symbolical drawing).

ommatidium, subunit of the compound eye of arthropods. The sensory part of the subunit, called the rhabdom, may be shared by several ommatidia, but each ommatidium has its own hexagonal lens, the facet.
·arthropod nervous system **12**:981g
·compound eye optics **14**:357e; illus.
·insect eye and vision **9**:618a; illus. 617

Ommatophoca rossi: *see* Ross seal.

ommochrome, one of a group of biological pigments (biochromes) conspicuous in the eyes of insects and crustaceans as well as in the changeable chromatophores (pigment-containing cells) in the skin of cephalopods. Although ommochromes, which are derived from the breakdown of the amino acid tryptophan, are responsible for the colours of insect eyes, they are not known to be involved directly in the biochemistry of photoreception. In the changing integumentary cells of cephalopods, however, they may contribute to adaptive responses.
·types, properties, and occurrence **4**:921g

Omnibook, U.S. periodical, founded 1938.
·magazine publishing history **15**:254g

omnibus: *see* trucks and buses.

omnidirectional kinship, kinship system in which individuals are free to choose the relatives they will ally themselves with.
·kinship relationship structures **10**:484a

omnipotence, an attribute of God connoting unlimited power.
·cross-cultural views of creator deity **5**:240a
·Origen's theological system **13**:735h
·Rāmānuja's doctrine on Brahman's will **13**:950g

omnium, bicycle-racing competition in which racers compete in several different events on a track.
·cycling competition types **5**:391g

omnivore, in biology, animal of wide food preferences, eating both animal and plant tissues.
·Australopithecine inferred diet **2**:439c
·bear, raccoon, and viverrid diets **3**:929f *passim* to 933g; illus. 941
·biological community interactions **4**:1028g
·Homo erectus opportunistic diet **8**:1034b

Ömnögovi, province of the Mongolian People's Republic.
·area and population table **12**:366

Omo hominids, some four or five species of early hominids described from the sequence of Omo Group sediments and volcanic ashes (three-fourths of a mile thick), of Pliocene and earlier Pleistocene age, that were exposed in the lower Omo Basin of southwestern Ethiopia. The hominid remains, including many teeth, jaws, skull parts, and some limb bones, have been recovered from nearly 90 localities in the time range of more than 3,000,000 to 1,000,000 years ago. The oldest part of the sequence affords evidence of a distinct hominid species of still unknown affinities. *Australopithecus africanus* occurs between 3,000,000 and 1,900,000 years ago and is in part coexistent with *Australopithecus robustus* (or *boisei*), which occurs from 2,100,000 to perhaps 1,500,000 years ago. A hominid that is dentally like *Homo habilis* (also classified *Australopithecus africanus*) from Olduvai Gorge occurs at about 1,850,000 years ago, and traces of *Homo erectus* are found at just over 1,000,000 years ago.
·Australopithecine fossil discovery table **2**:437
·characteristics and significance **11**:423a
·Ethiopian fossil remains **6**:1006f

Omo Homo sapiens fossils, remains of three individuals (Omo I, II, III) found in 1967 by R.E.F. Leakey in sedimentary deposits of the Kibish Formation of an ancient delta of the Omo River in Ethiopia, north of Lake Rudolf. The human remains were associated with bones of buffalo, reedbuck, a primitive elephant, and a small monkey; a few stone tools were found with Omo I. Dating is difficult, but a date of about 130,000 years ago is possible. Omo II, best preserved of the skulls, is that of an elderly person, has thick bones with heavy muscle markings, and is long-headed, with a receding forehead, moderately developed brow ridges, a large occipital torus and flat nuchal area for attachment of powerful neck muscles, a well-developed mastoid process, and thickened zygomatic process; the widest part of the skull is low, on the temporals. Omo I is a younger, more lightly built, and more modern-looking individual and includes an incomplete cranium and much of the face and postcranial skeleton. The skull vault is high, with a somewhat receding forehead, moderate brow ridges, reduced occipital torus and rounded nuchal area, a large mastoid process, and thickened zygomatic process. The widest part of the skull is high on the parietals. The face is robust, the mandible has a well-developed chin eminence, and the teeth are large but modern. The postcranial skeleton does not fall outside the range of variation for modern man. Omo III consists of two skull fragments, similar to, but later in time than, Omo I. All three individuals are believed to be early representatives of *Homo sapiens*. Omo II, somewhat more primitive looking, has been compared to Solo man, Vértesszőllős man, and Kanjera man; Omo I is reminiscent of the Swanscombe skull and the Maghārat as-Skhūl remains from Mt. Carmel. The marked degree of morphological variation between Omo I and II is not unexpected from studies of other groups of early *H. sapiens*.
·African skull and jaw finds comparison **1**:286h; illus.
·description of fossils and site **8**:1048a
·types and characteristics **11**:426e

Omomyidae, prosimian family of the order Primates.
·primate evolution, fossils, and classification **14**:1026b *passim* to 1029c

Omoo (1847), full title OMOO: A NARRATIVE OF ADVENTURES IN THE SOUTH SEAS, novel by Herman Melville.
·style and adventures **11**:873f

omophorion (vestment): *see* pallium.

Omori Fusakichi (1868–1923), Japanese seismologist.
·seismology and seismograph history **16**:489g

Omo River, in southwestern Ethiopia, rises in the highlands of Kefa province and flows southward for about 400 mi (644 km) into the north end of Lake Rudolf. The lower Omo Valley is rich in wildlife and is the site of important fossil hominid remains.
8°48′ N, 37°14′ E
·map, Ethiopia **6**:1001
·rift lake geography and hydrography **6**:116d; map 119

Omortag, 9th-century Bulgarian king.
·settlement with Byzantines **3**:559b

Omosudidae, family of hammerjaw fishes of the order Salmoniformes.
·classification and general features **16**:191f

Omotic languages: *see* Cushitic languages.

Ōmoto-kyō, English RELIGION OF GREAT FUNDAMENTALS, religious movement of Japan that had a large following in the period between World War I and World War II and that served as a model for numerous other sects in that country.

The teaching of Ōmoto is based on divine oracles transmitted through a peasant woman, Deguchi Nao, whose healing powers attracted an early following. Her first revelation in 1892 foretold the destruction of the world and the appearance of a messiah who would usher in the new heaven on earth.

The doctrine was systematized and organized by her son-in-law, Deguchi Onisaburō (1871–1948), who denounced armament and war and identified himself as the leader who would establish the new order. He attracted more than 2,000,000 believers in the 1930s but aroused the hostility of the government, which twice, in 1921 and again in 1935, arrested him and destroyed Ōmoto-kyō temples and buildings at its headquarters in Ayabe, near Kyōto. He was released on bail in 1942 and initiated the revival of the movement in 1946 under the name Ōmoto-Aizen-en (Great Foundation of Love of Goodness Garden). The sect was known by several names but has reverted to its most commonly used name, Ōmoto-kyō.

Though the membership of the sect in 1970 was estimated at only 140,975 believers, its importance may be measured by the number of other "new religions" of Japan that owe their original inspiration to Ōmoto-kyō. These include Seichō-no-ie (Household of Growth) and Sekai Kyūsei-kyō (Religion of World Messianity), both founded by former disciples of Onisaburō. Ōmoto-kyō emphasizes the universal character of religion. It promotes the use of the international language Esperanto and sponsors an organization called ULBA (Universal Love and Brotherhood Association).
·extermination and revival **10**:114g

omphacite, one of the solid solution series of the pyroxenes, essentially iron-magnesium aluminum silicates that contain calcium and sodium. Omphacite is most common in certain metamorphic rocks.
·formula and metamorphic occurrence **12**:7h; table 5
·occurrence, structure, and chemistry **15**:318e *passim* to 322b

Omphalea, genus of tropical shrubs or trees of the family Euphorbiaceae, consisting of 15 species; 12 are native to the Americas, 3 to the Old World. *O. triandra*, the Jamaican cobnut or pop nut, is native to the West Indies and cultivated in Europe. It grows to about 3.5 metres (11.5 feet) and bears yellow nuts that are edible if the poisonous embryo is removed. Juice from the fruit blackens and is used in making ink and glue. *O. diandra*, native to Colombia, bears edible oily seeds that are also used as hog feed. Large hunter's nuts from *O. megacarpa* are a stimulating, nutritious food popular in the West Indies.

Omri, also spelled ʿAMRI (reigned 876–869 or *c.* 884–*c.* 872 BC), king of Israel, the father of Ahab. Omri is mentioned briefly and unfavourably in the Bible (I Kings 16; Micah 6:16), but is thought by modern scholars to have been one of the most important rulers of the northern kingdom. His name appears frequently in Assyrian inscriptions, and he is known to have conquered Moab, formed an alliance with Tyre, and moved the capital of Israel to Samaria.
·alliance with Tyre **17**:946b
·northern kingdom reign **2**:914f
·Old Testament basis in history **2**:896h

Omsk, administrative region (*oblast*), west central Russian Soviet Federated Socialist Republic. It covers an area of 53,900 sq mi (139,700 sq km) in the basin of the middle Irtysh River. Its entire surface is an extremely flat plain with numerous lakes, of which Lake Tenis is the largest. Many southern lakes are saline. In the north is a dense, swampy forest, or taiga, of pine, fir, spruce, and birch; this yields southward to forest-steppe, with groves of birch, and finally to true steppe. The forest-steppe and steppe have rich soils and are intensively cultivated. Much land was plowed up in the Virgin and Idle Lands Campaign of the 1950s. Agriculture dominates the economy, and the towns, apart from Omsk city, the *oblast* headquarters, are small food-processing centres. Grains, especially spring wheat, are the main crop; flax, sunflowers, and mustard are also important. Around Omsk city, market gardening is significant. Livestock husbandry and dairying are highly developed, with large numbers of cattle and sheep. Some timber is extracted in the north. Pop. (1977 est.) 1,920,000.

Transporting timber in the north of Omsk *oblast*, Russian S.F.S.R.
Novosti Press Agency

Omsk, administrative centre, Omsk *oblast* (region), Russian Soviet Federated Socialist Republic, on the Irtysh River at its junction with the Om. Omsk, founded in 1716 at the eastern end of the Ishim fortified line between the Tobol and the Irtysh, developed as an agricultural centre and became a city in 1804. Its military function as the administrative headquarters of the Siberian Cossacks lasted until the late 19th century. In 1918–19 it was the seat of the anti-Bolshevik government of Adm. A.V. Kolchak.

Monument to Lenin at Omsk, Russian S.F.S.R.
Novosti Press Agency

The building of the Trans-Siberian Railroad in the 1890s and Omsk's position as a transshipment point on the Irtysh led to rapid commercial growth. Industrial growth was given great impetus during World War II, since which time its population has more than trebled. Engineering, especially the production of agricultural machinery, dominates a wide range of industry. Pipelines from the Volga-Urals and West Siberian oilfields supply the refinery and petrochemical industry, which makes synthetic rubber and tires. Other industries include the manufacture of cotton and woollen textiles, cord, footwear, and leather goods and food processing. Timber working is also carried on. Among the cultural and educational facilities of Omsk are agricultural, engineering, medical, and veterinary institutes and other research and higher educational establishments. Pop. (1970 prelim.) 821,000.
55°00′ N, 73°24′ E

·map, Soviet Union **17**:322
·population and resources **17**:333d

Ōmura, city, Nagasaki Prefecture (*ken*), Kyushu, Japan, facing Ōmura-wan (Ōmura Bay), on the western slopes of Tara-dake (Mt. Tara). In early historic times it was a post station and later developed as a port and castle town. It became a base for trade with Portugal and a centre of Christianity in the late 16th century. The city is now an industrial centre, producing processed foods and pearls farmed in the bay. Ōmura contains the Nagasaki Airport and a base of the Japanese Self-Defense Force. Pop. (1970) 56,538.
32°54′ N, 129°57′ E

·map, Japan **10**:36

Ōmura Masujirō (b. 1824—d. 1869), Japanese scholar and soldier popularly regarded in Japan as the founder of the modern Japanese Army.

Ōmura was the son of a physician of the Chōshu clan in Sūo (now Yamaguchi Prefecture). After studying Confucian ethics, at the age of 19 he began studying Rangaku (Dutch, or Western, learning) and medicine. When he was 23, he went to Osaka to study western medicine at the Tekijyuku, a school founded by the Dutch-language scholar and physician Ogata Koan.

In 1850 he returned home to practice medicine but had little success, and in 1853 he became an instructor in Western learning for the Uwajima clan of Iyo (now Ehime Prefecture). He spent some time in Nagasaki studying Western naval science before going to Edo (now Tokyo) in 1856. There he became an instructor at Bansho-Shirabesho, the government's Western Literature Research Office, and later at the national military academy. During this period he studied English under James Curtis Hepburn, an American missionary, who later devised a romanized system for the Japanese language and who was then working for the Japanese government. Ōmura also studied Western military strategy.

After returning to his clan in 1861, Ōmura applied his knowledge of the Western military sciences as an adviser to the clan military organization. He gained fame as a strategist during the battles between the Choshū clan and the forces of the shogunate, the military dictatorship in 1864 and 1865, before the Meiji Restoration of direct imperial rule (1867–68) ushered in the modern era.

In 1869 he was appointed minister of military affairs and planned the adoption of a conscription system for the new Imperial Army and the complete elimination of the samurai (knights) as a warrior class. While he was in Kyoto inspecting sites for military schools, he was assassinated by samurai opposed to his reform plans.

Ōmura was posthumously accorded the Junior Grade of Second Court Rank, and his son, Hirondo, was made a viscount in 1888. A statue of Ōmura in front of the Yasukuni Shrine—dedicated to the spirits of all Japanese soldiers—in Tokyo depicts him as the "father" of the Imperial Army that evolved in the Meiji period.

Ōmuta, city, Fukuoka Prefecture (*ken*), northern Kyushu, Japan, on the east coast of the Ariakeno-umi (Ariakeno Sea). It is a coal-mining centre, some of Japan's finest bituminous coal being extracted from the Miike coalfield. The artificial harbour has modern coal-handling facilities. Ōmuta has been an important industrial city since 1917, especially in the manufacture of chemicals. Other industries include coke ovens, a zinc refinery, a ferroalloy steel mill, fireproof brick works, a cotton mill, and a synthetic petroleum plant. Pop. (1970) 175,143.
33°02′ N, 130°27′ E

·map, Japan **10**:36

on (Japanese: "pronunciation"), one of two alternate readings (the other is *kun*) for a *kanji* (Japanese: "character"). The ambiguity of a *kanji* arises from the fact that it has two values: the meaning of the original Chinese character and a Chinese pronunciation of the character. In the *on* reading, the character is pronounced as it would be in Chinese, and the sounds are interpreted as forming a Japanese word or part of a Japanese word.

Ona, South American Indians inhabiting the island of Tierra del Fuego, of whom fewer than 50 remained in the 1960s. They were historically divided into two major groups: Shelknam and Haush. They spoke different dialects, linguistically classified in the Macro-Pano-Tacanan group, and had slightly different cultures. The Ona were hunters and gatherers who subsisted chiefly on guanaco, small herds of which were stalked by bowmen; on various small animals; and on shellfish, cormorants, and berries.

They were organized in patrilineal bands of 40 to 120 members, each claiming territorial rights to a well-defined hunting area. The men took their wives from other bands. The nomadic life of the Ona resembled that of the Patagonian and Pampean hunters more than that of their immediate neighbours of the Chilean archipelago except for social and religious ceremonials. The Ona celebrated male initiation rites, *klóketen;* secrets were revealed by the older men to the younger, and women were excluded from them. The rites were based on a myth that told how the men had overturned a previous regime dominated by women. They believed in a supreme being, who sent punishment and death for wrongdoing. Shamans, who aided hunters and cured sickness, derived their power from the spirits of deceased shamans who appeared to them in dreams.

The Ona had little aesthetic life. Their technology, like that of neighbouring peoples, was very simple.

·geographic distribution and socioeconomic structure **17**:116e; map 117
·hunting band organization **17**:114f; map 113
·nomadic cultural characteristics **8**:1159e
·racial typing and characteristics **14**:847f

Oña, Pedro de (b. 1570?, Los Confines, Chile—d. 1643?, Lima), the first poet of major significance to be born in Chile. After studying at the University of San Marcos in Lima, Peru, he entered the army and served in several battles against rebellious Indians. His most famous work is *Primera parte de Arauca domado* (1596; "First Part of The Araucan Conquest"), a verse epic in rhymed couplets depicting the deeds of the Marquis of Canete, Viceroy of Peru from 1556 to 1560, based in part on the famous *La Araucana* (1569, 1578, 1589; "The Araucan") of the Spanish poet Alonso de Ercilla. Although by no means approaching the stature of Ercilla's masterpiece, Oña's poem brought him immediate success and marked him as the finest poet of his day in Chile. Among his other well-known works are *El Ignacio de Cantabrice* (1639; "Ignatius of Cantabria"), a religious poem about St. Ignatius Loyola, and *Temblor de Lima en 1609* ("The Earthquake of Lima in 1609").

On Actors and the Art of Acting (1875), critical work by George Henry Lewes.
·nature of acting **1**:58h

On a Dream, sonnet by John Keats.
·Keats's period of poetic intensity **10**:413g

onager (*Equus hemionus onager*), subspecies of the wild ass of Asia that ranged from northwest Iran to Soviet Turkistan; sometimes another name for the Asian wild ass

Onager (*Equus hemionus onager*) and foal
Kenneth W. Fink—Bruce Coleman Inc.

(*Equus hemionus*). Pale-coloured and small, it has a short erect mane and fairly large ears. It was domesticated in ancient times but was replaced by the domestic horse and donkey. It now is found in limited numbers and may be approaching extinction. *See also* ass.

·development of agriculture **1**:326d
·distribution and population decline **14**:82e
·draft animal domestication in Asia **5**:970g
·draft animal early use **8**:657e
·history of wagons and carriages **19**:521a
·Syrian onager distribution and history **14**:82f

onager (weapon): *see* catapult.

On Aggression (1966), book by Konrad Lorenz.
·aggression and moral responsibility **12**:875e
·environmental modification of instinct **11**:107c

Onagraceae, the evening primrose family of dicotyledonous flowering plants, belonging to the myrtle order (Myrtales), that contains 21 genera and 640 species concentrated in the temperate region of the New World. The family is characterized by flowers with parts mostly on the plan of four (four sepals, four petals, four or eight stamens), but there are some exceptions. The ovary is inferior (*i.e.*, below the flower proper). In the temperate zone the family is best known by genera such as *Epilobium*, including the great willow herb or fireweed (*E. angustifolium*, so-called because it becomes readily established on newly burned areas), occurring in cooler parts of the world and disseminated by means of a tuft of hairs at the tip of each seed. Another well-known genus is *Oenothera*, with about 80 species, some of which are grown in gardens. Most of its members are yellow- or white-flowered; some species are evening bloomers, hence the name evening primrose; others are day bloomers with names such as suncup. The genus has been of great importance in studies in genetics and evolution.

Fuchsia, with about 100 species, is largely tropical and subtropical; but some species are widely used in gardens and as potted plants indoors. Fuchsias differ from the the other members of the family by having fleshy fruit. *Clarkia*, native of western North America and Chile, with about 35 species, is well-known in gardens. The flowers range from purplish red to pink and lavender and are often blotched or flecked. *Lopezia*, with 17 species ranging from Mexico to Panama, has a small highly specialized flower with only two stamens (male parts), a sterile, petaloid stamen enfolding a fertile one. *Lopezia* species are grown as garden annuals or in the greenhouse.

In wet places, especially in warmer parts of both the Old and New worlds, is another large day-blooming genus, *Ludwigia*, 75 species of water and marsh plants ranging from annual herbs to large shrubs; the flowers are yellow, the petals falling away easily. Some other genera of the family are *Boisduvalia; Circaea*, enchanter's nightshade, with hooked bristles on the fruits; *Gaura*, with small nut-like, indehiscent fruits; *Gayophytum*, thread-stemmed annuals with minute flowers; and *Hauya* of Mexico and Central America, shrubby or treelike, with large white to pinkish flowers.

·range, life cycle, uses, and classification **12**:773a

On Agriculture (160 BC), work by Cato.
·Rome's economic crisis **15**:1100b

Onam, Hindu festival in Kerala State, India.
·Kerala's cultural uniqueness **10**:435f

on and ho-on (Japanese: "favour" and "return of favour"), two elements of a reciprocal value system characteristic of Japanese religions and society. The system reflects a family hierarchy in which the patriarch determines the relationships with each member of his group and is himself responsible to his ancestors and to his social and political superiors in the national hierarchy. The emperor is responsible to his ancestors and to the gods. Semidivine or divine status is afforded the highest ranking superiors, both deceased ancestors and living persons of exceptional merit.
·Japanese cosmological outlook **10**:111d

On Architecture (Vitruvius): *see* De architectura.

Onassis, Jacqueline Bouvier Kennedy (b. 1929), widow of U.S. president John F. Kennedy; subsequently married to international businessman Aristotle Onassis (1968).
·marriages and public life **10**:416h

Oñate, Juan de (b. 1550?, New Spain, now Mexico—d. 1630), conquistador who established the colony of New Mexico for Spain. During his despotic governorship he vainly sought the mythical riches of North America and succeeded instead in unlocking the geographical secrets of the southwestern U.S.

Son of wealthy parents in Zacatecas, New Spain, Oñate gained added status when he married a granddaughter of Hernán Cortés. His request to conquer and govern New Mexico was approved in 1595, but it was not until three years later (January 1598) that his expedition of 400 settlers finally began its northern journey. Crossing the Rio Grande at El Paso in July 1598, he established headquarters at that river's confluence with the Chama at San Juan. From there he sent out small parties in all directions to search for treasure—which did not exist. Disillusioned, many settlers wanted to return to New Spain, but Oñate refused to let them go and executed several of the leading malcontents. His treatment of the Indians was even more brutal.

To please his followers and to mollify the crown, Oñate set out in June 1601 to find the legendary treasure of quivira (in what is now central Kansas) but returned in November empty-handed and found, moreover, that most of his colony had departed during his absence. In a last attempt to recover his prestige, he led (Oct. 7, 1604) 30 soldiers on an expedition west to the Colorado River and south to the Gulf of California. Though he gained a great deal of information, he still found no gold. He resigned in 1607 and later stood trial for his crimes while governor. Found guilty of cruelty, immorality, and false reporting, he was exiled from the colony, heavily fined, and deprived of his titles. Appeals brought a reversal of his sentence (1624) but not restoration to office.
·New Mexico discovery and colonization **13**:3b

On Baile's Strand, play by W.B. Yeats, first performed 1904, published 1905.
·Yeats's involvement in the Abbey Theatre **19**:1077a

onça, unit of measure in Portugal equivalent to 28.688 grams.
·weights and measures, table 5 **19**:734

once, unit of measure in France equivalent to 30.59 grams (old).
·weights and measures, table 5 **19**:734

Once and Future King, The (1958), novel by T.H. White.
·public recognition of the novel **13**:297b

Onchi Kōshirō (1892–1955), Japanese maker of woodcuts and printmaker.
·20th-century Japanese printmaking **14**:1096a

onchocerciasis (medicine): *see* filariasis.

Oncholaimida, order of the class Nematoda, phylum Aschelminthes (wormlike animals).
·classification and general features **2**:142f

On Christian Doctrine (*c.* 1658–60), translation of DE DOCTRINA CHRISTIANA, treatise by John Milton.

Oncidium, a genus of 350 to more than 750 species (depending on the authority consulted) of tropical American and Caribbean orchids, family Orchidaceae, that vary greatly in size and shape. Most species grow on other plants and have yellow flowers that range in width from 6 millimetres (about ¼ inch) to more than 10 centimetres (about 4 inches). The flowers of many species are borne on spikes or in long sprays. *Oncidium papilio*, the butterfly orchid, and *O. kramerianum*, a similar species, have one petal and two sepals modified into long, thin extensions. Other species are known by the common names bee orchid, tiger orchid, mule-ear orchid, and dancing ladies because of their coloration and appearance.
·bee territorial rival simulated as pollination lure **13**:652f
·deceptive mimicry in bee-like flowers **14**:746b
·house plants and their care **8**:1121c

Oncidium kramerianum
Walter Chandoha

Oncken, Johann Gerhardt (1800–84), German Baptist leader.
·Baptist expansion in Europe **2**:716a

oncogenic virus, any virus associated with inducing tumours. There is much dispute about the possible viral origin of tumours. It is not always clear whether a virus isolated from a tumour has actually caused the tumour or is merely coincidentally present. Many viruses, such as the poxviruses, cause proliferation of cells that is limited in extent and normally followed by regression. No one class of viruses can be considered "tumour viruses"; some are deoxyviruses (with deoxyribonucleic acid, or DNA) from several different virus families; others are riboviruses (with ribonucleic acid, or RNA). Papillomas, or warts, are benign tumours, many of which are known to be caused by viruses (*see* papovavirus). There is evidence that certain animal leukemias are viral in origin; human leukemias are also suspected of being viral. Certain adenoviruses of humans can cause tumours in newborn hamsters.
·animal experiments **19**:171e

oncolite, concretionary grain from 10 to 30 millimeters in diametre, components of some limestones.
·size, structure, and limestone textures **16**:466h

Oncomeris flavicornis (insect): *see* stink-bug.

On Contradiction, major theoretical work by Mao Tse-tung; written in 1937 and published in 1952. In it Mao discusses the law of contradiction in things and the law of the unity of opposites.
·analysis and revolutionary objectives **4**:388c
·Mao's dialectic theories **11**:467d

oncopod 13:568, any member of three small invertebrate groups—Onychophora, Tardigrada (water bears), and Pentastomida.

The text article covers natural history, form and function, and evolution, and includes an annotated classification of the oncopods.

REFERENCES in other text articles:
·arthropod classification problems **2**:70c
·circulatory system anatomy **4**:622a
·phylogenic position of onychophorans **14**:382h
·social parental behaviour patterns **16**:938a

RELATED ENTRIES in the *Ready Reference and Index:*
onychophoran; pentastomid; tardigrade

Oncorhynchus: *see* salmon.

Oncorhynchus gorhuscha: *see* pink salmon.

Oncorhynchus nerka: *see* sockeye salmon.

Oncothecaceae, flowering plant family of the order Theales.
·classification and general features **18**:211e

oncotic pressure, the pressure exerted by blood plasma proteins on the capillary wall.
·fluid changes in inflammation **9**:560d

Ondatra zibethica (rodent): *see* muskrat.

Ondes Martenot, also called ONDES MUSICALES ("musical waves"), electronic musical instrument demonstrated in 1928 in France by the inventor Maurice Martenot. Oscillating radio tubes produce electric pulses at two supersonic sound wave frequencies. They, in turn, produce a lower frequency within audible range that is equal to the difference in their rates of vibration and that is amplified and converted into sound by a loudspeaker. Many timbres, or tone colours, can be created by filtering out upper harmonics, or component tones, of the audible notes.

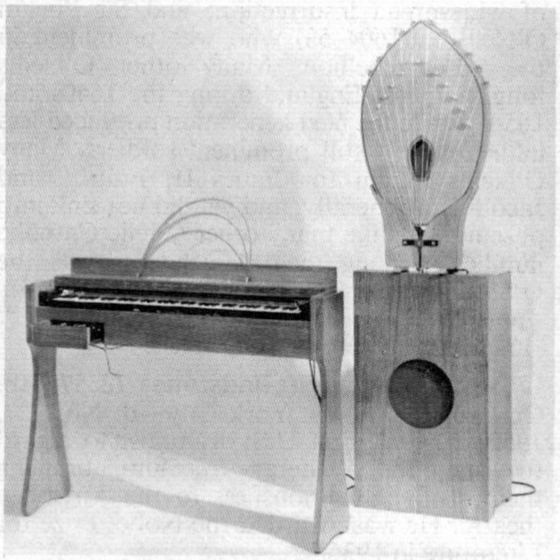

Ondes Martenot
Photo Lauros

In the earliest version, the player's hand approaching or moving away from a wire varied one of the high frequencies, thus changing the lower frequency and altering the pitch. Later, a wire was stretched across a model keyboard; the player touched the wire to vary the frequency. A version also exists in which the frequency changes are controlled from a functioning keyboard. Works for the Ondes Martenot include those by the French-born Swiss composer Arthur Honegger, the French composer Darius Milhaud, and the U.S. composer Samuel Barber.
·structure, operation, and composition **6**:673g

Ondo, town, Ondo Province, Western State, southwestern Nigeria, at the southern edge of the Kukuruku Hills (altitude 940 ft [287 km]) and the intersection of roads from Ife, Akure, and Okitipupa. A collecting point for cocoa and palm oil and kernels, it is a local market centre (yams, cassava, maize [corn], poultry, fish, fruits, palm produce, pumpkins, okra) for the Ondo branch of the Yoruba people and the location of a branch office of the Federal Ministry of Trade. The site of the Adeyemi College of Education, an advanced teacher-training college, and St. Helen's Teacher Training College (Anglican), it also has Anglican, Roman Catholic, and government secondary schools, a vocational institute, several hospitals, and a maternity clinic.

Ondo Province covers an area of 8,162 sq mi (21,139 sq km), which includes mangrove-swamp forest near the Bight of Benin, tropical rain forest in the centre, and wooded savanna on the gentle slopes of the Kukuruku Hills. The chief products are cotton and tobacco from the north, cocoa from the centre, and rubber (around Okitipupa) and timber (teak and hardwoods) from the south and east; palm oil and kernels are cultivated for export throughout the province. Although an agricultural-based economy prevails, the province's predominantly Yoruba population has traditionally lived in large urban centres; several of the market towns, including Ado-Ekiti (the largest), Akure (the capital), Effon-Alaiye, Ikare, Ikere-Ekiti, Ilawe, Oka-Akoko, Ondo, and Owo (*qq.v.*), have more than 50,000 inhabitants. Pop. (1971 est.) town, 89,861; (latest census) province, 2,728,000.
7°04′ N, 4°47′ E
·map, Nigeria **13**:86

Öndörhaan, also spelled UNDUR KHAN, town, administrative headquarters of Hentiy province (*aymag*), Mongolian People's Republic. Situated on the Kerulen River, 180 mi (290 km) east of Ulaanbaatar, in the east central part of the country, the town is the main transportation centre of Hentiy *aymag*. Coal mining is important to the economy; the coalfield in the Mörön Gol (river) Valley, 50 mi from the town, has a productive coal seam up to 15 ft thick. Latest census 7,900.
47°19′ N, 110°39′ E

One, Eleatic, in Eleatic philosophy, the assertion of Parmenides of Elea that Being is one (Greek *hen*) and unique and that it is continuous, indivisible, and all that there is or ever will be.

His deduction of the predicate one from his assertion that only Being exists is not adequately explicit; thus, later thinkers felt it necessary to fill in his argument. Aristotle, for example, wrote: "Claiming that besides Being that which is not is absolutely nothing, he thinks that Being is of necessity one, and there is nothing else." Aristotle suggested that, to Parmenides, Being must be all that there is (because other than Being there is only Not-Being); and there can therefore exist no second other thing. Moreover, one can ask what could divide Being from Being other than Not-Being? But because for Parmenides (as opposed later to the Atomists), Not-Being cannot be, it cannot divide Being from Being. It follows, then, that Being is whole, continuous, and "not divisible, since it is all alike."

The consequent oneness of Being was thus recognized throughout antiquity as a fundamental tenet of the Eleatic school. Plato, in his dialogue the *Parmenides*, wrote that a number of the arguments of Zeno of Elea concerned this very issue, which he approached deviously by demonstrating the absurd consequences of the opposite assertion that the many are. Plato himself insisted that such abstractions (or forms) as justice itself and piety itself are each a one as opposed to the many "happenings" to which the Greeks had tried to restrict them. Thus, justice itself could not happen; only events that instigate justice happen. Justice simply is and as such remains eternally changeless. It is thus a one and not a many; a being and not a happening.

Plato's treatment became a principal source of the Neoplatonist interpretation, advanced in the 3rd century AD, of a divine one out of which all reality progressively emanates, a view that arose, as Plato's seems not to have done, from a deeply mystical source.

In time, within Plato's Academy (his school in Athens) the meanings of all of the early terms used to talk about the "forms" came under scrutiny; and among them "one" and "being" remained prominent—terms that, in consequence, long retained a place in the intellectual life of Athens.
·Parmenides and monism **6**:525d

One, None and a Hundred Thousand (1933), translation of UNO, NESSUNO E CENTOMILA (1925–26), a novel by Luigi Pirandello.
·theme and style **14**:469f

O'Neal, Jeffrey Hamet, 18th-century Irish porcelain painter and miniaturist.
·Chelsea ceramic painting production **14**:913g

one-design class, yacht-racing division in which all boats eligible to compete are built to the same basic measurements. A test of the relative abilities of the skippers, the one-design concept has been applied to nearly every type of sailing vessel used in racing (even iceboats). The first to become popular was the "Star," a 22-foot 8½-inch (6.9-metre) keel sloop developed from an earlier design by William Gardner in 1911. The Star Class Association of America was formed in 1915 and the International Star Class Yacht Racing Association in 1923. The class was admitted to Olympic Games competition in 1932.

Other one-design classes followed similar patterns of growth. After World War II rising costs forced the decline of larger racing yachts built in accordance with the older rating rule (*q.v.*) and encouraged the building of identical yachts, which are more economical. By the 1970s there were probably more than 200 one-design classes active throughout the world, many with their own international organizations. One-design classes competing in the Olympic Games during the 1960s were the Star, Finn monotype, Flying Dutchman, and Dragon. After 1968, a new policy dictated that at least one class would be changed for each Olympiad. For 1972 the Soling class replaced the 5.5-metre, and the Tempest class was added.

One-Eleven, twin-jet short-range transport aircraft built by British Aircraft Corporation Ltd.
·short-haul jet development **18**:635h

Onega, Lake 13:570, Russian ONEZHSKOYE OZERO, in the northwestern European Soviet Union, occupies parts of the Karelian Autonomous Soviet Socialist Republic and of the Leningrad and Vologda *oblasti* of the Russian S.F.S.R. between Lake Ladoga and the White Sea. It has an area of 3,753 sq mi (9,720 sq km) and is the second largest lake in Europe after Ladoga. Onega is important for its fisheries and as a transport link between the Baltic and White seas.

The text article covers the lake's physiography, geology, hydrography, and fisheries.
61°30′ N, 35°45′ E

REFERENCE in other text article:
·map, Soviet Union **17**:322

one gene-one enzyme hypothesis, an idea advanced in the early 1940s that each gene controls the synthesis or activity of a single enzyme (a catalytic protein). The concept has been amply verified in principle, but has undergone considerable sophistication since then. It has been supplanted by the hypothesis that, essentially, a segment of genetic material controls a segment of an enzyme.
·gene action in organism development **7**:987g
·metabolic pathway research **11**:1026a

Oneglia (Italy): *see* Imperia.

Oneg Shabbat (Hebrew: Joy of Sabbath), an informal sabbath (or Friday evening) gathering of Jews in a synagogue or private home to express outwardly the happiness inherent in the sabbath holiday. Now more social than religious, the group entertains itself with music, drama, community discussions, lectures, or the singing of religious melodies—all in keeping with the biblical injunction, "and call the sabbath a delight" (Isa. 58:13). Usually refreshments are provided to complement the congenial atmosphere and perpetuate in spirit the Talmud's recommendation to eat three full meals that day.

one-horned rhinoceros: *see* rhinoceros.

one-horse shay, also called a CHEER (for chair) or WHISKY, U.S. carriage, an open two-

One-horse shay, *c.* 1870; in the Henry Ford Museum, Dearborn, Mich.
Owned by the Henry Ford Museum

wheeled vehicle. Its chairlike body, seating the passengers on one seat above the axle, was balanced on a square wooden spring attached to the shafts. Early one-horse shays had fixed standing tops, later ones folding tops. Oliver Wendell Holmes's poem "The Deacon's Masterpiece," a satire on Calvinism, paints a whimsical picture of a "one-hoss" shay that was so perfectly built that it lasted for 100 years and then fell apart all at once.

Oneida, Iroquoian-speaking North American Indian tribe of what is now central New York state and one of the original five nations of the Iroquois League (*q.v.*). Like the other Iroquois tribes, the Oneida were semi-sedentary and practiced maize (corn) agriculture. Longhouses sheltered families related through maternal descent. They were divided into three clans, each having three representatives in the confederation. Each community also had a local council that guided the chief, or chiefs. The least populous of the confederates, the Oneida during the 17th century had only one palisaded town of 60 to 100 longhouses; the town was destroyed by a French-Canadian expedition in 1696. Thereafter the community divided into Oneida (Upper Castle) and Canawaroghere. In the early 18th century a village of North Carolina Tuscarora joined the Oneida, becoming the sixth nation of the Iroquois League, and former Oneida enemies in the Carolinas became the targets of war parties for a generation.

The Oneida supported the colonist cause in the American Revolution and consequently felt the depredations of the pro-British Iroquois under the Mohawk chief Joseph Brant. They retired within American lines, where they served as scouts. Returning to their homes after the war, they took in remnants of the Mohegan (*q.v.*) and were compensated by the U.S. for their losses. In the following years the Oneida divided into factions resulting from disagreements over Quaker missions, their traditional religion, and the sale of lands. By 1833 those who had not settled at Oneida on the Thames River, Ontario, emigrated to Green Bay, Wis.; a few families remained at Oneida and Onondaga, N.Y. Oneida descendants were estimated to number 3,000 in the 1970s, with major concentrations in Canada, Wisconsin, and central New York state.

·Woodlands Indian culture **6**:169b

Oneida, city, Madison County, central New York, U.S., on Oneida Creek, 6 mi (10 km) southeast of Oneida Lake. Founded in 1834 by Sands Higinbotham, it developed as a depot and supply point for the Utica and Syracuse (later New York Central) Railroad. Growth was influenced by the Oneida Community, an experiment in communal living founded in 1848 by John Noyes; in 1881 it was reorganized as a stock company that produced leading lines of silverware (still a major industry). Oneida Limited, which retains some cooperative features, has large factories at Oneida and nearby Sherrill. Local manufactures also include wood products, burial vaults, and dairy equipment. Colgate University (founded 1819) is in Hamilton, 18 mi (30 km) south of the city. Inc. village, 1848; city, 1901. Pop. (1980) 10,810.
43°06′ N, 75°39′ W

Oneida Community, also called PERFECTIONISTS and BIBLE COMMUNISTS, a utopian religious community that developed out of a Society of Inquiry established by John Humphrey Noyes and some of his disciples in Putney, Vt., in 1841. As new recruits arrived, the society turned into a socialized community.

Noyes had experienced a religious conversion during a revival in 1831, when he was 20 years old. He then gave up law studies and attended Andover Theological Seminary and Yale Divinity School. His acceptance and preaching of the doctrine of perfectionism, the idea that after conversion one was free of all sin, was considered too unorthodox, and he was denied ordination. He also became convinced that the Second Coming of Christ was not an event of the future but had already occurred within a generation of Christ's ministry on earth. But it was Noyes's ideas concerning sexual union that made him notorious. He considered sexual union very important but rejected monogamy and the idea that one man and one woman should become closely attached to each other. The application of his views led to the practice of complex marriage in his community, in which every woman was the wife of every man and every man was the husband of every woman. Noyes also believed that Socialism without religion was impossible and that the extended family system devised by him could dissolve selfishness and demonstrate the practicality of perfectionism on earth.

In 1847, at a time when revivalist belief in a new coming of Christ was at its height, Noyes proclaimed that the Spirit of Christ had earlier returned to earth and had now entered into his group at Putney. This proclamation, together with the practice of complex marriage, aroused the hostility of the surrounding community, and the group left Putney to found a new community at Oneida, N.Y.

For the next 30 years Oneida flourished. The community, which in the early years numbered about 200 persons, earned a precarious existence by farming and logging before the arrival of a new member who gave the community a steel trap that he had invented. Manufacture and sale of Oneida traps, which were considered the best in the land, became the basis of a thriving group of industrial enterprises that included silverware, embroidered silks, and canned fruit.

The community was organized into 48 departments that carried on the various activities of the settlement, and these activities were supervised by 21 committees. The women worked along with the men; for practical reasons they cut their hair short and wore trousers or short-skirted tunics. Though marriage was complex, the Perfectionists denied the charge of free love. Sexual relations were strictly regulated, and the propagation of children was a matter of community control. Those who were to produce children were carefully chosen and paired. Children remained with their mother until they could walk but were then placed in a common nursery.

The central feature of the community was the custom of holding criticism sessions or cures, a practice that Noyes had discovered in his seminary days at Andover. They were attended by the entire community at first and, later, as the community grew, were conducted before committees presided over by Noyes. For those subjected to criticism it was a nerve-racking ordeal, yet the sessions probably had some therapeutic value as a means of releasing feelings of guilt and aggression. The criticism sessions were also a shaming technique that enforced social control and were a highly successful device for promoting community cohesion.

Hostility mounted in the surrounding communities to the Perfectionists' marriage arrangements, and in 1879 Noyes advised the group to abandon the system. As the reorganization of the community began, the entire Socialist organization of property in Oneida also was questioned. Noyes and a few adherents went to Canada, where he died in 1886. The remaining members set up a joint stock company, known as Oneida Community, Ltd., which carried on the various industries, particularly the manufacture of silver plate, as a commercial enterprise.

·Holiness ideal and antinomianism **8**:994c

O'Neill, Irish family most prominent in Ulster although other branches also existed. Tracing their descent from the early Irish king Niall of the Nine Hostages (d. AD 405), the O'Neills derived their name from a later king, Niall Glúndubh (d. 919). O'Neill is thus one of the oldest hereditary surnames in Europe. The O'Neills were independent until the mid-16th century, when Con Bacach, chief of the O'Neills (created earl of Tyrone for life), led resistance to English encroachments in Ireland. Meanwhile, intra-family feuds were widespread among the O'Neills. Among other members of the family were Hugh O'Neill (*c.* 1540–1616), 2nd earl of Tyrone, "the great earl," who won several victories over the English, but procrastinated at a crucial moment of widespread insurrection; and Sir Phelim O'Neill (*c.* 1604–53) who was prominent in the 1641 rebellion. Many other O'Neills fought against England during the 1640s and 1650s, while the next generation produced less influential but still prominent soldiers. Many O'Neills fought for James II, France, and Jacobitism generally, and yet did not sink into obscurity, unlike many other Gaelic Catholic families. Among their descendants was the U.S. playwright Eugene O'Neill (1888–1953).

·influence on Eugene O'Neill **13**:571d
·Irish political development **3**:284e

O'Neill, Eugene (Gladstone) 13:571 (b. Oct. 16, 1888, New York City—d. Nov. 27, 1953, Boston), first U.S. dramatist to regard the stage as a literary medium, bringing themes of high seriousness to the American theatre. He was awarded the Nobel Prize for Literature in 1936.

Abstract of text biography. As the son of an actor, O'Neill experienced an insecure childhood. He studied at Princeton University for one year (1906–07) and spent the next six years as a seaman, living the life of a derelict on several of the world's waterfronts. He contracted tuberculosis and, while confined to a sanitarium (1912–13), began to write plays. His first to be produced was a one-act sea play, *Bound East for Cardiff* (1916). It was followed by his first full-length play, *Beyond the Horizon* (1920), awarded a Pulitzer Prize. Other prize-winning plays were *Anna Christie* (1922), *Strange Interlude* (1928), and *Long Day's Journey into Night* (posthumously, 1956). Immensely important on Broadway in the 1920s and 1930s, O'Neill became the only U.S. playwright to be awarded the Nobel Prize for Literature (1936). *The Iceman Cometh* (1946) is considered to be among his greatest works.

REFERENCES in other text articles:
·literary style and works **10**:1225a
·tragedy worthy of theatre **18**:587a

O'Neill, Hugh, 2nd earl of Tyrone (b. *c.* 1540—d. July 20, 1616, Rome), Irish rebel known as "The Great Earl" who, from 1595 to 1603, led an unsuccessful Roman Catholic uprising against English rule in Ireland. The defeat of O'Neill and the conquest of his province of Ulster was the final step in the complete subjugation of Ireland by the English.

Although born into the powerful O'Neill family of Ulster, Hugh grew up in London. In 1568 he returned to Ireland and assumed his grandfather's title of earl of Tyrone. By cooperating with the government of Queen Elizabeth I, he established his base of power, and in 1593 he replaced Turlough Luineach O'Neill as chieftain of the O'Neills. Skirmishes between Tyrone's forces and the English in 1595 were followed by three years of fruitless negotiations between the two sides.

In 1598 Tyrone reopened hostilities. His victory (August 14) over the English in the Battle of the Yellow Ford on the Blackwater River, Ulster, sparked a general revolt throughout the country. Pope Clement VIII lent moral support to Tyrone's cause, and in September 1601, 4,000 Spanish troops arrived at Kinsale, Munster, to assist the insurrection. But these reinforcements were quickly surrounded at Kinsale, and Tyrone suffered a staggering defeat (December 1601) while attempting to break the siege. He continued to resist until forced to surrender on March 30, 1603, six days after the death of Queen Elizabeth.

Elizabeth's successor, King James I, allowed Tyrone to keep most of his lands, but the chieftain soon found that he could not bear the loss of his former independence and prestige. In September 1607 Tyrone, with Rory O'Donnell, earl of Tyrconnell, and about 100 northern chieftains, secretly embarked on a ship bound for Spain. The vessel was blown off course and landed in the Netherlands. From here the refugees made their way to Rome, where they were acclaimed by Pope Paul V. This "flight of the earls" signalled the end of Gaelic Ulster; thereafter the province was rapidly anglicized. Outlawed by the English, O'Neill lived in Rome the rest of his life.
·Irish rebellions under Elizabeth I **3**:287e

O'Neill, John (1834–78), Irish-American leader of the U.S. branch of the Irish nationalist organization known as the Fenians, or Irish Republican Brotherhood. In an attempt to strike at British power, he led two abortive attacks on Canada.

O'Neill, Owen Roe (b. *c.* 1590—d. Nov. 6, 1649), rebel commander during a major Roman Catholic revolt (1641–52) against English rule in Ireland. His victory at Benburb, Ulster, on June 5, 1646, was the only significant rebel triumph of the war.

A nephew of the renowned Irish chieftain Hugh O'Neill, 2nd earl of Tyrone (died 1616), Owen Roe served with distinction for about 30 years in the Spanish Army before returning to Ireland in late July 1642, nine months after the outbreak of the insurrection. He immediately replaced Sir Phelim O'Neill as commander in the north, but he soon came into conflict with the other leaders of the Catholic confederacy. O'Neill advocated the complete independence of Ireland from England, while his colleagues favoured a settlement providing for religious liberty and an Irish constitution under the English crown. After routing the army of England's Scottish ally, Gen. Hector Munro, at Benburb, O'Neill helped the papal nuncio, Giovambattista Rinuccini (*q.v.*), force the confederacy to rescind a peace it had concluded with the English. Nevertheless, O'Neill and the other members of the Catholic faction eventually had to ally with the English Anglican royalists against the English Independent (radical Puritan) parliamentarians. He died three months after the parliamentarian general Oliver Cromwell arrived in Ireland.

O'Neill, Sir Phelim (b. *c.* 1604—d. 1653), Roman Catholic rebel who initiated a major revolt (1641–52) against English rule in Ireland. Elected a member of the Irish Parliament in 1641, O'Neill appeared to be a supporter of King Charles I. Nevertheless, on Oct. 22, 1641, he seized the strategically important Charlemont castle, Ulster, and then created confusion by claiming that Charles had authorized this act. O'Neill's followers proceeded to massacre hundreds of England's colonists in Ulster, but after besieging Drogheda, County Louth, for several months they were compelled to withdraw (April 1642). This and other failures caused Phelim to lose his command to his kinsman and rival, Owen Roe O'Neill. After Owen Roe's death in 1649, Phelim sought unsuccessfully to regain his former position, but he continued to fight bravely until the final defeat of the rebel cause in 1652. The next year he was tried by the English for treason and executed.

O'Neill, Shane (b. *c.* 1530, Ireland—d. June 2, 1567), Irish chieftain who, from 1559 to 1567, led a revolt against English rule in Ireland. He succeeded his father, Con Bacach (the Lame), as chieftain of the O'Neills of Ulster in 1559, and shortly afterward his supporters killed his major rival, Matthew, Con's illegitimate son. The refusal of England's Queen Elizabeth I to recognize his claim to the chieftainship caused O'Neill to take up arms against the English.

After a period of intermittent fighting, O'Neill travelled to London in January 1562 to carry on negotiations with Elizabeth and formally submitted to her authority. Nevertheless, upon his return to Ireland in May 1562, he pursued an independent course; soon the English provoked him to renew hostilities. He extended his power in Ulster by defeating his neighbours, the MacDonnells of Antrim, at Ballycastle, Ulster, in 1565, and he then attempted to obtain support for his uprising from Mary, Queen of Scots, and from France. He was declared a traitor by the English in August 1566, but before English troops could engage him in battle his army was annihilated at Farsetmore, Ulster (1567), by his traditional enemies, the O'Donnells of Tyrconnell. He took refuge with the MacDonnells, who slew him in a quarrel.
·Irish rebellions under Elizabeth I **3**:287b

oneiromancy, form of divination based on the interpretation of dreams.
·practice and nature **5**:919f

One May Spin a Thread Too Finely (1848), play by Ivan Turgenev.
·Turgenev's play-writing career **18**:779d

On Encountering Sorrow, in Chinese LI SAO, ode by Ch'ü Yüan.
·Chinese poetry development **10**:1052e

One of Our Conquerors (1891), novel by George Meredith.
·cryptic monologue style **11**:925e

Oneonta, city, Otsego County, east central New York, U.S., in the Catskill foothills, on the Susquehanna River, within the town (township) of Oneonta. The first white settlers were John Vanderwerker (1775) and Aaron Brink (1780), and the community was originally known as McDonald's Mills or Bridge (for James McDonald, 1808), and Milfordville (1817). Renamed Oneonta (Indian: "place of open rocks") in 1832, it was incorporated as a village in 1848. Railroad shops were built after the arrival of the Albany and Susquehanna Railroad in 1865. The Brotherhood of Railroad Trainmen originated (1883) in a side-tracked caboose at Oneonta, which became an important rail centre.

It is the home of a state university college (1889) and of Hartwick College (Lutheran; 1928). Although no longer a railway hub, it remains a busy distribution point and has diversified industries. Pop. (1980) 14,933.
42°27′ N, 75°04′ W
·map **18**:United States of America, Plate 15

Oneota, prehistoric North American Indian culture, the archaeological remains of which are found predominantly in Illinois and Missouri.
·decorative art forms **1**:680f

Onesimus (fl. 1st century AD), Phrygian (Asia Minor) slave converted to Christianity on whose behalf St. Paul wrote his letter to Philemon, the slave's master. A play on words is found in the text (verse 11) based on the Greek name Onesimus, meaning "useful." According to tradition, he suffered martyrdom.
·episcopacy attainment speculation **2**:967b
·St. Paul's activities in prison **13**:1093f

Onesquethaw Stage, lowermost division of Middle Devonian rocks and time in North America (the Devonian Period began about 395,000,000 years ago and lasted about 50,000,000 years). The Onesquethaw Stage precedes the Cazenovia Stage and follows the Deerparkian Stage of the Lower Devonian. One of the most familiar formations of the Onesquethaw Stage is the Onondaga Limestone Formation, a marine limestone with a rich invertebrate fauna, of New York and Ohio. During Onesquethaw time, the Appalachian landmass was low, and seas were clear and shallow.

one-step (dance): *see* fox-trot.

One Thousand Guineas, one of the English Classic horse races, established in 1814. Run at Newmarket, Suffolk, the over one-mile event is open only to three-year-old fillies. For winners since 1949, *see* sporting record.

One Thousand Seven Hundred and Thirty Eight (1738), later known as EPILOGUE TO THE SATIRES, title of two dialogues by Alexander Pope.
·Pope's works **14**:798c
·satirist's justification of his art **16**:272c

One Ton Cup, international racing trophy for sailing yachts of about one-ton displacement. From 1907 to 1955 the cup was the object of a major competition for 20-foot (6-metre) yachts, but with the decline of that class the cup was put up for challenge in the 1960s by the Cercle de la Voile de Paris, a French yacht club, for boats rated up to 22 feet (7 metres) by the measurement formula of the Royal Ocean Racing Club of Great Britain. Competing nations could enter up to three yachts each, with the winning yacht determined by performance in a series of races. The first three challenges consisted of three races, the first and third of 30 miles (48 kilometres) around a closed course and a second, counting double, a distance race of up to 300 miles (500 kilometres), run without handicap. In 1968 two more short races were added. A new rating of 27.5 feet (8.4 metres), by rules of the International Yacht Racing Union, was adopted for the 1971 event. *Major ref.* **2**:1169c

one-to-one correspondence (mathematics): *see* isomorphism.

Onezhskoye Ozero (Soviet Union): *see* Onega, Lake.

On First Looking into Chapman's Homer, sonnet by John Keats, first published in *The Examiner* in 1816.
·Keats's mature sonnets **10**:412g

On First Principles, Latin DE PRINCIPIIS, Greek PERI ARCHŌN, 3rd-century work by the Greek theologian Origen.
·Alexandrian school influence **13**:1081a
·Origen's doctrinal writings **13**:735e

Onganía, Juan Carlos (1914–), general and president (1966–70) of Argentina.
·economic and political program **1**:1150c

Ong Boun, also spelled ONG BUN, variously known as KING SIRIBUNYASARN or KING SIRIBUNYASAN and by the royal title PHRA MAHA BUNYA-SAYA-SETHATHIRATH (b. *c.* 1730—d. 1781), king of the Laotian principality of Vien Chang (now Vientiane) whose imprudent domestic and foreign policies led to the complete subjugation of all the Laotian states by Siam (now Thailand).

Ong Boun was the son and successor of King Ong Long (Ong Rong, or King Phra Saya Sethathirath II). At his father's death, Ong Boun's claim was disputed, and he assumed the throne in 1760 with the help of Phra Vor (Vorarat) and Phra Ta, elder statesmen who had helped quell rebellions and defend the kingdom for a decade. They expected compensation for their services, but instead Ong Boun reserved coveted offices for members of the royal family.

Ong Boun followed his father's foreign policy of allying Vien Chang to Burma, which had undertaken massive campaigns against the more powerful Southeast Asian states, especially Siam. When Ong Boun ascended the throne, the Siamese nation had been nearly obliterated by the Burmese; during his reign, however, Siam recouped its forces under the leadership of Phra Taksin (later king of Siam). The other Laotian principality, Luang Prabang, allied itself with the Siamese, becoming increasingly more powerful, but Ong Boun, defying Phra Taksin and assisting the Burmese, angered the Siamese.

Meanwhile, Phra Vor and Phra Ta rebelled and attempted to set up rival kingdoms. Phra Vor gained the sponsorship of the Siamese king and, when Ong Boun moved against the rebels and Phra Vor was slain (1778), the Siamese used this as a pretext to invade Vien Chang. Siamese forces seized Ong Boun's capital in 1779, set up a military government, and carried off the Laotian treasures—the statue of the Prabang Buddha and the Phra Kaeo (Emerald Buddha) image—to Bangkok. Ong Boun and one of his sons fled the city, but the rest of the royal family was taken to Bangkok. Ong Boun took refuge either at Kham Keut (a village in the Kammon Plateau of Laos) or in Annam (now central Vietnam).

Ong Boun was granted clemency by the Siamese monarch and permitted to return to Vien Chang to live out his last days. In a further gesture of benevolence, Phra Taksin permitted one of Ong Boun's sons, Chao Nan, to govern in Vien Chang. By 1782, however, Vien Chang and the rest of Laos had become vassals of the Siamese kingdom. Although the rulers continued to be of Laotian descent, the independence of the Laotian states had ended.

Onge, negrito people living on the island of Little Andaman, 900 miles (1450 kilometres) off the east coast of India.
·Australoid racial characteristics **14**:844g
·racial type description **17**:125h; map 126

Ongyoku chikaragusa (1762, "Musical Aid"), Japanese music book, aided in creating a more accurate rendering of fingering positions for the samisen.
·samisen notational systems **12**:688g

On Heroes, Hero-Worship, and the Heroic in History (1841), a book by Thomas Carlyle.
·Carlyle's reverence for heroic strength **3**:924a

oni, in Japanese folklore, a type of demonic creature often of giant size, great strength,

Oni, disguised as a begging monk converted to Buddhism, wood figurine, Edo period (1603–1867); in the Musée Guimet, Paris

By courtesy of the Musee Guimet, Paris

and fearful appearance. They are generally considered to be foreign in origin, perhaps introduced into Japan from China along with Buddhism. Cruel and malicious, they can nevertheless be converted to Buddhism. Though *oni* have been depicted in various ways in Japanese legend and art, sometimes as women also, they are characteristically thought of as pink, red, or blue-grey in colour, with horns, three toes, three fingers, and on occasion with three eyes.
·loss of status under Buddhism **10**:100c

Oniad family, a dynasty of Jewish high priests during the Second Temple Period in Palestine.
·Judaean theocracy **10**:310e

Onias IV (2nd century BC), a deposed Jewish high priest who established a temple at Leontopolis in Egypt.
·Diaspora temple rivaling Jerusalem **10**:313a

Onighlo, mining site in Dahomey, Africa.
·limestone deposit site **5**:422e

Onin (Nigeria): *see* Lagos.

On Indolence (1819), an ode by John Keats.
·Keats's period of poetic intensity **10**:413g

On Intelligence (1871), translation of DE L'INTELLIGENCE (1870), work on psychology by Hippolyte Taine.
·Taine's scientific methodology **17**:993c

Ōnin War (1467–77), civil war in the central Kyōto region of Japan, which was a prelude to a prolonged period of domestic strife (1490–1573). It led to the end of the manorial system and hastened the rise of the great territorial magnates, or daimyo.

The war originated in rivalry between Hosokawa Katsumoto, prime minister (1452–64) for the shogun Ashikaga Yoshimasa, and Yamana Mochitoyo, whose family were powerful landowners in the western Honshu region. Yoshimasa's wife gave birth to an infant son in 1465, the year after the shogun had designated his brother Yoshimi as his heir apparent. Yoshimi was allied with Hosokawa, and Yoshimasa's wife turned to Yamana for help in having her son gain his rightful position. Warfare erupted between the two sides in 1467. The ancient city of Kyōto was severely damaged in the fighting, which soon spread throughout the country, as local clans took sides in hopes of gaining more territory for themselves.

Although the war ended in a stalemate in 1477, the Hosokawa did eventually win control of the government, but fighting in the provinces continued for another 100 years, eroding all pretense of central control over the outlying regions.
·military and political history **10**:68d

onion (*Allium cepa*), hardy, herbaceous biennial plant of the lily family (Liliaceae), or its edible bulb or the food flavouring derived therefrom. Onion has a characteristic pungent aroma and sharp taste; it is used as a spice for many foods, particularly meats, sausages, vegetables, and salads, and as a vegetable. Probably originating in the eastern Mediterranean region and western and middle Asia, the onion is unknown in the wild state, having been cultivated since prehistoric times. It is now grown the world over, but chiefly in the temperate zones.

The edible part consists of thickened leaf bases arising from the stem plate at the base of the bulb. The upper part of the leaf is hollow and cylindrical. A tuft of shallow, fibrous roots emerges from the stem plate. In the second season of growth, a smooth seedstalk rises 20 to 50 inches (½ to 1½ metres) with a large globular umbel of small white flowers on top. The seeds are small, irregular, angular, and usually black. Two types of onion produce no seed: those propagated by bulblets formed instead of seeds in the umbel, and those propagated only by division of a vegetative cluster of plants. The Welsh onion, *Allium fistulosum*, native to China, forms no enlarged bulb.

Most varieties of onions are sensitive to length of day and night. Bulbing varieties adapted to summer culture in high latitudes will not form bulbs during the short days of winter in low latitudes. Certain varieties that form large bulbs during the short days of low latitudes will form only small bulbs during the long days of high latitudes.

Onion (*Allium cepa*)

Walter Chandoha

Varieties grown in the northern U.S. need a mild, cool climate. Spanish and Egyptian varieties tolerate hot days of spring but not the midsummer heat of low latitudes. The latter types are sown in autumn in regions having little or no winter freezing. Northern bulbing varieties are firm fleshed, long keeping, and very pungent. The Bermuda type, grown in the south for spring harvest, is less firm, mild, and can be stored several weeks but not several months.

Discovery of cytoplasmically inherited male sterility in the onion in 1925 led to a commercially feasible method of producing F_1 hybrid seed of onion in 1944 and later of certain other plants. After 1950 substantial quantities of seed for growing superior F_1 hybrid varieties became commercially available in the United States. Most onions are grown by sowing seed directly in the field, but many are grown from transplants. Some are propagated by planting tiny mature bulbs called sets, which were grown from thickly sown seed the preceding year.

Nonbulbing onions for use in the fresh green state may be harvested as soon as they are large enough. Sometimes bulbing onions are harvested for immediate use before bulbs form. Green onions, or scallions, are sold with the fresh green tops attached. Bulb onions are mature for harvesting soon after the necks weaken and the tops fall to the ground. They are pulled from the soil and dried in the field until the necks are dry, then the tops are removed and the bulbs packed for shipment or storage. Onions keep best in dry, well-ventilated storage at about 33° F (1° C).

Onion powder is the spice consisting of the ground product of dehydrated, trimmed onion bulbs. Onion salt is onion powder mixed with free-running salt. Dehydrated flake onion and dehydrated instant minced onion are available. Dehydrated onion possesses the characteristic aroma and taste of fresh onion.

Onion contains a number of volatile sulfur compounds including methyl disulfide, methyl trisulfide, methyl-*n*- propyl trisulfide, *n*-propyl disulfide, and *n*-propyl trisulfide.
·development of agriculture **1**:326h
·domesticated plant centres of origin **5**:938c
·history, classification, and cultivation **19**:43a; tables 44
·seedling morphology and germination, illus. 2 **16**:481
·spice history, use, production, and region of origin **17**:503e; tables 504

onion couch (herbage): *see* oat grass.

Onions, Oliver, in full GEORGE OLIVER ONIONS (b. 1873, Bradford, Yorkshire—d. April 9, 1961, Aberystwyth, Wales), novelist and short story writer whose first work to attract attention was *The Story of Louie* (1913), the last part of a trilogy later published as *Whom God has Sundered*, in which he achieved a successful combination of poetry and realism. Of his other novels, the greatest success was perhaps *The Story of Ragged Robyn* (1945), a tale of 17th-century England. His *Poor Man's Tapestry* (1946) earned him the James Tait Black Memorial Prize. Onions was married to the Welsh-born novelist Berta Ruck.

Oniscus: *see* sow bug.

Onitsha, port, capital of Onitsha Province, East-Central State, southern Nigeria, on the east bank of the Niger River just south of its confluence with the Anambra. Traditionally founded by adventurers from Benin (nearby, to the west) in the early 17th century, it grew to become the political and trading centre of the small Ibo Kingdom of Onitsha. Its monarchical system (rare among the Ibo people) was patterned after that of Benin. An Onitsha *obi* ("king") negotiated in 1857 with William Balfour Baikie (who explored the Niger in the steamer "Dayspring") for the establishment of a British trading post in the town.

Modern Onitsha remains the chief entrepôt port for goods coming upstream from the Niger Delta and those transported downstream from towns on the Niger and Benue rivers. Roads lead to the town from Enugu and Owerri, and the completion in 1965 of the 4,606 ft (1,404-m) bridge to Asaba, on the opposite bank of the Niger, provides Onitsha with Eastern Nigeria's only direct road link to Benin City and Lagos. Palm oil and kernels are the most important local exports, but yams, cassava, maize (corn), citrus fruits, palm produce, rice, eddoes (cocoyams), fish, and beef are traded in the Onitsha market. The market building, formerly the largest and most modern in Nigeria, was destroyed in 1968 in the Nigerian Civil War (1967–70), but it is being rebuilt.

Onitsha's first mission (Anglican) and Western school were established by the Rev. J.C. Taylor, a freed Ibo slave who was on the "Dayspring." The town is the site of the Roman Catholic Holy Trinity Cathedral (1935) and the Anglican All Saints Cathedral (1952). Its oldest secondary schools are the Dennis Memorial Grammar School (1925; Anglican), St. Charles Teacher Training College (1929; Roman Catholic), and Christ the King College (1933; Roman Catholic); but it also has several newer mission, private secondary, and commercial-training schools. The government sponsors a handicraft centre and several hospitals. Onitsha is also known for the annual Ofala Festival, which honours the *obi*.

Industries include tire retreading, sawmilling, printing, soft-drink bottling, and the production of phonograph records. A textile plant is located on the industrial estate south of the town near the bridge, and a steel mill is planned for the site in the 1970s.

Onitsha Province, whose area covers 1,821 sq mi (4,716 sq km), has wooded savanna in the east and forested areas along the bank of the Niger. It is mainly inhabited by the Ibo people, and its chief urban centres are Onitsha, Awka (*q.v.*), and Ihiala. Pop. (1971 est.) town, 197,062; (latest census) province, 1,491,782.

6°09′ N, 6°47′ E

·map, Nigeria **13**:86
·Niger River physiography **13**:97d; map 98

Onitsha market literature, a 20th-century genre of sentimental, moralistic novellas and pamphlets produced by a semiliterate school of writers (students, fledgling journalists, taxi drivers) and sold at the bustling Onitsha market in eastern Nigeria. Among the most prolific of the writers are Felix N. Stephen, Speedy Eric, Thomas O. Iguh, and O. Olisah, the latter two having also written chapbook plays about prominent literary figures.

The Onitsha writings have two distinct characteristics: a fascination with westernized urban life, and the desire to warn the newly arrived against the corruption and dangers that accompany it. Typical titles are "Rose Only Loved My Money," "Drunkards Believe Bar as Heaven," "Why Some Rich Men Have No Trust in Some Girls," "How to Get a Lady in Love," and "How John Kennedy Suffered in Life and Death Suddenly." Sentimental novelettes, political tracts, and "how to" guides on writing love letters, handling money, and attaining prosperity all have achieved great commercial success, and booksellers hawk these cheap, locally produced pamphlets (which are printed on handpresses and average 45 pages in length) at Onitsha alongside farmers and fishermen, cattlemen from the north, and cocoa merchants from the west.

Although the Onitsha pamphlets are of little literary value, they serve the dual educational function of improving the English of their broad, semiliterate audience and of addressing themselves to the immediate problem of how to live in a big city and how to reconcile rural values with a confusing cluster of new temptations and styles of living. Unfortunately, traditional mores are often only halfheartedly upheld, and the old folk back in the village often become symbols of outdated ideas and are laughed at for their illiterate pidgin English. Thus, the dangerous city is secretly the object of great admiration for most Onitsha writers, and no sense of nostalgia over a lost African past such as is found in Nigeria's top literary figures has its place in their pamphlets.

As a literary phenomenon, the Nigerian chapbooks, similar in many ways to the chapbooks of 17th- and 18th-century England, are important for the close relationship of writer and audience without reference to an outside world, and this subliterary genre seems likely to persist alongside the mainstream of Nigerian literature.

Onkelos, *c.* 1st-century-AD Palestinian Jewish scholar.

·Targum's form, growth, and authority **2**:886h

onkos, a headdress used in classical Greek drama.

·costume conventions of Greek drama **17**:560a

On Liberty, by the English political philosopher John Stuart Mill (1859).

·censorship in 19th-century England **3**:1088h
·defense of individual liberty **14**:270h
·democratic ideals and wife's assistance **12**:198h
·Victorian Age attitudes **3**:268h

On Melancholy (1819), an ode by John Keats.

·Keats's period of poetic intensity **10**:413g

On-Myō-dō (Japanese: the Way of On-Myō [Chinese Yin-Yang]), a system of belief introduced into Japan from China holding that harmony in the universe results from a balance between two contrary and complementary cosmic principles, the Yin and the Yang (negative, dark, feminine opposed to positive, light, masculine). Their interaction produces matter composed of five elements—wood, fire, earth, metal, and water. The five elements in turn are associated with other sets of five, such as the planets, directions, seasons, and signs of the zodiac. The arts of divination and astrology based on the Yin-Yang system evolved as attempts to avoid calamity and to insure harmony by conforming to the natural order of things.

On-Myō beliefs entered Japan in early times with other aspects of religious Taoism. A government bureau, the On-Myō-ryō, existed as early as AD 675 to advise the government on control of the calendar and on divination but later fell into disuse. Yin-Yang notions permeated every level of Japanese society and persist even into modern times, as evident in the widespread belief in lucky and unlucky days and directions and in consideration of the zodiac signs when arranging marriages.

onna-de (Japanese calligraphy): *see* hiragana.

onna-e ("female painting"), in 11th- and 12th-century, Japanese art paintings done by women.

·feminine-written literary use **19**:228d

onna-moji ("female letters"), 10th- and 11th-century Japanese writings done by women in the kana syllabary.

·feminine-written prose use **19**:228c

Onn bin Ja'afar, Dato (b. 1895, Johore Bahru, Malaya—d. Jan. 19, 1962, Johore Bahru), Malayan political leader who played a leading role in the Merdeka (independence) movement and the establishment of the Federation of Malaya, forerunner of the present independent nation of Malaysia.

Born in the sultanate of Johore, north of Singapore, Onn bin Ja'afar was educated in England and served for a time as a government officer in Johore. Turning then to journalism, he edited two Malay newspapers, the *Lembaga Melayu* and the *Warta Malaya*, the first independent Malay daily. After World War II, he became extremely active in Malayan politics. In 1946, when the British published proposals for a Malayan Union—one that would transfer political power from the sultans to a central government in Kuala Lumpur and that would grant all people in Malaya, regardless of race or religion, equal rights as citizens—Onn bin Ja'afar led the protest against this Union, holding that undermining the power of the sultans and giving the economically dominant Chinese and Indians a part in the government would lead to the "extinction" of the Malay race. Convening a meeting of more than 40 Malay organizations in March 1946 to oppose the Union, Onn bin Ja'afar founded the United Malays National Organization (UMNO), the first political party representing purely Malay interests. When the plan for Union was eventually withdrawn, the Sultan of Johore appointed him prime minister (Mentri Besar) of his state, and in February 1948 he became Member for Home Affairs for the Federation of Malaya.

Although known as an advocate of specifically Malay interests, Onn bin Ja'afar in 1951 resigned from UMNO because it rejected his proposal that membership be open to persons of all races. He was replaced by Tunku Abdul Rahman, later prime minister of Malaysia. Onn bin Ja'afar formed two political parties on his own, the Independence of Malaya Party and the Party Negara (National Party) in 1953–55; but, when neither party gained popular support against Rahman's new Alliance Party, he was eclipsed from Malayan political life.

Onnes, Heike Kamerlingh: *see* Kamerlingh Onnes, Heike.

On New Democracy, political essay written by Mao Tse-tung in 1940, which outlines the type of government the Communists were planning to establish after they came to power. The essay, usually rendered into English as "On New Democracy," exerted a tremendous influence on moderate elements in China because of its assertion that members of the Chinese middle class would be allowed an important role in the future Communist state (in Marxist theory, power is held by the proletariat alone in Communist states).

China, Mao explained, was too underdeveloped to be able to implement a Socialist state—unlike the Soviet Union. A more important priority for the country, he said, was the replacement of feudalism by an industrial society. To that end the post-revolutionary society had to be governed by a coalition of four classes: the proletariat, the peasantry, the petty bourgeoisie, and the national bourgeoisie (those capitalists who did not cooperate with but helped resist the Japanese invaders of China). The leadership of this coalition would of course be held by the proletariat and their party, the Communists; but the other groups would have a strong voice in the government of the country and their parties would continue to function. Moreover, the economy was to be divided into three sectors: the state economy, consisting of government-controlled large industries; the agricultural economy, which would divide the holdings of the larger landholders, assign land to all peasants, and then eventually develop this land into collective farms; and the private economy, in which small and medium-sized capitalists would be allowed to operate.

After taking power in 1949, the Communist government implemented the "New Democracy" and became a coalition, giving considerable power to non-Communist elements and allowing many capitalists to continue to run their own businesses. The new constitution of 1954 gave less power to non-Communist elements; and in 1955, as the Communists began to cooperatize all land, they announced that China had entered the Socialist phase of its development, in which most property was to be held collectively. Some capitalists were, however, still allowed to operate within the framework of the Chinese economy.

·Chinese 20th-century philosophy **4**:421f
·ideological content **4**:388f
·Mao's analysis of Communist front **11**:467e

Onoclea sensibilis, species of the fern family Polypodiaceae (class Leptosporangiopsida).

·reproductive system variations **15**:720e

Onoe Kikugorō V (1844–1903), Japanese actor.

·cropped-hair play performance **5**:479f

Onomasticon, 10-volume encyclopaedia by Julius Pollux, a Greek scholar and grammarian of the 2nd century AD, containing rhetorical material (*e.g.*, collections of synonyms and compounds), the technical terms of a wide variety of subjects, and literary citations. Of special note is the information about music and theatre, which includes a detailed catalogue of Greek comic and tragic theatrical masks. Editions include those by Wilhelm Dindorf (1824) and by Erich Bethe in the three-volume Teubner *Lexicographi Graeci* (1900–37).

·costume conventions of Greek drama **17**:560a
·encyclopaedias as reflections of culture **6**:783f
·theatrical design in ancient Greece **17**:530g

onomastics, in the broadest sense, the study of names in all languages and time periods and in all their aspects. In a more limited sense, onomastics is the study of personal names, while toponymy (*q.v.*), or toponomastics, is the study of place-names. *Major ref.* **12**:815a

onomatopoeia, word formation based on the imitation of natural sounds; *e.g.*, English "whisper," "bang," "hiss." The word may be either the name of the sound itself, as "moo" or "crash," or the name of the source of the sound, as "cuckoo" or "peewit." Interpretation of a sound varies from language to language (*e.g.*, English "cock-a-doodle-do" and Spanish *cucurucu* for a rooster's crow) and also within the same language (*e.g.*, English "puff, puff," American "choochoo" for the sound of a steam engine). In philosophical debates in ancient Greece, onomatopoeic words were cited as an argument for the "naturalness" of language or the appropriateness of words to their meaning; in no language, however, do onomatopoeic words comprise more than a very small proportion of the total number of words.

Used broadly, onomatopoeia refers to any combination of imitative sounds and rhythms that strongly reinforce the sense of a passage in prose or poetry. An example is Matthew Arnold's description of the tide in "Dover Beach":

Listen! you hear the grating roar
Of pebbles which the waves draw back, and fling,
At their return, up the high strand,
Begin, and cease, and then again begin,
With tremulous cadence slow, and bring
The eternal note of sadness in.

A theory that language originated in the imitation of natural sounds is called the bowwow theory.

·meaning and sound features in language **10**:651c
·naturalist–conventionalist debate on language origins **10**:993b
·prosodic elements and Pope's view **15**:74b

Onomichi, city, Hiroshima Prefecture (*ken*), Honshu, Japan, facing the Inland Sea. The city's port opened in 1168 and served for about 500 years as a rice trans-shipment centre and port of call for trade with China. The port's commercial significance declined somewhat during the Tokugawa era (1603–1867) but has since revived. Onomichi now offers steamship services to ports of northern Shikoku and islands in the Inland Sea. The city has a shipbuilding yard and a motor factory.

Onomichi and its industrial channel, Japan
Photos Pack—EB Inc.

The Senko-ji, a Buddhist temple founded in the 9th century, is located on the side of a hill that commands a fine view of the city and coast and contains an observatory and a planetarium. Pop. (1975) 102,951.
34°25′ N, 133°12′ E

·map, Japan **10**:37

Onondaga, a tribe of Iroquoian-speaking North American Indians who lived in what is now New York state. The Onondaga (meaning On the Mountain) inhabited villages of wood and bark longhouses occupied by related families; they moved these houses periodically to plant new gardens, to seek firewood, and to be nearer fish and game. They grew maize (corn), beans, squash, sunflowers, and tobacco. A council of adult males in each community guided the village chiefs. In the 17th century they numbered about 1,700.

The Onondaga tribe, one of the original five nations of the Iroquois League (*q.v.*), was the political and geographical centre of the league. With 14 seats in the council, the Onondaga furnished the chairman and the archivist.

In the 18th century most of the Onondaga returned to their ancestral valley. A sizable faction settled along the St. Lawrence River, while others removed to Grand River in Ontario. The population of the Onondaga reservation in New York in the 1970s was more than 1,000.

·jewelry forms and European influence **10**:182f
·Woodlands Indian culture **6**:169b; map

Onondaga Limestone Formation, division of Middle Devonian rocks found in New York, Pennsylvania, Ohio, Maryland, Virginia, and West Virginia (the Devonian Period began about 395,000,000 years ago and lasted about 50,000,000 years); it was named for exposures studied in Onondaga County, New York. The Onondaga Limestone extends from eastern New York to central Ohio and consists of a gray, coral-bearing limestone, about 21 metres (70 feet) thick, in which nodules of chert frequently occur. Important exposures occur in the Catskill Mountains, in the Finger Lakes region, and in the region of Lake Erie. The Onondaga contains a rich marine-invertebrate fauna.

Ono-no Imoko (7th century AD), Japanese ambassador to China, founder of the Ikenobō school of floral art.

·flower arranging traditional styles **7**:417h

Ono Tōfū (b. 894, Japan—d. 964, Japan), calligrapher known as one of the *sanseki* ("three best writing brushes") who, along with Fujiwara Yukinari and Fujiwara Sukemasa, perfected the style of writing called *jōdai-yō* ("ancient style").

Ono was the son of a high government official. His writing, which departed from the traditional Chinese style, may be regarded as the model for subsequent Japanese calligraphy. His extant works include *Chishō daishi shigō chokusho* ("Imperial Rescript on the Posthumous Name for Chishō the Great Teacher"), dated 927, owned by the Tokyo National Museum; *Byōbu jōdai* ("Ancient Folding Screen"), a poem dated 928 and owned by the Imperial Household; *Gyokusen-cho* ("Album of the Pure Spring") owned by the Imperial Household; and *Haku-shi santai-shi kan.*

On Our Selection (1899), collection of humorous sketches written by Arthur Hoey Davis under the pseudonym Steele Rudd (*q.v.*).

On Perspective in Painting, Latin DE PROSPECTIVA PINGENDI (1474–82), treatise by Piero della Francesca.

·Euclidean-Albertian method **14**:454h

On Practice, major work by Mao Tse-tung written in 1937 and published in 1950. In it Mao points out that theory depends on practice and that truths are discovered, verified, and developed through practice.

·Chinese 20th-century philosophy **4**:421f
·Mao's dialectic theories **11**:467d
·Mao's emphasis on pragmatic knowledge **4**:387h

On Providence, Latin DE PROVIDENTIA, essay by the 1st-century-AD Jewish philosopher Philo of Alexandria.

·content and influence **14**:246b

On Religion: Speeches to Its Cultured Despisers (1893), German ÜBER DIE RELIGION. REDEN AN DIE GEBILDEN UNTER IHREN VERÄCHTERN (1799), work by Friedrich Schleiermacher.

·religious experience investigation **15**:622e
·Schleiermacher and the Romantics **16**:346a

ons, unit of measure in The Netherlands equivalent to 100 grams, or 3.2 troy ounces.

·weights and measures, table 5 **19**:734

Onsager, Lars (b. Nov. 27, 1903, Kristiania, now Oslo—d. Oct. 5, 1976. Coral Gables, Fla.), chemist whose development of a general theory of irreversible chemical processes gained him the Nobel Prize for Chemistry in 1968. His early work in statistical mechanics attracted the attention of the Dutch chemist Peter Debye, under whose direction Onsager studied at the Federal Institute of Technology, Zürich (1926–28). He then went to the U.S. and taught at Johns Hopkins University, Baltimore, and Brown University, Providence, R.I. He received his Ph.D. from Yale (1935), where he became professor of theoretical chemistry in 1945. His explanation of the movement of ions in solution as related to turbulences and fluid densities had a major effect on the development of physical chemistry and has been described as providing the fourth law of thermodynamics.

·thermodynamic theory research **18**:310c

Onslow, coastal town, northwest Western Australia, near the mouth of the Ashburton River. Founded in 1883 and officially proclaimed a town in 1885, it was named for either Sir Alexander Onslow, former chief justice of South Australia, or a hydrographic surveyor, Capt. Arthur Onslow of HMS "Howe." With the discovery of the Ashburton goldfield (1889), the town assumed importance. In 1926, after being severely damaged by cyclones, Onslow was moved to its present location on Beadon Bay. Situated on the North West Coastal Highway to Perth (890 mi [1,430 km] southeast), it serves the Barrow Island petroleum field and a highly mineralized hinterland, including the iron deposits at Deepdale (60 mi east). Pop. (1971) 349.
21°39′ S, 115°06′ E
·map, Australia **2**:400

Ontake-san, English MOUNT ONTAKE, rising to an elevation of 10,049 ft (3,063 m) on the boundary of Gifu and Nagano prefectures, central Honshu, Japan. A compound volcano with a heavy snow mantle in winter, it is second only to Fujiyama in elevation and popular esteem.
35°53′ N, 137°29′ E
·map, Japan **10**:36

Ontario 13:573, second largest province of Canada (area 412,582 sq mi [1,068,582 sq km]). It is bordered by Hudson and James bays to the north, Quebec to the east, the St. Lawrence River–Great Lakes chain to the south, and Manitoba to the west. The capital is Toronto. Pop. (1975 est.) 8,226,000.
The text article covers the province's history, landscape, people, economy, transportation, administration and social conditions, cultural life and institutions, and future prospects.
REFERENCES in other text articles:
·administration and social conditions **3**:728a *passim* to 732f
·area and population table **3**:721; map 723
·educational structure and influence **6**:367d
·geographic features and population composition **3**:713h *passim* to 723c
·Gunflint Chert Precambrian fossils **7**:556g
·map, Canada **3**:716
·Toronto layout features and cultural role **18**:520g

Ontario, city, San Bernardino County, southern California, U.S., in the Los Angeles metropolitan area. Named for Ontario in Canada, it was settled in 1882 by George and William Chaffey, who irrigated the land for citrus and vineyard cultivation. After the arrival of the Santa Fe Railroad in 1887, Ontario became a fruit processing and shipping point. Industrial development includes the manufacture of electrical appliances, aircraft parts, steel, and plastics. The Ontario Motor Speedway (1970) is the scene of the annual California "500" auto race. Ontario International Airport serves the area east of Los Angeles. Inc. city, 1891. Pop. (1980) 88,820.
34°04′ N, 117°39′ W
·metropolitan population density map **18**:930

Ontario, city, Malheur County, eastern Oregon, U.S., at the juncture of the Snake and Malheur rivers. A gateway to the Oregon cattle country, it grew after the building of the Union Pacific Railroad in 1884 and was named for the Canadian province. It has food-processing industries based on the produce (potatoes, sugar beets, alfalfa, onions, corn [maize]) of the Owyhee and Malheur irrigated region. A tourist-service centre, it is close to an area of rugged canyon terrain. Lake Owyhee (created by Owyhee Dam, 1928–32) and Cherry Creek are nearby. Treasure Valley Community College was opened in 1962. Inc. 1914. Pop. (1980) 8,814.
44°02′ N, 116°58′ W
·map, United States **18**:908

Ontario, Lake, smallest and most easterly of the Great Lakes of North America, bounded on the north by Ontario (Canada) and on the south by New York (U.S.). The lake is roughly elliptical; its major axis, 193 mi (311 km) long, lies nearly east to west, and its greatest width is 53 mi. The total area of the lake's drainage basin is 27,200 sq mi (70,400 sq km), exclusive of the lake surface area, which is 7,550 sq mi (19,550 sq km). The Niagara River is the main feeder of the lake; others include the Genesee, Oswego, and Black rivers from the south and the Trent River from the north. The 30-mi-wide eastern extremity of the lake is crossed by a chain of five islands, where the lake discharges into the St. Lawrence River near the city of Kingston, Ont. With a mean surface height of 245 ft (75 m) above sea level, the lake has a mean depth of 283 ft, and its deepest point is 802 ft. A general surface current (8 mi a day) flows toward the east and is strongest along the south shore. The Welland Canal (navigational) and the Niagara River (natural) serve as connections with Lake Erie. Lake Ontario is linked with the New York State Barge Canal at Oswego, N.Y., and with Georgian Bay via the Trent Canal at Trenton, Ont. The Rideau Canal runs northeastward in Ontario from Kingston to Ottawa.
The land to the north of Lake Ontario spreads out into broad plains, which are intensively farmed. The Niagara Escarpment, or Lake Ridge, extends eastward along the southern shore (3 to 8 mi inland) from the Niagara River to Sodus, N.Y. Industry is concentrated around the port cities of Toronto and Hamilton, Ont., and Rochester, N.Y. Other important ports include Kingston, Ont., and Oswego, N.Y. The lake freezes only near the land, and in consequence its harbours are icebound from mid-December to mid-April.
Lake Ontario was visited by Étienne Brûlé, a French scout, and by Samuel de Champlain in 1615. The Iroquois Indians, allies of the British, held the Ontario region; but during the late 17th and early 18th centuries a temporary peace allowed the French to build forts including Fort-Frontenac (1673), where Kingston now stands. The French and Indian War led to British control, and the American Revolution (1775–83) hastened settlement, trade, and shipping in the region.
43°40′ N, 78°00′ W
·Great Lakes physical characteristics **8**:302b; table 301
·heat budget, current period, and vertical physical and chemical distributions **10**:607h; illus. 606
maps
·Canada **3**:717
·North America **13**:177
·United States **18**:909

Ontario International Airport, in Ontario, Calif., serving nearby Los Angeles.
·passenger statistic projections **11**:111e

On the Art of the Theatre (1911), collection of essays by the innovative stage designer Edward Gordon Craig. The central essay, called "The Art of the Theatre," had appeared earlier (1905).
·scenographic concepts **5**:232a

On the Art of War, Italian DELL'ARTE DELLA GUERRA (1520), work by Niccolò Machiavelli.
·content and style **11**:229f
·Renaissance political philosophy **15**:665g

On the Boiler (1939), prose pamphlet by William Butler Yeats.
·Yeats's admiration for Mussolini **19**:1077g

On the Chersonese, oration delivered by Demosthenes in 341 BC.
·Philip II attack **5**:579d

On the Contemplative Life, treatise by Philo of Alexandria.
·content and influence **14**:245h

On the Crown, oration delivered by Demosthenes in 330 BC.
·Aeschines' defeat and exile **5**:579g

On the Death of a fair Infant (written 1628), poem by Milton.
·subject, mode, and use of English **12**:205c

On the Divine Names (1920), English translation of *De divinis nominibus*, 5th- or 6th-century work attributed to Pseudo-Dionysius the Areopagite.
·Christian stress on God's ineffability **4**:546f *passim* to 550a

On the Duty of Civil Disobedience (Thoreau): *see* Civil Disobedience.

On the Embassy to Gaius, essay by Philo of Alexandria.
·content and influence **14**:246c

On the Essence of Laughter (1855), essay by Charles Baudelaire.
·comedy distinguished from the grotesque **4**:960g

On the Eternity of the World, essay by Philo of Alexandria.
·content and influence **14**:246b

On the Eve, Russian NAKANUNE (1860), novel by Ivan Turgenev.
·Turgenev's increasing pessimism **18**:780c

On the History of Religion and Philosophy in Germany, German ZUR GESCHICHTE DER RELIGION UND PHILOSOPHIE IN DEUTSCHLAND (1834–35), work by Heinrich Heine.
·revolutionary potential of German heritage **8**:744f

On the Idea of Comedy and the Uses of the Comic Spirit (delivered as a lecture and published in a periodical, 1877; separately published as *An Essay on Comedy, and the Uses of the Comic Spirit*, 1897), work of criticism by George Meredith.
·comedy as socially corrective **4**:961b

On the Jews, title of works by the Hellenistic Jewish authors Pseudo-Hecataeus (2nd century BC), who wrote of conditions in Palestine *c.* 300 BC, and Artapanus (*c.* 100 BC), whose purpose was to prove that the foundations of Egyptian culture were established by Abraham, Jacob, Joseph, and Moses; also of a work by Alexander Polyhistor (*q.v.*; d. *c.* 35 BC), whose extensive quotations of earlier writers are preserved in the later works of Josephus, Clement of Alexandria, and Eusebius of Caesarea.
·Diaspora apologetics **10**:313c

On the Kings in Judaea, title of works by the Hellenistic Jewish writer Demetrius, who lived during the reign (221–205 BC) of Ptolemy IV, a history of Israel from Jacob to Demetrius' own time; and by Eupolemus, the first significant Greco-Jewish historian, covering the period from Moses (perhaps the creation) to his own day (158–157 BC). Fragments from both are preserved in the monograph *On the Jews* by Alexander Polyhistor (*q.v.*; d. *c.* 35 BC), quoted by Josephus, Clement of Alexandria, and Eusebius of Caesarea.
·Diaspora apologetics **10**:313c

On the Life of Moses, work by Philo of Alexandria.
·content and influence **14**:246c

On the Morning of Christ's Nativity (first published in *Poems*, 1645), poem by Milton.
·theme and stylistic excellence **12**:205d

On the Nature of Things, Latin DE RERUM NATURA, by Lucretius, exposition of the atomic theory of Epicurus in Latin hexameters.
·atomic concept development **2**:332h
·cosmology representative of Atomism **18**:1007b
·philosophy, language, and style **11**:173g
·Roman speculative science **16**:367e
·world view importance in explication **2**:52c

On the Navy Boards, oration delivered by Demosthenes in 354 BC.
·Athenian democracy and foreign policy 5:578e

On the Origin of Species by Means of Natural Selection (1859), book by Charles Darwin in which his theory of evolution was first described. It presented the thesis that different species of plants and animals were not fixed from the beginning of the world but developed in response to such external factors as geography, food supplies, or available mates. Although the *Origin of Species* was not the first work to offer the hypothesis of evolution, it was the first to abandon all attempts to limit evolutionary mutability of species by the religious concept of special creation, as, for example, J.-B. Lamarck had done. Thus, it cast doubt on cherished beliefs in man's superiority, the unchangeable nature of the universe, and a God who had created the world exactly as it was known. Darwin's suggestion that only those species best adapted to their environment would survive was deemed a cruel, atheistic interpretation of nature. (The previous notion of natural selection —again, not an idea originated by Darwin— was that it eliminated atypical individuals rather than tended to create new species.) The work provoked a storm of religious opposition, but, because it was so well conceived and painstakingly constructed, being supported by over 20 years of data gathering and observation that had begun with Darwin's naturalist's voyage (1831–36) on the HMS "Beagle," it found illustrious defenders in T.H. Huxley and other scientists.

The Variation of Animals and Plants under Domestication (1868) followed and expanded the material found in the first chapter of the *Origin of Species*. In this work, Darwin introduced his theory of pangenesis, adapted from Herbert Spencer, in which portions (gemmules) of body cells carry the characteristics of the organism and are modified by natural selection. This theory was necessary to carry to a logical conclusion the evolutionary process put forth in the *Origin of Species*. The correct answer to the problem of natural selection came almost 35 years later with the rediscovery and development of Gregor Mendel's work on individual genetic variations, which had gone unnoticed since 1866.
·archaeological importance of evolution 1:1079d
·biological sciences development 2:1024a
·Darwin's evolutionary proofs 7:8f
·Darwin's impact on science and religion 5:494c
·faunal sequence explanation 6:82e
·Haeckel's evolutionary interpretations 8:542c
·Lyell's geological research 11:209e
·physical anthropology contributions 1:974b
·Rationalist attacks on natural law 10:717h
·Rationalist challenge to faith 15:531b
·Social Darwinism's ideological roots 5:366a
·social science influence 16:984c
·T.H. Huxley's defense of evolution 9:72c

On the Peace (346 BC), oration by Demosthenes.
·Philocrates' treaty denunciation 5:579c

On the Revolutions of the Celestial Spheres (1952), original Latin DE REVOLUTIONIBUS ORBIUM COELESTIUM, *libri VI* (1543), book by Copernicus espousing the theory of a moving Earth. *See also* Copernican system.
·Copernican theory of the heavens 5:145b
·impact on astronomical observation 14:386d
·science development in Renaissance 16:369e

On the Rocks (1933), play by George Bernard Shaw.
·composition and style 16:658a

On the Sensations of Tone, study by H.L.F. von Helmholtz (1821–94).
·musical consonance physical basis 17:37f

On the Special Laws, an exposition of the laws in the Pentateuch, by the 1st-century-AD Jewish philosopher Philo of Alexandria.
·content and influence 14:245h

On the Spectacles (AD 80), poetry of Marcus Valerius Martialis.
·Martial's weak early poetry 11:546e

On the Theology of the Church, a work by the Christian theologian and bishop, Eusebius of Caesarea (260–339).
·Eusebius and homoousian controversy 6:1131b

On the Trinity (1873), original Latin DE TRINITATE (written 400–416), a treatise by St. Augustine of Hippo in which he set forth the notion that true knowledge of God is acquired through his image in the human soul.
·knowledge of the soul and God 2:366d
·Neoplatonism in Augustine's theology 14:543h

On the Vernacular Tongue, translation of DE VULGARI ELOQUENTIA, defense of a hypothetical language by Dante (1265–1321).
·tragic style's proper subject matter 18:588h

On the Worship and Love of God (1801), English translation of DE CULTU ET AMORE DEI (1745), a work by the Swedish mystic Eman.
·Swedenborg's theory of creation 17:856a

On This Island (1937), also published as LOOK, STRANGER! (1936), a poetry collection by W.H. Auden.
·verse style and popularity 2:363g

On Time (1645), poem by John Milton.
·religious theme 12:205g

ontogeny, the name for all the developmental events occurring from the time of sexual reproduction to the end of an organism's life. Ontogeny begins with the changes in the egg at the time of fertilization and includes developmental events to the time of birth or hatching and afterward—growth, remolding of body shape, and development of secondary sexual characteristics.
·Haeckel's theory of Metazoan origins 14:381a
·homology as evidence of phylogeny 14:377b
·lepidopteran larval primitiveness 10:826e

ontology, the theory or study of Being as such; *i.e.*, of the basic characteristics of all reality. Though the term was first coined in the 17th century, ontology is synonymous with metaphysics or "first philosophy" as defined by Aristotle in the 4th century BC. Because metaphysics came to include other studies (*e.g.*, philosophical cosmology and psychology), ontology has become the preferred term for the study of Being. It was brought into prominence in modern philosophy by Christian Wolff a German Rationalist, for whom it was a deductive discipline leading to necessary truths about the essences of beings. His great successor Immanuel Kant, however, presented influential refutations of ontology as a deductive system and of the ontological argument for God's necessary existence (as supreme and perfect being). With the 20th-century renovation of metaphysics, ontology or ontological thought has again become important, notably among Phenomenologists and Existentialists, among them Martin Heidegger.
·Anselm's proof of God's existence 15:601c
·argumentative dissociation usage 15:804c
·Aristotle's philosophy of logic 1:1167d
·creation ex nihilo solution of Kabbala 10:186g
·dualism in Greek body–soul concepts 5:1066h
·Eckehart's stages of union of being 6:187g
existence
·Buddhist thought on human suffering 3:426b
·Existentialist theories of man 7:73a
·intentionality's intentional inexistence 12:225g
·Kant on ontological argument 10:391c
·mind as metaphysical entity 12:229c
·ontology and predication in logic 11:75c
·Realist views of knowledge object 15:539d
·Existential theories of Being 7:73f
·formal–material distinction 12:34c
·God's existence proof from very idea 18:266d
·Heidegger Existentialist Phenomenology 8:738g
·intuitionist cognitivist meta-ethics 6:983a
·Jewish philosophical thought 10:210b
·logical individuation and predication 11:75b
·logic history from antiquity 11:71a
·mereology development as extension 11:36h
·Nāgārjuna's explanations of Buddhism 12:808h
·Phenomenology and related movements 14:210h
·Tendai view of interdependent universe 10:102e
·value and naturalistic meta-ethics 6:985a

Ontong Java Islands, also called LORD HOWE ISLANDS, atoll in the British Solomon Islands, a dependency of New South Wales, southwest Pacific Ocean, 160 mi (257 km) north of Santa Isabel Island. A large coral formation, 20 mi by 50 mi, it was discovered by the Dutch navigator Abel Tasman (1643) and was renamed Lord Howe by Capt. John Hunter of the British Navy in 1791. Passages through the encircling reef into its lagoon are difficult. Its Polynesian inhabitants trade in copra. Pop. (1971 prelim.) 223.
5°20′ S, 159°30′ E

Ontowirjo, Raden Mas (Javanese military leader): *see* Dipo Negoro, Pangeran.

On Translating Homer (1861), work of Matthew Arnold containing some of his lectures.
·Matthew Arnold's classicism 2:37h

Ó Nuallain, Brian: *see* O'Brien, Flann.

Onverwacht Series, division of Early Precambrian rocks in the Swaziland region of southern Africa (the Precambrian began with the formation of the Earth's crust about 4,600,000,000 years ago and ended 570,000,000 years ago). The Onverwacht Series is well known from exposures in the Komati Valley in the eastern Transvaal region, South Africa, where Onverwacht rocks consist of dark, andesitic lavas, dolomitic limestones, cherts, and jaspers as well as serpentines, gabbros, and peridotites. Many of the rocks have been intensely deformed by metamorphic processes; the results of these processes are observed as locally abundant schists and marbles. Rocks of the Onverwacht Series underlie those of the Fig Tree Series and form the basement rocks in the region of their occurrence.

Radiometric dating techniques have established the age of the Onverwacht Series at about 3,700,000,000 years. Algae-like forms have been discovered and studied in the Onverwacht rocks of sedimentary origin; studies of the hydrocarbon compounds in the rocks have also been carried out. The Onverwacht Series possibly contains the earliest known traces of living organisms on Earth. Indeed, it is possible that the transition from nonliving to living material is recorded within the Onverwacht. Further study, it is hoped, will elucidate the actual steps in this transition.

On War (1873), English translation of VOM KRIEGE (1832), work by Carl von Clausewitz.
·critical approach to strategy problems 4:698b
·strategy as influenced by Clausewitz 19:560h

On Wit and Humor (1819), essay by William Hazlitt.
·theory of comedy 4:958h

Onychomys: *see* grasshopper mouse.

onychophoran, any of about 90 species of free-living, elongated, mainly tropical, terrestrial invertebrates belonging to the Onychophora, usually considered a class. In evolutionary development, onychophorans are considered to lie between annelid worms and arthropods (*e.g.*, insects, crustaceans); a common genus is *Peripatus*. Onychophorans range

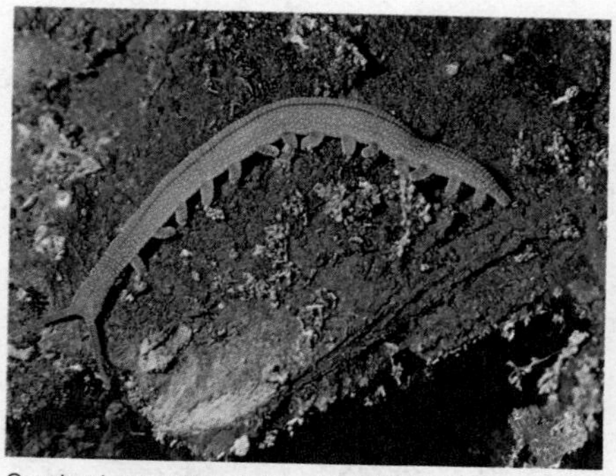

Onychophoran (*Peripatoides novaezealandiae*)
J. Green—G.R. Roberts

in size from 14 to 150 millimetres (about 0.6 to 6 inches), have 14 to 44 pairs of legs, and a soft, furrowed, velvety skin. They live in moist places and eat insects.
·circulatory system anatomy **4**:622a
·optical mechanism properties **14**:360e
·phylogenic position **14**:382h
·problematic classification **2**:70c
·rain forest undergrowth phenomena **10**:343b
·skeletal structures and functions **16**:821c
·social parental behaviour patterns **16**:938a
·traits, behaviour, and classification **13**:568e

Onygenales, order of fungi of the class Ascomycetes (division Mycota).
·classification and general features **12**:766e

onyx, striped, semiprecious variety of the silica mineral agate (*q.v.*) with white and black alternating bands, largely used in carved cameos and intaglios because the layers could be cut to show a colour contrast between the design and the background. Other varieties include carnelian onyx, with white and red bands, and sardonyx, with white and brown

Onyx from Yavapai County, Arizona
Floyd R. Getsinger—EB Inc.

bands. The chief localities of onyx are India and South America. The name comes from the Greek *onyx* ("fingernail") because of the similar colour banding of the stone and fingernails. The name was used by the Romans for a variety of stones including alabaster, chalcedony, and what is now known as onyx marble.

Onyx is one of the 12 stones mentioned in the Bible (Ex. 28:20; 39:13) as adorning the breastplate (*ḥoshen*) of Yahweh's high priests. Its properties are the same as those of quartz (*see* silica minerals).
·chalcedony formation and properties **16**:753d
·comparison with onyx marble **11**:487a
·gemstone and commercial colouring **7**:975a

Onyx River, glacial stream in Antarctica.
·flow and course **1**:953c

oocyst, encapsulated zygote, typical in sporozoans (phylum Protozoa). Encapsulation allows the zygote to develop undisturbed within the host organism. The zygote often undergoes fission to produce forms called sporozoites, which infect other hosts when released.
·protozoan life cycles **15**:122g

oocyte (biology): *see* ovum.

Oodnadatta, town, north central South Australia, on the intermittent The Neales River. Founded in 1890, it was once the chief supply centre for central Australia; and as the northern terminus of the Central Australian Railway, it was the starting point for Afghan camel caravans bound for the desert interior. When the railway was extended to Alice Springs (280 mi [450 km] north-northwest) in 1929, Oodnadatta began to decline. It now functions as a cattle marshalling station, dependent on artesian wells, with its poor hinterland yielding little produce. The Australian Inland Mission maintains its headquarters in the town, the Aboriginal name of which means "blossom of the Mulga," in reference to local species of wattle bushes. Pop. (1971 prelim.) 234.
27°33′ S, 135°28′ E
·map, Australia **2**:400

oogamy (reproduction): *see* isogamy.

oogenesis, growth process in which the primary egg cell (or ovum) becomes a mature ovum. In any one generation, the egg's development starts before the female that carries it is even born; 8 to 20 weeks after the fetus has started to grow, cells that are to become mature ova have been multiplying, and by the time that the female is born, all of the egg cells that the ovaries will release during the active reproductive years of the female are already present in the ovaries. These cells, known as the primary ova, number around 400,000. The primary ova remain dormant until just prior to ovulation, when an egg is released from the ovary. Some egg cells may not mature for 40 years; others degenerate and never mature.

The egg cell remains as a primary ovum until the time for its release from the ovary arrives. The egg then undergoes a cell division. The nucleus splits so that half of its chromosomes go to one cell and half to another. One of these two new cells is usually larger than the other and is known as the secondary ovum; the smaller cell is known as a polar body. The secondary ovum grows in the ovary until it reaches maturation; it then breaks loose and is carried into the fallopian tubes. Once in the fallopian tubes, the secondary egg cell is suitable for fertilization by the male sperm cells.
·egg structure fertilization **7**:255d
·meiotic divisions in human embryogenesis **6**:742c
·polar body size and position on ovum, illus. 1 **5**:626

oogonium, the specialized cell that functions in sexual reproduction of algae and fungi to produce the egg(s); roughly comparable to the archegonium of ferns, mosses, and some gymnosperms, and to the pistil of higher plants.
·algae sexual reproduction **1**:490e
·animal tissue comparisons **18**:450b
·prenatal formation of human ovarian follicles **6**:742c

Ōoka Tadasuke (b. 1675, Japan—d. 1751, Japan), most famous judge of the Tokugawa period (1603–1867). Appointed to office by Yoshimune (reigned 1716–45), shogun (hereditary military dictator) of Japan, Ōoka soon gained a reputation as one of the most able and incorruptible officials of the realm. As a reward, Yoshimune also appointed him the head of a small hereditary fief. Ōoka's wisdom and fair-mindedness in arriving at decisions while serving on the bench made him a legendary figure, much celebrated in popular stories.

oölite, ovoid or spherical crystalline deposit with a concentric or radial structure; most are composed of calcium carbonate, but some are composed of silica, siderite, calcium phosphate, iron silicate, or iron oxide. Oölite diameters range from 0.25 to 2 millimetres, with most being in the 0.5- to 1-millimetre range; oölitic bodies with diameters greater than 2 millimetres are called pisolites.

The term oölite has been applied both to the concretionary bodies and to the rock composed largely of such structures; to avoid ambiguity, these structures sometimes have been called oöids, oöliths, or ovulites and the term oölite reserved for the rock. The term also is used in an adjectival sense, such as oölitic limestone or oölitic chert. False oölites bear superficial resemblance to oölites but are devoid of a regular internal structure.

Calcareous oölites form where cold oceanic waters flow onto warm shallow banks, as in the Bahamas. The carbonate is precipitated on bits of shell, quartz grains, or other nuclei. They also are known to form in springs and caves, as cave pearls.
·deformation by metamorphism, illus. 6 **12**:6
·description and theories of origin **10**:981d; illus.
·size, structure, and limestone textures **16**:466h

oolong, a tea that is partially fermented before drying and combines the characteristics of black and green teas.
·tea preparation and classification **18**:18a

Oomycetes, a class of fungi (division Mycota) distinguished by the production of asexual motile cells (zoospores) with an anterior, whiplike structure (flagellum) and a posterior, feathery flagellum. Sexual reproduction between distinct sex cells is followed by formation of an oospore. Economically important genera occur as saprophytes (living on decaying matter) or parasites (living on or in another organism) in water (*e.g.*, *Saprolegnia*, the water molds, *q.v.*); as parasites on higher plants, *Aphanomyces* (*q.v.*; which causes root rot of pea) and *Phytophthora* (which causes root rots and foliage blights); and as obligate parasites on higher plants (*Plasmopara*, downy mildews, and *Albugo*, white rusts).
·classification and general features **12**:765h

Oonopidae: *see* jumping spider.

Oorlams, displaced Khoikhoi who moved from Cape Colony to South West Africa in the 19th century.
·South West African migration and impact **17**:289g

Oort, Jan Hendrik (b. April 28, 1900, Franeker, Neth.), astronomer who, as did Bertil Lindblad of Sweden, advanced a hypothesis leading to the now generally accepted view that the Milky Way rotates in its own plane around the centre of the Galaxy. Oort was appointed astronomer to the Leiden Observatory in 1924 and became director in 1945. He worked chiefly on galactic dynamics and galactic structure. When Linblad advanced the theory of the rotation of the galactic system in 1925, Oort modified it in 1927 to conform better with accumulated observations and developed the theory substantially into the form used thereafter.

Oort's subsequent work, as well as that of the school of astronomy he developed in The Netherlands, was directed toward strengthening and testing the Lindblad–Oort theory. The discovery in 1951 of the 21-centimetre radio waves generated by hydrogen in interstellar space provided him with a new method for mapping the spiral structure of the Galaxy.

In 1950 Oort proposed that comets originate from a vast cloud of small bodies that orbits the Sun at a distance of one light-year. In 1956 he and Theodore Walraven, also of The Netherlands, made the first extensive investigation of polarized light rays—those that vibrate more in certain directions than in others—from the Crab Nebula. They showed that these rays were produced by electrons moving in circular paths in strong magnetic fields. Most starlight is produced by electrons when they change their orbits about an atomic nucleus.

From 1958 to 1961 Oort was president of the International Astronomical Union, of which

he had been general secretary from 1935 to 1948. Earlier, in 1953, he was made a foreign associate of the U.S. National Academy of Sciences.
· Galaxy rotational variations 7:846d
· orbital motions of stars within Galaxy 18:1013f

Oos-Londen (South Africa): *see* East London.

oospore, thick-walled resting algal or fungal cell formed by the fusion of two unlike gametes (egg and sperm) to produce the zygote that gives rise to the next generation.

Oosterbeek, village, Gelderland Province, Netherlands, forms part of Renkum (*q.v.*).
· map, The Netherlands 12:1060

Oost-Vlaanderen (Belgium): *see* East Flanders.

Ootacamund, administrative headquarters, Nīlgiris district, Tamil Nadu state, southern India, in the Nīlgiri Hills, at about 7,500 ft (2,300 m) above sea level. It is sheltered by several peaks including Doda Betta (8,649 ft [2,637 m]), the highest point in Tamil Nadu. Founded by the British in 1821, it was used as the official government summer headquarters for the Madras Presidency until Indian independence in 1947. The town is now primarily a tourist resort, but it also contains tea-processing and textile industries, schools, and one college affiliated with the University of Madras. Pop. (1971 prelim.) 63,003.
11°25′ N, 76°43′ E
· map, India 9:278

Oothcaloga (Georgia, U.S.): *see* Calhoun.

ootheca, a firm-walled and distinctive egg case.
· orthopteran egg-laying habits 13:744a

opah, or MOONFISH (*Lampris regius*), large marine fish of the family Lampridae (order Lampridiformes), widely distributed in warm oceans. A deep-bodied fish with a small, toothless mouth, the opah grows to a length

Opah (*Lampris regius*)
Painting by Richard Ellis

of about 2 metres (7 feet) and a weight of 300 kilograms (660 pounds). It is distinctively and attractively coloured, blue above and rosy below, with scarlet fins and jaws and round white spots on the body. Although uncommon, it is valued as food.
· classification and general features 2:273c

opal, silica mineral extensively used as a gemstone, a sub-microcrystalline variety of cristobalite (*q.v.*; *cf.* lussatite). In ancient times opal was included among the noble gems and was ranked second only to emerald by the Romans. Many superstitions have centred about this stone; in the Middle Ages it was supposed to be lucky, but in modern times it has been regarded as unlucky.

Opal is fundamentally colourless, but such material is rarely found. Disseminated impurities are common and impart various dull body colours ranging from the yellows and reds due to iron oxides to black from manganese oxides and organic carbon. The milkiness of many white and gray opals is due to an abundance of tiny gas-filled cavities. Black opal, with a very dark gray or blue to black body colour, is both rare and highly prized. White opal, with light body colours, and fire opal, characterized by yellow, orange, or red body colour, are much more common.

Precious opals are translucent to transparent and are distinguished by a combination of milky to pearly opalescence and an attractive play of many colours. These colours flash and change as a stone is viewed from different directions and are caused by interference of light along minute cracks and other internal inhomogeneities.

Opal is deposited from circulating waters as nodules, stalactitic masses, veinlets, and encrustations and is widely distributed in nearly all kinds of rocks. It is most abundant in volcanic rocks, especially in areas of hot-spring activity. It also forms pseudomorphs after wood and other fossil organic matter, and after gypsum, calcite, feldspars, and many other minerals that it has replaced. As the siliceous material secreted by organisms such as diatoms and radiolarians, opal constitutes important parts of many sedimentary accumulations.

The finest gem opals have been obtained from Queensland and New South Wales in Australia; the Lightning Ridge field is famous for superb black stones. Deposits of white opal in Japan, fire opal in Mexico and Honduras, and several varieties of precious opal in India, New Zealand, and the western U.S., also have yielded much gem material. Most of the precious opal marketed in ancient times was obtained from occurrences in what is now Czechoslovakia. Various forms of common opal are widely mined for use as abrasives, insulation media, fillers, and ceramic ingredients.

Fire opals usually are facet cut, but most other precious opals are finished *en cabochon* because their optical properties are best displayed on smoothly rounded surfaces. Undersized fragments are used for inlay work, and small pieces scattered throughout a natural matrix are commonly sold under the name root of opal. Because opal may crack or lose its colour if it dries, many finished stones are protected by water or films of oil until they are sold. Opals absorb liquids very readily. An extremely porous variety, known as hydrophane, can absorb surprising quantities of water and will adhere to the tongue; it is almost opaque when dry but nearly transparent when saturated. Light-coloured stones are often dyed to resemble rarer, more deeply coloured varieties.
· diatom concentration of silica 6:715b; table 714
· formation, structure, and properties 16:754d; table 752
· gem characteristics and value 7:973e; illus.
· marine sediment's biogenic origin 11:497c
· South Australia's resource strength 17:210a

opalescence: *see* iridescence.

Opalglas (opal glass ware): *see* Beinglas.

opaline glass, generally used in reference to opaque glass or crystal, either white or coloured, made in France roughly between 1810 and 1890. Opaline resembles the lattimo, or milk glass (*q.v.*), of 16th-century Venice and the opaque, white glass produced near London in the 18th century.

The main centres of production were Creusot, Baccarat, and Saint-Louis; smaller factories included Bercy, La Villette, Belleville, and Choisy-le-Roi. Items made of opaline included bowls, vases, boxes, cups, and decanters as well as objects used by perfumers and hairdressers.

The earliest colours used were turquoise blue, yellow, and pink (the latter not produced after 1840). Under Louis-Philippe and Napoleon III, opaline was made in more vivid

Opaline glass bowl made at Choisy-le-Roi, Fr., 1827; in the Musée National de Céramique, Sèvres, Fr.
By courtesy of Musee Ceramique, Sevres, Fr.

colours, in imitation of Bohemian glass. It was also produced in the form of crystal, semi-crystal, glass, and pâte-de-riz (glass made by firing glass powder in a mold), the latter a Bohemian innovation. Sky blue—a colour invented in Bohemia in 1835—was copied at Baccarat and Saint-Louis around 1843; the glass used was generally pâte-de-riz. Ultramarine blue was most frequently used between 1845 and 1850. Some bicolour (white and blue) opaline was made by Baccarat in 1850. Purple opaline was made in small quantity around 1828 at the Paris factory of Bercy and also outside the capital at Choisy-le-Roi. Various greens were also made, from almond and sea green between 1825 and 1830 to less subtle shades of leaf green in later years. A type of fluorescent colour, invented in Bohemia in 1830, was produced eight years later at Choisy-le-Roi.

Decoration included gilding, painting, and transfer printing (*q.v.*). From 1840 onward copies of Chinese and Japanese porcelain were made in opaline glass.

opalinid, any of about 150 ciliated protozoans of the superclass Opalinata. The nuclei of opalinids vary in number from two (*e.g.*, *Zelleriella* to many (*e.g.*, *Cepedea*); the cilia (short, hairlike proportions) are arranged in slanting, longitudinal rows. Species of the genus *Opalina* range from 90 to 500 microns (0.004 to 0.02 inch) in length. Reproduction is sexual by fusion of gametes (syngamy) or asexual by longitudinal splitting with distribution of the nuclei. Opalinids inhabit the intestines of amphibians (*e.g.*, salamanders, newts) and some reptiles and fishes. They do not harm their host. Distribution is by encystment after reproduction; the cyst escapes in host feces and is ingested by another host. Opalinids are found worldwide, although species vary with location. One species, *Zelleriella opisthocarya*, is itself parasitized by another protozoan, *Entamoeba paulista*.

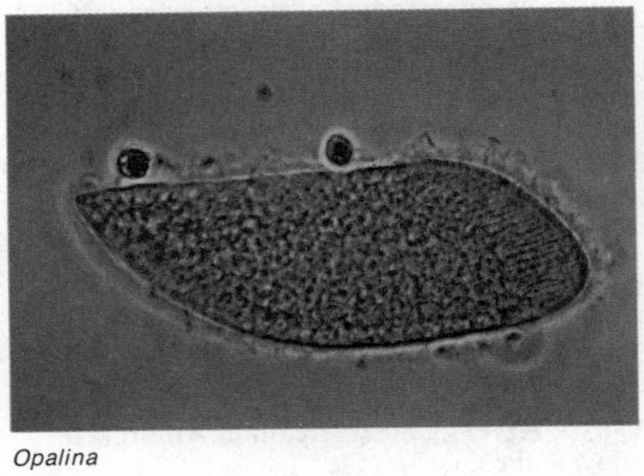

Opalina
J.M. Langham

The taxonomic position of opalinids is uncertain. Sometimes they are classified as a superclass of the flagellate subphylum Sarcomastigophora; as members of the superclass Mastigophora; or as ciliates. Formerly considered a separate group, they were called Protociliata.
· protozoan features and classification 15:128a

Opa Locka, city, Dade County, southern Florida, U.S. Primarily residential and a northern part of Greater Miami, its development was promoted by Glenn H. Curtiss, an aviation magnate, whose preference for Islāmic architecture is reflected in the early buildings. The place-name was derived from *opatishawockalocka*, a Seminole word meaning "high, dry hummock." Inc. 1926. Pop. (1980) 14,460.
25°54′ N, 80°15′ W

opaqueness: *see* diaphaneity.

Oparin, Aleksandr Ivanovich 13:577 (b. March 3, 1894, north of Moscow), biochemist, is most noted for his studies on the origin of life.

Abstract of text biography. Oparin studied plant physiology, obtained his doctorate, and left Russia at the time of the revolution. When he returned, a biochemical institute was established in his honour in 1935; he directed it from 1946. Oparin's premises on how life arose from chemical matter have greatly stimulated research.

His works include *The Origin of Life on Earth*, 3rd ed. (1957); *Life: Its Nature, Origin, and Development* (1961); and *Genesis and Evolutionary Development of Life* (1968), all English translations of books originally in Russian.

REFERENCES in other text articles:
·life's origin in hydrogen-rich atmosphere **10**:901b
·theoretical biology **2**:1023b

Oparo (Pacific Ocean): *see* Rapa.

Op art, or OPTICAL ART, international branch of mid-20th-century geometric nonobjective art that deals with optical illusion. Achieved through the systematic and precise manipulation of colours and forms, the effects of Op art can be based either on perspective illusion or on chromatic tension; in painting, the dominant medium of Op art, the surface tension is usually maximized to the point at which an actual flickering is perceived by the human eye. To the extent that Op art is intrinsically concerned with colour, line, and overall pictorial structure, it has evolved from such other 20th-century styles as Orphism, Constructivism, Suprematism, and Futurism —particularly the latter because of its reliance on dynamism. It also shares with 19th-century Neo-Impressionism the theory of simultaneous chromatic contrast employed by such painters as Georges Seurat and Camille Pissarro. Op artists of the 1950s and 1960s thus differ from other contemporary painters working with hard-edged geometric forms in their opposition to the creation of singular imagery that is based upon the perfect coincidence of colour and shape on canvas.

Op painters such as Victor Vasarely, Bridget Riley, Richard Anuskiewicz, Larry Poons, Tadasky, and Jeffrey Steele have created dynamic nonrepresentational surfaces through both colour and form. By devising a complex and paradoxical optical space through the illusory manipulation of such simple repetitive forms as parallel lines, checkerboard patterns, and concentric circles or by creating chromatic tension from the juxtaposition of complementary (chromatically opposite) colours of equal intensity, Op artists create the illusion of movement, preventing the viewer's eye from resting long enough on any one part of the surface to be able to interpret it literally. "Op art works exist," according to one writer, "less as objects than as generators of perceptual responses." These works, which can be mass-produced by industrial means, always depend on the participation of the viewer to succeed.

Op art goals are shared by the French Groupe de Recherche d'Art Visuel (Group on Experimentation in the Visual Arts) and by the Chilean-born artist Jesus Raphael Soto. These artists have made large-scale Op sculptures that employ light and motors, as well as sculptural materials, to create the illusion of movement in space that is basic to all Op art.
·colour theory experiments **13**:872f
·modern visual art history **19**:483h

"Vega," Op art painting by Victor Vasarely, oil, 1957; in the artist's collection
By courtesy of Victor Vasarely

Ópata, remnant Indian tribe of Sonora, Mex.; their Uto-Aztecan language is now extinct. Since the 17th century they have accepted Spanish culture and have been gradually assimilated into the rural Sonoran culture. They are subsistence farmers and wage labourers. Although they are Roman Catholic, traces of aboriginal religious practices survive.
·loss of language and identity **13**:245d; map 246

Opatija, Italian ABBAZIA, one of the best known coastal resorts in Istria, republic of Croatia, Yugoslavia, situated on the Kvarner (gulf) of the Adriatic Sea. The town's name derives from the old Benedictine *opatija* (abbey) of S. Giacomo (James) al Palo, situated in the main park. Besides remains of medieval walls and the town gate, there are striking villas built by Austrian and Hungarian nobility.

Austrian before World War I, Opatija was ceded to Italy in 1919 and returned to Yugoslavia after World War II. The Opatija Riviera developed as a tourist and vacation centre in the latter half of the 19th century, stimulated by the Trieste–Rijeka railway in 1873; tourists in the 1970s numbered 50,000 or more annually. Pop. (1971) mun., 27,118.
45°21′ N, 14°19′ E

Opava, German TROPPAU, Polish OPAWA, town, Severomoravský *kraj* (Northern Moravia Region), Czechoslovakia, on the Opava River, northwest of Ostrava, from which it is separated by part of the wooded Oderské vrchy (Odra Hills).

First recorded as Oppavia in 1195, it was a principate and fief of the Bohemian crown in the early 14th century and later became capital of Austrian Silesia. In 1820, after the Napoleonic Wars, representatives of Prussia, Austria, and Russia convened there for the Congress of Troppau. Many historic buildings were destroyed in World War II. Surviving in the Horní náměstí (the Upper Square) is the 237-ft (72-m) town hall tower. In the Dolní náměstí (Lower Square) is the restored 17th-century Jesuit Church of St. George and the building of the former Silesian Diet. The Gothic Church of St. Mary was built by the Teutonic Knights.

The town is now a market centre with good rail and road connections to other parts of Czechoslovakia and Poland. Manufactures include clothing, machinery, railway cars and foodstuffs. Pop. (1970 prelim.) 50,194.
49°56′ N, 17°54′ E
·map, Czechoslovakia **5**:412

Opdyke, Neil D. (b. Feb. 7, 1933, Frenchtown, N.J.), geophysicist known for his paleomagnetic determinations (paleomagnetism is the magnetic polarization of rocks with respect to the Earth's magnetic field at some previous time).

Opdyke became a resident scientist for the Lamont-Doherty Geological Observatory at Columbia University in 1964. His investigations include magnetic measuring techniques and the use of paleontological (fossil) evidence in determining paleomagnetic data. He reported evidence of faunal (animal) extinctions that coincide with reversals of the magnetic poles and suggested that removal of the Earth's magnetic screen (which filters radiation) produces mutations and accelerates faunal evolution.

Opel, Fritz von (b. May 4, 1899, Rüsselsheim, Hesse, now in West Germany—d. April 8, 1971, Sankt Moritz, Switz.), automotive industrialist who took part, with Max Valier and Friedrich Wilhelm Sander, in experiments with rocket propulsion for automobiles and aircraft. He was a grandson of Adam Opel, who founded (1862) at Rüsselsheim a firm bearing his name that manufactured bicycles, sewing machines, refrigerators, air compressors, and (from 1898) automobiles. The world's first rocket-propelled car, the Opel-Rak 1, was initially tested on March 15, 1928. Opel himself test-drove an improved version, the Opel-Rak 2, on May 23 of that year. On Sept. 30, 1929, he piloted the second rocket airplane to fly, a Hatry glider fitted with 16 Sander solid-fuel rockets.
·rocket-powered aircraft invention **15**:941h
·rocket research in Germany **7**:398d

Opelika, city, seat of Lee County, eastern Alabama, U.S., 15 mi (24 km) west of the Chattahoochee River. The first white settlers went into the area following the signing of a final treaty with the Indians in 1832. *Opelika* is a Creek Indian word meaning "large swamp," although there is no evidence of a swamp in the vicinity. The original settlement grew up around a Methodist Meeting House (*c.* 1836). The arrival of the Montgomery and West Point Railroad in 1848 contributed to the early growth of the community, which developed as a trade centre for cotton, beef, and dairy, poultry, and timber products. Manufactures are diversified and include textiles, magnetic tape, plastics, television tubes, tires, concrete products, and cardboard boxes. Inc. town, 1854; city, 1899. Pop. (1980) 21,896.
32°39′ N, 85°23′ W
·map, United States **18**:908

Opelousas, city, seat of St. Landry Parish, south central Louisiana, U.S., on the Gulf Coastal Plain. Founded in 1720 as a French garrison and trading post and named for the Opelousas Indians, it served as capital of Atakapas Territory during Spanish rule and was a sanctuary for Acadians exiled from Nova Scotia. The site of the State Supreme Court until 1819, it was incorporated as a town in 1821 and was temporary Confederate capital of Louisiana during the Civil War. Its agricultural-based economy, which depended largely on cotton and cattle, has been augmented by oil and gas (discovered in 1929 at Port Barre). Opelousas is associated with sweet potatoes and holds a "Yambilee" (yam festival) each October. Its Jim Bowie Museum displays Bowie mementos and French and Indian relics. Inc. city, 1898. Pop. (1980) 18,903.
30°32′ N, 92°05′ W
·map, United States **18**:908

openbill, or OPEN-BILLED STORK: *see* stork.

Open Brethren: *see* Plymouth Brethren.

opencast mining: *see* strip mining.

open cluster, also known as GALACTIC CLUSTER, in astronomy, contains as many as a thousand young (*i.e.*, Population I) stars in a grouping held together by mutual gravitation. Several hundred open clusters, including the Pleiades and the Hyades, are known to exist relatively near the Sun; many thousands more are thought to exist in other parts of the Galaxy. Open clusters have also been identified in several external galaxies.

The stars within each cluster are thought to have been formed at approximately the same time and place. The brightest are blue. *Cf.* globular cluster.
·Galaxy distribution **7**:838d
·H–R and colour–magnitude diagrams **17**:594g; illus. 593
·interstellar matter and apparent size **9**:791g
·structure and composition **17**:606g; illus.

Open Craps, or MONEY CRAPS, dice game, variant of Craps (*q.v.*), in which players bet among themselves instead of against the house, although a house banker is present to serve as arbiter and accept bets that a player is unable to place with another player. The banker usually charges a small percentage of such bets.

Open Door policy, statement of principles initiated by the U.S. (1899, 1900) for the protection of equal privileges among nations trading with China and in support of Chinese territorial and administrative integrity. The statement was issued in the form of circular notes dispatched by U.S. Secretary of State John Hay to Britain, Germany, France, Italy, Japan, and Russia.

The principle of equal access to trade with China had been stipulated in the treaties of Nanking and Wanghia (1842–44). After the first Sino-Japanese War (1894–95), the scramble for "spheres of influence" in China—primarily by Russia, France, Germany, and Great Britain—not only violated the Open Door principle but also threatened the complete subjection of China to foreign rule. A new interest in foreign markets had emerged in the U.S. following the economic depression of the 1890s. The U.S. also had just gained the Philippines, Guam, and Hawaii as a result of the Spanish–American War and was becoming increasingly interested in China, where U.S. textile manufacturers had found markets for cheap cotton goods.

The 1899 Open Door notes, written jointly by Secretary Hay's adviser W.W. Rockhill and A.E. Hippisley, a former commissioner in the Chinese Maritime Customs Service, provided that: (1) each power should maintain free access to a treaty port or to any other vested interest within its sphere; (2) only the Chinese government should collect taxes on trade; and (3) no power having a sphere should be granted exemptions from paying harbour dues or railroad charges. The replies from the various nations were evasive, but Hay interpreted them as acceptances.

In reaction to the presence of European armies in North China to suppress the Boxer Rebellion, Hay's second circular of 1900 stressed the importance of preserving China's territorial and administrative integrity.

Japan violated the Open Door principle with its presentation of Twenty-one Demands to China (1915). The Nine-Power Treaty after the Washington Conference (1921–22) reaffirmed it. The Manchurian crisis of 1931 and the war between China and Japan in 1937 led the U.S. to adopt a rigid stand in favour of the Open Door policy, including the cutting off of supplies to Japan. Japan's defeat in World War II and the Communist victory in China's civil war (1949), which ended all special privileges to foreigners, made the Open Door policy meaningless.
·China's unified preservation **4**:364f
·major provisions and support **18**:982f
·United States immigration systems **13**:195f
·Western rivalry in China **4**:898g

open-end investment company: *see* mutual fund.

open-field system, basic community organization of cultivation in European agriculture for 2,000 years or more. Its best-known medieval form consisted of three elements: individual peasant holdings in the form of strips scattered among the different fields; crop rotation; and common grazing. Crop rotation was by the two-field system (*q.v.*) in the earlier age and by the three-field system (*q.v.*) in the later centuries; in either case some of the commonly held fields were always fallow and used for common grazing. The system was especially well adapted to the feudal manorial social system, in which the lord's holdings were intermixed and cultivated with those of the peasants. As society grew more complex and a market economy began to appear, the open-field system tended to give way to individual farming, permitting progressive peasants to farm as they pleased without having to conform to the old restrictive pattern.
·medieval agricultural technology **1**:332a; illus.

open-hearth process, also known as SIEMENS–MARTIN PROCESS, major steelmaking technique that up to the 1970s had accounted for the major part of all steel made in the world. William Siemens, a German living in England in the 1860s, seeking a means of increasing the temperature in a metallurgical furnace, resurrected an old proposal for using the waste heat given off by the furnace; passing the fumes from the furnace through a duct of brick checkerwork, he heated the brick to a high temperature, then used the same duct for the introduction of air into the furnace; the air, thus preheated, materially increased the flame temperature of the furnace. The first to use the device to produce steel were Pierre and Émile Martin of Sireuil, France, in 1864, using a charge of pig iron with the addition of some wrought-iron scrap. The ores most readily available in both Britain and the United States were especially well suited to the open-hearth process, the product of which proved superior to that from the Bessemer furnace. Gaseous fuel, either natural or produced from coal, is used; both air and fuel are preheated before charging into the furnace along with iron ore, steel scrap, and limestone flux. The furnace itself is made of highly refractory materials that contain lime and magnesia to aid in removing impurities. Capacities of open-hearth furnaces run to as high as 600 tons, and they are usually installed in groups, so that the massive auxiliary equipment needed to produce the gaseous fuel and preheat the gas and fuel can be efficiently employed.

In the 1970s the open-hearth process was being widely replaced by the newer basic oxygen process (*q.v.*).
·description and operation **17**:647b; illus.
·design and applications **16**:732e
·steelmaking from scrap **11**:1067g
·steel manufacturing development role **18**:42a

open-heart surgery, surgical operation upon the heart with the part to be repaired in direct view of the operating surgeon.
·mechanical requirements and applications **3**:895a; illus.
·techniques and early development **17**:823e

opening of the mouth ceremony, in Egyptian religion, rite performed on statues of the deceased, the mummy itself, or statues of a god located in a temple. The ceremony, which symbolized the death and regeneration concept of the Osiris myth (in which the dismembered god Osiris was pieced together again and infused with life), was performed on a

Opening of the mouth ceremony, from the Book of the Dead, Hunefer Papyrus; in the British Museum
By courtesy of the trustees of the British Museum

statue in the sculptor's workshop, but on a mummy at the tomb entrance. By this rite the statue or mummy was believed to be endowed with life and power so that he might enjoy the daily funeral service conducted before his tomb. In the case of temple statues, the ceremony was included in the daily temple ritual.
·Egyptian reanimation rites **5**:535e

open market operations, purchases and sales of government securities and sometimes commercial paper by the central banking authority for the purpose of regulating the money supply and credit conditions on a continuous basis.

Open market operations can also be used to stabilize the prices of government securities, an aim that conflicts at times with the credit policies of the central bank. When the central bank purchases securities on the open market, the effects will be (1) to increase the reserves of commercial banks, a basis on which they can expand their loans and investments; (2) to increase the price of government securities, equivalent to reducing their interest rates; and (3) to decrease interest rates generally, thus encouraging business investment. If the central bank should sell securities, the effects would be reversed.

Open market operations are customarily carried out with short-term government securities (in the U.S., quite often Treasury bills). Observers disagree on the advisability of such a policy. Supporters believe that dealing in both short-term and long-term securities would distort the interest-rate structure and therefore the allocation of credit. Opponents believe that this would be entirely appropriate because the interest rates on long-term securities have more direct influence on long-run investment activity, which is responsible for fluctuations in employment and income.
·central banking and the economy **2**:710a
·foreign-exchange effect on monetary policy **7**:25d
·monetary policy stabilization tools **7**:324c
·money market and central bank activity **12**:357d
·money-supply control by central banks **12**:352g
·public-debt effects on economy **15**:187e

open-pit mining: *see* strip-mining.

open-plan teaching, in education, division of curriculum into large areas, making all teaching resources available in a common teaching space.
·theory and practice **13**:1102a

open set, of real numbers, any set A of real numbers that, together with every element a, contains an interval $(a - \epsilon, a + \epsilon)$ for sufficiently small positive ϵ.
·algebraic geometry fundamentals **7**:1072g
·algebraic topology fundamentals **18**:504g
·Euclidean geometry principles **7**:1110g
·real analysis principles **1**:785e
·topological group theory **18**:490b
·topological space definition **18**:510e

open shop, establishment in which eligibility for employment and retention on the payroll are not determined by membership in a labour union.
·trade union membership in postwar era **18**:566a

open space planning, in urban planning, that portion of a community site given over to roads, parks, and other land not containing the buildings.
·positive design and future prospects **18**:1063d

open stage, site of a type of theatrical production performed on a raised stage surrounded on three sides by an audience. A popular form of modern staging, this type of production largely originated with the platform stage of the Elizabethan theatre. The Festival Theatre in Chichester, Sussex, and the Shakespearean Festival Theatre at Stratford, Ont., are two important mid-20th-century examples of open-stage theatres.
·advantages for contemporary theatre **18**:215c
·playhouse shape and dramatic style **5**:987c
·Tieck's reaction to pictoral realism **17**:543h

Open University, institution of higher education in Great Britain designed for part-time attendance by adults. Officially opened in May 1970, it is located on a 70-acre site at the new city of Milton Keynes, Buckinghamshire. There are no academic prerequisites for enrollment in Open University, the aim of which is the extension of educational opportunities to all. Courses, centrally organized by the staff, are conducted by various means, including television, correspondence, study groups, and residential courses or seminars.
·broadcasting extension use **3**:314a
·founding and goals **18**:888c
·higher education potentialities **8**:860c

opera 13:578, a Western theatrical form consisting of a dramatic text (libretto) combined with music, usually singing with instrumental accompaniment. A complex and often costly variety of entertainment, it has attracted audiences, with varying degrees of popularity, for five centuries.

TEXT ARTICLE covers:
Italian origins **13**:579c
Early opera in France 581f
Early opera in Germany and Austria 581h
The "reform" 582e
Opera in England 583b
Viennese masters 583d
France, 1752–1825 584c
Italy in the first half of the 19th century 584h
French grand opera 586a
German Romantic opera 586d
Verdi 587d
Wagner and his successors 588b
Later opera in France 588g
Later opera in Italy 589f
Russian opera 590e
Later opera in Germany and Austria 591d
Nationalist opera 592c
Recent developments 592h

REFERENCES in other text articles:
·Auden libretto revitalization **2**:364b
·Baroque development **18**:226a
·Beethoven's Fidelio **2**:797h
·Calderón de la Barca's contribution **3**:593f
·castrati's role in Baroque era **16**:790b
·Classical and Romantic eras **12**:711h
·comic spirit's musical expression **4**:966e
·composite musical genres **12**:727h
·costume design in French Baroque period **17**:562c
·counterpoint as expressive device **5**:215a
·decline in England and rise of oratorio **8**:603h
·development and impact on theatre **12**:695g
·Donizetti's career and works **5**:953g
·dramatic and musical feature emphasis **18**:257c
·dramatic literature's role **5**:988b
·dramatic text subordination **5**:986h
·economic dependence on selective audiences **2**:111f
·German contemporary trends **8**:67a
·Gluck's emphasis on drama **8**:212a
·Gounod's development of French style **8**:258c
·Haydn's Esterháza productions **8**:682b
·Italian, French, and English Baroque **12**:709a
·Italian literary influence **10**:1159f
·modern developments and renewal **12**:667e
·Monteverdi's theory and development **12**:404b
·orchestration of Baroque masters **13**:645f
·origin and political function **18**:223b
·performance media in complex dimension **12**:739c
·Prokofiev's contemporary influence **15**:33f *passim* to 36b
·Puccini's musico-dramatic style **15**:257g
·Rameau's life and works **15**:500b
·Rimsky-Korsakov's main works **15**:852d
·Rossini's Italian and French styles **15**:1159f
·school styles of art theory **2**:129c
·stylistic comparisons in Baroque **12**:718e
·television adaptation and effect **18**:125c; table
·theatre and stage design influence **18**:246e
·tragic style in music **18**:592e
·United Kingdom cultural life **18**:890f
·Venetian historic presentations **19**:75b
·Verdi and growth of music drama **19**:82d
·visual arts relation to other arts **19**:246e
·Vivaldi's style and works **19**:494f
·Wagnerian music-drama synthesis **19**:517b
·Weber's Romantic trend **19**:713d
·wind instrument use in Baroque period **19**:856a

RELATED ENTRIES in the *Ready Reference and Index: for*
German opera: see cavatina; leitmotiv; Singspiel
Italian opera: Camerata; castrato; intermezzo; opera buffa; opera seria; verismo
opera associations: Covent Garden; La Scala; Metropolitan Opera Association; Paris Opera; Vienna State Opera
operatic genre: ballad opera; comic opera; masque; opera comique; tonadilla; zarzuela
vocal types: aria; cabaletta; recitative
other: libretto; overture

Opéra, in full THÉÂTRE NATIONALE DE L'OPÉRA, the Paris opera house designed by Charles Garnier. The building, considered one of the masterpieces of the Second Empire style, was begun in 1861 and opened with an orchestral concert on Jan. 5, 1875. The first opera performed there was Jacques Halévy's work *La Juive* on Jan. 8, 1875.
The Opéra also houses the Académie Nationale de Musique, which had been founded in 1669–71 during the reign of Louis XIV.
·electric lighting installation **18**:227c
·style, size, and ornamentation **13**:1014f; map 1005
·Verdi commissions and premieres **19**:83f

opera, Chinese, musical drama of China, known generically as *hsi ch'ü* (each of the many varieties is also specifically named). Although traceable to earlier times, regional forms of music drama flourished during the Sung dynasty (960–1279) and were broadly divided into northern and southern styles. From the ensuing Yüan dynasty (1279–1368) to the present, literally hundreds of varieties developed, later styles often borrowing elements from earlier ones. They differ from each other especially in their instrumentation and in the voice quality used (*e.g.*, raspy or nasal in Peking opera, relaxed and open in Cantonese opera). Choruses, acrobats, and dancers occur in some forms. Rhythm plays a prominent role in setting dramatic atmosphere. Arias tend to be either stereotyped melodic patterns that are varied in performance or complete standard melodies having recognized, emotional import and used from opera to opera, an older approach suited especially to texts of rigid poetic structure.
·acting traditionalism **18**:252h
·classical theatre style **17**:533h
·development of form **12**:675b
·East Asian literary history **10**:1056c
·Ming dynasty's dramatic contribution **4**:353e
·Yüan dynasty's classic contributions **4**:345b

Opera and Drama translation of OPER UND DRAMA (1850), study by Richard Wagner.
·outline of aesthetic ideals **19**:518e

opera buffa, genre of comic opera originating in Naples in the mid-18th century. It developed from the intermezzi, or interludes, performed between the acts of serious operas. Opera buffa plots centre on two groups of characters: a comic group of (usually) five male and female personages, and a pair (or more) of lovers. The dialogue is sung. The operatic finale, a long, formally organized conclusion to an opera act, including all principal personages, developed in opera buffa. The earliest opera buffa still regularly performed is Giovanni Battista Pergolesi's *La serva padrona* (1733; *The Maid as Mistress*). Opera buffa is distinct from French opéra bouffe, a general term for any light opera.
·development since Mozart and Haydn **13**:583e *passim* to 586a
·interfusion with opera seria **13**:581d
·melodic shape of style **12**:718f
·origin, development, content, and style **12**:702b
·popular music sources in 20th century **14**:810b
·Rossini's stylistic innovations **15**:1160a

opéra comique, French form of opera in which spoken dialogue alternates with self-contained musical numbers. The earliest examples of opéra comique were satirical comedies with interpolated songs, but the form later developed into serious musical drama distinguished from other opera only by its spoken dialogue.
The opéra comique developed in the early 18th century out of the *comédies de vaudeville,* farcical entertainments performed at fairs. Their characters derived from those of the improvised Italian *commedia dell'arte* and they included popular songs, or vaudevilles, which were given new, frequently satirical words. In 1715 the various performing groups were combined in Paris as the Théâtre de l'Opéra-Comique.
In the mid-18th century the writer Charles-Simon Favart brought a higher literary level to the opéra comique texts, and newly composed songs began to be added, eventually replacing the popular vaudevilles. Plots began to centre on characters from everyday life. This emphasis was influenced by Jean-Jacques Rousseau's theories of the noble, simple life. He himself composed an early example of opéra comique, *Le Devin du village* (1752; *The Village Soothsayer*), which the 12-year-old Mozart parodied in *Bastien und Bastienne*.
Lesser 18th-century composers such as Nicolas Dalayrac, Egidio Duni, Pierre Monsigny, and François Philidor specialized in opéra comique. Gluck, writing for audiences in Vienna that favoured the French genre, was the only great composer of that era to devote himself extensively to it. The opéras comiques of this period were characterized by social comment, light plots of romance or intrigue, and tuneful music. The tradition continued in the late 18th and early 19th centuries in the work of André Grétry, François Boieldieu, and Daniel Auber, who treated more serious and romantic subjects and made a more evocative use of the orchestra.
Also characteristic of this period was the "rescue opera" with its plot of political tyranny defeated. Toward 1830 the opéra comique developed into serious music drama approximating grand opera and gradually lost its satirical character. Georges Bizet's *Carmen* (1875) is a late, isolated example of opéra comique, possessing spoken dialogue, but dealing with a tragic theme.
·Donizetti's career and works **5**:954b
·Gluck's evolution from vaudeville comedy **8**:213b
·origin, development, and style **12**:702d
·pervasive influence of Italian opera **12**:712c
·representative scores and composers **13**:584d

Opera dei congressi (1875), organ of the Catholic Labour Movement in Italy.
·economic and social program **9**:1165a

Opera Drama Studio, Russian experimental opera company founded in 1935 by Konstantin Stanislavsky.
·Stanislavsky's last years **17**:582d

Opera nella quale si insegna a scrivere (1554), script of Vespasiano Amphiare.
·calligraphic styles development **3**:659b

operant conditioning: *see* conditioning.

Opera Philosophica et Mineralia (1734), a work by the Swedish mystic Emanuel Swedenborg.
·development of philosophy of nature **17**:855c

opera seria, style of Italian opera dominant in 18th-century Europe except France. It emerged in the late 17th century, notably in the work of Alessandro Scarlatti (1660–1725) and other composers working in Naples, and is thus frequently called Neapolitan opera.

The primary musical emphasis of opera seria was on the solo voice and on bel canto, the florid vocal style of the period. Chorus and orchestra played a circumscribed role. High voices were cultivated, both in women and in the castrati, or eunuch male sopranos. Music and text were divided into recitative (simply accompanied dialogue sung with speech rhythms), which advanced the dramatic action, and arias, solos that reflected a character's feelings and also served as vehicles for vocal virtuosity. Arias characteristically took the da capo form (ABA), the first section (A) being repeated after the B section, but with improvised embellishments.

Apostolo Zeno (1668–1750) and Pietro Metastasio (1698–1782) were the leading masters of the required libretto style, which presented characters from classical mythology or history and avoided diversionary comic episodes. Among the examples of opera seria are *Rinaldo*, by George Frideric Handel (1685–1759), *Demofoonte*, by Niccolò Jommelli (1714–74), *Didone abbandonata* (*Dido Abandoned*), by Nicola Porpora (1686–1768) and *Artaserse*, by Johann Adolf Hasse (1669–1783).
·bel canto's melodic shape in comparison **12**:718e
·Neapolitan origin and later development **13**:580h *passim* to 585b
·origin and development in Naples **12**:709c
·stylistic reactions in 18th century **12**:711h

Opéras-Minutes (1927–28), musical work by Darius Milhaud.
·jazz and parodistic elements **13**:589e

Operas Portuguesas (1733–41), plays by António José da Silva.
·content and significance **10**:1176a

Operation A (1944), an unsuccessful Japanese defense plan to coordinate land and sea forces in an attempt to stop Allied advances in the Pacific late in World War II.
·Allied capture of the Mariana Islands **19**:1004f

operational fatigue: *see* combat fatigue.

Operation Barbarossa, code name given to the invasion of the Soviet Union by Germany in World War II. Beginning on June 22, 1941, the German Army overran the western areas of the soviet Union, later to be stalled at the Siege of Leningrad, and defeated at the Battle of Stalingrad.

Operation Breadbasket, the economic arm of the Southern Christian Leadership Conference, founded by Martin Luther King, Jr.
·Chicago segregation reform programs **4**:213h
·Martin Luther King's role in creation **10**:473d

Operation Crossroads, U.S. atomic weapons tests conducted July 1946 in the Bikini area of the Pacific.
·Bikini nuclear tests and research **2**:988e

Operation Deep Freeze, U.S. program for the study of Antarctica (1955–56).
·Ross Ice Shelf importance **15**:1158g

Operation Highjump, U.S. Naval Antarctic expedition conducted in 1946 and 1947. It involved 4,800 men, 13 ships, 33 aircraft, and an assortment of tractors, landing craft, cargo carriers, and jeeps. About 60% of the coastline of Antarctica was photographed from the air.
·Antarctic expedition headquarters **15**:1158h
·exploration and equipment **1**:962h
·land discovery claims **3**:542f

Operation Overlord: *see* Normandy Invasion.

Operation Pan America, cooperative program for Latin American economic development.
·Kubitschek's proposition for adoption **3**:148g

Operation Sea Lion, code name for the proposed invasion of the British Isles by Nazi Germany during World War II. The plan, after being setback by the poor showing of the Luftwaffe in the Battle of Britain, was shelved for good when Hitler decided to invade the Soviet Union in June 1941.
·RAF and the Battle of Britain **19**:984d

operations on sets, a procedure that constructs new sets from other sets. Union, intersection, and difference are all operations on sets.

operations research **13**:594, or OPERATIONAL RESEARCH, the application of scientific methods to the management of organized military, governmental, commercial, and industrial systems. It is distinguished from systems engineering in that it focusses on systems in which human behaviour is important.

The text article covers the history of operations research, which began as a conscious technique in the British Royal Air Force in the late 1930s. It also treats the essential characteristics of operations research; the stages of its application from problem formulation to model-testing and solution; prototype problems and associated techniques such as allocation, inventory, replacement and maintenance, and queuing; and some of the problems on its frontiers.

REFERENCES in other text articles:
·analogue computer operation and use **4**:1049c
·bureaucracy and scientific management **3**:491b
·chemical synthesis analysis **4**:163c
·coal mining methods and technique development **4**:777a
·computer simulation programs **4**:1057b
·control systems applications **5**:129f
·economic productivity and physical capital **15**:28b
·food service efficiency planning **7**:498a
·historical growth of systems approach **17**:970d
·human-factor study in procedure design **8**:1168g
·industrial monitoring instrumentation **9**:639f
·industrial safety programs **16**:140e
·mass production and management functions **11**:596b
·mine design engineering **12**:254h
·operational analysis of weapon systems **11**:84d
·optimization theory and method **13**:628e
·postal systems improvement studies **14**:891d
·production planning and statistical tools **15**:27e
·ship construction planning **16**:693h
·statistical theory and method **17**:615d
·steel testing method **17**:656f
·systems organization in auto industry **2**:531g
·telecommunications systems technology **18**:94f

RELATED ENTRIES in the *Ready Reference and Index:*
game theory; inventory control; management science; programming, mathematical; queuing theory

Operation Torch, code name for the Allied plan in World War II for the invasion of North Africa that took place on November 7–8, 1942; it ultimately led to the invasion of Italy and the collapse of Nazi Germany.

Operation Windmill (1947–48), U.S. naval Antarctic expedition.
·ground verification of data **1**:964a

operator, in mathematics, any symbol that indicates an operation to be performed. Examples are $\sqrt{x}$ (which indicates the square root of x is to be taken) and d/dx (which indicates a differentiation with respect to x is to be performed).

As a synonym for function, the word indicates the particular operation of the function, the association of a set of objects (the independent variable) with another set of objects (the dependent variable). The domain of the independent variable is mapped onto its image in the range of the dependent variable. An operator may be a transformation, map, or mapping.
·Fourier analysis fundamentals **1**:749g
·functional analysis fundamentals **1**:758h
·linear and multilinear algebra theory **1**:511d
·notation and function in logical systems **11**:40b; table
·topological group theory **18**:491e

operator, in physics, sequence of mathematical manipulations to be performed on suitable mathematical formulas to convert them into new formulas. Usually designated by a letter of the alphabet or some arbitrary symbol, operators themselves may be applied repeatedly, so that a multiple operator may constitute a number of quite sophisticated mathematical operations.

Operators are used in physics as the mathematical representations of physical processes. The formulas to which they apply in turn represent conditions, or states, of physical systems and are frequently called states themselves. Thus the application of an operator to a formula or state generally parallels the action of a physical process on the actual state of a physical system, even though the mathematical manipulations that constitute the operator may have no obvious resemblance to the corresponding physical process.

An operator corresponding to a physical process of measurement, such as those of weight, position, energy, temperature, height, and so on, is called an observable. Although the action of any operator when applied to a state is typically to change the system into an entirely new state, each observable has certain privileged states, called eigenstates, that are not changed into new states by its application but are simply multiplied by a constant. This constant, or number, gives the value that the corresponding physical measurement would yield if carried out on a physical system in the corresponding eigenstate.

On the other hand, a physical system need not be in a condition that can be represented by an eigenstate of the given observable. In that case, application of the observable alters the state, and, correspondingly, performance of the physical measurement would alter the physical state, and no definite value of the measured quantity would result.

operator in Hilbert space, any continuous or discontinuous linear operator from a Hilbert space to itself. If T is a continuous linear operator on a Hilbert space H, its adjoint is the uniquely determined continuous linear operator T^*, defined by the equation $(T^*x, y) = (x, Ty)$ (for symbols, *see* Hilbert space) for all x and y in H; and T is said to be normal if $TT^* = T^*T$, self-adjoint if $T = T^*$, and unitary if $T^* = T^{-1}$.

operators, theory of, study of the continuous or discontinuous linear operators between topological vector spaces, with particular attention to the dual operators.
·von Neumann quantum theory relationship **12**:1067a

operculum, general term for a covering lid or flap. In bony fishes, some immature amphibians, and aquatic invertebrates, the operculum covers and protects the gills. In barnacles it is the moveable plates that form the shell. In gastropods the horny plate used to close the shell opening when the entire animal is within the shell is called the operculum; and in spiders it covers the spiracles.

·bryozoan jaw evolution 3:357c
·moss morphology and function 3:353f; illus. 352
·perch bones, illus. 1 7:332
·protective and locomotive functions in gastropods 7:952e *passim* to 954e

operetta, a musical-dramatic production similar in structure to an opera but characteristically having a romantically sentimental plot interspersed with songs, orchestral music, and rather elaborate dancing scenes, along with the spoken dialogue.

The operetta originated in part with the tradition of popular theatrical genres such as of the commedia dell'arte that flourished in Italy from the 16th to the 18th centuries and the *vaudeville* of France. In the 19th century the term operetta came to designate stage plays with music that were generally of a farcical and satiric nature. The most successful practitioner of this art was Jacques Offenbach (1819–80) whose *Orphée aux enfers* (1858; *Orpheus in the Underworld*) and *La Belle Hélène* (1864) used the guise of Greek mythology to express a satirical commentary on contemporary Parisian life and mores. In England, from the late 1870s, the team of Sir William S. Gilbert and Sir Arthur Sullivan, influenced by Offenbach's works, established their own part in the genre with such familiar works as *H.M.S. Pinafore*, *The Pirates of Penzance*, and *Iolanthe*, among many others.

In Vienna around 1870, Johann Strauss the Younger was producing operettas of a more romantic and melodious type, such as *Die Fledermaus*, which in many respects spanned the differences between operetta and opera. Toward the end of the 19th century, perhaps influenced by the gentler quality of Viennese operetta, the French style became itself more sentimental and less satirical, stressing elegance over parodic bite. Viennese successors to Strauss, such as Franz Lehár (Hungarian by birth), Oscar Straus, and Leo Fall, and French composers such as André Messager contributed to the evolution of operetta into what is now called musical comedy.

The operetta traditions of Austria, France, Italy (whose operatic composer Giacomo Puccini made one contribution, *La rondine*), and England began to wane but found new life in the United States. Victor Herbert (1859–1924), Reginald De Koven (1859–1920), and Sigmund Romberg (1887–1951) were all significant transitional figures adding to U.S. musical life with such operettas as, respectively, *Babes in Toyland*, *The Highwayman*, and *The Student Prince*.

The overlapping in the United States of operetta and so-called musical comedy (*q.v.*) has been the result of shifting points of view, public taste, and social and political change. But within the range of works that might be regarded as just short of serious opera and hardly recognizable as comedy are George Gershwin's *Porgy and Bess* (1935), Kurt Weill's *Threepenny Opera* (1928), Rodgers and Hammerstein's *Oklahoma!* (1943), Jerome Kern's *Show Boat* (1927), and Leonard Bernstein's *West Side Story* (1957) and *Candide* (1956). Perhaps the most successful of all modern operettas is Frederick Loewe and Alan Jay Lerner's *My Fair Lady* (1956), a stage work that combines a libretto based on George Bernard Shaw's *Pygmalion* with distinctive music, social comment, and the demonstrated capacity to enthrall the public.

·development by German Romanticists 13:587b
·origin and international development 12:699h
·popular music sources in 20th century 14:810b
·Yiddish theatre 19th-century repertoire 10:201c

Operina da imparare di scrivere littera cancellarescha, La, by Ludovico degli Arrighi.

·writing manual development 3:657g

operon, concept first elucidated (1961) in the bacterium *Escherichia coli* to explain the control of gene activity. An operon is a region of a chromosome consisting of (1) so-called structural genes, which direct the synthesis of catalytic proteins (enzymes) involved in the formation of a cell constituent (*e.g.*, the amino acid arginine) or the utilization of a nutrient (*e.g.*, the sugar lactose), and (2) an operator gene, which responds to a molecule called a repressor. The operator gene can exist in two states, open and closed. When open, the genes it controls are functional, and proteins are produced. The operator gene is closed whenever it interacts with the repressor. The synthesis of repressor, thought to be a protein, is directed by a regulator gene located on the chromosome close to—but not adjacent to—the operon. The repressor is neutralized by a specific substance, called an inducer, which prevents the interaction between the repressor and the operator gene; the operator is thus turned on, and the structural genes direct the synthesis of the enzymes.

·gene action control mechanisms 7:990d; illus.

Operophtera brumata, species of winter moth of the family Geometridae (order Lepidoptera).

·population fluctuations and mortality 14:833a; illus. 832

Opet, Beautiful Feast of (Egyptian religion): *see* Taurt, Beautiful Feast of.

Opheodrys: *see* green snake.

Ophichthidae, family of snake eels of the order Anguilliformes.

·characteristics and classification 1:900d

ophicleide, brass wind instrument with a cup-shaped mouthpiece and padded keys, the bass version of the old keyed bugle. The name (from Greek *ophis*, "serpent" and *kleides*, "keys") alludes to its improvement on the military band "upright serpents" (now-obsolete S-shaped bass instruments sounded by

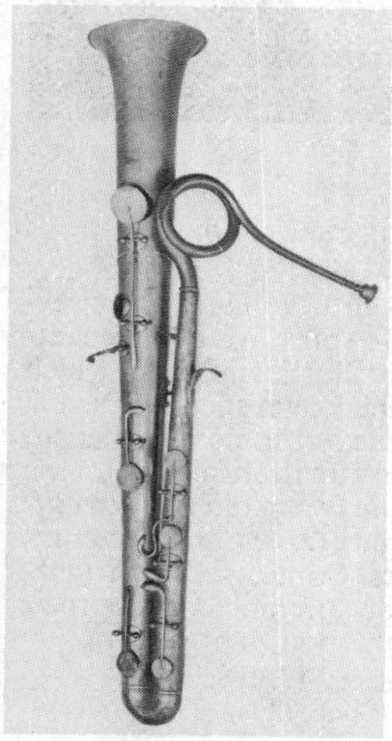

Belgian ophicleide; in the Musee Instrumental du Conservatoire Royal, Brussels

By courtesy of the Musee Instrumental, Brussels; photograph, © A.C.L., Brussels

vibration of the lips against a cup mouthpiece) by providing 11 brass keys to replace open finger holes. It was normally built in C or B♭ with the same compass (three octaves) as the euphonium and with a similar tone. Invented in 1817 by Jean Asté, known as Halary, it was extensively used in French and British bands and orchestras until replaced by the tuba near the end of the 19th century.

Ophidia (animal suborder): *see* Serpentes.

Ophidiidae (fish family): *see* cusk eel; brotula.

ophidiophobia, the condition of being fearful of snakes and other organisms with a similar mode of locomotion.

·avoidance behaviour pattern 2:542a

Ophioglossaceae, only family in the fern order Ophioglossales, a primitive group not closely related to other ferns. The family contains four genera and about 70 to 90 species and is characterized by leaves (fronds) that are divided into two parts, a sterile green blade and a fertile spike with spore-producing structures (sporangia) embedded in its tissues.

Rattlesnake fern (*Botrychium virginianum*)

Louise K. Broman from Root Resources—EB Inc.

Most species produce only one such frond each season. The genera are distinguished mainly by the position and structure of the sporangia.

Ophioglossum (adder's-tongue ferns), with 30 to 50 tropical and temperate species, has sporangia in two rows near the tip of a usually unbranched, narrow, fertile spike.

Botrychium (grape fern), with about 40 species distributed throughout the world, has both the sterile and fertile portions of the leaf branched, the latter with sporangia in small grapelike clusters that are arranged in a long, loose spike.

The moonwort, or moon fern *Botrychium lunaria*, is named for the long sterile portion of its single frond 7–15 centimetres (about 3–6 inches) long, which bears several pairs of close-set, crescent or fan-shaped leaflets (pinnae). The rattlesnake fern (*Botrychium virginianum*) has thin textured, lacy-cut, and nonleathery leaves.

Helminthostachys, with one species (*H. zeylanica*) in Sri Lanka (Ceylon) and regions extending from the Himalayas to Queensland in Australia, has sporangia in small groups on both sides of the fertile spike.

Rhizoglossum, also with a single species in South Africa, has separate sterile and fertile fronds, the latter similar to the fertile spike of *Ophioglossum*.

·fern characteristics and classification 7:246d
·reproductive system comparisons 15:720c

Ophiophagus hannah (snake): *see* cobra.

Ophir, an unidentified region, famous in Old Testament times for its fine gold. The geographical list of Gen. 10 apparently places it in Arabia, but, in the time of Solomon (*c.* 920 BC), Ophir was thought of as being overseas. Gold, almug (or algum) wood (*i.e.*, sandalwood), ivories, monkeys, and peacocks were procured there. Many areas of the Arabian Peninsula have been proposed as the site of Ophir; the principal alternative locations overseas are East Africa and India.

That many Egyptian pharaohs reported sending naval expeditions to Punt (Somaliland) for monkeys, ivory, frankincense, and slaves lends credence to an East African site. There is some similarity between the Solomonic expeditions and those of the Egyptians, and the equation of Somaliland with Ophir is plausible. The other East African possibility is Zimbabwe in Rhodesia, the site of the famous stone-built ruins about 200 miles inland from Sofala, where there are gold mines. The ruins at Zimbabwe, however, do not appear to be earlier than the 9th century AD.

The Jewish historian Josephus and St. Jerome evidently understood that India was the location of Ophir, which they spelled Sophir. That spelling would seem to represent Sopārā, or Śūrpāraka (an ancient port north of Bombay). Although there have been no archaeological excavations at Sopārā, there is no inherent improbability in locating Ophir in India. The Hebrew words for the products of Ophir can be derived from Indian languages; furthermore, sandalwood and peacocks are commonly found in India, whereas, at least in modern times, they do not exist in East Africa.

·identification with Sopārā and Śūrpāraka **9**:355d

Ophisaurus (lizard): *see* glass snake.

Ophites, a Gnostic sect—*i.e.*, a group of religious dualists who believed that matter was evil and the spirit good and that salvation was attained through esoteric knowledge, or gnosis. The sect flourished in the Roman Empire during the 2nd century AD. Though they were Christians, their reinterpretation of basic doctrines in terms of a radical dualism classed them as heretics. According to their elaborate system of cosmogony, the aeons (powers) that ruled over the spheres around the Earth had been begotten from an ineffable principle of Light. When the aeon Ialdabaoth (Gnostic name for Yahweh, the God of the Old Testament) boasted that he alone was God, the aeon Sophia (wisdom) created man so that Ialdabaoth would forget his power by breathing the spirit of life into man. When Ialdabaoth did not lose his power, however, Sophia determined to transmit gnosis to Adam and Eve by means of the serpent. Reversing biblical values, the Ophites (from the Greek *ophis*, serpent) regarded the serpent as their pneumatic, or spiritual, principle because it had given man the secret knowledge that his spirit had originally derived from the unknown God. The task of the true Gnostic was to escape his earthly prison and ascend to the highest heaven, there to be reunited with the primal Light.

For the accomplishment of this heavenly journey, the Ophites used magical formulas and symbols to overcome the hostile aeons who ruled the realms separating earth from heaven. The Ophites would not admit anyone into their ranks who had not first cursed the man Jesus, for they believed in a spiritual Christ who, like the serpent, had taught the saving gnosis.

Closely related to the Ophites were the Naassenes, who took their name from the Hebrew word (*naḥash*) for serpent. They used the *Gospel of Thomas*, a purported collection of secret sayings of Jesus, and like the Ophites emphasized Christ's spiritual existence, referring to him as the "Living One." An extreme asceticism led to a condemnation of all earthly things as inimical to one's true nature. The Naassenes used language similar to that of the mystery religions to describe the odyssey of the Gnostic spirit from the "lesser mysteries" of carnal existence to the "greater mysteries" of ascension to the highest heaven. Also like the Ophites, they based their system on an allegorical and dualistic reinterpretation of select biblical texts.

·Adam and Eve in antinomian Gnosticism **4**:553d

ophitic texture, descriptive term for igneous rocks in which lath-shaped, sometimes radiating, plagioclase feldspar crystals occur within individual anhedral augite (pyroxene) crystals. In its typical development, the lengths of the plagioclase laths do not exceed the diameters of the pyroxene grains, and they appear to be enclosed in a continuous mass of pyroxene; when the lengths of the laths exceed the size of the pyroxenes, the texture can be called subophitic. Some petrographers make a distinction on the basis of the relative amounts of plagioclase and augite in the rock. In this case, ophitic texture has augite in excess of the plagioclase included within it; but, when the plagioclase is in excess, with the augite filling the interstices between the laths, the texture is diabasic. Rocks commonly showing ophitic texture, sometimes called ophites, include gabbro, diabase, and basalt.

·igneous rock characteristics **9**:204f

Ophiuchus (Greek, Latin: "serpent bearer"), constellation of the equatorial zone.

·constellation table **2**:226

Ophiuroidea (marine invertebrate): *see* brittle star.

Ophryodendron (protozoan): *see* suctorian.

Ophrys, a genus of orchids, family Orchidaceae, that contains approximately 30 species of plants native to Eurasia and North Africa. All have metallic-coloured, hairy flowers that resemble insects. Each plant is less than 30 centimetres (1 foot) tall and bears several flowers on a single spike. Male insects attempt to copulate with the flowers, which resemble females of their own species. During this process, pollen sacs become attached to the insect's body and are transferred to the next flower visited. The fly orchid (*O. insectifera*) and the bee orchid (*O. apifera*) are common European species. Some species of *Ophrys* are known as spider orchids because their flower lips resemble the bodies of spiders.

Ophrys
Ingmar Holmasen

·mimicry of female insects **12**:218c
·O. apifera imitation of bee, illus., **12**:Mimicry, Plate I
·pollination adaptation **2**:1052d
·pollination by pseudocopulation **13**:654d

ophthalmia neonatorum, in medicine, gonorrhea infection of the eyes in newborn infants.

·disease transmission theory **9**:543a

ophthalmic artery, in human anatomy, the artery supplying blood to the eye and adjacent structures.

·structure and function in human eye **7**:94h

ophthalmic nerve, in human anatomy, branch of the trigeminal nerve supplying the eyesocket, the forehead skin, and part of the nasal cavity.

·anatomic relationships and branches **12**:1019a; illus. 1017

ophthalmology, the medical specialty that treats diseases and disorders of the eye. Board requirements, examinations for specialization and practice, and residencies vary from country to country.

·cryosurgical cataract removal **5**:320e
·visual tests and examination **7**:124c

Ophthalmosaurus, extinct genus of Jurassic and Cretaceous icthyosaurs of England.

·fossil reptiles and eras, illus. 11 **7**:571

ophthalmoscope, an instrument for inspecting the retina of the eye.

·eye examination techniques **7**:124e
·Helmholtz' invention and research **8**:752f

Ophüls, Max (b. May 6, 1902, Saarbrücken, Saarland—d. March 26, 1957, Hamburg, W. Ger.), motion-picture director whose mastery of fluid camera movement gave his films the lyrical flow that became a stylistic characteristic. He was one of the first truly international directors, sensitive to national differences and to the human qualities common to all his characters. Ophüls was an actor, stage director, and producer in Germany and Austria from 1921 to 1930. His first famous film was *Liebeli* (1932). A bittersweet love story set in Vienna, it exemplified the narrative excellence that characterized his subsequent films. In Italy he directed *La signora di tutti* (1934); for French audiences he made *La Tendre Ennemie* (1936), *Sarajevo* (1940), and a French version of *Liebeli;* releases in the United States between 1947 and 1949 included *The Exile* (1947), *Letter from an Unknown Woman* (1948), *Caught* (1949), and *The Reckless Moment* (1949).

Returning to France in 1950 he directed the stylishly witty *La Ronde* (1950) and *Le Plaisir* (1952), considered two of his finest pictures.

Between 1925 and 1941 Ophüls was also a writer and producer for German and French radio stations.

Opie, Amelia, *née* ALDERSON (b. Nov. 12, 1769, Norwich, Norfolk—d. Dec. 2, 1853, Norwich), long known for *Father and Daughter* (1801), a novel blending morality and pathos in relating the seduction of the heroine and her father's resultant insanity; the work influenced the development of the 19th-century popular novel. Mrs. Opie's life was less sombre and restricted than her works would suggest. She had many friends among the radical intellectuals who supported the French Revolution, free thought, and free love. In 1798 she married John Opie, a talented, self-taught painter, and continued to write.

Amelia Opie, engraving by an unknown artist
Radio Times Hulton Picture Library

She produced 13 works of prose and 5 of verse between 1790 and 1834. She later became torn between Quaker asceticism and love of society, in which she cut a lively figure.

Opie, Eugene L(indsay) (1873–1971), U.S. pathologist.

·discovery of cause of diabetes **11**:835d

Opie, John (b. May 1761, St. Agnes, Cornwall—d. April 9, 1807, London), portrait and historical painter popular in England during the late 18th century. He received art instruction from John Wolcot ("Peter Pindar") in Truro from about 1775; and in 1781 Wolcot successfully launched him in London as a "Cornish wonder," a self-taught genius. Opie attempted fashionable portrait painting but was most at ease with unsophisticated subjects, where his gifts for depicting rough textures in strong chiaroscuro could best be displayed, as in "The Peasant's Family" (1783–84; Tate Gallery, London) or the rugged portrait of "Lloyd Kenyon, 1st Baron Kenyon" (1789; Lord Kenyon Collection). The works of Rembrandt, Caravaggio, and Velázquez were strong formative elements in his art. In 1786 he was commissioned to paint seven illustrations for John Boydell's Shakespeare Gallery. His first exhibited historical work was the "Assassination of James I of Scotland" (1786), followed by "The Murder of Rizzio" (1787), which secured his election in

John Opie, self-portrait, 1785; in the National Portrait Gallery, London
By courtesy of the National Portrait Gallery, London

1787 as a member of the Royal Academy. He was made a professor of painting at the academy in 1805. Just before his death Opie delivered four lectures on painting to the academy students that were remarkable for their lucid exposition. They were published in 1809. Opie also wrote a life of Reynolds, in Wolcot's edition of Pilkington, and *An Enquiry into the Requisite Cultivation of the Arts of Design in England.*

Öpik, Ernst Julius (b. Oct. 23, 1893, Port Kunda, now in Estonian S.S.R.), astronomer best known for his studies of meteors and meteorites. In the early 20th century he devised the double-count method of tallying meteors, in which two observers work simultaneously. He also made pioneering studies of planetary atmospheres and interiors of double stars and of the Moon.

In 1916 Öpik joined the staff of the Tashkent Observatory (now in Uzbek S.S.R.), and from 1921 to 1944 he worked at the Astronomical Observatory in Tartu, Estonian S.S.R. The research he performed during the early 1920s elucidated the theory of the entry of high-speed bodies into the atmosphere and was fundamental to the understanding of ablation, the peeling back of meteor surfaces during vaporization. His findings were of prime importance in rocket and missile design for developing nose cones and heat shields that would withstand the heat and frictional forces encountered during re-entry. He also contributed to cometary studies and proposed that a reservoir of comets orbit the Sun, providing the source of those few comets that assume orbits sufficiently eccentric to bring them so close to the Sun that they are visible.

Öpik was a professor at the Baltic University in Germany (1945–48) before joining the staff of the Armagh Observatory in Northern Ireland, where he later became director. From 1956 he was visiting professor of astrophysics at the University of Maryland, College Park, dividing his time equally between Armagh and Maryland.

Opiliaceae, family of flowering plants of the order Santalales.
·characteristics and classification **16**:228g

Opilioacariformes, order of mites (subclass Acarina).
·characteristics and classification 1:22f; illus. 19

Opiliones (arthropod): *see* harvestman.

opinion sampling: *see* sampling, statistical.

Opis, lost city of Babylonia, in the southern part of modern Iraq, scene of the decisive defeat of Nabonidus, last king of Babylon, by Cyrus of Persia in 539 BC. The theory that Opis is to be identified with Akshak (*q.v.*) appears to be incorrect; neither is there any proof that Opis can be identified with Seleucia (Tall 'Umar). It was perhaps located on a canal that joined the Tigris River near Khafajah in the Baghdad area.
·Alexander the Great and army mutiny **1**:472a

opisthobranch, any marine gastropod of the approximately 2,000 species of the subclass Opisthobranchia. These gastropods, sometimes called sea slugs, either breathe through gills, which are located behind the heart, or through the body surface. The shell and mantle cavity are reduced or lacking. Larval asymmetry may give way to bilateral symmetry in the adult through a partial untwisting of the embryonic viscera (detorsion). Reproduction is hermaphroditic—*i.e.*, both male and female reproductive organs occur in one animal.

Major groups include nudibranchs (sea slugs), pteropods (sea butterflies), and sea hares (*qq.v.*).
·habits, anatomy, and classifications **7**:947h

Opisthocomus hoazin (bird): *see* hoatzin.

Opisthognathidae, family of jawfishes, order Perciformes.
·classification and general features **14**:55a

Opisthopora, order of oligochaete worms of the phylum Annelida.
·characteristics and classification **1**:936f; illus. 935

Opisthoproctidae, family of barrel-eye fish of the suborder Argentinoidei, order Salmoniformes.
·classification and general features **16**:191d; illus. 186

opisthorchiasis, infestation with liver flukes of the genus *Opisthorchis.*
·zoonoses, table 9 **5**:878

Opisthorchis (liver fluke): *see* fluke.

opisthosoma, the posterior portion of the body of an arthropod.
·arachnid body segmentation **1**:1061d

Opisthotropis (mountain water snake): *see* water snake.

Opitz (von Boberfeld), Martin (b. Dec. 23, 1597, Bunzlau, Silesia, now Bołeslawiec, Pol. —d. Aug. 20, 1639, Danzig), poet and literary theorist who introduced Renaissance poetic theories into Germany. He studied at Frankfurt an der Oder, Heidelberg, and Leiden, where he met Daniel Heinsius. He led a wandering life in the service of various territorial nobles. In 1625, as a reward for a requiem poem on the death of Charles Joseph of Austria, he was crowned laureate by the emperor Ferdinand II, who later ennobled him. In 1629 he was elected to the Fruchtbringende Gesellschaft, the most important of the literary societies that aimed to reform the German language. He went to Paris in 1630, where he made the acquaintance of Hugo Grotius, Dutch poet, jurist, and classical scholar. He lived from 1635 until his death at Danzig (Gdańsk), where Władysław IV of Poland made him his historiographer and secretary.

Opitz was the head of the so-called First Silesian school of poets and during his life was regarded as the greatest German poet. He was the "father of German poetry," at least in respect of its form. His *Aristarchus sive de Contemptu Linguae Teutonicae* (1617) defended his native tongue. His influential *Buch von der deutschen Poeterey*, written in 1624 and based on the work of Joseph Scaliger, Pierre Ronsard, and Daniel Heinsius, established rules for the "purity" of language, style, verse, and rhyme. It insisted upon word stress rather than syllable counting as the basis of German verse and recommended the alexandrine. The scholarly, stilted, and courtly style introduced by Opitz dominated German poetry until the middle of the 18th century. Opitz' poems follow his own rigorous rules. They are mostly didactic and descriptive—formal elaborations of carefully considered themes—containing little beauty and less feeling. The generation of poets who built upon his work far outshone him. His *Trostgedichte in Widerwärtigkeit des Krieges* (1633) praised Christian stoicism. He translated from Heinsius, Grotius, Seneca, and Sophocles; partly translated from the text by O. Rinuccini the libretto of *Dafne*, the first opera in German; introduced the political novel (John Barclay's *Argenis*) into Germany; and edited (1638) the German version of Sir Philip Sidney's *Arcadia* and the 11th-century *Annolied.* Opitz' *Opera Poetica* appeared in 1646.
·contribution and influence **18**:343f
·literary style and influence **10**:1158a

opium, narcotic drug obtained from the immature fruits of the opium poppy (*Papaver somniferum*; *see* poppy), family Papaveraceae, by collecting and drying the juice from slightly incised fruits. The white juice coagulates and turns brown after exposure to air, and some types of opium appear black. Raw opium is marketed as lumps, cakes, or bricks that may be powdered or further treated.

Opium poppy (*Papaver somniferum*)
J.E. Downward

The legitimate uses of opium are medical and include extraction of purified opium alkaloids (*e.g.*, morphine, codeine; *qq.v.*) and manufacture of alkaloid derivatives (*e.g.*, dihydromorphinone, dihydrocodeinone; *qq.v.*). Opium, either raw or purified as alkaloids and their derivatives (such as heroin; *q.v.*), is also used illicitly.

The active principles of opium reside in its alkaloids, the most important of which is morphine. Opium alkaloids are of two types, depending on chemical structure and action. Morphine, codeine, and thebaine, which represent one type, act upon the nervous system. They are analgesic, narcotic, and potentially addicting compounds. Papaverine, noscapine (formerly called narcotine), and most of the other opium alkaloids are not analgesic, narcotic, or addicting; instead they act to relax involuntary (smooth) muscles. For many years morphine has been the physician's mainstay for the relief of severe pain, although powerful synthetic substitutes are now available.

In the treatment of pain the opium alkaloids

are given orally, rectally, or by injection. For the symptomatic treatment of diarrhea, opium is used orally in the form of its alcoholic tincture, laudanum, and as the diluted and camphorated tincture of opium, paregoric. In ancient times, the drug was made into pills or added to beverages.

In the 1st century AD, Dioscorides, whose *De Materia Medica* was the leading text on pharmacology for centuries, described modern opium. Assyrian herb lists and medical texts, as translated from cuneiform writings, refer to both the opium poppy plant and opium; the latter also was known as "lion fat." The growth of poppies for their opium content spread slowly eastward from Greece and Mesopotamia. Apparently opium was unknown in either India or China in ancient times, and its widespread cultivation in these countries is a comparatively recent development. Knowledge of the opium poppy first reached China about the 7th century AD, but Japan probably did not begin cultivating it until the 15th century.

Opium smoking, a custom of the Far East, did not begin until after the discovery of America, where the practice of pipe smoking originated. It was reported as a problem in China about the middle of the 17th century. Between World Wars I and II the illicit cultivation of the poppy for opium became established in the mountains of western Mexico. Later, it was begun to some extent in Peru and Ecuador.

The cultivation of opium, both licit and illicit, is carried on chiefly in Asia. Two major opium-producing and opium-exporting countries in the world are India and Turkey. The medical needs of the world have exceeded 750 tons annually, in spite of the advent of synthetic drugs that often could be substituted for opium and its alkaloids.

The habitual use of opium produces physical and mental deterioration and shortens life. In acute poisoning through the overdosage of opium, respiratory depression, which otherwise may be fatal, can be treated with levallorphan or nalorphine (*qq.v.*).

·alkaloid early isolation **1**:595c
·cultic use in ancient Eastern Mediterranean **14**:201f
·drug uses, control, and addiction **5**:1048b
·effects on nervous system **12**:992d
·narcotics analgesic derivatives **12**:842a
·Papaverales derivatives and medical use **13**:963f
·poppy flower, fruit, and seed, illus., **14**:Poisonous Animals and Plants, Plate III

opium trade, in Chinese history, traffic that developed in the 18th and 19th centuries in which Western nations, mostly Britain, brought opium grown in India, and to a lesser extent in Turkey, to China and used the profits from its sale to purchase items such as tea and silk, which were desired in the West.

Opium was first introduced into China by Turkish and Arab traders in the late 7th or early 8th century. Used as a drug to relieve tension and pain, it existed in limited quantities until the 17th century, when the practice of smoking tobacco spread from America to China. Some people mixed opium and tobacco, and opium smoking soon became a fad all over China. Opium addiction increased, and opium importations grew rapidly. By 1729 it had become such a problem that the Yung-cheng emperor (1723–35) prohibited the sale and smoking of opium. This failed to hamper the trade, and in 1796 the Chia-ch'ing emperor outlawed opium importation and cultivation. In spite of this, however, the opium trade continued to flourish.

Early in the 18th century the Portuguese found that they could import opium from India and sell it in China at a considerable profit. By 1773 the British had discovered the trade, and in that year they became the leading suppliers on the Chinese market with the establishment by the British East India Company of a monopoly on opium cultivation in the Indian province of Bengal, where they developed a method of growing the product cheaply and abundantly. Other Western nations also joined in the trade, including the Americans, who brought in Indian as well as Turkish opium.

The East India Company did not carry the opium itself but, because of the Chinese ban, farmed it out to "country traders," private traders licensed by the company to bring goods from India to China. The country traders sold the opium to smugglers along the coast. The gold and silver the traders received from these sales were then turned over to the East India Company representative in the South China port of Canton in exchange for a bill of exchange payable in British money in London. In China the company used the gold and silver they thus received to purchase tea and silks, which could be sold in England.

The amount of opium imported into China increased from around 200 chests a year in 1729 to about 1,000 in 1767 and to around 10,000 a year between 1820 and 1830. By 1838 it had grown to some 40,000 chests, and the balance of payments for the first time began to run against China and in favour of Britain, which had previously had to export gold and silver to buy Chinese products.

Smuggling boats covered the coast to receive the opium shipments from the foreign vessels, and a whole network of opium distribution was formed throughout the country, often with official connivance. Meanwhile, levels of opium addiction grew so high that it began to affect the Imperial troops and official classes. Efforts of the Ch'ing dynasty (1644–1911) to enforce the opium restrictions resulted in the trading conflict between Britain and China known as the first Opium War (1839–42). This war did not legalize the trade, but it did halt Chinese efforts to stop it. In the second Opium War (1856–60) the trade was finally legalized, although a small import tax was now levied on opium. By that time opium imports had already grown to 50,000 to 60,000 chests a year, and they continued to increase rapidly for the next 30 years.

By 1906, however, the importance of opium in the China trade had decreased, and the Ch'ing government was able to begin a crackdown on importation and smoking. In 1907 China signed the "Ten Years' Agreement" with India, whereby China agreed to forbid native cultivation and consumption on the understanding that the export of Indian opium would decline in proportion and cease completely in ten years. The trade was thus almost completely stopped by 1917.

·British economic imperialism **4**:898a
·Indian decline in production **9**:411d
·Lin Tse-Hsü's blocking of British **10**:1015b

Opium Wars, two trading wars in the mid-19th century in which Western nations gained commercial privileges in China; the first Opium War (1839–42) was between China and Britain, the second Opium War (1856–60), also known as the "Arrow" War, or the Anglo-French War in China, was fought by Britain and France against China.

At the beginning of the 19th century, British traders began illegally importing opium into China. In 1839 the Chinese government attempted to put a stop to this opium trade and confiscated all opium warehoused at Canton by British merchants. The antagonism between the two sides increased a few days later when some drunken British sailors killed a Chinese villager and the British government, which did not trust the Chinese legal system, refused to turn the guilty men over to the Chinese courts.

Hostilities broke out, and the small British forces were quickly victorious. The Treaty of Nanking, signed Aug. 29, 1842, and the British Supplementary Treaty of the Bogue, signed Oct. 8, 1843, provided for payment of a large indemnity by China, cession of five ports for British trade and residence, and the right of British citizens to be tried by British courts. Other Western countries quickly demanded and were given similar privileges.

In 1856 the British, seeking to extend their trading rights in China, found an excuse to renew hostilities when some Chinese officials boarded the ship "Arrow" and lowered the British flag. The French joined the British in this war, using as their excuse the murder of a French missionary in the interior of China.

The allies began military operations in late 1857 and quickly forced the Chinese to sign the Treaty of Tientsin (1858), which provided residence in Peking for foreign envoys, the opening of several new ports to Western trade and residence, the right of foreign travel in the interior of China, and freedom of movement for Christian missionaries. In further negotiations in Shanghai later in the year, the importation of opium was finally legalized. The Chinese, however, refused to ratify the treaty, and the allies resumed hostilities, captured Peking, and burned the emperor's summer palace. In 1860 the Chinese signed the Peking Convention, in which they agreed to observe the Treaty of Tientsin.

·background and dynastic disintegration **4**:358c
·British penetration of China **4**:898a
·Canton's danger and salvation **3**:781h
·Chinese loss of Macau and Hong Kong **11**:221h
·control of opium to 20th century **5**:1051e
·Hupeh port openings **9**:55c
·Japanese apprehensive reaction **10**:77e
·Lin Tse-Hsü's provocation of British **10**:1015b

Opius concolor (insect): *see* braconid.

Oplegnathidae, family of fishes of the order Perciformes.

·classification and general features **14**:54d

Opler, Marvin K(aufmann) (1914–), U.S. anthropologist and sociologist.

·social evaluation of homosexuality **16**:604h

Opobo, formerly EGWANGA, fishing and oil-palm port, Uyo Province, South-Eastern State, southern Nigeria, in the eastern Niger Delta, near the mouth of the Imo (Opobo) River. It lies at a break in the mangrove swamps and rain forest and at the terminus of roads from Port Harcourt, Oron, and Ikot Ekpene. A traditional trading centre (yams, cassava, fish, palm produce, maize [corn], eddoes [cocoyams]) for the Ibibio people, it served in the 19th century as a collecting point for slaves. In 1870 Jubo Jubogha, a former Ibo slave and ruler of the Anna Pepple House of Bonny (28 mi [45 km] west-southwest), came to Egwanga and founded the Kingdom of Opobo, which he named for Opubu the Great, a Pepple king (reigned 1792–1830). Called Chief Jaja by Europeans, he destroyed the economic power of Bonny and made Opobo the master of the eastern delta oil-palm trade until he was deported in 1887 by the British, who established a trading post at Opobo Town, 4 mi southwest, across the Opobo River.

Although modern Opobo is known for boatbuilding, a sandbar partially blocks the entrance to its port from the Gulf of Guinea. The town has a Methodist-sponsored secondary school, a government hospital, and a maternity clinic. Pop. (1971 est.) 42,860.
4°35′ N, 7°34′ E

·map, Nigeria **13**:86

Opole, *województwo* (province), southwestern Poland, surrounded by the provinces of Wrocław on the west, Poznań on the north, Łódź on the northeast, and Katowice on the east. Czechoslovakia lies to the south. Its area is 3,689 sq mi (9,554 sq km). Physiographically, Opole ranges from sandy plains and forests in the northeast to the Sudety (Sudeten) foothills in the southwest. The Oder River crosses it southeast–northwest; other rivers are the Nysa Kłodzka and the Mała Panew. The economy is based on agricultural products, cementworks, chemical and textile production, lumber milling, and metallurgical works. One-third of the population is urban, concentrated around Opole city, the capital; other centres are Racibórz, Kędzierzyn, Nysa, and Brzeg. Pop. (1970 prelim.) 1,057,000.

Opole, German OPPELN, capital, Opole *województwo* (province), southwestern Poland, on the Oder River. It is an important river port and rail link between Wrocław and Górny Śląsk (Upper Silesia); its economy depends on cement industries and iron foundries.

Opole began as the home of the Slavic Opolanie tribe; the earliest mention of it was in the 9th century. In 1202 it became capital of the Opole principality, which included the entire Górny Śląsk region. The town passed to Bohemia (1327), the Habsburgs (16th century), and Prussia (1742); it returned to Poland in 1945. A regional museum and many notable historic buildings are located there. Pop. (1970 prelim.) 86,500.
50°41′ N, 17°55′ E
·map, Poland **14**:626

Opomyzidae, family of flies of the order Diptera.
·classification and features **5**:824g

Opon (Philippines): *see* Lapu-Lapu City.

Oporto (Portugal): *see* Porto.

opossum, any of about 66 species of New World mammals constituting the family Didelphidae of the superorder Marsupialia. For ordinal relatives in American tropics, *see* rat opossum; for Australasian marsupials of similar name (possum), *see* phalanger.

Common opossum (*Didelphis marsupialis*)
Robert J. Ellison—National Audubon Society

The best known and the only species occurring north of Mexico is the common opossum (*Didelphis marsupialis*). It ranges from lower eastern Canada and Puget Sound southward (except in western mountains and deserts) to Argentina; the only other member of that genus, Azara's opossum (*D. azarae*), is in South America. The common species may be 100 centimetres (40 inches) long. The pelage varies from grayish-white (northern regions) to nearly black (warm regions). It has a pointy white face, beady black eyes, round black ears, stout body, and naked prehensile tail, which is about half the total length. There are five sharp-clawed toes on each foot, except that the innermost rear toe is clawless and opposable and used for grasping branches. There are 50 teeth.

Largely arboreal, in woodlands near water, the common opossum eats almost anything. It usually dens in a hollow tree. If surprised on the ground, it may feign death ("play possum"). It is hunted for its meat and its fur (used as cheap trim).

An opossum may have as many as 25 young at a time (average 10), after only 12 to 16 days' gestation (average 12.5). The young are born blind, naked, and grublike—no larger than a honeybee, and weighing 2 grams (7/100 ounce). Using their clawed forelimbs, they struggle toward the mother's fur-lined pouch: those that reach the pouch seek out a nipple—there usually are 13 of them—and achieve a firm oral attachment as the nipple swells. After four or five weeks in the pouch the young spend an additional eight or nine weeks clinging to the mother's back. The notion that the opossum gives birth through its nose probably comes from the female's habit of putting her face into the pouch to clean it just before giving birth.

The water opossum, or yapok (*Chironectes minimus*, sometimes *panamensis*), found from Mexico to Argentina, is the only marsupial adapted to a semi-aquatic life: it has webbed hindtoes, dense oily fur, and a pouch opening that can be tightened to keep the young dry. This carnivore has a head and body length of 30 centimetres and a 38-centimetre naked tail. The dark upperparts are broadly striped.

The gray four-eyed opossum (*Philander opossum*) and the brown four-eyed, or rat-tailed, opossum (*Metachirus nudicaudatus*) have a pair of large whitish spots over the eyes. Both occur in Central and South America; they are rat sized, with big heads and long tails. The latter species is pouchless; this is the case (or nearly so) in all the remaining opossum species.

The thick-tailed opossum, or little water opossum (*Lutreolina crassicaudata*), of South America east of the Andes is found chiefly along watercourses but may enter cities. As long as 70 centimetres, including its 30-centimetre tail, it resembles a weasel and is fiercely carnivorous. Woolly opossums include the two species of *Glironia*, of the northern Andes, *Dromiciops australis*, of Chile, and the three species of *Caluromys*, from southern Mexico to Brazil.

The smallest didelphids are the shrewlike, small-eyed, rather short-tailed species of *Monodelphis*, of South America (one, *M. melanops*, in Panama); some are only 15 centimetres long, tail included. The most abundant didelphids are the 40 species of *Marmosa*, sometimes called mouse, or murine, opossums; distributed from northern Mexico to Argentina, they sometimes reach North America accidentally in bunches of bananas.
·attack and defense patterns **1**:296b
·classification and general features **5**:318d; illus. 312
·estuary growth and place in food chain **6**:974e
·eye adaptation for night vision **14**:354d; illus.
·fur origin and characteristics table **7**:814
·traits and behaviour **11**:538f; illus. 539

opossum shrimp, any member of the crustacean order Mysidacea. Most of the 450 known species live in the sea; a few live in brackish water; and fewer still live in freshwater. Most are 1 to 3 centimetres (about 0.4 to 1.2 inches) long. The name opossum shrimp derives from the females' brood pouch, in which young larvae spend several weeks.

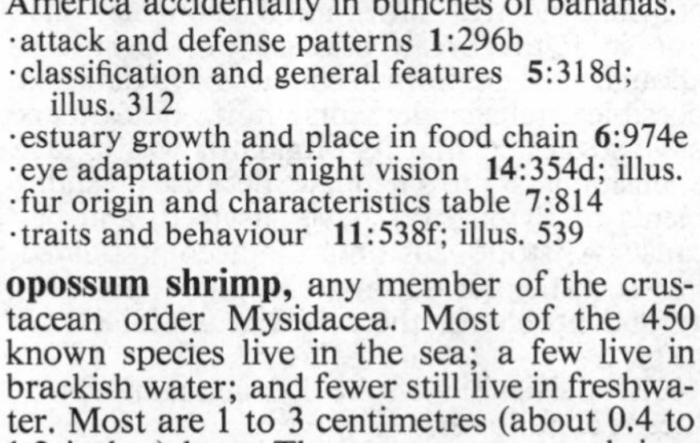

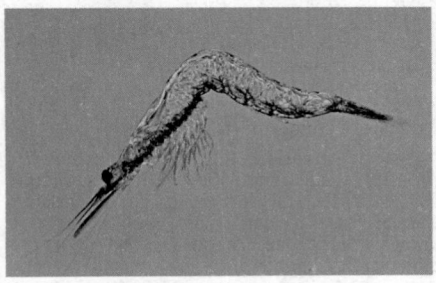

Opossum shrimp (Mysidacea)
William H. Amos—Helen Wohlberg, Inc.

Most species live in cold water, often at great depths. Some burrow into or crawl along the bottom; others creep among vegetation. Certain species swim in the open water, occasionally forming swarms consisting of great numbers of individuals. The freshwater species *Mysis relicta*, which is common in cold lakes of North America, Great Britain, and northern Europe, is an important food for lake trout in the Great Lakes. Some species, such as *Heteromysis cotti* of the Canary Islands, live in caves and either are blind or have poorly developed eyes.
·body plan, illus. 2 **5**:312

Opostegidae, family of moths of the order Lepidoptera.
·classification and general features **10**:828e

Opous (ancient Greek city): *see* Opus.

Oppel, Albert (b. Dec. 19, 1831, Hohenheim, Württemberg, now in West Germany—d. Dec. 22, 1865, Munich), geologist and paleontologist, professor at Munich from 1861, one of the most important early stratigraphers. In studying the Swabian Jura he discovered that paleontologic and lithologic zones need not be identical or even mutually dependent. His use of ammonite fossils in dating Jurassic rocks (136,000,000 to 190,000,000 years old) has been followed to the present.
·Jurassic strata and name derivations **10**:354d
·time scale development and zone divisions **7**:1068a
·zone concept introduction **17**:719a

Oppeln (Poland): *see* Opole.

Oppenheim, E(dward) Phillips (b. 1866, London—d. Feb. 3, 1946, St. Peter Port, Guernsey), internationally popular author for more than 50 years of novels and short stories dealing with international espionage and intrigue. Quitting school at 17 to help in his father's leather business, Oppenheim wrote in his spare time. His first novel, *Expiation* (1886), and subsequent thrillers caught the fancy of a wealthy New York businessman who bought out the leather business at the turn of the century and made Oppenheim a high-salaried director. He was thus freed to devote the major part of his time to writing. The novels, volumes of short stories, and plays that followed, totalling more than 150, were peopled with sophisticated heroes, adventurous spies, and dashing noblemen. Among his well-known works are *The Long Arm of Mannister* (1910), *The Moving Finger* (1911), and *The Great Impersonation* (1920).

Oppenheim, Lassa Francis Lawrence (b. March 30, 1858, Windecken, near Frankfurt am Main—d. Oct. 7, 1919, Cambridge, Cambridgeshire), jurist, law teacher in Germany, Switzerland, and (from 1895) England who was best known for his positivist approach to international law. Moving from Basel, Switz., to London, he joined the faculty of the newly organized London School of Economics and Political Science in 1895, and in 1908 he became Whewell professor of international law at Cambridge, succeeding John Westlake, whose papers he edited (published 1914). Oppenheim's most important book is *International Law: A Treatise* (2 vol., 1905–06; 1st vol., 7th ed., 1960; 2nd vol., 8th ed., 1960), which remained in print in the early 1970s. In this work he elaborated an international jurisprudence based on specific agreements and customs among nations rather than on theoretical prescriptions. Although he emphasized the supremacy of national laws and national sovereignty over international law, he came, during and after World War I, to believe in the necessity for the League of Nations.

Oppenheim, Moritz (1800?–1882), German painter.
·Heine portrait illus. **8**:744

Oppenheimer, Sir Ernest (b. May 22, 1880, Friedberg, now in West Germany—d. Nov. 25, 1957, Johannesburg, S. Af.), industrialist, financier, and one of the most successful leaders in the mining industry in South Africa and Rhodesia. He became a junior clerk at the age of 16 with Dunkelsbuhlers & Company, London diamond brokers. In 1902 he moved to Kimberley, S. Af., where he served as a Dunkelsbuhlers' representative. In 1917, with considerable backing from the financier J.P. Morgan, he formed the Anglo American Corporation of South Africa, Ltd., to exploit the east Witwatersrand goldfield.

Sir Ernest Oppenheimer
Popperfoto

Two years later he formed Consolidated Diamond Mines of South West Africa, Ltd. This diamond prospecting corporation was so successful that he gained control of the De Beers Consolidated Mines, which once dominated the world diamond market, and in 1930 established The Diamond Corporation, Ltd.

In 1929 Oppenheimer formed the Rhodesian Anglo American Corporation to exploit the rich copper deposits in Northern Rhodesia. His last project was the pioneering of new goldfields in the Orange Free State, S. Af.

Oppenheimer served as mayor of Kimberley from 1912 to 1915 and was a member of the Union of South Africa Parliament from 1924 to 1938. A philanthropist and an outstanding figure in South African life, he furthered Commonwealth studies at Oxford University. Oppenheimer was one of the richest men in the world, his success lying in his business acumen and his courage in undertaking mining enterprises of vast scope. He was knighted in 1921.

Oppenheimer, J. Robert **13**:602 (b. April 22, 1904, New York City—d. Feb. 18, 1967, Princeton, N.J.), theoretical physicist and science administrator, noted as director of the Los Alamos (N.M.) laboratory during development of the atomic bomb.

Abstract of text biography. Oppenheimer graduated from Harvard University in 1925 and began doing atomic research at the Cavendish Laboratory at the University of Cambridge. He received his doctorate at the University of Göttingen in 1927 and soon returned to the United States to teach physics at the University of California at Berkeley and the California Institute of Technology. In 1943 he was instructed to establish and administer a laboratory to carry out the Manhattan Project designed to harness nuclear energy for military purposes. It resulted in the first nuclear explosion on July 16, 1945, at Alamogordo, N.M. In 1947 Oppenheimer became head of the Institute for Advanced Study at Princeton University and from 1947 to 1952 served as chairman of the General Advisory Committee of the Atomic Energy Commission. He was presented the Enrico Fermi Award of the Atomic Energy Commission in 1963.

REFERENCES in other text articles:
·atomic bomb project **13**:325d
·collapsed star theory **15**:587e
·technological acceleration problems **18**:22h

Opperman, Daniel C., U.S. Pentecostal leader and one of the organizers of the Pentecostal conference in Hot Springs, Ark., in 1941.
·Assembly of God organization **14**:32e

Opperman, D.J. (1914–), South African author.
·South African literature development **10**:1232g

Oppian, name given to the authors (now generally regarded as two persons) of two (or three) didactic poems in Greek. Oppian of Cilicia of Corycus (or Anazarbus) in Cilicia, southern Anatolia, flourished in the reign of the Roman emperor Marcus Aurelius (AD 161–180), to whom he presented his poems. His poem on fishing (*Halieutica*) has little poetic merit. A poet of Apamea in Syria, possibly not named Oppian, wrote a poem on hunting (*Cynegetica*) of about 2,150 lines, dated AD 211 or later.

Oppland, *fylke* (county) in south central Norway; bisected by Gudbrandsdalen (Gudbrand's Valley), it has an area of 9,773 sq mi (25,312 sq km) and extends from Lakes Mjøsa and Randsfjorden northward to the high Jotunheimen, Dovrefjell, and Rondane mountains (*qq.v.*) Much of the *fylke* is made up of high plateaus; large areas of the mountainous north are virtually uninhabited. Population is strung out along the principal valleys, where farming (livestock, grains, potatoes, fruit [in the south]) is the most important occupation. Industry (timber and wood-products, metal-processing, glass) is centred at Lillehammer (the county seat) and Jøvik. Tourism is vital to the economy; scenic Gudbrandsdalen and the high northern peaks are major attractions. Pop. (1971 est.) 172,479.
·area and population table **13**:265
·map, Norway **13**:266

opportunity cost: *see* cost.

opposed-piston engine, an engine in which cylinders are placed opposite each other.
·gasoline engine design principles **7**:931f; illus.

opposites, doctrine of, in Pythagoreanism, doctrine that the world is composed of opposites (*e.g.*, wet–dry, hot–cold) and is generated by the imposition of limit upon the unlimited.
·Pythagorean concept of harmony **15**:322h *passim* to 325b

opposites, table of, in Pythagorean philosophy, a set of 10 pairs of contrary qualities. The earliest reference to the table is in Aristotle, who said that it was in use among some contemporary Pythagoreans. But Aristotle provided no real information about its function in Pythagorean practice or theory nor about its origin. Some scholars have detected possible archaic elements in it, but others have suggested that its originator was in fact Speusippus, Plato's nephew. Because no statements of Pythagoras have survived, and because Aristotle customarily accommodated Pre-Socratic philosophy to his own terminology and problems, the problem is difficult to resolve.

Aristotle's table of the Pythagorean opposites is as follows:

Limited	Unlimited
Odd	Even
Unity	Plurality
Right	Left
Male	Female
At Rest	In Motion
Straight	Curved
Light	Darkness
Good	Evil
Square	Oblong

Aristotle remarked that Alcmaeon of Croton, a medical writer, also had pairs of contraries as the first "principles" of things and also of most human things, but he did not know whether contemporary Pythagoreans influenced Alcmaeon in this regard or vice versa.

Aristotle associated moral prestige with the left-hand column, because the "good" things appear in that column. The table had some currency among Aristotle's contemporaries, perhaps in the Academy (Plato's school in Athens), but his references are made merely in the interest of supporting certain views of his own.

Aristotle's formal table has 10 members, because the Pythagoreans considered 10 the "perfect" number. But the pairs varied in different authors. Possibly no list or set number of opposites became canonical among the Pythagoreans.

opposition. The idea of opposition is treated under the following titles: Cartesianism; dualism, religious; Idealism; Kantianism; logic, formal; and Platonism and Neoplatonism. The titles of these articles indicate the fields of scholarship or thought in which the idea of opposition plays an important role.

opposition, in astronomy, occurs when two celestial bodies appear in opposite directions in the sky. The Moon, when full, is said to be in opposition to the Sun; the Earth is then approximately between them. A superior planet (one with an orbit farther from the Sun than Earth's) is in opposition when Earth passes between it and the Sun. The opposition of a planet is a good time to observe it, because the planet is then at its nearest point to the Earth and in its full phase. The planets Venus and Mercury, whose orbits are smaller than Earth's, can never be in opposition to the Sun.
·conditions for Martian observation **11**:519f

opposition, square of, in traditional logic, a diagram exhibiting four forms of a categorical proposition (*q.v.*), or statement, with the same subject and predicate, together with their pairwise relationships:

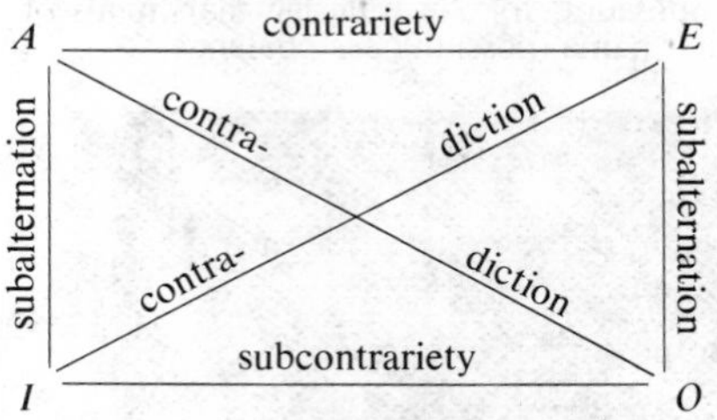

in which *A*, *E*, *I*, and *O* are of the forms "Every *S* is *P*," "No *S* is *P*," "Some *S* are *P*," and "Some *S* are not *P*." As shown on the square, "Every swan is white" is the contrary of "No swan is white" and the contradictory of "Some swans are not white." Conclusions drawn from one of these forms to another (as in subalternation) are said to be obtained by immediate inference. *Major ref.* **17**:891c

Oppressed Nationalities, Congress of (April 8–10, 1918), meeting at Rome of representatives of minority nationality groups, mainly from the Habsburg empire; the delegates produced an unofficial document, known as the Pact of Rome, that claimed the right of self-determination for subject peoples and specifically approved the union of Serbs, Croats, and Slovenes in a single, independent state.
·Austrian democratic liberation movement **2**:475e
·South Slav's cooperation **2**:632f

oprichnina, private court or household created by Tsar Ivan IV the Terrible (1565) that administered those Russian lands (also known as *oprichnina*) that had been separated from the rest of Muscovy and placed under the Tsar's direct control; the term also refers generally to the economic and administrative policy that divided the Russian lands into two parts and established the new court.

The *oprichnina* land area was located in northern and central Muscovy and was created by the forcible removal of boyars (upper nobility) from their estates; the boyars were either executed or relocated on *zemshchina* territory (*i.e.*, the remainder of the land), which continued to be ruled by the traditional boyar council.

The term *oprichnina* also refers to this reign of terror; which was conducted by the *oprichniki*, members of the Tsar's new court, who

were primarily drawn from the lower gentry. The terror culminated with the proscription of the entire population of Novgorod and the sack of that northern city, which opposed Muscovite dominance (1570). The policy reduced the boyars' political power, disrupted the Russian economy, and contributed to the centralization of the Muscovite state. After 1572, when the *oprichniki* were disbanded, the term *dvor* (court) replaced *oprichnina*.
·formation and function under Ivan the Terrible **9**:1180d
·origin, function, and pernicious nature **16**:46a *passim* to 47b

Ops, in Roman religion, an obscure goddess (originally perhaps of the earth's fertility) with an ancient shrine in the Regia, the office of the *pontifex maximus*, or chief priest, which only he and the Vestal Virgins might enter. She was early equated with the Greek goddess Rhea, wife of Saturn, and like her was later identified with Cybele. She also had connections with the rustic god Consus, as her title, Consiva, and the dating of her festivals demonstrate.

Optic, Oliver: *see* Adams, William Taylor.

optical activity, the ability of a substance to rotate the plane of polarization of a beam of light that is passed through it. (In plane-polarized light, the vibrations of the electric field are confined to a single plane.) The intensity of optical activity is expressed in terms of a quantity, called specific rotation, defined by an equation that relates the angle through which the plane is rotated, the length of the light path through the sample, and the density of the sample (or its concentration if it is present as a solution). Because the specific rotation depends upon the temperature and upon the wavelength of the light, these quantities also must be specified. The rotation is assigned a positive value if it is clockwise with respect to an observer facing the light source, negative if counterclockwise. A substance with a positive specific rotation is described as dextrorotatory and denoted by the prefix *d* or (+); one with a negative specific rotation is levorotatory, designated by the prefix *l* or (−).

Optical activity was first observed in quartz crystals in 1811 by a French physicist, François Arago; another French physicist, Jean-Baptiste Biot, found in 1815 that liquid solutions of tartaric acid or of sugar are optically active, as are liquid or vaporous turpentine. Louis Pasteur was the first to recognize that optical activity arises from the dissymmetric arrangement of atoms in the crystalline structures or in individual molecules of certain compounds.
·alkaloid synthesis reactions **1**:601d
·amino acid isomeric properties **15**:82h
·carbohydrate optical properties **3**:825b
·light polarization properties **10**:933b
·molecular structure and stereoisomerism **12**:313d
·protein structure analysis approach **15**:88f

optical antipode (chemistry): *see* enantiomorph.

Optical art: *see* Op art.

optical brightener, also called FLUORESCENT WHITENING AGENT, organic compound that can absorb electromagnetic waves shorter than those of visible light and emit waves in the visible range. Such compounds absorb ultraviolet from daylight and emit visible blue, which acting with yellow on a fabric surface will yield white. They are widely used in household laundry detergents. *Major ref.* **16**:916f

optical crystallography, branch of crystallography that deals with the optical properties of crystals. It is of considerable interest theoretically and has the greatest practical importance. The science of petrography is largely based on the study of the appearance of thin transparent sections of rocks in a microscope fitted with two polarizing calcite prisms; in the absence of external crystalline form, as with the minerals in a rock, a mineral often may be readily identified by the determination of some of its optical properties.

According to their action on transmitted plane-polarized light, all crystals may be assigned to one or another of the five groups enumerated below, which correspond to the six systems of crystallization (in the second group two systems are included together). The several symmetry classes of each system are optically the same, except in rare cases:

1. Optically isotropic crystals (isometric system), which exhibit only one index of refraction for light of each colour
2. Optically uniaxial crystals (tetragonal and hexagonal systems), which exhibit double refraction and yield two refractive indices for light of each colour, one parallel to the optical axis and one perpendicular to the optical axis
3. Optically biaxial crystals (all of which exhibit three principal refractive indices, one along each of the mutually perpendicular optical axes) in which the three optical axes correspond to the three crystallographic axes (orthorhombic system)
4. Optically biaxial crystals in which only one of the three optical axes corresponds to a crystallographic axis (monoclinic system)
5. Optically biaxial crystals in which there is no fixed relation between the optical and crystallographic axes (triclinic system)

·principles and techniques **5**:343h

optical engineering **13**:603, branch of technology concerned with design, construction, and testing of equipment originally relating to vision and the formation of images and now broadened to encompass many other aspects of the transmission, detection, recording, and measurement of light and other electromagnetic radiations.

The text article covers the scope and development of optical engineering, design problems in optical engineering, and the manufacture and testing of optical devices.

REFERENCES in other text articles:
·colour scanner separation process **14**:303a
·communications systems design **18**:96f
·glass characteristics and homogeneity **8**:211a
·glassmaking history **8**:200c
·industrial monitoring instrumentation **9**:638a
·Leeuwenhoek's microscopy methods **10**:773c
·lighthouse systems design **10**:954a
·lighting device development **10**:960d
·microscope theory, types, and construction **12**:127f
·military detection technology **19**:599c
·photocathode image conversion process **14**:300b
·photographic technology **14**:328a
·telescopes and auxiliary devices **18**:97f
·television technology **18**:105c

RELATED ENTRIES in the *Ready Reference and Index:*
binoculars; contact lenses; eyeglasses; Fresnel lens; prism; stereoscope

optical fibre bundle: *see* fibre optics.

optical illusions: *see* illusions and hallucinations.

optical isomerism (chemistry): *see* isomerism, optical.

optical mineralogy: *see* mineralogy; optical crystallography.

optical model, in physics, description of atomic nuclei as similar to cloudy crystal balls in that, when struck by a beam of particles, they partially absorb the beam, partially scatter it, and partially transmit it in a way analogous to the behaviour of light. The optical nuclear model has proved very successful in explaining nuclear reactions in which the incident (striking) particles have energies of about 10^6 to 10^9 electron volts.

optical phenomena, atmospheric: *see* airglow; Aurora Australis; Aurora Borealis; auroras; Cellini's halo; corona, atmospheric; fogbow; halo; mirage; parhelion; rainbow.

optical pumping, in physics, the use of light energy to raise the atoms of a system from one energy level to another. A system may consist of atoms of which the individual magnetic fields are randomly oriented. When optically pumped, the atoms will undergo a realignment of individual magnetic fields with respect to the direction of the light beam; that is, there will be a rearrangement of magnetic energy levels; and, in some cases, the bulk of the atoms will be oriented to generate a magnetic field throughout the system.

More familiarly, optical pumping takes place in laser action, in which the energy of electrons is raised by letting them absorb photons of light. The electrons remain at the higher energy level until they are triggered to release their stored energy in the form of a laser beam, in which the light waves all have the same wavelength and vibrate in unison.
·atomic spectrum development **2**:340a
·laser light production **10**:686f

optical sound recording, use of an optical system for registering sound on photographic film; it is the technique most widely used in making the sound track (*q.v.*) of motion pictures.
·De Forest's sound-on-film development **5**:553f
·modern printing techniques **12**:549f
·motion picture beginnings **12**:541h
·sound recording systems **17**:57e

optic atrophy, degeneration of the optic (second cranial) nerve, which carries visual data from the retina of the eye to a relay station in the centre of the brain (the lateral geniculate body) for transmission to a cortical area at the back of the brain. The atrophy may be a hereditary defect (called Leber's disease) affecting males, primarily between the ages of 15 and 25 years, and causing loss of central vision. There is sometimes some recovery of vision in Leber's disease, but the recovery is rarely complete. Optic atrophy may also be caused by physical injury, as from a blow to the head; by glaucoma (*q.v.*); by a tumour that presses on the nerve; by poisons such as wood alcohol, quinine, or arsenic; or by disease of the retina. *Major ref.* **7**:121e

optic axis, Latin AXIS OPTICUS, in vertebrates, an imaginary line drawn from the centre of the visual field to the central point of the eye.
·human visual physiology **7**:98d
·vertebrate optical properties **14**:354h; illus.

optic cup, in embryology, the double-walled cup formed by invagination of the optic vesicle of the embryo's brain. The cup develops into the retina and the iris, but not the lens, of the eye.
·animal eye development **5**:634c
·eye origins and development in man **6**:751c

optic foramen, opening in the sphenoid bone through which the optic nerve and ophthalmic artery pass; the bone at this point forms part of the eye socket.
·anterior cranial fossa structure **16**:814f
·structure and function **7**:91g

Opticks (1704), treatise in which Sir Isaac Newton explained optical phenomena in terms of corpuscles that give rise to waves in the course of their travel.
·light theories and experimental method **14**:388b *passim* to 390e
·Newton's life and writings **13**:18a
·theory of colour's physical origin **4**:913f

optic nerve, in human anatomy, the second cranial nerve, serving the sense of sight. *Major ref.* **12**:1018; illus. 1017
·cranial nerve origins and development **6**:751a
·disease symptoms and causes **12**:1048d
·eye anatomy and physiology **7**:95g; illus. 93
·eye diseases **7**:121d
·foramen of anterior cranial fossa **16**:814f
·morphology and physiological responses **14**:365e
·tests for functional disorders **12**:1042b

optic neuritis, inflammation of the optic (second cranial) nerve, the nerve that carries visual data from the retina of the eye to a relay station in the centre of the brain for transmission to a cortical area at the back of the brain. Most instances of optic neuritis occur as a result of multiple sclerosis (*q.v.*), a disease of the brain and spinal cord in which hard patches in the nerve-fibre sheaths interfere with the transmission of impulses. Other causes include inflammation of the brain and spinal cord as a result of such infections as smallpox or measles and poisoning by such substances as wood alcohol or lead. Optic neuritis may be centred in the optic disk, the point of entrance of the nerve and of blood vessels into the eyeball (this type is called papillitis), or it may be in the nerve shaft behind the eyeball (retrobulbar, or axial, neuritis). The effect may be in the nerve fibres or only in the sheath enveloping the nerve, and it may extend to adjacent areas of the retina. The chief effects of the inflammation are a blind spot (a scotoma, usually in the centre of the visual field), pain in the eyeball, and headache on the affected side. The optic nerve usually recovers from the inflammation, but there may be some residual degeneration of the nerve fibres.

·visual effects of nerve inflammation **7**:121d

optic papilla, also PAPILLA NERVI OPTICI, or DISCUS NERVI OPTICI, in anatomy, a round white disk at the back of the eyeball through which the optic nerve and retinal blood vessels pass.

·human eye anatomy **7**:96f

optic recess, or RECESSUS OPTICUS, in anatomy, a depression in the floor of the third ventricle of the brain.

·human nervous system, illus. 3 and 5 **12**:999

optics, geometrical, that branch of optics characterized by the use of geometrical methods to determine the formation of images. The wave–particle duality of light is ignored so that diffraction, polarization, and interference are not accounted for. Light is considered to travel along a straight line (rectilinear propagation) in a homogeneous substance, its direction being diverted only by reflection or refraction when it encounters another substance. Most optical problems concerned with mirrors, prisms, and lenses can be solved by using the principles of geometrical optics.

The nature and properties of light itself are the province of physical optics; the mechanisms of vision and photoreception are treated in physiological optics; and the analogies between optical systems and electronic circuitry are the concern of information theory. *Major ref.* **13**:608f

·optical study divisions **15**:402b
·physics principles and methods **14**:425e

optics, principles of 13:608, the rules that govern the image-forming properties of lenses, mirrors, and other devices that make use of light.

TEXT ARTICLE covers:
Historical background of geometrical optics **13**:608f
Reflection and refraction 609g
Ray-tracing methods 610h
Paraxial, or first-order, imagery 611f
Optical systems 613a
Lens aberrations 614c
Image brightness 615f
General considerations of optics and information theory 616f
Image formation 617d
Partially coherent light 618b
Optical processing 619a
Holography 620c
Nonlinear optics 621f

REFERENCES in other text articles:
·astronomical spectroscope design **2**:235h
·atomic base of colour and luminescence **2**:342c
·glass properties and light transmission **8**:198d
·Hamilton's discoveries and influence **8**:588e
·history after Newton **14**:389d
·hologram image recording **8**:1010c
·human eye anatomy and function **7**:100b
·Kepler's research and writings **10**:431g
·lens design and optical engineering **13**:603g; illus. 604
·lighting device development role **10**:960d
·light properties and theory **10**:928e
·mathematical concepts and formulations **14**:408c
·microscope and theory of magnification **12**:128h
·motion-picture lens systems **12**:544d
·Newton's theory of colour **13**:17h
·optical study divisions **15**:402b
·photographic image considerations **14**:307d
·photographic lens design **14**:333d
·photoreceptive mechanisms in animals **14**:354b
·physics principles and methods **14**:425e
·polarization of starlight **9**:792h
·scientific revolution of 17th century **14**:387d
·spectra dispersion methods **17**:459g
·telescope classifications and principles **18**:97a
·wave theory development **11**:797g

RELATED ENTRIES in the *Ready Reference and Index: for*
basic concepts: see aberration; aperture, relative; axis, optical; diopter; image, optical; lens; magnification; mirror; optics, geometrical; pupil
other related entries: fibre optics; moiré pattern; stereoscopy

optic tract, or TRACTUS OPTICUS, in anatomy, the portion of each optic nerve between the chiasma and the diencephalon proper.

·anatomic interrelationships **12**:1018e; illus. 998

optic vesicle, or VESICULA OPHTHALMICA, an outpouching of each lateral wall of the forebrain of a vertebrate embryo from which the nervous structures of the eye develop.

·embryonic origin and later developments **5**:633f; illus. 631

Optimates and Populares, two principal political groups during the later Roman Republic from about 150 to 27 BC. The members of both groups were of the wealthier classes. The Optimates were the conservative majority in the Senate, representing a few influential families. They generally controlled elections for public offices and state finances. Their opponents, the Populares, were for the most part businessmen of more recent wealth who sought greater political and social status and posed as champions of the rights of the poor in their search for political allies.

·Cicero's political alignment and results **4**:607e
·Pompey's opposition and alliance imposition **14**:793h

optimization, mathematical theory of 13:621, concerns the mathematical description of a system or a problem in such a way that the application of rigorous procedures to this representation results in the best performance of the system or in the best solution of the problem within the framework of the relevant limitations and variables.

TEXT ARTICLE covers:
The theory of games **13**:622c
Linear and nonlinear programming 688c
Cybernetics 632f
Control theory 634f

REFERENCES in other text articles:
·automata theory **2**:500a
·combinatorics theory and method **4**:948c
·maximizing in economic measurement **11**:745b
·von Neumann's game theory **12**:1067d

RELATED ENTRIES in the *Ready Reference and Index: for*
cybernetics: see algorithm; cybernetics; encoding of information; probabilistic automata
game theory: expectation, mathematical; game theory; inference, statistical; matrix
linear and nonlinear programming: convexity; decision theory; programming, mathematical

optimum programming (mathematics): *see* programming, mathematical.

option (stock): *see* stock option.

optokinetic nystagmus, regular to-and-fro movements of the eyes directed at a moving object.

·eye movement comparisons **7**:99b
·movement perception and visual stability **14**:45c

optometry, a profession concerned with the care of the eyes. Optometrists examine the eyes and related structures to determine the presence of vision problems, eye disease, or other abnormalities and prescribe and adapt lenses or other optical aids; they may use visual training to preserve or restore maximum efficiency of vision.

Optype, in "cold" typesetting, process that uses optical distortion to justify lines or to magnify, reduce, or set a line in italics.

·optical justification method **14**:1062e

Opuntia, a cactus genus, family Cactaceae, native to the New World, featuring glochids —small bristles with backward facing barbs —found in no other genus. Stems of chollas (*see* cholla) are composed of series of cylindroid joints; those of prickly pears (*see* prickly pear) are composed of flat joints, stem segments arising one from the end of another.

Prickly pear (*Opuntia vulgaris*)
John H. Gerard

Opuntia grows from the Peace River in western Canada almost to the tip of South America. In the Northern Hemisphere, it is the most northern ranging cactus. The most cold-hardy forms are small, some with joints only 2½ to 5 centimetres (1 to 2 inches) long. In contrast, *O. megacantha*, the commonly cultivated prickly pear of Mexico, is treelike, reaching 5 meters (about 16 feet) with a woody trunk and joints 40 to 60 centimetres long or more.

·features, distribution, and life cycle **3**:573b

Opus, also spelled OPOUS, in ancient Greece, the chief city of the Locri Opunti. Its site may have been at modern Atalándi or at Kiparíssi. Homer in his *Iliad* mentioned Opus, and Pindar devoted his ninth Olympian ode mainly to its glory and traditions. By the 5th century BC, Opus gave its name to some of the eastern Locrians. Locri Opunti fought with the Greeks at Thermopylae but surrendered and joined the Persians; later they supported Sparta during the Peloponnesian War. Opus went over to the Romans in 198 BC.

opus Alexandrinum, a type of decorative pavement mosaic work widely used in Byzantium in the 9th century in which tiny, geometrically shaped pieces of coloured stone and glass paste were arranged in intricate geometric patterns dotted with large disks of semiprecious stones. The technique was first introduced to southern Italy in 1071 at Monte Cassino. In the 12th century several variations of *opus Alexandrinum* evolved at local centres in Italy, including the well-known Cosmati work (*q.v.*) of Rome.

opus anglicanum, Latin term used internationally for "English work"—that is, embroi-

Opus anglicanum cope, English, 14th century; in the Victoria and Albert Museum, London

By courtesy of the Textile Department, the Victoria and Albert Museum, London

dery (*q.v.*) done in England between *c.* 1250 and *c.* 1350 and of a standard unsurpassed anywhere.

The technical skill shown by English workers in handling gold—*i.e.*, silver gilt thread—is unequalled. Gold is used in large expanses as background for figures that are embroidered in coloured silks. Another characteristic of English work is the general vivacity of expression and pose in the figure modelling of features; the use of spiral stitchery, for example, to suggest rotund cheeks and black, popping eyes. Minutely observed birds and animals, clearly based on contemporary animal drawings, figured largely in the decorative schemes. Opus anglicanum was famous throughout Europe, and liturgical vestments in this type of embroidery were given and sold to churches abroad, where they were much prized; several popes commissioned such vestments. Opus anglicanum has consequently survived all over Europe wherever historic vestments are treasured; there are also examples in the U.S. in the Metropolitan Museum of Art, New York City. In England the largest collection is in the Victoria and Albert Museum, London, which possesses, among other examples, several famous copes, including the Syon cope (late 13th century) and the Butler-Bowden cope (early 14th century).

Opuscula sacra, English SACRED WORKS, 6th-century theological work by the Roman scholar Boethius.
·Boethius use of logic **16**:353f

Opuscules mathématiques, English WORKS ON MATHEMATICS, (1761–80), multi-volume work by Jean Le Rond d'Alembert.
·d'Alembert's mathematical principles **1**:464f

Opus Dei (Latin: God's Work), Roman Catholic international organization of chiefly lay men and women whose members seek personal Christian perfection and strive to conform to and promote Christian ideals in their lives and works. There are separate organizations for men and women under a president general, who resides in Rome. Priests comprise only a small percentage of the membership, which is active in some 80 countries.

Opus Dei was founded in 1928 (women's branch in 1930) by Josémaría Escrivá de Balaguer (died 1975), a priest with a background in the law, and was fully approved by the Holy See in 1950. During the 1950s it developed into what many regard as an elitist group, although it claims members from all walks of life. There are three categories of members (in both the men's and women's organizations), Numeraries, Associates (both unmarried), and Supernumeraries (who may be married). Most Numeraries are persons with high academic degrees or social position, and they must be prepared to devote a large part of their time to the organization. Members attend regular meetings and spend five consecutive days each year in religious retreat. "Cooperators," who are not members, help in the organization's activities.

Though Opus Dei imposes no political ideology, members of the organization became a political force in Spain following Francisco Franco's decision in 1956 to pursue a program of economic development. Opus Dei counted many highly educated men of ability among its members, and it was to them, the so-called technocrats, that Franco turned for help. Two economic ministries were entrusted to members of Opus Dei, and other members have held ministerial posts and other positions in the government. Members are also active in banking and other commercial enterprises.

The organization's many charitable and educational activities include operation of vocational, trade, home arts, and agricultural centres in various parts of the world, as well as high schools, residence halls for university students, and schools of business administration. Opus Dei founded (1952) the University of Navarre, which has come to be regarded by many as the best university in Spain, and it operates institutions of higher learning in Kenya, Japan, and Mexico.
·influence and goals **17**:442e

opus incertum, in ancient Roman buildings, type of facing used on concrete walls.
·Roman wall construction techniques **19**:302a

opus interassile, metalwork technique developed in Rome and widely used during the 3rd century AD, especially appropriate for making arabesques and other nonrepresentational ornamental designs. Probably of Syrian origin, the technique consists of piercing holes in the metal to create an openwork design suggesting lacework. *Opus interassile* was often used for large wheels placed next to the clasps of loop-in-loop chains. The Roman *opus interassile* technique survived in certain Byzantine and early Christian designs, such as crescent-shaped earrings.
·Roman jewelry-making development **10**:171b

Roman *opus interassile* bracelet, 4th century AD; in the Staatliche Museen Preussischer Kulturbesitz, Berlin

By courtesy of the Staatliche Museen, Preussischer Kulturbesitz Antikenabteilung, Berlin

opus mixtum, in ancient Roman building, type of facing used on concrete walls.
·Roman wall construction techniques **19**:302b

Opus Oxoniense, also called ORDINATIO, work by John Duns Scotus.
·Lombard Scholasticism distorted **16**:355e

opus quadratum, in ancient Roman building, type of facing used on concrete walls.
·Roman wall construction techniques **19**:302a

opus reticulatum, in ancient Roman building, type of facing used on concrete walls.
·Roman wall construction techniques **19**:302a

opus sectile, type of mosaic work in which figural patterns are composed of pieces of stone or, sometimes, shell or mother-of-pearl cut in shapes to fit the component parts of the design, thereby differing in approach from the commoner type of mosaic in which each shape in the design is composed of many small cubes (tesserae) of stone or glass. Although portable stone mosaic works of similar technique were produced in the Near East as early as 3000 BC, the term *opus sectile* properly refers to an art that began in the Hellenistic world, perhaps first in Italy, and continued as a European decorative tradition. *Opus sectile* first appeared in Rome in Republican times (before the 2nd century BC) as pavement in simple geometrical and floral designs. From the 1st century AD there was also a regular production of small pictures of the *opus sectile* type.

Tiger attacking a calf, detail of an *opus sectile* wall from the Basilica of Junius Bassus, Rome, 4th century AD; in the Capitoline Museum, Rome

SCALA, New York

Both traditions continued as important pavement- and wall-decorating arts throughout the Roman era. A fine example of pictorial *opus sectile* from the late antique period is a picture composed of coloured marbles of a tiger attacking a calf, from a wall in the Basilica of Junius Bassus, Rome (4th century; Capitoline Museum, Rome). Early Christian churches in Rome and Ravenna were decorated with both types of *opus sectile*. In medieval Europe the ornamental *opus sectile* of antiquity evolved into more specialized arts, notably the intricate and severely geometrical Byzantine *opus Alexandrinum* and its descendants, Roman Cosmati work and other similar Italian arts. Pictorial *opus sectile* gained great sophistication in the Renaissance with monumental compositions of marble inlay in Italian churches and reached its climax with the Florentine *commesso* (*q.v.*) work of the 17th century, in which shaped pieces of highly coloured stone were joined together to form pictures that rival painting in their realism. Geometrical *opus sectile* continued to be the major form of floor decoration in Italian churches throughout the Middle Ages and Renaissance.

opus signinum, type of simple, unpatterned or roughly patterned pavement mosaic that was commonly used in Roman times. It was composed of river gravel, small pieces of stone, or terra-cotta fragments cemented in lime or clay.

Opus signinum was the prevalent form of pavement in Roman houses from the 1st century BC to about the 2nd century AD, when it was rapidly superseded in main rooms by patterned pavement mosaics made up of small shaped pieces of stone, ceramic, or glass, or tesserae.

opus tessellatum, mosaic technique involving the use of tesserae (*q.v.*) of uniform size applied to a ground to form pictures and ornamental designs. *Opus tessellatum* was the most commonly used technique in the production of Hellenistic, Roman, early Christian, and Byzantine mosaics. Evolving from the supplementary use of stone tesserae to achieve colour intensity in earlier pebble mosaics, *opus tessellatum* came to be used for entire mosaic floors in most areas of the eastern Mediterranean by at least the beginning of the 2nd century BC. The earliest mosaics in *opus tessellatum* were composed of stone and marble tesserae, but, in the course of the 2nd century, tesserae of coloured glass were introduced for special colour effects. In the Hellenistic period (3rd to 1st centuries BC) in cities in Greece, Africa, Sicily, and Italy, pictorial mosaics of great virtuosity were produced in *opus tessellatum*; more commonly, however, *opus tessellatum* was reserved for decorative borders surrounding *emblēmata*, or central figural panels executed in *opus vermiculatum*, a finer mosaic work using much smaller tesserae (*see* emblēma; opus vermiculatum). In the 1st century BC, with the rise of the Roman Empire, Italy became the centre of mosaic

Mythological figure, possibly Dionysos, riding a panther, a Hellenistic *opus tessellatum emblēma* from the House of Masks on Delos, Greece, 2nd century BC

Dimitri Papadimos

production; there and in the rest of the empire *opus tessellatum* continued to be used in a mainly secondary, decorative role whenever *opus vermiculatum* could be afforded. Beginning with the 1st century AD, however, figural *opus tessellatum* was increasingly used to cover whole floors, and by the early Christian period it had become the dominant technique. With the widespread use of monumental wall mosaics that began with that era, *opus tessellatum* entirely replaced *opus vermiculatum*, being much better suited, with its large tesserae and rougher visual effect, to viewing at a distance. Glass tesserae were used almost exclusively for these wall mosaics, and glass *opus tessellatum* remained the common mosaic technique throughout the Middle Ages.

Opus testaceum, most common wall construction during the ancient Roman Empire.
·Roman wall construction techniques **19**:302b

opus vermiculatum, a type of mosaic work frequently used in Hellenistic and Roman times, in which part or all of a figural mosaic is made up of very small, closely set tesserae (cubes of stone or glass) that permit fine gradations of colour and an exact following of figure contours and outlines. The name *vermiculatum* ("wormlike") refers to the undulating rows of tesserae that characterize this work. *Opus vermiculatum* was generally used for *emblēmata*, or central figural panels, which were surrounded by geometrical or floral designs in *opus tessellatum*, a coarser mosaic technique with larger tesserae; occasionally *opus vermiculatum* was used only for faces

Tragic and comic masks, Roman *opus vermiculatum emblēma* found on the Aventine, Rome, 3rd century AD; in the Capitoline Museum, Rome

SCALA, New York

and other details in an *opus tessellatum* mosaic (*see* opus tessellatum). The earliest known example of *opus vermiculatum*, *c.* 200 BC, is an emblēma showing a personification of the city of Alexandria (Greco-Roman Museum, Alexandria). By the 1st century BC, Romans had adopted the technique or at least imported Greek artists to work in it; a number of fine *opus vermiculatum* pieces from this period have been found at Pompeii, including a magnificent large *emblēma* with many figures, usually identified as a scene of the Battle of Issus between Alexander the Great and the Persian king Darius III (Museo Nazionale, Naples). This work probably copies a famous Greek painting from the 4th century BC; with its thousands of chromatically blended tesserae and its complete subordination of the natural properties of the stone and glass medium to plastic pictorial effect, it well illustrates the primary objective of *opus vermiculatum:* to paint in stone.

Although its use decreased steadily after the 1st century AD, *opus vermiculatum* continued to be the major technique for finer pictorial mosaics in the Roman world until the 4th century. Thereafter the style of floor mosaics changed to a more impressionistic one that took advantage of the crystalline and reflective qualities of stone and glass and was better suited to the coarser *opus tessellatum*. With the advent of widespread use of mosaic decoration for walls and vaults in the early Christian period, *opus vermiculatum* was entirely abandoned in favour of an increasingly impressionistic *opus tessellatum* that was visually effective at a distance.
·mosaic art's technical development **12**:466f; illus. 467
·Roman mosaic forms and styles **19**:315h

Oquendo, Antonio de, 17th-century Spanish admiral.
·Dutch naval victory under Maarten Tromp **18**:716e

Oquirrh Mountains, also called OQUIRRH RANGE, extend about 30 mi (50 km) southward from the southern end of the Great Salt Lake, Utah, U.S.
40°30′ N, 112°10′ W
·Utah's ore deposits **18**:1102f

or, in heraldry, the metal colour gold.
·heraldic colour and design **8**:787d; illus.

oracle (Latin *oraculum* from *orare*, "to pray" or "to speak"), a divine communication delivered in response to a petitioner's request; also, the seat of prophecy itself. Oracles were a branch of divination but differed from the casual pronouncements of augurs by being associated with a definite person or place; for example, the oracles of Zeus originated at Dodona, Olympia, or Siwa, while those of the Sibyl were in general circulation, but their provenance was unknown.

Oracular shrines were numerous in antiquity, and at each the god was consulted by a fixed means of divination. The method could be simple, such as the casting of lots or the rustling of tree leaves, or more sophisticated, taking the form of a direct inquiry of an inspired person who then gave the answer orally. One of the most common methods was incubation, in which the inquirer slept in a holy precinct and received an answer in a dream.

The most famous ancient oracle was that of Apollo at Delphi, located on the slopes of Mt. Parnassus above the Corinthian Gulf. Traditionally, the oracle first belonged to Mother Earth (Ge) but later was either given to or stolen by Apollo. At Delphi the medium was a woman over fifty, known as the Pythia, who lived apart from her husband and dressed in a maiden's clothes. Though the oracle, at first called Pytho, was known to Homer and was the site of a Mycenaean settlement, its fame did not become Panhellenic until the 7th and 6th centuries BC, when Apollo's advice or sanction was sought by lawmakers, colonists, and founders of cults. The Pythia's counsel was most in demand to forecast the outcome of projected wars or political actions.

Consultations were normally restricted to the seventh day of the Delphic month, Apollo's birthday, and were at first banned during the three winter months when Apollo was believed to be visiting the Hyperboreans in the north, though Dionysus later took Apollo's place at Delphi during that time. According to the usual procedure, sponsors were necessary, as was the provision of a *pelanos* (ritual cake) and a sacrificial beast that conformed to rigid physical standards. The Pythia and her consultants first bathed in the Castalian spring; afterwards, she drank from the sacred spring Cassotis and then entered the temple. There she apparently descended into a basement cell, mounted a sacred tripod, and chewed leaves of the laurel, Apollo's sacred tree. While in her abnormal state the Pythia would speak, intelligibly or otherwise. Her words, however, were not directly recorded by the inquirer; instead they were interpreted and written down by the priests in what was often highly ambiguous verse.

In addition to Delphi there were less frequented oracles at Thebes, Tegyra, and Ptoon in Boeotia, at Abae in Phocis, Corope in Thessaly, and on Delos, Apollo's birthplace. In Anatolia his oracles at Patara, Branchidae, Claros, and Grynium were also well known, though none rivalled Delphi's reputation.

The oracle of Zeus at Dodona in northwestern Greece was regarded as the oldest. At Dodona the priests (later priestesses) revealed the god's will from the whispering of the leaves on the sacred oak, a sacred spring, and from the striking of a gong. Zeus also prophesied from his altar at Olympia, where priests divined from offerings, as well as the oasis of Siwa in Libya, originally an oracle of the Egyptian god Amon.

Oracles delivered through incubation were believed to come from chthonian (underworld) powers. Thus invalids slept in the hall of Asclepius, the god of medicine, at Epidaurus and claimed to receive cures through dreams. At the oracle of the hero Amphiaraus at Oropus in Attica, consultants slept on skins, while visitors to the oracle of Trophonius (son of Erginus the Argonaut) at Levádhia slept in a hole in the ground. Incubation was also practiced at the oracle of Dionysus at Amphicleia, while an oracle for consulting the dead existed beside the river Acheron in central Greece.

Oracles in the formal sense were generally confined to the classical world; the Egyptians, however, divined from the motion of images paraded through the streets, and the Hebrews from sacred objects and dreams. Babylonian temple prophetesses also interpreted dreams. In Italy the cult of the Sibyl reached Cumae from Erythrae in Anatolia, but details of the oracle are generally unknown. The lot oracle of Fortuna Primigenia at Praeneste was popular and was consulted even by the emperors. The goddess Albunea possessed a dream oracle at Tibur (Tivoli), and the incubation rites of the god Faunus resembled those of the Greek hero Amphiaraus.

·Delphic evaluation of Socrates **16**:1003a
·hermeneutics of biblical prophecy **7**:63a
·Inca methods and belief **9**:261a
·prophetic divination types **15**:62f
·Ramesside institution **6**:478h
·sacrificial altar symbolism **16**:132b
·water's prophetic powers **12**:882f
·witch detection **19**:897c
·Yoruba Ifa poetry body **1**:238c

oracle bones, more than 100,000 inscribed tortoise shells and animal bones discovered mostly between 1928 and 1937 at An-yang, Honan, China. The sharply engraved Chinese characters, as yet only partly deciphered, are the earliest known examples of Chinese script and prove that China's written language has a history of at least 4,000 years. The bones, originally used for divination, date from the Shang dynasty (*c.* 1766–*c.* 1122 BC) and provide information about ancient Chinese rulers, battles, folk religion, and religious rites.
·Chinese excavations and inscriptions **4**:300e

Oracles of Hystaspes, a pre-Christian text, widely circulated in the Hellenistic world, containing elements of the myth of Mithra.
·Iranian origin and Mithra's role **9**:871h

Oradea, Hungarian NAGY-VÁRAD, German GROSSWARDEIN, capital and chief town of Bihor district (*județ*), northwestern Romania. It is situated 8½ mi (14 km) from the Hungarian frontier on the Crişul Repede River, where it leaves the western foothills of the Transylvanian Alps and flows onto the Hungarian Plain.

Oradea on the Crişul Repede River, Romania
By courtesy of "Carpati" Romanian National Tourist Office

Archaeologists have discovered vestiges of several ancient settlements in the locality. Neolithic implements have been found in the Seleņ district; there are remains of Dacian, Scythian, and Roman artifacts elsewhere. One of the first feudal states in the area, a principality ruled by Prince Menumorut (9th–10th centuries), was centred on a citadel at Biharea, northwest of Oradea.

The citadel of Oradea was erected between 1114 and 1131, destroyed by the Tartars in 1241, and rebuilt in the 15th century under the Corvinus dynasty. Between 1660 and 1692 the town was occupied by the Turks; it then became Hungarian until ceded to Romania in 1919. Since World War II, Oradea has become an important industrial centre, producing machine tools, mining equipment, chemicals, processed foods, and footwear.

There is a state theatre, puppet theatre, philharmonic orchestra, regional library, and museum. Five miles east of Oradea are the spas of Băile 1 Mai (Băile Felix) and Băile 9 Mai (Băile Victoria). Pop. (1970 est.) 137,662.
47°03′ N, 21°57′ E
·map, Romania **15**:1048

Orage, Alfred Richard, originally ALFRED JAMES ORAGE (b. Jan. 22, 1873, Dacre, Yorkshire—d. Nov. 6, 1934, Hampstead, London), editor and social thinker, known as an exponent of guild socialism (based on self-government in industry).

Orage became an elementary school teacher at Leeds, Yorkshire, in 1893, lectured on theosophy, and in 1900 helped found the avant-garde Leeds Arts Club. He moved to London in 1906 and became joint editor in 1907 of *The New Age*, a guild socialist publication of which from 1909 on he was the sole editor and dominant spirit. A diverse corps of political writers and literary figures crystallized around him.

After World War I Orage became a supporter of the Social Credit theories of Major Clifford Hugh Douglas, who advocated government-created consumer credit to make up for what he believed to be a permanent deficiency in purchasing power. Orage also became a pupil of the Russian mystic George Gurdjieff, spending most of the 1923–30 period lecturing in behalf of his institute Le Prieuré in France. He returned to England in 1930 and established *The New English Weekly* as the organ of the Social Credit movement.

Orage wrote *Nietzsche in Outline and Aphorism* (1907), *Friedrich Nietzsche: The Dionysian Spirit of the Age* (1911), *Readers and Writers* (1922), and *Social Credit and the Fear of Leisure* (1935). *Political and Economic Writings* (1935) was a posthumous collection.
·Pound's financial backing **14**:932a

Oraibi, or OLD ORAIBI, Indian pueblo (village), Navajo County, northeastern Arizona, U.S., on the narrow, rocky Third Mesa of the Hopi Indian Reservation. The unofficial capital of the reservation and occupied continuously since pre-Columbian times, it lies at an elevation of nearly 6,500 ft (1,980 m). It was the site of the San Francisco Mission (1629–80). After 1906, dissenting Hopi residents founded the nearby pueblos of Hotevilla and Bacobi. At the base of Third Mesa is lower Oraibi (Kyakatsmovi), with a trading post and a Hopi elementary school. Pop. (1970 est.) about 100.
35°53′ N, 110°37′ W

Oraisons funèbres (1669), a collection of orations by Jacques-Bénigne Bossuet.
·Bossuet's writing skills **3**:54c

oral cavity, the interior of the mouth.
·human digestive system anatomy **5**:789d
·vertebrate digestive system comparisons **5**:784c

oral contraceptives, or BIRTH CONTROL PILLS, pills containing synthetic hormones that prevent ovulation. Although they are highly effective, there are several medical hazards that may be associated with their continued use.
·evaluation of effectiveness **2**:1068f

orale (liturgical garment): *see* fanon.

oral evidence, in law, evidence given by word.
·witness and testimony laws **7**:3e

Oral Law, in Judaism, that part of religious law not contained in Scripture, collected in the Mishna and discussed in Talmudic commentary.
·Jewish philosophical thought **10**:208d

oral pathology, the science dealing with diseases of mouth structures and especially with the structural and function changes in them that are caused by or that cause disease.
·disease treatment role **5**:596d

oral stage, in psychoanalytical theory, the phase of human development, during the first postnatal year, when the infant's mouth is his chief organ for emotionally charged contact and when the mother and her breast constitute his most important external object.
·autonomic function modification **12**:1036h
·psychological study of learning **15**:149f

oral surgery, dental specialty that deals with the diagnosis and surgical treatment of the diseases, injuries, and defects of the human jaw and associated structures. The most common oral surgery is tooth extraction. Other dental problems that require the skill of an oral surgeon include treatment of cysts (liquid- or semisolid-filled sacs), tumours, lesions, and infections of the mouth and jaw. More complex problems that are dealt with by the oral surgeon include jaw and facial injuries, cleft palate, and cleft lip. Both dentists and physicians refer patients to an oral surgeon for treatment of such defects. Oral surgery has special problems because of (1) the limited access afforded by the lips and the cheeks; (2) the movement of the tongue and the lower jaw; (3) the fact that the oral cavity opens into the pharynx (the passageway for air and food); and (4) the fact that the area is continually being flooded with saliva and is inhabited by the largest number and greatest variety of micro-organisms found in the human body.

To become an oral surgeon requires three years of postgraduate study after acquisition of a degree in dentistry.
·distinctive features of practice **5**:596e

oral tradition, the aggregate of customs, beliefs, and practices that were not originally committed to writing but contribute to the cultural continuity of a social group and help shape its views.
·African myth and folktale development **1**:237d
·Amerindian rendition, themes, and use **1**:659a
·anthropology's use in cultural analysis **1**:969e
·art preservation techniques **2**:120c
·Australian Aborigine flexibility **2**:428c
·biblical origins research **7**:62c
·California Indians ritual and art forms **3**:622d
·Ceylonese historical myth of island **4**:1d
·children's literature propagation of folk material **4**:228e
·comedic techniques and narrative style **9**:6c
·early Christian sources of authority **4**:537f
·epic poetry traditions and forms **6**:906g
·folk literature origin theories **14**:1035c
·folk literature's unique feature **7**:454f
·folk music transmission **7**:466h
·Greek and Roman literature development **10**:1090f
·Grimm's tale collections **8**:427e
·Halakha in Hellenistic Jewish sects **10**:313a *passim* to 314h
·Hindu mythological tradition **8**:928d
·Hindu sacred scripture tradition **8**:933a
·Homeric tradition of oral poetry **8**:1018c
·Jewish and Christian attitudes **4**:497e
·Jewish canonization of Mishna tradition **10**:285a
·Jewish revelation concepts of Torah **17**:1006c
·medieval vernacular literature **10**:1099f
·Mesopotamian literary history **11**:1007b
·music in medieval Europe **12**:715g
·mythology's relationship to literature **12**:798d
·Oceanian peoples' art **13**:454b
·performance accessibility and genre origins **10**:1046a
·poet's status in preliterate cultures **2**:97b
·popular literary approach distinction **14**:804g
·postapostolistic deterioration **2**:939e
·preservation on recording tape **10**:654b
·primitive religion **14**:1041h
·Qur'ānic traditional variation **15**:343d
·Roman popular theatre origins **18**:220e
·sacred scripture formulation concepts **16**:126f
·short story evolution from tale **16**:711g
·Slavic culturolinguistic heritage **16**:870d
·textual reconstruction from manuscripts **18**:190c
·vagabond artist's occurrence and status **2**:107e
·Vedic text and chanting formula **17**:151f
·Welsh cultural blending in literature **19**:529c
·western Sudan narrative literature **19**:799f

Oran, French OUAHRAN, *wilāyah* (province), département, northwestern Algeria. With an area of 6,486 sq mi (16,800 sq km), it extends from the Mediterranean coast south across the Tell Atlas to the High Plateaus. Main towns include Oran (*wilāyah* capital), Sidi bel Abbès, Aïn Temouchent, and Sig (*qq.v.*). Pop. (1970 est.) 1,075,000.

·Abdelkader's victories over French 1:8a
·map, Northern Algeria 1:560
·North African ancient culture 13:146a; maps

Oran, Arabic WAHRAN, French OUAHRAN, Mediterranean capital of Oran *wilāyah* (province), Algeria, between Pointe Mers el-Kébir and Pointe Canastel. With adjacent Mers el-Kébir (*q.v.*), it is the nations's second port after Algiers. Founded at the beginning of the 10th century by Andalusian merchants as a base for trade with the North African hinterland, it developed commercially because of its sea connections with Europe. It became the

The Santa Cruz citadel of Oran, Alg., overlooking the Mediterranean Sea
E.P.H. Inc.—EB Inc.

port for the kingdom of Tlemcen in 1437 and served as an entrepôt for trade with the Sudan. In 1492 and 1502 Oran received colonies of Spanish Muslims, refugees from forcible conversion to Christianity. Thereafter it began to decay and, with Mers el-Kébir, became a centre for pirates. It was occupied by the Spanish in 1509. For the next two centuries Oran was contested by the various Mediterranean powers until it fell to the Turks in 1708. Piracy made control tenuous, and the city reverted to Spain (1732). Devastated by an earthquake in 1790, it was evacuated and returned (1792) to the Turks, who settled a Jewish community there. In a state of decline, it was occupied in 1831 by the French, who developed it as a modern port. An Allied objective during World War II, Oran was captured by U.S. forces on Nov. 10, 1942. Surviving the bloodshed and violence before and after Algeria's independence (July 3, 1962), it has become an important commercial centre.

Modern Oran ("Ravine") is divided into three main sections: La Blanca, the old Spanish city on the hill; La Marine, near the sea; and La Ville Nouvelle, built on the terraces on the right bank of Raz el-Aïn Ravine. The old port and La Blanca, on the plateau above it, are crowned by the Turkish citadel of Santa Cruz, modified by the Spanish and French. The Spanish quarter, with its narrow streets, contains the former Cathedral of Saint-Louis (rebuilt by the French in 1838), the Porte de Canastel (reconstructed in 1734), and the fountain in the Place Emerat (1789). In the Turkish part of the old town is the Great Mosque (Grande Mosquée du Pasha) built in 1796 with money obtained by ransoming Spanish captives. To the east lies the Château Neuf, former residence of the beys of Oran and later a French army headquarters. Near the kasbah, which surrounds the old Spanish castle, are the mosque of Sīdī al-Hawwārī, a 15th-century scholar and monk; the former barracks of the Janissaries; and the harem of the beys. The former French sector spreads across the ravine and far outside the second city wall (1866; now largely demolished) into suburbs including Saint-Eugène, Gambetta, Eckmühl, Choupot, and Boulanger. Between the Jewish cemetery and the public park is the Village Nègre (1845). The Université d'Oran was opened in 1965. Other institutions include the Musée Municipal (Roman and Punic exhibits), the Musée de Tlemcen (Islāmic art), and the Bibliothèque Aubert.

Oran is an international port of call. Greatly enlarged after 1848, its artificial harbour has a jetty over 3,000 yd (2,700 m) long and five large basins covering an area of about 330 ac (134 ha). It is connected by rail to Algiers, Morocco, and Béchar, and its airport lies beyond the village of La Senia. The industrial part of Oran, in the outlying south-southeastern districts, contains food-processing and diversified manufacturing plants, including some heavy industry. Principal exports are wine, cereals, vegetables, and fruits. A 400-mi (650-km) pipeline from Hassi-R'Mel in the Sahara transports natural gas to Oran and Arzew. Latest census 325,807.
35°43′ N, 0°43′ W
·map, Northern Algeria 1:560

orang (ape): *see* orangutan.

Orange, city, east central New South Wales, Australia, on the slopes of Mt. Canobolas. In 1828 the original settlement on Blackman's Swamp was renamed by Sir Thomas Mitchell in memory of the Prince of Orange, his commander during the Peninsular War. It grew after gold was discovered (1851) at nearby Ophir. Farming replaced mining, and Orange is now the centre of a fruit-growing (mainly cherries), mixed-farming, and grazing area. It has stockyards and abattoirs, and light industrial development includes the manufacture of electrical appliances. It was proclaimed a town in 1860, a municipality in 1885, and a city in 1946. Pop. (1971 prelim.) 23,143.
33°17′ S, 149°06′ E
·map, Australia 2:400

Orange, town, Vaucluse *département*, southeastern France, situated in a fertile plain on the left bank of the Rhône River, north of Avignon. The town has grown up round the Roman monuments for which it is famous. The semicircular theatre, probably built during the reign of the first Roman emperor, Augustus (27 BC–AD 14), is the best preserved of its kind. The tiered benches (partly rebuilt), which rise on the slopes of a slight hill, originally seated 1,100. The magnificent wall that constitutes the back of the theatre is 334 ft (102 m) long and 124 ft (38 m) high. An imposing statue of Augustus, about 12 ft high, stands in the central niche. The triumphal arch, one of the largest built by the Romans, about 61 ft high, has fine sculptures evoking the victories in the 1st century BC of the Roman general and statesman Julius Caesar.

Roman theatre, Orange, Fr.
Victor Englebert—De Wys Inc.

Orange is a market town; its main industries include the manufacture of brooms and food processing (jam, canned fruit). It derives its name from Arausio, a Gaulish god. Under Augustus' rule it became a prosperous city. In the 5th century it was pillaged by the Visigoths (a westerly division of the Teutonic peoples known as the Goths). The town became an independent countship in the 11th century, and later passed into the possession of the House of Nassau. The French king Louis XIV captured it and pulled down the fortifications in 1660. It was ceded to France in 1713 by the Treaty of Utrecht. Latest census 17,852.
44°08′ N, 4°48′ E
·map, France 7:584

Orange, city, Orange County, southern California, U.S., on the Santa Ana River. Part of Rancho Santiago de Santa Ana, it was founded as Richland in 1868, laid out in 1871, and renamed in 1875 for its orange groves. It subsequently developed with the Los Angeles metropolitan area and acquired some light manufacturing. Chapman College (established in Los Angeles, 1861) was relocated there in 1954. Inc. city, 1888. Pop. (1980) 91,788.
33°47′ N, 117°51′ W

Orange, town (township), New Haven County, Connecticut, U.S., immediately west of New Haven, on the Housatonic River. Originally a part of Milford Colony (bought from the Paugusset Indians and settled in 1639), it was known as North Milford. In 1822 the latter joined with a portion of New Haven to be incorporated as the town of Orange, named for William III, prince of Orange. In 1921 West Haven seceded from Orange to become a separate town. Orange's oldest house was built by Richard Bryan in 1720 and is an example of a Connecticut colonial "salt box" with a long steep roof and large kitchen. Development has been mainly residential with some diversified manufacturing. Pop. (1980) 13,237.
41°17′ N, 73°02′ W

Orange, city, Essex County, New Jersey, U.S., just west of Newark. Named Mountain Plantations when it was settled in 1678, it was later renamed to honour William, prince of Orange, who became King William III of Great Britain. Orange was a part of Newark until 1806, when it became a separate community. In 1861–63 it was separated from East Orange, South Orange, and West Orange, municipalities, which, together with Maplewood, comprise a suburban community known as "The Oranges," which are primarily residential suburbs of New York City and Newark, the first commuters having arrived with the completion of a railroad in the 1830s. Orange has been a centre for hat making since 1785; other light industries produce pharmaceuticals, electrical equipment, foods, business machines, and clothing. Inc. town, 1860; city, 1872. Pop. (1980) 31,136.
40°46′ N, 74°14′ W

Orange, city, seat (1852) of Orange County, southeastern Texas, U.S., deepwater port on the Sabine River canalized to connect with the Gulf Intracoastal Waterway. With Beaumont and Port Arthur it forms the "Golden Triangle" industrial complex. Settled in 1836 as Green's Bluff, it was known as Madison in 1852 but was renamed (1856) either for the orange groves along the river or for Orange, N.J. An early rice, lumber, and shipbuilding centre, it boomed during World War I when shipyard construction became a major industry. After World War II the U.S. Navy maintained a naval station and "mothball fleet" there. Located in a major gas and oil field area, its key industries include petrochemicals, synthetic rubber, steel fabrication, lumber, cement, and shipbuilding. Inc. 1881. Pop. (1980) 23,628.
30°01′ N, 93°44′ W
·map, United States 18:908

orange, any of several species of small trees or shrubs of the genus *Citrus* of the family Rutaceae and their nearly round fruits, which have leathery and oily rinds and edible, juicy inner flesh. The species of orange most important commercially are the China orange, also called the sweet, or common, orange; the mandarin orange, some varieties of which are called tangerines (*q.v.*); and the sour, or Seville, orange, which is less extensively grown. The tree of the sweet orange often grows to a height of 6 metres (20 feet) and sometimes at-

Orange (*Citrus*)

By courtesy of Florida Department of Commerce

tains 10 metres (33 feet). The broad, glossy, evergreen leaves are medium sized and ovate; petioles (leafstalks) have narrow wings. Flowers are very fragrant. Although the usual shape of the sweet-orange fruit is round, certain varieties are greatly elongated and others much flattened. The pulp of the sweet orange is agreeably acidulous and sweet, the peel is comparatively smooth, and the oil glands are convex.

Oranges are believed native to the tropical regions of Asia, especially the Malay Archipelago; along with other citrus species, they have been cultivated from remote ages. Orange culture probably spread from its native habitat to India, the east coast of Africa, and from there to the eastern Mediterranean region. Contributing to the spread of orange cultivation were the Roman conquests, the development of the Arab trade routes, and the expansion of Islām. By the time Columbus sailed, orange trees were common in the Canary Islands. Today oranges are cultivated in subtropical and tropical America, northern and eastern Mediterranean countries, Australia, and South Africa.

Oranges thrive best where the trees are chilled somewhat by occasional light frosts in winter. The trees are semidormant at that season, and temperatures just below freezing will not harm trees or fruit unless frost occurs early, before the trees have finished their annual growth. On the coldest sites, the orchards are heated.

The orange thrives in a wide range of soil conditions, from extremely sandy soils to rather heavy clay loams; it grows especially well in intermediate types of soil. Orange orchards are generally planted in relatively deep soil where drainage is good. The orange trees are usually budded on stocks grown from the seed of selected trees. The seeds are sown in well-prepared soil in a lath house; after about 12 months' growth there, the seedlings are removed to a nursery. After about 12–16 months in the nursery, the trees are usually large enough to bud. When the budded tops are one to two years old, the trees are large enough to plant in the orchard.

The culture of intercrops, such as beans, tomatoes, or melons, helps to provide favourable conditions for the young orange trees for the first five or six years, until they reach the age of profitable production. The growth of cover crops makes use of seasonal rainfall for production of organic matter to be incorporated into the soil. In many areas where oranges are grown, it is necessary to supplement the rainfall with irrigation; this is generally the practice in Texas, California, Israel, Spain, Morocco, and parts of South Africa. Orange trees bear abundantly from 50 to 80 years or even more, and some old orange trees whose age must be reckoned by centuries still produce crops. Oranges are picked when fully ripe, for, unlike some deciduous fruits, they do not ripen or improve in quality after being picked.

The sweet and mandarin oranges are the principal species produced commercially in the following countries, listed in order of importance: the U.S., Brazil, Japan, Spain, Italy, Israel, India, Mexico, Argentina, and Morocco. World production of oranges is approximately 700,000,000 boxes (32 kilograms [71 pounds] each) annually.

Prior to 1920 the orange was considered principally as a dessert fruit. The spread of orange-juice drinking, in contrast with eating of the fresh fruit, significantly increased per capita consumption. Another important factor was the growing appreciation of the dietary value of citrus fruit; oranges are rich in vitamin C and also provide some vitamin A.

The most important product made from oranges in the U.S. is frozen concentrated juice, which accounts for nearly 40 percent of the crop. Essential oils, pectin, candied peel, and orange marmalade are among the important by-products. Sour, or Seville, oranges are raised especially for making marmalade. Stock feed is made from the waste material left from processing.

·citrus industry by-products **11**:626a
·flavouring extract production **17**:506d
·fruit farming economics 7:753g; tables 754
·Italian production and problems **9**:1099e
·Rutales order characteristics **16**:103a; illus. 104

Orange, William IV, prince of: *see* William IV.

Orange, William VI, prince of (king of The Netherlands): *see* William I.

Orange II, an acid dye.
·azo dyestuff preparation **5**:1115d

Orange, councils of, two church synods held in Orange, Fr., in 441 and 529. The first, under the presidency of St. Hilary of Arles, dealt mainly with disciplinary matters. The second, and by far the more important, was concerned with refuting the Semi-Pelagianism of Faustus of Riez. It was attended by 15 bishops and was under the presidency of Caesarius of Arles. Caesarius had sought the aid of Rome against Semi-Pelagianism, and in response Pope Felix IV had sent certain passages concerning grace and free will, drawn chiefly from the writings of Augustine and Prosper of Aquitaine. The synod approved 25 of them and adopted a supplementary statement reaffirming the Augustinian doctrines of corruption, human inability, prevenient grace, and baptismal regeneration. Its decrees were later confirmed by Pope Boniface II, and they became the Roman Catholic norm for doctrines on grace, predestination, and free will.

Orange, Fort, Dutch fort (1624–64) built near the present site of the capitol in Albany, N.Y.
·European settlement in New York **13**:21f

Orange, House of, princely dynasty deriving its name from the medieval principality of Orange, in old Provence, but chiefly important in the history of the Netherlands. The lords of Orange, vassals of the Holy Roman emperors from the 12th century, early began to style themselves princes. In the 16th century, through a marital alliance with the German House of Nassau, the House of Orange became involved in the history of the Netherlands.

In 1544 a count of Nassau became prince of Orange as William I. William led the Netherlands' revolt against Spain from 1568 to his death in 1584 and held the office of stadholder in four of the rebelling provinces. This was the start of a tradition in the Dutch Republic whereby the stadholderships were for long periods monopolized by the princes and counts of Orange-Nassau supported by an enduring Orange "party" composed of nobles, orthodox Calvinist leaders, artisans, and peasants, against the rivalry of the patriciate of Holland. The gifted 16th- and 17th-century stadholders were followed by less effective Orange leaders in the 18th century. The last stadholder fled to England in 1795 as the republic collapsed.

The next titular prince of Orange became King William I of the Kingdom of The Netherlands in 1815, beginning the royal dynasty of the present Netherlands state.
·Dutch Republic leadership conflicts **11**:144e
·Frederick Henry's life and achievements 7:706d

Orangeburg, city, seat of Orangeburg County, central South Carolina, U.S., on the North Fork of Edisto River. In 1735 Germans, Swiss, and Dutch established a settlement, naming it for William, prince of Orange. The Donald Bruce House (*c.* 1735), on nearby Middlepen Plantation, served as Revolutionary headquarters for Gov. John Rutledge, Gen. William Moultrie, and Lord Rawdon, and during the Civil War as headquarters for local Federal forces.

Section of the Edisto Memorial Gardens on the North Fork of the Edisto River, Orangeburg, S.C.

Milt and Joan Mann from CameraMann

A basic agricultural economy has given way to light diversified industry and educational services. Orangeburg is the seat of Claflin University (1869), South Carolina State College (1896), and Southern Methodist College (founded 1956 in Greenville). Edisto Memorial Gardens have test sections affiliated with the American Rose and Camellia societies. The Orangeburg National Fish Hatchery (established 1912) occupies 20 ac (8 ha) of ponds. Inc. 1883. Pop. (1980) 14,933.
33°30′ N, 80°52′ W
·map, United States **18**:908

Orange Free State 13:638, Afrikaans ORANJE VRYSTAAT, second smallest (area 49,866 sq mi [129,152 sq km]) of the four provinces of the Republic of South Africa, bounded by Natal and the Kingdom of Lesotho (east), Cape of Good Hope (south and west), and the Transvaal (north). The capital is Bloemfontein. Pop. (1970) 1,649,306.

The text article covers the province's history, physiography, soils, climate, vegetation, animal life, population, administration, social conditions, economy, transportation and communications, and culture.

REFERENCES in other text articles:
·Boer–native conflict and British role **17**:285a; map
·British annexation and imperial status **3**:304c; map 305
·map, South Africa **17**:62
·population density **17**:67f; table
·Transvaal alliance and British rule **18**:685c

Orange Range (New Guinea): *see* Djajawidjaja Mountains.

Orange River 13:640, Afrikaans ORANJERIVIER, longest river of southern Africa, rises in Lesotho near the Mont aux Sources in the Drakensberg range and flows across the Republic of South Africa; it forms the southern boundary of South West Africa and empties into the Atlantic Ocean at Alexander Bay, South Africa, after a course of 1,300 mi (2,100 km).

The text article covers the river's course, its riverine population, history, hydrology, navigability, bridges, dams, and future projects.
28°41′ S, 16°28′ E

REFERENCES in other text articles:
- African continent drainage pattern **1**:191e
- map, South Africa **17**:62
- Namib Desert soils and drainage **12**:820b
- source and flow direction **10**:834g
- South Africa drainage system **17**:61b

orangeroot (plant): *see* Hydrastis.

orangery, a garden building designed for the wintering of exotic shrubs and trees, primarily orange trees. The earliest orangeries were practical buildings that could be completely covered by planks and sacking and heated in the cold season by stoves; such buildings existed in Britain and France as early as the second half of the 16th century. The great period of the orangery, when few great gardens were without one, extended from the latter half of the 17th century into the early 18th century. Great numbers of orange trees were fruited in what had become the most elaborate architectural feature of princely gardens and favourite promenades in winter and early spring. Many famous orangeries survive, notably those at the gardens of Versailles and Kew House.

Orangerie at Kew House, Greater London

British Crown Copyright reproduced with permission of the Controller of Her Britannic Majesty's Stationery Office

Oranges, War of the (1801), brief conflict in which France and Spain fought against Portugal; it was brought about by Portugal's refusal in 1800 to accept Napoleon's demands to become a political and economic extension of France and to cede to France the major part of its national territory.

In April 1801, French troops arrived in Portugal, and on May 20 they were bolstered by Spanish troops under the command of Manuel de Godoy. In a battle that was disastrous for Portugal, Godoy took the town of Olivenza, near the Spanish frontier. Following his victory, Godoy picked oranges at nearby Elvas and sent them to the Queen of Spain with the message that he would proceed to Lisbon. Thus, the conflict became known as the War of the Oranges.

After Olivenza, Portugal negotiated a treaty with France and Spain—the Peace of Badajoz (June 1801)—ending the invasion. Portugal agreed to close its ports to English ships, to give commercial concessions to France, to cede Olivenza to Spain and part of Brazil to France, and to pay an indemnity. The treaty was antedated, however, because of the receipt of a message from Napoleon on the day it was signed, which ordered the French negotiators to divide Portugal between France and Spain.
- Spain's alliance with France **17**:436b

Orange Society, an Irish sectarian and political society, named after the Protestant William of Orange, who, as King William III, had defeated the Catholic king James II; the society was formed in 1795 to maintain Protestantism and the Protestant succession. Enmity between Catholics and Protestants had always been endemic in Ireland and was much exacerbated in the 17th century by the introduction into Ulster of Presbyterian settlers, by the rebellion of 1641, and by the war of 1688–91, when the Catholic king James II attempted to maintain in Ireland the power he had lost in England. Inter-sectarian feeling became especially bad again in the 1790s, especially in County Armagh, where Protestants, known as the "Peep o' Day Boys," attacked their Catholic neighbours. After a major confrontation in 1795, known as the Battle of the Diamond, the Orange Society was formed as a secret society, with lodges spreading throughout Ireland and ultimately into Great Britain and various British dominions. In 1835, with the Orange Society in mind, the House of Commons petitioned the king to abolish societies that were secret and that excluded persons on the ground of religion. Some official attempts were made to discourage the provocative Orange processions, the most notable of which is held annually on July 12, the anniversary of the Battle of Aughrim, at which William III's generals were finally victorious in Ireland. The Orange Society strengthened resistance in Ulster to the Irish Home Rule Bill of 1912 and has continued as a bastion of Protestant Unionist opinion.

Orangeville, town, seat of Dufferin County, southeastern Ontario, Canada, on the headwaters of the Credit River. Established in 1832 as the The Mills around a sawmill and flour mill built by James Greggs 40 mi (64 km) northwest of Toronto, it was later renamed after a local property owner, Orange Lawrence. Manufactures include automotive parts, wire and foundry ware, knitted goods, flour, veterinary supplies, and dairy products. Pop. (1971) 8,074.
43°55′ N, 80°06′ W

Orange Walk, administrative district in Belize (formerly British Honduras).
- area and population table **3**:308

Orange Walk, administrative headquarters of Orange Walk district (area 1,829 sq mi [4,737 sq km]), northwestern Belize (formerly British Honduras), on the west bank of the New River. Established in early colonial times, it was pillaged by hostile Indians in 1872. During the late 19th and early 20th centuries, it conducted a thriving trade in mahogany. The town declined after demand for mahogany lessened. Rubber gathering, sugarcane cultivation, and rum distilling are the main economic activities. Its inhabitants are a mixture of Mennonites, Maya Indians, and Creoles. Pop. (1970) town, 5,698; district, 17,041.
17°15′ N, 88°47′ W
- map, British Honduras **3**:307

Orangoutan Brother and Sister, The (1875), play by U Ku.
- popular theatre style creation **17**:246d

orangutan (Malay: "man of the woods"), large manlike ape (*Pongo pygmaeus*), family Pongidae, restricted to lowland swamp forests in Borneo and a small part of Sumatra.

Like the related gorilla and chimpanzee, the orangutan (or orang) has a short, thickset body, long arms, and short legs. It differs in having a shaggy, reddish coat, greater disproportion between arm and leg lengths, and in having a differently shaped skull. Its ears are small but humanoid. The male orang may be about 137 centimetres (4½ feet) tall and weigh about 75 kilograms (165 pounds) when mature. It is strikingly different from the female not only in being considerably larger but also in having cheek flaps of fatty tissue and an air sac that forms a baglike swelling hanging from the throat.

The orangutan is arboreal and feeds mainly on fruit. In the wild, it lives alone or in small groups and each night constructs a nest in the trees for sleeping. A single young is born after a gestation period of about 275 days and is nursed by the mother, which carries it at her breast. Sexual maturity is attained at eight years in the female, ten years in the male. Life span, at least in captivity, may exceed 30 years. The orangutan is remarkably silent; among its few vocalizations are grunts and lip-smacking.

Orangutan (*Pongo pygmaeus*)

Russ Kinne—Photo Researchers

By nature, the orangutan is a placid, deliberate animal. It is intelligent, and in captivity it has shown considerable ingenuity and persistence, with a particular ability to manipulate mechanical objects.

The *Red Data Book* lists the orangutan as a rare animal that could quickly become extinct. Factors contributing to the decline in its population include hunting and the destruction of its habitat by man.
- human blood type comparison **2**:1149b
- traits, behaviour, and classification **14**:1014h

Oranian stone tool industry: *see* Ibero-Maurusian stone tool industry.

Oranienbaum (U.S.S.R.): *see* Lomonosov.

Oranjemund, town in extreme southwest South West Africa; it is the site of diamond fields. Pop. (1970 prelim.) 2,594.
28°38′ S, 16°24′ E
- Namib Desert and coastal mining **12**:820h

Oranjestad, seaport and chief town of Aruba Island, in the Netherlands Antilles, on the island's western coast, 80 mi (130 km) west-northwest of Willemstad on Curaçao. It is a free port and a petroleum processing and shipping centre. The enclosed harbour, with two basins, has modern cargo-handling and fuelling equipment. Oranjestad has brightly coloured buildings, fine residential sections, and a modern sports arena, Wilhelmina Stadium. Latest pop. est. 14,720.
12°33′ N, 70°06′ W

orant, in Christian art, a figure in a posture of prayer, usually standing upright with raised arms. The motif of the orant, which seems to reflect the standard attitude of prayer adopted by the first Christians, is particularly important in Early Christian art (*c.* 2nd century–*c.* 6th century) and especially in the frescoes (*q.v.*) that decorated Roman catacombs from the 2nd century on. Here many of the characters in Old Testament scenes of divine salvation of the faithful, the most commonly represented narrative subjects of the catacombs, are shown in the orant position. The most frequent use of the orant in the catacombs, however, was as an abstract representation of the soul of the deceased. The reason for depicting the soul in the attitude of prayer has been widely disputed, but it has been plausibly suggested that the orant is a symbol of faith rather than of supplication; this explanation is consistent with its concurrent use in Old Testament scenes in which deliverance is already accomplished and with the general spirit of confidence and expectation that characterized the art of the catacombs. By extension, when it is identified with no particular individual, the orant can be taken as a symbol of the church itself; in the miniature art of early medieval manuscripts and ivories and in Byzantine art, a female orant figure in certain contexts can be satisfactorily explained only as representing the church. In Byzantine art also, the Madonna orant, or *blacherniotissa*, was one of the major types of the Virgin. Used to decorate the main apse of a number of churches, the Madonna orant stood as an intercession with Christ on behalf of the congregation.

Orant, fresco in the crypt of "La Velata," Catacomb of Priscilla, Rome, late 3rd century
EDI Studio, Barcelona

Oraon, aboriginal people of Chota Nāgpur in the state of Bihār in India. They call themselves Kurukh and speak a Dravidian language akin to Gondi and other tribal languages of central India. They once lived farther to the southwest on the Rohtās Plateau, but were dislodged by other populations and migrated to Chota Nāgpur, where they settled in the vicinity of Munda-speaking tribes.

Speakers of Oraon number about 1,140,000, but in urban areas, and particularly among Christians, many Oraon speak Hindi as their mother tongue. The tribe is divided into numerous clans associated with animal, plant, and mineral totems. Every village has a headman and a hereditary priest; a number of neighbouring villages constitute a confederation, the affairs of which are conducted by a representative council.

An important feature of the social life of a village is the bachelors' dormitory for unmarried males, an institution found among many other tribes of the area, including the Ho, the Kharia, and the Gonds. The Oraon call it *jonkerpa* or *dhumkuria.* The bachelors sleep together in the *dhumkuria*, which is usually on the outskirts of the village. There is a separate house for the girls.

The dormitory institution serves in the socializing and training of the young; it is a means of inculcating traditional usages in social and ceremonial duties, economic pursuits, and sexual behaviour.

The traditional religion of the Oraon includes the cult of a supreme god, Dharmes, the worship of ancestors, and the propitiation of tutelary deities and spirits. Hinduism has influenced the ritual and certain beliefs. Many Oraon, including the majority of the educated, have become Christians.

·Christian percentage within population **2**:986b
·Indian racial types and distribution **14**:846e
·South Asian peoples and cultures **17**:125h; map 126

orarion, also spelled ORARIUM, the original name of the clerical vestment now called a stole (*q.v.*).

ora serrata retinae, in human anatomy, a structure of the retina of the eye.

·structure and function in human eye **7**:95a; illus. 93

Oraşul Stalin (Romania): *see* Braşov.

Oratio Dominica: *see* Lord's Prayer.

Oration on the Dignity of Man, Latin ORATIO DE HOMINIS DIGNITATE (1486), by Pico della Mirandola.

·embodiment of Humanism **14**:262e
·Renaissance Christian tradition **15**:665c

Orator (*c.* 55 BC), work on oratorical principle and practice by Cicero.

·oratorical qualifications and goals **4**:609f

Oratorians, informal name given to members of the Roman Catholic societies called Institute of the Oratory of St. Philip Neri and the French Oratory (*qq.v.*).

oratorio, large-scale musical composition for solo voices, chorus, and orchestra on a sacred or semi-sacred subject, not intended for liturgical use. The principal schools are the Italian, essentially a form of religious opera; the German, developed from treatment of the Passion story; and the English, synthesized by the composer George Frideric Handel from several forms. The term oratorio derives from the oratory of the Roman church in which, in the mid-16th century, St. Philip Neri instituted moral musical entertainments, which were divided by a sermon, hence the two-act form common in early Italian oratorio.

The earliest surviving oratorio is *La rappresentazione di anima e di corpo* (*The Representation of Soul and Body*) by Emilio del Cavaliere, produced in 1600 with dramatic action, including ballet. Many similar, sometimes spectacular, works followed. Toward the mid-17th century Giacomo Carissimi introduced a more sober type with Latin text based on the Old Testament. His oratorios are short, simple, and free from extravagance. The most memorable episodes are those in which narrative is interrupted and characters express their emotions. Latin and Italian types continued in use, but the vernacular Italian *oratorio volgare*, sung by virtuoso singers, was more popular and flourished until the late 18th century. Stage action was abandoned in the 18th century.

German oratorio begins with Heinrich Schütz, a composer whose style is a blend of German and Italian elements. His oratorios, confined to Gospel subjects, show great powers of emotional expression and anticipate those of J.S. Bach in vigorous treatment of the choruses. In the *Easter Oratorio* (published 1623) Schütz retains the old convention of setting the words of each character for two or more voices. His oratorios achieve a balance between austerity and exuberance, but by the late 17th century this balance had been disturbed. Passion oratorio texts of this period often abandon biblical words for a mixture of rhymed paraphrase and lyrical commentary of a more or less sentimental nature.

Bach's two great Passion oratorios, the *Passion According to St. John* (first performed 1724) and the *Passion According to St. Matthew* (1729), restored the balance attained by Schütz, though they are written on a greater scale and enriched by introduction of the later Italian aria. Bach, besides increasing the significance of the chorale, or congregational hymn, emphasized the narrative.

Handel's oratorios are essentially theatrical. Influenced by opera, masque, even Greek tragedy, they were performed by opera singers in theatres (though ecclesiastical prejudice forbade stage action) and have no connection with the church. Handel's achievement has been distorted by the concentration of posterity on the atypical oratorios with biblical themes, *Israel in Egypt* (1739) and *Messiah* (1742). Handel's successors imitated his style but mistook his aim; thereafter, English oratorio remained undistinguished for a century and a half.

After Bach and Handel, oratorio on the Continent, apart from the works of Haydn, ceased to represent a vital, creative tradition. Haydn's *Creation* (*Die Schöpfung;* 1798) shows the influence of Handel's oratorios and Mozart's operas, fusing these epic and dramatic elements with Haydn's own mature mastery of symphonic style to make the work a masterpiece. Haydn called *The Seasons* (*Die Jahreszeiten;* 1801) an oratorio, though its content is secular and its form a loosely articulated series of evocative pieces. Beethoven's single oratorio, *Christus am Ölberg* (*Christ on the Mount of Olives*; 1803), does not succeed, nor do most of those occasioned by the 19th-century large halls, choral societies, and festivals, especially in Germany and England.

Mendelssohn's *Elijah* (1846) is one of the few 19th-century oratorios still performed. Mendelssohn's promotion of the revival of Bach's music and his experience of Handel's music led him to attempt a fusion of the two styles. *Elijah* is remarkable for the vitality of the choruses, but *St. Paul* (1836) has been criticized as expressing no religious emotion except in terms of respectable complacency.

Germany produced little of consequence after Mendelssohn, unless *Ein deutsches Requiem* (*A German Requiem;* 1868), a setting of texts from Luther's Bible by Brahms, is classed as an oratorio. The two oratorios of Franz Liszt, *Christus* (composed 1855–56) and *Die Legende von der heiligen Elisabeth* (*The Legend of St. Elizabeth;* 1873), combine devotional and theatrical elements on the grandest scale. Italian oratorio remained in abeyance after the 18th century, and Slavic composers produced few oratorios. Perhaps the only French oratorio of major importance is *L'Enfance du Christ* (1854) by Hector Berlioz, a series of theatrical tableaus.

A masterpiece of 20th-century English oratorio is Sir Edward Elgar's *Dream of Gerontius* (1900). The poem by Cardinal Newman on which it is based has a dramatic framework within which the music could expand without becoming disorderly. Igor Stravinsky's opera-oratorio *Oedipus Rex* (1927), with a Latin text, was most successful in the opera house. The Swiss Frank Martin was one of the most active oratorio composers in the mid-20th century. Many large-scale works, generally secular in content, have come out of the Soviet Union and eastern European Communist countries and China. An especially notable oratorio is the *St. Luke Passion* of the Polish composer Krzysztof Penderecki. *See also* Passion music.

·composite musical genres **12**:727h
·counterpoint of Baroque period **5**:215a
·departure from Renaissance style **12**:709f
·Handel's life and works **8**:604a
·Haydn's Creation and Seasons **8**:683c
·principal composers and works **4**:445b

oratory 13:641, rationale and practice of persuasive public address.

The text article covers the principles and types of oratory and oratory as a reflection of its audience.

REFERENCES in other text articles:

·acting skill requirements **1**:59h
·Cicero's reputation and contribution **4**:609b
·Classical esteem for rhetorician **2**:97h
·Demosthenes' rhetorical style **5**:578f
·flourish in 4th-century Greece **8**:372a
·Greek and Roman literature development **10**:1092h
·Greek law sources **8**:399b
·Hellenistic survival and importance **6**:326f
·literary merit **10**:1042b
·Lucian's career and profession's status **11**:172h

- ·Melanesian oral literature **13**:455c
- ·Quintilian's ideas of public speaking **15**:341b
- ·radio broadcasting adaptations **18**:123f; table 125
- ·relationship to expository prose **10**:1077d
- ·Roman educational preparation and use **6**:328c
- ·Sophist curriculum **17**:11e
- ·Tacitus' rejection and reasons **17**:983e
- ·Woodlands Indian cultivation **6**:170h

Oratory of Saint Philip Neri, Institute of the, Latin INSTITUTUM ORATORII S. PHILIPPI NERII, Roman Catholic society of common life, without vows, founded by St. Philip Neri at Rome in 1575, approved in 1612, and confederated and re-approved in 1942. Each congregation, composed of priests and lay brothers (called Oratorians), is autonomous.

orb, an emblem of royal power usually made of precious metal and jewels and consisting of a sphere surmounted by a cross. The ball as a symbol of the cosmos, or of the universe as a harmonious whole, is derived from the ancient Romans, who associated it with Jupiter and hence with the emperor as his earthly repre-

Orb of the Holy Roman Empire, 12th century; in the Hofburg Treasury, Vienna
Lessing—Magnum

sentative. Christians adapted the symbol by setting a cross above the ball to signify the world dominated by Christianity. Rulers were often depicted with the orb, but the first to hold it in hand at his coronation was the Holy Roman emperor Henry II in 1014; thereafter the "imperial apple" became an important emblem of the royal power invested in the monarch.

orbicular muscle of the eye, Latin MUSCULUS ORBICULARIS OCULI, the sphincter muscle that closes the eyelids, as in sleep or winking.
- ·structure and function in human eye **7**:92a; illus. 93

orbicular muscle of the mouth, Latin MUSCULUS ORBICULARIS ORIS, the complex muscle that closes and moves the lips.
- ·human digestive system anatomy **5**:789d

orbicular texture: *see in* spherulite.

Orbigny, Alcide (-Charles-Victor) Dessalines d' (b. Sept. 6, 1802, Couëron, Fr.—d. June 30, 1857, near Saint-Denis), founder of the science of micropaleontology. During eight years of travel in South America (1826–34) he studied the people, natural history, and geology of the continent. He summarized these studies in *Voyage dans l'Amérique méridionale* (10 vol., 1834–47; "Journey into South America") and drew up the first comprehensive map of that continent (1842). The most important result of his work was the founding of the science of stratigraphical pa-

Orbigny, engraving by an unknown artist
Boyer—H. Roger-Viollet

leontology, which was based on his observations of exposed fossil-bearing strata in the Paraná Basin. He realized that the distinct layers of sedimentary rock must have been deposited in water at successive periods of time and that these periods could be determined by dating the fossils found in each layer, and thus was the first to divide geological formations into stages of deposition. He believed, however, that each stage represented an independent fauna, the result of a special act of creation. His position thus differed radically from the evolutionary theory advanced by Charles Darwin, who had explored much of South America and observed many of the same phenomena during the time that Orbigny was present there.

Orbigny's study of small marine fossils, pollen, grains, and spores found in sedimentary rocks, for the purpose of dating stages, represented the beginning of the science of micropaleontology, a discipline that is of great practical value in petroleum exploration. In 1850 Orbigny undertook the detailed assignment of stages represented by Jurassic Period fossils in geologic formations of northwestern Europe. His *Paléontologie française* (14 vol., 1840–54), although never completed, is a monumental work.
- ·Jurassic stage name origins **10**:354d; table 355
- ·stage concept introduction **17**:718e
- ·time scale development and divisions **7**:1068a

Orbiniida, order of polychaete worms of the class Polychaeta, phylum Annelida.
- ·characteristics and classification **1**:936b; illus. 935

orbit, in anatomy, the socket of the eye.

human
- ·eye anatomy and physiology **7**:91g
- ·fractures caused by explosions **4**:1043e
- ·inflammatory conditions and tumours **7**:117b
- ·protective function of skull **16**:813h
- ·primate sensory evolution trend **11**:420d

orbit, in astronomy, the path of a body revolving around an attracting centre of mass, as a planet around the Sun or a satellite around a planet. In the 17th century, Johannes Kepler and Isaac Newton discovered the basic physical laws governing orbits; in the 20th century, Albert Einstein's general theory of relativity appeared to supply a more exact description.

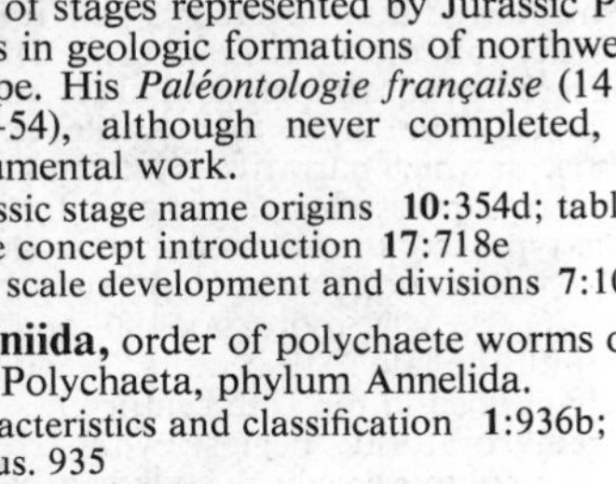

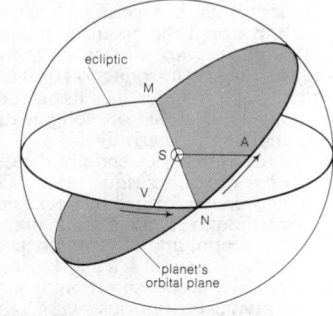

Planet's orbital plane in relation to the ecliptic

The orbit of a planet, if unaffected by the attraction of another planet, is elliptical; some elliptical orbits are very nearly circles, others are much elongated. In theory, some bodies may follow a parabolic or hyperbolic path. The orbit of a body approaching the solar system from a very great distance, curving once around the Sun, and receding again, is practically such an open curve.

In determining the elements (see below) of the orbit of a body, at least three positions of the body should be measured. Observations should be spread evenly in time and should extend over a considerable arc of the orbit. Further measurements are necessary to account for the effects of minor disturbing forces, such as planetary attractions, irregularities of mass within the body at the centre of the orbit (mascons), and, in the case of some artificial satellites, atmospheric drag.

An orbit is completely described by six geometric properties called its elements; from them the planet's future positions can be calculated. The elements are (1) the inclination of the orbit plane and (2) the longitude of the ascending node, which fix the orbit plane; (3) the semimajor axis, (4) the eccentricity and (5) the longitude of perihelion (or perigee or periastron), which fix the size and shape of the orbit in the orbit plane; and (6) the time of perihelion (or perigee or periastron), which locates the body in the orbit. These are explained below.

The Sun occupies one of the two foci of the ellipse of the orbit of a planet. A line drawn through the point of the planet's closest approach to the Sun (perihelion) and farthest retreat (aphelion) passes through the Sun and is called the line of apsides or major axis of the orbit; one-half the length of this line is the semimajor axis, equivalent to the planet's mean distance from the Sun. The eccentricity of an elliptical orbit is the amount by which it deviates from a circle; it is found by dividing the distance between the focal points of the ellipse by the length of the major axis. To predict the position of the planet at any time it is necessary to know the time when it passed through any definite position; *e.g.*, its time of perihelion passage.

The inclination, or tilt, of a planet's orbit is measured in degrees of arc from the plane of the Earth's orbit, called the ecliptic. S, at the centre of the drawing, represents the Sun. The points where the two orbital planes intersect (as projected in imagination upon the celestial sphere) are called the nodes, shown as M and N. V is the vernal equinox, a point on the ecliptic from which several celestial coordinates are measured. The angle VSN, in degrees of arc, is the longitude of the ascending node, *i.e.*, of the point where the moving planet passes north of the plane of Earth's orbit. M, the descending node, is where the planet passes from north to south. The sum of the angles subtended at S by the arcs VN and NA is called the longitude of the perihelion. It defines the direction of the major axis in the plane of the orbit.
- ·cometary orbits and perturbations **4**:971g
- ·Copernican theory in historical perspective **5**:145b
- ·Earth climatic change theories **4**:740c
- ·eclipse alignments and variations **6**:189f
- ·eclipsing binary star light curves **17**:591f
- ·Eudoxus' explanation **6**:1021g
- ·Gauss's calculation techniques **7**:966h
- ·interplanetary magnetic field **9**:787a
- ·Kepler's planetary motion studies **10**:432h
- ·Lagrangian point theory **8**:288a
- ·Laplace and theory of gravitation **10**:680g
- ·Martian orbital elements **11**:519d; table
- ·Mercury studies and changes in data **11**:916b; table
- ·meteor and comet orbit sharing **12**:37b
- ·Moon's periods and inclination **12**:415f
- ·Neptune and satellite orbits **12**:964h; tables 963
- ·Newton–Hooke planet motion controversy **13**:19b

·planetary motion law development **11**:757a
·planetary motion theories **14**:384f *passim* to 389c
·Poincaré's mathematical theory **14**:605e
·satellite orbit control system **16**:263a
·spacecraft orbital flight **17**:359h
·star cluster motion and orbit **17**:606d
·stellar dynamical parallax **13**:996g
·theoretical development since Aristotle **8**:286h
·theory, variations, and calculations **2**:250d

orbital, in chemistry and physics, strictly a mathematical expression, called a wave function, that describes properties characteristic of no more than two electrons in the vicinity of an atomic nucleus or of a system of nuclei as in a molecule. Orbitals are commonly regarded as regions in space about the nucleus that can be occupied by no more than a pair of electrons. The shape of an electron's orbital often is depicted as a three-dimensional figure that represents a region within which there is a 95 percent probability of finding the electron.

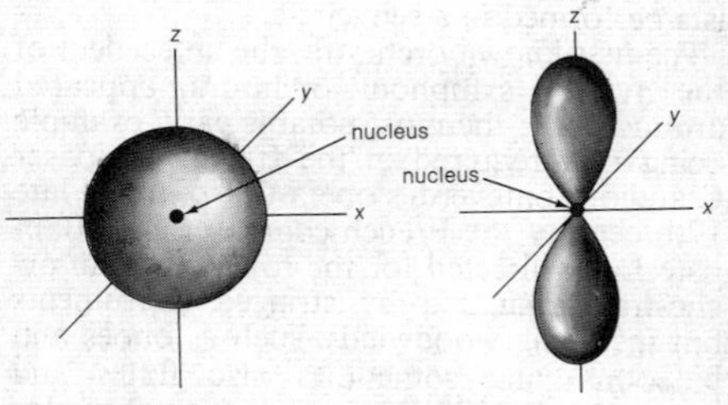

Electron orbitals in atoms: (left) *s* orbital; (right) *p* orbital

Atomic orbitals are commonly designated by a combination of numerals and letters that represent specific properties of the electrons associated with the orbitals—for example, 1*s*, 2*p*, 3*d*, 4*f*. The numerals, called principal quantum numbers, indicate energy levels as well as relative distance from the nucleus. A 1*s* electron occupies the first energy level, or shell, nearest the nucleus. A more energetic 2*s* electron spends most of its time farther away from the nucleus. The letters, *s*, *p*, *d*, *f*, *g*, *h*, *i*, and so forth, designate the shape of the orbital. (The shape is a consequence of the magnitude of the electron's angular momentum, resulting from its angular motion.) An *s* orbital is spherical with its centre at the nucleus. Thus a 1*s* electron is almost entirely confined to a spherical region around the nucleus with a very high probability of being near the edge of the sphere. A *p* orbital has the approximate shape of a pair of lobes on opposite sides of the nucleus, or a somewhat dumbbell shape. An electron in a *p* orbital has equal probability of being in either half. The shapes of the other orbitals are more complicated. The letters *s*, *p*, *d*, *f* originally were used to classify spectra descriptively into series called sharp, principal, diffuse, and fundamental, before the relation between spectra and atomic electron configuration was known.

No *p* orbitals exist in the first energy level, but there is a set of three in each of the higher levels. These triplets are oriented in space as if they were on three axes at right angles to each other and may be distinguished by subscripts, for example, $2p_x$, $2p_y$, $2p_z$. In all but the first two principal levels there is a set of five *d* orbitals and a set of seven *f* orbitals, appearing in all but the first three levels, all with complicated orientations. (The orientation of orbitals in space about the nucleus is a consequence of the vector nature, or direction, of the electron's angular momentum and its related magnetic properties as implied by the magnetic quantum number.)

Only two electrons, because of their spin, can be associated with each orbital. An electron may be thought of as having either a clockwise or a counterclockwise spin about its axis, making each electron a tiny magnet. Electrons in full orbitals are paired off with opposite spins or opposite magnetic polarities. Thus, in an atom that has all of the fourth-level orbitals occupied, there are 32 electrons: a pair of 4*s* electrons, six 4*p* electrons, 10 4*d* electrons, and 14 4*f* electrons. *Major ref.* **18**:602f; illus. 603

·actinide element atomic structure **1**:64h
·atomic electron concept development **6**:666e; illus.
·atomic spectra periodic properties **17**:463h
·boron group structures **3**:44e
·Broglie electron orbit theory **3**:323e
·carbon group hybrid bonding **3**:842c
·chemical bonding and electronic structure **4**:87b; table
·halogen bonding capacities **8**:561f
·ligand-field theory **18**:609h
·nitrogen structure and bond formation **13**:122f
·noble gas bonding and valence electrons **13**:141h
·organic nitrogen compound structure **13**:694e
·organometallic bonds and structures **13**:718a
·periodic law and electronic structure **14**:79d
·radiation interactions with atoms **15**:392d
·reaction rate and shell availability **4**:155e
·sulfur atom characteristics **13**:707f

orbital angular momentum (physics): *see* momentum.

orbital electron capture (physics): *see* electron capture.

orbital quantum number: *see* LS coupling.

orbital velocity, velocity sufficient to cause a natural or artificial satellite to remain in orbit. Inertia of the moving body tends to make it move on in a straight line, while gravitational force tends to pull it down. The orbital path, elliptical or circular, thus represents a balance between gravity and inertia. A cannon fired from a mountaintop will throw a projectile farther if its muzzle velocity is increased. If velocity is made high enough the projectile never falls to the ground. The surface of the Earth may be thought of as curving away from the projectile, or satellite, as fast as the latter falls toward it. The more massive the body at the centre of attraction, the higher is the orbital velocity for a particular altitude or distance. Near the surface of the Earth, if air resistance could be disregarded, orbital velocity would be about eight kilometres (five miles) per second. The farther from the centre of attraction a satellite is, the weaker the gravitational force and the less velocity it needs to remain in orbit. *See also* escape velocity.

·planetary orbit and motion laws **11**:757h
·spacecraft orbital flight **17**:359h

Orbiting Astronomical Observatory (OAO), any of a series of three U.S. research satellites launched between April 8, 1966, and Aug. 21, 1972.

·research capabilities and launchings **17**:364c; table 365

Orbiting Geophysical Observatory (OGO), any of six U.S. research satellites launched between Sept. 4, 1964, and June 5, 1969.

·design, instrumentation, and research **17**:364d; table

Orbiting Solar Observatory (OSO), any of a series of eight U.S. research satellites launched between March 7, 1962, and June 21, 1975.

·development, design, and research **17**:363f; table 364

Orbitoidacea, superfamily of extinct foraminiferans of Cretaceous and Tertiary age.

·fossil era and structure **7**:558b

orbitosphenoid bone, also called LESSER WING OF SPHENOID BONE, one of two triangular, pointed, thin plates projecting from the sphenoid bone of the skull.

·human skeletal interrelationships **16**:814f; illus.

Orbost, coastal town, Victoria, Australia, in East Gippsland district just above the mouth of the Snowy River. Named after a settlement on the isle of Skye, Scotland, it was proclaimed a town in 1885 and a shire in 1892. It is a commercial centre for a region devoted to raising dairy and beef cattle, maize (corn), and vegetables. Orbost has sawmills and butter- and food-processing plants and is also a resort serving East Gippsland National Park. Pop. (1976 prelim.) 2,789.
37°42′ S, 148°27′ E

orb weaver, any spider of the family Araneidae (Argiopidae or Epeiridae) of the order Araneida, a large and widely distributed group noted for their orb-shaped webs. More than 2,500 species are known. Notable among them are the silk spiders (subfamily Nephilinae), so-called because of the great strength of their silk, which is sometimes used in the manufacture of textiles. The garden spiders (subfamily Argiopinae), common in grassy areas, are brightly coloured—yellow and black or red and black.

Golden garden spider (*Argiope aurantia*), an orb weaver
John H. Gerard—EB Inc.

·classification and general features **1**:1073d

Orcagna, Andrea, original name ANDREA DI CIONE (b. *c.* 1308—d. *c.* 1368), the most prominent Florentine artist of the mid-14th century. The son of a goldsmith, Orcagna was the leading member of a family of painters, which included three younger brothers: Nardo (died 1365/66), Matteo, and Jacopo (died after 1398) di Cione. He matriculated in the *arte dei medici e speziali* in 1343–44 and was admitted to the guild of stonemasons in 1352. In 1354 he contracted to paint an altarpiece for the Strozzi Chapel in the left transept of Sta. Maria Novella, in Florence. This polyptych (signed and dated 1357) shows the forceful handling of the figures is strongly individual, as is the attempt to treat the panels of the polyptych as a unitary scheme. The sur-

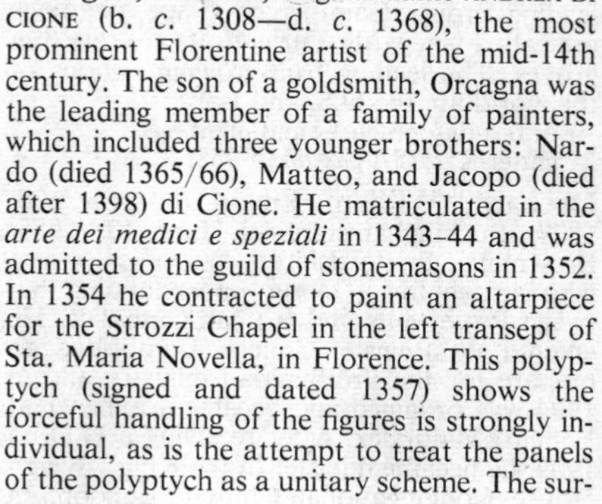

Altarpiece of "The Redeemer," polyptych by Andrea Orcagna, 1357; in the Strozzi Chapel, Sta. Maria Novella, Florence
SCALA, New York

viving section of a fresco of the "Triumph of Death" in Sta. Croce has also been ascribed to Orcagna. In September 1367 he received the commission from the Arto del Cambio for an altarpiece of the patron of the guild, St. Matthew, with four scenes from his life. In August 1368 the execution of this picture (now in the Uffizi, Florence) was taken over by Jacopo di Cione on account of the illness of his brother. Orcagna is assumed to have died in this year.

As a sculptor, Orcagna is known through a single work, the tabernacle in the guild oratory of Or San Michele, of which he became superintending architect by 1356. This is a decorative structure of great complexity, supported on four octagonal piers and heavily encrusted with coloured inlay. Its principal sculptural features are, on the front and sides, a number of hexagonal reliefs with scenes from the life of the Virgin, and, at the back, a large relief of the Dormition and Assumption of the Virgin, signed and dated 1359. The large relief is among the most notable surviving examples of the expressive art that sprang up in Tuscany after the Black Death. There are marked differences of quality in the figurated parts of the tabernacle, and some of these may be due to Orcagna's brother Matteo.

It is known that Orcagna was employed as architect in the Duomo in Florence in 1357 and 1364–67. In 1358 he became architect of the cathedral at Orvieto, where he was engaged in 1359–60 with his brother Matteo in supervising the mosaic decoration of the facade.

orchard, a planting of fruit or nut trees; also, the trees themselves. Orchards are common the world over; in the tropics, fruit, especially mangoes and bananas, is grown in small orchards for home or local consumption. Since the end of World War II, tropical orchards have become more commercial, growing large quantities of high-quality fruit for export. In the Northern Hemisphere, orchards are generally larger and more commercial; apples, grapes, and oranges (in subtropical areas) are leading crops. Commercial grape plantings are called vineyards; citrus fruits are raised in groves. The leading fruit-growing nations of the world are the U.S. and Italy.

·fruit farming practices and planting patterns **7**:757f *passim* to 758f

Orchard, William Edwin (b. Nov. 20, 1877, Buckinghamshire—d. June 12, 1955, Brownhills, Staffordshire), ecumenical priest who strove for a closer understanding between Protestants and Roman Catholics. He entered Westminster College, Cambridge, to prepare for the Presbyterian ministry and in 1904 was ordained and became a minister at Enfield, Middlesex. After receiving a D.D. in 1909, he became minister of the King's Weigh House Congregational Church, London, in 1914.

Throughout World War I, Orchard's preaching attracted large congregations. The courage of his ministry was shown by his braving a hostile mob in Trafalgar Square, London, to conduct a prayer meeting aimed at ending the war. Seeking a worldwide Christianity, he introduced Roman Catholic thought and practices into his services and attempted a rapprochement with the Church of England, a plan that collapsed after prolonged negotiations.

Becoming a Roman Catholic in 1932, he was ordained in 1935. He preached and lectured in the United States, and in 1943 he became a psychological consultant in Gloucestershire. His numerous works include the popular *The Temple* (1913) and its sequel, *Sancta Sanctorum* (1955; "The Most Holy Place").

orchard grass, also known as COCKSFOOT GRASS (*Dactylis glomerata*), perennial pasture, hay, and forage grass of the family Poaceae. It has flat leaf blades and open, irregular, stiff-branched panicles (flower clusters). Orchard grass grows in dense clusters, or tussocks, about 0.6 to one metre (2 to 3 feet) tall. It is widely cultivated throughout temperate North America, Eurasia, and Africa.

Orchard grass (*Dactylis glomerata*) showing (top) form and (bottom) seed heads

(Top) G.R. Roberts, (bottom) Grant Heilman—EB Inc.

Orchardson, Sir William Quiller (b. March 27, 1832, Edinburgh—d. April 13, 1910, London), a British portraitist and painter of historical and domestic genre.

After studying at the Trustees' Academy in Edinburgh from 1850 to 1857, Orchardson began to do black-and-white illustrations, chiefly for *Good Words*, after the Pre-Raphaelite manner. He evolved a personal style characterized by thinly hatched strokes in fluid pigment, predominantly golden in tone with relieving touches of brighter colour. After exhibiting at the Royal Scottish Academy, he went to London in 1862, exhibiting at the Royal Academy from 1863. He was elected academician in 1877 and knighted in 1907. Two of his more famous paintings, "Napoleon on Board the Bellerophon" (1880) and "Her Mother's Voice" (1888), are in the Tate Gallery, London.

Orchelimum: *see* meadow grasshopper.

Orchésographie, book about 16th century dance (especially French), written by Thoinot Arbeau (an anagram pen name of Jehan Tabourot), a priest from Langres, Fr. The first edition was published in 1588 and a second edition was brought out in 1596. Arbeau's dance descriptions are written with such clarity that the dances can be reconstructed today.

·dance style's social significance **14**:801e
·Western dance descriptions **5**:461b

Orchestia: *see* sand flea.

orchestra, instrumental ensemble of varying size and composition. Although applied to various ensembles found in Western and non-Western music, orchestra in an unqualified sense usually refers to the typical Western music ensemble of bowed string instruments complemented by wind and percussion instruments and which, in the string section at least, has more than one player per part. The word stems from the Greek *orchēstra*, the part of the ancient Greek theatre in front of the proscenium where the dancers and instrumentalists performed in a semicircle.

The first known orchestra, the antecedent of the modern symphony orchestra, appeared around 1600, the most notable early example being that required in the Italian composer Claudio Monteverdi's opera *Orfeo*. In the late 17th century the French composer Jean-Baptiste Lully directed for the royal court an orchestra dominated by stringed instruments but including woodwinds, such as oboes and bassoons, and sometimes also flutes and horns. In the 18th century in Germany, Johann Stamitz and other composers in what is known as the Mannheim school established the basic composition of the modern symphony orchestra: four sections consisting of woodwinds (flutes, oboes, and bassoons), brass (horns and trumpets), percussion (two timpani), and strings (first and second violins, violas, cellos and double basses). Clarinets were adopted into the orchestra during this period, while earlier mainstays, such as the harpsichord, lute, and theorbo (a bass lute), were gradually dropped.

The 19th century was a fertile period for the orchestra. Woodwinds were increased from two to typically three or four of each instrument, and the brass section was augmented by a third trumpet, third and fourth horns, and the inclusion of trombones. Composers such as Hector Berlioz, Richard Wagner, Nikolay Rimsky-Korsakov, and—into the 20th century—Richard Strauss, Gustav Mahler, and Igor Stravinsky added their imagination and skills to producing orchestras of unprecedented size and tonal resources. The large orchestra typical of the late 19th through mid-20th

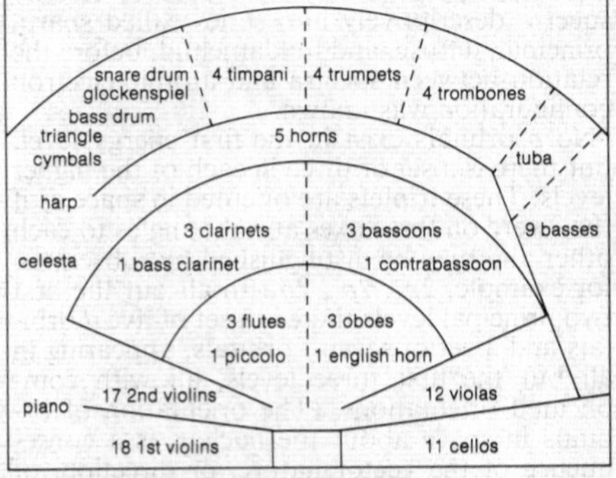

Full symphony orchestra.
Number and position of instruments is typical but may vary with musical requirements and conductor's preference

centuries incorporates an average of 100 performers and may include a wide variety of instruments and devices required in specific works. In the 1920s another trend emerged, becoming especially prominent by midcentury: many composers turned toward smaller, chamber-size ensembles, sometimes maintain-

ing and sometimes discarding the traditional instrumental subdivisions.
·concerto role with soloists **4**:1064g
·development from Classical era **12**:711e *passim* to 713e
·instrumental combinations and technique **13**:644a *passim* to 647f
·tuning disparity in early ensembles **18**:743b

orchestration and instrumentation 13:643, arts dealing with musical instruments and their capabilities of producing various timbres or colours. Instrumentation is the art of combining instruments in any sort of musical composition. Orchestration is a somewhat narrower term since it is frequently used to describe the art of instrumentation as specifically related to the symphony orchestra.

The text article covers types of instrumentation; history and development of Western instrumentation; non-Western instrumentation; and arrangement and transcription.

REFERENCES in other text articles:
·Debussy's innovative approach **5**:541d
·Gabrieli's innovations **7**:823d
·instrumental idiom development **4**:24b
·Japanese gagaku performance regulation **12**:682d
·jazz styles development **10**:121g
·Peking opera performance **12**:744d
·Romantic and 20th-century approaches **12**:720b *passim* to 721b
·Sammartini's symphonic writing style **17**:911f
·string ensemble configurations **17**:742f
·symphony orchestra's development **12**:711e *passim* to 713e
·wind section use in Western music **19**:857f

RELATED ENTRIES in the *Ready Reference and Index:*
arrangement; band; conducting; orchestra; score

Orchestre de la Suisse Romande, founded in Geneva in 1918 by the Swiss conductor Ernest Ansermet and led by him until 1967. Under Ansermet's guidance the Orchestre de la Suisse Romande became one of the world's great symphonic ensembles and introduced works—not at the time widely accepted—by such modern composers as Debussy, Stravinsky, Bartók, and Berg.

orchestrini di camera, a group of small instruments related to the harmonium, were invented and made by W.E. Evans of London. Designed to imitate the tone of the clarinet, oboe, flute, horn, and bassoon, they were intended primarily to be used as substitutes for those instruments in orchestral performances when players of the actual instruments were not available.

Orchha, a former Rājput princely state of central India, was founded about 1500. In the early 17th century, it was systematically devastated by the forces of the Mughal emperor Shāh Jahān following the rebellion of the Bundēla chief Jujhār Singh. Tehri (now Tīkamgarh; *q.v.*) was chosen as the capital in 1783. Orchha was part of the Central Indian Agency under British rule. In 1948, following the achievement of Indian independence, it was merged into Vindhya Pradesh (later Madhya Pradesh) as the district of Tīkamgarh.

Orchha, historic town, Tīkamgarh district, Rewa division, Madhya Pradesh, India, on the Betwa River. The town, surrounded by thick jungle that long made it impregnable, was founded in 1531 and served until 1783 as the capital of the former Orchha princely state. An island in the Betwa, approached by a causeway, contains a large 17th-century fort and palace. Other buildings of historic interest are several temples and a palace of Jahāngīr, an excellent example of Hindu domestic architecture. There are also several cenotaphs of the Orchha rulers. Two fairs are held annually. Orchha declined with the transfer of the capital to Tīkamgarh in 1783.
25°21′ N, 78°39′ E

orchid, common name for all members of the family Orchidaceae, a group of attractively flowered plants that comprises the order Orchidales (*q.v.*). There are from 400 to 800 genera of orchids, with at least 15,000 to as many as 35,000 species. The word orchid is derived from the Greek word (*orchis*) for testicle, because of the shape of the root tubers in some species of the genus *Orchis*. Orchids are found throughout most of the nonpolar world and are especially abundant in tropical regions. These nonwoody perennial plants grow in soil or on other plants. Those attached to other plants often are vinelike and have a spongy root covering called the velamen that absorbs water from the surrounding air. Most species manufacture their own food, but some live on dead organic material or are helped to obtain nourishment by a fungus living in their roots.

Odontoglossum grande
Sven Samelius

An orchid may have one of two growth patterns, sympodial or monopodial. Most orchids are sympodial; that is, they develop a new stem each year along a horizontal axis. The stem often has a swollen, bulblike region termed a pseudobulb. A monopodial orchid has one erect stem that grows taller each year, adding more leaves and flowers. Flowers are borne singly or in erect or pendent clusters. They range in sizes from about 2 millimetres (about 0.1 inch) to 38 centimetres (15 inches) in diameter.

All orchids have the same bilaterally symmetrical flower structure, with three sepals, but the flowers vary greatly in colour and shape. One of the petals, called the lip, often is very distinct in shape and colour from the other petals. The lip usually is the lowest part of the flower, although it is the uppermost part in the developing bud, which turns around its axis as it grows in a process termed resupination. A club-shaped structure in the centre of the flower, known as the column, results from the fusion of male and female reproductive parts. Most orchid species have one stamen (male reproductive organ) at the top of the column, rarely two at the sides. The pollen grains, contained within lobes at the top of the stamen, are grouped into mealy or waxy masses termed pollinia. These packets usually are transferred from one flower to another by insects or birds, although some species are wind- or self-pollinated. Many orchids have highly developed mechanisms (structures, scents, etc.) to ensure cross-pollination between plants. The flowers of some species resemble female insects so closely that male insects try to mate with them (a process called pseudocopulation) and thus carry pollen between flowers.

Polystachya bella
A to Z Botanical Collection—EB Inc.

More than 2,000,000 seeds may be contained in the seedpod produced by a single orchid flower. The size of these seeds caused some botanists to give the orchid order the name Microspermae. An orchid seed contains little nutritive material and needs the help of a fungus to germinate and obtain food.

The only economically important product derived from an orchid is the flavouring agent vanilla, which is obtained from the seedpod of several species of the genus *Vanilla*. Many folk medicines, local beverages, and foods are prepared from parts of orchid plants.

The ornamental genera *Cattleya*, *Cymbidium*, *Vanda*, and *Laelia* are commonly grown for hybridization. Many thousands of hybrids have been developed for use as garden or greenhouse ornamentals and in the commercial flower trade. Species of *Pleurothallis*, *Lepanthes*, and *Stelis* are popular among horticulturists because of their extremely small size. *Major ref.* **13**:648c
·Darwin's theory of adaptation **5**:494f
·embryo formation and development **5**:662c
·house plants and their care **8**:1121c
·mimicry of bee **4**:927c
·mimicry of female insects **12**:218b; illus., **12**:Mimicry, Plate 1
·Tertiary evolution inference **18**:153f

Orchidales 13:648, the orchid order of flowering plants, containing the family Orchidaceae, which includes about 400 to 800 genera with 15,000 to 35,000 species (depending on the authority consulted). Many species are cultivated as ornamentals and for the cut-flower trade. Vanilla is the only economically important product derived from an orchid.

The text article covers general features, form and function, natural history, and evolution of the orchid order and includes an annotated classification of the group.

REFERENCES in other text articles:
·angiosperm features and classification **1**:884d
·artificial light effect on flowering **14**:352e
·Iridales features resemblance **9**:891c
·lady slipper seeds, illus., **16**:Seed and Fruit, Plate 1
·Liliales evolutionary relationships **10**:974e
·mimicry of female insects **12**:218b; illus., **12**:Mimicry, Plate 1
·pollination by bees **14**:746b
·pollination function of flower symmetry **14**:380h
·pseudocopulation of wasps **2**:806d

RELATED ENTRIES in the *Ready Reference and Index: for*
common plants: see bird's-nest orchid; bucket orchid; butterfly orchid; coralroot; donkey orchid; dragon's-mouth; fairy slipper; frog orchid; greenhood; jewel orchid; ladies' tresses; lady's slipper; lizard orchid; man orchid; moth orchid; orchid; rein orchid; spider orchid; sun orchid; twayblade
general terms: Microspermae; pollinium; pseudocopulation
plant genera: Bulbophyllum; Calanthe; Calopogon; Cattleya; Coelogyne; Cymbidium; Dactylorhiza; Dendrobium; Disa; Epiden-

drum; Laelia; Lycaste; Masdevallia; Maxillaria; Odontoglossum; Oncidium; Ophrys; Orchis; Pleurothallis; Pogonia; Serapias; Vanda; Zygopetalum

orchid cactus: *see* leaf cactus.

orchil, or ARCHIL, a violet dye obtained from some lichens by fermentation. It is also the term for any lichen that yields orchil (*Roccella*, *Lecanora*, *Ochrolechin*, and *Evernia*) and refers to any colour obtained from this dye.
·lichen sources of litmus **10**:883d

Orchis, a genus of orchids, family Orchidaceae, that contains about 35 to 100 species (depending on the authority consulted) native to Eurasia and North America. Each plant bears a single flower spike with many flowers and has egg-shaped, lobed, or forked root tubers. Most species have several leaves at the base. The petals and sepals often form a helmetlike structure, and the flower lip usually is several lobed. The monkey orchid (*O. simia*) and the soldier, or military, orchid (*O. militaris*) are two European species the flowers of which resemble helmeted human figures. The root tubers of the early purple orchid (*O. mascula*) and several other species contain a nutritive starch. In southern Europe they are softened by soaking to produce a drink called salep. The green-winged orchid (*O. morio*) is widely distributed throughout Eurasia. Other Eurasian species of *Orchis* include some known as marsh orchids and others called spotted orchids. The showy orchis (*O. spectabilis*) is the most well-known of the three North American species of *Orchis*. It has pink or purple flowers and ranges in height from 6 to 20 centimetres (2 to 8 inches).
·salep derivation and food uses **13**:649f

orchitis, inflammation and swelling of the testes as a result of infection or physical injury. The testes are located in the scrotum of the male; they produce sperm cells for reproduction. Connected to the back of each testis is the epididymis structure; this serves as a storage duct for sperm awaiting release. The tubules that produce the sperm are called seminiferous tubules; the tube that conducts sperm away from the testes and epididymis is the spermatic cord. Covering the body of the testicular tissue is a thick, white fibrous coat known as the tunica albuginea. The rich blood supply and lymphatic supply in the testicle prevent most infections from obtaining a strong foothold in this organ. Infections can spread from elsewhere in the body by way of the blood stream, lymphatic channels, or the spermatic cord to the epididymis and testes. Organisms causing inflammation can be bacterial, viral, fungal, or parasitic, and inflammation can come from chemical or physical injury. The usual symptoms of orchitis are high fever, sudden pain in the testicle, nausea, vomiting, swelling, tightness, and tenderness of the gland upon touching. Fluids that may accumulate around the testes may contain pus or blood. The scrotum is generally red and thickened.

Orchitis may result from infections and other diseases elsewhere in the body. Mumps is probably the systemic disease most likely to affect the testes; it is caused by a virus. Permanent damage is rare. Usually only one testis is influenced, with sometimes the epididymis. Impotence and sterility are the worst permanent effects of orchitis. Usually the symptoms are chills, nausea, vomiting, and testicular swelling. The orchitis subsides spontaneously in 10 days or less; in severe cases of swelling and edema, relief may be obtained by surgical drainage, which can also reduce some of the tissue destruction.

Physical injuries, such as those caused by blows, are generally followed by infections when severe. The injury lowers the resistance to bacteria. Enlargement, bruises, and most of the infectious symptoms appear. Chemicals such as iodine, lead, and alcohol have on occasion caused testicular injury. Treatment for most orchitis is administration of antibiotics, bed rest, support of the testes, use of compresses, and surgical relief or drainage when required.

Orchoë (ancient Mesopotamian city): *see* Erech.

Orchomenus, ORCHOMENOS in literature, ERCHOMENOS on coins and in inscriptions, the name of two cities in ancient Greece.

Orchomenus, a Boeotian town on a promontory on the north of the Copiac plain. The northernmost Mycenaean fortified town, it was a seat of the Minyae dynastic family and controlled a large part of Boeotia. In the archaic period, Orchomenus was a member of the Calaurian League, but political supremacy in Boeotia passed to Thebes. Among the first Boeotian cities to coin money (*c.* 550 BC), it was famed in legend for its wealth. The worship of the Charites or Graces was an important cult.

Orchomenus became the headquarters of the oligarchic exiles who freed Boeotia from Athenian control (447/446), and by the 4th century its policy was anti-Theban. After repeated sackings by the Thebans in the 4th century, Orchomenus was left to obscurity and the encroaching waters of Lake Copias.

The excavations of H. Schliemann (late 19th century) and A. Furtwängler and H. Bulle (early 20th century) showed Orchomenus to have been an important Neolithic and Bronze Age site with a Late Bronze Age *tholos*, or "beehive," temple and palace.

Orchomenus, an Arcadian town about nine miles north-northwest of Mantineia that held some sovereignty over all Arcadia until late in the 7th century BC. In the 5th century it was overshadowed by Mantineia and in 370 lost possessions to the new Arcadian capital, Megalopolis. In the 3rd century it joined successively Sparta, the Aetolian League, and the Achaean League (*c.* 235).
·growth and importance in Archaic Period **8**:345e; map 326
·Schliemann's archaeological discovery **16**:349a

Orcinus orca: *see* killer whale.

Orconectes: *see* crayfish.

Orcus, in Roman religion, the kingdom of the dead or its ruler. The term originally may have meant "a storage vessel" and, later, "a subterranean repository for the dead"; but that is not borne out by the earlier literary evidence, in which Orcus is always a person. As king of the underworld, he was frequently indistinguishable from Dis; he could, however, also be a demon of death who destroyed living men. He was too menacing and insubstantial to have a cult or to be represented in the visual arts.

Orczy, Baroness (Emmuska) (b. 1865, Tarna-Eörs, Hung.—d. Nov. 12, 1947), novelist chiefly remembered as author of *The Scarlet Pimpernel*, one of the greatest popular successes of the century.

The only child of Baron Felix Orczy, a noted composer and conductor, she was educated in Brussels and Paris, then studied art in London. She later exhibited some of her work in the Royal Academy. She became famous in 1905 with the publication of *The Scarlet Pimpernel*, set in the times of the French Revolution, and relating the swashbuckling adventures of the "elusive" Sir Percy Blakeney, whose mission was to smuggle French aristocrats out of the country to safety. Baroness Orczy produced sequels—*The Elusive Pimpernel* (1908), *The Way of the Scarlet Pimpernel* (1933)—which were less successful than the original. She also wrote several detective stories, including *Lady Molly of Scotland Yard* (1910) and *Unravelled Knots* (1925).

ordeal, a trial or judgment of the truth of some claim or accusation by various means based on the belief that the outcome will reflect the judgment of supernatural powers and that these powers will ensure the triumph of right. Although fatal consequences often attended an ordeal, its purpose is not punitive.

There are several main types of ordeal: ordeals by divination, physical test, and battle. A Burmese ordeal by divination involves two parties being furnished with candles of equal size and lighted simultaneously; the owner of the candle that outlasts the other is adjudged to have won his cause. Another form of ordeal by divination is the appeal to the corpse for the discovery of its murderer. The ordeal of the bier in medieval Europe was founded on the belief that a sympathetic action of the blood causes it to flow at the touch or nearness of the murderer.

The ordeal by physical test, particularly by fire or water, is the most common. In Hindu codes a wife passed through fire to prove her fidelity to a jealous husband; traces of burning would be proof of guilt. Water is often believed to reject the guilty and accept the innocent, hence the old English usage of ducking suspected witches.

In ordeal by combat, or ritual combat, the victor wins not by his own strength but because supernatural powers have intervened on the side of the right, as in the duel in the European Middle Ages in which the "judgment of God" was thought to determine the winner. If still alive after the combat, the loser might be hanged or burned for a criminal offense or have a hand cut off and property confiscated in civil actions.
·English feudal trial procedures **8**:766a
·evidence and appeal to supernatural **7**:1c
·feudal Europe's legal evolution **6**:1120e
·Iranian ritual of fire and water **9**:872e
·jury trial as replacement **10**:360h
·medieval legal system development **12**:152f
·passage rite practices **13**:1050d
·ritual rebirth as plant or animal **1**:915e
·social responses to possession **5**:919h
·weight lifting as test of manhood **8**:516d

Ordelaffi, noble Italian family that ruled the town of Forlì and neighbouring places in the Romagna during most of the 14th and 15th centuries. Little is known of their rise; a reference in Dante's *Inferno* indicates that Forlì had passed effectively under their control by the early 14th century. In 1307 Scarpetta Ordelaffi became head of the city with the title *capitano del popolo* ("captain of the people.") They were aggressively Ghibelline (pro-imperial) and during the 14th century added Forlimpopoli and Cesena to their dominion. Eventually the Guelf (papal) faction organized a campaign against them that led to three years of war (1356–59), including the stubborn defense of Cesena by Francesco Ordelaffi and his no less resolute wife, Cia Ubaldini, before they won. Even then, though Francesco lost Forlì, it was recovered in 1376 by his son Sinibaldo. A popular rising in 1405 led to another dispossession of the Ordelaffi by the papal party, followed by another recovery; through the remainder of the century the family alternately seized and lost its dynastic estate, culminating in the reign of Pino III Ordelaffi, distinguished for his patronage of the arts and his murderous violence. Having seized the throne by the murder of his brother Cecco III, he killed his first wife, his mother, and his second wife before being himself murdered by his third wife, Lucrezia Pico, in 1480. Pope Sixtus IV reclaimed Forlì and gave it to his nephew; except for a momentary restoration in 1503–04, the Ordelaffi disappeared from the history of Forlì and Italy.

Ordenações Afonsinas: *see* Afonsine Ordinances.

Ordenancas Reales, Castilian juridical publication of 1485. *See* Libro de Montalvo.

order (architecture): *see* orders of architecture.

order (taxonomy): *see* taxon.

order, in mathematics, a relationship exemplified by the "less than" relationship of an inequality (*q.v.*). Order if represented by the symbol "*" is: (1) not symmetric—if $A * B$ then $B * A$ cannot be true; (2) transitive—if $A * B$, $B * C$, then $A * C$; (3) trichotometric—if A is not equal to B, then $A * B$, or $B * A$. In algebra, a set S is called well-ordered if every subset of S contains a first (or least) element.
·algebraic structure theory **1**:519d
·axiomatic basis of measurement **11**:740h
·Euclidean geometry principles **7**:1102a

order and chaos (philosophy): *see* chaos and order.

ordered field, in mathematics, field that has positive and negative elements; *i.e.*, a collection of elements called the positive elements in which the sum and product of two positive elements are again positive and such that any non-zero element of the field is either a positive element or the negative of a positive element. *Major ref.* **1**:539b
·complex analysis fundamentals **1**:720b
·number theory principles **13**:363f
·real analysis principles **1**:777c

ordered pair, in mathematics, a set containing two members, called the first and second. A common example of an ordered pair is the set of Cartesian coordinates (x,y) of a point in the XY-plane.
·algebraic geometry fundamentals **7**:1072e
·Cartesian product spaces **18**:511d
·complex analysis fundamentals **1**:720b
·set theory equivalence relation **16**:570f

Orderic Vitalis (b. Feb. 16, 1075, near Shrewsbury—d. *c.* 1142), monk of Saint-Évroult in Normandy, a historian who in his *Historia ecclesiastica* left one of the fullest and most graphic accounts of Anglo-Norman society in his own day.

The eldest son of Odelerius of Orléans, the chaplain to Roger de Montgomery, earl of Shrewsbury, he was baptized with the name of Orderic in Atcham church on Easter Eve, 1075. He learned his letters from the priest Siward in the Church of St. Peter and St. Paul, Shrewsbury; and was sent to Normandy in 1085 to become a monk at Saint-Évroult, where he was given the name Vitalis. There, apart from a few visits to other monasteries, including Cluny, Cambrai, Crowland, and Worcester, he passed the remainder of his life. Most of his time was spent in the scriptorium, teaching calligraphy, copying books, and later composing epitaphs and other occasional verses and, above all, history.

He began his historical work before 1109 by transcribing the *Gesta Normannorum ducum* of William of Jumièges with lengthy interpolations of his own, chiefly relating to the history of Norman families connected with Saint-Évroult. Not later than 1115, at the command of his abbot, he began a history of his own monastery and its patrons, which gradually expanded into a general history of the church and incorporated a chronological outline of events from the birth of Christ, originally intended as a separate work. He worked on his history, periodically revising the early parts, until June 1141.

He made critical use of all the works of contemporary historians that he was able to borrow, including the histories of William of Poitiers, William of Jumièges, and Florence of Worcester for English and Norman affairs, and Baudry of Bourgueil and Fulcher of Chartres for the First Crusade. His account of William the Conqueror's campaigns in 1067–71, based on William of Poitiers, has the value of a contemporary narrative, because the last books of William's *Gesta Guillelmi ducis Normannorum et regis Anglorum* have not survived in the original. Otherwise the *Historia ecclesiastica* is most valuable for Norman, English, and French history in the period 1082–1141. Orderic's handling of the life of Christ, based partly on St. Augustine's *De consensu Evangelistarum* and partly on the universal history of Marianus Scotus, has a fullness and individuality unusual at that date.

Order Number 1 (March 14, 1917), during the Russian Revolution, directive issued by the Petrograd Soviet placing military authority in soldiers' committees and removing it from the Provisional Government and military officers. The order undermined discipline and contributed to the Russian surrender in World War I.
·Russian World War I withdrawal **19**:958b

Order of Geneva (religious manual): *see* Common Order, Book of.

orders (in religion): *see* holy orders; religious communities, Anglican; religious orders of men, Roman Catholic; religious orders of women, Roman Catholic.

orders in council, in Great Britain, regulations issued by the sovereign on the advice of the Privy Council; in modern practice, however, an order is issued only upon the advice of ministers, the minister in charge of the department concerned with the subject matter of the order being responsible to Parliament for its contents. An order is signed by the clerk to the Privy Council, who is responsible for making sure that it is in correct form.

In modern practice, there are two distinct types of order in council: that issued under the royal prerogative and that made under a power conferred by a statute. An example of the first type is the order declaring a state of war to be at an end, since the power to make war and peace is a matter of the royal prerogative. Most orders in council, however, are issued to implement legislation passed by Parliament; for example, the Ministers of the Crown (Transfer of Functions) Act, 1946, arranged for the redistribution of ministerial functions and the dissolution of government departments to be effected by order in council, confirmed by a resolution of both houses of Parliament.

Orders in council, the modern equivalent of medieval ordinances and the proclamations of the Tudor sovereigns, were first issued during the 18th century. Historically, the best known are those issued in November and December 1807, which imposed a blockade on Napoleonic Europe by the British and, in response, the decree by which the French might seize any neutral ship that complied with the British regulations.
·Continental System retaliation measures **7**:727f

orders of architecture, architectural units, each consisting of a column with its base and capital (the most distinguishing characteristic of a particular order) and, above, an entablature (*q.v.*) composed of three parts: the lintel, called the architrave, the frieze, and the cornice. There are five major orders: Tuscan, Doric, Ionic, Corinthian, and Composite (*qq.v.*).

Greek architecture developed two distinct orders, the Doric and the Ionic, together with a third (Corinthian) capital, which, with modifications, were adopted by the Romans in the 1st century BC.

Although distinguishable by capital, there are many separate elements that make up the complete order. At the bottom is the top step of the structure called the stylobate. Above this is the plinth, on which the base of the column rests. The column itself is composed of the shaft, sometimes articulated with fluting (semicircular depressions) and cinctures (narrow, vertical flat bands). At the top of the shaft, but still below the capital, is the necking; in the Greek Doric order this form consists of the hypotrachelion (groove), annulets (flat strips), and the trachelion (groove). On top of the shaft is the echinus (an ovolo, or rounded convex, molding) and the abacus (a flat slab) on which the lintel, or architrave, rests. The volutes (spiral scrolls) of the Ionic capital and the bell of acanthus leaves on the Corinthian capital occur between the echinus and the abacus. Resting on the abacus is the architrave, bottom element of the tripartite entablature. In the Corinthian order, the architrave is stepped, composed of projecting fascia (bands) alternating with moldings. Immediately above the architrave is a projecting band called the taenia above which is the frieze. The Doric frieze has alternating vertical, slightly projecting slabs (triglyphs) and depressions (metopes). Under the triglyph, beneath the taenia and parallel to it, there is a band called the regula from which small drops (guttae) project. The Ionic and Corinthian frieze is carved or plain with a row of toothlike projections (dentils) under the cornice. The Tuscan cornice is composed of a bed molding surmounted by a corona and a cymatium (*see also* molding). The sloping profile of the gabled roof is called the raking cornice.

The Tuscan order has an unfluted shaft and a simple echinus–abacus capital. This order is the most solid appearing, and Vitruvius (who in the 1st century BC wrote a handbook for Roman architects, *De architectura*) therefore placed it at the bottom of the hierarchy.

The Doric order differs from the Tuscan order in having a more elaborate base, a fluted shaft, and a more articulated capital, which may or may not be carved with rosettes or egg and dart. The frieze has metopes and triglyphs, and the top may be denticular or mutular. The Roman forms of the Doric order have smaller proportions and appear lighter and more graceful than their Greek counterparts.

The Ionic column has more flutes than does the Doric and has volutes on its front and rear faces, which droop below the carved echinus.

The Greeks as well as the Romans regarded the Corinthian as only a variant capital to be substituted for the Ionic. First appearing on the choragic Monument of Lysicrates (Athens, 335/334 BC; *see* choragic monument), it was raised to the rank of an order by Vitruvius. The capital is an inverted bell that is covered with acanthus leaves. Small scrolls or rampant animal figures appear at the corners. The remainder of the order is essentially Ionic.

The Composite order, which in the Renaissance period was ranked as a separate order, is a late Roman development of the Corinthian. The lower part of the capital is Corinthian and is surmounted by Ionic volutes canted at a 45° angle at the corners. A monumental example is on the Arch of Titus in the Forum Romanum.
·furniture adaptation and period use **7**:785f
·Greek architectural evolution **19**:287b
·Indian use in various styles **17**:173g
·Renaissance use of five orders **19**:380d
·Roman architectural developments **19**:302d

Ordinalia, 15th-century Cornish dramatic literary work.
·content and literary significance **10**:1115e

ordinal numbers, in mathematics, quantities that denote positions in an order or set (*i.e.*, first, second, third, . . . as opposed to one, two, three, . . .). Two well-ordered sets have the same ordinal number if there exists a one-to-one order-preserving correspondence between them. Finite ordinals are denoted by positive integers; the ordinal number of the set of finite ordinals is symbolized by the Greek letter omega, ω; successive ordinals by $\omega + 1$, $\omega + 2$, ... *See* number; cardinal numbers; transfinite number.
·real analysis principles **1**:776g
·set theory ordering relations **16**:572f

Ordinance 50, act passed in the Cape Colony, now part of South Africa, in 1828 to secure legal rights for nonwhite servants. It specifically allowed Cape Coloureds to hold property, abolished the immobilizing pass system, and introduced safeguards in the master–servant relationship. Passed at a time when the abolition of the slave trade created a demand for indigenous labour, the ordinance greatly disturbed colonists who feared consequent desertion, vagrancy, and labour shortages. Attempts to introduce laws against vagrancy in 1828 and 1834 were, however, disallowed by the British government. Though Ordinance 50 was an ostensible reason for the Great Trek—the emigration of Afrikaners from Cape Colony—it probably had little long-term effect on the supply and powerlessness of Coloured labour in the colony. In 1841 the law was largely incorporated in a Masters and Servants Ordinance, which brought all servants under common laws and, among other provisions, made desertion a criminal offense.

·basic provision and white reaction **17**:284b

Ordinances of the Holy Apostles Through Clement: *see* Apostolic Constitutions.

Ordinari post tijdender, Swedish newspaper begun in 1645 and considered to be the oldest continuously published paper in the world. It survives in the 1970s, however, in the form of an official bulletin called *Post-och inrikes tidningar*.

·newspaper publishing history **15**:239b

ordinary, OR HONOURABLE ORDINARY, in heraldry, a class of charges on the field, often used and hence "ordinary."

·heraldic figures and design **8**:788a; illus. 787

ordinary differential equation, in mathematics, an equation relating a function f of one variable to its derivatives. (The adjective "ordinary" here refers to those differential equations involving one variable, as distinguished from such equations involving several variables, called partial differential equations.)

The derivative, written f' or df/dx, of a function f expresses its rate of change at each point; that is, how fast the value of the function is increasing or decreasing as the value of the variable is increased or decreased. For the function $f = ax + b$ (representing a straight line), the rate of change is simply its slope—that is, $f' = a$. For other functions, the rate of change varies along the curve of the function, and the precise way of defining and calculating it is the subject of differential calculus. The derivative of a function is again a function, because the rate of change varies along the curve. Therefore, the derivative of the derivative can also be calculated, $(f')'$ or simply f'' or d^2f/dx^2, and is called the second-order derivative of the original function. Higher-order derivatives can be similarly defined.

The order of a differential equation is defined to be that of the highest order derivative it contains. The degree of a differential equation is defined as the power to which the highest order derivative is raised. The equation $(f''')^2 + (f'')^4 + ff = x$ is an example of a second-degree, third-order differential equation. A first-degree equation is called linear if the function and all its derivatives occur to the first power, and if the coefficient of each derivative in the equation involves only the independent variable x. An equation is called homogeneous if each term contains the function or some derivative. The equation $xf'' + af' + bf = 0$ is a homogeneous linear differential equation. Some equations, such as $f' = x^2$, can be solved by merely recalling which function has a derivative that will satisfy the equation, but in most cases the solution is not obvious by inspection, and the subject of differential equations consists partly of classifying the numerous types of equations that can be solved by various techniques.

Differential equations do not always have solutions, and the greater part of research involves investigating this question. *Major ref.* **5**:738a

·history of mathematics **11**:652h
·mathematical calculation theory **11**:689g
·numerical analysis fundamentals **13**:390d

ordinary-language philosophy, the analysis and use of nontechnical language as a proper and capable vehicle for conveying all thought, including philosophical reflections. The basic source for the school is the later writings of Ludwig Wittgenstein, followed by the contributions of John Langshaw Austin, Gilbert Ryle, John Wisdom, and other British philosophers.

·basis in study of linguistic rules **14**:882b
·development within Analytic philosophy **1**:800h
·intuitionist meta-ethics criticism **6**:983c
·natural language as philosophical tool **16**:507d
·noncognitivist meta-ethical theories **6**:986h

ordinary ray (optics): *see* refraction, double.

ordinary shares: *see* common stock.

Ordinatio Imperii (817), ordinance by which Louis the Pious determined the division of the Frankish empire among his sons.

·Carolingian succession regulation **11**:930c

ordination, in Christian churches, a rite for the dedication and commissioning of ministers. The essential ceremony consists of the laying of hands of the ordaining minister upon the head of the one being ordained, with prayer for the gifts of the Holy Spirit and of grace required for the carrying out of the ministry. The service also usually includes a public examination of the candidate and a sermon or charge concerning the responsibilities of the ministry.

Christianity derived the ceremony from the Jewish custom of ordaining rabbis by the laying on of hands (the *Semikha*). In the Old Testament, Moses ordained Joshua (Num. 27: 18, 23; Deut. 34:9), and in the New Testament the seven were ordained by the Twelve Apostles (Acts 6:6) and Barnabas and Paul were commissioned by prophets and teachers at Antioch (Acts 13:3). According to the Pastoral Letters (I Tim. 4:14; II Tim. 1:6), ordination confers a spiritual gift of grace. The oldest ordination prayers extant are contained in the *Apostolic Tradition* of Hippolytus of Rome (*c.* AD 217). In medieval times, the Latin rites were elaborated by the addition of various prayers and of such ceremonies as the anointing of hands, clothing the ordinand with the appropriate vestments, and presenting him with the symbols pertinent to his rank; *e.g.*, the Gospels to a deacon and the chalice and paten with the bread and wine to a candidate for the priesthood. The rites of ordination in the Roman Catholic Church were considerably simplified in 1968.

In churches that have retained the historic episcopate, the ordaining minister is always a bishop. In Presbyterian churches, ordination is conferred by ministers of the presbytery; in Congregational churches, by persons chosen by the local congregation.

According to Eastern Orthodox and Roman Catholic theology, ordination (holy orders) is a sacrament essential to the church, and it bestows an unrepeatable, indelible character upon the person ordained. *See also* holy orders.

·Christian doctrine of Holy Spirit **4**:483d
·Congregationalist beliefs **4**:1130e
·monastic ritualized status distinctions **12**:339f
·passage rites of social status **13**:1046g
·Pastoral Letters' statement of office requirements **2**:966e
·Protestant rites and duties of ministers **15**:102g
·Roman Catholic priesthood **15**:990h
·Roman Catholic sacraments **15**:999d
·sacramental status in Christianity **16**:117g

Ordino, municipality in Andorra.

·parish area and population table **1**:865

ordnance, general term designating military supplies and equipment, especially weapons, and the materials and tools required for the maintenance of these items. The branch of service charged with ordnance procurement is generally termed the Ordnance Corps, but quartermaster and other designations have been used. *See also* supply, military.

·weapons and delivery systems history **19**:683d
·weapons procurement, repair, and inventory control **11**:83f

Ordo Domus Sanctae Mariae Teutonicorum: *see* Teutonic Knights.

Ördögi Kísértetek, English ON THE TEMPTATIONS OF THE DEVIL (16th century), work by the Hungarian Péter Bornemisza.

·literature of the Renaissance **10**:1145c

Ordóñez, Bartolomé (b. *c.* 1490, Burgos, Spain—d. 1520, Carrara, Italy), sculptor, one of the originators of the Spanish school of Renaissance sculpture. Influenced by the masters of the Italian Renaissance, he evolved his own pure style, which was greatly imitated after his early death.

A member of a wealthy family, he apparently studied under Andrea Sansovino in Florence, though not much is known of his early years. It is known that he collaborated with Diego de Silóe on the "Caraccioli Altarpiece" (1514–15; S. Giovanni a Carbonara) and

Tomb of Joan the Mad and Philip I the Handsome, in the Royal Chapel, Granada, Spain, by Bartolomé Ordóñez

A. Gutierrez—Ostman Agency

worked on the marble tomb of Andrea Bonifacio (*c.* 1518; SS. Severino e Sosia), both in Naples, and probably established himself in Barcelona about 1515. He was commissioned by the Barcelona cathedral in 1517 to make wooden reliefs for the choir stalls and marble reliefs for the *trascoro* (a screen wall at the rear of the choir). In 1519 he moved to Carrara to acquire marble for the *trascoro*, setting up a workshop to execute the reliefs, but he died prematurely the next year.

Ordóñez knew the work of Donatello, Leonardo da Vinci, and Michelangelo, and, like his masters, he was able to animate the human figure and create an ordered space in his works. "The Adoration of the Magi," the principal panel of the "Caraccioli Altarpiece," is a splendid example of his mastery of Renaissance style in its clear organization of figures, careful perspective, and distinct rhythm. This panel and his other masterpieces profoundly influenced the major Neapolitan sculptors of the 16th century, such as Merliano da Nola and Santacroce, and also affected the sculptural style in Flanders through the work of his collaborator Jehan Mone.

Ordonnance Cabochienne (1413), series of reforms issued in Paris by the Burgundians.
·Burgundian reforms in Hundred Years' War **9**:19e

Ordos, group of Mongolian-speaking peoples in China.
·Altan Khan's territorial expansion **12**:373f

Ordos Desert, Western conventional for Chinese O-ERH-TO-SSU, Pin-yin romanization O-ER-DO-SU, on a plateau in the southern section of the Inner Mongolian Autonomous Region (*tzu-chih-ch'ü*), China. The Ordos fills the area inside the great northern bend of the Huang Ho (Yellow River), and is bounded by the provincial boundaries with Shensi Province (*sheng*), and with the Ningsia Hui Autonomous Region, a frontier that follows closely the line of the Great Wall of China. Structurally, the Ordos is the northern part of the great raised basin-platform that occupies northern Shensi, where its peneplained surface (*i.e.,* worn down by erosion to a nearly flat plain) is masked by massive deposits of loess (wind-blown silt). This basin consists of immense thicknesses of largely undisturbed sedimentary rocks of Carboniferous (345,000,000 to 280,000,000 years ago) and Jurassic periods (190,000,000 to 136,000,000 years ago). These include rich coal strata, particularly along the eastern border of the basin, and the whole basin plateau has great potential as an oil-producing area.

Generally speaking the surface features of the Ordos comprise undulating hills and plains. There are some higher ridges: the Arhiso Shan (mountains) in the northwest, which overlook the Huang Ho, represent the raised western edge of the basin structure, while in the southeast the ridge of the Pai-yü Shan constitutes the northern limit of the drainage basin of the Wei Ho. The general elevation of the plateau is about 3,600 ft (1,100 m), and the ridges rarely rise above 6,500 ft (2,000 m). Much of the area, particularly the lower-lying depressions, is covered with shifting sands; blown by the strong prevailing northwesterly winds of winter, they are constantly encroaching on the territory of northern Shensi bordering the desert. There are very few streams. The climate is extremely arid, the country receiving less than 10 in (250 mm) of rain annually. The only sizeable river is the Tu-ssu-tu Ho, flowing west into the Upper Huang Ho. In the south of the Ordos are great numbers of salt pools and lakes with no drainage outlet; many of these have dried up, leaving deposits of salt and soda behind. Vegetation is extremely sparse, particularly in the drier northern and western sections. In the lake basins there are salt-meadows with sedge swamps along the seasonal watercourses. The vegetation gradually improves in the wetter east and south, where much of the surface, apart from the shifting sand dunes, is covered with drought-resistant grasses and sparse shrubs. The whole area is very sparsely populated, human life being generally supported only by nomadic herds of sheep, goats, and horses. The population is almost entirely Mongol. Where, in some marginal areas, Han (*i.e.,* northern) Chinese have attempted to plant crops, the excessive alkalinity of the poor soils has caused a major problem. To prevent the spread of the sand dunes, the Chinese government in the 1960s planted a wide belt of drought-resistant trees along the southern and eastern edges of the desert.
·archaeological excavations and discovery **2**:201f
·excavations and culture discoveries **4**:298a
·map, China **4**:262
·Siberian metalwork similarity **3**:1132f; illus. 1133

Ordovician Period 13:656, span of geological time that began 500,000,000 years ago and lasted 70,000,000 years; the Ordovician followed the Cambrian Period and preceded the Silurian Period.

The text article treats the classification, correlation, and geographical distribution of Ordovician rocks, which are widely recognized in the continents of the Northern Hemisphere, in the South American Andes, in Australia, and in parts of New Zealand, but which have not been found in Africa south of the Sahara, peninsular India, or Antarctica. It also deals with Ordovician life, including stratigraphically important fossils and faunal realms, and with the paleogeography and climate of the Ordovician Period.

REFERENCES in other text articles:
·African continent development **1**:182e; map 181
·Agnatha evolution illus. **1**:310
·animal fossil records of major groups **7**:557d
·Asian paleogeography **2**:153f; map 154
·Australian geological history **2**:385d
·Cambrian boundary controversy **3**:689h
·conodont fossil record **5**:26b
·continental margin evolution illus. **12**:582
·coral appearance and reef development **5**:163e
·European features **6**:1039b
·fish evolutionary trends **7**:336h; illus. 339
·geological time scale, illus. 2 **5**:499
·geologic history and fossil record **6**:13f
·North American geological history **13**:180d
·plant fossil records of major groups **7**:574e
·plant organ evolution **13**:734b
·rocks, life, and strata correlations **13**:916e; table 919
·sedimentary rock occurrence **16**:473a
·Silurian life lineages **16**:769a
·South American marine transgression **17**:76h; map 79
·time scale improvement by Lapworth **7**:1067f

RELATED ENTRIES in the *Ready Reference and Index: for*
Australian stages: see Bendigonian Stage; Bolindian Stage; Castlemainian Stage; Chewtonian Stage; Darriwilian Stage; Eastonian Stage; Gisbornian Stage; Lancefieldian Stage; Yapeenian Stage
Baltic-Scandinavian series: Harju Series; Oeland Series; Virju Series
British series: Arenig Series; Ashgill Series; Bala Series; Borrowdale Volcanic Series; Caradoc Series; Llandeilo Series; Llanvirn Series; Snowdon Series; Tremadoc Series
Chinese series: Chientang-kiang Series; Ichang Series; Neichia-shan Series
North American series: Canadian Series; Champlainian Series; Cincinnatian Series
North American stages: Black Riveran Stage; Chazyan Stage; Edenian Stage; Maysvillian Stage; Richmondian Stage; Trentonian Stage
rock formation: Deepkill Shale Formation; Eureka Quartzite Formation; Martinsburg Shale Formation; Normanskill Shale Formation; Pogonip Limestone Formation; Queenston Delta; Queenston Shale Formation; Trenton Limestone Formation; Utica Shale Formation
uplift and structures: Cincinnati Arch; Findlay Arch; Kankakee Arch; Logan's Line; Nashville Dome; Taconic orogeny

Ord River, in the Kimberley Plateau region, northeastern Western Australia, rises in the Albert Edward Range and follows an easterly and northerly course for 300 mi (500 km) to Cambridge Gulf. Chief tributaries are the Denham, Stirling, Panton, Wilson, Bow, Nicholson, and Elvire. Its upper reaches cut

Ord River Diversion Dam, Western Australia
Authenticated News International

through deep gorges, which give way to grasslands and forests along its middle course and to alluvial plains in its lower valley. It was discovered in 1879 by Alexander Forrest and was named for Sir Harry Ord, governor of Western Australia (1877–80). The Ord River Project, built in the 1960s, includes a service centre (Kununurra Township), main storage dam with hydroelectric power in the Carr Boyd Range, a spillway, and diversion tunnels. It is designed to prevent seasonal flooding and to impound water for irrigating large areas formerly subject to drought.
15°30′ S, 128°21′ E
·map, Australia **2**:400

Ordu, port, capital of Ordu *il* (province), northern Turkey, on the Black Sea. It lies at the mouth of Melet Irmağı (river) on the eastern slopes of Boztepe (1,800 ft [550 m]), which protects it against storms from the northwest. Ordu is the site of ancient Cotyora, founded by Greek colonists from Sinope (modern Sinop) in the 5th century BC, and is the place from which the survivors of Xenophon's Ten Thousand (Greeks who went to Asia to seek their fortunes) embarked from Sinope and Heraclea Pontica (modern Ereğli in Zonguldak *il*). Ordu is now a centre for hazelnut processing and exporting. The town is on the Samsun–Trabzon coastal road about 100 mi (160 km) west of Trabzon, and is linked with Sivas via the Kelkit Valley.

Ordu *il* (2,317 sq mi [6,001 sq km]) is rugged, well-forested, and humid. Its fertile coastal strip produces a variety of agricultural products, including maize (corn) and hazelnuts. Livestock is raised and grain is grown in the deep valleys of the interior. Small deposits of copper and zinc are worked near the coast. Pop. (1970 prelim.) town, 117,449; *il*, 607,319.
41°00′ N, 37°53′ E
·map, Turkey **18**:784
·province area and population, table 2 **18**:787

Ordyn-Nashchokin, Afanasy Lavrentyevich (b. Pskov province, Russia—d. 1680/81, Monastery of St. John the Evangelist, near Pskov), statesman and diplomat who became the chief adviser on foreign affairs to Tsar Alexis of Russia (ruled 1645–76).

The son of a petty landowner, Ordyn-Nashchokin received a good education in the relatively cosmopolitan environment of Pskov; during the reign of Michael (ruled 1613–45), he participated in the work of ambassadorial commissions that defined the Russo-Swedish borders and gained a reputation as a talented administrator. In 1654, when war broke out between Poland–Lithuania and Russia, he successfully defended the Russian borders with Lithuania and Livonia from attack, and after Russia concluded a truce with Poland so that Alexis could concentrate his military operations against Sweden (1656), Ordyn-Nashchokin was made *voyevoda* (governor) of the conquered town of Kokenhausen on the Dvina River; he subsequently became the virtual ruler of all the Livonian lands seized by Russia.

In 1658 Ordyn-Nashchokin arranged an armistice with Sweden, but, convinced that Russia should direct its policy toward increasing its power in the Baltic Sea region, he strongly urged Alexis to end the renewed war against Poland even at the price of sacrificing the Ukraine. Alexis, however, overruled his plan, concluded the Peace of Kardis (1661) with Sweden that restored the prewar territorial distribution, and pursued his war against Poland until 1666, when he called Ordyn-Nashchokin from his post as *voyevoda* of Pskov (which he had held since 1665) to conclude a peace settlement with Poland. After eight months of negotiations, Ordyn-Nashchokin and the Poles agreed upon the Truce of Andrusovo (January 1667), which placed the Ukraine east of the Dnieper River, as well as the city and region of Kiev, under Russian control. Following his diplomatic success, Ordyn-Nashchokin was promoted to the rank of boyar, appointed minister of foreign affairs, and also made head of several other departments, including the Ukrainian department (Malorossiysky Prikaz).

Assuming the role of Alexis' chief adviser, Ordyn-Nashchokin not only involved himself in foreign policy but also, foreshadowing Peter I the Great (ruled 1682–1725), advocated using western Europe as a model for Russian development, sharply criticized traditional Muscovite society and government, and took an active interest in Russia's domestic—particularly economic—affairs. He promulgated a trade ordinance protecting Russian merchants from both foreign competition and native bureaucrats (1667), advanced the prospect of trade with Persia and Central Asia, and promoted interest in the shipbuilding industry.

Nevertheless, as Ordyn-Nashchokin continued to view expansion into the Baltic region as the major objective of Russian foreign policy and to favour a policy of friendship with Poland, which precluded an attempt to seize control of the remainder of the Ukraine, he came into conflict with the Tsar, who dismissed him from the Ukrainian department in 1669 and from the Foreign Office in 1671. In February 1672 Ordyn-Nashchokin took monastic vows and subsequently only briefly resumed his lay career to conduct negotiations with the Poles in 1679.

Ordzhonikidze, capital of the Severo-Ossetian Autonomous Soviet Socialist Republic, Russian Soviet Federated Socialist Republic, on the Terek River and the northern slopes of the Caucasus. Founded as Vladikavkaz in 1784, it was designed as the key fortress to hold the Georgian Military Highway through the Terek Valley and the Ossetian Military Highway along the Ardon Valley, the two main routes across the Caucasus. In 1860 it became a town and in 1875 the terminus of a railway from Prokhladny on the Rostov–Baku line. The town was known as Dzaudzhikau (1944–54). Industrial development has been considerable: nonferrous metals, electrical equipment, vehicle parts, and foodstuffs are produced. Ordzhonikidze has medical, agricultural, teacher-training, and mining institutes and three scientific research institutes. Pop. (1970) 236,000.
43°03′ N, 44°40′ E

Ordzhonikidze, Grigory Konstantinovich, nicknamed "SERGO" (b. Oct. 27 [Oct. 15, old style], 1886, Goresha, Georgia, now in the U.S.S.R.—d. Feb. 18, 1937, Moscow), Communist leader who played major roles in bringing Georgia under Soviet rule and in industrializing the Soviet Union. Having joined the Bolshevik faction of the Russian Social Democratic Workers' Party in 1903, Ordzhonikidze was active in the revolutionary movement, participating in the revolution of 1905 in the Caucasus, serving as a member of the Baku Party committee (1907), attending the party school run by Lenin at Longjumeau near Paris (1911), helping organize the Prague party conference held in January 1912, and becoming a member of the party's central committee (1912). In April 1912, however, he was arrested for the third time; he resumed his activities only after the imperial Russian government had been overthrown (February 1917, O.S.) and he had returned from exile in Siberia to Petrograd (modern Leningrad).

Ordzhonikidze then became a member of both the executive committee of the Petrograd Soviet (the revolutionary council of workers and soldiers that rivalled the authority of the provisional government) and of the Bolshevik Party committee. After the Bolsheviks seized power (October 1917, O.S.), he became commissar extraordinary for the Ukraine area (1918), a member of his party's Central Committee (1921), and chairman of the Central Committee's Caucasian bureau (1921), which had been created to establish Soviet rule in the Caucasus. Despite Lenin's objections to his brutal methods, which were approved by Josef Stalin, and the opposition of the local Communist organizations, Ordzhonikidze founded an effective Soviet government in Georgia, then merged Georgia with Armenia and Azerbaidjan to create the Transcaucasian Federal Republic, which joined Russia, Belorussia, and the Ukraine to form the Soviet Union (December 1922).

During the intraparty power struggles of the mid-1920s, Ordzhonikidze generally supported Stalin. Although he incurred the hostility of Lavrenti Beria, who as chief of the secret police in Transcaucasia forced him to transfer to the northern Caucasus (1926), Ordzhonikidze nevertheless advanced in 1926 to become a candidate member of the Central Committee's Politburo, chairman of the party's central control commission, which was responsible for discouraging dissension among party members, and commissar for worker-peasant inspection. In 1930 he became a full member of the Politburo.

Having helped organize the development of Soviet industry during the First Five-Year Plan (1928–32), Ordzhonikidze became commissar for heavy industry in 1932. While the Second Five-Year Plan was in effect, however, he demonstrated his increasing opposition to Stalin by insisting that the rate of industrial growth be reduced (1934). During the 1930s he also displayed his disapproval of Stalin's terroristic policies by intervening on behalf of victims of the Great Purge. Although his sudden death in 1937 was officially attributed to natural causes, Nikita Khrushchev later charged (1956) that Stalin had driven Ordzhonikidze to commit suicide.

ore, mineral aggregate that contains sufficient quantities of metallic and some nonmetallic substances to be of economic importance and from which those substances may be separated. Originally the term applied only to metallic minerals, but it has subsequently been broadened to include such nonmetallics as sulfur, calcium fluoride (fluorite), and barium sulfate (barite) that have been deposited in the host rock after its formation. Such industrial rock deposits as gypsum, salt, or limestone are not ores because they form rock beds and do not therefore require separation from associated country rock (rock enclosing the ore deposit) and gangue (unwanted rock and minerals).

·Bronze Age ore reduction **8**:611f
·deposit types, processes, and sites **13**:661g
·fluorine production from fluorite **8**:563d
·magmatic emplacement and assimilation **9**:224b

Oreads (Greek mythology): *see* nymph.

Oreamnos americanus: *see* mountain goat.

ore boil, a part of the open-hearth steel production process.

·open-hearth heat production **17**:648c

Örebro, town and *län* (county) in south central Sweden. The town, seat of the *län*, is on Svartälven (Svart River) near its entrance into Hjälmaren (Lake Hjalmar). One of Sweden's oldest towns, it was already a commercial centre in the 13th century and played a prominent part in Swedish history. It was the residence of Engelbrekt Engelbrektsson, leader of a rebellion against Denmark in 1434, and the birthplace of Olaus and Laurentius Petri, 16th-century church reformers. Of the several important assemblies held there, the most notable was that of 1810, at which the French field marshal Jean Bernadotte was elected heir to the Swedish throne as Charles XIV John.

Örebro Castle on an island in Svartälven (Svart River), Sweden
Refot

Largely rebuilt since a fire in 1854, Örebro has a modern appearance, but its imposing historic buildings include a 16th-century Swedish Renaissance castle on an island in the river, used partly as a museum and partly as the governor's residence; a 13th-century Gothic church; and the 15th-century Kungsstugan (King's House), one of the best-preserved wooden buildings in Sweden. The University of Örebro, affiliated with the University of Uppsala, was founded in 1970. There is also a school of social work and public administration, founded in 1967.

The town is known also for its shoe and biscuit manufacture. It has good rail and boat communications and is situated at the junction of national highways.

Örebro *län* (area 3,340 sq mi [8,650 sq km]) is comprised of the *landskap* (province) of Närke and parts of those of Västmanland and Värmland. It has many lakes and is drained by several rivers. Mineral deposits include iron, zinc, and copper; and lumbering, papermaking, steel, and metal smelting are important industries. Pop. (1970) 115,454 (town); 276,790 (*län*).

·area and population table **17**:846
·map, Sweden **17**:848

Orectolobidae, family of shallow-water sharks. Most species are native to the Indo-Pacific and the Red Sea, but one, the nurse shark (*q.v.*), inhabits the Atlantic ocean.

·Australia's resources **2**:397b; illus. 396
·classification and general features **16**:498g

ore deposits 13:661, natural concentrations of metals, metalliferous minerals, and some important nonmetallic substances; the ore in these deposits can be separated from the associated rock and mined at a profit.

The text article deals with the nature, genesis, classifications, and Earth processes involved in the formation of ore deposits. It also treats the distribution of the various types of ore deposits throughout the world.

REFERENCES in other text articles:

·alkali minerals and production **1**:582g *passim* to 587c
·aluminum ores, mining, and processing **1**:641g
·carbonate rocks as mineral hosts **10**:980a
·chromite ore classification and processing **4**:570c
·clay mineral occurrence and composition **4**:700c
·continental shelf economic values **5**:115e
·copper history and classification **5**:148c; table 149
·Devonian rock crops **5**:671e
·element abundance for profitable mining **6**:706f; table
·formation, types, and minerals **12**:243e
geographic regions
·African metal distribution **1**:199a
·Asian reserves **2**:172b
·Baffin Island economic potential **13**:259e
·European reserves **6**:1050d; illus.
·Hungary's limited resources **9**:26a
·North American mineral resource regions **13**:192e; map 198
·Red Sea's natural resource variety **15**:545e
·Sahara desert location and quantity **16**:150h
·geological forms and composition **7**:1054d
·gold in African conglomerate placers **4**:1113b
·gold ores and mining **8**:237a
·gravimetric density measurements **6**:22g
·igneous rock association **6**:26d
·iron ore composition and distribution **9**:894f; tables 895
·iron quality and availability **17**:640h
·lead ore weathering and processing **10**:728a
·magnesium sources and processing **11**:302f
·magnetic exploration of iron deposits **15**:946h
·mercury mining and production **11**:921h
·metallurgical extraction and processing **11**:1063f
·metamorphism and element concentration **12**:2c
·mineral exploration geophysical methods **7**:80f
·native element occurrence and formation **12**:857c
·near surface copper oxidation **7**:1032a
·nickel discovery and exploration **13**:71d
·oil shale diagenesis and metal concentration **13**:536b
·origin speculation in history **6**:75e
·pegmatites and hydrothermal veins **9**:225b
·Permian rock types and distribution **14**:96b
·phosphate mineral occurrence in nature table **14**:287
·platinum mining and processing **14**:529h
·Precambrian mineral locations **6**:13a
·prospecting, exploration, and mining **12**:247h
·resource distribution and renewability **5**:46b; illus.
·rutile and ilmenite mining and processing **18**:455f
·Silurian rock crops **16**:769e
·silver mineral occurrence **16**:777h
·steel production problems and solution **18**:42b
·sulfide mineral origin and properties **17**:785f; illus. 786
·sulfur occurrence and mining techniques **17**:791g; illus. 792
·tin mining and recovery techniques **18**:427d
·uranium ore mining **18**:1035a
·zinc ore associations and mining **19**:1147c

RELATED ENTRIES in the *Ready Reference and Index: for*

deposit types and characteristics: see cockade ore; gangue; gossan; hydrothermal ore deposits; metallogenic provinces; nugget; ore; porphyry copper; protore; tenor
enrichment processes: lateral secretion; metasomatic replacement; paragenesis; pneumatolytic processes; supergene sulfide enrichment
structures: boxwork

ore dressing, treating crude ores to mechanically separate out the valuable minerals. Formerly applied only to ores of precious metals such as gold and silver, ore-dressing processes came to be used to recover other metals and nonmetallic minerals and such materials as graphite, sulfur, mica, feldspar, asbestos, and fluorspar.

The primary operations are crushing; comminution, or grinding; and beneficiation, or concentration. Other important operations are sizing and classification, settling and filtering, drying and heat treating, and agglomerating or pelletizing.

Most ores must be crushed to free the valuable minerals, sometimes from huge boulder size into fine powders.

Comminution is customarily carried out by primary and secondary crushers, followed by fine grinders consisting of rotating cylindrical mills that contain steel balls (ball mill), rods (rod mill), or lumps of rock, ore, or flint pebbles (pebble mill). Mills may be operated either wet or dry.

In beneficiation, the simplest method of concentration is handpicking to remove either the rich material or the waste material from a moving table or conveyor belt. Flotation (*q.v.*), or sink and float methods, may be used to separate materials of different buoyant properties in water. Gravimetric methods of concentration utilize the differences in the densities of the wanted and unwanted materials to effect their separation. Jigging is a method of concentrating heavy minerals by using an open box, the jig, with a perforated bottom through which pulsating water currents are forced. Crushed ore fed into the top is stratified by the action of the water currents, the heavier minerals settling to the bottom. Another method uses shaking tables, also called sand or slime tables, depending on the particulate size of the material they treat. They are inclined slightly from the horizontal and operated with a reciprocating action that moves the heavy minerals to the end of the table, while water washes the lighter minerals over the side into a container below. Pneumatic jigs and tables operate on the same principles but are applied to mineral ores of a light, fluffy nature, such as asbestos. Magnetic properties may be the basis for separation of minerals containing iron; minerals having electrostatic properties may be separated by an electric field. Ordinary screening devices may be used on many ores in which the valuable mineral is either finer or coarser, or softer or harder, than the gangue, or ore residue.

Sizers, or classifiers, are machines used to grind to at least the fineness of dissemination of the desired mineral particles. Screens are used in various forms for sizing and classifying, with and without water; some are heated to facilitate the flow of materials and prevent sticking. Hydraulic classification depends on the different rates of settling of mixed sizes of grains in water. In air classification, air is the medium instead of water. Centrifugal classifiers use centrifugal force to separate coarse and fine particles.

Settling and filtering remove water from the mixture. Drying is usually in a rotary kiln, an inclined rotating cylinder with a burner at one end. Heat treating or roasting may be used to change the form or characteristic of a mineral in the ore to make it easier to concentrate. Pyrite, for example, is made magnetic by roasting to drive off sulfur.

Agglomeration, the formation into tough lumps of material that cannot be smelted as fine particles, may be carried out by fusing the material at high temperature, variously called sintering, pelletizing, and briquetting. A binder such as starch, molasses, or bentonite may be mixed with the fine ore and the mixture heated or subjected to pressure.

·aluminum Bayer refining process **1**:642d
·gravity concentration of minerals **11**:1064d
·industrial ceramics manufacture **3**:1155c
·iron flotation and sintering processes **9**:895c
·mineral concentration processes **11**:1063g
·petroleum conservation methods **5**:50f
·zinc froth flotation process **19**:1147e

oregano, or ORIGANUM, flavourful dried leaves and flowering tops of any of various perennial herbs of the mint family (Lamiaceae or Labiatae), particularly *Origanum vulgare*, called wild marjoram in northern and central Europe, widely used to season many foods. The name is derived from the Greek *oros*, "mountain," and *ganos*, "joy." Oregano has long been an essential ingredient of Latin cooking. Pliny the Elder thought it a remedy for bad digestion. The aroma, strong and aromatic, and the taste, warm, pungent, and bitter, are particularly appreciated in tomato dishes, meats, fish, eggs, cheese, beans, Mexican dishes such as chili con carne, and Italian dishes such as pizza. Italians call it the mushroom herb but use it with many other foods as well. The Spanish word *orégano* means marjoram, and the herbs are sometimes used interchangeably.

Native to the hills of the Mediterranean countries and western Asia, the herbs were brought to the Western Hemisphere in early times and are naturalized in parts of Mexico and the United States.

All varieties contain essential oil. In some, the principal component of the oil is thymol, in others carvacrol; both have the empirical formula $C_{10}H_{14}O$.

·Lamiales commercial importance **10**:620b
·spice use, region, and demand, tables 1, 2, and 4 **17**:504

Oregon **13**:672, state of the U.S. Pacific Northwest, admitted to the Union in 1859 as the 33rd state. Occupying an area of 96,981 sq mi (251,180 sq km), it is bounded by Washington (north), Idaho (east), Nevada and California (south), and the Pacific Ocean (west). Its capital is Salem. Pop. (1980) 2,632,663.

The text article, after a brief overview of the state, covers its history, natural and human landscape, people, economy, administration, social conditions, and cultural life and institutions.

REFERENCES in other text articles:

·administration problems and results **19**:618c
·area and population, table 1 **18**:927
·British and U.S. trade **19**:618c
·Great Basin Indian cultures **13**:204g; map 205
·map, United States **18**:908
·mountain range geological development **13**:824d
·political territory division **9**:186b
·Polk territorial rights settlement **14**:733f
·territorial expansion 1822–54 map **18**:966

Oregon, city, seat of Ogle County, northern Illinois, U.S., on the Rock River. It was founded in the 1830s by John Phelps, a sawmiller. Near Lowden State Park (immediately north) is the site of Eagle's Nest Camp, a retreat used by Lorado Taft and other artists from 1898 to 1942; the 66-ac (27-ha) tract was acquired in 1951 by Northern Illinois University for a field campus. Taft's "Soldiers' Monument" is in the courthouse square, and on the river bluffs stands his Black Hawk statue (1911), commemorating the American Indian. White Pines Forest State Park is 9 mi (14 km) west. Oregon has an agricultural-based economy with some manufacturing (chiefly pianos and road-building equipment). Inc. town, 1843; city, 1869. Pop. (1980) 3,559.
42°01′ N, 89°20′ W

Oregon, city, eastern suburb of Toledo, Lucas County, northwestern Ohio, on the east bank of the Maumee River and facing Maumee Bay (Lake Erie). Formerly Oregon Township, it was incorporated as a village in August 1957 and became a city four months later. Its western section along the Toledo line is densely populated, and the bay shore around Harbor View has scattered settlements; but some of its area (about 28 sq mi [73 sq km]) contains farmland. Within the city is Ohio's largest concentration of oil refineries, petrochemical plants, and tank farms. Other activities are based on electric-generating and food-processing plants. Pop. (1980) 18,675.

Oregon, USS, late-19th-century U.S. battleship.

·naval ship design **12**:892a

Oregon Caves National Monument, in southwestern Oregon, U.S., lies in the Siskiyou Mountains near the California border. Established in 1909, it is a single cave comprised of a series of chambers joined by subterranean corridors on four levels. Formed by the dissolving of limestone by groundwater, they contain many beautiful stalagmites, stalactites, and other fantastic formations. On the surface above and around the caves are forests of Jeffrey pine, with many trees from 100 to 180 ft (30 to 55 m) high and from 200 to 400 years old. The monument occupies an area of 480 ac (194 ha).

Oregon City, seat (1843) of Clackamas County, northwestern Oregon, U.S., at the Willamette Falls (40 ft [12 m] high) and the juncture of the Clackamas and Willamette rivers. It forms part of a tri-city complex that includes Gladstone and West Linn. In 1829–30 John McLoughlin of the Hudsons Bay Company settled the site at an Indian village on a narrow plain backed by high cliffs. His house (1845–46) is preserved as a national historic site. Laid out in 1842 and incorporated in 1849, Oregon City became the first territorial capital. It flourished as a supply point during the California gold rush, and published (1846) one of the first newspapers (*Oregon Spectator*) west of the Mississippi River.

Locks now bypass the falls, which supply power for paper and woollen mills. Dairying, fruit growing, and tourism are further economic factors. A municipal free elevator (built 1915, replaced 1955) lifts pedestrians 90 ft up from the river (business) to the cliff (residential) sections of the city.

Oregon City was the birthplace of poet Edwin Markham (1852–1940). Pop. (1980) 14,673.
45°21′ N, 122°36′ W
·map, United States **18**:908

Oregon grape, common name for several species of the genus *Mahonia*, evergreen shrubs of the barberry family (Berberidaceae).

Oregon grape (*Mahonia aquifolium*)
G.E. Hyde from the Natural History Photographic Agency—EB Inc.

M. aquifolium, the principal species with the common name Oregon grape, is native to the Pacific Coast of North America and bears yellow flowers and small, blue, edible berries.
·Ranunculales pollination mechanism **15**:510b

Oregon Question, dispute over ownership of the Pacific Northwest involving Spain, Russia, the U.S., and Great Britain, all of which had established claims based on exploration or settlement by their nationals. Spain first vacated its claims by the Nootka Sound Convention (1790) with Britain and the Transcontinental Treaty (1819) with the U.S. The U.S. and Great Britain, in the Convention of 1818, established a joint claim over "Oregon Country," eventually defined to lie below latitude 54°40′ N, above latitude 42° N, and west of the Continental Divide. Russia later abandoned its claim to the area in separate treaties with the U.S. and Great Britain (1824–25). Using the slogan "Fifty-four forty or fight" (*q.v.*), the Democrats won the 1844 presidential election on a platform that demanded exclusive U.S. control of the area. U.S. preoccupation with the Mexican War (1846–47) and British troubles in Ireland, however, paved the way for the Oregon Treaty (1846), a compromise by which British navigation rights on the Columbia River were guaranteed and the land boundary was drawn along latitude 49° N. Final delineation of the marine portion south of Vancouver Island was arbitrated in 1872. *See also* Nootka Sound controversy.

"Ridiculous Exhibition; or, Yankee-Noodle putting His Head into the British Lion's Mouth," cartoon by John Leech, 1846, on the Oregon boundary dispute
The Granger Collection

·Adams' boundary negotiation and opinion **1**:79d
·Ashburton's diplomatic mission **13**:1107g
·Polk presidential campaign stance **14**:733f
·Polk role and U.S. acquisition **18**:967b
·U.S.–Canadian boundary settlement **3**:739c

Oregon Trail, in U.S. history, one of the great emigrant routes to the Northwest, running from Independence, Mo., to the Columbia River region of Oregon. It crossed about 2,000 miles (3,200 kilometres) of rugged terrain, including desert and Indian territory. First used by fur traders and missionaries, the trail was suddenly in the 1840s thick with the wagon trains of about 12,000 emigrants to Oregon. Some 1,000 settlers joined the "great migration" led by Marcus Whitman (1843). Hordes of gold seekers also used the eastern portion of the trail to California in the late 1840s. Beginning in 1847, thousands of Mormons followed a route later called the Mormon Trail, which frequently coincided in Wyoming with the Oregon Trail.
·Missouri western expansion role **12**:284b
·settlers' northwestern movement **19**:618b
·Wyoming western settlement role **19**:1052b

Oregon Trail, The (1849), work by Francis Parkman.
·title change and popularity **13**:1019g

Oregon Treaty (1846): *see* Oregon Question.

Oregon yew: *see* western yew.

O'Reilly, John Boyle (b. June 28, 1844, near Drogheda, County Louth—d. Aug. 10, 1890, Hull, Mass.), journalist who championed the Irish republican cause both in Ireland and in the United States.

At 19 when O'Reilly was serving in the 10th Hussars, stationed near Dublin, he was recruited as a secret republican agent for enrolling Irish soldiers from the British Army by the Fenian leader John Devoy. O'Reilly's subversive activity was discovered in 1866, and he was sentenced to be shot, but the penalty was commuted to 23 years penal servitude. In 1867 he was deported to Western Australia; from there he escaped to the United States. Within seven years he and John Devoy successfully rescued the remaining Irish prisoners in Western Australia.

O'Reilly, engraving by an unknown artist
By courtesy of the National Library of Ireland, Dublin

O'Reilly was a gifted journalist, being first editor and, later, part owner with the archbishop of Boston of the Roman Catholic weekly *Pilot* in Boston. He reported Fenian activities and supported the Irish republicans. He was, however, convinced of the incompetence of the Fenian organization and believed the name Fenianism discredited the Irish cause.

O'Reilly published several volumes of verse and a novel of convict life in Australia, *Moondyne* (1889).

Orekhovo-Zuyevo, city, Moscow *oblast* (administrative region), western Russian Soviet Federated Socialist Republic, east of Moscow, on the Klyazma River. Formed in 1917 through the amalgamation of several industrial villages, it is now one of the largest textile cities of the U.S.S.R., specializing in cotton. Chemicals and engineering are also important. Peat is extracted in the vicinity. Pop. (1970 prelim.) 120,000.
55°49′ N, 38°59′ E

Orellana, Francisco de (b. *c.* 1490, Trujillo, Spain—d. *c.* 1546, Amazon River), Spanish soldier and first explorer of the Amazon River.

After participating with Francisco Pizarro in the conquest of Peru in 1535, Orellana moved to Guayaquil and was named governor of that area in 1538. When Pizarro's half brother, Gonzalo, prepared an expedition to explore the unknown regions east of Quito, Orellana was appointed his lieutenant. In April 1541 he was sent ahead of the main party to seek provisions, taking a brigantine with 50 soldiers. He reached the junction of the Napo and Marañón rivers, where his group persuaded him of the impossibility of returning to Pizarro. Instead, he entered upon an exploration of the Amazon system. Drifting with the current, he reached the mouth of the river in August 1542. Proceeding to Trinidad, he finally returned to Spain, where he told of hoards of gold and cinnamon and of encounters with tribes led by women resembling the Amazons of Greek mythology—a comparison that is presumed to have led him to name the river the Amazon.

Orellana sought the right to explore and exploit the lands he had discovered. Because the Spanish crown was involved in controversy with Portugal over the ownership of this area, it could provide him only with some assistance but no official support. His return to the Amazon proved a disaster. Ships and men were lost on the passage to America, and Orellana's vessel capsized near the mouth of the great river and he was drowned.
·Amazon River exploration and naming **1**:652h

Orem, city, Utah County, north central Utah, U.S., at the base of Mt. Timpanogos, on the high benchlands (plateau), near Utah Lake, just north of Provo. It was settled in 1861 and named at its incorporation (1919) for Walter C. Orem, president of the Salt Lake and Utah Electric Interurban Railroad. Manufactures include electronic and ski equipment. The Geneva plant of U.S. Steel is 3 mi west. The city is also a shipping point for

fruits and vegetables grown in the surrounding irrigated area. Pop. (1980) 52,399.
40°19′ N, 111°42′ W

Ore Mountains, Czech KRUŠNÉ HORY, German ERZGEBIRGE, range of hills bounding the Bohemian Massif, extending for 100 mi (160 km) along the East German–Czechoslovakian border, reaching an average width of 25 mi. The Bohemian (southeastern) side of the range has a steep scarp face (2,000 to 2,500 ft [600–750 m] high in places); the outer slope to the northwest is gradual. The highest summits, Klínovec (4,081 ft [1,244 m]) on the Czech side and Fichtelberg (3,983 ft) on the German side, are in the centre of the range. Loučná (3,136 ft) is at the northeastern end and Špičák (3,658 ft) at the southwestern end. The name Ore Mountains rightly suggests the tradition of mineral wealth, worked by generations of small groups of craftsmen: gold and silver, lead and copper, tungsten (wolfram), and pitchblende. These ores attracted medieval immigrant groups of German miners from the northwest, who, until their expulsion after World War II, gave the whole area a predominantly German character and tradition. To the original mining economy the Germans added forestry, furniture making, textile industries, and some farming. The main feature of settlement on both sides of the range was small-scale towns. After 1945 the region saw the supplanting of an almost wholly German population by an almost wholly Czech one. Certain parts, such as the western extension into German territory, suffered large population losses. After World War II the uranium deposits at Jáchymov (Czechoslovakia) and Aue (East Germany) were developed. Large quantities of brown coal are mined from around Chomutov and Most, Czechoslovakia, in the Bílina River Valley.

Road communications across the Ore Mountains are good. There are also railway routes, but the sinuous and often dead-end tracks on the Bohemian side show the obstacle of the great scarp face. The numerous mineral springs and winter sports resorts have aided the development of the tourist industry.
50°30′ N, 13°15′ E
·formation and composition **8**:7d
·map, German Democratic Republic **8**:8

Orenburg, *oblast* (administrative region), western Russian Soviet Federated Socialist Republic, occupies an area of 47,900 sq mi (124,000 sq km) across the southern end of the Ural Mountains. It stretches from the limestone plateaus of the Obshchy Syrt in the west, across the low Urals ridges, to the flat Turgay Plateau in the east. Most of the *oblast* lies in the feather-grass and fescue steppe; in the north and northwest are groves of birch and pine, especially in the Buzuluk pine forest nature reserve. Much of the steppe is plowed up, particularly as a result of the Virgin and Idle Lands Campaign of the 1950s, and agriculture is important, principally spring wheat, corn (maize), millet, and sunflowers—but the economy is dominated by the mining and industrial area at the southern end of the Urals, centred on Orenburg city, the *oblast* headquarters. Many minerals are exploited: oil and gas near Buguruslan, copper at Mednogorsk, iron ore at Khalilovo, nickel and cobalt at Novotroitsk and Svetly, coal at Dombarovsky, and salt at Sol-Iletsk. Heavy industry—iron and steel, petrochemicals, and engineering—is highly developed. Pop. (1970 prelim.) 2,050,000.

Orenburg, called CHKALOV from 1938 to 1957, city and administrative centre of Orenburg *oblast* (region), western Russian Soviet Federated Socialist Republic, on the Ural River at the Sakmara confluence. Founded as a fortress in 1735 at the Ural-Or confluence, where Orsk (*q.v.*) now stands, it was moved to its present site in 1743. It was originally the military centre of the Ural Cossacks, and its commercial importance grew with trade to Central Asia, especially after the railway from Kuybyshev was built in 1871–73. Modern Orenburg has major engineering industries, producing heavy-industrial and agricultural machinery; it manufactures a range of consumer goods and foodstuffs. The city has teacher-training, medical, and agricultural institutes. Pop. (1970 prelim.) 345,000.
51°45′ N, 55°06′ E
·map, Soviet Union **17**:322

orenda, Iroquoian term for spiritual energy or power believed to be inherent in animate and inanimate natural objects.
·definition and usage **12**:878a
·Woodlands Indian world view **6**:172d

Orense, the only landlocked province in Galicia, northwestern Spain; it has an area of 2,810 sq mi (7,278 sq km). The principal river system is the Miño-Sil, the fertile valleys of which produce maize (corn) and grapes for wine. The Sil is harnessed for hydroelectric power. The Ribeiro area is famous for its white wine. There is also considerable pig breeding and potato growing. Industries include chemical manufacture; and tin, wolfram, and granite deposits are worked. Tourism contributes to the economy; large lakes offer sailing and fishing facilities; and Peña Trevinca (6,660 ft [2,030 m]), the region's highest peak, is the site of one of Spain's better winter skiing resorts. The provincial capital, Orense, is the only large centre, and the population is predominantly rural. Pop. (1970) 413,733.
·area and population table **17**:389

Orense, capital of Orense province, Galicia, northwestern Spain, on the eastern bank of the Río Miño, south-southeast of La Coruña. Its name derives from its hot springs, known to the Romans as Aquae Originis or Urentae, and now utilized mainly for domestic supply. The residence of the Suebi (Suevi) tribes in the 6th and 7th centuries, the town was destroyed by the Moors in 716 and rebuilt by Alfonso III of Asturias *c.* 877. The Miño is crossed at Orense by one of the most remarkable bridges in Spain, built by Bishop Lorenzo in 1230 but frequently repaired since then; it has seven arches and a central span of 150 ft (45 m). The town has three parts: the medieval, the area of 19th-century expansion, and the modern perimeter. Medieval family mansions include those of the Oca and the Valladares (now a casino). The Capilla del Cristo, or Christ's chapel (16th century), in the Gothic cathedral (founded 572; rebuilt in the 13th century) contains a crucifix venerated throughout Galicia. The former episcopal palace houses the Provincial Archaeological Museum. The town has sawmills, flour mills, iron foundries, and some light industries. Pop. (1970) 73,379.
42°20′ N, 7°51′ W
·map, Spain **17**:382

Oreocincla (bird): *see* ground-thrush.

Oreoica gutturalis: *see* bellbird.

Oreopithecus, extinct genus of primates found as fossils in late Miocene deposits in East Africa and early Pliocene deposits in southern Europe (the Miocene Epoch preceded the Pliocene Epoch and ended 7,000,000 years ago). *Oreopithecus* is best known from complete but crushed specimens found in coal deposits in Europe. The relation of the genus to other primates has been a matter of some debate and confusion; *Oreopithecus* appears to combine primitive and advanced features that, on one hand, seem to ally it with the Old World monkeys and, on the other, with the advanced, manlike apes. It is probable that *Oreopithecus* represents a specialized side branch of primate evolution that did not give rise to more advanced forms; it is generally included in a separate ape family, the Oreopithecidae. *Oreopithecus*, an inhabitant of swampy regions, was about 1.2 metres (4 feet) tall and had relatively long arms; it is estimated that *Oreopithecus* weighed about 40 kilograms (90 pounds). The skull was small and the teeth were specialized; it probably ate soft plant foods. It is doubtful that *Oreopithecus* habitually stood erect.
·skeletal traits and classification **14**:1027e

Oreortyx pictus (bird): *see* quail.

Oreosomatidae, fish family of the order Zeiformes, class Actinopterygii, phylum Chordata.
·classification and general features **2**:273b

Oreotragus oreotragus (antelope): *see* klipspringer.

Oresme, Nicole d' (b. *c.* 1325, Allemagne, Fr.—d. July 11, 1382, Lisieux), Roman Catholic bishop, Aristotelian scholar, and economist whose work prepared some basis for the development of modern mathematics and science and of French prose, particularly scientific vocabulary.

After studying theology in Paris, Oresme became bursar in the Collège de Navarre in the University of Paris from 1348 to October 1356, then master until he resigned in December 1361. He was canon (1362) and dean (1364) of Rouen, Fr., and preached before Pope Urban V on Christmas Eve 1363.

By 1370 Oresme had been appointed chaplain to King Charles V the Wise of France, who introduced notable changes in financial matters in accordance with Oresme's theories of the lawfulness of tax and its necessary permanence coupled with the indispensable stability of the coinage. Oresme regarded the coin as a definite weight of precious metal, its fineness guaranteed by the issuing authority; he viewed coins as belonging to the public, not to the prince, who had no right to vary their standard, weight, or bimetallic ratio. Furthermore, his economic policy took account neither of credit nor of bills of exchange, although they were in general use by the 14th century.

Because Charles was ardently interested in books and in men of learning who would be especially beneficial to his government, he asked Oresme (*c.* 1375) to translate Aristotle for him. Oresme's translations from the current Latin versions of Aristotle's *Ethics*, *Politics*, and *Economics* are considered an important contribution to the development of the French language. He was elected bishop of Lisieux in November 1377 and consecrated in January 1378.

In mathematics Oresme helped lay the foundation that later led to the discovery of analytical geometry: he possibly found the logical equivalence between tabulation and graphing and, in a way, he proposed the use of a graph for plotting a variable magnitude the value of which depends on that of another; the systematic theoretical basis for this possibility later evolved in the work of René Descartes. In science, Oresme made a major contribution to kinematics (the principles and laws of motion) by proving geometrically the Merton theorem—*i.e.*, the space traversed in a given period by a body with uniformly accelerated motion is the same as if the body moved uniformly at its speed for the middle instant of the period. He represented qualities and motions as two-dimensional figures; his proof showed the equality of a right triangle representing the uniform acceleration and a rectangle representing the uniform motion. Apparently he held that the velocity of falling bodies was directly proportional to time (but he did not apply the Merton theorem to the acceleration of falling bodies, as Galileo essentially did some two centuries later).

Oresme's *Traité de la sphère* ("Treatise on the Sphere") and *Livre du ciel et du monde* ("Book on the Sky and the World") reveal his original scientific concepts. Against black magic and the claims of astrologers to predict the future, he wrote *Livre de divinacions* ("Book on Divinations"). He taught against Aristotle by advocating the possibility of several universes and, more specifically, against the Aristotelian theory expressed in *De caelo* ("On the Heavens") that the heavens move around a stationary Earth. Oresme's theory of earthly motion preceded Copernicus. His celebrated treatise *De moneta* (*c.* 1360; "On Coinage"), first printed in 1484 and frequently reissued in the 17th century, is directed against any debasement of the coinage. On the basis of this work, Oresme has been called the greatest medieval economist.

George William Coopland's *Nicole Oresme and the Astrologers: A Study of His Livre de divinacions* appeared in 1952, followed by Charles Johnson's *The De Moneta of Nicholas Oresme and English Mint Documents* in 1956.

·analytic geometry foundations **1**:773g
·French Aristotelian influence **1**:1159h

Oresteia (performed 458 BC), trilogy of tragic dramas by Aeschylus. His latest work and the only complete trilogy of Greek dramas that has survived, it tells the story of the house of Atreus. The first play, *Agamemnon*, portrays the victorious return of that king from the Trojan war and his murder by his wife, Clytemnestra, and her lover, Aegisthus (*see* Agamemnon). The second play, *Choephoroi* (*The Libation Bearers*), deals with Agamemnon's daughter Electra and his son Orestes (*see* Electra; Orestes). Orestes avenges his father's murder by killing his mother and her lover. The third play, *Eumenides*, describes Orestes driven by the Furies, for though he was required to avenge his father's death, a matricide is infamous in the eyes of the gods. He is finally absolved by the goddess Athena.

·criticism and extra-esthetic factors **2**:88d
·ethics and moral force **18**:581a
·Eugene O'Neill's modern
  interpretation **13**:572e
·war theme and harmonious resolution **1**:148h

Orestes, in Greek mythology, son of Agamemnon, king of Mycenae (or Argos), and his wife, Clytemnestra. According to Homer, Orestes was away when his father returned from Troy to meet his death at the hands of Aegisthus, his wife's lover. On reaching manhood, Orestes avenged his father by killing Aegisthus and Clytemnestra. His conduct was regarded as exemplary, in accordance with the moral code of the heroic age.

Orestes being purified by Apollo after his acquittal by the court of the Areopagus, with the placated Eumenides nearby, detail of a 5th-century-BC Greek vase; in the Louvre
Alinari-Mansell

According to the poet Stesichorus, Orestes was a small child at the time of Agamemnon's murder and was smuggled to safety by his nurse. Clytemnestra was warned of impending retribution by a dream, and Orestes, for the crime of matricide, was haunted by the Furies (Erinyes) after her death. In Aeschylus' trilogy the *Oresteia*, Orestes acted in accordance with Apollo's commands; he posed as a stranger with tidings of his own death, and, after killing his mother, he sought refuge from the Furies at Delphi. Prompted again by Apollo, he went to Athens and pleaded his case before the Areopagus. The jury divided equally, Athena gave her deciding vote for acquittal, and the Furies were placated by being given new worship as Eumenides (kindly goddesses).

In Euripides' *Iphigeneia in Tauris* some of the Furies remained unappeased, and Orestes was ordered by Apollo to go to Tauris and bring the statue of Artemis back to Athens. Accompanied by his friend Pylades, he reached his goal, but they were arrested because it was the local custom to sacrifice all strangers to the goddess. The priestess in charge of the sacrifice was his sister Iphigeneia (*q.v.*); they recognized each other, and all escaped together, bringing the statue with them. Orestes inherited his father's kingdom, adding to it Argos and Lacedaemon. He married Hermione, daughter of Helen and Menelaus (*qq.v.*), and eventually died of snakebite.

The story of Orestes was a favourite in ancient art and literature. Aeschylus' *Oresteia* showed its dramatic potentialities, and these were further exploited by Sophocles and Euripides. Aspects of the story were also featured in the work of many later European dramatists, such as Voltaire's *Oreste*, Goethe's *Iphigenie auf Tauris*, Eugene O'Neill's *Mourning Becomes Electra*, and Jean-Paul Sartre's *Les Mouches*, and, in opera, Gluck's *Iphigénie en Tauride* and Richard Strauss's *Elektra*.

·posthumous sacred power **8**:823e

Orestes (d. August 476, Pavia, Italy), regent of Italy and minister to Attila, king of the Huns; he obtained control of the Roman army in 475 and made his own son Romulus, nicknamed Augustulus, the last Western Roman emperor.

Of barbarian origin, Orestes' family had been Roman citizens for a few generations. Orestes married the daughter of Count Romulus of Passau, after whom he named his son. In 474 Julius Nepos (*q.v.*), the Byzantine supreme magistrate in Italy, proclaimed himself emperor; a year later Orestes, commander of Nepos' barbarian troops, deposed him and caused the troops to acclaim the 14-year-old Romulus emperor. In 476, however, the troops mutinied, proclaiming as king one of their own number, Odoacer, besieging and killing Orestes in Pavia, and exiling Romulus. *See also* Romulus Augustulus.

Øresund (Baltic Sea): *see* Sound, The.

Oretes, the name by which the Greeks called the ODRAS, or ODDAKĀS, an indigenous people of what is now the state of Orissa in India; by extension, it was also the name of the territory they occupied. They appear early in Sanskrit literature and are mentioned in the law code, the *Manu-smṛti*, of the 1st century BC. They were visited by the Chinese Buddhist pilgrim Hsüan-tsang in the 7th century AD.

·Orissa as known by ancient Greeks **13**:739c

orfe (fish): *see* ide.

Orfeo, in full LA FAVOLA D'ORFEO, English THE FABLE OF ORPHEUS, opera in five acts and a prologue composed by Claudio Monteverdi and first performed in Mantua on Feb. 24, 1607 (the score was published in 1609). It preserved many independent 16th-century musical forms, including madrigals, instrumental pieces, and songs, yet the work has a unity that gives it a claim to be the first great example of the operatic form.

·dramatic expression and unity **12**:404b
·dramatic function of orchestration **13**:645f
·musical and dramatic innovations **13**:580b

Orfeo ed Euridice, English ORPHEUS AND EURYDICE, opera in four acts by Cristoph Gluck with a libretto by Ranieri Calzabigi. It was first performed at the Burgtheater in Vienna on Oct. 5, 1762.

·Angiolini's choreographic role **2**:649f
·Don Juan dance scene incorporation **12**:702f
·embodiment of opera reform
  principles **13**:582g
·music in subservience to drama **8**:213b
·reaction against opera seria style **12**:712b
·reaction to vocal exhibitionism **16**:790c

Orff, Carl (b. July 10, 1895, Munich), a principal composer after World War II, known particularly for his operas and dramatic works and for his innovations in music education. Orff studied at the Munich Academy of Music and with the prominent German composer Heinrich Kaminski and later conducted in Munich, Mannheim, and Darmstadt. In 1924 in Munich he founded, with the German gymnast, teacher, and writer Dorothee Günther, the Günther School for gymnastics, dance, and music. Orff edited some 17th-century operas and in 1937 produced his secular oratorio *Carmina Burana* (*q.v.*). Intended to be staged with dance, it was based on a manuscript of medieval poems. This rugged, successful work led to others inspired by Greek theatre and by medieval mystery plays, notably *Catulli carmina* (1943; *Songs of Catullus*) and *Trionfo di Afrodite* (1953; *The Triumph of Aphrodite*), which form a trilogy with *Carmina Burana*. Other works are an Easter cantata, *Comoedia de Christi Resurrectione* (1956); a musical play, *Oedipus der Tyrann* (1959); a nativity play, *Ludus de nato infante mirificus* (1960); and an opera, *Prometheus* (1968). Orff's system of music education, largely based on group performance with percussion instruments, has been widely adopted.

·opera-like dramatic works **13**:592a
·text choice for choral works **4**:447e

Orffyreus, real name JOHANN ERNST ELIAS BESSLER (1680–1745), German physicist.

·perpetual motion wheel invention **14**:103c

Orford, Horace Walpole, 4th earl of (1717–97): *see* Walpole, Horace, 4th earl of Orford.

Orford, Robert Walpole, 1st earl of (1676–1745): *see* Walpole, Robert, 1st earl of Orford.

orfray (embroidery): *see* orphrey.

organ (biology): *see* organs and organ systems, animal; organs and organ systems, plant.

organ 13:676, keyboard musical instrument in which wind is fed into pipes, causing them to sound.

The text article covers the parts, mechanism, and production of sound, the history of the organ to 1800, and developments after 1800.

REFERENCES in other text articles:
·aerophone principle of sound
  production **17**:38h
·ancient origin and later usage **12**:729f
·keyboard instrument development **10**:437a
·mean-tone temperament emergence **18**:742b
·music history and development **12**:707e
·orchestration role **13**:645a
·sound production by pipes **17**:29g
·synagogue use and music style **10**:207b
·varieties and operation principles **19**:854a

RELATED ENTRIES in the *Ready Reference and Index: for*
organ builders: see Cavaille-Coll, Aristide; Hope-Jones, Robert; Schnitger, Arp; Willis, Henry
organ parts: diapason; pipe; stop; tracker action
organ types: barrel organ; calliope; electronic organ; harmonium; hydraulis; melodeon; organ, electric; pipe organ; portative organ; positive organ; regal

organ, electric, pipe organ whose mechanical action utilizes electricity; also, an electronic organ (*q.v.*).

·history and construction **13**:677a

organal voice, also called VOX ORGANALIS, melody combined with *vox principalis* to form organum music.

·contrapuntal scheme of organum **5**:213h

organbird, any of several unrelated species that produce vibrant fluting tones. New Zealand's organbird is the kokako (*q.v.*). A butcherbird of Australia and a wren (*q.v.*) of South America are sometimes called organbirds.

organ culture (biology): *see* cell culture.

organelle, any of the specialized structures within a cell (*q.v.*) that perform a specific function (*e.g.*, mitochondria, ribosomes, endoplasmic reticulum). Organelles in unicellular organisms are the equivalent of organs in multicellular organisms. The contractile vacuole of protozoans, for example, extracts fluid wastes from the cell and eliminates them from the organism, as does the kidney, an organ.
·animal organ systems' evolution **13**:725b
·excretory mechanism in Protozoa **7**:47a
·laser sensitivity differences **15**:391c
·membrane functions in cell **11**:878f
·protozoan nervous systems **12**:976c
·theory of origin from independent cells **14**:378e

organic geochemistry: *see* biogeochemistry.

organic halogen compounds 13:682, substances composed of molecules in which one or more atoms of the elements fluorine, chlorine, bromine, and iodine are joined to atoms of carbon. Very few members of this class are found in nature, but numerous synthetic organic halogen compounds are used as solvents, refrigerants, propellants, anesthetics, insecticides, and plastics.

The text article covers the nomenclature and classification of organic halogen compounds and their general chemical and physical properties; continues with a survey of major subdivisions of the class—alkyl, alkenyl, alkynyl, and aryl halides; and concludes with a summary of technological and analytical aspects, including their commercial uses and methods by which they can be separated and identified and their structures can be determined.

REFERENCES in other text articles:
·alkane synthesis and reactions **9**:84a
·bromine reactions with hydrocarbons **4**:109b
·carbanion-metal ion pair preparation **3**:819c
·carbene formation precursors **3**:822a
·carboxylic acid functional groups **3**:868e
·conformation and reaction mechanisms **4**:1090g
·dye intermediate manufacture by halogenation **5**:1100g
·fluoroplastic properties and uses **14**:524b
·Halon fire extinguisher use **7**:321c
·organometallic preparation **13**:715g
·plastics production and uses **14**:514b; illus.
·propylene chlorination mechanism **4**:154b
·substitution mechanism of methyl iodide **12**:308b

RELATED ENTRIES in the *Ready Reference and Index: for*
chemical warfare agents: see chloroacetophenone, alpha-; chloropicrin; phosgene; tear gas; thioether
pesticides: aldrin; benzene hexachloride; chlordan; chlorophenol; chloropicrin; DDT; dichlorobenzene; methoxychlor; methyl bromide; toxaphene
solvents: carbon tetrachloride; chlorobenzene; dichlorobenzene; ethylene chloride; methyl chloride; methylene chloride; tetrachloroethylene; trichloroethylene
other: chlorotrifluoroethylene; ethyl chloride; ethylene bromide; Freon; halocarbon; iodoform; polychlorinated biphenyl; tetrafluoroethylene; vinyl fluoride; vinylidene chloride

organicism, in biology, the theory that life and living processes are the expression of an activity that is possible only by virtue of the condition of autonomous organization of a living system rather than because of its individual components. As such, it is directly opposed to vitalism and mechanism (*qq.v.*).
·biophilosophy theories **12**:873g

organic lake, any lake formed by the accumulation of plant material or the action of animals. This class of lakes includes those dammed by dense plant growth, such as in Silver Lake in Nova Scotia, those formed by the accumulation of coral debris, and lakes caused by beaver dams, as well as man-made lakes.
·formation processes **10**:604a

organic matter, material containing carbon derived from living organisms. It is included within a large variety of naturally occurring substances in varying stages of alteration. These range from decaying vegetation to some soils, peat and the several kinds of coals, and tars, asphalts, and crude oil.
·agricultural production requirements **1**:350e
·vegetable farming soil management **19**:49b

organic nitrogen compounds 13:693, substances made up of molecules that contain at least one atom of the element carbon and one of nitrogen. Organic nitrogen compounds are essential and often major components of all known living organisms and also include many drugs and medicinal agents, explosives, dyestuffs, and synthetic resins and fibres.

The text article treats chemical bonding in nitrogen and its compounds, the classification of organic nitrogen compounds, the amines and their derivatives, compounds with bonds between two nitrogen atoms, and those with bonds between atoms of nitrogen and oxygen.

REFERENCES in other text articles:
·alkaloid chemical structure **1**:595b
·dye manufacturing processes and raw materials **5**:1100e
·dyestuff development and chemistry **5**:1106h
·fixation and denitrification cycles **2**:1040f
·free radical resonance stabilization **15**:421f
·heterocycle structure and chemistry **8**:832e
·nitrile structures and preparation **3**:873b
·nucleotide structure and derivatives **13**:331a
·nylon and polyimide production and uses **14**:516a
·nylon production and nomenclature **7**:264a
·organic sulfur acid reactions **13**:712c
·plastics production and uses **14**:512f
·protein catabolism reactions **11**:1031f
·substitution mechanism of nitrobenzenes **4**:152g

RELATED ENTRIES in the *Ready Reference and Index: for*
classes of compounds: see amine; azo compound; diazo compound; diazonium salt; nitrile; oxime
individual compounds: aniline; benzidine; ethanolamine; nitrobenzene; nitroglycerin; PETN; trinitrotoluene; urea

organic phosphorus compounds 13:701, substances of which the molecules contain at least one atom of each of the elements carbon and phosphorus. The best known members of the class are a group of insecticides and chemical warfare agents (the nerve gases) and the biologically essential nucleic acids and nucleotide coenzymes; other organic phosphorus compounds are used as solvents and flame-retarding agents and in the preparation of complex chemical compounds.

The text article covers the general properties of organic phosphorus compounds, including electronic configuration, molecular structure, chemical bonding, and chemical reactivity, and continues with a survey of major classes of these compounds: organic derivatives of phosphorus acids, trivalent organic phosphorus compounds, and pentavalent organic phosphorus compounds.

REFERENCES in other text articles:
·industrial environment risks **9**:529f
·insecticide uses of organophosphates **14**:141b
·lake productivity cycle **10**:606d
·nucleotide structure and derivatives **13**:331a
·pesticide research in 20th century **1**:345c
·phosphorus production and use **4**:133f

RELATED ENTRIES in the *Ready Reference and Index:*
malathion; parathion; tetraethyl pyrophosphate; tributyl phosphate

organic psychosis, a severe mental disorder caused by brain damage or structural impairment.
·types, characteristics, and causes **5**:861b

organic solidarity (sociology): *see* mechanical and organic solidarity.

Organic Statute of 1832: *see* Congress Kingdom of Poland.

organic sulfur compounds 13:706, a family of chemical substances the molecules of which contain one or more atoms of sulfur combined with carbon and hydrogen, and often with oxygen, nitrogen, and other elements. Many organic sulfur compounds are important natural constituents of animal, vegetable, and mineral substances, and numerous synthetic members of this family are useful as medicinals, insecticides, solvents, and other products of economic value.

The text article covers the nomenclature, properties, sources, reactions, and applications of the major classes of organic sulfur compounds, namely, thiols, sulfides, disulfides, and polysulfides; thiocarbonyl compounds; sulfoxides and sulfones; sulfonic, sulfinic, and sulfenic acids; and esters of inorganic sulfur-containing acids.

REFERENCES in other text articles:
·heterocycle structure and chemistry **8**:832e
·micro-organism reduction process **2**:1041d
·petroleum purification processes **14**:184f
·soil organisms and plant nutrition **16**:1016b

RELATED ENTRIES in the *Ready Reference and Index:*
mercaptan; mustard oil; sulfonic acid; sulfoxide; thioether; thiol; xanthate

organic unity, in literature, a structural principle, first discussed by Plato (in *Phaedrus*, *Gorgias*, and *The Republic*) and later described and defined by Aristotle. The principle calls for internally consistent thematic and dramatic development, analogous to biological growth, which is the recurrent, guiding metaphor throughout Aristotle's writings. According to the principles, the action of a narrative or drama must be presented as "a complete whole, with its several incidents so closely connected that the transposal or withdrawal of any one of them will disjoin and dislocate the whole." The principle is opposed to the concept of literary genres—standard and conventionalized forms that art must be fitted into. It assumes that art grows from a germ and seeks its own form and that the artist does not interfere with its natural growth by adding ornament, wit, love interest, or some other conventional expectation.

Organic form in poetry was a preoccupation of the German Romantics and was also claimed for the novel by Henry James in *The Art of Fiction* (1884).
·theatrical convention and Romanticism **17**:544a

Organisation de l'Armée Secrète (OAS), English SECRET ARMY ORGANIZATION, an extremist organization of French Algerians, opposed to the creation of an Algeria independent of France, which conducted a terrorist campaign against Muslim Algerians in 1961–62.

The French Algerians rejected French president Charles de Gaulle's support of the nationalist aspirations of the Muslim Algerians and sought instead the integration of Algeria into France. This attitude was demonstrated by a French settlers' uprising in January 1960 and an abortive military revolt in April 1961 led by generals Raoul Salan, Edmond Jouhaud, Maurice Challe, and André Zeller. Challe and Zeller surrendered, but Salan and Jouhaud went underground to lead the Organisation de l'Armée Secrète, which initiated a terrorist campaign in both Algeria and France. Algerian Muslims were killed; town halls, schools, and hospitals were bombed; banks were robbed; street riots were incited; and an attempt was made to assassinate de Gaulle on Sept. 8, 1961.

The efforts of the OAS proved fruitless as a cease-fire agreement was signed by de Gaulle with the Algerian provisional government in March 1962, and Salan was captured in Algiers on April 20. The great majority of the French population of Algeria started a mass exodus immediately after the cease-fire, ignoring the OAS order to stay. With the proclamation of an independent Algeria on July 3,

1962, the OAS cause was lost, and the organization eventually died out.
·Algerian nationalism growth **13**:164g
·organizer, purpose, and methods 7:679a

Organisation du travail, L' ("The Organization of Labor"), essay by Louis Blanc that appeared serially in *Revue du Progrès* in 1839.
·Blanc's outline of Socialist principles **2**:1104d

organistrum (stringed instrument): *see* hurdy-gurdy.

Organización Regional Interamericana de Trabajadores (ORIT), or INTER-AMERICAN REGIONAL ORGANIZATION OF WORKERS, Latin American labour organization that in 1969 consisted of about 28,500,000 members in 39 countries and territories. ORIT was organized in January 1951 as a regional organization for the Latin American members of the International Confederation of Free Trade Unions (*q.v.*), which had been established in 1949. At the time of ORIT's founding, the bulk of its members was made up by most of the union groups formerly affiliated with the Confederación Interamericana de Trabajadores (CIT), a democratic organization opposed to Communism but subject to political attack for its strong U.S. orientation.

The aims of the new organization included land reform, opposition to totalitarianism, and support for organizing efforts in areas where unionism was weak. One of its well-known activities, which began in the 1950s was the sponsorship of a training school for trade union leaders.
·trade unionism in Latin America **18**:570d

organization, in the social sciences, an arrangement of individuals or groups into a coherent whole, with a complex of functional interrelationships and a system of overall administration.
·bureaucratic characteristics of formal group **3**:484h
·social unit and subunit differentiation **16**:960f

organization, military: *see* armed forces.

Organization, Pact of (1933), concluded between Germany and its partners in the Little Entente.
·German militaristic growth **19**:974d

organizational relations (sociology): *see* industrial and organizational relations.

Organization for Economic Cooperation and Development (OECD), international organization founded in 1961 to stimulate economic progress and world trade. Members included Austria, Belgium, Canada, Denmark, Finland, France, the Federal Republic of Germany, Greece, Iceland, Ireland, Italy, Japan, Luxembourg, The Netherlands, Norway, Portugal, Spain, Sweden, Switzerland, Turkey, the United Kingdom, and the United States. In a broad sense it represents an extension of the Organisation for European Economic Co-operation, set up in 1948 to coordinate efforts to restore Europe's economy under the Marshall Plan. One of the fundamental purposes of the OECD is "to achieve the highest sustainable economic growth and employment and a rising standard of living in member countries, while maintaining financial stability, and thus to contribute to the development of the world economy." This aim is to be accomplished in part by liberalizing international trade and capital movements. A second major goal is the coordination of economic aid to less developed countries.

The group is essentially a consultative assemblage and decisions are not binding on individual members. The organizational structure of the OECD is similar to that of the North Atlantic Treaty Organization, the main feature being that each member is represented by a permanent delegation on the council. A secretary general chosen for a five-year term heads the permanent staff.
·customs unions in history of trade **5**:378d
·foreign aid allocations and distribution **7**:522f
·international educational assistance **9**:737g
·public administration and theory of change **15**:186b

Organization for European Economic Co-operation (OEEC), organization set up in 1948 to coordinate efforts to restore Europe's economy under the European Recovery Program (Marshall Plan). In 1961 it was superseded by the Organization for Economic Co-operation and Development, which included non-European members.
·international cooperation and trade **7**:33e
·U.S. aid for post war reconstruction **7**:523b

Organization of African Unity (OAU), intergovernmental organization, established May 25, 1963, to which, in mid-1973, all independent African states (except South Africa and Rhodesia) belong. Its charter defines its aims as the promotion of African unity, the coordination and harmonization of policies and programs among African countries on a basis of nonalignment, and the defense of the independence and sovereignty of African states.

The OAU's major practical achievements were mediation in the Algerian–Moroccan dispute (1964–65) and in the Somali–Ethiopian and Kenya–Somali border disputes (1965–67). Efforts to mediate in the civil war in Nigeria (1968–70) proved unavailing. The OAU maintains the "Africa group" at the UN through which many of its efforts at international coordination are channelled. The OAU has also brought about the joint cooperation of African states in the work of the "Committee of 77," which acts as a caucus of developing nations within the UN Conference on Trade and Development (UNCTAD).

The principal organ of the OAU is the annual assembly of heads of state and government. Between these summit conferences policy decisions are in the hands of a council of ministers, composed of foreign ministers of member states. The OAU's headquarters are in Addis Ababa, Eth.
·Ethiopian postwar influence in Africa **6**:1011g
·refugee problems and solutions **15**:570b
·Somali boundary crisis statement **6**:104a

Organization of American States (OAS), organization of 23 independent states of the Western Hemisphere. In mid-1973 it included all sovereign states of the region except Cuba, which was expelled from the OAS in 1962, and Canada.

The OAS Charter was signed on April 30, 1948, at the conclusion of the Ninth Pan-American Conference held in Bogotá. The aims of the organization are to strengthen the peace and security of the Western Hemisphere, to ensure peaceful settlement of disputes among member states, to provide for collective security, and to permit cooperation in economic, social, and cultural matters. The OAS is largely anti-Communist in its orientation.

Among the organs of the organization, the most important is the Inter-American Conference, meeting every five years. Supplementing the Conference, the Meeting of Consultation of Foreign Ministers serves as the executive body in the event of an attack or an act of aggression within the territory. The third organ, in permanent session, is the Council; composed of an ambassador from each member state, it acts as the executive committee of the OAS. In addition, specialized committees deal with technical matters. The OAS General Secretariat is in Washington, D.C.

The founding of the OAS was based on the general acceptance of the principles of the U.S. Monroe Doctrine by the countries of the Western Hemisphere, especially the principle that an attack upon an American state by another state would be considered as an attack upon all. The OAS attempted to "continentalize" the Monroe Doctrine, creating obligations for the other states without restricting the right of the U.S. to take immediate action in self-defense.

Important decisions on regional security taken by the OAS include the support extended to Pres. John F. Kennedy in 1962 in the quarantine against the Russian shipment of missiles to Cuba, and, in 1965, to support the U.S. intervention in the Dominican Republic. In the economic and social field, the most notable achievement was the adoption by the OAS of the Charter of Punta del Este (1961), establishing the Alliance for Progress.
·constituent agreements of regional nature **9**:731e
·development and project approval basis **9**:739e
·Honduras–El Salvador dispute settlement in 1969 **3**:1113g
·North American regional alliances **13**:196b
·U.S. creation and control efforts **9**:757b; map 752

Organization of Labour, The (essay by Louis Blanc): *see* Organisation du travail, L'.

Organization of the U.S. Executive Branch, Commissions on: *see* Hoover Commissions.

organization theory, the analysis of the behaviour of organizations, particularly of large formal organizations such as bureaucracies, factories, corporations, labour unions, and armies.
·authority in uninodal and multinodal organizations **13**:601d
·bureaucratic method of management **3**:485b
·group dynamics in systems approach **17**:974a
·logistics of military staffs **19**:587c
·research-laboratory organization structure **15**:742g
·work organization development **19**:932d

organized crime, complex of highly centralized criminal enterprises set up for the purpose of engaging in illegal enterprises. Although Europe and Asia have had their international rings of smugglers, jewel thieves, and drug traffickers, crime operated as a major industry is primarily a U.S. phenomenon. There, it is so vast an operation that it has been compared to a cartel of legitimate business firms.

The tremendous growth in crime in the United States during Prohibition (1920–33) led to the formation of a national organization. After repeal put an end to bootlegging—the practice of illegally manufacturing, selling, or transporting liquor—criminal overlords turned to other activities and became even more highly organized than they had been during Prohibition. The usual setup was a hierarchical one with different "families," or syndicates, in charge of operations in many of the major cities. At the head of each family was a boss who had the power of life and death over its members. *See also* Mafia.

Wherever organized crime existed, it sought protection from interference by the police and the courts. Accordingly, large sums of money have been expended by syndicate bosses in an attempt to gain political influence on both local and national levels of government. Additionally, profits from various illegal enterprises have been invested in legitimate business. Although it is difficult to estimate the profits of organized crime, in 1967 a federally sponsored study of such crime in the United States concluded that the income from gambling and various other rackets amounted to more than $8,000,000,000 per year, nearly twice the amount derived from all other kinds of criminal activity combined.

In addition to the illegal activities—principally gambling and narcotics—that have provided the syndicate's chief source of income, they may also engage in nominally legitimate enterprises, such as loan companies (known in underworld parlance as "the juice racket") that charge usurious rates of interest and collect from delinquent debtors through threats and violence. Also, real estate firms, dry cleaning establishments, and vending machine operations—all legally constituted business—when operated by the syndicate may include in their activities the elimination of competition through coercion and assassination.

It is generally believed that the power of organized crime in the United States rests, ultimately, not on violence but on political protection and on the ordinary citizen's feeling of impotence in the face of criminals who have that protection. Another important contribution to the continuing prosperity of syndicate operations is that gambling, which has been called the base for some of the uglier forms of organized crime, is not an activity of which large numbers of U.S. citizens disapprove.

·Las Vegas gambling possible involvement **12**:1078g
·structure and extent of activities **5**:270d

organ of Corti, in the ear, a complex arrangement of sensory cells—called hair cells because of their hairlike projections—and supporting cells that receives sound vibrations transmitted from the air to the eardrum membrane, then along the chain of three small bones in the middle ear to the liquid in the inner ear. The hair cells for the organ of Corti convert the vibrations that they receive from the liquid to electrical impulses that are conveyed to the brain via the vestibulocochlear nerve. The organ of Corti rests along a spiral platform of bone and membrane that extends through the twisting channel of the snailshell-like cochlea of the ear (*q.v.*). A cross section of the organ shows an arch or tunnel formed by two rows of pillar cells, or rods. These provide the major support of Corti's organ. They separate a row of larger, somewhat pear-shaped inner hair cells on the inside of the tunnel from several rows of smaller cylindrical outer hair cells on the outer side.

·animal hearing organs **17**:43e
·annelid nervous system **12**:980e
·biomedical models, table 1 **5**:866
·cranial nerve distribution **12**:1020b
·structure and function **5**:1123h; illus.

organogenesis, series of organized integrated processes that transforms an amorphous mass of cells into a complete organ. The cells of an organ-forming region undergo differential development and movement to form an organ primordium, or anlage. Organogenesis continues until the definitive characteristics of the organ are achieved. Concurrent with this process is histogenesis (*q.v.*); the result of both processes is a structurally and functionally complete organ. The accomplishment of organogenesis ends the period during which the developing organism is called an embryo and begins the period in which the organism is called a fetus.

·animal embryonic development **5**:633b; illus. 632
·plant growth and development **5**:664c

organomercurial, any of a class of chemical compounds in which a covalent bond exists between atoms of carbon and mercury. The class includes several useful pesticides and medicinal substances.

organometallic compounds 13:714, substances of which the molecules contain chemical bonds between atoms of carbon and those of metals, a class that does not include the ionic salts of metals and organic acids, which show quite different properties. The most familiar organometallic compound is tetraethyl lead, which has been added to gasoline for internal-combustion engines; other members of the class include catalysts for making polyethylene and related plastics and reagents useful in synthesis and analysis of organic compounds. Still others occur as intermediates in important industrial processes.

The text article covers the history of organometallic compounds, the nature of chemical bonds in these substances, and the preparation, reactions, analysis, and applications of organometallic compounds of the main-group chemical elements and of the transition elements.

REFERENCES in other text articles:
·alkali metals and organic reactions **1**:585a
·alkyl halide formation and reactions **13**:686f
·alkyne reaction with sodium **9**:88c
·aluminum compound structure and uses **3**:49e
·bonding structure and types **4**:103b
·carbene production reactions **3**:822b
·classification and compound composition **4**:95c
·coordination compound formations **5**:140a
·free radical decomposition and detection **15**:422d
·gold compounds in ceramics and drugs **8**:239g
·Grignard reagent preparation **1**:592c
·ion pair formation and bonding **3**:818h
·mercury compound toxicity **19**:1145f
·metalloprotein composition and functions **15**:94a
·molecular structure types and variation **12**:311f
·tin compound synthesis and uses **18**:433a
·transition element chemistry **18**:607f

RELATED ENTRIES in the *Ready Reference and Index:*
ferrocene; Grignard reagents; tetraethyl lead; Ziegler–Natta catalyst

Organon, collective name given to six treatises on logic by Aristotle, so called because logic was viewed as a basic instrument (*organon*) of learning. Their titles are *Categoriae, De interpretation, Analytica priora, Analytica posteriora, Topica*, and *Sophistici elenchi*.

·Boethius' translation and commentary **2**:1180g
·editing and arrangement **1**:1167b
·logic history from antiquity **11**:57h
·Porphyry's Isagoge as an introduction **1**:1156h

organophosphorus compound: *see* organic phosphorus compounds.

organotin compounds: *see* tin compounds.

organotroph (biology): *see* nutritional type.

organ pipe cactus (*Lemairocereus thurberi*), family Cactaceae, native from southern Arizona in the United States to Venezuela and Columbia and the West Indies. The name is applied also to a few other species of *Lemairocereus* and other *Cereus*-like cacti that have several to many tall columns arising candelabra-like from the base or not far above it.

L. thurberi is characteristic of warmer parts of the Sonoran Desert, in Arizona, Baja California, and Sonora, Mexico. It and most other *Lemairocereus* species are valued for their delicious fruit. Cuttings are often planted closely in rows for hedges or fences. Where *Lemairocereus* species are native, the wood is used for fuel and in construction.

Lemairocereus species vary from treelike, 10 or more metres (33 or more feet) high, to shrubby thickets of 2 to 3 metres high. *Lamairocereus* is sometimes placed with *Cereus*.

Organ Pipe Cactus National Monument, in southwestern Arizona, U.S., at the Mexican border, 12 mi (19 km) south of Ajo. Established in 1937 with an area of 517 sq mi (1,339 sq km), it preserves segments of the mountainous Yuma, or Sonoran, Desert and is named for the organ-pipe cactus (found in the U.S. only in this locality and so called because its branches resemble organ pipes). Desert ironwood, ocotillo, and numerous other desert plants are also found there. Wildlife includes Gila monsters (venomous lizards), pronghorn antelope, coyotes, and a variety of birds. Portions of the El Camino del Diablo (Devil's Highway), the historic Spanish route along which hundreds of miners and pioneers lost their lives, may still be seen.

organ-pipe coral (marine animal): *see* Tubipora.

organs and organ systems, animal 13:722, various tissues—not necessarily similar—that are grouped together into structural and functional units. The bodies of some of the simple multicellular animals generally have few clearly distinct organs. Most larger, more advanced, animals, however, characteristically have numerous distinct organs, which, in turn, may be organized into groups of organs that cooperate as a functional complex. Such a complex is called an organ system.

The text article covers specialized organ systems, interrelationships between them, and their development and evolution.

REFERENCES in other text articles:
·Aristotle's biological treatises **1**:1168e
·blood cells and circulation **2**:1121f
·circulatory system comparisons **4**:619h
·crustacean structural variations **5**:315b
·digestive system comparisons **5**:782f
·embryonic formation of organs **5**:631c
·endocrine–nervous interactions **2**:812g
·evolution of organization levels **14**:381g
·growth rate patterns **8**:441f
head
·bivalve evolutionary trends **2**:1085c
·burrowing use adaptations **11**:19e
·human cranial nerve distribution **12**:1017e; illus.
·human development from birth through adolescence **5**:653d; illus.
·human embryonic growth and graded development **6**:746h
·human musculoskeletal adaptation **12**:637b
·insect appendage anatomy **9**:614d; illus.
·joint sites and characteristics **10**:253b; illus.
·mammalian braincase specializations **11**:407a
·skin senses and early classification **16**:548d
·spinal nerve distributions **12**:1023b
·homeostatic feedback relationships **8**:1017a
·human cardiovascular system anatomy **3**:875g; illus. 876
·human digestive system anatomy **5**:789b
·human reproductive system structures **15**:690h; illus. 691
·human respiratory system structures **15**:764a
·human reticulo-endothelial system **15**:780g
·immunological response systems **9**:249c
·joint anatomy and physiology in vertebrates **10**:252f; illus. 253
·muscle contraction mechanisms **12**:620g; illus. 622
·muscle system functions within organs **12**:637e
·myriapod structural comparisons **12**:770g
·oncopod structural variations **13**:569c
·ostariophysian respiratory variations **13**:761c
·physiological demands of hibernation **5**:964a
·platyhelminth anatomic comparisons **14**:549c
·pressure and temperature adaptations **14**:995c
·primate structural variations **14**:1022g
·repiration and respiratory systems **15**:751f
·reproductive system comparisons **15**:702b
·sex organ evolution **16**:588b
·skeletal structures and functions **16**:818e
·sound receivers and sound-making organs **17**:39d
·tissue and fluid types **18**:443h
·toxin reaction sites and effects **14**:621f
·vertebrate integumentary system **9**:667e

organs and organ systems, plant 13:726, structures such as leaves, stems, and roots by which the plant relates to and exploits the environment.

The text article covers the economic importance of plant organs, their development and physiology; the organ systems of vascular plants, the organs of non-vascular plants, and the evolution of plant organs and organ systems.

REFERENCES in other text articles:
·aging processes and effects **1**:300a
·angiosperm evolution **1**:879b
·bulbous plant types **7**:904b
·conifer form and function **5**:4f
·cotyledon development **18**:451b
·environmental respiratory adaptations **12**:774h
·evolution and homologous structures **7**:8g
·fern form and function **7**:240g
·formation and development **5**:664c
·growth rates and meristematic centres **8**:441d
·life-span and meristems and flowers **10**:914f
·malformations of plant organs **11**:380e
·morphologic patterns **12**:454a
·movements, stimuli, and mechanisms **17**:672d
·plant adaptations for specific niche **7**:10g

·reproduction by asexual structures 15:716g
stoma
·agricultural damage effects 1:360h
·Alismales leaf structure 1:577b
·angiosperm structure and function 1:879d
·conifer shoot form and function 5:5a
·desert modifications 5:617b
·excretion in photosynthetic plants 6:720f
·grass order distinguishing features 14:591f
·hydrologic element transformations 9:107c
·integumentary structures and dynamics 9:665c; illus.
·lichen pores and function 10:886a
·organ activity in plants 3:1063c
·plant internal transport system 14:502f
·plant respiratory regulation mechanism 17:674c
·Rosales anatomical distinctions 15:1152c
·stem tissue organization 13:728c
·structure, location, and function 13:729e; illus.
·types, development, and function 18:452g
·terrestrial existence adaptation 18:144g
·tree growth and internal structure 18:690g
·Upper Paleozoic shoot and leaf evolution 13:922h
·wetland metabolic adaptations 17:841a
RELATED ENTRIES in the *Ready Reference and Index:*
flower; guard cell; inflorescence; leaf; root system

Organt (1789), epic poem published anonymously by Louis de Saint-Just.
·style and themes 16:170g

organum, medieval Latin musical term denoting (1) any musical instrument, later specifically an organ; or (2) a polyphonic (many-voiced) setting, in certain specific styles, of Gregorian chant (9th–15th century). In its earliest written-down form, found in the treatise *Musica enchiriadis* ("Musical Handbook"; *c.* 900), two melodic lines moved simultaneously, note against note. Sometimes the second, or "organal," voice doubled the chant melody, or "principal voice," exactly a fourth or a fifth lower (as G or F below C, etc.). In others the two voices started in unison but moved to wider intervals during each phrase. Both melodies might in turn be doubled at the octave, making three- or four-voice polyphony. Such polyphony, during the 9th to 11th century, was probably spontaneously produced by specially trained singers (*e.g.*, at the cathedrals of Chartres and Fleury in France and Winchester in England).

In more elaborate forms of organum a freely composed melody was sung note against note above the plainchant. In manuscripts from the abbeys of Santiago de Compostela, Spain (*c.* 1137; 22 compositions), and Saint-Martial of Limoges, France (*c.* 1150; 64 compositions), an important principle emerges—that of composing above the plainsong (called "tenor") a second melody ("duplum") having many more notes and falling into regular rhythmic patterns, or "rhythmic modes." Parisian composers in the late 12th century, associated with Notre-Dame, brought the style to its greatest floridity. One of them, Léonin, is believed to have composed organal settings of the chant melodies for the Graduals, Alleluias, and Responsories in the masses for all the major feasts, collected in the *Magnus Liber* ("Great Book"; *c.* 1170). They contained contrasting sections, with both voices rhythmically patterned ("discantus" style) alternating with sections in which the chant notes were prolonged to accommodate the many notes sung above them ("organal" style). Around 1200 the composer Pérotin modified this collection and wrote florid organum and discantus for three and four voices (the first known four-voice compositions in Western music).
·Central Asian folk style 3:1124g
·contrapuntal elaboration of chant 5:213h
·harmony's elaboration in chant 8:648b
·perfect intervals in polyphony practice 12:716f
·polyphonic tradition of West 12:747b
·polyphony's origin and development 12:705c
·South Asian classical music development 17:153g

orgasm, also called CLIMAX, physiological state of heightened sexual excitement and gratification that is followed by relaxation of sexual tensions and the body's muscles.

Generally the differences between the male and female orgasm are that the climax in the female can be psychologically interrupted more easily than can the male response, and the male's orgasm is usually accompanied by ejaculation of semen; both male and female experience momentary muscular contractions during the orgasm, but the female's effects are usually longer in duration. As the ejaculation is essential for fertilization and the male responses are usually more rapidly induced, the male probably achieves orgasms more consistently during intercourse than does the female. Once the female attains an orgasm, however, she remains sexually excited longer and may experience several successive orgasms, whereas the male is ordinarily unable to experience a second orgasm except after a waiting period.
·sexual response pattern 16:594h

Orgburo, agency of the Soviet government created in 1919 to supervise party organization.
·Bolshevik government structure 16:71c

Orgueil meteorite, involved in the controversy on whether organic matter in meteorites is evidence of extraterrestrial life. From a meteoric fall on the village of Orgueil, near Toulouse, Fr., on the night of May 14, 1864, some 20 fragments of the carbonaceous chondrite (*q.v.*) type were recovered. Examination soon after the fall showed that the meteorite contained hydrogen, carbon, and oxygen and that its substance resembled peat and lignite, which are produced on Earth from living matter. Further examination four years later revealed hydrocarbons much like those of petroleum. The origin of those organic substances in the meteorite, and others since found in Orgueil and in other carbonaceous chondrites, remains uncertain.

In 1962, an examination of parts of the meteorite that had lain sealed in a museum case for almost a century disclosed an attempted 19th-century hoax. Seeds, bits of the European reed *Juncus conglomeratus*, and fragments of gravel and coal were found embedded in the meteorite. They must have been painstakingly placed there, since the substance of the meteorite had been restored around them in such a way as to rule out accidental contamination. The apparent attempted hoax is thought to have been connected with the vehement debate going on in France during 1864 over the possibilities of life evolving from nonliving matter.
·meteorite occurrence and mass, table 4 12:47

Orhan, also spelled ORKHAN, known as ORHAN GAZI (d. *c.* 1360), the second ruler of the Ottoman dynasty, which had been founded by his father, Osman I; Orhan's reign (*c.* 1324–60) marked the beginning of Ottoman expansion into the Balkans.

Under Orhan's leadership, the small Ottoman principality in northwestern Anatolia continued to attract *gazis* (warriors for the Islāmic faith) from surrounding Turkish emirates fighting against Byzantium. In 1326 the Byzantine town of Brusa (later Bursa) fell to the Ottomans, followed by the conquests of Nicaea (modern İznik) in 1331 and Nicomedia (modern İzmit) in 1337.

Turning to the neighbouring Turkmen states, Orhan annexed the principality of Karası, weakened by dynastic struggles (*c.* 1345), and extended his control to the extreme northwest corner of Anatolia. In 1346 the Ottomans became the principal ally of the future Byzantine emperor John VI Cantacuzenus by crossing over into the Balkans to assist him against his rival John V Palaeologus.

As John VI's ally, Orhan married Theodora, John's daughter, and acquired the right to conduct raids in the Balkans. His campaigns provided the Ottomans with an intimate knowledge of the area, and in 1354 they seized Gallipoli as a permanent foothold in Europe.

Orhan's reign also marked the beginning of the institutions that transformed the Ottoman principality into a powerful state. In 1327 the first silver Ottoman coins were minted in Orhan's name, while the Anatolian conquests were consolidated and the army was reorganized on a more permanent basis. Finally, Orhan built mosques, *medreses* (theological colleges), and caravanseries in the newly conquered towns, particularly the Ottoman capital, Bursa, which later became a major Islāmic centre.
·Ottoman territorial expansion 13:771e

Orhan Veli Kanik (b. 1914, Bekoz, Istanbul —d. Nov. 14, 1950, Istanbul), poet who was one of the most innovative poets in 20th-century Turkish literature.

The son of an orchestra conductor, he was educated at the Galatasaray lycée of Istanbul and at the Faculty of Literature of Istanbul University. After working briefly as a teaching assistant at Galatasaray, he then went to work for the Turkish postal administration in Ankara (1936–42) and served as a reserve officer in the Turkish Army (1942–45). Because he had a good command of French, he worked for the Ministry of Education in the translation office for two years and later translated the works of several major French poets and playwrights. In 1950 he was editor of the literary review *Yaprak* ("Folio").

Orhan Veli first wrote under the pen name Mehmet Ali Sel and published his early poems in the avant-garde literary review *Varlik* ("Existence"). He gradually turned away from traditional poetic forms and in 1941 published a volume of poetry, *Garip* ("Strange"), in collaboration with two other well-known poets, Oktay Rifat (1914) and Melih Cevdet Anday (1915). The work revolutionized Turkish literature, creating a break with everything associated with Turkish poetry to that time; conventional metre, rhyme, language style, and themes were discarded. In the introduction to the work the poets declared that poetry was for the masses not just for the privileged educated few as it had been in the past. Orhan Veli felt that it was necessary to start afresh, and, not only rebelling against the past, he was highly critical of his more conservative contemporaries who continued to use classical poetic metres and themes and who were not concerned with directing their art to the people. Introducing everyday spoken Turkish, with its rich idiom, and making use of folk poems and popular song motifs, he encountered violent opposition, but by the time of his death his work and reputation were firmly established. Other works included *Vazgecemediğim* (1945; "I Cannot Give Up"); *Destan Gibi* (1946; "Like an Epic"); *Yenisi* (1947; "The New One"); and *Karşi* (1949; "Across"). English translations of poems selected from all his works appear in *I Am Listening to Istanbul*, translated by Talât Sait Halman (1971).

Orhon inscriptions (732), also called TURKISH RUNES, inscriptions on two monuments that relate the origin and the history of the Turks.
·Central Asian discovery and language significance 3:1123b

Oribe, Manuel (Ceferino) (b. Aug. 27, 1792, Montevideo—d. Nov. 12, 1857, Montevideo), second president of Uruguay (1835–38), previously a member of the Treinta y Tres Orientales, 33 nationalists who successfully fought (1825–28) for Uruguayan independence. Although he had been allied with José Fructuoso Rivera, the first president of Uruguay, their ambitions eventually clashed. For some years the nation experienced civil war between the Blanco (White) and Colorado (Red) factions of gaucho soldiers, led, respectively, by Oribe and Rivera. From 1843 to 1851 Oribe, with aid from Argentina, besieged Rivera in Montevideo. Eight years after Oribe's death the Colorados finally triumphed.

·Argentine territorial expansion **1**:1145h
·Blancos leader in Uruguayan politics **18**:1098g

Oribe ware, type of Japanese ceramics, usually glazed in blue or green, and first appearing during the Keichō and Genna eras (1596–1624). The name Oribe is derived from Furita Oribe, a pupil of Sen Rikyu, under whose guidance it was first produced.

Some Oribe utensils and functional objects were made in standard ceramic shapes and forms. Others, however, were deliberately deformed by a distortion and imbalance to create a new aesthetic sensibility. The blue-green vitriol glazes have the lustre of fine glass, and the decorative motifs, drawn in an iron glaze, have the same imaginative and modernistic feeling found in contemporary textiles and lacquerware. Many of the motifs are exotic,

Oribe cake plate, Edo period, early 17th century; in the Seattle Art Museum

By courtesy of the Seattle Art Museum, Eugene Fuller Memorial Collection; photograph, Earl Fields

probably deriving from foreign imports arriving at the port of Sakai (just south of Ōsaka), which was also the original home of Sen Rikyu.

·Japanese pottery **19**:236g; illus.
·Seto-Mino wares **14**:927b

oribi (*Ourebia ourebia*), swift African antelope, family Bovidae (order Artiodactyla), living on sub-Saharan grasslands in pairs or small herds. The oribi is a graceful animal with a silky coat, large ears, and a short, bushy tail. It stands about 50–66 centimetres

Oribi (*Ourebia ourebia*)

Lloyd McCarthy—Tom Stack and Associates

(20–26 inches) at the shoulder and is yellowish to reddish brown with white underparts. There is a bare, dark spot beneath each ear and a tuft of long hair on each "knee." The male has slim, spikelike horns.

·scent gland location **2**:77f

oriel, in architecture, bay window in an upper story, supported from below by projecting

Oriel window, the Great Gateway of Hampton Court Palace, Richmond upon Thames, London, designed by Henry Redman, *c.* 1520

A.F. Kersting

corbels or brackets of stone or wood. Usually semihexagonal or rectangular in plan, oriels first became prevalent early in the 15th century. They were often placed over gateways or entrances to manor houses and public buildings in the late Gothic and Tudor periods. They became popular again during the revivals of these styles in the 19th and early 20th centuries.

Orient, term, now seldom used, referring to that portion of the world east of Europe; Asia in general and particularly eastern Asia, or the Far East (*q.v.*).

·origin and East Asian application **19**:174b

orient, faint play of colours on the surface of a pearl (*q.v.*).

Oriental, Cordillera, or EASTERN CORDILLERA, name applied to a number of mountain ranges in Spanish-speaking countries, notably the Andean mountain ranges in Colombia, Ecuador, Bolivia, and Peru.
6°00′ N, 73°00′ W

·Andes location, elevation, and features **1**:858e
·Bolivian relief features **3**:1c
·geographic, demographic, and economic features **4**:864d *passim* to 865h
·map, Bolivia **3**:3
·map, Colombia **4**:868
·map, Peru **14**:129

Oriental button (infection): *see* Oriental sore.

Oriental canon law: *see* canon law, Oriental.

Oriental del Uruguay, República (country, South America): *see* Uruguay.

Oriental draw (archery): *see* Mongolian draw.

Orientales, Les (1829), collection of poetry by Victor Hugo.

·Hugo's display of technical mastery **8**:1133a

Oriental fruit moth: *see* olethreutid moth.

Oriental Jews, Hebrew BENE HA-MIZRAḤ ("Sons of the East") or ʿADOT HA-MIZRAḤ ("Communities of the East"), popular designation for approximately 1,500,000 Diaspora Jews who have lived for the most part in North Africa and the Middle East and whose ancestors did not reside in either Germany or Spain. They are thus distinguished from two other major groups of Diaspora Jews—the Ashkenazim ("German") and the Sefardim ("Spanish").

In the Arab lands of Morocco, Algeria, Tunisia, Libya, Egypt, Yemen (Aden) and Yemen (Ṣanʿāʾ), Jordan, Lebanon, Iraq, and Syria, Oriental Jews speak Arabic as their native tongue. In Iran, Afghanistan, and Bukhara they speak Persian, whereas in Kurdistan (a region extending into modern Turkey, Iraq, Iran, and Soviet Armenia) their language is a variant of ancient Aramaic.

Oriental Jews also migrated to India, other parts of Central Asia, and China. In some Oriental Jewish communities (notably those of Yemen and Iran), polygyny has been practiced. Following the establishment of the state of Israel in 1948, almost all Yemenite, Iraqi, and Libyan Jews and major parts of the Indian, Turkish, Tunisian, Algerian, Moroccan, and Syrian Jewish communities migrated to Israel. Absorbing the Oriental Jews, with their unique culture and generally lower levels of education, proved a major challenge to Israeli society.

·Israel's dual rite tradition **9**:1060g
·musical tradition and history **10**:206a

Oriental lacquer, varnish resin derived from a tree indigenous to China, *Rhus vernicifera*, commonly known as the varnish tree (*q.v.*). The manufacturing process was introduced into Japan and remained secret for centuries. A milklike emulsion secured from the tree is concentrated by evaporation to a viscous liquid. When this is applied as a thin film, it hardens in about a day to form a tough skin. The composition is peculiar in that it will dry only in a dark, moist atmosphere; when exposed to light and heat, the varnish remains tacky. It contains a skin irritant, somewhat similar to that in poison ivy, *Rhus toxicodendron. See also* lacquer. *Major ref.* **10**:575d

·Rutales economic importance **16**:103d

Oriental Lowestoft: *see* Lowestoft porcelain.

Oriental Mindoro, province occupying the eastern portion of Mindoro, Philippines. It has an area of 1,685 sq mi (4,365 sq km). Calapan, the provincial capital, is across Verde Island Passage from Batangas province, Luzon, and has regular shipping connections with Manila and nearby ports. The other population centres of Pola, Pinamalayan, Bongabong, Roxas, and Mansalay are small ports and market centres. Pop. (1975) 388,744.

·area and population table **14**:236

Oriental Project (Russian history): *see* Greek Project.

Oriental rat flea: *see* flea.

Oriental region, or INDIAN REGION, one of the six zoographic regions of the world, biologically defined on the basis of its characteristic animal life. It encompasses tropical Asia and the Indo-Australian transitional zone, consisting of Celebes, the Moluccas, Lesser Sunda, and the West Papuan islands. The analogous vegetational division is called the Indo-Malaysian subkingdom of the Paleotropical kingdom. The Oriental region includes a large variety of vertebrate animals, among them a variety of pheasants, snakes, monkeys, buffalo, and deer, as well as the Asian elephant, jungle fowl, leopard, tiger, and tapir. Conspicuous plants of the region are dipterocarp trees, teak, ebony, loquat, mango, and many spice plants.

·Asian animal life **2**:170f
·characteristic life and conditions **2**:1004d
·prehistoric locales of early man **14**:839f

Oriental sore, also called DELHI BOIL, ALEPPO BOIL, OR ORIENTAL BUTTON, and CUTANEOUS, OR DERMAL, LEISHMANIASIS, protozoan infection caused by the flagellate *Leishmania tropica* and transmitted by the bites of sand flies (*Phlebotomus* species); it is endemic in areas around the Mediterranean, in central and northeastern Africa, and in southern and western Asia.

Moist- or dry-type cutaneous ulcers are produced by different strains of *L. tropica*, and both may be found on the same patient. They heal spontaneously after many months but usually leave disfiguring scars.

·zoonoses, table 9 **5**:878

orientatio, in ancient Roman town planning, the orientation of the streets.

·Roman urban design process **18**:1067d

orientation, strictly, the fixing or directing of something so as to face the east. The word is used in architecture to express the position of a building in relation to an east–west axis. In Mesopotamia and Egypt, as well as in pre-Columbian Central America, the important features of a building, such as entrances and passages, faced east, in the direction of the rising sun. Orientation, however, varies according to religious and practical considerations. Muslims turn, in their prayers, toward Mecca, and depending on their geographical location, therefore, some believers turn eastward, some west, some north, some south. Mosques are oriented so that the *miḥrāb*, or prayer niche, faces Mecca.

Christian churches have usually been oriented with the apse or high altar placed at the east end, but this orientation was not always favoured. In early Christian churches, architects commonly oriented churches to the west; in the basilica of Old St. Peter's in Rome (4th century), for example, the apsed transept was at the west end.

Orientation is frequently planned to take maximum advantage of the daily and seasonal variations of the sun's radiation. Optimum orientation of a structure is, in the end, a compromise between its function, its location, and the prevailing environmental factors of heat, light, humidity, and wind.

orientation diagram, any plot of directional data, principally used in the physical and earth sciences. Such diagrams generally portray the frequency of orientation of a particular attribute; examples include plots of wind direction and intensity and the angle of inclination of stratigraphic bedding or stream-bed pebbles to the horizontal.

Oriente, largest of the three traditional regions of Bolivia, including all of the country east of the Andes. It is sparsely populated and little developed; the main urban centre is Santa Cruz (*q.v.*).

·geographic and socio-economic features **3**:5e

Oriente, former province, eastern Cuba. Cuba's largest province in area (14,132 sq mi [36,602 sq km]), Oriente contained the island's highest mountain, Pico Turquino, 6,542 ft (1,994 m), in the Sierra Maestra.

In 1976 Oriente province was dissolved and five new provinces were created from its former territory: Granma, Guantánamo, Holguín, Las Tunas (including part of the former Camagüey province), and Santiago de Cuba.

orienteering, an outdoor competitive sport that combines athletic ability with map-reading and direction-finding skills.

Contestants race on foot over a cross-country course several miles in length and usually laid out in a forest or woodland setting. Participants use a compass and a map of the course provided just before the event. They usually start at one-minute intervals and must check in at control points shown on the map, although the route between points is left to the individual. Because control points may be from a few hundred yards to a mile apart, intervening terrain often makes the choice of route critical.

In some races the points must be taken in specified order, and the runner who covers the course in the shortest time is the winner. In others, contestants try to reach as many control points as possible within a limited time; points are scored according to difficulty, and the competitor with the highest score, less any penalty for exceeding the time limit, is the winner.

The sport originated about 1920 in Sweden, where it is now highly popular among people of all age groups. European championships were first held in 1962 and world championships in 1966. Two books on the subject are John Disley, *Orienteering* (1967), and Gordon Pirie, *The Challenge of Orienteering* (1968).

Orient Express, railway service that connected Paris and Istanbul from 1883 to 1977. Its trains were noted for their luxury, especially in the period between the World Wars. The service was romanticized in novels such as *Orient Express* (1932) by Graham Greene and *Murder on the Orient Express* (1934) by Agatha Christie. The service was ended because of the decline in the numbers of passengers, especially in eastern Europe.

·Istanbul's international rail service **9**:1072g

orifice meter, or ORIFICE PLATE, device for measuring the rate of flow of a liquid.

·industrial process instrumentation **9**:636e

oriflamme (from Medieval Latin *aurea flamma*, literally "golden flame"), a banner or ensign that inspires great devotion or courage. The oriflamme of the abbey church of Saint-Denis, near Paris, became a symbol of the French monarchy in the Middle Ages.

·Suger's support of monarchy **17**:776g

origami: *see* paper folding.

origanum (plant): *see* oregano.

Origen 13:734, Latin ORIGENES ADAMANTIUS (b. *c.* 185, probably Alexandria, Egypt—d. *c.* 254, Tyre, modern Ṣūr, Lebanon), the most influential and seminal theologian and biblical scholar of the early Greek Church.

Abstract of text biography. After the martyrdom of his father in 202, Origen earned money by teaching grammar and then became head of the catechetical school of Alexandria. About 212 he learned Hebrew and began to compile his *Hexapla*, a synopsis of several versions of the Old Testament. While still in Alexandria he wrote his lost *Miscellanies*, *On the Resurrection*, and *On First Principles* and began his commentary on St. John.

In about 229–230 Origen was ordained presbyter at Caesarea Palestinae, where he lived and taught for several years. During the persecution of Christians under the emperor Decius (250) he was imprisoned and tortured. Origen's expository writings on the Bible include, in addition to his commentary on John, commentaries on the Song of Solomon, Isaiah, Jeremiah, Ezekiel, Romans, Matthew, and Luke. His major work on doctrine was *On First Principles* (completed before 231), and *Contra Celsum* (*c.* 248) was his great vindication of Christianity against pagan attack.

REFERENCES in other text articles:
·Christian dogma on universal salvation **4**:490f
·Christian education development **6**:333g
·classification of canonical writings **2**:940f
·Eusebius of Caesarea as disciple **6**:1130b
·exegetical contributions **7**:66g
·Gregory of Nazianzus' editing of works **8**:420d
·Hexapla methodology and influence **2**:887e
·influence on medieval exegesis **4**:539h
·Justinian's attempt to eradicate heresy **10**:365a
·mystery religions and Christianity **12**:784h
·patristic and heretical influence **13**:1080g
·Pauline authenticity of Hebrews **2**:967h
·Platonism and Christianity synthesis **14**:543a
·St. Jerome's translations **10**:137g
·salvation theory influence on St. Gregory of Nyssa **8**:421g
·Stoicism and Christian thought **17**:700b
·typological-allegorical exegesis **4**:498f
·Universalist eschatology **18**:860c

Original Dixieland Jass Band, early 20th-century group of white jazz musicians.

·jazz's Southern growth after Storyville edict **10**:122d

Original Poems for Infant Minds (1804), book of verse for children.

·poetry for child's entertainment **4**:233a

original sin, in Christian doctrine, the condition of sin into which each human being is born; also, the origin (*i.e.*, the cause, or source) of this state. Traditionally, the origin has been ascribed to the sin of the first man, Adam, with the consequent transmission of his guilt by heredity to his descendants.

The doctrine has its basis in the Bible. Although the human condition (suffering, death, and a universal tendency toward sin) is accounted for by the story of the Fall of the first man in the early chapters of the book of Genesis, the Old Testament says nothing about the transmission of hereditary sin to the entire human race. In the Gospels also there are no more than allusions to the notion of the fall of man and universal sin. The main scriptural affirmation of the doctrine is found in the writings of the Apostle Paul and particularly in Rom. 5:12–19, a difficult passage in which Paul establishes a parallelism between Adam and Christ, stating that whereas sin and death entered the world through Adam, grace and eternal life have come in greater abundance through Christ.

Through the centuries, church councils (*e.g.*, the Council of Trent in the 16th century) and theologians have articulated definitions and speculative explanations of the various points of the doctrine.

Many points, nevertheless, remain the subject of much controversy; *e.g.*, the existence of only one original set of parents and their Fall from some prior state, the explanation of how a person could be in a guilty condition before any act of his or her own and resulting from an act of a previously deceased person, and the very nature of the sinful state, which is sin only in an analogous sense insofar as it is not a personal act.

·Christian doctrine of liberation **4**:489c
·Christian views of man's status **4**:521a
·conservative view of human nature **5**:63a
·dualist contrast of previous sin **5**:1069e
·Duns Scotus' Mariological teaching **5**:1083c
·early Christian theory of polytheism **15**:615f
·Eastern Orthodox view of guilt and freedom **6**:144a
·Edwards' defense theory **6**:442a
·Eliade's mythological study **15**:626d
·Genesis account of the Fall **2**:899e
·Gnostic antinomian Adam and Eve myth **4**:553d
·Islām and Christian theology **9**:913f
·Jansenist interpretation of Augustine **15**:1013g
·Jewish adaptation of Eden myth **10**:191f
·malevolent spiritual beings **1**:872g
·Manichaean theological position **11**:445d
·Mary's role in reversing Eve's decision **11**:561g
·Niebuhr's theology and social analysis **13**:74f
·Pelagian rejection of doctrine **2**:367c
·Roman Catholic doctrine **15**:995g
·salvation concepts in Judaism and Christianity **16**:202d *passim* to 203h
·Scotist criticism of Aristotle **14**:260e

Origin and Goal of History, The (1953), German VOM URSPRUNG UND ZEIT DER GESCHICHTE (1949), by Karl Jaspers.

·civilization and world unity **10**:117d

origin of a coordinate system, the point at which all the coordinates are zero. In Cartesian coordinates, this is the point at which the coordinate axes intersect.
·analytic geometry fundamentals **7**:1077c

Origin of Civilization and the Primitive Condition of Man, The, a book by the English anthropologist John Lubbock (1834–1913).
·evolutionary scheme of religion **15**:618g

Origins of Contemporary France, The, translation of ORIGINES DE LA FRANCE CONTEMPORAINE, LES (1876–93), historical work by Hippolyte Taine.
·Taine's historical causality theory **17**:993e

Origo Gentis Langobardorum, a late-7th-century tract on the origin of the Lombards, a Germanic tribe.
·Germanic myth of origin of Lombards **8**:34d

Orihuela, town, Alicante province, Valencia, southeastern Spain, in the fertile Vega (flat lowland) del Segura, just northeast of Murcia city. The town dates back to 1500 BC and was the Roman Orcelis. Captured by the Moors in 713, it was finally liberated by the Christians in 1264. It was sacked during the disturbances at the beginning of Charles V's reign (1520) and again in the War of the Spanish Succession (1706). Orihuela suffered several epidemics of plague, was partly destroyed by an earthquake in 1829, and has often been flooded by the Río Segura. The old part of the town is north of the Segura, the new on the south. Historic buildings include the 14th-century cathedral; the church of Santiago (once a mosque; rebuilt in the 18th century); the 14th-century church of Santas Justa y Rufina, with an 18th-century facade; and the Colegio de Santo Domingo (1516–1701), the former university. There is a diocesan museum of sacred art.

Local agriculture is important and is assisted by a remarkable irrigation system left by the Moors. Its effectiveness resulted in the proverb "Rain or no rain, corn in Orihuela." Oranges, lemons, potatoes, pepper, hemp, cotton, maize (corn), oats, wheat, almonds, and dates are the chief products. Orihuela is also famous for its carnations. Pop. (1970) 44,938.
38°05′ N, 0°57′ W
·map, Spain **17**:382

Orillia, town, Simcoe County, Ontario, Canada, north of Toronto, between Lakes Couchiching and Simcoe.

The name, probably derived from the Spanish *orilla* ("border," "shore," or "bank"), was suggested by Sir Peregrine Maitland, lieutenant governor of Upper Canada (1818–28), who had served in Spain. The townsite was surveyed in 1839, a few years after an earlier settlement called The Narrows had been established. Orillia Corporation built the first municipally owned hydroelectric plant in Canada on the Severn River in 1902. Lumbering, once important, has given way to light manufacturing.

The house of Stephen Leacock, Canadian humorist, who lived in Orillia for many years, is a national literary shrine. A monument commemorating the visit by Samuel de Champlain to the area in 1615 stands in Couchiching Beach Park. Inc. village, 1867; town, 1875. Pop. (1971) 24,040.
44°47′ N, 79°25′ W
·map, Canada **3**:716

O-ring, a flat ring of synthetic rubber used as a gasket in sealing a joint against high pressures.
·face seal construction **11**:256a; illus. 255

Orinoco River **13**:737, Spanish RÍO ORINOCO, a major stream of South America, rises in the Sierra Parima and flows through Venezuela for 1,336 mi (2,150 km) to enter the Atlantic near Trinidad. It has a drainage basin of 366,000 sq mi (948,000 sq km).

The text article covers the river's course, climate, vegetation, animal life, and riverine population, as well as the history of its exploration, its navigation and river crossings, and its economic development.
8°37′ N, 62°15′ W
REFERENCES in other text articles:
·Columbus geographic misidentification **4**:941d
·delta, tides, and discharge table **15**:868
·discharge and drainage area **15**:877c
·drainage area, course, and flooding **17**:84d
·Humboldt exploration system-link proof **8**:1190d
·hydroelectric power potential **18**:771b
·length and drainage **19**:59a
·map, Colombia **4**:866
·map, South America **17**:77

Oriol, Pierre: *see* Petrus Aureoli.

oriole, any of 24 birds of the Old World genus *Oriolus*, family Oriolidae, or, in the New World, any of the 30 species of *Icterus*, family Icteridae. Both are families of perching birds (order Passeriformes). Males of either group typically are black and yellow or black and red, with some white. Females tend to be plainer. They are shy and not easily seen in the treetops, but may be detected by their loud whistling and jarring notes. All are insect eaters (*Oriolus* species also take much fruit) in woodlands and gardens, chiefly in warm regions.

(Top) Golden oriole (*Oriolus oriolus*), (bottom) Baltimore oriole (*Icterus galbula*)

(Top) H. Schrempp—Bruce Coleman Inc., (bottom) R. Austing—Bruce Coleman Inc.

The only European species is the 24-centimetre (9½-inch) golden oriole (*O. oriolus*), breeding eastward to central Asia and India. It is yellow, with black eye-mark and wings. The African golden oriole (*O. auratus*) is similar. The maroon oriole (*O. traillii*) of the Himalayas to Indochina is one of several black and red Asian forms. Northern Australia has the yellow oriole (*O. flavicinctus*), strictly a fruit-eater.

Among the icterids is the well-known Baltimore oriole (*I. galbula*), breeding in North America east of the Rockies; it is black, white, and golden-orange. In the west is the closely related Bullock's oriole (*I. bullockii*). The orchard oriole (*I. spurius*), black and chestnut, occurs over the eastern U.S. and Mexico. Among brilliant tropical forms are the apaulet oriole (*I. cayanensis*), from the Guianas to Argentina, and the troupial (*q.v.*; *I. icterus*), so called from its song, from northern South America and the West Indies.
·classification and general features **13**:1063f
·golden oriole migratory routes **12**:180b
·Western black-headed and yellow orioles, illus., **13**:Passeriformes, Plates II and IV

Oriolidae, family of forest orioles and figbirds of the order Passeriformes.
·classification and general features **13**:1060c

Orion (abbreviated Ori), major constellation lying at about 5 hours 30 minutes right ascension (the coordinate on the celestial sphere analogous to longitude on the Earth) and zero declination (at the celestial equator), named for the Greek mythological hunter. Traditionally, in many cultures, when Orion rose at dawn it was taken as a sign of approaching summer; in the evening, as a sign of winter and storms; and when it rose about midnight it heralded the season of grape picking. One of the most conspicuous constellations, Orion contains many bright stars. One of these, Betelgeuse (Alpha Orionis), a variable, is easily distinguished by its yellowish-red colour; the others are white, B-type suns. The total brightness of Rigel, in the hunter's leg, when measured over all visible light is greater than that of Betelgeuse. The third brightest star is Bellatrix. Orion's belt of three bright stars lies nearly on the celestial equator. His sword, south of the belt, contains the great Orion Nebula (M42), visible to the naked eye, an emission nebula containing hundreds of irregularly variable T Tauri stars. Faint extensions of this nebula have been photographed filling practically the whole constellation. The multiple star Theta Orionis, also known as the Trapezium, is near the centre of the nebula, the distance of which from the solar system is estimated at about 1,500 light-years.
·Arabic translations of Greek star names **2**:228h; table
·star cluster distance and age **17**:607g
·worship in hunting cultures **12**:881e

Orion (1893), essay by Bal Gangadhar Tilak.
·Tilak's calculation of Vedic antiquity **18**:407c

Orion Nebula (NGC 1976, M 42), bright diffuse nebula, faintly visible to the naked eye in the sword of the hunter's figure in the constellation Orion. The nebula lies more than 1,000 light-years from Earth and contains very hot (O-type) young stars in a grouping called the Trapezium. Radiation from these stars excites the nebula to glow. It was discovered in 1610 by the French scholar Nicolas-Claude Fabri de Peiresc and independently in 1618 by the Swiss astronomer Johann Cysat. It was the first nebula to be photographed (1880), by Henry Draper in the United States.
·emission spectra features **2**:243b
·external galaxy properties **7**:832f
·Huygens' discovery of components **9**:75b
·infrared source research **9**:582d
·interstellar nebulae light emissions **9**:791c
·nebula structure and properties **12**:930f
·radio emission properties **15**:473f; table 474

Orisha Oko, a god of the Yoruba people of southwestern Nigeria and eastern Dahomey.
·Yoruba peoples beliefs and deities **13**:90d

Oriskany, village in Whitestown town (township), Oneida County, central New York, U.S., on the Mohawk River near the mouth of Oriskany Creek, and on the New York State Barge Canal. The village was founded in 1802 by Col. Gerrett Lansing near the site (now a state park) of a battle fought during the 1777 Saratoga campaign of the American Revolution. The name derives from an Indian village, Oriska (Place of Nettles),

which once occupied the area. The state's first woollen cloth factory was founded in Oriskany in 1811 and an iron foundry in 1856. Light manufactures include felt and dies. Inc. 1914. Pop. (1980) 1,680.
43°09′ N, 75°20′ W

Oriskany, Battle of (Aug. 6, 1777), in the U.S. War of Independence, bloody struggle between British troops and American defenders of the Mohawk Valley, contributing to the failure of the British campaign in the North. British troops under Lt. Col. Barry St. Leger were marching eastward across northern New York state to join with British forces at Albany. En route, they arrived at Ft. Stanwix (also called Ft. Schuyler, now Rome, N.Y.) and demanded its surrender. Attempting to come to the fort's rescue, 800 colonial militiamen under Gen. Nicholas Herkimer were ambushed two miles west of Oriskany Creek by a force of about 1,200 British and their Iroquois allies. The battle that followed resulted in heavy casualties for both sides. St. Leger was unable to capture the fort and retreated to Oswego on August 22.
·British strategy **19**:604c

Orissa 13:739, constituent state of India. Occupying an area of 60,178 sq mi (155,860 sq km) in the eastern part of the country, it is bounded by Bihār (north), West Bengal (northeast), the Bay of Bengal (southeast), Andhra Pradesh (south), and Madhya Pradesh (west). The capital is Bhubaneswar. Pop. (1974 est.) 23,455,000.
The text article covers Orissa's history, landscape, population, administration, social conditions, economy, and cultural life.
REFERENCES in other text articles:
·Bihār's union and separation **2**:984f
·classical and folk performing arts **17**:159d
·conflicts with Vijayanagar **9**:375b
·Patna's rule and Indian political regions **13**:1076d
·province area and population table **9**:288

Orissi (Indian dance): *see* Odissi.

Oristano, town and archiepiscopal see, Oristano province, western Sardinia, Italy, near the mouth of the Tirso River (Riu de su Campo), northwest of the city of Cagliari. It was founded in the 11th century by the people of Tharros, a Punic city, the ruins of which are nearby. There are also Roman remains. In its early days it was the capital of Arborea, one of the *giudicati*, each under separate family control, into which Sardinia was divided. There is a monument in the town to Eleanora d'Arborea, who ruled from 1383 to 1404 and was an important figure in Sardinian history. The Tower of St. Christopher dates from 1291, and the cathedral, largely rebuilt in the 18th century, from 1288. The archives of Arborea are housed in the local town hall. It is an agricultural and fish-canning centre (especially eel and mullet) and it also has potteries and netting and embroidering factories. Pop. (1975 est.) mun., 27,937.
39°54′ N, 8°35′ E
·map, Sardinia **16**:244

ORIT: *see* Organización Regional Interamericana de Trabajadores.

Orius insidiosus (insect): *see* flower bug.

Oriya language, Indo-Aryan language of the eastern group spoken by about 20,000,000 persons mainly in the state of Orissa, India; Oriya is one of the 14 regional languages recognized by the Indian constitution. A direct descendant of the Ardhamāgadhī Prākrit spoken in the ancient kingdom of Magadha, it is now most closely related to Maithili, Assamese, and Bengali. Oriya has not changed greatly since the 14th century, the time of the earliest known inscriptions in the language. It shows less foreign influence (Muslim and British) than most Indo-Aryan languages because its speakers were among the last to be conquered. Oriya's literary style borrows heavily from Sanskrit. In grammar, Oriya distinguishes between rational and nonrational beings and objects. Like Bengali, it uses the plural verb forms instead of the singular to show respect to a rational being.
·Indian scripts and alphabets, table 3 **1**:623
·literature and comparative phonology and grammar **9**:447b *passim* to 448g
·modern Indo-Aryan language, table 1 **9**:440; map 442
·Orissa's linguistic cohesion **13**:739b
·poetry and prose literature **17**:143g
·prevalence and literature **9**:286b

Orizaba, city, west central Veracruz state, east central Mexico. It stands at 4,211 ft (1,284 m) above sea level in a fertile, well-drained, and temperate valley of the Sierra Madre Oriental, over which towers Citlaltépetl (also called Orizaba), a snowcapped extinct volcano. The town was founded by Spaniards in the 16th century on the former site of an Aztec garrison called Ahuaializapan (Pleasant Waters) to guard strategic routes linking the port of Veracruz and Mexico City. Chartered as a city in 1774, Orizaba was licensed under crown monopoly to produce tobacco and was one of the first Mexican textile centres. Its public buildings reflect its long colonial past. It is an agricultural (tobacco, corn [maize], sugarcane, and cereals) and industrial centre (chiefly textile mills, tobacco factories, and a brewery) and a tourist resort. It also houses the Regional Technical Institute of Orizaba (1957). It is accessible by highway and railroad. In August 1973 a severe earthquake, centred near the city, caused many deaths and widespread destruction. Pop. (1975 est.) 108,283.
18°51′ N, 97°06′ W
·map, Mexico **12**:69

Orizaba, Pico de (Mexico): *see* Citlaltépetl.

Ørjasaeter, Tore (b. March 3, 1886, Skjåk, Nor.—d. Feb. 29, 1968, Skjåk), regional poet who carried on the tradition of the ballad and of folk and nature lyrics. He expressed great attachment to farm life and its traditions as well as to the mountains and the sea, each of which plays a symbolic role in his writings. His concern with the conflict between the individual and his heritage is the underlying theme of his main work, the poetic trilogy *Gudbrand langleite* (1913–27).

Orkhan (Ottoman sultan): *see* Orhan.

Orkhon Turks (Mongolia): *see* T'u-chüeh.

Orkney, earls of, a Scottish title derived from the Norwegian earls, or jarls, who ruled the Orkney Islands from the 9th until the mid-14th century, when the title passed to Sir Henry Sinclair. Sinclair's grandson resigned it to King James III, who acquired sovereignty over the islands in 1468. The earldom was revived in 1581 for Robert, an illegitimate son of James V; his son Patrick (died 1615) was a notable tyrant in the Orkneys. The title was later held by Hamiltons, passing by marriage to the Fitz-Maurice family, who hold it today.

Orkneyinga saga, a history of the earls of Orkney from about 900 to 1200.
·kings' saga perfection **16**:146d

Orkney Islands, group of more than 70 islands and islets (only about 20 of which are inhabited), formerly an insular county of Scotland, lying about 20 mi (32 km) north of the northernmost tip of the Scottish mainland, across the strait known as the Pentland Firth. Since the administrative reorganization of 1975, they form one of three Islands areas (*q.v.*).
The landscape of the islands has been fashioned (by glacial erosion of the underlying sandstone, limestone, and igneous rocks) into areas of low, undulating hills, covered over in large areas by fertile glacial drift deposits. Westerly winds and gales account for the active marine erosion that has produced the spectacular cliffs of Hoy and for the general scarcity of trees.
The Orkneys were the Orcades of classical literature. There remains much evidence of prehistoric occupation at various periods: underground houses, circles, standing stones, and earth houses, the earliest dating from the Stone and Bronze ages. Skara Brae, an underground village in West Mainland Island, is one of the most complete European relics of the Late Neolithic Period. A Roman fleet is known to have reached the Orkneys shortly before AD 85. Norse raiders arrived in the late 8th century and colonized the islands in the 9th century; thereafter the islands were ruled by Norway and Denmark. Celtic missionaries had arrived in the 7th century, but the Norsemen were not finally converted until much later. The Norwegian king Haakon died in Orkney after his defeat at the Battle of Largs (1263). Kirkwall cathedral (dedicated to St. Magnus), one of the most complete of Scotland's Norman churches, was mainly built by Norsemen during the 12th century. Orkney and Shetland passed into Scottish rule in 1472 in compensation for the nonpayment of the dowry of Margaret of Denmark, queen of James III.
The largest island of the Orkneys is Mainland, or Pomona, which is divided into East Mainland and West Mainland; they are connected by a narrow strip of land about a mile wide between Kirkwall and Scapa Flow. The island is comparatively low, undulating country, generally intensively cultivated but with much moorland and several lochs. The streams are short, but fishing for brown trout is good. The small islands of Burray and South Ronaldsay, to the south of East Mainland, are now joined to it by causeways built on the Churchill Barriers that were constructed during World War II to prevent submarines from entering the naval base at Scapa Flow. It was in Scapa Flow, after World War I, that the German fleet surrendered, scuttled itself, and sank. To the north of Mainland lie the North Isles, generally flat and intensively cultivated.
Orkney is a prosperous farming area despite its fragmentation. It is in essence completely different from the crofting, or peasant, economy of such islands as Lewis in the Outer Hebrides. Orkney is essentially an area of small, owner-occupied farms averaging about 35 ac (14 ha), using modern mechanical methods to achieve high productivity. Each year more land is claimed for agriculture, but much peat and moor remain.
The main agricultural products are beef cattle and eggs, although the raising of pigs and the production of milk (largely for cheese) have both greatly increased. Orkney produces more beef cattle than any other part of the Scottish Highland region and is also among the foremost egg-producing regions. Some fodder crops are grown, but much is imported. Because of the importance of agriculture, the fishing industry has not been developed to the same extent as in the neighbouring Shetlands.
There are only two towns on Mainland: Kirkwall, a royal burgh (chartered town), and Stromness, a small burgh on the southwest. Kirkwall is the seat of the islands area council, which carries out the responsibilities of both region and district authority except for fire and police services, for which it combines with the Highland (*q.v.*) region. Both towns are picturesque, with narrow main streets. In Kirkwall, in addition to St. Magnus Cathedral, there are several fine old houses and the ruins of the Bishop's Palace and that of the Scottish earls.
Connections between Orkney and the Scottish mainland are good, with daily air services to Kirkwall from Aberdeen and Inverness and steamer connections with Aberdeen, Leith, and Shetland. Pop. (1971 prelim.) former Orkney County 17,254 (Mainland,

6,535; South Ronaldsay, 1,006; Westray, 866; Sanday, 609; Hoy and Walls, 548; Stronsay, 453; Shapinsay, 353; Rousay, 256; Eday, 170; North Ronaldsay, 146).
·map, United Kingdom **18**:866
·Neolithic plumbing artifacts **14**:575a
·Scotland's history and cultures **3**:232g
·United Kingdom population density map **18**:875
·Viking invasions and settlements **16**:306d; map 305

Orlamünde, a historic town in Thuringia, Gera *Bezirke* (district), East Germany. Latest pop. est. 2,000.
50°47′ N, 11°31′ E
·Karlstadt's conversion of community **11**:193g

Orlando, city, seat (1856) of Orange County, central Florida, U.S. Settlement began about 1844 around Ft. Gatlin, a U.S. army post. First called Jernigan, the name was changed in 1857 to honour Orlando Reeves, an army sentry killed locally during the Seminole Wars. The South Florida Railroad arrived in 1880 and was extended to Tampa in 1883. Orlando's citrus-based economy is augmented by tourism, the insurance business, and the manufacture of missile components and electronic equipment.

Orlando Naval Training Center, McCoy Air Force Base (Strategic Air Command), and a navy underwater sound reference laboratory are local installations. Educational facilities include Rollins College (1885) in nearby Winter Park, Florida Technological University (1968), and Valencia Community College (1967). Walt Disney World, a 27,000 ac (11,000 ha) entertainment-recreation centre, 15 mi (24 km) southwest of Orlando, opened in 1971. Inc. 1875. Pop. (1980) city, 128,394; metropolitan area (SMSA), 700,699.
28°32′ N, 81°23′ W
·map, United States **18**:908

Orlando (1928), novel by Virginia Woolf.
·historical novel techniques **13**:285f

Orlando, Vittorio Emanuele (b. May 19, 1860, Palermo—d. Dec. 1, 1952, Rome), Italian statesman and prime minister during the concluding years of World War I and head of his country's delegation to the Versailles Peace Conference. Educated at Palermo, he made a name for himself with writings on electoral reform and government administration before being elected to the Chamber of Deputies in 1897. He served as minister of education in 1903–05 and of justice in 1907–09, resuming the same portfolio in 1914. He favoured Italy's entrance into the war (May 1915), and in October 1917, in the crisis following the defeat of Italy's forces at the Battle of Caporetto by the Austrians, he became prime minister, successfully rallying the country to a renewed effort.

After the war's victorious conclusion, Orlando went to Paris and Versailles, where he had a serious falling out with his allies, especially Pres. Woodrow Wilson of the United States, over Italy's claims to formerly Austrian territory. On the question of the port of Fiume, which was contested by Yugoslavia after the war, Wilson appealed over Orlando's head to the Italian people, a manoeuvre that failed. Orlando's inability to get concessions from the Allies rapidly undermined his position, and he resigned on June 19, 1919. On December 2 he was elected president of the Chamber of Deputies. In the rising conflict between the workers' organizations and the new Fascist Party of Benito Mussolini, he at first supported Mussolini, but when the Socialist leader Giacomo Matteotti was assassinated by the Fascists, he withdrew his support. (The murder marked the beginning of Mussolini's dictatorship over Italy.) Orlando opposed the Fascists in local elections in Sicily and resigned from Parliament in protest against Fascist electoral fraud (1925).

Orlando remained in retirement until the liberation of Rome in World War II, when he became a member of the consultative assembly and president of the Constituent Assembly elected in June 1946. His objections to the peace treaty led to his resignation in 1947. In 1948 he was elected to the new Italian Senate and in the same year was a candidate for the presidency of the republic (an office elected by Parliament) but was defeated by Luigi Einaudi.
·World War victory **9**:1167c

Orlando furioso, romantic epic by the Italian Renaissance poet Ludovico Ariosto, who worked on it for nearly 30 years, from *c.* 1502 or 1503 to the end of his life, in 1533. In its first edition (1516), the poem consisted of 40 cantos; in the third edition (1532), it was extended to 46 cantos, and Ariosto's style achieved its perfection.

Furioso consists of a number of episodes derived from the epics, romances, and heroic poetry of the Middle Ages and early Renaissance. The poem, however, achieves homogeneity by the author's skill and economy in handling the various episodes. It is possible to identify three principal nuclei round which the various stories are grouped: Orlando's passion for Angelica, the war between Christians and pagans near Paris, and the love between Ruggiero and Bradamante. Sensual love is the prevailing sentiment; but it is tempered by the author's ironic attitude and artistic detachment. The metrical form of the poem is the ottava, according to a tradition that continued from Boccaccio to Politian and Boiardo. The poem enjoyed immediate popularity all over Europe and greatly influenced the literature of the Renaissance.
·adaptation by early opera librettists **13**:579f
·literary sources **15**:1024a
·literature of the Renaissance **10**:1133c
·Orlando's idenification with French Roland **1**:1151h
·Renaissance literary forms and themes **15**:667a
·style, themes, and revisions **1**:1151c

Orlando innamorato (1483), epic by Matteo Maria, conte Boiardo, the first poem to combine the Arthurian and Carolingian traditions of romance. Its hero is the Roland of the Charlemagne legends.
·Renaissance literary forms and themes **15**:667a

Orlando Paladino (1782), in English KNIGHT ROLAND, opera by Joseph Haydn.
·heroic–comic style of drama **8**:682c

orle, in heraldry, a number of small charges arranged to form a border within the edge of a field.
·heraldic design elements **8**:788b; illus. 7787

Orléanais, a French province or military government of the 17th and 18th centuries, centred at Orléans and corresponding roughly to the modern *départements* of Loiret, Loir-et-Cher, and Eure-et-Loir, with parts of Essonne and Sarthe.

The *gouvernement* of Orléanais in 1789

Orleanists, constitutional monarchists in 19th-century France who supported the July Monarchy (1830–48) of Louis-Philippe, of the Orléans branch of the House of Bourbon. Anti-republican and anti-Bonapartist, the Orleanists also opposed the Legitimist supporters of Charles X, Louis-Philippe's deposed predecessor. The Orleanist monarchy appealed strongly to the prosperous bourgeoisie, to academics and intellectuals like the Doctrinaires, and to Protestants who resented the reactionary Catholicism of Charles X.

The foremost representatives of Orleanism in power were Casimir Perier, Jacques Laffitte, Adolphe Thiers, Albert, duc de Broglie, and François Guizot. Eventually, the Orleanists split into the conservative Parti de la Résistance (Perier, Guizot), standing for the consolidation of the dynasty and limitation of the franchise, and the more liberal Parti du Mouvement (Laffitte), advocating the spread of liberalism abroad and progressive extension of the franchise. The latter, under the leadership of Odilon Barrot, became after 1831 the "dynastic left" in the chamber of deputies.

The Orleanists supported Louis-Philippe's grandson and heir, Louis-Philippe Albert, comte de Paris, after the fall of the July Monarchy (1848) and during the Second Republic and Second Empire. The demise of the Second Empire, in 1870, offered another chance for a restoration of the monarchy, but the Third Republic was born while the Orleanists and Legitimists were still arguing over a candidate. After the direct male line of the elder Bourbons died out in 1883, most of the Legitimists joined with the Orleanists in fruitlessly supporting the Comte de Paris for the throne.
·activities through Third Republic **7**:663f

Orléans, capital of Loiret *département*, north central France, south southwest of Paris. The city stands on the banks of the Loire River in a fertile valley on the edge of the Beauce plain. The Loire divides the town into two unequal parts. To the south lies the small Saint-Marceau quarter, a market gardening centre. The main part of the city stands on the northern bank of the Loire. The old quarter, surrounded by pleasant wide boulevards and quays along the river, was largely destroyed during World War II. It has been rebuilt in keeping with the style of the old 18th-century town, with consideration for the imperatives of modern traffic. Beyond the boulevards new districts were being built in the 1970s along the main roads leading out of the town.

Orléans is the centre of a modern road network; the railway junction just outside the city at Les Aubrais is one of the most important in France. The university, founded in 1305, was abolished during the French Revolution, but the new one was established at la Source (source or springs of the Loire River) in 1962. Traditionally a centre for market gardening and horticulture (Orléans roses are famous), it has benefitted from the decentralization of Paris, which took place after World War II, and has developed new industries. These include textiles, food processing (nearly half France's production of vinegar), and the manufacture of machinery (automobile accessories, agricultural equipment).

The Sainte-Croix cathedral, begun in the 13th century, was largely destroyed by the Protestants in 1568. Henry IV, king of France from 1589–1610, gave funds for its reconstruction, and it was faithfully rebuilt (17th–19th centuries) in Gothic style. The 18th century towers were damaged in World War II but were later restored. The cathedral is about the same size as Notre-Dame of Paris. The stone and brick Renaissance Hôtel de Ville (1549–1555) was restored and enlarged in the 19th century. Orléans, which derives its name from the Roman Aurelianum, was conquered by the Roman general and statesman

Julius Caesar in 52 BC. It became an intellectual capital under Charlemagne, emperor from 800 to 814, and in the 10th and 11th centuries it was the most important city in France after Paris. In 1429, during the Hundred Years' War (1337–1453), after it had been besieged for seven months by the English, the French national heroine St. Joan of Arc (called the Maid of Orléans) and her troops delivered it. The victory continues to be celebrated annually (*see* Orléans, Siege of). Orléans was a Huguenot (Protestant) centre during the 16th-century Wars of Religion, but the Catholics took control of the city in 1572 after the Massacre of St. Bartholomew's Day in which about 1,000 Protestants were killed. It was occupied in 1870 by the Prussians after a long siege. The city was severely bombed in World War II. Many buildings of historical and artistic interest were destroyed, including the Musée Jeanne-d'Arc and the church of St. Paul. Pop. (1971 est.) 102,200.
47°55′ N, 1°54′ E
·Frankish kingdom boundary fluctuations **11**:927d; map 926
·map, France **7**:584

Orléans, duc d', title closely associated with the French royal house from the 14th century. From the 17th century it was held by the branch of the House of Bourbon that became the ruling family of France in the person of King Louis-Philippe (reigned 1830–48).
·accession to French throne after 1830 revolt **3**:82h
·heraldic badge, illus. 5 **8**:786

Orléans, Anne-Marie-Louise d', duchesse de Montpensier: *see* Montpensier, Anne-Marie-Louise d'Orléans, duchesse de.

Orléans, Canal d', France, one of the waterways (45 mi [72 km] long) connecting the Seine and Loire rivers.
·Loire River navigability **11**:88e

Orléans, Charles, duc d': *see* Charles, duc d'Orléans.

Orléans, Council of (511), Frankish church council summoned and dominated by Clovis, king of the Franks, extended the King's temporal and spiritual authority.
·Clovis' summoning and result **4**:762e

Orléans, François-Ferdinand-Philippe-Louis-Marie d', prince de Joinville: *see* Joinville, François-Ferdinand-Philippe-Louis-Marie d'Orléans, prince de.

Orléans, Gaston de France, duc d' (b. April 25, 1608, Fontainebleau, Fr.—d. Feb. 2, 1660, Blois), prince who readily lent his prestige to several unsuccessful conspiracies and revolts against the ministerial governments during the reign of his brother, King Louis XIII (ruled 1610–43), and the minority of his nephew, Louis XIV (ruled 1643–1715).

Gaston de France, duc d'Orléans, engraving by N. de Poilly (1675–1747)
By courtesy of the Bibliotheque Nationale, Paris

The third son of King Henry IV (ruled 1589–1610) and Marie de Médicis, Gaston was at first known as the Duc d'Anjou. As the only surviving brother of Louis XIII, he was known as "Monsieur" from 1611. He first came into conflict with royal authority in 1626, when Marie de Médicis and Louis XIII's powerful chief minister, the Cardinal de Richelieu, attempted to force him to marry Marie de Bourbon-Montpensier. Several nobles, including the Duchesse de Chevreuse and her lover, the Marquis de Chalais, encouraged him to resist the marriage and drew him into a plot to assassinate Richelieu. Richelieu discovered the conspiracy and had Chalais beheaded; but Anjou, as heir presumptive to the throne, escaped prosecution. He went through with the marriage (August 1626) and was created duc d'Orléans; nine months later his wife died in childbirth.

When Marie de Médicis was exiled from Paris by Louis in February 1631 for demanding Richelieu's dismissal, Orléans declared his support for the Queen Mother and began raising troops; but he fled to the duchy of Lorraine in April. In January 1632 he secretly married Marguerite, sister of Charles IV, duc de Lorraine. A few days later Louis XIII's troops invaded Lorraine and forced Orléans to flee to the Spanish Netherlands. He re-entered France with a small army in July to join a revolt led by the powerful Duc de Montmorency, governor of Languedoc. On the suppression of the uprising, Orléans was pardoned; but after the execution of Montmorency in November, he again withdrew to the Spanish Netherlands. Richelieu allowed him to return to France in 1634. Orléans campaigned for Louis XIII against the Spaniards in Picardy in 1636, but the King continued to refuse to recognize his marriage to Marguerite. The birth of the dauphin Louis (later King Louis XIV) in 1638 quashed his hopes of succeeding to the throne. He was further humiliated by the exposure of his complicity in the Marquis de Cinq-Mars's plot against Richelieu (1642).

In accord with the provisions of the will of Louis XIII, Orléans became lieutenant general of the kingdom on the accession of young Louis XIV. He helped the Queen Mother, Anne of Austria, to become sole regent; but she proceeded to appoint Richelieu's protégé, Cardinal Jules Mazarin, as first minister. When the aristocratic uprising known as the Fronde broke out in 1648, Orléans at first supported Mazarin; in 1651, however, he joined the coalition of princes that forced Anne to dismiss the minister. Exiled by Louis XIV upon the recapture of Paris by government forces in 1652, Orléans was formally reconciled with the King four years later. G. Dethan's *Gaston d'Orléans* appeared in 1959.
·conspiracies against Louis XIII **7**:632g

Orléans, House of: *see* Orléans, duc d'.

Orléans, Jean d', comte de Dunois: *see* Dunois, Jean d'Orléans, comte de.

Orléans, Louis, duc d' (b. March 13, 1372, Paris—d. Nov. 23, 1407, Paris), younger brother of King Charles VI, initiated the power struggle with the dukes of Burgundy that became the dominating factor in 15th-century France. Known for his ambition and his love of pleasure, he was said to have had a liaison with the Queen as well as with other ladies.

Louis was at first titled comte de Valois; in 1386 Charles granted him Touraine, which he exchanged in 1392 for the duchy of Orléans. In 1386 he married his cousin Valentina Visconti, daughter of the Duke of Milan, who brought as part of her dowry lands in northern Italy and awakened Orléans's ambitions for founding a kingdom there. Her hereditary right to Milan furnished her descendants, the kings Louis XII and Francis I, with a pretext for the wars they undertook in Italy.

Orléans sat on his brother's council. When Charles VI went mad, a power struggle developed between Orléans and his uncle Philip the Bold, duke of Burgundy. When Philip died in 1404, the rivalry continued with his son John the Fearless, culminating in Orléans's assassination by John's agents in 1407. A long feud ensued between the Armagnacs, partisans of Orléans's heirs, and the Burgundians. Orléans was the father of the poet Charles d'Orléans (1394–1465), head of the Armagnacs after his father's death and grandfather of Louis XII.
·civil war involvement and assassination **7**:624f
·control of royal council and desire for war **9**:19c
·military and diplomatic ambitions **6**:1082g
·murder by John the Fearless of Burgundy **10**:243g

Orléans, Louis, duc d' (d. 1550), second son of Henry II of France.
·Rabelais's account of birth celebration **15**:347d

Orléans, Louis-Charles-Philippe-Raphaël d', duc de Nemours: *see* Nemours, Louis-Charles-Philippe-Raphaël d'Orléans, duc de.

Orléans, Louis-Philippe-Joseph, duc d', called PHILIPPE ÉGALITÉ (b. April 13, 1747, Saint-Cloud, Fr.—d. Nov. 6, 1793, Paris), Bourbon prince who became a supporter of popular democracy during the Revolution of 1789. The cousin of King Louis XVI (ruled 1774–92) and the son of Louis-Philippe (later duc d'Orléans), he became duc de Chartres in 1752 and succeeded to his father's title in 1785. Orléans's hostility to Louis XVI's queen, Marie-Antoinette, caused him to live away from the royal court of Versailles.

During the conflicts that arose between Louis XVI and the nobles over the crown's financial policies in 1787, Orléans was temporarily exiled to his estates for challenging the King's authority before the Parlement of Paris (one of the high courts of justice). He was elected a representative for the nobles to the States General, which convened on May 5, 1789. In the ensuing struggle within the States General, Orléans supported the unprivileged Third Estate (bourgeoisie) against the two privileged orders (nobles and clergy). On June 25 he and a small group of nobles joined the Third Estate, which had already (June 17) proclaimed itself a National Assembly. Orléans's Paris residence, the Palais-Royal, became a centre of popular agitation, and he was viewed as a hero by the crowd that stormed the Bastille on July 14.

Philippe Égalité, lithograph by Joseph Traviès de Villers (1804–59)
H. Roger-Viollet

On returning from a mission to England in July 1790, Orléans took a seat in the National Assembly. He was admitted to the politically radical Jacobin Club in 1791. After the fall of the monarchy in August 1792, he renounced his title of nobility and accepted the name Philippe Égalité from the Paris Commune, one of the popular Revolutionary bodies. Elected to the National Convention (the third successive Revolutionary legislature), which convened in September 1792, Égalité supported the radical democratic policies of the Montagnards against their more moderate Girondin opponents. Nevertheless, during the trial of Louis XVI by the Convention, the Girondins attempted to confuse the issues by accusing the Montagnards of conspiring to put Égalité on the throne. Égalité voted for the execution of Louis, but he fell under suspicion when his son Louis-Philippe, duc de Chartres, defected to the Austrians with the French commander Charles-François du Périer Dumouriez on April 5, 1793. Accused of being an accomplice of Dumouriez, Égalité was arrested on April 6 and was sent to the guillotine in November. The Duc de Chartres reigned as King Louis-Philippe from 1830 to 1848. E.S. Scudder's biography of Égalité, entitled *Prince of the Blood*, was published in 1938.

Orléans, Louis-Philippe-Robert, duc d' (b. Feb. 6, 1869, Twickenham, Middlesex—d. March 28, 1926, Palermo, Sicily), pretender to the French throne during the Third Republic.

Louis-Philippe-Robert, duc d'Orléans, engraving by Dujardin after a photograph, 1890

By courtesy of the Bibliotheque Nationale, Paris

The eldest son of Louis-Philippe-Albert, comte de Paris, Orléans was banished from France in 1886 as a threat to the republican regime. Returning in 1890, he was arrested and given a prison sentence, but was released after a few months and escorted out of the country.

Considered by most French royalists as their rightful king after his father's death (September 1894), Orléans had no children by his marriage (Nov. 5, 1896) to the Austrian archduchess Maria Dorothea Amalia, so that when he died his pretensions passed to his cousin Jean, duc de Guise.

Orléans, Philippe I de France, duc d' (b. Sept. 21, 1640, Saint-Germain-en-Laye, Fr.—d. June 9, 1701, Saint-Cloud), younger brother of King Louis XIV (reigned 1643–1715), who prevented him from exercising political influence but tolerated him as an overtly respected and covertly despised figure at court.

The son of King Louis XIII and Anne of Austria, Philippe was titled duc d'Anjou until he succeeded his uncle Gaston de France as duc d'Orléans in 1660. Orléans married (March 1661) his cousin Henrietta, sister of King Charles II of England, but he soon avoided her and became involved in a succession of homosexual relationships. Henrietta died suddenly and in circumstances that caused scandal in 1670. In the following year Orléans was married to Elizabeth Charlotte, daughter of the Elector Palatine.

Orléans proved to be a courageous soldier. He distinguished himself fighting in the Spanish Netherlands in the War of Devolution (1667–68), and during the Dutch War (1672–78) he won an important victory over William of Orange at Cassel (April 11, 1677). Allegedly jealous of his brother's military success, Louis gave him no further commands. Two of Orléans's daughters by his first marriage became queens. Philippe, his son by his second marriage, inherited the dukedom of Orléans and served as regent for young King Louis XV from 1715 to 1723.

·patronage of Molière's theatre company **12**:322f
·relationship of Houses of Bourbon and Orléans **3**:80g; table

Orléans, Philippe II, duc d' (b. Aug. 2, 1674, Saint-Cloud, Fr.—d. Dec. 2, 1723, Versailles), regent of France for the young King Louis XV from 1715 to 1723. He attempted, with only limited success, to restore to the nobles the political powers they had lost during the reign of King Louis XIV (1643–1715).

The son of Philippe I, duc d'Orléans, and Charlotte Elizabeth of the Palatinate, Philippe d'Orléans was known as the Duc de Chartres during his father's lifetime. Although he served with the French army against the English and Dutch in the War of the Grand Alliance (1689–97), his uncle, Louis XIV, excluded him from the high military commands to which he considered himself entitled. The Duc de Chartres retaliated by studiously neglecting his wife, Françoise-Marie de Bourbon, the King's favourite legitimized daughter. His irreverence, habitual drunkenness, and licentious behaviour had earned him an unsavoury reputation by the time he succeeded to his father's title in 1701. Nevertheless, he was given military commands in Italy (1706) and Spain (1707–08) during the War of the Spanish Succession (1701–14).

As premier prince of the blood royal, Orléans became regent for the five-year-old Louis XV upon the death of Louis XIV (Sept. 1, 1715). Through the provisions of his will, however, Louis XIV had left the effective power in the hands of his own two legitimized bastard sons in order to prevent Orléans from dismantling the system of absolute royal despotism. If the sickly Louis XV had died, the legitimized princes would have rejected Orléans's claim to the throne in favour of the claim of Louis XIV's grandson, King Philip V of Spain. Hence, in order to assert his authority as regent and advance his dynastic ambitions, Orléans induced the Parlement (high court of justice) of Paris to annul Louis XIV's will (Sept. 12, 1715). He then proceeded to institute an experimental system of conciliar government—known as *la polysynodie*—designed to destroy the authority of the secretaries of state and restore political power to the high nobility. Seven councils, each headed by a leading noble, were established, and the whole conciliar network was placed under the control of a council of regency appointed and presided over by Orléans. Nevertheless, the new system proved so cumbersome and inefficient that the Regent dissolved it in September 1718 and reinstated the secretaries of state.

Orléans's foreign policy was also tied to his dynastic interests. In 1716 he had his foreign minister, the abbé (later Cardinal) Guillaume Dubois (who in 1722 became first minister), conclude with Great Britain, France's traditional enemy, an alliance that secured British support against Philip V's claim to the succession to the French throne. France and Great Britain went to war with Spain in 1719, and in the following year Philip V was forced to renounce his French claims and recognize Orléans as Louis XV's heir.

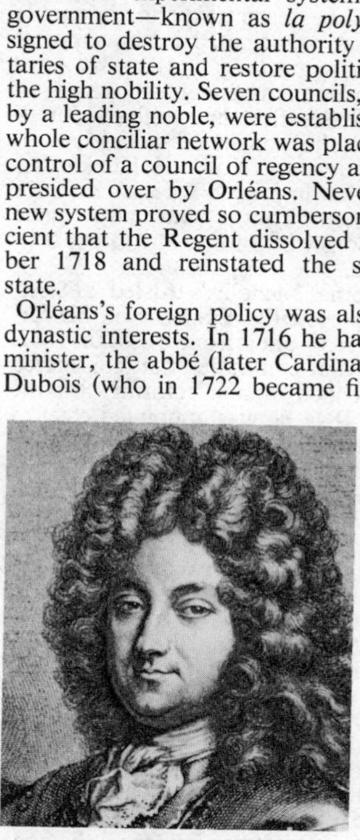

Philippe II, duc d'Orléans, detail of an engraving by C. DuFlos (1665–1727), after a painting by R. Tournières

H. Roger-Viollet

Meanwhile, Orléans had to grapple with the acute fiscal problems that had resulted from the costly wars of Louis XIV. In 1717 he entrusted the reform of French finances to a Scottish banker, John Law, whose innovations led to a financial disaster three years later that severely discredited Orléans's regime.

In ecclesiastical affairs Orléans at first sided with the Jansenists (a dissident party within the French Roman Catholic Church) in their struggle against the Society of Jesus (the Jesuits), but by 1722 he was taking a firmly anti-Jansenist line.

Orléans's regency ended when Louis XV came of age in February 1723. Upon the death of Dubois in August, the Duc himself became first minister; he died only four months later. Philippe Erlanger's biography of Orléans, *Le Régent*, was published in 1938.

·claim to Louis XV's throne **6**:1095e
·regency for Louis XV **3**:83a

Orléans, Siege of (Oct. 12, 1428–May 8, 1429), the military turning point of the Hundred Years' War between France and England. The siege was begun by Thomas de Montacute, earl of Salisbury, after the English conquest of Maine, a border region between the zone recognizing Henry VI of England as king of France and the zone recognizing the dauphin, Charles VII; but Salisbury's enterprise was contrary to the advice of Henry VI's regent in France, John, duke of Bedford, who argued for an advance into Anjou instead. Salisbury captured some important places upstream and downstream from Orléans and also the bridgehead fort on the south bank of the Loire opposite the city itself, then died of a wound on Nov. 3, 1428. His successor in command, William de la Pole, earl of Suffolk, did nothing to promote the operation until December, when John Talbot (later earl of Shrewsbury) and Thomas Scales arrived to stimulate him. Impressive siegeworks, including forts, were then undertaken. Weeks went by; a French attempt to cut the besiegers' line of supply was defeated (Battle of the Herrings, Feb. 12, 1429); and the defenders, under Jean d'Orléans, comte de Dunois (bastard son of Charles VII's late uncle Louis, duc d'Orléans), were envisaging capitulation when Joan of Arc, at Chinon, persuaded Charles VII to send an army to relieve the city. Diversionary action against one of the English forts enabled Joan, from Chézy, five miles upstream, to enter Orléans with supplies on April 30. In the following week the principal English forts were stormed, and Suffolk then raised the siege.

·cannon use by English and French **19**:577b
·Hundred Years' War turning point **9**:20b
·Joan of Arc's victory **10**:226f

Orleans, Territory of, created in 1804 by the Louisiana Purchase (*q.v.*) and the forerunner of the state of Louisiana (established in 1812).

·boundaries and Union entrance petition **11**:125g

Orléansville (Algeria): *see* el-Asnam.

Orley, Bernard (BERNAERT, BAREND) **van** (b. 1492?, Brussels—d. 1542, Brussels), Flemish painter of religious subjects and portraits and designer of tapestries. Son of the painter Valentin van Orley, he entered the employ of Margaret of Austria, regent of the Netherlands, in 1515, and three years later was appointed court painter. The German painter Albrecht Dürer made a portrait of him in 1521.

Orley's earliest important work, painted about 1512, was an altarpiece of saints Thomas and Matthew, of which the centrepiece is in the Kunsthistorisches Museum, Vienna, and the wings in the Musées Royaux des Beaux-Arts, Brussels. From 1516 to 1522 he followed the style of the Flemish painter Jan Mabuse but after that was influenced by the Venetian painter Raphael, whose tapestry cartoons were in Brussels for many years; both influences may be seen in an altarpiece representing the "Patience of Job" (1521), now in the Musées Royaux des Beaux-Arts, Brussels. Of Orley's portraits, that of Georg Zelle, Musées Royaux des Beaux-Arts, Brussels, is the only surviving one that is signed and dated (1519). Tapestries designed by Orley are the "Hunts of Maximilian" (Louvre) and the "Victory of Pavia" (Naples). His paintings in the United States include the well-known "Virgin and Child with Angels" (Metropolitan Museum of Art, New York City) and works at the National Gallery of Art, Washington, D.C.

·tapestry design innovations **17**:1062a

"Banquet of the Children of Job" from the series "The Virtue of Patience," panel painting by Bernard van Orley; in the Musées Royaux des Beaux-Arts, Brussels

By courtesy of the Musees Royaux des Beaux-Arts, Brussels

Orlice Mountains, Czech ORLICKÉ HORY, German ADLER GEBIRGE, a subgroup of the Sudeten mountains in northwestern Bohemia, Czechoslovakia, forming part of the frontier with Poland for a distance of 25 mi (40 km). They comprise mostly crystalline rocks, like most of the northern highland rim of Bohemia. The highest point is Velká Deštná, at 3,658 ft (1,115 m).
50°20′ N, 16°30′ W

Orlon: *see* acrylic compounds.

Orlov, Aleksey Fyodorovich, Prince (b. Oct. 19 [Oct. 8, old style], 1786, Moscow—d. May 21 [May 9, O.S.], 1861, St. Petersburg, modern Leningrad), military officer and statesman who was an influential adviser to the Russian emperors Nicholas I (ruled 1825–55) and Alexander II (ruled 1855–81) in both domestic and foreign affairs. The nephew of Catherine II the Great's lover, Grigory Grigoryevich Orlov, and the illegitimate son of Count Fyodor Grigoryevich Orlov, who had helped Grigory place Catherine on the throne (1762), Aleksey was educated under Catherine's general supervision. In 1804 he entered the army and, during the Napoleonic Wars, took part in all the Russian campaigns after 1805. But he opposed the radical ideas adopted by many Russian officers, including his brother Gen. Mikhail Fyodorovich Orlov, and in 1825, having become the commander of a cavalry regiment, helped suppress the uprising of the Decembrist movement, which hoped to establish a constitutional regime. As a reward, Nicholas I made him a count.

Later, Orlov fought in the Russo-Turkish war of 1828–29, attained the rank of lieutenant general, and led the Russian delegation that concluded the peace treaty of Adrianople (1829). He then participated in the suppression of the Polish uprising of 1830–31. After becoming both commander in chief of Russia's Black Sea fleet and ambassador to Turkey (1833), he concluded a defense alliance with Turkey (Treaty of Hünkâr İskelesi; 1833) that improved Russia's defenses on its southern frontier but also made Russia's relations with France and Great Britain more tense.

Having become Nicholas' trusted adviser, Orlov accompanied the Emperor on his foreign tour in 1837 and, from 1839 to 1842, served on a secret committee that considered and recommended minor reforms for the peasantry. In 1844 he was appointed chief of the third department of the imperial chancellery; Orlov thus became responsible for the security police force and, by spending a great deal of time with the Emperor, attained a high degree of influence over him and his policies.

In 1854, after the Crimean War began, Nicholas sent Orlov on an unsuccessful mission to Vienna to convince Austria to remain neutral. After the war, Orlov attended the peace conference and helped negotiate the Treaty of Paris (1856). When he returned to Russia, the new emperor, Alexander II, made him a prince, named him president of both the state council and the council of ministers, and, in 1858, appointed him chairman of a committee to investigate the problems of emancipating the serfs. Despite his great influence, the conservative Orlov was unable to prevent the emancipation, which was proclaimed several months before his death.

Orlov, Aleksey Grigoryevich, Count (b. Oct. 5 [Sept. 24, old style], 1737, Lyutkino, Tver [Kalinin] Province, Russia—d. Jan. 5, 1808 [Dec. 24, 1807, O.S.], Moscow), military officer who played a prominent role in the coup d'etat that placed Catherine II the Great on the Russian throne. Having entered the cadet corps in 1749, Orlov became an officer in the Russian guards as well as a close adviser to his brother Grigory Grigoryevich Orlov, who around 1760 became the lover of Catherine, wife of Emperor Peter III (ruled 1762). The Orlov brothers, supported by the guards, planned to overthrow the unpopular Peter; on the night of July 9 (June 28, O.S.), 1762, Aleksey Orlov brought Catherine from her residence at Peterhof, outside St. Petersburg (modern Leningrad), to the guards' barracks. From there a military escort accompanied her into St. Petersburg, where she was solemnly proclaimed empress of Russia by the Archbishop of Novgorod. Aleksey Orlov then proceeded to Peter's palace at Oranienbaum, received his abdication, arrested him, and transported him to the village of Ropsha. Several days later, while still under Orlov's supervision, Peter was killed (July 16 [July 5, O.S.]).

Immediately after the coup d'etat, Orlov was promoted to the rank of major general, and, in 1769, during the Russo-Turkish War of 1768–74, he was placed in command of the Russian fleet, which destroyed the superior Turkish fleet near Çesme (Chesme, located on the Aegean coast of Anatolia) on July 6, 1770. Although Orlov's actual role in this victory was minor and he subsequently refrained from forcing his way through the Dardanelles strait, he was welcomed in St. Petersburg as a hero and given the title Count Chesmenski.

After the war, in order to prevent Yelizaveta Alekseyevna Tarakanova, a potential pretender to the throne, from presenting a serious threat to Catherine, Orlov seduced Tarakanova, lured her onto his ship at Livorno, Italy, and had her imprisoned at the Shlisselburg Fortress, near St. Petersburg (1775). After this incident, Orlov resigned from the army (1775), retired to his estate at Lyutkino, and devoted himself to horse breeding. He was later recalled to St. Petersburg, however, by Emperor Paul I (ruled 1796–1801), who succeeded Catherine. Orlov was forced to carry the crown of Peter III in a procession transferring the late emperor's body to a place of honour in the Cathedral of St. Peter and St. Paul.

Count Aleksey Grigoryevich Orlov, oil painting by an unknown artist

Novosti Press Agency

Orlov, Grigory Grigoryevich, Count (b. Oct. 17 [Oct. 6, old style], 1734, Lyutkino, Tver [Kalinin] Province, Russia—d. April 24 [April 13, O.S.], 1783, Neskuchnoye, near Moscow), military officer and lover of Catherine II, empress of Russia from 1762 to 1796; he organized the coup d'etat that placed Catherine on the Russian throne and subsequently was her close adviser. Having entered the cadet corps in 1749, Orlov became an artillery officer and fought in the Battle of Zorndorf (1758) during the Seven Years' War (1756–63). In 1759, after escorting a Prussian prisoner of war to St. Petersburg (modern Leningrad), he was introduced to the Grand Duke Peter and his wife, Catherine; around 1760 Orlov became Catherine's lover.

After Peter ascended the Russian throne (1762), Orlov and his brother, Aleksey Grigoryevich, planned a coup d'etat, overthrew Peter, and made Catherine Russia's empress. Grigory was then given the title of count, promoted to the rank of adjutant general, and made director general of engineers and general in chief. He also began to study natural science and was one of the founders of the Free Economic Society (1765), which was organized to modernize the country's agricultural system.

Count Grigory Grigoryevich Orlov, oil painting by an unknown artist

Novosti Press Agency

While Catherine was composing her "Instruction" for the legislative commission that was to devise liberal government reforms and formulate a new legal code, Orlov acted as her consultant, and, later, when he was a member of the commission (1767–68), he strongly urged the passage of reforms that would improve the condition of the serfs; the commission, however, adjourned without making any substantial proposals. In 1772 Catherine sent Orlov as her chief delegate to a peace conference to end the Russo-Turkish War that had begun in 1768, but he advocated the liberation of Christian subjects from Turkish rule, as well as the dismemberment of the Ottoman Empire, and thereby failed in his mission; peace was not concluded until 1774.

Around 1772, Orlov also ceased to be Catherine's lover; he subsequently left Russia (1775) and married a cousin (1777). After his wife's death (1782), he lost his sanity and returned to his estate in Russia.

·Catherine the Great's coup d'etat **3**:1006a
·horse racing and Orlov-trotting breed **8**:1101f

Orlov diamond, rose-cut gem from India, one of the Romanov crown jewels; it is shaped like half an egg, with facets covering its domed surface, and the underside is nearly flat. It weighs nearly 200 carats. According to legend, it was once used as the eye of an idol in a Brahman temple in Mysore and was stolen by a French deserter, who escaped with it to Madras. Others contend that the authenticated history of the Orlov extends to the middle of the 18th century, when the stone (believed to be the long-missing Great Mogul diamond; *q.v.*) belonged to Nāder Shāh, king of Persia. After his assassination it was stolen and sold to an Armenian millionaire named Shaffrass. In either case, it was purchased in 1774 by Count Grigory Grigoryevich Orlov, who in an unsuccessful attempt to regain favour gave it to Catherine II the Great. Catherine had it mounted in the Romanov sceptre, and it is now part of the Soviet Union's Diamond Fund (which contains the tsarist regalia) in Moscow.

·diamond sources **7**:971e

Orm, also called ORMIN (fl. *c.* 1200), Augustinian canon, author of an early Middle English book of metrical homilies on the Gospels, to which he gave the title *Ormulum*, "because Orm made it." The work (dated on linguistic evidence *c.* 1200) is of little literary interest but of great value to the linguist, for Orm—who clearly wished to spread sound teaching, derived mainly from works of Gregory the Great, Bede, and Aelfric—invented an individual and remarkably consistent orthography based on phonetic principles. Intended to help preachers when reading his work aloud, it shows, for example, the quantity (length) of the vowels by doubling a consonant after a short vowel in a closed syllable, and it distinguishes by three separate symbols sounds that in the Anglo-Celtic or insular script of Old English were all represented by a single symbol.

·English spelling reform attempt **6**:879e

Ormazd (god): *see* Ahura Mazdā.

Ormea, Carlo Vincenzo Ferrero di Roasio, marchese d' (b. April 5, 1680, Mondovì, Italy—d. May 29, 1745, Turin), Piedmontese statesman who as minister under both Victor Amadeus II and Charles Emmanuel III played a leading role in the internal and external affairs of the Piedmontese–Sardinian kingdom.

A member of a noble but poor family, Ormea attracted attention by his gifts at the court of Victor Amadeus, who made him first count of Roasio and then marquess of Ormea (1722). The King also appointed him minister of finances and of the interior, where he instituted important reforms. Ormea obtained papal recognition for Victor Amadeus as king of Sardinia (December 1726) and then concluded with the papacy a concordat favourable to the King (May 1727).

When Victor Amadeus abdicated in favour of his son Charles Emmanuel (1730), Ormea was appointed minister of foreign affairs as well as of the interior (1732). He helped Charles Emmanuel by the arrest of the old king when Victor Amadeus tried to revoke his abdication (1731). During the War of the Polish Succession (1733–38), Ormea engineered an alliance with France, and in the War of the Austrian Succession (1740–48) he concluded an alliance with Austria. By the Treaty of Worms, he obtained from the empress Maria Theresa lands in Piacenza and in the Ticino in Italian Switzerland. When the new pope Clement XII nullified the concordat of 1727, Ormea was instrumental in obtaining a new concordat in 1741. Finally, in 1744, he succeeded in lifting the French siege of the city of Coni (now Cuneo).

Ormin (medieval homilist): *see* Orm.

Ormizd (ORMAZD): *see* Hormizd I; Hormizd II; Hormizd IV.

Ormoc, city and port, Leyte province, western Leyte, Philippines, at the head of Ormoc Bay, an inlet of the Camotes Sea. It serves the only commercial sugarcane district in the eastern Visayas. Rice, copra, and sugar are exported, and sugar, rice, and corn (maize) milling are important. Ormoc has an airport and is the headquarters of Tongonan Hot Spring National Park.

During World War II Ormoc was Leyte's largest Japanese stronghold and supply base; it fell to the U.S. general Douglas MacArthur's forces on Dec. 10, 1944. From its war-torn ruins rose the modern city. Inc. city, 1947. Pop. (1970) 84,563.
11°00′ N, 124°37′ E

·map, Philippines **14**:233

ormolu (French *dorure d'or moulu*, meaning literally "gilding with gold paste"), gold-coloured alloy of copper, zinc, and sometimes tin, in various proportions but usually containing at least 50 percent copper; used in mounts (ornaments on borders, edges, and as angle guards) for furniture, especially 18th-century furniture, and for other decorative purposes. Its gold colour may be heightened by immersion in dilute sulfuric acid or by burnishing.

The earliest ormolu appears to have been produced in France in the mid-17th century,

Secretary decorated with ormolu mounts, marquetry, and intarsia, French, *c.* 1770; in the Wallace Collection, London

By courtesy of trustees of the Wallace Collection, London

and France always remained the main centre of manufacture, though fine examples were also produced in other countries during the 18th and 19th centuries. To fashion ormolu, a model is made in wood, wax, or some other suitable medium; a mold is formed and the molten alloy is poured into it. The cast alloy is then chased (ornamented with indentations) and gilded. True ormolu is gilded by a process whereby powdered gold is mixed with mercury, and the resulting paste is brushed onto the cast form. The whole is then fired at a temperature that causes the mercury to evaporate, leaving a gold deposit on the surface. Finally, the gold is burnished or matted to give the greatest effect of metallic brilliance. (During the second half of the 19th century, pieces were gilded by a process of electrolysis, and these are often inaccurately referred to as ormolu.) Master craftsmen who worked in ormolu include Jean-Jacques Caffieri, Pierre Gouthière, and Pierre-Philippe Thomire in France and Matthew Boulton in England.

·Régence style development **7**:801c; illus.

Ormond Beach, city, Volusia County, northeast Florida, U.S., on the Halifax River (lagoon). Primarily a resort, it has about 4 mi (6 km) of compact white sand, part of a reef that continues southward for more than 20 mi along the Atlantic coast to Ponce de Leon Inlet. In 1874 a colony from Connecticut settled the site and called it New Britain. When incorporated as a town in 1880, it was renamed for a Capt. James Ormond, who had arrived from the Bahamas in 1815 and lived on a Spanish land grant. Henry M. Flagler, a railroad pioneer and resort promoter, bought and enlarged the Hotel Ormond (built in 1875), and several large estates developed including John D. Rockefeller's winter home, the Casements. Early in the 20th century, Henry Ford, Ransom E. Olds, Louis Chevrolet, and others tested automobiles on nearby Daytona Beach, marking the beginning of the Daytona Beach speed trials. Ormond became a city in 1930 and was renamed Ormond Beach in 1949. Pop. (1970) 14,063; (1980) 128,394.
29°17′ N, 81°02′ W

Ormonde, earls, marquesses, and dukes of, titles held by the Irish family of Butler, the earldom from 1328, the dukedom from 1682 to 1758, and the marquessate (extinct in 1758, revived 1825). James Butler (*c.* 1305–38) was created earl of Ormonde by Edward III. Afterward Ormondes served in the chief offices

of the government of Ireland and were generally loyal to the English crown. Among them were James (*c.* 1392–1452), 4th earl (the White Earl), famous as scholar, warrior, and antiquarian; John (d. 1478), 6th earl, a famous scholar who spoke every European language and served Edward IV as ambassador; and Thomas (1531–1614), the 10th earl (the Black Earl), raised as a Protestant at the English court, who fought for England against rebels in his own country, pacified Munster, and was lieutenant governor in 1597. James (*see* Ormonde, James Butler, 12th earl and 1st duke of) was the most famous Butler of all and was the first duke. The Ormonde dukedom and marquessate became extinct in 1758 but the marquessate was revived in 1825 for James, the 19th earl. *See also* Butler.
·Ireland's feudal nobility and conflicts **3**:286b *passim* to 288g

Ormonde, James Butler, 12th earl and 1st duke of (b. Oct. 19, 1610, London—d. July 21, 1688, Kingston Lacy, Dorset), Anglo-Irish Protestant who was the leading agent of English royal authority in Ireland during much of the period from the beginning of the English Civil War (1642–51) to the Revolution of 1688. Born into the prominent Butler family, he grew up in England and in 1632 succeeded to the earldom of Ormonde.

1st Duke of Ormonde, detail of a painting after Sir Peter Lely, *c.* 1665; in the National Portrait Gallery, London
By courtesy of the National Portrait Gallery, London

He began his active career in Ireland in 1633 by offering his services to Lord Deputy Thomas Wentworth (later earl of Strafford). Upon the outbreak of the Roman Catholic rebellion in Ireland in 1641, Ormonde was appointed a lieutenant general in the English Army. He defeated the rebels of the Catholic Confederacy at Kilrush, Munster (April 15, 1642), and at New Ross, Leinster (March 18, 1643). Those triumphs, however, did not prevent the confederates from overrunning most of the country. Ormonde's attempts to conclude a peace were blocked by a Catholic faction that advocated complete independence for Ireland. The situation deteriorated further, and in July 1647 Ormonde departed from Ireland, leaving the Protestant cause in the hands of the Parliamentarians, who had defeated King Charles I in the English Civil War.

Returning to Ireland in September 1648, Ormonde concluded a peace with the confederacy (January 1649); he then rallied Protestant royalists and Catholic confederates in support of Charles II, son and successor of Charles I. For several months most of Ireland was under Ormonde's control. But the Parliamentarian general Oliver Cromwell landed at Dublin in August 1649 and swiftly conquered the country for Parliament. Ormonde fled to Charles II's court-in-exile in Paris in December 1650, and for the next 10 years he was one of Charles's closest advisers.

When Charles II returned to England in the Restoration of 1660, Ormonde was made commissioner for the treasury and the navy. Appointed lord lieutenant of Ireland in 1662, he made vigorous attempts to encourage Irish commerce and industry. Nevertheless, his enemies at court persuaded Charles to dismiss him in 1669. He was restored to royal favour in 1677 and again appointed lord lieutenant of Ireland. Although he was created a duke in the English peerage in 1682, he was recalled from Ireland in 1684 as a result of new intrigues at Charles's court. His career is recounted in W. Burghclere's *Life of James, First Duke of Ormonde* (1912).
·Irish involvement in Civil War **3**:288g

Ormonde, James Butler, 2nd duke of (b. April 29, 1665, Dublin—d. Nov. 16, 1745, Avignon, Fr.), Irish general, one of the most powerful men in the Tory administration that governed England from 1710 to 1714. The grandson of the Irish statesman James Butler, 1st duke of Ormonde, he inherited his grandfather's title in 1688 and fought in the wars of King William III. Ormonde served Queen Anne as lord lieutenant of Ireland from 1703 to 1707 and from 1710 to 1713. In 1711 he succeeded John Churchill, duke of Marlborough, as commander in chief of the British forces in the War of the Spanish Succession against the French (1701–13). Nevertheless, soon after he landed in the Netherlands, he was secretly instructed not to join England's allies in offensive operations while the Tory government was trying—unknown to the Allies and the Whigs—to come to terms with the French. Because Ormonde maintained ties with the Jacobites, who upheld Stuart claims to the English throne, he was removed from his command on the accession of the Hanoverian king George I in 1714. In June 1715 the Duke was impeached by the Whigs for his complicity in the secret Tory negotiations. He fled to France in August and shortly thereafter attempted, without success, to land in England during an abortive Jacobite rebellion. He settled in Spain and later lived at Avignon.

Ormuri language, Iranian language spoken in the northern stretches of the Afghanistan–Pakistan border region.
·Indo-Iranian languages distribution map **9**:442

Ormuz (Iran): *see* Hormuz.

Ormuz, Strait of (Asia): *see* Hormuz, Strait of.

Ormyridae, family of insects of the order Hymenoptera.
·characteristics and classification **9**:132f

ornament, architectural, elements used to decorate or embellish architectural structures.
·Art Nouveau movement **19**:464f; illus.
·Coptic sculpture developments **19**:344g
·furniture adaptation and period use **7**:785f
·Georgian visual art forms and styles **19**:341h
·Gothic church decoration **19**:365d
·Greek architecture of Archaic period **19**:288h
·Indian styles and materials **17**:173d
·Islāmic architectural history **9**:991a
·Melanesian board carvings **11**:865f
·neo-Babylonian, Arabian, Anatolian, and Iranian visual arts **19**:264g
·Renaissance Plateresque style use **19**:392d
·Rococo interior design **19**:414d
·Roman visual art forms and styles **19**:306g
·Sullivan's theories and works **17**:795c
·types, uses, and developments **1**:1108h; illus. 1104

ornamentation, in music, the embellishment of a melody, either by adding notes or by modifying rhythms. In European music, ornamentation is added to an already complete composition in order to make it more pleasing. This concept is foreign to ancient and much modern Oriental music, in which boundaries between ornamentation, improvisation, and composition are impossible to define. *See* improvisation; melody type.

Ornamentation varies greatly in different ages and countries. Its traditional vocabulary reflects and often influences musical styles. Some styles of ornamentation result from technical limitations of an instrument; others reflect the desire to add variety to repetitions. Most creatively, ornamentation is linked with improvisation and, therefore, with composition. When a piece is transferred from one medium to another, the instrumental style and ornamentation appropriate to the new medium may alter the character of the music.

Until the late 18th century, performers learned to improvise florid embellishment in order to heighten the expressive power of music. But badly executed ornaments cause confusion, and critics complained that ornamentation was sometimes debased by a tasteless display of virtuosity. Vocal ornamentation in sacred music was opposed by medieval churchmen as detrimental to the purity of the chant. All that is known of early medieval ornamentation is that some notational signs signified ornaments and that the vocal trill was known from at least the 3rd century. The first notated dances, dating from the 13th century, show features of a purely instrumental style of ornamentation. In 14th-century Italian secular music a fundamental technique of ornamentation arose, that of diminution or division; *i.e.*, dividing the basic melody notes into groups of shorter notes. This technique became codified, and the performer could choose one of several diminution patterns to ornament a phrase. Diminutions were generally cadential (*i.e.*, performed at the end of a section), and the practice became a feature of the 18th-century concerto (*see* cadenza).

In the 15th century the first theoretical works dealing with ornamentation appeared, followed in the 16th century by many guides to ornamentation, mostly by Italian authors and directed toward amateurs. In these works vocal ornamentation was conceived as abstract musical expression rather than as an expression of literary ideas. It was primarily concerned with reflecting the *mood* of the text, not with underlining individual words. Therefore, the singer's approach to diminution was basically similar to the instrumentalist's.

Early in the 17th century there was a decisive change in vocal and instrumental styles of composition, and two distinct national styles of ornamentation, Italian and French, were founded. Vocal ornamentation was used expressly to heighten the emotional content of the words. To achieve this, a new, emotionally expressive style of melodic writing developed, together with a rhythmically mannered vocabulary of vocal ornamentation. In Italy, although diminution was still practiced, the new style of ornamentation was reserved for solo vocal music.

The principles of diminution were preserved in the 17th-century French style of vocal ornamentation associated with the *airs de cour* (accompanied solo songs, or airs). They also survived in the varied repeats found in harpsichord and lute music. Early 17th-century French lute music used many small ornaments for purposes of articulation and accentuation, as well as rhythmic modifications of the written notes. These ornaments became important features of harpsichord music, while rhythmic modifications were incorporated in later instrumental styles.

Following the ornamented vocal style of *c.* 1600, the Italian instrumental style remained florid. Elaboration of solo works in the mid-18th century required great skill on the performer's part, as it was customary for the composer to write only a skeleton of the melody to be filled out by the performer. But the gymnastics practiced by virtuosi of the late 18th and early 19th centuries led ultimately to debasement of the Italian style.

French and Italian styles of ornamentation remained distinct throughout most of the 18th century. Thus, J.S. Bach, not born to either style, could use both at will. In the works of Haydn and Mozart, written ornaments were incorporated in a manner that announces the absorption of ornaments into the accepted musical language. In the 19th century many ornaments became an integral part of the

musical language without being left to the performer's discretion, except in Italian opera. Thus, many phrases in works of Chopin and Wagner can be traced back to earlier forms of ornamentation.
·Baroque vocal improvisation **19**:30f
·medieval root of later bel canto style **16**:789g
·notational shorthand for performance **12**:733h
·Palestrina's use of plainsong **13**:932c

Orne, *département*, northwestern France, created from parts of the historic province of Normandy (*q.v.*), the county of Perche, and the duchy of Alençon. Its area of 2,355 sq mi (6,100 sq km) is separated from the English Channel by the *départements* of Manche on the west and Calvados on the north. Hilly in most parts, especially in the southwest and east, Orne is the watershed between rivers flowing to the Channel and the Atlantic Ocean. Most of the land lies above 600 ft (180 m). The highest point in Orne and in the whole of Normandy is 1,368 ft (417 m) in the Forêt (forest) d'Écouves, north of the ancient market town of Alençon (*q.v.*), Orne's capital, which is situated on the Sarthe River (*q.v.*) on the southern boundary. The Sarthe, which springs from headwaters north of Mortagne-au-Perche (one of the most picturesque small towns in France), is one of 20 rivers and 800 streams rising in the *département*. The Orne River (*q.v.*) rises near the ancient cathedral city of Sées and flows northwestward through the market town of Argentan, seriously damaged in 1944 during the Battle of Normandy.

Orne, predominantly agricultural, has a temperate climate with moderate rainfall. Most of the farming land is used for horse and cattle breeding. Butter and cheese, particularly Camembert (the name of a village in the northeast), are among the chief products. Apple trees abound, and the local cider is famous. A stud farm founded under Louis XIV is situated near Argentan. Textiles are still manufactured and some light industries have been developed. Alençon, Argentan, and Mortagne-au-Perche are the administrative centres of the three *arrondissements* of the *département*, which is in the educational division of Caen. Pop. (1972 est.) 294,000.
·area and population table **7**:594

Orneodidae, family of feather-winged moths, order Lepidoptera.
·classification and general features **10**:829e

Orne River, Normandie region, northern France, 94 mi (152 km) long, flowing through Orne and Calvados *départements* to empty into the English Channel 8 mi (13 km) north-northeast of Caen. It rises in the Collines (hills) du Perche, east of the cathedral city of Sées, after which it flows northwest through the market town of Argentan and then westward through Putanges-Pont-Écrepin, below which it is dammed. Its course then runs through the Saint-Aubert gorges to Pont-d'Ouilly and Thury-Harcourt, traversing some of the most beautiful parts of a region sometimes called the Norman Switzerland. It crosses pastureland to Caen, which is connected with the sea by a canal running parallel to the Orne and its estuary, along its left bank. Limestone from the formations that flank the lower course of the river has been used to construct historic buildings in England, including the Tower of London and Norwich Cathedral.
48°39′ N, 0°14′ E
·map, France **7**:584

ornithine, an amino acid formed as an intermediate compound during the synthesis of arginine, a component of proteins. It is important in protein metabolism.
·nicotine synthesis experiments **1**:606b
·nitrogen disposal adaptations **11**:1032e

Ornithischia: *see* dinosaur.

Ornithodelphia (mammal group): *see* Prototheria.

Ornithogalum, genus of plants in the family Liliaceae, about 100 species of bulbous herbs, native to Eurasia and Africa. The leaves are grouped at the base of the plant, and the yellow or white bell- or star-shaped flowers are borne in clusters at the top of a leafless stalk.

Ornithogalum
Klaus Fiedler—Bruce Coleman Ltd.

Each flower is on a short stalk, with a bract (leaflike structure) below it. Star-of-Bethlehem (*O. umbellatum*), a common garden ornamental, has white-marked leaves and white star-shaped flowers. There is a wide green band on the outside of three segments of each flower.

Ornitholestes, or, more properly, COELURUS, relatively small, lightly built dinosaur found as fossils in Late Jurassic deposits of North America (the Jurassic Period began 190,000,000 years ago and lasted 54,000,000 years). *Ornitholestes* is relatively well-known from a complete skeleton found in Wyoming. It was a small dinosaur, only about two metres (six feet) long. The skull, neck, and tail were long, and the neck was apparently very flexible. The forelimbs were well developed and ended in fingers longer and slimmer than are expected in dinosaurs, indicating that *Ornitholestes* sought rather quick moving and elusive prey. It has been suggested that *Ornitholestes* may have preyed upon the early birds, hence the name, which means "bird robber," but it is equally probable that it ate small, speedy lizards and even early mammals. The hindlimbs were well developed, with strong running muscles; *Ornitholestes* was a biped capable of rapid movement, running with the neck and tail outstretched as counterbalances to the body.

Ornitholestes represents a successful adaptive development; similar forms are present in many other regions of the world. It is probable that *Ornitholestes*, a small, active predator, filled an eco-niche later filled by the mammals. *Ornitholestes* probably inhabited the undergrowth regions of the forests present in the Late Jurassic of North America. The genus appears to have persisted into the Early Cretaceous Period.

ornithology, the scientific study of birds. Among the most familiar of the wild animals that coexist with man, birds have attracted his attention from prehistoric times. Most of the early writings on birds are more anecdotal than scientific, but they represent a broad foundation of knowledge, including much folklore, on which later work was based. In the Middle Ages many treatises dealt with the practical aspects of ornithology, particularly falconry and game-bird management. From the mid-18th to the late 19th century the major thrust in ornithology was the description and classification of new species, as scientific expeditions made collections in tropical areas rich in bird species. By the early 20th century the large majority of birds were known to science, although the biology of many species was virtually unknown. In the latter half of the 19th century much effort was devoted to the study of the internal anatomy of birds, primarily for its application to taxonomy. Anatomical study was overshadowed in the first half of the 20th century by the rising fields of ecology and ethology (the study of behaviour), but underwent a resurgence in the 1960s and 1970s, with more emphasis on the functional adaptations of birds.

Ornithology is one of the few scientific fields in which nonprofessionals make substantial contributions. Much research is carried out at universities and museums, which house and maintain the collections of bird skins, skeletons, and preserved specimens upon which most taxonomists and anatomists depend. Field research, on the other hand, is conducted by both professionals and amateurs, the latter providing valuable information on behaviour, ecology, distribution, and migration.

Although much information about birds is gained through simple, direct field observation (usually aided only by binoculars), some areas of ornithology have benefitted greatly from the introduction of new instruments and techniques. Bird banding (or ringing), first performed early in the 19th century, is now a major means of gaining information on longevity and movements. Banding systems are conducted by a number of countries and each year hundreds of thousands of birds are marked with numbered leg bands. The study of bird movements has been greatly aided by the use of sensitive radar. Individual bird movements are also recorded on a day to day basis by the use of minute radio transmitters (telemeters) worn by the bird or implanted inside. Visual markings, such as plumage dyes and plastic tags on the legs or wings, allow visual recognition of an individual bird without the difficult task of trapping it, and allow the researcher to be aided by amateur bird watchers in recovering his marked birds.
·bird characteristics and behaviour **2**:1053a
·falconiform life span calculations **7**:146d
·pair formation studies in doves **4**:934d

Ornithomimus (dinosaur): *see* Struthiomimus.

Ornithonyssus bacoti, species of mite of the subclass Acarina (phylum Arthropoda).
·mite and tick diversity, illus. 1 **1**:19

ornithophily, pollination by birds.
·bird pollination in angiosperms **14**:746h

ornithopter, machine designed to fly by the flapping of its wings in imitation of birds. The wooden bird said to have been made *c.* 400 BC by Archytas of Tarentum is one of the earliest examples; the Greek myth of Daedalus and Icarus involves man's use of wings in the manner of birds. In the late 15th century Leonardo da Vinci made many drawings and models of such aircraft. Despite continuing efforts, extending to the present, no ornithopter design has been successful.
·aircraft design and development **7**:380g

Ornithorhynchidae (mammal family): *see* platypus.

ornithosis, a viral disease of birds, resembling and perhaps related to psittacosis (*q.v.*) and transmissible to man. Chickens, pheasant, ducks, turkeys, and caged birds are susceptible and often show no symptoms. Acute cases are marked by respiratory infection and generalized wasting. Both psittacosis and ornithosis are chronic infections in many aviaries, pet shops, and other places in which birds are kept, and both are the concern of public health: even short-term exposure to infected animals or carcasses may result in influenza-like or pneumonia-like diseases in man. Birds given antibiotic-treated feed may resist overt disease but may still carry the virus.
·common diseases of poultry, table 6 **5**:875
·human infection from pigeons **4**:933c

·human respiratory system
  involvement **15**:770g
·psittacosis cause and quarantine laws **15**:139c
·transmission to man by birds **2**:1053g

oro-antral fistula, in anatomy, hole leading from the maxilla sinus to the mouth cavity.
·tooth extraction effects on sinuses **16**:807b

Orobanchaceae, family of broomrapes of the plant order Scrophulariales.
·parasitic features and classification **16**:413g

Orobanche (plant genus): *see* broomrape.

Orobie Alps, Italian ALPI OROBIE, part of the Alpine zone of Lombardy, northern Italy, south of the Valtellina (valley of the upper Adda River). Pizzo di Coca (10,010 ft [3,052 m]) is the highest peak.
46°00′ N, 10°00′ E
·folk culture patterns **1**:628b
·map, Italy **9**:1088

Orochis, a Tungus people of the Soviet Far East living near the mouth of the Amur River.
·nomadic life before colonization
  period **19**:495g
·Soviet Union nationalities distribution,
  table 3 **17**:339

Orocovis, town and municipality, central Puerto Rico in the Cordillera Central. The town is 24 mi (39 km) southwest of San Juan in a tobacco growing region. Pop. (1970) town, 3,684.
18°14′ N, 66°23′ W
·area and population table **15**:261
·map, Puerto Rico **15**:262

Orodes II, Parthian WRWD, Pahlavi WYRWD or WYRWY (d. 37/36 BC), king of Parthia (reigned *c.* 57–37/36 BC), who helped his brother Mithradates III murder their father, Phraates III, and in turn supplanted Mithradates. When Mithradates occupied Seleucia and Babylon, Orodes stormed those towns, immediately executing his brother. No less ruthless to his attendants, he put to death the general who in 53 BC crushed the Romans under the triumvir Marcus Licinius Crassus Dives at Carrhae in northern Mesopotamia. Parthian raids into Roman Syria were checked by the death of Pacorus, Orodes' favourite son and perhaps joint king. Orodes, stunned by the loss, was murdered in turn by another son, Phraates IV.
·Parthian triumph over Rome **9**:843f

orogeny, a mountain-building event, generally one that occurs in geosynclinal areas. In contrast to epeirogeny (*q.v.*), an orogeny tends to occur during a relatively short time in linear belts and results in intensive deformation. Accompaniments of orogeny include folding and faulting of strata, development of angular unconformities, and the deposition of clastic wedges of sediments in areas adjacent to the orogenic belt. Igneous intrusion and regional metamorphism frequently accompany the orogenic event.

Orogenies may result from continental collisions, the underthrusting of continents by oceanic plates, continental rifting, the overriding of oceanic ridges by continents, and other causes.
·African geological history **15**:843c
·Canadian Shield history **6**:11f
·climatic and topographic changes **4**:741b
·Cretaceous tectonic episodes **5**:250c
·Elburz Mountains' structural evolution **6**:523c
·extrusive igneous rock formation **9**:215h
·geological formation of Europe **6**:1036f
·Jurassic activity and geographic
  change **10**:360b
·mountain building and tectonism **12**:577h;
  illus. 578
·mountain range and belt features **12**:588e
·Pacific island arcs and fault zones **13**:837e
·Precambrian dating and shield areas **7**:1069e
·Pyrenees Hercynian origin and
  structure **15**:316c
·tectonic processes and effects **14**:434a
·Tertiary worldwide activity **18**:151f
·Triassic and Late Paleozoic activity **18**:696f
·waterfall height and uplift rates **19**:641a

orographic precipitation, rain, snow, or other precipitation produced when moist air is lifted as it moves over a mountain barrier. As the air rises and cools, orographic clouds form and serve as the source of the precipitation, most of which falls upwind of the mountain ridge. Some also falls a short distance downwind of the ridge and is sometimes called spillover. Commonly, on the lee side of the mountain range the quantity of rain is low, and the area is said to be in a rain shadow. Very heavy annual precipitation often occurs where a prominent mountain range is oriented across a prevailing wind from a warm ocean.
·cloud formations near hills and
  mountains **4**:758g
·historic theories **6**:81d
·Malayan–Australian monsoon **12**:392d
·precipitation generation and
  movements **4**:721h

Orohippus, genus of fossil horse, family Equidae, order Perissodactyla.
·horse ancestry and evolution **14**:87c

Oromazes (Zoroastrian deity): *see* Ahura Mazda.

Oromocto, town, Sunbury County, south central New Brunswick, Canada, on the St. John River at the mouth of the Oromocto River. The area was first settled in 1776 by William Hazen, and a blockhouse (Ft. Hughes) was built as a defense against revolutionaries from Massachusetts. Shipbuilding thrived (1834–78) but declined with the introduction of steel ships. The name is derived from a Malesite Indian word for deep water. Oromocto has become almost entirely a centre of military operations since Camp Gagetown, the Canadian Army's largest training project, was established in 1952. Inc. 1956. Pop. (1971 prelim.) 11,518.
45°51′ N, 66°29′ W

Oron, or IDUA ORON, town, Uyo Province, South-Eastern State, southeastern Nigeria, at the mouth of the Cross River and the terminus of roads from Uyo and Opobo. A coastal trade centre (yams, cassava, fish, palm oil and kernels) for the Ibibio people, it is the site of a hospital, a Methodist teacher-training college, and several secondary schools. Oron has a museum (1959) that houses a notable collection of ancestral carvings. There is ferry service across the river's mouth to Calabar, the state capital, 12 mi (19 km) northeast. Pop. (1971 est.) 41,294.
4°50′ N, 8°14′ E
·map, Nigeria **13**:86

Orono, town, Penobscot County, southern Maine, U.S., on the Penobscot River, 8 mi (13 km) north of Bangor. Settled about 1775, it was known as Stillwater and Old Town before acquiring in 1840 its present name honouring Joseph Orono, an Indian chief who befriended the Americans during the American Revolution. Mainly residential, the town is the seat of the University of Maine (1865). Light manufactures include textiles and wood and paper products. Inc. 1806. Pop. (1980) 10,578.
44°53′ N, 68°40′ W

Albert B. Nutting Hall, Department of Forestry, University of Maine in Orono
Mark Sexton

Orontes River, Arabic NAHR AL-ʿĀSĪ, southwestern Asia, drains a large part of the northern Levant into the Mediterranean. From its source in al-Biqāʿ of central Lebanon, it flows northward between the parallel ranges of the Lebanon and Anti-Lebanon mountains into Syria, where it has been dammed to form the Lake of Homs. Northwest of Ḥamāh the Orontes crosses the fertile al-Ghāb, once a swampy depression, and enters Turkey, where it bends westward and empties into the sea near Samandag. Largely unnavigable for most of its 250-mi (400-km) length, it is, nonetheless, an important source of irrigation water, especially between Homs and Ḥamah and in the al-Ghāb. Major tributaries include the Kura Su and the Odi Meidani. Homs, Ḥamāh, and the ancient Greek city of Antioch (Antakya) are the largest riparian settlements.
36°02′ N, 35°58′ E
·geography and utilization **10**:765f
·location and course **17**:920b
·map, Syria **17**:921
·map, Turkey **18**:784

Orontium aquaticum (plant): *see* Arales.

oropendola, any of a dozen tropical American birds of the family Icteridae (order Passeriformes) that are larger than caciques but of similar habits. Oropendolas weave hanging nests—up to 1.8 metres (6 feet) long—in tall isolated trees. They nest colonially: males stand guard by day but roost apart, and females construct the nests—sometimes 100 in a single tree—and raise the young. Males are about 30 to 50 centimetres (12 to 20 inches) long; females are considerably smaller. Both sexes are mainly black, sometimes with touches of reddish or brown. They have rounded yellow tails and heavy bills swollen at the base to form frontal shields. Most widely distributed species is the crested oropendola (*Psarocolius*, formerly *Ostinops*, *decumanus*) from Panama to Argentina.
·classification and general features **13**:1063f

oropharynx, the portion of the passage for food that extends from the back of the mouth to the level of the larynx, or voice box.
·human alimentary canal anatomy **5**:792a
·human respiratory pathway **15**:764g

Oropus, modern SKÁLA OROPOÚ, ancient Greek seaport on the Gulf of Euboea at the border between Attica and Boeotia, seat of the oracle of Amphiaraus. Athens probably acquired it in the 6th century BC, but both Boeotia and Eretria controlled it for long periods in and after the 4th century. Finally, the Romans restored it to Athens. Latest census 540.
38°20′ N, 23°46′ E
·map, Greece **8**:314

Orosius, Paulus (b. probably Braga, Spain; fl. 414–417), defender of early Christian orthodoxy, theologian, and author of the first world history by a Christian. As a priest he went *c.* 414 to Hippo (now Annaba, Alg.), where he met St. Augustine and where he wrote his earliest work, *Commonitorium ad Augustinum de errore Priscillianistarum et Origenistarum* ("Reminder to Augustine Concerning the Error of the Priscillianists and the Origenists").

In 415 Augustine sent him to Palestine, where he immediately opposed Pelagianism, a heretical doctrine by the theologian Pelagius minimizing the role of divine grace in man's salvation. At a synod summoned that July by Bishop John of Jerusalem, Orosius ineffectively accused Pelagius of heresy. Soon afterward he wrote *Liber apologeticus contra Pelagianos* ("Apology Against the Pelagians").

Early in 416 he returned to Augustine, who asked him to compose a historical apology of Christianity, *Historiarum adversus paganos libra VII* (Eng. trans. by I.W. Raymond, 7

Books of Histories Against the Pagans, 1936). In this world history, he focussed on the catastrophies that befell mankind before Christianity, arguing against the contention that the calamities of the Roman Empire were caused by its Christian conversion. J. Svennung's *Orosiana* appeared in 1922.
·historiography in Christian thought **8**:948g

Óros Óthris, mountains in central Greece. 39°02′ N, 22°37′ E
·geographic features **8**:313a

orotic aciduria, hereditary metabolic disorder characterized by an anemia with many large immature red blood cells, low white blood cell count, retarded growth, and the urinary excretion of large quantities of orotic acid, an intermediate in purine metabolism. It is thought that the disease is caused by a deficiency in two enzymes: orotidylic pyrophosphorylase and orotidylic decarboxylase. The disorder is extremely rare; it is transmitted recessively, and carriers of the trait can be detected by an examination of their white blood cells. The administration of pyrimidines usually brings about the remission of the anemia.
·pyrimidine metabolism disturbances **11**:1060a

Orotiña, Central American Indian tribe.
·Costa Rican population and assimilation **5**:211b

Oroville, city, seat (1856) of Butte County, north central California, U.S., on the Feather River, in the Sacramento Valley, at the foot of the Sierra Nevada. It originated in 1850 as a gold-mining camp known as Ophir City. By 1872 the lure of gold (Spanish *oro*, whence Oroville) had attracted large numbers of prospectors, including Chinese from other parts of the state. After the decline of gold mining, there was extensive cultivation of citrus fruit and olive groves in the area.

Oroville is now a shipping point for semitropical fruit and has one of the nation's largest olive canning factories. Tourist attractions include the Chinese Temple (1863) and the Judge C.F. Lott Home (1856) containing period furnishings.

Oroville Dam (*q.v.*) on the Feather River is 6 mi (10 km) northeast. Also nearby are Feather Falls in Plumas National Forest and the Feather River Hatchery. Pop. (1980) 8,683. 39°31′ N, 121°33′ W
·map, United States **18**:908

Oroville Dam, earth-filled dam on the Feather River, California, U.S., completed in 1968 by the state of California. The dam, 770 feet (234 metres) high and 6,920 feet (2,109 metres) long at its crest, has a volume of 80,300,000 cubic yards (61,400,000 cubic metres) and forms a reservoir of 3,500,000 acre-feet (4,300,000,000 cubic metres) capacity. The first and key unit of the Feather River project, planned to serve extensive areas in central and southern California hundreds of miles distant, Oroville Dam provides irrigation water, flood control, and 440 megawatts of hydroelectric power capacity.
·dam cross-sectional design **5**:445d; illus.

Oroville Dam

By courtesy of Department of Water Resources, State of California

Orozco, José Clemente 13:741 (b. Nov. 23, 1883, Ciudad Guzmán, Mex.—d. Sept. 7, 1949, Mexico City), pre-eminent artist of modern Mexico who is considered the most important 20th-century muralist to work in fresco.

Abstract of text biography. Born into a prominent family, Orozco became obsessed with art at an early age. His preparations for careers as an agronomist and an architectural draftsman were abandoned when he lost his left hand in 1900 in a laboratory accident. He then turned his full attention to painting. Through his acquaintance with Gerardo Murillo, Orozco began to explore indigenous artistic traditions. He became an artist-propagandist for the revolutionary cause of 1914 and was forced to leave for the U.S. in 1917 due to a reaction of critics and moralists to the exhibition of his painting "House of Tears." Upon his return in 1920, the government commissioned him and other artists like Diego Rivera to paint murals, thereby initiating the Mexican muralist movement. Under criticism he left for the U.S. (1927–32), where he painted an important series of frescoes at Dartmouth College, Hanover, N.H., making a brief trip to Europe in 1932. Internationally established as a muralist, Orozco returned to Mexico in 1934. The profundity and emotional range of the imagery in his later murals, such as those in Guadalajara (1937–39 and 1949), were expressive of his strong social and spiritual convictions.

REFERENCES in other text articles:
·Hospicio Cabañas ceiling frescoes, illus., **13**:Painting, Art of, Plate III
·Mexican mural painting **19**:481g
·Mexican nationalistic culture movement **12**:86c

Orpen, Sir William (Newenham Montague) (b. Nov. 27, 1878, Stillorgan, County Dublin—d. Sept. 29, 1931, London), British painter, an outstanding portraitist who was also an official artist during World War I.

Orpen studied at the Dublin Metropolitan School of Art and at the Slade School, London. He was elected an associate of the Royal Academy in 1910 and academician in 1919. He first exhibited at the New English Art Club, of which he became a member in 1900, his early work being marked by pre-occupation with spacing and silhouette and the use of quiet harmonies of gray and brown with a note of vivid red or blue. He soon turned to the use of bright colour and the study of light, seen in a series of brilliant portrait interiors such as the "Hon. Percy Wyndham" (1907) and "Myself and Venus" (1910; Pittsburgh). About this time he became well known for his vigorously characterized portraits. Orpen received an appointment as official artist, and in 1918 an exhibition of his war pictures was held in London. Many of these are now in the Imperial War Museum.

"Leading the Life in the West" (self-portrait), oil on canvas by Sir William Orpen; in the Metropolitan Museum of Art, New York

By courtesy of the Metropolitan Museum of Art, New York, gift of George F. Baker, 1914

Orpen was created knight commander of the Order of the British Empire in 1918. He wrote *An Onlooker in France* (1921) and *Stories of Old Ireland and Myself* (1924).

Orphan, The, ancient Chinese ballad of the *yüeh-fu* genre from the Han dynasty (206 BC–AD 220).
·subject matter **10**:1053b

Orphans of the Storm (1922), film by D.W. Griffith.
·plot and techniques **12**:518c

orpharion (stringed instrument): *see* cittern.

Orphée (1950), play by Jean Cocteau.
·tragedy in contemporary theatre **4**:816b

Orpheus, ancient Greek legendary hero with a superhuman skill in music and song; he also became the patron of a religious movement dependent on a body of sacred writings said to be his own. Traditionally, Orpheus was the son of a Muse (probably Calliope, the patron of epic poetry) and Oeagrus, a Thracian river god (other versions give Apollo); his home was Thrace. He joined the expedition of the Argonauts, where he used his bewitching music in various ways (*e.g.*, he saved the Argonauts from the music of the Sirens by countering it with the even more beautiful music of his lyre); he also performed certain religious functions connected especially with initiation and purification. In his most popular myth he descended to Hades in an unsuccessful attempt to restore to life his wife, Eurydice, who had died from a snakebite. Orpheus' music charmed the gods of the underworld, and he was allowed to return to earth with Eurydice, provided he did not look back to see her until they reached the earth. He looked back too soon and lost her forever.

Orpheus himself was later killed by the women of Thrace. According to the earliest account, the wine god Dionysus urged his followers, the Maenads, to tear Orpheus to pieces in a Bacchic orgy because he preferred the worship of the rival god Apollo. His head, still singing, and his lyre floated on to Lesbos, where an oracle of Orpheus was established.

Orpheus was believed to be the founder of Orphism and to have laid down its doctrines in sacred texts. According to Orphic belief, the primal god of Love and Light (Eros-Phanes) sprang from an egg laid by Chronos

(Time) and created a world containing gods and men. Zeus, however, swallowed Phanes with his creation and brought a new world into being. Dionysus, son of Zeus, was killed and eaten by the Titans, the wicked sons of Earth (Ge). Zeus destroyed the Titans with a thunderbolt, and from the soot arose the human race, which therefore combined an earthly (Titanic) nature that had to be suppressed and a heavenly (Dionysiac) nature that had to be cultivated. That was accomplished by living an Orphic life, which included abstention from meat, wine, and sexual intercourse.

"Orpheus Charming the Beasts," mosaic by an unknown Roman artist; in the Museo Archeologico Nazionale, Palermo, Italy

Alinari

Orphic eschatology laid great stress on rewards and punishments after death. The soul was a divine essence and achieved its true life only after the death of the body. To achieve full freedom it had to undergo a cycle of incarnations, being reborn into a higher or lower form of life according to its previous merits.

Orphism was in many ways opposed to the prevailing current of religious ideas in classical Greece. It lacked moderation and ignored the Hellenic advice to man to remember his mortality and not strive to emulate the gods. It was dogmatic, with an authoritative priesthood and sacred writings. Orphism exalted the life of the next world, whereas most Greeks preferred to live in the present. While the Olympian religion was bound up with the common life of the close-knit city-state, Orphism was personal and stood outside the social and political order. Thus Orphism never became popular, and its importance lies in the influence it exercised over a few leading thinkers, such as Empedocles and Plato. Through Plato and Neoplatonism it influenced Christian thought.

The romantic story of Orpheus himself had a much wider appeal. In the Middle Ages it was transformed into an English tale of *Sir Orfeo* (which has a happy ending). It appears in Chistoph Gluck's opera *Orfeo ed Euridice*, in the 18th century, and in Jean Cocteau's drama and motion picture *Orphée*, in the 20th.

·folkloric themes in mythology **8**:404b
·musician as divinely endowed **2**:97g
Orphic religion
·Archaic Greek religion **8**:333d
·cosmological significance of man **12**:799g
·dualism in body–soul mysticism **5**:1066h
·epigraphic texts' significance **6**:923a
·Greek ascetic practices **2**:136e
·Homeric epics incorporation **8**:1171d
·man's dualistic nature and reincarnation **5**:534a *passim* to 535a
·mystery cult beliefs and practices **12**:779f
·sacramental means to immortality **16**:116b
·salvation from recurring birth **16**:202b
·war of good and evil **14**:786g

Orpheus und Eurydike (1923), play by Oskar Kokoschka.
·theme and adaptation **10**:500e

Orphic religion (ancient Greece): *see* Orpheus.

Orphism, in painting, name given by the French poet Guillaume Apollinaire in 1912 to a trend in Cubism that gave priority to colour. He described Orphic Cubism as "the art of painting new structures out of elements which have not been borrowed from the visual sphere, but have been created entirely by the artist himself, and been endowed by him with

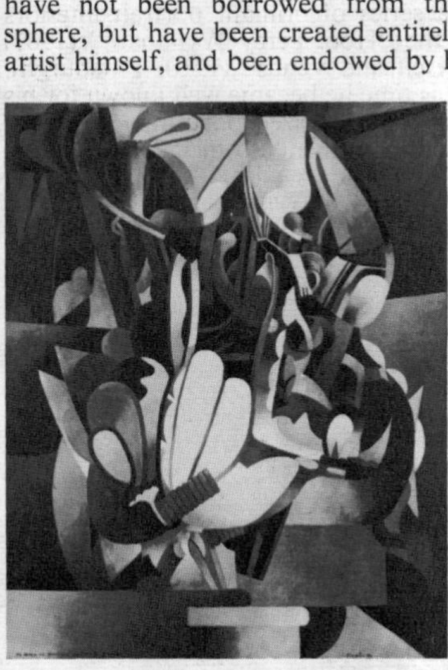

"I See Again in Memory My Dear Udnie," Orphic painting by Francis Picabia, 1913; in the Museum of Modern Art, New York

By courtesy of the Museum of Modern Art, New York, Hillman Periodicals Fund; permission S.P.A.D.E.M. 1971 by French Reproduction Rights, Inc.

fullness of reality. The works of the Orphic artist must simultaneously give a pure aesthetic pleasure, a structure which is self-evident, and a sublime meaning, that is, the subject. This is pure art." Apollinaire's use of the word Orphic recalls both the Symbolist painters' use of the term Orphic art in reference to Paul Gauguin's orchestration of colour and the poetry of Orpheus, the legendary poet and singer. Among the painters working in this style, Apollinaire noted Robert Delaunay (*q.v.*), Fernand Léger, Francis Picabia, and Marcel Duchamp. In the attempt to approximate music, Delaunay led the way in transforming the visual into abstract colour harmonies.

One of the resources Delaunay used to arrive at a way of integrating colour and Cubism was a book on simultaneous contrasts (*De la loi du contraste simultané des couleurs*, 1839), by the chemist Michel-Eugène Chevreul. Unlike the Neo-Impressionist painter Georges Seurat, who had employed these theories during the 1880s, Delaunay was interested in applying them in an abstract way, exploring the effects of colour and light when they are not bound to an object. In his abstract work "Simultaneous Composition: Sun Disks" (1912–13; Museum of Modern Art, New York City), superimposed circles of colour have their own rhythm and movement; the cosmic aura of the work is enhanced by the round format of the painting.

Another painter associated with Orphism (though not mentioned by Apollinaire) was František Kupka (*q.v.*), a Czech who lived in Paris. Possibly Kupka was aware of Delaunay's disk paintings when he painted his "Disks of Newton (Study for Fugue in Two Colors)" in 1912 (Philadelphia Museum of Art). As the musical analogy implicit in the title suggests, the vibrating colour orchestrations on the canvas seem to create visual music in the eye of the beholder.

It was Delaunay's canvases, however, that deeply impressed August Macke, Franz Marc, and Paul Klee, who visited his Paris studio in 1912; this exposure had a decisive influence on their subsequent work. Orphism also influenced the development of German Cubism.
·modern visual art history **19**:480c

orphrey, also spelled ORFRAY and ORFREY, highly elaborate embroidery work, or a piece of such embroidery. More specifically the term refers to an ornamental border, or embroidered band, of very elaborate work, especially as used on ecclesiastical vestments.
·German textile industry history **18**:171f

orpiment, an arsenic sulfide (As_2S_3) mineral. Typical occurrences are as a hot-springs deposit, an alteration product (especially from realgar), or as a low-temperature product in hydrothermal veins. It is found in Copalnic, Romania; Andreas-Berg, E.Ger.; Valais, Switz.; and Çölemerik, Tur. For detailed physical properties, *see* table under sulfide minerals.

Orpiment (from *auri* + *pigmentum*, "golden paint") was used as an artist's pigment in the ancient Near East, but it never gained much attention from Western artists till the 18th century, when production of artificial arsenic trisulfide was begun. Because of its extreme toxicity, it was abandoned, except for a very fine grade called king's yellow, which was used until cadmium yellow (principally cadmium sulfide) became available.
·physical properties and realgar oxidation **17**:789d

orpine (plant): *see* Crassulaceae.

Orpington, former urban district of the county of Kent, England; since 1965, part of Bromley (*q.v.*).

Orr, Bobby (1948–), Canadian hockey player considered by many the best defenseman in the history of the game. Playing for the Boston Bruins, he was named the National Hockey League's most valuable defense-

Orr (number 4), 1968

Canada Wide—Pictorial Parade

man for six consecutive seasons (1967–73) and its most valuable player for three (1969–72).

Orrefors glass, important 20th-century glass, manufactured in the south of Sweden,

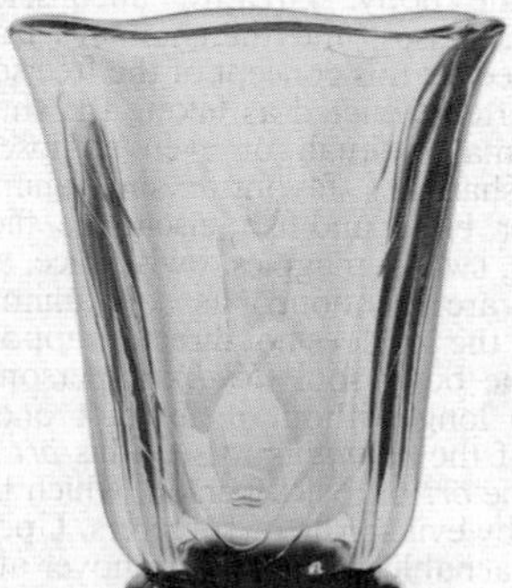

Orrefors glass vase, Swedish, 1930; in the Victoria and Albert Museum, London

By courtesy of the Victoria and Albert Museum, London; photograph, A.C. Cooper Ltd.

at Orrefors, since 1917. Orrefors' fame rests mainly on the quality of the crystal, the elegant functionalism of its shapes, and the quality of its ornamentation, which combines modern designs and a revival of the 18th-century excellence in engraving technique.

·designers and ware characteristics **8**:194g

orrery, mechanical model of the solar system used to demonstrate the motions of the planets about the Sun, probably invented by George Graham (died 1751) under the patronage of Charles Boyle, 4th earl of Orrery. In use for several centuries, the device was formerly called a planetarium (a name now applied to the projection of an artificial sky on the interior of a dome). The orrery presents a perspective of the planets as viewed from outside the solar system. The time scale may be relatively quite accurate, with the Earth completing a year's rotation in about 10 minutes; but the sizes and distances are necessarily relatively inaccurate. The sizes of the bodies are large compared with the scale of distances.

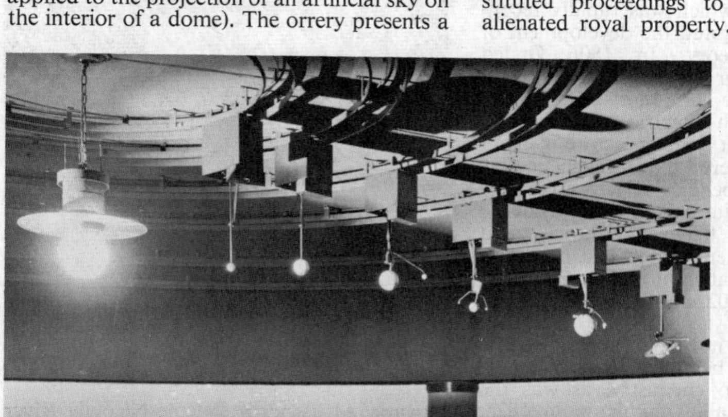

Copernican orrery showing the grouping of the major planets in relation to the Sun; in the Hayden Planetarium, American Museum, New York

By courtesy of the American Museum of Natural History, New York

Orrery, Roger Boyle, 1st earl of (1621–1679), Irish magnate and author prominent during the English Civil War, Commonwealth, and Restoration periods. Boyle took the Parliamentary side in the Civil War and became a confidential adviser of Oliver Cromwell; yet when Charles II was restored to the throne in 1660, he also became a popular member of the King's circle, where he was known as a poet and playwright. He wrote *Parthenissa* (1676), a romance in the French style, and introduced rhymed heroic drama into England. Created earl of Orrery in 1660, he was made a privy councillor and lord president of the council of Munster in the same year. In 1669 he successfully defended himself before Parliament on charges of having tried to seize the lord lieutenantship of Ireland.

orris oil, yellowish semisolid fragrant essential oil obtained from the roots of the Florentine iris and used chiefly as a flavouring agent and in perfumes.

·economic importance of irises **9**:890f

orrisroot, fragrant rootstock of any of several European plants of the genus *Iris* used in perfumery and medicine.

·economic importance of irises **9**:890f

Orry, Jean (b. Sept. 4, 1652, Paris—d. Sept. 29, 1719, Paris), economist whose broad financial and governmental reforms in early-18th-century Spain helped to further the implementation of centralized and uniform administration.

Louis XIV of France, whose grandson had just succeeded to the Spanish throne as Philip V (November 1700), sent Orry to Spain in 1701 to report on the finances of that kingdom. Orry drew up detailed memoranda advising not only the centralization of financial administration but also a thoroughgoing reform of the governmental system in which political power would be transferred from the royal councils, dominated by nobles with strong vested interests, to a number of ministers, similar to the French secretaries of state, loyal to the crown.

Orry was first put in charge of Spain's military finance. He reorganized and increased tax collection and devised various expedients to pay for troops and provisions for the War of the Spanish Succession (1701–14). He also instituted proceedings to recover stolen or alienated royal property. Shortly after May 1705 a secretaryship of war and finance was created, an initial step in Orry's governmental reform program.

Orry was recalled to France in the summer of 1706 and returned to Spain in April 1713. He and the royal favourite, Madame des Ursins, then became the real rulers of the country. Orry continued his efforts to bring financial administration under the control of the central government. He also packed the royal councils with new members whose votes would support his policies and created four new secretaries of state who reported to him. Meanwhile, local government was centralized by the division of Spain into 21 provinces, each governed by an intendant responsible to the *veedor general*, who was Orry. Before his reforms could be established, however, Orry was dismissed and ordered to leave Spain (Feb. 7, 1715).

Though certain of Orry's reforms did not survive intact after his departure, his financial reorganization, destruction of the power of the royal councils, and creation of secretaries of state and intendants had a significant impact on future Spanish governmental administration.

Or San Michele, church of Florence, completed in the 15th century.

·sculpture and contributing artists **19**:407a *passim* to 408f

Orsay, Alfred-Guillaume-Gabriel, comte d' (1801–52), French adventurer and dandy, of Bonapartist persuasion. From 1830 to 1849 he led fashion in London and spent the fortune of Lady Blessington and her family.

Orsha, city, Vitebsk *oblast* (administrative region), Belorussian Soviet Socialist Republic, on the Dnepr River. From the time it was first mentioned in 1067, it has always been a major focus of routes—frequently attacked and destroyed. Today Orsha is an important railway junction on the Moscow–Warsaw and Leningrad–Odessa lines, with other lines to Lepel and Krichov, and has linen, clothing, machine-building, and food-processing industries. Pop. (1970) 101,000.
54°31′ N, 30°26′ E

Orsi, Paolo (b. Oct. 18, 1859, Rovereto, Austria, now in Italy—d. Nov. 9, 1935,

Orsi

By courtesy of the Antichita della Sicilia Orientale

Rovereto), archaeologist who pioneered in the excavation and research of sites, from the prehistoric to the Byzantine, in Sicily and southern Italy. A large part of present knowledge of Sicilian art and civilization, especially in the Siculan (pre-Greek) period, is the result of his work. Appointed director of the museum at Syracuse, Sicily, in 1888, he devoted himself to explorations, discovering the Siculan culture from excavations of cemeteries all over the island and laying the groundwork for the chronology of its four periods. His meticulous excavations of Greek cities throughout Sicily and in the southern Italian provinces of Magna Graecia uncovered many new sites and extended known sites, including Syracuse and Gela in Sicily and Croton and Locri on the mainland. He organized his finds in the museums of Syracuse and Reggio di Calabria and published 300 titles. He also edited *Bullettino di paletnologia italiana* and *Archivia storico della Calabria e Lucania*.

Orsini, one of the oldest, most illustrious, and for centuries most powerful of the Roman princely families. Their origins can be traced to an Ursus de Baro, recorded at Rome in 998; they became important when Giacinto Bobo-Orsini was elected Pope Celestine III (1191–98) and, through nepotism, founded the territorial fortunes of the family. The Orsini assumed Guelf (papal party) leadership in Rome against the rival Ghibelline (imperial party) Colonna family. In 1241 Matteo Rosso Orsini, as senator (chief of government) of Rome, saved the city from capture by the Holy Roman emperor Frederick II and the Colonna. Several Orsini served as cardinals in the next few decades, and one became pope, as Nicholas III, in 1277. Acquisition of lands and lordships in Angevin Naples, rewards of their Guelf partisanship, led several branches of the family to take root in southern Italy. In accordance with their tradition, most of the Orsini supported Boniface VIII, pope from 1294 to 1303, in his attacks on the Colonna, but Cardinal Napoleone Orsini sided with the Colonna and King Philip IV the Fair of France, who was embroiled with the Pope over taxes on the French clergy. In 1305 Cardinal Orsini promoted the election of a French pope, Clement V, who in 1309 moved the papal residence to Avignon, Fr., where it remained until 1377.

In succeeding centuries the Orsini's history was closely involved with the annals of Rome and its neighbour states. Apart from a brief interval of Borgia supremacy, when the Orsini were dispossessed of their castles and three of them were murdered, they retained their dominant place in the Roman aristocracy, providing soldiers, statesmen, and prelates to the church. In 1629 they were created princes of the Holy Roman Empire, and in 1718 they were raised to the princely dignity at Rome. In 1724 Pierfrancesco Orsini was elected pope as Benedict XIII.

The family survives in the Orsini dukes of Gravina, descendants of Matteo Rosso Orsini, who received their ducal title from Pope Pius IV in 1560. From the 16th century an Orsini customarily held the office of prince assistant to the pontifical throne.

·Medici marital association **11**:819c

Orsini, Felice (b. Dec. 10, 1819, Meldola, Italy—d. March 13, 1858, Paris), Italian nationalist revolutionary and conspirator who tried to assassinate the French emperor Napoleon III. A follower of the Italian revolutionary leader Giuseppe Mazzini, Orsini participated in the uprisings in Rome in 1848–49, thereafter serving as Mazzini's agent in Switzerland, Hungary, and England. After a daring escape from an Austrian prison in Mantua in 1855, he went to London and wrote two accounts of his adventures—*The Austrian Dungeons in Italy* (1856) and *Memoirs and Adventures of F. Orsini Written by Himself* (1857)—which were extremely popular with the British public. Orsini broke with Mazzini in 1857 and, emotionally disturbed, began to plot the assassination of Napoleon III, impelled by the notion that the Emperor's death would trigger in France a revolution that would spread to Italy. On the night of Jan. 14, 1858, he and two accomplices threw bombs at the carriage of Napoleon and Empress Eugénie as they were going to the opera in Paris; although several persons were killed, the intended victims were unhurt. Orsini was arrested and executed.

Ironically, following Orsini's attack, Napoleon, remembering the pro-Italian sympathies of his youth, was prompted to declare war on Austria in 1859, from which Italy's independence followed.

·attempted assassination of Napoleon III **3**:1032c

Orsini, Giovanni Gaetano: *see* Nicholas III.

Orsini, Pierfrancesco: *see* Benedict XIII.

Orsini Castle, 16th-century castle in Bomarzo, Italy.

·Mannerist influence on landscaping **7**:894f

Orsk, city, Orenburg *oblast* (administrative region), western Russian Soviet Federated Socialist Republic, at the confluence of the Ural and Or rivers. It was founded in 1735 as the fortress of Orenburg (*q.v.*), which was moved downriver in 1743. Orsk is now a major industrial centre, with a large oil refinery using petroleum piped from the Emba and Mangyshlak fields on the Caspian. Other products include nickel and cobalt, heavy-metallurgical and mining machinery, electrical equipment, synthetic alcohol, and processed meat. Pop. (1970 prelim.) 225,000.
51°12′ N, 58°34′ E

·automobile-trailer factory construction **16**:95f
·map, Soviet Union **17**:322

Ørsted, Anders Sandøe (1778–1860), Danish statesman.

·Danish 19th-century political growth **16**:324c

Ørsted, Hans Christian (b. Aug. 14, 1777, Rudkøbing, Den.—d. March 9, 1851, Copenhagen), physicist and chemist who discovered that current flowing through a wire can deflect a magnetized compass needle, a phenomenon the importance of which was rapidly recognized and which inspired the development of electromagnetic theory. In 1806 Ørsted became a professor at the University of Copenhagen, where his first physical researches dealt with electric currents and acoustics. During an evening lecture in April 1820, Ørsted discovered that a magnetic needle aligns itself perpendicularly to a current-carrying wire, definite experimental evidence of the relationship between electricity and magnetism. This phenomenon had been first discovered by the Italian jurist Gian Domenico Romagnosi in 1802, but his announcement was ignored.

Ørsted, detail of a lithograph by Kaufmann after a drawing by C.A. Jensen

By courtesy of the trustees of the British Museum; photograph, J.R. Freeman & Co. Ltd.

Ørsted's discovery, in 1820, of piperidine, the poisonous agent in hemlock, was an important contribution to chemistry, as was the preparation of metallic aluminum in 1825. He was an inspiring teacher and lecturer and wrote numerous popular articles. In 1824 he founded a society devoted to the spread of scientific knowledge among the general public. Since 1908 this society has awarded an Ørsted Medal for outstanding contributions by Danish physical scientists. In 1932 the name oersted was adopted for the physical unit of magnetic field strength.

·aluminum isolation **1**:641c
·electricity and magnetism experiments **6**:647e
·electric motor development **6**:610c
·instrumentation history and devices **9**:632b
·magnetic properties research **11**:311e
·physical science history **14**:390b
·science and natural philosophy **16**:373b

Ors y Rovira, Eugenio d' (1882–1954), Spanish essayist, art critic, and influential novelist whose main recurrent themes were concerned with the place of reason and intelligence in life and philosophy, with the concepts of space–time and civilization, and with passion and restraint.

Orszàgh, Pavol (Slovak author): *see* Hviezdoslav.

ört, a Cheremis shadow or shape soul that is detachable and can wander about outside the body; it is most often considered a personification of consciousness. The concept of a free soul is common to all Finno-Ugric peoples. The Votyak *urt* and the Zyryan *ört*, as well as the soul of the Lapp shaman, *noiade*, can leave the body and visit places far distant from the body. Dreams, unconsciousness, severe illnesses, and the shaman's traces are explained by this concept of the free soul. The *ört* is often depicted as taking the shape of a bird, small animal, or even an insect. The Lapp shaman's favourite soul animals are reindeer, birds, and fish; elsewhere, flies, mosquitoes, swans, magpies, owls, mice, and butterflies are mentioned as soul animals. Although the *ört* does not directly support life as does the body soul (*lélek*), a person cannot survive long without it. In fact one of the tasks of the *noiade* is to send his *ört* to fetch back the *ört* of a sick person, which has been stolen by evil spirits or sorcerers. Upon death the detachable soul is said to hover about the place where the body has been buried. The Ostyak soul, *iles*, has its abode in the head of its bearer, which explains the earlier custom of taking scalps from the slain enemy, thereby rendering them harmless.

Orta, Lake, Italian LAGO D'ORTA, sometimes called LAGO CUSIO, in Novara province, Piemonte (Piedmont) region, northwestern Italy, lies just west of Lake Maggiore, from which it is divided by the Monte Mottarone. About 8 mi (13 km) long and 3/4 mi wide, it has an area of 7 sq mi (18 sq km). Its greatest depth is 469 ft (143 m), and the surface is 951 ft (290 m) above sea level. It is the remnant of a much larger sheet of water by which the waters of the Toce River flowed south toward Novara. At its north end the Nigoglia River flows out of it northward to Lake Maggiore. The lake has tourist resorts along its shores, including Omegna, Orta San Giulio, and the island of San Giulio.
45°49′ N, 8°24′ E

Island of San Giulio, Lake Orta, Italy

SCALA, New York

Ortalis vetula (bird): *see* curassow.

ortaoyunu, 18th- and 19th-century theatrical production of the Ottoman empire.

·history and theatrical style **9**:978g; illus. 979

Ortega y Gasset, José (b. May 9, 1883, Madrid—d. Oct. 18, 1955, Madrid), philosopher and humanist who greatly influenced the cultural and literary renaissance of Spain in the 20th century. As professor of metaphysics at Madrid (1910), he early diverged from neo-Kantianism in *Adán en el paraíso* (1910; "Adam in Paradise"), *Meditaciones del Quijote* (1914; "Quixote's Meditations"), and *El tema de nuestro tiempo* (1923; Eng. trans., *Modern Theme*, 1931).

Ortega y Gasset
© Gisele Freund

He saw man's individual life here and now as the basic reality: reason as a function of life ("vital reason" or "historical reason") is substituted for absolute reason, and for absolute truth the perspective of each individual ("I am I, and my circumstance"). He shared the preoccupation of his generation with the "problem of Spain," and his writings were deliberately "circumstantial" and published in periodicals—he founded *España* (1915), *El Sol* (1917; "The Sun"), and *Revista de Occidente* (1923; "Magazine of the West"). He spent the troubled years between 1936 and 1945 as a voluntary exile in Europe and Argentina, returning to Spain at the end of World War II. In 1948 he founded the Instituto de Humanidades in Madrid. Of his other works, the best known are *España invertebrada* (1922; Eng. trans., *Invertebrate Spain*, 1937) and *La Rebelión de las masas* (1929; Eng. trans., *The Revolt of the Masses*, 1932). An account of his philosophy is given by J. Ferrater Mora (1957).
·Existential crisis in man's development 7:78e
·philosophy in nonfictional prose **10**:1081b
·Spanish literary role **10**:1239b

Ortelius (WORTELS), **Abraham** (b. April 14, 1527, Antwerp—d. July 4, 1598, Antwerp), cartographer and map, book, and antiquary dealer who published the first modern atlas, *Theatrum orbis terrarum* (1570; *Theatre of the Whole World*, 1606).

Ortelius, detail of an engraving from *Theatrum orbis terrarum*, 1584 edition
By courtesy of the trustees of the British Museum; photograph, J.R. Freeman & Co. Ltd.

Trained as an engraver, around 1554 Ortelius set up his book and antiquary business. About 1560, under the influence of the great German geographer of the Renaissance Gerardus Mercator, Ortelius became interested in map making. Within a decade he compiled maps of the world on a heart-shaped projection (1564), of Egypt (1565), and of Asia (1567), as well as the first edition of the *Theatrum*, which contained 70 maps, derived from 87 authorities and engraved in a uniform style. Enlarged and kept up to date in successive editions until late 1612, the *Theatrum* appears to have been the most popular atlas of its time. Appointed geographer to Philip II of Spain (1575), Ortelius also assembled a fine collection of coins, medals, and antiques and published a number of writings. A facsimile of the *Theatrum* was published in 1964.
·atlas influenced by Mercator **11**:915e
·evaluation of Bruegel **3**:340a

Orthalicus, genus of neotropical snails of the class Gastropoda.
·dentition and geographic region 7:950e

Ortheziidae, family of coccids of the order Homoptera (sapsucking insects).
·characteristics and classification **8**:1043a

orthicon, camera tube similar to but more sensitive than an iconoscope in which the charges are scanned by a low-velocity beam to eliminate the secondary emission that reduces picture quality at low-light levels.
·design and operation principles **18**:111h; illus. 112

Orthis, extinct genus of articulate brachiopods of Paleozoic age.
·fossil brachiopods and eras, illus. 5 7:563

orthoarsenic acid: *see* arsenic acid.

orthoboric acid: *see* boric acid.

orthochlorite: *see* chlorite.

orthoclase, a common alkali feldspar mineral, potassium aluminosilicate ($KAlSi_3O_8$); it usually occurs as variously coloured, frequently twinned crystals in granite. Orthoclase is used in the manufacture of glass and ceramics; occasionally, transparent crystals are cut as gems. Orthoclase is primarily important as a rock-forming mineral, however, and is abundant in alkali and acidic igneous rocks, in pegmatites, and in gneisses. For detailed physical properties, *see* table under feldspars.

Orthoclase from Serra de Peneda, Portugal
Emil Javorsky—EB Inc.

The feldspar minerals are mixtures of sodium, potassium, and calcium aluminosilicates; and any feldspar may be classed by its percentage of each of these three pure compounds, called end-members. The name orthoclase is applied to the system's potassium-bearing end-member; its symbol is *Or*.

Orthoclase and the system's sodium-bearing end-member, albite (sodium aluminosilicate; $NaAlSi_3O_8$), form the alkali feldspars, a solid-solution series in which sodium-bearing and potassium-bearing molecules intermingle; thus, there is a continuous chemical variation between the two end-members. Because the intermediate members, called orthoclase–microperthites, cannot blend homogeneously, they take the form of microscopic intergrowths of distinct crystals of the pure sodium and potassium end-members.

Orthoclase has an intermediate degree of ordering exhibited by the aluminum and silicon atoms in its aluminosilicate crystal framework, falling between the fully ordered arrangement of microcline and the random arrangement of high-sanidine. *Major ref.* 7:212d
·Bowen's reaction series, illus. 7 and 8 **9**:210
·metamorphic occurrence **12**:7a; table
·optical properties, table 2 7:216
·structure and atomic ordering **16**:762e
·weathering products **19**:704f

orthoconglomerate (geology): *see* conglomerates and breccias.

ortho-cousin: *see* cross-cousin.

orthodontics, division of dentistry dealing with the prevention and correction of irregularities of the teeth—generally referred to as straightening of crooked teeth, or correcting a bite, or correcting malocclusion, physiologically unacceptable contact of opposing dentition, which may be due to imperfect development, loss of teeth, or abnormal growth of jaws. Of significance to the orthodontist is the sequence of eruption (emergence of the tooth from its developmental crypt into the oral cavity), because such knowledge helps to determine the position of the teeth in the arch. Human bone responds best to tooth movement before the age of 18, and consequently orthodontic work is usually more beneficial to a child than an adult. Generally speaking, oral health and physical appearance are the two most important reasons for orthodontic treatment, because abnormal mental attitudes often develop because of dentofacial malformation.

The practice of orthodontics has existed since early antiquity, but the more elaborate and modern methods of treatment came about as recently as the early 20th century. In the United States, particularly, development and recognition of orthodontics as a specialty was encouraged by the formation of the American Society of Orthodontists (ASO) in 1901 (now American Association of Orthodontists [AAO]). Training in orthodontics is a two-year postgraduate course open only to dentists who have a minimum of two years of general practice. There was a great need in the 1970s for expanded training facilities at a postgraduate level.
·distinctive features of practice **5**:595g

orthodox (from Greek *orthodoxos*, "of the right opinion"), true Christian doctrine and its adherents as opposed to heterodox or heretical doctrines and their adherents. The word was first used in the early 4th century by the Greek Fathers. Because almost every Christian group believes that it holds the true faith (though not necessarily exclusively), the meaning of "orthodox" in a particular instance can be correctly determined only after examination of the context in which it appears.

It forms part of the official title of the Greek-speaking church (Eastern Orthodox Church) and those in communion with it. Also including orthodox as part of their titles are some of the smaller Eastern churches, which separated from the rest of Christendom in the 5th century as a result of the Monophysite controversy concerning the question of two natures in Christ.

Within Judaism, Orthodox Judaism represents a form of religious belief and practice that adheres most strictly to ancient tradition. Orthodox Judaism, consequently, rejects the view held by modern Reform Judaism that the Bible and other sacred Jewish writings contain not only eternally valid moral principles but also historically and culturally conditioned interpretations of the Law that may be legitimately abandoned. For Orthodox Jews, therefore, the Law is immutably fixed for all times and remains the sole norm of religious observance.

Orthodox is also applied to a certain type of Protestantism that is usually quite conservative in its interpretation of Scripture. In a nonreligious sense, the accepted views held by any unified body of opinion or in any field of study are referred to as orthodox.

Orthodox, Baptistery of the (*c.* 440), baptistery in Ravenna, Italy.

·Byzantine mosaic art developments **19**:327h

orthodox caliphs (Islām): *see* khulafā' ar-rāshidūn, al-.

Orthodox Catholic Church: *see* Eastern Orthodoxy.

Orthodox Church in America: *see* America, Orthodox Church in.

Orthodox Jewish Congregations of America, Union of, official federation of Jewish Orthodox synagogues in the U.S. and Canada; its counterpart organization for rabbis is the Rabbinical Council of America.

The union was established in New York City in 1898 to foster Orthodox beliefs and practices. To pursue its goals, the union sponsors numerous elementary and secondary day schools oriented toward Orthodoxy and supports some 15 Orthodox institutes of higher learning (yeshivas). It also publishes the quarterly *Perakim* and two bi-monthlies, *Jewish Life* and *Jewish Action*. The union's main auxiliary unit, Women's Branch (established 1924), publishes *Hachodesh* and operates the Hebrew Teachers Training School for Girls. The National Conference of Synagogue Youth was set up in 1954. Many manufactured foods that meet the requirements of Jewish dietary laws (*kashrut*) bear the union's mark of approval.

·Reform–Orthodox conflict in U.S. **10**:326e

Orthodox Judaism, the religious tenets of those Jews who adhere most strictly to traditional beliefs and practices. Jewish Orthodoxy resolutely refuses to accept the position of Reform Judaism that the Bible and other sacred Jewish writings contain not only eternally valid moral principles but also historically and culturally conditioned adaptations and interpretations of the Law that may be legitimately discarded in modern times. In Orthodox Judaism, therefore, both the Written Law (Torah, first five books of the Old Testament) and the Oral Law (codified in the Mishha and interpreted in the Talmud) are immutably fixed for all times and remain the sole norm of religious observance.

Orthodox Judaism has resisted modern pressures to modify its observance and has held fast to such things as daily worship, dietary laws (*kashrut*), the traditional prayers and ceremonies, regular and intensive study of the Torah, and the separation of men and women in the synagogue. It also enjoins strict observance of the sabbath and religious festivals and does not permit instrumental music during communal services.

Despite such seeming inflexibility, Orthodox Judaism is marked by considerable variety. Neo-Orthodoxy, for example, a late-19th-century development under the leadership of Samson Raphael Hirsch, sanctioned modern dress, the use of the vernacular in sermons, and a more positive view of modern culture. Within the Orthodox movement there are also the Ashkenazi (German) and Sefardic (Spanish) rites and the warmly pious Ḥasidim.

All Jewish groups—Orthodox, Conservative, and Reform—consider themselves and each other as adherents of the Jewish faith. This fact, however, has not deterred Orthodox rabbis from challenging the legitimacy of certain non-Orthodox marriages, divorces, and conversions on the grounds that they violate prescriptions of Jewish law.

In the U.S., many Orthodox synagogues have joined together to form the Union of Orthodox Jewish Congregations of America. Most Orthodox rabbis are affiliated with the Rabbinical Council of America, the Union of Orthodox Rabbis of the United States and Canada, or the Rabbinical Alliance of America. Yeshiva University, in New York City, composed of a rabbinical seminary and departments for secular studies, is one of the leading centres of Orthodox Judaism in the U.S. In the State of Israel, Orthodoxy is the official form of Judaism and has considerable power and status exercised through the Chief Rabbinate of Israel.

·festival disputes on modern practice **10**:222a
·legal influence in Israeli state **17**:1013d
·modern European movements **10**:324b
·modern forms and self-concept **10**:301a
·U.S. communities **10**:326c

Orthodox Rabbis of the United States and Canada, Union of, an organization founded in New York City in 1902 to foster traditional Orthodox practices, such as strict observance of the sabbath and the dietary laws (*kashrut*). By controlling the appointment of Orthodox rabbis to various congregations, the union also hopes to insure that Orthodox Jews within their congregations will observe religious laws governing marriage and divorce. Union members consist almost exclusively of European-trained, Yiddish-speaking rabbis who elect the officials of their organization at an annual meeting.

The Rabbinical Council of America, a parallel organization, has similar aims, but its members are mostly English-speaking, American-trained rabbis.

orthodoxy, correct religious belief, according to an authoritative norm; *i.e.*, tradition, doctrine, dogma, or creed. In Orthodox Judaism the emphasis has been as much or more on correct practice as on correct belief. Since views of right belief vary, there are varying orthodoxies within the same religion; *e.g.* Roman Catholic and Lutheran orthodoxies in Christianity.

·censorship implications **3**:1083h
·Creed apologetical value **5**:244g
·doctrines of various patristic authors **13**:1079c
·early Christian authority problems **4**:538a
·Islāmic theological standards **9**:1012a
·Islām's tolerance of differences **9**:916c
·liturgical misunderstanding in 17th-century Greece and Russia **6**:157e
·North African Sunnī-Shī'ah conflict **13**:157c
·Ṣūfī apologetic writings **9**:943g

Orthodoxy, Autocracy, and Nationality, Russian PRAVOSLAVIYE, SAMODERZHAVIYE, I NARODNOST, in Russian history, slogan created in 1832 by Count Sergey S. Uvarov, minister of education 1833–49, that came to represent the official ideology of the imperial government of Nicholas I (reigned 1825–55) and remained the guiding principle behind government policy during later periods of imperial rule, particularly during the 1880s.

Uvarov presented the phrase in a report to Nicholas on the state of education in the Moscow university and secondary schools (*gimnazii*). In the report he recommended that the state's future educational program stress the value of the Orthodox Church, the autocratic government, and the national character of the Russian people; he considered these to be the fundamental factors distinguishing Russian society and protecting it from the corrupting influence of Western Europe, which he believed had been demoralized by liberalism, secularism, and the French revolution. But the practical efforts made to promote the principles of Orthodoxy, Autocracy, and Nationality generally reinforced the repressive character of Nicholas' regime.

As the official ideology became the basis of Russian education, the study of theology and the classics, as well as vocational training, received much emphasis. Philosophy, however, was considered to be the main medium through which corrupting Western ideas were transmitted to Russian students; it therefore was virtually eliminated from the curricula. Outside the schools, strict censorship was imposed on all publications—liberal and conservative—that were critical of the system of autocracy.

Furthermore, official adherence to the slogan "Orthodoxy, Autocracy, and Nationality" gave an impetus (not entirely approved of by the Emperor) to the cause of the Russian nationalists, many of whom were employed in government and in other influential positions. Interpreting the term "narodnost" to mean "nationalism" rather than "nationality," they used their authority to institute russification policies in schools in non-Russian areas of the empire, to pressure non-Orthodox religious groups to convert, and to enact various restrictive and discriminatory measures that suppressed non-Russian nationality groups. The nationalists also encouraged the government to support other Slavic peoples' efforts to achieve national autonomy and, thereby, contributed to the developing rivalry between Russia and Austria (one of Russia's chief allies) for dominance in the Slavic-peopled Balkans.

·Russian nationalism official sanction **16**:60d

Orthodoxy, Feast of, also called ORTHODOX DAY, celebrated on the first Sunday of Lent by the Eastern Orthodox Church and Eastern Catholics of the Byzantine Rite to commemorate the return of icons (sacred images) to the churches (843) and the end of the long iconoclastic controversy. Fear of idolatry had led to an official proscription against icons in 730. The restoration was effected by Empress Theodora after the death of her iconoclast husband, Theophilus.

orthogenesis, OR STRAIGHT-LINE EVOLUTION, a concept that successive members of an evolutionary series become increasingly modified in an undeviating direction. Ortho-evolution, orthoselection, aristogenesis, undeviating evolution, and rectilinear evolution are synonymous or related terms.

That evolution frequently proceeds in orthogenetic fashion is undeniable, though many striking features developed in an orthogenetic group appear to have little if any adaptive value and may even be markedly disadvantageous. Work in genetics has shown that very small mutations may have a definite survival value and that the action of a gene may extend to more than one trait. The development of disadvantageous structures (*e.g.*, the huge antlers of the extinct Irish elk), therefore, may be explained as a concomitant of the development of other advantageous structures or functions.

·physical anthropology theories **1**:974d

orthogneiss (petrology): *see* gneiss.

orthogonality, in mathematics, generally qualities of right angles or a reference to some type of rectangular transformation. Families of curves or surfaces are said to exhibit orthogonality when perpendicularity is involved; a matrix is orthogonal if it is equal to its inverse; and in vector analysis, an orthogonal complement of a vector is the set of all vectors perpendicular to it. Two vectors are defined as orthogonal, however, when their scalar product equals zero.

·algebraic structure theory **1**:525h
·combinatorics theory and method **4**:948b
·combinatorics theory and method **4**:947f
·Fourier analysis fundamentals **1**:743e
·physical theory formulations **14**:398f
·vector and tensor analysis principles **1**:793c

orthogonal polynomials, infinite collection of special polynomials $P_n(x)$, with the subscript n indicating the degree of the polynomial. Their importance derives from their being solutions of differential equations and from the possibility of representing any (continuous) function as a (possibly infinite) sum of these polynomials, a device often useful in the differential equations of physics and engineering.

The simplest example of these polynomials are the Legendre polynomials. The Legendre polynomials can be obtained by calculating the nth derivative of $(x^2-1)^n/2^n n!$. The polynomial $P_n(x)$ satisfies the so-called second-order Legendre differential equation. They are orthogonal on the interval from −1 to +1, meaning that the integral of the product of any two such functions from −1 to +1 is zero. They can also be constructed from the polynomial series 1, x, x^2, x^3 ⋯ by starting with the first term and requiring that each succeeding term $p_n(x)$ be an nth-degree polynomial orthogonal to all previously found polynomials.

There are other classes of orthogonal polynomials, such as Chebyshev and Hermite polynomials, which involve intervals other than −1 to +1, or weight functions, which are functions by which the product $p_n(x)p_m(x)$ is multiplied in the integral.

·differential equation principles **5**:762e

orthogonal trajectory, family of curves that intersect another family of curves at right angles (*see* Graph). Such families of mutually orthogonal curves occur in such branches of physics as electrostatics, in which the lines of force and the lines of constant potential are orthogonal; and in hydrodynamics, in which the streamlines and the lines of constant velocity are orthogonal.

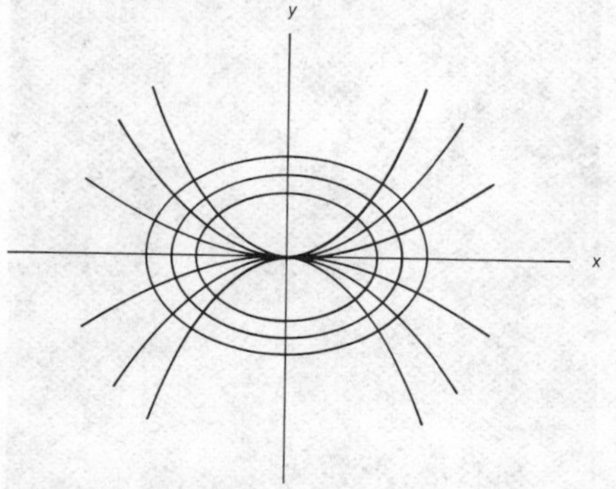

Orthogonal trajectories

In two dimensions, a family of curves is given by $y = f(x, k)$, in which the value of k, called the parameter, determines the particular member of the family. Two lines are perpendicular if their slopes are negative reciprocals of each other. To apply this to two curves, their tangents at the point of intersection must be perpendicular. The slope of the tangent to a curve at a point, called its derivative, can be found using calculus. This derivative, written as y', will also be a function of x and k. Solving the original equation for k in terms of x and y and substituting this expression into the equation for y' will give y' in terms of x and y, as some function $y' = g(x, y)$.

As noted above, a member of the family of orthogonal trajectories, y_1, must have a slope satisfying $y'_1 = -1/y' = -1/g(x, y)$, resulting in a differential equation that will have the orthogonal trajectory as its solution. To illustrate, if $y = kx^2$ represents a family of parabolas, then $y' = 2kx$, and using $k = y/x^2$ gives $y' = 2y/x$. For the orthogonal curve, $y'_1 = -1/y' = -x/2y$, which is a differential equation that can be solved to give the solution $y^2 + (x^2/2) = k$, which represents a family of ellipses orthogonal to the family of parabolas (*see* Graph).

orthographic projection, a common method of representing three-dimensional objects, usually by three two-dimensional drawings, in each of which the object is viewed along parallel lines that are perpendicular to the plane of the drawing. For example, an orthographic projection of a house typically consists of a top view, or plan, and a front view and one side view (front and side elevations).

·azimuthal projection modifications **11**:476d; illus.
·drafting and descriptive geometry **5**:973f

orthography, the representation of the sounds of a language by means of written or printed symbols.

·alphabet improvement attempts **1**:627c
·English developments and problems **6**:879d
·English pronunciation and written language **10**:658g
·English revisions after Normans **6**:881b
·hieratic rigidity and evolution **8**:856a
·hieroglyphic method and characteristics **8**:854e
·Romance standardization problems **15**:1044c
·Scandinavian adaption of Latin letters **8**:29a
·standardization effect of dictionaries **5**:720a
·Webster's spelling reform principles **19**:720e

orthomorphic projection, having the same scale along both the meridian and the parallel at any point and having meridians and parallels at right angles so that the shapes of small areas around that point are true to the shape of the corresponding areas on the earth.

·navigational charts contrasted **12**:902f

orthonectid, any of a group of rare parasites (*i.e.*, organisms deriving nourishment from the body of another living organism) of various marine invertebrates; they are sometimes included in the Mesozoa, a group regarded as intermediate between Protozoa (single-celled animals) and Metazoa (multicellular animals). The parasitic orthonectid larva consists of a cytoplasmic mass containing numerous nuclei. It develops into a free-swimming adult.

·mesozoan parasitic behaviour **11**:1013a

orthonormal basis in a Hilbert space H is any collection $\{e_\alpha\}$ (for symbol, *see* number sequence) of elements of H such that $(e_\alpha, e_\beta) = \delta(\alpha, \beta$[beta]) (*see* Hilbert space for symbol) in which δ (delta) is the Kronecker delta function, and such that $(x, e_\alpha) = 0$ for all α (alpha) if and only if $x = 0$.

·linear and multilinear algebra theory **1**:515f
·vector and tensor analysis principles **1**:793d

orthonormal functions, measurable real- (or complex-) valued functions f and g on a measured space X such that $\int_X [f(x)]^2 dx = 1$, $\int_X [g(x)]^2 dx = 1$ (*see* integration [for symbol]), and $\int_X f(x)g(x)dx = 0$.

orthopedics, medical specialty concerned with the preservation of the health of, and restoration to health of, diseased and injured parts of the skeletal system—bones, joints, tendons, ligaments, and associated structures. Board requirements, examinations for specialization and practice, and residencies vary from country to country.

·surgery types and techniques **17**:821g

orthophosphoric acid: *see* phosphoric acid.

orthopteran 13:742, common name for members of four related insect orders: cockroaches and mantids (Dictyoptera); grylloblattids (Grylloblattodea); walking sticks (Phasmida); and katydids, crickets, camel crickets, pygmy sand crickets, grasshoppers, and locusts (Orthoptera).

The text article covers orthopteran general features, importance, natural history, and form and function. Information on evolution, paleontology, and classification are also included.

REFERENCES in other text articles:
·characteristics, classification, and evolution **9**:619a; illus. 618
·hearing and sound-making organs **17**:40b; illus. 41
·reproductive behaviour patterns **15**:686b
·social parental behaviour patterns **16**:938d

RELATED ENTRIES in the *Ready Reference and Index:*
camel cricket; cockroach; cone-headed grasshopper; cricket; grasshopper; ice bug; Jerusalem cricket; katydid; leaf insect; leaf-rolling grasshopper; locust; long-horned grasshopper; mantid; meadow grasshopper; mole cricket; pygmy grasshopper; pygmy sand cricket; shield-backed grasshopper; short-horned grasshopper; walkingstick

orthoptic curve, in mathematics, the locus of the points of intersection of tangents to a given curve (or a pair of curves) meeting at a constant angle is an isoptic curve of the given curve or curves. When the constant angle is right, the isoptic curve is said to be the orthoptic curve.

·analytic geometry fundamentals **7**:1092h

orthopyroxene, series of common silicate minerals in the pyroxene family. They typically occur as fibrous or lamellar (thin-plated) green masses in igneous and metamorphic rocks and in meteorites.

Hypersthene from Labrador

By courtesy of the Field Museum of Natural History, Chicago; photograph, John H. Gerard—EB Inc.

In these minerals, magnesium is replaced by iron in the molecular structure; thus magnesium silicate ($MgSiO_3$) is replaced by ferrous iron silicate ($FeSiO_3$). The series includes:

enstatite	0 to 10% Fe
bronzite	10 to 30% Fe
hypersthene	30 to 50% Fe
ferrohypersthene	50 to 70% Fe
eulite	70 to 90% Fe
ferrosilite	90 to 100% Fe

All except the theoretical end-member ferrosilite occur naturally. The magnesium-rich varieties commonly occur in ultrabasic igneous rocks, the iron-rich varieties in metamorphosed iron-rich sediments. Orthopyroxenes are essential constituents of norite; they also are characteristic of charnockite and granulite. Aside from olivine, magnesium-rich (less than 30 percent iron) orthopyroxene is the commonest silicate in meteorites; it is a major constituent of most chondrites and an important component of mesosiderites and calcium-poor achondrites. For detailed physical properties, *see* pyroxenes.

The orthopyroxene series crystallizes in the orthorhombic system (three crystallographic axes unequal in length and at right angles to each other). An analogue crystallizing in the monoclinic system (three crystallographic axes unequal in length with one oblique intersection), the clinoenstatite–clinoferrosilite series is found largely in meteorites (achondrites, chondrites, and mesosiderites).

·hornfel metamorphic equilibrium **15**:949g
·hypersthene formula and metamorphic occurrence **12**:6h; table5
·pyroxene structure and composition **15**:318h *passim* to 320h
·silicate structure and chemistry **16**:759c

orthoquartzite (petrology): *see* quartzite.

orthorhombic system, one of the six crystal systems to which a given crystalline solid can be assigned. Crystals in this system are referred to three mutually perpendicular axes that are unequal in length. If the atoms or atom groups in the solid are represented by points and the points are connected, the resulting lattice will consist of an orderly stacking of blocks, or unit cells. The orthorhombic unit cell is distinguished by three lines called axes of 2-fold symmetry about which the cell can be rotated by 180° without changing its appearance. This characteristic requires that the angles between any two edges of the unit cell be right angles but the edges may be any length. Alpha-sulphur, cementite, talc, arago-

nite, enstatite, topaz, staurolite, barite, cerussite, marcasite, and enargite crystallize in the orthorhombic system.
·amphibole magnesium–iron ratios **1**:709a
·crystal structures and patterns **5**:345f
·mica crystal structures **12**:95b

orthosilicates: *see* nesosilicates.

orthostatic hypotension, in medicine, low blood pressure occurring when the patient is in a standing position.
·fatigue in unpleasant situations **7**:192a

ortho-sulfobenzoic acid imide: *see* saccharin.

Orthotomus (bird): *see* tailorbird.

orthowater: *see* anomalous water.

Orthurethra, order of land snails, class Gastropoda.
·characteristics and classification **7**:956f

Ortigão, José Duarte Ramalho (b. Nov. 24, 1836, Porto, Port.—d. Sept. 27, 1915, Lisbon), essayist and journalist who began his career as a teacher of French and as a contributor to the *Jornal do Porto* ("Porto Journal") at the age of 19. In 1868 he moved to Lisbon to take up an appointment in the office of the Academia Real das Ciências (Academy of Sciences). In Lisbon he continued writing assiduously for Portuguese journals and established contact with the progressive intellectuals and writers Antero de Quental, Oliveira Martins, Eça de Queirós, and others. Ortigão and his lifelong friend, Queirós, started the satirical review *As Farpas* ("The Darts") in 1871, and after the departure overseas of Queirós late in 1872, Ortigão produced the review alone until 1888. In his hands, *As Farpas* gradually became less satirical and more didactic and descriptive, a vehicle for disseminating doctrines of humanitarianism, positivism, aesthetic realism, and physical fitness.

A robust, athletic figure, Ortigão travelled widely throughout his life. His writings reveal his mastery of Portuguese prose, his remarkable descriptive power, and his intense love of, and concern for, the welfare of his native land. His outstanding book is probably *A Holanda* (1885; "Holland"), in which he praises the mode of life and achievements of the Dutch people and upholds them as a model for the Portuguese. With advancing years his political outlook became more conservative; he was opposed to the revolution of 1910, which overthrew the monarchy and established a republic, and, in protest, resigned his public appointments as keeper of the Royal Ajuda Library and secretary to the Academia Real das Ciências.

Ortigueira, city, La Coruña province, Galicia, northwestern Spain, northeast of La Coruña city, on the Ría de Santa Marta de Ortigueira, an inlet of the Bay of Biscay, near the northernmost point of the Iberian Peninsula. The city is a summer resort with sardine fisheries and a coastal trade. Other activities include boatbuilding, fish salting, and the manufacture of linen and chinaware. Pop. (1970 prelim.) 17,559.
43°41′ N, 7°51′ W
·map, Spain **17**:382

Ortiz, Roberto (1886–1942), Argentinian president (1938–40).
·presidency and reform attempts **1**:1149b

ortolan, or ORTOLAN BUNTING (*Emberiza hortulana*), Eurasian garden and field bird of the subfamily Emberizinae, family Fringillidae (order Passeriformes). It grows fat in autumn, when large flocks gather for migration to northern Africa and the Middle East, and at that season it is a table delicacy. The bird is 16 centimetres (6½ inches) long, with streaked brown back, grayish head and breast, pale yellow throat, and pinkish belly.

Ortolan (*Emberiza hortulana*)
K.J. Carlson—Ardea London

Orton, Edward, Jr. (1863–1932), U.S. potter who set up a university-level department of ceramics in 1894 and helped found the American Ceramic Society in 1898.
·ceramics department at Ohio State University **14**:917b

Orton, Joe, in full JOHN KINGSLEY ORTON (b. Jan. 1, 1933, Leicester, Eng.—d. Aug. 9, 1967, London), playwright whose work is commonly labeled "black comedy" and has had great influence on the development of the uninhibited modern "comedy of manners." Finding people "profoundly bad, but irresistibly funny," Orton delighted in offending the tastes of conventional audiences. His humour was callous, gay, and in deliberate bad taste; it treated death as the biggest joke of all.

Orton was an actor before he became a playwright, beginning his literary career as a radio dramatist with *The Ruffian on the Stair* (1964). That same year his award-winning first play, *Entertaining Mr. Sloane*, opened in London; its comedy lies in the disparity between its anarchic, brutal action (murder, blackmail, sexual perversion) and its sculptured epigrams and ostentatiously genteel dialogue. This same technique was even more successful in *Loot*, first produced at the Cambridge Arts Theatre in February 1965. Dissatisfied with his first version, Orton radically revised *Loot* before its London opening in 1966. An outrageous black farce, *Loot* is ostensibly about the funeral arrangements for one Mary McLeavy. But it is basically a satire on police corruption. Orton's original program note quoted G.B. Shaw: "Anarchism is a game at which the police can beat you." The point of *Loot* is precisely that.

Orton's final play, *What the Butler Saw*, was produced posthumously in 1969. While it achieves moments of glittering brilliance, it appeared in need of the same kind of reworking that *Loot* had received. Orton in 1967 was battered to death by his male lover, a less successful writer, who immediately afterward committed suicide.
·literary style and works **10**:1222g

Ortona, formerly ORTONA A MARE, town, Chieti province, Abruzzi region, central Italy, on a promontory 230 ft (70 m) above sea level, on the Adriatic coast, southeast of Pescara. An ancient settlement, it was placed by the 1st-century-BC Greek geographer Strabo and the 1st-century-AD Roman scholar Pliny the Elder in the territory of the Frentani, a clan that allied itself with Rome in the 4th century BC. Ortona later became a Roman municipality. It was severely damaged by earthquakes on several occasions. In the 18th century it was annexed to the Kingdom of Naples and was subsequently absorbed into the Kingdom of Italy. Monuments include the cathedral, rebuilt after damage in World War II, and the Aragonese castle (1452).

A commercial and fishing port and seaside resort, Ortona manufactures bricks, and macaroni; vines are cultivated and grapes exported. Pop. (1971 prelim.) mun., 20,660.
42°21′ N, 14°24′ E
·map, Italy **9**:1088

Ortygia, island on which the majority of the settlement of Syracuse, Sicily, was historically and is contemporarily located.
·archaeological remains and architecture **17**:919f

Oruro, department, west central Bolivia, bounded west by Chile. Established in 1826, its 20,690 sq mi (53,588 sq km) lie entirely on the cold, high, Andean plateau known as the Altiplano. The Río Desaguadero, which drains Lake Titicaca to the south, empties into Lago (lake) de Poopó. The latter's only outlet is the Río Lacajahuira, which disappears below the surface within a few miles. Mining is the basis of Oruro's economic life: in mineral wealth (tin, zinc, wolfram, silver, bismuth, and gold) the department is almost as notable as Potosí department. Despite semi-arid conditions, traditional agriculture and livestock raising are practiced by rural inhabitants, who are chiefly Indians. Principal crops are potatoes, quinoa, cañahuí, and barley. Llama and alpaca are the most important livestock, followed by cattle, sheep, and mules. A road and a railroad traverse the department's eastern sector, passing through Oruro city, the departmental capital. Pop. (1971 est.) 352,600.

Tin mining in Oruro department, Bolivia
Stephanie Dinkins—Photo Researchers

·area and population table and map **3**:6
·map, Bolivia **3**:2

Oruro, capital, Oruro department, central Bolivia, lies at 12,150 ft (3,702 m) above sea level, 30 mi (48 km) north of Lago (lake) de Poopó. Founded in 1606 as Real Villa de San Felipe de Austria (Royal Town of St. Philip of Austria), Oruro rose to prominence during the colonial period as the centre of a rich silver-mining region. It lost importance with the decline of silver production in the 19th century but regained status with the development of tin mining. Wolfram and copper are also worked nearby. The city possesses a technical university (1892) and a refinery that processes much of the nation's tin. The hub of Bolivia's railway system, it is accessible by road and by air and can be reached from La Paz, the national capital. Pop. (1970) 119,700.
17°59′ S, 67°09′ W
·map, Bolivia **3**:2
·population and economy **3**:5g

Orussidae (insect family): *see* wood wasp.

Orūzgān, also spelled URUZGAN, *velāyet* (province) in central Afghanistan, 12,563 sq mi (32,537 sq km) in area, with its capital at Oru. It is bounded by the provinces of Bāmīān (northeast), Ghaznī (east), Zābol and Qandahār (south), Helmand (west), and Ghowr (northwest). A rough, mountainous region drained by the Helmand River, Orūzgān is

relatively isolated, having no airfields or major roads. Pop. (1970 est.) 527,821.
·area and population table **1**:169
·map, Afghanistan **1**:167

Orvieto, town, Terni province, in the Umbria region of central Italy, located on an isolated rock on the Paglia River opposite the mouth of the Chiana River. An Etruscan and later a Roman city (Urbs Vetus, from which its Italian name is derived), Orvieto was the seat of a Lombard duchy and of a Tuscan countship before becoming an independent commune in the 12th century. After much civil conflict and strife with neighbouring cities, it passed under the dominion of the papacy in 1448.

Its cathedral, one of the most celebrated in Italy, was begun in 1290 to commemorate the miracle at Bolsena, a town just to the southwest, where in 1263 a priest witnessed the miraculous appearance of drops of blood on a Host that he was consecrating; a large silver shrine in the Cappella (chapel) del Corporale contains the Holy Corporal (linen altar cloth) from Bolsena. The cathedral is richly decorated with the work of many medieval sculptors and painters, notably the frescoes by Luca Signorelli and Fra Angelico in the Cappella Nuova.

Cathedral of Orvieto, Italy
SCALA, New York

The town's many fine 13th-century houses and palaces include the episcopal palace, the Palazzo del Popolo, and the Palazzo dei Papi, containing the civic museum with many works of art and a collection of antiquities from the nearby Etruscan necropolis of Volsinii. Also notable are the Churches of S. Andrea (11th–12th centuries) and S. Domenico (1233–64); the old fortress (1364), which has been converted into public gardens; and the disused St. Patrick's Well, or Pozzo di S. Patrizio (1527–40).

Orvieto is an agricultural centre noted for its white wine; its handicraft industries are represented by wrought iron, ceramics, and lace. It is linked to Rome and Florence (via Arezzo) by rail and road. Pop. (1971 prelim.) mun., 25,195.
42°43′ N, 12°07′ E
·cathedral's Gothic facade design **19**:372f
·map, Italy **9**:1088
·pottery styles and development **14**:906a

Orvieto ware, Italian maiolica (tin-glazed earthenware) produced originally at Orvieto, in Umbria, from the 13th century onward. It was copied from, or inspired by, the faience produced in Paterna, Spain. The most common colours of Orvieto ware are the green and manganese purple of their Spanish prototype, though sometimes blue and yellow were added. The style of decoration is Gothic, sometimes with a Middle Eastern flavour. The most common shape is that of a *boccale*, or

Orvieto maiolica *boccale*, first half of the 15th century; in the Victoria and Albert Museum, London
By courtesy of the Victoria and Albert Museum, London; photograph, EB Inc.

jug, that has a lip characteristically large and out of proportion with its size. Orvieto ware has almost become a generic term for any pottery in this style.

Orwell, George 13:750, pseudonym of ERIC ARTHUR BLAIR (b. 1903, Motihāri, now in Bihar state, India—d. Jan. 21, 1950, London), novelist, essayist, and critic famous for his savagely angry satirical novels *Animal Farm* and *Nineteen Eighty-four*.

Abstract of text biography. Orwell was educated at Eton College (1917–21) and served as assistant district superintendent in the Indian Imperial Police in Burma (1922–27). He revolted against imperialism and found his political reorientation as an anarchist and later as a Socialist. After returning to Europe, he lived in great poverty in Paris and London and described his experiences in his first book, *Down and Out in Paris and London* (1933) and in *The Road to Wigan Pier* (1937). Orwell's anti-Communism resulted from experience of Communism and its methods that he acquired while fighting in the Spanish Civil War and described in *Homage to Catalonia* (1938). From this period also derived both the anti-Stalinism expressed in his fantasy *Animal Farm* (1945) and the distrust of all political parties that inspired *Nineteen Eighty-four* (1949), an elaborate satire on modern politics prophesying a world perpetually laid waste by warring dictators.

REFERENCES in other text articles:
·English literature development **10**:1219e
·novel as philosophical vehicle **13**:282d
·satiric humour by social denunciation **9**:8f

Ory, Kid, real name EDWARD ORY (b. Dec. 25, 1886, Laplace, La.—d. Jan. 23, 1973, Honolulu), trombonist, composer who was perhaps the first musician to codify, purely by precept, the role of the trombone in classic three-part contrapuntal jazz improvisation.

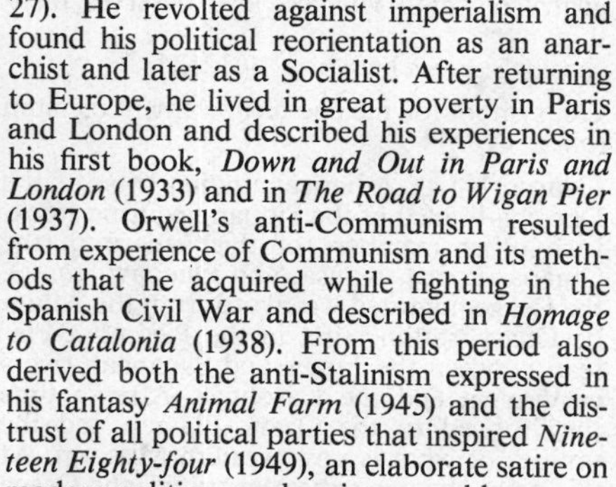

Kid Ory
By courtesy of *Down Beat*

He began to play as a child on homemade instruments. By 1911 he was a bandleader in New Orleans; and the cornettists and trumpeters in this group comprise the authentic line of succession: Mutt Carey, King Oliver, Louis Armstrong.

In 1919 Ory moved to California, forming a new band in Los Angeles. After five years he joined King Oliver in Chicago and by the end of the 1920s had become a prolific jazz recording musician. In 1930 he retired from music to run a successful chicken farm, but on his comeback in 1939 he enjoyed even greater success. He worked with clarinettist Barney Bigard (1942), and trumpeter Bunk Johnson (1943), and his motion-picture credits include *Crossfire* (1947), *New Orleans* (1947), and *The Benny Goodman Story* (1956). A musician of rough, almost coarse candour and naïve sensibilities, he must be seen in the context of the early days of jazz, which he influenced heavily. His outstanding jazz composition is "Muskrat Ramble" (1926).

Oryān (Persian poet): *see* Bābā Ṭāher.

Orycteropus afer: *see* aardvark.

Oryctolagus: *see* rabbit.

Oryol, *oblast* (administrative region), western Russian Soviet Federated Socialist Republic, occupies an area of 9,550 sq mi (24,700 sq km) on the rolling hills of the Central Russian Upland, into which are cut many broad, shallow river valleys. The greater part is in the basin of the upper Oka River. The *oblast*, centred on Oryol city, lies on the boundary of the mixed forest and forest-steppe zones. The soils indicate a former widespread forest cover, but this has been almost entirely cleared since the 16th century, and only small groves of oak or pine remain. Intensive soil erosion has resulted, and the hillsides are greatly cut up by ravines. The economy is mainly agricultural; only 39 percent of the 1970 population lived in the small towns. Rye, buckwheat, oats, and corn (maize) are the main crops, together with hemp, potatoes, and sugar beet. Pop. (1970 prelim.) 931,000.

Oryol, city and administrative centre of Oryol *oblast* (region), western Russian Soviet

Monument to the Soviet tankmen who died liberating the town of Oryol, Russian S.F.S.R.
Vance Henry—Globe

Federated Socialist Republic, on the headwaters of the Oka River at the Orlik confluence. Founded in 1564 as a fortress against Tatar attacks, it was the scene of heavy fighting during World War II. The city centre, with a street pattern of ring roads and radials and with a mixture of old and new buildings, lies on the high left bank of the Oka. South of the Orlik and across the Oka lie the newer residential areas and industries, which include a range of engineering, clothing, and food processing. The house of the novelist Ivan Turgenev is preserved as a museum. There are teacher-training and engineering institutes. Pop. (1970 prelim.) 232,000.
52°59′ N, 36°05′ E
·map, Soviet Union **17**:322

oryx, any of three large antelopes of the genus *Oryx*, family Bovidae (order Artiodactyla). Oryxes live in herds on deserts and dry plains.

The beisa and gemsbok, races of the species *O. gazella*, inhabit eastern and southern Africa; the scimitar-horned oryx (*O. dammah*) lives in northern Africa; the Arabian oryx (*O. leucoryx*) is of the deserts of Arabia and Iraq. Oryxes are stocky animals 102–120 centimetres (40–47 inches) tall at the shoulder. They have a mane and a tufted tail and have dark patches on the face and forehead, a dark streak on either side of the eye, and dark markings (varying with the species) on the body and legs. The coat is grayish brown in the beisa and gemsbok, whitish in the scimitar-horned oryx, and white in the Arabian oryx. Horns, present in both sexes, are long,

Arabian oryx (*Oryx leucoryx*)

Rod Moon—National Audubon Society

sharp-tipped, and straight or curved. The Arabian and scimitar-horned oryxes are listed as endangered in the *Red Data Book* (*q.v.*); the Arabian oryx is critically endangered because of indiscriminate hunting by man.

The beisa is sometimes classified as *O. beisa*, the scimitar-horned oryx as *O. tao* or *O. algazel*.

·desert melon as food, illus., **16**: Seed and Fruit, Plate II
·distribution and water needs **2**:75c

Oryzaephilus surinamensis, species of saw-toothed grain beetle.

·cereal grain destruction **3**:1162c

Oryza sativa: *see* rice.

Oryziatidae, family of fish called medakas of the order Atheriniformes.

·classification and distribution **2**:273f

Oryzomys: *see* rice rat.

Orzeszkowa, Eliza (b. ELIZA PAWŁOWSKA, May 25, 1841, Milkowszczyzna, Pol.—d. May 18, 1910, Grodno, now in Belorussian S.S.R.), novelist, one of the most popular in Poland of her day. In her 20 volumes of short stories and novels, she campaigned for better treatment of the Jews and the peasantry and for education that would prepare women for independent lives. Her writings are animated by the insurgents' ideals in the ill-fated uprising of 1863: social justice and equality, individual freedom, and the brotherhood of man.

Born to a family of gentry, she was married at the age of 17 to a landowner, Piotr Orzeszko. When the marriage was annulled 11 years later, she settled in Grodno, where in 1879 she opened a bookshop and publishing house. In 1878 she had published *Meir Ezofowicz*, a novel that presented a lurid picture of Jewish life in a small town in Belorussia and preached

Eliza Orzeszkowa, woodcut by J. Holewiński (1848–1917)

By courtesy of the Muzeum Narodowe, Krakow, Pol.

not so much toleration as the assimilation of the Jewish community. The Russian authorities closed down her publishing and bookselling operation in 1882, placing her under police surveillance for five years. She remarried in 1894, but her husband died two years later.

Her well-known peasant novels include *Dziurdziowie* (1885), which presented a shocking picture of the ignorance and superstition of poor farmers; and *Cham* (1888; "The Boor"), the tragic story of a humble fisherman's love for a neurotic and sophisticated city girl. Considered her masterpiece, *Nad Niemnen* (1888; "On the Banks of the Niemen") depicts Polish society in Lithuania. *Bene nati* (1892; "Well Born"), which describes the impoverished gentry of small villages, also deserves mention.

·positivist prose literature **10**:1252d

Os, symbol for the chemical element osmium (*q.v.*).

Osage, North American Indian tribe of the Dhegiha branch of the Siouan linguistic stock. Like other members of this subgroup (the Omaha, Ponca, Kansa, and Quapaw [*qq.v.*]), the Osage migrated westward from the Atlantic Coast, settling first in the Piedmont Plateau between the James and Savannah rivers in Virginia and the Carolinas. After a time they moved to the Ozark Plateau and the prairies of what is now western Missouri. At this point the five tribes separated, the Osage remaining in villages on the Osage River, where Jacques Marquette recorded their location in 1673. They remained there until the early 19th century when they ceded their Missouri lands to the U.S. and moved west to the Neosho River Valley in Kansas.

Cler-mont, chief of the Osage, painting by George Catlin, 1834; in the National Collection of Fine Arts, Washington, D.C.

By courtesy of the National Collection of Fine Arts, Smithsonian Institution, Washington, D.C.

Osage culture was of the prairie type, marked by the characteristic combination of village agriculture and buffalo hunting. Other important game animals were deer, bears, and beaver. Their villages consisted of longhouses covered with mats or skins and arranged irregularly about an open space used for dances and council meetings. Tepees were used during the hunting season. Osage tribal life centred on religious ceremonials in which clans were divided into symbolic sky and earth groups, with the latter further subdivided to represent dry land and water. The Osage were remarkable for their poetic rituals. Among them was the custom of reciting the history of the creation of the universe to each newborn infant.

After settlement on the Kansas reservation, the Osage were notable for their rejection of white culture; they continued to dress in skins and discouraged the use of whiskey.

Following the Civil War, pressure on the U.S. government to open all Indian lands to white settlement resulted in the sale of the Kansas reservation. The proceeds were used to purchase land in Indian Territory (present-day Oklahoma). The discovery of oil on the Osage reservation in the late 19th century, and an agreement with the U.S. by which all mineral rights on the reservation were to be retained by the tribe, with royalties divided on a per capita basis, made the Osage a uniquely prosperous people. In the 1970s they numbered about 5,000.

·Plains Indian culture **13**:223g; map 224

Osage orange (*Maclura pomifera*), a thorny tree with large, yellow-green wrinkled fruit

Osage orange (*Maclura pomifera*)

John H. Gerard—EB Inc.

and a milky sap that can produce dermatitis in man. Known also as bowwood and *bois d'arc*, it is the only species of its genus in the mulberry family (Moraceae). Native to the south central United States, it has been planted extensively farther north, being hardy in New England. Planted as a hedge and kept pruned, it forms an effective spiny barrier. The hard yellow-orange wood, formerly used for bows and war clubs by the Osage and other Indian tribes, is now used for railway ties and fence posts. The wood yields a yellow dye. Attempts have been made to prepare an edible meal or flour from the fruit, which was long considered poisonous.

Osage River, rises as the Marais des Cygnes ("swan marshes") in the Flint Hills near Eskridge, Kan., U.S. It becomes the Osage (named for the Osage Indians) after its junction with the Little Osage near Rich Hill, Mo., and then flows east through the Ozark

highlands to the Missouri River near Jefferson City. The 500-mi- (800-km-) long river drains 15,300 sq mi (39,625 sq km). Near Bagnell Dam, which impounds Lake of the Ozarks, it has an average discharge of 10,000 cu ft (280 cu m) per second. The dam was built in 1931 to produce electricity for St. Louis. In the 1950s the U.S. Congress authorized an Osage basin flood-control, water-conservation, recreation, and power plan involving four reservoirs in Missouri and five in Kansas.
38°35′ N, 91°57′ W

Osagian Series, major stratigraphic division of Mississippian rocks in North America that were laid down during the Mississippian Period (the Mississippian began about 345,000,000 years ago and lasted about 20,000,000 years); the Osagian overlies rocks of the Meramecian Series and underlies the Kinderhookian. Osagian rocks reflect a major marine transgression. Extensive outcrops in the Mississippi Valley region consist largely of limestones and bedded chert deposits. The chert commonly forms lenses and nodules as well as bedded deposits. The Boone Chert is especially prominent and in Missouri contains lead and zinc ores.

Osa Gulf (Pacific Ocean): *see* Dulce, Gulf of.

Ōsaka, urban prefecture (*fu*), Honshu, Japan, bordered by the prefectures (*ken*) of Hyōgo (northwest), Nara (east), and Wakayama (south), and Ōsaka-wan (Ōsaka Bay; southeast). It covers an area of 716 sq mi (1,854 sq km) and includes the industrial city of Ōsaka and numerous industrial and residential suburbs. Ōsaka-fu does not, however, include the port of Kōbe, which lies in Hyōgo Prefecture. Pop. (1970) 7,620,000.
34°30′ N, 135°30′ E
·development and aspects **13**:752a
·map, Japan **10**:36
·population and prefecture, table 2 **10**:45

Ōsaka Asahi: *see* Japanese newspapers.

Ōsaka–Kōbe Metropolitan Area 13:751, second largest urban and industrial agglomeration in Japan, on Ōsaka-wan (Ōsaka Bay) at the eastern end of the Inland Sea. It includes the former national capital of Kyōto and many satellite industrial and residential cities. Pop. (1970) 14,886,005.

The text article surveys the history of the Ōsaka area and provides a general description of it, including its topography, street plan, demography, and economic life.
34°45′ N, 135°30′ E
REFERENCES in other text articles:
·area and population, tables 1 and 2 **10**:45
·expressway construction in Japan **15**:901d
·Kabuki theatre traditional production **10**:369f
·metropolitan area's development **13**:751h

Ōsaka Mainichi: *see* Japanese newspapers.

Ōsaka Nippo: *see* Japanese newspapers.

Osa Peninsula, Spanish PENÍNSULA DE OSA, Puntarenas province, southern Costa Rica, bounded on the northwest by Coronado Bay, on the west by the Pacific Ocean, and on the east by the Gulf of Dulce. Costa Rica's second largest peninsula, Osa measures about 20 mi (30 km) northeast–southwest and about 35 mi northwest–southeast. The generally low-lying terrain, rising to an elevation of 2,566 ft (782 m) at Tigre Hill, is used for livestock raising. The principal town on the peninsula is the port of Puerto Jiménez, on the Gulf of Dulce. No major highways or railways lead onto the peninsula. Pop. (1972 est.) 24,375.
8°35′ N, 83°33′ W

osar (geology): *see* esker.

Osasco, city, southeastern São Paulo state, Brazil, on the Rio Tietê; it forms a part of the (northwestern) São Paulo metropolitan area. Industries include meat packing and the production of railroad cars. Pop. (1970 prelim.) 283,203.
23°32′ S, 46°46′ W

Osawatomie, city, Miami County, eastern Kansas, U.S., on the Marais des Cynges River at the mouth of Potawatomie River. Founded in 1854 with support of the New England Emigrant Aid Company, Osawatomie was the site for John Brown's free-state operations in Kansas Territory. In retaliation for Brown's slaying of four pro-Southern settlers at Potawatomie River, the abolitionist stronghold was invaded on Aug. 30, 1856, by a party of about 400 Missourians. Brown and 40 of his followers fled, and the town was ransacked and burned. The 23-ac John Brown Memorial State Park located there commemorates this skirmish and Brown's career. The name Osawatomie combines the names of the Osage and Potawatomi Indians. The town is near oil and gas fields and is a trading centre of an agricultural region. Osawatomie State (Mental) Hospital was established in 1863. Inc. 1883. Pop. (1980) 4,459.
38°31′ N, 94°57′ W

Osborn, Henry Fairfield (b. Aug. 8, 1857, Fairfield, Conn.—d. Nov. 6, 1935, Garrison, N.Y.), paleontologist, museum administrator, greatly influenced the art of museum display and the education of paleontologists in the United States and Great Britain. At Princeton University Osborn made profitable studies of brain anatomy while serving as assistant professor of natural sciences (1881–83) and professor of comparative anatomy (1883–90).

Henry Fairfield Osborn
By courtesy of the American Museum of Natural History, New York

He spent the greater part of his career in New York City, as professor of biology (1891–96) and zoology (1896–1935) at Columbia University, but devoted most of his attention to the city's American Museum of Natural History. As curator of the department of mammalian (later changed to vertebrate) paleontology (1891–1910) and president of the museum (1908–35), Osborn accumulated one of the world's finest vertebrate-fossil collections. He introduced a highly successful instructional approach to museum display and was an effective popularizer of paleontology.

Osborn proposed the valuable concept of adaptive radiation, postulating that a primitive plant or animal in many cases evolves into several species by scattering over a large land area and adapting to different ecological niches. Osborn also served as vertebrate paleontologist (1900–24) and senior geologist (1924–35) with the U.S. Geological Survey. His works include *From the Greeks to Darwin* (1894), *The Age of Mammals* (1910), and *Origin and Evolution of Life* (1917).

Osborne, Dorothy (b. 1627, Chicksands Priory, Bedfordshire—d. February 1695, Moor Park, near Farnham, Surrey), wife of the statesman and diplomat Sir William Temple, remembered for the letters she wrote to him before their marriage. Regarded among the finest in English, they are simply written in an easy, conversational style and present an interesting picture of the life of a young English gentlewoman in the Commonwealth period (1649–60). Lively and tender, they are full of good sense, humour, and keen observation.

The daughter of Sir Peter Osborne, until 1646 lieutenant governor of Guernsey, in the Channel Islands, Dorothy Osborne met William Temple in 1647, and, despite opposition from both families, they married in 1655.

Dorothy Osborne, detail of an oil painting by Sir Peter Lely (1618–80); in the Broadlands Collection
By courtesy of the Courtauld Institute of Art, London

Thereafter she became a devoted wife, as a few surviving letters from later years testify. She bore him nine children of whom seven died in infancy. A friend of Queen Mary, she was buried in Westminster Abbey.

Temple preserved the group of letters written to him during their prolonged courtship between December 1652 and October 1654, and they remained in manuscript until the 19th century. They were sold to the British Museum in 1891. The letters well fulfill the requirements she laid down for herself: "All letters, methinks, should be free and easy as one's discourse, not studied as an oration, nor made up of hard words like a charm."

Osborne, John (James) (b. Dec. 12, 1929, London), playwright and film producer whose *Look Back in Anger* (performed 1956) ushered in the new movement in British drama that was to bring it again to the forefront of world theatre and made him known as the first of the "angry young men." *Look Back in Anger* dealt with an educated hero from a working-class background, rebelling against the social privilege most frequently depicted in the well-crafted plays of the time. Both a commercial and critical success, the play blazed a path that other playwrights were quick to follow.

The son of a commercial artist and a barmaid, Osborne used insurance money from his father's death in 1941 for a boarding-school education at Belmont College, Devon. He hated it and left after striking the headmaster. He went home to his mother in London and briefly tried trade journalism until a job tutoring a touring company of juvenile actors introduced him to the theatre. He was soon acting himself, later becoming an actor-manager for various repertory companies in provincial towns and also trying his hand at playwriting.

Osborne made his first appearance as a London actor in 1956, the same year *Look Back in Anger* was produced by the English Stage Company. Although the form of the play was not revolutionary, its content was unexpected. On stage for the first time were the 20- to 30-year-olds of Great Britain who had not participated in World War II and found its aftermath shabby and lacking in promise. The hero, Jimmy Porter, although the son of a worker, has through the state educational system reached an uncomfortably marginal position on the border of the middle class from which he can see the traditional possessors of privilege holding the better jobs and threatening his upward climb. Jimmy Porter continues to work in a street market and vents his rage on his middle class wife and her middle class friend. No solution is proposed for Porter's frustrations, but Osborne makes the audience feel them acutely.

Osborne's next play, *The Entertainer* (1957), projects a vision of a contemporary Britain diminished from its days of self-confidence. Its hero is a failing comedian, and Osborne uses the decline of the music hall tradition as a metaphor for the decline of a nation's vitality. In 1958 Osborne and director Tony Richardson founded Woodfall Film Productions, which produced motion pictures of *Look Back in Anger* (1959); *The Entertainer* (1959); and, from a filmscript by Osborne that won an Academy Award, *Tom Jones* (1963), based on the novel by Henry Fielding.

Luther (1961), an epic play about the Reformation leader, again showed Osborne's ability to create an actably rebellious central figure. His two *Plays for England* (1962) include *The Blood of the Bambergs*, a satire on royalty, and *Under Plain Cover*, a study of an incestuous couple playing games of dominance and submission.

The tirade of Jimmy Porter is resumed in a different key by a frustrated solicitor in Osborne's *Inadmissible Evidence* (1964), but the problems seem more petty and arbitrary. *A Patriot for Me* (1965) portrays a homosexual Austrian officer in the period before World War I and shows Osborne's interests in the decline of empire and the perils of the nonconformist. *West of Suez* (1971) revealed a measure of sympathy for a type of British colonizer whose day has waned and antipathy for his ideological opponents, who are made to appear confused and neurotic.

Having come to the stage initially as an actor, Osborne is noted for his skill in providing actable roles. He is also significant for restoring the tirade—or passionately scathing speech—to a high place among dramatic elements. His most significant contribution, however, is his reorientation of British drama from well-made plays depicting upper class life to vigorously realistic drama of contemporary life.

·English theatre development **10**:1222f

Osborne, Sir Thomas, 1st earl of Danby: *see* Leeds, Thomas Osborne, 1st duke of.

Osborne, Thomas Mott (b. Sept. 23, 1859, Auburn, N.Y.—d. Oct. 20, 1926, Auburn), penologist whose inauguration of self-help

Thomas Osborne

By courtesy of the Osborne Association, New York

programs for prisoners through Mutual Welfare Leagues functioned as a model for humanitarian programs by later penologists. Osborne served two terms on the Auburn Board of Education and in 1903 was elected mayor of Auburn, serving one term.

In 1913 he became chairman of the New York State Commission on Prison Reform, a post that inspired him to spend a week in Auburn Prison as "Tom Brown" to learn about conditions firsthand. Convinced thereby that (in the British statesman W.E. Gladstone's phrase) "it is liberty alone that fits men for liberty," he founded a Mutual Welfare League of the Auburn prisoners, who assumed such responsibilities as forming committees to judge violators of prison rules and to plan entertainment events.

Osborne was warden of Sing Sing State Prison (now Ossining Correctional Facility), Ossining, N.Y., from 1914 to 1916 and, from 1917 to 1920, commander of the Portsmouth Naval Prison in New Hampshire; he instituted a Mutual Welfare League in both places. His administration at Sing Sing was a stormy one, culminating in an indictment by the Westchester County Grand Jury for perjury and neglect of duty. The charges, however, were dismissed. Osborne wrote many books on penology and was the founder of a national society for dissemination of penal information.

Osborne Beds, division of Oligocene rocks in Great Britain (the Oligocene Epoch began about 38,000,000 years ago and lasted about 12,000,000 years). The Osborne Beds, which overlie the Upper Headon Beds and underlie the Bembridge Beds, occur in the Hampshire Basin region but are absent from the London Basin. They consist of terrestrial marls and limestones that grade into sandstones and contain a fossil fauna dominated by freshwater molluscan forms such as the genera *Planorbis*, *Viviparus*, and *Limnaea*. Fossils from the sandstones seem to indicate that brackish-water conditions prevailed in some areas during Osborne time. In the Whitecliffe Bay region, greenish clays and sands occur. The Osborne Beds have yielded large quantities of fossil remains of Oligocene reptiles and mammals. The Osborne Beds are included in the Lattorfian Stage, a major, standard division of Oligocene rocks and time.

Oscan, one of the Italic languages closely related to Umbrian and Volscian and more distantly related to Latin and Faliscan. Spoken in southern and central Italy, it was probably the native tongue of the Samnite people of the central mountainous region of southern Italy. Oscan was gradually displaced by Latin and apparently became completely extinct by the end of the 1st century AD. Modern knowledge of Oscan comes from some 250 documents and inscriptions written in several alphabets: a rustic or colonial Latin alphabet, the Greek alphabet, and a native alphabet derived from Etruscan. Although similar to Latin, Oscan shows a series of different sound shifts (Oscan *ausum:* Latin *aurum* "gold"; Oscan *fircus:* Latin *hircus* "he-goat"; Oscan Pompilius: Latin Quintilius, a family name) and a divergent vocabulary.

·Italic group interrelationships **9**:1074c; illus.
·location and relationship to Latin **15**:1033a

Oscans, Italic tribe that first settled Pompeii and Herculaneum.

·Campania's earliest settlement **14**:789f

OSCAR, or ORBITING SATELLITES CARRYING AMATEUR RADIO, low-budget communications satellite system begun in the 1960s.

·satellite for low power communication **16**:267d

Oscar, a golden statuette awarded by the U.S. Academy of Motion Picture Arts and Sciences for artistic and professional achievement.

·artistic achievement recognition **12**:496f

Oscar I, christened JOSEPH-FRANÇOIS (b. July 4, 1799, Paris—d. July 8, 1859, Stockholm),

Oscar I, detail from an oil painting by Sophia Adlersparre, 1847; in Krageholm Castle, Sweden

By courtesy of the Svenska Portrattarkivet, Stockholm

king of Sweden and Norway from 1844 to 1859, whose early liberal outlook and progressive ideas on such issues as fiscal policy, freedom of the press, and penal reform fortuitously coincided with a period of social, political, and industrial change. After his accession (March 8, 1844) he furthered various reforms, although his attitude was paternalistic. Especially after the 1848 revolutions elsewhere in Europe he became increasingly conservative, particularly on constitutional issues. He became ill in 1857, and for the next two years his functions were performed by his son, the future Charles XV.

·reign and accomplishments **16**:326a

Oscar II (b. Jan. 21, 1829, Stockholm—d. Dec. 8, 1907, Stockholm), king of Sweden from 1872 to 1907 and of Norway from 1872 to 1905. An outstanding orator and a lover of music and literature, he published several

Oscar II, detail from an oil painting by Emil Osterman, 1904; in Gripsholm Castle, Sweden

By courtesy of the Svenska Portrattarkivet, Stockholm

books of verse and wrote on historical subjects. In home politics he proved a conservative; in foreign policy he favoured Scandinavian cooperation and after 1866 supported Germany in the hope of strengthening Sweden against Russia, encouraging the Germanophile trend that characterized Swedish political and cultural life from the 1870s until the outbreak of World War I. He tried hard to maintain the union of Norway with Sweden and was much grieved when he was obliged to abdicate the Norwegian throne in 1905. By his marriage (1857) to Sophie of Nassau he had four sons; the eldest succeeded him as Gustav V.

·reign and accomplishments **16**:326g

Osceola (b. *c.* 1804, Georgia—d. Jan. 30, 1838, Charleston, S.C.), Indian leader during

Osceola, detail of a lithograph by George Catlin, 1838

By courtesy of the Library of Congress, Washington, D.C.

the Second Seminole War, which began in 1835 when the U.S. government attempted to force the Seminole Indians off their traditional lands in Florida and into the Indian territory west of the Mississippi River. Osceola (also known by his English father's name, Powell) moved from Georgia to Florida and led the young Indians who opposed the Treaty of Payne's Landing (1832), by which only some

Seminole chiefs agreed to submit to removal from Florida. In 1835 he and a group of braves murdered Charley Emathla, a chief who was preparing to emigrate with his people, and Gen. Wiley Thompson, the U.S. Indian agent at Ft. King.

For the next two years, U.S. troops attempted to crush Seminole opposition. The Indians withdrew into the Everglades and fought back, employing guerrilla tactics. In October 1837 Osceola and several other chiefs went to St. Augustine under a flag of truce to attend a parley with Gen. T.S. Jesup. By special order of the General, the Indians were seized and imprisoned. Osceola was removed to Ft. Moultrie at Charleston, S.C., where he died. The war continued until 1842, but only sporadically after Osceola's death.

Osceola, city, southern seat (1832) of Mississippi County (the northern seat is Blytheville), northeastern Arkansas, U.S., on the Mississippi River. It was founded in 1830 by William B. Edrington, who bartered the site (probably Plumb Point) from the Indians and developed it as a refuelling station for riverboats. It was named (1833) for the famed Seminole Indian chief and developed as a processing–shipping point for crops (especially cotton and, later, soybeans) grown on rich alluvial deposits from the Mississippi. Food processing and light industry support the economy. Inc. 1838. Pop. (1980) 8,881. 35°42′ N, 89°58′ W

oscillation (physics): *see* vibrations; wave motion.

oscillation wave, surface-water wave in which each water particle involved moves in an essentially closed orbit that does not move so that only the wave form advances. Oscillation waves in shallow water shape the bottom sediment into stationary ripples that are symmetrical, exhibiting sharp peaks and rounded troughs.
- origin and sea form **13**:494h

oscillator, any of various electronic devices that produce alternating electric current, commonly employing tuned circuits and amplifying components such as thermionic vacuum tubes. Oscillators used to generate high-frequency currents for carrier waves in radio broadcasting often are stabilized by coupling the electronic circuit with the vibrations of a piezoelectric crystal, usually quartz.
- antenna and frequency selection **1**:966c
- electronic control of alternating current **6**:685g
- laser as amplifier and oscillator **10**:687c
- radar transmitter instruments **15**:375c
- radio reception and transmission **15**:428c
- sympathetic vibration theory **19**:667h
- transistor circuit design and operation **16**:519f

Oscillatoria, a genus of blue-green algae found commonly in a variety of freshwater environments, including hot springs. This unbranched filamentous alga, occurring singly or in tangled mats, derives its name from rhythmic oscillating motion that probably results from secretion of mucilage. Reproduction is by fragmentation in which dead concave cells (separation disks) separate sections of the filament (hormogonia). When present, the mucilage sheath is very thin.

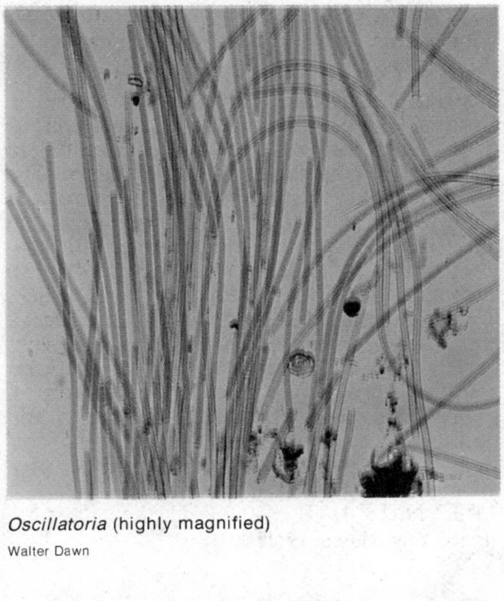

Oscillatoria (highly magnified)
Walter Dawn

oscillograph, instrument for indicating and recording time-varying electrical quantities, such as current and voltage. The two basic forms of the instrument in common use are the electromagnetic oscillograph and the cathode-ray oscillograph; the latter is also known as a cathode-ray oscilloscope (*q.v.*), which, strictly speaking, is purely an indicating instrument, while the oscillograph can make permanent records.

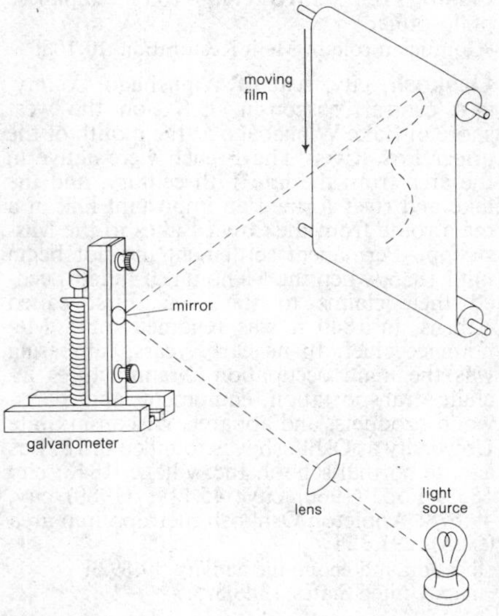

Oscillograph
From *Applied Electrical Measurements* by I.F. Kinnard. Copyright (1956)

The operation of an electromagnetic oscillograph, like the operation of a d'Arsonval galvanometer, depends on the interaction of the field of a permanent magnet and a coil of wire through which an electric current is flowing.

Some oscillographs are provided with a pen arm, attached to the coil, that traces an ink record on a moving paper chart. The commonest device of this nature is the electrocardiograph, which employs a coil of fine wire with many turns and is used for studying heart action.

The light beam oscillograph (*see* illustration) has much less weight to move than the pen writing instrument and so responds satisfactorily to higher frequencies, about 500 hertz, or cycles per second, compared with 100 hertz for the pen assembly. It utilizes a U-shaped coil of one turn to which a small mirror is attached. A beam of light is reflected from the mirror onto a photographic film moving at a constant speed. The cathode-ray oscillograph (or oscilloscope) makes use of a sharply focussed electron beam to display the relationship between two or more variable quantities on a luminescent screen similar to that used in television and can be used at frequencies in the megahertz range.
- role in measurement systems **11**:732e

oscilloscope: *see* cathode-ray oscilloscope.

Oscines (bird suborder): *see* songbird.

Osco-Umbrian, language group of the Italic branch of Indo-European, includes Oscan, Umbrian, and the minor dialects of central Italy—Marsian, Marrucinian, Paelignian, Sabine, Vestinian, and Volscian. Oscan, the language imposed by the Samnites on the Osci of Campania, is known from over 200 inscriptions dated between 200 and 89 BC. Umbrian, known chiefly from the Iguvine Tables (*q.v.*), diverges from Oscan in several phonological features. The Osco-Umbrian languages have much in common with Latin-Faliscan (*q.v.*), the other subdivision of Italic.
- Italic group interrelationships **9**:1074c; illus.
- location and relationship to Latin **15**:1033a

Osee (king of Israel): *see* Hoshea.

Osei Tutu (d. 1712), founder and first ruler of the Ashanti nation (in present-day Ghana) who as chief of the small state of Kumasi came to realize (about 1680–90) that a fusion of the small separate Ashanti kingdoms was necessary to withstand their powerful Denkyera (Denkyira) neighbors to the south. Earlier, he had been a hostage in the Denkyera court but had escaped eastward to the powerful state of Akwamu, where he was exposed to new ideas of political and military organization.

When Osei Tutu returned to Kumasi, some Akwamu accompanied him. One was a priest, Okomfo Anokye, who is usually given credit for introducing the legendary Golden Stool, which, according to Ashanti tradition, was brought down from heaven by the priest and as the repository of the spirit of the nation became the symbol of the mystical bond between all Ashanti. With a spiritual as well as practical basis for unity, the other Ashanti kingdoms merged with Kumasi, and Osei Tutu led their combined forces in a successful war against the Denkyera in *c.* 1698/99–1701.

More wars followed, both to consolidate and to extend Ashanti conquests. During Osei Tutu's reign as Asantehene (king of Ashanti), the area of Ashanti approximately tripled, bringing Ashanti into contact with the coast and the important slave and gun trade, and beginning its turbulent 200-year existence as a powerful and warlike nation.

Osgood, Charles (1916–), U.S. psychologist.
- semantic scale development **11**:739d

Osgood, Samuel Stillman (1808–85), U.S. painter.
- Poe portrait illus. **14**:597

Osh, *oblast* (administrative region), southwestern Kirgiz Soviet Socialist Republic, with an area of 28,500 sq mi (73,900 sq km). It is mountainous territory, which frames the Fergana Valley on the north, east, and south, and varies in altitude from 1,650 ft (500 m) to over 23,000 ft (7,000 m) on the frontier with Tadzhikistan. The climate is continental and dry. The population, 31 percent of which is urban, lives mainly in the foothill valleys, in which cotton is grown on irrigated land. The *oblast* accounts for most of the mineral extraction in Kirgiziya, including coal, oil, and gas; it has the most important mercury and antimony mines in the Soviet Union. Other crops besides cotton are fruit, grain, and tobacco, and there are thousands of acres of nut (including walnut) and wild-fruit forests in the Fergana and Chatkal ranges. Sheep are raised on the steppe and alpine pastures. The communities are Osh, the administrative centre, Dzhalal-Abad, Uzgen, Mayli-Say, and the coal-mining centres of Kyzyl-Kiya, Kok-Yangak, Sulyukta, and Tash-Kumyr. Besides the Kirgiz, who live mainly in the mountains, there are many Uzbeks in the foothill valleys and Russians and Ukrainians in the towns. Pop. (1970) 1,233,000.

Osh, city and administrative centre of Osh *oblast* (region), Kirgiz Soviet Socialist Republic, at an altitude of 3,300 ft (1,000 m) on the Akbura River where it emerges from the Alay foothills. First mentioned in writings of the 9th century, it was destroyed by the Mongols in the 13th century and subsequently rebuilt. In the 15th century, before the sea routes were discovered, it was an important post on the trade routes to China and India. Now it has a variety of industrial undertakings, including silk and cotton textiles and food processing,

and is the starting point of the Osh–Khorog road, the main Pamirs Highway. The city has a teacher-training institute, a branch of the Frunze Polytechnic Institute, a theatre, a museum, and a botanical garden. Takht-i-Suleyman (Solomon's Throne), a hill in the western part of the city, has long been a Muslim place of pilgrimage. Pop. (1970) 120,000.
40°33′ N, 72°48′ E
·map, Soviet Union **17**:322

O'Shaughnessy, Arthur (William Edgar) (b. March 14, 1844, London—d. Jan. 30, 1881, London), poet best known for his much-anthologized "Ode" ("We are the music-makers"). He was strongly influenced by the work of Algernon Charles Swinburne and the artists and writers of the Pre-Raphaelite group. He published four volumes of verse and is representative of many Victorian poets for whom a concentration on musicality and emotions was more important than intellectual content.

Oshawa, originally called SKEA'S CORNERS, city, Ontario County, southeastern Ontario, Canada, on the north shore of Lake Ontario, northeast of Toronto. Founded as a settlement on the military Kingston Road in 1795, it was renamed Oshawa—an Indian word referring to a stream crossing—in 1842, when a post office was established there. The city, a port of entry and a major manufacturing centre, is the home site of General Motors of Canada. There are also woollen mills, foundries, and plants that manufacture machine parts, fabricated metals, glass, plastics, pharmaceuticals, furniture, leather, and electrical appliances. Inc. village, 1850; town, 1879; city, 1924. Pop. (1971) 91,587.
43°54′ N, 78°51′ W
·map, Canada **3**:716

O'Shea, William Henry and Katharine Page, the latter *née* WOOD, afterward MRS. CHARLES STEWART PARNELL (respectively b. 1840, Dublin—d. April 22, 1905, Brighton, Sussex; b. Jan. 30, 1846, Cressing, Essex—d. Feb. 5, 1921, Littlehampton, Sussex), husband and wife from 1867 to 1890, whose relationship with the Irish nationalist leader Charles Stewart Parnell led to a divorce scandal that terminated Parnell's career, divided Irish opinion, and delayed the granting of Home Rule by Great Britain to Ireland.

O'Shea retired from the British Army in 1862 with the rank of captain. He and his wife had three children but are said to have ceased marital relations several years before 1880, when she and Parnell became acquainted. From 1881 Mrs. O'Shea and Parnell lived together at Eltham, near London. Neither she nor O'Shea, who did not object to this arrangement, contemplated divorce during the lifetime of her aunt, Mrs. Benjamin Wood, on whom the O'Sheas were financially dependent.

In the meantime, O'Shea was elected to the British House of Commons in 1880 as a Home Rule member from County Clare, and in the same year he supported Parnell's successful campaign for leadership of the Irish Nationalist Party. Although he helped obtain Parnell's release from prison for having attacked the Irish Land Act of 1881, Parnell came to mistrust him. In 1885 O'Shea claimed to have negotiated an agreement between Parnell and Joseph Chamberlain, at that time president of the Board of Trade, for a local government plan in substitution for Home Rule. In 1886 Parnell and Chamberlain arranged O'Shea's election to Parliament from Galway as a Home Ruler, but O'Shea (as Chamberlain evidently expected) thereupon refused to support a Home Rule bill sponsored by the prime minister William Ewart Gladstone. Throughout that decade, Mrs. O'Shea was the intermediary for correspondence between Parnell and Gladstone on the Irish problem.

Mrs. Wood, who died in 1889, left her considerable property to her niece, Mrs. O'Shea; but other relatives contested the will. When O'Shea saw that he could not share in the estate and had no further reason for preserving the appearance of marriage, he filed a petition for divorce on Dec. 24, 1889, charging adultery and naming Parnell as corespondent. No defense was offered, and the divorce was granted on Nov. 17, 1890. Parnell was blackguarded by English Nonconformists and by the Irish Catholic hierarchy and lost his political leadership. He married Mrs. O'Shea in June 1891, four months before his death.
·Parnell political alliance and rift **13**:1021d

Oshin, late-10th-century Armenian noble who established himself at Lambron.
·Armenian dynastic succession **18**:1043a

Ōshio Heihachirō (1796–1837), Japanese philosopher.
·Confucian role in Meiji Restoration **10**:105f

Oshkosh, city, seat of Winnebago County, east central Wisconsin, U.S., on the west shore of Lake Winnebago at the mouth of the upper Fox River. The French were active in the area from the late 17th century, and the lake and river formed an important link in a main route from the Great Lakes to the Mississippi. Permanent settlement did not begin until 1836, when the Menominee Indians ceded their claims to the area. First called Athens, in 1840 it was renamed for a Menominee chief. In its early years, lumbering was the main occupation. Manufactures include transportation equipment and parts, wood products, and apparel. Wisconsin State University at Oshkosh was founded in 1871 as a state normal school. Inc. village, 1846; city 1853. Pop. (1960) city, 45,110; (1980) city, 49,678; Appleton-Oshkosh metropolitan area (SMSA), 291,325.
·location and economic activity **19**:892h
·map, United States **18**:908

Oshmyanka Hills, Russian OSHMYANSKAYA VOZYSHENNOST, upland area in the Lithuanian S.S.R., usually below 1,000 ft (305 m).
54°20′ N, 26°00′ E
·Lithuanian physical geography **10**:1264h

Oshogbo, town, Ibadan Province, Western State, southwestern Nigeria, on the Oshun River and on the railroad from Lagos, 182 mi (293 km) to the southwest; it lies at the intersection of roads from Ilesha, Ede, Ogbomosho, and Ikirun and is served by a local airport. Originally settled by the Ilesha (Ijesha, a subtribe of the Yoruba) from Ibokun, 12 mi east, it remained a small town subservient to the Ijesha Kingdom of Ilesha, to the southeast, until it was greatly enlarged in the early 19th century by an influx of Oyo–Yorubas fleeing from the Muslim Fulani conquerors (from Ilorin) of the Oyo Empire. In 1840 Oshogbo was the scene of a battle that proved the turning point in the Fulani–Yoruba wars. Armed with European rifles bought from coastal tribes, infantrymen from Ibadan decisively defeated the Fulani cavalrymen; this victory made Ibadan, 50 mi southwest, the largest and most powerful city of the Yoruba people. Oshogbo continued to pay tribute to Ibadan until 1951, when it became the capital of the Oshun Division of the province.

The present Yoruba inhabitants of Oshogbo are ruled by an *oba* ("king") who holds the traditional title of *ataoja* ("he who stretches out his hand and takes the fish"), first given to Laro, one of the town's founders, who, according to legend, fed the fish of the Oshun and in return received a liquid believed efficacious against sterility in women. The Oshun River and its personification and namesake, the goddess Oshun (a Yoruba heroine deified for her role in saving Oshogbo), are honoured at an annual festival in August. Two chalk- and camwood-covered shrines are connected with this worship—the Ile Oshun (at the *oba*'s market), in which are stored the idols of the cult, and the Ojubo Oshun (on a bend of the river at Laro's original settlement), which is the centre of the worship.

With the construction of the railway in 1906 from Lagos, the town became a major collecting point for cocoa and palm oil and kernels. Weaving and dyeing of cotton cloth, cotton ginning, and tobacco growing are local occupations; trade is primarily in yams, cassava, maize (corn), beans, pumpkins, okra, palm produce, and cotton.

Oshogbo is the site of a teacher-training college, a vocational school, a commercial institute, and Baptist, Roman Catholic, private, and government secondary schools. Several hospitals, a government health office, and a maternity clinic serve the town. Next to the *oba*'s market is the central mosque and the town hall. Pop. (1971 est.) 252,583.
7°47′ N, 4°34′ E
·map, Nigeria **13**:86

Osiān, town in Rajasthan state, India, noted for its temples.
·temple group construction and style **17**:178b

Osiander, Andreas (b. ANDREAS HOSEMANN, Dec. 19, 1498, Gunzenhausen, Brandenburg, now in West Germany—d. Oct. 17, 1552, Königsberg, now Kaliningrad region, U.S.S.R.), theologian who helped introduce the Protestant Reformation to Nürnberg. The son of a blacksmith, he was educated at Leipzig, Altenburg, and the University of Ingolstadt. Ordained in 1520, he helped reform the imperial free city of Nürnberg on strictly Lutheran principles and in 1522 won over Albert von Hohenzollern, grand master of the Knights of the Teutonic Order, to the Lutheran movement. Osiander also helped write the influential Brandenburg–Nürnberg Church Order (1532) and compiled the liturgically conservative Pfalz–Neuberg Church Order (1543). By substituting his own preface in 1543 to Nicolaus Copernicus' *De revolutionibus orbium coelestium, libri VI* ("Six Books on the Revolutions of the Celestial Orbs"), which introduced Copernican theories in a purely hypothetical manner, he helped keep this controversial work off the *Index of Forbidden Books* until the next century.

In 1548, when the Emperor compelled Nürnberg to accept the Augsburg Interim, a provisional imperial religious ordinance, Osiander fled, first to Breslau and then to Königsberg, where despite his lack of a theological degree he was appointed professor primarius of the new university's theological faculty (1549). The envy of his colleagues and apparently his own stubborn personality produced a violent controversy the next year. One Lutheran faculty and synod after another declared its opposition to Osiander's depreciation of forensic justification of sinners, which stressed duty and responsibility and his exaggerated stress on the indwelling of Christ himself as the essential factor in justification. In addition to his *Harmoniae Evangelicae* (1537), Osiander wrote several treatises expounding his theological views, which his followers, the Osiandrists, continued to promote until 1567.
·Copernican theory publication **5**:146c

Osijek, German ESSEG, Hungarian ESZEK, industrial town and agricultural centre in Croatia, Yugoslavia, on the Drava River. A river port, it also has good rail connections to all parts of Yugoslavia and to Hungary. The upper, or old, town centres on the fortress; the lower, or new, town is the commercial and main residential area. Industries include textiles, tanneries, and the manufacture of soap and agricultural machinery. North of Osijek, in a triangular area bounded by the Drava and Danube rivers and the Hungarian frontier, is a giant state farm and agricultural combine, producing cereals, fodder crops, sugar beet, dairy produce, livestock, and poultry. At nearby Borovo is the largest footwear factory in Yugoslavia and a rubber-producing plant. Pop. (1971 prelim.) 93,912.
45°33′ N, 18°41′ E
·map, Yugoslavia **19**:1100

Osimo, town, Ancona province, Marche (The Marches) region, central Italy. Originally called Auximum, the town was a Roman provincial capital, and has a 13th-century cathedral and a Renaissance civic palace. Local manufactures include musical instruments and textiles. Pop. (1971 prelim.) mun., 23,877.
43°29′ N, 13°29′ E

Osinniki, city, Kemerovo *oblast* (administrative region), central Russian Soviet Federated Socialist Republic, at the confluence of the Kandalep and Kondoma rivers. It is a coal-mining centre in the Kuznetsk Basin that developed in the 1930s, and it supplies coal to the Kuznetsk metallurgical complex located in Novokuznetsk. A college of mining technology is located in the city, which was incorporated in 1938. Pop. (1970) 62,000.
53°37′ N, 87°21′ E

Osiris, one of the most important gods of ancient Egypt. The origin of Osiris is obscure, for it is not certain whether he was originally a local god of Abydos, in Upper Egypt, or of Busiris, in Lower Egypt, or whether he was the personification of chthonic fertility or simply a deified hero. By about 2400 BC, however, Osiris clearly played a double role: he was both a god of fertility and the personification of the dead king. The myths concerning Osiris originated when the functions of his dual role were combined with the Egyptian dogma of divine kingship. According to Egyptian belief, the king at death became Osiris, god of the underworld. The dead king's son, the living king, was Horus, god of the sky. Osiris and Horus, therefore, were father and son. The goddess Isis was the mother of the king and was thus the mother of Horus and wife of Osiris. The god Seth was considered the murderer of Osiris and adversary of Horus.

Osiris, bronze figurine of the Late Period; in the Ägyptisches Museum, Berlin
By courtesy of the Staatliche Museen Preussischer Kulturbesitz, Berlin

According to the most traditional form of the myth, Osiris was slain or drowned by Seth, who tore the corpse into 14 pieces, which he flung over the Earth. Eventually, Isis and her sister Nephthys found and buried all the pieces, thereby giving new life to Osiris, who from that point onward remained in the underworld as ruler and judge. His posthumous son, Horus, then successfully fought against Seth and became the new king of Egypt. Thus, the idea of divine kingship became established in mythical dogma.

Osiris was not only regarded as ruler of the dead but also as the power that granted all life from the underworld, from sprouting vegetation to the annual flood of the Nile. All those buried with Egyptian ritual hoped to participate in that life-giving power, and from about 2000 BC onward the Egyptians believed that every man, not just the deceased kings, became identified with Osiris at death. The process of becoming Osiris, however, did not imply resurrection, for even Osiris did not rise from the dead. Instead, the process was a claim to live on in the hereafter and in one's descendants on Earth. Having become the god of every dead person, Osiris' cult soon spread throughout all of Egypt, often joining with the cults of local fertility and underworld deities.

The idea that immortality could be gained by following Osiris was maintained through certain cult forms, which, during Hellenistic times, were transformed into the Osiris mysteries. In earliest times, however, the festivals were comprised of processions and nocturnal rites and were celebrated at the temple of Abydos. Because the festivals took place in the open, public participation was permitted, and by the end of the 3rd millennium BC it became fashionable to be buried on the processional road at Abydos or to erect a stela there as a representative of the dead and thereby participate in the blessings of Osiris.

Osiris festivals symbolically repeating the fate of the god were celebrated annually in various towns throughout Egypt. The central feature of the festivals was the construction of the "Osiris garden," a mold in the shape of Osiris, filled with soil and various drugs. The mold was moistened with the water of the Nile and sown with grain. Later, the sprouting grain symbolized the vital strength of Osiris.

At Memphis, the holy bull, Apis, was regarded as a representation of Osiris. The bull was later called Osiris-Apis, which eventually became the name of the Hellenistic god Sarapis. Within Greek mythology itself, Osiris was intimately connected with the god Dionysus.

Representations of Osiris are rare before the New Kingdom (1567–1085 BC), when he was shown as a mummy with his arms crossed on his breast, one hand holding a crook, the other a flail. He wore a narrow, plaited beard, and on his head was the *atef* crown, composed of the white crown of Upper Egypt and two red feathers.

·brewing's mythical origin **3**:158f
·dualism in celestial conflict **5**:1066e
·Egyptian pantheon myths and cultic influence **6**:506b *passim* to 509b
·Egyptian 5th-dynasty personal religion **6**:467f
·judgment and resurrection **5**:535a
·mystery cults and divine kingship **12**:780e
·mythological function **18**:219f
·personal religion of 12th dynasty **6**:470c
·pharaoh as high priest and divine descendant **14**:1008g
·polytheism and hero worship **14**:787b
·salvific functions and attributes **16**:203a

Oskaloosa, city, seat (1844) of Mahaska County, southeastern Iowa, U.S., between the Des Moines and Skunk rivers. Settled by Quakers in 1843, it takes its name (meaning "the last of the beautiful") from a wife of the Indian chief Osceola. Iowa's first coal was mined near there by Welsh miners in 1870; as the mines were depleted, the city gradually became an agricultural-trade centre. Manufacturing is mainly farm based. Oskaloosa is the home of William Penn College (1873), and Vennard College (1910) is at adjacent University Park. Lake Keomah State Park is 4½ mi east. Inc. 1853. Pop. (1980) 10,629.
41°18′ N, 92°39′ W
·map, United States **18**:908

Osler, Sir William 13:754 (b. July 12, 1849, Bond Head, Ontario—d. Dec. 29, 1919, Oxford, Eng.), physician and professor of medicine who practiced and taught in Canada, the United States, and Great Britain and whose book *The Principles and Practice of Medicine* (1892) has been a leading textbook in the field of medicine.

Abstract of text biography. Osler was educated at Trinity College, Toronto, Toronto Medical School (entered 1868), and McGill University, where he received a medical degree in 1872. He identified platelets in the blood in 1873. In 1875 he was appointed professor at McGill Medical School and in 1878 as physician to the Montreal General Hospital. He was appointed professor of medicine at Johns Hopkins University Medical School in 1888 and as regius professor of medicine at Oxford University in 1904.

Osler's disease: *see* telangiectasia, hemorrhagic.

Oslo 13:756, known as CHRISTIANIA, 1624–1877, and as KRISTIANIA, 1877–1925, capital and largest city of Norway, forming also a separate *fylke* (county); it lies at the head of Oslo Fjord leading into the southeast of the country from the Skagerrak, a strait that links the North and Baltic seas via the Kattegat. It is the economic, transportation, and cultural centre of Norway. Pop. (1971 est.) 481,204.

The text article surveys Oslo's historical development and the site (including the demography and economy), topography, institutions, and services of the contemporary city.
59°55′ N, 10°45′ E

REFERENCES in other text articles:
·area and population table **13**:265
·building design temperature, table 1 **8**:713
·Håkon V's centralization of royal power **16**:310a
·immigration centre function **13**:264b
·map, Norway **13**:266

Oslofjorden, or OSLO FJORD, on the Skagerrak (strait) penetrating the southern coast of Norway for 60 mi (100 km) from about Fredrikstad to Oslo. With an area of 766 sq mi (1,984 sq km), the fjord occupies a glacier-formed depression, or graben, that has been partially filled and partially re-excavated. Its forested shoreline, dotted with numerous towns and seaports, is one of the most densely populated areas of Norway and carries considerable shipping to and from Oslo. The northern part splits into several smaller fjords, including Sandefjordsfjorden, Dramsfjorden, Vestfjorden, and Bunnefjorden. The fjord has many islands, the largest and most famous of which is Jeløya, near Moss (*q.v.*). All major rivers of southeastern Norway flow into Oslofjorden.
59°20′ N, 10°35′ E

Osman I, also called OSMAN GAZI (b. 1258—d. *c.* 1326, Söğüt, Tur.), ruler of a Turkmen principality in northwestern Anatolia who is

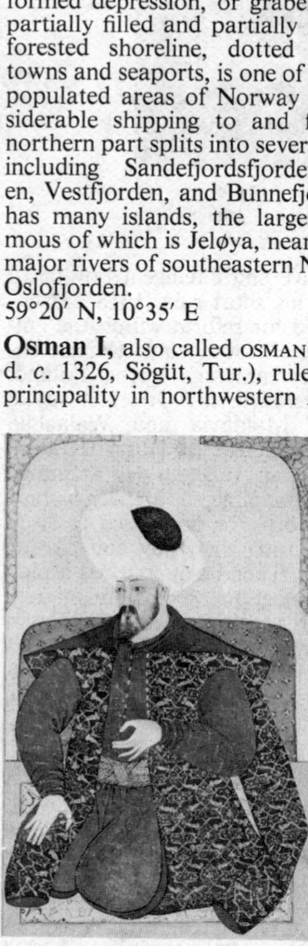

Osman I, miniature from a 16th-century manuscript illustrating the dynasty; in Istanbul University Library (Ms. Yildiz 2653/261)
By courtesy of Istanbul University Library

regarded as the founder of the Ottoman Turkish state. Both the name of the dynasty and the empire that the dynasty established are derived from the Arabic form (ʿUthmān) of his name.

Osman was descended from the Kayı branch of the Oğuz Turkmen. His father, Ertugrul, had established a principality centred at Söğüt. With Söğüt as their base, Osman and the Muslim frontier warriors (*gazis*) under his command waged a slow and stubborn conflict against the Byzantines, who sought to defend their territories in the hinterland of the Asiatic shore opposite Constantinople. Osman gradually extended his control over several fortresses, including Yenişehir, which provided the Ottomans with a strong base to lay siege to Bursa and Nicaea (now İznik), in northwestern Anatolia. The greatest success of Osman's reign was the conquest of Bursa shortly before his death.

·encroachment in Byzantium **3**:568d
·Ottoman Empire founding and conflicts **13**:771d

Osman II, also called GENÇ OSMAN ("young Osman"), in full OSMAN OGLU AHMED I (b. Nov. 15, 1603, Istanbul—d. May 20, 1622, Istanbul), Ottoman sultan who came to the

Osman II, miniature, mid-17th century; in the Topkapı Saray Museum, Istanbul

By courtesy of the Topkapi Saray Museum, Istanbul

throne as an active and intelligent boy of 14 and who during his short rule (1618–22) understood the need for reform within the empire. Ambitious and courageous, Osman undertook a military campaign against Poland, which had interfered in the Ottoman vassal principalities of Moldavia and Walachia. Realizing that his defeat at Hotin (Khotin, Ukrainian S.S.R.) in 1620 largely stemmed from the lack of discipline and the degeneracy of the Janissary corps, he proceeded to discipline them by cutting their pay and closing their coffee shops. Then he announced a plan to go on a pilgrimage to Mecca, but his real purpose was to recruit a new army in Egypt and Syria to break the power of the Janissaries. Hearing of this scheme and already resentful because of Osman's previous policies, the Janissaries revolted, deposed Osman on May 19, 1622, and strangled him the next day.

·social and economic reforms **13**:782g

Osman III (b. Jan. 2, 1699, Istanbul—d. Oct. 30, 1757, Istanbul), Ottoman sultan whose short reign (1754–57) was domestically and externally uneventful. His more than a half century of living in the seclusion required for brothers of sultans left him nervous, untrusting, and conservative when he succeeded Mahmud I. Osman's first act as a ruler was to abolish the tax paid by officeholders to the new sultan. In his attempts to curb the powers of his grand viziers, he made frequent changes in this office—often by executions. Severe with women, he forbade them to wear colourful clothes and ordered that they stay indoors four days of the week; he also regulated the dress of his Christian subjects. His reign was marked by two major fires in Istanbul (1755 and 1756).

Osmānābād, administrative headquarters, Osmānābād district, Mahārāshtra state, western India, north of Sholāpur. Part of the ancient Yādava Hindu kingdom, it fell to Bahmanī and Bijāpur Muslims in the 14th and 16th centuries and was later incorporated into the territories of the Niẓāms of Hyderābād. It joined the Indian Union in 1947. Cotton ginning and pressing are its chief industries. It has two colleges affiliated with Marāthwādā University.

Osmānābād district (5,495 sq mi [14,233 sq km]) borders on Mysore state. It occupies the Osmānābād plateau, which is drained by the Mānjra River. Despite favourable annual rainfall, the district is sparsely populated. Most of the people are engaged in agriculture; the chief crops are millet, pulses, and oilseeds. Some cotton is grown and is the basis of the only large-scale industry. Osmānābād town, Lātūr, and Tuljāpur (a Hindu pilgrimage centre) are the chief towns. Pop. (1971 prelim.) town, 27,258; district, 1,892,683.

·map, India **9**:278

Osman Ali, also called UṢMĀN ʿALĪ KHĀN, MĪR (b. April 6, 1886, Hyderābād, India—d. Feb. 24, 1967, Hyderābād), *niẓām* (ruler) of Hyderābād in the period 1911–48 and constitutional president until 1956. Once possibly the richest man in the world, he ruled over a state the size of Italy.

After a private education, Osman Ali succeeded his father, Maḥbūb ʿAlī Khān, the sixth *niẓām*, on Aug. 29, 1911. Encouraging financial reform, he led the state to an enviable credit position; it issued its own currency notes and coins and acquired ownership of a major railway network. In 1918 he patronized the founding of Osmania University, Hyderābād. Unlike some neighbouring princes, he maintained the feudal character of his state and showed little interest in the increasing voice of the Hindu majority among his people, although he spent considerable sums to improve their living conditions. In World War II his state provided naval vessels and two Royal Air Force squadrons; in 1946 he was awarded the Royal Victorian Chain.

Supported by the Majlis Ittehad al-Muslimin (movement for Muslim unity) with its private army, the Razākārs, Osman Ali refused to submit to Indian sovereignty in 1947 when Britain withdrew. Appealing to the special alliance he claimed with the British, he placed his case for the full independence of his state before the United Nations. He rejected an Indian ultimatum that he surrender his authority but, in September 1948, was obliged to yield to Indian troops. He was made president (*rajpramukh*) of the state but had to accept the advice of Cabinet ministers responsible to an elected legislature until his state was absorbed by neighbouring states in the 1956 general reorganization of boundaries. He then lived in splendid retirement with 3 wives, 42 concubines, 200 children, 300 servants, and aging retainers, including a private army. He provided pensions for some 10,000 princelings and serfs of his former empire and aided Muslim refugees from Palestine. He was created Knight Grand Commander of the Star of India in 1911 and Knight Grand Cross of the British Empire in 1917.

·Hyderābād and modern India **9**:76e

Osman Dinga (b. *c.* 1840, Sawakin, The Sudan—d. 1926, Egypt), a leader of the Mahdist revolt that broke out in The Sudan in 1883. His father was a merchant of Kurdish descent; his mother, a member of the local Hadendowa tribe. Before the revolt of the Mahdī, he traded in slaves. In 1877, however, the Egyptian government, which had nominal authority in The Sudan, began to take serious measures against the slave trade, adversely affecting his prosperity. He was jailed for a while and later joined an ecstatic mystical order. When in 1883 he learned of the advent of Muḥammad Aḥmad, the Mahdī, he joined him and thereafter became a devoted follower. The Mahdī, being possessed of a keen judgment, soon recognized Osman's great potential as a leader and gave him the mission of raising the rebellion in the Red Sea hinterland. The Beja tribesmen who populated the area had until then been peaceful. They did not speak Arabic and had never been ruled by an Arab; they thus quickly gave their allegiance to Osman, who was their kinsman and through years of friendly commercial dealings with them had come to know their language and their ways. With his Beja tribal warriors, Osman destroyed two Egyptian columns near Tokar in November and December 1883, while Tokar itself, the chief city in the region, fell to him several months later. From then until 1891 Osman directed Mahdist activities in the eastern Sudan and thus protected the Mahdī's eastern borders from Egyptian forces. After a period of inactivity, however, an Anglo-Egyptian force (Great Britain had occupied Egypt in 1881) recaptured Tokar in February 1891, and, abandoned by all of his allies, Osman had to flee to the mountains. He remained a general in the Mahdī's service but did not play a decisive role in the battles that led to the defeat and death of the Mahdī in November 1899. Osman then fled, trying to reach the Hejaz. He was captured in the Red Sea hills in January 1900 and was imprisoned until 1908. Thereafter he lived in Egypt. In 1924 he made a pilgrimage to the Muslim holy city of Mecca.

Osmania University, founded 1918 in Hyderābād, India.

·founding and growth **9**:77a

Osman Nuri Paşa (b. 1832, Tokat, Tur.—d. April 14, 1900, Istanbul), Ottoman paşa and *muşir* (field marshal) who became a national hero for his determined resistance at Plevna (modern Pleven, Bulg.) during the Russo-Ottoman War of 1877–78. After graduation from the military academy of Istanbul, Osman entered the cavalry in 1853 and served in the Crimean War (1853–56). Later, he took part in the campaigns in Lebanon (1860) and Crete (1866–69) and in the suppression of an insurrection in Yemen (1871). He was given command of an army corps at Vidin in 1876, and, following his successes against the Serbian Army, he was promoted to the rank of *muşir*. During the Russo-Ottoman War, after the Russians had crossed the Danube in July 1877, Osman entrenched himself at Plevna on the right flank of the Russian line of communications and maintained his position until December 9, when, compelled to cut his way out, he was wounded and forced to capitulate. This famous defense earned him the title of *gazi* ("victor in the holy war") and, after his return from imprisonment in Russia, he was appointed marshal of the sultan's court. Later, Osman served as war minister on four occasions.

Osmanthus (plant): *see* tea olive.

Osmeña, Sergio (b. Sept. 9, 1878, Cebu City, Phil.—d. Oct. 19, 1961, Manila), statesman, founder of the Nationalist Party (Partido Nacionalista), and president of the Philippines from 1944 to 1946.

Osmeña was educated in the Philippines, receiving a law degree in 1903. He was also editor of a Spanish newspaper, *El Nuevo Día*, in Cebu City. In 1904 the U.S. colonial administration appointed him governor of the province of Cebu and *fiscal* (district attorney) for the provinces of Cebu and Negros Oriental. Two years later he was elected governor of Cebu. In 1907 he was elected delegate to the Philippine National Assembly and founded the Nationalist Party, which came to dominate Philippine political life.

Osmeña remained leader of the Nationalists until 1921, when he was succeeded by Manuel Quezon, who had joined him in a coalition. Made speaker of the House of Representatives in 1916, he served until his election to the Senate in 1923. In 1933 he went to Washington, D.C., to secure passage of the Hare-Hawes-Cutting independence bill, but Quezon differed with Osmeña over the bill's provision to retain U.S. military bases after independence. The bill was superseded by the Tydings–McDuffie Act of March 1934, making the Philippines a commonwealth with a large measure of independence. The following year Osmeña became vice president, with Quezon as president. He remained vice president during the Japanese occupation, when the government was in exile in Washington, D.C. On the death of Quezon in August 1944, Osmeña became president. He served as president until the elections of April 1946, when he was defeated by Manuel Roxas, who became the first president of the independent Republic of the Philippines.

·Philippine postwar election candidacy **14**:244b

Osmeridae (fish family): *see* smelt.

osmiridium (mineral): *see* iridosmine.

osmium (from Greek *osmē*, "odour"), symbol Os, chemical element, one of the platinum metals of transition Group VIII of the periodic table, densest naturally occurring element. A gray-white metal, osmium is very hard, brittle, and difficult to work, even at high temperatures. Of the platinum metals it has the highest melting point, so fusing and casting are difficult. Osmium wires were used for filaments of early incandescent lamps before the introduction of tungsten. It has been used chiefly as a hardener in alloys of the platinum metals, though ruthenium has generally replaced it. A hard alloy of osmium and iridium has been used for tips of fountain pens and phonograph needles, and osmium tetroxide is used in certain organic syntheses.

Pure osmium metal does not occur in nature. Though rare, osmium is found in native alloys with other platinum metals: in siserskite (up to 80 percent), in iridosmine (*q.v.*), in aurosmiridium (25 percent), and in slight amounts in native platinum. The English chemist Smithson Tennant discovered the element together with iridium in the residues of platinum ores not soluble in aqua regia. He announced its isolation (1804) and named it for the unpleasant odour of some of its compounds.

Of the platinum metals, osmium is the most rapidly attacked by air. The powdered metal, even at room temperature, exudes the characteristic odour of the poisonous, volatile tetroxide, OsO_4. Because solutions of OsO_4 are reduced to the black dioxide, OsO_2, by some biological materials, it is sometimes used to stain tissues for microscopic examinations. Osmium exhibits oxidation states from 0 to +8 in its compounds, with the exception of +1; well-characterized and stable compounds contain the element in +2, +3, +4, +6, and +8 states. Ruthenium is the only other element known to have a valence of 8. All compounds of osmium are easily reduced or decomposed by heating to form the free element as a powder or sponge. Natural osmium consists of a mixture of seven stable isotopes: osmium-184 (0.018 percent), osmium-186 (1.59 percent), osmium-187 (1.64 percent), osmium-188 (13.3 percent), osmium-189 (16.1 percent), osmium-190 (26.4 percent), osmium-192 (41.0 percent).

atomic number	76
atomic weight	190.2
melting point	3,000° C (5,432° F)
boiling point	about 5,000° C (9,032° F)
specific gravity	22.48 (20° C)
valence	2, 3, 4, 6, 8
electronic config.	2-8-18-32-14-2 or $(Xe)4f^{14}5d^{6}6s^{2}$

Major ref. **18**:624a

·atomic weight and number table **2**:345
·geochemical abundances, table 1 **6**:702
·platinum metal group property, table 3 **12**:855
·production and uses **14**:529g
·transition properties and reactions **18**:606d; tables 601

osmometer, apparatus for measuring osmotic pressure.

·molecular-weight determination **12**:320c

osmoregulation, in biology, maintenance by an organism of an internal balance between water and dissolved materials regardless of environmental conditions. In many marine organisms osmosis (the passage of molecules through a membrane) occurs without any need for regulatory mechanisms because the cells have the same osmotic pressure as the sea. Other organisms, however, must actively take on, conserve, or excrete water or salts in order to maintain their internal water-mineral content.

·annelid worm excretion mechanisms and salt balances **1**:934b
·human fluid and electrolyte imbalance **7**:429f
·seawater salinity and marine life **13**:497g

osmosis, the spontaneous passage or diffusion of water or other solvents through a semipermeable membrane (one that blocks the passage of dissolved substances—*i.e.*, solutes). The process, important in biology, was first thoroughly studied in 1877 by a German plant physiologist, Wilhelm Pfeffer. Earlier workers had made less accurate studies of leaky membranes (*e.g.*, animal bladders) and the passage through them in opposite directions of water and escaping substances, processes that the 19th-century French physiologist René-Joachim-Henri Dutrochet named endosmose (inward movement) and exosmose (outward movement). The more general term osmose (now osmosis) was introduced in 1854 by a British chemist, Thomas Graham.

If a solution is separated from the pure solvent by a membrane that is permeable to the solvent but not the solute, the solution will tend to become more dilute by absorbing solvent through the membrane. This process can be stopped by increasing the pressure on the solution by a specific amount, called the osmotic pressure. The Dutch-born chemist Jacobus Henricus van't Hoff showed in 1886 that, if the solute is so dilute that its partial vapour pressure above the solution obeys Henry's law (*i.e.*, is proportional to its concentration in the solution), then osmotic pressure varies with concentration and temperature approximately as it would if the solute were a gas occupying the same volume. This relation led to equations for determining molecular weights of solutes in dilute solutions through effects on the freezing point, boiling point, or vapour pressure of the solvent.

·animal adaptation to salinity changes **6**:974f
·barrier separation characteristics **4**:160h
·body fluid balancing effect **7**:429f
·colloid history and discovery **4**:854d
·dehydration and cellular fluid diffusion **5**:560h
·drug absorption mechanisms **5**:1043f
·excretory process spontaneity **7**:45f *passim* to 48a
·fish relations with environment **7**:335d
·geological membranes and equilibrium **7**:1034f
·historical theories and experiments **2**:1035c
·ion-exchange membrane permeability **9**:802b
·mussel adaptation to lake environment **10**:615e
·plant internal transport system **14**:501d
·plant water transport mechanisms **13**:731b
·plasma ion content regulation **2**:1122b
·plasma proteins and water passage **2**:1114e
·solution colligative properties **16**:1051e
·thermodynamic solution properties **18**:304g; illus.
·water desalting in the membrane process **19**:652b

osmotic pressure, force created across a semipermeable membrane separating two solutions of different concentrations. It results in the passage of water from a region of greater concentration to a region of lesser concentration. *See* osmosis.

·animal adaptation to salinity changes **6**:974g
·barrier separation characteristics **4**:161a
·blood plasma volume consequences **7**:429f
·circulation and plasma water retention **2**:1131e
·definition and geological systems **7**:1034h
·dehydration and extracellular fluid **5**:560h
·excretory system energy requirements **7**:45f
·hormonal secretion influence **6**:811b
·hydrologic element transformations **9**:107e
·kidney regulation of fluid distribution **7**:55f
·lymph flow and filtration **11**:212d
·molecular-weight determination **12**:320b
·plasma ion content regulation **2**:1122b
·renal tubular function **7**:38e
·solution colligative properties **16**:1051d; illus.
·thermodynamic solution properties **18**:304g
·water movement across cell membrane **11**:879e

Osmund, Saint (d. Dec. 3 or 4, 1099, England), Norman priest, was chancellor of England (*c.* 1072–78) and bishop of Salisbury (1078–99). According to a 15th-century document, he was William the Conqueror's nephew. He certainly accompanied the Normans to England, where he was William's chaplain and one of the compilers of Domesday Book. A late document states, probably inaccurately, that he was Earl of Dorset. He completed and consecrated the cathedral at Old Sarum, Wiltshire, in 1092 and organized a cathedral chapter of secular canons similar to Norman chapters, which was copied by other English cathedrals. His liturgical reforms became the basis for the later "Old Sarum" liturgy used throughout the British Isles. After Osmund was canonized on Jan. 1, 1457, his remains were moved from Old Sarum to Salisbury Cathedral. His feast day is December 4.

Osmunda, fern genus of the family Osmundaceae, with divided fronds and often growing to a height of 1.5 metres (5 feet). The matted fibrous roots of these abundant ferns are called osmunda fibre, osmundine, or orchid peat; they are broken up and used as a rooting medium for epiphytic orchids; *i.e.*, those that derive moisture and nutrients from the air. For information on the *Osmunda* species, *see* Osmundaceae.

Osmundaceae, the royal fern family, only family of the fern order Osmundales (suborder Osmundineae in some classification sys-

Cinnamon fern (*Osmunda cinnamomea*)

Shunji Watari—EB Inc.

tems). A primitive group consisting of three present-day genera of large ferns (*Osmunda, Todea,* and *Leptopteris*), the family contains about 20 species; 5 to 10 extinct genera date from the Late Permian Period (225,000,000 to 280,000,000 years ago). *Thamnopteris* and *Zalesskya* are the earliest known members of the family. The family is characterized by spore-producing structures (sporangia) that are either scattered or in clusters (sori) on the lower sides of leaflets (pinnae) or on both sides of special fertile regions of some leaves (fronds), but the sori are without the membranous covering (indusium) found in many other fern families. The genera are distinguished by the disposition of the sporangia and sori.

Osmunda, with about 12 species distributed in wet areas from Canada and Europe into the tropics, has sporangia on special fertile pinnae. The royal fern, or flowering fern (*O. regalis*), for example, produces cylindrical fertile pinnae at the tips of the fronds that are densely covered with sporangia and give the appearance of a cluster of flowers. The cinnamon fern (*O. cinnamomea*) has separate fertile fronds that turn a rich cinnamon colour as the spores mature. The interrupted fern (*O. claytoniana*) produces small fertile pinnae midway along the fronds. These ripen to a dark-brown colour and eventually drop off, producing the gaps in the frond that give the plant its common name.

The genus *Todea,* represented by one species (*T. barbara*) of Africa, Australia, and New Zealand, has sporangia on the backs of ordinary green pinnae.

Leptopteris, with seven species distributed in New Guinea, Polynesia, and New Zealand, has sporangia positioned as in *Todea,* but its thin, filmy leaves are only two cell layers thick.

Economically, the roots and rhizomes (horizontal stems) of *Osmunda* species are the source of a fibre (osmundine, or Osmunda fibre) used as a growing medium for orchids and other epiphytes. The cinnamon fern and the interrupted fern are popular as greenhouse plants.

·characteristics and classification **7**:246f

Osmylidae, family of osmylidflies of the order Neuroptera.

·classification and distinguishing features **12**:1069h

Osnabrück, city, Niedersachsen (Lower Saxony) *Land* (state), northwestern West Germany, on the canalized Hase River between the Teutoburger Wald (forest) and the Wiehengebirge.

Originally a Saxon settlement where Charlemagne established a bishopric in 785, it was chartered in 1171 and was a member of the Hanseatic League, known for its "Osnaburg" linen. The city accepted the Reformation in 1543 and has been predominantly Protestant since. The Peace of Westphalia, signed there in 1648, stipulated that the bishopric was to be held alternately by Catholics and Protestants. Ernest Augustus I, the first Protestant bishop, was the father of George I of England, whose brother became the second bishop. The see was secularized and given to Hanover in 1803, but it was re-established as a Roman Catholic bishopric in 1858.

The palace of the elector bishops (1667–90) has survived. Despite widespread destruction in World War II—in which the historic town hall (1487–1512) with its peace hall (Friedenssaal) and the Gothic St. Mary's Church (1280–1324) were damaged—these landmarks survived. Other medieval buildings include the 13th-century Romanesque cathedral and St. John's and St. Katherine's churches. There are town houses of the 13th–19th centuries, one of which was the birthplace of the writer and statesman Justus Möser (1720–94). In the vicinity are many old moated castles, such as Haus Gesmold, and spas, such as Melle (saline springs).

Osnabrück is a major rail junction with steel and cable works and factories producing machinery, auto equipment, hardware, chemicals, textiles, and paper. Pop. (1974 est.) 163,674.

52°16′ N, 8°02′ E

·map, Federal Republic of Germany **8**:47

OSO-1, U.S. unmanned satellite launched March 7, 1962, and in operation almost 18 months.

·space exploration, table 2 **17**:364

Osorno, province, southern Chile, bordering Argentina on the east and the Pacific Ocean on the west. Created in 1940 with territory

Osorno Volcano and the falls on the Petrohué River, in Osorno province, Chile

Arthur Griffin—EB Inc.

taken from Llanquihue and Valdivia provinces, Osorno, with an area of 3,566 sq mi (9,236 sq km), lies in the temperate rain forest zone and spans the coastal mountain range, the interior valley, and the Andean cordillera. Agriculture is the economic mainstay, and wheat, oats, sugar beets, and potatoes are the principal crops; cattle raising and dairying are important. Eastern Osorno is famous for its lakes (Puyehue, Rupanco) and mountain scenery (notably Morro Oscuro and Cerro Puntiagudo), lakeside thermal springs, fishing, and skiing facilities. This region is, however, volcanic, and activity began again with the disastrous earthquakes of May–June 1960. Chile's main longitudinal highway and railroad run the length of Osorno, passing through the city of Osorno, the provincial capital, and Río Negro, the second provincial town. Development of a port at Caleta Mansa (Mansa Bay) is expected to decrease the high cost of transporting goods to other parts of the country. Pop. (1970) 160,125.

·area and population table **4**:251

Osorno, capital of Osorno province, southern Chile, lying at the junction of the Damas and Rahue rivers, 40 mi (64 km) inland from the Pacific coast.

It was founded in 1553 under the name Santa Marina de Gaete. This settlement failed, but it was refounded, effectively, in 1558 by García Hurtado de Mendoza, who named it Ciudad de San Mateo de Osorno in honour of his grandfather, the Conde de Osorno. The settlement came under attack by Araucanian Indians in 1599 and was devastated in 1602. After unsuccessful attempts in 1723, 1744, and 1750, it was repopulated in 1796 by order of Ambrosio O'Higgins (the father of Bernardo O'Higgins).

Osorno's greatest growth followed the influx of German colonists, who began arriving in the mid-19th century and subsequently influenced the cultural life and architecture of the city. The opening of the Santiago–Puerto Montt railroad in 1895 alleviated Osorno's isolation. The city is also linked by road and ferry to San Carlos de Bariloche, in Argentina. Its industries include grain and lumber milling as well as milk and meat processing. Tourism is an added economic asset, for Osorno is a gateway to Chile's famed lake district. Pop. (1970) 68,815.

40°34′ S, 73°09′ W

·map, Chile **4**:248

Ospedale degli Innocenti (1419–26), foundling hospital in Florence. The loggia across the facade was designed by Brunelleschi.

·architecture and design **19**:381b

os penis (bone): *see* baculum.

osphradium, in most aquatic mollusks, sensory organ, probably olfactory, testing the purity of the water passing to the gills.

·prototypical molluscan function **12**:328f

·snail anatomy and function **7**:954d

Osphronemidae (fish family): *see* gourami.

Ospina Pérez, Mariano (1891–1976), president of Colombia, 1946–50.

·presidency and widespread violence **4**:876c

osprey (*Pandion haliaetus*), often called FISH HAWK in North America, a large, long-winged hawk, about 65 centimetres (26 inches) long, that lives along seacoasts and larger interior waterways, where it catches fish.

It belongs to the family Pandionidae (sometimes considered a subfamily, Pandioninae, of the family Accipitridae). It is brown above and white below, with some white on the head. An osprey flies over the water, hovers above its prey, and then plunges feet first to seize a fish in its long, curved talons. With grip secured by sharp spicules on the underside of the toes, the bird carries its prey to a favourite perch to feed. Sometimes, after feeding, an osprey flies low over the water, dragging its feet as if to wash them.

Throughout its wide breeding range, which extends to all the continents except South America, where it occurs only in winter, the osprey nests singly or in colonies in tall trees, at ground level on small islands, or on ledges of cliffs. The North American population of this species has declined greatly since 1900, especially since 1950, apparently because of the effects of DDT residues. Exterminated from the British Isles by 1910, the osprey reappeared there as a successfully breeding species in 1959.

Ospreys (*Pandion haliaetus*) at nest

Peter L. Ames

The nest is a bulky structure, up to 2 metres (6.5 feet) across, composed of haphazardly arranged sticks. Two to four boldly marked eggs are laid; downy young hatch in about five weeks and are fed by both parents. The young birds fledge in six to eight weeks.

·distribution of predators **5**:910d

·falconiform habits and natural history **7**:146d; illus. 150

·feeding behaviour and diet selection **7**:211c

os priapi (bone): *see* baculum.

Osraighe (ancient kingdom, Ireland): *see* Ossory.

os resectum, a Roman burial custom in which only a severed finger joint of a cremated corpse was buried.

·symbolism of dismembered burial **5**:536g

Osroëne, also spelled OSRHOENE, ancient kingdom in northwestern Mesopotamia, located between the Euphrates and Tigris rivers and lying across the modern frontier of Turkey and Syria. Its capital was Edessa (modern Urfa, Turkey). The name of the kingdom appears to have been ultimately derived from a certain Osroes of Orhai, who founded the state about 136 BC. Although Osroes was probably of Iranian origin, the rulers after him were Arabs.

Osroëne commanded the strategic east-west highway that followed the southern edge of the Kurdish plateau; it also controlled part of the trade route from Anatolia to Mesopotamia known as the old Persian royal road. Osroëne was, therefore, in a strong position during wars between Rome and Parthia from the 1st century BC to the 2nd century AD, and it formed alliances at different times with one or the other. Finally, the Roman emperor Trajan deposed Abgar VII, king of Osroëne, after quelling a Mesopotamian revolt of AD 116, and foreign princes occupied the throne. In AD 123, however, Maʿnu VII, brother of Abgar, became king under the protection of the emperor Hadrian. Thereafter the state maintained some autonomy until 216, when the emperor Caracalla occupied Edessa and abolished the kingdom.

Under its Arab dynasties, Osroëne became increasingly influenced by Aramaic culture and was a centre of national reaction against Hellenism. By the 5th century Edessa had become the headquarters of Chaldean Syriac literature and learning. In 608 Osroëne was taken by the Sāsānid Khosrow II, and in 638 it fell to the Muslims.

Oss, municipality (*gemeente*), Noord-Brabant Province, south central Netherlands, east-northeast of 's-Hertogenbosch. A food-processing town noted for margarine and meat products, it also manufactures pharmaceuticals—especially insulin and vitamins—electrical equipment, wool, boxes, and metalware. Mainly Roman Catholic, it was chartered in 1399. Pop. (1971 est.) 41,047.
51°46′ N, 5°31′ E
·map, The Netherlands **12**:1060

Ossa, Modern Greek ÓSSA, mountain massif, Lárisa *nomós* (department), eastern Thessaly, Greece, on the Gulf of Thérmai separated on the north from the Olympus massif by the Vale of Tempe (Témbi). Rising from a broad, steep-sided plateau to a pyramidal peak of 6,489 ft (1,978 m), the mountain is noted in mythology for the attempt of the Aloads, sons of the sea god Poseidon, to climb to heaven by placing Ossa on Olympus and the Pelion mountains on Ossa.
39°49′ N, 22°42′ E
·map, Greece **8**:314

Ossa, Mount, highest peak (5,305 ft [1,617 m]) of Tasmania, Australia, in the central highlands. At the northern end of the rugged Ducane Range, Mt. Ossa, along with several other peaks surpassing 5,000 ft, lies within Cradle Mountain-Lake St. Clair National Park. Its slopes are deeply gouged by glacial corries (cirques). The name, with the adjacent Mts. Pelion and Achilles, is taken from Greek mythology.
41°54′ S, 146°01′ E
·map, Australia **2**:400

Osservatore Romano, L', Italian newspaper, originally founded as the papal organ in Rome in 1849.

Ossetes, people speaking an Iranian language and living in the Severo-Ossetian Autonomous Soviet Socialist Republic and the Yugo-Ossetian Autonomous *oblast* in the Caucasus Mountains. They are thought to be the descendants of the ancient Alani, a Scythian tribe.
·Iranian myth sources **9**:868g *passim* to 870a
·naming patterns **12**:818g
·Soviet Union nationalities distribution, table 3 **17**:338

Ossetic language, eastern Iranian language spoken in the northern Caucasus by the Ossetes, who number about 400,000. There are two major dialects: (1) eastern, called Iron, and (2) western, called Digor. The majority of the Ossetes speak Iron, which is the basis of the literary language now written in the Cyrillic alphabet. Ossetic is the modern descendant of the language of the ancient Alani, a Sarmatian people, and the medieval As. It preserves many archaic features of Old Iranian, such as eight cases and verbal prefixes. The phonology of the language has been greatly influenced by the non-Indo-European languages of the Caucasus, and the present vocabulary has many loanwords from Russian. There are many folk epics in Ossetic; the most famous are the tales about hero warriors, the Narts. The literary language was established by the national poet Kosta Khetagurov (1859–1906).
Major ref. **9**:450h
·Indo-Iranian languages distribution map **9**:442
·name structure and order **12**:818g
·relationship to Digor dialect **9**:451f

Ossett, industrial town in West Yorkshire (until 1974 in the West Riding of Yorkshire), England. In Domesday Book (1086), the record of William I the Conqueror's land survey of England, the village of Osleset is shown as part of the manor of Wakefield. For centuries it was important for handloom weaving, but in the 19th century this was replaced by manufacture of the wool products known as shoddy and mungo. Today these textile trades are still important, together with carpet manufacture and a little light industry. Pop. (1971 prelim.) 17,181.
53°41′ N, 1°35′ W

Ossian, Scottish Gaelic name for OISÍN, the Irish warrior-poet of the Fenian cycle of hero tales about Finn and his war band, the Fianna Éireann. The name became known throughout Europe in 1762, when the Scottish poet James Macpherson "discovered" the poems of Oisín and published the epic *Fingal* and the following year *Temora*, supposedly translations from 3rd-century Gaelic originals. Actually, although based in part on genuine Gaelic ballads, the works were largely the invention of Macpherson and were full of similarities to Homer, Milton, and the Bible. These so-called poems of "Ossian" won wide acclaim and were a central influence in the early Romantic movement. Goethe was one of their many admirers, but they aroused the suspicions of some critics, such as Samuel Johnson. They infuriated Irish scholars because they mixed Fenian and Ulster legends indiscriminately and because Macpherson claimed the Irish heroes were Caledonians and a glory to Scotland's past, rather than Ireland's. The Ossianic controversy was finally settled in the late 19th century, when it was demonstrated that the only Gaelic originals Macpherson produced were translations in a barbarous Gaelic of his own English compositions. The name Ossian, popularized by Macpherson, superseded Oisín, though they are often used interchangeably. The term Ossianic ballads (*q.v.*) refers to genuine late Gaelic poems that form part of the common Scots-Irish Gaelic tradition and should not be confused with the romanticized epics of "Ossian." *See also* Macpherson, James.

Ossianic ballads, Irish Gaelic lyric and narrative poems dealing with the legends of Finn and his war band, named after Oisín, the chief bard of the Fenian cycle of sagas. These poems belong to a common Scots-Irish Gaelic tradition: some are found in the Scottish Highlands, others in Ireland, but their subjects are of Irish origin. Consisting of over 80,000 lines, they were formed from the 11th to the 18th century, although their themes of pursuits and rescues, monster slayings, internecine strife, elopements, and magic visitors go back to an earlier period (*c.* 3rd century AD). The tone of the Ossianic ballads is strikingly different from the earlier Fenian literature, which reflected a mutual respect between pagan and Christian tradition. The Ossianic ballads, usually introduced by a dialogue between Ossian and Patrick, are stubbornly pagan and anti-clerical, full of lament for the glories of the past and contempt for the Christian present. St. Patrick is often portrayed as a bigoted cleric. The earliest collection of these late ballads was made by Sir James MacGregor between 1512 and 1526 and is known as *The Book of the Dean of Lismore*.

ossicles (anatomy): *see* Weberian apparatus.

Ossietzky, Carl von (b. Oct. 3, 1888, Hamburg—d. May 4, 1938, Berlin), journalist and pacifist, winner of the Nobel Prize for Peace for 1935. In 1912 Ossietzky joined the German Peace Society but was conscripted into the army and served throughout World War I. In 1920 he became the society's secretary in Berlin. Convinced that "nothing was more devastating for peace and democracy than the omnipotence of the generals," Ossietzky helped to found the Nie Wieder Krieg (No More War) organization in 1922. He became editor of the *Weltbühne*, a liberal political weekly, in 1927, where in a series of articles he unmasked the Reichswehr leaders' secret preparations for rearmament. Accused of treason, Ossietzky was sentenced in November 1931 to 18 months' imprisonment, but was amnestied in December 1932. When Hitler became chancellor, Ossietzky had resumed his editorship. Steadfastly refusing to flee Germany, he was arrested on Feb. 28, 1933, and sent to Papenburg concentration camp near the Dutch frontier. Suffering from tuberculosis, he was transferred in May 1936 to a prison hospital and then to a private hospital, where he died.

On Nov. 24, 1936, Ossietzky was awarded the Nobel Prize for Peace for 1935. The award to Ossietzky was interpreted as an expression of worldwide censure of Nazism. Hitler's reply was a decree of Jan. 30, 1937, forbidding Germans to accept any Nobel Prize.

ossification: *see* bone formation.

Ossining, village in the Town (township) of Ossining, Westchester County, southeastern New York, U.S., on the east bank of the Hudson River. The site was part of a land grant made in 1680 to Frederick Philipse by Charles II and known as Philipsburg Manor. It was included in Tory lands confiscated by New York State in 1779 and later sold mainly to patriot tenant farmers. Two hamlets, Sparta and Hunters Landing, developed and these were incorporated as the Village of Sing Sing (for the Sin Sinck Indians) in 1813. Sing Sing was part of the Town of Mount Pleasant until 1845 when the Town of Ossining was formed. It became a boatbuilding centre from which farm produce was shipped to New York City. In 1901 the village name was changed to Ossining to avoid too close identification with Sing Sing State Prison (established there in 1824—renamed Ossining Correctional Facility in 1969). Manufactures include plumbing and electrical equipment, wallpaper, drugs, and office furniture. Pop. (1980) village, 20,196; town, 30,680.
41°10′ N, 73°52′ W

ossis hyoidei: *see* hyoid bone.

Ossius of Córdoba: *see* Hosius of Cordoba.

Ossory, also written OSRAIGHE, an ancient kingdom of Ireland that won for itself a semi-independent position as a state within the kingdom of Leinster, probably in the 1st century AD. In the 9th century it was ruled by an able king, Cerball, who allied himself with the Norse invaders and figured in later centuries as an ancestor of some important families in Iceland. When surnames were introduced, the dynasts descended from him in Ireland were known as Mac Gillápadraig, a name transformed under Norman influence into Fitzpatrick. In the 11th century they contended for the kingship of Leinster but were soon overwhelmed by the south Leinster family of MacMurrough. In feudal times the Butlers became the most powerful lords in that area. The modern diocese of Ossory, with its see at Kilkenny, indicates the extent of the ancient state.

Ostade, Adriaen van (b. Dec. 10, 1610, Haarlem, Neth.—buried May 2, 1685, Haarlem), painter and printmaker of the Baroque period known for his genre pictures of Dutch peasant life. He also did religious subjects, portraits, and landscapes. Van Ostade was a prolific artist, executing between 800 and 1,000 small-scale works in oil, usually on wood panels. He also worked in watercolour, did spirited pen drawings, and produced about 50 etchings. His works won him much popularity during his lifetime and he became a fairly wealthy man. In 1662 he was made president of the Haarlem painters' guild.

Ostade and the Flemish painter A. Brouwer may have been pupils of Frans Hals around 1627, although his style was not a major influence on either of them. There is a much closer resemblance between the paintings of the two young painters than between their pictures and those of any older master. Brouwer was the most important influence in shaping Ostade's style. Ostade delighted in scenes of low peasant life, such as tavern brawls, usually in dimly lit interiors with a single source of light illuminating a principal group; *e.g.*, "Carousing Peasants in an Interior" (*c.* 1638; Alte Pinakothek, Munich). He treated these themes with a broad and vigorous technique

"Carousing Peasants in an Interior," oil painting by Adriaen van Ostade, *c.* 1638; in the Alte Pinakothek, Munich, W. Ger.

By courtesy of the Alte Pinakothek, Munich; photograph, Blauel

in a subdued range of colours that often borders on monochrome and used a considerable element of caricature to underline the coarseness of his peasant types. Ostade's colour schemes in his early period of the 1630s are largely confined to a range of neutral bluish-grays and browns, sometimes enlivened by a single note of bright colour. From the 1640s on, he gradually adopted a brighter palette, and his subjects, still mostly from peasant life, tend to become less ribald and grotesque. In the works of his maturity (1650–70) are found more outdoor settings such as peasants by a cottage door or figures making merry outside an inn; *e.g.*, "The Itinerant Fiddler" (1672; Mauritshuis, The Hague, Neth.).

·genre painting and etching **14**:1090c

Ostade, Isack van (b. 1621, Haarlem, Neth. —d. Oct. 16, 1649, Haarlem), genre and landscape painter of the Baroque period, especially noted for his winter scenes and depictions of peasants and travellers at rustic inns. He was a pupil of his brother Adriaen, whose manner he followed so closely that some of his early works have been confused with those of the elder Ostade. Too accomplished and individual an artist to remain an

"Rest at the Farm House," oil painting by Isack van Ostade; in the Frans Halsmuseum, Haarlem, The Netherlands

By courtesy of the Frans Halsmuseum, Haarlem, The Netherlands; photograph, Blauel

imitator, he soon branched out into a style that was more ambitious both in scale and in complexity of composition.

In the 1640s, his most distinguished period, he did a small number of winter landscapes, with sleighers and skaters; they can be ranked among the finest of all Dutch paintings of this type. His most characteristic pictures depict figures resting outside an inn or a cottage with carts and horses. These works, reminiscent of compositions by Salomon van Ruysdael, show a keen grasp of design in the disposition of the figures, together with a sense of vivacity. He excells in rendering misty or smoke-laden atmosphere.

Since he died at such an early age (28), Isack van Ostade had few if any pupils, yet his influence on the succeeding generation of Haarlem painters was by no means negligible. Philips Wouwerman in particular seems to have owed much to him, apparently deriving his subject matter in general, as well as his particular favourite motif of a gray or white horse, directly from Ostade's example.

Ostād Moḥammadī: *see* Moḥammadī.

Ostaijen, Paul van (b. Feb. 22, 1896, Antwerp—d. March 18, 1928, Miavoye-Anthée area, near Namur, Belgium), poet and man of letters whose avant-garde writings in Flemish were influential in Belgium and Holland. While a clerk in the municipal service (1914–18), he began to contribute to newspapers and periodicals. His first volume of verse, *Music-Hall* (1916), introduced modern city life as a subject for poetry. His second, *Het Sienjaal* (1918), showed the influence of the war and of German Expressionism and inspired the Humanitarian Expressionist movement in Flanders. Compromised as a political activist, van Ostaijen went into exile in Berlin (November 1918–21). The political and artistic climate there and the hardships he endured made him a nihilist: he took up Dadaism as a writer of poetry in rhythmic typography (*Bezette Stad*, 1921) and of grotesque prose. But he soon developed a poetic system of his own, an "organic expressionism," aiming at a "pure poetry" that gave up personal and humanitarian confessions. Words were freed from their traditional syntactic relationships and images replaced by associations. These concepts were embodied in "Het eerste boek van Schmoll" (part of *Gedichten*, 1928), containing his best and most original poems.

His essays on art and literature and his criticism are also important (*Krities proza*, 2 vol., 1929–31). His creative prose (*e.g.*, *Vogelvrij*, 1927; *De bende van de stronk*, 1932; *Diergaarde voor kinderen van nu*, 1932) consists mainly of grotesque sketches showing keen imagination; they are concerned less with telling a story than with capturing whimsical associations. By its lucidity, stubborn analysis of a theme, and underlying restlessness, this prose sometimes recalls that of Kafka. Van Ostaijen was Kafka's first foreign translator, publishing five of his short prose pieces in Flemish in 1925.

After his return to Flanders, van Ostaijen worked in the book trade and then became an art dealer in Brussels (1925–26).

·Belgian Expressionist literature **10**:1245e

O Star: *see* Harvard classification system.

Ostariophysi 13:757, superorder of about 6,000 species of teleost fishes containing 2 orders: Cypriniformes (*e.g.* characins, carps, minnows) and Siluriformes (catfishes). The Ostariophysi form the majority of freshwater fishes. Many species provide man with food, sport, or (as aquarium pets) entertainment. Some, such as the piranhas, may be harmful.

The text article covers the structure, behaviour, and importance to man of the Ostariophysi, including sections on anatomy, physiology, and such behavioral aspects as reproduction, feeding, and defense. An annotated classification gives the distribution and distinguishing features of each recognized family.

REFERENCES in other text articles:
·examples and significance **7**:339h; illus.
·hearing function of swim bladder **17**:44b; illus.
·social parental behaviour patterns **16**:940a
·water depth sensitivity of swimbladder **11**:804h

RELATED ENTRIES in the *Ready Reference and Index: for*
common fishes: see bitterling; bleak; bream; bullhead; candiru; carp; catfish; characin; chub; dace; danio; dorado; electric catfish; electric eel; goldfish; gudgeon; hatchetfish; ide; knife fish; loach; madtom; mahseer; minnow; pencil fish; piranha; roach; rudd; squawfish; sucker; tench; tetra; tiger fish; wels; white cloud
families of fishes: Callichthyidae; Ictaluridae; Siluridae; Trichomycteridae
genera of fishes: Barbus; Labeo; Rasbora
order: Cypriniformes

Östberg, Ragnar (1866–1945), Swedish architect.

·town hall architectural design **19**:466g

Osteichthyes, fish class containing all of the bony fishes, including the great majority of food and game fishes. Some authorities separate the members of this class into the ray-finned fishes (class Actinopterygii) and the fleshy-finned fishes (class Sarcopterygii). They are characterized by a bony skeleton, paired fins, lidless eyes, red blood cells with nuclei, and gills covered by an operculum.

·Chondrichthyes relationship **16**:497f
·Chordata classification and features **4**:451e
·Devonian fish evolution **5**:678a
·embryonic bone origins **5**:635d
·embryonic discoidal cleavage, illus. 3 **5**:627
·fossils, eras, and traits **7**:568h; illus.
·poisonous animal table 7 **14**:615a
·reproductive behaviour patterns **15**:686g
·skeletal comparisons of vertebrates **16**:823h *passim* to 825f

osteitis deformans: *see* Paget's disease of bone.

osteitis fibrosa cystica (disease): *see* parathyroid adenoma.

Ostend, Flemish and French OSTENDE, municipality, West Flanders province, northwestern Belgium, on the North Sea and at the end of the Ghent-Brugge Canal. A fishing village since the 9th century, it was fortified in 1583 and became the last Dutch stronghold in Belgium, falling to the Spanish in 1604 after a three-year siege. It entered a period of prosperity when the Holy Roman emperor Charles VI of Austria founded the Ostend Company (1722), which was dissolved in 1731. Commercial activity resumed under the emperor Joseph II (1780–90).

After Belgian independence (1830), Ostend developed as a fashionable seaside resort, later patronized by Leopold II. It served as a

The harbour, Ostend, Belg., with the railway station in the foreground

Pier Giorgio Sclarandis—Black Star

major German submarine base in World War I until the sinking of the British blockship "Vindictive" sealed the port (1918). During World War II it was severely damaged. Most of its public buildings have been rebuilt, and the city survived storm floods in 1953 that broke the dike between Ostend and Knokke.

A thriving resort and Belgium's most important fishing port, its industries include fish curing, oyster culture, shipbuilding, and tobacco and soap manufacturing. Landmarks include the Vismijn, or Minque (fish market), the 3-mi (5-km) Digue (promenade), the Kursaal (casino), the Chalet Royal, the Thermal Institute (for hydropathic and electrotherapeutic treatment), and the racecourse. Connected with England by cross-Channel boat and by air services (airport at Raversijde), Ostend is the railroad "gateway to Europe." The painter James Sydney Ensor (1860–1949) lived and worked there. Pop. (1971 est.) 56,167. 51°13′ N, 2°55′ E

·map, Belgium **2**:818

Ostend Company, trading company that operated from the Austrian Netherlands from 1722 to 1731. Founded by the Holy Roman emperor Charles VI, it was an attempt to cash in on the riches being won by the Dutch and English East India companies and stemmed from Charles VI's awareness of the importance of foreign trade and the recent acquisition (1714) by Austria of the port of Ostend. The initial charter was to run for 30 years while trade was to be with the East and West Indies and with Africa. In return, the imperial treasury was to receive 3 to 6 percent of the profits. At first trade flourished, two settlements being founded in India while much smuggling into England occurred. The English and Dutch, however, feared trade rivalry; and their feelings were exacerbated by Spain's support for the venture (1725), which introduced political elements. In 1727 Charles VI, aiming for international recognition of his daughter Maria Theresa's eventual succession, suspended the company for seven years because of opposition from France, Russia, and Prussia as well as from Britain and the United Provinces. In 1731 the Treaty of Vienna dissolved the company in return for outright recognition of the Pragmatic Sanction (Maria Theresa's right of succession). Nevertheless, unofficial trading activities continued until 1744, when the company's servants lost their last Indian settlement.

·Charles VI economic policies **11**:156e
·Hapsburg maritime interests **2**:457d
·Indian colonial trade history **9**:394f

Ostend Manifesto (Oct. 18, 1854), communication from three U.S. diplomats to Secretary of State William L. Marcy, advocating U.S. seizure of Cuba from Spain; marked the high point of the U.S. expansionist drive in the Caribbean in the 1850s. After Pierre Soulé, U.S. minister to Spain, had failed in his mission to secure the purchase of Cuba (1853), Marcy assigned James Buchanan, minister to England, and John Y. Mason, minister to France, to confer with Soulé at Ostend, Belg. Their dispatch urged U.S. seizure of Cuba, if the U.S. possessed the power and if Spain refused the purchase. This action stemmed from fear that Negro slaves might take over Cuba, as they had Haiti, and provide a dangerous example for blacks enslaved in the U.S. South. Their proposals, couched in intemperate language, were rejected, and when contents of the dispatch leaked out, the Republican press branded it as a "manifesto" appealing to Southern opinion for partisan reasons.

ostensorium (religious receptical): *see* monstrance.

osteoarthritis, degenerative disease of the joints, apparently a consequence of the aging process. It is also thought to be a stress disease associated with weight bearing, postural or orthopedic abnormality, or accidental injury that causes chronic irritation of a bone joint. In its early stages there is softening and roughening of the joint cartilage; later the cartilage is destroyed, and the bared bone is deprived of its protective cover. The exposed bone becomes hard, and the joints show evidence of the system's attempts at regeneration of destroyed tissue. There is pain but not necessarily in proportion to the amount of damage. There is stiffness of the joints, but this disappears with movement. Osteoarthritic changes are fairly common in women after the menopause, but persons in all age-groups and of both sexes may have the disorder. Physical therapy, with emphasis on heat and exercise; analgesic medication; and injection of cortisone into painful joints have served to relieve the symptoms of osteoarthritis.

Studies reported early in 1973 indicate that the initial damage leading to osteoarthritis is not in the joint itself but in relatively soft bone near the joint. This bone normally serves to cushion the joint but suffers multiple microfractures from repeated impacts and loses its resiliency.

·bone remodelling in joints **3**:24d
·joint degeneration diseases **10**:261h
·predisposing conditions **5**:22h
·symptoms and incidence **5**:862e

osteoblast, cell responsible for the synthesis of new bone, whether in initial bone formation or remodelling of previously formed bone. They usually exist as a layer on the surface of developing bone. Osteoblasts differentiate from osteogenic cells of the inner, cellular layer of the periosteum, which covers the surface of most bones. An adequate blood supply is necessary for the differentiation of these cells; in its absence, they become chondroblasts and produce cartilage. The cells of the endosteal layer, which lines the bone marrow cavity, also can produce osteoblasts under certain circumstances, as in the healing of a fracture.

Structurally, an osteoblast is a large cell with a considerable quantity of cytoplasm, dominated by the internal network of endoplasmic reticulum and Golgi apparatus and other morphology characteristic of a cell actively engaged in synthesizing proteins for export outside the cell. The material secreted by osteoblasts is known as osteoid, the organic component of bone not yet calcified. The bone surface on which osteogenesis is occurring is covered with a layer of osteoid. The osteoblast does not play a direct role in the mineralization of the newly formed osteoid; only the organic components of bone are synthesized in this cell type.

Eventually the secretion of bone precursors surrounds the osteoblast. As calcification occurs, the cells are trapped and can no longer lay down bone. Under such conditions, they are termed osteocytes (*q.v.*).

·animal tissue comparisons **18**:448d
·bone matrix synthesis **3**:19c
·connective tissue types and bone formation **5**:17a
·sources, function, and properties **16**:828f

osteochondritis dissecans, in medicine, the separation of joint cartilage from the bone.

·knee joint injuries **10**:263g

osteochondroma, also known as EXOSTOSIS, solitary lesions partly of cartilage and partly of bone. Exostoses are common and may develop following trauma (injury) or may have a hereditary basis. At least one type, occurring in the external ear canal (external auditory exostosis) occurs with varying frequency in different populations and is of interest to anthropologists. Exostoses are not serious unless they interfere with function. Rarely, a solitary one will become malignant in adulthood; it is morphologically identical with the lesions produced in osteochondromatosis.

Osteochondromatosis (hereditary multiple exostosis, diaphyseal aclasis) is a relatively common disorder of skeletal development in children in which bony protrusions develop on the long bones, ribs, and vertebrae. If severe, the exostoses may halt bone growth, and dwarfing will result. Pressure on tendons, blood vessels, or nerves may cause other disability. Normally, such lesions cease growing at the end of puberty; reactivation of growth in adulthood may indicate malignant change, which occurs in 5 to 15 percent of cases.

osteochondrosis, also known as EPIPHYSEAL ISCHEMIC NECROSIS, poorly understood but relatively common orthopedic disorder of children in which the epiphysis (growing end) of a bone dies and then is gradually replaced over a period of years. The immediate cause of bone death is loss of blood supply, but why the latter occurs remains unclear. The commonest form, coxa plana, or Legg–Calvé–Perthe's syndrome, affects the hip and most often begins at about age six. It is four times more frequent in boys. Crippling may result, and degenerative joint disease is a complication of middle age.

·Legg-Calve-Perthes disease changes in juvenile hip **10**:263h

osteoclast, large, multinucleate cell the primary function of which is bone resorption, the dissolution and reassimilation of bone materials. Bone is a dynamic tissue, continuously being turned over, broken down and restructured in response to such influences as structural stress and the body's requirement for calcium. The osteoclasts are the mediators of the continuous destruction of bone.

Osteoclasts are characteristically seen in small depressions at the surface of bones. These pits, called Howship's lacunae (after an English surgeon, John Howship), are presumed to be the result of osteoclastic activity. The osteoclast is an extrordinarily large cell with from 5 to 20 nuclei present. The surface facing the bone is a very specialized membrane that is thrown into many folds that penetrate the cavities of the bone as they are being hollowed out. This surface formerly was known as a brush border. Portions of the deep indentations that lie between the villous projections may be pinched off and incorporated into the cell, contributing to its vesicular (granular) appearance. The origin of osteoclasts is the layer of osteogenic cells at the surface of the bone. These cells also have the potential to give rise to osteoblasts (bone-forming cells), depending on the external conditions. It is also thought that wandering macrophages may fuse to become osteoclasts, since dead bone chips, which contain no living cells, develop an osteoclast layer when implanted in tissue.

The resorption of bone involves the destruction of both the mineral matrix and the embedded collagen (protein) fibres. Histochemical tests have revealed the presence in osteoclasts of enzymes that may be responsible for the destruction of collagen fibres. Such enzymes are associated with the activities of lysosomes (minute cell bodies). Destruction of the mineral matrix is probably accomplished through the osteoclasts capacity to lower the pH alkalinity in their environs by secreting hydrogen ions. Under these conditions, the mineral salts of bone are much more soluble and are thus dissolved away.

The function of the osteoclast is closely related to the parathyroid gland, which serves to regulate the body's circulating calcium level. An important mechanism for accomplishing this end is the deposition and resorption of bone. If the serum calcium level drops, parathyroid hormone is secreted into the bloodstream. Upon reaching the osteogenic cells of the periosteum, the hormone stimulates them to differentiate into osteoclasts and initiate the resorption process.

·animal tissue comparisons **18**:448g
·connective tissue types and bone resorption **5**:17a
·structure, function, and resorption of bone **3**:19c *passim* to 23g

osteoclastoma, or GIANT CELL TUMOUR OF BONE, moderately common bone-forming tumour of bones affecting young adults; it shows a predilection for the knee region but may involve the wrist, hand, foot, jaw, or vertebrae. It is frequently very rapid growing and locally destructive but metastasizes (*i.e.*, seeds itself elsewhere in the body) late. Irradiation has been known to cause osteoclastomas to convert to osteosarcomas (*see* osteosarcoma). With effective treatment (block resection or amputation) the cure rate approximates 50 percent. *See also* tumours, bone-related.

osteocyte, a cell that lies within the substance of fully formed bone. It occupies a small chamber called a lacuna, contained in the calcified matrix of bone. Osteocytes derive from osteoblasts, or bone-forming cells, and are essentially osteoblasts surrounded by the products they secreted. Cytoplasmic processes of the osteocyte extend away from the cell toward other osteocytes in small channels called canaliculi. By means of these canaliculi nutrients and waste products are exchanged to maintain the viability of the osteocyte.

The existence of the osteocyte is quiescent; it is no longer actively engaged in synthesizing bone. It has been suggested that the osteocyte may function in calcium removal from bone when the body calcium level drops too low.

·animal tissue comparisons **18**:448d
·bone cell types and functions **3**:19c
·connective tissue types and bone matrix **5**:16h
·structure and function of bone **3**:23g

osteodontokeratic tool industry, name (from Greek *osteo-*, "bone"; *odont-*, "tooth"; *keras*, "horn") given by R. Dart to accumulations of bones, teeth, and horns found with the remains of the slender australopithecine *Australopithecus africanus* (originally named *A. prometheus*) at Makapansgat, S.Af., which show evidence of alteration for use as tools and of wear. Dart has identified axes, daggers, digging tools, flakes, lissoirs (leatherworking implements), saws, scoops, scrapers, and bones into which notches were worn (perhaps used for smoothing thongs) at Makapansgat. Many anthropologists believe early man or man-ape made tools of such readily available materials as bone, teeth, and horns before discovering the manufacture of tools from stone.

Later usage has tended to broaden the sense of osteodontokeratic industry to include bone-tool manufacture by other fossil men. At Sterkfontein, S.Af., and Olduvai Gorge (Bed I), Tanzania, lissoirs have been found associated with slender australopithecines; such tools, aged about 2,000,000 years, suggest these primitive hominids had a more complex culture than was previously thought. *Homo erectus* had an osteodontokeratic industry; evidence for it exists at sites such as Chou-k'ou-tien, China, and Torralba, Spain. At the latter site, elephant tusks were used to fashion blades, cleavers, hand axes, scoops, scrapers, and spatulas. In the upper Paleolithic, bone and antler were used to make points, harpoons, eyed needles, hairpins, and pendants; teeth were used for necklaces. It is not known whether the osteodontokeratic industry represents a tradition evolving slowly from earliest times or a habit reinvented several times in several places. The study of wear marks on such tools under the microscope should provide more information on both their manufacture and use.

osteogenesis imperfecta, hereditary disease characterized by thin-walled, extremely fracture-prone bones deficient in osteoblasts (bone-forming cells) as well as by malformed teeth, blue scleras (whites of the eyes), and progressive deafness. Two distinct forms of the disease occur: in the early form, the result of a recessive gene, the child at birth suffers from countless fractures, and life expectancy is short; a late, milder form (osteogenesis imperfecta tarda), the result of a dominant gene, develops in childhood and is typified by single fractures from trivial stress. In both forms, the tendency to fracture lessens at puberty.

·diseases of animals, tables 1 and 5 **5**:866
human
·bone diseases causing fractures **3**:27c
·congenital skeletal disorder **2**:1073e
·forms, symptoms, causation, and incidence **5**:18f

osteogenic sarcoma: *see* osteosarcoma.

Osteoglossomorpha 13:763, superorder of primarily primitive freshwater fishes, including the elephantsnout fish, mormyr, butterfly fish, pirarucu, and arawana.

The text article covers the natural history and form and function, and includes an annotated classification of this group of fishes.

REFERENCES in other text articles:
·classification and characteristics **7**:343d
·evolutionary significance **7**:339h; illus.
·hearing mechanism development **17**:44a

RELATED ENTRIES in the *Ready Reference and Index:*
bony tongue; mooneye; mormyr; Notopteridae

Osteoglossum bicirrhosum, a species of bony tongue fish of the order Osteoglossi formes of the class Actinopterygii.

·reproduction and classification **13**:763h

osteoid, having a bone skeleton.

·bone formation mechanisms **16**:828g

Osteolepis, extinct genus of lobe-finned fish generally regarded as very primitive although it survived into later Devonian time (395,-000,000 to 345,000,000 years ago) and was contemporaneous with more advanced relatives. Its body was covered with large rhomboid scales; the upper lobe of the tail was more strongly developed than the lower lobe. An advanced trait of *Osteolepis* is the general bone pattern in the skull and jaws, a pattern ancestral to that of early amphibians.

Osteolepis, model

By courtesy of the trustees of the British Museum (Natural History); photograph, Imitor

osteoma, common, a small mass of new bone found mainly on membrane bones (those without cartilaginous models during development) of the skull. Osteomas usually appear in late childhood or young adulthood; they are self-limiting and usually single. They do not become malignant and need be treated (by excision) only if they interfere with normal function.

·cause and symptoms in ear **5**:1134c

osteomalacia, progressive loss of calcium and phosphorus from the bones in adult humans. The condition may occur after several pregnancies or in old age, resulting in softening and curving of the bones and increased susceptibility to fractures.

Depletion of the bone minerals may be caused by prolonged deficiency of calcium in the diet, lack of dietary vitamin D (or its precursor, ergosterol), impaired function of one of the body organs involved in the absorption or metabolism of the bone minerals or vitamin D, or too frequent ingestion of mineral oil in which vitamin D dissolves but is not absorbed from the intestines.

Dietary histories of cases of osteomalacia frequently disclose multiple nutrient deficiencies. Therapy consists of the administration of a well-balanced diet high in protein and calcium and supplemented in moderation with vitamin D concentrates or fish-liver oils.

·bone mineralization deficiencies **3**:24g
·nutritional calcium deficiencies **13**:418g
·vitamin D deficiencies in adults **13**:410a

osteomyelitis, infection of bone tissue, usually occurring in childhood, most commonly caused by *Staphylococcus aureus*. The infectious organism reaches the bone via the bloodstream or by extension from a local injury and produces an inflammation with destruction of the cancellous (porous portion) bone and marrow, loss of blood supply, and bone death. Living bone around the infected area walls it in, forming a sequestrum, the contents of which are gradually resorbed as the lesion is repaired. In chronic osteomyelitis, infection remains active in sequestra, and periodic drainage to the surface via sinus tracts may occur. Symptoms include fever, chills, and severe bone pain; later, swelling and redness may develop around the area of infection. Formerly a disease with high mortality, osteomyelitis today is usually controlled with antibiotics. Osteomyelitis may occur as a complication of many diseases such as typhoid, syphilis, tuberculosis, or sickle cell anemia; in the middle-aged, spinal osteomyelitis may be associated with urinary bladder infection.

·bone diseases and injuries **3**:26e; illus.

osteon, also called HAVERSIAN SYSTEM, the characteristic organizational unit of compact bone. It is quite evident in a cross section of a long bone (*e.g.*, the femur) as a pattern of many groups of concentric circles. At the centre of each group of circles is a longitudinal hollow passage called a haversian canal (after Clopton Havers, a 17th-century English physician). This structure contains small blood vessels responsible for the blood supply to osteocytes (bone cells). The blood vessels arise either in the periosteum or in the marrow cavity. They are connected with the longitudinal haversian canals by means of transverse passages called Volkmann's canals (named for the German physiologist Alfred Volkmann). Both haversian and Volkmann's canals are lined with cells continuous with those of the lining (endosteum) of the marrow cavity.

The haversian canals are surrounded by concentric rings (haversian lamellae) with small chambers called lacunae. The lacunae are the cavities in the bone matrix in which osteocytes are found. The lacunae are connected with others in all three dimensions by minute passages called canaliculi. Nutrients and waste products travel through the canaliculi between the osteocytes of various lamellae and the haversian canal. The extent of the osteon is defined by a line circumscribing the outer lamella called the cementing line. There are no lacunae in the cementing line.

The entire bone is not organized into osteons. Since the osteon is cylindrical, close packing still leaves spaces between osteons. These spaces are filled with remnants of former haversian systems, now called interstitial lamellae. The periphery of the shaft and the area adjacent to the marrow cavity also do not contain haversian systems. The lamellae in each of these regions are concentric with the centre of the marrow cavity and are known as circumferential lamellae.

The structure of the haversian system is closely related to bone development. Since the calcified matrix of bone does not expand, there is no possibility of internal growth for the shafts of long bones; an osteon once formed cannot increase in size. Therefore, all growth must occur by adding new layers on surfaces of bone. The inner layer of the periosteum contains osteogenic cells (capable of bone formation) and blood vessels. As osteogenic cells become osteoblasts (bone-forming cells) they deposit bone matrix on the bone surface, causing ridges and depressions to be formed around blood vessels. The ridges are gradually built up over the blood vessel, eventually enclosing it in a tunnel. The inner surface of the tunnel is the region of the future cementing line. The osteoblasts within the tunnel continue to proliferate and lay down bone matrix. Each time a new layer of osteoblasts is formed the diameter of the haversian canal is decreased and a new lamella develops. The osteoblasts are trapped in lacunae of the bone matrix and become osteocytes. Eventually, the haversian canal space is only slightly larger than the vessel that occupies it. During the formation of the osteon, the blood vessel retains a connection to the periosteum, which runs perpendicular to the haversian lamellae. This passage becomes a Volkmann's canal. If a bone could be dissected into separate osteons, it would be seen that osteons are not all perfect cylinders like a bundle of drinking straws. The pattern of the blood vessels in the periosteum governs the orientation of the forming osteons. Since the vessels branch and do not run in straight lines, the full-formed haversian systems also follow this pattern. *See also* bone remodelling.

·connective tissue types **5**:16g; illus.

osteonecrosis, or NECROSIS OF BONE, death of bone tissue that may be the result of infection, as in osteomyelitis, or deprivation of blood supply, as in fracture, dislocation, caisson disease, or radiation sickness. In all cases, blood circulation in the affected area ceases, bone cells die, and the marrow cavity becomes filled with debris. Surrounding bone reacts to resorb and replace necrotic bone over a period of months or years. When the damage is widespread orthopedic care may be required.

·skeletal abnormalities due to hormones **3**:25c *passim* to 26d

osteopathic medicine 13:765, school of medical practice that places greater emphasis than orthodox medicine upon the relationship between the musculo-skeletal structure and organ function.

The text article surveys the origin and development of osteopathy and covers training in osteopathy, the legal status of osteopathy, and osteopathic research.

osteopenia, in medicine, a condition of low density in bone.

·causes and symptoms **3**:24d *passim* to 25c

osteopetrosis: *see* marble bone disease.

osteoporosis, a disease characterized by insufficient production of bone matrix, the basic material from which bone develops, or by serious reduction in bone calcium content. In acute osteoporosis, large amounts of calcium are excreted in the urine and may lead to grave kidney complications. This disease is most commonly associated with the postmenopausal state in women, when decreased secretion of estrogen (female sex hormone) changes normal metabolic function; but it is also attributed to malnutrition and simple disuse. So osteoporosis can be considered as a disorder of tissue metabolism and only secondarily as a deficiency of calcium and phosphorus.

In osteoporosis, the calcified mass of all bones decreases because bone resorption (normal loss of substance) continues at a regular rate, while formation practically ceases, and thus demand exceeds supply. The body responds to depletion by stimulating osteoblastic (bone-producing) cell activity so that bone mass is restored to some extent but seldom in sufficient quantity. In the malnutrition often associated with eating habits of the elderly, all protein tissues are depleted, and lack of vitamin C results in deficient protoplasm production, thus adding to the natural atrophy, or wasting away, of bone and other tissue that occurs in older persons. Sometimes hyperthyroidism (overactivity of the thyroid gland) will cause osteoporosis in younger people because it increases the rate of metabolism and promotes excessive activity that in turn places added stress on the bones and increases bone tissue depletion. Only rarely is osteoporosis seen in children, and when it appears it is usually the result of serious metabolic disorder.

The disease is most common in women over the age of fifty. The severity of symptoms has little correlation to the amount of osteoporosis seen on X-ray examination. About 50 percent of those patients X-rayed will show grossly decreased bone mass; 30 percent will reveal previously undetected fractures of the vertebrae in the spinal column, but only 10 percent will have experienced pain or other signs related to these fractures. Artificial or surgically induced menopause usually leads to a more severe degree of bone destruction, in which spontaneous fractures of the spine and pelvis are fairly common. Only occasionally are bones of the skull and extremities (arms and legs) involved. Sometimes the disease causes repeated formation of kidney stones.

Osteoporosis requires extended treatment. Usually the disease has been present for a long time before a diagnosis is made. Steroid hormone therapy, which stimulates bone formation, is effective, and the combination of female (estrogen) and male (androgen) hormone therapy in suitable ratio also stimulates normal bone tissue regrowth without unwanted side effects. High-protein diet and increased fluid intake is helpful in improving general good health and prevents, to some degree, kidney function complications. There is some evidence that strontium lactate, a compound found in milk, increases the mineralization of bone matrix. Some studies indicate that a diet high in calcium, phosphorus, and vitamin D helps, but there is no evidence that this stimulates bone cell growth.

It is not known to what extent the atrophy that accompanies old age is caused by underfunction of the hormone-producing glands (gonads). This underfunction may be a factor in osteoporosis, for a higher incidence of that disease occurs at an earlier age in women than in men, who usually experience much later in life a climacteric—the group of physical and mental changes associated with decreased sexual activity in old age.

Patients suffering from osteoporosis are usually instructed to avoid inactivity and immobilization. Generally, however, they wear a brace or other device to provide adequate support to the pelvis and back, thus preventing vertebral collapse and spontaneous fractures.

·aging's effect on skeletal system **1**:308g
·atrophy of bone in aging process **2**:352e
·biomedical models, table 1 **5**:866
·endocrine system disorders **6**:818e
·idiopathic bone disease **3**:25g
·intersexuality's physical traits **15**:698d
·nutritional calcium deficiency **13**:418g
·racial propensity for bone degeneration **15**:354f

osteosarcoma, or OSTEOGENIC SARCOMA, the most common bone-forming malignant tumour of bone, affects males more than females, occurs mostly under age 30, and affects mainly the large long bones, with a predilection for the knee area. Major symptoms include pain (intermittent, at first, later severe and constant), swelling, limitation of joint motion, a high frequency of pathological fractures, and eventually fever and general debilitation. Metastases occur early and death usually results from the spread of the disease to the lung. The average length of life after diagnosis is 18 months; the five-year survival rate is less than 10 percent. Treatment usually involves amputation of the affected limb. Osteosarcoma that occurs over age 50 is frequently associated with Paget's disease of bone (*q.v.*). *See also* tumours, bone-related.

osteosclerosis, abnormal density or hardening of bone.

·bone structure changes **3**:24f

Osteostraci, order of extinct fishes (class Agnatha) with one nostril and the head and gills enclosed in a bony shield.

·characteristics and classification **7**:340d; illus. 339
·fossils, eras, and traits **7**:568c
·general features of Agnatha **1**:311b

osteosynthesis (medicine): *see* internal fixation.

Österbotten in Swedish, POHJANMAA in Finnish, lowland plain covering about 70 percent of Vaasan *lääni* (Vaasa province), southwestern Finland, along the Gulf of Bothnia. Also known as the Ostrobothnian plain, Österbotten is about 60 mi (100 km) wide and 160 mi long. It consists of flat, sand- and clay-soil plains broken by rivers and bog areas. It is drained mainly by the Lapuanjoki, Kyrönjoki, and Isojoki (rivers), which flow to the Gulf of Bothnia. The lowlands are divided between agricultural developments and forested areas. The Swedish-speaking rural farmers produce turnips, winter wheat, and hay. Dairy cattle are also raised. The pine forests, which cover approximately 65 percent of the region, have not been exploited to any great extent. The city of Vaasa (*q.v.*) is the primary port and economic centre for the area. Kokkola and Jakobstad (*qq.v.*; Pietasaari) also serve as important ports. Seinäjoki is the main city of the Österbotten's inner region. It has extensive road and rail linkage to the port cities mentioned above and with the remainder of Finland.

·map, Finland **7**:304

Østerdalen, narrow valley of southeast Norway, in Hedmark *fylke* (county). It extends in a general north–south orientation from the eastern flanks of the Dovrefjell (Dovre Mountains) and is approximately 75 mi (120 km) long. The Glåma, Norway's longest river, flows through the valley. Lumbering, agriculture (grains, hay), and livestock raising are principal economic activities. Rena, at the junction of the Rena and Glåma rivers near the valley's south end, has paper and cardboard mills, powered by hydroelectricity from dams on the Glåma. Other places of importance in the valley are Tynset and Alvdal, which are *herredskommuner* (rural municipalities), and Koppang. The area has been continuously inhabited since the Stone Age. Fine fishing in the Glåma attracts many tourists.

Östergötland, *län* (county) of southeastern Sweden, between Vättern (lake) and the Baltic Sea. It has an area of 4,079 sq mi (10,566 sq km) and consists of the *landskap* (province) of Östergötland and a small part of that of Södermanland. Lakes dot the countryside, which is drained by the Motala Ström (stream) and other rivers. Although partly wooded, it supports agriculture; mineral deposits include iron, zinc, and copper, and industries range from textile weaving to stone quarrying. Most of the major towns, including Linköping, the capital, are in the lowland crossed by the Göta Kanal. Pop. (1970) 382,205.

·area and population table **17**:846
·map, Sweden **17**:848

Österhaninge, *socken* (parish) in the *län* (county) of Stockholm, east central Sweden, on Södertörn, the easternmost peninsula of the *landskap* (province) of Södermanland, just south of Stockholm. Encompassing the communities of Handen, Vega, Jordbro, Vendelsö, Sandemar, Årsta, Tyresta, Söderby, and

Stegsholm, it stretches from Drevviken (lake) on the north to the Gulf of Bothnia on the south and includes Gålö, an island in the Stockholm archipelago, separated from the mainland by Horsfjärden (bay). Except for open, level land in the southwest, the parish consists mostly of rolling, forested heights, making it an attractive residential area for Stockholm and environs, with which it has excellent rail and bus connections. Outstanding recreational facilities are found at Årsta and Tyresta and on Gålö, where the University of Stockholm maintains an ecological station. In the northeastern part, at Stegsholm, there is an agricultural school. Among the historic buildings in the area is a medieval church, a rectangular granite structure dating from the 13th century. Pop. (1970) 29,485.

Osterman, Andrey Ivanovich, Count, originally HEINRICH JOHANN FRIEDRICH OSTERMAN (b. July 9, 1687, Bochum, Westphalia, now in West Germany—d. June 11 [May 31, old style], 1747, Berëzovo, Siberia), statesman who dominated the conduct of Russia's foreign affairs from 1725 to 1740. Having come to Russia in 1704, Osterman was appointed by Peter I the Great to be an interpreter for the Russian Foreign Office (1708) and was given the rank of secretary in 1710. He assisted in negotiating a peace settlement with the Turks in 1711 and subsequently played a major role in the peace conferences with Sweden (1718 and 1721) that preceded the conclusion of the Great Northern War (1721). In 1723 he signed a treaty with Persia by which Russia gained some territory along the shore of the Caspian Sea, including the cities of Baku and Derbent. For these diplomatic successes Osterman was made a baron and vice president of the Foreign Office.

Osterman, engraving by an unknown artist after a portrait by I. Argunov
Novosti Press Agency

After Peter died and Catherine I ascended the throne (1725), Osterman became vice chancellor, a member of the Supreme Privy Council (which became the effective ruling body of Russia), postmaster general, and president of a special commission for commerce. Thus he became involved in the state's economic and financial concerns as well as master of its foreign affairs. He maintained his influence during the reign of Peter II (ruled 1727–30), and, as a reward for helping Anna Ivanovna retain her autocratic powers when she became empress (1730), he was made a count and Anna's "first cabinet minister" (1731). During Anna's reign (1730–40) Osterman strictly adhered to an alliance with Austria, guided Russia through the War of Polish Succession (1733–38) and the Russo-Turkish War of 1736–39, concluded an Anglo-Russian commercial treaty in 1734, and generally raised Russia's prestige as a European power. But he was obliged to return some territory to Persia in 1732 and gained only a strip of steppe land between the Bug and Donets rivers for Russia as a result of the Turkish war.

After Anna died, Osterman helped his colleague Burkhard Münnich overthrow Ernst Biron, the regent for the infant emperor Ivan VI (Nov. 19–20 [Nov. 8–9, O.S.], 1740); Osterman then became admiral general. But after he and Münnich quarrelled and thereby weakened the ruling clique, the French ambassador, who strongly objected to Osterman's persistently pro-Austrian policy, intrigued with Elizabeth, the daughter of Peter the Great. On Dec. 6 (Nov. 25, O.S.), 1741, they overthrew Ivan, the regent Princess Anna Leopoldovna, and their chief advisers, including Osterman, who was banished to Siberia.

Osterode, also called OSTERODE AM HARZ, town, Niedersachsen (Lower Saxony) *Land* (state), northeastern West Germany, at the southwest foot of the Oberharz (Upper Harz mountains) northeast of Göttingen. The residence of the dukes of Braunschweig-Grubenhagen in the 14th–15th centuries, it has numerous medieval half-timbered houses and buildings. The 16th-century market church and the town hall (1552) are notable. The sculptor Tilman Riemenschneider was born in the town (*c.* 1460). Osterode, near the Naturpark Harz and the Söse River reservoir, is a popular resort and manufactures chemicals, textiles, machinery, and furniture. Pop. (1970 est.) 16,757.
51°43′ N, 10°14′ E
·map, Federal Republic of Germany **8**:46

Österreichischer Werkbund (artists' association): *see* Deutscher Werkbund.

Österreichische Volkspartei, English AUSTRIAN PEOPLE'S PARTY, Catholic political party of Austria appealing to farmers and businessmen. Since 1945 it has been one of the two main parties, governing for 20 years in coalition with the Socialist Party. From 1966 to 1970 it had a majority in the national assembly and formed the government. In the 1970 elections it yielded control to the Socialists.

Östersund, town, seat of the *län* (county) of Jämtland, northwestern Sweden, on the west shore of Storsjön (lake). It was founded in 1786 by King Gustav III. Although primarily an agricultural and tourist centre, it has some industry, producing chemicals, machinery, furniture, and leather goods. The Jämtland Läns Museum houses archaeological and cultural exhibits; Fornbyn Jämtli is an open-air museum of many 15th–18th-century buildings from the area, notably Pilgrimsstugan (1424). Near the bridge that connects the town with Frösön, an island in Storsjön, is Sweden's northernmost runic stone, dating from the 11th century and telling of Jämtland's conversion to Christianity. Pop. (1970) 49,588.
63°11′ N, 14°39′ E
·map, Sweden **17**:848

Ostertagia, a genus of parasitic worm of the order Strongylorida (class Nematoda).
·parasitic diseases of animals, table 2 **5**:870

Østfold, *fylke* (county), extreme southeast Norway, extending from Oslofjorden (west) to the Swedish border (east). Its total area is 1,614 sq mi (4,180 sq km). The hilly landscape, with forests to the north and east, rises gradually to about 800–1,000 ft (240 m–300 m). The principal rivers are the Glåma (*q.v.*) and the Tistedalselva, flowing north–south through the glaciated topography. The Glåma, longest river of Norway, discharges into the Skagerrak at Fredrikstad. The *fylke*, smallest in Norway (except for the independent urban communes of Oslo and Bergen) is perhaps the nation's oldest inhabited region. Rock drawings and mounds throughout the area are relics of the Stone Age, and numerous stone churches date from shortly after Norway's conversion to Christianity in the 10th and 11th centuries AD. Østfold is, in its economy, essentially suburban to Oslo; the chief towns—Moss (the county seat), Fredrikstad, Sarpsborg, and Halden—are all within 60 mi (100 km) of Oslo, the nation's capital. These communities engage in manufacturing (wood products, pulp, chemicals, rubber) and food processing. Moss and Fredrikstad have important shipyards. The rural areas of the south produce large quantities of vegetables and dairy products for the Oslo market. Østfold's coast and offshore islets are a popular resort area. Pop. (1971 est.) 221,386.
·area and population table **13**:265
·map, Norway **13**:266

Ostfriesische Inseln (West Germany): *see* East Frisian Islands.

Ostia, modern OSTIA ANTICA, Italy, ancient Roman military base at the mouth of the Tiber; it was a port of republican Rome and a commercial centre under the empire (after 27 BC). The Romans considered Ostia their first colony and attributed its founding to their fourth king, Ancus Marcius (7th century BC). Archaeologists have found on the site a fort of the mid-4th century BC but nothing older.

Ruins of a Roman colony, Ostia, Italy
Authenticated News International

Ostia became a naval station and a major fleet base during the Punic Wars (264–201). It was the major port for republican Rome until its harbour, partly obstructed by a sandbar, became inadequate for large vessels. During the empire Ostia was a commercial and storage centre for Rome's grain supplies and a service station for vessels going to Portus (*see* Portus). At the height of Ostia's prosperity in the early 2nd century AD, its population was approximately 50,000. New buildings included tall brick apartment buildings and numerous temples. Ostia suffered from the decline of the Roman economy beginning in the 3rd century, and barbarian raids of the 5th and following centuries. It was abandoned after the erection of Gregoriopolis, site of Ostia Antica, by Pope Gregory IV (827–844). Although the Roman ruins were quarried for building materials in the middle ages and for sculptors' marble in the Renaissance, about two-thirds of the Roman town, after long archaeological excavation, can now be seen.
·mosaic art examples **12**:467e; illus.
·Tiber navigation problems **18**:372e

ostinato (Italian: "obstinate"), in music, short melodic phrase repeated throughout a composition, sometimes slightly varied or transposed to a different pitch. Ostinati appear from time to time in Western compositions from the 13th century onward, as in the motet *Emendemus in melius* (*Let Us Change for the Better*), by Cristóbal de Morales (*c.* 1500–53), and in the *Concerto*, Opus 38 (first performed, 1925), of Paul Hindemith (1895–1963). Use of an ostinato was particularly common in 16th-century dance pieces, notably in the bass line, where it is called a basso ostinato, or ground bass (*q.v.*).
A rhythmic ostinato is a short, constantly repeated rhythmic pattern.
·concerto grosso variation forms **4**:1068g
·Southeast Asian musical antiquity **17**:238c
·strophic variation forms **12**:727a
·structural integration for complexity **12**:717b

ostium, in anatomy, opening into a passageway or chamber, such as the openings in the arthropod heart; those on the surface of a sponge that regulate the flow of water and capture food; and the openings of the fallopian tube from the ovary (*q.v.*).
·mucus drainage in human sinus **16**:807a
·sponge adaptations for water transport **14**:851c; illus. 852

Østlandet, unofficial traditional region, southeastern Norway, embracing the *fylker* (counties) of Østfold, Akershus, Hedmark, Oppland, Buskerud, Vestfold, Telemark, and Oslo. With an area of 36,550 sq mi (94,663 sq km), it ranges from the highest mountains in Norway, Jotunheimen, to coastal lowlands adjacent to the Skagerrak and Oslofjorden. The region is quite mountainous, especially in the western and northern parts, and is heavily forested. The eastern part is the centre of Norway's timbering industry. The area is drained through great valleys—by the Hallingdelselvi, Lågen, and Glåma rivers (the Glåma is the longest in Norway)—into Oslofjorden. Many lakes, including the Mjøsa, the largest in Norway, are located in the region.

The numerous cities and towns—including Oslo, the national capital—give Østlandet nearly one-half of Norway's population; it has much of the country's industrial capacity as well. The mountain scenery, winter-sports areas, summer resorts along the lakes and coasts, and the city of Oslo make Østlandet a popular tourist destination. Transportation routes crisscross the lowlands and penetrate the interior via the valleys, rivers, and lakes. Pop. (1971 est.) 1,910,039.
·settlement and economic activity **13**:264b

Ostomidae: *see* bark-gnawing beetle.

Ostpolitik, foreign policy formulated by Willy Brandt, who became West Germany's chancellor in 1969. In conjunction with this policy, which aimed at improving Germany's relations with its Communist neighbours, West Germany signed treaties with the Soviet Union (August 1970) and Poland (December 1970) and sought improved relations with East Germany.
·German relations with the East **8**:124g
·Polish boundary settlement **14**:654e

Ostraciontidae: *see* boxfish.

ostracism, political practice in ancient Athens whereby a prominent citizen who threatened the stability of the state could be banished without bringing any charge against him. (A similar device existed at various times in Argos, Miletus, Syracuse, and Megara.) At a fixed meeting in midwinter, the people decided, without debate, whether they would hold a vote on ostracism (*ostrakophoria*) some weeks later. Any citizen entitled to vote in the assembly could write another citizen's name down, and, when a sufficiently large number wrote the same name, the ostracized man had to leave Attica within 10 days and stay away for 10 years. He remained owner of his property. Ostracism must be carefully distinguished from exile (*q.v.*) in the Roman sense, which involved loss of property and status and was for an indefinite period (generally for life).

Ostracism is said by Aristotle, in his *Constitution of Athens,* to have been introduced by Cleisthenes in his reform of the Athenian constitution after the expulsion of Hippias (*c.* 508 BC), but the first use of it seems to have been made in 488–487 BC, when Hipparchus, son of Charmus of Collytus, was ostracized. After Hipparchus, four more men, the last of them being Aristides, were ostracized before the amnesty in 481, preceding the invasion of Xerxes I. The institution was invoked less frequently after the Persian Wars, falling into disuse after it was used ineffectively, probably in 417, to resolve the political impasse caused by the rivalry of Nicias and Alcibiades.
·introduction of measure **8**:344f

Ostracoda: *see* mussel shrimp.

ostracoderm, a small, extinct, fishlike Paleozoic vertebrate, members of which belonged to several orders particularly abundant in Late Silurian and Early Devonian formations of Europe and North America (about 400,000,000 years ago).

Jaws were not yet developed, and paired appendages were often absent. These are primitive characteristics that show that they were allied to the living Cyclostomata—hagfish and lampreys—with which they are often grouped to form the vertebrate class Agnatha. Ostracoderms carried bony armour; internal bony areas also are sometimes present.

There are three major orders: Osteostraci, Anaspida, and Heterostraci. In the Osteostraci (Cephalaspid-like form), such as *Cephalaspis*, the head and the gill region were covered by a broad crescent-shaped shield of bone. Dorsally, there were paired orbits, a median eye, and, anterior to this (as in lampreys), a median opening leading to the nasal organ and hypophysis. Areas of small checkered, or tessellated, plates, to which large nerves led, are thought to represent electric organs or pressure-sense organs. The "head" region is ossified internally; delicate dissection and sectioning has revealed cavities for brain, nerves, and blood vessels of a pattern broadly comparable to that of lampreys. The underside of the head region was covered by a series of small plates with about 10 round gill openings at either margin. The mouth was small. Internally there was a large branchial or gill chamber; the animal appears to have been a filter feeder after the fashion of lower chordates. In many osteostracans, there were paired structures behind the shield in the position of pectoral fins.

The Anaspida include small spindle-shaped (or fusiform) fishes with a narrower and deeper form than that of osteostracans. There was no expanded head shield, and this region was covered by a series of small oat-shaped scales. No internal structures are known, but the pattern of openings for sense organs and gills was similar to that of the Osteostraci.

In the Heterostraci (Pteraspid-like form), the anterior part of the longer, slender body was enclosed in a set of large plates that were fused to a variable degree. In contrast with the other two orders of the group, the small paired eyes were laterally placed. There was no dorsal nostril opening; the nares may have been paired and placed at the corners of the mouth opening. The mouth was a transverse ventral slit, bounded posteriorly by small, movable plates, suggesting a mud-grubbing mode of feeding. No internal structures have been preserved, but impressions inside the plates indicate the presence of large gill chambers. There was a single external gill opening on either side. Possibly related to the Heterostraci are *Thelodus* and other genera, in which no plates or large scales were present; instead, the whole body was covered with minute scales.
·Agnatha evolution illus. **1**:310
·Devonian fish evolution **5**:675h
·fossils, eras, and traits **7**:568b

ostracon, potshard or limestone flake used in antiquity, especially by the ancient Egyptians,

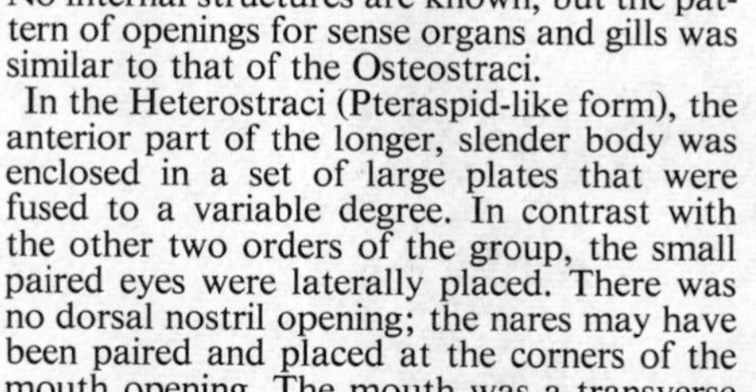

Limestone ostracon with a drawing of a cat bringing a boy before a mouse magistrate, New Kingdom Egypt, 20th dynasty (1200–1085 BC); in the Oriental Institute, University of Chicago

By courtesy of the Oriental Institute, University of Chicago

Greeks, and Hebrews, as a surface for drawings or sketches, or as an alternative to papyrus for writing as well as for calculating accounts.

Of considerable artistic merit, the drawings on ostraca, which are usually coloured, depict scenes from nature and everyday life or scenes in which animals seem to parody human actions (it has been conjectured that the latter illustrated popular fables).
·New Testament inscription and letter classification **2**:942g

Ostrava, city, Severomoravský *kraj* (Northern Moravia region), Czechoslovakia, between the Ostravice and Oder rivers above their confluence at the southern edge of the Upper Silesian coalfield. It was founded *c.* 1267 as a fortified town by Bruno, bishop of Olomouc, to protect the entry to Moravia from the north. Its castle was demolished in 1495. Historic buildings include the 13th-century St. Wenceslas' Church and the Old Town Hall tower (1687).

Called the iron heart of Czechoslovakia, it is surrounded by a rich, black-coal basin that has made it a centre of heavy industry, with a long tradition dating from 1830, when the first blast furnace was built at the Vítkovice ironworks. Some of the coal pits extend into the city limits, and their derricks are common features of the skyline.

The conurbation of Greater Ostrava occupies an area of more than 400 sq mi (1,000 sq km). The region receives a steady influx of workers, and many housing estates and new towns, such as Poruba and Havířov, have been built there. Most planned development is east of the Ostravice River, in Slezská Ostrava (the Silesian part of Ostrava). Settlements west of the Ostravice are in Moravská (Moravian) Ostrava.

The population of the region is employed predominantly in mining (at Ostrava, Karviná, Orlová) and in metalworking (at Vítkovice, Kunčice, Třinec). Manufactures also include mining machinery at Opava, railway cars at Studénka, and automobiles at Kopřivnice. The coal mining also supports chemical (ammonia and nitrate fertilizers) and power industries.

Ostrava is linked by rail and road to all parts of Czechoslovakia and Poland. It is on the electrified rail line, and the Ostrava airport operates services to Prague. The city has several theatres, including a fine opera house, a philharmonic orchestra, and an art gallery. Pop. (1970 prelim.) city, 278,737; (latest est.) Greater Ostrava 520,000.
49°50′ N, 18°17′ E
·map, Czechoslovakia **5**:412
·population and area **5**:414d

Ostrava-Karviná coalfields, in northeastern Moravia, Czechoslovakia.
·output and reserves **5**:415h

Ostrea: *see* oyster.

ostrich (*Struthio camelus*), largest living bird, flightless and found in Africa. It belongs to the family Struthionidae, order Struthioniformes. The adult male may be 2.5 metres (nearly 8 feet) tall—almost half of its height is neck—and weight 155 kilograms (345 pounds); the female is somewhat smaller. The ostrich's egg, averaging about 150 millimetres (6 inches) in length by 125 millimetres (5 inches) in diameter and weighing up to 1.35 kilograms (3 pounds), is presently the world's largest. The male is mostly black but has white plumes in the wings and tail; females are mostly brown. The head and most of the neck, reddish to bluish in colour, is lightly downed; the legs, including the powerful thighs, are naked. The head is small, the bill short and ducklike; the big brown eyes have thick black lashes.

The ostrich lives in flocks of 5 to 50, usually

in the company of grazing animals. The ostrich relies on its strong legs—uniquely two-toed, with the main toe developed almost as a hoof—to escape its enemies, chiefly man and the larger carnivores. A frightened ostrich can achieve a speed of 65 kilometres per hour (40 miles per hour). If cornered it can deliver dangerous kicks.

Ostriches live mainly on plant matter but take some animal food; they can go without water for long periods. Breeding males emit roars and hisses as they fight for a harem of three to five hens. The communal nest scraped in the ground may contain 15 to 60 shiny, whitish eggs. The male sits by night; the females take turns by day. The chicks hatch in about 40 days and when a month old can keep up with running adults. To escape detection, chicks as well as adults may lie on the ground with neck outstretched; a habit that may have given rise to the legend that the ostrich buries its head in the sand when danger threatens. Ostrich plumes adorned the helmets of medieval European knights, and, in the 19th century, such plumes were sold for women's finery. This demand led to the establishment of ostrich farms in South Africa, the southern U.S., Australia, and elsewhere, but the trade collapsed after World War I. The hide provides a soft, fine-grained leather. Ostriches have been trained for saddle and sulky racing, but they are bad-tempered and tire easily. They do well in captivity and may live 50 years.

Ostriches (*Struthio camelus*); at left is male

David C. Houston—Bruce Coleman Ltd.

The ostrich is typical of a special group of flightless birds (*see* ratite). The forms, differing slightly in skin colour, size, and egg features, formerly were considered separate species but are merely races of *S. camelus*. Most familiar is the North African ostrich, *S. c. camelus*, ranging, in much reduced numbers, from Morocco to The Sudan; the Syrian ostrich, *S.c. syriacus*, of Syria and Arabia became extinct in 1941. Fossil ostriches are known from lower Pliocene rock (about 7,000,000 years old) from southern Russia, India, and north central China. Parasitology suggests that the ostrich may have originated in South America: it and the rhea carry a louse found on no other birds.

·evolutionary vestiges of flight **7**:9b
·fashion use of plumes **5**:1028g

ostrich feather, in Egyptian religion, amulet signifying truth, justice, and order. The amulet's purpose was perhaps to serve as an aid to its wearer at death, when his heart would be weighed against an ostrich feather. It was the emblem both of Shu (the god of light, air, and supporter of the sky) and of Maat (the goddess of truth and justice), but other gods often

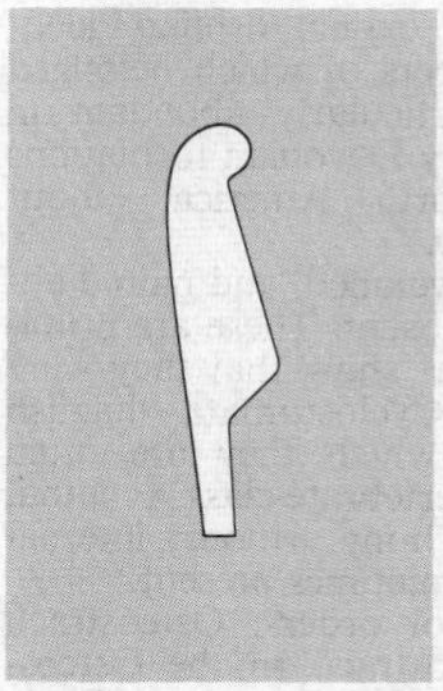

Ostrich feather

were portrayed wearing the ostrich feather in combination with some other head ornament.

Ostrihom (Hungary): *see* Esztergom.

Ostrogorsky, Moisey (Yakovlevich) (b. 1854, Grodno—d. 1919), Russian political scientist known for his pioneering study of comparative party organization. Ostrogorsky studied law at St. Petersburg, and after working for a number of years in the Russian Ministry of Justice studied at the École Libre des Sciences Politiques in Paris until 1885. He produced histories of Russia that were used in schools and, as a result of his studies in Paris, wrote in French a treatise on the rights of women in public law in 1892.

Ostrogorsky spent many years in the United States and Britain where he studied political parties, his major scholarly concern. In 1902 he published *Democracy and the Organization of Political Parties* (originally written in French). Having returned to Russia he was elected to the first Duma in 1906 and played a major role in the caucus of his Constitutional Democratic Party, but left active politics after its dissolution.

Although Ostrogorsky's work included such things as a recommendation that political parties be replaced by single issue leagues and a belief in an atomic and rational citizenry that would make possible democracy, which he defined as the unmediated and pure rule of the people, he also made many realistic and productive contributions to political analysis and influenced several serious students of politics. He showed the pathological tendencies of democratic mass parties toward bureaucratic-oligarchic organization, a theme that has been developed by his successors. He made the first major effort at comparative analysis of political systems through his studies of the U.S. and Britain. He presented a detailed and authoritative account of the party systems in the two societies. Finally, he offered valuable hypotheses about electoral behaviour and the formation of opinion.

Ostrogoths (Germanic people): *see* Goths.

Ostrov, resort village in the Moravian Karst (*q.v.*), Czechoslovakia. It lies in a picturesque region of limestone formations. Latest pop. est. 1,893.
50°17′ N, 12°57′ E
·map, Czechoslovakia **5**:412

Ostrovsky, Aleksandr Nikolayevich (b. April 12 [March 31, old style], 1823, Moscow —d. June 14 [June 2, O.S.], 1886, Slykovo), Russian dramatist who is generally considered the greatest representative of the Russian realistic period.

Ostrovsky; detail of an oil painting by V.G. Perov, 1871; in the State Tretyakov Gallery, Moscow

State Tretyakov Gallery, Moscow

From 1843 to 1848 Ostrovsky was employed as clerk at the Moscow juvenile court. He wrote his first play, *Kartiny semeynogo schastya* ("Scenes of Family Happiness") in 1847. His next play, *Bankrot* ("The Bankrupt"), later renamed *Svoi lyudi sochtemsya* (Eng. trans., *It's a Family Affair, We'll Settle It Among Ourselves, 1917*), written in 1850, provoked an outcry because it exposed bogus bankruptcy cases among Moscow merchants and brought about Ostrovsky's dismissal from the civil service. The play was banned for 13 years.

Ostrovsky wrote several historical plays in the 1860s. His main dramatic work, however, was concerned with the Russian merchant class and included two tragedies and numerous comedies. His *Snegurochka* (1873; "The Snow Maiden") was adapted as an opera by Rimsky-Korsakov in 1880–81.

Ostrovsky was closely associated with the Maly ("Little") Theatre, Moscow's only dramatic state theatre, where all his plays were first performed under his supervision. He was first president of the Society of Russia Playwrights, founded on his initiative in 1874, and in 1885 became artistic director of the Moscow imperial theatres.

·Russian literature of the 19th century **10**:1208h

Ostrovsky, Nikolay (1904–36), Soviet author.
·Soviet Union cultural history **17**:353g

Ostrov Vrangelya (Russian S.F.S.R.): *see* Wrangel Island.

Ostrowiec Świętokrzyski, town, Kielce *województwo* (province), southeastern Poland, on the Kamienna River, a tributary of the Vistula. It lies in the Wyżyna Małopolska (Polish Uplands) just north of the Góry Świętokrzyskie (Holy Cross Mountains), is noted for its iron industry, and has road connections with Lublin and Kielce. The town began *c.* the 15th century, developing during the 19th century after the establishment of its ironworks. Other industries include food processing and the production of ceramics and building materials. Pop. (1970 prelim.) 50,000.
50°57′ N, 21°23′ E
·map, Poland **14**:626

Ostrów Wielkopolski, capital of a *powiat* (county), Poznań *województwo* (province), west central Poland. A rail junction and indus-

trial town, it produces machine tools and railroad cars, lumber, ceramics, and textiles. The town, which lies in the south of the great Polish plain, was first chronicled in the 13th century but received municipal rights only in the 18th. It passed to Prussia in 1793 and was returned to Poland in 1918. Pop. (1970 prelim.) 49,500.
51°39′ N, 17°49′ E
·map, Poland **14**:626

Ostrya (tree): *see* hop-hornbeam.

Ostryopsis (tree): *see* Betulaceae.

Ostsee (Europe): *see* Baltic Sea.

Ostuni, town, Brindisi province, Puglia (Apulia) region, southern Italy. It has a 15th-century cathedral with an unusual Gothic facade. Local commerce is mainly agricultural. Pop. (1971 prelim.) mun., 31,488.
40°44′ N, 17°35′ E

Ostwald, Wilhelm (b. Sept. 2, 1853, Riga, now in the Latvian S.S.R.—d. April 4, 1932, near Leipzig, now in East Germany), chemist who almost solely organized physical chemistry into a nearly independent branch of chemistry and who won the 1909 Nobel Prize for Chemistry for his work on catalysis, chemical equilibrium, and reaction velocities. Strongly philosophical in his approach to science, he preferred energy as the explanation for all physical phenomena and refused to believe in atoms.

Wilhelm Ostwald
Bavaria-Verlag

He took his doctorate from the University of Dorpat (now in Tartu, Estonian S.S.R.) in 1878 and taught at Riga before going to the University of Leipzig (1887–1906). He was quick to espouse the theories of Svante August Arrhenius and Jacobus Henricus van't Hoff, with whom he placed physical chemistry on a firm basis. It was probably as author and editor, however, that he most helped to advance the science. He wrote *Lehrbuch der allgemeinen Chemie* (2 vol., 1885–87; "Textbook of General Chemistry"), and other influential texts, and was chiefly responsible for the founding (1887) of the *Zeitschrift für physikalische Chemie* ("Journal of Physical Chemistry"), long the most influential publication in the field. In 1889 he began issuing an important series of reprints of significant papers in physics and chemistry that had appeared up to that time.

He began his laboratory researches with studies on the dynamics of reactions in solution, and then turned to electrochemistry. In 1894 he gave the first modern definition of a catalyst and turned his attention to catalytic reactions. His process for the conversion of ammonia to nitric acid, patented in 1902, became of great industrial importance.

Following his resignation from the University of Leipzig, he wrote on the philosophy of science and, in the book *Grosse Männer* (1909; "Great Men"), he investigated the psychological causes of scientific productivity. He published a three-volume autobiography (1926–27). Toward the end of his life one of his many activities, painting, led him to investigate colour from physical and psychological viewpoints.

·acid–base theory development **1**:46a
·catalysis and reaction equilibrium **3**:1000h
·Positivist rejection of atomic theory **14**:878c
·science as rational panacea **16**:391g

Ostwald, (Carl Wilhelm) Wolfgang (1883–1943), German chemist who devoted his career to the study of colloid chemistry.

Ostyak language: *see* Khanty language.

Ostyaks and Voguls, also known respectively as KHANTS and MANSI, western Siberian peoples, living mainly in the Ob River Basin; they are grouped together as the Ob-Ugrians, for they belong to the Ugric branch of the Uralic language family. They are descended from people from the south Ural steppe who moved into this region about the middle of the 1st millennium AD. Although the term Ostyak has been applied to other groups, in precise usage it refers only to the Khants.

The Ostyaks and the Voguls have the same kind of habitat, economy, organization, and traditions. Their principal sources of subsistence are hunting (traditionally with bows and arrows and spears, later with guns), trapping, and fishing (with nets, weirs, seines, and traps); reindeer herding was usually a subsidiary occupation and was probably borrowed from the neighbouring Nentsy in the 15th century. The Ob-Ugrians traditionally had either nomadic-type or settled dwellings according to their subsistence pattern. At summer hunting sites they generally lived in tents; their permanent winter homes were wooden huts. Boats, skis, and some horse or reindeer sleds provided transportation.

The Ostyaks and the Voguls were formerly divided into tribes consisting of local territorial groupings. Each individual, regardless of tribe, belonged to one of two phratries, and was expected to marry outside his phratry. A phratry consisted of several clans, each with a name or names of an ancestor or ancestor hero, a sign or brand to identify clan property, internal organization, an ancestor cult, and a sacred site.

Under Soviet administration the Ostyaks and the Voguls have been settled on collective farms. In addition to the development of the aboriginal economy, such new forms as animal husbandry, fur farming, and agriculture have been introduced.

·cultural patterns and social structure **6**:132g
·culture and present conditions **16**:725a
·economy, physical type, and origin **1**:1127a; map 1124
·geographic distribution map **2**:194
·religio-cultural history **7**:310c
·shamanic healing rituals **16**:640c
·Soviet Union nationalities distribution **17**:333c; table 338
·Ural Mountains traditional cultures **18**:1034a

O'Sullivan, Timothy H. (b. *c.* 1840, New York City—d. Jan. 14, 1882, Staten Island), photographer best known for his Civil War subjects and for his landscapes of the American West. He learned photography at Mathew B. Brady's gallery in New York, and during the Civil War he photographed on many fronts as one of the team sent out by Brady. On two occasions his camera was knocked down by shell fragments. One of his best known pictures, "Harvest of Death," showing Confederate dead at Gettysburg, was taken in the early morning of July 4, 1863. From 1867 to 1869 he was official photographer on the United States Geological Survey of the 40th Parallel, which began at Virginia City, Nev. (where he photographed the mines), and worked eastward. In 1870 he went to Panama as part of a team to survey for a canal across the isthmus. In 1871, 1873, and 1874 he was associated with a series of surveys in southwestern U.S. On the recommendation of Brady and Alexander Gardner, another Washington, D.C. photographer, he was appointed chief photographer for the Department of Treasury in 1880.

Timothy H. O'Sullivan in Panama, 1870, self-portrait (detail of a stereograph)
By courtesy of the George Eastman House, Rochester, New York

·historic and scenic photography **14**:313g; illus.

O'Sullivan, William (1931–), U.S. physicist.
·Echo communication satellite development **16**:262b

Osumi, Japanese satellite put into orbit on Feb. 11, 1970.
·launching and characteristics **17**:366a; table 364

Ōsumi-guntō, archipelago, Kagoshima Prefecture (*ken*), Japan, lying south of the Ōsumi-hantō (Ōsumi Peninsula) of Kyushu. It consists of the two larger islands of Tanega-shima (Tanega Island) and Yaku-shima and several smaller isles, with a combined area of about 475 sq mi (1,230 sq km). The chief town is Nishinoomote on the northwest coast of Tanega-shima. In 1543 the Portuguese landed on Tanega-shima and introduced the first guns into Japan. Pop. (1970) 121,685.

Osuna, town, Sevilla province, Andalusia, southern Spain, at the foot of a hill at the edge of an extensive plain, east-southeast of Sevilla city. Of Iberian origin, the town became the Roman Urso. It supported Pompey against Julius Caesar, who later made it a colony. In the Middle Ages it was known as Ursona or Orsona, and the Muslims called it Oxuna. Conquered by Ferdinand III (the Saint) in 1240, it came eventually to the Giron family. In 1562, Pedro Tellez Giron, 5th count of Ureña, was created 1st duke of Osuna. The town was prosperous in the 17th and 18th centuries. The many fine 16th- to 18th-century buildings include the Capilla (chapel) del Santo Sepulcro, where the dukes of Osuna are buried, and the Colegiata (Collegiate Church; 1534–39), with a Baroque portal of the "Crucifixion" by José de Ribera. The former university (1549–1820) now houses the Instituto Nacional de Enseñanza Media, a high school.

Agriculture is the main occupation; but flour, olive oil, unslaked lime, and gypsum are produced, and esparto is processed. Pop. (1970) 21,669.
37°14′ N, 5°07′ W
·map, Spain **17**:382

Osu promontory, site of Christianborg castle in Accra, Ghana.

Oswald, Saint (b. *c.* 605—d. 641, Maserfeld, probably present-day Oswestry, Shropshire), Anglo-Saxon king of Northumbria from 633 to 641; he restored Christianity to his kingdom and gained ascendancy over most of England. His father, King Aethelfrith (died 616), had united the two ancient Northumbrian kingdoms of Bernicia and Deira. Expelled from Northumbria upon the accession of his uncle Edwin in 616, Oswald and his brother

Oswiu took refuge in Iona in the Hebrides, where they were converted to Christianity.

After Edwin was killed fighting King Cadwallae of Gwynedd (in northern Wales) and Penda of Mercia in 632, Northumbria was again divided into two parts, and the Northumbrian Church collapsed. The next year Oswald defeated and killed Cadwallae near Hexham (in present-day Northumberland). He then ascended the Northumbrian throne, united his kingdom, and asserted his authority over all the peoples of southern England. In order to revive the church, he brought the Celtic monk Aidan from the island of Iona and made him bishop of Northumbria. In 641 the pagan Penda defeated and killed Oswald at Maserfeld. The dead King was venerated as a martyr of the Northumbrian Church, and it was believed that his remains worked miracles. His feast day is August 5.

·Mercian territorial conflict **3**:201a

Oswald, Lee Harvey (b. Oct. 18, 1939, New Orleans—d. Nov. 24, 1963, Dallas), presumed assassin of U.S. Pres. John F. Kennedy in Dallas on Nov. 22, 1963. A former U.S. Marine who had lived (1959–62) in the Soviet Union, Oswald proclaimed himself a sympathizer with the Cuban Communist government headed by Fidel Castro. While driving in an open car past the Texas School Book Depository, where Oswald was employed, the President was mortally wounded by two rifle bullets and Texas Gov. John B. Connally was seriously wounded by a third, all evidently fired from the sixth floor of the depository building. Having been arrested for the shooting, Oswald himself was shot to death two days later in the basement of the Dallas police headquarters by Jack Ruby, a night club owner. The Warren Commission, which investigated the assassination, concluded that neither Oswald nor Ruby had been involved in a conspiracy, but each had acted on his own. Oswald refused to admit his guilt.

·Kennedy assassination and Oswald murder **10**:418d

·Kennedy assassination role **18**:996h

Oswald of York, Saint (b. *c.* 925, Britain—d. Feb. 29, 992, Worcester), Anglo-Saxon archbishop who was a leading figure in the 10th-century movement of monastic and feudalistic reforms. Of Danish parentage, he, under the spiritual direction of his uncle, Archbishop St. Odo of Canterbury, entered the monastery of Fleury, Fr., then a great centre of reformed Benedictinism. Returning just after Odo's death (June 958), Oswald was, in 961, consecrated bishop of Worcester by the celebrated Archbishop St. Dunstan of Canterbury.

Soon after his appointment, Oswald founded a small Benedictine monastery at Westbury-on-Trym, Gloucestershire. About 965, when King Edgar (Eadgar) of the Mercians and Northumbrians ordered the establishment of many new monasteries, Oswald founded Ramsey Abbey, Huntingdonshire, on a site provided by Aethelwine, ealdorman of East Anglia. From Ramsey, which had close ties with Fleury and became a great religious centre, Oswald founded several other Benedictine houses, including those at Winchcombe, Gloucestershire, and at Pershore, Worcestershire. He also brought monks from Ramsey to his cathedral at Worcester, where they gradually replaced the secular clerks.

In 972 Oswald was transferred to the archbishopric of York, being allowed to retain the see of Worcester, where he mainly resided. As an ecclesiastical landlord, he practiced the leasing of land to certain men and to their heirs on condition that they perform various services for him. He created leasehold tenures limited to three generations for tenants who owed him various services, especially riding services as messengers and escorts. Some of the estates so granted were extensive and must have been held by people of importance and of noble birth who had perhaps done fealty to Oswald. Thus, the relationship of lord with client and the connection of tenure with service and fealty were already known in Anglo-Saxon England.

A near-contemporary life of Oswald notes his esteemed goodness. His support of Dunstan's apostolate and his collaboration with Bishop St. Aethelwold of Winchester, Hampshire, in establishing religious centres rank Oswald among the chief contributors to Anglo-Saxon monastic reform. His feast day is February 28. The early lives of Oswald were edited by J. Raine in *The Historians of the Church of York* (1879–94; 3 vol.). *St. Oswald and the Church of Worcester*, British Academy Supplemental Papers no. 5, appeared in 1919.

·monastic reform and scholarship **3**:203e

Oswald the Rabbit, cartoon character created by Walt Disney.

·film use and distribution **5**:896g

Oswego, port-city, seat (1816) of Oswego County, north central New York, U.S., on Lake Ontario at the mouth of the Oswego River. The name derives from Osh-we-geh, Iroquois, meaning "pouring out place." It was the site of two forts which were strategically important during the French and British colonial wars. A British fur-trading post, founded there in 1722 and fortified (1727) as Ft. Oswego, was the western terminus of the water route connecting the Mohawk and Hudson rivers with Lake Ontario. The second fort, Ontario, was built in 1755; it was destroyed by the French in 1756, was rebuilt in 1759, and was ceded to the U.S. in 1796 by the British, who recaptured it in the War of 1812. Reconstructed in 1839, Ft. Ontario is now a New York state historical site and museum.

Permanent settlement of the site dates from 1796. In 1841 "Vandalia," one of the first steamboats with a screw propeller, was built there. The opening of the Oswego Canal in 1828 (linking Lake Ontario to the Erie Canal) stimulated Oswego's commercial growth, but by the 1880s railroad competition had practically killed the port and forced the city to industrialize. The port, the most easterly on the Great Lakes, revived when it became the northern terminus of the New York State Barge Canal System (completed 1917). With the opening of the St. Lawrence Seaway in 1959, Oswego became a world port, handling principally cement, wood pulp, coal, and grains. Varied manufactures now include boilers, textiles, paper, machinery, clothing, aluminum, and sheet metals. Major power installations, including the Nine Mile Point Nuclear Station, make it the hydro-atomic, and steam-electric-power centre of central New York.

The State University College at Oswego originated in 1861 as a normal (teacher's) school. Inc. village, 1828; city, 1848. Pop. (1870) 20,910; (1980) 19,793.
43°28′ N, 76°31′ W

·map, United States **18**:908

Oswego (Oregon, U. S.): *see* Lake Oswego.

Oswego Canal (New York, U.S.): *see* New York State Barge Canal System.

Oswestry, market town in the county of Salop, England, near the border of the principality of Wales. It lies in a scenic setting in the foothills of the Berwyn Mountains between Wat's Dyke (*c.* 700) and Offa's Dyke (*c.* 784), defensive earthworks formerly separating England and Wales. "Old" Oswestry, an Iron Age hill fort with complicated defenses reflecting a long history, stands 1 mi (1.6 km) from the town. Oswestry is thought to derive its name from Oswald, king of Northumbria, a saint who was killed by Penda, king of Mercia, in 642 at the Battle of Maserfelth (or Maserfeld) near the present town. The scene of much border warfare between Welsh and English, the town was twice burned to the ground in the Middle Ages. On Castle Bank are the ruins of a castle built by Madog ap Maredudd, Welsh king of the adjacent region of Powys. A grammar school was founded there in 1407 and was moved to larger premises in 1776, but the old building still stands. For centuries Oswestry has been a market centre for Welsh goods, especially wool, and the modern town has a large cattle market and also light industry. Pop. (1971 prelim.) 30,320.
52°52′ N, 3°04′ W

·map, United Kingdom **18**:866

Oświęcim, German AUSCHWITZ, town, Kraków *województwo* (province), southern Poland, at the confluence of the Vistula and Soła rivers. A rail junction and industrial centre, the town became known as the site of an infamous Nazi concentration camp, Auschwitz-Birkenau (Oświęcim-Brzezinka), established 1940. It consisted of three main camps—Zasole, Brzezinka (Birkenau), and Dwory—in which between 1,000,000 and 5,000,000 people were massacred. The Oświęcim State Museum, founded there in 1946, serves as a memorial to those victims of World War II. A chemical factory built by the Dwory prisoners was rebuilt after the war and is now a major industrial plant.

Oświęcim State Museum, founded in 1946 on the site of the Auschwitz concentration camp, Poland
Gianni Tortoli—Photo Researchers

The town began in the 12th century as a fortress settlement; it received municipal rights in the 13th century. It served as the capital of a sovereign duchy that in 1307 swore allegiance to Bohemia. Annexed to Poland in 1457 and passed to Austria in 1772, it was returned to Poland in 1918. After World War II a new industrial town was built. A few historic buildings remain. Pop. (1970 prelim.) 39,600.
50°03′ N, 19°12′ E

·map, Poland **14**:626

·Nazi concentration camp **14**:629c

Oswiu, also spelled OSWY (d. 670), Anglo-Saxon king of Northumbria from 655 to 670, during the period of Northumbrian ascendancy in England. His father, King Aethelfrith (died 616), had united the two ancient Northumbrian kingdoms of Bernicia and Deira, but, after the death of Oswiu's brother, King Oswald, in 641, Northumbria was again divided, Oswiu assuming control of Bernicia. For 13 years he was subordinate to King Penda of Mercia. Finally, in 655 Penda invaded Bernicia and was killed by Oswiu's forces in the Battle of the Winwaed near Leeds in modern Yorkshire. Oswiu then reunited Northumbria and became overlord of southern England. He annexed northern Mercia but gave southern Mercia to Penda's son Peada. Peada was murdered in 656, and a revolt by Mercian nobles in 657 brought an end to Oswiu's rule in southern England. In 664 Oswiu,

a staunch Christian, helped reconcile differences in modes of worship between the Celtic churches and the Roman Church at the Synod of Whitby. Upon his death he was succeeded by his son Ecgfrith.
·Mercian territorial conflict 3:201b

Ōta, city, Gumma Prefecture (*ken*), Honshu, Japan, on the Tone-gawa (Tone River). During the Tokugawa era (1603–1867) it was a post town (rest stop) on the Nikkō-Kaida road and a temple town for the Daiko-in Temple. Japan's first civil aircraft manufacturing plant was established in Ōta in 1918. During World War II, munitions factories moved to Ōta, and the population subsequently grew. Industrial products now include automobiles, aircraft, electrical machinery, rubber, plastics, and knitted clothing. The city's agricultural area produces flowers and vegetables. Pop. (1970) 98,257.
36°18′ N, 139°22′ E
·map, Japan 10:36

Otači (Buddha): *see* Bhaiṣajyaguru.

Otago, historic region and former province, southern South Island, New Zealand. It is now merely a statistical area used for the collection of data. Pop. (1971) 183,000.
·area and population table 13:47
·geography and climate 13:44a
·19th-century educational structure 6:368f

Otaheite gooseberry: *see* Phyllanthus.

Otakar I, sometimes spelled OTTOKAR, properly PŘEMYSL OTAKAR I (b. *c.* 1155—d. Dec. 15, 1230), king of Bohemia from 1198, who won both Bohemia's autonomy from the German king and the hereditary rights to the Bohemian crown for his house of Přemysl.

Initially confirmed as duke of Bohemia in 1192 by the Holy Roman emperor Henry VI, Otakar was deposed the following year, but subsequently regained possession of the fief of Bohemia in 1197. He obtained the title of king in 1198 and almost total autonomy for Bohemia from the emperor Philip of Swabia. His title was subsequently confirmed by Frederick II (1212), who thereby all but extinguished the control of the empire in Bohemian affairs. Otakar's reign thus established the basis of a strong Bohemian state, which was to reach the height of its power later in the 13th century.
·Bohemian political and economic growth 2:1186g

Otakar II, sometimes spelled OTTOKAR, properly PŘEMYSL OTAKAR II (b. 1230—d. Aug. 26, 1278, Dürnkrut, now in Austria), king of Bohemia from 1253, who briefly established his crownland as the most powerful state of the Holy Roman Empire.

The son of King Wenceslas I of Bohemia, Otakar was elected duke of Austria in November 1251 and succeeded his father as king of Bohemia and Moravia in September 1253. In 1254 he conducted a crusade against the heathens of East Prussia, where later the Teutonic Knights named their citadel of Königsberg after him. He also conducted another crusade against the Lithuanians (1266–67). He seized Styria (1260) from the Hungarians and in 1269 took possession of Carinthia, Carniola, and Istria. His domains then stretched from Silesia to the Adriatic, and he stood as the strongest prince of the Holy Roman Empire. His fortunes changed soon after the election of Rudolf of Habsburg as emperor (1273). After having incurred the enmity both of rival princes and of his own nobility, Otakar was first divested of his rights to Austria, Styria, and Carinthia by the Diet of Regensburg (1274), then placed under the ban of the empire (June 1276). Finally Rudolf invaded Austria and forced him to renounce all his territories save Bohemia and Moravia (Treaty of Vienna, November 1276). Two years later, in an attempt to reassert his rights, Otakar marched on Vienna, but was killed at the Battle of Dürnkrut.
·Bohemian territorial expansion 2:1187a; map
·German throne struggle 8:79b
·political rise and fall 2:451g

Otakar IV (d. 1192), last of the independent rulers of Styria, which on his death passed to the Babenbergs of Austria.
·Babenberg territorial gains 2:451b

Otariidae, family of mammals of the order Carnivora, suborder Pinnipedia, including the eared seals. *See* seal; sea lion; fur seal.
·breeding, traits, and anatomy 3:937f *passim* to 939h
·characteristics and classification 3:943c; illus. 941a

Otaru, city, Hokkaido, Japan, on Ishikari-wan (Ishikari Bay) of the Sea of Japan. Its name is a corruption of the Ainu word *otarunai*, meaning "sandy beach." Otaru developed as a modern town in the late 19th century. Provided with a good natural harbour, it is now the second most important seaport after Hakodate and the largest industrial and commercial city on the west coast of Hokkaido. The city is also a recreation centre for Asarigawa Spa, Otamoi Park, and the Otaru Aquarium, one of the largest in Japan. Pop. (1970) 191,856.
43°13′ N, 141°00′ E
·map, Japan 10:36

Otavalo, town, Imbabura province, northern Ecuador, in the Andean highlands at an altitude of 8,441 ft (2,573 m), in the centre of the Ecuadorian Lake Region. It was originally settled by the Otavalo Indians, later conquered by the Incas, and became a Spanish-controlled settlement in the 16th century. Largely destroyed in the 1868 earthquake, the town has since been rebuilt.

The surrounding land, owned in small parcels by the Otavalo Indians, produces coffee, sugarcane, cotton, cereals, potatoes, fruit, and livestock. The main economic activity, however, centres on the weekly Indian market, famous for its cotton and woollen textiles (ponchos, carpets), leather goods, and native jewelry. The weavers of the villages near Otavalo are among the most prosperous Indians in the country. There is a nearby health resort with thermal springs. Otavalo is connected by rail and the Pan-American Highway to Quito. Pop. (1972 est.) 9,194.
0°14′ N, 78°16′ W
·map, Ecuador 6:286

otavite, cadmium carbonate, a mineral.
·occurrence and crystal properties 3:834h; table

Ŏtdâr Méanchey, also spelled ODDAR MEANCHEY, province (*khêt*), northern Cambodia (Khmer Republic). Principally an extension of the central Cambodian plain, it is drained by the O (river) Spéan Kméng (formerly Stung Sraeng), a principal affluent of the Tonle Sap. Bounded on the north by the steep escarpment of the Chuŏr Phnum (mountains), Dângrêk, which separate Cambodia from Thailand, the province is highest in the southeast, where rolling hills reach 330–660 ft (100–200 m). Although economically it is one of the least developed provinces of Cambodia, considerable rice cropping is carried on in the Spéan Kmeng alluvial lowlands and tributary system. Phumi Sâmraông (formerly Samrong), the small provincial seat, lies 150 ft (45 m) above sea level and has a small hospital and airport. The province lacks improved road links with other parts of the country. Among the few known minerals is alluvial gold.
·area and population table 3:678

Otello, opera in four acts by Giuseppe Verdi, with a libretto by Arrigo Boito, based on Shakespeare's *Othello*. The opera was first performed at La Scala in Milan on Feb. 5, 1887.
·premiere after 16-year silence 13:588a
·Verdi–Boito collaboration and first performances 19:84c

Otfrid, also spelled OTFRIED (fl. 9th century), monk of Weissenburg in Alsace and the first German poet whose name is known. He was trained in the monastery school of Fulda under Rabanus Maurus, who directed the school from 802 to 824. Otfrid's fame rests on his *Evangelienbuch* (*c.* 870; "Book of the Gospels"), a poem of 7,416 lines, which is extant in three good contemporary manuscripts. It is an exceptionally valuable document not merely linguistically as the most extensive work in the South Rhine Franconian dialect of Old High German, but also theologically as an introduction to early Christian thought in Germany. In German literary history it is also a milestone since it is the first poem to depart from traditional German alliterative verse and to use end rhymes.

The *Evangelienbuch* is a selective paraphrase of the Gospels, interposed by short passages of commentary. In a Latin dedication, Otfrid describes his concern over treating the life of Christ in the barbarous German tongue and explains that he did so to combat the native love for vernacular hero poetry. The work, which occupied him for a number of years, shows a development from crude attempts at rhyming to a skillful and graceful style of versification.

Othello (first performance 1604–05), tragedy by Shakespeare dealing with the marriage of a noble Moor, Othello, to a Venetian lady, Desdemona, and the destruction of that marriage through jealousy. Othello's suspicions, aroused and carefully nurtured by the villain Iago, eventually overwhelm him and lead him to murder his blameless wife.
·literature of the Renaissance 10:1141f
·temporal scheme 18:254f
·theme and character analysis 16:625d

other-directed (sociology): *see* inner-directed and other-directed.

Othman (3rd Muslim caliph): *see* ʿUthmān ibn ʿAffān.

Otho, in full MARCUS SALVIUS OTHO (b. AD 32—d. April 16, 69, near Cremona, Italy), Roman emperor from January to April 69. He was born into a family that had held the consulship under Augustus. Otho married Poppaea Sabina, but when the emperor Nero took Poppaea for his mistress—she later became his wife—Otho was sent from Rome to govern Lusitania (58). For ten years he ruled this province with integrity. Then, in 68 Otho joined the rebellion against Nero led by Galba, governor of the neighbouring province of Tarraconensis. He had hoped to be designated Galba's successor, but when Galba disappointed him by adopting Lucius Piso Licinianus (January 69), Otho prepared to seize power. The Praetorian Guard rebelled, Galba and Piso were murdered in the forum, and Otho was acclaimed emperor (January 15).

Before Galba's death, however, the legions in Germany had declared for Aulus Vitellius, whose troops were already moving toward Italy. Acting with speed and determination, Otho sent a naval expedition to Narbonensis (a region in southern Gaul), summoned the Danube legions, and himself marched out on March 14. Although substantial forces joined Otho from Illyricum, by early April the Vitellian forces were far stronger. Experienced advisers counselled delay, but Otho insisted on action. His army was completely defeated east of Cremona, and Otho committed suicide.

Otho, in German OTTO (b. June 1, 1815, Salzburg, Austria—d. July 26, 1867, Bamberg, now in West Germany), first king in modern Greece (1832–62), governed his country autocratically until he was forced to become a constitutional monarch in 1843. Attempting to increase Greek territory at the expense of Turkey, he failed and was overthrown.

The second son of King Louis I of Bavaria,

Otho was chosen king of Greece by the great powers at the conference of London in May 1832. The Greek National Assembly confirmed his selection in August 1832, and he arrived in Greece on Feb. 6, 1833, accompanied by several Bavarian advisers. He instituted a new legal code and organized a regular army, but the Bavarians' absolutist rule and heavy taxation led to discontent, which was appeased by the resignation of Otho's chancellor, Joseph Ludwig von Armansperg, in 1837. After failing to annex Crete in 1841, an attempt that alienated Great Britain, the Greeks staged a revolt in 1843. Otho, a Roman Catholic in an Eastern Orthodox country, was forced to grant a constitution specifying that his eventual successor be Orthodox. A Greek oligarchy now replaced the former Bavarian one. The King toyed with the "Great Idea," the re-establishment of the former Byzantine Empire with its capital at Constantinople; but his intervention against Turkey in the Crimean War (1853–56) merely provoked a Franco-British occupation of the Piraeus, and he failed to gain any additional territory for Greece. Otho's backing of

Otho, king of Greece, painting by an unknown artist; in the Historical and Ethnological Museum, Athens

Dimitri Papadimos

Austria in the Italian War of Independence (1859) further damaged his prestige. He was finally deposed in a revolt on Oct. 23, 1862, and returned to Bavaria.

·nationalistic reform program **2**:626h

Otho, Valentin (*c.* 1550–1605), German mathematician.

·history of mathematical tables **11**:650b

Otho the Great (1819), play by John Keats in collaboration with Charles Brown.

·Keats's collaboration with Charles Brown **10**:413g

otic ganglion, in anatomy, part of the ninth cranial nerve, situated near the cartilaginous portion of the auditory tube.

·anatomic relationships and functions **12**:1020e
·location, autonomic roots, and distribution **12**:1027f; table

Otididae (bird family): *see* bustard.

Oti River, in West Africa, rises in the southern plain of Upper Volta and meanders southward, briefly flowing along the Togo–Dahomey border; it cuts south-southwest across northern Togo and then forms the Ghana–Togo border for about 60 mi (100 km), before continuing southward through Ghana to empty into Lake Volta (created in the dammed Volta River). It is approximately 320 mi (520 km) long, and its basin is about 500 ft (150 m) above sea level. The river may have once been a tributary of the Niger. Its major riparian towns are Sansanné-Mango (Togo) and Nambiri (Ghana).
8°40′ N, 00°13′ E

·map, Togo **18**:472
·Togo physical geography **18**:471e
·Volta River's contributing sources **19**:516e

Otis, Elisha Graves (b. Aug. 3, 1811, Halifax, Vt.—d. April 8, 1861, Yonkers, N.Y.), inventor of the safety elevator. He worked as a

Elisha Otis, engraving by an unknown artist

By courtesy of Otis Elevator Co.

builder in Troy, N.Y., in 1830, and later, while employed as a master mechanic in a bedstead factory in Albany, N.Y., invented several labour-saving machines. As a result, his firm sent him to Yonkers, N.Y., in 1852 to build a new factory and to install its machinery. There he designed and installed the first elevator equipped with an automatic safety device to prevent it from falling if the lifting chain or rope broke. The next year he set up a small elevator shop and sold his first machine on Sept. 20, 1853. It hauled freight. Orders were few until May 1854, when, at the Crystal Palace in New York City, he demonstrated his elevator by riding the platform high in the air and ordering the rope cut. In 1856 he installed the first safety elevator for passenger service in a store in New York City. On Jan. 15, 1861, he patented a steam elevator, an invention that laid the foundation for the business that his two sons, Charles and Norton, carried on after his death.

·passenger elevator development **6**:716b

Otis, Harrison Gray (b. Oct. 8, 1765, Boston—d. Oct. 28, 1848, Boston), Federalist political leader who championed the Hartford Convention resisting mercantilist policies and the War of 1812. A successful Boston lawyer, Otis served in the U.S. House of Representatives (1797–1801), the Massachusetts legislature (1802–17), and the U.S. Senate (1817–22). From 1829 to 1832 he was mayor of Boston. A leader in the Hartford Convention (1814–15), Otis drafted its final report and remained for years (to the detriment of his political career) a champion of the Hartford resolutions in favour of states' rights.

Otis, Harrison Gray (1837–1917), U.S. soldier and journalist, served in the Union army during the Civil War and moved to California in 1876. In 1882 he purchased a substantial interest in the *Los Angeles Times* and by 1886 had full control of the paper. Under his active leadership the *Times* contributed much to the growth of southern California.

·Los Angeles Times conservatism **11**:111c

Otis, James (b. Feb. 5, 1725, West Barnstable, Mass.—d. May 23, 1783, Andover), American political activist whose incisive writing and speaking made a signal contribution to that body of legal doctrine underlining the historic rights of Englishmen in the period leading up to the American Revolution.

Son of the elder James Otis, who was already prominent in Massachusetts politics, the younger Otis moved his law practice from Plymouth to Boston in 1750. His reputation was built mainly upon his famous challenge in 1761 to the British-imposed writs of assistance—general search warrants designed to enforce more strictly the trade and navigation laws in North America. So much opposition was aroused in Massachusetts, where the legality of the writs was vigorously questioned, that the Superior Court in Boston consented to hear the case in February, with Otis delivering the chief argument. He focussed on the fundamental relationship between the English colonists in America and the home government, arguing that such writs, even if authorized by Parliament, were null and void. In harking back to fundamental British constitutional law, Otis offered the colonists a basic doctrine upon which publicists could draw for decades to come. At this time he also reportedly coined the euphonious, oft-quoted phrase, "Taxation without representation is tyranny."

Otis was elected in May of the same year as a representative to the General Court (state legislature), to which position he was re-elected nearly every year thereafter during his active life. In 1766 he was chosen speaker of the house, though this choice was negated by the royal governor of the province.

In September 1762 Otis published *A Vindication of the Conduct of the House of Representatives of the Province of Massachusetts Bay* in defense of that body's action in sending the governor a message (drafted by Otis) rebuking him for asking the assembly to pay for ships not authorized by them—though sent to protect New England fisheries against French privateers. He also wrote various state papers addressed to the Colonies to enlist them in the common cause or sent to the government in England to uphold the rights or set forth the grievances of the colonists. His influence at home in controlling and directing the movement of events toward freedom was universally felt and acknowledged, and few Americans were so frequently quoted, denounced, or applauded in Parliament and the

James Otis, the Younger, portrait by J. Blackburn, 1755; in the Library of Congress, Washington, D.C.

By courtesy of the Library of Congress, Washington, D.C.

British press before 1769. In 1765 Massachusetts sent him as one of its representatives to the Stamp Act Congress in New York City, and there he was a conspicuous figure, serving on the committee that prepared the address sent to the House of Commons.

After being struck on the head during an altercation with a crown officer in 1769, Otis was rendered harmlessly insane almost continually until his death. He did have occasional lucid intervals, however, serving as moderator at a Boston town meeting as late as 1778.

·conservatism of American Revolution **5**:66b
·John Adams support of writs of assistance **1**:75h
·Parson's Cause argument basis **18**:954c

otitid fly, sometimes called PICTURE-WINGED FLY (family Otitidae of the order Diptera) because the wings are spotted or banded with black, brown, or yellow. These small flies are common in moist places. Little is known about the larvae; some are parasites, and some are plant feeders that may damage cultivated plants.

otitis externa, dermatitis of the external auditory canal and sometimes also of the exposed ear. Skin is dry, scaling, and itchy; there may be foul-smelling watery or purulent discharge, pain, fever, and intermittent deafness. Predisposing factors include excessive

perspiration, trauma, allergy, underwater swimming and diving, and a warm, damp environment. The infection, which may be recurrent, is usually bacterial in origin.
·causation, symptoms, and treatment **5**:1133g
·common diseases of domestic cats, table 5 **5**:874

otitis interna, inflammation of the internal ear. *See* labyrinthitis.

otitis media, acute or chronic inflammation of the middle ear. The inflammation may be due to allergic disease of the middle ear or to infection with a virus or with bacteria. Allergic otitis media, if not complicated by bacterial invasion, usually subsides after elimination of the substance to which the person is allergic. Viral meningitis is usually an extension of common cold virus to the ear and usually subsides with disappearance of the cold. Acute bacterial otitis media causes earache, fever, and suppuration (discharge of pus). Treatment includes administration of antibiotics. Chronic otitis media may be relatively benign and respond to local medical treatment, or it may invade the bone and require surgical treatment.
·aerospace flight condition and symptoms **1**:143d
·cause, symptoms, complications, and treatment **5**:1129 *passim* to 1134h

Otjiwarongo, town and magisterial district, northern South West Africa. The town, at a railroad junction, is a distribution centre for a cattle raising region. Pop. (1970) town, 8,018. 20°29′ S, 16°36′ E
·district area and population table **17**:303
·map, South West Africa **17**:301

Otlet, Paul (1868–1944), Belgian lawyer who, with Henri-Marie Lafontaine (Belgian international lawyer, winner of the 1913 Nobel Prize for Peace), devised the Universal Decimal Classification (UDC; first published 1899) of subject groups for library collections.
·library classification systems **10**:870a
·universal bibliography project **2**:978e

Oto, North American Indian people of the Chiwere branch (including the Missouri and Iowa [*qq.v.*]) of the Siouan linguistic family. In their historic past the Oto, together with the Iowa and the Missouri, separated from the Winnebago and moved southwest. In 1673, when contacted by the Jacques Marquette expedition, they were some distance up the Des Moines River in present-day Iowa. By 1804 they were living near the mouth of the Platte River. In 1830 they ceded all their land in Missouri and Iowa to the U.S. and ultimately sold off their remaining land in Kansas and Nebraska. In 1882 they were removed to Indian Territory (present-day Oklahoma). In the early 1970s several hundred of them were reported in Oklahoma, most of them of mixed blood.
·Plains Indian culture **13**:223h; map 224

Otoceratacea, extinct family of ammonites of Permian and Triassic age.
·extinctions survived and new evolutions **7**:562c

Otocyon megalotis: *see* bat-eared fox.

otocyst, in vertebrate embryos, structure from which the ear develops; in certain invertebrates—*e.g.*, mollusks, flatworms, the otocyst is a sac that seems to serve in perception of motion and balance.
·human ear evolution and embryology **5**:1131g
·inner ear origins and specializations **6**:751e
·molluscan placement and function **12**:329b

otoko-e, Japanese prose illustration of the 12th century.
·masculine-written style and literary example **19**:228d

otolaryngology, a single medical specialty consisting of the knowledge of the ear and treatment of its disorders and of the throat, pharynx, larynx, nasopharynx, and tracheobronchial system. Board requirements, examinations for specialization and practice, and residencies vary from country to country.
·cryosurgical tonsillectomy **5**:320e
·surgery of the drum and stapes **11**:840a
·techniques and fields of treatment **17**:822h

otolith, one of the small crystals of calcium carbonate that rest on the otolithic membrane, a delicate structure without cells that covers the sensory patches called maculae in the utricle and saccule, chambers in the vestibule of the inner ear. The hair cells of the maculae are sensory receptors that detect changes in the position of the head. *See also* proprioception.

Oto-Manguean languages, a phylum of American Indian languages made up of the following language families and groups: Oto-Pamean, Popolocan, Mixtecan, Zapotecan, Chinantecan, and Chiapanec-Manguean. The Tlapanec and Huave language groups are sometimes also included in Oto-Manguean. The living languages of these groups are spoken in Mexico, although languages of the Chiapanec-Manguean group, all of which are extinct, were spoken along the western coast of Central America from El Salvador through Costa Rica.

There are more than 1,000,000 speakers of Oto-Manguean languages, the most important of which are Otomí, of the Oto-Pamean family, spoken by about 300,000 persons in the Mexican states of Hidalgo, México, Veracruz, Querétaro, and adjacent states; Mixtec dialects, of the Mixtecan family, spoken by some 250,000 persons in the states of Guerrero, Puebla, and Oaxaca; Zapotec dialects (or languages), of the Zapotecan family, spoken by about 300,000 persons in Oaxaca; and Mazahua, of the Oto-Pamean family, spoken by about 100,000 persons in the states of Michoacán and Mexico. Characteristic of many Oto-Manguean languages is the use of a complex system of pitches or intonations to distinguish otherwise identical utterances.
·geographical endemicity and sub-groups **11**:954f
·grouping theories since 1891 **11**:960e; map 957
·language families and use **12**:164h
·Meso-American distribution **10**:672a
·Meso-American language families **11**:935c
·Meso-American typological comparison **11**:962h

Oto Melara, Italian weapons manufacturer.
·rate of fire, weight, and crew **8**:498a

Otomí, Middle American Indian population living in the central plateau region of Mexico. The Otomí peoples speak seven Otomían languages: Mazahua, Matlatzinca, Ocuiltec, Chichimec Jonaz, Northern and Southern Pame, and Otomí proper. A rather large number of modern Otomí no longer speak an Otomían language but continue to consider themselves Otomí. All the Otomí peoples are culturally similar.

Their subsistence is based on farming and livestock raising; staple crops are corn, beans, and squash. Fields are cleared by slash-and-burn methods, and planting is done with a *coa*, a sort of combination hoe and digging stick. The less conservative Otomí also plant cash crops such as wheat and barley, which are cultivated using plow and oxen. The maguey (Mexican century plant) is also cultivated for a variety of uses. Sheep, goats, chickens, turkeys, and hogs are the most commonly raised livestock. Settlements vary in composition from the concentrated central village with surrounding farmlands to the dispersed type in which each family lives on its land and only public buildings are congregated. Crafts include spinning, weaving, pottery, basketry, and rope making. Dress varies from completely traditional to completely modern. Common dress in conservative areas consists of white cotton shirt and pants, serape, sandals, and hat for men and long tubular skirt, embroidered cotton blouse, and shawl (*rebozo*) or cape (*quechquemitl*) for women.

Ritual kinship institutions, based on a godparent relationship between the adults of one family and a child of another, is a central and essentially universal custom. Close ties exist between the parents and godparents of a child, and a series of ritual obligations obtain between them. The Otomí are Roman Catholic, and, although certain identifications between Christian figures and pre-Christian gods exist, the major religious rituals, myths, and ceremonies are basically Christian.
·Aztec deities and religious beliefs **2**:549d
·flying acrobat dance characteristics **1**:675c
·Meso-American Indian distribution map **11**:955

Otomían languages, Oto-Pamean language group of central Mexico, including Mazahua and four distinct languages called Otomí.
·Meso-American languages table **11**:958e

Otomí language, an American Indian language of the Oto-Pamean family; Oto-Pamean is a subdivision of the Oto-Manguean languages (*q.v.*), a language phylum spoken widely in Mexico. Otomí is spoken by about 300,000 persons in the central Mexican states of Hidalgo, Veracruz, México, Guanajuato, and Querétaro. Neighbouring languages are Pame to the north and the closely related Mazahua in the southern part of the Otomí speech area, as well as the non-Oto-Manguean Nahuatl to the southeast, Tarascan to the west, and Totonac, Tepehua, and Huastec to the east.

In phonology Otomí is characterized by the use of nasalized vowels and a tone or pitch accent system. It does not make much use of compound words, in contrast with many of its neighbours. Although prefixes and suffixes are used to indicate grammatical categories, words are generally short. Some grammatical categories are marked by modification of the initial consonant or consonant cluster of the verb stem, a process sometimes called simulfixation.
·Meso-American comparative features **11**:962g

Oto-Pamean languages, Meso-American Indian language stock containing the Chichimec, Pame, Matlatzinca, and Otomí languages and language groups.
·member languages **11**:960c
·Meso-American languages table **11**:958e; map 957

otosclerosis, disease of the bone enclosing the inner ear that causes fixation of the base of the stirrup, or stapes, in the oval window, an opening into the inner ear; this fixation prevents the conveyance of sound vibrations to the inner ear. The stirrup is one of the chain of minute bones in the middle ear that transmit sound vibrations from the eardrum membrane.
·hearing threshold comparisons **5**:1126a
·surgical treatment since 1876 **11**:840a
·symptoms, incidence, and treatment **5**:1135f

ototoxic drug, substance having a bad effect on the inner ear's organs or nerve.
·hearing function effects **5**:1136f

Otrante, Joseph Fouché, duc d': *see* Fouché, Joseph, duc d'Otrante.

Otranto, town and archiepiscopal see, Lecce province, Puglia (Apulia) region, southeastern Italy, on the east coast of the Salentine Peninsula (the "heel" of Italy), on the Strait of Otranto (40 mi [64 km] wide), opposite Albania. It is the easternmost town in Italy and is an old port of communication with Greece. The Greek settlement of Hydrus, it was known as Hydruntum by the Romans, under whom it was only less important than Brundisium (now Brindisi) as a port of embarkation. Taken by the Norman Robert Guiscard in 1068, it was destroyed by the Turkish fleet in 1480 and never recovered its previous importance. The castle, built by Alfonso II of

Aragon, king of Naples, in 1485–98, was made famous by Horace Walpole's novel *The Castle of Otranto* (1765). Also notable are the cathedral, consecrated in 1088, and the small Byzantine church of S. Pietro.

Modern Otranto is an agricultural centre, fishing port, and bathing resort. Pop. (1978 est.) 4,612.
40°09′ N, 18°30′ E
·Byzantine medieval mosaic art **12**:471g
·map, Italy **9**:1089

Otranto, Strait of, channel in the Mediterranean Sea, extends for 47 mi (76 km) between the capes of Otranto (southeast Italy) and Linguetta (west Albania); it links the Adriatic and Ionian seas.
40°00′ N, 19°00′ E
·map, Albania **1**:418

Otrepyev, Yury: *see* Dmitry, False.

Otric, 10th-century master of the cathedral school at Magdeburg, Germany.
·debates with Pope Sylvester II **17**:898h

Ōtsu, capital, Shiga Prefecture (*ken*), southern Honshu, Japan, on the shore of Biwa-ko (Lake Biwa). A castle town established by Toyotomi Hideyoshi, a general important in the reunification of Japan in the 16th century, it is situated at the junction of ancient highways, including the Tōkaidō Highway (Tokyo–Kyōto) route. Ōtsu has long been a gateway to Kyōto and a centre of transportation. The city contains the Ishiyama-dera (Ishiyama Temple), known for its rock formations. The temple is associated with Murasaki Shikibu, author of the 11th-century novel *Genji monogatari* (*The Tale of Genji*), considered to be the greatest work of Japanese classical literature. Pop. (1978 est.) 204,233.
35°00′ N, 135°52′ E
·map, Japan **10**:37

Ott, Mel, full name MELVIN THOMAS OTT (b. March 2, 1909, Gretna, La.—d. Nov. 21, 1958, New Orleans), professional baseball player, first man to hit 500 home runs in the National League. A compact (5-foot 9-inch, 170-pound), left-handed hitter, Ott played the outfield and third base for the New York Giants of the National League from 1926 to 1947 and managed the team from 1942 to 1948. He set National League career records for most home runs, runs scored, runs batted in (all eventually broken), and bases on balls. His National League home run record of 511 was first surpassed by Willie Mays in 1966.

Ott, who never played in the minor leagues, joined the Giants at the age of 17. In 1929 he hit 42 home runs and batted in 151 runs. He drove in at least 100 runs in each of nine seasons and hit 30 or more home runs in each of eight years. His career batting average was .304. Ott was elected to the Baseball Hall of Fame in 1951.

ottava rima, Italian stanza form composed of eight 11-syllable lines, rhyming *abababcc*. It originated in the late 13th and early 14th centuries and was developed by Tuscan poets for religious verse and drama and in troubadour songs. The form appeared in Spain and Portugal in the 16th century. It was used in 1600 in England (where the lines were shortened to 10 syllables) by Edward Fairfax in his translation of Torquato Tasso. In his romantic epics *Il filostrato* (written c. 1338) and *Teseida* (written 1340–41) Boccaccio established ottava rima as the standard form for epic and narrative verse in Italy. The form acquired new flexibility and variety in Ludovico Ariosto's *Orlando furioso* (*c.* 1507–32) and Tasso's *Gerusalemme liberata* (published 1581). In English verse ottava rima was used for heroic poetry in the 17th and 18th centuries but achieved its greatest effectiveness in the work of Byron. His *Beppo* (1818) and *Don Juan* (1819–1824) combined elements of comedy, seriousness, and mock-heroic irony, exploiting the form in the manner of the Italian masters. Shelley employed it for a serious subject in *The Witch of Atlas* (published 1824).
·Ariosto's use in "Orlando furioso" **1**:1151g
·Boccaccio's literary style **2**:1173g

Ottaviani, Alfredo (1890–1979), Vatican ecclesiastic.
·Vatican position defined **14**:487a

Ottawa, Algonkian-speaking Indians whose territory included what are now part of the Ottawa River, the French River, Georgian Bay, northern Michigan, and adjacent areas. According to tradition, the Ottawa, Ojibwa, and Potawatomi were formerly one tribe, having migrated from the northwest and separated at what is now Mackinaw, Mich. The earliest known location of the Ottawa was on Manitoulin Island. They were widely known as traders, their location enabling them to become middlemen in intertribal commerce; their canoes travelled as far west as Green Bay, Wis., and as far east as Quebec. The Ottawa were semi-sedentary, living in agricultural villages in summer and separating into family groups for winter hunts. Planting and harvesting crops were female occupations; hunting and fishing were the responsibility of men. Ottawa villages, situated along waters navigable by canoe, were sometimes palisaded for protection.

In the late 17th century the tribe comprised four, or possibly five, major divisions, which were subdivided into local bands; they are believed to have had several clans distributed among the bands. Attacked by the Iroquois, the Ottawa fled, some joining the Potawatomi at Green Bay, others finally scattering throughout the lower peninsula of Michigan, Wisconsin, and northern Illinois.
·Michigan's history **12**:104g
·Pontiac's Detroit plot **5**:620d
·religious dance symbolism **1**:671b

Ottawa 13:766, capital of Canada and seat of Carleton County, southeastern Ontario, at the confluence of the Ottawa, Gatineau, and Rideau rivers. Its metropolitan area lies astride the Ontario–Quebec border. Pop. (1976) city, 304,462; (1978 est.) metropolitan area, 726,400.

The text article surveys the location and physical features of the city, its history, and the contemporary demography, economic life, political institutions, services, and cultural life and recreation.
45°25′ N, 75°42′ W
REFERENCES in other text articles:
·botanical garden table **3**:64
·building design temperature, table 1 **8**:713
·map, Canada **3**:717

Ottawa, city, seat (1831) of La Salle County, north central Illinois, U.S., at the confluence of the Fox and Illinois rivers. The site was visited by French explorers and missionaries in the 17th century; the town was laid out in 1830. Originally called Carbonia, from coal deposits nearby, it was renamed Ottawa for the Indian tribe. Situated in a rich agricultural area, it developed as a grain and trading centre, with the building of elevators and mills, small factories, and shops along the river. Its growth was stimulated by completion of the Illinois and Michigan Canal (1848) and the arrival of the Rock Island Railroad (1853). The opening of the Illinois Waterway (1933) increased navigational facilities to the Chicago area. Local industries are based on nearby deposits of silica sand, clay, coal, and gravel. Chief products are glass and plastic materials. A monument marks the site of the first of the Lincoln–Douglas debates (Aug. 21, 1858). Starved Rock State Park is nearby. Inc. town, 1837; city, 1853. Pop. (1980) 18,166.
41°21′ N, 88°51′ W
·map, United States **18**:909

Ottawa, city, seat (1864) of Franklin County, eastern Kansas, U.S., on the Marais des Cygnes River. It was founded in 1864 near the Ottawa Baptist Mission, which had been established (1837) on lands given (1832) to the Ottawa Indians in exchange for their Ohio lands. When the Indians were moved to Oklahoma (1867), settlers rushed to the site; prosperity followed construction (1872) of railroad machine shops.

Ottawa is now the trading centre for a grain, poultry, and livestock area; manufactures include textiles, plastic and metal products, and mobile homes. It is the seat of Ottawa University (1865). Of interest are the Ottawa Indian Burial Grounds and the Centennial Cabin and Old Depot museums. Inc. 1866. Pop. (1980) 11,016.
38°37′ N, 95°16′ W
·map, United States **18**:909

Ottawa Agreements (1932): *see* imperial preference.

Ottawa River, in east central Canada, the chief tributary of the St. Lawrence River. It rises in the Laurentian Plateau of western Quebec and flows swiftly westward to Lake Timiskaming and then southeastward, forming for most of its course the Quebec–Ontario provincial border before it joins the St. Lawrence west of Montreal. Throughout its total course of 696 mi (1,120 km), the river widens to form innumerable lakes, the largest being Grand Victoria, Simard, Timiskaming, Allumette, Chats, and Deschenes. The Ottawa and its main tributaries, including the Rouge (150 mi long), Lièvre (205), Gatineau (240), Coulonge (135), Rideau (123), Mississippi (105), and Madawaska (130) rivers, drain an area of over 55,000 sq mi (142,000 sq km).

Discovered in 1613 by the French explorer

Log boom being towed on Lake Timiskaming, an expansion of the Ottawa River, Quebec
George Hunter—Publix

Samuel de Champlain and named after an Ottawa band of Algonkian Indians that once inhabited the area, the river became a favourite route of explorers, fur traders, and missionaries to the Upper Great Lakes. In the 19th century the Rideau Canal, linking Ottawa with Lake Ontario, was completed, and lumbering became the dominant economic activity along the river. The river is no longer a major transportation artery, but it has become an important source of hydroelectric power; several generating plants and an atomic energy plant at Chalk River supply electricity for much of Quebec and Ontario. Riverine cities include Pembroke and Ottawa in Ontario and Hull in Quebec.
45°20′ N, 73°58′ W
·Champlain navigation and significance **3**:734f
·Great Lakes formation and drainage **8**:301h
·map, Canada **3**:717
·Ontario's early settlement **15**:331a
·Ottawa's metropolitan growth **13**:767d

otter, any of several species of semi-aquatic mammals in four genera of the weasel family (Mustelidae). They have the same general proportions as a weasel—the lithe, slender

River otter (*Lutra canadensis*)
Kenneth W. Fink—Root Resources

body, long neck, small ears, and short legs. The head is flattened, and the base of the tail is almost as thick as the body. Few other animals produce a fur so highly valued by man and so durable; the darker furs of northern animals are the most prized.

Otters swim easily with webbed feet, and can travel underwater for 0.4 km (¼ mi) without surfacing for air. They prefer to travel by water but, their short legs notwithstanding, can travel on land faster than a man can run. Their food consists of all manner of small aquatic animals, including fish, which they catch sometimes by teamwork; they also prey on other small mammals. A litter of one to five young is born after a gestation of 61–63 days.

Unlike almost all other wild animals, otters are playful as adults. A favourite sport is sliding down a steep bank of mud or snow and plunging into water or a snowdrift. Otters are intelligent, friendly, and inquisitive. When obtained young, they can be trained readily.

African small-clawed otter (*Aonyx philippsi*) of western and central Africa, principally in rain forests and mountain streams; also called Liberian otter; considered as three species (*Paraonyx philippsi*, *P. congica*, and *P. microdon*) by some authors; length about 95 cm (38 in.), including the 35-cm (14-in.) tail; weight about 7 kg (15 lb); shining, dark-brown fur, pale markings on throat and face; claws, blunt and short on the partly webbed forefeet and entirely webbed hindfeet.

Central American otter (*Lutra annectens*) of Central and South America; also called southern river otter; coat, yellowish to reddish brown with grayish brown underparts.

Clawless otter (*Aonyx capensis*) of central and southern Africa, generally near slow-moving water; also called African (or cape) clawless and giant African otter; length, 95–100 cm (38–40 in.) exclusive of the flattened, 55-cm (22 in.) tail; weight, 14–27 kg (31–59 lb); fur, brown with pale chin and throat patches; claws lacking except for rudimentary claws on third and fourth hindtoes.

Common otter: Eurasian otter or river otter.

Eurasian Otter (*Lutra lutra*) of Eurasian and North African rivers; also called common and Old World otter; length, 56–83 cm (22–33 in.), exclusive of the 36–55-cm (14–22-in.) tail; shoulder height, about 30 cm (12 in.); weight, 6–15 kg (13–33 lb); fur, brown, paler below, white on cheeks and throat.

Giant (Brazilian giant) otter (*Pteronura brasiliensis*), very rare species confined to slow-flowing rivers and streams of South America; probably hunting for its pelts has decreased its numbers; also called saro and margin-tailed, or flat-tailed, otter for its flattened, ridged tail; feet, completely webbed; fur, brown with a large whitish chest patch; probably the largest otter, attaining a length of 1–1.5 m, excluding the 0.7-m tail.

Hairy-nosed otter (*Lutra sumatrana*) of southern Asia, named for its finely haired nose pad; length about 130 cm (52 in.), including the 50-cm (20-in.) tail; coat, reddish brown with whitish throat, chin, and cheeks.

Oriental small-clawed otter, *Aonyx cinerea* separated as *Amblonyx cinerea* by some authors), of Southeast Asia; also called Asian clawless and Indian small-clawed otter; sometimes tamed and used to catch fish; weight 2.7–5.4 kg (6–12 lb); length 56–61 cm (22–24 in.), excluding the 31-cm (12-in.) tail; fur, dark brown, paler below, with whitish throat and face markings.

River otter (*Lutra canadensis*) of North American lakes and streams; also called land, common, North American, and Virginia otter; head and body length, 65–75 cm (26–30 in.); tail length, 30–50 cm (12–20 in.); weight, 5–12 kg (11–26 lb); fur, glossy, dark brown, usually paler ventrally, with contrasting whitish throat and muzzle markings.

Sea (great sea) otter (*Enhydra lutris*), rare, completely marine species of the North Pacific, usually in kelp beds; floats on its back with a stone on its chest, opening mollusks by smashing them on the stone; hindfeet large, broad, flipperlike; forefeet reduced; coat (the most expensive otter fur) thick, lustrous, reddish to dark brown, often grizzled; head and body, 76–120 cm (30–48 in.); tail length, 25–37 cm (10–15 in.); weight, 16–41 kg (35–90 lb); hunted almost to extinction by 1910, now fully protected and gradually increasing in numbers.

Smooth-coated otter (*Lutra perspicillata*) of Southeast Asia, separated as *Lutrogale perspicillata* by some authors; also called smooth, or smooth Indian, otter and simung; coat, sleek reddish to blackish brown, often lighter ventrally and marked by whitish face and throat patches; length 66–74 cm (26–30 in.) exclusive of the flattened, 43–46-cm (17–18-in.) tail.

·California sea otter tool usage ability **10**:735a
·feeding specificity on mollusks **7**:209b
·food's effect on body coloration **4**:916b
·fur origin and characteristics table **7**:814
·pet ownership responsibilities **14**:151d
·tool use and fur value **3**:932b; illus. 931

Otter Creek, originates in Mt. Tabor, north Bennington County, Vermont, U.S., and flows north and west to Lake Champlain, near Ferrisburg after a course of about 100 mi (160 km). In its upper course, Otter Creek, the longest river in the state, flows between the Taconic and Green Ranges.
44°13′ N, 73°17′ W

otterhound, dog breed first described in the 14th century. Developed to hunt otters, it resembles a rough-coated bloodhound and has a large head, pendulous ears, and a dense, shaggy, water-resistant coat. Its webbed feet make it an excellent swimmer. It stands 61 to 66 centimetres (24 to 26 inches), weighs 25 to 30 kilograms (55 to 65 pounds), and is usually blue gray or yellowish brown with black-and-tan markings.

otter shrew, any of the three species of west equatorial African mammals composing the subfamily Potamogalinae of the tenrec (*q.v.*) family (Tenrecidae). Some authors separate them as the family Potamogalidae (of the order Insectivora). They are carnivorous and

Otter shrew (*Potamogale velox*)
Painting by Don Meighan

semi-aquatic, in streams and estuaries. All are long bodied, with laterally flattened tails, used for propulsion underwater, and dense brown and white fur. The largest species is *Potamogale velox*, often called giant water shrew; it may be 64 centimetres (25 inches) long, including its 29-centimetre (11-inch) tail. It has skin flaps on the inner sides of the hindfeet. The two species of the genus *Micropotamogale* (including *Mesopotamogale*) are smaller.

·anatomy, habits, and classification **9**:623b; illus. 622

otter trawl, fishing trawl using otter boards to spread the net and drawn usually by trawlers that handle the fish caught.

·commercial fishing gear innovations **7**:357g; illus. 354

Ottery Saint Mary, market town in the county of Devon, England, sited on the River Otter at the foot of Blackdown Hill. St. Mary's Church, consecrated in 1259, was rebuilt in 1337–42; fine Tudor buildings include Cadhay House and Knightstone Manor. Agricultural trade comprises the town's main economic activity. Pop. (1971 prelim.) 5,824.
50°45′ N, 3°17′ W

Ottilien (New Guinea): *see* Ramu River.

Öttingen–Schrattenhofen faience, German tin-glazed earthenware made in Bavaria in the 18th and 19th centuries. The factory was first established at Öttingen in 1735 and two years later was moved to Schrattenhofen. The ware is characteristic of much produced in Bavaria—*e.g.*, cylindrical beer tankards—and the decoration is likewise Bavarian in the Rococo style. The factory also produced less ornate ware and, in later years, like many German faience centres, it produced a cream-coloured earthenware inspired by the Wedgwood prototype in England.

Otto (king of Greece): *see* Otho.

Otto I the Great, Emperor 13:768 (b. Nov. 23, 912—d. May 7, 973, Memleben, Ger.), German king and Holy Roman emperor, consolidated the German *Reich* by his suppression of rebellious vassals and his decisive victory over the Magyars. His use of the church as a stabilizing influence created a secure empire and stimulated a cultural renaissance.

Abstract of text biography. Beleaguered by internal problems with treacherous relatives, he crushed insurrections and twice forgave his younger brother Henry for plotting against him (939 and 941). He directed the foundation of the monastery in Magdeburg (937) and bishoprics in Denmark (968) to strengthen his rule. After quelling the rebellion of his son Liudolf he ended the Magyar threat at the Battle of the Lechfeld, near Augsburg (955). He was crowned Holy Roman emperor by Pope John XII (Feb. 2, 962), who by treaty accorded him privileges in church affairs. Having replaced John XII with Pope Leo VIII (December 963), he solidified relations with the Eastern Empire by marrying his son Otto II to the Byzantine princess Theophano (972).

REFERENCES in other text articles:
·Bohemia's German orientation **2**:1186b
·cultural Renaissance attempts **8**:1174h
·German-Slav victory over Magyars **2**:450d
·Hungarian defeat at Augsburg **8**:72c
·Italian intervention success **9**:1125h
·Low Countries political intervention **11**:135c
·Nicephorus II's opposition **13**:65c
·Poland's development and independence **14**:638c
·regulation of church administration **15**:1002h
·relations with Byzantium **3**:562b

Otto I (*c.* 1120–1183), first Wittelsbach duke of Bavaria (from 1180), founded the dynasty that reigned in Bavaria until 1918.

·Frederick Barbarossa's grant of Bavaria **2**:774e
·Munich's founding and growth **12**:617c

Otto I (b. 1164—d. April 30, 1207, Oudekamp, now in The Netherlands), count of Gelderland and Zutphen, who tried to expand his domain south to include the counties of Brabant and Limburg (on the present Belgium–Netherlands border) and the bishopric of Liège (now in Belgium).

Son of Count Henry of Gelre (Gelderland) and Agnes of Arnstein, Otto I became count at his father's death in 1182. Seeking to increase his territorial power by absorbing ecclesiastical lands, he besieged the bishop of Utrecht at Deventer in 1188 but was forced to raise the siege when ordered by the Holy Roman emperor Frederick I Barbarossa to accompany him on the Third Crusade to Jerusalem. On returning from the crusade in 1191, the Count undertook to reform the administration of justice in his lands. From 1195 to 1202 he was engaged in a series of wars against the dukes of Brabant and the counts of Holland over control of the election for the bishopric of Utrecht, to which he ultimately succeeded in electing his son Otto. In 1202 he and Count Dirk VII of Holland were captured by Duke Henry I of Brabant and not released until ransomed by their families late that year. The Count of Gelderland also had to agree to a marriage between his son and heir, Gerhard III, and Brabant's daughter Margaretha. This marriage, which took place in 1206, united the two formerly hostile families in friendship until 1283, when they waged war over possession of the duchy of Limburg.

Otto II (b. 955—d. Dec. 7, 983, Rome), German king from 961 and Holy Roman emperor from 967, sole ruler from 973, son of Otto I and his second wife, Adelaide. Otto continued his father's policies of promoting a strong monarchy in Germany and of extending the influence of his house in Italy. In 961 he was

Emperor Otto II enthroned, miniature from his gospel, Reichenau school, *c.* 975; in the treasury of Aachen Cathedral, Germany

Foto Ann Munchow

crowned co-regent king of Italy and Germany with his father and was made co-regent emperor in 967. On April 14, 972, he married the Byzantine princess Theophano. At his father's death in 973 he was accepted without opposition as successor, although revolts in the duchy of Bavaria and in Lorraine occupied the early years of his reign. Bavaria, the most independent of the duchies, rebelled in 974, under the leadership of its duke, Henry II the Quarrelsome, Otto's cousin. It was not until 978 that Bavaria was pacified, the same year that Lothair, king of France, invaded Lorraine. In 979 Otto received the submission of Bohemia and Poland, and in 980 Lothair renounced his claim to Lorraine. Having thus secured his German dominions, Otto marched into Italy in 980, where German rule had been maintained by an imperial party headed by Hugh, marquis of Tuscany. Otto invaded southern Italy and was decisively defeated there by the Arabs in 982. In 983 he summoned a diet at Verona, where his young son, Otto III, was crowned German king. Otto II died in 983 while attempting to bring Venice under imperial control. His absence from Germany had occasioned revolts along its borders, and after his defeat in Calabria in 982 the German position east of the Elbe collapsed because of a revolt by the Danes and an invasion by the Slavs. Nonetheless, Otto left a firmly established realm to his son and successor Otto III.

·Mediterranean sphere of action **8**:73h
·Otto I's consolidation of power **13**:768f
·Pope Sylvester II and Otric **17**:898g
·southern Italian expansion **9**:1126e

Otto II the Lame (b. *c.* 1220—d. Jan. 10, 1271, Cleves, now in West Germany), count of Gelderland and Zutphen, Neth., who encouraged the growth of new towns and industry and added the town of Nijmegen to his domain.

Son of Gerhard III of Gelre (Gelderland) and Margaretha, daughter of Duke Henry I of Brabant, Otto II succeeded his father in 1229, his mother serving as guardian. When he came of age in 1234, he took part in a crusade against the Stedingers, a heretical Christian sect located in Weser (now in West Germany). He supported the claim of his cousin, Count William II of Holland, to the throne of Germany, and in 1247 William gave him the town of Nijmegen for his loyalty and financial support. After William's death (1256), several Holland nobles asked him to replace the Count's widow as governor for the two-year-old Count Floris V. After defeating her supporters (1263), however, Otto declined the governorship in favour of the young count's uncle. In a war with Cologne, he imprisoned the city's archbishop, for which he was excommunicated (1270).

Otto III (b. July 980—d. Jan. 23, 1002, near Viterbo, Italy), German king and Holy Roman emperor who planned to recreate the glory and power of the ancient Roman Empire in a universal Christian state governed from Rome, in which the pope would be subordinate to the emperor in religious as well as in secular affairs.

Son of the Holy Roman emperor Otto II and Empress Theophano, Otto III was elected German king in June 983 and crowned at Aachen in December, shortly after his father's death. But the child king was seized by Henry II the Quarrelsome, the deposed duke of Bavaria, in an attempt to secure the regency, if not the throne, for himself. In May 984, however, Henry was forced by the imperial diet to turn the child over to his mother, who served as regent until her death in 991; Otto's grandmother, the dowager empress Adelaide, assumed the regency until the King came of age in 994.

In 996, heeding an appeal by Pope John XV for help in putting down a rebellion led by the Roman noble Crescentius II, Otto crossed the Alps. Declared king of Lombardy at Pavia, he reached Rome after the Pope's death, whereupon he secured the election of his 23-year-old cousin, Bruno of Carinthia, as Gregory V, the first German pope. Gregory, who crowned Otto emperor on May 21, 996, was driven from Rome after the Emperor's return to Germany by Crescentius, who then installed John XVI as pope. The Emperor marched back into Italy in late 997; taking Rome in February 998, he executed Crescentius, deposed John, and reinstated Gregory.

Otto then proceeded to make Rome his official residence and the administrative centre of the empire. Instituting elaborate Byzantine court ceremonies and reviving ancient Roman customs, he assumed the titles "the servant of Jesus Christ," "the servant of the apostles," and "emperor of the world" and saw himself as the leader of world Christianity. When Gregory V died (999), Otto had the Frenchman Gerbert of Aurillac, his former tutor who agreed with his concept of a theocratic emperor, installed as Pope Sylvester II.

In 1000 Otto made a pilgrimage to the tomb of the mystical archbishop Adelbert of Prague at Gniezno, which he established as the archbishopric of Poland. When in January 1001 Tibur, Italy, rebelled against Otto, he laid siege to the town, forced its surrender, and then pardoned its inhabitants. Angered by this

Otto III, Holy Roman emperor, detail from a miniature, Reichenau school, *c.* 998; in the Bayerische Staatsbibliothek, Munich (Codex Monacensis Graecus 4453)

By courtesy of the Bayerische Staatsbibliothek, Munich

action, the Romans, who wanted the rival town destroyed, rebelled against the Emperor (February 1001) and besieged his palace. After placating the rebels momentarily, Otto withdrew to the monastery of St. Apollinaris, near Ravenna, to do penance. Unable to regain control of the imperial city, he requested military support from his cousin Henry of Bavaria, who was to succeed him as German king and later as emperor. Shortly before the Bavarian troops arrived at his headquarters, Otto died.

·church financial power **8**:72h
·Gospel Book page, illumination
illus., **19**:Visual Arts, Western, Plate IV
·Italian politics and revival of Rome **9**:1126e
·Polish metropolitanate establishment **14**:638e
·Pope Sylvester II's alliance **17**:899a
·regulation of church administration **15**:1002h

Otto IV, or OTTO OF BRUNSWICK (b. *c.* 1175 or *c.* 1182, either in Germany or at Argentan, Normandy, now in France—d. May 19, 1218, Harzburg Castle, Saxony, now in East Germany), German king and Holy Roman emperor, candidate of the German anti-Hohenstaufen faction, who, after prevailing against two Hohenstaufen kings, was finally deposed.

A member of the Welf dynasty, Otto was a son of Henry the Lion of Brunswick and Matilda, daughter of Henry II of England. Brought up at the court of his uncle Richard I of England, Otto was made earl of York in 1190 and count of Poitou and duke of Aquitaine in 1196. Under both kings Richard and John, English diplomatic and financial help were to be of great assistance to Otto in his struggles with the Hohenstaufens.

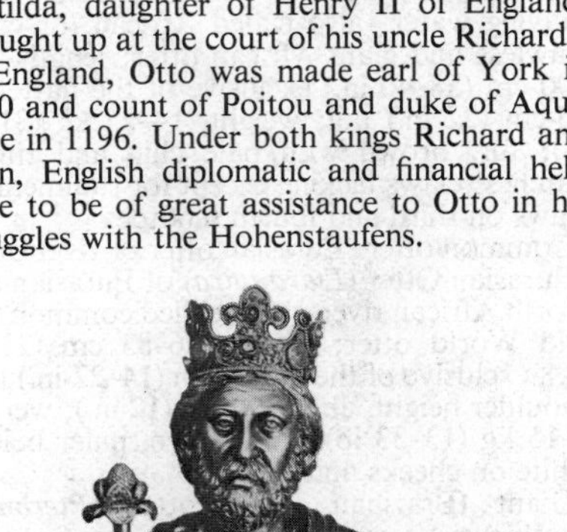

Otto IV, detail of a statue on the Shrine of the Three Kings, *c.* 1200; in the treasury of Cologne Cathedral

Foto Rathschlag, Cologne

When the Hohenstaufen Holy Roman emperor Henry VI died in September 1197, because his heir, Frederick, was an infant, the German princes favouring the Hohenstaufens elected Frederick's uncle, Philip of Swabia, as German king in March 1198. The opposing party, led by Archbishop Adolf of Cologne, however, elected Otto in 1198.

War ensued between the two factions. In 1201 Otto obtained the support of Pope Innocent III after agreeing to the papacy's territorial claims in central Italy. In 1204, however, some of Otto's chief supporters in Germany, including Archbishop Adolf, went over to Philip's side. When, in early 1208, Otto held only the Welf allodial (freely held under no fiefdom) lands in Brunswick, even Pope Innocent recognized Philip as king.

When in June 1208 Philip was murdered by a German count to whom he had refused to give one of his daughters in marriage, many of Philip's former supporters made overtures to Otto, who agreed to a new election. Chosen king at Frankfurt in November 1208, he strengthened his position by his bethrothal to Philip's 10-year-old daughter Beatrix. The pope recognized Otto again after the king reaffirmed the papacy's claims in central Italy.

When in August 1209 Innocent received Otto at Viterbo, Italy, he refused to concede to the church all the lands that the papacy had been claiming from the empire, but he agreed not to claim suzerainty over Sicily, of which the young Frederick II of Hohenstaufen had in 1198 been crowned king as a vassal of the papacy, because the pope's policy aimed at preventing a reunion of the German and Sicilian crowns. Otto was crowned emperor in Rome on October 4, 1209.

Soon, however, it became evident that Otto did not intend to keep his word. After occupying Tuscany, he invaded the mainland part of Frederick's kingdom of Sicily. Disregarding his excommunication by Innocent, Otto in November 1210 conquered southern Italy. By the time Apulia had fallen, an assembly of princes at Nürnberg declared him deposed and invited Frederick to take his place.

When Otto returned to Germany in March 1212, in order to retain the support of at least part of the Hohenstaufen faction, he married Philip's daughter Beatrix, but lost that support when she died within three weeks of their marriage. Frederick, who arrived in Germany in September 1212, soon prevailed in the southern duchies, but Otto and his supporters held out against him in the lower Rhine district and northeastern Germany. In alliance with his uncle, King John of England, Otto then invaded France, which supported Frederick. Disastrously defeated at the Battle of Bouvines (July 27, 1214), Otto was deserted by nearly all his supporters. He was formally deposed as king in 1215. By the time of his death, three years later, his power was confined again to his Brunswick dominions.

·attempt to conquer Italy and Sicily **7**:700b
·Innocent III's papal support for king **9**:605h
·Sicilian kingdom renunciation **9**:1132d
·struggle for the throne **8**:77h

Otto IV, 13th-century count of Franche-Comté.
·treaties with Philip IV **3**:497h

Otto, Nikolaus August (b. June 10, 1832, Holzhausen, now in W.Ger.—d. Jan. 26, 1891, Cologne), engineer who developed the four-stroke internal-combustion engine, which offered the first practical alternative to the steam engine as a power source. Otto built his first gas engine in 1861. Three years later he formed a partnership with the German industrialist Eugen Langen, and together they developed an improved engine that won a gold medal at the Paris Exposition of 1867.

In 1876 Otto built an internal-combustion engine utilizing the four-stroke cycle (four strokes of the piston for each explosion). Although the four-stroke cycle was patented in 1862 by the French engineer Alphonse Beau de Rochas, since Otto was the first to build an

Nikolaus Otto, *c.* 1868
Ullstein Bilderdienst

engine based upon this principle, it is commonly known as the Otto cycle. Because of its smooth-running reliability, its efficiency, and its relative quietness, Otto's engine was an immediate success. More than 30,000 of them were built during the next ten years, but in 1886 Otto's patent was revoked when Beau de Rochas' earlier patent was brought to light.

·De Rochas and the four-stroke cycle **2**:515a
·four-stroke engine development **8**:705g
·gasoline engine development **18**:40f
·internal-combustion engine **7**:930a
·mechanical energy availability **6**:856b

Otto, Rudolf 13:769 (b. Sept. 25, 1869, Peine—d. March 6, 1937, Marburg, both now in West Germany), theologian, philosopher, and historian of religion, exerted worldwide influence through his pioneering work of man's experience of the holy.

Abstract of text biography. Otto studied at the University of Erlangen and Göttingen and was appointed to the faculties of Göttingen (1897–1914), Breslau (1914–1917), and Marburg (1917–1929). Simultaneously, he was a member of the Prussian parliament (1913–18) and in 1918 of the Constituent Chamber. He began his inquiry into the holy with *Die Anschauung vom heiligen Geiste bei Luther* (1898; "The Perception of the Holy Spirit by Luther"), expanded in *Naturalistische und religiöse Weltansicht* (1904; *Naturalism and Religion*, 1907). An extensive world trip (1911–12) prompted him to set his ideas in a larger context. In 1917 he published his most important work, *Das Heilige* (*The Idea of the Holy*, 1923). Three major publications followed: *West-Östliche Mystik* (1926; *Mysticism East and West*, 1932); *Die Gnadenreligion Indiens und das Christentum* (1930; *India's Religion of Grace and Christianity*, 1930); and *Reich Gottes und Menschensohn* (1934; *The Kingdom of God and Son of Man*, 1938).

REFERENCES in other text articles:
·aesthetic–mystic experience comparison **1**:157f
·Christian concept of transcendence **4**:477f
·Christianity's place in history **4**:529a
·dread and attraction of the holy **15**:605f
·experiential approach to religion **15**:647d
·influence on various religious scholars **15**:624h
·mystical research **15**:621d
·mythology as a religious phenomenon **12**:794b
·psychological revelation of Kant's a priori **10**:397c
·ritual as expression of sacred realm **15**:864e
·sacred reality and human perception **16**:122h
·spiritual realm analysis **15**:592f

Ottobeuren, Abbey of, Benedictine abbey in Germany built in 1744 by J.M. Fischer.
·Baroque Bavarian Rococo architecture **19**:418h; illus.

Ottoboni, Pietro: *see* Alexander VIII.

Otto cycle, four-stroke cycle for internal-combustion engines.
·discovery and development **8**:705g

Otto Hahn, West German nuclear-powered merchant ship.
·nuclear ship experiment **16**:686d

Ottokar (Bohemian kings): *see* Otakar I; Otakar II; Otakar IV.

ottoman, a deeply upholstered seat of any shape, with or without a back, introduced into Europe in the late 18th century from Turkey, where, piled with cushions, it was the central piece of domestic seating. One of the early versions was designed as a piece of fitted furniture to go entirely around three walls of a room, and from this evolved a smaller version, designed to fit the corner of a room. As the 19th century progressed, ottomans became circular or octagonal, either with arms radiating from the centre, which divided the seating space into sections, or with a central, padded column, which often supported a plant or statue and against which one could

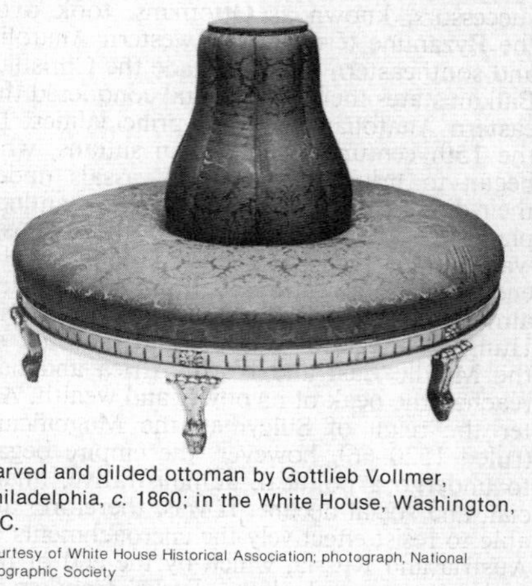

Carved and gilded ottoman by Gottlieb Vollmer, Philadelphia, *c.* 1860; in the White House, Washington, D.C.
Courtesy of White House Historical Association; photograph, National Geographic Society

lean. The growth of club life stimulated the proliferation of ottomans, many of which also came to have hinged seats underneath for holding magazines and the like. The ottoman footstool, a closely allied piece of furniture, was an upholstered footstool on four legs, which could also be used as a fireside seat.

Ottoman carpets, carpets handwoven under the earlier Ottoman sultans of Turkey. Extremely fine, handsome carpets—of wool on a foundation of silk, having floral patterning, often with schemes of large or small circular medallions—and comparable prayer rugs were made for the court, possibly at Bursa in the 16th century. Coarser, all-wool examples

Detail of an Ottoman carpet from Turkey or Cairo, late 16th century; in the Metropolitan Museum of Art, New York
By courtesy of the Metropolitan Museum of Art, New York, bequest of George Blumenthal, 1941

were made in Cairo after the conquest in 1517 and probably also at one or more sites in Anatolia. In due course many of these rugs were exported to southern Europe, where they have been preserved. Although they are mentioned in old records, all-silk examples do not seem to have survived.

Ottoman Empire and Turkey, history of the 13:771 A major Muslim power that controlled southeastern Europe, the Middle East, and North Africa for centuries, the Ottoman Empire had disintegrated by the time of World War I; its possessions formed separate states, and its centre was reorganized as the republic of Turkey.

In the 13th–14th centuries, Osman I, a Muslim prince of northwestern Anatolia, and his successors, known as Ottomans, took over the Byzantine territories of western Anatolia and southeastern Europe, made the Christian Balkan states their vassals, and conquered the eastern Anatolian Turkmen principalities. In the 15th century the Ottoman sultans, who began to bring their Balkan vassals under their direct rule, also conquered Constantinople (1453) and extended their authority eastward to the Euphrates River (1468). By the end of the 16th century, their empire included almost all of the Balkans, a large portion of Hungary in central Europe, and the bulk of the Middle East and North Africa and had reached the peak of its power and wealth. After the reign of Süleyman the Magnificent (ruled 1520–66), however, the empire began to undergo a political, administrative, financial, and social decline. It was, therefore, unable to resist effectively the encroachments of Austria and Russia, which by the end of the 18th century pushed the Turks' frontiers in Europe back to the Danube River and seized its lands on the northern Black Sea coasts. At that time the central government also lost much of its authority to local provincial rulers; and despite efforts to reform the central administration and army, the empire lost control of Egypt as well as of much of the Balkans (19th century). Although the Young Turk Revolution (1908) tried to revitalize the empire, it continued to suffer military and territorial losses in the Balkans; and after World War I, it also lost its Arab provinces and part of Asia Minor. Mustafa Kemal (later Atatürk) then declared the creation of the state of Turkey (1921) and obtained the abolition of the sultanate (1922) and a favourable revision of the peace settlement (1923). Under his autocratic presidency (1923–38), the Turkish Republic fostered Turkish nationalism and secularism and imposed its firm control over the economy. After World War II Turkey received U.S. military and economic aid and aligned itself with the West.

TEXT ARTICLE covers:

REFERENCES in other text articles:

RELATED ENTRIES in the *Ready Reference and Index: for*

Ottoman Public Debt Administration (OPDA), organization established in 1881 to collect the public debt of the Ottoman Empire.

·formation and economic program 13:787g

Ottonian art, art produced during the reigns of the German Ottonian emperors and their first successors from the Salic House (950–1050).

As inheritors of the Carolingian tradition of the Holy Roman Empire, the German emperors also assumed the Carolingian artistic heritage, the conscientious revival of late antique and Early Christian art forms (*see* Carolingian art). Ottonian art later developed a style of its own, however, distinct from the Carolingian tradition. This was particularly true in painting, ivory carving, and sculpture. Ottonian illuminators were less concerned with naturalism and more with expression through sober, dramatic gesture and heightened coloration. Ivory carving continued to be produced for liturgical purposes; as can be seen in scenes from the ivory plaques of the "Magdeburg Antependium" (*c.* 970), carvings have a characteristic restraint, the narrative is conveyed through simple gestures and enlivened by an original kind of decoration such as that in the strongly patterned background. An important development in Ottonian art was that of

Ottonian ivory plaque from the "Magdeburg Antependium," *c.* 970; in the Metropolitan Museum of Art, New York

By courtesy of the Metropolitan Museum of Art, New York; gift of George Blumenthal, 1941

large-scale sculpture. Stone sculpture continued to be rare, but wooden crucifixes such as the over-life-size "Gero Crucifix" (before 986; Cathedral of Cologne) and wooden reliquaries covered with gold leaf began a return to sculpture in the round. Bronze casting, an antique art practiced also by the Carolingians, flourished. Its most impressive manifestation was in relief-covered bronze doors commissioned by Bishop Bernward of Hildesheim (died 1022) for his cathedral.

Ottonian architecture was more conservative, expanding and elaborating Carolingian forms rather than developing a new style. The westwork, or fortress-like construction with towers and inner rooms through which one entered the nave, and outer crypt, or chapel complexes below and beyond the eastern apse (projection at the end of the church), were retained and enlarged; the Carolingian double apses (projections at each end of the nave) were elaborated with double transepts. Ottonian architecture was more regulated than Carolingian, with simple interior spaces and a more systematic layout. St. Michael's (founded *c.* 1001), Hildesheim, exemplifies this regularity, with two crypts, two apses, and two transepts, each with a crossing tower.

The achievements of Ottonian artists provided background and impetus for the new monumentality distinguished as Romanesque (*q.v.*).

·copperwork on Catholic liturgy objects **11**:1095a
·enamelwork techniques and tradition **6**:776b
·stylistic evolution from Carolingian **11**:1104c
·Western Christian visual art styles **19**:351c; illus. 121

Ottonian Privilege, Latin PRIVILEGIUM OTTONIANUM (962), treaty concluded between Emperor Otto I the Great and Pope John XII.

·Otto I's Italian campaigns **13**:768f

Otto of Freising (b. *c.* 1111—d. Sept. 22, 1158, Morimond, Champagne, France), German bishop and author of one of the most important historico-philosophical works of the Middle Ages. He entered (1132 or 1133) the Cistercian monastery at Morimond in eastern Champagne and became its abbot in 1138 but immediately was called as bishop to Freising in Bavaria. As half-brother of the Hohenstaufen German king Conrad III and as uncle of Frederick I Barbarossa, Otto influenced the policy of the *Reich*, and was present at the imperial diet of Besançon in the County of Burgundy (1157).

Otto's *Chronica sive historia de duabus civitatibus* is a history of the world from the beginning to 1146. Following St. Augustine, it interprets all secular history as a conflict between the *civitas Dei* ("the realm of God") and the world; and it views its contemporary period as that in which Antichrist (the principal personage of power opposed to Christ) is to appear. His second work, the *Gesta Friderici*, deals with the house of Hohenstaufen and with the deeds of Frederick Barbarossa up to 1156.

·historiographic works and methodology **8**:950a

Otto of Nordheim (d. Jan. 11, 1083), duke of Bavaria and also a leading noble in Saxony, the most implacable opponent of the German king Henry IV.

In 1061, Agnes of Poitou, regent for her young son Henry IV, invested Otto with the duchy of Bavaria. The following year, however, he helped Archbishop Anno of Cologne to kidnap Henry IV, an act that deprived Agnes of the regency. From then until the end of Henry's minority, Otto played a prominent part in the government of the German state. He led an expedition against the Hungarians in 1063, went with Anno to Italy to settle the schism between Pope Alexander II and the antipope Honorius in 1064, and helped to secure the dismissal of the powerful archbishop Adalbert of Bremen as guardian and adviser of the young king in 1066. Along with other Saxon nobles, he did not hesitate to take advantage of Henry's minority to usurp part of the king's demesne.

In 1070 Otto was accused of complicity in a plot to murder the king. Required to confront his accuser in ordeal by battle, he asked for a safe-conduct, and, when this was refused, declined to present himself. The duchy of Bavaria was taken from him, and a diet of Saxon nobles deprived him of his Saxon possessions as well. He promptly rebelled, and held out for a number of months in Saxony. Taken prisoner in 1071, he was restored to his lands in Saxony in 1072.

Shortly after the Saxon uprising against Henry IV broke out in 1073, Otto assumed its leadership. The short-lived Peace of Gerstungen (1074) stipulated Otto's restoration to Bavaria. But when Henry resumed war against the Saxons in June 1075, Otto was taken prisoner again. Around Christmas of that year, however, Henry not only pardoned Otto, but also gave him a high administrative post in Saxony.

Nevertheless, after the excommunication and deposition of Henry by Pope Gregory VII over the investiture of bishops (1076), Otto rejoined the Saxon rebels. As soon as his restoration to Bavaria was assured, he assented to the election of Rudolf of Rheinfelden as German king in opposition to Henry (1077). A skillful fighter, Otto inflicted losses on Henry's forces in 1078 and in January 1080 and won the battle on the Elster River in October of that year; but Rudolf received a mortal wound in the battle. The forces opposing Henry then elected Hermann of Salm as antiking, but Hermann's chief military support collapsed with Otto's death less than three years later.

·Henry IV's rebellion solution **8**:761e

otto of rose (essential oil): *see* attar of roses.

ottrelite (mineral): *see* chloritoid.

Ottumwa, city, seat (1844) of Wapello County, southeastern Iowa, U.S., on the Des Moines River. Settled in 1843 as Louisville, it was renamed (1845) Ottumwa, an Indian word meaning "rippling waters." Following a damaging flood (1947), the city recovered its position as a commercial and manufacturing centre with a locally financed program of self-help, "Operation Bootstrap." Meat-packing and the manufacture of farm equipment are the chief industries. Ottumwa is the home of Iowa Technical Institute (1962) and Ottumwa Heights College (1925). Inc. town, 1851; city, 1857. Pop. (1960) 33,871; (1980) 27,381. 41°01′ N, 92°25′ W

·map, United States **18**:908

Ottweiler porcelain, true, or hard-paste, German porcelain produced in the Rhineland from 1763 onward. The factory was started by Étienne-Dominique Pellevé, a porcelain maker from Rouen, Fr., under the patronage of Prince Wilhelm Heinrich of Nassau-Saarbrucken. The Ottweiler factory was situated within the prince's garden. Few specimens of Ottweiler porcelain are known. After 1789 the works produced only a kind of stoneware called English Stone porcelain.

Ottweiler hard-paste porcelain coffee jug, *c.* 1765; in the Victoria and Albert Museum, London

By courtesy of the Victoria and Albert Museum, London; photograph, EB Inc.

Otway, Thomas (b. March 3, 1652, Trotton, near Midhurst, Sussex—d. April 14, 1685, London), dramatist and poet, one of the forerunners of sentimental drama through his presentation of human emotions in an age of heroic but artificial tragedies. His masterpiece, *Venice Preserved*, was one of the greatest theatrical successes of his period. He studied at Winchester College and at Oxford but left in 1671 without taking a degree. He went to London where he was offered a part by Aphra Behn in one of her plays. He was overcome by stage fright, and his first performance was his last.

His first play, a rhyming tragedy called *Alcibiades*, was produced at the Duke's Theatre at Dorset Garden in September 1675. The part of Draxilla in this play was created by the famous actress Elizabeth Barry, and Otway fell violently in love with her. Six unsigned love letters, said to be addressed to Mrs. Barry, were published in a collection that appeared in 1697, 12 years after Otway's death. His second play, *Don Carlos*, produced in June 1676, had an immense success on the

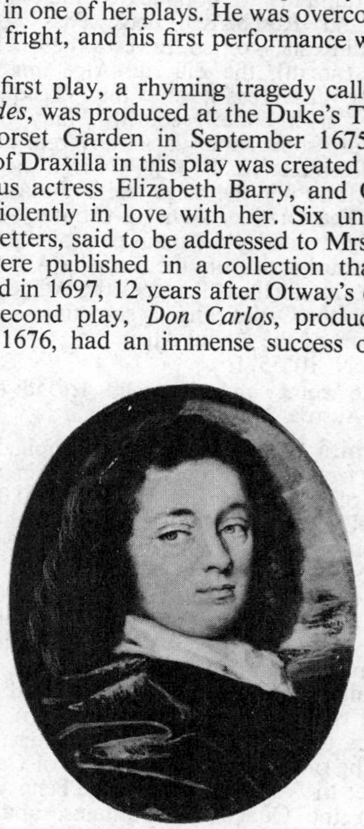

Otway, miniature by Thomas Flatman, *c.* 1675; in the Victoria and Albert Museum, London

By courtesy of the Victoria and Albert Museum, London

stage and is the best of his rhymed heroic plays. *Titus and Berenice*, adapted from Molière, and *The Cheats of Scapin*, adapted from Jean Racine, were published together in 1677.

In 1678 Otway obtained a commission in an English regiment serving in the Netherlands, and he was abroad when his first comedy, *Friendship in Fashion*, was staged. His next play, *Caius Marius*, a curious mixture of a story from Plutarch with an adaptation of *Romeo and Juliet*, was staged in 1679. He published his powerful, gloomy autobiographical poem, *The Poet's Complaint of His Muse*, in 1680.

Otway's most memorable dramatic work was done in the last years of his short life. In the spring of 1680 his fine blank verse domestic tragedy *The Orphan* had great success on the stage. On March 1 in the same year his best comedy, *The Souldier's Fortune*, probably drawn from his military experience, was produced. *Venice Preserved*, also written in blank verse, was first performed at the Duke's Theater in 1682. Until the middle of the 19th century it was probably revived more often than any poetic play except those of Shakespeare. The plot is founded on the Abbé de Saint-Réal's historical novel, *La Conjuration des Espagnols contre la république de Venise en l'année 1618* (1674). Dryden, who wrote the prologue, was generous in his praise. "Nature," he wrote, "is there, which is the greatest beauty."

Another comedy, *The Atheist* (printed 1684), some poems, and *The History of the Triumvirates*, a piece of hack work published posthumously in 1686, complete the list of Otway's writings.

Otway Basin, land depression in Melbourne, Australia.

·formation, relief, and composition **2**:387c

Otzaki, archaeological site in Thessaly, Greece.

·Sesklo archaeological discoveries **2**:613b; map 612

Ötztal Alps, German ÖTZTALER ALPEN, Italian ALPI VENOSTE, eastern segment of the Central Alps lying mainly in the southern Tirol (western Austria) and partly in northern Italy. The mountains are bounded by the Rhaetian Alps and Reschenscheideck Pass (Italian Passo di Resia, west-southwest), the Inn River Valley (north), the Zillertal Alps (*q.v.*) and Brenner Pass (east), and the Val d'Adige (Adige River Valley, south). Many of the peaks are snow- and glacier-covered, including Wildspitze (12,382 ft [3,774 m]), the highest point both in the range and in the Austrian Tirol. The Ötztaler Ache, a tributary of the Inn River, divides the main part of the range to the southwest from the Stubaier Alpen section to the northeast. Across the Adige River in Italy, the Ortles range is sometimes considered part of the Ötztal Alps.
46°45′ N, 10°55′ E

·Alpine geology and geography **1**:634d; map
·map, Austria **2**:442

Ouachita Geosyncline, name applied to a linear trough in the Earth's crust in which rocks of Paleozoic age (from 225,000,000 to 570,000,000 years old) were deposited along the southern margin of North America, from Mississippi to eastern Mexico. Most of the belt is buried by undisturbed, younger (Cretaceous and Cenozoic) rocks of the Mississippi Embayment and the Gulf Coastal Plain, but marginal parts of the belt are exposed in the Ouachita Mountains of Arkansas and Oklahoma, the Marathon uplift of western Texas, and scattered remnants in northeastern Mexico. The oldest exposed rocks are of Cambrian age; the youngest are Middle Pennsylvanian, in the Ouachita Mountains, and Late Pennsylvanian, in the Marathon uplift. Rocks of Cambrian through Devonian age consist of dark, siliceous shales, sandstones, and cherts, which indicate slow deposition over a long period of time. Mississippian through Pennsylvanian rocks, on the other hand, consist of thick sequences of shales and sandstones deposited rapidly in a subsiding trough.

Deformation of the geosyncline probably began during Early Paleozoic time in the buried interior portions of the geosyncline, but the marginal exposed portions were not deformed until post-Middle Pennsylvanian time in the Ouachita Mountains and post-Late Pennsylvanian in the Marathon uplift. Deformation, based on the evidence now available, seems to have shifted from the interior portions of the geosyncline northward to the marginal portions through time. The name Ouachita orogeny is applied to the event that resulted in the folding and northward thrusting of the exposed marginal part of the geosyncline.

The Ouachita Geosyncline may represent a southward continuation of the Appalachian Geosyncline, which was displaced westward by the opening up of the Gulf of Mexico in Early Mesozoic time.

·Appalachian mountain-building process **13**:181c
·Silurian rocks and paleogeography **16**:770b

Ouachita Mountains, range that continues the Ozark Plateau, extending approximately 225 mi (360 km) east to west from Little Rock, Ark., to Atoka, Okla., and north to south, approximately 50–60 mi from the Arkansas River Valley to the northern margin of the Coastal Plain. The highest elevation (2,950 ft [899 m]) is Rich Mountain in Le Flore County, Okla., near the Arkansas line. Hot Springs National Park lies in the Ouachita Mountains. The word Ouachita is derived from an Indian tribal name.
34°40′ N, 94°25′ W

·Appalachian mountain-building process **13**:181c
·inhabitants and farming **2**:6e
·location and Appalachian origin **18**:907e; map 906
·map, United States **18**:908
·topography and economic activity **13**:543a

Ouachita National Forest, in Arkansas and Oklahoma, U.S., including parts of the Ouachita and Kiamichi mountains and lying south of the Arkansas River. Established as Arkansas National Forest in 1907 and renamed in 1926, it has an area of 3,708 sq mi (9,605 sq km), mostly in Arkansas. The forest is drained by the Fourche la Fave and Ouachita rivers and their lake systems, including Lake Ouachita (52 mi [84 km]) long, formed by Blakely Mountain Dam northwest of Hot Springs National Park (the forest headquarters). Large deposits of novaculite (siliceous rock used for whetstones) are embedded in mountain ridges. Scenic areas are at Blowout and Crystal mountains, Dutch Creek, and Lake Winona. The 55-mi Talihina Scenic Drive follows the crests of Winding Stair and Rich mountains from near Talihina, Okla., to Mena, Ark.

Ouachita orogeny, name applied to the mountain-building event that resulted in the folding and faulting of exposed strata in the Ouachita Geosyncline in the southern portion of the United States in Arkansas, Oklahoma, and the Marathon uplift region of West Texas. The deformation is Late Paleozoic in age, probably culminating in Late Pennsylvanian and Early Permian (about 280,000,000 years ago) time. The orogeny resulted in a northward and westward compression in the geosynclinal strata onto adjacent platform rocks.

Ouachita River rises in the Ouachita Mountains of west central Arkansas, U.S., and flows east, then south, southwest, and southeast, joining the Red River in Louisiana after a course of 605 mi (973 km). The lower 57 mi of the Ouachita (from its confluence with the Tensas River) is known as the Black River (*q.v.*). Most of its 25,000-sq-mi (65,000-sq-km) drainage basin lies in the upper Coastal Plain of Arkansas and Louisiana and the alluvial valley of the Mississippi. Chief tributaries are the Boeuf and Tensas rivers (*qq.v.*) entering from the east, Bayou Bartholemew from the west, and the Saline River (*q.v.*) from the north.

The Ouachita has been a navigation route since the late 18th century. Six locks and dams were built prior to 1924. There are three multipurpose dams (hydropower, flood control, recreational facilities) on the upper Ouachita within the Ouachita Mountains: Blakely Mountain (1955) and Carpenter (1931) dams near Hot Springs National Park, impounding Lakes Ouachita and Hamilton, and Remmel Dam (1924), impounding Lake Catherine.

Chief riparian cities are Arkadelphia and Camden, Ark. (the latter linked to the Ouachita by a channel [1950]), and Monroe, La. Formerly called the Washita River, the name Ouachita is derived from that of an Indian tribe.
31°38′ N, 91°49′ W

Ouaddaï, *préfecture* in eastern Chad, Central Africa, whose capital is Abéché. Its area of 29,435 sq mi (76,240 sq km) of savanna grasslands roughly corresponds to the formerly independent Ouaddaï Muslim sultanate. Its Muslim inhabitants, the Maba, are primarily a Negroid, Sudanic people. The region has long been important as a trade and cultural link between North and Equatorial Africa and West Africa and the Middle East, being crossed by caravan and pilgrimage routes. From the 1850s the Sanūsīyah Islāmic brotherhood remained the dominant political and religious force until the French conquest of the area. The brotherhood fiercely resisted the French against whom a holy war, *jihād*, was declared in 1908 by the Sultan of Ouaddaï. In 1912 the French abolished the sultanate, but sporadic resistance continued. A famine in 1913–14 devastated the population.

Chad and Ouaddaï politics since independence in 1960 have been dominated by tensions between the Muslim, nomadic north and the more populous, sedentary Christian, or animist south. Muslim northerners have virtually been excluded from government and administration at all levels, and banditry, long prevalent in Ouaddaï and eastern Chad under the French, has evolved into guerrilla warfare against the southern-dominated government. Pop. (1970 est.) 344,000.

·geographic and population features **4**:14b; table 15
·map, Chad **4**:13

Ouagadougou, capital and largest town of Upper Volta, West Africa. It is the terminus for the railway from Abidjan, Ivory Coast, linking landlocked Upper Volta with the Atlantic Ocean. It is also on a main east–west road across Africa that connects with Niamey

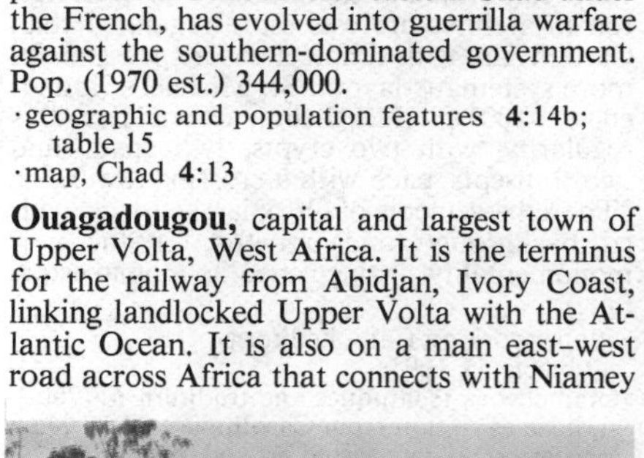

French embassy building, Ouagadougou, Upper Volta
Walter Weiss—Ostman Agency

(Niger) in the east and Bobo Dioulasso and Bamako (Mali) in the west. A road going south links the town with Tamale, Kumasi, Accra, and Trema in Ghana. An international airport is near the capital. Ouagadougou is said to have been founded *c.* AD 1050 as the seat of the *morho naba* ("big lord") of the ancient and numerous Mossi people. The *morho naba* still lives there, though his powers have been greatly eclipsed by the French colonial

and post-independent administrations. Groundnuts (peanuts) and shea-butter products are the primary exports. A technical boarding school and college are located in the town. Pop. (1970 est.) 124,779.
12°22′ N, 1°31′ W
·administration, population, transportation, and culture **18**:1019c *passim* to 1021b
·Ivory Coast railway system **9**:1185d
·map, Africa **1**:179
·origin theory and location **19**:764h; map 765

Ouahran (Algeria): *see* Oran.

Ouaka, *préfecture*, Central African Republic, bordered by Zaire across the Ubangi (Oubangui) River to the south. The capital is Bambari, on the Bangui-Buta road, which crosses the *préfecture* (west to east). Agricultural products include cotton, wax, sisal, and groundnuts (peanuts). There is an airfield at Bambari. The Ouaka River, which crosses the *préfecture* (northeast to southwest), is navigable to the Ubangi River (*c.* 150 miles).
·area and population table **3**:1104
·map, Central African Republic **3**:1102

ouananiche: *see* Atlantic salmon.

Ouaphris (Egyptian king): *see* Apries.

Ouargla, capital of Oasis *wilāyat* (province), Algeria, on the western edge of a *sebkha*

The Saharan museum in Ouargla, Alg.
Shostal

(large, enclosed basin) in the Sahara. One of the oldest settlements in the Sahara was made by the Ibāḍīyah, a Muslim heretical sect, at nearby Sedrata in the 10th century (ruins remain). In the 11th century they fled to Ghardaïa (*q.v.*), and the Ouargla site was settled by Berbers and black Africans. The town remained autonomous but for a brief period of Turkish control in the 16th century. The French gained possession of Ouargla in 1872, and the present town was built around Ft. Lutaud to the south after 1928.
Ouargla is walled with six gates, an arcaded marketplace, and a Saharan museum. It is surrounded by date palm groves and fruit and vegetable gardens irrigated by numerous wells, tapped from the underground Oued Mya. There is a trade in livestock, woollen carpets, and basketry. Hassi Messaoud, with its valuable deposits of oil and natural gas, lies 50 mi (80 km) east-southeast. Latest census 18,206.
31°57′ N, 5°20′ E
·map, Northern Algeria **1**:560

Ouarzazate, town and province of south central Morocco, on the Saharan side of the

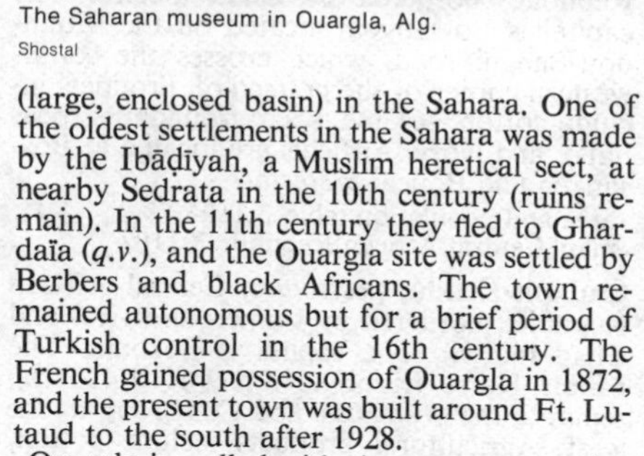
The fortress, Ouarzazate, Mor.
Ed Scully—Photo Trends

Haut (High) Atlas. The town, situated in the valley of the Oued Ouarzazate near its juncture with the Oued Drâa, originated as a military post during the French occupation (1932–56). Still a military centre with a fortress, it is also an important oasis and road junction linked to Marrakech by way of Tizi (pass) n' Tichka.
Ouarzazate province, extending from the crests of the Haut (High) Atlas southward to the borders of the Sahara, is an arid region of 21,506 sq mi (55,700 sq km) inhabited only in the valleys, chiefly those of the Dadès and Drâa. Its greatest economic resource lies in the manganese mines of Imini and the cobalt mines of Bou-Azzer. The agricultural potential of the Oued Drâa valley was enhanced in the early 1970s with the completion of a dam 10 mi (16 km) downstream from Ouarzazate. Pop. (1971) town, 11,142; province, 522,376.
·area and population table and map **12**:444
·map, Morocco **12**:446
·town's economic aspects **12**:448a

Ouatchi Plateau, area of loams and clayey sands behind the coastal lagoons of Togo.
·Togo physical geography **18**:471d

Oubangui-Chari: *see* Central African Republic.

Oubangui River (Africa): *see* Ubangi River.

Ouchy, Treaty of: *see* Lausanne, Treaty of.

oud (stringed instrument): *see* ʿūd.

Oud, Jacobus Johannes Pieter (b. Feb. 9, 1890, Purmerend, near Amsterdam—d. April 5, 1963, Wassenaar, near The Hague), architect notable for his pioneering role in the development of modern architecture. He was educated in Amsterdam and at the Delft Technical University. He worked with a number of architects; then in 1916 he met Theo van Doesburg. With van Doesburg he helped to found the influential review *De Stijl* in 1917. Oud made important contributions to the de Stijl movement, which in architecture meant achieving a balance through the use of contrasting planes and volumes, horizontal and vertical lines, and primary colours. Among his important theoretical experiments in the de Stijl idiom were a plan for houses at Scheveningen (1917) and a plan for a factory at Purmerend (1919). Cubelike forms were emphasized in his hotel at Noordwijkerhout (1917) and the Allegonda villa at Katwijk (1917).
In 1918 Oud was appointed housing architect to the city of Rotterdam. There his housing blocks of Spangen (1918) and Tuschendijken (1920) had a severity that contrasted strongly with the picturesqueness and elaboration of details associated with the works of the school of Amsterdam led by Michel de Klerk. His Café de Unie (1924–27, destroyed in 1940) and Kiefhoek estate (1925–27), both in Amsterdam, emphasized de Stijl principles, although by then he was tending toward separation from the movement. His book *Höllandische Architektur* (1926) gave him an international reputation. Other notable projects during the 1920s were the housing estates of Oud-Mathenesse (1922) and Hook of Holland (1924).
Following a long illness Oud again became active in the late 1930s. Among his late works are his Shell Building (1938) in The Hague, the Bio-Children's Convalescent Home (1952–60) near Arnhem, and the Congress Hall (completed in 1968) in The Hague.
·De Stijl movement in architecture **19**:468a

Oudenaarde, French AUDENARDE, municipality, East Flanders province, west central Belgium, on the Scheldt (Schelde) River, south of Ghent. A prosperous tapestry-making centre in the Middle Ages, its industry declined in the 15th century with the success of the Gobelin tapestry weavers (trained in Oudenaarde), many of whom later went to Paris.

Town hall, Oudenaarde, Belg.
Nels—Club Iris

Landmarks include the town hall (1526–36) with its five-story belfry, the 13th-century Cloth Hall, the Church of St. Walburga with its carillon, and the Church of Our Lady of Pamele (1325). The old bishop's residence (1600) was the birthplace of Margaret of Parma, natural daughter of Charles V and Johanna van der Gheenst.
Beer and textiles are the main products of Oudenaarde, which includes the outlying towns of Bevere, Edelare, Eine, Ename, Leupegem, Nederename, and Volkegem. Pop. (1971 est.) 22,019.
50°51′ N, 30°36′ E
·economic fluctuations in 17th century **11**:155f
·map, Belgium **2**:818

Oudenaarde, Battle of (July 11, 1708), victory over the French won by the Duke of Marlborough and Prince Eugene of Savoy during the War of the Spanish Succession; it eventually led to the Allied (Anglo-Dutch-Austrian) recapture of Ghent and Bruges, which had been captured by the French on July 4–5. It was fought north of the town of Oudenaarde, between an Allied army of 80,000 men under Marlborough and Eugene and a French army of 85,000 men under the marshal Louis-Joseph, duc de Vendôme, and Louis, duc de Bourgogne. The French were preparing to besiege Oudenaarde and were caught off guard. The Allied army, which had marched 50 miles in 65 hours, crossed the Scheldt River on July 11 and immediately attacked before the French could deploy properly. The French command had been divided: Bourgogne had wanted to retreat and only at the last moment consented to Vendôme's plea to stand and fight. All afternoon a bitter and confused battle raged. Unnoticed by the French, Marlborough sent a Dutch force on a long detour to the west. It struck the French right flank while Eugene pressed against the French left. By the time darkness forced a halt, the French had lost 6,000 killed or wounded and another 9,000 captured. The Allies suffered about 4,000 casualties. The next day Vendôme rallied the defeated army and repulsed the Allies at Ghent. Marl-

borough recaptured Ghent and Bruges in January 1709, and the French withdrew to their own border.
·Austria's threat to Paris **2**:456f

Oudh (India): *see* Ayodhyā.

Oudinot, Nicolas-Charles (b. April 25, 1767, Bar-le-Duc, Fr.—d. Sept. 13, 1847, Paris), general, administrator, and marshal of France in the Napoleonic Wars whose career illustrates the opportunities to rise in the French Army after the Revolution.

The son of a businessman, Oudinot joined France's royal army in 1784, but, since commoners were barred from promotion, resigned in 1787. After the French Revolution, however, he became the leader of Meuse volunteers (1792) and was transferred to the regular army the following year, rising to general of brigade (1794) for his heroic resistance at Kaiserslautern. General of division (1799) and chief of staff under André Masséna, Oudinot fought in Switzerland and Italy and then commanded an elite division of grenadiers (1805–07) in fighting at Austerlitz and Ostrolenka.

Oudinot was promoted to marshal after the Battle of Wagram (1809) and was created duke of Reggio in 1810. After serving as administrator in Holland (1809–12) and fighting in the Russian campaign, he was badly defeated in 1813 at Grossbeeren, Ger., after which he was superseded by Michel Ney. After Napoleon's abdication in 1814, Oudinot rallied to Louis XVIII, remaining loyal to him during the Hundred Days (1815). He served in Spain in 1823 and was governor of the Invalides (veterans' hospital) from 1842 until his death.

Oudry, Jean-Baptiste (b. March 17, 1686, Paris—d. April 30, 1755, Beauvais, Fr.), Rococo painter, tapestry designer, and illustrator, considered one of the greatest animal painters of the 18th century. He first studied

"The Calling of the Hounds," tapestry by Jean-Baptiste Oudry, 1742–45; in the Palazzo Pitti, Florence
SCALA, New York

portrait painting with Nicolas de Largillière, a portraitist of Parisian society, through whom he made many connections. His early portraits are often arcadian in setting and tender and sentimentally charming in the Rococo tradition. Also in his early career he executed many still lifes that were used as decorative inserts for panelled rooms. After he was made a member of the French Royal Academy in 1719, his work consisted largely of animal paintings, tapestry designs, and book illustrations.

In 1734 Oudry was made head of the Beauvais tapestry works. Some of his designs brought the company world fame, such as those for the tapestry series "Country Amusements" (1730), "Moliere's Comedies" (1732), and "The Fables of La Fontaine" (1736). The designs for the last series were related to the 277 illustrations Oudry did for a four volume edition of the *Fables*. Other book illustrations included those for editions of *Don Quixote* and *Le Roman comique*. In 1736 he was made inspector general of the Gobelins tapestry factory and designed a series of tapestries (1736–49) depicting the hunts of Louis XV. He was also commissioned to paint the dogs of the king's pack and was appointed official painter of the royal hunts. Oudry's tapestries, like his paintings, were highly regarded for their tonal subtlety and lively study of nature. His services were sought not only by Louis XV but by Tsar Peter the Great of Russia, the Queen of Sweden, and the Prince of Mecklenburg-Schwerin.
·Gobelin tapestry factory directorship **17**:1063f

oued (hydrology): *see* ephemeral stream.

Ouémé, *département* in Dahomey.
·population growth 1961–68 table **5**:422

Ouémé River, also known as WEME RIVER, rises in the Atacora massif in northwest Dahomey. It is about 310 mi (500 km) in length and flows south, being joined by its main affluent, the Okpara, on the left and by the Zou on the right, and then divides into two branches, one discharging into Lac (lake) Nokoué in the Niger Delta near Cotonou, and the other into Lagune (lagoon) de Porto-Novo. Rain forests grow along the shores; navigation, although impeded by rapids, is possible during the rainy season. Freshwater fish, dried, smoked, and salted, are exported to Nigeria and Togo. Millet, sweet potatoes, and yams are cultivated, and the Ouémé Valley development scheme is Dahomey's largest single project for improving agriculture.
6°29′ N, 2°32′ E
·map, Dahomey **5**:421

Ouenza, town, Annaba *wilāyat* (province), northeastern Algeria, on the eastern border with Tunisia. The nearby Djebel (mount) Ouenza (4,226 ft [1,288 m]) is the site of extensive iron ore deposits making Ouenza one of Algeria's leading mining centres. Latest census 29,069.
35°57′ N, 8°04′ E
·Algerian mining centre **1**:566b
·map, Northern Algeria **1**:560

Ouessant Island, French ÎLE D'OUESSANT, also called USHANT ISLAND, a rocky island, Finistère *département*, off the western tip of Bretagne, western France. The island, about 5 mi (8 km) long and 2 mi wide, has an area of 6 sq mi (15 sq km). Its lighthouse, Phare de Creac'h, marks the south entrance to the English Channel, the north entrance light being at Land's End, England. Lampaul, the little port that is the capital of Ouessant, is the chief settlement of fishermen; its fields, which cover only a small fraction of the island, traditionally have been worked by the fishermen's wives. A large but indecisive action was fought off Ouessant in July 1778 between British and French fleets. Latest census 1,814.
48°28′ N, 5°05′ W
·map, France **7**:584

Ouest, department, Haiti.
·area and population **8**:550; table 5

Oughtred, William (b. March 5, 1574, Eton, Buckinghamshire—d. June 30, 1660, Albury, Surrey), mathematician and Episcopal minister who invented the earliest form of the slide rule, two identical linear or circular logarithmic scales held together and adjusted by hand. Improvements involving the familiar inner rule with tongue-in-groove linear construction came later. In 1604 Oughtred became vicar of Shalford, Surrey, and subsequently rector of Albury. Although his years in the ministry included the period of the Commonwealth, when more than 8,000 clerics were deprived of their charges, he was permitted to continue in his parish.

Oughtred, detail of a watercolour by G.P. Harding after a portrait by W. Hollar, 1644; in the National Portrait Gallery, London
By courtesy of the National Portrait Gallery, London

Oughtred's most important published work was the *Clavis Mathematicae* (1631; "The Keys to Mathematics"), which included a description of Hindu–Arabic notation and decimal fractions and a considerable section on algebra. He experimented with many different algebraic symbols and was responsible for the use of the symbol "::" in writing a proportion and the symbol "×" for multiplication. His work on slide rules was an adaptation to a physical scale of the tabular logarithms of John Napier of Scotland. His early form of circular slide rule was invented before 1632 and the pair of rectilinear, relatively slidable members by 1633. His claim of priority of the circular rule was contested by one of his former students, Richard Delamaine the elder. Oughtred's *Trigonometria* (1657) treated plane and spherical trigonometry.
·history of calculatory device and table **11**:653f
·mathematical calculation theory and use **11**:683c

Ouham, *préfecture*, central Central African Republic, bordered by Chad (north). The capital is Bossangoa, located on the Moundou-Bangui road, which crosses the southwestern corner of the *préfecture*. Products include cotton, sesame, wax, groundnuts (peanuts), and ivory. Airfields are located at Bossangoa and Bouca. *préfecture*,
·area and population table **3**:1104
·map, Central African Republic **3**:1102

Ouham-Pendé, *préfecture*, Central African Republic, bordered by Cameroon (west) and Chad (north). The capital is Bozoum. The Monts Karre (rising to 4,659 ft [1,420 m]) separate the *préfecture* and Cameroon to the west. Agricultural products include cotton, sesame, groundnuts (peanuts), and livestock. Airfields are located at Bozoum and Paoua. Roads connect the capital, Bozoum, with Cameroon, Chad, and other parts of the Republic.
·area and population table **3**:1104
·map, Central African Republic **3**:1102

Ouham River, formerly called BAHR SARA, stream of central Africa; one of the main headwaters of the Chari River (*q.v.*). It rises in two main branches in the elevated plateau country of the western Central African Republic, flows north, crossing the international frontier into Chad, and joins the Chari just north of Fort-Archambault. The Ouham's length, from its longest (eastern) branch to its junction with the Chari, is estimated at 420 mi (676 km); it is navigable for commercial traffic in its lower course.
9°18′ N, 18°14′ E
·map, Chad **4**:13

Ouida, pseudonym of MARIA LOUISE RAMÉ OR DE LA RAMÉE (b. Jan. 1, 1839, Bury St. Edmunds, Suffolk—d. Jan. 25, 1908, Viareggio, Italy), English novelist, famous for her extravagant melodramatic romances of fashionable life. Her father was a teacher of French, and the pseudonym "Ouida" derived from a childhood version of "Louisa." Her first novel, *Granville de Vigne* (renamed *Held in Bond-*

age, 1863), was first published serially in 1860. Her accounts of high-society life were often wildly inaccurate, particularly in details of sports and professions, but a stirring narrative style and a refreshing lack of sermonizing caught the public's fancy and made her extraordinarily popular. *Strathmore* (1865) and *Chandos* (1866) were followed by *Under Two Flags* (1867), with a gallant, aristocratic hero who, falsely accused of his younger brother's crime, joins the French Foreign Legion. After travelling in Italy, Ouida settled at Florence in 1874, and, among many subsequent novels, *Moths* (1880) was one of her best. She was the author of a number of animal stories, of which *A Dog of Flanders* (1872) was long a children's favourite. Reckless extravagance reduced her to acute poverty in later life.

Ouidah, also spelled WHYDAH, town in Atlantique *département*, southwestern Dahomey, on the Gulf of Guinea of West Africa's Atlantic coast. It is primarily only of historical importance, having been the main port of the Kingdom of Abomey in the 18th and 19th centuries. Portuguese, French, Dutch, Danish, British, and Americans all vied for a share of the slave and palm-oil trade made available through Ouidah by the efficiently organized and centralized kingdom. In 1893 the area came under French control. Some of the old forts, a cathedral, and a temple of the Abomey traditional religion remain. Ouidah is connected by road and railway to Cotonou, 20 mi (32 km) east, the major port and commercial centre of Dahomey. Coconut-, palm-, and coffee-growing areas surround Ouidah. Pop. (1971 est.) 27,000.
6°22′ N, 2°05′ E
·European slave trade centre **5**:422b

Ouija board, in occultism, a device ostensibly used for obtaining messages from the spirit world. The name derives from the French and German words for "yes" (*oui* and *ja*). The Ouija board consists of an oblong piece of wood with letters of the alphabet inscribed along its longer edge in a wide half-moon. On top of this, a much smaller, heart-shaped board is placed, mounted on casters, which enable it to slide freely. Each participant lightly places a finger on the small board, which then slides about because of the resultant pressure. The letters pointed out by the apex of the board may in some instances spell out words or even sentences. In the late 19th century, when the Ouija board was a popular pastime, it was fashionable to ascribe such happenings to discarnate spirits; more recent interpretation has emphasized that the collective nature of the experiment probably liberates subconscious thoughts and emotions that direct the Ouija board.

Ouimet, Francis (b. May 8, 1893, Brookline, Mass.—d. Sept. 2, 1967, Newton), amateur golfer whose prowess did much to remove the British upper-class aura from the game and to popularize it in the U.S. After starting as a caddie and working in a dry-goods store to earn his expenses, he gained a limited recognition until the 1913 U.S. Open championship. In that event he tied the English professionals Harry Vardon and Ted Ray and then defeated them in the playoff. That victory gave golf an impetus in the U.S. that has accelerated ever since. Ouimet won the U.S. Amateur championship in 1914 (when he also won the French Amateur) and 1931. He played on the U.S. Walker Cup team continuously from 1922 through 1936 and was nonplaying captain from 1936 through 1949, excluding the war years. Elected captain of the Royal and Ancient Golf Club of St. Andrews in 1951, he was the first non-Briton to receive this honour.
·championship tournament
record **8**:247e

Oujda, city of eastern Morocco and capital of Oujda province, near the Algerian border. Founded in 944 by Zanātah Berbers, it was fought over by Berbers, Arabs, and Turks and destroyed and rebuilt so often that it was called Medinet el-Haira, "City of Fear." Peace finally came after French occupation (1907). The Moroccan and Algerian railways meet at Oujda, the main function of which is as a frontier post. It is also a tourist centre. There are traces of ancient walls, but its appearance is generally modern, with wide avenues and parks. Oujda is near Sidi Yahya oasis, a legendary burial place of John the Baptist and site of the Battle of Isly, where the French defeated the Moors in 1844. Pop. (1971) 175,532.
34°40′ N, 1°54′ W
·map, Morocco **12**:446
·physical layout and composition **12**:448a
·province area and population table **12**:444; map 448

Oullins, town, industrial suburb of Lyon, Rhône *département*, southeast central France. It has two 16th-century châteaus (Grand-Perron and Petit-Perron), and an 18th-century palace built by Cardinal Pierre de Tencin. Latest census 26,520.
45°43′ N, 4°48′ E
·map, France **7**:584

Oulu, long form OULUN LÄÄNI (Oulu province), Swedish ULEÅBORG, in central Finland, bounded on the west by the Gulf of Bothnia and on the east by the U.S.S.R. It has a land area of 21,895 sq mi (56,707 sq km). Founded in 1776, when the former province of Ostrobothnia (now Österbotten) was replaced by the *läänit* (provinces) of Oulu and Vaasa, Oulu included all of Finnish Lapland until 1938 when the *lääni* of Lappi was created out of the northern portion. Level along the coast, it rises in the east to forested hills; the large Oulujärvi (lake) is situated in its south central part. Economic activities, dominated by agriculture (mostly barley with some oats) and forestry, include iron mining at Otanmäki, cattle raising, and the manufacture of wood products. Principal towns are Oulu (the administrative centre), Kajaani, and Raahe. Pop. (1970 prelim.) 403,206.
·area and population table **7**:303
·map, Finland **7**:304

Oulu, Swedish ULEÅBORG, capital of Oulun *lääni* (Oulu province), west central Finland, at the mouth of the Oulujoki (river) on the Gulf of Bothnia. During the Middle Ages a trading post was located on the site. In 1590 the prospering settlement was fortified, and town rights were granted in 1610. The fortress was destroyed by an explosion in 1793, and the city was almost completely destroyed by fire in 1822; but it became one of Finland's major commercial centres in the 19th century. An important seaport, the city specialized in the export of wood tar; the tar depots and harbour facilities were destroyed, however, during the Crimean War by the British. During World War II, many sections of the city were destroyed and postwar building has modernized it considerably. Oulu has been the seat of a bishopric since 1900 and its cathedral was built in 1830–32, incorporating the remains of an earlier church destroyed in 1822. The city is an important educational centre, with a university (founded 1959), a summer university, and the district hospital. Industry includes lumber, flour, and cellulose mills; shipyards; fisheries; tanneries; and a foundry. The Merikoski (rapids), on which the city is located, provide hydroelectric power and are also a major tourist attraction. Oulu is connected by air, rail, and sea to the rest of Finland. Pop. (1970 prelim.) mun., 85,500.
65°01′ N, 25°28′ E
·map, Finland **7**:304

Oum er-Rbia, Oued, chief river of central Morocco, rising in the Moyen (Middle) Atlas and flowing generally westward for 345 mi (555 km) to the Atlantic Ocean near Azemmour. Although not navigable, it is a perennial river and a major source of hydroelectric power and irrigation: dams include Afourer, Kasba Zidania, Im Fout, Daourat, Sidi Saïd Maachou, and Bine el-Ouidane (on the Oued el-Abid). The Tessaout and el-Abid, both of which join the Oum er-Rbia from the south, are the main tributaries. Agricultural products include citrus fruits, wheat, grapes, cotton, and flax.
33°19′ N, 8°21′ W
·length and regularity **12**:445e
·map, Morocco **12**:446

ounce, or SNOW LEOPARD (*Leo uncia*), attractive, long-haired cat, family Felidae, grouped with the lion, tiger, and others as one of the big, or roaring, cats. The ounce inhabits the mountains of Central Asia, ranging from an altitude of about 1,800 m (about 6,000 ft) in the winter to about 5,500 m (about 18,000 ft) in the summer. Its soft coat, consisting of a

Ounce (*Leo uncia*)
Kenneth W. Fink—Root Resources

dense, insulating undercoat and a thick outer-coat of hairs about 5 cm (2 in.) long, is pale grayish with dark rosettes and a dark streak along the spine. The underparts, on which the fur may be 10 cm (4 in.) long, are uniformly whitish. The ounce attains a length of about 2.1 m (7 ft) including the 0.9-m (3-ft) tail; it stands about 0.6 m (2 ft) at the shoulder and weighs 23–41 kg (50–90 lb). It hunts at night and preys on various animals, such as marmots, wild sheep, and domestic livestock. Its litters of two to four young are born after a gestation period of about 93 days.

The ounce has often been placed, with the other big cats, in the genus *Panthera*. Because of certain skeletal features, it has also been separated by some authorities as the sole member of the genus *Uncia*.

Oundle, market town in Northamptonshire, England, on the River Nene. The manor was granted to the feudal landowner John, earl of Bedford, after the Dissolution of the Monasteries under Henry VIII in the 1530s. The Church of St. Peter, with its crocketed spire, has work in Early English, Decorated, and Perpendicular styles. Oundle School, a well-known public (independent, fee-paying) school for boys founded in 1556 under the will of Sir William Laxton, lord mayor of London, was granted a royal charter in 1930. The town itself, small and residential in character, with buildings of local gray limestone, has a twice-yearly fair. Pop. (1971 prelim.) 3,741.
52°29′ N, 0°29′ W

Oun Kham (b. 1811/16—d. Dec. 15, 1895), ruler of the Laotian principality of Luang Prabang in 1872–87 and 1889–94, who turned his region over to France as an act of friendship and gratitude.

When Chinese bandits attacked Luang Prabang in 1885, Oun Kham was unable to resist them effectively. The Siamese sent an army to defend the area and appointed two of their own as administrators; they lowered Oun Kham from sovereign status to that of governor. In 1887 the Siamese army left, and the Chinese overwhelmed Luang Prabang. Oun Kham took refuge at Paklay, near the Siamese border, with the assistance of the French resident of Vientiane, Auguste Pavie. Pavie quickly ingratiated himself with Oum Kham, who felt that the Frenchman had saved his life —a gesture that was not forgotten.

His health in grave condition after his escape, Oun Kham spent two years in Bangkok, the Siamese capital. He was reinstalled as sovereign in Luang Prabang in 1889 and reigned until 1894. Pavie continued to cultivate good relations with the King, and in 1893 he secured Luang Prabang as a French protectorate.

Ouolof (people): *see* Wolof.

Ouologuem, Yambo (b. 1940, Mali), writer highly acclaimed for his first novel, *Le devoir de violence* (1968; Eng. trans., *Bound to Violence*, 1971), which received the Prix Renandot. Critics claim that the type of epic he created about a fictitious Sudanese empire (the mythical empire of Nakem, ruled by Berber and Jewish peoples) is a new form for an African writer—one that combines historical narrative, legend, verbal acrobatics, African rhythms, and a troubador style into a pessimistic recounting of seven centuries of Saif dynasty rule, replete with violence, sordidness, and excesses. Colonial administrators become mere pawns of the Saif as do African people in the novel. The African's lot would seem to be a legacy of violence and, in modern times, a duty of violence towards white misconceptions of blacks that impose on him a slave mentality and character. Bitterness about white attitudes appear also in some of his poems, and *Lettre à la France nègre* (1968) attacks the "noble" sentiments that have been expressed by paternalistic French liberals about Africa.

·philosophical presentation style **1**:239g

Our Country in Danger, French revolutionary club and newspaper founded by Auguste Blanqui in 1870.

·Blanqui's radical patriotism **2**:1106f

Ourebia ourebia (antelope): *see* oribi.

Ourém, João Fernandes Andeiro, conde de: *see* Andeiro, João Fernandes, conde de Ourém.

Our Father (prayer): *see* Lord's Prayer.

Ourinhos, city, south central São Paulo state, Brazil, lies at 1,568 ft (478 m) above sea level on the Rio Paranapanema, near the border of Paraná state. Once called Jacarèzinho, the city was made the seat of a municipality in 1948. Principal crops of the region include coffee, alfalfa, cotton, rice, and millet. Industrial plants in Ourinhos process these products and also manufacture liquor, metal goods, and ammunition. The city is linked by railroad and highway to the state capital, São Paulo, 220 miles (350 km) east, and to neighbouring urban centres in São Paulo and Paraná states. It also has an airfield. Pop. (1970 prelim.) 40,773.

22°59′ S, 49°52′ W

·map, Brazil **3**:124

Our Knowledge of the External World (1914), book by Bertrand Russell.

·Positivist theory of perception **14**:878h

Our Mutual Friend (serialized, 1864–65; published, 1865), novel by Charles Dickens.

·scope and criticism of corrupt society **5**:710e

Ouroboros, emblematic serpent of ancient Egypt and Greece represented with its tail in its mouth continually devouring itself and being reborn from itself. A Gnostic and alchemical symbol, Ouroboros expresses the unity of all things, material and spiritual, which never disappear but perpetually change form in an eternal cycle of destruction and re-creation.

In the 19th century, a vision of Ouroboros

Crowned dragon as tail eater, illustration from Eleazar's *Uraltes Chymisches Werk*, 1760

By courtesy of The Beinecke Rare Book and Manuscript Library, Yale University

gave the German chemist Friedrich August Kekule von Stradonitz the idea of linked carbon atoms forming the benzene ring.

Ouro Prêto (Portuguese: Black Gold), city in southeastern Minas Gerais state, Brazil, on the lower slopes of the Serra do Oro Prêto, a spur of the Serra do Espinhaço, at 3,481 ft (1,061 m) above sea level, in the Rio Doce drainage basin.

Within a decade of its founding in 1701 as a mining settlement, it had become the centre of the greatest gold rush in the Americas to that date. It still resembled a boom town when it was given city status in 1711 with the name Vila Rica. It was made capital of the newly created Minas Gerais captaincy in 1720. In 1823, after Brazil's independence was won from Portugal, Ouro Prêto was named capital of Minas Gerais province. In 1897, however, because of transportation difficulties the capital was transferred to Belo Horizonte (40 mi [64 km] northwest), adding to the economic decline that had already begun in Ouro Prêto.

Although it has a respected mining school, a few factories, and some agriculture, Ouro Prêto lives largely in the past. In 1933 it was decreed a national monument and the surrounding region a national park, so that the city's elaborate (mostly late-18th-century) public buildings, churches, and houses might be preserved or restored; these make the place a veritable open-air museum. The old colonial governor's palace houses the National School of Mines (founded 1876) and a museum that contains an outstanding collection of minerals native to Brazil. The massive colonial penitentiary contains the Museum of the Inconfidência, dedicated to the history of gold mining and culture in Minas Gerais. The colonial theatre, restored in 1861–62, is the oldest in Brazil. The city has many Baroque churches. Religious architecture and sculpture attained great perfection in the city under the skillful hands of António Francisco Lisboa, better known as Aleijadinho. The church of São Francisco de Assis and the facade of the church of Nossa Senhora do Carmo are probably his masterpieces. Pop. (1970 prelim.) 24,050.

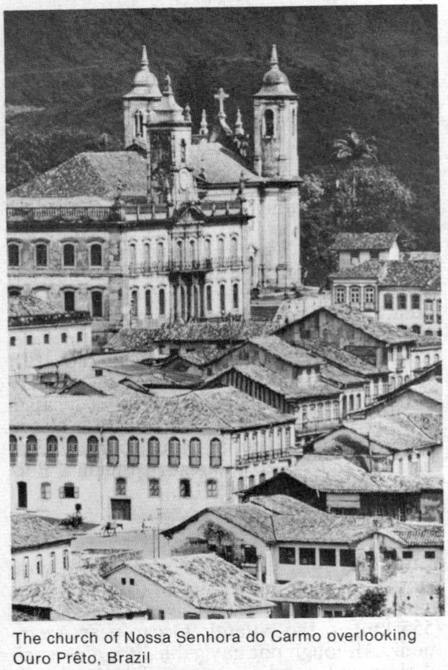

The church of Nossa Senhora do Carmo overlooking Ouro Prêto, Brazil

John Lewis Stage—Photo Researchers

20°23′ S, 43°30′ W

·historical attraction significance **12**:223h

·map, Brazil **3**:124

Ourselves (political organization): *see* Sinn Fein.

Ōu-sammyaku, English Ōu RANGE, forms the backbone of northeastern Honshu, Japan and extends for 310 mi (500 km) south from Aomori Prefecture (*ken*) to Fukushima Prefecture. Geologically, dominant Tertiary sediments are occasionally interrupted by intrusions of the basement granitic and gneissic core. These intrusions, such as Waga-dake (Mt. Waga), frequently attain much higher elevations than the surrounding formations. The margins of the mountains drop down by fault scraps to the Kitakami-gawa (Kitakami River) valley in the east and a row of longitudinal basins in the west.

The altitude of the range is greatly modified by the overlapping of the Nasu Volcanic Zone. From north to south the overtowering volcanic groups, each bearing the name of its major peak, are Hakkōda-san, Iwate-yama, Sugawa-dake, Funagata-yama, Zaō-san, Azuma-yama, and Bandai-san. The eruption of Bandai-san in 1888 resulted in debris accumulation on its northern flank and the consequent formation of numerous lakes, thereby greatly altering the drainage pattern of the entire area.

A salient feature of the Ōu-sammyaku is the row of depressions along its axis. Significant among them are, from north to south, the Hanawa and Shizukuishi basins, the Waga-kawa Valley, and the Onikōbe and Inawashiro basins.

38°45′ N, 140°50′ E

·map, Japan **10**:36

Ouse, an English river name, cognate with the Sanskrit word for water. The Great Ouse is a very important river system, draining the East Midlands at the Fens, a reclaimed area. It rises 5 mi (8 km) west of Brackley, Northamptonshire, and flows past Buckingham, Bedford, Huntington, and St. Ives to Earith and thence via the Fens to the Wash, a shallow inlet of the North Sea. For the first 100 mi it follows an irregular, meandering course, its gradient falling from 20 ft per mi (4 m per km) above Buckingham to 2 ft per mi toward Earith. From Earith to its mouth, a distance of 35 mi, the course is almost entirely artificial, having been straightened and having had its flow controlled by sluices. The average gradient here is only 4 in. per mi. Parts of the upper valley are followed by the Grand Union Canal. Locks make the river navigable upstream to Bedford. Coarse fishing and gravel extraction are important.

The River Ouse in Sussex is a short river, rising on the southern side of the central Weald region and now reaching the English Channel at Newhaven, via a gap in the South Downs. Like other Sussex rivers, it flows transverse to the direction of folding of the rocks and is thought to be superimposed. It is navigable for small vessels to Lewes. Its headwaters, dammed to form ponds, once provided power for the former Wealden iron industry.

The Ouse is also the name given to that part of the Yorkshire Ouse River system from the junction of the Swale and Ure near Boroughbridge as far as the junction with the Trent below Goole. It is believed to have captured a number of streams, namely the Swale, Ure, Nidd, Wharfe, Aire, and Calder, originally flowing eastward down the flank of the Pennines directly to the North Sea.
50°47′ N, 0°03′ E

ousel (bird): *see* ouzel.

Ousmane, Sembene (b. 1923, Ziguinchor-Casamance, Senegal), writer whose historical-political novels and work as a film director since the mid-1960s have gained him an international reputation. He was awarded the literature prize at the Festival of Negro Arts in Dakar in 1966 for his short novels *Le Mandat* and *Vehi-ciosane* (1965), and his film version of the former won a prize at the Venice Film Festival and was highly praised at the New York Film Festival in 1969.

Ousmane grew up in Senegal and worked first as a fisherman and then as a manual laborer in Dakar. Convinced that he must live in France in order to achieve success as a writer, he moved to Marseille; and his first novel, *Le Docker noir* (1956), records his experiences there as dock worker and trade union leader. *Les Bouts de bois de Dieu* (1960; Eng. trans., *God's Bit of Wood*, 1962), which exemplifies his thesis that a writer should stay as close to reality and to the people as possible, is a fictionalized account of the hardships of workers and their families during the Dakar–Niger railway strike of 1947–48. A later novel, *L'Harmattan* (vol. 1, *Référendum*, 1964), the first of a proposed trilogy, recreates the events surrounding an African nation's referendum on the question of independence or continued colonial rule.

Ousmane's short stories and excerpts from his novels have been widely anthologized, and he has directed a short feature film on Dakar (*Barom Sarret*) as well as adaptations of his own stories. All of his work attempts to present realistically the conditions under which African peoples must live until they themselves make an effort to change their lot.

Ouspensky, Peter (1878–1947), Russian philosopher.
·mysticism and psychology **12**:791e

Out (1964), novel by Christine Brooke-Rose.
·prophetic fantasy in the novel **13**:289e

Outaouacs, also called OUTAOUAIS, Canadian Indian tribe.
·Ottawa's name origins **13**:767c

Outardes River, in Côte-Nord (North Shore) region, east central Quebec province, Canada, rising in the Otish Mountains and flowing southward for 300 mi (483 km) through Lake Pletipi to the St. Lawrence River, 18 mi southwest of Baie-Comeau. Named after the numerous wild geese for which it is famous, the Outardes River, with its many rapids and falls, attracted hydroelectric development in the 1930s and, in the 1960s, the Manicouagan-Outardes Project of Hydro-Quebec.
49°04′ N, 68°25′ W

Outback, in Australian and New Zealand usage, a term applied to rural areas or the back country generally.
·physical geography and sociological aspects **2**:399g

outboard motorboat: *see* motorboat.

outbreeding (biology): *see* inbreeding.

Outcast, The (1925), English translation of L'ESCLUSA (written, 1893; published 1901), novel by Luigi Pirandello.
·wry nature of realistic style **14**:469e

outcaste (Hindu caste): *see* untouchables.

Outcast of the Islands, An (1896), novel by Joseph Conrad.
·publication and Wells' assessment **5**:30d

Outcault, Richard Felton (b. Jan. 14, 1863, Lancaster, Ohio—d. Sept. 25, 1928, Flushing, N.Y.), cartoonist and creator of the "Yellow Kid," a comic cartoon series influential in the development of the comic strip.

Outcault studied art in Cincinnati, Ohio, and Paris and later contributed to *Judge* and the old *Life*, humour magazines that had begun publication in the early 1880s. By 1885 he was drawing comic cartoons based on life in the slums for the rejuvenated *New York World*, purchased by Joseph Pulitzer in 1883. Outcault's drawing of an urchin wearing a nightshirt was selected for a colour-production test conducted by the *World* on Feb. 16, 1896. The bright yellow-clad figure attracted such wide attention that the urchin was named the "Yellow Kid." Almost from the first, slangy messages appeared on the nightshirt. Outcault was hired away from the *World* later that year by William Randolph Hearst, owner of *The New York Journal*. Pulitzer outbid Hearst, and then Hearst outbid Pulitzer, at which point Pulitzer gave up and hired George Luks to draw the "Yellow Kid." The press war and the shenanigans over Outcault's services resulted in the expression "yellow journalism" for sensational and unscrupulous publishing. The success of the "Yellow Kid" led to the introduction of many other comics.

In 1897 Outcault left the *Journal* for *The New York Herald*, where in 1902 he created "Buster Brown," his second important cartoon character. Neat and prissy in appearance, Buster was a mischief maker who carried out his pranks in a genteel setting far removed from the tough, vigorous slum of the "Yellow Kid." The strip is remembered chiefly for the use of the name Buster Brown in advertising a wide range of products.
·comic strip style and influence **3**:920b

outcrop, the portion of a rock stratum that is exposed at the surface of the Earth. As used in geology, any rock formation or other unit is mapped as an outcrop even if not exposed at the ground surface, provided that it is covered only by soil, glacial drift, alluvium, or other surficial deposits that are not classified as younger rock strata of the geological column.
·Precambrian rock exposures **14**:953f

Outer Banks, or THE BANKS, chain of islands extending along the coast of North Carolina from Virginia to South Carolina. Generally covered with sand dunes, the islands range from a few feet to over 100 ft (160 m) in height. They are inhabited by some fishermen and farmers, and the area attracts bird hunters and sports fishermen. The Atlantic Intracoastal Waterway threads its way between Outer Banks and the mainland.
35°10′ N 76°00′ W
·coastal feature result of sea level rise **4**:798d
·North Carolina coastal geography **13**:231d

Outer Court, structure of the regular offices of the Chinese government during the Han dynasty.
·Han dynasty's officialdom hierarchy **4**:312b

outer ear: *see* external ear.

Outer Himalayas, lowest section of the Himalayan mountain ranges, extend southeastward across north Pakistan, north India, Nepal, and into Sikkim. They lie between the Lesser Himalayas (north) and the plains of India (south) and have an average height of 3,000 to 4,000 ft (900 to 1,200 m).
28°00′ N, 82°30′ E
·Himalayan system **8**:883a; map 882

Outer Mongolia: *see* Mongolian People's Republic.

Outer Space Treaty (1966), international treaty signed by 63 nations to regulate activities in outer space and on celestial bodies.
·international space law principles **17**:377b

outflow, neural, flow of nerve impulses from the central nervous system to the periphery or from groups of nerve cell bodies (ganglia).
·autonomic system interrelationships **12**:1030e; illus. 1027
·central nervous system structures **12**:1003g

Out Islands, collective name given to all the islands that make up the Bahamas apart from New Providence Island. Extending eastward off the Florida coast to just north of Hispaniola, there are about 3,000 islands and rocks, with a combined area of about 4,000 sq mi. Just over 20 of the islands are permanently inhabited. Pop. (1970) 64,076.

Outjo, town and magisterial district, north central South West Africa. The town is a railroad terminus in a cattle raising region. Pop. (1970) 2,515.
20°08′ S, 16°08′ E
·district population and area table **17**:303
·map, South West Africa **17**:301

outlawry, act of putting one beyond the protection of the law for his refusal to become amenable to the court having legal jurisdiction. This deprivation of legal benefits was invoked when a defendant or person was in civil or criminal contempt of court; and, in cases of alleged treason or the commission of a felony (referred to as major outlawry), it amounted to a conviction as well as an extinction of civil rights. In England, on proof of the mere fact of major outlawry, the offender was sentenced to death and was often killed on sight or during the effort to arrest him. Conviction for major outlawry also effected the immediate forfeiture of all property and possessions to the crown and prevented the receipt of any property. In civil proceedings it was formally abolished in England in 1879. Under English law outlawry can still be invoked only for one accused of criminal charges.

In other countries outlawry in civil actions was virtually unknown, but manifestations of it, ranging from informal social ostracism to formal statutory proscription, were used as a criminal sanction. Conviction did not always result in sentence of death, but often the punishment involved transportation or exile for the offender, thereby completely stripping him of the benefits of his native land.

Some societies practiced a social form of outlawry on people not even accused of an offense but characterized by some manner of physical or mental abnormality. In India, for example, persons affected with leprosy were placed under ban and disability and driven from their communities to live in leper colonies, without the ordinary benefits of society.
·Anglo-Saxon law in early England **4**:998d
·Germanic legal punishment **8**:32f

outline drawing, schematical representation of an object, made by defining its outline with

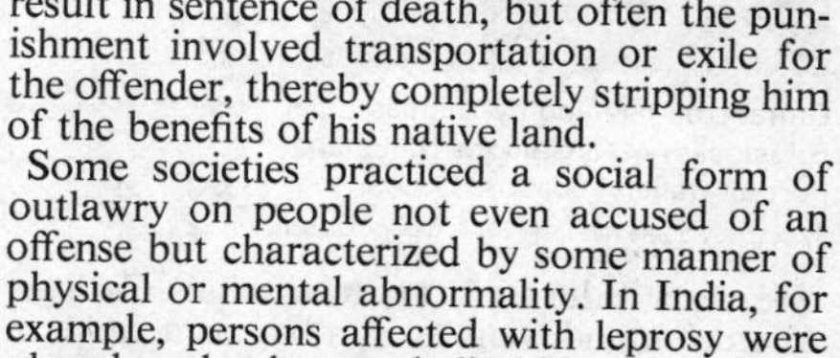

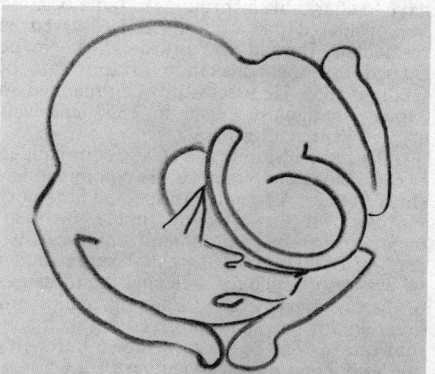

"Dog Curled Up," lithographic crayon by John Flannagan (1895–1942); in the Addison Gallery of American Art, Andover, Mass.

By courtesy of the Addison Gallery of American Art, Phillips Academy, Andover, Mass.

a line of consistent width and weight. The internal details are disregarded completely, and neither colouring nor shading is used. It is virtually a linear silhouette (*q.v.*) and is to be distinguished from a contour drawing (*q.v.*). Outline drawings are used almost exclusively in the teaching of art.

Outline of History, The (1920; revised 1931), popular general history by H.G. Wells.
· world instability theme **19**:758e

Outlines of Pyrrhonism, text by the 3rd-century-AD Latin author Sextus Empiricus.
· skepticism of Pyrrhonists and tropes **16**:831a

Out of the Cradle Endlessly Rocking, poem by Walt Whitman.
· prosodic elements in Whitman's poetry **15**:72e

Outokumpu, town, copper-mining centre in Kuopio *lääni* (province), southeastern Finland. Although Outokumpu's greatest source of income is copper, gold and silver are also mined. Pop. (1972 est.) 10,610.
62°44′ N, 29°01′ E
· map, Finland **7**:305
· resource and national income **7**:306c

Outram, Sir James, Baronet (b. Jan. 29, 1803, near Butterley, Derbyshire—d. March 11, 1863, Pau, Fr.), English general and political officer known, because of his reputation for chivalry, as "the Bayard of India" (after the 16th-century French *bon chevalier*).

Outram, oil painting by Thomas Brigstocke, *c.* 1863; in the National Portrait Gallery, London

By courtesy of the National Portrait Gallery, London

He was educated at Marischal College, Aberdeen, and went to Bombay as a cadet in 1819. After serving with distinction in the early stages of the First Afghan War (1839–42), he was appointed political agent in Sind. Though dismissed on the appointment to Sind of Sir Charles Napier, he persuaded the independent chieftains of Sind to accept a harsh new treaty. According to its terms his prize money amounted to 30,000 rupees, which he gave to charitable institutions in India because he considered the war unjust. He served as resident at Baroda and Lucknow, where he carried out the annexation of the state of Oudh in 1856. He successfully commanded an expedition against Persia in 1857 and was created lieutenant general.

In the Indian Mutiny of 1857 he commanded two divisions and resumed his commissionership of Oudh. Appointed to succeed Sir Henry Havelock at Cawnpore (Kānpur), he magnanimously refused command until the final capture of Lucknow. As chief commissioner he was responsible for softening the measures of the first viceroy, Lord Canning, against the great landowners, and thus securing their submission. In 1858 he was awarded a baronetcy and appointed military member of the governor general's council. In 1860 he returned to England. Outram is buried in Westminster Abbey, and a full-length bronze figure of him stands on the Thames Embankment near Charing Cross, London.

Outremer (French: Overseas), term denoting the crusader states established in the Near East in the 12th and 13th centuries.
· Latin Kingdom administration **5**:304e

Outremeuse, Jean d' (1338–99), author of two romanticized but fascinating historical works. The first, *La Geste de Liège*, is a leisurely account, partly in prose, partly in verse, of the mythical history of his native city. *Ly Myreur des Histors* ("The Mirror of History") is even more ambitious, purporting to be a history of the world from the Flood up to the 14th century.

D'Outremeuse was no accurate historian, but his fictionalized accounts of the past offer insights into the workings of a medieval mind. It is also possible to discover, amidst a great deal of pure invention, unique evidence about the author's time and especially about literature in his age.

Outremont, city, Montréal region, southern Quebec province, Canada, in the centre of Île de Montréal, adjoining Montreal city. Originally called Côte-Sainte-Catherine, it was renamed in 1875 for its location in relation to Montreal—on the far side of Mont-Royal. The city, a part of the Montreal Metropolitan Corporation, is now primarily a high-density residential suburb. Inc. town, 1895; city, 1915. Pop. (1971) 28,552.
45°31′ N, 73°38′ W

outside decorator, English, like the German Hausmaler (*see* Hausmalerei), a decorator who obtained white porcelain pieces from a factory and painted them in his studio. There were many outside decorators in the second half of the 18th century, but only a few of their names are known, and the attribution of much of their work is not certain. Very few signed or even initialled their work, and those who did did not do so consistently. When a piece is signed, however, it is likely to be the work of an outside decorator, because decorators employed at the factory were not encouraged to add their signatures to the factory's mark. William Duesbury was the first outside decorator in England; in a studio he maintained in London between 1750 and 1753, he decorated wares that came from almost every factory in existence in England at

Worcester porcelain vase painted and signed by Jeffrey Hamet O'Neale, 1769

By courtesy of the Worcester Royal Porcelain Company

the time. Another well-known decorator was James Giles, also in London, who was active between 1760 and 1776, and who himself employed several painters. Decorations such as the "dishevelled birds" and sliced fruit found on Chelsea and Worcester have been attributed to his studio, as have Kakiemon (*see* Kakiemon ware) patterns on Worcester and Bow.

Another identified outside decorator is Jeffrey Hamet O'Neale, who first worked at Chelsea but from 1758 worked independently. Some of his work on Worcester is signed. Other outside decorators included Fidèle Duvivier, who, after working at Tournai (Belgium) and Chelsea, decorated independently for Chelsea, Worcester, Derby, and New Hall; and John Donaldson, who decorated for Worcester and sometimes signed his work with the monogram JD.

The relationship between the outside decorators and the porcelain factories in England appears to have been far smoother—more in the nature of collaboration than of competition—than was the case with their counterparts in Germany.

Outsider, The (Camus): *see* Stranger, The.

outwash plain, deposit of sand and gravel formed by the fusion of several alluvial fans built at the terminus of a glacier by braided meltwater streams. An outwash plain may attain a thickness of 100 metres (328 feet) at the edge of a glacier, although the thickness is usually much less; it may also extend many miles in length. For example, outwash deposits from the Wisconsin Glaciation can be traced to the mouth of the Mississippi River, 1,120 kilometres (696 miles) from the nearest glacial terminus.

The sheet of outwash may be pitted with undrained kettles or dissected by postglacial streams. Outwash plains are commonly cross-bedded with units of alternating grain size. The ordinarily gentle slope causes the larger material to be dropped nearest the glacier, while the smaller grain sizes are spread over greater distances. Striated pebbles are uncommon because the striations are worn away during transport.

Outwash plains are the largest of the fluvioglacial deposits and provide a considerable source of eolian material.

When confined within valley walls, the outwash deposit is known as a valley train.
· braided stream formation **15**:883a
· formation and characteristics **8**:173h; illus. 172

Ouvéa (New Caledonia): *see* Uvéa, Île.

ouvrage à la Chine, imitation lacquerwork done in France in the late 17th and 18th centuries.
· Gobelins factory ware **10**:579e

Ou-yang Hsiu **13**:796, Pin-yin romanization OU-YANG XIU, courtesy name YUNG-SHU, literary name TSUI-WENG, canonized name WEN-CHUNG (b. 1007, Mien-yang, Szechwan Province, China—d. 1072, Honan), poet, historian, and statesman, reintroduced the simple "ancient style" in Chinese literature and sought to reform Chinese political life through classical Confucian principles.

Abstract of text biography. Recognized early (before 1030) for his literary brilliance, he began a long career in civil service as judge and counsellor in various provinces of China. He was demoted several times for criticism of bureaucratic policies but each time was reinstated. His writings include "New History of the Five Dynasties," recording the political chaos of the 10th century, and the "New History of the T'ang Dynasty." Ou-yang's character and opinions were esteemed by the emperor Sung Jen Tsung, who appointed him his chronicler. Hsiu's campaign against florid style set a new course in Chinese literature.

REFERENCE in other text article:
· prose reform **10**:1055d

Ouyen, town, Mallee district, northwest Victoria, Australia. It was founded in 1904 and connected to Melbourne (240 mi [390 km] southeast) by rail two years later. Situated at the junction of the Calder, Ouyen, and Henty highways, with links to Melbourne and Adelaide, it is the commercial centre of a region of

grain and sheep farming, and it is the administrative headquarters of Walpeup Shire. The name is derived from an Aboriginal term meaning "wild duck" or "ghost waterhole." Pop. (1971 prelim.) 1,562.
35°04′ S, 142°20′ E

ouzel, also spelled OUSEL, old name for the European blackbird (*see* blackbird), now applied to a closely related thrush of similar appearance, the ring ouzel (*Turdus torquatus*),

Ring ouzel (*Turdus torquatus*)
Drawing by John P. O'Neill

family Turdidae (order Passeriformes). The ring is a white crescent on the breast of this blackish bird, 24 centimetres (9½ inches) long, which breeds locally in uplands from Great Britain and Norway to the Middle East. For a related bird in Mexico, sometimes called black ouzel, *see* robin.The dipper (*q.v.*) is often called water ouzel.

Ovaja (South Indian poet): *see* Pampa.

Ovalau, largest island (40 sq mi [104 sq km]) of central Fiji, South Pacific. One of a volcanic group lying west of the Koro Sea, it is rugged, rising to Mt. Nade-Laivalau (2,053 ft [626 m]), but contains a fertile, well-watered central basin. Levuka (*q.v.*), capital of Lomaiviti Province and onetime capital of Fiji, is the main town and port. Pop. (1971 est.) 6,544.
17°40′ S, 178°48′ E
·map, Fiji 7:295

oval window (anatomy): *see* middle ear.

Ovambo (people): *see* Ambo.

Ovamboland, also AMBOLAND, tribal reserve (area 16,202 sq mi [41,544 sq km]), South West Africa, borders Angola (north) and extends westward from the Okavango River. Its main feature is Oponono Lake, a salt water depression. It was established in 1968 as a "homeland area" for the Ovambo (Ambo), a Bantu race who practice agriculture and stock-raising. The administrative headquarters are at Olukonda. Pop. (1970) 295,508.
·map, South West Africa **17**:301
·vegetation transition, area, and population **17**:301c; table 303

Ovando, Nicolás de (b. *c.* 1451, Brozas, Spain—d. *c.* 1511), Spanish military leader and first royal governor of the West Indies, first to apply the encomienda system of Indian forced labour, which became widespread in Spanish America, and founded a stable Spanish community in Santo Domingo that became a base and model for later settlement.

The son of a noble family, he grew up close to the court of Ferdinand and Isabella and was among the companions of the heir apparent to the throne. As a knight of the military Order of Alcántara, Ovando helped to reform the order and as a reward for his services was chosen to replace Francisco de Bobadilla as governor of the Spanish colonies in the West Indies. He arrived in Santo Domingo in 1502 with more than 2,000 colonists and the largest fleet that had ever sailed to the New World.

The natives of Santo Domingo, however, were reluctant to work for the Spanish colonists, and Ovando, with royal authority, established the paternalistic encomienda system. Intended to offer the Indians food and security in exchange for their labour, it quickly became a means for simple and brutal exploitation. Perhaps fearing him as a rival, Ovando let Christopher Columbus linger for a year without help in Jamaica, where the explorer had run aground on his fourth voyage to America. On learning of Ovando's harsh treatment of the Indians, the authorities in Spain recalled him in 1509. He returned to Spain, where he wrote his memoirs and published a map of Santo Domingo.
·Columbus Española admittance refusal **4**:942b

ovarian artery, one of two arteries in the female running from the aorta to the ovaries. They correspond to the testicular arteries in the male.
·human anatomic location **15**:695g
·human cardiovascular system anatomy **3**:883b

ovarian follicle, in anatomy, the pocket of cells or sac that encloses the female sexual cell —oocyte or ovum—in the peripheral tissues of the ovary. The follicle in its several stages has been labelled primordial, primary, secondary, and mature. The primordial follicle is inactive, with a single layer of cells enclosing the immature oocyte. In the primary stage the follicle becomes active: the oocyte begins to enlarge, and the follicle develops into stratified layers of cells. In the secondary stage the oocyte has become a mature ovum, but the follicle continues to grow, with the formation of a cavity, called an antrum, filled with liquid. The mature follicle, a tense sac that bulges the surface of the ovary, takes 10-14 days to develop. When the follicle bursts, a corpus luteum (*q.v.*) forms on the site.
·animal reproductive system comparisons **15**:710d
·animal tissue comparisons **18**:450b
·estrous cycle interactions **11**:403a
·hormonal effects on ovulation **6**:803e
·hormone secretion in mammals **8**:1083e
·menstruation effects of ovarian function **11**:908e

primary ovarian follicle
·human maturation sequence **15**:695h
·oogenesis and menstrual cycles **6**:742c

ovaries, in zoology, the female reproductive organs in which sex cells (eggs or ova) are produced. The usually paired ovaries of female vertebrates produce both the sex cells and the hormones necessary for reproduction. In some invertebrate groups such as coelenterates formation of ovaries is associated with the seasons. Many invertebrates have both ovaries and testes in one animal, and some species undergo sex reversal. *See also* egg, gonad, ovum.

Ovaries of the newborn and young child are a mass of elongated tissue; as the female reaches adolescence, the ovaries gradually enlarge and change their shape. The adult ovaries are almond-shaped and are about 4 centimetres (1.6 inches) long, 2 centimetres (0.8 inch) wide, and 1.5 centimetres (0.6 inch) thick; the two ovaries weigh from 4 to 8 grams (0.15 to 0.3 ounce). The ovaries are attached to the uterus and the fallopian tubes by several ligaments. The surfaces of the ovaries are usually uneven and have areas of scar tissue. Hollow balls of cells—follicles—containing immature egg cells are present in the ovaries at birth; there are usually 150,000 to 500,000 follicles at this time. When the female reaches adolescence and young adulthood, the number has been reduced to only about 34,000. As a woman ages, the follicles gradually diminish in number until, at menopause and the cessation of reproductive powers, the few remaining follicles degenerate. During the active child-bearing years of a woman, normally between the ages 13 and 50, only 300 to 400 of the follicles undergo maturation. In about every four weeks of the active reproductive years, one follicle from only one of the two ovaries matures; the egg inside the follicle is extruded from the ovary into the rest of the reproductive tract for fertilization. If the egg is not fertilized by the male sperm, it passes from the body during the process of menstruation.

The ovaries also function as endocrine glands by secreting hormones into the bloodstream. One hormone produced, estrogen, which is secreted by the ovarian follicle, controls the development of the secondary sex characteristics such as enlargement of the breasts, growth of pubic hair, and the increased amount of fat on the hips and buttocks; estrogen also stimulates growth of the uterine lining during the menstrual cycle. The other hormone produced, progesterone (or corpus luteum hormone), is secreted from the cells of the corpus luteum. Progesterone helps the fertilized egg to secure itself to the uterus and to develop into an embryo.

The centre of the ovary, called the medulla, is a core of connective tissue consisting of blood vessels, lymphatic ducts, and nerve fibres. The thick layer covering the medulla is the cortex. This contains the follicles and ova. As a follicle matures, it enlarges and migrates to the surface of the ovary. When an egg is discharged from a follicle, blood and yellow cells move into the empty follicular cavity to fill it; this tissue becomes the corpus luteum. If the egg is fertilized, the corpus luteum remains until the end of pregnancy; during this time the corpus luteum secretes progesterone. If the ovum is not fertilized, the corpus luteum becomes a whitish scar mass, known as corpus albicans, which, usually, eventually disappears. The spindle-shaped cells surrounding the follicles in the cortex form the supporting structure, or stroma. As a follicle matures, the stroma cells closest to it form a two-layered wall around the follicle that gives added protection to the developing egg. After the egg leaves the follicle, the stroma cells help form part of the corpus luteum. The outermost layer of the ovaries is a thin tissue known as the germinal epithelium; this layer serves as a "skin" that holds the contents of the cortex and medulla intact; it also supplies some of the stromal cells around the follicle.

After menopause, the ovaries shrink in size and usually consist of old fibrous tissue. The production of estrogen drops considerably but does not totally cease. Benign and malignant tumours of the ovaries can occur in either young or old women.

human
·cancer types and prognosis **3**:768d; table 767
·development and decline of function **16**:596a
·diseases, disorders, and treatments **15**:698d
·embryonic origin, hormones, and feedback control **6**:845b; illus. 840
·endocrine system disorders **6**:832g
·genetically determined disorders **7**:1004a
·glandular status and sex differences **16**:588b
·homeostatic control mechanisms **8**:1015f
·hormonal influence on function **18**:284g
·hormonal secretions and functions **6**:803c; illus. 800
·hormone production and target, table 3 **5**:859
·human anatomy and functions **15**:695g; illus. 693
·lactation preparation and initiation **10**:582h
·menopause and endocrine function **11**:907b
·menstruation and ovarian function **11**:907h
·origins and differentiation **6**:752h
·physiologic changes during pregnancy **14**:969e
·primary sex difference and gametes **16**:585g *passim* to **16**:591c

invertebrate
·annelid worm anatomy **1**:929b; illus. 933

·insect multiple egg production **9**:616g; illus. 615
·nematode reproductive system **2**:141d; illus. 140
·spider internal anatomy, illus. 2 **1**:1070
vertebrate
·animal tissue comparisons **18**:449g
·behaviour and endocrine influences **2**:813d
·embryonic origin and development **5**:638a
·estrous cycle interactions **11**:403a
·hormone secretion in mammals **8**:1083e
·monotreme reproductive techniques **12**:385d
·perch internal anatomy, illus. 1 **7**:332
·reproductive system comparisons **15**:710a; illus. 703
·viviparous nourishment in fish **7**:332d

ovariole, one of the tubes of which the ovaries of most insects are composed.
·animal reproductive system comparisons **15**:705b

ovary, in botany, the enlarged basal portion of the female flower parts (pistil; *q.v.*), which contains the portion of the plant (carpels; *q.v.*) bearing the ovules (potential seeds). An inferior ovary is partially or completely embedded in the receptacle (*q.v.*), which bears the floral organs; the more primitive superior ovary is elevated and free of the receptacle below it. Eventually the ovary develops into the fruit of the seed plant. *See also* hypogyny; epigyny.
·angiosperm flower parts **1**:880d; illus.
·Aristolochiales flower structure **1**:1153c
·Asterales flower structure **2**:215a; illus. 214
·Bromeliales structural diversity **3**:326b
·Euphorbiales flower structure **6**:1029d
·Fagales flower development **7**:142b
·Gentianales position variations **7**:1019d
·Lamiales structure and function **10**:621c
·Laurales flower forms **10**:709f
·orchid modifications and function **13**:649g *passim* to 651g
·Ranunculales pollination mechanism **15**:510b
·reproductive systems in angiosperms **15**:722h; illus.
·tissue culture illus. **18**:441
·Zingiberales reproductive system **19**:1153e

Oven (people): *see* Tungus.

oven (industry): *see* furnace.

oven, baking, a heated enclosure of varying construction used for baking.
·baking history and development **2**:597b

ovenbird, any of several species of small birds, named for building a domed nest with a side entrance, especially *Seiurus aurocapillus*, a wood warbler (family Parulidae, order Passeriformes) of North America east of the Rockies; it winters south to Colombia. Brownish-olive above, with a spotted breast, white eye ring, and black-edged orange crown, the bird looks like a small thrush. Its call, "tee-cher," is repeated with increasing intensity in dank woods. The ovenbird walks rather than hops, as do most other wood warblers. Its nest is a dome of grass placed on the ground.

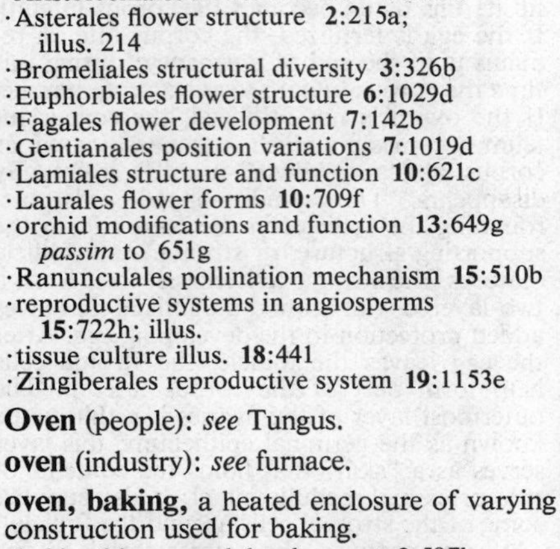

Ovenbird (*Seiurus aurocapillus*)
Jack Dermid

The term ovenbird is also used broadly for members of the tropical American family Furnariidae (*q.v.*) and especially for members of the genus *Furnarius* (also known by the Spanish name *hornero*, "baker"). They are 15–20 centimetres (6–8 inches) long, reddish-brown, and thrushlike, common in open country throughout most of South America. On a branch, post, or roof ledge, the hornero builds an ovenlike nest of mud and grass, about 30 centimetres high, with an enclosed nest chamber.
·classification and general features **13**:1058h
·pale-legged ovenbird, illus., **13**:Passeriformes, Plate I
·social behaviour patterns **16**:935e

Overami (king of Benin): *see* Ovonramwen.

Overbeck, Johann Friedrich (b. July 3, 1789, Lübeck, Ger.—d. Nov. 12, 1869, Rome), Romantic painter devoted to depicting Christian religious subjects, who was leader of a group of German artists known as the Lucas Brotherhood, or the Nazarenes. In 1806 Overbeck entered the Academy of Vienna, where, disappointed in the academic approach to teaching, he and Franz Pforr in 1809 founded the Lucas Brotherhood. They sought to revive the medieval artists' guilds and to renew the arts through Christian faith (in 1813 Overbeck joined the Roman Catholic Church). For artistic inspiration they turned to Albrecht Dürer and to Italian Renaissance art, particularly the works of Perugino and early Raphael.

Overbeck, self-portrait with his family, oil on panel, 1820–22; in the Museen für Kunst und Kulturgeschichte, Lübeck, W. Ger.
By courtesy of the Museen fur Kunst und Kulturgeschichte der Hansestadt, Lubeck, W. Ger.

In 1810 the Lucas Brotherhood went to Rome. Followers now included Peter von Cornelius, Julius Schnorr von Carolsfeld, Philipp Veit, and Wilhelm von Schadow. The Nazarene style was characterized by precise outlines; clear, bright colours; and an emphasis on Christian symbolism. Communally, the brotherhood executed the frescoes of "Joseph Sold by His Brethren" at the Casa Bartholdy (1816) and the interior pavilion (1817–29) at the Villa Massimo in Rome. In the Portiuncula Chapel at Assisi Overbeck painted his "Rose Miracle of St. Francis" (1829), usually considered his major work. Other important paintings are "Christ's Entry into Jerusalem" (1809–24; destroyed in Lübeck, 1942), "Italia and Germania" (1811–28; Neue Pinakothek, Munich), and portraits like "Vittoria Caldoni" (1821; Neue Pinakothek, Munich).

As he advanced in years, Overbeck's painting became pallid and stereotyped. Yet these late works greatly influenced Christian devotional art of the 19th century and the paintings of the Pre-Raphaelite Brotherhood. His more vital early pictures and drawings, however, were rediscovered and appreciated early in the 20th century.
·Nazarene group and Romanticism **19**:456a

overblowing, blowing through the tube of a wind instrument to produce harmonics.
·overtone generation **19**:848f

Overbury, Sir Thomas (baptized June 18, 1581, Compton Scorpion, Warwickshire—d. Sept. 15, 1613, London), poet and essayist, victim of a famous intrigue at the court of James I. His poem *A Wife*, which pictured the virtues that a young man should demand of a woman, played a large role in the events that precipitated his murder.

Overbury, detail of an oil painting by Cornelius Johnson, 1613; in the Bodleian Library, Oxford
By courtesy of the curators of the Bodleian Library, Oxford

Overbury was educated at Oxford and entered the Middle Temple, London, in 1598. Having travelled in the Low Countries, he later wrote his posthumously published *Observations in His Travailes Upon the State of the XVII Provinces* (1626). In 1606 he became secretary and close adviser to Robert Carr, the king's favourite who was to become earl of Somerset. Overbury was knighted in 1608. It was said that "Overbury governed Carr and Carr governed the King."

In 1611 Carr became enamoured of Frances Howard, wife of the Earl of Essex. Overbury, fearing that Carr's marriage would diminish his influence, bluntly stated his opinion of the Countess to Carr and circulated his poem at court, where it was interpreted as an attack upon Lady Essex. This incurred the displeasure of the King and enabled the Countess' relatives to have Overbury sent to the Tower. The offended Countess secretly arranged to have him slowly poisoned.

Now earl of Somerset, Carr and the Countess were married shortly thereafter. The scandal came to light a year later; the accomplices were hanged and the Earl and his Countess were disgraced.

Overbury's *A Wife* was published in 1614 and went through several editions within a year because of Overbury's posthumous publicity. Its real literary value lies in the *Characters*, ultimately 82, that were added to the second and subsequent editions. These prose portraits of Jacobean types, drawn with wit and satire, give a vivid picture of contemporary society and are important as a step in the development of the essay. A few were by Overbury, but most were contributed by John Webster, Thomas Dekker, and John Donne.

Overcoat, The (1956), English translation of SHINEL (1842), Russian author Nikolay Gogol's immortal tale about the colourless life of a poor clerk, Akaki Akakiyevich, which assumes a new vitality with the acquisition of a new overcoat. At once pathetic and outrageously funny, the short story mingles realism with fantasy in its attention to the details of ordinary life and thus achieves a more profound effect than mere social satire.

·short story theme and technique **16**:715h
·theme and impact on Russian literature **8**:235c

overdraft, the drawing upon a bank of more than is on deposit. In some countries banks grant their customers an overdraft privilege, allowing them to overdraw their accounts and charging interest on such overdrafts until they are paid off. The overdraft privilege thus amounts to a means of granting loans as they are desired, without separate formality.

·commercial bank operations **2**:707f

overglaze colours, in ceramics, additional glaze on porcelain over vitrifiable colours.

·pottery decoration techniques **14**:896e

overhand knot, simple knot used to make a knot on a rope or as the starting point for another knot, such as a square knot or surgeon's knot.

overhead cost: *see* cost.

Overijssel, province (*provincie*), northeastern Netherlands, extends northward "beyond the IJssel," a distributary of the Rhine, from Gelderland to Drenthe and Friesland and lies between West Germany (east) and the IJsselmeer or the Zuiderzee (west). Drained by the IJssel, Vecht, Zwarte Water, and Regge rivers and the Twente, Overijssel, and numerous smaller canals, it occupies an area of 1,516 sq mi (3,927 sq km). Its capital is Zwolle. First known as the lordship of Oversticht, a part of the secular domain of the bishops of Utrecht, it was sold to Charles V in 1527 and was incorporated in the Dutch dominions of the Habsburgs. Overijssel was one of the seven original United Provinces of the Netherlands. In medieval times its Hanseatic towns—Kampen, Deventer, and Zwolle (*qq.v.*)—were among the most important in the Netherlands until the ascendancy of Amsterdam *c.* 1500. The Northeast Polder was added administratively to the province in 1962.

Most of Overijssel is a varied glaciated delta with sandy soil and low hills, originally covered with heath, patches of woodland, and moist swampy meadows. High peat regions once extended to the northeast. The largely coastal area north of Zwolle consists of low peat, partly covered with clay. This northwestern part is primarily meadowland supporting cattle and dairying; in the sand regions there is cattle rearing and dairying based on a type of mixed farming. The central Salland district has some orchards. The region of high peat in the northeast has been reclaimed from the sea for farming and specializes in cereals and potatoes.

The province has become highly industrialized. The Twente district in the southeast, where cotton spinning, weaving, and bleaching came into prominence in the 19th century, is one of the principal centres of the Dutch textile industry. The main centres are Enschede, Almelo, Hengelo (*qq.v.*), and Oldenzaal. Other important industrial centres are Deventer, Kampen, and Zwolle. There are two national parks (1934, 1957) in the northwest, preserving peat bogs and reed culture and forming sanctuaries for waterfowl. Pop. (1971 est.) 932,946.

·government, area, and population **12**:1062g; table
·map, The Netherlands **12**:1060
·political, commercial, and urban growth **11**:134g

Øverland, Arnulf (b. April 27, 1889, Kristiansund, Nor.—d. March 25, 1968, Oslo), poet and Socialist famous for the role his poems played in the Norwegian resistance movement during the German occupation in World War II. He made his debut with a volume called *Den ensomme fest* (1911; "The Lonely Feast") and was immediately acclaimed for his style, his painstaking elimination of adjectives, his clarity and economy. All his life he was an uncompromising defender of the suppressed, but not until after World War I, in his *Brød og vin* (1919; "Bread and Wine"), did he develop a radical opposition to bourgeois society and to Christianity and recognize a need to make his poetry into a social weapon.

Øverland

By courtesy of the Norwegian Information Service, New York

His poems of the 1930s are intended to alert Norwegians to the danger of Fascism and Nazism. The best known of these is "Du må ikke sove!" (1937; Eng. trans., *You Must Not Sleep!*, 1943). The poems he wrote and distributed secretly, in 1940, directed against the Nazi occupation, led to a four-year imprisonment in a German concentration camp. When he was liberated in May 1945, the Norwegian government presented him with the old home of their great national poet, Henrik Wergeland, as an expression of gratitude.

Overland Mail: *see* Southern Overland Mail.

Overland Monthly, U.S. magazine published 1868–1935.

·magazine publishing history **15**:251b

Overland Park, city, Johnson County, eastern Kansas, U.S., southern suburb of Kansas City, near the Missouri border. Settled in 1906, it lies on the old Santa Fe Trail and was platted as a stop on an inter-urban railway. The city is now mainly residential, with some light industry. Inc. city, 1960. Pop. (1980) 81,784.
38°59′ N, 94°40′ W

Overland Trail, in U.S. history, any of several land routes leading westward toward California, used during the 19th century.

·Wyoming western settlement role **19**:1052b

Overlord, Operation: *see* Normandy Invasion.

overpotential, also called OVERVOLTAGE, excess potential needed to discharge an ion from an electrode over and above the electrode's equilibrium potential.

·electrochemical potential and current **6**:644c

Overseas Press, Japanese KAIGAI SHIMBUN (1865–66), one of the first Japanese newspapers.

·free press tradition in Japan **15**:242c

Overseas Private Investment Corporation, U.S. government agency established in 1970.

·U.S. foreign aid through private investment **7**:524a

Oversticht (Netherlands): *see* Overijssel.

overstringing, in piano construction, an additional row of strings placed over the original one.

·piano construction development **10**:444h

over-the-counter market, trading in stocks and bonds that does not take place on stock exchanges, most significant in the U.S., where requirements for listing stocks on the exchanges are quite strict. It is often called the "off-board market," and sometimes the "unlisted market," though the latter term is misleading because some securities traded over-the-counter are listed on an exchange. Such trading is most often accomplished by telephone, telegraph, or leased private wire.

In this market, dealers frequently buy and sell for their own account and usually specialize in certain issues. Schedules of fees for buying and selling securities are not fixed, and dealers derive their profits from the markup of their selling price over the price they paid. The investor may buy directly from a dealer willing to sell stocks or bonds that he owns or with a broker who will search the market for the best price.

Bonds of the U.S. government (treasuries), as well as many other bond issues and preferred-stock issues, are listed on the New York Stock Exchange but have their chief market over-the-counter. Other U.S. federal government obligations, as well as state and municipal bonds, are traded over-the-counter exclusively.

A third market has developed due to the increased importance of institutional investors, such as the mutual funds, who deal in large blocks of stock. Trading is done in shares listed on the exchanges but takes place over-the-counter; this permits large-quantity discounts not possible on the exchanges, where brokerage fees are fixed.

Much of the regulation of the over-the-counter market is effected through the National Association of Securities Dealers, Inc., created in 1939 by an act of Congress to establish rules of conduct and protect members and investors from abuses.

Although retail prices of over-the-counter transactions are not publicly reported, the NASD began publishing interdealer prices for the issues on its national list in February 1965.

·securities trading and market operations **16**:451h

Overton, Richard (fl. 1642–63), English pamphleteer and satirist.

·Leveller religious and political views **3**:245c

overtone, faint tone sounding above the fundamental tone when a string or air column vibrates simultaneously as a whole, producing the fundamental (or first partial, or first harmonic); if it vibrates in sections it produces overtones (upper partials, or harmonics). The listener normally hears the fundamental pitch clearly; with concentration he can hear the faint overtones.

Harmonics are a series of overtones resulting when the partial vibrations are of equal sections (*e.g.*, halves, thirds, fourths). As the vibrating sections become smaller, the harmonics are higher in pitch and successively closer together. The frequencies of the upper harmonics form simple ratios with the frequency of the first harmonic, or fundamental (*e.g.*, 2:1, 3:1, 4:1).

Some musical instruments the sounds of which result from the vibration of metal, wood, or stone bars; from cylinders; from plates (*e.g.*, cymbals, bells, marimbas), or from membranes (drums) produce nonharmonic overtones, or partials—that is, tones the frequencies of which (and, therefore, the pitches of which) lie outside the harmonic series. *See also* combination tone.

·African homophonic part-singing **1**:246f
·electronic music equipment **6**:676c
·instrumental design and tone colour **12**:729d
·medieval perfect interval theory and continental music practice **12**:717d
·musical sound's tonal coloration **17**:35c; illus. 37
·organ sound production systems **13**:677g
·stringed instrument sound production **17**:740b
·vocal registers in singing **17**:481g
·wind instrument generation **19**:848f

overture, musical composition, originally preceding an opera, but also used in the suite and as an independent instrumental work.

The earliest operas opened with a sung prologue or a short instrumental flourish, such as the trumpet "Toccata" that opens Claudio Monteverdi's *Orfeo* (1607). Subsequent 17th-century operas were sometimes preceded by a short instrumental piece called a sinfonia, sonata, or, often in Venice, canzona.

The first significant use of a full-scale overture was made by Jean-Baptiste Lully (*q.v.*), as in his opera *Thésée*. His musical form, known as the French, or Lullian, overture, opens with a slow section in dotted rhythms, followed by a quick section in fugal style; it often concluded with a slow passage that sometimes was expanded into a full third section—either a repetition of the initial slow section or a dance form such as a minuet or gavotte. Lully's overture form was widely copied by composers not only of operas (Purcell in *Dido and Aeneas*) but also of oratorios (Handel in *Messiah*).

The Italian overture became firmly established after 1680 in the operas of Alessandro Scarlatti. It is in three sections, the first and third in quick time and the second in slow (allegro-adagio-allegro). It provided the model for the earliest symphonies, which consisted of three movements, as in the works of C.P.E. Bach and Jiří Antonín Benda.

A more modern form of the opera overture was established by Gluck, who in the dedication of his opera *Alceste* (1767) declared that the overture should prepare the audience for the plot of the play. Mozart in his overtures also set the emotional tone of the drama to follow. Similar thematic anticipation occurs in Beethoven, Weber, and Wagner.

Another trend, particularly in French operas by Daniel Auber and François Boieldieu (late 18th and early 19th centuries), was established by the overture made up of a potpourri of tunes from the opera—a form common in musical comedies and operettas. In Italy during the same period, the overture simply served to attract the audience's attention.

Many overtures of the 18th and 19th centuries were derived from the sonata form. But toward the end of the 19th century the overture was frequently replaced by a short prelude in free form, leading directly into the opening scene; *e.g.*, in Wagner's *Lohengrin* and in Verdi's *Aida*.

The concert overture, based on the style of overtures to romantic operas, became established in the 19th century as an independent work in one movement. It took either the classical sonata form or the free form of a symphonic poem. Examples include Mendelssohn's *Hebrides* overture and Sir William Walton's *Portsmouth Point* overture. Such works were also written for performance on special occasions; *e.g.*, Brahms's *Academic Festival Overture*. Other works, such as Mendelssohn's *Overture to A Midsummer Night's Dream* and Beethoven's overture to Goethe's *Egmont*, originally were intended to be performed as an introduction to a spoken play.

·French opera **13**:581g
·Western music development **12**:709b *passim* to 713f

Overweg, Adolf (b. July 24, 1822, Hamburg—d. Sept. 27, 1852, Maduari, in modern Chad), German geologist, astronomer, and traveller and the first European to circumnavigate and map Lake Chad, in Central Africa. Overweg was also a member of a pioneering mission to open the Central African interior to regular trade routes from the north.

The expedition, headed by James Richardson and sponsored by the British government, left Tripoli, in Libya, in the spring of 1850 and crossed the Sahara southward. Early in 1851 the group split up, and Overweg went on alone by way of Zinder (in present south central Niger) to Kukawa (northeast Nigeria), where he joined Heinrich Barth (*q.v.*), the expedition's scientist (and, after the death of Richardson, leader). The two spent 18 months exploring southward to Adamawa emirate (Nigeria) and the Benue River, around Lake Chad and to the southeast, until Overweg's death.

Ovetum (ancient city, Spain): *see* Oviedo.

Ovibos moschatus: *see* musk-ox.

Ovid 13:797, name in full PUBLIUS OVIDIUS NASO (b. March 20, 43 BC, Sulmo, modern Sulmona, Italy—d. AD 17, Tomis, modern Constanța, Romania), Roman poet whose work had immense influence on European literature and was an example of supreme technical accomplishment. The arch-poet of love, he raised the subject to epic stature in his masterpiece, the *Metamorphoses*.

Abstract of text biography. Educated at schools of rhetoric in Rome, he early abandoned an official career for poetry. His major poems were the *Amores* (*Loves*), beginning about 20 BC, the *Ars amatoria* (*c.* 1 BC), and the *Metamorphoses* (AD 1–8), a long poem in 15 books, a collection of stories ranging in time from Creation to the death and deification of Julius Caesar. He was banished in AD 8 by Augustus, partly because of passages in the *Ars amatoria* that were offensive to the Emperor. In Tomis, a remote corner of the empire on the Black Sea, he continued to write, notably the *Tristia* (*Sorrows*).

REFERENCES in other text articles:
·literary style and contributions **10**:1097b
·love portrayal's influence on the romance **15**:1021d
·textual problems of manuscripts **18**:191f

oviducts: *see* fallopian tubes.

Oviedo, province, coextensive with the northern half of the historic Kingdom of Asturias (*see* Asturias, Kingdom of), northern Spain; its area of 4,079 sq mi (10,565 sq km) is largely mountainous, with a rugged coastline dented by *rías* (inlets) of the Bay of Biscay. The main river is the Nalón, though the Sella and Navia are also important. Oak, chestnut, and apple trees abound. Maize (corn) and rye are grown, and the province is one of Spain's largest producers of potatoes. It also has a substantial cattle and dairy industry.

The wealth of Oviedo, however, is in its coalfields, which extend throughout the Nalón Basin and cover more than 1,000 sq mi (2,600 sq km). A great industrial complex has been built up at Avilés. Mieres is a busy mining and smelting centre. Gijón's seaport, Puerto del Musel, is Spain's foremost coal-exporting port. There is an armaments factory at Trubia. The provincial capital, Oviedo, is a cultural and communications hub. Pop. (1980 est.) 1,145,825.

·area and population table **17**:389

Oviedo, ancient OVETUM, capital of Oviedo province, northern Spain, on a hill surrounded by mountains and a fertile plain. It lies 18 mi (29 km) southwest of Gijón. Founded as a monastery by Fruela I in 757, it became the capital of the Kingdom of Asturias (*q.v.*) in 810. It was one of the few Spanish towns never conquered by the Moors during the Middle Ages. Outstanding landmarks of the city include the cathedral (begun in 1388, on the site of the original monastery); the bishop's palace (*c.* 1500–1700); and the Convento de San Vicente (1493), which now houses the provincial museum.

The economy of Oviedo relies heavily on the mining (coal and iron) in its environs. Industry includes food processing and some light manufacturing. Pop. (1980 est.) 168,613.
43°22′ N, 5°50′ W
·map, Spain **17**:382

Ovimbundu, African tribe numbering about 2,300,000 in 1975 and inhabiting the tree-studded grasslands of the Benguela highlands in Angola. They speak a Bantu language, Umbundu; they are distinct from the smaller Mbundu group that speaks Kimbundu. The ruling families of the Ovimbundu entered the highlands from the northeast in the 17th century, subduing and incorporating the indigenous cattle-keeping peoples. They divide into 22 chiefdoms, about half of which were tributary to a larger chiefdom before effective Portuguese occupation in the 20th century. Each chiefdom had a paramount chief, council, and subchiefs.

A household usually comprises the male head, his several wives, and dependent children. The kinship system features double descent, land being inherited in the paternal line and movable property in the maternal. Initiation schools exist for boys and girls of certain families only. Agriculture is the chief economic activity, main crops being corn (maize) and beans. Most Ovimbundu men and boys hunt, but there are also professional hunters. Domestic animals include cows, sheep, and goats; oxen are used for transport. Cattle are a measure of wealth, but few families own large herds. Beeswax was and still is an important item of trade.

Ovimbundu groups (under the names Mambari, Viye, or Bailundu) were traders with other African peoples and with the Portuguese. Each trading caravan had a professional leader and diviner. Trade agreements linking the independent chiefdoms led to development of regional specialization, such as metalwork among the Viye and cornmeal production among the Ciyaka and Bailundu. Large-scale trading activities declined with the suppression of the slave trade and the construction of the Benguela Railway in 1904.

·Angolan distribution of Mbundu language **1**:891d
·Portuguese Angolan control **17**:288h

ovinnik, in Slavic folk religion, spirit that inhabits the drying house on each farm.

·attributes and propitiation **16**:874d

oviparity, expulsion of undeveloped eggs rather than live young. The eggs may have been fertilized before release, as in birds and some reptiles, or are to be fertilized externally, as in amphibians and many lower forms. In general, the number of eggs produced by oviparous species greatly exceeds the number of offspring from species that bear their young live, but the chances of survival are diminished because of the lack of maternal protection. *Cf.* viviparity.

·animal reproductive system comparisons **15**:714g
·animal tissues and fluids **18**:449h
·arachnid egg development **2**:67h
·oncopod reproductive variations **13**:569a
·Perciformes breeding patterns **14**:48e
·reptile reproduction types **15**:728d
·Selachii reproduction **16**:496h

ovipositor, structure at the posterior end of the abdomen of a female insect, used for depositing eggs.

·cicada injury to trees through use **8**:1037e
·dragonfly egg laying **13**:508d
·flies' adaptation for egg deposition **5**:820g
·homopteran structure and function **8**:1040e
·hymenopteran forms and uses **9**:130d; illus.

Oviraptor, genus of small, light predaceous dinosaurs found as fossils in Late Cretaceous deposits of eastern Asia (the Cretaceous Period began 136,000,000 years ago and lasted 71,000,000 years). *Oviraptor*, a small animal approximately 1.3 metres (4 feet) long, was a biped supported by two long, well-developed hindlimbs. The forelimbs were long and slender, with long, clawed fingers clearly suited for grasping, ripping, and tearing. *Oviraptor* had a relatively short skull, with very large eyes surrounded by a bony ring. It possibly was capable of stereoscopic vision and may have been able to judge distances quite well; it apparently was more dependent upon sight than upon smell for procuring food. In-

Oviraptor philoceratops, specimen from Djadochta Cretaceous beds, Shabarkh Uso, Outer Mongolia

By courtesy of the American Museum of Natural History, New York

stead of teeth, the jaws were probably sheathed with a horny, beaklike covering. The remains of *Oviraptor* have been found in association with the nests of other dinosaurs, and it has been suggested that it ate dinosaur eggs.

Ovis, genus of hoofed mammals, family Bovidae, including the domestic sheep (*Ovis aries*) and several wild forms, among them the bighorn (*q.v.*), or mountain sheep, the argali (*q.v.*), and the mouflon (*q.v.*).

Ovonramwen, also called OVERAMI (d. Jan. 1914, Calabar, Nigeria), West African ruler who was the last independent oba (king) of the 500-year-old Kingdom of Benin (in present Nigeria). Ovonramwen tried to maintain his independence in the face of increasing British pressure but was able to delay for only a few years the annexation of his kingdom by the colony of Nigeria.

Called Idugbowa until he took the title Ovonramwen upon becoming oba, Ovonramwen succeeded to a kingdom much reduced by growing British commercial and colonial encroachment from its greatest extent (*c.* 1700). He attempted to seal Benin to Europeans but by 1892 was forced to sign a protection treaty with the British administration. Disputes over trade along the Benin River (1892–94) led to a campaign against Benin; the murder of the British acting consul general in January 1897 led to a full-scale military expedition, which captured Benin City in February 1897. Ovonramwen surrendered to the British in August and died in exile.

ovoviviparity (animal reproduction): *see* viviparity.

Ovruch, centre of a *rayon* (district), Zhitomir *oblast* (administrative region), Ukrainian Soviet Socialist Republic. Ovruch was first mentioned in documents in AD 977, when it was known as Vruchy. The town was incorporated in 1795. Today Ovruch is a centre of varied industries, including food processing and flax spinning. Latest census 11,536.
51°21′ N, 28°49′ E

ovulation, release of a mature egg from the female ovary; the release enables the egg to be fertilized by the male sperm cells. Normally, in human beings, only one egg is released at one time; occasionally, however, two or more erupt during the menstrual cycle. The egg erupts from the ovary on the 14th to 16th day of the approximately 28-day menstrual cycle. If fertilization does not occur, the egg is passed from the reproductive tract during menstrual bleeding, which starts about two weeks after ovulation. Occasionally, cycles occur in which an egg is not released; these are known as anovulatory cycles.

Prior to eruption from the ovary, an egg first must grow and mature. Until stimulated to grow, the primary egg cell passes through a period of dormancy that may last several years. The egg cell is surrounded by a capsule of cells known as the follicle. The follicular wall serves as a protective casing around the egg and also provides a suitable environment for egg development. As the follicle ripens, the cell wall thickens and a fluid is secreted to surround the egg. The follicle migrates from within the ovary's deeper tissue to the outer wall. Once the follicle reaches the surface of the ovary, the follicular wall thins. Pressure caused by the follicle and fluid against the ovary's surface causes bulging of the ovarian wall. When the follicle ruptures, the egg and fluid are released along with some torn patches of tissue. The cells, fluid, and egg are directed into the nearby fallopian tubes, each of which serves as a passageway by which the egg reaches the uterus and as a site for fertilization of the released egg by sperm.

The hormones that stimulate ovulation are produced in the pituitary gland; these are known as the follicle-stimulating hormone (FSH) and luteinizing hormone (LH). If the egg is not fertilized within about 24 hours, it begins to degenerate. After the egg leaves the ovary, the walls of the follicle again close, and the space that was occupied by the egg begins to fill with new cells known as the corpus luteum. The corpus luteum secretes the female hormone progesterone, which helps to keep the uterine wall receptive to a fertilized egg. If the egg is not fertilized, the corpus luteum stops secreting progesterone about nine days after ovulation. The uterine wall then begins to slough off the excess tissue, and menstrual bleeding ensues. The corpus luteum is eventually replaced by other ovarian tissue, known as the corpus albicans, and the once active site now becomes scar tissue. If the egg becomes fertilized, progesterone continues to be secreted, first by the corpus luteum and then by the placenta, until the child is born. Progesterone blocks the release of more hormones from the pituitary gland, so that further ovulation does not normally occur during pregnancy.

·animal reproductive system comparisons **15**:711e
·animal tissues and fluids comparisons **18**:450b
·copulation as cause in insectivores **9**:622d
·copulation as trigger **2**:813h
·estrous cycle interactions **11**:403a
·follicular collapse and egg release **6**:742h
·hormonal regulation in man **6**:803f
·human anatomic consequences **15**:696b; illus.
·infertility factors **15**:699c
·menstrual cycle events **11**:908f
·progesterone production in mammals **8**:1083h
·reproductive events in humans **14**:968c

ovule, plant structure that develops into a seed when fertilized. In gymnosperms (conifers and allies) the ovules lie uncovered on the scales of the cone. In angiosperms (flowering plants), one or more ovules are enclosed by the ovary (portion of the carpel, or female reproductive organ). Each ovule is attached by its base to the stalk (funiculus) that bears it. A mature angiosperm ovule consists of a food tissue covered by one or two future seed coats. A small opening (the micropyle) in the integuments at the apex of the ovule permits the pollen tube to enter and discharge its sperm nuclei into the embryo sac, a large oval cell in which fertilization and development occur. Variations in form and position of the ovule are significant in plant classification: orthotropous ovules stand out straight into the cavity of the ovary; campylotropous ovules are at right angles to the funiculus; anatropous ovules are directed back toward the funiculus. Intermediate forms also occur.

·angiosperm structure and reproduction **1**:876h; illus. 880
·Asterales flower structure **2**:215a
·Caryophyllales structural uniqueness **3**:975a
·Fagales seed development **7**:142b
·gene concept development **7**:982b
·gymnosperm reproduction features **8**:521d; illus. 520
·orchid development and fertilization **13**:650a
·Piperales classification distinction **14**:467f
·plant reproduction and development **5**:660g
·plant sexual systems **15**:717d; illus. 718
·pollen transfer in higher plants **14**:743g; illus. 744
·Primulales distinctive flower structure **14**:1048e; illus.
·reproductive systems in seed plants **15**:720h; illus. 722
·Rhamnales structure and location **15**:795c
·seed and fruit development **16**:480d

ovum, a small, single cell released from the female reproductive organs, the ovaries (*q.v.*), which is capable of developing into a new organism of the same species when fertilized (united) with a male sperm cell.

The outer surface of each ovary is covered by a layer of cells (germinal epithelium); these surround the immature egg cells, which are present in the ovaries from the time of birth. A hollow ball of cells, known as the follicle, encompasses each ovum. It is within the follicle that the ovum gradually matures. It takes approximately four months for a follicle to develop once it is activated. Some follicles lie dormant in the ovaries for 40 years before they mature; others degenerate and never develop. During a woman's child-bearing ages, 300 to 400 follicles mature and emit eggs capable of being fertilized. By the time a woman reaches menopause, most of the remaining follicles have degenerated.

A follicle-stimulating hormone (FSH), secreted into the bloodstream by the pituitary causes ovum growth. After the egg matures, a second hormone from the pituitary, luteinizing hormone (LH), is liberated; this causes the egg's release (ovulation).

As the ovum develops, the walls of the follicle expand by adding new cells. The follicle and ovum slowly migrate through the tissue of the ovary until they cause a bulge in the surface of the organ. The hollow cavity between the egg and the follicular wall usually contains a fluid secreted by the follicular cells. This keeps the ovum moist and provides a suitable growing environment. When the ovum erupts from the ovaries, some of the follicular cells still adhere to it. The ovum is captured and guided by the fallopian tubes (*q.v.*). Muscular contractions of the fallopian tubes move the egg to the cavity of the uterus (*q.v.*). A mature follicle is known as a graafian follicle. As many as 15 follicles may mature in the ovaries just before ovulation, but only one egg is usually released. The remaining mature follicles degenerate.

The ovum itself has a central nucleus that contains the female's genetic material; this, with the genetic material in the sperm cell, determines the inherited characteristics of the child. Surrounding the nucleus is a cell plasma, or yolk, that contains nutritional elements essential to the developing egg cell.

In humans, an egg is usually ovulated once every month. There is considerable variation among other animals. Rabbits do not release eggs until after they have mated; rats ovulate every four days whether they mate or not. In the female dog, an egg is released only twice each year.

If an egg does not become fertilized within 24 hours of its eruption, it tends to degenerate. After the egg is fertilized it undergoes a series of cell divisions. Failure of a fertilized egg to divide properly may result in identical twins, which look alike and are of the same sex, or Siamese twins, which remain physically attached at some joint. Fraternal twins result when two separate eggs are released and independently fertilized.

·chordate embryonic development **4**:450f
·disease causation mechanisms **5**:849h; illus.
·fertilization and sex cell role **7**:254f
·functions as basis of sex difference **16**:585g
·gene concept development **7**:982b
·genetic contribution and structure **8**:805g
·Harvey's fertilization theory **8**:662f
·hereditary material transmission **7**:994c
·human ovulation and fertilization **14**:968c
·human prenatal development stages **8**:1137g
·induced ovulation and zygote transplant **1**:907b
·insect fertilization through shell **9**:617c
·man's genetic contributor **7**:996h

oocyte
·animal tissue comparisons **18**:450b
·bryozoan development in brood chamber **3**:356b
·human maturation sequence **15**:695h; illus. 696
·radiation-induced mutation **15**:380d
·reproduction and embryogenesis through gastrula stage **5**:625h; illus. 626
·reproductive cell structure and function **3**:1062b

secondary oocyte
·human oogenetic structure **15**:696c
·oogenesis and cytoplasmic allotments **6**:742d
·sex determination and multiple embryos in hymenopteran insects **9**:127b; illus. 128
·sex determination and parthenogenesis **16**:591f

Zona Pellucida
·fertilization and egg envelope **7**:255f
·human anatomic description **15**:696d
·ovulation and follicular collapse **6**:742h; illus. 743

Owain Cyfeiliog (*c.* 1130–97), Welsh warrior-prince of Powis and poet of distinct originality in a period of highly structured poetry. *Hirlas Owain* ("The Drinking Horn of Owain"), the only poem that remains of his compositions, is noteworthy for its dramatic presentation. It is set in court, where his warriors, weary from battle, are gathered at the banquet table. Each stanza begins with instructions to the cupbearer to pour a drink for a hero; he then bestows praise on the man as the drink is poured. After ruling over the people of Powis from 1149 to 1195, Owain retired to the Cistertian monastery of Strata Marcella (Ystrad Marchell), which he had established in 1170. He died and was buried there, despite his previous excommunication (1188) for failing to support the Third Crusade. As prince of Powis he was known for his sympathetic attitude toward the English.

·bardic literary tradition **10**:1114c

Owain Gwynedd (d. 1170), king of Gwynedd.

·Welsh political development **3**:231a

Owatonna, city, seat of Steele County, southeastern Minnesota, U.S. Settled in the early 1850s as a trading post on a river known to the Indians as Owatonna (meaning "straight"), it was the site of the state's first known health spa, now in Mineral Springs Park. Owatonna State School for handicapped children was founded in 1886. Louis Sullivan, the Chicago architect, designed the National Farmers' Bank Building (1908). Owatonna developed as a trade, industrial, and transportation centre for a mixed-farming area with many cooperative creameries and a high butter production. Jewelry, tools, and farm equipment are among its manufactures. Inc. town, 1854; city, 1957. Pop. (1980) 18,632.
44°05′ N, 93°14′ W

National Farmers' Bank Building designed by Louis Sullivan, 1908, Owatonna, Minn.

Milt and Joan Mann from CameraMann

Owen, Alun (Davies) (b. Nov. 24, 1926, Liverpool, Lancashire), dramatist for radio, television, screen, and stage whose work often reflects the cultural and religious conflicts of the city where he was born. Of Welsh origin, he attended school in Wales and Liverpool and began his theatrical training as assistant stage manager in repertory (1942), and then became a stage and screen actor. He started writing for radio and television in 1957, quickly proving his sharp ear for dialogue and his gift for characterization. His television plays sometimes concentrated on the seamier aspects of city life, as in *No Trams to Lime Street* (1959). His quartet of plays, televised as *Male of the Species* (1969), with Lawrence Olivier, Paul Scofield, Sean Connery, and Michael Caine, was immensely successful. Owen's stage plays include *Progress to the Park* and *The Rough and Ready Lot* (both perf. 1958), and *A Little Winter Love* (1964). Among his screen credits is the script for *A Hard Day's Night* (1964).

Owen, Daniel (b. Oct. 20, 1836, Mold, Flintshire—d. Oct. 22, 1895, Mold), writer, considered the national novelist of Wales, a natural storyteller, whose works, set in his own time, introduced a wealth of vivid and memorable characters that have given him a place in his national literature comparable to that of Dickens in English.

The son of a coal miner and the youngest of six children, he received little formal education and at the age of 12 was apprenticed to a tailor. In 1864 he started to preach and in the following year he enrolled in Bala Calvinistic Methodist College but returned home before completing the course. He resumed preaching and soon began writing for publication.

His works include the novels *Hunangofiant Rhys Lewis* (1885; "Autobiography of Rhys Lewis"); *Profedigaethau Enoc Huws* (1891; "The Trials of Enoc Huws"); *Y Dreflan, ei Phobl a'i Phethau* (1881; "Dreflan, Its People and Its Affairs"), which describes the life around the Welsh chapel. *Offrymau Neilltuaeth* (1879; "Offering of Seclusion") is a volume of sermons and portraits of Methodists; *Y Siswrn* (1888; "The Scissors") is a collection of poems, essays, and stories. Besides the vigour of his diction, his works contain pungent humour and freedom from didacticism, qualities not generally found in 19th-century Welsh literature.

Owen, Goronwy (b. Jan. 1, 1723, Llanfair Mathafarn Eithaf, Anglesey—d. July 1769, Brunswick, Va.), clergyman and poet who revived classicism in modern Welsh literature. He reintroduced the *cywydd* and the *awdl*, poetic forms used by the ancient Welsh bards, with their traditional correctness but with fresh content. It was while he was at Donnington, Shropshire, serving as master of the local school and curate of Uppington, that he attracted attention as a poet. Other poets gathered around him, establishing a classical school of poetry that is still alive. In 1757, despite his excessive drinking, he obtained an appointment, through the efforts of friends, as headmaster of the grammar school attached to the College of William and Mary, in Williamsburg, Va. After losing this mastership ("for riotous living"), he became minister of St. Andrew's, Brunswick County, where he remained until he died.

Among his best known poems are "The Day of Judgment," "The Gem or the Precious Stone," "The Lineage and Attributes of the Muse," and "*Cywydd* in Answer to Huw the Red Poet."

·Welsh literature development **10**:1180b

Owen, John (b. 1616, Stadhampton, Oxfordshire—d. Aug. 24, 1683, London), Puritan minister, prolific writer and controversialist, frequent preacher before the English Parliament, advocate of Congregationalism, and aide to Oliver Cromwell, the lord protector of England from 1653 to 1658. Appointed rector of Fordham, Essex, in 1642, he was made vicar at nearby Coggeshall in 1646 after preaching a notable sermon before Parliament the same year. At Coggeshall he came out in favour of Congregational autonomy in church government; his compendium of principles of church polity was published as *Eschol: . . . or Rules of Direction for the Walking of the Saints in Fellowship* (1648). His frequent preaching before Parliament led to his attachment to Oliver Cromwell, whose policies against the monarchy Owen began to support. The day after the execution of King Charles I by Cromwell's partisans in January 1649, Owen again preached in Parliament and then accompanied Cromwell on his military ventures to Ireland and Scotland (1649–50).

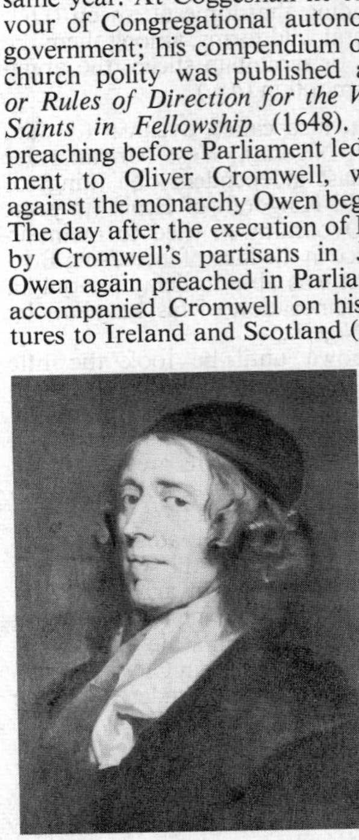

John Owen, oil painting by an unknown artist; in the National Portrait Gallery, London

By courtesy of the National Portrait Gallery, London

As chancellor of Oxford, Cromwell appointed Owen vice chancellor in 1652, a post he held until 1657. Also dean of Christ Church Cathedral (1651–60), he was elected in 1654 to represent Oxford in Parliament, but he was later disqualified because of his clerical vocation. Reserved in his support of Cromwell, Owen opposed plans to offer the English crown to him and avoided participation in Cromwell's installation in the office of lord protector in 1653. Owen abandoned politics on the restoration of the monarchy in 1660, when the House of Commons removed him from his position as Christ Church dean.

Among his works are historical treatises on religion, several studies of the doctrine of the Holy Spirit, and defenses of Nonconformist,

or Puritan, views. An edition of his *Works* fills 24 volumes (1850–55; W.H. Goold, ed.).
·influence and persecution **4**:1128a
·Puritan guidance under Cromwell **15**:306b

Owen, Sir Richard 13:800 (b. July 20, 1804, Lancaster, Lancashire—d. Dec. 18, 1892, London), anatomist and paleontologist who is remembered for his many contributions to the study of fossil animals.

Abstract of text biography. Owen studied medicine and set up practice in London until 1856, when he became superintendent of the natural history department of the British Museum. He bitterly opposed Darwin's thesis of evolution. Some of his views were challenged by his contemporaries. Among his publications were *Memoir on the Pearly Nautilus* (1832) and *On the Anatomy of Vertebrates* (1866–68).

REFERENCES in other text articles:
·Darwin's theories **5**:494d
·homology and analogy concepts **19**:1165b

Owen, Robert 13:800 (b. May 14, 1771, Newtown, Montgomeryshire—d. Nov. 17, 1858, Newtown), Welsh manufacturer turned reformer who was one of the most influential utopian Socialists of the early 19th century.

Abstract of text biography. Having become the superintendent of a large Manchester cotton mill by the age of 19, Owen quickly rose to be a manager and partner in the firm and induced his partners to purchase the New Lanark mills in Lanarkshire. He made many improvements in the lives of the people at the mills, including better housing, sanitation, and infant care. New Lanark became a place of pilgrimage for statesmen and social reformers, as well as a commercial success.

By 1817 Owen's thought had turned toward more basic consideration of the economic system and the need for the subordination of machinery to man. He recommended a system of cooperative communities in which work and the enjoyment of its results would be shared, and several experimental communities were founded, including one in the U.S. at New Harmony (*q.v.*), Ind. (1825). During the 1820s the growth of labour unions and the emergence of a working-class point of view caused Owen's doctrines to be widely accepted as an expression of workers' aspirations. In the unions, Owenism stimulated the formation of self-governing workshops, but government and employer resistance ended the movement after a few months. After 1834 Owen devoted himself to preaching his educational, moral, rationalist, and other reform ideas.

REFERENCES in other text articles:
·attack on bad institutions **14**:692g
·food service for industrial labour **7**:496d
·Indiana utopian religious community **9**:303f
·industry's concern for workers' conditions **9**:497c
·New Lanark preschool education **14**:990c
·pre-Marxist socialist thought **16**:965h
·trade union organization in Britain **18**:564e

Owen, Wilfred (b. March 18, 1893, Oswestry, Shropshire—killed in action Nov. 4, 1918, France), poet noted for his anger at the cruelty and waste of war and his pity for its victims. He also is significant for his technical experiments in assonance, which were particularly influential in the 1930s. He was educated at the Birkenhead Institute and matriculated at the University of London; after an illness in 1913, he lived in France. He had already begun to write and, while working as a tutor near Bordeaux, was preparing a book of "Minor Poems—in Minor Keys—by a Minor," which was never published. These early poems are consciously modelled on Keats.

In 1915 Owen enlisted in the Artists' Rifles. The experience of trench warfare brought him to rapid maturity; the poems written after January 1917 are full of anger at war's brutality, an elegiac pity for "those who die as cattle," and a rare descriptive power. In June 1917 he was invalided home and while in a hospital near Edinburgh met Siegfried Sassoon, who shared his feelings about the war and who became interested in his work. Reading Sassoon's poems and discussing his own work with him revolutionized Owen's style and his conception of poetry. Despite the plans of well-wishers to find him a staff job, he returned to France in August 1918 as a company commander. He was awarded the military cross in October and was killed a week before Armistice Day.

Published posthumously by Sassoon, his single volume of *Poems* contains the most poignant English poetry of the war. The fragmentary preface has been much quoted:

> Above all, this book is not concerned with Poetry, The subject of it is War, and the pity of
> War. The Poetry is in the pity. All a poet can do is warn.

The last three lines were used by Benjamin Britten as a motto for his *War Requiem* (first performed 1962), which also employed other poetry of Owen in its choral passages. Among his better known poems are "Anthem for Doomed Youth," "Strange Meeting," "Futility," "Arms and the Boy," and "Greater Love." Biographies of Owen are *Journey from Obscurity*, 3 vol. (1963–65), by his brother Harold Owen, and *Wilfred Owen* (1974) by Jon Stallworthy.

Owendo, deepwater port, Estuaire province, northwestern Gabon, on the north shore of the Gabon Estuary; it serves the national capital, Libreville (9 mi [15 km] north-northwest), and was designed to handle ore vessels. It has a seaplane base and road connections with Libreville, Cocobeach, Médouneu, and Kango. The Belinga–Owendo railway carries iron ore from Belinga in the Mekambo district (and timber and agricultural products from Belinga, Makokou, Booué, Alembé, and Kango) to the coast for export. In Owendo, sawmills and a plywood factory process hardwoods (notably okoumé) for export, and there is a pelletization factory for iron ore.
0°17′ N, 9°30′ E
·map, Gabon **7**:821

Owen Falls, on the Victoria Nile just northwest of Jinja, Uganda, below the river's outlet from Lake Victoria. The falls are the site of Owen Falls Dam, 2,725 ft (830 m) long and 100 ft (30 m) high, which was completed in 1954, transforming Lake Victoria into a reservoir. The fall from the lake is harnessed by a hydroelectric installation to provide power for Uganda's industry.

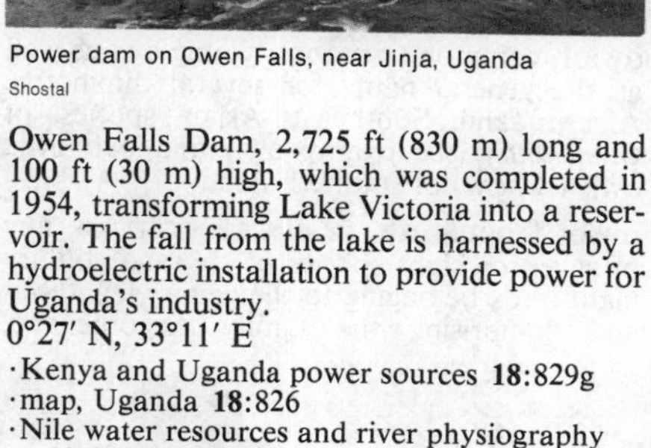

Power dam on Owen Falls, near Jinja, Uganda
Shostal

0°27′ N, 33°11′ E
·Kenya and Uganda power sources **18**:829g
·map, Uganda **18**:826
·Nile water resources and river physiography **13**:107g; map 103
·power and flood control potential **6**:118d; map 119

Oweniida, order of segmented worms of the class Polychaeta (phylum Annelida).
·characteristics and classification **1**:936d; illus. 935

O-wen-k'o, ethnic group in northeastern China.
·Heilungkiang settlement history **8**:743a

Owens, Jesse, real name JAMES CLEVELAND OWENS (b. Sept. 12, 1913, Danville, Ala.—d. March 31, 1980, Tucson, Ariz.), one of the greatest track-and-field athletes, who set a world record in the running broad jump (also called long jump) that stood for 25 years and won four gold medals in the 1936 Olympic Games in Berlin. It was believed that, because Owens was black, Adolf Hitler walked out of the stadium rather than congratulate him; historians later found that the slight was probably unintentional.

Owens, 1936
Wide World Photos

As a student in a Cleveland high school, Owens won three events in the 1933 National Interscholastic Championships, Chicago. In one day, May 25, 1935, while competing for Ohio State University (Columbus) in a Western Conference (Big Ten) track-and-field meet at the University of Michigan (Ann Arbor), Owens equalled the world record for the 100-yd dash (9.4 sec) and broke the world records for the 220-yd dash (20.3 sec), the 220-yd low hurdles (22.6), and the running broad jump (26 ft 8¼ in. [8.13 m]). The last of these marks was finally broken on Aug. 12, 1960, by Ralph Boston of the U.S. As a member of the U.S. team in the 1936 Olympic Games, Owens tied the Olympic record in the 100-m run (10.3 sec), broke Olympic and listed world records in the 200-m run (20.7 sec) and the running broad jump (26 ft 5¼ in. [8.05 m]; his world-record leap in 1935 had not yet been officially accepted), and ran the final segment for the world-record-breaking U.S. 400-m relay team (39.8 sec). For a time Owens held alone or shared the world records for all sprint distances recognized by the International Amateur Athletic Federation.

After retiring from competitive track, Owens engaged in boys' guidance activities, made goodwill visits to India and the Far East for the U.S. Department of State, served as secretary of the Illinois State Athletic Commission, and worked in public relations.
·running and long jump records **18**:548h

Owensboro, city, seat (1815) of Daviess County, on the Ohio River in northwestern Kentucky, U.S. Founded about 1800, it was known to early flatboat men as Yellow Banks, from the colour of its riverbanks. The town, laid out in 1816, was first named Rossborough after David Ross, a large property owner, and later changed to Owensboro to honour Col. Abraham Owen, a veteran of early Kentucky wars. During the Civil War, the city was headquarters for the Federal Camp Silas B. Miller. A Confederate attack was repelled in 1862, but, in August 1864, guerrillas burned part of the town.

The city is the centre of a rich oil and agricul-

tural (tobacco, corn, wheat, soybeans, and fruit) region. Manufactures include bourbon whiskey, alloy steel, chemicals, furniture, electronic products, and cigars. It is the site of Kentucky Wesleyan (1858) and Brescia (1925) colleges and the Natural Science Museum. Mt. St. Joseph Academy (1874) is nearby. Annual events include the Festival of the Arts, Square Dance Festival, and the Owensboro Hydroplane Regatta. Inc. town, 1817; city, 1866. Pop. (1930) city, 22,765; (1980) city, 54,450; metropolitan area (SMSA), 85,949.
37°46′ N, 87°07′ W
·map, United States **18**:909

Owenson, Sydney (Irish novelist): *see* Morgan, Sydney, Lady.

Owen Sound, city, Grey County, Ontario, Canada, west of Toronto, on Owen Sound (an inlet of Georgian Bay of Lake Huron). It was named for Capt. W.F. Owen of the Royal Navy, who charted the Great Lakes, including the bay, in 1815. Originally it was settled as Sydenham in 1841, incorporated as the town of Owen Sound in 1857, and became a city in 1920. In addition to being a resort and grain-shipping port, it manufactures marine engines, boats and tugs, machinery, and electronic and communications equipment. Pop. (1971) 18,469.
44°34′ N, 80°56′ W
·map, Canada **3**:717

Owens River, in eastern California, rises in the Sierra Nevada and flows generally southeastward into Owens Lake.
36°31′ N, 117°57′ W
·Los Angeles water supply system **11**:108e

Owen Stanley Range, segment of the central highlands of New Guinea, occupying the southeast "tail" of the island. The range rises abruptly from the coastal plain to a height of 9,000 ft (2,750 m) and extends for 200 mi (300 km). Highest point of the 25–70-mi-wide massif and of the Papuan portion of Papua New Guinea is Mt. Victoria, soaring to more than 13,000 ft. Rainfall on the forested slopes gives rise to several rivers, including the Kemp Welch and Yodda (flowing south) and the Musa (north). The range is named after British Capt. Owen Stanley, who explored the coast of New Guinea from 1845 to 1850. In 1942 Japanese forces began an overland crossing of the range in an attempt to capture Port Moresby. They were met by Allied troops and, after a prolonged fight, had to concede their first land defeat of World War II.
9°20′ S, 147°55′ E
·New Guinea mountain chains and volcanic activity **12**:1088d
·Papuan climate influence **2**:432f

Owen Wingrave (1971), opera written for television by Benjamin Britten, with libretto by Myfanwy Piper.
·television adaptations from other media **18**:125c

Owerri, town, seat of Owerri Province, East Central State, southern Nigeria, at the intersection of roads from Aba, Onitsha, Port Harcourt, and Umuahia. It is the chief trade centre (yams, cassava, cocoyams, maize [corn], and palm products) for a region of modified rain forest that also yields rubber for export. The town is the seat of an advanced teacher-training college and several government, mission, and private secondary schools; it is also known for its handicraft centres.

One of the most densely populated areas of Nigeria, the province (area 2,158 sq mi [5,589 sq km]) is inhabited by the predominantly Christian Ibo people. Owerri is its largest urban centre, but Oguta, Okigwi, and Orlu are also important market towns. Pop. (1971 est.) town, 25,675; (1963) province, 2,310,513.
5°29′ N, 7°02′ E
·map, Nigeria **13**:86

ʿOwfī (d. 1230), Persian writer.
·stories and biographical writings **9**:966a

owl, common name for the usually nocturnal birds of prey that form the order Strigiformes. The three extant families in the order are Strigidae (typical owls), Tytonidae (barn owls and grass owls), and Phodilidae (bay owls). Although owls bear some likeness to hawks and eagles (order Falconiformes) and were once placed with them in the same order, they are not closely related. Unlike other birds of prey, owls have virtually noiseless flight, the butterfly-like flapping of wings being muffled by a velvet-like surface on the flight feathers. Owls are protectively coloured, generally brownish. Many species show two phases of coloration, one in which the brown tends toward red, the other in which it tends toward gray. The females usually are larger than the males. Hearing and vision are acute. Owls are numerous but often go unnoticed because of their nocturnal habit. Owls nest in buildings, holes in trees, or nests abandoned by other birds. Some nest on the ground or in holes in the ground. The eggs are usually nearly round. *Major ref.* **17**:734c
·caprimulgiform bird comparison **3**:806g
·ear anatomy and use in hunting **17**:48e
·Falconiformes' convergent evolution **7**:150d
·predation on rodents **15**:973c
·territorial behaviour and breeding **14**:837e

RELATED ENTRIES in the *Ready Reference and Index:*
barn owl; bay owl; burrowing owl; eagle owl; elf owl; fish owl; hawk owl; horned owl; laughing owl; little owl; long-eared owl; pygmy owl; scops owl and screech owl; short-eared owl; snowy owl; spectacled owl; wood owl

Owl and the Nightingale, The, a late 12th- or early 13th-century English poem, some 2,000 lines long, written in fluent imitation of a commonly used French metre, the octosyllabic couplet, which was soon to be established as the standard metre for narrative and discursive writing in English. The poem is written as a debate (a popular device in both Latin and French poetry) between the two birds, and the poet ranges over a number of topics including witchcraft, the church, and marriage, giving expression to a wisdom based on experience rather than on schooling. It is difficult to say whether the birds have any consistent symbolism. The gravity of the owl contrasts with the gaiety of the nightingale, and suggestions as to the meaning of their respective "roles" have included theology and art, monasticism and life in the world, winter and summer, and Anglo-Saxon poetry and French poetry. The poet, though he never fully adopts the view of either the owl or the nightingale, seems to incline toward the latter. The poem is sometimes attributed to Nicholas de Guildford.
·theme, style, and literary significance **10**:1108f

owlet, common term for a young owl as well as the general name for several diminutive African and Southeast Asian species of *Glaucidium* (*see* pygmy owl) and two little owls (*Athene*) of southern Asia.

owlet frogmouth, or OWLET NIGHTJAR, any of seven or eight species of shy and solitary night birds belonging to the genus *Aegotheles* and comprising the family Aegothelidae, closely related to frogmouths, in the order Caprimulgiformes. These inhabitants of Australia's forests resemble small owls with very wide mouths nearly hidden by long bristles; they also perch like owls, but have tiny feet. They eat insects, which they catch either on the wing or by pouncing from a branch. Their call is a soft churring or whistling. They lay three to five eggs in a hole in a tree or sandbank.

The best known species is the 22-centimetre little *A. cristatus*, of Australia (where it is often called moth owl); it is green-glossed gray above and brown below. Other species, 19–30 centimetres long, occur in New Guinea, New Caledonia, and the Moluccas. *Major ref.* **3**:806f

Owlet frogmouth (*Aegotheles cristatus*)
Painting by Gene M. Christman

owlet moth, sometimes called MILLER, any of the more than 20,000 species in the cosmopolitan family Noctuidae (order Lepidoptera), having powdery, dusky wings. This large group is divided into many families by some authorities.

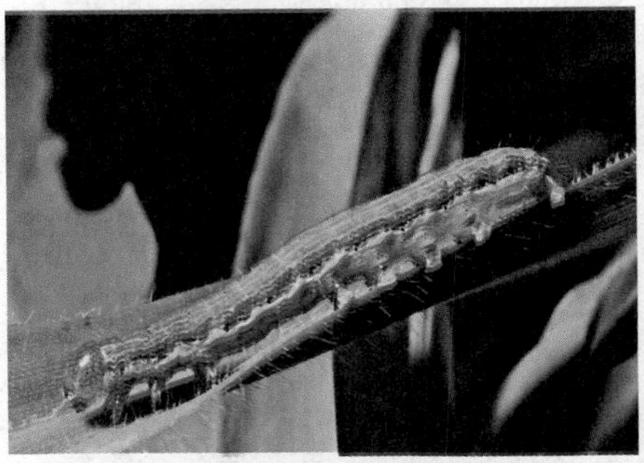

Army worm, larva of the owlet moth *Pseudaletia unipuncta*
William E. Ferguson

The wingspan of these triangular-shaped, stout-bodied moths ranges from 8 to 305 millimetres (⅓ to 12 inches). Although most have dull coloration, some tropical species are bright and iridescent. Owlet moths are mainly night fliers, and many are attracted to lights. Hearing organs on the thorax consist of a tightly stretched membrane that is protected by an expanded hood. Most adults feed on fruits, sap, or sweet fluids using well-developed mouthparts. Some species migrate northward after breeding in tropical regions.

Many species have protective coloration: the underwing moth (*Catocala*) blends into tree bark.

The larvae vary from dull to colourful and from smooth to hairy. Many species feed on foliage and seeds, others bore in stems and fruits, and a few prey on scale insects. Larvae of some species known as cutworms (*e.g.*, the black cutworm, *Agrotis ipsilon*) attack such plants as corn, grasses, tomatoes, and beans at night, severing roots and stems near ground level. Larvae of other species may eat foliage or fruits; still others (*e.g.*, the glossy cutworm, *Crymodes devastator*) live underground and feed on plant roots. The larvae of *Pseudaletia unipuncta*, called army worms, travel along the ground in large groups, destroying corn, small grains, sugarcane, cotton, and other crops. The name army worm is also generally applied to caterpillars of several other lepidopteran species that may migrate to new feeding grounds in large groups. The corn earworm, the destructive larval stage of the cosmopolitan moth *Heliothis zea*, is also known as the cotton bollworm, tomato fruitworm, vetch worm, or tobacco budworm, depending upon its host.

Many larvae pupate underground with cocoons; others make strong silken cocoons incorporating wood chips, larval hairs, and other material.
·classification and general features **10**:830a
·startle colour markings, illus., **4**:Coloration, Biological, Plate 4
·underwing moth adult, illus., **10**:Lepidoptera, Plate 4

owl-faced monkey, or HAMLYN'S MONKEY (*Cercopithecus hamlyni*), arboreal guenon found in heavy forest of the Congo basin. The owl-faced monkey is greenish gray with black underparts and forelimbs and silver gray on the lower back and base of the tail. The distinguishing feature is a white streak that runs the length of the nose and gives it an owllike appearance. *See also* guenon.

owlfly, large insect with membranous wings and long, clubbed antennae; any member of the neuropteran family Ascalaphidae. The larva camouflages itself with debris or hides beneath bark to await prey. The adults are found mainly in the tropics.
·classification and distinguishing features **12**:1070d

owl jugs (ceramics): *see* Eulenkrug.

owl monkey: *see* durukuli.

owners' equity (finance): *see* net worth.

ownership: *see* property, law of.

Owo, town, Ondo Province, Western State, southwestern Nigeria, at the southern edge of the Kukuruku Hills (altitude 1,130 ft [344 m]) and at the intersection of roads from Akure, Kabba, Benin City, and Siluko. A major collecting point for cocoa, it also serves as a market centre (yams, cassava, maize [corn], rice, palm oil and kernels, pumpkins, okra) for the Owo-Ifon branch of the Yoruba people. Cotton and teak are cultivated in the surrounding area, which was originally covered with dense tropical rain forest. Owo has Anglican, Methodist, New Church, Roman Catholic, government, and private secondary schools; and it is the site of St. John's Teacher Training College (Anglican), a government trade institute, several hospitals, and a maternity clinic. Pop. (1971 est.) 97,198.
7°18′ N, 5°30′ E
·map, Nigeria **13**:86
·visual art of West Africa **1**:265f

Owon (Korean painter): *see* Chang Sung-ob.

Owosso, city, Shiawassee County, Michigan, U.S., on the Shiawassee River. Settled in 1835 as a lumber centre, it has turned to agriculture and diversified manufacturing. The first log cabin (built 1836) is maintained as a historical museum, and Curwood Castle, studio of the adventure writer James Oliver Curwood, is there. It was the birthplace of Republican leader Thomas E. Dewey. Inc. city, 1859. Pop. (1980) 16,455.
43°00′ N, 84°10′ W

Owo-Yoruba, people of western Nigeria.
·traditional arms design illus. **2**:34

Owstoniidae, a family of bandfishes of the order Perciformes.
·classification and general features **14**:53b

Owyhee River, formed by the junction of several forks in the southwest corner of Idaho, U.S., flows northwest across the Oregon boundary, north through Malheur County, and empties into the Snake River south of Nyssa, Ore., after a course of 300 mi. The Owyhee Dam (1932) impounds the Lake Owyhee. The river was named Owyhee (an early spelling of Hawaii) in memory of Hawaiians killed near the stream in 1819.
43°46′ N, 117°02′ W

ox (*Bos taurus*, or *B. taurus primigenius*), a domesticated form of the large horned mammals that once moved in herds across North America and Europe (whence they have disappeared) and Asia and Africa, where some still exist in the wild state. South America and Australia have no wild oxen.

The castrated male of *B. taurus* is a docile form especially useful as a draft animal in many underdeveloped parts of the world.
·African livestock practices **1**:204a
·carriages use for transport power **19**:521a
·draft work suitabilities and history **5**:970b
·harness and saddlery history **8**:657e
·longevity comparison, table 1 **10**:913

Ox 100, trade name of a magnetic alloy.
·magnetic properties table 1 **11**:335

oxacillin, a penicillase-resistant semisynthetic penicillin.
·antibiotic action and spectrum **1**:988a

oxalacetate, or OXALOACETATE, a four-carbon compound produced during catabolism (*q.v.*) in living cells.
·catabolism oxidation phase **11**:1023g

oxalic acid, a colourless, crystalline, toxic organic compound belonging to the family of carboxylic acids. Oxalic acid is widely used as an acid rinse in laundries, where it is effective in removing rust and ink stains because it converts most insoluble iron compounds into a soluble complex ion. For the same reason, it is the chief constituent of many commercial preparations used for removing scale from automobile radiators.

The formula of oxalic acid is $(COOH)_2$; its usual form is that of the crystalline hydrate, $(COOH)_2 \cdot 2H_2O$. Known as a constituent of wood sorrel as early as the 17th century, oxalic acid was first prepared synthetically by a Swedish chemist, Carl Wilhelm Scheele, in 1776. It is manufactured by heating sodium formate in the presence of an alkali catalyst, by oxidizing carbohydrates with nitric acid, by heating sawdust with caustic alkalies, or by fermentation of sugar solutions in the presence of certain molds.
·Begoniales chemical substances **2**:802h
·chemiluminescent efficiency **11**:179h

Oxalis, genus containing about 800 species of small herbaceous plants in the family Oxalidaceae, native primarily to southern Africa and tropical and South America. A few South American species have edible tubers or roots, but most members of the genus are familiar as garden ornamentals. The name is derived from the Greek word *oxalis* ("acid") because the plants have an acidic taste. The common wood sorrel (*O. acetosella*) of eastern North America and Great Britain is a small, stemless plant with clover-like three-parted leaves. The leaves arise from a creeping, scaly rootstock, and the flowers are borne singly on a stalk that arises from the leaf axil. The flowers have five white, purple-veined petals. The fruit is a capsule that splits open by valves. The seeds have a fleshy coat, which curls back elastically, ejecting the true seed. The leaflets, as in other species of the genus, fold back and droop at night. Besides the wood sorrel, about 20 other species occur in North America, among which are the yellow wood sorrel (*O. stricta*), of the eastern United States and Canada, with yellow flowers; the violet wood sorrel (*O. violacea*), of the eastern United States, with rose-purple flowers; the redwood wood sorrel (*O. oregana*), of the coast redwood belt from California to Oregon, with pink to white flowers; and *O. cernua*, known as Bermuda buttercups, with showy yellow flowers, native to south Africa and naturalized in Florida and the Bermudas. Another yellow-flowered kind is the weedy, creeping oxalis (*O. corniculata*). Both *O. stricta* and *O. corniculata* are widely naturalized in the old world. The tubers of *O. tuberosa*, the oca of South America, and the roots of *O. deppei*, a bulbous Mexican species, are edible.
·propagation and distribution **8**:1d

Oxandra lanceolata, commonly known as LANCEWOOD, species of plant of the family Annonaceae of the order Magnoliales.
·timber characteristics and economic use **11**:341e

oxbird, colloquial name for certain small sandpipers (family Scolopacidae, order Charadriiformes), especially the dunlin (*q.v.*). In Africa the buffalo weaver (*q.v.*; family Ploceidae, order Passeriformes) and the oxpecker (family Sturnidae, order Passeriformes) are called oxbirds.

oxbow lake, small lake located in an abandoned meander loop of a river channel. It is generally formed as a river cuts through a meander neck to shorten its course, causes the old channel to be rapidly blocked off, and

Oxbow lakes formed by the Mudjatik River, northern Saskatchewan

By courtesy of the National Air Photo Library, Department of Energy, Mines, and Resources

then migrates away from the lake. If only one loop is cut off, the lake formed will be crescent shaped, whereas if more than one loop is cut off, the lake will be serpentine or winding. Eventually, oxbow lakes are silted up to form marshes and finally meander scars, marked by different vegetation or the absence of cultivation. The lakes commonly are filled with clay-sized sediment that is less easy to erode than surrounding material and thus may cause a more complex meandering system in its parent stream.

Oxenford, John (1812–77), English critic and dramatist.
·Iconoclasm in German philosophy **16**:359h

Oxenstierna, Axel, Count 13:802 (b. June 16, 1583, near Uppsala, Swed.—d. Aug. 28, 1654, Stockholm), chancellor of Sweden for more than 40 years during which Sweden emerged as a great power in Europe.

Abstract of text biography. Educated at Rostock and other German universities, he became a member of the council of state (1609). He was appointed chancellor in 1612 by King Gustavus Adolphus. Oxenstierna's contributions in administrative reform included drafting of the "parliamentary law" of 1617, which stabilized the constitution of the Riksdag. He negotiated the Truce of Altmark with Poland in 1629. In 1631 the King called him to Germany, and after the death of Gustavus in 1632, he was director of Swedish policy in the Thirty Years' War. The terms obtained by Sweden under the Peace of Westphalia (1648) justified his policies. Upon his return to Sweden (1636), he participated in the regency's government; and, until 1644, when Queen Christina attained her majority, he was the real ruler of the country.

REFERENCES in other text articles:
·Gustav Adolf government collaboration **8**:503f
·Queen Christina's chancellor **4**:564d
·regency and foreign policy **16**:318d
·Thirty Years' War policies **8**:92e
·Thirty Years' War role **18**:336b *passim* to 339g

Oxenstierna, Bengt Gabrielsson, Count (b. July 16, 1623, Morby Castle, Sweden—d. July 12, 1702, Stockholm), statesman who, as the principal foreign policy adviser of King Charles XI, established a virtually neutral foreign policy for Sweden, breaking the existing alliance with France and forming ties with the Netherlands, England, and the Holy Roman Empire.

Bengt Oxenstierna, a relative of Gustavus II Adolphus's chancellor Axel Oxenstierna, began his career as a diplomat at the Congresses of Osnabrück and Nürnberg, which were held in connection with the Peace of Westphalia

Bengt Oxenstierna, detail from a portrait by David Klöcker von Ehrenstrahl, 1690; in Gripsholm Castle, Sweden

By courtesy of the Svenska Portrattarkivet, Stockholm

(1648), which ended the Thirty Years' War. After serving as president of the tribunal at Wismar (now in East Germany), one of Sweden's German possessions, he joined (1655) the Polish campaign of King Charles X and fought with distinction in the defense of Toruń (1658). A councillor of state from 1654, he helped negotiate the Treaty of Oliva (1660), by which Poland ceded to Sweden its last Baltic territories.

After diplomatic service in Livonia, Wismar, and Vienna, Oxenstierna helped negotiate the treaties of Nijmegen (1678, 1679), which concluded the Dutch War (1672–78), in which Sweden had fought on the French side. Appointed head of the chancellery (1680) in succession to Count Johan Gyllenstierna, Oxenstierna soon assumed control of Sweden's foreign affairs. By negotiating an alliance with the Netherlands and the Holy Roman emperor in the Treaty of The Hague (1681), he reversed Sweden's long-standing policy of alliance with France.

Recognizing the threat to the European balance of power posed by the personal alliance of England and the Netherlands under William III in 1688, Oxenstierna helped maintain Sweden's neutrality during the ensuing War of the Grand Alliance (1689–97) between France and the major European powers. He gained a mediating role for Sweden in the Treaty of Rijswijk (1697), which concluded the war. With the accession of Charles XII in 1697, Oxenstierna's influence declined greatly. After the outbreak of the Northern War (1700–21), Charles disregarded Oxenstierna's chancellery and made his decisions in the field.

Oxenstierna, Johan Gabriel (1750–1818), Swedish writer.
·Swedish literature development **10**:1176e

Oxenstierna, Jon Bengtsson (1417–67), Swedish archbishop.
·rebellion against Charles VIII **16**:314a

oxetane, four-membered-ring heterocycle containing oxygen.
·synthesis and chemical properties **8**:838g

oxeye, in the sense of big-eyed, the name of a flower (daisy; *q.v.*) and, colloquially in Britain, of certain small sandpipers (especially the dunlin; *q.v.*) and the great tit (titmouse). *See also* tit. It is also used to refer to the Pacific tarpon.
·economic importance and breathing behaviour of Pacific tarpon **6**:729e

Oxford, the county town (seat) and from 1889 to 1974 a county borough of Oxfordshire, England, with a cathedral, the oldest university in England (often called a *studium generale* after 1168), and one of England's newest major institutions of higher education, Oxford Polytechnic (founded 1970). It is also an important industrial centre. Situated between the Upper River Thames (known in Oxford as the Isis) and the Cherwell, just north of their confluence, the town was first occupied in Saxon times as a fording point. Earlier peoples had spurned the valley lowlands in favour of the drier uplands to the north and south. Oxford became a Thames *burg* built to defend the northern frontier of Wessex from Danish attack. The first written mention of the town was in the Anglo-Saxon Chronicle (912), when it was observed that Edward the Elder "held Lurdenbryg [London] and Oxnaford and all the lands pertaining thereto." Except for the Saxon Romanesque tower of St. Michael's Church in Cornmarket Street, little remains of the Saxon settlement.

Robert d'Oilly was appointed first Norman governor and was responsible for building Oxford Castle, of which all that remains today is the motte (mound) and the tower of the Church of St. George in the Castle. The site today is occupied by the local prison. Robert also built Oxford's first bridges (Magdalen, Folly, and Hythe). The Normans constructed a stone wall around the settlement. This wall enclosed an area of approximately 95 ac (38 ha). Little now remains except a few short sections, such as that in the grounds of New College.

Established as a diocese in 1542, the first Oxford see was Osney Priory (destroyed), but in 1546 this designation was bestowed on St. Frideswide Priory, the "chapel" of Christ Church College and the smallest cathedral in England.

Oxford is known as the "City of Spires," most of which belong to the university and its various colleges. The college buildings were mostly built in the 15th, 16th, and 17th centuries. The earliest colleges were University College (1249), Balliol (1263), and Merton (1264). Oxford remained a market centre, but this function declined in importance from the 13th to the 16th century; its subsequent history became the history of the university, although there was always a certain antipathy between "town and gown." This found its most violent expression in the Massacre of St. Scholastica's Day in 1355.

In the English Civil War of the mid-17th century Oxford's strategic importance made the city the Royalist headquarters to which the king retired after his defeats at Edgehill, Newbury, and Naseby. In May 1646 Lord Fairfax besieged the city, which finally surrendered to him on June 24th. The town became an important stagecoach junction point and a considerable number of coaching inns are still found. During the 18th century a canal network linking Oxford with various parts of the country was also developed, and in 1835 the Great Western Railway from London to Bristol was begun.

In 1801 Oxford still depended very largely on the university for a livelihood, but, by the beginning of the 20th century, printing and publishing were also firmly established; and the manufacture of preserves (especially marmalade) was also important. Subsequently, English industrial magnate William Morris (later Lord Nuffield) started a motor-car industry at Cowley, just outside the city, and today this, together with associated heavy and electrical engineering enterprises, is the main industrial concern in the local economy. In 1926 a pressed-steel factory for car bodies was also set up in Cowley, and in 1929 the city's boundaries were extended to include this industrial quarter (increasing the city's area from 7,719 ac [3,124 ha] to 8,785 ac [3,555 ha]). Pop. (1971) 108,805.
51°46′ N, 1°15′ W
·map, United Kingdom **18**:866

Oxford, city, seat of Lafayette County, northern Mississippi, U.S. Originating as a trading post, it was incorporated in 1837 and named for the English seat of learning, reflecting the townspeople's early desire for a university. The University of Mississippi (Ole Miss), chartered 1844, was opened 1848 and occupies more than 1800 ac (727 ha). It served as a hospital during the Civil War when the city was occupied by Federal forces (December 1862–August 1864). In the fall of 1962 Oxford was riot torn over the enrollment of a black student, James H. Meredith.

The city is also an agricultural-trade centre (cotton, corn, and cattle). The former home of William Faulkner, where he wrote his Yoknapatawpha County tales, is on Garfield Street; the author's medals and prizes are displayed in the Mary Buie Museum on the Ole Miss campus. The Oxford Pilgrimage, an annual spring event, exhibits antebellum homes and historic landmarks. The Sardis Reservoir and Holly Springs National Forest are nearby. Pop. (1980) 9,882.
34°22′ N, 89°32′ W
·map, United States **18**:908

Oxford, village, primarily a university community, Butler County, southwestern Ohio, U.S. Bounded south and east by Fourmile (Tallawanda) Creek and its tributaries, Oxford is located in rolling farmland that supports wheat, corn, and livestock. In 1803 Oxford Township was ceded by Congress to the State of Ohio to be held in trust for "the endowment of an academy and other seminaries of learning." In 1810 the site was laid out in accord with an act (1809) of the State Assembly that chartered Miami University. Western College for women (chartered 1853) began as a female seminary. Rapid post-World War II growth of the university and the establishment of an atomic-energy project at nearby Ross has caused a population influx and an expansion of the original square mile boundary.

Cloisters of Magdalen College, University of Oxford, England, with the Bell Tower (left) and Founder's Tower (right)

A.F. Kersting

William Holmes McGuffey, while a professor at Miami University, compiled the first of his *Eclectic Readers*, and his house has been restored as a museum. Hueston Woods State Park with Acton Lake is 4 mi (6 km) north. Inc. village, 1830. Pop. (1960) 7,828; (1980) 17,655.
39°30′ N, 84°44′ W

Oxford, earls of, an English title held (1142–1703) by the de Vere family. The statesman Robert Harley (died 1724) and his descendants were earls of Oxford and Mortimer (1711–1853); and H.H. Asquith, prime minister (1908–16), and his descendants held the title of earl of Oxford and Asquith from 1925. Notable Vere earls include the 9th, Robert (died 1392), a supporter of Richard II; the 13th, John (died 1513), who fought for the Lancastrians in the Wars of the Roses; and the 17th, Edward (died 1604), a lyric poet and dramatist regarded by some as the author of Shakespeare's works.

Oxford, Robert Harley, 1st earl of (b. Dec. 5, 1661, London—d. May 21, 1724, London), statesman who headed the Tory ministry from 1710 to 1714. Coming from a Presbyterian family, he was first elected to Parliament in 1688. Within several years he became, with Paul Foley, leader of a coalition of Whigs and moderate Tories opposed to the government of King William III. Harley was speaker of the house from 1701 to 1705 and secretary of state from 1704 to 1708. During this period Harley, along with John Churchill, 1st duke of Marlborough, and Lord Treasurer Sidney Godolphin, dominated the government of Queen Anne (ruled 1702–14) and directed the war against the French (War of the Spanish Succession, 1701–14).

1st Earl of Oxford, detail of an oil painting by Sir Godfrey Kneller, 1714; in the National Portrait Gallery, London

By courtesy of the National Portrait Gallery, London

Although Harley became the Queen's favourite, his anti-Whig attitudes brought him into conflict with his two colleagues, who in February 1708 forced him to resign. He then allied with the Tories, while the Whigs occupied all major government offices. In 1710 public dissatisfaction with the Whig-directed war enabled Anne to dismiss Godolphin and install Harley as chancellor of the exchequer at the head of a Tory ministry. Created earl of Oxford and lord high treasurer in 1711, Harley was the most powerful man in England, but he had a dangerous rival in Secretary of State Henry St. John, 1st Viscount Bolingbroke. Oxford's major accomplishments during his ministry were the formation of the South Sea Company (1711) and the conclusion of a favourable peace at Utrecht. Nevertheless, Bolingbroke triumphed in the struggle for power, and the Queen dismissed Oxford from office on July 27, 1714, five days before her death. Upon the accession of the anti-Tory monarch George I, elector of Hanover, Oxford was imprisoned until acquitted of charges of treason in July 1717. His life is recounted in O.B. Miller's *Robert Harley, Earl of Oxford* (1925).

·Bolingbroke's cooperation and opposition **2**:1204g
·career under Anne and George I **3**:249g
·Defoe's service as intelligence agent **5**:551h
·Marlborough's political alliance **11**:516b
·Swift's Tory allegiance **17**:858a
·Walpole's Tory opposition **19**:534d

Oxford, Robert de Vere, 9th earl of (b. 1362—d. 1392, Louvain, in present-day Belgium), favourite of King Richard II of England (ruled 1377–99) during that ruler's minority. He led the group of courtiers who unsuccessfully supported Richard's efforts in 1385–87 to wrest control of the government from powerful nobles. Through his mother a descendant of King Henry III (ruled 1216–72), de Vere succeeded to his father's earldom in 1371. After the accession of his close friend Richard II, Oxford, who was already great chamberlain by hereditary right, became a privy councillor and Knight of the Garter. He was made marquess of Dublin—the first Englishman to be granted the title marquess—in 1385 and duke of Ireland in 1386.

Oxford's elevation caused much resentment among the King's ambitious enemies, such as his uncle Thomas of Woodstock, duke of Gloucester. Oxford further enraged Gloucester by divorcing the duke's niece in 1387. Further, Oxford and his Royalist Party acquired a reputation for frivolity and incompetence. On Nov. 17, 1387, Gloucester demanded the arrest of Oxford and other leading Royalists. Oxford organized an army in northwest England, but his force was routed by Gloucester at Radcot Bridge, Oxfordshire, on December 20. He escaped in disguise to the Netherlands and died in exile. As a result of Oxford's defeat, Richard was forced to submit to the merciless Parliament of 1388 and to the five lords appellant who controlled the realm until 1389, when the King asserted his authority by proclaiming his minority at an end.

Oxford, John de Vere, 13th earl of (b. Sept. 8, 1442—d. March 10, 1513), English soldier and royal official, a Lancastrian leader in the Wars of the Roses, helped to restore the deposed King Henry VI (1470) and later (1485) to secure the English throne for the last surviving male claimant from the house of Lancaster, Henry Tudor, earl of Richmond, afterward King Henry VII.

He was the second son of John de Vere, 12th earl, who, with his eldest son, Aubrey, was executed (February 1462) under the Yorkist king Edward IV. Several years later, the younger John de Vere fled to France with the "kingmaker," Richard Neville, earl of Warwick. Returning with Warwick in a successful attempt to restore Henry VI (September–October 1470), he was made constable of England, supplanting John Tiptoft, earl of Worcester, who had put de Vere's father and brother to death and was in turn executed by de Vere. After leading the Lancastrian vanguard in the Battle of Barnet, Hertfordshire (April 14, 1471), in which Warwick was killed and the Yorkists were victorious, de Vere was again exiled to France. Once more returning to Britain, he captured the island of St. Michael's Mount, Cornwall (1473), but surrendered after a siege and was imprisoned. On escaping (August 1484), he joined Henry Tudor, who was preparing to invade Wales and then England from France. For his service as commander of the right wing in Henry's victory at Bosworth Field, Leicestershire (Aug. 22, 1485), de Vere was again restored to his title and estates and was made chamberlain and admiral of England. Subsequently, he fought in the victory of Henry VII's army at Stoke, Nottinghamshire (June 16, 1487), the last battle of the Wars of the Roses, and crushed the 7th Baron Audley's Cornish rebels at Blackheath, south of London (1497).

Oxford, Edward de Vere, 17th earl of (b. April 12, 1550, Castle Hedingham, Essex—d. June 24, 1604, Newington, Middlesex), lyric poet and dramatist, patron of the acting company Oxford's Men, who became, in the 20th century, the strongest candidate proposed (next to Shakespeare himself) for the authorship of Shakespeare's plays. He studied at Cambridge and succeeded to the earldom in 1562. He was the ward of Queen Elizabeth's principal minister, William Cecil (later Lord Burghley), whose daughter, Ann Cecil, he married in 1571. He travelled on the Continent (1574–76) and became for awhile estranged from his wife and Lord Burghley. Because of his extravagance he fell into disgrace at court but was restored to favour in 1583. In 1586 he was granted an annuity by the Queen, perhaps for his services in maintaining the company of actors he had taken over from the Earl of Warwick in 1580.

17th Earl of Oxford, detail of an oil painting after a portrait by an unknown artist, 1575; on loan to the National Portrait Gallery, London

By courtesy of the Duke of Portland, K.G.; photograph, National Portrait Gallery, London

In his youth he had written some plays, none of which is extant. He was a notable patron of writers and employed John Lyly, the author of the novel *Euphues*, as his secretary for many years. The obscurity of Oxford's later life may be explained by his immersion in literary activities.

The Oxfordian theory of Shakespearean authorship, first advanced in 1920 in *"Shakespeare" Identified in Edward de Vere, the Seventeenth Earl of Oxford*, a study by J. Thomas Looney, rapidly gained adherents. It was strengthened in 1928 by Bernard Mordaunt Ward's biography *The Seventeenth Earl of Oxford, 1550–1604*. In 1947 Percy Allen published *Talks with Elizabethans Revealing the Mystery of "William Shakespeare,"* in which he describes contacts made through a spiritualist medium with Shakespeare, Francis Bacon, and Oxford, who informed him of their collaboration in the plays in which Oxford had the chief hand.

Oxford's death date (1604) has proved a major embarrassment to the advancement of the Oxfordian theory, because according to standard chronology, 14 of Shakespeare's plays, including many of the most important ones, were staged after that time.

Oxford, Provisions of, a plan of reform accepted, in return for the promise by his barons of financial aid, by the English king Henry III in 1258. It can be regarded as England's first written constitution.

Henry, bankrupted by a foolish venture in Sicily, summoned Parliament in the spring of 1258 (the Easter Parliament, or the so-called Mad Parliament). In return for a badly needed grant of revenue, Henry grudgingly agreed to abide by a program of reform to be formulated by a 24-man royal commission, half of whom were to be chosen by the king, half by the baronial party. The report of the commission (issued *c.* June 10) is known as the Provisions of Oxford.

The Provisions, confirmed by an oath of "community" of the magnates, were to remain in effect for 12 years and provide the machinery through which the necessary reforms could be accomplished. The government was placed under the joint direction of the king and a 15-member baronial council that was to advise the king on all important matters. All high officers of the realm were to swear allegiance to the king and the council. Parliament was to meet three times a year to consult on further reforms. A justiciar was appointed (for the first time since 1234) to oversee local administration, and the majority of sheriffs were replaced by knights holding land in the shires that they administered.

Annulled by papal bulls in 1261 and 1262 and by Louis IX of France in the Mise of Amiens (January 1264), the Provisions were restored by baronial action in 1263 and, in modified form, in 1264 but finally annulled by the Dictum of Kenilworth (October 1266).

·Louis IX's judgment of validity **7**:619b
·Montfort role in coercion of Henry III **12**:409d
·terms and repercussions **3**:210f

Oxford, University of, coeducational, privately controlled institution of higher learning, one of the archetypal Western universities, dating from the mid-12th century. It was modelled on the University of Paris (*See* Paris I à XIII, Universités de) and developed somewhat along the same lines: the university was divided into faculties of theology, law, medicine, and the arts. For a time during the Middle Ages the masters of arts were divided into nations (*see* university), but, unlike the continental universities, Oxford came to consist of only two nations—North (Scottish scholars) and South (Welsh, Irish, English, and Continentals). After a faction fight in 1274 it was decided that there should be only one nation at Oxford.

In the early years of the university, disputes between the students and the townspeople were frequent. The most renowned "town-and-gown" riot occurred in 1354, when a fierce battle fought with bows and arrows lasted two days. The university faction was defeated, and a number of students were killed. The result was that mayors, bailiffs, and 60 burghers of Oxford were required annually to make a religious observation and pay reparations to the university, a tradition that lasted until 1825. In addition, the jurisdiction of the university's chancellor was extended to cover both civil and criminal cases involving a scholar. For a long period also the university retained a share in the general government of the town of Oxford. Until 1868 the university controlled the night police—representing the ancient "watch"—and they still send representatives to the Oxford city council.

The various colleges of Oxford were originally merely endowed boardinghouses for impoverished scholars. They were intended primarily for masters or bachelors of arts who needed financial assistance to enable them to continue study for a higher degree. The earliest of these, University College, was endowed for the support of two masters of arts studying theology. By 1280 University College was supporting four masters, and John de Balliol had endowed a small foundation for "artists," Balliol College, and Walter de Merton had founded the much more elaborate Merton College.

During its early history Oxford's reputation was based on theology and the arts. But it also gave more serious treatment to the physical sciences than the University of Paris; Roger Bacon (*c.* 1214–94), after leaving Paris, conducted his scientific experiments and lectured at Oxford.

During the 13th and 14th centuries influential Franciscans of Oxford, in addition to Bacon, included such men as John Duns Scotus and William of Ockham. John Wycliffe (*c.* 1330–84) spent most of his life as a resident Oxford doctor. Although a smaller university with fewer foreign students, Oxford during the 14th century was the seat of far more rigorous and original scholarship than the continental universities.

During the Renaissance Desiderius Erasmus carried the new learning to Oxford through his lectures there. Toward the close of the 18th century, written examinations gradually supplemented the old oral examinations, and thereafter the range of studies themselves extended. Toward the end of the 19th century the direction of a proportion of college revenues to the use of the university led to the growth of a regular resident body of professors. Among its faculties are humanities, law, physical and biological sciences, mathematics, social studies, theology, and medicine. In the early 1970s enrollment was about 11,000.

·Bodleian library history and function **10**:861f
·competitive rowing introduction **2**:1158c
·cricket competition significance **5**:261g
·curriculum and Puritan changes **11**:12f
·football playing regulation **2**:275e
·higher education's autonomy in England **8**:859e
·liberal movement in 17th century **19**:1021a
·Matthew Arnold's symbol of culture **2**:36g
·medieval origin and colleges **6**:338a
·Penn's religious reaction and consequence **14**:24c
·philosophy after World War II **1**:806d
·Scholasticism as philosophical movement **14**:258h

Oxford Clay Formation, division of Jurassic rocks in Great Britain. (The Jurassic Period began about 190,000,000 years ago and lasted about 54,000,000 years.) The formation is found elsewhere in Europe and is known by regional names. The Oxford Clay is about 180 metres (600 feet) thick in southern England and consists of fossiliferous clay deposits with inclusion of sandy material. It overlies beds of the Kellaways Clays, underlies the Corallian Beds, and is placed in the lower part of the Oxfordian Stage and the upper part of the underlying Callovian Stage—a stage representing a smaller division of rocks and time than a geologic period. Marine fossils are well preserved in the Oxford Clay and include both invertebrate and vertebrate remains. Ammonoid cephalopods (fossil mollusks), such as the genera *Kosmoceras* and *Cardioceras*, are common in the deposits and are useful for stratigraphic correlation. Fossil marine reptiles are also well preserved: *Ichthyosaurus*, an extinct porpoise-like animal; *Plesiosaurus*, which often attained great size; and *Pliosaurus*. In many regions of its exposure, the Oxford Clay is employed in brick manufacture and is economically important.

Oxford English Dictionary, The (OED), definitive historical dictionary of the English language, consisting of 12 volumes plus a one-volume supplement. Published in 1933, the dictionary is a corrected and updated revision of *A New English Dictionary on Historical Principles*, which was published in 10 volumes from Feb. 1, 1884, to April 19, 1928, and which was designed to provide an inventory of words in use in English since the middle of the 12th century (and in some cases even earlier). Arranged in order of historical occurrence, the definitions in the OED are illustrated with about 5,000,000 dated quotations from English literature and records. The aim of the dictionary (as stated in the 1933 edition) is "to present in alphabetical series the words that have formed the English vocabulary from the time of the earliest records down to the present day, with all the relevant facts concerning their form, sense-history, and etymology."

The publication of the dictionary was first suggested to the Philological Society (London) in 1857 and the collection of materials began soon thereafter. In 1878, contact was made with Clarendon Press of Oxford concerning a printing agreement, which was concluded in March of 1879. Editorial work also began in 1879, with the appointment of James Murray, who was at that time president of the Philological Society, as editor in chief; Murray, during his term as editor, was responsible for approximately one-half of the dictionary, including the letters *a* through *d*, *h* through *k*, *o*, *p*, and *t*. Succeeding editors include Henry Bradley, William Alexander Craigie, and C.T. Onions.

A micrographically reproduced two-volume edition of the original 12-volume OED and 1933 supplement appeared in 1971, entitled *The Compact Edition of the Oxford English Dictionary*.

A Supplement to the Oxford English Dictionary, a work treating those words that came into use in the English-speaking world after the preparation of the OED), began to be compiled in 1955 under the editorial direction of R.W. Burchfield. Volume 1 (*A–G*) was published by the Clarendon Press in 1972; Volume 2 (*H–P*) was scheduled for publication in 1975, and Volume 3 (*Q–Z*) in the late 1970s.

·compilation and revisions **5**:717c *passim* to 719g
·English dictionary development **6**:883d

Oxford Group (revivalistic movement): *see* Moral Re-armament.

Oxfordian Stage, worldwide, standard division of Jurassic rocks and time. (The Jurassic Period began about 190,000,000 years ago and lasted approximately 54,000,000 years.) The stage was named for exposures in the region of Oxford. It is the lowest stage of the Upper Jurassic; rocks of the Oxfordian overlie those of the Callovian Stage and underlie rocks of the Kimmeridgian Stage. The Oxfordian has been further divided into zones (shorter spans of time), characterized by the presence of distinct fossil ammonites, mollusks related to the modern pearly nautilus.

·rock sequence table **10**:355

Oxford Movement, 19th-century movement centred at Oxford University that sought a renewal of Catholic thought and practice within the Church of England in opposition to the Protestant tendencies of the church. An immediate cause of the movement was the change that took place in the relationship between the state and the established Church of England from 1828 to 1832. Laws that required members of municipal corporations and government-office holders to receive the Eucharist in the Church of England were repealed, and a law was passed that removed most of the restrictions formerly imposed on Roman Catholics. For a short time it seemed possible that the Church of England might be disestablished and that it might lose its endowments. Consequently, many loyal Anglicans wished to assert that the Church of England was not dependent on the state and that it gained its authority from the fact that it taught Christian truth and its bishops were in the apostolic succession (the doctrine that bishops can trace their authority and office back in an unbroken line to the Apostles). The movement rapidly became involved in theological, pastoral, and devotional problems.

Leaders of the movement were John Henry Newman (1801–90), clergyman, and subsequently a convert to Roman Catholicism and a cardinal; Richard Hurrell Froude (1803–36), clergyman; John Keble (1792–1866), clergyman and poet; and Edward Pusey (1800–82), clergyman and professor of Hebrew at Oxford.

The ideas of the movement were published in 90 *Tracts for the Times* (1833–41), 24 of which were written by Newman, who edited the entire series. The Tractarians asserted the doctrinal authority of the catholic church to be absolute, and by "catholic" they understood that which was faithful to the teaching of the early and undivided church. They believed the Church of England to be such a catholic church.

Some of the movement's followers gradually moved closer to the beliefs of the Roman Catholic Church, and controversies over the Tractarians' ideas developed. In 1845 Newman joined the Roman Catholic Church, and, subsequently, several others also joined.

Keble and Pusey remained active leaders of the movement, which gradually spread its influence throughout the Church of England. Some of the results were increased use of ceremony and ritual in church worship, the establishment of Anglican monastic communities for men and for women, and better educated clergy who were more concerned with pastoral care of their church members.

Oxford Propositions, proposals of Parliament for peace negotiations with King Charles I. The propositions, made early in the English Civil War, were rejected by the King.

Oxfordshire, also known by its abbreviation OXON, English county bounded north by Warwickshire and Northamptonshire, west by Gloucestershire and Wiltshire, south by Berkshire, and east by Buckinghamshire. In the local government reorganization of 1974 Oxfordshire's boundaries were extended to include a large area previously in Berkshire.

The county consists of two upland areas divided by a broad vale, about 10 mi (16 km) wide. The North Oxfordshire Heights, rising to 700 ft (210 m) at Edgehill in the northeast of the county, are developed on oolitic limestone and related strata of the Jurassic period (150,000,000 years old). The Berkshire Downs and White Horse Hill are developed on Cretaceous (100,000,000-year-old) chalk. The intervening clay vale stretches from northeast to southwest. It is divided into the Oxford Clay Vale and the White Horse Vale by an outcrop of Corallian limestone, giving rise to the Oxford Heights.

Oxfordshire lies almost entirely within the Thames Basin. The river flows northeastward along the Oxford Clay Vale, receiving the Rivers Windrush, Evenlode, and Cherwell from the north and the Ock and its tributaries from the south. There is an elbow of capture (*i.e.*, where the drainage system has become connected to a former portion of a neighbouring system) to the east of Oxford, and the river then flows south through the Goring Gap. There is little glacial drift (material deposited by former glaciers) except in the northeast corner of the county. Gravel deposits, both plateau (North Leigh, Combe, Tiddington) and flood plain (Bampton, Oxford, Dorchester) are important economically.

Numerous Paleolithic and Mesolithic artifacts have been recovered from the floodplain gravels that border the Thames. Neolithic tools and pottery have similarly been located at many points in the county. A number of long barrows and the Rollright Stones on the Oxfordshire–Warwickshire border also date from this period. The major archaeological monument in the county, dating from the ensuing Iron Age, is the Uffington White Horse, carved into the chalk of the White Horse Hill. It is 360 ft long with a maximum height of 130 ft. Dorchester and Alchester, situated on the Roman road from Silchester to Watling Street and Towcester, were the most important sites in Roman Oxfordshire. Subsequent Saxon settlement in the county was concentrated at valley sites along the line of the Thames and its major tributaries, and Oxfordshire was successively part of the Anglo-Saxon kingdoms Wessex and Mercia. During the 10th and 11th centuries the area was overrun by the Danes. At the time of Domesday Book (1086), the record of William I the Conqueror's land survey of England, the county was fairly well populated, the major centres being Oxford itself, Wallingford, Abingdon, and Bampton. All were incipient towns with regular markets. The medieval period is commemorated by numerous ecclesiastical and domestic buildings. Iffley church, just south of Oxford, is one of the best examples of pure Romanesque style in England; Adderbury, south of Banbury, has a cruciform Decorated style church, and that at Minster Lovell is pure Perpendicular style. Secular buildings include Broughton Castle (14th century), Stonor Park, Stanton Harcourt (1450), Chastleton, and Blenheim Palace (early 18th century), built near Woodstock for the Duke of Marlborough, a member of one of the great political dynasties of England. The county saw action during the English Civil War (1642–51). The towns of Oxford, Banbury, and Wallingford were all besieged by Parliamentary forces at some time, and Oxford was the Royalist headquarters.

The economy of modern Oxfordshire is basically agricultural. The North Oxfordshire Heights are important for sheep and arable farming, mostly on large farms. From medieval times until quite recently wool was a mainstay of the economy. The clay vale is mainly sown to grass, milk and beef being produced. The White Horse Vale and the northern slope of the Downs are noted for fruit production.

Ironstone is mined near Banbury, and clay, sand, and gravel are also worked in various parts of the county. Cowley, a suburb of Oxford, is the major industrial centre, producing motor vehicles and pressed steel. Banbury, with light engineering, and Witney, with blanket manufacture, are also important centres. Paper mills are located at Wolvercote, Shiplake, Sandford, and Eynsham, using pure stream water. Pop. (1971 est. census adjusted for 1974 area) 504,000.
51°50′ N, 1°15′ W

oxidase, enzyme that catalyzes oxidation. *See also* oxidoreductase.

oxidation, any of a class of chemical reactions in which the number of electrons associated with an atom or a group of atoms is decreased. The electrons lost by the substance oxidized are taken up by some other substance, which thereby is said to be reduced (*i.e.*, brought to a lower oxidation state).

The term oxidation originally denoted chemical combination of a substance with oxygen, usually with the formation of an oxide of that substance or of one or more of its constituent elements. Examples include the reaction of oxygen with iron to form iron oxide or with methane, a compound of carbon and hydrogen, to form carbon dioxide and water (hydrogen oxide). Exactly analogous reactions occur if, instead of oxygen, sulfur or many other elements are used; and the concept of oxidation has been broadened to include the entire class of reactions.

oxidation number, also called OXIDATION STATE, in chemistry, a value assigned to an element that represents the relative electrical charge on the atoms of that element in a chemical compound. The number is equal to the excess or deficiency of electrons associated with the atoms of the element in the compound as compared to those associated with the atoms in uncombined form. The sign of the number is either plus or minus, corresponding respectively to a deficiency or an excess of electrons.

The oxidation number is equivalent numerically to the valence, or combining capacity of the element, although the valence is usually not associated with a plus or minus sign. In monatomic ions, the oxidation number of the element is equal to the electrical charge of the ion. In covalent compounds, the shared electron pair forming the chemical bond usually is assigned to the more electronegative of the two atoms. The sum of the oxidation numbers of the atoms of a neutral molecule is equal to zero, and that for a polyatomic ion is equal to its electric charge.

Certain elements assume the same oxidation number in different compounds, whereas others, notably the nonmetals and the transition elements, are able to assume a variety of oxidation numbers. In the nomenclature of inorganic compounds, it is accepted practice to indicate the oxidation number of an element (particularly those with several oxidation numbers) as a roman numeral in parenthesis immediately after the element name. *Major ref.* 13:803h

oxidation potential (chemistry): *see* oxidation number.

oxidation–reduction reactions 13:803, a large and diverse class of chemical processes mostly involving the transfer of oxygen atoms, hydrogen atoms, or electrons from one substance to another. Many of these reactions are familiar: fire, the corrosion and dissolution of metals, the browning of fruit, respiration, and photosynthesis.

The text article treats general aspects of oxidation–reduction (redox) reactions, including their major classifications and theoretical interpretation, the historical origins of the concept of such processes, and examples of them, and covers particulars of the theory of redox reactions, including oxidation states, half reactions, redox potentials, oxidation–reduction equilibria, and the rates and mechanisms of reactions belonging to this class.

REFERENCES in other text articles:
·aging influences in cells **1**:304f
·aldehyde and ketone behaviour **1**:460b
·alkaloid structure determination **1**:599b
·atmospheric oxidation reactions **2**:309b
·catabolic pathways and processes **11**:1026e
·chemical reaction type classification **4**:145c
·chemiluminescent reaction of luminol **11**:179g
·combustion reaction mechanism **4**:954e
·coordination compound bonding **5**:141h
·corrosion chemical processes **11**:1076e
·cotton bleaching process control **7**:276b
·dye manufacturing processes for intermediates **5**:1100f
·electrochemical processes and products **6**:640b
·free radical reaction mechanism **15**:423c
·fuel cell designs and reactions **2**:768h
·glass decolorizing process **8**:209h
·gun propellant composition **2**:656a
·halogen oxidizing properties **8**:561c
·metabolic cycle chemistry **10**:896c
·Nernst equation and phase diagram use **7**:1030d; illus. 1031
·noble gas oxidation by fluorine **13**:141b
·oxidizing and reducing agent classification **4**:96e
·photosynthetic electron flow **14**:368f; illus. 370
·potassium chloride electron transfer **13**:811f
·seawater biochemical cycles **9**:124h
·water and the electromotive series **19**:636h
·weathering processes **19**:704g

oxidation state: *see* oxidation number.

oxide, any of a large and important class of inorganic compounds in which oxygen is combined with another element. Nearly all the elements form oxides, which vary in properties from those of typical metal oxides—crystalline solids containing the oxide ion, O^{2-}, that react with water to form alkalies or with acids to form salts—to those of typical nonmetal oxides—volatile compounds in which the oxygen atoms are covalently linked to the nonmetal atom and that react with water to form acids or with alkalies to form salts. Thus, calcium, a metal, forms calcium oxide (CaO), which reacts with water to form calcium hydroxide, a strong alkali, and with hydrochloric acid to form calcium chloride, a salt; sulfur, a nonmetal, forms sulfur trioxide (SO_3), which reacts with water to form sulfuric acid, a strong acid, and with sodium hydroxide to form sodium sulfate, a salt. Oxides, such as those of aluminum, zinc, or tin, that form salts by reacting with either acids or alkalies, are called amphoteric; for example, aluminum oxide (Al_2O_3) reacts with hydrochloric acid to form aluminum chloride and with sodium hydroxide to form sodium aluminate.

Certain organic compounds react with oxygen or other oxidizing agents to produce substances called oxides. Thus, amines, phosphines, and sulfides form amine oxides, phosphine oxides, and sulfoxides, respectively, in which the oxygen atom is covalently bonded to the nitrogen, phosphorus, or sulfur atom. The so-called olefin oxides are cyclic ethers.
·alkali metal chemistry **1**:582a *passim* to 587e
·alkaline earth basicity trend **1**:589d
·aluminum oxide film protection **1**:644b
·carbon group element compounds **3**:844f
·crustal and upper mantle abundances, tables 1 and 2 **5**:120
·element classification based on reaction **4**:117a
·ferromagnetism and electron interaction **7**:254c
·glass composition and properties **8**:208b; table
·glass properties and manufacture **8**:196f
·halogen group compounds **8**:565h; table 569
·igneous rock composition, illus. 1 **9**:202
·inorganic compound classification **4**:100h
·Lewis acid–base reactions **1**:48g
·luminescence reactions **11**:180h
·nitrogen group compounds **13**:127d
·phosphorus–oxygen pi bonds **13**:701h
·phosphoryl compound preparation **13**:705b
·photoemission and metallic oxides **14**:298e
·rare-earth chemical properties **15**:519a
·transition element chemistry **18**:611g
·uranium compound production **18**:1036b
·xenon compound chemical properties **13**:142d

oxide facies: *see* geochemical facies.

oxide minerals, naturally occurring inorganic compounds that have structure based on an oxygen-atom framework, often dense packed, in which smaller positively charged metal atoms (cations) occur in the interstices. The oxides are distinguished from such oxygen salts as sulfates, arsenates, borates, phosphates, silicates, etc., all of which possess some readily definable negative complex or group containing oxygen and a metal ion. Some taxonomic mineralogists include the hydroxides with the oxides, but their structures are more reminiscent of the halides and oxyhalides.

Oxide minerals can be broken into two categories: simple oxides and complex oxides. The simple oxides are binary compounds of metal cations (*M*) and negatively charged oxide ion (O^{2-}); for the general composition M_rO_s, the *r* metal cations have a total positive charge that exactly balance the total negative charge of the *s* oxide anions ($s \times -2$). Complex oxides involve several cations, often of mixed charge. Some of these compounds are very complex and their distinction from oxygen salts is often arbitrary; thus, the heteropolyvanadates, heteropolytungstates, and heteropolymolybdates may be classed either as complex oxides or as oxygen salts. Even the distinction between simple and complex oxides is not clear, because a simple oxide often may be the basis for a more complicated structure involving more than one kind of cation in an ordered array; for example, ilmenite, $Fe^{2+}Ti^{4+}O_3$, is structurally derived from hematite, $Fe^{3+}Fe^{3+}O_3$, and for obvious similarity is classed with the latter compound.

The simple oxides that occur naturally are relatively inert; highly reactive oxides are not observed because they would have long reacted in mineralogical systems to form complex oxygen salts. Simple oxides can crystallize over a range of conditions, but many have formed as high-temperature dissociation products, *e.g.* periclase, manganosite, and wüstite, which derive from the thermal decomposition of carbonates. Noteworthy simple oxides include ice; cuprite, occasionally an ore of copper; and the oxides of trivalent metals such as hematite and corundum. Hematite crystallizes over a wide range of conditions and is the most important ore of iron; it constitutes the red colouring matter in sedimentary rocks. Corundum, a very hard substance with a dense-packed oxygen structure like hematite, is found in high-grade thermally metamorphosed assemblages. Quadrivalent oxides (those in which the cation has a charge of +4) are of considerable importance. Silica minerals (low quartz, high quartz, cristobalite, tridymite, melanophlogite, coesite, opal) are usually included with the silicate framework structures, but the high-pressure, octahedrally coordinated form stishovite has the same atomic structure as the oxide minerals rutile, pyrolusite, and cassiterite; pyrolusite and cassiterite constitute valuable ores of manganese and tin respectively.

A mineral group transitional between the simple and complex oxides is the spinel group; some 150 natural and synthetic compounds have structures like the dense-packed oxygen framework of spinel. Most spinels have formed at high temperature, high pressure, or both. Important compounds include magnetite, a valuable ore of iron; and ringwoodite, which has been inferred to make up a considerable portion of the upper mantle of the Earth.

The complex oxides include a large number of compounds, but only a few are fairly common, and many still require further study. Noteworthy are the niobates and tantalates, such as niobite–tantalite, which occurs in some pegmatites and which is a niobium and tantalum ore. Also included are many compounds based on the niobite structure, as polycrase, one of several ores marketed for the rare-earth series of elements.

Finally, there are the tungsten bronzes, heteropolyvanadates, and similar very complex oxides. These compounds involve a densely clustered arrangement of fragments of simpler oxides immersed in a matrix of larger and more loosely held cations and water molecules. Inclusion in the oxide group is somewhat arbitrary, but they show many properties in common and their chemistry is better understood through knowledge of simpler oxide structures.
·intrusive igneous rock minerals **9**:220g
·mineralogy, chemistry, and occurrence **12**:237a

oxidized ore zone (geology): *see* supergene sulfide enrichment.

oxidizing agent (chemistry): *see* oxidation.

oxidoreductase, one of the classes of enzymes (biological catalysts) recognized by the International Union of Biochemistry (IUB) in 1964. The overall reaction catalyzed by this large group of more than 200 enzymes, commonly known as dehydrogenases, or oxidases, is the transfer of hydrogen. Many oxidoreductases catalyze the removal of hydrogen atoms and electrons (negatively charged particles) from the compounds on which they act. Substances called coenzymes, associated with the enzymes and necessary for their activity, accept the hydrogen and electrons, which eventually are transferred to oxygen. Others of this group catalyze such reactions as the oxidation of aldehydes and ketones to carboxylic acids and the dehydrogenation of amino acids.
·catalytic action properties **15**:95f
·classification and reactions **6**:897f; table 898

oxime, any of a class of nitrogen-containing organic compounds usually prepared from hydroxylamine and an aldehyde, a ketone, or a quinone. Oximes have the structure

$$\begin{matrix} X \\ & \!\!>\!C=N-OH, \\ Y \end{matrix}$$

in which X and Y are hydrogen atoms or organic groups derived by removal of a hydrogen atom from an organic compound. Because most oximes are readily obtainable solids having easily determined melting points, they are useful in identifying liquid aldehydes and ketones.

Oximes can also be made by the action of hydrogen-donating reagents upon certain nitro compounds or by the isomerization of nitroso compounds. The oximes obtained from aldehydes (aldoximes) can be dehydrated to form nitriles. Other useful chemical reactions of oximes include conversion to amines (by treatment with hydrogen or other reducing substances) and to amides (by the action of strong acids or of phosphorus pentachloride). The latter conversion is called the Beckmann rearrangement, after Ernst Otto Beckmann, the German chemist who discovered it in 1886. A large-scale application of this rearrangement is the transformation of cyclohexanone oxime to caprolactam, the starting material for nylon 6.
·properties and reactions **13**:699h

oxirane (chemistry): *see* ethylene.

Oxit, trade name of a magnetic alloy.
·magnetic properties, table 1 **11**:335

Oxlahuntiku, in Mayan religion, thirteen gods who preside over the heavens.
·Mayan deities and cosmology **11**:720g

Oxide minerals

name formula	colour	lustre	Mohs hardness	specific gravity	habit	fracture or cleavage	refractive indices or polished section data	crystal system space group	remarks
anatase TiO_2	brown to indigo blue and black; also variable	adamantine to metallic adamantine	5½–6	3.8–4.0	pyramidal or tabular crystals	two perfect cleavages	$\omega = 2.561$ $\epsilon = 2.488$ extremely variable	tetragonal $I\frac{4}{a}md$	strong dispersion; has the same chemical composition as but different symmetry than rutile and brookite
boehmite $AlO(OH)$	white, when pure		3½–4	3.0–3.1	disseminated or in pisolitic aggregates	one very good cleavage	$\alpha = 1.64–1.65$ $\beta = 1.65–1.66$ $\gamma = 1.65–1.67$	orthorhombic Amam	has the same chemical composition as but different symmetry than diaspore
brookite TiO_2	various browns	metallic adamantine to submetallic	5½–6	4.1–4.2	only as crystals, usually tabular	subconchoidal to uneven fracture	$\alpha = 2.583$ $\beta = 2.585$ $\gamma = 2.700–2.741$	orthorhombic Pcab	has the same chemical composition as but different symmetry than anatase and rutile
brucite $Mg(OH)_2$	white to pale green, gray, or blue	waxy to vitreous	2½	2.4	tabular crystals; platy aggregates; fibrous or foliated massive	one perfect cleavage	$\omega = 1.56–1.59$ $\epsilon = 1.58–1.60$	hexagonal $C\bar{3}m$	pyroelectric
cassiterite SnO_2	reddish or yellowish brown to brownish black	adamantine to metallic adamantine, usually splendent	6–7	7.0	repeatedly twinned crystals; crusts and concretions	one imperfect cleavage	$\omega = 1.984–2.048$ $\epsilon = 2.082–2.140$ light gray; strongly anisotropic	tetragonal $P\frac{4}{m}nm$	
chromite $FeCr_2O_4$	black	metallic	5½	4.5–4.8	granular to compact massive	no cleavage; uneven fracture	$n = 2.08–2.16$ brownish gray-white; isotropic	isometric Fd3m	sometimes feebly magnetic; forms solid solution series with magnesiochromite in which magnesium replaces iron in the molecular structure
chrysoberyl $BeAl_2O_4$	variable	vitreous	8½	3.6–3.8	tabular or prismatic, commonly twinned, crystals	one distinct cleavage	$\alpha = 1.746$ $\beta = 1.748$ $\gamma = 1.756$	orthorhombic Pmnb	
columbite $(Fe,Mn)Cb_2O_6$	iron black to brownish black; often with iridescent tarnish		6–6½	5.2 (columbite) to 8.0 (tantalite)	prismatic crystals, often in large groups; massive	one distinct cleavage	brownish gray-white; weakly anisotropic	orthorhombic Pbcn	forms a solid solution series with tantalite in which tantalum replaces niobium in the magnetic structure; paramagnetic
corundum Al_2O_3	red (ruby); blue (sapphire); also variable	adamantine to vitreous	9 (a hardness standard)	4.0–4.1	pyramidal or barrel-shaped crystals; large blocks; rounded grains	no cleavage; uneven to conchoidal fracture	$\omega = 1.767–1.772$ $\epsilon = 1.759–1.763$	hexagonal $R\bar{3}c$	asterism frequently noted; fluorescent or phosphorescent; the only natural form of alumina
cuprite Cu_2O	various shades of red	adamantine to earthy	3½–4	6.1	octahedral, cubic, or capillary crystals; granular or earthy massive	conchoidal to uneven fracture	$n = 2.849$ bluish white; anomalously anisotropic and pleochroic	isometric Pn3m	
delafossite $CuFeO_2$	black	metallic	5½	5.4–5.5	tabular crystals; botryoidal crusts	one imperfect cleavage	rosy brown-white; strongly anisotropic; distinctly pleochroic	hexagonal $R\bar{3}m$	
diaspore $HAlO_2$	white, grayish white, colourless; variable	brilliant vitreous	6½–7	3.2–3.5	thin, platy crystals; scaly massive; disseminated	one perfect cleavage, one less so	$\alpha = 1.682–1.706$ $\beta = 1.705–1.725$ $\gamma = 1.730–1.752$	orthorhombic Pbnm	dimorphous with boehmite
euxenite $(Y,Ca,Ce,U,Th)(Cb,Ta,Ti)_2O_6$	black	brilliant submetallic to greasy or vitreous	5½–6½	5.3–5.9	prismatic crystals; massive	conchoidal to subconchoidal fracture	$n = 2.06–2.25$	orthorhombic	forms a solid solution series with polycrase in which titanium replaces niobium and tantalum in the molecular structure; radioactive; metamict
franklinite $ZnFe_2O_4$	brownish black to black	metallic to semimetallic	5½–6½	5.1–5.2	octahedral crystals; granular massive		$n \sim 2.36$ white; isotropic	isometric Fd3m	weakly magnetic; forms solid solution series with

Oxide minerals (continued)

name formula	colour	lustre	Mohs hardness	specific gravity	habit	fracture or cleavage	refractive indices or polished section data	crystal system space group	remarks
franklinite (continued)									magnesioferrite, magnetite, jacobsite, and trevorite in which magnesium, iron, manganese, and nickel respectively replace zinc in the molecular structure
gibbsite $Al(OH)_2$	white; grayish, greenish, reddish white	vitreous	2½–3½	2.3–2.4	tabular crystals; crusts and coatings; compact earthy	one perfect cleavage	$\alpha = 1.56–1.58$ $\beta = 1.56–1.58$ $\gamma = 1.58–1.60$	monoclinic $P\frac{2_1}{n}$	
goethite $HFeO_2$	blackish brown (crystals); yellowish or reddish brown	adamantine-metallic	5–5½	3.3–4.3	prismatic crystals; massive	one perfect cleavage, one less so	$\alpha = 2.260–2.275$ $\beta = 2.393–2.409$ $\gamma = 2.398–2.515$ gray; strongly anisotropic	orthorhombic Pbnm	has the same chemical composition as but different symmetry than lepidochrocite
hausmannite $MnMn_2O_4$	brownish black	submetallic	5½	4.8	pseudo-octahedral crystals; granular massive	one nearly perfect cleavage	$\omega = 2.43–2.48$ $\epsilon = 2.13–2.17$ gray-white; distinctly anisotropic	tetragonal $I\frac{4}{a}md$	
hematite Fe_2O_3	steel gray; dull to bright red	metallic or submetallic to dull	5–6	5.3	tabular crystals; rosettes; columnar or fibrous massive; earthy massive; reniform masses	no cleavage	$\omega = 2.90–3.22$ $\epsilon = 2.69–2.94$ anisotropic; weakly pleochroic; often shows lamellar twinning	hexagonal $R\bar{3}c$	
ilmenite $FeTiO_3$	iron black	metallic to submetallic	5–6	4.7–4.8	thick, tabular crystals; compact massive; grains	no cleavage; conchoidal fracture	$n \sim 2.7$ grayish white; anisotropic	hexagonal $R\bar{3}$	
lepidochrocite $FeO(OH)$	ruby red to reddish brown	submetallic	5	4.0–4.1	flattened scales; isolated rounded crystals; massive	one perfect cleavage, one less so	$\alpha = 1.94$ $\beta = 2.20$ $\gamma = 2.51$ gray-white; strongly anisotropic and pleochroic	orthorhombic Amam	has the same chemical composition as but different symmetry than goethite
litharge PbO	red	greasy to dull	2	9.1–9.2	crusts; alteration product on massicot	one cleavage	$\omega = 2.665$ $\epsilon = 2.535$	tetragonal $P\frac{4}{n}mm$	has the same chemical composition as but different symmetry than massicot
magnetite $FeFe_2O_4$	black to brownish black	metallic to semimetallic	5½–6½	5.2	octahedral crystals; granular massive		$n = 2.42$ brownish gray; isotropic	isometric Fd3m	strongly magnetic; good electrical conductor; forms solid solution series with magnesioferrite, franklinite, jacobsite, and trevorite in which magnesium, zinc, manganese, and nickel respectively replace ferrous iron in the molecular structure
manganite $MnO(OH)$	dark steel gray to iron black	submetallic	4	4.3–4.4	prismatic crystals, often in bundles; fibrous massive	one very perfect cleavage, two less so	$\alpha = 2.25$ $\beta = 2.25$ $\gamma = 2.53$ brownish gray-white; anisotropic; weakly pleochroic	monoclinic $B\frac{2_1}{d}$	
massicot PbO	sulfur to orpiment yellow	greasy to dull	2	9.6	earthy or scaly massive	two cleavages	$\alpha = 2.51$ $\beta = 2.61$ $\gamma = 2.71$	orthorhombic	has the same chemical composition as but different symmetry than litharge
periclase MgO	colourless to grayish; also green, yellow, or black	vitreous	5½–6	3.6–3.7	irregular, rounded grains; octahedral crystals	one perfect cleavage	$n = 1.730–1.746$	isometric Fm3m	
perovskite $CaTiO_3$ (often containing rare earths)	black; grayish or brownish black; reddish brown to yellow	adamantine to metallic	5½	4.0–4.3	cubic crystals	uneven to subconchoidal fracture	$n = 2.30–2.38$ dark bluish gray	monoclinic? (pseudo-cubic) $P\frac{2_1}{m}$	ferroelectric

Oxley, John (Joseph William Molesworth) (b. 1783, Kirkham Abbey, Yorkshire—d. May 26, 1828, New South Wales, Australia), British naval officer who became an important figure in the development of eastern Australia. As surveyor general of New South Wales (from 1812), he twice led parties of explorers into the interior of that colony (1817, 1818). Although these expeditions contributed to topographic and hydrographic knowledge, his pessimism concerning the habitability of the countryside unnecessarily discouraged settlement. Later (1823–24) he followed the east coast about 700 miles (1,127 km) northward from Sydney, discovering the mouth of the Brisbane River.

·Australian colonial exploration **2**:415a
·Australian river flow observation **7**:1044h

Oxnard, city, Ventura County, California, U.S., near the Pacific Coast. Founded in 1898, it developed around a sugar-beet factory financed by Henry Oxnard. The surrounding alluvial plain was the basis for agricultural industries. With the development of harbour facilities at adjacent Port Hueneme and nearby military installations, the city grew rapidly and acquired diversified manufactures, including chemicals, plastics, precision instruments, paper, electronics, and petroleum products. Oxnard Air Force Base is 5 mi northeast. Inc. 1903. Pop. (1950) city, 21,567; (1980) city, 108,195; Oxnard–Simi Valley–Ventura metropolitan area (SMSA), 529,899.
34°12′ N, 119°11′ W

·map, United States **18**:908

oxo halide, any chemical compound that is both an oxide (*q.v.*) and a halide (*q.v.*).

·acidity and molecular structure **1**:53a
·halogen oxidizing properties **8**:563c; table 568
·phosphorus orbital and bond strength **13**:123b

Oxon (England): *see* Oxfordshire.

oxpecker, or TICKBIRD, either of the two species of the African genus *Buphagus*, of the family Sturnidae (order Passeriformes). Both species—the yellow-billed (*B. africanus*) and the red-billed (*B. erythrorhynchus*)—are brown birds 20 centimetres (8 inches) long, with wide bills, stiff tails, and sharp claws. They cling to cattle and big-game animals to remove ticks and maggots from their hides; when alarmed, the birds hiss, alerting their hosts to possible danger. Though they rid animals of pests, oxpeckers also take blood from the sores, which may be slow to heal.

·classification and general features **13**:1062g
·feeding behaviour **13**:1055c; illus.

Oxudercidae, a family of fish of the order Perciformes.

·classification and general features **14**:55c

Oxus River (Asia): *see* Amu Darya (River).

Oxus Treasure, Achaemenid Persian metalwork dating from the 5th to 4th centuries BC found in 1877 on a bank of the Oxus River (now Amu Darya) near Daryā-ye Qondūz, in Kataghan province of Afghanistan (this region was a part of Bactria at the time the treasure was supposedly buried). The collection today is in London in the British Museum and in the Victoria and Albert Museum.

·Achaemenian metalwork **19**:271d; illus.
·griffin armlet, illus., **3**:Central Asian Peoples, Arts of, Plate 1

Oxybelis: *see* vine snake.

Oxycarenus hyalinipennis (insect): *see* lygaeid bug.

Oxyechus vociferus (bird): *see* killdeer.

oxygen (from Greek *oxys*, "sharp, acid," and *-genēs*, "born"; that is, acid-former), symbol O, nonmetallic chemical element of Group VIa of the periodic table; colourless, odourless, tasteless gas, most plentiful element in the Earth's crust, essential to life; its most important compound is water.

Oxygen was discovered (about 1772) by a Swedish chemist, Carl Wilhelm Scheele, who obtained it by heating potassium nitrate, mercury(II) oxide, and many other substances. An English chemist, Joseph Priestley, independently discovered (1774) oxygen by the thermal decomposition of mercury(II) oxide and published his findings the same year, three years before Scheele published. A French chemist, Antoine Lavoisier, first recognized the gas as an element (1775–77), coined the present name, and in opposition to the phlogiston theory explained combustion as a union of oxygen with the burning material.

Oxide minerals (continued)

name formula	colour	lustre	Mohs hardness	specific gravity	habit	fracture or cleavage	refractive indices or polished section data	crystal system space group	remarks
psilomelane $BaMnMn_8O_{16}(OH)_4$	iron black to dark steel gray	submetallic to dull	5–6	4.7	massive; crusts; stalagtites; earthy masses			orthorhombic	
pyrochlore $NaCaCb_2O_6F$	brown to black (pyro); pale yellow to brown (micro)	vitreous or resinous	5–5½	4.2–6.4	octahedral crystals; irregular masses	subconchoidal to uneven fracture	$n = 1.93–2.02$	isometric Fd3m	forms a solid solution series with microlite in which tantalum replaces niobium in the molecular structure
pyrolusite MnO_2	light steel gray to iron black	metallic	2–6	4.4–5.0	columnar or fibrous massive; coatings and concretions	one perfect cleavage	cream-white; distinctly anisotropic; very weakly pleochroic	tetragonal $P\frac{4_2}{m}nm$	
rutile TiO_2	reddish brown to red; variable	metallic adamantine	6–6½	4.2–5.5	slender to capillary prismatic crystals; granular massive; as inclusions, often oriented	one distinct cleavage	$\omega = 2.556–2.651$ $\epsilon = 2.829–2.895$	tetragonal $P\frac{4}{m}nm$	photosensitive; has the same chemical composition as but different symmetry than anatase and brookite
spinel $MgAl_2O_4$	various	vitreous	7½–8	3.55 (pure $MgAl_2O_4$)	octahedral crystals; round or embedded grains; granular to compact massive		$n = 1.715–1.725$	isometric Fd3m	forms a solid solution series with hercynite, gahnite, and galaxite in which iron, zinc, and manganese respectively replace magnesium in the molecular structure
tenorite CuO	steel or iron gray to black	metallic	3½	5.8–6.4	thin aggregates or laths; curved plates or scales; earthy masses	conchoidal fracture	light gray-white; strongly anisotropic; pleochroic	monoclinic $C\frac{2}{c}$	
thorianite ThO_2	dark gray to brownish black and bluish	hornlike to submetallic	6½	9.7–9.9	rounded cubic crystals	uneven to subconchoidal fracture	$n \sim 2.20$ (variable) isotropic	isometric	radioactive
uranite UO_2	steel to velvet black; grayish, greenish	submetallic to greasy or dull	5–6	6.5–8.5 (massive); 8.0–10.0 (crystals)	crystals; massive; dendritic aggregates of crystals	uneven to conchoidal fracture	light brownish gray; isotropic	isometric	radioactive

The occurrence of oxygen by weight in the atmosphere is 23 percent, in seawater 85.8 percent, and in the Earth's crust 46.6 percent.

During respiration, animals and lower plants take oxygen from the atmosphere and return to it carbon dioxide, whereas by photosynthesis, higher (green) plants assimilate carbon dioxide in the presence of sunlight and evolve free oxygen. Almost all the free oxygen present in the atmosphere is the result of photosynthesis. About 3 parts of oxygen by volume dissolve in 100 parts of fresh water at 20° C (68° F) and slightly less than this in seawater. Dissolved oxygen is essential for respiration in fish and other marine life.

Below −183° C (−297° F), oxygen is a pale blue liquid; it becomes solid at about −218° C (−360° F). Gaseous oxygen on Earth and in the lower atmosphere consists almost entirely of molecules of two atoms, O_2. Triatomic oxygen, O_3, called ozone (*q.v.*), and monatomic oxygen, O, are more predominant in the upper atmosphere, where ozone shields the Earth from the Sun's ultraviolet radiation and water vapour molecules are split by sunlight into hydrogen gas and oxygen atoms. Pure oxygen is 1.1 times heavier than air.

The chief source of commercial oxygen is the atmosphere, from which it is separated by the fractional distillation of liquid air. Of the main components of air, oxygen has the highest boiling point (−183° C [−297° F]) and therefore is less volatile than nitrogen (b.p. −196° C [−321° F]) and argon (b.p. −186° C [−303° F]). Commercial oxygen or oxygen-enriched air is gradually replacing ordinary air in steelmaking and other metallurgical processes and in the chemical industry for the manufacture of such substances as acetylene, ethylene oxide, and methanol. Medical applications of oxygen include use in oxygen tents, inhalators, and pediatric incubators. Oxygen-enriched gaseous anesthetics ensure life support during general anesthesia.

Oxygen has a valence of two and forms a large range of covalently bonded compounds, among which are oxides of nonmetals, as water (H_2O), sulfur dioxide (SO_2), and carbon dioxide (CO_2); organic compounds such as alcohols, aldehydes, and carboxylic acids; common acids such as sulfuric (H_2SO_4), carbonic (H_2CO_3), and nitric (HNO_3); and corresponding salts, such as sodium sulfate (Na_2SO_4), sodium carbonate (Na_2CO_3), and sodium nitrate ($NaNO_3$). Oxygen is present as the oxide ion, O^{2-}, in the crystalline structure of solid metallic oxides as calcium oxide, CaO; metallic superoxides, such as potassium superoxide, KO_2, contain the O^{2-} ion, whereas metallic peroxides, such as barium peroxide, BaO_2, contain the O_2^{2-} ion. Metallic oxides are generally basic, whereas most nonmetallic oxides are acidic. Some oxides, such as those of aluminum, Al_2O_3, and zinc, ZnO, exhibit both acidic and basic behaviour and are called amphoteric.

Natural oxygen consists of a mixture of three stable isotopes: oxygen-16 (99.759 percent), oxygen-17 (0.037 percent), and oxygen-18 (0.204 percent). Four artificially prepared radioactive isotopes are known of mass numbers 14, 15, 19, and 20. The longest lived, oxygen-15 (positron emitter of 124-second half-life), has been used to investigate respiration in mammals.

atomic number	8
atomic weight	15.9994
melting point	−218.4° C (−361.1° F)
boiling point	−183.0° C (−297.4° F)
density (1 atm, 0° C)	1.429 g/l
valence	2
electronic config.	2-6 or $1s^22s^22p^4$

oxygenator, an artificial lung. *See also* artificial organs.

oxygen cycle, in biology, the process through which gaseous oxygen, free in the atmosphere or dissolved in water, is taken in by organisms for use in respiration (*see* respiration, cellular), released to the atmosphere and the water as a waste product in the form of carbon dioxide, taken up in this form and used by plants in the formation of carbohydrates, and returned once again to the atmosphere and the water as gaseous oxygen, derived from the breakdown of water molecules in the photosynthetic process. Most atmospheric oxygen has resulted from this food-making action of green plants. The oxygen cycle becomes more complex if the oxygen stored in many chemical combinations in organic and inorganic compounds is considered to be part of the cycle.

Man's combustion of fossil fuels and removal of natural vegetation has decreased the atmospheric oxygen level, and the contamination of the waters by oil spills, pesticides, and industrial wastes has adversely affected oxygen-producing aquatic plant life. Increased plant growth because of irrigation and large-scale cultivation, however, has partly offset the oxygen loss in some areas of the world.

oxygen group elements and their compounds **13**:809, the five chemical elements oxygen, sulfur, selenium, tellurium, and polonium, comprising Group VIa, sometimes called the chalcogens, of the periodic classification, and the substances composed of them in combination with each other and with other elements.

Oxygen group elements in the periodic table 811b
Oxygen 813d
Sulfur 816c
Selenium 817c
Tellurium 817h
Polonium 818b
Compounds of the chalcogens 818c

REFERENCES in other text articles:
·acidity trends in the periodic table 1:52h
·organic sulfur compound chemistry 13:706e; table 707
·periodicity in properties of elements 14:78d

RELATED ENTRIES in the *Ready Reference and Index: for*
elements: see oxygen; polonium; selenium; sulfur; tellurium
oxygen allotropes and compounds: ozone; hydrogen peroxide; oxide
sulfur compounds: hydrogen sulfide; sulfuric acid; sulfur oxide

oxygen lance, an iron pipe that when supplied with oxygen through a hose burns and furnishes heat to cut thick metal.
·basic oxygen process 17:646a

oxyhemoglobin, in hematology, the bright red pigment in the red blood cells formed by the combination of hemoglobin with oxygen in the lungs or gills.
·blood coloration due to oxygenation 2:1112c
·respiratory gas transport mechanisms 15:750e

oxyhornblende (mineral): *see* basaltic hornblende.

oxymoron (rhetoric): *see* paradox.

Oxynotidae, commonly known as PRICKLY DOGFISH, a family of fish belonging to the suborder Squaloidei of the order Selachii of the class Selachii.
·classification and general features 16:499c

oxyntic cell (biology): *see* parietal cell.

Oxyopidae: *see* lynx spider.

Oxyrhynchus, modern BEHNESA, Egyptian village on the western edge of the Nile Valley, in al-Minyā *muḥāfaẓah* ("governorate"); formerly the capital of the 19th nome (province) of Upper Egypt. It is best known for the numerous papyri uncovered there, first by B.P. Grenfell and A.S. Hunt (1897–1907), and later by Italian scholars early in the 20th century. The papyri, dating from about 250 BC to AD 700, and written primarily in Greek and Latin but also in demotic Egyptian, Coptic, Hebrew, Syriac, and Arabic, include religious texts (*e.g.,* miracles of Sarapis, early copies of the New Testament, and such apocryphal books as the *Gospel of Thomas*), and also masterpieces of Greek classical literature. Among the papyri were texts once considered lost; for example, selections of early Greek lyric poetry; Pindar; the dramatists, including Menander and Callimachus, besides innumerable prose works of oratory or history, such as those of the Oxyrhynchus historian.

Oxyruncus cristatus (bird): *see* sharpbill.

oxytetracycline (antibiotic): *see* tetracycline.

oxytocin: *see* pituitary gland.

Oxytricha (protozoan): *see* hypotrich.

Oxyura (duck): *see* stifftail.

Oxyuranus scutellatus (snake): *see* taipan.

Oxyurida, an order of invertebrates of the class Nematoda of the phylum Aschelminthes.
·classification and general features 2:143a

oyako-kankei, or OYABUN-KOBUN (Japanese: "parent-child relation" and "boss-follower," respectively), in Japan, the customary paternalistic relation between a patron and his client or, in modern times, between an employer or foreman and his workers.
·Japanese industrial organization 6:129f
·kinship in symbolic alliances 10:482h

Oyama, city, Tochigi Prefecture (*ken*), Honshu, Japan, on the Omoi-gawa (Omoi River). A castle town during the Middle Ages, it became a post station (rest stop) and river port during the Tokugawa era (1603–1867). The transport centre of southern Tochigi Prefecture, Oyama is the hub of three major railways. Communication facilities and proximity to Tokyo made the city an industrial suburb after World War II. Major industries include the manufacture of mining and transport equipment and the refining of aluminum. The commercial sector of the economy has shown only slow growth; dried gourd shavings are a special product of the surrounding region. The Oyama Radio Transmitting Station, one of the largest in the Orient, is located outside the city. Pop. (1970) 105,346.
36°18′ N, 139°48′ E
·map, Japan 10:36

Ō-yama-tsumi-no-mikoto (god): *see* Yama-no-kami.

Oyapock River, Portuguese RIO OIAPOQUE, northeastern South America, rises in the Tumuc-Humac Mountains and flows north-

Saramacao, an Indian village near the mouth of the Oyapock River
P. Braun

east for 311 mi (500 km) to empty into the Atlantic near Cape Orange. It forms the border between French Guiana and the Brazilian territory of Amapá. Near its mouth are the ports of Saint-Georges (French Guiana) and Oiapoque and Ponta dos Índios (Brazil).
4°08′ N, 51°40′ W

Oyashio, also known as KURIL CURRENT, surface oceanic current flowing southwest along the Kamchatka Peninsula and the Kuril Islands. Meeting the Kuroshio Extension east of Japan, part of the cold, less saline Oyashio water sinks below the Kuroshio and continues southward; the confluence of these currents is marked by fogbanks. The Oyashio is thought to transport about 15,000,000 cubic metres (530,000,000 cubic feet) of water per second.

Oyem, capital of Woleu-Ntem *région*, northern Gabon, on a plateau (altitude about 3,000 ft [910 m]); it has road connections to Bitam, Minvoul, and Mitzic. The *région* is populated by Fang (Pahouin) people, direct descendants of the migrant Fang tribesmen, who came from Cameroon in the 18th century. Cocoa and coffee, grown on mixed plantations, are the most important cash crops and are trucked via Bitam to the Cameroon ports of Kribi and Douala (230 mi [370 km] northwest) for export. Rubber and potatoes are also cultivated. Oyem has a hospital, Catholic and Protestant missions, an agricultural school, a government secondary school, and a customs station. Pop. (1970 prelim.) 7,385.
1°37′ N, 11°35′ E
·map, Gabon 7:820

oyer and terminer, legal term of Anglo-French origin, meaning "to hear and determine," applied in England to one of the commissions by which a judge of assize (*q.v.*) sits. Originally the commission of oyer and terminer was used during times of insurrection. In modern times the judges of assize and other so designated persons are commanded to inquire into all treasons, felonies, and misdemeanours committed in the counties specified in the commission and to hear and determine them according to law. In the United States, oyer and terminer is the name given to several state courts of criminal jurisdiction.

Oyo, capital of Oyo Province, Western State, southwestern Nigeria, at the intersection of roads from Ibadan, Ilorin, Iseyin, and Iwo. It was declared the new seat of the *alafin* of Oyo (the political leader of all Yoruba people) by Alafin Atiba in the mid-1830s, after Old Oyo, also called Katunga (80 mi [129 km] north-northeast), the capital of the Oyo Empire, was completely destroyed by Muslim Fulani conquerors from Ilorin (60 mi northeast). New Oyo was aligned with Ibadan (32 mi south) in the mid-19th-century Yoruba civil wars. Following an invasion by Dahomeyan forces in 1887, the Alafin of Oyo joined with Lagos against the French and, in the treaty of 1888, placed all of Yorubaland under British protection.

Although the coronation of a new *alafin* retains some of the traditional pomp of the old empire, the *alafin* has only nominal sovereignty over other Yoruba chiefs. From the *ida oranyan* ("sword of state") given to him by the *oni* ("king") of Ife, the spiritual head of the Yoruba people, he derives the spiritual authority for his rule. At nearby Koso is the Shango shrine to the Yoruba god of thunder and lightning, which plays a ceremonial role in the installation of a new *alafin.*

The economy of modern Oyo is based chiefly on agriculture and handicrafts. Products include tobacco (for the cigarette factory at Ibadan), teak, and cotton. The town is a traditional centre of cotton spinning, weaving, and dyeing (with locally grown indigo). It is also famous for carved calabashes (gourds), leatherwork (especially cushions) in goatskins and sheepskins, wood carving, and mat making. Most of its artisans are individual entrepreneurs, but its leatherworkers are organized into a cooperative craft society. Local trade is primarily in yams, maize (corn), guinea corn, cassava, poultry, okra, and beans.

Calabash carving, Oyo, Nigeria
J. Allan Cash—EB Inc.

By the 1860s a Yoruba Mission (Anglican) was established in Oyo, which is now the site of St. Andrew's College (Anglican; founded 1897), one of the oldest teacher-training institutes in Nigeria. The town also has Baptist, Roman Catholic, and private secondary schools, a government vocational centre, and several hospitals.

Oyo Province covers an area of 9,695 sq mi (25,110 sq km). It is inhabited mainly by the Yoruba people, who are followers of Christianity, Islām, and the traditional Yoruba religion. In the two densely populated eastern divisions, Ife, Ila, and Ilesha (*qq.v.*) are the largest urban centres and the chief agricultural entrepôts; cocoa is the most important cash crop, but cotton and tobacco are also significant exports.

Within Oyo Division, apart from Oyo town, are the large market towns of Iseyin and Shaki (*qq.v.*). Cotton, tobacco, teak, and swamp rice are the chief exports; handicrafts and dyed cloth are commercially important for Oyo and Iseyin. Pop. (1971 est.) town, 135,785; (latest census) province, 1,882,000.

·central power control problems **19**:776c
·Ibadan's pioneer settlers **9**:140e
·map, Nigeria **13**:86

Oyo Empire, Yoruba state north of Lagos, in present-day Nigeria, that dominated, during its apogee (1650–1750), most of the countries between the Volta River in the west and the River Niger in the east.

According to traditions, Oyo derived from a great Yoruba ancestor and hero, Oduduwa, who came from the east to settle at Ile-Ife and whose son became the first *alafin*, or ruler, of Oyo. Linguistic evidence suggests, however, that of two waves of immigrants who came—probably from the Central Sudan—into Yorubaland between 700 and 1000, the second settled at Oyo in the open country north of the Guinea forest. This second state became preeminent among all Yoruba states because of its favourable trading position, its natural resources, and the industry of its inhabitants.

Early in the 16th century Oyo was a minor state, powerless before its northern neighbours Borgu and Nupe—by whom it was conquered in 1550. The power of Oyo was already growing, however, by the end of the century, thanks to the *alafin* Orompoto, who used the wealth derived from trade to establish a cavalry force and to maintain a trained army.

Oyo subjugated the kingdom of Dahomey in the west in two phases (1724–30, 1738–48) and traded with European merchants on the coast through the port of Ajase (Porto-Novo). As Oyo's wealth increased so did its leaders' political options—some wished to concentrate on amassing wealth; others advocated the use of wealth for territorial expansion. This difference was not resolved until the *alafin* Abiodun (reigned approximately 1770–89) conquered his opponents in a bitter civil war and imposed an unmitigated policy of economic development based primarily on the coastal trade with European merchants.

Abiodun's neglect of everything but the economy weakened the army, and thus the means by which the central government maintained control. His successor, the *alafin* Awole, inherited local revolts, an administration tenuously maintained by a complex system of public service, and a decline in the power of tributary chiefs. The decline was exacerbated by quarrels between the *Alafin* and his advisors; it continued throughout the 18th century and into the 19th, when Oyo began to lose control of its trade routes to the coast. Oyo was invaded by the newly risen Fon of Dahomey, and soon after 1800 it was captured by militant Fulani Muslims from Hausaland in the northeast.

·political consolidation as a result of trade increase **19**:771d; map 765
·sacred kingship, taboos, and politics **8**:474h

Oyomei (philosopher): *see* Wang Yang-ming.

Ōyōmeigaku, a school of Neo-Confucian studies that developed in Japan during the Tokugawa reign (1603–1867) and that played an important part in the modernization of Japan. The school was based on the teachings of the Chinese scholar Wang Yang-ming (called in Japanese Ōyōmei). He held self-knowledge to be the highest kind of learning and laid great emphasis on introspection and an intuitive perception of the truth, which was thereupon to be acted upon. Nakae Tōju was the pioneer of Ōyōmeigaku; some of the late Tokugawa reformers were greatly influenced by the school.

·Chinese roots and Meiji influence **10**:105e
·Tokugawa adoption of Confucian ethics **10**:73b

Oyono, Ferdinand (b. 1929, Ngoulémakong, Cameroon), comic writer whose two best known works—*Une Vie de boy* (1956; Eng. trans., *Houseboy*, 1966), hailed by critics as a masterpiece of modern African literature, and *Le Vieux Nègre et la médaille* (1956; Eng. trans., *The Old Man and the Medal*, 1967), written while he was studying law and administration in Paris—reflect his own experiences as a youth in French Cameroon. *Houseboy*, in diary form, depicts with brutality as well as with humour the life of a houseboy in the service of the French district commissioner; *The Old Man and the Medal* satirizes colonialism through the eyes of a God-fearing and loyal old villager, who completely reverses his opinion of the white man on the very day that he is to receive a medal for his "service" (*i.e.*, sacrifices) to France. Both novels illustrate sobering as well as amusing elements of colonial rule, and Oyono's indictment of paternalistic missionaries and administrators is devastating. A third novel, *Chemin d'Europe* (1960; "Road of Europe"), tackles the somewhat different problem of a young man who is better educated than his peers but still lacks the skills needed to assure him of success. In each book the hero first confronts the world with naïve enthusiasm but soon must accept the bitter reality of the subordinate position in which he finds himself.

Oyono, praised by critics in Paris in the 1950s for his skill as an actor on stage and on television, has since 1960 served as a diplomat on assignments to Paris, Rome, and the United Nations and as ambassador to Belgium and to Liberia.

Oyrat, peoples speaking western dialects of the Mongol language group. In the 13th century the western Mongols were enemies of the eastern Mongols of the Genghis Khan empire. During the following centuries the western Mongols maintained a separate existence under a confederation known as the Dörben Oyrat (Four Confederates, from which the name Oyrat is derived); at times they were allies, at times enemies, of the eastern Mongols in the Genghis Khan line. Part of the western Mongols remained in their homeland, northern Sinkiang, or Dzungaria, and western Mongolia. Another part of the Oyrat confederation, including all or some of the Torgut, Khoshut, Dörbed, and other groups, moved across southern Siberia to the southern Urals at the beginning of the 17th century. From there they moved to the lower Volga; and for a century and a half, until 1771, they nomadized both to the east and west of this region. During the course of the 18th century they were absorbed by the Russian empire, which was then expanding to the south and east. In 1771 those on the left bank, to the east of the Volga, returned to China. The right-bank Kalmyks (*q.v.*), comprising the contemporary Torgut, Dörbed, and Buzawa, remained in Russia.

Considerable numbers of Oyrat still live in the Sinkiang and Tsinghai regions of northwest China, where an estimated 100,000 speak Oyrat dialects; another 50,000 speakers live in the western portions of the Mongolian People's Republic, where they have been dominated by the numerically preponderant Khalkhas (*q.v.*).

·Chinese relation and western migrations **9**:600f
·geographic distribution map **2**:194
·K'ang-hsi's Dzungar conquest **10**:380f
·literary language and script survival **1**:639e
·Ming dynasty's defeat and reassertion **4**:347e
·Tibet invasion, hegemony, and dispersal **12**:373e *passim* to 374h
·Uzbek and Kazakh relation **18**:794h

Oyrat language, member of the Mongolian language group (a subfamily of the Altaic languages). Spoken by some 75,000 persons in the Mongolian People's Republic and by perhaps 65,000 more in China, Oyrat is not currently a written language. It is most closely related to the Kalmyk (Kalmuck) language of the Kalmyk A.S.S.R., but it uses Mongol (Khalkha) as its literary language. *See* Mongolian languages.

·affiliation and distribution, table 2 **1**:636
·literary language and script survival **1**:639e

oyster, any member of the families Ostreidae (true oysters) or Aviculidae (pearl oysters), bivalve mollusks found in temperate and warm coastal waters of all oceans. Bivalves known as thorny oysters (*Spondylus*) and saddle oysters (*Anomia*) are sometimes included in the group.

True oysters have been cultivated commercially since pre-Christian times as food. Pearl oysters also have long been valued for the precious pearls (*q.v.*) that often develop in them.

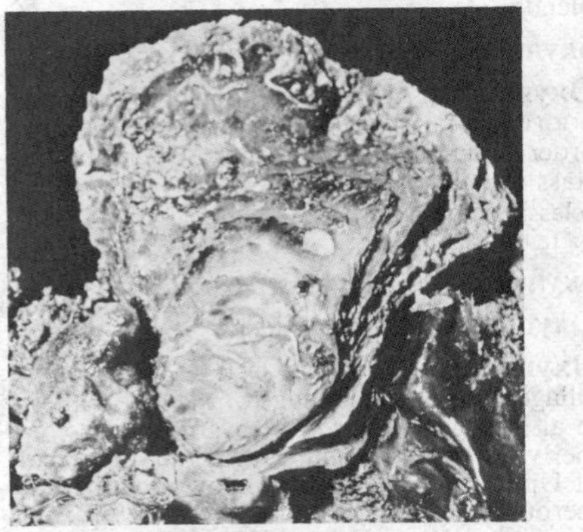

European flat oyster (*Ostrea edulis*)
G. Tomsich—Photo Researchers

The two valves of the oyster shell, which differ in shape, have rough surfaces that are often a dirty gray. The upper valve is convex, or higher at the middle than at the edges. The lower valve, fixed to the bottom or to another surface, is larger, has smoother edges, and is rather flat. The inner surfaces of both valves are smooth and white.

The valves are held together at their narrow ends by an elastic ligament. A large central muscle serves to close the valve against the pull of the ligament. As the valves are held slightly open, tiny hairlike structures (cilia) draw water inward by means of wavelike motions. Two to three gallons may pass through the oyster in an hour. Minute organic particles, filtered from the water, serve as food.

Oysters, in turn, are eaten by invertebrates such as starfishes and snails, as well as fishes, including skates. A common enemy is the oyster drill (*Urosalpinx cinera*), a widely occurring snail that drills a tiny hole through the oyster shell with its tongue, then sucks out the living tissue.

Oysters breed in the summer. The eggs of some species are released into the water before fertilization by the sperm; the eggs of others are fertilized within the female. The young are released as ciliated spheres known as spat, which swim for several days before attaching themselves permanently to a site. Edible oysters are ready for harvesting in three to five years.

True oysters (family Ostreidae) include species of *Ostrea*, *Crassostrea*, and *Pycnodonte*. Common *Ostrea* species include the European flat, or edible, oyster, *O. edulis;* the Olympia oyster, *O. lurida;* and *O. frons. Crassostrea* species include the Portuguese oyster, *C. angulata;* the North American, or Virginia, oyster, *C. virginica;* and the Japanese oyster, *C. gigas.* Pearl oysters (family Aviculidae) are mostly of the genus *Meleagrina,* sometimes called *Pinctada* or *Margaritifera.*

O. edulis occurs from the coast of Norway to waters near Morocco, through the Mediterranean Sea, and into the Black Sea. It is hermaphroditic, *i.e.,* with functional reproductive organs of both sexes in the same individual, and attains lengths of about eight centimetres (about three inches). *O. lurida,* of the Pacific coastal waters of North America, grows to about 7.5 centimetres (3 inches). *C. virginica,* native to the Gulf of St. Lawrence to the West Indies and about 15 centimetres (6 inches) long, has been introduced into Pacific coastal waters of North America. Unlike *O. edulis,* individuals of *C. virginica* are either male or female; the sex of the individual, however, may alternate several times within a season or a lifetime. Up to 50,000,000 eggs may be released by the female at one time. Commercially, *C. virginica* is the most important North American mollusk. *C. angulata* occurs in coastal waters of western Europe. *C. gigas,* of Japanese coastal waters, is among the largest oysters, attaining lengths of about 30 centimetres (one foot).

Oysters are shucked and eaten raw, canned, or smoked; small quantities are frozen. Popular varieties include the blue point and lynnhaven—forms of *C. virginica* (harvested, respectively, from the Blue Point, Long Island, and Lynnhaven Bay, Va., regions); as well as the colchester of Britain; and the marennes of France. The colchester and marennes are forms of *O. edulis.*

Pearls are formed in oysters by the accumulation of calcium-containing material around a solid piece of foreign matter that has become lodged inside the shell. Pearls formed in edible oysters are lustreless and of no value. The best natural pearls occur in a few Oriental species, particularly *Meleagrina vulgaris,* native to the Persian Gulf. This species is found mainly at depths of 8 to 20 fathoms (48 to 120 feet). Pearls are taken mostly from oysters more than five years old. Cultivated pearls are grown around bits of mother-of-pearl inserted manually into the oyster. Most cultivated pearls are grown in Japanese coastal waters.

·aquaculture area and method **7**:361f
·crab predation and parasitism **5**:543b
·C. virginica estuary and salinity change indications **6**:969d
·egg production capability **14**:827f
·features, behaviour, and cultivation **2**:1085b; illus. 1086
·feeding mechanisms and behaviour **7**:208h
·gold-lip pearl shell mother-of-pearl source **2**:1085g

Haematopus ostralegus
·charadriiform bill adaptations, illus. 3 **4**:40
·reaction to supernormal, egg, illus. 2 **2**:807
·territorial behaviour and breeding **14**:837e
·Jurassic forms and bivalve evolution **10**:357d
·lunar transits and activity cycle **14**:73b
·Ostrea edulis cultivation and sexuality **2**:1085e
·pearl culture process in Japan **7**:976f
·sex alteration influences **15**:704c
·whelk predation threat **2**:1046g

Oyster Bay, town (urbanized township), Nassau County, southeastern New York, U.S., occupies 108 sq mi (280 sq km) extending from the north to south shores on central Long Island and comprises more than 30 incorporated villages and unincorporated communities. The first settlers, led by Peter Wright, Samuel Mayo, and the Rev. William L. Leverich, arrived at Oyster Bay Harbor from Rhode Island in 1653. The first town meeting was held in 1660, and the town was granted a governor's patent in 1667. During the Revolutionary War, Raynham Hall (1738, now a museum) served as British Army headquarters, and Sally Townsend, who lived there, provided information that led to the capture of Maj. John André. Other colonial landmarks include Wisteria House at Oyster Bay, Young's Home at Bethpage, Friends Meeting House at Matinecock, and Tryon House and Carman Homestead at Massapequa Park. By the early 19th century the town was essentially rural, although the whaling industry flourished. With the arrival of the trolley car and the Long Island Rail Road at the turn of the century, a number of large estates were built by business tycoons such as L. Tiffany, A. Weeks, C. Theirot, W. Coe, J. Schift, G. Maxwell, and F.W. Woolworth. The village of Oyster Bay gained fame through its most notable resident, Pres. Theodore Roosevelt, whose three-story mansion "Sagamore Hill" (built 1880) became the summer White House (1901–09); it is now a national historic site.

The town continued to be almost entirely rural-residential until it experienced a pre-World War II growth of the aircraft industry at Bethpage and Farmingdale. It now has a broad-based diversified economy with planned industrial parks at Bethpage, Farmingdale, Hicksville, Jericho, Plainview, Syosset, and Woodbury. Educational institutions include the State University of New York Agricultural and Technical Institute (established 1912) at Farmingdale, the State University of New York Center for International Studies (1968) at Oyster Bay, the State University of New York (1968) at Old Westbury, and the C.W. Post College of Long Island University (1955) at Brookville. The Nassau County Charter of 1936 preserved the rights of existing incorporated villages but denied the right of unincorporated communities to incorporate. Villages include Massapequa Park (*q.v.*) and Oyster Bay Cove. Important unincorporated communities are Oyster Bay Cove "village," Jericho, Massapequa, East Massapequa, Hicksville, Plainview, and South Farmingdale. Pop. (1980) 305,750. 40°52′ N, 73°32′ W

oyster cap (fungus): *see* Agaricales.

oystercatcher, shorebird with a long, orange-red bill flattened like a knife. Oystercatchers constitute the genus *Haematopus,*

European oystercatcher (*Haematopus ostralegus*)
Stephen Dalton—EB Inc.

family Haematopodidae (order Charadriiformes). Found in temperate to tropical parts of the world, oystercatchers are stout-bodied birds 40 to 50 centimetres (16 to 20 inches) long, with thick pinkish legs, long pointed wings, and a long, wedge-shaped bill. Their plumage varies from black and white, including a bold white wing patch, to entirely black.

Oystercatchers feed largely on mollusks (such as oysters, clams, and mussels), attacking them as the tide ebbs, when their shells are exposed and still partially open.

These birds nest on the ground, usually laying their two to four eggs in the sand.

There are four species. The European oystercatcher (*H. ostralegus*), of Europe, Asia, and Africa, is black above and white beneath. The American oystercatcher (*H. palliatus*), of coastal regions in the Western Hemisphere, is dark above, with a black head and neck, and white below. The black oystercatcher (*H. bachmani*), of western North America, and the sooty oystercatcher (*H. fuliginosus*), of Australia, are dark except for the pinkish legs.

·characteristics and classification **4**:33e; illus. 40
·egg-brooding critical stimuli **2**:807d; illus.
·feeding specificity on mollusks **7**:209b
·territorial behaviour and breeding **14**:837e

oyster crab: *see* pea crab.

oyster drill (snail): *see* murex.

oystering, in furniture making, the use of transverse sections cut from the branches of certain trees, such as lignum vitae, olive, fruit,

Scriptore with oyster marquetry of prince wood, English, late 17th century; in the Victoria and Albert Museum
By courtesy of the Victoria and Albert Museum, London

and various saplings, to form a veneer with a pattern similar to that of an oyster shell. Of Dutch origin, the technique became prevalent in England in the late 17th century.

oyster nut, a gourd seed native to East Africa that is both consumed locally and exported as a dessert nut.

·fruit farming economics **7**:753c; table 755

oyster plant (*Rhoeo discolor*): *see* Commelinales.

oyster plant (*Tragopogan porrifolius*): *see* salsify.

oystershell scale (*Lepidosaphes ulmi*), a scale insect (order Homoptera) that resembles a miniature oystershell. There are three "races," each of a different colour and with a distinct life history. The gray oystershell scale has one generation per year and is found on lilacs, beeches, maples, willows, and many ornamentals. The brown oystershell scale has two generations per year and occurs on fruit trees. The yellow-brown oystershell scale also

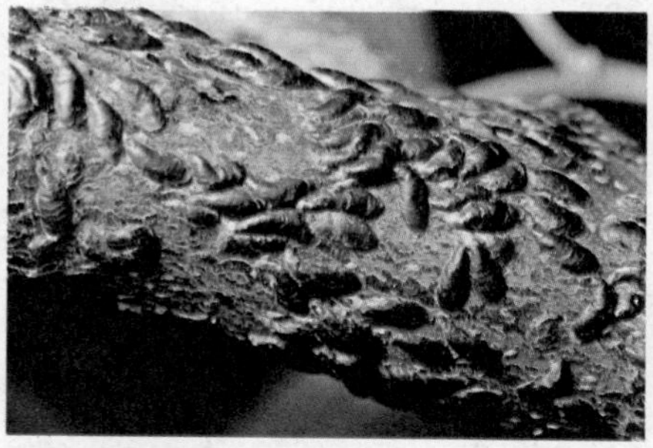

Oystershell scale (*Lepidosaphes ulmi*)
E.S. Ross

has two generations a year and lives on birches and poplars. Control is by dormant spray and natural enemies—*i.e.*, birds, mites, and parasitic wasps.
·homopteran life cycle comparison **8**:1038c

Ozaki Kōyō, original name OZAKI TOKUTARŌ (b. Dec. 16, 1867, Tokyo—d. Oct. 30, 1903, Tokyo), novelist, essayist, and haiku poet, one of the pioneers of modern Japanese literature. In 1885, with a group of friends, he formed the *Kenyūsha*, a magazine and literary association that exercised a major influence in the development of the novel for nearly 20 years. Through his study of Tokugawa period (1603–1867) literature, he led a revival of interest in the 17th-century writer Ihara Saikaku, whose sharp perceptions he blended with his own poetic aesthetic to create a style of romantic realism. Ozaki was active in the movement to create a new colloquial literary language. He excelled in an elaborate style that was well suited to his love themes and descriptions of women. Early works such as *Ninin bikuni iro zange* (1889; "Amorous Confessions of Two Nuns") and *Kyara makura* (1890; "The Perfumed Pillow") reflect his interest in 17th- and 18th-century literature. Later he displayed a more realistic tendency in *Tajō takon* (1896; "Tears and Regrets") and *Kokoro* (1903; "The Heart"). His masterpiece was *Konjiki yasha* (1897–1902; Eng. trans., *The Gold Demon*, 1917), which portrayed the social cost of modernization when the power of money wins over human affection and social responsibility. Ozaki's guidance was eagerly sought by young writers. Two of his best-known disciples were the romantic short-story writer Izumi Kyōka and the naturalistic novelist Tokuda Shūsei.

Ozaki Yukio (b. 1858, Kanagawa Prefecture, Japan—d. Oct. 7, 1954, Tokyo), noted democratic politician who was elected to the Japanese House of Representatives 24 consecutive times and is considered the "father of parliamentary politics" in that country.

Originally a journalist, Ozaki joined the government as a follower of the politician and later prime minister Ōkuma Shigenobu. When Ōkuma resigned in 1881 as a result of the cabinet's failure to adopt his radical proposals for the creation of a new constitution, Ozaki followed him into opposition. In 1898 Ozaki was back in the government, serving as education minister in the new Ōkuma cabinet. He was forced to resign, however, after a "slip" in which he referred to the Imperial Japanese state as a republic. In 1904 he became mayor of Tokyo, and in 1912 he led the members of the Rikken Seiyūkai party into the streets to rally popular support against the oligarchical cabinet of the former general Katsura Tarō. Within a few months the movement that Ozaki had helped form resulted in the fall of Katsura's government and the gradual creation of a cabinet responsible to the majority party in the Japanese Diet, or parliament.

In 1915, while serving as minister of justice in Ōkuma's new cabinet, Ozaki denounced the bribery and corruption carried on by Ōkuma during the election. He thereafter refused to affiliate with any faction or party but remained until his death a powerful force, always fighting for the expansion of democratic politics in Japan. He was especially active in the struggle for universal manhood suffrage, which was established in 1925.

Ozama River, stream in the Dominican Republic that rises in the Cordillera Central and flows *c.* 65 mi (105 km) east and south to the Caribbean.
18°28′ N, 69°53′ W
·drainage and flow **5**:943f
·map, Dominican Republic **5**:944

Ozamiz, city, on Panguil Bay in northwestern Mindanao, Philippines. Incorporated in 1948, it is the largest population centre in Misamis Occidental province and was the site of early Spanish fortifications. Pop. (1975) 71,559.
8°08′ N, 123°50′ E
·map, Philippines **14**:233

Ozanam, Antoine-Frédéric (1813–53), French historian, a leader in the 19th-century Catholic revival in France and founder (1833) of the Société de Saint-Vincent-de-Paul.

Ozark, city, seat of Dale County, Alabama, U.S. It was known as Woodshop until renamed in 1851 for the Ozark Indians. Following World War II its economy was boosted by the expansion of nearby Ft. Rucker as an aviation centre, comprising Hanchey Army Heliport and Cairns, Shell, and Lowe Army airfields, a complex that includes an Army aviation museum. Ozark is a shipping centre for livestock, peanuts, pecans, corn, cotton, and timber. It is the site of the Alabama Institute of Aviation Technology; Wallace Junior College (1965) is at nearby Napier Field. Inc. 1870. Pop. (1980) 13,188.
31°28′ N, 85°38′ W
·map, United States **18**:908

Ozark Mountains, or OZARK PLATEAU, heavily forested group of highlands in south central U.S., extending southwestward from St. Louis, Mo., to the Arkansas River. They occupy an area of about 50,000 sq mi (130,000 sq km) of which 33,000 sq mi are in Missouri, 13,000 in northern Arkansas, and the remainder in southern Illinois and southeastern Kansas. The Ozarks and the adjacent Ouachita Mountains represent the only large area of rugged topography between the Appalachians and the Rockies. The highest peaks, many exceeding 2,000 ft (600 m), are in the Boston Mountains (*q.v.*) in Arkansas. The highest point in Missouri is Taum Sauk Mountain (1,772 ft [540 m]), west of Ironton, in the St. Francois Mountains. The Ozark region, characterized by many underground streams and springs, is drained by the Osage, Gasconade, White, and Black rivers. Lake of the Ozarks provides power and recreation facilities. Taneycomo Lake, Bull Shoals Lake, and Table Rock State Park are also recreation areas.

Tourism, one of the region's chief industries, was given impetus by Harold Bell Wright's novel *The Shepherd of the Hills* (1907), which romanticized the Missouri Ozarks. Other economic assets include timber (mainly hardwoods), agriculture (livestock, fruit, and truck farming), and lead and zinc mining.

The word Ozark is probably a corruption of Aux Arc, name of a French trading post established in the region in the 1700s.
37°00′ N, 93°00′ W
·Appalachian mountain-building process **13**:181c
·country music origins **14**:811a
·farming, social classes, and tourism **2**:6b *passim* to 8c
·location and physical disadvantages **18**:906h; map
·map, United States **18**:908
·topography and economic activity **12**:284c *passim* to 287d

Ozark National Forest, embraces parts of the Ouachita and Boston mountains in northwestern Arkansas, U.S.; it is drained by tributaries of the Arkansas River and surrounded by large reservoirs. Established in 1908, it covers a total area of 2,339 sq mi (6,058 sq km). Apart from its main section (devoted primarily to timber, watershed, and wildlife protection), there are five smaller divisions: Magazine Mountain, Arkansas's highest point, 2,753 ft (839 m); Boston Mountains (*q.v.*), encompassing Devil's Den State Park; Lake Wedington; Henry Koen Experimental Forest; and Sylamore (Blanchard Springs). Natural bridges are at Alum Cove and Hurricane Creek. Mulberry and Buffalo rivers are noted for float fishing. Headquarters are at Russellville.
·Arkansas physical environment **2**:6b

ozarkodiniform, conodonts (small fossils that are toothlike in form and structure) that have a prominent, centrally located denticle flanked on either side by smaller, less pointed denticles. In some forms, the row of denticles may be straight, whereas in others it is curved. Ozarkodiniform conodonts are similar to the genus *Ozarkodina*, a long persisting form that first appeared during the Middle Ordovician and survived to the Late Triassic (the Ordovician Period began 500,000,000 years ago, and the Triassic Period ended 190,000,000 years ago).

Other ozarkodiniform genera include *Prionodus*, *Bryantodus*, and *Plectospathodus*. These and others resemble *Ozarkodina* but are modified to varying degrees. *Ozarkodina* appears to represent a type of development from which later, more complexly structured conodonts may have been derived. The ozarkodiniforms occur, as do other conodonts, only in marine rocks. Some forms were very widespread but restricted within a narrow time range and thus are useful as index fossils and for correlating rocks, sometimes over long distances. Ozarkodiniforms are especially useful in studies of the Silurian Period (between 395,000,000 and 430,000,000 years ago).

Ozarks, Lake of the, south central Missouri, U.S., is one of the largest man-made lakes in the United States. It is impounded by Bagnell Dam, built across the Osage River (1931) to provide hydroelectric power for the St. Louis area. Covering an area of 93 sq mi (242 sq km), the lake is 125 mi (200 km) long and has a shoreline of about 1,300 mi. In the scenic Ozark Mountains (*q.v.*), the lake, with facilities for fishing and water sports, is a popular recreation and resort area. There are several limestone caverns nearby, and Lake of the Ozarks State Park includes most of the Grand Galize arm of the lake, with 89 mi of shoreline.
38°12′ N, 92°38′ W
·Missouri natural environment **12**:284h

Ozawa Jisaburō (1888–1966), Japanese admiral in World War II.
·Philippine Sea naval battle **19**:1004g

Öz Beg, conventionally spelled UZBEK (reigned 1313–41), Mongol leader and khan of the Golden Horde, or Kipchak empire, of southern Russia, under whom it attained its greatest power. A convert to Islām, he also welcomed Christian missionaries from Western Europe into his realm. Öz Beg encouraged the predominance of the princes of Moscow among his Christian vassals; his name survives today in that of the Uzbek people of the Soviet Union.
·Golden Horde hegemony and alliances **16**:42f
·Golden Horde prosperity **9**:599g

Ózd, town, Borsod-Abaúj-Zemplén *megye* (county), northern Hungary. It is 19 mi (30 km) west-northwest of Miskolc in the hill country to the north of the Bükk highland, near the frontier with Czechoslovakia. Formerly a small village on the south bank of Hangony stream, just above its confluence with the Sajó River, where small quantities of iron had been made since the 18th century, it has developed rapidly as an industrial settlement and iron and steel producing centre. Pop. (1960) 34,137; (1970) 39,224; (1978 est.) 40,035.
48°14′ N, 20°18′ E
·map, Hungary **9**:22

Ozenfant, Amédée (1886–1966), French painter who founded Purism (*q.v.*) along with Le Corbusier.
·Le Corbusier introduction and collaboration **5**:168d
·Purism development **19**:468f

Ozias (king of Judah): *see* Uzziah.

Ozidi of Atazi, The (1966), play by John Pepper Clark (*q.v.*).
·ritual theme distinction **1**:240e

ozier pattern, molded basket-weave pattern introduced in the 1730s on Meissen porcelain (*q.v.*) tableware. It was probably one of the numerous inventions of the famous modeller Johann Joachim Kändler.

Painted porcelain dish with an *alt-ozier* border, Copenhagen, *c.* 1780; in the Victoria and Albert Museum, London

By courtesy of the Victoria and Albert Museum, London; photograph, EB Inc.

There are four basic types of ozier molding: the *ordinair-ozier*, a kind of zigzag basketweave; the *alt-ozier* ("old ozier"), which has radial ribs; the *neu-ozier* ("new ozier"), the ribs of which resemble the curves of an S, appearing around 1742; and the *Brühlsches Allerei-Dessin* ("Brühl's varied design"), a pattern of basketwork and molded motifs, such as shells and flowers, surrounded by Rococo scrollwork. Like much else that originated at Meissen, ozier molding was copied by other porcelain factories, such as those at Berlin, Sudwigsburg, Chantilly, Copenhagen, and Chelsea.

Ozma, Project, unsuccessful first attempt to receive radio signals generated by hypothetical intelligent beings living near stars other than the Sun. The project involved about 150 hours of intermittent observation between April and July of 1960. A special receiver was used, attached to the 26-metre- (85-foot-) diameter radio telescope of the U.S. National Radio Astronomy Observatory at Green Bank, W.Va. The two stars chosen (Epsilon Eridani and Tau Ceti, both about 11 light-years from the Earth), are the nearest stars that closely resemble the Sun and were therefore thought to be the nearest with a reasonable likelihood of having inhabited planets. Additional time and improved equipment would have been necessary to extend the search to more distant stars. Frank Donald Drake, director of the search, named the project for the princess of Oz, an imaginary, marvelous, and distant place described in a series of stories by the U.S. writer L. Frank Baum. The search was carried out at wavelengths near 21 centimetres. That is the wavelength of a signal generated naturally by interstellar hydrogen and would presumably be familiar, as a kind of universal standard, to anyone attempting interstellar radio communication.

ozokerite (Greek *ozocerite*, "odoriferous wax"), naturally occurring, light-yellow to dark-brown mineral wax composed principally of solid paraffinic hydrocarbons (compounds chiefly of hydrogen and carbon linked in chains). Ozokerite usually occurs as thin stringers and veins filling rock fractures in areas of mountain building. It is believed to have separated from paraffin-base petroleum and forms when the petroleum containing it percolates through the rock fissures; in Utah this process is exposed in fissures cut by mine drifts. Large deposits occur in Galicia (in modern Poland), Romania, the U.S.S.R., and Utah.

The deposits in Galicia and Utah have been mined, but production dropped after 1940 because of competition from paraffin wax cooled from distilled petroleum. Mined ozokerite is purified by boiling in water (its melting point is 58°–100° C [130°–212° F]); the wax rises to the surface and is refined with sulfuric acid and decolorized with charcoal. Ozokerite has a higher melting temperature than typical synthetic petroleum wax, a desirable property in the manufacture of carbon paper, leather polishes, cosmetics, electrical insulators, and candles.

Ozolua (d. 1504), African king, the greatest warrior-king of Benin, in present Nigeria. He was able to extend the boundaries of Benin almost to their widest extent, from the Niger River in the east virtually to Lagos in the west. Tradition calls him the first ruler in West Africa to have had contact with the Portuguese explorers who were just then exploring the west coast of sub-Saharan Africa.

The youngest son of another great Benin ruler, Ewuare the Great, Ozolua (called Okpame before his accession to the throne) embarked on his systematic reduction of surrounding peoples from the moment he was named oba (king) in 1481. Known as "The Conqueror," he bound together the area he subjugated by a complicated network of marriage and diplomatic obligations and brought the Benin kingdom to its widest extent. He encouraged trade with the Portuguese (*c.* 1500) and allowed them to establish missionary stations.

ozone, triatomic allotrope O_3, of oxygen which accounts for the distinctive odour of the air after a thunderstorm or around electrical equipment. An irritating, pale blue gas that is explosive and toxic, even at low concentrations, ozone occurs naturally in very small amounts in the Earth's stratosphere, where it absorbs solar ultraviolet radiation, which otherwise could cause severe damage to living organisms on the Earth's surface. Ozone usually is manufactured by passing an electric discharge through a current of oxygen or dry air. The resulting mixtures of ozone and original gases are suitable for most industrial purposes, although purer ozone may be obtained from them by various methods; for example, upon liquefaction, an oxygen–ozone mixture separates into two layers, of which the denser one contains about 75 percent ozone. The extreme instability and reactivity of concentrated ozone makes its preparation both difficult and hazardous.

Ozone is 1.5 times as dense as oxygen; at −112° C (−170° F) it condenses to a dark blue liquid, which freezes at −251.4° C (−420° F). The gas decomposes rapidly at temperatures above 100° C (212° F) or, in the presence of certain catalysts, at room temperatures. Although it resembles oxygen in many respects, ozone is much more reactive; hence, it is an extremely powerful oxidizing agent, particularly useful in converting olefins into aldehydes, ketones, or carboxylic acids. Because it can decolorize many substances, it is used commercially as a bleaching agent for organic compounds; as a strong germicide, it is used to sterilize drinking water as well as to remove objectionable odours and flavours.

·agricultural production hindrances **1**:361a
·alkene unsaturation identification **9**:86f
·atmosphere protective shield **2**:322h
·atmospheric composition, table 8 **6**:710
·atmospheric ozone formation **2**:308h
·atmospheric spectra absorption **2**:233h
·climate and ultraviolet radiation **4**:740a
·life protection from ultraviolet solar flux **10**:904a
·molecular quantum-mechanical analysis **4**:92e
·oxygen's allotropic forms **13**:813e
·photochemical reactions and processes **14**:291f
·plant disease and pollutants **5**:886d; illus. 887
·properties and applications **8**:727f
·radiation diminution capacity **15**:390c
·toxin reaction site and effect, table 4 **14**:622
·ultraviolet radiation absorption **2**:317a; table 318
·urban pollutants and human health **18**:1050e *passim* to 1051g

ozonide, any of a class of chemical compounds formed by reactions of ozone (*q.v.*) with other compounds. Organic ozonides, often made from olefins (*q.v.*), are unstable, most of them decomposing rapidly into oxygen compounds, such as aldehydes, ketones, and peroxides, or reacting rapidly with oxidizing or reducing agents. A few inorganic ozonides are known, containing the negatively charged ion O_3^-: an example is potassium ozonide (KO_3), an unstable, orange-red solid formed from potassium hydroxide and ozone; upon heating, it decomposes into oxygen and potassium superoxide (KO_2).

ozonosphere, region in the upper atmosphere between about 10 and 50 kilometres (6 and 30 miles) altitude, in which there are appreciable concentrations of ozone and in which the thermal structure is to a large degree determined by the radiative properties of ozone.

Ozone is a slightly bluish gas the molecules of which consist of three oxygen atoms; it has the formula O_3. It is always present in trace quantities in the Earth's atmosphere, but its largest concentrations are in the ozonosphere. There it is formed primarily as a result of shortwave solar ultraviolet radiation (wavelengths shorter than $2,420 \times 10^{-8}$ centimetre), which dissociates normal molecular oxygen (O_2) into two oxygen atoms. These oxygen atoms then combine with nondissociated molecular oxygen to yield ozone. Ozone, once formed, is also destroyed by solar ultraviolet radiation of wavelengths less than $3,000 \times 10^{-8}$ centimetre. When photochemical equilibrium exists, the amounts of ozone present are such that the production rate is equal to the destruction rate.

Because of strong absorption of solar ultraviolet radiation by molecular oxygen and ozone, radiation capable of producing ozone cannot reach the lower levels of the atmosphere; and photochemical production is not significant below about 20 kilometres (10 miles). This absorption of solar energy is very important in producing a temperature maximum at about 50 kilometres (30 miles), called the stratopause or the mesopeak. Also, the presence of the ozone layer in the upper atmosphere, with its accompanying absorption, effectively blocks almost all solar radiation of wavelengths less than $2,900 \times 10^{-8}$ centimetre from reaching the Earth's surface. This effect is very important for the existence of life on Earth.

Even though the ozone layer is about 40 kilometres (25 miles) thick at the high altitudes at which it occurs, the atmosphere is very tenuous; and the total amount of ozone, compared to more abundant atmospheric gases, is quite small. If all of the atmospheric ozone in a vertical column through the entire atmosphere were compressed to sea-level pressure, it would form a layer only a few tenths of a centimetre thick.

·climatic variation with height **4**:718b
·insulation from sterilization radiation **6**:711a
·jet stream spring motion **10**:164b

Ozoyong, son of the Dragon God of the Eastern Sea.

·Korean dance play **5**:474d

Ozu Yasujirō (b. Dec. 15, 1903, Tokyo—d. 1963), motion-picture director who originated the *shomin-geki*, a genre of film dealing with lower middle class Japanese family life. Because of the centrality of domestic interrelationships in his films, painstakingly detailed character portrayals, and the pictorial beauty of his images, Ozu is considered the most typically Japanese of all directors and has received more honours in his own country than any other director. Raised in Tokyo, Ozu became an assistant cameraman for the Shochiku Motion Picture Company, Tokyo, in 1923. By the mid-1920s he was a director, but not until the early 1930s did he establish his reputation by such outstanding *shomin-geki* silent comedies as *I Graduated, But. . .* (1931) and *Umarete wa mita kevedo* (1932; *I Was Born, But . . .*). Ten years later *Toda-ke-no-kyodai* (1941; *The Toda Brother and His Sisters*), a consideration of Japanese attitudes toward motherhood, was his first box-office success.

Ozu made no films from 1942 to 1947. In 1947 *Nagaya shinshi roku* (*The Record of a Tenement Gentleman*) initiated a series of pictures in which a further refinement of style was combined with a concern for postwar conditions. Plot was almost eliminated, while atmosphere and detailed character studies became preeminent. He almost totally abandoned such devices as camera movement in favour of straight pictorial shots. *Banshun* (1949; *Late Spring*), *Bakushu* (1951; *Early Summer*), *O-chazuke-no-aji* (1952; *The Flavour of Green Tea and Rice*), *Tokyo monogatari* (1953; *Tokyo Story*), and *Soshun* (1956; *Early Spring*) exemplify this style and helped to establish Ozu as an internationally prominent director. Such later films as *Early Autumn* (1961) and *An Autumn Afternoon* (1962) show Ozu's mastery of the decorative use of colour in motion pictures.

P (astronomy): *see* Pluto.

P, symbol for the chemical element phosphorus (*q.v.*).

P-51B, twin-engine World War II U.S. long-range fighter.
·World War II balance of power **19**:999c

Pa, chemical symbol for the element protactinium (*q.v.*).

Pa, Chinese feudal state that was absorbed by the Ch'in dynasty near the end of the 3rd century BC.
·incorporation into Shu Kingdom **4**:586f

Pa-an, capital of Kawthule, or Kawthoolei, (formerly Karen) State, Lower Burma. On the right bank of the Salween River, 27 mi (43 km) north of Moulmein, it has an airfield and is linked by road west to Thaton. Latest census 4,139.
16°53′ N, 97°38′ E
·map, Burma **3**:505

Paar, an Austrian family that in the late 15th century developed a letter-carrying service that operated on a national scale.
·national postal systems development **14**:884g

Paarl, town, Cape Province, Republic of South Africa, on the Groot-Berg River, between the Paarl Mountain and the Drakenstein Range. Founded in 1690 by Huguenots,

Fruit gardens and vineyards in the Paarl Valley, Cape Province, S. Af.
By courtesy of the South African Tourist Corporation

who introduced viticulture, it sprawls along the river bank for 8 mi (13 km). Known for its vineyards and orchards, it is a centre for wine-making and also produces citrus fruits, tobacco, and olives. Pop. (1970 prelim) 48,597 (30% white).
33°45′ S, 18°56′ E
·map, South Africa **17**:62

Paasche index, index developed by German economist Hermann Paasche for measuring current price or quantity levels relative to those of a selected base period. It differs from the Laspeyres index (*q.v.*) in that it uses current-period weights; that is, in computing the index, a commodity's price relative (ratio of current price to base-period price) is weighted by the commodity's relative importance to all purchases in the current period. The index is arrived at by taking the ratio of the weighted purchase value of a group of current-period commodities valued at current prices to the value of those same commodities at base-period prices and multiplying by 100.

The Paasche price index tends to understate price increases since it already reflects some of the change in consumption patterns with which consumers respond to price increases (increased consumption of goods that show little or no price change).

Paasikivi, Juho Kusti (b. Nov. 27, 1870, Tampere, Fin.—d. Dec. 14, 1956, Helsinki), prime minister of Finland and president, who

Paasikivi, detail of a painting by Eero Järnefelt, 1931; in the collection of Kansallis-Osake-Pankki, Helsinki
By courtesy of Kansallis-Osake-Pankki, Helsinki

believed that Finland's only chance for survival lay in friendly relations with the Soviet Union and, therefore, pursued a lifelong policy of making concessions to Finland's huge neighbour.

After studying law and history, Paasikivi taught at the University of Helsinki and then entered business. A political realist who took the view that small nations could not permanently hope to oppose the power politics of large ones, he campaigned for a constitution as a "complier" of the Old Finnish Party. A member of the Finnish Cabinet from 1908 to 1909, he resigned when Russia illegally attempted to carry out the Russification of his country, which at that time was part of the tsarist empire. As the first prime minister of the newly independent Finland (1918), Paasikivi advocated friendship with the Soviet regime and warned against trying to take advantage of Russia's temporary weakness. He also favoured a pro-German foreign policy and a monarchy for Finland.

During the 1938–39 diplomatic crisis, he advocated acceding to Soviet demands and successfully worked to bring the subsequent Russo-Finnish War (1939–40) to a speedy conclusion. Maintaining contacts with Soviet officials during the renewed conflict from 1941 to 1944, he conscientiously enforced the peace conditions while holding the post of prime minister (1944–46). From March 1946 to February 1956, Paasikivi served as president of the Finnish Republic and was instrumental in regaining Porkkala (1955), leased to the Soviet Union for a naval base in 1944. Perhaps Finland's greatest statesman, he never hesitated to yield on secondary issues, but he remained uncompromising over his country's independence.
·coalition government leadership **16**:335h

paauw (bird): *see* bustard.

Paavolainen, Olavi (1903–64), Finnish writer.
·Tulenkantajat movement participation **10**:1259c

PABA: *see* para-aminobenzoic acid.

pabbajjā, in Pāli, PRAVRAJYĀ in Sanskrit, Buddhist rite of ordination by which a layman becomes a novice (Pāli *sāmaṇera;* Sanskrit *śrāmaṇera*). The ceremony is also the preliminary part of higher ordination, raising a novice to a monk (*see* upasampadā).

In some Theravāda (Way of the Elders) countries such as Burma, the rite is normally held for every Buddhist boy, usually on reaching the age of puberty. In Tibet and China, a probationary period of study was required before the candidate became a novice, during which he did not receive tonsure and was not exempt from military service.

Details of the ceremony vary from country to country. It consists essentially of the candidate coming before an assembly of 10 (in some cases less) ordained monks and asking for admission as a novice to the order. His head and face are shaven, and he presents the upper and lower robes of the novice for consecration by the officiating abbot or senior monk. The candidate puts on the monastic robes and returns. He then asks for the threefold refuge (in the Buddha, the teaching, and the order) and the ten precepts (ethical code, *see* sīla) to be administered to him. The rite is concluded with his obeisance to the senior monks and his request for forgiveness of his faults.

The novice lives in the monastery for a period varying from a few days to several months and accompanies the monk on the daily alms rounds, but he is not allowed to participate in the fortnightly recitation of the *pātimokkha* (recitation of the rules of monastic discipline).
·ordination rite evolution **3**:394d

Pabianice, town and suburb of Łódź city, in Łódź *województwo* (province), central Poland, in the Łódź highlands on the Dobrzynka River. The second most important town in the Łódź industrial region, it lies on the Łódź-Wrocław rail line and is a major textile centre. The oldest community in the region, it was first settled in the 11th century and was granted town rights in 1297. Because it lay on the trade route between Kraków and Gdańsk (Danzig) it prospered. A late-16th-century Renaissance castle, built by the canons, now houses a museum. Pop. (1970 prelim.) 62,300.
·map, Poland **14**:626

Pābna, also spelled PUBNA, administrative headquarters of Pābna district, Rājshāhi division, Bangladesh (formerly East Pakistan), on the Ichāmati River, a tributary of the Padma (Ganges). An industrial centre, it has jute mills and is noted for its hosiery and handloomed products. Historical remains include the Hindu temple of Jor Bāṅgla and the Pābna Jubilee tank (water reservoir; excavated, 1887). Pābna was incorporated a municipality in 1876; it has Jinnah Park, a mental hospital, and two government colleges affiliated with the University of Rājshāhi.

Pābna district (area 1,877 sq mi [4,861 sq km]) lies within the angle formed by the confluence of the Padma and Jamuna rivers. Its wide alluvial plain is intersected by a network of streams, and many villages are accessible only by boat during the rainy season. The soil, enriched by flood deposits, supports rice, jute, sugarcane, and pulses. Pop. (latest census) city, 40,792; (1971 est.) district, 2,115,714.
·map, Bangladesh **2**:688

Pabst, G(eorge) W(ilhelm) (b. Aug. 27, 1885, Bohemia—d. 1967), motion-picture director, pre-eminent among the explorers of the new realism who made German films among the most artistically successful of those produced in the 1920s. Pabst's films are marked by a technical competence in incorporating documentary footage into fictional sequences; by an effective use of experimental camera angles to create mood; and by powerful editing that gave meaning to each shot, creating as well smooth transitions between scenes.

Pabst was educated in Vienna and at 20 began a career as a stage actor in Zürich. He performed in Salzburg, Berlin, and New York City before turning to the cinema. His first successful film as a director was *The Joyless Street* (*Die Freudlose Gasse*, 1925), which became internationally famous as a harshly realistic portrayal of life in inflation-ridden postwar Vienna. His second well-known film was *Secrets of a Soul* (*Geheimnisse einer Seele*, 1926), an objectively realistic consideration of psychoanalysis. *The Love of Jeanne Ney* (*Die Liebe der Jeanne Ney*, 1927) incorporated documentary shots to heighten realism. The picture is most highly praised, though, for its photography and the smooth cutting of one scene into another. With those three films Pabst became an internationally prominent director.

His films of the late 1920s and '30s contained

a stronger emphasis on the interrelationship between social conditions and the individual. Outstanding motion pictures of this type were *Crisis* (*Abwege*, 1928), *Pandora's Box* (*Die Büchse der Pandora*, 1929), and *Diary of a Lost One* (*Tagebuch einer Verlorenen*, 1929). Others were *Westfront 1918* (1930), a strongly pacifist statement, *The Beggar's Opera* (*Die Dreigroschenoper*, 1931), and *Comradeship* (*Kameradschaft*, 1931), in which a disaster exposes the social conditions in a mining district.

By the mid 1930s the overall quality of Pabst's films was declining. He moved to Paris, and attempted a ponderous three-language version of *Don Quixote* (1933) as well as several melodramas. Returning to Germany at the outbreak of World War II, he continued directing films such as *Comedians* (*Komödianten*, 1941) and *Paracelsus* (1943). His most outstanding postwar film was *The Last Act* (*Der Letzte Akt*, 1954), a restaging of the final days of the Hitler regime.

·street films and their themes **12**:524h
·themes and techniques **12**:528b

PAC: *see* Pan-African congresses.

paca, or SPOTTED CAVY (*Cuniculus paca*), stout-bodied, tailless rodent, family Dasyproctidae (order Rodentia), found chiefly in lowland forests from Mexico to Brazil. A white-spotted, brown animal, large for a rodent, the paca may attain a length of about 75

Paca (*Cuniculus paca*)
Lloyd G. Ingles

centimetres (29 inches). It has a relatively large head and bony swellings on its cheekbones that serve as resonating chambers in sound production. The paca is nocturnal and eats leaves, roots, and fruit, occasionally damaging sugarcane or other crops. It lives in a burrow, swims well, and when pursued heads for water in an attempt to escape. The female usually bears one young per litter.

The mountain paca (*Stictomys*, or *Cuniculus*, *taczanowskii*) is a highland paca found in the Andes. It is smaller than the lowland form and has thicker fur. Both species are locally valued as food. For false paca, *see* pacarana.

·classification and general features **15**:979d
·feeding behavior and life span **15**:973a

Pacaraima Mountains, Portuguese SERRA PACARAIMÃ, Spanish SIERRA PACARAIMA, in Guyana, PAKARAIMA MOUNTAINS, a southern tabular upland of the Guiana Highlands in Brazil, Venezuela, and Guyana, forms the drainage divide between the Orinoco Valley (north) and the Amazon Basin (south). Extending for 250 mi (400 km) in an east–west direction, the mountains mark the borders between Brazil and southeastern Venezuela and between Brazil and west central Guyana. Mt. Roraima (9,094 ft [2,772 m]) is the highest peak. The rivers that rise on the plateau tops pour over the cliffed edges in spectacular waterfalls, such as the Kaieteur Falls in Guyana.

5°30′ N, 60°40′ W
·location and elevation **8**:506h
maps
·Brazil **3**:124
·Guyana **8**:507
·South America **17**:77

pacarana, or BRANICK'S RAT (*Dinomys branickii*), rare South American rodent of the valleys and lower slopes of the Andes Mountains. The only living member of the family Dinomyidae (order Rodentia), the pacarana is a diurnal, terrestrial rodent that eats leaves, fruit, and other vegetation. It is heavy bodied and has small ears, a relatively large head, and coarse, white-spotted, black or brown fur. Large for a rodent, it attains a length of about 90 to 100 centimetres (35 to 39 inches) including its thick, hairy tail.

·classification and general features **15**:979d

Pacasmayo, seaport town, La Libertad department, northwestern Peru. It is connected by road with Chiclayo (north) and Trujillo (south) and by rail with Guadelupe and Chilete, and is an agricultural shipping centre. Pre-Incan pottery has been found in a nearby valley. Pop. (1972 prelim.) 15,381.

7°20′ S, 79°35′ W
·map, Peru **14**:128
·pre-Incan pottery discoveries **1**:843d

Pacatnamú, large ancient Andean town of the Chimú Empire, in what is now Peru.

·Chimú cultural centres **1**:846e; map 840
·development and design **18**:1070e

Pacatus Drepanius, Latinius, first name also spelled LATINUS (fl. *c.* AD 390), Gallo-Roman orator and poet, the author of an extant panegyric addressed to Theodosius I at Rome in 389 after the defeat of the usurper Maximus. He was a friend of Symmachus, the champion of paganism, and of the Christian poet Ausonius. It is uncertain whether Pacatus was pagan or Christian; in his speech he denounced Maximus' persecution of the Priscillianist heretics. In 390 Pacatus received the proconsulship of Africa and later held other high offices.

Paccard, Michel-Gabriel, 18th-century French doctor who, in 1786, was the first to ascend Mt. Blanc.

·ascent of Mont Blanc for prize money **12**:585d

paccaya (Buddhist philosophy): *see* pratyaya.

pacceka-buddha (Buddhism): *see* pratyeka-buddha.

pace, a Roman measure of length equal to 5 feet, or 1.544 metres, in the Greek system of measurement. A thousand paces made up the Roman mile.

·Roman linear measurement system **19**:728g

Pace, Luigi da, 16th-century Italian artist who did the mosaics in the Chigi Chapel of Sta. Maria del Popolo, Rome, 1576.

·Chigi Chapel mosaics, illus., **12**:Mosaic, Plate VI
·mosaic work in Roman church **12**:472h

Pacelli, Eugenio: *see* Pius XII, Pope.

pacemaker, artificial cardiac device that, by means of electrical impulses, stimulates the heart muscle to contract at regular intervals when the heart's own pacemaker has failed.

·digestion and intestinal motions **5**:776d
·heartbeat regulation mechanism **3**:879g
·plutonium as power source **1**:68b
·surgical treatment of heart block **3**:896h; illus.

Pacem in Terris (1963), an encyclical by Pope John XXIII.

·significance of document **15**:1017c

pacer, horse trained to use a two-beat gait in which legs move in lateral pairs and support the animal alternately on the right and left legs.

·breeding history and characteristics **8**:1102d

Pachacamac, creator deity worshipped by the pre-Inca maritime population of Peru; it was also the name of a pilgrimage site in the Lurín Valley (south of Lima) dedicated to the god and revered for many centuries. After the Incas conquered the coast, they did not attempt to replace the ancient and deeply rooted worship of Pachacamac but instead incorporated him into their own pantheon. Pachacamac was believed to be a god of fire and a son of the sun god; he rejuvenated the world originally created by the god Viracocha and taught men the crafts. Pachacamac was also believed to be invisible and thus was never represented in art.

The ruins of the shrine in the Lurín Valley include several pyramids and temples and are partially restored. The site may have served as the central city of a coastal "kingdom" from *c.* 1000 to *c.* 1440.

Pachacamac, a large pre-Columbian ruin located in the Lurin Valley on the central coast of present-day Peru. The earliest major occupation and construction of Pachacamac dates to the Early Intermediate Period (*c.* 200 BC–AD 600) and to a culture generally known as Early Lima (Maranga, Interlocking style). The terraced adobe pyramid and temple known as the Temple of Pachacamac belongs to this time and culture, and Pachacamac's fame as the seat of an oracle probably began in the Early Intermediate Period. During the Middle Horizon (AD 600–1000) it continued as a major centre and place of pilgrimage and was probably the principal establishment of the Huari Empire on the coast. In late pre-Columbian times the Inca constructed the large Temple of the Sun at the site, and the Oracle of Pachacamac, to which the early Spanish explorers refer, probably was associated with a shrine in this temple. The shrine and temple were sacked by Francisco Pizarro's soldiers during the Spanish conquest (*c.* 1532).

·development and design **18**:1070g
·Huari pottery varieties **1**:845e

Pachacuti (PACHACUTEC) **Inca Yupanqui** (reigned 1438–71), Inca emperor in northwestern South America, an empire builder who, because he initiated the swift, far-ranging expansion of the Inca state, has been likened to Philip II of Macedonia. (Similarly, his son Topa Inca Yupanqui is regarded as a counterpart of Philip's son Alexander III the Great.) Pachacuti first conquered various peoples in what is now southern Peru and then extended his power northwesterly to Quito, Ecuador. He is said to have devised the city plan adopted for his capital, Cuzco (in present southern Peru).

·civil war and conquests **1**:849a; table 847
·godly protection of Viracocha **9**:260a

Pacha-Mama, in Peruvian traditions, an Andean earth-mother figure.

·earth cult survivals **12**:879d

Pacheco, Huari site in Nazca Valley, Peru.

·pre-Incan pottery development **1**:845b; map 840

Pacheco, Francisco (b. 1564, Sanlúcar de Barrameda, Spain—d. 1654, Seville), painter, teacher, and scholar. An undistinguished artist, he is best remembered as the teacher of both Velázquez and Alonso Cano and as the author of *Arte de la pintura* (1649), a treatise on the art of painting that is the most important document for the study of 17th-century Spanish art.

Moving to Seville early in his life, he studied painting under Luis Fernández, learning primarily by copying the work of Italian Renaissance masters. After visiting (1611) Madrid and Toledo, where he studied the work of El Greco, he returned to Seville and opened an academy. His instructions were marked by an emphasis on academic correctness. The official censor of the Inquisition in Seville, he concerned himself with the proper way of depicting religious themes and images.

His paintings, such as the "Last Judgement" (1614) in the convent of Santa Isabel and the "Martyrs of Granada" (Granada), are highly imitative and rigid works, monumental but unimpressive. Although Velázquez became Pacheco's son-in-law, he was uninfluenced by his father-in-law's art.

Pacheco's *Arte de la pintura*, in addition to chapters on iconography and the theory and practice of painting, includes a series of biographies of contemporary Spanish painters that is most valuable to scholars.

·Velázquez' kinship and early career **19**:53h

Pacheco Pereira, Duarte (fl. late 15th–early 16th century), Portuguese explorer whom the poet Camões called "Aquiles Lusitano" (the "Portuguese Achilles"). In 1488, after exploring the southwestern coast of Africa, he joined, on its return voyage, the expedition of Bartolomeu Dias that had discovered the Cape of Good Hope. He sailed with Pedro Álvares Cabral on a voyage resulting in the discovery of Brazil (April 22, 1500). Later he defended the Portuguese trading station at Cochin, in India, against attacks by the ruler of Calicut. In 1520–22 he was military governor in Portuguese East Africa (Mozambique). A well-educated man, he wrote a valuable account of Portuguese exploring and empire-building, *Princípio do Esmeraldo "de Situ Orbis"* . . . (modern editions 1892, 1903).

·defense of Portuguese position at Cochin **11**:464g

Pachelbel, Johann (baptized Sept. 1, 1653, Nürnberg, now in West Germany—d. March 3, 1706, Nürnberg), composer, known for his works for organ, and one of the great organ masters of the generation before J.S. Bach. He held posts as organist in Vienna, Stuttgart, and other cities. In 1695 he was appointed organist at St. Sebalduskirche in Nürnberg, where he remained until his death.

All Pachelbel's work is in a contrapuntally simple style. His organ compositions show a knowledge of Italian forms derived from Frescobaldi through J.J. Froberger. Of special importance are his chorale-preludes, which did much to establish the chorale melodies of Protestant North Germany in the more lyrical musical atmosphere of the Catholic south.

·organ music development **13**:680d

Pacher, Michael (b. *c.* 1435, Austrian Tirol—d. 1498, Salzburg?), late Gothic painter and wood-carver, one of the earliest artists to introduce the principles of Renaissance painting into Germany. Little is known of his early life, but he is thought to have gone to Italy, where he was much impressed by the experiments in perspective of two eminent northern Italian artists of the Renaissance, Jacopo Bellini and Andrea Mantegna. That trip must have occurred sometime before Pacher began work on the altarpiece of the Pilgrimage Church at Sankt Wolfgang, in Upper Austria (centre completed in 1479; wings completed in 1481). The large figures placed close to the picture plane and seen from a low viewpoint, the deep architectural perspective, and the dramatic foreshortening in such scenes as the "Expulsion of the Money Changers from the Temple" and the "Nativity" betray knowledge of Mantegna's frescoes in the Church of the Eremitani in Padua. Pacher, however, rejected Mantegna's static compositions in favour of a dynamic sense of movement. In contrast to the painted wings, the carved and painted centre of the altarpiece, showing the "Coronation of the Virgin," exhibits no Italian characteristics. Instead, its intricate carving that accentuates minute detail, the bright polychrome and sweeping draperies are wholly northern in spirit.

The "Expulsion of the Money Changers from the Temple," panel from the altarpiece by Michael Pacher, 1478–81; in the Pilgrimage Church of Sankt Wolfgang, in Upper Austria

Meyer Erwin—EB Inc.

In the "Altarpiece of the Church Fathers" (*c.* 1483; Alte Pinakothek, Munich) Pacher uses direct and reflected light to create a convincing spatial ambience within a shallow depth. His narrow niches are dominated by the four monumental figures of the Fathers of the Church. The back of the altarpiece exhibits scenes from the life of St. Wolfgang and is notable for its attenuated male nude, whose idealized form and sharp outline again reflect Pacher's knowledge of Mantegna's art.

Such late works as the "Betrothal of the Virgin" and the "Flagellation" (both *c.* 1484; Museum Mittelalterlicher Österreichischer Kunst, Vienna) repudiate his early dynamic compositions and introduce a new, static serenity. The faces and drapery are more idealized and more monumental than in his early works, and the figures are emphasized at the expense of the architectural background.

·Gothic painting developments **19**:376g

Pa Chin, pseudonym of LI YAO-T'ANG, also called LI FEI-KAN (b. 1904, Ch'eng-tu, Szechwan, China), anarchist writer whose novels and short stories achieved widespread popularity in the 1930s and '40s. The pen name Pa Chin was formed from the Chinese equivalents of the first and last syllables, respectively, of Bakunin and Kropotkin, the names of two Russian anarchists whom Li greatly admired.

Born to a wealthy gentry family, Li received a traditional Confucian education as well as training in more modern subjects such as foreign languages and literatures. While in school he developed socialist convictions and an interest in writing. Li's first novel, *Mieh-wang* ("Extinction"), appeared with great success in 1929, when he returned to China after two years of study in France. During the next four years Li published seven novels, most of them dealing with social concerns and attacking the traditional family system. Best known of these was the novel *Chia* ("The Family"), the first volume of the autobiographical trilogy *Chi-liu* ("Three Parts of the Torrent"), which was completed in 1940 with the publication of the second and third volumes, *Ch'un* ("Spring") and *Ch'iu* ("Autumn"). In these and other novels the influence of foreign writers, notably Turgenev and Zola, is apparent.

Li's work was frequently attacked by the Communists both for its content and its style, even though his numerous magazine articles and political activities on behalf of the left helped to create the emotional climate that allowed the intellectuals to accept the Communist revolution. For this reason, after the establishment of the People's Republic of China in 1949, Li was judged politically reliable and was elected to important literary and cultural organizations. Although he formally renounced his anarchist ideas in the late 1950s, he was never able to fully adapt himself to the new society. During the Great Proletarian Cultural Revolution (1966–69) he was labelled a counterrevolutionary and sharply criticized.

Li's works include more than 20 novels, several volumes of short stories, a collection of essays, translations of Soviet novels and treatises, and countless magazine articles. He also served as the editor of Chinese journals.

Pachino, town, Siracusa province, southeastern Sicily, Italy. Industries include production of wine and olive oil and canning of tuna fish. There are salt mines in the district. Pop. (1975 est.) mun., 23,671.
36°42′ N, 15°06′ E

Pachisi, board game, called the national game of India by the British games historian R.C. Bell.

Four players in opposing partnerships of two attempt to move pieces around a cross-shaped track. Moves are determined by throws of cowrie shells or dice. Each player has four pieces, which begin at the centre space, move down the middle track nearest the player, and counterclockwise around the outer track of the board. The partnership whose pieces first complete the course by returning to the centre space is the winner.

Indian Pachisi board of cloth with painted wood pieces and cowrie shells as dice; in the collection of R.C. Bell

R.C. Bell

Marked squares along the course represent castles in which the occupying pieces cannot be captured. An occupied castle is open to the player's other pieces or those of his partner but closed to those of his opponents. Pieces resting on other squares are captured and sent back to the centre to begin again if an opposing piece lands on the square they occupy.

Pachisi, with slight modifications, has been patented and marketed under the names Ludo in Great Britain and Parcheesi in the United States.

·rules of play and board design **2**:1150e; illus.

Pachmann, Vladimir von, also called VLADIMIR DE PACHMAN (b. July 27, 1848, Odessa, Ukraine—d. Jan. 6, 1933, Rome), pianist known for his performances of Chopin. He studied in Vienna and made his debut in 1869 in Odessa. Though his early concerts were successful, he was extremely self-critical and withdrew for long periods of study. He later toured widely in Europe and the U.S. Pachmann's performances were almost exclusively devoted to works of Chopin, which he played in an intimate, miniature style. His playing was noted for its fine pianissimo shadings and for its smooth touch. His concerts were enlivened by his eccentric gestures, muttered comments, and remarks addressed to the audience.

Pachomius, Saint (b. *c.* 290, probably in Upper Egypt—d. 346), founder of Christian cenobitic (communal) monasticism, whose rule (book of observances) for monks is the earliest extant.

Of Egyptian origin, Pachomius encountered Coptic, or Egyptian, Christianity among his cohorts in the Roman emperor Constantine's North African army and, on leaving the military *c.* 314, withdrew alone into the wilderness at Chenoboskion, near his Thebian home. Soon after, he joined the hermit Palemon and a colony of solitaries (anchorites) in the same area at Tabennisi, on the east bank of the Nile. With a talent for administration, Pachomius built the first monastic enclosure, replacing the scattered hermits' shelters, and he drew up a common daily program providing for proportioned periods of work and prayer patterned about a cooperative economic and disciplinary regimen.

This Rule was the first instance in Christian monastic history of the use a cenobitic, or uniform communal, existence as the norm and to depart from the individualistic, exclusively contemplative nature of previous religious life. Pachomius, moreover, instituted a monarchic monastic structure that viewed the relationship of the religious superior's centralized authority over the community as the symbolic image of God evoking obedient response from man striving to overcome his egocentrism by self-denial and charity. By the time he died, Pachomius had founded 11 monasteries, numbering more than 7,000 monks and nuns.

Though none of Pachomius' manuscripts have survived, his life and bibliography have been preserved by the 5th-century historian Palladius in his *Lausiac History*. The Rule of Pachomius is extant only in the early-5th-century Latin translation of St. Jerome.

·Christian monasticism development **4**:500g
·monastic cenobitism organization **12**:338b

Pachuca, in full PACHUCA DE SOTO, capital city, Hidalgo state, east central Mexico. One of the first settlements in New Spain, it lies in a rich mining district in the Sierra Madre Oriental, 7,959 ft (2,426 m) above sea level. Its first silver mine was discovered in 1534, although it is said that some of the mines were known to pre-Columbian Indians. The nearby Real del Monte mine, begun in 1739 and still in operation, producing 10 percent of Mexico's silver, is one of the most extensive mining properties in the world. The patio, or Mexican, process of separating silver from the ore by amalgamation with quicksilver was perfected in Pachuca by Bartolomé de Medina in the 16th century, and the Pachuca tank used in the cyanide process was developed there in the 20th century. The government has sought to counteract declining mineral production by increasing industrialization. Industries include smelting works and numerous metallic ore reduction plants. Pachuca has a school of mines and metallurgy, founded in 1877, and it houses the Autonomous University of Hidalgo (1961). It is accessible by railroad and highway. Pop. (1970) 83,892.
20°07′ N, 98°44′ W

·colonial design and expansion problems **12**:70f
·map, Mexico **12**:68

Pachycephala (bird): *see* thickhead.

Pachycephalosaurus, genus of large and unusual dinosaurs found as fossils in Late Cretaceous deposits of North America (the Cretaceous Period began 136,000,000 years ago and lasted 71,000,000 years). *Pachycephalosaurus*, which grew to be about 9 metres (30 feet) long, was a biped with very strong hindlimbs and much less developed forelimbs. The unusual and distinctive feature of *Pachycephalosaurus* is the high, domelike skull formed by a thick mass of solid bone grown over the tiny brain. The growth of bone obliterated normal openings found in the skull of related forms. Abundant bony knobs in front and at the sides of the skull further added to the unusual appearance. *Pachycephalosaurus* and closely related forms thus are known as the bone-headed dinosaurs; most are much smaller than *Pachycephalosaurus*, such as *Stegoceras*, which grew to a length of about two metres (six feet).

Debate has centred on the adaptive significance of the great mass of bone atop the skulls of the bone-heads. It has been suggested that the bony skull was employed as a battering ram to ward off attacks by predatory forms or in combat with other bone-heads, perhaps for mates or territory. It has also been suggested that it may have been related to some disfunction of the pituitary gland; yet it is hard to imagine how such a trait, if related to pituitary disfunction, could have become established in several different genera.

Pachycormiformes, an extinct order of fish of the class Actinopterygii of the phylum Chordata.

·characteristics and classification **7**:342g; illus. 339

pachyderm, any member of a thick-skinned mammal group (including various species of elephant, rhinoceros, hippopotamus, walrus, and pig) in an obsolete 19th-century classification. In current usage this term usually refers to an elephant (*q.v.*).

Pachydiscus seppenradensis, a species of fossil ammonite mollusk of the family Pachydiscidae (class Cephalopoda).

·shell size **3**:1149e

Pachymeres, George (b. 1242, Nicaea, now Iznik, Tur.—d. *c.* 1310, Constantinople, now Istanbul), considered the outstanding Byzantine liberal arts scholar of the 13th century, whose chronicle of the Palaeologus emperors constitutes the primary historical source for that period.

With the fall in 1262 of the Latin Eastern Empire (established at the conquest of Constantinople in 1204 by the Flemish count Baldwin I) and the return of the Byzantine emperor Michael VIII Palaeologus, Pachymeres went to Constantinople and was ordained to the Greek Orthodox ministry. In addition to ecclesiastical and political functions, he taught the liberal arts at the patriarchal academy of the basilica of Hagia Sophia (Holy Wisdom).

Strongly opposed to union with the Latin Church, Pachymeres recorded with studied neutrality the tumultuous upheavals marking the reigns of two Palaeologus emperors, the pro-unionist Michael VIII and the anti-unionist Andronicus II. This chronicle, the *Hrōmaikē historia* ("Roman"; *i.e.*, Eastern, "History"), a 13-volume continuation of the work of George Acropolites, the 13th-century statesman and historian, is Pachymeres' principal work. Described by modern scholars as a unique eyewitness record of this period, *Hromaikē historia* emphasizes the theological nature of the events it describes, a characteristic that marked subsequent Byzantine chronicles. Thus, Pachymeres depicts the period of the two Palaeologus emperors in the light of the East–West dispute over ecclesiastical authority and orthodoxy; *i.e.*, Eastern patriarchal autonomy versus Western papal supremacy. His impartiality is shown by his objective treatment of John Beccus, the late-13th-century theologian–patriarch of Constantinople, who collaborated in a temporary union with the Western Church. The admixture of classical Homeric style, theological language, and personal neologisms, however, produced a difficult text that required two revisions for greater clarity. Its turgid style notwithstanding, *Hrōmaikē Historia* is particularly valuable for its accounts of Latin military campaigns (under the title of Christian Crusades) throughout Byzantium; the construction of frontier defenses against Slavic and Turkish incursions; and the Byzantine feudal nobility's growth, by astute manipulation of land deeds at the expense of centralized imperial authority.

Writing on a wide range of subjects, Pachymeres also composed a theological treatise on the doctrine of the Trinity (one God in three persons). Mediating the controversy between the Greek and Latin speculative interpretation of the Holy Spirit's relationship to the Father and the Son, he proposed a compromise formula suggested by the 8th-century Greek Church Father John of Damascus.

Pachymeres' lectures at Constantinople's academy produced notes that later formed the *Syntagma tōn tessarōn mathēmatōn* ("Compendium of Four Mathematics"), a type of classical handbook on four liberal arts disciplines: mathematics, music, geometry, and astronomy. The *Syntagma*, with its innovative use of Arabic numbers, became the standard academic text in Greek Byzantine culture.

Other works include a compendium of the philosophy of Aristotle, of which only the book on logic has been published; a paraphrase of texts from the 5th-century Neoplatonist Pseudo-Dionysius the Areopagite; and a series of exercises in rhetoric. The *Hrōmaikē historia* is contained in Pachymeres' edited works in the series *Patrologia Graeca*, vol. 3, 4, 143, 144 (1866). The *Syntagma* is available in the critical edition by P. Tannery and C. Stéphanou (1940).

Pachyptila (bird): *see* prion.

Pachyramphus (bird): *see* becard.

Pacifastacus: *see* crayfish.

Pacific, Atlantic, and Mediterranean suites, division of the rocks of the Tertiary and Recent periods into groups according to their petrographic characteristics. The Atlantic and Pacific suites were defined on the basis of apparent differences in the rock types surrounding these ocean basins; the Pacific suite was typified by calcic and calc-alkalic rocks, whereas the Atlantic suite had a more alkaline nature. The Atlantic suite was subdivided later, such that soda-rich rocks were called the Atlantic suite, and potash-rich rocks were named the Mediterranean suite. Somewhat different tectonic characteristics were attributed to these three basins, and they were called provinces with the same names.

More recent data have shown that the distinction between these three provinces is not so clear as originally believed. The tectonics of each province are complex, and the rocks of each are more variable than the classification into three magma types would indicate. Undersaturated alkaline rocks (Atlantic type) do tend to be associated with regions of crustal stability, and oversaturated calcic rocks (Pacific type) are more typical of folded belts bordering the continents; but, because neither province can be limited to such areas and because rock types of all three provinces may occur in one province, some authors have abandoned the use of these terms.

Pacific, War of the (1879–84), conflict involving Chile, Bolivia, and Peru; resulted in Chilean annexation of valuable disputed territory on the Pacific coast. It grew out of a dispute between Chile and Bolivia over control of a part of the Atacama Desert that lies between the 23rd and 26th parallels on the Pacific coast of South America. The territory contained valuable mineral resources, particularly sodium nitrate.

National borders in the region had never been definitively established; the two countries negotiated a treaty that recognized the 24th parallel as their boundary and that gave Chile the right to share the export taxes on the mineral resources of Bolivia's territory between the 23rd and 24th parallels. But Bolivia subsequently became dissatisfied at having to share its taxes with Chile and feared Chilean seizure of its coastal region where Chilean interests already controlled the mining industry.

Peru's interest in the conflict stemmed from its traditional rivalry with Chile for hegemony on the Pacific coast. Also, the prosperity of the Peruvian government's *guano* (fertilizer) monopoly and the thriving nitrate industry in Peru's Tarapacá Province were related to mining activities on the Bolivian coast.

In 1873 Peru agreed secretly with Bolivia to a mutual guarantee of their territories and independence. In 1874 Chilean–Bolivian relations were ameliorated by a revised treaty under which Chile relinquished its share of export taxes on minerals shipped from Bolivia, and Bolivia agreed not to raise taxes on Chilean enterprises in Bolivia for 25 years. Amity was broken in 1878 when Bolivia tried to increase the taxes of the Chilean Antofagasta Nitrate Company over the protests of the Chilean government. When Bolivia threatened to confiscate the company's property, Chilean armed forces occupied the port city of Antofagasta, on Feb. 14, 1879. Bolivia then declared war on Chile and called upon Peru for help. Chile declared war on both Peru and Bolivia (April 5, 1879).

Chile occupied the Bolivian coastal region (Antofagasta Province) easily and then took the offensive against more powerful Peru. Naval victories at Iquique (May 21, 1879) and Angamos (Oct. 8, 1879) enabled Chile to control the sea approaches to Peru. A Chilean army then invaded Peru. A United States attempt at mediation failed in October 1880, and Chilean forces occupied the Peruvian capital of Lima the following January. Peruvian resistance continued for three more years, with U.S. encouragement. Finally, on Oct. 20, 1883, Peru and Chile signed the Treaty of Ancón, by which Tarapacá Province was ceded to the latter.

Chile was also to occupy the provinces of Tacna and Arica for ten years, after which a plebiscite was to be held to determine their nationality. But the two countries failed for decades to agree on what terms the plebiscite was to be conducted. This diplomatic dispute over Tacna and Arica was known as the Question of the Pacific. Finally, in 1929, through the good offices of the United States, an accord was reached by which Chile kept Arica; Peru reacquired Tacna and received $6,000,000 indemnity and other concessions.

During the war Peru suffered the loss of thousands of people and much property, and at its end a seven-month civil war ensued; the nation foundered economically for decades thereafter. In 1884 a truce between Bolivia and Chile gave the latter control of the entire Bolivian coast (Antofagasta Province) with its nitrate, copper, and other mineral industries; a treaty in 1904 made this arrangement permanent. In return Chile agreed to build a railroad connecting the Bolivian capital of La Paz with the port of Arica and guaranteed freedom of transit for Bolivian commerce through Chilean ports and territory. But Bolivia continued its attempt to break out of its landlocked situation through the La Plata river system to the Atlantic coast, an effort that led ultimately to the Chaco War (1932–35).

Ancon, Treaty of
- Chilean acquisition of Atacama Desert **2**:255a
- Peru–Chile dispute settlement **14**:134g

- Bolivian territory and economy affected **3**:10g
- Chilean victory and repercussions **4**:256e
- Chilean victory and results **2**:255a
- Tacna-Arica dispute, Ancón treaty, and 1930 outcome **14**:134g

Pacific anticyclone, atmospheric eddy occurring northeast of Hawaii.
- Hawaii climate influences **8**:674a

Pacification of 1917, Dutch political compromise providing state support for religious schools and universal male suffrage.
- religious education conflict settlement **11**:153d

Pacific Coast Mountains (North America): *see* Pacific Coast Ranges.

Pacific Coast Ranges 13:824, major physical feature of western North America, running parallel to the coasts of the U.S. states California, Washington, and Oregon for 4,500 mi (7,242 km) and extending both north into Canada and south into Mexico. The ranges include many high points, including Mt. Rainier (14,410 ft [4,392 m]) in the Cascade Range and Mt. Logan (19,524 ft [5,951 m]) in the St. Elias Range.

The text article covers the history of the study of the region, and the relief divisions, geological history, climate and vegetation, and human development of the Pacific Coast Ranges.

40°00′ N, 123°30′ W

REFERENCES in other text articles:
- California mountain system linkage and elevation features **3**:615d
- Canadian physiographic features **3**:714e
- Cordilleran mountain-building process **13**:181f
- Cretaceous and Cenozoic orogeny **18**:152c
- map, United States **18**:908
- Oregon range landform features **13**:673a
- regional gravity anomalies **6**:23c; illus.
- sectional formation variation **18**:914c; map 906
- Washington mountain range features **19**:618e
- Western Cordillera and Intermontaine regional formation and features **18**:913g

Pacific Coast Stock Exchange, in San Francisco, California, was established in 1957 as the consolidation of the San Francisco and the Los Angeles Stock Exchanges.
- San Francisco financial importance **16**:220g

Pacific Fur Company: *see* American Fur Company.

Pacific Great Eastern Railway: *see* British Columbia Railway.

Pacific Grove, resort and residential city, Monterey County, western California, U.S., on Monterey Bay adjoining Monterey. Founded in 1874 by Methodists as a religious retreat, the city remains a centre for conferences of religious and other groups. Pacific Grove is the northern terminus of the scenic Seventeen-Mile Drive from Carmel. The famous Butterfly Trees on Lighthouse Avenue are covered each winter by monarch butterflies that migrate from Canada and Alaska. Point Pinos Lighthouse is on the bay. The city is the site of the Hopkins Marine Station of Stanford University and has a natural-history museum. The Feast of Lanterns and the Butterfly Festival are annual events. Inc. 1889. Pop. (1980) 15,755.

36°38′ N, 121°56′ W

Pacific Gyral, clockwise surface oceanic current over the Canada and Beaufort deeps in the Beaufort Sea (Arctic Ocean). Little is known about the Pacific Gyral because its currents pile ice against the coasts of Canada and Alaska, making navigation difficult.

Pacific high, or HAWAIIAN HIGH, large, atmospheric high-pressure centre over the eastern Pacific Ocean, west of North America. The ocean's low summer temperatures, relative to those of the continents, cause the high to expand and bring dry weather to the North American west coast; in winter, the high weakens and contracts and shifts southward slightly. Its July mean sea-level pressure is 1,026 millibars (30.3 inches of mercury).
- wind systems and mid-Pacific climate **19**:868c; illus. 865

Pacific Islanders Protection Act (Britain, 1872): *see* blackbirding.

Pacific Island Labourers' Act (1901), legislation of the new Commonwealth of Australia that provided for the deportation by 1906 of all Kanaka (South Pacific islands) labourers, thus ensuring the breakup of the plantation system on which Australia's sugar industry had been based (*see* Kanaka Question). An early expression of the commonwealth's anti-Asian immigration policy (*see* White Australia Policy), the act was conceived in response to a long-standing demand of Queensland's white labourers and small farmers for abolition of cheap Kanaka labour and for the breakup of the large sugar-growing estates. The act called for the abolition of Kanaka recruitment after 1904 and the deportation of all Kanakas by the end of 1906. A 1906 amendment to the act exempted from deportation certain categories of Kanakas, including those resident in Australia before September 1879, those who owned land in freehold, and those who were married to non-Kanaka women. As expected, the deportation of the "black" labourers led to the displacement of the large estates by small holdings, which the commonwealth government undertook to subsidize.

Pacific Islands 13:826, broadly, all the islands in the Pacific Ocean, more specifically, the Melanesia, Micronesia, and Polynesia groupings. In the stricter usage, the islands exist mainly in the area bounded by 12° N and 25° S and 130° E and 130° W. Exceptions include the Mariana Islands, extending northward; the Hawaiian Islands, lying on the Tropic of Cancer to the northeast; New Zealand to the south; and Easter Island far to the southeast. There are more than 10,000 islands, with a land area of a little less than 500,000 sq mi (1,300,000 sq km).

The text article, which deals with the islands included in the narrower usage, covers their ecosystems, including island types, climate, soils, vegetation, and animal life; people and population, including aboriginal groupings, historical associations, and population dynamics; and political and economic systems in the islands, including administrative groupings, communication networks, and economic development.

REFERENCES in other text articles:
- cuisine ingredients, methods, and menu **7**:944f
- forestry and world timber use **7**:533h; tables 534
- Micronesian geocultural fragmentation **12**:122b
- Oceania's diverse physical features **13**:443f
- rain forest varieties, characteristics, and locations **10**:337c; map
- Tasman's voyages and discoveries **17**:1070h
- U.S. territorial administration **18**:1003c *passim* to 1006d
- wood and wood production, table 2 **19**:924
- wood products consumption, graph 8 **19**:924

Pacific Islands, Trust Territory of the 13:831, United Nations strategic area trusteeship administered by the United States, consisting of more than 2,000 islands in the Pacific Ocean north of the Equator and situated almost entirely in Micronesia. The Caroline, Mariana (except Guam), and Marshall islands are the principal groups. (For statistical details, *see* p. 666.)

The text article covers the territory's physical geography, climate and vegetation, animal life, landscape under human settlement, people and population, economy, transportation, administration, social conditions, and prospects for the future.

REFERENCES in other text articles:
- acquisition, administration, and population **18**:1003f
- animals' biogeographic characteristics **2**:1005e
- Asian geography **2**:159f
- Bikini resettlement after A-bomb tests **2**:989b
- map, Australia and Oceania **2**:383
- Melanesian culture and society **11**:864g
- Micronesian response to administration **12**:126c
- politics, area, and population **13**:829g; table 830
- U.S. political administration **13**:448a
- wood product world production, table 2 **19**:924

Pacific mackerel (*Pneumatophorus diego*), important food fish of the Pacific coast of North America.
- Perciform fish commercial importance **7**:348e

Pacific Mail Steamship Company, steamship lines in service between California and Panama (1847–81).
- San Francisco shipping importance **16**:220f

Pacific maritime air, vast body of air that originates over the North Pacific Ocean and dominates the weather conditions of the west coast of North America in both summer and winter. The type of weather to be expected from Pacific maritime air depends largely on its trajectory, whether cyclonic (counterclockwise) around a deep low-pressure area centred in the Gulf of Alaska or anticyclonic (clockwise) around the Pacific high-pressure cell centred at 30° N, 135° W in winter and 38° N, 150° W in summer. The cyclonically moving air is usually accompanied by high winds, showers and squalls, low ceilings, and poor visibility, affecting primarily the portion of the coast north of San Francisco (40° N). The air flowing around the Pacific high is much more stable and is usually accompanied by stratiform clouds and fog, fair to poor visibility, and a strong subsidence inversion below 4,000 ft (1,200 metres). As the Pacific maritime air moves eastward across the continent, it loses much of its moisture on the windward slopes of the mountain ranges and is gradually transformed into a continental air mass. When this air is caught up in the circulation around a semipermanent high-pressure cell that overlies the Great Basin area of the western U.S. in the fall and winter, mild temperatures, clear skies, and little vertical mixing may result.

Pacific National Exhibition, annual agricultural event held in Vancouver, British Columbia.
·British Columbia's cultural life **3**:300h

Pacific North Equatorial Current: *see* equatorial currents.

Pacifico, David: *see* Don Pacifico Affair.

Pacific Ocean **13**:836, largest of the world's oceans, extends from the Antarctic region to the Arctic and lies between Asia and Australia to the west and North and South America to the east. It has an area, excluding adjacent seas, of about 64,000,000 sq mi (166,000,000 sq km). The north to south distance from Bering Strait to Antarctica is more than 9,600 mi (15,500 km). The Pacific attains its greatest breadth, 11,500 nautical mi, along the parallel of 5° N between Colombia and Malaysia.

The text article covers the ocean's relief, principal ridges and basins, islands, geology, climate, temperature and salinity, hydrology, marine life, bottom deposits, economic resources, resource exploitation, history, trade and communications, and prospects for the future.

REFERENCES in other text articles:
·area, volume, depth, and marginal seas **13**:482g; table 484
·Bering Sea in geographical and hydrological relation **2**:846c; map 845
·calcium carbonate saturation **7**:1032g
·Cenozoic volcanism and earthquakes **6**:17f
·China Sea physiography and hydrography **4**:405e; map
·Cretaceous coastal mountain building, volcanism, and rock series **5**:250c; table 248
discovery and exploration
·Balboa's discovery and significance **10**:692c; map 701
·Balboa's sighting and claim **2**:610f
·Cook's voyages of discovery **5**:130h; map
·Magellan's discovery of extensive size **18**:652b
·Magellan voyage route and experiences **7**:1041h
·iceberg and sea ice extent **9**:155h; illus. 159
islands
·arc composition and evolution **9**:1026a; map
·Indonesian islands' structure **9**:458b
·Pacific Islands Trust Territory **13**:831d
·types, distribution, and peoples **13**:826b
·manganese nodules metals' reserves, table 7 **13**:504
·North American continent evolution **13**:178b; maps 176
·ocean basin structure and composition **13**:433c
·ocean current systems **13**:439f; illus. 438
·paleogeography and fossil distribution **13**:909a
·physiography and elevation **6**:47h; illus. 42
·ridge occurrence and features **13**:474g
·Tertiary volcanic activity **18**:151g
·volcanic distribution and plate motion **12**:579c
·wave velocity and amplitude **19**:658e

TRUST TERR. OF THE PACIFIC ISLANDS

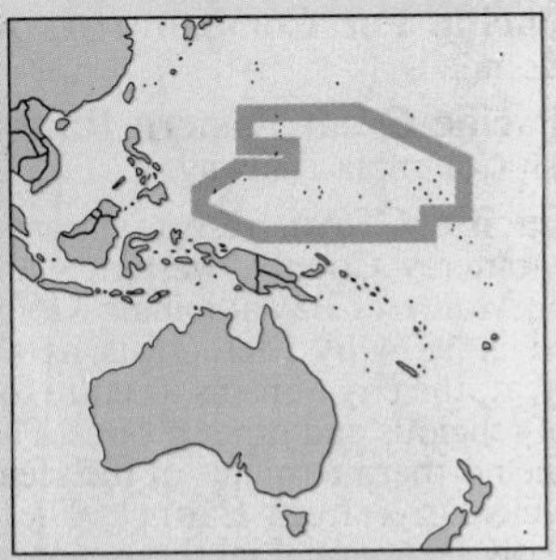

Official name: Trust Territory of the Pacific Islands under United States Administration.
Location: northern Pacific.
Political status: trust territory (United States).
Official language: English.
Official religion: none.
Area: 700 sq mi, 1,813 sq km.
Population: (1967 census) 91,448; (1971 estimate) 107,000.
Capital: Saipan.
Monetary unit: 1 United States dollar (U.S. $) = 100 cents.

Demography
Population: (1971 estimate) density 152.9 per sq mi, 59.0 per sq km; urban–rural distribution—no data available; (1970) male 51.29%, female 48.71%; (1970) under 15 43.0%, 15–29 25.7%, 30–44 13.4%, 45–59 10.2%, 60–74 5.2%, 75 and over 2.4%.*
Vital statistics: (1970) births per 1,000 population 34.9, deaths per 1,000 population 5.7, natural increase per 1,000 population 29.2; life expectancy at birth—no data available; (1969) major causes of death (per 10,000 population)—malignant neoplasms 6.2; influenza and pneumonia 6.0; diseases of the heart 4.4; accidents, all types 4.1.
Ethnic composition: Micronesian except for about 1,000 Polynesians on the islands of Kapingamarangi and Nukuoro and a scattering of other racial groups. *Religious affiliation* (mid-1960s): approximately 50% Roman Catholic, the remainder predominantly Protestant; no exact figures available.

National accounts
Budget (1969–70). Revenue: U.S. $52,894,456 (grants from U.S. Congress 89.9%, unobligated funds brought forward 6.3%, territorial taxes 1.6%, direct U.S. appropriation 1.1%). Expenditures: U.S. $50,832,957 (public works, maintenance, operations, and rehabilitation 22.7%; education 21.4%; transport and communications 13.3%; health 10.6%; administration 9.8%; resources and development 6.9%). *Total national debt:* no data available. *Tourism* (1969). Receipts from visitors: U.S. $906,484. Expenditures by nationals abroad: no data available.

Domestic economy
Gross national product (GNP; at current market prices, 1970): U.S. $40,000,000 (U.S. $360 per capita).
Origin of gross domestic product: no data available.
Production (metric tons except as noted). Agriculture, forestry, hunting, fishing (1969–70): coconuts 15,897; copra 12,800; cocoa 14; vegetables 838; citrus fruit 79; breadfruit 2,279; bananas 1,658; taro 2,461; yams, sweet potatoes, and tapioca 2,405; swine 19,875 head; fish catch 368.
Energy: (1970) installed electrical capacity 20,740 kW, production—no data available.
Persons economically active: (1967) employable population 41,000 (44.8%), unemployed—no data available.
Price and earnings indexes: no data available.
Land use (1970): agricultural and under permanent cultivation 42.8%, forested 22.1%, meadows and pastures 11.2%, other 23.8%.*

Foreign trade
Imports (1969–70): U.S. $20,920,318 (foodstuffs 33.4%, of which, rice 6.8%, canned meat 5.2%; petroleum, oil, and lubricants 15.4%; building materials 11.1%; machinery 7.6%; clothing and textiles 7.4%; milk 5.8%). *Major import sources:* United States 48.1%, Japan 31.5%.
Exports (1969–70): U.S. $4,176,003 (copra 64.3%, fish 23.7%, handicrafts and shells 3.5%, meat 3.2%). *Major export destination:* Japan 66.9%.

Transport and communication
Transport. Railroads (1970): none. Roads (1970): total length 512 mi, 824 km (paved 103 mi, 166 km; unpaved 409 mi, 658 km). Vehicles (1970): passenger cars 2,696, trucks and buses 2,348. Merchant marine (1970): vessels (over 1,000 gross tons) none. Air transport: (1970) passenger mi 59,793,000, passenger km 96,228,000; short ton-mi cargo 1,174,988, metric ton-km cargo 1,715,453; (1971) airports with scheduled flights 6.
Communication. Daily newspapers (1970): none. Radios (1969): total number of receivers 36,000 (1 per 2.5 persons). Television (1971): receivers 1,500 (1 per 60.6 persons); broadcasting stations 1. Telephones (1971): 5,680 (1 per 16 persons).

Education and health

Education (1969–70)†:	schools	teachers	students	student–teacher ratio
primary (age 6 to 14)	217	1,210	28,360	23.4
secondary (age 12 to 16)	21	260	5,186	19.9
teacher training	...	...	2,129	...

College graduates: none. *Literacy* (1960): total population literate (over 14) 70–75%.
Health: (1970) doctors 50 (1 per 1,819 persons); (1969) hospital beds 502 (1 per 181 persons); daily per capita caloric intake—no data available (FAO recommended minimum requirement 2,610 calories).

*Percentages do not add to 100.0 because of rounding. †Higher education is received outside of the country.

Pacific Scandal (1872–73), charges of corruption against Canadian Prime Minister John Macdonald in awarding the contract for a transcontinental railroad; the incident resulted in the temporary downfall of Macdonald's Conservative administration.

One of the conditions under which British Columbia entered the Dominion of Canada (1871) was that a railway to link that province with the east be constructed within 10 years. In 1872 a contract for construction of such a railway was awarded to a syndicate headed by Sir Hugh Allan, a Canadian shipowner and financier. Allan was a heavy contributor to the Conservative campaign in the 1872 election, and Macdonald's Liberal opponents accused him of having awarded the contract in return for this financial support (April 1873). The charges led to the resignation of the Macdonald government on November 5 and to the cancellation of the contract. In the election of January 1874, the Conservatives were badly beaten.

Pacific South Equatorial Current: *see* equatorial currents.

Pacific tarpon (flower): *see* oxeye.

Pacific yew (tree): *see* western yew.

pacifism and nonviolent movements **13**:845, are aimed at abolishing or minimizing the use of violence in human affairs. Pacifism is taken here to embrace the sum of all endeavours for realizing a lasting, or if possible a perpetual, peace among peoples, in the belief that such peace is historically possible; and nonviolent movements refers here to sects or movements of small minorities convinced that the individual ethic of "negative actions" (nonresistance, sufferance) can be transmitted to the collective arena.

The text article covers the relations of the two movements and the genesis and dynamics of war and peace, including inherent conflict and its control and limiting of the scope of war (both geographically and demographically); and it traces pacifism through the history of man—in Greek, Roman, medieval Christian, and modern times. It then deals with nonviolent movements in modern times, including that of the Protestant peace sects, Gandhi's nonviolent activism, the United States civil rights movement, and tendencies to return to violence. A critical evaluation in the light of ethical and pragmatic principles follows, with some final perspectives on the problem of violence.

REFERENCES in other text articles:
·Amarna revolution speculation **6**:474f
Anabaptist positions **15**:552d
·Mennonite precepts of love and way of the cross **11**:904g *passim* to 905d
·Menno's influence **11**:906a
·worship effects of Mennonite stance **19**:1015e
·Black Muslim's political beliefs **2**:1094d
·Bose's relationship to Gandhi **3**:53b
·Brethren church beliefs and practices **3**:156h
·Crusades social and religious milieu **5**:298f
·Diesel's social philosophy **5**:726a
·early Christians and military service **4**:536c
·Egypt 18th-dynasty peace party theory **6**:472e
·Einstein's wartime resistance and leadership **6**:511h *passim* to 513a
Gandhi
·Hindu ideological basis **8**:919c
·initiation of satyagraha **7**:876b
·political redirection of Hinduism **8**:900d
·strategy for independence **12**:945f
·Garrison's prewar policy **7**:913e
·Jain principles of ahiṃsā **10**:10e
·Martin Luther King's role in the civil rights movement **10**:471h
·Mo-tzu philosophy **12**:577c
·Niebuhr's responsible politics **13**:74h
·Quaker anti-war position in colonies **7**:743c *passim* to 743g
·Quaker principles **7**:745b
·religious support for social action **15**:610a
·Tilak's resistance to British in India **18**:406f
·Vitoria conscientious objection theory **19**:493g

RELATED ENTRIES in the *Ready Reference and Index: for*
nonviolent movements: see civil disobedience; pariah; psychological warfare
pacifist problematics: conscientious objector; conscription; just war

pacing (horse gait): *see* harness racing; pacer.

pacinian corpuscle, oval, onion-like structure serving as the terminal capsule of certain sensory nerve endings, particularly found in the deeper skin and subcutaneous tissues of the hands and feet. They are thought to be involved in the sensation of pressure and also occur in and around muscles, joints, ligaments, and tendons. They are named for the 19th-century Italian anatomist Filippo Pacini, who first described them.
·pressure reception in vertebrates **11**:802f
·skin senses and nerve terminals **16**:549a; illus. 550
·structure and function in man **18**:447b

Paciola, Lucas, 15th-century Italian painter.
·Leonardo's scientific studies **10**:811c

Pacioli, Lucas (1450–1520), Italian monk who wrote the pioneer work on double-entry bookkeeping, dated 1494.
·algebraic method development **11**:662g
·bookkeeping by double-entry system **3**:37e

pack, in zoology, social group of cooperatively-hunting predators.
·animal social behaviour patterns **16**:942e
·dog suitability for domestication **5**:929c

Pack, Otto von (b. 1480?—d. Feb. 8, 1537, Brussels), German politician whose intrigues and forgeries almost caused a general war between Germany's Catholic and Protestant princes in 1528.

A Saxon nobleman, Pack studied law at the University of Leipzig, after which he entered the service of George, duke of Saxony. By 1519 most important governmental matters were entrusted to him, and he represented his ruler at the Reichstage (imperial diets) from 1522 to 1526. His perpetual lack of funds, however, soon led him into a number of fraudulent schemes. The most serious of these became known as the Pack Affair (Packsche Händel). After a meeting between the emperor Ferdinand I and a number of Catholic princes at Breslau (1527), Pack reported to Philip the Magnanimous, landgrave of Hesse, that an offensive alliance had been formed against Germany's Protestant rulers. Philip immediately formed a defensive league with the elector John the Steadfast of Saxony (1528) and attacked the cities of Würzburg and Bamberg. Simultaneously, he published a copy of the alleged Catholic treaty, provided by Pack. The document was immediately exposed as a forgery, but Philip, unconvinced, protected the culprit until 1529. After being expelled from Hesse, Pack became a fugitive until captured and beheaded in Brussels almost seven years later.

packaging 13:854, art and technology of preparing a product for convenient transport, storage, and sale.

The text article covers the many forms and materials of containers for such general products as food and beverages; special packaging for fragile and hazardous materials; labelling and decoration; and packaging machinery and manufacturing techniques.

REFERENCES in other text articles:
·aluminum tank resistivity to acid **1**:644c
·coffee's special needs for aroma protection **4**:820c
·container ship design **16**:683e; illus.
·convenience-food packaging **7**:484d
·cosmetics industry manufacturing **5**:199a
·distilled liquor requirements **5**:904b
·egg container variations in other nations **6**:444b
·electroplating of tin cans with chromium **6**:693e
·film material production and use **4**:132b
·food preservation technology **7**:495d
·food quality control requirements **7**:488f
·hydrogen wet and dry holders **7**:927c
·jute and competitive materials **7**:278b
·meat freshness and protection **11**:752f
·milk storage problems and practices **5**:434e
·nylon plastics production and uses **14**:516c
·ray detection for liquid level gauging **15**:455f
·semiconductor package design **16**:516h
·spice environmental control **17**:506h
·textile industry and yarn production **18**:174a
·tin physicochemical properties and uses **18**:429b *passim* to 432a
·vegetables premarketing operations **19**:52c
·warehousing and space utilization **17**:711h

RELATED ENTRIES in the *Ready Reference and Index:*
aerosol container; barrel; bottle; drum

pack animals: *see* draft animals.

Packard, Martin E., 20th-century U.S. physicist.
·nuclear magnetic-resonance discovery **11**:306b

packen, measure of weight in U.S.S.R., equivalent to 1,083.38 pounds avoirdupois.
·weights and measures, table 5 **19**:734

packet, a passenger boat carrying mail and cargo on a regular schedule.
·trade influence on ship design **18**:665c

pack gun, a light weapon developed in the second half of the 19th century for use in mountain warfare. Pack guns could be broken down for carriage by packhorses or mules.
·introduction and use **8**:490d

pack ice: *see* icebergs and pack ice.

packing, manner in which solid units are arranged so that each is held in place by contact with surrounding units. Atoms exhibit packing when they combine in a solid substance (*see* crystal structure), and all larger units follow similar patterns. Packing may be disorderly, or it may be systematic and thus repetitive; six basic packing types are known, each based on a different arrangement of equal spheres. All types of packing, from systematic to random, are exhibited in nature, but generally the closest packing—that is, the one with the smallest pore spaces (void areas)—is preferred when particle size is uniform. In clastic sediments (those formed from pre-existing fragments), packing influences porosity and permeability.
·conglomerate clast–matrix ratios **4**:1110h; illus. 1111
·sedimentary rock properties **16**:468h

packing, in mathematics, a general term for a type of problem in combinatorial geometry that involves placement of figures of a given size or shape within another given figure—with greatest economy or subject to some other restriction. The problem of placement of a given number of spheres within a given volume of space is an example of packing problems.
·combinatorics theory and method **4**:948b *passim* to 951b
·Euclidean geometry principles **7**:1112d
·number theory principles **13**:375b

packing fraction, measure of the loss or gain of total mass of a group of nucleons when they form an atomic nucleus.
·isotopes and nuclear stability **9**:1055f

pack rat: *see* wood rat.

Pacorus, Parthian PKWR, sometimes called PACORUS I (d. 38 BC), a Parthian prince, son of King Orodes II (reigned *c.* 57–37/36 BC); he apparently never ascended the throne. In the summer of 51 BC he was sent to invade Syria with an army commanded by Osaces, an older warrior. Osaces, however, was killed in battle, and early the next year Orodes, learning that one of his satraps was conspiring to make Pacorus king, recalled his son. In 45 Pacorus intervened in Roman politics by leading a Parthian force to help one of Pompey's generals, who was besieged in Apamea (a city in northwestern Mesopotamia) by Augustus' forces.

Orodes later decided to support the refugee republican general Quintus Labienus; thus Pacorus led an army into Syria and Palestine while Labienus occupied Cilicia, in southwestern Anatolia, and overran southern Anatolia. In 39 Mark Antony sent Publius Ventidius against Labienus, who was defeated and killed. Pacorus returned to Syria, was lured into battle by Ventidius, and was also defeated and killed. His head was displayed in the cities of Syria to convince them of the futility of hoping for Parthian support against the Romans.
·Syrian surprise conquest for Parthians **9**:844a

Pacorus II, Parthian PKWR II, king of Parthia in ancient Persia (reigned AD 78–*c.* 115/116). Little is actually known of his reign,

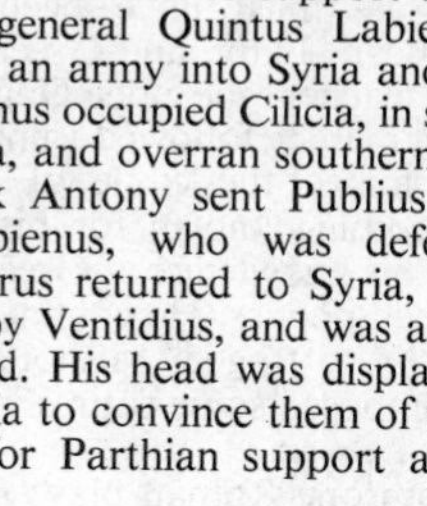

Pacorus II, coin, 2nd century AD

which seems to have been filled with rebellions and the rule of counterkings (Artabanus IV, Osroes, and Vologases II). In 110 Pacorus sold the Parthian client kingdom of Osroëne to Abgar VII, son of Izates, ruler of Adiabene. It is uncertain whether Pacorus was alive when the Roman emperor Trajan invaded Mesopotamia (114–115).

Pacta conventa (1098), agreement between the Hungarian king Coloman (Kálmán) and

Croatian representatives after Coloman had defeated the Croatians in battle. They accepted him as their king and he promised to respect their rights, which were outlined in detail in subsequent guarantees.
·Croatian national development **2**:619b

pacta sunt servanda, in contract law, doctrine by which informal promises were binding; in international law, the customary principle that valid treaties should be executed.
·contract law and influence of canon law **5**:124h

Pacte de Famille (French: Family Compact), the name by which three defensive alliances (1733, 1743, and 1761) between France and Spain are known, so called because both nations were ruled by members of the Bourbon family. The Pactes de Famille generally had the effect of involving Spain in European and colonial wars on the side of the French Bourbons (*e.g.*, the Seven Years' War, 1756–63; the U.S. War of Independence, 1775–83; and the first French Revolutionary War, 1793–95), but ceased to be effective after the dynasty was overthrown in France in the 1790s. *Major ref.* **3**:83b
·Charles III and colonial power balance **4**:57a
·Spain's fear of Britain **17**:434a

Pactum mutuae successionis (1703), Habsburg agreement whereby if one brother's male line died out the other's was to succeed it.
·Charles VI and Habsburg diplomacy **8**:96e

pactus (Latin: "agreement"), in early Germanic law, a name often given to compilations of laws, indicating that they were arrived at by agreement between the king and the people.

Pacuvius, Marcus (b. 220 BC, Brundisium—d. *c.* 130, Tarentum), considered the greatest Roman tragic dramatist before Accius. Bearer of an Oscan name and probably educated at Tarentum, he must have been equally at home in Oscan, Latin, and Greek, as was his uncle and teacher, the poet Quintus Ennius. As a young man he followed Ennius to Rome, where he joined the circle of the younger Scipio, becoming known for his painting as well as for his knowledge of Greek dramatists and of Greek poetics. He confined himself almost entirely to tragedy, although he is said to have composed some satires in the manner of Ennius.

Apart from one Roman play, *Paullus* (celebrating the victory of Lucius Aemilius Paullus over Perseus of Macedonia in 168 BC), 12 plays, translated from Greek originals, have survived in title only, and these may represent his entire output. Ingenious plots and those that gave ample scope for argument seem to have appealed to him. He did not follow his originals slavishly: Cicero praises him for having reduced the moanings of the wounded Odysseus, which he thought excessive in Sophocles; in another Sophoclean play he inserted a passage from Euripides that was altogether alien to the spirit of Sophocles.

Pacuvius was admired by Varro for his elevated style, more sedate than that of Ennius; Cicero considered him the greatest Roman writer of tragedy up to that time. His plays continued to be produced until the end of the Roman Empire.

pada, genre of religious song used in South India.
·Vaiṣṇava bhakti poets **17**:141h

Pädagogisches Skizzenbuch (Paul Klee): *see* Pedagogical Sketchbook.

padam, in the classical *bhārata-nāṭya* dance drama of India, songs that make up the fifth stage of the performance.
·bhārata-nāṭya dancer's interpretations **17**:160e

padān, a cotton veil worn to cover the nose and mouth in some Zoroastrian ceremonies.
·sacred clothing for initiation rites **3**:1179g

Padang, town, capital of Sumatera Barat (West Sumatra) province, Indonesia. The chief port on Sumatra's west coast and centre of the old Minangkabau society descended from Malay peoples, it was one of the earliest Dutch settlements (*c.* 1606) in Sumatra, and warehouses and a small fort were erected in 1667. The town prospered during the 19th century with the opening up of the highlands' mineral wealth, tourist traffic, and construction of coastal and inland railways. The port, formerly Emmahaven, at the mouth of the Padang River, is 5 mi (8 km) south of the town on Teluk Bayur (*teluk*, "bay"). Originally a bunker port for coal from the Umbilin coalfields, it now ships principally coffee and copra. There is an airport and Andalas University. Pop. (1971 prelim.) 196,339.
0°57′ S, 100°21′ E
·map, Indonesia **9**:460

Padang Highlands, region near the west coast, part of the Pegunungan (mountains) Barisan of Sumatera Barat (West Sumatra) province, Sumatra, Indonesia. Highest among several volcanoes is Gunung (mount) Merapi (9,485 ft [2,891 m]). A favourite resort area because of its climate, the region has superb scenery, the sources of three major rivers (the Kampar, Inderagiri, and Batanghari), and the Umbilin coalfields. Good roads connect with Padang, Medan, and Pakanbaru. The two major towns of the region are Bukittinggi and Sawahlunto, both connected by rail to Padang. The region produces rice, coffee, coconuts, tobacco, and tea and is homeland to the skillful, enterprising Minangkabau people.

Padārthatattvanirūpaṇa, an Indian philosophical text by Raghunātha Śiromaṇi (*c.* 1475–*c.* 1550).
·revision of philosophical categories **9**:327h

padauk, common name of several species of tropical trees of the genus *Pterocarpus*. Padauks of the Indo-Malaysia region tend to be larger than related species elsewhere. They are highly prized as shade trees and for their red or reddish-brown wood. The blood-red sap is used commercially; a red dyewood known as "Red Saunders," obtained from the padauk, was formerly exported in quantity from India.

Padaung (people): *see* Karen.

padāvalī, Bengali poetic genre.
·form and representative works **17**:143d

Padda opyzivora (bird): *see* Java sparrow.

Paddington, former metropolitan borough of London; since 1965, part of Westminster (*q.v.*).

paddlefish, or DUCKBILL CAT, archaic freshwater fish with paddlelike snout, wide mouth,

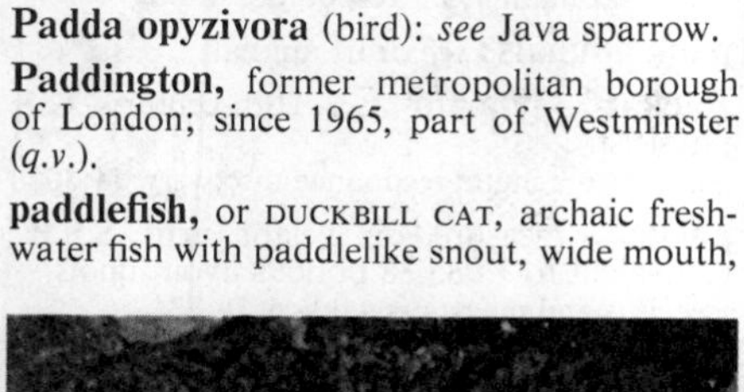

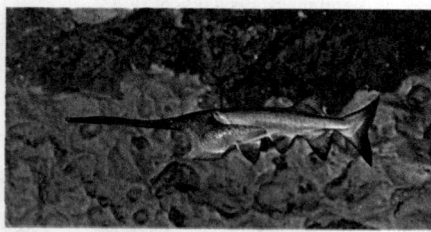

Paddlefish (*Polyodon spathula*)
Russ Kinne—Photo Researchers

smooth skin, and cartilaginous skeleton. A relative of the sturgeon, it is of the family Polyodontidae and the order Acipenseriformes. It feeds with mouth gaping open, gill rakers straining plankton from the water. The American paddlefish (*Polyodon spathula*), also called spoonbill, is greenish or gray and averages about 18 kilograms (40 pounds). It lives in open waters of the Mississippi Basin. The other known species (*Psephurus gladius*), a larger fish with more slender snout, inhabits the Yangtse River Basin. The flesh of both species is somewhat like catfish; the roe can be made into caviar.
·Chinese habitation **2**:170e
·traits, behaviour, and classification **4**:436f; illus.

paddle tennis, a small-scale form of tennis similar to a British shipboard game of the 1890s. Frank P. Beal, a New York City official, introduced paddle tennis on New York playgrounds in the early 1920s. It became popular, and national championship tournaments are still held in the United States. Platform tennis, a later development, is sometimes called paddle tennis.

Instead of rackets, short-handled, rectangular wooden bats, or paddles, are used with a slow-bouncing ball of sponge rubber. Courts at first were 39 by 18 feet (11.9 by 5.5 metres), about one-fourth the size of a regulation tennis court. Adults use a court measuring 44 by 20 feet.

Rules and scoring are similar to tennis, except that adults are allowed only one serve. If it is a fault, the server loses the point. Children may take two serves overhand and play on a smaller court.

paddle wheel, method of ship propulsion once widely employed but later almost entirely superseded by the screw propeller. Early experiments with steam-driven paddles acting as oars led several inventors, including Robert Fulton, to mount the paddles in a wheel form, either at the stern or at the side of the vessel. The device has a high degree of efficiency and

Paddle-wheel steamboat
By courtesy of the U.S. Corps of Engineers

is competitive even with modern propellers; its supplanting by the latter was due principally to two defects: the paddle wheel's vulnerability to damage in storms and its emergence from the water when the ship rolled heavily, which made steering difficult. For inland navigation these defects were insignificant, and paddle-wheel steamers long continued to operate on many rivers. *Major ref.* **16**:681f

Paddock, Charles William (1900–43), U.S. athlete.
·sprinting finish techniques **18**:543h

paddy, or PADI, also PADDY FIELD or RICE PADDY, a wet field on which rice is grown.
·China's soil distribution and use **4**:267b
·cultivation and milling procedures **3**:1165f; world production table

Paderborn, town, Nordrhein-Westfalen (North Rhine-Westphalia) *Land* (state), northwestern West Germany, on the Pader River—a small affluent of the Lippe formed from rain seepage on the slope of the Eggegebirge—which emerges from below the cathedral in about 200 springs. Paderborn was the birthplace of the Holy Roman Empire when Charlemagne met Pope Leo III there in 799 to discuss the founding of a German nation. Excavation of Charlemagne's palace began in 1964. Paderborn has been the seat of a bishopric from 805; it joined the Hanseatic League in the 13th century. It was ruled by

The cathedral (left) and Abdingshofkirche (right), Paderborn, W.Ger.
Toni Schneiders—Bruce Coleman Inc.

prince-bishops from *c.* 1100 until 1802, when it passed to Prussia under an agreement with France.

Massive destruction in World War II greatly altered the town's appearance, but some old buildings survived and many have been restored. Particularly notable are the three-gabled Renaissance town hall (1613–16), the Baroque Franciscan church (1681) with a fine facade by Antonio Petrini, and the cathedral (11th–13th centuries) with a typically Westphalian tower and a monumental carved portal. Other buildings include several 11th–13th century churches, the classical *Gymnasium* (high school; 1612), the philosophy and theology academy, and the Jesuit church (1682–86). The diocesan museum contains the "Madonna" of Bishop Imad, an important 11th-century sculpture.

A road and rail junction and cultural centre, Paderborn is the market and export centre for the surrounding agricultural region; Paderborn bread, cattle, and beer are well-known. Cement, iron, and timber are the chief industrial products. Pop. (1970 est.) 68,700.
51°43′ N, 8°45′ E

·map, Federal Republic of Germany **8**:46

Paderewski, Ignacy (Jan) (b. Nov. 18, 1860, Kuryłówka, Podolia province in Russian Poland—d. June 29, 1941, New York City), Polish pianist, composer, and statesman, who persuaded Pres. Woodrow Wilson to include a paragraph on Polish independence in his famous Fourteen Points (*q.v.*) and who was prime minister of Poland in 1919.

Paderewski
EB Inc.

The son of a steward of the property of a Polish landowner, he studied music from 1872 at the Warsaw Conservatory and from 1878 taught piano there. In 1880 he married one of his pupils, Antonina Korsak, who died in childbirth the following year. Encouraged by the actress Helena Modrzejewska (Modjeska), he studied in Vienna from 1884 to 1887 under Theodor Leschetizky (Leszetycki), of whose method he became the principal exponent. During this period he also taught at the Strasbourg Conservatory. Between 1887 and 1891 he made his first public appearances as a pianist, in Vienna, Paris, London, and New York. Thereafter he impressed most critics, notably George Bernard Shaw, as the leading pianist of his time, remarkable for both his musical culture and his mind. His personality on the concert platform, like that of Liszt, his predecessor among piano virtuosos, generated a mystical devotion. Chopin (whose works he edited), Bach, Beethoven, and Schumann were the chief composers of his repertory. In 1898 he settled at Riond Bosson near Morges in Switzerland and the following year married Helena Gorska, née Baroness von Rosen. In 1901 his opera *Manru*, dealing with life in the Tatra Mountains, was given at Dresden. In 1909 his *Symphony in B Minor* was given at Boston, and in the same year he became director of the Warsaw Conservatory.

Throughout his life Paderewski was a staunch patriot. In 1910, on the 500th anniversary of the Battle of Grunwald, he had presented the city of Cracow with a monument commemorating the victory of the Poles over the Teutonic Order. During World War I he became a member of the Polish National Committee, presided over by Roman Dmowski, and was appointed its representative to the United States. During 1916 and 1917 he frequently urged Pres. Woodrow Wilson to use his influence to restore an independent and united Poland, with the result that Wilson included the independence of Poland in his tentative peace message of Jan. 22, 1917, and as the thirteenth of his Fourteen Points of Jan. 8, 1918.

In December 1918, Paderewski visited Paris and London, where A.J. Balfour encouraged him "to go to Poland to unite the Polish hearts." By agreement with Dmowski in Paris, he left for Gdańsk (Danzig) and later visited Poznań and Warsaw, where Józef Piłsudski was provisional head of state with a left-wing government. In Paris, however, the Polish National Committee was recognized by the Allies as representing the Polish nation. Persuaded by Paderewski of the necessity of forming a broad national government, Piłsudski asked him to form in Warsaw a government of experts free from party tendencies. This was formed on Jan. 17, 1919. Paderewski reserved the portfolio of foreign affairs for himself and appointed Dmowski first Polish delegate at the Paris Peace Conference.

His premiership was not a success. As a virtuoso Paderewski was accustomed to flattery, and he resented criticism. His ambition was to be elected president of the Polish Republic, but he was supported by no political party. On Nov. 27, 1919, he resigned the premiership and returned to Riond Bosson. He never revisited Poland. In 1921 he resumed his musical career, giving concerts in Europe and the United States mainly for war victims. At the beginning of World War II, in October 1939, a Polish government-in-exile, formed in Paris with Gen. Władysław Sikorski as prime minister, offered Paderewski the chairmanship of the Polish National Council. After the French capitulation in 1940, he went to the United States.

·Polish self-determination **14**:651a

Paderno Dugnano, town, Milano province, Lombardy (Lombardia) region, northern Italy. A northern suburb of Milan city, it produces textiles, glass, aluminum, and furniture. Pop. (1971 prelim.) mun., 34,774.
45°34′ N, 9°10′ E

Padilla, Juan (b. *c.* 1500, Andalusia, Spain—d. 1542, Herington?, Kan.), first Christian missionary martyred within the territory of the present U.S. After serving as a soldier, he joined the Franciscans in Andalusia. He went to Spanish Mexico in 1528, and in the following year accompanied an expedition to Nueva Galicia (northwestern Mexico). There he spent most of his remaining years, except for a trip to Tehuantepec, in southern Mexico, with the Spanish conqueror Hernán Cortés in 1533. He founded the first Franciscan friaries at Zapotlán and Tamazula, and at Tulantizingo, where he became abbot.

In 1540–41 he accompanied the Spanish explorer Francisco Vázquez de Coronado in his fruitless quest for a legendary kingdom of riches called Quivira, probably in modern Kansas. The disappointed Coronado and his company returned to Mexico, but Padilla decided to go back to Quivira with some companions. After working for many months among the Wichita Indians, he was on his way to visit the Guas tribe but was ambushed by them. His companions escaped to Mexico.

·Kansas early explorations **10**:383b

Padilla, Juan de (b. 1490?, Toledo, Spain—d. April 24, 1521, Villalar), aristocratic military leader of the Castilian Comunidades (*Communeros*) in their unsuccessful revolt (1520–21) against the government of the Habsburg emperor Charles V (King Charles I of Spain), whose defeat permitted the restoration of absolutist Habsburg rule in Castile.

Juan de Padilla, lithograph by an unknown artist
By courtesy of the Biblioteca Nacional, Madrid

Padilla was a member of an ancient noble family of Toledo. Charles, who came to the Spanish throne in 1516, had inflamed national opinion by his appointing to high posts foreigners who carried out arbitrary and exploitative actions. Demands soon arose for the imposition of traditional Castilian constitutional checks on royal power. Padilla had personal grievances against Charles as well and took part in dissident activities in Toledo in late 1519 and early 1520. Summoned in April 1520 to appear before the King at Santiago, Padilla instead took up arms in support of a popular uprising in Toledo.

A circular letter from Toledo to other Castilian cities in revolt invited them to meet at Avila. When the municipalities, supported by the nobles and clergy, set up the Junta Santa (a revolutionary junta) there (July–August 1520), Padilla was named captain general of its forces, and on August 29 he took Tordesillas, thereby assuring the junta's control over Charles's mother, the hereditary queen Joan the Mad, who had been living there since she had gone insane in 1506.

The junta soon alienated the nobility by its popular demands, and Charles cleverly moved to secure their loyalty. It also courted defeat in the field by replacing Padilla with Don Pedro Girón, an important nobleman. After Charles's troops had recovered Tordesillas (December 5) and Girón had defected,

the Junta Santa recalled Padilla. Padilla's reappointment was received with a great outpouring of popular enthusiasm. He occupied Torrelobatón on Feb. 28, 1521. Seven weeks later, however, on the advance of royal forces, he attempted to retreat but was defeated and captured at Villalar (April 23, 1521). He was executed the next day along with other leaders of the revolt.
·comunero revolt and fall of Tordesillas **17**:425b

Padjelanta National Park, in Norrbotten *län* (county), northwestern Sweden, adjoins Norway (west) and Sarek National Park (east). It is the largest of the Swedish national parks, with an area of 756 sq mi (1,958 sq km), and was established in 1962. Its wide mountainous area contains several lakes, the largest of which are Virihaure, Vastenjaure, and Salojaure, as well as valleys and glaciers. Some species of its alpine flora are not found elsewhere in Sweden; *e.g.*, the sandwort *Arenaria humifusa*, the cinquefoil *Potentilla hypartica*, and the felwort *Gentianella aurea*. Among its fauna are the wolverine, Arctic fox, and brown bear; its rich birdlife includes the golden eagle, merlin, rough-legged buzzard, and lesser white-fronted goose.
67°28′ N, 16°41′ E
·map, Sweden **17**:849

padlock, a removable lock.
·invention and distribution **11**:10d

Padma 'byung-gnas: *see* Padmasambhava.

Padma dkar-po, a medieval Tibetan Buddhist scholar and monk of the Bka'-brgyud-pa (Kagyurpa) order.
·Buddhist philosophic system **3**:439d

Padmapāda (*c.* 9th century), Indian Vedāntic philosopher.
·philosophical writings and influence **9**:330b

Padmapāṇi (Buddhist mythology): *see* Avalokiteśvara.

Padma River, main channel of the Ganges River below its bifurcation into the Bhagirathi and Padma rivers in Rājshāhi division, Bangladesh (formerly East Pakistan). Flowing southeastward, it forms the boundary between Rājshāhi and Kushtia and Farīdpur divisions. After receiving the Jamuna (Brahmaputra) River near Rājbāri, it continues southeastward between Dacca and Farīdpur districts to join the Meghna River through a channel 2 mi (3 km) wide, known as the Kirtimasa. The combined streams continue south to the Bay of Bengal as the Meghna.

The Padma is navigable for its entire 190-mi course by river steamer. Its main tributary is the Mahānanda; its principal distributary, the Madhumati. The Ganges-Kobadak Project is designed to irrigate about 2,000,000 ac (800,000 ha) in Kushtia, Jessore, and Khulna districts.
23°22′ N, 90°32′ E
·confluence and mouth **3**:104g; map 105
·map, Bangladesh **2**:689

Padmasambhava, also called GURU RIMPOCHE, Tibetan SLOB-DPON and PADMA 'BYUNG-GNAS, meaning "the Lotus-Born" (fl. 8th century), Indian Buddhist mystic who introduced Tantric Buddhism to Tibet and who is credited with establishing the first Buddhist monastery there.

A native of Udyāna (now Swat, Pak.), an area famed for its magicians, Padmasambhava was a Tantrist and a member of the Yogācāra sect, and taught at Nalanda, a centre of Buddhist studies in India. He was invited to Tibet in 747 by King Thī-srong-detsan and arrived at Samye (Bsan-yas), where he is said to have exorcised demons that were inhibiting the construction of a Buddhist monastery by causing earthquakes. He supervised the completion of the monastery in 749.

The Tibetan Buddhist sect Rnying-ma-pa (the Old Order) claims to follow most closely Padmasambhava's teachings, emphasizing Tantric ritual, worship, and Yoga. Texts basic to the sect's teachings, said to have been buried by Padmasambhava, began to be found around 1125. He also had many Tantric books translated from the original Sanskrit into Tibetan.
·Buddhism in Tibet **3**:388a
·Buddhism's ascendancy in Tibet **3**:410h
·'cham Tibetan origin **3**:1129b

Padmāvatī (*c.* 1540), epic poem in Hindi by Jāyasī.
·literary style **17**:143b

Padova (Italy): *see* Padua.

Padova, Università degli Studi di, English UNIVERSITY OF PADUA, coeducational state institution of higher learning in Padua, Italy. Founded in 1222, the university is the oldest in Italy after Bologna; among its teachers have been famous philosophers, Humanists, and scientists, including Galileo, whose relics are preserved in a museum connected with the university. Among its faculties are jurisprudence, political science, economics and commerce, statistical sciences, philosophy and letters, education, medicine, science, pharmacy, engineering, and agriculture. In the mid-1970s enrollment was about 37,000.

Padre Island National Seashore, lies along the Gulf Coast of Texas, U.S., extending south from Corpus Christi to Port Isabel. Authorized in 1962, it is actually a barrier reef 113 mi (182 km) long and up to 3 mi wide, separated from the mainland by Laguna Madre. Padre Island consists largely of grassy dunes and a broad beach that yields shellfish such as clams and marine snails. The area is well-known for its mackerel, sailfish, and tarpon fishing and for its variety of birds, particularly the heron, tern, white pelican, and frigate bird.

Padri War (1821–37), an armed conflict in Minangkabau (Sumatra) between reformist Muslims and local chieftains assisted by the Dutch. In the early 19th century the puritan Wahhābīyah sect of Islām spread to Sumatra, brought by pilgrims who entered the island through Pedir, a northern port. The Padris objected to local institutions that were not in accordance with the pure teaching of Islām. This jeopardized the power of the local chiefs, whose authority was based on traditional practices. In the ensuing conflict between the Padris and local chiefs, the Padris, using Bondjol as their base, launched guerrilla war against the chiefs. The Dutch, afraid of the influence of the Muslim reformists, sided with the chiefs but were still engaged in the Java War (1825–30) and thus unable to send troops to crush the Padris till the end of that war. Tuanku Imam Bondjol, the leader of the Padris, surrendered to the Dutch in 1832 but soon renewed his rebellion. The war continued till 1837, when the Dutch seized Bondjol.
·Dutch influence extension **9**:485g

Padstow, seaport and market town near the north (Atlantic) coast of the county of Cornwall, England, on the estuary of the River Camel. St. Petroc, patron saint of Cornwall, is said to have landed at Padstow and to have died there in the 6th century; the ancient name of the place was Petrocstow (Petroc's Church). The town had been incorporated by 1592, by which time it was a major seaport. The statesman Sir Walter Raleigh, once warden of Cornwall, lived at Raleigh's Court on the South Quay. Abbey House, North Quay, is a 15th-century building, while Prideaux Place (1598) is a fine Elizabethan manor. Padstow's industries include fishing and sand dredging. Pop. (latest census) 2,675.
50°33′ N, 4°56′ W
·map, United Kingdom **18**:867

Padua, Italian PADOVA, capital of Padova province, Veneto region, northern Italy, on the Fiume Bacchiglione, west of Venice.

Prato della Valle and the cupolas of the church of Sta. Giustina, Padua, Italy
J. Allan Cash

The Roman Patavium, founded, according to legend, by the Trojan hero Antenor, it was first mentioned in 302 BC, according to the Roman historian Livy, who was born there (59 BC). The town prospered greatly and, in the 11th–13th centuries, was a leading Italian commune. The poet Dante lived there, and St. Anthony of Padua is buried there. It was governed by the Carrara family from 1318 to 1405, when it passed to Venice, which held it until 1797. Under Austrian dominion from 1815 to 1866, it was active in the Risorgimento (movement for Italian independence); a rising took place there in February 1848. It was heavily bombed in World War II, and the frescoes by Andrea Mantegna in the Church of the Eremitani were almost completely destroyed.

The Capella degli Scrovegni (1303–05) contains famous frescoes by Giotto, and the Scuola del Santo has frescoes by Titian. The cathedral (rebuilt 1552) has a Romanesque baptistery. The basilica of S. Antonio (1232–1307) contains the tomb of the saint and has statues and reliefs by Donatello on the high altar. In the piazza before the basilica is Donatello's magnificent equestrian bronze statue (set up in 1453) of the Venetian condottiere Erasmo da Narni (called Gattemelata). Other notable secular landmarks include the Palazzo della Ragione (1218–19; rebuilt 1306); the Palazzo del Capitano (1532), now the university library; the Loggia della Gran Guardia; and the 16th–17th-century Palazzo il Bo, the nucleus of the university. Founded in 1222, the university is the oldest in Italy after Bologna (*see* Padova, Università degli Studi di). The civic museum has a fine art gallery as well as historical and archaeological exhibits, libraries, archives, and collections of sculpture and coins. The botanical garden, which dates from 1545, is the oldest in Europe.

An important rail and road junction, the city is a lively agricultural, commercial, and industrial centre. Manufactures include electrical and agricultural machinery, motorcycles, chemicals, and artificial and synthetic textiles. Pop. (1973 est.) mun., 234,203.
45°25′ N, 11°53′ E
·Donatello's residence and works **5**:952g; illus. 951
·Livy's political and academic environs **11**:3d
·Mantegna's formative years **11**:462d
·map, Italy **9**:1088
·province area and population table **9**:1094
·Renaissance Humanism **15**:664b
·Renaissance political development **9**:1140d

Padua, University of (Italy): *see* Padova, Università degli Studi di.

Paducah, city, seat of McCracken County, southwestern Kentucky, U.S., at the confluence of the Ohio (there bridged to Brookport, Ill.) and Tennessee rivers. The site, known as Pekin, was part of a grant to George Rogers Clark, soldier and frontiersman. At his death his brother William, co-leader of the Lewis and Clark Expedition, received the land, laid out the town in 1827, and named it for Paduke, a Chickasaw Indian chief who lived in the vicinity. During the Civil War, because of its strategic river facilities, the city was occupied by Union forces under Gen. Ulysses S. Grant and was raided by Gen. Nathan B. Forrest, a Confederate cavalry leader.

Paducah is now an important market for tobacco, strawberries, corn, livestock, and coal; it has diversified industry. Located in one of the world's greatest power-generating areas, its growth has been greatly stimulated by the Tennessee Valley Authority and Atomic Energy Commission projects. Recreational facilities provided by nearby Kentucky Lake and Kentucky Dam Village State Park have attracted tourists. Paducah Community College was founded in 1932. The city was the birthplace of the humorist Irvin S. Cobb and Vice Pres. Alben W. Barkley. Inc. city, 1856. Pop. (1930) 33,541; (1980) 29,315.
37°05′ N, 88°36′ W
·map, United States **18**:908

Padus (river, Italy): *see* Po River.

Paean, in Greek religion, the physician of the gods. It is not known whether he was originally a separate deity or merely an aspect of Apollo. In later poetry Paean was invoked independently as a health god. The word paean (*q.v.*) is still used for any song of joy or triumph.

paean, solemn choral lyric of invocation, joy, or triumph, originating in ancient Greece where it was addressed to Apollo in his guise as Paean (*q.v.*), physician to the gods. Paeans were sung at banquets following the boisterous dithyrambs, at the festivals of Apollo, and at public funerals. It was the custom for them to be sung by an army on the march and before going into battle, when a fleet left the harbour, and after a victory.

Paeans were later addressed to other gods as well as to men like the 5th-century BC Spartan commander, Lysander, who were more or less deified for their achievements.

paedogenesis, also spelled PEDOGENESIS, reproduction by sexually mature larvae, usually without fertilization. The young may be eggs, such as produced by *Miastor*, a genus of gall midge flies, or other larval forms, as in the case of some flukes. This form of reproduction is distinct from neotenic reproduction (*see* neoteny) in its parthenogenetic nature (*i.e.*, no fertilization occurs) and the eventual maturation or metamorphosis of the parent organism.

paedomorphosis, also spelled PEDOMORPHOSIS theory concerning evolution suggesting that larval stages and developmental phases of existing organisms may give rise, under certain conditions, to wholly new organisms by abbreviation of the life cycle.
·evolution and embryological development **7**:18h
·salamander developmental processes **18**:1085g

p'aegwan munhak, Korean literature recorded by official scribes of the late Chosŏn period.
·origin and meaning **10**:1062g

Paekche, one of three kingdoms into which ancient Korea was divided before 660. Occupying the southwestern tip of the Korean peninsula, Paekche is traditionally said to have been founded in 18 BC in the Kwangju area by a legendary leader named Onjo. In any case, by the 3rd century AD, during the reign of King Koi (234–286), Paekche emerged as a fully developed kingdom. By the reign of King Kŭnch'ogo (346–375), it had established control over the whole Han River basin in central Korea and was carrying on dealings with China and Japan.

In the late 5th century, the northern Korean kingdom of Koguryŏ deprived Paekche of its territory in the Han River basin, and it moved its capital south to Ungjin (present Kongju). In the reign of King Sŏng (523–554), the kingdom was forced to move its capital even further south to Sabi (present Puyŏ), as more of its territory was occupied by Koguryŏ.

The kingdom was divided into five administrative districts. There were 16 official grades in the central government, and the 6 officials of the first grade formed a kind of Cabinet. The highest ranking official, called *sangjwapyong*, was elected every three years.

Buddhism flourished, and many temples were built. Confucianism also prospered, producing a large number of eminent scholars.

In an attempt to contain Koguryŏ's attacks and recover some of its lost territory in the Han River basin, Paekche allied itself with the other southern Korean state, known as Silla. But it eventually lost this territory to Silla. In 660 its defeat by the allied forces of Silla and the Chinese T'ang dynasty (668–907) brought an end to its rule. Eight years later Silla's forces defeated the northern Korean state of Koguryŏ and united the Korean peninsula under the Unified Silla dynasty (668–935).
·early Korean music and dance **5**:474b
·Japanese cultural relations **10**:59d *passim* to 60f
·literary history **10**:1061d
·origins and political development **10**:507f; map
·Seoul's historical location **16**:555f

Paekche style, Korean visual arts style characteristic of the Paekche kingdom (18 BC–AD 660) of the Three Kingdoms period. Paekche art reveals technical maturity and at the same time a warm, human quality, the latter perhaps reflecting the influence of the art of the Chinese southern dynasties during the Six Dynasties period. These qualities are clearly discerned in Paekche Buddha statues, with their unique, expressive "Paekche smile," their relaxed poses, and their soft modelling. Even after the fall of the Paekche kingdom, the Paekche style survived in the southwestern region of the Korean peninsula and continued well into the Koryŏ period (935–1392).
·Korean visual arts features and development **19**:208b *passim* to 209e
·religious sculptural style **10**:533h

Paektu-san, mountain in North Korea.
42°00′ N, 128°03′ E
·elevation and geological distinction **10**:516g

Paeligni, an ancient people of central Italy, whose territory lay inland on the eastward slopes of the Apennines. Though akin to the Samnites (*q.v.*), they formed a separate league with their neighbours the Marsi, Marrucini, and Vestini (*qq.v.*). This league appears to have broken up after the Second Samnite War (304 BC), when each tribe came into an alliance with the Romans that lasted until the Social War (91 BC onward). This war ended when the Paeligni and the other allies were finally granted Roman citizenship.

The Paeligni's oldest Latin inscriptions probably date from shortly after the Social War, although the Paelignian dialect doubtlessly lasted to about 50 BC. Similar dialects were spoken by the Marrucini and Vestini; together they formed a group known as Northern Oscan.

paella, Spanish food specialty.
·preparation and provincial variations **7**:945g

paenula (liturgical vestment): *see* chasuble.

Paeon (Greek mythology): *see* Aetolus.

Paeonia, the land of the Paeonians, originally including the whole Axius (Vardar) Valley and the surrounding areas, corresponding to parts of what is now northern Greece, southern Yugoslavia, and western Bulgaria. The Paeonians, probably of mixed Thraco-Illyrian origin, were weakened by the Persian invasion (490 BC), and those tribes living along the Strymon River fell under Thracian control. The growth of Macedonia forced the remaining Paeonians northward, and in 358 BC they were defeated by Philip II of Macedonia. The native dynasty, however, continued to be highly respected: about 289 BC, King Audoleon received Athenian citizenship, and his daughter married Pyrrhus, king of Epirus. Under the Romans, Paeonia was included in the second and third districts of Macedonia. By AD 400, however, the Paeonians had lost their identity, and Paeonia was merely a geographical term.

Paeonia is also the name of an *eparkhía* in the *nomós* of Kilkís, Greece, with its capital at Gouménissa.
·Philip of Macedonia's campaigns **14**:225h

Paeoniales, an order of dicotyledonous flowering plants containing 1 family (Paeoniaceae, the peony family), 1 genus (*Paeonia*), and about 33 species distributed in Europe, Asia, and western North America. They are perennial (long-lived) herbs or sometimes shrubby plants up to about two metres (about six feet) tall that grow from stout rootstocks. The leaves are alternately produced along the stems, lack the basal appendages called stipules, and are divided into three lobes, each lobe being further divided into three smaller lobes. The flowers are radially symmetrical, bisexual, and large, with 5 sepals, 5 petals (sometimes 10), and an indefinitely large number of stamens (male pollen-producing structures). The female parts are superior (*i.e.*, positioned above the attachment point of the other flower parts) and consist of two to five separate, large, more or less fleshy pistils or ovaries containing many ovules, which develop into large seeds that are at first red in colour, later turning a shining black and bearing a fleshy appendage called an aril.

Japanese double tree peony (horticultural variant of *Paeonia suffruticosa*)
Roche

The order is considered to be related to the order Dilleniales, although traditionally it has been placed near the buttercup family (Ranunculaceae), a position still defended by some authorities.

Economically, the group is important for the many ornamentals it contains, which go by the name peony (*q.v.*). *Paeonia officinalis* of southern Europe was once cultivated as a medicinal herb and is occasionally still used as such.
·angiosperm features and classification **1**:883c

Paeonius (fl. 450–400 BC), Greek sculptor, native of Mende in Thrace, a contemporary and follower of the sculptors Phidias and Polyclitus who is famous for his statue of the Nike, or "Winged Victory" (*c.* 420 BC; Archaeological Museum, Olympia) found in Olympia in 1875. An inscription on its pedes-

tal states that the statue commemorated a victory of the Messenians and the Naupactians over an unnamed enemy, probably the Spartans. The inscription also states that Paeonius won a competition for the construction of the *akrōtērion* (the ornamental device at the peak or corner of a gable) for a temple.
·sculpture style of Classical Greece **19**:295a

Paer, Ferdinando (b. June 1, 1771, Parma, Italy—d. May 3, 1839, Paris), composer who, with Cimarosa and Zingarelli, was one of the principal composers of Italian opera buffa of his period. He produced his first opera, *Orphée et Euridice*, in Parma in 1791. From 1797 to 1802 he was in Vienna, where his most successful opera, *Camilla*, was produced in 1799. He was in Dresden from 1802 to 1807 and then went to Paris, where he became chapelmaster to Napoleon, conducted at the Opéra-Comique, and (1812–27) directed the Italian Opera. His most successful opera of this period was *Le Maître de chapelle* (1821; *The Chapelmaster*). In addition to his 43 operas he also composed religious and chamber music and secular cantatas.
·opera style transition **13**:585a

Paeroa, town, Ohinemuri County, northern North Island, New Zealand, on the Ohinemuri River near its junction with the Waihou. Its name is derived from a Maori word meaning "long ridge of hills." The town was founded in the early 1880s as a port for the Ohinemuri goldfield, 5 mi (8 km) southeast. Mining was shifted to the underground Komata Reefs (6 mi northeast) from 1891 to the 1930s. Gazetted a borough in 1915, Paeroa was regularly served by river shipping until 1947. The town is a hub of rail lines and highways to Auckland and Tauranga. Pop. (1975 est.) 3,750.
37°23′ S, 175°41′ E
·map, New Zealand **13**:45

Paesiello, Giovanni (Italian composer): *see* Paisiello, Giovanni.

Paestum, Greek POSEIDONIA, ancient city in Lucania, Italy, 22 miles southeast of modern Salerno and five miles south of the Silarus (modern Sele) River, noted for its Greek ruins and for what are believed to be the only examples of classical Greek wall painting. Founded probably *c.* 600 BC by colonists from Sybaris, it became a flourishing town by 540. Paestum came under Lucanian domination from *c.* 390 until 273, when Rome made it a Latin colony. The city supported Rome during the Second Punic War. The gradual silting up of the mouth of the Silarus created a malarial swamp, and Paestum was finally deserted after being sacked by Muslim raiders in AD 871.

The site, rediscovered in the 18th century, contained pottery and excellently preserved walls and temples. Its best known buildings are the so-called Temple of Ceres (in fact dedicated to Athena), the basilica probably dedicated to Hera, and a temple of Hera called the Temple of Neptune. In July 1969 a farmer uncovered the limestone roof of an ancient Lucanian tomb that contained frescoes in the early classical style.
·red figure painting **19**:295f

The so-called Temple of Ceres at Paestum
Alinari

Paetus, Thrasea (Roman senator): *see* Thrasea Paetus, Publius Clodius.

Páez, Indians of the southern highlands of Colombia. The Páez speak a Chibchan language very closely related to that of the now extinct Pijao and Coconuco (*see* Chibchan languages).

The Páez inhabit the high mountains and plateaus, their chief crop being potatoes. Many also grow such nontraditional crops as wheat and coffee. Each family farms its own land, but the lands of the church are cultivated by communal labour. Most planting is done with digging sticks. Settlements are dispersed, each family living on its own land. Houses are made of poles, sometimes being double walled with mud and stones between.

Clothing formerly consisted simply of a small woollen blanket, but after the Conquest rough cotton shirts and later trousers and shirts were introduced for men and skirts and ponchos for women. Modern crafts include pottery, weaving, and basketry. Before Spanish rule, stone and gold and copper were worked. Polygyny was also common, but Roman Catholicism has enforced monogamy. Traditional puberty rites and menstrual taboos continued to be observed well into the 20th century. The Páez were estimated to number 16,000 in the 1970s.
·agricultural and economic features **3**:1107c; map
·geographic distribution and socio-economic structure **17**:117h; map

Páez, José Antonio (b. June 13, 1790, Aricagua, Venez.—d. May 7, 1873, New York City), soldier and politician, a leader in Venezuela's independence movement and its first president. In the crucial early years of Venezuelan independence, he served his country as a moderate dictator.

José Antonio Páez, detail of a portrait by an unknown artist
By courtesy of the Library of Congress, Washington, D.C.

Páez was a part-Indian *llanero*, one of the horsemen of the plains. Beginning as a ranch hand, he quickly acquired both land and cattle. In 1810 he joined the revolutionary movement against Spain as the leader of a band of *llaneros*. Becoming chief Venezuelan commander to Simón Bolívar, the liberator of northern South America, Páez and his men helped secure victories at Carabobo (1821) and Puerto Cabello (1823) that resulted in the complete withdrawal of the Spanish. In 1826, after rebelling against the authority of Gran Colombia, of which Venezuela was a province, Páez was appointed military and civilian head of his country. In 1829 he successfully led the movement that resulted in Venezuela's becoming a sovereign nation.

He was elected president in 1831 and controlled the country either as chief executive or as a power behind titular presidents until 1846. He usually respected the constitution, permitted limited freedom of the press, and promoted agriculture and industry. He curbed the power of the church in secular affairs but supported its religious authority.

In 1846 his own candidate for president turned against him, and he was imprisoned and later forced into exile. He returned to Venezuela in 1861, ruling for a short period as a severely repressive dictator, only to be forced again into exile in 1863. He spent most of his remaining years in New York City, where he published his autobiography in 1867–69.
·New Granada liberation and civil war **2**:1208c
·Venezuela's first independent government **19**:68g

Páez (Xaramillo), Pedro, also PERO PÁEZ (b. 1564, Olmedo, Spain—d. May 20, 1622, Gorgora, Eth.), learned Jesuit priest who, in the tradition of Frumentius—founder of the Ethiopian Church—went as a missionary to Ethiopia, where he became known as the second apostle of Ethiopia. Páez entered the Society of Jesus in 1582 and sailed for Goa, in India, in 1588. En route to Ethiopia (1589) he was captured by Turkish pirates and enslaved until 1596, when he returned to Goa. He finally reached Ethiopia in 1603. There he learned two of the main languages, translated a catechism, and wrote a treatise on the theological errors of the Ethiopian Church. He also wrote a history of the country, included in the Portuguese work *Biblioteca Historica de Portugal e Brasil* (vol. 5, 1945–46; "Historical Library of Portugal and Brazil"). Páez succeeded in converting the formerly Monophysite King Susenyos of Ethiopia to orthodoxy, and for a while most of Ethiopia was Roman Catholic. Páez was the first European to visit Lake Tana, the source of the Blue Nile in northwestern Ethiopia, where he died of fever.
·Portuguese religious policy in Ethiopia **6**:163e

Pagalu, formerly ANNOBÓN, volcanic island in the Gulf of Guinea, occupies an area of 6.5 sq mi (17 sq km) and rises to an altitude of 2,200 ft (671 m). A part of Equatorial Guinea (formerly Spanish Guinea), the island is administered from Macías Nguema Biyogo (formerly Fernando Po). Fishing and lumbering activities are centred in San Antonio, the chief settlement. Pop. (latest est.) 1,436.
1°25′ S, 5°36′ E
·Equatorial Guinea resources and economy **6**:949c

Pagan 13:860, a village in Burma on the Irrawaddy River, was the capital of the Burmese kingdom from the 11th to the end of the 13th century. The old city's site is covered with historic buildings, many of them Buddhist shrines that are important examples of Southeast Asian architecture.

The text article covers Pagan's history from its founding about 849. As the capital of Burma it was the focus of a road network by which it commanded a large, fertile region. The walled city probably then contained royal, aristocratic, administrative, and religious buildings, with the populace living outside. Pagan became an important centre of Buddhist learning. In 1287 it was captured by Mongol conquerors and thereafter never recovered its former importance. Pop. (latest census) 2,825.
21°10′ N, 94°51′ E

REFERENCES in other text articles:
·Buddhist arts and spirit of reverence **17**:232e
·foundation, Buddhist evangelism, and fall **3**:511f
·temple architecture and iconography **17**:253h *passim* to 255e; illus.

Paganelli, Bernardo (pope): *see* Eugenius III.

paganica, cross-country Roman game played with a bent stick and a ball.
·golf comparison **8**:242e

Paganini, Niccolò (b. Oct. 27, 1782, Genoa—d. May 27, 1840, Nice, Fr.), composer and principal violin virtuoso of the 19th century. A popular idol, he inspired the Romantic mystique of the virtuoso and revolutionized violin technique. After initial study with his father, he studied with a local violinist, G. Servetto, and then with the celebrated Giacomo Costa. He made his first appearance in 1793 and then studied with Alessandro Rolla and Gaspare Ghiretti at Parma, Italy. In 1797, accompanied by his father, he toured Lombardy, where with each concert his reputation grew. Gaining his independence soon after, he indulged excessively in gambling and romantic love affairs. At one point he pawned his violin because of gambling debts; a French merchant lent him a Guarneri violin to play a concert and, after hearing him, gave him the instrument.

Paganini, etching by Luigi Calamatta after a drawing by J.-A.-D. Ingres, 1818
The Granger Collection, New York

Between 1801 and 1807 he wrote the *24 Capricci* for unaccompanied violin, displaying the novel features of his technique, and the two sets of six sonatas for violin and guitar. He reappeared in Italy as a violinist in 1805 and was appointed director of music at Piombino by Napoleon's sister, Élisa Bonaparte Baciocchi. He later gave recitals of his own compositions in many towns in Italy and in 1815 formed his long attachment with the dancer Antonia Bianchi.

In 1828 Paganini had great success in Vienna, and his appearances in Paris and London in 1831 were equally sensational. His tour of England and Scotland in 1832 made him a wealthy man. In 1833 he settled in Paris, where he commissioned Berlioz to write his symphony *Harold en Italie*. Paganini thought the challenge of its viola solo was too slight, however, and he never played it. Following the failure of the Casino Paganini, a gambling house in which he had invested, he went to Marseille in 1839, then to Nice.

Paganini's romantic personality and adventures created in his own day the legend of a Mephistophelean figure. Stories circulated that he was in league with the devil and that he had been imprisoned for murder; his burial in consecrated ground was delayed for five years. He was long regarded as a miser, but a more accurate portrait would consider his desire to be free from a train of dependent followers and their importunities for his largesse. His gift of 20,000 francs to the struggling composer Berlioz was an act of generosity seemingly uncharacteristic; possibly Paganini, recognizing a worthy talent, thought it was his duty to come to the composer's aid.

His violin technique, based on that of his works, principally the *Capricci*, the violin concertos, and the sets of variations, demanded a wide use of harmonics and pizzicato effects, new methods of fingering and even of tuning. In performance he improvised brilliantly. He was also a flamboyant showman who used trick effects such as severing one or two violin strings and continuing the piece on the remaining strings. His technical innovations became the basis for later virtuosi, notably Pablo Sarasate and Eugène Ysaÿe. His other works include 6 violin concertos, of which the first, in D major, is especially popular; 12 sonatas for violin and guitar; and 6 quartets for violin, viola, cello, and guitar. The influence of his virtuosity extended to orchestral as well as to piano music. His influence on Liszt was immense. Themes from the *Capricci* inspired works by Liszt, Schumann, Brahms, and Rachmaninoff.

·Berlioz' musical success **2**:855g
·Liszt's technique adaptations for piano **10**:1035c

paganism, practices and beliefs that are incompatible with monotheism; it thus often designates religions that are neither Christian, Jewish, nor Islāmic.

·benevolent nature of pagan deities **15**:134c
·Christian competition in Roman Empire **13**:1078d
·Christianity and classical culture **4**:538g
·Christian support of state persecution **4**:590g
·Constantine's partial toleration **5**:73e
·Frankish conversion opposition **11**:933f
·Julian's personal and political support **10**:333c
·Neoplatonist defense of pagan theology **14**:542a
·patristic attitudes and apologetics **13**:1080b
·St. Ambrose's opposition **1**:657d

Pagan Min (d. 1880, Mandalay, Burma), king of Burma (1846–53) who suffered defeat in the Second Anglo-Burmese War, after which Rangoon and the province of Pegu in Lower Burma were annexed by the British. Pagan Min deposed his father, the insane king Tharrawaddy, in 1846. Although Pagan Min was not one of Burma's more enlightened monarchs, he acted with tact and restraint during the crisis preceding the war. Part of his undoing was the aggressive policy of Lord Dalhousie, the governor general of India.

In 1851 Pagan Min's governor in Rangoon, Maung Ok, charged the captains of two British merchant ships with murder, embezzlement, and evading customs fees. They were forced to pay him several hundred rupees before being allowed to return to Calcutta, where they requested compensation. Dalhousie sent an emissary with a letter to the King requesting compensation that amounted to £920 and the dismissal of Maung Ok. Pagan Min agreed to replace Maung Ok, but the emissary's lack of tact and ignorance of Burmese protocol made it impossible for the new governor to deal with him. On Jan. 6, 1852, the British were evacuated and the harbour blockaded. Three days later British warships began firing on the city.

On Feb. 7, 1852, Pagan Min protested to Dalhousie against the acts of aggression in Rangoon, expressing hope that the governor general would repudiate them. A few days before, the governor of Rangoon had offered to pay the compensation for the two ship captains. On February 13, however, Dalhousie sent an ultimatum to the King, demanding an indemnity of £100,000. Pagan Min refused to answer the ultimatum, which expired on April 1, and a few days later British troops entered Burmese territory. Rangoon was taken, and, by December 1852, Lower Burma was occupied.

On Feb. 18, 1853, Pagan Min was deposed by his brother, Mindon Min, who favoured reconciliation with the British.

Pagasaí, Gulf of, Greek PAGASITIKÓS KÓLPOS, classical GULF OF PAGASAE, large inlet of the Aegean Sea, Magnisía *nomós* (department), Thessaly, Greece. Known also as the Gulf of Vólos, it is almost landlocked by a fishhook prong of the Magnesia peninsula, which forms the Dhíavlos (strait) Tríkkeri. At the head of the gulf is Vólos, the primary port of Thessaly. It lies on the site of ancient Iolcos and its port, Pagasae, from whence is derived the gulf's present name. In Greek myth the king of Iolcos, Pelias, dispatched Jason from Pagasae in the ship "Argo" to search for the Golden Fleece.
39°15′ N, 22°51′ E

maps
·Aegean civilizations **1**:112
·modern Greece **8**:314

page, in medieval Europe, youth of noble birth who left his home at an early age to serve an apprenticeship in the duties of chivalry in the family of some prince or man of rank. Beginning as assistants to squires who attended knights and their ladies, pages were trained in arms and in the art of heraldry and received instruction in hunting, music, dancing, and such other accomplishments as befitted their social status. Later, pages were promoted to squires and from that status were frequently advanced to knights.

In Great Britain, the term pages of honour still designates boys from 13 to 17 years of age who act as ceremonial attendants to the sovereign. In the United States, "page" refers to young people who are appointed to wait upon legislators in the Congress or other legislatures; also, the term may designate someone who carries messages or performs other light duties in clubs, hotels, or theatres.

·apprenticeship period **1**:1019b
·medieval duties and pastimes **6**:339d

Page, Sir Earle (Christmas Grafton) (b. Aug. 8, 1880, Grafton, Australia—d. Dec. 20, 1961, Sydney), Australian statesman, co-leader of the federal government (1923–29) in coalition with Stanley Melbourne Bruce (*q.v.*; later 1st Viscount Bruce of Melbourne). As head of the Country Party (1920–39), he was a spokesman for the party's goal of rural economic development.

Sir Earle Page
By courtesy of the Australian Information Service

A physician in New South Wales, Page entered the federal Parliament in 1919 as one of the first Country Party members and assumed party leadership the following year. He formed a coalition with the Nationalist Party to create the Bruce–Page ministry of 1923–29, which was noted for its economic program. As federal treasurer in the ministry, he was responsible for the National Insurance Bill, coordination of federal loan policy, and strengthening of the commonwealth bank. Although he served in the federal Cabinet for the next three decades, his influence was greatest in the 1920s.

Page was minister of commerce (1934–39, 1940–41) under Joseph Lyons and Robert Menzies, and in 1934 he established the Australian Agricultural Council, which sought government emphasis on rural production. As minister of health under Menzies (1949–56), he introduced a comprehensive national health plan. Page became the first chancellor of the University of New England, Australia's only rural university, in 1955 and remained in Parliament until 1961. His autobiography, *Truant Surgeon*, was published in 1963.

Page, Sir Frederick Handley (b. Nov. 15, 1885, Cheltenham, Gloucestershire—d. April 21, 1962, London), British aircraft designer and civil aviation pioneer who built the Handley Page 0/400, the world's first twin-engine bomber and one of the largest planes used in World War I. Trained as an electrical engineer, Page turned his interest to flight and in 1909 founded Handley Page, Ltd., the first British aircraft manufacturing corporation.

Frederick Page
Camera Press—Publix

During World War I he produced the first twin-engine bomber, which was capable of carrying 1,800 pounds of bombs. He then designed the V-1500 four-engine bomber, built to fly from England to Berlin with a bomb load of three tons. The war ended before it was used. Handley Page Transport, Ltd., was formed in 1919 to pioneer airline flights to France, Belgium, The Netherlands, and Switzerland but later merged to form Imperial Airways.

Page's company manufactured transports and the Halifax heavy bomber during World War II. His Victor B.2, a long-range medium bomber, which carries the Blue Steel missile, has been deployed with the Royal Air Force Bomber Command since early 1962. Handley Page Aircraft, Ltd., closed on Feb. 27, 1970.

Page, The, journal published by Edward Gordon Craig from 1898 to 1903.
·publication and contents **5**:232c

Page, Thomas Nelson (b. April 23, 1853, Oakland plantation, Hanover County, Va.—d. Nov. 1, 1922, Oakland), author whose work fostered romantic legends of the Southern plantation. He attended Washington College (now Washington and Lee University), taught for a year, and in 1874 graduated in law from the University of Virginia. He practiced until 1893, when he moved to Washington, D.C., and devoted himself to writing and lecturing. He first won notice with the story "Marse Chan" in the *Century Illustrated Magazine*. This and similar stories were collected in what is probably Page's most characteristic book, *In Ole Virginia, Marse Chan, and Other Stories* (1887), reflecting his formative years amid the glamorous life of the old regime and the tumults of the Civil War. His essays and social studies, including *Social Life in Old Virginia* (1897) and *The Old Dominion—Her Making and Her Manners* (1908), have the same tone as his fiction. From 1913 to 1919 Page was ambassador to Italy. His other works include *Two Little Confederates* (1888), a children's tale; *The Burial of the Guns; and Other Stories* (1894); *The Old Gentlemen of the Black Stock* (1897); *Red Rock* (1898), which told of Southerners rebelling against Reconstruction; and a biography of Robert E. Lee (1911). The Plantation edition of his works (12 vol.) was published in 1906. His brother Rosewell published a biography in 1923.

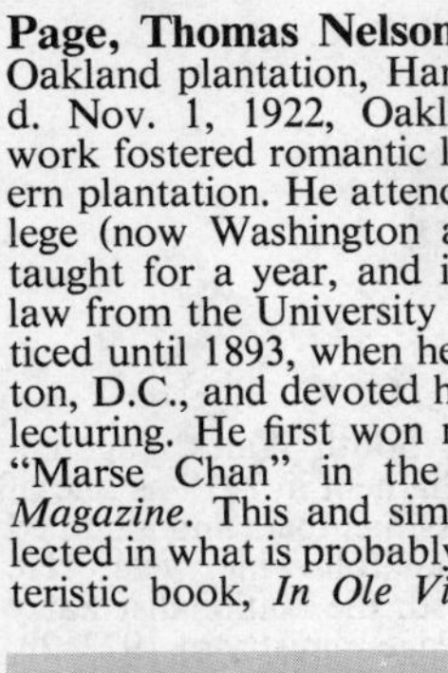

Thomas Page
By courtesy of the Library of Congress, Washington, D.C.

Page, Walter Hines (b. Aug. 15, 1855, Cary, N.C.—d. Dec. 21, 1918, Pinehurst), journalist, book publisher, author, and diplomatist who, as U.S. ambassador to Great Britain during World War I, worked strenuously to maintain close relations between the two countries while the U.S. remained neutral and who, from an early stage of the war, urged U.S. intervention on an unwilling Pres. Woodrow Wilson.

Page worked as a journalist in various parts of the U.S. in the 1880s and '90s and from 1898 to 1899 was editor of *The Atlantic Monthly*. In January 1900 he and Frank N. Doubleday founded the publishing house of Doubleday, Page and Company (afterward Doubleday and Company, Inc.) and the magazine *The World's Work*, which he edited until 1913. In 1911 he was one of the first to propose Woodrow Wilson as a presidential candidate. One of Wilson's first acts after his inauguration in March 1913 was to appoint Page ambassador to Great Britain.

Walter Hines Page, detail of a portrait by P.A. de Laszlo (born 1869); in the collection of the Department of Archives and History, North Carolina
By courtesy of the Department of Archives and History, North Carolina

A firm believer in Anglo-American superiority in cultural and political matters, Page at first worked amicably with both Wilson and the British government and was largely responsible for the repeal of a U.S. Panama Canal toll schedule that the British considered discriminatory. By the outbreak of war in August 1914 he had become popular with the official class and the public in Great Britain. Unlike Wilson, however, Page soon viewed the war as an attempt by imperial Germany to rule Europe and to substitute Prussian militaristic autocracy for the democratic ideal. Outwardly conforming to U.S. neutrality, Page expressed his disagreement with Wilson's policy of noninvolvement in private messages to the President. When the British steamship "Lusitania" was sunk by a German submarine (May 7, 1915), with the loss of more than 100 American lives, Page called for a U.S. declaration of war. He insisted then and later that U.S. intervention at that time would have resulted in a swift victory for the Allies. In April 1917, when Wilson did ask Congress to declare war on Germany, he used arguments that he had been hearing from Page for two and a half years.

Always in precarious health and further weakened by his labours as ambassador, Page became so ill in August 1918 that Wilson acquiesced in his retirement. Page died shortly after returning home.

An authoritative work on his career is Burton J. Hendrick's *Life and Letters of Walter H. Page* (3 vol., 1922–25), supplemented by *The Training of an American: The Earlier Life and Letters of Walter H. Page, 1855–1913* (1928), also by Hendrick.

Page, William (b. Jan. 23, 1811, Albany, N.Y.—d. Oct. 1, 1885, Tottenville, Staten Island, N.Y.), painter in the Romantic style,

William Page, self-portrait, oil on canvas; in the Detroit Institute of Arts
By courtesy of the Detroit Institute of Arts

known for his sedate portraits of prominent American and British Victorians. He was trained and initially influenced by the famed inventor and Romantic painter Samuel F.B. Morse. From 1849 to 1860 he lived in Rome, where he painted portraits of friends such as Robert and Elizabeth Barrett Browning. His best known works, "Self-Portrait" (1860; Detroit Institute of Arts) and "Portrait of Mrs. William Page" (1860–61; Detroit Institute of Arts), typify the serene dignity of his likenesses, his monumental and sculptural handling of the figure, and his use of warm, resonant tonalities of dark colours.

Pageant, U.S. magazine founded in 1944.
·magazine publishing history **15**:254h

pageant and parade 13:861, entertainments, often in the open air, involving spectacle that is sometimes extravagantly devised and usually used as a means of expressing national, communal, or other kinds of group purpose or identity.

The text article covers the varieties of pageants and parades in different periods and different parts of the world.

REFERENCES in other text articles:
·advertising design considerations **1**:109d
·armour parade-use origins **2**:29h
·bullfighting spectacle and ceremony **3**:476a
·choreography of Renaissance spectacles **4**:452g
·circus development and importance **4**:638g
·floral decorations usage **7**:414f
·forms, appeal, and communal purpose **18**:257a
·Jewish dance and theatre origins **10**:199e
·medieval structure and special effects **18**:242h
·Roman theatres' construction and uses **18**:237e
·Shi'ite passion plays **9**:980f
·staging conventions of medieval drama **17**:536c
·theatre costumes of Renaissance **17**:560h

pageant drama, loosely unified drama with resplendent parade.
·origins and distinction from drama **13**:861f

Paget, parish in Bermuda.
·area and population table **2**:858

Paget, Henry William, 1st marquess of Anglesey: *see* Anglesey, Henry William Paget, 1st marquess of.

Paget, Sir James, Bart. (b. Jan. 11, 1814, Yarmouth, Isle of Wight—d. Dec. 30, 1899, London), surgeon, physiologist, considered (with Rudolf Virchow) a founder of the science of pathology. During his first year (1834) at St. Bartholomew's Hospital, London, he discovered in human muscle the parasitic worm (*Trichinella spiralis*) that causes trichinosis. A professor of anatomy and surgery (1847–52), vice president (1873–74) and president (1875) of the Royal College of Surgeons, he rendered excellent descriptions of breast cancer, an early indication of breast cancer known as Paget's disease (1874; an inflammatory cancerous condition around the nipple in elderly women), and osteitis deformans (1877; a bone inflammation known as Paget's disease of bone). Also named for him is Paget's abscess, one recurring about the remains of a former abscess. He was one of the first to recommend surgical removal of bone-marrow tumours (myeloid sarcoma) instead of amputation of the limb.

Paget
Radio Times Hulton Picture Library

A surgeon of international repute, he served as surgeon extraordinary (1858–67), serjeant surgeon extraordinary (1867–77), and serjeant surgeon (1877) to Queen Victoria. Among his works are *Lectures on Tumours* (1851), *Lectures in Surgical Pathology* (1863), and *Clinical Lectures and Essays* (1875).

Paget, Violet: *see* Lee, Vernon.

Paget's disease of bone, also called OSTEITIS DEFORMANS, moderately common chronic disease of middle age, characterized by local disorganized bone-destructive processes alternating with bone-constructive activity; the disease leads to deformity, fracture, and imbalance in calcium metabolism and carries with it an increased risk of cancer. The long bones, vertebrae, pelvis, and skull are most commonly affected, in men more often than in women. In the bone-destructive stages, bones soften and become a site for the pooling of blood, which may lead to heart or circulatory trouble; calcium builds up in the blood as it is lost from bones, sometimes resulting in kidney stones or systemic calcium poisoning. In bone-constructive stages, bones are dense and brittle and fracture easily. There is no generally accepted treatment for the disease, which is named for Sir James Paget, who first described it.
·bone diseases **3**:26a
·causation and neurological symptoms **12**:1044d
·race types with propensity for disease **15**:354e

paging systems, office communications systems used to locate persons by means of a bell or light code or of speakers that call out their names.
·varieties for office use **13**:514f

pagliacci, I, opera in prologue and two acts by Ruggero Leoncavallo, one of the figures associated with the *verismo (q.v.)* school, of which this opera is an outstanding example. It was first performed at the Teatro dal Verme in Milan on May 21, 1892.
·popularity and verismo elements **13**:589g

Pagninus (PAGNINI, PAGNINO), **Santes** (b. Oct. 18, 1470, Lucca, Italy—d. Aug. 24, 1536, Lyons, Fr.), Dominican scholar whose Latin version of the Hebrew Bible—the first since St. Jerome's—greatly aided other 16th-century scriptural translators. In 1487 he joined the Dominicans at Fiesole, Italy, where he became a disciple of Girolamo Savonarola. In 1516 he went to Rome, where Pope Leo X encouraged his work. From 1523 to 1526 he lived in Avignon, then settled in Lyons, where in 1528 he published his Latin translation of the whole Bible, apparently the first to divide chapters into numbered verses. In 1529 Pagninus issued a Hebrew lexicon, *Thesaurus linguae sanctae* ("Thesaurus of the Sacred Language"), which was frequently republished.

Pagninus' translation was remarkably literal, so, despite his inelegant, even crude style, his Bible was reprinted several times. Although more accurate than the Vulgate, and hence more useful to other translators needing help with Hebrew or Greek, Pagninus' version was not intended to supersede the Vulgate except for purely scholarly purposes; it is now chiefly of historical interest.

Pagnol, Marcel (b. Feb. 24, 1895, Aubagne, Fr.—d. April 18, 1974, Paris), playwright and film maker who depicted life in southern France with realism and simplicity. He is perhaps best known for his film trilogy of the Marseille waterfront; Pagnol first wrote *Marius* (1931) and *Fanny* (1932) as plays and then adapted them for the screen, while *César* (1937) was written as a screenplay in 1936.

Pagnol became the first film maker to be admitted to the Académie Française (1946). His autobiography was published as *La Gloire de mon père* (1957), *Le Château de ma mère* (1958; both translated as *The Days Were Too Short*, 1960), and *Le Temps des secrets* (1960; *The Time of Secrets*, 1962).

pagoda, in the Far East, a towerlike, storied structure of stone, brick, or wood usually associated with a temple complex. The pagoda derives from the *stūpa* (*q.v.*) of ancient India. Perhaps the most celebrated pagoda in India was that erected by Kaniṣka I near Peshāwar in the 2nd century AD to enshrine a collection of relics of the Buddha. It was the inspiration for the later pagodas of China, Korea, and Japan, in which the design always consisted of the repetition of a basic story unit (circular, square, polygonal) in regularly diminishing proportions. Each unit had its own projecting roof and the whole structure was capped by a prominent mast and disks.

The pagoda, like the *stūpa*, was at first thought of as an architectural diagram of the cosmos. The great pillar that runs up the core of the structure is symbolic of that invisible world axis joining the centres of earth and heaven. The Japanese still refer to the four columns at the corners of a wooden pagoda as the pillars of the sky. The separate stories, diminishing in size as they mount upward, may be thought of as the many terraces of the mythical world mountain. The disks that crown the pagoda correspond to the various heavens of the gods. The cosmic diagram, thus fixed in architectural forms, was thought to be animated by the precious relics enshrined within. This concept of the building and its animation by the enshrining relics probably originated in Vedic India.
·Chinese, Japanese, and Korean architecture **19**:184g; illus. **19**:Visual Arts, East Asian, Plates 10, 11, 13
·iron use in construction **11**:1116f
·religious function of architecture **1**:1091d; illus. 1092

pagoda tree, any of several trees of erect, conical form suggesting a pagoda, particularly *Sophora japonica*, commonly called Japanese pagoda tree. A member of the pea family (Fabaceae), it is native to East Asia and is sometimes cultivated in other regions as an

Pagoda tree (*Sophora*)
G.R. Roberts

ornamental. It grows 12–22 m (about 40–75 ft) tall. The alternate, compound leaves consist of 7 to 17 leaflets. The yellowish-white flowers, about 1 cm long, grow in loose, showy clusters 30–35 cm (12–14 in.) long. The fruit is a pod 5–7.5 cm long.

Pagodroma nivea, species of petrel (*q.v.*).

Pago Pago, formerly PANGO-PANGO, port, southeast Tutuila island, administrative capital since 1899 of American Samoa, in the southern Pacific, at the head of an inlet forming a deeply indented, landlocked harbour. The site was chosen in 1872 by Comdr. R.W. Meade, who negotiated facilities for a coaling station for the U.S. Navy from the Samoan high chief Mauga. It remained an active naval base from 1900 to 1951 and is now a regular port of call for all types of vessels. Canned tuna is the dominant export. Pago Pago International Airport (formerly Tafuna), built partly on a fringing reef and opened in 1964, has stimulated tourist traffic. The town is no longer the shabby place depicted by Somerset Maugham in his short story "Rain" but has assumed a modern look, with new homes, roads, and usual amenities. It has worldwide radio and telegraph communications. Pop. (1970) 2,451.

Pago Pago harbour beneath Mt. Matafao (right)
David Moore—Black Star

14°16′ S, 170°42′ W
·map, Samoa **16**:206
·Samoan geography and culture **16**:205f

Pagophilus groenlandicus: *see* harp seal.

Pagurus, a genus of hermit crab (*q.v.*).

pagus, (pl. *pagi*), Latin equivalent of German *gau*, a village community among the ancient Germanic peoples, which became a basic land unit in medieval Europe; the word survives in the modern French *pays* and Italian *paese*.
·ancient German society and land tenure **8**:42g
·Frankish administrative institutions **11**:932e
·Low Countries administrative institutions **11**:133d
·medieval legal system development **12**:152e

Pahang, state (*negeri*), eastern West Malaysia (Malaya), bounded by the states of Terengganu (formerly Trengganu) and Kelantan (north), Perak, Selangor and Negeri Sembilan (formerly Negri Sembilan [west]), and Johor (formerly Johore [south]). Its eastern coastline stretches for 130 mi (209 km) along the South China Sea. West Malaysia's largest state (area 13,886 sq mi [35,963 sq km]), it occupies the vast Sungai (River) Pahang Basin, enclosed by the Main Range to the west and the eastern highlands to the north.

A Chinese chronicle by Cha Ju Kua (*c.* 1225) mentions Pahang as subject to the Sumatran kingdom of Śrivijaya. After the 15th century it was part of the kingdom of Malacca and later came under the control of Johore. The representatives from Johore eventually established an independent sultanate, which received British protection through a treaty negotiated in 1887. Pahang became one of the Federated Malay States in 1895 and after World War II joined the Federation of Malaya.

Although most of the state is dense jungle, its central plains are intersected by numerous rivers, and a 20-mi wide coastal expanse of alluvial soil extends from Kuantan (*q.v.*; the capital) to Mersing, Johor. This coastal area includes the deltas and estuarine plains of the Kuantan, Pahang, Rompin, Endau, and Mersing rivers.

Pahang is thinly settled, its population consisting of Malays, Chinese, and semi-nomadic Aboriginals. Malay farmers and fishermen live along the rivers and coast. Chinese dominate the larger towns to the west—Bentong, Jerantut, Temerloh, and Kuala Lipis (until 1957, the state capital). Pekan, the residence of the sultan of Pahang, is in the Sungai (River) Pahang Delta.

The state is linked by road to Kuala Lumpur and Singapore and spur roads connect the larger towns. The centrally located Gemas–Kelantan railway ends in Kelantan in the north. Kuantan is the peninsula's most important east coast port; riverine transport, though highly localized, is important in the roadless interior.

Rubber estates are located along the Pahang River, the railway, and the major roads. Rice is extensively farmed in the coastal deltas. Other products include coconuts, tobacco, gutta-percha (a tough latex derivative), rattan, and hemp. The comprehensive Jengka Triangle Project of the 1970s has undertaken the clearing of more than 450 sq mi of jungle forest (lying between Maran, Temerloh, and Jerantut) for oil-palm and rubber plantations and the resettling of thousands of people in more than 100 new villages. There are large iron ore reserves at Rompin, gold is mined at Raub, and at Sungai Lembing one of Malaya's major mines for deep-vein tin has been in operation since 1888.

Two hill stations, Cameron Highlands and Bukit Fraser (*qq.v.*; Fraser's Hill), are in the western portion of the state. Taman Negara (national park), with an area of 1,677 sq mi and site of Gunong Tahan (7,185 ft [2,189 m]), highest mountain of the Malay Peninsula, is in the northeast corner. The Kerau Wildlife Reserve in the centre of the state has an area of 161,280 ac (65,252 ha). Pop. (1970 prelim.) 503,131.

Pahang, Sungai, in Pahang state, West Malaysia (Malaya), is the longest river on the Malay Peninsula; it rises in two headstreams, the Jelai and Tembeling, about 10 mi (16 km) north of Jerantut and flows south past Temerloh, paralleling the Main Range to Mengkarak, where, at the break of slope between the mountains and the plains, it abruptly turns eastward. The river then completes its 271-mi course, through alluvial plains more than 20 mi wide, to the South China Sea at Pekan.

Navigable upstream by shallow-draft boats for about 250 mi, the Pahang was a vital link in the porterage route between the east and west coasts during the 15th and 16th centuries. Settlers later moved upriver, establishing rubber and coconut plantations along its banks. Deforestation projects have led to heavy flooding during the monsoon season (November–February).
3°32′ N, 103°28′ E
·map, Malaysia **11**:370

Pahang Civil War (1857–63), a complicated succession dispute between rival Malay contenders for the Pahang throne during which Britain began to contest Siamese hegemony in Malaya. In 1857 Bendahara Tun Ali died, leaving two sons whose claims to succession were both backed by outside interests. Tun Mutahir, the oldest son, was assisted by the *temenggong* of Johore for reasons of self-interest and family connections. Wan Ahmad, the younger son, received aid from the Sultan of Trengganu, the Siamese, and the former sultan of Lingga. These supporters sought to expand their individual influence in Pahang. The hostilities, as in other Malay wars of this era, consisted of infrequent raids and ambushes and more lengthy battles near stockades.

In 1862, when Siamese warships were sent to aid Wan Ahmad, they were dispersed by a British vessel, supporting Tun Mutahir. The civil war petered out in 1863, when Tun Mutahir died.

Pahari, also known as PARBATE, and KHASIYA, or KHASA, people of mixed descent who comprise about half the population of Nepal. They speak an Indo-European language sometimes called Nepali, but which bears no relation to the Tibeto-Burman tongues of many other ethnic groups in Nepal. The Pahari are North Indian in their religious and cultural institutions. Their numbers in Nepal are estimated at more than 4,800,000.

The majority of the Pahari belong to the high Hindu caste groups of Brahmins and Kṣatriya. There are also low-caste Pahari known as Ḍom, many of whom are goldsmiths, leatherworkers, metalworkers, tailors, musicians, drummers, and sweepers. Most of the high-caste Pahari are farmers.

People usually marry within their caste group, although there is some intermarriage between closely-ranked caste groups such as Brahmins and Kṣatriya. Traditionally the family of the groom paid a bride price to the family of the bride, in contrast to the Indian custom of dowry. The extended family is common, including under one roof parents, unmarried children, and married sons with their wives and children.
·Himachal Pradesh culture **8**:881b

Pahari woman of Pokhara, Nepal
W.H. Hodge

Pahari language ("language of the mountains"), group of Indo-Aryan dialects spoken by more than 1,000,000 persons in the lower ranges of the Himalayas. Three divisions are distinguished: Eastern Pahari, represented by Nepali of Nepal; Central Pahari, spoken in the north of Uttar Pradesh; and Western Pahari, found around Simla in Himachal Pradesh. The most important dialect is Nepali (Naipali), also called Khas-kura and Gorkhali (Gurkhali). Because most of the inhabitants of Nepal speak a form of Tibeto-Burman speech, Nepali has borrowed many Tibeto-Burman idioms that Central and Western Pahari do not have. The Nepali language was brought to Nepal by the Gurkha conquerors in 1768. The chief Central Pahari dialects are Garhwali and Kumauni. Western Pahari includes a great number of dialects, of which the most important are Sirmauri, Kiunthali, Jaunsari, Chameali, Churahi, Mandeali, Gadi, and Kuluhi. Pahari dialects have several linguistic features in common with Rajasthani and Kashmiri (*qq.v.*).
·derivation and classification **12**:954a
·modern Indo-Aryan language, table 1 **9**:440; map 442

Pahari painting, miniature painting and book illustration that developed in the independent states of the Himalayan foothills in India, made up of two markedly contrasting schools, the bold intense Basohli and the delicate and lyrical Kangra. Pahari painting—sometimes referred to as Hill painting (*pahārī*, "of the hills")—is closely related in conception and feeling to Rajasthani painting and shares with the Rājput art of the plains a preference in subject for the legends of the cowherd god, Kṛṣṇa (Krishna).

Rādhā dancing before Kṛṣna, Pahari painting in the Kāngra style, *c.* AD 1780; in the Lalbhai collection, Ahmadābād, Gujarāt, India
P. Chandra

The earliest known paintings in the hills, *c.* 1690, are in the Basohli idiom, a style that continued at numerous centres until about mid-18th century. Its place was taken by a transitional style sometimes referred to as pre-Kangra, which lasted *c.* 1740–75. During the mid-18th century, a number of artist families trained in the late Mughal style apparently fled Delhi for the hills in search of new patrons and more settled living conditions. The influence of late Mughal art is evident in the new style, which appears as a complete rejection of the Basohli school. Colours are less intense, the treatment of landscape and perspective is generally more naturalistic, and the line is more refined and delicate.

By 1770 the lyrical charm of the Kangra school was fully developed. It reached its peak during the early years of the reign of one of its important patrons, Rājā Sansār Chand (1775–1823).

The school was not confined to the Kangra state but ranged over the entire hill area, with many distinctive idioms. As the states were small and often very close to each other it is difficult to assign a definitive provenance to much of the painting.

The life and loves of Lord Kṛṣṇa (Krishna) as expressed in the poetic works the *Bhāgavata-Purāṇa* and the *Gītagovinda* make up the commonest theme of the paintings, together with other Hindu myths, hero–heroine, and *rāgamālā* (musical modes) series and portraits of hill chiefs and their families.

After 1800 the school began to decline, though painting of inferior quality continued to be done through the remainder of the 19th century. *Major ref.* **17**:203e

·style characteristics, illus., **17**: South Asian Peoples, Arts of, Plates 6 and 7

Pahiatua, administrative headquarters, Pahiatua County, south North Island, New Zealand, at the confluence of the Mangatainoka River and Mangaramarama Creek, 80 mi (130 km) northeast of Wellington. It was founded in 1881 by Scandinavian immigrants and gazetted a borough in 1892. The town, which derives its name from a Maori word meaning "dwelling place of the God," was almost totally destroyed in 1897 when a fire occurred in the surrounding Forty Mile Bush Forest. Pahiatua now serves a dairy, mixed, and fat-lamb farming area and has various light industries. On the Napier–Palmerston North State Highway, it is linked to the North Island Main Trunk Railway by a 1.5-mi spur. Pop. (1973 est.) 2,620.
40°27′ S, 175°50′ E

Pahjois-Karjalan lääni (Finland): *see* Pohjois-Karjala.

Pahlavī (Iran): *see* Bandar-e Pahlavī.

Pahlavi, or PEHLEVI, ruling dynasty of Iran, which came to power in 1925. The founder of the dynasty was Reza Khan (ruled 1925–41 as Reza Shah Pahlavi of Iran; *q.v.*).

Pahlavi (PEHLEVI) **alphabet,** writing system of the Persian people from the 2nd century BC until the advent of Islām (7th century AD); the Zoroastrian sacred book, the Avesta, is written in a variant of Pahlavi called Avestan. The Pahlavi alphabet developed from the Aramaic alphabet and occurs in at least three local varieties: northwestern, Pahlavik, or Arsacid; southwestern, Parsik, or Sāsānian (in both monumental and cursive forms); and eastern, known only in the cursive form. All were written from right to left. Of the 22 letters in Aramaic, most came to represent more than one sound in Pahlavi; several were not used at all, and one evolved into two letters in Pahlavi. Northwestern Pahlavi had 20 letters, and southwestern had 19. Avestan, a cursive script, has 50 distinct letters and was perhaps separately invented, patterned after Pahlavi.

A peculiarity of Pahlavi was the custom of using Aramaic words in writing to represent Pahlavi words; these served, so to speak, as ideograms. An example is the word for "king," in Pahlavi *shāh*, which was consistently written *m-l-k* after the Aramaic word for "king," *malka*, but read as *shāh*. A great many such ideograms were in standard use, including all pronouns and conjunctions and many nouns and verbs, making Pahlavi quite difficult to read.

·Iranian modifications of Aramaic script **9**:456f

Pahlavi Dam, or DEZ DAM, an arch dam across the Dez River in Iran, completed in 1963. The dam is 668 feet (204 metres) high, 787 feet (240 metres) wide at the crest, and has a volume of 608,000 cubic yards (465,000 cubic metres). Until the late 1960s it was the largest Iranian development scheme; it is one of 14 major projects in Khūzestān province.

·dam design and dimensions **5**:444a

Pahlavi (PEHLEVI) **language,** major form of the Middle Persian language (*see* Persian language), which existed from the 3rd to the 10th century and was the official language of the Sāsānian Empire (AD 226–652). It is attested by Zoroastrian books, coins, and inscriptions. Pahlavi books were written in a confusing writing system of Aramaic origin called the Pahlavi alphabet. The major part of Pahlavi literature is religious, including translations from and commentaries on the Avesta. Little has survived from pre-Islāmic times, and the *Bundahishn* and *Dēnkart*, both Zoroastrian religious works, date from the Islāmic period. Manuscripts were preserved by the Parsis (Zoroastrians) of Bombay and elsewhere. Pahlavi was superseded by Modern Persian, written in the Arabic alphabet.

·Iranian linguistic relationships **9**:450g
·source text critical problems **9**:453c
·Zoroastrian later Avestan texts **19**:1173a

pahoehoe lava: *see* lava.

Pahouins: *see* Fang.

Pa Hsien (Chinese: Eight Immortals), a heterogeneous group of holy Taoists, each of whom earned the right to immortality and had free access to the Peach Festival of Hsi Wang Mu, Queen Mother of the West. Though unacquainted in real life, the eight are frequently depicted as a group—bearing gifts, for instance, to Shou Hsing, god of longevity, to safeguard their position as immortals.

In Chinese art they sometimes also stand alone or appear in smaller groups. Four of them, for example, recline beneath a pine tree: Chung-li Ch'üan and Lü Tung-pin are drinking wine heated by Li T'ieh-kuai, while Lan Ts'ai-ho entertains them on a flute. Lists vary, but the other four immortals are most commonly identified as Chang Kuo-lao, Han Hsiang, Ts'ao Kuo-chiu, and Ho Hsien-ku. *Major ref.* **17**:1052b

·ceramic figures and symbolic motifs **14**:918g
·magical powers and myths **4**:413e

Pa Hsien, the Eight Immortals, Chinese painting of the 18th century; in the Musée Guimet, Paris

Giraudon

Pai (people): *see* Min-chia.

Pai, town and district, Mae Hong Son province, northwestern Thailand, on the Nam Mae (stream) Pai, southeast of the 460-sq-mi (1,200-sq-km) Lum Nam Pai Game Sanctuary, created 1972, preserving elephant and gaur. Pop. (1970) district, 14,549.
19°25′ N, 98°26′ E

·map, Thailand **18**:199

Pai-ch'eng, also known as T'AO-AN, Pin-yin romanization, respectively, BAI-CHENG and TAO-AN, city, northwest Kirin Province (*sheng*), China. It is a county-level municipality and the administrative centre of Pai-ch'eng Area. This region was originally a hunting ground reserved for the Mongols and was not opened for legitimate colonization by the Chinese till 1902; it remains an area of extensive agriculture with pastoral activities playing a major role.

Pai-ch'eng was first established as a county seat, called Ching-an, in 1904; it remained a place of minor importance until the opening of the railway from Ch'i-ch'i-ha-erh to Ssu-p'ing in 1920. In 1930 another line was opened to Wu-lan-hao-t'e (now K'o-erh-ch'in-yu-i-ch'ien-ch'i, in Kirin), enabling Pai-ch'eng to become the market centre for the Mongolian border area; another line to the east was constructed by the Japanese in the 1930s.

P'ai-cheng had a population of about 20,000 at the end of World War II and had a small generating plant and a paper mill but little industry. Since 1949 more small-scale industry has been established, based on local agriculture. Pai-ch'eng, however, remains essentially an administrative and commercial centre. Latest pop. est. 70,000.
45°22′ N, 122°47′ E

paidagōgos, in ancient Greek cultures, a slave whose duties were to educate children in conduct, good manners, and morals and to act as a lesson coach.

·Hellenistic educational role and pedagogy **6**:325e

paideia, system of education and training in classical Greek and Hellenistic (Greco-Roman) cultures that included such subjects as gymnastics, grammar, rhetoric, music, mathematics, geography, natural history, and philosophy. In the early Christian era the Greek paideia, called humanitas, served as a model for Christian institutions of higher learning, such as the Christian school of Alexandria in Egypt, which offered theology as the highest and culminating science of their curricula.

paid-in capital, in accounting, portion of owners' equity representing the amounts paid to the corporation in exchange for shares of the company's preferred and common stock.

·accounting and balance-sheet relationships **1**:36e

Paid on Both Sides, verse play by W.H. Auden published with *Poems* (1930).

·source, theme, and artistic philosophy **2**:363f

PAIGC: *see* Partido Africano da Independência da Guiné e Cabo Verde.

Paige, Satchel (b. LEROY ROBERT PAIGE, July 7, 1906?, Mobile, Ala.), professional baseball pitcher who earned legendary fame many years before entering the major leagues in 1948, after the unwritten rule against black players was relaxed. A right-handed, loose-jointed "beanpole" standing 6 feet 3½ inches, Paige had considerable pitching speed and developed a comprehensive mastery of slow-breaking deliveries (one of which was known as the "eephus ball").

In his later years Paige, a humorous man, derived much amusement from the controversy about his age; his birth date is sometimes placed as early as Dec. 18, 1899. He was surely well past his prime in 1948 when Bill Veeck signed him for the Cleveland Indians, but he helped to spark that team to American League pennant and World Series victories that year. When Veeck moved to the St. Louis Browns, Paige joined that team and was its most effective relief pitcher from 1951 through 1953.

Paige, 1942
UPI Compix

Prior to his major league career, Paige was a pitcher for various teams in the Negro Southern Association and the Negro National League. Wearing a false red beard, he also played for the bearded House of David team. A true "iron man," he pitched in the Caribbean, Central America, and South America during the northern winter. As a barnstormer he would travel as many as 30,000 miles a year while pitching for any team willing to meet his price. In 1935 he pitched every day for 29 days.

Despite the colour bar, Paige faced the best major league players in exhibition games before 1948. He once struck out Rogers Hornsby, probably the greatest right-handed hitter in baseball history, five times in one game. In Hollywood, Calif., in 1934 Paige scored a spectacular 1–0 victory in 13 innings over Dizzy Dean, who won 30 games for the St. Louis Cardinals that year.

paigeite (mineral): *see* ludwigite.

Paignton, town and holiday resort in the county of Devon, England. It faces Tor Bay and the English Channel and in 1961 was amalgamated with Torquay and Brixham to form the urban district of Torbay. The red-sandstone parish Church of St. John dates from the 15th century, although its 90-ft (27-m) tower is a little earlier. Another medieval tower is found at the old Bishop's Palace. Near the church is Kirkham House, built in the 15th century and now under the care of the Department of the Environment. The town's main attractions for tourists are its sands, long esplanade, and zoo. Latest census 30,292.
50°26′ N, 3°34′ W
·map, United Kingdom **18**:866

Pai Ho, river in Hopeh Province, northern China, rises near the Great Wall near Kuyüan and flows generally southeast past Tunghsien, east of Peking, to join the Yungtin Ho (river) after a course of 300 mi (480 km).
40°22′ N, 116°19′ E
·Peking water supplies **14**:10d

pai-hua (Chinese "colloquial language"), vernacular style of Chinese adopted as a written language in a movement to revitalize the Classical Chinese literary language and make it more accessible to the common people. Started in 1917 by the philosopher and historian Hu Shih, the *pai-hua* literary movement succeeded in making *pai-hua* the language of textbooks, periodicals, newspapers, and public documents, thus causing a definite change in Chinese cultural life.
·Chinese intellectual revolution **4**:368f
·classical change and advantages **6**:388d
·Hu Shih's literary reform **9**:66b

Pai-i, also called PA-I or P'O-I, ethnic group inhabiting the hot river valleys of southwest Yunnan Province in China. The Pai-i are part of the Tai (*q.v.*) cultural group of China and Southeast Asia. They spread southward from their centres in Szechwan and the Yangtze Valley two millennia ago, following the southern tributaries of the Yangtze into the Yunnan lake basins. Subsequently, under pressure from the Chinese, the Pai-i moved farther southwest into the river basins of the China–Burma frontier region. Those that settled across the border in the Shan Plateau are called the Shan tribes of Burma.

Although the Pai-i in Yunnan were compelled to acknowledge Chinese suzerainty, they were ruled generally by their own hereditary local chieftains. Many of them retained virtual autonomy in local affairs until after the Communists achieved power in China, when the Pai-i were organized into a Tai autonomous district. The district had a population of about 470,000 in the 1960s.

The Pai-i live by rice agriculture and stock raising; they use the buffalo as a draft animal. Like the Burmese, they adhere to the Theravada (southern) branch of Buddhism; on the other hand, the Pai-i have adopted a number of Chinese ways—for example, in burial customs.

Päijänne, Lake, located in parts of the *läänit* (provinces) of Keski-Suomi, Häme, and Mikkeli, south central Finland. It has an area of 421 sq mi (1,090 sq km), making it the largest single Finnish lake. It has a maximum depth of 305 ft (93 m) and is about 85 mi (135 km) long and between 2 and 18 mi wide, broken by thousands of islands. Jyväskylä, at the north tip of the lake, and Heinola, on a southeastern branch of the lake, are the principal towns. They are connected by ship service with the major city of Lahti to the south of Lake Päijänne via the Vesijärven Kanava (canal) and lake. The Päijänne lake system is drained southward to the Gulf of Finland by the Kymijoki (river). The irregular shoreline around Lake Päijänne is heavily forested and supports important timber operations that utilize the lake as a means of transport. Numerous villages dot the shore of the lake and many private villas are on the quiet bays off its southern end.
61°35′ N, 25°30′ E
·map, Finland **7**:304

paile, in heraldry, a figure of the ordinary class of charges on the upper half of a saltire and half a pale.
·heraldic design elements **8**:788c

Pai-lien chiao, also known as WHITE LOTUS SOCIETY, religious sect in China during the Ch'ing dynasty (1644–1912).
·Ch'ing's religiopolitical dissent **4**:357b

paille-maille (game): *see* pall-mall.

Pai Lu Tung Academy (Chinese: "White Deer Grotto Academy"), near Ku-lung, Kiangsi province, China.
·Kiangsi province history **10**:458e

Pai Marire (religio-military cult): *see* Hau-hau Movement.

pai-miao, a brush technique in Chinese painting that produces a finely controlled, supple ink outline drawing without any colour or wash (diluted ink or paint applied in broad sweeps) embellishment. It is commonly used for figure painting, in which precise description is important. Outline painting of more brittle articulations to define areas subsequently filled in with colour is called *kou-le.* Painting without outline but rather with forms achieved by washes of ink and colour is known as *mo-ku*, or "boneless."
·ink brush drawing techniques **5**:1010c

pain, any disagreeable sensation not associated with one of the special senses (*i.e.*, bad taste, bad smell, unpleasant sounds, are not thought of as instances of pain).
·alkaloid use in alleviation **1**:596a
·analgesic agents and action **1**:717g
·anesthesia and insensitivity to pain **1**:866h
·childbirth analgesia **13**:1038a
·diagnosis from symptoms **5**:685f
·drug effects on nervous system **12**:992d
·drugs used as anesthetics and analgesics **5**:1045d
·headache causative mechanisms **8**:684f
·heart disease symptoms **3**:888f
·joint sensitivity and innervation **10**:258f
·narcotic response to severity and degree of pain **12**:841h
·relief of disease symptoms **18**:280e
·respiratory disease symptom complex **15**:767d
·throbbing sensation in inflammation **9**:560e
·treatment by autonomic denervation **12**:1040a
·treatment by nerve surgery **12**:1004g

pain, theories of 13:865, attempt to explain the experience usually associated with injury or some other type of damage to the body. Since another person's pain cannot be directly observed, inferences regarding it are drawn from the objective behaviour of the subject.

The text article contains sections on the manifestations of pain (*e.g.*, verbal complaints and avoidance behaviour); on neurophysiological and psychological theories of pain; on methods used to modify or abolish the experience (*e.g.*, with drugs or hypnosis); and on masochism.

REFERENCES in other text articles:
·brain function and structure **6**:766d
·diagnosis of physical symptoms **5**:685f
·Epicurean psychology and ethics **6**:912a
·fish sensory ability **7**:336f
·human and animal reception **11**:802b
·reflex elicitation hierarchies **12**:1015d
·sensory awareness as mind attribute **12**:226e
·skin senses and repetitive stimulation **16**:550b
·spinal cord transmission pathways **12**:1009g

Paine, Robert Treat (1731–1814), U.S. politician, jurist, member of the Continental Congress (1774–78), and signer of the Declaration of Independence. Paine was speaker of the Massachusetts Provincial Assembly (1777), a judge of the Massachusetts Supreme Court (1790–1804), and in 1780 was one of the founders of the American Academy of Arts and Sciences.

Paine, Thomas 13:867 (b. Jan. 29, 1737, Thetford, Norfolk—d. June 8, 1809, New York City), political journalist who was one of the greatest political pamphleteers in history.

Abstract of text biography. Early hardships as a sailor, teacher, and exciseman partially explain Paine's lifelong sympathy for the poor and unfortunate and his emigration to America on Benjamin Franklin's recommendation. His first employment there was editing the *Pennsylvania Magazine;* he also began publishing numerous articles of his own. The pamphlet for which he is most widely known, "Common Sense" (1776), provided the most persuasive argument for independence from England for many. His greatest contribution during the Revolutionary War was the publication of 16 "Crisis" papers (1776–83).

During his stay in Europe between 1787 and

1802, Paine published *Rights of Man* (1791), which originated as a response to Edmund Burke's attack on the French Revolution and grew into a proposal for the elimination of poverty, illiteracy, unemployment, and war. As a result of the fears of revolution generated by his work, he was indicted for treason in England, but managed to escape to France, where he was elected to the revolutionary National Convention. The first part of *Age of Reason* (1794) was published during Paine's year in prison while Robespierre was in power. In 1802 Paine returned to the United States. He found that his contributions had been largely forgotten.

REFERENCES in other text articles:
- ·American literature development **10**:1168c
- ·British reaction to French Revolution **3**:259b
- ·censorship in 18th-century England **3**:1088g
- ·conservative–progressive split **5**:66c
- ·Erskine's defense on treason charge **6**:958d

Painesville, city, seat of Lake County, northeastern Ohio, U.S., near the mouth of the Grand River and Lake Erie. The site, first settled permanently by Gen. Edward Paine with a party of 66, was laid out around 1805; it was known variously as The Opening, Oak Openings, and Champion (for Henry Champion, original owner of the plot). In 1816 the community was renamed to honour Paine and was incorporated as a village in 1832. Jonathan Goldsmith, an architect of the Western Reserve period, built many elegant homes there in the 1820s, some of which survive.

The Cleveland, Painesville and Ashtabula (now Penn Central) Railroad came through in 1853, and the nursery business, now extensive, began in 1854. Lake Erie College (founded as Willoughby Seminary for women in 1847) was moved to Painesville in 1856. The village remained mainly residential and became a city in 1902. Since 1940 it has developed industrially as part of Lake Erie's "chemical shore." Pop. (1980) 16,391.
41°43′ N, 81°15′ W

Painlevé, Paul (b. Dec. 5, 1863, Paris—d. Oct. 29, 1933, Paris), politician, mathematician, and patron of French aviation who was prime minister at a crucial period of World War I and again during the 1925 financial crisis.

Educated at the École Normale Superieure and the University of Paris, where he received his doctorate in mathematics in 1887, Painlevé taught at the universities of Lille and Paris and the École Polytechnique. He took special interest in the infant science of aviation, becoming a theoretician of heavier-than-air flight. He was the first Frenchman to fly with Wilbur Wright, at Auvours in 1908, and the following year created the first course in aeronautical mechanics at the École Aeronautique.

Becoming interested in politics, Painlevé was elected to the Chamber of Deputies from a Paris constituency in 1906. He served as minister of education and minister of inventions in the wartime government of Aristide Briand, and, as war minister from March to September 1917, made the controversial decision to replace Gen. Robert-Georges Nivelle with Gen. Philippe Pétain after the costly failure of

Painlevé, drawing by A. Bilis, 1930
By courtesy of the Bibliotheque Nationale, Paris

Nivelle's offensive in May. In September 1917 he formed his own ministry and the following month agreed to the establishment of the Supreme Allied Council at Versailles, choosing as the French representative Gen. Ferdinand Foch, who later became Allied commander. Painlevé resigned in November, however, and was succeeded as prime minister by Georges Clemenceau.

Painlevé was one of the founders of the Cartel des Gauches, a coalition of Socialists and radicals, which defeated the rightist Bloc National in the general elections of 1924. He became prime minister in April 1925 but resigned in November because neither his ministers nor French financial interests could agree on a solution to the financial crisis engendered by the devaluation of the franc. Subsequently, he served as war minister in the governments of Aristide Briand and Raymond Poincaré and was air minister in 1930–31 and 1931–32.

Although not an outstanding political leader, Painlevé was internationally recognized as a brilliant mathematician. He was elected a member of the Académie des Sciences in 1900.

pain nerve (biology): *see* nerves and nervous systems.

paint: *see* paints, varnishes, and allied products.

paint brush (plant): *see* Indian paint brush.

Painted Colonnade, Greek STOA POIKILE, hall in Olympia, Cyprus.
·Zeno of Citium and Stoicism **17**:699a

painted cup (plant): *see* Indian paint brush.

Painted Desert, section of the high plateau in north central Arizona, U.S., extending from

Painted Desert, Arizona
David Muench—EB Inc.

the Grand Canyon in a southeasterly direction along the north side of the Little Colorado River to Holbrook. It is approximately 150 mi (240 km) long and 15 to 50 mi wide and covers an area of 7,500 sq mi (19,400 sq km). The name was first used in 1858 by a government explorer, Lieut. Joseph C. Ives, to describe the brilliantly coloured shales, marls, and sandstones, which are banded with vivid red, yellow, blue, white, and lavender. At times the air glows with a pink mist or purple haze of desert dust. Elevations range from 4,500 ft (1,370 m) to 6,500 ft. The surface is rolling, broken by isolated buttes, and bounded on the north by vermilion cliffs, rising to broad, flat-topped mesas. Marks of volcanic activity are abundant and widely scattered. The region is barren and arid, with 5–9 in. (127–229 mm) annual precipitation and temperature extremes of −25° to 105° F (−31° to 41° C). Part of the eastern section is within the Petrified Forest National Park (94,189 ac [38,118 ha]) and contains the Black Forest, one of the four remarkable areas of petrified trees of Mesozoic (Triassic) Age, about 170,000,000 years old. Navaho and Hopi Indian reservations occupy a large part of the Painted Desert, and these tribes use the variegated, brightly coloured sands for their famous ceremonial sand paintings.
36°00′ N, 111°20′ W

painted lady (plant): *see* Indian paint brush.

painted snipe, boldly marked marsh bird with snipelike body and bill. Painted snipes

Painted snipe (*Rostratula benghalensis*)
Peter Slater—Photo Researchers

are about 25 centimetres (10 inches) in length and are brown and white in colour. There are two species, comprising the family Rostratulidae (order Charadriiformes).

The Old World painted snipe (*Rostratula benghalensis*) ranges from Africa to Australia and Japan and has yellowish "spectacles" around the eyes.

The South American painted snipe (*Nycticryphes semicollaris*) is a darker bird with a yellow-striped back.

In both species the female is larger and brighter in colour than the male. She courts the male, and he undertakes most of the nesting duties. Painted snipes nest on the ground, the Old World painted snipe laying four eggs, the South American species laying two eggs. The downy young readily take to the water.
·characteristics and classification **4**:33f; illus. 39

painted turtle (*Chrysemys picta*), brightly marked North American turtle, family Emydidae, found from southern Canada to northern Mexico. Sometimes kept as a pet, the painted turtle is a smooth-shelled reptile with a shell about 10 to 18 centimetres (4 to 7 inches) long. It has red and yellow markings on its relatively flat, black or greenish-brown upper shell. The painted turtle usually lives in

Painted turtle (*Chrysemys picta*)
Leonard Lee Rue III—National Audubon Society

quiet, shallow bodies of fresh water, especially those with thickly planted mud bottoms. It feeds on plants, small animals, and some carrion. It often basks in large groups on logs and other objects and in many areas it hibernates during the winter.
·hearing range of turtles **17**:48a

painter (cat): *see* puma.

Painter, town, Accomack County, Virginia, U.S., on the Delmarva Peninsula. Named for an official of the Pennsylvania Railroad, it is situated on the Penn Central and on the main north-south road connecting Maryland to the north with Norfolk, Va., to the south via the Chesapeake Bay Bridge-Tunnel. Inc. 1950. Pop. (1980) 321.
37°35′ N, 75°47′ W

Painter, Theophilus Shickel (b. Aug. 22, 1889, Salem, Va.—d. Oct. 5, 1969, Fort Stockton, Tex.), zoologist and cytologist who first identified individual genes in the chromosomes of fruit flies.

He received a Ph.D. degree from Yale (1913) and was a member of the faculty there (1913–16). In 1916 he joined the faculty of the University of Texas, where, in 1946, he became president. Painter early realized that the unusually large cells of the salivary glands of *Drosophila* fruit flies are particularly well suited for studies of genes and chromosomes. In 1933 he published a drawing of a section of a *Drosophila* chromosome showing more than 150 bands; precise loci, or positions, of genes could, for the first time, be determined by means of these bands.

Painter, William (b. *c.* 1540—d. February 1594, London), English author whose collection of tales, *The Palace of Pleasure*, based on classical and Italian originals, was a source book for many Elizabethan dramatists. Educated at St. John's College, Cambridge, he was ordained in 1560. In 1561 he became a clerk of the ordnance in the Tower of London, a position in which he appears to have amassed a fortune out of the public funds. In 1591 his son Anthony confessed that he and his father had abused their trust, but Painter retained his office until his death.

The first volume of *The Palace of Pleasure*, which appeared in 1566, contained 60 tales. It was followed in the next year by a volume including 34 new stories. An improved edition (1575) contained seven more new stories. To its popularity, and that of similar collections, is due the high proportion of Elizabethan plays with Italian settings.

The early tragedies *Appius and Virginia, a Tragedy*, by John Webster, and *The Tragedy of Tancred and Gismund*, by Robert Wilmot, were taken from Painter's book, and it was also the source for Shakespeare's *Timon of Athens* and *All's Well That Ends Well* (and probably for details in *Romeo and Juliet* and *The Rape of Lucrece*), for Beaumont and Fletcher's *Triumph of Death*, and for James Shirley's *Loves Crueltie*.

painting, art of 13:869, expression of ideas and emotions, with the creation of certain aesthetic qualities, in a two-dimensional visual language.

TEXT ARTICLE covers:
Elements and principles of design **13**:869h
Techniques and methods 875e
Tempera 876h
Fresco 877f
Oil 878d
Watercolour 879a
Ink 879d
Gouache 879e
Encaustic 879f
Casein 879g
Synthetic mediums 879h
Other mediums 880b
Mixed mediums 880h
Mural painting 881a
Easel and panel painting 881e
Miniature painting 881f
Manuscript illumination and related forms 881h
Scroll painting 882c
Screen and fan painting 882d
Panoramas 882g
Modern forms 882g
Imagery and subject matter 883a
Symbolism 885b

REFERENCES in other text articles:
·African visual art forms and styles **1**:254e
·Amerindian stylistic directions **1**:692e; illus.
ancient, Western
·Aegean civilization contributions **1**:118d
·early Christian forms and styles **19**:321g
·Egyptian visual art history **19**:249g *passim* to 255e
·Greek visual arts development **19**:285b
·Roman visual art forms and styles **19**:314e
·Stone Age styles and themes **17**:704d; illus.
·arms decoration with colour **2**:33a
·Australian Aboriginal bark designs **2**:428f
Baroque
·Caravaggio's use of light **3**:816e
·Dutch 17th-century themes and moods **11**:149h
·Gainsborough's style and themes **7**:823f
·Hals's brushstroke technique **8**:576g
·major artists, styles, and themes **19**:422b
·Rembrandt's use of chiaroscuro **15**:653c
·Rubens' style and contributions **16**:1a
·Van Dyke's style and major works **19**:24b
·Velázquez' technique and adaptations **19**:53g; illus.
Central Asian
·Nepalese and Tibetan styles **3**:1140f *passim* to 1142g
·Turkistan mural paintings **3**:1134e
·classification as visual art **2**:82h
·comic depiction of common life **4**:965e
·critical and aesthetic approaches **2**:43b
·drawing's similarities and differences **5**:995d
East Asian
·Chinese landscape tradition **8**:1123a
·Chinese visual arts development **19**:176f *passim* to 207a
·Japanese visual arts development **19**:215f *passim* to 243c
·Korean visual arts development **19**:208h *passim* to 215d
·Ma Yüan's landscapes **11**:723h
·Ming dynasty's artistic philosophy **4**:353b
·Sesshū as height of sumi-e style **16**:567f
·Taoist doctrines and techniques **10**:534a
·Eastern and Western Christian developments **4**:502e; illus. 485
folk art
·media and decorative works **7**:472e; illus.
·U.S. national folk art **7**:478h
·interior design styles and use **9**:702c
Islāmic peoples
·Islāmic artistic prohibitions **9**:923f
·visual arts development **9**:994g *passim* to 1009c
·Jewish religious principles **10**:299b
medieval
·Coptic frieze designs **19**:345a
·Giotto's career, works, and style **8**:161f
·Gothic visual art forms **19**:367g
·Romanesque mural painting and illumination **19**:360h
·van Eyck's contributions **7**:89f
modern
·Cezanne's perspective, colour, and form **4**:10g
·Gauguin's primitivism and use of colour **7**:958c
·Impressionism and the visual process **13**:284c
·Kandinsky's theories of abstraction **10**:376e
·Matisse's colour and line **11**:699a
·modern visual art development **19**:473g
·Modigliani's vocation and studies **12**:298g
·Picasso's development and diversity **14**:440g
·Pollock's action painting development **14**:748d
·U.S. dominance of abstract art **18**:941h
Neoclassicism and Romanticism
·David's life and works **5**:519g
·Delacroix's style and development **5**:565c
·Ingres's classical heritage **9**:583e
·Romanticism's major exponents **19**:454e
·Romantic style development **6**:1070a
·photography aesthetics development **14**:312c
·pottery decoration techniques **14**:896c
·preservation and restoration techniques **2**:59g
·professional status and training of artist **2**:93d *passim* to 95a
Renaissance
·Alberti's development of perspective **1**:428e
·Bellini's use of tempera and oils **2**:828e
·Correggio's contribution and techniques **5**:190a
·El Greco's use of colour and distortion **8**:306g
·Leonardo's career **10**:809h
·Lippi's artistic eclecticism **10**:1022f
·major artists and styles **19**:397b *passim* to 406e
·Mantegna's experiments in illusionism **11**:462a
·Michelangelo's sculptural figures **12**:98f
·perspective in theatrical scenery **18**:223b
·Raphael's life and works **15**:512a
·sculpture's use of paint **16**:431e
South Asia
·Ceylonese major works **17**:206f
·Indian style development **17**:197e
·Jaina forms and media **10**:13g
·South Asian styles, illus., **17**:South Asian Peoples, Arts of, Plates
Southeast Asia
·Southeast Asian styles, illus., **17**:Southeast Asian Peoples, Arts of, Plates
·styles and iconography **17**:258c
·stained glass technique and design **17**:567a
·stylistic movements in the 19th century **6**:1076a
·visual arts development in West **19**:246g
·Western styles, illus., **19**:Visual Arts, Western, Plates

RELATED ENTRIES in the *Ready Reference and Index: for*
mediums and tools: see casein painting; Claude Lorrain glass; distemper, whitewash, and calcimine; encaustic painting; frottage; gouache; maulstick; muller; tempera painting; watercolour
painting surfaces: easel painting; fresco painting; mural painting; panel painting; sizing
techniques and styles: camaieu; diorama; fresco painting; grisaille; impasto; mural painting; panorama; plein air painting; sfumato; tenebrism; tondo; veduta
other: bloom; fête champêtre; limner; pentimento

Painting, Photography, Film (1925), book of photographs collected by László Moholy-Nagy.
·camera as means of discovering form **14**:321c

paint pot (geology): *see* mud volcano.

Paint Rock, town, seat of Concho county, central Texas, U.S., on the Concho River about 30 mi (50 km) east of San Angelo. It is situated at an altitude of about 1,640 ft (500 m) and is named for the approximately 1,500 Indian pictographs found on a nearby river bluff, dating from prehistoric times to the appearance of Christian missions in the vicinity. Pop. (1980) 256.
31°31′ N, 99°55′ W

paints, varnishes, and allied products 13:886, coatings applied to protect and enhance interior and exterior surfaces and objects.

The text article covers historical development, paint manufacture, pigments and other colorants, varnishes and other paint binders, films, paint application, economics, and future of the coatings industry.

REFERENCES in other text articles:
·art deterioration and preservation **2**:60f
·Asterales commercial importance **2**:213g
·chemical industry technology **4**:132d
·conifer commercial uses **5**:3b
·fine arts use **13**:876g
·floor-covering manufacture **7**:410d
·homopteran lac excretion and use **8**:1037c
·luminous calcium sulfide production **3**:586d
paints
·aluminum pigment uses **1**:646c
·automobile body construction **2**:520d
·Bessemer's gold paint **2**:870g
·colloidal polymeric substances **4**:859a
·corrosion prevention and paint pigment **11**:1077c
·crystallographic identification method **5**:346a
·fire control capabilities **7**:314f
·lead pigment production **10**:730c
·lead poisoning causation **5**:852c
·luminous paint and radioisotopes **11**:180e
·mercury pigments and mildew-proofing **11**:923b
·pneumatic sprayer and airbrush **14**:584d
·testing of radiation effect on material **11**:629h
·zinc coating and galvanizing of metals **19**:1149e *passim* to 1150d
·sunflower seed oil importance **2**:213g

varnishes
·chemical modification of oils 14:517c
·fibre development from varnish solution 7:258c
·woodwork finishing techniques 3:956a

RELATED ENTRIES in the *Ready Reference and Index: for*
paints and varnishes: see black varnish; bronzing; Brunswick black; drying oil; lacquer; luminous paint; shellac
other: lac; spray gun and airbrush; varnish tree

Paipai, also known as AKWA' ALA, North American Indian tribe of Mexico living in Baja California and speaking a language of the Yuman branch of the Hokan linguistic stock.
·language, habitation pattern, and area 13:245f; map 246

pair bonding, the mutual attraction that the two sexes of a given species have for one another. Pair bonds may be of brief duration, as among many fishes and a few birds, or they may last a breeding cycle, a season, or a lifetime.
·alcid billing display 4:38f
·animal society types 16:940f
·bird coupling advantages 16:589g
·ciconiiform mating ritual 4:612d
·communication effects 4:1011a
·falconiform display and partnership duration 7:147f
·gruiform courtship displays 8:445e
·gull courtship feeding 4:37e
·kinship structure development 10:478e
·mating and parental advantages 16:589g
·owl songs and calls 17:734h
·pigeon displays and behaviour 4:934f; illus.
·tern's fish flight display 4:38b
·waterfowl displays and bond maintenance 1:941a

paired-associate learning, technique for studying learning and retention in which items (usually words, nonsense syllables, or numbers) are learned in pairs and the subject is later tested on his ability to give the second member of the pair when the first is presented.
·transfer of training similarity 18:597g

Pair of Blue Eyes, A (serialized, 1872–73; published, 1873), a novel by Thomas Hardy.
·serial publication 8:645g

pair production, formation or materialization of two electrons, one negative and the other positive (positron), from a pulse of electromagnetic energy travelling through matter, usually in the vicinity of an atomic nucleus. Pair production is a direct conversion of radiant energy to matter. It is one of the principal ways in which high-energy radiation, such as strong X-rays and gamma rays, is absorbed in matter. For pair production to occur, the electromagnetic energy, in a discrete quantity called a photon, must be at least equivalent to the mass of two electrons. The mass m of a single electron is equivalent to 0.51 million electron volts of energy E as calculated from the equation formulated by Albert Einstein, $E = mc^2$, in which c is a constant equal to the velocity of light. To produce two electrons, therefore, the photon energy must be at least 1.02 million electron volts. Photon energy in excess of this amount, when pair production occurs, is converted into motion of the electron–positron pair. If pair production occurs in a radiation detector, such as a cloud chamber, to which a magnetic field is properly applied, the electron and the positron curve away from the point of formation in opposite directions in arcs of equal curvature. In this way pair production was first detected (1933).

Pair production does not occur in free space but only in the vicinity of a mass that is charged, such as an atomic nucleus or an electron. The charged body provides both the electromagnetic field or environment needed for this reaction and the mass required to take up the recoil. In accord with the laws of conservation of energy and momentum, an atomic nucleus absorbs only a minute amount of energy and momentum because of its relatively large size; but an electron recoils with great energy of motion because of its lightness. In fact, twice the energy, or 2.04 million electron volts, is required to produce an electron–positron pair in the vicinity of an electron than near a nucleus. The positron that is formed quickly disappears by reconversion into energy in the process of annihilation with another electron in matter.

Internal pair production, a species of gamma decay (*q.v.*), occurs when an unstable nucleus that has at least 1.02 million electron volts of excess energy directly ejects an electron–positron pair created within its own electromagnetic field without first producing a gamma photon.
·cosmic particle production 5:206f
·gamma ray matter interactions 15:439h
·matter and antimatter production 11:703e
·radiation interactions with atoms 15:392g
·radiation particle conversion 15:405e
·subatomic particle theory 13:1023f
·X-ray absorption processes 19:1059d

pair skating: *see* figure skating.

Pais, Abraham (1918–), U.S. physicist.
·subatomic particle research 13:1031b

Pais, Ettore (1856–1939), Italian disciple of the German historian Theodor Mommsen and author of a multi-volume history of the ancient Roman Republic (1898–1931).

Paiśācī: *see* Prākrit languages.

Pai-se, also known as PO-SE, Pin-yin romanization, respectively, BAI-SE and BO-SE, city in the west of the Kwangsi Chuang Autonomous Region (*tzu-chih-ch'ü*), China. Pai-se is a county (*hsien*) seat and the administrative headquarters of the extensive Pai-se Area (*ti-ch'ü*), which includes 12 counties on the borders of Yunnan and Kweichow provinces. Pai-se is on the Yu Chiang (river), which flows southeast to Nan-ning, and is situated at its junction with its tributary, the Ssu-ch'eng Ho. It is at the limit of navigation on the Yu Chiang for small craft and is also at the centre of a highway network radiating to the north and west. Transport routes also lead into the neighbouring provinces of Yunnan and Kweichow, linking them with Nan-ning and central Kwangsi. Until comparatively recent times, Pai-se was in the territory of non-Chinese tribes and was only loosely controlled by the Chinese. A subdistrict (*t'ing*), Pai-se was set up and fortified in 1730 as a garrison among the tribes, but not until 1875 was a regular civil administration established. During the late 19th century, Pai-se became a trading centre, and a considerable colony of merchants from Canton settled there. The goods collected for export include kapok (floss used as stuffing), ramie (a textile fibre), aniseed, edible fungi, and various herbs. In the 19th and the early 20th centuries, it was a centre of the opium traffic, with processed opium from Yunnan and Kweichow being collected here by Cantonese merchants for shipment to Nan-ning, Canton, Hong Kong, and Shanghai. Since 1949 some minor industry has developed, including sugar refineries, tobacco curing, rice milling, and ceramic manufacture. Latest pop. est. 24,000.
23°54′ N, 106°37′ E
·urban commercial role 10:551g

Pai shang-ti hui, Chinese religious organization founded by Feng Yün-shan and Hung Hsiu-ch'üan.
·founding and doctrinal inspiration 9:44c

Paisiello (PAESIELLO), **Giovanni** (b. May 9, 1740, Taranto, Italy—d. June 5, 1816, Naples), composer of operas admired for their robust realism and dramatic power. His father, a veterinary surgeon who intended him for the legal profession, enrolled him, at the age of five, at the Jesuit school in Taranto. When his talent for singing became obvious, he was placed in the Conservatorio di S. Onofrio at Naples. Paisiello's earliest efforts in composition were for the church. For the theatre of the conservatory he wrote some intermezzi, one of which attracted so much notice that he was invited to write two operas, *La Pupilla*, for Bologna, and *Il Marchese Tulipano*, for Rome. His reputation established, he settled for some years at Naples, where he produced a series of successful operas. In 1776 Paisiello was invited by the empress Catherine II to St. Petersburg, where he remained for eight years.

Among the works he produced for Catherine was *Il Barbiere di Siviglia* (*The Barber of Seville*, 1782), which some consider his masterpiece, on a libretto by Giuseppe Petrosellini, after Beaumarchais' comedy *Le Barbier de Séville*.

Paisiello, sculpture by P. Pierantoni, 1817; in the Palazzo dei Conservatori, Capitoline Museum, Rome
By courtesy of Palazzo dei Conservatori, Musei Capitolini, Rome

In 1784 Paisiello left Russia and, after a brief sojourn in Vienna, where he composed for Joseph II, entered the service of Ferdinand IV of Naples. During his 15 years as music director there, he composed several of his best operas, including *La Molinara* (1788) and *Nina* (1789). After many vicissitudes resulting from political and dynastic changes, he was invited to Paris in 1802 by Napoleon. Paisiello conducted the music of the court in the Tuileries; the Parisian public, however, received his opera *Proserpine* (1803) without enthusiasm. Disappointed at the failure of his only opera with a French libretto, he asked to return to Italy, pleading his wife's delicate health. On his arrival at Naples, Paisiello was re-instated in his former appointment by Joseph Bonaparte and Joachim Murat, but he was unable to meet the demands for new works. The power of the Bonaparte family was tottering, and Paisiello's fortunes fell with it.

Paisiello is known to have composed about 100 operas. His church music comprises about 40 masses and many smaller works. His instrumental music includes symphonies, a harp concerto, string quartets, and sonatas for harp and for violin and cello. In the 20th century, *Il Barbiere* and *La Molinara* were revived, and several of his operas and piano concerti, string quartets, and keyboard pieces were republished.

Paisley, large burgh, industrial centre, and county town (seat) of Renfrew, Scotland, situated on the River White Cart, a tributary of the Clyde. St. Mirren, an Irish monk, is known to have built a church there in the 6th century, but Paisley eventually developed as a small village clustered around a Cluniac abbey founded in 1163. The original abbey was burned down in 1307, and the present building dates from the 15th century. The nave (restored 1933) is still used as a parish church. Parts of the abbey buildings were also incorporated in the 17th-century palace of Paisley, which is now restored as a 20th-century war memorial.

By the early 18th century, Paisley had developed into a manufacturing centre for the hand-loom weaving of linen. At the end of the 18th century the new town was laid out over much of the ground that once belonged to the

abbey. During the early 19th century, Paisley became famous for its Paisley Shawls, copies in silk and cotton of the Asian shawls sent back by Scottish soldiers serving in India. These shawls are now rare items, and a priceless collection is on show in the Paisley museum. During the early 19th century, the manufacture of linen thread gave way to that of cotton, and Paisley became one of the greatest thread-manufacturing centres in the world and the fifth largest town in Scotland. The town's modern industry is more varied and includes the production of chemicals and dyes; engineering, shipbuilding, and food-processing industries; and textile and thread manufacturing. A government-sponsored industrial estate, opened in 1937, contains more than 150 factories. Paisley has many fine buildings, including the town hall, public library and museum, the Coats Observatory, the Thomas Coats Memorial Church, and a modern College of Technology. Pop. (1971 prelim.) 95,403.
55°50′ N, 4°26′ W
·map, United Kingdom **18**:866

paisley, textile pattern owing its name to the manufacture at the town of Paisley, Renfrewshire, of Paisley shawls. When, *c.* 1800, patterned shawls made from the soft fleece of the Kashmir goat began to be imported to Britain from India, machine-woven wool equivalents were made at Paisley to supply the insatiable demand that had been created for "cashmere" shawls. Paisley shawls, in fine wool and sober colouring, were beautiful in their own right.

Paisley shawl, English, 19th century; in the Victoria and Albert Museum, London

By courtesy of the Victoria and Albert Museum, London; photograph, A.C. Cooper

Their rich, abstract, curvilinear patterns, modified from their Kashmir counterparts and deriving ultimately from Mughal art, have continued to be widely adopted in modern textiles, especially for clothing. A motif resembling an enlarged comma (well-known in Mughal decorative art) is the one by which most people recognize a paisley pattern.

Pai-t'ou Shan, also PAEKTU-SAN, mountain on the Chinese-Korean frontier.
42°00′ N, 128°03′ E
·Ch'ang-pai Shan physical features **4**:261c

pai-t'ung, an alloy of copper, nickel, and zinc that was made by the Chinese as early as 200 BC. The alloy is now called nickel–silver.
·nickel production development **13**:71d *passim* to 73b

Paiute, two distinct American Indian groups that speak languages of the Numic (formerly

Paiute woman weaving a basket, 1873

By courtesy of the Smithsonian Institution, Washington, D.C., Bureau of American Ethnology

called Plateau) branch of Shoshonean. The Southern Paiute, who speak Ute, at one time occupied southern Utah, northwestern Arizona, southern Nevada, and southeastern California, the last group being known as Chemehuevi. The Spaniards who traversed some of the Paiute territories in the 16th and 17th centuries left them undisturbed. Although encroached upon and directed into reservations by the U.S. government in the 19th century, the Southern Paiute had comparatively little friction with whites; and many stayed scattered in the territories, working on the ranches of whites or remaining on the fringes of white settlements.

The Northern Paiute, who have also been designated Mono (*q.v.*) in California and Paviotso in Nevada and have been known more loosely as Diggers, occupied east central California, western Nevada, and eastern Oregon. An offshoot, the Bannock (*q.v.*), lived with the Shoshoni in southern Idaho, where they were buffalo hunters. After 1840, with the rush of European prospectors and farmers and the consequent despoiling of their already meagre supply of food plants, the Northern Paiute acquired guns and horses and fought at intervals with the whites until 1874, when the last Paiute lands were appropriated by the U.S. government.

The Northern and Southern Paiute were traditionally simple food collectors who subsisted primarily on seed, pine nuts, and small game, although many Southern Paiute planted small gardens. They occupied temporary brush shelters, wore little or no clothing except rabbitskin blankets, and made a variety of baskets for gathering and cooking food. Families were loosely affiliated through intermarriage; but there were no formal bands or territorial organizations, except in the more fertile areas such as the Owens Valley in California. Little of the old customs survive, except for shamanism. In the early 1970s the Northern and Southern Paiute lived largely near or on reservations, numbering about 4,000.
·Basin Indian culture and religion **13**:204h
·dance forms and ritual use **1**:674b
·Idaho settlement patterns **9**:187e
·Southern Paiute culture and present status **18**:1101g

Paiva, Afonso de, 15th-century Portuguese traveller sent by John II to visit Guinea and Abyssinia by an overland route.
·Abyssinian mission and search for Prester John **5**:230h

Paiwan, aboriginal people of Taiwan.
·Taiwanese aboriginal population **17**:998d

Paix des Dames: *see* Cambrai, Treaty of.

Paixhans, Henri-Joseph (1783–1854), French artillery officer.
·naval artillery design history **12**:890h

Pai-yen (Mongol military leader): *see* Bayan.

Pai-yin T'ai-lai (China): *see* T'ung-liao.

Pai Yüeh, Tai people who established the first settlement on the site of Canton, China.
·Canton's settlement and political adjustments **3**:781d

Pajalu (Asian kingdom): *see* Kadiri, Kingdom of.

pajamas, also spelled PYJAMAS, loose, lightweight trousers worn in the East or a loose two-piece suit of silk, cotton, or synthetic material worn for sleeping or lounging. Men's pajamas appeared in the Western world about 1870, after returning British colonials brought

Man wearing pajamas, illustration from the *Catalogue of Welch Margetson,* English, 1910

By courtesy of Welch Margetson

back with them the pajamas worn by the Hindus. At the beginning of the 20th century, pajamas were introduced as women's sleepwear and around 1920 as at-home evening wear.
·style origin and popularity **5**:1032c

Paján Mountains, also called CHONGÓN, COLONCHE, and PUCA MOUNTAINS, segment of the Ecuadorian Andes.
1°25′ S, 80°36′ W
·volcanic origin and geologic age **6**:285d

Pajjusaṇa (religious festival): *see* Paryuṣaṇa.

Pajou, Augustin (b. Sept. 19, 1730, Paris—d. May 8, 1809, Paris), sculptor and decorator known mainly for his portrait busts of figures, such as his patroness, Madame du Barry (Louvre, Paris), and for directing the decoration of the Versailles opera house.

Pajou, a student of the sculptor Jean-Baptiste Lemoyne, won the Prix de Rome (1748) and spent a dozen years in Italy. He was elected to the Paris Academy in 1760. He executed bas-reliefs and small decorative figures in bronze, silver, and marble and later did work on the court of the Palais Royal, Paris, and the cathedral at Orléans. A directive from King Louis XVI for the creation of statues honouring great Frenchmen led him to do many busts, including those of such persons

"Psyche Abandoned," marble sculpture by Augustin Pajou; in the Louvre, Paris
Giraudon

as Lemoyne and the naturalist Georges Buffon (Louvre) and Descartes and Bossuet (Institut de France, Paris). Appointed keeper of the king's antiquities (1777), he was commissioned to complete the Fountain of the Innocents, Paris, in the manner of Jean Goujon. Pajou's "Psyche Abandoned" (1791; Louvre) offers an example of his graciously seductive style.

Pakaha, biblical PEKAH (d. 732 BC), king of Israel from *c.* 737 BC.
·Tiglath-pileser's Assyrian empire **18**:401h

Pakaraima Mountains (South America): *see* Pacaraima Mountains.

Pak Dogol, in Malay puppet theatre, a clown character.
·Malaysian dramatic role **17**:248e

Pak-hoi (China): *see* Pei-hai.

Pakhto language: *see* Pashto language.

Pakhtūnwalī, or PASHTŪNWALĪ, meaning WAY OF THE PASHTUNS, code of honour of the Pashtuns of Afghanistan and Pakistan.
·moral and social obligations **13**:257c

Pak In-no, Korean poet of the later Chosŏn period.
·kasa style **10**:1063b

Pakiser, Louis Charles, Jr. (b. Feb. 8, 1919, Denver, Colo.), geophysicist known for his studies of crustal thickness of the Earth in the United States and of seismic velocities in the crust and upper mantle.

Pakiser became a member of the U.S. Geological Survey in 1952, chief of the Office for Earthquake Research and Crustal Studies from 1967 to 1970, and research geophysicist thereafter. His work includes investigations of heat flow, tectonic activity, and volcanism in the western U.S.; in 1967 Pakiser estimated the average composition of the Earth's crust.

Pakistan **13**:892, country in southern Asia, is bounded by Afghanistan and the Soviet Union (north), by China (northeast), by India (east and southeast), by the Arabian Sea (south), and by Iran (west). (For statistical details, *see* pages 684–685.) *See also* Indian subcontinent, history of the.

TEXT ARTICLE covers:
Relief and drainage **13**:894d
Soils and climate 895e
Vegetation and animal life 895h
Traditional regions 896b
The landscape under human settlement 896d
Ethnic groups 896h
Linguistic groups 897c
Religious groups 897h
Demography 898d
Resources 899c
Sources of national income 899g
Management of the economy 901a
Transportation and communications 902d
The structure of government 902f
Social conditions 904b
Cultural life and institutions 904c
Prospects for the future 904h

REFERENCES in other text articles:

agriculture, forestry, and fishing
·agrarian reform **10**:641f
·cotton production **7**:276d
·grain farming with high-yield seeds **1**:316e

art, archaeology, and architecture
·folk visual art forms **7**:480c
·music, dance, theatre, and visual arts **17**:131c
·Baluchistan's geography, culture, and institutions **2**:677e

commerce, industry, and mining
·China's trade relationship **4**:280f; table
·coal production and reserves, table 5 **4**:781
·petroleum production statistics, table 1 **14**:176
·trade union membership **18**:570b

culture and education
·education administration and problems **6**:428e
·education system reform and progress **6**:404f
·English use as official language **6**:885g
·Indo-Iranian languages distribution map **9**:442
·Iranian dialects and location **9**:451c
·magazine publishing **15**:253b
·social organization and religious base **17**:125g; map 126
·South Asian language area survey **10**:664f

economics, finance, and currency
·foreign aid from OECD countries **7**:522e; table
·property taxation practices **15**:60h
·public and private enterprise patterns **15**:198g
·spice import, export, and value, table 3 **17**:506

government
·armed forces statistics, table 2 **2**:16
·Islāmic law in contemporary reform **9**:941c
·political geography and commerce **2**:177f
·Jammu and Kashmir **10**:30h
·Karachi's organization and institutions **10**:400a
·Northwest Frontier Province **13**:256a

physical geography
·Asian physical and human geography **2**:146c
·Himalayas' role in weather **8**:884e
·Hindu Kush boundary **8**:921e
·Indus River course and utilization **9**:492c; illus.
·map, Asia **2**:149
·monsoon influences and climate **12**:390e
·Salt Range physiography and geology **16**:199c
·Thar Desert features and implications **18**:206e

religion
·Christian denominational demography map **4**:459
·education under Islāmic doctrine **6**:428e
·Sind resources, demography, and culture **16**:781b

social issues
·caste rankings' relative unimportance **3**:987e
·Islāmic factional problems **9**:937c

sports and recreation
·cricket popularity and Test matches **5**:262c
·falconry practices and quarries **7**:152f

transportation and communications
·inland waterway development plans **3**:762d
·newspaper publishing statistics table **15**:237
·postal system origins and development **14**:889e
·railway systems data table **15**:482

pakkā, meaning "Perfected," in north India, a class of cooked foods served at intercaste feasts.
·caste ranking use at village feast **3**:986e

Pakokku, administrative headquarters, Pakokku District, Magwe Division, southwestern Upper Burma, on the Irrawaddy River below its junction with the Chindwin. A trade centre for the Chindwin and Yaw river valleys, it deals in timber and palm sugar and is the head of downstream Chindwin navigation. It has a diesel electric plant, and the model village of Kyauksauk is immediately northwest.

The district (area 5,345 sq mi [13,843 sq km]) lies southwest of Mandalay between the Irrawaddy River (east) and the Chin Hills (west). Its eastern portion is characteristic of Burma's dry zone, with undulating gravelly and sandy land. The Chindwin and Irrawaddy rivers provide alluvium and are utilized for irrigation. To the west, over the Shinmataung and Tangyi ridges, the region is drained by the Yaw and Myittha rivers. Peanuts (groundnuts), millet, and sesame are the principal crops. In the riverine areas sugar is produced from the toddy palm; rice, gram, peas, beans, and maize (corn) are grown, the latter primarily for its husk, which is used for cheroot wrappers under the name of *yawpet*. The western forests yield teak. In the Yaw Valley, cutch, a yellow dye, is extracted from a small acacia tree. The Yenangyat oil field is in the south of the district; in 1927 the Lanywa field was created on a sandbank reclaimed from the Irrawaddy. Major riverine towns include Gangaw and Tilin on the Myittha and Pauk and Seikpyu on the Yaw. The inhabitants are mainly Burmese. Pop. (latest census) town, 30,943; district, 50,122.
21°20′ N, 95°05′ E
·map, Burma **3**:505

Pakse, seat of Sedone province, in the southern panhandle of Laos on the Houei (river) Sédone. Before 1970, Pakse functioned as the chief port of entry of Laos and was a part of Champassak province. East of Pakse begins the rolling Plateau des Bolovens, nearly 3,300 ft (1,000 m) high, for whose products—teak, tea, cinchona, kapok, and cardamom—Pakse is the distributing centre. Industries include several sawmills, manufacture of brick and tile, and an ice plant; there is also an agricultural experimental station, a criminal court of appeals, and a secondary school. In 1970 the Selabam Dam of the Mekong River Valley Plan opened on the lower Sédone, providing electricity for Pakse and irrigation for the district. Pakse is linked by road to the Thailand border and to Cambodia. Pop. (1970 est.) 37,000.
15°07′ N, 105°47′ E
·map, Laos **10**:675

Pak Tai, traditional region of Thailand.
·linguistic and economic tradition **18**:201f

Paktīā, formerly SAMT-E JUNŪBĪ, or SOUTHERN, PROVINCE, in eastern Afghanistan, occupies an area of about 6,086 sq mi (15,762 sq km) and is bounded east by Pakistan, north by Nangarhār and Lowgar, and west and south by Ghaznī provinces. Most of the land is mountainous and forested, and the climate is mild in summer but cold in winter. The only large towns besides Gardēz (*q.v.*), the provincial capital, are Matūn and Orgūn.

Khowst, in central Paktīā, has long been a trouble spot, and the fierce tribesmen there have at times threatened both Kābul, the national capital, and the Indus Valley, even in the 20th century. The British marched to Kābul through this area in 1878 during the Second Afghan War, and, during the Third Afghan War, an Afghan army used the same route to attack the British fort at Thal. The people of western Paktīā are Ghilzays, but numerous small, independent, and warlike tribes also live in the province. Most of the people are engaged in agriculture, usually nomadic or semi-nomadic stock raising, but some lumbering is carried on, part of it for export. Although Gardēz has road connections with Kābul and Ghaznī, Paktīā lies off the main routes and is rarely visited. There are airfields at all three large towns, primarily for military purposes. Pop. (1970 est.) 732,779.

·area and population table 1:169
·map, Afghanistan 1:167

pa kua (Confucianism): *see* trigram.

Pakubuwono I (d. 1719), ruler of Mataram, in Java, from 1704 to 1719.
·Indonesian territorial favours to Dutch **9**:484d

pa-ku wen, Chinese literary genre.
·definition and usage **10**:1051e

Pal, Bipin Chandra (b. Nov. 7, 1858, Poil, India—d. May 20, 1932), Indian journalist and an early leader of the nationalist movement. By his contributions to various newspapers and through speaking tours, he popularized the concepts of *swadeshi* (exclusive use of Indian-made goods) and *swarāj* (Indian self-rule).

Though originally considered a moderate within the Indian National Congress, by 1919 Pal had moved closer to the more militant policies of Bal Gangadhar Tilak, one of the leading nationalist politicians. In later years Pal allied himself with fellow Bengali nationalists who resented the cult of personality surrounding Mahatma Gandhi, the most popular nationalist leader. Pal's overriding concern in his writings from 1912 to 1920 was to achieve confederation of the different regions and different communities within India. After 1920 he remained aloof from national politics but continued to contribute to Bengali journals.

Pāla, an important dynasty that ruled in Bihār and Bengal, India, from the 8th to the 12th century. Its founder, Gopāla, was a local chieftain who rose to power in the mid-8th century during a period of anarchy. His successor, Dharmapāla (reigned *c.* 770–810), greatly expanded the kingdom and for a while was in control of Kannauj. Pāla power was maintained under Devapāla (reigned *c.* 810–850), who carried out raids in the north, the Deccan, and the peninsula; but thereafter the dynasty declined in power, and Mahendrapāla, the Gurjara-Pratihāra emperor of Kannauj in the late 9th and early 10th centuries, penetrated as far as northern Bengal. Pāla strength was restored by Māhīpāla I (reigned *c.* 988–1038), whose influence reached as far as Vārānasi (Benares), but on his death the kingdom again weakened.

Rāmapāla (reigned *c.* 1077–1120), the last important Pāla king, did much to strengthen the dynasty in Bengal and expanded its power in Assam and Orissa; he is the hero of a Sanskrit historical poem, the *Rāmacarita* of Sandhyākara. On his death, however, the dynasty was virtually eclipsed by the rising power of the Senas, although Pāla kings continued to rule in southern Bihār for 40 years. The main capital of the Pālas appears to have been Mudgagiri (Monghyr) in eastern Bihār.

The Pālas were supporters of Buddhism, and it was through missionaries from their kingdom that Buddhism was finally established in Tibet. Under Pāla patronage a distinctive school of art arose, of which many noteworthy sculptures in stone and metal survive.
·Buddhist monastic patronage **3**:407d
·origins and military expansion **9**:361b

Pāla bronzes: *see* Eastern Indian bronzes.

palace, originally a royal residence, as for a king or emperor, the word being derived from the Palatine Hill in Rome, where the emperors of Rome built their residences. Later, the residences of bishops and archbishops in England, France, and Spain came to be known as palaces, and eventually the name was given to many large and imposing buildings, both public and private. Thus, in the United States, for example, there are colonial governors' palaces in Williamsburg, Va.; Santa Fe, N.M.; and San Antonio, Texas; as well as museums such as the California Palace of the Legion of Honor in San Francisco.

The earliest known palaces are those built behind the temple of Karnak in Thebes by King Thutmose III of Egypt (reigned 1504–1450 BC). There are a few remains of a palace erected by Amenhotep III (reigned 1417?–1379? BC), also at Thebes, which had a rectangular outer wall enclosing a labyrinth of small, dark rooms and courtyards. Much larger palaces were erected at Nimrūd, Nineveh, and Khorsabad in Assyria. The palace of Sargon II (reigned 721–705 BC) at Khorsabad (Dur Sharrukin), extending over more than 25 acres (10 hectares), is built on a platform in the city wall and contains two huge, central courts and a disorganized mass of smaller courts and rooms.

The architects of ancient Babylon achieved more symmetry in the palaces they designed for their kings, using hallways and repeated groupings of rooms. In the 4th, 5th, and 6th centuries BC, vast Persian palaces were built at Susa and at Persepolis, where the residences of three kings (Darius I, Xerxes I, and Artaxerxes III) perch on three low platforms raised upon a main platform that is reached by a double staircase. All of these Eastern palaces were used not only as residences but also for governmental and religious purposes, as were the Cretan palaces at Phaestus and Knossos, the latter having several stories and featuring a grand staircase three stories high. More than 1,000,000 square feet (90,000 square metres) of the Palatine Hill in Rome were devoted to splendid residences built between AD 3 and 212 by such Roman emperors as Augustus, Tiberius, Caligula, and Septimius Severus. Ruins of these remain. A superb Roman palace was built in AD 300 by Diocletian at Split, in what is now Yugoslavia. At Constantinople, the Sacred Palace is a conglomeration of Byzantine churches, schools, and residences, covering 400,000 square yards (330,000 square metres).

During the Middle Ages, palace building declined, but in Renaissance Italy every prince had his *palazzo*, such as the Pitti Palace in Florence and the many splendid palaces lining the Grand Canal in Venice. In France royal *palais* were built, as were palaces of justice (courthouses) and of public assembly. Famous Spanish *palacios* include El Escorial outside Madrid, the Alhambra in Granada, and the Alcázar in Seville. There are three royal palaces—Buckingham, St. James's, and Whitehall—in London. *See also* desert palace; Forbidden City.
·ancient Near East architecture **19**:262e
·Ch'in and Han architectural features **19**:181g
·Islāmic palace-cities **9**:989e
·Minoan and Mycenaean architecture **19**:274g
·Roman residential architecture **19**:305c

Palace School, or ACADEMIA PALATINA, 9th-century centre of learning organized by Charlemagne at Aachen.
·Western Christian art developments **19**:349d

Palace style (1450–1375 BC), Minoan pottery style.
·Mycenaean influence on Minoan pottery **19**:275g

Palacio Valdés, Armando (b. 1853, Entralgo, Spain—d. February 1938, Madrid), one of the most popular 19th-century Spanish novelists, distinguished by his optimism, his charming heroines, his realism and also his rather un-Spanish qualities of moderation and simplicity. His novels provide his best autobiography, particularly *Riverita* (1886), *Maxi-*

PAKISTAN

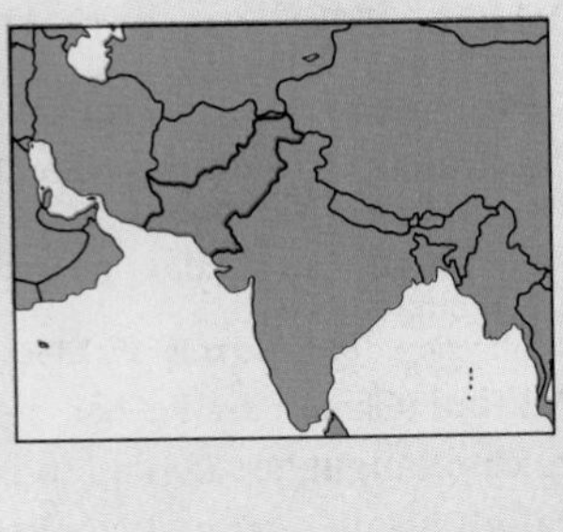

Official name: Islāmī Jamhūrīya-e-Pākistān (Urdu), Islāmic Republic of Pakistan.
Location: southern Asia.
Form of government: federal republic.
Official language: Urdu.
Official religion: Islām.
Area: 307,374 sq mi, 796,095 sq km.
Population: (1972 census) 64,892,000; (1975 estimate) 70,260,000.
Capital: Islāmābād.
Monetary unit: 1 Pakistan rupee (PakRs.) = 100 paisa.

Demography
Population: (1975 estimate) density 228.6 per sq mi, 88.3 per sq km; urban 26.9%, rural 73.1%; male 51.66%, female 48.3%; under 15 46.5%, 15–64 50.5%, 65 and over 2.9%.*
Vital statistics: (1970–75) births per 1,000 population 47.4, deaths per 1,000 population 16.5, natural increase per 1,000 population 30.9; (1975) life expectancy at birth—male 52.4, female 52.1; major causes of death—no data available, but the major diseases are cholera, tuberculosis, typhoid, dysentery, malaria, trachoma, and typhus.
Linguistic composition (1961): Punjabi 66.4%, Sindhi 12.6%, Pashto 8.5%, Urdu 7.6%, Baluchi 2.5%, Brahui 0.9%, Gujarati 0.6%, other 1.0%.*† *Religious affiliation* (1961): Muslim 97.2%, Christian 1.4%, scheduled caste 1.0%, caste Hindu 0.5%, other less than 0.1%.

National accounts
Budget (1974–75 estimate). Revenue: PakRs. 14,590,090,000 (customs duties 40.7%, excise duties 20.6%, personal income tax 6.1%, general turnover tax 4.8%, corporation income tax 1.8%). Expenditures: PakRs. 20,951,800,000 (national defense 26.6%, loans and advances to local authorities 9.9%, interest on public debt 7.7%, tax and grant transfers to local authorities 7.4%, education and health 2.4%). *Total national debt* (1974): PakRs. 57,860,000,000. *Tourism* (1974). Receipts from visitors: U.S. $20,750,000; expenditures by nationals abroad—no data available.

Domestic economy
Gross national product (GNP; at current market prices, 1974): U.S. $8,770,000,000 (U.S. $130 per capita).

Origin of gross domestic product:	1961				1973–74		1972	
	value in 000,000 PakRs.‡	% of total value	labour force	% of labour force	value in 000,000 PakRs.§	% of total value	labour force	% of labour force
agriculture, forestry, hunting, fishing	7,695	43.2	7,643,904	59.9	28,404	36.7	10,515,285	56.9
mining, quarrying	81	0.5	21,692	0.2	460	0.6	79,369	0.4
manufacturing	2,276	12.8	1,708,567	13.4	11,501	14.9	2,222,111	12.0
construction	612	3.4	261,749	2.1	2,923	3.8	610,374	3.3
electricity, gas, water	99	0.6	24,969	0.2	1,118	1.4	65,096	0.4
transport, storage, communications	1,065	6.0	361,269	2.8	5,683	7.3	861,981	4.7
trade	2,251	12.6	877,253	6.9	11,250	14.5	1,745,714	9.4
banking, insurance, real estate	247	1.4	17,800	0.1	1,748	2.3	149,638	0.8
ownership of dwellings	858	4.8	...	...	2,868	3.7	...	...
public administration, defense	1,145	6.4	392,459	3.1	5,488	7.1	...	...
services	1,478	8.3	1,166,504	9.1	5,938	7.7	1,285,464	7.0
other	...	...	286,858	2.2	...	...	946,198	5.1
total	17,807	100.0	12,763,024	100.0	77,381	100.0	18,481,230	100.0

mina (1887; Eng. trans., 1888), and *La novela de un novelista* (1921). He experienced an early predilection for science, and his work reveals a temporary phase of Naturalism, notably *La espuma* (1890; *The Froth*, 1891) and *La fe* (1892; *Faith*, 1892). *Marta y María* (1883), with its biblical Martha and Mary theme, has perhaps a greater claim to profundity than most of his work. Local colour of Asturias, his native province, abounds in *Marta y María*, as it does in his other Asturian novels, *José* (1885; Eng. trans., 1901), a realistic picture of the sea, whose epic note seems an echo of José María de Pereda's *Sotileza*, and *La aldea perdida* (1903). Unlike Pereda, he set his novels in different parts of Spain: *Riverita* in Madrid, *La alegría del capitán Ribot* (1898; *The Joy of Captain Ribot*, 1900) in Valencia, and *La hermana San Sulpicio* (1889; *Sister Saint Sulpice*, 1890) in Andalusia. The courtship of the Galician and the young Sevillian nun is set against a striking background of local colour and gaiety. Excessive sentimentality in his novels is mitigated by sincerity and humour.

·Spanish novel development **13**:294f

Palacký, František (b. June 14, 1798, Hodslavice, Moravia—d. May 26, 1876, Prague), the founder of modern Czech historiography and a leading figure in the political life of 19th-century Bohemia.

He early came into contact with the resurgence of national feeling that had begun to influence Czech and Slovak intellectuals. His early writings were concerned with aesthetics. In 1823 he settled in Prague, where he was enabled by noble patronage and by an advantageous marriage to devote himself to his scholarly and patriotic interests. In 1827 he became editor of the journal of the Bohemian museum, in which he published articles on aesthetics and on the Czech language (arguing against any far-reaching changes).

In 1832 he began his magnum opus, a history of the Czech nation in Bohemia and Moravia to 1526. Published as *Geschichte von Böhmen* (5 vol., 1836–67) and *Dějiny národu českého* (1848–76), the work shows a clear conception of the nature of Czech history, which Palacký held to consist in "the constant contact and conflict between the Slavs on the one hand and Rome and the Germans on the other." Thus the Hussite period became the central episode of Czech history, epitomizing the national and the religious struggle.

As a politician, Palacký supported the Austro-Slavic conception of a federal Austria, composed of nationalities with equal rights. He was chairman of the Prague Slavic congress in 1848 and attended the constituent assembly that met in Kroměříž (Kremsier) in 1848–49. After the failure of the revolutionary movements Palacký retired from active politics until 1861, when he became a deputy in the Reichsrat. In his *Idea státu rakouského* (1865; "Idea of the Austrian State"), he propounded a federalism based not on nationalities but on the historic provinces of the Habsburg empire. His influence on Czech political thought and historiography was immense. The liberal nationalism of Tomáš Masaryk and his generation owed much to Palacký.

·constitutionalist movement leadership **2**:1193f
·Czech independence movement **2**:464g
·Masaryk's historical writings **11**:572d

Palade, George E(mil) (b. Nov. 19, 1912, Iaşi, Rom.), cell biologist who developed tissue-preparation methods and conducted electron microscopy studies that resulted in the discovery of several cellular structures. With Albert Claude and Christian de Duve he was awarded the Nobel Prize for Physiology or Medicine in 1974.

Palade received a degree in medicine from the University of Bucharest in 1940 and remained there as a professor until after World War II. He emigrated to the United States in 1946 and began work at the Rockefeller Institute in New York.

Palade performed many studies on the internal organization of such cell structures as mitochondria, chloroplasts, the Golgi apparatus, and others. His most important discovery was that microsomes, bodies formerly thought to be fragments of mitochondria, are actually parts of the endoplasmic reticulum (internal cellular transport system) and have a high ribonucleic acid (RNA) content. They were subsequently named ribosomes. He became a naturalized citizen of the U.S. in 1952 and in 1958 a professor of cytology at Rockefeller Institute, which he left in 1972 to direct studies in cell biology at Yale University Medical School. In 1964 he received the Warren prize of Massachusetts General Hospital, Boston, and shared the Passano Award with K.R. Porter in the same year. He received the Albert Lasker Basic Research Award in 1966.

Pala d'Oro, 11th-century Byzantine altar screen of cloisonné enamel and precious stones in St. Mark's, Venice.

·Byzantine designs **19**:334e
·Byzantine enamelwork tradition **6**:776b; illus.

Palaeanodon, extinct genus of the mammalian order Edentata.

·characteristics and era **6**:301e

Palaearctic subregion: *see* Holarctic region.

Palaelodidae, extinct family of birds of the order Ciconiiformes.

·classification and fossil record **4**:614g

Palaemonias ganteri: *see* shrimp.

palaeo . . .: For words beginning thus, *see* under "paleo . . .," except as below.

Palaeociconiidae, extinct family of birds of the order Gruiformes.

·classification and fossil record **8**:448h

Palaeoctopus newboldi, extinct species of mollusk of the order Octopoda, class Cephalopoda.

·fossil record of Octopoda **3**:1153d

Palaeodus, extinct genus of primitive, fishlike animals found as fossils in European rocks of Early Ordovician age (500,000,000 to 430,000,000 years old). Primitive in structure, the genus lacked jaws and possessed a well-developed external shield of bony armour. Taxonomically, *Palaeodus* is placed in the order Heterostraci, the oldest known vertebrates.

Palaeohypnum: *see* moss.

Palaeologus, Byzantine family that became prominent in the 11th century and the members of which married into the imperial houses of Comnenus, Ducas, and Angelus. Michael VIII Palaeologus, emperor at Nicaea in 1259, founded the dynasty of the Palaeologi in Constantinople in 1261. His son Andronicus II (reigned 1282–1328) and his grandson Michael IX (died 1320) succeeded Michael as co-emperors. Michael IX's son Andronicus III (1328–41) left the throne to his infant son John V (1341–91), whose rule was disputed by John VI Cantacuzenus (1347–54) and later by his grandson, John VII (1390). John V was succeeded, however, by his second son, Manuel II (1391–1425). John VIII (1425–48) was a son of Manuel II, and his brother Constantine

Production (metric tons except as noted). Agriculture, forestry, hunting, fishing (1974): sugarcane 23,911,000, wheat 7,629,000, paddy rice 3,277,000, corn (maize) 675,000, sorghum 315,000, millet 280,000, chick-peas 575,000, cottonseed 1,280,000, rapeseed 293,000, tobacco 65,700, barley 140,000; livestock (number of live animals): cattle 13,154,000, buffalo 10,199,000, sheep 18,072,000, goats 12,749,000, camels 827,000; roundwood 8,815,000 cu m‖. Mining, quarrying (1974–75): coal 1,104,000¶; natural gas 4,020,000,000 cu m¶; crude petroleum 384,000; limestone 2,864,000; gypsum 303,000; rock salt 412,300. Manufacturing (1974–75): cotton yarn 351,000; cotton textiles 607,903,200 m; art silk and rayon cloth 8,094,300 m; sugar, refined 503,500; chemical fertilizers 726,600; cement 3,319,400; mild steel products 222,500; sea salt 138,200; tires and tubes 7,304,000 pieces; cigarettes 26,804,000,000 units; beer 2,908,700 litres.

Energy: (1970) installed electrical capacity 1,850,000 kW; (1971–72) production 7,630,000,000 kWhr (123 kWhr per capita).

Persons economically active (1972): 18,481,230 (30.0%), unemployed 373,766 (2.0%).

Price and earnings indexes (1971 = 100):	1972	1973	1974	1975
consumer price index	105.2	126.9	164.0	198.2

Land use (1973): total area 80,394,000 ha (agricultural and under permanent cultivation 24.1%; meadows and pastures 6.2%; forested 3.2%; built-on, wasteland, and other 66.4%).*

Foreign trade

Imports (1973–74): PakRs. 13,569,562,000 (food and live animals 18.0%, of which, wheat 11.4%, tea 2.5%; chemicals 15.4%, of which, fertilizers, manufactured 6.6%; petroleum, crude and partly refined 7.8%; universal plates and sheets of iron and steel 4.2%; road motor vehicles 4.0%; aircraft 3.3%; textile and leather machinery 1.8%; telecommunications apparatus 1.6%). *Major import sources:* United States 25.4%, Japan 8.3%, West Germany 7.7%, United Kingdom 7.0%, Saudi Arabia 6.6%, China 4.2%, The Netherlands 3.8%, Canada 3.8%, Kuwait 3.7%.

Exports (1973–74): PakRs. 10,161,215,000 (rice 20.7%; textile yarn and thread 18.4%; cotton fabrics 13.9%; floor coverings and tapestries 5.3%; leather 4.1%; cotton 4.1%; clothing 4.0%; fish, fresh and simply preserved 1.8%). *Major export destinations:* Hong Kong 11.0%, Indonesia 9.2%, United Kingdom 6.8%, Japan 6.2%, United States 5.3%, Italy 4.8%, West Germany 4.6%, Saudi Arabia 3.9%.

Transport and communications

Transport. Railroads (1974): length 7,915 mi, 12,738 km; (1973–74) passenger-mi 7,209,000,000, passenger-km 11,601,000,000; short ton-mi cargo 5,029,800,000, metric ton-km cargo 7,343,300,000. Roads (1972–73): total length 22,219 mi, 35,757 km (paved 12,365 mi, 19,899 km; unpaved 9,854 mi, 15,858 km). Vehicles (1975): passenger cars 188,205, trucks and buses 84,392. Merchant marine (1975): vessels (100 gross tons and over) 84, total deadweight tonnage 649,716. Air transport: (1974) passenger-mi 1,146,800,000, passenger-km 1,845,600,000; short ton-mi cargo 65,000,000, metric ton-km cargo 95,000,000; (1976) airports with scheduled flights 16.

Communications. Daily newspapers (1972): total number 71, total circulation and circulation per 1,000—no data available. Radios (1973): total number of receivers 1,033,000 (1 per 65 persons). Television (1972): receivers 129,000 (1 per 500 persons). Telephones (1973): 195,000 (1 per 340 persons).

Education and health

Education (1972–73):	schools	teachers	students	student/teacher ratio
primary (age 5–10)	48,507	111,408	4,441,322	39.9
secondary (age 10–14)	6,829	79,024	1,316,428	16.7
vocational	160	1,580	23,450	14.8
teacher training	246	1,389	36,508	26.3
higher	423	12,017	246,811	20.5

College graduates (per 100,000 population, 1973): 45. *Literacy* (1961): total population literate (age 5 and over) 5,380,308 (16.3%); males literate 4,260,586 (23.9%), females literate 1,119,722 (7.4%).

Health: (1974) doctors 17,194 (1 per 3,967 persons), hospital beds 33,307♀ (1 per 2,048 persons); (1970) daily per capita caloric intake 2,280 calories (FAO recommended minimum requirement 2,300 calories).

*Percentages do not add to 100.0 because of rounding. †Excluding frontier regions and non-Pakistanis. ‡Factor cost of 1959–60. §Current factor cost. ‖1973. ¶1973–74. ♀In hospitals and dispensaries only.

XI (1449–53) became the last Byzantine emperor. Other brothers were Demetrius and Thomas, despots of the Morea until 1460. Thomas died at Rome in 1465; his daughter Zoe married Ivan III of Russia. Another branch of the family, descended from Theodore, son of Andronius II, held the marquisate of Monteferrat from 1305 to 1533.
·Byzantine mosaic art development **12**:471g
·Michael VIII and Istanbul's return to Byzantine Empire **9**:1070f
·religious and political situation **6**:154e

Palaeoloxodon, a genus of extinct mammals belonging to the family Elephantidae of the order Proboscidea.
·species, traits, and distribution **15**:1f

Palaeomastodon, a genus of extinct elephant of the order Proboscidea.
·body traits and distribution **15**:3h; illus.

Palaeomerycidae, a family of extinct members of the mammalian order Artiodactyla.
·classification and general features **2**:80a

Palaeomyrmedon, an extinct genus of mammals of the order Edentata.
·traits and era **6**:302e

Palaeonisciformes, order of extinct bony fishes, superorder Chondrostei, that dominated freshwaters during the Paleozoic. They were succeeded in the Early Mesozoic by the subholostean and holostean fishes. Members of typical genera, such as *Palaeoniscus* of the Permian, were herring-like but had hard and shiny ganoid scales, a heterocercal tail (the upper lobe larger), a single dorsal fin, and long jaws. Fishes of such genera as *Tarrasius*, with an eellike median fin, and *Cornuboniscus*, with a fleshy lobe in each pectoral fin, were variant forms.

The subholosteans, a group of more advanced fishes typified by the genus *Redfieldia*, were the representative ray-finned fishes of the Triassic, with features of both the Palaeonisciformes and the later holost fishes—*e.g.*, gars.

The Palaeonisciformes may be considered the ancestral stock of the fishes of the superorders Chondrostei, Holostei, and Teleostei. Chondrostean descendants include the sturgeon, bichir, and paddlefish.
·body features, evolution, and classification **4**:436h
·characteristics and classification **7**:342b
·evolutionary importance and anatomy **7**:338g

Palaeoptera, group of primitive Paleozoic insects.
·fossils, traits, and importance **7**:565g

Palaeoscincus, genus of Late Cretaceous armoured herbivorous dinosaurs (the Cretaceous Period ended 65,000,000 years ago). *Palaeoscincus*, heavily protected by bony armour, was a massive animal that may have weighed as much as 3½ tons and was rather clumsy in appearance. The armour was clearly a protection against predators of the time. The teeth were poorly developed, and the brain was very small and primitive.

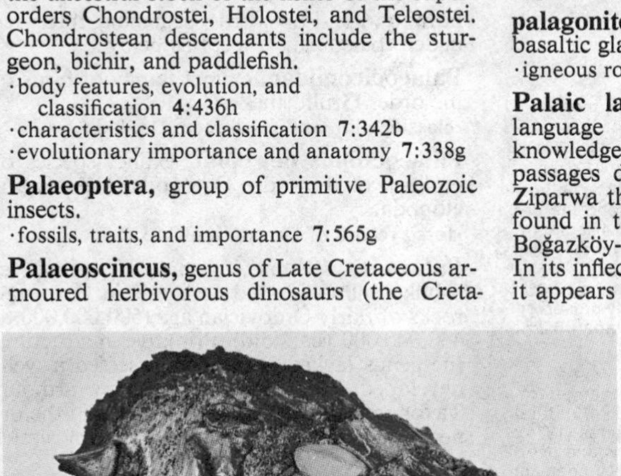

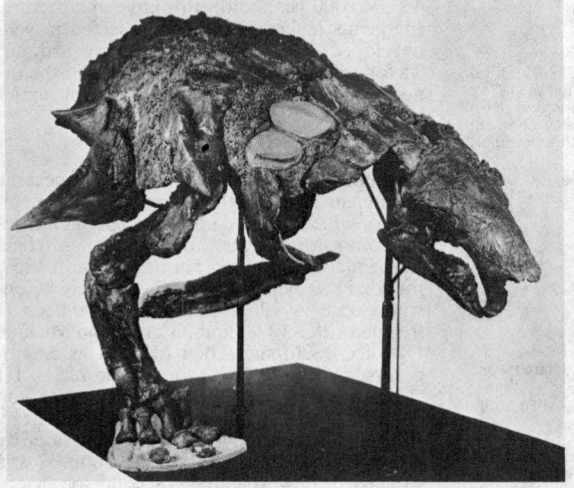

Palaeoscincus, skeleton
By courtesy of the American Museum of Natural History, New York

Palaeospondyliformes, an extinct order of fish belonging to the class Placoderni of the phylum Chordata.
·characteristics and classification **7**:341a

Palaeospondylus, enigmatic fossil vertebrate genus, very fishlike in appearance but of uncertain relationships. *Palaeospondylus* is only found at one locality: in the Middle Devonian Old Red Sandstone rocks in the region of Achannaras, Scot. (the Devonian Period began 395,000,000 years ago and lasted 50,000,000 years). Hundreds of specimens are known, yet the position of this genus in relation to other fishlike vertebrates is still poorly understood. *Palaeospondylus* was very small,

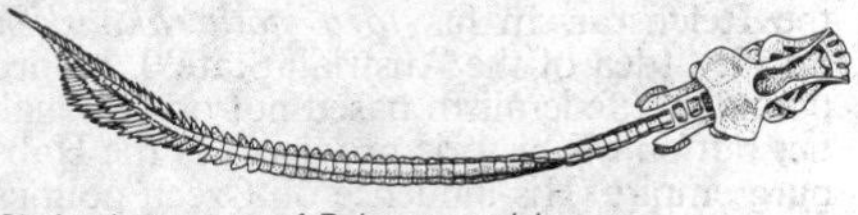

Skeletal structure of *Palaeospondylus*
Reprinted from *Vertebrate Paleontology* by A.S. Romer, by permission of the University of Chicago, copyright 1933, 1945, 1966; all rights reserved

only about five centimetres (about two inches) long. Unlike most of the contemporary forms of the Middle Devonian, the skeleton was very well ossified, and no dermal armour was present, a feature prominent among the placoderms. A well-developed caudal, or tail, fin was present; plates occur in the pectoral and pelvic regions and have been interpreted as representing the supporting structures for paired fins, although no trace of the fins themselves has been found. The skull, which is very unusual and distinctive, consists of many elements that are difficult to interpret precisely. It is uncertain whether *Palaeospondylus* represents an advanced or degenerate form. It has been suggested that the genus actually represents the larvae of some fishlike form, but this hypothesis is unlikely.

palagonite, amorphous alteration product of basaltic glass.
·igneous rock classification **9**:208a; table 207

Palaic language, ancient Indo-European language of northwest Anatolia. Modern knowledge of the language comes from 21 passages dealing with the cult of the deity Ziparwa that appear in the cuneiform tablets found in the ruins of the Hittite archives at Boğazköy-Hattusas (now in modern Turkey). In its inflectional systems and pronoun forms, it appears to be very close to the Hittite and Luwian languages, with which it is placed in the Anatolian subgroup of the Indo-European language family. *See also* Hittite language; Luwian language.
·Anatolian linguistic history **1**:831h
·Anatolian subgroup characteristics **1**:834b

Palaiopreveza (Greece): *see* Nicopolis Actia.

palais à volonté, neutral stage setting without particularized detail, used as the typical background for tragedies in the 17th-century French theatre, the Comédie Française.
·staging at Comédie-Française **17**:542a

Palais-Cardinal, now known as the PALAIS-ROYAL, opera and ballet theatre built (1637) by Jacques Le Mercier under Richelieu.
·ballet history influence **2**:648f

Palais des Machines (1889), exhibition hall for machinery designed by Ferdinand Dutert and Victor Contamin for the Paris International Exhibition of 1889.
·trussed arch design **19**:462g

palaistra, ancient Greek school of gymnastics.
·organization and purpose **6**:323f

Palamas, Saint Gregory **13**:905 (b. Nov. 11/14, 1296, Constantinople—d. 1359, Thessalonica, modern Thessaloníki, Greece), Orthodox monk, theologian, and intellectual leader of Hesychasm, a monastic mystical method of prayer.

Abstract of text biography. After becoming a monk at Mt. Athos, Greece, in 1316, Palamas studied and reflected on the scriptures and the writings of the Church Fathers for 25 years, and became a master of contemplative prayer. When raids by the Turks (1325) interrupted his monastic life, he fled to Thessalonica and Macedonia, where he was ordained a priest in 1335. Returning to Mt. Athos (1331), he was chosen religious superior of a neighbouring convent (1335), from which he resigned a short time later. From 1332 to about 1357 Palamas engaged in theological disputes with various Latin and Greek theologians and certain Humanists, especially those who attacked Hesychasm. After a civil war in the Byzantine Empire, in which the Hesychast controversy played a part, Palamas was appointed bishop of Thessalonica (1347). In 1368, nine years after his death, he was acclaimed a saint and named "Father and Doctor of the Orthodox Church."

REFERENCES in other text articles:
·Eastern Christian theology and Hesychasm **6**:145e
·Hesychast defense against Humanists **6**:155d

Palāmau, district, Bihār state, northeastern India. Its area (4,926 sq mi [12,757 sq km]) consists of lower spurs of the Chota Nāgpur Plateau, drained by tributaries of the Son River and the North Koel River. Rice, corn (maize), and oilseeds are the major crops, and forest products (including lac) are important. Coal, bauxite, dolomite, and iron ore deposits are worked. Daltonganj is the district headquarters. Pop. (1971 prelim.) 1,501,320.

Pālamcottah (India): *see* Pālayankottai.

palamé, measure of length in Greece, equivalent to 25.4 millimetres.
·weights and measures, table 5 **19**:734

Palamedes, in Greek legend, the son of Nauplius, king of Euboea; he was one of the heroes of the Trojan War. During the siege of Troy he alternated with two other Greek heroes, Odysseus and Diomedes, in leading the army in the field, but his ability aroused their envy. In the epic version, they drowned him while fishing or persuaded him to seek treasure in a well, which they thereupon filled with stones. In the tragic version, Agamemnon (king of Mycenae, or Argos), Diomedes, and Odysseus had an agent steal into his tent and conceal a letter that contained money and purported to come from King Priam of Troy.

They then accused Palamedes of treasonable correspondence with the enemy, and he was stoned to death.

Palamedes had a reputation for sagacity, and the ancients attributed a number of inventions to him, including the alphabet, numbers, weights and measures, coinage, and the practice of eating at regular intervals. These abilities may reflect his name (Greek *palame*, "hand"), but he is now generally considered to be a personification of Phoenician culture.

Palana, urban settlement and centre of Koryak national *okrug* (area), Kamchatka *oblast* (administrative region), far eastern Russian Soviet Federated Socialist Republic, on the west coast of Kamchatka Peninsula on the Palana River, 5 mi (8 km) from its mouth on the Sea of Okhotsk. The national area was formed in 1930. The settlement has a regional museum. Latest pop. est. 1,500.

·map, Soviet Union **17**:322

Pālanpur, administrative headquarters, Banās Kāntha district, Gujarāt state, west central India, in the lowlands between the Arāvalli Range and the Kāthiāwār Peninsula. The former capital of the princely state of Pālanpur, it is now a trade and processing centre for agricultural produce and a rail and road junction. Pālanpur is also known for its handicrafts. Pop. (1971 prelim.) 47,766.
24°10′ N, 72°26′ E

·map, India **9**:278

Pāla painting: *see* Eastern Indian painting.

Pālār River, in southern India, rises near the Ponnaiyār River, southwest of Chintāmani, Mysore state, and flows 183 mi southeastward through Tamil Nadu state to the Bay of Bengal, south of Sadras. Its major tributaries are the Ponnai and Cheyyār rivers.

The flow of the Pālār is irregular, with considerable variations from year to year. Although it generally does not flood, heavy rains have caused the river to remain in flood for six months. The river has been dammed for irrigation, especially in North Arcot and Chingleput districts of Tamil Nadu. The largest towns along its banks are Vellore, Arcot, and Chingleput.
12°28′ N, 80°09′ E

palas, a flat-surfaced handwoven rug from the Caucasus, Turkistan, or Persia. The Caucasian *palas* is a slit tapestry in technique, the Shirvan (*q.v.*) variety designed without a border as a series of transverse bands carrying bold polygonal ornaments in vivid colouring. A Karabagh rug (*q.v.*) may be planned with diagonal rows of highly geometric palmette forms within a narrow border on all sides. A Kurdish *palas* might have a honeycomb pattern of ornamented hexagons with no real border or a set of transverse bands much narrower than those in the Shirvan *palas* (*see* Kurdish rugs). Turkmen *palasy*, usually of Yomud workmanship, are brocadings of several types, the most common showing a diamond grid with a narrow border on all sides and long aprons at both ends (*see* Yomud carpets). Much of the ground shows through between and around the brocaded motifs. The *palas* is usually all wool but is sometimes made of goat hair.

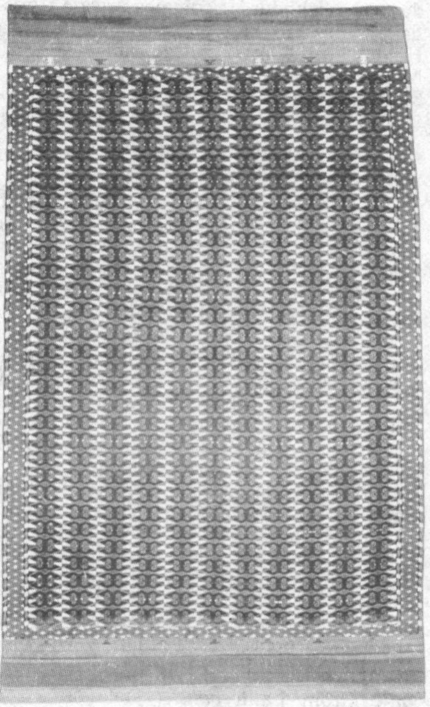

Yomud Palas from Russian Turkistan, *c.* 1900; in the H. McCoy Jones Collection

Collection of H. McCoy Jones; photograph, Bruce A. Humphrey

palatal consonant, a consonant sound produced by raising the blade, or front, of the tongue toward or against the hard palate just behind the alveolar ridge. The German *ch* sound in *ich* and the French *gn* (pronounced *ny*) in *agneau* are palatal consonants. English does not contain any purely palatal consonants, except for the *y* sound (a semivowel) in "you." (The *sh* sound in "ship" and the *zh* sound represented as *z* in "azure" are usually classified as palato-alveolar sounds.)

·Romance innovation **15**:1039d; table 1040
·Sinitic versus Tibeto-Karen phonology **16**:800e
·Slavic phonology development **16**:870g; table 871

palatalization, the production of consonants with the blade, or front, of the tongue drawn up farther toward the roof of the mouth (hard palate) than in their normal pronunciation. Palatalized consonants in Russian are pronounced as if attempting simultaneously to pronounce a particular consonant and a *y* sound; in English, the *ny* in "canyon" approximates a palatalized sound. Palatalized consonants may be distinguished from palatal consonants, in which the front of the tongue and the hard palate form the primary articulation.

Palatalization also refers to the process of sound change in which a nonpalatal consonant, like *k*, changes to a palatal consonant, like *ch* or *sh*; *e.g.*, French *chaîne* (pronounced with an initial *sh* sound) developed from Latin *catena* (pronounced with an initial *k* sound).

·Eurasian language union hypothesis **18**:1029e
·phonetic articulatory description **14**:277b
·Slavic phonological development **16**:870f; table 871

palate, in vertebrate anatomy the roof of the mouth, separating the oral and nasal cavities. It consists of an anterior hard palate of bone and, in mammals, a posterior soft palate that has no skeletal support and terminates in a fleshy, elongated projection called the uvula.

The hard palate, which comprises two-thirds of the total palate area, is a plate of bone (containing maxillary, premaxillary, palatine, and occasionally pterygoid bones) covered by a moist, durable layer of mucous membrane tissue. The mucous membrane is strongly attached to the bone and is capable of withstanding abrasion by food; it also secretes small amounts of mucus. This layer forms several ridges that help grip food while the tongue agitates it during chewing. The hard palate provides space for the tongue to move freely and a rigid floor to the nasal cavity so that pressures within the mouth do not close off the nasal passage. In many lower vertebrates the hard palate bears teeth.

The soft palate is composed of muscle and connective tissue, which give it both mobility and support. This palate is very flexible. When elevated for swallowing and sucking, it completely blocks and separates the nasal cavity and nasal portion of the pharynx (*q.v.*) from the mouth and oral part of the pharynx. While elevated, the soft palate creates a vacuum in the oral cavity, which keeps food out of the respiratory tract.

The first well-developed palates are found in the reptiles, although only in the form of a hard partition. Palates similar to those in humans occur only in birds and some mammals. With a few whales the mucous membrane forms toughened plates known as baleen or whalebone.

In the human abnormality of cleft palate, the separation between the nose and mouth is incomplete, causing food to enter the nose. This condition can be corrected surgically.

·crocodilian features and evolution **5**:288h
·human cranial nerve distribution **12**:1019a; illus. 1017
·human digestive system anatomy **5**:789g; illus. 791
·mammalian skull specializations **11**:407b
·phonetic study of speech production **14**:276b; illus. 275

soft palate
·human respiratory pathway **15**:764g
·speech production physiology **10**:649b
·speech defects from oral malformation **17**:491c
·vertebrate structural comparisons **5**:787e

Palatina, Cappella (*c.* 1140–71), palace chapel built in Sicilo-Byzantine style in Palermo, Sicily.

·Byzantine influence on medieval mosaics **12**:470h

Palatinate, German PFALZ, two historic states of Germany: The Rhenish Palatinate (Rheinische Pfalz) or Countship Palatine of the Rhine (Pfalzgrafschaft bei Rhein), now divided between the Rheinland-Pfalz, Baden-Württemberg, and Hessen lands of the Federal Republic of Germany; and the Upper Palatinate (Oberpfalz), in what is now Bavaria. The Count Palatine of the Rhine was the foremost secular prince of the Holy Roman Empire and one of the seven electors who chose the emperor. Perhaps the most famous holder of the title was Count Palatine Frederick V, whose claim to the throne of Bohemia was a major issue in the early phase of the Thirty Years' War. *See also* Rheinland-Pfalz.

·French destruction and its consequences **11**:130e
·Protestant and Catholic rivalry in 1600s **15**:112g
·Reformed Church destruction attempt **15**:559g

Palatine, village, northwestern suburb of Chicago, Cook County, Illinois, U.S. The community, established in 1855 when a Chicago and North Western Railway siding and depot was put in, was named for Palatine, N.Y., original home of one of the early settlers. Although there are some light industries, Palatine is mainly residential. William Rainey Harper College was established there in 1965. Inc. 1869. Pop. (1970) 25,904; (1980) 32,166.

palatine (from *palatinus*, "belonging to the palace"), the name of diverse officials found in numerous countries of medieval and early modern Europe. Originally the term was applied to the chamberlains and troops guarding the palace of the Roman emperor. In Constantine's time (early 4th century), the designation was also used for the senior field force of the army that might accompany the emperor on his campaigns. During the early European Middle Ages the term applied to various officials among the Germanic peoples. The most important of these was the count palatine, who in Merovingian and Carolingian times (5th through 10th century) was an official of the sovereign's household, in particular of his court of law. The count palatine was the official representative at court proceedings such as oath takings or judicial sentences and was in charge of the records of such proceedings. At first he examined cases in the king's court and was authorized to carry out the decisions; later he had his own court in which he was allowed certain discretion in making decisions. In addition to his judicial responsibilities, the count palatine had administrative functions dealing with the king's household.

Under the German kings of the Saxon and Salian dynasties (919–1125), the function of the counts palatine corresponded to those of the Carolingian *missi dominici*, who were representatives of the king in the provinces, responsible for the administration of the royal domain and for the disposition of justice in certain duchies, such as Saxony and Bavaria, and, in particular, Lotharingia (Lorraine). When other palatine rights were absorbed by ducal dynasties, local families, or, in Italy, bishops, with little of the authority retained, the count palatine of Lotharingia, whose office had been attached to the royal palace at Aachen from the 10th century onward, became the real successor to the Carolingian count palatine. From his office grew the Countship Palatine of the Rhine, or simply the Palatinate, which, from the time of the emperor Frederick I Barbarossa (died 1190), became a great territorial power (*see* Palatinate). The term palatine recurs in the 14th century, when the emperor Charles IV instituted a court body of household counts palatine, but they had only voluntary jurisdiction and some honorific functions.

In England the term palatinate or county palatine was applied in the Middle Ages to counties the lords of which, whether lay or ecclesiastical, exercised powers that were normally reserved to the crown. There were also palatine provinces among the English colonies in North America: Lord Baltimore was granted palatine rights in Maryland in 1632, as were the proprietors of Carolina in 1663.

The word *palatinus* and its derivatives also translate the titles of certain great functionaries in eastern Europe, such as the Polish *wojewoda* (voivode), the military governor of a province. In addition, the word paladin was used in post-Carolingian literature to apply to the companions of Charlemagne.
·Hungarian absentee administration **9**:33a

palatine aponeurosis, thin, fibrous plate of the soft palate, that serves as attachment for palate muscles.
·human digestive system anatomy **5**:789g

Palatine Chapel, also called PALACE CHAPEL, imperial chapel and burial place of Charlemagne in Aachen (now in West Germany). The most important extant example of Carolingian architecture, it was begun in 790 and consecrated a cathedral in 805. The chapel's octagonal shape and two super-imposed galleries were modelled after the Byzantine style of S. Vitale at Ravenna. The dome, however, is in the Germanic style; rising to 101.5 feet (30.9 metres), it was influential in later Romanesque and Gothic architectural styles. The interior is decorated with Classical columns; the monumental bronze doors and bronze grilles were executed in the Classical style, probably by Lombard artisans. Charlemagne's tomb is marked by a stone slab over which hangs a bronze chandelier presented by Frederick I Barbarossa in 1168.

Palatine Hill, Italian MONTE PALATINO, one of the seven hills of Rome and traditionally the site of the earliest settlement in the city.
Major ref. **15**:1075f; map 1068
·Romulus and Remus legend **15**:1085g

palatine raphe, ridge in the middle of the hard palate.
·human digestive system anatomy **5**:789g

Palatino, Giovanni Battista, 16th-century Italian calligrapher.
·writing manual significance **3**:658b; illus.

Palation: *see* Miletus.

Palatka, city, seat (1849) of Putnam County, north central Florida, U.S. James Marver established a trading post (1820) on the site of a Seminole village called Pilatka (Pilotaikita, Pilaklikaha), an Indian term meaning "Crossing Over" or "Cow's Crossing." During the Second Seminole War (1835–42), Ft. Shannon was built. The settlement, incorporated as the town of Pilatka in 1851, came under fire from gunboats in 1864 and was occupied by Federal troops. After the Civil War, it developed as a river port and winter resort with rail connections and was chartered as a city in 1872. To avoid confusion with Picolata, the post office changed the city's name to Palatka.

Mixed agriculture and the paper industry are basic economic activities, supplemented by light manufacturing and tourism. St. Johns River Junior College was opened there in 1958. The Ravine Gardens are known for their brilliant colour, and an azalea festival is held in March. Pop. (1980) 10,175.
29°39′ N, 81°38′ W
·map, United States **18**:909

Palauan, major language of the Palau Islands of the western Carolines, part of the Trust Territory of the Pacific Islands. It is classified as belonging in the eastern branch of the Austronesian (Malayo-Polynesian) family of languages; like Chamorro, spoken in the Mariana Islands, it is considered to be of the Indonesian type of languages, with closest relations to the Philippine languages. Palauan, spoken by about 12,000 persons, is characterized by a small phonemic inventory and the use of phonemic stress.
·Austronesian languages **2**:486h
·Micronesian cultural diversity **12**:122f
·Pacific Islands' linguistic groups **13**:834c

Palau (PELEW) **Islands,** group, western end of the Caroline chain (part of the United Nations Trust Territory of the Pacific Islands) in the western Pacific, 550 mi (880 km) east of the Philippines. They include the volcanic islands of Babelthuap, Koror (*qq.v.*), and Arakabesan; the coral islands of Angaur, Peleliu, and Urukthapel; and Kayangel atoll. A major Japanese naval stronghold in World War II, the group fell to U.S. forces in 1944. It now comprises an administrative territorial district with its capital at Koror. Pop. (1973) 12,674.
7°30′ N, 134°30′ E
·area and population table **13**:834
·map, Trust Territory of the Pacific Islands **13**:833
·Micronesian cultural patterns **12**:122b
·Oceanian peoples and cultures **13**:468e

Palauli, political district, Savai'i Island, Western Samoa.
·Samoan area and population table **16**:206

Palaung, hill people of the Shan Plateau in the Shan State of Burma. They were estimated to number about 150,000 in the 1960s. They speak dialects of the Palaungic branch of Austro-Asiatic languages, quite distinct from the Tai languages of the Shan, with whom they live closely intermingled. Their main crops are rice and tea. Shan-type Buddhism coexists with the worship of spirits.
·Burmese ethnic regions and languages **3**:504e

Palaungic languages, branch of the Mon-Khmer subfamily of the Austro-Asiatic family of languages, spoken in Burma, Thailand, and Yunnan Province of China.
·classification and characteristics of Austro-Asiatic languages **2**:481d; map 484

Palawan, most southwesterly large island and province of the Philippines. The island is long and narrow and trends northeast–southwest between the South China and Sulu seas. It has an area of 4,550 sq mi (11,785 sq km), a maximum width of 24 mi (39 km), and a mountainous backbone that runs its entire 270-mi length, with Mt. Mantalingajan (6,840 ft [2,085 m]) in the south as its highest peak. The Balabac–Bugsuk group of islands off the southern tip is a remnant of a land bridge that once connected Palawan and Borneo; for this reason the animal life and vegetation are more closely related to those of Borneo than to those of the other Philippine islands. The long, irregular coastline is generally coral fringed with numerous offshore islets. A discontinuous coastal plain that seldom extends more than 5 mi inland supports most of the island's population. It has the only all-weather road, constitutes the main agricultural area, and is best developed on the east coast south of Puerto Princesa (*q.v.*), the principal port and provincial capital.

Palawan province has the nation's lowest population density, 40.3 per square mile, and most of the island is the forest homeland of the Batah, Palawan, and Tagbanuas peoples. Christian migrants (Visayans, Tagalogs, Ilocanos, and Bicolanos) have settled in the north and east. There are some Moro (Muslim) villages in the south. Scattered settlement and shifting agriculture predominate, with rice as the principal food crop. Corn (maize), beans, and sweet potatoes are also grown. Large-scale commercial fishing operations are carried out at Puerto Princesa and Taytay and on Coron and Dumaran islands.

Palawan province (area 5,751 sq mi) is composed of the main island and about 1,800 smaller islands and islets, of which the principal groups are the Calamians (north), the Dumaran–Cuyo group (northeast), and the Balabac–Bugsuk group. Culion Island in the Calamians is a leper colony. Mineral wealth includes manganese and guano in the Calamians and mercury and chromite near Puerto Princesa. Pop. (1975 est.) province, 279,299.
9°30′ N, 118°30′ E
·area and population table **14**:236; map 235
·map, Philippines **14**:233

Palawan Trough, submarine trench in the China Sea.
7°00′ N, 115°00′ E
·China Sea physiography and hydrography **4**:406f; map 405

Pālayankottai, also called PĀLAMCOTTAH, city, Tirunelveli district, Tamil Nadu state, southern India, across the Tāmbraparni River from its twin city, Tirunelveli. Formerly the district administrative headquarters, it is now a residential and educational centre for its industrial neighbour. It contains private Christian schools and three Christian colleges and a Hindu liberal arts college affiliated with Madurai University. Pop. (1971) 70,070.
8°43′ N, 77°44′ E
·map, India **9**:279

Palazzo: *see under* substantive word.

Palazzolo Acreide, town, Siracusa province, southeastern Sicily, Italy, in the Monti Iblei, west of Syracuse. The successor to the Syracusan colony of Acrae (founded nearby in 664 BC), which was ravaged by the Muslims in the 9th century, the town was ruled by a succession of families in the Middle Ages, later passing to the Kingdom of the Two Sicilies and eventually to the Kingdom of Italy. It was largely destroyed by the earthquake of 1693, and most of the buildings date from the 18th century. On the site of Acrae (Akrai) are the remains of a Greek theatre and council house. The *templi ferali* ("temples of the dead"), carved in the rock, contain Greek inscriptions and votive niches. The Santoni are 12 life-size rock carvings of deities, including Cybele, dating from the 3rd century BC. The Palazzo Iudica houses objects from the ruins.

Palazzolo Acreide has a hydroelectric plant, and olives, grain, citrus fruits, and almonds are grown. Pop. (1975 est.) mun., 9,896.
37°03′ N, 14°54′ E

pale (from Latin *palus*, "stake"), district separated from adjacent country by definite boundaries or distinguished by a different legal and administrative system. In imperial Russia Empress Catherine II the Great created a pale (Jan. 3, 1792 [Dec. 23, 1791, old style]) for the Jews in the southwestern territories annexed from Poland in 1772. The Jews were forbidden to live or travel outside this "Pale of Settlement," which by the 19th century included all of Russian Poland, Lithuania, Belorussia, most of the Ukraine, the Crimea, and Bessarabia.

During the 1860s a few exceptions were made to this restriction, permitting some Jews (*e.g.*, certain classifications of merchants and artisans, those with higher educations, and those who had completed their military service) to cross the boundary of the pale and settle in any part of the empire except for Finland and after 1891 the city and province of Moscow. Nevertheless, the census of 1897 indicated that most of the Jews remained confined to the pale (almost 5,000,000 lived within it; only about 200,000 lived elsewhere in European Russia).

Other examples of pales include the English pales in Ireland and France. "The Pale" in Ireland (so named in the late 14th century) was established at the time of Henry II's expedition (1171–72) and consisted of the territories conquered by England, where English settlements and rule were most secure; the Pale existed until the entire country was subjugated under Elizabeth I (reigned 1558–1603). Its area, which varied considerably depending upon the strength of the English authorities, included parts of the modern counties of Dublin, Louth, Meath, and Kildare during the reign of Henry VIII (1509–47). The Calais pale in northern France (1347–1558) extended from Gravelines to Wissant on the coast and stretched inland from six to nine miles.

·English settlements in Ireland **3**:286c

pale, in heraldry, vertical band in a shield somewhat less than one-third of its width.

·heraldic design elements **8**:788a; illus. 787

palea, in botany, one of the chaffy scales on the receptacles subtending the disk flowers in the heads of many composite plants.

·grass order flower structures **14**:590d

Palearctic Region, biogeographic region in the Earth's Northern Hemisphere, encompassing Europe, Asia north of the Himalayas, Iran, Turkey, and the Mediterranean coast of Africa.

·African vegetation and wildlife **1**:196h
·Asian animal life **2**:170a
·Polish plant and animal life **14**:628c
·prehistoric locales of early man **14**:839f

Palearctic subregion: *see* Holarctic region.

Palecanus occidentalis: *see* pelican.

pale crepe, nearly white rubber with a crinkly surface, prepared by a special chemical treatment.

·colour control and production process **15**:1175h

Pale Fire (1962), novel by Vladimir Nabokov.

·Expressionistic tradition in the novel **13**:285b

Palembang, capital, Sumatera Selatan (South Sumatra) province (*daerah tingkat I*), Indonesia, on the Sungai (river) Musi (*q.v.*). Sumatra's largest city, it was once the capital (7th century) of the Hindu Sumatran kingdom of Śrivijaya and long the chief town of Palembang sultanate. In 1617 the Dutch East India Company set up a trading post there and in 1659 built a fort. Intermittently (1811–14; 1818–21) under British suzerainty, the sultanate was finally abolished by the Dutch (1825). Occupied by Japan during World War II, the city was temporarily (1948–50) capital of the autonomous state of South Sumatra until included in the Republic of Indonesia (1950).

The Great Mosque in Palembang, Sumatra, Indonesia
Richard Allen Thompson—EB Inc.

Important landmarks are the Great Mosque (1740; minaret 1753), tombs of several sultans, a museum, the town hall, Sukarno General Hospital (1959), a sports hall, a centre for training in public administration, Universitas Negeri Sriwidjaja, a Methodist school (1959), and the provincial parliament building. The town is accessible to ocean traffic on the Musi and has considerable trade with ports on the Malay Peninsula, Thailand, and China as well as other Indonesian ports. Exports include rubber, coffee, timber, petroleum products, coal, tea, spices, resin, rattan, cinchona, and pepper. There are also shipyards, iron foundries, machine shops, rubber plants, and a fertilizer factory. The suburbs of Sungaigerong and Pladju, to the east, have large oil refineries. Served by rail and road, the town also has an airport. Latest census 474,971.
3°00′ S, 104°45′ E

·map, Indonesia **9**:460
·size and character **9**:465g

Palencia, inland province, Old Castile, northern Spain, bounded by the provinces of Santander (north), Burgos (east), Valladolid (south), and Valladolid and León (west). Formed in 1833, it has an area of 3,100 sq mi (8,029 sq km). The north is traversed by the Cordillera (mountains) Cantábrica, rising to 6,644 ft (2,025 m) in the Sierra del Brezo. The remainder of Palencia, the fertile Tierra de Campos, belongs to the great Castilian tableland. In the south is a marsh or lake, known as Laguna de la Nava; and the principal rivers are the Pisuerga and Carrión. The mountainous district abounds in minerals, but only coal and small quantities of copper are worked. The Canal de Castilla (built 1753–1832), on which the provincial capital, Palencia, is located, connects the province with Valladolid and is used for irrigation as well as transport.

Wheat and other cereals, vegetables, sugar beet, hemp, and flax are grown; sheep raising is extensive; and there are manufactures of linen and woollen stuffs, oil, porcelain, leather, paper, and rugs. Apart from Palencia city, the chief centres are Venta de Baños, Barruelo de Santullán, Dueñas, and Paredes de Nava. Pop. (1970) 198,763.

·area and population table **17**:389

Palencia, capital of Palencia province, Old Castile, north central Spain, on the Tierra de Campos (plain) southwest of Burgos. Called the Pallantia by the ancient Greek geographers Strabo and Ptolemy, it was the chief town of the Vaccaei, an Iberian tribe. Its history during the Gothic and Moorish periods is obscure, but it was the seat of the Castilian kings and their Cortes (courts) in the 12th and 13th centuries. The university founded there in 1208 by Alfonso IX was removed in 1239 to Salamanca. The Gothic cathedral, begun in 1321, completed in 1504, and dedicated to San Antolín, occupies the site of a church erected by Sancho III of Navarre and Castile (1026–35) over the cave of San Antolín, which is still shown. The cathedral contains El Greco's "St. Sebastian" and other valuable paintings, old Flemish tapestry, and magnificent carved woodwork and stonework. Portions of the hospital of San Lázaro are said to date from the time of El Cid, the Spanish soldier-hero celebrated in Spain's epic poem, *El cantar de mío Cid*, who there married Ximena in 1074.

Palencia is an important communications centre. Its economy is based on the manufacture of iron, rugs, alcohol, leather, soap, porcelain, linen, cotton, wool, machinery, and matches. Pop. (1970) 58,370.
42°01′ N, 4°32′ W

·map, Spain **17**:382

Palenque, also known as GUARINE, Indian tribe of northern Venezuela at the time of the Spanish Conquest (16th century). The Palenque were closely related to the neighbouring Cumanagoto (*q.v.*); their language probably belonged to the Arawakan family. They were a tropical forest people known to eat human flesh, to be warlike, and to live in settlements surrounded by palisades (*palenques*). The Patángoro (*q.v.*) of Colombia were also sometimes called Palenque because of their fortified settlements.

Palenque, modern name for a ruined ancient Mayan city of the Classic Period (*c.* AD 300–900) in what is now Chiapas state, Mexico, about 80 miles (130 kilometres) south of Ciudad del Carmen. Its original name was lost, and thus it was named after the neighbouring village of Santo Domingo del Palenque. By the 1960s, tourists could visit the site, which formerly had been overgrown by jungle. The

The watchtower and Great Palace with the North Group ruins in the background, Palenque
Georg Gerster—Rapho Guillumette

Palenque builders used plaster to obtain a smooth finish unlike the usual Mayan tooled limestone construction. They used carving, however, on the interior walls; the best examples are on tablets affixed to the walls with plaster. Stucco and terra-cotta images have been found. The so-called Great Palace shows three parallel walls housing two corridors covered with pointed vaults of the Palenque style.

One of the largest and best preserved structures, the Temple of Inscriptions, is noted for its hieroglyphic inscriptions. In 1952 a crypt was discovered under it, in which were the jade-ornamented remains of what may have been a ruler priest of the early 8th century AD. The small Temple of Beau Relief is noted for a large stucco bas-relief of a beautifully modelled, enthroned figure.

·Classic Mayan architecture **11**:944h; map 935
·Mayan religious sculpture **11**:720h

paleoanthropology, or HUMAN PALEONTOLOGY, is the interdisciplinary study of the origins and development of early man. Fossils are assessed by the techniques of physical anthropology, comparative anatomy, and the theory of evolution. Artifacts, such as bone and stone tools, are identified and their significance for the physical and mental development of early man interpreted by the techniques of archeology and ethnology. Dating of fossils by geological strata, chemical tests, or radioactive decay rates requires knowledge of the physical sciences.

·hominid fossil classification **8**:1030f
·Homo sapiens fossil analysis **8**:1044f; illus. 1045
·human lineage and fossils **11**:420h

paleobotany, scientific discipline that is concerned with all aspects of fossil plants, including their description and classification, occurrence and distribution, and origins and evolutionary trends through geological time.
·fossil types and fossil history **7**:574c
·geological forms and feature studies **7**:1064g
·pollen stratigraphic evidence **14**:734c
·Upper Carboniferous index fossils **3**:859a

Paleocaucasian languages: *see* Caucasian languages.

Paleocene Epoch, major worldwide division of Early Tertiary rocks and time that began about 65,000,000 years ago and lasted about 11,000,000 years; the earliest division of the Tertiary Period, it precedes the Eocene Epoch and follows the Cretaceous Period. Because marine rocks of the Paleocene Epoch are limited in occurrence, much of the information about the Paleocene comes from terrestrial deposits. In Europe, three major divisions of the Paleocene are recognized; from oldest to youngest these divisions are the Danian, Montian, and Thanetian stages. In North America, especially the San Juan Basin region of New Mexico and southern Colorado, where Paleocene continental deposits are well developed, a threefold division of the Paleocene also is recognized. The Puercan (named for rocks near Puerco, N.M.), Torrejonian (named for exposures near Torrejon, N.M.), and Tiffanian (named for rocks near Tiffany, N.M.) stages represent lower, middle, and upper Paleocene rocks, respectively. The Paleocene record of North America affords the most complete picture of Paleocene life and environments; elsewhere, Paleocene animals, especially mammals, are lacking, rare, or of late Paleocene age. Late Paleocene faunas are known from the regions of Cernay, Fr.; Gashato, Mongolia; and the Río Chico region of Patagonian Argentina.

The Paleocene of North America was characterized by a general warming trend in climatic conditions, with little or no frost; seasonal variations that existed probably consisted of alternating dry and wet seasons. Among the most prominent features of Paleocene vertebrate faunas are the complete absence of dinosaurs and other reptilian groups that were dominant during the Cretaceous and the rapid expansion and evolution of the mammals. Paleocene mammals include representatives of many groups or orders that are still extant, although the Paleocene forms are mostly archaic or highly specialized. In terms of proportions and relative abundance, however, Paleocene faunas are dominated by mammals that have no living representatives. Paleocene mammalian faunas include Cretaceous forms such as opossum-like marsupials and especially the archaic and unusual multituberculates, animals that subsisted on a herbivorous diet and had teeth very similar in some respects to those of the later, more advanced rodents. The condylarths are very important elements of Paleocene faunas and include forms that were trending toward a herbivorous diet while still retaining primitive traits allying them to their ancestral, insectivore–carnivore progenitors. Primates became relatively abundant in the middle Paleocene and displayed characteristics intermediate between the insectivores and lemurs, especially in terms of dental anatomy.

Late in the Paleocene, trends in mammalian evolution were clearly toward larger forms and more varied assemblages. The primitive mammalian carnivores, the creodonts, appear late in the Paleocene, as do large herbivores, ancestral rodents, and the first tarsioid primates. The Gashato fauna from Mongolia contains the remains of the earliest known hare, *Eurymylus*, and among Paleocene mammals from South America are many early representatives of animals that dominated later Tertiary faunas in the region. In general, what is known of Paleocene faunas on a worldwide scale indicates close relationships between North American and western European faunas, a fact explained perhaps by a land connection between the regions or by closer, if not contiguous, connections.
·African fossil record **1**:183d
·animal evolutionary forms **3**:1082b *passim* to 1083a
·Black Sea area geologic history **2**:1097d
·geological time scale, illus. 2 **5**:499
·lagomorph origin in geologic time **10**:590d
·nomenclature adoption and type deposits **18**:151c
·North American geological history **13**:178d
·primate ancestry and evolution **14**:1026a
·tool discovery and classification **8**:606c

paleoclimates, climates of the geologic past. Because the historical record of climate is limited to the last few centuries, most conclusions regarding past climates must be reached indirectly, using biological, lithogenetic (rock-formation), or morphological (structure of organisms) evidence. Hot climates, for example, are thought to be indicated by the presence of red coloration in sediments, aragonite–lime deposits in caves, thick limestone formations, coral reefs, and remnants of large reptiles and tropical plants. Glacier moraines, thick masses of boulder and rubble, lack of chemical weathering, and the presence of conifers provide evidence of cold climates by analogous argument. Evidence of arid climates is given by salt deposits, rain-pitted soil, silicification, wind ripples, plants with small, light-coloured leaves, and well-preserved animal tracks. Finally, humid climates are indicated by dry lake beds, peat bogs and coal seams, and the remnants of tree ferns.

On the basis of such evidence, it has been established that during the past 600,000 years there have been a series of at least four glacier advances (ice ages), the last ending about 11,000 years ago in the United States. Along with these advances came periods of unusual wetness in most of the world's subtropical deserts and periods of near-aridity in the present-day tropical jungles.
·African rift valley morphology **15**:843a
·Antarctic ice sheet geologic record **1**:955e
·Carboniferous subtropics and glaciers **3**:854f
·climate geological and biological basis **2**:324e
·climate indicators and history **4**:731d; table 736
·Cretaceous climate reconstruction **5**:252b
·desert regions climatic changes **5**:614a
·evaporite deposits and arid climate **6**:1132f
·foraminiferan coiling as indicator **7**:557f
·fossil and rock indications of ancient climate **13**:907e *passim* to 911e
·Holocene changes and vegetation, illus. 1 **8**:1000
·Holocene evidence interpretations **8**:999f; table 1000
·indicators in belemnoid fossils **7**:562f
·Jurassic climate indications **10**:360d; illus.358
·loess formation conditions **11**:26c
·Paleozoic environment and faunal changes **13**:926h
·Paleozoic rock record **6**:14c
·playa and saline-flat origins **14**:555f
·Pleistocene climate indications **14**:560c
·pollen stratigraphy applications **14**:742d
·Precambrian glaciation **14**:959b
·Triassic rock and animal distribution **18**:697a
·Upper Carboniferous sedimentation **3**:859h
·varved deposit analysis inference **19**:36a

paleoclimatology, study of climate through geologic time. A large number of fields are involved, but the basic material is drawn mainly from geology and paleobotany, whereas speculative attempts at explanation have come largely from astronomy, physics, meteorology, and geophysics. The ultimate, and probably unachievable goal of the paleoclimatologist is to explain completely the variations in climate for all parts of the world and for all portions of the history of the Earth, beginning with the time of its formation. Most research in paleoclimatology centres on explaining (1) the warmth of the Northern Hemisphere land masses during at least 90 percent of the last 570,000,000 years, (2) the semiperiodic occurrence of widespread glaciation at intervals of about 250,000,000 years, and (3) the irregular advances and retreats of the ice sheets during the glacial periods, termed ice ages and interglacials, respectively. The warmth of the past can be largely explained by continental drift; until about 150,000,000 years ago, both North America and Europe were much closer to the Equator than they are today. The glacial periods and ice ages are much more difficult to explain, and no completely satisfactory theory has been presented.
·carbonate sediment climatic conditions **10**:984f
·climate geological and biological basis **2**:324e
·Tertiary conditions and animal life **18**:155h

paleocurrent, ancient current of wind or water, the direction and regime of which can be deduced from the interpretation of sedimentary structures. Such structures as cross bedding, ripple marks, striations, and current lineation, as well as dune type, heavy mineral distribution, and the like, can be used to determine the former direction of current flow. Other information sometimes gleaned from the study of paleocurrents includes turbulence, velocity, and other flow characteristics and the rock type of the source area.
·sedimentary rock ripple marks **13**:909e; illus.

paleoecology, scientific discipline that is concerned with all aspects of the relationships between fossil organisms and their ancient life environments. These relationships are also treated by paleontology and biostratigraphy, but many specialists prefer the term paleoecology because of the widespread use of "ecology" in reference to study of modern groups of organisms and their environments.
·pollen stratigraphy applications **14**:742a

paleoentomology, the study of fossil insects.
·insect lineage problems **1**:1023h

Paleogene Period, lower of two divisions of the Cenozoic Era; it is the interval of geological time beginning about 65,000,000 years ago, spanning the next 39,000,000 years, and preceding the Neogene Period. The Paleogene Period includes the Paleocene, Eocene, and Oligocene epochs and their corresponding series of rocks; it was defined in Europe, where it is widely recognized. In North America, where the classical subdivision of the Cenozoic Era into the Tertiary Period and Quaternary Period is employed, this usage has not gained similar recognition.
·nomenclature adoption **18**:151d
·rocks, climate, and plant and animal life **3**:1080f

paleogeographic map, cartographic representation of the positions of lands and seas in the geological past. One of the principal goals of historical geology is the reconstruction of ancient environments, and, accordingly, paleogeographic maps are available for much of the world for each of the periods of geological time. As is true of any map, the accuracy of a paleogeographic map cannot exceed that of the data used in its construction.

paleogeography 13:906, interpreted reconstruction of portions of the Earth's surface at specific times in the geologic past. Paleogeographic maps are visual summaries of a wide variety of complex geological information and provide a series of relatively instantaneous views of the Earth as it appeared throughout geologic history.

The text article provides an overview of paleogeography and covers the kinds and application of paleogeographic data, including sections on biological, petrological, and geophysical and geochemical information.

REFERENCES in other text articles:
·Arabian Sea foraminifera deposits **1**:1060d
·Azov and Black Sea geological history **2**:547e
·Black Sea area ancient sea and lake **2**:1096g
·Cambrian lands, seas, and oceans **3**:692f; illus. 693

·carbonate sediments and sea levels **10**:984g
·climate and geography relation **4**:731a; table 736
·conodonts' stratigraphic uses **5**:26g
·Cretaceous marine transgressions **5**:249a; illus. 250
·cyclothem strata, theories, and significance **5**:396a
·Devonian geographic features **5**:672c; illus.
·evaporite depositional conditions **6**:1132g
·faunal sequence theory **6**:81g
·geological history of Earth **6**:15a
·Jurassic orogenies and transgressions **10**:360a; illus. 358
·Lake Eyre's geological evolution **7**:125g
·landform evolution concepts and theories **10**:624a
·Lower Carboniferous lands and seas **3**:855e; maps 856a
·Mesozoic landmasses and mountains **11**:1013h
·Ordovician continents and drift theory **13**:660f; figure 661
·Permian fossils and continental drift **14**:98g
·Pleistocene beaches and placer deposits **13**:503a
·Pleistocene faunal and floral regions **14**:568c
·Pleistocene glacial landforms **8**:164b
·pollen stratigraphy applications **14**:742a
·Precambrian basins and coastlines **14**:958c
·principles and methods of reconstruction **6**:8g
·sedimentary facies and land reconstruction **16**:462c; map
·Silurian land and sea changes **16**:772f; illus. 773
·Tertiary land–sea distribution **18**:155c
·Triassic land emergence **18**:696e; map 694
·Upper Carboniferous geography **3**:856h
·Upper Paleozoic ocean and land areas **13**:927h

paleography 13:911, study of ancient and medieval handwriting. The primary tasks of the paleographer are to read the writings of the past correctly and to assign them a date and place of origin. As a rule paleography deals with Greek and Latin scripts and their derivatives, excluding Egyptian, Hebrew, Middle, and Far Eastern scripts.

The text article describes the types of writing materials used in antiquity and the Middle Ages and the different styles of scripts.

REFERENCES in other text articles:
·diplomatics accessory skill and basis **5**:809a
·epigraphic relation and major concern **6**:915e
·formal studies of writing **19**:1042b
·historiographic method development **8**:958b
·New Testament manuscript dating **2**:942c
·textual criticism methodology **18**:192c
·Western and Eastern calligraphy remains **3**:645h; illus.

paleohydrology, science concerned with hydrologic systems as they existed on the Earth during previous periods of Earth history. Changing hydrologic conditions are inferred from the evidence of the alteration, deposition, and erosion in rocks from these periods. Paleohydrology also deals with the changes in the floral and faunal assemblages through geologic time that have been greatly influenced by hydrologic change.

Paleolithic, ancient cultural stage or level of development in man; in some parts of the world, a basically Paleolithic culture level still persists. The Paleolithic is characterized by distinctive stone tool types that are simple and relatively crude in the Early Paleolithic but become more complex and sophisticated in later Paleolithic time. The Paleolithic, also known as the Old Stone Age, essentially began with the appearance of the first hominids or manlike forms such as the australopithecines. The earliest stone tools, about 2,500,000 years old, are simple pebble tools and are associated with australopithecines. More sophisticated Paleolithic tools, though still relatively crude, are the chopper-chopping tools that have a wide distribution in the Eastern Hemisphere. It is likely that, apart from stone tools, the earliest hominids used tools fabricated from wood and bone, sometimes with little alteration. The wooden tools were not preserved in the geological record, but studies indicate the presence of bone tools in association with the australopithecines and probably the more advanced *Homo erectus*.

In the Middle Pleistocene (the Pleistocene Epoch began about 2,500,000 years ago and lasted until about 10,000 years ago) a new and distinctive tool type emerged, the hand axe. Hand axes are large stone tools that were used for a variety of purposes and are roughly heart-shaped. Hand axes have a very wide distribution in the Old World, and the development of various hand-axe cultures can be traced through space and time. The earliest hand axes are assigned to the Abbevillian culture; a later, more refined culture is the Acheulian. Parallel, and often intrinsic components of hand-axe implement cultures were the flake cultures in which flakes of flint, perhaps produced by the making of hand axes, were worked and used as special tools.

In Europe, an early flake culture was the Clactonian, which eventually evolved into the Mousterian culture, a cultural assemblage associated with the familiar Neanderthal people. A further development of the Middle Paleolithic was the prepared core technique for making flaked tools associated with the Levalloisian culture. It was later combined with the Mousterian into the Levalloisio-Mousterian culture found in association with the later Neanderthaloid peoples, as well as with more modern types.

Upper Paleolithic cultures are typified by the Perigordian, Aurignacian, and Magdalenian cultures as well as many regional cultures of the Old World and the most anciently known cultures of the New World. Upper Paleolithic cultures are associated with the remains of essentially modern man. They are characterized by their greater sophistication and specialization. A greater variety of tool types used for a greater variety of purposes is found in Upper Paleolithic assemblages. Similarly, Upper Paleolithic cultures contain abundant remains of art, either as paintings found on the walls of caves or even as sculpture work. The paintings are very naturalistic and some are highly coloured and sophisticated.

·Aegean early cultures **1**:113b
·archaeological proof of mankind's age **1**:1079c
·artifact classification and archaeological time scale **5**:501d; illus. 500
·burial customs **5**:533b
·Central Asian visual arts evidence **3**:1130g
·cereal milling evidence **3**:1157c
·Ceylonese prehistoric cultures **4**:1f
·Chinese age evidence **19**:174c
·Chinese fossil discoveries **4**:297h
·clothing origins **5**:1015h
·Cro-Magnon tools, dwellings, and art **5**:289f
·Early Stone Age African developments **1**:286b
·East African community evidence **6**:91b
·Egyptian climate and cultures **6**:463d
·European culture and artistic style **17**:702c
·Geneva human settlement beginnings **7**:1011a
·hominid fossil deposits **8**:1046c
·Iranian tool industries **9**:830a
·Japanese cultures and artifacts **10**:57e
·man's extinction due to overpopulation **7**:21f
·North African stone tool quality **13**:145h
·religious practices and beliefs **14**:984g *passim* to 988e
·rope making innovations by primitive man **15**:1145c
·Sahara desert relics and man **16**:150a
·Scandinavian peoples and cultures **16**:304h
·seasonal ritual food supply control **7**:198h
·Southern African civilization features **17**:274f
·Spain's primitive culture and art **17**:401d
·Syrian and Palestinian prehistory **17**:927b
·technological developments and impact **18**:26e
·tool and toolmaking history **8**:606g; illus. 608

Paleolithic art, earliest of all art, produced during the latter part of the Old Stone Age, the Upper Paleolithic Period. Consisting of small sculpture and monumental cave painting, engraving, and relief, mostly of animals, Paleolithic art was the work of hunters, as farming and domestication of animals did not appear until the Neolithic Period (New Stone Age). It was produced in several locations in the Mediterranean region, but it survives in quantity only in two major areas, eastern Europe and certain parts of Spain and France.

Small, portable arts, clay figurines and carvings in bone and ivory, flourished especially in eastern Europe, where sculpture was the dominant tradition. Most works from this area are simple, realistic clay figurines of animals. More striking, however, are many carved statuettes of women, called Venus figures, which are stylized to emphasize parts of the body connected with sexuality and fertility and often so schematized that breasts and hips are the only features depicted. The function of these small arts seems to have been to reduce nature to a portable size and so gain a measure of control over it. The maker of an animal figurine had, by extension, power over the animal it represented; the Venus figure gave its possessor mastery over the fertility force it embodied.

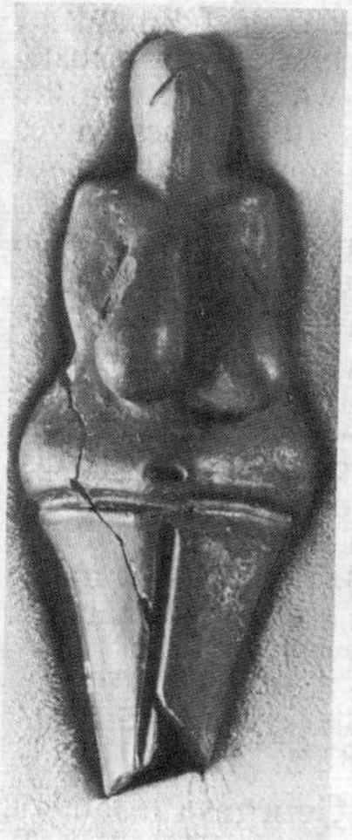

"Venus of Věstonice," Upper Paleolithic period clay statuette from Dolni Věstonice, Mikulov, Czechoslovakia, Aurignacian culture (*c.* 28,000–*c.* 22,000 BC); in the Moravian Museum, Brno, Czech.

From W. and B. Forman, *Prehistoric Art*, Spring Books, London

Monumental arts found their best expression by far in western Europe (the province of the so-called Franco-Cantabrian school; *q.v.*), where the inner walls of limestone caves that served as human habitation provided a sheltered field for painting, engraving, and relief. In addition to much small carving of fine quality, these caves have preserved a complete sequence of graphic art, from its beginnings in simple finger tracings in clay, aimless at first and then in abstract designs, to vastly sophisticated polychrome paintings of dynamic naturalism and exquisite design. The finger tracings and early painted hand prints stencilled on cave walls seem to reflect an instinctive desire in man to make a personal mark on the universe, to attempt to possess it and to subject its chaos to his sense of order. When it was observed that lines could form images of things in nature, the image itself seems to have become a means of annexing part of nature to the self. That the image was taken as magic reality by Old Stone Age man is suggested by the absence of narrative scenes or formal compositions, apparently ruling out anything but a symbolic function for these pictures. Moreover, there is evidence of a wishful subjection of the image to its creator's will: some animals are injured by painted arrows or the marks of ritual spear thrusts; others are depicted without heads and thus helpless before the hunter. Unlike its living counterpart, the image of an animal could neither flee nor resist. If image was reality, then the artist could affirm his power over the living species in the act of "creating" the animal. Thus cave art from the beginning seems to have been, for the man who produced it, an effective means of dealing with a complex universe: standing as a half-way point between man and the outside world, it was primarily an act of taking possession. Nature itself was often made to participate in this process, and thereby strengthen it, through the incorporation of natural features, stalactites and bulges in the cave wall, as part of the image.

The importance of such an art to a hunting people that had very little control over nature but depended completely upon it is obvious. The skill with which the works were executed indicates a kind of professional status for artists, perhaps a partial exemption from other tasks crucial to survival. It is thought that some of these animal pictures played a vital role in rituals conducted to invoke success in the hunt and to promote fertility of the animals hunted. Some caves are decorated with hundreds of images created over thousands of years by successive generations of artists. Each generation perhaps was inspired by the accumulated magic of the site, for these caves seem to have been long-standing centres of hunting cults.

Finally, a striking feature is the almost total absence of the human figure in Franco-Cantabrian cave art and its virtual limitation to Venus figures in other areas. Such human figures as do appear in cave art are almost always disguised in some way, either combined with animal forms or crudely drawn, with distorted, masklike faces. Possibly the enormous power of art made men reluctant to subject themselves to its control. For the two major phases of Paleolithic art, *see* Aurignacian art; Magdalenian art. *Major ref.* **17**:702c

·archaeological time scale **5**:501e; illus. 500
·Cro-Magnon tools, dwellings, and art **5**:289g
·naturalistic painting **13**:877g

Paléologue, Maurice-Georges (b. Jan. 13, 1859, Paris—d. November 1944, Paris?), French diplomat and writer who encouraged the Franco-Russian Alliance. He entered the diplomatic service at an early age and became deputy-director (1909) and director (1911) of affairs in the foreign office. Shortly before World War I he was appointed ambassador to St. Petersburg (now Leningrad) and retained this post until 1917. During the war he consolidated the Franco-Russian alliance and sought to ensure effective military action on the part of Russia. In 1920 he was secretary-general of the ministry of foreign affairs. His *La Russie des Tsars pendant la grande guerre* (1921–22) records his diplomatic experiences in St. Petersburg.

paleomagnetism, study of the history of the Earth's magnetic field using the evidence of permanent rock magnetism, called natural remanent magnetism (*see* remanent magnetism). The basic assumption involved is that the measured principal component of remanent magnetism of a rock gives the orientation of the Earth's magnetic field at the time (or shortly after) the rock was formed. Remanent magnetization can arise in igneous rocks and in detrital (particulate) sedimentary rocks; in the latter case, magnetite-bearing sandstones are especially suitable.

Paleomagnetism has provided important evidence of the occurrence of polar wandering and continental drift and has been used to locate the continents and subcontinents in relation to each other during particular intervals of time. The entire crust of the Earth has been active, and the geomagnetic poles have wandered slowly; frequently, during geological time, they have switched polarity. It is often difficult to interpret the data from rock samples because a fixed spatial reference point through time is generally lacking. *Major ref.* **15**:945b

·chronology and correlation methods **8**:999b
·continental drift evidence **13**:929a
·Earth's magnetic field variations **6**:27d
·geological sciences studies **7**:1060a
·geologic interval and polarity reversal **13**:907c
·polar wandering and magnetic reversals **17**:724h
·rock magnetism detection and measurement **15**:962f

Paleomastodon, genus of extinct proboscidean mammals of Oligocene age.

·fossil mammal evolution, illus. 13 **7**:573

Paleomoropus, genus of fossil chalicotheres of the order Perissodactyla.

·horse relatives' evolution **14**:87g

paleontology, also spelled PALAEONTOLOGY, scientific discipline that overlaps biology and geology, focussing on fossil plants and animals, their position in the geological time scale, and their relationships to modern living species. In its geological aspect, paleontology is mutually interdependent with stratigraphy and historical geology, fossils being a major means by which sedimentary strata are identified and correlated with one another. As a branch of biology, paleontology deals with the time course of the appearance, modification, and extinction of groups of animals, plants, and protozoa. *Major ref.* **7**:1064b

·biological sciences classification **2**:1014h
·conodonts as index fossils **5**:26d
·distribution of species and fossil data **5**:914e
·evolutionary biology and biophilosophy **12**:874e
·fossil evidence for evolution and paedomorphosis consequences **7**:10c
·fossil record of major life-forms **7**:555h

invertebrate

·Porifera evolution **14**:853g
·primitive wingless insect evidence **1**:1025e
·paleogeographic dating **13**:907d
·pollen stratigraphic evidence **14**:734c
·sedimentary facies maps usage **16**:462c; illus.
·stratigraphic and paleontological development **6**:79b
·theoretic influences and developments **19**:1166f
·Upper Carboniferous index fossils **3**:859a

vertebrate

·Agassiz's fossil fish study influence **1**:290c
·Cuvier's animal evolution studies **5**:389g
·hominid fossil classification **8**:1030f
·Homo sapiens fossil analysis **8**:1044f; illus. 1045
·prehistoric man's major breeding grounds **14**:840b
·primate ancestry and evolution **14**:1025e
·Romer's evolutionary research **15**:1133h
·Simpson's mammalian evolution studies **16**:778e
·whale evolutionary controversy **19**:809b

RELATED ENTRIES in the *Ready Reference and Index: for*
animals: see fossil insect; fossil invertebrate; fossil tracks, trails, and burrows; fossil vertebrates; micropaleontology; paleoanthropology
plants: fossil plants; palynology
other: stratigraphy

paleopallium, in the lowest vertebrates, cerebral hemisphere of the brain that functions as an association area for impulses related to the sense of smell. The paleopallium corresponds to the pyriform lobe in mammals, a V-shaped formation deep in the forebrain.

·nervous system evolution **12**:991d; illus.

paleosalinity, total salt content per unit mass of an ancient body of water, determined by chemically analyzing the sedimentary rocks that were deposited in it. Paleosalinities are sometimes deduced from analyses of ancient evaporite assemblages, salt deposits the precipitation of which is partly governed by water salinity.

·marine life dependence on salinity **13**:497g
·ocean, atmosphere, and rock interaction **13**:477a
·shale boron ratio **13**:911c

Paleosiberian, any of the peoples of northeastern Siberia who are believed to be remnants of earlier and more extensive populations pushed into this area by later Neosiberians. The Paleosiberians include the Chukchi (*q.v.*), Koryak, Kamchadal, Yukaghir (*q.v.*), and Ket (*q.v.*). The Chukchi and Koryak are traditional reindeer breeders and hunters; maritime groups are sea-mammal hunters and fishers. The Kamchadal are sedentary fishers and the Yukaghir were formerly hunters. *Major ref.* **1**:1127d

·ethnolinguistic groups and traditions **6**:133b
·origins, languages, and groupings **16**:93h
·Siberian linguistic cultural traits **16**:725a

Paleosiberian languages **13**:914, languages spoken in northern Asia (Siberia) that belong to four genetically unrelated groups—Yeniseian, Luorawetlan, Yukaghir, and Gilyak. The Yeniseian group contains at least four languages—Ket, Kott, Arin, and Assan—of which only Ket is still in use. The Luorawetlan group is usually divided into five languages: Chukchi, Koryak, Kamchadal, Aliutor, and Kerek. The only living language of the Yukaghir group is Yukaghir proper (or Odul), although the extinct Omok and Chuvan languages also belonged to this group. Gilyak is an individual language unrelated to any of the other Paleosiberian groups.

The text article discusses the classification of the languages, their linguistic characteristics, and their writing systems.

REFERENCES in other text articles:
·Asian ethnic language distribution **2**:177c
·language areas and genetic affiliations **10**:666c
·Soviet Union nationalities distribution table **17**:339

RELATED ENTRIES in the *Ready Reference and Index:*
Gilyak language; Luorawetlan languages; Yeniseian languages; Yukaghir language

Paleosuchus (reptile): *see* caiman.

paleotemperature, surface temperature during the geologic past, as measured indirectly, using various minerals, fossils, rock types, and geochemical-isotope ratios. Certain corals, for example, can tolerate temperatures only within a definite range. Glaciated boulders, carried Equatorward by icebergs, may be found in water for which the mean midsummer temperature does not exceed 10° C (50° F).

The commonest geochemical-isotope ratio used is that of oxygen-16 to oxygen-18, which is partly dependent on temperature. This ratio, as measured in carbonate shell matter of marine organisms, indicates the surrounding water temperature at the time the matter was secreted. The ^{16}O:^{18}O ratio has been used to provide evidence of past ice ages and to demonstrate the occurrence of an unusually rapid rise in temperature in the North Atlantic Ocean and elsewhere about 11,000 years ago.

·climate indicators and history **4**:731c; table 736
·Cretaceous climate evidence **5**:252c
·crust and ocean formation **13**:476f
·foraminiferan and belemnoid fossils as indicators **7**:557f
·fossil assemblages' climatic indication **13**:907f
·Holocene evidence interpretations **8**:999f
·ice sheets and oxygen isotope ratios **9**:182g
·playa and saline-flat origins **14**:555f
·Pleistocene climate indicators **14**:560d
·pollen stratigraphy applications **14**:742d
·Upper Paleozoic marine faunal changes **13**:926h

paleothere, also spelled PALAEOTHERE, one of an extinct group of mammals of the order Perissodactyla.

·horse ancestry and evolution **14**:88e

Paleotropical (PALAEOTROPICAL) **kingdom,** one of the six primary floristic zones of the Earth.

·characteristic life and conditions **2**:1003f; illus. 1001

Paleotyrrhenian Stage (geology): *see* Milazzian Stage.

paleowinds, ancient surface winds as deduced from geologic evidence. There are two methods commonly used to estimate past wind directions. The first consists of determining the direction of movement of large quantities of wind-transported dust or soil (loess). A thick loess deposit, with depths up to 40 metres (120 feet), covers large parts of Nebraska, Kansas, Iowa, Missouri, and Illinois. From the pattern of its distribution, it has been determined that the deposit was laid down by strong winds from the west, probably during the Pleistocene Epoch.

The second method of deducing paleowinds is based on the study of the structure of former sand-dune deposits. When the wind direction is relatively constant, a dune usually has a simple structure, with the steepest (slip-face) slope on the leeward side.

The role of winds in shaping the terrain was apparently much more important in the past than it is today. The great fossil dune beds in the Colorado Plateau bear witness to this fact.

·Pleistocene wind direction evidence **14**:566h
·sandstone bedding directions **4**:732a
·wind deposits and formations **19**:846h

Paleozoic Era, Lower **13**:916, division of Earth history that began at the end of the Precambrian, 570,000,000 years ago, and lasted 175,000,000 years; as generally used, the Lower Paleozoic Era includes the Cambrian, Ordovician, and Silurian periods. Lower Paleozoic rocks bear the first abundant record of life-forms, characterized by the evolution and abundance of marine invertebrate faunas; the Silurian Period witnessed the dawn of animal life on land.

The text article covers the rocks, life-forms, stratigraphic correlation, and environments of the Lower Paleozoic.

REFERENCES in other text articles:
·African continent development **1**:182d; map 181
·animal fossil records of major groups **7**:557a
·Appalachian orogeny **1**:1016f
·Asian continent formation **2**:151f
·Australian geological history **2**:385b; map 382
·boundary problem studies **17**:723a
·Cambrian rocks, life, and evolution **3**:689f; illus. 693
·climate changes and glaciation **4**:731e
·conodont fossil record **5**:26b
·continental drift and coast development **6**:45b
·geological history, climate, and life **6**:13b
·geological record history **7**:1066c; illus.
·mountain building by folding **12**:579f; illus. 581
·Ordovician rocks, life, and environment **13**:656h; illus.
·ore deposits and mineralizing activity **13**:671f
·plant fossil records of major groups **7**:574e
·sedimentary rock occurrence **16**:472h
·Silurian rocks, life, and environment **16**:767h; illus.
·Tien Shan region geological history **18**:393g
·worldwide folding distribution, illus. 9 **12**:9

Paleozoic Era, Upper **13**:921, division of Earth history that began 395,000,000 years ago and lasted until the beginning of the Mesozoic Era, 225,000,000 years ago. Generally, the geologic periods included in the Upper Paleozoic Era are, from oldest to youngest: the Devonian, Carboniferous (Mississippian and Pennsylvanian in North America), and Permian. The Upper Paleozoic is distinguished by more highly evolved plants and animals. The first reptiles and first insects appeared then.

The text article covers the rocks, life-forms, sequence of faunal changes, stratigraphic correlation, and environments of the Upper Paleozoic.

REFERENCES in other text articles:
·African continent development **1**:182d; map 181
·animal fossil records of major groups **7**:557h
·annelid parasites of sea lilies **1**:931g
·Asian continent formation **2**:151g
·boundary problem studies **17**:723d
·carbonate sedimentation **10**:984e
·continental drift and coast development **6**:45b
·continental drift and paleogeography **5**:109a; illus.
·coral forms and reef development **5**:163c
·cyclothem strata, theory, and importance **5**:396a
·Devonian rocks, life, and environment **5**:671e; illus.
·European features **6**:1039a
·geological history, climate, and life **6**:13b
·geological time scale, illus. 2 **5**:499
·glaciation of present desert areas **5**:603b
·Lower Carboniferous rocks and life **3**:852g
·mountain-building processes **12**:590e *passim* to 592c
·North American geological history **13**:180f; map 198
·oil shale, sea fauna, and environment **13**:538f
·Permian life, rocks, and climate **14**:96a
·plant fossil records of major groups **7**:574f
·Red Sea floor development **15**:545c
·sedimentary rock occurrence **16**:473a
·Upper Carboniferous Earth history **3**:856c
·worldwide folding distribution, illus. 9 **12**:9

Palermo, district, Buenos Aires.
·architectural style **3**:448d

Palermo **13**:930, ancient PANORMUS, capital of the autonomous region of Sicily in the Italian Republic and an important port since antiquity, was one of the most cosmopolitan cities of the medieval Mediterranean world.

The text article covers Palermo's history from its foundation by the Phoenicians. The city decayed under the Roman Empire, subsequently prospering after it was conquered by the Arabs in 831. Palermo enjoyed its "golden age" during the Norman era (1072–1194), during which it was the capital of the Kingdom of Sicily. The court of the Hohenstaufen Holy Roman emperor Frederick II at Palermo was renowned throughout western Europe, but under succeeding Hohenstaufen, Angevin, and Aragonese rulers the city declined. A revival occurred in the 15th and 16th centuries, and from 1860, when Palermo was liberated from the Spanish Bourbons by Garibaldi, it has prospered.

REFERENCES in other text articles:
·Byzantine influence on medieval mosaics **12**:470h
·map, Sicily **16**:728
·province area and population table **9**:1094
·Roger II's court **15**:984f
·weaving in Middle Ages **18**:171c

Palermo Stone, one of the basic sources of information about the chronology and cultural history of Egypt during the first five dynasties (*c.* 3100–*c.* 2345 BC). Named for the Sicilian city where it has been preserved since 1877, the black basalt stone is one of six existing fragments, all similar in scale and arrangement, that probably originally stood in Egyptian temples or other important buildings. It is

The Palermo Stone, first side
By courtesy of the National Museum of Archaeology, Palermo

inscribed on both sides with horizontal lines of hieroglyphic text, the top row listing the names of predynastic rulers. The following rows, each headed by the name of a different king, are divided into compartments, each compartment signifying one year. Within the compartments the hieroglyphs always list one or more memorable events of that year. Thus the original monument was apparently a year-by-year record of all the kings from the 1st through the 5th dynasty, although the last name preserved on the stone is that of Neferirkare, the third of the nine kings of the 5th dynasty.

·historiographic importance **6**:462c

Palés Matos, Luis (b. 1898, Guayama, P.R. —d. Feb. 23, 1959, San Juan), poet, considered by many to be Puerto Rico's most distinguished lyric poet, who enriched the vocabulary of Spanish poetry with words, themes, symbols, images, and rhythms of African and Afro-American folklore and dance.

Palés Matos wrote his first poetry, collected in *Azaleas* (1915), in imitation of the fashionable Modernist trends but soon found his own direction in his personal interpretation (as a white man) of black culture. His poems, published in periodicals, on black themes firmly established his literary reputation and gave impetus to the developing concern of Spanish-Americans with their African heritage.

Palés Matos, unlike some of his contemporaries and disciples in what became known as the Negro poetry movement, did not strive for authenticity. He preferred to evoke a culture as a poet rather than as a sociologist. For this freely inventive approach to black themes, he was sometimes criticized by those more concerned with accuracy than with poetic merit; his ironic, often skeptical note has been interpreted by some as condescension. His mastery of poetic form and language is acknowledged, however, even by those who find his approach offensive. Although Palés Matos was best known and most influential for his "Negro poetry," his reflective and introspective personality found expression in poetry of many other moods and themes. *Poesía, 1915–56* (1957), a collection of much of his poetry, reveals his more personal side as a lyric poet and as a melancholy man, ill at ease in the modern world.

Palestine, the name of a territory on the eastern Mediterranean coast, occupied in biblical times by the kingdoms of Israel and Judah and, in the 20th century, the scene of conflicting claims between Jewish and Arab national movements. Also called the Holy Land, it is sacred in varying degrees to Judaism, Christianity, and Islām. For Judaism, Palestine, called Erez Yisra'el (Land of Israel), has traditionally been the land promised by God, a uniquely sacred place, and the seat of national independence. For Christianity, it is the scene of the life and ministry of Jesus and the Apostles, with especially revered places. For Islām, certain sites, associated with the Prophet Muḥammad, are holy places. A local Palestinian Arab nationalism has developed during the period of the Zionist settlement (*see* Zionism) and especially since the establishment of the State of Israel; it claims Palestine as the homeland and domain of the Arab peoples who have inhabited it since the Muslim conquest in the 7th century.

The name Palestine is derived from the Greek Palaistina, which comes from the Hebrew Pleshet (Land of the Philistines), a small coastal area northeast of Egypt, also called Philistia. The Romans used the term Syria Palaestina in the 2nd century BC for the southern third of the province of Syria, including the former Judea. The name Palestine was revived as an official title when the British were given a mandate (restricted to the territory west of the Jordan River) after World War I.

Palestine's frontiers have fluctuated widely throughout history, but it has usually embraced the territory from the Mediterranean and the coastal plain (west), through the transitional zone of ha-Shefela, to the hill country of Judaea and Samaria (*qq.v.*). The Wilderness of Judaea (Midbar Yehuda) slopes down to the Jordan River Valley, the northern section of the East African Rift System. In the south is the Negev (*q.v.*), a dry, rugged area ending at the Gulf of Aqaba. In the north the broad, fertile Plain of Esdraelon (*q.v.*) divides Samaria (south) from the hill country of Galilee (*q.v.*), the highest and best watered part of Palestine, as its boundaries are described here. In the east of Galilee lie the harp-shaped Sea of Galilee and the now drained H̱ula Valley (*see* H̱ula, 'Emeq). Kings David and Solomon, however, ruled (*c.* 1000) over a kingdom that included much of modern Lebanon and Syria, extending to the Euphrates River.

Settled since early prehistoric times, Palestine has been held by virtually every power of the Near East, among them Egypt, Assyria, Babylonia, Persia, Alexander the Great and his successors (the Ptolemies and Seleucids), the Romans, Byzantines, Umayyads, ʿAbbāsids, Fāṭimids, crusaders, Ayyūbids, Mamlūks, and Ottoman Turks. After World War I Palestine was administered by Great Britain under a mandate of the League of Nations; the mandate incorporated the Balfour Declaration (*q.v.*) of 1917, which stated that British policy favoured the establishment of a national home for the Jewish people in Palestine. British administration, however, satisfied neither the majority Arabs nor the growing Jewish population. After World War II the British continued to enforce strict regulations against Jewish immigration. Britain's position in Palestine grew untenable, and the problem was turned over to the United Nations, which recommended (Nov. 29, 1947) the establishment of separate Arab and Jewish states in Palestine. On May 14, 1948, the British left Palestine and the State of Israel was proclaimed. (For the ensuing wars with the Arab states, and Israeli territorial gains, *see* Arab-Israeli wars.) The Palestine Liberation Organization (*q.v.*), which by the 1970s was recognized by third-world countries as speaking for the Palestinians, announced that its goal was to reconstitute Palestine as an independent country of Muslims, Christians, and Jews. *Major ref.* **17**:926f

·Ben-Gurion role in Israeli liberation **2**:836f
·Churchill's 1922 White Paper **4**:597a
·Hashemite Kingdom of Jordan **10**:270c
·Israeli republic **9**:1059b

Palestine, city, seat of Anderson County, eastern Texas, U.S., near Lake Palestine (Blackburn Crossing Reservoir) and between the Neches and Trinity rivers. Settlement developed around Ft. Houston (1836) and the Old Pilgrim Church (1830s), established by Primitive Baptists from Illinois and said to be the first Protestant church in Texas (a replica stands on the site). The original townsite was laid out as the county seat by Johnston Shelton in 1846 and named for Palestine, Ill., the hometown of the Rev. Daniel Parker and of Kenneth L. Anderson, vice president of Texas. The community is now an agricultural-marketing centre for a region in which oil and gas production are also significant. The Scientific Balloon Flight Station of the National Center for Atmospheric Research is just to the west. Inc. 1871. Pop. (1980) 15,948.
31°46′ N, 95°38′ W
·map, United States **18**:908

Palestine, history of: *see* Syria and Palestine, history of.

Palestine Liberation Organization (PLO), Arabic AL-MUNAẒẒAMĀT TAḤRĪR FILASṬĪN, umbrella political organization that is the recognized representative of the world's 3,000,000 Palestinians (those Arabs living in mandated Palestine before 1948 and their descendants). It was formed in 1964 by the leaders of various Palestinian groups. Membership within the PLO has varied with the re-organization and internal disagreements of its constituent bodies. Major groups associated with the PLO include al-Fatah, the name of which is an acronym in reverse for Taḥrīr Filasṭīn (Palestine Liberation); the Popular Front for the Liberation of Palestine (al-Jabha al-Shaʿbīyah li-Taḥrīr Filasṭīn); and the Popular Democratic Front for the Liberation of Palestine (al-Jabha al-Shaʿbīyah al-Dimuqrāṭīyah li-Taḥrīr Filasṭīn). Terrorist organizations connected with the PLO before 1973 are the Black September group of al-Fatah and the PFLP–General Command.

In 1969 Yasir Arafat, leader of al-Fatah, the largest and richest Palestinian group, was named chairman of the PLO. From 1973 he advocated withdrawal from international terrorism and acceptance of the PLO as a government-in-exile. In 1974 the Arab League recognized the PLO as the representative of all Palestinians, against the claims of King Hussein of Jordan. In November 1974 the PLO became the first nongovernmental organization to address a plenary session of the United Nations General Assembly. The PLO was admitted to full membership in the Arab League in 1976.
·origins and guerrilla tactics **17**:962c

The Wilderness of Judaea west of the Dead Sea (foreground), and the mountains of Moab (background), in Palestine
By courtesy of the Ministry of Culture and Information, Jordan

Palestinian religions: *see* Syrian and Palestinian religions.

Palestrina (Italy): *see* Praeneste.

Palestrina (1917), opera by Hans Pfitzner.
·conservative compositional style **13**:591f

Palestrina, (Giovanni Pierluigi da) **13**:931 (b. *c.* 1525, Palestrina, Italy—d. Feb. 2, 1594, Rome), foremost among the Italian composers of the 16th century. His mastery of contrapuntal composition was supreme in his time and enormously influential for later generations.

Abstract of text biography. Leaving Palestrina in boyhood, he filled a series of church musical appointments in Rome. He became director of the Julian Chapel choir of St. Peter's in 1551, publishing his first book of masses in 1554. He directed the choir of St. John Lateran, 1555–60, became musical director at Sta. Maria Maggiore in 1561, and returned to St. Peter's in 1571. In the meantime he had also served Cardinal Ippolito d'Este and had written music for Guglielmo Gonzaga, duke of Mantua, for use in the ducal chapel. His wife and two of his three sons having died in the 1570s, he married a wealthy widow in 1581 but continued to serve virtually as the pope's official composer. Much of his music was published in his later years, and in 1592 he was honoured by fellow composers with 16 settings of the Vesper Psalms written in his praise.

REFERENCES in other text articles:
·contrapuntal-imitative style **5**:214e
·exemplification of modal counterpoint **12**:717f
·Gounod's musical style **8**:258d

Paley, William (b. July 1743, Peterborough, Huntingdon and Peterborough—d. May 25,

Paley, engraving by Ridley (18th century) after a portrait by S. Drummond (1765–1844)
Radio Times Hulton Picture Library

1805, Bishopwearmouth Without, Durham), Anglican priest, Utilitarian philosopher, and author of influential works on Christianity, ethics, and science, among them the standard exposition in English theology of the teleological argument for the existence of God.

His major works are *The Principles of Moral and Political Philosophy* (1785), the subject of lectures at the University of Cambridge; *A View of the Evidence of Christianity* (1794), which was required reading for entrance to Cambridge until the 20th century; and *Natural Theology* (1802), based on John Ray's *Wisdom of God Manifested in the Works of the Creation* (1691). In *Natural Theology* Paley expounded that form of the teleological argument for the existence of God comparable to the argument that the existence of a watch implies the existence of a watchmaker. The book strongly influenced Charles Darwin.
·teleological anti-evolutionary philosophy **7**:14e

Pālghāt, town and district in central Kerala state, India. The town, headquarters of the district, lies on the Ponnāni River in a break in the Western Ghāts range known as the Pālghāt Gap. Its location has always given the town strategic and commercial importance. It is a marketplace for grain, tobacco, textiles, and timber; its industries include tobacco processing, rice milling, weaving, and light manufacturing. In Pālghāt are Government Victoria College (established 1888) and an engineering college. Across the river, to the north, is the rail junction of Olavakod. Pālghāt has an ancient fort, captured by the British temporarily in 1783 and permanently in 1790.

Palghāt district, 1,982 sq mi (5,133 sq km) in area, mostly consists of a stretch of coastal plain between the Ghāts and the Arabian Sea; the hills of the Ghāts extend into the district's southeastern corner. Ponnāni, 50 mi (80 km) to the west, is its outport. Pop. (1971 prelim.) town, 95,765; district, 1,683,436.

·map, India **9**:278

Pālghāt Gap, major break in the Western Ghāts mountain range, in southwestern India. Located between the Nilgiri Hills (north) and the Anaimalai Hills (south), it is about 20 mi (32 km) wide and straddles the Kerala–Tamil Nadu border, serving as a major communication route between these two states. Highways and rail lines through the gap connect Pālghāt in Kerala with Coimbatore and Pollāchi in Tamil Nadu. Pālghāt Gap also influences southern India's climate; the southwest monsoons as well as storms from the Bay of Bengal cross the mountains through the opening. 10°45′ N, 76°45′ E

Palgrave, Francis Turner (b. Sept. 28, 1824, Great Yarmouth, Norfolk—d. Oct. 24, 1897, London), critic and poet, editor of the influential anthology *The Golden Treasury.*

Palgrave, chalk drawing by Samuel Lawrence, 1872; in the National Portrait Gallery, London

By courtesy of the National Portrait Gallery, London

Palgrave spent many years in the education department of the civil service and from 1885 to 1895 was professor of poetry at Oxford. He was a friend of many notables of the time: the statesman William Gladstone (to whom in 1846 he was assistant private secretary) and the poets Robert Browning, Alfred Tennyson, and Matthew Arnold. Of his original verse, *Visions of England* (1880–81) is the best known. His greatest service to poetry, however, was his compilation of *The Golden Treasury of English Songs and Lyrics* (1861), a comprehensive, well-chosen anthology, carefully arranged in its sequence. Palgrave's choice of poems was made in consultation with Tennyson. The *Anthology* had great influence on the poetic taste of several generations and was of particular value in popularizing Wordsworth. Notable omissions (within its historical limits) were the Metaphysical poets of the 17th century and the Neoclassical poets of the 18th century. The original selections were modified in later editions.

Pāli, town and headquarters, Pāli district, Rājasthān state, India, just north of the Bāndi River, a tributary of the Lūni. Chiefly an agricultural market centre, it is connected by road and rail with Beāwar and Jodhpur. Industries include textile and oil mills, cotton printing and dyeing, copper working, and ivory and sandalwood handicrafts. A trade centre in ancient times, Pāli is divided into an ancient and modern quarter; it has several historic temples. Pāli also has a hospital and one college affiliated with the University of Rājasthān.

Pāli district (area 4,792 sq mi [12,411 sq km]), formerly a part of Jodhpur princely state, comprises a tract of plain bordered east by the Arāvalli Range and drained by the Lūni River and its tributaries. The district has oil and textile mills, metalworks, and cotton-ginning factories. The chief crops include wheat, sorghum (jowar), oilseeds, and cotton. Pop. (1971 prelim.) town, 49,814; district, 964,854.

·map, India **9**:278

Paliau cult, a 20th-century cargo cult in the Admiralty Islands of Melanesia, founded by the messianic prophet Paliau.

·new tribal cargo cults **18**:704f

Palibrotha (Indian state): *see* Patna and Pāṭaliputra.

Palici, ancient pair of local Sicilian gods who presided over the twin geysers still called Lago dei Palici, near Palagonia. The site became an asylum for escaped slaves, hence its importance as a symbol during the Sicilian slave revolts during the second half of the 2nd century BC. The Palici were only local, volcanic gods, divine derivatives of the geysers that they represented, but the mythographers made them the offspring of Zeus or Hephaestus.

Palikao, Charles-Guillaume-Marie-Apollinaire-Antoine Cousin-Montauban, comte de: *see* Cousin-Montauban, Charles-Guillaume-Marie-Apollinaire-Antoine, comte de Palikao.

Pāli language, sacred language of the Theravāda Buddhist canon, a Middle Indo-Aryan language of north Indian origin. On the whole, Pāli seems closely related to the Old Indo-Aryan Vedic and Sanskrit dialects but is apparently not directly descended from either of these. Its use as a Buddhist canonical language came about because the Buddha opposed the use of Sanskrit, a learned language, as a vehicle for his teachings, and encouraged the use of vernacular dialects. In time, his orally transmitted sayings spread through India to Ceylon (*c.* 3rd century BC), where they were written down in Pāli (1st century BC), a literary language of rather mixed vernacular origins. Pāli eventually became a revered, standard, and international tongue. The language and the texts, known collectively as *Tipiṭaka* (Sanskrit *Tripiṭaka*), were brought to Burma, Thailand, Cambodia, Laos, and Vietnam, where they are still used. Pāli died out as a literary language in mainland India in the 14th century. *Major ref.* **3**:433d

·Anglo-German resource use **3**:403e
·Buddha and contemporary usage **9**:285f
·Buddhist mythology textual origins **3**:419c
·Burmese contributions to scripture **3**:512b
·characteristic changes from Sanskrit phonology and grammar **9**:444e *passim* to 446a
·literary influence in South Asia **17**:135b
·Pagan Buddhism education **17**:232e
·research of Pāli Text Society **15**:617g

Palilia (ancient Roman festival): *see* Parilia.

Pāli literature, the canonical texts and accompanying commentaries, collectively called the *Tipiṭaka* (Sanskrit, *Tripiṭaka*), of the Theravāda Buddhist scriptures. They originated in North India in the first few centuries of Buddhism (from *c.* 500 BC) and, according to tradition, were brought to Ceylon in the 3rd century by Mahinda (Mahendra), son of the emperor Aśoka. From Ceylon they were carried to Burma and Thailand. At an unknown period after the introduction to Ceylon the use of Pāli died out in India.

·Buddhist canon internal differences **16**:127b
·literary history and development **17**:135b
·researches of Pāli Text society **15**:617g

Palimé, town, southwest Togo, West Africa, in the plateau region. It is in a coffee and cocoa producing area and lies on a government-owned national railway line. Pop. (1971 est.) 17,600.
6°54′ N, 0°38′ E

·coastal climatic conditions **18**:471f
·map, Togo **18**:472
·urban settlement, transportation, and government **18**:472c *passim* to 474b

palimpsest, a manuscript in roll or codex form carrying a text erased, or partly erased, underneath an apparent additional text. The underlying text is said to be "in palimpsest," and even though the parchment or other surface is much abraded the older text is recoverable in the modern laboratory by such scientific means as the use of ultraviolet light. The motive for making palimpsests usually seems to have been economic—reusing parchment was cheaper than preparing a new skin. Another motive may have been directed by Christian piety, as in the conversion of a pagan Greek manuscript to receive the text of a Father of the Church.

·ancient book re-use method **13**:912b
·early New Testament text example **2**:941g

Pa-lin Ai-hsin (China): *see* T'ung-liao.

Palinurus: *see* lobster.

Palio, horse races of medieval origin held annually in Italy. In Siena it is staged on July 2 and on August 16 in the main square. The riders in medieval costume represent districts of the city and compete for a standard.

·origin and celebration **9**:1113c

Palisa, Johann (b. Dec. 6, 1848, Troppau, Silesia, now Opava, Czech.—d. May 2, 1925, Vienna), astronomer noted as a discoverer of minor planets, a total of 121, of which he found 83 by visual observation through 1891, when the photographic plate first was used for that purpose. An Austrian naval officer detailed (1872–80) to the observatory at Pola (now Pula, Yugos.), he was subsequently (1880–1919) on the Vienna Observatory staff. He prepared star catalogs published in 1899, 1902, and 1908.

palisade cell, in botany, an elongated, photosynthetic (food-producing), parenchyma (*q.v.*) cell lying below and at right angles to the surface of a plant leaf. The palisade cell layer is above the spongy parenchyma layer in the mesophyll (*q.v.*), the parenchyma between the epidermal layers of a leaf.

·conifer leaf form and function **5**:5d
·mesophyll structure and function **13**:729e; illus.

Palisades, The, sandstone bluffs 200 to 540 ft (60–165 m) high along the west side of the Hudson River, southeastern New York and northeastern New Jersey. They are an extension of the Catskill Mountains. Rising vertically from near the water's edge, they are characterized by uplifts, faults, and columnar structure developed by slow cooling of molten material near the end of the Triassic Period (225,000,000–190,000,000 years ago).

The Palisades Interstate Park Commission, established in 1900, comprises more than a dozen park units along the river. They occupy a total area of 62,407 ac (25,255 ha), mostly in New York but also including one park (2,405 ac) in New Jersey. Linking the various units is the 42-mi (68-km) Palisades Interstate Parkway, extending northward from George

Washington Bridge, Fort Lee, N.J., to Bear Mountain Bridge, N.Y. Facilities for hiking, swimming, fishing, boating, camping, picnicking, and skiing are available. Palisades Interstate Park Commission headquarters are at Bear Mountain, N.Y.

Palisades orogeny, name applied to the episode of faulting, basaltic extrusions and intrusions, and deposition of arkosic (feldspar-rich) sediments during Late Triassic time (the Triassic Period began 225,000,000 years ago and ended 190,000,000 years ago) in fault-trough basins in the Appalachian Geosyncline, from South Carolina northward to the Bay of Fundy in Canada. The basins are in alignment with the structural trends of the Appalachians, and several of the more prominent isolated basins (Connecticut Valley, New York–Virginia, and basins in North Carolina) may originally have been linked together to form a rift valley along the east coast of North America.

The Palisades orogeny may have resulted from the initial rifting of the North American Plate from the African and European plates in Early Mesozoic time.

·age determination of basalt **13**:906g
·sill formation by magma emplacement **9**:224g

Palissy, Bernard (b. 1510, Agen, Lot-et-Garonne, Fr.—d. 1589, Paris), French Huguenot potter and writer, particularly associated with decorated rustic ware, a type of lead-glazed earthenware sometimes mistakenly called faience (tin-glazed earthenware).

Palissy began as a painter of glass, but, after journeys in the south and in the Ardennes brought him into contact with great Humanists, he settled as a surveyor and potter in Saintes, near La Rochelle. Persecuted as a Protestant, he was imprisoned until the constable of Montmorency employed him in the decoration of the Château d'Ecouen. His appointment, about 1565, as "inventor of rustic pottery to the king and the queen-mother" enabled him to work in Paris. In 1570, helped by his sons, he built a pottery grotto for Catherine de Médicis in the garden of the Tuilerie.

From 1575, in Paris, Palissy gave public lectures on natural history, which, published as *Discours admirables* (1580; Eng. trans. *Admirable Discourses* by Aurèle la Rocque, 1957), became extremely popular, revealing him as a writer and scientist, a creator of modern agronomy, and a pioneer of the experimental method, with scientific views generally more advanced than those of his contemporaries. After seeing a white glazed cup, probably Chinese porcelain, he determined to discover the secrets of its manufacture. His early researches are described in *De l'art de la terre*.

As the struggle against Protestants grew, Palissy took refuge in the homes of the Princess of Sedan and Robert de la Marck, in eastern France, returning to Paris in 1575. Imprisoned in the Conciergerie for religious reasons in 1588, he was transferred to the Bastille, where he died.

Palissy's pottery generally consists of oval or circular dishes, ewers, and sauceboats, decorated with plants and animals and allegorical and mythological scenes. Some of his pottery had marbled reverse surfaces, and some pieces were reproductions of objects by such leading French metalworkers of the 16th century as François Briot.

Palissy probably did not use the potter's wheel. His best known pieces were apparently pressed into a mold and finished by modelling or the application of ornament molded in relief. His authentic productions bear no signature or mark. His molds were used later during the 17th century at Avon near Fontainebleau and at Manerbe, Calvados, where a few lead-glazed earthenware statuettes were made. Between 1840 and 1870 copies were executed by Jean-Charles Avisseau of Tours and by Georges Pull of Paris.

·heresy and execution **17**:717d
·hydrologic concept evolution **9**:103d
·lead-glazed ceramic ware production **14**:907b
·water source theories **6**:80b

Palissy ware: *see* Rustic ware.

Paliurus spina-christi (shrub): *see* Christ's thorn.

Pālkonda Hills, a series of ranges in southern Andhra Pradesh state, southern India. The hills trend northwest to southeast and form the central part of the Eastern Ghāts. Geologically they are relics of ancient mountains formed during the Cambrian Period (500,000,000 to 570,000,000 years ago) that were subsequently eroded by the Penner River and its tributaries. The Punchu and Cheyyeru rivers join in a spectacular confluence in a gorge in the corridor between the Velikonda and the Pālkonda Hills. Formed of quartzites, slates, and lavas, the Pālkondas reach an elevation of 3,000 ft (900 m) in the south. The valleys between the mountains are drained by many streams, many of which, having been dammed for storage tanks, provide irrigation for cultivation. The mains crops are sorghum (jowar) and peanuts (groundnuts).
14°05′ N, 78°30′ E

Palk Strait, sometimes called PALK BAY, inlet of the Bay of Bengal, between southeastern India and northern Sri Lanka (formerly Ceylon) and bounded on the south by Rāmeswaram Island, Adams (Rama's) Bridge (a chain of shoals), and Mannar Island. The strait is 40–85 mi (64–137 km) wide and 85 mi (137 km) long. It receives several rivers, including the Vaigai (India), and it contains many islands of Sri Lanka. The port of Jaffna, the commercial centre for northern Sri Lanka, has a brisk trade with south India (limited to small ships).
9°30′ N, 79°30′ E

·India's geographical proximity **17**:519e
·map, India **9**:278
·map, Sri Lanka **17**:520

Pālkuriki Sōmanātha, 13th-century writer in Telugu and Kannada.

·writing style and principal works **17**:141c

P'alkwanhoe (Korean: Assembly of P'alkwan), the most important of Korea's ancient national festivals, a ritualistic celebration that was essentially Buddhist in form but tinged with elements of Taoism and superstitious folk beliefs. Some historians think P'alkwanhoe was originally a state-sponsored cultural festival that developed from the harvest festivals of earlier days. The festival, which seems to have been firmly established in AD 551 at a time when Buddhism was recognized as the state religion, was conducted by Buddhist priests and apparently included prayers for the welfare of the state. During the festival, lamps were lit, incense was burned, the royal palace was elaborately decorated, and there was joyous singing and dancing. The king took an active part by receiving congratulations from foreign merchants, provincial ministers, and ordinary citizens and dispensed food and even wine, which was forbidden at other times. The royal P'alkwan treasury (P'alkwanbo) took care of all expenses but sometimes relied on contributions from the aristocracy.

The festival still survives in certain rural areas of Korea as an expression of folk religion and includes prayers to heaven, mountains, rivers, and the dragon.

pall, also called PAILE, in heraldry, ordinary which is the upper half of a saltire and the lower half of a pale, roughly forming a Y-shaped figure on the shield.

·heraldic design elements **8**:788c

Palladianism, style of architecture based on the writings and buildings of the Humanist and theorist from Vicenza, Andrea Palladio (died 1580). Perhaps the greatest architect of the later 16th century and certainly the most influential, Palladio felt that architecture could be governed both by reason and by certain universal rules reflected in the buildings of Classical antiquity. In his own work he strived to incorporate the Classical qualities that he found in ancient Roman architecture, thereby providing a practical application for his theories.

Palladianism was especially popular in England, where its impact was felt in two successive phases, early in the 17th century and in the 18th century. The first great English disciple was Inigo Jones. Upon his return from a trip to Italy (1613–14), Jones created a Palladian style in London based upon the knowledge he had acquired from his study of Palladio's writings and from his own first-hand examination of ancient and Renaissance architecture. Outstanding among the preserved examples are the Queen's House at Greenwich (completed 1635), the Banqueting House at Whitehall (1619–22), and the Queen's Chapel at St. James Palace (1623). Jones's works were not copies of Palladio's buildings but, rather, re-creations in the same spirit.

At the beginning of the Georgian period (1714–1830), a second and more consuming interest in Palladio developed. Partly as a reaction to the grandiose architecture of the later Stuarts, the newly-powerful Whigs expressed a desire to return to a more rational and less complicated style. Their wish coincided with the publication of an English translation of Palladio's treatise, *I quattro libri dell' architettura* (1570; *Four Books on Architecture*, 1715), and the first volume of Sir Colin Campbell's study of Classical buildings in Britain, *Vitruvius Britannicus* (1715). Campbell, the first practitioner of the new English Palladianism, built Houghton Hall in Norfolk

Holkham Hall, by William Kent, Palladian style, begun 1734, Norfolk, Eng.

A.F. Kersting

(begun 1722) and Mereworth Castle in Kent (*c.* 1722), both of which attest to his considerable talents. The wealthy amateur architect Richard Boyle, 3d Earl of Burlington, and his protégé William Kent complete the triumvirate responsible for the second phase of the style. Burlington's home, Chiswick House (begun 1725), was designed by him as a reinterpretation of Palladio's Villa Rotonda. Holkham Hall, Norfolk (begun 1734), was built by William Kent, an architect who is also credited with having invented the English landscape garden. Palladianism in England lasted until around 1760.

·Fischer von Erlach's adaptations **7**:329a
·impact on furniture size and design 7:801g
·Jones's architecture as movement incentive **10**:266f
·popularity of Palladio's architecture **13**:935b
·Robert Adam's form of Neoclassicism **1**:71h

Palladian window, in architecture, three-part window composed of a large, arched central section flanked by two narrower, shorter sections having square tops. This type of window, popular in 17th- and 18th-century Engish versions of Italian designs, was inspired by the so-called Palladian motif, similar three-part openings having been featured in the work of the 16th-century Italian architect Andrea Palladio; his Basilica at Vicenza, designed in 1546, was especially rich in these. Because the motif was first described in the work *L'architettura* (1537), by the Italian architect Sebastiano Serlio, it is also known as the Serlian motif, or Serliana, and the window derived from it may be called a Serlian window. It is also sometimes referred to as a Venetian window.

Palladio, Andrea 13:933, christened ANDREA DI PIETRO DELLA GONDOLA (b. Nov. 30, 1508, Padua—d. August 1580, Vicenza), the greatest architect of 16th-century northern Italy, one of the most influential figures in Western architecture.

Abstract of text biography. After working for various sculptors in his early years, Palladio in about 1540 built his first villa, the Villa Godi at Lonedo, and his first palace in Vicenza. His first major public commission was the reconstruction of the 15th-century town hall in Vicenza (1546; finished 1617). He published *Le antichità di Roma* in 1554; in 1556 a new edition of Vitruvius' *De architectura*, in collaboration with Daniele Barbaro; and in 1570 *I quattro libri dell'architettura*. His designs for Venetian churches include the facade for S. Francesco della Vigna, S. Giorgio Maggiore (1566; completed 1610), and Il Redentore (1576; completed 1592).

REFERENCES in other text articles:
·architectural spatial expression illus. **1**:1105
·architectural theory model **9**:710g
·Jones influenced by classic Roman style **10**:266a
·stylistic diffusion of artistic canons **2**:133f
·Teatro Olimpico's odeum style **18**:243h; illus. 244
·theatre architecture of Renaissance **17**:537h
·truss adaptation to bridge design **3**:177f
·Venetian church and Villa Capra design **19**:388g; illus. 389
·Venetian church designs **19**:75a

palladium (after the asteroid Pallas), symbol Pd, chemical element, lightest and lowest melting of the platinum metals of transition Group VIII of the periodic table, used especially as a catalyst (a substance that speeds up chemical reactions without changing their products) and in alloys. A precious, gray-white metal, palladium is extremely ductile and easily worked. Palladium is not tarnished by the atmosphere at ordinary temperatures. Thus, the metal and its alloys serve as substitutes for platinum in jewelry and in electrical contacts; the beaten leaf is used for decorative purposes. Relatively small amounts of palladium alloyed with gold yield the best white gold. Palladium is used also in dental alloys. The largest use of the pure metal is for electrical contacts in telephone equipment. Palladium coatings, electrodeposited or chemically plated, have been used in printed-circuit components.

Native palladium, though rare, occurs alloyed with a little platinum and iridium in Colombia (district of Chocó), in Brazil (Itabira, Minas Gerais), in the U.S.S.R. (Ural Mountains), and in South Africa (the Transvaal). For mineralogical properties, *see* table under native elements. Palladium also occurs up to 37 percent alloyed with native platinum. It is associated too with a number of gold, silver, copper, and nickel ores. Palladium is generally produced commercially as a by-product in the refining of copper, and nickel ores. Palladium was first isolated (1803) from crude platinum by the English chemist and physicist William Hyde Wollaston.

Surfaces of palladium are excellent catalysts for chemical reactions involving hydrogen and oxygen, such as hydrogenation of unsaturated organic compounds. Under suitable conditions, palladium absorbs more than 900 times its own volume of hydrogen; it expands and becomes harder, stronger, and less ductile in the process. A metallic or alloy-like hydride is formed from which the hydrogen can be removed by increased temperature and reduced pressure. Because hydrogen passes rapidly through the metal at high temperatures, heated palladium tubes impervious to other gases function as semipermeable membranes and are used to pass hydrogen in and out of closed gas systems or for hydrogen purification.

Palladium is attacked more readily by acids than any of the other platinum metals. It dissolves slowly in nitric acid to give palladium nitrate, $Pd(NO_3)_2$, and with concentrated sulfuric acid it yields palladium sulfate, $PdSO_4 \cdot 2H_2O$. A series of palladium compounds can be prepared with the normal +2 oxidation state; numerous compounds in the +4 state and a few in the 0 state are also known. Among the transition metals palladium has one of the strongest tendencies to form bonds with carbon. All palladium compounds are easily decomposed or reduced to the free metal. An aqueous solution of potassium tetrachloropalladate(II), K_2PdCl_4, serves as a sensitive detector for carbon monoxide or olefin gases because a black precipitate of the metal appears in the presence of exceedingly small amounts of those gases. Natural palladium consists of a mixture of six stable isotopes: palladium-102 (0.96 percent), palladium-104 (10.97 percent), palladium-105 (22.23 percent), palladium-106 (27.33 percent), palladium-108 (26.71 percent), and palladium-110 (11.81 percent).

atomic number	46
atomic weight	106.40
melting point	1,552° C (2,826° F)
boiling point	2,927° C (5,301° F)
specific gravity	11.97 (0° C)
valence	2, 4
electronic config.	2-8-18-18 or (Kr)$4d^{10}$

Major ref. **18**:625d
·abundance and physical properties, tables 1 and 2 **18**:601
·atomic weight and number table **2**:345
·geochemical abundances, table 1 **6**:702
·gold production hazard **8**:239f
·production and uses **14**:529g
·solar abundances, table 2 **17**:803
·structure and physical properties **12**:855a; table

Palladium, in Greek religion, an image of the goddess Pallas (Athena), especially the archaic wooden image of the goddess that was preserved in the citadel of Troy as a pledge of the safety of the city. It was said that Zeus, the king of the gods, threw it down from heaven when the city of Ilium (Greek Troy) was founded, and that the Greek warriors Odysseus and Diomedes carried it off from the temple of Athena, thus making the capture of Troy possible. Many cities in Greece and Italy claimed to possess the genuine Trojan Palladium, but it was particularly identified with the figure brought to Italy by the hero Aeneas and preserved in the shrine of the goddess Vesta at Rome. The Palladium was a common subject in Greek art, as was its theft in literature. The story of its fall from heaven perhaps signifies that the Palladium was originally a baetylus, or sacred stone.

palladium(II) chloride, a dark-brown, crystalline or powdery inorganic compound ($PdCl_2$) prepared by dissolving palladium in a mixture of hydrochloric and nitric acids and used mostly as a catalyst in reactions of unsaturated organic compounds.

·catalytic oxidation of ethylene **3**:1002a
·palladium compound chemistry **18**:625g

Palladius (b. *c.* 363, Galatia, now Ankara —d. before 431, Aspuna, near Ankara), monk, bishop, and chronicler whose *Lausiac History*, an account of early Egyptian and Middle Eastern Christian monasticism, provides the most valuable single source for the origins of Christian asceticism.

Palladius took up the ascetical life himself, first at the Mount of Olives, outside Jerusalem, the scene of Christ's passion, then in Egypt in the Nitrian desert, now Wādī an-Naṭrūn, to avail himself of the advice of the 4th-century pioneer monks Macarius and Evagrius Ponticus. Returning to Palestine *c.* 399 because of poor health, he was named bishop of Helenopolis in Bithynia, near modern Istanbul.

Soon after 400, Palladius began an extended defense of his articulate theological mentor St. John Chrysostom, patriarch of Constantinople, against charges of heresy. Enemies both at the rival theological school of Alexandria, Egypt, and at Constantinople's imperial court, embarrassed by Chrysostom's moral exhortations and envious of his office, accused him of doctrinal errors attributed to the 3rd-century theologian Origen regarding Christ's position subordinate to the Godhead and the doctrine of the pre-existence of souls. For supporting Chrysostom at Byzantium and at Rome, the Eastern Roman emperor Arcadius exiled Palladius for six years, during which, *c.* 408, he wrote his *Dialogue on the Life of St. John Chrysostom.* Styled after the manner of Plato's *Phaedo*, it provides data with which to reconstruct the political–theological controversy.

In 413, after his banishment was lifted, Palladius became bishop of Aspuna in Galatia, Tur., and during 419–420 composed his chronicles on "The Lives of the Friends of God," referring to the earliest Christian ascetics in various wilderness areas of Egypt and Asia Minor. This *Lausiac History*, dedicated to Lausus, chamberlain of Emperor Theodosius II, is a fusion of personal experiences with secondary accounts of desert monasticism, written in the critical spirit of Evagrius Ponticus. Although sometimes credulous in repeating legendary narratives modelled after the classical Greek form of heroic epic, Palladius also exhibits a sober humanism that avoids pious ascetical theory, as in his reaction to monastic vanity: "To drink wine with reason is better than to drink water with pride." After previous doubts, 20th-century scholarship has verified the authenticity of the *Lausiac History* as well as part of a treatise on ascetical ideals of India. Palladius died before the general Council of Ephesus in 431.

·Ireland's religious development **3**:284g

Pallanza (Italy): *see* Verbania.

Pallas, second-largest known minor planet and the second to be discovered by Heinrich Wilhelm Matthäus Olbers on March 28, 1802. Thought to be nearly spherical (some minor planets are elongated "splinters"), it has a diameter of about 470 kilometres (about 290 miles).

Pallas, Peter Simon (b. Sept. 22, 1741, Berlin—d. Sept. 8, 1811, Berlin), naturalist who advanced a theory of mountain formation and, by age 15, had outlined new classifications of certain animal groups. In 1761 he went to England to study natural-history collections and to make geological observations. Appointed professor of natural history at the Imperial Academy of Sciences, St. Petersburg (now Leningrad), in 1768, about that time Pallas also joined a scientific expedition to Russia and Siberia. For the next six years he travelled across the length and breadth of the vast empire. He found a wide distribution of mammoth and rhinoceros fossils, including some with their hairy hides preserved, in the Siberian ice. He returned to St. Petersburg in 1774 with a great amount of data and many fossil specimens, but he had ruined his health. He published his major findings from the expedition in three volumes, *Reise durch verschiedene Provinzen des russischen Reichs* (1771–76; "Journey Through Various Provinces of the Russian Empire"). His chief geo-

Pallas, engraved portrait
Bruckmann—Art Reference Bureau from Staatsbibliothek, Berlin

logical contribution, based largely on his study of the Ural and Altai mountain ranges of Siberia, was to recognize a temporal sequence of rocks from the centre to the flanks of a range.
·rock strata study in Urals **17**:716g

Pallas Athene (goddess): *see* Athena.

pallasite, stony iron meteorite (*q.v.*) containing about 50 percent olivine as well as kamacite, plessite, taenite, and troilite. The olivine is in single crystals larger than those in any other meteorite type and may form aggregates. The olivine is usually swathed by kamacite that does not show the Widmanstätten pattern (bands of kamacite with narrower bands of taenite, the meshes being a mixture of the two); kamacite forms a large part of the metal found in pallasites. The centres of large areas of metal, however, are able to develop Widmanstätten structure.
·meteorite structure and composition **12**:45g

Pallas's cat, also called STEPPE CAT or MANILL (*Felis manul*), small, long-haired cat (family Felidae) native to deserts and rocky, mountainous regions from Tibet to Siberia. The Pallas's cat is a soft-furred animal about the size of a house cat and is pale silvery gray or light brown in colour. The end of its tail is ringed and tipped with black, and some individuals have vague, dark markings on the body. The fur of the underparts is about twice as long as that of the upperparts and possibly represents an adaptation to the cat's habitual lying and crouching on cold ground. Head and body length ranges from 45–60 cm (18–24

Pallas's cat (*Felis manul*)
Tierbilder Okapia—Frankfurt am Main

in.) with an additional 23–30 cm (9–12 in.) for the tail; weight ranges from 2.5 to 3.5 kg (5.5–7.7 lb). The Pallas's cat is distinguished by a broad head with high-set eyes and low-set ears. It has been suggested that the positioning of these features is an adaptation for peering over rocky ledges; the supposition is that the cat thus exposes only a small part of itself to its prey of small mammals (such as pikas and rodents) and birds.

Pallava, early 4th-century to late 9th-century southern Indian dynasty whose members originated as indigenous subordinates of the Sātāvahanas in the Deccan, then moved into Andhra, and thence to Kāñcī (Kānchipuram in modern Tamil Nadu state), where they became rulers. Their genealogy and chronology are highly disputed. The first group of Pallavas was mentioned in Prākrit (a simple and popular form of Sanskrit) records, which tell of King Viṣṇugopa, who was defeated and then liberated by Samudra Gupta, the emperor of Magadha, about the middle of the 4th century AD. A later Pallava king, Siṃhavarman, is mentioned in the Sanskrit *Lokavibhāga* as reigning from AD 436.

The Pallavas were the emperors of the Dravidian country and rapidly adopted Tamil ways. Their rule was marked by commercial enterprise and a limited amount of colonization in Southeast Asia, but they inherited rather than initiated Tamil interference with Ceylon.

The Pallavas supported Buddhism, Jainism, and the Brahminical faith and were patrons of music, painting, and literature. Their greatest monuments are architectural, in particular the Shore Temple, the various other temples carved from granite monoliths, and the Varāha cave (7th century) at Mahābalipuram (Māmallapuram), once a flourishing port. The Pallava ruler Siṃhaviṣṇu's mother (mid-6th century) may have been a Christian. Mahendravarman I wrote (*c.* 620) the *Mattavilasaprahasana*, a farce in Sanskrit ridiculing the manners of his day.

In general the Pallava rulers were ineffective in withstanding military pressure from the forces of the Western Cālukya dynasty, and their capable feudatories, the Cōlas, gradually ousted them from power. In about 880 the Pallava dominions passed under the rule of the Cōla kings.
·artistic view of government functions **17**:132b
·military and political history **9**:359h; map 357

Pallavicinia (liverwort): *see* Jungermanniales.

Pallavicino, Nicolò, 17th-century Italian banker.
·Rubens' meeting and future patronage **16**:2c

Pallavicino, Oberto: *see* Pelavicino, Oberto.

Pallca, archaeological site of Coast Chavín culture in the Casma Valley, Peru.
·Chavín pyramid architecture **1**:842h

Pallenberg, Max (1877–1934), Austrian actor.
·commedia style of Reinhardt's work **4**:986f

Pallene, modern KASSANDRA, westernmost peninsula of Chalcidice, Greece.
·Peisistratus' final power seizure **13**:1110b

pallet, a portable platform designed for handling by a forklift truck or crane and used in the storage or movement of materials.
·materials-handling systems **11**:617a

pallium (biology): *see* mantle.

pallium, or PALL, a liturgical vestment worn over the chasuble by the pope, archbishops, and some bishops in the Roman Catholic Church. It is bestowed by the pope on archbishops and bishops having metropolitan jurisdiction as a symbol of their participation in papal authority. It is made of a circular strip of white lamb's wool about two inches wide, is decorated with four black crosses, and is placed over the shoulders. Two vertical bands, each decorated with a cross, extending from the circular strip in the front and back, give the pallium a Y-shaped appearance.

The pallium probably developed from the ancient Greek himation, called pallium by the Romans, a common outer garment formed from a rectangular piece of cloth draped around the body as a mantle or folded and carried over the shoulder when not needed for warmth. Gradually, the pallium became narrower and resembled a long scarf. The Y-shaped pallium probably developed during the 7th century.

Emperor Henry II flanked by two bishops wearing palliums, 11th century miniature; in the Staatsbibliothek Bamberg, Bamberg, Ger.
Hirmer Fotoarchiv, Munchen

The use of the pallium by church officials developed from the secular tradition of emperors and other high officials wearing a special scarf as a badge of office. The pallium was worn by many bishops in the 4th and 5th centuries, and in the 6th century the pope was conferring it as a symbol of distinction. Since the 9th century, an archbishop cannot exercise his metropolitan jurisdiction until he has received the pallium from the pope. He can wear it only within his own province; only the pope can wear it anywhere.

The equivalent vestment in the Eastern churches is the omophorion, a long, white silk or velvet embroidered scarf, worn by bishops celebrating the holy liturgy.

pall-mall, French PAILLE-MAILLE (from *palla* [of Germanic origin], "ball," and Latin *malleus*, "mallet"), an obsolete game of French origin, resembling croquet. Sir Robert Dallington in his *Method for Travell* (1605) wrote: "Among all the exercises of France, I prefer none before the Paille-Maille." James I recommended it as a proper game for Prince Henry, and it was actually introduced into England in the reign of Charles I (1625–49) or perhaps a few years earlier. Thomas Blount's *Glossographia* (1656) described it as "a game wherein a round bowle is with a mallet struck through a high arch of iron (standing at either end of an alley) which he that can do at the fewest blows, or at the number agreed on, wins. This game was heretofore used in the long alley near St. James's and vulgarly called Pell-Mell." The pronunciation here described as "vulgar" afterward became classic, a famous London street having been named after a pall-mall alley. A mallet and balls used in the game were found in 1845 and are now in the British Museum: the mallet resembles that used in croquet, but its head is curved; the balls are of boxwood and about one foot in circumference. The 17th-century diarist Samuel Pepys described the alley as of hard sand "dressed with powdered cockle-shells." The length of the alley varies, the one at St. James being close to 800 yards long.

·billiards history **2**:989h

palm, common name for any flowering plant of the order Arecales and of the single family in the order: Arecaceae (Palmae). Many of the 2,600 known species are economically important. Palms are chiefly tropical and subtropical trees, shrubs, and vines, usually with a tall columnar trunk. The trunk is crowned

Doum palm (*Hyphaene thebaica*)
Gerald Cubitt

by very large pleated, fan-shaped, or feather-shaped leaves with stout sheathing and often prickly petioles (stems) the persistent bases of which frequently clothe the trunk. The small, usually unisexual flowers are produced in very large clusters. The stem, or trunk, may vary from the length and width of a pencil to a height of about 60 metres (about 200 feet) and a diameter of about one metre. The leaves may vary in length from several centimetres to more than nine metres. Seeds may be smaller than a match head or the size of a large melon, weighing as much as 9 kilograms (20 pounds).

Among the most important palms are:

Arenga pinnata (*saccharifera*), the sugar palm, occurs in Malaysia. It grows about 12 metres tall and frequently has 20–28 feather-shaped leaves. Sugar, wine, and arrack, a distilled liquor, are processed from the sap. Sago, a starch, is made from the pith. The leaves yield a moisture-resistant fibre.

Attalea cohune (cohune palm), occurring in Central America, grows about 18 metres tall and has erect, plume-shaped leaves. Oil from the seeds is used in soap. The related *A. funifera* of the Amazon region of South America yields a water-resistant fibre.

Borassus flabellifer (palmyra palm), occurring in tropical Asia, grows 20 metres tall and has fan-shaped leaves. Fibre from various parts of the plant are made into brooms, hats, and mats. The fruits and seeds are edible.

Chrysalidocarpus lutescens, native to Madagascar, sometimes grown indoors as an ornamental, grows to 10 metres and has feather-shaped leaves about 60 centimetres long.

Royal palm (*Roystonea regia*)
E.R. Degginger—EB Inc.

Coccothrinax argentea (*garberi*), biscayne palm, or silver palm, is a stemless species native to the southeasternmost United States. The fan-shaped leaves are silvery beneath.

Cocos nucifera, coconut palm, originated in Malaysia but has been widely distributed throughout the tropical coastal regions of the world. The tree grows about 30 metres tall and has feather-shaped leaves. The nuts—40 to 100 are produced each year—grow to 25 centimetres (10 inches) in diameter. The fibre of the nut husk, is called coir (*q.v.*). The white meat of the nut is eaten raw or shredded and dried for use in confections. When dried for industrial purposes, it is called copra (*q.v.*). Liquid in the core of the nut, known as coconut milk, is a tasty white beverage. Palm wine, arrack, and vinegar are made from the flower buds. Baskets and mats are made from the leaves. The trunk yields a useful timber.

Copernica cerifera (carnauba palm), occurring in tropical South America, grows to about 10 metres tall and has fan-shaped leaves. The trunk is swollen near the base. Carnauba wax, used in polishes, varnishes, and candles, is obtained from the leaves.

Hyphaene thebaica (doum palm), an African species, is unusual because of its frequently-branched stem.

Lodoicea maldivica (*callipyge*), commonly called coco de mer or double coconut, occurring in the Seychelles, islands of the Indian Ocean, grows about 30 metres tall. Its nuts, perhaps the largest (nine kilograms), require about 10 years to mature. They are not commercially valuable, but water vessels and platters are made from the shell.

Phoenix dactylifera (date palm), native to the Near East where it has been cultivated for its fruit since about 6000 BC, grows about 30 metres tall and has feathery leaves. A tree may bear as much as 250 kilograms (550 pounds) of dates (*see* date palm) annually and continues bearing for 100 years or more.

Roystonea regia (royal palm), an erect, beautiful species native to the southeastern United States, the West Indies, and tropical America, grows to 30 metres tall and has graceful feathery leaves and a smooth, pale gray trunk resembling concrete in colour and texture. It is often grown as an ornamental.

Sabal palmetto (cabbage palmetto), occurring in the southeastern United States and the West Indies, grows to about 24 metres tall and has fan-shaped leaves. The water-resistant trunk is used as wharf piling; the trees are commonly grown for shade and as ornamentals along avenues. The buds are edible; mats and baskets are sometimes made from the leaves; and stiff brushes are made from the stems. *S. texana*, a similar species, occurs in the southwestern U.S. and in Mexico.

·alcoholic beverages source, table 1 **5**:901
·Amazon varieties and uses **1**:654c
·basketry in religious ritual **2**:761d
·domesticated sugar palm centres of origin **5**:938b
·economic uses of sugar palm **1**:1131h
·forestry and tree products **7**:529a
·fruit and nut farming, table 1 **7**:755
·house plants and their care **8**:1120f
·repellant type and animal use **12**:215a
·stem tissue organization **13**:728g
·Washington and Talipot palms, illus. **18**: Tree, Plate II

palm, measure of length in The Netherlands, equivalent to one decimetre.

·Egyptian linear measurement system **19**:728c; table

Palma, also PALMA-DE-MALLORCA, capital of the Balearic Islands comprising Baleares province, Spain, in the western Mediterranean Sea; the city lies on the southwestern coast of Bahía (bay) de Majorca (Mallorca) in the centre of the island of Palma, which is 10 mi (16 km) wide. Little is known of Palma before 123 BC, when the Romans conquered Majorca, making the archipelago a Roman province. Attacked by the Vandals in the 5th century, it became part of the Byzantine Empire a century later. In the 8th century it fell to the Arabs, and in 1229 it was conquered by James I, who united it with the crown of Aragon. On his death it became independent but was again incorporated into Aragon by Peter IV in the 14th century. In 1469 it became part of the Spanish monarchy upon the marriage of Ferdinand II of Aragon and Isabella I of Castile.

The old quarters have many notable homes of the 16th and 18th centuries. Historic buildings include the Gothic cathedral (1230–1601); Bellver Castle, on the hill of the same name (14th century); La Lonja, the former exchange, now a museum (early 15th century);

Palma (capitol of Majorca) and Palma Bay with the Cathedral in the background
Keystone

Almudaina Palace, former residence of the Arab dynasty, and now the captain general's headquarters (restored in the 12th and 16th centuries); the Sea Consulate (Consulado del Mar; 17th century); bishop's palace (17th century); and the town hall (16th century) housing the Archives of the old Kingdom of Majorca. The modern part, with its fine buildings, promenades, and gardens, stretches along the coast for 7 mi. Palma's cultural facilities include a section of the University of Barcelona and art museums and galleries.

The city's economy is varied with tourism and the manufacture of furniture, footwear, and fabrics as the most important factors. Palma's many craftsmen produce embroidery, pottery, artistic glasswork and ironwork, palmetto and raffia basketwork, and olive woodcarving. Palma is linked to the mainland by frequent air and steamer services. Pop. (1970) 287,038.
39°34′ N, 2°39′ E
·map, Spain **17**:382

palma, Meso-American carved stone artifact associated with the ritual ballgame and similar in function to the *hacha.*
·function theories and evidence **1**:685f; illus. 686

Palma, Jacopo, also called PALMA VECCHIO, originally JACOPO NEGRETI (b. *c.* 1480, Serinalta, Italy—d. July 30, 1528, Venice), Venetian painter of the High Renaissance, noted for the craftsmanship of his religious and mythological works. He may have studied under Giovanni Bellini, the originator of the Venetian High Renaissance style.

"Three Sisters," oil on wood panel by Jacopo Palma, early 16th century; in the Staatliche Kunstsammlungen, Dresden
By courtesy of the Staatliche Kunstsammlungen, Dresden

Palma specialized in the type of contemplative religious picture known as the *sacra conversazione* (a group of historically unrelated sacred personages grouped together). To his late-15th-century subject matter he applied the idyllic vision of Giorgione in colour and fused soft-focus effects. Palma's particular refinement of the Giorgionesque technique was his use of transparent glazes, most of which later deteriorated. Monumental figures, loose technique, and blond tonality characterize his finest work, such as the "Sta. Barbara Altarpiece" (*c.* 1510; Sta. Maria Formosa, Venice). Palma developed an ideally feminine, blonde, pretty type, which may be seen in such works as the "Three Sisters" (Staatliche Kunstsammlungen, Dresden). This work, along with many of his later paintings, shows the influence of Lorenzo Lotto. Sixty-two of Palma's works remained unfinished at his death and were finished by his pupils. Presumably this accounts for the variable quality of his work.

Palma, Ricardo (b. Feb. 7, 1833, Lima, Peru—d. Oct. 6, 1919, Lima), writer best known for his legends of colonial Peru, one of the most popular collections in Spanish-American literature. At the age of 20 he joined the Peruvian Navy and in 1860 was forced by political exigencies to flee to Chile, where he devoted himself to journalism. Six years later he returned to Lima to join the revolutionary movement against Spain. He also took part in the War of the Pacific (1881) and during the Chilean occupation courageously protested against the wanton destruction of the famous National Library by Chilean troops. After the war Palma was commissioned to rebuild the National Library; he remained its curator until his death. In 1887 he founded the Peruvian Academy.

Palma's literary career began in his youth with light verses, romantic plays, and translations from Victor Hugo. His *Anales de la inquisición de Lima* (1863, "Annals of the Inquisition of Lima") was followed by several volumes of poems. His fame derives chiefly from his charmingly impudent *Tradiciones peruanas* (1872, "Peruvian Traditions")—short prose sketches that mingled fact and fancy about the pageantry and intrigue of colonial Peru. His sources were the folk tales, legends, and racy gossip of his elders, in addition to historical bits gleaned from the National Library. The first six volumes of this series appeared between 1872 and 1883; they were followed by *Ropa vieja* (1889, "Old Clothes"), *Ropa apolillada* (1891, "Moth-Eaten Clothes"), *Mis últimas tradiciones* (1906, "My Last Traditions") and *Apéndice a mis últimas tradiciones* (1910).
·Latin-American 19th-century literature **10**:1204g
·Peruvian art development role **14**:133d

Palma, Tomás Estrada: *see* Estrada Palma, Tomás.

Palma di Montechiaro, town, Agrigento province, south central Sicily, Italy, in an almond-growing and sulfur-mining district. Pop. (1971 prelim.) mun., 20,903.
37°11′ N, 13°46′ E

Palmae (plant family): *see* palm.

Palma Soriano, city, south central Oriente province, eastern Cuba. Lying on the Río Cauto, on the northern slopes of the Sierra Maestra, Palma Soriano is a commercial and manufacturing centre for the agricultural and pastoral hinterland, which yields sugarcane, cacao, coffee, corn (maize), fruits, and cattle. Coffee, soft drinks, and furniture are the main industrial products. Manganese is found in the vicinity. Palma Soriano is on the central highway and a major railroad and has an airfield. Pop. (1970 prelim.) 41,188.
20°13′ N, 76°00′ W
·map, Cuba **5**:350

Palm Beach, town, Palm Beach County, southeastern Florida, U.S., on a narrow barrier beach between the Atlantic (east) and Lake Worth (west). The latter, actually a lagoon (part of the Atlantic Intracoastal Waterway), is bridged to West Palm Beach (*q.v.*). Settled in 1873 as Palm City, it was renamed in 1887 and developed as a resort after Henry Flagler extended the Florida East Coast Railroad to West Palm Beach in 1894 and opened his Royal Poinciana Hotel. Known as the American Riviera, it was frequented by wealthy and famous personages and remains one of the most luxurious winter resorts in the U.S., with palatial hotels, clubs, private estates, and yacht facilities. It is strictly zoned and has no manufacturing. The University of Palm Beach (1926) is in West Palm Beach. Inc. 1911. Pop. (1980) 9,729.
26°42′ N, 80°02′ W

View of Palm Beach, Fla.
S. Aarons—Photo Researchers

palm chat (*Dulus dominicus*), songbird of Hispaniola (Haiti and the Dominican Republic) and nearby Gonâve Island, which may belong in the waxwing family (Bombycillidae, order Passeriformes) but is usually separated as the family Dulidae. This 20-centimetre (8-inch) bird, with stout bill and plumage that is greenish-brown above and whitish, with dark streaking, below (sexes alike), feeds in flocks on berries and flowers. They build a large communal nest in a tree, with a private-entrance chamber for each of up to 30 pairs.
·classification and general features **13**:1062d

Palm chat (*Dulus dominicus*)
Painting by H. Jon Janosik

palm chestnut (*Guilielma gasipaes*), a nut used principally as a source of food; it probably originated in tropical South America.
·fruit and nut farming, table 1 **7**:755

Palmdale, city, Los Angeles County, southwestern California, U.S., at the southern end of Antelope Valley and west of the Joshua (Palm) Trees State Park. Settled in the 1880s, it was a small farming community until after 1950, when, with nearby Lancaster, it became a focus for industrial development, chiefly aircraft assembly and electronic research. Inc. 1962. Pop. (1970) 8,511; (1980) 12,277.
34°35′ N, 118°07′ W

Palme, Île de, also known as PRASLIN ISLAND, one of the Seychelles group in the Indian Ocean.
4°19′ S, 55°44′ E
·Seychelles history, geography, and population **16**:611c; table

Palme, Olof (b. Jan. 30, 1927, Stockholm), prime minister of Sweden who became internationally known as one of the leading critics of U.S. involvement in Vietnam.

An active member of the Social Democratic Party from the early 1950s, Palme entered the Swedish Parliament in 1958. Long a close associate of Tage Erlander, Sweden's Social Democratic prime minister from 1946 to 1968, Palme joined the Social Democratic government in 1963 as minister without portfolio. In 1965 he advanced to the post of minister of communication and in 1967 to the dual post of minister of education and ecclesiastical affairs. He succeeded Erlander as party secretary and as prime minister in 1968. Soon afterward his attacks on U.S. war policy in Vietnam and his support for U.S. army deserters who sought refuge in Sweden led to strained relations between his country and the U.S.

Palme resigned in September 1976 when, after 44 years as the majority party in the Swedish parliament, the Social Democrats were defeated in a general election.

·Social Democratic Party leadership **16**:332f

Palmela, Pedro de Sousa Holstein, duque de (b. May 8, 1781, Turin, Piedmont—d. Oct. 12, 1850, Lisbon), Portuguese liberal statesman. Palmela served as minister of foreign affairs (1817–20). After King John VI's death (1826), he allied himself with the Liberal Party and supported the accession of Maria II to the throne. Created *duque* in 1833, Palmela served as prime minister from 1842 to 1846.

Palmén, Erik Herbert (1898–), Finnish meteorologist and oceanographer who explored the interaction of the atmosphere with the oceans and seas. Particular research areas included the structure and energy conversion of cyclones.

Palmer, city, southern Alaska, U.S., on the Matanuska River. Established *c.* 1916 as a station on the Matanuska branch of the Alaska Railroad, it was supposedly named for George Palmer, a late 19th-century trader. In the 1930s Palmer became the seat of the Alaska Rural Rehabilitation Corporation, a supply centre for farm families moving to Alaska from the Midwestern U.S. The city, 40 mi (64 km) northeast of Anchorage, on the railroad and on the Glenn Highway, grew as a market for agricultural products of the Matanuska Valley. It is the site of an experimental station of the University of Alaska. Inc. city, 1951. Pop. (1980) 2,141.
61°36′ N, 149°07′ W

Palmer, Arnold (Daniel) (b. Sept. 10, 1929, Youngstown, Pa.), professional golfer, first to earn $1,000,000 in tournament prize money. From 1954, when he became a professional, through 1975 he had won 61 tournaments sanctioned by the Professional Golfers' Association of America (PGA), a total exceeded only by Sam Snead's 84 and Ben Hogan's 62. As the leading figure in world golf from the late 1950s through the middle 1960s, he attracted a vast following known as "Arnie's Army."

The son of a greenskeeper, Palmer attended Wake Forest (N.C.) University and served in the U.S. Coast Guard. He turned professional after winning the 1954 U.S. Amateur championship. In addition to four victories in the Masters Tournament (Augusta, Ga.; 1958, 1960, 1962, 1964), he placed first in the U.S. Open on one occasion (1960) and won the British Open for two consecutive years (1961–62).

Arnold Palmer
Golf Magazine

An astute businessman, he served as president of Arnold Palmer Enterprises, a highly successful organization that became a division of the National Broadcasting Company.

·championship career record **8**:247g

Palmer, E(dward) H(enry) (b. Aug. 7, 1840, Cambridge, Cambridgeshire—d. Aug. 11, 1882, Wādī Sidr, Egypt), orientalist, distinguished as a linguist and as a traveller, among whose many translations is a version of the Qur'ān—the sacred scripture of Islām—that, despite some inaccuracies, conveys the true atmosphere of the culture of the desert.

E.H. Palmer, engraving by M. Klinkicht, 1883, after a portrait by J. Bell
By courtesy of the trustees of the British Museum; photograph, J.R. Freeman & Co. Ltd.

He early showed remarkable linguistic ability; in 1867 he was elected fellow in Oriental studies at the University of Cambridge. In 1868–69 he joined an ordnance survey expedition following the route taken by the Israelites from Egypt through the Sinai Desert to Jerusalem; in 1870 he accompanied Charles Tyrwhitt Drake, an explorer, on a further desert exploration. Both journeys he described in *The Desert of the Exodus*, 2 vol. (1871). The same year he published *Jerusalem, the City of Herod and of Saladin*, a Muslim view of the history of the city. He was professor of Arabic at Cambridge during 1871–81. In 1882 he was asked by the British government to enlist the sheikhs' support for the proposed British occupation of Egypt and to take measures ensuring the safety of the Suez Canal. His first mission was successful, but he was ambushed and killed on a second. His many publications include *Oriental Mysticism* (1867) and *The Song of the Reed and Other Pieces* (1877), which include translations from the Persian and Arabic as well as original poems.

Palmer, Roundell, 1st earl of Selborne: *see* Selborne, Roundell Palmer, 1st earl of.

Palmer, Samuel (b. Jan. 27, 1805, London—d. May 24, 1881, Redhill, Surrey), painter and etcher of visionary landscapes who was a disciple of William Blake. Palmer's father, a bookseller, encouraged him to become a painter. By 1819 he had already exhibited small landscape studies at the Royal Academy. The works that survive from 1819–21 are able but conventional. In the following years, however, there are signs of a profound change in his thinking, perhaps connected with his conversion from the Baptist faith to a personal form of High Anglicanism and with his discovery of medieval art.

A sketchbook of 1824 (British Museum), rediscovered in 1956, already shows all the elements of his visionary style: a mystical but precise depiction of nature and an overflowing religious intensity, united by a vivid re-creation of the pastoral conventions. In October 1824 the painter John Linnell took him to see William Blake, who encouraged Palmer in the mystical direction he was taking and provided examples of his own work for Palmer to follow. The most striking of these models were Blake's illustrations to Thornton's *Virgil* (1821). Blake's influence can be seen clearly in the "Repose of the Holy Family" (1824–25) and the series of sepia drawings of 1825 (Ashmolean Museum, Oxford). Palmer shared his reverence for Blake with a small group of other painters, including Linnell, George Richmond, and Edward Calvert.

In 1826 Palmer visited Shoreham in Kent, and the following year he settled there. His Shoreham paintings became more naturalistic but were still charged with visionary intensity. The years 1827–30 were his most productive, but from 1830 onward his work shows unmistakable signs of artistic decline. As his religious fervour faded, the precarious balance between realism and vision was lost. He left Shoreham for London in 1834, and expeditions to Wales and Italy confirmed the break with his own past. He continued to paint in an unexceptional pastoral style until his death.

The closest parallel to Palmer's nature mysticism can be found in the work of the German Romantic painter Caspar David Friedrich, but his real forebears are writers rather than painters. He read with enthusiasm the writings of the German mystic Jakob Böhme, the pastoral poems of John Milton, and above all the works of John Bunyan, whose "Countrey of Beulah" is the nearest equivalent to Palmer's "Valley of Vision."

The esteem accorded Palmer's Shoreham works in the 1960s was shown by the high prices paid at London auctions for pastiches executed by Tom Keating, an English painter and art restorer.

·Blake's influence **19**:454g

Palmer, Timothy (b. 1751, Newburyport, Mass.—d. 1821), pioneer builder of covered timber truss bridges. A millwright, he was also a self-taught carpenter and architect, and in 1792 he built the Essex-Merrimack Bridge over the Merrimack River near Newburyport. Composed of two trussed arches meeting at an island in the river, the bridge remained in use for more than a century and was the prototype of the numerous bridges he later built throughout New England.

Palmer's most noted work was the completely enclosed Permanent Bridge (*c.* 1806) over the Schuylkill River at Philadelphia. In use until destroyed by fire in 1875, the Permanent Bridge proved the value of, and set the style for, covered bridges in the U.S.

Palmer, Vance, pseudonym of EDWARD VIVIAN PALMER (b. Aug. 28, 1885, Bundaberg, Queensland—d. July 15, 1959, Australia), author of novels, short stories, and plays whose range, scope, and construction have earned him a high place in 20th-century Australian literature. His work is also noted for disciplined diction and frequent understatement. He is considered a founder of Australian drama.

Born and educated in Queensland, Palmer published his first work in English magazines when only 17 years old. Two years later he went to London to become a writer, meeting with some success. He returned, however, by way of Finland, Russia, Siberia, and the East and spent several years working at a variety of jobs in the Australian Outback. He next took up writing again, travelling to London and the U.S., then serving with Australian forces during World War I. From 1922 to 1926 he and his wife, Nettie (*née* Janet Higgins, also a writer), helped organize the Pioneer Players, a theatrical company in Melbourne specializing in Australian drama.

Of his novels, *The Passage* (1930), set in the Caloundra area of Queensland, is considered the best. It describes the life of a family and the subtle links between its members and their environment. *Golconda* (1948) deals with the conflict between miners and management in the Mount Isa area of Queensland; it is the first volume of a political trilogy that includes *Seedtime* (1957) and *The Big Fellow* (1959). He also wrote several plays on political themes. His short stories have been collected in four volumes: *Separate Lives* (1931); *Sea and Spinifex* (1934); *Let the Birds Fly* (1955); and *The Rainbow Bird* (1956). These often resemble character sketches, depicting ordinary men and women, tending to be undramatic and understated. He also wrote two volumes of ballad-like poetry, of which *The Forerunners* (1915) is considered the best, and several volumes of essays and literary criticism.
·Australian literary contributions **2**:418f

Palmer, Volney (1799–1864), advertising agent.
·advertising industry history **1**:107a

Palmer, William Waldegrave, 2nd earl of Selborne: *see* Selborne, William Waldegrave Palmer, 2nd earl of.

Palmer Archipelago, also called ANTARCTIC ARCHIPELAGO, island group off the northwest coast of the Antarctic Peninsula, from which it is separated by Gerlache and Bismarck straits. The archipelago, which includes the islands of Anvers (46 mi [74 km] long by 35 mi wide), Liège, Brabant, and Wiencke, was discovered in 1898 by the Belgian explorer Adrien de Gerlache. Argentina and the United Kingdom have operated research stations in the islands, which are claimed by both these countries and Chile.
64°10′ S, 62°00′ W

Palmer Land, broad southern part of the Antarctic Peninsula, Antarctica. It is mountainous and entirely covered by ice.
71°30′ S, 65°00′ W
·international agreements and location **1**:963a
·map, Antarctica **1**:950

Palmer Peninsula (Antarctica): *see* Antarctic Peninsula.

Palmerston, Lord 13:935, full name HENRY JOHN TEMPLE, 3RD VISCOUNT PALMERSTON (b. Oct. 20, 1784, London—d. Oct. 18, 1865, Brocket Hall, Hertfordshire), Whig-Liberal statesman whose long career, including more than 30 years as foreign secretary or prime minister, made him a permanent embodiment of British nationalism.

Abstract of text biography. Palmerston was educated at Harrow School, the University of Edinburgh, and St. John's College, Cambridge. In 1802 he succeeded to his father's title and estates as 3rd Viscount Palmerston. He entered Parliament and became a junior lord at the Admiralty in 1807, and in 1809 took the office of secretary at war, which he held for nearly 20 years. As foreign secretary (1830–34, 1835–41, and 1846–51) and prime minister (1855–58 and 1859–65) he was an influential figure in European affairs, supporting national movements when he felt they were in accord with British interests, and was generally conspicuous for his rather belligerent attitude in foreign policy.

REFERENCES in other text articles:
·British 19th-century political growth **3**:264f
·Cobden's promotion of free trade **4**:811d
·Gladstone opposition to foreign policy **8**:178h
·Victoria and foreign policy **19**:107e

Palmerston, also called AVARAU, atoll of the northern Cook Islands (*q.v.*), a dependency of New Zealand in the southwest Pacific Ocean. A coral formation, it has a land area of about 500 ac (200 ha) and a lagoon that lacks clear passages to the open sea. Covered with coconut and pandanus groves, it exports copra. Its inhabitants are mixed Polynesian and English descendants of William Marsters, who settled the island in 1862. They speak English with a Gloucestershire accent. Pop. (1976) 86.
18°04′ S, 163°10′ W
·map, Pacific Islands **2**:433

Palmerston North, city, south North Island, New Zealand, on a terrace beside the Manawatu River. The settlement, named after Lord Palmerston, prime minister of England, was founded in 1866 and declared a town two years later. Made a borough (1877) and a city (1930), it lies within Kairanga County. Junction of road and rail lines to Wellington (87 mi [140 km] southwest) and Auckland (339 mi northwest), it is a communications, commercial, and service centre for the pastoral and mixed farming Manawatu Plain and its bordering hills. Industries include food processing, printing, brewing, the manufacture of brick, tile, footwear, clothing, fertilizer, and pharmaceutical supplies, general and electrical engineering works, and motor and tractor assembly plants. The Royal New Zealand Air Force jet engine testing facility, workshops, and aircraft assembly factory are there. The city has become a university and research centre for Massey University, Queen Elizabeth Technical College, botanical research stations, a veterinary school, a teachers' college, a dairy research institute, and the Department of Scientific and Industrial Research. Pop. (1976) 57,931.
40°21′ S, 175°37′ E
·map, New Zealand **13**:45

Palmgren, Selim (b. Feb. 16, 1878, Pori, Fin.—d. Dec. 13, 1951, Helsinki), pianist and composer who helped establish the nationalist movement in Finnish music. He studied at the Helsinki Conservatory in 1895 and with Ferruccio Busoni in Germany (1899–1901). In 1909 he became conductor at Turku, where he produced his opera *Daniel Hjort* (in Swedish, 1910; revised in 1929 for performance in Finnish). He toured widely as a pianist and as accompanist to his wife, the singer Maikki Pakarinen. He taught at the Eastman School of Music, Rochester, N.Y. (1923–26), became a music critic in Helsinki, and taught composition at the Sibelius Academy in Helsinki (1939–51). Palmgren is best known for his small piano pieces, among them the "Finnish Lyric Pieces," inspired by folk songs. In his larger piano works, notably his five piano concerti, he was influenced by Franz Liszt.

Palmgren
Wide World Photos

Palmieri, Luigi (1807–96), Italian physicist.
·seismometer invention **16**:489b

Palmira, city, Valle del Cauca department, southwestern Colombia, 3,300 ft (1,000 m) above sea level. Founded in 1688, the city has long been an important agricultural and livestock-raising centre. Now the second largest city in Valle del Cauca, Palmira is referred to as the "agricultural capital of Colombia." The city houses an agricultural experiment station and a college of agronomy. Palmira is accessible by highway and railroad from Cali, the departmental capital, and from other cities in the Cauca Valley. Pop. (1973 prelim.) 140,481.
3°32′ N, 76°16′ W
·map, Colombia **4**:866

palmistry, also called CHIROMANCY, or CHIROSOPHY, character reading and divination of the future by interpretation of lines and undulations on the palm of the hand. Although there is no scientific support for the contention that these structures have psychic or occult predictive meaning, the human hand does show evidence of the person's occupation, habits, and (by implication) temperament, interests, and personality.

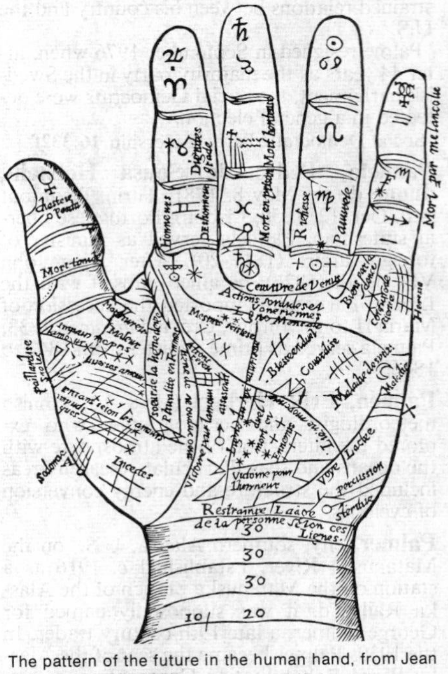
The pattern of the future in the human hand, from Jean Belot's *Oeuvres*, 1649
The Mansell Collection

palmitic acid: *see* fatty acid.

palmo, unit of linear measure, equivalent in Portugal to 0.22 metre, or 8.7 inches, in Spain to 0.209 metre, or 8.2 inches.
·weights and measures, table 5 **19**:734

palm oil: *see* oil palm.

Palm Springs, city, Riverside County, southern California, U.S., in the Coachella Valley, at the foot of Mt. San Jacinto (10,804 ft [3,293 m]). Known as Agua Caliente for its hot springs, it was by 1872 a stage stop between Prescott, Ariz., and Los Angeles. In 1884 Judge John Guthrie McCallum established the Palm Valley Colony on the site that later developed as a model desert resort. Incorporated as a city in 1938, it includes within its boundaries lands leased from the Agua Caliente Reservation (organized in a unique checkerboard pattern under an agreement with the Southern Pacific Railroad whereby alternate squares of land were allotted to the Agua Caliente band of Mission Indians). The Joshua Tree National Monument is immediately northeast. Pop. (1980) 32,271.
33°50′ N, 116°33′ W
·map, United States **18**:908

palm sugar, brown sugar made from the juice of palms.
·production in tropical Asian countries **17**:775c

Palm Sunday, in the Christian Church, first day of Holy Week and the Sunday before Easter, commemorating Jesus' triumphal entry into Jerusalem. The name derives from the blessing and procession of palms (leaves of the date palm or twigs from locally available trees). These special ceremonies were taking place toward the end of the 4th century in Jerusalem and are described in the *Pere-*

grinatio Etheriae. In the West, the earliest evidence of the ceremonies is found in the Bobbio Sacramentary (8th century). During the Middle Ages the ceremonies were elaborated: the procession went from a church in which the palms were blessed to another in which the liturgy was sung. The principal feature of the liturgy that follows the procession is the chanting by three deacons of the account of the Passion of Christ (Matt. 26:36–27:54). Musical settings for the crowd parts are sometimes sung by the choir. After the reform of the Roman Catholic liturgy for Holy Week in 1955, the ceremonies were somewhat simplified. The day is now called Second Passion Sunday or Palm Sunday.

In the Byzantine liturgy the Eucharist on Palm Sunday is followed by a procession in which the priest carries the icon representing the events commemorated. In the Anglican churches some of the traditional ceremonies were revived in the 19th century, but in most Protestant churches the day is celebrated without the traditional ceremonies.

Palmyra, ancient Syrian city, in Ḥimṣ *muḥāfaẓah* (governorate). The name Palmyra is the Greek and Latin form of Tadmor, the pre-Semitic name of the site, still in use in modern times. Although Tadmor and its inhabitants are mentioned as early as the 19th century BC on a Cappadocian tablet, the city did not attain prominence until the 3rd century BC, when the Seleucids probably made the road through Palmyra one of the routes of east-west trade. Two centuries later, this trade had reached international proportions.

The Temple of Bel at Palmyra
H. Roger-Viollet

Although at first autonomous, Palmyra came under Roman control at least by the time of the emperor Tiberius (AD 14–37). The emperor Hadrian visited (*c.* AD 129) the city, which thereafter became a *civitas libera* (free city). Later it was granted the title of *colonia*, with exemption from taxes, by Caracalla. The 3rd century AD was the great age of Palmyra.

When the Sāsānians supplanted the Parthians in Iran and southern Mesopotamia (AD 227), the road to the Persian Gulf was soon closed to Palmyrene trade. These difficulties plus the instability of the Roman Empire favoured the setting up of the personal rule of the family of Septimius Odenathus. Odenathus the Younger (probably the son of Septimius), brought his family, of Arab origin into world history. He was appointed governor of Syria Phoenice by the emperor Valerian, but it was apparently Gallienus (AD 253–268) who conferred on him the title of *corrector totius Orientis* ("governor of all the east"). Both Odenathus, however, and his eldest son, the heir apparent, were assassinated, reputedly at the command of Odenathus' wife, Zenobia.

Zenobia governed effectively, and in 270 the armies of Palmyra entered Anatolia, she and her son Vaballathus shortly thereafter proclaiming themselves Augusti. The emperor Aurelian, however, regained Anatolia and Palmyra (AD 272).

The city remained the chief station on the *strata Diocletiana*, a paved road that linked Damascus to the Euphrates. But in 634 it was taken by Khālid ibn al-Walīd in the name of the first Muslim caliph, Abū Bakr (AD 632–634). Modern Palmyra, situated on the Kirkuk (Iraq)–Tripoli (Lebanon) pipeline and at the junction of the motor routes through the Syrian Desert, has become a town of 12,722 (1970 prelim.) inhabitants.

The language of Palmyra was Aramaean; it had two systems of writing: a monumental script and a Mesopotamian cursive—reflecting the city's position between east and west. The great bilingual inscription known as the Tariff of Palmyra and the inscriptions carved below the statues of the great caravan leaders are sources of knowledge of the organization and nature of Palmyra's trade. The Palmyrenes exchanged goods with India via the Persian Gulf route and also with such cities as Coptos on the Nile, Rome, and Doura-Europus in Syria.

The principal deity of the Aramaeans of Palmyra was Bol (probably Baal, Lord). Bol soon became Bel by assimilation to the Babylonian Bel-Marduk, both of whom presided over the movements of the stars: the Palmyrenes associated Bel with the sun and moon gods, Yarhibol and Aglibol. Another heavenly triad formed around the Phoenician god Baal Shamen, the "lord of heaven," more or less identical with Hadad. A monotheistic tendency emerged in the 2nd century AD with the cult of an Unnamed God, "he whose name is blessed forever, the merciful and good."

The ruins at Palmyra clearly reveal the network plan of the ancient city. Along the principal street, oriented east–west, a double portico is ornamented with three nymphaea. To the south are the agora, the Senate House, and the theatre. Other ruins include a vast complex called Diocletians' Camp and the chief Palmyrene sanctuary, dedicated to Bel, Yarhibol, and Aglibol. In architecture, the Corinthian order marks almost all the monuments, but the influence of Mesopotamia and Iran is also clearly evident.

·Arabian kingdoms' choice of pantheons **1**:1058c
·art of ancient Near East **19**:272d
·climate, economy, and Classical impact **17**:920f *passim* to 923b
·independence of Roman control **17**:951d
·map, Syria **17**:921
·significance of collapse for tribes **1**:1045b

Palmyra Atoll, also called SAMARANG, one of the northern Line Islands in the west central Pacific Ocean, 1,000 mi (1,600 km) southwest of Hawaii. It comprises 50 islets with a combined area of 4 sq mi (10 sq km) and an average height of only 6 ft (2 m) above sea level. Discovered (1802) by the American ship "Palmyra," the island was annexed by the Kingdom of Hawaii in 1862 and by Britain in 1889. By an act of the U.S. Congress (1898), Palmyra was included with the Hawaiian Islands and then annexed in 1912. The atoll, once a producer of copra, is now under the administration of the U.S. Department of the Interior. There are no permanent inhabitants.
5°52′ N, 162°06′ W
·map, U.S. Outlying Territories **18**:1004

Palmyric (PALMYRENE) **alphabet,** Semitic script used in Palmyra, a city on the trade routes between Syria and Mesopotamia, from the 3rd to 2nd century BC until shortly after the conquest of the city by the Romans in AD 272. Developed from the Aramaic alphabet, Palmyric had 22 letters and was written from right to left. It occurred in two forms: a rounded, cursive form derived from Aramaic *c.* 250 BC and a decorative monumental script developed from the cursive form in the 1st century BC.

Palmyric inscriptions have been found in Palmyra, Palestine, Egypt, and elsewhere in North Africa and from as far afield as the Black Sea coast, Hungary, Italy, and England. The earliest surviving Palmyric inscription dates from 44 BC; the last dates from AD 274.

Palni Hills, eastward extension of the Western Ghāts, Madurai district, Tamil Nadu state, southern India. A continuation of the Anaimalai Hills in Kerala state, the Palnis are about 45 mi (72 km) wide and 15 mi long. In the south, the hills terminate abruptly in steep slopes.

The upper Palnis, in the west, consist of rolling hills covered with coarse grasses; dense forests grow in the valleys. Peaks include Vandaravu, 8,380 ft (2,553 m); Vembādi Shola, 8,221 ft; and Karunmakadu, 8,042 ft. The town of Kodaikānal is located in a high basin averaging 7,000 ft above sea level. Hill villages specialize in the cultivation of vegetables and fruits such as potatoes, beans, root crops, pears, and peaches. There are also bauxite mines.

The lower Palnis, in the east, form a confused jumble of peaks averaging 3,000–5,000 ft above sea level, and separated by steep wooded valleys. Teak trees have been extensively planted. Important cash crops include coffee, plantain, cardamom, citrus fruit, and turmeric.
10°20′ N, 77°35′ E
·map, India **9**:278

Palo Alto, city, Santa Clara County, California, U.S., on the west shore of San Francisco Bay. Gaspar de Portolá's 1769 expedition is said to have camped near El Palo Alto (meaning "the tall [redwood] tree"). The site was developed in 1891 as a "dry" village for Stanford University, and deeds still prohibit liquor sales. The city received its name from Sen. Leland Stanford's "Palo Alto" farm. Stimulated by the university and urban growth of the west bay shore area, it developed research-oriented light industries including aerospace, communications, and electronics. Inc. 1939. Pop. (1950) 25,475; (1970) 56,181; (1980) 55,225.
37°27′ N, 122°09′ W
·map, United States **18**:908

Palo Alto, Battle of, the first clash (May 8, 1846) in the Mexican War, fought at a small site in southeastern Texas about 9 miles (14.5 kilometres) northeast of Matamoros, Mex. Mexican troops had crossed the Rio Grande to besiege Ft. Brown and to threaten Gen. Zachary Taylor's supply centre. General Taylor and his army met the invaders at Palo Alto with superior artillery. Despite the greater numbers and crack cavalry units of the Mexican army, commanded by Gen. Mariano Arista, the Mexicans suffered heavier casualties. Disheartened by their lack of success, they retired the next day to a defensive position farther south.

Palomar Mountain Observatory (California, U.S.): *see* Hale Observatories.

Palomino, type of horse distinguished by its colour—some shade of yellow or gold with a

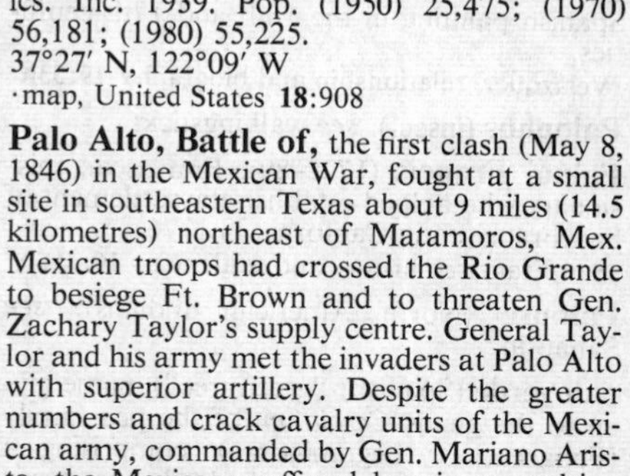

Palomino
Sally Anne Thompson—EB Inc.

white or silver mane and tail. The colour does not breed true. Horses of proper colour, proper saddle horse type, and from at least one registered parent of several light breeds can be registered. This colour is popular for pleasure and parade classes. Their type and use depend upon their breeding and training. They may conform to the breed types of several light breeds, such as Arabian or American Quarter Horse. Two associations, the Palomino Horse Breeders of America, established in 1941, and the Palomino Horse Association, established in 1936, register Palominos.

Palomino (de Castro y Velasco), Antonio (b. 1655, Bujalance, Spain—d. August 1726, Madrid), painter, scholar, and author, the last court painter of King Charles II of Spain.

In 1688 Palomino was appointed court painter and continued to concentrate on easel work until 1699. Thereafter he assisted Luca Giordano in the fresco decoration of El Escorial and continued to execute numerous large frescoes in churches in Madrid, Salamanca, Córdoba, Granada, and El Paular. Influenced both by Carreño and Coello, he specialized in elaborate allegorical paintings that were marked by effects of light and a dignified elegance, as is evident in the representative "St. Michael" (Kansas City, Mo.).

He is most important for his writings. *El Museo pictórico y escala óptica* (1715–24; "The Pictorial Museum and Optical Scale") consists of two major volumes, one on the theory and the other on the practice of painting. Bound together with the second volume is a collection of the lives of eminent Spanish painters and sculptors and of artists from other countries who worked in Spain. Modelled on Vasari's biographies of Italian artists, it is the most valuable source for the history of Spanish painting in the 16th and 17th centuries.

·Velázquez' relationship and biography **19**:53h

Palophus (insect): *see* walkingstick.

Palóu, Francis (1722–89), Franciscan missionary who helped establish the settlement of San Francisco in California in 1776.

·San Francisco history and settlement **16**:218b

Palouse (North American Indians): *see* Sahaptin.

paloverde (Spanish: "green tree"), name given to the genus *Cercidium* of the pea family (Fabaceae or Leguminosae), comprising a small group of trees and shrubs scattered through the arid regions of the southwestern United States, Mexico, Central America, and Venezuela. Three species are native to the United States; two become treelike. Blue paloverde (*C. floridum*) is a grotesque tree 4½ to 6 metres (15 to 20 feet) high, found in desert areas of southern California, Arizona, and Mexico, including the Baja California peninsula. It is usually a short-trunked, intricately branched tree, with smooth, conspicuously green bark and minute leaves that quickly wither and fall. The bright yellow flowers, borne in clusters, are followed by cylindrical, beanlike pods about 7.6 centimetres (3 inches) long. The paloverde is a characteristic woody plant along washes in the Colorado desert. Border paloverde (*C. macrum*), a Mexican tree, grows only as far north as southeastern Texas. It is readily distinguished from the blue paloverde by its flattened, podlike fruits.

palpation, medical diagnostic examination with the hands to discover internal abnormalities. By palpation the physician may detect enlargement of an organ, excess fluid in the tissues, a tumour mass, a bone fracture, or, by revealing tenderness, the presence of inflammation (as in appendicitis). Irregular heartbeat or vibrations of the chest can sometimes be diagnosed.

·basic clinical techniques **5**:688h
·veterinary diagnostic methods **5**:871f

palpebral conjunctiva, in human anatomy, membrane on the inner side of the eyelids.

·structure and function in human eye **7**:92b

palpigrade, any of the 36 species of the order Palpigradi of the arthropod class Arachnida. They resemble tiny scorpions—body length is 0.8 to 2.6 millimetres (0.03 to 0.1 inch)—and they have a long telson, or tail. They live under logs, stones, and dead leaves. Three species are found in California and Texas; others are found in South America and in the Old World.

·classification and general features **1**:1065e

Palpimanidae, family of about 100 species of spiders (order Araneida).

·classification and general features **1**:1073b

palpus, in zoology, segmented process attached to a mouthpart of an arthropod. The palpi are used to sense taste and direction.

·chemoreceptive structures of insects **4**:180d

palsas, low hills of perennially frozen peat that form in permafrost areas.

·permafrost formation and size **14**:94c

Palsgraf v. Long Island Railroad Co. (1928), U.S. tort case.

·tort law concerning negligence **18**:527f

palstave, type of prehistoric implement, usually of cast bronze, that is shaped like a chisel or ax head.

·cast axhead hafting design developments **8**:616a

palsy (disease): *see* paralysis.

Palta, Ecuadorian Indian ethnolinguistic group that lived in the Andean highlands at the time of the Spanish Conquest (16th century). The Palta language probably belonged to the Arawakan language family. Although the Ecuadorian highlands are still inhabited by persons of Indian descent, the languages, cultures, and tribal affiliations existing at the time of the conquest have disappeared and little is known of them. The Palta appear to have moved into the highlands from the tropical forests to the east not long before the conquest. They were mainly farmers who grew corn (maize), potatoes, beans, squash, avocados, and tropical fruits. Settlements were dispersed, each family living on its own farmland; houses were made of mud and thatch. Little is known about Palta crafts, religion, or social structure.

·geographic distribution and socioeconomic structure **17**:117h; map

Palúa (port, Venezuela): *see* Ciudad Guayana.

Pałuba (1903), psychological novel by Karol Irzykowski.

·Young Poland movement literature **10**:1252h

Paludan, (Stig Henning) Jacob (Puggaard) (b. Feb. 7, 1896, Copenhagen—d. Sept. 26, 1975, Birkerod, near Copenhagen), novelist and conservative critic whose work expressed a mistrust—based on the fear of Americanization of European culture—of Danish society and of the generation that followed World War I. He was the leading critic of the conservative Copenhagen newspaper *Dagens Nyheder* and was the editor of *Hasselbalchs Kulturbibliotek*, a book series that popularized arts and letters. Of the several books he translated into Danish, the most notable is Sinclair Lewis' *Dodsworth.* His foremost contribution, however, is that of his novels. *Fugle omkring fyret* (1925; *Birds Around the Light*, 1928), *Markerne modnes* (1927; "The Ripening Fields"), and his monumental epic novel *Jørgen Stein* (1932–33; Eng. trans., 1966) were among his most widely known and translated works.

Paludan-Müller, Frederik (b. Feb. 7, 1809, Kerteminde, on the Island of Fyn, Den.—d. Dec. 28, 1876, Copenhagen), poet who achieved early acclaim in the Danish Romantic movement for his Byronic epic *Danserinden* (1833; "The Danseuse"). Later, after he was rescued from a mental and religious crisis by a happy marriage, he became a moralist

Paludan-Müller
By courtesy of the Royal Library, Copenhagen

and a critic of Romantic values. His *Adam Homo* (1841 and 1848), a lengthy satirical epic in three parts, is counted among the most important works of Danish literature. Its autobiographical hero, Adam Homo, is a worldly success who suffers the loss of his soul. He is saved only by the devotion of his jilted sweetheart Alma. Adam Homo is said to have been Ibsen's model for the character of Peer Gynt.

Paludicella (bryozoan genus): *see* gymnolaemate.

Paludrine, trade name for derivatives of biguanide used as antimalarial drugs.

·malaria control in World War II **11**:82f

Palus (North American Indian tribe): *see* Sahaptin.

Paluy cult, religious movement among the Igorot peoples of the Philippines; it was founded *c.* 1896 by the prophet Angsui.

·new tribal religious movements **18**:704c

palygorskite (mineral): *see* attapulgite.

palynology, scientific discipline that is concerned with pollen, spores, and seeds and their description, classification, and utilization in a wide variety of stratigraphic, paleoclimatic, and archeologic problems. Palynology has, in particular, compiled much information about environmental changes during the Pleistocene Epoch (2,500,000 to 10,000 years ago). Analysis of the pollen record in lake and bog sediments has in many instances revealed a pattern of floral changes that reflects the climatic fluctuations associated with Pleistocene history. Applied to more recent events, palynology has served to clarify patterns of human settlement and land use in Europe and elsewhere.

·chronological principles and use **8**:999d
·geological forms and feature studies **7**:1064g
·stratigraphic evidence of microfossils **14**:734d; illus. 735

palynomorphs, organic microfossils such as pollen and spores.

·pollen stratigraphic evidence **14**:734g; illus. 735

pama (snake): *see* krait.

pamaquine, synthetic chemical drug introduced into medicine in 1926. It is related to both quinine and quinacrine and is used in treating malaria. It was the first of a series of important synthetic antimalarial drugs to be derived from 6-methoxyquinoline, which is a constituent of the naturally occurring drug quinine.

Pamaquine occurs as an oil. The pamoate salt, pamaquine pamoate, was used successfully in the treatment of malaria, although toxic reactions led to its displacement in therapy by related but less toxic drugs, such as chloroquine, primaquine, and amodiaquin.

Toxic effects include blood diseases such as methemoglobinemia and leukopenia as well as toxic hepatitis.

The chemical formula for pamaquine is $C_{19}H_{29}N_3O$.

Pamban Island, India, in the Palk Strait, an inlet of the Bay of Bengal.
9°17′ N, 79°17′ E
·Ceylon's geographical proximity **17**:519e

Pamean languages, Oto-Pamean language group of central Mexico, including Northern Pame, Southern Pame, Matlazinca or Pirinda, and Ocuiltec or Atzingo.
·Meso-American languages table **11**:958e

Pamela: or, Virtue Rewarded (1740), first novel of the English author Samuel Richardson. Epistolary in form, the novel is considered to be the first modern English novel of character. The story concerns a virtuous servant girl who resists all her master's attempts at seduction, her virtue being finally rewarded by marriage to him. Richardson's exhaustive treatment of his heroine's feelings and states of mind shows psychological insight, but the book's questionable moral values led to many parodies, the most noteworthy of which were *An Apology for the Life of Mrs. Shamela Andrews* and *Joseph Andrews* both by Henry Fielding. Richardson wrote a continuation of his story, in two volumes, called *Pamela in Her Exalted Condition* (1741), in which the heroine wins over those who had disapproved of the match.
·epistolary novel tradition **13**:286h
·plot, characters, and style **15**:829b
·source and theme **10**:1165h
·theme and Fielding's satirization **7**:292a

Pamir, German sailing vessel lost at sea in 1958.
·sailing ship training use **16**:162e

Pamir languages, group of Iranian languages spoken in the Pamir region of northeast Afghanistan and northwest Pakistan whose continued existence is threatened by the ongoing extension of modern Persian; the major languages (or dialects) of the group include Munji, Ormuri, and Parachi.
·Indo-Iranian languages distribution map **9**:442

Pamir mountain area 13:938, highland region of Central Asia, centred in the Tadzhik Soviet Socialist Republic of the Soviet Union. Its highest peaks, all exceeding 20,000 ft (6,000 m) include Communism, Lenin, and Karl Marx.

The text article covers the relief, geology, climate, plant and animal life, population, and industry of the area.

REFERENCES in other text articles:
·Asian geography **2**:159a
·location and geographical features **17**:325d
·map, Asia **2**:148
·map, Soviet Union **17**:322
·Marco Polo voyage map **14**:758
·mountain range unification **6**:45e
·rockfall in Bartang River valley **6**:64b
·Tadzhik ranges and highest peak **17**:985e
·Turkistan geographic importance **18**:792b
·vegetation, grazing, and land forms **17**:986c

Pamlico, Algonkian-speaking Indians who lived along the Pamlico River, in what is now Beaufort County, N.C., when first encountered by Europeans. These sedentary agriculturalists were almost destroyed by smallpox in 1696, and in 1710 the 75 survivors lived in a single village. They joined with part of the Tuscarora (*q.v.*) and other tribes in a war against white settlers (1711–13); at the close of the war those Tuscarora under treaty with the English agreed to exterminate the Pamlico. The surviving remnant were probably incorporated as slaves to the Tuscarora.

Pamlico River, actually the estuary (38 mi long and 1–5 mi wide) of the Tar River (*q.v.*) in North Carolina, U.S. It originates below Washington and flows into Pamlico Sound.
35°20′ N, 76°30′ W

Pamlico Sound, a very shallow body of water along the east shore of North Carolina, U.S., separated from the Atlantic Ocean by narrow barrier beaches of which Cape Hatteras is the easternmost. The sound extends 80 mi (130 km) south, then southeastward, from Roanoke Island, and is 8–30 mi wide. It receives the Tar-Pamlico and Neuse-Trent rivers, while the main inlets from the ocean are Ocracoke and Hatteras. Numerous swans, geese, and ducks nest along the coastal waters, and there is some commercial fishing, especially for oysters. The name is derived from the local Indian tribe, the Pamtecough.
35°20′ N, 75°55′ W
·continental shelf forms and features **5**:116c
·map, United States **18**:908

Pampa, also called ĀDIPAMPA, NADOJA, UPADHAYAYA, OJHA, OJA, JHA, and OVAJA (fl. 940), South Indian poet and literary figure called *ādikavi* (first poet) in the Kanarese language (Kannada), who created a style that served as the model for all future works in Kannada.

Although Pampa's family had been orthodox Hindus for generations, his father, Abhirāmadevarāya, along with his whole family, was converted to the Jaina faith. True to his rearing, Pampa cared little for material possessions and gave freely of what he had. He esteemed his guru, Devendramuni, and his royal patron, Arikēsarī, highly and lauded both in his writings.

Pampa's great work was the *Ādipurāna* ("First or Original Scriptures"), in which Jaina teaching and tenets are expounded. Another epic is the *Pampa-Bhārata* (*c.* 950; Bharata is both the ancient name for India and the name of a famous king), in which Pampa likens his royal master to the mythical hero Arjuna in the *Mahābhārata* ("Great Bharata").
·sacred and secular epics **17**:140c

Pampa, city, seat of Gray County, northern Texas, U.S. In the northeastern Panhandle, it is the centre of an oil-producing, wheat-growing, and cattle-raising area. Its economy is based mainly on petroleum, natural gas, chemicals, and related industries. It is headquarters for one of the world's largest producers of carbon black and oil-field equipment. Other activities include meat-packing and clothing manufacturing. Named for the supposed resemblance of the surrounding prairie lands to the Argentine Pampa, it was incorporated as a city in 1912. Pop. (1980) 21,396.
35°32′ N, 100°58′ W
·map, United States **18**:908

Pampa, La (province, Argentina): *see* La Pampa.

Pampa de Comas (Peru): *see* Comas.

Pampa de las Cuevas (Peru): *see* Cuevas.

Pampanga, province of central Luzon, Philippines, bounded by Manila Bay (south) and the provinces of Bataan (southwest), Zambales (west), Tarlac and Nueva Ecija (north), and Bulacan (east). Largely a plain, its area of 842 sq mi (2,181 sq km) is drained by the Pampanga River. The cultivation of rice and sugarcane, the manufacture of nipa palm products, and fishing are the main occupations. Candaba Swamp, on the Pampanga–Bulacan border, is a huge, shallow lake during the wet season, but during the dry season its bed serves as the nation's principal melon-producing district. The inhabitants are mainly the Pampangeños, who represent the seventh largest Philippine ethno-linguistic group. The chief towns are San Fernando (*q.v.*; the provincial capital), Guagua, Lubao, and Angeles. Clark U.S. Air Force Base is near Angeles. Municipal ports are located at Sexmoan and Masantol. Pampanga has long been a focal point for unrest, as in the rebellion against Spain (1896–98) and in the Communist-inspired Hukbalahap movement of the post-World War II period. Pop. (1970) 907,275.
·area and population table **14**:236

Pampangan, seventh largest cultural-linguistic group of the Republic of the Philippines. The Pampangan live principally in the agricultural province of Pampanga in the central plain of Luzon, but also inhabit portions of Tarlac, southern Nueva Ecija, and northeastern Bataan. Their region, extending north from Manila Bay, has a high population density; there are large numbers of tenant farmers as well as many landless workers.

The Pampangan language is closely related to others of the central Philippines, all of which belong to the Austronesian (Malayo-Polynesian) family of languages.

Pampanga River, Spanish RÍO GRANDE DE PAMPANGA, in Luzon, Philippines, rises in several headstreams in the Caraballo Mountains and flows south for *c.* 120 mi (190 km) to empty into northern Manila Bay in a wide, swampy delta. The Candaba Swamp, covering more than 200 sq mi (500 sq km) when flooded, has been formed north of the delta where the Angat River joins the Pampanga. Other major tributaries are the Chico Pampanga and the Lubao. There is a large-scale irrigation project on its lower course, which is also the site of extensive fishponds.
14°46′ N, 120°40′ E
·map, Philippines **14**:233

Pampas, singular PAMPA, vast plain extending westward across central Argentina from the Atlantic coast to the Andean foothills, bounded by the Gran Chaco (north) and Patagonia (south). The name comes from a Quechua Indian word meaning "flat surface," and South Americans use it in the singular. It has a gradual slope from northwest to southeast, from about 1,640 ft (500 m) above sea level at Mendoza to 66 ft at Buenos Aires. Apart from a few sierras in the northwest and south, most of the region appears perfectly flat. Several smaller plains in other parts of South America, such as the desert of northern Chile, are also referred to by the same term.

Cattle herd on the Pampas in Santa Fe state, Argentina
Carl Frank—Photo Researchers

The Argentine Pampas cover an area of 295,000 sq mi (760,000 sq km) and are divided into two distinct zones. The dry Pampa in the west, comprising most of La Pampa province, is largely barren, with great saline areas, brackish streams, and sandy deserts. The humid Pampa (Pampas) in the east is temperate, well-watered, and considered the economic heart of the nation and the main source of its wealth. The soil consists chiefly of fine sand, clay, and silt washed down toward the Atlantic by the great rivers or blown in dust storms from the west. Periodically cool winds from the south meet warm air from the tropical north, creating violent gales accompanied by heavy rain in the neighbourhood of Buenos Aires. These storms are known as pamperos. Characteristic animals of the Pampas include foxes, skunks, small herds of guanaco (*Lama guanacoe*), vizcachas (*Lagostomus tridactyla*), bush dogs (*Speothos*), and many bird species related to the sparrows, hawks, and waterfowl of the North American prairies.

Since the middle of the 19th century, the region has been transformed. Previously the

Spaniards had introduced cattle and horses but made no attempt toward land development. The animals were rounded up by the gauchos (cowboys) who were celebrated for their horsemanship, hardiness, and lawlessness. After liberation from Spain (1816) and the pacification of the wild Indians who roamed the plains, landowners began to employ immigrants (chiefly Italians) to cultivate their estancias (ranches), sowing alfalfa for fodder, maize (corn), and finer pastures. They fenced their lands and imported pedigreed sheep and cattle from Great Britain. Railways were built across the Pampa, the gauchos gradually became peons (labourers), and horses were replaced by tractors. The southeastern area between Mar del Plata and Tandil, being relatively cool and containing much swampy land, has been devoted to the breeding of high-grade sheep and cattle, while the western belt (from Bahía Blanca to Santa Fe) has been cultivated principally for alfalfa and wheat. Around Rosario, maize and flax are the chief crops and some livestock is raised. The vicinity of Buenos Aires has been developed to supply the capital with vegetables, fruit, and milk.

The Pampas served as background in Argentina's gauchesque literature, including such notable works as José Hernández' *El gaucho Martín Fierro* (1872) and Ricardo Güiraldes' *Don Segundo Sombra* (1926), and also as the theme for a great deal of Argentina's musical folklore.

·Argentine cattle grazing illus. **17**:90
·climatic characteristics **3**:447a
·ecosystem types and distribution **18**:146c
·formation, physiography, and vegetation **17**:82b; map 88
·geographic features and settlement **1**:1135b *passim* to 1138c
·Indian cultural and economic patterns **17**:112g *passim* to 115h
·location, soil, and precipitation **8**:284f
·map, Argentina **1**:1136
·map, South America **17**:77
·nomad cultures distribution map **17**:113
·Spanish colonial cattle industry growth **10**:696f

pampas cat (*Felis colocolo*), small cat, family Felidae, native to South America. It is about 60 centimetres (24 inches) long, including the 30-centimetre (12-inch) tail. The coat is long haired and grayish with brown markings which in some individuals may be indistinct. Little is known about the habits of the pampas cat. It is reported to live in thick shrubbery and to hunt birds and small animals at night.

pampas grass (*Cortaderia selloana*), one of about six species of tall, reedlike South American grasses comprising the genus *Cortaderia* (family Poaceae). Female plants bear silvery, plumelike flower clusters about 30 to 90 centimetres (1 to 3 feet) tall. Pampas grass is cultivated as a lawn ornamental in warm parts of the world.

Pampas grass (*Cortaderia selloana*)
A.M. Wettach—Shostal

Pampatherium, genus of extinct armadillo of the family Dasypodidae of the order Edentata.

·size, diet, and era **6**:301h

Pampean Group, major division of Pleistocene time and deposits in Argentina (the Pleistocene Epoch began about 2,500,000 years ago and ended about 10,000 years ago). The Pampean Group, also the name given to a faunal age, the Pampean, is still incompletely known. Pampean deposits consist of silts and sands that are often fossiliferous, containing the remains of toxodonts, an extinct mammal that grew to relatively large size; giant armoured animals, glyptodonts, extinct forms related to the modern armadillos; carnivores; and others.

The Pampean Group has been divided into several smaller units. From oldest to youngest, these are the Ensenada Formation, the Buenos Aires Formation, and the Luján Formation. The Pampean Group appears to span the entire Pleistocene Epoch and overlies the Chapadmalal Formation, which is of Pliocene age. The Pampean underlies the Querandí Formation, which is of Holocene age. The Pampean is also correlated with the Belgrano Formation, a marine unit that underlies another marine unit, the La Plata Formation, which itself is correlated with the Holocene Querandí Formation.

pampero, cold, irregular wind in Argentina and Uruguay, where it blows from the south or southwest. A passing cold front causes the pampero, which brings heavy rain and a temperature drop.

·effect on the Rio de la Plata **14**:525g
·Gran Chaco climatic characteristics **8**:276b
·Uruguayan climatic effects **18**:1094e
·wind direction and climatic effect **3**:447b

Pamphagidae, family of insects of the order Orthoptera.

·classification and characteristics **13**:749g

Pamphili, Eusebius: *see* Eusebius of Caesarea.

Pamphili, Gian Battista: *see* Innocent X.

Pamphiliidae, family of sawflies of the order Hymenoptera.

·characteristics and classification **9**:132a

Pamphilus (d. AD 310), teacher of Eusebius of Caesarea.

·Eusebius of Caesarea as respected friend **6**:1130b

pamphlet, a word first used in a 14th-century text to distinguish a brief booklet from a book. After the invention of printing, short unbound or loosely bound booklets were called pamphlets. Since polemical and propagandist works on topical subjects were circulated in this form, the word came to be used to describe them. Librarians and bibliographers generally describe them as any short work, unbound or bound in paper covers. Although the word tract is almost synonymous, it generally describes religious publications.

Pamphlets were widely used in England, France, and Germany during the religious controversies in the 16th century. Martin Luther was one of the earliest and most effective pamphleteers. Authors during the Elizabethan age used pamphlets for romantic fiction, autobiography, and social and literary criticism. In France pamphlets satirized the morals of the court and the chief ministers. At the time of the Restoration in England in 1660, the flow of pamphlets was checked, their range restricted to some extent by newspapers and periodicals. During the Revolution of 1688, however, pamphlets increased in importance as political weapons. The development of party politics gave employment to pamphleteers, including such writers as Joseph Addison, Richard Steele, Matthew Prior, Francis Atterbury, and Jonathan Swift.

The pamphlet continued to be powerful throughout the 18th century. In North America, pre-Revolutionary political agitation stimulated the beginning of extensive pamphleteering; foremost among the writers of political pamphlets was Thomas Paine (*q.v.*), whose "Common Sense" appeared in January 1776. After the United States was founded, another wave of pamphleteering was caused by the proposal of a new constitution in 1787. From this material there emerged *The Federalist Papers* (*see* Federalist, The), contributions made to the discussion of government by the revolutionary pamphleteers Alexander Hamilton, John Jay, and James Madison. Noted pamphleteers of 18th-century France —Voltaire, Rousseau, Montesquieu, and Diderot—used pamphlets to express the philosophy of the Enlightenment. The pamphlet once again became a powerful polemic weapon with the arrival of the French Revolution. The most complete collection of Revolutionary pamphlets can be found in the Bibliothèque Nationale, Paris. Edmund Burke's pamphlet *Reflections on the Revolution in France* (1790), one of the most remarkable produced during the Revolution, provoked many replies, the most famous being Thomas Paine's "Rights of Man" (1791–92).

In 19th-century France Paul-Louis Courier wrote polemic masterpieces. In England the pamphlet played a part in all political movements of the 19th century. Most notable were pamphlets on Chartism, Irish Home Rule, and the Oxford Movement. At the turn of the century, Fabian Society members George Bernard Shaw, Beatrice Webb, and Graham Wallas propagated political doctrine in a series of pamphlets.

In the 20th century the pamphlet has been used for information rather than controversy, chiefly by government departments and learned societies.

·newspaper publishing history **15**:236e

Pamphylia, ancient maritime district of southern Anatolia, originally a narrow strip of land that curved along the Mediterranean between Cilicia and Lycia, but that under Roman administration included large parts of Pisidia to the north. The Pamphylians, a mixture of aboriginal inhabitants, immigrant Cilicians, and Greeks, never acquired great political significance and ran the gauntlet of

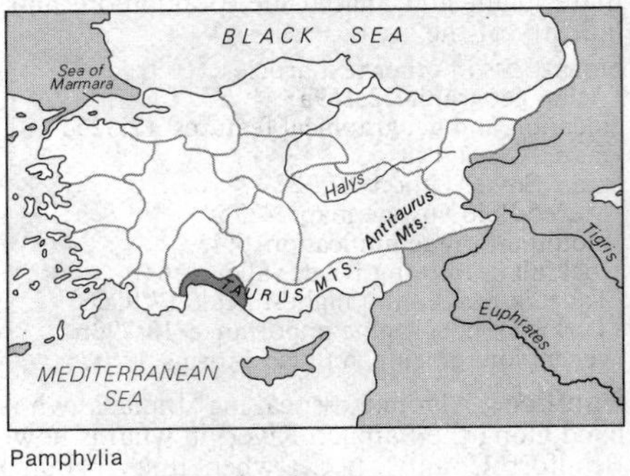

Pamphylia
From W. Shepherd, *Historical Atlas*, Harper & Row, Publishers (Barnes & Noble Books), New York; revision copyright © 1964 by Barnes & Noble, Inc.

Anatolian conquerors: Phrygians, Lydians, Persians, Alexander the Great and his successors, and, finally, the Romans. In the 1st century BC, they joined with Pisidians and Cilicians in piratical raids on Mediterranean shipping. The Pamphylians became largely Hellenized in Roman times and have left memorials of their civilization at Perga, Aspendus, and Side.

·Greek contact and settlement **1**:823c

Pamplona, city of Norte de Santander department, northeastern Colombia, in the Andean Cordillera Oriental at an elevation of

7,200 ft (2,195 m), on the Río Pamplonita. Founded in 1548, it was famed during the colonial era for its mineral production. Though it has been damaged by earthquakes (most severely in 1644 and 1875), much colonial architecture survives. Particularly noteworthy are the cathedral and the former monasteries of San Francisco, Santo Domingo, and San Agustín. The city's industries include textile mills, breweries, and distilleries. Gold and coal are mined in the vicinity. Pamplona lies on the Pan-American Highway, 45 mi (72 km) southeast of Cúcuta, the departmental capital. Pop. (1972 est.) 32,890.
7°23′ N, 72°39′ W
·map, Colombia **4**:866

Pamplona, capital of Navarra province, northeastern Spain, on the western bank of the Río Arga in the fertile La Cuenca region, just south of Bayonne, Fr. According to tradition, it was founded in 75 BC by Julius Caesar's rival Pompey (Gnaeus Pompeius Magnus) as a military settlement during his campaign against Quintus Sertorius, leader of a revolt against Rome. The city's first name was Pompeiopolis, or Pompaelo (corrupted by the Moors to Banbalūnah). It was almost derelict after Moorish and Frankish invasions and the final dismantling of its defenses by the Frankish king Charlemagne in 778. Pamplona was made capital of the kingdom of Navarre by Sancho III of Navarra (1000–35), his new foundation being known as the Ciudad de la Navarrería. In 1512 the armies of Ferdinand the Catholic entered Pamplona, and Navarra was incorporated into Castile. The citadel built by Philip II of Spain in 1571 made Pamplona the most strongly fortified town of the north. After the First Carlist War (1833–39), Pamplona ceased (1841) to be the capital of the Navarre kingdom but became capital of the new Navarre province.

The medieval core of the town, La Navarrería, is dominated by the cathedral, mostly 14th- to 15th-century French Gothic but with Romanesque remnants and a Neoclassical facade. Notable, too, is the Gothic church (13th–14th century) in the old district of San Saturnino or Cernín (*i.e.*, San Saturninu, who traditionally evangelized the city). Other important buildings include the Cámara de Comptos (royal treasury, *c.* 1364); the Casa Consistorial (1741, with Baroque facade); and the Diputación Provincial (Neoclassical) with the Archivo General de Navarra adjoining. The centre of the city, linking old with new, is the porticoed Plaza del Castillo. Pamplona has various museums and institutions of higher education.

The city's chief tourist attraction is the Fiesta de San Fermín (honouring St. Fermin, its first bishop), described in Ernest Hemingway's novel *The Sun Also Rises* (1926). Starting on July 6, the eve of the saint's festival, the fiesta lasts until the 14th, with daily bullfights preceded each morning by the famous *encierro* ("enclosing") of the bulls, when they are driven through the streets behind crowds of skillfully dodging men and boys.

Situated in an irrigated cereal-producing area, Pamplona is a flourishing agricultural centre. The city's ancient crafts of wineskin, sandal, rope, and pottery making coexist with the manufacture of kitchen ware, liquor, paper, and chemicals, and the milling of flour and sugar. Industrialization has produced a suburban belt of factories and workers' dwellings. Pamplona is important for communications between Spain and France. Pop. (1970) 147,168.
42°49′ N, 1°38′ W
·map, Spain **17**:382

Pam River, in Tibet, headwater of the Mekong River.
·Mekong River sources **11**:861b

Pan, Greek deity associated by the Romans with Faunus. Originally an Arcadian deity, his name is a Doric contraction of *paon* ("pasturer") but was commonly supposed in antiquity

Pan, terra-cotta statuette from Eretria, *c.* 300 BC; in the Staatliche Museen zu Berlin, East Germany

By courtesy of the Staatliche Museen zu Berlin

to be connected with *pan* ("all"). His father was generally said to be Hermes; his mother, however, was often named Penelope, probably not the wife of Odysseus but commonly identified with her, and consequently one or another of the characters in the *Odyssey* was sometimes called his father. Pan was represented as more or less bestial in shape, generally having the horns, legs, and ears of a goat; in later art the human parts of his form were much more emphasized. His activities were those of a giver of fertility, and he was thus represented as vigorous and lustful. He haunted the high hills and his chief concern was with flocks and herds, not with agriculture. Like a shepherd he was a piper, and he rested at noon. Pan was insignificant in literature, aside from Hellenistic bucolic, but he was a very common subject in ancient art. His rough figure was antithetical to, for example, that of Apollo, who represented culture and sophistication; hence the story of their musical contest.

pan (geography): *see* playas, pans, and saline flats.

Pan (ape): *see* chimpanzee.

Pan, or PANGUINGUE, card game, expanded form of the Mexican game Cooncan, or Conquian, and one of the earliest of the Rummy games. Pan is popular in the western United States, where it is played as a gambling game in many clubs. Eight packs of 40 cards are used, ranking K (high), Q, J, 7, 6, 5, 4, 3, 2, A. The game is best with 6 or 7 players, although as many as 15 may play. Each player is dealt ten cards, five at a time. The rotation is to the right, as in Cooncan, but unlike most other card games. The remainder of the pack is placed face down on the table to form the stock, and the top card is turned face up beside it to begin the discard pile.

The object of the game is to meld 11 cards. After the deal, players may decide whether to stay in the game or drop the hand; if they drop, they usually must pay a forfeit.

Melds, as in Rummy, are either sequences of three or more cards in the same suit or groups of three or more cards of the same rank. In Pan, groups of aces or kings (noncomoquers) are valid regardless of suits; groups of other ranks (comoquers) must be either all of one suit or all of different suits. Certain melds, called conditions, entitle the player to collect from all other players. Valles, or value cards, are 3s, 5s, and 7s. Conditions and their usual collections are a group of valles of one suit (2 units); a group of nonvalles of one suit (1); low sequence of 3–2–A (1); and high sequence of K–Q–J (1). In some games conditions in spades collect double.

In play, each player in turn (again, in rotation to the right) draws one card from the top of the stock or the discard pile. Some rules forbid drawing from the discard pile; others allow it only if the card drawn may be melded at once. After drawing, the player may meld or add (lay off) as many cards as he wishes to his previous melds. Then he must discard one card. When a player has melded all ten cards of his original hand, he must continue to draw and discard until he can meld or lay off the card drawn.

Players may split or borrow cards from previous melds to form new ones, providing that they leave valid melds. Conditions formed by splitting or borrowing collect as if they were entirely new.

The first player to meld 11 cards wins the deal and collects a previously established sum from all players who did not drop. He also collects from them again for all of his conditions and takes the forfeits of players who did drop.

p'an, type of Chinese bronze vessel produced during the Shang (*c.* 1766–*c.* 1122 BC) and, more commonly, during the Chou (*c.* 1122–231 BC) dynasties. A low bowl or pan used as a serving dish or for ceremonial washing, the *p'an* is generally circular and supported on a

Bronze *p'an*, late Warring States, *c.* 3rd century BC; in the Avery Brundage Collection, San Francisco

Center of Asian Art and Culture, the Avery Brundage Collection, San Francisco, California

low ring base. Sometimes there are two handles, placed vertically to the rim, and occasionally there are legs attached to the ring base. The bronze *p'an* shape has a Neolithic (*c.* 3000–1500 BC) pottery predecessor. The base and the narrow exterior surfaces of the bowl support a limited series of decorative motifs, the broad, flat interior of the vessel is often used for a more elaborate design or for a long inscription. *See also* Chinese bronze ritual vessels and implements.
·origin, description, and purpose **19**:178c

pan, in film making, the rotation of a motion picture camera to achieve a panoramic effect or to keep a moving object in view. The camera remains mounted in a fixed position while it sweeps the scene horizontally or vertically. A combination of both movements can also be used—*e.g.*, when a character is being followed as he climbs a staircase. Panning was used as early as Edwin S. Porter's *The Great Train Robbery* (1903).
·Griffith and early cinema **12**:516b
·motion pictures and camera movement **12**:501h

panaca, royal corporation to which ancient Inca rulers belonged.
·Inca political organization **1**:847c; table

Panaetius (*c.* 180–109 BC), Rhodian Greek philosopher, became a protege of the Roman statesman Scipio Aemilianus and implanted Stoicism in Rome before succeeding his teacher, Antipater of Tarsus, as head of the Stoa in Athens in 129.
·adaptation of Stoic philosophy **14**:255h
·Aristotelianism as an influence **1**:1156e
·Stoic growth and themes **17**:699e

Pan-African congresses, series of international meetings of prominent world blacks. The first congress (London, 1900) was mainly attended by delegates from the U.S., the West Indies, and Britain; its main achievement was to popularize the idea of pan-Africanism. The

second congress (Paris, 1919), organized by the U.S. separatist W.E.B. Du Bois and attended mostly by U.S. and French blacks, was concerned with improving the post-World War I colonial governments. The fifth congress (Manchester, 1945) which included many Africans of diverse backgrounds, rejected colonialism of all forms and advocated immediate independence for African peoples. The Pan-African ideal was continued by the Organization of African Unity, founded in 1963.
·Du Bois's influence **5**:1076a
·Kenyatta's role at fifth congress **10**:431c

Pan-African Freedom Movement, formed in 1958 for East and Central African economic co-operation.
·organization and Nyerere influence **6**:104h

Pan-Africanist Congress (PAC), organization of Africans formed in 1958 in South Africa and banned in 1960.
·African militancy **17**:295f

Panaji, also spelled PANJIM, administrative capital, Goa, Daman, and Diu union territory, western India, on the Mandovi River. It was a tiny village until the mid-18th century,

Church in Panaji, in Goa, Daman, and Diu union territory, India
picturepoint–Publix

when repeated plagues forced the Portuguese to abandon their capital of Velha Goa (Old Goa, or Ela). It became the capital of Goa in 1843. The town contains colonial houses and plazas, and, by law, all the houses are whitewashed annually. Chiefly an administrative centre, it is growing in commercial importance; an industrial estate has been developed nearby. Pop (1971) 34,953.
15°29′ N, 73°50′ E
·map, India **9**:279

Panama **13**:940, Central American republic occupying the Isthmus of Panama and lying between the Caribbean Sea (north) and the Pacific Ocean (south); it is bordered by Colombia (east) and Costa Rica (west).

The text article covers Panama's natural environment, regions of settlement, ethnic and linguistic groups, demography, resources and economic activity, transportation and communications, structure of government, services and social conditions, cultural life, and prospects for the future. *See also* Latin America and the Caribbean, Colonial; Central American states, history of.

REFERENCES in other text articles:
·armed forces statistics, table 2 **2**:16
·canal and Canal Zone features **13**:945b; map
·Chocó Indians' traditional society **17**:120e
·Christian denominational demography map **4**:459
·gross national debt percentage, table 4 **15**:193
·Indian visual art styles and media **1**:686f
·map, North America **13**:177
·merchant fleet and shipping statistics **18**:673f
·newspaper publishing statistics table **15**:237
·Panama Canal sovereignty negotiations **3**:759e

Panamá, province, on the Pacific coast of the Republic of Panama. Its area of 4,360 sq mi (11,292 sq km) is divided by the Panama Canal Zone, approximately three-fourths of the province lying to the east of the zone. As originally formed in 1719, it covered the entire eastern part of the Isthmus of Panama. About 35 percent of the national population lives in urban centres of the province (within a 25-mi radius of the Canal Zone). The province produces a variety of crops for domestic consumption and is the site of the country's leading industries. The provincial seat is at Panama City. Pop. (1973 est.) 659,580.
·area and population table **13**:942

Panama, Declaration of (Oct. 2, 1939), issued by the foreign ministers of the American republics (including the U.S.), meeting at the Panama Conference at the beginning of World War II. They proclaimed a safety zone in American waters for inter-American shipping and made a general declaration of neutrality in the European war. The zone began at the U.S.–Canadian border, both east and west, and covered the shipping lanes of the entire American continent southward, being broadened in the Pacific to include the Galápagos Islands. On October 4 the participants in the European conflict were formally notified of the declaration and asked to respect the neutrality of the individual nations.
·background and provisions **3**:1117b

Panama, Gulf of, Spanish GOLFO DE PANAMÁ, inlet of the Pacific Ocean, borders the southern side of the Isthmus of Panama and is 115 mi (185 km) across at its widest point and 100 mi long. It is shallow and separates the mountain ranges of western Panama from the beginning of the Colombian Serranía de Baudó. Its western part is indented as Parita Gulf, its northern as the Bay of Panama, and its eastern as San Miguel Gulf. The Pearl Islands (*q.v.*), which have important fisheries, are in the gulf, and Panama City is the main urban centre on the gulf shore.
8°00′ N, 79°10′ W
·map, Panama **13**:941

Panama, Isthmus of, Spanish ISTMO DE PANAMÁ, land link extending about 400 mi (644 km) from the border of Costa Rica to that of Colombia in an east–west direction between North and South America and separating the Caribbean Sea (Atlantic Ocean) from the Gulf of Panama (Pacific Ocean). The narrowest part of the Americas (30–120 mi wide), it is occupied by the Republic of Panama and the Panama Canal Zone. The terrain alternates between mountains and coastal plains.

The isthmus was first inhabited by Indians, migrating from the Andes and from the West Indies. The Spanish explorer Rodrigo de Galván Bastidas was the first European to visit the area (1501). The following year Christopher Columbus landed on the north coast and named Portobelo (Beautiful Harbour). During colonial times, the isthmus, crossed by the Cruces Mule Trail, was a source of friction between the Spanish and English, but despite constant attacks by English pirates, it remained in Spanish hands until independence early in the 19th century. Following the California Gold Rush of 1849, the Transisthmian Railway was constructed, and the towns of Portobelo and Colón experienced a tremendous economic boom. The opening of the Panama Canal in 1914 resulted in a heavy

PANAMA

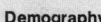

Official name: República de Panamá (Republic of Panama).
Location: Central America.
Form of government: republic.
Official language: Spanish.
Official religion: Roman Catholic.
Area: 33,659 sq mi (land area 29,208 sq mi), 87,176 sq km (land area 75,650 sq km).
Population: (1970 census) 1,428,082; (1971 estimate) 1,474,910.
Capital: Panama City.
Monetary unit: 1 balboa = 10 centesimos.

Demography
Population: (1971 estimate) density 50.5 per sq mi, 19.5 per sq km; (1970) urban 47.6%, rural 52.4%; (1970) male 50.68%, female 49.32%; (1970) under 15 43.4%, 15–29 26.1%, 30–44 15.2%, 45–59 9.6%, 60–74 4.3%, 75 and over 1.3%.*
Vital statistics: (1970) births per 1,000 population 36.0, deaths per 1,000 population 6.8, natural increase per 1,000 population 29.2; (1965–70) life expectancy at birth—64.3; (1970) major causes of death (per 100,000 population)—senility without mention of psychosis, ill-defined and unknown causes 129.6; ischemic heart disease 62.0; pneumonia 47.3; enteritis and other diarrheal diseases 45.4.
Ethnic composition (mid-1960s): mulatto 72%, African Negro 14%, European 12%, Indian and other 2%.
Religious affiliation (1968)†: Roman Catholic 91.5%, other 8.5%.

National accounts
Budget (1970). Revenue: 223,445,600 balboas (income tax 24.4%, import duties 16.5%, taxes on production and sales 10.2%, profits of the state's enterprises 7.5). Expenditures: 249,225,900 balboas (capital expenditures financed from loan funds 16.4%, education 15.0%, interest on public debt 10.5%, government and justice 10.2%, health 7.8%, current and capital transfers 7.3%, public works 5.9%). *Total national debt* (1970): 285,456,200 balboas. *Tourism* (1970). Receipts from visitors: U.S. $41,980,000. Expenditures by nationals abroad: U.S. $23,810,000.

Domestic economy
Gross national product (GNP; at current market prices, 1970): U.S. $1,060,000,000 (U.S. $730 per capita).

Origin of gross domestic product (at 1960 market prices):	1960				1970			
	value in 000,000 balboas	% of total value	labour force	% of labour force	value in 000,000 balboas	% of total value	labour force	% of labour force
agriculture, forestry, hunting, fishing	94.8	24.9	155,690	46.2	167.7	18.5	159,800	35.0
mining, quarrying	1.1	0.3	450	0.1	2.3	0.3	500	0.1
manufacturing	48.9	12.8	25,514	7.6	155.6	17.2	51,200	11.2
construction	22.8	6.0	14,364	4.3	57.1	6.3	26,400	5.8
electricity, gas, water	8.4	2.2	1,683	0.5	24.1	2.7	4,300	0.9
transport, storage, communication	18.8	4.9	10,002	3.0	52.1	5.8	17,600	3.9
trade	35.2	9.2	30,721	9.1	124.2	13.7	59,400	13.0
banking, insurance, real estate	10.0	2.6	...	...	33.5	3.7	...	...
ownership of dwellings	31.4	8.2	...	...	61.2	6.8	...	...
public administration, defense	11.4	3.0	...	...	24.2	2.7	...	...
services	98.4	25.8	67,663	20.1	202.5	22.4	113,800	24.9
persons employed in Canal Zone	...	...	18,848	5.6	...	...	23,700	5.2
other	...	...	12,034	3.6	...	...	...	...
total	381.2	100.0*	336,969	100.0*	904.5	100.0*	456,700	100.0

population migration to the Canal Zone. The strategic importance of the isthmus accounts for much of Panama's turbulent history.
9°20′ N, 79°30′ W
·map, Panama **13**:941
·paleogeography and fossil vertebrates **13**:908a
·Panama history **3**:1116g

Panama Canal **13**:945, interoceanic waterway measuring 51 mi (82 km) that connects the Atlantic and Pacific oceans through the Isthmus of Panama. It was owned and operated by the United States until the Panama Canal treaties (ratified 1977–78) provided for its operation by a Panama Canal Commission until Dec. 31, 1999. On that date Panama will assume full responsibility for its management, operation, and maintenance. The treaties also abolished the Panama Canal Zone.

The text article covers the canal's history, waterway, navigation and maintenance, capital improvements, traffic, Panama Canal Commission, property valuation and transfers, tolls, and future prospects.
9°00′ N, 79°37′ W

REFERENCES in other text articles:
·Colombian loss of Panama **4**:875h
·construction problems and achievements **3**:756b
·early construction plans **3**:1116g
·Lesseps' construction difficulties **10**:837g
·man's effect on physiographic features **14**:432b
·map, Panama **13**:941
·ocean connection importance **18**:653b
·organization and administration role **13**:942b

Panama Canal Zone
·establishment and political problems **3**:756c
·sociopolitical and geographical features **13**:940c *passim* to 944g
·Theodore Roosevelt acquisition role **15**:1143e
·U.S. acquisition by treaty **3**:1117a
·pre-construction negotiation **18**:982g
·shipping industry impact **18**:666e
·U.S. jurisdiction limits **13**:940d

Panama Canal Convention: *see* Hay–Bunau-Varilla Treaty.

Panama City, capital of the Republic of Panama and of Panamá province, in Central America. The city is located near the Pacific entrance of the Panama Canal, on the Bay of Panama.

The site was originally an Indian fishing village; the name Panama means "many fish." The old city (Panamá Viejo) was founded in 1519 by Gov. Pedro Arias de Avila and was made the seat of both secular and ecclesiastical authority. From the Andean countries of South America, bullion was shipped northward by sea to Panama and from there was carried across the isthmus by pack animals to Nombre de Dios or Portobelo on the Caribbean coast for shipment to Spain. The city prospered until the depredations of pirates and privateers curtailed trade.

In 1595 Sir Francis Drake tried unsuccessfully to send a force across the isthmus to sack old Panama; in 1671, however, Henry (afterward Sir Henry) Morgan completely destroyed it. The new city (Panamá Nuevo) was rebuilt 5 mi (8 km) west of the old site in 1674 by Alonso Mercado de Villacorta, a Spanish conquistador. Political and economic decline followed, and in 1751 the city and area became part of New Granada and eventually part of Colombia.

During the 19th century, Panama was the scene of much disorder, and in 1903 independence from Colombia was declared there, and the city was made the national capital. In the Hay–Bunau-Varilla Treaty of 1903, the United States was given the right to keep order in the city and to maintain hygiene. Both rights were yielded in treaties of 1936 and 1959, respectively.

Panama City cathedral
Charles May—Shostal

Following the opening of the canal (1914), Panama City developed rapidly. The title to the water and sewer systems, built by the U.S., was turned over to the government of the republic in 1942, and in 1953 their management was also transferred. The city was the site of Latin American congresses in 1826, 1939, and 1959.

Panama City is no longer a port; the harbour facilities lie in adjacent Balboa, and many canal employees live in Ancón. The city's economy is largely dependent on canal traffic and on providing services for canal personnel. Industries include breweries, oil refineries, steel-rolling mills, and clothing and wood factories. Panama City is linked with Colón by the canal, the Ferrocarril de Panama (Panama Railroad), and the Transisthmian Highway and with David and Chepo by the Carretera Interamericana (Pan-American Highway). It is served by an airport at Tocumen, 17 mi from the city.

Although the city is essentially modern, it retains many impressive reminders of colonial times, including several plazas; the cathedral (begun 1673), which contains Bartolomé Murillo's painting of the Virgin of the Rosary; and the San Francisco church (now renovated). Modern buildings include the Palace of Justice, La Presidencia, the National Palace, and the hotel El Panamá. Panama City is the seat of the national university (founded 1935), and the University of Santa Maria la Antigua (1965). The Gorgas Memorial Laboratory of Tropical and Preventive Medicine was established there in 1929. Pop. (1980 prelim.) city, 610,384.
8°58′ N, 79°31′ W
·map, North America **13**:177
·map, Panama **13**:941
·political and economic importance **13**:942d
·University of Panama enrollment and cultural importance **13**:944d

Panama City, seat of Bay County, northwest Florida, U.S., port of entry on St. Andrew Bay (Gulf of Mexico). The first settlement (*c.* 1765), known as "Old Town," was a fishing village later called St. Andrew.

In 1909 Panama City, which was then a village, merged with St. Andrew and Millville to form the present city. During the American Revolution the area was settled by British Loyalists, who established indigo plantations and engaged in the lumbering and naval stores

Production. Agriculture, forestry, hunting, fishing (metric tons except as noted, 1969–70): bananas 900,000,‡ sugarcane 1,009,200, husked rice 182,150, maize (corn) 96,455, coffee 5,665, cattle 1,187,700 head, pigs 195,300 head, fish catch 55,727, dried kidney beans 5,410, chickens and hens 2,928,700 head, eggs 172,042 dozens, milk 16,033 hectolitres. Manufacturing (gross value in 000 balboas, 1969): tobacco and beverages 34,301, of which, cigarettes 8,584, beer 5,576, carbonated beverages 6,346; paper and paper products 25,139; cereals and cereal preparations 20,284, of which, flour 4,760, rice 4,490; nonmetallic mineral products 17,152; clothing 12,499; meat and meat products 7,468; refined sugar 7,186; brown sugar 6,117. Construction (gross value in 000 balboas, 1970): residential 30,283, nonresidential 8,578.

Energy (1969): installed electrical capacity 163,961 kW, production 773,782,923 kW-hr (542 kW-hr per capita).

Persons economically active (1970): 456,700 (32.0%), unemployed 23,800 (5.2%).

Price and earnings indexes (1963 = 100):	1964	1965	1966	1967	1968	1969	1970	1971
consumer price index§	102.4	102.9	103.1	104.5	106.2	108.1	111.3	113.3
monthly earnings index	106.1	109.7	116.9	121.5	128.4	134.0	...	...

Land use (1961): forested 80.5%; meadows and pastures 11.0%; agricultural and under permanent cultivation 7.5%; built-on, wasteland, and other 1.0%.

Foreign trade

Imports (1970): 322,511,487 balboas (petroleum, crude and partly refined for further refining 26.0%; chemicals 12.3%, of which, medicinal and pharmaceutical products 3.3%, essential oils and perfume materials, and toilet, polishing, and cleansing preparations 2.1%; machinery other than electric 9.5%; road motor vehicles 8.8%, of which, passenger motor cars other than buses 4.5%; textile yarn, fabrics, made-up articles, and related products 7.9%, of which, textile fabrics, woven, other than cotton fabrics 4.0%; electrical machinery, apparatus, and appliances 7.6%; paper and paperboard 6.2%‖). *Major import sources:* United States 39.1%, Venezuela 18.6%, Japan 6.3%, West Germany 3.1%, United Kingdom 2.5%, Costa Rica 1.7%, Netherlands 1.5%.

Exports (1970): 106,853,516 balboas (bananas 56.9%; petroleum products 20.1%; shrimps, fresh and simply preserved 9.5%; sugar 4.6%; meat of bovine animals, fresh, chilled or frozen 2.3%; coffee, ground 1.6%). *Major export destinations:* United States 62.2%, West Germany 16.3%, Netherlands 4.1%, Canada 3.9%, Panama Canal Zone 3.3%, Costa Rica 2.1%.

Transport and communication

Transport (1970). Railroads: length 396 mi, 637 km; passengers 543,551; metric tons cargo 14,414. Roads: total length 4,230 mi, 6,807 km (paved 1,123 mi, 1,807 km; earth 2,476 mi, 3,985 km; gravel 631 mi, 1,015 km). Vehicles: passenger cars 45,526, trucks and buses 14,827. Merchant marine: vessels (over 1,000 gross tons) 615, total deadweight tonnage 8,907,000. Air transport: inbound passengers 428,227, outbound passengers 378,626; inbound cargo 19,775 metric tons, outbound cargo 15,186 metric tons; airports with scheduled flights 6.

Communication. Daily newspapers (1970): total number 7, circulation per 1,000 population 92, total circulation 130,000. Radios (1965): total number of receivers 500,000 (1 per 2.5 persons). Television: (1969) receivers 125,000 (1 per 11 persons); (1970) broadcasting stations 2. Telephones (1970): 85,088 (1 per 17 persons).

Education and health

Education (1970):	schools	teachers	students	student–teacher ratio
primary (age 7 to 12)	1,784	8,448	255,287	30.2
secondary (age 13 to 18)	71	2,458	54,040	22.0
vocational, teacher training	120	1,282	24,667	19.2
higher	2	592	8,947	15.1

College graduates (per 100,000 population, 1970): 421. *Literacy* (1970): total population literate (10 and over) 778,542 (79.3%), males literate 396,275 (79.6%), females literate 382,267 (79.1%).

Health (1970): doctors 857 (1 per 1,666 persons); hospital beds 5,237 (1 per 273 persons); daily per capita caloric intake 2,370 calories (FAO recommended minimum requirement 2,370 calories).

*Percentages do not add to 100.0 because of rounding. †Includes Panama Canal Zone. ‡1969. §Panama City. ‖Commodity breakdown is based on 1969 total imports valued at 239,635,000 balboas.

industries. Saltworks on St. Andrew Bay, established to serve the Confederacy, were destroyed by Union raids from the sea in 1863. During World War II the city became a shipbuilding and war industrial centre, and the population grew rapidly. Its landlocked, deepwater harbour is on the Intracoastal Waterway. Tyndall Air Force Base and the U.S. Navy Mine Defense Laboratory are nearby. Fish, paper, chemicals, and tourism are the chief economic factors. Panama City is the seat of Gulf Coast Junior College (1957). Pop. (1980) 33,346.
30°10′ N, 85°41′ W
·map, United States **18**:908

Panama disease, also called BANANA WILT, a devastating disease caused by the soil-inhabiting fungus *Fusarium oxysporum* form species *cubense*, which is widespread in Asia, Africa, Australia, Pacific islands, Caribbean, Central and South America, and wherever susceptible

Banana trees afflicted with Panama disease
W.H. Hodge

banana cultivars, such as 'Gros Michel,' are grown. Described in 1904 from Hawaii, Panama disease was observed 15 years or more earlier in tropical America and the West Indies. Some 20,000 acres (8,000 hectares) of bananas in Panama were abandoned by 1910, increasing to 50,000 acres by 1926. In Costa Rica, Panama, Guatemala, and Honduras 91,000 acres were lost to this disease between 1915 and 1926, with another 50,000 acres between 1930 and 1935. The *Fusarium* fungus invades young roots or root bases, often through wounds. Some infections progress into the rhizome (rootlike stem) followed by rapid invasion of the rootstock and leaf bases. Spread occurs through vascular bundles, which become discoloured brown or dark red, and finally purplish or black. The outer edges of older leaves turn yellow. Within a month or two all but the youngest leaves turn yellow, wilt, collapse, and hang downward covering the trunk (pseudostem) with dead brown leaves. All aboveground parts are eventually killed, although fresh suckers form at the base. These later wilt and the entire stool dies, usually within several years.

The best long-range control is to breed and grow highly resistant cultivars such as 'Cavendish,' 'Lacatan,' and 'Robusta.' *See* fusarium wilt.

Panama Scandal, the exposure of corruption in the French Chamber of Deputies; an episode much exploited in propaganda by the enemies of the Third Republic. To overcome a financial crisis in 1888, the French Panama Canal Company (Compagnie Universelle du Canal Interocéanique), originally sponsored by Ferdinand de Lesseps, needed to float a lottery loan to raise money. The required legislative approval was received from the Chamber of Deputies in April and from the Senate in June 1888. Although French investors contributed heavily, the company collapsed in February 1889 as a result of corruption and mismanagement. A judicial inquiry into the affairs of the Panama Canal Company was opened after some delay; in the autumn of 1892 two newspapers, *La Libre Parole* and *La Cocarde*, accused the government of complicity with the directors of the company. A Royalist deputy, Jules Deldhaye, further charged that "more than 150" parliamentarians had taken bribes to vote for the lottery loan in 1888. A parliamentary commission of inquiry was set up, and on Nov. 28, 1892, Émile Loubet's government was forced to resign.

The bribery had been managed by three men: Baron Jacques de Reinach, a financier, who died on Nov. 19, 1892, presumably by suicide, and two adventurers, Léopold Arton (properly Aaron) and Cornélius Herz, who subsequently fled abroad. Charles Baïhaut, a former minister of public works, confessed to having received money and was sentenced in March 1893 to five years' imprisonment; the other parliamentarians were acquitted for lack of proof. Georges Clemenceau, an associate of Herz (through whom he was alleged to have received money from the British), was discredited and temporarily retired from political life.
·investigation, trial, and consequences **7**:669f

Pan-American conferences, various meetings between representatives of some or all of the independent states of the Western Hemisphere (Canada usually excluded). Between 1826 and 1889, several meetings between American states were held to discuss problems of common defense and juridical matters. The First International Conference of American States (1889–90), held largely as the result of the efforts of the United States secretary of state James G. Blaine, established the International Union of American Republics (later called the Pan-American Union), with its headquarters in Washington, D.C. Subsequent conferences dealt with such matters of common concern as arbitration of financial and territorial claims, extradition of criminals, codification of international law, copyrights, patents and trademarks, and the status of aliens and diplomatic personnel. The Inter-American Conference for the Maintenance of Peace, held in 1936 at the request of Pres. Franklin D. Roosevelt, at Buenos Aires, adopted a draft treaty for the peaceful resolution of conflicts between American states; conferences held in 1938 (at Lima), 1945 (at Chapultepec in Mexico City), and 1947 (at Quitandinha, near Petrópolis, Brazil) considered the problems of hemispheric defense, reciprocal assistance, and solidarity. The Ninth International Conference of American States, at Bogotá (1948), led by the U.S., reconstituted the Pan-American organization as the Organization of American States (*q.v.*; OAS). The OAS established as one of its chief goals the prevention of the spread of Communism in the Americas; in the 1960s it was active in attempting to isolate the Fidel Castro regime in Cuba.
·Andes location and connections **1**:860h
·congress of 1826 **2**:1208b
·highway construction and operation **15**:900b

Pan-American Games, Spanish JUEGOS DEPORTIVOS PAN-AMERICANOS, quadrennial sports event for the nations of the Western Hemisphere, patterned after the Olympic Games and sanctioned by the International Olympic Committee.

The Pan-American Games had their inception at a meeting of the Pan-American Congress at Buenos Aires in 1940, attended by representatives of the national Olympic committees of 16 countries.

Buenos Aires was chosen as the site of the first games, scheduled to be held in 1942, the 450th anniversary of the discovery of America by Columbus. Because of World War II, however, they were not held until 1951. Delfo Cabrera, Argentina's 1948 Olympic marathon champion, opened the games before 100,000 spectators as he circled the track, carrying his country's flag. Some 2,000 athletes represented 20 Western Hemisphere nations in a program of 19 sports: baseball, basketball, boxing, cycling, equestrian events, fencing, gymnastics, pentathlon, polo, rowing, shooting, soccer, swimming and diving, tennis, track and field, water polo, weight lifting, wrestling, and yachting. Judo, synchronized swimming, and volleyball were added later.

Argentina and the United States, which had close to half the entries, dominated the first competition. The second games were held in Mexico City in 1955, the third in Chicago in 1959, and the fourth in São Paulo, Braz., in 1963. U.S. dominance continued through the early 1970s, reaching almost embarrassing proportions during the fifth games at Winnipeg, Canada, in 1967, where U.S. athletes won gold medals in 120 of 171 events.
·volleyball competition expansion **19**:511b
·yacht classes and selection of teams **2**:1170c

Pan-American Health Organization, division of the World Health Organization.
·public health services history **15**:204g

Pan-American Highway, a network of highways connecting North and South America. Originally conceived (1923) as a single route, the concept grew to include a great number of designated highways in participating countries. The Inter-American Highway, from Nuevo Laredo, Mex., to Panama City (3,350 miles [5,390 kilometres]), is a part of it. The Mexican section was entirely built and financed by Mexico, while the sections through the smaller Central American countries were built with U.S. assistance. The whole system, when completed through Chile, Argentina, and Brazil, will total nearly 16,000 miles (26,000 kilometres).
·Chilean route and length **4**:253b
·El Salvador's contribution **6**:734b
·Honduras section and branch **8**:1057f
·Panama link at Thatcher Ferry Bridge **13**:946c
·Peruvian transportation importance **14**:132d
·road types and mileage **17**:101h
·Santiago as central Chilean link **16**:233a
·Venezuelan route and length **19**:66d

Panamint, also called KOSO, North American Indian tribe of the Numic division of the Uto-Aztecan linguistic family.
·Basin Indian culture and religion **13**:204h; map 205

Panamint Range, group of mountains lying mainly in Inyo County, eastern California, U.S., and forming the western wall of Death Valley. Elevations average 6,000 to 11,000 ft (2,000–3,000 m); Telescope Peak (11,049 ft) is the highest point. Some ghost mining towns are found within the range.
36°30′ N, 117°20′ W

Panathenaea, in Greek religion, an annual Athenian festival of great antiquity and importance. It was eventually celebrated every fourth year with special splendour, probably in deliberate rivalry to the Olympic Games. The festival consisted solely of the sacrifices and rites proper to the season (mid-August) in the cult of Athena, the city protectress. At the Great Panathenaea, representatives of all the dependencies of Athens were present, bringing sacrificial animals. After the presentation of a new embroidered robe to Athena, the sacrifice of several animals was offered. The great procession is the subject of the frieze of the Parthenon. The Athenian statesman Pericles (*c.* 495–429 BC) introduced a regular musical contest in place of the recitation of rhapsodes (portions of epic poems adapted for recitation), which were a long-standing accompaniment of the festival. The contest took place in the odeum, originally built for the purpose by Pericles himself.

In addition to major athletic contests, many of which were not in use at Olympia, several minor contests also were held between the Athenian tribes.

·black-figure victory vases **14**:899h
·Greek religious festivals **8**:409f
·Homeric epics inclusion **8**:1171b
·Peisistratus' additional attractions **13**:1110e

panautomorphic texture (geology): *see* panidiomorphic texture.

Panax schinseng (plant): *see* ginseng.

Panay, island, westernmost of the Visayas, central Philippines, surrounded by the Sibuyan, Visayan, and Sulu seas; the Guimaras Strait to the southeast separates it from Negros. Roughly triangular shaped, it has an area of 4,446 sq mi (11,515 sq km). A rugged, almost unpopulated mountain range parallels its western coastline. Between that range and a hilly eastern portion, a densely populated, intensely farmed (sugarcane, rice) fertile central plain extends for about 95 mi (153 km) from the northern to the southern coasts. A wide lowland on the southeast is formed by the deltas of the Jalaud, Jaro, and Sibalom rivers.

There are large concentrations of fishponds in the north and east, and mineral deposits include coal and copper. The inhabitants are primarily of the Hiligaynon (Ilongo) ethnolinguistic group, and nomadic Negritos live in the mountainous areas. The island is divided into four administrative provinces, and its chartered cities are Roxas and Iloilo (*qq.v.*). Pop. (1970) 2,144,544.
11°10′ N, 122°30′ E

·map, Philippines **14**:233
·population density map **14**:235

pancake ice, pancake shaped ice sheets one to six feet in diameter, formed in polar regions.

·stage in sea ice formation **9**:158d

Pañcala, ancient Indian tribe of the Vedic period.

·tribal structure and territory **9**:347a; map 350

pañcama-grāma-rāga, Indian melodic scale.

·Western scale comparison table **17**:154

Pāñcarātra cult, an early Hindu group that worshipped the deified sage Nārāyaṇa (who came to be identified with Lord Viṣṇu) and that, in merger with the Bhāgavatas (*q.v.*), formed the earliest sectarian movement within Hinduism. The new group was a forerunner of modern Vaiṣṇavism, or the worship of Viṣṇu.

The Pāñcarātras originated in the Himalayan region perhaps in the 3rd century BC. The name of the cult is attributed to a sacrifice continuing for five days (*pañca-rātra*) performed by Nārāyaṇa by which he obtained superiority over all beings and became all beings.

The Pāñcarātra doctrine was first systematized by Śāṇḍilya (*c.* AD 100), who composed several devotional verses about the deity Nārāyaṇa; that the Pāñcarātra system was also known in South India is evident from 2nd-century-AD inscriptions. By the 10th century, the sect had acquired sufficient popularity to leave its influence on other groups, though criticized by Śaṅkara and other orthodox figures as nonmonastic and non-Vedic.

The Pāñcarātras developed an elaborate doctrine of emanations (*vyūhas*) from the one god, Viṣṇu. According to this theory of evolution, first Śakti, the female aspect of Viṣṇu, was made manifest, then Vāsudeva (Kṛṣṇa), from whom proceeded Saṅkarṣaṇa (another name for Kṛṣṇa's half brother, Balarāma), from whom emanated Pradyumna (Kṛṣṇa's son), from whom evolved Aniruddha (Kṛṣṇa's grandson). Each of the *vyūha*s also correspond to one of the four quarters of the universe and to aspects of human personality.

·Lakṣmī as liberator of souls **8**:897d
·philosophical texts and doctrines **9**:332d
·philosophy in the Mahābhārata **9**:317h

pañca-sīla (Buddhism): *see* sīla.

Pañca-tantra, OR PANCHATANTRA (Sanskrit: "Five Chapters"), a collection of Indian animal fables, which has had extensive circulation both in the country of its origin and throughout the world. In Europe the work was known under the name *The Fables of Bidpai* (after the narrator, an Indian sage, Bidpai, called in Sanskrit Vidyāpati), and one version reached there as early as the 11th century.

In theory, the *Pañca-tantra* is intended as a textbook of *artha* (worldly wisdom); the aphorisms tend to glorify shrewdness and cleverness more than the helping of others. The original text is a mixture of Sanskrit prose and stanzas of verse, with the stories contained within one of the five "frame stories." The introduction, which acts as an enclosing frame for the entire work, attributes the stories to a learned Brahmin named Viṣṇuśarman, who used the form of animal fables to instruct the three dull-witted sons of a king.

The original Sanskrit work, now lost, may have originated at any time between 100 BC and AD 500. It was translated into Pahlavi (Middle Persian) by the Persian royal physician Burzoe in the 6th century. Although this work also is lost, a Syriac translation of it has survived, together with the famous 8th-century Arabic translation by Ibn al-Muqaffaʿ known as *Kalīlah wa Dimnah* after the two jackals that figure in the first story. The *Kalīlah wa Dimnah* led on to various other versions, including a second Syriac version and an 11th-century version in Greek, the *Stephanites kai Ichnelates*, from which translations were made into Latin and various Slavic languages. The 17th-century Turkish translation, the *Hümayun-name*, was based on a 15th-century Persian version, the *Anwār-e Suhaylī*.

In Europe a version was written in Latin hexameters by the fabulist Baldo, probably in the 12th century, and in the 13th century a Spanish translation was made on the orders of Alfonso X of Leon and Castile. It was the 12th-century Hebrew version of Rabbi Joel, however, that became the source of most European versions. First translated into Latin by John of Capua as the *Liber Kelilae et Dimnae* or the *Directorium vitae humanae*, it led to various European versions including another Latin version, the *Liber de Dina et Kalila* by Raimond of Béziers, in the 14th century and the *Buch der Beispiele der alten Weisen* by Antonius von Pforr in the 15th century. Sir Thomas North's *The morall philosophie of Doni* (1570) is a translation of A.F. Doni's 16th-century Italian version.

The *Pañca-tantra* stories also travelled to Indonesia through Old Javanese written literature and possibly through oral versions. In India, the *Hitopadeśa* ("Good Advice"), composed by Nārāyaṇa in the 12th century and circulated mostly in Bengal, appears to be an independent treatment of the *Pañca-tantra* material.

·fables as vehicles of instruction **7**:138f
·folklore origins in Benfey's theory **7**:462h
·Indian and Western versions **17**:138c
·Indian tales **16**:712d

pañcāyat, caste, the most important adjudicating and licensing agency in the self-government of an Indian caste. There are two types: permanent and impermanent. The permanent *pañcāyat* is found most commonly in northern Indian castes with a single, well-defined occupation; in functional castes in trade or with allied occupations; in nonfunctional but respectable castes; and in nonfunctional castes of low status. Such a *pañcāyat* may be of the entire caste, the endogamous subcaste, or a local section (often indistinguishable from the *berādarī*, or family brotherhood).

Literally, a *pañcāyat* (from Sanskrit *pañca*, "five"), consists of five members, but usually there are more; the *pañcāyat* has a policy committee, however, often numbering five.

Most *pañcāyat*s have a permanent head (*sarpañc*, "head of the five"), who is a permanent member; the position is often hereditary. Nonhereditary committeemen are selected on the basis of merit. Meetings are held on a ritual occasion, such as a marriage or funeral; by special summons, heralded by the caste summoner or the caste barber; or on set occasions, such as an annual festival.

The *pañcāyat* sits as a court of law. The culprit pleads guilty or not guilty. If guilty, he is sentenced forthwith. If not, the evidence is aired, discussed, and adjudged and a sentence is issued. Cases are heard in open meetings in which all members of the caste group concerned are entitled to take part. Any evidence that has any conceivable bearing on the case is admissible; it can be produced by either party, by onlookers, or even by members of the council. Everyone has the chance to say everything he wants to say; every hidden influence, every cherished loyalty or carefully nourished spite is exposed to the gaze of the whole caste group.

Types of offenses adjudicated in meetings of the *pañcāyat* are breaches of eating, drinking, or smoking restrictions; infractions of marriage rules; breaches of a caste's customs in feast; breaches of its trade rules; the killing of certain animals, notably cows; causing injury to a Brahmin; and, less commonly, criminal and civil cases actionable before a court of law and offenses already tried by a court of law. *Pañcāyat*s of Muslim castes try only a few of the offenses, as the rest fall under *fiqh*, or Islāmic law.

Penalties take the form of fines (paid by distributing sweets to a caste group or by contributing to a caste fund), the obligation to offer a feast to the *berādarī* or to Brahmins, and temporary or permanent excommunication. Pilgrimage and self-humiliation are sometimes levied, but physical punishment is now uncommon.

An impermanent council has no official agent to convene meetings; the person offended must do so at his own cost, and this procedure is quite rare. The higher ranking caste groups, such as the Brahmins, most Rājputs, and some merchant classes, have no *pañcāyat*s at all. This is in part because of their dispersion over a wide geographic area; customs regulating marriage between castes also can present difficulties in the summoning of a council. Among these castes public opinion suffices to castigate the offender.

The passing of the Evidence Act by the British in 1872, with its strict rules of admissible evidence, led to a bypassing of the *pañcāyat* by some caste members who began to take their cases directly to the state court (*see* Indian Evidence Act). Some castes try cases that have come up before a state court or retry them after the verdict of the state court has been given.

The historical relation between the caste *pañcāyat* and the "village *pañcāyat*" is not clear. The French sociologist Louis Dumont is inclined to consider the latter as something of a myth inspired by a romantic notion of "village community" among the Europeans. In any case, he argues, the village *pañcāyat*, insofar as it existed as an official body, would have been the caste *pañcāyat* of the dominant caste in the village. The Congress Party in India has made a point of creating village *pañcāyat*s as local instruments of government, the so-called *pañcāyat rāj*, or government by *pañcāyat*s.

·Gujarāt rural administration **8**:479h
·Rājasthān's pioneering of system **15**:497a
·Tamil Nadu's grass roots polity **17**:1015a
·West Bengal's local polity model **19**:787h

Pančevo, town, southwestern autonomous region of Vojvodina, republic of Serbia, Yugoslavia. It is a nodal point for rail and road commerce and a port on the Danube River, a few miles from Belgrade. Heavy industries include chemicals, fertilizer, petroleum refining, glass, metal, and electrical goods. The town was first documented in the 12th century. Freed from the Turks in 1717, it was under Austrian rule until incorporated in 1920 into the Kingdom of Serbs, Croats, and Slovenes (Treaty of Trianon), later Yugoslavia. Pop (1971 prelim.) 54,300.
44°52′ N, 20°39′ E
·map, Yugoslavia **19**:1100

Panchakosi, Hindu sacred road in Vārāṇasi, Uttar Pradesh state, India.
·Vārāṇasi and Hindu tradition **19**:26f

Pan Ch'ao (b. AD 31, China—d. 101, China), famous Han dynasty (206 BC–AD 220) general and colonial administrator who re-established Chinese control over Central Asia. The brother of the famous historian Pan Ku (31–92), Pan Ch'ao early tired of literary pursuits and turned to military affairs. In 73 he was dispatched with a handful of troops on a mission to pacify the Hsiung-nu tribes who had been raiding China's northwestern borders. By playing on the internal dissensions among the various tribes, he quickly succeeded in pacifying the area. His efforts were frustated, however, by his recall three years later.

Several years elapsed before he was permitted to resume his mission, but he soon had the entire Tarim Basin (in modern Sinkiang Province) under his control. Made *Tu hu* (protector general) of the western regions in 91, he expanded his conquests across the Pamirs to the shores of the Caspian Sea. Only Parthia (in modern Iran) separated him from the outer reaches of the Roman Empire, and he sent an envoy to contact Roman authorities. The man, however, turned back after reaching the Persian Gulf.

In 101 Pan Ch'ao's famous scholar sister, Pan Chao, successfully petitioned the Emperor to allow Pan Ch'ao to return home, where he died a month later. Two of his sons maintained Chinese control in Central Asia for a brief period.
·Pan Ku defense **13**:948a

Pan Chao (b. *c.* AD 45, China—d. *c.* 115, China), China's most famous woman scholar. Daughter of a prominent family, she married at the age of 14, but her husband died while she was still young. She never remarried, devoting herself instead to literature and the education of her son. Her father, Pan Piao (AD 3–54), apparently had begun a history of the Former Han dynasty (206 BC–AD 8). After his death, Pan Chao's brother Pan Ku (AD 31–92) attempted to revise and amplify the work. He was arrested by government officials and charged with tampering with dynastic records, a serious offense to the history-conscious Chinese. Pan Chao obtained an imperial audience and pleaded her brother's case before the Emperor. After reading the writings in question, the Emperor gave Pan Ku a post as official historian and ordered him to complete the work. The resulting *Han shu* ("Book of Han") is one of the most famous history works ever written and the model for all future dynastic histories in China. Pan Chao, who assisted her brother with the work during his lifetime, was commissioned by the Emperor to complete it following Pan Ku's death. She added several tables and the treatise on astronomy.

Because of her reputation as a scholar and an exemplary widow, Pan Chao was made a lady in waiting to the Empress. In 101, while in the palace, she wrote the memorial to the throne that enabled her other brother, the famous general Pan Ch'ao, to return to the capital after 30 years of extraordinary military and colonial service in Central Asia. Pan wrote many beautiful poems and essays, the most famous of which is *Nü shih* (106; "Lessons for Women").

Panchatantra (Indian animal fables): *see* Pañca-tantra.

Pañchen (PAṆ-CHEN) **Lama,** title of the line of reincarnated lamas in Tibet who head the influential Tashilhunpo monastery (near Zhikatse) and who until recent times were second only to the Dalai Lamas in spiritual authority within the dominant Dge-lugs-pa sect.

The title Pañchen (a short form of the Sanskrit-Tibetan Paṇḍita Chen-po, "great scholar") was the title traditionally given to head abbots of the Tashilhunpo monastery, who were chosen for their maturity and learning. In the 17th century the fifth Dalai Lama declared that his tutor, Blo-bzang chos-kyi-rgyal-mtshan (1570–1662), who was the current Pañchen Lama, would be reincarnated after his death in a child. He thus became the first of the line of reincarnated lamas, reappearing as Blo-bzang-ye-shes (1663–1737), Blo-bzang-dpal-ldan-ye-shes (1737–1780), Blo-bzang-bstan-pa'i-nyi-ma (1781–1854), Bstan-pa'i-dbang-phyug (1854–1882), and Chos-kyi Nyi-ma (1883–1937). They were each regarded as physical manifestations of the "self-born" Buddha Amitábha. (Sometimes the three lamas who preceded Blo-bzang chos-kyi- rgyal-mtshan as abbots of Tashilhunpo are also included in the list of reincarnations.)

Disagreements between the government of the Dalai Lama and the Tashilhunpo administration over tax arrears led to the Pañchen Lama's flight to China in 1923. A boy born in Tsinghai Province of China in 1938 of Tibetan parents, Bskal-bzang Tshe-brtan, was recognized as his successor by the Chinese government but without having gone through the usual exacting tests that determine rebirth. He was brought to Tibet in 1952 under Communist military escort and enthroned as head abbot of Tashilhunpo. The Pañchen Lama remained in Tibet in 1959 after the popular revolt and the Dalai Lama's flight into exile, but his refusal to denounce the Dalai Lama as a traitor brought him into disfavour with the Communist regime.
·Buddhist incarnation and role **3**:411b
·relation to Dalai Lama and Chinese rule **18**:381g

Panchimalco, town, San Salvador department, southern El Salvador, in the Pacific coastal range, just south of San Salvador. Grain, coffee, and sugarcane are grown, and poultry is raised. The population is made up primarily of descendants of Pipil Indians, who are noted for their handwoven textiles and for their traditional (pre-Columbian) dress and customs. Panchimalco's colonial Baroque church has exceptional wood carvings. Pop. (1971 prelim.) 2,663.
13°43′ N, 89°12′ W

Pānch Mahāls, district, in Gujarāt state, west central India, bounded by Rājasthān (northeast) and Madhya Pradesh (east) states. Its 3,486-sq mi (9,029-sq km) area rises from lowlands into foothills of the Vindhya Range and is largely rough and wooded. The valleys produce pearl millet, maize (corn), cotton, and gram (a legume). Manganese is mined near Shivrājpur. Godhra (*q.v.*;the district headquarters), Dohad, and other principal towns are served by a railway and highways. Pop. (1971 prelim.) 1,846,452.

panchromatic film, photographic film sensitive to light of all the colours in the visible spectrum.
·film colour sensitivity extension **14**:335e

pancratium, Greek PANKRATION, ancient Greek sports event that combined boxing and wrestling, introduced at the XXV Olympiad (652 BC). Contests were savage, with hitting, kicking, twisting of limbs, strangling, and struggling on the ground allowed. The only recognized fouls were biting and gouging. A contest ended when one of the fighters acknowledged defeat.
·boxing in Olympics **3**:91h
·introduction and rules **2**:274g
·wrestling history and styles **19**:1025e

pancreas, a compound gland common to all vertebrates; it functions both as an exocrine gland discharging digestive enzymes into the gut and as an endocrine gland secreting insulin and glucagon, vital in carbohydrate (sugar) metabolism, into the bloodstream. The term also designates a gland found in many invertebrates the primary function of which is the secretion of digestive enzymes.

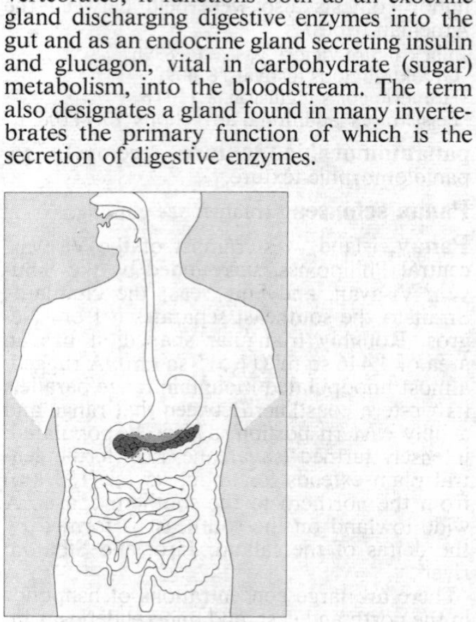
Pancreas

In man, the pancreas lies beneath the stomach in the curve of the duodenum, the upper portion of the small intestine, to which it is attached. A large main duct, the duct of Wirsung (*see* Wirsung, duct of), collects pancreatic juice and empties into the duodenum, usually in common with the termination of the common bile duct at the ampulla of Vater. In many individuals a smaller duct (duct of Santorini) also empties into the duodenum. Enzymes active in digestion of carbohydrate, fat, and protein flow through these ducts continuously and at an increased rate when food is present in the small intestine. About 41 fluid ounces of digestive juices are secreted daily. Flow is controlled by the vagus nerve and by the hormones secretin and pancreozymin, produced in the intestinal mucosa.

When food enters the duodenum, secretin and pancreozymin are released into the bloodstream by the duodenum's secretory cells. When these hormones reach the pancreas, its cells are stimulated to produce and release large amounts of digestive enzymes, which then flow into the intestine. As the enzymes reach the intestine, the duodenum stops producing its hormones, and the pancreas returns to its normal enzyme production level.

The cells that produce digestive enzymes are called acinar cells (Latin *acinus*, "grape"), so named because the cells aggregate to form bundles appearing much like a cluster of grapes. The base of the cell has fine tubules (endoplasmic reticulum) that produce the secretory granules. These granules are carried from the tubules to a more complex tubular apparatus (Golgi) that concentrates the secretions. The Golgi encase the enzymes in a thin membrane and send them to the apex of the cell. Here, the enzyme granules pass through the acinar cell wall into a complicated network of ducts that eventually reaches the small intestine.

Located between the clusters of acinar cells are scattered patches of another type of secretory tissue collectively known as the islands (or islets) of Langerhans, named for the 17th-century German pathologist Paul Langerhans. The islets are responsible for the secretion of insulin and glucagon, which control the amount of sugar stored in the body. Unlike the acinar tissue, however, the islets of Langerhans secrete their substances directly into the bloodstream. Insulin stimulates the body's cells to remove sugar from the bloodstream and utilize it. With a shortage of insulin, a condition termed diabetes mellitus, the sugar remains in the blood and liver tissue and is not metabolized. Too much insulin reduces the amount of sugar in the blood. Glucagon has the opposite effect of insulin; it releases stored sugar and increases the blood-sugar level, acting as a control mechanism when the normal body produces too much insulin.

The pancreas may be the site of acute and chronic infections, tumours, and cysts. Should it be removed surgically, life can be sustained by the administration of insulin and of potent pancreatic extracts. If only a small portion of the pancreas is wounded or removed, the pancreatic cells will multiply until sufficient new tissue has been regenerated to replace the old. *See also* pancreatitis.

comparative zoology
·animal tissue comparisons **18**:447e
·drug extraction from animal organs **14**:192g
·embryonic origin and developments **5**:639f
·hormone secretion in vertebrates **8**:1080c
·proinsulin production of insulin **15**:96g
·structure, function, and embryonic origin **6**:843f; illus. 841
·digestion mechanisms in vertebrates **5**:786d; illus. 784
human **5**:795e; illus. 791
·aging's impairment of endocrine system **1**:308c
·anatomy, blood supply, innervation, and hormones **6**:811f; illus. 800
·atrophy from duct obstruction **2**:353g
·Bernard's research on function **2**:860b
·cancer types and prognoses **3**:767h; table
·diabetes symptoms and treatment **6**:836c
·digestion and pancreatic enzymes **5**:777a
·digestive disorder causes and symptoms **5**:771c
·drug effects on function **18**:284c
·duodenum as site of disease symptoms **5**:800b
·embryonic origins from foregut **6**:753e
·pregnancy's effect on size and secretion **14**:975a
·vitamin involvement in pancreatic disease **5**:860h
·X-ray examination **15**:464d

pancreas of Asellius, or ASELLI'S PANCREAS, also called NODI LYMPHATICI MESENTERICI, or MESENTERIC LYMPH NODES, lymph nodes lying at the root of the mesentery.

·lymph node comparisons in mammals **11**:211a

pancreatic islets (biology): *see* islands of Langerhans.

pancreatic juice, also called SUCCUS PANCREATICUS, the liquid secretion of the pancreas.

·composition and digestive functions **5**:777a

pancreatic proteolytic enzymes: *see* proteolytic enzymes, pancreatic.

pancreatitis, inflammation of the pancreas. Development of the disorder has been associated with intake of alcohol and with obstruction of pancreatic ducts. The process of inflammation starts with the escape of activated pancreatic enzymes into the tissues of the pancreas. These digestive juices cause chemical irritation, with edema, or collection of fluid, and with congestion of the blood vessels. Often the inflammation then subsides, but occasionally there is bleeding, necrosis of pancreatic tissue, and formation of pus. Infection may set in. With recovery the necrotic areas are replaced with scar tissue.

The onset of pancreatitis may bring severe pain, most acute when the affected person is lying on his or her back. There may be slight fever, and the blood pressure may be somewhat higher than usual. If the attack is severe, the skin may be cold and moist, the pulse feeble and rapid, and the temperature below normal. Treatment of acute pancreatitis is directed toward control of pain, prevention or alleviation of shock, inhibition of the secretion of pancreatic juices, and avoidance of infection. Lost fluids and salts are replaced.

In chronic pancreatitis, with repeated attacks, much of the pancreas may be destroyed, with resultant deficiency in the amounts of pancreatic juices secreted. Islet cells of the pancreas may also be destroyed, so that the secretion of insulin is depleted and diabetes mellitus develops. Management includes a low-fat diet, abstinence from overeating and from intake of alcohol, the administration of pancreatic extracts, and control of diabetes if it has developed. *Major ref.* **5**:803e

·biomedical models, table 1 **5**:866
·common diseases of dogs, table 4 **5**:873
·physiological shock causes **16**:701b

pancreozymin (hormone): *see* cholecystokinin/pancreozymin.

panda, name given to two species of East Asian carnivores. The bearlike, black and

(Top) Giant panda (*Ailuropoda melanoleuca*); (bottom) lesser panda (*Ailurus fulgens*)

W. Suschitzky

white panda popular in zoos is the giant panda (*Ailuropoda melanoleuca*). Armand David, a Jesuit missionary, discovered some panda furs in 1869, but no European observed a live giant panda until the Stötzner Expedition of 1913–15. One of the rarest large mammals, the giant panda is classified by different authorities as either a relative of the raccoon (family Procyonidae) or as an aberrant bear (family Ursidae). It inhabits bamboo forests and is known only from the mountains of central China and eastern Tibet.

Growing to a length of 1.5 metres (5 feet) and a weight of about 160 kilograms (350 pounds), the stubby-tailed giant panda has a dense white coat marked with black on the ears and limbs, over the shoulders, and around the eyes. It feeds at night on bamboo, grasping the young stems and leaves with the aid of a special thumblike structure on its front foot. In addition to bamboo, it eats the leaves and roots of herbs, as well as flowers and some small animals. The giant panda is mainly terrestrial and lives alone except when breeding. One or two young are born in January. Su-Lin, first of the very few giant pandas to be seen in the West, reached the United States as an infant in 1936 and was a popular attraction at the Brookfield Zoo, near Chicago, until his death in 1938.

The lesser (red, or common) panda (*Ailurus fulgens*) is a small, attractive member of the raccoon family. It ranges from the eastern Himalayas to western China. Sometimes called bear cat or cat bear, it has soft, thick fur—rich reddish brown above and black underneath; the face is white, with a stripe of red brown from each eye to the corners of the mouth, and the bushy tail is faintly ringed. The head and body length of the lesser panda is 50–65 centimetres (20–26 inches); the tail, 30–50 centimetres (12–20 inches) long; and the weight ranges from 3–4.5 kilograms (6.6–10 pounds). It lives high in the mountains among rocks and trees and climbs with agility. It is nocturnal and may live alone, in pairs, or in family groups. The diet consists mainly of fruit and other plant material. The litters generally contain one or two young born in spring after a gestation period of about 130 days. The lesser panda is gentle and easily tamed but usually resents being handled.

·anatomy and traits **3**:929g *passim* to 931g
·Asian distribution **2**:170e
·classification and general features **9**:942f

pandāl, a tent or pavilion in which the Hindu marriage ceremony is performed.

·ritual importance for marriage ceremony **3**:1180a

Pandanales, an order of monocotyledonous flowering plants containing 1 family (Pandanaceae, the screw-pine family), 3 genera, and about 700 species of trees, shrubs, and vines. The genus *Pandanus* (600 species) produces from the trunk and branches stiltlike aerial prop roots that support the plants and give them a distinctive appearance. The main root usually decomposes and disappears, leaving the plant entirely supported by these stout, slanted flying buttress roots. The genus *Freycinetia* (100 species) consists of shrubby vines that climb by means of aerial roots produced from the stem like the brace roots of *Pandanus*, but they are much more slender. The genus *Sararanga* (two species) consists of trees that lack both aerial roots and the spiral leaf arrangement found in the other plants of the order. In nearly all members of the order, numerous long, narrow, parallel-veined, palmlike leaves with spiny margins and midribs are produced in tufts at the branch tips in three or four close, twisted ranks around the stem, forming the screwlike helices of leaves that give the common name screw-pine to these plants. The plants grow along seacoasts and in marshy places and forests of tropical and subtropical regions, especially in Asia and Africa.

The flowers are simple, petalless, usually densely clustered and are either male or

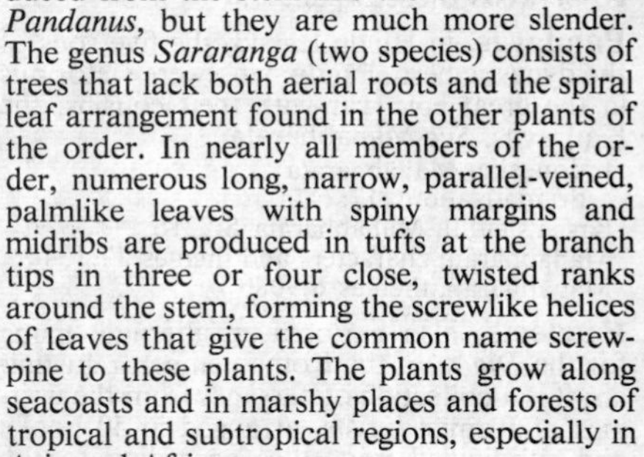

Screw-pine (*Pandanus tectorius*)

G.R. Roberts

female, the sexes being produced on different plants. The fruits of many are heavy ball-shaped or conelike aggregates produced by the coalescence of the developing ovaries of many adjacent flowers. Often there are hollow spaces inside the fruits that aid in distribution by floating. Fruit-eating birds are also thought to distribute the seeds of some.

Much use is made of the leaves for thatching, mats, hat making, ropes, twine, sails for small boats, baskets, and fibre products, especially from the textile screw-pine (*Pandanus tectorius*). Fibres are also obtained from the aerial roots. The fruits and seeds of many species are edible (*e.g.*, *P. utilis* and the Nicobar Islands breadfruit, *P. leram*). A small number of species are grown as greenhouse subjects (*e.g.*, *P. pygmaeus*, *P. veitchi*, and *P. utilis*). The candelabrum, or chandelier, tree (*P. candelabrum*) is especially favoured as an outdoor ornamental in warm regions throughout the world and as a conservatory plant and houseplant.

The order is considered to be related to the cattail order (Typhales) and the Panama-hat-palm order (Cyclanthales), but the relationships are not clear.

·angiosperm features and classification **1**:884g
·Pandaceae classification and general features **6**:1030e
·Polynesian uses of pandanus **14**:780a
·P. veitchii as house plant **8**:1120e
·screw-pine prop roots, illus., **18**:Tree, Plate II

Pandarus, in Greek legend, son of Lycaon, a Lycian. In the *Iliad* he broke the truce between the Trojans and the Greeks by treacherously wounding Menelaus, the king of Sparta; he was finally slain by the warrior Diomedes. In the medieval tale of Troilus and Cressida, as well as in Shakespeare's play by the same name, Pandarus acted as the lovers' go-between; hence "pander."

Pāṇḍavas, in Hindu legend, the five sons of the dynastic hero, Pāṇḍu, who were victorious in the great epic war with their cousins, the Kauravas. *See* Mahābhārata.

·Indonesian Mahābhārata dramatizations **17**:247a
·Kṛṣṇa's aid in Mahābhārata **8**:931b
·Mahābhārata characters and themes **17**:134c
·Mahābhārata themes **6**:908b

Pandects, also PANDECTAE, alternate name for the *Digest* of the Roman emperor Justinian; it is a collection of passages from the writings of Roman jurists, arranged in 50 books and subdivided into titles according to the subject matter (*see also* Justinian code). In AD 530 Justinian entrusted its compilation to the jurist Tribonian with instructions to appoint a commission to help him. The Pandects were published in AD 533 and given statutory force.

Early in the 19th century the term Pandectists was applied to the historical school of Roman-law scholars in Germany who resumed the scientific study of the Pandects. The leader of the school was Friedrich Karl von Savigny. In the course of the century extensive treatises were produced, notably by Georg Friedrich Puchta, Heinrich Dernburg, and Bernhard Windscheid.

·Poliziano's historiographic researches **8**:952d
·purpose and scope of codification **15**:1056e

pandemic: *see* epidemic.

Pandemos (goddess): *see* Aphrodite.

Pander, Christian Heinrich (1794–1865), German anatomist, influential in founding the modern study of embryology; his observation that the germinal membrane of the fertilized egg forms three layers during the embryo's early development led him to propose the concept of germ layers. He also studied the development of the chick embryo with the German embryologist Karl Ernst von Baer.

·chick embryonic development **2**:582c
·germ layer concept's introduction **19**:1164c

Panderma (Turkey): *see* Bandırma.

Panderma rugs, rugs handwoven at Panderma (or Bandırma), a town in Turkey on the southern shore of the Sea of Marmora, usually as imitations of Ghiordes prayer rug designs (*see* Ghiordes carpets). The enterprise was begun early in the 20th century, perhaps with weavers from Ghiordes, though it is usually described as an Armenian establishment. Panderma imitations are usually more finicky in their draftsmanship than the originals, with over-elaboration of some areas, such as the sides of the prayer-niche design, and a differing colour range, including pastel shades and opaline effects. As in less plausible counterfeits made elsewhere, there may be a general hardness of effect, in contrast with the true Ghiordes products.

Anatolian Panderma rug designed to imitate a Ghiordes prayer rug, 20th century; in a private collection in New York state

New York state private collection; photograph, Otto E. Nelson—EB Inc.

pandermite (mineral): *see* priceite.

Pandharpur, religious and administrative town, Sholāpur district, Mahārāshtra state, western India, on the Bhīma River, west of Sholāpur town. Easily reached by road and rail, it is visited throughout the year by thousands of Hindu pilgrims. Four major annual festivals are held in honour of the deities Viṭhoba, an incarnation of Viṣṇu (Vishnu), and his consort, Rukmiṇī. The main temple was built in the 12th century by the Yādavas of Devagiri. The town is also associated with the Mahārāshtra poet-saints devoted to the Bhakti cult. Pop. (1971 prelim.) 53,634.
17°39′ N, 75°20′ E

pandiatonicism, in music, term introduced by Nicolas Slonimsky to describe the 20th-century technique of using the diatonic scale instead of the chromatic scale as a tonal basis without conventional harmonic limitations.

·harmony of Stravinsky and Les Six **8**:654b

Pandit, Vijaya Lakshmi, *née* SWARUP KUMARI NEHRU (b. Aug. 18, 1900, Allahābād, India), political leader and diplomat, one of the world's leading women in public life in the 20th century. She was the daughter of Motilal Nehru, Indian nationalist leader, and sister of Jawaharlal Nehru, the first prime minister of independent India. Privately educated in India and abroad, in 1921 she married Ranjit S. Pandit (died 1944), a fellow Congress worker. In her family's tradition she became an active worker in the Indian nationalist movement and was imprisoned three times by the British authorities in India. She entered municipal government in Allahābād (western India) before entering the legislative assembly of the United Provinces (later Uttar Pradesh) and becoming minister for local self-government and public health (1937–39), the first Indian woman to hold a cabinet portfolio.

Vijaya Pandit, 1955

Keystone

With the coming of Indian independence, Mrs. Pandit entered on a distinguished diplomatic career, leading the Indian delegation to the United Nations (1946–48, 1952–53) and serving as India's ambassador to Moscow (1947–49) and to Washington and Mexico (1949–51). In 1953 she became the first woman president of the UN General Assembly. From 1954 to 1961 she was Indian high commissioner (ambassador) in London and concurrently ambassador to Dublin. She served as governor of the state of Mahārāshtra from 1962 to 1964. In November 1964 she became a member of the Indian Lok Sabha (Parliament), representing the constituency formerly represented by her brother, Jawaharlal Nehru.

Panditārādhya Caritra, 13th-century Telugu text by Pālkuriki Sōmanātha on the life of the Saiva saint Paṇḍitārādhya.

·theme and diverse subjects **17**:141c

Pandjari River (Western Africa): *see* Oti River.

Pandji, called INAO in Burma, Thailand, Cambodia, and Laos, group of stories and plays popular in Indonesia and Malaysia and based on similar Indian stories of the Paṇḍava family.

Pando, department, northern Bolivia, bounded north and east by Brazil and west by Peru. Created in 1938, the area of 24,644 sq mi (63,827 sq km) lies in the Amazon Basin, where there is considerable rain, heat, and humidity. It is watered by many streams, the largest of which is the Madre de Dios River (*q.v.*). The main economic resources are forest products: rubber, quinine, Brazil nuts, and hardwoods. Crops include rice, sugarcane, manioc, bananas, and corn (maize). Cobija (*q.v.*), the capital, can be reached by air, but, otherwise, transportation is by river. Isolation, poor communications, and sparse population hinder development of the region. Pop. (1971 est.) 33,200.

·area and population table and map **3**:6
·map, Bolivia **3**:2

Pandolpho (bishop): *see* Pandulph.

Pandora (Greek: All-giving), in Greek mythology, the first woman. After Prometheus, a fire god and divine trickster, had stolen fire from heaven and bestowed it upon mortals, Zeus, the king of the gods, determined to counteract this blessing. He accordingly commissioned Hephaestus (a god of fire and patron of craftsmen) to fashion a woman out of earth, upon whom the gods bestowed their choicest gifts. She had or found a jar—the so-called Pandora's box—containing all kinds of misery and evil. Zeus sent her to Epimetheus, who forgot the warning of his brother Prometheus and made her his wife. Pandora afterward opened the jar, from which all manner of evils flew out over the earth. According to another version, Hope alone remained inside, the lid having been shut down before she could escape. In a later story, the jar contained not evils but blessings, which would have been preserved for the human race had they not been lost through the opening of the jar out of curiosity by man himself.

·Hesiod's account of the first woman **8**:830f

pandora (stringed instrument): *see* cittern.

Pandora's Box (1892–1901), play by Frank Wedekind.

·dramatic use of the grotesque **4**:964g

Pandorina morum, species of green algae (phylum Chlorophyta).

·protozoan reproductive variation **15**:123g

Pandulph, also PANDULF or PANDOLPHO (b. Rome—d. Sept. 16, 1226, Rome), papal legate to England and bishop of Norwich who was deeply involved in English secular politics. Pope Innocent III sent him to England in an effort to secure King John's acceptance of Stephen Langton as archbishop of Canterbury. When the negotiations failed, John was excommunicated, and England was placed under papal interdict. On May 15, 1213, however, Pandulph accepted John's personal submission and surrender of the country as a fief of the Pope, whose vassal the King became. John also permitted Langton to assume the see of Canterbury. Allying himself with John, Pandulph used ecclesiastical censures, including excommunication, to avert a threatened French invasion of England and suspended Archbishop Langton for refusing to excommunicate the barons and extracted Magna Carta (charter of liberties) from the King (June 19, 1215). For these services John rewarded Pandulph with the see of Norwich. After John's death (Oct 18/19, 1216), Pandulph was prominent in the regency for the boy king Henry III until 1220 or 1221, when Langton induced Innocent's successor, Pope Honorius III, to recall him.

Pandulph III (b. *c.* 987—d. 1049), prince of Capua, prominent Lombard leader who alternately employed and fought against the Normans in the early years of their conquest of southern Italy.

Deserting his own Lombard people in 1019, Pandulph gave his allegiance to the Byzantines, aiding the Greek general Boiannes when he invaded southern Italy in 1021 and handing over the Lombard leader Dattus of Bari to be executed. The Holy Roman emperor Henry II made a punitive expedition to Italy to avenge Dattus, besieging Capua in 1022 and capturing Pandulph, whom he imprisoned in Germany, giving the throne of Capua to another Lombard lord.

Released by Henry's successor, Pandulph set to work to recover his principality, enlisting allies, including the Norman soldier of fortune Ranulph Drengo. Capua fell after a long siege (1026), and, when an opportunity presented itself the following year, Pandulph seized Naples, from where he also controlled Salerno, ruled by his sister. But Ranulph Drengo deserted him and helped Naples' former ruler, Duke Sergius, retake his city.

When the first Hauteville brothers, Normans who in less than 100 years conquered southern Italy, arrived on the scene, they enlisted as mercenaries in Pandulph's service, facilitating new aggressions on his part. He seized Gaeta (northwest of Naples), threatening the rich territories of the abbey of Monte Cassino. In 1036, however, Pandulph was accused of attempting to rape the niece of Gaimar V of Salerno, who appealed to the emperor Conrad II for help. When Conrad invaded southern Italy, Pandulph fled to a castle east of Capua and thence to Constantinople, where his former Byzantine allies threw him in prison. In 1041 he was allowed to return to Italy, and four years later a new emperor, Henry III, restored Capua to him. He was soon once more embroiled in war with Gaimar of Salerno and died amid the shifting contentions of Lombards and Normans.

Pandulph Ironhead (d. March 981), prince of Capua and Benevento and an important ally of the Holy Roman emperor Otto I, whose acquisition of Spoleto and Salerno unified all the Lombard states of central and southern Italy.

Co-ruler with his father, Landulph II, from 944, Pandulph successfully defended Capua against attack by Pope John XII. After Landulph's death in 961, Pandulph ruled with his brother Landulph III. In 963 he welcomed Otto, the newly crowned emperor, to Capua and became his vassal. Four years later Otto invested him with the duchy of Spoleto.

When Otto invaded Byzantine Apulia (the "heel" of Italy) in 968, Pandulph supported him, taking over the fighting in 969 when Otto was called to northern Italy. During the siege of Bovino Pandulph was captured by the Byzantines and taken to Constantinople. After the assassination of Emperor Nicephorus Phocas (969), Pandulph persuaded the new emperor, John Tzimisces, to negotiate with Otto, and he was sent back to Italy to assist in peace talks that resulted in the marriage of the Byzantine princess Thephano to the German emperor's son, the future Otto II.

When a rebellion unseated Salerno's Prince Gisulph, Pandulph helped him regain his throne (974), and in return Gisulph made Pandulph's son, also named Pandulph, his heir; when the younger Pandulph became prince of Salerno in 977, Pandulph Ironhead annexed Salerno, thus uniting the Lombard states of Benevento, Capua, Spoleto, and Salerno. After his death his lands were divided among his sons, dissipating the Lombard principality.

·Otto I and Italian expansion **9**:1126e

Panduvasudeva, 5th-century-BC king of Ceylon of the Vijaya dynasty.

·Ceylonese Mahāvaṃsa settlement account **4**:1h

Pāṇḍya, a Tamil dynasty of the extreme south of India of unknown antiquity (they are mentioned by Greek authors in the 4th century BC). The Roman emperor Julian received an embassy from a Pāṇḍya *c.* AD 361. The dynasty revived under Kaḍuṅgōn in the early 7th century AD and ruled from Madura or farther south until the 16th century. The small but important (9th–13th century) dynasty of Pāṇḍya of Ucchangi, a hill fort south of the Tungabhadra River, may have originated from the Madura family.

The Pāṇḍya kings were called either Jatavarman or Maravarman. From being Jains they became Śaivas (worshippers of Śiva) and are celebrated in the earliest Tamil poetry. They ruled extensive territories, at times including the Cēra (or Kerala) country, the Cōḷa country, and Ceylon through collateral branches subject to Madura. The "Five Pāṇḍyas" flourished from the 12th to 14th century and eventually assumed control of all the plains of the extreme south as far north as Nellore (1257). Family quarrels, however, and Muslim invasions, from 1311 onward, culminating in the foundation of the Madura sultanate, weakened Pāṇḍya influence. By 1312 control over Kerala was lost and by the mid-16th century all their territories had passed into other hands.

·Ceylonese tradition and history **4**:1g *passim* to 4d

·Rājput dynastic histories **9**:363e

panegyric, eulogistic oration or laudatory discourse that originally was a speech delivered at an ancient Greek general assembly (*panegyris*), such as the Olympic and Panathenaic festivals. Speakers often took advantage of these occasions, when Greeks of various cities were gathered together, to advocate Hellenic unity. With this end in view and also to gratify their audience, they tended to expatiate on the former glories of Greek cities; hence came the encomiastic associations that eventually clung to the term panegyric. The most famous ancient Greek panegyrics to survive intact are the *Panegyricus* (*c.* 380 BC) and the *Panathenaicus* (*c.* 340 BC), both by Isocrates.

Akin to panegyric was the *epitaphion*, or funeral oration, ancient and modern examples being Pericles' funeral speech as recorded by Thucydides, a panegyric both on war heros and on Athens itself, and Abraham Lincoln's Gettysburg Address.

In the 2nd century AD, Aelius Aristides, a Greek rhetorician, combined praise of famous cities with eulogy of the reigning Roman emperor. By his time panegyric had probably become specialized in the latter connection and was, therefore, related to the old Roman custom of celebrating at festivals the glories of famous men of the past and of pronouncing *laudationes funebres* at the funerals of eminent persons.

Another kind of Roman eulogistic speech was the *gratiarum actio* ("thanksgiving"), delivered by a successful candidate for public office. The *XII Panegyrici Latini*, an ancient collection of these speeches, includes the *gratiarum actio* delivered by Pliny the Younger when he was nominated consul by the emperor Trajan in AD 100. Late Roman writers of the 3rd to the 5th century indiscriminately praised and flattered the emperors in panegyrics that were sometimes written in verse.

Although primarily a literary form associated with classical antiquity, panegyric continued to be written on occasion in the Middle Ages, often by Christian mystics in praise of God, and in the Renaissance and Baroque periods, especially in Elizabethan England, in Spain during the *siglo d'oro*, and in France under the reign of Louis XIV.

·Isocrates' theme and content **9**:1031g

panēgyris (pl. *panēgyreis*, Greek: "gathering"), in Greek religion, an ancient assembly that met on certain fixed dates for the purpose of honouring a specific god. The gatherings varied in size from the inhabitants of a single town to great national meetings, such as the Olympic Games. The religious aspect of the meetings was by far the most important, and included prayers, feasts, and processions. The populace, however, was probably more attracted to the amusements, games, fairs, and festive orations (panegyrics) that occurred at the gatherings.

panel chair: *see* wainscot chair.

panel heating: *see* radiant heating.

panelling, in architecture and design, decorative treatment of walls, ceilings, doors, and furniture consisting of a series of wide, thin sheets of wood, called panels, framed together by narrower, thicker strips of wood. The latter are called styles (the external vertical strips), muntins (the internal vertical strips), and rails (the horizontal strips).

Simple panelling on doors was used in Classical architecture, both Greek and Roman, as it was in the transitional Italian Romanesque interiors. Its extensive use on walls and furnishings, however, began in the Gothic period. The richness and warmth of interior wood panelling is a highly characteristic aspect of the Tudor and Elizabethan styles of decoration in England. Early Tudor walls are profusely carved, often in fielded panels, in which the central area is raised above the framing. One particularly popular form of fielded panel was the linenfold, featuring stylized carvings that represent vertically folded linen; Hampton Court Palace near London contains many superb examples. In the English Renaissance, panelling became simpler; in the France of Kings Louis XIV and XV, it was lavish and ornate; and in the Italian Renaissance, architects restricted its use to ceilings. In 17th-century New England, panelling was used but without decoration; in the 18th century it became more decorative, especially in the Southern colonies.

Salon de la Princesse in the Hôtel de Soubise, Paris, Rococo style panelled room designed by Germain Boffrand (begun 1732)

Wayne Andrews

While in all of these historical instances panelling was almost always either oak or pine, in the 20th century an enormous variety of materials is used: solid wood (walnut, mahogany, birch, redwood), plywood (a thin wood veneer on a plywood base), vinyl with surface imitating wood grain, hardboard, or pressed wood, pegboard, and even translucent materials such as lucite.

·furniture adaptation in the Middle Ages **7**:784d
·human comfort factors **8**:712f
·interior design historical use **9**:710a; illus.
·panel furniture origin and Renaissance use **7**:796e
·stained glass and architectural traditions **17**:575c
·wood panelling craftsmanship **9**:695g

panel painting, painting executed on a rigid support—ordinarily wood or metal—as distinct from painting done on canvas. Before canvas came into general use at the end of the 16th century, the panel was the support most often used for easel painting (*q.v.*). A variety of woods has been used, including beech, cedar, chestnut, fir, larch, linden, white poplar, mahogany, olive, dark walnut, and teak. Wooden panels were usually boiled or steamed to remove gum and resin and thereby prevent splitting, then coated with size (a glutinous material, to fill the pores in the surface) and with gesso (a mixture of glue and gypsum, chalk, or whiting), on which the painting was executed. Metals used for panel paintings include silver, tin, and even lead and zinc.

During the Middle Ages, especially in Russia, paintings were executed on panels over which leather had been stretched.

·Byzantine visual art forms and styles **19**:330f
·themes and decorative functions **13**:881e

Front of the Wilton Diptych, "Richard II Presented to the Virgin," panel paintings by an anonymous artist of the French school, 15th century; in the National Gallery, London

By courtesy of the trustees of the National Gallery, London

panentheism (philosophy): *see* pantheism and panentheism.

Paneth, Friedrich Adolf (b. Aug. 31, 1887, Vienna—d. Sept. 17, 1958, Vienna), chemist who with George Charles de Hevesy introduced radioactive tracer techniques (1912–13). Following study at Munich, Glasgow, and Vienna, he held positions at the Radium Institute, Vienna, and in Prague, Hamburg, Berlin, and Königsberg. Upon the rise of the Nazis he went to the Imperial College of Science and Technology, London (1933–38), and then became professor of chemistry at Durham (1939). In 1953 he returned to West Germany as director of the Max Planck Institute at Mainz.

Between 1918 and 1922 Paneth prepared hydrides of bismuth, lead, and polonium with radioactive isotopes. Beginning in 1929 he furnished proof of the brief existence of the methyl and ethyl free radicals. His microanalytical work in rare gases led him to study the composition of the atmosphere and to conclude that the composition of air is constant at least to an altitude of approximately 38 miles (about 60 kilometres). His measurement of helium from the radioactive decomposition of earth rocks and meteorites led to methods for ascertaining their age.

Paneth cell, specialized type of epithelial cell found in the mucous membrane lining of the small intestine and of the appendix, at the base of tubelike depressions known as Lieberkühn glands. Named for a 19th-century Austrian physician, Joseph Paneth, the Paneth cell has one nucleus at its base and densely packed secretory granules throughout the rest of its body. The cells' shape is either narrow, pyramidal, or columnar.

Their function is not totally known, nor is the manner in which they discharge their granules. They are thought to secrete the enzyme peptidase, which breaks peptide molecules into amino acids suitable for assimilation by the body. In man, the granules are found to contain carbohydrates, proteins, and radioactive zinc. In mice, a specific protein (lysozyme), known to destroy some bacteria, is believed to be present in the granules. This suggests that the Paneth cell might also have an antibacterial function.

·human digestive system anatomy **5**:794b

Panevėžys, city and regional economic centre, north central Lithuanian Soviet Socialist Republic, on the Nevėžis River. First mentioned in 1503 in the writings of Alexander, grand prince of Lithuania (1492–1506) and king of Poland (1501–06), it was chartered as a district town in 1842.

Agricultural trade is important; the leading industry is food processing (especially sugar refining). There are steel mills, glassworks, and a large flax-processing plant. The city has schools of technology, music, and medicine and is the home of the Panevėžys Drama Theatre (founded 1940, new building completed 1967), which has become a celebrated Lithuanian national institution. Pop. (1973 est.) 84,000.
55°44′ N, 24°21′ E

·population and regional importance **10**:1265d

Panfilov, formerly DZHARKENT, city, administrative centre of the Panfilovsky *rayon* (district) in the Taldy-Kurgan *oblast*, Kazakh S.S.R. It was renamed in 1942 for Maj. Gen. I.V. Panfilov, a World War II hero. The city has cotton ginning and metalworking industries. Pop. (1970) 19,173.
44°10′ N, 80°01′ E

Pangaea (landmass): *see* Gondwanaland.

Pangalos, Theodoros (b. Jan. 11, 1878, Salamís, Greece—d. Feb. 26, 1952, Athens), soldier and statesman who for eight months in 1926 was dictator of Greece.

After service in World War I and the ill-starred Greek campaign in western Turkey (1921–22), he was appointed minister of war shortly after the abdication of King Constantine (1922). He directed the military court that condemned those responsible for the rout of Greek forces at Afyon, Tur., in August 1922 and the later massacre of Greeks in Smyrna (now Izmir, Tur.). In 1923 he also served as commander in chief in Thrace. In June 1925 he staged a coup and had himself installed as prime minister, and on Jan. 3, 1926, he proclaimed himself dictator. In April he procured his own election as president but was finally deposed in a coup by his own Republican Guard (Aug. 22, 1926). His arbitrary rule brought an eight-month suspension of Parliament, a near war with Bulgaria (October 1925), and half-comic attempts to regulate public morality. After his retirement from public life he was sentenced to two years' imprisonment in a building scandal (1930). In World War II he was accused of having collaborated with the Germans and Italians, but the charges remained unsubstantiated.

Pangani, town, northeast Tanzania, at the mouth of the Pangani River, on the Pemba Channel of the Indian Ocean. It was once a slave-trading depot at the terminus of Arab caravan routes; its ancient buildings and narrow lanes are now falling into decay. It is an important commercial centre, exporting sisal, copra, cotton, and sugar. Pop. (latest census) 2,955.
5°26′ S, 38°58′ E

·map, Tanzania **17**:1027

Pangani River, in northeast Tanzania, flows about 250 mi (400 km) from Kilimanjaro southeast into the Indian Ocean northwest of the island of Zanzibar. Pangani Falls, just west of the town of Pangani, is an important source of hydroelectric power.
5°26′ S, 38°58′ E

·hydroelectric power complex **17**:1031f
·map, Tanzania **17**:1027

Pangasiidae, a family of Asian catfish of the order Siluriformes of the superorder Ostariophysi.

·classification and general features **13**:762h

Pangasinan, province, central Luzon, Philippines, bounded by the Lingayen Gulf and the

South China Sea (west) and the provinces of La Union, Nueva Vizcaya, and Benguet (north), Nueva Ecija (east), and Tarlac and Zambales (south). It includes Santiago and Cabarruyan islands in the Lingayen Gulf and has an area of 2,073 sq mi (5,368 sq km). Drained by the Agno River, the province is basically agricultural (rice, corn [maize], coconuts, fruits). It is inhabited by Pangasinenses (members of the eighth largest Philippine ethno-linguistic group) and Ilocanos from northern Luzon. Its name is based on the word *asin* ("salt") because of the salt industry along the Lingayen Gulf. The provincial capital, Lingayen, was the site of U.S. landings during World War II. Dagupan (*q.v.*), the chief port, is a chartered city. The towns of Binmaley, Mangaldan, and Calasiao are in the northern portion of the Agno River plain, while Manaoag, San Carlos, and Bayambang are inland population centres. Pop. (1970) 1,386,143.

·area and population table **14**:236

Pangasinan, eighth largest cultural-linguistic group in the Republic of the Philippines. They occupy the central area of the province of Pangasinan in Luzon. They are predominantly Roman Catholic. There has been considerable intermarriage with the Ilocano, who in the 1960s constituted about half of the total provincial population. Their language is closely related to others of the central Philippines, all of which belong to the Austronesian (Malayo-Polynesian) family of languages.

The area is one of the richest agricultural regions of the Philippines. The chief crop is rice, much of which goes by rail to the Manila markets. Minor crops are maize, mangoes and other fruits, sugarcane, tobacco, and coconuts.

pangenesis (evolutionary theory): *see* gemmule.

Pan-Germanism, movement whose goal has been the political unification of all people speaking German or a Germanic language. Some of its adherents favoured the unification of only the German-speaking people of central and eastern Europe and the Low Countries (Dutch and Flemish being regarded as Germanic dialects). The movement had its roots in the desire for German unification stimulated by the war of liberation (1813–15) against Napoleon I and fanned by such early German nationalists as Friedrich Ludwig Jahn and Ernst Moritz Arndt. Advocates of the Grossdeutschland solution wished also to include the Germans of the Austrian Empire in one German nation. Others wished also to include the Scandinavians. Writers such as Friedrich List, Paul Anton Lagarde, and Konstantin Franz argued for German hegemony in central and eastern Europe—where German domination in some areas had begun as early as the 9th century AD with the *Drang nach Osten* (expansion to the East)—to ensure European peace. The notion of the superiority of the "Aryan race" proposed by Joseph-Arthur, comte de Gobineau, in his *Essai sur l'inégalité des races humaines* (1853–55; Eng. trans. *Essay on the Inequality of Human Races*, 1907) influenced many Germans to extol the Nordic, or German, "race."

The Pan-German Movement was organized in 1894, when Ernst Hasse, a professor at Leipzig and a member of the Reichstag (parliament), set up the *Alldeutscher Verband* (Pan-German League) on the basis of the loosely organized *Allgemeiner Deutscher Verband* (General German League) founded in 1891. Its purpose was to heighten German nationalist consciousness, especially among German-speaking people outside Germany. In his three-volume work *Deutsche Politik* (1905–07), Hasse called for German imperialist expansion in Europe. Georg Ruter von Schönerer and Karl Hermann Wolf articulated Pan-Germanist sentiments in Austria-Hungary and also attacked Slavs, Jews, and capitalism. These ideas did much to mold the mind of Adolf Hitler. Under the Weimar Republic (1919–33), Pan-Germanists continued to press for expansion; the most articulate and active force toward that end was Hitler and the Nazi Party. Expansionist propaganda was buttressed by a theory called geopolitics, which made history subject to a kind of geographical determinism. The expansionism preached by Munich professor Karl Haushofer, together with Ewald Banse, author of *Raum und Volk im Weltkriege* (1932); and Hans Grimm, author of *Folk ohne Raum* (1926) was put into practice by Hitler in his annexation of Austria and the German-speaking area of Czechoslovakia and in the demands he made on Poland that led to the outbreak of World War II. Defeat in 1945 not only brought an end to the Third Reich and its European hegemony but also resulted in the expulsion of Germans from formerly German areas of Eastern Europe, the loss of a large portion of territory on Germany's eastern frontier, and the division of the remaining German territory into two states. Since then Pan-Germanism has diminished in influence.

·Austrian nationalities struggle **2**:470f
·Hitler foreign policy development **8**:968a
·Stresemann's expansionist policies **17**:732f

Pang-fou, also called PANG-PU, Pin-yin romanization, respectively, BANG-FOU and BANG-BU, a city in north central Anhwei Province (*sheng*), China, with autonomous sub-provincial-level municipality (*shih*) status. The name Pang-fou is mentioned in the early 1st millennium BC in connection with the myths surrounding the culture hero Emperor Yü. But, throughout most of Chinese history, it was merely a small market town and port on the middle course of the Huai Ho (river). The city comprises two parts—greater Pang-fou, on the south bank of the Huai, and little Pang-fou, on the northern bank.

Its modern growth began with the construction in 1912 of the great trunk railway from Tientsin to P'u-k'ou, opposite Nanking, on the Yangtze River (Ch'ang Chiang)—a route that crossed the Huai. The river traffic on the Huai made Pang-fou the natural collecting centre for the agricultural produce, especially grain, cotton, peanuts (groundnuts), and soya beans, from much of northern Anhwei. Pang-fou's importance as a communication centre was further increased with the completion in 1944 of a railway linking it to Ho-fei and to the Huai-nan coalfield. In addition it is also the centre of a road network, connecting it with K'ai-feng in Honan to the northwest and with Ho-fei to the south.

Since 1949, particularly since the improvement of the Huai Ho system and the restoration of the Yün Ho (Grand Canal), Pang-fou's position as the chief commercial centre of the middle Huai Ho Valley has been consolidated. Industrial growth, however, was comparatively slow. There are coal mines at Huai-yüan, to the northwest, and copper mines have been reported opened in the vicinity. Industrial capacity, however, remained minimal as late as 1963. Latest pop. est. 330,000. 32°58′ N, 117°24′ E

·machine-accessories production **1**:903b
·map, China **4**:262

Pang Hsün, 9th-century Chinese rebel leader.

·T'ang dynasty internal rebellion **4**:328a

Pangkor, Pulau (Malaysia): *see* Dindings.

Pangkor Engagement (1874), treaty between the British government and Malay chiefs in Perak; the first step in the establishment of British dominion over the Malay states. In January 1874 Gov. Andrew Clarke of the Straits Settlements, prompted by the local trading community, organized a meeting between British, Malay, and Chinese leaders to settle a Perak succession dispute and to stop warfare between Chinese secret societies. Named after Pangkor Island, off the Perak coast, the engagement adjudicated these issues. The complicated Perak succession controversy was settled in favour of Raja Abdullah, the candidate supported by Lower Perak chiefs, who had been passed over in the 1871 succession. Ismail, the Upper Perak contender, absent from the meeting, was pensioned off with an annual allowance and was granted the honorific title of *sultan muda*. In return for British backing, Abdullah agreed to accept a British resident (adviser) with broad powers at his court. The Chinese-secret-society issue was settled in the separate Chinese Engagement (*q.v.*). Similar agreements were later signed with other Malay states, achieving de facto British rule of the Malay Peninsula by 1914.

pangolin, or SCALY ANTEATER, any of the armoured placental mammals of the order Pholidota. Pangolin, from the Malayan meaning "rolling over," refers to this animal's habit of curling into a ball when threatened. About eight species of pangolins, usually considered in the genus *Manis*, family Manidae, are found in tropical Asia and Africa. Pangolins are 30 to 90 centimetres (1 to 3 feet) long exclusive of the tail and weigh from 5 to 27 kilograms (10 to 60 pounds). Except for the sides of the face and underside of the body, they are covered with overlapping brownish scales composed of cemented hairs. The head is short and conical, with small, thickly lidded eyes and a long, toothless muzzle; the tongue is wormlike and extensile, up to 25 centimetres (10 inches) in length. The legs are short, and the five-toed feet are armed with sharp claws. The tail, about as long as the body, is used to grasp with and forms, with the hind legs, a tripod for support.

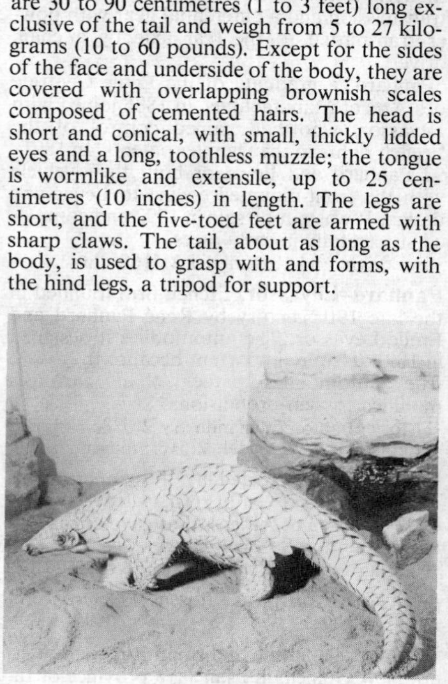

Indian pangolin (*Manis crassicaudatus*)
By courtesy of the New York Zoological Society

Some pangolins, such as the African black-bellied pangolin (*Manis longicaudata*) and the Chinese pangolin (*M. pentadactyla*), are almost entirely arboreal; others, such as the giant pangolin (*M. gigantea*) of Africa, are terrestrial. All are nocturnal and able to swim a little. Terrestrial forms live in burrows. Pangolins feed mainly on termites but also eat ants and other insects. They locate prey by smell and use the forefeet to rip open nests.

The means of defense are the emission of a odorous secretion from large anal glands and the ploy of rolling up, presenting erected scales to the enemy. Pangolins are timid and live alone or in pairs. Apparently usually one young is born at a time, soft scaled at birth and carried on the female's back for some time. Life-span is about 12 years.

Pangolins were once grouped with the true anteaters, sloths, and armadillos in the order Edentata, mainly because of superficial likenesses to South American anteaters. Pangolins differ from edentates, however, in many fundamental anatomical characters.

The earliest fossil Pholidota are bones indistinguishable from those of the African giant pangolin, found in a cave in India, and dating to the Pleistocene Epoch (beginning 2,500,000 years ago).

·evolutionary relationships, illus. 6 **11**:414
·relation to Edentata **6**:303c

Pango-Pango (Tutuila): *see* Pago Pago.

Pang-pu (China): *see* Pang-fou.

pang-tzu ch'iang, also known as CLAPPER OPERA, type of Chinese opera of the Ming dynasty.
·string instrumental accompaniment **12**:675f

Panguingue (card game): *see* Pan.

Pangwa, a people of southern Tanzania and Malawi, of the Nyasa cluster of Tanganyika Bantu.
·creation myth **1**:237f

Panhard, René (b. 1841, Paris—d. 1908, La Bourbole, Fr.), automobile engineer and manufacturer who, with Émile Levassor, produced the first vehicle with an internal-combustion engine mounted at the front of the chassis rather than under the driver's seat. Their vehicle became the prototype of the modern automobile. It had a sliding gear transmission and a differential gear with power transmitted to the rear axle by a chain drive.

Panhard, a graduate of the École Centrale des Arts et Manufactures, in 1886 joined with Levassor, who had gained control of the French rights to the Daimler patents. In 1891–92 Panhard and Levassor built their vehicle with the front-mounted engine to Levassor's design. It was put on sale in 1892 and competed successfully in early races.
·firm origin and 1891 model **2**:516f; illus.

Panhard–Levassor, French firm founded in the late 19th century by René Panhard and Émile Levassor. The automobiles it designed in 1891–94 were important because they were true automobiles rather than carriages modified for self-propulsion.
·history of automotive industry **2**:528c
·origins and 1891 model **2**:516f; illus.

Panhellenion, created by the emperor Hadrian in the 2nd century AD, a federation of Greeks, based at Athens, that gave equal representation to all Greek cities.
·Hadrian's creation and significance **8**:540d

panhypopituitarism (disease): *see* Simmonds' disease.

Paniai, lake, in the Sudirman Range of western New Guinea, in Irian Jaya province of Indonesia.
3°50′ S, 136°15′ E
·formation and elevation **12**:1088g

panic, in economics, acute financial disturbance, such as widespread bank failures, feverish stock speculation followed by a market crash, or a climate of fear caused by economic crisis or the anticipation of such crisis. The term is applied only to the violent stage of financial convulsion and does not extend to the whole period of a decline in the business cycle.

Until the 19th century, economic fluctuations were largely connected with shortages of goods, market expansion, and speculation, as when stock speculation reached panic proportions in 1720 in both France and England (*see* South Sea Bubble). Panics in the industrialized societies of the 19th and 20th centuries, however, reflect the increasing complexity of advanced economies and the changed character of their instability. A financial panic has quite often been a prelude to a crisis that extended beyond commercial activities into sectors of consumption and capital-goods industries.

The Panic of 1857 in the United States, for example, was the outcome of a number of developments, including the railroads' defaulting on their bonds, the resultant decline in the value of rail securities, and the tying up of bank assets in nonliquid railroad investments. Its effects were also complex, including not only the closing of many banks but also a sharp increase in unemployment in the U.S. and a money-market panic on the European continent. The Panic of 1873, which began with financial crises in Vienna in June and in New York City in September, marked the end of the long-term expansion in the world economy that had begun in the late 1840s. The great panic, however, was the crisis in 1929, which rocked the U.S. economy and shattered world economic relations (*see* Great Depression).
·business cycles and economic history **3**:537b
·capital redistribution during depression **3**:801c
·central bank operations **2**:708d
·contract performance in periods of changing economic conditions **5**:127c

panicle (botany): *see* inflorescence.

panicum, common name for 500 to 600 species of forage and cereal grasses in the genus *Panicum* (family Poaceae), distributed throughout tropical and warm temperate regions. These plants are annuals (mostly weeds) and perennials; many are tufted or have underground stems. Of the more than 150 species found in the U.S., only about 40 percent have a haploid, or half normal, number of chromosomes (9 as compared with the diploid, or normal, number of 18). About 70 to 80 percent of all grass species are haploid.

Panicum
Syndication International—Photo Trends

Many species of *Panicum*, known as millet (*q.v.*), are cultivated in Europe and Asia as crop plants and in the U.S. for forage, hog feed, and birdseed. Guinea grass (*P. maximum*), a tall African grass, also is cultivated for forage, especially in tropical America and southern North America. Para grass (*P. purpurascens*), also native to Africa, has been introduced into wet regions of the southeastern U.S. as a forage grass. It is propagated by sectioning stems and stolons (horizontal root-forming stems), which develop into new plants. Switch grass (*P. virgatum*), is an erect, tough perennial, 1 to 2 metres (about 3 to 6.5 feet) tall, which grows in clumps; its spikelets may be reddish. A major constituent of tall grass prairie in North America, switch grass is a valuable forage grass and is sometimes used for erosion control because its thick underground stems send up new plants.

Witchgrass (*P. capillare*), a tufted annual, is a common weed in fields and areas disturbed by fire, grazing, or construction; its large, purplish flower clusters break off and are blown by the wind. Vine mesquite grass (*P. obtusum*) is planted for erosion control in the southwestern U.S.
·classification and characteristics **14**:586a *passim* to 592d

panidiomorphic (PANAUTOMORPHIC) **texture,** a descriptive term for igneous rocks in which the constituents are well-formed crystals; because this texture is well developed in lamprophyres, it also is called lamprophyric texture. Originally the term was used for rocks in which all of the constituents had crystal faces; in practice, however, the term is applied much more freely than the abundance of good crystals in a rock would warrant. The development of such a texture requires special conditions not commonly achieved during the crystallization of magmas. Although good crystals are not uncommon in many rocks, they are usually surrounded by a groundmass that preserves the crystal faces.

panier (dress design): *see* farthingales.

Pānihāti, town, Twenty-four Parganas district, Jalpaiguri division, West Bengal state, India, just east of the Hooghly River. Connected by road and rail with Calcutta, it is a rice trade centre; its major industries include cotton milling, tanneries, and the manufacture of chemicals, pottery, cement, glass, paint, and rubber goods. With the southern suburb of Āgarpārā, it was constituted a municipality in 1900, when it was separated from Barrackpore (*q.v.*) municipality. Pop. (1971) 148,046.
22°42′ N, 88°23′ E

panike (Baltic religion): *see* gabija.

Panikerveetil, Ghiverghis, later called MAR IVANIOS (1882–1953), priest and bishop among the Christians of St. Thomas who effected a union with Rome.
·union with Rome in 1930 **6**:164b

Panikkar, Kavalam Madhava (b. June 3, 1895, Travancore, Kerala, India—d. Dec. 10, 1963, Mysore), Indian statesman, diplomat, and scholar. Educated at the University of Oxford, he read for the bar at the Middle Temple, London, before returning to India, where he taught at Aligarh and Calcutta universities. He turned to journalism in 1925 as editor of the *Hindustan Times*.

Panikkar entered political life in the service of the Indian princes, becoming secretary to the chancellor of the Chamber of Princes (organization of rulers of the princely states). He also served as the foreign minister of the state of Patiala and as foreign minister and later as chief minister of the state of Bikaner (1944–47). After India gained its independence, he was entrusted with greater responsibilities as ambassador to China (1948–52), Egypt (1952–53), and France (1956–59). Late in life, he returned to the academic world and was vice chancellor of the University of Mysore at the time of his death.

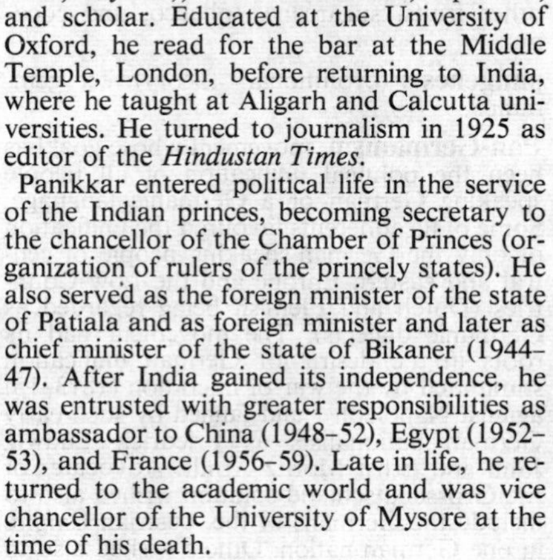

Panikkar
Camera Press—Publix

Panikkar's interest in European influence on Asia was reflected in his studies of the Portuguese and the Dutch in Malabar (in South India) and especially in his *Asia and Western Dominance* (1953). *In Two Chinas* (1955) revealed his sympathy with Communist China. He also wrote plays and novels.

Panin, Nikita Ivanovich, Count (b. Sept. 29 [Sept. 18, old style], 1718, Gdańsk, Pol.—d. April 11 [March 31, O.S.], 1783, St. Petersburg, now Leningrad), statesman who served as a chief diplomatic adviser to Catherine II the Great of Russia (ruled 1762–96). Son of the Russian commandant at Pärnu (Pernau), Estonia, Panin entered the Russian army in 1740, was appointed Russia's minister to Denmark in 1747, and was then transferred to Sweden, where he served from 1748 to 1760, officially acting as a major opponent of the pro-French party in Sweden and personally developing liberal political views and an appreciation of constitutional forms of government.

When Russia reversed her foreign policy in 1756 and entered the Seven Years' War as an ally of France and Austria, his position became increasingly difficult; he was about to retire in 1760 when Empress Elizabeth (ruled 1741–62), recognizing him as one of the most learned and accomplished gentlemen of Russia, recalled him to St. Petersburg to supervise the education of the grand duke Paul, son of her heir, the future Peter III (ruled 1762), and his wife, the future Catherine II (ruled 1762–96).

Although Panin urged that Paul be named emperor and that Catherine serve only as regent when Peter was overthrown in 1762, he became a trusted adviser to Catherine, particularly in foreign affairs, and was given the formal position of head of the foreign college (department of foreign affairs) in 1763. In that capacity he developed the concept of the "Northern Accord," an alliance system involving Russia, Prussia, Poland, Sweden, and, perhaps, Great Britain aimed against the Franco-Austrian bloc, and tried to direct Russia's foreign policy toward forming that alliance system.

Panin, detail of a portrait by A. Roslin, 1777
Novosti Press Agency

In conjunction with that concept, however, Panin advocated the development of Poland into a strong, independent state that would maintain friendly relations with Russia. This position brought him into conflict with Frederick II of Prussia, with whom Panin had cultivated close relations, as well as with Catherine, both of whom preferred that Poland remain weak and subservient. Upon Catherine's insistence, Panin first implemented her plan to place her former lover Stanisław Poniatowski on the Polish throne and effectively subordinate Poland to Russia (1764), then participated in the negotiations with Prussia and Austria (1770–71) that culminated in the first partition of Poland (1772).

Despite the failure of his grand scheme, Panin continued to urge close Russo-Prussian relations. But Catherine preferred to improve Russia's relations with Austria and, as she succeeded, Panin's position of influence declined. She finally dismissed him in May 1781, after they quarrelled over her plan (1780) to organize the protection of neutral shipping against British interference during the American Revolution.

Panin, Joseph: *see* Joseph of Volokolamsk, Saint.

Pāṇini (fl. 6th or 5th century BC), Indian grammarian, author of *Aṣṭādhyāyī* ("Eight Chapters"), the oldest known grammar of Sanskrit and perhaps the oldest extant grammar in the world.

·grammar scholarship precision and impact on Western studies **8**:266d
·language and writing studies **19**:1044a
·Sanskrit description and observations **9**:439f *passim* to 444b

Panini, Giovanni Paolo: *see* Pannini, Giovanni Paolo.

Panioniom, location of the festival of the Ionic cities of ancient Greece, founded in the early 7th century.
·formation and function **8**:346f

Pānīpat, town, Karnāl district, Haryana state, India, connected by road and rail with Delhi (south) and Ambāla (north). Wool and

The wheat market at Pānīpat, Haryana, India
Baldev—Shostal

cotton milling, saltpetre refining, and the manufacture of glass, electrical appliances, and bricks are the chief industries. The plain of Pānīpat was the site of three decisive battles in Indian history in the 16th and 18th centuries. Constituted a municipality in 1867, Pānīpat has three colleges affiliated with Panjab University. Pop. (1971 prelim.) 88,017.
29°25′ N, 76°59′ E
·Akbar's accession to the throne **1**:400c
·Bābur's defeat of Ibrāhīm Lodī **9**:378f
·map, India **9**:278
·Muslim domination end **8**:663d

Pānīpat, Battles of (1526, 1556, 1761), three battles, important in North Indian history, fought at Pānīpat, a level plain suitable for cavalry movements, about 50 miles north of Delhi.

The first battle (April 21, 1526) was between the Mughal chief Bābur, then ruler of Kābul, and Sultan Ibrāhīm Lodī of Delhi. Although the Sultan's army outnumbered the Mughals', it was unused to the wheeling tactics of the cavalry and suffered from deep divisions. Ibrāhīm was killed, and his army was defeated. This marked the beginning of the Mughal Empire in India.

The second battle (Nov. 5, 1556) ended in a victory for Bayrām Khān, the guardian of the young Mughal emperor Akbar, over Hemū, the Hindu general of an Afghān claimant who had proclaimed himself independent. It marked the restoration of Mughal power after the expulsion of the emperor Humāyūn by Shēr Shāh the Afghān in 1540.

The third battle (Jan. 14, 1761) ended the Marāthā attempt to succeed the Mughals as rulers of India and marked the virtual end of the Mughal Empire. The Marāthā army, under the Bhāo Sahib, the uncle of the peshwa (chief minister), was trapped and destroyed by the Afghān chief Aḥmad Shāh Durrānī. This began 40 years of anarchy in northwest India and cleared the way for later British supremacy.

Pan-Islāmism, the ideal of an Islām united under a caliph who could oppose the advance of Christian powers in Muslim lands, propagated by Muslim leaders in the 19th century. It originated mainly as a result of European encroachments on Muslim lands in the 19th century and partly in Islām's realization of its own stagnation.

Pan-Islāmism was the dominant ideology of the Muslim world of the 19th century before the rise of nationalism. Its patron, Abdülhamid II, the Ottoman sultan and caliph (reigned 1876–1909), conducted an extensive campaign of Pan-Islāmic propaganda that alarmed the European powers, though his emissaries were often ill-chosen and the success of their efforts appeared slight. Perhaps the greatest monument to the Pan-Islāmic ideal was the Hejaz Railway, built by private funds, partly provided by Sultan Abdülhamid himself.

The most outstanding exponent of the movement was Jamāl ad-Dīn al-Afghānī, who preached his doctrine in several Muslim countries. His teachings reached almost every corner of the world and were echoed in centres as far afield as Shanghai. Another advocate of Pan-Islāmism, Abdullah Suhrawardi, founded in 1903 a Pan-Islāmic society of London, which attempted to unify the two major branches of Islām, the Sunnah and the Shīʿah, and cleverly used the annual conferences at Mecca during the pilgrimage for Pan-Islāmic propaganda.

The fall of Abdülhamid in 1909 marked the decline of Pan-Islāmism. His failure to achieve Islāmic unity and to protect Islām from western encroachment prompted the new generation to turn to Western constitutionalism and nationalism, in the hopes that they might create a strong Ottoman state. Nationalism proved to be incompatible with the internationalism of Islām, however, and after World War I, the Ottoman Empire was broken up into a number of regimes. In 1922 the Turks at first reduced caliphal powers to spiritual powers and in 1924 abolished the caliphate itself. While the need for the restoration of the caliphate was expressed in the creation of the Indian Khilāfah movement and two caliphate congresses held in 1926 in Cairo and Mecca, the problem remained unresolved.

After World War II, the newly independent Muslim states realized the influence of their new numbers in international councils. They then adopted a neo-Pan-Islāmism that aimed not at the unity of all Muslim peoples under one central authority but at the coordination of their activities within the international community. The religious approach to foreign affairs was rejected as impracticable, and secular standards were adopted to enable the integration of Muslim countries into the larger world community.
·origin and political application **13**:788f

Panizzi, Sir Anthony, given name ANTONIO GENESIO MARIA PANIZZI (b. Sept. 16, 1797, Brescello, Italy—d. April 8, 1879, London), Italian patriot and man of letters who became famous as a librarian at the British Museum and played a part in the unification of Italy.

Panizzi, detail of an oil painting by G.F. Watts; in the National Portrait Gallery, London
By courtesy of the National Portrait Gallery, London

In 1822 Panizzi was forced into exile to avoid arrest as a revolutionary. He arrived in England in 1823 and, after teaching Italian at Liverpool, became professor of Italian at University College, London (1828–37). In 1831 he was named assistant librarian at the British Museum and became principal librarian in 1856. As a librarian and administrator, Panizzi combined vision with attention to detail, and he was responsible for the reorganization and for the new spirit of energy and concern for scholarship that made the museum one of the world's great centres of culture. He planned and began work on the general catalogue; secured strict enforcement of the 1842 Copyright Act; drew up a report on the library's deficiencies that led to an increased grant for book purchases in 1845; improved staff conditions by insisting on the museum's recognition as a branch of the civil service; and was responsible, through his friendship with Thomas Grenville, for the bequest of the Grenville library in 1846. He is best remembered, however, for designing and supervising the building of the Reading Room, opened in May 1857.

Although he became a British citizen in 1832, Panizzi continued to further the cause of Italian liberty through his friendship with influential Liberal statesmen in England, with Thiers in France, and with the Italian leaders. After the unification of Italy, he declined invitations from Garibaldi and Cavour to return as senator or as a member of the Council of Public Instruction, preferring to continue to serve as "unofficial ambassador" in London.

Panizzi's literary works include editions of Boiardo's *Orlando innamorato* and Ariosto's *Orlando furioso* (1830–34) and of Boiardo's minor poems (1835). In his later years he was a close friend of Prosper Mérimée. He retired in 1866 and was knighted in 1869.

·library history, function, and design **10**:860b; illus. 864
·library science technical development **10**:867d

Pañjāb (Indian state): *see* Punjab.

Panjabi language: *see* Punjabi language.

Panjim (India): *see* Panaji.

Panjnad River, Punjab province, Pakistan, formed just below Uch by successive junctions of the Sutlej, Beās, Rāvi, Jhelum, and Chenāb rivers. The Panjnad (literally Five Rivers) flows 44 mi (71 km) southwest to its junction with the Indus near Mithankot, forming in its course part of the boundary between Muzaffargarh, Bahāwalpur, and Rahīmyār Khān districts. A barrage located just after its junction with the Chenāb is part of the Sutlej Valley irrigation project.
29°18′ N, 71°02′ E

P'an-keng, or PAN-KENG (fl. *c.* 14th century BC), Chinese emperor of the Shang dynasty (*c.* 1766–*c.* 1122 BC).
·Shang dynasty relocation **4**:302c

Pankhurst, Emmeline, *née* GOULDEN (b. July 14, 1858, Manchester—d. June 14, 1928, London), militant champion of woman suffrage whose 40-year campaign achieved complete success in the year of her death, when British women obtained full equality in the franchise. Her daughter Christabel Harriette (afterward Dame Christabel) Pankhurst (1880–1958) also was prominent in the woman suffrage movement.

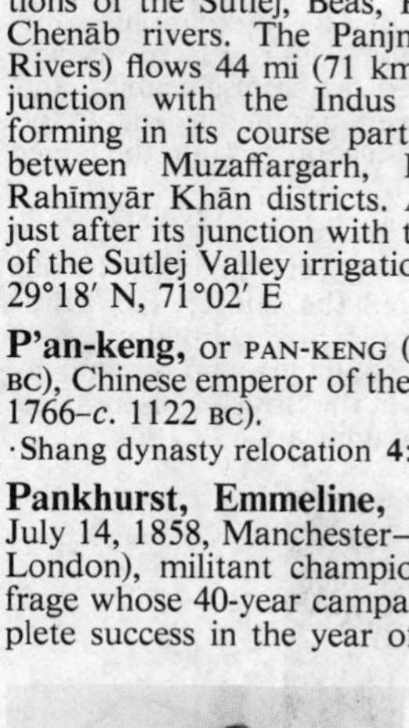

Emmeline Pankhurst in prison clothes, 1908
Radio Times Hulton Picture Library

In 1879 Emmeline Goulden married Richard Marsden Pankhurst, lawyer, friend of John Stuart Mill, and author of the first woman suffrage bill in Great Britain (late 1860s) and of the Married Women's Property acts (1870, 1882). Ten years later she founded the Women's Franchise League, which secured (1894) for married women the right to vote in elections to local offices (not to the House of Commons). From 1895 she held a succession of municipal offices in Manchester, but her energies were increasingly in demand by the Women's Social and Political Union (WSPU), which she founded in 1903 in Manchester. The union first attracted widespread attention on Oct. 13, 1905, when two of its members, Christabel Pankhurst and Annie Kenney, thrown out of a Liberal Party meeting for demanding a statement about votes for women, were arrested in the street for a technical assault on the police and, after having refused to pay fines, were sent to prison.

From 1906 Mrs. Pankhurst directed WSPU activities from London. Regarding the Liberal government as the main obstacle to woman suffrage, she campaigned against the party's candidates at elections, and her followers interrupted meetings of Cabinet ministers. In 1908–09 Mrs. Pankhurst was jailed three times, once for issuing a leaflet calling on the people to "rush the House of Commons." A truce that she declared in 1910 was broken when the government blocked a "conciliation" bill on woman suffrage. From July 1912 the WSPU turned to extreme militancy, mainly in the form of arson directed by Christabel from Paris, where she had gone to avoid arrest for conspiracy. Mrs. Pankhurst herself was imprisoned, and, under the Prisoners (Temporary Discharge for Ill-Health) Act of 1913 (the "Cat and Mouse Act"), by which hunger-striking prisoners could be freed for a time and then reincarcerated upon regaining their health to some extent, she was released and re-arrested 12 times within a year, serving a total of about 30 days. With the outbreak of World War I in 1914, she and Christabel called off the suffrage campaign, and the government released all suffragist prisoners.

During the war Mrs. Pankhurst, who previously had made three tours of the U.S. to lecture on woman suffrage, visited the U.S., Canada, and Russia to encourage the industrial mobilization of women. She lived in the U.S., Canada, and Bermuda for several years after the war. In 1926, upon returning to England, she was chosen Conservative candidate for an east London constituency, but her health failed before she could be elected. The Representation of the People Act of 1928, establishing voting equality for men and women, was passed a few weeks before her death.

Mrs. Pankhurst's autobiography, *My Own Story*, appeared in 1914. *The Life of Emmeline Pankhurst* (1935) was written by her second daughter, E. Sylvia Pankhurst.

pankration (sport): *see* pancratium.

P'an Ku, central mythological figure in Chinese Taoist legends of creation. P'an Ku, the first man, is said to have come forth from chaos (an egg) with two horns, two tusks, and a hairy body. Some accounts credit him with the separation of heaven and earth, setting the sun, moon, stars, and planets in place, and dividing the four seas. He shaped the earth by chiselling out valleys and stacking up mountains. All this was accomplished from P'an Ku's knowledge of *yin-yang*, the passive feminine and active masculine principles that permeate all being.

Another legend asserts that the universe derived from P'an Ku's gigantic corpse. His eyes became the sun and moon, his blood formed rivers, his hair grew into trees and plants, his sweat turned to rivers, and his body became soil. The human race, moreover, evolved from parasites that infested P'an Ku's body. These creation myths date from the 3rd to the 6th century. Artistic representations frequently depict P'an Ku as a dwarf clothed with leaves.

P'an Ku holding the *yin-yang* symbol, 19th-century European print after a Chinese drawing; in the British Museum
By courtesy of the trustees of the British Museum

·origin of heaven and earth **4**:411h

Pan Ku 13:947, Pin-yin romanization BAN GU (b. probably AD 32, Ch'ang-an, modern Sian, China—d. AD 92), scholar-official of the Later Han dynasty and one of China's most noteworthy historians.

Abstract of text biography. Following the example of his father, Pan Piao, Pan Ku undertook the study of China's ruling dynasties and, aided by his brother, a highly placed general, was appointed official historian. After 16 years of work, he completed the *Han shu*, or *The History of the Former Han Dynasty*, which became the model most frequently used by later Chinese historians. When he was in his mid-40s, however, Pan Ku abandoned his historical work and joined the staff of Tou Hsien, a general who was campaigning against barbarian tribes north of China. When Tou Hsien fell into disfavour, Pan Ku was implicated and was sent to prison, where he died.

REFERENCES in other text articles:
·biographical literature of China **2**:1008c
·historical works **10**:1053d

pan ku, drum used in Peking opera.
·unique acoustical properties **12**:675g

pankus, also written PANKUSH, Hittite word meaning "whole community," used to describe the citizenry that passes judgment.
·Indo-European relationship to Hittites **1**:818a

panleucopenia (disease of cats): *see* feline distemper.

panmixis, also spelled PANMIXIA, in biology, a system of mating in which the choice of partners is random.
·gene pool subdivisions and mating **8**:811g

pan movement, in politics, an organized effort to unify a geographic area, linguistic group, nation, race, or religion. Pan movements have arisen variously as nationalistic movements against the domination of an imperial power, as justifications for gaining international political ends, and as romantic utopian dreams.

The concept of the pan movement is generally applied to movements in the 19th and 20th centuries among divided peoples, especially those in Europe and Asia. Pan-Slavism, Pan-Germanism, and Pan-Turkism were militant nationalist movements of a racist and imperialist type. Pan-Islāmism was a reaction against European colonialism. In the present, Pan-Africanism and Pan-Arabism are more largely ideological bases for united fronts against common enemies than they are real social movements. Since the final years of the 19th century, Pan-Americanism has been dominated by the United States government, some claim for imperialistic purposes, others claim simply to promote international understanding.

P'anmunjŏm, village, Korea, in the demilitarized zone established after the Korean War; 5 mi (8 km) east of Kaesŏng and 3 mi south of the 38th parallel on the Kyŏngŭi high road (from Seoul to Sinŭiju). It was the location of the truce conference held for two years (1951–53) between representatives of the United Nations forces and the opposing North Korean and Chinese armies during the war. After the armistice, signed there July 27, 1953, both the liaison officers and the guards of the four neutral nations comprising the Neutral Nations Supervisory Commission (Sweden, Switzerland, Poland, and Czechoslovakia) were located there. In 1968 the U.S. intelligence ship "Pueblo" was seized off the North Korean coast by North Korean patrol boats and its officers and crew were incarcerated and charged with espionage. P'anmunjŏm was then used as the negotiation site between the United States and North Korea, and the crew were released through the village. Subsequently, it has served as a meeting place for conferences between North and South Korea, including Red Cross conferences to establish means of communication and contact between people on either side of the truce line.
37°57′ N, 126°40′ E
·Korean War negotiations and obstacles **10**:514a
·map, North Korea **10**:518

Panmure, Fox Maule, 2nd Baron: *see* Dalhousie, Fox Maule Ramsay, 11th earl of.

Panmycin (antibiotic): *see* tetracycline.

Panna, town and district, Rewa division, Madhya Pradesh state, India. The town, the district headquarters, is a trade centre for agricultural products, timber, and cloth fabrics; handloom weaving is the major industry. The town grew in importance when Chhatrasal, ruler of Bundelkhand, made it his capital in 1675. Buildings of historical importance include the marble-domed Swami Pran Nath temple (1795) and Shri Baldeoji temple. Constituted a municipality in 1921, Panna has a college and a law school affiliated with Awadesh Pratap Singh University.

Swami Pran Nath temple in Panna, Madhya Pradesh, India
Baldev—Shostal

Panna district (area 2,715 sq mi, or 7,031 sq km), constituted in 1948, comprises major areas of the former princely states of Panna and Ajaigarh. It consists of a hilly region known as the Panna Range, a branch of the Vindhya Range. The name Panna ("jewel") is derived from the important diamond mines located there; they have been worked since the 17th century. Rice, wheat, sorghum, and oilseeds are the chief crops; there are several fisheries. Pop. (1971 prelim.) town, 24,383; district, 428,121.
·map, India **9**:278

Pannartz, Arnold (d. *c.* 1476), German printer who, with Konrad Sweynheym, introduced printing into Italy.
·typography development role **18**:814a; illus. 816

paññatti (Buddhist philosophy): *see* prajñapti.

Panneton, Philippe, pseudonym RINGUET (b. April 30, 1895, Trois-Rivières, Que.—d. Dec. 29, 1960, Lisbon), French-Canadian novelist whose best known works present the individual caught in the transition from primitive rural to modern urban life. Panneton

Panneton
Andre Larose

practiced medicine in Montreal and taught medicine at the Université de Montréal. He was a co-founder of the French-Canadian Academy. From 1956 until his death, Panneton served as Canadian ambassador to Portugal. *Trente arpents* (1938; Eng. trans., *Thirty Acres*, 1940), Panneton's major work, deals with the plight of the small French-Canadian farmer forced by the economic and social upheavals of the late 19th and early 20th centuries into migration to the city. In other novels, such as *Fausse monnaie* (1947; "False Money") and *Le Poids du jour* (1948; "The Heaviness of the Day"), he again studied displaced peasants. He also published a volume of short stories and two historical sketches.
·literary themes and works **10**:1229e

pannier (dress design): *see* farthingales.

pannier, in saddlery, a pack consisting of two bags or cases for carriage by a pack animal.
·sidesaddle development **8**:657h

panning, in geology, simple method of separating particles of greater specific gravity from earth or gravels by washing in a pan with water, using a circular agitating motion. It is one of the principal techniques of the individual prospector for gold and diamonds in placer (alluvial) deposits.
·gold products and production **8**:237h
·metallurgical concentration of minerals **11**:1064b

Pannini (PANINI), **Giovanni Paolo** (b. 1691, Pracenza—d. 1765, Rome), was the foremost painter of Roman topography in the 18th century. His real and imaginary views of the ruins of ancient Rome embody precise observation and tender nostalgia, combining elements of late classical Baroque art with those of incipient Romanticism.

His early education included instruction in the art of perspective, and he may have studied *quadratura* (scenic perspective or design) with Ferdinando Galli Bibiena (1657-1743). He probably began painting in Piacenza, but his early activity remains entirely conjectural. Pannini setted in Rome in 1711, and shortly thereafter entered the studio of Benedetto Luti (1666–1724).

In 1718-19 Pannini was admitted into the Academy of St. Luke. His reception piece, "Alexander Visiting the Tomb of Achilles" (1719; Rome, Academy of St. Luke), is typical of his earlier easel paintings, having small figures dwarfed by an elaborate architectural construction derived from Bolognese theatrical scenography. Many of his canvases prior to 1730 feature explicit historical or religious subjects.

His frescoes at the Villa Patrizi (1718–25, later destroyed) established Pannini's fame in this field. Later decorations include those at the Palazzo Alberoni (*c.* 1725; now Palazzo del Senato), displaying his talent as a quadraturist, and at S. Croce in Gerusalemme (*c.* 1725–28), where his "Triumph of the Holy Cross" continued the tradition of late Baroque illusionistic ceiling painting.

Toward 1730 Pannini began to specialize in the depiction of Roman topography. His scenes fall into several types. The *vedute dal vero* are exact renderings of particular views. Those of contemporary Rome, such as "Piazza del Quirinale" (1743; Palazzo del Quirinale, commissioned by Benedict XIV), are akin to the Venetian *vedute* of Canaletto. Roman antiquities are featured in others, as in the "View of the Roman Forum" (1735). In his famous *vedute ideale* (*e.g.*, "*The Colosseum and Other Monuments*," *1735*), Pannini combined views of various famous ancient monuments into imaginary compositions. Foregrounds are animated by small lively figures, monumental sculpture, and ruined architectural fragments. A variation of the *veduta ideale* is the *capriccio*, smaller in size, having, as in "Roman Ruins with Preaching Apostle" (1753; National Gallery, Dublin), a dominant figure subject, frequently an unspecified orator. The architecture functions more as a frame, often depicting imaginary monuments.

To satisfy tourists' demands for his paintings, Pannini frequently repeated subjects, yet always retained his spontaneity by varying composition and details. Stylistic changes are gradual. In paintings of the 1740s, the monuments recede from the picture plane, increasing the effect of spaciousness, and the clear Roman light becomes somewhat subdued. His delicate brushwork suggests his awareness of French Rococo painting. The "Celebrations in the Piazza Navona" (1729; Louvre, Paris) was the first of many large scenes recording contemporary Roman events. Pannini's *oeuvre* included interiors of Roman buildings, old and new; most famous are the several versions depicting the Pantheon and St. Peter's.

As both artist and friend, Pannini maintained a close relationship with the French community in Rome. He was admitted into the French Academy in 1732, and subsequently became its professor of perspective. His greatest pupil was Hubert Robert (1733-1808), whose more imaginative paintings of ruins, with heavier atmosphere and less rigorous perspective, represent a climax of early Romanticism. In 1754 Pannini became principal of the Academy of St. Luke. He painted little after 1760.

Pannonia, a province of the Roman Empire, corresponded to present western Hungary, with parts of eastern Austria and northern Yugoslavia. The Pannonians were mainly of Illyrian stock with some Celts in the western part of the province. The Roman conquest of

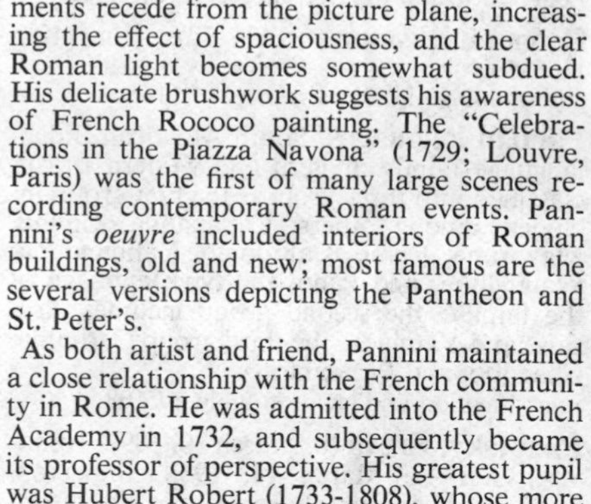

Pannonia in the time of Augustus
Adapted from R. Treharne and H. Fullard (eds.), *Muir's Historical Atlas: Ancient, Medieval and Modern*, 9th ed. (1965); George Philip & Son Ltd., London

the area began in 35 BC under Octavian (later the emperor Augustus) and was completed in 14 BC with the capture of Sirmium (Sremska Mitrovica, Yugos.), the key town of the Sava Valley. The Pannonian tribes, joined by the Dalmatians, revolted in AD 6, posing the gravest threat to Italy since Hannibal's invasion. After the revolt was put down, Pannonia was organized as a separate province and garrisoned with three legions. The emperor Trajan divided the province about AD 106. The western and northern district constituted Pannonia Superior, which was the focal point of the Roman wars with the Marcomanni in the reign of Marcus Aurelius (161–80), who died at Vindobona (Vienna). The southern and eastern districts were organized as Pannonia Inferior under Diocletian (reigned 284–305). Pannonia Superior was divided into Pannonia Prima and Pannonia Ripariensis or Savia, Pannonia Inferior into Valeria and Pannonia Secunda. The inhabitants of Pannonia retained their own culture into the 2nd century AD, but Romanization did proceed rapidly, especially in the west. In the 1st century AD, Emona (Ljubljana, Yugos.) and Savaria (Szombathely, Hung.) were made Roman colonies; and Scarbantia (Sopron, Hung.) and other cities were made *municipia* (self-governing communities). Pannonia was the birthplace of several Roman emperors of the 3rd century, and the province provided large numbers of troops for the Roman army. The grave barbarian threat in the 4th century AD forced the Romans to withdraw after AD 395. From that time, Pannonia ceased to exist as a separate unit.

·Augustus' Bohemia plan disruption **2**:371e
·Bohemian ecclesiastical development **2**:1185g
·Theodoric and the Ostrogoths **18**:270h

Pannonius, Janus (1434–72), Hungarian Humanist poet.

·literature of the Renaissance **10**:1145b

Panoan languages, South American Indian language family of Peru and western Brazil, classified into three groups: the first group includes, among others, Capanahua, Culino, Mayoruna, Remo, Catoquino, Yahuanahua, Waninahua, and Pano, the type language of the family; the second group includes Arazaire and Yamiaca; the third group Caripuna, Chacobo, and Pacahuara.

·classification and location table **17**:108

Panofsky, Erwin (b. March 30, 1892, Hanover, Ger.—d. March 14, 1968, Princeton, N.J.), art historian whose writings are distingushed for their variety of subject, critical penetration, erudition and rich allusiveness to literature, philosophy, and history. Panofsky was the historian of many iconographic, stylistic and theoretical aspects of medieval and Renaissance art; he also wrote the classic account of Albrecht Dürer and a definitive history of early Netherlandish painting. He received the degree of doctor in philosophy from the University of Freiburg in Breisgau and was professor at the University of Hamburg from 1926 to 1933. He first went to the United States in 1931 as visiting professor at New York university, New York, and in 1935 became professor of art history at The Institute for Advanced Study, Princeton, N.J.

Among Panofsky's major works in English are *Studies in Iconology: Humanistic Themes in the Art of the Renaissance* (1939); *The Codex Huygens and Leonardo da Vinci's Art Theory*, Studies of the Warburg Institute, vol. xiii (1940); *Albrecht Dürer*, 2 vol. (1943), 3d ed. (1948), also republished, with full text and illustrations but without the handlist of Dürer's works, as *The Life and Art of Albrecht Dürer* (1955); (ed. and trans.) *Abbot Suger on the Abbey Church of St. Denis and Its Art Treasures* (1946); *Gothic Architecture and Scholasticism* (1951); *Early Netherlandish Painting, Its Origin and Character*, 2 vol. (1953); *Meaning in the Visual Arts* (1955), a collection of nine of Panofsky's most important articles and essays on a wide variety of subjects; with Dora Panofsky, *Pandora's Box: the Changing Aspects of a Mythical Symbol* (1956); *Renaissance and Renascences in Western Art* (1960); *The Iconography of Correggio's Camera di San Paolo*, Studies of the Warburg Institute, vol. xxvi (1961); and *Tomb Sculpture* (1964).

·sculptural principle of axiality **16**:422h

Panopea: *see* clam.

panopticon, architectural form for a prison designed by Jeremy Bentham in the late 18th century. It consisted of a circular, glass-roofed, tanklike structure with cells along the external wall facing toward a central rotunda; guards stationed in the rotunda could keep all the inmates in the surrounding cells under constant surveillance. Although Bentham's novel idea was not incorporated in the plans for penal institutions built at that time, its design had some influence on future construction. For example, a prison incorporating the essential features of the panopticon was erected in the United States at Stateville, near Joliet, Ill., in the early 20th century.

·Bentham's prison reform statement **2**:838e
·prison design and reform **14**:1099a

Panorama, British television news magazine.

·television news magazine development **18**:126d

Panorama, Italian periodical founded in 1961.

·magazine publishing history **15**:253f

panorama, in the visual arts, continuous narrative scene or landscape painted to conform to a flat or curved background, which surrounds the viewer or is unrolled before him. Panoramas are usually painted in a broad and direct manner, akin to scene, or theatrical, painting. Popular in the late 18th and 19th centuries, the panorama was essentially the antecedent of the stereopticon and of motion pictures, especially animations and the process called Cinerama. The true panorama is exhibited on the walls of a large cylinder, the earliest version about 60 feet (18 metres) in diameter and later ones as large as 130 feet (40 metres) in diameter. The viewer, who stands on a platform in the cylinder centre, turns around and successively sees all points of the horizon. The effect of being surrounded by a landscape or event may be heightened in various ways: filling the space between the viewer and the cylinder walls with three-dimensional objects that gradually blend into the picture or the use of indirect lighting to give the illusion that light is emanating from the painting itself.

The first panorama was executed by the Scottish painter Robert Barker, who exhibited in Edinburgh in 1788 a view of that city, followed by panoramas of London and battle scenes from the Napoleonic Wars. Another early panorama painter, the American John Vanderlyn (1775–1852), painted in 1816–19 "The Palace and Gardens of Versailles" (preserved in New York's Metropolitan Museum of Art), exhibiting it until 1829 in a rotunda he built on a leased corner of City Hall Park in New York City. By the mid-19th century panoramas became a widespread, popular form of entertainment. Among the major works of this period was Henri Philippoteaux's "Siege of Paris," depicting an event in the Franco-Prussian War. His son Paul painted the panorama "The Battle of Gettysburg" (1883), exhibiting it in several American cities before its permanent installation in Gettysburg, Pa. At mid-century the rolled panorama, a kind of portable mural, became a popular amusement and educational device. Accompanied by a lecture and often music, the painting, on canvas and wound between two poles, would slowly be unrolled behind a frame or revealed in sections. Sometimes theatrical realism was utilized in the form of real steam, smoke, and sound effects. Among the longest and most ambitious of these rolled panoramas was one 1,200 feet (370 metres) long (deceptively advertised as three miles in length), depicting the landscape along the entire course of the Mississippi River, by the American John Banvard.

The term is also used for a continuous painted backdrop surrounding a theatrical audience. The first theatrical panorama was invented as a major scenic innovation by Jacques-Mandé Daguerre in 1787.

·historical development in painting **13**:882g
·staging and scene design development **17**:543c

Panormus (Sicily): *see* Palermo.

panorpoid complex, in entomology, group that probably gave rise to the scorpionflies (Mecoptera), flies (Diptera), fleas (Siphonaptera), caddisflies (Trichoptera), and butterflies and moths (Lepidoptera).

·evolutionary position and descent **9**:619b; illus. 618
·fly ancestral connection from fossil record **5**:823b
·lepidopteran unique insect order **10**:827b

pan-Orthodox Conferences, various meetings of Eastern Orthodox churches since 1923, attempting to discuss common issues.

·ecumenical purposes and achievements **6**:296d

Pano-Tacanan languages, superfamily of South American Indian languages, grouping the Panoan and the Tacanan languages. Because of the great complexity in the language relationships of the Americas, especially

Panorama of the battle of Gettysburg, painting by Paul Philippoteaux, 1883; at Gettysburg National Military Park, Pa.

Lane Studio—Walter B. Lane

South America, linguists customarily group American Indian languages in larger taxa than would be considered appropriate elsewhere.
·classification and location table **17**:108

Pan Piao (b. AD 3, Fu-feng, China—d. 54, China), eminent official of the Han dynasty (206 BC–AD 220) who is reported to have begun the famous *Han shu* ("Book of Han"), considered the Confucian historiographic model on which all later dynastic histories were patterned.

Pan Piao intended the work to supplement the *Shih-chi* ("Historical Records") of the famous historian Ssu-ma Ch'ien (*c.* 145–85 BC) and to cover the period from 104 BC, the last year covered by Ssu-ma. Pan died before the writing was completed, at which point it was taken over by his son Pan Ku. While Pan Ku is credited with the major responsibility for the *Han shu*, he did not live to finish the work, ultimately completed by Pan Piao's daughter Pan Chao, China's most famous woman scholar. Pan Piao's other son was Pan Ch'ao, the famous Han general who restored much of Central Asia to Chinese control.
·court life and retirement **13**:948a

panpipe, or SYRINX, wind instrument consisting of cane pipes of different lengths tied in a row or held together by wax (metal, clay, or wood instruments are also made) and generally closed at the bottom. They are blown across the top, each providing a different note.

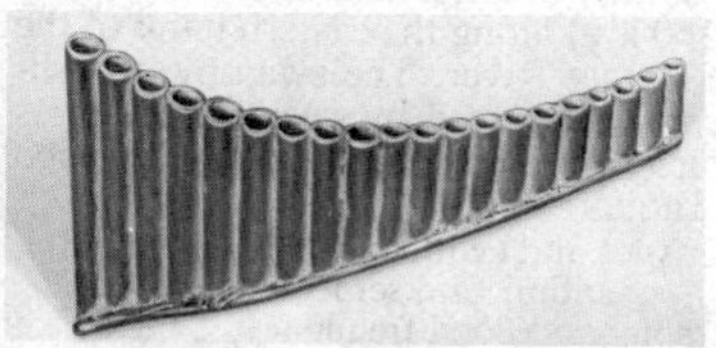

Romanian panpipe; in the Horniman Museum, London
By courtesy of the Horniman Museum, London

The panpipe is widespread in Neolithic and later cultures, especially in Melanesia and Aboriginal South America. In the Greek legend of Pan the invention of the instrument is ascribed to the nymph Syrinx. In Europe it has been mainly a shepherd's instrument and has so endured in the Pyrenees. In Romania, however, it is played among professional *lăutari* (fiddlers); their panpipe, the *nai*, has from 19 to 22 pipes tuned diatonically (*i.e.*, to a seven-note scale), semitones being made by tilting the pipes toward the lips.
·African flute types and performance **1**:249e
·Solomon Islands music **13**:459c

Pan-p'o-ts'un, one of the most important sites yielding remains of the Painted Pottery, or Yang-shao, culture of late Neolithic China. Located in the northwestern Chinese province of Shensi, Pan-p'o-ts'un was excavated by members of the Chinese Academy of Sciences in 1953 and 1955.

The large Neolithic settlement was situated on a low river terrace and contained multi-shaped clay huts, with floor levels often below the ground. Each hut had an earthen pillar in the middle to support a thatched roof, which was reinforced with clay. All dwellings contained several fireplaces and a number of storage areas. Several kilns were found on the site, as well as a number of fine specimens of coloured red and gray bowls and jars. Some coarse sandy ware decorated with black geometric figures has also been found.

Most of the Pan-p'o-ts'un people's tools were bone, though they also had some polished and chipped stone implements. They were agriculturalists whose primary grain was millet. Bones of pigs, dogs, and sheep have been found around the village, indicating the presence of domestic animals. Children were buried in small urns, adults in rectangular pits.
·excavation implications for Yang-shao **4**:299g

panpsychism (from Greek *pan*, "all"; *psychē*, "soul"), a philosophical theory asserting that a plurality of separate and distinct psychic beings or minds constitute reality. Panpsychism is distinguished from hylozoism (all matter is living) and pantheism (everything is God). For Gottfried Wilhelm Leibniz, the 17th-century German philosopher and a typical panpsychist, the world is composed of atoms of energy that are psychic. These "monads" have different levels of consciousness: in inorganic reality they are sleeping, in animals they are dreaming, in man they are waking; God is the fully conscious monad.

In 19th-century Germany, Arthur Schopenhauer asserted that the inner nature of all things is will—a panpsychistic thesis; and Gustav Theodor Fechner, founder of experimental psychology and ardent defender of panpsychism, contended that even trees are sentient and conscious. The American Josiah Royce, an absolute Idealist, not only followed Fechner in affirming that heavenly bodies have souls but adopted a unique theory that each species of animal is a single conscious individual—incorporating into itself the individual souls of each of its members.

Among other 20th-century philosophers, Alfred North Whitehead may fittingly be called a panpsychist inasmuch as in his philosophy each "actual entity" is capable of "prehensions" that involve feelings, emotions, consciousness, and so on.
·panentheism in Fechner and Whitehead **13**:954a
·Spinozistic metaphysical system **17**:510b

Pan-Scandinavianism, also SCANDINAVIANISM and SCANDINAVISM, an unsuccessful 19th-century movement for Scandinavian unity that enflamed passions during the Schleswig-Holstein crises. Like similar movements, Scandinavianism received its main impetus from philological and archaeological discoveries of the late 18th and the 19th century, which pointed to an early unity. It was also spurred by the rise of Pan-Germanism and by a general fear of Russian expansion. Generally a middle class and student movement calling for varying forms of cultural and political unity, Scandinavianism was a significant force from 1845 to 1864. It clashed with Pan-Germanism over the Schleswig-Holstein question, and Swedish and Norwegian volunteers joined the Danes during the Schleswig War (1848–50). When Sweden-Norway refused to join Denmark after hostilities over the duchies again erupted in 1864, however, Scandinavianism became bankrupt. Thereafter it remained strong only among the Swedish minority in Finland. There has been a resurgence of Pan-Scandinavian sentiment in the latter part of the 20th century.
·Danish and Swedish nationalism in the 19th century **16**:325a *passim* to 326g

Pan-shan (Chinese writer and statesman): *see* Wang An-shih.

Pan-shan ware, a type of Chinese Neolithic painted pottery. The name is that of the site in

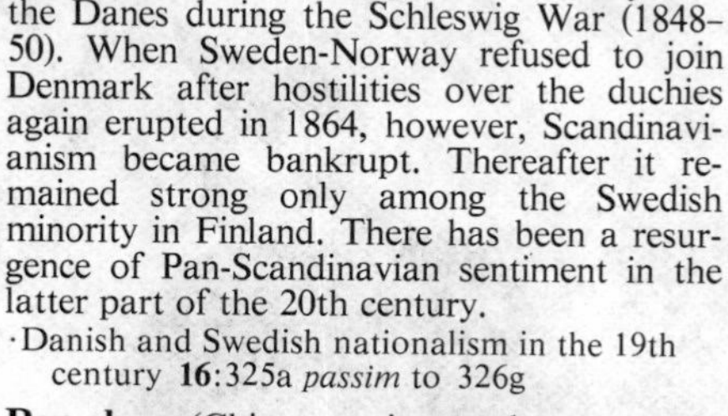

Pan-shan urn, Neolithic painted pottery found in Kansu province; in the Museum of Fine Arts, Boston
By courtesy of the Museum of Fine Arts, Boston, Hoyt Collection

the Kansu Province of North China in which this pottery was found in a grave in 1923. As with all Neolithic ware, the dating is conjectural; but Pan-shan ware is generally considered to be from between 2500 and 2000 BC; some authorities extend the limits as far back as 3000 BC, while others believe them to be as late as the early Shang dynasty, *c.* 1500 BC. Most of the specimens are urns, some quite large; and a few deep bowls have been found. The body is a reddish brown; the decoration, mostly in black pigment probably applied with a brush, consists of geometric or stylized figures of men, fish, and birds; and there is no glaze. Some of the wares were probably shaped on a slow, or hand-turned, wheel. The handles are set low on the body of the urns, and the lower part of the body is left undecorated—as with most Greek Proto-Geometric funerary ware, with which there is a certain likeness. The paucity of Neolithic Chinese pottery at the time of the discovery gave the find an importance out of proportion to its size. Since the 1950s, however, the large amount of archaeological activity in China has placed Pan-shan in a larger framework of Neolithic Chinese ware.
·Chinese pottery development and designs **14**:919a
·excavations and ornamental design **4**:299d

Pan-Slavism, 19th-century movement that recognized a common ethnic background among the various Slav peoples of eastern and east central Europe and sought to unite those peoples for the achievement of common cultural and political goals. The Pan-Slav movement originally was formed in the first half of the 19th century by West and South Slav intellectuals, scholars, and poets, whose peoples were at that time also developing their senses of national identity. The pan-Slavists engaged in studying folk songs, folklore, and peasant vernaculars of the Slav peoples, in demonstrating the similarities among them, and in trying to stimulate a sense of Slav unity. As such activities were conducted mainly in Prague, that city became the first Pan-Slav centre for studying Slav antiquities and philology.

The Pan-Slavism movement soon took on political overtones, and in June 1848, while the Austrian Empire was weakened by revolution, the Czech historian František Palacký, convened a Slav congress in Prague. Consisting of representatives of all Slav nationalities ruled by the Austrians, the congress was intended to organize cooperative efforts among them for the purpose of compelling the Emperor to transform his monarchy into a federation of equal peoples under a democratic Habsburg rule.

Although the congress had little practical effect, the movement remained active, and by the 1860s it became particularly popular in Russia, to which many pan-Slavs looked for leadership as well as protection from Austro-Hungarian and Turkish rule. Russian Pan-Slavists, however, altered the theoretical bases of the movement. Adopting the Slavophil notion that western Europe was spiritually and culturally bankrupt and that it was Russia's historic mission to rejuvenate Europe by gaining political dominance over it, the Pan-Slavists added the concept that Russia's mission could not be fulfilled without the support of other Slav peoples, who must be liberated from their Austrian and Turkish masters and united into a Russian-dominated Slav confederation.

Although the Russian government did not officially support this view, some important members of its foreign department, including its representatives at Constantinople and Belgrade, were ardent Pan-Slavists and succeeded in drawing both Serbia and Russia into wars against the Ottoman Empire in 1876–78.

After the Russo-Turkish war of 1877–78,

however, the political influence of Pan-Slavism subsided, and, when efforts were made in the early 20th century to call new Pan-Slav congresses and revive the movement, the nationalistic rivalries among the various Slav peoples prevented their effective collaboration.

·Alexander II's Balkan policies **1**:477a
·cultural symbol and literary exponents **16**:870a
·Decembrists nationalist orientation **16**:60e
·Ottoman imperial decline in the Balkans **2**:627g
·Prague Congress of 1848 **2**:465d
·Russia Balkan policy reaction **16**:65g
·World War I origins and settlement **19**:942g

pansophism, universal knowledge or pretension of such knowledge.

·Comenius' harmony explanation **4**:968e
·educational philosophy **6**:349g

p'ansori, type of Korean oral folk literature of the Yi dynasty (1392–1910) known as "story singing."

·dance stylization and instrumental accompaniment **12**:680a
·Korean literary history **10**:1060g *passim* to 1063e

pansy, common name for a popular cultivated hybrid violet (*Viola tricolor* variety *hortensis*) of the family Violaceae. Native to Europe,

Pansy (*Viola tricolor*)
Kitty Kohout—Root Resources

the pansy is one of the oldest cultivated flowering plants. It is an annual or a short-lived perennial and grows about 15 to 30 centimetres (6 to 12 inches) tall. It has heart-shaped or rounded leaves at the base and oblong or oval leaves growing from the stems. The velvety flowers, usually in combinations of blue, yellow, and white, are about 2.5 to 5 centimetres (1 to 2 inches) across and have five petals. Four petals are in pairs; the fifth has a short spur. The plant grows best in rich soil in a damp, cool climate.

The cultivated pansy is a hybrid of *V. tricolor* with such other *Viola* species as *V. cornuta*, the tufted pansy, and *V. lutea* variety *suedetica*, the mountain pansy. The wild pansy (*V. tricolor*), also known as the field pansy, johnny-jump-up, heartsease, and love-in-idleness, has been introduced to North America. The flowers of this form are mostly purple and less than 2 centimetres (0.8 inch) across.

Pantaenus, 2nd-century Greek Stoic philosopher, teacher of St. Clement of Alexandria, and the first recorded president of the Christian Catechetical school in Alexandria.

·career and St. Clement's conversion **4**:710g

Pantágoro (people): *see* Patángoro.

Pantagruel (book by Rabelais): *see* Gargantua and Pantagruel.

pantaleon (musical instrument): *see* dulcimer.

Pantaléon, Jacques: *see* Urban IV.

Pantaleone di Mauro (b. *c.* 1030—d. *c.* 1071), merchant and statesman of Amalfi (south of Naples), whose farsighted efforts to thwart the Norman conquest of southern Italy were frustrated by local power struggles.

A member of an old patrician family and son of Mauro, a wealthy merchant known for his founding of churches and hospitals, both in Amalfi and in pre-Crusades Muslim Jerusalem and Antioch, Pantaleone presided for many years over the Amalfian colony in Constantinople. In 1062 he tried to establish a common front against the Normans and Pope Alexander II among the Holy Roman emperor Henry IV, the Byzantine emperor Constantine X Ducas, and the antipope Honorius II. To promote the entente, the Lombard prince Gisulph II of Salerno, although an old enemy of Amalfi, visited the Byzantine emperor in Constantinople, where Pantaleone was his host. When the projected alliance failed to materialize, Gisulph began to wage pirate warfare against Amalfi, in which one of Pantaleone's nephews was killed and another taken prisoner. In 1071 an attempt at peace led only to the release of Pantaleone's nephew without ransom; two years later Amalfi placed itself under Norman protection, ending its existence as an independent state.

The first Italian businessman of the Middle Ages of whom any information survives, Pantaleone is known not only for his diplomatic activities but also for his philanthropy, donating such artistic monuments as the Church of St. Michael on Monte Gargano, in Apulia, and the bronze doors of St. Paul's Outside the Walls at Rome.

Pantaloon, Italian PANTALONE, stock character of the 16th-century Italian commedia dell'arte; he was a cunning and rapacious yet often deceived Venetian merchant. The name is thought to be derived from the phrase *pianta leone* (Italian: "plant the lion") referring to the Lion of St. Mark, the emblem of the Venetian flag.

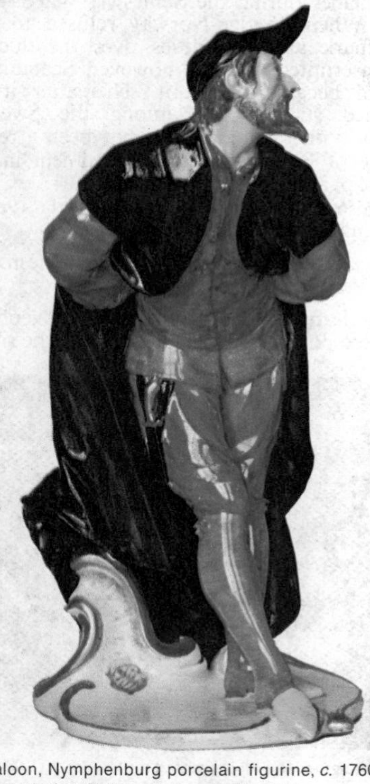

Pantaloon, Nymphenburg porcelain figurine, *c.* 1760; in the Bayerisches Nationalmuseum, Munich
By courtesy of the Bayerisches Nationalmuseum, Munich

Pantaloon dressed in a tight-fitting red vest, red breeches and stockings, a pleated black cassock, slippers, and a soft brimless hat. Later Pantaloons sometimes wore long trousers ("pantaloons"). His mask was gaunt and swarthy with a large hooked nose, and he had a disorderly gray goatee.

The humour of the role stemmed from Pantaloon's avarice and his amorous entanglements. An abject slave to money, he would starve his servant until he barely cast a shadow. If he discharged him, he made certain to do so before dinner. If married, he was a foil for his wife, who was young, pretty, disrespectful, and completely untrustworthy, and for the intrigues and deceits of his daughters and servant girls. Although anxious about his reputation, he engaged in flirtations with young girls who openly mocked him.

In the Italian commedia, Pantaloon was frequently paired with Dottore (*q.v.*) as a parent or guardian of one of the lovers. The French Pantaloon evolved from Pantalone when the commedia dell'arte companies played in France. In Elizabethan England, Pantaloon came to mean simply an old man. In 18th-century London, Pantaloon, minus his long coat, was one of the characters of the harlequinade (*q.v.*), the English pantomime version of the commedia dell'arte.

·commedia character development **4**:981h
·stock role and mask use **18**:223e

Pantanal, floodplain in southern Mato Grosso State, southwestern Brazil, extending about 100 mi (160 km) along the eastern bank of the upper Paraguay River. The swampy, marshland region is traversed by several tributaries of the Paraguay including the São Lourenço and the Taquari.

·characteristics and economic activity **3**:129d
·features, vegetation, and settlement **13**:992b
·physiography and flood frequency **17**:81h; map

p'an t'ao (Chinese: "flat peach"), in Chinese Taoist mythology, the peach of immortality that grew in the garden of Hsi Wang Mu, Queen Mother of the West. When the fruit ripened every 3,000 years, the event was celebrated by a sumptuous banquet attended by the Eight Immortals.

Hsi Wang Mu presented the *p'an t'ao* to favoured mortals such as Emperor Mu Wang (10th century BC) and the Han dynasty emperor Wu Ti (140–86 BC). The first Ming dynasty emperor (14th century AD) is said to have been presented with a *p'an t'ao* stone identified, by ten engraved characters, as formerly belonging to Wu Ti.

Flat peaches from Chekiang Province were sent each year to the imperial palace in Peking before the founding of the Chinese Republic (1911).

Pantelleria Island, Italian ISOLA DI PANTELLERIA, ancient Cossyra, Italian island in the Mediterranean Sea between Sicily and Tunisia; it forms part of Trapani province, Sicily. Of volcanic origin, it rises to 2,743 ft (836 m) at the extinct crater of Magna Grande, and has an area of 32 sq mi (83 sq km). The last eruption (underwater to the west of the island) took place in 1891, but hot mineral springs and fumaroles testify to continued volcanic activity. The island is fertile but lacks fresh water. A fortified Neolithic village (*c.* 3000 BC) has been excavated on the west coast, with remains of huts, pottery, and obsidian tools. To the southeast are tombs, known as *sesi*, similar to the *nuraghi* of Sardinia, comprising rough lava towers with sepulchral chambers in them. After a considerable interval, during which the island probably remained uninhabited, the Phoenicians established a trading station there in the 7th century BC. Later controlled by the Carthaginians, it was occupied by the Romans in 217 BC. Under the Roman Empire it served as a place of banishment. About AD 700 the Christian population was annihilated by the Arabs, from whom the island was taken by the Norman Roger II of Sicily in 1123. The Spanish Requesens family were princes of Pantelleria from 1311 until the town of Pantelleria was sacked by the Turks in 1553. The island's strategic situation in the narrow passage separating the eastern and western Mediterranean induced the Italian government of Benito Mussolini to fortify it as a base, from which Allied convoys were attacked in World War II. The installations and the town of Pantelleria were destroyed by intensive Allied air assault in 1943.

The main occupations are fishing and farming, and sweet wine and raisins are exported. The chief town, Pantelleria, is on the northwest, on the sole harbour; there is also a penal colony there. Pop. (1971 prelim.) mun., 8,094.
36°47′ N, 12°00′ E

Panthay, name given in southwest China to the Hui or Chinese Muslims. Most Chinese Muslims are engaged in agriculture, although a few are merchants.
·East Asian cultural patterns **6**:122h
·Yunnan use as revolutionary base **19**:1113f

pantheism and panentheism 13:948, cognate views of the relationship between God and the world that stress his all-embracing inclusiveness as compared with his separateness in traditional theism. In a sense, they are both versions of theism because they emphasize the immanence, or indwelling presence, of God. Pantheism stresses the identity between God and the world and panentheism the inclusion of the world within God while viewing him also as more than the world.

The text article covers the nature and significance of pantheism and panentheism; the distinctions between hylozoistic, immanentistic, monistic (absolutistic and relativistic), acosmic, identity of opposites, and emanationistic pantheisms; Hindu, Buddhist, and ancient Near Eastern doctrines; and Western doctrines, including those of the Pre-Socratics, Plato, Stoicism, Neoplatonism, medieval scholars, Giordano Bruno, Benedict de Spinoza, the German Idealists, Gustav Fechner, A.N. Whitehead, and Charles Hartshorne.

REFERENCES in other text articles:
·Bolivian Indian preservation **3**:6c
·formal and material atheistic forms **2**:261b
·Froebel pedagogical basis **6**:360g
·God's finite contingencies concept **18**:265c
·Hegelian development and criticism **8**:733c
·Hindu growth from Ṛgveda polytheism **8**:930c
·Islāmic mystical beliefs **9**:918a
·Jewish philosophical thought **10**:215h
·metaphysical investigation of creation **5**:243c
·monotheism distinguished **12**:383a
·monotheistic personalism contrasted **12**:381f
·mystical conception of God and nature **12**:789b
·nature hymn attitudinal elements **14**:950c
·nature in religious study **12**:877f
·Romanticism in the visual arts **19**:445c
·Spinozistic metaphysical system **17**:510b
·Stoicism and naturalism **17**:701a
·Ṣūfī forms and heterodoxy **9**:943f *passim* to 945c

pantheon, building for the worship of all the gods revered in a certain locality; hence, also a building honouring famous men or national heroes; specifically, the name of two famous buildings, one of which is in Rome, the other in Paris.

The Roman Pantheon was begun in 27 BC by the statesman Marcus Vipsanius Agrippa, probably as a building of the ordinary classical temple type—rectangular with a gabled roof supported by a colonnade on all sides. It was completely rebuilt by the emperor Hadrian in about 118–119 AD, with some alterations made in the early 3rd century by the emperors Lucius Septimius Severus and Caracalla. It is a circular building of concrete faced with brick, with a great concrete dome rising from the walls and a front porch, probably reassembled from Agrippa's building by Severus or Caracalla, of Corinthian columns supporting a gabled roof with triangular pediment.

Pantheon, Rome, begun by Agrippa in 27 BC, completely rebuilt by Hadrian *c.* AD 118–*c.* 128
Frederico Arborio Mella

Beneath the porch are huge bronze double doors, 24 feet (7 metres) high, the earliest known large examples of this type.

The Pantheon at Rome is remarkable for its size, its construction, and its design. The dome is the largest built until modern times, measuring about 142 feet (43 metres) in diameter and rising to a height of 71 feet (22 metres) above its base. There is no external evidence of brick arch support inside the dome, except in the lowest part, and the exact method of construction has never been determined. Two factors, however, are known to have contributed to its success: the excellent quality of the mortar used in the concrete and the careful selection and grading of the aggregate material, which ranges from heavy basalt in the foundations of the building and the lower part of the walls, through brick and tufa (a stone formed from volcanic dust), to the lightest of pumice toward the centre of the vault. In addition, the uppermost third of the drum of the walls, seen from the outside, coincides with the lower part of the dome, seen from the inside, and helps contain the thrust with internal brick arches. The drum itself is strengthened by huge, brick arches and piers set above one another inside the walls, which are 20 feet (6 metres) thick.

The porch is conventional in design, but the body of the building, an immense circular space lit solely by the light that floods through the 27-foot "eye," or oculus, opening at the centre of the dome, was revolutionary; possibly this was the first of several great buildings of antiquity that were designed to favour the interior rather than the exterior. In contrast with the plain appearance of the outside, the interior of the building is lined with coloured marble; the walls are marked by seven deep recesses, screened by pairs of columns whose modest size gives scale to the immensity of the rotunda. Rectangular ceiling coffers, or indentations, were cut in the ceiling probably under Severus and decorated with bronze rosettes and molding.

The Pantheon was dedicated in 609 AD as the church of the Sta. Maria Rotonda, which it remains today. The bronze rosettes and moldings of the ceiling and other bronze embellishments have disappeared in the course of time, and a frieze of stucco decoration was applied to the interior directly beneath the dome in the late Renaissance. Otherwise, the building exists entirely in its original form.

The Panthéon at Paris was begun in 1759 by the architect Jacques-Germain Soufflot as the church of Sainte-Geneviève to replace a much older church of that name on the same site. It was secularized during the French Revolution and dedicated to the memory of great Frenchmen, receiving the name Panthéon. Its design exemplified a general movement (Neoclassicism) to return to a strictly logical use of classical architectural elements. The Panthéon is a cruciform building with a very high dome over the crossing and lower saucer-shaped domes (covered by a sloping roof) over the four arms. Like that of the Roman Pantheon, the facade is formed by a porch of Corinthian columns and triangular pediment attached to the ends of the eastern arm. The interior is decorated with mosaics and paintings of scenes from French history, some of which were executed by Puvis de Chavannes. The pediment has sculptures by Pierre-Jean David d'Angers of post-Revolutionary patriots. The Panthéon was reconsecrated and resecularized several times during the 19th century, serving as a church in 1828–30 and in 1851–70. Today it is a civil building.
·architectural space composition **1**:1107c; illus.
·architectural splendour and history **15**:1080e
·brick in early construction **3**:163c
·Hadrian's rebuilding significance **8**:541a
·masonry dome construction **3**:454c
·Nepalese and Tibetan design comparison **3**:1140e
·Palladio's use of Roman motifs **13**:934d

Pantheon (Sainte-Geneviève) of Paris
·Gothic construction theory application **19**:450b
·Neoclassical architectural developments **19**:435c
·power of style and history **13**:1017d; map 1005
·Roman circular temple architecture **19**:303b
·Roman design durability **11**:587f

panther (mammal): *see* leopard; puma.

Panther, German medium tank developed in 1943.
·tank development in World War II Germany **17**:1021b

Panthera, invalid genus name formerly used for the big, or roaring, cats (*Leo*): the jaguar, leopard, lion, tiger, ounce, and clouded leopard (*qq.v.*).

Pantholops, commonly called TIBETAN ANTELOPE, a genus of the family Bovidae of the order Artiodactyla.
·distribution and scent glands **2**:75e

pantile, in architecture, curved roofing tile shaped like a flattened S. Pantiles, made of fired and sometimes glazed clay, are laid in mortar, with the downward curve of one tile overlapping the upward curve of the next. First used by the architects of ancient Rome, they have retained their precise original shape.

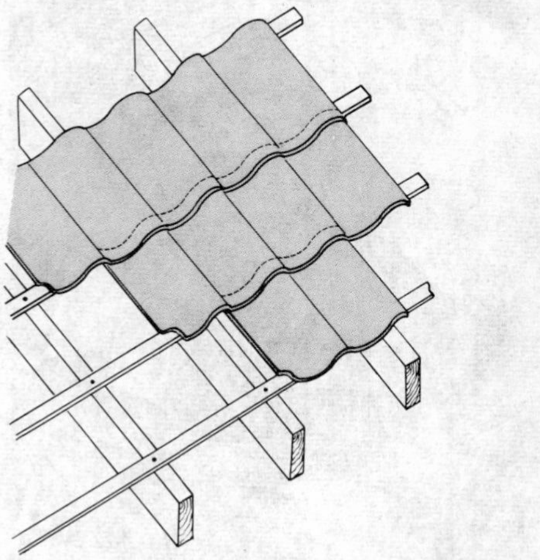

Pantiles
From M.S. Briggs, *Everyman's Encyclopaedia of Architecture*. E.P. Dutton & Co., and J.M. Dent & Sons, Ltd.

Most popular in buildings erected on the shores of the Mediterranean Sea, they are now used by architects who wish to give a Mediterranean flavor to a building. A distinction is sometimes made between the pantile and the S-tile, the latter being more rounded and more like the conventional letter S.

Pantin, town, a northeastern industrial suburb of Paris, in Seine-Saint-Denis *département*, north central France. Manufactures include steel, flour, machine tools, electrical equipment, cotton thread, and cigarettes. Latest census 47,580.
48°54′ N, 2°24′ E

panting, a form of cooling, used by many mammals, most birds, and some reptiles. It depends on the evaporation of water from internal body surfaces. As the animal's body temperature rises, its respiration rate increases sharply; cooling results from the evaporation of water in the nasal passages, mouth, lungs, and (in birds) air sacs. Like other forms of evaporative cooling (*e.g.*, perspiration [*q.v.*]), panting expends large amounts of water, which must be replaced if the animal is to maintain effective heat regulation.
·temperature regulation means in animals **14**:997g

Pantjasila, literally FIVE PRINCIPLES, the Indonesian state philosophy, first formulated by the Indonesian nationalist leader Sukarno on June 1, 1945, in a speech delivered to the preparatory committee for Indonesia's independence, which was sponsored by the Japanese during their World War II occupation. Sukarno argued that the future Indonesian state should be based on the Five Principles: Indonesian nationalism; internationalism, or humanism; consent, or democracy; social prosperity; and belief in one God. The statement was not well received by the Japanese authorities, but independence preparations for Indonesia were continued. Before Indonesia's independence was declared, the Japanese had already surrendered. The Five Principles have since become the blueprint of the Indonesian nation. In the constitution of the Republic of Indonesia promulgated in 1945, the Five Principles were listed in a slightly different order and in different words: the belief in one God, just and civilized humanity, Indonesian unity, democracy under the wise guidance of representative consultations, and social justice for all the peoples of Indonesia.

Pantocrator (from Greek: Ruler of the Universe), in Christian art, a representation of Christ as the almighty, combining in one person the Creator and the Saviour. The type of

Christ Pantocrator, apse mosaic in the Cathedral of Cefalù, Italy, 12th century
Hans Hinz, Basel, Switz.

the Pantocrator is derived from Early Christian (*c.* 2nd century–*c.* 6th century) representations of Christ as judge, which, in contrast to the typical youthful Early Christian image of Christ, depict him as an older, bearded figure. In its definitive form, however, the Pantocrator is exclusive to Byzantine art. Here Christ, bearded, mature, with an exceedingly stern expression, is shown in rigid frontality, usually in bust, raising his right hand in a gesture of benediction or admonition and holding a bound book of the Gospels in his left. The most important use of the Pantocrator, represented sometimes in fresco (*q.v.*) but more often in mosaic, was as the apical image of Byzantine church iconographic schemes, which present in their decoration a hierarchy of the universe, from the earthly realm of the congregation, up through the saints on the walls, to God and his archangels in the central dome or principal apse (domed semicircular end of the nave). All the power of the vital, rhythmic line and transcendent spirituality characteristic of Byzantine art was brought to bear in this awesome image, which is one of its finest expressions.

Pantodonta, extinct order of the class Mammalia.
·evolutionary relationships, illus. 6 **11**:414

Pantodontidae: *see* butterfly fish.

pantograph, instrument for duplicating a motion or copying a geometric shape to a reduced or enlarged scale. It consists of an assemblage of rigid bars adjustably joined by pin joints; as the point of one bar is moved over the outline to be duplicated, the motion is translated to a point on another bar, which makes the desired copy according to the predetermined scale. In the figure the links 2, 3, 4, and 5 are connected by pin joints at O, A, B, and C. Joint O is fixed to a support, while

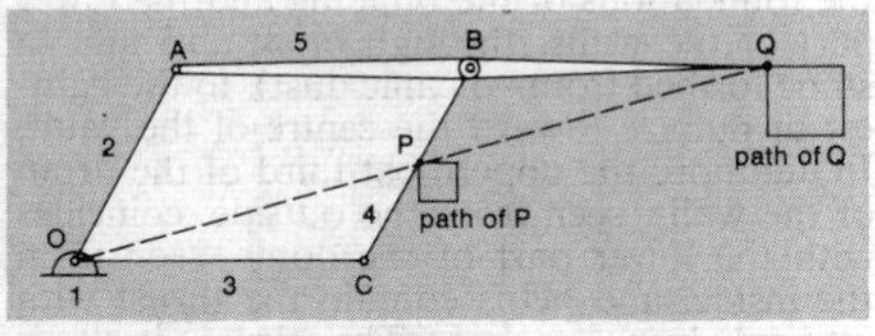

Pantograph

joints A, B, and C are free to move. Link 5 is a solid bar continuing on to Q. Point P is the guided point and is usually fixed on link 4. As P is guided on a specific path, such as the square in the figure, point Q will follow a similar path on an enlarged scale. Conversely, if point Q is guided, point P will follow a similar path on a reduced scale.

The links in a pantograph may be arranged in other ways, but they all contain a parallelogram. Pantographs are used for reducing or enlarging engineering drawings and maps and for guiding cutting tools over complex paths. Artists specializing in miniatures use pantographs to achieve greater detail in their finished works.
·drawing devices for correct perspective **5**:1003c

pantomime: *see* mime and pantomime.

pantomimus (pl. *pantomimi*), a dancer who performed dramatic scenes in dumb show, acting all the characters in a story in succession, using only masks, body movement, and rhythmic gestures. The *pantomimus*, whose name means "player of every role" or "imitator of all persons and things," was the central figure of an entertainment that became fashionable in Rome during the reign of Augustus and remained popular throughout the history of the Roman Empire.

The pantomime differed from its equally popular sister form, mime, in two ways: its themes were usually loftier, avoiding the farce and coarse humour that were common in mime; and, unlike the mime actor, the *pantomimus* wore various masks, which identified his characters but deprived him of the use of facial expressions. Thus his art was primarily one of posture and gesture, in which hand movements were particularly expressive and important.

The *pantomimus*, dressed like a tragic actor in a cloak and long tunic, usually performed solo, accompanied by an orchestra that included cymbals and other rhythm instru-

Drawing of an ancient Roman pantomimus wearing a mask and tunic
Historical Pictures Service, Chicago

ments, flutes, pipes, and trumpets. The libretto of the piece was sung or recited by a chorus, and was usually adapted from a well-known tragedy, although any historical or mythological story might be chosen. Both the music and the librettos of the pantomimes were generally considered to be of little artistic value, although noted poets such as Lucan and Statius occasionally wrote for them. The talent and skill of the *pantomimus* himself were of supreme importance, and the greatest performers enjoyed the favour of wealthy patricians and even emperors, such as Nero and Domitian. The early Christians decried the sensual, sometimes lascivious gestures of the dancers, and St. Augustine himself denounced the pantomime as being more morally dangerous than the Roman circus. Despite such opposition, the *pantomimi* enjoyed enormous popularity and success throughout the Roman Empire, and many were able to amass considerable fortunes.
·mime and pantomime in ancient Rome **12**:212a

Pantophthalmidae, a family of flies belonging to the order Diptera.
·classification and features **5**:823g

Pantopoda (marine animal): *see* pycnogonid.

pantothenic acid, a water-soluble vitamin essential in animals. Pantothenic acid, a growth-promoting substance for yeast and certain bacteria, appears to be synthesized by the intestinal flora in the higher animals. The vitamin, although widespread in nature—especially in yeasts, liver, kidney, and eggs—does not occur in a free form in animal tissues.

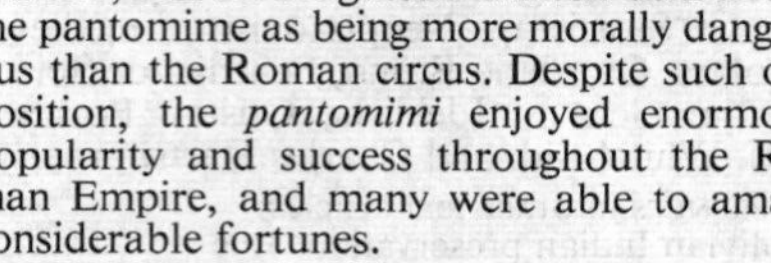

The nature of the bound form was clarified through the discovery and synthesis (1947–50) of the compound pantetheine, which contains pantothenic acid combined with the compound thioethanolamine. Pantetheine is part of two larger compounds (coenzyme A and acyl-carrier protein) that promote a large number of synthetic and degradative reactions essential for the growth and well-being of animals. In the absence of pantothenic acid (or of its dietary equivalents: pantetheine, coenzyme A, or acyl-carrier protein), experimental animals fail to grow, show skin lesions, and frequently show a graying of the hair. All animals studied thus far require the vitamin, but a dietary deficiency severe enough to lead to clear-cut disease has not been described in man.

Pantothenic acid, discovered in 1933, was first synthesized in 1940. The compound is a nitrogen-containing hydroxyacid that is highly soluble in water but very insoluble in oils. Its chemical formula is $C_9H_{17}NO_5$.
·coenzyme biosynthesis, table 3 **6**:898
·mental illness involvement **5**:861d
·milk product content, table 5 **5**:428
·nutrient of varied organisms, table 5 **13**:406
·vitamin activation and coenzymes **19**:489e; table

Pantotheria, extinct mammalian order in the subclass Theria that existed in North America and Europe from the Middle Jurassic to the Lower Cretaceous. Pantotheres had long slender jaws with many cheek teeth.
·fossil record and era **7**:572d
·Melanodon body plan, illus. 5 **11**:413

Pan troglodytes: *see* chimpanzee.

Pan-Turianism, political philosophy based on 19th century theory of the common origin of Turkish, Mongol, Tungus, Finnish, Hungarian, and other languages.
·origin and political impact **13**:789f

Pan-Turkism, late 19th- and early 20th-century political movement which aimed at the political union of all Turkish speaking peoples in the Ottoman Empire, Russia, China, Iran, and Afghanistan, in one state. The movement which began among the Turks in Crimea and on the Volga, won only limited support among the Ottoman Turks, and its aims were not realized.
·origin and political impact **13**:789f
·Turkistan nationalist movements **18**:796h

Pánuco River, in Veracruz state, east central Mexico. Formed by the junction of the Moctezuma and Tamuín rivers on the San Luis Potosí–Veracruz state line, the Pánuco meanders generally east-northeastward past the town of Pánuco to the Gulf of Mexico about 6 mi (10 km) below Tampico (*q.v.*). Just upstream from Tampico and Ciudad Madero (*q.v.*), the Pánuco is joined by the Tamesí, which forms the Veracruz–Tamaulipas border. Principal headstreams of the Pánuco include the Santa María, which arises in the inland plateau near San Luis Potosí and becomes the Tamuín as it descends from the Sierra Madre Oriental, and the Moctezuma, which flows through the mountains from southern Querétaro state. The river system (316 mi long including the Santa María) has considerable economic importance. It has served to drain Texcoco (*q.v.*) and other interior lakes via a system of tunnels and channels; its waters are used to irrigate the fertile La Huasteca lowlands; and its lower course is navigable (ocean vessels can be accommodated at Tampico).
22°16′ N, 97°47′ W

Panuridae (bird): *see* parrotbill; reedling.

Panyassis (fl. 5th century BC), Greek epic poet from Halicarnassus, on the coast of Asia Minor. The Roman rhetorician Quintilian stated that some later critics regarded Panyassis' work as being second only to Homer. His chief poems, extant only in fragments, were the *Heracleia*, describing the mythical adventures of the hero Heracles (Hercules), and the *Ionica*, relating the founding of Ionic Greek colonies in Asia Minor.

panzer division, a mechanized unit of the German army used for rapid attack.
·tank success and increased production **17**:1020h; illus. 1021

Panzerfaust, a German smoothbore, recoilless rifle used effectively against enemy tanks during World War II.
·recoilless weapons of World War II **19**:687e

pao, Chinese term for a gazette or newspaper, applied originally to an authorized court circular issued during the T'ang dynasty (AD 618–907).
·newspaper publishing history **15**:236c

Pao-chang tai-fang lu, translated as CRITICAL DESCRIPTION OF THE CALLIGRAPHIES OF MI FEI, records and essays by the Chinese painter Mi Fei (1051–1107).
·painting aesthetics and criticism **12**:174d

Pao-chi, Pin-yin romanization PAO-JI, city in western Shensi Province (*sheng*), China. It is a county- (*hsien-*) level municipality (*shih*), and the administrative centre of the Pao-chi Area (*ti-ch'ü*). Situated on the north bank of the Wei Ho (river), it has been a strategic and transportation centre since early times, controlling the northern end of a pass across the Tsinling Shan (mountains), the only practicable route from the Wei Valley into Szechwan Province and the upper valley of the Han Chiang (river). It is also at the western end of the intensively cultivated Wei Valley and is at the centre of a network of routes into Kansu Province and the Ningsia Hui Autonomous Region. Surrounded by mountains to the south, north, and west, it was the major western defensive outpost of the metropolitan district around Sian in early times. It was known as Ch'en-ts'ang County from the 3rd century BC to the end of the 3rd century AD, when its name was changed to Wan-ch'uan County. In the 5th century its old name was revived. Under the T'ang dynasty (618–907) in the 7th century, it was first given the name Pao-chi, which it has retained ever since; at the same time the county seat was moved to its present site from its former position some 8 mi (12 km) to the northeast.

Pao-chi's modern importance has resulted from its improved communications. The Lunghai Railway was extended from Sian to Pao-chi on the eve of the war in 1937 and was subsequently extended westward to T'ien-shui (Kansu) by 1947. Since 1949 this railway has been extended to Lan-chou (Kansu), where it links with the trunk line into central Asia and with the northern line to Pao-t'ou (Inner Mongolia) and Peking. In 1958 a further rail link was completed from Pao-chi southwest to Ch'eng-tu (Szechwan), where it links with the various new railways of the Southwest.

In the early 1970s, Pao-chi was an important commercial centre, collecting goods from a wide area, and had begun to develop some industry, in particular, cotton textiles and light engineering. Latest pop. est. 180,000.
34°22′ N, 107°14′ E
·map, China **4**:262
·railway network statistics **4**:285g

pao-chia, traditional Chinese system of collective neighbourhood responsibility, utilized by the government to maintain order and control through all levels of society, while employing relatively few officials. Under the *pao-chia* system, a certain number of households were formed into a *chia;* and several *chia* were combined into a *pao*. The community as a whole was made responsible for the good behaviour of all of its residents.

A collective neighbourhood guarantee system was first instituted by the legalist leaders of the Ch'in dynasty (221–206 BC). It was revived in a different form during the Northern Wei dynasty (386–534 BC) but did not take on the name by which it is now known until the Sung dynasty (960–1279), when a *pao-chia* system was instituted by the great reformer Wang An-shih as a military measure. Under Wang's scheme, each *pao-chia* was made responsible for supplying the government with a certain number of trained and armed militiamen.

During the Ming dynasty (1368–1644), the *pao-chia* system often coincided with the *li-chia* system, which had been established for the collection of land and labour taxes. But it also began to assume the separate function of overseeing the moral conduct of members of the community. The Ch'ing dynasty (1644–1911) perfected the system. Under the Ch'ing, a *pao-chia* unit ideally consisted of 100 families formed into a *chia* and 10 *chia*s formed into a *pao*, all under the supervision of an elected chief. The chief of each unit was responsible for preserving the public order; he also maintained the local census records and acted as an intelligence agent for the central government. *Pao-chia* organization began to deteriorate around the middle of the 19th century, when central control over local government began to erode.

The institution was revived by the Japanese when they occupied Taiwan after 1895 in an attempt to suppress anti-Japanese resistance on the island. Chiang Kai-shek also attempted to use the *pao-chia* in 1934 during his campaigns against the Chinese Communists.

Pao-ch'ing (China): *see* Shao-yang.

Pão de Açúcar, English SUGAR LOAF, landmark overlooking the entrance of the Baía (bay) de Guanabara, in southeastern Brazil. Named for its shape, the conical, granitic peak (1,325 ft [404 m]) lies at the end of a short range between Rio de Janeiro and the Atlantic. At its base is the fortress of São João. A cable car runs from its summit to the adjacent Morro da Urca (Urca Hill), near the foot of which is the Federal University of Rio de Janeiro, formerly the University of Brazil (1920).
22°57′ S, 43°09′ W
·formation and height **17**:81d

Pao-ji (China): *see* Pao-chi.

Paola, also spelled PAWLA OR PAULA, town, eastern Malta, just south of Valletta and adjacent to Tarxien (southeast). Founded in 1626 by the Grand Master of the Order of the Knights of St. John of Jerusalem, Antoine de Paule, it remained a small village until the late 19th century, when it grew rapidly as a residential district for workers from the adjacent Grand Harbour dockyards. It has a well-preserved Neolithic temple and the Hal Saflieni Hypogeum (catacombs). Pop. (1971 est.) 12,248.
35°53′ N, 14°31′ E
·map, Malta **11**:391

Paoli, Pasquale (b. April 26, 1725, Stretta di Morosaglia, Corsica—d. Feb. 5, 1807, London), statesman and patriot who was responsible for ending Genoese rule of Corsica and for establishing enlightened rule and reforms.

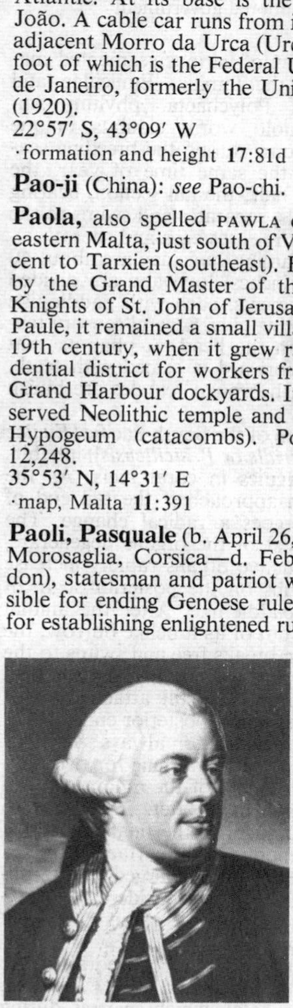
Paoli, detail of a portrait by Henry Bembridge, 1768
The Mansell Collection

The son of Giacinto Paoli, who led the Corsicans against Genoa from 1735, Pasquale followed his father into exile at Naples in 1739, studying at the military academy there and preparing to continue the fight for Corsican independence. In 1755 he returned to Corsica and, after overcoming the Genoese faction, was elected to executive power under a constitution more democratic than any other in Europe. For the next nine years, under the principles of enlightened despotism, he transformed Corsica, first by suppressing the system of vendetta and substituting order and justice, then by encouraging mining, building up a naval fleet, and instituting national schools and a university. At the same time he continued the war, first against Genoa and after 1764 against Genoa's ally, France. France bought Corsica in 1768 and invaded the island and defeated the nationalists in 1769. Paoli fled to England, received a pension from George III and lived in London for the next 20 years.

Appointed lieutenant general and military commandant during the French Revolution, Paoli returned to Corsica in July 1790. Breaking with France in 1793, he once more led the fight for independence and, with British naval support, expelled the French in 1794. He then offered the sovereignty of Corsica to George III, who accepted and sent Sir Gilbert Elliot as viceroy. Elliot in turn chose not Paoli but Pozzo di Borgo as his chief adviser. Disappointed and not wishing to cause internal strife, Paoli retired to England in 1795, where he received a British government pension.

·Corsican independence movement **12**:831f
·Corsica's constitutional government role **5**:191h

paolo worm, any of various segmented marine worms of the families Eunicidae and Nereidae (class Polychaeta, phylum Annelida). The paolo worm exhibits unique breeding behaviour: during the breeding season, always at the same time of year, the worms break in half; the tail section, bearing reproductive cells, separates and swims to the surface, where it releases eggs and sperm.

Adults of the family Eunicidae are about 40 centimetres (16 inches) long and are divided into ringlike segments, each with paddle-like appendages bearing gills. Several sensory tentacles grow from the head. A pharynx that may be thrust forward is armed with teeth. Males are reddish brown; females are bluish green.

The paolo worm of the South Pacific (*Eunice viridis* [*Palolo viridis* or *P. siciliensis*]) inhabits crevices and cavities in coral reefs. As the breeding season approaches, the tail end of the body undergoes a radical change. The muscles and most of the organs degenerate, and the reproductive organs rapidly increase in size. The limbs on the posterior segment become more paddle-like. After the animal backs part way out of its tubelike burrow, the posterior section breaks free and swims to the surface as a separate animal, complete with eyes. The anterior end, still attached to its tube, regenerates a new posterior end.

The free-swimming section always makes its appearance in the early morning for two days during the last quarter of the moon in October. Twenty-eight days later, it appears in even greater numbers in the final quarter of the November moon. At the surface of the sea the sperm and eggs are discharged, and fertilization occurs. Paolo tails, considered a delicacy by the Polynesians, are gathered in vast numbers during swarming.

Widely distributed in the rock coral of the West Indies is the Atlantic paolo (*E. furcata*, or *E. schemocephala*), which swarms during the last quarter of the June–July moon. The Japanese paolo (*Tylorrhynchus heterochaetus*), also considered a food delicacy, occurs in the coastal waters of Japan.

Paolo worm (*Eunice*)
Jacques Six

·Eunice viridis social behaviour and breeding patterns **16**:937h
·Leodice viridis reproductive mechanism and food use **1**:928c *passim* to 930e
·migration and reproductive habits **12**:177f
·reproduction and tidal cycle **14**:70f
·reproductive behaviour pattern **15**:684a

Pao-p'u-tzu (alchemist): *see* Ko Hung.

Pao-sheng-fo (Buddha): *see* Ratnasambhava.

p'ao-style robe, garment worn by Chinese men and women from the Han dynasty (206 BC–AD 220) to the end of the Ming dynasty (1644). The widesleeved robe was girdled about the waist and fell in voluminous folds around the feet. From the T'ang period (618–907) certain designs, colours, and accessories were used to distinguish rank; the emperor, for example, wore a dark-coloured *p'ao* on which the 12 imperial symbols were displayed, and officials wore a red *p'ao* with large squares containing symbolic birds or animals ("mandarin squares") on the breast. When the Manchus overthrew the Ming, it was decreed that a new style of dress should replace the *p'ao*. The style, which had been adopted by the Japanese court in the 8th century, has been basically retained in the Japanese kimono.

P'ao-style robe on the poet T'ao Yüan-ming (365–427), ink drawing on paper by Wang Chung-yu, 14th century; in the Imperial Museum, Peking
Editions Cercle d'art, Paris

·early use, ornamentation, and spread **5**:1035d; illus.

Pao-ting, Pin-yin romanization BAO-DING, city, Hopeh Province (*sheng*), China. It is a county- (*hsien-*) level municipality and the administrative centre of the Pao-ting Area (*ti-ch'ü*). It is situated on the edge of the North China Plain at the foot of the Wu-hui Ling section of the T'ai-hang Shan (mountain range) and stands on the T'ang Shui, a tributary of the Ta-ch'ing Ho. Situated on the main road from Peking through western Hopeh, it is southwest of the capital, roughly midway between Peking and Shih-chia-chuang. To the west, a route leads into northern Shansi via the Lung-ch'üan Pass.

Pao-ting is in an area of old-established settlement. Before the Ch'in dynasty (221–206 BC) it was part of the state of Chao. During the period to 581 AD, counties of various names were established in the district and formed parts of a variety of higher administrations. In 581 the Sui dynasty (581–618) changed the county's name to Ch'ing-yüan, which it retained until 1958. The area was of major strategic importance from early times. During the T'ang dynasty (618–907) it was the headquarters of one of the armies guarding the northeastern frontier against the Khitan, a Ural-Altaic people, and it later became a key garrison for government forces defending access to Shansi against the autonomous provinces of Hopeh. During the Five Dynasties (907–960) and the early years of the Sung dynasty (960–1126) it was a military prefecture on the contested border between the Sung and the Liao in the north. Under the Yüan (Mongol) dynasty (1279–1368), the area it administered became Pao-ting Circuit (*lu*). The transfer of the capital to Peking in Yüan and Ming (1279–1644) times meant a reversal of its strategic role so that it became the chief defensive bastion protecting Peking against attack from the south or incursions over the passes of the T'ai-hang Shan. Under the Ming, it was the administrative centre of the Pao-ting Prefecture (*fu*), and under the Ch'ing dynasty (1644–1911) it became even more important. It was both the seat of the provincial government of Chihli, and also the alternative seat, with Tientsin, of the military governor of Chihli. The city was heavily fortified, with walls more than 5 mi (8 km) in circumference, enclosing the government offices of the province, the military governor's offices, extensive barracks, and a military academy. In the late 19th century its population was estimated at between 70,000 and 100,000.

Although it was primarily an administrative city, with a large consumer population and extensive service industries, it was also a notable centre of learning. Under the Ming and Ch'ing it had many well-known schools, and in the reign of the emperor Yung-cheng (1723–35) a famous library, the Lien-ch'ien Shu-yüan, was founded there, which later became the Hopeh Library.

Being a communication centre, it also had commercial importance. It was the centre of a rather dense road network and in 1905 was joined to Peking and Tientsin, and later to Hankow (Han-k'ou, or Wu-han), by the Peking to Wu-han railway. It was also a commercial centre, collecting grain, wool, cloth, cotton, cottonseed oil, and various agricultural products.

The city maintained its administrative importance both under the Japanese occupation before and during World War II and under the Communist regime that came to power in 1949. Until 1958 it remained the provincial capital and the seat of the Hopeh People's Assembly. In that year the provincial administration was transferred to Shih-chia-chuang, and the name of the city was formally changed from Ch'ing-yüan to Pao-ting. The city has continued to grow, nearly doubling its population between 1948 and 1958. This growth, however, has been largely non-industrial. There are a number of light industrial

Market near a pagoda in Pao-ting, China.
Hedda Morrison

plants, mostly small scale, as well as a medium-sized thermal generating plant. In the drive for fertilizer production in the mid-1960s, an ammonium carbonate plant was built there. Pop. (latest est.) 250,000.
38°52′ N, 115°29′ E
·history and cultural and commercial features **8**:1069h
·map, China **4**:263

Pao-t'ou, Pin-yin romanization BAO-TOU, city in the Inner Mongolian Autonomous Region of China. An independent sub-provincial-level municipality, Pao-t'ou is situated on the north bank of the Huang Ho (Yellow River) on its great northern bend. The river and its upper tributaries are navigable westward as far as Hsi-ning in Tsinghai Province and Lan-chou in Kansu Province, but southward the main stream is impeded by rapids.

Pao-t'ou is of comparatively recent origin. Although the region was colonized and garrisoned during the T'ang dynasty (618–907), it was afterward occupied by Mongol tribes, and as late as the 1730s Pao-t'ou was merely a hamlet. As the Ch'ing dynasty (1644–1911) strengthened its grip on the Mongol border regions, Pao-t'ou gradually developed into a market town. It was walled in 1871 and eventually given the status of an administrative county in 1925.

The modern growth of Pao-t'ou began with the construction of a railway link with Peking, completed in 1922. It grew rapidly into a major commercial centre for trade with Mongolia and with Northwest China, controlling a marketing area including most of what is now Ningsia Hui Autonomous Region, Kansu, Tsinghai, and parts of the Mongolian People's Republic. Exports were mostly hides, wool, and felt; chief imports were cloth, grain, drugs, and tea. The wool and hides collected by local merchant firms and by traders from Peking and Tientsin were transported to Tientsin for export.

The area along the northern loop of the Huang Ho had been colonized by Chinese settlers from the 1880s onward, and Pao-t'ou became the major commercial centre for this Chinese community also. By 1932 the county was estimated to have more than 300,000 people. During the Japanese occupation (1937–45) Pao-t'ou was a centre of the autonomous government of Meng-chiang. The Japanese began the development of light industry there, and also discovered rich coal and mineral deposits nearby.

After 1949 Pao-t'ou was completely transformed. Its rail link with Peking, destroyed during the Chinese Communist Revolution in 1949, was restored in 1953 and double-tracked in the late 1950s. In 1955 construction was begun of a line following the Huang Ho to Lan-chou, where it now connects with other rail links to Szechwan Province, to central China, and to Urumchi in the Sinkiang Uighur Autonomous Region. Under the First Five-Year Plan (1953–57), Pao-t'ou was the site of a major integrated iron and steel complex, based on the rich iron ore deposits at Pai-yün-o-po to the north, with which it has been linked by rail; on coking coal from Shih-kuai-kou in the Ta-ch'ing Shan; and on local limestone. The new complex was part of the move to relocate heavy industrial centres away from the coastal zone. By 1975 Communist sources claimed an annual production of 1,500,000 tons of finished steel and 1,100,000 tons of pelletized steel. The completion of the industrial installation was announced in 1961, but full operation was not achieved until the late 1960s, allegedly because of the withdrawal of Soviet advisers and nondelivery of Soviet equipment.

Pao-t'ou also has an aluminum industry, based on the use of large thermal generating plants, and local sugar refining. By the 1970s Pao-t'ou had become one of China's chief industrial centres and constituted a major industrial base not merely for Inner Mongolia and the Northwest but for China as a whole. Although the city's growth has been phenomenal, some of it is attributable to the expansion of the municipal area to include the coal mines to the east and the iron and steel complex to the west. Pop. (1975 est.) 1,400,000.
40°40′ N, 109°59′ E
·industrialization and growth of population **4**:270e; table
·map, China **4**:263

Pao-t'ou carpets, rugs and carpets woven in Pao-t'ou, in the Inner Mongolian Autonomous Region of China, noted for their high quality of workmanship and materials. The designs usually consist of landscapes or religious symbols and are executed in fine wool dyed blue, brown, red, and beige. The foundation weave is of cotton.

PAP (political party in Singapore): *see* Peoples' Action Party.

Pápa, town, Veszprém *megye* (county), northwest Hungary, on the northwest edge of the Bakony Mountains, alongside the Tapolca, a tributary of the Rába. Its interesting and historic old houses, churches, museums, and libraries attract many visitors annually. The former Esterházy Castle, surrounded by a 180-ac (70-ha) park, was built between 1773 and 1784, using some of the stones from its medieval predecessor. There are also the parish church (1774–83), the Protestant College (founded 1531, present building dating from 1797), the Franciscan church (1764), and the Benedictine church (1737–42). Hotels, a swimming beach, and entertainment places serve the tourist industry.

The local soils are fertile; grain and beets are specialties. Industry is light and consumer-oriented (shoes, cigars, and textiles). Pápa is also a local rail junction. Pop. (1976 est.) 31,730.
47°19′ N, 17°28′ E
·map, Hungary **9**:22

papacy 13:954, the system of central government of the Roman Catholic Church, the largest of the three major branches of Christianity, presided over by the pope, the bishop of Rome. As the successor of St. Peter, the pope has supreme legislative, executive, and judicial powers over the universal church, a Roman Catholic doctrine officially defined and promulgated at the first Vatican Council in 1870 and reaffirmed at the second Vatican Council in 1964.

TEXT ARTICLE covers:
The papal office **13**:954h
The instruments of papal government 955c
The early bishops of Rome to Leo I 955g
Gregory the Great 956d
The early medieval papacy 956f
The Hildebrandine papacy and the Investiture Conflict 957b
The papacy at its height: the 12th and 13th centuries 957g
The crisis of the late Middle Ages: Boniface VIII to the Council of Trent 958c
The papacy in the modern world: Trent to the first Vatican Council 959a
From the first Vatican Council to the second Vatican Council 959f
The contemporary papacy 960a
The theory of papal authority 960d

REFERENCES in other text articles:
church issues
·alienation of East after Chalcedon **4**:542g
·apostolic development of hierarchy **13**:1078h
·Constantinople and Rome disagreements **9**:1070a
·Cyprian's view of primacy **5**:401d
·East–West Christian split over authority **6**:142e *passim* to 143f
·evolution and doctrinal foundation **4**:491g
·Innocent III's conception of papal rule **9**:605d
·legalism in Western Christianity **4**:476e
·Lutheran contention of fallibility **11**:197a
·Maistre's heirarchical absolutism **5**:64f
·medieval theocratic claims **4**:509f
·Old Catholic Churches and infallibility **13**:552h
·Peter's authority in apostolic church **14**:153d
·Protestant Reformation issues **15**:109c
·Protestant rejection of papal authority **15**:103f
·Roman Catholic concept of continuity **4**:465c
·sacred kingship traditions **16**:121f
·Sarpi's view of papal authority **16**:251f
·vestments and papal authority **15**:636a
history
·Alexander III's solidification of authority **1**:466h
·Alexander VI's political manoeuvring **1**:467h
·Babylonian Captivity and French support **7**:618f
·Boniface VIII's European power struggle **3**:32d
·Borgia political and financial use **3**:41g
·Byzantine–Frankish competition in Italy **6**:153g
·Cavour's dissolution of temporal power **3**:1032h
·Charlemagne's aid in expansion **4**:44e
·Charles III's repression of authority **4**:57b
·Cromwell and the English Reformation **5**:296c
·Crusade revenue squandering **4**:462d
·Crusades and religious revival **5**:298d
·diplomatics and chancery features **5**:808c
·Duns Scotus' defense against the kings **5**:1083d
·Eastern church unions after 1439 **6**:162c
·ecclesiastical reforms of Gregory I **8**:415e
·English medieval jurisdiction conflicts **3**:205f
·English Reformation cause and effect **3**:223b
·Frankish emperors' political relation **11**:932c
·Frankish Empire partnership **4**:464b
·Frederick I's conflict **7**:697g
·French Revolution reaction **6**:1099g
·Gregory VII's claim of sovereignty over Spain **17**:408f
·Gregory VII's reforms **8**:417c
·Gregory IX's authority dispute and defense **8**:419a
·Henry III's coronation and control **8**:759h
·Henry IV's Investiture Conflict and relationship with reform popes **8**:761b
·hierarchical role development **12**:143c
·Innocent IV and medieval politics **9**:606h
·Investiture Controversy and Henry V **8**:762g
·John of England's controversy with Innocent III **10**:237d
·John XXII politico-religious conflicts **10**:233e
·John XXIII's style and significance **10**:234d
·Julius II's temporal power enhancement **10**:333h
·Leo IX's power expansion **10**:804g
·Leo X's influence on position **10**:805g
·Leo XIII's election and policies **10**:807c
·medieval authority and schism **15**:1002b
·medieval church government **12**:154c
·medieval reforms and the German church **8**:73h
·Michael VIII and Roman religious union **12**:96g
·nature and development **15**:986b
·Nicholas V's Humanism support and politico–religious conciliation **13**:66h
·Otto I's Italian intervention **13**:768f
·Papal States origins and power **9**:1121b
·Paul III's Counter-Reformation program **13**:1087a
·Paul VI's activity and contributions **13**:1089b
·Philip IV's Christian authority conflict **14**:224b
·Photius' relations with Rome **14**:290e
·Pius V's Counter-Reformation enforcement **14**:481h
·Pius IX's shaping of modern pontificate **14**:483b
·Pius XII's impact on position **14**:486b
·political intrigues with Franks **4**:469e

·Portuguese defiance in 13th century **14**:866e
·pre-schism church authority **4**:537c
·Reformation and church secularization **15**:547d
·Roman decay and restoration **15**:1069e
·Roman Empire power vacuum **4**:511h
·Scottish conflict in 14th century **3**:237g
·secular authority in Middle Ages **4**:591c
·Sylvester II's reorganization **17**:899d
·tactical diversion for political choice **11**:191e
·Urban II's church reform continuation **18**:1044e
·Vatican City governmental operation **19**:36d
·Vitoria's political authority limitation **19**:493f
·Wolsey's ambition and Henry's divorce **8**:770c

RELATED ENTRIES in the *Ready Reference and Index: for*
authority: see infallibility, papal; motu proprio; primacy, papal
history: antipope; Avignon papacy; Donation of Constantine; Vatican Council, first
papal decrees: brief, papal; bull; encyclical, papal; papal documents
representatives and delegations: apostolic delegate; conclave; consistory; legate, papal; nuncio; Roman Curia

Papadiamadis, Alexandros (1851–1911), Greek author.
·pastoral themes of major works **10**:1257b

Papadiamantópoulos, Yánnis (Greek-French poet): *see* Moréas, Jean.

Papadopoulos, Dimitrios (patriarch): *see* Dimitrios.

Papadopoulos, Giorgios (1919–), retired Greek army officer, prime minister in the military government (1967–73) of Greece; became president following the abolition of the monarchy in June 1973 and was unseated in a military coup in November.

Pāpag (Persian prince): *see* Pāpak.

papagallo, or ROOSTERFISH, common name of fishes of the family Nematistiidae, order Perciformes.
·classification and general features **14**:54f

papagayo, strong winter wind on the west coast of Central America, especially in the Golfo (Gulf) del Papagayo of northwestern Costa Rica. It blows from the northeast for three or four consecutive days, is dry and cold, and brings clear weather. The papagayo occurs when a cold air mass crosses the Cordillera de Guanacaste and descends their western slopes.

Papago, North American Indians who call themselves the "Bean People" and who traditionally inhabited the desert regions of Arizona and northern Sonora, south of the Pima Indians (*see* Pima). The Papago speak a Uto-Aztecan language that is little more than a dialectal variant of Piman, and culturally they are similar to the Pima (*see also* Uto-Aztecan languages). There are, however, certain outstanding dissimilarities. The drier, harsher habitat of the Papago made intensive farming difficult and greatly enhanced their reliance on wild foods. Similarly, the lack of water necessitated a sort of seasonal nomadism, whereby the Papago spent the summer in "field villages" and the winter in "well villages."

The Papago did not have irrigated fields like those of the Pima but practiced flash-flood farming. After the first rains, seeds were planted in the alluvial fans at the mouths of washes that marked the maximum reach of the water after flash floods. Because the floods that provided water for the crops could be heavy while they lasted, it was necessary for the seeds to be planted deeply, four to six inches usually. Crude reservoirs to impound runoff waters along the flood channels, and some ditches and dikes, were constructed by Papago men. Women were responsible for gathering wild foods.

The shifting residential pattern and the wide dispersal of the Papago fields made large villages and tribal political organization impossible. The largest organizational unit appears to have been a group of related villages. Villages tended to be composed of several families related through the male line. The Papago have had much less contact with whites than the Pima, and they have retained some elements of aboriginal culture. In the 1970s they numbered about 8,300 located on two reservations in southern Arizona (the Papago and Ak Chin reservations) and a few hundred more in scattered villages in northwestern Sonora.
·alcoholic beverage manufacture **1**:442c
·American Indian local races **15**:349b
·Arizona income and residence **2**:3b
·Christian-influenced tribal cults **18**:702e
·habitation and cultural patterns **17**:305g; map
·numbers and habitation area **13**:245e; map 246
·rattle use in ritual **1**:665b

Papagos, Alexandros (b. Dec. 9, 1883, Athens—d. Oct. 4, 1955, Athens), soldier and statesman who late in life organized a political party and became premier (1952–55) of Greece.

Papagos
Dimitri Papadimos

Papagos, commissioned in 1906, saw his first service in the Balkan Wars (1912–13). He took part in the Greek invasion of Turkey (1919–22), won promotion to the rank of major general (1927), and became corps commander and minister of war (1935); the following year he was named chief of staff. Although at the time of the Italian attack on Greece (October 1940) he conducted, as commander in chief, a passive, basically defensive campaign, he nonetheless succeeded in driving the Italians back into Albania. His defenses soon crumbled, however, against the later German onslaught (April 1941), and he was taken to Germany as a hostage. Liberated in 1945, he directed postwar operations in Greece against Communist guerrillas and was appointed field marshal in 1949.

In May 1951 Papagos resigned as military commander in chief to form a new political party, the Greek Rally, which soon became the strongest political force in Greece. Enjoying wide popularity and modelling himself after Charles de Gaulle, Papagos led his party to a decisive victory in the elections of November 1952 and became premier. He died in office.
·governmental stabilization program **2**:638g

papain, a protein-digesting enzyme obtained from the milky juice of the papaya, the fruit of *Carica papaya.* Its action resembles that of pepsin, a protein-digesting enzyme found in animals. Papain is used in biochemical research involving the analysis of proteins, in preparations of various remedies for indigestion, and in the manufacture of meat tenderizers.
·derivation and use **7**:752g
·immunoglobulin molecule fragmentation **9**:251d; illus.
·meat tenderizer use **17**:506c

Pāpak, also spelled BĀBAK and PĀPAG (fl. AD 208–222), Persian prince and father of Ardashīr I, founder of the Sāsānian dynasty. *See also* Sāsān.
·Sāsānian pre-dynastic location **9**:846b

Pāpak (9th-century Iranian religious leader): *see* Bābak.

papal documents, a generic designation for formal pronouncements that emanate directly from the pope or from one of his authorized representatives in the Roman Curia. They may be directed to Roman Catholics as members of a universal church, to a specific group, or even to an individual; they may be used for doctrinal, pastoral, social, disciplinary, or administrative purposes. Historically, a great many different names have been given to papal documents depending upon their content and form. Various classifications—of which the most important are briefly described below—are still in use today, although the names are not always used consistently.

An *apostolic* or *papal constitution* is a most solemn pronouncement issued by a pope in his own name concerning either doctrinal or disciplinary matters of a serious nature. A *motu proprio* is a less formal document drawn up at a pope's own initiative and personally signed by him; it can be instructional, administrative, or disciplinary. An *encyclical letter* is a formal pastoral letter written by a pope for the entire church (although John XXIII addressed *Pacem in Terris* to "all men of good will"), relating to doctrinal, moral, or disciplinary matters; it is authoritative but not necessarily infallible in nature. An *encyclical epistle* is addressed to part of the church—that is, to the bishops and faithful of a particular country or area—and it may pertain to specific conditions in that locality. *Chirographi* (autograph letters) are handwritten letters from a pope, ordinarily addressed to a cardinal. *Decrees* are executive orders issued by a pope, an ecumenical council, or, most commonly, one of the departments of the Roman Curia; they have binding force in the whole church or for the concerned parties. A *rescript* is a reply by a pope or a department of the Curia to a request or question of an individual.

Papal documents may receive an additional name by reason of their appearance. A *papal bull*, the most solemn form in which a document is issued, is a parchment to which a leaden seal (*bulla*) bearing the image of SS. Peter and Paul and the name of the reigning pope is attached; it is used for documents that announce such things as a canonization, the appointment of a bishop, or the definition of a doctrine as a matter of Catholic belief. A *papal brief*, dealing with matters of lesser importance, is sealed with red wax, upon which is impressed the fisherman's ring of the pope.
·medieval university prestige **6**:337a
·13th-century division and distinctions **5**:810f

papal election: *see* conclave.

papal infallibility: *see* infallibility, papal.

Papalist Confutation: *see* Confutation.

Papaloapan River, Spanish RÍO PAPALOAPAN, in Veracruz state, southeastern Mexico, is formed by the junction of several rivers near the Veracruz–Oaxaca border and meanders generally northeastward for 76 mi (122 km) to Alvarado Lagoon, 10 mi (16 km) south-southeast of Alvarado. The chief headstreams include the Santo Domingo, Chichicatiapa, and San Cristóbal, which rise in the Sierra Madre Oriental. Since 1947 the Papaloapan Basin has been developed and colonized by the government. Swampy lowlands have been drained and reclaimed, dams for flood control and hydroelectric power built, farmlands apportioned, and settlers moved in from elsewhere in Mexico. The project's success has

led to development of similar schemes in other parts of the gulf lowlands. The Papaloapan system is navigable for 150 mi (240 km) upstream from Alvarado Lagoon.
18°42′ N, 95°38′ W
·map, Mexico **12**:68
·poor basin drainage **12**:66f

papal primacy: see primacy, papal.

Papal States, territory of central Italy over which the pope had sovereignty from 756 to 1870. Included were the modern Italian regions of Lazio, Umbria, Marche, and part of Emilia-Romagna, although the extent of the territory, along with the degree of papal control, varied over the centuries.

The Papal States in 1815

As early as the 4th century, the popes had acquired considerable property around Rome (called the Patrimony of St. Peter). From the 5th century, with the breakdown of Roman imperial authority in the West, the popes' influence in central Italy increased as the people of the area relied on them for protection against the barbarian invasions. When the Lombards threatened to take over the whole peninsula in the 750s, Pope Stephen II (q.v.; sometimes III) appealed for aid to the Frankish ruler Pepin III the Short. On intervening, Pepin "restored" the lands of central Italy to the Roman see, ignoring the claim of the Byzantine (East Roman) Empire to sovereignty there. This Donation of Pepin (754) provided the basis for the papal claim to temporal power, and in the Treaty of Pavia (756) the Lombard king Aistulf ceded territory in northern and central Italy. The pope thus became ruler of the area around Ravenna, the Pentapolis (along the Adriatic from Rimini to Ancona), and the Roman region. By alliance with the Normans in the late 11th century, the Duchy of Benevento was acquired in 1077.

Through the Middle Ages, the popes were able to maintain their sovereignty over this territory despite the rise of local feudal lords in the 9th and 10th centuries and, more importantly, despite a clash with the German Holy Roman emperors that lasted from the Investiture Controversy of the mid-11th century until the 14th century. Relations with the emperors were exacerbated by controversy over the allodial lands of Countess Matilda of Tuscany, donated (1102) to the papacy, but finally left (1111) to the emperor Henry V. But papal sovereignty was more nominal than real. The rise of commune governments, especially in the Romagna, weakened the popes' authority. With the transfer of the papal residence from Rome to Avignon (1309–77), local independence prevailed in the Papal States, a situation that continued through the end of

the Great Schism in 1417. Many towns nominally held as vicariates granted by the pope were in fact ruled by local families.

From the mid-15th century, the Renaissance popes sought to reestablish papal authority in central Italy. Under Julius II (pope from 1503 to 1513), the States reached their definitive boundaries, stretching from Parma and Bologna in the north, along the Adriatic coast, through Umbria, to the Campagna, south of Rome. These popes, however, failed in their attempt to make the papacy a force in international politics, and, by the end of the 16th century, the papal territory was merely one of a number of petty Italian states.

In the 17th and 18th centuries, the trend toward centralization, begun by the Renaissance popes, continued, although the clerical-run government made little progress in improving the backward economic condition of the Papal States. When the French, under Napoleon, secured domination of the Italian peninsula in the late 1790s, the States were taken from the pope in 1798–99 (to be included in the Cisalpine and Roman republics) and again in 1808–09 (to be included in the Italian kingdom and the French Empire). Liberal ideas introduced during the French Revolution continued to play a role after the restoration of the States to the pope by the Congress of Vienna (1815). Revolts occurred in the States in 1830–31 and again in 1849, when another short-lived Roman Republic was established.

Through the Risorgimento (movement for Italian unification during the 19th century), the existence of the Papal States proved an obstacle to national union both because they divided Italy in two and because foreign powers intervened to protect papal independence. After Austria's defeat in 1859, the papal territories of Romagna, Umbria, and Marche voted to join the Italian kingdom. With the withdrawal of French troops from Rome in 1870, the remaining papal territory—the area around Rome—was taken by Italian forces, and Rome was made capital of Italy. The question of the pope's relation to the Italian state was unsettled until the Lateran Treaties of 1929 set up an independent Vatican City state.

·Borgia family attempt to control **3**:41h
·diplomacy and wars from 1494 **6**:1082b; map 1097
·formation and political power **9**:1121b
·Garibaldi's Risorgimento invasions **7**:908h passim to 910c
·Gregory VII's defense against Normans **8**:417g
·Innocent III and feudal power of papacy **9**:605e
·Julius II and restoration activity **10**:334c
·origin of papal claims to Italian lands **14**:35h
·papal policy effects after 1815 **13**:959d
·Pius IX's power struggle **14**:483h
·Pope Gregory I as founder **8**:416g
·Ravenna's decline **15**:534d
·Renaissance political history **9**:1139a
·revolutionary acts during Austrian war **3**:1032e
·Roman Catholicism and political theory **15**:986d
·Spanish hegemony and church reform **9**:1151d

Papandreou, Georgios (b. Feb. 13, 1888, Kaléntzi, Gr.—d. Nov. 1, 1968, Athens),

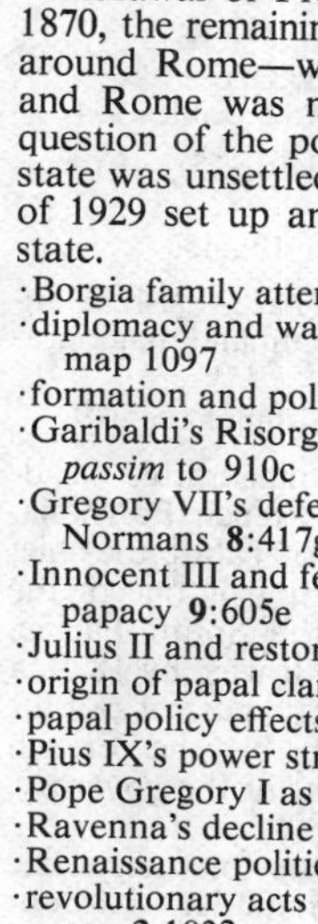

Papandreou

Greek republican politician who served three times as prime minister. Papandreou headed a Greek government in exile during World War II and held power for a few months after the Germans evacuated the country in 1944. He was again premier, as head of the reformist Centre Union Party in 1963 and 1964–65, until forced out of office in a conflict with King Constantine II (q.v.). Papandreou was arrested following the military coup of 1967; his son, the economist Andreas Papandreou, went into exile and continued criticism of the Greek military regime after his father's death.

Papanicolaou's stain, also called PAP SMEAR, laboratory method of staining smears of various body secretions, from the respiratory, digestive, or genitourinary tract, for the examination of cast-off body cells, to detect the presence of cancer. In the examination of the uterine cervix, the lower narrow end of the uterus, the Pap smear is notably reliable in detecting cancer in its pre-invasive, presymptomatic stage. For such a Pap smear, two specimens are usually taken for laboratory staining and examination, one consisting of vaginal secretions, obtained by suction (aspiration) or with a spatula, and the other of scrapings of the surface of the cervix, at the site where cancerous growth frequently originates. While the cervical scrapings provide material for highly accurate interpretations, the vaginal smear gives reliable results as well and may reveal malignant cells not only from the cervix but also from the endometrium (the mucous coat of the uterus) and the ovaries.
·cervical cancer fatality prevention **3**:768d
·diagnosis of cervical cancer **5**:695c
·uterine cancer detection **15**:701e

Papantla, in full PAPANTLA DE OLARTE, city, north central Veracruz state, east central Mexico. Formerly known as Papantla de Hidalgo, the city lies at 978 ft (298 m) above sea level in the hills dividing the Cazones and Tecolutla river basins. Corn (maize), beans, tobacco, and fruits flourish in the hot, humid climate, but the city is best known as Mexico's largest producer of vanilla, almost all of which is exported. Cattle and pigs are also raised in the area, and petroleum fields are nearby. The ruins of Tajin, a Totonac Indian sacred city, are 6 mi (10 km) west of Papantla. The city is accessible by road from Veracruz, 177 mi (285 km) to the southeast, and from Mexico City, 197 mi (317 km) to the southwest. Traditional Indian dress, dances, and folklore have been preserved by the population, which is largely Indian. Pop. (1970) 26,773.
20°27′ N, 97°19′ W
·map, Mexico **12**:68

Papareschi, Gregorio: see Innocent II.

Papaveraceae, poppy family of flowering plants (in the order Papaverales) that consists of approximately 26 genera and 200 annual, biennial, and perennial species, mostly herbaceous, but including some woody, small trees and shrubs, such as those of the genus *Bocconia.* The family is outstanding for its many garden ornamentals and pharmaceutically important plants. Species are native to temperate and tropical regions, but most are found in the Northern Hemisphere.

All species have bisexual, regular, cup-shaped flowers with one superior pistil (female structure) and many stamens (male parts). They have 2 or 3 conspicuous, separate sepals and 4 to 12 or more separate petals. The fruit is a capsule, the leaves are usually deeply cut or divided into leaflets, and the sap is coloured. Some species contain protopine and other alkaloids.

Opium, from which morphine, heroin, codeine, and papaverine are derived, is from the opium poppy (*Papaver somniferum*), which is native to Asia Minor. Numerous members of the family are valuable ornamental plants, including about 50 species of the genus *Papaver* (poppy). Other genera of the Papaveraceae distinguished for their ornamental species include: *Meconopsis* (Welsh poppy), *Eschscholzia* (California poppy), *Hunnemannia*, *Dendromecon* (bush poppy), *Stylophorum*, *Chelidonium* (celandine), *Sanguinaria* (bloodroot), *Platystemon* (creamcups), *Romneya*, *Macleaya*, *Stylomecon*, *Bocconia*, and *Eomecon*.

The genera *Argemone* (prickly poppy), *Glaucium* (horned poppy), and *Papaver* contain weedy species.

·classification and general features **13**:965f

Papaverales 13:963, the poppy and fumitory (or bleeding heart) order, containing 3 families, 44 genera, and 625 species of herbaceous and woody plants that are native throughout the temperate world but sparingly found in the tropics. Many species, such as the opium poppy, are important drug sources; others are garden ornamentals.

The text article covers the economic significance, natural history, form and function, evolution, and classification of the Papaverales.

REFERENCES in other text articles:

·alkaloid sources in plant kingdom **1**:597b

·angiosperm features and classification **1**:882f

RELATED ENTRIES in the *Ready Reference and Index: for*

common plants: see bleeding heart; bloodroot; bush poppy; California poppy; celandine; creamcups; Dutchman's-breeches; fumitory; golden cup; horned poppy; poppy; prickly poppy; squirrel corn; Welsh poppy

other: Corydalis; Fumariaceae; Hypecoaceae; Papaveraceae

Papaver somniferum (plant): *see* opium.

papaw (tree): *see* pawpaw.

papaya, succulent fruit of a large plant (*Carica papaya*) of the family Caricaceae, barely a tree, since its palmlike trunk, though up to eight metres tall, is not as woody as a typical tree. The plant bears no lateral branches but is crowned by deeply lobed leaves, sometimes 60 centimetres (2 feet) across, borne on hollow petioles 60 centimetres long. Normally, the species is dioecious, male and female flowers being produced on separate plants; but hermaphroditic forms are known, and numerous irregularities in the distribution of the sexes are common. Male flowers are borne in clusters on stalks 90 centimetres (3 feet) long; the flowers are funnel shaped, about 2.5 millimetres (0.1 inch) long, whitish, the corolla five-lobed, with ten stamens in the throat. The female flowers are considerably larger, on very short stalks, and are often solitary in the leaf axils; they have five fleshy petals that are united toward the base and a large cylindrical or globose superior ovary that is crowned by five fan-shaped sessile stigmas.

The fruit is commonly spherical to cylindrical in form, 75–500 millimetres (3–20 inches) or even more in length, sometimes weighing as much as 9 or 11.5 kilograms (20 or 25.5 pounds). In general character it strongly resembles a muskmelon. The very juicy flesh is deep yellow or orange to salmon coloured, about 2.5 millimetres thick. Along the walls of the large central cavity are attached the numerous round, wrinkled, black seeds, the size of peas.

Though its origin is rather obscure, the papaya may represent the fusion of two or more species of *Carica* native to Mexico and Central America. Today it is cultivated throughout the tropical world and into the warmest parts of the subtropics.

The papaya fruit is slightly sweet, with an agreeable musky tang, more pronounced in some varieties and in some climates than in others. It is a popular breakfast fruit in many countries and is also used in salads, pies, sherbets, juices, and confections. The unripe fruit can be cooked like squash.

The unripe fruit contains a milky juice in which is present a protein-digesting enzyme known as papain, which greatly resembles the animal enzyme pepsin in its digestive action.

Papaya (*Carica papaya*)
Grant Heilman—EB Inc.

This juice is used in the preparation of various remedies for indigestion and in the manufacture of meat tenderizers.

Papayas are usually grown from seed. Their development is rapid, fruit being produced before the end of the first year. Under favourable conditions, a plant may live five years or more.

·alkaloid derivative **1**:602e

·development of agriculture **1**:330c

·fruit farming economics **7**:752f; tables 754

Pape, Jean-Henri (1784–1875), French piano maker.

·piano felt hammer invention **10**:445c

Papebroch, Daniel van (1628–1714), Danish-Flemish Jesuit theologian and hagiographer.

·diplomatics standards establishment **5**:807f

Papeete, capital and administrative headquarters of Tahiti and of French Polynesia, lies on the northwest coast of Tahiti, the chief island of the Society group; it is one of the largest urban centres in the South Pacific. With an excellent harbour, it was, by 1829, a place of trade and a favourite port of call for whalers. After annexation by the French (1880), it was made the seat of the governor, becoming a commune in 1890.

Papeete is now a major stop for transpacific shipping and airlines with modern harbour

Quayside near the main street of Papeete, Tahiti
Charles R. Meyer—Photo Researchers

facilities and a jet airport. Copra, sugarcane, mother-of-pearl, vanilla, and coffee are exported. It is a major tourist base serving both Tahiti and the other French Polynesian islands. The appearance of the town is distinctively French. Pop. (1971) 25,342.
17°32′ S, 149°34′ W

·Oceanian trade community characteristics **13**:446a

·population and economy **7**:717g

·tourist boom **14**:784b

Papen, Franz von (b. Oct. 29, 1879, Werl, now in West Germany—d. May 2, 1969, Obersasbach), German statesman and diplomat who played a leading role in overthrowing the Weimar Republic and in helping Adolf Hitler to become German chancellor in 1933.

The scion of a wealthy Catholic landowning family, Papen began his career as a professional soldier. At the beginning of World War I, he was military attaché in Washington but, implicated in cases of espionage and sabotage, he was recalled in 1915 at the request of the U.S. government. Until the end of the war he served as chief of staff of the 4th Turkish Army in Palestine. Returning after the war to Germany, Papen, a monarchist, decided to enter politics. From 1921–1932, he was a deputy in the Reichstag (federal lower house), belonging to the ultra-right wing of the Catholic Centre Party. An advocate of Franco-German understanding, he himself had no political following. His elevation to the chancellorship (June 1, 1932), engineered by President Paul von Hindenburg's adviser Gen. Kurt von Schleicher, came as a complete surprise to the public.

Papen
Camera Press—Pix

Papen established a rightist, authoritarian government without a political base in the Reichstag. Determined to assure acceptance of his government by the Nazis, the second largest party in Parliament, he lifted the ban on the Nazis' paramilitary Sturmabteilung (SA, June 15) and deposed the Sozialdemokratische Partei Deutschlands (German Social Democratic Party) government (July 20). In foreign affairs, he achieved the virtual cancellation of Germany's reparations obligations under the Treaty of Versailles. Hitler, however, who wanted to rule Germany himself, remained in opposition. When Papen attempted to wear down Nazi political strength through repeated elections, Schleicher, his defense minister, wishing to establish a broad national front, induced a number of Cabinet ministers to reject Papen's policies; Papen thereupon resigned and was, on December 4, succeeded by Schleicher.

Chagrined at his ouster, Papen came to terms with Hitler (Jan. 4, 1933) and persuaded Hindenburg to appoint the Nazi leader to the chancellorship. As vice chancellor, Papen, whose associates received a majority of the ministerial posts, hoped to restrain the Nazis. Though he soon realized how mistaken he had been, he continued to serve Hitler. Almost a victim of the purge of Ernst Röhm and his SA of June 30, 1934, during which Hitler rid himself also of other encumbrances, Papen was dismissed three days later and sent as ambassador to Austria (1934–38), for whose annexation to Germany he worked. He then became ambassador to Turkey (1939–44), where he attempted to keep that country out of an alliance with the Allies.

Papen was arrested by the Allies in April 1945 and placed on trial as a war criminal. Found not guilty by the Nürnberg tribunal of conspiracy to prepare aggressive war, he was sentenced to eight years' imprisonment by a German court as a major Nazi, but in 1949, on his appeal, was released and fined. Papen's memoirs, *Der Wahrheit eine Gasse* (Eng. trans., *Memoirs*), appeared in 1952.

·Hindenburg and parliamentary crisis **8**:119a
·Hindenburg's concessions to Nazis **8**:888c

paper and paper production **13**:966, covers the substance commonly used for writing or printing or for wrapping and the manufacturing process.

TEXT ARTICLE covers:
Historical development of papermaking **13**:966d
Fibre sources 967d
Processes for preparing pulp 969g
Manufacture of paper and paperboard 972a
The world paper industry 974f
Paper properties and uses 974h

REFERENCES in other text articles:
·African resource development **1**:210f
·ancient writing use **13**:912c
·automated papermaking machines **2**:508c
·cellulose source alternates **10**:972g
·Chinese folk art paper use **7**:480g
·clay mineral industrial uses **4**:706b
·contribution to pollution **16**:582f
·drawing paper development **5**:995f
·dye requirements and application processes **5**:1104c
·Han dynasty's discovery and use **4**:314g
·manuscript use in Middle Ages **3**:650h
·Montgolfiers' innovations of 1700s **12**:409h
·origin, spread, and document use **5**:808g
·packaging purposes, materials, and styles **13**:854g
·paperboard characteristics, measurement, and types **13**:975a *passim* to 976g
·Poales unusual products **14**:586c
·police evidence examination procedure **14**:676c
·printing history and development **14**:1052g *passim* to 1059a
·printing press operation **14**:1066d *passim* to 1073b
·printing's invention and influence **18**:34h
·publishing history and development **15**:224a
·resin fortification of paper **14**:517e
·salvage techniques and by-products **11**:625g
·wood pulping process in manufacturing **19**:924b; illus. 8
·world production, table 2 **19**:924

RELATED ENTRIES in the *Ready Reference and Index*:
calendering; cylinder machine; Fourdrinier machine; kraft process; pulp, paper; sulfite process

paperbacks, books (*q.v.*) published with soft covers at modest cost. They have served to expand enormously the distribution of printed matter among the general public of countries with high literacy percentages.

·economics of novel publication **13**:297d
·history and development **15**:231g
·origin and popular market **2**:121f

paperbark tree, common name for *Melaleuca leucadendron*, a species of the family Myrtaceae of the order Myrtales.

·Myrtales economic importance **12**:773f

paper birch (*Betula papyrifera*), also called canoe birch, silver birch, and white birch, ornamental, shade, and timber tree of the family Betulaceae, native to northern and central North America.

Usually about 18 metres tall but occasionally reaching 40 metres, the tree has ovate, dark-green, sharp-pointed leaves about ten centimetres long. The bark, brown at first, whitens and peels into paper-thin layers, marked by narrow horizontal pores, or lenticels. On the copper-coloured inner bark, the pores are bright orange. Short, pendulous branches and their numerous flexible twigs create a lacy silhouette in winter.

The western paper birch (*B. papyrifera* variety *commutata*) of Canada and the western U.S. is about 30 metres tall, with orange-brown to nearly white bark; the smaller northwestern paper birch of western North America (variety *subcordata*), is 18 metres high and has orange-brown to silver-gray bark, purplish, red-brown twigs, and small, heart-shaped leaves, about six centimetres long; the mountain paper birch (variety *cordifolia*), with white bark, is a small, sometimes shrubby tree of Canada and the eastern and midwestern U.S. In the Alaska paper birch (variety *humilis*) the nearly triangular leaves are about four centimetres long, the bark white to red brown; the Kenai birch (variety *kenaica*), found in Alaska from sea level to altitudes of 665 metres, is rarely 12 metres tall and has white bark, tinged orange or brown.

Paper birch (*Betula papyrifera*)
E.H. Ketchledge

Paper birch is fast growing but short-lived and susceptible to borers when cultivated south of its natural range. The close-grained, almost white wood is used for turned articles, woodenware, pulp, and fuel. North American Indians and early settlers used the thin, water-impervious bark for roofing, canoes, and shoes.

·size range and distribution **2**:872c

paperbone, common name for *Scopelosauridae*, a family of fish belonging to the suborder Myctophoidei of the order Salmoniformes.

·classification and general features **16**:191f

paper bush: *see* Thymelaeales.

paper chasing (sport): *see* cross-country running.

paper chromatography, a technique for separating dissolved chemical substances through the use of sheets of paper. It is an inexpensive but powerful analytical tool, especially useful when the sample quantities are small.

The method consists of applying the test solution or sample as a spot near one corner of a sheet of filter paper. The paper is initially impregnated with some suitable solvent to create a stationary liquid phase. An edge of the paper close to the spot is then immersed in another solvent in which the components of the mixture are soluble in varying degrees. The solvent penetrates the paper by capillary action (caused by the attractive forces between the paper and solvent molecules) and, in passing over the sample spot, carries along with it the various components of the sample. The components move with the flowing solvent at velocities that are dependent on their solubilities in the stationary and flowing solvents. Separation of the components is brought about if there are differences in their relative solubilities in the two solvents. Before the flowing solvent reaches the farther edge of the paper, both solvents are evaporated, and the location of the separated components is identified, usually by application of reagents that form coloured compounds with the separated substances. The separated components appear as individual spots on the path of the solvent. If the solvent flowing in one direction is not able to separate all the components satisfactorily, the paper may be turned 90° and the process repeated using another solvent. As many as 16 components may be separated using the two-dimensional technique. Paper chromatography has become standard practice for the separation of complex amino acid mixtures and of peptides. It has also been widely used in the separation of carbohydrates, steroids, purines and a long list of simple organic compounds. Inorganic ions can also readily be separated on paper.

·biochemistry research techniques **2**:997a
·chemical analysis separation methods **4**:79c
·partition chromatography development **4**:566c

paper coal: *see* dysodile.

paper cut, also called CARDBOARD CUT, relief printing process using cardboard or paper materials.

·printmaking technique and history **14**:1076d

paper folding, art of folding objects out of paper without cutting, pasting, or decorating. Its early history is not known, though it seems to have developed from the older art of folding cloth.

In Japan, where it is called origami, paper folding has reached its greatest development, with hundreds of traditional folds and an extensive literature dealing with the art. Japanese folds divide roughly into two categories: figures used in ceremonial etiquette (such as *noshi*, folded decorations attached to gifts); and, birds, animals, fish, insects, flowers, human figures, furniture, and other objects. Some of the animals have amusing action features; best known are the bird that flaps its wings when its tail is pulled and the frog that hops when its back is tapped. Akira Yoshizawa of Tokyo is considered the greatest of modern paper folders. He wrote several books on origami and created a large number of new, often fantastically complex, figures possessing great realism and delicate beauty.

"Peafowl," origami by Akira Yoshizawa, 1942; in the artist's collection, Tokyo
Photograph, Nobuyuki Masaki

Paper folding also has flourished in Spain and South America. Miguel de Unamuno, Spanish writer and philosopher, made a hobby of paper folding. He invented many new animal constructions and wrote his *Amor y pedagogía* (1902), a humorous essay on the art. In South America, Vicente Solórzano Sagredo of Argentina was the leading expert on paper folding and the author of the most comprehensive manuals on the art in Spanish. George Rhoads of Evanston, Ill., and Giuseppe Baggi of New York also achieved distinction in this art.

Apart from the Oriental tradition, the folding of coloured papers into ornamental designs was introduced by Friedrich Froebel into the kindergarten movement that he initiated in Germany in the 19th century. Later, the Bauhaus, a famous German school of design, stressed the folding of paper as a method of training students for commercial design. The use of folded paper in mathematical recreations is similarly independent of origami. Particularly intriguing are A.H. Stone's flexagons (1939), a variety of paper structures that alter their faces in curious ways when properly flexed.

·flexagon figure construction **13**:353e

Paphiopedilum (orchid): *see* lady's slipper.

Paphlagonia, ancient district of Anatolia adjoining the Black Sea, bounded by Bithynia in the west, Pontus in the east, and Galatia in the south. The Paphlagonians were one of the most ancient peoples of Anatolia. Passing under the rule of Lydia and Persia, they submitted to Alexander the Great (333 BC), after which they enjoyed a measure of independence. In the 2nd and 3rd centuries BC Paphlagonia was gradually absorbed by the expanding Pontic kingdom on its eastern border.

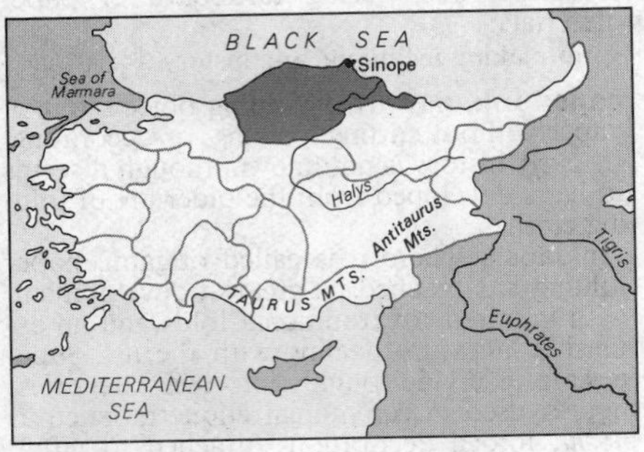

Paphlagonia

From W. Shepherd, *Historical Atlas*, Harper & Row, Publishers (Barnes & Noble Books), New York; revision copyright © 1964 by Barnes & Noble, Inc.

When the Pontic kingdom under Mithradates VI was destroyed by Pompey in 65 BC, the coastal districts of Paphlagonia (including its capital at Sinope) were attached to Roman Bithynia while the interior regions were left under native rulers. Upon the extinction of the native dynasty (*c.* 6 BC), the remainder of the territory was incorporated into the Roman province of Galatia. In the 4th century AD, the emperor Domitian made Paphlagonia a separate Roman province.

·Greek colonies and conquests and Hellenistic kingdoms maps **8**:335 *passim* to 380
·Mithradates VI's military career **12**:288b

Paphos, the name of a modern town and administrative district and of two ancient cities on the west coast of Cyprus. The older ancient city (Greek Palaipaphos) was located at modern Pírgos (Kouklia); New Paphos, which had already superseded Old Paphos in Roman times, was ten miles farther west. New Paphos and Ktima together form modern Paphos.

Paphos, settled by Greek colonists in the Mycenaean period, contained a famous temple of Aphrodite and was the legendary site where Aphrodite was born from the sea foam. In Hellenic times Paphos was second only to Salamis in extent and influence among the states of Cyprus. The Cinyrad dynasty ruled Paphos until its final conquest by Ptolemy I of Egypt (294 BC). Old Paphos dwindled in influence after the fall of the Cinyradae, the foundation of New Paphos, and the Roman conquest of Cyprus (58 BC). It was finally deserted after the 4th century AD.

New Paphos, the port town of Old Paphos, became the administrative capital of the whole island in Ptolemaic and Roman times and head of one of the four Roman districts. The city was attacked and destroyed by Muslim raiders in AD 960.

·area and population table **5**:403
·map, Cyprus **5**:402

Papiamento, also spelled PAPIAMENTU, creole language based on Spanish, spoken on the islands of Curaçao, Aruba, and Bonaire, in the Caribbean Sea. Papiamento is apparently based on a Spanish pidgin or creole language, with early influences from Portuguese and, more recently, strong Dutch influences (Dutch is the official language of Curaçao). Twenty-five percent of the vocabulary of Papiamento is of Dutch origin; the remainder is primarily from Spanish or Portuguese. Although Papiamento has no official status, it is widely used on Curaçao and is more often recognized as a "real" language than formerly. As is usual with pidgins and creoles, Papiamento's grammar and syntax have become changed and simplified from those of Spanish, the parent language. An example of a sentence in Papiamento is: *E máma ta'a mand' e jú bái bende piská*, Spanish *La mamá mandaba al hijo que vaya a vender pescado*, "The mother sent the boy to go and sell fish."

·Caribbean Creole dialect groups **3**:904f
·classification and number of speakers **15**:1030d

Papias (fl. early 2nd century AD), bishop of Hierapolis, Phrygia (near modern Erzurum, Tur.), whose work "Explanation of the Sayings of the Lord," although extant only in fragments, provides important apostolic oral source accounts of the history of primitive Christianity and of the origins of the Gospels.

According to the 2nd-century theologian Irenaeus, bishop of Lyons, whose work "Against the Heresies"—according to some scholars—depends partly on the text of Explanation, Papias was a companion of Polycarp of Smyrna (Turkey) and had known the Apostle John. The 4th-century church historian Eusebius of Caesarea critically records that Papias derived his material not only from John the Evangelist but also from John the Presbyter, through whose influence he had infected early patristic theologians with a false Judeo-Greek millenarianism, the apocalyptic teaching that Christ would reappear to transform the world into a 1,000-year era of universal peace, and had implicated Christ in fantastic parables. Eusebius' antipathy to Papias consequently led him to edit severely the latter's text and preserve only short excerpts.

Papias' interpretation of the Gospels was used by Eastern and Western Christian theologians down to the early 4th century. He claimed that Mark the Evangelist's record of Christ was entirely an interpretation of St. Peter's preaching. About Matthew, Papias observed that he "compiled the oracles in the Hebrew language [or, a Hebrew dialect]; but everyone translated them as he was able." Early interpreters disagreed whether this statement meant that the Gospel According to St. Matthew was originally written in Hebrew or that only certain Hebraic idioms were used. Papias maintained that a fifth Gospel also existed, to the Hebrews, as well as additional extraordinary parables attributed to Christ that differ from the regular Gospel accounts. This belief, together with his antimillenarianism, prompted Eusebius of Caesarea to assert that the Book of Revelation was not the work of John the Evangelist but of the second John, whom Papias was supposed to have known. Such conflicting testimony continues to raise problems about the formation of the Gospel texts, the existence of an Aramaic version of Matthew, the identity of the two Johns, and other aspects in the history of the primitive church.

The severe criticism that Eusebius levelled at Papias, motivated largely by the latter's realistic millenarianism, in the opinion of modern historians, can be tempered by Eusebius' difficulty in grasping Papias' mentality, the singular practical and intellectual attitudes distinctive of both, and the changed situation of the church evolving over the three centuries separating the two men. The varied backgrounds characterizing Papias and Eusebius rendered the latter practically incapable of understanding the nature of millenarianism in the primitive church and thus complicated his appreciation of Papias' simple but intense faith experience.

·canon oral tradition degeneration **2**:939f
·Johannine letters literary sources **2**:971b
·Mark Gospel authorship **2**:951d

Pa-Pien Chiang (South east Asia): *see* Black River.

papier-mâché, repulped paper that has been mixed with glue or paste so that it can be molded. The art of making articles of papier-mâché, beautifully decorated in Oriental motifs and handsomely lacquered, was known in the East centuries before its introduction in Europe. Molded paper products were first made in France in the early part of the 18th century and, later, in Germany and England. Different processes were used; for instance, several sheets of paper glued together could be pressure molded into such articles as trays and furniture panels. Although production has declined since the 19th century, papier-mâché is still used for toys, masks, model scenic materials, and the like.

·folk sculpture use **7**:472g
·furniture use in Victorian England **7**:783b
·hobby materials and uses **8**:979g
·sculptural uses **16**:426g
·Tibetan mask use **3**:1141b

papiers collés (art): *see* collage.

papiers decoupés (art): *see* collage.

Papilionidae, cosmopolitan family of butterflies (order Lepidoptera) including the swallowtail butterfly, bird-winged butterfly, and parnassian.

Representative Papilionidae.
(Top) Giant swallowtail (*Papilio cresphontes*) and (bottom) parnassian butterfly (*Parnassius apollo*)

(Top) Ray Glover—National Audubon Society, (bottom) W. Zept from the Natural History Photographic Agency—EB Inc.

The swallowtail butterfly, found worldwide except the Arctic, is named for the characteristic taillike extensions of the hindwings, although many species are tailless. Colour patterns vary; many species have yellow, orange, red, green, or blue markings on an iridescent black, blue, or green background. Sexual and seasonal differences in coloration also occur. Many swallowtails mimic the coloration and patterns of butterflies that are protected by a bad taste.

The large, smooth, brightly coloured larvae feed on foliage. Black and yellow eyelike spots on the thorax of some larvae resemble the head of a snake. Many have scent glands and discharge a bad-smelling substance when disturbed.

The bird-winged butterflies (*Troides*, sometimes *Ornithoptera*) are large, beautiful butterflies with long, graceful forewings. Most species occur in the Indo-Australian area. The male's velvet black wings are marked with iridescent blue, green, or gold. The females are larger and duller coloured than the males.

The parnassian (*Parnassius*), also called apollo, found in alpine regions in Asia, Europe, and North America, is a medium-sized butterfly, generally with translucent white, yellow, or gray wings with dark markings and usually a red or orange spot on the hindwing. Unlike most butterflies, parnassians pupate inside cocoon-like webs, usually constructed among leaves or in rubbish piles. They are prized among butterfly collectors because of their coloration and high mountain habitat. Parnassians are sometimes separated into their own family, Parnassiidae.

·classification and general features **10**:830e
·concealing and startle patterns, illus., **4**:Coloration, Biological, Plates III and IV
·swallowtail larva and pupa, illus., **10**: Lepidoptera, Plates II and III

papilla amphibiorum (anatomy): *see* amphibian papilla.

papilla basilaris (anatomy): *see* basiler papilla.

papillary muscles, nipple-like muscles, variable in number, that project into the cavities of the ventricles (lower chambers of the heart). The free edges of the flaps, or cusps, making up the valves between the upper and lower chambers are anchored to the papillary muscles by many slender cords, called the chordae tendineae. In the part of the heart cycle called systole, when the walls of the ventricles contract to force blood out through the aorta into the general circulation and into the pulmonary artery to the lungs, the papillary muscles also contract. They pull on the free edges of the cusps and prevent the valves from being forced open by the pressure in the ventricles.

papilledema, swelling of the structure through which the optic nerve enters the eyeball.

·intracranial pressure changes **7**:121d

papilloma, non-cancerous lobed or branched tumour of a lining tissue (epithelium).

·ocular tumour conditions **7**:117h

papillomavirus (virus): *see* papovavirus.

papillon, breed of toy dog known from the 16th century, when it was called a dwarf spaniel. A fashionable dog, it was favoured by Madame de Pompadour and Marie Antoinette, and it appeared in paintings by some of the Old Masters. The name papillon (French: "butterfly") was given to the breed in the late 19th century, when a variety with large, flaring ears resembling the wings of a butterfly came into vogue. There is another variety of papillon, with drooping ears. A slender, graceful dog with a plumed tail, the papillon stands 28 centimetres (11 inches) or less and weighs up to 5 kilograms (11 pounds). The coat is soft, full, and usually white with patches of black or of pale tan to dark reddish brown.

Papillon
Sally Anne Thompson—EB Inc.

Papillons (1832), piano cycle by Robert Schumann.

·component pieces **16**:364g

Papin, Denis (b. Aug. 22, 1647, Blois, Fr.—d. *c.* 1712, London), physicist who invented the pressure cooker and suggested the first cylinder and piston steam engine. Though his design was not practical, it was improved by others and led to the development of the steam engine, a major contribution to the Industrial Revolution. Papin assisted the noted Dutch physicist Christiaan Huygens with his air-pump experiments and went to London in 1675 to work with the English physicist Robert Boyle.

In 1679 Papin invented his steam digester (pressure cooker), a closed vessel with a tightly fitting lid that confines the steam until a high pressure is generated, raising the boiling point of the water considerably. A safety valve of his own invention prevented explosions. Observing that the enclosed steam in his cooker tended to raise the lid, Papin conceived of the use of steam to drive a piston in a cylinder, the basic design for early steam engines; he never built an engine of his own, however.

Papin, detail of an engraving by an unknown artist, *c.* 1689
H. Roger-Viollet

In 1705 the German physicist and philosopher Gottfried Wilhelm Leibniz sent Papin a sketch of the first practical steam engine, built by Thomas Savery of England. That sketch stimulated Papin to further work, culminating in his *Ars Nova ad Aquam Ignis Adminiculo Efficacissime Elevandam* (1707; "The New Art of Pumping Water by Using Steam"). In 1709 he built a man-powered paddle-wheel boat that successfully demonstrated the practicability of using the paddle-wheel in place of oars on steam-driven ships. Later that same year Papin returned to London, where he lived in obscurity until his death.

·automotive technology **2**:514e
·steam engine development **18**:35h
·steam engine history **8**:704b
·steam propulsion proposal **18**:654c

Papineau, Louis Joseph (b. Oct. 7, 1786, Montreal—d. Sept. 23, 1871, Montebello, Que.), politician who was the leader of the French-Canadians in Lower Canada (now Quebec) in the period preceding an unsuccessful revolt against the British government in 1837.

Papineau was elected a member of the House of Assembly of Lower Canada in 1808. During the War of 1812 against the United States, he served as an officer in the Canadian militia. He became speaker of the house in 1815 and was already recognized as leader of the French-Canadian Party in its struggle against the English-dominated government of Lower Canada. In 1820 he was appointed a member of the executive council by the governor, Lord Dalhousie, but he resigned three years later, realizing that he had no real influence. Papineau went to England in 1822 to speak out in behalf of the French-Canadians, and he thereafter remained bitterly opposed to British government in Canada. Lord Dalhousie refused to confirm Papineau's speakership in 1827 and resigned when the house supported Papineau.

Papineau
By courtesy of the Public Archives of Canada

To achieve reforms for French-Canadians, Papineau began to work with William Lyon Mackenzie, leader of the Reform Party in Upper Canada (now Ontario). In 1834 Papineau inspired the 92 Resolutions, a statement of French-Canadian demands and grievances, which was passed by the assembly. Lord Gosford, the governor, was authorized in 1837 to reject the demands and to appropriate provincial revenues without the assembly's consent. Papineau protested with inflammatory speeches. Hostilities broke out that November, and Papineau was forced to escape to the United States. He went to Paris in 1839 and remained there until 1844, when a general amnesty was granted.

During his absence, the British Parliament had united Upper and Lower Canada, as Canada West and Canada East (Act of Union, 1840). Papineau sat in the House of Commons in 1848–54, but he never regained his former dominance or his leadership of the French-Canadians. He agitated for the redivision of Canada and for independence from Great Britain, then retired to private life in 1854.

·French-Canadian nationalism **15**:331c

Papini, Giovanni (b. Jan. 9, 1881, Florence—d. July 8, 1956, Florence), journalist, critic, poet, and novelist, one of the most outspoken and controversial Italian literary figures of the early and mid-20th century. He was influential first as a fiercely iconoclastic editor and writer, then as a leader of Italian Futurism, and finally, after his reconversion in 1920 to Roman Catholicism, as a prolific (though sometimes unorthodox) spokesman for religious belief.

Educated at the University of Florence, Papini worked for a time as a museum clerk and a teacher of Italian but soon became a literary leader in Florence. He was a founder of an influential Florentine literary magazine, *Leonardo* (1903), dedicated to total intellectual freedom and the highest literary aims. During this period he wrote several violently anti-traditionalist prose works, such as *Il crepuscolo dei filosofi* (1906; "The Twilight of the Philosophies"), in which he expressed disenchantment with traditional philosophies. *Leonardo* was discontinued in 1907, and Papini moved on to the staffs of *L'Anima* and *La Voce*. Then he wrote one of his best known and most frequently translated books, the autobiographical novel *Un uomo finito* (1912; Eng. trans., *A Man—Finished;* U.S., title, *The Failure*, both 1924), a candid account of his early years in Florence and his desires for ideological certainty and personal achievement.

Papini had already become an enthusiastic adherent of Futurism, the frenzied militant, anti-traditional, experimental literary movement founded by Filippo Tommaso Marinetti, and he founded another Florentine periodical, *Lacerba* (1913), to further its aims. The magazine lasted two years, and, though Papini followed Marinetti in becoming a fervent Fascist, he later lost interest in the Futurist movement.

In 1920 Papini was reconverted to the Roman Catholicism in which he had been reared. A number of religious works followed, notably *Storia di Cristo* (1921; Eng. trans., *The Story of Christ*, 1923), a vivid and realistic recreation of the life of Jesus; *Pane e vino* (1926; Eng. trans., *Bread and Wine*, 1923), a volume of religious poetry; and *Sant' Agostino* (1929; Eng. trans., *St. Augustine*, 1930). Some of his later works were not uncritical of the church, however; for example, *Lettere agli uomini di papa Celestino VI* (1946; Eng. trans., *Letters of Pope Celestine VI to All Mankind*, 1948) and *Il diavolo* (1953; Eng. trans., *The Devil*, 1954), both of which contained unorthodox views.

Among Papini's many other books (he wrote more than 60) are three early collections of literary essays, the best known of which is *Ventiquattro cervelli* (1912; Eng. trans., *Four and Twenty Minds*, 1970), a discussion of major European literary giants including, rather characteristically, an essay on Papini himself. He also published some early poetry and short stories; a biography of Dante, *Dante vivo* (1933; Eng. trans., *Dante Living*, 1935), an opinionated but often insightful work that won the Mussolini Prize; a *Storia della letteratura italiana* (1937; "History of Italian Literature"); and also a biography (1949) of Michelangelo that met with a rather mixed reception.

Critical estimates of Papini vary widely. An abrasive personality (he has been called an "Italian Mencken"), he has been blamed for occasional lapses into stupidity and overgeneralization and especially for an arrogance that one critic has called neo-Promethean. Papini's unquestionable strengths, however, are a vigorous, colourful style and great imaginative power.

·pragmatism influence by
James **14**:943e

Papinian, full name AEMILIUS PAPINIANUS (b. *c.* AD 140, probably at Emesa, now Homs, Syria—d. 212), Roman jurist who posthumously became the definitive authority on Roman law, possibly because his moral high-mindedness was congenial to the world view of the Christian rulers of the postclassical empire. His creative understanding of the law does not quite justify his great reputation. The most important of his works are two collections of cases: *Quaestiones* (37 books) and *Responsa* (19 books). In the postclassical law schools the third-year students, who were called Papinianistae, used the *Responsa* as the basis of the curriculum. The Law of Citations (AD 426) of the emperor Theodosius II made Papinian predominant among five classical jurists whose works were to be authoritative in legal proceedings. His books were written in precise and elegant Latin.

Papinian held high public office under the emperor Lucius Septimius Severus (reigned AD 193–211). He was killed at the order of Severus' son and successor, Caracalla, perhaps for refusing to supply a legal excuse for the new emperor's murder of his brother and political rival, Geta.

Papinius Statius, Publius: *see* Statius.

Papio (monkey): *see* baboon; hamadryas.

Papoonan, 18th-century North American Indian prophet.

·North American new tribal religious
movements **18**:702a

papovavirus, also called PAPILLOMAVIRUS, a group of viruses responsible for a variety of abnormal growths in animals: warts (papillomas) in humans, dogs, and other animals; tumours (polyomas) in mice; and vacuoles (open areas) in cells of monkeys. The virus particle lacks an outer membrane; is cubical, about 45 nanometres (nm; 1 nm $= 10^{-9}$ metre) across; is covered with 42 subunits called capsomeres; and contains deoxyribonucleic acid (DNA). Papovaviruses develop in the nuclei of cells, in which they can be seen in apparent crystalline arrangements.

·infectious diseases of animals, table 2 **5**:868

pappataci fever, also known as PHLEBOTOMUS FEVER, THREE-DAY FEVER, or SAND FLY FEVER, acute, infectious, febrile disease caused by a virus and producing temporary incapacitation. It is transmitted by the bloodsucking female sand fly, *Phlebotomus papatasii*, and is prevalent in the moist subtropical countries of the Eastern Hemisphere lying between latitude 20° and 45° N, particularly around the Mediterranean Sea, in the Middle East, and in parts of India. It breaks out in epidemic form during the summer season following the breeding of this species of fly, but the reservoir for the virus between epidemics is unknown. The sand fly becomes infected as a result of biting an infected person when the virus is circulating in the patient's blood; *i.e.*, from 48 hours before until 24 hours after the onset of fever. The virus then requires seven to ten days to incubate, after which the sand fly remains infected for life.

Man becomes infected from the bites of infected female sand flies. The virus multiplies and becomes widely disseminated throughout the body; and within two and one-half to five days after exposure, there is suddenly a feeling of lassitude, abdominal distress, and dizziness, followed within one day by a chilly sensation and a rapid rise in temperature during the next day or two to 102°–104.5° F (38.8°–40.3° C). As in dengue, there are severe frontal headache and postorbital pain, intense muscular and joint pains, and a flushed appearance of the face but no true rash or subsequent scaling. During the first day of fever there is an accelerated pulse. Usually after two days the temperature slowly returns to normal; only rarely is there a second episode of fever. Following the febrile period there is great fatigue and weakness, accompanied by slow pulse and frequently subnormal blood pressure. Convalescence may require a few days or several weeks, but the prognosis is always favourable. Treatment is entirely symptomatic.

Sand flies breed in vegetation within a few hundred feet of human habitations. These breeding places are difficult to discover, hence larvicidal control is impractical. The bloodsucking females feed only from sunset to sunrise and only at ground level, so that sleeping above the ground floor provides moderately good protection. Ordinary mosquito netting and screening are useless, because unfed female flies can pass through their 18-mesh squares. Insect repellents, such as dimethyl phthalate, when applied to exposed skin, will keep sand flies away for a few hours, but the use of insecticide sprays on verandas, on screens, around doors and windows, and within habitations will readily kill all adult sand flies that alight on the sprayed surfaces. With this procedure an epidemic can be rapidly ended.

Pappenheim, Gottfried Heinrich, Graf zu (b. May 29, 1594, Treuchtlingen, Bavaria —d. Nov. 17, 1632, Leipzig), German cavalry commander conspicuous early in the Thirty Years' War. Originally a Lutheran and destined for diplomacy, he studied law but changed his profession and religion to become a soldier. He served with the Catholic League, headed by the elector Maximilian I of Bavaria, and proved a tempestuous cavalry officer, always charging ahead of his men, frequently wounded, and ruthless. Idolized by his regiment of cuirassiers, the Pappenheimers, he became colonel in 1623, and fought in the Bohemian War of 1620; against Ernst von Mansfeld (1621–22); and with the Spaniards in Lombardy and with the Grisons (1623–26). Recalled by Maximilian, he quelled a rebellion of Upper Austrian peasants in 1626. After conquering Wolfenbuttel (1627) in the Danish War, he showed great courage in storming Magdeburg. He skillfully covered Tilly's retreat and executed independent actions against the Swedes in northwestern Germany. Early in November 1632 Wallenstein sent Pappenheim, by this time an imperial field marshal, toward Westphalia and the lower Rhine. On the eve of the Battle of Lutzen, however, Pappenheim was recalled to Saxony, where he was mortally wounded soon after his arrival.

Pappus of Alexandria (fl. *c.* AD 320), the last great Greek geometer whose *Synagoge* (*c.* AD 340; "Collection") incorporates a wealth of Greek mathematical writings, many of which are no longer available in any other form, and whose efforts to arrest the general decay of mathematics were unsuccessful. The *Synagoge* is made up of eight books, but the first and part of the second are lost. His other works include commentaries on the *Analemma* (on an astronomical instrument) of Diodorus; on Ptolemy's *Almagest* (the classical astronomical work of his day), *Planisphaerium*, and *Harmonica;* and on Euclid's classical geometry *Elements*. One of Pappus' own theorems is still cited as the basis of modern projective geometry.

The *Synagoge* contains a systematic account of the most important works in ancient Greek mathematics, with historical annotations, improvements and alterations of existing theorems and propositions, and original material. This work was intended as a guide to be used with the original works. Included are systematic introductions to each book, setting forth clearly the contents and general scope of the topics to be treated.

Book 1 covers arithmetic, and the existing fragment of Book 2 sets forth a system of continued multiplication coupled with the expression of large numbers in terms of tetrads (powers of 10,000). Book 3 contains problems in plane and solid geometry, including the famous problem of finding two mean proportionals between two given lines. Pappus gave several solutions of this problem, one of them his own, and included a method of approximating continually to a solution, the significance of which he apparently failed to appreciate. The study of the arithmetic, geometric, and harmonic means and the problem of representing all three in one geometrical figure served as an introduction to a general theory of means. He distinguished among 10 kinds of means with examples. Book 3 also reveals how each of the five regular polyhedra may be inscribed in a sphere.

Included in Book 4 are various theorems on the circle that circumscribes three given circles tangent to one another. Also considered are certain properties of various curves, including the Spiral of Archimedes, the conchoid of Nicomedes (fl. *c.* 240 BC), and the quadratrix of Hippias of Elis (fl. *c.* 430 BC). Proposition 30 describes the construction of a curve of double curvature called by Pappus the helix on a sphere. The area of the surface included between this curve and its base is found by the classical method of exhaustion equivalent to integration. The rest of the book concerns the trisection of any angle and the solution of problems by means of special curves.

Book 5 concerns the areas of different plane figures and the volumes of different solids; the 13 semiregular polyhedra discovered by Archimedes; and the surface and volume of a sphere.

Book 6 comments on problems of geometry and astronomy treated by Theodosius of Bithynia, Autolycus of Pitane, Aristarchus, and Euclid.

Book 7 explains the terms analysis and synthesis and the distinction between theorem and problem. Also the works of Euclid, Apollonius of Perga, Aristaeus, and Eratosthenes of Cyrene, 33 in all, are enumerated, as well as the famous problem of Pappus, which inspired René Descartes and the theorems rediscovered by and named after Paul Guldin (1577–1643) of Switzerland.

Book 8 deals principally with mechanics; interspersed are some questions on pure geometry.

Pappus' commentary on Euclid's theory of irrational numbers is extant in an Arabic translation and traces the historical development of the theory of irrationals.

·conic section study **7**:1079g
·description of Euclid's works **6**:1020g
·mathematics history **11**:642a
·projective geometry development **7**:1120e

Pappus'–Pascal's theorems, mathematical statements that originated in Pappus' *Synagoge* (*see* Pappus of Alexandria), important in the development of geometry. The most famous, rediscovered by Paul Guldin, state the methods for finding the volume generated by a surface rotated about a line and the area generated by a curve rotated about its centre. Both methods make use of, or can be used to find, the centroid. Another theorem, sometimes called Pascal's theorem, is an early example of the principle of duality. Yet another theorem concerns the creation of lines of harmonic progression. A proposition of great interest concerns the construction of a parallelogram containing the same total area as two given parallelograms.

·projective geometry development **7**:1120e *passim* to 1121h

paprika, spice made by grinding the large red fruits of the *Capsicum annuum.* Sweet and semisweet paprikas are mildly pungent, usually preferred in temperate climates; pungent paprika is a hot spice, usually preferred in tropical and subtropical zones. The colour of paprika varies from a bright rich red in first-quality products to a dull brick red in products of inferior quality.

Production methods vary in different countries and districts of cultivation. After picking, paprika pods are cured and dried in the sun or in artificially heated chambers. In California, pods are not cured but are dried with artificially heated forced air under controlled conditions, a process that requires only hours, in contrast to days for the older method.

First-quality sweet paprika is prepared from pods divested of seeds, placenta tissue, calyces, and stems. First-quality semisweet paprika, in addition to the pericarps (fleshy walls) of the pods, includes a low percentage of seeds and placenta tissue. First-quality pungent paprika consists of pericarps, seeds, and placenta tissue. Low-quality pungent paprika may include all parts of the pod including calyx and stem.

·spice use and sources, tables 1 and 2 **17**:504
·vegetable products and processing **19**:46e

Pap smear (medicine): *see* Papanicolaou's stain.

Papua (former external territory of Australia): *see* Papua New Guinea.

Papua, Gulf of, inlet of the Coral Sea (southwest Pacific) indenting the southeast coast of New Guinea. About 225 mi (360 km) wide, it extends 95 mi into south central New Guinea. From west to east it is entered by the Fly, Bamu, Turama, Kikori, Purari, Lakekamu, and Vanapa rivers.
8°30′ S, 145°00′ E

·map, Australian External Territories **2**:433

Papuan (Malay *papuwah,* "woolly-haired"), term applied by early European navigators to the inhabitants of New Guinea and adjacent islands; they speak both Austronesian (Malayo-Polynesian) and Papuan languages. The racial composition of the islands is complex, and the term Papuan must be used cautiously when intended to indicate a racial grouping. Evidence suggests that there were two immigrant races, as well as isolated enclaves of aborigines with unique languages and blood-group patterns. Some Melanesian groups occupied the tip of the eastern coast of New Guinea and mixed with the Papuans. There is a considerable range of physical variation, as in stature (ranging from the medium height of coastal peoples to the very short Negritos of the central mountains) and skin colour (from dark brown to reddish white).

The cultures of the Papuans are varied, with considerable local specialization. Most groups are gardeners, practicing subsistence cultivation, the staple food varying according to region (taro, sweet potato, yam, banana, or sago). Coast peoples also rely on fishing, and hunting for marsupials and birds is important in many regions. Pigs are raised for food, ceremonial feasts, and trade; they are an important symbol of wealth and prestige.

Gardening techniques vary. The people of the lowlands practice rough shifting cultivation—the use of a plot of land for a year or two, followed by a long fallow period. There is more intensive cultivation in the highlands, where gardens are used for longer periods and are prepared more systematically. Many Papuans now participate in a cash economy in which they work as wage labourers or producers of such cash crops as coffee, cocoa, and copra.

On and near the coast, Papuans live in hamlets and villages of several hundred persons. In other areas, homestead patterns prevail. The family is the basic unit of production and consumption. The lineage, a group of persons who trace their descent from a common ancestor, is usually the most important social and ceremonial unit and generally owns the gardening land. Villages usually have several lineages, each with its own leader, based on personal influence and wealth; the leaders form a village council.

Beliefs in spirits associated with natural objects and in spirits of the dead are widespread, as are the practices of magic and sorcery. Almost everywhere boys are initiated into men's secret cults. *See also* cargo cults.

·Australoid racial characteristics **14**:844e
·mask design, structure, and use **11**:581f
·physical characteristics and diffusion **11**:864h
·property ownership and death customs **9**:585h

Papua New Guinea, an independent parliamentary state and a member of the Commonwealth of Nations, situated in the southwest Pacific Ocean and separated from Australia by the Torres Strait. It is composed of the eastern part of the great island of New Guinea, the Bismarck Archipelago, the Trobriand Islands, Woodlark Island, the Louisiade Archipelago, the D'Entrecasteaux Islands (*qq.v.*), and part of the Solomon Islands, including Buka and Bougainville (*qq.v.*) islands. In area it is 178,260 sq mi (461,690 sq km), and the population was estimated to be 2,756,500 in 1975. The capital and largest city is Port Moresby (*q.v.*), on the south coast of New Guinea.

Papua New Guinea became independent on Sept. 16, 1975, being the former Australian external territory of Papua (in the southeastern part of New Guinea) and the UN Trust Territory of New Guinea (in the northeast), the two having been jointly administered by Australia since World War II.

Most of the new nation is on mainland New Guinea, where the terrain ranges from extensive swampy lowland plains to the high central mountains, rising to 14,793 ft (4,509 m) in Mt. Wilhelm. The larger outlying islands, such as Bougainville, New Ireland, Manus, and New Britain, are predominantly high volcanic types fringed by low-lying coral formations. The whole country is subject to temperatures, precipitation, and humidity that are uniformly high throughout the year. The distribution of rainfall, usually exceeding 60 in. (1,500 mm) everywhere except in a portion of the south coast, is controlled by the effect of relief on the prevailing winds; precipitation may range from more than 300 in. in some mountainous parts of New Guinea to 40 in. at Port Moresby. Most of New Guinea is clothed with dense rain forest, and the soils are thin, washed out, and of low fertility. Some good volcanic and alluvial soils are found in the lowlands and outlying islands.

The name Papua was given to the south coast of New Guinea by the Portuguese navigator Jorge de Meneses, who sailed along it in 1526–27. In 1883 Queensland filed claim to Papua to block German control, and the following year a British protectorate was proclaimed, strengthened in 1885 by an agreement with the Dutch concerning the western boundary (the Netherlands then controlling the part of New Guinea that now belongs to Indonesia. In 1906 Papua became an Australian territory; Australia's status as the administering power was reaffirmed by the Australian Papua and New Guinea Act of 1949–73. It was administered under provision of the Australian Commonwealth Department of External Territories and the joint Papua New Guinea House of Assembly, but actual government operation fell largely within the sphere of the local districts, each with its administrator and public service officers. On Dec. 1, 1973, Papua New Guinea became self-governing in the first step toward full independence, which came in 1975.

The new nation of Papua New Guinea has great possibilities for development (*see* below), but it also faces many problems. Some of these have to do with the extreme ethnic and linguistic diversity of its people, which appears to make the creation of a sense of national identity and unity very difficult. Even as the state was created, Bougainville was declaring its independence as the "Republic of the North Solomons."

The country is divided into 18 districts, six in the former territory of Papua (Central, containing Port Moresby, and Gulf, Milne Bay, Northern, Southern Highlands, and Western), 11 in the former trust territory (Bougainville, Eastern Highlands, East New Britain, East Sepik, Madang, Manus, Morobe, New Ireland, Western Highlands, West New Britain, and West Sepik), and one, Chimbu, lying on the border between Papua and New Guinea.

For the people of Papua New Guinea, *see* Papuan. Roughly 90 percent of the people are villagers who exist by subsistence farming and small cash crops. The official languages are English, Police Motu, and Pidgin English; various Papuan and Melanesian languages are generally spoken, and the lingua franca is Pidgin English.

In 1974 about 236,000 children were receiving primary education and 29,000 secondary. More than 2,800 students were in higher education. The University of Papua New Guinea, opened in 1966, had 1,300 students in the mid-1970s.

The monetary unit is the kina, at par with the Australian dollar. The budget for 1975–76 showed revenues of 408,100,000 kinas (including grants of 210,000,000 kinas by Australia) and expenditures of 408,100,000 kinas.

Papua New Guinea is considered to be rich in scarcely tapped natural resources: timber, tuna and other fish, hydroelectric power, and, above all, copper, and possibly oil and natural gas. It has been exporting copper since 1972, and in 1974 extracted 193,000 metric tons. Gold and silver are also produced in some quantity, and several natural gas wells large enough to be commercially successful have been discovered. Industries include the manufacture of paint, industrial gases, concrete, and twist tobacco, as well as brewing, boatbuilding, and the assembly of electrical appliances; all of them are on a small scale and employ fewer than 16,000 persons.

The chief agricultural products are cocoa, coffee, copra, cassava, taro, yams, and rubber, mostly consumed domestically, though some copra, coffee, tea, cocoa, and crude rubber are exported. (Australia and Japan are the chief trading partners.) Cattle, pigs, and chickens are also raised for food. About 28,400,000 cu ft (804,500 cu m) of logs were harvested in 1972–73.

Exports of prawns are becoming important in the fisheries, and giant perch is taken in commercial quantities on the south coast. Pearl culture enterprises have been started, and there is a small export trade in marine shell. Tuna exports began in 1970.

·art materials and characteristics **13**:463e; illus. 452
·language types and grammars **13**:977b
·map, Australian External Territories **2**:433
·Melanesian peoples and cultures **11**:864g
·mountain ranges, soil, and climate **12**:1088c
·New Guinea Trust Territory history and features **12**:1090b
·Oceanian peoples' history **13**:443d
·politics, area, and population **13**:829g; table 830
·population, climate, and government **2**:431h *passim* to 436c
·song style and food ritual **16**:792c

Papuan languages 13:977, a group of some 700 languages spoken in an area centred on New Guinea. Some of these languages (350–450 of them) have been shown to be related and are known as the Central New Guinea macrophylum; the remaining 250–350 languages are of doubtful or unknown affiliation.

The text article covers the number and variety of Papuan languages, their genetic relationships, the major groupings of languages, the number of speakers, and the complexities of grammatical structures seen in the group.

REFERENCES in other text articles:
·Austronesian influence **2**:490b *passim* to 492a
·complexity and geographic distribution **13**:469f
·distribution and Austronesian contacts **11**:865b
·heritage and development **13**:828e
·language areas and affiliations **10**:669b
·New Guinea usage **12**:1090h

papule (Latin *papula*, "pimple"), a small, circumscribed, solid elevation of the skin. It may be round or irregularly shaped, domelike or flat topped, and with or without a smooth surface.

·industrial environment diseases **9**:532a

Papyri, Villa of the, building excavated at Herculaneum.

·excavations in the 18th century **14**:790h

Papyridae mutica (mollusk): *see* cockle.

papyrology, the care, reading, and interpretation of ancient documents written on papyrus, which is of prime importance in Egyptian, Near Eastern, and Classical archaeology.

Most papyrus documents have been found in Egypt, where the papyrus plant was cultivated for the manufacture of writing material, and the dry climate favoured preservation. Papyrus fragments have been found dating from as early as *c.* 2600 BC, and there are several important documents from the New Kingdom (1567–1085 BC)—*e.g.*, the Edwin Smith Papyrus, a medical text—but the majority of them date from Hellenistic and Roman times (4th century BC–6th century AD) and are written either in Egyptian demotic script, Greek, or Latin. Since they began to be collected in the late 18th and early 19th centuries, they have become an important source of information about the ancient Mediterranean world and an invaluable aid to the study of Classical literature and ancient religions. More than 2,500 papyrus copies of Greek and Roman literary works have been discovered, many of them previously unknown and some known only from references in ancient authors. One of the most spectacular of these discoveries was a manuscript of Aristotle's *Constitution of Athens*, found by an American missionary in Egypt in 1890. New biblical manuscripts have also come to light, and the papyrus scrolls found in the Dead Sea area since the late 1940s have been an outstanding aid to the study of ancient Judaism and early Christianity.

·epigraphic disciplines **6**:915e

papyrus, *Cyperus papyrus*, the paper reed, a plant cultivated in ancient times in the Nile Delta region in Egypt and chiefly important for the writing material made from its stem. The stem also provided material used in the manufacture of boats, sails, mats, cloth, and cords; the root was employed as fuel; and the pith was a common food. *See also* Cyperales.

plant
·Congo River and tributaries' grassy borders **4**:1126b
·marsh types and characteristic flora **17**:839c
·Okavango River plant communities **13**:541a
·rift lake shoreline vegetation **6**:118b

writing material
·ancient uses and manufacture **13**:911h
·calligraphic remains and forms **3**:646d; illus.
·origin and European document use **5**:808f
·printing and publishing history **15**:222g
·production and use **13**:966c

papyrus column, in Egyptian religion, amulet that conveyed freshness, youth, vigour, and the continuance of life to its wearer. The

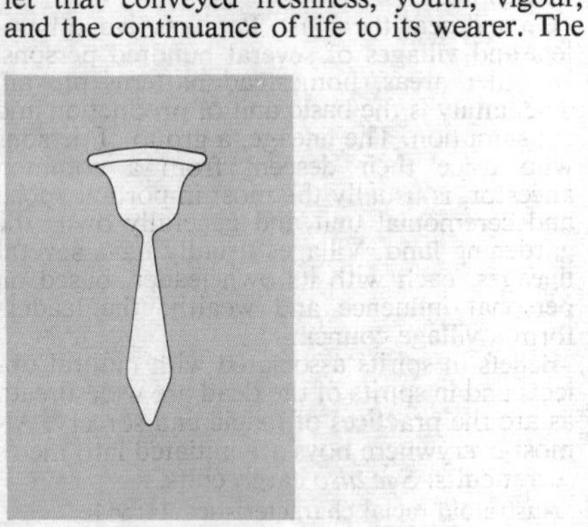

Papyrus column

amulet, made of glazed ware or various types of stone, was shaped like a papyrus stem and bud. Its significance was perhaps derived from its ideographic value; for, just as the plant itself was vigorous and growing, so also would the wearer of the papyrus column amulet possess these qualities.

Paquet, Louis-Adolphe (1859–1942), Canadian author.

·Canadian literature development **10**:1228g

Paquier, Claudius Innocentius du, 18th-century Dutch ceramist.

·Vienna hard-porcelain factory style **14**:910g

PAR (El Salvador): *see* Partido Acción Renovadora.

PAR, abbreviation for PRECISION-APPROACH RADAR, also called GROUND-CONTROLLED APPROACH (GCA), an aircraft landing system in which the controller gives the pilot oral instructions regarding the aircraft heading and glide path as shown on two radar screens.

·aircraft landing procedure function **18**:643c

para, in old Finnish religion a spirit who is believed to bring all kinds of wealth to the farm lucky enough to harbour him; the term is derived from the Swedish *bjära*, "bearer." The basic belief underlying the *para* concept is that there is only a limited amount of good available to all members of society and any one individual or family succeeds at obtaining it only at the expense of others. What the *para* brings to one farm disappears from another, whether it be grain, milk, or butter. The *para* can appear in the form of animals that may be seen frequently around the farmstead, such as a snake, dog, or rabbit. It can also be constructed by a farmwife envious of her neighbours. One typical form consists of a spindle wrapped with yarn for a body and a communion wafer for a heart. This creation was spun on the floor while an incantation was recited for the birth of the *para*.

Pará 13:978, state of northern Brazil, bounded by Guyana, Surinam, and the Territory of Amapá (north), by the Atlantic Ocean (northeast), by the states of Maranhão and Goiás (east), by Mato Grosso (south), and by Amazonas (west). The Amazon River crosses the state to enter the Atlantic via its enormous delta. The area of Pará is 481,872 sq mi (1,248,042 sq km). The capital is Belém. Pop. (1976 est.) 2,544,300.

The text article covers the state's history, natural environment, the contemporary state (population, administration and social conditions, economy, transportation and communications, and cultural life), and future prospects.

REFERENCES in other text articles:
·area and population table **3**:133
·map, Brazil **3**:125

Pará (city, Brazil): *see* Belém.

Para (Judaism): *see* sabbaths, special.

para, measure of weight in Sabah (in northern Borneo) equivalent to 90 pounds avoirdupois, or 40.8 kilograms.

·weights and measures, table 5 **19**:734

para adumma (Judaism): *see* red heifer.

para-aminobenzenesulfonamide (drug): *see* sulfanilamide.

para-aminobenzoic acid (PABA), a vitamin-like substance and a growth factor required by several types of micro-organisms. *Para*-aminobenzoic acid is used in the manufacture of the vitamin folic acid. The drug sulfanilamide is effective in treating some bacterial diseases because it competes with PABA for a position in a molecule required by the bacteria for reproduction.

Para-aminobenzoic acid has not been established as an essential nutrient for vertebrates.

The chemical formula for *para*-aminobenzoic acid is $C_6H_4COOHNH_2$. Found in brewer's yeast, it is one of three structural arrangements (isomers) of aminobenzoic acid.

·drug inhibition of bacterial growth **4**:191d
·enzyme inhibition mechanisms **6**:900g
·vitamin function for bacteria **13**:405h; table 406
·vitamin-like substances **19**:492b

para-aminopropiophenone (PAPP), drug used to increase the resistance of an animal body to external radiation.

·radiation protection chemicals, table 10 **15**:386

para-aminosalicylic acid, or sometimes AMINOSALICYLIC ACID, chemotherapeutic drug used in combination with isoniazid or the antibiotic streptomycin to treat tuberculosis. *Para*-aminosalicylic acid (PAS), which is administered orally, is only slightly anti-tuberculotic when used alone. It was introduced in the treatment of tuberculosis in 1946. The use of *para*-aminosalicylic acid in combination with isoniazid or streptomycin helps reduce or delay the development of resistant strains of the tubercle bacillus.

The chemical formula for para-aminosalicylic acid is $C_7H_7NO_3$.
·antituberculotic drugs and resistance **4**:192a
·pulmonary tuberculosis treatment **15**:771g

para-aortic body, in the human nervous system, collection of sympathetic nerve cells found along the abdominal aorta.
·autonomic nerve supply **12**:1032e

Parablastoidea, extinct class of the invertebrate phylum Echinodermata.
·classification and anatomical features **6**:185c

parable: *see* fable, parable, and allegory.

parabola, open curve, a conic section produced by the intersection of a right circular cone and a plane parallel to an element of the cone. As a plane curve, it may be defined as the path (locus) of a point moving so that its distance from a fixed line (the directrix) is equal to its distance to a fixed point (the focus).

The vertex of the parabola is the point on the curve that is closest to the directrix; it is equidistant from the directrix and the focus. The vertex and the focus determine a line, perpendicular to the directrix, that is the axis of the parabola. The line through the focus parallel to the directrix is the latus rectum (straight side).

The parabola is symmetric about its axis, moving farther from the axis as the curve recedes in the direction away from its vertex. When rotated about its axis, the parabola forms a paraboloid (*q.v.*).

The parabola is the path, neglecting air resistance and rotational effects, of a projectile, such as a hand-thrown baseball or a bullet fired from a gun, propelled outward into the air for a short distance. The parabolic shape is seen in certain bridges, forming arches, and in suspension-bridge cables that support a uniformly loaded road bed.

For a parabola the axis of which is the x axis and with vertex at the origin, the equation is $y^2 = 2px$, in which p is the distance between the directrix and the focus. The parameter of the curve is therefore, p.
·analytic geometry fundamentals **7**:1081b
·cometary orbital characteristics **4**:971h
·Fermat generalization equation **7**:235c

parabola of Descartes, also called TRIDENT OF NEWTON, in mathematics, the curve described by the equation $xy = cx^3 + dx^2 + ex + f$.
·analytic geometry fundamentals **7**:1088e

parabolic dune (landform): *see* crescentic dune.

parabolic equations, class of partial differential equations arising from diffusion phenomena, as in the heating of a slab. The simplest such equation in one dimension, $u_{xx} = u_t$, governs the temperature distribution at the various points along a thin rod from moment to moment. The solutions to even this simple problem are complicated, but they are constructed largely from a function called the fundamental solution of the equation, given by an exponential function, $\exp[(-x^2/4t)/t^{1/2}]$. To completely determine the solution to this type of problem, the initial temperature distribution along the rod and the manner in which the temperature at the ends of the rod is changing must also be known. These additional conditions are called initial values and boundary values, respectively, and together are sometimes called auxiliary conditions.

Also in the analogous two- and three-dimensional problems, the initial values and boundary values must be known. The differential equation in two-dimensions is, in the simplest case, $u_{xx} + u_{yy} = u_t$, with an additional u_{zz} term added for the three-dimensional case. These equations all assume the medium is of uniform composition throughout, while, for problems of non-uniform composition or for some other diffusion-type problems, more complicated equations may arise. These equations are also called parabolic in the given region if they can be written in the simpler form described above by using a different coordinate system. An equation in one dimension the higher-order terms of which are $au_{xx} + bu_{xt} + cu_{tt}$ can be so transformed if $b^2 - 4ac = 0$. If the coefficients a, b, c depend on the values of x, the equation will be parabolic in a region if $b^2 - 4ac = 0$ at each point of the region.
·differential equation principles **5**:756g
·numerical analysis fundamentals **13**:391b

parabolic geometry: *see* geometry, Euclidean.

parabolic reflector, polished surface the cross-section of which has the shape of a parabola. Radiation of certain wavelengths—such as light, heat, sound, or microwaves—parallel to the axis of such a surface converges at a single point (the focus); conversely, radiation emanating from the focus is converted into a parallel beam along the axis of the reflector. Applications of this property are used in automobile headlights, solar furnaces, radar, and radio relay stations.
·analytic geometry fundamentals **7**:1081g
·antenna and radiation focussing **1**:967f
·parabolic cylinder structure **18**:102e
·radio telescope operation **15**:467g
·satellite radio transmission **16**:265c; illus.

paraboloid, in its simplest form, an open surface generated by rotating a parabola (*q.v.*) about its axis. If the axis of the surface is z and the vertex is at the origin, the intersections of the surface with planes parallel to the xz and yz planes are parabolas (*see* Figure, top). The intersections of the surface with planes parallel to and above the xy plane are circles. The general equation of such a paraboloid is $x^2/a^2 + y^2/b^2 = z$, in which a and b are both positive.

If $a = b$, intersections of the surface with planes parallel to and above the xy plane produce circles, and the figure generated is the paraboloid of revolution. If a is not equal to b, intersections with planes parallel to the xy plane are ellipses, and the surface is an elliptical paraboloid.

If b is negative, cutting planes parallel to xz and yz produce parabolas of intersection, and cutting planes parallel to xy produce hyperbolas. Such a surface is a hyperbolic paraboloid (*see* Figure, bottom).

A circular or elliptical paraboloid surface may be used as a parabolic reflector.

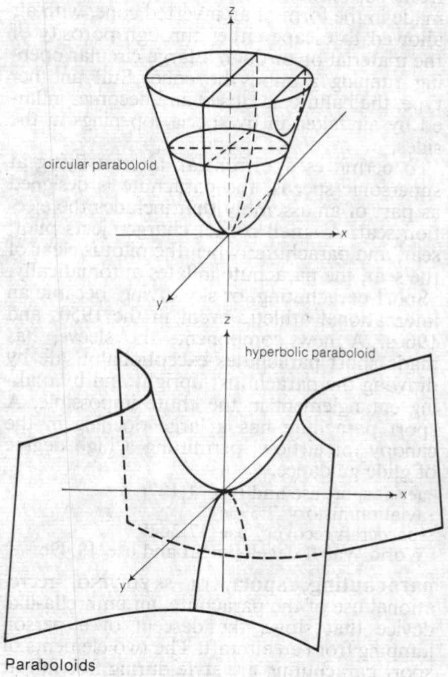

Paraboloids

Paracanthopterygii **13**:979, superorder of bony fishes comprised of six orders and containing about 1,160 species. Better known forms include the anglerfishes and the commercially valuable codfishes.

The text article covers the natural history, form and function, evolution and paleontology, and classification of the Paracanthopterygii.

REFERENCES in other text articles:
·commercial importance and habits **7**:347c
·evolutionary significance and classification **7**:340a; illus. 339

RELATED ENTRIES in the *Ready Reference and Index:*
anglerfish; batfish; beardfish; bib; brotula; burbot; cave fish; clingfish; cod; cusk; cusk eel; eelpout; frogfish; Gadidae; goosefish; grenadier; haddock; hake; ling; pearlfish; pirate perch; pollock; toadfish; trout-perch; whiting

Paracas, name applied to the culture that was centred on the Paracas peninsula, in

Embroidered cloak used to bury the dead, Paracas Necrópolis culture *c.* 200 BC–AD 200; in the Linden-Museum, Stuttgart, West Germany
Ferdinand Anton

the present-day southern Peruvian department of Ica, during the Early Horizon Period and the Early Intermediate Periods (*c.* 900 BC–AD 400). The Paracas culture's earlier phase, called Paracas Cavernas, is related to the Chavín culture (*c.* 1000–400 BC). The pottery of the period is not well fired and was sometimes painted after firing. The Paracas cultures of the middle Early Intermediate Period (*c.* AD 1–400) are referred to as the Paracas Pinilla and the Paracas Necrópolis phases. These periods show an improvement in pottery making. The Paracas Necrópolis people were named for and described by the study of cemeteries discovered at Cerro Colorado. The people wrapped the mummified corpses, along with funeral offerings, in embroidered cloaks, which are among the finest of examples of the art of textile-making. The multicoloured designs on these textiles bear a definite relationship to those of painted pottery of the Nazca culture. The Paracas also engaged in artificial deformation of the skull by binding the skull in infancy. *See also* Andean pottery; Andean textiles.
·funerary feline images **9**:259e
·mass burial chambers **6**:738a
·pre-Incan pottery design **1**:843b; map 840

Paracel Islands, Chinese HSI-SHA, archipelago in the South China Sea, about 150 mi (240 km) southeast of Hainan. The 15 scattered, low, coral islands and reefs have a total land area of 1.2 sq mi (3 sq km). The islands came under French control in the 1930s. They were occupied by Japan in 1939–46 and then passed to the People's Republic of China. Their control has been disputed by Taiwan and Vietnam.

Paracelsus 13:982, real name PHILIPPUS AUREOLUS THEOPHRASTUS BOMBAST VON HOHENHEIM (b. Nov. 10/14, 1493, Einsiedeln, now in Switzerland—d. Sept. 24, 1541, Salzburg, Austria), physician and alchemist. Paracelsus established the role of chemistry in medicine.

Abstract of text biography. In 1507 Paracelsus became a vagrant scholar and is said to have studied at the universities of Basel, Tübingen, Vienna, Wittenberg, Leipzig, Heidelberg, and Cologne. He graduated from the universities of Vienna and Ferrara and served as an army surgeon in Italy in 1521. In 1527–28 he lectured at the University of Basel. He published *Die grosse Wundartzney* ("Great Surgery Book") in 1536 and a clinical description of syphilis in 1530. Because his ideas were controversial and his manner was argumentative, Paracelsus frequently had to move from one area to another. He died under mysterious circumstances while in the service of the prince-archbishop Duke Ernst of Bavaria.

REFERENCES in other text articles:
·essential oil extraction and quinta essentia **13**:533c
·influence on modern chemistry **14**:387h
·laudanum introduction **5**:1053a
·medical chemistry and alchemy **1**:435a
·medicine in the Renaissance **11**:829e
·science development in Renaissance **16**:369g

Paracelsus (1835), a long poem by Robert Browning.
·Browning's popularity and style **3**:334e

paracetaldehyde (drug): *see* paraldehyde.

Parachi language, Iranian language of the Pamir group, spoken in the Pamir Mountains in northern Afghanistan.
·Indo-Iranian languages distribution map **9**:442

parachute, umbrella-like device for slowing the descent of a body falling through the atmosphere. Originally conceived for human use either as a sport or to provide a safe escape from a disabled aircraft, parachutes have found wide employment in war and peace for safely dropping supplies and equipment as well as personnel; a spectacular recent use has been to slow a returning space capsule during re-entry into the Earth's atmosphere.

Parachutes guiding the Apollo 14 spacecraft as it approached touchdown in the South Pacific Ocean, Feb. 9, 1971
By courtesy of the National Aeronautics and Space Administration

The parachute was invented at virtually the same time as the balloon but independently of it. The principle had been recognized by several writers, including Leonardo da Vinci; the first man to demonstrate it in action was Louis-Sébastien Lenormand of France in 1783. Lenormand jumped from a high tower; a few years later, other French aeronauts jumped from balloons; André-Jacques Garnerin was the first to use a parachute regularly, making a number of exhibition jumps, including one of about 8,000 feet (2,400 metres) in England in 1802.

Early parachutes were made of canvas; later, silk was employed. The first successful descent from an airplane was by Capt. Albert Berry of the U.S. Army in 1912. But in World War I, although parachutes were used with great frequency by observers escaping from captive balloons, they were considered impractical for airplanes, and only in the last stage of the war were they finally introduced. In World War II, however, parachutes were extensively employed for a variety of purposes, including landing special troops for combat, supplying isolated or inaccessible troops, infiltrating agents into enemy territory, stabilizing and retarding airborne weapons, and in decelerating aircraft during landing. With the increased speed of aircraft the ejection seat was developed, which automatically opened the pilot's chute after he had cleared the aircraft.

Modern man-carrying parachutes are made of nylon and assembled in a pack containing the parachute canopy, a small pilot parachute that assists in opening the canopy, and suspension lines, attached to a harness worn by the user. The canopy is given extraordinary strength by fabrication from up to 28 separate panels, or gores, each made of smaller sections, sewn together in such a way that a tear will usually be confined to the section in which it originates. The direction of the weave in each section adds further strength. The pack is fitted to the parachutist's back or front and opened by a ripcord that can be activated manually, by an automatic timing device, or by a line fastened to the aircraft. The harness is so constructed that deceleration, gravity, and wind forces are transmitted to the wearer's body with maximum safety and minimum discomfort.

Several forms of parachute have been developed for special purposes. The ring or ribbon parachute, invented in Germany during World War II, is composed of a number of concentric rings of fabric with openings that permit some airflow; such a chute has high aerodynamic stability and performs heavy-duty functions well, as in dropping heavy cargo loads or braking aircraft in short landing runs. Gliding parachutes have been designed to take advantage of the natural glide potential of chutes in general through manipulation of the suspension lines.

Parachutes designed for opening at supersonic speeds have radically different contours from conventional canopy chutes; they are made in the form of an inverted cone, with air allowed to escape either through porosity of the material or through a large circular opening running around the cone. Still another type, the ballute, is closed and becomes inflated by air taken in by special openings in the sides.

To permit escape from an aircraft flying at supersonic speeds, the parachute is designed as part of an assembly that includes the ejection seat. A small rocket charge ejects pilot, seat, and parachute; when the pilot is clear of the seat, the parachute inflates automatically.

Sport parachuting, or sky diving, became an international athletic event in the 1950s and 1960s. A new component, the sleeve, has made sport parachutes exceptionally safe by drawing the parachutist upright and by making entanglement in the chute impossible. A sport parachute has a large opening in the canopy for airflow, permitting a high degree of glide guidance.
·aerial sport use and type **1**:127f
·aviation history **7**:393e
·spacecraft recovery use **17**:362f
·World War II development and use **18**:49c

parachuting, sport, or SKYDIVING, recreational use of the parachute, an umbrella-like device that slows the descent of a person jumping from an aircraft. The two elements of sport parachuting are style during free fall (it is this element to which the term skydiving is usually applied)—the period after exit from the aircraft and before the opening of the parachute—and accuracy in landing. By spreading and arching his body, a parachutist can hold a stable position during descent in free fall, or he can make turns, loops, and barrel rolls and increase or decrease his rate of descent. By combining these techniques a parachutist may catch up to another parachutist during free fall and actually pass a baton for a free-fall relay event.

Sport parachutes that give the parachutist control of his direction and a horizontal speed of 10 miles (16 kilometres) per hour or more have permitted improved standards of accuracy in landing. Distance is measured from the exact centre of the target to the point of impact of the parachutist.

Jumper with a Parafoil parachute
Jim Larsen

Sport parachutes have large holes that permit the air to escape and drive the parachute in the direction opposite the hole, much like a low-power jet engine. The parachutes may be rotated by a light pull on a control knob that regulates the direction of the escaping air. The curved surface of the parachute moving through the air gives lift like that of an airplane wing. This lift effect greatly reduces the landing shock.

A device called the sleeve that controls the deployment of the parachute canopy is perhaps the main technological development behind the growth of sport parachuting. The sleeve is a three-way safety factor. It draws the parachutist upright during deployment and thereby virtually eliminates the opening shock. It controls the canopy during deployment and makes it impossible for a man to wrap up in the parachute while it opens. The sleeve also lessens the possibility that the canopy will remain closed by removing the pilot chute pressure from the apex of the canopy during the opening.

An outgrowth of informal competition for accuracy, sport parachuting came into its own at the first world championship meet in Yugoslavia in 1951, with five countries participating under the sponsorship of the Fédération Aéronautique Internationale. World championship meets are held every two years. *See* sporting record.

Improved equipment and techniques created an amazing safety record for the sport. The Telsan technique of parachuting instruction permits persons who have never before seen a parachute, and with only four hours of instruction, to make a static line jump, during which the parachute opens automatically. In France 100,000 student jumps were made without a fatality. Strict international regulations condemn unsafe practices. Sport parachutists are required to open their parachutes at a safe altitude of about 2,200 feet (670 metres).

The sport of parachute jumping is usually governed in each country by the parachute branch of the national aeronautic club.
·aerial sport development and form **1**:127f; illus. 128

paraclete (religion): *see* Holy Spirit.

paraconformity (geology): *see* unconformity.

Paracrinoidea, fossil class of the invertebrate phylum Echinodermata.
·classification and anatomical features **6**:185b

Paracryphiaceae, family of flowering plants of the order Saxifragales.
·classification system conflicts **16**:299c

parade: *see* pageant and parade.

Parade, ballet in one act centred around the parade of a travelling circus, with choreography by Léonide Massine, scenario by Jean Cocteau, music by Erik Satie, and scenery and costumes by Pablo Picasso. Especially innovative were the music (incorporating sounds of typewriters and airplane engines) and the Cubist costumes. *Parade* was first performed by Sergey Diaghilev's Ballets Russes at the Théâtre du Châtelet in Paris on May 18, 1917.
·Surrealism's stylistic development **19**:480g

Parade, La (1887–88), painting by Georges Seurat.
·Golden Mean proportion use illus. 1 **13**:870

Parade's End, tetralogy of novels (published individually 1924–28; collectively, 1950) by Ford Madox Ford.
·Impressionism in the novel **13**:284d

Paradies, (Pietro) Domenico (Italian musician): *see* Paradisi, (Pietro) Domenico.

Parādip, principal port of Orissa State, India, on the Bay of Bengal. Developed after 1958, it was being enlarged in the 1970s to handle 2,000,000 tons of freight traffic annually. Pop. (1971) 6,705.
20°14′ N, 86°39′ E
·map, India **9**:279
·Orissa's industrial development **13**:741b

Paradisaeidae (bird family): *see* bird of paradise.

paradise, place of exceptional happiness and delight. It is often used as a synonym for heaven and for the Garden of Eden before the expulsion of Adam and Eve.
·Manichaean cosmological system **11**:445f
·millennialist prophecies **12**:200f
·mythological themes and myth types **12**:800a
·salvific implications in religion **16**:201b

paradise bird: *see* bird of paradise.

Paradise Formation, sedimentary rocks that were laid down in southeastern Arizona during the Mississippian Period (the Mississippian began about 345,000,000 years ago and lasted about 20,000,000 years); the Paradise was named for exposures studied near the abandoned mining camp of Paradise, near Bisbee, Ariz. In the Chiricahua Mountains of southeastern Arizona, the formation consists of about 40 metres (135 feet) of black and gray crystalline limestones that weather to an olive and yellow colour. The limestones alternate with sandstones, shales, cross-bedded calcareous sandstones, and sandy limestones. Fossil evidence shows that the formation should be included in the upper Meramecian and lower Chesterian Series of the Mississippian.

Paradise Lost (1667), masterpiece of the English Puritan poet John Milton and one of the great literary epics. Its theme is the Fall of man. It closely follows the conventions of the Classical epic and is notable for its characterization of the fallen angel Lucifer, who dominates the work.
·Aeneid structural and stylistic impact **19**:153e
·allegoric mode and themes **7**:137h
·content and significance **10**:1150d
·epic example **6**:906f
·Haydn's setting in The Creation **8**:683d
·literary art forms **10**:1048a
·prosody and stylistic determinants **15**:73b
·Ptolemaic cosmos utilization **2**:42a
·theology, characterization, and imagery **12**:207c *passim* to 208f

paradise nut, also called MONKEY POT and SAPUCAIA NUT, edible seed of various sapucaias, especially in Brazil and Guyana.
·fruit farming economics **7**:753c; table 755

Paradise Regained (1671), poem by John Milton, a sequel to his great epic *Paradise Lost* but less ambitious in scope and more simple and austere in language. It deals with the temptation of Christ in the desert by Satan.
·literary style and significance **10**:1150e
·religious theme and mood **12**:208a

Paradisi (PARADIES), **(Pietro) Domenico** (1707–91), Italian composer, harpsichordist, and teacher of singing who composed operas and keyboard works.
·sonata evolution **12**:711g

paradox, apparently self-contradictory statement, the underlying meaning of which is revealed only by careful scrutiny. The purpose of a paradox is to arrest attention and provoke fresh thought. The statement of the architectural principle "Less is more" is an example.

Paradoxical statements are often used for irony or satire; for example, Francis Bacon's saying, "The most corrected copies are commonly the least correct." In George Orwell's anti-utopian satire *Animal Farm* (1945), the first commandment of the animals' commune is revised into a witty paradox: "All animals are equal, but some animals are more equal than others." But paradox has a function in poetry that goes beyond mere wit or attention-getting. Modern critics view it as a device, integral to poetic language, encompassing the tensions of error and truth simultaneously, not necessarily by startling juxtapositions but by subtle and continuous qualifications of the ordinary meaning of words. When a paradox is compressed into two words as in "loud silence," "lonely crowd," or "living death," it is called an oxymoron.
·infinite series and Zeno paradox **13**:348e
·logical paradox examples **13**:356g
·logic history from antiquity **11**:57f
·mathematical foundations **11**:632c
·mathematics history from antiquity **11**:641c
·optimization theory and method **13**:623c
·pantheistic application to the Deity **13**:950a
·set theory axiomatic necessity **16**:571c

paradoxes of Zeno, statements made by the Greek philosopher Zeno of Elea, a 5th-century BC disciple of his fellow Eleatic Parmenides, designed to show that any assertion opposite to the monistic teaching of Parmenides leads to contradiction and absurdity. Parmenides had argued from reason alone that the assertion that only Being *is* leads to the conclusions that Being (or all that there is) is (1) one and (2) motionless. The opposite assertions, then, would be that, instead of only the One Being, many real entities in fact are, and that they are in motion (or could be). Zeno thus wished to reduce to absurdity the two claims, (1) that the many are and (2) that motion is.

Plato's dialogue, the *Parmenides*, is the best source for Zeno's general intention, and Plato's account is confirmed by other ancient authors. Plato referred only to the problem of the many, and he did not provide details. Aristotle, on the other hand, gave capsule statements of Zeno's arguments on motion; and these, the famous and controversial paradoxes, generally go by names extracted from Aristotle's account: the "Achilles" (or "Achilles and the tortoise"); the "dichotomy"; the "arrow"; and the "stadium."

The "Achilles" is designed to prove that the slower mover will never be passed by the swifter in a race. The "dichotomy" is designed to prove that an object never reaches the end. Any moving object must reach halfway on a course before it reaches the end; and, because there is an infinite number of halfway points, a moving object never reaches the end in a finite time. The "arrow" endeavours to prove that a moving object is actually at rest. The "stadium" tries to prove that, of two sets of objects travelling at the same velocity, one will travel twice as far as the other in the same time.

If, in each case, the conclusion seems necessary but absurd, it serves to bring the premise (that motion exists or is real) into disrepute, and it suggests that the contradictory premise, that motion does not exist, is true; and indeed, the reality of motion is precisely what Parmenides denied. *See also* One, Eleatic.
·basis for plausibility **14**:252c
·Eleatic theory of Being **6**:526g
·infinite series and Zeno paradox **13**:348e
·logic history from antiquity **11**:57g
·Rationalist rejection of change and motion **15**:528h

Paradoxe sur le comédien (written 1773–78; published 1830), essay by Denis Diderot.
·acting theory and criticism **5**:724e

paradoxical cold and heat, sensation of cold when a cold spot on the skin—*i.e.*, a spot normally sensitive to cold—responds to a warm stimulus or a sensation of heat when a warm spot responds to a cold stimulus.
·cold sensations and warm stimuli **18**:331e
·illusions of coldness and warmth **9**:242h
·skin senses and thermal stimulation **16**:549h

Paradoxides, extinct genus of trilobites found as fossils in Middle Cambrian rocks of North America and western Europe (the Cambrian Period began 570,000,000 years ago and lasted 70,000,000 years). *Paradoxides*

Paradoxides

By courtesy of the trustees of the British Museum (Natural History); photograph, Imitor

has a well-developed head region terminating laterally in pointed spines that vary in development, species to species; the tail region is poorly developed. The body is well segmented, and the axial lobe tapers to the minuscule pygidium (tail). Some species of *Paradoxides* attained large size and were the giants of the Cambrian seas. *Paradoxides* is useful in correlating Middle Cambrian rocks and time.

Paradoxides Series, Middle Cambrian rocks that generally are referred to by this name in western Europe and Scandinavia and, sometimes, with reference to North America (the Cambrian Period began about 570,000,000 years ago and lasted about 70,000,000 years). In North America, the Middle

Cambrian is known as the Albertan Series. The Paradoxides Series is characterized by the fossil occurrence of trilobites of the family Paradoxididae and a fauna that includes other trilobites, such as the genera *Agnostus* and *Eodiscus*. The type area of the Paradoxides Series is in Wales, where it comprises the Solva, Menevian, and a portion of the Harlech Grits. In England, the genus *Agnostus* is prominent in the Upper Comley Beds at Nuneaton.
·Cambrian stratigraphic correlations **13**:918c; table

Paradox of Acting, The (1957), translation of PARADOXE SUR LE COMÉDIEN (1773), prose work by Denis Diderot.
·problem of consistent performance **1**:60c

Paradoxornis flavirostris (bird): *see* parrotbill.

Paradoxurus (mammal): *see* civet.

paraffin, colourless or white, somewhat translucent, hard wax consisting of a mixture of solid straight-chain hydrocarbons ranging in melting point from about 48° to 66° C (120° to 150° F). Paraffin is obtained from petroleum by dewaxing light lubricating oil stocks. It is used in candles, wax paper, polishes, cosmetics, and electrical insulators. It assists in extracting perfumes from flowers, forms a base for medical ointments, and supplies a waterproof coating for wood. In wood and paper matches, it helps to ignite the matchstick by supplying an easily vaporized hydrocarbon fuel.

Paraffin was first produced commercially in 1867, less than 10 years after the first petroleum well was drilled, though limited amounts had been distilled earlier from bituminous shales. Paraffin precipitates readily from petroleum on chilling. Technical progress has only made the separations and filtration more efficient and economical. Purification methods have been added consisting of chemical treatment, decolorization by adsorbents, and fractionation of the separated waxes into grades by distillation, recrystallization, or both. New crude oils have been discovered with higher wax content.

Synthetic paraffin was introduced commercially after World War II as one of the products obtained in the Fischer-Tropsch reaction. Snow-white and harder than petroleum paraffin, synthetic paraffin has a unique character and high purity that make it a suitable replacement for certain vegetable waxes and as a modifier for petroleum waxes and for some plastics, such as polyethylene. Synthetic paraffins may be oxidized to yield pale-yellow, hard waxes of high molecular weight that can be saponified with aqueous solutions of organic or inorganic alkalies, such as borax, sodium hydroxide, triethanolamine, and morpholine. These wax dispersions serve as heavy-duty floor wax, as waterproofing for textiles and paper, as tanning agents for leather, as metal-drawing lubricants, as rust preventives, and for masonry and concrete treatment.
·metal sintering and paraffin binders **11**:1074h

paraffin hydrocarbons, or ALKANE, the generic name given to the saturated hydrocarbons having the general formula C_nH_{2n+2}, C being a carbon atom, H a hydrogen atom, and *n* an integer. The paraffins are major constituents of natural gas and petroleum. Paraffins containing fewer than 5 carbon atoms per molecule are usually gaseous at room temperature, those having 5 to 15 carbon atoms are usually liquids, and the straight chain paraffins having more than 15 carbon atoms per molecule are solids. Branched-chain paraffins have a much higher octane number rating than straight-chain paraffins and therefore they are the more desirable constituents of gasoline. The hydrocarbons are immiscible with water but are soluble in absolute alcohol, ether, and acetone. All paraffins are colourless.
·ammonium dynamite development **7**:85d
·carbonium ion stability and hyperconjugation **3**:861h
·conformation of aliphatic compounds **4**:1089h
·free radical reaction mechanism **15**:422d
·heterocycle comparative chemistry **8**:833b
·ion pair bond stability **3**:819b
·nucleophilic substitution mechanisms **4**:151f
·organic halogen compound classification **13**:683c
·petroleum composition and properties **14**:167c
·sodium in Wurtz synthesis **1**:585b
·structural determinants of phase **12**:315d
·structure, nomenclature, and properties **9**:81b

paraffin oil: *see* kerosine.

paraformaldehyde (chemistry): *see* formaldehyde.

Parafusulina, genus of extinct fusulinids (single-celled animals with a hard, complexly constructed shell) whose fossils are found in Permian marine rocks (the Permian Period began 280,000,000 years ago and lasted 55,000,000 years). *Parafusulina* is more specifically restricted to the Leonardian and Guadalupian stages, smaller divisions of Permian rocks and time, and is thus an excellent index or guide fossil. The shell is characterized by distinct flutings, and the details of internal structure are best studied in thin section.

paragenesis, the sequence in which the minerals are formed in an ore deposit. Variations in the pressure and temperature and in the chemical constituents of a hydrothermal solution will result in the precipitation of various minerals at different times within the same ore deposit. The general sequence of deposition is gangue minerals (silicates and carbonates) first; oxide minerals next, with the sulfides and arsenides of iron, nickel, cobalt, and molybdenum contemporaneous with or closely following the oxides, and the lead and zinc sulfides following them; and lastly the native metals and tellurides followed by the antimony and mercury sulfides. The paragenesis at any particular location may be complicated where the ore deposit has been formed by more than one period of hydrothermal activity.
·sulfide mineral formation and solution **17**:791c; illus.
·variables and mineral deposition order **13**:666d; illus. 664

paragneiss (petrology): *see* gneiss.

Paragominas, town, Para state, Brazil. Pop. (1970 prelim.) 1,726.
3°00′ S, 47°30′ W
·land improvement measures **1**:654d

paragonimiasis, infection caused by *Paragonimus westermani*, or lung fluke, a parasitic worm some 8 to 12 millimetres (0.31 to 0.47 inch) long. The worm lives in the lungs of the infected individual, where it produces small cysts with fibrous walls. It is common in Japan, Korea, China, the Philippines, and Indonesia, and has also been reported in parts of Africa and South America. It is acquired by eating undercooked crab or crayfish harbouring the fluke larvae. The pulmonary lesions and symptoms resemble those of tuberculosis in many respects. Definitive diagnosis is obtained by finding the fluke eggs in the sputum, which may be bloodstained and purulent. In heavy infestations, lesions may also be found in the liver, skeletal muscle, and brain. Drugs effective against the fluke include thiobisdichlorophenol, chloroquine, and emetine hydrochloride. In the absence of reinfection, gradual recovery takes place after the worms die. Prevention consists of the thorough cooking of shellfish; salting, pickling, or soaking in rice wine is usually not effective in killing the infective larvae.
·zoonoses, table 9 **5**:878

paragonite, a mica mineral similar to muscovite, a basic silicate of sodium and aluminum; a member of the common mica group. It was thought to be an uncommon mineral, but experiment and investigation have shown that its occurrence is widespread in metamorphic schists and phyllites, in gneisses, in quartz veins, and in fine-grained sediments. It seems probable that much paragonite has been mistaken for muscovite. Fine-grained paragonite, like muscovite, is called sericite or white mica. For chemical formula and detailed physical properties, *see* table under micas.
·characteristics, occurrence, and synthesis **12**:93f; tables
·dioctahedral crystal structure **16**:761f
·map, United States **18**:908

Paragould, city, seat of Greene County, northeastern Arkansas, U.S. Named for J.W. Paramore and Jay Gould, officials of two railroads (St. Louis Southwestern and Missouri Pacific), it developed as a lumbering centre. Now an industrial and agricultural centre, its manufactures include wood products, textiles, and flour. Inc. 1882. Pop. (1980) 15,214.
36°03′ N, 90°29′ W

Para grass: *see* panicum.

Paraguaçu River, in central and eastern Bahia state (*estado*), eastern Brazil, arising in the Chapada Diamantina and flowing northward and then eastward for approximately 300 mi (500 km). It empties into Baía de Todos os Santos (All Saints Bay), just below Maragogipe. The river is navigable from its mouth for only about 25 mi (40 km) as far as Cachoeira. The region around its upper course yields black industrial diamonds. Principal riverine towns, apart from Cachoeira, are Andaraí and Itaetê.
12°45′ S, 38°54′ W
·map, Brazil **3**:124
·source and basin economy **2**:593c

Paraguaná Peninsula, Spanish PENÍNSULA DE PARAGUANÁ, Falcón state, northwestern Venezuela, between the Caribbean Sea on the east and the Golfo de Venezuela on the west. Of low elevation and infertile, the peninsula is sparsely populated, but the development of the petroleum industry, especially in the 1950s and 1960s, has given Paraguaná great economic importance. Pipelines lead from the oil fields on the eastern shore of Lake Maracaibo to the large oil refineries at Amuay and Punta Cardón on the western side of the peninsula, where coastal indentations permit easy access by deep-draft tankers. In the 1960s Punto Fijo emerged as the peninsula's major urban centre. Coro, the state capital, lies at the base of the isthmus linking the peninsula to the mainland and is connected by highways with the oil-refining centres of the peninsula and with Venezuela's principal highland cities.

Paraguarí, department, southern Paraguay. The territory, 3,187 sq mi (8,255 sq km) in area, is drained by the Río Tebicuary, a tributary of the Paraguay River, and by Laguna Verá, the nation's largest lake. Northern Paraguarí contains part of the forested extension of the Brazilian Highlands that reach westward to Asunción. Southern Paraguarí consists of rich agricultural lowlands producing tropical subsistence and cash crops. Population is well distributed, and there are many processing and marketing centres. Near Caapucú, the principal centre of southern Paraguarí, are important iron ore reserves. The department is served by the main Asunción–Villarrica railway, which passes through Paraguarí (*q.v.*), the departmental capital, and by the Asunción–Encarnación highway. Pop. (1972 prelim.) 210,592.
·area and population table **13**:987
·map, Paraguay **13**:986

Paraguarí, capital, Paraguarí department, southern Paraguay. It lies on the southern slopes of the forested extension of the Brazilian Highlands that reach westward to Asunción. Originally a Jesuit mission, the city was formally organized in 1775. In 1811, when Paraguay stood aside from the Argentine

colonies in their revolt against Spain, Paraguarí was the scene of an important battle in which the Argentines were repulsed and Paraguay's independence was secured. Paraguarí is now the commercial and manufacturing centre of a fertile and active agricultural hinterland. Cotton, tobacco, sugarcane, oranges, rice, maize, hides, and petitgrain (a base for perfume made from bitter orange leaves) are among its products. Ceramic works, tanneries, and food-processing plants are located in the area. The city is also the headquarters of Paraguay's artillery regiment and school. Santo Tomás grottoes, on a nearby hill, are noted for their hieroglyphic inscriptions, presumably the work of early indigenous peoples; one long cavern is a centre of Good Friday pilgrimage. Paraguarí is accessible by railway or highway from Asunción, Villarrica, and Encarnación. Pop. (1975 est.) 5,020.
25°38′ S, 57°09′ W
·map, Paraguay **13**:986

Paraguay 13:984, landlocked republic, south central South America, bordered by Bolivia to the northwest and north, Brazil to the east, and Argentina to the southeast, south, and west. (For statistical details, *see* pp. 744–745.)

The text covers Paraguay's landscape, people, economy, administration and social conditions, and cultural life and institutions.

REFERENCES in other text articles:
·armed forces statistics, table 2 **2**:16
·Christian denominational demography map **4**:459
·economic and political status **13**:991f
·Gran Chaco geographical features **8**:275a
·gross domestic product by sector, table 1 **17**:98
·language characteristics and use **17**:109g
·map, South America **17**:77
·mestizo riverine population **13**:993a
·newspaper publishing statistics table **15**:237
·Paraná Basin structure **14**:527f
·Paraná River navigation **13**:1001d
·rain forest varieties, characteristics, and locations **10**:338d; map 337
·South American political divisions map **17**:98
·Triassic Paraná Basin **18**:694g
·urban population percentage growth, table 2 **17**:103

Paraguay, history of 13:990. Frequently in conflict with its neighbours, Paraguay endured political instability for a century before a dictatorship was established in 1954.

The text article covers the era from the end of the colonial period to the present. Freed from Spain in 1810, Paraguay soon (1814) became a dictatorship under José Gaspar Rodríguez Francia, who closed the country to the outside world until his death in 1840. A pressing national issue was maintaining independence from Argentina, a goal that was finally achieved in 1852. Ruled from 1840 to 1870 by Carlos Antonio López and his son, Francisco Solano López, Paraguay became embroiled with Brazil, Argentina, and Uruguay in the Paraguayan War (1864–70), which resulted in loss of territory and great loss of life. The Liberal Party and the Colorado Party vied for power, and rarely did a president finish a term in office. From 1932 to 1935 Paraguay fought the Chaco War with Bolivia, gaining three-fourths of the territory in dispute. In 1936 there began a series of military coups that lasted until 1954, when Gen. Alfredo Stroessner took over the government. Under his rule some modernization took place, and the constitution of 1967 (amended in 1977) reinstated the Congress and granted certain civil liberties. In the early 1970s Paraguay remained free of the terrorism and guerrilla activity present in so much of South America, but the nation's standard of living remained among the lowest on the continent. *See also* Latin America and the Caribbean, colonial.

REFERENCES in other text articles:
·Argentine liberation resistance **10**:704c
·Chaco War and ensuing territorial gains **3**:11h
·La Plata viceroyalty establishment **1**:1143h
·Paraguayan War defeat and results **3**:145h

Paraguayan tea: *see* maté.

Paraguayan War, also called WAR OF THE TRIPLE ALLIANCE (1864–70), the bloodiest conflict in Latin-American history, fought between Paraguay and the allied countries of Argentina, Brazil, and Uruguay.

Paraguay had been involved in boundary and tariff disputes with its more powerful neighbours, Argentina and Brazil, for years. The Uruguayans had also struggled to achieve and maintain their independence from those same powers, especially from Argentina.

In 1864 Brazil helped the Uruguayan Colorado leader to unseat his Blanco opponent, whereupon the dictator of Paraguay, Francisco Solano López, believing that the regional balance of power was threatened, went to war with Brazil. Bartolomé Mitre, president of Argentina, then organized an alliance with Brazil and Colorado-controlled Uruguay (the Triple Alliance), and together they declared war on Paraguay on May 1, 1865.

López' action, following his buildup of a 50,000-man army, then the strongest in Latin America, was viewed by many as aggression for self- and national aggrandizement; but as the war wore on, many Argentines and others saw the conflict as Mitre's war of conquest.

At the opening of the war, in 1865, Paraguayan forces advanced through Argentina northward into the Brazilian province of Mato Grosso and southward into the province of Rio Grande do Sul. Logistical problems and the buildup of the allied troop strength, which soon outnumbered Paraguay's by 10 to 1, then forced the Paraguayans to withdraw behind their frontiers. In June 1865, Brazilian naval forces defeated a Paraguayan flotilla on the Paraná River at Riachuelo, near the Argentine city of Corrientes; by January 1866 the allies had blockaded the rivers leading to Paraguay. In April, Mitre led an allied invading force into southwest Paraguay but was prevented from advancing for two years. Fierce battles were fought; the most notable, won by the Paraguayans at Curupayty in September 1866, inhibited any allied offensive for nearly a year. Both sides suffered heavy losses in the campaign.

In January 1868 Mitre was replaced as commander in chief by the Brazilian marquês (later duque) de Caxias. In February, Brazilian armoured vessels broke through Paraguayan defenses at the river fortress of Humaitá, near the confluence of the Paraná and Paraguay rivers, and pressed on to bombard Asunción, the capital. In the campaign of Lomas Valentinas in December the Paraguayan army was annihilated. López fled northward and carried on a guerrilla war until he was killed on March 1, 1870.

The war left Paraguay prostrate; its prewar population of about 525,000 was reduced to about 221,000 in 1871, of which only about 28,000 were men. During the war the Paraguayans suffered not only from the enemy but also from malnutrition, disease, and the domination of López, who tortured and killed countless numbers. Argentina and Brazil annexed about 55,000 square miles of Paraguayan territory: Argentina took much of the Misiones region and part of the Chaco between the Bermejo and Pilcomayo rivers; Brazil enlarged its Mato Grosso province from annexed territory. They both demanded a large indemnity (never paid) and occupied Paraguay until 1876. Meanwhile, the Colorados had gained control of Uruguay and retained it until 1958.

·anti-Paraguay alliance outcome **3**:145h
·Argentine intervention and results **1**:1146g
·development and outcome **13**:990h

Paraguay River 13:991, Portuguese RIO PARAGUAI, fifth largest river of South America and principal tributary of the Paraná, with a length of 1,584 mi (2,550 km). Rising in the Mato Grosso region of Brazil at 980 ft (300 m) above sea level, it crosses Paraguay to empty into the Paraná near the Argentine border.

The text article surveys the river's physiography, hydrography, climate, vegetation and animal life, history, navigation, economic resources, and prospects.
27°18′ S, 58°38′ W

REFERENCES in other text articles:
·basin physiography and course **17**:81h
·Bolivia border proximity **3**:1f
·Brazilian drainage significance **3**:128d
·geographic features and importance **13**:984f
·Guató tribal life style **17**:113h
maps
·Argentina **1**:1137
·Brazil **3**:124
·Paraguay **13**:986
·Paraná River and tributaries **13**:1000
·South America **17**:77

Paragymnomma, genus of flies.
·orchid pollination by pseudocopulation **13**:654g

Parahippus, genus of Miocene horses. Its teeth, more advanced than those of the Oligocene fossil *Mesohippus*, indicate a change from forest browsing to feeding on grasses.
·traits and evolutionary position **7**:573d; illus.

Parahoplites, fossil genus of ammonite cephalopods (mollusks) of the Lower Cretaceous Period. They are a distinctive feature of deposits of the period, such as the Aptian and Lower Greensand stages and the Miyakoan Series.

parahormone, substance that is not a true hormone but resembles a hormone in its effect on the functioning of an organ.
·evolution in vertebrates **8**:1074g

Paraíba 13:993, historically known as PARAHYBA and PARAHYBA DO NORTE, state of northeastern Brazil, with an area of 21,765 sq mi (56,372 sq km), on the Atlantic coast. It borders the states of Rio Grande do Norte (north), Ceará (west), and Pernambuco (south). Its capital is João Pessoa. Pop. (1977 est.) 2,785,300.

The text article covers Paraíba's history, physiography, climate, vegetation, population, economy, and transportation.

REFERENCES in other text articles:
·area and population table **3**:133
·map, Brazil **3**:125

Paraíba do Sul River, Portuguese RIO PARAÍBA DO SUL, in eastern Brazil, is formed by the junction of the Paraibuna and Paraitinga rivers, east of São Paulo, between Mogi das Cruzes and Jacareí. It then flows east-northeastward, receiving tributaries from the Serra da Mantiqueira and the Serra do Mar and forming part of the border between Minas Gerais and Rio de Janeiro states. From its initial elevation of 5,000 ft (1,500 m), the river descends gradually until it reaches São Fidélis, where it emerges through a series of falls to the coastal plain and enters the Atlantic Ocean near São João da Barra after a course of 700 mi (1,100 km).

The Paraíba do Sul has long played a vital role in the social and economic life of Brazil, for its lower course is navigable and several large cities, including Volta Redonda, are located on its banks. Some of its tributaries, notably the Piraí, have been used for power generation and irrigation.
21°37′ S, 41°03′ W
·map, Brazil **3**:125
·source and flow **3**:128g
·valley climatic characteristics **15**:853c

Paraibuna (Brazil): *see* Juiz de Fora.

Paraíso, El, pre-Inca ceremonial building in the Chillón Valley, Peru.
·pre-Incan architecture **1**:841d

Paraiulidae: *see* millipede.

parakeet, also spelled PARRAKEET, seed-eating parrot of small size and slender build, with long, tapering tail. In this sense the name is given to some 115 species in 30 genera and has influenced another parrot name, lorikeet (*see* parrot). To indicate size only, the name is sometimes extended to little parrots with short, blunt tails, as the hanging parrots, or bat parrotlets, *Loriculus* species, popular cage birds in their native area, India to Malaya and the Philippines.

Budgerigar (*Melopsittacus undulatus*)
Bruce Coleman Ltd.

Parakeets occur worldwide in warm regions; they are particularly abundant from India to Australia and the Pacific Islands. Typically they form large flocks and may be serious pests in grainfields. Most species lay four to eight eggs in a tree hole. Dozens of colourful kinds are kept as pets. All are highly active and need much room; most are pugnacious—notably when paired—toward other birds; and a few become good, though small-voiced, mimics. The most popular caged parakeet is the budgerigar, or shell parakeet, *Melopsittacus undulatus*.

Mistakenly called lovebird, this 19-centimetre (7½-inch) parakeet has hundreds of colour mutations from the green and yellow basic stock; but cheek spots and close barring on the upper parts usually persist. Sexes look alike but may differ seasonally in colour of the cere, the bare skin at the base of the bill. Budgerigars are seed eaters; in the wild, they form large flocks in Australia's grasslands. They breed colonially, in tree holes, laying six to eight eggs twice a year. Most budgerigars are hardy, surviving for 5 to 10 years.

The Australian parakeet, or rosellas, *Platycercus* species, has scalloped back and underparts, black shoulders, distinctive cheek and throat markings, and a long, broad tail that is centrally greenish or bluish with a blue and white margin. The seven species, averaging 18 centimetres (7 inches) in length, are also called harrakeets.

The smaller broad-tailed parrots are the five species of *Psephotus*, which have no specific group name. Female rosellas are duller than males. Popular caged birds, rosellas are hardy and prolific but notoriously quarrelsome with other species. Many colour varieties and generic hybrids are known in the wild as well as in aviaries.
·imprinting to wrong sex object **2**:811f
·pet ownership pleasures **14**:150e
·traits, behaviour, and classification **15**:138b; illus. 140

Parakou, capital of Borgou *département*, central Dahomey, West Africa. It is the terminus of the misnamed Benin–Niger Railway, which was originally planned to extend all the way to the Niger River. At present the railway runs northward from Cotonou, Dahomey's major port and commercial centre on the Gulf of Guinea coast, to Parakou, whence goods must be transported by road to the navigable Niger River and into landlocked Niger. An extension of the railway from Parakou to Dosso, Niger, was planned in the 1970s. Latest pop. est. 18,000.
9°21′ N, 2°37′ E
·map, Dahomey **5**:421
·national trade and communications role **5**:422b

Cotton harvest near Parakou, Dahomey
EB Inc.

Parākramabāhu I, also called PARĀKRAMABĀHU I THE GREAT (b. *c.* 1123, Punkhagama, Ceylon, now Sri Lanka—d. 1186, Polonnaruva), Sinhalese king of Ceylon from 1153 who united the island under one rule, reformed Buddhist practices, and sent successful expeditionary forces to India and Burma.

The son of Manabharana (one of Ceylon's four regional lords), who controlled the south and who died while Parākrama was still a boy, Parākrama succeeded his father's successor, Siri Megha, the de facto ruler of Ceylon. He won and maintained control only after several battles and counter revolutions.

Parākramabāhu designed a government of 12 provincial governors, princes, army generals, and leading merchants. He reformed the Buddhist establishment by expelling lax monks, and by building new temples. He allowed Hindus freedom of worship.
·Ceylonese early kingdoms **4**:2h *passim* to 4f

Parakramabahu II (reigned 1236–70), Ceylonese king of the Dambadeniya kingdom.
·Ceylonese history of early kingdoms **4**:3h

Parakrama Samudra, giant reservoir constructed in Ceylon in the 12th century.
·Ceylonese early water systems **4**:3f

paraldehyde, or PARACETALDEHYDE, colourless liquid of disagreeable taste and pungent odour used in medicine as a sedative–hypnotic drug and in chemistry in the manufacture of organic chemicals. When administered as a medicine, it is largely excreted by the lungs and gives an unpleasant odour to the breath. It is most useful for recalcitrant cases and is an older drug for treatment of acute alcoholic dementia.

It is produced for commerce by polymerizing acetaldehyde with a trace of sulfuric acid; with concentrated acid, this reaction is accompanied by the generation of considerable heat. The resulting liquid is neutralized with calcium carbonate and purified by fractional distillation. Paraldehyde boils at 124° C (255° F) and melts at 12.5° C (54.5° F). Its chemical formula is $C_6H_{12}O_3$.
·psychiatric treatment usage **15**:143a
·synthetic production by polymerization **14**:196d
·traits, use, and effects **16**:458c

PARAGUAY

Official name: República del Paraguay (Republic of Paraguay).
Location: South America.
Form of government: republic.
Official language: Spanish.
Official religion: Roman Catholic.
Area: 157,048 sq mi, 406,752 sq km.
Population: (1962 census) 1,819,103; (1970 estimate) 2,395,614.
Capital: Asunción.
Monetary unit: 1 guarani = 100 centimos.

Demography
Population (1970): density 15.3 per sq mi, 5.9 per sq km; urban 35.7%, rural 64.3%; male 49.45%, female 50.55%; under 15 46.4%, 15–29 26.7%, 30–44 13.4%, 45–59 8.5%, 60–74 3.9%, 75 and over 1.0%.*
Vital statistics: (1970) births per 1,000 population 44.6, deaths per 1,000 population 10.8, natural increase per 1,000 population 33.8; (1965–70) life expectancy at birth—male 57.4, female 61.3; (1969) major causes of death (per 100,000 population)—senility without mention of psychosis, ill-defined and unknown causes 101.5; enteritis and diarrheal diseases 46.3; malignant neoplasms, including neoplasms of lymphatic and hematopoietic tissue 33.1; pneumonia 33.0.
Ethnic composition (mid-1960s): mestizo 74%, white 21%, Amerindian 3%, Negro 1%, other 1%. *Religious affiliation* (1967): Roman Catholic 95.1%, other 4.9%.

National accounts
Budget (1971). Revenue: 8,288,000,000 guaranis (internal revenue 32.1%, customs duties 18.4%, exchange surcharge on imports 11.0%, income tax 10.6%). Expenditures: 8,836,600,000 guaranis (defense 20.5%, education 14.8%, Ministry of Interior 9.3%, interest on public debt 7.3%, public works and communication 7.1%, finance 4.7%, health 3.4%). *Total national debt* (1970): U.S. $81,700,000.† *Tourism* (1968). Receipts from visitors: U.S. $8,100,000. Expenditures by nationals abroad: U.S. $3,400,000.

Domestic economy
Gross national product (GNP; at current market prices, 1970): U.S. $630,000,000 (U.S. $260 per capita).

Origin of gross domestic product (at current market prices):	1962				1970		1969	
	value in 000,000 guaranis	% of total value	labour force	% of labour force	value in 000,000 guaranis	% of total value	labour force	% of labour force
agriculture, forestry hunting, fishing	16,770	36.9	320,857	54.7	24,024	32.1	...	56
mining, quarrying	46	0.1	476	0.1	83	0.1	...	‡
manufacturing	7,152	15.8	88,486	15.1	12,498	16.7	...	16‡
construction	1,015	2.2	19,475	3.3	2,076	2.8	...	3
electricity, gas, water	306	0.7	1,209	0.2	840	1.1	...	§
transport, storage, communication	1,876	4.1	14,622	2.5	2,950	3.9	...	3§
trade	10,403‖	22.9	41,458	7.1	18,291	24.4	...	...
ownership of dwellings	1,641	3.6	...	...	...	...	...	...
public administration, defense	1,624	3.6	...	...	...	...	...	...
services	4,561	10.0	87,091	14.9	14,160¶	18.9	...	22
other	...	...	12,741	2.2	...	...	...	...
total	45,394	100.0*	586,415	100.0*	74,921	100.0	697,000	100

Paralepididae (fish): *see* barracudina.

paraliageosyncline (geology): *see* geosyncline.

Paralithodes camtschatica: *see* king crab.

parallax, the apparent displacement of a stationary point or object with respect to its background when viewed from two positions; *e.g.*, by the left eye and right eye.
- ·dependence on angle of viewed object **17**:380a
- ·depth perception mechanism 7:115c; illus.
- ·measurement system error **11**:731e

parallax, astronomical 13:993, the difference in direction between two apparent positions of an astronomical body as observed from two widely separated points, used as a measure of the body's distance.

The text article covers lunar, solar, and stellar parallaxes and the direct and indirect methods of measuring parallaxes.

REFERENCES in other text articles:
- ·Bessel's correction for 61 Cygni **2**:870c
- ·direct determination and distance error **17**:586b
- ·Herschel's proof of earth revolution **8**:826g
- ·Hipparchus on size of Moon and Sun **8**:942a
- ·historical attempts at measurement **3**:101a
- ·light aberration discovery **10**:949f
- ·refracting telescope measurement **18**:99e
- ·stellar distance measurement **2**:250b
- ·trigonometric and photometric methods **7**:835e
- ·Venus transit determination for Sun **6**:194b

RELATED ENTRIES in the *Ready Reference and Index*:
astronomical distances; astronomical unit; light-year; parsec

parallel, imaginary line extending around the Earth parallel to the Equator; it is used to indicate latitude. The 38th parallel, for example, has a latitude of 38° N or 38° S. *See* latitude and longitude.

parallel bars, gymnastic apparatus developed in the early 19th century, especially use-

Parallel bars
Stewart Fraser—Colorsport

ful in improving upper-body strength. The two bars, made of wood, are oval in cross section, 3.5 metres (138 inches) long, 1.7 metres (67 inches) high, and 42 to 48 centimetres (16.5 to 19 inches) apart. Height and width of the bars are usually adjustable. In competitive performances, movements combine swings, vaults, strength, and balance, although swings and vaults must predominate. Movements below the bars and the release and regrasping of the bars are also required.

Uneven (asymmetric) parallel bars, used in women's competition, are of the same dimensions and construction as the men's parallel bars, except that the top bar is 2.3 metres (90.5 inches) above the floor, while the lower bar is 1.5 metres (59 inches) high. This apparatus is one of the latest to be developed; it was first used in international competition at the 1936 Olympic Games and allows a great variety of movements, although hanging and swinging exercises predominate. The performer strives for smoothness in her routine and equal use of both bars. *See also* sporting record.
- ·men's and women's gymnastic exercises **8**:514d

Parallèlement (1889), collection of poetry by Paul Verlaine.
- ·themes and literary merit **19**:85f

parallel evolution, the evolution of geographically separated groups in such a way that they show morphological resemblances. A notable example is the similarity shown by the marsupial mammals of Australia to the placental mammals elsewhere. Through the courses of their evolution they have come to remarkably similar forms, so much so that the marsupials are often named for their placental counterparts (*e.g.*, the marsupial "wolf," "mole," "mice," "cats").
- ·marsupial radiation in protected region **7**:19e
- ·orchid ancestral and recent groups **13**:655c *passim* to 659f
- ·perissodactyl and artiodactyl traits **14**:81d
- ·rodent structural adaptations **15**:977g

parallelism, component of literary style in both prose and poetry, in which coordinate ideas are arranged in phrases, sentences, and paragraphs that balance one element with another of equal importance and similar wording. The repetition of sounds, meanings, and structures serves to order, emphasize, and point out relations. In its simplest form parallelism consists of single words that have a slight variation in meaning: "ordain and establish" or "overtake and surpass." Sometimes three or more units are parallel; for example: "Reading maketh a full man, conference a ready man, and writing an exact man" (Francis Bacon, "Of Studies"). Parallelism may be inverted for stronger emphasis; *e.g.*, "I have changed in many things: in this I have not" (John Henry Newman, *Apologia pro Vita Sua*, 1864). Parallelism lends wit and authority to the antithetical aphorism; *e.g.*, "We always love those who admire us, but we do not always love those whom we admire" (La Rochefoucauld, *Maximes*, 1665).

Parallelism is a prominent figure in Hebrew poetry as well as in most literatures of the ancient Near East. The Old Testament and New Testament, reflecting the influence of Hebrew poetry, contain many striking examples of parallelism, as in the following lines from the Psalms: "but they flattered him with their mouths; they lied to him with their tongues" (Psalms 78:36); "we will not hide them from their children, but tell to the coming generation the glorious deeds of the Lord" (78:4).
- ·Hebrew poetry types **2**:923a

parallelism, psychophysical, in the philosophy of mind, a theory that excludes all causal interaction between mind and body inasmuch as it seems inconceivable that two substances as radically different in nature

Production (1970). Agriculture, forestry, hunting, fishing (metric tons except as noted): cassava 1,549,000♀; sugarcane 744,000; bananas 250,000♀; maize (corn) 200,000; sweet potatoes 94,000♀; wheat 35,000; pineapples 34,000♀; citrus fruits 33,000; rice 32,000; cattle 5,800,000 head; hogs 980,000 head; horses 730,000 head; forest products 1,036,300,000 guaranis; meat, cleaned for consumption 4,668,523,000 guaranis. Manufacturing (gross value in 000 guaranis): wheat flour 1,271,500, cotton fabrics 1,071,000, preserved meat 931,905, sugar 880,000, cotton fibres 610,300, frozen meat 598,599, beer 525,400, tung oil 401,000.
Energy (1969): installed electrical capacity 110,000 kW, production 203,000,000 kW-hr (88 kW-hr per capita).
Persons economically active: (1969) 697,000 (30%), unemployed—no data available.

Price and earnings indexes (1964 = 100):	1965	1966	1967	1968	1969	1970	1971
consumer price index♂	103.8	106.8	108.3	109.0	111.5	110.5	116.0
earnings index	...	...	...	...	...	...	...

Land use (1967): forested 50.5%; meadows and pastures 24.6%; agricultural and under permanent cultivation 2.3%; built-on, wasteland, and other 22.6%.

Foreign trade

Imports (1971): 8,836,600,000 guaranis (iron and steel products 7.2%; chemicals and pharmaceutical products 6.0%; boilers, motors, and steam engines 6.0%; crude petroleum 5.9%; wheat and wheat products 5.2%; cigarettes 5.2%; buses and trucks 5.2%; whiskey 4.8%; electrical appliances 3.1%; cars, jeeps, and farm trucks 2.5%; parts for cars and trucks 2.5%). *Major import sources:* United States 25.5%, Argentina 14.4%, West Germany 11.6%, United Kingdom 9.9%, France 2.8%, Italy 2.0%, Sweden 1.8%.
Exports (1971): 8,057,300,000 guaranis (meat and meat preparations 31.9%; sawn beams 9.1%; tobacco 7.3%; logs, including palm trees 6.8%; tung oil 5.7%; perfumeries 3.6%; quebracho extract 3.4%; seeds for industrial use 2.8%; leather 2.3%; fruits and vegetables 2.1%). *Major export destinations:* Argentina 27.4%, United States 16.0%, Netherlands 7.7%, United Kingdom 5.6%, West Germany 5.5%, France 4.6%, Belgium 4.5%, Spain 3.7%.

Transport and communication

Transport. Railroads: (1970) length 274 mi, 441 km; (1968) passenger mi 17,000,000, passenger km 28,000,000; (1970) short ton-mi cargo 20,719,951, metric ton-km cargo 30,250,533. Roads (1971): total length 9,915 mi, 15,956 km (paved 374 mi, 602 km; gravel and crushed stone 630 mi, 1,014 km; earth, graded and drained 2,497 mi, 4,019 km; unimproved 6,413 mi, 10,321 km). Vehicles (1969): passenger cars 7,816, trucks and buses 9,970. Merchant marine (1970): vessels (over 1,000 gross tons) none. Air transport: (1968) passenger mi 19,000,000, passenger km 30,580,000; short ton-mi cargo 2,270,000, metric ton-km cargo 3,320,000; (1971) airports with scheduled flights 3.
Communication. Daily newspapers (1969): total number 9, circulation per 1,000 population 40,□ total circulation 93,000.□ Radios (1970): total number of receivers 169,000 (1 per 14 persons). Television (1971): receivers 25,000 (1 per 95 persons); broadcasting stations 1. Telephones (1971): 23,649 (1 per 101 persons).

Education and health

Education (1969):	schools	teachers	students	student–teacher ratio
primary (age 7 to 13)	2,896	12,951	415,791	32.1
secondary (age 13 to 19)	298	1,121	35,402	31.6
vocational	156	3,386	11,891	3.5
teacher training	44	1,047	4,115	3.9
higher	2	663◇	7,593	...

College graduates: no data available. *Literacy* (1962): total population literate (15 and over) 732,159 (74.5%), males literate 377,765 (81.0%), females literate 354,394 (68.7%).
Health: (1968) doctors 1,386 (1 per 1,610 persons); (1968) hospital beds 4,753 (1 per 470 persons); (1970) daily per capita caloric intake 2,730 calories (FAO recommended minimum requirement 2,540 calories).

*Percentages do not add to 100.0 because of rounding. †External debt only. ‡Manufacturing includes mining, quarrying. §Transport, storage, communication includes electricity, gas, water. ‖Includes banking, insurance, real estate. ¶Includes finance, insurance, real estate, business services, government services. ♀1969. ♂Asunción only. □Refers to four dailies only. ◇National University of Asunción only.

could influence one another in any way. Mental and physical phenomena are seen as two series of perfectly correlated events; the usual analogy is that of two synchronized clocks that keep perfect time. Thus, for parallelism, the mental event of a man's wishing to raise his arm is followed immediately by the physical event of his arm being raised, yet there is no need to postulate any direct causal connection.

Parallelism is usually associated with Gottfried Wilhelm Leibniz, a 17th-century German philosopher, scientist, and mathematician who maintained that perfect correlation between mind and body was ensured by the Creator at the beginning of time in a "pre-established harmony."

Parallelism has been criticized on the grounds that a refusal to postulate causal connections in the face of constant correlation conflicts with the empirical procedures recognized in modern science, which call for the supposition of a cause wherever the coefficient of correlation between two sets of phenomena approaches 1. The case for parallelism, however, has been said to depend more on the validity of the arguments discrediting the possibility of interaction between mind and body than upon statistical theory.

·Bergson's attack on determinism **2**:843f
·mind and body as substantial attributes **12**:19e

parallel lines, in geometry, lines that lie in the same plane but do not intersect.

·Euclidean geometry principles **7**:1100f
·historical development of geometry **11**:655c
·non-Euclidean geometries and models **7**:1114f

Parallel Lives (first transcribed AD 105–115), 50 biographies of eminent Greeks and Romans (soldiers, legislators, orators, and statesmen) by the Greek author Plutarch. Most are composed in pairs (one Greek and one Roman subject of equal weight). Each biography emphasizes the moral implications of the man's character more than the accomplishments of his career. Comparisons between the lives are discussed in a number of shorter essays. Rich in personal anecdotes, humanity, and wisdom, the biographies are noteworthy for their dramatic and narrative skill.

·content and significance **10**:1094d

parallel motion, in music, two voices moving simultaneously and remaining the same interval apart.

·African homophonic part-singing **1**:246c

parallelogram, in geometry, a quadrilateral, or four-sided, plane figure with the property that the opposite sides are parallel. This definition is equivalent to saying that the opposite sides are of the same length or again equivalent to having equal opposite angles. Squares, rectangles, and rhombuses are special cases of parallelograms.

·Euclidean geometry principles **7**:1106f

parallelogram law, rule for obtaining geometrically the sum of two vectors by constructing a parallelogram. A diagonal will give the requisite vector sum of two adjacent sides. The law is commonly used in physics to determine a resultant force or stress acting on a structure.

·mechanics force principles **11**:764c
·vector and tensor analysis principles **1**:791d

parallel perspective (visual arts): *see* perspective.

parallel postulate, of Euclidean geometry, states that through a given point there exists exactly one line parallel to a given line. This postulate does not hold true for all geometries.

·axiomatic method applications **11**:631b
·Euclidean geometry principles **7**:1100a
·historical development of geometry **11**:655d
·Lobachevsky's non-Euclidean geometry **11**:9c
·non-Euclidean geometry development **7**:1113c
·Riemann's comprehension of limitation **15**:840f

parallel skiing, form of Alpine ski racing in which two skiers race simultaneously against each other, instead of singly for best time, as in most other competition. Races consist of an agreed number of runs over roughly equal parallel courses, with the racers alternating courses after each run.

parallel slope retreat, theory of landmass reduction that postulates that slopes retreat parallel to themselves leaving behind a very gently sloping surface at their foot. Although usually credited to Walther Penck, the theory was originally proposed by Kirk Bryan (1888–1950) and Lester King, who worked in the semi-arid areas of the U.S. and southern Africa, respectively.

In arid areas where rainfall usually occurs as thundershowers, successive layers tend to be washed from the slopes leaving the angle of the slope essentially the same. Although it has been pointed out that in humid areas creep tends to cause a decline in slope angle, parallel retreat is also observed in some cases. Such differences in lithology as porosity and consolidation also produce marked differences in hillslope development. It is hoped that further field observations will provide information on the relative importance of parallel retreat in landmass reduction.

·hillslope development mechanisms **8**:877b; illus. 879

paralysis, or PALSY, medical term usually implying the loss or impairment of voluntary muscular power. For paralysis from psychiatric causes, *see* hysteria.

Most of the commonly encountered diseases that produce paralysis can be divided into two main groups depending on whether they (1) entail structural alterations in nervous or muscular tissue or (2) lead to metabolic disturbances in neuromuscular function.

Some act in a systematic way and affect one of the three elements in the motor system (upper and lower neuron and muscle) more or less extensively and exclusively. More often, however, one element or neighbouring portions of two of the three elements are involved over a limited extent by a single focal lesion.

The most common cause of hemiplegia (paralysis of the muscles of the lower face, arm, and leg on the side opposite the main lesion) is damage to the pyramidal tract in one hemisphere of the brain from obstruction (blood clot or thrombosis) or rupture (cerebral hemorrhage) of a major cerebral artery. Brain tumour is another but less common cause of hemiplegia and develops and increases in severity gradually over a period of weeks or months. When the lesion is in the left hemisphere in a right-handed person, the resulting right hemiplegia is often associated with one of the various forms of aphasia (*q.v.*).

Bilateral hemiplegia with pseudobulbar palsy results from diffuse, bilateral brain disease such as occurs in severe cerebral arteriosclerosis or cerebral vascular syphilis. The terms cerebral palsy and spastic diplegia refer to bilateral hemiplegia resulting from prenatal developmental brain defects or from injury to the brain at birth.

The spinal cord is rarely the site of vascular obstruction or hemorrhage. The more common causes of damage to the pyramidal tracts in the cord include deformities of the spinal column from bone and joint disease and from injury to the spine with fracture and dislocation, spinal cord tumours, and a number of inflammatory and degenerative diseases and changes associated with pernicious anemia. One of the most common causes of progressive spastic paraplegia in persons past middle age is spinal degenerative arthritis, with protusion of an intervertebral disk cartilage into the lower cervical portion of the spinal canal.

Of the diseases that attack lower motor neurons and result in flaccid paralysis with muscular wasting, the most common are poliomyelitis and polyneuritis, the former affecting the cell bodies of bulbar and spinal motor neurons and the latter affecting their peripheral processes. Bell's palsy is a peripheral neuritis of unknown cause affecting a single nerve trunk—the facial nerve—and resulting in paralysis of all the muscles of one side of the face: the facial lines are smoothed out, the forehead cannot be wrinkled or the eye closed, and the corner of the mouth droops. In the majority of cases, recovery eventually occurs.

Amyotrophic lateral sclerosis is a rare, chronic, idiopathic progressive disease of the nervous system.

Diseases that result in paralysis through primary changes in muscle tissue are fewer than the above. Of the conditions belonging in this category, progressive muscular dystrophy is the only one apparently confined to the muscles. This is a familial, hereditary disease characterized by progressive, symmetrical muscular weakness and wasting. One rare variety has its onset before puberty, is more common in boys, and usually progresses to severe disability within a few years. It is known as pseudohypertrophic muscular dystrophy. The other types of dystrophy, in general, begin in adolescence or young adult life, and the two sexes are about equally affected. The progress of these other forms is slow; and life expectancy is not necessarily shortened, nor is severe disability inevitable.

Muscular weakness without structural alteration in nerve or muscle tissue may be a symptom of disturbances in metabolism arising from a wide variety of causes. Among such conditions are diseases of the endocrine glands, certain intoxications, and several metabolic defects.

The most common example of a metabolic disorder in neuromuscular function of unknown cause is myasthenia gravis. In this condition there is muscular weakness, without atrophy, which may be mild or severe and either generalized or restricted to a few muscle groups. Some of the muscles innervated by cranial nerves are affected in almost every case. The weakness of myasthenia gravis results from a localized defect in the chemical processes involved in the transmission of impulses from motor nerve endings to muscle fibres. Although the cause of this defect and its precise nature are unknown, several drugs facilitate the transmission of impulses from nerve to muscle. One of these, neostigmine, proved to benefit most patients but does not correct the basic, unknown defect. *Major ref.* **12**:1052c

·botulism complications **9**:554e
·diphtheroid toxicity in nervous system **9**:550b
·lower and upper motor neuron paralyses **12**:1010a
·mineral metabolic disturbances **11**:1060e
·narcoleptic auxiliary symptoms **16**:881e
·poliomyelitis sequelae **12**:1053f

paralysis, infantile: *see* poliomyelitis.

paralysis agitans: *see* Parkinson's disease.

paralytic ileus, intestinal blockage due to paralysis of the bowel wall.

·burn wound complications **3**:522a

paralytic shellfish poisoning, poisoning caused by eating shellfish that have been feeding on toxic microscopic plants.

·symptoms and nature of poison **14**:609h; table 612a

paramagnetic mineral: *see* mineral magnetism.

paramagnetism, kind of magnetism characteristic of materials weakly attracted by a strong magnet, named and extensively investigated by the British scientist Michael Faraday beginning in 1845. Most elements and some compounds are paramagnetic. Strong paramagnetism (not to be confused with the ferromagnetism of the elements iron, cobalt, nickel, and other alloys) is exhibited by compounds containing iron, palladium, platinum, and the rare-earth elements. Such compounds have some inner electron shells that are incomplete, causing their unpaired electrons to spin like tops and orbit like satellites, thus making the atoms a permanent magnet tending to align with and hence strengthen an applied magnetic field.

Strong paramagnetism decreases with rising temperature because of the de-alignment produced by the greater random motion of the atomic magnets. Weak paramagnetism, independent of temperature, is found in many metallic elements in the solid state, such as sodium and the other alkali metals, because an applied magnetic field converts the spin of some of the loosely bound conduction electrons. The value of susceptibility (a measure of the relative amount of induced magnetism) for paramagnetic materials is always positive, typically about $^1/_{100,000}$ to $^1/_{10,000}$ for weakly paramagnetic substances and about $^1/_{10,000}$ to $^1/_{100}$ for strongly paramagnetic substances. *Major ref.* **11**:324d

·atomic structure and properties **2**:342h
·free radicals and electron resonance **15**:423d
·low-temperature properties **11**:162g
·rare-earth physical properties **15**:520g
·rock magnetization and atomic alignment **15**:943c
·solid state magnetic properties **16**:1040h

paramahaṃsa: *see* sannyāsin.

paramāṇu (Hindu philosophy): *see* aṇu.

Paramanuchit, or PARAMANUJITA JINORASA (b. 1791—d. Dec. 9, 1852), prince-patriarch of the Siamese Buddhist Church who was a prolific writer on patriotic and moralistic themes in verse and prose. He became abbot of Watphra Jetubon and was later created *Krom Somdec-phra Paramanujit*, prince-patriarch of the church.

Paramanuchit's masterpiece is the *Taleng Phai*, a heroic epic of the struggle of King Naresvara of Ayutthaya to liberate his country from Burmese rule and of his famous single combat with the crown prince of Burma in 1590. Its tone is patriotic but never chauvinistic, and the Burmese are depicted in a chivalrous and sympathetic manner. His concluding section of the *Samuddhaghosa*, a folktale adapted from a collection called the *Paññāsajātaka*, which had been left unfinished since the 18th century, is distinguished for the beauty of its descriptive passages. His prose—*e.g.*, the *Pathomasombodhi*—is equally valued for its eloquence and descriptive power. He also contributed to the collection of literary inscriptions on stone at Watphra Jetubon under the patronage of King Rama III, by writing classic models of Siamese poetry that still remain. Notwithstanding the conservative monastic and celibate seclusion of his adult life, Prince Paramanuchit was a versatile writer with liberal ideas.

·Thai court poetry **17**:235c

Paramāra, Central Indian ruling dynasty of the 10th and 11th centuries.

·Rājput dynastic history **9**:362b

Paramaribo, largest town, capital, and chief port of Surinam (formerly Dutch, or Netherlands, Guiana); it lies 9 mi (15 km) from the Atlantic on the Suriname River, which is tidal at that point. It originated as an Indian village that became a French settlement (*c.* 1640) and was later the site of an English colony planted in 1651 by Lord Willoughby of Parham, a status it retained until Dutch rule began in 1816. Since World War II the town has grown considerably. Tourism and commercial and small industrial enterprises have developed, including a notable brewery.

Paramaribo is built on a shingle reef that forms a plateau 16 ft (5 m) above the river at low tide. Access from the sea is limited by a sandbar that allows a depth of about 20 ft (6 m). The broad streets, often shaded by flowering trees, are laid out in grid pattern. Most buildings are made of wood, and much of the distinctive Dutch colonial architecture remains; the canals particularly provide a flavour of The Netherlands. Paramaribo has the

Government House, Paramaribo, Surinam
EB Inc.

Surinam Museum and an extensive library, as well as the botanic gardens and government house. The 17th-century Ft. Zeelandia is nearby. An airport, 25 mi south, and a railroad serve the town, which is also an administrative district. Pop. (1971 prelim.) 102,297.

·district area and population table **17**:826
·map, Surinam **17**:824
·physical geography, urban settlement, and transportation **17**:824e *passim* to 827a

Paramārtha (6th century AD), Indian Buddhist missionary and translator.

·Yogācāra Buddhist teachings in China **3**:382g

paramārtha-satya (Buddhist philosophy): *see* saṃvṛti-satya.

Paramatrailokanatha (king of Siam): *see* Trailok.

Paramattha Mañjūsā (Pāli: Jewel Box of the True Meaning), Buddhist commentary by Dhammapāla, *c.* 5th century AD.

·Hīnayāna syncretistic philosophy **3**:436a

Paramecium, genus of free-living protozoans of the holotrichous order Hymenostomatida. There are at least eight well-defined species; all can be cultivated easily in the laboratory. Although they vary in size, most *Paramecium* species are about the size of the period at the end of this sentence. The basic shape varies, depending on the species; *P. caudatum* is elongated and gracefully streamlined, *P. bursaria* resembles a footprint. The term paramecium is also used to refer to individual organisms in a *Paramecium* species.

These microscopic single-celled organisms

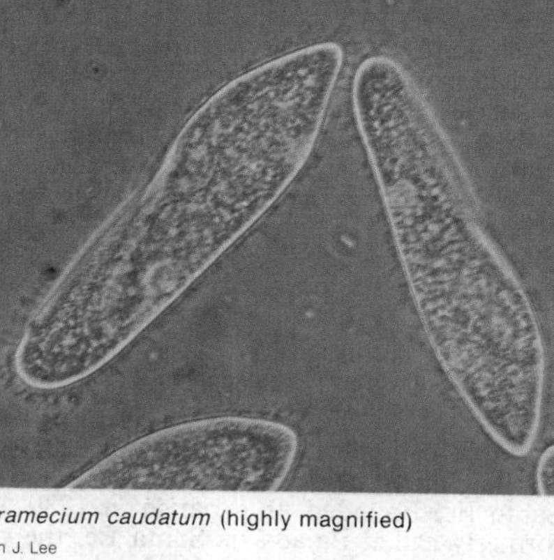

Paramecium caudatum (highly magnified)
John J. Lee

are completely covered with fine hairlike filaments (cilia) that beat rhythmically to propel them and to direct bacteria and other food particles into their mouths. On the ventral surface an oral groove runs diagonally posterior to the mouth and gullet. Digestion takes place within the food vacuole, and the waste material is excreted through the anus.

A thin layer of clear, firm cytoplasm (ectoplasm) lies directly beneath the flexible body membrane (pellicle) and encloses the inner, more fluid portion of the cytoplasm (endoplasm), which contains granules, food vacuoles, and crystals of different sizes. Embedded in the ectoplasm are spindle-shaped bodies (trichocysts) that may be released by chemical, electrical, or mechanical means. Originally believed to be a defense reaction, they appear to be extruded as a reaction to injury or for use as an anchoring device.

A paramecium has two, occasionally three, contractile vacuoles located close to the surface near the ends of the cell. They function in regulating the water content within the cell and may also be considered excretory structures since the expelled water contains metabolic wastes.

Paramecia have two kinds of nuclei: a large ellipsoidal nucleus called a macronucleus and one or more small nuclei called micronuclei. The organism cannot survive without the macronucleus; it cannot reproduce without the micronucleus. The macronucleus is the centre of all metabolic activities and, like the micronucleus, contains genes that bear hereditary information. The micronucleus is necessary for conjugation.

The most common type of reproduction in *Paramecium* is asexual binary fission in which a fully grown organism divides into two daughter cells. *Paramecium* also has several types of sexual reproduction. Conjugation (cross-fertilization) consists of the temporary union of two animals and the exchange of micronuclear elements. Without the rejuvenating effects of conjugation, a paramecium ages and dies. Only mating types, or genetically compatible organisms, can unite in conjugation. *P. aurelia* has 34 hereditary mating types that form 16 distinct mating groups, or syngens. Autogamy (self-fertilization) is a similar process that occurs in one animal. In cytogamy, another type of self-fertilization, two animals join together but do not undergo nuclear exchange.

Besides their utility in general study and for teaching purposes, paramecia have been widely used for research in cytogenetics, nutrition, serology, radiation biology, and other fields of biology.

·biological reproduction systems **15**:677d
·chemoreceptors and food selection **4**:177d
·cilia coordination theories **12**:976d
·circulation patterns and functions **4**:619c
·conjugation between unlike populations **16**:587f
·digestive system structures **13**:722h
·nutrient intake and digestion **5**:781d
·oxygen consumption table, 1 **15**:751
·P. aurelia and bursaria reproduction **15**:122b
·P. aurelia cytoplasmic inheritance of killer trait **8**:805c
·reproductive behaviour pattern **15**:683d

paramedical personnel, trained personnel who assist physicians in the diagnosis and treatment of patients.

·China's barefoot doctors **4**:295f
·Soviet paramedical practice **11**:843d

Paramesvara (Cambodian ruler): *see* Jayavarman II.

Paramesvara, after conversion to Islām MEGAT ISKANDAR SHAH (d. 1424, Malacca, now Melaka, Malaysia), founder of Malacca (*see* Melaka), which became the most powerful and wealthy maritime trade centre in 15th-century Southeast Asia.

Following the *Sejarah Melayu* (*Malay Annals*), most scholars have assigned the years 1403 to 1424 to Paramesvara's reign in Malacca. One, however, has argued, instead, that Paramesvara came to power in 1388 or 1389 as ruler of Palembang (a Sumatran kingdom); three years later fled in the face of a Javanese

attack to the island of Tumasik (now Singapore), where he remained for six years; and then moved on to found Malacca in 1399 or 1400. The city of Malacca was located on a fine natural harbour, and Paramesvara established relations with the Thai kingdom of Ayutthaya and in 1405 with Ming China. It was not until the 1430s that Malacca achieved its position as pre-eminent trading centre for Southeast Asia, but the trade pattern established in the early years and particularly the cordial relations with China, whose fleets made Malacca a port of call, provided the basis for Malacca's later greatness.
·Malayan struggles for power **11**:365f

parameter, in mathematics, a variable for which the range of possible values identifies a collection of distinct cases in a problem. Any equation expressed in parameters is a parametric equation. The general equation of a straight line in slope-intercept form, $y = mx + b$, in which m and b are parameters, is an example of a parametric equation. When values are assigned to the parameters, such as the slope $m = 2$ and the y-intercept $b = 3$, and substitution is made, the resulting equation, $y = 2x + 3$, is that of a specific straight line and is no longer parametric.

In statistics, the parameter in a function is the variable sought by means of evidence from samples. The resulting assigned value is the estimate or statistic.

In the calculus of variations, parametric representation of arcs is made *See also* variable.
·dimensional analysis theory **14**:422f
·statistical theory and method **17**:616c
·systems-design changes **17**:974e

pāramitās, in Mahāyāna (Great Vehicle) Buddhism, the perfections, or virtues, the practice of which leads to enlightenment. The six virtues are generosity (*dāna-pāramitā*, "perfection of giving"); morality (*śīla-pāramitā*); perseverance (*kṣānti-pāramitā*); vigour (*vīrya-pāramitā*); meditation or concentration (*dhyāna-pāramitā*); and wisdom (*prajñā-pāramitā*). Some lists expand the virtues to ten, by adding skill in the means of helping others (*upāya* [*kauśalya*]*-pāramitās*); profound resolution to produce enlightenment (*praṇidhāna-pāramitā*); perfection of the ten powers (*bala-pāramitā*); and practice of transcendent knowledge (*jñāna-pāramitā*). The cultivation of the six (or ten) *pāramitā*s is considered to be the appropriate training for a *bodhisattva*, or Buddha-to-be.
·Buddhist ethical thought **3**:390h
·Mahāyāna boddhisattva ideal **3**:380h

paramnesia, the illusion of remembering of events that had not been previously experienced.
·memory errors and illusions **11**:889h

paramorph, pseudomorph formed by the alteration of the molecular arrangement of a substance without an accompanying change in its chemical composition. *See* pseudomorph.

Paramount, city, Los Angeles County, California, U.S. Once part of the Rancho Santa Gertrudes, it was laid out as Clearwater by a commercial tract company in 1867. Dairying and hay marketing were early activities. Its southern portion formed the separate community of Hynes in 1892, and the two were joined in 1949 as Paramount. Residential and industrial growth has been tied to expansion of the Los Angeles metropolitan area. Inc. city, 1957. Pop. (1980) 36,407.
33°53′ N, 118°09′ W

Paramount Pictures Corporation, one of the most successful of the Hollywood motion-picture studios, known for its production of light, family type films. Established in 1914 when W.W. Hodkinson's film-distributing firm offered Adolph Zukor's Famous Players Company, Jesse Lasky Feature Play Company, and other producers an outlet for their movies, it quickly rose to prominence by introducing the first "big Western," *The Covered Wagon* (1923), the story of the westward journey of the '49ers, and by opening branches in Britain and France. *The Ten Commandments* (1923; 1956) and *The King of Kings* (1927), Biblical epics directed by Cecil B. deMille, were produced under Paramount's auspices. Paramount was declared bankrupt in 1933 but was reorganized two years later. The studio built up a reputation for producing light entertainment with such films as *Going My Way* (1944) and the "road" comedies of Bob Hope, Bing Crosby, and Dorothy Lamour; *e.g.*, *Road to Zanzibar* (1941), *Road to Rio* (1947).

In the 1950s Paramount introduced VistaVision, a widescreen process that retained the colour and image clarity of the smaller screen, an important development in the transition to the wide screen. The company merged with Joseph E. Levine, Inc., in the 1960s. Later, Gulf & Western Industries took over control of the corporation.
·Eisenstein production problems **6**:517e
·history and image **12**:529h

Paramus, borough, Bergen County, northeastern New Jersey, U.S., immediately northeast of Paterson. Settled by Dutch colonists in 1666, the name was derived from a Lenni Lenape Indian word, *peremessing* ("a place abounding in wild turkey"). An important transportation centre since the American Revolutionary War, the community is the site of several large shopping areas. Its manufactures include electronic equipment and cosmetics. Vegetable growing in the area is important, with celery the main crop. A point of interest is an 1873 one-room schoolhouse featured by the Paramus Historical and Preservation Society. Inc. 1922. Pop. (1980) 26,474.
40°57′ N, 74°04′ W

Paramyidae, family of mammals of the order Rodentia.
·classification and general features **15**:977h

paramylum, starchlike carbohydrate, food reserve in some algae and protozoans. The size, shape, and number of paramylum granules vary among species, and may be used to some extent in taxonomy.

paramyosin, a protein found in muscle fibres of the adductor muscle of mollusks such as clams, scallops, and oysters. The paramyosin-containing fibres are in those adductor muscles that hold the two shells of the animals closed.
·invertebrate smooth muscle **12**:632g
·mollusk muscle tissues **12**:641a

paramyosin smooth muscle, contractile tissue type found only in mollusks, the muscle part that holds the shells together.

Paraná 13:997, state, southern Brazil, with an area of 77,048 sq mi (199,554 sq km). It is bordered by the Atlantic Ocean (east), by Argentina (southwest), by Paraguay (west), and by the states of Santa Catarina (south), Mato Grosso (northwest), and São Paulo (north and northeast). The capital is Curitiba. Pop. (1970 prelim.) 6,997,682.

The text article covers Paraná's history, physiography, climate, vegetation, population, administration, economy, and transportation.

REFERENCES in other text articles:
·area and population table **3**:133
·map, Brazil **3**:124

Paraná, capital of Entre Ríos province, eastern Argentina, near the Río Paraná, opposite Sante Fe. Founded as a parish in 1730 and formerly called Bajada de Santa Fe, the city had little importance until 1853, when it was made capital of the Argentine Confederation. Until 1862, while Buenos Aires was separated from the confederation, Paraná was the residence of the federal authorities. This boosted its economic, cultural, and population growth. Development was sustained after it was made the provincial capital in 1882. Because of flood dangers, Paraná (Guaraní Indian for "father of the rivers") stands on high ground 2 mi (3 km) from the riverbank and is linked by rail and road to its port, Bejada Grande, which handles the region's agricultural produce. The city has two national historic monuments—the Cathedral of Paraná

The cathedral of Paraná, Arg.
Editorial Photocolor Archives

(1883), which houses the image of Our Lady of the Rosary, and the building of the Senate of the Argentine Confederation (1858). Other notable buildings include the home of Gen. Justo José de Urquiza (Argentina's first president), the Bishop's Palace, and the Museum of Entre Ríos. Pop. (1970 prelim.) 127,635.
31°45′ S, 60°30′ W
·map, Argentina **1**:1136

Paraná Basin, region of sedimentary deposition in eastern South America, especially well known and studied in the states of Santa Catharina and Paraná, in southern Brazil. The sequence of rocks in the Paraná Basin is similar to sequences in South Africa and is Permo-Triassic in age (190,000,000 to 280,000,000 years ago). Evidence for several periods of continental glaciation has been noted in the Permian portion of the sequence of strata, whereas a Middle Triassic age is indicated for the Rio do Rasto beds. The Rio do Rasto contains a reptilian fauna dominated by the genera *Cephalonia* and *Scaphonyx*, closely related to forms found in Great Britain.
·area, location, and geology **17**:75f; map76
·flood basalt structure **14**:527f
·Triassic sedimentation in Brazil **18**:694f

Paranaguá, port, southeastern Paraná state, Brazil, on the Baía (bay) de Paranaguá, at the foot of the coastal Serra do Mar, 18 mi (29 km) from the open Atlantic. It was founded in 1585 by Portuguese explorers. Surviving colonial landmarks include the fort of Nossa Senhora dos Prazeres (1767), the Baroque Museum of Archaeology and Popular Art (formerly the Colegio dos Jesuitas), and a 17th-century fountain.

By the mid-20th century Paranaguá had become Brazil's largest coffee-exporting port as well as the chief port (hides, paper, maté, lumber, bananas, sugar) of Paraná state. Industry includes sawmilling, woodworking, coffee roasting, and processing maté (an aromatic tea). Paranaguá is linked to Curitiba, the state capital (65 mi inland), by rail and road, and serves as a free port for Paraguay. Pop. (1970 prelim.) 51,510.
25°31′ S, 48°30′ W
·map, Brazil **3**:124

Paranaíba River, Portuguese RIO PARANAÍBA, in south central Brazil, arises on the western slopes of the Serra da Mata da Corda and flows west-southwestward for about 600 mi (1,000 km) collecting eight sizable tributaries along its course to join the Grande River (*q.v.*) and form the Paraná River. It constitutes the border between Minas Gerais and Goiás

states and briefly separates Minas Gerais from Mato Grosso state. Diamond washings are along its course.
20°07′ S, 51°05′ W
·map, Brazil **3**:124
·waterfalls and tributaries **13**:999b; map 1000

Paraná lava fields, extend over southern Brazil, southeastern Paraguay, and northeastern Argentina.
25°00′ S, 53°00′ W
·location, area, and geology **17**:75f; map 76

Paranapanema River, Portuguese RIO PARANAPANEMA, rises south of São Paulo in the Serra do Paranapiacaba, southeastern Brazil, and flows in a west-northwesterly direction for 560 mi (900 km) before entering the Paraná River at Pôrto São José. After receiving the Itararé, it forms part of the São Paulo–Paraná state border. There are numerous rapids along its course, which is navigable only for the last 50 mi. Dam-flood control projects are near Piraju and Jacarèzinho. Coffee and cotton are grown in the river basin, which occupies part of the fertile Paraná Plateau.

Tributaries include the Rio das Cinzas and Rio Tibagi, the latter having an important hydroelectric station near Monte Alegre.
22°40′ S, 53°09′ W
·map, Brazil **3**:124
·source and border importance **13**:998b

Paraná pine, also called BRAZILIAN PINE or CANDELABRA TREE (*Araucaria angustifolia*), an important evergreen timber conifer of the family Araucariaceae, native to the mountains

Paraná pine (*Araucaria angustifolia*)
E. Aubert de la Rue

of southern Brazil. The Paraná pine grows to 30 metres (100 feet) high and bears branches in a circle about the stems. As the tree matures, the lower branches drop off, leaving a long, bare trunk with a crown of upturned branches tufted at the ends.
·location, species, and associations **17**:87e; map 88

Paraná Plateau, one of the world's largest lava plateaus, lies mostly in southern Brazil (Rio Grande do Sul and São Paulo states) but its diabase formations (solidified sheets of lava rock) also appear in Uruguay, Argentina, and Paraguay. Where the diabase is exposed at the surface, it weathers into a dark purple-coloured soil known as *terra roxa*, famous as a producer of coffee. The plateau is dissected by rivers, between which the surface is flat-topped.
·geologic features **18**:1094a
·lava composition and height **15**:862a

Parañaque, town, Rizal province, central Luzon, Philippines, on the southeastern shore of Manila Bay. Its site was occupied by small vegetable farms until the mid-20th century,

Fishing settlement at Parañaque, Luzon, Philippines
Morton Beebe—Photo Researchers

when expanding urbanization transformed the town into a southern suburb of Manila. The Manila International Airport to the east occupies Nichols Field, a former U.S. air base. Parañaque has long been noted for intricate hand embroidery, which continues as a household industry. Fishing from the rafts mounted with *salambaos* (large nets) remains an important activity. The Manila Bay Beach Resort, a national park, is there. Pop. (1970) 97,214.
14°30′ N, 120°59′ E

Paraná River **13**:999, Portuguese RIO PARANÁ, rises on the plateau of southeast central Brazil and flows generally south to the point where, after a course of 2,485 mi (4,000 km), it joins the Uruguay River to form the extensive Río de la Plata Estuary of the Atlantic. South America's second longest river (after the Amazon), it drains parts of southeastern Brazil, Paraguay, eastern Bolivia, and northern Argentina.

The text article covers the river's physiography, climate, vegetation, animal life, human ecology, cartographic history, hydrology, navigation, principal crossings, economic resources, and prospects for the future.
33°43′ S, 59°15′ W

REFERENCES in other text articles:
·basin area and sediment types **17**:75f
·Brazilian drainage significance **3**:128d; map 140
·delta, tides, and discharge table **15**:868
·geographic features and importance **13**:984g
maps
·Argentina **1**:1136
·Brazil **3**:124
·South America **17**:77
·Paraná state related features **13**:997f *passim* to 999a
·São Paulo tributaries and flow **16**:236h

Parandowski, Jan (1895–), Polish author.
·themes of major works **10**:1253e

Parangaba, city, northern Ceará state (*estado*), northeastern Brazil, immediately southwest of Fortaleza, the state capital. Until the 1940s it was a small cotton-producing centre on the site of an old Indian village, Parangaba (formerly Porangaba), but has since experienced phenomenal suburban growth. Pop. (1970 prelim.) 164,332.
3°45′ S, 38°33′ W

paranoid reactions, a group of psychotic disorders characterized by systematic delusions. The word paranoia was used by the ancient Greeks, apparently in much the same sense as the modern popular term insanity. Since then it has had a variety of meanings. Toward the end of the 19th century it came to mean a delusional psychosis, in which the delusions develop slowly into a complex, intricate, and logically elaborated system, without hallucination and without general personality disorganization. Sometimes the fixed delusional system, usually persecutory or grandiose, is more or less encapsulated, thus leaving the rest of the personality relatively intact. Though a great many patients with paranoia have to be hospitalized, some do not, and, among these, an occasional one succeeds in building up a following of persons who believe him to be a genius or inspired. In contemporary psychiatric practice, the term paranoia is generally reserved for all rare, extreme cases of chronic, fixed, and highly systematized delusions. All the rest are called paranoid states; *i.e.*, states resembling paranoia but less severe. Some psychiatrists, however, have come to doubt the validity of paranoia as a diagnostic category, claiming that what has in the past been considered paranoia is actually a variety of schizophrenia.

Paranoid states are relatively common psychotic disorders, characterized by persistent delusions and by behaviour and emotional responses that are consistent with the delusional ideas. Hallucinations are absent; and there is no general personality disorganization, such as that commonly seen in schizophrenia. Paranoid states may develop gradually or appear suddenly; they may remain chronic or clear up. Complete recovery is not rare; a person who was distrustful before his illness, however, is likely to remain distrustful afterward.

Persecutory paranoid state. Individual susceptibility to paranoid developments varies greatly. The person most vulnerable to a persecutory paranoid state is the tense, insecure, suspicious person who has little basic trust in other persons, who has always found it difficult to confide in others, who tends to be secretive, who has few close friends, and who is addicted to solitary rumination.

A chief contributing factor is an exaggerated tendency to self-reference; *i.e.*, to misinterpret remarks, gestures and acts of others as intentional slights or as signs of derision and contempt directed at him. It is normal to assume occasionally that criticism, contempt, or derision is directed at oneself when actually it is not. But the average person is able to shrug it off, after a brief period of resentment, or to challenge it, and thus find out his error of interpretation.

Self-reference becomes paranoid delusion when a person persists in believing that he is the target of hostile actions or insinuations, aimed at him by some enemy or band of enemies, when this is actually not the case. The identifying marks of delusional conviction are (1) readiness to accept the flimsiest evidence in support of the belief and (2) inability to entertain seriously any evidence that contradicts it. It is this biased selection of available evidence that gives to paranoid development its appearance of irresistible progression.

When apparent persecution reaches a sufficient degree of intensity and complexity, it is natural to assume an organized source. The search for some unifying explanation leads many paranoid patients to conclude that the "plot" is being engineered by certain specific persons, some of them actual persons who can be pointed out, some of them imaginary. Such an imagined community of alleged conspirators is called a paranoid pseudo-community.

Other paranoid states. In addition to the common persecutory type of paranoid reaction, a number of others have been described, most notably paranoid grandiosity, or delusions of grandeur. This is much less common than delusions of persecution, and when it occurs the paranoid disorder is usually more severe. Unlike the grandiose delusions in mania and in schizophrenia, paranoid grandiosity tends to be well organized, relatively stable, and persistent. The complexity of delusional conviction varies from rather simple beliefs in one's alleged talent, attractiveness, or inspiration to highly complex, systematized beliefs that one is a great prophet, author, poet, inventor, or scientist. The latter extreme belongs to classical paranoia.

BIBLIOGRAPHY. N. Cameron, "The Paranoid Pseudo-community Revisited," *Amer. J. Sociol.*, 65:52 (1959), and "Paranoid Conditions and Paranoia," *American Handbook of Psychiatry* (1959); Aubrey Lewis, "Paranoia and Paranoid: A Historical Perspective," *Psychological Medicine*, 1:2–12 (1970).

·amphetamine-produced psychosis **5**:1057g
·attitudinal changes in paresis **2**:361h
·psychotic delusional systems **15**:177c

paranoid schizophrenia: *see* schizophrenia.

Parāntaka I (reigned 907–955), Indian king of the Cōla dynasty.
·Cōla military expansion **9**:363a

Paranthropus, genus assigned by Robert Broom to a robust form of australopithecine found at Kromdraai and Swartkrans, S.Af. The remains are known as *Australopithecus robustus* to scholars, who do not consider it a separate genus from other australopithecines. Finds from East Africa (*Zinjanthropus*, *Meganthropus*) and Asia (*Meganthropus*) are classed with *Paranthropus* (or *A. robustus*) by some scholars. *Paranthropus* remains are known from the late Pliocene to middle Pleistocene, a stretch of perhaps 4,000,000 years. *Paranthropus* is characterized by a small cranial capacity; heavy browridges; frequent development of sagittal and nuchal (on the occipital) crests on the skull; massive jaws; cheek teeth large, but canines and incisors very small, long; apelike ischium (posteroventral portion of the pelvis) with short lower limb, and possibly mobile foot. *Paranthropus* is believed to have been herbivorous, to have walked erect, but also to have climbed trees and to have preferred wet climates. Tools and remains of *Homo erectus* have been found in association with remains of *Paranthropus*, demonstrating coexistence of two hominid species. Much controversy exists as to whether or not *Paranthropus* belongs in the line of evolution to man. Competition with the more successful toolmaking *Homo erectus* populations may have led to the eventual extinction of the robust australopithecines.
·African veld habitat and fossil record **19**:57g
·morphology, behaviour, classification, and fossil record **2**:437b
·taxonomic status of fossils **11**:422h

para nut: *see* brazil nut.

Paraonyx (mammal): *see* otter.

paraphrase, musical, in Renaissance music, use of an elaborated plainsong melody from one composition in another, usually a mass or motet but also in keyboard works. The melody is frequently broken up, with new notes interpolated between each of its notes; occasionally the melody may be condensed. The paraphrased melody may appear in one voice part of the new composition, as in the motet *Alma redemptoris mater* (*Beloved Mother of the Redeemer*), by Guillaume Dufay, or in all voice parts through the technique of melodic imitation, as in the *Missa pange lingua* (mass on the plainsong hymn "Pange lingua" ["Sing, My Tongue"]), by Josquin des Prez.

paraphysis, a sterile filament associated with the reproductive structures of some algae and fungi; possibly functions in the dissemination of spores.
·fern reproductive system **7**:244h; illus.

Parapinaces (Byzantine emperor): *see* Michael VII Ducas.

Parapithecidae, fossil primate family of the order Primates.
·classification and fossil record **14**:1029g

Parapithecus, genus of fossil Oligocene apes (order Primates).
·primate ancestry and evolution **14**:1026d

paraplegia, paralysis of the legs and lower part of the body. Often it involves loss of sensation (of pain, temperature, vibration, and position) as well as loss of motion. It may also include paralysis of the bladder and bowels. Paraplegia may be caused by injury to or disease in the lower spinal cord or peripheral nerves or by such brain disorders as cerebral palsy. Some paraplegics are able to lead noninstitutionalized lives on crutches. A few can be taught to walk in braces. Quadriplegia is the same condition applied to both arms and both legs. *See also* paralysis.

Parapriacanthus ransonneti, species of luminous fish of the order Perciformes.
·bioluminescent chemical reactions **2**:1032a

Parapsida, extinct group of reptiles in which the skull had a single opening.
·reptile skull types, illus. 2 **15**:732

parapsychological phenomena, theories of 13:1002 Parapsychological phenomena are putative events of an extrasensory or extrakinetic nature, sometimes referred to by the more neutral term psi phenomena.

The text article covers the various types of extrasensory perception (ESP), clairvoyance, telepathy, and precognition, with illustrative examples and a discussion of informal and formal investigation of ESP. The evidence for psychokinesis—levitation, poltergeist activity, and the like—is then considered. The article concludes with a section on theories developed to account for parapsychological phenomena.

REFERENCES in other text articles:
·argument against Materialism **11**:614e
·miracles in world religion **12**:269g
·prophetic ecstasy **15**:62d
·Schopenhauer's investigation and essays **16**:359g
·spiritualist explanation **17**:512g

RELATED ENTRIES in the *Ready Reference and Index:*
clairvoyance; extrasensory perception; lycanthropy; precognition; psychical research; psychokinesis; telepathy

pararammelsbergite, nickel arsenide, a mineral.
·sulfide mineral physical properties **17**:788g

Pará River, Portuguese RIO PARÁ, name applied to the channel of the Amazon Delta that passes to the south and east of Marajó Island, in northeastern Pará state, northern Brazil. It carries a small part of the discharge of the Amazon River, eastward and northward to the Atlantic Ocean, off Cabo Maguarinho. Its width varies from 5 to 40 mi (8 to 64 km), and its entire 200-mi length is navigable. Because it receives the Tocantins River (*q.v.*) from the south, the Pará is often called an estuary of that river. Belém, capital of Pará state, lies on the right bank, near the mouths of the Guamá and Guajará rivers. The tidal bore of the Amazon is strong on the Pará.
1°30′ S, 48°55′ W

Pararthropoda (invertebrate): *see* oncopod.

Para rubber (*Hevea Brasiliensis*), South American rubber tree.
·tree use and sustained yield forestry **7**:528c

parasambhogakāya, the referential aspect of the *sambhoga-kāya*, the second aspect of the Threefold Body of the Buddha (*tri-kāya*).
·Buddhist mystical existence-forms **3**:417d

parasang, measure of length in Iran, equivalent to 3.88 miles.
·weights and measures, table 5 **19**:734

Paraschwagerina, extinct genus of fusulinid foraminiferans (protozoans with a relatively large shell readily preservable in the fossil record), the fossils of which are restricted to marine rocks; the animal probably formed in clear water, far from the shoreline. The various species are excellent index or guide fossils for the Early Permian (the Permian Period began 280,000,000 years ago) and allow the correlation of sometimes widely separated rock units.

Parasemionotiformes, order of extinct fishes (subclass or infraclass Chondrostei) containing two families that existed during the Lower Triassic.
·classification and general features **4**:439a
·structure and families **7**:342f

Parasha (1843), long poem by Ivan Turgenev.
·Turgenev's early works **18**:779a

Parasite, The, translation of KOLAX, 4th-century-BC play by Menander.
·Terence's sources for plays **18**:143d

Parasitica, collective name formerly given to parasitic Hymenoptera of the suborder Apocrita (*q.v.*). The rest of the Apocrita, which were known as Aculeata, are stinging, nonparasitic forms. Distinctions between Parasitica and Aculeata were difficult to define, and the names are no longer used in a taxonomic sense.
·Hymenoptera behaviour and larvae **9**:126a *passim* to 131a

parasitism, relationship between two species of plants or animals in which one benefits at the expense of the other, usually without killing it.

Relationships in which the host is killed by the parasite are referred to as parasitoidism. Parasitoidism occurs in some Hymenoptera (ants, wasps, and bees), Diptera (flies), and a few Lepidoptera (butterflies and moths): the female lays her eggs in or on the host, upon which the larvae feed on hatching.

Parasites may also become parasitized; such a relationship is known as hyperparasitism. A protozoan living in the digestive tract of a flea living on a dog is a hyperparasite.

The cuckoo and the cowbird do not build nests of their own but deposit their eggs in the nests of other species and abandon the eggs. This form of parasitism is called brood parasitism.

The exploitation of one species by another, as, for example, some ants that make slaves of another species, is known as social parasitism.

diseases and infestations
·amoebic dysentery and treatment **5**:801f
·anemia from fish tapeworm infestation **2**:1136a
·blowfly myiasis of livestock **9**:610g
·cat internal and external parasites **3**:999a
·chemotherapeutic drugs for infections **18**:285g
·chemotherapeutic treatment of disease **4**:189e
·digestive disorders from infection **5**:770f
·disease and biotic interactions **5**:838b
·diseases of animals, tables 2, 5, 7, 8, and 9 **5**:867
·disease transmission and symptoms **9**:544c
·dog infestations and transmission **5**:934a
·ecological effects of dam projects **6**:199g
·human disease causation and progression **5**:858b
·lice feeding off birds and mammals **14**:373f
·malaria and mosquito life cycle **9**:557d
·pest control use and results **14**:144d *passim* to 147c
·pet diseases and hazards to man **14**:152a
·Platyhelminthes infestation effects **14**:546c
·protozoan pathogens in man and animals **15**:120g
·sex change influence in crabs **15**:705a
·skin invasion by lice and mites **16**:846h
·tissue culture demonstration **18**:439b
·trematode infestation in human liver **10**:1274e
·Trichinella spiralis in human body **9**:555e
·trichinosis' causes and symptoms **12**:636a
·virus life cycle **19**:165c
·virus origin and nature **14**:377d *passim* to 379a
·waterfowl susceptability and mortality **1**:944f

dispersal mechanisms and hosts
·angler fish male as adjunct to female **16**:589e
·anglerfish male–female relationships **13**:980h
·annelid worm fossil and recent types **1**:931f
·bivalve larval development on fish **2**:1086h

·brood parasitism exhibited by cuckoos **14**:776b
·chemoreception and host finding **4**:176g
·cleaning behaviour function and angler fish reproduction **13**:500e
·coastal community animal life **4**:806f
·crabs harbouring vectors **5**:543c
·crustacean-sponge associations **14**:850h
·cuckoo behavioral polymorphism **14**:776b
·cuckoo nesting and mimicry of host **5**:360b
·cyst formation as survival mechanism **5**:960f
·dispersal of parasites through hosts and carriers **5**:912g
·echiurid male's life in female uterus **6**:186f
·ecosystem food web **18**:147h
·evolutionary relationships among hosts **7**:10a
·flea host dependence **16**:808a
·flies' role in life cycle of trypanosome **5**:819h
·Great Lakes predators and food chains **8**:303d
·Homoptera in parasitic and hyperparasitic relationships **8**:1039c
·homopterans as hosts for wasps **8**:1039d
·larval specialization advantages **5**:640d
·lepidopteran parasitic predators **10**:823b
·mesozoan dependence on marine invertebrates **11**:1013a
·mimicry's functions and evolution **12**:214a
·nematode larvae and host penetration **2**:139b
·reproductive behaviour in barnacles and insects **15**:684g
·schistosome life cycle **10**:615h
·soil organisms and animal diseases **16**:1014c
·spiny-headed worm habitat **1**:18f
·symbiosis and feeding adaptations **4**:1028g
·symbiotic relationships in echinoderms **6**:181c
·tick simple reactions to host **2**:805h; illus. 806
·Trichoptera parasitized by hymenoptera **18**:709f

other specializations

·acarine mouthpart modifications **1**:1063a
·arthropod specialized forms **2**:67e
·barnacle cyprid metamorphosis **4**:642e; illus. 641
·bee and wasp adaptations **9**:126f *passim* to 129d
·catfish interspecies relations **18**:82e
·evolutionary modification of habitat **7**:10a
·flatworm muscular specializations **12**:642a
·leech anatomy, habits, and taxonomy **1**:928d; illus.933
·pigment derivation from host **4**:918d
·tick and mite traits **1**:19h

plants

·algae damage to tea plants **1**:487g
·broomrape and witchweed adaptations **16**:413g
·dodder response to host plant presence **17**:673e
·endoparasitic slime mold diseases **16**:889c
·forest devastation by fungi **7**:537g
·fungal nutritional sources **12**:763d
·grass order adaptations **14**:589c
·live oak as host, illus., **18**:Tree, Plate III
·moss and fungus associations **3**:354b
·Nepenthales trap exploitation **12**:960g
·pitcher-plant dependents **16**:254d
·Polemoniales relationships **14**:660a
·rain forest Rafflesia parasite of vines **10**:343g
·rust fungi host control **14**:143h
·sandalwood plant's specialized structures **16**:227f
·tree fungi transmission in forest **7**:537g
·viral and bacterial plant parasitism **5**:886f
·weed control by parasitic plants **19**:727b
·white-pine rust life cycle **16**:294g

parasitoidism (biology): *see* parasitism.

parasitology, the study of animal and plant parasitism as a biological phenomenon. Parasites occur in virtually all major animal groups and in many plant groups, with hosts as varied as the parasites themselves. Many parasitologists are concerned primarily with particular taxonomic groups and should perhaps be considered students of those groups, rather than parasitologists per se; others are interested in parasitism as an evolutionary phenomenon and work with a number of taxonomic groups. The science has a number of branches (*e.g.*, veterinary, medical, or agricultural parasitology).

The history of parasitology is scattered among a number of other disciplines, especially zoology. Many highly evolved parasites remained essentially unknown or misunderstood until the advent of the microscope in the mid-17th century. A pioneer in the field of intestinal parasitology was the mid-19th century Belgian biologist P.J. van Beneden, who unravelled the life history of tapeworms and many other groups.

·biological classification systems **4**:688e
·biological development types **5**:644d
·biotic interaction and natural balance **2**:1046h; table 1045
·negative interactions of populations **14**:838b
·protozoan virulence studies **15**:122c

Paráskhos, Akhilléfs (b. March 6, 1838, Návplion, Greece—d. Jan. 26, 1895, Athens), Greek poet, was the central figure of the Greek Romantic school of poetry in its second and last period (*c.* 1850–80). His models were Alfred de Musset, Victor Hugo, and Lord Byron, but he fell short of their achievement. His manner is unrestrained and his language grandiloquent, owing much to the Phanariote poets, whose tradition he continued. He touched on all the usual Romantic subjects, but love and patriotism were his favourites. In his numerous lyrics he made use of both "refined" Greek, inherited from the Byzantine scholars, and the spoken language, but his vocabulary remained as limited as his ideas. Perhaps no other modern Greek poet was more admired by his contemporaries. His poems were published in Greek in two volumes (1881, 1904).

parasol mushroom: *see* Agaricales.

parasol pine: *see* umbrella pine.

Paras Pathar, translated as THE PHILOSOPHER'S STONE (1958), film by Satyajit Ray.
·Satyajit Ray's satirical films **15**:538b

Paraśurāma (Sanskrit: "Rāma with the axe"), sixth of the ten *avatāra*s (incarnations) of the Hindu god Viṣṇu (Vishnu). The *Mahābhārata* ("Great Epic of the Bharata Dynasty") and the *Purāṇas* ("ancient stories") record that Paraśurāma was born to the Brahmin sage Jamadagni in order to deliver the world from the arrogant oppression of the baron or warrior caste, the Kṣatriyas. He

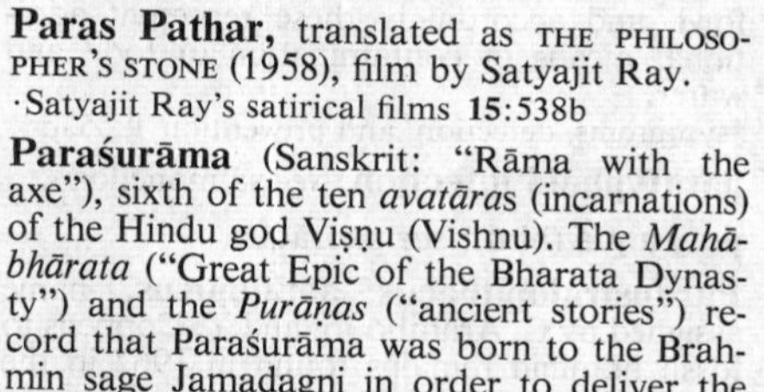

Paraśurāma (centre), miniature painting, Basohli style, early 18th century; in a private collection
Pramod Chandra

killed all the male Kṣatriyas on earth twenty-one successive times (each time their wives survived and gave birth to new generations) and filled the lakes with blood. Scholars view the legend as reflecting strife between the two classes of society in pre-Buddhist India. Paraśurāma is the traditional founder of Malabar and is said to have bestowed land there on members of the priestly caste whom he brought down from the north in order to expiate his slaughter of the Kṣatriyas. He is sometimes said to have lived on earth during the lifetime of the seventh *avatāra*, Rāma, and to have expressed some jealousy of the younger incarnation. Paraśurāma is depicted in painting and sculpture as a bearded sage with matted hair, dressed in the skin of the black deer, and carrying the *paraśu*, or battle axe, and other weapons of war in his hands.
·Vishnu playing card illus. **3**:901a

Paraśurāmeśvara, *c.* 8th-century Indian temple.
·construction and wall decoration **17**:176e

parasympathetic nervous system: *see* autonomic nervous system.

parasympatholytic agent, agent that antagonizes the effects of the parasympathetic nervous system's impulses or mimics a cessation of those impulses.
·types and action mechanisms **12**:1035d

parasympathomimetic drug, any drug that mimics the stimulation of parasympathetic nerve fibres, including drugs, such as acetylcholine, methacholine, and pilocarpine, that stimulate gastric or salivary secretion.
·salivary flow regulation **5**:788b
·types and activity sites **12**:1035b

Paratettix: *see* pygmy grasshopper.

parathion, the organic phosphorus compound with systematic name *O,O'*-diethyl *O''*-*p*-nitrophenyl phosphorothioate, a well-known insecticide that is also extremely toxic to humans. The compound acts in mammals, as in insects, as a cholinesterase inhibitor, cholinesterase being the enzyme that controls the normal functioning of the nervous system. In humans the typical symptoms associated with cholinesterase inhibition include nausea, excessive salivation, vomiting, muscle twitching, convulsion, and coma. Death occurs by respiratory failure. The specific antidote for poisoning by parathion and other organophosphorus insecticides is atropine. Parathion and similar insecticides must be handled with great care because the substance is toxic if swallowed, inhaled, or absorbed through the skin.

Parathion is prepared by a sequence of reactions using phosphorus trichloride, sulfur, sodium ethoxide, and sodium *p*-nitrophenate. It forms as a yellowish liquid boiling at 375° C (707° F) and solidifying at 6° C (43° F). It is miscible in all proportions with most organic solvents except paraffin hydrocarbons but is practically insoluble in water. Parathion may be rendered nontoxic by application of an alkaline solution.
·lethal dosage comparisons **14**:619d

parathormone: *see* parathyroid glands.

parathyroid adenoma, also called HYPERPARATHYROIDISM, OSTEITIS FIBROSA CYSTICA, or VON RECKLINGHAUSEN'S DISEASE OF BONE, uncommon disorder characterized by loss of mineral materials from the skeleton, the development of brown cystic bone tumours and of kidney stones, and progressive kidney insufficiency. Increase in the number (hyperplasia) of secretory cells of one or more of the parathyroid glands results in an excess of parathormone in the circulation. The action of parathormone removes calcium from the bones; it may then be deposited elsewhere, as in kidney stones. Symptoms include chronic tiredness and sleepiness, weakness, loss of appetite, constipation, nausea, thirst, and sometimes personality changes. Pain accompanies weakening of bones and in 25 percent of cases, so-called brown tumours develop in the ends of long bones; pathological fractures are not uncommon. The teeth become loose in their sockets, and the lamina dura, or compact bone lining of the sockets, disappears. The disease is twice as frequent in women as in men and usually begins in middle age. Persons with pre-existing peptic ulcers are more likely to develop hyperparathyroidism. Treatment usually includes surgical excision of the hyperplastic parathyroid.

parathyroid glands, endocrine glands occurring in all vertebrate species from amphibia upward, usually located close to and behind the thyroid gland and secreting parathormone, a hormone that regulates and maintains a normal calcium level in the blood serum. Human parathyroid tissue is brownish red, and the tiny (6 × 4 × 22 millimetres; one millimetre = 0.039 inch) glands may number as few as two and as many as eight on each side of the thyroid. Their embryonic origin is from the third and fourth pharyngeal pouches. Microscopically, they are made up of closely packed epithelial cells separated by thin fibrous bands; occasionally the cells are arranged in circles with an open centre (alveolar arrangement), which may contain a colloid material.

In the latter half of the 19th century, the parathyroids were recognized as playing an important physiological role when it became apparent that the convulsive seizures and death that sometimes followed experimental thyroid operations were due to the inadvertent removal of the parathyroid glands. In 1908 it was discovered that removal of the parathyroids was followed by a fall in the calcium concentration of the blood serum and that administration of calcium salts prevented or corrected the ill effects of the operation. In 1925 a method was developed for preparing a physiologically active extract of the parathyroid with which experimental animals could be tested.

The exact action of the internal secretion of these glands is not clear. It is believed that the parathyroid hormone plays an important role in stabilizing the calcium concentration of the body fluids—a very important function, since a lowering of the calcium ion concentration results in a condition of increased excitability of nerves and muscles known as tetany, which results in muscular spasms, convulsions, and sometimes dementia. Under normal conditions a small drop in the calcium concentration of the body fluids results in increased activity of the parathyroid glands, which raises the calcium concentration by mobilizing some of the skeletal calcium.

On the other hand, a rise in body fluid calcium concentration above the normal is counteracted by a reduction or cessation of secretion of parathyroid hormone. The internal secretion of the parathyroids also affects the metabolism of phosphorus, an excess of the hormone resulting in a lowering of inorganic phosphate concentration in the blood serum and an increased excretion of phosphate in the urine. Reduced parathyroid function is accompanied by a rise in the inorganic phosphate of the serum and a lessened urinary output of phosphate. Both overfunction and underfunction of the parathyroid glands produce important disease entities.

Along with the roles of these hormones in calcium metabolism, vitamin D enhances calcium and phosphate absorption from the gut; cortisol, from the adrenal gland (*q.v.*), seems to oppose this action of vitamin D. Parathyroid hormone appears to play a role in the regulation of magnesium metabolism, possibly increasing the excretion of that electrolyte.

·anatomy, cellular characteristics, and hormones **6**:813h; illus. 800
·animal tissue comparisons **18**:447e
·bone metabolic regulation **3**:24a
calcitonin
·bone and serum calcium ion level control **3**:21b
·calcium regulation in the plasma **2**:1115e
·pharmaceutical sources in fish **6**:848d
·source, chemical nature, and function **6**:814e
·calcium release in renal disease **7**:57g
·chief-cell function and response to blood calcium **6**:842g
·disease symptoms and treatment **6**:826h
parathormone
·bone and serum calcium ion level control **3**:21b
·calcium regulation in the plasma **2**:1115e
·function and characteristics **15**:96g
·hormone secretion by chief cells **6**:814a
·hormone secretion in land vertebrates **8**:1079g
·muscle disorders with hormone imbalance **12**:634g
·neural symptoms of endocrine diseases **12**:1044a
·renal function influenced by hormones **7**:38f
·source and site of action, table 3 **5**:859
·vertebrate structure, function, and embryonic origin **6**:842g; illus. 841

parathyroid tetany, disorder involving intermittent muscular spasms, due to low calcium in the body fluids, following removal of the parathyroid glands.

·causation and neurological symptoms **12**:1044a

Para ti, Argentinian weekly women's magazine founded in 1922.

·magazine publishing history **15**:253c

paratroops, soldiers trained and equipped to parachute from an airplane, primarily on combat missions.

·air tactics and World War II **7**:401e

Paratropidae, family of spiders of the order Araneida (class Arachnida).

·classification and general features **1**:1072f

paratuberculosis: *see* Johne's disease.

paratyphoid fever, infectious disease similar to typhoid, though usually milder, caused by any of several organisms: *Salmonella paratyphi* (paratyphoid A), *S. schottmulleri* (paratyphoid B), or *S. hirschfeldii* (paratyphoid C). The means of infection, spread, clinical course, pathology, diagnosis, prevention, and treatment are similar to those for typhoid.

Whereas typhoid and paratyphoid A are diseases of man only, the paratyphoid B organism has been found in other animals and fowl, and accordingly these represent additional means of contamination of food and water.

·symptoms, detection, and prevention **9**:553b

paratyphoid infection: *see* salmonellosis.

parauque (bird): *see* pauraque.

Paraustralopithecus aethiopicus, name assigned by C. Arambourg and Y. Coppens to fossil hominid remains found in 1967 in the Omo region of southwest Ethiopia. *See* Omo australopithecines.

·Australopithecine fossil discovery table **2**:437

Parautoptic lock, also called NEWELL LOCK, burglar-proof lock developed by Day and Newell, a New York firm, in the mid-19th century.

·design and construction **11**:11b

paravaccinia, also called MILKER'S NODULES, a disease in man caused by a virus and characterized by reddish-blue nodules on the hands and face.

·zoonoses table, 9 **5**:877

paraventricular nucleus, cluster of nerve cells in the part of the brainstem called the hypothalamus; like the supraoptic nucleus, it manufactures the hormones oxytocin and vasopressin, which the posterior pituitary stores and releases.

·autonomic nervous system relationships **12**:1029e
·hormone secretion function **6**:811e

Paraxerus: *see* squirrel.

paraxonia, in zoology, a condition in which the axis of symmetry exists between the third and fourth digits, as in even-toed ungulates.

·artiodactyl limb adaptations **2**:76b

Parazoa, in zoology, name sometimes used to denote the grade of organization represented by the sponges, in contradistinction to Protozoa and Metazoa.

·differentiating characteristics **14**:381f
·sponge classifications and phylogeny **14**:855b

Parbate (people): *see* Pahari.

Parbhani, administrative headquarters, Parbhani district, Mahārāshtra state, western India, on the Manmād-Hyderābād railway, about 10 mi (16 km) south of the Dudna River. Its name refers to the Prabhāvatī temple, which was forcibly converted to a mosque during the Mughal period. Now an administrative and commercial centre, the town has little industry.

Parbhani district occupies 4,847 sq mi (12,554 sq km) in the Godāvari River Valley and is drained by the Godāvari and three of its major tributaries—the Penganga, Dudna, and Pūrna. The river valleys are separated by eroded plateau ranges. The district is bounded by remnant plateaus of the Ajanta Hills (north) and by the Bālāghāt Range (south). The economy is almost wholly agricultural; the chief crops are jowar (sorghum) and bajra (pearl millet) and cotton. Most of the cotton is transported to cities outside the district, but some is locally processed. Cotton manufacture and the processing of vegetable oils are the major industries. A hydroelectric power and irrigation project on the Pūrna River and an industrial estate at Hingoli were being developed in the early 1970s. The sacred Godāvari River and the Śiva Jyotirliṅga shrine at Aundah attract large numbers of pilgrims. Pop. (1971 prelim.) town, 61,477; district, 1,503,724.
19°16′ N, 76°47′ E

·map, India **9**:278

Parc Cenedlaethol Bannau Brycheiniog (Wales): *see* Brecon Beacons National Park.

parcel post, a mail service handling packages.

·international postal services **14**:886c

Parcheesi (board game): *see* Pachisi.

parchment, material on which writing is inscribed, consisting of the processed skins of certain animals, chiefly sheep, goats, and calves. The name apparently derives from Pergamum (modern Bergama, Tur.), where parchment is said to have been invented in the 2nd century BC. Skins had been used for writing material even earlier, but a new, more thorough method of cleaning, stretching, and scraping made possible the use of both sides of a manuscript leaf, leading to the supplanting of the rolled manuscript by the bound book (codex).

Parchment made from the more delicate skins of calf or kid or from stillborn or newly born calf or lamb came to be called vellum, a term that was broadened in its usage to include any especially fine parchment. The vellum of most early manuscripts, through the 6th century AD, is of good quality. After this, as demand increased, a great amount of inferior material came on the market, but by the 12th century, when large numbers of manuscripts were being produced in western Europe, a soft, pliant vellum was in vogue. In Constantinople, a sumptuous form was produced at an early date by dyeing the material a rich purple and lettering it in silver and gold, a practice condemned as a useless luxury in a well-known passage of St. Jerome. The purple dye was subsequently abandoned, but the practice of "illuminating" parchment manuscripts in gold, silver, and other tints flourished throughout the Middle Ages.

In modern usage, the terms parchment and vellum may be applied to a type of paper of high quality made chiefly from wood pulp and rags and frequently having a special finish.

·ancient writing use and source **13**:912a
·book publishing origins **15**:222h
·early New Testament text use **2**:941g
·European production and document use **5**:808f
·furniture use in Renaissance Italy **7**:791d
·Roman calligraphy materials and use **3**:652e

parchment worm, common name for members of the genus *Chaetopterus* (especially *C. variopedatus* of the Atlantic and Pacific oceans), a group of segmented worms of the class Polychaeta (phylum Annelida) that live in U-shaped tubes on the sea bottom. The tubes are lined with parchment-like material.

The animal grows to a length of about 25 centimetres (10 inches).
·bioluminescence mechanism and host function for commensals **1**:931f
·bioluminescent chemical reactions **2**:1032b
·feeding mechanisms and behaviour **7**:209a

Parcoblatta pennsylvanica: *see* cockroach.

par conditio creditorum, in bankruptcy law, principle giving creditors equal treatment in the liquidation of insolvent estates.
·bankruptcy and liquidation of estates **2**:697b

Parc Zoologique de Paris: *see* Paris Zoo.

pard: *see* leopard.

pardah (Islām): *see* ḥaram.

pardalote (bird): *see* diamondbird.

Pardo Bazán, Emilia, condesa de (b. Sept. 16, 1852, Corunna, Spain—d. May 12, 1921, Madrid), author of novels, short stories, and literary criticism. Pardo Bazán attained early eminence with her polemical essay *La cuestión palpitante* (1883; "The Critical Issue"). It discussed Zola and Naturalism, made French and Russian literary movements known in Spain, and started an important literary controversy in which she championed a brand of Naturalism that affirmed the free will of the individual. Her finest and most representative novels are *Los Pazos de Ulloa* (1886; *The Son of a Bondwoman*, 1908) and its sequel, *La madre naturaleza* (1887; "Mother Nature")—studies of physical and moral ruin among the Galician squirearchy, set against a beautiful, natural background and a moral background of corrupting power. By no means a purely regional writer, she was nevertheless most successful when dealing with her native Galicia. Pardo Bazán was professor of Romance literature at the University of Madrid. In 1916 she was accorded the distinction—unusual for a woman—of a chair of literature.
·Spanish literature of the 19th century **10**:1202g

pardon, in law, release from guilt or remission of punishment. In criminal law the power of pardon is generally exercised by the chief executive officer of the state. Pardons may also be granted by a legislative body, often through an act of indemnity, anticipatory or retrospective, for things done in the public interest that are illegal.

A pardon may be full or conditional. It is conditional when its effectiveness depends on fulfillment of a condition by the offender, usually a lesser punishment, as in the commutation of the death sentence.

The effect of a full pardon is unclear in some jurisdictions. In England it is said that a full pardon clears the person from all infamy, removing all disqualifications and other obloquy, so that a pardoned person may take action for defamation against anyone who thereafter refers to him as a convict. In the United States the matter is much less clear, although the Supreme Court has held that a pardon blots out guilt and makes the offender "as innocent as if he had never committed the offense." Some states in the U.S. have held that a pardon does not remove the disqualification from holding public office and that a pardoned offender may still be refused a license to engage in a business or profession. The difficulty stems from lack of differentiation between pardons granted for reasons of clemency and those granted from a belief in the accused's innocence. Continental European and Latin American countries generally have detailed statutory provisions governing the law of pardon.

Pardosa: *see* wolf spider.

Pardubice, German PARDUBITZ, town, Východočeský *kraj* (Eastern Bohemia region), Czechoslovakia, at the confluence of the Labe (Elbe) and Chrudimka rivers, east of Prague. Originating in the 13th century as a trade mart, it received civil rights in 1340 and by 1490 had become a possession of the Czech Pernštejn family, who renovated it in Renaissance style during the 16th century. The town was razed by Swedish troops in 1645. Its square (náměstí Viléma z Pernštejna) is an architectural showplace, with a row of outstanding patrician houses, a 16th-century Gothic castle, and the Green Gate (Zelená brána, 1507). Kunětická hora, 4 mi (6 km) northeast, is a cone-shaped basaltic hill (1,006 ft [305 m]), site of a prehistoric burial ground and topped by a 15th-century castle ruin.

Pardubice is known for horse racing, particularly its Grand Pardubice Steeplechase, and for motorcycle track meets. Industries include engineering, sugar refining, brewing, and, since World War II, oil refining. The town is an important road and rail junction and a cultural and administrative centre. Pop. (1970 est.) 70,777.
50°02′ N, 15°47′ E
·map, Czechoslovakia **5**:412

Paré, Ambroise (b. 1510, Bourg-Hersent, Fr.—d. Dec. 20, 1590, Paris), one of the most notable surgeons of the Renaissance, regarded by some medical historians as the father of modern surgery.

Paré, detail of an engraving by an unknown artist, 1582
H. Roger-Viollet

About 1533 Paré went to Paris, where he soon became a barber-surgeon apprentice at the Hôtel-Dieu. He was taught anatomy and surgery and in 1537 was employed as an army surgeon. By 1552 he had gained such popularity that he became surgeon to the king; he served four French monarchs: Henry II, Francis II, Charles IX, and Henry III.

At the time Paré entered the army, surgeons followed the practice of treating gunshot wounds with boiling oil since such wounds were believed to be poisonous. On one occasion, when Paré's supply of oil ran out, he treated the wounds with an ointment that turned out to be a mixture of egg yolk, rose oil, and turpentine. The next day he found that the wounds he had treated with the ointment were healing better than those treated with the boiling oil. Sometime later he reported his findings in *La Méthod de traicter les playes faites par les arquebuses et aultres bastons à feu* (1545; "The Method of Treating Wounds Made by Harquebuses and Other Guns"), which was ridiculed by the more scholarly physicians because it was written in French rather than in Latin. Another of Paré's innovations that did not win immediate medical acceptance was the reintroduction of the tying of large arteries to replace the method of searing vessels with hot irons to check hemorrhaging during amputation.

Unlike most surgeons of his time, Paré resorted to surgery only when he found it absolutely necessary. He was one of the first surgeons to discard the practice of castrating patients who required surgery for a hernia. He introduced the implantation of teeth, artificial limbs, and artificial eyes made of gold and silver. He invented many scientific instruments, popularized the use of the truss for hernia, and was the first to suggest syphilis as a cause of aneurysm (swelling of blood vessels).
·medicine in the Renaissance **11**:829b
·surgical technique development **17**:816c

Parecis Mountains, Portuguese SERRA DOS PARECIS, in Rondônia territory and Mato Grosso state, west central Brazil. Rising out of the tropical rain forests of Rondônia, near the Bolivian border, the range extends southeastward for 500 mi (805 km) to the vicinity of Diamantino, Mato Grosso. Its northwestern section consists of rolling plateaus, which rise to over 2,300 ft (700 m) above sea level in the southeast. On its northern and western slopes arise the Juruena and Guaporé rivers, both tributaries of the Amazon; from the southern flanks come headwaters of the Paraguay River.
13°00′ S, 60°00′ W
·map, Brazil **3**:124

paregoric, camphorated opium tincture, narcotic drug used in medicine as a cough suppressant and as a mild anodyne for the treatment of diarrhea. In early medical writings the term paregoric sometimes was used in reference to soothing medicaments in general. The tincture that is official in the *British Pharmacopoeia* and the *United States Pharmacopeia* contains about 0.4 percent opium (which amounts to 0.04 percent morphine) and about 45 percent alcohol. The preparation is made from tincture of opium (laudanum) or from powdered opium. The formula has been changed only slightly from time to time since the early 1700s.
·discovery and use **5**:1053a

Pareinae: *see* snail-eating snake.

Pareja, Juan de, sometimes called EL ESCLAVO, Spanish meaning the Slave (b. *c.* 1605, Seville, Spain—d. *c.* 1670, Madrid), painter and student of Velázquez.

A mulatto, Pareja was once believed to be Velázquez' slave. This legend has been discredited by a letter from Seville dated May 12, 1630, asking permission to go to Madrid to continue his studies as a painter with his brother. Later, Pareja probably became Velázquez' assistant and accompanied him on his second visit to Italy (1649–51), where Velázquez painted his portrait. The portrait was said to have been exhibited in the Pantheon to the admiration of all the painters in Rome.

According to early writers, Pareja painted portraits in the manner of Velázquez, but his only known portrait, of José Rates (private collection, Granada, Spain), is a crude reflection of Velázquez' style. From other works Pareja appears to have been a mediocre follower of the Madrid school. The "Calling of St. Matthew" (1661; Prado, Madrid) contains a self-portrait based on the portrait by Velázquez.
·Velázquez' realistic portraiture **19**:55f

Pare Mountains, range in northeast Tanzania, eastern Africa. Of volcanic origin, the mountains extend between Kilimanjaro and Usambara mountains and rise to 6,000 ft (1,880 m).
4°00′ S, 37°45′ E
·map, Tanzania **17**:1026
·Tanzanian geographical features **17**:1025g

parenchyma, in plants, a tissue typically composed of cells that are living, thin-walled, of about equal diameters in all directions, usually 14-sided, and unspecialized in structure and therefore adaptable, with differentiation, to various functions. Parenchyma may be compact or have extensive spaces between the cells. It is often called ground or fundamental tissue and makes up the mesophyll (internal layers) of leaves, and the cortex (outer layers), and pith (innermost layers) of stems and roots; it also forms the soft tissues of fruits. Cells of this type are also associated with xylem (wood) as wood rays, with phloem (bast or food-conducting cells) as transfer cells (*see* phloem), and with both xylem and phloem as bundle sheaths, the cells that surround the vascular strands.

parent, one who has begotten offspring or occupies the role of mother or father. In Western societies, parenthood, with its several obligations, rests strongly on biological relatedness; that is, sexual reproduction. This is not the case in all societies: in some, a distinction is made between a biological parent and social parent, with the former producing the child and latter raising the child and acting as a mother or father in as affective or legal a sense as biological parents are expected to do in Western society. This distinction is particularly common in the case of fathers, and anthropologists have developed appropriate terms: a "genitor" is a biological father, and a "pater" is a social one.

parental care, in animals, generally considered to include all behaviour that enhances the survival of offspring. It varies from such simple acts as burying eggs to the prolonged and elaborate relationship between parent and young found in many mammals. There is a strong inverse relationship between the number of young produced and the amount of care given them.

Parentalia, Roman religious festival held in honour of the dead. The festival, which began at noon on February 13 and culminated on February 21, was essentially a private celebration of the rites of deceased family members. It was gradually extended, however, to incorporate the dead in general. During the days of the festival, all temples were closed and no weddings could be performed. On the last day a public ceremony, the Feralia, was held, during which offerings and gifts were placed at the graves and the anniversary of the funeral feast was celebrated.

parentela, in law, the line of blood relatives or the kin of a person by descent.

Parents and Teachers, National Congress of, commonly known as the PTA, noncommercial, nonpartisan organization concerned with the educational, social, and economic well-being of children. The PTA was founded in the United States on Feb. 17, 1897, as the National Congress of Mothers; membership was later broadened to include teachers, fathers, and other citizens. The organization had enrolled about 1,500,000 persons by 1930, after which time membership, on the average, doubled each decade, numbering over 10,000,000 in the 1970s. There are 52 state branches, including one in the District of Columbia and one in Europe to serve dependents on military bases. Within the national framework, the approximately 41,000 local PTA's have a large measure of autonomy with which to design programs suited to their individual needs.

The stated purposes of the National Congress are to promote the welfare of children and youth in home, school, church, and community; to raise the standards of home life; to secure adequate laws for the care and protection of children and youth; to bring into closer relation the home and school, so that parents and teachers may cooperate intelligently in the training of the child; and to develop between educators and the general public such united efforts as will secure for every child the highest advantages in mental, social, and physical education. Thus, the National Congress has made its position known on a wide range of issues, including legislation affecting child labour and federal aid to education; teachers' training, salaries, and standards of employment; community use of school buildings and facilities; the necessity of raising the quality of the mass media; and the need for adequate safety education, special services for disadvantaged children, and preventive programs against juvenile delinquency. Publications include *The PTA Magazine*, *National PTA Bulletin*, manuals designed to help local organizations, and other publications of concern to parents and teachers.

Parentucelli, Tommaso: *see* Nicholas V, Pope.

Parerga und Paralipomena (1851), book by Arthur Schopenhauer.

paresis, also known as SYPHILITIC MENINGOENCEPHALITIS or GENERAL PARALYSIS OF THE INSANE, psychosis caused by widespread destruction of brain tissue occurring in some cases of late syphilis. Mental changes include gradual deterioration of personality, impaired concentration and judgment, delusions, loss of memory, disorientation, and apathy or violent rages. Convulsions are not uncommon, and while temporary remissions sometimes occur, untreated paresis is eventually fatal. It occurs most frequently in men between 35 and 50 years of age. Malarial treatment, effective because the fever destroys syphilitic micro-organisms, was initiated in 1917 by the Austrian physician Julius Wagner von Jauregg; it has been supplanted by the use of antibiotics.

Pareto, Vilfredo (b. July 15, 1848, Paris—d. Aug. 20, 1923, Geneva), Italian economist and sociologist, known for his theory on mass and elite interaction as well as for his application of mathematics to economic analysis. Born while his father was in exile, Pareto went to Italy when his father returned with his Parisian wife in 1858. After his graduation from the University of Turin (1869), where he had studied mathematics and physics, Pareto became an engineer and later a director of an Italian railway and was also employed by a large ironworks.

Residing in Florence, he wrote many periodical articles in which he first analyzed economic problems with mathematical tools. He also began studying philosophy and politics, thus equipping himself to deal critically with sociological and humanitarian issues. Chosen to succeed Léon Walras in the chair of political economy at the University of Lausanne, Switz., in 1893, Pareto continued and sharpened Walras' mathematical approach to political economy.

Pareto's first work, *Cours d'Économie Politique* (1896–97), included his famous but much criticized law of income distribution, a complicated mathematical formulation in which Pareto attempts to prove that the distribution of incomes and wealth in society is not random and that a consistent pattern appears throughout history, in all parts of the world and in all societies.

In his *Manuale d'economia politica* (1906), he further developed his theory of pure economics and his analysis of ophelimity (power to give satisfaction); he also introduced "curves of indifference," analytical instruments that did not become popular until the 1930s.

Believing that there were problems that economics could not solve, Pareto turned to sociology, writing what he considered his greatest work, *Trattato di sociologia generale* (1916; Eng. trans., *Mind and Society*, 1963), in which he inquired into the nature and bases of individual and social action. He concluded that all societies are composed of diverse social groupings, each of which is structured according to the abilities of its members to perform necessary social functions. These apparently congenital abilities can, however, be improved through active use; they will decay if not used. Those of superior ability, he argued, actively seek to confirm and aggrandize their social position. Thus social classes are formed. In an effort to rise into the elite of the upper strata, privileged members of the lower class groups continually strive to use their abilities and thus improve them; the opposite tendency obtains among the elite. As a result, the best equipped persons from the lower class rise to challenge the position of the upper class elite. There thus occurs a "circulation of elites." Pareto also declared all history to be "the succession of aristocracies."

Pareto further inquired into the methodology of economics and sociology and the degree to which physical science methods are applicable in the study of man's behaviour. He distinguished ideal or social ends from the individual wants of economics, thereby contributing to the analysis of "welfare." He also developed a cyclical theory of social change.

Because of his theory of the superiority of the elite, Pareto sometimes has been associated with fascism.

pareve (Yiddish: "neutral"; sometimes pronounced *par-vay*), in the observance of Jewish dietary laws (*kashrut*), those foods that may be eaten indiscriminately, with either meat dishes or with dairy products—two general classes of food that may not be consumed at the same meal. Fruits and vegetables are classified as *pareve* unless cooking or processing alters their status. In modern times, cakes and similar foods are classed as *pareve*, provided they are made with vegetable oil (rather than butter) and with "neutral" liquids substituted for milk.

parfleche, tough, folded rawhide carrying bag made by the Plains Indians of North America; more loosely applied, the term also refers to any article made of rawhide.

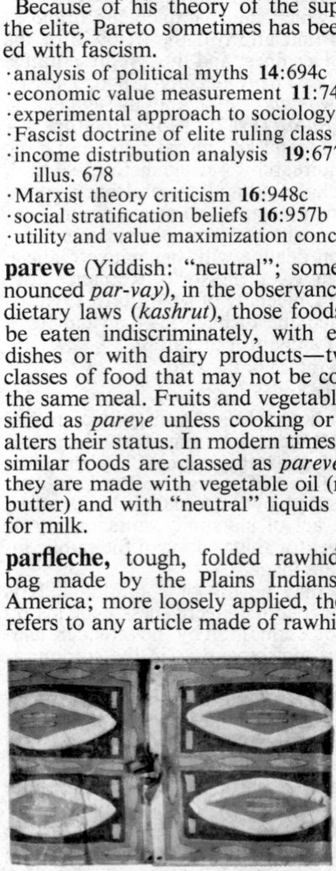

Painted Arapaho parfleche, 1860–75; in the Museum of the American Indian, Heye Foundation, New York

Museum of the American Indian, Heye Foundation, New York

The Plains Indians, among them the Dakota (Sioux), Cheyenne, Blackfeet, Crow and Comanche, had an abundant source of hides in the buffalo they hunted but, as they were nomadic tribes, they had little opportunity to tan the skins. Parfleche, or rawhide, was prepared by cleaning and dehairing the skin and then by stretching it and allowing it to dry in the sun. This process created a stiff but durable leather that was used for many items, including bags, thongs, and war shields.

The parfleche bag, or trunk (valise), was assembled by folding the two ends of a long, rectangular piece of rawhide over to meet and form a kind of envelope. The two flaps were thonged together, and the whole was used in tandem with another, similar parfleche, one strapped to each side of a horse. The maximum dimensions of the parfleche were generally 2 feet (60 centimetres) by 3 feet (90 centimetres).

The large flat surface of the parfleche bag was invariably painted with colourful, basically geometric, abstract designs; a sharpened porous buffalo bone served as an effective paint brush. Sometimes the rawhide was incised to highlight a design.

Párga, port of Préveza *nomós* (department), on the Ionian Sea opposite the island of Paxos (Paxoí), Greece. In 1447 it welcomed the Venetians, who built (1572) the mole that forms the present harbour, over which stands

The harbour, at Párga, Greece

R.G. Everts—Rapho Guillumette

a Venetian fortress. For two centuries quasi-independent under Venice, it came under Russian protection in 1800 after capture by a Russian fleet. Napoleon forced the Russians out in 1800, but in 1814 the citizens expelled the French garrison and accepted British protection. In 1815, however, England invoked the Russo-Turkish Convention of 1800, by terms of which Párga reverted to Turkey, provided that no mosque be built or Muslim settle there. Rather than submit to Turkish rule, the Pargiotes elected in 1819 to migrate to the Ionian Islands, and the Turkish government was constrained to pay them compensation. A few families returned in 1822. Párga was taken by the Greeks in the Balkan Wars (1912–13) and annexed to Greece with most of Epirus in 1913. Pop. (1971 prelim.) 11,284.
39°17′ N, 20°23′ E
·map, Greece **8**:314

pargasite (mineral): *see* hornblende.

pargyline, drug that reduces hypertension.
·use and MAO inhibitor action **17**:693g

Parhae, state established in the 8th century among the Tungus tribes of northern Manchuria (Northeast Provinces) and northern Korea by a former Korean general named Tae Cho-yang. The ruling class consisted largely of the former aristocrats of the northern Korean state of Koguryŏ, which had occupied most of northern Korea and Manchuria before it was conquered by the southern Korean state of Silla in 668. Parhae was considered the successor state to Koguryŏ.

Known as P'o-hai to the Chinese, Parhae, like Silla, became a tributary state of the Chinese T'ang dynasty (618–907) and was prevented by the T'ang from developing friendly relations with Silla. Its trade and cultural relations were largely with the nomadic tribes of the north and with Japan and China. Parhae appears to have enjoyed high prosperity, as evidenced in a name given to it in Korean in its heyday, *Haedong-songguk*, "the prosperous country of the East." The territory at this time extended from the Sungari and Amur rivers in northern Manchuria down to the northern half of Korea.

Parhae bore a strong cultural resemblance to Koguryŏ. The surviving Buddhist images and stone lanterns suggest that Buddhism played a predominant role in the life of the Parhae people. The government administration was modelled after the T'ang bureaucracy.

Parhae's rule was brought to an end in 927, when it was conquered by the Mongolian-speaking Khitan tribes of Central Asia, who were soon to form the Liao dynasty (947–1125) on China's northern borders.
·foundation and expansion **11**:435g
·origins and rivalry with Silla **10**:508b
·T'ang loss of power in Korea **4**:326c

Parham, Charles Fox (1873–1929), founder of Bethel Bible College.
·Pentecostal teachings and their impact **14**:31c

Parhasius, 4th-century-BC Greek painter.
·painting in late Classical Greece **19**:297c

parhelion, atmospheric optical phenomenon appearing as luminous spots 22° on each side of the Sun and at the same elevation as the Sun; it is often called mock sun or sun dog. Usually, the inner edges closest to the Sun will appear reddish. Other colours are occasionally visible, but more often the outer portions of each spot appear whitish.

Parhelia are a refraction phenomenon that occurs when the Sun or Moon shines through a thin cloud composed of hexagonal ice crystals falling with their principal axes vertical, as opposed to the halo phenomenon that occurs when the principal axes are randomly arranged in a plane perpendicular to the Sun's or Moon's rays. As in the case of the halo, the refraction is through a 60° prism angle, resulting in the component colours of the solar spectrum each being bent through a slightly different angle. The red end of the spectrum, being bent the least, appears on the inside, with the blue, when visible, appearing on the outside.

Paria, Gulf of, inlet of the Caribbean Sea, lying between the Venezuelan coast (including the mountainous Paria Peninsula) and Trinidad. Extending about 100 mi (160 km) east–west and 40 mi north–south, it is linked with the Caribbean (north) by the islands of Dragon's Mouth and with the Atlantic (south) by the Serpent's Mouth (both 10 mi wide). It receives the San Juan River and several arms of the Orinoco River Delta, including the Caño Mánamo. Gulf ports, including San Fernando and Port of Spain (Trinidad) and Cuira, Irapa, and Pedernales (Venezuela), handle shipments of petroleum, iron ore, bauxite, lumber, and agricultural products. Columbus, while on his third voyage (1498), probably first sighted South America when he sailed into the Gulf of Paria.
10°20′ N, 62°00′ W

pariah, a generic term applied by Westerners to the low caste groups of Hindu India, which were formerly known as "untouchables" but were renamed by the great social reformer Mahatma Gandhi as Harijans (children of God). The word pariah (originally derived from Tamil *paṛaiyar*, "drummer") once referred to the Paraiyan, a Tamil caste group of labourers and village servants of low status, but the meaning was extended to embrace many groups outside the so-called clean caste groups, with widely varying degrees of status. The differences in status derive from dietary habits, occupational association with polluting materials, or disapproved customs such as widow remarriage. Though the Indian government passed legislation aimed at improving the lot of lower caste groups, old ideas of purity and pollution persisted, and the notion of untouchability continued in Hindu thinking.
·serfdom and Indian caste system **16**:857h

Parian Chronicle, also called MARMOR PARIUM (Latin: Parian Marble), document inscribed on marble in the Attic Greek dialect containing an outline of Greek history from the reign of Cecrops, legendary king of Athens, down to the archonship of Diognetus at Athens (264/263 BC). The years are reckoned backward from the archonship of Diognetus and further specified by the reigns of kings or the archons of Athens. The author gave little attention to constitutional history or battles but recorded the dates of the establishment of festivals, of the introduction of various kinds of poetry, the births and deaths of the poets, and of their victories in contests of poetic skill. One large fragment, bought at Smyrna in the early 17th century, is at the Ashmolean Museum, Oxford; another, found on Paros in 1897, is now in the Paros Museum.
·chronology of Greek history **4**:578g
·historiographic stage and location **6**:918g

Parian ware, porcelain introduced about 1840 by the English firm of Copeland & Garrett, in imitation of Sèvres (*see* Sèvres porcelain) biscuit (unglazed porcelain). Its name is derived from its resemblance to Parian marble. A great many figures, some extremely large, were made in this medium. Most of them consist of either sentimental subjects or quasi-erotic nudes, which were popular in Vic-

Parian ware figure of Musidora, Staffordshire, 1857; in the Victoria and Albert Museum, London

By courtesy of the Victoria and Albert Museum, London, and Spode Limited

torian art. In the U.S., Parian ware was manufactured by Norton and Fenton.
·porcelain of the Sèvres tradition **14**:916a

paricá (hallucinogenic snuff): *see* cohoba.

Paricutín, volcano, western Michoacán state, west central Mexico, just north of the volcano Pico de Tancítaro and 20 mi (32 km) west-northwest of Uruapan. It is one of the youngest volcanoes on Earth. On Feb. 20, 1943, it began to erupt in an open field. The fire, lava, and ashes destroyed and buried two villages and hundreds of homes. In the first year the volcano's cone had risen 1,475 ft (450 m) from the base (at 7,480 ft [2,280 m] above sea level) and had buried the village of Paricutín. Its peak reached an elevation of 9,210 ft (2,808 m) in 1952 when the eruption finally ended.
19°28′ N, 102°15′ W
·map, Mexico **12**:68

Paridae (bird family): *see* tit; chickadee.

parietal bone, cranial bone forming part of the side and top of the head. In front each parietal adjoins the frontal bone; in back, the occipital bone; and below, the temporal and sphenoid bones. The parietals are marked internally by meningeal blood vessels and externally by the temporal muscles. They meet at the top of the head (sagittal suture) and form a roof for the cranium. The parietal bone forms in membrane (*i.e.*, without a cartilaginous precursor); the sagittal suture closes between ages 22 and 31. In primates with large jaws and well-developed chewing muscles (*e.g.*, gorilla, baboon), the parietals may be continued upward at the midline to form a sagittal crest. Among early hominids, *Paranthropus* (*q.v.*; also called *Australopithecus robustus*) sometimes had a sagittal crest.
·reptile skull joint types **15**:733a
·skeletal relations in cranium **16**:813h; illus.

parietal cell, also called OXYNTIC CELL or DELOMORPHOUS CELL, in biology, one of the cells that are the source of the hydrochloric acid and most of the water in the stomach juices. The cells are located in glands in the lining of the fundus, the part of the stomach that bulges above the entrance from the esophagus, and in the body, or principal part, of the stomach.
·digestion and gastric secretion **5**:774a
·human digestive system anatomy **5**:793b

parietal lobe, section of the cerebrum high in the side of each hemisphere of the brain; each parietal lobe is above a temporal lobe, in back of a frontal lobe, and in front of an occipital lobe.
·anatomic interrelationships **12**:1002b
·cortex lobes and surface, illus. 2 **15**:159

parietal pleura, serous (moisture-exuding) membrane that lines the chest.
·function in breathing **15**:748f
·human respiratory system anatomy **15**:765g

Parietaria, genus of flowering plants of the order Urticales.
·pollination and dispersal mechanisms **18**:1091a

Parilia, also called PALILIA, ancient Roman festival celebrated annually on April 21 in honour of the god and goddess Pales, the protectors of flocks and herds. The festival, basically a purification rite for herdsmen, beasts, and stalls, was at first celebrated by the early kings of Rome, later by the *pontifex maximus*, or chief priest. During the festival, the Vestal Virgins first distributed the ashes of the calves of the Fordicidia (*q.v.*), the blood of the October Horse (*see* Mars), and bean straw. Animals and people were then sprinkled with water; the stalls were cleaned, adorned with wreaths, and, together with the animals, fumigated. Sacrifices of cakes, millet, and milk were made, and prayers were recited to Pales; finally, the celebrants jumped over a bonfire three times to complete the purification. An open-air feast ended the festival.
According to later tradition, April 21 was the day on which Romulus began building the city of Rome and was thus celebrated as the *dies natalitius* of the city.

Parima Mountains, Spanish SIERRA PARIMA, Portuguese SERRA PARIMA, range in northern Brazil and southern Venezuela, is an outlying range of the Guiana Highlands (*q.v.*) and extends south-southeastward for about 200 mi (320 km), separating Venezuela from Roraima territory (Brazil). Its peaks, largely unexplored, reach 5,000 feet (1,500 m) above sea level. Headstreams of the Orinoco River rise on the western flanks, and headstreams of the Rio Branco descend from the eastern slopes. The range connects with Pacaraima Mountains (*q.v.*) in the northeast.
3°00′ N, 64°20′ W
·map, Brazil **3**:124

pari-mutuel (French *pari*, "bet"; *mutuel*, "mutual"), method of wagering introduced in France about 1870 by Parisian businessman Pierre Oller; subsequently it became one of the world's most popular methods of betting on horse races. Most systems are operated by the racetrack, although in France a national pari-mutuel system with offtrack branches was established in 1891. In pari-mutuel betting, the player buys a ticket on the horse he wishes to back. The payoff to winners is made from the pool of all bets on the various entries in a race, after deduction of an operator's commission. The system has the advantages of always giving the operator a profit and allowing any number of bettors to win.
An important innovation in pari-mutuel betting came in the 1920s with the development of the totalizator, a mechanical device for issuing and recording betting tickets. Modern totalizators calculate betting totals and current odds on each horse and flash these figures to the public at regular intervals. They may also display race results, payoff amounts, running times, and other information. Increasingly sophisticated equipment has encouraged introduction of a variety of combination bets, such as the daily double (picking winners in two specified races, usually the first two), exacta (picking the first two finishers in a race in precise order), and many others.
Pari-mutuel betting is still most practiced in horse racing but has an important place in other sports as well, most notably dog racing and jai-alai.
·horse racing, totalizators, and betting pools **8**:1103e
·jai alai gambling in the United States **10**:7c
·payoff adjustment reasons and laws **7**:868f

pariṇāma (Sanskrit: "maturation"), in Hindu philosophy, an organic change of a particular object into something else that has the same degree of reality. The stock example is milk turned into curds. According to several schools of philosophy (notably, Bhedābheda and Viśiṣṭādvaita; *qq.v.*) the change of the supreme being, Brahman, into the phenomenal world is an example of such a *pariṇāma*, so that the resulting world has the same degree of reality as the cause. The Nondualist (Advaita) school of Vedānta, however, argues that the change is not organic but, rather, a distortion and that the produced world has a lower degree of reality than Brahman (*see* vivarta).

parināmanā, in some forms of Buddhism, the transfer of merits from a Buddha, or *bodhisattva*, to a sentient being.
·Buddhist Pure Land salvation doctrine **3**:408g

Parini, Giuseppe (b. May 22/23, 1729, Bosisio, Italy—d. Aug. 15, 1799, Milan), prose writer and poet remembered for a series of beautifully written Horatian odes and particularly for *Il giorno*, a masterful satiric poem on the selfishness and superficiality of the Milanese aristocracy.
Of humble origins, Parini was educated by the Barnabites in Milan. A volume of Arcadian verse, *Alcune poesie di Ripano Eupilino* (1752), brought him into literary circles; the following year he joined the prestigious Milanese Accademia dei Trasformati.
In 1754 Parini was ordained priest and entered the household of Duke Gabrio Serbelloni as tutor to the Duke's oldest son. He remained there until 1762, unhappy and badly treated (the Duke called him "that peasant from Bosisio"); but he won ample revenge, first in *Dialogo sopra la nobilità* (1757), a discussion between the corpse of a nobleman and the corpse of a poet about the true nature of nobility, and next through his masterpiece, the satiric poem *Il giorno* (Eng. trans., *The Day*, 1927), which appeared in four books: *Mattino* (1763), *Mezzogiorno* (1765), *Vespro* (1801), and *Notte* (1801).
Written, as one critic said, with "stifled wrath" and a subtle viciousness, *Il giorno* is a minutely particularized account of a day in the life of a Milanese nobleman, which begins with his wakening and continues with the visits of his dancing, music, and French teachers, his hairdresser, jeweler, and miniaturist, through the countless trivial events of the day. No damaging detail is excluded—no superficiality, no minute particular of dress, no fawning gesture of a servant. Classical and historical allusions are constantly brought in to give ironic reinforcement of the nobleman's opinion of himself. And against the foreground of this self-indulgent and cushioned life is a contrast with the lives of the peasants, the true nobility.
The first two parts of *Il giorno* brought Parini literary renown; he became editor of the *Gazzeta di Milano* and then a humanities professor in the Palatine and Brera schools. In Milan he met the young Mozart, who composed an operatic score for his play *Ascanio in Alba* (opera performed 1771). When the French took Milan in 1796, Parini, rather uncomfortably, held a government post for three years. In 1899, a century after his death, a national monument was erected to him in Milan.
The most important of Parini's other works are his odes (*Odi*, published 1795), composed over a period of about 20 years. Written in a pure Horatian style, they deal with personal, civil, social, and political themes. Parini also wrote several literary tracts and an aesthetic treatise, *Dei principi generali e particolari delle belle lettere* (1801).
The moral force of Parini's personality was as evident in his dealings with people as it was in his works. When someone once berated him for kindness to an Austrian prisoner, Parini retorted, "I would do as much for a Turk, a Jew, an Arab; I would do it even for you if you were in need." Clearly, Parini was a man who could not be bought, and that quality of integrity, coupled with consummate literary skill, is the source of his continuing appeal.
·Italian literature development **10**:1175b

Parintintin (people): *see* Kawaíb.

Paris, also known as ALEXANDROS (Greek: Defender), in Greek legend, son of King Priam of Troy and his wife, Hecuba. Exposed upon birth, he was either nursed by a bear or found by shepherds. He was raised as a shepherd, unknown to his parents. As a young man, he entered a boxing contest at a Trojan festival, in which he defeated Priam's other sons. After his identity was revealed, he was received home again by Priam.
As a shepherd Paris delivered the "judgment," which formed a popular theme of ancient art. Rejecting offers of kingly power from the goddess Hera and military might from the goddess Athena, he accepted the offer of the goddess Aphrodite to help him win the most beautiful woman alive. His seduction of Helen (the wife of Menelaus, king of Sparta) and refusal to return her started the Trojan War. During the war Paris seems to have had a secondary role: a good warrior

The Judgment of Paris, Hermes leading Athena, Hera, and Aphrodite to Paris, detail of a red-figure kylix by Hieron, 6th century BC; in the Staatliche Museen Antikenabteilung, West Berlin

By courtesy of Staatliche Museen Antikenabteilung, West Berlin

but inferior to his brother Hector and to the Greek leaders whom he faced. Symbolically, Menelaus defeated Paris in single combat; but Aphrodite rescued him, and the war continued.

Near the end of the war, Paris shot the arrow which, by the god Apollo's help, caused the death of the Greek hero Achilles. Paris himself, soon after, received a fatal wound from an arrow shot by the archer Philoctetes.

·Homeric treatment of Trojan War **8**:1021a

Paris, town, Brant County, southeastern Ontario, Canada, at the confluence of the Nith and Grand rivers, west of Hamilton. Originally known as The Forks of the Grand River, it was founded by Hiram Capron and renamed in 1836 for the extensive deposits of gypsum, the source of plaster of Paris, in the vicinity. In addition to its gypsum quarries the town has woollen mills and manufactures alabastine (gypsum) and cement products, kitchen cupboards, refrigerators, graders and road equipment, screen doors, and knitted goods. Pop. (1971) 6,483.
43°12′ N, 80°23′ W

Paris 13:1004, historic capital and dominant city of France and the nucleus of a major metropolitan agglomeration. Founded in prehistoric times on an island (now Île de la Cité) in the Seine River, about 233 mi (375 km) upstream from its mouth, the city and its extensions now cover much of the Île-de-France region at the centre of the Paris Basin. Pop. (1971 est.) city, 2,496,600; metropolitan region, 10,270,400.

The text article, after surveying the character of Paris, provides a detailed treatment of the contemporary topography and its historical, social, and institutional associations.
48°52′ N, 2°20′ E

REFERENCES in other text articles:
·air pipe system **14**:584g
·anarchist action in 1968 insurrection **1**:812g
·aqueduct construction and history **1**:1039e
·art schools and movements **2**:101c
·Blanche of Castile's Latin Quarter intervention **2**:1105d
·book publishing history **15**:225c
·boulevard design **19**:460h
·building design temperature, tables 1 and 3 **8**:713
·city government form **4**:651b
·food riots and fall of Bastille **7**:649b
·Gothic visual art developments **19**:374a
·immigration **7**:593d; area and population table 594
·map, France **7**:584
·medieval improvement and administration **7**:616g
·Olympic Games event change **2**:279c
·opera premieres and composers **13**:581f *passim* to 589c
·population change from 1870–1925 map **6**:237
·rebuilding and rise as social center **7**:638d
·restaurant origin and development **15**:778c
·science during Enlightenment **16**:372d
·stock exchange operations **16**:449f *passim* to 452a
·street pavement in Middle Ages **8**:695a
·tapestry from the Middle Ages to 20th century **17**:1060f
·urbanization and population density **18**:1075c *passim* to 1076b
·urban transportation history and problems **18**:658f
·Viking raids and French tribute **7**:613b

Paris, city, seat of Bourbon County, north central Kentucky, U.S., on the South Fork of Licking River, in the Bluegrass region. First settled *c.* 1775, it was founded as Hopewell (1789) and was called Bourbontown before it was renamed Paris (1790) in appreciation of French aid during the Revolutionary War. Bourbon whiskey was first distilled there in 1790. A few miles east is Cane Ridge Meeting House (1791), where in 1804 Barton W. Stone started a movement called the New Lights, which merged in 1832 with the "Campbellites" to become the Disciples of Christ, or Christian Church. The basic farm economy (livestock, thoroughbred horses, seed processing) is supplemented by the manufacture of textiles and machinery. Inc. city, 1862. Pop. (1980) 7,935.
38°13′ N, 84°14′ W

Paris, city, seat (1844) of Lamar County, northeastern Texas, U.S., on a ridge between the Red and Sulphur rivers. Laid out in 1845 and named for Paris, Fr., it developed after the arrival of the railroad in 1876. The city was replanned after a disastrous fire in 1916. A shipping point for cotton, grain, and livestock of the Blacklands Belt, it also has some light manufacturing. Paris Junior College was established in 1924. The Gambill State Wildlife Refuge on Lake Gibbons is 4 mi (6 km) northwest. Inc. town, 1874; city, 1905. Pop. (1980) 25,498.
33°40′ N, 95°33′ W
·map, United States **18**:908

Paris I à XIII, Universités de, English UNIVERSITIES OF PARIS, consists of 13 faculties comprising coeducational, state-financed, autonomous institutions of higher learning located primarily at Paris. The universities were founded in 1970 under France's 1968 Orientation Act reforming higher education. One of the provisions of this act empowered a university centre such as Paris to create one or more autonomous universities combining arts and letters with sciences and technical studies, or, if preferred, concentrating on a particular field of specialization. The structure of the universities is based on academically and administratively independent teaching and research faculties called units. Paris I includes units of economics, law, modern languages, and art; Paris II, law, technology, and economic sciences; Paris III, theatre studies and English, Latin American, and South Asian languages and civilization; Paris IV, art and archaeology, Latin language and literature, musicology, and applied humanities; Paris V, pharmaceutics and biological sciences; Paris VI, mathematics, physics, and Earth sciences; Paris VII, medicine, physical and biological sciences, English, and Far Eastern studies; Paris VIII, Anglo-American languages, literature, and civilization, French, English, and German literature, sociology, arts, and political economy; Paris IX, business studies and applied economics, business information science, and mathematics; Paris X (at Nanterre), economics, history, sociology, and Romance languages; Paris XI (at Sceaux), mathematics, physics, chemistry, and medicine; Paris XII (at Val-de-Marne), medicine, law, and letters; Paris XIII (at Saint-Denis), technology and letters and humanities. Paris I through XIII replaces the former University of Paris, one of the archetypal European universities, founded *c.* 1170. It grew out of the cathedral schools of Notre-Dame and, like most other medieval universities, was a kind of corporate company including both professors and students. With papal support, Paris became the great transalpine centre of orthodox theological teaching. During the 1220s mendicant orders—Dominicans and Franciscans—began teaching at Paris. At the end of the 13th and during the 14th century it was the most celebrated teaching centre of all Christendom, particularly in theology. Among its famous professors were Alexander of Hales, Bonaventura, Albertus Magnus, and Thomas Aquinas.

The fully developed university was divided into four faculties: three "superior," theology, canon law, and medicine; and one "inferior," arts. The head of each faculty was the dean; the rector, in the first instance head of the faculty of arts, eventually became the head of the collective university.

In the course of the 16th and 17th centuries this democratic structure from the Middle Ages was largely superseded by an oligarchic development. The Tribunal of the university—the rector, deans, and subordinate officials called proctors—came to occupy a position somewhat similar to that of the heads of colleges at Oxford and Cambridge. Almost as much as the English universities, Paris came to be virtually reduced to a federation of colleges, though at Paris the colleges were less independent of university authority, and the smaller colleges sent their members to receive instruction in the larger ones.

The famous Sorbonne was really the most celebrated college of Paris; it was founded by the theologian Robert de Sorbon *c.* 1257. Its close connection with the faculty, and the use of its hall for disputations, led to the word Sorbonne becoming a popular term for the theological faculty of Paris. The present site of the Sorbonne, off the Boulevard Saint-Michel, dates from 1627 and houses the faculty of letters (26,029 students in 1963) and is also the administrative quarters of the educational district (*académie*) of which Paris is the centre.

With the French Revolution (1789–99) and Napoleon's subsequent reorganization of all France's institutions, the University of Paris became one of the academies of the newly created University of France. Among its several faculties were some that were abandoned (*e.g.*, theology in 1886), and others, such as science and pharmacy, that were to be created. Teaching was secular—that is, independent of political or religious doctrine.

At mid-20th century (when the University of France, as a central organizing body, had given place to the Ministère de l'Instruction Publique) the University of Paris included mainly the faculties of law, medicine and pharmacy, science, and letters and had again become a pre-eminent scientific and intellectual centre. The most distinguished professors lectured there, and there were more than 600 professorial chairs. The number of students had grown from nearly 12,000 in 1885 to more than 115,000 in the 1960s. Students of both sexes came from all parts of France and from

many foreign countries. In some areas the university curriculum underwent considerable change. A student of medicine, for instance, proceeded directly to his doctorate without any intervening change of status; students of pharmacy or at the various institutes took their own special diplomas; and the old examinations were being progressively superseded by competitions.
·administrative revisions **8**:866d
·Aristotelianism and Christian philosophy **1**:1159a
·Blanche of Castile's intervention **2**:1105d
·censorship and academic freedom **3**:1086a
·early development and difficulties **7**:622d
·faculty organization origins **8**:864d
·foundation by Abelard **13**:1011e
·founding as step in cultural history **8**:1175c
·Joan of Arc's trial arrangements **10**:227h
·medieval origin, degree program, and prestige **6**:337f *passim* to 338g
·medieval student food service program **7**:496g
·primacy in French higher education **8**:857g
·Scholasticism as philosophical movement **14**:258h *passim* to 261a
·Scholastic philosophical centre **16**:355c
·Sorbonne participation in May 1968 crisis **7**:679f
·15th–16th-century French publishing **15**:225b
·17th-century religious controversy **6**:350g

Paris, (Bruno-Paulin-)Gaston (b. Aug. 9, 1839, Avenay, Fr.—d. March 6, 1903, Cannes), the greatest French philologist of his age. After a thorough education in German

Gaston Paris
H. Roger-Viollet

universities and at the École des Chartes in Paris, he succeeded his father as professor of French medieval literature at the Collège de France. He was one of the founders and directors of *Revue critique* and of *Romania*, the leading journal devoted to French philology. A scholar of enormous erudition and exemplary thoroughness, he is also remarkable for his efforts to present the findings of research in a form suitable for the general reading public. He became a member of the Académie des Inscriptions in 1876 and of the Académie Française in 1896.
·textual editing methodology **18**:194d

Paris, Matthew (d. 1259), English Benedictine monk and chronicler known only through his voluminous and detailed writings, which constitute one of the most important sources of knowledge of events in Europe between 1235 and 1259.
·historiography in the Middle Ages **8**:950c
·Mongols barbaric reputation account **7**:1013g

Paris, Observatoire de, the national astronomical observatory of France, under the direction of the Academy of Sciences. It was founded by Louis XIV at the instigation of J.-B. Colbert, and construction at the site in Paris began in 1667. Contemporary architectural aesthetics prevailed over functional needs, and no dome was built, despite the objections of Giovanni Domenico Cassini, who was the first of four generations of his family to hold the post of director.
The observatory was enlarged in 1730, 1810, 1834, 1850, and 1951. The Paris building now houses the headquarters of the International Time Bureau, which standardizes the time determinations of the world's observatories. In 1926 the solar observatory at Meudon, on the outskirts of Paris, was taken over by the Observatoire de Paris. A radio astronomy station is maintained at Nançay, about 100 miles (160 kilometres) south of Paris.

Paris, Pact of: *see* Kellogg–Briand Pact.

Paris, treaties of, a number of major international peace treaties negotiated in Paris.
By the Treaty of Feb. 10, 1763, which marked the end of the Seven Years' War (with two preliminary years, known in the New World as the French and Indian War), France ceded its territory on mainland North America east of the Mississippi River (including Canada) to Great Britain; Spain ceded Florida to Britain but in return received the Louisiana Territory and New Orleans from the French. Though unpopular with the British public, which would have preferred France's rich sugar-producing islands of the West Indies to Canada, the 1763 treaty is often thought to mark the beginning of Britain's imperial greatness.
The Treaty of Sept. 3, 1783, ended the U.S. War of Independence. Great Britain recognized the independence of the United States (with western boundaries to the Mississippi River) and ceded Florida to Spain. Other provisions called for payment of U.S. private debts to British citizens, U.S. use of the Newfoundland fisheries, and fair treatment for American colonials loyal to Britain.
The Treaty of May 30, 1814, was concluded between defeated France and the victorious Allies (Great Britain, Austria, Prussia, Russia, Sweden, and Portugal) and marked the end of Napoleon's domination of Europe. France under the restored Bourbon dynasty received generous terms.
The Treaty of Nov. 20, 1815, imposed on the French by the Allies after Napoleon's brief return to power and final defeat at Waterloo, reduced France to its 1790 boundaries. The French had to pay a large indemnity and support an army of occupation.
The Treaty of March 30, 1856, ending the Crimean War, guaranteed the integrity of Ottoman Turkey and obliged Russia to surrender southern Bessarabia, at the mouth of the Danube. The Black Sea was neutralized, and the Danube River was opened to the shipping of all nations.
By the Treaty of Dec. 10, 1898, which ended the Spanish–American War, Spain agreed to the independence of Cuba and ceded the Philippine Islands, Puerto Rico, and Guam to the United States.
For a discussion of the treaties ending World War I signed in various Parisian suburbs, *see* Paris Peace Conference.
The Treaties of Feb. 10, 1947, were imposed by the victorious Allies on nations (Italy, Romania, Hungary, Bulgaria, and Finland) allied with Germany during World War II. They were forced to pay indemnities, and some of them lost territory.

1763
·background and significance **6**:1097h
·British and French diplomatic failures **2**:459c
·British gains in North America **4**:890a
·English dominance of the New York region **13**:21h
·French decline in India **4**:887f
·French North American mainland loss **3**:737a
·French view of English attitude **7**:644h
·Louisiana Territory cession to Spain **13**:6h
·Martinique returned to France **11**:548b
·Pitt's diplomatic policy **14**:477a
·Quebec surrender to England **15**:336g
·Seven Years' War colonial settlement **16**:580c
·Spain's colonial decline **17**:434g

1783
·American independence acknowledgement **19**:154d
·British Canadian control confirmation **3**:302h
·Continental Congress ratification **11**:566e
·Franklin's preliminary negotiation **7**:695g
·Indiana in Northwest Territory gain **9**:303e
·U.S.–Canadian boundary delineation **3**:739b
·Wisconsin ceded to United States **19**:891g

1814
·anti-French alliance's terms **2**:462b
·British achievement of goals **3**:992e
·British territorial gains **3**:303d
·Germany's structure as a confederation **12**:63f
·wars of liberation culmination **8**:104b

1815
·French territorial loss and indemnity **7**:662e
·Geneva territorial expansion **7**:1011g
·Metternich's conservative diplomacy **2**:463f
·Wellington and the Napoleonic Wars **19**:756b

1856
·Austria's threat to Russia **2**:466e
·Balkan independence movements **2**:627c
·Cavour and Italian diplomacy **9**:1161a
·Cavour's discussion of Italian union **3**:1032a
·Danube River supervising commission **5**:488g
·diplomatic background and significance **6**:1107d

1898
·Cuban independence granted **5**:357c
·Philippine stipulation and ratification **14**:242d
·provisions and Philippine acquisition question **18**:982c
·Spanish–American War and land claims **18**:1004d

1947
·Finland's military services **7**:308c
·Hungarian reparations and occupation **9**:41f

Paris, Treaty of (1259), treaty between Henry III of England and Louis IX of France, in which France regained all claims to Normandy.
·French territorial gain confirmation **7**:617b

Paris, Treaty of (1327), treaty between France and England in which the British lost Agenais and Bazadais to the French.
·English territorial loss and indemnity **7**:619f

pariṣad, ancient Indian institution of the Pre-Mauryan states that acted as a legislative and executive body.
·meeting procedure and jurisdiction **9**:349a

Paris Basin, geographical region of France, occupying a lowland area around Paris. Geologically it comprises the centre of a structural depression that extends between the ancient Armorican Massif (west), the Massif Central (south), and the Vosges, Ardennes, and Rhineland (east). The area, which forms the nucleus of France, is drained largely by the Seine River and its major tributaries converging on Paris.
·formation and characteristics **7**:583h
·geological time based on fossil discoveries **7**:1067b
·Seine river course from source to sea **16**:488d
·Tertiary sedimentary sequences **18**:151a

Paris Codex, also known as CODEX PERESIANUS, original manuscript of Mayan hieroglyphic writing, containing compilations of astronomical, calendrical, and liturgical lore.
·extant Mayan codices **11**:719f

Paris Commune (history): *see* Commune of Paris.

Paris Commune, gas-turbine-powered ship launched by the Soviet Union in the late 1960s.
·merchant ship turbine design **18**:673g

Paris Conservatoire: *see* Conservatoire National d'Art Dramatique.

Paris Exposition of 1889, unprecedentedly successful exposition that occupied an area of 72 acres, was centred on the Eiffel Tower and had two long galleries devoted to some 5,000 exhibits of fine art, and a third gallery given over to some 55,000 industrial exhibits. Other remarkable features were its Palais des Machines, its central dome, and its illuminated fountains.

parish, in some Christian church polities, geographical unit served by a pastor; it is a subdivision of a diocese. In the New Testament, the Greek word *paroikia* means sojourning, or temporary residence. In the very early church, the parish was the entire body of Christians in a city under the bishop, who stood in the same relationship to the Christians of the entire city as does the parish priest to the parish in modern times. In the 4th century, when Christianity in western Europe spread to the countryside, Christians in an important village were organized into a unit, called a parish, with their own priest under the jurisdiction of the bishop of the nearest city.

In Anglo-Saxon England the first parish churches were founded in important administrative centres. They were called minsters, and subsequently old minsters, to distinguish them from the later village churches. When the Church of England became independent of Rome during the 16th century, it retained the parish as the basic unit of the church.

The parish system in Europe was essentially created between the 8th and 12th century. The Council of Trent (1545–63) reorganized and reformed the parish system of the Roman Catholic Church to make it more responsive to the needs of the people.

In civil government, the parish is the lowest unit of government in England. In the United States, Louisiana is divided into parishes, the equivalent of counties in other states.

·hierarchical development **12**:146d
·medieval church government **12**:155b
·Protestant England and Methodism **15**:114a
·Roman Catholic unit **15**:990h

Parisien Libéré, Le, French daily newspaper, founded in Paris in 1944.

·French press influence **7**:610d
·publishing history **15**:245h

Paris-Match, (1949–), French weekly magazine, successor to *L'Illustration* (1843–1944).

·magazine publishing history **15**:254a

parison, gob of partially shaped or molded glass.

·bottle production processes **8**:202g

Paris Opéra, formally ACADÉMIE NATIONALE DE MUSIQUE, one of the most venerable operatic institutions in the world. The opera house (formally the Théâtre National de l'Opéra) built in 1875 was the 12th home of the Académie Royale de Musique, which was established under a patent granted by Louis XIV in 1669. The first performance was *Pomone* (1671), by two holders of the patent, the composer Robert Cambert and the poet Pierre Perrin.

In the 17th and 18th centuries the Opéra was dominated by a series of operatic giants. Jean-Baptiste Lully, who profoundly influenced the development of French opera, ruled the Opéra from 1672 until his death in 1687. In 1733 Jean-Philippe Rameau, Lully's equal in the history of French opera, began his 30 years as the leading operatic figure in France, with *Hippolyte et Aricie*. Christoph Gluck, the leader of the movement for operatic reform, was associated with the Opéra from 1773 to 1779.

The French Revolution of 1789 led to a series of operas on revolutionary subjects. In the middle and late 19th century, grand opera, exemplified by Giacomo Meyerbeer, flourished. The Opéra underwent a decline in the 20th century, and attempts to rejuvenate it began in mid-century. Its administration was joined with that of the Opéra-Comique, which traditionally stages works with spoken dialogue. A ceiling by the artist Marc Chagall was installed in 1964.

·ballet history in France **2**:648g
·Gluck's Paris performances **8**:213e
·theatrical electrification **17**:554f

Paris Opéra Ballet, ballet company established in 1661 by Louis XIV as the Académie Royale de Danse and amalgamated with the Académie Royale de Musique in 1671. The company dominated European theatrical dance of the 18th and early 19th centuries. Its artists developed the basic techniques of classical ballet: Pierre Beauchamp, the company's first director, codified the five basic ballet positions, and the virtuosos Jean Balon, Louis Duport, Marie Camargo, and Gaetano and Auguste Vestris extended the range of dance steps, especially the jumps and leaps.

In 1832 the company opened the era of Romantic ballet by presenting Filippo Taglioni's *La Sylphide*. Dancers of this period included Jules Perrot, Arthur Saint-Léon, Fanny Elssler, and Carlotta Grisi, who created the title role in *Giselle* at the Paris Opéra in 1841.

The company's decline at the end of the 19th century was arrested by Jacques Rouché, director of the Paris Opéra and Opéra-Comique from 1914 to 1944. After the successful avant-garde productions of the Diaghilev Ballets Russes at the Opéra, Rouché engaged as guest artists Michel Fokine, Anna Pavlova, and Bronisława Nijinska and in 1930 appointed Sergey Lifar director of the company. Principal performers under Lifar included Yvette Chauviré, Solange Schwarz, Marjorie Tallchief, Michel Renault, and George Skibine. Lifar resigned in 1958 and was succeeded by a number of directors.

·French ballet history **2**:648f

Paris Peace Conference (1919–20), the meeting that inaugurated the international settlement after World War I.

Although hostilities had been brought formally to an end by a series of armistices—that of Salonika (Thessaloníki) with Bulgaria on Sept. 29, 1918, that of Mudros with Turkey on October 30, that of Villa Giusti with Austria-Hungary on November 3, and that of Rethondes with Germany on November 11—the conference did not open till Jan. 18, 1919. This delay was attributable chiefly to the British prime minister, David Lloyd George, who chose to have his mandate confirmed by a general election before entering into negotiations.

Lloyd George's arrival in Paris was followed on Jan. 12, 1919, by a preliminary meeting of the French, British, U.S., and Italian heads of government and foreign ministers—respectively Georges Clemenceau and Stephen Pichon; Lloyd George and Arthur James Balfour; Woodrow Wilson and Robert Lansing; and Vittorio Emanuele Orlando and Sidney Sonnino—at which it was decided that they themselves, with the Japanese plenipotentiaries, would constitute a Supreme Council, or Council of Ten, to monopolize all the major decision making. In March, however, the Supreme Council was, for reasons of convenience, reduced to a Council of Four, numbering only the Western heads of government, as the chief Japanese plenipotentiary, Prince Saionji Kimmocho, abstained from concerning himself with matters of no interest to Japan. The foreign ministers continued to meet as a Council of Five, dealing with secondary matters.

The five Great Powers likewise controlled the Supreme Economic Council, created in February 1919 to advise the conference on economic measures to be taken pending the negotiation of peace. Specialized commissions were appointed to study particular problems: the organization of a League of Nations and the drafting of its Covenant; responsibility for the war and guarantees against a renewal of it; reparations; international labour legislation; international ports, waterways, and railroads; financial questions; economic questions of a permanent sort; aviation; naval and military matters; and territorial questions.

Major products of the conference were (1) the Covenant of the League of Nations, submitted in a first draft on Feb. 14, 1919, and finally approved, in a revised version, on April 28; (2) the Treaty of Versailles, presented at last to a German delegation on May 7, 1919, and signed, after remonstrances, on June 28; (3) the Treaty of Saint-Germain, presented to an Austrian delegation in a rough draft on June 2, 1919, and in a fuller version on July 20 and signed on September 10; and (4) the Treaty of Neuilly, presented to a Bulgarian delegation on Sept. 19, 1919, and signed on November 27.

There had been wrangling among the Allies over both the German treaty and the Austrian: on the one hand the Americans and the British resisted French demands affecting Germany's western frontier and the Polish demand, supported by France, for Danzig (Gdańsk), while the Americans also objected to Japanese claims to Germany's special privileges in Shantung, China; on the other, the Italians and the Yugoslavs quarrelled over the partition of Austria's former possessions on the Adriatic.

The formal inauguration of the League of Nations on Jan. 16, 1920, brought the Paris conference to an end, before the conclusion of treaties with Turkey or with Hungary. *Major ref.* **19**:966e

·Australian interest achievement **2**:420c
·Balkan territorial rearrangement **2**:633a
·Clemenceau's leadership **4**:709g
·Lawrence's lobby for Arab independence **10**:726c
·preliminary agreements and Wilson leadership compromises **18**:987c

Versailles Treaty

·Belgian neutrality abolition **11**:159d
·Danish boundary settlement **16**:329h
·French opposition and provisions **7**:672c
·German concessions and humiliation **8**:116h
·German reaction to harsh terms **6**:177e
·Hitler's struggle to abolish **8**:968b
·Ho Chi Minh's petition **8**:981f
·human rights and establishment of ILO **8**:1185c
·Keynes's critique of participants and policy **10**:447e
·Lloyd George's role in peace settlement **11**:8e
·May Fourth Movement protest **4**:368g
·missile research stimulation in Germany **7**:398d
·Polish boundary settlement **14**:651b
·Stresemann's successful opposition **17**:733b
·war crimes definition and punishment **19**:554h
·Weizmann's role in Arab–Jewish pact **19**:737c
·Wilson's diplomatic triumphs and defeats **19**:838h

Paris Postal Conference, (1863), meeting attended by delegates of 15 European and American postal administrations, which formulated principles to simplify the exchange of mail among nations.

·Universal Postal Union origins **14**:886a

Paris Psalter, 10th-century illuminated Byzantine manuscript in the Bibliothèque Nationale, Paris.

·Byzantine visual art forms and styles **19**:332g; illus.

Paris qui dort (1923), also called THE CRAZY RAY, first film by the French film maker René Clair.

·René Clair's early films **4**:681h

Paris Sketch Book, The (1840), two-volume collection of articles about France by William Makepeace Thackeray.

·Thackeray's journalism **18**:196d

Paris Symphonies, collective name for Symphonies 82–87 (1785–86) by Joseph Haydn, commissioned by a Parisian concert organization.

·stylistic characteristics **17**:913b

Paris ware, faience (tin-glazed earthenware) and porcelain ware produced in the Paris region from the 16th century. In Paris most faience workshops were situated in the Faubourg Saint-Antoine, but of the wares produced little is known before the 18th century. Paris faience was greatly influenced by Rouen, but what was painted red on Rouen was painted on ochre yellow on Paris. This ware often is confused with Saint-Cloud, for both use the famous radiating pattern of Rouen.

The hard-paste porcelain industry owed its existence to a breach in the Sèvres porcelain monopoly after 1766. The major factories were under the protection or ownership of high-ranking noblemen, just as Sèvres was under that of the king. They are known by the names of those protectors and of the streets on which they were situated. The Clignancourt factory of Monsieur was the most important after Sèvres, of which it is reminiscent in decor; it was opened in 1771. The factory of the duc d'Angoulêmes, rue de Bondy, was among the better known in 1781–1819. Its ceramist enjoyed an especially high reputation during the empire. It is renowned for its biscuit (unglazed porcelain). The duc de Berry's factory in rue Fontaine-au-Roy was active in 1771–1841. It produced, among other things, medallions in the likeness of members of Louis XVIII's family. Among the factories not under such ownership was one in the rue de Crussol; its English potter in 1789 asked permission to print on porcelain, glass, and faience. In general all Paris porcelain is rather more transparent than Sèvres, and its paste is of an extraordinary whiteness.

Paris Zoo, comprising the Ménagerie du Jardin des Plantes and the Parc Zoologique de Paris, both services of the French National Museum of Natural History. Founded in 1793, when the Museum of Natural History was reorganized into an institute of natural sciences, the Jardin des Plantes, originally a botanical garden, became the first public zoo in France. The compact 6.5-hectare (16-acre) area, with formal 18th-century landscaping, was retained when the Jardin was improved between 1918 and 1939. It holds more than 1,800 specimens of 480 animal species, including the rare Przewalski horse and the onager. Annual attendance is about 640,000.

In 1934 the Parc Zoologique, a modern 17-hectare (42-acre) zoo with spacious natural-habitat surroundings, was opened in a wooded area, the Bois de Vincennes. Its landmark is the Grand Rocher, a 71-metre (236-foot) high artificial mountain with winding paths for wild sheep. An elevator inside the rock carries visitors to its summit for an outstanding view of the city. The zoo has more than 1,100 specimens of 250 species. It has had notable success in breeding the okapi and giraffe. Annual attendance is about 1,500,000.

·Jardin des Plantes location, museum, and menagerie **13**:1017c; map 1005

parity, mathematical transformation that converts the abstract expression for an object or a process into its mirror image. A slowly spinning ball, for example, which looks just like its reflected image in a mirror, is said to have even parity. The two can be superimposed in thought so that they are indistinguishable, both spinning in the same direction. A spinning cone, however, which can always be distinguished from its mirror image (one spins clockwise, the other spins counter-clockwise) is said to have odd parity. A left-handed glove reflected in a mirror looks right-handed. A glove has odd parity.

In a much more abstract way, in physics, the mathematical expressions for subatomic particles and their interactions may be reflected by changing to their negatives all the variables that signify position in space. This mathematical transformation amounts to space inversion or reflection in an imaginary mirror. If the final formulation is identical with the original, its parity is even. If the final formulation is the negative of the original, its parity is odd. Again, odd parity means the two expressions are distinguishable; right can be distinguished from left and clockwise spin can be distinguished from counterclockwise spin.

Until 1956 it was thought that when an isolated system of fundamental particles interacts, the overall parity remained the same, or was conserved. This conservation of parity implied that, for fundamental physical interactions, it is impossible to distinguish right from left and clockwise from counterclockwise. The laws of physics, it was thought, are indifferent to mirror reflection and could never predict a change in parity of a system.

In 1956 the Chinese-born physicists Tsung-Dao Lee and Chen Ning Yang proposed that parity is not always conserved. For subatomic particles, three basic interactions are important: electromagnetic, strong, and weak. Lee and Yang showed that the evidence for parity conservation applies only to the first two interactions and not to the weak interaction. The fundamental laws governing weak interactions should not be indifferent to mirror reflection, and, therefore, weak interactions should show some measure of built-in right- or left-handedness that might be experimentally detectable. The following year (1957) it was conclusively proven that the electrons ejected along with antineutrinos from certain unstable cobalt nuclei in the process of beta decay, a weak interaction, are predominantly left-handed. The spin vector of these electrons is opposite to their direction of travel; that is, their spin rotation is that of a left-handed screw. Nevertheless, it is believed, because of strong theoretical grounds called the CPT theorem (*q.v.*), that, when the operation of parity reversal P is joined with two others, called charge conjugation C and time reversal T, the combined operation does leave the fundamental laws unchanged. *Major ref.* **5**:36f

·conservation violation and beta decay **15**:445g
·electron selective emission process **6**:668h
·nuclear momentum and radiation emission **13**:344g
·radiation's quantized states **6**:655c
·subatomic particle conservation laws **13**:1029h; table 1028

parity, in economics, exchange rate between currencies of two countries making purchasing power of both currencies substantially equivalent.

·money market and gold exchange standard **12**:357f

Parity Amendment (1949), Philippine constitutional amendment giving the United States equal rights in exploiting Philippine natural resources.

·Bell Trade Act provision **14**:244e

parity check, in information theory, coding technique used in message transmission to provide a simple means of detecting errors.

·algebraic structure theory **1**:537g
·information error correction coding **9**:577d
·mathematical calculation theory and use **11**:694c

parity prices, in economics, prices that represent a parity, or equality, in purchasing power, as between different periods, countries, or currencies.

·agricultural price-support programs **1**:319d
·exchange rate contrasted with purchasing power **14**:1002e
·farm price-support programs **17**:755a
·foreign-exchange operations and problems **7**:24c *passim* to 28c
·money conversion on gold-exchange standard **12**:351b

Parivāra (Pāli: "Appendix"), the last section of the *Vinaya Piṭaka*, a Buddhist sacred scripture and part of the *Tripiṭaka*.

·contents and monastic function **3**:433f

park, a large area of ground set aside for recreation. The earliest parks were those of the Persian kings who dedicated many square miles to the sport of hunting; by natural progression such reserves became artificially

Hyde Park, London
A.F. Kersting

shaped by the creation of riding paths and shelters until the decorative possibilities became an inherent part of their character. A second type of park derived from such open-air public meeting places as that in ancient Athens, where the functions of an exercising ground, a social concourse, and an athletes' training ground were combined with elements of a sculpture gallery and religious centre. Modern parks are of two sorts: large tracts of enclosed ground commonly attached to private houses until the 18th century and now adapted for public recreational use, and parks especially made for public enjoyment and often paid for by public funds.

·Edinburgh's urban design **6**:306g
·landscape design elements and examples **7**:884f; illus.
·Olmsted's continuous system **3**:58e
·Paris' parks and Seine banks **13**:1018d
·Viennese woods and sports park **19**:115d

Park, Charles Frederick, Jr. (b. Dec. 18, 1903, Wilmington, Del.), geologist known for his extensive explorations for mineral deposits. He was a member of the U.S. Geological Survey from 1931 until 1946, when he became a professor at Stanford University, California. He became dean of the school of science there in 1950 and a consultant to the Bethlehem Steel Corporation in 1952.

Park's work includes explorations for iron and manganese ore and research concerning the localization and zoning phenomena of ore deposits.

Park, Mungo (b. Sept. 10, 1771, Fowlshiels, near Selkirk, Scot.—d. *c.* Jan. 1806, near Bussa on the Niger, now in Nigeria), Scottish explorer of the Niger.

Mungo Park, miniature after Henry Edrige; in the National Portrait Gallery, London
By courtesy of the National Portrait Gallery, London

Educated as a surgeon at the University of Edinburgh, Park was appointed a medical officer in 1792 on a vessel engaged in the East India trade. His subsequent studies on the plant and animal life of Sumatra won for him the backing of the African Association to explore the true course of the Niger. Beginning his exploration at the mouth of the Gambia River on June 21, 1795, Park ascended that river for 200 miles to Pisania (now Karantaba, The Gambia), a British trading station. Hampered by fever and formidable hardships, he crossed the unknown territory of the upper Sénégal Basin. He was imprisoned by an Arab chief for four months but escaped on July 1, 1796, to continue his journey with little more than a horse and a compass. On July 20 he reached Ségou (now in Mali) on the Niger, where he journeyed downstream for 80 miles to Silla. Finally forced to turn back for lack of supplies, Park, travelling on foot, took a more southerly route on his return. After traversing mountainous country, he arrived at Kamalia in Mandingo country, where he lay dangerously ill with fever for seven months. With the assistance of a slave trader, he reached Pisania on June 10, 1797. He returned to Britain to write an account of his adventures, *Travels in the Interior Districts of Africa* (1797), which became a popular success.

Two years later Park married and practiced medicine in Peebles, Peeblesshire, until asked by the government to head a second expedition to the Niger. Commissioned a captain, he led a party of 40 Europeans to Pisania and, on Aug. 19, 1805, with only 11 survivors, reached Bamako (now in Mali) on the Niger. Resuming the journey by canoe, he and his companions reached Ségou, where the local ruler gave him permission to continue his voyage down the unexplored river. Hoping to reach the coast at the end of January 1806, he set sail with eight companions from Sansanding, a little below Ségou, on Nov. 19, 1805. Reports that the expedition had met with disaster soon reached the settlements on The Gambia. In 1812, after inquiries made by the government, it was learned that when the explorers reached the rapids at Bussa, about 1,000 miles below Sansanding, they were attacked by natives, and Park was drowned.

·Niger exploration and fate **7**:1043g
·Niger River mapping **13**:98g
·West Africa exploration **1**:206g

Park, Robert E(zra) (b. Feb. 14, 1864, Luzerne County, Pa.—d. Feb. 7, 1944, Nashville, Tenn.), sociologist noted for his work on ethnic minority groups, particularly the U.S. black population, and on human ecology, a term he is sometimes credited with coining.

Park studied under the philosophers John Dewey (at the University of Michigan), William James, and Josiah Royce (both at Harvard), and the sociologist Georg Simmel (in Germany). All his graduate work was done after 11 years' experience as a newspaper reporter in various large cities, where his interest in social problems was stimulated. He taught at Harvard (1904–05), the University of Chicago (1914–33), and Fisk University, Nashville, Tenn. (1936–43).

In 1906 Park wrote two magazine articles about the oppression of the Congolese by Belgian colonial administrators. Turning to the study of the black population in his own country, he became secretary to Booker T. Washington and is said to have written most of Washington's book *The Man Farthest Down* (1912). He believed that a caste system produced by sharp ethnic differences tends, because of the division of labour among the castes, to change into a structure of economic classes.

Robert E. Park
By courtesy of Fisk University News Bureau

With Ernest W. Burgess, Park wrote a standard text, *Introduction to the Science of Sociology* (1921; 2nd ed., 1929). In *The Immigrant Press and Its Control* (1922), Park argued that foreign-language newspapers in the long run would promote assimilation of immigrants. Three volumes of his *Collected Papers*, edited by Everett C. Hughes and others, were published between 1950 and 1955.

·collective behaviour theory development **4**:842c
·sociological research on urban areas **16**:996d
·urbanization's sociological impact **16**:983c
·urban society theory **11**:602b

Park, Thomas (b. Nov. 17, 1908, Danville, Ill.), animal ecologist known for his experiments with beetles in analyzing population dynamics.

Using two species of flour beetles, *Tribolium confusum* and *T. castaneum*, Park studied the effects of competition caused by overcrowding. By analyzing birth and death rates, he found that in any mixed population one of the species always declined in numbers and became extinct. The other species, while responding to its external conditions, increased in numbers in a characteristic percentage of tests. Overcrowding always led to a decrease in the birth rate of the less fit species with an increase in disease, malformations, and death rate. Some scientists think that the implications of Park's experiments on insects may be applied to human populations as well.

After earning a Ph.D. from the University of Chicago in 1932, Park taught at Johns Hopkins University, Baltimore, and at the University of Chicago. He wrote, with others, *Principles of Animal Ecology* (1949). The authors applied principles first formulated in studies of plant ecology to animal relationships in an evolutionary perspective.

parka, hip-length, hooded jacket made of caribou, seal, or other fur, worn as an outer garment by the Arctic Eskimos. Men's and women's parkas are basically the same except

Eskimos in parkas
Brown Brothers

for an extra hood in which the Eskimo woman can wrap a small child. The modern parka is often adapted for such sports as skiing.

·design, function, and origins **1**:1125c

Park Chung Hee (b. Nov. 14, 1917, region of Taegu, Korea—d. Oct. 26, 1979, Seoul), president of the Republic of Korea (South Korea) from 1963 to his death. Park served in the Japanese army during World War II and became an officer in the Korean army when Korea was freed from Japanese rule after the war. He was made a brigadier general during the Korean War and was promoted to general in 1961. In the same year he led a bloodless coup that overthrew the Second Republic, and two years later he became president of the Third Republic.

At home Park maintained a policy of guided democracy; in foreign affairs he continued his predecessors' close relations with the United States, sending Korean troops to fight on the U.S. side in Vietnam. His regime achieved a remarkable economic growth (more than 10 percent per year), transforming an impoverished, largely rural society into an industrial nation with exports of naval vessels, automobiles, and television sets. Democracy, however, was curtailed, with restrictions on personal freedoms, expansion of the central intelligence agency, and a new constitution (1972) that gave Park sweeping powers. He was assassinated, after several earlier unsuccessful attempts, by the head of the central intelligence agency.

·military rule and presidency **10**:514h

Park City, town of the Old West preserved in Salt Lake City, Utah, using the original buildings and furnishings.

·Salt Lake City preservation of Old West **18**:1105e

Parker, Sir Peter Parker, 1st Baronet (1721–1811), British naval officer who became admiral of the fleet (1799) and was an early patron of Lord Nelson.

Parker, Charlie, in full CHARLES PARKER, JR., also known as "BIRD" or "YARDBIRD" (b. Aug. 29, 1920, Kansas City, Kan.—d. March 12, 1955, New York City), considered by most

Charlie Parker, 1949
Wide World Photos

jazz musicians the greatest alto saxophonist and by many the greatest jazz improviser. A professional musician from the age of 17, Parker first played with bands in Kansas City, Mo. In New York City, with Kenny Clarke, Dizzy Gillespie, and Thelonious Monk, he participated in the famous jam sessions at Minton's Play House that gave rise to the bebop (*q.v.*) movement. His first New York recordings, with Lloyd ("Tiny") Grimes in 1944 and especially with Dizzy Gillespie in 1945 (*e.g.*, "Hot House," "Salt Peanuts"), won him early fame. From that time on, young musicians considered him the most original and most representative soloist of the new school.

He spent six months in Camarillo State Hospital, California, for treatment of narcotics addiction. Resuming his activities in 1947, he formed a quintet with Max Roach and Miles Davis; their recordings were widely acclaimed after Parker's death and reissued many times.

In Parker's last years, darkened by sickness, he did not capture the widespread favour of the public. He lived as an outcast whose presence was felt only indirectly—through his blues themes, which everybody was playing ("Now's the Time" and "Billie's Bounce" exhibit the flexibility of his improvised paraphrases), and through his ever-growing influence on the new jazzmen. The most famous saxophonists—Theodore ("Sonny") Rollins, John Coltrane, Ornette Coleman—were marked by his influence, which can also be found in the style of many pianists and trumpet players. By the time of his death he had become a legend, as noted by the popular phrase, "Bird is God."

·harmonic and rhythmic style traits **10**:125d

Parker, Dorothy (b. Aug. 22, 1893, West End, N.J.—d. June 7, 1967, New York City), writer who employed wit, precision, and an acute sensitivity to expose the stupidities and cruelties of the urban milieu—particularly New York from the 1920s to midcentury. Her reputation largely rests on her short stories, although she also wrote verses of merit in a bittersweet and minor key. She also collaborated on a number of film scripts and three plays.

Dorothy Parker, 1939
Culver Pictures

Her life-style in the 1920s, when she epitomized the woman liberated from conventions who could hold her own at drinking or wisecracking with any man, was nationally influential; and her barbed wit was so legendary that humorous remarks tended to be attributed to her whether she had said them or not.

She grew up in New York, where—after graduation from Miss Dana's School in Morristown, N.J.—she worked on the magazine *Vanity Fair*. She and two other writers for the magazine, Robert Benchley, the humorist, and Robert Sherwood, then a drama critic and later to become a playwright, formed the nucleus of the Algonquin Round Table, an informal luncheon club held at New York's Algonquin Hotel. The club achieved fame for the talents of its members drawn chiefly from the worlds of journalism and the theatre.

Discharged from *Vanity Fair* in 1920 for the acerbity of her drama reviews, she became a free-lance writer. She initiated a personal kind of book reviewing in *The New Yorker* magazine as "Constant Reader." Starting in 1927 and appearing intermittently until 1933, some of these reviews have been collected in *A Month of Saturdays* (1971). Her first volume of verse, *Enough Rope*, was a best seller when it appeared in 1926, going into eight printings. The two other books of verse that followed—*Sunset Gun* (1928) and *Death and Taxes* (1931)—were collected with it in *Collected Poems: Not So Deep as a Well* (1936).

In 1929 she won the O. Henry Award for the best short story of the year with "Big Blonde," a compassionate account of an aging party girl. *Laments for the Living* (1930) and *After Such Pleasures* (1933) were collections of her short stories, combined and augmented in 1939 as *Here Lies*. Characteristic of both the stories and verses is a view of the human situation as simultaneously tragic and funny. Among her more notable stories are "Lady with a Lamp," "Glory in the Daytime," "A Telephone Call," "You Were Perfectly Fine," "Diary of a New York Lady," "Soldiers of the Republic," "Clothe the Naked," and "The Lovely Leave."

In 1933 she and her second husband, Alan Campbell, went to Hollywood to collaborate as film writers, receiving screen credits for more than 15 films, including *A Star is Born*, nominated for an Academy Award. She became active in left-wing politics, disdained her former role as a smart woman about town, reported from the Spanish Civil War, and discovered that her beliefs counted against her employment by the studios in the fervour of anti-Communism that seized Hollywood after World War II. She wrote book reviews for *Esquire* magazine and collaborated on two plays, *The Coast of Illyria* (first performance 1949), about the English essayist Charles Lamb, performed briefly in Dallas and London, and *The Ladies of the Corridor* (1953), about lonely widows in side-street New York hotels, which had a short run on Broadway. An earlier play, *Close Harmony*, written with Elmer Rice, also had a short New York run in 1924.

Parker, Eric, real name FREDERICK MOORE SEARLE (b. Oct. 9, 1870, East Barnet, Hertfordshire,—d. Feb. 13, 1955, Hambledon, Surrey), editor, journalist, and writer whose literary output consisted of works on field sports, cricket, dogs, natural history, and gardens.

Parker was educated at Eton and at Merton College, Oxford. He became a schoolmaster but at the age of 30 entered journalism. He became editor of *The Country Gentleman* (1902–07). During World War I he was a captain in the Queen's Royal West Surrey Regiment. After the war he resumed his journalistic career as editor in chief of *Fields* magazine (1929–37). His books include *A Book of Zoo* (1909); *Promise of Arden* (1912), a novel about the life of a child; *Eton in the Eighties* (1914), a book of reminiscences; *Playing Fields* (1922), the story of life at prep school at Eton; *The History of Cricket* (1950); and *Surrey Gardens* (1954).

Parker, Francis (Wayland) (b. Oct. 9, 1837, Bedford, N.H.—d. March 2, 1902, Chicago), a founder of progressive elementary education in the U.S. and organizer of the first parent-teacher group at Chicago. At age 16 he began to teach and five years later became school principal at Carrolton, Ill. (1858). He was commissioned a lieutenant in the Union Army (1861) and rose to the rank of lieutenant colonel.

Teaching in various places after the Civil War, he experimented with teaching methods in an attempt to change the rigid formalism prevalent in U.S. schools. In 1872 he went to Germany to study educational methods pioneered by Johann F. Herbart and others.

Returning to the U.S. (1875), he became school superintendent for Quincy, Mass. He brought science, arts, and crafts into the curriculum and advocated pupil self-expression, socialized activity, and a humanized, informal instruction stressing children's individuality. After he became supervisor of the Boston school system (1880), he was appointed principal of the Cook County Normal School at Chicago (1883), which became noted for its liberalizing influence on American education.

Francis Parker
By courtesy of the Chicago Historical Society

In 1899 an endowment made it possible for Parker to establish a private normal school, the Chicago Institute, which two years later became associated with the University of Chicago on his becoming the first director of the University's School of Education. A private progressive school in Chicago bears his name.

·progressive education experiments **6**:373g

Parker, Sir (Horatio) Gilbert (b. Nov. 23, 1862, Camden East, Ont.—d. Sept. 6, 1932, London), prolific novelist of popular adventure and historical romances whose most widely known work was *The Seats of the Mighty* (1896), a novel of the 17th-century conquest of Quebec. From 1885 to 1889 he travelled widely in Australia and the South Seas, after which he settled in London and began writing his spirited stories and novels, in which he skillfully combined energetic action, vivid characterizations, and rich local colour with accuracy of historical detail. His first success was *Pierre and His People* (1892). Among his 33 volumes were *The Battle of the Strong* (1898), a historical tale of the Channel Islands during the Napoleonic Wars; *The Right of Way* (1901), a novel of violence set in contemporary Montreal; and *The Weavers* (1907), a melodramatic story of imperialist intrigue in England and Egypt. In politics Parker became a prominent imperialist and was a member of Parliament from 1900 to 1918. He was knighted in 1902, made a baronet in 1915, and a privy councillor in 1916.

·Canadian novel tradition **13**:292c

Parker, Horatio William (b. Sept. 15, 1863, Auburndale, Mass.—d. Dec. 18, 1919, Cedarhurst, N.Y.), composer, conductor, and teacher, prominent member of the turn-of-the-century Boston group of U.S. composers. He studied in Boston and Munich. Returning to New York, he taught at the National Conservatory of Music, then directed by Dvořák. In 1894 he became professor of music at Yale, where he was active in choral conducting. He also founded the New Haven Symphony Orchestra.

Horatio Parker
By courtesy of the Yale University Archives, Yale University Library

Parker's principal compositions are his choral works, which include his masterpiece, the oratorio *Hora Novissima* (1893), the ode *Hymnos Andron*, and the morality *The Dream of Mary*. He also wrote two operas, *Mona* (1912) and *The Fairyland* (1915), as well as organ works, piano pieces, chamber music, orchestral works, and a book, *Music and Public Entertainment* (1911).

Parker, Sir Hyde (b. 1739—d. March 16, 1807), British admiral who as commander of the Baltic Fleet in the Battle of Copenhagen

(April 2, 1801) sent a signal for withdrawal that was ignored by his subordinate Horatio (afterward Viscount) Nelson, the real winner of the battle.

The second son of Vice Adm. Sir Hyde Parker, he fought in the U.S. War of Independence, breaking through the American defenses on the Hudson River on July 12–18, 1776 (the Tappan Sea Raid). After serving as commander in chief at Jamaica (1796–1800), he was placed in charge of a fleet that sailed March 12, 1801, to demolish the second Armed Neutrality, a league formed (Dec. 16, 1800) by Russia, Denmark, Sweden, and Prussia to protect their merchant shipping from search by the British Navy. At Copenhagen, Nelson's squadron of smaller ships did most of the fighting. After several hours Parker signalled Nelson to withdraw, but Nelson put his telescope to his blind right eye so that he could claim he had not seen the order. It is sometimes said that Parker's order was discretionary and that Nelson's gesture was merely a joke or self-dramatization. When the Danes had yielded, Parker declined to sail up the Baltic against Russia, for which he was removed from active service.

Parker, Matthew (b. Aug. 6, 1504, Norwich, Norfolk—d. May 17, 1575, Lambeth, London), Church of England archbishop of Canterbury (consecrated 1559) and moderate reformer under Queen Elizabeth I, carried out a religious settlement in which the Church of England maintained a distinct identity apart from Roman Catholicism and Protestantism, thus alienating the Puritans, who sought complete integration with the Protestant Reformation. He supervised the formulation of the *Thirty-nine Articles* (the Anglican summation of doctrine), initiated liturgical reforms, and wrote several scholarly treatises on English church history.

·historiographic methods and purpose **8**:954d
·library history and function **10**:858f
·Puritan rebellion against his Advertisements **15**:304g

Parker, Quanah (b. 1845?, near Wichita Falls, Texas—d. Feb. 23, 1911, near Ft. Sill, Okla.), aggressive Comanche leader who, after mounting a short but unsuccessful war against white invaders in southeast Texas (1874–75), settled down peacefully to become the Indians' main spokesman and leader in that area for 30 years.

Quanah was the son of Chief Peta Nocone and Cynthia Ann Parker, a white woman captured by the Comanches as a child. Quanah added his mother's surname to his own. He was a member of the fierce Kwahadi band—particularly bitter enemies of the buffalo hunters who had appropriated their best land on the Texas frontier. In order to stem the onslaught of Comanche attacks on settlers and travellers, Indians were assigned to reservations in the area (1867). Parker and his band, however, refused to cooperate and continued their raids on settlements and hunters. In June 1874 Parker gathered some 700 warriors from among the Comanche, Cheyenne, and Kiowa and attacked about 30 white buffalo hunters quartered at Adobe Walls, Texas. The U.S. military retaliated in force. Troops were called in from all directions, but Parker's group held out on the Staked Plains for almost a year before he finally surrendered at Ft. Sill.

Eventually agreeing to settle down on the reservation in southwestern Oklahoma, Parker persuaded other Comanche bands to conform, and peace reigned at last on the Texas plains. During the next three decades he was the main interpreter of white civilization to his people, encouraging education and agriculture and becoming a successful businessman while maintaining his own Indian cultural ways and beliefs.

Parker, Theodore (b. Aug. 24, 1810, Lexington, Mass.—d. May 10, 1860, Florence), Unitarian theologian, pastor, scholar, and social reformer active in the anti-slavery movement. Theologically, he repudiated much traditional Christian dogma, putting in its place an intuitive knowledge of God derived from man's experience of nature and insight into his own mind. He resembled Ralph Waldo Emerson and other New England Transcendentalists in his emphasis on intuition but differed in the way he tempered his romanticism with rationalist and scientific interest. He combined his belief in intuition, for example, with a critical and historical study of religion.

Although Parker passed the entrance examination for Harvard College in 1830, he had no funds to attend. He was allowed, however, to take the examinations for his course of study without enrolling and was granted an honorary degree. He then attended Harvard Divinity School, from which he graduated in 1836. The next year he was ordained pastor of the Unitarian Church in West Roxbury, Mass.

By 1841 he had formulated his liberal religious views and had incorporated them in the sermon "The Transient and Permanent in Christianity." The transient, to him, was Christianity's theological and scriptural dogma, and the permanent was its moral truths. The following winter he elaborated his position in lectures published as *A Discourse of Matters Pertaining to Religion*. Opposition to his liberalism increased and he soon resigned his pastorate. His supporters founded the 28th Congregational Society of Boston and installed him as minister.

Believing that the moral truths of Christianity had application to contemporary social problems, Parker worked for prison reform, temperance, women's education, and other such causes. He made impassioned speeches against slavery, helped fugitive slaves to escape, and wrote an abolitionist tract, *A Letter to the People of the United States Touching the Matter of Slavery* (1848). He also served on the secret committee that aided the abolitionist John Brown.

Parker, William Henry (1902–   ), Los Angeles police chief.

·Black and Chicano criticism **11**:111g

Parkersburg, city, seat (1801) of Wood County, western West Virginia, U.S., at the confluence of the Ohio (there bridged to Belpre, Ohio) and Little Kanawha rivers. Settled *c.* 1785 as Neal's Station on a land tract originally purchased by Alexander Parker of Pittsburgh, it was first chartered by Virginia in 1820 and rechartered by West Virginia in 1863. The discovery in the 1890s of the nearby Burning Springs oil field stimulated industrial growth. Manufactures are well diversified and include oil-well equipment, glass and porcelain products, rayon, shovels, iron and steel, and chemicals. The city is also an agricultural-marketing centre. The Ohio Valley College (1960) and a branch of West Virginia University are in the city. Blennerhassett Island in the Ohio River, 2 mi (3 km) south, was the home of Harman Blennerhassett, a wealthy Irishman who supposedly plotted with Aaron Burr to seize the Southwest and set up an empire; they were acquitted of treason after their plot was discovered in 1806. Inc. city, 1863. Pop. (1950) 29,684; (1980) 39,967.
39°17′ N, 81°32′ W

·map, United States **18**:908

Parkes, town, east central New South Wales, Australia, in the Lachlan River Valley. Originally known as Bushman's, it was founded (1862) as a reef- and alluvial-gold centre. Proclaimed a municipality (1883), it was renamed after Sir Henry Parkes, a state premier (1871–91). A commercial centre for a sheep-, grain-, fruit-, and poultry-farming area of the Western Slopes region, it is a rail junction on the Newell Highway, with air connections to Sydney (185 mi [298 km] southeast). Industries include iron foundries, steel fabrication works, sawmills, joineries, rail workshops, and agricultural machinery plants. One of the world's largest (210 ft [64 m]) bowl-shaped radio telescopes, operated by the Commonwealth Scientific and Industrial Research Organization, is at Alectown (15 mi north). Pop. (1971 prelim.) 8,849.
33°08′ S, 148°11′ E

·radio telescope of large aperture **18**:102c

Parkes, Alexander (1813–1890), British chemist and inventor who discovered (1846) the cold vulcanization process, especially important in the manufacture of thin-walled rubber articles. He also did work that led to the invention (1870) of the first synthetic plastic material, called Celluloid.

·plastic composition and award **18**:47d
·plastic name and composition **14**:511c

Parkes, Frank Kobina (b. FRANCIS ERNEST KOBINA PARKES, 1932, Korle Bu, Ghana), journalist, broadcaster, and widely anthologized poet whose style and great confidence in the future of Africa owe much to the Senegalese poet David Diop.

Parkes was educated in Accra, Ghana, and Freetown, Sierra Leone. He worked briefly as a newspaper reporter and editor and in 1955 joined the staff of Radio Ghana as a broadcaster. He was president of the Ghana Society of Writers and published a volume of poems, *Songs from the Wilderness* (1965).

His poetry, a rhythmic free verse with much repetition of words and phrases, tends to romanticize and glorify all that is African, from the blackness of African skin to indigenous music, dancing, and ritual. He recalls his continent's past sufferings, exhorts the reader to do something about oppression of blacks that still exists (in South Africa, for example), and criticizes world powers for their concern with atomic weapons and the moon landings rather than with human needs. He admonishes colonial administrators of the past for the legacy they have left behind them. A great faith, similar to Diop's, in the ability of Africans to bring about a glorious future through their own efforts is revealed.

Parkes, Harry (1828–1885), British diplomat.

·Japanese relations problems **10**:78f

Parkes, Sir Henry (b. May 27, 1815, Stoneleigh, Warwickshire—d. April 27, 1896, Sydney, Australia), the dominant political figure in Australia during the second half of the 19th century. In his five terms as premier of New South Wales between 1872 and 1891, he worked for Australian federation, free trade, and improvement of education.

Sir Henry Parkes, 1888
Collection of the National Library of Australia

Parkes became politically prominent in 1849 as a spokesman for ending transportation of convicts to Australia from England. The following year he launched the *Empire*, a newspaper he ran until 1858 and through which he campaigned for fully representative government. He first held public office in 1854 and served almost without interruption as a representative, minister, and premier until 1895.

Parkes's educational work resulted in the Public Schools Act of 1866 and the Public Instruction Act of 1880, which introduced compulsory free education and severed connections between the church and the public schools. In his ministries between 1872 and 1887 he established New South Wales as a free-trade colony. In his fourth administration (1887–89) he carried through measures to improve railways and public works and to limit Chinese immigration.

Parkes first spoke for federation in 1867 and later presided over the National Australasian Convention in 1891. He withdrew support from the resulting Commonwealth of Australia Bill, however, and federation was postponed until 1901. After the elections of 1891 Parkes lost his position of political leadership. His autobiography, *Fifty Years in the Making of Australian History*, appeared in 1892.

Parkesine, trade name for the first synthetic plastic. It was exhibited by Alexander Parkes in 1862.

·chemical composition and importance **18**:47d

Park Forest, village, southern residential suburb of Chicago, Cook County, Illinois, U.S. Developed after World War II, it attracted widespread interest because its planners assumed responsibility for all phases of community development. It was designed by Elbert Peets for American Community Builders, Inc., primarily for middle-income families, to include rental and privately owned dwellings as well as schools, churches, shopping centres, municipal services, and an industrial park. Park Forest received national attention when William H. Whyte, Jr., wrote a series of articles (published 1956 as *The Organization Man*) about the manners, morals, and home life of young executives, based on research done in that community. Inc. 1949. Pop. (1970) 30,638; (1980) 26,222.

Pārkham, archaeological site in northern India.

·yakṣa image size and style **17**:189c

Parkhurst System (teaching method): *see* Dalton Plan.

Parkinson's disease, also known as SHAKING PALSY, or PARALYSIS AGITANS, a relatively common chronic malady of the central nervous system that produces such striking symptoms that almost any observant person can recognize it at a glance. The stooped posture, the slowness of movement, the carriage of the arms in front of the body, the quick short-stepped gait (as if to keep from falling), the fixity of facial expression, and the tremor of the hands are the characteristic signs.

The onset of the disease usually occurs in late adult life, but it may begin as early as the third decade. The course is slowly progressive over 10 to 20 or more years. The first symptom may be the scuffing of one foot in walking, a sense of heaviness of a limb, or a gentle tremor of one hand; the other symptoms follow in slow procession. The handwriting becomes small, and this and other manual skills are gradually lost. Speech is poorly articulated, and swallowing and chewing are laborious. Locomotion becomes increasingly difficult, and ultimately the patient finds it an effort even to arise from bed or a chair or to walk; and there is a tendency to lose balance and to fall. In the advanced stages, the patient is greatly handicapped in all voluntary movements but usually is not paralyzed. An unexpected call for action may momentarily excite the patient to perform some movement with surprising facility. The senses and the intellect are not damaged.

There is a slight tendency for more than one member of a family to be affected. The nerve cells in certain of the basal ganglia of the brain (the substantia nigra, locus caeruleus, the globus pallidus, and their afferent and efferent nerve connections) degenerate. The affected nerve cells often contain a cytoplasmic inclusion body (Lewy body). In a closely related disease with almost identical symptoms (*i.e.*, postencephalitic parkinsonism), a virus is believed to attack the same parts of the brain.

The observation was made in the mid-20th century that dopa (dehydroxyphenylalanine) or structurally related substances are depleted in the brain of the patient with Parkinson's disease and that its symptoms can be alleviated by the replacement of a normal metabolite of the brain. In the late 1960s, L-dopa was used experimentally on patients with parkinsonism; the results were remarkable but not without undesirable side-effects. The drug was approved for sale on a prescription basis in the U.S. in 1970.

·biomedical models, table 1 **5**:866
·cryogenic surgery with freezing probe **5**:320d
·speech and voice pattern irregularities **17**:490a
·symptoms, causation, and treatment **12**:1049h
·ultrasonic wave technique of treatment **18**:843b

Parkman, Francis 13:1019 (b. Sept. 16, 1823, Boston—d. Nov. 8, 1893, Jamaica Plain, Mass.), historian noted for his classic seven-volume history of the Anglo-American struggle for North America.

Abstract of text biography. After studying history and law at Harvard, Parkman made tours of Europe and North America (1844–46). In 1849, after returning from the West, he began his literary career with the publication of a series of recollections of the Oregon Trail. He then began (in 1851) to write historical works and biographies covering various aspects of the settlement of North America; the series of works, known as *England and France in North America*, was completed in 1893.

REFERENCE in other text article:
·American literature of the 19th century **10**:1189e

Park Range, segment of the Rocky Mountains, extends south-southeastward for about 200 mi (320 km) from Carbon County, Wyo., to northwestern Park County, Colo., U.S. The range lies largely within Medicine Bow, Pike, Arapaho, Routt, and White River national forests and includes the Mosquito (Colorado), Gore (Colorado), and Sierra Madre (Wyoming) subranges. Many peaks surpass 14,000 ft (4,300 m), with Mt. Lincoln (14,284 ft) the highest point. Major highways cut through Vail (10,603 ft) and Rabbit Ears (9,426 ft) passes, leading to popular winter-sports areas. The headstreams of the North and South Platte rivers rise in the range, which has extensive mineral deposits.
40°00′ N, 106°30′ W

Park Ridge, city, northwestern suburb of Chicago, Cook County, Illinois, U.S. Founded in 1856 as Pennyville (later called Brickton), it developed as a residential community after the arrival of the Chicago and North Western Railway (1856). It was renamed (1873) in the belief that it included the highest ridge in the county. Park Ridge is known for its special educational facilities, which include Park Ridge School for (dependent, adolescent) Girls (1877), Park Ridge Military Academy, and two Montessori schools. The Modern Music Masters, an international music honour society, was organized there in 1936. Chicago O'Hare International Airport is nearby. Inc. village, 1873; city, 1910. Pop. (1970) 42,614; (1980) 38,704.

parkway: *see* expressway.

parlando-rubato, European folk music singing style in which the words are stressed and metric and rhythmic patterns are irregular.

·folk music element absorption **7**:469d

Parlement, the supreme court under the *ancien régime* in France. It developed out of the *Curia Regis*, or King's Court, in which the early Capetian kings periodically convened their principal vassals and prelates to deliberate with them on feudal and political matters. It also dealt with the few legal cases submitted to the king as sovereign judge.

Throughout the 12th century and in the first decades of the 13th, the *Curia Regis* grew in importance, and professional advisers, *consiliarii*, were added to its membership. Meanwhile, by a slow process, the judicial sessions came to be differentiated from its meetings for other business; by the middle of Louis IX's reign (1226–70) these judicial sessions were being described as *curia regis in parlemento* ("speaking") or Parlement. A system of appeal also grew up, with the Parlement hearing appeals against the judgments of *baillis* (representatives of the royal administration in the provinces); and cases concerning the royal towns were likewise decided by the Parlement. Furthermore, the expansion of the royal domain enlarged the competence of the *curia in parlemento*, which moreover could serve politically to strengthen the royal power by means of its *arrêts* (final decisions), since these expressed the king's law with incontestable authority.

Louis IX had his *curia in parlemento* installed in a special Chambre aux Plaids, or pleading chamber, on what is now the site of the modern Palais de Justice in Paris. The Grand Chambre, as the Chambre aux Plaids grew to be called, remained the core of Parlement, although other chambres grew up along side it. Originally parties were required to make their statements in person, but eventually the Grand Chambre admitted certain written documents. Other chambres were the Chambre des Enquêtes (*q.v.*; inquiry) and the Chambre des Requêtes (*q.v.*; petitions), both instituted in the 14th century; the Chambre de la Tournelle (the criminal chamber), formally instituted in the 16th century, but in existence much earlier; and the Chambre de l'Édit (set up in the 16th century to deal with Huguenot affairs, but finally abolished in 1669).

Vacant seats in the Parlement in the later Middle Ages were supposed to be filled by election or co-optation; but from the 14th century members had resigned in favour of their sons or of someone willing to pay a specified price. In 1552 venality was formally recognized by the crown. Attempts to abolish it later in the century came to nothing; and in 1604 the "annual right," or *paulette* (devised by financier Charles Paulet), was established, enabling officeholders to ensure the hereditability of their offices by paying one-sixtieth of its purchase price every year. The office of premier president, heading Parlement, however, could be acquired only by a nominee of the crown.

Originally there was only one Parlement, that of Paris, but later others were created for the provinces. The provincial Parlements were organized on lines similar to that of Paris and claimed to possess equal powers. But the Parlement of Paris had jurisdiction over nearly half of the kingdom.

The political pretensions of the Parlements were based on their registration of the king's edicts and letters patent. Before registering a measure, the Parlements examined it to see whether it conformed with the principles of law and justice and with the interests of the king and realm; if it did not, they withheld registration and addressed remonstrances to the king. If the king wished to force registration, he had to either send a *lettre de jussion*, ordering it, or come in person, to hold a *lit de justice*, at which his actual presence suspended any delegation of authority to his magistrates; but the right of remonstrance remained a counterbalancing influence in relation to the royal power—though only a negative influence insofar as the courts had no right of initiative in political matters.

During the 16th and early 17th centuries the Parlements took up a course of systematic opposition. Although this was restricted under Louis XIV, it was resumed in the 18th century. By that time opposition of the members was motivated, to a large extent, by anxiety to maintain their own privileges; but it served to focus more general feelings of political and social discontent. At the same time the Parlements were looked upon as a source of privilege and reaction and were swept away early in the French Revolution (1789).

- ·ascendancy after Louis XIV's death **11**:123e
- ·bureaucratic defeat of local autonomy **3**:486c
- ·censorship in publishing and theatre **3**:1087g
- ·enlargement by Francis I **7**:628h
- ·exile to provinces by Maupeou **7**:646e
- ·Fronde demands and their settlement **7**:633d
- ·Louis XIV's curbing of criticism **7**:636a
- ·medieval judicial institutions **12**:159f
- ·organization as a distinct entity **7**:617c *passim* to 618a
- ·power and prestige development **7**:640c
- ·Protestant magistrate additions **7**:631h

Parlement of Foules (*c.* 1382), a poem of some 700 lines by Geoffrey Chaucer, written in rime royal stanzas, about the poet's dream that he had attended an argumentative St. Valentine's Day meeting of the birds, who were assembled to choose their mates.

- ·style, sources, theme, and evaluation **4**:64a

Parléř, Petr (1330–1399), best known member of a famous German family of masons. At the age of 23 he was called by King Charles IV of Bohemia to Prague to continue the cathedral church of St. Vitus. Seemingly influenced by English late Gothic, he built complicated vaults with hanging bosses and ribs rising free through space; these vaults were the first real net vaults on the Continent. He was also the first to use an even number of sides for the polygon of a choir (at Kuttenberg, Czech., in 1360). His sculptural work and vault innovations greatly influenced subsequent architecture.

- ·Charles IV bust illus. **4**:47
- ·Gothic architectural developments **19**:376a

Par les champs et par les grèves (1886; "Over fields and shores"), work by the French author Gustave Flaubert.

- ·author's account of journey with du Camp **7**:379a

Parleyings with Certain People of Importance in Their Day (1887), book by Robert Browning.

- ·Browning's dramatic poems **3**:335d

Parliament (from Old French *parlement*, Latin *parliamentum*), the name of the original legislative assemblies of England, Scotland, and Ireland, and successively of those of Great Britain and the United Kingdom, became also that of some national and provincial legislatures in countries that were once British colonies. The British Parliament consists of the sovereign, the House of Lords, and the House of Commons.

Modern Parliaments have developed from the fusion, during the reign (1272–1307) of Edward I, of two English governmental institutions. One of these, sometimes described as a *colloquium*, was a meeting of the Magnum Concilium, or Great Council, comprising the lay and ecclesiastical magnates, summoned to treat with the king on the affairs of the realm. Often, in practice, they were asked to agree to the levying of specific taxes. The Norman Magnum Concilium, in feudal terms a gathering of the king's tenants in chief, was not greatly dissimilar from the old Anglo-Saxon Witan, a meeting of the king's wise men. The second, and newer, institution was the *Curia Regis*, the King's Court, or Council, a much smaller body of semiprofessional advisers; at those of its meetings that came to be called *concilium regis in parliamento* ("the king's council in Parliament"), judicial problems might be settled that had proved beyond the scope of the ordinary law courts dating from the 12th century. Joint meetings of the two bodies were held when the king wanted them and were attended by those explicitly summoned. The *Curia Regis* members were preeminent and, indeed, often remained to complete business after the magnates had been sent home; the proceedings of Parliament were not formally ended until they had accomplished their tasks. To about one in seven of these meetings Edward, following precedents from his father's time, summoned knights from the shires and burgesses from the towns to appear with the magnates.

Early in the 14th century the practice developed of the lords spiritual and temporal debating together in one chamber, or "house," and the knights and burgesses debating in another. Strictly speaking, there were, and still are, three houses: the king and his council, the lords spiritual and temporal, and the commons. But the Lancastrian kings were usually forced to take all their councillors from among the lords, and under the Tudors it became the practice to find seats among the Commons for privy councillors who were not lords. Meanwhile, the greater cohesion of the Privy Council achieved in the 14th century separated it in practice from Parliament; and the decline of Parliament's judicial function led to an increase in its legislative activity, originating now not only from royal initiative but by petitions, or "bills," framed by groups within Parliament itself. Bills, if assented to by the king, became acts of Parliament; eventually, under Henry VI, the assent of the Lords and Commons became also necessary. Under the Tudors, though it was still possible to make law by royal proclamation, the monarchs rarely resorted to such an unpopular measure, and all major political changes were effected by acts of Parliament.

Along with these developments was added that of keeping a Parliament in being for several sessions, and there thus grew up a class of almost professional parliamentarians, some of whom were used by the king to secure assent to his measures and others who would disagree with some of those measures and encourage the Commons to reject them, though the firm idea of a formed "opposition" did not develop until much later.

In the 17th century the Parliament became a revolutionary body, and was the centre of resistance to the King during the English Civil War (1642–51). The Restoration period (1660–88) saw the development of the Whig and Tory factions, ancestors of the later political parties. After the Glorious Revolution of 1688, William III chose his council, or officers of state, from among these party members in Parliament—at first from both parties and then, finding this unworkable, from the party commanding a majority in Commons. Under Queen Anne this council, or Cabinet, as it came to be known, became a distinct policy-making body, usually meeting alone without the Queen. Subsequently, under the first two Georges, who were politically ineffectual, Robert Walpole, as leader of the Whigs, of Commons, and of the Cabinet, became the real head of government, the "prime" minister; he set the principle that the Cabinet must act as a unit. Later, particularly after 1830, the party system became entrenched, and all members of Parliament began using a party label. Effective power was passing from the monarch, and the power of the House of Lords, too, would be diminished in the late 19th and early 20th centuries.

- ·budget appropriation procedure **3**:444e
- ·copyright law historical development **5**:153g
- ·England's governmental tradition **6**:871a
- ·government types and political power **5**:89b

<u>history</u>

- ·communitas regni and representative government **3**:210c *passim* to 211g
- ·Edward I's use to strengthen monarchy **6**:434f
- ·exclusion of Jews **5**:898d
- ·George III and 18th-century power struggle **3**:500a
- ·Great Chain of Being concept **3**:226e
- ·Henry VIII's reformation participation **8**:771c *passim* to 771g
- ·history and development of power **5**:96h
- ·Ireland's political development **3**:286b
- ·James II and the Glorious Revolution **10**:23a
- ·medieval governmental structures **12**:158d
- ·Oliver Cromwell's reorganization of government **5**:292a *passim* to 295a
- ·origin and developments **11**:103a
- ·political party growth under George III **7**:1126c
- ·reform movement of the 1830s **19**:756g
- ·Scottish institution's feudal nature **3**:236h
- ·Thomas Cromwell's political theory **5**:296f
- ·Tudor and Stuart political development **3**:228d

- ·individualistic concept of representation **6**:529c
- ·Northern Ireland legislative powers **13**:241b
- ·oratory used in issue debates **13**:643b
- ·Palace of Westminster Gothic Revival design **19**:447h
- ·powers and composition **7**:604b
- ·School of Design establishment **2**:94f
- ·Scotland representation and committees **16**:408f
- ·United Kingdom governmental structures **18**:885b

Parliamentary Party (opponents of Charles I during English Civil War): *see* Roundhead.

Parma, Alessandro Farnese, duke of: *see* Farnese, Alessandro, duke of Parma.

Parma, capital of Parma province, in the Emilia-Romagna region of northern Italy, on the Parma River, northwest of Bologna. Founded by the Romans along the Via Aemilia in 183 BC, Parma was important as a road junction; its trade flourished, and it obtained Roman citizenship. It became an episcopal see in the 4th century and was later destroyed by the Ostrogoth king Theodoric. The city was rebuilt in the Middle Ages and was ruled by its bishops from the 9th century. Parma enjoyed communal liberty in the late 12th and 13th centuries, until its involvement in the struggles between the Holy Roman Empire and the papacy in the early 14th century led to its subjugation by a series of lordships. Created a duchy by Pope Paul III, it was granted in 1545 to the Farnese dukes and passed later to the Austrians, from whom it was taken by Napoleon, who in 1815 gave it to his second consort, Marie Louise of Austria. In 1831 and 1848 it took part in the risings for independence and in 1861 became part of united Italy (*see also* Parma and Piacenza, Duchies of). During World War II the city was extensively damaged by Allied bombardment.

Famous natives of Parma include the music conductor Arturo Toscanini and the artists Benedetto Antelami, Correggio (Antonio Allegri), and Parmigianino (Francesco Mazzola). The printer and typeface designer Giambattista Bodoni worked and died there.

The city's imposing Romanesque cathedral, rebuilt after an earthquake in the 12th century, contains magnificent works by Antelami and Correggio, and there are sculptures by Antelami and others of his school in the nearby baptistery (1196–1260). The church of S. Giovanni Evangelista (1494–1510) has frescoes by Correggio and arabesques by Michelangelo Anselmi. The church of Sta. Maria della Steccata (1521–39), the burial place of the Farnese family, is in the form of a Greek cross with a cupola displaying frescoes by Parmigianino. The 16th-century abbey of S. Paolo, with the Camera della Badessa (Room of the Abbess), has been splendidly decorated by Correggio. Notable secular landmarks include the Palazzo della Pilotta (begun 1583), residence of the Farnese dukes, containing the picture gallery, the Biblioteca Palatina (Palatine Library), and the National Museum of Antiquities; the partly ruined Palazzo Ducale (1564); and the Farnese Theatre (1618), all of which were restored after World War II. The university was founded in the 11th century and reorganized in 1601 by Ranuccio I Farnese.

Parma is an important rail and road junction on the main routes from Milan to Bologna. Its economy is mainly agricultural. Parmesan cheese is world famous. Machinery, pharmaceuticals, fertilizer, shoes, and alcohol are also made. Pop. (1971 prelim.) mun., 177,485. 44°48′ N, 10°20′ E

- ·map, Italy **9**:1088

Parma, city, Cuyahoga County, northeast Ohio, U.S., a southern suburb of Cleveland. Settled by New Englanders in 1816, it was known as Greenbriar until 1826, when it became the township of Parma, named for the Italian town and province. A small section seceded to form Parma Heights in 1912, and in 1924 the remainder of the township became the village of Parma. After a proposal for annexation to Cleveland was defeated in 1931, Parma was organized (1932) as a city. Manufactures include automotive parts, tools and dies, and metal stampings. Pop. (1950) 28,897; (1970) 100,216; (1980) 92,548.
41°22′ N, 81°43′ W

Parma and Piacenza, Duchy of, the north Italian cities of Parma and Piacenza, with their dependent territories, detached from the Papal States by Pope Paul III in 1545 and made a hereditary duchy for his son Pier Luigi Farnese (died 1547). They were retained by the Farnese family until its extinction in 1731, when they passed to the Spanish Bourbons in the person of Don Carlos (the future Charles III of Spain). Except for one brief interruption, the Spanish Bourbons controlled the duchy until 1808, when it was formally annexed to France as the *département* of Taro.

In 1814 the Congress of Vienna gave the duchy to Napoleon's consort, Marie-Louise. With her death, in 1847, Parma and Piacenza were restored to the Bourbons, whose reign was periodically troubled by revolution and assassination. Louise of Bourbon-Berry, regent for her infant son Robert, transferred her powers to a provisional government on June 9, 1859, which paved the way for the annexation of Parma and Piacenza to Piedmont-Sardinia in March 1860. Piedmont-Sardinia became part of the Kingdom of Italy in 1861.

·House of Bourbon acquisition 3:82c; table 83

parmak, Turkish unit of linear measure equivalent to one decimetre, or 3.9 inches.

·weights and measures, table 5 19:734

Parmelia (lichen): *see* crottle; skull lichen.

Parmenides (b. *c.* 515 BC), Greek philosopher of Elea, in southern Italy, founder of Eleaticism, one of the leading pre-Socratic schools of Greek thought. His general teaching has been diligently reconstructed from the few surviving fragments of his principal work, a lengthy two-part verse composition. He held that the multiplicity of existing things, their changing forms and motion, are but an appearance of a single eternal reality ("Being"), thus giving rise to the Parmenidean principle "all is one." His relation to the opposing philosophical school of Heracleitus ("all is change") is controverted. He also introduced the method of rational proofs as the basis for assertions. One of Plato's dialogues, the *Parmenides*, deals with Parmenides' thought. An English translation of his extant writings was edited with a critical commentary by L. Tarán (1965).

Parmenides, dialogue of Plato, generally considered to be one of his last seven, dealing chiefly with the Eleatic philosophy of Parmenides. *Major ref.* 14:536d

·reality of Forms 12:16a

Parmenio (b. *c.* 400 BC—d. 330, Ecbatana, now Hamadan, Iran), Macedonian general usually considered the best officer in the service of Philip II and his son Alexander the Great. During the reign of Philip, Parmenio won a great victory over the Illyrians (356). In 336 he was sent with Amyntas and Attalus, his son-in-law, to Asia Minor to make preparations for the conquest of Asia. In the confusion that followed Philip's murder, he declared for Alexander and assisted in the murder of members of the faction opposed to Alexander. Parmenio became Alexander's second in command throughout the conquest of Persia and commanded the left wing of the army at the battles of Granicus, Issus, and Gaugamela. When Alexander continued eastward after the conquest of the Persian Empire, he left Parmenio in Media to guard his communications. During the campaign, Philotas, Parmenio's son, was charged with conspiring to murder Alexander, tried, and put to death. Though it is likely that Philotas was innocent, Alexander had Parmenio murdered.

·Alexander III's trust and later rivalry 1:469d *passim* to 470g

Parmentier, André, also called ANDREW PARMENTIER (b. July 3, 1780, Enghien, Belg.—d. Nov. 26, 1830), Belgian-born U.S. horticulturist, responsible for exhibiting many plant species in America. He was the son of a linen merchant and was educated at the University of Louvain. His brothers were all horticulturists, the eldest being director of the Duc d'Arenberg's park at Enghien. In 1824 André Parmentier lost his capital in speculation and emigrated to New York, where he established a commercial nursery and botanical garden. He imported plants and contributed to horticultural journals. Although he designed and laid out grounds, it is as a plantsman that he is remembered.

Parmesan, a very hard cheese first made in Italy in the Middle Ages.

·production stages and content 5:433a; table

Parmigianino, also called PARMIGIANO, byname of GIROLAMO FRANCESCO MARIA MAZZOLA, OR MAZZUOLI (b. Jan. 11, 1503, Parma, Italy—d. Aug. 24, 1540, Casalmaggiore, Cremona), painter who was one of the first artists to react against High Renaissance classicism and initiate the Mannerist style. There is no doubt that Correggio was the strongest single influence on his early development, but he probably was never a pupil of that master painter. The influence is apparent in Parmigianino's first important work, the "Mystic Marriage of St. Catherine" (*c.* 1521). About 1522–23 he executed two series of frescoes: one series in two side chapels of S. Giovanni Evangelista, in Parma, executed contemporaneously with Correggio's great murals on the dome and pendentives of that church; and the other, representing the "Legend of Diana and Actaeon," on the ceiling of a room in the castle of Fontanellato just outside Parma. The scheme of the latter decoration recalls Correggio's work in the Camera di San Paolo in Parma.

Parmigianino, self-portrait from a convex mirror, oil on convex panel, 1524; in the Kunsthistorisches Museum, Vienna

By courtesy of the Kunsthistorisches Museum, Vienna

In 1524 Parmigianino moved to Rome, taking with him three specimens of his work to impress the pope, including the famous portrait that he had painted of himself, reflected in a convex mirror, on a convex panel. His chief painting done in Rome is the large "Vision of St. Jerome" (1527). Although this work shows the influence of Michelangelo, it was Raphael's ideal beauty of form and feature, rather than Raphaelesque motives or compositions, that he found sympathetic and that influenced his entire *oeuvre*. While at work on the "Vision of St. Jerome" in 1527 he was interrupted by soldiers of the imperial army taking part in the sack of Rome, and he left for Bologna. There he painted one of his masterpieces, the "Madonna with St. Margaret and Other Saints," which shows a new fluency of linear rhythm and a new technical virtuosity. In 1531 he returned to Parma, where he remained for the rest of his life, the principal works of this last period being the "Madonna dal Collo Lungo" (1534; "Madonna of the Long Neck") and the frescoes on the vault preceding the apse of Sta. Maria della Steccata.

Parmigianino was perhaps the first Italian artist to practice etching. He used the etching needle with the freedom of a pen rather than as a substitute for the engraver's burin. His etchings were usually reproductions of his drawings, which enjoyed great popularity. In all probability he used etching as a method of satisfying the demand for his drawings.

He was one of the most remarkable portrait painters of the century outside Venice. Some of his best portraits are in Naples, in the Museo e Gallerie Nazionali di Capodimonte, including the "Gian Galeazzo Sanvitale" (1524) and the portrait of a young woman called "Antea" (*c.* 1535–37).

The style that he developed was among the most brilliant expositions of one of the two major aspects of Mannerism—the decorative aspect (the other, the expressionist aspect, having been developed in Florence chiefly by Pontormo). This involved a reaction against many of the principles of High Renaissance art, especially its dependence on nature and its basis in stability and clarity of design.

Parmigianino's works are distinguished by ambiguity of space composition, by distortion and elongation of the human figure, and by the pursuit of what the art historian Vasari called "grace"; that is to say, a rhythmical, sensuous beauty beyond the beauty of nature.

·Roman reception and style 19:404a

Parnaíba, port city, northwestern Piauí state, northeastern Brazil, on the Rio Igaraçu, an outlet of the Rio Parnaíba, 9 mi (14 km) upstream from the Atlantic Ocean. Founded in 1761 and given city status in 1884, Parnaíba is the most important trade and distributing centre of the river valley. The chief products shipped from Parnaíba and its outport, Luís Correia (just to the northeast), are carnauba wax, cotton, babassu oil (similar in properties and use to coconut oil), sugar, cattle, and hides. The city is also accessible by road and air. Pop. (1970) 57,030.
2°54′ S, 41°47′ W

·Map, Brazil 3:125

Parnaíba River, Portuguese RIO PARNAÍBA, in northeastern Brazil, rises in the Serra da Tabatinga and flows north-northeastward for 1,050 mi (1,700 km) to empty into the Atlantic Ocean, forming a delta at its mouth. In addition to marking the border between the states of Maranhão and Piauí, the Parnaíba

has great economic importance. Although its middle and upper reaches are interrupted by waterfalls, it is navigable by shallow-draft vessels from its mouth at least as far south as the junction of the Rio Canindé. Important river ports include Piauí's three major cities, Teresina (the state capital), Floriano, and Parnaíba.
3°00′ S, 41°50′ W
·map, Brazil **3**:124
·navigability and flow **3**:128f; map 140
·transportation and power importance **14**:440c

Parṇaśabarī, Tibetan LO-MA-GYON-MA, Japanese HIYŌI, a Buddhist goddess distinguished by the girdle of leaves which she wears. She is apparently derived from an aboriginal deity, and one of her titles is Sarvaśavarāṇām Bhagavātī, or "goddess of all the Śavaras" (a tribe in eastern India). She is invoked to fight disease and epidemics, and is represented with a smiling but irritated expression, stamping on personified figures of fever and smallpox.

Parnasse contemporain, Le (1866–76), publication containing the collected poems of the French Parnassian poets.
·Verlaine's first poetry publication **19**:84h

Parnassia, commonly called GRASS OF PARNASSUS, genus of flowering plants in the family Parnassiaceae, about 50 species of low perennial herbs distributed throughout the Northern Hemisphere. The plants grow in tufts and bear white, greenish-white, or yellow flowers. Five sterile stamens bearing nectar glands alternate with five fertile stamens in each flower. Grass of Parnassus is occasionally planted in damp, shady places near bodies of water.
·distribution, features, and classification problems **16**:292g
·P. palustris false nectar droplets and fly attraction **12**:216e

parnassian (butterfly): *see* Papilionidae.

Parnassians, group of French poets headed by Leconte de Lisle, who stressed restraint, objectivity, technical perfection, and precise description as reaction against the emotionalism and verbal imprecision of the Romantics. The poetic movement led by the Parnassians that resulted in experimentation with metres and verse forms and the revival of the sonnet paralleled the trend toward Realism in drama and the novel that became evident in the late 19th century. Initially taking their themes from contemporary society, the Parnassians later turned to the mythology, epics, and sagas of exotic lands and past civilizations, notably India and ancient Greece, for inspiration. The Parnassians derived their name from the anthology to which they contributed: *Le Parnasse Contemporain* (3 vol., 1866, 1871, 1876), edited by Louis-Xavier de Ricard and Catulle Mendès and published by Alphonse Lemerre. Their principles, though, had been formulated earlier in Théophile Gautier's preface to *Mademoiselle de Maupin* (1835), which expounded the theory of art for art's sake, in Leconte de Lisle's preface to his *Poèmes antiques* (1852), and in *La Revue Fantaisiste* (1860), founded by Mendès. Gautier's *Émaux et camées* (1852), a collection of carefully worked, formally perfect poems, pointed to a new conception of poetry and influenced the works of major Parnassians such as Albert Glatigny, François Coppée, Léon Dierx, and José Maria de Heredia. Heredia, the most representative of the group, looked for precise details, double rhymes, sonorous words, and exotic names, and concentrated on making the 14th line of his sonnets the most striking.

The influence of the Parnassians was felt throughout Europe and was particularly evident in the Modernist movement of Spain and Portugal and in the Jeune Belgique (Young Belgium) movement.

In the late 19th century a new generation of poets, the Symbolists, followers of Stéphane Mallarmé and Paul Verlaine, themselves Parnassians in their youth, broke away from precise description in search of an art of nuance and musical suggestion.
·anti-Realist style **6**:1077a
·French literature of the 19th century **10**:1194c
·Verlaine's beginnings as poet **19**:84h

Parnassus, Mount, modern PARNASSÓS, barren limestone spur of the Pindus Mountains, central Greece, running northwest–southeast on the borders of Phocis, Fthiótis, and Boeotia *nomoí* (departments) and rising to a maximum elevation of 8,061 ft (2,457 m) in Mt. Parnassus, within sight of Delphi, and extending to Cape Opus on the Gulf of Corinth. In ancient times Parnassus was sacred to the Dorians and in mythology to Apollo and the Corycian nymphs. On a plateau between the summit and Delphi was the Corycian stalactite cave sacred to the nymphs and Pan. For

Sanctuary of Apollo near Mt. Parnassus, Greece
Sven Samelius

the Roman poets, Parnassus' Castalian spring was a source of inspiration; they favoured Parnassus over Mt. Helicon as the home of the Muses.
38°32′ N, 22°35′ E
·geographic and legendary significance **8**:313a
·map, Greece **8**:314

Parnell, Charles Stewart 13:1020 (b. June 27, 1846, Avondale, County Wicklow—d. Oct. 6, 1891, Brighton, Sussex), nationalist leader of the struggle for Irish Home Rule in the late 19th century.

Abstract of text biography. Elected to Parliament in 1875 as an advocate of Home Rule for Ireland, Parnell was chosen president of the Home Rule Confederation of Great Britain in 1877 and became the most conspicuous figure in Irish politics. He also became president of the Irish Land League (1879), and the following year he organized massive land agitation as well as obstruction of parliamentary business to press for Home Rule legislation. Parnell's subsequent parliamentary manoeuvres brought Gladstone to the office of prime minister and a proposal for Home Rule, entailing broad autonomy for Ireland before the House of Commons (1886). Nevertheless, when Lord Salisbury succeeded Gladstone, Parnell reduced his political activity; and after a scandal involving him and a colleague's wife broke out (1889), he lost his position as leader of the Irish parliamentary party.

REFERENCES in other text articles:
·Gladstone quarrel over O'Shea divorce **8**:180g
·Home Rule movement leadership **3**:272b
·Land League sponsorship **3**:291c
·Yeats' hope for Irish nationalism **19**:1076g

Parnell, Thomas (b. 1679, Dublin—d. 1718, Chester, Eng.), poet, essayist, and friend of Alexander Pope, who relied on Parnell's scholarship in his translation of the *Iliad*. Parnell's poetry, in heroic couplets, was esteemed by Pope for its lyric quality and stylistic ease. Among his best poems are "An Elegy to an Old Beauty" and "Night Piece on Death," said to have influenced Thomas Gray's "Elegy Written in a Country Church Yard." Parnell contributed to *The Spectator* and the *Guardian* and was a member, with Swift and Gay, of the literary club Scriblerus. After Parnell's

Thomas Parnell, detail of an engraving by an unknown artist
Radio Times Hulton Picture Library

death, Pope collected his poetry and published it in a volume called *Poems on Several Occasions* (1722). The work was republished in 1770 with additional poems and a life of Parnell by Oliver Goldsmith. A complete collection of Parnell's poetry can be found in *Minor Poets of the Eighteenth Century*, edited by H. l'A. Fausset (1930).

Parni, also called APARNI, one of three nomadic or semi-nomadic tribes in the confederacy of the Dahae living east of the Caspian Sea; its members founded the Parthian Empire. After the death of Alexander the Great (323 BC) the Parni apparently moved southward into the region of Parthia and perhaps eastward into Bactria. They seem to have adopted the speech of the native Parthians and been absorbed into the settled population. According to tradition Arsaces I was the first ruler of the Parthians and founder of the Parthian Empire; a governor under Diodotus, king of the Bactrian Greeks, he revolted and fled westward to establish his own rule (*c.* 239 BC). The ruling family of the Parni in Parthia became known as the Arsacid dynasty, and Parthian kings were called Arsaces.
·Antonius' invasion attitude and plans **1**:1000c
·Iranian tribal empire establishment **9**:840f
·Near Eastern Seleucid Empire demise **12**:914f

Parnicki, Teodor (1908–), Polish author.
·social realist works **10**:1254c

Párnis, Mount, Greek PÁRNIS (or PARNES) ÓROS, formerly OZEA, mountain massif just north of Athens, Greece. It rises to 4,636 ft (1,413 m) and its slopes afford summer pasture and carry some forests of fir.
38°11′ N, 23°42′ E
·Athens' topography **2**:262g
·map, Greece **8**:314

Parnu, Russian PYARNU, city, Estonian Soviet Socialist Republic, at the mouth of the Parnu River on Parnu Bay of the Gulf of Riga. First mentioned in 1251 as a member of the Hanseatic League, Parnu was successively controlled by the Teutonic Knights, the Poles, the Swedes and finally the Russians. It is now significant as a port, holiday resort, and centre of light industry. Pop. (1970) 46,000.
58°24′ N, 24°32′ E

Paroaria coronata (bird): *see* cardinal.

parochial education, education offered institutionally by a religious group; especially, in the United States, education in elementary and secondary schools that are maintained by Roman Catholic parishes or other religious bodies, that are separate from the public school systems, and that provide instruction based on sectarian principles.
·educational economics and financing **6**:314h
·education system, curriculum, and funds **6**:428h

parody (Greek *parodeia*, "a song sung alongside another"), in literature, a form of satirical criticism or comic mockery that imitates the style and manner of a particular writer or school of writers so as to emphasize the weakness of the writer or the overused conventions of the school. Differing from burlesque by the depth of its technical penetration and from travesty, which treats dignified subjects in a trivial manner, true parody mercilessly exposes all the tricks of manner and thought of its victim yet cannot be written without an almost loving appreciation of the work that it ridicules. Although it is sometimes employed for comic effect, as in *The Ingoldsby Legends* (1840–47) by R.H. Barham, an exaggerated imitation of the conventions of medieval legend making, parody is more generally satirical. An anonymous poet of ancient Greece, for example, imitated the epic style of Homer in *Batrachomyomachia* (*The Battle of the Frogs and Mice*), one of the earliest examples of parody; Aristophanes parodied the dramatic styles of Aeschylus and Euripides in *The Frogs*; Chaucer parodied the chivalric romance in "The Tale of Sir Thopas" (*c.* 1375), as did Cervantes in *Don Quixote* (1605); Rabelais parodied the Scholastics in *Gargantua and Pantagruel* (1532–34); Shakespeare mimicked Christopher Marlowe's high dramatic style in the players' scene in *Hamlet* and was himself parodied by John Marston, who wrote a travesty of *Venus and Adonis* entitled *The Metamorphosis of Pigmalions Image* (1598); the 2nd Duke of Buckingham in *The Rehearsal* (1671) and Sheridan in *The Critic* (1779) both parodied the heroic drama, especially Dryden's *Conquest of Granada* (1670); John Phillips in *The Splendid Shilling* (1705) caught all the superficial epic mannerisms of Milton's *Paradise Lost* (1667); Racine parodied Corneille's lofty dramatic style in *Les Plaideurs* (1668, "The Litigants"); Fielding parodied Richardson's sentimental novel *Pamela* (1740–41) in *Shamela* (1741) and *Joseph Andrews* (1742) and mimicked the heroic play in *Tom Thumb* (1730).

In England the first collection of parodies to score a wide success was *Rejected Addresses* (1812) by Horace and James Smith; it is a series of dedicatory odes on the reopening of the Drury Lane Theatre in 1812, written in the manner of various contemporary poets such as Scott, Byron, Southey, Wordsworth and Coleridge. Later in the 19th century, Victorian parodists satirized their contemporaries, particularly Robert Browning and the Pre-Raphaelites. Unique among the Victorians is Lewis Carroll, whose parodies preserve verses that would otherwise not have survived—*e.g.*, Robert Southey's "Old Man's Comforts" (the basis for "You Are Old, Father William") and the verses of Isaac Watts that gave rise to "How Doth the Little Crocodile" and "The Voice of the Lobster."

In the United States, too, during the 19th century, the poems of Poe, Whitman, Whittier, and Bret Harte were mimicked by their contemporaries, particularly by the poet and translator Bayard Taylor. Because of the variety of accents of 19th century immigrants, the individual characteristic of U.S. parody is the play on dialect—*e.g.*, Charles G. Leland's *Hans Breitmann's Ballads* (1914) is a parody of the German poets Heine and Uhland in macaronic German-American. Among more modern parodists Samuel Hoffenstein is outstanding for his carefully damaging versions of A.E. Housman and the Georgian poets.

The art of parody has been encouraged in the 20th century by such periodicals as *Punch* and *The New Yorker* and by journals that have offered prizes for parodies on their competition pages. The scope of parody has been widened to take in the far more difficult task of parodying prose. One of the most successful examples is Sir Max Beerbohm's *Christmas Garland* (1912), a series of Christmas stories in the style and spirit of various contemporary writers, most notably Henry James. Another innovation is double parody, invented by Sir John Squire in the period between World Wars I and II; it is the rendering of the sense of one poet in the style of another—*e.g.*, Squire's version of Thomas Gray's "Elegy Written in a Country Churchyard" written in the style of Edgar Lee Masters' *Spoon River Anthology* resulted in "If Gray Had Had to Write His Elegy in the Cemetery of Spoon River Instead of in That of Stoke Poges." Also outstanding among modern parodists have been Sir Arthur Quiller-Couch, H.D. Traill, and G.H. Vallins.

parody, musical, technique of musical composition used in the Renaissance; in modern usage, humorous imitation of a serious composition.

The Renaissance technique of parody was the creative reworking of several voice parts of a pre-existent composition to form a new composition, frequently a mass. The earliest known parody masses are from the late 14th century, but the procedure became common in the 15th and 16th centuries. The composer of a parody mass used as his model a vocal work such as a chanson, madrigal, or motet, freely reorganizing and expanding the original material, often inserting new sections between borrowed, modified passages. A parody mass is known by the name of its model, as *Missa Malheur me bat*, by Josquin des Prez, a reworking of Jean d'Okeghem's chanson *Malheur me bat* (*Misfortune Struck Me*).

The process of parody was also utilized in arrangements of vocal works for lute or keyboard, as in Peter Philips' arrangement for virginal (harpsichord) of the chanson *Bon Jour, mon coeur* (*Good Day, My Heart*), by Orlando di Lasso.

Musical parody in the modern, humorous sense usually appears in music either as a humorous application of new text to a pre-existent vocal piece or as tongue in cheek imitation of a given musical style. Among the most successful examples of musical parody are Mozart's *Ein musikalischer Spass* (*A Musical Joke*; K. 522, completed 1787), deliberately breaking technical conventions and concluding with glaringly wrong notes, and the absurd repetitions in quick tempo of the word amen by the chorus in Hector Berlioz' oratorio *L'Enfance du Christ* (*The Childhood of Christ*; Opus 25, 1854).

parole (French: "speech"), in Saussurean linguistics, one of the three aspects of language (the other two being *langue* and *langage*). *Parole* is defined as the manifestation of the language in the individual speakers, including the sum total of their idiosyncracies; *e.g.*, lisps, idioms, ungrammatical utterances, and coined words.

parole, form of supervised conditional liberty from prison granted prior to the expiration of the sentence. As a form of correctional treatment, parole is designed to enhance the protection of the community through the supervision and rehabilitation of selected offenders following their release from prison. The modern use of parole as a correctional method stems from a change in penal philosophy to emphasize reform and rehabilitation rather than retribution and punishment.

Parole systems are usually administered by the ministry of justice, although in Mexico and South Africa the program is run by the ministry of welfare. In a few countries, parole is a function of the judiciary.

Eligibility for parole is governed by statutes that provide either definite or indeterminate sentences (*q.v.*) and define offenses for which parole may be granted. In some jurisdictions, eligibility for parole is prohibited by statute for offenders convicted of such serious crimes as narcotics peddling, armed robbery, kidnapping, rape, or murder.

Parole supervision ranges from little more than a periodic police check to intensive supervision by trained personnel. Conditions of parole vary widely but usually define minimum standards of conduct, delimit freedom of movement, and require the parolee to report regularly to a parole officer. Violation of the conditions of parole may constitute grounds for parole revocation and reincarceration.

paronychia, inflammation of the skin folded over the nail of a finger or toe.

Paropia, genus of leafhoppers of the insect order Homoptera.

Páros, one of the Cyclades islands in the Aegean Sea, Greece, separated from Náxos on the east by a channel 4 mi (6 km) wide. With an area of 75 sq mi (194.5 sq km), it is formed by a single peak, Profítis Ilías (classical Marpessa), 2,530 ft (771 m) in height, which slopes evenly on all sides to a maritime plain that is broadest on the northeast and southwest sides. The island is mainly composed of marble. On a bay on the northwest lies the capital, Páros (or Paroikía,), occupying the site of the ancient and medieval capital. The small harbour is excelled by that of Náousa on the north side. White, semitransparent Parian Marble (Paria Marmara), used for sculpture and quarried from subterranean pits on the north side of Mt. Marpessa, was the chief source of wealth for ancient Páros. Several of the marble tunnels have survived.

Páros shared the Early Bronze Age culture of the Cyclades. Traditionally it was first colonized by Arcadians and then by Ionians. In the 7th century BC Parian colonies were sent to Thasos and to Parium on the Sea of Marmara and in 385 to the island of Pharos (Hvar, Yugoslavia) in the Adriatic. In 490 Páros joined the Persians and sent a force to Marathon; in retaliation, its capital was attacked by an Athenian fleet under Miltiades. Páros also sided with Persia's Greek mercenary, Xerxes I, but after the Battle of Artemisium (480) its contingent remained in Kíthnos. After 480 a member of the Delian League, it joined the Second Athenian Confederation in 378. On its political decline it passed to the Ptolemies of Egypt and thence to Roman rule. Following the brief Latin conquest of Constantinople (AD 1204), Páros was subject to Venice, becoming in 1389 an independent duchy. In 1537 it was taken by the Turks and was annexed to Greece in 1830 after the War of Greek Independence.

Recent excavations have been carried out by the German School. A most important 17th-century find was the Parian Chronicle, a marble inscription giving an account of artistic milestones in early and classical Greece. North of the capital is a Delian sanctuary of Apollo and Artemis. The present economy depends largely on locally grown cereals, grapes, figs, olives, and tobacco. Separated from Páros on the southwest by a channel, 1.4 mi (2 km) wide, is the once-attached Andíparos (Antiparos), the ancient Oliarus. Pop. (1971) capital, 1,955; island, 6,776.
37°08′ N, 25°12′ E

parosteal sarcoma, an uncommon malignant tumour of the periosteum (growth-capable surface of bones) that occurs in young adults and shows a predilection for the large long bones and especially the knee. Symptoms are mild—a mass may be felt, but pain may not be present, and fractures seldom occur. The lesion grows slowly and spreads late; a cure may often be effected with adequate treatment. *See also* tumours, bone-related.

parotid gland, largest of the three paired major salivary glands (*q.v.*).
·digestive impairment due to disease **5**:802e
·human digestive system anatomy **5**:791b

parotitis, epidemic: *see* mumps.

Parousia (religion): *see* Last Judgment.

paroxysmal atrial tachycardia, sudden, intermittent attacks of over-rapid heartbeat, originating in the atrium of the heart.
·symptoms, course, and treatment **4**:226a

paroxysmal dyspnea, acute difficulty in breathing, following upon the lung congestion caused by left heart failure.
·heart failure symptom **3**:894e

Parque Güell, park in Barcelona, designed (1900–02) by Antonio Gaudí.

Parquet, in France, the department of the public prosecutor.
·organization and membership **7**:606d

parquetry: *see* veneering.

Parr, Catherine: *see* Catherine (Parr).

Parr, Thomas (d. 1635), celebrated English centenarian reputed to have been born in 1483, making him 152 years old at the time of his death in London.
·life-span study and autopsy by Harvey **10**:912f

parrakeet: *see* parakeet.

Parramatta, city, New South Wales, Australia, on the 15-mi-long (24-km) Parramatta River (which enters Port Jackson harbour). Founded in 1788 by Gov. Arthur Phillip as a western agricultural outlying farm colony of Sydney and called Rose Hill, it was renamed Parramatta, an Aboriginal word meaning Plenty of Eels and Head of River, when it was proclaimed a town in 1790. Declared a municipality (1861), it became a city in 1938 and was expanded (1948) to include Granville, Dundas, and Ermington-Rydalmere. It serves a region with plant nurseries and mixed vegetable farms and is industrialized to include motor-vehicle body assembly, flour milling, and textile, paint, tile, tire, and asbestos manufacture. Parramatta, the second oldest white settlement in Australia (after Sydney), has many historic buildings, including Elizabeth Farm House (1793; the nation's oldest home still standing), Experiment Farm Cottage (1798), and the Kings School (1832). Pop. (1971 prelim.) 110,717.
33°49′ S, 151°00′ E

Parratt, Sir Walter (b. Feb. 10, 1841, Huddersfield, Eng.—d. March 27, 1924, Windsor), organist who exerted great influence by his understanding of Bach. At age 11 he was organist at a local church, and later held positions as organist of Magdalen College, Oxford (1872) and St. George's Chapel, Windsor (1882); professor of music, Oxford (1908–18); and teacher of organ at the Royal College of Music, London (1883–1923). In 1893 he became organist to Queen Victoria. His few compositions include incidental music, and organ and choral works. As an organist, by insisting on accurate phrasing and simple registration, he helped restore the original style to the works of Bach.

Parrett, River, flows through the county of Somerset, England. It rises in the south of the county near Crewkerne on the boundary with the county of Dorset, then flows northwestward to the town of Bridgwater. Finally it enters Bridgwater Bay and the Bristol Channel. The river's two major tributaries are the Isle and the Yeo. For much of its 35-mi course the Parrett flows through the Somerset Levels, a flat alluvial area subject to frequent flooding. Very little arable farming is practised in the area. Withy (tough, flexible reed such as osier) beds are found along the river.
51°13′ N, 3°01′ W
·map, United Kingdom **18**:866

Parrhasius (fl. 5th century BC, Athens), one of the greatest painters of Greece. Parrhasius was born in Ephesus, Ionia (now part of Turkey), and later settled in Athens. He was certainly distinguished as a painter and is said to have been interested in the study of proportion. Many of his drawings on wood and parchment were preserved and highly valued by later painters for purposes of study. His picture of Theseus adorned the Capitol in Rome; other works are chiefly mythological groups. A picture of the Demos, the personified people of Athens, is famous.

Parri, Feruccio (1890), Italian prime minister in 1945.
·political and economic disunity **9**:1170d

Parrington, Vernon L(ouis) (b. Aug. 3, 1871, Aurora, Ill.—d. June 16, 1929, Winchcombe, Gloucestershire), U.S. literary historian and teacher who greatly influenced U.S. historical and literary thought. He grew up in Emporia, Kan., and was educated at the College of Emporia and Harvard University. He taught English and modern languages at the College of Emporia (1893–97), at the University of Oklahoma (1897–1908), and at the University of Washington, Seattle (1908–29). Influenced by William Morris and John Ruskin, by the critical principles of Taine, and by the political program of the Populists, Parrington reappraised U.S. literary history in *Main Currents in American Thought*, 2 vol. (1927), which won the Pulitzer Prize for history in 1928. A third volume with the subtitle *The Beginnings of Critical Realism in America*, incomplete at his death, was edited by E.H. Eby and was published in 1930. Parrington, a Jeffersonian liberal, objected to aestheticism and pedantry, emphasized economic influences, and defined literature as any writing successfully presenting important ideas or experiences. Notwithstanding objections to his political liberalism, his economic determinism, and his summary literary judgments of such writers as Poe and Henry James, his work became an important landmark in U.S. literary history. He also wrote *The Connecticut Wits* (1926) and *Sinclair Lewis, Our Own Diogenes* (1927).

parrot, any bird of the family Psittacidae, order Psittaciformes.

Classification of psittaciform birds is problematic; the entire group is under frequent taxonomic review. Nomenclature is vexed by

Rainbow lorikeet (*Trichoglossus haematodus*)
Bruce Coleman Ltd.

inaccurate use of scientific names by aviculturists and dealers and by vague application of traditional popular group names. There are about 300 species distributed in approximately 75 to 80 genera and 6 subfamilies, as follows:

Strigopinae, comprising the owl parrot, *Strigops habroptilus*, a rare New Zealand bird once thought extinct, survives as a scant population on South Island.

Nestorinae, two species in the genus *Nestor*. The kea, *N. notabilis*, occasionally attacks sheep to get at the fat around the kidneys. The kaka, *N. meridionalis*, a gentler forest bird, is often kept as a pet. Both are from New Zealand.

Loriinae, about 60 species in 15 genera; Australia, New Guinea, and many Pacific islands. These are the lories (with short tails) and lorikeets (with longer, pointed tails). All have a slender, wavy-edged beak and a brush-tipped tongue for extracting nectar from flowers and juices from fruits.

Kea (*Nestor notabilis*)
M. F. Soper—Bruce Coleman Inc.

Micropsittinae, six species in the genus *Micropsitta*, on New Guinea and nearby islands. These are the pygmy parrots, smallest members of the family. They live in forests, where they live on insects and fungi.

Cacatuinae, about 17 species in 5 genera; Australia, New Guinea, and nearby islands. The group includes the large cockatoo (*q.v.*) species and the cockatiel, *Nymphicus hollandicus*, a smaller bird. They are crested and have heavy beaks for cracking nuts.

Psittacinae, about 220 species in 60 genera; worldwide in warm regions. In this varied assemblage the tongue is blunt; the birds eat seeds, buds, and some fruit and insects. Many members of the subfamily are known simply as parrots but some have group names (*see* conure; lovebird; macaw; parakeet).

Among all the psittaciform birds, the gray parrot, *Psittacus erithacus*, of Africa is unsurpassed as a talker; the male may perfectly echo human speech. Captive birds are alert and, for a parrot, relatively good-tempered. Individuals are said to have lived 80 years. About 33 centimetres (13 inches) long, the bird is light gray except for its squared, red tail and bare, whitish face; sexes look alike. Common in the rain forest, gray parrots eat fruits and seeds; they damage crops but are important propagators of the oil palm.

Equally good as mimics are the Amazon parrots. The 26 species of *Amazona*—often simply called parrots—are chunky birds, mostly 25 to 40 centimetres (10 to 16 inches) long, with slightly erectile crown feathers and a rather short, squared tail. Their predominantly green plumage is marked with other bright colours, chiefly on the upper parts; sexes look alike. Amazon parrots live in rain forests from Mexico to northern South America. They are difficult to breed and may be aggressive as well as squawky.

Common in aviaries is the blue-fronted Amazon, *A. aestiva*, of Brazil, which has a blue forehead, yellow or blue crown, yellow face, and red shoulders. *A. ochrocephala*, of Mexico and from Ecuador and Brazil, has some yellow on head and neck, a red wing patch, and yellow tail tip.

Other remarkable parrots include the caiques, *Pionites* species, small, short-tailed South American birds similar to conures in build and habits.

The night parrot (or night parakeet), *Geopsittacus occidentalis*, a nearly extinct Australian bird, feeds at night on spinifex grass seeds and dozes under a tussock by day. Its nest, in a bush, is a twig platform entered by a tunnel. Equally unusual is the ground parrot (or ground parakeet), *Pezoporus wallicus*, rare and local in wastelands of coastal southern Australia and western Tasmania. Formerly hunted with dogs, it runs in the grass, flushes like a quail, and makes a sudden deceptive pitch. It eats seeds and insects; its nest is a leaf-lined depression under a bush.

Parrot is alternatively the name of birds described under other names. Thus, the Australian gray parrot is a cockatoo; the burrowing parrot, a conure; the cockatoo parrot, the cockatiel; the owl parrot, the kakapo. For sea parrot (not a psittacid), *see* puffin. *Major ref.* **15**:138b; illus.

- counting ability study **10**:743h
- foot adaptation for climbing **11**:22a
- movement repertory fixity **2**:805g
- pet ownership inconveniences **14**:150e
- protective coloration mechanisms **4**:928e
- psittacosis and disease transmission **9**:539a

parrotbill, or CROW-TIT, any of 14 species of the songbird family Panuridae (order Passeriformes) that have a deep and compressed bill like a parrot's. They occur in brushy grasslands of central and eastern Asia. A typical species is Gould's parrotbill (*Paradoxornis flavirostris*); 18 centimetres (7 inches) long, it is brown above and white below, with a heavy-looking head and black markings around the eyes and in the ear region. Some of the smaller species, formerly separated as *Suthora*, are brightly coloured; an example is the 11-centimetre (4½-inch) vinous-throated parrotbill (*P. webbiana*), a garden bird in Chinese cities.

Vinous-throated parrotbill (*Paradoxornis webbiana*)
Painting by H. Douglas Pratt

- classification and general features **13**:1061a

parrot fever: *see* psittacosis.

parrot fish, any of about 80 species of fishes of the family Scaridae (order Perciformes) found on tropical reefs. Parrot fishes are elongated, usually rather blunt headed and deep bodied, and often very brightly coloured. They have large scales and a characteristic birdlike beak formed by the fused teeth of the jaws. The beak is used to scrape algae from coral reefs and is strong enough to leave noticeable scars in the coral. The fish grind their food and bits of coral with platelike teeth in their throats.

Parrot fishes range to a length of about 1.2 metres (4 feet) and weight of about 20 kilograms (45 pounds). They are variable in colour, the male of a species often differing considerably from the female, and the young may differ from the adult.

Parrot fishes are edible but are not, as a group, of great economic importance. The surf, or rivulated, parrot fish (*Callyodon fasciatus*) is an Indo-Pacific representative of the family; it grows to 46 centimetres (18 inches)

Parrot fish (*Calotomus*)
Douglas Faulkner

or more and the male is green and orange or red, the female blue and yellow. Atlantic species include the rainbow parrot fish, which grows to about 90 centimetres (35½ inches) and is bright orange and green with a blue beak, and the queen parrot fish (*Scarus vetula*), which grows to about 50 centimetres (19¾ inches) and is blue with green, red, and orange if male but reddish or purplish with a white stripe if female.

- classification and general features **14**:54g
- migration and methods of navigation **12**:183f
- teeth and feeding **7**:334c

Parrott, Robert Parker (b. Oct. 5, 1804, Lee, N.H.—d. Dec. 24, 1877, Cold Spring, N.Y.), inventor who developed the rifled cannon known as the Parrott gun, the most formidable cannon of its time. Parrott was graduated from the U.S. Military Academy, West Point, N.Y., in 1824 but resigned from the army in 1836 to become superintendent of the West Point Foundry. In 1861 he patented both a method of building stronger cannon by shrinking bands of wrought iron around a cast breech and a projectile suitable for muzzle-loading rifled cannon. The projectile had an encircling brass ring that expanded upon firing to fit the rifling grooves of the barrel. Parrott guns were widely used on land and at sea during the U.S. Civil War.

Parrsboro, town, Cumberland county, western Nova Scotia, Canada, on the north shore of Minas Basin. Named after John Parr, former governor of Nova Scotia, the town is a lumber-, pulp-, and coal-shipping port and resort centre. Industries include shipbuilding, fishing, and the manufacture of furniture. Amethysts and other semiprecious stones are found in the vicinity. Inc. 1889. Pop. (1971) 1,807.
45°24′ N, 64°20′ W

Parry, Sir (Charles) Hubert (Hastings) (b. Feb. 27, 1848, Bournemouth, Hampshire —d. Oct. 7, 1918, Rustington, Sussex), composer, writer, and teacher, influential in the revival of English music at the end of the 19th century. While at Eton, where he studied composition, he took the bachelor of music degree from Oxford (1867). Among his later teachers, the pianist Edward Dannreuther particularly influenced him.

Sir Hubert Parry, detail of a chalk drawing by W. Rothenstein, *c.* 1897; in the National Portrait Gallery, London
By courtesy of the National Portrait Gallery, London

Parry's *Scenes from Prometheus Unbound* (1880) was the first of a series of choral works that showed his gift for the massive effects that characterized English music of the rest of the 19th century. Among his works are *Blest Pair of Sirens* (1887) for chorus and orchestra; the oratorios *Judith* (1888), *Job* (1892), and *King Saul* (1894); and his *Songs of Farewell* (1916–18). His unison song "Jerusalem" (1916), a setting of words from William Blake's *Milton*, became almost a second national anthem during and after World War I. His other works include five symphonies, *Symphonic Variations*, chorale preludes for organ, motets, and many songs.

In 1883 Parry was appointed choragus (festival conductor) of Oxford and joined the staff of the Royal College of Music, London, becoming its director in 1894. In 1900 he became professor of music at Oxford. He was knighted in 1898 and created a baronet in 1903. His writings on music include *Studies of Great Composers* (1886), *The Evolution of the Art of Music* (1896), *Johann Sebastian Bach* (1909), and *Style in Musical Art* (1911).

- anthem composing principles **4**:445a

Parry, Milman (1902–35), U.S. scholar noted for his studies of Homer.

- Homeric scholarship in oral tradition **8**:1019c

Parry, Sir William Edward (1790–1855), English rear admiral and Arctic explorer who repeatedly attempted, without success, to discover the Northwest Passage to the Orient.

Parry Island (Cook Islands): *see* Mauke.

Parry Islands, archipelago in Franklin District, Northwest Territories, Canada, part of the Queen Elizabeth Islands, in the Arctic Ocean, south and west of Ellesmere Island. Major islands are Devon, Cornwallis, Bathurst, Melville, and Prince Patrick (*qq.v.*).
75°30′ N, 106°00′ W

- map, Canada **3**:716

Parry Sound, town, seat of Parry Sound District, southeastern Ontario, Canada, on the east shore of Georgian Bay of Lake Huron, at the mouth of the Seguin River. Named in honour of the Arctic explorer Sir William Parry, the town was founded in the mid-19th century by W.H. Beatty, a British land surveyor. Its deepwater harbour on landlocked Parry Sound and its position 120 mi (190 km) north of Toronto on two transcontinental railroads and the Trans-Canada Highway have fostered the town's development as a merchandising, distributing, and shipping centre for the surrounding lumbering and mining region. A gateway to the Thirty Thousand Islands of Georgian Bay (*q.v.*), Parry Sound is a popular summer resort. Inc. 1888. Pop. (1971) 5,842.
45°21′ N, 80°02′ W

- map, Canada **3**:717

Parsa (ancient city of Persia): *see* Persepolis.

Parsa (ancient region of Persia): *see* Persis.

parsec, an astronomical unit of distance, equal to 3.262 light-years, 206,265 astronomical units, 3.0856×10^{13} kilometres, or 1.917×10^{13} miles. It is defined as the distance at which the radius of the Earth's orbit sub-

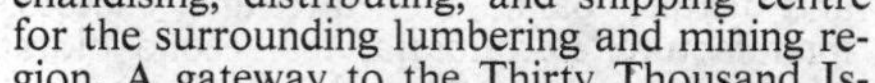

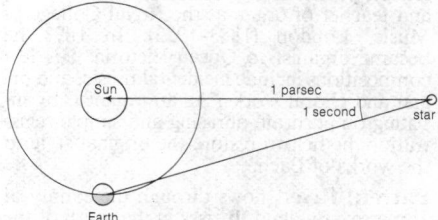

Parsec. The angle shown is actually much greater than one second (1″) of arc.
From *Dictionary of Astronomical Terms* by Ake Wallenquist, translated and edited by Sune Engelbrekson. Copyright © 1966 by Sune Engelbrekson. Reproduced by permission of Doubleday & Company, Inc.

tends an angle of one second of arc; thus a star at a distance of one parsec would show a stellar parallax of one second, and the distance of an object in parsecs is the reciprocal of its parallax in seconds of arc.
·parallax unit and distance equivalent **13**:996a
·stellar distance measurement **2**:250b
·weights and measures, table 5 **19**:734

Parseeism: *see* Zoroastrianism and Parsiism.

Parseval's formula, also called PARSEVAL'S EQUALITY or PARSEVAL'S THEOREM, in mathematics, an expression of the integral of the square of a function that can be represented by a Fourier series: the integral may be rendered as the sum of the squares of the Fourier coefficients. The theorem has numerous corollaries, one of which amounts to a proof that the energy transported by electromagnetic radiation must equal the sum of the energies of the component waves.
·Fourier analysis fundamentals **1**:742f
·real analysis principles **1**:779f

Parsifal, opera in three acts by Richard Wagner, with libretto by the composer, based on the epic poem *Parzival* (*c.* 1200–10) by Wolfram von Eschenbach. The opera was first performed on July 26, 1882, at Bayreuth.
·ethical tone of Wagnerian aesthetic **13**:588e
·harmony undermined by chromaticism **8**:653f
·personal and religious symbolism **19**:520a

Parsiism: *see* Zoroastrianism and Parsiism.

parsimony, law of: *see* Ockham's razor.

pars intercerebralis, in insect anatomy, group of cell bodies of neurosecretory neurons in the brain.
·neurosecretory system function **6**:846a

pars intermedia, in anatomy, the tissue between the anterior and posterior lobes of the pituitary gland.
·endocrine system interrelationships **6**:839h; illus. 840
·hormone production and neural control **6**:810a; table 801
·hormone secretion **8**:1074h; illus. 1075

Parsippany–Troy Hills, township, Morris County, northeastern New Jersey, U.S., extending eastward from the Appalachian hills to the Passaic River swamps.

Early settlers of the site were the missionaries Abraham and Zackariah Baldwin; Zackariah's tombstone is in the old Parsippany Cemetery. Local iron-ore deposits attracted other settlers. About 1713 John Cobb established a forge at Forge Pond in Troy. In the mid-18th century, David and Samuel Ogden established the Boone Town Iron Work, the site of which is now covered by the Jersey City Reservoir. Historic houses of the township include Beverwyck (home of Lucas von Beverhoudt and a meeting place for George Washington and his aides) and the home of William Livingston, New Jersey's first governor. Parsippany, which has had more than 50 different spellings, is derived from Parsippanong, an Indian name for a local stream, meaning perhaps "the Place Where the Waters Rush Through." The name Troy appeared on pre-Revolutionary maps, but its origin is unknown. Originally, Parsippany and Troy Hills were included in Whippanong Township (renamed Hanover in 1740). They amalgamated and were incorporated in 1928 when Hanover Township was divided into smaller units. Mainly residential, the community has some light manufacturing including chemicals and cosmetics. Pop. (1980) 49,868.
40°52′ N, 74°26′ W

Parsis: *see* Zoroastrianism and Parsiism.

pars legitima, in Roman law, safeguard against disinheritance.
·inheritance law development **9**:587h

parsley (*Petroselinum crispum* or *Petroselinum sativum*), hardy biennial herbs of the family Apiaceae, or Umbelliferae, native to Mediterranean lands. Parsley leaves were used by the ancient Greeks and Romans as a flavouring and garnish for foods. The compound leaves—deep green, tender, and curled or deeply frilled—that develop in a cluster the first season of growth are used fresh or dried today, the pleasant, mildly aromatic flavour being popular in fish, meats, soups, sauces, and salads.

Parsley is often the principal ingredient of *bouquet garni* and *fines herbes*.

In the second season of growth, seed stalks rise about three feet (one metre) tall and are topped by compound umbels of small, greenish-yellow flowers followed by tiny fruits, or seeds, similar to those of a carrot but without spines. Parsley seedlings are small and weak; they emerge with difficulty from heavy, crusty soils.

Parsley contains less than 0.5 percent essential oil, the principal component of which is

Parsley (*Petroselinum crispum*)
Shunji Watari—EB Inc.

the pungent, oily, green liquid called apiol, $C_{12}H_{14}O_4$.

Hamburg parsley, or turnip-rooted parsley (*P. crispum* var. *tuberosum*), is grown for its large, white, parsnip-like root, popular in Europe.
·spice use, region, and demand, tables 1 and 2 **17**:504
·vegetable history, classification, and cultivation **19**:43a; tables 1, 2, and 4

parsley piert (*Aphanes arvensis*), a small annual herb of the rose family (Rosaceae) native to Europe. It grows to a height of 5 to 20

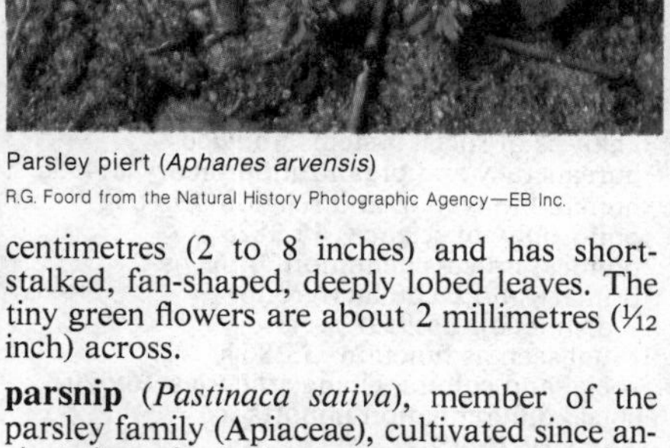

Parsley piert (*Aphanes arvensis*)
R.G. Foord from the Natural History Photographic Agency—EB Inc.

centimetres (2 to 8 inches) and has short-stalked, fan-shaped, deeply lobed leaves. The tiny green flowers are about 2 millimetres (1⁄12 inch) across.

parsnip (*Pastinaca sativa*), member of the parsley family (Apiaceae), cultivated since ancient times for its large, tapering, fleshy white root, edible and with a distinctive flavour. The root is found on roadsides and in open places in Great Britain and throughout Europe and temperate Asia. It was introduced in the Americas early in the 17th century and has become extensively naturalized in North America.

Parsnip seed is sown in the spring, thinly in

Parsnip (*Pastinaca sativa*)
G.R. Roberts

rows about a half metre apart, and the plants are thinned to stand five to seven centimetres (two to three inches) apart in the row. At the end of summer the solids of the root consist largely of starch, but a period of low temperature changes much of the starch to sugar. The root is hardy and not damaged by hard freezing of the soil. It is sweet in flavour and is usually served as a cooked vegetable.
·history, classification, and cultivation **19**:43c

Parsons, city, Labette County, southeastern Kansas, U.S. Founded in 1870, Parsons developed as a railroad division point for the Missouri–Kansas–Texas Railroad. During World War I the population reached 18,000, but it declined when labour disputes caused the railroad to relocate its repair shops.

The city is now a shipping centre for grain, dairy products, and livestock, and there is diversified industry. The Kansas Army Ammunition Plant is located there. Neosho County State Lake and Neosho Waterfowl Refuge are nearby. Inc. 1871. Pop. (1980) 12,898.
37°20′ N, 95°16′ W
·map, United States **18**:909

Parsons, Sir Charles Algernon (b. June 13, 1854, London—d. Feb. 11, 1931, Kingston, Jamaica), engineer whose invention of a multi-stage steam turbine revolutionized marine propulsion. He entered the Armstrong engineering works at Newcastle upon Tyne in 1877. In 1889, after working for several other companies, Parsons established his own works at Newcastle for the manufacture of steam turbines, dynamos, and other electrical apparatus.

The turbine Parsons invented in 1884 utilized several stages in series; in each stage the expansion of the steam was restricted to that extent that allowed the greatest extraction of kinetic energy without causing the turbine blades to overspeed. Parsons' turbine was fitted with a condenser in 1891 for use in electric generating stations, and in 1897 it was successfully applied to marine propulsion in the "Turbinia," a ship that attained a speed of 34½ knots, extraordinary for the time. The turbine was soon used in warships and other steamers.

In addition to the chairmanship of C.A. Parsons and Company, Parsons held directorial positions on the boards of several other electrical supply and engineering companies. He was made a fellow of the Royal Society (1898), was awarded the Royal Society's Rumford Medal (1902), and was president of the Institute of Marine Engineers (1905–06) and of the British Association (1919–20). He was knighted in 1911 and given the Order of Merit in 1927.

In addition to his turbine, Parsons invented a mechanical reducing gear, which, when placed between the turbine and a screw propeller, greatly improved the efficiency of both. He also invented nonskid automobile chains. A collection of his scientific papers and addresses was published posthumously in 1934.

·steamship engine development **16**:680f
·steam turbine development **18**:766f; illus.
·steam turbine invention **18**:39h

Parsons, Elsie (Worthington) Clews (b. Nov. 27, 1875, New York City—d. Dec. 19, 1941, New York City), sociologist and anthropologist whose studies of the Pueblo and other Indians of the southwestern United States remain standard references.

After receiving her Ph.D. in sociology from Columbia University (1899), Elsie Parsons taught for several years at Barnard College, New York City. Her earlier writings reflect concern over restrictions imposed on women in many cultures and periods. *The Old-Fashioned Woman* (1913), containing her views on post-Victorian society, includes a discussion of sexual relations. Since the subject matter was scandalous at the time, she published the work under the pseudonym John Main. Though she advocated women's rights, her fundamental concern came to be the individual's right of expression.

After a visit to the American Southwest (1915), where she met the anthropologists Franz Boas and Pliny E. Goddard, Elsie Parsons began a 25-year career of field study and writing on the Indians of the Americas. She collected a vast amount of Pueblo data that led to useful and valid syntheses of knowledge, culminating in *Pueblo Indian Religion*, 2 vol. (1939). Her interest in all possible influences on Pueblo peoples led her to investigations among Indians of the Great Plains and of Mexico, Peru, Ecuador, and the Caribbean. The Zapotec Indians of the state of Oaxaca, in Mexico, were the subject of her widely acclaimed work *Mitla: Town of the Souls* (1936). The results of her Andean researches appeared in *Peguche, Canton of Otavalo* (1945). She also did considerable work on the folklore of New World black people.

She believed that professional anthropology was obliged to educate the public about its knowledge and insights so that laymen might better evaluate opinions channelled through mass communications. At the close of her career, she became the first woman to be elected president of the American Anthropological Association, but she did not live to deliver her inaugural address, which dealt with the abuse of anthropology to further racist schemes.

Parsons (PERSONS), **Robert** (b. June 24, 1546, Nether Stowey, Somerset—d. April 15, 1610, Rome), Jesuit who, with Cardinal William Allen, organized Roman Catholic resistance in England to the Protestant regime of Queen Elizabeth I. He favoured armed intervention by the continental Catholic powers as a means of restoring Catholicism in England, and he probably encouraged the numerous plots against the Queen's life.

Early in 1575 Parsons was forced to resign his teaching position at Oxford University because his sympathies lay with the proscribed Roman Catholic religion. He went to Rome and there, on July 4, 1575, entered the Society of Jesus. In 1580 Parsons and his colleague Edmund Campion re-entered England to minister to English Catholics.

After Campion's arrest in July 1581, Parsons returned to the Continent and was assigned by William Allen—an influential English Catholic living abroad—the task of directing from abroad the Jesuit mission to England. In 1588 he was sent to Spain, where he spent nearly nine years establishing seminaries for

Robert Parsons, engraving by an unknown artist, 1622

By courtesy of the trustees of the British Museum; photograph, J.R. Freeman & Co. Ltd.

English priests in Valladolid, Seville, and Madrid. He died at the English College in Rome.

Parsons wrote many incisive works. His *Christian Directorie* (1585) became a devotional classic.

·"School of Atheism" accusation of Raleigh **2**:261d

Parsons, Talcott (b. Dec. 13, 1902, Colorado Springs, Colo.—d. May 8, 1979, Munich, W.Ger.), influential sociologist. Parsons called himself an "incurable theorist," for his work was concerned with a general theoretical system for the analysis of society rather than with narrower empirical studies.

After receiving his B.A. from Amherst (Mass.) College in 1924, Parsons studied at the London School of Economics and at Heidelberg University, receiving his Ph.D. in 1927. He joined the faculty of Harvard University as an instructor in economics; he began to teach sociology in 1931, became full professor in 1944, and was appointed chairman of the new department of social relations in 1946, retiring in 1973. He served as president of the American Sociological Society in 1949.

In his first major work, *The Structure of Social Action* (1937), Parsons drew on elements from the works of several European writers (Alfred Marshall, Vilfredo Pareto, Émile Durkheim, and Max Weber) to develop a common systematic theory of social action based on a voluntaristic principle; *i.e.*, the choices among alternative values and actions must be at least partially free. In *The Social System* (1952) he turned his analysis to large-scale systems and the problems of social order, integration, and equilibrium (*see* social equilibrium). He advocated a structural-functional analysis; *i.e.*, a study of the ways in which the interrelated and interacting units that form the structures of a social system contribute to the development and maintenance of that system (*see* functionalism).

Other works by Parsons include *Essays in Sociological Theory* (rev. ed. 1954); *Structure and Process in Modern Societies* (1960); *Societies: Evolutionary and Comparative Perspectives* (1966); *Sociological Theory and Modern Society* (1968); and *Politics and Social Structure* (1969).

·analysis of social systems **16**:995c
·bureaucracy and organization theory **3**:495c
·human motivation and religion **15**:605g
·philosophy of science **16**:382a
·political process definition **14**:697g
·primary and secondary group distinction **16**:959f
·ritual seen as function **15**:864c
·social and cultural change theories **16**:920f
·social differentiation importance theory **16**:956e
·social structure theory emphasis **16**:992c

Parsons, William: *see* Rosse, William Parsons, 3rd earl of.

Parson's Cause, dispute involving Anglican clergy in colonial Virginia, arising (1755, 1758) when laws commuted clerical salaries, previously paid in tobacco, to currency at the rate of twopence a pound when tobacco was selling at sixpence a pound. A royal veto (1759) encouraged the clergy to sue for back pay. In the most publicized case (1763), Patrick Henry defended a Hanover County parish against a suit by the Rev. James Maury, assailing the crown interference and inducing the jury to return only one penny damages for the plaintiff. After a general twopenny act (1769) that reflected going rates, the clergy gave up their protest.

·American leadership arguments **18**:954c
·Patrick Henry's natural rights advocacy **8**:775g

Pārśvanātha (Sanskrit: "Lord Serpent"), or PARŚVA, 23rd Tīrthaṅkara (*q.v.*), or saint, of the present age, according to the Jaina religion of India. Pārśvanātha was the first Tīrthaṅkara for whom there is historical evidence, but what is known of his life is intricately interwoven with myth and legend. He is said to have preceded by about 250 years Mahāvīra, the most recent of the Tīrthaṅkaras, who died probably in 527 BC. Mahāvīra's parents followed the teachings of Pārśvanātha, and Mahāvīra himself is said to have joined the religious order founded by Pārśvanātha for some time. The four vows that Pārśvanātha made binding on members of his community (not to take life, not to steal, not to lie, not to own property) became, with the addition of the explicitly stated vow of celibacy introduced by Mahāvīra, the five great vows (*mahāvratas*) of later Jainism. Pārśvanātha allowed monks to wear an upper and lower garment, while Mahāvīra himself gave up clothing. The two sets of views were eventually reconciled, and the followers of Pārśvanātha were won over to Mahāvīra's reforms.

Pārśvanātha, stone sculpture from Shahdol district, Madhya Pradesh, India, c. 10th century; in a private collection

Pramod Chandra

The legends surrounding Pārśvanātha emphasize his association with serpents. His mother is said to have seen a black serpent crawling by her side before his birth, and in sculpture and painting he is always identified by a canopy of snake hoods shown over his head. According to accounts in the Jaina text the *Kalpa-sūtra*, Pārśvanātha once saved a family of serpents that had been trapped in a log in an ascetic's fire. The snake, later reborn as Dharaṇa, the lord of the underworld kingdom of *nāgas* (snakes), sheltered Pārśvanātha from a storm sent by an enemy demon.

·history of Jainism **10**:8b
·Mahāvīra's religious sources **11**:347d
·rule formulation in Jainism **12**:341c

Partai Nasional Indonesia: *see* Indonesian Nationalist Party.

Partāpgarh, also PARTĀBGARH, more correctly PRATĀPGARH, town in Chittorgarh district, Rājasthān state, India. Partāpgarh is an agricultural market centre, with handloom weaving and cotton-ginning industries. The town was founded in 1689 and was the capital of the former princely state of Partābgarh (founded in the 15th century), which became part of the state of Rājasthān in 1948. Historic monuments include a palace and several ancient Jain and Hindu temples. Partābgarh has one college affiliated with the University of Rājasthān. Pop. (1971) 17,402. 24°02′ N, 74°47′ E

Partāpgarh, also PARTĀBGARH, more correctly PRĀTAPGARH, district, Uttar Pradesh state, northern India. Part of the Ganges alluvial plain, it is 1,440 sq mi (3,730 sq km) in area and is bounded on the southwest by the Ganges River and drained by one of its tributaries, the Sai. The district is fertile and partially forested, although there are small, barren saline areas. Rice, barley, millets, and sugarcane are grown, and hemp and hides are produced. Salt, potassium nitrate, and limestone are mined. Belā, the district headquarters, lies on the Sai River at a junction of roads and rail lines. It is a trade centre for agricultural products. Pop. (1971) 1,422,707.
·aboriginal peoples habitat **15**:496d

Partatua, also spelled BARTATUA (fl. 7th century BC), ruler of the Scythians.
·Scythian Middle East empire **16**:438f

partbook, the usual form in which vocal or instrumental polyphonic music was handwritten or printed in the 15th and 16th centuries. Each partbook contained the notation of only one voice, or part. The parts of madrigals, however, were sometimes published crosswise on single sheets, which allowed each of the singers seated around a rectangular table to sing from his particular part. Most commonly there were four partbooks: *cantus* (also *discantus* or *superius*), *altus*, *tenor*, and *bassus;* additional parts were either indicated *quinta vox*, etc., or were subdivisions of one of the principal parts—*e.g.*, *cantus* I and *cantus* II.
·Japanese use as mnemonic device **12**:682e
·singing practice before modern printing **4**:448a

Partch, Harry (b. June 24, 1901, Oakland, Calif.—d. Sept. 3, 1974, San Diego), visionary and eclectic composer and instrument builder, largely self-taught, whose compositions are remarkable for the complexity of their scores (each instrument has its own characteristic notation, often involving 43 tones to each octave) and their employment of unique instruments of his invention. Partch's early works are mainly vocal, based on texts collected during his travels as a hobo during the Depression (*The Letter, a Depression Message from a Hobo Friend*, 1943; *8 Hitchhiker Inscriptions from a California Highway Railing*).

Later his interest in mythology and the occult led him to the magical sounds of common materials such as light bulbs and bowls. Instruments such as the boo (bamboo marimba, 1955–56), marimba eroica (1951–55, the largest plank 8 feet [2.4 metres] long), cloud-chamber bowls, mazda marimba, and many others resulted; some of these were exhibited at the San Francisco Museum of Art (1966) and at the Whitney Museum of American Art in New York.

Typical of his works of the 1950s are *Oedipus* (1951; Partch's first large dramatic work), the theatre pieces *Plectra and Percussion Dances* (1952), the dance satire *The Bewitched* (1955), and the filmtrack of *Windsong* (1958). The enormous suite *And on the Seventh Day Petals Fell on Petaluma* (1963–64, revised 1966) comprises 23 one-minute duets and trios among 20 instruments, followed (by means of electronic dubbing) by 10 quartets and quintets and a final septet. The traditional process of development is ignored; musical ideas are simply stated, then abandoned.

Later Partch was involved with "tactile" theatre pieces, which have the nature of rituals. In 1949 he summarized his esoteric theories in a book, *The Genesis of a Music*. In 1953 he began issuing his own recordings, and in 1966 he won an award from the National Institute of Arts and Letters.
·scale of 43 tones **12**:748f

Parteciaco, Agnello, also spelled ANGELO PARTECIPAZIO (d. 827, Venice), doge of Venice, founder of a dynasty that produced seven doges between 810 and 942, as well as many bishops and church officials.

Agnello, opposing a faction that had placed Venice under the control of Charlemagne's son Pepin, Frankish king of Italy, moved the government from the island of Malamocco (now Lido) to its present site on the Rialto group of islands, where political independence could be more easily maintained. He undertook the building of many bridges connecting the islands and began the construction of the first Doges' Palace. A merchant as well as a statesman, he obtained important commercial privileges from the Byzantine emperors Leo V the Armenian and Michael II. He was succeeded by his sons Giustiniano and Giovanni I. Giustiniano is known to economic historians because of his will, which contained large bequests of pepper and other spices, demonstrating that Venice was already engaged in large-scale trade with the Levant in the early 9th century. In 828, during Giustiniano's reign, the remains of St. Mark were smuggled out of Alexandria, Egypt, and the building of a basilica was begun on the site of the present St. Mark's to house the relics. During the rule of Orso I (864–881), many reforms were accomplished, including a reorganization of the national church.

Partenkirchen (West Germany): *see* Garmisch-Partenkirchen.

parterre, the division of garden beds in such a way that the pattern is itself an ornament. It is a sophisticated development of the knot garden, a medieval form of bed in which various types of plant were separated from each other by dwarf hedges of box, thrift, or any low-growing controllable hardy plant. As the patterned area became of greater importance in the 16th century, it became necessary to make it more permanent and precise than was possible with plants. The hedges were replaced by wooden or leaden shapes or by lines of shells or coal, and the areas between were filled with coloured sand or stone chips. The design and making of parterres was a principal gardening skill in the late 17th century, and writers distinguished many sorts, one of which was a plain bowling green of turf. At the end of the 16th century, the English philosopher Francis Bacon was the first of many to complain of the artificiality of these gardens, and, with the advent of the *jardin anglais* (*q.v.*) in the 18th century, the elaborate parterre disappeared until the 19th century, when it returned in the form of "carpet-bedding."

Sixteenth-century parterre, Villa Lante, Bagnaia, Italy
Peter Coats

parterre de broderie (garden design): *see* broderie.

Parthaunisa (ancient Parthian city): *see* Nisa.

Parthenium argentatum (plant): *see* guayule.

Parthenius of Nicaea (fl. 1st century BC, Rome), Greek poet and grammarian, described as the "last of the Alexandrians."

Born in Nicaea (now İznik, Tur.), Parthenius was captured in the third Mithriadatic war and taken to Italy, where he became Virgil's teacher in Greek. His collection of 36 love stories made for the poet Cornelius Gallus has survived, and fragments from two funeral poems, one on his wife Arete, have come to light in papyri. He also wrote an encomium of the same lady in three books. His poems were favourite reading of the emperors Tiberius and Hadrian.

parthenocarpy, development of fruit without fertilization. The fruit resembles a normally produced fruit but is seedless. Varieties of pineapple, banana, cucumber, grape, orange, grapefruit, persimmon, and breadfruit exemplify naturally occurring parthenocarpy. Seedless parthenocarpic fruit can be induced in nonparthenocarpic varieties and in naturally parthenocarpic varieties out of season by a type of artificial pollination with dead or altered pollen or by pollen from a different type of plant. The application of synthetic growth substances in paste form, by injection or by spraying, also causes parthenocarpic development. Many new varieties of fruit have been produced in this manner. *Major ref.* **15**:725d
·persimmon fruit production features **6**:175a
·seed and fruit development **16**:481e

Parthenocissus quinquefolia (plant): *see* Virginia creeper.

Parthenocissus tricuspidata (plant): *see* Boston ivy.

parthenogenesis, biological reproduction that involves development of a female (rarely a male) gamete (sex cell) without fertilization. It occurs commonly among lower plants and invertebrate animals, particularly rotifers, aphids, ants, wasps, and bees. An egg produced parthenogenetically may be haploid (*i.e.*, with one set of dissimilar chromosomes) or diploid (*i.e.*, with a paired set of chromosomes). *Major ref.* **15**:706e
·aphid reproduction and life cycle **8**:1038c; illus.
·aphid sex distribution factors **14**:826g
·branchiopod reproduction variations **3**:114e
·earthworms and allies **1**:929e
·honeybee reproductive behaviour **2**:792e

·insect reproduction types **9**:612e
·lizard reproduction and hybridization **16**:283g
·orthopteran species with females only **13**:744d
·plant reproductive cycle variations **15**:724e
·reproduction and egg activation **7**:254h
·reproductive process in aphids **15**:677h
·seasonal appearance in Daphnia **16**:587b
·sex determination and artificial causes **16**:592b
·tick reproduction without males **1**:20c
·variant types in Hymenoptera **9**:127d

Parthenon, the chief temple of the Greek goddess Athena on the hill of the Acropolis at Athens. Built in the mid-5th century BC, it is generally considered to be the culmination of the Doric order, the simplest of the three classical Greek architectural orders, or systems of proportion and decoration. The name Parthenon refers to the cult of Athena Parthenos (Athena the Virgin) that was associated with the temple.

Parthenon, on the Acropolis, Athens, by Ictinus and Callicrates, 447–432 BC
Alison Frantz

Directed by the Athenian statesman Pericles, the Parthenon was built by the architects Ictinus and Callicrates under the supervision of the sculptor Phidias. Work began in 447 BC, and the building itself was completed by 438 BC. The same year a great gold and ivory statue of Athena, made by Phidias for the interior, was dedicated. Work on the exterior carvings and decoration of the building continued until 432 BC.

Although the Parthenon has suffered damage over the centuries, including the loss of most of its sculpture, its basic structure has remained intact. It is a rectangular white marble building in the Doric style. A colonnade of fluted, baseless columns with square capitals stands on a three-stepped base and supports an entablature, or roof structure, consisting of a plain architrave, or band of stone; a frieze of alternating triglyphs (vertically grooved blocks) and metopes (plain blocks with relief sculpture, now partly removed); and, at the east and west ends, a low triangular pediment, also with relief sculpture (now mostly removed). The colonnade, consisting of 8 columns on the east and west and 17 on the north and south, encloses a walled interior rectangular chamber, or cella, originally divided into three aisles by two smaller Doric colonnades closed at the west end just behind the great cult statue. The only light came through the east doorway, except for some that might have filtered through the marble tiles in the roof and ceiling. Behind the cella, but not originally connected with it, is a smaller, square chamber entered from the west. The east and west ends of the interior of the building are each faced by a portico of six columns. Measured by the top step of the base, the building is 101.34 feet (30.89 metres) wide and 228.14 feet (69.54 metres) long.

The Parthenon embodies an extraordinary number of architectural refinements, which combine to give a plastic, sculptural appearance to the building. Among them are an upward curvature of the base along the ends and repeated in the entablature; an imperceptible, delicate convexity (entasis) of the columns as they diminish in diameter toward the top; and a thickening of the four corner columns to counteract the thinning effect of being seen at certain angles against the sky.

The sculpture decorating the Parthenon rivalled its architecture in careful harmony. The metopes over the outer colonnade were carved in high relief and represented, on the east, a battle between gods and giants; on the south, Greeks and centaurs; on the west, probably Greeks and Amazons. Those on the north are almost all lost. The continuous, low-relief frieze around the top of the cella wall, representing the annual Panathenaic procession of citizens honouring Athena, culminated on the east end with a priest and priestess of Athena flanked by two groups of seated gods. The pediment groups, carved in the round, show, on the east, the birth of Athena and, on the west, her contest with the sea-god Poseidon for domination of the region around Athens. The entire work is a marvel of composition and clarity, which was further enhanced by colour and bronze accessories.

The Parthenon remained essentially intact until the 5th century AD, when Phidias' colossal statue was removed and the temple transformed into a Christian church; by the 7th century, certain structural alterations in the inner portion had also been made. The Turks, after their capture of Athens in 1458, adopted the Parthenon as a mosque, without material change except for the raising of a minaret at the southwest corner. During the bombardment of the Acropolis in 1687 by Venetians fighting the Turks, a powder magazine located in the temple blew up, destroying the centre of the building. In 1801–03, a large part of the sculpture that remained was removed, with Turkish permission, by the English nobleman Lord Elgin and sold in 1816 to the British Museum (London). Other sculptures from the Parthenon are now in the Louvre, in Copenhagen, and elsewhere, but many are still in Athens.
·building uses **2**:58g
·history and architecture **2**:262h *passim* to 266f
·mythological motifs in sculpture **8**:406c
·style types and concept of Classicism **2**:131d
·visual art of Classical Greece **19**:293g

Parthenopean Republic, short-lived state established in Naples with the aid of French Revolutionary forces in 1799.
·French Revolution satellite countries **7**:724a
·Napoleonic expansion map **6**:1101
·Nelson's conquest and reprisals **12**:948h
·origins and administration **9**:1156d

Parthenope investigatoris: *see* spider crab.

Parthia, ancient land corresponding roughly to the modern region of Khorāsān in Iran; the term is sometimes also used in reference to the Parthian Empire (247 BC–AD 224). The first certain occurrence of the name is as Parthava in the Bīsitūn inscription (*c.* 520 BC) of the Achaemenian king Darius I, but Parthava may be only a dialectal variation of the name Parsa (Persian). Nothing is known of the history of Parthia while it was part of a satrapy of the Achaemenian Empire. It was joined to Hyrcania (present Gorgān, Iran) in the time of Alexander the Great, and the two remained together as a province of the Seleucid kingdom. During the reigns of Seleucus I (312–281 BC) and Antiochus I Soter (281–261) the Parni (Aparni) nomads probably moved from Central Asia into Parthia and seem to have adopted the speech of the Parthians and been absorbed into the settled population.

Traditionally, the first ruler of the Parthians and founder of the Parthian Empire, Arsaces I, was a governor under Diodotus, king of the Bactrian Greeks, who revolted and fled westward to establish his own rule. By 200 BC Arsaces' successors were firmly established along the southern shore of the Caspian Sea. Later, through the conquests of Mithradates I (reigned 171–138 BC) and Artabanus II (reigned 128–124 BC), all of the Iranian Plateau and the Tigris-Euphrates Valley came under Parthian control. The Parthians, however, were troubled by nomad attacks on their northeastern borders and also by the threat of Roman domination. Their most famous victory over Roman forces was at Carrhae (Harran) in 53 BC. Although one of their capitals, Ctesiphon, was later occupied by the Romans, the Parthians were successful in at least setting a limit to Roman expansion eastward.

The earliest Parthian capital was probably at Dara (modern Abivard); one of the later capitals was Hecatompylos, probably near modern Dāmghān. The empire was governed by a small Parthian aristocracy, which successfully made use of the social organizations established by the Seleucids and which tolerated the development of vassal kingdoms. Although not an inventive people, the Parthians' control of most of the trade routes between Asia and the Greco-Roman world brought them great wealth, which they used on their extensive building activities. The empire lacked tight internal control, however, and in AD 224 Ardashīr, a local ruler in southern Iran, revolted and established the Sāsānian Empire.
·Antiochus III territorial expansion **1**:993g
·Armenian and Roman invasions **18**:1041e
·clothing styles **5**:1019c
·design of towns **18**:1066h
·Greek conquests and Hellenistic kingdoms maps **8**:374
·historical development and territory **9**:841c; map 842
·inscription sources for study **9**:453d
·Iranian nomad and noble as detriment **9**:840b
·Marcus Aurelius and the Eastern wars **11**:492e
·Mesopotamian conquest and rule **11**:990b
·Roman foreign policy of Claudius I **4**:697a
·Roman rivalry over Syria **17**:950d
·Saka invasion and settlement **18**:792d
·Seleucid Kingdom relationship **16**:501g
·Tiberius' recovery of legion standards **18**:370b
·visual art history of Iran **19**:271g
·visual arts preservation and features **3**:1133f; illus. 1134
·war tactics used by Alexander the Great **19**:575a

Parthian language, Middle Iranian language spoken in the ancient province of Parthia (the northeastern corner of modern Iran); it was the official language of the Arsacid period (2nd century BC to 3rd century AD). Among the earliest records of the language are more than 2,000 ostraca (inscribed pottery fragments), largely records of wine deliveries dating from the 1st century BC, which were discovered in Soviet excavations (1949–58) at Nisa, an Arsacid capital near present-day Ashkhabad in the Turkmen S.S.R. Parthian is also attested by inscriptions of the first Sāsānian kings (224–303), which were accompanied by a Middle Persian version. Manichaean Parthian literature is a very rich source for the language and includes the outstanding hymn cycles of the poet Mar Ammo (second half of the 3rd century). Parthian script was derived from the Aramaic alphabet.
·Iranian linguistic relationships **9**:450g

partial (music): *see* overtone.

partial derivative, in mathematics, rate of change of a function of several variables with respect to changes in one only; that is, in the case when all variables except one are held constant. Given a function $f(x, y) = z$, the partial derivative of z with respect to x may be denoted by x_z, holding y constant. For example, if $z = 2x^2y + 3$, then $z_x = 4xy$ and $z_y = 2x^2$. Second partial derivatives and those of higher orders may also be taken.
·differential equation principles **5**:752d
·differential geometry principles **7**:1094c
·thermodynamic properties theory **18**:295b

partial differential equation, in mathematics, equation relating a function of several variables to its partial derivatives. A partial derivative of a function of several variables expresses how fast the function changes when one of its variables is changed, the others being held constant (*see* ordinary differential equation). The partial derivative of a function is again a function, and if $f(x, y)$ denotes the original function of the variables x and y, the partial derivative with respect to *x*—*i.e.*, when only *x* is allowed to vary—is written as $f_x(x, y)$, $\partial f/\partial x$, or $f_1(x, y)$, in which the numerical subscript corresponds to the position of the variable in the parentheses. The operation of finding a partial derivative can be applied to a function that is itself a partial derivative of another function to get what is called a second-order partial derivative, written as $f_{xy}(x, y)$, $\partial^2 f/\partial y \partial x$, or $f_{12}(x, y)$, in the case in which the partial derivative with respect to *y* of the function $f_x(x, y)$ is to be found. The order and degree of partial and ordinary differential equations are defined in the same way.

In general, partial differential equations are difficult to solve, but techniques have been developed for the simpler classes. Partial differential equations find their widest applicability in the science of physics. *Major ref.* **5**:752d

·deformation kinematics and tensors **5**:555g
·Fourier analysis fundamentals **1**:748g
·functional analysis fundamentals **1**:765c
·mathematics history from antiquity **11**:643e
·numerical analysis fundamentals **13**:391a
·physical theory formulations **14**:399c

partial pressure (physics): *see in* Dalton's law.

participation, in Platonic metaphysics, the notion that explains the being, or the existence, of the world in terms of the transcendent ideas. It is the relation between a particular (something that is in the world) and the Form that it exemplifies.

·antinomies of third man **12**:15h
·classification's ontological basis **4**:693h

particle, in grammar, a unit of speech that expresses some general aspect of meaning or indicates a function or relationship within a sentence, such as an article, preposition, or conjunction. In some languages, such as Chinese and Tibetan, particles constitute one of the major grammatical classes.

·Mandarin and Cantonese grammar features **16**:800h *passim* to 801h
·Tibetan postpositive use **16**:806a

particle, in physics, a body of negligible dimensions but definite mass. The particle is one of the basic concepts of classical mechanics, for which Newton's laws of motion were written. If a body does not rotate or if rotational effects can be neglected, the body can be treated as if all its mass were concentrated in a single particle at the centre of gravity of the body. If rotational effects cannot be neglected, the body must be treated as a system of particles comprising a rigid body, using extensions of Newton's equations. Whether a body should be treated as a particle or a rigid body depends on the dimensions of the body compared with the distances travelled and the nature of the paths traversed.

·differential equation of projectile motion **5**:739c
·gas theory origins **7**:918h
·mathematical concepts **14**:393c

particle accelerators: *see* accelerators, particle.

particle board, a wood product manufactured by gluing together flakes, shavings, or splinters.

·wood products, processes, and uses **19**:923e

particle physics, scientific discipline concerned with the origin, properties, and fate of fundamental, or subatomic, particles. *See* particles, subatomic.

·principles and research methods **14**:426b
·quantum theory and nuclear structure **11**:800b

particles, elementary: *see* particles, subatomic.

particles, subatomic **13**:1022, also called ELEMENTARY PARTICLES, the fundamental units of matter and energy.

TEXT ARTICLE covers:

Atomic structure and nuclear forces **13**:1022e
Negative energy states and quantum field theory 1023b
Yukawa mesons and strong interactions 1023g
Theoretical development 1025a
Dawn of a new age 1026b
Four basic forces 1026c
Four classes of particles 1027d
Conservation laws and quantum numbers 1027h
Spectroscopy of the hadrons: the quark model 1030h
Experiments 1032f
Relations between the interactions 1033g
Undiscovered particles 1035a

REFERENCES in other text articles:

·acceleration capabilities and processes **1**:23e
·atmospheric electron behaviour **2**:311f
·Atomism of Dalton **2**:350e
·big-bang cosmological model **18**:1008d
·biological effects of radiation **15**:378h
·biological hazard of accelerators **15**:383h
·cosmic ray composition and origin **5**:202g
·cosmological theory and quantum physics **12**:869d
·crystal defects and particle interaction **9**:806f
·electron properties **6**:665a
·fission product characterization **13**:304a
·fundamental interactions, symmetries, and conservation laws **5**:34e; table
·Heisenberg and indeterminacy principle **8**:745g *passim* to 746f
·interplanetary matter composition **9**:785h; table 786
·interstellar matter and absorption spectra **9**:790f
·magnetic field interactions **11**:317f
·magnetic moment and angular momentum **11**:305c
·Materialist theory of matter **11**:611b
·matter–antimatter production and reactions **11**:703c
·neutron discovery, decay, and reactions **12**:1070f
·nuclear fusion reaction types **13**:307e
·nuclear structure and properties **13**:334b
·Oppenheimer's early research **13**:602e
·photon discovery and properties **6**:653g
·physical constant measurement theory **5**:75g
·physics principles and research **14**:426b
·quantum theory development **11**:793b
·radiation detection methods **15**:392a
·radiation's particulate components **15**:399f
·rationalist causality and indeterminacy **15**:531f
·relativity theory applications **15**:587e
·Sun's ionized gases and radiation **17**:804e
·thermodynamic systems and properties **18**:313h
·Yang's study of parity violation **19**:1071g

RELATED ENTRIES in the *Ready Reference and Index: for*

classification of particles: see antiparticle; baryon; bootstrap hypothesis; boson; Eightfold Way; fermion; hadron; heavy ion; hyperfragment; hyperon; lepton; meson; resonance particle; strange particle
field particles: graviton; intermediate vector boson; photon; virtual particle; W-particle
specific particles: alpha particle; antideuteron; antineutron; antiproton; beta particle; deuteron; muon; neutrino; nucleon; positron; proton; quark; triton

particle theory: *see* corpuscular theory.

Parti Communiste Français (PCF), English FRENCH COMMUNIST PARTY, French branch of the international Communist movement, commanding about 20 percent of the electorate in France. Founded in 1920 by the left wing of the French Socialist Party, the PCF did not gain significant votes until 1936, when it affiliated with Léon Blum's leftist Popular Front coalition government. In 1945 the PCF won some 25 percent of the vote, and in 1946 it took part in the Fourth Republic's first government. After May 1947, when the Communists were dismissed from the Cabinet as a result of hardening political attitudes, the PCF did not participate in any administration, though it commanded a large representation in the National Assembly.

When Gen. Charles de Gaulle became president of the Fifth Republic in 1958, the PCF lost ground. In September 1965, the party lent its support to other left-wing parties to form the Fédération de la Gauche Démocrate et Socialiste (Federation of the Democratic and Socialist Left), which succeeded in keeping de Gaulle from an absolute majority in the first round of the 1965 election; it disbanded in 1968. In 1972 the PCF and the Socialist Party agreed upon a "common program of government," which included an undertaking to abide by the processes of democratic elections. The PCF in 1976 emphasized its commitment to a particularly French and democratic route to power.

Auxiliary organizations of the PCF are the Communist Youth Movement (Mouvement de la Jeunesse Communiste; MJC), the Union of French Communist Students (Union des Étudiants Communistes de France; UECF), and the Union of French Women (Union des Femmes Françaises; UFF). Controlled by Communist influence is the General Confederation of Labour (Confédération Générale du Travail; *q.v.*), the largest union organization in France.

·Corsican following **5**:193e
·formation, Blum's split, and policies **7**:673c
·French opposition parties **7**:605g
·ideological and organizational attempts **4**:1022h

Parti Communiste Indochinois (PCI): *see* Indochinese Communist Party.

Particular Baptists, church association absorbed in 1891 in the Baptist Union of Great Britain and Ireland (*q.v.*).

particulate radiation, radiation of subatomic particles.

·biological effects of radiation **15**:378g; table 379
·disease causation and symptoms **5**:853g
·industrial hazard prevention **16**:143b

Partido Acción Nacional, English NATIONAL ACTION PARTY, established 1939, chief minority political party in Mexico.

·ideology and success **12**:75d

Partido Acción Renovadora (PAR), English RENEWAL ACTION PARTY, minority political party of El Salvador.

·ideology shift in 1960s **3**:1113f

Partido Africano da Independência da Guiné e Cabo Verde (PAIGC), English AFRICAN PARTY FOR THE INDEPENDENCE OF GUINEA AND CAPE VERDE, political party founded in 1956 by African nationalists to work for the independence of Portuguese colonial territories.

·Portuguese Guinea reorganization claims **14**:876f

Partido Autonomista Nacional (PAN), English NATIONAL AUTONOMIST PARTY, alliance of Argentine political groups loyal to Pres. Julio Argentino Roca in his first term (1880–86). Dissension during Roca's second term (1898–1904), however, led to the alliance's demise.

·composition and support of Roca **1**:1147c

Partido Blanco (political party): *see* Partido Nacional.

Partido Comunista de Cuba (PCC), English COMMUNIST PARTY OF CUBA, the only political party permitted to function in Cuba under the constitution of 1976. Formed in 1925 by Cuban and non-Cuban, Moscow-trained Communists, the PCC supported the dictator Fulgencio Batista in the 1940s and '50s, though it was suppressed during 1954–59. In 1961 it merged with Fidel Castro's victorious 26th of July Movement and smaller revolutionary groups under the name Integrated Revolutionary Organizations (Organizaciones Revolucionarias Integradas). The latter was succeeded in 1963 by the Unified Party of the Socialist Revolution (Partido Unificado de la Revolución Socialista), which in turn was dissolved in 1965 and the new PCC formed. Its first congress was held in 1975.

·Cuban political parties **5**:354g

Partido de Conciliación Nacional (PCN), English NATIONAL CONCILIATION PARTY, in El Salvador, political party formed by a military junta in the early 1960s and in the late '70s still the country's dominant party.
· El Salvador's political parties **3**:1113e

Partido de la Izquierda Revolucionaria (PIR), English LEFT-WING REVOLUTIONARY PARTY, Marxist and largely pro-Soviet political party formed in Bolivia in the early 1940s and dissolved in 1950.
· establishment, duration, and dissolution **3**:12c

Partido de la Revolución Mexicana, original name of the Mexican political party now called the Partido Revolucionario Institucional (*q.v.*).

Partido del Orden, English PARTY OF ORDER, in Argentina, governing political party in the province of Buenos Aires during the 1820s.
· economic and political reforms **1**:1144e

Partido Demócrata Cristiano (Chile): *see* Christian Democratic Party.

Partido Nacional, English NATIONAL PARTY, Chilean right-wing coalition formed in 1965 after the rightist electoral losses in the 1965 elections.
· formation of right-wing coalition **4**:258f

Partido Nacional, also called PARTIDO BLANCO, English WHITE PARTY, one of the two major political parties of Uruguay.
· Uruguayan political factional disputes **18**:1098g
· Uruguay's political parties **18**:1097g

Partido Nacionalista, English NACIONALISTA (NATIONALIST) PARTY, one of the two principal political parties of the Philippines.
· 20th-century domination and duration **14**:243d *passim* to 244d

Partido Obrero de Unificación Marxista (POUM), English WORKER PARTY OF MARXIST UNIFICATION, in Spain, anti-Stalinist Socialist party prominent on the Republican side in the early stages of the Spanish Civil War.
· Barcelona rebellion **17**:441h

Partido Republicano Genuino, English GENUINE REPUBLICAN PARTY, in Bolivia, a political party formed in the 1920s by dissident members of the Republican Party.
· establishment and rise to power **3**:11f

Partido Revolucionario Institucional (PRI), English INSTITUTIONAL REVOLUTIONARY PARTY, leading political party of Mexico. It was founded in 1929 as the Partido de la Revolución Mexicana (National Revolutionary Party) and took its present name in 1946.
· founding and growth **12**:86e *passim* to 87g
· political dominance and ideology **12**:75c

Partido Revolucionario de Unificación Democrática (PRUD), English REVOLUTIONARY PARTY OF DEMOCRATIC UNIFICATION, in El Salvador, political group that dominated political life during the 1950s.
· political domination in 1950s **3**:1113c

Partido Unificado de la Revolución Socialista, the name for a short time for the political party now called the Partido Comunista de Cuba (*q.v.*).

Partidul Comunist Român (PCR), English COMMUNIST PARTY OF ROMANIA, founded in 1921, the only political party of Romania.
· Romanian political parties **15**:1053g

Parti du Peuple Algérien (PPA), English ALGERIAN PEOPLE'S PARTY, political party organized in 1937 by Messali Hadj, with a platform calling for Algerian independence from France. The PPA developed from an earlier movement that was originally Communist and then nationalist—the Étoile Nord-Africaine (North African Star)—formed in Paris *c.* 1924 and dissolved by the French government in 1937.

The PPA, organized by cells, soon gained a considerable following among Algerians in France and in Algeria itself. By 1941 it had nearly 3,000 members, especially among the poor and the working classes. In the same year the party was officially proscribed. The PPA then went underground until 1946, when Messali Hadj formed the Mouvement pour le Triomphe des Libertés Démocratiques (*q.v.*; Movement for the Triumph of Democratic Liberties), which officially absorbed the PPA in 1953.
· Algerian nationalist movements **13**:164d

Partie de campagne, Une, English A DAY IN THE COUNTRY (made 1936, released 1946), film by Jean Renoir.
· Renoir's impressionistic cinematography **15**:674a
· theme and techniques **12**:529d

Partij van de Arbeid, English LABOUR PARTY, one of the major political parties of The Netherlands, founded in 1946 and representing various social democratic, left-wing, and progressive Roman Catholics and Protestants
· postwar political groups **11**:154d.

parting, in metallurgy, method of separating silver from bullion or from doré (gold–silver bars) by placing them in a bath of hot, concentrated sulfuric acid or strong nitric acid to dissolve the silver. Since all gold ores contain some silver and silver ores some gold, the mixture of silver and gold must be purified and afterward parted. The silver forms water-soluble compounds, silver sulfate or silver nitrate, leaving a residue that is filtered off and treated for its gold content. The clear solution, containing the silver compounds, is treated with ferrous sulfate or copper or iron to precipitate the silver, which is then washed, dried, and melted down to give silver of 99.5 percent purity, or 995 fine.
· gold assay methods **8**:239d
· silver extraction processes **16**:777c

Partinico, town, Palermo province, northwestern Sicily, Italy, at the foot of Mt. Cesarò. Agriculture and wine production are the main local occupations. Partinico was the birthplace of a notorious bandit, Salvatore Giuliano. Pop. (1975 est.) mun., 26,177.
38°03′ N, 13°07′ E
· map, Italy **9**:1089

Parti Ouvrier, English WORKER PARTY, French Marxist political party founded by Jules Guesde.
· history and evolution **16**:967c

Parti Populaire Français, English FRENCH POPULAR PARTY, 20th-century Fascist group.
· Fascist organizations in France **7**:187h

Parti Populaire Syrien, French name of the Syrian Social Nationalist Party (*q.v.*).

Parti pour la Liberté et le Progrès, Flemish PARTIJ VOOR VRIJHEID EN VOORUITGANG, English PARTY OF FREEDOM AND PROGRESS, in Belgium, major political party of the 20th century.

Parti Républicain Radical et Radical-Socialiste, commonly referred to in English as RADICAL PARTY or RADICAL-SOCIALIST PARTY, in France, the oldest, least disciplined, and most amorphous of the political parties.

The first French "radical" party was active in the Revolution of 1848. In the 1870s, the more reformist wing of the Republican Party, led by Georges Clemenceau among others, became known as the Radicals. The party played an important part in administrations of the late 19th and early 20th centuries. In the 1930s the Radicals began to lose ground. Although they won control of the government in the 1932 election, the Socialist Party won the popular vote. In 1936 the Radicals were reduced to participation in the Socialist Party's coalition government, Léon Blum's Popular Front.

After World War II the Radicals' popularity further declined. In the 1940s and early '50s, they formed with other groups the Rassemblement des Gauches Républicaines (RGR; Assembly of Republican Leftists), which never won more than 11 percent of the vote in legislative elections. Until 1958, however, the Radicals played disproportionately important roles in the governments of the Fourth Republic, since party fragmentation in the National Assembly made the politically central Radical group important.

Under Gen. Charles de Gaulle's Fifth Republic, founded in 1958, the Radicals continued both to lose votes and to hold key political positions. In 1965 the Radicals supported François Mitterrand, the presidential candidate of the all-left Fédération de la Gauche Démocrate et Socialiste (Federation of the Democratic and Socialist Left). In the 1970s its share of votes cast continued to decline, though it was still represented in the government.
· French political parties **7**:605h
· role in French politics **7**:669c *passim* to 677g

Parti Rouge, English RED PARTY, radical party formed in Lower Canada (now Quebec) about 1849 and inspired primarily by the French-Canadian patriot Louis Joseph Papineau.

In general the Parti Rouge advocated a more democratic system of government, with a broadly based electorate, and the abolition of the old feudal laws that still survived in Quebec. It also opposed the political influence of the Roman Catholic clergy in French Canada.

In later years the party became more moderate, and in the 1860s it merged with the Liberal Party of Quebec. Sir Wilfrid Laurier, who later became prime minister of Canada, began his political career as a member.

Partisans, Serbo-Croatian PARTIZANI, Yugoslav guerrilla force led by Tito and his Communists in World War II against the Axis powers and the royalist resistance force, the Chetniks. The Partisans provoked seven enemy offensives, thus drawing large numbers of enemy forces from other Allied fronts; their final victory was achieved with the aid of the Soviet Union. During the war the Partisans held two political conferences (Bihać, November 1942; Jajce, November 1943) at which they established local and federal provisional governments for liberated areas; the network of Partisan-controlled local governments contributed to the Communists' political success after the war. The loyalty to Tito and the sense of nationalism developed among the Partisans during the war enabled Tito to withstand Stalin's political attacks in 1948.
· Balkan resistance movements **19**:985h
· Chetnik organization dispute **2**:636d

Parti Socialiste, English SOCIALIST PARTY, French Marxist party that supports a directed economy; it was particularly important under the Fourth Republic from 1946 to 1958.

Founded in 1905 as the Section Française de l'Internationale Ouvrière (SFIO), it grew quickly in the early years of the 20th century. The Russian Revolution of 1917, however, produced a crisis for the party, and in 1920 its left wing separated to form the Parti Communiste Français (PCF; French Communist Party). In 1936 the SFIO, then France's strongest party, played the central role in Léon Blum's Popular Front government.

In 1945 the SFIO won more than 20 percent of the vote in national elections and participated in a tripartite government with the PCF and the Christian Democratic Mouvement Républicain Populaire (MRP). Later, the SFIO took part in a government of parties supporting the constitution of the Fourth Republic against the attacks of the PCF and Gen. Charles de Gaulle's nationalist Rassemblement du Peuple Français (Assembly of the French People). The growth of other parties, however, cost the SFIO support, and after 1946 it usually won only about 15 percent of the vote.

The Socialist Party led a confused existence under de Gaulle's Fifth Republic, and dissent over whether to ally with parties to the left or to the right of the Socialists, including Gaullist parties and the PCF, caused party splits. In 1965 an all-left coalition, which included the PCF, pushed the presidential election into a second-round runoff between de Gaulle and the leftist candidate, François Mitterrand. In 1969 the SFIO became the Parti Socialiste.

A new Socialist–Communist alliance in 1972 was hailed as the most significant event for the French left since the split in 1920, and it nearly won the presidency for Mitterrand in 1974 (49.19 percent of the final vote). Later that year midterm elections gave substantial gains to the Socialists at the expense of the Communists, leading to friction that continued to develop until a near breakdown in 1977 and the alliance's failure to win a majority in the parliamentary elections of 1978. Though the largest and fastest growing political party in France, the Parti Socialiste suffered internal dissension in 1979 with a strong challenge to Mitterrand's leadership by Michel Rocard.

·Convention of François Mitterrand **7**:605h
·Corsica's radical legislative majority **5**:193f
·evolution and role **16**:972b
·formation and cabinet
  nonparticipation **7**:670a

Parti Socialiste Belge, Flemish BELGISCHE SOCIALISTISCHE PARTIJ, English BELGIAN SOCIALIST PARTY, one of Belgium's major political parties; it participated in several coalition governments in the 1950s and 1960s.

partita (music): *see* suite.

Partitas (published 1726–31), six keyboard works by Johann Sebastian Bach; also an alternative title for Bach's six sonatas for solo violin (*c.* 1720).

·harmonic contrast and modulation **8**:650c

partition, in heraldry, one of numerous divisions in a coat-of-arms.

·heraldic shield divisions **8**:788d; illus. 788

partition, in mathematics and logic, division of a set of objects into a family of subsets that are mutually exclusive and jointly exhaustive; that is, no element of the original set is present in more than one of the subsets, and all the subsets together contain all the members of the original set.

A related concept, central to the mathematical topics of combinatorics and number theory, is the partition of a positive integer; that is, the number of ways that an integer n can be expressed as the sum of k smaller integers. For example, the number of ways of representing the number 7 as the sum of 3 smaller whole numbers ($n = 7$, $k = 3$) is 4 ($5 + 1 + 1$, $4 + 2 + 1$, $3 + 3 + 1$, and $3 + 2 + 2$).

·algebraic structure theory **1**:520c
·classification and theory of domain **4**:691f
·combinatorics theory and method **4**:944d
  passim to 953e
·number theory principles **13**:366a
·probability theory and method **14**:1114d

partition function, in statistical mechanics, mathematical expression of the effect of the temperature upon the way the total energy of a physical system, such as a quantity of a gas, is distributed (partitioned) among the individual particles (*e.g.*, molecules) that comprise it. Alternatively, the partition function expresses the distribution of a population of particles among the discrete energy states available to them. *See also* distribution function.

·gas energy distribution **7**:918d

Partito Comunista Italiano (PCI), English ITALIAN COMMUNIST PARTY, Italy's second largest political party and western Europe's largest Communist party.

Dissidents of the Italian Socialist Party's extreme left wing founded the PCI in January 1921. The new party matured quickly, sending deputies to parliament before Benito Mussolini's Fascists outlawed all political parties in 1926. After that year, the PCI went underground to establish an organization that later proved important to the Italian Resistance.

After World War II, the PCI joined five other anti-Fascist parties in coalition governments until May 1947, when the Christian Democrat premier Alcide De Gasperi excluded both the PCI and the Partito Socialista Italiano (PSI) from a new government. The PCI's consistent success at the polls ensured that it would continue to influence Italy's political life. In particular, the Communists' ability to win votes away from the PSI's left wing affected the policies of that important party.

In 1956, when the revelation of Joseph Stalin's crimes was followed by the Soviet Union's suppression of the Hungarian revolt, PCI leader Palmiro Togliatti (*q.v.*) helped dissociate the party from the Soviet Union. After Togliatti's death in 1964, the PCI nearly split into "Russian" and "Italian" wings over this concept, but the secretary general from 1972, Enrico Berlinguer, kept Italy's second largest political party intact.

·ideological and organizational
  attempts **4**:1022h
·membership and opposition power **9**:1108c
·Milanese party strength and influence **12**:192d
·Socialist factional splintering **9**:1167g

Partito Liberale Italiano (PLI), English ITALIAN LIBERAL PARTY, Italian political party.

·origin and aims **9**:1108d

Partito Popolare Italiano (Italian political party, 1919–26): *see* Democrazia Cristiana.

Partito Repubblicano Italiano (PRI), English ITALIAN REPUBLICAN PARTY, anticlerical social reform party that began in the 19th century when radicals fought for a unified Italy under a republican form of government. Although it had only a small following in the years after World War II, its position in the centre of the Italian political spectrum enabled it to take part in many coalition governments.

·origin and affiliation **9**:1108d

Partito Socialista Democratico Italiano (PSDI), English ITALIAN SOCIAL DEMOCRATIC PARTY, anti-Communist reform party advocating economic planning and nationalization of some industries; as a centre party, it was able to join many Italian governments in the decades after World War II.

In early 1947, Socialists who opposed the Italian Socialist Party (Partito Socialista Italiano, PSI) for its cooperation with the Partito Comunista Italiano (Italian Communist Party, PCI) seceded to form the Partito Socialista dei Lavoratori Italiani (Socialist Party of Italian Workers, PSLI). In 1951 the PSLI and other anti-Communist Socialist groups founded the PSDI, which participated in centre governments after 1954.

As the PSI moved away from its Communist ally during the 1950s, its platform came to resemble that of the PSDI. In 1963 the PSI took part in government, and in October 1966 the PSDI rejoined under PSI's name. The reunion lasted only a short time; after the PCI's share of the vote increased to 26.9 percent in the 1968 parliamentary election, the question of a government including Communists arose. The former Social Democrats who opposed Communist participation left the PSI in July 1969 and formed the Unitary Socialist Party (PSU). The PSU took the name of Social Democrat again in the spring of 1970. *See also* International, Socialist.

·Italian political evolution **9**:1171f *passim* to
  1172h

Partito Socialista Italiano (PSI), English ITALIAN SOCIALIST PARTY, Italy's traditional Socialist party. In 1947 it was split by a factional struggle over the question of collaboration with the Italian Communist Party (PCI). The anti-Communists withdrew to establish the Italian Social Democratic Party (Partito Socialista Democratico Italiano; PSDI), while the PSI, led by Pietro Nenni (*q.v.*), formed an alliance with the Communists.

In the late 1950s the PSI moved away from the Communists and closer to the position of the PSDI. In 1966 the PSDI rejoined the PSI, but a new split occurred again in 1969 over the question of Communist participation in the government. This led to the resignation of Nenni and the reorganization of the PSI under the leadership of Francesco de Martino, replaced in 1976 by Bettino Craxi.

·De Gasperi and the left **9**:1170g *passim*
  to 1173a
·evolution and role **16**:972c
·origins and orientation **9**:1165b

Partizani (Yugoslav guerrillas): *see* Partisans.

Partizansk, formerly SUCHAN, city, Primorsky (Maritime) *kray* (territory), far eastern Russian Soviet Federated Socialist Republic, in the valley of the Partizanskaya River. It was formed as Suchan in 1932 by the amalgamation of mining settlements that developed near mine shafts in a bituminous coal basin, and was renamed in 1972. A thermal power station serving the region is located in the northern suburb of Uglekamensk (formerly Severny Suchan). Partizansk has clothing and haberdashery factories and a mining college. Pop. (1974 est.) 49,000.
43°08′ N, 133°09′ E

partners' desk: *see* desk.

partnership, voluntary association of two or more persons for the purpose of managing a business enterprise and sharing its profits or losses. In the usual partnership, each general partner has full power to act for the firm in carrying on its business; thus, partners are at once proprietors and also agents of their copartners. Not only is each partner individually liable to third persons for the obligations incurred for the firm but is equally liable for obligations incurred by copartners when they are acting within the scope of the firm's business.

If a partner has paid or been required to pay creditors of the firm from personal assets, other partners may be expected to contribute on an equal or some other agreed-upon basis. If copartners have become insolvent, however, this remedy to the problem of unlimited personal liability may be inadequate. The alternative of restricting a partner's liability to third persons on a pro rata basis or of limiting it to the property held in common never gained foothold in the common law. This has been one factor restricting the partnership form of business to small enterprises.

Unlike the corporation, the partnership is generally regarded merely as an aggregation of persons doing business under a common name and not as a legal person separate and apart from its shareholders. The implication is that the earnings of the partnership will be taxed only as personal earnings of the partners. Although corporations are usually organized to have perpetual existence, partnerships may be dissolved at any time upon withdrawal of a partner and by operation of law upon the death of a partner. Dissolution may be avoided by issuing transferable shares, but this device is not feasible except by a large organization. *Cf.* limited liability.

·business enterprise forms **5**:182f
·legal aspect of business associations **3**:530d

Partnership Pinochle (game): *see* Pinochle.

Parton, James (1822–91), U.S. writer, especially of biographies.

·American biographical literature **2**:1012g

Partonopeus de Blois, anonymous French romance of the late 12th century. Its story, which is based on the classical tale of Cupid and Psyche, tells of Partonopeus, a count of Blois, who by means of magic is carried off to a castle. There an enchantress comes to him by night, but, although he loves her, he is forbidden to look upon her for two and a half years. He takes a lantern, however, and she is revealed as Melior, heiress to the throne of Byzantium. Rejected by her, Partonopeus runs wild in the woods but eventually wins his beloved's hand after a tournament, which the poem describes in great detail. *Partonopeus*, which was written in couplets, enjoyed widespread popularity and was adapted in many other languages.

partridge, name given to many small game birds native to the Old World and belonging to the family Phasianidae (order Galliformes). They are larger than quails, with stronger bills and feet. (For New World birds erroneously called partridges locally, *see* grouse; quail. For dwarf partridges of India called bush quail and for the Mexican bird called long-tailed partridge, *see* quail.)

(Top) gray partridge (*Perdix perdix*), (bottom) chukar (*Alectoris graeca*)

(Top) Eric Hosking, (bottom) Ellen Trueblood

The typical partridge of Europe is the gray partridge (*Perdix perdix*), called Hungarian (or hun) partridge in North America, where it was introduced in 1889 (Virginia) and again, much more successfully, in 1908–09 (Alberta). It ranges throughout the British Isles and across Europe—chiefly in farmlands—to the Caspian region. The gray partridge has a reddish face and tail, gray breast, barred sides, and a dark U shape on the belly; sexes look alike. The hen lays about 15 eggs in a grassy cup in grainfields or hedges. A large male is 30 centimetres (12 inches) long and may weigh ⅓ kilogram (¾ pound).

In the rock partridges (*Alectoris*), both sexes have red legs and bill, and the male has blunt leg spurs. The chukar (*A. graeca*), stocked in many countries, is native from southeastern Europe to India and Manchuria (Northeast Provinces). It has a brown back with strongly barred sides and a black-outlined whitish throat. The crested wood partridge, or roulroul (*Rollulus roulroul*), of Malaysia has an iridescent blue-green body, red feet and eye region, and crimson crest.

Francolins are partridges with leg spurs. The 5 Asian and about 35 African species of *Francolinus* are prized game birds, 25–40 cm (10–16 in.) long, with big bills and strong legs; most are plain brown, but some are patterned in black, white, or reddish.

The snow partridge (*Lerwa lerwa*) of high mountains of south central Asia resembles a ptarmigan in appearance and habits.

·traits, behaviour, and classification **7**:854a

Partridge, John (1644–1715), British astrologer.

·Swift's role in career termination **17**:857h

partridgeberry (*Mitchella repens*), North American plant of the madder family (Rubiaceae), growing in dry woods from southwestern Newfoundland to Minnesota and southward to Florida and Texas. It is evergreen, with nearly round, 18-millimetre (0.7-inch) leaves, often variegated with white lines; a slender, often whitish, trailing stem; and white flowers, often borne in pairs, which are replaced by scarlet, edible but almost tasteless berrylike drupes. The flowers occur in long-styled and short-styled forms, as in the primrose. The plant, also called checkerberry, squawberry, teaberry, running box, two-eyed berry, squaw vine, and twinflower, is a good wild-garden subject for shady places. It is popular in winter terrariums because of its diminutive size and attractive colour contrast of berries and leaves.

part-singing, polyphonal performance in which singers perform parts in their assigned ranges.

·culture's effect on performance style **16**:791d

Parts of Holland, The (England): *see* Holland.

Parts of Kesteven, The (England): *see* Kesteven.

Parts of Lindsey, The (England): *see* Lindsey.

parts of speech, in grammar, classifications into which the words of a language can be divided according to their function or form or both. The eight traditional parts of speech for languages like English and Latin are nouns, pronouns, adjectives, verbs, adverbs, prepositions, conjunctions, and interjections. Most Indo-European languages share this general configuration, but it is by no means universal. Nouns and verbs are the only categories that all languages distinguish in some way. There are wide differences among languages in the number and composition of their classifications, languages like Chinese and Tagalog having fewer parts of speech. In Yana, an American Indian language, words corresponding to English adjectives are verbs, and traditional adverbs and prepositions are nouns or verb affixes. Traditional definitions, such as "a noun is the name of a person, place or thing," are often imprecise, incorrect, or incomplete.

adjective
·English word order principles **6**:877c
·Germanic inflectional innovations **8**:17g
·Japanese conjugation system **10**:95c

adverb
·English word order principles **6**:877d

grammatical features
·Altaic–Indo-European comparison **1**:637d
·categorization by modistae **8**:267e
·definition by distribution **8**:271b
·description and distinction **8**:273a
·English functional flexibility **6**:875b
·Esperanto free derivation processes **9**:742e
·Papuan grammatical intricacy **13**:977d
·pidgin grammatical peculiarities **14**:453b
·semantic implications **16**:511e
·Sino-Tibetan lack of distinctions **16**:799f
·system and function in language **10**:645a
·tagmemic syntactic description **10**:1004d

noun
·Eskimo–Aleut adverbial case system **6**:964b
·Greek declensional innovations **8**:392g
·logic history from antiquity **11**:58a
·names as classed subset **12**:814d
·prefixes indicating possessive **13**:211a
·tagmemic syntactic description **10**:1004d

preposition
·Meso-American relational particle use **11**:963b

pronoun
·Chari-Nile inclusive and exclusive **1**:228b
·Eskimo–Aleut adverbial case system **6**:964b
·honorific complexity in Japanese **10**:95c
·meaning distinctions in languages **10**:651b

verb
·Armenian development of auxiliaries **2**:24b
·Celt tense and declension peculiarities **3**:1065h *passim* to 1066e
·Dravidian pronominalization process **5**:992d
·Eskimo–Aleut syntactic relationships **6**:964a
·Germanic modification of tense–aspect **8**:17h
·Greek morphological originality **8**:395d
·Hamito-Semitic typological patterns **8**:591d
·Indian linguistic philosophy **9**:319d
·Melanesian pidgin verb forms **14**:453b
·Old English morphological system **6**:880e
·person, aspect, and evidential forms **13**:210h
·structuralist analytical difficulties **10**:999d

parturient paresis (animal disorder): *see* milk fever.

parturition, human 13:1036, process of bringing forth a child from the uterus.

The text article covers the stages of labour, relief of pain in labour, operative obstetrics, accidents during labour, natural childbirth, and puerperium or the postnatal period characterized by involution of the uterus.

REFERENCES in other text articles:
·age, size, and weight of newborn infant **6**:748e
·Australian Aborigine spirit incarnation **2**:426c
·birth canal injury and repair **17**:822a
·birth defects and related abnormalities **2**:1073a
·bone fracture during delivery **3**:29e
·brain size and fetal development **7**:20e
·circulatory system changes in infant **4**:631f
·complications from placental disease **14**:982b
·heart changes in infant **3**:877c
·hypnosis as an analgesic **9**:139b
·infant prematurity and birth injuries **4**:220d
·lactation trigger in humans **10**:583b
·oxytocin's effect on uterus **6**:811e
·pain alleviation by narcotics **12**:843f
·passage rite forms and beliefs **13**:1046a
·pelvic joint adaptability **10**:253f
·premature birth due to brain size **7**:20e
·primate birth canal comparisons **14**:1017e
·reproductive system infections **15**:700b
·respiration disorders in infants **15**:766g
·sagittal suture function **10**:253d
·Semmelweis' study of puerperal fever **16**:529e
·Sinkaietk Indian birth lodges **13**:228h

RELATED ENTRIES in the *Ready Reference and Index:*
cesarean section; natural childbirth; presentation

party, in law, one individual, firm, or corporation that constitutes the plaintiff or defendant in a lawsuit.

·procedure and capacity to sue **15**:7a

party kings: *see* mulūk aṭ-ṭawā'if.

Party of Unity (Hungarian political party): *see* Smallholders' Party.

Party of Work: *see* Liberal Party of Hungary.

party per bend, also called PER BEND, in heraldry, division of the shield in a coat-of-arms from the dexter corner of the top diagonally.

·heraldic shield design **8**:788e; illus. 789

party per chevron, also called PER CHEVRON, in heraldry, division of the shield in a coat-of-arms chevronwise across the middle.

·heraldic shield design **8**:788e; illus. 789

Parulidae (bird): *see* woodwarbler.

parure, a matched set of jewelry consisting of such pieces as earrings, bracelet, brooch, necklace, and ring. By mid-17th century,

Coral parure, *c.* 1830; in the Musée des Arts Décoratifs, Paris
Arnoldo Mondadori Editore

jewellers had developed a delicate technique of placing gems in light and elegant leafy settings of gold and silver; with the development of this style, the forms of jewels tended to become stereotyped, and, by the end of the century, the characteristic jewels had become the parure. About 1700, parures consisted of earrings, brooch, necklace or clasp, ring, and sometimes shoulder brooches or buckles, all set with diamonds, either alone or in combination with rubies, topazes, sapphires, or emeralds. In the 18th century, both Louis XIV and Louis XV had parures of great splendour, most made of diamonds and including shoe buckles, coat decorations, insignia, and sword hilts. For state occasions, the 19th-century Napoleonic court imitated the parures of the *ancien régime*, with the addition of a jewelled coronet of classic form. Parures of semiprecious stones were made for everyday wear and for the less affluent.

Paru River, Portuguese RIO PARU, in northern Brazil, arises on the southern slopes of the Tumuc-Humac Mountains, on the Surinam border, and flows for about 500 mi (800 km) south-southeastward through Pará state. It empties into the Lower Amazon River just above Almeirim. The Paru is navigable for 50 mi above its mouth.
1°33′ S, 52°38′ W
·map, Brazil **3**:124

Parus major (bird): *see* tit.

Parvān, *velāyet* (province) in eastern Afghanistan, 3,456 sq mi (8,951 sq km) in area, with its capital at Chārīkār (*q.v.*). It is bounded by the provinces of Baghlān, Takhār, Badakhshān (north), Laghmān (east), Kāpīsā, Kābul, and Vardak (south), and Bāmīān (west). Parvān comprises a chain of picturesque valleys, drained by the Qondūz and Panjshēr rivers. Only a small part of the province is cultivated, mostly under irrigation. The chief crops are cotton, rice, wheat, and barley; cotton textiles are produced near Chārīkār. Coal is mined from the Panjshēr and Ghowr Band valleys and iron ore from the Ghowr Band. Silver deposits exist in the Panjshēr Valley but are not rich enough to be profitably mined. At Chārīkār cutlery, farm equipment, and other metal products are manufactured. An all-weather road connects Parvān with Kābul, the nation's capital, and with Peshāwar, Pakistan. Pop. (1970 est.) 887,127, mainly Tadzhik (Tajik), Ḥazāra, and Uzbek.
·area and population table **1**:169
·map, Afghanistan **1**:167

Parva naturalia, Latin title given to a collection of treatises by Aristotle that covers such topics as sensation, memory, sleep, dreams, life and death, and youth and old age.
·biological and psychological inquiries **1**:1168h
·dreams from sensory movement **5**:1011g

Pārvatī (Sanskrit: "daughter of the mountain"), the wife of the Hindu god Śiva (Shiva). Pārvatī is the benevolent aspect of the goddess Śakti, and is sometimes identified with Umā. The legendary account of her marriage relates that she won Śiva's notice only after severe ascetic discipline. The couple had two children, the elephant-headed Gaṇeśa and the six-headed Skanda. She is often represented in sculpture with Śiva—as an attendant figure, or looking on as he performs a miraculous feat, or engaged in a game with him in their mountain kingdom Kailāsa—and is always depicted as a mature and beautiful woman.

Pārvatī, bronze image, early Cōla period, 10th century AD; in the Freer Gallery of Art, Washington, D.C.
By courtesy of the Smithsonian Institution, Freer Gallery of Art, Washington, D.C.

The *Tantra*s—texts of sects worshipping Śiva—are written as a discussion between Pārvatī and Śiva.
·classical dance temperament inspiration **17**:160c
·Hindu ascetic and fertility archetype **8**:894g; illus.
·mythology and association with Śiva **8**:931g; illus.
·Rājasthān's festival worship **15**:497f

parveh (Judaism): *see* pareve.

parvis, in architecture, enclosed area in front of a church. In France the word is often applied to all of the open spaces that surround a church or cathedral and that are, in turn, surrounded by balustrades or low walls. The parvis formerly outside of St. Paul's Cathedral in London was famous as a gathering place for lawyers. The term is sometimes used incorrectly to refer to a room above the porch of a church.

Parvīz (Persian ruler): *see* Khosrow II of Persia.

Paryphanta, genus of carnivorous snails in the mollusk class Gastropoda.
·traits, behaviour, and classification **7**:952h

Paryuṣaṇa, in Sanskrit, PAJJUSAṆA in Prākrit, a popular eight-day festival in Jainism, a religion of India. It generally is celebrated among members of the Śvetāmbara sect from the 13th day of the dark half of the month Bhādrapada (August–September) to the 5th day of the bright half of Bhādra. Among Digambaras, a corresponding festival is called Daśalakṣaṇa, and it begins immediately following the Śvetāmbara Paryuṣaṇa.

Paryuṣaṇa closes the Jaina year. Jainas make confessions at the meetinghouse so that no quarrel is carried over into the new year, and many lay members temporarily live the lives of monks, an observance called *poṣadha*. The fourth day of Paryuṣaṇa coincides with the birth anniversary of Mahāvīra.

The last day of the festival, Bhadra-śukla-pañcamī ("fifth day of the bright fortnight of Bhādra"), is also an ancient Indian festival day known to Hindus as Ṛṣi-pañcamī ("the fifth of the seers"), the day on which Hindus pay homage to the seven seers, who are identified with the seven stars of the constellation Ursa Major, then visible. On that day Jainas distribute alms to the poor and take out a Jina (saviour) image in a procession that is headed by an ornamental pole called *Indra-dhvaja* ("staff of Indra"). The *Kalpa-sūtra*, a sacred text that describes the lives of the Jinas, is read before the laity by monks, and the miniature paintings illustrating the incidents are shown and revered. The last day is a day of fasting, though the very pious will observe a fast throughout the eight-day festival.
·practices and principles **10**:11e

Parzival (early 13th century), verse epic of almost 25,000 lines by the German poet Wolfram von Eschenbach, adapted from the French *Perceval* of Chrétien de Troyes. It is exemplary of the way in which the German poets rendered the worldly Anglo-French romances of King Arthur and the Knights of the Round Table into more earnest and religious works, and is perhaps the earliest example of the *Bildungsroman* (educational novel) in German literature, relating the personal development of a young knight and his adventures in quest of the Holy Grail.
·court epic tradition **10**:1116c

PAS (drug): *see* para-aminosalicylic acid.

Pas, The (Manitoba, Canada): *see* The Pas.

Pasadena, city, Los Angeles County, California, U.S., in the San Gabriel Valley, at the base of the San Gabriel Mountains. Once part of Rancho San Pasqual, it was founded in 1874 by Thomas B. Elliott as the Indiana Colony, adopting the name of Pasadena (Chippewa: "crown of the valley") in 1875. Growth as a winter resort and citrus centre was stimulated by the Santa Fe Railroad, and later freeway construction brought it within easy commuting distance to Los Angeles.

Based on the California Institute of Technology (1891), which includes the Jet Propulsion Laboratory operated in conjunction with the National Aeronautics and Space Administration, the city has become a centre of research and light manufacturing, chiefly scientific and precision instruments and electronic, aircraft, and missile components.

Pasadena City (junior) College was founded in 1924. The city is the home of the State Theatre of California (formerly Pasadena Community Playhouse). The New Year's Day Tournament of Roses (first introduced in 1890) features a televised parade and the Rose Bowl football classic between the champion teams of west coast and midwestern U.S. universities. Inc. 1886. Pop. (1980) 119,374.
34°09′ N, 118°09′ W
·map, United States **18**:908

Pasadena, city, Harris County, southeastern Texas, U.S., bordering Houston (west) between the Houston Ship Channel and the NASA Clear Lake area. Founded in 1895 by J.H. Burnett, its Spanish name meaning "land of flowers" was inspired by blooming fields along Vince's Bayou. Rapid post-World War II growth was stimulated by adjacent industrial development, particularly petrochemicals and aerospace. Pasadena is the seat of San Jacinto (junior) College (1961) and the Texas

Chiropractic College. Inc. 1929. Pop. (1950) 22,483; (1980) 112,560.
29°42′ N, 95°13′ W

Pasadenan orogeny, name applied to a period of folding and thrust faulting of rock strata in the Coast Ranges of California in middle Pleistocene time (the Pleistocene Epoch began about 2,500,000 years ago and ended 10,000 years ago). This period marks the final disappearance of older, Tertiary depositional troughs in the Coast Range area and probably is only one of a series of deformational events related to the movement of the Pacific Plate in relation to the North American Plate in western California. *See further* plate tectonics.

Pa Sak, Mae Nam, river in central Thailand, rises in the northern portion of the Thiu Khao Phetchabun, a mountain range, and flows south through a narrow valley for 319 mi (513 km). It empties into the Mae Nam Lop Buri at Phra Nakhon Si Ayutthaya. Lomsak, Phetchabun, and Sara Buri are the main towns on its banks. Below Sara Buri town, the Pa Sak is dammed for irrigation.
14°11′ N, 100°40′ E

Pasargadae, first dynastic capital of the Achaemenian Empire, situated northeast of Persepolis in modern southwest Iran. Traditionally, Cyrus II the Great (reigned 559–529 BC) chose the site because it lay near the scene of his victory over Astyages the Mede (550). The name of the city may have been derived from that of the chief Persian tribe, the Pasargadae.

Tomb of Cyrus II the Great at Pasargadae
By courtesy of the Oriental Institute, the University of Chicago

The majestic simplicity of the architecture at Pasargadae reflects a sense of balance and beauty that was never equalled in either earlier or later Achaemenian times. The principal buildings stand in magnificent isolation, often with a common orientation but scattered over a remarkably wide area. The dominant feature of the citadel is a huge stone platform, projecting from a low, conical hill. Two unfinished stone staircases and a towering facade of rusticated masonry were evidently intended to form part of an elevated palace enclosure. An abrupt event, however, brought the work to a halt, and a formidable mud-brick structure was erected on the platform instead. It is possible that the building represents the famous treasury surrendered to Alexander the Great in 330 BC.

To the south of the citadel was an extensive walled park with elaborate, irrigated gardens surrounded by a series of royal buildings. One building, designed as the sole entrance to the park, is notable for a unique four-winged, crowned figure that stands on a surviving doorjamb; the figure appears to represent an Achaemenian version of the four-winged genius (guardian spirit) found on palace doorways in Assyria.

Farther to the south, the tomb of Cyrus still stands almost intact. Constructed of huge, white limestone blocks, its gabled tomb chamber rests on a rectangular, stepped plinth, with six receding stages. In Islāmic times the tomb acquired new sanctity as the supposed resting place of the mother of King Solomon. At the extreme southern edge of the site, an impressive rock-cut road or canal indicates the course of the ancient highway that once linked Pasargadae with Persepolis.

After the accession of Darius I the Great (522 BC), Persepolis replaced Pasargadae as the dynastic home.

·architecture of Achaemenian period **19**:270e
·artistry as effectively Persian **9**:837g; map 834
·urban geographic location map **9**:868

Pasay, city, Rizal province, central Luzon, Philippines, on the eastern shore of Manila Bay. A major residential suburb of Manila (immediately north), it is well-known for the nightclubs that line the waterfront along Roxas (formerly Dewey) Boulevard. Pasay is densely populated and highly commercialized. Araneta University (1946) is located in the city. Both the domestic and international airports are on its outskirts. Inc. city, 1947. Pop. 1970) 206,283.
14°33′ N, 121°00′ E
·map, Philippines **14**:233

Pascagoula, city, seat of Jackson County, southeastern Mississippi, U.S., on Pascagoula Bay of Mississippi Sound, at the mouth of Pascagoula River. The settlement developed around the Old Spanish Fort (one of the oldest existing structures in the Mississippi Valley), built in 1718 by the Frenchman Joseph Simon de la Pointe. It thrived in the 19th century as a lumber-shipping port. The Pascagoula River is known locally as the Singing River because of strange humming sounds audible in its vicinity. Legends have linked the "singing" with the death chant of the Pascagoula Indians who chose to commit mass suicide in its waters rather than suffer extinction at the hands of the Biloxi tribe.

A seaport and fishing and shipbuilding centre, the city also has diversified industries producing kraft paper, petroleum, chemicals, and metal products. The huge Bayou Casotte Industrial Park is immediately east. Inc. village, 1892; city, 1904. Pop. (1980) 29,318.
30°23′ N, 88°31′ W
·harbour accomodation capabilities **12**:278e
·map, United States **18**:908

Pascal, Blaise **13**:1041 (b. June 19, 1623, Clermont-Ferrand, Fr.—d. Aug. 19, 1662, Paris), mathematician, physicist, religious philosopher and writer, was the founder of the modern theory of probabilities. His ideas on inner religion influenced Rousseau, Bergson, and the Existentialists.

Abstract of text biography. At the age of 17 Pascal published an essay on mathematics that was highly regarded in the academic community and praised by Descartes. He invented the first digital calculator (1642–44) to assist his mathematician father in local administration. Further studies in geometry, hydrodynamics, and hydrostatic and atmospheric pressure led him to invent the syringe and the hydraulic press and to discover Pascal's law of pressure (1647–54). He entered the convent of Port-Royal in 1654, where he wrote *Les Provinciales*, a defense of Jansenism against the Jesuits, and the *Pensées*. Pascal spent his last years in scientific research and good works.

REFERENCES in other text articles:
·anticipation of Existentialist position **7**:73h
·argument on Roman Catholic authenticity **1**:314a
·Catholic reaction to Skepticism **6**:890g
·computer history and early machines **4**:1046c
·digital calculating machine **13**:512c
·eternal truths and man's ego **1**:976f
·Fermat probability theory **7**:235g
·fluid mechanics development **11**:780f
·French literature development **10**:1156a
·French theological literature **10**:1082c
·Huygens' association and correspondence **9**:74h
·Jansenist defense and papal rejection **10**:34c
·mathematics history from antiquity **11**:643c
·projective geometry development **7**:1120e
·Skepticism's impossibility **16**:832b
·Stoicism and reason **17**:701e
·theological inadequacy of metaphysics **4**:560d

Pascal, Carlo (1866–1926), Italian scholar of Latin.
·textual editing dangers of conjecture **18**:192b

Pascal's principle, or PASCAL'S LAW, in fluid (gas or liquid) mechanics, states that in a fluid at rest in a closed container a pressure change in one part is transmitted without loss to every portion of the fluid and to the walls of the container. The principle was first enunciated by Blaise Pascal (1623–62), a French scientist, mathematician, and religious writer.

Pressure is equal to force per unit area, or the force divided by the area on which it acts. According to Pascal's principle, in a hydraulic system a pressure exerted on a piston produces an equal increase in pressure on another piston in the system. If the second piston has an area ten times that of the first, the force on the second piston is ten times greater, though the pressure is the same as that on the first piston. This exemplifies the hydraulic press, based on Pascal's principle, which is utilized in such applications as hydraulic brakes.

Pascal also discovered that the pressure at a point in a fluid at rest is the same in all directions; the pressure would be the same on all planes passing through a specific point. This fact is also known as Pascal's principle, or law.
·early work with hydraulics **13**:1041f
·fluid statics equations **11**:783h
·hydraulic machine principles **9**:77d

Pascal's theorem (geometry): *see* Pappus'-Pascal's theorems.

Pascendi Dominici Gregis ("Feeding the Lord's Flock"), antimodernist encyclical issued by Pope Pius X in 1907.
·Pius X's thought on Modernism **15**:1016h

Pasch, Georg (1661–1707), German philosopher and mathematician.
·historical development of geometry **11**:658g

Paschal, also spelled PASCAL, Latin PASCHALIS (d. 692, Italy), antipope against both the rival antipope Theodore and the legitimate pope St. Sergius I during 687. After the death of Pope Conon in 687, the Roman populace proceeded to enthrone both Paschal, then an archdeacon, and the archpriest Theodore. No agreement could be reached, and neither Paschal nor Theodore would renounce their claims. To resolve the dispute, the higher clergy, supported by the Roman army, elected the priest Sergius. Among those who supported Sergius was Paschal's patron, John Platyn, the imperial deputy at Ravenna; having been bribed by Paschal into influencing his original nomination, Platyn was also bribed with gold (reportedly 100 pounds) to support Sergius, who was consecrated on Dec. 15, 687. Theodore ceded, but Paschal refused to submit and was deposed and imprisoned in a monastery until his death.

Paschal I, Saint (b. Rome—d. Feb. 11, 824, Rome), pope from 817 to 824. A priest who had served in the Curia, Paschal was an abbot when elected pope immediately after the death of his predecessor, Stephen V (VI), on Jan. 26, 817. Paschal's pontificate was continually embroiled in the problem of relating the papacy to the recently founded Frankish Empire under Charlemagne's son and successor, Louis I the Pious, who forcibly imposed on the church an unprecedented reform and reorganization of monasteries and dioceses while concurrently arranging the empire and trying to reconcile the safeguarding of Christian order and unity.

Paschal secured from Louis the independence of the Roman see, its suzerainty over the states of the church, and the right of Romans to freedom of election. In 823 he crowned Louis's son Lothair I as co-emperor, a deed that was signficant because it initiated the handing of a sword by the pope to the emperor as a symbol of the temporal power that was to suppress evil. Meanwhile, in Rome an anti-Frankish movement was developing, which Paschal supposedly joined. Some of his servants executed at the Curia two leaders of the Frankish party accused of plotting against Paschal and of favouring imperial control of Rome. Louis ordered an investigation at

St. Paschal I, detail from a 9th century mosaic; in the apse of the church of Sta. Prassede, Rome

Alinari

which Paschal was forced to clear himself by an oath of purgation. The exact proceedings of this investigation are clouded by intrigue and the argument that no mortal can judge a pontiff. It is known, however, that Paschal was hated, and the emotions aroused by the executions caused considerable trouble that necessitated firmer supervision of Rome by the imperial court.

Paschal was further faced with the revival of Iconoclasm (destruction of images) in the East under the Byzantine emperor Leo V the Armenian. The Eastern abbot Theodore Studites, leading defender of orthodoxy and of the veneration of icons, appealed to the Pope, who dispatched legates to Constantinople. Paschal's intervention proved unsuccessful, but he did supply refuge for the Greek monks who fled to Rome.

Paschal's contribution to the building activity in Rome typifies the period that followed Charlemagne's consecration as Holy Roman emperor. Sta. Prassede and the annexed chapel of S. Zeno, both containing magnificent mosaics, were his work; he also built Sta. Maria in Domnica and rebuilt Sta. Cecilia. He was responsible for the translation of the relics of many martyrs, including those of St. Cecilia, from the catacombs to Rome. It is believed that he was canonized for his building and not for his character. His feast day is May 14.

·medieval mosaic art style sources **12**:471d

Paschal II (b. RANIERUS, at Bieda di Galeata, near Ravenna—d. Jan. 21, 1118, Rome), pope from 1099 to 1118. He entered a monastery as a boy and was made cardinal by Pope St. Gregory VII *c.* 1080. He was legate to Spain under Pope Urban II, whom he was elected to succeed on Aug. 13, 1099.

Although Paschal fostered the First Crusade and followed Gregory's great policies of church reform, his pontificate was dominated by the Investiture Controversy—the long conflict between popes and secular rulers over control of ecclesiastical appointments. In 1107 settlements on the issue of lay investiture were made with kings Henry I of England and Philip I of France (who was excommunicated for his unsanctioned marriage to Bertrada in 1100 but absolved in 1104).

Paschal's struggles with the Holy Roman emperors Henry IV and Henry V, however, proved inconclusive. After unsuccessful negotiations in 1106, 1107, and 1110, he officially condemned Henry V, who invaded Italy. They met at Sutri, where Henry renounced the right to investiture, and Paschal agreed to have the German church return all lands and rights received from the crown—an agreement that, when promulgated at St. Peter's in Rome on Feb. 12, 1111, caused a tumult among the German bishops. They felt deprived of power, and their protests killed the pact. A popular rising forced Henry to leave Rome temporarily, and he took Paschal as prisoner. After two months of harsh captivity, Paschal consented to Henry's demands on royal investiture of bishops, and on April 13, 1111, he crowned Henry as Holy Roman emperor.

Strong opposition arose in the Curia against Paschal. A council declared invalid the privilege he had granted Henry, and, against his will, Archbishop Guido of Vienne excommunicated the Emperor. Paschal finally revoked the privilege in 1112 and renewed his earlier condemnations of regal investiture in 1116. The problem remained unsolved until 1122, when Pope Calixtus II concluded the Concordat of Worms, which secured peace between the church and the empire.

·Crusades of 1101–07 **5**:300h
·Henry IV's final papal negotiation **8**:762d
·investiture compromise failure **9**:1130a
·Investiture Controversy and Henry V **8**:763a
·lay investiture ruling **15**:1003h

Paschal III (b. GUIDO OF CREMA, d. Sept. 20, 1168, Rome), antipope from 1164 to 1168. Against Pope Alexander III, he was one of the original supporters of the antipope Victor IV, whom he succeeded on April 22, 1164, becoming the second antipope set up by the Holy Roman emperor Frederick I Barbarossa. Elected through the influence of Rainald of Dassel, Frederick's chancellor and vicar in Italy, he won only limited allegiance in the empire. By imperial command in 1165 he canonized Charlemagne at Aachen, a decree never confirmed by the church, although Charlemagne is now regarded as having been informally beatified.

Paschal was enthroned when Rome was seized by Frederick, whom Paschal crowned (for a second time) in August 1167, together with his wife, Béatrix. After a sudden outbreak of pestilence destroyed the imperial army, Frederick retreated to Germany in the spring of 1168, accompanied by Paschal.

·Charlemagne's canonization **4**:46h
·Frederick I's reluctant endorsement **7**:698e

Paschal candle, or EASTER CANDLE, ritual candle displayed by some Christian churches during the Easter season. It is inscribed and dedicated during the Easter Vigil.

·lighting devices of cultic significance **3**:1177d

Paschal controversies, in the Christian Church, disputes concerning the correct date for observing Easter (Greek Pascha). The earliest controversy was over the question of whether Easter should always be celebrated on a Sunday or on the actual day of the Jewish lunar month (14th of Nisan) on which the Paschal lamb was slaughtered. The latter practice, followed by the church in the Roman province of Asia, was generally condemned at the end of the 2nd century because it meant celebrating Easter when the Jews were keeping Passover.

Later controversies concerned the different methods of calculating the paschal moon, until in the 6th century the computations of Dionysius Exiguus were generally accepted in the West. The Celtic Church, however, did not accept this method until the 7th century (*see* Whitby, Synod of), and there were some difficulties in Gaul in the 8th century.

In the Eastern Orthodox Church, Easter is often observed on a later Sunday than in the Western Church, partly because it adheres to the Julian calendar for the movable year. In the West the subject has ceased to be a matter of dispute, and the second Vatican Council stated in 1963 that there was no objection in principle to observing Easter on a fixed Sunday (probably early in April).

Paschal lamb, in Judaism, the lamb sacrificed at the first Passover, on the eve of the Exodus from Egypt, the most momentous event in Jewish history. In early Jewish history, an unblemished year-old lamb sacrificed in the Temple of Jerusalem on the 14th of Nisan to commemorate the eve of the Exodus was later eaten by the family. For those who had been impeded from visiting the Temple at the prescribed time, a second Passover festival was permitted a month later. In modern times, Jews use a roasted shank bone at the seder (*q.v.*) meal as symbolic of the Paschal lamb. Christians, applying the symbolism to Christ, see him as the spotless Lamb of God who by his death freed mankind from the bonds of sin.

Paschaltide, or EASTERTIDE, a worship season in the Christian Church, the 50-day period from Easter until Pentecost (Whitsunday). It is a time of rejoicing following the Easter celebration of the Resurrection of Christ.

Paschasius Radbertus, Saint (b. *c.* 785, Soissons, Fr.—d. *c.* 860), abbot, theologian, and author whose monograph *De corpore et sanguine Christi* ("Concerning Christ's Body and Blood") later became the dominant interpretation of the Eucharist. Abandoned as an infant, he was raised by the monks of St. Peter's, Soissons. Later, he joined the Benedictine abbey of Corbie, near Amiens, under St. Adalhard the Elder (abbot of Corbie, 814–821) and his brother and successor, St. Wala, whose lives Paschasius was to write. Well read in the Scriptures and patristic works, he was ordained deacon and subsequently became novice master and headmaster at Corbie and at the daughter abbey of New Corbie, Westphalia (now in Höxter, W.Ger.), which in 822 he had assisted in founding. Under Paschasius' leadership the Corbie schools became famous.

He was elected, *c.* 843, fourth abbot of Corbie. During his office there were disturbances in the monastery. His plans for reform were opposed, and his *De corpore* (written in 831 and revised in 844, when he presented it to King Charles II the Bald of the West Frankish kingdom) was seriously challenged by the monk Ratramnus (*q.v.*), who *c.* 850 wrote his famous eucharistic treatise *De corpore et sanguine Domini* ("Concerning the Lord's Body and Blood") partially in reply to Paschasius. Ratramnus showed marked independence of thought, and Paschasius was further criticized by Rabanus Maurus, abbot of Fulda and later archbishop of Mainz.

The chief differences between their eucharistic concepts lay in emphasis, Paschasius' on realism and Ratramnus' and Rabanus' on more spiritual conceptions. For Paschasius, the bread and wine on the altar become, after consecration, Christ's true body and blood, whereas for Ratramnus the bread and wine are symbolical of Christ's body and blood. Furthermore, Ratramnus opposed Paschasius' view that the true body and blood are identical with the natural body and blood visible during Christ's life on earth and now reigning in heaven.

Paschasius attended the synods of Paris (847) and Quercy (849). He resigned his abbacy *c.* 851 and retired to the monastery of Saint-Riquier, to write in peace, although his last years were supposedly spent at Corbie. He wrote 12 books of commentary on Matthew, an exposition of Psalm 44, five books on Lamentations, and several minor works. During succeeding centuries his eucharistic views were dominant, particularly during the 11th-century eucharistic controversy associated with the noted theologian Berengar of Tours, who was condemned at the Council of Vercelli in 1050 for sympathizing with Ratramnus' views (then falsely attributed to the Irish philosopher and theologian John Scotus Erigena). Modern theologians, however, recognize faults in Paschasius' doctrine. His feast day is April 26. H. Peltier's *Pascase Radbert, abbé de Corbie* appeared in 1938, followed by C. Gliozzo's *La dottrina in Paschasio Radberto e Ratramno, monaci di Corbia* ("The Doctrine of Paschasius Radbertus and Ratramnus, Monks of Corbie") in 1945.

Paschen series (physics): *see* spectral line series.

Pascin, Jules (b. JULIUS PINCAS, 1885, Vidin, Bulg.—d. 1930, Paris), painter of the school of Paris renowned for his delicate draftsmanship and sensitive studies of women. Born of Italian-Serbian and Spanish-Jewish parents, he spent a number of years in Austria and Germany working for such satirical journals as the *Lustige Blätter* and *Simplicissimus.* In 1905 he moved to Paris where he continued to produce tragically satirical drawings of the underworld. At the outbreak of World War I he was away from France. He travelled for a while in the United States, where he became a citizen, and Cuba, returning to Paris in 1920. There he began to create a series of large-scale, representational, and very sensitively drawn biblical and mythological paintings, as well as portraits. Later he turned to the material for which he is generally known, the delicately toned, thinly painted, but poetically bitter and ironic studies of women, generally prostitutes. These suggest an analogy to Henri de Toulouse-Lautrec, but Pascin's characters have an individual grace and perverse tenderness that bespeak a personal identification with these creatures of sorrow. On the eve of an important one-man show of his work in 1930, Pascin hanged himself.

Pasco, department of central Peru, stretching from the Andes eastward to the Amazon Basin. Created in 1944, it occupies an area of 8,438 sq mi (21,854 sq km). Western Pasco, a mountainous and rugged area, is drained by the headwaters of the Río Huallaga. Eastern Pasco, on the steep, rain-drenched eastern slopes of the Andes and the forested plains beyond, is drained by the Río Pachitea.

Western Pasco is one of the world's great mining regions. Silver ores at Cerro de Pasco (*q.v.*), the departmental capital, were discovered in 1630. Copper is now more important than silver, and numerous other minerals, including lead, zinc, gold, vanadium, and bismuth, are mined. Pop. (1972 prelim.) 21,854.

·area and population table **14**:131

Pasco, city, seat of Franklin County, southeastern Washington, U.S., at the confluence of the Snake and Columbia rivers, opposite Kennewick and immediately southeast of Richland. The city was established in 1880, when the Northern Pacific Railway (now Burlington Northern) reached that point; it became the county seat *c.* 1890. It is a busy river port, as well as a rail centre. Inc. 1891. Pop. (1980) 17,944.

46°14′ N, 119°06′ W

·map, United States **18**:908

Pascoli, Giovanni (b. Dec. 31, 1855, San Mauro di Romagna, Italy—d. April 6, 1912, Bologna), classical scholar and poet whose graceful and melancholy lyric poems, perfect in form, rhythmic in style, and innovative in wording, have been an important influence on subsequent Italian poetry, particularly on the *crepuscolari* ("twilight poets"), a group of despondent Italian poets active in the early 20th century.

Pascoli had an extremely painful childhood: his father was mysteriously assassinated when he was 12, his mother died when he was 13, and five other children in the family died by the time he reached adulthood. As a result, Pascoli grew up in great poverty. He also experienced a long period of psychological duress while studying on a scholarship at the University of Bologna under the great poet Giosuè Carducci. Pascoli was arrested and imprisoned for a few months in 1879 for preaching political anarchy. Following his imprisonment he took his younger siblings to live with him, and from 1882 began a career of teaching, first in secondary schools and then in various Italian universities, as professor of Greek, Latin, and Italian literature. In 1905 he was appointed to the chair of Italian literature at the University of Bologna.

Pascoli's first literary work, a great success, was *Myricae* (published as book 1891; "Tamarisks"), a volume of short, delicate, musical lyrics inspired by nature and domestic themes and reflecting the psychological unrest of his student years. Some easing of inner turmoil is apparent in his next volume, usually considered his best, *Canti di Castelvecchio* (1903, definitive edition, 1907; "Songs of Castelvecchio"), a collection of moving evocations of his sad childhood and celebrations of nature and family life. Subsequent volumes include the classically inspired and more formal *Poemi conviviali* (1904) and two collections influenced by Virgil's *Georgics*, Carducci's work, and the French Symbolists, *Primi poemetti* (1904, originally published as *Poemetti*, 1897) and *Nuovi poemetti* (1909). Pascoli's Latin poems won poetry prizes and exhibited a fluent skill; Gabriele D'Annunzio considered him (though some would dissent) the finest Latin poet since the Augustan age. During his later years Pascoli wrote several nationalistic and historic poetic works, notably *Poemi del Risorgimento* (1913). He also translated poems of Wordsworth, Shelley, and Tennyson.

Though usually simple in theme and subject, Pascoli's poems have a distinctive formal refinement, an unusual mastery of rhythm and imagery, and an innovative vocabulary that includes dialectal forms, archaic words, and the purely auditory sounds of birds and small children. An Italian literary award, the Pascoli Prize, was established in 1962 to commemorate the 50th anniversary of his death.

·Italian literature of the 19th century **10**:1201g

Pascua, Isla de (Pacific Ocean): *see* Easter Island.

Pas d'acier, Le, one-act ballet created by Sergey Prokofiev in collaboration with Sergey Diaghilev, first performed in 1927.

·social and historical theme **15**:35b

Pas-de-Calais, *département* in northern France, extending southeast from the English Channel and separated from Belgium by Nord *département*. Created from the historic province of Artois (*q.v.*) and a part of Picardy, it has an area of 2,563 sq mi (6,639 sq km). The coastline runs north from the boundary of Somme *département* at the Authie River, past Le-Touquet-Paris-Plage and Boulogne (*qq.v.*), to Cap Gris-Nez on the Strait of Dover (French, Pas de Calais). It continues east-northeast past Calais (*q.v.*) to the estuary of the Aa River bordering Nord. Low and marshy to the south and northeast, the coast has high chalk cliffs around Cap Gris-Nez and Cap Blanc-Nez, facing the cliffs of Dover in England across the English Channel. Extending inland from the Boulogne region, the chalk hills of Artois rise to 700 ft (210 m) and are the watershed of several rivers flowing north to Flanders and south to the Canche, which enters the Channel at Le Touquet-Paris-Plage.

The climate is mild with moderate rainfall. Agriculture thrives: dairy farming and market gardening are intensively pursued in the coastal lowlands, on which large areas have been reclaimed and canalized. Inland, cattle are raised, and sugar beets, cereals, and fodder are grown.

The eastern half of the *département*, which embraces part of the coal basin extending across northern France into Belgium, is highly industrialized. The greatest number of pits is in the Béthune–Liévin–Lens–Hénin–Liétard area, in which coking plants, blast furnaces, steel mills, metalworks, and chemical installations are concentrated. The area is densely populated. Pas-de-Calais is skirted by the Lille–Paris motorway, which passes east of Arras, the capital, in which such industries as textiles and food processing long have been established. Textile, metal, and cement industries are among those in the Calais-Boulogne region. Calais, which, with Boulogne, receives most of the surface traffic from England, is France's major passenger harbour, while Boulogne is France's major fishing harbour.

The *département* has seven *arrondissements:* Arras, Béthune, Boulogne-sur-Mer, Calais, Lens, Montreuil, and Saint-Omer. It is in the educational division of Lille. Pop. (1972 est.) 1,400,600.

·area and population table **7**:594

pas de deux, ballet term denoting a dance for two performers. The strictly classical pas de deux followed a fixed pattern: a supported *adagio*, a solo variation for the male dancer, a solo variation for the female dancer, and a coda in which both participants displayed their virtuosity.

pas d'élévation (French: "high steps"), all jumping and leaping movements in classical

Grand jeté, pas d'elevation, from Enrique Martinez's "Coppelia," performed by the American Ballet Theatre

Jack Mitchell

ballet. The steps are admired for the height (*élévation*) at which they are performed and for the dancer's ability to ascend without apparent effort and to land smoothly. Dancers famed for aerial manoeuvres of this kind include Jean Balon, a French dancer of the late 17th century whose soaring leaps reputedly inspired the term ballon, and Nijinsky, reportedly an early master of the *entrechat-dix* (jump with five leg crossings). *Pas d'élévation* include cabriole, entrechat, and jeté (*qq.v.*).
·ballet history and development **2**:649c
·Nijinsky's legendary leaping ability **13**:101b

pasha, Turkish PAŞA, the highest title of civil and military officials in the Ottoman Empire.
·Ottoman rule in North Africa **13**:160e

Pashto language, also called PUSHTU, PAKHTO, or AFGHAN, Eastern Iranian language spoken by about 17,775,000 (1976 est.) Pashtuns in eastern Afghanistan and northern Pakistan. Its dialects fall into two main divisions: the southern, which preserves the ancient *sh* (as in "Pashto") and *zh* sounds, and the northern, which has *kh* (as in "Pakhto") and *gh* sounds instead. Written in a modified Arabic alphabet, Pashto shows strong Indian influence, many Arabic and Persian loanwords, and numerous archaic Iranian features. It has been attested from the beginning of the 16th century and became of significance in diplomacy after the creation of the Afghan state in the 18th century. In 1936 Pashto was declared the national language of Afghanistan, and instruction in it is now compulsory. Persian is the second language.

Pashto literature exists certainly from the 17th century, less certainly from the 11th. The national poet of Afghanistan, Khushḥāl Khān (1613–94), chief of the Khaṭak tribe, wrote spontaneous and forceful poetry of great charm. His grandson Afḍal Khān was the author of a history of the Pashtuns. Popular mystical poets were ʿAbd ar-Raḥmān and ʿAbd al-Ḥamīd in the late 17th or early 18th century, and Aḥmad Shāh Durrānī, founder of the Afghan nation, was himself a poet. The Pashto Academy (Pashto Ṭolana) publishes a variety of literary works.
·Afghan official language distribution **1**:168e
·Baluchistan's linguistic groups **2**:678d
·dialects and locations **9**:451h
·Indo-Iranian languages distribution map **9**:442
·Islāmic poetic literature **9**:968e
·offical status in Afghanistan **9**:454b
·Pakistan's linguistic groups **13**:897d

Pashtun, also spelled PAKHTUN, formerly called PATHAN (a term considered derogatory), Persian AFGHAN, name applied to the Pashto-speaking tribes of southeastern Afghanistan and northwestern Pakistan. All these people call themselves Pashtuns (pronounced Pakhtun in the north), and though a distinction has sometimes been made between "Afghan" and "Pathan," it results only from the use of the Persian term in the west and the Indianized form of their own name in the east.

The Pashtuns believe themselves to have originated in Afghanistan and to be descended from a common ancestor. Several tribes are known to have moved from Afghanistan to Pakistan between the 13th and 16th centuries. Each tribe, consisting of kinsmen who trace descent in the male bloodline from a common tribal ancestor, is divided into clans, subclans, and patriarchal families. Tribal genealogies establish rights of succession and inheritance and the right to use tribal lands and to speak in tribal council. Disputes over property, women, and personal injury can result in blood feuds between families or clans.

Most tribesmen are sedentary farmers, combining cultivation with animal husbandry; some are migratory herdsmen and caravaneers. Large numbers of them have always been attracted to military service.

There are estimated to be about 11,625,000 Pashtuns in Afghanistan and 6,150,000 in Pakistan. They comprise about 60 tribes of varying size and importance and occupying particular territories. In Afghanistan, where Pashtuns are the predominant ethnic group, the main tribes— or, more accurately, federations of tribes—are the Durrānī south of Kābul and the Ghilzay east of Kābul.

In Pakistan, Pashtuns predominate north of Quetta between the Sulaimān Range and the Indus River. In the hill areas the main tribes are, from south to north: the Kākaṛ, Shērānī, and Ustarāna south of the Gumal River; the Maḥsūd, Darwēsh Khēl, Wazīrī, and Biṭanī between the Gumal River and Thal; the Tūrī, Bangash, Ōrakzay, Afrīdī, and Shinwārī from Thal to the Khyber Pass; and the Mahmand, Utmān Khēl, Tarklānī, and Yūsufzay north and northeast of the Khyber.

The settled areas include lowland tribes subject to direct administration by the provincial government. The main tribes there are, from south to north: the Banūchī and Khaṭak from the Kurram River to Nowshera; and the Khalīl and Mandāṇ in the Vale of Peshawar.

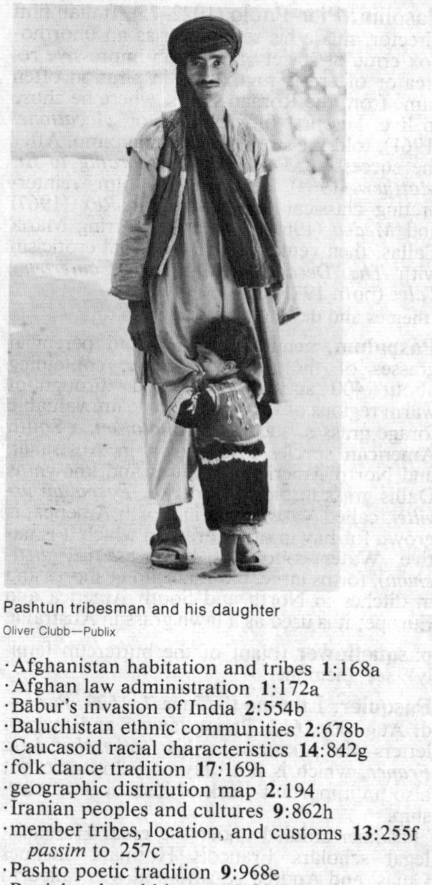
Pashtun tribesman and his daughter
Oliver Clubb—Publix

·Afghanistan habitation and tribes **1**:168a
·Afghan law administration **1**:172a
·Bābur's invasion of India **2**:554b
·Baluchistan ethnic communities **2**:678b
·Caucasoid racial characteristics **14**:842g
·folk dance tradition **17**:169h
·geographic distritution map **2**:194
·Iranian peoples and cultures **9**:862h
·member tribes, location, and customs **13**:255f *passim* to 257c
·Pashto poetic tradition **9**:968e
·Punjab cultural history **15**:288b
·racial type description **17**:125h; map 126
·Ranjit Singh's Punjab victories **15**:506b
·Sikh struggle for autonomy **16**:744h

pashtūnwalī, also spelled PAKHTŪNWALĪ, honour code of the Pashtuns of southeastern Afghanistan and northwestern Pakistan.
·moral and social obligations **13**:257c

Pashupati, town, central Nepal, in the Kāthmāndu Valley on the Bāghmati River, just east of Kāthmāndu. Regarded as the holiest place in Nepal, it is the site of an ancient Śaivite (*i.e.*, devoted to the Hindu god Śiva) temple of Paśupatinātha (Pashupatinath). The temple is built in pagoda style with gilt roof, and the banks of the Bāghmati are paved for several hundred yards. There are also numerous other shrines in the vicinity. The Śivarātri festival in February or early March attracts Hindu pilgrims from India and other foreign countries. Pious Hindus also go there to die, in the belief that they will find salvation if they

The Paśupatinātha Temple at Pashupati, near Kāthmāndu, Nepal
J. Allan Cash—EB Inc.

die with their feet in the sacred waters of the river at Pashupati.
27°42′ N, 85°22′ E

Pašić, Nicola **13**:1043 (b. Dec. 31 [Dec. 19, old style], 1845, Zaječar, Serbia—d. Dec. 10, 1926, Belgrade), statesman and one of the founders of the Kingdom of the Serbs, Croats, and Slovenes (later Yugoslavia), Pan-Serb nationalist, and leader of Serbia's Radical Party.

Abstract of text biography. Returning to Serbia (1873) after graduating from the Zürich Polytechnikum, Pašić joined a Socialist group. After participation in wars against Turkey (1876–78), he entered politics. In 1881 he helped found the Radical Party. Forced to flee to Bulgaria (1883) for plotting against King Milan Obrenović, he remained in exile until 1889. Returning to Serbia, he served as prime minister (1891–92) and Serbian minister to St. Petersburg in 1893. He left Serbia again (1899) following further attempts on Milan's life but returned in 1903 and supported the Karageorgević dynasty, in the person of King Peter I. Pašić served as premier and as minister for foreign affairs (1904–05; 1906–08; premier 1909–11). Reinstated as premier in 1912, he led Serbia through three wars; against Turkey (1912), against Bulgaria (1913), and in World War I (1914–18). Although denied the premiership of the new Kingdom of the Serbs, Croats, and Slovenes (formed Dec. 1, 1918), he was one of the new state's delegates to the Peace Conference at Versailles (1919). Appointed premier in 1921, he formed a Radical Cabinet. He was forced to resign in March 1926.

REFERENCES in other text articles:
·Austro-Hungarian antagonism **19**:944b
·Balkan political development **2**:631f *passim* to 632f

Pasig River, in the Philippines, a 14-mi-long (23-km) outlet of Laguna de Bay (*see* Bay, Laguna de) flowing north-northwest through the market town of Pasig and bisecting Manila. It empties into Manila Bay between the North and South harbours. The wharves and quays at the river's mouth served the early inter-island trade during the Spanish colonial period. At that time the Pasig was home for a large barge- and raft-dwelling population. The shallow and sluggish stream is spanned by nine bridges and is navigable by small craft; its port functions now, however, have become minimal.
14°36′ N, 120°58′ E
·Manila's features **11**:448g; map 449

Pasiphae (Greek mythology): *see* Minos; Minotaur.

Pasiphaeidae, family of shrimp of the order Decapoda, class Crustacea.
· anatomic characteristics and classification **5**:545c

Pasiteles (fl. 1st century BC), Greek sculptor, notable for having written a book, in five volumes, about works of art throughout the world. None of Pasiteles' sculpture has survived.

Little is known about Pasiteles. He was born in a Greek city in southern Italy and became a Roman citizen in 90/89. He made an ivory and gold statue of Zeus for the temple of Metellus. It is believed that he was one of the originators of exact copying of statuary by means of plaster casts and the pointing machine, which was invented about this time. He also worked from nature, however, as is shown in Pliny's story that while sketching a lion he was almost killed by a panther.

Paskevich, Ivan Fyodorovich (b. May 19 [May 8, old style], 1782, Poltava, Ukraine—d. Feb. 1 [Jan. 20, O.S.], 1856, Warsaw), military officer and administrator in the Russian government who suppressed the Polish insurrection of 1830–31. Having entered the Russian army through the imperial institution for pages in 1800, he gained combat experience fighting against the Turks (1806–12) and the French (1812–14) and became one of the emperor Nicholas I's closest associates.

Paskevich, lithograph by Antoine Maurin (1793–1860)
Novosti Press Agency

After the revolutionary Dekabrists tried to establish a constitutional regime in Russia at the time of Nicholas' accession to the throne, Paskevich participated in their trial; later, appointed governor and military commander in chief of the Caucasus (1827), he treated the Dekabrist exiles under his jurisdiction with particular severity. After the Russo-Persian war broke out in 1826, he seized the military initiative from the Persians and captured the fortress of Erivan (Yerevan; October 1827) and was rewarded with the title count of Erivan. With successive victories he forced the Persians to cede the provinces of Nakhichevan and Erivan (*i.e.*, Persian Armenia) to Russia (1828; Treaty of Turkmanchay).

Immediately afterward, with the onset of the Russo-Turkish War of 1828–29, Paskevich captured the strategic Turkish strongholds that controlled the chief route linking Transcaucasia with Asia Minor, enabling Russia, when it concluded the Treaty of Adrianople with the Turks (1829), to annex territory around the mouth of the Danube River and in eastern Asia Minor. Promoted to the rank of field marshal (1829), he subdued the mountaineers of Daghestan (in the eastern Caucasus; 1830) and was preparing an assault against the Circassians when he was transferred to Poland (June 1831) to command the Russian forces suppressing the Polish rebels. Despite his overcautiousness and indecisiveness, Paskevich defeated the rebels and was given the title prince of Warsaw. He was subsequently appointed viceroy of Poland and from 1832 to 1856 ruled dictatorially, trying to Russify the country both culturally and administratively.

When the Hungarian Revolution broke out in March 1848 and the Austrian government requested military assistance from Russia, Paskevich commanded the Russian troops that invaded Hungary in June 1849. Although his forces suffered badly from disease, and his leadership was less effective than it had been during the Polish uprising, the rebels were finally suppressed; hoping to receive better treatment from the Russians than from the Austrians, they surrendered directly to Paskevich at Világos (Aug. 13, 1849). For a brief period during the Crimean War he commanded the Russian armies in the western war zone (April–June 1854), but after being defeated by the Turks at Silistria (June 8, 1854) he was relieved of his post.

Pasoeroean (Indonesia): *see* Pasuruan.

Pasolini, Pier Paolo (1922–75), Italian film director, made his reputation as an unorthodox critic of society and as an impressive recreator of erotic myth. His inspiration often came from the Roman slums, where he chose to live. His first film as director, *Accattone!* (1961), told the story of a Roman pimp. After the success of *The Gospel According to St. Matthew* (1964), he made two films reinterpreting classical myth, *Oedipus Rex* (1967) and *Medea* (1969), the latter starring Maria Callas, then ventured into medieval eroticism with *The Decameron* and *The Canterbury Tales* (both 1971).
· themes and development **12**:535e

Paspalum, genus of annual and perennial grasses of the family Poaceae, containing about 400 species distributed throughout warm regions of the world. Some are valuable forage grasses, such as *P. dilatatum*, a South American species also grown in Australian and North American pastures and known as Dallis grass in North America. *Paspalum urvillei*, called Vasey grass in North America, is grown for hay in other areas in which it is native. Water couch, or knotgrass (*P. distichum*), forms large, flat mats along shores and in ditches in North and South America and Europe; it is used as a lawn grass in Australia.

pasqueflower (plant of the buttercup family): *see* anemone.

Pasquier, Étienne (b. June 7, 1529, Paris—d. Aug. 30, 1615, Paris), lawyer and man of letters who is known for his *Recherches de la France*, which is not only encyclopaedic but also an important work of historical scholarship.

Pasquier studied under the great Humanist legal scholars François Hotman, Jacques Cujas, and Andrea Alciato and was called to the bar at Paris (1549) and began to practice law there. In 1557 he married a wealthy young widow whom he had defended in court.

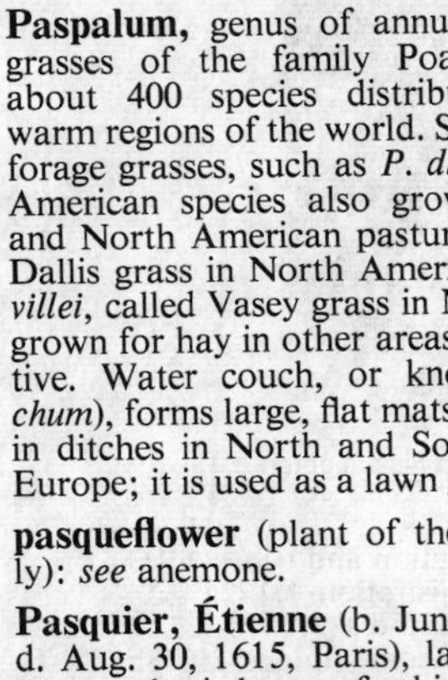

Étienne Pasquier (1529–1615), oil painting by Henri de Rudder; in the Musée National de Versailles et des Trianons, France
Cliche Musees Nationaux, Paris

He became ill in 1560 and convalesced in Amboise and Cognac, where he began work on his *Recherches* (first volume published 1560), with which he was occupied, off and on, for the next 40 years.

Pasquier hoped that his work would show the people of France the glory of their history and institutions. He wrote in French and consulted original sources, primarily court and government documents, in preference to relying on chronicles. Literary criticism was added later, as were materials from specific periods of French history. With other Humanists and lawyers, Pasquier soon developed a sustained correspondence, which was published in 1619. Providing a vivid commentary on the political and military aspects of the Wars of Religion (1562–98), it contains discussions of historical and literary problems.

In 1565 Pasquier defended the University of Paris in a suit instituted by the Jesuits, who wished to gain the right to teach there. The decision in the case was "delayed" until 1594 when the university pressed the case again and won. Although a moderate in most respects, Pasquier spent much of his life fighting the Jesuits. His *Catéchisme des Jésuites* (1602; The Jesuit Catechism) was bitterly satirical. The university trial brought him fame, and he became counsel for many important clients, primarily in cases involving property disputes. He became a commissioner at the assize court at Poitiers in 1579 and at Tours in 1583, and in 1585 Henry III appointed him advocate general in the Chambre des Comptes at Paris.

Pasquier retired from forensic work in 1604 to devote full time to his writing, publishing many more books of the *Recherches*. During this period he also wrote *L'Interprétation des "Institutes" de Justinien* (1847), a work that was as much about French law as about Roman law. Near the end of his life, disillusioned by the assassination of Henry IV (1610), he turned to biblical exegesis. He wrote some minor poetry in the style of the Pléiade and some excellent literary criticism.
· historiographic study of feudalism **8**:955a
· literature of the Renaissance **10**:1135a

Pasquier, Étienne (-Denis), duc de (b. April 21, 1767, Paris—d. July 5, 1862, Paris), statesman and the last chancellor of France. A descendant of the celebrated 16th-century

The duc de Pasquier, detail of an engraving after a portrait by an unknown artist, 19th century
By courtesy of the Bibliotheque Nationale, Paris

lawyer and man of letters Étienne Pasquier, he became a counsellor in the Paris Parlement in 1787. During the Revolution his father, also a counsellor, was guillotined, and he himself was arrested as a Royalist (1794). He was set free during the Thermidorian reaction and was later created baron (1808) by the emperor Napoleon and appointed to the council of state and to the prefecture of police (1810). On the restoration of the monarchy in 1814 Louis XVIII made him director of highways and bridges. He later served as minister of justice and foreign minister and was created duke in 1821. Nine years later he was made president of the Chamber of Peers, which enabled him to sit as supreme judge in political trials. Pasquier was appointed chancellor of France when that office was revived in 1837. He was created duc in 1844, and the hereditary succession to the title was secured for his adopted son, E.-A.-G. d'Audiffret-Pasquier. Pasquier retired from public life on the Revolution of February 1848, which replaced the monarchy with the Second Republic (1848–52).

pasquinade, a brief and generally anonymous satirical comment in prose or verse that ridicules a contemporary leader or national event. Pasquinade is derived from "Pasquino," the popular name for the remains of an ancient Roman statue unearthed in Rome in 1501. "Pasquino," supposedly named after a local shopkeeper near whose house or shop the statue was discovered, was the focus for bitingly critical political squibs attached to its torso by anonymous satirists. These pasquinades and their imitations, some ascribed to important 16th century writers such as Aretino, were collected and published. After the 16th century, the vogue of posting pasquinades died out, and the term acquired its more general meaning.

passacaglia (Italian, from Spanish *passacalle*, or *pasacalle*, "street song"), musical form of continuous variation in $\frac{3}{4}$ time; and a courtly dance. The dance, as it first appeared in 17th-century Spain, was of unsavoury reputation and possibly quite fiery. In the French theatre of the 17th and 18th centuries, it was a dance of imposing majesty. Little is known of the actual dance movements and steps. Musically, the passacaglia is nearly indistinguishable from the contemporary chaconne; contemporary writers called the passacaglia a graver dance.

Both dances gave rise to musical forms. Baroque composers used the two names indiscriminately, writing rondeaux (pieces with recurring refrains) as well as variation forms under both titles (*see* chaconne). Musicians conflict and hedge in defining the two forms. One opinion is that the chaconne is a series of variations over a short repeated theme (ostinato) in the bass—a basso ostinato, or ground bass—whereas in the passacaglia the ostinato may appear in any voice. Another view is that the passacaglia uses an ostinato normally in the bass but possibly in any voice; but the chaconne consists of variations over a harmonic ground: like a jazz riff, a series of chords that underlies the variations. Such a series may imply a constant bass line (of the chords), but merely as a component of the harmony.

Examples of passacaglias include Bach's *Passacaglia and Fugue, in C Minor*, for organ; Walter Piston's *Passacaglia* for piano; and the music of Act I, scene 4, of Alban Berg's opera *Wozzeck*.

The dance's original name survives in the *pasacalle*, a lively folk dance for couples popular in western South America.

·dance-form influence on 18th century **12**:718f
·variation forms related to ground bass **19**:28g

Passacaglia and Fugue in C Minor (1708–17), organ work by Johann Sebastian Bach.

·ground bass principle **12**:727a

passage, in horsemanship, causing the horse to walk sideways.

·haute école airs of Lippizaner horses **15**:838f

passage grave, Neolithic burial place consisting of a distinct passageway leading to a polygonal chamber, all of which was covered by a round tumulus. Megalithic in size and sometimes, as in England, containing several chambers, the passage graves usually served as family or collective tombs. The passage grave is believed to have originated in the Iberian Peninsula, spreading northward by means of a sea route to Brittany, the British Isles, and Denmark.

·Irish prehistoric burial practices **3**:283d

passage rites 13:1044, ceremonial events, existing in all historically known societies, that mark the passage from one social or religious status to another. Many of the most important and common rites are connected with the biological crises of life—birth, maturity, reproduction, and death; other rites celebrate changes that are wholly cultural, such as initiation into societies composed of people with special interests.

The text article covers the nature, significance, and functions of passage rites; classifications of rites according to life-cycle ceremonies, ceremonies of social transformation, and ceremonies of religious transformation; symbolic aspects of the ceremonies; passage rites in the context of the social system, their psychological aspects, and in the context of the religious system; and, finally, the primary passage rites (birth rites, initiation rites, marriage rites, and death rites).

REFERENCES in other text articles:

·African artistic expression **1**:234e
·African mourning dances **1**:252a
·African oral tradition in puberty rites **1**:237e
·American Indian rattle use **1**:664h
·American Subarctic Indian customs **1**:696b
·Amerindian puberty rite features **1**:673e *passim* to 675a
·Anatolian circumcision customs **1**:828f
·Australian Aborigine initiation rituals **2**:426d
·Baltic ceremonies of beginnings **2**:666g
·Buddhist monastic and other ceremonies **3**:394d
·burial customs in primitive society **6**:739b
·California Indians puberty rites **3**:621e
·Chinese ceremonies marking maturity **4**:424h
·churching of women **6**:1128a
·Congo adolescent initiation customs **4**:1122e
·dietary customs and social life **5**:729f
·drama's religious origins **18**:257g
·drugs in heightening of puberty ordeal **14**:201a
·economic exchange in primitive societies **6**:279e
·Egyptian view of time **18**:412e
·familial roles of the adolescent **7**:156e
·folk celebrative arts **7**:474d
·folklore and socio-cultural patterns **7**:464c
·Hindu and Zoroastrian parallel **8**:908f
·Hindu beliefs and practices **8**:900g
·Hindu kin role in death ritual **17**:128d
·Jain–Hindu common practices **10**:12c
·Javanese ritual selamatan **17**:227b
·Jewish concepts and practices **10**:296b
·Jewish wedding dances **10**:199g
·Manichaean initiatory rituals **11**:447c
·man's nature, afterlife, and burial **5**:533a
·Mashriq birth and circumcision rites **11**:575d
·mask use in initiation ritual **11**:581c; illus. 579
·Melanesian manhood initiation **11**:868g
·Mexican Indian children's rites **13**:247a
·Micronesian feasting occasion **12**:125c
·monastic ordination and dispensation **12**:339f
·mystery cult initiations in Roman times **12**:781h
·mythological concept of transformation **12**:802b
·Near East fertility motif in antiquity **16**:115h
·North American Plateau Indian practices **13**:228h
·Northwest Coast Indians customs **13**:252h
·Polynesian rites and customs **14**:782e
·primitive asceticism **2**:137a
·primitive societies and ritual celebrations **8**:1160c
·primitive symbolization of life crisis **14**:1046b
·puberty rites cultural significance **8**:1158a
·Pueblo Indian ceremonies **17**:308c
·religious education through ritual **15**:641c *passim* to 642e
·religious experience and life **15**:650f
·ritual objects for initiation, marriage, and death ceremony **3**:1179f
·ritual rebirth as plant or animal **1**:915e
·ritual typology and significance **15**:865h
·Roman Catholic sacrament of confirmation **15**:997f
·sacrality and primitive initiation **16**:124b
·sacred significance and practices **7**:200e
·seclusion and ritual purification **15**:301d
·shamanic visionary and symbolic rituals **16**:638f
·Shintō devotional practices **16**:674d
·Sikh practices and beliefs **16**:746g; illus. 747
·Sotho circumcision social importance **10**:835c
·South American forest culture practices **17**:122e
·South American nomad practices **17**:115d
·Ṣūfī monastic initiation ceremony **9**:947b
·Tibetan marriage and death customs **18**:377f
·Vedic sacralization procedures **16**:130d
·western Sudan initiation ceremonies **19**:798c
·wind instrument symbolic use **19**:851f
·Wiradjuri totem transmission to novice **18**:530d

Passage to India (1871), poem by Walt Whitman, first published in part in 1868 in *Atlantic Monthly*.

·triple inspiration and themes **19**:820h

Passage to India, A (1924), major novel by E.M. Forster about the barriers, not wholly insuperable, to understanding between individuals, especially those from different national backgrounds.

Passaic, city, Passaic County, New Jersey, U.S., on the Passaic River. Established by the Dutch in 1678 as a fur-trading post 9 mi (14.5 km) north of Newark and originally called Acquackanonk, it was named Passaic (Indian for Peaceful Valley) in 1854. During the American Revolution it was occupied by George Washington's troops; and following their retreat, Lord Cornwallis, British general, was quartered there. Passaic thrived as a river port until the completion of the Morris Canal between Newark and Phillipsburg (1831) and the building of the railroad reduced river commerce. With the construction of a dam (*c.* 1850), Passaic became a textile centre. With industrial expansion, the population grew from 6,532 in 1880 to 54,773 in 1910, the increase including large numbers of eastern European immigrants, especially Hungarians, Slovaks, and Poles. Once a leading woollen producer, Passaic's last mill ceased operation *c.* 1955. The city was the scene of serious labour struggles, notably textile strikes (1926) against a wage cut and involving the right of free assembly. Still an industrial city, its chief products include rubber goods, communication equipment (television tubes and receivers), textile machinery, clothing, and handkerchiefs. Inc. 1873. Pop. (1980) 52,463.
40°52′ N, 74°08′ W

Passaic River, rising near Morristown, southeastern Morris County, northeastern New Jersey, U.S. It flows south past Millington, then north and east to Paterson and its falls (70 ft [21 m] high), from which point it turns south and east past Passaic and Newark and into Newark Bay. Some 80 mi (130 km) long and with a drainage area of 935 sq mi (2,422 sq km), it has been intensively developed as a source of power and of water. Its most serious of many floods occurred in 1903. Major tributaries are the Whippany, Rockaway, Pequannock, Wanaque, and Ramapo rivers. The name is derived from the Algonkian word for valley.
40°43′ N, 74°07′ W

Passalidae (beetle family): *see* bess beetle.

Passamaquoddy, Algonkian-speaking Indians who lived on Passamaquoddy Bay, St. Croix River, and Schoodic Lake, on the boundary between what are now Maine and

New Brunswick. They belonged to the Abnaki (*q.v.*) confederacy, and their language was closely related to that of the Malecite (*q.v.*). They depended on hunting and fishing for subsistence; birch bark and wood were used for manufacture. Villages, consisting of conical dwellings and a large council house, were sometimes palisaded. A tribal council of the war chief, the civil chief, and representatives of each family decided most important matters; a general council of the entire tribe decided war matters.

The pressure of white settlement restricted their territory, and in 1866 they were settled mainly at Sebaik, on the south side of the bay, and on Lewis island. The Passamaquoddy and the Penobscot (*q.v.*) send to the Maine state legislature a representative who serves without a seat or vote and is permitted to speak only on matters of tribal concern. In 1969 there were two Passamaquoddy reservations in Maine and a total tribal population of 1,057.

·Woodlands Indian culture **6**:169b

Passamaquoddy Bay, inlet of the Bay of Fundy (Atlantic Ocean), between southwestern New Brunswick, Canada, and southeast Maine, U.S., at the mouth of the St. Croix River. Deer Island and Campobello Island are in its southern part. The bay has an immense tidal flow with about 70,000,000,000 cu ft (2,000,000,000 cu m) entering and leaving twice daily on the turn of the tide.
45°06′ N, 66°59′ W

·electric power project and opposition **11**:356g
·tidal flow, range, and power project **7**:780h; map 781

Pass and Out (card game): *see* Draw Poker.

Passant, Le (1869), play in French by François Coppée.

·Bernhardt's famous performance **2**:862h

Passarge, Siegfried (b. Feb. 26, 1866, Königsberg, East Prussia, now Kaliningrad, U.S.S.R.—d. June 26, 1958, Bremen, W.Ger.), geographer and geomorphologist known for his studies of southern Africa.

A professor at Breslau and Hamburg Universities (1908–35), Passarge studied the climate and physical morphology of Africa. He wrote *Die Kalahari* (1904), *Südafrika* (1908), *Physiologische Morphologie* (1912), *Die Grundlagen der Landschaftskunde*, (3 vol. 1919–20), *Vergleichende Landschaftskunde* (4 vol., 1921–30), *Geographische Völkerkunde* (1933), and *Die Deutsch Landschaft* (1936).

Passarowitz, Treaty of (July 21, 1718), a pact signed at the conclusion of the Austro-Turkish (1716–18) and the Venetian–Turkish (1716–18) wars at Passarowitz (now Požerevac, Yugos.). By its terms the Ottoman Turks lost substantial territories in the Balkans to Austria, thus marking the end of Ottoman westward expansion.

In 1715 the Ottomans forced Venice to surrender the Morea (the Peloponnesus Peninsula, Greece), the major Venetian gain under the Treaty of Karlowitz (1699), and threatened Venetian possessions in Dalmatia and the Ionian Islands. At this point Austria intervened by concluding an alliance with Venice (1716). In ensuing hostilities the Ottomans suffered a series of disastrous defeats at the hands of the Habsburg general Prince Eugene of Savoy. In 1718, at the initiation of Great Britain and Holland, whose eastern Mediterranean trade was disrupted by the war, a treaty was concluded at Passarowitz that provided for a 24-year peace between the Ottoman Empire and Austria and that gave to Austria the Banat of Temesvár (the last important Ottoman stronghold in Hungary), Little Walachia, and Belgrade with parts of northern Serbia. The pact stipulated that Venice surrender the Morea to the Ottomans while retaining the Ionian Islands and making gains in Dalmatia. At the same time an Austro-Turkish commercial treaty was signed, granting Austria commercial privileges in the Ottoman Empire.

·Charles VI and Habsburg gains **8**:96c
·Ottoman territorial concessions **13**:783e
·Prince Eugene of Savoy's victories **2**:457b

Passau, town, Bavaria (Bayern) *Land* (state), southeastern West Germany, port at the confluence of the Danube, Inn, and Ilz rivers, on the Austrian frontier. Originating as the Celtic settlement of Bojodurum, it was later the site of a Roman camp, Castra Batava, and was made an episcopal see in 739. The bishops became princes of the Holy Roman Empire in 1217 and ruled Passau until 1803, in spite of citizens' revolts for municipal freedom. Fires in 1662 and 1680 caused great damage and subsequent rebuilding gave the town a Baroque character. It is dominated by the Oberhaus fortress (1219) and the Cathedral (1668), which incorporates the remains of an earlier Gothic structure. The Cathedral contains one of the largest church organs in the world, with 17,000 pipes (1928). The bishops' palace (1712–30) and numerous fine churches in varied styles recall the era of the prince-bishops. The Gothic town hall (1298–1389) has paintings depicting episodes in the town's past, including its association with the Nibelungen legends. The Niedernburg convent (founded 8th century) contains the tomb of Gisela, the first queen of Hungary.

Passau, W. Ger., showing St. Paul's Church (left) and the cathedral (left centre)
Emil Bauer—Bavaria-Verlag

Passau was an important medieval trade and shipping centre. The Inn salt trade and the making of knife and sword blades were traditional occupations. It is now the economic, cultural, and communications centre of southeastern Bavaria. Industries include a bell foundry, brewing, and the manufacture of gears, optical instruments, textiles, and tobacco. There is also a tourist trade and a steamer service to Vienna. Pop. (1970 est.) 31,600.
48°35′ N, 13°28′ E

·map, Federal Republic of Germany **8**:46
·Moravian ecclesiastical development **2**:1185f

pass band, frequency band that is transmitted with maximum efficiency by a filter or circuit.

·acoustic filter operation **17**:26b

Passchendaele, Battle of: *see* Ypres, Battles of.

passement, old French name for lace, superseded in general use around mid-17th century by the term dentelle, which is still in use. *See also* point.

passenger pigeon (*Ectopistes migratorius*), migratory bird hunted to extinction by man. Billions of these birds inhabited eastern North America in the early 1800s; migrating flocks darkened the skies for days. As settlers

Passenger pigeon, mounted (*Ectopistes migratorius*)
Bill Reasons—National Audubon Society

pressed westward, however, passenger pigeons were slaughtered by the million yearly and shipped by railway carloads for sale in city markets. From 1870 the decline of the species became precipitous, and it became officially extinct when the last representative died on Sept. 1, 1914, in the Cincinnati, Ohio, zoo.

The passenger pigeon resembled the mourning dove and the Old World turtledove but was bigger (32 centimetres [about 13 inches]), with longer pointed tail, pinkish body, and blue-gray head. Its single white egg was laid in a flimsy nest of twigs; more than 100 nests might occupy a single tree. Its natural enemies were hawks, owls, weasels, skunks, and arboreal snakes.

The pigeon sometimes foraged in newly planted grainfields but otherwise did little damage to crops. Its greatest legacy to man was the impetus its extinction gave to the conservation movement. A monument to the passenger pigeon, in Wisconsin's Wyalusing State Park, declares: "This species became extinct through the avarice and thoughtlessness of man."

·behavioral characteristics **4**:932e
·extinction of species **19**:1161g
·social behaviour patterns **16**:933e

passepied, in England PASPY, lively dance of Britanny adopted *c.* 1650 by French and English aristocrats, who, during the century of its popularity, frequently danced it dressed as shepherds and shepherdesses. As a court dance the passepied lost its original chain formations and became, like the minuet, a couple dance with figures. Its name (French: "passing feet") probably refers to its characteristic step: the feet crossed and recrossed while gliding forward, one foot often striking the other.

The music, which begins with an upbeat in

fairly rapid $\frac{3}{4}$ or $\frac{3}{8}$ time, appears occasionally among the optional movements, or *galanteries*, of the suite, notably in Bach's *Partita in G Major* and English *Suite No. 5*.

Passerat, Jean (b. Oct. 18, 1534, Troyes, Fr.—d. Sept. 14, 1602, Paris), poet, author of some elegant and tender verse, and one of the contributors to the "Satire Ménippée," the manifesto of the moderate royalist party in support of Henry of Navarre's claim to the throne. He studied at the University of Paris, became a teacher at the Collège de Plessis, and in 1572 was made professor of Latin at the Collège de France, where he wrote scholarly Latin works and commentaries on Catullus, Tibullus, and Propertius. He also composed poetry, some of it inspired by the Italian Catarina Delbene, his best pieces being his

Passerat, detail of a portrait by an unknown artist
H. Roger-Viollet

short ode "*Du premier jour de mai*" ("On the First Day of May") and a charming villanelle "*J'ai perdu ma tourterelle*" ("I Have Lost My Turtle Dove"). His exact share in the "Satire Ménippée" (1594) is variously stated, but it is generally agreed that he wrote much of the verse. His lines "*Sur la journée de Senlis,*" in which he commends the duc d'Aumale's ability in running away, became a celebrated political song.

Passerculus sandwichensis: *see* sparrow.

Passer domesticus: *see* house sparrow.

passeree, unit of volume used in Bengal, which is equivalent to about 300 cubic inches (5 litres).

·weights and measures, table 5 **19**:734

Passerella iliaca: *see* sparrow.

Passeres: *see* songbird.

Passeriformes 13:1052, largest order of birds, containing more than one-half of all known species and most of the highest forms. Passeriform birds are generally subdivided as suboscines, several suborders containing about 1,100 species, and oscines, or songbirds (suborder Passeres), containing over 4,000 species. The passeriforms range in size from minute wrens and sunbirds to crows and birds of paradise. They are the true perching birds, with four toes, three directed forward and one backward.

The text article covers the birds' distribution, behaviour, morphology, evolution, and classification.

REFERENCES in other text articles:
·avoidance behaviour factors **2**:542a
·identification functions of birdsong **4**:1014c

RELATED ENTRIES in the *Ready Reference and Index: for*
common birds: see accentor; amakihi; antbird; ant pipit; apapane; asity; avadavat; babbler; bananaquit; becard; bellbird; bell-magpie; bird of paradise; bishop; blackbird; blackcap; bluebird; bluethroat; bobolink; bowerbird; brambling; broadbill; buffalo weaver; bulbul; bullfinch; bunting; bushtit; butcherbird; cacique; cage bird; canary; cardinal; catbird; chaffinch; chat; chat-thrush; chickadee; chiffchaff; chough; cisticola; cock of the rock; cordon bleu; cowbird; creeper; crossbill; crow; cuckoo-shrike; currawong; diamondbird; dickcissel; dipper; drongo; elaenia; emu-wren; fairy bluebird; fairy wren; false sunbird; fantail; fieldfare; finch; fire finch; flat bill; flowerpecker; flycatcher; forktail; fruit crow; Galápagos finch; gallito; gnatcatcher; gnatwren; goldfinch; grackle; grass finch; greenfinch; grosbeak; ground-thrush; hawfinch; helmet shrike; honeycreeper; honeyeater; house sparrow; hypocoly; iiwi; jackdaw; Java sparrow; jay; junco; jungle babbler; kingbird; kinglet; kiskadee; kokako; lark; laughing-thrush; linnet; lyrebird; magpie; magpie-robin; mamo; manakin; mannikin; martin; meadowlark; minivet; mockingbird; monarch; munia; myna; nightingale; nightingale-thrush; nun; nutcracker; nuthatch; organbird; oriole; oropéndola; ortolan; ouzel; ovenbird; oxpecker; palm chat; parrotbill; peppershrike; pewee; phoebe; pipit; pitta; plant cutter; plush-capped finch; prinia; quelea; rail-babbler; raven; redstart; redwing; reedling; robin; rockfowl; rook; rose finch; saddleback; scimitar-babbler; scrub-bird; scythebill; seedeater; serin; sharp bill; shrike; shrike-vireo; silverbill; siskin; sitella; skylark; social weaver; song-babbler; songlark; spade bill; sparrow; standardwing; starling; stonechat; sunbird; swallow; swallow-tanager; tailorbird; tanager; tapaculo; thickhead; thrasher; thrush; tit; tit-babbler; tityra; towhee; tree creeper; troupial; tyrannulet; tyrant flycatcher; umbrella bird; vanga-shrike; verdin; vireo; wagtail; wall-creeper; warbler; wattleeye; waxbill; waxwing; weaver; weaverfinch; wheatear; whinchat; whipbird; white-eye; whitethroat; whydah; woodcreeper; woodswallow; woodwarbler; wren; wren-babbler; wrenthrush; wrentit; wren-warbler; yellowhammer
bird families: Aegithalidae; Bombycillidae; Callaeidae; Campephagidae; Carduelidae; Corvidae; Cotingidae; Cracticidae; Drepanididae; Emberizidae; Fringillidae; Furnariidae; Grallinidae; Mimidae; Muscicapidae; Ploceidae; Remizidae
other: Cardinalinae; Leiothrix; songbird; suboscine

Passerina (bird): *see* bunting.

Passfield, Sidney Webb, Baron: *see* Webb, Sidney and Beatrice.

Passfield White Paper (1930), published by a British commission under Lord Passfield (Sidney Webb) recommending that Jews be forbidden to acquire more Palestinian land while Palestinians were still landless and unemployed. It was never enforced.

·recommendations for Palestine **17**:958d

Passiflorales, an order of dicotyledonous flowering plants containing 5 families, 27 genera, and about 850 species of herbs, shrubs, trees, and vines, mostly of warm regions. The largest genus in the order is *Passiflora*, the passion-flower (*q.v.*) genus, which has about 500 species, many of which are highly prized ornamental vines grown for their showy, unusual flowers (*e.g.*, the wild passion-flower or maypop, *P. incarnata;* and *P. caerulea*). Many also produce edible fruits, such as the giant granadilla (*P. quadrangularis* and *P. macrocarpa*); sweet calabash, sweet cup, or pomme d'or (*P. maliformis*); the yellow granadilla, or belle apple (*P. laurifolia*); and the purple granadilla (*P. edulis*). Another important member of the order is the papaya (*Carica papaya*, family Caricaceae), a columnar tree with large leaves in a bunch at the top like palm trees, source of the papaya fruit of the tropics. *Passiflora* and *Carica* are the only genera cultivated to any extent.

Purple granadilla (*Passiflora edulis*)
E. Lastovica

The order is considered to be evolutionarily derived from the violet order (Violales). The families are Passifloraceae (12 genera and 600 species), Turneraceae (7 genera and 120 species), Malesherbiaceae (1 genus with 35 species), Achariaceae (3 genera and 3 species), and Caricaceae (4 genera and 55 species).

The plants of the order are characterized by the presence of radially symmetrical male, female, or bisexual flowers with three to five sepals, petals, and stamens (male pollen-producing structures) and a usually one-chambered, superior ovary (*i.e.*, the female structure positioned above the attachment point of the other flower parts) composed of three to five carpels (ovule-bearing segments) with indefinitely numerous ovules attached to the inner ovary walls. Nearly all species (except Malesherbiaceae and Caricaceae) have seeds that bear a fleshy appendage called an aril. The flower is also distinctive in most species in having a gynophore or androphore, a pedestal-like structure in the centre of the flower that carries the reproductive parts of both sexes. In the passion-flower family there is an additional whorl of tendril-like structures in the flower called the corona. The fruits are capsules or berries.

·angiosperm features and classification **1**:883c

Passion, in Christianity, the suffering and death of Jesus Christ, from the events in the Garden of Gethsemane on the eve of his arrest to his entombment.

·historical reconstruction of events **10**:153c

Passion de Semur, 13th-century French medieval passion play.

·medieval dramatic literature **10**:1103g

passion-flower, members of the genus *Passiflora* (family Passifloraceae), about 500 species of tendril-bearing, herbaceous vines with characteristic flowers. Some are important as ornamentals; others are grown for their edible fruits.

The wild passion-flower, passion vine, or maypop (*P. incarnata*) climbs about 3 to 9 metres (10 to 30 feet) high and has pink and white flowers about 4 to 7½ centimetres (1½ to 3 inches) across, and a yellow, berrylike, edible fruit about 2 inches long. The yellow passion-flower (*P. lutea*) is a smaller plant with greenish-yellow flowers and purple fruits.

Some highly perfumed passion fruits are eaten as delicate dessert fruits, as the giant granadilla (*P. quadrangularis*). The purple granadilla (*P. edulis*) and the yellow granadilla (*P. laurifolia*), as well as the wild passion-flower, are widely grown in tropical America for their fruit. *Passiflora maliformis* is the sweet calabash of the West Indies. The size of these fruits usually does not exceed that of a hen's egg, but that of the giant granadilla is like a gourd and may weigh up to seven or eight pounds.

The passion-flower blossom consists of a receptacle (expanded tip of the flower stalk) that varies in form from a shallow saucer shape to a long cylindrical or trumpet-shaped tube, producing at its upper border five sepals, five petals, and many threadlike or membranous outgrowths from the tube, which constitute the most conspicuous and beautiful part of the flower, called the corona. From the base of the inner part of the tube, at the centre of the flower, rises a structure called the gynophore, a characteristic feature of the family. The gynophore is a stalk surrounded below by a small cuplike outgrowth and bearing above the middle a ring of five stamens (the male pollen-producing structures). Above the ring of stamens is the female structure, or ovary, at the top of which arise three widely spreading armlike structures, the styles. Each style ends in a button-like stigma, the pollen-receptive surface, giving each style–stigma unit an appearance rather like a stout, large-headed spike or nail. The ovary, which has a single internal compartment, contains numerous seeds arranged in three groups and ripens into a berrylike or capsular fruit.

Passion-flower (*Passiflora caerulea*)
Grant Heilman—EB Inc.

The passion-flower blossom is often used to symbolize events in the last hours of the life of Christ, the Passion of Christ, which accounts for the name of the group. Thus, the corona represents the crown of thorns; the styles represent the nails used in the crucifixion; the stamens represent the five wounds; and the five sepals and five petals represent 10 of the apostles, excluding Judas, who betrayed Jesus, and Peter, who denied him three times on the night of his trial.
·fruit and nut farming, table 1 **7**:754

passionfruit, edible fruit of the passionflower.
·fruit and nut farming, table 5 **7**:766

Passionists, also called CONGREGATION OF THE PASSION, in full CONGREGATION OF THE DISCALCED CLERKS OF THE MOST HOLY CROSS AND PASSION OF OUR LORD JESUS CHRIST (C.P.), a religious order of men in the Roman Catholic Church, founded by Paolo Francesco Danei (now known as St. Paul of the Cross) in Italy in 1720 to spread devotion to the sufferings and death on the Cross of Jesus Christ. In regions where the church is established this apostolate (religious activity) is fulfilled especially by the preaching of missions and retreats; in other regions foreign missions are conducted. The members of the order follow an austere rule of life that calls for common recitation of the liturgical office, three days of fasting each week, and other penances. Their habit consists of a black tunic and mantle with a leather belt and rosary. The tunic and mantle have a heart-shaped badge, bearing a white cross and three nails with the inscription *Jesu XPI Passio* ("Passion of Jesus Christ"). For current membership, *see* table under religious orders of men, Roman Catholic. A women's branch of the order, the Passionist Sisters, or Sisters of the Most Holy Cross and Passion of Our Lord Jesus Christ, was established in 1852.

Passion music, musical setting of the suffering and Crucifixion of Christ, based either on biblical texts or poetic elaborations. Dating from the 4th century onward, they range from unaccompanied plainsong to compositions for soloists, chorus, and orchestra. In the medieval Passion the deacon sang the entire text. A range of 11 notes was divided into three parts: the lowest four notes were used for the part of Christ, the middle register for the Evangelist, and the top four notes for the *turba* ("crowd"), which comprised all the other characters. Each of the vocal ranges was distinguished by a characteristic method of performance.

From the 15th century onward, the three parts often were sung by three deacons; in consequence, the dramatic nature of the text was heightened, and the congregation could follow the narrative easily. In the 13th century the Passions were adapted as music-drama. Two versions are found in the famous German manuscript *Carmina Burana*. Later Passion plays abound, and they tended to become longer and more complex. In the early 15th century, wealthy establishments had small choirs capable of singing the *turba* parts. One of the first composers to set this music polyphonically (for more than a single melodic part) was the Burgundian Gilles Binchois (*c.* 1438). The type of Passion in which plainsong alternated with polyphony was set by fine composers throughout Europe.

Latin and German Passion texts were used in Germany early in the Protestant Reformation. The Lutheran composer Johann Walther created a setting of the Passion according to St. Matthew (*c.* 1550) that was still popular in 1806. Other German Passions adopted a style called motet Passion because the entire text is set polyphonically, as in a motet. The 16th-century French composer Antoine de Longaval, who made extensive use of the plainsong formulas was more concerned with declamation of the text than with elaborate polyphony. Among the Germans, Jacob Handl and Leonhard Lechner produced dignified settings.

The Longaval setting inspired motet Passions by 16th-century Franco-Flemish composers, whereas Antonio Scandello, an Italian working at Dresden, produced a hybrid setting of the Passion according to St. John in German. He amalgamated the two types by setting the *turba* music for five voices, contrasting this with the single line of the Evangelist and with three-part settings of the words of Peter, Pilate, and other characters, while the words of Jesus are in four-part harmony.

The solo vocal and many-part choral styles of Italian Baroque music were strongly influential in Germany. The St. Matthew Passion setting of Thomas Selle (1599–1663) uses a double chorus extensively, while his setting of the St. John Passion incorporates instruments and a "distant choir." Contrast between the interlocutors is achieved by assigning particular instruments or groups to different characters. Chorales, or hymn tunes, were introduced into the German Passions by Johann Theile and Johann Kuhnau. The three Passions by the celebrated composer Heinrich Schütz return to the more austere type.

Settings of the Passion were rare in 17th-century Italy and France, for elaborate music was unwelcome during Holy Week. The St. John Passion setting of Alessandro Scarlatti is a strictly liturgical work that follows the text with scrupulous accuracy and refrains from undue elaboration. In France, Marc-Antoine Charpentier's Passion displays an intensity of emotion and contrast of colour.

Hamburg witnessed early attempts at operatic settings of the Passion, based on new libretti paraphrasing Biblical texts. These rhymed, sentimental accounts appealed to German audiences but were not entirely approved by the clergy. The reaction to this trend came with Christian Heinrich Postel's version of the St. John Passion, set by Handel in 1704, and with the *St. John* and *St. Matthew Passions* by J.S. Bach. Bach's Passions made the texts important and dignified and wedded to them music of remarkable fervour, heightening the drama by interplay of choral and instrumental forces alternating with vocal solos.

C.P.E. Bach wrote two Passions challenged in popularity only by Karl Heinrich Graun's *Der Tod Jesu* (*Jesus' Death*), famous even outside Germany. Throughout the Classical and Romantic periods, the Passion written as an oratorio was usual, commonly using a large orchestra and chorus. Haydn and Beethoven set fashions in the writing of Passion oratorios. The English composer Sir John Stainer's *The Crucifixion* (1887) achieved great popularity. In the 20th century the *St. Luke Passion* of Krzysztof Penderecki, a Polish composer, was acclaimed.

Passion of Anna, The (1969), film by Ingmar Bergman.
·theme and techniques **12**:537b

Passion of Joan of Arc, The (1929), film by Carl Dreyer.
·plot and techniques **12**:526f

Passion play, a religious drama of medieval origin dealing with the suffering, death, and Resurrection of Christ. Early Passion plays (in Latin) consisted of readings from the Gospel with interpolated poetical sections on the events of Christ's Passion and related subjects, such as Mary Magdalene's life and repentance, the raising of Lazarus, the Last Supper, and the lament of the Virgin Mary.

Christ before Pilate and Herod, scene from 1960 performance of the Passion play of Oberammergau
Bavaria-Verlag, Munich

Use of the vernacular in these interpolations led to the development of independent vernacular plays, the earliest surviving examples being in German. Such plays were at first only preludes to dramatic presentations of the Resurrection. The introduction of Satan (which became typical of German and Czechoslovak plays), and thus of introductory representations of the fall of Lucifer and the Fall of man (as in the early 14th-century Vienna Passion), and of scenes from the Old Testament and of the Last Judgment, led to development of cyclic plays similar to the Corpus Christi cycles. The great Celtic Passion cycles of Cornwall and Brittany, and the St. Gall Passion play (which begins with the entry of St. Augustine, who introduces the Old Testament prophets and patriarchs, and also includes the marriage at Cana) exemplify this type of Passion play.

The Tirol plays early formed a separate group, representing only scenes from the Passion and Resurrection; and the Bohemian plays, such as the St. Eger Passion, developed from a simpler version of the Vienna Passion, were also distinct in style and incident.

The earliest Passion plays of France and Flanders are thought to have their source in a nondramatic narrative poem of the 13th century, the *Passion des jongleurs*. These plays became highly elaborated in the course of their development, culminating in performances (Mons, 1501; Valenciennes, 1547) lasting more than a week. Confraternities were founded for performance of Passion plays, the most famous being the Confrérie de la Passion (1402).

Passion plays were also performed in Spain, Italy, and elsewhere, with local variations.

By the 16th century, many of the Passion plays, debased by secular influences, had degenerated into mere popular entertainments, full of crude slapstick and buffoonery. Many were forbidden by ecclesiastical authorities, and many more were suppressed after the Reformation.

The most famous of the Passion plays to survive into the 20th century is that performed at Oberammergau, in the Bavarian Alps. According to tradition, the play has been presented every 10 years since 1634, in fulfillment of a vow made after the village was spared an epidemic of plague. It remains an entirely local production, with villagers taking all the parts and singing in the chorus. Traditional Passion plays have also been revived in villages in the Austrian Tirol. In northern Spain, during Lent and Holy Week, a Catalan Passion play is performed by villagers; and in Tegelen, in The Netherlands, a modern play by the Dutch poet Jacques Scheurs is given every five years.

·Islāmic Shiʿite drama **9**:980d
·medieval dramatic literature **10**:1103g
·origins and festival performance **18**:257g
·pageant local origin **13**:865d
·puppet presentation basis **15**:294c
·Shiʿite religious festivals **9**:917b; illus.

passive immunity, resistance to disease or poison due to acquiring of preformed antibodies from another organism.

·infectious diseases and antibody action **9**:535d

passive resistance: *see* civil disobedience.

passive voice (grammar): *see* voice.

pȧssjo, the sacred area in a Lapp *kota*, or tent, found directly behind the central hearth; it was furnished with a separate entrance and sometimes set off with poles to separate it from the living space in the rest of the *kota*. The *pȧssjo* held the cooking utensils, dishes, and food of the household, as well as all objects of value, such as the men's hunting weapons, which the women were not allowed to touch. The Lapp shaman, the *noiade*, also stored his magic drum, the *kobdas*, and other magic implements there. The *pȧssjo* was strictly forbidden to women. Bear hunters left for and returned from a hunt through the *pȧssjo* door, after which the women spat alder juice upon them. The dead were also removed through this back door. The entire Lapp *kota* was a microcosmic representation of the ordered cosmos in the Lapp's world view. In such an arrangement the *pȧssjo* represented the centre of the universe, its most sacred locality.

Passo Fundo, city, northern Rio Grande do Sul state, southern Brazil, lies near the headwaters of the Rio Passo Fundo at 2,326 ft (709 m) above sea level. It was founded in 1857 and given city status in 1890. The city is a service centre for an agricultural and livestock-raising area. In addition to flour mills, meat and maté- (tea-) processing plants, there is some lumbering and sawmilling. Passo Fundo, 140 mi (225 km) northwest of Pôrto Alegre, the state capital, is accessible by railway, road, and air. Pop. (1970 prelim.) 69,135.
28°15′ S, 52°24′ W
·map, Brazil **3**:124

Passos, city in west central Minas Gerais state, Brazil, on the Rio da Bocaina near the Rio Grande, at 2,388 ft (728 m) above sea level. It was made a seat of a municipality in 1848 and became a city 10 years later. Rice, millet, sugarcane, cotton, coffee, and livestock are processed in the city and transported by rail and road to Belo Horizonte, the state capital, 183 mi (295 km) east-northeast. Pop. (1970 prelim.) 39,184.
20°43′ S, 46°37′ W
·map, Brazil **3**:124

Passout (card game): *see* Draw Poker.

Passover (Judaism): *see* Pesaḥ.

Passy, Frédéric (b. May 20, 1822, Paris—d. June 12, 1912, Paris), economist, advocate of international arbitration, co-winner (with Jean-Henri Dunant, founder of the Red Cross) of the first Nobel Peace Prize (1901). After serving as auditor for the French Council of State (1846–49), he devoted himself to writing, lecturing, and organizing on behalf of various economic reforms and philanthropies. An ardent free trader, he belonged to the 19th-century liberal tradition of the British economists Richard Cobden and John Bright, whom he knew personally.

Passy, 1901
H. Roger-Viollet

Passy's work for peace began during the Crimean War (1853–56). His plea for peace in the periodical *Le Temps* (1867) helped to avert war between France and Prussia over Luxembourg. In the same year he founded the Ligue Internationale de la Paix, later known as the Société Française pour l'Arbitrage entre les Nations. After the Franco-German War (1870–71) he proposed independence and permanent neutrality for Alsace-Lorraine. As a member of the French Chamber of Deputies (from 1881), he successfully urged arbitration of a dispute between France and The Netherlands concerning the French Guiana–Surinam boundary. He assisted in founding the International Parliamentary Union (1889) and remained active in the peace movement for the rest of his long life.

pasta, starchy food preparations frequently associated with Italian cuisine (*pasta alimentaria*) and made from semolina, the granular product obtained from the endosperm of a type of wheat called durum, containing a large proportion of gluten (elastic protein). It is formed into ribbons, cords, tubes, and various special shapes, all originally developed for specific characteristics, such as ability to retain heat, absorb liquid, or hold sauces.

In commercial processing, the semolina, mixed with warm water, is kneaded into a smooth, stiff dough and extruded. The dough, moved forward while it is being compacted and mixed, is forced through perforated plates, or dies, that form it into the desired shape. Hollow tubular forms, such as macaroni, result when the perforations are small and contain steel pins; smaller holes without pins produce spaghetti; flat ribbonlike types are made by slitted perforations. Shell forms are produced by a special die; small fancy shapes are produced by rotary knives slicing the dough as it emerges from the die. The formed dough is next dried, reducing moisture content from about 31 percent to approximately 12 percent. Drying is carefully regulated, as very rapid drying may result in cracking, and very slow drying may produce stretching or encourage the growth of mold or of organisms that produce souring.

Doughs may be coloured with spinach juice, producing green pasta; with beet juice, resulting in red types, and with eggs, adding bright-yellow colour. Eggs are frequently added to homemade pastas.

Pastas are prepared by boiling and may be cooked until firm and resilient to the bite (*al dente*) or until very tender. Uncooked products keep their freshness three to six months.

Among the popular cord forms are spaghetti ("little string"), a finer type called spaghettini, and the very fine vermicelli ("little worms"). Tubular types include macaroni, shaped into tubes of ½-inch (1¼-centimetre) diameter, and such variations as the small elbow-shaped pieces called *dita lisci*, and the large, fluted, elbow-shaped pieces called rigatoni. Ribbon types include the wide lasagna and the narrow linguini. Farfels are ground, granulated, or shredded. The wide variety of special shapes includes *farfalloni* ("large butterflies"), *lancette* ("little spears"), *fusilli* ("spindles"), and *riccioline* ("little curls").

·production techniques and problems **3**:1169g

Past and Present (1843), book by Thomas Carlyle.

·Carlyle's idea of the hero **3**:924a
·social organization theory **6**:1071h

Pastaza, province, eastern Ecuador, in El Oriente, the forested lowlands of Ecuador east of the Andes. It was created from part of former Napo-Pastaza province in 1959 and its boundaries have not been finally delimited because of a boundary dispute with Peru. Most of the terrain is tropical rain forest; the province is populated almost entirely by Indians who subsist by hunting and gathering and by primitive shifting (slash-and-burn) agriculture. The provincial capital, Puyo (*q.v.*), is a missionary settlement in the western part of the province. Pop. (1971 est.) 22,800.

·area and population table **6**:288
·map, Ecuador **6**:286

paste, a heavy, very transparent flint glass that simulates the fire and brilliance of gemstones, because it has relatively high indices of refraction and strong dispersion (separation of white light into its component colours). From a very early period the imitation of gems was attempted. The Romans in particular were very skillful in the production of coloured-glass pastes, which copied especially emerald and lapis lazuli. With an increasing demand for jewelry, the number of imitations steadily increased. In 1758 the Viennese goldsmith Joseph Strasser succeeded in inventing a colourless glass paste that could be cut and that superficially approached the sparkle of genuine diamond; the products of this paste are called strass stones.

Before 1940 most imitation gems were made from glass with a high lead content. Such glasses were called paste, because the components of the mixture were mixed wet to ensure a thorough and even distribution. Colourless paste is commonly formulated from 300 parts of silica (silicon dioxide, SiO_2), 470 of red lead (a lead oxide, Pb_3O_4), 163 of potassium carbonate (K_2CO_3), 22 of borax (a sodium borate, $Na_2B_4O_7 \cdot 10H_2O$), and 1 of white arsenic (arsenic oxide, As_2O_3). Pigments may be added to give the paste any desired colour: chromium compounds for red or green, cobalt for blue, gold for red, iron for yellow to green, manganese for purple, and selenium for red.

Pastes are softer than ordinary or crown glass but have a higher index of refraction and dispersion that give them great brilliancy and fire. The cheaper paste imitations are pressed or molded, but, on the better quality stones, the facets are cut and polished. Molded-glass imitations can be easily identified with a hand lens, because the edges between the facets are rounded whereas cut glass has sharp edges.

Cut paste stones may be distinguished from real ones in several ways: (1) paste has air bubbles, natural stones do not; (2) paste is a poor conductor of heat, and so paste stones feel warm to the touch; and (3) paste, like all glass, has an easy conchoidal fracture, yielding brilliant curved surfaces particularly on the girdle (the widest part) of mounted stones near the mounting prongs. Other differentiation methods involve hardness (paste is softer than real stones and will not scratch ordinary glass), index of refraction (1.50–1.80, less than diamond at 2.42), specific gravity (between 2.5 and 4.0, depending on the amount of red lead used), and isotropic character (because paste has the same properties in all directions, it shows only single refraction and no dichroism, whereas most natural stones are partially doubly refractive and dichroic).

paste, in pharmacy, external medicament that is stiffer and less greasy than an ointment.
·colloids properties **4**:857d
·pharmaceutical preparation methods **14**:197d

pastel, dry drawing medium executed with fragile, finger-size sticks. These drawing crayons, called pastels, are made of powdered pigments combined with a minimum of nongreasy binder, usually gum tragacanth or, from the mid-20th century, methyl cellulose. Made in a wide range of colour values, the darkest in each hue consists of pure pigment and binder, the others having varying admixtures of inert whites. Once the colours are applied to paper, they appear fresh and bright. Because they do not change in colour value, the final effect can be seen immediately. Pastel remains on the surface of the paper and thus can be easily obliterated unless protected by glass or a fixative spray of glue size or gum solution. Fixatives, however, have a disadvantage in that they tend to change the tone and flatten the grain of pastel drawings. When pastel is applied in short strokes or linearly, it is classed as drawing; when it is rubbed, smeared, and blended to achieve painterly effects, it is often regarded as a painting medium. The latter technique was principally used until the late 19th century, when the linear method came to be preferred. Special papers for pastel have been made since the 18th century with widely varying textures, some like fine sandpaper, with a flocked or suedelike finish, prominently ribbed or strongly marked by the drying felts.

Portrait of a youth from the Le Blond family, pastel drawing by Rosalba Carriera (1675–1757); in the Accademia, Venice, Italy
SCALA, New York

Pastels originated in northern Italy in the 16th century and were used by Jacopo Bassano and Frederico Barocci. The German artist Hans Holbein the Younger and Jean and François Clouet (French) did pastel portraits in the same period. The greatest popularity of the medium came in the 18th century, when it was primarily used for portraiture. Rosalba Carriera (Italian), Jean-Baptiste Chardin, François Boucher, Maurice-Quentin de La Tour, Jean-Baptiste Perronneau (all French), Jean-Étienne Liotard (Swiss), and Anton Raphael Mengs (German) were among the major masters of pastel. Largely revived and revitalized in the last third of the 19th century by the French artist Edgar Degas, pastels figure importantly in the work of such artists as Auguste Renoir, Henri de Toulouse-Lautrec, Odilon Redon, Gustave Moreau, Édouard Vuillard, Pierre Bonnard (all French), Mary Cassatt (U.S. expatriate), and Paul Klee (Swiss).
·drawing mediums and techniques **5**:997d
·drawing technique, illus., **5**:Drawing, Plate 2
·fine arts use **13**:880b

pastel-manner engraving: *see* engraving.

paste mold, iron mold lined with adherent carbon that is used to shape a circular glass object as it is blown.
·glass production processes **8**:203a

Pasternak, Boris (Leonidovich) (b. Feb. 10, 1890, Moscow—d. May 30, 1960, Peredelkino, near Moscow), poet whose novel *Doctor Zhivago* helped win him the 1958 Nobel Prize for Literature but aroused so much opposition in the Soviet Union that he declined the honour. An epic of wandering, spiritual isolation, and love amid the harshness of the Russian Revolution and its aftermath, the novel became an international best seller but circulated only in secrecy and translation in his own land.

Pasternak grew up in a cultured Jewish household. His father, Leonid, was an art professor and a portraitist of novelist Leo Tolstoy, poet Rainer Maria Rilke, and composer Sergey Rachmaninoff, all frequent guests at his home, and of Lenin. His mother was the pianist Rosa Kaufman.

Young Pasternak himself planned a musical career, though he was a precocious poet. He studied musical theory and composition for six years, then abruptly switched to philosophy courses at Moscow University and the University of Marburg (Germany). Physically disqualified for military service, he worked in a chemical factory in the Urals during World War I. After the Revolution he worked in the library of the Soviet commissariat of education.

In 1917 he brought out a volume of lyrics, *Poverkh baryerov* ("Over the Barriers"), that reflected Symbolist influences. Though avant-garde and esoteric by Russian standards, they were successful. From 1933 to 1943, however, the gap between his work and the official modes (such as Socialist Realism) was too wide to permit him to publish, and he feared for his safety during the purge trials of the late 1930s. One theory is that Stalin spared him because Pasternak had translated poets of Stalin's native Georgia. His translations, which were his main livelihood, included

Pasternak
Cornell Capa—Magnum

renderings of Shakespeare, Goethe, English Romantic poets, Paul Verlaine, and Rilke.

Although Pasternak hoped for the best when he submitted *Doctor Zhivago* to a leading Moscow monthly in 1956, it was rejected with the accusation that "it represented in a libelous manner the October Revolution, the people who made it, and social construction in the Soviet Union." The book reached the West in 1957 through an Italian publishing house that had bought rights to it from Pasternak and refused to return it "for revisions." By 1958, the year of its English edition, the book had been translated into 18 languages.

In the Soviet Union, the Nobel Prize brought a campaign of abuse. Pasternak was ejected from the translators' union and thus deprived of his livelihood. Public meetings called for his deportation; he wrote Premier Nikita S. Khrushchev, "Leaving the motherland will equal death for me." Suffering from cancer and heart trouble, he spent his last years in his home at Peredelkino.

Pasternak's works in English translation include short stories, the autobiographical *Okhrannaya Gramota* (1931; Eng. trans., *Safe Conduct*, 1958), and the full range of his poetic output, which ended on a note of gravity and quiet inwardness.

BIBLIOGRAPHY. Donald Davie and Angela Livingstone (eds.), *Pasternak* (1970); Henry Gifford, *Pasternak, a Critical Study* (1977); Olga R. Hughes, *The Poetic World of Boris Pasternak* (1974); Olga Ivinskaya, *A Captive of Time* (1978); Mary F. and Paul Rowland, *Pasternak's Doctor Zhivago* (1967).
·Khrushchev's repression of works **10**:457d
·major poetic works and Doctor Zhivago **10**:1250a
·novel changes in U.S.S.R. **13**:293f

pastes, confections made by evaporating fruit with sugar or by flavouring a gelatin, starch, or gum arabic preparation.
·candy production methods and ingredients **4**:1084a

Pasteur, Louis 13:1066 (b. Dec. 27, 1822, Dôle, Fr.—d. Sept. 28, 1895, Saint-Cloud, near Paris), chemist and microbiologist whose scientific contributions were among the most varied and important in history.

Abstract of text biography. Pasteur earned his doctorate of sciences in 1847, and the following year he presented before the Paris Academy of Sciences a paper expounding his theory of molecular asymmetry. He was named dean of the science faculty at the University of Lille in 1854, and he was director of scientific studies at the École Normale Supérieure in Paris from 1857 to 1867. He was elected to the Academy of Sciences in 1862 and the French Academy in 1882. His work on fermentation saved both the wine and beer industries through pasteurization, a process also used for milk. The silk industry benefitted from his isolating the bacilli of two distinct silkworm diseases. He originated and was the first to use vaccines for anthrax, chicken cholera, and rabies. The Pasteur Institute was established in 1888 for the research, prevention, and treatment of rabies, and he served as its head until his death.

REFERENCES in other text articles:
·biological sciences development 2:1022h
·disease cause theories and importance 18:43c
·enzymatic action as attribute of cell 3:1059g
·germ theory development 8:1114f
·history of medicine and surgery 11:832a
·life origin theories 10:900d
·medical-scientific discoveries 11:809g
·microbiology history and development 12:109h *passim* to 111c
·micro-organism and fermentation study 2:993h
·optical activity discoveries 9:1036a
·optical isomer separation 12:313c

Pasteurella: *see* eubacteria.

pasteurellosis, or SHIPPING FEVER, a bacterial disease of cattle and sheep, caused by *Pasteurella* species. It commonly attacks animals under stress, as in shipping (hence its alternate name). Fever is followed by respiratory difficulty, which may lead to pneumonia and more severe symptoms. Treatment includes isolation, rest, and antibiotic therapy. Some immunity may be gained from antiserums and other preventive preparations.
·infectious diseases of animals, table 2 5:867

Pasteur Institute (1888), Paris research centre.
·foundation and nature of research 13:1067h

pasteurization, heat-treatment process that destroys pathogenic micro-organisms in certain foods and beverages. It is named for French scientist Louis Pasteur, who in the 1860s demonstrated that abnormal fermentation of wine and beer could be prevented by heating the beverages to about 57° C (135° F) for a few minutes. Pasteurization of milk, widely practiced in several countries, notably the United States, requires temperatures of about 62° C (143° F), maintained for 30 minutes, or, alternatively, heating to a higher temperature, 72° C (161° F), and holding for 15 seconds. The times and temperatures have been worked out to destroy the *Mycobacterium tuberculosis*, one of the most heat resisting of the non-spore-forming micro-organisms capable of causing human disease. The treatment also destroys most of the potential spoilage micro-organisms and so prolongs the keeping time of food.

Pasteurization of some solid foods involves a mild heat treatment, the exact definition of which depends on the food. Radiation pasteurization refers to the application of small doses of beta or gamma rays to foods to enhance keeping quality. *Major ref.* 5:429e
·bacterial contamination of milk 2:572d
·discovery and economic importance 13:1067e
·egg processing methods 6:444c
·infectious disease prevention methods 9:546h
·nutritional vitamin C loss 13:421d
·soft drink preparation 16:1010g

pasticcio, in music, a work consisting of contributions by two or more composers; also, an operatic medley of melodies by various composers.
·Neapolitan and ballad opera 13:581a *passim* to 582b

pastiche, composite fraudulence of a work of art in which the forger combines various parts of another artist's work to form a new composition of convincing presentation.
·forgery in the visual arts 2:91d

Pastinaca sativa (plant): *see* wild parsnip.

Pasto, capital of Nariño department, southwestern Colombia, at 8,510 ft (2,594 m) above sea level at the base of extinct Volcán Galeras (13,999 ft [4,267 m]). Founded in 1539, it was a royalist stronghold during the revolution against Spain. Although now less important as a trade centre than it was in the colonial era, Pasto controls traffic between Ecuador and the Cauca Valley and is the commercial centre for the surrounding agricultural and mining area. The University of Nariño was established in Pasto in 1904. The city lies on the Pan-American Highway, 76 mi (122 km) from the Ecuadorian border and is linked by road

Galeras Volcano and mountain fields near Pasto, Colom.
Victor Englebert

and railway with the Pacific port of Tumaco. Pop. (1972 est.) 111,100.
1°13′ N, 77°17′ W
·map, Colombia 4:866

Pasto, Nudo de, also called MACIZODE PASTO, mountain knot formed in Colombia by the merging of the terminal ranges of the Andes.
1°00′ N, 77°30′ W

Paston Letters, the largest surviving collection of 15th-century English correspondence, invaluable to historians and philologists, preserved mainly in the British Museum, London; some of the letters are derived from the circle of the career soldier Sir John Fastolf (*c.* 1378–1459), and some from that of his neighbours in eastern Norfolk, the Paston family. Because the letters have survived, the Pastons and the Fastolf entourage are among the best known of their class in the 15th century. The Pastons involved in the letters include William (died 1444), who became a justice of the Court of Common Pleas; his son John I (died 1466), a London lawyer; John's two sons, John II (died 1479) and John III (died 1503), both of whom were knighted; and their respective wives and children. The collection, of more than 1,000 letters, contains instructions, information, local and national news, and gossip; through all this, the characters of the writers emerge vividly.

It is not known how the Paston Letters were kept from the 15th to the 18th century; but in 1735 the antiquary Francis Blomefield explored the muniment room at Oxnead, the family seat in Norfolk, and retrieved those letters that he adjudged "of good consequence in history." After belonging to various antiquarians, the letters eventually reached either the Bodleian Library, Oxford, or the British Museum.

The collection remains of outstanding interest to philologists as illustrations of the capacity of the English language at a crucial period in its development. For historians, the letters are a primary source for the political history of 15th-century England and also for the domestic history of medieval English provincial society.

The most complete edition is that by James Gairdner, *The Paston Letters* (6 vol., 1904).
·autobiographical literary forms 2:1009f
·literary and historical value 10:1110f
·medieval legal processes description 12:160a

pastor, a title, from the Latin word meaning "shepherd," applied in general to Christian clergymen serving a local church or parish.
·Baptist position and limited authority 2:716d
·Protestant early issues of church structure 15:110e

Pastor, Ludwig Freiherr von (b. Jan. 31, 1854, Aachen, now in West Germany—d. Sept. 30, 1928, Innsbruck, Austria), author of one of the monumental papal histories, *Geschichte der Päpste seit dem Ausgang des Mittelalters*, 16 vol. (*History of the Popes from the Close of the Middle Ages*, 1886–1933). While a student, he became acquainted with the leading historians of his day. Pastor became a lecturer at the University of Innsbruck (1881), where, in 1887, he was appointed professor of modern history. He subsequently became director (1901) of the Austrian Historical Institute, Rome, and Austrian ambassador (1920) to the Vatican. He was knighted by Emperor Francis Joseph of Austria in 1908 and created a baron in 1916.

Pastor's works include more than a dozen monographs, the most famous being his *History of the Popes*, which was translated into all major languages (Eng. ed., 1891–1953). In 1881 Pastor caused Pope Leo XIII to open the Vatican archives, heretofore unavailable to scholars; he also consulted archives all over Europe. His *History* emphasized objective scholarship, treated dark periods of the papacy with frankness, and concentrated on individual popes rather than on the papacy as an institution. Another major work includes his editing of *Geschichte des deutschen Volkes* (8 vol., 1893–1926; "History of the German People"), by one of his former teachers, Johannes Janssen.

Pastor, Tony, in full ANTONIO PASTOR (b. May 28, 1837, New York City—d. Aug. 26, 1908, Elmhurst, N.Y.), impresario and comic singer, considered the father of American vaudeville because of his influence in making variety a respectable and popular family entertainment. An entertainer from the age of six, Pastor appeared at P.T. Barnum's American Museum in New York City as a child

Tony Pastor
Culver Pictures

prodigy, in minstrel shows, and in the circus before he first performed in a variety show in 1861. He opened his own variety theatre in New York City in 1865. At the time, variety featured coarse humour and was considered entertainment only for men or for women of questionable reputation. When Pastor opened his Fourteenth Street Theatre (New York City) in 1881, he advertised it as "the first specialty and vaudeville theatre of America, catering to polite tastes, aiming to amuse, and fully up to current times and topics." His unexpected success encouraged other theatre managers to adopt his code of prohibitions. Clean variety soon became America's most popular form of entertainment.

Pastor Aeternus, a papal decree issued July 18, 1870, that outlines the conditions for a formal statement on faith or morals to qualify as infallible pronouncement.

·document's central thought **15**:1015h
·papal primacy and judicial supremacy **13**:961a

Pastoral Care (*c.* 901), English translation by King Alfred the Great of the REGULAE PASTORALIS LIBER (*c.* 591) of Pope St. Gregory I the Great, the chief textbook of bishops during the Middle Ages.
·literary merit and use **8**:416h
·translation by Alfred the Great **1**:486e

pastoral counselling, advice given by clergymen to individuals for their general spiritual development or to solve spiritual problems.
·Christian developments from early times **4**:518d

pastoral elegy (poetic form): *see* elegy.

pastoralism (herding): *see* nomadism; transhumance.

pastoralists, religion of: *see* agriculturalists and pastoralists, religion of.

Pastoral Letters, those writings of the New Testament that are principally concerned with the responsibilities of church leaders and church discipline, namely, the First Letter of Paul to Timothy, the Second Letter of Paul to Timothy, and the Letter of Paul to Titus. If they actually were written by Paul (and there is some doubt about this), they date from very late in his life. *See also* Pauline Letters; Timothy, letters of Paul to; Titus, Letter of Paul to. *Major ref.* **2**:966b
·St. Luke's disputed authorship **11**:178c
·St. Paul and Apostolic writings **13**:1090d

pastoral literature, a class of literature that presents the society of shepherds as free from the complexity and corruption of city life. Many of the idylls written in its name are far remote from the realities of any life, rustic or urban. Among the writers who have used the pastoral convention with striking success and vitality are the classical poets Theocritus and Virgil and the English poets Spenser, Herrick, Milton, Shelley, and Matthew Arnold.

The pastoral convention sometimes uses the device of "singing matches" between two or more shepherds, and it often presents the poet and his friends in the (usually thin) disguises of shepherds and shepherdesses. Themes include, notably, love and death. Both tradition and themes were largely established by Theocritus, whose *Bucolics* are the first examples of pastoral poetry. The tradition was passed on, through Bion, Moschus, and Longus, from Greece to Rome, where Virgil (who transferred the setting from Sicily to Arcadia, in the Greek Peloponnese, now the symbol of a pastoral paradise) used the device of alluding to contemporary problems—agrarian, political, and personal—in the rustic society he portrayed. His *Eclogues* exerted a powerful effect on poets of the Renaissance, including Dante, Petrarch, and Boccaccio in Italy; Pierre de Ronsard in France; and Garcilaso de la Vega in Spain. These were further influenced by medieval Christian commentators on Virgil and by the pastoral scenes of the Old and New Testaments (Cain and Abel, David, the Bethlehem shepherds, and the figure of Christ the good shepherd). During the 16th and 17th centuries, too, pastoral romance novels (by Jacopo Sannazzaro, Jorge de Montemayor, Miguel de Cervantes, and Honoré d'Urfé) appeared, as in the 15th and 16th centuries did the pastoral drama (by Politian, Beccari, Tasso, and Guarini).

In English poetry there had been some examples of pastoral in the earlier 16th century, but the appearance in 1579 of Edmund Spenser's *Shepheardes Calender*, which imitated not only classical models but also the Renaissance poets of France and Italy, brought about a vogue for the pastoral. Sir Philip Sidney, Thomas Lodge, Greene, Nash, Marlowe, Drayton, Dekker, Donne, Raleigh, Heywood, Campion, Browne, Drummond, and Phineas Fletcher all wrote pastoral poetry. (This vogue was subjected to some satirical comment in Shakespeare's *As You Like It*—itself a pastoral play.) The first English novels, by Greene and Lodge, were in the pastoral mode. Apart from Shakespeare, playwrights who attempted pastoral drama included Lyly, Peele, Fletcher, Jonson, Day, and Shirley.

The climax of this phase of the pastoral tradition was reached in the unique blend of freshness and learned imitation achieved by the poetry of Herrick and Marvell. Later 17th-century work, apart from that of Milton, was more pedantic. The 18th-century revival of the pastoral mode is chiefly remarkable for its place in a larger quarrel between those Neoclassical critics who preferred "ancient" poetry and those others who supported the "modern." This dispute raged in France, where the "ancient" sympathy was represented in the pastoral convention by René Rapin, whose shepherds were figures of uncomplicated virtue in a simple scene. The "modern" pastoral, deriving from Bernard de Fontenelle, dwelled on the innocence of the contemporary rustic (though not on his miseries). In England the controversy was reflected in a quarrel between Alexander Pope and Ambrose Philips, though the liveliest pastorals of the period were by John Gay, whose mode was burlesque (and whose *Beggar's Opera* is ironically subtitled "A Newgate Pastoral"—Newgate being one of London's prisons).

A growing reaction against the artificialities of the genre, combined with new attitudes to the natural man and the natural scene, resulted in a sometimes bitter injection of reality into the rustic scenes of such poets and novelists as Burns, Crabbe, Wordsworth, Clare, George Eliot, Thomas Hardy, George Sand, Émile Zola, B.M. Bjørnson, and Knut Hamsun. Only the pastoral elegy survived, through Shelley and Matthew Arnold.

In the time since Wordsworth, poets have sometimes revived the pastoral mode, though usually for some special purpose of their own—often ironic, as in the eclogues of Louis MacNeice, or obscure, as when W.H. Auden called his long poem *The Age of Anxiety* "a baroque eclogue." *See also* elegy.
·Milton's contribution in Lycidas **12**:205h
·origin and literary influence **15**:1024c
·pastoral play definition and theatrical scenery **18**:223b
·rural utopian tradition **13**:287a
·Spenser's Shepheardes Calender **17**:494f

pastoral staff (insignia of bishops): *see* crosier.

Pastoral Symphony (completed 1808), popular name for SYMPHONY NO. 6 IN F MAJOR, symphony by Ludwig van Beethoven.
·programmatic structure **17**:914b

pastorela, European-influenced Middle American Indian dance-drama.
·characteristics and influences **1**:675d

Pastoureaux (French: Shepherds), the participants in two popular outbreaks of mystico-political enthusiasm in France in 1251 and 1320. The first Pastoureaux were peasants in northeastern France who were aroused in 1251 by news of reverses suffered by King Louis IX in his first crusade against the Muslims. Accusing the nobles, clergy, and bourgeoisie of indifference to the King's fate, they began pillaging churches and towns. The regent of France, Blanche of Castile, who initially supported the movement, easily had the Pastoureaux put down and dispersed.

More serious was the mass rising of the Pastoureaux in 1320, directed against Philip V, whom they blamed for not undertaking a crusade. The Pastoureaux, led on by unfrocked priests and charlatans, converged on Paris. There they held the King besieged and helpless while they sacked the city and expanded their ranks with convicts released from the prisons. Still clamouring for a crusade they marched, about 40,000 strong, southwestward into the Garonne Valley, indulging in pogroms against Jews and lepers on the way. They were finally routed by the seneschal of Carcassonne; scattered bands still roamed through southern France in 1322.
·origin, course, and royal suppression **7**:617f

Pastrana (Borrero), Misael (1923–), Colombian politician, president of Colombia 1970–74.
·urban opposition to National Front **4**:877a

Pastry War, a brief and minor conflict between Mexico and France in 1838, arising from the claim of a French pastry cook living in Tacubaya, near Mexico City, that some Mexican army officers had damaged his restaurant. A number of foreign powers had pressed the Mexican government without success to pay for losses some of their nationals claimed they had suffered during several years of civil disturbances. France decided to back up its demand for 600,000 pesos by sending a fleet to Veracruz, the principal Mexican port on the Gulf of Mexico. After bombarding the fortress of San Juan de Ulúa, situated on a reef outside the harbour, and occupying the city for a short time, the French won a guarantee of payment through the good offices of Great Britain and withdrew their fleet. The most important domestic result of the conflict was the further enhancement of the prestige and political influence of the dictator Antonio López de Santa Anna, who lost a leg in the fighting.

pasture, green foliage crop, usually grass, grown for livestock feed and eaten by livestock in the field without being harvested.
·animal feed nutritive values **1**:910h
·conservation method and cycling time **5**:44d
·grass order vegetation types **14**:586a
·Kentucky distinction and use **10**:420f
·livestock production management method **5**:55f; illus. 56

Pāśupatas, perhaps the earliest Hindu sect to worship the god Śiva (Shiva) as the supreme deity; it gave rise in turn to numerous subsects that flourished in Gujarāt and Rājasthān, at least until the 12th century, and also travelled to Java and Cambodia. The sect takes its name from Paśupati, an epithet of Śiva meaning "Lord of Cattle," which was later extended to convey the meaning "lord of souls."

The Pāśupata sect is mentioned in the Indian epic the *Mahābhārata*. Śiva himself was believed to have been the first preceptor of the system. According to legends contained in later writings such as the *Vāyu-Purāṇa* and the *Liṅga-Purāṇa*, Śiva revealed that he would make an appearance on Earth during the age of Lord Viṣṇu's appearance as Vāsudeva-Kṛṣṇa. Śiva indicated that he would enter a dead body and incarnate himself as Lakulin (or Nakulin or Lakulīśa, *lakula* meaning "club"). He foretold that he would have four pupils—Kuśika, Gārgya, Maitreya, and Kauruṣya—who, after having been initiated into the doctrine, would reach Śiva's heaven and would thereafter not return (*i.e.*, would not be reborn). Inscriptions of the 10th and 13th centuries appear to corroborate the legend, as they refer to a teacher name Lakulin, who was believed by his followers to be an incarnation of Śiva, and to his four disciples. On analogy with the Vāsudeva cult, some historians place the rise of the Pāśupatas as early as the 2nd century BC, while others prefer the 2nd century AD as a date of origin.

According to the Pāśupatas, Śiva revealed five categories of the soul's obtaining release from the bonds of earthly existence: (1) *kārya*, or effect (that which is not independent); (2) *kāraṇa*, or cause (that which is independent); (3) *yoga*, or path (consisting of two types, one involving cessation from action); (4) *vidhi*, or rule (conduct); and (5) *duḥkhānta*, or final deliverance (of two kinds, one the total destruction of misery and the other the attainment of miraculous powers).

The simple ascetic practices adopted by the

Pāśupatas included the thrice-daily smearing of their bodies with ashes, meditation, and chanting the symbolic syllable "om." The sect apparently included lay householders as well as ascetics. The school fell into disrepute when some of the mystical practices were distorted. Out of the Pāśupata doctrine developed two extreme schools, the Kālāmukhas (Black-faced) and the Kāpālikas (worshippers of Kāpālin, the skull bearer; *i.e.*, Śiva), as well as one moderate sect, the Śaivas (also called the Siddhānta school). The Pāśupatas and the extreme sects were called Atimārgika (schools away from the path) to maintain their distinction from the more rational and acceptable Śaivas, whose development led into modern Śaivism. *See also* Kāpālikas and Kālāmurkhas.

Paśupati, in Hindu cosmology, a form of Śiva bearing the epithet "Lord of Beasts."
·Śiva's association with Varuṇa **8**:894c

Pasuruan, also spelled PASOEROEAN, port, Djawa Timur (East Java) province (*daerah tingkat I*), Java, Indonesia, on Selat (strait) Madura. It was the capital of a Dutch residency which by transferring to Malang in 1934, precipitated the industrial decline of the town, with much of its trade being diverted to Probolinggo. The town has institutes of forestry and copper mining, a research institute for pulmonary diseases, a hospital, and a number of schools. Industries include rice milling, tanneries, light engineering, shipbuilding, and cabinet making. A railway passes through Pasuruan. Latest census 63,408.
7°38′ S, 112°54′ E
·map, Indonesia **9**:460

Pataecidae, family of mail-cheeked fish in the order Scorpaeniformes (class Actinapterygii).
·classification and general features **16**:400e

patagium, in biology, an extension of skin such as that found between the limbs of flying squirrels and flying lizards, or the flaps of skin on the surface of a bird's wing that keeps the flight feathers from twisting during flight. The term patagia refers to lateral projections on the backs (thorax) of some insects.
·gliding animal anatomy and technique **11**:22d
·rodent locomotive adaptations **15**:971h

Patagona gigas: *see* hummingbird.

Patagonian Desert 13:1068, essentially a semi-arid and scrub plateau, in southern Argentina, is the largest desert in the Americas, with an area of about 260,000 sq mi (673,000 sq km). Its approximate boundaries are the Río Colorado in the north, the Atlantic Ocean in the east, the Río Coig (Coyle) in the south, and the Andes in the west.

The text article surveys Patagonia's physiology, geology, different types of landscape and geomorphological features, rivers and soils, climate, vegetation and animal life, population, resources, transport facilities, and future prospects.

REFERENCES in other text articles:
·Andes course and geography **1**:856d
·Andes soil and flora characteristics **1**:859c
·aridity causation **5**:604g
·desert location and landscape **13**:1068c
·geographic features and settlement **1**:1135c *passim* to 1138h
·Indian cultural and economic patterns **17**:112g *passim* to 115h
·Magellan circumnavigation discovery **7**:1041h
·map, Argentina **1**:1136
·map, South America **17**:77
·nomad cultures distribution map **17**:113
·physical features **17**:74c; map 81
·plateau structure **14**:527f
·solo song as hunting people hallmark **16**:791g

Patagonian Shield, ancient Precambrian shield in South America.
·geological features and separation **6**:46g

Patagonian Theatre, 18th-century London puppet theatre.
·puppet theatre presentations **15**:294f

Pāṭaliputra (India): *see* Patna and Pāṭaliputra.

Pātan (Nepal): *see* Lalitpur.

Pātan, town, Mehsāna district, Gujarāt state, west central India, on the Saraswati River in the lowlands between the Arāvalli Range and the Gulf of Cambay. Once capital of the Chāvada and Solaṅki dynasties (720–1242), it was sacked in 1024 by Maḥmūd of Ghazna. Pātan is now a commercial centre for agricultural produce; industries include cotton milling, weaving, embroidering, and wood and ivory carving. Pottery and swords are also manufactured in the town, which is served by a railroad. Pop. (1971 prelim.) 17,473.
23°52′ N, 72°07′ E
·map, India **9**:278

patanas, grasslands of Sri Lanka (formerly Ceylon).
·Ceylon's eastern highlands **17**:521d

Patángoro, sometimes called PANTÁGORO, Indian people of western Colombia, apparently extinct since the late 16th century. They spoke a language of the Chibchan family. The Patángoro were agricultural, raising corn (maize), sweet manioc (yuca), beans, avocados, and some fruit. Land was cleared by slash-and-burn methods, and planting was done with digging sticks by the sisters of the man who owned the field. Fishing was an important food source, but hunting was not; and there were no domesticated animals except possibly tamed fledglings. Their villages of 50 to 100 houses, located in high places, were sometimes fenced by wooden palisades for defense purposes. Clothing was minimal: men went naked, and women wore a small cotton apron. Skull deformation was practiced, and feathers, beads, and (rarely) gold ornaments were worn. Little is known about Patángoro crafts, although evidently pottery was made. Marriage consisted of a trade between two men of their sisters, and most men had several wives, who were often themselves sisters. Marriages were ended without formality if the husband or the wife's brother so wished; in such a case the divorced wife was returned in exchange for the sister originally traded. The Patángoro recognized several deities, the most important of which was Am, a wind god.

Their methods of warfare were cruel. They fought continually with their neighbours and killed and ate their prisoners.
·tribal distribution map **3**:1107

Patañjali, also called GONARDĪYA and GONIKĀPUTRA (fl. 2nd century BC or 5th century AD), author or one of the authors of two great Hindu classics: the first, *Yoga sūtras*, a categorization of Yogic thought arranged in four volumes with the titles "Psychic Power," "Practice of Yoga," "Samadhi" (transcendental state induced by trance), and "Kaivalya" (liberation); and the *Mahābhāṣya* ("Great Commentary"), which is both a defense of the grammarian Pāṇini against his chief critic and detractor Kātyāyana and a refutation of some of Pāṇini's aphorisms.

The *Yoga sūtras* seems to span several centuries, the first three volumes apparently written in the 2nd century BC and the last book in the 5th century AD. Authorities therefore tend to credit more than one author writing under this name, although there is wide variance in opinion. There is a possibility that many men used this name, as it was used by the authors of a number of other works on such diverse subjects as medicine, metrics, music, and alchemy. The name itself is obviously a pseudonym, since it denotes no caste and implies divine descent from the Great Serpent, Śeṣa.
·Hindu and Greek gnostic parallels **8**:913f
·Sanskrit use in Middle Indo-Aryan era **9**:446c
·Yoga-sūtras' philosophical influence **9**:320h

Pātan-Somnāth (India): *see* Somnāth.

Patarines, also called PATARELLI, a medieval reform movement of lay craftsmen, tradesmen, and peasants organized in Milan in the mid-11th century to check the papacy's moral corruption and temporal powers. Viewed by the church as heretical, the Patarines, though short-lived in terms of organized activities, became an impetus for a large number of religious reform movements that arose during the decline of the feudal system and the beginnings of the aspirations to power of the peasant and middle classes.
·church corruption and secular protest **9**:1129b
·Henry IV's Investiture Conflict stimulus **8**:761f

patas monkey (*Erythrocebus patas*), long-limbed quadrupedal monkey, family Cercopithecidae, also called, because of its colour and habits, red guenon and Hussar, military, and dancing red monkey. The adult patas monkey has a shaggy red coat set off by a white moustache and white underparts. It is about 50–70 centimetres (20–28 inches) long excluding the tail of about the same length.

Patas monkey (*Erythrocebus patas*)
George Schaller

Omnivorous and predominantly terrestrial, it lives in bands in the grass and scrub regions of Central Africa. Single young are born, possibly only at a certain time of year, after a gestation period estimated at 170 days. The patas monkey is said to be a good pet but is somewhat delicate in captivity.
·reproductive behaviour and habitat **14**:1017c

Patavium (Italy): *see* Padua.

Patay, Battle of (June 18, 1429), a major victory for the French over the English in the Hundred Years' War. In May 1429, when they had to raise the Siege of Orléans, the English forces had retired to their three principal strongholds on the Loire, Jargeau (upstream from Orléans), Meung, and Beaugency (both downstream). Incited to the offensive by Joan of Arc, the French army under the Duc d'Alençon took Jargeau on June 12 and proceeded to besiege Beaugency. Meanwhile, two English commanders, John Talbot and Sir John Fastolf, were approaching the Loire with reinforcements from Janville. When they heard, however, that the French, having taken Beaugency as well as Jargeau, were advancing in strength against Meung, they began a withdrawal back toward Janville; but just south of Patay (nearly halfway between Meung and Janville) the French overtook them. The French cavalry, led by La Hire, Étienne de Vignolles, and Jean Poton de Xaintrailles, attacked promptly, before Talbot had time to post his archers effectively for the defense of Fastolf's outnumbered troops. The English were routed, and Talbot was taken prisoner. The victory paved the way for the advance of Charles VII into France north of the Loire for his long-overdue coronation at Reims.
·Joan of Arc's victory over English **10**:226h

Patayan (HAKATAYAN) **culture,** centred in the desert region around the lower Colorado River and probably dating from about AD 600 to historic times. Its earliest stage marks the first appearance of pottery in this region. These Indians practiced floodplain farming.

Patcham Limestones, division of Jurassic rocks in the Kutch region of India, along the coast from Bombay to Karachi. (The Jurassic Period began about 190,000,000 years ago and lasted about 54,000,000 years.) The

Patcham Limestones are divided into an Upper and Lower Patcham. The Upper Patcham is a coralline limestone characterized by the ammonite genera *Macrocephalites*, *Procerites*, and *Sivajiceras;* the Lower Patcham is a shelly limestone characterized by different species of *Macrocephalites*. The Patcham underlies the Chari Group and overlies rocks of the Kuar Bet Beds.

·rock sequence table **10**:357

patch box, small, usually rectangular, sometimes oval, box used as a receptacle for beauty patches. Especially in the 18th century, fashionable women (and sometimes men) pasted onto their faces black patches of gummed taffeta, to emphasize the beauty or whiteness of the skin. The patches varied in form and design from simple spots, stars, or crescents to elaborate representations of animals, insects, or figures.

Early American silver patch box by William Rouse, *c.* 1690–1705; in the Yale University Art Gallery

By courtesy of the Yale University Art Gallery, the Mable Brady Garvan Collection

There was a language of patches: a patch at the corner of the eye could indicate passion, one in the middle of the forehead could express dignity. Women sometimes carried their patch boxes (which might also contain rouge) with them. A gift of a patch box could be a costly expression of admiration, for they were usually of gold, sometimes enamelled or painted with scenes of *l'amour* and encrusted with jewels. Mme de Pompadour reputedly kept on her dressing table a special patch box, made in the shape of a swan and enamelled naturalistically.

Patchen, Kenneth (b. Dec. 13, 1911, Niles, Ohio—d. Jan. 8, 1972, Palo Alto, Calif.), experimental poet, novelist, painter, and graphic designer.

Itinerant in his youth and only occasionally a student, Patchen worked at many jobs before beginning to write and paint. He published many collections of verse from 1936, notably *Collected Poems* (1968), and several novels, including *The Journal of Albion Moonlight* (1941), *Memoirs of a Shy Pornographer* (1945), and *See You in the Morning* (1948). He also wrote plays and other works, all of which exhibit a combination of high idealism, abhorrence of violence, isolation from the mainstream of American thought, and shock at materialistic secularism. In occasionally sentimental verse and drawings, he celebrated the joy and freedom he felt in life, frequently in an experimental style.

patch panel, in theatrical lighting, device that makes possible temporary connection and control of a group of stage lights.

·stage lighting's technical development **17**:555c

patch reef: *see* coral islands, coral reefs, and atolls.

patch test, method of identifying substances to which a person may be hypersensitive.

·allergic reactions to foreign proteins **1**:609b

pa te (Chinese: "eight virtues"), Chinese list of virtues generally identified as: *chung* ("loyalty"), *hsiao* ("filial piety"; *q.v.*), *jen* (*q.v.*; "benevolence"), *ai* ("love"), *hsin* ("sincerity"), *i* ("righteousness"), *ho* ("harmony"), and *p'ing* ("peace"). It is also possible to read the virtues two by two, thereby obtaining four complex concepts.

The origin of the *pa te* is uncertain, and lists have varied through the ages. The Taoist sage Chuang-tzu spoke of eight virtues in the 4th century BC, the same number cited by the K'ang-hsi emperor (reigned 1661–1722). Such early sages as Confucius, Mencius, and Tseng-tzu often emphasized single virtues but with the understanding that single virtues do not flourish alone.

A severely derogatory Chinese expression, *wang pa*, is sometimes interpreted as meaning "forget the eight," suggesting that a person who has forgotten the eight virtues is worthy of nothing but contempt.

The *pa te* are often associated with the *ssu wei* ("four directions"), the cornerstones of Chinese society, said to provide a moral defense for the nation. The *ssu wei*, which may have been known about a century before the time of Confucius (whose dates are 551–479 BC), are *li* ("propriety"), *i* ("righteousness"), *lien* ("modesty"), and *tz'u* ("sense of shame").

pâte de riz (French: "rice paste"), alabaster glass, a type of semi-opaque glass of a slightly grayish colour resembling that of rice water. It was invented in Bohemia and produced from 1840 onward. Well made, it can be a fine glass, but since it contains no lead, it has no ring. It was copied in France from 1843; at first, because of the cost, it was used only for luxury wares, but by 1870 quite ordinary articles were made in *pâte de riz*.

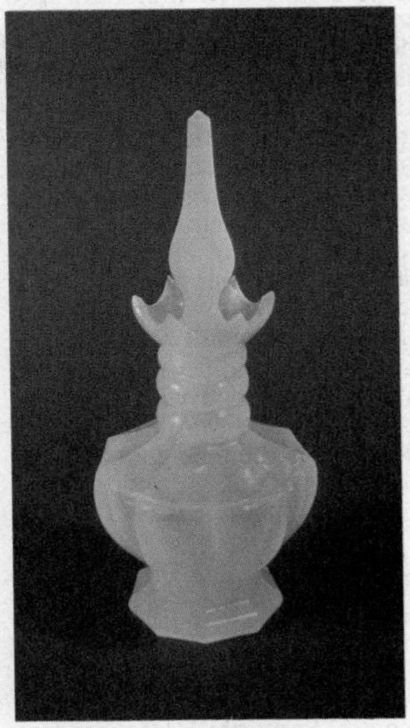

Pâte de riz glass flacon made at the Saint-Louis glass factory, France, 1844; in the Musée National de Céramique, Sèvres, Fr.

By courtesy of the Musee Ceramique, Sevres, Fr.

pâte de verre (French: "glass paste"), in glassmaking, powdered glass fired in a mold.

·technique and use **8**:194e

Pategi, town, Kwara State, west central Nigeria, on the south bank of the Niger River opposite the town of Mureji and the mouth of the Kaduna River and at the end of a road that has connections to Lafiagi, Jebba, and Ilorin. Founded in the late 16th century by the *etsu Nupe* ("king of the Nupe"), the town became the capital of the Pategi emirate in 1898. Idrisu Gana, the leader of the Kede (a subgroup of the Nupe), had given aid to the Royal Niger Company in its conquest of Bida, a Fulani-dominated Nupe town (28 mi [45 km] north-northeast), in 1897; and, in return, the company recognized him as the *etsu Nupe* and the first emir of Pategi. Most of the present inhabitants of the emirate are Muslim Nupe (*q.v.*) people.

A collecting point for the rice grown on the floodplains of the Niger and for dried fish, it is also a market centre for rice, yams, guinea corn, millet, maize (corn), sugarcane, kola nuts, peanuts, palm produce, fish, and cotton. The weaving of cotton cloth and of raffia mats is traditionally important. Served by a government craft school, Pategi also has a health office and a maternity clinic and dispensary. Pop. (latest census) 5,399.

8°44′ N, 5°44′ E

·map, Nigeria **13**:86

Patel, Pierre, the Elder (b.1605—d. Aug. 5, 1676, Paris), French artist, known for his landscape paintings. With Eustache Le Sueur he decorated the Hôtel Lambert, and he decorated the apartments of Anne of Austria in the Louvre. He was a founding member (1648) of the Académie Royale de Peinture et de Sculpture. His son, Pierre Patel the Younger (1648 or 1654–1705), was also a landscape painter.

·Claude Lorrain's influence **4**:695g

Patel, Vallabhbhai Jhaverbhai **13**:1069, called SADAR ("Leader") PATEL (b. Oct. 31, 1875, Nadiād, Gujarāt, India—d. Dec. 15, 1950, Bombay), barrister and statesman, one of the leaders of the Indian National Congress during the struggle for Indian independence.

Abstract of text biography. After studying law in India and England, Patel became the leading barrister in criminal law at the Ahmadābād bar. In 1917, having been influenced by Gandhi, he changed his style and appearance and dressed in the white cloth of the Indian peasant. He was municipal president of Ahmadābād (1924–28). In 1928 he led the landowners of Bārdoli in their resistance against increased taxes. During the 1930s and '40s he was repeatedly imprisoned by the British. In the first three years of Indian independence (1947–50) he was deputy prime minister, minister of home affairs, minister of information, and minister of states.

REFERENCES in other text articles:

·Congress deliberations on Pakistan **9**:422b

·Gandhi and Congress Party factions **7**:877c

Patella (snail): *see* limpet.

patella, also called KNEECAP, triangular bone in the tendon of the quadriceps extensor femoris muscle that helps provide stability for the knee joint. The ligamentum patellae joins the apex of the triangle to the tuberosity of the tibia, or shinbone, which may be felt below the movable kneecap at the front of the knee joint. The patella articulates behind with the femur, or thighbone.

·human skeleton, illus. 1 **16**:813

·Lister's work on surgical antisepsis **10**:1034b

patellar reflex: *see* knee-jerk reflex.

Patenier, Joachim (de): *see* Patinir, Joachim (de).

patent ductus arteriosus, persistence of a channel that shunts blood between the pulmonary artery and the aorta. Normally, after birth the pulmonary artery carries blood depleted of oxygen and laden with carbon dioxide from the right lower chamber of the heart to the lungs, where the excess carbon dioxide is removed from the blood and replaced with oxygen. Before birth the fetus depends upon its mother's circulation for this function and not on its own lungs. Consequently, a shunt carries blood from the right side of the heart over into the aorta for distribution into the general circulation. Persistence of the open passage is a common congenital defect that ordinarily causes no symptoms. It is diagnosed from characteristic abnormalities of the heart sounds. If the passageway is large, it can have serious effects. The left side of the heart tends to become enlarged. Abnormally high pressure in the pulmonary artery may direct sufficient oxygen-poor blood to the aorta and the general circulation to deprive parts of the body of adequate oxygen during exertion or even when the affected person is resting. The oxygen deprivation is indicated by cyanosis—bluish discoloration—of the feet. Treatment of patent ductus arteriosus is surgical, the ligation—tying off—of the duct.

·anatomic description **3**:887g
·surgical treatment procedure **3**:895h

patent flour, a high-grade wheat flour consisting wholly of endosperm of sound wheat grains, usually with the outer parts of the endosperm removed.

·content purity due to milling technique **3**:1164c

patent law 13:1071, the law relating to government grants of the exclusive right to make, use, or sell a new and useful product, commodity, process, or improvement.

The text article covers the history of patents, the processes of granting patents, and the international conventions and other developments relating to patents.

REFERENCES in other text articles:
·auto industry technological controversy **2**:528e
·Bell's patent and telephone specifications **18**:84d
·copyright law theories and comparisons **5**:152d
·government research-contract problem **15**:743h
·perpetual-motion machine patent application restriction **14**:105a
·Soviet restrictions and rights **17**:319d
·technology development results **18**:45b
·telephone industry decisions **18**:85b
·trademark and patent distinctions **18**:558d

patent leather, hard, smooth leather with a glossy surface created by application of daub and varnish. *See* leather and hides.

patent-note hymnals: *see* shape-note hymnals.

patent sail, an early-19th-century improvement in windmill construction which permitted the shutters on all the sails to be controlled simultaneously by a lever inside the mill.

·windmill improvement role **18**:38f

Patents and Designs Act (1907), an act providing that a British patent could only be retained to protect manufacture carried on in Great Britain.

·Lloyd George's legislative reforms **11**:7b

Pater (Latin: "Father"), in Mithraism, the highest initiatory degree.

·mystery cult initiatory structure **12**:782a

Pater, Walter Horatio (1839–94), English critic and essayist, celebrated for his painstak-

Pater, drawing by Simeon Solomon, 1872; in the Horne Museum, Florence
By courtesy of the Museo Horne, Florence

ingly fastidious style. His highly personal criticism of painting and of literature were halfway between scholarship and original artistic creation.

·aesthetic principles impact on Wilde **19**:824g
·English literature of the 19th century **10**:1186f

patera, in architecture, small disklike ornament decorated in low relief in one of a wide variety of forms and often sunk below the level of the surrounding surface. Originally a patera was a flat, saucer-like, handleless vessel

Detail of patera from the doorway of the north porch of the Erechtheum, the Acropolis, Athens, designed by Mnesicles, 5th century BC
Alison Frantz

used by the ancient Romans for drinking and pouring libations at their festivals. Paterae, which recur throughout classical and neoclassical designs for furniture, as well as on interior and exterior walls, often feature an acanthus leaf motif. When a stylized rose pattern is employed, the patera may be called a rosette.

Paterculus, Velleius: *see* Velleius Paterculus.

paterfamilias, head of the patriarchal social unit in ancient Rome.

·Rome's family structure **15**:1086f

Paterinida, order of branchiopods of the class Inarticulata.

·classification and general features **3**:100c

Paterna ware, tin-glazed earthenware (*q.v.*) produced in the 14th and 15th centuries at

Paterna ware albarello from Spain, 14th century; in the Cleveland Museum of Art
By courtesy of the Cleveland Museum of Art, in memory of Mr. and Mrs. Henry Humphreys, gift of their daughter, Helen; purchase from the J.H. Wade Fund

Paterna, near Valencia in eastern Spain. Although pottery was produced in Paterna as early as the 12th century under the Almohads, it was not famous until the reign of the Naṣrids (1230–1492), the last Islāmic dynasty of Spain. Like the works of the other great Hispano-Moresque pottery centres, Valencia, Manises, and Málaga, the stylistic origins of Paterna ware may be traced ultimately to the Middle East. Paterna ware is somewhat plainer in style, however, than the lustreware (pottery painted with metallic pigments) produced by these other cities, but the decorative effects are highly refined. Representational and abstract designs are usually combined in a rather formal, geometric manner. In spite of occasional Gothic motifs, Paterna ware has a strong Oriental quality, particularly evident in its stylized representations of animal figures. Greens, blues, manganese violets, and browns are the favourite colours painted on a white background. The most common surviving forms of Paterna ware are large plates and bowls, examples of which may be seen in the Louvre, in Paris.

·tin-glazed pottery wares **14**:905d

Paternò, town, Catania province, eastern Sicily, Italy, at the southwest foot of Mt. Etna, overlooking the Fiume (river) Simeto, just northwest of Catania. It is believed to occupy the site of the ancient Siculan town of Hybla Maior or Hybla Geleatis. Paternò suffered heavily from Allied bombing in World War II. It is dominated by the restored Norman castle (1073, rebuilt 14th century), and there are several medieval churches. It is a holiday resort with hot mineral springs, and citrus fruits and grapes are cultivated. Pop. (1971 prelim.) mun., 44,877.
37°34′ N, 14°54′ E

·map, Italy **9**:1088
·map, Sicily **16**:728

Pater Noster: *see* Lord's Prayer.

paternoster lakes: *see* glacial valley.

pater patriae (father of the country), in ancient Rome, a title originally accorded (in the form *parens urbis Romanae*, or parent of the Roman city) to Romulus, Rome's legendary founder, and to Marcus Furius Camillus, who led the city's recovery after its capture by the Gauls (*c.* 390 BC). The senate conferred it on Cicero and Julius Caesar in the 1st century BC, and it was thereafter borne by most of the Roman emperors. Various later Western statesmen (*e.g.*, the first U.S. president, George Washington) were honoured with this title in imitation of the Romans.

·Cosimo Medici's noteworthy life **11**:818c

Paterson, city, seat (1837) of Passaic County, northeastern New Jersey, U.S., on the Passaic River northwest of New York City. It was founded after the American Revolution by advocates of American industrial independence from Europe who saw the falls of the Passaic, which drop 70 ft (21 m), as the best potential industrial site on the Atlantic Seaboard. The enterprise was chartered by the New Jersey legislature in 1791 as the Society for Establishing Useful Manufactures (SUM); the city was named for Gov. William Paterson, one of the framers of the U.S. Constitution.

A successful enterprise, SUM ultimately sold waterpower and building space to private manufacturers. The earliest industries were cotton mills, and Samuel Colt produced the first Colt revolvers there in 1836. By 1837, when the locomotive industry was established, machine manufacturing had become important. The silk industry was introduced in 1839, and linen thread manufacture was begun in 1864. The city was the scene of many labour disputes, but by the mid-20th century it had become a centre of widely diversified industrial activity, including textiles, machines, machine tools, and chemicals.

Falls on the Passaic River at Paterson, N.J.
George E. Jones III—Photo Researchers

Rutgers, the state university, has a branch in Paterson as does Seton Hall University. Paterson State College (established as Paterson City Normal School in 1855) is nearby. Paterson Museum is known for its collection of New Jersey rocks and Indian relics. One of the first modern submarines, which sank in the Passaic River in 1878, was recovered in 1927 and placed on exhibit in West Side Park.

Lambert Castle (1891) in the Garret Mountain Reservation houses the Passaic County Historical Society Museum. Inc. 1851. Pop. (1980) 137,970.
40°55′ N, 74°10′ W
·map, United States **18**:908

Paterson (5 vol., 1946–58), poem by William Carlos Williams.
·poetic structure innovations **10**:1044d

Paterson, A(ndrew) B(arton), also called BANJO PATERSON (b. Feb. 17, 1864, Narrambla, New South Wales—d. Feb. 5, 1941, Sydney), poet and journalist noted for the internationally famous song "Waltzing Matilda." He achieved great popular success in Australia with *The Man from Snowy River and Other Verses* (1895), which sold more than 100,000 copies before his death, and *Rio Grande's Last Race and Other Verses* (1902), which also went through many editions.

Educated as a lawyer, he practiced in Sydney until 1900, then became a journalist, covering the Boer War in South Africa and travelling on assignment to China and the Philippines. He became editor of the *Sydney Evening News* in 1904 but left this post two years later to edit the Sydney *Town and Country Journal*. He later took up ranching; but when World War I broke out, he travelled to Europe for the *Sydney Morning Herald* and later served with the armed forces in France and Egypt. After the war, he spent the rest of his life as a journalist.

The Man from Snowy River and Other Verses was a popular success at once, selling 10,000 copies in its first year of publication. In 1905 he published a collection of popular Australian songs, *The Old Bush Songs: Composed and Sung in the Bushranging*, and *Digging and Overlanding Days*, another success. The famous "Waltzing Matilda" appeared in 1917 as part of a collection of verses entitled *Saltbush Bill, J.P., and Other Verses*. He also produced several other volumes of verse, including one for children (*The Animals Noah Forgot*, 1933), and some short stories.

Paterson, Sir Alexander (b. Nov. 20, 1884—d. Nov. 7, 1947, London), penologist who modified the progressive Borstal system of English reformatories for juvenile offenders to emphasize its rehabilitative aspects. Before he became a prison commissioner (1922–47), Paterson had worked with discharged Borstal boys and was therefore well qualified to undertake reform of the system, emphasizing special location and treatment on reformatory lines of prisoners from age 16 to 21 selected from the ordinary prisons, implemented in 1902 by Sir Evelyn Ruggles-Brise at Borstal, Kent. Among Paterson's innovations were the introduction of the Borstal house system, in which groups of delinquents live in individual houses, each with its own trained and dedicated housemaster and house staff who try to influence the boys by good example and a training program that includes hard but interesting work, extended education, and sports. Paterson emphasized that rehabilitation consists of sparking a drive for reform within the delinquent rather than imposing it upon him.

Paterson, William (b. April, 1658, Tenwald, Dumfries—d. Jan. 22, 1719), founder of the Bank of England, writer on economic issues, prime mover of an unsuccessful settlement at Darién on the Isthmus of Panama. After travelling in Europe and the West Indies, where he gained experience as a merchant, he returned to England and tried unsuccessfully to induce the government of King James II to back an expedition to Darién.

By 1686 Paterson was a London merchant and a member of the Merchant Taylors' Company. In 1694 he organized the Bank of England, an institution long desired by the London merchants. He withdrew as a director the next year, following a policy disagreement. After an unsuccessful attempt to organize a rival bank in London, Paterson resumed efforts to start a colony at Darién. Along with a group of Scottish and English merchants seeking investment outlets, he secured in 1695 the passage by the Scottish Parliament of the Act for a Company Trading to Africa and the Indies. Paterson was deprived of his position in the company by the directors because he was suspected of being involved with a loss of company funds, although his guilt was never proved. He nevertheless accompanied the expedition in 1698 as a private citizen.

Paterson lost much of his financial investment in the affair. His wife and child died at Darién, and he was forced to return to England after falling gravely ill. Thereafter, Paterson continued agitation for new expeditions to the West Indies, and he advocated the parliamentary union of Scotland and England. Beginning in 1701, he recommended that the government employ the sinking-fund method of retiring the national debt, whereby deposits are regularly made in a fund for this purpose. His proposals provided the basis of Robert Walpole's sinking fund established in 1716. Shortly before his death, the British government paid him an indemnity for his losses incurred in his ill-fated expedition.

Paterson, William (1745–1806), jurist, one of the framers of the U.S. Constitution, and senator (1789–90) and governor (1790–93) of New Jersey. He also served as an associate justice of the U.S. Supreme Court from 1793 to 1806.

Paterson, William (1755–1810), British traveller and governor of New South Wales.
·Orange River explorations **13**:641b

pâte-sur-pâte, literally "paste on paste," a method of porcelain decoration in which a relief design is created on an unfired, unglazed

Plaque with pâte-sur-pâte decoration by Marc-Louis Solon, Sèvres, Fr., *c.* 1870; in the Victoria and Albert Museum, London

By courtesy of the Victoria and Albert Museum, London; photograph, EB Inc.

body by applying successive layers of white slip (liquid clay) with a brush. The technique was first employed by the Chinese in the 18th century. It was introduced in Europe around 1850 at Sèvres where it was perfected by Marc-Louis Solon, who later worked for the Minton (*see* Minton ware). The technique was also used in the U.S., at the Rookwood factory in Cincinnati, Ohio.
·19th-century pottery improvements **14**:916f

patet, in the music of Java and Bali, the concept of mode, which serves as a framework for melodies. Three *patet* may be generated by each of the music's scale systems, *slendro*, which has five tones, and *pelog*, which has seven tones, two of them auxiliary. Each *patet* emphasizes different notes of the scale and is associated with certain melodic formulas suitable for beginning or ending a piece, with certain times of day and with parts of a theatrical performance.

path, in mathematics, has essentially the same meaning in some instances as in the general physical usage; in others, more specialized meanings. In the kinematic sense (1), a path is described by a particle moving in space during a certain interval of time. In astronomy (2), the path of a meteor (its trail) or of a celestial object is the projection of its position, more especially, of the position of its centre of gravity, or projection of a continuous series of its positions on the celestial sphere, as seen by an observer on Earth. Also in astronomy (3), the path of totality of an eclipse is the narrow track of the central part of the moving shadow. In aerospace technology (4), the path of a satellite (its track) is the projection of its orbital plane upon the Earth's surface, hence the locus of the subsatellite point. Because of the Earth's rotation, the path projected by a single orbital pass of a subdiurnal (less than 24-hour orbit) satellite is always an open curve. The shape of this path, plotted on a map of the Earth's surface made by cylindrical projection, is sinusoidal. In hydrodynamics (5), the paths of the elements of a moving fluid are called streamlines. Also in fluid dynamics, and more generally in mechanics and astronomy, is the useful related concept hodograph (Greek *hodos*, "path"), a curve defined by the acceleration vectors of a moving particle. Thus in celestial mechanics, if the orbit of a planet or a comet be considered as in a Newtonian, 2-body field, its hodograph is a circle.

The customary mathematical definition of path is somewhat more rigorous than the physical one; and for two paths to be considered identical in the latter sense, not only must the point-locations of the paths coincide, but so must the times of visitation. For a path C, an inverse path (denoted by C^{-1}) may be formed by traversing C in the reverse direction. A closed path, having the same initial and terminal points, is called a loop. In real analysis, it is shown that the line integral between two points is independent of the path, or that the line integral around any closed path is zero. Paths are also important in topology.
·Euclidean geometry principles **7**:1103b
·physical theory formulations **14**:406c

Pathamcetiya, temple at Nagara Pathama (now Nakhon Pathom), Thailand, finished in the early 20th century.
·Chinese influence on Thai architecture **17**:258g

Pathan, Hindi play produced in 1946 by Prithvi Raj Kapoor.
·plot and Prithvi production **17**:167f

Pathans (people): *see* Pashtuns.

pathasalas, also known as TOLS, Brahminical school in India.
·enrollment and instruction type **6**:320b

Pathé, Charles (b. Dec. 25, 1863, Paris—d. Dec. 26, 1957, Monte-Carlo, Monaco), pioneer motion-picture executive who controlled a vast network of production and distribution facilities that dominated the world film market during the first years of the 20th century. With his brother Émile, he founded Pathé Frères (Pathé Brothers, 1896) in Paris, a company that manufactured and sold phonographs and phonograph cylinders. The company placed the Kinetoscope, Thomas A. Edison's newly invented viewing device, in theatres throughout France. Using the camera developed by Louis and Auguste Lumière, Pathé Frères filmed numerous short subjects, the majority of which are sensational criminal adventures, melodramatic love stories, and comic anecdotes. In 1909 Pathé produced his first "long film," *Les Misérables*, a four-reel screen version of the novel by Victor Hugo.

Pathé

H. Roger-Viollet

That same year he originated the *Pathé Gazette* in France (U.S.: 1910; U.K.: 1911). Identified by the symbol of the crowing rooster, it was an internationally popular newsreel (*q.v.*) until 1956. In 1914 Pathé Frères released from its studios in the United States the first episodes of *The Perils of Pauline*, one of the earliest and best remembered screen serials. The company also began publishing the screen magazine *Pathé Pictorial.*

Pathé Frères, with production facilities in France, England, and the United States and distribution offices throughout the world, was an enormously lucrative company. Profits on some pictures were 50 to 100 times the original cost of production.

In 1917 Pathé began to sell the company's equipment, production studios, and exhibition circuits. He retired in 1929, but the company remained in existence as a leading film distributor.

·musical recordings and phonographs **12**:693f

Pathelin, La Farce de maistre Pierre, best known of the medieval French farces. An anonymous work written about 1470 in octosyllabic couplets, it displays the witty and nonsensical dialogue and preposterous situations characteristic of later French comedy. In the farce the rascally lawyer Pathelin, the central character, tricks the foolish draper Joceaume out of a length of cloth by feigning madness when the draper comes to collect payment. Aignelet, Joceaume's shepherd, steals some sheep from his master, then hires Pathelin to defend him in court. Pathelin advises him to answer only "Baa," like a sheep, to all questions. During the ensuing courtroom scene, Joceaume jumbles his complaints against Pathelin and Aignelet so badly that the judge must repeatedly plead, "Revenons à ces moutons" ("Let us come back to these sheep"), an expression that has remained in the French language to mean "let's get back to the subject." Finally the judge dismisses the case, but the tables are turned on Pathelin when he tries to collect from the shepherd and receives the answer, "Baa."

Pather Panchali (1955), film by Satyajit Ray.

·India's motion pictures **12**:538b
·Satyajit Ray's Bengali trilogy **15**:538a

pathetic fallacy, term coined by John Ruskin in *Modern Painters* (1843–60) to describe the poetic practice of attributing human emotion or responses to nature or inanimate objects. The practice is a form of personification that is as old as poetry, in which it has always been common to find flowers smiling or dancing, angry or cruel winds, brooding mountains, moping owls, or happy larks. In some classical poetic forms such as the pastoral elegy, the pathetic fallacy is actually a required convention. In Milton's "On The Morning of Christ's Nativity," all aspects of nature react fittingly to the event of Christ's birth.

The Stars with deep amaze
Stand fixt in steadfast gaze

Ruskin allowed that violent feelings produce "a falseness in all our impressions of external things" and that an inspired poet distraught with grief might project his internal feeling on his surroundings, but he considered the excessive use of the fallacy the mark of an inferior poet. The pathetic fallacy is still used by modern poets. Robert Frost uses it with great charm in "Stopping by the Woods on a Snowy Evening":

My little horse must think it queer
To stop without a farmhouse near

Pathet Lao, English LAO COUNTRY, left-oriented nationalist group in Laos. Founded in 1950, it joined with the Viet Minh in armed resistance to French rule in Indochina. In 1956 a legal political wing, the Lao Patriotic Front (Neo Lao Hak Xat), was founded and participated in several coalition governments. In the 1960s and early '70s the Pathet Lao (renamed Lao People's Liberation Army in 1965) fought a civil war against the U.S.-backed Vientiane regime, winning effective control of the northern and eastern parts of the country. In 1975 it gave way to the Lao People's Revolutionary Party.

·army strength and support **10**:676g
·establishment and temporary recognition **10**:673a
·Laotian opposition to French conciliation **10**:678g

Pathfinder, U.S. news magazine, published 1894–1954.

·magazine publishing history **15**:253d

Pathfinder, The (1840), in full THE PATHFINDER: OR, THE INLAND SEA, one of James Fenimore Cooper's "Leatherstocking" stories, set in the Lake Ontario region in 1760, at the time of the French and Indian War.

·theme and character development **5**:133f

pathogenesis: *see* disease.

pathology, medical specialty concerned with the essential nature of disease, especially the structural and functional changes in the cells, tissues, and organs caused by the disease. Board requirements, examinations for specialization and practice, and residencies vary from country to country.

·autopsy in clinical diagnosis **2**:536a
·diagnosis of tumour types **5**:695b
·disease classification systems **5**:863b
·forensic medicine fields of study **11**:814c
·Harvey's direct study and lecture use **8**:661h
·historical development **5**:684f
·history of medicine in Europe **11**:830h
·inflammatory response of diseased tissue **9**:559d
·instrumentation for laboratory analysis **9**:640g
·Müller's cell study and contribution **12**:615f
·Virchow's revolutionary work **19**:150c
·yellow fever and epidemiology **15**:546f

pathos, quality of human experience or its representation in art that evokes pity, sympathy, and sorrow in the spectator or reader. Distinct from the grander passions of tragedy, pathos is evoked especially by the helpless or those who suffer undeservedly. Portrayed in art unsuccessfully, pathos is bathos (*q.v.*) and provokes laughter at the ridiculous excess of emotion. Pathos also may become sentimentality when an artist presumes on an audience's stock responses to orphans, animals, the aged, or the oppressed to arouse pity. Genuine pathos, however, has a respectable place in art; Honoré Daumier's painting "The Third-Class Carriage" evokes a powerful sympathy for the poor, and Robert Burns's poem "To a Mouse" dramatizes the bond between all of nature's creatures.

·tragic theory of individual emotion **4**:960d

Pathum Thani, also called PRADUM, administrative headquarters of Pathum Thani province (*changwat*), south central Thailand, on the west bank of the Mae Nam (river) Chao Phraya. It is a rice-collecting and milling centre. The province, with an area of 569 sq mi (1,497 sq km), occupies the low, well-irrigated plains of the Chao Phraya and is intensively farmed in rice. Fishing is a secondary economic activity. Pop. (1972 est.) town, 37,807; (1970) province, 233,861.
14°01′ N, 100°32′ E

·area and population table **18**:202
·map, Thailand **18**:199

Patiāla, city, district, and division, Punjab state, northwestern India. The city, the district's headquarters, lies on a major rail line, as well as on a branch of the Sirhind Canal. Founded in 1763 as the capital of the princely state of the same name, Patiāla is a trade and industrial centre; weaving, cotton ginning, distilling, and manufacturing are among its industries. Punjabi University (established 1962) and 10 affiliated colleges are located in the city, as are an old fort and a modern sports stadium.

Patiāla district, 1,770 sq mi (4,583 sq km) in area, is a dry region watered only by a few *cos* (seasonal streams). Wheat, cotton, corn, and gram are the chief crops grown. The princely state of Patiāla, of which the present district was a part, was the most important in the Punjab. It merged with independent India in 1948, and the district became part of the reorganized Punjab state in 1966. Besides Patiāla, other important towns are Nābha, Samāna, and Rājpura.

Patiāla division is one of Punjab's two major divisions. It comprises four districts: Patiāla, Bhatinda, Rūpar, and Sangrūr. Pop. (1971) city, 151,041; district, 1,215,100; division, 4,224,889.

·map, India **9**:278

Patiāla and East Punjab States Union (PEPSU), state of the Indian Union, consisting of Patiāla and the other states (mostly Sikh) in the east Punjab (Pañjāb). The raja of Patiāla, as head of the largest state, became the rajpramukh, or governor. PEPSU was formed in 1948 as part of the integration of Indian states with the Indian Union. The Sikhs disliked it because their population ratio was 49 percent, just short of a majority, and because they felt the union was not economically viable. In 1956, on the recommendation of the States Reorganization Commission, PEPSU was united with the Punjab state. That union was later divided into a Sikh-controlled state of the Punjab and a Hindu-controlled state of Haryana.

·Punjab absorption of states **15**:285e

Patía River, in Cauca and Nariño departments, southwestern Colombia. It rises southwest of Popayán and flows generally westward for about 200 mi (322 km) before emptying into the Pacific Ocean.
2°13′ N, 78°40′ W

·map, Colombia **4**:869
·volume of water and rapid flow **4**:865a

paṭicca-samuppāda (Buddhist philosophy): *see* pratītya-samutpāda.

Patience (card game): *see* Solitaire.

Patience, in full PATIENCE OR BUNTHORNE'S BRIDE, operetta in two acts, composed by Sir Arthur Sullivan with libretto by Sir W.S. Gilbert (*qq.v.*). It was first performed at the Opera Comique in London in 1881.

·Bunthorne characterization sources **19**:824g

Patillas, town and municipality, southeast Puerto Rico. The town, near the coast just east of Guayam, lies in an irrigated area of sugar plantations. Pop. (1980 prelim.) town, 3,148; mun., 17,820.
18°00′ N, 66°01′ W

·area and population table **15**:261
·map, Puerto Rico **15**:263

pātimokkha, Sanskrit PRĀTIMOKṢA, Pāli term for a Buddhist monastic code, a set of 227 rules that govern the activities of the monk and nun. The *pātimokkha* ("that which is binding") is contained in the *Vinaya Piṭaka*, that part of the Pāli canon concerned with discipline and arranged for monks and for nuns according to the severity of the offense—from those that require immediate and lifelong expulsion from the order, temporary suspension, or various degrees of restitution or expiation to those that require confession only. Also given are rules for settling disputes within the monastic community. The entire *pātimokkha* is recited during the *uposatha*, or fortnightly assembly of Theravāda (Way of the Elders) monks.

A comparable set of 250 rules is contained in the Sanskrit canon of the Sarvāstivādins (holders of the doctrine that "all is real") tradition that was widely known in northern Buddhist countries. The Mahāyāna (Great Vehicle) tradition in China and Japan more generally rejected those rules that were not applicable locally and substituted disciplinary codes that differed from sect to sect and sometimes from monastery to monastery.

·monastic formation and discipline **3**:405g
·monastic rules and usage **3**:392c

patina: *see* desert varnish.

Patineṇ-Kīlkkaṇakku, major collection of Tamul poetry written *c.* 4th–7th century AD.

·principle texts and themes **17**:139c

Patinir (PATINIER or PATENIER), **Joachim (de)** (b. *c.* 1485, Bouvignes or Dinant, Belg.—d. Oct. 5, 1524, Antwerp), painter, the first Western artist known to have specialized in landscape painting. Little is known of his early life, but his work reflects an early knowledge of the painting of Gerard David, the last of the Early Netherlandish painters. It has also been hypothesized that he studied under Hieronymus Bosch, the painter of fantastic allegories and landscapes.

Patinir seems to have made a practice of supplying landscape settings for figure compositions painted by other Flemish masters, but the only known example of his collaborations is the "Temptation of St. Anthony" (*c.* 1520–24; Prado, Madrid), in which Quentin Massys painted the figures. He did not, however, paint pure landscape pictures and all his work has a nominal religious subject. Its novelty, anticipated in different vein by Bosch, lay in the fact that the religious motif in such works as the "Flight into Egypt" (1515–20; Musée Royal des Beaux-Arts, Antwerp), the "St. Christopher" (*c.* 1515–24; Prado, Madrid) and the "St. Jerome" (Prado, Madrid) was much reduced in scale and immersed in the phenomena of the natural world. The basic elements of his landscape style—the high viewpoint overlooking vast tracts, where earthy brown foregrounds merge into woodland and meadow greens and again into the hazy blues of distant mountains—do not differ from those of his predecessors, particularly Gerard David. Yet the picturesque melancholy with which he invests the woods and rivers and the great ghostly rocks that jut up abruptly in the middle distance of such paintings as his "Baptism of Christ" (*c.* 1515–20; Kunsthistorisches Museum, Vienna) and his "Crossing the Styx" (*c.* 1520–24; Prado, Madrid) strike a personal note that won Patinir instant success and many imitators.

Patiño, José (*c.* 1666–1736), Spanish statesman, served King Philip V efficiently in various appointments from 1707 and was from 1726 to his death minister for the navy and for the colonies, with control also over financial and foreign affairs. His naval reorganization was a conspicuous success.

Patinopecten, fossil genus of the discoasters of the family Pectinidae.

·Tertiary evolution and index fossils **18**:154a

patio process, or MEXICAN PROCESS, a method of reducing silver from its ore that was used from the 16th to early in the 20th century; the process was apparently common to Latin America before the arrival of the Europeans.

The silver ore was crushed and ground by mule power in arrastras, shallow circular pits paved with stone. Large blocks of stone attached by beams to a central rotating post were dragged around the arrastra, reducing the ore to a fine mud. It was then spread over a courtyard or patio, sprinkled with mercury, salt, and copper sulfate, and mixed by repeatedly driving mules over it. Chemical reactions freed the silver from its compounds and caused it to unite with the mercury. When the amalgamation was complete, the material was agitated with water in large tubs and the mud run off through plug holes. The amalgam remaining at the bottom was collected and treated to drive off the mercury. The process, especially suitable for the silver ores of the dry, barren areas of Mexico, was responsible for a large proportion of the world's silver production for 350 years, until it was finally displaced by the cyanide process early in the 20th century.

Paṭisambhidā-magga, one of 15 sections of the *Khuddhaka Nikāya*, itself the fifth of five divisions of the *Sutta Piṭaka*, a Buddhist sacred scripture.

·content and traditional use **3**:434e

Patjitanian stone tool industry: *see* chopper-chopping tool industry.

Pātkai Range, mountains, Nāgāland, India. 27°00′ N, 96°00′ E

·Nāgāland's physical geography **12**:806c

Patkoi Hills (Burma): *see* Chin Hills.

Patkul, Johann Reinhold von (b. July 27, 1660, Stockholm—d. Oct. 10, 1707, Kazimierz, Pol.), Baltic German diplomat who played a key role in the initiation of the Northern War (1700–21).

Born to the Livonian German gentry, Patkul entered the Swedish army in Livonia in 1687. After serving as a representative of the Livonian landowners to the Swedish court in 1690–91, Patkul was arrested and sentenced to death for sedition by the Swedes in 1694 for airing the Livonians' grievances over land questions. He escaped to western Europe, however, via Courland.

Making the acquaintance of highly placed Saxon officials in 1698, Patkul gained an audience in the following year with King Augustus II of Poland (who was also the elector of Saxony), during which he interested the King in a Saxon–Russian alliance against Sweden. Patkul then led negotiations that resulted in the Saxon–Polish–Russian–Danish coalition, which started the Northern War against Sweden in 1700. Patkul entered the Russian diplomatic and military service in 1703, and thereafter he tried unsuccessfully to bring Prussia into the war. In 1707, after angering the Saxons by intriguing with Austria, he was delivered to the Swedish forces in Poland and tortured to death at Kazimierz for desertion and treason.

Patmore, Coventry (Kersey Dighton) (b. July 23, 1823, Woodford, Essex—d. Nov. 26, 1896, Lymington, Hampshire), poet and essayist whose allusive poetry reflects a deep knowledge and understanding of 17th-century metaphysical poetry, unusual in one of his day. His best poetry is in *The Unknown Eros and Other Odes*, containing mystical odes of divine love and of married love, which he saw as a reflection of Christ's love for the soul.

An independent-minded Victorian, with a waggish sense of humour and a love of paradox, Patmore left prudery to what he called the "Puritan Half-believers." After his father fled to France to escape his creditors, Patmore obtained a position in the library of the British Museum, London, and worked there for 19 years. He published a vast novel in verse, telling the story of two marriages, beginning in the 1850s with *The Angel in the House*, consisting of *The Betrothal* (1854) and *The Espousals* (1856), and continuing with *The Victories of Love* (1863), consisting of *Faithful for Ever* (1860) and *The Victories of Love* (1863). Interspersed with lyrical "preludes" that form a philosophical commentary on the narrative, they were appreciated by a wide audience for their subtle wit, poetry, and psychological insight. A further section was abandoned on the death of his wife, Emily, in 1862.

Patmore, detail of an oil painting by J.S. Sargent, 1894; in the National Portrait Gallery, London

By courtesy of the National Portrait Gallery, London

In 1864 Patmore became a Roman Catholic and married Marianne Byles. Together they translated *St. Bernard on the Love of God* (1881). Meanwhile, *The Unknown Eros* had appeared in 1877, but, despite the originality of the poems (and what has been called "incandescent austerity"), they were not widely appreciated. *Amelia* (1878) virtually ended his poetic output, and in later years he concentrated on essays—original and provocative—on literature, art, philosophy, and politics, chiefly for the *St. James's Gazette*. (These were later partly collected in *Principle in Art*, 1889, and *Religio Poetae*, 1893). Marianne died in 1880, and Patmore married Harriet Robson in 1881. His last work was a collection of aphorisms, *The Rod, the Root, and the Flower* (1895). Patmore's seminal study of *English Metrical Law* (1857) was greatly admired by Gerard Manley Hopkins, a poet well-known for his own metrical innovations. Books on Patmore include J.C. Reid's *The Mind and Art of Coventry Patmore* (1957) and E.W. Gosse's *Coventry Patmore* (1969).

Pátmos, smallest and most northerly of the original 12, or Dodecanese, Greek islands, only 11 sq mi (28 sq km) in area. The barren, arc-shaped island consists of three deeply indented headlands joined by two narrow isthmuses; its maximum elevation is near the centre in Óros (mountain) Áyios Ilías (883 ft [269 m]). Several islets belonging to Pátmos form a semicircle on the east, strongly suggesting that in prehistoric times Pátmos was shattered by the explosion of a giant volcano and is now partially submerged. The only evidence of active vulcanism is a hot-air vent near Psallídha. An ancient acropolis lies on the northern isthmus. The chief town, Pátmos, stands on a ridge in the south central sector.

Successively settled by Dorians and Ionians, Pátmos received scant mention by such ancient writers as Thucydides (5th century BC), Strabo (fl. early 1st century AD), and Pliny (1st century AD). Under the Romans it was a place for exiles, the most noted of whom was John, author of the Fourth Gospel, sent there according to tradition *c.* AD 95. Both the Gospel and the Revelation to John are said to have been written there by John.

During the Middle Ages, Pátmos appears to have been deserted, probably because of Saracen raids. In 1088 the Byzantine emperor Alexius I Comnenus granted the island to an abbot, who founded a monastery dedicated to

St. John on the southern part of the island. Its library contains a celebrated collection of manuscripts and printed books begun by St. Christodoulos. The autonomy of the monastery was confirmed under Venetian rule (1207–1537); during the Turkish occupation (1537–1912) annual tribute was required from the monks. The port of Skála grew out of the original settlement around the monastery. Lacking permanent watercourses but having numerous springs, the island yields grapes, cereals, and vegetables, though not enough for domestic needs. Sponge fishing is the main economic activity. Pátmos is the seat of a school of theology founded in 1669. Pop. (1971) 2,432.
37°20′ N, 26°33′ E
·map, Greece **8**:314

Patna and Pāṭaliputra **13**:1076, Patna is the capital of Bihār state in northern India; Pāṭaliputra, the ancient capital of the Maurya and Gupta empires, occupied approximately the same site.

The text article recounts Pāṭaliputra's founding in the 5th century BC by the King of Magadha. His son made it the capital, which it remained until the 1st century BC. The second Magadha dynasty, the Maurya, ruled in the 3rd and early 2nd centuries BC, until the city was sacked in 185 by Indo-Greeks. The Śuṅga dynasty then began, ruling until about 73 BC. Pāṭaliputra remained a centre of learning, and in the 4th century AD became the Gupta capital. It declined and was deserted by the 7th century. The city was refounded as Patna by an Afghan ruler in 1541 and again rose to prosperity under the Mughal Empire. It passed to the British in 1765. Extensive archaeological excavations have been made in the vicinity. Pop. (1971 prelim.) 474,349.
25°36′ N, 85°06′ E

REFERENCES in other text articles:
·administration in Mauryan times **9**:352b
·ancient flooding and modern development **2**:984f
·chronological source materials **4**:574c
·map India **9**:278
·yakṣa and yakṣī sculptures **17**:186c

Pa-tok (board game): *see* Co.

paṭolā, type of silk sari (characteristic garment worn by Indian women) of Gujarati origin, the warp and weft being tie-dyed (*see* bāndhanī work) before weaving according to a predetermined pattern. It formed part of the trousseau presented by the bride's maternal uncle. Although extant *paṭolās* of Gujarāt do not predate the late 18th century, their history certainly goes back to the 12th century, if not earlier. The technique was also adopted by the weavers of Andhra Pradesh, especially at Pochampalli, where coarse cotton yarn was used as weaving material. Dancing girl, elephant, parrot, pipal leaf, floral spray, watercress, basketwork, diaper (overall diamond pattern) with a double outline, and flowers were employed as patterns on a deep-red ground. The extraordinary laboriousness of the work and the high cost of production led to decreased demand and the decline of this important craft.

Detail of a *Paṭolā* sari from Gujarāt, late 18th century; in the Prince of Wales Museum of Western India, Bombay
M. Chandra

The technique of *paṭolā* weaving was not confined to India but was also known in Indonesia, where it was called *ikat*.

Paton, Alan (Stewart) (b. Jan. 11, 1903, Pietermaritzburg, Natal, now in South Africa), one of the foremost writers in South Africa, who became, through circumstances and conscience, an eminent but reluctant politician.

In 1935 Paton gave up teaching to take charge of the Diepkloof Reformatory for delinquent urban African boys, near Johannesburg.

Paton, 1961
United Press International

Leaving Diepkloof, he published the novel *Cry, the Beloved Country* (1948), which made a tremendous impact. Both it and his next novel, *Too Late the Phalarope* (1953), are written in Paton's characteristic balanced, economical, rhythmic prose, which has, especially in dialogue, a singing psalmodic tone. The Diepkloof period provided material for some short stories.

In 1953 the Liberal Party of South Africa was formed to offer a nonracial alternative to apartheid; Paton was its national president until its enforced dissolution in 1968. His active opposition to the policy of apartheid led to confiscation of his passport in 1960.

His work for the liberal cause included a fortnightly column, "The Long View," for the liberal journal *Contact*. These pieces, along with some public speeches, were collected in *The Long View* (1968). Mainly commentaries on people and affairs, they are diverse in tone: indignant, witty, compassionate, profound.

Paton worked for a long period on *Hofmeyr* (1964), a massive biography of the brilliant parliamentarian and cabinet minister. Over the years he has also written verse. It is, however, as a novelist and as "South Africa's conscience," that he is known and respected.
·African novel tradition **13**:293b

Patos, city, west central Paraíba state, northeastern Brazil, on the Rio Espinharas at 804 ft (245 m) above sea level. Given a city rank in 1903, Patos is a commercial centre for an agricultural hinterland, yielding principally cotton and beans. The city's varied industries include shoe factories, cotton mills, and millet-processing and vegetable-oil factories. Goods are transported by rail and road to João Pessoa (the state capital) to the east, to Recife, and to other communities in Paraíba and neighbouring Pernambuco and Rio Grande do Norte states. Pop. (1970 prelim.) 39,850.
7°01′ S, 37°16′ W
·map, Brazil **3**:124

Patos de Minas, city in west central Minas Gerais state, Brazil, at 2,808 ft (856 m) above sea level in the highlands. Made a seat of a municipality in 1866, it gained city status in 1892 with the name of Patos, which was lengthened in 1944. Agriculture (beans, millet, manioc, rice, coffee, and oranges) and livestock raising are the main source of income. Dairy products, jerked beef, and hog byproducts are processed in the city, which is linked by air and by circuitous roads with railroad connections (north and south) to Belo Horizonte, the state capital, 314 mi (506 km) east-southeast. Pop. (1970 prelim.) 42,215.
18°35′ S, 46°32′ W
·map, Brazil **3**:124

Patos Lagoon, Portuguese LAGOA DOS PATOS, shallow lagoon—the largest in Brazil and the second largest in South America—in Rio Grande do Sul state. It is 180 mi (290 km) long and up to 40 mi wide, with an area of more than 3,900 sq mi (10,100 sq km), and is separated from the Atlantic by a sandbar 20 mi wide in the north and narrowing in the south, dotted with smaller lagoons. It receives the Rio Jacuí (via the Rio Guaíba) in the north and the Lagoa (lagoon) Mirim overflow (via the Canal de São Gonçalo) in the south. A one-mile-wide channel leads to the Atlantic at the city of Rio Grande in the south. The dredged channel allows vessels to ply between Rio Grande and Pôrto Alegre, the state capital. The waters of the Lagoa dos Patos (meaning "lake of the ducks") are fished, and rice is cultivated on the western shore.
31°06′ S, 51°15′ W
·map, Brazil **3**:124

Patos Pass, route through the Andes, at the Argentine–Chile border.
·Andes location and elevation **1**:857c

Pátrai, also called PATRAE OR PATRAS, capital, Achaea *nomós* (department), and chief port of the Peloponnese (Pelopónnisos) and the third

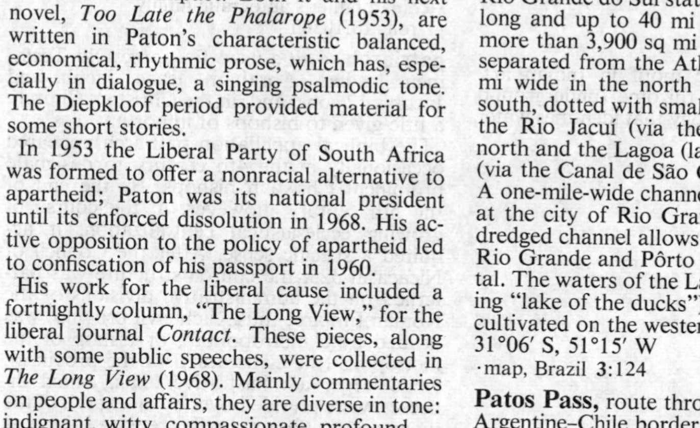
The harbour front, Pátrai, Greece
C.J. Coulson—Photo Trends

largest in Greece, on the Patraïkós Kólpos (gulf).

A legendary federation of three villages—Aroë, Antheia, and Mesatis—Pátrai received its name from the Achaean leader Patreus and became one of the 12 cities of Achaea. The ancient city lay some distance from the shore. About 280 BC it helped to form the anti-Macedonian Achaean League and was briefly a commercial rival to Corinth. After the Battle of Actium (31 BC), the Roman emperor Augustus colonized it, and as such it prospered commercially until about the 3rd century AD. St. Andrew, the first disciple of Christ, is said to have been crucified there.

In the 8th and 9th centuries its population was increased by refugees from the Slavic invasion of the Peloponnese; St. Andrew was confirmed as patron for his supposed role in resisting the combined Slavic and Saracen attack of 805 or 807. In the Byzantine Empire, Pátrai was noted for its silk industry. In 1205 it became a Frankish barony and the seat of an autonomous Latin archbishop, who later sold it to Venice (1408). It was long contested by Venetians and Turks. At Pátrai the War of Greek Independence began in 1821, inspired by Archbishop Germanos; in 1828 the Turks burned the city before retreating, and the current grid plan dates from the reconstruction.

Since 1899 seat of a metropolitan bishop of the Orthodox Church, Pátrai was previously an archbishopric. The chief exports are currants, sultanas, tobacco, olives and olive oil, figs, citrons, wine, brandy, hides, and valonias. An important port of call on shipping lanes between Greece and the West, it is linked by rail to Corinth, Athens, and Kalámai. The port is overlooked by a Byzantine-Turkish-Venetian fortress on the site of the ancient acropolis. Pop. (1971) 112,228.
38°15′ N, 21°44′ E
·map, Greece **8**:314

patralatā, decorative motif in Indian art, consisting of a lotus rhizome (underground plant stem). A cosmology that identifies water

Sandstone *patralatā* from the Great Stūpa at Sānchi, Madhya Pradesh, *c.* 1st century BC
M. Chandra

as the source of all life had a great influence on early Indian art, and, of its visual symbols, the lotus is the most important and has been a dominant motif in Indian decoration from the earliest times. The *patralatā*, with flowers issuing from a central undulating stem, is found carved on temples at Bhārhut (2nd century BC) and Sānchi (1st century BC). Relatively naturalistic in the earlier monuments, the motif was progressively stylized, finally culminating in rich, foamlike foliated scrolls that have little resemblance to the lotus plant.

The *patralatā* also appears in the Islāmic art of India, in which it is assimilated to the arabesque motif.

patria potestas, in Roman family law, power that the father exercised over his children and his more remote descendants in the male line, whatever their age, as well as over those brought into the family by adoption. This power meant originally not only that he had control over the persons of his children, amounting even to a right to inflict capital punishment, but that he alone had any rights in private law. Thus, acquisitions of a child became the property of the father. The father might allow a child (as he might a slave) certain property to treat as his own, but in the eye of the law it continued to belong to the father.

Patria potestas ceased normally only with the death of the father; but the father might voluntarily free the child by emancipation, and a daughter ceased to be under the father's *potestas* if she came under her husband's *manus* (*q.v.*).

The system had been modified by classical times. The father's power of life and death had shrunk to that of light punishment; and sons could keep as their own what they earned as soldiers (*peculium castrense*). By Justinian's day (527–565), the rules of *peculium castrense* were extended to many sorts of professional earnings; and in other acquisitions, such as property inherited from the mother, the father's rights were reduced to a life interest.
·Roman father's autocratic family role **15**:1056h

patriarch, a title used for some Old Testament leaders (Abraham, Isaac, Jacob, and Jacob's 12 sons) and, in the Christian Church, a title given to bishops of important sees.

The biblical appellation patriarch appeared occasionally in the 4th century to designate prominent Christian bishops. By the end of the 5th century, however, in the course of growing ecclesiastical centralization, it acquired a specific sense. After the Council of Nicaea in 325, the church structure was patterned on the administrative divisions of the Roman Empire; thus, each civil province was headed by a metropolitan, or bishop of the metropolis (the civil capital of the province), while larger administrative units, called dioceses, were presided over by an exarch of the diocese, a title gradually replaced by patriarch.

Some patriarchs, referring to "ancient privileges" and traditions, exercised authority over several dioceses: the bishop of Rome over the entire West; the bishop of Alexandria over the dioceses of Egypt, Libya, and Pentapolis; and, after the Council of Chalcedon (451), the bishop of Constantinople over the dioceses of Pontus, Asia, and Thrace.

Controversy over the growth of major ecclesiastical centres contributed to the schism between East and West. Rome maintained that only "apostolic sees," those originally established by apostles, had the right to become patriarchates. The East, however, always took for granted that primacies were based on such empirical factors as the economic and political importance of cities and countries. Constantinople, the new imperial capital and the ecclesiastical centre of the East, had no claims to apostolicity, but new jurisdictional rights were bestowed upon it at Chalcedon (451) for the explicit reason that it was "the residence of the emperor and the senate."

Five patriarchates, the pentarchy, were the first to be recognized by the legislation of the emperor Justinian (reigned 527–565), later confirmed by the Council in Trullo (692): Rome, Constantinople, Alexandria, Antioch, and Jerusalem, though after the Muslim invasions of Egypt and Syria in 638–640 the bishops of Rome and Constantinople were alone in possessing any real power. Despite Constantinople's efforts to resist any proliferation of patriarchates, new centres emerged in the Slavic centres of Preslav (932), Tkhovo (1234), Peć (1346), and Moscow (1589). At present there are nine Orthodox patriarchates: Constantinople, Alexandria, Antioch, Jerusalem, Moscow, Georgia, Serbia, Romania, and Bulgaria; except in the title, there is no difference between a patriarch and any other head of an autocephalous (independent) church.

In Roman Catholicism, especially since the second Vatican Council, some effort has been made to restore the dignity of the Eastern rite patriarchs as effective signs of collegiality, balancing Roman centralization.
·Alexandrian church origins **6**:487a
·Byzantine background of Schism **6**:152f *passim* to 154b
·Byzantine position in state **4**:511f
·canon law origins in early Church **3**:773g
·Eastern Orthodox church authority **6**:142f
·investiture by Eastern emperor **4**:591e
·Istanbul role as ecclesiastical centre **9**:1070a
·medieval papal hierarchical conflicts **12**:143d
·Ottoman political use of office **6**:155h
·pre-Schism church authority **4**:537c
·religious concepts and covenant form **10**:303a
·see rivalry after Constantinople I **4**:541b
·Third Rome theory and implications **16**:47d

patriarchal caliphs: *see* khulafāʾ ar-rāshidūn, al-.

Patriarch Palace, early-17th-century palace built within the Kremlin in Moscow.
·history and architecture **12**:482b

patriarchy, a hypothetical social system based on the absolute authority of the father or an elderly male over the family group. Inspired by the classical social Darwinism of the 19th century, the pioneering anthropologists Lewis Henry Morgan and Henry Maine envisioned cultures as having developed through evolutionary stages, one of which was patriarchy. Maine felt that all status or relationship in the earliest societies derived from a patriarchal kinship system and that all decisions of social consequence were the arbitrary judgments of a quasi-tyrannical patriarch. Sometimes patriarchy also includes in its meaning *patria potestas*, the system in which power to govern members of even the extended family rested in the hands of a father and his kin.

Although Morgan did undertake ethnographic work of nonliterate societies, Maine based his conclusions almost entirely on records of ancient Greece and Rome. In the 1970s, anthropologists had largely disproved such evolutionary schemes and had found absolute male authority to be rare even in patrilineal descent systems. The word patriarchy, therefore, has fallen into disuse among social scientists as a technical or categorical term.
·Arab family structure **11**:575a
·Baltic familial and religious function **2**:666f
·Christian attitudes and traditions **4**:522e
·familial power distribution in modern society **7**:161e
·Japanese religious based family structure **10**:111d
·medieval and Renaissance family life **18**:1076d
·Mesopotamian legal rights of family head **5**:370b
·Roman family and patronage system **4**:536d
·Roman patria potestas changes **15**:1056h

Patrice Lumumba Battalion, Congo guerrilla organization that fought in the Congolese civil war in the 1960s.
·Che Guevara's organization role **8**:465b

Patrice Lumumba People's Friendship University, coeducational state institution of higher learning in Moscow, founded in 1960.

It was named for the Congolese premier after his death in 1961 and serves primarily students from developing countries. The university was organized at the behest of Soviet trade unions and various committees for cultural exchange. It is administered by a university council headed by the dean and made up of faculty members, representatives of the organizations responsible for founding the university (*i.e.*, trade unions, the Soviet Committee of Solidarity with Countries of Africa and Asia, the Youth Committee, the Council of Soviet Societies of Friendship with Foreign Countries, and the minister of higher education), and student representatives.

As at all Soviet universities, the students are fully financed by the government, including initial transportation to the Soviet Union and their return after graduation. Their stipend, though, is more than twice that of the average Soviet student.

There are six faculties: engineering; agriculture; medicine; physics, mathematics, and general science; economics and international law; and history and philosophy. There is a strong emphasis on the first three subjects; only about 30 percent of the students are in the humanities. All courses are for six years, the first year being preparatory, during which the student must learn Russian, the language of instruction. Methods used for teaching Russian have been so successful that graduates find they are qualified for teaching and translating jobs as well as for work in their field of specialization.

In 1970 there were over 4,000 students. Included were approximately 1,000 Soviet citizens representing all major nationalities in the Soviet Union. Students from 85 other countries were apportioned approximately as follows: 800 from African countries; 770 from the Middle East; close to 1,000 from Latin America; and over 500 from Southeast Asia.
·history, enrollment, and scholarships **12**:485a

patricians, privileged citizen class in early Rome. Probably originating as leaders of the rudimentary Roman senate, they came to monopolize the magistracies and priesthoods in the period before *c.* 400 BC. Because their political influence was reduced by the plebeians (*see* plebeians), patricians at the end of the early Republic retained exclusive control only of the old priesthoods, the office of *interrex*, or provisional consul, and perhaps that of *princeps senatus*, or senate leader. In the late Republic (*i.e.*, to the 1st century BC), society became less stratified and distinctions between patricians and plebeians lost political importance; many patricians became plebeians by adoption. During the empire (after 27 BC), patrician rank was a prerequisite for ascent to the throne, and only the emperor could create patricians. Necessary for the continuation of ancient priesthoods, patricians had few privileges other than reduced military obligations. After Constantine's reign (306–337), *patricius* was a nonhereditary title of honour, ranked third after the emperor and consuls. By derivation, *patricius Romanorum* was the title of the patron of the Roman Catholic Church, conferred by the pope on emperors from Charlemagne in the 9th century to Frederick I (Barbarossa) in the 12th.
·Caesar's family position and later political role **3**:576a
·economic and social struggle **15**:1066g
·Rome's social inequality **15**:1086f

patricios, Argentine army corps created in 1810.
·creation and distinction **3**:450a

Patrick, Saint **13**:1076 (fl. 5th century in Britain and Ireland), Roman Catholic bishop and patron saint of Ireland, credited with bringing Christianity to Ireland and probably responsible in part for the Christianization of the Picts and Anglo-Saxons. He is known only from two short works, the *Confessio*, a spiritual autobiography, and his *Epistola*, a denunciation of British mistreatment of Irish Christians.

Abstract of text biography. Patrick was captured at age 16 by Irish raiders but returned to Britain after a period of slavery. In Britain he had a dream in which the Irish begged him to return. Despite misgivings, he departed for Ireland and began a successful missionary career. The stories that Patrick drove the snakes out of Ireland and used the shamrock (Ireland's national flower) to explain the Trinity are unsubstantiated by facts.
REFERENCES in other text articles:
·Ireland's religious development **3**:284g
·snake banishment legend **9**:881h

patrilineal descent (kinship): *see* descent.

patrilocal residence (sociology): *see* residence.

Patriocetidae, extinct family of baleen whales (order Cetacea).
·classification and fossil record **19**:810d

Patriot, The (1774), an essay by Samuel Johnson.
·theme of essay **10**:249h

Patriote Party, 19th-century French-Canadian political party led by Louis Joseph Papineau.
·French-Canadian nationalism **15**:331c

Patriotic Union Party, formerly the PEOPLE'S PARTY, a political party of Liechtenstein which in 1970 won its first political majority in 32 years.
·Liechtenstein party system **10**:892d

Patriot Movement, 18th-century Dutch organization with a democratic and Enlightenment influenced political philosophy.
·theoretical base and political realization **11**:150e

Patriots, an 18th-century British political faction with Whig principles that was in opposition to the government of Robert Walpole.
·Britain's 18th-century political growth **3**:254a

patristic literature **13**:1077, the writings of the Fathers (bishops and teachers) of the early Christian Church from the late 1st to the early 8th century AD. Both orthodox and heretical writings are included because some Christian writers were of questionable orthodoxy, others deliberately left the church, and the orthodox Fathers cannot be properly understood in isolation from their heterodox contemporaries.

The text article covers the writings of the ante-Nicene period (before AD 325), including those of the Apostolic Fathers, Gnostic writers, Apologists, and other writers from the late 2nd to the early 4th century, and the writings of the post-Nicene period (after AD 325), including those of the Nicene Fathers, the Cappadocian Fathers, monastic literature, the schools of Antioch, Edessa, and Nisibis, the Chalcedonian Fathers, the non-Chalcedonian Fathers, the post-Nicene Latin Fathers, and later Greek writers. The article concludes with an assessment of patristic literature as a whole.
REFERENCES in other text articles:
·aid to opposition of Luther's position **11**:194f
·Basil the Great's contribution **2**:747f
·Byzantine liturgy origins **6**:162h
·canonicity problems and discussions **2**:883d
·canon law sources in early texts **3**:774a
·Christ, sacraments, and healing **4**:516e
·Christian heritage of Logos concept **4**:478e
·Christian self-definitions **4**:460a
·Church's worldly and spiritual power and definition of orthodoxy **4**:536g *passim* to 541e
·classical and Christian scholarship **8**:1173e
·Eastern Christian understanding of Trinity **6**:145b
·Erasmus' scholarly criticisms **6**:952e
·Eusebius and Augustine on the state **4**:511b
·Eusebius of Caesarea's life and doctrine **6**:1130c
·exegesis, Christmas, and monasticism **4**:498e
·exegetical allegorism and literalism **7**:66g
·Greek and Christian philosophy harmony **6**:333f
·Greek mythology acceptance **4**:552g; illus. 553
·Gregory I's life and career **8**:415e
·Gregory of Nazianzus' preaching **8**:420f
·Gregory of Nyssa and Trinity doctrine **8**:421f
·Hellenistic influences **4**:467h
·historiography in Christian thought **8**:948f
·Ignatius and Clement I on hierarchy **4**:537a
·Ignatius' letters and doctrinal stands **9**:200a
·Irenaeus' defense of scripture, bishops **9**:889c
·Mary seen as Old Testament Eve parallel **11**:561g
·millenarian Christianity de-emphasis **12**:201g
·Nestorian debate evolution **12**:1058a
·normative classifications of religion **15**:628g
·Origen's controversial theology **13**:734f
·pacifism of Tertullian **13**:848b
·papal supremacy **13**:960e
·Philo of Alexandria's contribution **14**:245c
·Platonist philosophy influence **14**:257f
·Reformed Church's qualified acceptance **15**:561e
·Saint John Chrysostom's life and works **4**:583c
·Satan figure attributes **4**:480c
·Stoic influence on Christianity **17**:699h
·St. Paul's life and writings **13**:1090c
·Tertullian's contribution **18**:160d
·theological systematization and defeat of Gnostics **8**:215h
·theology and anti-intellectualism **4**:514b
·transmission of manuscript by hand **18**:190a
·Unitarian thinking **18**:860b
RELATED ENTRIES in the *Ready Reference and Index:*
Ambrosiaster; Apologists, early Christian; Apostolic Constitutions; Apostolic Fathers; Barnabas, Letter of; Clement, First Letter of; Clementine Literature; Didache; Diognetus, Letter to; Ecclesiastical History; Hippolytus, Canons of Saint; Peregrinatio Etheriae; Polycarp, Martyrdom of; Testamentum Domini

Patroclus (Greek mythology): *see* Achilles.

Patroclus (minor planet 617): *see* Trojan planets.

patronage in the arts: *see* arts, social and economic aspects of the.

patronage system (U.S.): *see* spoils system.

patronato real, the royal patronage under which the Spanish church operated in colonial America.
·Spanish colonial religious powers **10**:697f

patron saint, a saint to whose protection and intercession a person, a society, a church, or a place is dedicated. The choice is often made on the basis of some real or presumed relationship with the persons or places involved. St. Patrick, for example, is the patron saint of Ireland because he is credited with bringing Christianity to the Irish people. In some cultures national or local gods are the equivalent of patron saints; *e.g.*, in China K'uei Hsing is the patron of scholars because he reputedly passed his civil service examination with great distinction and will assist others to do the same.
·body and health protection **11**:828b
·Catholic and Orthodox practices **4**:501f
·local deity heritage **16**:166c
·pagan relics in Christian practice **4**:541f
·providential care objects **15**:136e
·Slavic communal banquet tradition **16**:875e

patronymic, name derived from that of a father or paternal ancestor, usually by the addition of a suffix or prefix. For example, the Scottish name MacDonald originally meant son of Donald, and the English name Johnson is derived from son of John. In Russian society everyone is referred to by a patronymic as well as a first name and surname—*e.g.*, Ivan Mikhaylovich Petrov is Ivan the son of Mikhail Petrov; his son will have the patronymic Ivanovich, and his daughter, Ivanovna, meaning daughter of Ivan. In Iceland, patronymics rather than family names are

used almost exclusively; thus, husbands and wives, as well as their offspring, all have different last names.
·English, Brythonic, and Greek patterns **12**:818c
·forms and patterns **12**:815f

Päts, Konstantin (b. Feb. 23 [Feb. 11, old style], 1874, Pärnu district, Estonia—d. Jan. 18, 1956, Kalinin Oblast, Russian S.F.S.R.), Estonian statesman who served as the last president of Estonia before its incorporation into the Soviet Union in 1940.

Päts, 1938
By courtesy of the Estonian Legation, London

Of peasant stock, Päts was educated in the law but began a career in journalism in 1901, when he founded the Estonian-language newspaper *Teataja* ("Announcer") in Tallinn. *Teataja* reflected Päts's socialistic leanings, and in this sense it differed from the Estonian daily *Postimees* ("Mailman"), published in Tartu, which stressed cultural matters. In 1904 Päts was part of an Estonian–Russian slate of candidates that won the Tallinn municipal elections, dealing the powerful local German interests a serious blow. Päts became deputy mayor of Tallinn. During an Estonian rising in connection with the Russian Revolution of 1905, Päts, although he had called for restraint, was sentenced to death and had to flee Estonia. He was not able to return until 1910, at which time he served a brief prison term.

Active in the movement for Estonian independence after 1917, Päts became head of a provisional government when independence was declared in February 1918. Almost immediately, he was arrested by the German occupation authorities, but he resumed his post after the armistice of November 1918.

In 1921–22, 1923, and 1932–33 Päts served as *riigivanem* (equivalent to president and prime minister) of Estonia. After a new constitution providing for a stronger executive was approved by referendum in 1933, Päts learned of a planned coup d'etat by the Fascist "Vaps" movement, which had sponsored the constitution. He arrested the leaders of the movement and assumed the powers of a dictator.

Päts's authoritarian regime lasted until the Soviet Union occupied Estonia in June 1940. He was deported to Russia at the start of the occupation and died there.
·nationalist reform government **2**:673f *passim* to 675b

Patsayev, Viktor Ivanovich (b. June 19, 1933, Aktyubinsk, Kazakh S.S.R.—d. June 30, 1971, in space, probably over Iran), Soviet cosmonaut, design engineer on the Soyuz 11 mission, in which he, Georgy T. Dobrovolsky, and Vladislav N. Volkov remained in space a record 24 days and created the first manned orbital scientific station by docking their Soyuz 11 spacecraft with the unmanned Salyut station launched two months earlier. The three were found dead in their space capsule after it made a perfect landing in Kazakhstan. The deaths were caused by decompression of the capsule resulting from a leak when a hatch was improperly closed.

While in the space station, they had conducted meteorological and plant-growing experiments.
·manned space flight, table 3 **17**:368

patshak, Ostyak word for a type of ghost, comparable to the Lapp *äppäräs* (*q.v.*).

Pattani, province of southwestern Thailand, on the east coast of the Malay Peninsula. It occupies an area of 777 sq mi (2,013 sq km) and has a 72-mi (116-km) coastline on the Gulf of Thailand. Salt production and fishing are important in the coastal towns of Yaring, Sai Buri, and Pattani (the provincial capital). One of Thailand's smallest provinces, it was a larger political unit before a revolt in 1800.

Pattani is drained by the Pattani and Sai Buri rivers. Sandy ridges, remnants of old offshore sandbars, alternate with strips of clay soils. The ridges are the location of coconut groves and settlements, and the lowlands are filled lagoons ideal for rice and rubber cultivation. There are tin reserves. The population is mainly Muslim, and the culture of the area is oriented toward that of Malaysia, 65 mi south.

Pattani town, located at the mouth of the Pattani River, was one of the first Thai seaports opened to international trade, in the 16th century. Its port, which also serves Yala province, exports rubber and tin. Pop. (1972 est.) town, 26,243; (1970) province, 330,217.
·map, Thailand **18**:199
·province area and population table **18**:202

Patte, Pierre (1723–1814), French architect.
·theatre design theories after Vitruvius **18**:247e

patterned ground, generally symmetrical surface pattern of soil and rock material, formed in a perennially cold climate. The two types of patterned ground, sorted and nonsorted patterns, are both associated with frozen ground but are formed by different processes.

Patterned ground produced in a flat surface by freeze–thaw action near Dundas, Greenland
By courtesy of the U.S. Army Cold Regions Research and Engineering Laboratory, Hanover, N.H.; photograph, Arturo Corte

By the process of frost action, mounds may be heaved up on the ground surface while at the same time larger rock fragments migrate to the surface. Because of the pull of gravity, the larger fragments may slide away from the centres of upheaval and accumulate around them. These sorted accumulations may take the form of stone circles, polygons, or stripes (if located on a slope); intersecting patterns may be called stone nets. Although formed naturally, these patterns are remarkably regular in shape; the individual polygons may range in size from a few centimetres to several metres (one inch to 10–15 feet).

The nonsorted patterns are formed by ice wedging. When frozen ground is subjected to extreme cold for extended periods of time, it may shrink and crack; the colder it becomes, the more cracks are formed per unit area. Cracks of this sort remain open and collect frost until warming occurs. Repeated freezings and thawings add to the ice wedge and enlarge the crack until it disturbs the adjacent soil bedding, heaving the material into mounds without regard for particle size.

The absence of vegetation and the saturation of the soil by meltwater provide environments conducive to the formation of patterned ground, although these factors are not requirements.

Patterned ground commonly occurs in tundra, Arctic deserts, and high mountain regions. Relict or inactive features have been found in areas near the former edges of the Pleistocene ice sheets.
·formation, types, and characteristics **8**:175g
·ice wedges and polygonal ground **14**:92e; illus. 93
·Pleistocene permafrost evidence **14**:567g
·tundra features **18**:733c

pattern glass, sets of matching pressed glassware decorated with the same pattern. Produced in large quantities in the U.S. in 1840–80 by the larger glassworks, it was an offshoot of the U.S. invention (1820s) of mechanically pressed glass, which made glass production cheaper.

Pattern sets sometimes included a staggering number of pieces, ranging from sugarbowls to celery vases; from eggcups to wineglasses; and from butter dishes to spoon holders. More than 250 major patterns are known to have been made. Some popular patterns, known as camphor glass, combined the use of clear glass with an acid-finished design.

pattern poetry, verse in which the lines or typography are arranged to convey or extend the emotional content of the words. It is also known as shaped, Cubist, or concrete poetry. Of ancient (probably Eastern) origin, pattern poems are found in the *Greek Anthology*, where one poem was recorded in the shape of an ax, another as an egg.

Notable later examples are the wing-shaped "Easter Wings" and the altar-shaped "Altar" of the 17th-century English Metaphysical poet George Herbert.

In the 19th century, Stéphane Mallarmé employed different type sizes in *Un Coup de dés* (1897; "A Throw of Dice"). The representative Cubist poet is Guillaume Apollinaire, whose *Calligrammes* (1918), inspired by the attempts of Cubist painters to represent all aspects of a subject simultaneously, are visual evocations as well as poems; in a poem about rain, the words fall in long, slanting lines. The U.S. poet e.e. cummings, famous for his typographical eccentricities, was perhaps most successful in making visual innovations significant elements of his poems. Some concrete poets have constructed tangible poems out of iron and other durable materials.
·allegorical nature **7**:134f
·visual prosodic styles **15**:71h

Patterson, Floyd (b. Jan. 4, 1935, Waco, N.C.), professional boxer, first to hold the world heavyweight championship twice. He succeeded the retired champion Rocky Marciano by knocking out Archie Moore in five rounds in Chicago on Nov. 30, 1956; lost the title to Ingemar Johansson of Sweden by a three-round knockout in New York City on June 26, 1959; and regained the championship by knocking out Johansson in five rounds in New York on June 20, 1960. He was subsequently knocked out in one round by Sonny Liston in a title bout in Chicago on Sept. 25, 1962. Patterson later was defeated by Liston and by Muhammad Ali in his attempts to recapture the world championship and by Jimmy Ellis, World Boxing Association

Patterson (top) fighting Tom McNeeley, 1961
Wide World Photos

heavyweight champion, in a match for that version of the disputed world title.

Patterson, who was reared in Brooklyn, learned to box while in a school for emotionally disturbed children. He won several Golden Gloves titles in 1951 and 1952 and was the Olympic Games light-heavyweight champion in 1952. His first professional fight took place Sept. 12, 1952. When he won the heavyweight title he had lost only one professional fight, a disputed decision in favour of the clever and far more experienced Joey Maxim, a former 175-pound light-heavyweight champion.

Patterson, Joseph Medill (b. Jan. 6, 1879, Chicago—d. May 26, 1946, New York City), journalist, co-editor and publisher—with his cousin Robert Rutherford McCormick—of the *Chicago Tribune* from 1914 to 1925; he subsequently became better known as editor and publisher of the New York *Daily News*, the first successful tabloid newspaper in the U.S.

A *Tribune* staff member from 1901, Patterson was an Illinois state legislator (1903–04) and Chicago commissioner of public works (1905–06). During World War I he served as a war correspondent, in 1914–15, and, after the U.S. entered the war in 1917, as a combat officer. With McCormick he founded the New York *Daily News* (first published June 26, 1919), which, because of its sensationalism, soon attained a circulation of nearly 1,000,000, the largest among U.S. tabloids. Relinquishing to McCormick his authority over the *Tribune*, Patterson became sole editor and publisher of the *Daily News* in 1925. A mild Socialist as a young man, he later became more conservative, as did the *Daily News;* the paper switched from support of Pres. Franklin D. Roosevelt's policies to isolationist opposition.

·newspaper publishing history **15**:244a

Paṭṭhāna (Pāli: "Activations"), one of the seven Pāli sections—called *pakaraṇas*—of the Buddhist scripture *Abhidhamma Piṭaka.*

·philosophical contents **3**:434h

Patti, Adelina, originally ADELA JUANA MARIA PATTI (b. Feb. 19, 1843, Madrid—d. Sept. 27, 1919, Craig-y-Nos Brecknock, Wales), one of the great coloratura singers of the 19th century. She went to the U.S. as a child and appeared in concerts in New York City from age seven. She made her operatic debut as Lucia in Gaetano Donizetti's *Lucia di Lammermoor* in New York City in 1859. Two years later she sang Amina in Vincenzo Bellini's *La sonnambula* at Covent Garden, London, where she sang regularly until 1885. She sang many roles in the operas of Rossini, Bellini, Meyerbeer, Gounod, and others, and also in several of the early operas of Verdi.

Her voice was considered small, but remarkable for its wide range, evenness of production, and purity of quality. She achieved her greatest successes in comedy, notably in the roles of Dinorah in Meyerbeer's *Dinorah*, Zerlina in Mozart's *Don Giovanni*, and Rosina in Rossini's *Barbiere di Siviglia*, Rossini having arranged much of the music of this part for her. She had three marriages: in 1868 to Henri, marquis de Caux (divorced 1885); in 1886 to tenor Ernesto Nicolini (d. 1898); and in 1899 to a Swedish baron, Rolf Cederström.

Adelina Patti
By courtesy of the Victoria and Albert Museum, London; photograph, J.R. Freeman & Co. Ltd.

Pattison, Mark (1813–84), English scholar, rector of Lincoln College Oxford, memorable more for his devotion to an intellectual ideal rather than for positive literary achievements.

Patton, George S(mith) (b. Nov. 11, 1885, San Gabriel, Calif.—d. Dec. 21, 1945, Heidelberg, now in West Germany), U.S. Army officer and able tactician who proved himself an outstanding practitioner of mobile tank warfare in the European and Mediterranean theatres during World War II. His strict discipline, toughness, and self-sacrifice elicited exceptional pride within his ranks, and the General was colourfully referred to as "Old Blood-and-Guts" by his men.

A 1909 graduate of the United States Military Academy at West Point, N.Y., and a descendent of a Virginia family with a long military tradition, Patton became a keen student of the U.S. Civil War (1861–65)—particularly of its great cavalry leaders—and collected an outstanding military library. His continuing interest in past wars contributed to his concept of bold, highly mobile, armoured operations. His professional interest turned from the cavalry to the new tank arm as the result of battle experience with the U.S. tank corps in World War I. Between World Wars I and II, Patton forcefully espoused the cause of the tank. Having taken part in the North African campaign (1942), he commanded the U.S. 7th Army in Sicily, employing his armour in a rapid drive that captured Palermo (1943).

Patton, 1945
By courtesy of the U.S. Army

The apogee of his career came with the dramatic sweep of his 3rd Army across France in the summer of 1944 in a campaign marked by great initiative, ruthless drive, and disregard of classic military rules. Made operational on August 1, Patton's armoured units by the end of the month captured Mayenne, Laval, Le Mans, Reims, and Châlons. In December his forces played a strategic role in defending Bastogne in the massive Battle of the Bulge. By the end of January 1945 Patton had reached the German frontier; on March 1 he took Trier and cleared the entire region north of the Moselle River ten days later, trapping thousands of Germans. He then jumped the Moselle to join the 7th Army in sweeping the Saar and the Palatinate, taking 100,000 prisoners.

It was that kind of spectacular military thrust that caused authorities to overlook strong civilian criticism of some of Patton's methods, including his widely reported striking of a hospitalized, shell-shocked soldier in August 1943. (Patton publicly apologized for the incident.)

The controversial general died in a Heidelberg hospital after an automobile accident near Mannheim. His memoirs appeared posthumously under the title, *War As I Knew It* (1947).

·Allied advance across Europe **19**:1006g
·French Red Ball Express system **11**:81h

Patuca River, Spanish RÍO PATUCA, in northeastern Honduras, formed southeast of Juticalpa by the merger of the Guayape and Guayambre rivers. It flows northeastward for approximately 200 mi (320 km), emerging from the highlands and crossing the Mosquito Coast to empty into the Caribbean Sea at Patuca Point, in Gracias a Dios department. Near the river's mouth the Tom-Tom Creek branches to empty into Brus Lagoon. The course of the Patuca is interrupted by rapids in several places, most notably Portal del Infierno (Gate of Hell). Its navigable lower course is used to float logs cut from the dense tropical rain forests through which it flows. 15°50′ N, 84°18′ W

·map, Honduras **8**:1058

Patyn, William (English chancellor): *see* Waynflete, William of.

Patzinakoi (Turkic people): *see* Pecheneg.

Pau, capital of Pyrénées-Atlantiques *département*, southwestern France. The capital of the former province of Béarn, Pau is a spa and winter sports centre. It stands on the edge of a plateau 130 ft (40 m) above the valley of the Gave (stream) de Pau—the Pau torrent, which descends from the Pyrenees. The Boulevard des Pyrénées, more than 1 mi long, situated high above the valley, offers a magnificent panoramic view of the mountains. The castle, on a spur above the river, was the birthplace (1553) of Henry IV of France, who reigned from 1589–1610. Now a national museum, it contains a fine collection of the Gobelins tapestries. The house that was the birthplace (1763) of Marshal Jean Bernadotte who became Charles XIV of Sweden (1818–44) is also a museum. Latest census 71,865. 43°18′ N, 0°22′ W

·map, France **7**:584

Paucar Warai, Inca month equivalent to March in the Gregorian calendar.

·Inca month and festival table **9**:261

paucilithionite (mineral): *see* lepidolite.

Pau Cin Hau, religion of the Chin people, who inhabit the mountain ranges between Burma and Assam, India.

·Christian-influenced tribal worship **18**:704a

Paucituberculata, order of marsupial animals (class Mammalia).

·classification and general features **11**:545a

Paudorf Interstadial, division of late Pleistocene time in Europe (the Pleistocene Epoch began about 2,500,000 years ago and ended about 10,000 years ago). The Paudorf Interstadial, also known as the Paudorf-Arcy Interstadial, represents a transitory phase within an ice age, in this case the Würm Glacial Stage, of relatively moderate climatic conditions and temporary retreat or at least a halt to the advance of the ice. The Paudorf Interstadial has been dated at 33,000 to 25,000 years ago and thus lasted about 8,000 years; climatic conditions during the Paudorf were cool.

·hominid culture and geological period correlation table **8**:1051

Pauger, Adrien de, 18th-century French engineer who drafted New Orleans' first city plan, comprising the section now known as the Vieux Carré.

·New Orleans original design **13**:6g

Paul I, Saint (b. Rome—d. June 28, 767, Rome), pope from 757 to 767. Consecrated deacon by Pope St. Zacharias, he became a key member of the Curia under his brother Pope Stephen II (III), whom he was elected on April 26, 757, to succeed. He secured the support of the Frankish king Pepin the Short against the animosity of the Lombard king Desiderius and the Byzantine emperor Constantine V Copronymus.

In 763 Pepin mediated between Paul and Desiderius, who, allied with the Byzantines, had invaded the Papal States. Concurrently, Paul, heretofore loyal to Constantinople (now Istanbul), vigorously protested Constantine's revival of Iconoclasm (destruction of images). The ensuing Iconoclastic persecution caused an expulsion of many Greek monks, for whom Paul provided refuge in Rome. He is noted for transporting the relics of many saints from the catacombs to Roman churches and for his building projects, including the church of SS. Peter and Paul. His feast day is June 28.

·appeal to Pepin III for aid **14**:36b

Paul I, originally PAVEL PETROVICH (b. Oct. 1 [Sept. 20, old style], 1754, St. Petersburg, modern Leningrad—d. March 23 [March 11, O.S.], 1801, St. Petersburg), emperor of Russia from 1796 to 1801. Son of Peter III (ruled 1762) and Catherine II the Great (ruled 1762–96), Paul was reared by his father's aunt, the empress Elizabeth (ruled 1741–61).

Paul I, emperor of Russia, detail of a portrait attributed to J. Voille, *c.* 1800; in the collection of Mrs. Merriweather Post, Hillwood, Va.

By courtesy of Mrs. Merriweather Post, Hillwood, Va.

After 1760 he was tutored by Catherine's close adviser, the learned diplomat Nikita Ivanovich Panin, but the boy never developed good relations with his mother, who usurped the imperial crown from both her husband and her son in 1762 and, afterward, consistently refused to allow Paul to participate actively in government affairs.

Having married Sophia Dorothea of Württemburg (Russian name Maria Fyodorovna) in 1776 shortly after his first wife, Wilhelmina of Darmstadt (Russian name Nataliya Alekseyevna), died, Paul and his wife were settled by Catherine on an estate at Gachina (1783) where Paul, removed from the centre of government at St. Petersburg, held his own small court and engaged himself in managing his estate, drilling his private army corps, and contemplating government reforms.

Despite Catherine's apparent intention to name Paul's son Alexander her heir, Paul succeeded her when she died (Nov. 17 [Nov. 6, O.S.], 1796) and immediately repealed the decree issued by Peter I the Great in 1722 that had given each monarch the right to choose his successor and had provided the opportunity for Catherine to become empress; in its place Paul established a definite order of succession within the male line of the Romanov family (April 5, 1797, O.S.). Paul also, in an effort to strengthen the autocracy, reversed many of Catherine's policies; he re-established centralized administrative agencies she had abolished in 1775, increased bureaucratic control in local government, and denied the nobility its recently acquired rights to elect certain local officials, to gather in provincial assemblies, and to be exempt from direct taxation. In the process, however, he provoked the hostility of the nobles, and, when he introduced harsh disciplinary measures in the army and displayed a marked preference for his Gachina troops, the military, particularly the prestigious guards units, also turned against him.

Confidence in his ability dropped even among his trusted supporters because of a number of actions. He demonstrated an inconsistent policy toward the peasantry and rapidly shifted from a peaceful foreign policy (1796) to involvement in the second coalition against Napoleon (1798) to an anti-British policy (1800). By the end of 1800, he had manoeuvred Russia into the disadvantageous position of being officially at war with France, unofficially at war with Great Britain, without diplomatic relations with Austria, and on the verge of sending an army through the unmapped khanates in Central Asia to invade British-controlled India.

As a result of his inconsistent policies, as well as his tyrannical and capricious manner of implementing them, a group of highly placed civil and military officials, led by Count Peter von Pahlen, governor general of St. Petersburg, and Gen. Leonty Leontyevich, count von Bennigsen, gained the approval of Alexander, the heir to the throne, and on March 23 (March 11, O.S.), 1801, seized the Mikhaylovsky Palace and assassinated Paul in his bedchamber.

·life, reign, and assassination **1**:473d
·neurotic personality and family life **13**:67h
·reign and social policy failure **16**:57c
·Second Coalition defection **7**:724d

Paul I (b. Dec. 14, 1901, Athens—d. March 6, 1964, Athens), king of the Hellenes (1947–64) who helped his country against Communist guerrilla forces.

The third son of King Constantine of Greece, Paul left Greece with his father following Constantine's deposition in 1917. He refused the crown after the death of his brother, King Alexander (October 1920), but returned home in December 1920 upon Constantine's restoration to the throne. With the rise of republican feeling, however, he again left Greece (December 1923) and remained in exile until 1935, when his brother George was recalled as king. In 1938 Paul married his young cousin, the princess Frederika of Brunswick. He held officer's rank in the Greek Navy, Army, and Air Force and was a member of the army general staff at the outbreak of war with Italy (1940). In 1941 he escaped from occupied Greece and lived in Cairo and South Africa.

After the war, Paul again returned home and ascended the throne upon the death of George (April 1, 1947). At that time Greece received U.S. economic assistance and help in putting down the Communist insurrection. Though professing aloofness from politics, he occasionally intervened in domestic issues.

Paul II (b. PIETRO BARBO, Feb. 23, 1417, Venice—d. July 26, 1471, Rome), pope from 1464 to 1471. He was bishop of the Italian cities of Cervia and Vicenza before being made cardinal by Pope Eugenius IV in 1440. After services in the Curia under popes Nicholas V and Calixtus III, he became governor of Campania in 1456. Elected Pope Pius II's successor on Aug. 30, 1464, he immediately declared that "capitulations," or binding agreements that determined the subsequent conduct of elected prelates, could affect a new pope only as counsels, not as obligations, investing the papacy with an autocratic tone that was to persist throughout his pontificate.

Paul II, commemorative medallion from the Roman school, 1464–71

By courtesy of the National Gallery of Art, Washington, D.C., the Samuel H. Kress Collection

Paul impaired his relations with King Louis XI of France by his repeated condemnations of the Pragmatic Sanction of Bourges—a pronouncement, issued by King Charles VII of France in 1438, that established the liberties of the French Church, particularly the election of the French king's nominee for successors to vacant prelacies. He next turned his attention to the state of the Bohemian Church, which had been damaged by religious struggles with the Hussites (followers of the Bohemian religious reformer Jan Hus). Because the Council (1431–37) of Basel recognized the Hussites as a legitimate church released from papal censureship, Paul strove to abolish the Basel decree. He supported the Romanist (Catholic) party, which formed a confederacy against the king of Bohemia, George of Podebrady, a Hussite sympathizer.

On Dec. 23, 1466, Paul excommunicated George and declared him deposed for refusing to suppress the Utraquists, an independent national church that branched off from the Hussites and that Rome did not recognize. Paul furthermore forbade all Catholics to continue their allegiance to George. In March 1468 he persuaded King Matthias I Corvinus of Hungary to declare war against George, who, concurrently, gained Louis's support. After Matthias conquered much of Moravia, Paul crowned him king of Bohemia in March 1469, a triumphant gesture of his crusade against the Hussites.

Seeing the advancing Turks as a major threat to Christendom, Paul in 1468 began fruitless negotiations with the Holy Roman emperor Frederick III to mount a crusade against them. He opposed the domineering policy of the Venetian government in Italian affairs and promulgated, with the Romans' consent, new statutes for Rome. In 1466 he initiated a severe prosecution against the Fraticelli (Franciscan extremists) with plans to exterminate them and their associates.

Suspecting the Roman Academy and its founder, the Italian Humanist Julius Pomponius Laetus, of opposing Christian ideals and endorsing a materialistic vision of life inspired by an admiration for the ancient world, Paul dissolved the academy and arrested its members in February 1468, subjecting one of its leading Humanists, Bartolomeo Platina, to torture on additional charges of conspiracy. Thus, he incurred the enmity of the Humanists, who saw him as an enemy of letters. He was, however, a patron of scholars and also a collector of antiquities and a restorer of monuments. He is responsible for founding the first printing presses at Rome, where he had built the celebrated Palace of St. Mark (now the Palazzo Venezia), his principal residence from 1466. R. Weiss's *Un umanista veneziano: papa Paolo II* ("A Venetian Humanist: Pope Paul II") appeared in 1958.

- ·Bohemian reform opposition **2**:1190b
- ·church construction and restoration **15**:1074d

Paul III, Pope 13:1087, originally ALESSANDRO FARNESE (b. Feb. 29, 1468, Canino, Italy—d. Nov. 10, 1549, Rome), the last of the Renaissance popes and the first pope of the Counter-Reformation. The worldly Paul III was a notable patron of the arts and at the same time encouraged the beginning of the reform movement that was to affect deeply the Roman Catholic Church in the later 16th century.

Abstract of text biography. Born into an important Italian family, Alessandro became the protégé of Cardinal Rodrigo Borgia. After Borgia became pope (as Alexander VI), Alessandro was created a cardinal deacon (1493). His personal conduct was that of a Renaissance nobleman until his ordination as a priest (1519), after which he changed his private way of life and became identified with the reform party of the Roman Curia. Elected pontiff in 1534, he initiated church reform and called the Council of Trent in 1545.

REFERENCES in other text articles:

- ·Alexander VI religious sponsorship **1**:468c
- ·church reform importance **15**:1011c
- ·Erasmus' nomination as Deventer dean **6**:953h
- ·military and diplomatic goals **6**:1086d
- ·Nice Truce and Charles V **8**:89g
- ·papal reforms in post-Reformation era **13**:959a
- ·Spanish hegemony threat **9**:1151d
- ·Titian portraits and patronage **18**:459d
- ·Transcendant God edict and the New World **1**:980d

Paul IV (b. GIAN PIETRO CARAFA, June 28, 1476—d. Aug. 18, 1559, Rome), pope from 1555 to 1559, whose anti-Spanish policy renewed the war between France and the Habsburgs. Of noble birth, he owed his ecclesiastical advancement to the influence of his uncle Cardinal Oliviero Carafa.

Paul IV, detail from his tomb sculpture by Pirro Ligorio; in the church of Sta. Maria sopra Minerva, Rome

Alinari

Bishop of Chieti, Italy, Carafa served Pope Leo X as envoy to England and Spain. He resigned his benefices and, with St. Cajetan of Thiene (Gaetano da Thiene), founded the order of the Theatines (Congregation of Clerics Regular) in 1524 to promote clerical reform through asceticism and apostolic work. Having advised Leo's successors in matters of heresy and reform, he was appointed to Pope Paul III's commission for ecclesiastical reform, was made cardinal in 1536, and was responsible for a reorganization of the Roman Inquisition.

Despite his violent antipathies, austerity, uncompromising reformism, and exalted concept of papal authority, Carafa was elected pope on May 23, 1555, through the influence of Cardinal Alessandro Farnese. Even the veto of the Holy Roman emperor Charles V was ignored. When Paul's excessive violence in orthodoxy and reform was carried over into politics, his pontificate was destined to be strife ridden. He succumbed to the counsels of his nephews, whom he elevated, and to his hatred of the Habsburgs and of the Spaniards, whom he attempted to drive from Naples by allying with France in December 1555. Thus, he provoked war against Charles and King Philip II of Spain. The Spanish victory in August 1557 at Saint-Quentin, Fr., and the advance upon Rome by the Duke of Alba forced Paul to come to terms with Spain; peace was made on Sept. 12, 1557. He continued his animosity toward Spain and the Habsburgs, however, by refusing to recognize the abdication of Charles and the election of his brother Ferdinand I (1558) as successor on grounds that the imperial transaction was effected without papal approval.

Paul's handling of the Protestant question was as disastrous as his politics. He denounced as a pact with heresy the Peace of Augsburg, the first permanent legal basis for the existence of Lutheranism and Catholicism in Germany. He facilitated the ultimate victory of Protestantism in England by insisting upon the restitution of monastic lands that had been sold and by requiring Elizabeth I to submit her claims to the English throne to him. Furthermore, he ruined Cardinal Reginald Pole, archbishop of Canterbury, who had infuriated Paul by trying to prevent the conflict between France and the Habsburgs. In April 1557 Paul deprived Pole of his authority and in the following June, after England's declaration of war on France, summoned him to Rome on protests of heresy. Queen Mary I of England intervened, saving Pole from the fate suffered by his friend Cardinal Giovanni Morone, whom Paul imprisoned on illegitimate charges of unorthodoxy.

An enemy to conciliar methods, Paul did not reassemble the Council of Trent (which had been suspended since 1552), preferring instead to work through commissions or congregations. But without a council he stopped many ecclesiastical abuses in Rome, disciplined vagrant clergy, and introduced firmer asceticism in the papal court.

Under him, the Roman Inquisition, established in 1542, launched a reign of terror, alienating nearly all parties and the best minds of his age. Following the trend in the Roman Catholic Church that wrongly suspected Jews of influencing the Reformation to some degree, Paul in 1555 established the ghetto at Rome. He enforced perpetual wearing of the Jewish badge and drastic separation of Jews from Christians, excluding Jews from all honourable positions and occupations. The antagonisms he aroused proved fatal to his reforming cause. G.M. Monti's *Ricerche su Papa Paolo IV Carafa* ("Researches on Pope Paul IV Carafa") appeared in 1923.

- ·Catholic Church reform in 16th century **15**:1011a
- ·censorship of arts **12**:100e
- ·influence on Palestrina's career **13**:931f
- ·Jewish persecution in Rome **15**:1080c
- ·military and diplomatic ambitions **6**:1088b
- ·Pius V aided in Inquisition career **14**:482a
- ·public opinion and censorship **15**:210f
- ·Roman Inquisition establishment **15**:1012d
- ·Spanish threat and church reform **9**:1151d

Paul V (b. CAMILLO BORGHESE, Sept. 17, 1552, Rome—d. Jan. 28, 1621, Rome), pope from 1605 to 1621. A distinguished canon lawyer, he was papal envoy to Spain for Pope Clement VIII, who made him cardinal in 1596. He became vicar of Rome in 1603, and on May 16, 1605, was elected as Pope Leo XI's successor at a time when the Kingdom of Naples and the Venetian Republic were violating ecclesiastical rights.

One of his first acts was to excommunicate the recalcitrant minister of Naples for violating the *privilegium fori—i.e.*, the right of ecclesiastics to be judged in criminal cases not by civil courts but by church courts. In 1606 a conflict erupted between Paul and Venice over papal jurisdiction and ecclesiastical immunity within the republic, where the celebrated theologian Paolo Sarpi encouraged resistance to papal censures. The situation became critical when Paul's interdict (a severe form of papal censure, although not an excommunication) against Venice (May 1606) caused firmer defiance, led chiefly by Sarpi; fear of Venice's breaking with Rome and the risk of civil war in Italy induced the neighbouring states to intervene. Paul was prepared to appeal to arms, but a compromise was reached on April 21, 1607, mainly through France's mediation. Paul lifted the interdict and excommunicated Sarpi, against whom a murderous attack was made in the following October. Sarpi accused the Curia of instigating the assault, which Paul reprobated. He realized that the effect of interdicts was dead, and they were not used by the papacy against a sovereign state again.

Paul V, portrait bust by Gian Lorenzo Bernini, *c.* 1618; in the Borghese Gallery, Rome

Alinari

Earlier (Sept. 22, 1606), Paul expressly forbade the Roman Catholics of England to take the new oath of allegiance imposed on them by King James I. His contention with Venice, however, made him politically cautious, and he endeavoured to maintain peace between the Habsburgs and France. He considered another crusade against the Turks, though without success. He particularly feared an open breach of the Peace of Augsburg, the first permanent legal basis for the coexistence of Lutheranism and Catholicism in Germany. Thus, when in 1618 hostility between German Catholics and Protestants caused fighting that developed into the Thirty Years' War, Paul gave no support to the Catholic powers.

In doctrinal matters, he was surprisingly undogmatic. He encouraged missions, notably those in Latin America, and confirmed many new congregations and brotherhoods, including St. Philip Neri's Oratorians (approved 1613), a congregation of secular priests. He canonized SS. Charles Borromeo and Frances of Rome and beatified SS. Ignatius of Loyola and Francis Xavier. To preserve papal documents he founded the privy Vatican archives. In 1612 he authorized a new version of the *Rituale Romanum*, one of the Roman rite's liturgical books, which he promulgated on June 17, 1614.

Paul was guilty, however, of nepotism and is responsible for his family's inordinate wealth. He especially favoured his nephew Marcantonio Borghese, whom he created prince of Vivaro. His excessive fondness for display, which wasted funds needed for more crucial purposes, made him a spectacular patron of the arts and of building, including the chapel in the Basilica of Sta. Maria Maggiore, Rome, where he is buried.

- ·conflict with Venice **16**:251f
- ·Richelieu's early experience in Rome **15**:831b
- ·Venetian church and state conflict **9**:1151f

Paul VI, Pope 13:1088, originally GIOVANNI BATTISTA MONTINI (b. Sept. 26, 1897, Concesio, Italy—d. Aug. 6, 1978, Castel Gandolfo), 262nd pope of the Roman Catholic Church during a period including most of the second Vatican Council (1962–65) and the immediate postconciliar era, in which he issued directives and guidance to a changing Roman Catholic Church.

Abstract of text biography. Montini was ordained priest in 1920 and entered the Vatican diplomatic service soon thereafter, serving on the papal nuncio's staff in Warsaw (1923). Returning to Rome, he resumed work at the Vatican Secretariate of State, where he rose to ever higher posts during the next 30 years. He was appointed papal undersecretary of state in 1939 and acting secretary for ordinary (nondiplomatic) affairs in 1944. In November 1954 Pope Pius XII appointed him archbishop of Milan, and in 1958 Pope John XXIII named him cardinal. After John's death, Montini was elected pope (June 21, 1963) and chose the name Paul VI. He guided the second Vatican Council through its remaining sessions and was then confronted with carrying out its many decisions. He issued several encyclicals, some of which (such as those on artificial means of birth prevention, 1968, and clerical celibacy, 1967) aroused opposition. Paul also made a pilgrimage to the Holy Land, where he met Athenagoras, the Greek Orthodox ecumenical patriarch (1964), and visits to India (1964), to the United Nations in New York (1965), to Fátima, Port., and Istanbul and Ephesus, Tur. (1967), to Colombia (1968), to Switzerland and Uganda (1969), and to Asia (1970). He worked for social justice and church reunion.

REFERENCES in other text articles:
- birth control and traditional Catholic view **2**:1071d
- Catholic social teaching **15**:1001c
- celibacy for clergy reaffirmed **3**:1043e
- coat-of-arms in Vatican City illus. **19**:37
- ecumenical meetings with Athenagoras I **6**:295g
- papal authority issues **13**:960b

Paul, Acts of, apocryphal (noncanonical and unauthentic) Christian writing of the late 2nd century AD that purports to be an account of the travels and teachings of the Apostle Paul. It was composed in Greek by a presbyter of a church in Asia Minor who, though claiming to have written "out of love for Paul," was deprived of his office, probably because of the romancing character of the work. Doctrinally, he established a close relationship between sexual purity and salvation. He was quite orthodox in opposing the moral laxity of heretical Gnostic sects and in attacking their denial of the Resurrection. It was not until modern times that such writings as the *Acts of Paul and Thecla*, the *Martyrdom of Paul*, and the pseudo-correspondence between Paul and the Corinthians—formerly known only in fragments—were recognized as constituent parts of the *Acts of Paul*.
- New Testament Apocrypha **2**:973g

Paul, Bruno (1874–1968), German designer, critic, and art educator.
- synthesis of fine and applied arts **2**:95c

Paul, Jean, real name JOHANN PAUL FRIEDRICH RICHTER (1763–1825), German author.
- literary style and works **10**:1174c

Paul, John: *see* Jones, John Paul.

Paula (Malta): *see* Paola.

Paul and Thecla, Acts of, apocryphal (noncanonical) writing that was popular in the early Christian Church; it describes, unhistorically, the activities of Paul the Apostle in Asia Minor.
- Apocrypha literary form and content **2**:973g
- exemplary function in popular religion **4**:553h

Paul-Boncour, Joseph (b. Aug. 4, 1873, Saint-Aignan, Fr.—d. March 28, 1972, Paris), leftist politician who served as minister of labour, of war, and of foreign affairs, and who for four years was France's permanent representative to the League of Nations.

After receiving a degree in law from the University of Paris, Paul-Boncour practiced law, organized the legal council of the Bourses du Travail (syndicalist workers' associations), and from 1898 to 1902 was private secretary to Premier Pierre Waldeck-Rousseau. He was elected deputy from his native district in 1909 and served as minister of labour in 1911. He lost his seat in the Chamber in 1914 but was returned to the National Assembly after World War I as a Socialist. In 1931, however, he resigned from the Socialist Party and formed a new group, the Union Socialiste Républicaine, composed of independents. That same year he was elected senator and served until the establishment of Marshal Philippe Pétain's Vichy government in 1940.

Paul-Boncour
H. Roger-Viollet—Harlingue

Paul-Boncour was permanent delegate to the League of Nations from 1932 to 1936, minister of war in the 1932 cabinet of Édouard Herriot, premier from December 1932 to January 1933, and minister of foreign affairs from December 1932 to January 1934, from January to June 1936, and in March 1938. In July 1940 he voted against granting constitutional powers to Marshal Pétain and recommended continuation of the war against Germany from Algiers. A member of the Consultative Assembly in 1944, he led the French delegation at San Francisco and signed the United Nations Charter on behalf of France. He was a senator from 1946 to 1948.

Paul-Boncour's books *Le Fédéralisme économique* (1900; "Economic Federalism") and *Les Syndicats de fonctionnaires* (1906; "Unions of Civil Servants") showed his interest in trade unionism. He was also the author of *Art et démocratie* (1912; "Art and Democracy") and *Entre deux guerres: souvenirs sur la IIIe République* (1946; *Recollections of the Third Republic*, 1958).

Paulding, James Kirke (b. Aug. 22, 1778, Dutchess, now Putnam, County, N.Y.—d. April 6, 1860, Hyde Park), dramatist, novelist, and public official chiefly remembered for his early advocacy and use of native American material in literature. He held several public posts in New York and from 1838 to 1841 served as secretary of the navy. His literary work, however, overshadows his routine labours as a government official. At 18 he went to New York City, where he formed a lasting friendship with the Irving brothers. This association aroused his enthusiasm for literature, and he, with William and Washington Irving, founded the *Salmagundi* (1807–08), a periodical consisting mainly of light satires on local subjects. The outbreak of hostilities between England and America encouraged the assertion of Paulding's nationalism. He satirized England's conduct toward America during the war in *The Diverting History of John Bull and Brother Jonathan* (1812) and *The Lay of the Scottish Fiddle: A Tale of Havre de Grace* (1813), the latter a burlesque of Sir Walter Scott. The same spirit of nationalism found expression in two later satires also directed at the British: *A Sketch of Old England: by a New England Man* (1822) and *John Bull in America* (1825).

The advantages and hardships of western migration are the theme of "The Backwoodsman" (1818), a poem written to call the American author home in his search of literary themes. Novels such as *Koningsmarke, the Long Finne, a Story of the New World* (1823), *Westward Ho!* (1832), and *The Old Continental, or, the Price of Liberty* (1846) represent Paulding's attempts to employ the American scene in fiction. His popular play, *The Lion of the West* (first performed, 1831; first published, 1954), introduced frontier humour to the stage by depicting a character resembling Davy Crockett and helped during the 1830s to contribute to the growing legend of Crockett. In his *Life of Washington* (1835), once commended by Edgar Allan Poe, lies further evidence of Paulding's Americanism. Plain, even at times vulgar in style, he yet possessed a playful irony that he shared with the New York writers of his day.

Paulet, also spelled PAWLET, or POULETT, name, derived from Pawlett near Bridgwater in Somerset, of a well-known English family, different branches of which have held the baronies of St. John of Basing (from 1539), of Poulett of Hinton St. George (from 1627), and of Pawlet of Basing (1717–54); the earldoms of Wiltshire (from 1550) and of Poulet (from 1706); the marquessate of Winchester (from 1551); and the dukedom of Bolton (1689–1754). One of its best-known members was Sir Amias Paulet, who had charge of Mary Stuart, queen of Scots, from 1585 until her execution (February 1587).

paulette, in pre-Revolutionary France, royal edict of 1604 that resulted in making offices hereditary, a step in the creation of a permanent class of judicial magistrates, the *noblesse de robe*. The edict provided that, for an annual payment to the crown of one-sixtieth of its value, an office could be sold or bequeathed rather than revert to the crown on the death of the holder. The edict took its name from Charles Paulet who proposed the measure and obtained control of the collection of payments.

The *paulette* provided the crown with needed revenue, although it also diminished the king's power of appointment. The officeholders, desiring to gain complete disposal of their offices, were eager both to make the annual payment (*droit annuel*) and to ensure its renewal every nine years.
- origin and stipulations under Louis XIV and the ancien régime **7**:632b

Pauley, Edwin W(endell) (1903–), U.S. diplomat and businessman.
- Japanese post-war business **10**:88a

Pauley report (1945), postwar U.S. reparations report, not adopted, calling for the dismantling of Japanese industry.
- Japanese post-war settlement **10**:88a

Pauli, Wolfgang (b. April 25, 1900, Vienna—d. Dec. 15, 1958, Zürich), winner of the Nobel Prize for Physics in 1945 for his discovery (1925) of the Pauli exclusion principle (*q.v.*), which states that in an atom no two electrons can have the same energy. This principle clearly relates the quantum theory to the observed properties of atoms. When he was 20, Pauli wrote a 200-page encyclopaedia article on the theory of relativity. He was appointed a lecturer at the University of Hamburg in 1923, and the following year he proposed that a fourth quantum number, which may take on the numerical values $+\frac{1}{2}$ or $-\frac{1}{2}$, was needed to specify electron energy states. It was later found that the two values represent the two possible directions of spin for fermions. In 1925 he introduced his exclusion principle, which, when applied to electrons, immediately made clear the reason for the structure of the periodic table of the elements.

In 1928 Pauli became professor of theoretical physics at the Federal Institute of Technology, Zürich. Under his direction the institution became a great centre of research in theoretical physics during the years preceding World War II. In the late 1920s it was observed that when a beta particle (electron) is emitted from an atomic nucleus, there is generally some energy and momentum missing, a grave violation of the laws of conservation. Rather than allow these laws to be discarded, Pauli proposed in 1931 that the missing energy and momentum is carried away from the nucleus by some particle (later named the neutrino by the Italian-born physicist Enrico Fermi) that is uncharged and has little or no mass. Furthermore, the postulated particle had gone unnoticed because it interacts with matter so seldom that it is nearly impossible to detect. The neutrino was finally observed in 1956.

In 1940 Pauli was appointed to the chair of theoretical physics at the Institute for Advanced Study, Princeton University, and in 1946 he became a naturalized citizen of the U.S. Following World War II he returned to Zürich.

·atomic model contributions **2**:337g
·particle theory and quantum physics **12**:870b
·quantum theory development **11**:799d

Paulicians, a dualist Christian sect that originated in Armenia in the mid-7th century. It was influenced most directly by the dualism of Marcionism, a heretical movement in early Christianity, and of Manichaeism, a Gnostic religion founded in the 3rd century by the Persian prophet Mani. The identity of the Paul, after whom the Paulicians are called, is disputed.

The fundamental doctrine of the Paulicians was that there are two principles, an evil God and a good God; the former is the creator and ruler of this world, the latter of the world to come. From this they deduced that Jesus was not truly the son of Mary, because the good God could not have taken flesh and become man. Though recognizing the Scriptures as uniquely authoritative, they rejected the Old Testament and also the letters of St. Peter; they especially honoured the Gospel According to Luke and the letters of St. Paul. They rejected the sacraments, the worship, and the hierarchy of the established church.

The founder of the Paulicians seems to have been an Armenian, Constantine, who took the additional name of Silvanus (Silas; one of St. Paul's companions). He gave a more distinctively Christian character to the Manichaeism that at the time was prevalent in the Asian provinces of the Byzantine Empire. The sect seems to have started a widespread political and military rebellion within the empire shortly after its appearance. Between 668 and 698 Constantine III and Justinian II sent two expeditions to repress it. Constantine (Silvanus) was stoned to death, and his successor, Simeon (Titus), was burned alive. In the early 9th century Paulicianism was revived. It expanded into Cilicia and Asia Minor under Sergius (Tychicus), who made it strong enough to survive the persecution and massacre instigated by the emperor Michael I and the empress Theodora. The number and power of the Paulicians were at the greatest under Karbeas and Chrysocheir, the leaders in the third quarter of the 9th century. An expedition sent by Basil I in 872 broke their military power, but they survived in Asia at least until the Crusades. After the 9th century, their importance lay chiefly in Thrace, where many Paulicians had been forcibly located to serve as a frontier force against the Bulgarians. Paulician doctrines were disseminated among the Macedonians, Bulgarians, and Greeks, especially among the peasants, and it seems that they contributed to the development of the doctrines and practices of the Bogomils, another neo-Manichaean sect, who first appeared in Macedonia in the early 10th century.

·Basil I's persecution **3**:560h
·Basil I's wars and victory **2**:748c
·Christian mysticism in heretical form **4**:546h
·Manichaeism and Christian heresy **11**:444f

Pauli exclusion principle, assertion that no two electrons in an atom can be at the same time in the same state or configuration, proposed (1925) by the Austrian physicist Wolfgang Pauli to account for the observed patterns of light emission from atoms. The exclusion principle subsequently has been deepened and generalized to include a whole class of particles of which the electron is only one member.

Subatomic particles fall into two classes depending upon their statistical behaviour. Those particles to which the Pauli exclusion principle applies are governed by Fermi-Dirac statistics (*q.v.*) and as a class are called fermions. The nuclear particles, neutrons and protons, are also fermions, behaving according to the Pauli exclusion principle. When in a closed system, such as an atom for electrons or a nucleus for protons and neutrons, fermions are distributed so that a given state is occupied by only one at a time. The other class of particles, called bosons, because their behaviour is described by Bose-Einstein statistics (*q.v.*), do not obey the Pauli exclusion principle; large numbers of these particles may aggregate in the same state.

Particles obeying the exclusion principle have a characteristic value of spin, or intrinsic angular momentum, analogous to the spinning property of a turning top; their spin is always one-half fundamental unit or some negative or positive odd whole-number multiple of one-half. In the modern view of atoms, the space surrounding the dense nucleus may be thought of as consisting of orbitals, or regions, each of which comprises only two distinct states. The Pauli exclusion principle indicates that, if one of these states is occupied by an electron of spin one-half, the other may be occupied only by an electron of opposite spin, or spin negative one-half. An orbital occupied by a pair of electrons of opposite spin is filled: no more electrons may enter it until one of the pair vacates the orbital. An alternative version of the exclusion principle as applied to atomic electrons states that no two electrons can have the same values of all four quantum numbers.

·atomic spectra periodic properties **17**:463e
·electron occupancy of energy levels **6**:667f
·elementary particle statistics **5**:35b
·ionic crystal and electron repulsion **9**:805f
·metal conduction theory **11**:1089e
·neutron occupancy of energy levels **12**:1071h
·nuclear shell model **13**:338c *passim* to 339h
·orbital atomic model **2**:337g
·particle theory and quantum physics **12**:870b
·periodic law and electronic structure **14**:79d
·quantum theory development **11**:799d
·semiconductor energy band analysis **16**:525g
·subatomic particle theory **13**:1023b
·transition element structure **18**:603c

Pauline: A Fragment of a Confession (1833), the first published work of Robert Browning.

·Browning criticism by Mill **3**:334d

Pauline Letters, New Testament writings traditionally attributed to St. Paul the Apostle. Some are now known to have been written by someone else.

·authorship, content, and emphases **2**:958b
·Jesus doctrine and theology **10**:145g
·Muratorian Canon defense of canonicity **2**:940c
·soteriological conceptions **16**:202e
·St. Paul's life and teachings **13**:1090d

Pauling, Linus (Carl) **13**:1094 (b. Feb. 28, 1901, Portland, Ore.), chemist who contributed greatly to the understanding of molecular structures, particularly with regard to chemical bonding. Pauling received two Nobel Prizes, one for Chemistry in 1954 and the Nobel Peace Prize in 1962.

Abstract of text biography. He was educated at the California Institute of Technology, Pasadena (Ph.D. 1925), and in Europe. He made significant contributions in his work on chemical bonding, carried on from the 1930s, and other studies, and his efforts on behalf of the international control of nuclear weapons, against nuclear testing, and other campaigns for the cause of peace.

REFERENCES in other text articles:
·chemical concepts in hereditary disease **11**:1050c
·diagnosis historical development **5**:684g
·ionic crystal structure prediction **9**:806b

Paulinus, Saint (b. 584?, Rome—d. 644, Rochester, Kent), missionary who converted Northumbria to Christianity, became the first bishop of York, and was later made archbishop of Rochester. In 601 he was sent with SS. Mellitus (later first bishop of London) and Justus (later first bishop of Rochester) to England by Pope St. Gregory I the Great to assist Archbishop St. Augustine of Canterbury in his mission of converting England to Christianity. Paulinus was consecrated bishop at Kent (625) by Justus (then fourth archbishop of Canterbury) and escorted the daughter of King Aethelberht (Ethelbert) of Kent to the Northumbrian king Edwin. Paulinus converted and baptized Edwin (627), who made him first bishop of York, after which Paulinus' missions spread throughout Northumbria. In 632 Edwin was slain by the Anglo-Saxon kings Caedwalla (Cadwallon) and Penda, and Paulinus fled to Kent, where he became bishop of Rochester. He became archbishop in 634, when he received the pallium (*i.e.*, symbol of metropolitan jurisdiction) from Pope Honorius I. His feast day is October 10.

·Northumbrian mission activity **3**:200b

Paulinus of Nola, Saint, in full MEROPIUS PONTIUS ANICIUS PAULINUS (b. AD 353, Bordeaux—d. June 22, 431, Nola, Italy), bishop of Nola and one of the most important Christian Latin poets of his time. He became successively a Roman senator, consul, and governor of Campania, a region of southern Italy. Returning to Aquitaine he married and in 389 retired with his wife to Spain. The death of their only child, in 392, influenced them to sell their possessions in Gaul and Spain. In 395 Paulinus was ordained priest and with his wife settled at Nola to live an ascetic life devoted to charity.

Paulinus' act of renunciation caused his old master, the Latin poet and rhetorician Ausonius, to write reproaches in verse, to which Paulinus replied in poetical epistles. Paulinus' style generally echoes that of such classical authors as Virgil, Horace, and Ovid. His poems (395–407) on the feast day of St. Felix of Nola are particularly charming and are regarded as the chief source of Felix's life. Paulinus also promoted the saint's cult and built a basilica at Nola dedicated to him.

Some 50 of his extant letters correspond with famous contemporaries, including SS. Augustine and Jerome and the celebrated ascetic Sulpicius Severus. Paulinus' prose style is often rhetorical and exuberant: he could describe in dignified language his cold reception by Pope St. Siricius, or satirize the ignorance of those who could not understand the life of renunciation. About 409 Paulinus was consecrated bishop of Nola. His feast day is June 22. P. Fabre's *Essai sur la chronologie de l'oeuvre de S. Paulin de Nole* (1948; "Essay on the Chronology of the Works of St. Paulinus of Nola") was followed by his *S. Paulin de Nole et l'amitié chrétienne* (1949; "St. Paulinus of Nola and Christian Friendship.")

·patristic contributions **13**:1085h

Paulistas, the inhabitants of the city and state of São Paulo, Brazil. In the 17th century some of them were noted for aggressive expeditions (*bandeiras*) into the South American interior. In the early 18th century they were unable to prevent the influx of outsiders, called *emboabas*, into Minas Gerais province. Tensions between the two groups broke out in the War of the Emboabas (1708–09); the Paulistas were defeated and penetrated farther westward into Mato Grosso province.
·Brazil's colonial expansion **3**:144e
·São Paulo city history **16**:238b
·São Paulo state history **16**:236f

Paul Karageorgević, Prince (b. April 27 [April 15, old style], 1893, St. Petersburg, now Leningrad—d. Sept. 14, 1976, Paris), regent of Yugoslavia in the period just before World War II. When King Alexander I was assassinated (Oct. 9, 1934) Paul was appointed regent for his 11-year-old nephew Peter II. Although Paul's sympathies lay with the British–French entente, he was forced to align his country with the Axis powers. On March 23, 1941, two days after signing a treaty with Germany, Paul was deposed; he fled to Greece, where he was captured by British forces after the war. After internment in Kenya he was released and settled in Paris.
·foreign relations policy **2**:635e

Paullinia cupana (plant): *see* guarana.

Paullus (PAULUS) **Macedonicus, Lucius Aemilius** (b. *c.* 229—d. 160 BC), Roman general whose victory over the Macedonians at Pydna ended the Third Macedonian War (171–168 BC).

Paullus' father, a consul of the same name, had been killed fighting the Carthaginians at Cannae in 216. Praetor in 191 and consul in 182, Paullus campaigned against the Lusitanians in Spain (191–189) and the Ingauni in Liguria (181). As consul for a second time in 168, he decisively defeated the Macedonian king Perseus at Pydna (June 22). Paullus carried out the settlement with Macedonia and Greece, and on orders from the Senate he sacked the cities of Epirus. He was censor in 164. *See also* Pydna, Battle of.
·Perseus' fall at Pydna **15**:1094f
·Roman conquest of Macedonia **8**:385a
·Scipio Aemilianus family ties **16**:393f; illus. 394

Paulo Afonso, city, northeastern Bahia state, northeastern Brazil, on the São Francisco River, at the site of the Paulo Afonso Falls and Paulo Afonso National Park. Made a seat of a municipality in 1958, Paulo Afonso is the transportation and commercial centre for its agricultural hinterland. It is accessible by highway from Salvador, the state capital, about 310 mi (500 km) south, and from neighbouring communities in Bahia, Alagoas, and Pernambuco states. Pop. (1970) 38,265.
9°21′ S, 38°14′ W

Paulo Afonso Falls, Portuguese CACHOEIRA DE PAULO AFONSO, series of rapids and three cataracts on the São Francisco River along the border between Bahia and Alagoas in northeast Brazil. Lying 190 mi (306 km) from the river's mouth, the falls have a total height of 275 ft (84 m) and a width of less than 60 ft. With an average water discharge of 100,000 cu ft (3,000 cu m) per second, the falls are the site of a large hydroelectric station (at Três Marias Dam), which provides flood control and management of irrigation, power, and transportation throughout much of northeast Brazil. The falls form the central feature of Paulo Afonso National Park.
·dam's hydroelectric power capacity **2**:593g
·hydroelectric project importance **1**:408g
·map, Brazil **3**:125
·type, height, and discharge **19**:640d; table 638
·watercourse and drop **16**:235g

Paulo Afonso Falls and hydroelectric plant on the São Francisco River, Brazil
Carl Frank—Photo Researchers

Paulo Afonso National Park, Portuguese PARQUE NACIONAL DE PAULO AFONSO, located along the banks of the São Francisco River in the states of Alagoas, Bahia, and Pernambuco, in Brazil. It has an area of 41,500 ac (16,800 ha), and its principal attraction is Paulo Afonso Falls.

Paul of Aegina, Latin PAULUS AEGINETA (b. *c.* 625, Aegina—d. *c.* 690), Alexandrian physician and surgeon, the last major ancient Greek medical encyclopaedist, wrote the *Epitomēs iatrikēs biblio hepta*, better known by its Latin title, *Epitomae medicae libri septem* ("Medical Compendium in Seven Books"), containing nearly everything known about the medical arts in his time.

Based largely on the works of such earlier Greek physicians as Galen, Oribasius, and Aëtius, the *Epitome* greatly influenced the medical practice of the Arabs, who considered Paul among the most authoritative of Greek medical writers. The Persian master physician ar-Rāzī (Rhazes), drew extensively from the work in writing his *Kitāb al-Manṣūrī* (Latin *Liber Almansoris;* "Book to al-Manṣūr"), and Abū al-Qāsim (Latin Albucasis), one of Islām's foremost surgeons, borrowed heavily from the *Epitome*'s sixth (surgical) book in compiling the 30th chapter ("On Surgery") of his *at-Taṣrīf* ("The Method"). Thus Paul's work exercised an influence on Western medieval medicine when the Arabic works were adopted as primary references in Europe.

Besides his descriptions of lithotomy (surgical removal of bladder stones), trephination (removal of a disc of bone from the skull), tonsillotomy (removal of part of the tonsil), paracentesis (puncture of a body cavity in order to drain fluid), and amputation of the breast in the sixth book, Paul also devoted much attention in the *Epitome* to pediatrics and obstetrics. He dealt extensively with apoplexy and epilepsy, distinguished 62 different types of pulse associated with various diseases, and rendered one of the first known descriptions of lead poisoning. The complete Greek text of the *Epitomēs* was published in 1921–24 in the *Corpus Medicorum Graecorum.*
·poisonous animal and plant research **14**:607e

Paul of Samosata (fl. 3rd century AD), heretical bishop of Antioch in Syria and proponent of a kind of Dynamic Monarchian doctrine on the nature of Christ (*see* Monarchianism). The only indisputably contemporary document concerning him is a letter written by his ecclesiastical opponents, according to which he was a worldly cleric of humble origin who became bishop of Antioch in 260.

Paul held that it was a man who was born of Mary, through whom God spoke his Word (Logos). Jesus was a man who became divine, rather than God become man. A similar speculative Christology was found among the primitive Ebionites of Judaea; in Theodotus and Artemon of Rome (both of whom were excommunicated); and perhaps in other early Christian writers (and suggested by phrases in the New Testament such as Acts 2:36). The great biblical scholar Lucian of Antioch and his school were influenced by Paul. The 7th-century Paulicians of Armenia may have claimed to continue his traditions, hence their name.

Between 263 and 268 at least three councils were held at Antioch to debate the Bishop's orthodoxy. The third condemned his doctrine and deposed him. But Paul enjoyed the patronage of Zenobia, queen of Palmyra, to which Antioch was then subject, and it was not until late in 272, when the emperor Aurelian defeated Zenobia and brought Antioch under Roman imperial rule again, that the sentence of deposition could be executed.

Paul of Thebes, Saint, also called PAUL THE HERMIT (b. *c.* AD 230, Upper Egypt—d. *c.* 341), traditionally regarded as the first Christian hermit. The only life of Paul, the *Vita Pauli*, was written by St. Jerome, according to whom Paul fled to the desert around Thebes during the persecution of Christians (249–251) under the Roman emperor Decius. Thereafter, he lived a life of prayer and penitence in a cave, dying at the reputed age of 113. Jerome considered Paul to be the first Christian hermit, an honour that in modern times is generally accorded to St. Anthony of Egypt. It is said that Anthony visited Paul when the latter was 113 years old and later buried him, wrapped in the cloak given to Anthony by Athanasius, bishop of Alexandria. In art Paul is often represented with a palm tree, symbolizing the source of his sustenance, or with two lions, who allegedly dug his grave. His feast day is January 15.

Paul of the Cross, Saint, original name PAOLO FRANCESCO DANEI (b. Jan. 3, 1694, Ovada, Italy—d. Oct. 18, 1775, Rome), founder of the order of missionary priests known as Passionists (*q.v.*). In 1720 he dedicated his life to God and began to experience visions, in the last of which the Virgin Mary appeared to him. He was inspired by this to found a congregation devoted to the suffering of Christ on the cross, and his rule for the new order was approved in 1741 by Pope Benedict XIV and confirmed in 1769 by Clement XIV. Paul subsequently founded the Passionist Nuns at Corneto (modern Tarquinia), Italy; the order was approved by Clement XIV in 1770. By the time of his death, Paul had established 12 monasteries in Italy, and since then his institute has spread throughout the world. He was canonized in 1867 by Pope Pius IX, and his feast day is April 28.

Paul of Venice, 15th-century Augustinian theologian.
·logic history from antiquity **11**:60h

Paulsen, Friedrich (b. July 16, 1846, Langenhorn, Schleswig-Holstein, now in W. Ger. —d. Aug. 14, 1908, Berlin), philosopher and educator, perhaps best known for his theories of education. Educated at the major universities of Germany, he was a lecturer (1875–78) and professor of philosophy and pedagogy (1878–1908) at the University of Berlin. Drawing from the work of Immanuel Kant, Arthur Schopenhauer, and Gustav Theodor Fechner, he elaborated the theory of Panpsychism, emphasizing the connection between philosophy and contemporary life.

Paulsen's major work in the history of education is *Geschichte des gelehrten Unterrichts auf den deutschen Schulen und Universitäten vom Ausgang des Mittelalters bis zur Gegenwart* (1885; *The German Universities: Their Character and Historical Development*, 1895). His philosophical works include *System der Ethik* (1889; *A System of Ethics*, 1899), *Immanuel Kant: Sein Leben und seine Lehre* (1889; *Immanuel Kant: His Life and Doctrine*, 1902), and *Einleitung in die Philosophie* (1892; *Introduction to Philosophy*, 1895).
·Kant as metaphysician **10**:396h

Pauls Valley, city, seat (1907) of Garvin County, south central Oklahoma, U.S., south

of Oklahoma City on the Washita River. The first white settler in the river valley (1847) was Smith Paul (whence the city's name). Pauls Valley serves a farming (alfalfa, cotton, corn, broomcorn, fruit, and pecans) and dairying area. Economic activities include oil refining, cotton ginning, the manufacture of oil-field equipment and furniture, and food and animal-feed processing. The Pauls Valley State Hospital (originally built in 1915 as a boys reformatory) cares for mentally retarded children. Inc. 1899. Pop. (1980) 5,664.
34°44′ N, 97°13′ W

Paul the Apostle, Saint 13:1090 (b. in Tarsus in Cilicia, now in Turkey—d. between AD 62? and 68?, Rome), a 1st-century Jew who, after being a bitter enemy of the Christian Church, became its leading missionary and possibly its greatest theologian.

Paul, a Roman citizen whose formal education must have been strictly Jewish, was trained as a rabbi and learned the trade of tentmaking. Although he never met Jesus, he regarded him as a threat to Pharisaic Judaism and persecuted his followers. Converted through a vision on the road to Damascus, he accepted his call to be the Apostle to the Gentiles. After spending time in Arabia and in Damascus, he visited Peter and James in Jerusalem, returned to Cilicia, and eventually went with Barnabas to Antioch, where the idea of a planned mission first arose. Paul and Barnabas went to Jerusalem, consulted with the leaders of the Christians there, and reached agreement on future missionary policy. When Peter later visited Antioch, Paul insisted on disregarding the law that forbade Jews to eat with Gentiles.

Paul then began a series of three missionary journeys that took him to cities throughout Asia Minor and Greece. He maintained contact with the churches that he established by means of letters that taught, corrected, encouraged, and sometimes chided the young Christian communities. Paul paid his last visit to Corinth in AD 57 and then went to Jerusalem, where he was arrested. After being imprisoned at Caesarea for two years, he appealed to the Emperor. He arrived in Rome in AD 60 and was kept in custody for two years awaiting trial, during which time he wrote several letters. There is evidence that he died a martyr's death in Rome under Nero.

TEXT BIOGRAPHY covers:
Early life **13**:1090d
Conversion 1091a
Visits to Jerusalem and Antioch 1091b
First missionary journey 1091e
Second missionary journey 1091g
Third missionary journey 1092g
Arrest and imprisonment 1093d
Character 1093h

REFERENCES in other text articles:
·ascetic view of Christian life **2**:137e
·atheism and the letter to Titus **2**:259b
·Athens' Christianization **2**:268a
·biographical chronology reconstruction **2**:948d
·Christian and political participation **4**:509b
·Christian dogma judicial orientation **4**:476c
·Christian hermeneutical precedents **7**:64b
·Christianity's spread to the Gentiles **15**:1121g
·Christian limitation of love ethic **4**:525g
·Christ-mysticism of the early church **4**:545f
·church festival indifference **4**:601d
·circumcision dispute with Peter **14**:155f
·Cyprus' conversion to Christianity **5**:403b
·division between Judaism and Christianity **10**:216a
·ecumenical concept of mystical body **6**:293e
·elements of human nature **15**:152h
·Ephesian theatre use **18**:237a
·Eucharistic principles established **16**:117d
·exegetical allegorism **7**:66f
·Gentile mission and theology **4**:535e
·Hellenistic philosophy rejection **4**:468b
·Holy Spirit principle difficulties **4**:483g
·Jesus doctrine and theology **10**:145g
·life chronology and Letters' authorship **2**:957b
·Luke's relationship in tradition **11**:177e
·Malta's conversion to Christianity **11**:391g
·original sin and salvation **16**:202e
·position against women's equality **19**:909h
·prophetic office in apostolic church **15**:66a
·Protestant roots for Luther **15**:109c
·Protestant view of salvation **15**:101f
·revelation in Christ **15**:784f
·sainthood and prophetic reform **16**:167b
·Stoic influence on Christianity **17**:699h
·Torah relevance for Gentile Christians **4**:466d
·travelling prowess **4**:504d

Paul the Deacon, Latin PAULUS DIACONUS (b. *c.* 720, Cividale del Friuli, Italy—d. *c.* 799, Monte Cassino), Lombard historian and poet, whose *Historia Langobardorum* ("History of the Lombards") is the principal source of information about his people.

Born to a rich and noble family of Friuli, northeast of Venice, Paul spent many years at the Lombard court in Pavia, serving as councillor under King Desiderius. After the fall of the Lombard kingdom to Charlemagne, Paul and his brother were involved in an anti-Frankish plot; their property was confiscated, and his brother was carried off as a prisoner to France. Paul took refuge in Benevento in southern Italy at the court of Duke Arichis II, who had married Desiderius' daughter Adalberga, once Paul's pupil. Several years later, when Charlemagne was in Rome, Paul sent verses to him begging for pardon and for the release of his brother. Charlemagne responded by freeing Paul's brother but insisted that Paul become a member of his court at Aachen, where he took part in the Frankish king's palace school, along with the scholars Alcuin and Einhard, meeting with the King for learned discussions. In 786 Paul returned to Italy with Charlemagne, settling at the abbey of Monte Cassino, where he spent the rest of his life and wrote his history. Based on written sources and on oral tradition, which would otherwise have been lost, it covers the history of the Lombards to 744. His other works include a collection of homilies for the ecclesiastical year, a commentary on the Rule of St. Benedict, and a *Historia Romana*.

Paul the Hermit: *see* Paul of Thebes, Saint.

Paulus, Friedrich (b. Sept. 23, 1890, Breitenau, now in West Germany—d. Feb. 1, 1957, Dresden, now in East Germany), World War II German field marshal on the Eastern Front, whose capture at Stalingrad in early 1943 with his entire army became one of the turning points of World War II and contributed substantially to Germany's defeat.

After serving in World War I and as a staff officer early in World War II, Paulus became deputy chief of the German general staff (1940) and helped draft plans for the invasion of the Soviet Union. As commander of the 6th Army from early 1942, he led the drive on Stalingrad (now Volgograd). Surrounded in the city by a Russian counteroffensive beginning Nov. 19, 1942, the 6th Army surrendered on Feb. 2, 1943. The Stalingrad disaster put an end to Germany's offensive role in Russia. A tremendous blow to morale, it also deprived Germany of about 300,000 irreplaceable trained men. Captured by Soviet forces, Paulus agitated against Hitler among German prisoners of war and later testified at the Nürnberg War Crimes trials. After his release in 1953 he settled in East Germany.
·Stalingrad siege and Russian response **19**:995h

Paulus, H(einrich) E(berhard) G(ottlob) (1761–1851), German Orientalist and theologian.
·Schelling's Berlin lectures **16**:341b

Paulus Aegineta: *see* Paul of Aegina.

Paulus Macedonicus, Lucius Aemilius: *see* Paullus Macedonicus, Lucius Aemilius.

Paulus Venetus, born PAOLO NICOLETTI, 14th- and 15th-century Italian philosopher.
·Aristotelianism and the Renaissance **1**:1160a

Pauly, August von (1796–1845), German classical philologist.
·antiquities encyclopaedia collaboration **6**:792e

Paumgärtner Altarpiece, The (1502–04), painting by Albrecht Dürer.
·northern and Italian stylistic elements **19**:405d

Paumotu (French Polynesia): *see* Tuamotu Archipelago.

paunch: *see* stomach.

pauraque (formerly PARAUQUE), *Nyctidromus albicollis*, nocturnal bird of brushlands from southern Texas to northern Argentina, is a nightjar (*q.v.*; family Caprimulgidae). The pauraque is about 30 centimetres long, with rounded wings and a longish tail. It is mottled brown with a bold white bar on each wing; in the male the outer tail feathers are white.

pauropod, any member of the arthropod class Pauropoda, commonly grouped with several other classes as myriapods. The approximately 400 species, found worldwide in decaying logs and ground litter, eat fungi and rotting animal matter. They resemble tiny centipedes. The soft body has 12 segments; each segment bears a pair of short legs, a pair on one segment is inconspicuous. Four or five pairs of hairlike tactile organs project from the sides of the body, which is usually 0.5 to 1.0 millimetre (0.02 to 0.04 inch) long. Pauropods are the only arthropods with branched antennae. They lack eyes, tracheae, and a circulatory system.
·arthropod features **2**:69g; illus. 66
·characteristics and classification **12**:772c
·traits and behaviour **12**:768h; illus. 769

Pausanias (d. probably between 470 and 465 BC, Sparta), Spartan commander during the Greco-Persian Wars who was accused of treasonable dealings with the enemy. A member of the Agiad royal family, Pausanias was the son of King Cleombrotus I and nephew of King Leonidas. He became regent for Leonidas' son after the father was killed at Thermopylae (480). Pausanias commanded the allied Greek army that defeated the Persians at Plataea (479), and he led the Greeks in the capture of Byzantium (478).

While Pausanias was at Byzantium, his arrogance and his adoption of the Persian style of living offended the allies and raised suspicions of disloyalty. Recalled to Sparta, he was tried and acquitted of the charge of treason but was not restored to his command. When the Athenians separated from the Spartans to form the Delian League, Pausanias returned to Byzantium privately and held the city until expelled by the Athenians (probably in 477). Later, suspected of plotting to seize power in Sparta by instigating a helot uprising, he took refuge in the temple of Athena of the Brazen House to escape arrest. The Spartans walled in the sanctuary and starved him to death.

Although Herodotus doubted that Pausanias had colluded with the Persians, Thucydides, writing years after the events, was certain of his guilt. It is conceivable that the Spartans had made Pausanias a scapegoat for their failure to retain the leadership of Greece; nevertheless, some of his activities seem to justify suspicion.
·Greeks defeat of Persia at Plataea **8**:311e
·incrimination and death **8**:352c
·Philip of Macedonia assassination **14**:227c
·role in victory of Battle of Plataea **8**:350d

Pausanias (fl. AD 143–176; b. Lydia, now in Turkey), Greek traveller and geographer whose *Description of Greece* is an invaluable guide to ancient ruins. Before visiting Greece, he had travelled widely in Asia Minor, Syria, Palestine, Egypt, Macedonia, Epirus (now in Greece and Albania), and parts of Italy. His *Description* takes the form of a tour of Greece starting from Attica. It is divided into ten books: (1) Attica and Megara; (2) Corinth and Argolis; (3) Laconia; (4) Messenia; (5) and (6) Elis, including Olympia; (7) Achaea;

(8) Arcadia; (9) Boeotia; and (10) Phocis, including Delphi. The first book seems to have been completed after 143, but before 160–161. No event after 176 is mentioned in the work.

His account of each important city begins with a sketch of its history; his descriptive narration follows a topographical order. He gives a few glimpses into the daily life, ceremonial rites, and superstitious customs of the inhabitants and frequently introduces legend and folklore. Works of art are actually his major concern.

Inspired by interest in the ancient glories of Greece, he is most at home in describing the religious art and architecture of Olympia and Delphi. At Athens he is intrigued by pictures, portraits, and inscriptions recording the laws of Solon; on the Acropolis, the great bronze statue of Athena; and outside the city, the monuments of famous men and of Athenians fallen in battle. The accuracy of his descriptions has been proved by the remains of buildings in all parts of Greece.

The topographical part of his work shows his fondness for the wonders of nature: the signs that herald the approach of an earthquake; the tides; the icebound seas of the north; and the noonday sun, which at the summer solstice casts no shadow at Syene (Aswān), Egypt.

The famed anthropologist and classical scholar Sir James Frazer said of Pausanias: "without him the ruins of Greece would for the most part be a labyrinth without a clue, a riddle without an answer."

·accounts of hero cult activities **8**:823e
·man's effect on physiographic features **14**:431f

Paussidae, family of tropical beetles of the insect order Coleoptera.

·characteristics and classification **4**:834b

Paustovsky, Konstantin (Georgiyevich) (b. May 31, 1892, Moscow—d. July 14, 1968, Moscow), Soviet fiction writer best known for his short stories, which carried the pre-Revolutionary romantic tradition into the Soviet period.

A descendant of Ukrainian Cossacks, Paustovsky attended school in Kiev, St. Petersburg (now Leningrad), and Odessa. Before he began to write, he worked at various jobs; he also travelled a good deal, both in the Soviet Union and abroad.

He wrote novels, novellas, short stories, and historical and biographical fiction. The short novels *Kara-Bugaz* (1932) and *Kolhkida* (1934) brought him wide popularity. His works reveal a lyrical interest in nature and an intense curiosity about people; he has been described as one of the best craftsmen among the writers of the 1920s and 1930s. His main work, *Rasskaz zhizni* (1946–62; *The Story of a Life*, Eng. trans., 1964), published in several volumes, is an autobiographical cycle of reminiscences.

Because of his age and prestige, Paustovsky was able in the 1950s and 1960s to act as defender and protector of other Soviet writers who had been subjected to various degrees of official criticism.

Pauvre Christ de Bomba, Le (1956), novel by Mongo Beti.

·colonial disillusion theme **1**:239d

Pauxi pauxi (bird): *see* curassow.

pavane (possibly from Italian *padovana*, from "Padua," or from Spanish *pavo*, "peacock"), majestic processional dance of the 16th- and 17th-century European aristocracy. Until about 1650 the pavane opened ceremonial balls and was used as a display of elegant dress. Adapted from the *basse danse*, an earlier court dance, the pavane presumably travelled from Italy to France and England by way of Spain; in southern Spain it was performed in churches on solemn occasions.

Pavane from "The Romance of the Rose," Toulouse, 16th century; in the British Museum (Harley MS 4425, fol. 14v)

By courtesy of the trustees of the British Museum

The pavane's basic movement, to music in $\frac{2}{2}$ or $\frac{4}{4}$ time, consisted of forward and backward steps; the dancers rose onto the balls of their feet and swayed from side to side. A column of couples circled the ballroom, and the dancers occasionally sang. By about 1600, livelier steps like the *fleuret* (a brief lift of each foot before a step) made the dance less pompous. The pavane was customarily followed by its afterdance, the vigorous galliard. The *passamezzo* was a livelier Italian contemporary of the pavane.

The paired dances, pavane and galliard, were a forerunner of the instrumental dance suites of the 17th century, and pavanes appear in a few early suites—*e.g.*, the *padouanas* in some suites of Johann Hermann Schein. Later composers occasionally used the pavane as an instrumental piece; *e.g.*, Fauré (*Pavane for Orchestra*) and Ravel (*Pavane for a Dead Princess*).

·description and court introduction **14**:801c

Pavane (1969), novel by Keith Roberts.

·fiction of hypothesis **13**:289c

Pavelić, Ante (b. July 14, 1889, Bradina, Bosnia, now in Yugoslavia—d. Dec. 28, 1959, Madrid), nationalist leader and revolutionist who headed a Croatian state subservient to Germany and Italy during World War II.

As a practicing lawyer in Zagreb, Pavelić entered the nationalist Croatian Party of Rights. In 1920 he was elected city and county alderman at Zagreb. From 1927 to 1929 he was a representative in the Yugoslav Skupština (parliament), in which he vigorously opposed centralization of the country. When King Alexander assumed dictatorial power (1929), Pavelić fled to Italy and organized a group of Croatian terrorists known as the Ustashe (Insurgents). They achieved their greatest success in organizing the assassination of King Alexander in Marseilles, Fr., on Oct. 9, 1934.

After the conquest of Yugoslavia by Axis forces in April 1941, Pavelić was installed as head (*poglavnik*) of the Independent State of Croatia, which included Bosnia and part of Dalmatia. Under the Ustashi regime, whose slogan was "Za dom Spremni" ("Ready for the Fatherland"), a brutal program of oppression was conducted against the Orthodox Serbs and the Jews. With the defeat of his German sponsors in May 1945, Pavelić left Croatia and went into hiding in Austria and Italy, finally escaping to Buenos Aires in 1948. Demands for his extradition as a war criminal by Yugoslavia in 1957 were rejected by Argentina. Wounded in an attempt on his life that same year, Pavelić settled secretly in Spain.

·Fascist leadership in Croatia **7**:186h

Pavel Petrovich (Russian emperor): *see* Paul I.

pavement, in civil engineering, surfacing of road or similar area. The primary function of a pavement is to transmit loads to the subbase and underlying soil. Modern flexible pavements contain sand and gravel or crushed stone with a binder of bituminous material, as asphalt, tar, or asphaltic oil. Such a pavement has enough plasticity to absorb shock. Rigid pavements are of concrete, made up of coarse and fine aggregate and portland cement, and usually reinforced with steel rod or mesh.

·lighting problems due to improvements **10**:963b
·roadway construction and maintenance **15**:896b; fig. 892
·types, construction, and soil influence **16**:1013d

Pavese, Cesare (b. Sept. 9, 1908, Santo Stefano Belbo, Italy—d. Aug. 27, 1950, Torino), poet, critic, novelist, and translator, who, like Elio Vittorini, introduced many modern U.S. and English writers to Italy and whose own novels are distinguished for their poetic beauty, allusive power, and intense concentration on the problems of alienation and disillusionment in modern life. He is generally regarded as one of the most important Italian novelists of his time.

Pavese

Arnoldo Mondadori Editore

Pavese was born in a small town in which his father, an official, owned property; the family moved to Torino, where he attended high school and the university. Denied an outlet for his creative powers by Fascist control of literature, Pavese translated many 20th-century writers in the 1930s and '40s: the U.S. writers Sherwood Anderson, Gertrude Stein, John Steinbeck, John Dos Passos, Ernest Hemingway, and William Faulkner; a 19th-century writer who influenced him profoundly, Herman Melville (one of his first translations was of *Moby Dick*); and the Irish novelist James Joyce. He also published many critical articles on U.S. literature, posthumously collected in *La letteratura americana e altri saggi* (1951; Eng. trans., *American Literature, Essays and Opinions*, 1970). His work probably did more to foster the reading and appreciation of U.S. writers in Italy than that of any other single man.

A founder and, until his death, an editor of the publishing house of Einaudi, Pavese also edited the anti-Fascist review *La Cultura*. His work led to his arrest and imprisonment by the government in 1935, an experience later recalled in "Il carcere" (published in *Prima che il gallo canti*, 1949; Eng. trans. in *The Political Prisoner*, 1955) and the novella *Il compagno* (1947; Eng. trans., *The Comrade*, 1959). His first creative publication, a volume of lyric poetry, *Lavorare stanca* (1936; "To Work Is Tiring"), followed his release from prison. An initial novella, *Paesi tuoi* (1941; Eng. trans., *The Harvesters*, 1961), recalled, as many of his works do, the sacred places of childhood. Between 1943 and 1945 he lived with the partisans of the anti-Fascist Resistance in the hills of Piedmont.

The bulk of Pavese's work, mostly short stories and novellas, appeared between the end of the war and his death; most are concerned with the agonies and isolation of modern life, the search for answers in an inevitably destructive past. Partly through the influence of Melville, Pavese became preoccupied with myth, symbol, and archetypes. One of his most striking books is *Dialoghi con Leucò* (1947; Eng. trans., *Dialogues with Leucò*, 1965), poetically written conversations about the human condition, exploring the effect of an individual's past upon his present experience. The novel considered his best, *La luna e i falò* (1950; Eng. trans., *The Moon and the Bonfires*, 1950), is a bleak, yet compassionate story of a hero who tries to find himself by visiting the place in which he grew up. Several other works are notable, especially *La bella estate* (1949; Eng. trans. in *The Political Prisoner*, 1955), for which Pavese won the Strega Prize in 1950. Shortly after receiving the prize he committed suicide in a hotel room.

A Pavese Prize for literature was established in 1957, and some of Pavese's most significant work was published after his death, notably a volume of love lyrics that is considered to contain his best poetry, *Verrà la morte e avrà i tuoi occhi* (1951; "Death Will Stare at Me Out of Your Eyes"); the story collection *Notte di festa* (1953; Eng. trans., *Festival Night and Other Stories*, 1964); and the striking chronicle of his inner life, *Il mestiere de viviere, diario 1935–1950* (1952; Eng. trans., London, *This Business of Living*, New York, *The Burning Brand: Diaries 1935–1950*, both 1961), which one reviewer called "a document of strange, harrowing pathos." In her introduction to the work, the noted Italian novelist Natalia Ginzburg describes Pavese as a man who, visiting, would sit for hours, stolid and silent; and the diaries themselves, apparently not intended for publication, reveal a man inwardly tortured, given to addressing himself in the second person singular, warning himself not to "wallow in your own unhappiness."

Many collections of Pavese's work have appeared, including *Racconti* (1960; Eng. trans., *Told in Confidence and Other Stories*, 1971), a collection of much of his best fiction; *Poesie edite e inedite* (1962), edited by Italo Calvino; and *Lettere* (1966), which covers the period from 1924 to 1950. Pavese's *Opere* in 16 volumes was completed in 1968. A poetry collection in English, *A Mania for Solitude, Selected Poems 1930–1950*, was published in 1969.

·Italian literary role **10**:1238c

Pavia, capital of Pavia province, Lombardia (Lombardy) region, northern Italy, on the left bank of the Ticino River, above its junction with the Po, 20 mi (32 km) south of Milan,

The Certosa di Pavia, a Carthusian monastery completed in the 17th century, Pavia, Italy
SCALA, New York

with which it is connected by the Naviglio di Pavia (Pavia Canal). Pavia originated as Ticinum, a settlement of the Papiria tribe, which was conquered by Rome *c.* 220 BC and later became a key point in the Roman defense of upper Italy. Pillaged by the barbarians Attila in AD 452 and Odoacer in 476, it later became an important centre of Gothic resistance against the Byzantine Empire. From the 6th century, under the Lombards, it was a leading city of Italy, even after it fell to the Franks in 774. After a series of wars with Milan from the 11th to the 13th century, it was finally subdued by the viscounts of Milan and the Visconti of Brittany in the 14th century and became the political centre of Italy under Gian Galeazzo II Visconti, who founded the University of Pavia. The park of the Visconti Castle north of Pavia was the scene in 1525 of the defeat and capture of the French king Francis I by Emperor Charles V of Spain, aided by the Pavians and by Swiss militia; this battle demonstrated the superiority of firearms over cold steel and revolutionized military tactics. During the 18th century, Pavia was occupied by the Austrians, French, and Spaniards. It was one of the leading cities of Venetian Lombardy in the campaigns of the Risorgimento (movement for Italian political union) and was joined to the Kingdom of Italy in 1859.

The city still retains the ancient plan of the Roman *castrum* (fortified place), with main crossroads and a network of streets for *centuriae* (companies of soldiers). At its centre is the cathedral with its vast cupola; begun in 1488 by Cristoforo Rocchi and completed in 1898 according to his still extant model, the building has the form of a Latin cross. Among numerous other churches the most notable are S. Michele (1155, on the remains of a 7th-century foundation), the ancient Lombard cathedral where the medieval "kings of Italy" were crowned; S. Pietro in Ciel d'Oro (consecrated 1132), mentioned by the writers Dante, Petrarch, and Boccaccio, with a marble tomb (1362) containing the bones of St. Augustine of Hippo; S. Teodoro (12th century), decorated with 13th-century frescoes; and the Gothic churches of the Carmine (14th century) and S. Francesco (begun 1288). Secular buildings include the 12th- and 16th-century Broletto, or town hall; the Visconti Castle (1360–65) containing valuable artistic collections; and beautiful cloisters and palaces, one of which (Palazzo Malaspina) houses the Pinacoteca (art gallery). North of Pavia on the extreme boundary of the park of the Visconti is the Certosa di Pavia, a Carthusian monastery, the most celebrated religious monument in Lombardy; it was begun in 1396 by Bernardo da Venezia and continued by other notable artists in a transitional style between Gothic and Renaissance.

The University of Pavia, founded in 1361, is linked with the ancient law school, which dates back to 825. The colleges of Ghislieri and Borromeo, founded in the 16th century by Pope Pius V and St. Charles Borromeo, with the addition of the Cairoli, Castiglioni-Brugnatelli, Fraccaro, and Afro-Asiatic colleges, made Pavia the Oxford of Italy. It is particularly noted for the study of law, science, medicine, and surgery and has a central library of more than 400,000 volumes and 1,500 manuscripts.

A centre of communications, agriculture, and industry, the city manufactures sewing machines and has mechanical-engineering, ferrous-metalworking, chemical, and textile industries. Pop. (1971 prelim.) mun., 90,125. 45°10′ N, 9°10′ E

·Charlemagne's conquest of Lombards **4**:44g
·Charles V's victory and significance **4**:49b
·map, Italy **9**:1088
·province area and population, table 1 **9**:1094

Pavia, Battle of (Feb. 24, 1525), the decisive military engagement of the war in Italy between Francis I of France and the Habsburg emperor Charles V, in which the French army of 28,000 was virtually annihilated and Francis himself, commanding the French army, was taken prisoner. Francis was sent to Madrid, where, the following year, he concluded peace and surrendered French claims to Italy. The French army had been besieging the city of Pavia, 20 miles (30 kilometres) south of Milán, when the 23,000-man Habsburg army under Fernando Francisco de Avalos, marchese di Pescara, arrived to aid the 6,000-man garrison and lift the siege. A hasty French attack was on the point of encircling Pescara when 1,500 Spanish arquebusiers opened fire on the rear of the French cavalry and riddled the ranks of the French and their allied Swiss infantry. The French attacks thereafter, made by German and Swiss mercenary infantry, were routed. The Spanish counterattack, supported by the Pavia garrison, which joined in the battle, completely swept the French from the field, destroying Francis' army as a fighting force in the process. Spanish hegemony in Italy dates from this battle.

·French losses in Italy **9**:1148e

Pavia, Compact of (1329), an agreement that divided the House of Wittlesbach into Palatinate and Bavarian branches.

·Wittelsbach dynasty division **11**:117b

Pavia, Council of, council convened by Pope Martin V in 1423, later moved to Siena, Italy.

·ineffectiveness as reform assembly **15**:1008d

Pavía y Lacy, Manuel (b. July 6, 1814, Granada, Spain—d. Oct. 22, 1896, Madrid), general whose defeat in the Spanish Revolution of 1868 helped bring about the deposition of Queen Isabella II.

Pavía was encouraged to enter the military by his father, an infantry colonel, and eventually was admitted to the elite Guards regiment. When Isabella became queen in 1833, he fought for her against her uncle Don Carlos in the First Carlist War (1833–39) and in 1840 he was made marqués de Novaliches. He emigrated to France in 1841 and on his return in 1843 took part in the overthrow of the government of Gen. Baldemero Espartero.

Pavía was named minister of war (1847) in the cabinet of the conservative Gen. Ramón Narváez. Afterward he was captain general of Catalonia, where he attempted to stimulate economic development and also conducted military operations against Carlist rebels. In 1853 he reluctantly accepted the post of captain general of the Philippines, where in the following year he crushed the revolt of José Cuesta.

In the revolution that deposed Isabella, Pavía attempted to halt the rebel army of Gen. Francisco Serrano y Domínguez by seizing a strategic bridge at Alcolea. His forces were repulsed at the bridge, and he was badly wounded. His defeat (Sept. 28, 1868) opened the way to Madrid, and the following day the Queen fled into exile.

Pavía emigrated at the accession of Amadeus as king of Spain (December 1870) but returned after the collapse of the First Republic and the restoration of Alfonso XII (December 1874). Pavía then regained his honours.

Pavía y Rodríguez de Alburquerque, Manuel (b. Aug. 2, 1827, Cádiz, Spain—d. Jan. 4, 1895, Madrid), general whose coup d'etat ended Spain's First Republic (1873–74).

In 1865 Pavía joined the staff of Gen. Juan Prim, whom he supported in the unsuccessful uprisings of 1866 and, after two years in exile, in the successful revolution of 1868 that deposed Isabella II (1833–68). After the abdication of Amadeus (February 1873) and the proclamation of the First Republic, Pavía suppressed insurrection in the south of Spain and restored the authority of the central government. On three occasions during 1873 he served as captain general of Madrid.

Pavía supported Pres. Emilio Castelar y Ripoll from September 1873 to Jan. 3, 1874, when Castelar was defeated in the Cortes (National Assembly) and was forced to resign. Castelar had governed firmly and had the confidence of the army. Believing the return to power of more radical republicans would harm both the nation and the army, especially his own artillery corps, Pavía forcibly dissolved the Assembly and summoned Gen. Francisco Serrano y Domínguez to form a new government. During Serrano's year of

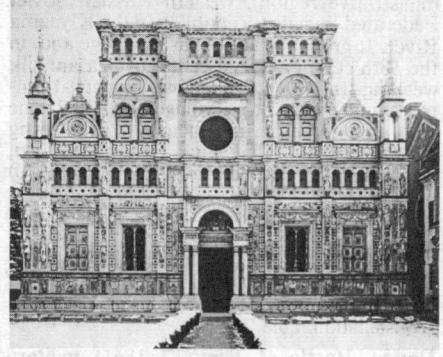

rule the First Republic existed in name only.
After the restoration of Alfonso XII (December 1874), Pavía was elected to the Cortes (1876). He was captain general of Catalonia (1880–81) and of New Castile (1885–86).
·military intervention for order **17**:438g

Pavie, Auguste (-Jean-Marie) (b. 1847, Dinan, Fr.—d. 1925, Thourie), explorer and diplomat, who is best known for his explorations of the Upper Mekong Valley and for having brought the kingdoms of Laos virtually singlehandedly under French control.
Pavie went to Cochinchina (now part of South Vietnam) as a sergeant in the marines in 1869 and subsequently worked in the Post and Telegraphic Department, directing construction of a telegraph line between Phnom Penh, the Cambodian capital, and Bangkok, the capital of Siam, in 1879 and another between Saigon and Bangkok in 1882. While working on the telegraph lines, he travelled throughout Siam, Cambodia, and Vietnam and gained an intimate knowledge of each country's customs and languages. The French government hoped to gain control of the Lao states lying to the east of the Mekong River and appointed Pavie vice consul in Luang Prabang (now the royal capital of Laos) in 1886. During the next five years he travelled throughout the Lao states, winning for France the allegiance of local chiefs and kings and frustrating Siamese attempts to dominate the region, traditionally under Siamese suzerainty.
From 1891 to 1893 Pavie served as consul general in Bangkok. In October 1893 he secured a treaty by which the Siamese agreed to cede the east bank of the Mekong to France, after a French blockade of Bangkok harbour had almost touched off war between the two countries. The disputed Lao territories had originally been under Vietnamese domination, and, with France's control of Vietnam, Pavie argued that the Laotian territories passed rightfully to France. He hoped the Mekong River would provide easy access to the potentially vast markets of Southwest China.
Before returning to France, Pavie conducted an expedition, defining Laos' borders with China, and with Upper Burma, which the British had annexed in 1886. He wrote *Mission Pavie: Indochina 1879–1895* (Paris, 1898–1919) and *À la conquête des coeurs* (1921).

pavilion (gemstones): *see* facet.

pavilion, a light temporary or semipermanent structure used in gardens and pleasure

Garden pavilion, Versailles
Edwin Smith

grounds. Although there are many variations, the basic type is a large, light, airy garden room with a high-peaked roof resembling a tent. Originally erected, like the modern canvas marquee, for special occasions such as fetes, garden banquets, and balls, it became more permanent; and by the late 17th century the term was used for any garden building designed for use on special occasions. Although many ornamental garden pavilions survive in old gardens, the modern use of the term is usually limited to buildings on sports grounds with accommodations for changing clothes and storing equipment.
The word pavilion has also been used in reference to an annex, or structure connected to a larger building, and to one of several buildings making up a complex.

Pavillard, Daniel, 18th-century Swiss Calvinist minister who at Christmas, 1754, converted Edward Gibbon to Protestantism.
·Edward Gibbon's spiritual growth **8**:153f

pavillon chinois (musical instrument): *see* jingling Johnny.

Pavlodar, *oblast* (administrative region), northern Kazakh Soviet Socialist Republic, with an area of 49,250 sq mi (127,500 sq km) along the middle course of the Irtysh River on the southern edge of the West Siberian Plain. Its lands consist mainly of flat steppe, which turns into semi-desert in the southwest. The climate is continental and dry. Pavlodar, the capital, and Ekibastuz form a rapidly growing industrial complex based on power generated from the rich Ekibastuz coal deposits; there is also gold mining at Maykain and salt production from the salt lakes. The *oblast* is a major grain producer—mainly wheat and millet—and sheep and cattle also are raised. In 1970 just over one-half of the population was rural. The most numerous nationalities are Russians, Kazakhs, Ukrainians, and Germans. The Kanal Irtysh-Karaganda starts near the new town of Yermak (founded 1961), the site of a large power station; there is navigation on the Irtysh. Pop. (1970 prelim.) 697,000.

Pavlodar, city and administrative centre of Pavlodar *oblast* (region), Kazakh Soviet Socialist Republic, and a port on the Irtysh River. The oldest *oblast* centre in northern Kazakhstan, it was founded in 1720 as Koryakovsky outpost on the Russian Irtysh fortified line, near salt lakes. It became the town of Pavlodar in 1861, but, although it did a substantial trade in salt and agricultural produce, its population was only about 8,000 in 1897. Since then and particularly since the mid-1960s, it has grown considerably to become a major industrial centre, with tractor, aluminum, and chemical plants. An oil refinery was scheduled to be completed in the mid-1970s. The city has industrial and teacher-training institutes. Pop. (1970 prelim.) 187,000.
52°18′ N, 76°57′ E
·map, Soviet Union **17**:322

Pavlograd, city and centre of a *rayon* (district), Dnepropetrovsk *oblast* (administrative region), Ukrainian Soviet Socialist Republic. A minor trading centre before the October Revolution and incorporated in 1797, it is now a major railway junction and centre of the west Donets Basin coal region. Its varied industrial base includes the manufacture of machinery for the chemical industry and for foundries and the production of bricks. There is a linen mill, and consumer industries include the processing of foodstuffs and production of clothes and furniture. Pop. (1970) 80,000.
48°32′ N, 35°53′ E

Pavlov, Ivan Petrovich 13:1095 (b. Sept. 26 [Sept. 14, old style], 1849, Ryazan, now in Russian S.F.S.R.—d. Feb. 27, 1936, Leningrad), physiologist known chiefly for his development of the concept of the conditioned reflex.
Abstract of text biography. Pavlov studied chemistry and physiology at the University of St. Petersburg (now Leningrad) beginning in 1870 and received his M.D. at the Imperial Medical Academy. From 1878 to 1888 he investigated cardiac physiology and blood pressure. He was appointed professor of physiology in the Imperial Medical Academy (1897). His research on gastrointestinal secretions in a normal animal were published in *Lektsi o rabote glavmykh pishchevaritelnykh zhelez* (1897; *The Work of the Digestive Glands*, 1902). In 1903 he was awarded the Nobel Prize. He was a critic of the Soviet government until the 1930s, although his research and laboratory were supported by government funds.

REFERENCES in other text articles:
·experiment in classical conditioning **2**:810f
·gastric secretion studies **5**:774e
·human and animal communication theory **19**:1043f
·hypnosis and neural inhibition **9**:134h
·psychology and conditioned reflexes **15**:156f
·reflex concept in psychology **14**:438h
·salivation experiment inferences **12**:977a
·sleep induction and maintenance **16**:883b
·stages and direction of classical conditioning **10**:755b
·theory of classical conditioning **10**:732c
·transfer of training in conditioning **18**:597b

Pavlova, Anna (Pavlovna) 13:1097 (b. Jan. 31, 1882, St. Petersburg, now Leningrad —d. Jan. 23, 1931, The Hague), Russian ballerina, most celebrated dancer of her time.
Abstract of text biography. She studied at the Imperial School of Ballet at the Mariinsky Theatre from 1891, joined the Imperial Ballet in 1899, and became a prima ballerina in 1906. In 1909 she went to Paris on the historic tour of the Ballets Russes. After 1913 she danced independently with her own company in the main cities of Europe.

REFERENCE in other text article:
·ballet popularization **2**:651f

Pavlovian conditioning (psychology): *see* conditioning.

Pavlovo, city and administrative centre of Pavlovo *rayon* (district) of Gorky *oblast* (region), western Russian Soviet Federated Socialist Republic, on the Oka River. Its metalworking industries are continuations of what was a long handicraft tradition in metal goods, though now the industry produces tractor and automobile parts as well. The city has a technical college devoted to the metalworking industry. Pop. (1970) 63,000.
55°58′ N, 43°04′ E

Pavlovsk, town, Leningrad *oblast* (administrative division), Russian Soviet Federated Socialist Republic.
53°20′ N, 82°59′ E
·origin, architecture, and restoration **10**:803b; map 798

Pavlovsky Posad, city, Moscow *oblast* (administrative region), western Russian Soviet Federated Socialist Republic, on the Klyazma River. It grew from a monastic village and, in the 18th century, was a centre of peasant silk weaving. In 1844 it became an industrial centre (*posad*) with other villages and had nine silk and three paper factories, employing 2,000 workers. It now has cotton, woollen, clothing, and ceramic industries. Pop. (1970) 66,400.
55°47′ N, 38°40′ E

Pavo (bird): *see* peacock.

Pavo (Latin: "peacock"), a constellation of the southern sky.
·constellation table **2**:226

Pavón, Battle of (Sept. 17, 1861), military clash at Pavón in the Sante Fe province of Argentina between the forces of the Argentine Confederation, commanded by Justo José de Urquiza, and those of Buenos Aires province, led by the governor, Bartolomé Mitre. Mitre's victory there marked the end of decades of internal armed conflict in Argentina.
Following the defeat of Mitre's Buenos Aires army at the Battle of Cepeda in 1859, Buenos Aires was constrained to join the confederation. But Mitre's forces won in a subsequent confrontation at Pavón, though not decisively, and Urquiza concluded that he now had little chance of success in his bid for national leadership. Thus a new national government

was set up, with the capital again at Buenos Aires (it had been moved to Paraná, in Entre Ríos province, in 1853, when Buenos Aires had seceded from the confederation), and Mitre became provisional president. When the Congress that was elected under the new government convened in May 1862, Mitre was chosen president for a six-year term.

pavor nocturnus (nightmare): *see* night terror.

Pavsner, Naum Neemia (Russian-born U.S. Constructivist): *see* Gabo, Naum.

Pawcatuck River, rises in Worden Pond and Great Swamp, South Kingstown, R.I., U.S., and flows generally southwestward, emptying into Little Narragansett Bay after a course of about 30 mi (50 km). It forms part of the boundary between Rhode Island and Connecticut. Several dams supply power for manufacturing plants. The name is derived from an Algonkian Indian word that probably means Open-divided-stream.
41°25′ N, 71°45′ W
·textile power sources **15**:809a

Pawhuska, city, seat of Osage County, northeastern Oklahoma, U.S. It was settled in 1872 and named for an Osage chief, Paw-Hu-Scah (Pah-Hue-Skah), or White Hair, and the first buildings were those of the Indian Agency (established 1873). Cattle and oil (discovered in 1897) provide the basis of the economy, which is augmented by cotton ginning and light manufacturing. Pawhuska is the tribal capital of the Osage Nation and the site of the Osage Tribal Museum. In 1909 the Rev. John Mitchell organized in the city what is claimed to be the first Boy Scout troop in the U.S. Inc. 1906. Pop. (1980) 4,771.
36°40′ N, 96°20′ W
·map **18**:United States of America, Plate 9

Pawla (Malta): *see* Paola.

pawn (law): *see* pledge.

pawnbroking, business of advancing loans to customers who have pledged household goods or personal effects as security on the loans. The trade of the pawnbroker is one of the oldest known to mankind; it existed in China 2,000 to 3,000 years ago. The forces that have nurtured pawning are need, habit, and convenience. Pawnshops have always been used by the poor, and from the Middle Ages to the 20th century they have also attracted the patronage of a declining aristocracy. In the 19th century the growing middle class also became principal borrowers.

Pawnbroking in the West may be traced to three different institutions of the Middle Ages: private pawnbrokers, public pawnshops, and *montes pietatis*. Usury laws in most countries prohibited the taking of interest, and pawnbroking was therefore carried on chiefly by classes exempt from these laws by religion or regulation. Their sometimes exorbitant interest rates, however, caused social unrest, which made public authorities aware of the need for alternative facilities for consumption loans. As early as 1198, Freising, a town in Bavaria, set up a municipal bank that accepted pledges and made loans against moderate interest charges. These public pawnshops enjoyed only a comparatively short existence; their moderate charges did not cover the risks incurred in this type of business.

The church also recognized the need for institutions to make lawful loans to indigent debtors; the Order of Friars Minor (Franciscans) in Italy in 1462 were the first to establish *montes pietatis* (*mons* denoted any form of capital accumulation), which were charitable funds for the granting of interest-free loans secured by pledges to the poor. Later, in order to prevent the premature exhaustion of funds, *montes pietatis* were compelled to charge interest and to sell by auction any pledges that became forfeit.

In the 18th century many states reverted to public pawnshops as a means of preventing exploitation of the poor. These suffered a decline toward the end of the 18th century because limitation of interest was thought to represent restriction, and the use of public funds seemed to stand for state monopoly. Most states returned again to a system of public pawnshops, however, after finding that complete freedom in pawning was harmful to debtors. At mid-20th century, the public pawnshop predominated in the majority of countries on the European continent, sometimes alone, sometimes side by side with private pawnbrokers. Public pawnshops were never established in the United States.

Modern developments have provided pawnshops with new functions. These include, for example, determining and certifying the precious-metal content of plate and other articles. In Great Britain and France, many persons have come to use pawnshops for depositing their valuables when leaving town because of the reasonable rates. Methods of regulating private pawnbrokers include licensing, bonding, fees, and numerous limitations by law on interest charges and redemption periods.

The importance of pawnshops as a credit source has declined in the 20th century. Social policies have helped to mitigate the financial needs resulting from temporary interruptions in earnings; operating expenses have risen; and installment credit and personal loans from banks have become widely available.
·commercial law and loan systems **4**:993e

Pawnee, North American Plains Indian people of Caddoan linguistic stock who lived on the Platte River, Nebraska, from before the 16th century to the latter part of the 19th. In the 19th century the Pawnee tribe was composed of relatively independent bands: the Kitkehahki, Chaui, Pitahauerat, and Skidi. Each of these was divided into villages, the basic social unit of the Pawnee people.

They lived in large, dome-shaped, earth-covered lodges but used skin tepees on buffalo hunts. The women raised corn, squash, and beans. They had developed the art of pottery making, but it declined after the introduction of horses in the 17th and 18th centuries.

An earthlodge in the Pawnee village on the Loup Fork, Nebraska; photograph by William Jackson, 1871
By courtesy of the Smithsonian Institution, Washington, D.C.

Class distinctions favoured chiefs, priests, and shamans. Each chief of a village or band had in his keeping a sacred bundle. Shamans had special powers to treat illness and to ward off enemy raids and food shortages. Priests were trained in the performance of rituals and sacred songs. Along with shamanistic and hunt societies, the Pawnee also had military societies.

The religion of the Pawnee was quite elaborate. They believed some of the stars to be gods and performed rituals to entreat their presence, but they also used astronomy in practical affairs. Corn was regarded as a symbolic mother through whom the sun god bestowed his blessing. Other important deities were Tirawa, the supreme power, and the morning and evening stars. For a time Pawnee religion included the sacrifice of a captive adolescent girl to the morning star, but this practice was ended in the 19th century.

Relations between the Pawnee and whites were peaceful, and many served as scouts in the armies of the frontier. They ceded most of their lands in Nebraska to the U.S. government by treaties in 1833, 1848, and 1857. In 1876 their last Nebraska holdings were given up, and they were moved to Oklahoma, where they remained. More than 2,300 Pawnee were reported to be living in the U.S. and abroad in 1979.
·peace dance development **1**:673g
·Plains Indian culture **13**:223f *passim* to 226f; map 224

pawpaw, also spelled PAPAW (*Asimina triloba*), deciduous tree or shrub of the custard-apple family (Annonaceae of the order Magnoliales), native in the United States, from the Atlantic coast north to New York and west to Michigan and Kansas. It may grow to 11.5 metres (38 feet), with pointed, broadly oblong, drooping leaves up to 30 centimetres (12 inches) long. The malodorous, purple five-centimetre (two-inch) flowers appear in spring. The edible, 7.7- to 13-centimetre long, potato-like fruits are almost black when ripe. They vary, depending on the variety, in size, time of ripening, and flavour. Some persons may develop a skin reaction after handling pawpaw fruits. The other seven species of *Asimina*, which are shrubby North American plants, include *A. speciosa* and *A. angustifolia;* both have large, yellowish-white blooms.

Cluster of unripened fruit of pawpaw (*Asimina triloba*)
John H. Gerard

·cultivation and variability **11**:342c

Pawtucket, city, Providence County, Rhode Island, U.S., on the Blackstone River (there bridged and known locally as the Pawtucket, or the Seekonk), just northeast of Providence and adjoining Central Falls. In the heart of the business district, the river plunges 50 ft (15 m) over a mass of rocks; the name Pawtucket is from an Indian (Algonkian) word meaning At the Falls. First settlement on the site was made in 1671 by Joseph Jencks, Jr., an ironworker, who set up a forge on the west side of the river near the falls. His manufactory, destroyed in 1676 during King Philip's (Indian) War, was rebuilt, and soon the village became a centre for ironmongers. In 1790 Samuel Slater built the first successful waterpowered cottonmill in North America, now restored and designated as a historic site. Pawtucket now has an economy based on the manufacture of electronic equipment, wire and cable products, textiles, toys, glass, and glass fibre.

The river has been continually improved by the federal government from 1867; there is a 16-ft channel all the way to Narragansett Bay. That part of Pawtucket east of the river was originally in Massachusetts and was trans-

ferred to Rhode Island and incorporated as a town in 1862; the section west of the river was annexed to Pawtucket from North Providence in 1874. Inc. 1885. Pop. (1930) 77,149; (1980) 71,204.
41°53′ N, 71°23′ W
·physical geography, settlement patterns, and ethnic composition **15**:809a

Pawtuxet River, Rhode Island, U.S., flows 28 mi (45 km) from Scituate into the Providence River.
41°45′ N, 71°45′ W
·mill village description **15**:809a

Pax, in Roman religion, personification of peace, probably recognized as a deity for the first time by the emperor Augustus, in whose reign much was made of the establishment of political calm. An altar of Pax Augusta was dedicated in 9 BC and a great temple of Pax completed by the emperor Vespasian in AD 75.

Pax, Cerro, mountain on the Ecuador–Colombia border, South America.
0°23′ N, 77°26′ W
·Andes location and elevation **1**:858c

Pax Americana, a term used to describe the post-World War II period in which American influence in world politics was dominant.
·U.S. attempts and limitations **9**:764a

Paxos, Modern Greek PAXOÍ, smallest of the seven major Ionian Islands of Greece, 8 mi (19 km) southwest of Párga on the coast of Epirus. A hilly mass of limestone covered with olive groves, it rises to about 750 ft (230 m). Gáïos on the east coast is the chief village and port. Papandi, the bishop's residence, stands near the centre with several quaint churches and belfries.
39°12′ N, 20°12′ E
·map, Greece **8**:314

Pax Romana (Latin: Roman Peace), a state comparative peace prevailing in the Mediterranean world under Roman rule from Augustus' reign (27 BC–AD 14) to the reign of Marcus Aurelius (AD 161–180).
·Augustus' creation and cultural heritage **2**:371h
·Jewish synthesis with Torah **10**:316b
·religiopolitical and judicial aspects **13**:846g

Pax Sinica, in Ch'ing China, period of domestic peace that lasted from the late 17th century to the end of the 18th century.

Paxton, Sir Joseph (b. Aug. 3, 1801, near Woburn, Bedfordshire—d. June 8, 1865, Sydenham, near London), landscape gardener and designer of hothouses, turned architect when he designed the Crystal Palace, which housed the Great Exhibition of 1851 in Hyde Park, London.

He was originally a gardener employed by the Duke of Devonshire, whose friend, factotum, and adviser he became. From 1826 he was superintendent of the gardens at Chatsworth, the Duke's Derbyshire estate; he built in iron and glass the famous conservatory there (1840) and the lily house for the duke's rare *Victoria regia* (1850). The lily house had a flat, ridge-and-furrow glass roof supported by cast-iron columns. Also in 1850, after a cumbersome design (chosen from among many by professional architects) had been officially accepted by the Great Exhibition's organizers, Paxton's inspired plan for a building of prefabricated elements of sheet glass and iron was substituted. His design, based on his earlier glass structures, particularly the lily house, covered four times the area of St. Peter's, Rome, and the grandeur of its conception was a challenge to mid-19th-century technology. Built within six months, it was at once recognized as marking a revolution in style. In 1854 its components were moved to Sydenham, where they remained (re-erected in a different form from the original) until destroyed by fire in 1936.

Paxton was a member of parliament for Coventry from 1854 until his death. During the period of his glass structures, he also built conventional masonry houses and laid out a number of public parks.
·architectural design innovations **19**:461g
·comparison with Nervi **12**:994d
·Crystal Palace design **18**:43g
·iron construction in Crystal Palace **17**:633f

Paya languages, complex of languages or dialects in northern Honduras, about which very little is known.
·Meso-American languages table **11**:959g; map 957

Paya Tak (Siamese king): *see* Taksin.

Payen, Anselme (b. Jan. 6, 1795, Paris—d. May 12, 1871, Paris), chemist who made important contributions to industrial chemistry and discovered cellulose, a basic constituent of plant cells.

Payen, the son of an industrialist, was put in charge of a borax-refining plant in 1815. At that time most borax was mined in the Dutch East Indies, but he discovered a process for producing borax from boric acid and thus broke the Dutch monopoly on borax. In 1820 he turned his efforts to refining beet sugar. Two years later he introduced the use of activated charcoal to filter out colouring impurities from beet sugar. Charcoal has since found numerous applications for its filtration and adsorption properties. In 1833 he discovered and isolated diastase, the first enzyme (organic catalyst) to be obtained in concentrated form. He then pursued the extensive analysis of wood and its components that culminated in the discovery of cellulose. He became professor of industrial and agricultural chemistry in 1835 at the École Centrale des Arts et Manufactures, Paris. Among his other contributions were studies of starch and bitumen, and the discovery of pectin and dextrin.

Pa-yen-k'a-la Shan, mountain range, Tibet.
32°20′ N, 97°00′ E
·Yangtze River valley **19**:1072h; map 1073

Payer, Julius von (1842–1915), Austrian Arctic explorer who, with Karl Weyprecht, in 1872–74 discovered Franz Josef Land.

Payette River, formed by confluence of North and South Forks in Boise National Forest, Boise County, western Idaho, U.S., flowing south and then west, past Emmett to join the Snake River near Payette at the Oregon line after a course of about 70 mi (110 km). Black Canyon Dam and Reservoir on the Payette and the Cascade Dam and Reservoir on North Fork are part of the Payette division of the Boise irrigation project. The river was named for a Hudson's Bay Company trapper.
44°05′ N, 116°57′ W

pa yin, Chinese classification of musical instruments based on the material used in making the instrument.
·construction material classification **12**:673b

payments, international: *see* exchange and payments, international.

Payne, John Howard (b. June 9, 1791, New York City—d. April 9, 1852, Tunis), playwright and actor, one of the most notable of the school of American playwrights that followed the techniques and themes of the European Romantic blank-verse dramatists. A precocious actor and writer, he wrote his first play, *Julia, or, The Wanderer*, when he was 15. The play was successful enough to cause him to be sent to Union College, Schenectady, N.Y., but family finances forced him to leave two years later. At 18 he made his first stage appearance in the play traditional for such debuts, John Home's *Douglas*. Although his portrayal of Young Norval was successful, Payne encountered much opposition from established actors, and in 1813, at the height of the War of 1812, he sailed for England. At first interned as an enemy national, he was later released and triumphed at Drury Lane as Young Norval, repeating his success in other European capitals. In Paris Payne met two men who were to have an important influence on his career: the actor Talma, who introduced him to French drama, from which many of his more than 60 plays were adapted; and Washington Irving, with whom he was to collaborate on two of his best plays.

The play considered Payne's finest, *Brutus: or, The Fall of Tarquin*, was produced at Drury Lane on Dec. 3, 1818. Although Payne received only £183 for it, *Brutus* was on the boards for 70 years and served as a vehicle for three of the greatest tragedians of the 19th century: Edwin Booth, Edwin Forrest, and Edmund Kean. Other important plays were *Clari: or, The Maid of Milan*, which included Payne's famous song "Home, Sweet Home"; *Charles the Second* (1824), written with Irving; and *Thérèse* (1821), a French adaptation. Because of weak copyright laws, Payne received little return from his successful plays, and in 1842 he accepted a consular post in Tunis.

Although Payne was no innovator, his plays were strong both in language and structure, and he exerted an important influence on later playwrights. The scholar Arthur Hobson

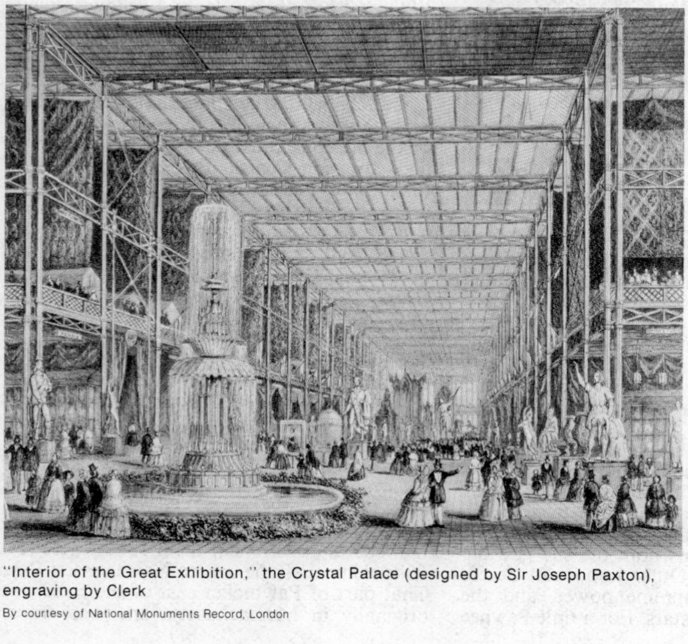

"Interior of the Great Exhibition," the Crystal Palace (designed by Sir Joseph Paxton), engraving by Clerk
By courtesy of National Monuments Record, London

Quinn suggested that *Brutus* may have been partially responsible for the emergence of the Romantic drama in France under Hugo.

Payne, Peter (b. *c.* 1380, Hough-on-the-Hill, Lincolnshire—d. *c.* 1455, Prague), theologian, diplomat, and follower of the early Reformer John Wycliffe; he was a leading figure in securing Bohemia for the Hussites.

At about the time Payne was principal of St. Edmund Hall, Oxford (1410–12), he joined the Lollards, and when the influential Lollard soldier Sir John Oldcastle was indicted in 1413, Payne felt it prudent to flee to Bohemia. There he supported the Utraquist Hussites. He became a central figure in the consistory that governed the Hussite church and was entrusted with several diplomatic missions. At the Council of Basel in 1433 he spoke out against state seizure of church property. Taken prisoner at the Battle of Lipany, in 1434, he was soon freed and took part in peace negotiations. With the return of the anti-Hussite king Sigismund to Bohemia, the Hussites were temporarily proscribed, and Payne was expelled from Prague. He was imprisoned for two years in Austria, then ransomed by fellow Hussites to return to Bohemia and participate in unification of the scattered Hussite church. Respected by all factions, he sought in vain to reconcile the extreme Taborites with the elected archbishop, Jan Rokycana. By 1448, when Payne went back to Prague, Rokycana's party was firmly established. Though he never learned Czech, Payne served the Hussites also through his theological works, listed in František M. Bartoš, *Literární činnost M. Jana Rokycany, . . . M. Petra Payna* (1928).

Payne–Aldrich Tariff: *see* tariffs, U.S.

Paysandú, department, western Uruguay, bounded on the west by Argentina. The territory of 5,446 sq mi (14,106 sq km) lies on the Uruguay River, which is navigable for vessels up to 14 ft (4 m) in draft. Although the riverside and hinterland areas of Paysandú are developing agriculturally, cattle and sheep ranching continues to be the major activity. Surrounding farms supply vegetables and poultry to the capital, Paysandú. The department is linked by highway, rail, and air services to riverine cities and to Montevideo. Pop. (1972 est.) 91,000.
·area and population table **18**:1096

Paysandú, capital, Paysandú department, western Uruguay, on the Uruguay River. The city was founded in 1772 by a priest, Policarpo Sandú, and 12 families of Christianized Indians, who translated the Spanish word *padre* (father) into the Guaraní Indian word *pay*, from which stems the city's (and the department's) name. Now Uruguay's third largest city, Paysandú has a relatively varied economy, with tanneries, textile factories, flour mills, distilleries, and breweries processing regionally produced raw materials. The port is active, for cargo destined for northwestern Uruguay must be transferred at Paysandú from oceangoing ships to the shallow-draft vessels that ply the upper Uruguay. Paysandú is linked also by rail, highway, and air services to Montevideo. Pop. (latest census) 52,472.
32°19′ S, 58°05′ W
·map, Uruguay **18**:1095

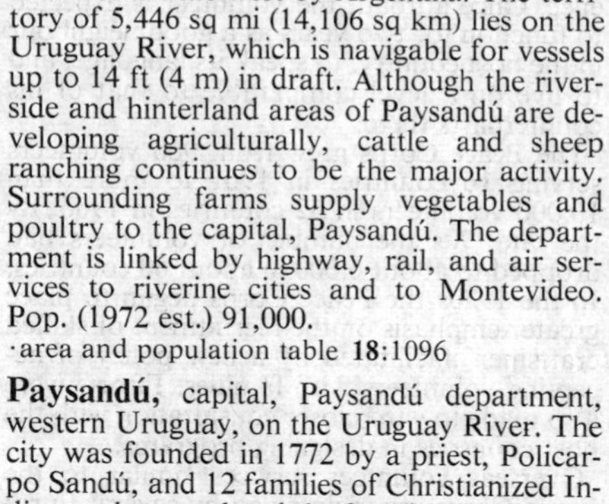
The cathedral at Paysandú, Uruguay
Walter Aguiar—EB Inc.

paysannat system, in the Belgian Congo (now Zaire) a land-settlement plan in which strips of cultivated land were alternated with bush and grassland, introduced in the 1930s.
·farm management in Zaire **7**:181a

Pays de la Loire, term referring to either the traditional *pays* ("country") of the southwest Paris Basin, France, or to the somewhat smaller modern planning region of the same name, composed of the five *départements* of Loire-Atlantique, Maine-et-Loire, Mayenne, Sarthe, and Vendée (*qq.v.*), having a combined area of 12,404 sq mi. Pop. (1974 est.) planning region, 2,694,400.
·area and population table **7**:594

Paz, Octavio (b. March 31, 1914, Mexico City), Mexican poet, writer, and diplomat, recognized as one of the major literary figures in Latin America since World War II. He founded, directed, and edited several literary reviews, including *Barandal* (1931), *Taller* (1939), and *El hijo pródigo* (1943). His poetic publications include *Luna silvestre* (1933), *Raíz del hombre* (1937), *Entre la piedra y la flor* (1941), *Piedra del sol* (1957; *The Sun Stone*, 1963), and *La estación violenta* (1958). Paz has also produced forceful prose such as *El laberinto de la soledad* (1950; *The Labyrinth of Solitude*, 1961), *¿Aguila o sol?* (1951; *Eagle or Sun?*, 1970), and *Posdata* (1970). Paz was awarded the International Poetry Grand Prix in 1963. An able diplomat, he served as the Mexican ambassador to India (1962–68).

Pazardzhik, also spelled PAZARDJIK, or PAZARDŽIK, town, Pazardzhik *okrŭg* (province), west central Bulgaria, on the upper Maritsa River. It is a rail junction and an industrial centre, specializing in textiles, rubber, furniture, engineering, and the processing of agricultural produce.

The National Museum in Pazardzhik has artifacts dating the settlement from 2000 BC. From its foundation by Russian Tatars, through the 15th and 19th centuries under Turkish rule, and until 1934, the town was called Tatar Pazardzhik. The Church of the Virgin Mary, which is half buried in the ground, contains masterpieces of Bulgarian carvings. Pop. (1971 est.) 65,051.
42°12′ N, 24°20′ E
·map, Bulgaria **3**:471
·province area and population table **3**:472

Paz Estenssoro, Víctor (b. Oct. 2, 1907, Tarija, Bolivia), founder and principal leader of the left-wing Bolivian political party Movimiento Nacionalista Revolucionario (MNR), served as president of Bolivia (1952–56 and 1960–64). His administration marked the beginning of a process of revolutionary social, economic, and political change in Bolivia.

Paz Estenssoro began his career as professor of economics at the University of San Andrés in La Paz. He was economic adviser to Pres. Germán Busch (1937–39) and in 1939 was elected to the Chamber of Deputies. In 1941 he and others established the MNR; when it seized power in 1952, Paz Estenssoro became president. During his administration the right to vote was extended to Indians, and the three largest tin companies in the country were expropriated by the government. Most fundamental of all, an agrarian reform law began the process of transferring the arable land of the central plateau to the Indians.

During 1956–60, Paz Estenssoro served as ambassador to the United Kingdom. He again became the MNR candidate for president in 1960 and won a decisive victory. During his second administration, his government reached an agreement with the U.S. government, the Inter-American Development Bank, and West German industrialists providing for a reorganization of the tin industry.

In the election of 1964, about 70 percent of the eligible voters cast their ballots for Paz Estenssoro. Nevertheless, he was overthrown by a military coup d'etat in early November

Paz Estenssoro
By courtesy of the Organization of American States

1964 and went into exile in Peru. He remained in Lima as a professor of economics at the university until August 1971, when he returned to Bolivia as an adviser to the government led by the right-wing president Hugo Banzer Suárez.
·MNR program and final dissolution **3**:12e

Pázmány, Péter (1570–1637), Hungarian statesman and theologian.
·literary style and works **10**:1162h

Paz Soldán, Mariano Felipe (1821–86), Peruvian historian, geographer, and statesman. His works include a great atlas of Peru (1861) and the first history of the country (begun in 1868).

Pazvantoglu, Osman (1758–1807), Bulgarian feudal lord and rebel.
·Balkan nationalistic movements **2**:626a

Pazyryk, Scythian burial site in a dry valley opening on the Bolshoy Ulagan River valley in the Kazakh S.S.R. The site, consisting of five large and nine smaller burial mounds and dating from about the 5th to the 3rd century BC, was excavated in 1929 and 1947–49. It is perhaps the richest source of information about the customs and artifacts of the Scythians before their westward migrations into western Asia and Europe. The site and its significance are described in S.I. Rudenko's *Frozen Tombs of Siberia: The Pazyryk Burials of Iron Age Horsemen* (1970).
·burial mound floor covering discoveries **7**:406d
·musical instruments, tomb preservation, and art **3**:1126g *passim* to 1139g
·Scythian excavations and research **16**:438b *passim* to 442a

Pazzi Chapel, in the 14th-century cloister of the church of Sta. Croce in Florence, designed by Brunelleschi in the early Renaissance style and built *c.* 1442–*c.* 1460 with the patronage of the Pazzi family.
·architect, plan, and domes **19**:381e; illus.
·Brunelleschi's spatial innovations **3**:344g

Pazzi conspiracy (April 26, 1478), an unsuccessful plot to overthrow the Medici rulers of Florence; the most dramatic of all political opposition to the Medici family. The conspiracy was led by the rival Pazzi family of Florence. In league with the Pazzi were Pope Sixtus IV and his nephew Girolamo Riario, who resented Lorenzo de' Medici's efforts to thwart the consolidation of papal rule over the Romagna, a region in north central Italy, and also the Archbishop of Pisa, Francesco Salviati, whom Lorenzo had refused to recognize. An assassination attempt on the Medici brothers was made during mass at the cathedral of Florence on April 26, 1478. Giuliano de' Medici was killed by Francesco Pazzi but

Lorenzo was able to defend himself and escaped only slightly wounded. Meanwhile, other conspirators tried to gain control of the government. But the people of Florence rallied to the Medici; the conspirators were ruthlessly pursued, and many (including the Archbishop of Pisa) were killed on the spot.

The failure of the conspiracy led directly to a two-year war with the papacy that was almost disastrous for Florence. But the most important effect was to strengthen the power of Lorenzo, who not only was rid of his most dangerous enemies but also was shown to have the solid support of the people.
·Lorenzo de' Medici's political opposition **11**:818h
·papal alliance **9**:1144h

Pb, symbol for the chemical element lead (*q.v.*).

PBI test (medicine): *see* protein-bound iodine.

P blood group system, one of the earliest systems found (1927), later shown to be more complex than originally believed. The system now is known to consist of genes designated P_1, P_2, p (formerly Tj^a, identified 1951) and P^k (identified 1959). P_1 is dominant to P_2 and p, which are believed to be alleles; P^k is recessive but occurs at a locus different from that of the other three genes. Another antigen, called Luke (identified 1965), is associated in an unknown fashion with the P system and also segregates independently. The frequency of phenotype P_1 is about 95 percent in West Africans, 78 percent in Europeans (except Finns, in whom the frequency is 70 percent), and 41 percent in Japanese; the phenotypes p and P^k are extremely uncommon. Anti-PP_1P^k and anti-P, though rare, may cause severe erythroblastosis fetalis or transfusion reactions; anti-PP_1P^k may be a cause of early abortion.
·discovery and antigens **2**:1144c; table
·Negroid blood composition **14**:843g

PC (logic): *see* propositional calculus.

PCB (chemistry): *see* polychlorinated biphenyl.

PCC (political party): *see* Partido Comunista de Cuba.

PCF (political party): *see* Parti Communiste Français.

PCI (political party): *see* Indochinese Communist Party; Partito Comunista Italiano.

PCM (electronics): *see* modulation.

PCN, abbreviation for PARTIDO DE CONCILIACIÓN NACIONAL, English NATIONAL CONCILIATION PARTY, in El Salvador, political party formed by a military junta in the early 1960s and in the late '70s still the country's dominant party.
·El Salvador's political parties **3**:1113e

P Cygni star, type of variable star with an irregular period.
·emission spectra characteristics **2**:241a

Pd, symbol for the chemical element palladium (*q.v.*).

pé, Portuguese unit of linear measure equivalent to one-third of a metre, or 13 inches.
·weights and measures, tables **19**:734

PE, abbreviation for PLASTIC EXPLOSIVE, demolition explosive introduced in World War II.
·military engineering history **6**:864f

pea, common name for several species of herbaceous annuals of the family Fabaceae, grown for their edible seeds (legumes), borne in pods. The favourite market and garden pea in North America, Europe, and parts of Asia is a variety of *Pisum sativum*.

The stems of the pea plant are hollow and trailing or climbing. Leaves are pinnately

Pea (*Pisum sativum*)
Walter Chandoha

compound, ending in tendrils that enable the plant to climb. The flowers are butterfly-like in shape and are coloured white or purple. The fruit is a one-celled, many-seeded pod, which splits into halves when ripe; the 5 to 10 seeds are attached by short stalks to the halves of the pod. Some varieties, called sugar peas, produce edible pods that are popular in the Orient; before the seeds enlarge appreciably, the flat pods are tender, succulent, and sweet. Split peas for soup consist of only the cotyledons of smooth peas harvested mature and dry. Dried peas are sometimes ground to make flour. Peas are marketed fresh, canned, or frozen.
·ancient cultivation in Thailand **1**:325b
·colour inheritance pattern **4**:912a
·crop rotation methods **1**:349h
·history, classification, and cultivation **19**:43c; tables 44
·Mendel's experiments and laws **8**:802g
·nitrogen-fixation cycle **2**:1040h
·nutritional protein and vitamin content **13**:420h
·Pisum sativum legume fruit structure **7**:129b
·radiation-induced improvement table **7**:482

Peabody, city, Essex County, northeastern Massachusetts, U.S. Originally part of Salem, it became part of Danvers in 1752 and was separately incorporated as the town of South Danvers in 1855. In 1868 it was renamed to honour the philanthropist George Peabody. Glassmaking began there as early as 1638, and tanneries were established before the American Revolution. One of the nation's major leather-processing centres, it also produces chemicals, fabricated metals, and wood products. Inc. city, 1916. Pop. (1980) 45,976.
42°32′ N, 70°55′ W
·map **18**:United States of America, Plate 15

Peabody, Elizabeth Palmer (b. May 16, 1804, Billerica, Mass.—d. Jan. 3, 1894, Jamaica Plain), educator and participant in the Transcendental movement, who opened the first kindergarten (*q.v.*) in America. Educated at a small private school by her gifted mother, as were her sisters Sophia (who married Nathaniel Hawthorne) and Mary (who married Horace Mann), she started her own school in Boston in 1820. From 1825 to 1834 she was secretary to William Ellery Channing, the early leader of Unitarianism in the United States; then she began an association with Bronson Alcott in his Temple School, of which she wrote in *Record of a School* (1835). Although overshadowed by Margaret Fuller, she was one of the leading feminine figures in the Transcendental movement (*see* Transcendentalists, New England). After two years with Alcott's school, she became involved in adult education in Boston.

In 1839 Peabody opened her West Street bookstore, which became a sort of club for the intellectual community of Boston; the early planners of the Brook Farm experiment in communal living met there. On her own printing press she published translations by Margaret Fuller and three of Nathaniel Hawthorne's earliest books. For two years she published and wrote articles for *The Dial*, the critical literary monthly of the Transcendental movement, and other periodicals.

In 1860 she opened in Boston the first kindergarten in the U.S. She went to Europe in 1867 to study Friedrich Froebel's methods and brought back several experienced German kindergarten teachers. She devoted herself thereafter to organizing public and private kindergartens and to lecturing and writing. Her numerous books included *Kindergarten Culture* (1870), *The Kindergartner in Italy* (1872), and *Letters to Kindergartners* (1886).

Peabody Conservatory of Music, formally PEABODY INSTITUTE OF THE CITY OF BALTIMORE, established in Baltimore in 1857 through benefactions of George Peabody and incorporated in 1858.
·Paris Conservatoire as model **2**:95h

Peace, The, Greek EIRENE (421 BC), play by Aristophanes.
·theme of war and peace **1**:1154h

Peace Commission of 1778: *see* Carlisle Commission.

Peace Corps, U.S. government agency of volunteers created by the Peace Corps Act of 1961. In 1971 it became a sub-agency of a new independent agency, ACTION, created to coordinate and strengthen volunteer programs both in the U.S. and abroad.

The purpose of the Peace Corps is to assist other countries in their development efforts by providing skilled workers in the fields of education, agriculture, health, trade, technology, and community development. Peace Corps volunteers are assigned to specific projects on the basis of their skills, education, and experience. Once abroad, the volunteer is expected to function for two years as a good neighbour in the host country, to speak its language, and to live on a level comparable to that of his counterparts there.

The Peace Corps grew from 900 volunteers serving 16 countries in 1961 to more than 10,000 volunteers in 52 countries in 1966. By the late '70s the number of volunteers had dropped to about 6,000 in about 60 countries. In the 1970s the Peace Corps began to place greater emphasis on the recruitment of skilled craftsmen, facilitated by a new policy of accepting volunteers with families. Efforts were also made toward closer consultation with the host countries in designing programs.

Overseas volunteer services similar to the Peace Corps are maintained by several European countries, including France, Germany, and Great Britain.
·educational effect on host and native country **9**:739b
·founding, support, and directorship **10**:418a

peaceful coexistence, in Communist ideology, the assertion that Communist and capitalist nations can coexist without war, even though carrying on intense political struggle.
Major ref. **4**:1026e
·Khrushchev's role **10**:455d
·Soviet pragmatism and ideology **9**:197b

Peace Mission, predominantly black 20th-century religious cult in the U.S., originated and headed by Father Divine.
·Father Divine's biography and beliefs **12**:943a

Peace of God and Truce of God, agreements that served as the basis for the Christian peace movement of the late 10th century in Europe, designed to abolish violence and private warfare and to guarantee protection to pilgrims and travellers. The Peace of God was first declared in 989 at a council held at Charroux, near Poitiers, France. It prohibited men from entering churches by force or plundering them, forbade the usurpation of a peasant's property, and upheld the rights of noncombatants. It was later extended to guarantee protection to merchants.

Appearing *c.* 1027 as an addition to the Peace of God, the Truce of God provided for periodic armistices between feuding parties, suspending private wars from Wednesday night to Monday morning in remembrance of Christ's sufferings. Bishops gathered the members of their dioceses together, commanded them to pledge an oath to keep the peace, and imposed spiritual penalties on those who refused. Temporal punishment was handled by sworn associations that established their own militia to enforce the agreements.

Though the peace-keeping efforts intensified in the 11th century, they were not particularly effective. Thus when Urban II (pope from 1088 to 1099) proposed at the Council of Clermont in 1095 that the feuding nobility enlist in a crusade to rescue the Holy Land from the Muslims, he pointed the peace movement in a new direction by purposely removing those who spread violence and anarchy in Europe.

·Crusades religious background **5**:298f
·ecclesiastical origin and provisions **7**:612f
·medieval church truces **6**:1120d

peace pipe: *see* sacred pipe.

peace pipe dance, also called CALUMET DANCE, American Indian dance that originated in the tobacco rite of such Northern Plains tribes as the Crow, Dakota, and Sioux.

·origin and development locale **1**:673g

Peace Policy, sometimes called GRANT'S PEACE POLICY (March 3, 1871), act of U.S. Congress ending the treaty-making rights of Indian tribes within national borders and placing their reservations under stricter jurisdiction of Indian agents and various religious denominations. After 1778 about 370 treaties had been negotiated with Indian tribes as though they were separate nations. In 1871 Pres. Ulysses S. Grant was induced to replace this fiction with simple agreements to be ratified by both houses of Congress.

More meaningful was the act's unprecedented disregard of the traditional separation of church and state; Grant was persuaded by humanitarian reformers that the Indians would be brought to terms more peacefully (hence the name Peace Policy) by religious influence than military coercion. Under this experimental policy, Christian missionaries assigned to various reservations suppressed Indian culture and civil liberties. Furthermore, the military still had to be called in to enforce orders.

Finally, the authority of the tribal hierarchy was replaced with that of the Indian reservation agencies as far as possible, and certain judicial matters were transferred to the jurisdiction of the federal courts. This trend continued through the next two decades.

Peace River, town, northwestern Alberta, Canada, 254 mi (409 km) northwest of Edmonton, on the Peace River just below its junction with the Smoky. It grew around Fort of the Forks (built 1792 by Sir Alexander Mackenzie) and Fort Dunvegan (where the Rev. J. Brick established an Anglican mission in 1881). A feature is the grave and statue of "Twelve Foot" Davis, who staked a 12-foot claim during the gold rush. The town is the see of an Anglican bishop whose diocese (Athabasca) extends to the Arctic Circle. Originally a fur-trading centre, the town's economy now depends largely on oil and gas production and on farming. Inc. village (Peace River Crossing), 1914; town, 1919. Pop. (1971) 5,039.
56°14′ N, 117°17′ W

·Alberta's modern urban centres **1**:424g
·map, Canada **3**:716
·settlement, agriculture, and dam **11**:266h

Peace River, in northern British Columbia and Alberta, Canada, forms the southwestern branch of the Mackenzie River system. From headstreams (the Finlay and Parsnip) in the Canadian Rockies of British Columbia, the Peace flows northeastward across the Alberta prairies, receiving its major tributaries (the Smoky and Wabasca) before joining the Slave River in Wood Buffalo National Park. Its total course (from the head of the Finlay) is 1,195 mi (1,923 km). The river, named for Peace Point, Alta., where the Cree and Beaver Indians settled their territorial dispute, became an important fur-trade route after it was explored by Sir Alexander Mackenzie (1792–93). Farming, the valley's economic mainstay during the early decades of the 20th century, is now supplemented by lumber, coal, petroleum, and natural gas. In 1968 the 600-ft (200-m) W.A.C. Bennett Dam near Hudson Hope, B.C., was completed, creating Peace River Reservoir (with a capacity of 248,000,000,000 cu ft [about 7,000,000,000 cu m]) and providing the valley with hydroelectric power and flood control. The Peace is navigable from the town of Peace River, Alta., to the Slave, except for a stretch of falls near Fort Vermilion.
59°00′ N, 111°25′ W

The Peace River at Taylor Flats, B.C.
By courtesy of the Canadian Government Travel Bureau, Ottawa; photograph, E. Bork

·map, Canada **3**:716
·topography and climate **3**:298a

Peace Tower (1916–27), tower reaching 291 ft (89 m) atop the Parliament building in Ottawa.

·Ottawa's urban structures **13**:767d; illus.

peach (*Prunus persica*), fruit tree of the rose family (Rosaceae), grown throughout the warmer temperate regions of both the Northern and Southern hemispheres.

Peach (*Prunus persica*)
Grant Heilman—EB Inc.

Small to medium-sized, the tree seldom reaches 6.5 metres (21 feet) in height. Under cultivation, however, it is usually kept between 3 and 4 metres (10 and 13 feet) by pruning. Leaves are glossy green, lance shaped, and long pointed; they usually have glands at their bases, which secrete a fluid that attracts ants and other insects. The flowers, borne in the leaf axils, are arranged singly or in groups of two or three at nodes along the shoots of the previous season's growth. The five petals, usually pink but occasionally white, five sepals, and three whorls of stamens are borne on the outer rim of the short tube that forms the base of the flower. The pistil consists of a single carpel with a relatively long style and an enlarged basal portion, the ovary, which becomes the fruit.

The peach develops from a single ovary that ripens into a fleshy, juicy exterior, making up the edible part of the fruit, and a hard interior, called the stone or pit. Of the two ovules in the ovary, usually only one becomes fertilized and develops into a seed, which is enclosed within the stone. This frequently results in one half of the fruit being slightly larger than the other, the two halves forming the slight longitudinal cleft typical of drupe fruits. The flesh may be white, yellow, or red. Varieties may be freestone types, which have stones that separate easily from the ripe flesh, or clingstones, which have flesh that adheres firmly to the stone.

The peach probably originated in China, then spread westward through Asia to the Mediterranean countries and later to other parts of Europe. The Spanish explorers brought the peach to the New World, and as early as 1600 the fruit was found in Mexico. Large-scale commercial peach growing did not begin until the 19th century, in the U.S. Early plantings were seedling peaches, inevitably variable, often of poor quality. The practice of budding superior strains onto hardy seedling rootstocks, which came later in the century, led to the development of large commercial orchards.

The peach does well on various soil types ranging from coarse-textured sand or gravelly loams and shales to silt loam, but in general it grows best on well-drained sandy or gravelly loams. On most soils the peach responds well to nitrogen-rich fertilizers or manures, without which satisfactory growth cannot be obtained.

Most peach varieties produce more fruits than can be maintained and developed to full size. Some shedding of fruitlets takes place naturally, about a month to six weeks after full bloom, but the number remaining may have to be reduced further by hand thinning.

Peach trees are relatively short-lived as compared with some other fruit trees. In some regions orchards are replanted after 8 to 10 years, while in others trees may produce satisfactorily for 20 to 25 years or more, depending upon their resistance to diseases, pests, and winter damage.

Worldwide, the peach is the third most important of the deciduous-tree fruits, ranking after the apple and the pear. The U.S., where the peach ranks second to the apple, produces about a third of the world's supply. Italy is second, with about one-fifth the world supply. France, Spain, Greece, Argentina, Japan, Turkey, Canada, South Africa, and Australia also produce substantial crops.

·fruit farming economics **7**:757a; tables 754
·fruit types and structure, illus. 3 **16**:482
·germination stimulants **5**:960e
·radiation induced improvement, table **7**:482

Peach, Charles William (b. Sept. 30, 1800, Wansford, Northamptonshire—d. Feb. 28, 1886, Edinburgh), naturalist and geologist who made valuable contributions to the knowledge of marine invertebrates and of fossil plants and fish. While in the revenue coast guard (1824–45) in Norfolk, his attention was attracted to seaweeds and other marine organisms, and he began to collect them. In Cornwall, Peach found fossils in some of the older rocks previously regarded as unfossiliferous. This discovery proved the presence of Bala beds (Ordovician strata, 430,000,000 to

500,000,000 years old) nearby. In 1841 he wrote a paper entitled "On the Fossil Organic Remains Found on the Southeast Coast of Cornwall," and in 1843 he gave an account of his discovery of fish remains in the Devonian slates (345,000,000 to 395,000,000 years old) near Polperro, Cornwall.

Peach was appointed to a position with customs at Fowey, Cornwall, in 1845, and four years later he went to Scotland. He studied the Old Red Sandstone (Devonian strata), the boulder clay of Caithness, and the Carboniferous plants (280,000,000 to 345,000,000 years old) of Scotland. During a stay at Durness, Sutherland, in 1854, he found the first fossils in the Cambrian limestone (500,000,000 to 570,000,000 years old). His contributions to natural history included the discovery of many new species of sponges, coelenterates, and mollusks.

Peacham, Henry (b. *c.* 1576, North Nimms, Hertfordshire—d. *c.* 1643), author best known for his *Compleat Gentleman* (1622), important in the tradition of courtesy books. Numerous in the late Renaissance, courtesy books dealt with the education, ideals, and conduct befitting a gentleman or lady of the court. Peacham was educated at Cambridge and was successively schoolmaster, travelling tutor, and author. Of his time as master of the free school at Wymondham, Norfolk, he wrote "whiles that it was free, Myselfe, the Maister, lost my libertie." He wrote on a variety of themes and also published some of his pen-and-ink drawings, but his chief work remained *The Compleat Gentleman.* It was a full expression of his theories on education, and its table of contents exhibits the wide range of his interests: cosmography, geometry, poetry, music, sculpture, drawing, painting, heraldry. Samuel Johnson drew the heraldic definitions for his *Dictionary* from the 1661 edition.

peach bloom, also called BEAN RED or CHIANG-TOU HUNG, a pinkish-red ceramic glaze used primarily on a pure white body.
·Ch'ing glazes and colour variety **14**:923d

peachblow glass, type of U.S. art glass made in the latter part of the 19th century by factories such as the Mount Washington Glass Works of New Bedford, Mass., and the New England Glass Company of Cambridge, Mass. The name is derived from a Chinese porcelain glaze called "peach-bloom." Peachblow is made with either a shiny or a mat finish (*see* satin glass). Its colours range from bluish white or cream to violet red or pink. The glass is sometimes made with a milk-white lining.

peach tree borer: *see* clearwing moth.

peacock, the name given to several resplendent birds of the family Phasianidae (order Galliformes). Strictly, the male is a peacock, and the female is a peahen; both are peafowl. Two species of *Pavo* are the blue, or Indian, peacock (*P. cristatus*), of India and Sri Lanka (Ceylon), and the green, or Javanese, peacock (*P. muticus*), from Burma to Java. The Congo peacock (*Afropavo congensis*) was discovered in 1936 after a search that began in 1913 with the finding of a single feather.

In both species of *Pavo*, the male has a 75-centimetre (30-inch) body and 150-centimetre (60-inch) tail, a lacy train in which each feather is tipped with an iridescent "eye," ringed with blue and bronze. In display the cock elevates the tail and brings it forward, enveloping his body as he struts and quivers, audibly rattling the quills and uttering loud screams.

The blue peacock's body is mostly metallic blue green. The green peacock, with train much like that of the blue, has a green-and-bronze body. Hens of both species are green and brown and almost as big as the male but lack the train and the head ornament. In the wild, both species live in open lowland forests,

Peacock (*Pavo cristatus*) displaying before peahen
Norman Tomalin—Bruce Coleman Inc.

flocking by day and roosting high in trees. The male forms a harem of one to five hens, each of which lays four to eight buffy or white eggs in a depression in the ground.

As ornamental birds, peacocks must be kept apart from other fowl, because of their bad disposition. Blue peacocks, though native to hot steamy lands, can survive northern winters; green peacocks, however, cannot tolerate much cold.

The Congo peacock is the only large phasianid in Africa. The cock is mainly blue and green, with a short rounded tail; the hen is reddish and green, with brown topknot.

Peacock, Thomas Love (b. Oct. 18, 1785, Weymouth, Dorset—d. Jan. 23, 1866, Lower Halliford, Middlesex), author who satirized the intellectual tendencies of his day in novels in which conversation predominates over character or plot. His best verse is interspersed in his novels.

Having made himself familiar with the Greek and Latin classics, he wrote four long poems of no great merit, published between 1804 and 1812. Peacock met Shelley in 1812, and the two became such close friends that Shelley made Peacock executor of his will. Peacock spent several months near the Shelleys at Great Marlow in 1817, a period of great importance to his development as a writer. The ideas that lie behind many of the witty dialogues in his books probably found their origin in the conversation of Shelley and his friends. Peacock's essay, *The Four Ages of Poetry* (1820), provoked Shelley's famous *A Defence of Poetry* (written 1821, pub. 1840).

Peacock, oil painting by H. Wallis, 1858; in the National Portrait Gallery, London
By courtesy of the National Portrait Gallery, London

Peacock considered his novels to be "comic romances." His characters are very nearly abstractions, fashioned to develop the opinions and conversations that form the main matter of the work. *Headlong Hall* (1816), the first of his seven novels, already sets the pattern of all of them: characters seated at table, eating and drinking, and embarking on learned and philosophical discussions in which many common opinions of the day are criticized.

In his best-known work, *Nightmare Abbey* (1818), romantic melancholy is satirized, with the characters Scythrop drawn from Shelley, Mr. Flosky from Coleridge, and Mr. Cypress from Byron. Ranked high among his other novels are *Crotchet Castle* (1831), over which the troubles of the time lie heavily, and *Gryll Grange* (1860), marked by the serenity of the end of Peacock's life, when he had ceased to worry about contemporary problems.

Peacock worked most of his life for the East India Company, the last 20 years as its chief examiner.
·English literature of the 19th century **10**:1184a
·Shelley's study of classics **16**:660e

Peacock Army Revolt, uprising against Caliph ʿAbd al-Malik (685–705) by one of his armies, suppressed by 701.
·military revolts against the Umayyads **3**:628g

peacock flower: *see* flamboyant tree.

peacock pine: *see* Japanese cedar.

Peacock Room (Whistler): *see* Freer Gallery of Art.

peacock worm: *see* sabellid.

pea crab, common name for any crab of the genus *Pinnotheres* (order Decapoda of the class Crustacea), living in certain bivalved mollusks as a commensal (*i.e.*, on or in another animal host but not deriving nourishment

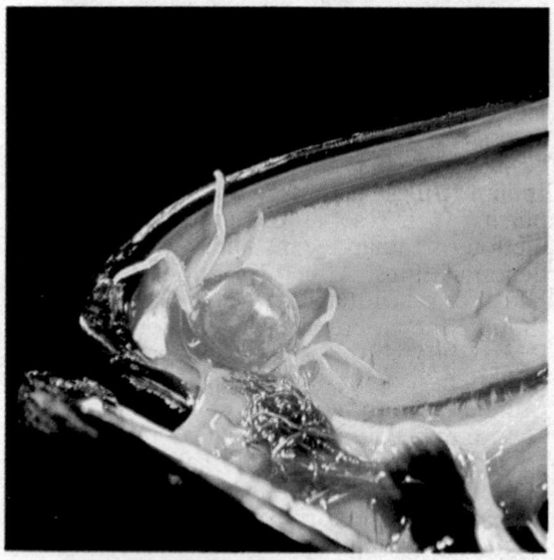

Pea crab (*Pinnotheres pisum*) in opened shell
Jane Burton—Bruce Coleman Ltd.

from it). Females of *P. ostreum*, also known as the oyster crab, are found in oysters of the Atlantic coastal waters of North America and are especially abundant in oysters of Chesapeake Bay. The body of the female is pinkish white and up to 2 centimetres (about 0.75 inch) across. An irregular stripe runs from front to back across the carapace, or back. Males, seldom seen, are smaller, dark brown, and usually free swimming. The female pea crab holds her eggs with the back legs until they hatch. The larvae leave their mollusk home and swim before settling in another mollusk shell.

P. maculatus, with a range similar to that of *P. ostreum*, is found in the shells of scallops, clams, and mussels. *P. pisum*, found in European coastal waters, lives in mussel and cockle shells.
·commensalism, parasitism, and classification **5**:546d
·symbiotic relationships in echinoderms **6**:181c

Peak District, hill area in north Derbyshire, England, forming the southern end of the Pennines, the upland "spine" of England. The northern half is dominated by high gritstone moorlands rising to Kinder Scout 2,088 ft (6,364 m). The limestone central plateau is cut through by scenic dales, notably those of the Rivers Wye and Dove. The Peak District National Park was formed in 1950–51, and its 542 sq mi (1,404 sq km) area includes parts of Cheshire, Derbyshire, Staffordshire, and South Yorkshire.

Peak Downs, district, northeast central Queensland, Australia, comprising rolling scrub- and grass-covered country studded with peaks of volcanic rock. Bounded by the Belyando (west) and Nogoa (east) rivers and drained by the Mackenzie River system, the Downs were once the source of gold and copper; cattle, sheep, grains, timber, and coal are now produced. Visited (1844–45) and named for the Peak Range, whose granite summits rise to 2,000 ft (600 m), by the explorer Ludwig Leichhardt, the district was pioneered by pastoralists in 1854. Principal settlements include Clermont, Blair Athol, Emerald, and Springsure.

Peake, Mervyn (b. July 9, 1911, China—d. Nov. 17, 1968, Oxford), novelist, poet, painter, playwright, and illustrator, best known for the bizarre Titus Groan trilogy of novels and for his illustrations of his novels and of children's stories.

Educated in China and in Kent, Peake went to art school and trained as a painter; but he was stricken with a progressive illness that made him increasingly helpless until his death.

His Titus Groan novels—consisting of *Titus Groan* (1946), *Gormenghast* (1950), and *Titus Alone* (1959)—display a gallery of eccentric and freakish characters in an idiosyncratic Gothic setting. Peake's drawings and paintings, particularly his illustrations for the novels and for children's books, are only a little less known, and his poem, *The Glassblowers* (1950), won a literary prize, together with *Gormenghast*. Peake also wrote a play, *The Wit to Woo* (performed 1957). He was made a Fellow of the Royal Society of Literature in 1950.

·literary style and works **10**:1222c

Peale, Charles Willson (b. April 15, 1741, Queen Annes County, Md.—d. Feb. 22, 1827, Philadelphia), painter best remembered for his portraits of the leading figures of the American Revolution and as the founder of the first major U.S. museum. Peale, who was a saddler, watchmaker, and silversmith, began his art career by exchanging a saddle for a few painting lessons from John Hesselius. In 1766 a group of Maryland patrons sent him to London, where he studied for three years with Benjamin West. Peale's ideas were firmly democratic, and it is recorded that he even refused to take off his hat when the coach of King George III passed by.

"The Artist in His Museum," oil painting by Charles Willson Peale, 1822; in the Pennsylvania Academy of the Fine Arts, Philadelphia

By courtesy of the Pennsylvania Academy of the Fine Arts, Philadelphia

On his return to America, Peale immediately became the fashionable portrait painter of the middle colonies. He moved to Philadelphia in 1775, entered wholeheartedly into the Revolutionary movement, and served with the city militia in the Trenton–Princeton campaign. From 1779 to 1780 he represented the "Furious Whig" party in the Pennsylvania assembly, an activity that damaged his professional career. He opened a portrait gallery of Revolutionary heroes in 1782 and in 1786 founded an institution intended for the study of natural law and display of natural history and technological objects. Known as Peale Museum, it grew to vast proportions and was widely imitated by other museums of the period and later by P.T. Barnum. Located in Independence Hall, the museum was a mélange of Peale's paintings, curious gadgets, and stuffed animals. Its most celebrated exhibit was the first complete skeleton of an American mastodon, unearthed in 1801 on a New York farm. Peale, who had accompanied the expedition, chronicled the excavation in his painting "Exhuming the Mastodon" (1806; Peale Museum, Baltimore).

In his long life, Peale painted about 1,100 portraits, including Washington, Franklin, Jefferson, and John Adams. Crisply outlined and firmly modelled, they paralleled the Neoclassical style developed in France by J.-L. David. His seven life portraits of Washington were repeated many times by himself and other painters of his family. Peale was also a master of *trompe l'oeil* painting, *e.g.*, "The Staircase Group" (1795; Philadelphia Museum of Art), a life-sized double portrait of his sons Raphaelle and Titian, intentionally framed in a real door jamb and with a projecting bottom step, is said to have deceived George Washington into doffing his hat to the boys' images.

·Romantic portraiture in America **19**:457h
·Rush portrait painting illus. **16**:31

Peale, Rembrandt (b. Feb. 22, 1778, Bucks County, Pa.—d. Oct. 3, 1860, Philadelphia), painter, writer, and portraitist of prominent figures in Europe and post-Revolutionary U.S. One of the sons of Charles Willson Peale, he studied first with his father, whose sculpturesque Neoclassical style is reflected in "Thomas Jefferson" (1805; New York Historical Society)—Rembrandt Peale's acknowledged masterpiece and the best existing portrait of Jefferson. Peale continued his training at the Royal Academy in London. Between 1808 and 1810 he went to Paris, where his work was admired by Jacques-Louis David, and he was offered the post of court painter to Napoleon.

A highly sensitive man, he gave up painting for eight years, apparently because of unfavourable criticism. Following his father's example, he opened a museum and portrait gallery in Baltimore, where he also established the first illuminating-gas works. He sold his museum in 1822; it is now known as the Peale Museum and is devoted to local history.

When he took up painting again he was ambitious to rise above portraiture, so he turned to formal subject pieces. "The Court of Death" (1820; Detroit Institute of Arts), a gracefully drawn and subtly illuminated allegory, was the culmination of this series. Peale exhibited this painting throughout the country, earning over $8,000 during the first year.

With equal vigour he promoted his portrait of George Washington (1823; Pennsylvania Academy of the Fine Arts), seeking to replace the popular accepted likeness of Washington, Gilbert Stuart's "Athenaeum" head (1796), with his own work. He had painted Washington from life in 1795, and of this later likeness —strong but somewhat idealized—he painted 76 replicas. Peale's painting and writing—*Notes on Italy* (1831), *Portfolio of an Artist* (1839)—occupied him for the remainder of his life.

·artistic exhibition and monetary reward **2**:100e
·Jefferson portrait illus. **10**:127

Pe-an (emperor of China): *see* Wang Yang-ming.

Peano, Giuseppe (b. Aug. 27, 1858, Cuneo, Italy—d. April 20, 1932, Turin), mathematician and a founder of symbolic logic whose interests centred on the foundations of mathematics and on the development of a formal logical language.

He became a lecturer of infinitesimal calculus at the University of Turin in 1884 and professor in 1890. He also held the post of professor at the Accademia Militare, Turin, from 1886 to 1901. His *Formulaire de mathematiques* (Italian *Formulario Mathematico;* "Mathematical Formulary"), published 1894 to 1908 with collaborators, was intended to develop mathematics in its entirety from its fundamental postulates using Peano's logic notation. This work, and others, profoundly changed the outlook of mathematicians and was a major influence upon later efforts to restructure mathematics, notably the program by the French mathematicians whose works appear under the pseudonym Nicolas Bourbaki. Part of Peano's logic notation was adopted by Bertrand Russell and Alfred N. Whitehead in their *Principia Mathematica* (3 vol., 1910–13).

Peano's *Calcolo differenziale e principii di calcolo integrale* (1884; "Differential Calculus and Principles of Integral Calculus") and *Lezioni di analisi infinitesimale* (2 vol., 1893; "Lessons of Infinitesimal Analysis") are two of the most important works on the development of the general theory of functions since the work of the French mathematician Augustin Cauchy (died 1857). In *Applicazioni geometriche del calcolo infinitesimale* (1887; "Geometrical Applications of Infinitesimal Calculus") Peano introduced the basic elements of geometric calculus and gave new definitions for the length of an arc and for the area of a curved surface. *Calcolo geometrico* (1888; "Geometric Calculus") contains his first work on mathematical logic.

Peano is also known as the creator of *Latino sine Flexione*, later called *Interlingua*, an artificial language. Based upon a synthesis of the vocabulary from Latin, French, German, and English, with a greatly simplified grammar, *Interlingua* was intended for use as an international auxiliary language. Peano compiled a *Vocabulario de interlingua* (1915) and was for a time president of the Academia pro Interlingua.

·genetic method application **11**:631g
·Interlingua grammar invention **9**:743c
·logic history **11**:69a
·Whitehead–Russell extrapolation of logic **19**:816f

Peano axioms, postulates set forth by the Italian mathematician Giuseppe Peano (1858–1932) concerning the definition of the positive integers as a set of elements.

·metamathematical method applications **11**:636d

peanut, also called GROUNDNUT, EARTHNUT, or GOOBER, despite its several common names,

Peanut (*Arachis hypogaea*)

G. Tomsich—Photo Researchers

is not a true nut but the pod, or legume, of *Arachis hypogaea* (family Fabaceae), which has the peculiar habit of ripening underground. It is a concentrated food; pound for pound, peanuts have more protein, minerals, and vitamins than beef liver; more fat than heavy cream; and more food energy (calories) than sugar. The plant is an annual, ranging from an erect or bunch form 450–600 millimetres (18–24 inches) high, with short branches, to a spreading, or runner, form 300–450 millimetres (12–18 inches) high with branches up to 600 millimetres (24 inches) long that lie close to the soil. The stems and branches are sturdy and hairy; leaves are pinnately compound with two pairs of leaflets. The flowers are borne in the axils of the leaves; what appears to be a flower stalk is a slender calyx up to 40 millimetres (1.6 inches) long; the golden-yellow petals are about 10 millimetres (0.4 inch) across. The pods are most commonly 25–50 millimetres (1–2 inches) long, with two or three seeds, oblong, roughly cylindrical with rounded ends, contracted between the seeds, and have a thin, netted, spongy shell. The seeds vary from oblong to nearly round; seed coat colours range from whitish to dark purple, but mahogany red, rose, and salmon predominate.

After pollination and the withering of the flower, an unusual stalklike structure called a peg is thrust from the base of the flower toward the soil. In the pointed tip of this slender, sturdy peg the fertilized ovules are carried downward until the tip is well below the soil surface. Only then does the tip start to develop into the characteristic pod. The pegs sometimes reach down 100 millimetres (4 inches) or more before their tips can develop fruits. The fruits appear to function as roots to some degree, absorbing mineral nutrients directly from the soil. The pods may not develop properly unless the soil in which they lie is well supplied with available calcium, regardless of the nutrients available to the roots.

Native to tropical South America, the peanut was at an early time introduced into the Old World tropics. India, China, West Africa, and the U.S. have become the largest commercial producers of peanuts.

Peanut growing requires at least five months of warm weather with rainfall (or irrigation equivalent) of 600 millimetres (24 inches) or more during the growing season. In Asia the peanut is grown under irrigation. The best soils are well-drained sandy loams underlain by deep, friable loam subsoils. At harvest, the entire plant, except the deeper roots, is removed from the soil. The nuts are best cured by allowing the harvested plants to wilt for a day, then placing them for four to six weeks in stacks built around a sturdy stake driven upright into the soil. The pods are placed toward the inside of each stack to protect them from weather.

The peanut is grown mainly for its edible oil, except in the U.S., where it is produced for grinding into peanut butter (half the harvested crop); for roasted, salted nuts; and for use in candy and bakery products. A small percentage of the U.S. crop is crushed for oil. In the southern U.S., the peanut is used extensively as feed for livestock. The tops of the plants, after the pods are removed, usually are fed as hay, although the entire plant may be so used.

·African distribution and production **1**:213a
·Carver's agricultural research **3**:973a
·development of agriculture **1**:328c
·domesticated plant centres of origin **5**:938e
·fruit and nut farming, table 1 **7**:755
·fruit development and habitat **7**:129b
·Gambian production and processing **7**:864b
·new food sources and production problem **7**:482e; table
·pre-Incan agricultural development **1**:841h
·seed and fruit dispersal **16**:486c; illus. 483
·synthetic fibre research **7**:263f

peanutworm, common name for any member of the invertebrate phylum Sipuncula (about 320 species), a group of rare, bottom-dwelling, sedentary, often spindle-shaped worms found on the bottoms of all oceans.

Peanutworm
Bucky Reeves—National Audubon Society

They range in length from a few millimetres to more than 300 millimetres (about one foot). The body consists of a muscular trunk and a slender anterior region that can be extended.

Most peanutworms burrow in the ocean bottom; some live on discarded seashells or in sponges or coral. They eat micro-organisms and organic debris. *Major ref.* **16**:809h

·circulatory system anatomy **4**:623f

pea picker's disease (contagious disease of animals): *see* leptospirosis.

pear, any of several species of *Pyrus*, especially *Pyrus communis*, of the rose family (Rosaceae), one of the most important fruit

Pear (*Pyrus communis*)
Grant Heilman—EB Inc.

trees of the world, cultivated in all temperate-zone countries of both hemispheres.

The pear tree is broad headed and up to 13 metres (about 43 feet) high at maturity; it is taller and more upright than the apple tree. The roundish to oval, leathery leaves, somewhat wedge-shaped at their bases, appear about the same time as the flowers, which are 25 millimetres (one inch) wide and usually white. The pear flower, similar to that of the apple, differs in that the bases of the five styles are separated.

Pears are generally sweeter and of softer texture than apples. The fruit is distinguished by the presence of hard cells in the flesh, the so-called grit, or stone cells, which are absent in apples. In general, pear fruits are elongate, being narrow at the stem end and broader at the opposite end, although some types are apple-shaped.

The common pear, probably of European origin, has been cultivated since long before the Christian Era. Thousands of varieties have been bred and named since ancient times in Europe alone. The pear was introduced into the New World by British and other Europeans as soon as the colonies were established. Also at an early date, Spanish missionaries carried the fruit to Mexico and California.

The pear is propagated by budding or grafting onto a rootstock. Many are grafted on seedling pears, usually of *Pyrus communis* origin. In Europe the main rootstock used is quince, which produces a dwarfed tree that fruits at an earlier age than most of the trees on pear rootstocks.

Pear trees are relatively long-lived (50 to 75 years) and may reach considerable size unless carefully trained and pruned. Within four to seven years of setting out, the tree begins to bear satisfactorily; at age 20 to 25 it should yield 25 to 45 bushels of fruit.

The pear is commercially the second most important of the world's deciduous fruit trees, exceeded only by the apple. In the U.S., however, the pear ranks third, after the apple and peach.

World production of table and dessert pears, excluding those used for perry, an alcoholic beverage prepared from fermented pears, is over 7,000,000 tons annually, more than half of which is produced in Europe. Italy is the world's leading pear producer, followed by China and the U.S. Other countries producing sizable quantities are France, Japan, Spain, West Germany, Turkey, Australia, Bulgaria, and South Africa.

In the U.S., Canada, and Australia, canners use about half the total commercial crop of fresh fruit; in South Africa canning accounts for 30 percent. In Europe canning is unimportant. About one-third of the total production of pears in France is used for making perry; in Germany, half; in Switzerland, about four-fifths. *Major ref.* **7**:758g; tables 756

·domesticated plant centres of origin **5**:938c

Pearic languages, group of the Austro-Asiatic language family of Southeast Asia including Chong, Pear (the type language), Samre, and Sa'och.

·Austro-Asiatic language distribution map **2**:484

Pea Ridge, Battle of, called in the South BATTLE OF ELKHORN TAVERN (March 7–8, 1862), U.S. Civil War clash in Arkansas, in which Federal forces were victorious.

·Civil War strategic result **4**:676f

pearl, a concretion formed by a mollusk consisting of the same material (called nacre or mother-of-pearl) as the mollusk's shell. Pearl-like, chitinous formations have been found in insects and hornlike formations in horn-bearing mammals, but the name pearl is restricted to concretions of mollusks; every mollusk endowed with a shell can produce pearls.

An unblemished pearl is one of the most ancient symbols of perfection. Pearls are mentioned in the literature of ancient India and China. Indian Vedic literature indicates that the pearl was known in India before the influx of the Aryans (*c.* 1500 BC). Archaic Greek and Etruscan jewelry (about 400 BC) featured borders of pearls surrounding a central setting of coloured gemstones. Pearls were so highly esteemed in classical Rome that only persons of a specified rank were permitted to wear them. The 1st-century Roman naturalist-philosopher Pliny the Elder speaks of pearls as

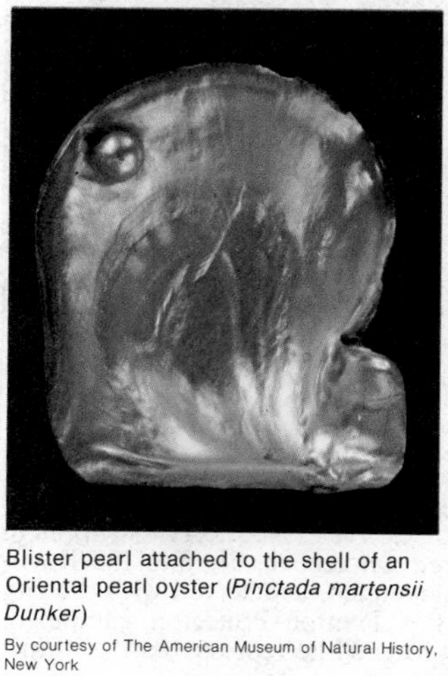

Blister pearl attached to the shell of an Oriental pearl oyster (*Pinctada martensii Dunker*)
By courtesy of The American Museum of Natural History, New York

"the most sovereign commodity in the whole world."

Pearls are characterized by their translucence and lustre and by a delicate play of surface colour called orient. The more perfect the shape (spherical or droplike) and the deeper the pearly lustre, the more highly the pearl is valued. Only those pearls produced by mollusks the shells of which are lined with mother-of-pearl are really fine pearls; pearls from other mollusks are either reddish or whitish, porcellaneous, or lacking in pearly lustre.

The chief component of the nacre that constitutes the pearl is aragonite (*q.v.*), one form of calcium carbonate ($CaCO_3$). Nacre also contains a small amount of conchiolin, the hornlike organic substance (albuminoid) that is the main constituent of the mollusk's outer shell.

The mollusk's shell-secreting cells are located in the mantle, or epithelium, of its body; when a foreign particle penetrates the mantle, the cells attach to the particle and build up more or less concentric layers of pearl around it. If the foreign substance penetrates deeply enough, a sac or cyst of tissue is first formed around it; the pearl building takes place within this sac. When the sac is not subjected to any deforming pressure, the pearl that develops inside it is either spherical or pearlike. Pearl cysts lodged in muscular tissue, however, assume irregular shapes; they are called baroque pearls. If the particle lodges between the shell and the mantle, the shell-secreting cells deposit a sacless pearl formation that is attached to the shell; these are often flat on one side and are called blister pearls.

Ranking first among Oriental pearls for superior form, lustre, and orient are those produced by the *mohar*, a variety of the *Pinctada martensii* species of saltwater mollusk. Found in the Persian Gulf with the richest harvest taken from the waters off the great bight that curves from the peninsula of Oman to that of Qatar, the pearls come from depths of 8 to 20 fathoms (48 to 120 feet). Pearls of fine quality are also fished near Bahrain.

Another important source of Oriental pearls produced by *Pinctada martensii* is the neighbourhood of Sri Lanka, particularly the Gulf of Mannar between South India and Sri Lanka. These pearls are marketed in Madras, India, together with African pearls, taken chiefly from the banks that lie in the coastal waters of East Africa.

In Southeast Asia, the pearls of Celebes are noted for their lovely colouring, whereas Australian waters yield pearls of a beautiful silvery white. The islands of the South Pacific also produce fine pearls. In the Americas, saltwater pearls, larger in size than Oriental pearls though less finely formed, have been fished in the Caribbean. The Gulf of California, the Gulf of Mexico, and the waters of the Pacific coast of Mexico have yielded dark-hued Pacific coast pearls with a metallic sheen, as well as white pearls of good quality.

Freshwater mussels in the temperate zone of the Northern Hemisphere have produced pearls of great value. The freshwater pearls of the U.S. have come principally from the Mississippi River. Pearling has declined greatly in Great Britain, but pearls from Scottish rivers and from the Conway River in northern Wales were once in great demand. Pearling is still a carefully fostered industry in central Europe, and the forest streams of Bavaria, in particular, are the source of choice pearls. Freshwater pearling in China has been known from before 1000 BC. In all pearl fisheries, however, production has declined greatly since the widespread introduction in the 1930s of cultured pearls (*see* pearl, cultured).

The colour of pearls varies with the mollusk and its environment. Colours range from black to white, with the rose of Indian pearls being valued most highly. Other colours are cream, gray, blue, yellow, lavender, green, and mauve. All occur in delicate shades. The surface of a pearl is rough to the touch.

Pearls come in a wide range of sizes. Those weighing less than ¼ grain (1 pearl grain = 50 milligrams = ¼ carat) are called seed pearls; as many as 9,000 seed pearls may together weigh one ounce. The largest naturally occurring pearls are the baroques; Henry Thomas Hope, the 19-century Amsterdam and London banker, owned a baroque pearl weighing 1,860 grains (about two-thirds of a pound).

Special care must be taken with pearls because they are comparatively soft (Mohs hardness 3½–4) and are easily damaged by acids (including that in perspiration) or scratching. They are also affected by heat.

Pearls noted for their size, beauty, and historical associations rank among the famous jewels of the world. La Reine des Perles, a 27.5-carat Oriental pearl, was among the crown jewels of France stolen in 1792. La Régente, an oval pearl weighing 337 grains, once was owned by the French imperial court.

·commercial value and sources **7**:351c
·economics of conspicuous consumption **5**:107c
·gemstone qualities and occurrence **7**:976f; illus.
·jewelry-making materials and usage **10**:165c; illus.
·mosaic art's technical development **12**:464h; illus. 473
·Philippines' biological resources **14**:235h

Pearl (late 14th century), an elegiac dream allegory written in Middle English by an unknown author, probably also the author of *Sir Gawayne and the Grene Knight* (*q.v.*) and called, consequently, the Pearl Poet, or the Gawain Poet.

·Middle English alliterative verse **10**:1109d

pearl, cultured, natural but cultivated pearl (*q.v.*) produced by a mollusk after the intentional introduction of a foreign object inside the creature's shell. The discovery that such pearls could be cultivated in freshwater mussels is said to have been made in China in the 13th century, and the Chinese have been adept for hundreds of years at cultivating pearls by opening the mussel's shell and inserting into it small pellets of mud or tiny bosses of wood, bone, or metal and returning the mussel to its bed for about three years to await the maturation of a pearl formation. The cultured pearls of China have been almost exclusively blister pearls (hemispherical pearls formed between the mussel and its shell), which require the addition of a half sphere of mother-of-pearl to create the assembled gem, called a pearl doublet.

The production of whole cultured pearls was perfected by the Japanese. The research that led to the establishment of the industry was started in the 1890s by Mikimoto Kōkichi, who, after long experimentation, concluded that a very small mother-of-pearl bead introduced into the mollusk's tissue was the most successful stimulant to pearl production. It possesses the added virtue of providing a pearl entirely of nacreous content.

Cultured pearls closely approximate natural pearls. If the covering of nacre is too thin, however, it will deteriorate upon prolonged contact with the acids of the human body and eventually will reveal the mother-of-pearl matrix. Japan has about 2,800 sea farms devoted to cultured pearls; a few were established off northern Australia in the 1960s, principally with Japanese collaboration, and by the mid-1970s were an established industry, producing pearl shell as well as pearls.

·aquaculture area and method **7**:362a
·economics of conspicuous consumption **5**:107c
·gemstones and Japanese industry **7**:976g
·Japanese production technique **2**:1085f

Pearl, Raymond (b. June 3, 1879, Farmington, N.H.—d. Nov. 17, 1940, Hershey, Pa.), one of the founders of biometry, the application of statistics to biology and medicine. As an instructor at the University of Michigan, Ann Arbor, where he had earned a Ph.D. in zoology (1902), Pearl recognized the advantages that would accrue from applying standard statistical procedures to biological problems. He served as head of the biology department at the Maine Agricultural Experimental Station (1907–18) and as chief of the statistical division of the U.S. Food Administration (1917–19). He was then invited to organize the department of medical statistics and biometry at the School of Hygiene and Public Health of Johns Hopkins University, Baltimore, Md.

Pearl

By courtesy of the Johns Hopkins University, Baltimore

Pearl founded the *Quarterly Review of Biology* (1926) and *Human Biology* (1929) and was the author of more than 700 articles and books, including *Introduction to Medical Biometry and Statistics* (1923), which became a prototype for such college texts.

pearl essence, a suspension of guanine crystals that is sprayed on such articles as beads and textiles to give them an iridescent sheen.

·sources and commercial use **7**:351b

pearleye, name often used for members of the fish family Scopelarchidae, order Salmoniformes.

·classification and general features **16**:191f

pearlfish, also called FIERASFER OR CUCUMBER FISH, any of about 27 species of slim, eel-shaped, marine fishes of the family Carapidae noted for living in the bodies of sea cucumbers, pearl oysters, starfishes, and other invertebrates. Pearlfishes are primarily tropical and are found around the world, mainly in shallow water. They are elongated, scaleless, and often transparent. The long dorsal and anal fins meet at the tip of the long, pointed tail. Most pearlfishes are about 15 centimetres (6 inches) or less in length. They penetrate sea cucumbers by way of the anus of the host, in some instances apparently feeding on its reproductive and respiratory organs.

·symbiotic relationships in echinoderms **6**:181c
·traits, behaviour, and classification **13**:981b

Pearl Fishers, The, English translation of LES PÊCHEURS DE PERLES, Romantic opera in three acts by the French composer Georges Bizet, with libretto by Michel Carré and Eugène Cormon, set in legendary Ceylon. The opera was first performed in Paris in 1863.

·dramatic and musical weaknesses **2**:1092f

Pearl Harbor, Honolulu County, southern Oahu Island, Hawaii, U.S. Ringed by ancient Hawaiian fishponds, it is virtually surrounded (west to east) by the cities of Ewa, Waipahu, Pearl City, Aiea, and Honolulu. The nerve centre of the U.S. Pacific Command, it has 10 sq mi (26 sq km) of navigable water and hundreds of anchorages and covers a land area of more than 10,000 ac (4,000 ha). Its four lochs are formed by the Waipio and Pearl City peninsulas and Ford Island. Pearl Harbor entrance connects its virtually landlocked bay with the Pacific Ocean.

The volcanic structure is that of a drowned river system formed by the banking of the Koolau Range lavas against the older Waianae Range. Waikele and Waiawa streams,

USS "Arizona" National Memorial in Pearl Harbor, Oahu, Hawaii

Charles Giugno—Pix from Publix

flowing off the Koolau Range, were deflected southward. Other large streams entered the bay, cutting deep canyons in the hard basalt. The harbour assumed its present level 11,000 years ago when the Ice Age ended, flooding the ancient valleys to form the lochs. Ford Island and Waipio Peninsula are the old divides extended by reefs and sediment.

Pearl Harbor, at the double estuary of the Pearl River, was called Wai Momi ("pearl waters") by the Hawaiians because of the pearl oysters that once grew there. They also referred to it as Puuloa, believing the harbour to be the home of the queen of the sharks, Kaahupahau, protectress of humans.

In 1840 Lt. Charles Wilkes of the U.S. Navy made the first geodetic survey and urged the dredging of the coral-bar entrance to the lochs. About 30 years later, Col. John McAllister Schofield further recommended that the U.S. secure harbour rights. A subsequent treaty (1887) granted the U.S. the exclusive use of the harbour as a coaling and repair station, but work was not begun until after 1898, when the Spanish-American War indicated its strategic value as a Pacific base. A naval station was established after 1908, and drydock was completed in 1919.

On Dec. 7, 1941, Japanese aircraft bombed military installations in Hawaii, touching off the Pacific phase of World War II. The U.S. Pacific Force, comprising nearly 100 naval vessels (including 8 battleships) and substantial naval and air forces, had been stationed at Pearl Harbor since April 1940. U.S. military casualties exceeded 3,000, of which over 2,000 were fatalities. All eight battleships were damaged; three were destroyed, and a fourth was capsized. The USS "Arizona" sank on the "day of infamy," with a loss of 1,102 sailors, the single greatest disaster of the attack; a white concrete-steel structure now spans the hull of the sunken ship, which was dedicated as a national memorial on May 30, 1962.

Present facilities at Pearl Harbor include a naval shipyard, supply centre, and submarine base. The naval shipyard on Waipio Peninsula and the Southeast Loch area has drydocks, two marine railways, auxiliary floating drydocks, and industrial shops equipped to handle repair, alteration, and construction. The naval supply centre is on Pearl City Peninsula. Pearl Harbor Entrance is bounded on the east by Hickam Air Force Base and on the west by a naval reservation, including housing for the Barbers Point Naval Air Station at nearby Ewa Beach. During the Korean and Indo-China conflicts of the 1950s, 1960s, and 1970s, the harbour complex was a staging area for forces and equipment bound for the combat zones.

21°22′ N, 157°58′ W

·groundwater origin and spring discharge **17**:516g

·map, Hawaii **8**:675

·shipyard and defense significance **8**:677f

Pearl Harbor Attack, aerial attack on the United States naval base at Pearl Harbor, Hawaii, on December 7, 1941, by the Japanese, which brought the U.S. into World War II. The attack culminated worsening relations between the United States and Japan that had extended over a decade. In November, after being economically strangled by U.S. efforts to stop petroleum and other war material from being shipped to Japan, the government of Premier Tōjō Hideki finally decided on war. The assault began at 7:55 on Sunday morning. Dive bombers, fighters, and torpedo planes destroyed three battleships (the "West Virginia," "California," and "Arizona"), and one (the "Oklahoma") was capsized.

A second wave swept into Pearl Harbor about one hour after the first. Although not as successful, it inflicted heavy damage on the battleship "Nevada," and three destroyers were reduced to wrecks. The Japanese inflicted on the U.S. Navy casualties to the number of 2,718, of which 2,000 were fatalities. Army casualties exceeded 600 men, of whom more than 200 were killed. To accomplish these results, the Japanese had sacrificed fewer than 100 men, 29 planes, and five midget submarines. Their task force escaped without being attacked.

Though they were successful in destroying the strength of the U.S. battleships, the Japanese missed the entire aircraft carrier fleet, which was at sea.

·attack and destruction **18**:992c

·battleship repair after attack **12**:894g

·cryptanalysis importance in World War II **5**:333f

·Japanese war strategy **10**:86a

·Sino-American resulting alliance **4**:374c

·U.S. naval losses during attack **19**:989g

Pearl Islands, Spanish ARCHIPIÉLAGO DE LAS PERLAS, group of islands belonging to Panama lying in the Gulf of Panama, consisting of 183 islands, of which 39 are sizable, and lying about 50 mi (80 km) southeast of Panama City. The most important islands include the mountainous Isla del Rey, on which the principal town, San Miguel, is located; San José; Pedro González; and Saboga. In the colonial era, pearl fishing was the principal economic activity; now the islands are visited by fishermen in search of mackerel, red snapper, sailfish, marlin, and other species abounding in the waters. Pop. (1970) 2,756.

8°20′ N, 79°02′ W

·map, Panama **13**:941

pearlite, principal component of both steel and cast iron. It is a mechanical mixture of ferrite, a solid solution of carbon in body-centred iron, and cementite, an iron-carbon compound having the formula Fe_3C.

·cast iron production **9**:897b

·structure and composition **17**:659e; illus.

pearl millet (grass): *see* Pennisetum.

Pearl of Great Price, The, scriptural work written in 1842 by Joseph Smith, Mormon founder and prophet.

·Mormon scriptures revealed to Smith **12**:443b

pearl perch, common name for members of the fish family Glaucosomidae (order Perciformes).

·classification and general features **14**:52d

Pearl River, southeastern United States, rises in east central Mississippi and flows southwestward, through Jackson, the capital of the state, then generally southward into Louisiana, past Bogalusa, emptying into Mississippi Sound on the Gulf of Mexico. West of Picayune, Miss., the river divides into two streams: East Pearl River, which enters the Sound near Grand Island, and West Pearl River, which parallels the East Pearl several miles to the west, entering the Rigolets, a tidal channel connecting Lake Pontchartrain with Lake Borgne (inlet of Mississippi Sound). Approximately 490 mi (789 km) long, the Pearl and its tributaries (Yockanookany and Strong rivers and the Bogue Chitto) drain about 7,600 sq mi (19,700 sq km). Locks on the West Pearl (1953) provide a 7-ft channel from the mouth to Bogalusa (58 mi upstream). Once a main transportation route for lumber below Jackson, the river is no longer important for navigation above Bogalusa. Chief river cities are Columbia, Monticello, and Jackson, all in Mississippi, and Bogalusa, in Louisiana. The Ross Barnett Reservoir north of Jackson provides water, flood and pollution control, and recreation facilities. The lower course of the Pearl and the East Pearl form the boundary between Mississippi and Louisiana. Prior to 1812 (when Louisiana was granted statehood) the river was the eastern boundary of the Republic of West Florida. Honey Island Swamp, lying in the mid-delta area southwest of Picayune, is noted for its wildlife and fishing.

30°11′ N, 89°32′ W

·map, United States **18**:909

pearls of Sluze, in mathematics, the curve described by the equation $y^n = k(a - x)^p x^m$, in which m, n, p are positive integers.

·analytic geometry fundamentals **7**:1090a

pearlstone (natural glass): *see* perlite.

pearl ware, earthenware with a white to bluish-white glaze, introduced by the English potter Josiah Wedgwood at the end of the 18th century. It eventually superseded Wedgwood's creamware (*q.v.*), which it resembles, at factories such as those in Staffordshire and Leeds, where it was made in quantity.

pearlwort (flower): *see* Caryophyllaceae.

pear psylla (pear sucker): *see* jumping plant louse.

Pearse, Patrick Henry (b. Nov. 10, 1879, Dublin—d. May 3, 1916, Dublin), leader of Irish nationalism, poet and educator, the first president of the provisional government of the Irish Republic proclaimed in Dublin on Easter Monday, April 24, 1916, and commander in chief of the Irish forces in the anti-British uprising that began on the same day. Exceedingly gentle in his personal relations, he became a symbol in Ireland of romantic revolutionary violence.

Pearse

Radio Times Hulton Picture Library

The son of an English sculptor and his Irish wife, Pearse became a director of the Gaelic League (founded 1893 for the preservation and extension of the Irish language) and edited (1903–09) its weekly newspaper *An Claidheamh Soluis* ("The Sword of Light"). To promote further the Irish language as a weapon against British domination, he published tales from old Irish manuscripts and a collection (1914) of his own poems in the modern Irish idiom. He founded St. Enda's College, near Dublin (1908), as a bilingual institution with its teaching based on Irish traditions and culture.

On the formation (November 1913) of the Irish Volunteers as a counterforce against the Ulster Volunteers (militant supporters of the Anglo-Irish union), Pearse became a member of their provisional committee, and he contributed poems and articles to their newspaper, *The Irish Volunteer.* Later (July 1914) he was made a member of the supreme council of the Irish Republican Brotherhood (IRB). After the Irish Volunteers split (September 1914), he became a leader of the more extreme Nationalist section, which opposed any support for Great Britain in World War I. He came to believe that the blood of martyrs would be required to liberate Ireland, and on that theme he delivered a famous oration at the burial (August 1915) of Jeremiah O'Donovan, known as O'Donovan Rossa, a veteran of Sinn Féin.

As an IRB supreme council member, Pearse helped to plan (January 1916) the Easter Rising. On Easter Monday, from the steps of the Dublin General Post Office, he delivered the proclamation of the Irish Republic, whereupon street fighting broke out. On April 29, when the revolt was crushed, he surrendered to the British. After a court-martial, he was shot by a firing squad.

Pearse's *Collected Works* appeared in 1917–22 (3 vol.) and again in 1924 (5 vol.), and his *Political Writings and Speeches* in 1952. *Patrick H. Pearse*, Desmond Ryan's English translation of Louis N. Le Roux's *Vie de Patrice Pearse*, was published in 1932.

pear-shaped quartic, in mathematics, the curve described by the equation $b^2y^2 = x^3(a - x)$.

·analytic geometry fundamentals **7**:1089h

pear slug: *see* sawfly.

Pearson, Arthur (1866–1921), British publisher.

·magazine publishing history **15**:249d

Pearson, George (1751–1828), British physician.

·utilization of Jenner's vaccine **10**:133g

Pearson, Hesketh (1887–1964), English biographer.

·biographer's interpretive freedoms **2**:1008b

Pearson, Karl (b. March 27, 1857, London—d. April 27, 1936, London), mathematician, one of the founders of modern statistics. Part of his multifaceted nature is revealed by his three-year law practice begun in 1881, his radical political activities in London, and the publication of two literary works, *The New Werther* (1880) and *The Trinity: A Nineteenth Century Passion-Play* (1882). In 1884 he was appointed professor of applied mathematics and mechanics at University College, London, where he taught, until his retirement in 1933, as Gresham professor of geometry (1891), head of the department of applied mathematics (1907), and Galton professor of eugenics (1911).

Pearson's lectures as professor of geometry evolved into *The Grammar of Science* (1892), his most widely read book and a classic in the philosophy of science.

Karl Pearson, pencil drawing by F.A. de Biden Footner, 1924

By courtesy of Professor D.V. Lindley; photograph, J.R. Freeman & Co. Ltd.

Stimulated by the evolutionary writings of Francis Galton and a personal friendship with Walter F.R. Weldon, Pearson became immersed in the problem of applying statistics to biological problems of heredity and evolution. His work in applying statistics to the biological and social sciences resulted in methods that are essential to every serious application of statistics. From 1893 to 1912 he wrote a series of 18 papers entitled *Mathematical Contributions to the Theory of Evolution*, which contained much of his most valuable work, including the chi-square test of statistical significance. He was a co-founder (with Galton and Weldon), editor of (1901–36), and major contributor to the statistical journal *Biometrika*. He was also editor of *The Annals of Eugenics* (1925–36).

Pearson's other works include *The Ethic of Free Thought* (1888); *The Chances of Death and Other Studies in Evolution* (1897); *The Life, Letters and Labours of Francis Galton* (1914, 1930); *Tables for Statisticians and Biometricians* (1914, 1931); *Tables of the Incomplete Gamma Function* (1922); and *Tables of the Incomplete Beta Function* (1934).

·correlation coefficient history **15**:156g
·misapplication of eugenics **6**:1023f
·probabilistic theory and method **11**:670e
·sociological use of statistical measures **16**:996e

Pearson, Lester B(owles) (b. April 23, 1897, Toronto—d. Dec. 27, 1972, Ottawa), politician, diplomat, and prime minister of Canada, who was prominent as a mediator in international disputes in 1963–68.

Lester Pearson, 1963

Canadian Press

Pearson served in World War I (1914–18) and lectured in history at the University of Toronto and at Oxford (1924–28). He joined the Canadian foreign service in 1928 and became first secretary in the Department of External Affairs. He served on two Royal commissions (1931) and as counsellor of the Canadian high commissioner's office in London (1935).

Recalled to Canada in 1941, Pearson then served as ambassador to the United States in 1945–46. He spoke for Canada at the United Nations in 1946–48; in 1947 he was chairman of the Political and Security Committee of the United Nations General Assembly, in which post he helped achieve the Palestine partition resolution. In 1948 he became secretary of state for external affairs in the Liberal government of Louis Saint Laurent and entered Parliament for Algoma East. In 1951 he was chairman of the North Atlantic Treaty Organization (NATO), and in 1957 he received the Nobel Peace Prize for his efforts to solve the Suez crisis of 1956. Pearson succeeded as leader of the Liberal Party in 1958 and became prime minister in 1963; he resigned as prime minister in 1968 and retired from politics in that year.

Pearson, Martin: *see* Peerson, Martin.

Pearson, Weetman Dickinson, 1st Viscount Cowdray: *see* Cowdray, Weetman Dickinson Pearson, 1st Viscount.

Pearsonian coefficient (statistics): *see* correlation coefficient.

Pearson's Magazine, British magazine founded in 1896.

·magazine publishing history **15**:252f

Peary, Robert Edwin (b. May 6, 1856, Cresson, Pa.—d. Feb. 20, 1920, Washington, D.C.), Arctic explorer usually credited with leading the first expedition to reach the North Pole (1909). He entered the U.S. Navy in 1881 and pursued a naval career until his retirement, with leaves of absence granted for Arctic exploration. In 1886, with his American Negro associate Matthew Henson, he travelled inland from Disko Bay over the Greenland ice sheet for 100 miles, reaching a point 7,500 feet above sea level. In 1891 Peary returned to Greenland with seven companions, including his wife and Dr. Frederick A. Cook, who in 1909 claimed to have reached the Pole before Peary. On this expedition Peary sledged 1,300 miles to northeast Greenland, discovered Independence Fjord, and found evidence of Greenland's being an island. He also studied the "Arctic Highlanders," an isolated Eskimo tribe who helped him greatly on later expeditions.

During his expedition of 1893–94 he again sledged to northeast Greenland—this time in his first attempt to reach the Pole. On summer trips in 1895 and 1896 he was mainly occupied in transporting masses of meteoric iron from Greenland to the U.S. Between 1898 and 1902 he reconnoitred routes to the Pole from Etah, in Inglefield Land, northwest Greenland, and from Fort Conger, Ellesmere Island, N.W.T. On a second attempt to reach the Pole he was provided with a ship built to his specifications, the "Roosevelt," which he sailed to Cape Sheridan, Ellesmere Island, in 1905. But the sledging season was unsuccessful owing to adverse weather and ice conditions, and his party reached only 87°6′ N. Peary returned to Ellesmere in 1908 for his third attempt and early the following March left Cape Columbia on his successful journey to the Pole. On the last stage of the trek he was accompanied by Henson and four Eskimo. Cook's claim to have arrived at the Pole in 1908, though generally discredited, marred Peary's enjoyment of his triumph. In 1911 he retired from the navy with the rank of rear admiral. His published works include *Northward over the "Great Ice"* (1898), *The North Pole* (1910), and *Secrets of Polar Travel* (1917).

·Arctic exploration activity **7**:1045b
·Arctic soundings off Greenland **1**:1119d

Peary Land, region, northern Greenland, extending about 200 mi (320 km) east and west along the Arctic Ocean, between Victoria Fjord and the Greenland Sea. The northernmost land region of the world (next to Kaffeklubben Island), ending at Cape Morris Jesup (*q.v.*), it is Greenland's largest ice-free part, with a generally mountainous surface rising to 6,398 ft (1,950 m). The coastline is deeply indented by fjords. Although the region is without human habitation, its vegetation supports herds of musk-oxen. It was explored in 1892, 1895, and 1900 by Robert E. Peary, U.S. Arctic explorer.

·map, Greenland **8**:412

Peasant Party: *see* Bulgarian Agrarian Union.

peasantry, small-scale agricultural producers who are part of a larger society and culture. They differ from other rural cultivators in being subject to the governance of outside power holders. This integration into a larger society is often considered the criterion for defining a peasantry, although some writers have stressed other features, such as self-sufficient agriculture or small-scale production. In peasant society, ultimate control of the means of production is usually not in the hands of the primary producers. Goods and services, rather than being exchanged directly, are supplied to a centre where they are redistributed. Surpluses tend to be transferred to rulers and other non-farmers. This power relationship is also expressed in the payment of rent in the form of labour, produce, or money. The power is often, though not always, concentrated in the city.

The peasant economy generally has a relatively simple technology and a division of labour by age and sex. The unit of production is the family or household, which has many nonproductive concerns, such as consumption, rearing of children, and religious and other ceremonial observances. The economic system is not governed solely by prices and profits. A piece of land, for example, is not merely a factor of production but an object of symbolic value as well.

Peasant culture has been characterized as the "little tradition" in contrast to the "great tradition" of the centres of civilization. Ideas and artifacts from the great tradition, including religious beliefs and practices, dress, furnishings, linguistic features, and forms of social organization, filter down to the peasant community and are integrated in the little tradition, usually in a modified or simplified form and after a considerable passage of time. Cultural elements also flow from the little tradition to the city, but to a lesser extent.

Peasants, originally MUZHIKI (1897), controversial story by Anton Chekhov about the sombre conditions under which the peasantry in the Russian central provinces were forced to live.

Peasants, The (1924–25), English title of novel *Chłopi* (1902–09) by Polish writer Władysław S. Reymont.

Peasants' Land Bank, Russian economic organization formed in 1882 to give financial aid to peasants seeking land.

Peasants' Revolt (1381), the first great popular rebellion in English history. Its immediate cause was the imposition of the unpopular poll tax of 1381, which brought to a head the economic discontent that had been growing since the middle of the century. The rebellion drew support from several sources and included well-to-do artisans and villeins as well as the destitute. Probably the main grievance of the agricultural labourers and urban working classes was the Statute of Labourers (1351), which attempted to fix maximum wages during the labour shortage following the Black Death.

The rising was centred in the southeastern counties and East Anglia, with minor disturbances in other areas. It began in Essex in May, taking the government by surprise. In June Essex and Kentish rebels under Wat Tyler marched toward London and the King, young Richard II. The Kentishmen entered London on the 13th where they massacred some Flemish merchants and razed the palace of the King's uncle, the unpopular John of Gaunt, duke of Lancaster. The government was compelled to negotiate. On the 14th Richard met with the men of Essex outside London at Mile End where he promised cheap land, free trade, and the abolition of serfdom and forced labour. During the King's absence, the Kentish rebels in the city forced the surrender of the Tower of London; the chancellor, Archbishop Simon of Sudbury, and the treasurer, Sir Robert Hales, both of whom were held responsible for the poll tax, were beheaded.

The death of Wat Tyler (left) and Richard II addressing the peasants (right), miniature from a manuscript of Jean Froissart's *Chronicles*, 15th century; in the British Museum

By courtesy of the trustees of the British Museum

The King met with Tyler and the Kentishmen at Smithfield on the following day. Tyler was treacherously cut down in Richard's presence by the enraged Mayor of London. The King, with great presence of mind, appealed to the rebels as their sovereign and, after promising reforms, persuaded them to disperse. The crisis in London was over, but in the provinces the rebellion reached its climax in the following weeks. It was finally ended when the rebels in East Anglia under John Litster were crushed by the militant bishop of Norwich, Henry le Despenser, on about June 25.

The rising lasted less than a month and failed completely as a social revolution. The King's promises at Mile End and Smithfield were promptly forgotten, and manorial discontent continued to find expression in local riots. But as a protest against the taxation of poorer classes it succeeded, insofar as it prevented further levying of the poll tax. *Major ref.* **3**:214c

Peasants' Revolt, also called PEASANTS' WAR, uprising (1524–25) in Germany during the early stages of the Reformation, following the Knights' War (1522–23) and inspired by the Protestant teachings of Luther, Calvin, and Zwingli; it sought to ameliorate conditions of peasant life, and force the restoration of customary rights abrogated by the nobility. Peasant bands pillaged the south German countryside and even won some adherence from local landowners and small towns. But the higher nobility were determined to put them down; Luther, at length exasperated at their excesses and their threat to order, published his pamphlet *Wider die räuberischen und mörderischen Rotten der andern Bauern* (1525; "Against the Rapacious, Murdering Hordes of Peasants"), which alienated many of his more radical followers.

In May 1525, combined forces of the Lutheran Prince Philip of Hesse and the Catholic Duke George of Saxony crushed the insurgents at Frankenhausen in Thuringia, after which their leader, Thomas Müntzer, was put to death.

Marxists have seen the revolt as a rudimentary proletarian revolution; others have pointed out that its religious reformist anticlericalism and its millennialism derived from the reformers' emphasis on personal righteousness and salvation.

Pease, Edward Reynolds (b. Dec. 23, 1857, Henbury Hill, Dorset—d. Jan. 5, 1955, Limpsfield, Surrey), writer, one of the founders and longtime secretary of the Fabian Society.

Born to a prosperous family, Pease left a business career and joined with Frank Podmore, a spiritualist and socialist writer, to found the Fabian Society in January 1884. It was named for the Roman consul Fabius Cunctator, known for his successful temporizing approach in the war against Hannibal. The Fabians sought a gradualist approach to socialism in Britain. Early members included such leading intellectuals as George Bernard Shaw, Beatrice and Sidney Webb, and Graham Wallas. Following the notions of William Morris, the socialist who stressed craftsmanship, Pease left the business world and became a cabinetmaker. In 1890 the society hired Pease as a nominally paid part-time secretary. The following year the position became full-time and was held by Pease until 1913, when he became honorary secretary until 1938. In 1900 he helped form the Labour Representation Committee that became the Labour Party in 1906, serving as the vigilant representative of the increasingly influential Fabian Society for 14 years.

Pease was the author of *The Case for Municipal Drink Trade* (1904) and the official *History of the Fabian Society* (1916; rev. ed., 1925).

peat, organic fuel that varies from a light, spongy material mainly composed of sphagnum moss in the upper layers of bogs to a dense, brown, more humified substance at the bog bottom. Peat is formed chiefly in temperate humid climates by the accumulation and partial decomposition of vegetable remains under conditions of deficient drainage. Vast accumulations occur in Europe, North America, and northern Asia, but they are worked only where coal is deficient.

Peat burns readily with a smoky flame and a characteristic odour. The ash is powdery and light, except in certain varieties that have a high content of sand and other inorganic matter. Peat is used for domestic purposes and forms a fuel suitable for boiler firing in either the briquetted or pulverized form; it also has been used in gas producers, and the coke from carbonized peat forms a suitable fuel for small producers such as are sometimes used for motor-transport purposes. In Ireland millions of tons are consumed annually; the Soviet Union, Sweden, East and West Germany, and Denmark also produce and use considerable quantities, and peat is used locally in England and Scotland.

Peat is usually hand-cut, although progress has been made in the excavation and spreading of peat by mechanical methods. Peat is cut by spade in the form of blocks, which are spread out on the bog to dry (peat in its natural state contains 90 to 95 percent water); when dry, these blocks weigh from three-quarters of a pound to two pounds each. In one method of mechanized winning, a dredger or excavator digs the peat from the drained bog and delivers it to a macerator, which extrudes the peat pulp through a rectangular opening; the pulp is then cut into blocks, which are spread upon the bog surface to dry. Maceration tends to yield more uniform shrinkage and a denser and tougher fuel; it also accelerates drying under unfavourable weather conditions. Hydraulic excavating can also be used, particularly in bogs that contain roots and tree trunks. The peat is washed down by a high-pressure water jet and the pulp run to a sump. There, after slight maceration, it is pumped to a draining ground in a layer about nine inches thick, which after partial drying is cut up and then dried completely.

Peat is the first step in the formation of coal. The humid climate of the Carboniferous Period (about 300,000,000 years ago), which favoured the growth of huge tropical seed ferns and giant nonflowering trees, created the vast swamp areas that comprise the coal beds of today. As the plants died and fell into the boggy waters, which excluded oxygen and killed bacteria, they partially decomposed but did not rot away. The vegetation was changed into peat, some of which was brown and spongy, some black and compact, depending on the degree of decomposition. The sea advanced and withdrew over such deposits, and new sediments were laid down. Under pressure the peat dried and hardened to become low-grade coal, or lignite; further pressure and time created bituminous coal; and even more extreme pressures, anthracite.

·agricultural production and use **1**:351g
·Alberta's soil variations **1**:424d
·coal formation processes **4**:793g
·composition and formation **6**:707f; table
·cyclothem sedimentation and compaction **5**:399h
·ecosystem decomposition limitations **1**:1034d
·Falkland deposit depth **7**:153g
·formation, distribution, and uses **17**:836g *passim* to 839f
·Irish usage and production **9**:881d
·Northern Ireland soil types **13**:238b
·rain forest soil types **10**:341a
·Scotland occurrence and origin **16**:404h
·Upper Carboniferous accumulation **3**:856e

peat moss, also called BOG MOSS, or SPHAGNUM MOSS, any of more than 300 species of plants of the order Sphagnales, comprising the family Sphagnaceae, which contains one genus, *Sphagnum.* The pale-green to deep-red plants, up to 30 centimetres (about 12 inches) tall, form dense clumps in ponds, swamps, and bogs and on lake shores from tropical to subpolar regions. The veinless phyllids (leaves) and caulid (stem) cortex contain many large interconnected storage cells, with external openings through which water enters; the plants can hold up to 20 times their weight in water.

Each spherical brown capsule, or spore case, shrinks as it dries, creating internal pressure that pushes off the lid and ejects the spores as far as 10 centimetres from the plant. The metabolic processes of growing peat moss cause an increase in the acidity of the surrounding water, thus reducing bacterial action and preventing decay. The plants also contain sphagnol, a phenolic compound with antiseptic properties.

Peat moss (*Sphagnum flexuosum*)
K.G. Preston-Mafham—The Natural History Photographic Agency

Peat moss forms several types of bogs in northern areas. Compression and chemical breakdown of dead plants and other vegetable debris cause formation of the organic substance known as peat, which is harvested and dried for use as fuel. Dried peat moss has been used for surgical dressings, diapers, lamp wicks, bedding, and stable litter. It is commonly employed as a packing material by florists and shippers of live aquatic animals, and as a seedbed cover by gardeners who value its ability to increase soil moisture, porosity, and acidity. Peat mosses are valuable in erosion control, and properly drained peat bogs provide useful agricultural land.

Some botanists believe peat mosses constitute a class; others consider them to be an order or a family.

·age of tufa-forming beds **10**:915a
·agricultural production and use **1**:351g
·bog formation properties **17**:837a
·bog in northern Wisconsin, illus., **18**:Terrestrial Ecosystem, Plate 3
·economic value and by-products **3**:352c

peat sampler, device for collecting uncontaminated samples of sediment from various kinds of deposits where fossil pollen and other organic remains are to be studied. Several instruments have been developed to retrieve controlled samples, and, although they are termed peat samplers, they are used to study many kinds of deposits other than peat. In general, peat samplers consist of closed sections of tubing that are forced into a sedimentary deposit to a required depth and then opened and filled. The tube or chamber may be filled either from the bottom or from the side. The Livingstone and the Dachnowsky peat samplers are of the bottom-filling type. They consist of a piston and surrounding jacket that are lowered to the desired depth within the deposit. The piston is retracted and the jacket lowered farther, whereupon the empty jacket is filled with material. Variations on these samplers have been developed; in the Kullenberg sampler, the piston is held stationary and sediment is retrieved by means of a created vacuum. The side-filling method is represented by the Hiller sampler, which is filled by a twisting motion that moves the chamber's outer covering to expose a series of openings in the inner portion. When filled, further turning closes the chamber; when the openings no longer coincide, the core is withdrawn.

Various problems arise in attempting to force the devices into resistant sediments; weights are frequently employed to achieve this. The Mackereth sampler uses hydrostatic and vacuum pressure to drive the sampler. Other developments in corer technology have provided samplers suited to particular tasks. Samplers have been devised to deal with frozen sediments encountered in arctic environments. Preventive measures must be taken to ensure that materials retrieved are not distorted; one preventive method gaining popularity in the 1970s involves the freezing of samples either after retrieval or while the sample is being taken. The handling of cores in transit also requires special techniques.

Peaucellier, Charles-Nicolas (1832–1913), French military officer and engineer who in 1873 invented a linkage, known by his name, capable of describing a circular arc of any radius, including an infinite one; that is, a straight line.

·straight-line mechanism **11**:242b; illus. 241

Peau de chagrin, La (1831), English THE WILD ASS'S SKIN (1949), novel by Balzac.

·philosophical theme and symbolism **2**:681d

pea weevil: *see* seed beetle.

pebble: *see* grade scale.

pebble chopper, or PEBBLE TOOL, primordial cutting tool, the oldest type of tool made by forerunners of modern man. The tool consists of a rounded stone struck a number of blows with a similar stone used as a pounder, which created a serrated crest that served as a chopping blade. The tool could be used as a crude hunting knife, to grub roots, and for other purposes.

·toolmaking technique and tool use **8**:608d; illus.

pebble heater, a heat-transfer device used in industrial processes requiring hot gases.

·aluminum refractory uses **1**:646h

pebble mosaic: *see* mosaic, pebble.

Peć, formerly IPEK, ancient PESCIUM, most populous town in the autonomous region of Kosovo, republic of Serbia, Yugoslavia. Lying on a small tributary of the Beli Drim River, between the North Albanian Alps (Prokletije) and the Mokra Gora (mountains), Peć is the terminus of a rail line from Niš. A majority of its inhabitants are Albanians. The town—which, with its mosques, narrow streets, and old Turkish houses, has an Oriental character—serves as a local market centre for agricultural produce. Industries are leatherworking, food processing, and handicrafts.

Peć was especially important as a religious centre and was from *c.* 1253 to 1766, with brief interruptions, the chief see of the Orthodox Church of Serbia. The patriarchal monastery, repeatedly ravaged and restored, consists of four churches with fine frescoes, library, and treasury. About 12 miles (19 kilometres) south of Peć is Dečani Monastery (1327–35), which has more than 1,000 frescoes and represents one of the finest extant examples of Serbian architecture and ornamentation. Pop. (1971 prelim.) 42,100.
42°40′ N, 20°19′ E

·map, Yugoslavia **19**:1101

Pecalongan (Indonesia): *see* Pekalongan.

pecan (*Carya illinoensis*), nut of the walnut family (Juglandaceae), native to temperate North America. The tree occasionally reaches a height of about 50 metres (160 feet) and a trunk diameter of 2 metres (7 feet). It has a deeply furrowed bark and compound leaves with 9–17 finely toothed leaflets, arranged in feather fashion.

The male flowers form hanging catkins; the female flowers are arranged in tight clusters at the ends of the shoots.

At maturity the fleshy hulls of the short-clustered fruits dry, split along suture lines, and separate into four approximately equal sections, thus gradually freeing the nuts. The nuts have brown, mottled shells, varying greatly in thickness; size varies from 100 to 500 per kilogram (45 to 225 per pound) and shape from long and cylindrical with pointed apex to short and roundish.

One of the finest nuts in flavour and texture,

the pecan has the highest fat content of any vegetable product and a caloric value close to that of butter. Its production is the basis of a considerable industry in the southeastern U.S.

Pecan (*Carya illinoensis*)
Grant Heilman—EB Inc.

Native pecan trees have been found in the U.S., from near the Rio Grande in Texas, in Nebraska, Iowa, Indiana, and occasionally Alabama. Limited cultivation of grafted varieties had begun in Louisiana by 1847; some important varieties were introduced before 1890. Georgia, Alabama, and Mississippi are today the most important producers of grafted pecan nuts. The pecan has been introduced into many countries without becoming important. It is cultivated to a limited extent in Australia and South Africa.
·economic importance and use **10**:329e
·fruit farming economics **7**:758b; tables 755
·Juglandales economic importance **10**:329c

peccary, New World counterpart of the swine, forming the family Tayassuidae (order Artiodactyla). Peccaries are also known as javelins, or javelinas, because of their spear-like upper canines.

Resembling small pigs with small, erect ears and almost no tails, peccaries reach a length of 75–90 centimetres (30–35 inches) and a weight of 15–30 kilograms (33–66 pounds). They are hunted for their hides and meat; although ferocious when molested, they are sometimes tamed by South American Indians.

Peccaries differ from true pigs (family Suidae) in certain skeletal and dental features. They also have a scent gland under the skin that opens on the ridge of the back and gives off a strong, musky odour; this gland is the source of the tale that they have two navels, one above and one below. Peccaries are found from Texas to Patagonia. They feed on a variety of plants, small animals, and carrion. They have a barklike alarm call and when disturbed make a rattling sound by chattering their teeth. Litters usually consist of two young, born after a five-month gestation period.

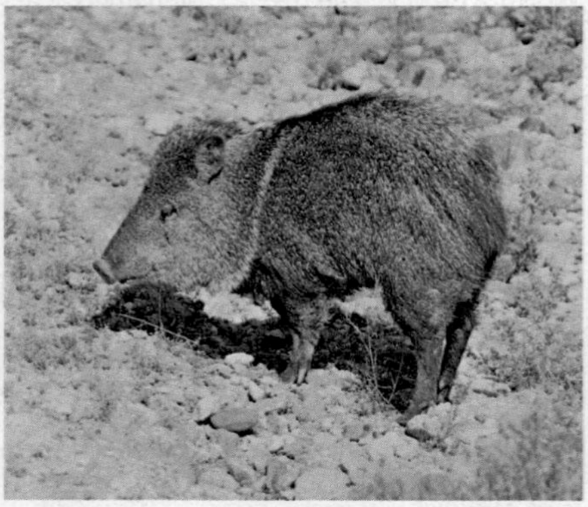

Collared peccary (*Dicotyles tajacu*)
Jen and Des Bartlett—Bruce Coleman Inc.

There are two species. The collared peccary (*Dicotyles*, or *Tayassu tajacu*) is dark gray with a white band across the chest and lives in deserts and forests in bands of about 5 to 25 individuals. The white-lipped peccary (*Tayassu pecari*) is slightly larger and darker, with a white area around the mouth. Found in wet, tropical forests, it lives in herds of 50 to more than 100 individuals.
·traits, behaviour, and classification **2**:70f

Pecci, Vincenzo Gioacchino: *see* Leo XIII, Pope.

Pecheneg, Byzantine PATZINAKOI, Latin BISSENI, Hungarian BESENYO, nomadic Turkic people who occupied the steppes north of the Black Sea (6th–12th century) and by the 10th century were in control of the lands between the Don and lower Danube rivers (after having driven the Hungarians out); thus they had become a serious menace to Byzantium. Originally inhabiting the area between the Rivers Volga and Yaik (Ural), the Pechenegs were attacked by the Khazars and the Oghuz (*c.* 889). They moved westward (especially as the Khazar state declined and could no longer impede the migration), driving the Hungarians into the Carpathian Basin and attacking Russian territory. Kept at bay by the Russians and the Hungarians, the Pechenegs repeatedly invaded Thrace (10th century); they increased the frequency and intensity of their raids (11th century) after Byzantium conquered Bulgaria (1018) and became an immediate neighbour of the Pechenegs. In 1090–91 the Pechenegs advanced to the gates of Constantinople, where Emperor Alexius I with the aid of the Kumans annihilated their army and effectively destroyed Pecheneg power. Important Pecheneg settlements were later established in Hungary, probably after their defeat by Byzantium. The main source on Pecheneg history is the *De administrando imperii* of the Byzantine emperor Constantine VII Prophyrogenitus.
·Alexius I Comnenus' defense against penetration **1**:483d
·invasions of Byzantine territory **3**:564c; map 563

Pechenga, called PETSAMO between 1919 and 1940, town, Murmansk *oblast* (administrative region), northwestern Russian Soviet Federated Socialist Republic, at the head of Pechenga Bay on the Barents Sea coast. Dating from the 16th century, the town was in northern Finland between 1919 and 1940 and was the terminus of the Arctic Highway from the Gulf of Bothnia. It is linked by rail to Murmansk, but its port functions, especially for the adjacent copper- and nickel-mining area, have largely been usurped by its outport of Linakhamari. Latest census 3,500.
69°33′ N, 31°07′ E

Pechera, *rayon* (district), Kiev, Ukrainian Soviet Socialist Republic.
·government organizations and buildings **10**:470e

Pêcheurs de perles, Les, translated THE PEARL FISHERS (1863), opera by George Bizet.
·dramatic and musical weaknesses **2**:1092f

pecheus, measure of length in Greece, equivalent to 0.648 metre.
·weights and measures table 5 **19**:734

Pech-Merle, archaeological site, cave with prehistoric wall paintings located east of Cahors, France.
·Aurignacian cave art description **17**:704f

Pech Morena (India): *see* Morena.

Pechora River, in the Russian Soviet Federated Socialist Republic, is 1,124 mi (1,809 km) in length and drains 124,500 sq mi (322,000 sq km). It rises in the Ural Mountains near Mt. Koyp. At first flowing south in a narrow, deep valley, it swings west and north across an extensive, level basin to enter the Barents Sea by a delta. Freeze-up extends from early November to early May. Navigation is possible as far as Ust-Unya; there is much timber rafting. In its basin are large deposits of coal, petroleum, and natural gas.
68°13′ N, 54°10′ E
·drainage basin and tributaries **18**:1033c
·geographical and climatic features **17**:327b
·map, Soviet Union **17**:322

The Pechora River, Russian S.F.S.R., along its upper course
Syndication International Ltd., London

Pechora Sea, Russian PECHORSKOYE MORE, lies to the north of European Russian Soviet Federated Socialist Republic, between Kolguyev Island to the west and the Yugorsky Peninsula to the east. To the north is Novaya Zemlya. The Pechora Sea is, in effect, a southeastern extension of the Barents Sea. Its average depth is 20 feet (6 m). In the southern part of the sea run the eastward-flowing Kolguyev Current and its extension, the Novaya Zemlya, the flow of which is interrupted by the inflow of the Pechora River. The Pechora Sea is blocked by floating ice from November until June. Cod, seals, and other marine life are exploited. The main port is Naryan-Mar on the Pechora, an important exporter of timber.

Pechstein, Max (b. Dec. 31, 1881, Zwickau, Ger.—d. June 29, 1955, Berlin), painter and printmaker who was a leading member of the group of German Expressionist artists known as Die Brücke (*q.v.*). He is best known for his paintings of nudes and landscapes. In 1906 when he joined Die Brücke, he was

"Indian and Woman," oil painting by Max Pechstein, 1910; in the collection of Morton D. May
By courtesy of Morton D. May

painting such works as "Still Life with Winter Cherries" (1906; Städtische Galerie im Landesmuseum, Hannover, now in West Germany), filled with the bright colours and thick impasto of Impressionism (*q.v.*). But his association with the members of Die Brücke and exposure to the works of the French Fauvist painter Henri Matisse led Pechstein to use jarring colour combinations, achieving a highly emotive effect, as in his "Horse Market at Moritzburg" (1910; Thyssen-Bornemisza Collection, Lugano, Switzerland) and his "Indian and Woman" (1910; Morton D. May Collection, St. Louis, Mo.).

In 1910, Pechstein joined the Neue Sezession (New Secession), an association of artists in Berlin. His works of this period, such as "Nude under the Tent" (1911; Bayerische Staatsgemälde-sammlung, Munich), have simpler compositions and more sombre colours. In 1914, he travelled to Palau in the South Pacific, where he painted exotic subjects in a deliberately primitive manner.

Back in Europe, he designed stained glass and mosaics and took a teaching position at the Berlin Academy. He was forced to resign when the Nazis declared his work "decadent," only to regain the post after World War II. His late work, however, lost much of the vigour of his earlier styles, becoming increasingly concerned with descriptive detail.

peck order (animal behaviour): *see* dominance hierarchy.

Pecock, Reginald (d. *c.* AD 1460), English theologian, a popularizer of rational argument, was known for his anti-Lollard views when he was made bishop of St. Asaph in 1444 and of Chichester in 1450. Charged with heresy in 1457, he died in confinement.

Pecos, city, seat (1883) of Reeves County, southwestern Texas, U.S., in the Pecos River Valley. It began in the 1880s as a station on the Texas and Pacific Railway and as a cow town at the intersection of old cattle and wagon trails. It developed as a livestock distribution and service centre and is credited with holding the first Texas rodeo in 1883 (now held annually each July).

In the 1940s commercial activities became more diversified when underground water was pumped for irrigation and oil and natural gas were tapped. Farming (especially cotton, cantaloupes, and vegetables), cattle ranching, oil and gas production (with more than 1,500 wells within a 50 mi [80 km] radius), and tourism are now major economic factors. Large automotive (tire) proving grounds are nearby. Inc. 1903. Pop. (1980) 12,855.
31°25′ N, 103°30′ W
·map, United States **18**:908

Pecos River, in the southwestern United States, rises in Mora County, north central New Mexico, in the Sangre de Cristo Mountains, and flows about 926 mi (1,490 km) through eastern New Mexico and west Texas, draining about 38,300 sq mi (99,200 sq km) before emptying into the Rio Grande. After leaving the mountains, the Pecos flows over desert-like land, and the stream channel is dry much of the year. Near Roswell the river widens into a basin, which closes somewhat to a broad, shallow valley at the Texas–New Mexico border. In the last 125 mi of its course, the river has cut a narrow canyon over 1,000 ft (300 m) deep. Dams controlling the river's flow and providing water for irrigation include Alamogordo Dam (1937); Avalon Dam (1907); McMillan Dam (1908); part of the Carlsbad Reclamation Project; and Red Bluff Dam (1936). Pecos tributaries include the Hondo, Gallinas, Felix, and Black rivers, all in New Mexico. Santa Rosa, Fort Sumner, Roswell, and Carlsbad, N.M., and Pecos, Tex., are important towns on or near the river. The river's name is a Spanish adaptation of an Indian word; its meaning is uncertain.
29°42′ N, 101°22′ W
·map, United States **18**:908
·New Mexico physical environment **13**:3f

Pécs, German FÜNFKIRCHEN or medieval Latin QUINQUE ECCLESINE ("five churches"), capital of Baranya *megye* (county), southwestern Hungary, lies at the southern foot of the wooded Mecsek Mountains, 135 mi (220 km) south-southwest of Budapest. It is one of the five city-county administrative units in Hungary. The site was occupied by the Roman town of Sopianae, which succeeded an Illyrian and Celtic settlement. In 1009 Stephen I, the first king of Hungary, made it a bishopric. The name Pécs appears in the late 11th century. The town has a large main square with a well-preserved mosque, which is now a Catholic church. The cathedral (founded in 1009 on the site of an old Roman church), was extensively renovated in the 1960s.

Cathedral at Pécs, Hung.
Salmer—Plessner International

Pécs is an old established trade and handicrafts town, and during the 14th and 15th centuries, it was also a great humanist centre. Many relics survive from the Turkish occupation (1543–1686). The earliest university in Hungary, founded in 1367 by Louis I, was abolished by the Turks. Reopened in 1922, it has a specialist faculty in medicine and law. In the 18th century, German immigrant miners came to work the local coal seams, and there remains one of the few German minorities in Hungary. In 1780 the city received its free royal charter. The Pécs–Komló coalfield, which supplies coking coal to Dunaújváros, formed the basis for a rapid development in the 19th and 20th centuries.

Industries include engineering, furniture, tobacco, china, brewing, and leatherworking. An oil refinery is supplied by pipeline from the Soviet Union to augment its Hungarian oil consumption. The local ceramic ware (majolica) factory is one of the best known features in Pécs. In the vicinity are extensive vineyards. The town has good road and rail connections with Dunaújváros, Budapest, and other cities. The marked rise in population in the 20th century was the result of the influx of Hungarian peasants from the countryside. Pop. (1920) 58,808; (1970 prelim.) 145,307.
46°05′ N, 18°13′ E
·area and population table **9**:25
·map, Hungary **9**:22

pectin, concentrated extract of a group of substances found in cell walls and intercellular tissues of certain plants that is capable of forming thick solutions; its chief use is in preparation of jellies, jams, and marmalade; its thickening properties also make it useful in the confectionery, pharmaceutical, and textile industries.

Pectic substances consist of an associated group of polysaccharides extractable with aqueous solutions of dilute acids. The chief sources are citrus waste and apple pomace (residue from cider presses). Very small amounts of pectin suffice in the presence of fruit acids and sugar to form a jelly.
·candy production use in jelly-making **4**:1083g
·digestion and intestinal flora **5**:779f
·Dipsacales biochemical substances **5**:817c
·food preservation technology **7**:494d
·production and commercial utilization **3**:831a
·wood structural components **19**:918g

Pectinidae: *see* scallop.

Pectinophora gossypiella, also known as PINK BOLLWORM, one of the insect species that attack cotton.
·cotton insect damage and control **7**:273f

pectoralis muscles, muscles that connect the ventral (front) walls of the chest with the bones of the upper arm and shoulder. There are two in man: pectoralis major and pectoralis minor.

The pectoralis major, the larger and more superficial, originates at the clavicle (collarbone), sternum (breastbone), the ribs, and a tendinous extension of the external oblique abdominal muscle. The pectoralis major extends across the upper part of the chest and is attached to a ridge at the rear of the humerus, the bone of the upper arm. Its major actions are adduction, or depression, of the arm (in opposition to the deltoideus muscle), and rotation of the arm forward about the axis of the body. When the raised arms are fixed (as in mountaineering), it assists the latissimus dorsi and teres major muscles in pulling the trunk up.

The pectoralis minor lies, for the most part, beneath the pectoralis major, arising from the middle ribs and inserted into (attached to) the scapula (shoulder blade). It aids in drawing the shoulder forward and downward (in opposition to the trapezius muscle).
·bird muscle specialization and wing movement **2**:1057h
·evolved anatomic modifications **12**:637a

pectus excavatum, a chest deformity caused by depression of the breastbone, or sternum. Pectus excavatum is generally not noticeable at birth, but becomes more evident with age unless surgically corrected.

In most instances the abnormality is due to a shortened central tendon of the diaphragm, the muscular partition between the chest and the abdominal cavity. In other instances it is thought to result from displacement of the heart to the left of mid-chest, or excessive pulling downward by the diaphragm. Corrective surgery is best performed in early childhood or infancy.

The heart and lungs are most affected by pectus excavatum. The heart is displaced to the left, there is more pressure on the heart, and the respiratory movements of the lungs are impaired. The effects include breathlessness upon exertion, pain around the heart, dizziness, and irregular heart beats. The deformity may also have a bad psychological effect.

Pedagogical Sketchbook, German PÄDAGOGISCHES SKIZZENBUCH (1925), influential treatise on the principles of the visual arts written by the Swiss artist Paul Klee, while Klee was an instructor at the Bauhaus (*q.v.*).
·Klee's teaching method at Bauhaus **10**:493h

pedagogy 13:1098, the science of teaching, involving the study of human learning processes and the application of learning principles to the development of educational goals and curricula and to teaching situations.

The text article covers the various components of teaching and schooling, the major theories of learning, the major theories of educational organization, and the characteristics of instructional media.

REFERENCES in other text articles:
·Agassiz's science methodology **1**:290f
·animation's educational usage **12**:551g
·Bernard de Chartes' medieval lesson plan **6**:336e
·classical Hindu education methods **6**:319e

·Comenius' general theory and language method reform **4**:968b
·Confucius' emphasis on the whole man **4**:1108h
·doctrine's religion development role **5**:927f
·education television applications **18**:122c
·elementary and secondary teaching **6**:697e
·Greek and Roman educational method **6**:322g
·higher education curricula **8**:863g
·instructional adaptation in education of exceptional **6**:433b
·language teachability **10**:654h
·Latin America Lancasterin system adoption **6**:401e
·learning theory and differing educational conceptions **6**:409e
·legal education and teaching methods **10**:773h
·Mann's public school reform program **11**:455d
·medical education and training **11**:810f
·medieval monastic discipline **6**:334d
·Muslim halqah methodology **6**:332e
·19th-century changes and reformers **6**:359d
·Pestalozzi teaching method development **14**:138b
·Pope Sylvester II's innovations **17**:899h
·preschool education development and comparison **14**:990e
·primitive and ancient Eastern educational methods **6**:317g
·radio educational use **15**:432f
·religious techniques and goals **15**:642a
·Renaissance humanistic education **15**:664b
·Renaissance humanistic variations and Reformation modifications **6**:343f
·Rousseau's contract theory **15**:1170e
·sensorimotor skill instruction **16**:544f
·17th–18th-century development **6**:349d
·Shintō accommodations in 6th century **16**:672d
·teacher training development and present organization **18**:4f
·20th-century theories and method development **6**:373c
·U.S. classroom use of dictionaries **5**:716e
·use of mass communication methods **6**:430d
·U.S. progressive methods test **6**:382a
·zoo as information source **19**:1161e

RELATED ENTRIES in the *Ready Reference and Index*:
audio visual education; discovery method; foreign languages, teaching of; Initial Teaching Alphabet; Montessori system; programmed learning; reading; teaching methods

pedalboard, organ mechanism, operated by the organists' feet, controlling the longer pipes.
·organ construction and mechanisms **13**:676f

pedal curve, in mathematics, the locus C_1 of the feet of the perpendiculars dropped from a fixed point O to the tangents of a given curve C is said to be the pedal curve of C for—or with respect to—the point O.
·analytic geometry fundamentals **7**:1092h

pedalfer, soil enriched in iron and aluminum. The name is derived from Greek *pedon*, "earth," and from the first letters of the word aluminum and the Latin word for iron: *ferrum*. Pedalfers form in humid areas, typically in forests.

pedal harp, harp in which pedals control a mechanism raising the pitch of given strings by a semitone (single action) or by both a semitone and a whole tone (double action).

The modern double-action pedal harp, the standard orchestral harp, covers six and a half octaves (three below and three and a half above middle C). Along the neck, or harmonic curve, are two sets of rotating brass disks; concealed inside the forepillar and in the deep metal plates running along both sides of the neck is a mechanism operated by seven pedals, one for each group of strings of a given pitch name. Depression of the pedal to the first notch shortens the appropriate strings by a semitone, to the second notch, by a whole tone. The shortening is effected by the rotating disks, which grip the string at the proper point. The harp is normally tuned diatonically (to a seven-note octave) in $C^\flat$ (flat); depressing all pedals to the first notch puts it into C, to the second notch, into $C^\sharp$ (sharp). Playing the pedal harp demands skilled coordination between the hands, which pluck the strings with the fleshy part of the finger tips, and the feet, which, with the pedals, select the necessary pitch changes for the strings.

Pedal harps arose in the 18th century in response to changing musical styles demanding a full chromatic (12-note) octave. In the 17th century small hooks were placed on the harp neck near each string; when turned, a hook shortened the string by a semitone. Besides interrupting the harpists's playing, however, the hooks pulled the strings out of plane and sometimes out of tune. In 1720 Celestin Hochbrucker, a Bavarian, attached the hooks to a series of levers in the forepillar (which thenceforth became hollow), controlled by seven pedals.

Around 1750 the Parisian harp maker Georges Cousineau replaced the hooks by metal plates that gripped the strings while leaving them in plane. Cousineau also expanded the chromatic capability of the harp by building instruments with 14 pedals; although unwieldy, the second seven raised the strings an additional semitone. In 1792 the Parisian maker Sébastian Érard substituted a rotating disk for the metal plates. In 1810 he produced a double action by adding a second set of disks controlled by the same pedals, thus virtually establishing the modern harp capable of playing in all major and minor keys.

Pedaliaceae, family of flowering plants of the order Scrophulariales.
·general features and classification **16**:417b

pedal point, or PEDAL TONE, in music, sustained note, ordinarily in the bass, over which changing harmonies are played. The term may derive from the low tones sustained by organ pedals, although a pedal point can occur in the middle voices or soprano. Pedal points are usually important notes in a key (normally the tonic and dominant; in the key of C, C and G) and they create tension as other harmonies are heard against them. Fugue No. 2 in J.S. Bach's *Well-Tempered Clavier*, Book I, ends with a pedal point on the tonic. In the sonata-allegro form used in symphonies and sonatas, pedal points on the dominant often appear in the retransition (the passage preceeding the recapitulation of the principal themes in the tonic key). This persistent dominant tone leads the listener to anticipate the eventual return to the tonic. An example occurs in the first movement of Mozart's *Symphony No. 41 in C Major (Jupiter)*.

Pedal points are special instances of the use of drone (*q.v.*) and are occasionally called bourdons.

Peddler's War (Brazil): *see* Mascates, War of the.

Pedernales, capital, Pedernales province, southwestern Dominican Republic, on the Caribbean coast just across from Anse-à-Pitre, Haiti. Founded in 1915, the town was named capital when Pedernales province was created in 1958. In addition to its administrative functions, it serves as a commercial centre for the surrounding agricultural region, which yields principally sugarcane, coffee, corn (maize), and tubers. It is accessible by secondary highway from Jimaní and Barahona. Pop. (1970 prelim.) 5,919.
18°02′ N, 71°44′ W
·map, Dominican Republic **5**:944
·province area and population table **5**:945

Pedersen, Christiern (*c.* 1480–1554), Danish Humanist, among the first to rediscover Denmark's national literary and historical heritage and to encourage the development of a vernacular style.
·literature of the Renaissance **10**:1144g

Pedersen, Holger (b. April 7, 1867, Gelballe, Den.—d. Oct. 25, 1953, Copenhagen), linguist of exceptional accomplishment in a number of fields, especially in Celtic grammar. After receiving his doctorate in 1897 with a masterly dissertation, *Aspirationen i Irsk* ("Aspiration in Irish"), he proceeded, as professor at the University of Copenhagen, to enrich language science with an enormous number of books and articles of high originality.

Trained in the exacting methodology of the Neogrammarian school of linguistics, he went far beyond its limits to become a participant in, or a critic of, most succeeding schools of linguistic thought, and he also anticipated some new trends. His Celtic researches appeared in many papers, in his monumental

Holger Pedersen
By courtesy of Det Kongelige Bibliotek, Copenhagen

Vergleichende Grammatik der keltischen Sprachen (2 vol., 1909–13; "Comparative Grammar of the Celtic Languages") and the *Concise Comparative Celtic Grammar* (1937), done in collaboration with H. Lewis. About 30 books in Danish, English, French, and German offer authoritative treatments of Albanian, Armenian, Russian, and Indo-European dialects; Lithuanian, Hittite, Tocharian, Czech, and Turkish phonology; the relationship of Indo-European to the Semitic and Finno-Ugric languages; and the origin of runes. A work on the history of linguistic science was reissued under a new title, *The Discovery of Language*, in 1962.
·Lycian affiliation with Hittite **1**:833f

Pedersen, Johannes Peder Ejler (b. Nov. 7, 1883, Illebolle, Den.—d. Sept. 7, 1951), Old Testament scholar and Semitic philologist, important for his conception of Israelite culture and modes of thought based on religio-historical and sociological studies. He matriculated at the University of Copenhagen in 1902 as a student of divinity. The Old Testament in particular aroused his interest, and he studied Semitic languages under Frants Buhl. A graduate in divinity (1908), he went abroad for three years, studying under Heinrich Zimmern, August Fischer, Christiaan Snouck Hurgronje, and Ignaz Goldziher. He was appointed docent in Old Testament exegesis at Copenhagen (1916–22) and then professor of Semitic philology (1922–50) in succession to Buhl. His doctoral thesis (1912) showed him to be an eminent philologist with an exceptional ability to enter into the spirit of the ancient Oriental trains of thought. These qualities are even more pronounced in his chief work, *Israel: Its Life and Culture*, in four volumes (1920–34; Eng. trans. 1926–40). These studies of ancient Israel marked a new departure in Scandinavian Old Testament research. Pedersen's conception of the importance of the cult led in many aspects to a break with Julius Wellhausen and his school, especially in his estimation of the narratives and the laws in the Pentateuch as sources for the history of Israel.

pedestal, in classical architecture, support or base for a column, statue, vase, or obelisk (*q.v.*). The name is also given to the vertical members that divide the sections of a balustrade. A single pedestal may also support a group of columns, or colonnade. A pedestal is divided into three parts: from bottom to top

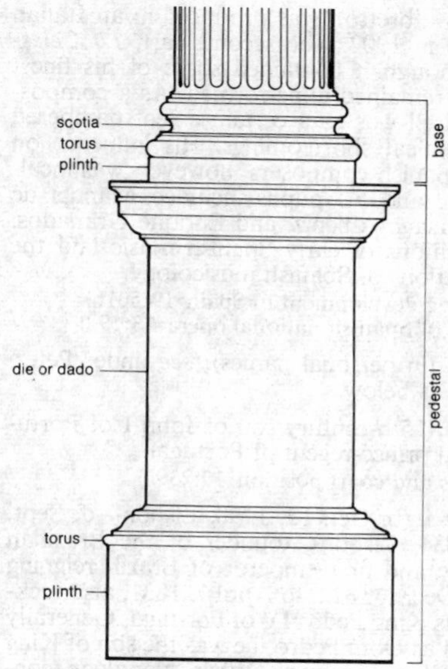

Corinthian order pedestal

From John Fleming, Hugh Honour, Nikolaus Pevsner, *The Penguin Dictionary of Architecture*. Copyright © John Flemming, Hugh Honour, Nikolaus Pevsner, 1966, 1972; Penguin Books Ltd.

the plinth (or foot), the die (or dado), and the cornice (cap, cap mold, or surbase).

Square, octagonal, or circular, the pedestal was first employed by the architects of ancient Rome to make a single column look more imposing; it was also featured in triumphal arches. In Renaissance Italy, architectural theorists decreed that the pedestal was an integral part of the order (classical stylistic unit; *see* orders of architecture) of the column and entablature and inseparable from it. At the same time, specific rules were established concerning the proportional height of pedestal to column: the higher the column is, the higher the pedestal must be. Renaissance columns, when extended horizontally, sometimes formed the sill of a window.

·construction and disadvantage **7**:789d

pedestal rock: *see* perched rock.

Pedetes (rodent): *see* springhare.

Pediaíos River (Cyprus): *see* Pedieas River.

Pediastrum, a genus of disk-shaped colonial green algae with peripheral hornlike projections, comprising part of the freshwater plankton. The number of cells per colony varies (2–128) depending on the species.

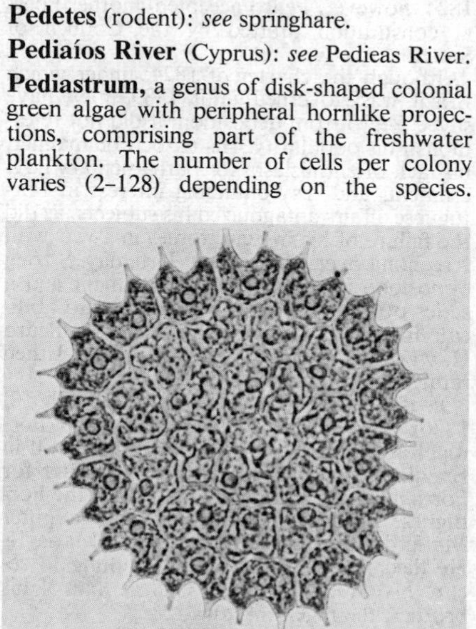

Pediastrum (highly magnified)
Winton Patnode—Photo Researchers

Young cells are uninucleate, whereas mature cells may have up to eight nuclei. During asexual reproduction the cell contents divide and form motile spores that arrange themselves into colonies before being liberated. Sexual reproduction is by gametes.

pediatrics, medical specialty concerned with the care of children and treatment of their diseases. Board requirements, examinations for specialization and practice, and residencies vary from country to country.

·childhood disease diagnosis **4**:218d
·medical and surgical practices **11**:842b

pedicab, three-wheeled bicycle with a hooded carriage body balanced on two of the wheels. The body may be placed in front or in back of the driver. Pedicabs are the successors to rickshas (*q.v.*) and are used in China, Japan, Vietnam, and other Asiatic countries. A specialized pedicab is the pedicab school bus.

Pedicab
UPI—Compix

pedicel, term used to refer to a short, stalklike structure, such as a segment of an insect's antenna, an abdominal segment of an ant, or the supporting stalk of a flower, leaf, or fruit.

animal
·Araneida body structure **1**:1070d; illus.
·orchid special characteristics **13**:649g
plant
·fruit types and structure, illus. 3 **16**:482
·hymenopteran egg laying **9**:130g

pedicellariae, minute stalked or unstalked pincherlike organ on the body surface of various inverterates of the phylum Echinodermata.

·echinoderm adaptations for defense **6**:182e

Pedicellina, a genus of the phylum Entoprocta—tiny aquatic invertebrates permanently attached to some object. *Pedicellina* often grows in tidal pools on seaweed. It lives in colonies, the individuals (zooids) interconnected by a flexible supporting stalk to an attachment structure (stolon). The zooids attain heights of 2–5 millimetres (about .08–0.2 inch).

·colony structure and reproduction **6**:895a; illus.

pedicle, brachiopod, an extension of the ventral body wall which holds brachiopods to the sea bottom.

·characteristics of brachiopods **7**:563d

pedicle graft, in medicine, a graft that includes the full thickness of the skin and the subcutaneous tissue attached by a pedicle, or narrow strip of tissue.

·plastic surgery techniques **17**:821f

Pedicularis (plant genus): *see* lousewort.

Pediculidae, family of human infesting lice of the insect order Phthiraptera.

·classification and distribution **14**:376b

Pediculoides ventricosus, species of mite (class Arachnida) that normally feeds on insects in stored grain but may attack human skin, causing groin itch.

·predator–prey interactions **14**:825e

pediculosis: *see* insect bite and sting.

Pediculus humanus: *see* human louse.

Pedieas (PEDIEOS) **River,** Greek PEDIAÍOS, Turkish PEDIYAS, in central and eastern Cyprus, rises in the Troödos range and flows in a northeasterly direction toward Nicosia, where it takes an easterly turn through the part of the central lowlands called the Mesaöria Plain toward Famagusta Bay. Although the longest (about 60 mi [100 km]) in Cyprus, the river is not navigable. Formerly emptying into the bay near the ancient city of Salamis, it now drains into the irrigation reservoirs near Akhyritou and Kouklia, west of Famagusta.
35°09′ N, 33°45′ E

pedigree, a record of ancestry or purity of breed. Studbooks (listings of pedigrees for horses, dogs, etc.) and herdbooks (records for cattle, swine, sheep, etc.) are maintained by governmental or private record associations or breed organizations in many countries.

In human genetics, pedigree diagrams are utilized to trace the inheritance of a specific trait, abnormality, or disease. A male is represented by a square or the symbol ♂, a female by a circle or the symbol ♀. Mating is shown by a horizontal line (marriage line) connecting a male symbol and a female symbol; offspring symbols are connected in a row (sibship line) beneath the mated pair. The offspring symbols appear from left to right in the order of birth and are connected to the marriage line by a vertical line. Possession of the character under study is shown by a solid or blackened symbol, and absence is shown by an open or clear symbol. Multiple births are designated by joining the individual symbols to the same point on the sibship line. Siblings not shown as individual symbols are indicated by a number within a large symbol for each sex.

·animal breeding assessment and use **1**:904e
·animal breeding for pet ownership **14**:151f
·chromosomal abnormality determination **5**:848g
·construction by inbreeding **5**:32b
·human genetics analyses **7**:998g; illus.
·plant breeding and hybrid populations **14**:498d
·stud books in horse racing **8**:1094e

Pedilanthus tithymaloides: *see* redbird cactus.

pediment, in architecture, triangular gable crowning a portice (area, with a roof supported by columns, leading to the entrance of a building) or a similar form used decoratively over a doorway or window. The pediment was

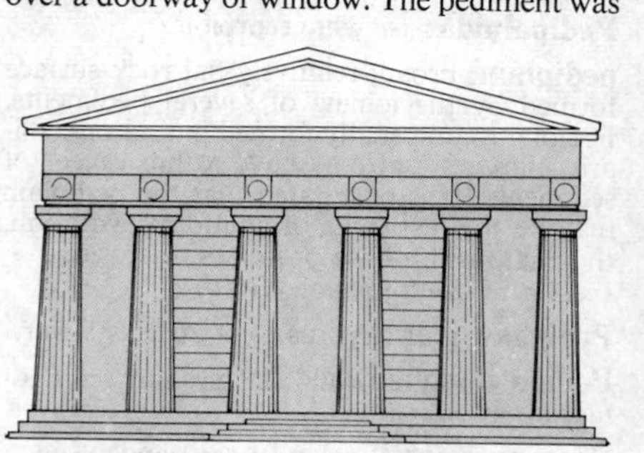

Greek temple pediment

the crowning feature of the Greek temple front. The triangular wall surface of the pediment, called the tympanum, rested on an entablature (*q.v.*), a composite band of horizontal moldings (*q.v.*) carried over the columns (*see* orders of architecture). The tympanum was often decorated with sculpture, as in the Parthenon (Athens, 447–432 BC), and was always crowned by a raking, or slanted, cornice. The Romans adapted the pediment as a purely decorative form to finish doors, windows, and especially niches (*q.v.*). Their pediments frequently appeared in a series consisting of alternating triangular and segmentally curved shapes, a motif revived by High Renaissance Italian designers; particularly fine examples are the window pediments of the piano nobile (*q.v.*; floor above the ground floor) of the Palazzo Farnese (Rome, begun in 1517), built by Antonio da Sangallo the Younger.

Following a late Roman precedent, in which the line of the raking cornice is broken before it reaches the apex, the designers of the Baroque period developed many varieties of fantastic broken, scrolled, and reverse-curved pediments, an example of which can be seen on the church of S. Andrea al Quirinale (Rome, 1658–70) by Gian Lorenzo Bernini.

In some cases the designers even reversed the direction of the form so that the high points of a broken pediment faced toward the outside of the composition rather than toward the centre; and in the extravagant Churrigueresque (*q.v.*), or late Renaissance, architecture of Spain, small sections of pediment were used as decorative motifs.

·Greek architecture and relief **19**:290d

pediments 13:1103, in geology, relatively flat surfaces of bedrock (exposed or veneered with alluvial soil or gravel) that occur at the bases of mountains or as plains having no associated mountains. Pediments, sometimes mistaken for groups of merged alluvial fans, are most conspicuous in basin-and-range-type desert areas throughout the world.

The text article covers the physical characteristics of pediments, their occurrence and distribution, and the several theories of origin.

REFERENCE in other text article:

·form and origin **5**:612d

RELATED ENTRIES in the *Ready Reference and Index*:

pediplain; rock fan; tor

Pedioecetes phasianellus (bird): *see* grouse.

pedion (crystallography): *see* form, crystal.

Pedionomus torquatus (bird): *see* plain wanderer.

pedipalp, one of the second pair of arachnid appendages, located on each side of the mouth and usually modified for seizing, crushing, or sensory functions.

·arachnid body structure and touch sense **1**:1061d

·Araneida copulation mechanisms **1**:1067e

·scorpion anatomy and use **16**:401h; illus.

·spider external anatomy, illus. 2 **1**:1070

Pedipalpida: *see* whip scorpion.

pediplain, broad, relatively flat rock surface formed by the joining of several pediments. Pediplains are usually formed in arid or semiarid climates and may have a thin veneer of sediments. It is postulated that the pediplain may be the last stage of landform evolution, the final result of the processes of erosion.

·pediment-like formation **13**:1105d

Pediyas River (Cyprus): *see* Pedieas River.

Pedma Jungne (Buddhist mystic): *see* Padmasambhava.

Pedn-an-Laaz (England): *see* Land's End.

pedocal, soil rich in calcium carbonate; the name is from Greek *pedon*, "earth," and Latin *calc-*, "lime." Pedocals form in arid or semiarid regions, accumulate because low rainfall permits the concentration of calcium carbonates, and are typical of areas covered by prairie vegetation.

·features and associated climate **13**:895f

pedodontics, dental specialty that deals with the care of children's teeth; *i.e.*, it is the dental counterpart of pediatrics in medical practice. The pedodontist is deeply concerned with prevention, which includes instruction in proper diet, use of fluoride, and practice of oral hygiene. The pedodontist's routine practice is concerned basically with caries (tooth decay) but includes influencing tooth alignment. Lengthy treatment may be required to correct incipient abnormalities in tooth position. Braces or other correctional devices may be used. The pedodontist needs patience and a basic knowledge of children's behavioural patterns, and a knowledge of the effects on the mouth of physical and mental diseases. A two-year postgraduate course leads to a diploma in pedodontics.

·distinctive features of practice **5**:596a

pedogenesis, formation of soil.

·loess formation processes **11**:27c

pedology, scientific discipline that is concerned with all aspects of soils, including their physical and chemical properties, the role of organisms in soil production and in relation to soil character, the description and mapping of soil units, and the origin and formation of soils. Accordingly, pedology embraces several subdisciplines that confine their focus to parts of these concerns, namely, soil chemistry, soil physics, and soil microbiology. Each of the latter employs a sophisticated array of methods and laboratory equipment not unlike that used in studies of the physics, chemistry, or microbiology of nonsoils systems. Sampling, description, and mapping of soils is considerably simpler, however. A soil auger is used to obtain core samples in places where no subsurface exposure can be found, and the soil units are defined, delineated, and mapped from the samples in a manner similar to procedures in stratigraphy. Such soils studies, in fact, overlap the concerns of the stratigrapher and Pleistocene geologist, both of whom may treat the soils layers as strata of the Pleistocene or Holocene epochs, which encompass the past 2,500,000 years of Earth history.

·geological discipline applications **7**:1063c

·soil properties and building consideration **16**:1011d

·study basis and specialist assistance **7**:1051d

pedophilia, an adult's preference or addiction for sexual relations with children. In almost all legal jurisdictions, sexual acts committed by an adult with a minor are deemed criminal.

·behaviour patterns and causes **16**:606h

Pedralbes, mountain, Spain.
42°58′ N, 2°49′ W

·medieval monastery location **2**:720f

Pedrarias Dávila: *see* Arias Dávilla, Pedro.

Pedrell, Felipe (b. Feb. 19, 1841, Tortosa, Spain—d. Aug. 19, 1922, Barcelona), composer and musical scholar who devoted his life to the development of a Spanish school of music founded on national folk songs and a great musical heritage from the past. When he was a choirboy, his imagination was first fired by contact with early Spanish church music. Though largely self-taught he composed several operas, mostly on national subjects. The first, *El último Abencerraje*, founded on a text by Chateaubriand, was produced in an Italian version in Barcelona in 1874. In 1891 he published his manifesto *Por nuestra música*, which attracted much attention; misunderstood as favouring Wagnerian reforms, it advocated a Spanish opera with musical roots in the Spanish folksong. He published an invaluable four-volume collection of folk songs, the *Cancionero musical popular español*. In his eight-volume *Hispaniae schola musica sacra* he edited, for the first time, a vast quantity of early Spanish church, stage, and organ music, including the keyboard works of Antonio de Cabezón and the complete works of Tomás Luis de Victoria. At the same time he was working on an operatic trilogy, the first part of which, *Los Pirineos* ("The Pyrenees"; to a Catalan libretto), was produced in an Italian version in 1902. The second part, *La Celestina*, though it contained some of his finest music, remained unperformed. As a composer, Pedrell was to a certain extent hampered by technical shortcomings. His influence on later Spanish composers, however, was incalculable, and his pupils included Manuel de Falla, Isaac Albéniz, and Enrique Granados. His editions of early Spanish music laid the foundations of Spanish musicology.

·art song development in Spain **19**:501h

·origin of Spanish national opera **13**:592f

Pedro (in personal names): *see* under Peter, except as below.

Pedro, 15th-century son of John I of Portugal and prince-regent of Portugal.

·travels and court position **10**:239h

Pedro I (b. Oct. 12, 1798, Lisbon—d. Sept. 24, 1834, Lisbon), founder of the Brazilian Empire and first emperor of Brazil, reigning from Dec. 1, 1822, to April 7, 1831, also reckoned as King Pedro IV of Portugal. Generally known as Dom Pedro, he was the son of King John VI of Portugal. When Napoleon conquered Portugal in 1807, Pedro accompanied the royal family in its flight to Brazil. He remained there as regent when King John returned to Portugal in 1821.

It is said that John advised Pedro to assume leadership of the Brazilian independence movement, if necessary, so that Brazil and Portugal might at least remain united under the Bragança dynasty. Pedro surrounded himself with ministers who counselled independence. When the Portuguese Cortês (Parliament), preferring colonial status for Brazil, demanded that Pedro return to Lisbon to "complete his political education," he issued a declaration of Brazilian independence (the *grito do Ipiranga*) on Sept. 7, 1822. Within three months he was crowned emperor.

Pedro's initial popularity waned because of widespread resentment of the influence of the Portuguese nobility at his court. In 1823, when the Brazilian Assembly was preparing a liberal constitution, the Emperor dissolved that body and exiled the radical leader José Bonifácio de Andrada e Silva. On March 25, 1824, however, Pedro accepted another liberal constitution drafted by the Council of State.

Although the charter of 1824, under which Brazil was governed until 1889, may have saved Pedro from deposition, it did not re-establish his popularity. His autocratic manner, his lack of enthusiasm for parliamentary government, and his continuing interest in Portuguese affairs antagonized his subjects, as did the failure of his military forces in a war with Argentina over what is now Uruguay. Strong opposition in the Brazilian Parliament and a series of local uprisings induced him to abdicate in 1831 in favour of his son Dom Pedro II, who was then five years old. Pedro I then returned to Portugal.

On the death of King John VI (March 10, 1826), Pedro I had become titular king of Portugal as Pedro IV. Two months later, still in Brazil, he issued a parliamentary charter for Portugal and conditionally abdicated the Portuguese throne in favour of his daughter Maria da Glória, the future Queen Maria II. He died in Portugal while attempting to secure his daughter's claim against that of his brother, the regent Miguel.

·Brazilian independence role **10**:705b

·Brazilian reign and accomplishments **3**:145b

·independence proclamation in São Paulo **16**:238c

·Portugal and Brazil in War of Two Brothers **14**:871b

Pedro I (1320–67), king of Portugal, reigned 1357–67.

·nobility revolt and dynastic war **17**:411b

Pedro II, formerly DOM PEDRO DE ALCÂNTARA (1825–91), second and last emperor of Brazil, ruled from 1840 to 1889.

·Amazon steamship line authorization **1**:652c
·political and social importance **3**:145e

Pedro II (b. April 26, 1648, Lisbon—d. Dec. 9, 1706, Lisbon), king of Portugal whose reign as prince regent (1668–83) and as king (1683–1706) was marked by the consolidation of royal absolutism and the reduction of the significance of the Cortes (National Assembly); at the same time he encouraged economic development and guided his nation through a troubled period in Europe.

After the death of his father, John IV, in 1656, Pedro's feebleminded and profligate elder brother Afonso VI brought Portugal to a very low condition. In November 1667 Afonso was sent into confinement in the Azores, and Pedro became regent. Shortly thereafter, his brother's marriage (1666) to Marie Françoise Elisabeth of Savoy-Nemours was annulled, and Pedro married her. He quickly made peace with Spain (Feb. 13, 1668), forgoing advantages that might have been expected from the Portuguese victories of 1663–65. When Afonso died on Sept. 12, 1683, Pedro became king.

In the last years of the 17th century, the goldfields of Brazil provided Pedro with great wealth and enabled him to govern without seeking revenue from the Cortes, which was not convoked after 1697. To stimulate Portuguese industry and commerce, Pedro concluded the Methuen Treaty (1703) with England, which agreed to reduce customs duties on Portuguese wines in return for favourable treatment of English woollen goods. The treaty largely resulted from Pedro's having finally adhered (May 1703) to the Anglo-Austrian side in the War of the Spanish Succession, though at first he had allied himself with France. Pedro died in the midst of the war, leaving his throne to John V, his son by his second wife, Maria Sophia of Palatinate-Neuburg, whom he had married in 1687, four years after the death of his first wife.

·Portuguese wealth in Brazilian mines **14**:870a

Pedro IV (1798–1834): *see* Pedro I.

Pedro V (b. Sept. 16, 1837, Lisbon—d. Nov. 11, 1861, Lisbon), king of Portugal who conscientiously and intelligently devoted himself to the problems of his country and whose short reign (1853–61) was characterized by advances in transportation and communication and his efforts to promote higher education and play an active role in external affairs.

Pedro succeeded his mother, Maria II, on Nov. 15, 1853; and while his father, Ferdinand of Saxe-Coburg-Gotha, acted as regent for two years, Pedro travelled (1854–55) to the more industrialized European nations. On his return to Portugal and assumption of full power, he was faced with successive, prolonged epidemics of cholera and yellow fever; and he worked assiduously to organize relief efforts. In the spring of 1858 he married Stephanie of Hohenzollern-Sigmaringen, but she died shortly after her arrival in Portugal.

During Pedro's reign Portugal achieved its first railway and its first telegraph line, both in 1856. Plans were also made for Atlantic cable services. The young king in 1859 founded the Curso Superior de Letras for teaching literature, philosophy, and history at the university level.

In foreign affairs Pedro succeeded in concluding the convention (1857) that temporarily reconciled the conflict between the papacy and the Portuguese national church over ecclesiastical jurisdiction in India and the Far East, and he concerned himself with the abolition of slavery in Portuguese possessions (1858). In October 1861 he fell ill with typhoid fever and died childless the following month. He was succeeded by his younger brother Luís, who became Luís I.

·Portuguese monarchical history **14**:871g

Pedro, often called PEDRO THE CONSTABLE (1429–66), constable of Portugal, son of Pedro, duque de Coimbra; he was a poet and from 1465 king of Aragon.

·literature of the Renaissance **10**:1137d

Pedro, duque de Coimbra (1392–1449), son of King John I of Portugal and younger brother of King Edward (Duarte), served as regent of Portugal from 1440, during the minority of Edward's son Afonso V. Forced out of office by the powerful Bragança family, he rebelled against Afonso's government until his death in battle at Alfarrobeira on May 20, 1449.

Pedro encouraged (as had John I and Edward) the voyages of discovery organized by his younger brother, Henry the Navigator, who had helped him obtain the regency.

·influence on Henry the Navigator and Afonso V **8**:777e
·Portugal under powerful Bragança family **14**:867e

Pedro Juan Caballero, capital, Amambay department, eastern Paraguay. It lies in the Cordillera de Amambay at 2,135 ft (651 m) above sea level, opposite Ponte Porã, Brazil. In addition to its administrative functions, Pedro Juan Caballero is the department's largest town and principal trade centre. The hinterland is utilized primarily for cattle ranching and coffee growing. The town is accessible by road from Concepción and by the Brazilian railroad that terminates in Ponte Porã. Pop. (1972 prelim.) 20,901.
22°34′ S, 55°37′ W

·map, Paraguay **13**:986

Pedrolino, French PIERROT, stock character of the Italian commedia dell'arte, a simpleminded and honest servant, usually a young and personable valet. One of the comic servants, or *zanni*, Pedrolino functioned in the commedia as an unsuccessful lover and a victim of the pranks of his fellow comedians. His costume consisted of a white jacket with a neck ruff and large buttons down the front, loose trousers, and a hat with a wide, floppy brim. Unlike most of the other stock characters, he played without a mask, his face whitened with powder.

Pedrolino, detail from "Actors of the Comédie-Italienne," oil painting by Nicolas Lancret, 18th century; in the Louvre, Paris
Giraudon

Pedrolino became tremendously popular in later French pantomimes as the naïve and appealing Pierrot. For 20 years at the Théâtre des Funambules, the great French mime Jean-Gaspard Deburau (1796–1846) played Pierrot as the pathetic, white-robed lover eternally mooning over the beautiful Columbine (*q.v.*). The clown hero of Ruggero Leoncavallo's opera *I pagliacci* (1892) was a later use of a Pierrot-like figure.

·commedia character development **4**:985a

peduncle, in botany, the stalk or stem of a single flower or the main stalk of a flower cluster (*see* inflorescence). In zoology, the term refers to the fleshy stalk attaching a barnacle (*q.v.*) or brachiopod to a solid object.

·cirriped anatomy, illus. 1 **4**:641
·palm flowers and inflorescence **1**:1133b

Peebles, former county, southeastern Scotland; since the reorganization of 1975 it constitutes the district of Tweeddale (*q.v.*; its former county name), of Borders (*q.v.*) region.

The Pentland Hills (about 1,700 ft [520 m]) lie north and south of the River Tweed. Moorland plateaus of 1,800–2,000 ft rise to Broad Law (2,723 ft). The climate is severe, a result of altitude and interior location. Temperatures are low, and rainfall ranges from 35 in. (900 mm) to 60 in. annually in the southwest. Antiquities include early Iron Age hill forts, Roman camps (*e.g.*, Lyne), medieval peel towers (15th-century Neidpath Castle, near the town of Peebles), and Traquair House, near Innerleithen, occupied by King William the Lion in 1209 and visited by Mary, Queen of Scots, in 1566.

Less than 20 percent of the district's total area is improved agricultural land; of this, more than one-third is under permanent pasture. Barley occupies 50 percent of the arable acreage, followed by turnips and fodder crops. Cultivation is confined to the better drained glacial soils of the flat valley floors. Livestock farming predominates, with sheep on the hills and beef cattle and arable farming on the lower land. Woollen goods and knitwear, the main manufactures, are produced at Peebles, Innerleithen (once a well-known spa), and Walkerburn. The scenery and good salmon and trout fishing in the Tweed are valuable assets that have led to an increase of tourism.

Peebles, small royal burgh (chartered town) and seat of the district authority of Tweeddale (*q.v.*), Borders region, Scotland, at the junction of Eddleston Water with the River Tweed. The town grew up under the shelter of the royal castle, which was a favourite residence of the Scottish kings when they hunted in nearby Ettrick Forest. Peebles was created a royal burgh in 1367 but declined following the union of the crowns of Scotland and England in 1603.

The modern town is an agricultural centre and has large woollen mills producing tweed and knitwear. The burgh consists of the new town on the south of the Eddleston and the old on the north. Portions of the town walls still exist, as do the cellars constructed underground in the 16th and 17th centuries to serve as hiding places during raids by lawless freebooters of the Border region. The old market cross still stands in the marketplace, but little survives of Crosskirk, erected in 1261 to contain a supposed relic of the True Cross. Pop. (1974 est.) 6,064.
55°39′ N, 3°12′ W

·map, United Kingdom **18**:866

Pee Dee River, rising as the Yadkin River in the Blue Ridge Mountains in northwest North Carolina, U.S. Flowing northeast, then southeast past Wilkesboro, Elkin, and Badin, it becomes the Pee Dee after a course of about 200 mi (320 km). As the Pee Dee, it continues for 230 mi, generally southeast into South Carolina, past Cheraw, being joined by the Little Pee Dee approximately 20 mi before emptying into Winyah Bay near Georgetown. As the Yadkin, the river is dammed to form High Rock and Badin lakes (by the Uwharrie National Forest); and as the Pee Dee, to form Tillery and Blewett Falls lakes. The Pee Dee,

in its lower course, is navigable for 90 mi. Pee Dee is the name of an Indian tribe.
33°21′ N, 79°16′ W
·map, United States **18**:908

Peekskill, city, Westchester County, southeastern New York, U.S., on the east bank of the Hudson River. Its name derives from Jan Peek, a Dutchman who established a trading post in 1654 at the point where a *kil* (Dutch for creek) joins the Hudson. An early river port and agricultural-trade centre, it was attacked and burned by the British during the Revolutionary War. From 1865 to 1910 it was a major producer of stoves, plows, and other foundry products. Yeast, gin, whiskey, electrical items, and stationery are now produced. The city is also a tourist base for nearby recreational areas, including Bear Mountain State Park. St. Peter's Church (1767) has been restored. Inc. village, 1839; city, 1940. Pop. (1980) 18,236.
41°17′ N, 73°55′ W

Peel, town on the west coast of the Isle of Man, one of the British Isles, on Peel Bay at the mouth of the River Neb, which forms the harbour. On the west side of the river mouth is Patrick's Isle, connected with the main island by a causeway; it is occupied by the ruined keep and guardroom of an ancient castle (the name Peel is Celtic for "fort"). Nearby are the remains of the cathedral of St. German. There are also ruins of the bishop's palace, palace of the lords of Man, and an ancient round tower. St. Patrick is said to have founded the first church on Man and a small chapel dedicated to him probably dates from the 8th or 10th century. Peel has a long established fishing industry and is a seaside resort. Pop. (1971 prelim.) 3,081.
54°13′ N, 4°40′ W
·map, United Kingdom **18**:866

Peel Castle at the entrance to Peel harbour, Isle of Man
Colour Library International

Peel, Sir Robert 13:1106 (b. Feb. 5, 1788, Bury, Lancashire—d. July 2, 1850), British prime minister and founder of the Conservative Party, was responsible for the 1846 repeal of the Corn Laws that had restricted imports.

Abstract of text biography. The son of a wealthy cotton manufacturer, Peel was educated at Harrow and at Oxford. He had a parliamentary seat as soon as he came of age (1809). He was appointed undersecretary for war and colonies (1810), and chief secretary for Ireland (1812). He was elected as member of Parliament for Oxford (1817), and in 1819 he was made chairman of the currency commission that brought about a return of the gold standard. In 1822 he became secretary of state and took a seat in the Cabinet, resigned in 1827 on the issue of Catholic Emancipation, but returned to office (1828) as home secretary and leader of the House of Commons. In 1834 he became prime minister. He resigned in 1846, following the repeal of the Corn Laws.

REFERENCES in other text articles:
·British 19th-century political growth **3**:264d
·Cobden's opposition to Corn Laws **4**:811b
·Disraeli's split of Conservative Party **5**:899b
·Gladstone's mentor in political career **8**:178d
·Irish emancipation opposition **3**:290g
·modern police organization concepts **14**:671g
·police force establishment **6**:1075c
·Russell opposition tactic and power rise **16**:38e
·Victoria's prime minister **19**:106b
·Wellington and Catholic Emancipation **19**:756d

Peel, Ronald Francis (Edward Waite) (b. Aug. 22, 1912, England), geographer and geomorphologist known for his studies of landforms of the Sahara. He was a faculty member at the University of Durham from 1935 until 1939 and from 1945 until 1946, when he moved to the University of Cambridge; he became a professor at Leeds (Yorkshire) University in 1951, and in 1957 he became a professor at the University of Bristol (Gloucestershire). He wrote *Geography* (1960), *British Geography* (1966), and *Advancement of Science* (1967).

Peel Commission (1936–37), British commission under Lord Peel that recommended the partition of Palestine and displacement of thousands of Palestinians from their homes.
·Palestine partition plan **17**:958e

Peele, George (b. 1556, London—d. 1596), dramatist, predecessor of Shakespeare, who experimented in many forms of theatrical art: pastoral, history, melodrama, tragedy, folk play, and pageant. His *The Arraignment of Paris* is one of the earliest mythological pastorals, and his *Device of the Pageant Borne Before Woolstone Dixi* is the earliest surviving complete lord mayor's show, the annual pageant produced for the inaugural ceremonies of the lord mayor of London.

Peele began his varied literary career while at Oxford by translating into English one of the plays of Euripides.

He also probably wrote at the university the first of his surviving works, a 485-line verse epitome of the *Iliad*, titled *The Tale of Troy* (published 1589).

In 1581 he moved to London but returned to Oxford in 1583, when Christ Church presented two spectacular plays by Gager, and Peele was hired as one of the technical directors.

About this time Peele had joined a group of Oxonians living just outside the London city wall and had begun to experiment with poetry in various metres. From this association with the so-called university wits comes a blank verse commendatory poem to the poet Thomas Watson and two mythological pastorals: *The Arraignment of Paris* (1584) and *The Hunting of Cupid* (1591). He then produced a series of pageants for the city, of which only *Descensus Astraeae* (1591) survives.

The Arraignment of Paris was produced for the courtiers, but the rest of Peele's life was devoted to writing for the popular stage. Of the many playhouse dramas he must have had a hand in, only four can be certainly ascribed to him: *The Battle of Alcazar* (1594), *The Old Wives' Tale* (1595; ed. by R.L. Blair, 1936), *Edward I* (1593), and *The Love of King David and Fair Bethsabe* (1599). In addition, Peele turned out commemorative poems to supplement a meagre income.

He lived and died a varied life fraught with the perils of poverty. His contemporaries praised him highly. Modern critics accord him a place, along with Robert Greene, Thomas Kyd, and Thomas Nashe, as an important early playwright with considerable technical skill. With Greene, he contributed to the development of dramatic blank verse and to the tone of idyllic romance of later comedy.
·literature of the Renaissance **10**:1140e

Peel River, in northern Yukon Territory and northwestern Mackenzie District of the Northwest Territories, Canada, is the northernmost tributary of the Mackenzie River. From its major headstream, the Ogilvie River, in the mountains of central Yukon Territory, the river flows generally northeastward for 365 mi (587 km) to join the Mackenzie near Fort McPherson, a fur-trading post and the only significant riverine settlement. Its upper course through Peel Plateau is characterized by canyons as deep as 1,000 ft (300 m); its lower valley, much of which consists of nature preserve and game sanctuary, is wide, with braided channels, gravel bars, and small wooded islands. The river was named for Sir Robert Peel, the British statesman.
67°42′ N, 134°32′ W
·map, Canada **3**:716

Peenemünde, village in *Bezirk* (district) Rostock, East Germany, lies at the northwestern end of Usedom Island in the estuarine mouth of the Peene River on the Baltic Sea coast. During World War II it was the site of the chief German research and testing facility for rockets and missiles (the so-called V-weapons). It was heavily bombed by the Royal Air Force in August 1943 and was captured by Soviet troops in April 1945.
·guided missile research **7**:402e
·rocket research and capture by Soviets **15**:929h

peep, collective name in America for about a dozen species of small nondescript sandpipers (*q.v.*); called stint in Britain. Some are also called oxbirds or oxeyes.

peeping tom, a secretive voyeur; a person who derives sexual satisfaction from watching from hiding places as others disrobe or engage in sexual acts. The term derives from the legendary Peeping Tom, a prying tailor who was struck blind (in some accounts, struck dead) for opening his window and watching Lady Godiva as she rode naked through Coventry to demonstrate against heavy taxes on the town. Though Godiva's ride supposedly took place in the 11th century and was recorded as early as the 13th, the legend of Peeping Tom was not added to the story until about the 17th century.
·behaviour pattern and causation **16**:608d

peep show, a children's toy and scientific curiosity, usually consisting of a box with an eyehole, through which the viewer sees a miniature scene or stage setting, painted or constructed in perspective. Peep shows of an earlier time are often the only accurate representation of the stage design and scenery of the period.

The earliest known peep shows are the perspective views said to have been painted in transparent colours on glass and lighted from behind for various effects, from sunshine to moonlight, by Leon Battista Alberti in 1437. Later models (some preserved in the Kunsthistorisches Museum in Vienna) have designs that are apparently patterned on Renaissance court masques and pageants, such as that of the discovery of Diana by Actaeon, with fully modelled figures set against a background painted in careful perspective.

In the 17th century, peep shows in their cabinets were often exhibited in the streets by itinerant showmen, and the device became a

Model of a peep show representing the discovery of Diana by Actaeon, by Christoph Margraf, 1596; in the Kunsthistorisches Museum, Vienna

By courtesy of the Kunsthistorisches Museum, Vienna

popular children's toy. Some, equipped with movable scenery and wooden or cardboard figures, developed into the juvenile theatres of the 19th century. The peep show was also the precursor of many types of optical toys, including the stereoscope and the magic lantern.

Peerage Act (1963), measure that allowed Lord Home to renounce his British peerage, win a seat in Parliament as Sir Alexander Frederick Douglas-Home, and become prime minister (October 1964).

Peerage Bill (1719), British legislation aimed at restricting the king's power to create peers.
·Britain's 18th-century political growth **3**:252b

peer group, combination of interacting persons of approximately equal status, usually of about the same age range.
·behaviour development in adolescence **8**:1145d
·dialectal pattern reinforcement **5**:700f
·educational promotion of social needs **6**:414c
·public opinion and attitude formation **15**:212d

Peer Gynt (published 1867; performed 1876), verse drama by Henrik Ibsen, a satiric fantasy directed against what the author felt was the narrowness of Norwegian life and the complacency of the Norwegian character. It follows the career of the legendary Norse folk hero, Peer Gynt, wholly unprincipled, buoyant, and yielding, content to take for his way of life the motto "Exist for Thyself." In the end, realizing that he has no firm identity, and threatened with being melted to anonymity in the Button Moulder's ladle, he finds his proper "shape" as an individual through Solveig's love for him.
·Ibsen's social criticism **9**:152h

Peer Gynt, two orchestral suites of 1876 by Edvard Grieg.
·suite style form **12**:727h

Peerless Corporation, U.S. company of the early 20th century that began as a manufacturer of washing machines, then produced automobiles until the 1930s.
·history of automotive industry **2**:528c

peewee (bird): *see* pewee.

peg-and-socket joint, also called GOMPHOSIS, in anatomy, a fibrous joint whose conical process is inserted into a socketlike portion.
·characteristics and functions **10**:253e

Pegasiformes (fish order): *see* dragonfish.

Pegasus, in Greek mythology, a winged horse that sprang from the blood of the Gorgon Medusa as she was beheaded by the hero Perseus (*q.v.*). With Athena's (or Poseidon's) help, another Greek hero, Bellerophon, captured Pegasus and rode him first in his fight with the Chimera (*q.v.*) and later while he was taking vengeance on Stheneboea (Anteia), who had falsely accused Bellerophon. Subsequently Bellerophon attempted to fly with Pegasus to heaven but was unseated and killed, the winged horse becoming a constellation in the sky and the servant of Zeus. Pegasus' story became a favourite theme in Greek art and literature, and in late antiquity Pegasus' soaring flight was interpreted as an allegory of the soul's immortality; in modern times it has been regarded as a symbol of poetic inspiration.

Pegasus, designation for a series of three artificial satellites launched by the U.S. in 1965.
·meteor penetration frequency study **12**:39f
·micrometeoroid detection and design **17**:366g; table 364

pegmatite, almost any wholly crystalline igneous or metamorphic (involving heat, pressure, and water to give more compactness and a more highly crystalline nature) rock that is at least in part very coarse grained, whose major constituents include minerals typically found in ordinary igneous rocks, and in which extreme textural variations, especially in grain size, are characteristic. Giant crystals, with dimensions measured in metres, occur in some pegmatites, but the average grain size of all such rocks is only eight to ten centimetres (three or four inches).

Most bodies of pegmatite are tabular, podlike (cigar-shaped), or irregular in form, and range in size from single crystals of feldspar to dikes (tabular bodies injected in fissures) hundreds of feet thick and nearly two kilometres long; many are intimately associated with masses of fine-grained aplite. Pegmatites occur in all parts of the world, and are most abundant in rocks of relatively great geologic age. Some are segregations within much larger bodies of intrusive igneous rocks; others are distributed satellitically in the rocks that surround such bodies; and still others are not recognizably associated with igneous rocks.

Granitic and syenitic pegmatite deposits are the chief source of commercial feldspar, sheet mica, and beryllium, tantalum-niobium, and lithium minerals. They also yield significant quantities of gem minerals, scrap mica, molybdenite, cassiterite, tungsten minerals, rare-earth minerals, and certain types of kaolin, either directly or as the sources of placer deposits. Economic lode concentrations generally occur in zoned pegmatite bodies (*i.e.*, those within which two or more different rock types are systematically disposed).

Pegmatites are little different from the common igneous rocks in major elements of bulk composition, and they range from acid to basic (silica-rich to silica-poor); granitic and syenitic types are most abundant. Quartz and alkali feldspars are the essential constituents; the most common varietal and accessory minerals are muscovite, biotite, apatite, garnet, and tourmaline. Many granitic pegmatites contain various minerals that bespeak unusual concentrations of the less abundant elements; *e.g.*, beryllium in beryl, chrysoberyl, and phenacite; boron in tourmaline and axinite; fluorine in apatite, micas, topaz, and tourmaline; lithium in lepidolite, spodumene, and several phosphate minerals; rare alkalies in pollucite, beryl, feldspars, and micas; tin in cassiterite; tungsten in wolframite; zirconium in zircon; and tantalum, niobium, uranium, thorium, and rare earths in many oxide and phosphate minerals. Ore minerals, chiefly sulfides and oxides, are widespread in pegmatites but rarely are abundant. The origin and behaviour of ore-forming fluids derived from magmas probably are intimately related to the processes responsible for development of pegmatites.

Three contrasting mechanisms together account for the origin of most pegmatites: (1) replacement of pre-existing nonpegmatitic rocks through the action of various fluids; (2) crystallization of silicate melts derived by partial fusion of pre-existing rocks; and (3) crystallization of residual fluids developed during late stages in the consolidation of intrusive magmas (molten materials). The first process is essentially metamorphic, the others mainly igneous. The presence of water and other volatile substances seems necessary and probably is common to all three processes; such constituents depress the temperature range of crystallization, participate directly in the formation of many minerals, and lower the viscosity of igneous melts, thereby promoting formation of large crystals. Experimental evidence indicates that the presence of a separate vapour phase is necessary for development of giant crystals.

Features indicating replacement of one mineral by another are widespread within many bodies of pegmatite. Most are attributable to attack of earlier-formed minerals either by residual liquid, by vapour separated from the liquid, or by liquid condensed from such vapour. The end stages of some pegmatite crystallization are marked by development of well-faced, transparent crystals, commonly as linings and partial fillings of cavities. Such occurrences have yielded handsome mineral specimens, as well as stones of gem quality.
·crystallization and mineralogy **12**:243c
·igneous rock classification **9**:207g; tables 203
·importance of crystals **14**:284c; table 287
·magma crystallization and element deposition **6**:705g
·origin, composition, texture, and ore **9**:225a
·silica occurrence and crystallization **16**:754h
·texture and spodumene crystals, illus. 2 and 9 **9**:203

pegmatitic texture, descriptive term for igneous rocks in which two minerals appear as mutually penetrating individuals throughout the rock. It is often interpreted as being the result of simultaneous crystallization of the two minerals at nearly the same growth rates, with neither forming crystal faces at the expense of the other. This texture is commonly exhibited by the dike rocks called pegmatites, which form late during the crystallization of the parent magmatic body, when crystals, liquid, and gas can coexist. Such rocks often are associated with an abundant vapour phase that enhances the growth of large mineral grains.

Pegolotti, Francesco Balducci (fl. 1315–1340), the Florentine author of a work, generally known as the *Pratica della mercatura* ("Practice of Marketing"), that provides an excellent picture of trade and travel in his day. He was a commercial agent in the service of the mercantile house of the wealthy and powerful Bardi family of Florence, visiting Antwerp, Brabant, now in Belgium (*c.* 1315–17), London (1317), and Cyprus (1324–27). He again visited Cyprus in 1335, obtaining trading privileges for the Florentines from Little Armenia, now in Turkey. Compiled between 1335 and 1343, the *Pratica* begins with a kind of glossary of foreign terms then in use for all kinds of taxes or payments on merchandise as well as entries for "every kind of place where goods might be bought or sold in cities." The work next describes some of the chief trade routes of the 14th century and many of the principal markets then known to Italian merchants; the imports, exports, and business customs of important commercial regions; and the comparative value of the leading moneys, weights, and measures. There is one manuscript of the *Pratica* in the Riccardian Library, Florence. The most interesting sections of the work appeared in English translation in Sir Henry Yule's, *Cathay and the Way Thither* (vol. 2, 1866).

Pegomyia hyoscyomi: *see* anthomyiid fly.

Pegu, former capital of the Mon kingdoms, giving its name to a district (*kayaing*) and division (*taing*) of Lower Burma. On the Pegu River, 47 mi (76 km) northeast of Rangoon, the town is surrounded by the ruins of its old wall and moat, which formed a square, with 1½-mi sides. On the Rangoon–Mandalay railway, it is the start of a branch line southeast along the Gulf of Martaban, an inlet of the Bay of Bengal, and has extensive road links in all directions. Pegu is a major rice- and timber-collecting centre and has numerous rice mills and sawmills.

Of its many pagodas, the ancient Shwemawdaw (Golden Shrine), 288 ft (88 m) high, is the most venerable. Said to contain two hairs of Gautama Buddha, it is of Mon origin and was severely damaged by an earthquake in 1930, but restoration was completed in 1954. The Shwethalyaung, a colossal reclining statue of Buddha (181 ft [55 m] long), is to the west of the modern town and is reputedly one of the most lifelike of all the reclining Buddha figures; allegedly built in 994, it was lost when Pegu was destroyed in 1757 but was rediscovered under a cover of jungle growth in 1881.

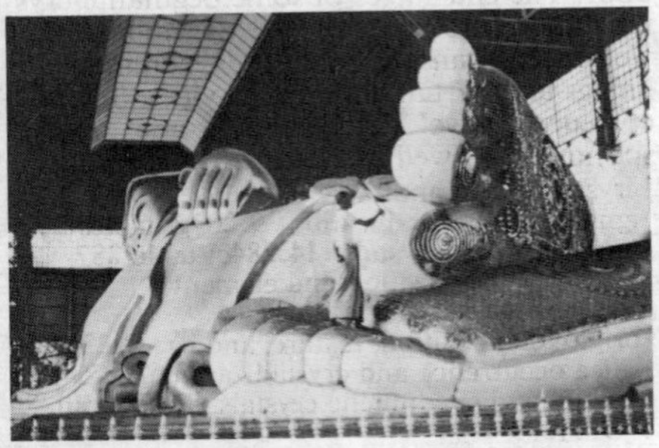

Reclining Buddha, Pegu, Burma

Slim Aarons—Photo Researchers

From the nearby Kalyani Sima (Hall of Ordination), founded by the Mon king Dhammazedi (1472–92), spread one of the greatest reform movements in Burmese Buddhist history. Its story is related in 10 stone inscriptions erected by the King close to the Sima. The Mahazedi, Shwegugale, and Kyaikpien are other notable pagodas.

Pegu town is said to have been founded in 573 by Mon emigrants from Thaton to the southeast, but the most likely date of its foundation as the capital of a Mon kingdom is 825. The earliest record of the kingdom shortly before 850 was by the Arab geographer Ibn Khurradādhbih, who called it Ramaññadesa (the Rmen, or Mon, land). In 1056, when the Burmese of Pagan conquered the kingdom, Thaton was its capital, and Pegu was little heard of until Pagan fell to the Mongols in 1287. When the Mons recovered their independence, Pegu became the capital of their new kingdom in 1369. Through nearby Martaban it functioned as a seaport, easily accessible from all parts of the alluvial plain. It was also a centre of Buddhist culture.

When in 1539 the Mon kingdom fell to the Burmese Toungoo dynasty, Pegu was made the capital of a united Burmese kingdom until 1599 and again from 1613 to 1634. The Burmese used it in the 16th century as a base for the invasion of Siam. Many Europeans visited it, including the Venetian trader Cesare Federici (1569) and the English merchant Ralph Fitch (1587–88), whose description detailed its magnificence.

After the Burmese moved their capital to Ava in 1635, Pegu became a provincial capital, but a Mon revolt in 1740 restored it as the capital of their short-lived kingdom. When in 1757 the Burmese king Alaungpaya invaded the Mon land, wiping out the last vestiges of independence, he destroyed Pegu but left the religious buildings intact. The British annexed the Pegu area in 1852, and in 1862, when the province of British Burma was created, the capital was moved from Pegu to Rangoon.

Pegu District was formed in 1883, with an area of 4,624 sq mi (11,717 sq km). It extends between the forested Pegu Yoma (west) and the Sittang River (east) and has a short coastline on the Gulf of Martaban. There is a major irrigation scheme; rice is practically the only crop and is exported through Rangoon. Pegu town is the district headquarters, and other important towns on the railway include Penwegon, Nyaunglebin, Daik-U, and Payagyi. The Pegu Sittang Canal, which crosses the district, is navigable for 85 mi with locks.

Pegu Division (area 19,223 sq mi [49,787 sq km]) lies east of the Irrawaddy. It comprises Hanthawaddy, Insein, Tharrawaddy, Pegu, and Prome districts. It formerly included Rangoon, which became a separate division after 1965. Pop. (latest census) town, 47,378; district, 171,362; (latest est.) division, 3,689,000.
17°20′ N, 96°29′ E

·Burmese tribal conflicts and kingdom **3**:511e; map 513
·Dalhousie's annexation for Britain **5**:439a
·division area and population table **3**:506
·map, Burma **3**:505

Péguy, Charles (b. Jan. 7, 1873, Orléans, Fr. —d. Sept. 5, 1914, near Valleroy), poet and philosopher who combined Christianity, socialism, and patriotism into a deeply personal faith that he carried into action. As a Christian, he voices a pristine and provincial faith in a modern world. As a social reformer, he championed Capt. Alfred Dreyfus, falsely convicted of treason by an anti-Semitic establishment. As a patriot, he died on the western front in World War I.

Péguy was born to poverty. His mother, widowed when he was an infant, mended chairs for a living. He attended the *lycée* at Orléans on a scholarship and in 1894 entered the École Normale Superieure in Paris, intending to teach philosophy.

It was the time of the Dreyfus affair. By 1895 Péguy was not only a Dreyfusard but also a socialist. He took leaves of absence from the normal school, foregoing an academic career. In 1897 he married and, with his wife's dowry, he started a bookstore that became a centre of pro-Dreyfus writings, including his own. To socialists who argued that their focus should be on the sufferings of society rather than those of one man, he argued, "A single injustice . . . suffices to make a break in the social body and in the social contract."

Besides running a bookstore, Péguy in 1900 began publishing a journal, *Cahiers de la Quinzaine* ("Fortnightly Notebooks"), to which leading talents of the day, including himself, contributed, that exercised a profound cultural influence. A favorite Péguy topic was his City of the Future, in which there would be no private wealth and injustice. Péguy's socialism has been described as more like St. Francis' than Karl Marx'. Simple in his humane faith, which he expressed in equally simple words, he wrote, "It is innocence that is full and experience that is empty."

Two of his most important works are about Joan of Arc, the maid of his native Orléans. The first (1897) is a socialist play. The second, essentially a philosophic poem, *Mystère de la charité de Jeanne d'Arc*, appeared in 1910. The meditative and devotional outpouring of Péguy's final years culminated in *Ève* (1913), a statuesque poem of 4,000 alexandrines, in which he views the human condition in the perspective of Christian revelation. There are several selections of Péguy's poetry and prose in English translation.

When World War I broke out, Péguy, then 41, went to the front as a lieutenant. Standing alone, with his field glasses to his eyes in a bright sun, he was shot in the forehead by retreating Germans. He had written a year earlier, "Blessed are those who died in a just war/Blessed is the wheat that is ripe and the wheat that is gathered in sheaves." Further information can be found in Y. Servais' *Charles Péguy: the Pursuit of Salvation* (1953); Marjorie Villiers' *Charles Péguy, A Study in Integrity* (1965).

Pegu Yoma, mountain range, north central Burma, extending 270 mi (435 km) north-south between the Irrawaddy and Sittang rivers and ending in a ridge at Rangoon. It averages about 2,000 ft (600 m), reaching its highest point in the north at Mt. Popa (4,981 ft), an extinct volcano.
19°00′ N, 95°50′ E

·Burmese mountain evolution **3**:503b
·map, Burma **3**:505

Pe-har, a popular Tibetan divinity, worshipped by Buddhists, particularly those of the Dge-lugs-pa ("Yellow Hat") sect as a *dharmapāla* ("defender of the faith"), whose oracles are transmitted through a state-appointed medium. He is also revered by adherents of Bon, a pre-Buddhist faith. He is chief of the "Five Great Kings" and is especially effective in affording protection against enemies. Many diverse traditions surround Pe-har. His name may possibly be derived from the Sanskrit *vihāra* ("monastery") probably because of his guardianship of the Samye monastery. After seven centuries there he moved to the Nechung monastery near Drepung, which is at present the principal centre

Pe-har, gilt bronze statuette from Tibet, 18th century; in the Musée Guimet, Paris

By courtesy of the Musee Guimet, Paris

of his cult. Pe-har is depicted with either one or three heads, white in colour, riding on a white lion, and wearing a broad-rimmed cane helmet.

Peh Kiangsu Canal, Kiangsu Province, China, from the Hung-tse Hu (lake) to the Yellow Sea.

·Anhwei navigation improvements **1**:902a

Pehlevi alphabet: *see* Pahlavi alphabet.

Pehowa, town, Karnāl district, Haryana state, India, on the Saraswati River. It is an important pilgrimage centre housing the Pirthudakeshwar (Pirthuveshwar) temples built by the Marāthās (18th century) in honour of the goddess Sarasvatī. The name is a corruption of the Sanskrit Pṛthūdaka (Pool of Pṛthu), the son of legendary Raja Vena. Excavations have revealed inscriptions dating to the 9th century AD. Pop. (1971 prelim.) 11,374.
29°59′ N, 76°35′ E

Pei, I(eoh) M(ing) (b. April 26, 1917, Canton), architect whose designs for large urban buildings and urban complexes reflect his sensitivity to the needs of the modern city and its inhabitants.

Pei went to the U.S. in 1935, enrolling initially at the University of Pennsylvania, Philadelphia, then transferring to the Massachusetts Institute of Technology, Cambridge, as a student of architectural engineering. He graduated in 1939 and, unable to return to China because of the outbreak of World War II, carried out various architectural contracts in Boston, New York, and Los Angeles. During World War II he worked with a unit of the National Defense Research Committee. From 1945 to 1948 he was an assistant professor at the Graduate School of Design of Harvard University.

In 1948 Pei joined the firm of Webb & Knapp, New York City, as director of the architectural division. Working closely with the real estate developer William Zeckendorf, head of the firm, Pei created such urban projects as the Mile High Center in Denver, Colo., and the Place Ville-Marie in Montreal.

National Center for Atmospheric Research by I.M. Pei, completed 1967, Boulder, Colo.

Pei formed I.M. Pei & Associates (later I.M. Pei and Partners) in 1955. Among the notable early designs of the firm were the Luce Memorial Chapel, Taiwan, which had walls that were typhoon resistant; the National Center for Atmospheric Research, Boulder, Colo., which, located near mountains, had a craggy, mountaintop appearance; and the Everson Museum of Art, Syracuse, N.Y., actually four buildings joined by bridges. For the Federal Aviation Agency, Pei designed a pentagonal control tower that was installed in many U.S. airports.

On the basis of a 1960 design competition Pei was selected to design the multi-airline terminal, including National Airlines, at John F. Kennedy International Airport, New York City. In 1964 he was also selected to design the John F. Kennedy Memorial Library at Harvard University.

In addition to his designs for public buildings, Pei has been active in urban renewal planning. His designs for areas of Philadelphia, Chicago, Washington, D.C., and New York City are considered by many to be outstanding for their beauty and economy.

Pei Chiang, also spelled PAI or PEH, Pin-yin romanization BEI JIANG, English NORTH RIVER, in central Kwangtung Province (*sheng*), southeastern China. It is formed by the union of the Wu Shui (river) and Cheng Shui in southern Hunan Province and flows about 217 mi (350 km) south to join the delta of the Hsi Chiang, or West River, west of Canton. For centuries the Pei has played an important role in the transport system between North and South China.
23°00′ N, 112°48′ E
·China's transport system map **4**:284
·Chu Chiang Delta **8**:1125d
·map, China **4**:262

Pei-ching, or PEI-P'ING (China): *see* Peking.

P'ei Chü, 7th-century Chinese official of the Sui dynasty.
·Sui dnyasty's policy with Turks **4**:321d

pei ch'ü, Chinese music-drama of Sung dynasty (960–1279).
·description of style **12**:675b

Peierls, Rudolf (Ernst) (1907–), German-born British nuclear physicist.
·nuclear weapons prediction **13**:326b

Pei-hai, Pin-yin romanization BEI-HAI, also called PAK-HOI, city and port in the Kwangsi Chuang Autonomous Region (*tzu-chih-ch'ü*), China. The city, an autonomous subprovincial-level municipality (*shih*), was in Kwangtung Province until 1965, when it became part of Kwangsi Chuang. It is on the northern shore of a small peninsula on the eastern side of Ch'in-chou Wan (bay) on the Gulf of Tonkin, immediately south of the delta of the Lien Chiang (river) and about 12.5 mi (20 km) south of Ho-p'u. Pei-hai was opened to foreign trade in 1876. Despite its poor harbour, badly exposed to northerly winds and impeded by sandbanks, Pei-hai became a moderately important port, the principal outlet for the trade of southern and western Kwangsi.

Later, the opening to trade of Wuchow on the Hsi Chiang in Kwangsi and of Meng-tzu on the Red River in Yunnan Province robbed Pei-hai of much of its importance, and it became no more than a minor port, much of its foreign trade being in the hands of French trading companies. Most of its trade was coastal, and only ships of under 3,000 tons could use the port. Pei-hai enjoyed a revival after 1937, when the Sino-Japanese War (1937–45) began, but in 1940 it was itself occupied by the Japanese. Since 1949 Pei-hai has flourished as one of the most important fishing ports of southern China. Although much of the fishing fleet was destroyed during World War II, after 1945 the fishing industry was rapidly rehabilitated. After 1949 Pei-hai developed a shipbuilding industry for small craft and also manufactured cables, sails, and nets; a canning industry was established and there are plants making such various fish products as fish-liver oil, dried fish, and glue. As the nearest Chinese port to North Vietnam, Pei-hai has traditionally had strong trading links with the Vietnamese port of Haiphong. Latest census 80,000.
21°29′ N, 109°05′ E
·urban location and commercial focus **10**:551g

Pei hai Park, near Peking, a recreational centre, the site of pleasure grounds, lakes, and buildings since the 12th century.
·Peking recreational facilities **14**:14b; illus.

Peine, town, Niedersachsen (Lower Saxony) *Land* (state), West Germany, on the Mittelland Kanal east-southeast of Braunschweig (Brunswick). After being founded in 1220 by Count Gunzelin of Wolfenbüttel, Peine belonged in turn to the duchy of Brunswick, the bishopric of Hildesheim (1260–1802), and the kingdom of Hanover, passing to Prussia in 1866. It is on the railway and truck road from Hannover to Berlin, and the airport at Eddesse is nearby. Iron and steel form the chief industry; machinery and footwear are made, and there is weaving, brewing, and food processing. Pop. (1970 est.) 31,000.
52°19′ N, 10°13′ E
·map, Federal Republic of Germany **8**:46

peine forte et dure (French: "strong and hard punishment"), in English law, punishment that was inflicted upon those who were accused of a serious crime and refused to plead either guilty or not guilty or upon those who challenged more than 20 prospective jurors. By the Statute of Westminster, 1275, the *peine* was "strong and hard punishment," but in 1406 pressing to death by heavy weights was substituted. An individual who chose to stand mute under the threat of *peine forte et dure* often did so to ensure that his goods and estates would be inherited by his family; if he was tried and convicted, they would pass directly to the crown. In treason cases *peine forte et dure* was not applicable, because standing mute in such cases meant a plea of guilty.

Peine forte et dure was rarely used in the American colonies. The few instances of its use helped to prompt the constitutional prohibition against cruel and unusual punishments.

Pei-p'an Chiang, English NORTH PAN RIVER, Kweichow Province, China, a tributary of the Hsi Chiang.
25°07′ N, 106°01′ E
·Hsi Chiang River system **8**:1125b

Pei-p'ing (China): *see* Peking.

Peipus, Battle of Lake, also called BATTLE OF LAKE CHUDSKOYE (April 5, 1242), victory of Aleksandr Nevsky of Novgorod over invading Teutonic Knights. In 1239 the Livonian Knights (Order of the Brothers of the Sword) began a military campaign in northwestern Russia to expand their territory and convert the Russians to Roman Catholicism. Interrupted by the Mongol invasion of Poland and Silesia (1241), the campaign was resumed by the Teutonic Knights (with whom the Livonian Knights were affiliated). In 1241 the knights captured Pskov, then proceeded against Novgorod in March 1242. But Nevsky led an army against them. Recovering all the territory seized by the knights, he engaged them in battle on the frozen Lake Peipus (Lake Chudskoye), known as the "battle on the ice." His victory forced the grand master of the knights to relinquish all claims to the Russian lands that he had conquered and substantially reduced the Teutonic threat to northwestern Russia.

Peipus, Lake, Russian CHUDSKOYE OZERO, Estonian PEIPSI JARV, forms part of the boundary between the Estonian Soviet Socialist Republic and Pskov *oblast* (administrative region) of the Russian Soviet Federated Socialist Republic. It is connected by the narrow Tyoploye Lake to a southern extension, Lake Pskov. Lake Peipus has an area of 1,400 sq mi (3,600 sq km), although this varies. The lake bottom, reaching a depth of about 50 ft (15 m), consists of gray mud; only in the south is it sandy. The banks are predominantly low-lying. The lake, which is frozen for six months of the year, forms the headwaters of the Narva River. In 1242 on the ice of Lake Peipus the Russians under Alexander Nevsky defeated the Germanic Teutonic Knights.
58°45′ N, 27°30′ E
·map, Soviet Union **17**:322

Peirce, Charles Sanders **13**:1108 (b. Sept. 10, 1839, Cambridge, Mass.—d. April 19, 1914, near Milford, Pa.), man of science, logician, and philosopher, is best known for his work on the logic of relations and on pragmatism as a method of research.

Abstract of text biography. Peirce studied at Harvard, where his father was professor of mathematics and worked for the Coast and Geodetic Survey for many years. He was a member of various learned societies and produced numerous papers but never wrote a book. His *Collected Papers* were published posthumously. Except for courses in logic at Johns Hopkins University (1879–84), he was never appointed to an academic post.

REFERENCES in other text articles:
·characterization of experience **12**:34b
·Duns Scotus' influence and philosophy **5**:1083c
·knowledge, thought, and science **6**:943d
·logical status of science concepts **16**:385e
·logic history from antiquity **11**:67f
·noncognitivist meta-ethical theories **6**:987e
·objective reality of cognitive object **15**:542b
·pragmatism development and history **14**:940d
·Pragmatist theory of meaning **14**:271c
·religious and secular experience **15**:648b

Peiresc, Nicolas-Claude Fabri de (b. Dec. 1, 1580, Belgentier, Fr.—d. June 24, 1637, Aix-en-Provence), antiquary, humanist, and influential patron of learning who emphasized the study of coins for historical research. Travels in Italy (1599–1602), studies at Padua, and acquaintance there with Galileo stimulated Peiresc's antiquarian interests. A senator at the parlement of Aix from 1605, he corresponded with the Flemish painter Peter Paul Rubens and many of the noted scholars of the day. Passionately interested in astronomy and in science in general, he discovered the Orion Nebula (1610) and was first to verify William Harvey's discovery of the circulation of blood. Sir Isaac Newton made use of his work on optics. Peiresc encouraged the legal studies of the Dutch jurist Hugo Grotius, on whose writings much of international law is based, and was largely responsible for the publication of a well-known political satire of the time, *Argenis*, by the Scottish poet John

Peiresc, engraving by J. Lubin (1637–95)

By courtesy of the trustees of the British Museum; photograph, R.B. Fleming

Barclay (1621). No published works by Peiresc are known, but the records of his correspondence indicate his catholicity.
·Orion Nebula discovery **12**:927b

Peirithous: *see* Pirithous.

Peisistratus 13:1109 (b. early 6th century BC —d. 527 BC), tyrant of ancient Athens and major figure in the city's development.

Abstract of text biography. A leading Athenian aristocrat, Peisistratus held power briefly twice in the city and gained definitive control in 546 BC when he defeated his rivals at the Battle of Pallene. He built numerous shrines and temples and fostered Athenian religious unity by promoting the cult of Athena as the city's chief deity. His extension of Athens' power and trade helped to make possible the city's later pre-eminence in Greece.

REFERENCES in other text articles:
·Athens artistic leadership **19**:288g
·Athens expansion under rule **2**:265g
·land reforms in ancient Greece **10**:638c
·life and accomplishments **8**:342g *passim* to 348e
·Solon's warnings against tyranny **16**:1046h
·struggle against Alcmaeonids **4**:707a

Pei-t'ou, also spelled PEITOW, town, T'ai-pei municipality, northern Taiwan, just northwest of Taipei, at the foot of the Ta-t'un Shan. It is a health resort with sulfur springs.
25°08′ N, 121°29′ E
·administration and recreation **17**:994b
·map, Taiwan **17**:996

Peixoto, Floriano (*c.* 1842–95), president of Brazil from 1891 to 1894.
·presidency and opposition **3**:146d

Pekah, Assyrian PAKAHA (d. 732 BC), king of Israel from *c.* 737 BC.
·Tiglath-pileser's Assyrian empire **18**:401h

Pekalongan, also spelled PECALONGAN, town and district, province of Djawa Tengah (Central Java), Java, Indonesia, situated on the northern coastal plain. The town, capital of the district, has a fort (1753) and a small harbour and is the main distributing centre for the area, exporting tea, rubber, and sugar, which is locally refined. The town is a main centre of batik production. Pekalongan district, with an area of 2,176 sq mi (5,636 sq km), was granted to the Dutch (1746) by the Sultan of Surakarta. The very fertile river valleys and coastal plain grow sugar, rice, kapok, cinchona, indigo, and corn (maize). Pop. (1971) town, 111,537; district 554,067.
6°53′ S, 109°40′ E
·map, Indonesia **9**:460

pekan (North American carnivore): *see* fisher.

Pekárna Cave, archaeological site in Moravia.
·Stone Age bone engravings **17**:704c

pekea nut: *see* souari nut.

Peker, Recep (1888–1950), prime minister of Turkey from 1946 to 1947.
·Democratic Party suppression **13**:792d

Pekin, city, seat of Tazewell County, central Illinois, U.S., on the Illinois River (bridged). The first settler (1824) was Jacob Tharp; the town was laid out in 1829 and in 1830 was named Pekin, the "new Celestial City," by Mrs. Nathan Cromwell, wife of a founder, in the belief (false) that it was directly opposite Peking, China, on the other side of the Earth. (Many of the older city streets are named for Mrs. Cromwell's friends—Ann Eliza, Cynthiana, Henrietta, Matilda, etc.) The dragon and other Chinese symbols are still commonly seen in the city. Pekin's first schoolhouse (Snell School) was fortified during the Black Hawk War as Ft. Doolittle. The town for many years remained a rough river port. Abraham Lincoln argued cases in its old courthouse, and the city was the birthplace and home of U.S. Sen. Everett M. Dirksen.

A shipping centre for grain, cattle, and coal, Pekin is served by several railroads and is on the Lakes-to-Gulf Waterway. Manufactures include corn products, alcohol, liquor, malt, steel tanks, barrels, burial vaults, and copper, brass, iron, and aluminum castings. The Spring Lake State Park is nearby. Inc. 1839. Pop. (1980) 33,967.
40°35′ N, 89°40′ W
·map, United States **18**:909

Pekin, a breed of large, active, creamy-white ducks of Chinese origin; now the chief duck breed for meat in the U.S.
·popularity and general features **10**:1286h

Peking 14:1, also spelled PEKIN, Western conventional for Chinese PEI-CHING, Pinyin romanization BEIJING, capital of the People's Republic of China; it is almost surrounded by Hopeh Province and is bordered at two points by Tientsin Municipality. It has a metropolitan area of 6,900 sq mi (17,800 sq km). Pop. (1975 est.) 8,487,000.
39°55′ N, 116°25′ E

TEXT ARTICLE covers:
History **14**:1d
Physical organization 2e
Transportation 5c
Demography 5h
Housing and architecture 6f
The economy 7h
Political and governmental institutions 9h
Public utilities 10d
Health 11b
Education 11f
Cultural life 12g
The media 13e
Recreation 14a

REFERENCES in other text articles:
·Catholic bishopric establishments map **15**:1019
·culinary specialties **7**:943g
·ethnolinguistic centre and population **4**:270g; table
·Forbidden City design and construction **19**:200e; illus., **19**:Visual Arts, East Asian, Plate 6
·map, China **4**:263
Peking Opera
·instrumentation and vocal style **12**:675g
·origin and development **5**:472f
·population and industrial development **8**:1069e
·railway network statistics **4**:284f
·Yung-lo's establishment of capital **19**:1112d

Peking, Treaty of (Nov. 14, 1860), agreement confirming the Treaty of Aigun (1858; *see* unequal treaties), by which China ceded to Russia all the territory north of the Amur River as well as a strip of Pacific coastline (which included the site on which Vladivostok was later built).
·Russian expansion in Manchuria **11**:437b
·Russian territorial expansion **16**:66a

Peking Convention (1860): *see* unequal treaties.

Peking duck, delicacy of Chinese cuisine.
·preparation and serving techniques **7**:943g

Pekingese, also spelled PEKINESE, breed of toy dog developed in ancient China, where it was held sacred and was kept as a palace dog by members of the imperial family. It was introduced to the West after 1860. The Pekingese has been known, both in the Orient and

Pekingese

Sally Anne Thompson—EB Inc.

in the West, as the "lion dog"—presumably because of its appearance, although it is also acclaimed as having a lionlike independence and courage. It stands about 15 to 23 centimetres (6 to 9 inches) and weighs up to about 6.5 kilograms (14 pounds). The celebrated "sleeve dogs" are very small Pekingese once carried by Chinese royalty in the sleeves of their robes. A long-haired dog, the Pekingese has a full mane and heavily haired thighs, forelegs, tail, and toes. Its head is broad and flat, with hanging ears and a short, wrinkled muzzle. The coat may be solid or variegated in colour, but there is always a black mask across the face.

Peking man, hominid fossils classified as belonging to the species *Homo erectus pekinensis*, formerly classified *Sinanthropus pekinensis*, from Chou-k'ou-tien cave near Peking. Peking man was identified as a new fossil hominid by Davidson Black in 1927 on the basis of a single tooth. Later excavations yielded 14 skullcaps, several mandibles, facial bones, and limb bones, and the teeth of about 40 individuals. All are dated to the Middle Pleistocene, perhaps 350,000 years ago. Peking man is characterized by a cranial capacity averaging 1,075 cubic centimetres (range 850–1,300 cubic centimetres, overlapping the range of modern man, whose average is 1,350), a skull flat in profile but with a small forehead, a sagittal ridge on top of the head for attachment of powerful jaw muscles, very thick skull bones, heavy browridges, an occipital torus, a large palate, and a large, chinless jaw. The teeth are essentially human, though the canines and molars are quite large, and the enamel of the molars is often wrinkled. The limb bones are indistinguishable from those of modern man. Core tools, primitive flaked tools, worked-bone tools, charred animal bones, and the remains of hearths found in association with these hominid bones show that Peking man had a well-developed communal culture, practiced hunting, and used fire domestically. Peking man postdates Java man (*q.v.*) and is considered more advanced in having a larger cranial capacity, a forehead, and nonoverlapping canines.

The bones were under study at the Peking Union Medical College in 1941, when, with Japanese invasion imminent, an attempt was made to smuggle them out of China and to the United States. The bones disappeared and have never been recovered, leaving only plaster casts for study. Renewed excavation in the caves, beginning in 1958, brought new specimens to light.

Peking Man (1975) by Harry L. Shapiro describes the original finding of the fossils and their significance and reconstructs the circumstances under which they vanished.
·characteristics and taxonomy **11**:424a
·discovery and significance **19**:174c

·fossil record and inferred behaviour **8**:1031a; illus. 1032
·Hopeh origin and habitation **8**:1069a

Peking Planetarium, in Peking, educational centre for the dissemination of general knowledge in astronomy and natural science, completed in 1957.
·astronomy education and exhibitions **14**:13c

Peking University, in Peking, institution of higher education founded in 1898. In 1952 it absorbed the humanities and social science departments of Tsinghua University and was reorganized. For three years during the anti-intellectual, anti-urban Great Proletarian Cultural Revolution of the late 1960s the university was closed; it reopened in 1970.

In order to be enrolled, students must be politically acceptable, physically fit, and at least 20 years old, and have approximately a high school education and three years' practical experience, either in the army or on a job. For older workers with revolutionary experience the university waives the formal education requirement. All students live in dormitories, and they receive a government stipend from which they must pay for their food. Tuition, books, equipment, and medical treatment are free. The university is organized around a work-study program. Since the Cultural Revolution, teachers have been required to work periodically in either a rural or an urban job for one to three years. About half of the teachers may be engaged in outside employment at any one time.

The university, which emphasizes science, is under the Ministry of Education.
·Ch'en Tu-hsiu's revolutionary activities **4**:194g
·Hu Shih's literary reform **9**:66h
·May Fourth Movement activity **4**:368f
·Peking academic district **14**:11h; map 4

Peking Upper Cave fossils, skeletal remains of seven or eight *Homo sapiens* individuals (three of them children), including three well-preserved skulls. They were found in a cave at Chou-k'ou-tien, China, above that in which the *Homo erectus* fossils known as Peking man were found. Fossil fauna, including bear, deer, hyena, and ostrich, and stone tools, bone needles, perforated teeth of fox and deer (perhaps for necklaces), polished beads and deer antlers, and painted stones were found in association with the human bones. A date of late Fourth (Würm) Glacial Period, or possibly early postglacial, has been assigned the finds. The skulls belonged to one elderly man and two younger women. The old man's skull has a fractured left temporal bone, one woman's has a spearlike wound in the left parietal, and several other bones show fractures, evidence indicating that the people, perhaps a family, died a violent death. Franz Weidenreich, after studying the skulls, suggested that the Upper Cave people belonged to three different racial groups; the old man was of Paleolithic European type, one woman of Melanesian type, and the other woman of Eskimo type. Later workers reject this interpretation: X.Z. Wu (1961) expressed the majority opinion when he said that the Upper Cave people were early Mongoloids, closely related to modern Eskimos and American Indians. The original specimens were lost during World War II; excellent casts made in the late 1930s and accompanying descriptions, however, have permitted continued study of the fossils.

Peking Zoological Gardens, on the western outskirts of Peking, founded in 1908 by the empress dowager Tz'u-hsi. With an area of 175 acres (70 hectares), it houses more than 300 species of animals in a landscaped park with many trees. Among the rare species in the zoo's collection are the golden monkey, wild yak, kiang (Tibetan wild ass), Thorold's deer, goral, and Szechwan sambar. Peking was the first zoo to breed the giant panda (Ming-Ming, born in 1963).
·Peking recreational facilities **14**:14f

Pekkanen, Toivo (1902–57), Finnish novelist.
·contributions to Finnish prose **10**:1259d

Peko, Estonian agricultural deity who aided the growth of grain, especially barley. Peko was represented by a wax image that was buried in a granary and brought out in early spring for a ritual of agricultural increase. An entire village might participate in such a ceremony, for which the food and beer were furnished in common. After the ceremonial feast, remaining food would be distributed among the poor, and the men would engage in ritual wrestling or fence jumping to determine who would be the host for Peko in the following year. The first one to get a bleeding wound would take Peko home and store him in his granary. The word Peko may derive from the name of the Swedish deity Beyggvir, in turn deriving from *bjugg* ("barley"), which in its earliest form was *beggwu*.

pelage, the hairy, woolly, or furry coat of a mammal, distinguished from the underlying bare skin. The pelage is significant in several respects: as insulation, as a guard against injury, and, in its colouring and patterning, as a species adornment for mutual recognition among species members, concealment from enemies, or, in the case of many males, as a sexual allurement to promote courtship and mating. *Cf.* plumage. *Major ref.* **11**:406a
·fur component **7**:811d
·mammalian skin appendages **9**:671c
·wool characteristics **7**:283f

Pelagianism, 5th-century Christian heresy taught by Pelagius (*q.v.*) and his followers that stressed the essential goodness of human nature and the freedom of the human will. Pelagius was concerned about the slack moral standards among Christians, and he hoped to improve their conduct by his teachings. Rejecting the arguments of those who claimed that they sinned because of human weakness, he insisted that God made human beings free to choose between good and evil and that sin is voluntary. Celestius, a disciple of Pelagius, denied the church's doctrine of original sin and the necessity of infant Baptism.

Pelagianism was opposed by Augustine, bishop of Hippo, who asserted that human beings could not attain righteousness by their own efforts and were totally dependent upon the grace of God. Condemned by two councils of African bishops in 416, and again at Carthage in 418, Pelagius and Celestius were finally excommunicated in 418; Pelagius' later fate is unknown.

The controversy, however, was not over. Julian of Eclanum (*q.v.*) continued to assert the Pelagian view and engaged Augustine in literary polemic until the latter's death in 430. Julian himself was finally condemned, with the rest of the Pelagian party, at the Council of Ephesus in 431. Another heresy, known as Semi-Pelagianism (*q.v.*), flourished in southern Gaul until it was finally condemned at the second Council of Orange in 529.
·British adherence **3**:198a
·Christian condemnation as heresy **4**:541a
·origin, tenets, and Catholic response **2**:367b

Pelagia of Antioch, Saint (d. *c.* 311, Antioch, now Antakya, Tur.), 15-year-old Christian virgin who, probably during the persecution of Christians by the Roman emperor Diocletian, threw herself from a housetop to save her chastity and died instantly. Her martyrdom was endorsed and praised by St. Ambrose and by St. John Chrysostom. Her feast day is June 9.

The memory of this historical Pelagia influenced two legends of fictitious Pelagias—Pelagia the Penitent (or Margarito) and Pelagia Margaret of Tarsus. Pelagia the Penitent was a prostitute of Antioch who experienced sudden conversion to Christianity and then lived her remaining life disguised as a man in a cave at Jerusalem. Pelagia of Tarsus, for refusing to marry Diocletian, was roasted to death. Both legends are associated with that of St. Margaret of Antioch (*q.v.*).

pelagic sediments, also called PELAGIC DEPOSITS, deposits on the bottom of the open ocean composed principally of materials that have been organically or inorganically precipitated out of seawater, with particles derived from continental erosion minor or altogether lacking. The most abundant components of pelagic sediments are the calcareous and siliceous remains of microscopic photosynthesizing plankton such as the calcareous coccolithophorids and siliceous diatoms, and zooplankton such as the calcareous foraminifers and siliceous radiolarians. Phosphates are organically precipitated in much smaller quantities, as skeletal apatite in fish.

Inorganic pelagic sediments include nodules and encrustations composed of the oxides of manganese, iron, and other metals; minute grains of calcium, barium, lead, and strontium sulfates; and silicates of the zeolite group. Where depositional rates are very slow, pelagic sediments may contain significant quantities of fine-grained quartz and feldspar, which were brought to sea as atmospheric dust, and microscopic spherical meteorites composed of iron and nickel or silicates. *Major ref.* **11**:498e
·ocean basin sediments **13**:436c

RELATED ENTRIES in the *Ready Reference and Index:*
coccolith ooze; diatomaceous ooze; foraminiferal ooze; pteropod ooze; radiolarian ooze

pelagic zone, the ecologic realm that includes the entire ocean water column. Of all the inhabited Earth environments, the pelagic zone has the largest volume, 1,370,000,000 cubic kilometres (330,000,000 cubic miles), and the greatest vertical range, 11,000 metres (36,000 feet). Pelagic life is found throughout the water column, although the numbers of individuals and species decrease with increasing depth. The regional and vertical distributions of pelagic life are governed by the abundance of nutrients and dissolved oxygen; the presence or absence of sunlight, water temperature, salinity, and pressure; and the presence of continental or submarine topographic barriers.

Pelagic life consists of three categories. The phytoplankton, which constitute the food base of all marine animals, are microscopic organisms that inhabit only the sunlit uppermost oceanic layer, using sunlight to photosynthetically combine carbon dioxide and dissolved nutrient salts. Zooplankton are the marine animals that rely mainly upon water motion for transport, although some forms such as jellyfish are feeble swimmers. Zooplankton subsist on phytoplankton and smaller zooplankton and are dominated in their numbers by small crustacean copepods and euphasiids. Nekton (*q.v.*), the free swimmers, are dominated by the bony and cartilaginous fishes, molluscans, and decapods, with rarer mammals and reptiles. *Major ref.* **13**:498b; illus. 485
·cephalopod distribution and life-styles **3**:1151h
·commercial fishing method **7**:351g
·fish feeding and adaptations **7**:331d
·plankton **14**:494b

Pelagie Islands, Italian ISOLE PELAGIE, group of islands in the Mediterranean Sea between Malta and Tunisia, south of Sicily; administratively they form the commune of Lampedusa in Agrigento province, Sicily, Italy. The group consists of the islands of Lampedusa (*q.v.*) and Linosa and the islet called Isolotto Lampione. Pop. (1977 est.) Lampedusa and Linosa mun., 4,574.
35°40′ N, 12°40′ E
·map, Italy **9**:1089

Pelagius (b. *c.* 354, probably Britain—d. after 418, possibly Palestine), monk and theologian whose heterodox theological system known as Pelagianism emphasized the primacy of human effort in spiritual salvation.

Coming to Rome *c.* 380, Pelagius, though not a priest, became a highly regarded spiritual director for both clergy and laymen. The rigorous asceticism of his adherents acted as a reproach to the spiritual sloth of many Roman Christians, whose moral standards greatly distressed him. He blamed Rome's moral laxity on the doctrine of divine grace that he heard a bishop cite from the *Confessions* of the eminent Latin Church Father, Augustine of Hippo, who in his prayer for continence beseeched God to grant whatever grace the divine will determined. Pelagius attacked this teaching on the grounds that it imperilled the entire moral law. He thus reasoned that if a man were not himself responsible for his good and evil deeds, there was nothing to restrain him from indulgence in sin. Pelagius soon gained a considerable following at Rome. Henceforth his closest collaborator was a lawyer named Celestius.

After the fall of Rome to the Visigoth chieftan Alaric in 410, Pelagius and Celestius went to Africa. There they encountered the hostile criticism of Augustine, who published several denunciatory letters concerning their doctrine, particularly Pelagius' insistence on man's basically good moral nature and on man's own responsibility for voluntarily choosing Christian asceticism for his spiritual advancement.

Pelagius left for Palestine *c.* 412. There, although accused of heresy at the synod of Jerusalem in 415, he succeeded in clearing himself and avoiding censure. In response to further attacks from Augustine and the Latin biblical scholar Jerome, Pelagius wrote *De libero arbitrio* ("On Free Will"), which resulted in the condemnation of his teaching by two African councils, in 416. In 417 Pope Innocent I endorsed the condemnations and excommunicated Pelagius and Celestine. Under Innocent's successor, Zosimus, Pelagius' case was again considered at Rome. At first Zosimus, on the basis of Pelagius *Libellus fidei* ("Brief Statement of Faith"), pronounced him innocent, but after renewed investigation at the council of Carthage in 418, Zosimus confirmed the council's nine canons condemning Pelagius. Nothing more is known of Pelagius after this date.

·Christian 5th-century free will debate **4**:541a
·free will doctrine and followers **2**:367b
·Saint Jerome and the Pelagian problem **10**:138b
·St. Augustine's opposition to doctrine **10**:33g
·Virgin Mary's sinlessness **11**:562e

Pelagius, 13th-century cardinal of Santa Lucia.

·Crusade military intervention **5**:307c

Pelagius I (b. Rome—d. March 4, 561, Rome), pope from 556 to 561. His ecclesiastical roles under popes St. Agapetus I, St. Silverius, and Vigilius were highly important in the history of the church. As a deacon, he accompanied Agapetus to Constantinople, now Istanbul, to help him dissuade the Byzantine emperor Justinian I from attempting the reconquest of Italy. Before he died at Constantinople, Agapetus appointed Pelagius nuncio. When the Byzantine empress Theodora, Justinian's wife, apparently effected the deposition and banishment in March 537 of Agapetus' successor, Silverius, Pelagius returned to Rome. After the deacon Vigilius was made pope, Pelagius went to Constantinople, where he counselled Justinian, returning to Rome as imperial representative.

In the church, a massive complication, subsequently called the "Three Chapters Controversy," arose in reaction to Justinian's edict of 544 against certain Nestorian writings (after the condemned heretical teachings of Patriarch Nestorius of Constantinople). The edict attempted to pacify the powerful, anti-Nestorian Monophysites (Christians who believed that Christ has only one nature rather than two, human and divine). Vigilius was summoned to Constantinople in 545 to ratify the edict, and during his absence Pelagius served as defender of Rome when it was captured in 546 by the Ostrogothic king Totila, whom he courageously persuaded to spare the Romans. Since the Goths had been warring with the Byzantines in Italy, Totila sent Pelagius on an unsuccessful mission to Constantinople to negotiate a settlement with Justinian.

Pelagius remained in Constantinople with Vigilius, whom he accompanied to Rome and to Constantinople in 552, where they refused to attend the council of 553 to settle the "Three Chapters Controversy." The council condemned the Nestorian writings and their authors. When, however, Vigilius decided, in 554, to sanction Justinian's edict and the council's condemnation of the Three Chapters, Pelagius withdrew his support of the Pope, for which he was excommunicated. To Justinian, Pelagius wrote letters against Vigilius, the Byzantine emperor, and to the Council of Constantinople. Imprisoned, he was not released until the death in 555 of Vigilius, whom he formally condemned in his *In defensione trium capitulorum* ("In Defense of the Three Chapters"). Pelagius was reconciled with Justinian and was elected, through imperial insistence, to succeed Vigilius in 555, being consecrated at Rome on April 16, 556.

Italy, however, was in chaos. The West had not accepted the decrees of the Council of Constantinople, and a schism immediately erupted that continued until 610. One of Pelagius' most urgent problems was to rebuild Rome, a task made easier because Justinian in 554 had promulgated his Pragmatic Sanction, confirming and increasing the pope's temporal power. In effect, Pelagius was the official protector of the civil population. By making his new rights resolute and by organizing the temporal government of papal sovereignty, Pelagius began the foundation of the papacy's political power. He then faced new problems. With the Eastern emperors no longer papal opponents, his role as spiritual head of the church shifted to concentrate on the danger of barbarian invasion and on the protection of the Italian peoples.

Despite his explicit correspondence, Pelagius was unable to prevent the bishops of Milan and Istria from schism because as pope he reversed his opinion and upheld the Council of Constantinople, arguing that the decrees of a general council could not be repudiated by a provincial council. His aim was church unification, and his power was set by the imperial government. In addition to his ecclesiastical labours, he was faced with the problem of alleviating the drastic aftermath of the Gothic invasions and wars. Pelagius' formative years and pontificate reveal the enormous difficulties of his time. Editions of his writings appeared in 1932 and 1956.

Pelagius II (b. Rome—d. Feb. 7, 590, Rome), pope from 579 to 590. Of Gothic descent, he was elected as Pope Benedict I's successor on Nov. 26, 579, without imperial confirmation. His pontificate was continually troubled by the Lombards, a Germanic people living in northern Italy, who were besieging Rome. The Lombard problem was crucial because it threatened not only Rome but also the Italian peoples, for whom the papacy was responsible as a result of temporal power granted the papacy in 554 by the Byzantine emperor Justinian I.

Pelagius sent the deacon Gregory (later Pope St. Gregory I the Great) as nuncio to Constantinople (modern Istanbul) for aid from the Byzantine emperor Tiberius II. Involved in wars with Persia, Tiberius was unable to help, and for the first time in papal history Pelagius appealed to the Catholic Franks. In a letter (580) to the Frankish bishop of Auxerre he declared it was the Franks' duty as Christians to defend Rome and Italy against the "deathly race" of the Lombards. Gregory persuaded Tiberius to approve Pelagius' unprecedented appeal and to grant the Franks subsidies. Halted in their advance, the Lombards took up a defensive position; but, when the Franks withdrew, the Lombards threatened again, and Pelagius made an appeal to Tiberius' successor, Maurice. The imperial representative in Italy, Exarch Smaragdus of Ravenna, finally negotiated peace in 585.

In the meantime, Pelagius tried unsuccessfully to end the long-standing schism in northern Italy, where certain bishops had broken with Rome over the "Three Chapters Controversy," a complicated dispute among the papacy, Justinian, and the Council (553) of Constantinople over the censuring of Nestorian writings (based on the condemned heretical teachings of Patriarch Nestorius of Constantinople). Despite Pelagius' efforts, the schism continued until 610.

Although relationships between Rome and Maurice were good, a dispute arose over St. John IV the Faster, bishop of Constantinople. Pelagius protested when John assumed the title—traditional at Constantinople since the 5th century—of ecumenical patriarch, which seemed to make him Pelagius' equal, if not his superior. Maurice supported John, and thus began a titular controversy between the Byzantine and Western churches, sharpened by Pelagius' refusal to accept the decrees of a Constantinopolitan council endorsed by John.

Pelagius was responsible for building projects in Rome, including a basilica adjacent to San Lorenzo fuori le Mura. He died in a plague that struck Rome after a disastrous flood.

Pelagornithidae, fossil family of birds of the order Pelecaniformes.

·pelecaniform classification **14**:19g

Pelamis (snake): *see* sea snake.

pelargonidin, a pigment giving a red or blue colour to certain flowers, *e.g.*, cornflowers and dahlias.

·properties and occurrence **4**:917h

pelargonium (plant): *see* geranium.

Pelasgi, also PELASGIANS, name used by the ancient Greeks for the pre-Hellenic (in modern terminology, "pre-Indo-European") people who occupied Greece before the 12th century BC. They were mentioned as a specific people by several Greek authors, including Homer, Herodotus, and Thucydides, and were said to have inhabited various areas, such as Thrace, Argos, Crete, and Chalcidice; in the 5th century BC the surviving villages apparently preserved a common non-Greek language.

It is uncertain whether any ancient people actually called themselves Pelasgi, and in later Greek usage their name was applied to all "aboriginal" Aegean populations.

Pelavicino (PALLAVICINO), **Oberto** (b. 1197, Palesine, Italy—d. May 8, 1269, Gisalecchio), leader of the Ghibelline (imperial) party in northern Italy and powerful supporter of the Holy Roman emperor Frederick II and his sons.

As a member of a great feudal family of Lombardy, Pelavicino fought at Frederick's side in 1238 against Brescia, near Milan, and the following year became imperial vicar (deputy of the emperor) in Lunigiana and Pontremoli, near Genoa. He acted as Frederick's representative in several north Italian cities, serving as podesta (chief magistrate) of Reggio in 1246 and at Cremona in 1249 and after 1249 as imperial vicar over the area from Pavia to Tuscany.

After Frederick's death (1250), he served in 1253 as imperial vicar in Lombardy for Frederick's son Conrad IV and, after Conrad's death (1254), took advantage of political turmoil to become lord of Pavia, Cremona, and Piacenza, allying himself with the Veronese tyrant Ezzelino da Romano against the Guelf supporters of the pope. In 1258 he quarrelled with Ezzelino over the possession of Brescia. Transferring his allegiance to Conrad's younger brother, King Manfred, he made an alliance with Azzo d'Este of Ferrara that contributed to Ezzelino's defeat by Guelf forces in 1259. The following year the Della Torre family, lords of Milan, made Oberto captain general for five years, with nominal control over several neighbouring cities. The invasion of Charles of Anjou's Guelf army in 1264–65 drove him out of Milan, and he died four years later, his power greatly diminished by the Ghibelline defeat.

Pelayo (d. *c.* 737) first king of the Christian Kingdom of Asturias (*q.v.*) in northern Spain, with its capital at Cangas de Onís. Asturias survived the period of Moorish hegemony to become the spearhead of the Christian Reconquista in the later Middle Ages. Pelayo, who became a popular figure in Spanish legend and a symbol of Christian resistance, was probably a Visigothic noble, but little is known about his life.
·Muslim defeat at Covadonga **17**:407d

Pele, Hawaiian goddess of fire.
·volcano origin myths **6**:75a

Pelé, byname of EDSON ARANTES DO NASCIMENTO (b. Oct. 23, 1940, Três Corações, Braz.), association football (soccer) player, in his time probably the most famous and possibly the best paid athlete in the world. In competition for the World Cup (Jules Rimet Trophy) he led the Brazilian national team to three victories (1958, 1962, 1970) and permanent possession of the trophy.

Pelé
A.F.P.—Pictorial Parade

After playing for a minor league club at Bauru, São Paulo state, Pelé (whose nickname apparently is without significance) was rejected by major league teams in the city of São Paulo. In 1956, however, he joined the Santos Football Club, which, with Pelé at inside left forward, won several South American clubs' cups and, in 1962, its first world club championship. On Nov. 20, 1969, in his 909th first-class match, he scored his 1,000th goal. A medium-sized man (5 feet 8 inches, 160 pounds), he combined kicking power and accuracy with a remarkable ability to anticipate other players' moves. Sometimes called "Pérola Negra" ("Black Pearl"), he became a Brazilian national hero.

Pelé announced his retirement in 1974 but in 1975 agreed to play through the 1977 season for the New York Cosmos of the North American Soccer League and to promote the game in the United States.
·soccer professionalism **2**:211a

Peléan-type eruption, a type of volcanic eruption (*q.v.*) similar to that which occurred in Martinique in 1902.

Pelecaniformes 14:15, an order of water birds including pelican, booby, cormorant, gannet, snakebird, frigate bird, and tropic bird.

The text article covers the general features of the pelecaniformes, their natural history, form and function, and evolution and classification.

RELATED ENTRIES in the *Ready Reference and Index:*
booby; cormorant; frigate bird; gannet; pelican; snakebird; tropic bird

Pelecanoididae, small family of birds, the diving petrels (*q.v.*).

Pelecinidae, family of insects of the order Hymenoptera.
·characteristics and classification **9**:132h

Pelecypoda, in biology, class of mollusks that includes all bivalves; *e.g.,* oysters and clams. Some authorities name the class Bivalvia (*q.v.*).

Pelée, Mount, French MONTAGNE PELÉE, active volcanic mountain on the Caribbean island of Martinique. Situated 15 mi (24 km) northwest of Fort-de-France, it is 4,583 ft (1,397 m) high. The Pelée (French: Bald Mountain) massif consists of volcanic ash and lavas. A gently sloping cone, it is scored with ravines and supports luxuriant forests. Minor eruptions occurred in 1792 and 1851, but on May 8, 1902, it destroyed the port of Saint-Pierre (*q.v.*), killing approximately 30,000 people.
14°48′ N, 61°10′ W
·eruption and deaths **9**:227d; table
·eruption in 1902 and results **19**:502h
·intrusive igneous core **9**:219g
·lava protrusion **9**:216d
·map, Martinique **11**:547
·Martinique's physical features **11**:547e

Pelee Island, in Lake Erie, southern Ontario, Canada. It lies near the Ohio boundary, a few miles south of Point Pelee National Park and has an area of 18 sq mi (47 sq km). Originally leased from the Indians by Thomas McKee in 1788, it was acquired in 1823 by William McCormick. Viticulture was practiced until 1855, when John Scudder drained marshes for raising vegetables and tobacco. Later soybeans became the leading crop. Middle Island, a rock off its southern coast, is the southernmost point of Canada. Pop. (1976) 275.
41°47′ N, 82°40′ W
·map, Great Lakes **8**:302

Pèlerinage de Charlemagne, 12th-century Old French chanson de geste.
·chansons de geste forms and themes **10**:1102c

Peletier, Jacques, also known as PELETIER DU MANS (b. 1517, Le Mans, Fr.—d. 1582, Paris), poet and critic whose knowledge and love of Greek and Latin poetry influenced the group of French poetic reformers known as La Pléiade. In the preface to his translation of Horace's *Ars Poetica* (1545) and in his *Art poétique française* (1555) he put forward his own program for the reform of French poetry. He insisted that poets must imitate the classics if French literature was to rise to great heights. In addition to lyric poetry, Peletier wrote major works on mathematics and spelling reform.
·literature of the Renaissance **10**:1134d

Peleus, in Greek mythology, king of the Myrmidons of Thessaly; he was most famous as the husband of Thetis (a sea nymph) and the father of the hero Achilles, whom he survived. When he and his brother Telamon were banished from Aegina, the kingdom of their father Aeacus, he went to Phthia to be purified by his uncle King Eurytion, whose daughter Antigone he married, receiving a third of Eurytion's kingdom. During the Calydonian boar hunt he accidentally killed Eurytion. He then went to Iolcus to be purified by King Acastus, whose wife Astydameia made advances to him. When he refused her, she told Antigone that he wanted to marry her daughter, causing Antigone to hang herself. Peleus later won the sea nymph Thetis by capture, and all the gods came to the wedding. But after she bore Achilles to him, she returned to the depths of the sea, later fetching Peleus to dwell with her.

Pelew (Caroline Islands): *see* Palau.

Pelham, the name, derived from Pelham in northeastern Hertfordshire, of an English family, different branches of which have held the baronies of Pelham of Laughton (1706–68) and Pelham of Stanmer (from 1762), the earldoms of Clare (1714–68), Chichester (from 1801), and Yarborough (from 1837), and the dukedoms of Newcastle upon Tyne (1715–68) and Newcastle-under-Lyme (from 1756). A branch also settled in New England; Herbert Pelham (died 1674) was treasurer of Harvard College.

Pelham, town, Hampshire County, west central Massachusetts, U.S. Pop. (1980) 1,112.
42°24′ N, 72°24′ W
·Massachusetts' historic sites **11**:595b

Pelham, Henry (b. 1696—d. March 6, 1754, London), prime minister of Great Britain from 1743 to 1754. A colourless politician, he worked for peace abroad and introduced important financial reforms.

Henry Pelham, detail of a portrait by John Shackleton, *c.* 1752; in the National Portrait Gallery, London
By courtesy of the National Portrait Gallery, London

First elected to Parliament in 1717, Pelham became a supporter of Robert Walpole (prime minister 1730–42), who helped him obtain appointments as lord of the treasury (1721), secretary for war (1724), and paymaster to the forces (1730). After Walpole resigned under pressure from the House of Commons in 1742, Pelham became prime minister and chancellor of the exchequer in a ministry that included his brother Thomas Pelham-Holles, duke of Newcastle, and John Carteret, a favourite of King George II.

Carteret's attempts to involve England more deeply in conflict with France and Prussia (War of the Austrian Succession, 1740–48) caused Pelham to dismiss him in 1744, shortly after Carteret had been created Earl Granville. When George II continued to push for the return of Granville, Pelham retaliated by calling for a mass resignation of the ministers on Feb. 11, 1746—the first such action in English history. Since Granville was unable to form a new ministry, Pelham returned to office three days later, bringing into his ministry William Pitt (later earl of Chatham), whom the King disliked. In 1748 Pelham signed the Treaty of Aix-la-Chapelle, which ended the war.
·Britain's 18th-century politics **3**:252g
·Pitt the Elder's political relations **14**:476d

Pelham-Holles, Thomas, 1st duke of Newcastle: *see* Newcastle, Thomas Pelham-Holles, 1st duke of.

Peliades (455 BC), play by Euripides.
·synopsis and significance **6**:1032a

Pelias, in Greek mythology, a king of Thessaly who imposed on his stepnephew Jason the task of bearing off the Golden Fleece. According to Homer, Pelias and Neleus were twin sons of Tyro (daughter of Salmoneus, founder of Salmonica in Elis) by the sea god Poseidon, who came to her disguised as the river god Enipeus, whom she loved. The twins were exposed at birth but were found and raised by a horse herder. Later, Pelias seized the throne and exiled Neleus.

Later legend relates that on Jason's return with the Fleece, his wife Medea, the enchantress, took revenge on Pelias by persuading his daughters, except for Alcestis, to cut up and boil their father in the mistaken belief that he would thereby recover his youth.

pelican (*Pelecanus*), any of seven living species comprising the family Pelicanidae (order Pelecaniformes). The pelican is a water bird notable for its distensible throat pouch. Young pelicans thrust their bills down the parent's gullet to take regurgitated food.

Pelicans inhabit lakes, rivers, and seacoasts of tropical and temperate regions in many parts of the world. They breed in colonies on islands. The one to four large, bluish-white eggs, often laid on a stick nest, hatch in about a month. The young mature in about three years. Though ungainly on land, adult pelicans are impressive in flight. Singly or in flocks they may soar far overhead. Sexes look alike; males are slightly larger. Best known are two species usually called white pelicans: *Pelecanus erythrorhynchos* of the New World and *P. onocrotalus* of the Old World. Reaching a

Brown pelican (*Pelecanus occidentalis*)

Norman Tomalin—Bruce Coleman Inc.

length of 180 centimetres (70 inches), with a wingspread of 3 metres (10 feet), and weighing up to 13 kilograms (30 pounds), they are among the largest of living birds.

·brown pelican guano production **14**:15b *passim* to 18e
·heraldic use and religious significance **8**:789e
·physics principles in wing structure **7**:544a

pelican flower: *see* birthwort.

Pelidnota punctata (beetle): *see* shining leaf chafer.

Péligot, Eugène-Melchior (1811–90), a French chemist known for work in connection with uranium.

·uranium element isolation **18**:1034f

Pelion, Mount, Modern Greek óros píLION, range on the Magnesia peninsula of southeast Thessaly, Greece, rising to 5,417 ft (1,651 m). Mt. Pelion (5,075 ft [1,547 m]), just northeast of Vólos, has a wooded western flank overlooking a gulf whose ancient ports were Iolcus and Pagasae. In Greek mythology it was the home of Centaurs. The ship "Argo" of the Argonauts allegedly was built of wood from its trees.
39°28′ N, 23°02′ E

Pélissier, Aimable-Jean-Jacques, duc de Malakoff (b. Nov. 16, 1794, Maromme, Fr. —d. May 22, 1864, Algiers), French general who distinguished himself in the conquest of Algeria and was the last French commander in chief in the Crimean War.

Pélissier; engraving by an unknown artist

H. Roger-Viollet

Educated at the military schools of La Flèche and Saint-Cyr, Pélissier was commissioned as an artillery second lieutenant in 1815. In 1823 he served in the Spanish campaign to suppress the revolution against Ferdinand VI and in 1828–29 fought against the Turks in the Peloponnese. After his first brief service in Algeria in 1830, he returned there in 1839 to take part in the campaign against the patriot emir of Mascara, Abdelkader. He fought with distinction, being promoted to general in 1846, and served as military commander of the coastal province of Oran from 1848 to 1851. During the 1852 coup d'etat of Napoleon III, he was interim governor of Algeria. Subsequently, he played a leading role in the subjugation of the tribes of southern Algeria.

In January 1855 Pélissier was given command of an army corps in the Crimea, defeating a Russian attack on the Traktir Ridge on August 16 and capturing the fort of Malakoff and the city of Sevastopol on September 8. Four days later he was made marshal of France and in July 1858 was created duc de Malakoff. From March 1858 to April 1859 Pélissier was French ambassador to London. In 1860 he was appointed governor of Algeria, a post he held at the time of his death.

Péłla, department, Macedonia, Greece.

·area and population table **8**:318

Pella, city, Marion County, south central Iowa, U.S., between the Des Moines and Skunk rivers. It was founded in 1847 by Dutch immigrants, who chose the name Pella (after the city in Jordan that served as a place of refuge to Christians from Jerusalem at the beginning of the Jewish revolt against Rome in AD 66) for their future settlement before they left The Netherlands. The city has a farm-based economy and is known for its annual tulip festival (held in May), its bologna, and bakeries. Central College (1853; affiliated with the Reformed Church) and the boyhood home of the Western lawman Wyatt Earp are there. Inc. 1855. Pop. (1980) 8,349.
41°25′ N, 92°55′ W

Pella, ancient capital of King Archelaus of Macedonia at the end of the 5th century BC and birthplace of Alexander the Great. Originally known as Bounomos, the city developed rapidly under Philip II, but after the defeat of the last Macedonian king by the Romans (167 BC) it sank to the status of a small provincial town.

The site of Pella, in northern Greece about 24 miles northwest of Thessaloníki, has long been known. Excavations by the Greek Archaeological Service begun in 1957 have revealed the rectangular grid plan of the town and large, well-built houses with colonnaded courts and rooms with mosaic floors portraying scenes of lion hunts and of Dionysus riding a panther.

·growth and importance under Antigonids **8**:381d
·map, Greece **8**:314
·mosaic floor design **12**:466d; illus.

Pellaea (plant): *see* cliffbrake.

pellagra (Latin: "rough skin"), nutritional disorder caused in large part by a deficiency of niacin, a member of the vitamin B complex (vitamin B_5), and characterized by skin lesions and by gastrointestinal and neurological disturbances—the so-called classical three Ds of pellagra: dermatitis, diarrhea, and dementia.

The skin lesions are the most characteristic and usually the earliest symptoms. They result from an abnormal sensitization of the skin to sunlight and tend to occur symmetrically on the exposed surfaces of the arms, legs, and neck. They may look at first like a severe sunburn, later becoming reddish brown, rough, and scaly.

Gastrointestinal symptoms usually consist of alternate constipation and diarrhea, with an accompanying inflammation of the mouth and the tongue, and fissuring and dry scaling of the lips and corners of the mouth.

Neurological signs appear later in most cases, when the skin and alimentary manifestations are prominent. The dementia, or mental aberrations, may include general nervousness, confusion, depression, apathy, and delirium. In humans, pellagra is seldom a deficiency of niacin alone; response to niacin therapy tends to be partial, whereas the therapeutic administration of multivitamins commonly brings swift recovery. Mild or suspected instances of niacin deficiency can be effectively treated with a well-balanced diet alone.

The breakthrough in the understanding of pellagra took place in 1937, when it was shown that the disorder known as black tongue in dogs could be cured by the administration of niacin (also called nicotinic acid) or the amide of niacin (nicotinic acid amide or nicotinamide). Pellagra is now seldom encountered in countries in which the population generally eats a well-balanced diet, but it still occurs widely where the diet is high in starchy foods and low in essential amino acids and vitamins. Corn (maize), for example, is low in both niacin and tryptophan, the latter being an amino acid that is converted to niacin in the body. Such foods as milk and eggs, although low in niacin, will protect the body from pellagra because their proteins contain sufficient tryptophan for the body synthesis of niacin. Pellagra can also be a side effect of chronic alcoholism.

·causation and symptoms **4**:224a
·cause discovery through experimentation **12**:279c
·causes, symptoms, and cures **13**:411a
·dietary niacinamide deficiency as cause **13**:419d
·Hartnup disease symptoms **11**:1056e

Pelléas et Mélisande (1892), play by Belgian playwright Maeterlinck.

·staging and nonillusionistic scenery **17**:548c

Pelléas et Mélisande, opera in five acts by the French composer Claude Debussy, with libretto based on Maurice Maeterlinck's poetic drama (1892). The opera was first performed on April 30, 1902, at the Opéra-Comique, in Paris.

·Debussy's Wagnerian influence **5**:541b
·integration of text and score **13**:589c

Pelleas und Melisande, Opus 5 (1902–03), symphonic poem for a large orchestra composed by Arnold Schoenberg and based on the drama by Maurice Maeterlinck.

·composition and first performance **16**:350c

Pellegrini, Carlo, pseudonym APE (b. March 1839, Capua, Italy—d. Jan. 22, 1889, London), caricaturist notable for his portraits of prominent Englishmen appearing in *Vanity Fair*. As a young man he was a part of Neopolitan society, whose members he caricatured in a good-natured way. Following an unhappy love affair and the death of a sister, he went to England in 1864 and turned his hand to cartooning. His first effort—a cartoon of Benjamin Disraeli—appeared in *Vanity Fair* in 1869, shortly before he adopted the signature "Ape." His second, of William Gladstone, appeared a week later. One of the best known is of the writer Thomas Carlyle, which appeared in 1870. His portraits were gently humorous, in keeping with his genial disposition.

Pellegrini, Carlos (1847–1906), Argentine president from 1890 to 1892.
·political and economic problems **1**:1147f

pellet bell (musical instrument): *see* rattle.

Pelletier, Pierre-Joseph (b. March 22, 1788, Paris—d. July 19, 1842, Paris), chemist who helped found the chemistry of alkaloids.

Pelletier was professor and from 1832 director of the École de Pharmacie, Paris. In 1817, in collaboration with the French chemist Joseph-Bienaimé Caventou, he isolated chlorophyll, the green pigment in plants that is essential to plant food manufacture by the process of photosynthesis. His interests soon turned to a new class of vegetable bases now called alkaloids, and he isolated emetine. With Caventou he continued his search for alkaloids, and in 1820 they discovered brucine, cinchonine, colchicine, quinine, strychnine, and veratrine. Some of these compounds soon found medicinal uses. Such applications marked the beginning of the gradual shift away from the use of plant extracts and toward the use of natural and synthetic compounds found in nature or formulated by the chemist.

In 1823 Pelletier published analyses of several alkaloids, thus providing a basis for alkaloid chemistry. He also did important studies of other compounds, including caffeine, piperine, and picrotoxin.

pelletization, in metallurgy, the process of forming a small, round, spherical body; frequently applied to metal ores, especially iron ore.
·clay mineral industrial uses **4**:706b
·iron beneficiation processes **9**:895d
·mineral agglomeration process **11**:1065b

Pellew, Edward: *see* Exmouth, Edward Pellew, 1st Viscount.

Pellia, a genus of about four species of liverworts in the order Jungermanniales. The greenish plant body (thallus), less than 1.5 centimetres (about 0.6 inch) wide, often is branched or lobed, with a notch at the end of each branch. The lobes may have slightly ruffled edges. *Pellia epiphylla*, a large species frequently discussed in biology texts as a typical liverwort, commonly forms patches up to 50 centimetres (about 20 inches) on damp banks throughout the Northern Hemisphere. Both male and female reproductive structures are borne on the same plant in this species, and usually only one sporophyte (asexual plant) develops, although several eggs may be fertilized. The sporophyte has a shiny, greenish-black, rounded spore case on a long stalk surrounded at its base by a ragged-edged collar.

Pellia epiphylla
A to Z Botanical Collection—EB Inc.

Pellicieraceae, family of flowering plants in the order Theales.
·classification and general features **18**:211c

pellicle, thin, protective envelope covering many protozoans, usually closely associated with the plasma membrane.
·cell shape and size **3**:1045c
·protozoan protective coverings **15**:125e

Pellico, Silvio (b. June 25, 1789, Saluzzo, Italy—d. Jan. 31, 1854, Turin), patriot, dramatist, and author of *Le mie prigioni* (1832; Eng. trans., *My Prisons*, 1853), memoirs of his sufferings as a political prisoner, which inspired widespread sympathy for the Italian nationalist movement, the Risorgimento. Educated at Turin, he later spent four years in France, returning to Italy in 1809 to begin his career as a poet and playwright. His romantic tragedy *Francesca da Rimini* (published 1818) was a success on its first performance (1815) and was followed by several others. He had already become one of the circle of Romantic revolutionary writers including Vincenzo Monti, Ugo Foscolo, Giovanni Berchet, and Alessandro Manzoni, and in 1818 he collaborated in founding a liberal and patriotic newspaper, *Il Conciliatore*, of which he became editor. After its suppression by the Austrian police (1819) he joined the Carbonari and, in October 1820, was arrested for treason. In 1822 he was sentenced to death, but the sentence was commuted to life imprisonment of which he served eight wretched years in prisons in Milan, Venice, and the infamous Spielberg (Spilberk) fortress (used as a political prison by the Habsburgs) in Brunn (now Brno, Czech.). From 1838 he lived with his wife in Turin. Of his plays, poetry, and prose works, *Le mie prigioni* is still widely read and translated for its simple, direct style, spiritual revelation, and Christian piety. According to the Italian statesman and political writer, Conte Cesare Balbo, its condemnation of Austrian persecution was more damaging to Austria than a defeat on the battlefield.
·Italian literature of the 19th century **10**:1200g

Pellico, detail of an oil painting by Luigi Norfini (1825–1909)
SCALA, New York

Pellipario, Nicola (d. *c.* 1542), Italian ceramist and painter.
·majolica decorative painting **14**:906d

pellitory (plant): *see* Urticaceae.

Pellorneum ruficeps (bird): *see* jungle babbler.

Pelloutier, Fernand (b. Oct. 1, 1867, Paris—d. March 13, 1901, Paris), a leading organizer and theoretician of the French labour movement who deeply influenced the philosophy and methods of anarcho-syndicalist labour unionism.

As a young journalist in the town of Saint-Nazaire, Pelloutier became a member of the Parti Ouvrier Français, the largest Marxist Socialist party in France at the time; but he left it in 1892 after the party's leader repudiated the idea of the general strike as romantic and impractical. Disillusioned by the intolerance and dogmatism of leftist party politics, he turned to anarchism and in 1895 became secretary of the Fédération des Bourses du Travail, an institution combining the functions of workers' clubs, employment exchanges, and local labour union federations. He criticized orthodox Marxists for relying upon the apparatus of the state, a bourgeois institution, as a means of changing society and asserted that the state would be replaced by a "voluntary and free association of producers." This association would be based upon the Bourses du Travail. Through them, Pelloutier believed, the workers would evolve communistic forms of production and create "a socialist state within the bourgeois state."

Pelloutier was a gifted organizer as well as a theoretician, and under his guidance the bourses grew in number until he claimed more than 250,000 members throughout France. In 1900 he founded the Office Nationale de la Statistique et de la Placement, for the purpose of getting satisfactory employment for workers and reducing job competition.

In his *Histoire des bourses du travail* (1902), Pelloutier defined the theory and practice of anarcho-syndicalism.
·Anarcho-Syndicalist development **1**:810c
·trade unionism's evolution **16**:968d

Pelloux, Luigi (Girolamo) (b. March 1, 1839, La Roche, Savoy, now in France—d. Oct. 26, 1924, Bordighera, Italy), Italian general and prime minister who brought his country to the brink of crisis by adopting an extremely repressive domestic policy that he attempted to promulgate with extraconstitutional methods.

After graduation from the military academy at Turin (1857), Pelloux fought in several battles against Austria, distinguishing himself as a brave and capable leader. He rose through the ranks and as major commanded the artillery that first breached Rome's Porta Pia, thus allowing the occupation of the city (1870), which the troops of a uniting Italy made the country's capital.

In 1880 Pelloux began his political career in the House of Deputies. Promoted to general in 1885, he was minister of war in three cabinets (1891–92, 1892–93, 1896–97). In 1896 he was made a senator. When disturbances broke out in Bari, where he was commander of the army corps, he recognized that the unrest arose from extreme economic need and refused to declare martial law, thus gaining the favour of the leftists. Similar outbursts in other Italian cities, however, led to the downfall of the government.

Invited to form a government (June 1898), Pelloux began correcting the excesses of the previous administration. Soon, however, his training as an army officer asserted itself, and he introduced a repressive bill that would have greatly curtailed civil liberties (February 1899). To avoid defeat on his foreign policy, which featured an unsuccessful military expedition to China, Pelloux resigned (March 1899) and formed a second, more conservative government.

Although the country was now quite calm, Pelloux attempted to make his earlier bill more repressive, thus finally uniting the left in opposition against him. Pelloux prorogued the chamber and tried to have the bill passed by royal decree. When the decree was ruled void by the Court of Cassation (February 1900), Pelloux had to resubmit his bill to a thoroughly hostile chamber. Forced to resign on June 18, 1900, he was given command of an army corps at Turin (1900–02).

·repressive decrees and resignation **9**:1165e

pellucid zone (anatomy): *see* zona pellucida.

Pelly River, in central Yukon Territory, Canada, one of the main headstreams of the Yukon River. It was discovered in 1840 by Robert Campbell, who named it after Sir John Henry Pelly, governor of the Hudson's Bay Company. Rising in the Mackenzie Mountains, the river flows 330 mi (530 km), receiving its two major tributaries, Ross and Macmillan rivers, before joining the upper course of the Yukon. It is navigable for small steamers for more than 200 mi except in the shallows of Bradens Canyon.
62°47′ N, 137°19′ W

·exploration, length, and drainage **19**:1107e *passim* to 1108e
·map, Canada **3**:716

Pelobatidae, family of frogs including the spadefoot toad (*q.v.*).

pelog: *see in* gamelan; patet.

Pelomedusidae, family of turtles commonly called side-necked turtle (*q.v.*).

Pelopia, in Greek legend, the wife of Atreus (*q.v.*).

Pelopidas (d. 364 BC, Cynoscephalae, Thessaly, Greece), Theban statesman and general responsible, with his friend Epaminondas, for the brief period (371–362) of Theban hegemony in mainland Greece. In 385 he served in a Theban contingent sent to support the Spartans at Mantineia, where he was seriously wounded but was saved by Epaminondas. Upon the seizure of the Theban citadel by the Spartans (382), Pelopidas fled to Athens and took the lead in a conspiracy to liberate Thebes. In 379 his party surprised and killed their chief political opponents and, by arousing the people, were able to force the Spartan garrison to surrender. In this and subsequent years he was elected chief magistrate of Thebes. Pelopidas was the leader of the Sacred Band, a picked infantry body of 300, which routed a large Spartan force at Tegyra (near Orchomenus) in 375 and distinguished itself in the defeat of Sparta at the decisive Battle of Leuctra (371). In 369, in response to a petition of the Thessalians, an army under Pelopidas drove Alexander, tyrant of Pherae, out of Thessaly. Later Pelopidas was seized by Alexander, and two expeditions from Thebes were needed to win his release. Finally Pelopidas defeated Alexander at Cynoscephalae (364) but was killed in the combat.

·Epaminondas' military support **6**:902g
·role in Theban rise **8**:363f

Peloponnese, also called PELOPONNESUS, Modern Greek PELOPÓNNISOS, large, mountainous peninsula of 8,278 sq mi (21,439 sq km), since antiquity a major region of Greece, joined to the rest of mainland Greece by the Isthmus of Corinth. The name, which is derived from Pelopos Nisos (Island of Pelops, a legendary hero), does not appear in Homer, who preferred to apply the name of Argos, a Mycenaean city-state, to the whole peninsula. The Mycenaean civilization flourished in the 2nd millennium BC at such centres as Mycenae, Tiryns, and Pylos. The city-state of Sparta was the major rival of Athens for dominion over Greece from about the 5th century BC until the Roman conquest in the 2nd century. By the 14th century AD the Peloponnese was known as the Morea ("Mulberry"), first applied to Elis, a northwestern mulberry-growing district, and was the site of the Despotate of Morea (*q.v.*). Patras (Pátrai), the major city, located in the north, has continued to gain commercial importance since the War of Greek Independence (1821–29), but the south has lagged behind the rest of Greece. Highways and railways link all the major regions of the Peloponnese except Laconia with the rest of Greece. *Major ref.* **8**:313b

·area and population table **8**:318
·Bronze Age civilization **1**:111g; map 112
·Epaminondas' four military invasions **6**:903a
·history of ancient Greece **8**:328d; maps 326, 335, 382
·jewelry-making development **10**:168d; illus. 170
·map, Greece **8**:314
·Peloponnesian War **14**:20e; map 21

Peloponnesian League, alliance of city-states of the Peloponnese in Greece, led by Sparta, which was formed in the 6th century BC and lasted till 366 BC, when it was dissolved after the defeat of Sparta at the Battle of Leuctra (371).

·formation, extent, and function **8**:340b *passim* to 364h
·Greek city-state defense system **14**:20f; map 21

Peloponnesian War 14:20, sometimes called SECOND, OR GREAT, PELOPONNESIAN WAR (431–404 BC), war between the two leading Greek city-states, Athens and Sparta, that broke the power of the Athenian empire and has traditionally been thought to mark the decline of Greek civilization.

The text article describes how the growing rivalry between Athens and Sparta led to the outbreak of war in the spring of 431 BC. The first 10 years of the conflict, known as the Archidamian War, ended inconclusively in 421 with the Peace of Nicias. The unstable truce broke down completely in 415, when Athens sent out a great armada to conquer Sicily. Spartan troops helped the Sicilians destroy the entire Athenian expeditionary force (413). As a result of the disaster, a group of oligarchs seized power in Athens (411), but they in turn were overthrown in a popular revolution that established a moderate democratic government known as the Five Thousand. A Spartan fleet, subsidized by the Persians, destroyed the Athenian navy at the Battle of Aegospotami in 405, and the following year Athens fell to the Spartans.

REFERENCES in other text articles:
·Alcibiades in Athenian politics **1**:436f
·causes, events, and effects **8**:356g
·censorship in ancient Greece **3**:1084c
·eclipse as decisive factor **6**:196b
·Pericles' strategy and results **14**:68f
·Persian role **9**:835f
·Persian role in Anatolian alliances **1**:824a
·Socrates' ethical admonitions as response **16**:1001d
·Thucydides' descriptive account **18**:359a
·war weariness in 5th-century Greece **13**:847e
·weapons systems of warships **19**:682e

Peloponnesian War, First (460–445 BC), struggle between Athens and the Peloponnesian League, led by Sparta.

·causes, events, and effects **8**:354a

Pelopónnisos: *see* Peloponnese.

Pelops, legendary founder of the Pelopid dynasty at Mycenae in the Greek Peloponnese, which was probably named for him. Pelops was a grandson of Zeus, the king of the gods. He was thought to have a shoulder of ivory because his father, Tantalus, had served his son up to the gods at a banquet; only the shoulder (which the goddess Demeter ate) needed to be replaced when they brought Pelops back to life.

According to Pindar, however, the sea god Poseidon loved Pelops and took him up to heaven; the ghastly feast was merely malicious gossip to account for his disappearance. Pelops, however, had to return to mortal life because his father had abused the favour of heaven by feeding mere mortals with nectar and ambrosia, of which only gods partook. Later, according to Pindar, Pelops strove for the hand of Hippodamia, daughter of King Oenomaus of Pisa, the district around Olympia. Oenomaus, who had an incestuous love for his daughter, had previously killed 13 suitors. He challenged Pelops to a chariot race, with Hippodamia the prize of victory and death the price of defeat. Though Oenomaus' team and chariot were the gift of his father, the god Ares, Pelops' chariot was a gift from Poseidon. Pelops won the bride and killed Oenomaus.

In more hostile versions, Pelops bribed Oenomaus' charioteer, Myrtilus, to remove the linchpins from Oenomaus' chariot. After his victory, for reasons that are given differently in different sources, he threw Myrtilus into the sea that afterward was called the Myrtoan. Myrtilus, or Oenomaus, was said to have uttered the curse that dogged the Pelopid house of Atreus (*q.v.*), the son of Pelops. Preparations for the chariot race are depicted in the east pediment of the Temple of Zeus at Olympia.

Peloridiidae, family of primitive insects of the order Homoptera.

·characteristics and classification **8**:1042d

Peloritani, mountain range, northeastern Sicily.
38°05′ N, 15°25′ E

·location and features **16**:727g
·map, Sicily **16**:728

pelota, an early handball game played in France and Spain, an ancestor of handball that evolved into jai alai, called *pelota vasca* in Spain.

·handball origins **8**:600b
·jai alai history and rules **10**:6g

Pelotas, coastal city, southeastern Rio Grande do Sul state, southern Brazil, on the left bank of the Canal de São Gonçalo. Founded in 1780 as São Francisco de Paula, it was raised to town status and renamed in 1830; it became a city in 1835 and is now the state's second largest community. It serves with the port of Rio Grande (25 mi [40 km] southeast) as a transfer point for ocean vessels that cannot cross the shallow Lagoa dos Patos to Pôrto Alegre fully loaded. It is also the chief port for the cattle-ranching area of southern Rio Grande do Sul. Pelotas is Brazil's largest producer of *xarque*, or jerked beef, and has food-processing and other factories. It is the site of the Sul Riograndense and Rural do Sul universities. Pop. (1970) 150,140.
31°46′ S, 52°20′ W

·map, Brazil **3**:125

Pelotas River, Portuguese RIO PELOTAS, also called RIO ALTO URUGUAI, major headstream of the Uruguay River (*q.v.*).
27°28′ S, 51°55′ W

·map, Brazil **3**:125

pelt, in furs, the animal skin with the hair forming the body covering remaining intact. In leather manufacture the term may be applied to a skin that has been stripped of hair or fur to prepare it for the tanning process.

·fur characteristics and preparation **7**:811h
·leather manufacturing and dehairing process **10**:761g

Peltaspermaceae: *see in* seed fern.

Peltephilidae, extinct family of the order Edentata that existed in South America.

·traits, diet, eras, and classification **6**:301h

Peltier, Jean-Charles-Athanase (b. Feb. 22, 1785, Ham, Fr.—d. Oct. 27, 1845, Paris), physicist who discovered that at the junction of two dissimilar metals, an electric current will produce heat or cold, depending on the direction of current flow. Called the Peltier effect, it is used in devices for measuring temperature and, with the discovery of new conducting materials, in refrigeration units of revolutionary design.

A clockmaker, Peltier retired when he was 30 years old to devote his time to scientific investigations. He discovered the effect named after him in 1834 and in 1840 introduced the concept of electrostatic induction, a method of charging a conductor by closely juxtaposing another charged object to attract all

Peltier, detail of a lithograph by Maurin

Giraudon

charges of one sign and then grounding the conductor to bleed off the other group of charges, leaving a net charge behind. He wrote numerous papers on atmospheric electricity, waterspouts, the boiling point at high elevations, and related phenomena.

·thermoelectric current **8**:706b
·thermoelectric effect discovery **18**:316a

Peltier effect, the cooling of one junction and the heating of the other when electric current is maintained in a loop of material consisting of two dissimilar conductors, generally two different metals. In a circuit consisting of a battery joined by two pieces of copper wire to a length of bismuth wire, a temperature rise occurs at the junction where the current passes from copper to bismuth, and a temperature drop occurs at the junction where the current passes from bismuth to copper. Discovered (1834) by the French physicist J.-C.-A. Peltier, this effect was used to produce in the 1960s commercial thermoelectric refrigerators of household size. *Major ref.* **6**:579f

·air conditioning applications **8**:724h
·explanation and discovery **8**:706b
·solid state thermoelectric properties **16**:1040b
·thermoelectric effects in solids **18**:315g
·thermoelectric power conversion **16**:529a
·thermoelectric refrigeration development **15**:566h

Peltigera canina (lichen): *see* dog lichen.

Pelton, Lester Allen (1829–1918), U.S. engineer.

·impulse turbine development **18**:768d; illus.

Pelton water turbine, also called PELTON WHEEL, a rotor driven by the impulse of a jet of water upon curved buckets fixed to its periphery; each bucket is divided in half by a splitter edge that diverts the water into two streams that fall clear of the rotor.

The Pelton turbine, patented by L.A. Pelton in 1889, is widely used in hydroelectric power generation.

·classification and operation **6**:623h
·design and development **18**:768d; illus.

Peltopleuriformes, extinct order of fishes of the subclass Chondrostei.

·Chondrostei classification and general features **4**:438g
·fish characteristics and classification **7**:342d

Pelucones (Chilean political group): *see* Pipiolos and Pelucones.

peludo (hairy armadillo): *see* armadillo.

Péluse, Gaspard Monge, comte de (French mathematician): *see* Monge, Gaspard, comte de Péluse.

Pelusios (genus of turtles): *see* side-necked turtle.

Pelusium, Greek PELOUSION, probably Egyptian SA'INU or PER-AMON (House of Amon), ancient Egyptian city on the most easterly mouth of the Nile (long silted up), about 20 miles southeast of Port Said, in the Sinai Peninsula. It is referred to in the Bible (Ezek. 30:15) as "the stronghold of Egypt" (the name being given in the King James Version as Sin, transliterated from the Hebrew). Under the later Egyptian dynasties, Pelusium was the main frontier fortress against Palestine and a customs post for Asiatic goods. In 525 BC the Persians, under Cambyses II, defeated the Saite dynasty of Egypt there. In Roman times it was a station on the route to the Red Sea. It is sometimes identified with Avaris, the capital of the Hyksos dynasty. The ruins date from the Roman period.
31°03′ N, 32°32′ E

pelvic girdle, or BONY PELVIS, basin-shaped complex of bones that connects the trunk and legs, supports and balances the trunk, and contains and supports the intestines, urinary bladder, and internal sex organs. The pelvic girdle consists of paired innominate ("unnamed") bones, commonly called the hipbones, connected in front at the pubic symphysis and behind by the sacrum. Each innominate is made up of three bones—the blade-shaped ilium (*q.v.*), above and to either side, which accounts for the width of the hips; the ischium (*q.v.*), behind and below, on which the weight falls in sitting; and the pubis (*q.v.*), in front. All three unite in early adulthood at a triangular suture in the acetabulum (*q.v.*), the cup-shaped socket that forms the hip joint with the head of the femur (thighbone). The ring made by the pelvic girdle functions as the birth canal in females. The pelvis provides attachment for muscles that balance and support the trunk and move the legs, hips, and trunk. In the infant the pelvis is narrow and nonsupportive. As the child begins walking, the pelvis broadens and tilts, the sacrum descends deeper into its articulation with the ilia, and the lumbar curve develops.

In the semi-erect apes, the centre of gravity falls near the shoulder, and the abdominal organs depend from the vertebral column. The ilium is elongated and somewhat spoon-shaped, and the pelvis is oriented horizontally. In a human being, when standing erect, the centre of gravity falls over the centre of the body, and the weight is transmitted via the pelvis from the backbone to the thighbone, knee, and foot. Morphological differences from apes include the following: the ilium is broadened backward in a fan shape, developing a deep sciatic notch posteriorly; a strut of bone, the arcuate eminence, has developed on the ilium diagonal from the hip joint (concerned with lateral balance in upright posture); the anterior superior iliac spine, on the upper front edge of the iliac blade, is closer to the hip joint; and the ischium is shorter. The pelvis of *Australopithecus africanus*, which is believed to be in the direct line of evolution to man and which lived in the Early Pleistocene, about 1,000,000 years ago, is clearly hominid. *Homo erectus* and all later fossil hominids, including Neanderthal man, had fully modern pelvises.

Sex differences in the pelvis are marked and reflect the necessity in the female of providing an adequate birth canal for a large-headed fetus. In comparison with the male pelvis, the female basin is broader and shallower; the birth canal rounded and capacious; the sciatic notch wide and U-shaped; the pubic symphysis short, with the pubic bones forming a broad angle with each other; the sacrum short, broad, and only moderately curved; the coccyx movable; and the acetabula farther apart. These differences reach their adult proportions only at puberty. Wear patterns on the pubic symphyses may be used to estimate age at death in males and females. *Major ref.* **16**:817b

·australopithecine form comparison **2**:438f
·birds' unique skeletal structure **2**:1056f
·dinosaur structural types, illus. 6 **15**:737
·fetal positioning and complications **13**:1036f
·hipbone in human skeletal development **16**:824c
·hominid adaptations for bipedalism **8**:1024c; illus. 1025
·Homo sapiens bipedal skeletal evolution **8**:1045f
·human pattern of australopithecines **11**:422g
·human reproductive organ site **15**:690h
·joint structures and functions **10**:253f
·organ changes during pregnancy **14**:970d
·perch skeletal anatomy, illus. 1 **7**:332
·pongid and hominid comparison **8**:1028c
·primate birth canal comparisons **14**:1017e
·sexual differences in body composition **5**:656b

Pelycosauria, extinct order of reptiles containing primitive synapsids and pelycosaurs, which existed from the Lower Pennsylvanian to the Middle Permian Period.

·Permian reptilian evolution **14**:97g
·reptile evolution and classifications **15**:736f

Pemba Island, Arabic JAZĪRAT AL-KHUḌRAH, in the Indian Ocean 35 mi (56 km) off the coast of East Africa, opposite the port of Tanga, a part of Tanzania. The island embraces 380 sq mi (984 sq km), being 42 mi (67 km) long and 14 mi (23 km) wide. As the Arabic name, which means Green Island, suggests, it is more fertile than its sister island, Zanzibar, 30 mi (48 km) to the southwest. Pemba is the world's major producer of cloves, and the island's economy is dependent upon the success of that crop.

Drying cloves on Pemba Island, Tanzania

Picturepoint—Publix

As in Zanzibar, the population and culture of the island have been greatly influenced by the infusion of peoples from mainland Africa, the Middle East, and the Indian subcontinent.

The administrative headquarters is at Wete on the western side of the island. Pop. (latest census) 164,321.
5°10′ S, 39°48′ E

·area and population table **17**:1030
·geographic and economic features **17**:1029b
·map, Tanzania **17**:1027
·political revolt and Nyerere reaction **6**:106a

Pemberton, town, southwest Western Australia, on Lefroy Brook, a tributary of the Warren River, near the coast. Founded in 1911, it was named after its first settler, and developed as a sawmilling centre, exploiting the fine karri and jarrah timber forests that blanket the area. Striking examples of these hardwood trees, which can grow to a height of 250 ft (76 m), are in the nearby groves of Carey Park, site of the well-known Gloucester Tree. Situated on a rail line to Perth (170 mi [270 km] north), Pemberton also serves local dairy, lamb, fruit, potato, and hop farms. Pop. (1971) 815.
34°28′ S, 116°01′ E

Pemberton, John C(lifford) (1814–81), Confederate general in the U.S. Civil War.

·Vicksburg defense activity and result **4**:678c

Pembroke, town, seat of Renfrew County, Ontario, Canada, northwest of Ottawa, on the Ottawa River at a point where it is entered by the Indian and Muskrat rivers. Algonquin Provincial Park lies a few miles to the west. The site was settled in 1828 by Peter White, later dividing into two sections—Campbellton and Mirimichi. A few years later the settlement combined under the name Pembroke (in honour of Sidney Herbert, son of the Earl of Pembroke). Its lumber-based economy is augmented by light manufacturing. Many ships were christened there during the early days of steamship navigation on the Upper Ottawa. Inc. village, 1856; town, 1877. Pop. (1971) 16,544.
45°49′ N, 77°07′ W
·map, Canada **3**:716

Pembroke, borough, county of Dyfed (until 1974 it was in the former Pembrokeshire), Wales, comprising the towns of Pembroke and Pembroke Dock (the latter about twice the size of the former), on Milford Haven.

Pembroke, incorporated in 1090 by royal charter, was a walled town built along a prominent narrow limestone ridge, at the west end of which was the castle that dominated the Haven, and was the seat of the earls of Pembroke in the 12th and 13th centuries. St. Mary's Church was founded in 1260, and nearby are the ruins of a Benedictine priory established in 1098: its church was fully restored in 1882. Pembroke is now mainly a small market town and tourist centre.

Pembroke Dock grew up around a naval dockyard that opened in 1814 and has since had a garrison function, even though the dockyard closed in 1926; most of the yard was then a Royal Air Force base until 1959. The town is still primarily industrial. Both town and dock have rail service. Pop. (1971 prelim.) 14,092.
51°41′ N, 4°55′ W
·map, United Kingdom **18**:866
·Norman impact on Wales **3**:230h
·Welsh landscape, tourism, and industry **19**:526c

Pembroke, William Marshal, 1st earl of (b. *c.* 1146—d. May 14, 1219, Caversham, Berkshire), regent of England during the first three years of the minority of King Henry III (ruled 1216–72), ended the civil war between the barons and the crown and restored stable government. During his long career Pembroke served four successive English monarchs as a royal adviser and agent and as a warrior of outstanding prowess.

Marshal's father, John (FitzGilbert) the Marshal (died 1165), fought for the empress Matilda (widow of the German emperor Henry V and daughter of Henry I of England) in her unsuccessful struggle to gain the throne of her cousin King Stephen (ruled 1135–54). After proving his bravery in warfare and in tournaments, Marshal became a guardian (1170) to Prince Henry, eldest son of King Henry II (ruled 1154–89). In 1187, four years after the prince's death, Marshal re-entered Henry II's service and fought beside him in France until the King died in 1189.

Upon the accession of Henry's third son, Richard I the Lion-Heart (ruled 1189–99), Marshal married the heiress of Richard de Clare, earl of Pembroke, thereby acquiring vast estates in England, Normandy, Wales, and Ireland. Richard set forth on a crusade in 1190, leaving William Longchamp in charge of the kingdom. In the following year Pembroke joined the opposition that drove Longchamp into exile. While Richard was held captive in Germany (1192–94), Pembroke struggled to prevent the King's brother, John, from seizing power in England.

Upon the death of Richard I in 1199, Marshal helped John succeed peacefully to the throne; Marshal was formally recognized as earl of Pembroke. By 1213 he had become the King's closest adviser, and he remained loyal to John during the disputes with the barons that led to the signing of the charter of liberties known as Magna Carta (June 1215). John died during the ensuing civil war with the barons, who had invited Louis of France (later King Louis VIII) to be their king. Designated *rector regis et regni* ("governor of the king and of the kingdom") for John's son, King Henry III, Pembroke defeated the English barons and French invaders and in September 1217 concluded a treaty with Louis that wisely granted amnesty to the rebellious barons. Biographies include those by Thomas Leckie Jarman (1930) and Sidney Painter (1933).

Pembroke, Richard de Clare, 2nd earl of, known as "STRONGBOW" (b. *c.* 1130—d. April 20, 1176, Dublin), Anglo-Norman lord whose invasion of Ireland in 1170 initiated the opening phase of the English conquest. The son of Gilbert de Clare, 1st earl of Pembroke, he succeeded to his father's estates in southern Wales in 1148. Pembroke had evidently lost these lands by 1168; it was probably in that year that he agreed to aid Dermot MacMurrough, king of Leinster, who had been expelled from his kingdom by Roderic (Rory O'Connor), high king of Ireland. King Henry II of England (ruled 1154–89) granted Pembroke permission to invade Ireland, and on Aug. 23, 1170, the Earl landed near Waterford. Waterford and Dublin quickly fell to the Normans. After the death of MacMurrough in May 1171, Pembroke was besieged in Dublin by Roderic, but in September his forces broke out and routed Roderic's army. In order to prevent Pembroke from setting himself up as an independent ruler, Henry II had him acknowledge royal authority over his conquests in Leinster. Pembroke helped the King suppress a rebellion in Normandy in 1173–74, and in return Henry granted him custody of Wexford, Waterford, and Dublin. By the time Pembroke died all Ireland had been committed to his care, but within Ireland his supremacy was recognized only in Leinster.
·Norman exploits in Ireland **3**:285h

Pembroke, Mary Herbert, countess of (b. Oct. 27, 1561, near Bewdley, Worcestershire—d. Sept. 25, 1621, London), patroness of the arts and scholarship and a notable translator. She was the sister of Sir Philip Sidney, to whom he dedicated *Arcadia.* After his death she published the poem and completed his verse translation of the Psalms.

In 1575 Queen Elizabeth I invited Mary to court, promising "a speciall care" of her. Two years later she married Henry Herbert, 2nd earl of Pembroke, and lived mainly at Wilton House, near Salisbury, Wiltshire. Their sons, William and Philip, were the "incomparable pair of brethren" to whom Shakespeare's First Folio (1623) was dedicated.

Wilton House was described by John Aubrey in his *Brief Lives* as ". . . like a College, there were so many learned and ingeniose persons." Among those who praised her for her patronage of poetry was Edmund Spenser, who dedicated his *Ruines of Time* to her, and Michael Drayton, Samuel Daniel, and John Davies. A lutanist, she inspired Thomas Morley's dedication of *Canzonets* (1593); and, in his dedication to her of *Pilgrimage to Paradise* (1592), Nicholas Breton likened her to the Duchess of Urbino, patroness in an earlier time to Baldassare Castiglione. In the chorus of contemporary praise, in which there was not a single discordant note, Lady Pembroke ranked after the Queen as the most admired of Elizabethan *femmes savantes.*

Lady Pembroke translated Robert Garnier's tragedy *Marc-Antoine* and Philippe Duplessis-Mornay's *Discours de la vie et de la mort* (both 1592) and elegantly rendered Petrarch's *Trionfo della morte* into terza rima.

Pembroke table, a light, drop-leaf table designed for occasional use, probably deriving its name from Henry Herbert, ninth earl of Pembroke (1693–1751), a noted connoisseur and amateur architect. The table has two drawers and flaps on either side that can be raised by brackets on hinges (known as "elbows") to increase its size. Provided with casters (it was often used for bedside meals), the legs of the common English versions, as illustrated by Thomas Sheraton and others, are X-shaped. In the United States, a distinctive type of support, incorporating a lyre, became very popular toward the end of the century. It is also known as a flap and elbow table.

Black and gold lacquer Pembroke table with casters, English, *c.* 1780; in the Victoria and Albert Museum, London

By courtesy of the Victoria and Albert Museum, London

pemmican, also PEMICAN, a concentrated food of North American Indians consisting of lean meat dried, pounded fine, and mixed with melted fat.
·food preservation technology **7**:489h

Pempheridae, family of sweepers of the fish order Perciformes.
·classification and general features **14**:53e

pemphigoid, bullous, OR BENIGN PEMPHIGUS, a chronic, generalized skin disorder characterized by an eruption of serum-filled vesicles (blisters). These vesicles form under the epidermis, the outermost, nonvascular layer of the skin, and have walls of stretched epidermal cells. The cause of bullous pemphigoid is not known. It occurs predominantly in elderly adults. Although debilitating, it is not fatal and responds well to treatment with corticosteroids.

pemphigus, a group of diseases characterized by vesicles (blisters) on the skin or mucous surfaces. Microscopically, there is a degeneration of the intercellular bridges of the cells of the epidermis, the outermost nonvascular layer of the skin, which results in a separation and destruction of skin cells. The clefts and splits within the degenerating skin layer form vesicles filled with a serum-like fluid containing fragments of dead cells. These vesicles eventually burst, leaving denuded and eroded skin areas. There are several clinical variants of pemphigus, depending on the acuteness of the disease and the type of lesions accompanying the vesicles. The most common form of pemphigus is pemphigus vulgaris; other forms are pemphigus erythematosus and pemphigus foliaceus. Variation of the level at which cell disintegration occurs within the epidermis may also help differentiate one form of pemphigus from another. In pemphigus vulgaris, cell destruction takes place just above the base of the epidermis, whereas in pemphigus erythematosus and pemphigus foliaceus, usually more benign types, this process occurs higher up within the epidermis. Pemphigus, formerly fatal within a few months or years of its onset, can now be relieved with the administration of corticoids or other suitable hormones. The cause of pemphigus has not yet been established, but evidence thus far suggests a virus.

Pemphredoninae: *see* wasp.

pen, tool for writing or drawing with a coloured fluid, such as ink. The earliest ancestor of the pen probably was the brush used by the Chinese by the 1st millennium BC. The Egyptians made pens from reeds of the genera *Calamus* and *Arundo* or from the hollow joints of bamboo. In Europe quill pens made from bird feathers were used from the 6th century until the mid-19th, when metallic pens and pen nibs (writing points) became common. Metallic pens were known in classical times (a bronze pen now in a Naples museum was found in the ruins of Pompeii) but were little used until the 19th century. In 1803 steel pens of a tubular design were sold in London; their edges met at a central slit and the sides were cut away as in the quill. Machine-made metallic pens were introduced in 1828 by John Mitchell of Birmingham, Eng. Birmingham was the chief centre of the industry for many years. In 1861 a U.S. company was established at Camden, N.J., by Richard Esterbrook, Jr., with craftsmen from Birmingham. Other companies began manufacture in the Camden area after World War I, and the centre of production shifted there. Stainless-steel pens were introduced in 1926.

The principle of the fountain pen was known in Paris as early as the mid-17th century, but a practical pen was not manufactured until L. E. Waterman of New York City introduced his model in 1884. In the fountain pen, writing fluid is contained in the holder and passes to the nib through capillary channels. The nib is covered with a cap when the pen is not in use.

Ball-point pens date from the late 19th century. Commercial models appeared in 1895, but the first satisfactory model was patented by Lazlo Biro, a Hungarian living in Argentina, whose pen became popular in Great Britain during the late 1930s. By the mid-1940s, the ball-point pen had been accepted all over the world. In ball-point pens, the writing tip is a ball housed in a socket that rotates freely when in contact with writing surface. The ball is constantly bathed in ink from a reservoir that may be a flexible, synthetic-resin sac inside a metal shell, or a metal or plastic tube, one end of which is open and attached to the writing tip. *Major ref.* **19**:1045a

·calligraphic tools and use **3**:646c
·classical use and materials **13**:912d
·drawing tool development and use **5**:998h
·osmiridium and ruthenium uses **14**:531b

pen, the horny, internal shell of a squid, imbedded in the mantel and often feather-shaped.

·squid anatomy and evolution **3**:1153d; illus. 1152

PEN, acronym of the International Association of Poets, Playwrights, Editors, Essayists and Novelists, founded in 1922.

·international organization's goal **2**:101g

Pena, Afonso (Augusto Moreira) (1847–1909), president of Brazil, 1906–09.

·presidency and economic stabilization **3**:146h

Pena di vivere così, English translation SUCH IS LIFE, a short story by Luigi Pirandello included in *Short Stories* (1959).

·psychological theme in literature **14**:469f

Penaeaceae, family of flowering plants in the order Myrtales.

·range, life cycle, uses, and classification **12**:773a

penal colony, distant or overseas settlement established for punishing criminals by forced labour and isolation from society. Such isolation is a traditional form of crime control; exile and banishment have been observed in some nonliterate societies, sometimes under conditions that made survival of the offender highly doubtful. Although a score of nations in Europe and Latin America transported their criminals to widely scattered penal colonies, such colonies were developed mostly by the English, French, and Russians. England shipped criminals to America until the American Revolution and to Australia into the middle of the 19th century. France established penal colonies in Africa, New Caledonia, and French Guiana (of which those in the latter, including Devil's Island, were still operating during World War II). French Guiana epitomized the worst features of penal colonies: torture and the underfeeding of prisoners assigned to hard labour were routine. The Siberian colonies maintained by the Soviet Union were initially organized under the tsars but were most widely employed from the Russian Revolution through the Stalin era. With modern means of communication, isolation has been increasingly difficult to maintain, and governments have turned to alternative means of crime control. Most penal colonies have been abolished.

·Australian settlements **2**:413g *passim* to 415g
·prison and rehabilitation methodology **14**:1098e
·Sydney, Australia's early history **17**:888f

Penal Laws, common name for laws passed against Roman Catholics in Britain and Ireland after the Reformation which penalized the practice of the Roman Catholic religion and imposed civil disabilities on Catholics. Various acts passed in the 16th and 17th centuries prescribed fines and imprisonment for participation in Catholic worship, and severe penalties, including death, for Catholic priests who practiced their ministry in Britain or Ireland. Other laws barred Catholics from voting, holding public office, owning land, bringing religious items from Rome into Britain, publishing or selling Catholic primers, or teaching.

Sporadically enforced in the 17th century and largely ignored in the 18th, the Penal Laws were almost completely nullified by the Roman Catholic Relief Act (1791), the Catholic Emancipation Act (1829), the Roman Catholic Charities Act (1832), and the Roman Catholic Relief Act (1926).

·Clarendon Code and test acts **3**:246g *passim* to 247h

penance (religion): *see* atonement; confession.

Penang (Malaysia): *see* Pinang.

Peñaranda, Enrique (1892–1970), Bolivian political and military figure.

·overthrow and political results **3**:12c

Peñarroya-Pueblonuevo, city, Córdoba province, Andalusia, southern Spain, northwest of Cordóba city. A railway junction in the Sierra Morena, the community is in an anthracite and bituminous coal-mining district. Other minerals worked are iron, silver, and lead. It has metal foundries and manufactures soap, paper, and chemical fertilizers. Pop. (1970) 15,649.
38°18′ N, 5°16′ W

·map, Spain **17**:382

Penarth, town, county of South Glamorgan (until 1974 it was in the former Glamorganshire), Wales. Now mainly an expanding dormitory suburb of Cardiff, the Welsh capital, 5 mi (8 km) to the north, Penarth is also a small seaside resort on the Bristol Channel, with impressive cliffs (especially Penarth Head, about 200 ft [60 m] high), a pebble beach, a pier, and attractive parks. Pleasure steamers provide summer services to other Bristol Channel resorts. The Turner House Art Gallery exhibits art collections of the National Museum of Wales. Penarth has rail service. Pop. (1973 est.) 24,180.
51°27′ N, 3°11′ W

Peñas, Gulf of, Spanish GOLFO DE PEÑAS, inlet of the southeast Pacific, Aysén province, Chile. It extends inland for 55 mi (89 km) and stretches 50 mi south from Taitao Peninsula to the Guayaneco Islands.
47°20′ S, 75°00′ W

·map, Chile **4**:248

Penates, more properly DI PENATES, household gods of the Romans and other Latin peoples. In the narrow sense, they were gods of the *penus*, "storeroom," or the *penetralia*, the innermost part of the house, but by extension their protection reached the entire household. They are associated with other deities of the house, such as Vesta and the Lares. The Penates are all or some specific group of deities with household connections, but their number and precise identity were a puzzle even to the ancients.

The Penates were worshipped privately as protectors of the individual household and also publicly as protectors of the Roman state. Each house had a shrine with images of them that were worshipped at the family meal and on special occasions. Offerings were of portions of the regular meal or of special cakes, wine, honey, incense, and more rarely, a blood sacrifice. The state as a whole worshipped them as the Penates Publici, about whose nature and origin there are various opinions. This state cult occupied a significant role as a focal point of Roman patriotism and nationalism.

·Roman spirit worship **15**:1063e

pencerdd, in the Welsh bardic system, an upper grade established under Gruffudd ap Cynan (d. 1137).

·Welsh bardic hierarchy **10**:1114b

Pen-ch'i, Pin-yin romanization BEN-CHI, also written BEN-XI, city in Liaoning Province, China, and an autonomous subprovincial level municipality controlling the two counties Pen-ch'i (also called Hsiao-shih) and Huanjen, in addition to the city itself. Pen-ch'i is situated some 45 mi (70 km) southeast of Mukden on the T'ai-tzu Ho (river). From the time of the Liao dynasty (947–1125), it was the centre of a small-scale iron industry, and coal began to be mined in the late 18th century. The startling modern growth of Pen-ch'i began with the establishment in 1905 of the Pen-ch'i Coal Mining Company with joint Chinese and Japanese capital. In 1911 the company began iron smelting and changed its name to the Pen-ch'i Coal and Iron Company. It was efficiently managed and remained important, but gradually became dominated by Japanese interests. Because of these economic developments, Pen-ch'i, originally a minor town subordinate to Liao-yang Superior Prefecture, was made an independent county in 1906.

After the establishment of the Japanese puppet state of Manchukuo in 1932, and the formulation of the Manchurian Industrial Development Plan in 1936, the Manchukuo government formed a new company in combination with the Ōkura Company to increase the iron and steel production. Much of the iron from Pen-ch'i had low phosphorus and sulfur content and was in demand for the munitions industry. In 1939 the enterprise was merged with the Manchurian Heavy Industry Company and began to produce special steels for the Japanese Navy. By 1943 it was producing more than 500,000 tons of pig iron and more than 1,000,000 tons of iron ore, and was supplying ore to An-shan (also in Liaoning Province) as well as to its own steelworks. In 1945–46 the occupying Soviet forces dismantled most of the equipment, but the plant was restored by 1950, and during the early 1950s much new equipment was installed by Soviet technicians. By 1957 iron production had reached the World War II level, and new local sources of ore were being exploited. The iron industry is closely integrated with the large iron and steel complex at An-shan, to which much of Pen-ch'i's pig iron production is transported. Since 1958 the steel output of Pen-ch'i has been greatly increased, in 1960 amounting to some 300,000 tons of ingot steel. In addition to its coal and iron mining and iron and steel industries, Pen-ch'i has large cement, chemical, and nonferrous alloy manufacturing industries. It also has two ther-

mal power stations. Pop. (1948) 321,000; latest census 449,000.
41°18′ N, 123°45′ E
·map, China **4**:262

pençik, tax prerogative of the beys during the period of the early expansion of the Ottoman Empire.
·Ottoman political system evolution **13**:775e

pencil, slender rod of a solid marking substance, such as graphite, enclosed in a cylinder of wood, metal, or plastic; used as an implement for writing, drawing, or marking. In 1565 the German-Swiss naturalist Conrad Gesner first described a writing instrument in which graphite, then thought to be a type of lead, was inserted into a wooden holder. Gesner was first to describe graphite as a separate mineral, and in 1779 the Swedish chemist Carl Wilhelm Scheele showed it to be a form of carbon. The name graphite is from the Greek *graphein*, "to write." The modern lead pencil became possible when an unusually pure deposit of graphite was discovered in 1564 in Borrowdale, Cumberland. The higher the ratio of clay to graphite, the harder is the lead of a pencil. Hardness of writing pencils is usually designated by numbers from 1, the softest, to 4, the hardest. Artists' drawing pencils range in a hardness designation generally given from 8B, the softest, to F, the hardest. The designation of the hardness of drafting pencils ranges from HB, the softest, to 10H, the hardest.

The darkness of a pencil mark depends on the number of small particles of lead deposited by the pencil. The particles are equally black regardless of the hardness of the lead; only the size and number of particles determine the apparent degree of blackness of the pencil mark. The degree of hardness of a lead is a measure of how much the lead resists abrasion by the fibres of the paper.
·production and various uses **19**:1046e

pencil, in projective geometry, all the planes passing through a given line. This line is known as the axis of the pencil. In the duality of solid geometry, the duality being a kind of symmetry between points and planes, the dual of a pencil of planes consists of a line of points. In a plane, in which there is a duality between points and lines, the dual of a line of points is a figure called a pencil of lines, consisting of all lines through a point.

pencil cedar (tree): *see* eastern red cedar.

pencil drawing, drawing executed with an instrument composed of graphite enclosed in a wood casing and intended either as a sketch for a more elaborate work in another medium, an exercise in visual expression, or a finished work. The cylindrical graphite pencil, because of its usefulness in easily producing linear gray-black strokes, became the successor of the older, metallic drawing stylus, with which late medieval and Renaissance artists and tradesmen sketched or wrote on paper, parchment, or wood.

Although graphite was mined in the 16th century, the use by artists of pieces of natural graphite, inserted in a *porte-crayon* (holder), is not known before the 17th century. Then minor graphite details were included in sketches, notably in landscape renderings by such Dutch artists as David Teniers the Younger and Aelbert Cuyp. During that century and most of the 18th, graphite was used to make preliminary sketch lines for drawings to be completed in other media. Drawings completely finished with graphite were exceptional; *e.g.*, a few 18th-century works by the English artists Thomas Gainsborough and George Romney.

Although pencil drawings were much less commonly produced by artists of those centuries than sketches in chalks, charcoal, and pen and ink, the use of graphite gradually increased among painters, miniaturists, architects, and designers. By the late 18th century, an ancestor of the modern pencil was constructed in the form of a rod of natural graphite fitted into a hollow cylinder of wood. Not until 1795, however, did the French inventor Nicolas-Jacques Conté devise a method of producing pencil rods from mixtures of graphite and clays, a true prototype of the modern graphite pencil. Conté's technical improvement made possible the production of fine pencils the strokes of which could be controlled, varying from type to type in softness and hardness, darkness and lightness. These excellent quality graphite pencils encouraged wider use by 19th-century artists, and pencil drawing became commonly used for studies and preliminary sketches. The graphite pencil could be used on almost any type of drawing surface, a fact that helped make it indispensable in the artist's studio.

Although graphite pencils provided a substantial range of light–dark effects and the opportunity for tonal modelling, the greatest masters of pencil drawing always kept the elements of a simple linearism or limited shading that were appropriate to pencil drawing. This concept of pencil drawing contrasted with that sometimes employed in the 18th and 19th centuries in which extensive tonal modelling of three-dimensional forms and elaborate effects of light and shade were produced by artists and miniaturists by rubbing the soft graphite particles with a stump, a tightly rolled piece of soft paper, or chamois.

The preciseness and clarity associated with the use of a moderately hard graphite pencil were developed in the highly selective draftsmanship of the 19th-century French Neoclassicist Jean-Auguste-Dominique Ingres. His figure sketches and portrait studies were the epitome of pencil drawing in which lucid contours and limited shading combined to create a spirit of elegance and restraint. Many artists throughout Europe accepted this manner, including such German draftsmen as Adrian

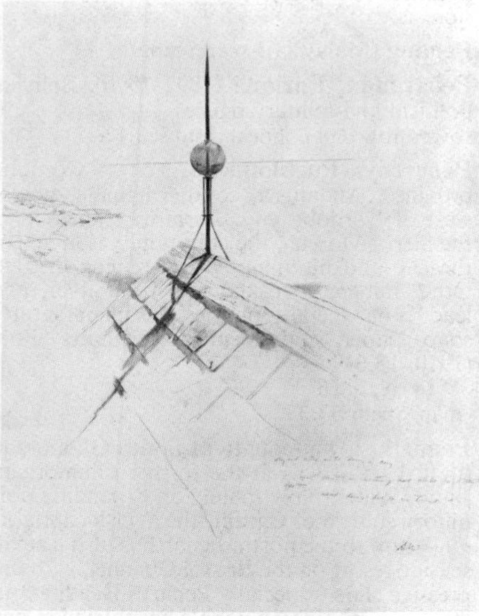

"Lightning Rod," pencil on white paper by Andrew Wyeth (1917–); in a private collection

Ludwig Richter, who preferred the hardest of pencils and sharpest of points to produce wirelike delineations of figures and landscapes. Softer and darker graphite pencils offered appropriate effects to artists whose tastes required more freedom and spontaneity. The sketches of the Romanticist Eugène Delacroix, created swiftly and filled with flamboyant and undetailed strokes, had a suggestiveness of dramatic figures and compositions. Van Gogh chose a broad carpenter's pencil for powerful, blunt strokes.

One of the most sensitive users of the graphite pencil in the 19th century was the French artist Edgar Degas. A master pastelist and draftsman with coloured chalks and charcoal, Degas created pencil drawings of warmth and charm that were quite unlike the cool, classic works of Ingres or the highly animated, sometimes violent sketches of Delacroix. Degas, with high selectivity, combined graciously fluid outlines with soft, limpid tonal shadings.

Artists of the 20th century continue to use the graphite pencil as a device for sketching and for making preliminary rehearsals of conceptions later carried out in painting or sculpture; *e.g.*, Henri Matisse, Amedeo Modigliani, Pablo Picasso, and others whose taste for basically linear conceptions is revealed in their graphic works.
·drawing technique, illus., **5**:Drawing, Plate II
·metalpoint development and use **5**:997f *passim* to 1009b; illus.

pencil fish, any of several slender South American fishes treated by some authorities as the family Hemiodontidae and by others as

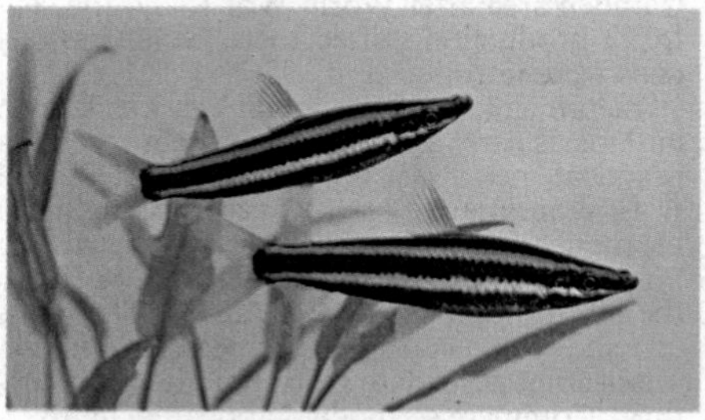

Pencil fish (*Anostomus anostomus*)
Gene Wolfsheimer

part of the characin family, Characidae. Pencil fishes are herbivores and inhabit slow, fresh water. Some habitually swim at an angle, tail down. The largest pencil fishes grow about 20 centimetres (8 inches) long. Several species are kept in home aquariums. Among these are *Nannostomus marginatus* and *Nannobrycon* (or *Poecilobrycon*) *unifasciatus*, both dark-striped fishes four to five centimetres long.
·classification and general features **13**:762d

Penck, Albrecht (b. Sept. 25, 1858, Leipzig, now in East Germany—d. March 7, 1945, Prague), geographer who exercised a major influence on the development of modern German geography, and geologist who founded Pleistocene stratigraphy (the study of Ice Age Earth strata, from 10,000 to 2,500,000 years ago), a favoured starting place for the study of man's prehistory. Professor of geography at the University of Vienna (1885–1906), he conducted research in the valleys of the Bavarian Alps that confirmed the four periods of Pleistocene glaciation—Günz, Mindel, Riss, and Würm. His findings were published, in collaboration with his assistant, Eduard Brückner, in *Die Alpen im Eiszeitalter* (3 vol., 1901–09; "The Alps in the Ice Age"). Penck also originated and promoted the 1:1,000,000-scale map of the Earth and published a pioneer work on geomorphology (the study of the Earth's surface features), a term he is believed to have introduced. From 1906 to 1926 he held the chair in geography at Berlin, where he was also director of the Institute of Oceanography. His work there embraced classification of climates, regional ecology, and political geography, notably the extent of German culture in Europe, and the refinement of the German geographer Friedrich Ratzel's concept of *Lebensraum* ("living space").
·climate classification **6**:89d
·river sediment movement study **14**:434g

Penck, Walther (b. 1888, Austria—d. 1923), geomorphologist noted for his theories of landform evolution.

Penck was a geologist for the Dirrecion General de Minas in Buenos Aires from 1912 until 1915, when he became a professor of mineralogy and geology at the University of Constantinople (now Istanbul). In 1918 he became a professor at the University of Leipzig (now in East Germany). His ideas of the dependence of landform evolution upon the mobility of the Earth's crust were a direct challenge to the accepted ideas of geomorphology of his time. His concept of parallel slope retreat stimulated the re-examination of some basic assumptions of the erosion cycle concept.

Penck wrote *Morphological Analysis of Land Forms* (1953).

·landform evolution and cycle of erosion **10**:628c
·landform evolution theories **8**:874b

Penda (d. 655), Anglo-Saxon king of Mercia from about 632 until 655, who made Mercia one of the most powerful kingdoms in England. In 628 Penda defeated a West Saxon people known as the Hwicce at the Battle of Cirencester (in present-day Gloucestershire) and annexed their territory. He and King Cadwalla (Cadwallon) of Gwynedd (in northern Wales) invaded Northumbria in 632 or 633 and defeated and killed the Northumbrian king Edwin. That victory carried Penda into the Mercian kingship, but in 633 he was forced to recognize Northumbrian overlordship. Penda did not recover his independence until 642, when his army killed King Oswald of Northumbria. He then proceeded to extend his power over an area corresponding to modern Cheshire, Shropshire, and Herefordshire. His son Peada had been made subking of Middle Anglia by 653. East Anglia was subjugated, and King Cenwalh was driven from Wessex for three years (645–648). In 655 Penda invaded Northumbria with forces drawn from many kingdoms, but he was slain by the Northumbrian king Oswin at the Battle of the Winwaed near Leeds (in present-day Yorkshire). Although Penda was a pagan, he allowed Peada to introduce Christianity into Middle Anglia.

·Mercian territorial expansion **3**:201a

pendant, an ornament suspended from a bracelet, earring, or, especially, a necklace. Pendants are derived from the primitive practice of wearing amulets or talismans around the neck. The practice dates from the Stone Age, when pendants consisted of such objects as teeth, stones, and shells.

The pharaohs of ancient Egypt wore pendants that were sometimes of huge dimensions, usually bearing commemorative or auspicious scenes in which the sovereign is being deified. Other pendants were in the shape of flies, winged scarabs, vultures, the eye of the god Horus, falcons, and sacred serpents. An exquisite example of an early gold pendant is that of two hornets clasped together, found in Mycenae and dating from the 17th century BC (Archeological Museum, Iráklion, Crete). Etruscan pendants were decorated with spindles and cylinders, figured, or in the shape of human heads. Greek and Hellenistic pendants usually formed the entire necklace. Pendants in the shape of a bulla (*q.v.*) are frequent in Roman necklaces, but there are also examples of cameos (*q.v.*), intaglios, and gold coins mounted as pendants.

During the Middle Ages, characteristic jewels were the reliquary, or devotional, pendant and the cross, chased or enamelled with religious subjects and often set in an architectural frame. One of the most famous early pendant reliquaries, which belonged to Charlemagne (cathedral treasury, Reims), contained relics of the true cross and the crown of thorns under a sapphire set with gold. In the 14th century, it was customary for noblemen to wear necklaces with pendants bearing heraldic subjects; pendants worn by women generally depicted sentimental subjects.

Toward the beginning of the 16th century, pendants became decorative rather than religious objects. The Renaissance artists created numerous beautiful crosses and figured pendants modelled in high relief and depicting numerous subjects, such as mermaids, tritons, animals and ships, and mythological and religious scenes. Often the irregular shapes of Baroque pearls (*q.v.*) were exploited and adapted for the bodies of human beings or animals, whose faces and limbs were modelled in gold and enamelled.

Art Nouveau pendant by L. Gautrait, *c.* 1900; in the Schmuckmuseum, Pforzheim, West Germany

By courtesy of the Schmuckmuseum, Pforzheim, Germany

In the Baroque period there was a return in pendants to engraved figures and intaglio cameo cutting, framed in geometric decorative designs containing gems and, later, in ribbons and floral designs done mainly in diamonds, rubies, emeralds, and pearls. Such pendants continued to be popular until the end of the 18th century.

The Empire style attached no great importance to pendants, and most of the rare examples consist of cameo medallions. In the 19th century, the Art Nouveau (*q.v.*) school created pendants with a lovely aesthetic line in which the most common motifs were women's figures and profiles, butterflies, peacocks, insects, and flowers.

·Sesostris III's memorial of conquests **10**:167g; illus. 168

Pendéli Óros (Greece): *see* Pentelicus, Mount.

pendeloque (gemstones): *see* drop cut.

Pendennis (1849–50), novel by William Makepeace Thackeray.

·snobbery analysis and deploration **18**:196f

pendentive, architectural term for a triangular segment of a spherical surface, filling in the upper corners of a room, in order to form, at the top, a circular support for a dome. The problem of supporting a dome over an enclosed square or polygonal space was of continually growing importance to the Roman builders of the late empire. It remained for the Byzantine architects, however, to recognize the possibilities of the pendentive and fully develop it. One of the earliest examples of the use of the pendentive is also one of the largest —that of Hagia Sophia (completed AD 537) at Istanbul. In the Romanesque period pendentives occur commonly in Western Europe in the domed churches of the Aquitaine in France, as in S. Front at Perigueux (begun 1120) and the cathedral of St. Pierre at Angoulême (1105–1128), but they occur only spasmodically in Italian churches. During the Renaissance and the Baroque the preference for domed churches, especially in Catholic Europe and Latin America, gave great importance to the pendentive. As a result of Byzantine influence, pendentives are frequent in Islāmic architecture. They are often decorated with stalactite work (*q.v.*) or sometimes, as in Iran, with delicate ribbing.

Romanesque pendentives supporting domes in the nave of the cathedral of St. Pierre at Angoulême, Fr., 1105–28

Archives Photographiques

A vaulting form in which the curve of the pendentive and dome is continuous, without a break, is known as a pendentive dome. *See also* squinch.

·Byzantine architectural developments **19**:327a

Penderecki, Krzysztof (b. Nov. 23, 1933, Debica, Poland), outstanding Polish composer of his generation, whose novel and masterful treatment of orchestration have won worldwide acclaim. Penderecki studied composition at the Superior School of Music in Kraków (graduated 1958), subsequently becoming a professor there. He first drew attention in 1959 at the third Warsaw Festival of Contemporary Music, where his *Strophes* for soprano, speaker, and ten instruments was performed. *Anaklasis*, premiered at the Donaueschingen Festival, and the now-classic *Threnody for the Victims of Hiroshima* for 52 strings, both in 1960, followed. A work of dramatic effect inspired by the atomic bombing of Hiroshima, the *Threnody* illustrates Penderecki's skilled and refined treatment of instruments, making use of quarter-tone clusters (close groupings of notes a quarter step apart), glissandi (slides), whistling harmonics (faint, eerie tones produced by partial string vibrations), and other extraordinary effects. These techniques were extended to Penderecki's vocal work *Dimensions of Time and Space* in 1961.

Penderecki

CAF, Warsaw

Penderecki's *Psalms of David* (1958) and *Stabat Mater* (1962) reflect a simpler, more linear trend (letting interwoven melodic lines predominate and determine harmonies) in his composition. The *Stabat Mater* combines traditional and experimental elements and led to his other well-known masterpiece, the *Passion According to St. Luke* (1963–66).

Penderecki selected the text for the *Passion* from the Old and New Testaments and the liturgy of Holy Week. In form the work resembles a Baroque Passion such as those by J.S. Bach, and Penderecki makes use of traditional forms such as the passacaglia (a variation form), chantlike freedom of metre, and a twelve-tone row (ordering of the 12 notes of the chromatic scale) based on the motif B-A-C-B♭ (in German notation, B-A-C-H) in homage to Bach. The *Threnody*, too, shows Penderecki's debt to traditional forms; one section is in strict melodic imitation. The 1962 *Canon* for 52 strings makes use also of polyphonic techniques (based on interwoven melodies) known to Renaissance composers. On the other hand, he makes some use of aleatoric (chance music) freedoms, percussive vocal articulation, nontraditional musical notation, and other devices that stamp him as a leader of the European avant-garde.

Pendergast, Thomas (1872–1945), U.S. politician.
·Truman early political career **18**:724h

Pendlebury (England): *see* Swinton and Pendlebury.

Pendleton, city, northeastern Oregon, U.S., on the Umatilla River, adjacent to the Umatilla Indian Reservation. On the Oregon Trail, it was founded (1869) by G.W. Bailey as the seat of Umatilla County and named for George Hunt Pendleton. It became a wheat and cattle centre after the arrival of the railroad (1889). Industries include food processing and lumber and woollen mills. It is headquarters for Umatilla National Forest and site of an Oregon State University agricultural experiment station and Blue Mountain Community College (1962). The Pendleton Round-Up (rodeo) is held annually in September. Inc. 1880. Pop. (1980) 14,521.
45°40′ N, 118°47′ W
·map, United States **18**:908

Pendleton Civil Service Act (Jan. 16, 1883), landmark U.S. legislation establishing the tradition and mechanism of permanent federal employment based on merit rather than on political party affiliation (the spoils system). Widespread public demand for reform was stirred after the Civil War by mounting incompetence, graft, corruption, and theft in government circles. When Pres. James A. Garfield was assassinated in 1881 by a disappointed office seeker, many reform candidates were elected to Congress the following year. In 1883 a comprehensive civil service bill was sponsored by Sen. George H. Pendleton of Ohio, providing for the open selection of government employees—to be administered by a Civil Service Commission—and guaranteeing the right of citizens to compete for federal appointment without regard to politics, religion, race, or national origin. Every president after Chester A. Arthur, who signed the bill into law, broadened its scope, and the percentage of federal employees covered was expanded from 10 percent in 1883 to 86 percent in the late 1960s.
·Arthur's support and provisions **18**:978d

Pend Oreille (PEND D'OREILLE) **Lake,** in Kaniksu and Coeur d'Alene national forests, northern Idaho, U.S. The largest lake in Idaho, it is about 40 mi (64 km) long, 4 mi wide, and covers an area of 125 sq mi (324 sq km); it is about 2,500 ft (762 m) deep. The Pend Oreille receives the Clark Fork River which becomes the Pend Oreille River when it leaves the lake.
48°10′ N, 116°11′ W
·map, United States **18**:908
·trading post establishment **9**:186e

pen drawing, work executed wholly or in part with pen and ink, usually on paper. Pen drawing is fundamentally a linear method of making images. In pure pen drawing in which the artist wishes to supplement his outlines with tonal suggestions of three-dimensional form, modelling must necessarily be effected by the close juxtaposition of a series of strokes forming areas of hatching or cross-hatching. Many pen studies, however, are produced with the substitution of tonal washes (a layer of colour spread evenly over a broad surface) laid onto the drawing with a brush, in which case the outlines or other important definitions of the figures or landscape are established by the pen lines. *See* wash drawing.

Inks of various types used in pen studies contributed additional diversity to the final effects. The prime requisites of inks for drawing were great fluidity and strong tinting power. Three types of ink were most frequently used. One was black carbon ink, made from extremely fine particles of the soot of burnt oils or resins in a solution of glue or gum arabic. The finest type of black carbon ink was known as Chinese ink and was the prototype of the modern black India ink. A brown ink popular with the old masters because of its warm, luminous colour qualities was known as bistre. It was prepared by boiling wood soot to obtain a liquid and transparent brown extract. The third important ink was an iron gall, or chemical, ink. Its principal ingredients were iron sulfate, the extract of gall nuts, and a gum arabic solution. It was, in fact, the common writing ink for centuries and was employed for most early drawings. Its colour when first applied to the paper was bluish-black, but it rapidly turned blackish and, over the years, a dull brown, as can be commonly seen in old handscript letters, documents, and drawings. Other inks, usually coloured inks made from natural or synthetic dyestuffs, were used rarely.

Pens are the oldest and most popular of all the drawing media of the Western artist, in part because of the variety of linear effects provided by the three basic types of pens and their adaptability to the changing styles of draftsmanship over many centuries. These three basic types are quill pens, cut from the wing feathers of fowls and birds; reed pens, formed and trimmed from stems of bamboolike grasses; and metal pens, fabricated from various metals, especially fine steel. Although the reed had been used in antiquity and in the Middle Ages, it was not employed for drawings until the Renaissance, when its fibrous structure and blunt point were found attractive to some draftsmen. The outstanding master of the reed pen, the Dutch artist Rembrandt, used it often in combination with the quill pen and washes to produce the richly suggestive atmospheric illusionism of his works. The reed pen never had the widespread popularity of quill or metal pens, but for special effects it has served artists admirably; for example, the 19th-century Dutch artist Vincent van Gogh in his last years used it in his drawings to produce the blunt, powerful strokes that were counterparts of the heavy brush strokes typical of many of his canvases.

"View of Arles," reed pen drawing by Vincent van Gogh, 1888–89; in the Museum Boymans-van Beuningen, Rotterdam, Neth.

By courtesy of the Museum Boymans-van Beuningen, Rotterdam, Neth.

Until the acceptance of the modern steel pen, most Western master draftsmen used quill pens. During the Middle Ages the quill pen was used for the fine delineations of images in manuscripts; its nibs, which could be sharpened to extreme fineness, permitted the craftsman to create small linear figures or ornamental decorations on the pages or along the borders of the parchment leaves. This characteristic, combined with the flexibility of the quill point, which responded to pressure for varying the widths of lines or forming accents, made it adaptable to the diverse personal styles of draftsmen from the 15th to the end of the 19th century.

"Nathan Admonishing David," drawing with reed pen, quill pen brush, and bistre ink by Rembrandt (1606–69), in the Metropolitan Museum of Art, New York

By courtesy of the Metropolitan Museum of Art, New York

The development of excellent steel pens by the Englishman James Perry in the 1830s and mass production by stamping pens from steel blanks led to the metal pen's supplanting the quill. Nevertheless, artists adopted the steel pen only reluctantly, and most drawings in pen and ink before the 20th century were made with quills. The steel pen is now used for drawing almost exclusively and is available in many shapes and sizes and degrees of rigidity or flexibility. It has become standard studio equipment of the illustrator, cartoonist, and designer. Pen drawings by such outstanding painters and sculptors as Pablo Picasso, Henri Matisse, and Henry Moore demonstrate the virtue the steel pen has in producing the sharp linear definition generally preferred by modern masters. *Major ref.* **5**: 999h *passim* to 1008h; illus.

·techniques and effects, illus., **5**:Drawing, Plate 1

Pendred's syndrome, hereditary condition in which deafness to high pitch is associated with goitre.

·cause and symptoms **6**:826e

pendulum, a body suspended so that it can swing back and forth under the action of gravity. Pendulums are utilized in regulating the movement of mechanical devices, especially clocks, because the interval of time for each complete swing to and fro, called the period, can be made constant. It is said that Galileo first noted (about 1583) the constancy of a pendulum's period by observing the movement of a swinging lamp in the Pisa cathedral. Christiaan Huygens obtained a patent (1657) on a clock regulated by the motion of a pendulum. The priority of invention of the pendulum clock has been ascribed to Galileo by some authorities and to Huygens by others, but Huygens solved the essential problem of making the period of a pendulum truly constant by devising a pivot that caused the bob to swing along the arc of a cycloid rather than that of a circle.

A simple pendulum is one composed of a body called the bob suspended at the end of a thread that is so light as to be considered without mass as compared to the mass of the bob. The period of a simple pendulum can be made longer by increasing the distance between the point of suspension and the middle of the bob. A change in the mass of the bob, however, does not affect the period. The period, on the other hand, is influenced by the position of the pendulum in relation to the Earth. Because the strength of the Earth's gravitational field is not uniform everywhere, a given pendulum swings faster and, therefore, has a shorter period at low altitudes than it has at high altitudes. In other words, the gravitational force per unit mass or, equivalently, the acceleration near the Earth that a body undergoes varies slightly and affects the behaviour of a pendulum. Mathematically, the period T of a simple pendulum is equal to 2π multiplied by the square root of the quotient of its length l divided by the acceleration g caused by gravity at that point:

$$T = 2\pi\sqrt{l/g}.$$

A simple pendulum with a length of one metre (39.4 inches) has a period of two seconds; each swing of the pendulum from one side to the other takes a second.

The period of a swinging pendulum is slightly affected by the angular displacement; that is, by the maximum angle the pendulum makes with the vertical rest position. For a displacement of 30° the period is 1 percent longer than given by the included formula. For amplitudes under 5° all periods are the same within 0.05 percent.

There are many other kinds of pendulums. A compound pendulum has an extended mass, like a swinging bar, that is not concentrated at a point as in the case of a simple pendulum, and is free to oscillate about a horizontal axis. Kater's pendulum, designed to measure the acceleration g caused by gravity, is a special reversible compound pendulum with a knife-edge support at a distance on each side of its centre of mass. If the knife edges are so adjusted that the pendulum has the same period when suspended from either one, its period is also described by the above formula for the simple pendulum in which l is the distance between the two points of suspension. From measurements of the period and length of Kater's pendulum, the acceleration caused by gravity can be calculated.

A spherical pendulum is one suspended from a pivot so that it may swing in any of an infinite set of vertical planes through the point of suspension. The pattern traced out by all the possible arcs the bob can make is a sector of a sphere. A simple spherical pendulum, the pivot of which is free to rotate while the pendulum is swinging, is called a Foucault pendulum (*q.v.*), used to demonstrate the rotation of the Earth on its axis.

A ballistic pendulum has a large wooden bob into which a bullet may be fired. By the resultant amplitude of the pendulum swing, the momentum and the speed of the bullet can be determined.

A Schuler pendulum is one that, once vertically suspended, remains aligned to the local vertical even when the point from which it is suspended is accelerated parallel to the Earth's surface. The principle of a Schuler pendulum is used in some inertial guidance systems to maintain a correct internal vertical reference even during acceleration.

Other devices that have constant repetitive movement are sometimes called pendulums. A torsion pendulum, for example, may consist of a relatively heavy mass attached to the end of a metal band, the other end of which is rigidly fixed. The mass is rotated in one direction, causing a slight twist in the metal band. The elastic restoring forces in the band build up and cause the suspended mass to slow down, stop, and rotate in the other direction. This twisting motion continues in successive clockwise and counterclockwise rotations, each pair of which constitutes a complete vibration of constant period. Torsion pendulums and gravity pendulums, when vibrating with small amplitudes, are specific examples of simple harmonic oscillators. *Major ref.* **11**:771d; illus.

·accuracy as time-measuring device **18**:415g
·Bessel's correction of seconds pendulum **2**:869h
·differential equation of motion **5**:737b
·dimensional analysis theory **14**:422h
·direct gravitation measurement **6**:21a
·Galileo's observation and clock idea **7**:851g
·gravitation theory development **8**:291e
·gravity measurement methods **6**:4g
·historical development of geometry **11**:661c
·Huygens' clock regulator use **9**:75b
·timekeeping usefulness and drawbacks **4**:744g; illus. 746
·types and uses in seismographs **16**:489c
·vibration detection principles **19**:103a
·vibratory motion theory **19**:667c

Pendzhikent, also spelled PYANJIKENT, PANJIKENT, and PYANDZHIKENT, Soviet Central Asia: *see in* Sogdian art.

penecontemporaneous fold (geology): *see in* fold.

Penedo, port city, Alagoas state, northeastern Brazil, on the north bank of the lower São Francisco River (bordering Sergipe state), 25 miles (40 kilometres) above its mouth on the Atlantic Ocean. Founded in the 16th century during the Portuguese conquest, it has developed a thriving trade in hides, rice, and cotton. There is light industrial development, including cotton spinning, weaving, vegetable-oil processing, and rice husking. Pop. (1970) 23,381.
10°17′ S, 36°36′ W

·establishment and historical importance **1**:408e
·map, Brazil **3**:124

Penelope, in Greek mythology, a daughter of Icarius of Sparta and the nymph Periboea and wife of the hero Odysseus. In the *Odyssey* is told the story of how, during her husband's long absence, many chieftains of Ithaca and nearby islands became her suitors. To spare herself their importunities she insisted that they wait until she had woven a shroud for Laërtes, father of Odysseus. Every night for three years, until one of her maids revealed the secret, she undid the piece that she had woven by day. She and her son Telemachus were finally relieved by the arrival of Odysseus. After the death of Odysseus, Penelope (according to later writers) married Telegonus, son of Odysseus and the sorceress Circe.

·Homeric treatment of Odysseus' return **8**:1021b

Penelope purpurascens (bird): *see in* curassow.

peneplain, gently undulating, almost featureless plain that, in principle, would be produced by fluvial erosion that, in the course of millions of years, would reduce the land almost to baselevel (sea level), leaving so little gradient that essentially no more erosion could occur. The peneplain concept was named in 1889 by William M. Davis, who believed it to be the final stage of his geomorphic cycle of landform evolution.

There has been much debate on the peneplain theory. The lack of present-day peneplains tends to discredit it, but some attribute this lack to geologically recent uplifting of the Earth's crust. Other geomorphologists question whether the Earth's crust has ever remained stable long enough for peneplanation to occur.

Criteria considered by its proponents to be evidence for the theory are (1) the accordant summits, or remnants of an uplifted, dissected peneplain; (2) the occurrence of uniform truncation of strata of varying erosional resistance; and (3) the presence of remnants of a mantle of residual soil formed on the peneplain. Examples cited as evidence are the Rocky Mountain Peneplain, the Schooley Peneplain of the Appalachians, and a buried peneplain seen in the strata of the Grand Canyon. Opponents of the theory hold that even if the examples cited do represent almost flat plains (which they consider unlikely), they were not necessarily formed by fluvial erosion within the confines of a geomorphic cycle.

·alluvial fan erosion-cycle model **1**:617c
·Ghana landscape **8**:136e
·landform evolution in Davis theory **10**:626h
·Ural Mountains geology **18**:1032f

Penetanguishene, town, Simcoe County, southeastern Ontario, Canada, on Penetang Harbour, at the southeast end of Lake Huron's Georgian Bay. The town (whose name is said to be derived from an Indian term meaning "white rolling sands") developed in the 1820s around a naval base built there in 1813. It is 3 mi (5 km) northwest of Midland. The base has since become a hospital. Industries include lumbering, tanning, and the manufacture of stoves, boxes, leather goods and shoes, concrete blocks, and truck bodies. A Canadian National Railway terminus and Great Lakes port, Penetanguishene is also a summer resort and centre of a district that produces seed potatoes. It is the site of one of Ontario's oldest historical attractions, the old garrison church of St. James-on-the-Lines, built in 1836. Inc. village, 1875; town, 1882. Pop. (1976) 5,460.
44°47′ N, 79°55′ W

penetrance, in genetics, the proportion of individuals in which a gene expresses itself in the bearer. Penetrance is influenced by neighbouring genes on the chromosome and by the external environment.

·gene expression and environment **8**:809f
·human heredity variable **7**:999d

Peneus River (Greece): *see* Piniós River.

Peneus setiferus: *see in* shrimp.

Penge, former urban district of the county of Kent, England; since 1965, part of Bromley (*q.v.*).

Pengelly, William (b. Jan. 12, 1812, East Looe, Cornwall—d. March 16, 1894, Torquay, Devon), educator, geologist, and a founder of prehistoric archaeology whose excavations in southwestern England helped earn scientific respect for the concept that early man coexisted with extinct animals, such as the woolly rhinoceros and mammoth. Supervising excavations at Brixham Cave in Devon (1858–59), he found flint tools deposited with extinct-animal bones, and his continued excavation at nearby Kent's Cavern (1865–83) demonstrated beyond any doubt that Paleolithic man had occupied the south Devon caves.
·archaeological proof of mankind's age **1**:1079c

P'eng Te-huai (b. 1898, Hsiang-t'an County, Hunan, China—d. 1974), military leader, one of the greatest in Chinese Communist history, and minister of national defense of China from 1954 until 1959, when he was removed for criticizing the military and economic policies of Mao Tse-tung. P'eng was a military commander under Chiang Kai-shek but separated from him in 1927 when Chiang attempted to rid the Kuomintang (Nationalist Party) of leftist elements. In 1928 P'eng became a Communist and soon afterward engaged in guerrilla activity and led a series of peasant uprisings. He became a senior military commander under Mao Tse-tung, participating in the Long March (1934–35), the Communist retreat of 6,000 miles from southeast to northwest China.

P'eng was the second-ranking man in the Communists' military hierarchy from the outbreak of the Sino-Japanese War in 1937 to 1954. He led Chinese forces in Korea and signed the armistice at P'anmunjŏm on July 27, 1953. In 1954 he became minister of national defense and a member of the Politburo of the Chinese Communist Party. In 1959, however, he criticized as impractical the policies of Mao Tse-tung's Great Leap Forward, which emphasized ideological purity over professional expertise in both the military forces and the economy. P'eng was deprived of office and of membership in the party and disappeared from view.

P'eng was "rehabilitated" in December 1978, under the post-Mao regime, and in a sympathetic article on him in *Jen-min jih-pao* (*People's Daily*) in March 1979 it was said that "the old man was criticized and lost his official posts because he said something true for the people. . . . He was a loyal official."
·Chinese Eighth Route Army leadership **4**:373f
·Lin's appointment to PLA leadership **10**:1014g
·Mao's forced concessions to orthodoxy **11**:468g
·military theory's ideological faults **4**:293h
·people's communes criticism and purge **4**:394g

Penguin, town, north Tasmania, Australia, at the mouth of Penguin Creek on Bass Strait. Founded in 1858 as a lumbering centre providing pit props for the gold mines of Victoria, it was proclaimed a town (1888) and a municipality (1908). The name stems from the flocks of penguins that once inhabited this stretch of coast. On the Bass Highway and a rail line to Launceston (60 mi [100 km] southeast), the town serves a section of the north coastal plain supporting intensive potato, pea, and dairy farming and market gardening. It also houses workers at an ilmenite-processing plant in Blythe (7 mi west). Many residents are Dutch immigrants who arrived after World War II. Pop. (1976) 2,558.
41°07′ S, 146°04′ E

penguin, bird, six genera and 18 species that constitute the family Spheniscidae, order Sphenisciformes. Penguins—of all birds the most fully adapted to water and extreme cold—are flightless and clumsy on land but at home in the water. They breed on islands in the sub-Antarctic and on cool Southern Hemisphere coasts of Africa, Australia, New Zealand, and South America. Only the Adélie penguin (*Pygoscelis adeliae*) and the emperor penguin (*Aptenodytes forsteri*) reach Antarctica itself; the Galápagos penguin (*Spheniscus mendiculus*) is confined to the tropics, off South America.

The Adélie, the best known penguin, has, like the others, a dark back and white belly. The species differ mainly in head pattern and in size, from 40 centimetres (16 inches) in the little blue, or fairy, penguin (*Eudyptula minor*) to almost 120 centimetres (4 feet) in the emperor. Sexes are alike in size and plumage. At sea for weeks at a time, flocks of penguins feed on fish, squids, and crustaceans. In turn, penguins are the prey of leopard seals and killer whales. Some species migrate long distances inland to ancestral nesting rookeries. The eggs, usually one or two, are brooded by both parents, who take no food during incubation. Young penguins are fed by regurgitation. Assemblages of half-grown young are often tended in crèches, or "kindergartens."

(Left) Emperor penguin (*Aptenodytes forsteri*) with chick, (right) Adélie penguin (*Pygoscelis adeliae*), female, incubating two eggs in nest
Michael C.T. Smith—National Audubon Society

Major ref. **17**:498b
·albatross evolutionary relationships **15**:18c
·Antarctic species and habits **1**:958b; illus.
·bird mortality rate, table 2 **14**:830
·diseases of animals, table 1 **5**:866
·emperor penguin mate identification **17**:48f
·Falkland Islands breeding grounds **7**:153h
·mating search preliminaries **16**:589h
·polar animal life **14**:656h; illus.
·swimming adaptations and movements **11**:18c

Penguin paperback, British pioneer softcover reprint book published at modest cost by Penguin Books, Ltd., founded by Allen Lane (*q.v.*) in 1935. Initial success led to Pelicans (serious nonfiction), topical Penguin Specials, and a Penguin Shakespeare (all 1937); Puffin Story Books (1941; a series that revolutionized children's literature), followed by Peacocks (for teen-agers) and in 1968 by Puffin Picture Books; Penguin Classics (1946) and Pelican Classics (1968); and many other series, from practical handbooks to the ambitious *Buildings of England* (1951–) and the *Pelican History of Art* (1953–).
·paperback history **15**:231g
·typography developments **18**:823c

Penibético Mountain System, Spanish SISTEMA PENIBÉTICO, also called CORDILLERA PENIBÉTICA, or BAETIC CORDILLERA, the Andalusian mountains of southern Spain. The northern mountains run about 360 mi (580 km) from Cabo Trafalgar to Cabo de la Nao. The central and southern ranges, the Penibaetic proper, extend a shorter distance from Estepona to Cabo de Gata. Separating the two systems is a complex series of structures, traceable in longitudinal corridors and high basins for 180 mi between Antequera and Baza and again between Lorca and the Guadalentín Valley. To the south, in the Penibaetic proper, the interior mountains include the Sierra Nevada, with the highest peak of the Iberian Peninsula, Cerro de Mulhacén, 11,411 ft (3,478 m). The lower, less continuous coastal ranges include the Sierras de Gador, de Almijara, and Alhamilla. Vegetation ranges widely, from subtropical at sea level to alpine higher up, within distances of only 20 to 30 mi.
37°00′ N, 3°30′ W
·map, Spain **17**:383

Pénicaud family, considered to be among the finest French enamellers active in Limoges during the 16th century. The members of the family are noted for their work in grisaille enamel, monochromatically painted enamel work intended to look like sculpture. Nardon Pénicaud (died Limoges, 1542/43), the first recorded member of the family, worked in the French Gothic style, but his brother or son, Jean I (fl. 1510–40), introduced motifs characteristic of the Italian Renaissance. He was also the first to extensively apply transparent enamel colours on copper. The existence of two other members of the Pénicaud family named Jean is disputed, although Jean III has often been cited as an important master of the grisaille technique. The last prominent enamellist of the family, Pierre, is considered a mediocre artist.

Peniche, town and municipality, Leiria district, Beira Litoral province, western Portugal, on the rocky Cabo Carvoeiro, southwest of Leiria. A fishing port and sardine-canning centre, it is noted for shellfish and lacework. The Berlengas and Farilhões islands are off the coast. Pop. (1970) town, 12,555; (1970 prelim.) mun., 21,046.
39°21′ N, 9°23′ W
·map, Portugal **14**:857

penicillin, antibiotic, the discovery of which in 1928 by Sir Alexander Fleming marked the beginning of the antibiotic era. Fleming observed that colonies of *Staphylococcus aureus* (the pus-producing bacterium) failed to grow in those areas of a culture that had been accidentally contaminated by the green mold *Penicillium notatum*. After isolating the mold, he found that it produced a substance capable of killing many of the common bacteria that infect human beings. This antibacterial substance, to which Fleming gave the name penicillin, was liberated into the fluid in which the mold was grown; this process is the basis of all commercial production of penicillin.

The several kinds of penicillin synthesized by various species of the mold *Penicillium* may be divided into two classes: biosynthetic penicillins (those formed during the process of mold fermentation) and semisynthetic penicillins (those in which the structure of a chemical substance—6-aminopenicillanic acid—found in all penicillins is altered in various ways). Because it is possible to change the characteristics of the antibiotic, different types of penicillin are produced for different therapeutic purposes.

Among the bacteria sensitive to penicillin are those that cause throat infections, pneumonia, spinal meningitis, gas gangrene, diphtheria, syphilis, and gonorrhea. In all these cases, penicillin acts by inhibiting the micro-organism's ability to synthesize a substance that is an essential ingredient of its cell wall, thereby making the internal components of the cell more vulnerable to changes in the surrounding medium of the host. The drug is not effective against all bacteria, however, because some have an inherent resistance to it, whereas others are capable of producing enzymes (biological catalysts) called penicillinases that can destroy penicillin.

·allergic reactions to antibiotics **1**:610c
·antibiotic research by Fleming **1**:986d
·chemotherapy and antibiotic development **4**:189a
·discovery and importance **18**:48a
·discovery by Fleming in 1928 **12**:756f
·disease causation mechanism **5**:856e
·drug action and effectiveness **5**:1047d
·drug effect on virus and bacteria **9**:533c
·genetic resistance of gonococcus **8**:814e
·industrial environment disease remedies **9**:532a
·joint destruction in venereal infections **10**:260a
·probenecid effects on kidney excretion **18**:284e
·renal tubular secretion **7**:38d
·representative chemical structure **8**:838h
·research of Fleming, Florey, and Chain **11**:833b

Penicillium, genus of about 250 species of blue or green mold fungus (division Mycota) of the form-class Deuteromycetes (Fungi Imperfecti). Those species for which the sexual phase is known are placed in the Eurotiales.

Penicillium notatum
Carlo Bevilacqua—SCALA

Found on foodstuffs, leather, and fabrics, they are of economic importance in the production of antibiotics (penicillin, *q.v.*), organic acids, and cheeses.

·competition exclusion in nature **2**:1048g
·Fleming's antibiotic research **1**:986d
·fungal growth illus. **12**:764
·mutant strain selection **12**:756a
·penicillin production and refining **14**:193a
·toxic microfungi, table 2 **14**:608

Penicuik, small burgh (town), county of Midlothian, Scotland, on the River Esk in the Pentland Hills. Situated in a formerly prosperous coal, iron, and oil-shale mining district, Penicuik was created a burgh in 1867. The town is now rapidly expanding following the introduction of several new industries in addition to the traditional waterpowered paper-making. Pop. (1971 prelim.) 10,216.
55°50′ N, 3°14′ W

Peninj Group (geology): *see* Olduvai Beds.

peninnite (mineral): *see* chlorite.

Peninsular Campaign (April 4–July 1, 1862), in the U.S. Civil War, large-scale but unsuccessful Union effort to capture the Confederate capital at Richmond, Va., by way of the peninsula formed by the York and the James rivers. Following the engagement between the ironclads "Monitor" and "Merrimack" at nearby Hampton Roads (March 9), Federal supplies and 100,000 troops were disembarked at Ft. Monroe under Maj. Gen. George B. McClellan. The first phase of the campaign, during which the North reached the town of White House, within striking distance of Richmond, concluded with the indecisive Battle of Seven Pines (*see* Seven Pines, Battle of; May 31–June 1). A second phase was characterized by three weeks of inactivity. The final phase ended triumphantly for the Confederate forces of Gen. Robert E. Lee, who forced the withdrawal of the Federal Army of the Potomac after the Seven Days' Battles (*q.v.*; June 25–July 1). Throughout the campaign, McClellan was unable to secure the additional troops he needed, due to the challenge of Confederate forces in the Shenandoah Valley. Thus Lee was able to play upon Pres. Abraham Lincoln's anxiety for the safety of Washington to break up the threatened combination against Richmond.

·Civil War strategy and battle tactics **4**:675f; map 676
·Lee's military strategy and effects **10**:770h

peninsulares, colonial residents of Latin America during the 16th to the early 19th century who had been born in Spain. The name refers to the Iberian Peninsula. Among the American-born in Mexico they were contemptuously called *gachupines* ("those with spurs") and in South America, *chapetónes* ("tenderfeet"). They enjoyed the special favour of the Spanish crown and were appointed to all of the leading civil and ecclesiastical posts under the colonial regime. As a result, the creoles, or persons of pure Spanish ancestry born in the Americas, were relegated to second class status, though they, in turn, enjoyed many advantages over Indians, Negroes, and those of mixed blood. *Peninsulares* were also given preference in commerce, while creoles were severely restricted in their business activities. Thus, there was mutual enmity between the two classes. With the achievement of independence from Spain in the early 19th century, the creoles moved into the first rank of Latin American society, and the *peninsulares* were, for the most part, driven out.

Peninsular War, also known as the PENINSULAR CAMPAIGN, in Spain, called the WAR OF INDEPENDENCE, (1808–14), that part of the Napoleonic Wars fought in the Iberian Peninsula, in which British troops (from 1809 commanded by Arthur Wellesley, later duke of Wellington) helped drive Napoleonic armies from Portugal, secured that country against attack, and later (1812–13) cooperated with Portuguese and Spanish forces in expelling the French from Spain, invading France itself in 1813–14. *Major ref.* **7**:728f; map 720

·British expedition and disaster **3**:992c
·guerrilla defense by Spain and Portugal **8**:459b
·insurrection against Bonaparte rule **12**:835g
·participants and leadership **3**:772d
·Spanish–English military tactics **17**:436d
·tactical system of Moore and Wellington **19**:579d
·Wellington field fortifications **6**:864b
·Wellington's military career **19**:755g

penis, the male organ through which sperm pass into the female reproductive tract. The corresponding structure in lower invertebrates is often called the cirrus.

The penis in man serves for the emission of urine during excretion and of semen (*q.v.*) during the reproductive process. It is anatomically divided into two continuous areas—the body, or external portion, and the root. The root of the penis begins directly below the bulbourethral glands (*q.v.*) with a long cylindrical body of tissue known as the corpus spongiosum (or corpus cavernosum urethrae). This tissue continues through the body of the penis until it reaches the tip, where it expands into a mushroom-shaped structure called the glans penis. Beginning alongside of the bulbourethral glands are a pair of long cylindrical bodies called the corpora cavernosa penis. These continue through the body of the penis, occupying the sides and upper portion directly above the corpus spongiosum; they terminate immediately before the glans penis.

The corpora cavernosa consist of empty spaces divided by partitions of tissue. The tissue consists of muscle, collagen (a fibrous protein), and elastic fibre. The corpora cavernosa are termed erectile tissue because, during sexual excitation, their fibrous tissue is expanded by blood that flows into and fills their empty spaces. The blood is temporarily trapped in the penis by the constriction of blood vessels that would normally allow it to flow out. The penis becomes enlarged, hardened, and erect as a result of this increased blood pressure; after intercourse the blood vessels again relax, allowing the return of normal blood flow. In the relaxed (or flaccid) state, the corpora cavernosa contain little blood and appear collapsed. There is an incomplete septum (fibrous wall) between the two corpora cavernosa. In several regions blood can pass through the septum.

The corpus spongiosum is also considered erectile tissue. This area, however, does not become as enlarged as the other two during erection, for it contains more fibrous tissue and less space; unlike the corpora cavernosa, the corpus spongiosum has a constant blood flow during erection. Running through the centre of the corpus spongiosum is the urethra, a common passage for semen and urine; the urethra ends in a slitlike opening at the tip of the glans penis.

The corpora cavernosa and corpus spongiosum are enclosed by a circular layer of elastic tissue. This in turn is covered by a thin layer of skin. The skin, which is slightly darker in colour than the rest of the body, is loose and folded while the penis is in a flaccid state. At the beginning of the glans penis, a circular fold of skin, commonly called the foreskin (or prepuce), extends forward to cover the glans. Frequently at birth or during early childhood, the foreskin is removed by an operation called circumcision.

·cirriped anatomy, illus. 1 **4**:641
·copulation in animal classes **16**:589b
corpus spongiosum penis
·animal reproductive system comparisons **15**:713e; illus.
·human anatomic interrelationships **15**:691b; illus.
·development and decline of function **16**:596b
·diseases, diagnoses, and treatment **15**:697a
·embryonic development of animals **5**:639a
·embryonic origins and development **6**:753b
·forking and bone in insectivores **9**:626g
·Khoisan pseudo-erection characteristic **10**:449a
·mammalian reproductive tract variations **11**:408d
·marsupial structural specializations **11**:542b
·Primate genitalia variations **14**:1025a
·reproductive development and maturation **5**:654h; illus. 655
·reptile types and erections **15**:734e
·size in sloth and armadillo **6**:301b
·snail anatomy and functions **7**:950h
·waterfowl adaptation for aquatic copulation **1**:945g

penis bone: *see* baculum.

penitential books, manuals used by priests of the Western Church, especially during the early Middle Ages, in administering ecclesiastical penance. (The name penance is applied to both a sacramental rite and acts performed in satisfaction for sins.) Penitentials contained (1) detailed lists of sins that the priest was to consider in assisting an individual penitent with his examination of conscience and confession during the rite and (2) corresponding penances or acts that were to be assigned to the penitent.

In the early church, the determination of the length and severity of these penances was left to the discretion of the local bishop or his delegate, the so-called priest penitentiary. In some instances, church councils and eminent ecclesiastics enacted canons that stipulated the penance to be done for certain grave sins. The penances were imposed as part of the ritual of public penance. When the rite of private penance—confession of a penitent to an individual confessor, normally a priest—began to replace public penance during the 6th century, the priests required guidelines for treating practical cases. The penitential books enjoyed great popularity among the clergy and played a significant role in the development of private penance.

The first penitential books appeared in Ireland and Wales, and the earliest extant compilations are probably those associated with St. David and various Welsh synods of the 6th century, though the *Canons of St. Patrick* (*c.* 450) are occasionally, and somewhat loosely, spoken of as the first penitential. Among the more important of the early books are those of St. Finnian of Clonard (*c.* 550), St. Columban (*c.* 600), and the influential penitential attributed to Theodore, archbishop of Canterbury (668–690). The Celtic penitentials were brought to the continent of Europe by missionary monks at an early date. Their introduction met with the opposition of ecclesiastics who favoured the older, traditional public penance, but there is considerable documentary evidence that penitential books were in use among the Franks by the late 6th century, in Italy by the late 8th century, and among the Spanish Visigoths by the early 9th century. Recognition that errors had crept into the penitential books and that they had imposed arbitrary penances, combined with the proscription of local councils and bishops, led to the decline in influence of these books. The ultimate effect of the penitentials and of the reaction against them was the official codification of disciplinary and penitential canons or laws.

Besides their importance in the history of theology and canon law, the penitentials are of value to the philologist as source material for comparative studies of Latin, Anglo-Saxon, Old Irish, and Icelandic forms; to the social historian for the vivid, often revolting picture they present of the manners and morals of barbarous peoples just coming under the influence of Christianity; and to the student of jurisprudence for the information they afford about the early history of the *wergild* (blood money), which defined in monetary terms the value of a man's life and was the basis for a system of compensation for wrongs by money payment.

penitentiary: *see* prisons and penology.

Penkovsky, Oleg Vladimirovich (b. April 23, 1919, Ordzhonikidze, Russia—d. May 1963, U.S.S.R.), colonel in the Soviet army intelligence directorate (GRU) and deputy chief of the foreign section of the State Committee for the Coordination of Scientific Research (1960–62), who was convicted of spying for the U.K. and the U.S.

Penkovsky became an intelligence officer after attending the Military Diplomatic Academy (1949–53) and served primarily in Moscow except while he was assistant military attaché in Ankara, Tur. (1955–56). In April 1961, through Greville M. Wynne, a British businessman, he offered his services to British intelligence. Between April 1961 and August 1962 Penkovsky passed more than 5,000 photographs of classified military, political, and economic documents to British and U.S. intelligence forces. He was arrested on Oct. 22, 1962, and executed for high treason soon after his trial. In 1965 his journal, *The Penkovskiy Papers*, was published in the U.S.

Penn, Irving (b. June 16, 1917, Plainfield, N.J.), photographer, influential for his incisive portraits and his innovations in colour photography. His early ambition was to be a painter. But at the age of 26 he took a job designing photographic covers for the fashion magazine *Vogue*. He soon developed a photographic style characterized by bold graphic design and brilliant contrast.

Irving Penn, 1960
Alexander Liberman

During his career, Penn photographed a large number of celebrities, sparring with each sitter to reveal his personality to the camera. In his early portraiture, he often used props to draw out the subject's personality. One of his most successful techniques was to pose his subjects between two walls that met at an acute angle to stimulate in him the feelings of security or of vulnerability. He also made a memorable series of portraits of the Indians of Cuzco, Peru, and a series of portraits, collectively called *Small Trades*, of labourers formally posed in their work clothes and holding the tools of their trade. Three hundred of his pictures were published in the photographic book, *Moments Preserved* (1960).

Penn is especially known for his innovations in colour photography. He often achieved very large grained colour through extreme enlargement and applied such romantic effects as image diffusion and soft focus to such unlikely subjects as industrial equipment.

Penn, Sir William (b. April 23, 1621, Bristol, Eng.—d. Sept. 16, 1670, London), British admiral and father of William Penn, the founder of Pennsylvania. In his youth he served at sea, and in the English Civil War (1642–51) he fought for Parliament, being appointed rear admiral of the Irish seas in 1647. He was arrested in 1648 on suspicion of corresponding with Charles I but was soon released. He fought in the First Anglo-Dutch War (1652–54) as vice admiral and then as general of the fleet. After secretly offering in 1654 to deliver the fleet to Charles II, then in exile, he sailed in command of the expedition sent by Oliver Cromwell to the West Indies, which captured Jamaica (May 1655) but failed to take Hispaniola. On his return he was briefly imprisoned, for reasons that are uncertain. At the Restoration (1660) he was knighted and appointed a commissioner for the navy. In the Second Dutch War (1665–67) he served as captain of the fleet with the Duke of York (afterward James II). Penn was the author of a code of naval tactics that was the basis of the "Duke of York's Sailing and Fighting Instructions," long the orthodox tactical guide of the navy.

·career vacillation and influence on son **14**:23h
·Pennsylvania charter and name **14**:25h

Penn, William **14**:23 (b. Oct. 14, 1644, London—d. July 30, 1718, Buckinghamshire), Quaker leader and advocate of religious freedom who founded the American Commonwealth of Pennsylvania.

Abstract of text biography. The son of the famous admiral, Sir William, Penn became a militant Quaker at the age of 21 and was imprisoned four times for his beliefs. In the 1670s he devoted himself to efforts in behalf of religious toleration and became involved in politics. Through his connections he secured from the crown a large tract of land in America (1674) and spent the remainder of his life developing a colony there organized according to his religious and political principles.

REFERENCES in other text articles:
·character summary of George Fox **7**:580e
·Delaware cession and Pennsylvania union attempts **5**:567d
·Pennsylvania charter and development **14**:25h
·Pennsylvania Hospital founding **8**:1114g
·Pennsylvania land grant and government **18**:949d
·Philadelphia's founding **14**:216b
·Philadelphia's planning aspects **18**:1081f
·promotion of migration to colonies **12**:187d
·Puritan idea of mandate from God **15**:307f
·Quaker Holy Experiment colony **7**:743f

Pennacook, Algonkian-speaking American Indians whose villages were located in what are now southern and central New Hampshire, northeastern Massachusetts, and southern Maine. Like other New England Algonkian tribes, they depended on hunting, fishing, and the cultivation of maize (corn). They were semi-sedentary, moving seasonally in response to changing food resources.

Smallpox and other causes reduced the Pennacook population from an estimated 2,000 in 1600 to 1,250 in 1674. In King Philip's War (*q.v.*) two of the constituent Pennacook tribes joined the hostile Indians against the colonists, but most remained friendly to the whites. The arrogance and treachery of the whites, however, subsequently caused the Pennacook to flee their territory, most removing to Canada and eventually settling at Saint-François-du-Lac. The remainder moved westward and eventually settled at Schaghticoke, Rensselaer County, N.Y.

·Woodlands Indian culture **6**:169b

pennant (flag): *see* armorial ensigns.

Pennant, Thomas (b. June 14, 1726, Downing, Flintshire—d. Dec. 16, 1798, Downing), naturalist and traveller, one of the foremost zoologists of his time. His books were valued for their highly readable treatment of the existing knowledge of natural history. His

Pennant, detail from a lithograph by an unknown artist
Radio Times Hulton Picture Library

volume on *British Zoology* (1766) stimulated zoological research, particularly in ornithology, in Great Britain, and his travel books presented valuable information on local customs, natural history, and antiquities. A careful observer, he kept elaborate journals on his tours of Scotland, Wales, England, and the Continent, made mostly on horseback.

Pennatulacea (marine animal): *see* sea pen.

Penn Center, multilevel complex of high-rise offices and hotels with interior courts and malls, west of Penn Square in Philadelphia.

·location and nature of the complex **14**:217b

Pennel, John (1940–), U.S. athlete, the first pole-vaulter to clear 16 feet.

·pole vault record improvements **18**:548e

Pennell, Joseph (b. July 4, 1857, Philadelphia—d. April 23, 1926, Brooklyn, N.Y.), etcher, lithographer, and writer, who was one of the major book illustrators of his time.

"Things that Tower—Coal Collieries," drypoint by Joseph Pennell (1857–1926); in the Metropolitan Museum of Art, New York City

By courtesy of the Metropolitan Museum of Art, New York, gift of David Keppel, 1917

Like his compatriot and friend J.M. Whistler, Pennell, after attending the Pennsylvania Academy of Fine Arts, went to Europe in 1884 and made his home in London. He produced numerous books (many of them in collaboration with his wife, Elizabeth Robins Pennell), but his chief distinction is as an original etcher and lithographer and notably as an illustrator. During his lifetime Pennell produced more than 900 etchings and mezzotints and more than 600 lithographs, on subjects ranging from the Panama Canal and Yosemite National Park to the factories of England and the temples of Greece. His publications include several books on drawing and printmaking, and his famous biography of Whistler, written with Mrs. Pennell (1908). Pennell moved back to the United States during World War I.

Pennell Bank, geologic feature, Ross Ice Shelf, Antarctica.
·geologic structure **15**:1159e

Penner (NORTHERN PENNER) **River,** rises on the Deccan Plateau 7 mi (11 km) west-southwest of Chik Ballāpur, Mysore state, southern India. It flows north into Andhra Pradesh state and turns east-southeast toward the Coromandel Coast, emptying into the Bay of Bengal near Nellore, about 350 mi from its source. The river is seasonal, becoming a torrent after the rains and a thin stream during dry periods.
14°35′ N, 80°11′ E
·map, India **9**:278

Penney, William (George) Penney, Baron, of East Hendred in the Royal County of Berkshire (b. June 24, 1909, Gibraltar), English atomic scientist who helped develop the British atomic bomb. Penney was engaged in atomic work for the Ministry of Home Security and the Admiralty during World War II; was principal scientific officer of the department of scientific and industrial research at the Los Alamos Scientific Laboratory, New Mexico, in 1944–45; and was official observer of the atomic bombing of Nagasaki. In 1953, one year after he was knighted, he was made director of atomic weapons research and development at Aldermaston, Berkshire. He became chairman of the U.K. Atomic Energy Authority in 1964. He was created a life peer in 1967.

Penn Hills, urban township, Allegheny County, southwestern Pennsylvania, U.S., it is an eastern suburb of Pittsburgh. Settled in 1770, it was established as Penn township in 1850 and was renamed Penn Hills township in 1958. Pop. (1980) 57,632.
40°28′ N, 79°53′ W

Penniman, Russell Sylvanus, 19th-century U.S. chemist.
·ammonium dynamite development **7**:85d

Pennine Alps, Italian ALPI PENNINE, French ALPES PENNINES, segment of the Central Alps along the Italian–Swiss border, bounded by the Great Saint Bernard Pass and the Mont Blanc group (southwest), by the Upper Rhône Valley (north), by Simplon Pass and the Lepontine Alps (*qq.v.*; northeast), and by the Dora Baltea River Valley (south). The highest point is Dufourspitze (*q.v.*; 15,203 ft [4,634 m]) in the Monte Rosa group; other important peaks include the Matterhorn and the Weisshorn. Most of the glaciers lie on the north slopes, including the well-known Gornergletscher near Zermatt, Switz. Mountain

The village of Courmayeur in the Pennine Alps, Italy

J. Alex Langley—DPI

climbing has long been the main activity of the region. The Swiss portion of the range is sometimes called the Walliser Alpen (German) or Alpes du Valais (French).
46°05′ N, 7°50′ E
·Alpine geology and geography **1**:634c; map
·map, Switzerland **17**:868

Pennines, major upland mass forming a relief "backbone" and watershed in the north of England, extending southward from Northumberland into Derbyshire. The uplands, with a short, steep western slope, dip gently eastward. They are surrounded on the east, west, and south by the Vale of York, the Lancashire and Cheshire plains, and the valley of the River Trent, respectively. On the north, the Tyne Gap and Eden Valley separate the Pennines from the Cheviots and the Lake District mountains.

The uplands are broken into numerous short ranges by valleys (often called dales); the main division is formed by the rivers Aire (flowing east) and Ribble (flowing west). The northern section of the Pennines is broader and generally higher than the southern. The highest points are Cross Fell (2,930 ft [893 m]), Whernside (2,419 ft), Ingleborough (2,373 ft), and Pen-y-Ghent (2,273 ft). In the southern section, heights of over 2,000 ft are rare, apart from Kinder Scout (2,088 ft), part of the scenic region known as Peak District of Derbyshire.

The geological structure of the Pennines consists of carboniferous limestone and Millstone Grit with some local shales. On the drier areas, heather moor predominates, while the wet, peaty areas are covered mostly with cotton grass. The summits of the hills are rounded or nearly flat, but geological structures and glacial action have helped to produce fine scenery in the dales. Water action has developed underground caverns and watercourses; *e.g.*, Ingleborough Cave near Clapham, Gaping Gill (over 350 ft deep), and Rowten Pot (365 ft). The stream draining Malham Tarn (brook), disappearing below ground and reappearing at the foot of the cliffs at Malham

Pen-y-Ghent in the northern section of the Pennines

Kenneth Scowen

Cove, is a tributary of the Aire. Derbyshire contains a remarkable series of caverns near Castleton. The River Wye disappears into Plunge Hole and traverses Poole's Hole, near Buxton. There are few lakes in the Pennines, but reservoirs in Millstone Grit areas supply the manufacturing regions of West Yorkshire and Lancashire.

The economy of the Pennines is based mainly on sheep farming and quarrying of limestone. The valleys contain numerous small market towns (*e.g.*, Hawes, Muker, and Grassington). Tourism has become an important element in the economy, helped by the designation of the Peak District, Yorkshire Dales, and Northumberland national parks. The Pennine Way, a right of way extending the length of the Pennines into Scotland for 250 mi, was opened in 1965, and Dales Way stretches from Wharfedale to the Lake District.

Prehistoric remains, such as the great circle at Arbor Low Hill, are numerous. The Roman Hadrian's Wall, a defensive line against the peoples of what was, in large part, to become Scotland, extends from Carlisle (in the west) to the North Sea mouth of the Tyne, along the northern edge of the Pennines.
·English physical geography **6**:867e
·map, United Kingdom **18**:866
·United Kingdom geographical features **18**:865f

Penning gauge, or COLD-CATHODE IONIZATION GAUGE, vacuum gauge widely used in industrial systems.
·vacuum gauge types and mechanisms **19**:17c

Pennington, Sir John (1568–1646), English admiral.
·Dutch victory at Battle of the Downs **18**:716f

Pennisetum, genus of the grass family (Poaceae), containing about 80 species of annual

Feathertop (*Pennisetum villosum*)

Hartmut Noeller—Peter Arnold

and perennial plants, native to tropical and subtropical areas. Kikuyu grass (*P. clandestinum*), a perennial, sod-forming species, is grown for pasturage in Central America. Several varieties of feathertop (*P. villosum*) and fountaintop, or fountain grass (*P. setaceum*, formerly *P. ruppelii*), both native to Ethiopia, are cultivated in North America as ornamentals. Pearl millet (*P. glaucum*), an annual species, which bears a cattail-like flower cluster, is cultivated in tropical areas for its edible grain. Napier grass, or elephant grass (*P. purpureum*), a tall African perennial, is cultivated for forage in Central America and as a lawn grass in North America.
·Kikuyu grass importation **19**:727e

pennon, a type of armorial ensign (*q.v.*).

Pennsauken, township, Camden County, southwestern New Jersey, U.S., immediately northeast of Camden, on the Delaware River. Settled in 1840, it developed as a river port. Its industries include an oil refinery and factories producing paperboard, fibre drums, barrels, enamelled iron, and metal sanitary ware. The name, formerly sometimes spelled Pensauken, is derived from an Algonkian word the meaning of which is uncertain. Inc. 1892. Pop. (1980) 33,775.
39°58′ N, 75°04′ W

Penn Square, in Philadelphia, site of the City Hall and centre of the gridiron of streets provided for in William Penn's original plans for the city.
·Philadelphia city plan **14**:217b; map 218

Pennsylvania **14**:25, officially COMMONWEALTH OF PENNSYLVANIA, Middle Atlantic state of the U.S., one of the 13 original states. Occupying an area of 45,333 sq mi (177,412 sq km), it is bounded on the north by Lake Erie and New York; on the east by New York and New Jersey; on the south by Delaware, Maryland, and West Virginia; and on the west by the Panhandle of West Virginia and by Ohio. Its capital is Harrisburg. Pop. (1980) 11,866,728.

The text article covers its history, natural and human landscape, people, economy, administration and social conditions, and cultural life and institutions.

REFERENCES in other text articles:
·Appalachian geology and ecology **1**:1016a
·area and population, table 1 **18**:927
history
·border dispute with Connecticut **5**:9h
·Civil War battle activity **4**:677g
·colonial education law **6**:358b
·colonial government, growth, and prosperity **18**:949d; map 951
·Delaware historical connections **5**:567b *passim* to 568c
·early U.S. agricultural specialties **18**:963a
·first commercial oil well **6**:854f
·Franklin's cultural and political contributions **7**:694d
·Penn's colonization and contribution **14**:24h
·post-Revolution state and national governments **18**:956e *passim* to 957f
·pre-Revolution political rivalry **18**:954g
·Quaker successes and failures **7**:743f
·Revolutionary War activities **19**:604a; map 603
·map, United States **18**:909
·Midland cultural origin and influence **18**:925c
·newspaper publishing history **15**:239d
·Philadelphia's importance **14**:216b
·Ridge and Valley appearance and mineral resources **18**:907e
·Susquehanna River illus. **13**:184
·town morphology and comparison **18**:920b

Pennsylvania, 19th-century U.S. steam warship.
·naval ship design history **12**:890h

Pennsylvania, University of, private, coeducational university located in Philadelphia, founded in 1740 as a charity school. Largely through the efforts of Benjamin Franklin and other leading Philadelphians, it became an academy in 1753, with Franklin as president of the first board of trustees. Two years later it was chartered as the College and Academy of Philadelphia. With the foundation in 1765 of the first medical school in North America, the institution became in fact a university, but it was not so called until 1779, when for a time it received state support. Since 1791 it has been privately endowed and controlled, although it continues to receive substantial state aid.

The university offers undergraduate and graduate study in arts and sciences, education, and engineering. Among the university schools are law, dentistry, medicine, social work, and fine arts, and the Wharton School of Finance and Commerce. University institutes include the Wistar Institute of Anatomy and Biology (the first anatomical institute in America devoted entirely to research, 1892) and the Henry Phipps Institute of Genetics and Community Diseases (1910). The University Museum (archaeology and ethnology) is a teaching and research organization. In the later 1970s total enrollment was more than 20,000.
·colonial curriculum distinctions **6**:358c
·computer age origins **14**:219b
·football victories of 1894–98 teams **7**:509d
·origin and distinctions **14**:29b

Pennsylvania Avenue, major thoroughfare of Washington, D.C., on which the White House is located.
·redevelopment proposals **19**:627b; map 624

Pennsylvania Dutch, 17th- and 18th-century German settlers (primarily from the Rhineland and south Germany) in Pennsylvania and their descendants. (The word Dutch is a rendering of the German word *Deutsch*, meaning "German"). Many of them in modern times have clung to their European culture and traditions, and they are known for their cooking and their decorative motifs, such as the hex signs they paint on their barns.
·folk visual art forms and motifs **7**:479a
·origin, settlement area, and contribution **14**:27c

Pennsylvanian Period, division of geologic time in North America that began about 325,000,000 years ago and lasted about 45,000,000 years; it follows the Mississippian Period, and precedes the Permian Period and is roughly equivalent to the Upper Carboniferous of European usage. Pennsylvanian rocks in North America are of great economic significance for the vast coal reserves and the large amounts of petroleum and natural gas they contain. In the U.S., five major coalfields are known. The largest, the Appalachian Field, extends from Pennsylvania to Alabama; it alone supplies about one-fourth of the coal production of the world. Other important coalfields are the Midcontinent Field, which extends from Iowa to Texas, the Illinois Field, and the Michigan Field.

During the Early Pennsylvanian, the North American continent was rimmed by rising mountain systems on the east and south and as far west as Texas. Canada was emergent, and a broad sedimentary basin developed between Canada and the mountainous borderlands. Marine waters swept eastward as a vast, shallow sea across the basin, and the shoreline receded and advanced. The Pennsylvanian is characterized by great lateral and vertical sedimentary variability and by cyclothems, sequences of rhythmically repetitive strata found in many regions. The Pennsylvanian fossil record is well documented for plants and animals. Moist lowlands were covered with forests of giant, treelike ferns and seed-bearing plants. Terrestrial animals were varied and abundant; the first reptiles appeared, and hundreds of species of Pennsylvanian insects are known, among them giant dragonflies and roaches. Similarly, Pennsylvanian marine faunas are diverse and abundant; especially prominent are the fusulinids, protozoans having hard shells useful for stratigraphic correlation.
·conodont fossil record **5**:26g
·geological forms and feature development **7**:1064h
·geological time scale, illus. 2 **5**:499
·geologic history, climate, and life **6**:14a
·pollen stratigraphy and evolution **14**:739h; illus. 740
·sedimentation, orogeny, and boundaries **3**:856d
·Upper Paleozoic geology and life **13**:921b

RELATED ENTRIES in the *Ready Reference and Index: for*
rock groups and formations: see Douglas Group; Gaptank Formation; Kansas City Group; Lansing Group; Marmaton Group; Shawnee Group
series: Allegheny Series; Atokan Series; Canyon Series; Cisco Series; Conemaugh Series; Desmoinesian Series; Lampasan Series; Missourian Series; Monongahela Series; Morrowan Series; Pottsville Series; Springeran Series; Virgilian Series

Pennsylvania Railroad Company, U.S. railroad company chartered in 1846; merged with the New York Central in 1968, to be retitled (1969) Penn Central Transportation Company; Penn Central in 1976 became part of Consolidated Rail Corporation (Conrail).
·Philadelphia–Pittsburgh line development **15**:480c

Pennsylvania system, penal method based on the principle that solitary confinement fostered penitence and encouraged reformation. The idea was advocated by the Philadelphia Society for Alleviating the Miseries of Public Prisons, whose most active members were Quakers. In 1829 the Eastern State Penitentiary, on Cherry Hill in Philadelphia, applied this so-called separate philosophy. Prisoners were kept in solitary confinement in cells about 16 feet high, nearly 12 feet long, and 7.5 feet wide (4.9 by 3.7 by 2.3 metres). An exercise yard, completely enclosed to prevent contact among prisoners, was attached to each cell. Prisoners saw no one except institution officers and an occasional visitor. Solitary penitence, however, was soon modified to include work. The Pennsylvania system spread until it predominated in European prisons. Critics in the U.S. argued that it was too costly and had deleterious effects on the minds of the prisoners. It was superseded in the U.S. by the Auburn system (*q.v.*). *Major ref.* **14**:1099b

Pennsylvania Turnpike, one of the earliest major limited-access express highways in the U.S., opened in 1938 as a toll road connecting Harrisburg and Pittsburgh.
·construction and operation **15**:900c
·size, location, and distinction **14**:28d

pennycress, common name for plants of the genus *Thlaspi* of the mustard family (Brassicaceae), named and sometimes grown for their round seedpods. Most of the 60 species are Eurasian, but a few are native to North and South America, mostly in mountain areas. Common pennycress, or field pennycress (*T. arvense*), has spikelike clusters of penny-shaped, notched pods topped by small, white, four-petalled flowers.

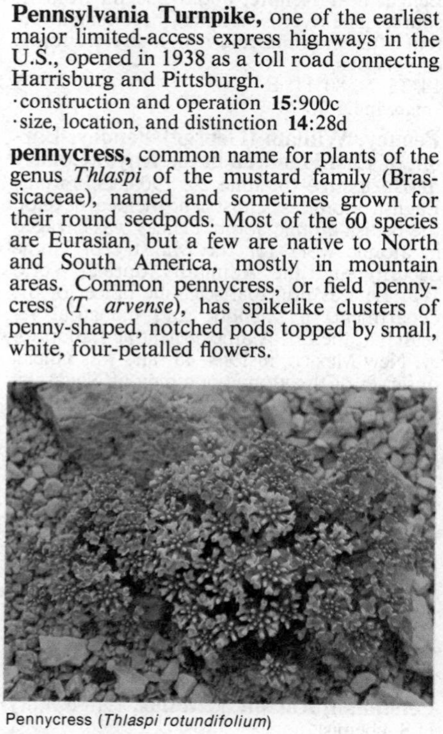

Pennycress (*Thlaspi rotundifolium*)
A.J. Huxley—EB Inc.

penny-farthing bicycle, also called ordinary bicycle and high wheeler bicycle, a bicycle with a large front wheel and a small rear wheel common from about 1870 to 1890.
·development and decline **2**:982b; illus. 981

Pennypack Park, in northeastern Philadelphia, a semi-wilderness setting, with bird-watching trails and an abundance of wildlife.
·natural setting and wildlife **14**:220d

Penny Post, British postal system carrying a letter for a penny; term applied to system established in London about 1680 and to the former system of Great Britain established in 1840.
·English public postal service origins **14**:885c

Pennyrile, also spelled PENNYROYAL, region, Kentucky.
·boundaries and unique cave formation **10**:420f

pennyroyal (herb): *see* Mentha.

pennywinkle (snail): *see* periwinkle.

pennywort (plant): *see* Crassulaceae.

Penobscot, Algonkian-speaking Indians who lived on both sides of the Penobscot Bay and throughout the Penobscot River Basin in what is now Maine. They were members of the Abnaki (*q.v.*) confederacy. Penobscot subsistence was based on hunting, fishing, and collecting, with seasonal movements following food resources. In winter small family groups lived in hunting camps within separate family territories, rights to which were inherited through the male line; larger camps and villages were inhabited during the summer. The office of tribal chief embodied little power, the individual acting generally as a tribal representative in ceremonies or in dealings with outsiders and sometimes adjudicating disputes.

Teepee-shaped wigwam of the Penobscot Indians of Maine
By courtesy of the American Museum of Natural History, New York

Europeans first encountered the Penobscot early in the 16th century; a French mission was established among them in 1688. The Penobscot assisted the French against the English in all the wars on the New England frontier until 1749, when they made peace with the English. As a result they did not remove to Canada with the other groups of the Abnaki confederacy, and they remain in their old territory to the present. The Penobscot and the Passamaquoddy (*q.v.*) send to the Maine state legislature a representative who has no seat or vote and is permitted to speak only on tribal affairs. In 1969, 840 persons were enrolled as tribal members in Maine.
·American Indian local races **15**:349b
·Woodlands Indian culture **6**:169b

Penobscot Bay, inlet of the North Atlantic Ocean, on the coast of south Maine, U.S., at the mouth of the Penobscot River. Lying 70 mi (110 km) northeast of Portland, it extends 35 mi inland and is 27 mi wide. The bay includes many islands and sheltered harbours. The once-thriving lumbering industry, centred to the north at Bangor on the Penobscot River, used the bay as an outlet; but the tourist industry is now the main economic activity. There is also some commercial fishing, especially nearer the ocean.
44°15′ N, 68°52′ W

Owl's Head Peninsula, Penobscot Bay
Mary M. Thacher—Photo Researchers

Penobscot River, Maine, U.S., the largest river in the state. Discovered by English voyagers in 1603, and in 1604 by Samuel de Champlain, it was named after the Penobscot Indians. The river valley became a bloody battleground for the French and British between 1673 and 1759 and between the British and Americans until 1815.

The Penobscot is formed by several headstreams draining numerous lakes that were created by melting glaciers; it is about 350 mi (560 km) in length. The western and eastern branches of the river flow together at Medway and run in a southeasterly direction to Penobscot Bay near Bucksport, where the river enters the Atlantic Ocean. The river's major tributary is the Mattawamkeag; Bangor, 23 mi from the ocean, is the head of navigation. Once an important source of salmon, the river has now become economically important to the lumbering and pulp and paper industries.
44°30′ N, 68°50′ W
·map, United States **18**:908

Penola, town, southeast South Australia, southeast of Adelaide. Founded in 1836, its Aboriginal name refers to the nearby "big swamp," part of the Murray River Basin, which extends northward along the coast. It is the fast-growing centre of a highly fertile agricultural district, which produces beef and dairy cattle, sheep, fruits, and table wines. There are also extensive pine plantations, which supply local sawmills. Pop. (1971 prelim.) 1,293.
37°23′ S, 140°50′ E

penology: *see* prisons and penology.

Penonomé, capital, Coclé province, west central Panama, on the Pacific coastal lowland. The original Spanish settlement was founded on the ruins of an ancient Indian town on the Zaratí River. The city is now a commercial centre through which the rubber, coffee, and cacao produced in the region are shipped; soap and Panama hats are manufactured as well. The city lies on the Pan-American Highway. Pop. (1970) 5,066.
8°31′ N, 80°21′ W
·map, Panama **13**:941

Penrhyn, most northerly of the Cook Islands, a dependency of New Zealand in the southwest Pacific Ocean. A coral atoll, it has a total land area of 4 sq mi (10 sq km) and a 40-mi (60-km) reef that surrounds a lagoon of 108 sq mi. Discovered in 1788, it was named (1822) for a British ship, the "Lady Penrhyn," that was taking convicts to Australia. Annexed to Britain in 1888, it came under New Zealand administration in 1901. The island is called Tongareva (Tonga in the Heavens) by its native populace. Copra and pearl shell are exported from the main village of Omoka. The large lagoon has good anchorage facilities with three passages to the open sea. Penrhyn has several schools, a hospital, and an airstrip, which was built during World War II. Pop. (1970 est.) 682.
9°00′ S, 158°00′ W

Penrith, city, east central New South Wales, Australia, on the Nepean River, a section of the Hawkesbury River. Founded in 1815, it was known as Evan and Castlereagh before being renamed after Penrith in Cumberland, England. It was declared a municipality in 1871 and a city in 1959. A suburb of Sydney (30 mi [48 km] east), to which it is linked by rail and the Great Western Highway, Penrith is also a resort and agricultural centre (dairying, fruits, vegetables, beef). Its industries include the manufacture of aluminum foil, concrete and building materials, plastics, textiles, and engineering and electrical products plants. Pop. (1971 prelim.) 60,242.
33°45′ S, 150°42′ E

Penrith, market town in the county of Cumbria (until 1974 it was in the county of Cumberland), England, on a main route to Scotland, at the foot of Penrith Beacon (937 ft [286 m]) overlooking the mountains of the scenic region known as the Lake District.

Penrith Castle was built in the 14th century as a defense against the Scottish raids and was dismantled during the mid-17th-century English Civil War. The parish Church of St. Andrew, of Norman foundation, has a 13th-century tower, but the body of the building is 18th-century.

The town, on the edge of the Lake District National Park, is now a tourist and agricultural centre, and a weekly livestock market is held.

Places of interest include the Giant's Grave (ancient hogsback stones and cross shafts) in the churchyard, and the Gloucester Arms (associated with Richard III of England [reigned 1483–85]).

The ruins of Brougham Castle, with a 12th-century keep, stand on the site of a Roman fort, 1½ mi to the southeast. Pop. (1971 prelim.) 11,299.
54°40′ N, 2°44′ W
·map, United Kingdom **18**:866

Penrose, Richard Alexander Fullerton, Jr. (b. Dec. 17, 1863, Philadelphia—d. July 31, 1931, Philadelphia), geologist known for his explorations for manganese and iron-ore deposits. He was a member of the Arkansas Geological Survey from 1889 until 1892, when he became a faculty member at the University of Chicago. From 1917 until 1923 he served on the National Research Council, Washington, D.C. He wrote *The Nature and Origin of Deposits of Phosphate of Lime* (1888); *The Geology of the Gulf Tertiary of Texas* (1889); *Manganese, Its Uses, Ores and Deposits* (1890); *The Iron Deposits of Arkansas* (1892); and *The Last Stand of the Old Siberia* (1922).

Penry, John (1559–93), Welsh Puritan, author of some of the most famous early Puritan treatises, most of which are violent and anti-episcopal in tone.

Penryn, market town, English Channel port, and borough in the county of Cornwall, England, lying at the head of the River Penryn's estuary. The town owed its development to the bishops of Exeter, within whose demesne (feudal tribute) lands it stood. A bishop granted the first charter (1265), and another bishop secured the rights to hold certain markets. Mary I (reigned 1553–58) gave parliamentary franchise to the burgesses in 1553 and James I (reigned 1603–25) granted and renewed the charter of incorporation, providing further markets. Yet another charter was given by James II (reigned 1685–88).

Penryn is the principal English port for the shipment of granite, which is extensively quarried in the neighbourhood and dressed and polished at Penryn. There are also engineering

works, boat repairing, and lumberyards. Pop. (1973 est.) 5,660.
50°09′ N, 5°06′ W

Pensacola, city, seat of Escambia County, extreme northwestern Florida, U.S., on Pensacola Bay. Discovered in 1516 and rediscovered in 1686, it became a Spanish fort (1698) and was ravaged during the French-Spanish colonial fighting of 1719–20. After the British gained control following the Seven Years' War, it became the capital of West Florida. During the Revolution it became a haven for Tories but in 1781 was taken by a Spanish force from New Orleans. In 1818 Gen. Andrew Jackson captured the city, accusing the Spanish of encouraging Indian raids against the U.S. After Florida was ceded to the U.S. in 1821, Pensacola acquired a federal navy yard in 1824. Although the city was seized by Confederates during the Civil War, Ft. Pickens on Santa Rosa Island remained in Federal hands, and in 1862 the Confederates evacuated the city. Lumbering and commercial fishing increased after the war, and industry began. The navy yard became a naval air station in 1913, and the large aviation training school helped the city's economy. The deepwater port of Pensacola, although important, suffers because of its proximity to Mobile, Ala. Tourism and chemical and wood-products industries are important economic factors. Pensacola is the seat of Pensacola Junior College (1948) and the University of West Florida (1967). The city's name was derived from that of the local Pansfalaya Indians. Inc. 1822. Pop. (1980) city, 57,619; metropolitan area (SMSA), 289,782.
30°25′ N, 87°13′ W
·Jackson's West Florida campaign **10**:2c
·map, United States **18**:908
·War of 1812 British military base **7**:424f

Pensées (French: "Thoughts"), a devotional work by the French mathematician and philosopher Blaise Pascal, published posthumously in 1670, which emphasizes man's weakness and the importance of believing in God's existence. *Major ref.* **13**:1042c
·French theological literature **10**:1082c
·skepticism's impossibility **16**:832b
·theme and influence **10**:1156b

Penseroso, Il, poem by John Milton, written probably in 1631, an invocation to Melancholy (or Contemplation), describing, by way of varied times and seasons, the pleasures of the meditative life. Like its companion poem, "L'Allegro," it is written in lines of seven or eight syllables.
·stylistic excellence **12**:205d

Penseur, Le, English THE THINKER (1880), sculpture by Auguste Rodin.
·inspirational sources and conception **15**:982f

Penshurst, village, county of Kent, England, at the confluence of the rivers Eden and Medway. The village contains some 15th-century timbered cottages and Penshurst Place, home of Sir Philip Sidney, the 16th-century poet, scholar, and soldier. The state rooms, including the hall (*c.* 1341) with open timber roof and minstrel's gallery, are open to the public. Pop. (1971) 1,620.
51°10′ N, 0°11′ E

pension, series of periodic money payments to a person who retires from employment because of age, disability, or the completion of an agreed span of time. The payments usually continue for the rest of the natural life of the recipient, and sometimes to a widow or other survivor. Military pensions have existed for many centuries; private pension plans originated in Europe during the 19th century.

Eligibility for and amounts of benefits are based on a variety of factors, including length of employment, age, earnings, and, in some cases, past contributions. Benefits are sometimes also arranged to complement payments from public social security programs. Although public and private pension plans have undergone parallel development in the U.S. and U.K., in other countries—*e.g.*, Italy and Sweden—the existence of social security programs paying generous retirement benefits has to some extent precluded significant development of private pension plans. In other cases, though, as in West Germany, private programs have been widely adopted, in spite of large social security benefits.

Pensions may be funded by making payments into a pension trust fund (or a pension foundation in some European countries) or by the purchase of annuities from insurance companies. Systems including employee contribution plans are less common in the United States than in other countries—*e.g.*, in France and Canada—perhaps reflecting the fact that employee contributions are not tax deductible in the U.S. as they are elsewhere. It is questionable whether the growth of pension funds represents an increase in national saving; many believe that their addition to total saving is largely offset by the decrease in saving in other forms that would have occurred in the absence of pension programs.

In plans known as multi-employer plans, various employers contribute to one central trust fund administered by a joint board of trustees. Such plans are particularly common in The Netherlands and France and in industries in the United States.
·baseball players' negotiations **2**:736a
·U.S. federal and private provisions **18**:939g
·welfare and security-program rationale **19**:746b
·workmen's compensation insurance **9**:649e

pensionary, also ADVOCATE, Dutch PENSIONARIS, a powerful political office in the Dutch Republic (United Provinces; 1579–1795). Pensionaries, originally the secretaries and legal advisers of the town corporations, were first appointed in the 15th century. They were members of the town delegations in the provincial States (assemblies). The pensionaries of the provinces of Holland and Zeeland were particularly influential and, by the end of the 16th century, virtually dominated certain city governments.

In Holland the nobility had its own pensionary who served as chairman of the States. This provincial office became a position of national power in the period 1586–1618, when Johan van Oldenbarnevelt, a former pensionary of Rotterdam, dominated the domestic and foreign policy of the republic. His power came not from his office but from the fact that he was the leader of the ruling oligarchy of Holland, the preponderant province. With the fall of Oldenbarnevelt in 1618, the office, renamed grand pensionary (or council pensionary [*raadpensionaris*]) in 1619, declined as that of the stadholder increased in power. In 1653, during the first stadholderless period (1650–72), the office again became ascendant with the appointment of Johan de Witt (*q.v.*), the leader of the ruling oligarchy. No succeeding grand pensionary equalled his power and prestige.

The office of grand pensionary (including the less important equivalent in Zeeland) was abolished with the fall of the republic in 1795. The title was briefly revived in 1805 but referred to a newly created national office.

Penstemon, the beard tongue genus of the figwort family (Scrophulariaceae; *q.v.*), containing 250 species native to North America, particularly the western United States. The flowers are usually large and showy, tubular, bilaterally symmetrical, and have four fertile stamens (male pollen-producing structures) and one sterile stamen (staminode). Many species and varieties are popular in home gardens.

pentaborane, liquid boron-hydrogen compound that ignites spontaneously in air.
·structure diagram, illus. 3 **3**:48

Pentaceratops, genus of extinct five-horned herbivorous dinosaurs found in Late Cretaceous rocks of North America and possibly eastern Asia (the Cretaceous Period began 136,000,000 years ago and lasted 71,000,000 years); it was a relative of the more familiar *Triceratops*. Especially well known from the Kirtland Shale of New Mexico, *Pentaceratops* had one horn on its snout, one above each eye, and one on each side of the large, bony neck frill. The frill served as an attachment area for powerful muscles that aided in chewing and controlling movements of the head. It also protected vulnerable areas from attack by predators.

The body and limbs were massive in order to support the great bulk of the animal. The forelimbs were shorter than the hindlimbs; the horned dinosaurs descended from bipedal dinosaurs and reverted to a quadrupedal mode of progression. The back had a characteristically arched appearance caused by the unequal development of the limbs.

pentachlorophenol (wood preservative): *see* chlorophenol.

pentachord, five-tone segment of the musical scale.
·church mode structure **12**:297b

Pentadactylos (Cyprus): *see* Kyrenia Mountains.

Pentadiplandraceae, family of flowering plants of the order Capparales.
·classification and general features **3**:806c

pentaerythritol tetranitrate (explosive): *see* PETN.

Pentaglottis sempervirens (plant): *see* alkanet.

pentagon, in geometry, a five-sided polygon. A regular pentagon has equal sides and equal angles.

Pentagon, a large five-sided building in Arlington County, Va., near Washington, D.C., serving as headquarters of the U.S. Department of Defense, including all three services—Army, Navy, and Air Force. Designed by George Edwin Bergstrom, it was built in

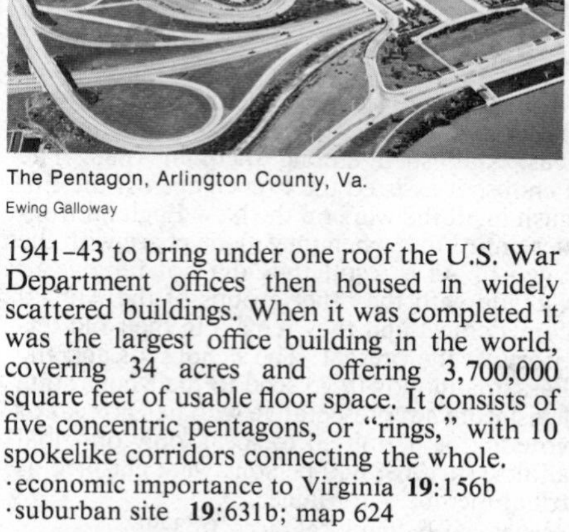

The Pentagon, Arlington County, Va.
Ewing Galloway

1941–43 to bring under one roof the U.S. War Department offices then housed in widely scattered buildings. When it was completed it was the largest office building in the world, covering 34 acres and offering 3,700,000 square feet of usable floor space. It consists of five concentric pentagons, or "rings," with 10 spokelike corridors connecting the whole.
·economic importance to Virginia **19**:156b
·suburban site **19**:631b; map 624

pentakosiomedimnoi, in ancient Athens, a propertied social class.
·status and functions **8**:342b

Pentameracea, superfamily of extinct articulate brachiopods.
·fossil brachiopods and eras, illus. 5 **7**:563

Pentamerida, invertebrate order of the phylum Branchiopoda.
·classification and general features **3**:100d

pentameter, line of verse containing five metrical feet. In English verse, in which pentameter has been the predominant metre since the 16th century, the preferred foot is the iamb; *i.e.*, an unstressed syllable followed by a stressed one, represented in scansion as ∪ ´.

Geoffrey Chaucer employed iambic pentameter in his *Canterbury Tales*, as early as the 13th century, although without the regularity that is found later in the heroic couplets of Dryden and Pope. Most English sonnets have been written in iambic pentameter, as in this example:

∪ ´ ∪ ´ ∪ ´ ∪ ´ ∪ ´
So long as men can breathe or eyes can see,
∪ ´ ∪ ´ ∪ ´ ∪ ´ ∪ ´
So long lives this and this gives life to thee.

(Shakespeare, Sonnet 18)

Shakespeare also used it in his blank verse tragedies.
·prosody and structural elements **15**:70b

pentane, any of three isomeric hydrocarbons with the formula C_5H_{12}.
·heating values of natural gas paraffins **12**:859a; table 860

Pentaphylcaceae, family of flowering plants of the order Theales.
·classification and general features **18**:211a

Pentapodidae, family of fish of the order Perciformes.
·classification and general features **14**:53c

Pentapolis (ancient cities): *see* Philistines.

Pentapora, genus of invertebrate animals of the phylum Bryozoa.
·bryozoan colony comparison **3**:355b

pentarchy, early Byzantine theory of church government according to which universal Christendom was to be directed by five patriarchal sees, under the auspices of a single universal empire. Formulated in the legislation of the emperor Justinian I (527–565), especially in his *Novella* 131, the theory received formal ecclesiastical sanction at the Council in Trullo (692), which ranked the five sees as Rome, Constantinople, Alexandria, Antioch, and Jerusalem.

Since the end of the 4th century, the five patriarchates were indeed the most prominent centres of the universal Christian church, enjoying a de facto primacy based on such empirical factors as the economic and political importance of their cities and countries. The church of Constantinople, the "New Rome," for example, occupied second rank because it was the capital of the empire.

According to the views of Roman bishops, however, only apostolic sees, churches actually founded by apostles, were eligible for primacy; this view thus excluded any patriarchal role for Constantinople. In fact, the popes always opposed the idea of pentarchy, gradually developing and affirming a universal ecclesiastical structure centred on Rome as the see of Peter. Byzantine imperial and conciliar legislation practically ignored the Roman view, limiting itself to the token recognition of Rome as the first patriarchal see. The tensions created by the opposing theories contributed to the schism between East and West.

The pentarchy lost its practical significance with the christological disputes of the 5th and 6th centuries, which separated the see of Alexandria from imperial Christendom, and after the Muslim domination of the Orthodox patriarchates of Alexandria, Antioch, and Jerusalem in the 7th century. The patriarch of Constantinople remained the only real primate of Eastern Christianity. On the other hand, the expansion of Byzantine Christianity into the Balkans and throughout eastern Europe led to the creation of new influential ecclesiastical centres in Bulgaria, Serbia, and Russia, with new and powerful patriarchates that would eventually compete with Constantinople and overshadow even more the ancient patriarchates of the East. The latter, however, preserved up to the present time a certain prestige of antiquity, safeguarded by the institutional conservatism of Eastern Christendom.

pentastomid, any of about 70 species of tiny parasites, primarily parasitic on reptiles, and belonging to the Pentastomida, usually considered a class. Most are tropical or subtropical. Pentastomids are considered to lie between annelids and arthropods in evolutionary development. They range from a few millimetres to 14 centimetres (about 6 inches) in length and lack respiratory, circulatory, and excretory organs.

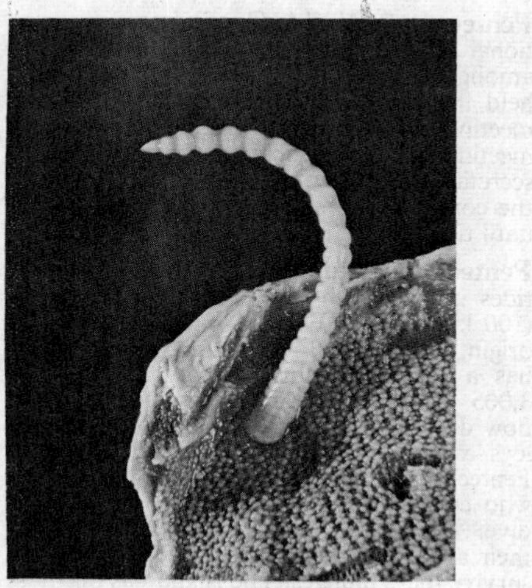

Pentastomid (*Armillifer moniliformis*) embedded in lung tissue of python host
Howard R. Hill

Porocephalus is parasitic in snakes and rodents; *Linguatula* parasitizes various mammals, including dogs; *Armillifer*, which is common in snakes, sometimes is a parasite of man.
·classification and general features **2**:70b
·traits, behaviour, and classification **13**:568e; illus.
·zoonoses, table 9 **5**:878

Pentateuch, the first five books of the Old Testament. *See* Torah.

pentathlon, athletic contest entailing five distinct types of competition (from the Greek *penta*, "five," and *athlon*, "contest"). In the ancient Greek Olympics, the pentathlon included a race the length of the stadium (about 200 yards or 180 metres), the long jump, discus throw, javelin throw, and a wrestling match between the two athletes who performed best in the previous four events. This Greek pentathlon was adapted for modern track and field competition by setting the sprint distance at 200 metres and by substituting a 1,500-metre run for the wrestling match. The event was included in the Olympic Games from 1912 through 1924.

A women's pentathlon—shot put, high jump, 80-metre hurdles, 200-metre dash, and long jump—was added to the program of the 1964 Olympic Games. The hurdles event was extended to 100 metres after the 1968 Games. *See also* sporting record.
·event order and Olympic changes **18**:552b
·introduction and composition **2**:274g

Pentatomidae, insect family of the order Heteroptera. For a general discussion of the family, *see* stinkbug; for *Murgantia histrionica*, *see* harlequin cabbage bug.

pentatonic scale, musical scale containing five different tones within an octave. It is thought that the pentatonic scale represents an early stage of musical development because it is found, in different forms, in most of the world's music. The most widely known form is anhemitonic (without semitones; *e.g.*, c–d–f–g–a–c′), the hemitonic form (with semitones; *e.g.*, c–e–f–g–b–c′) occurring less frequently. Pentatonic scales may have been used in ancient times to tune the Greek kithara (lyre), and some early Gregorian chant incorporated pentatonic melodies. A variety of pentatonic scales occur in the music of American Indians, black Africa, and Asia (*e.g.*, the Javanese five-tone *slendro*), as well as in many European folk melodies. In Western art music, 20th-century composers, such as Claude Debussy, have used pentatonicism for special effects.
·African scale structures and homophonic part-singing **1**:244c *passim* to 246e
·Chinese types, illus. 2 **12**:671
·derivation of diatonic scale **12**:748c
·dominance in non-Western music **16**:303f
·musical sound in scale organization **17**:38c

pentazocine, drug used as an analgesic.
·analgesic agents and action **1**:719b

penteconter, an ancient Greek galley with decks fore and aft and manned by 50 rowers.
·ship design history **12**:885f

Pentecost (Greek *pentecostē*, "50th day"), also called WHITSUNDAY, a major festival in the Christian Church, celebrated on the Sunday that falls on the 50th day after Easter. It commemorates the descent of the Holy Spirit on the disciples, which occurred on the Jewish Pentecost, after the death, resurrection, and ascension of Jesus Christ (Acts 2), and it marks the beginning of the Christian Church's mission to the world.

The Jewish feast was primarily a thanksgiving for the firstfruits of the wheat harvest, but the rabbis associated it with remembrance of the Law given by God for the Hebrews to Moses on Mt. Sinai. The church's transformation of the Jewish feast to a Christian festival was thus related to the belief that the gift of the Holy Spirit to the followers of Jesus was the firstfruits of a new dispensation that fulfilled and succeeded the old dispensation of the Law.

When the festival was first celebrated in the Christian Church is not known, but it was mentioned in a work from the Eastern Church, the *Epistola Apostolorum*, in the 2nd century. In the 3rd century, it was mentioned by Origen, theologian and head of the catechetical school in Alexandria, and by Tertullian, Christian priest and writer of Carthage.

In the early church, Christians often referred to the entire 50-day period following Easter as Pentecost. Baptism was administered both at the beginning (Easter) and end (the day of Pentecost) of the season. Eventually, Pentecost became a more popular time for Baptism than Easter in northern Europe, and in England the feast was commonly called White Sunday (Whitsunday) for the special white garments worn by the newly baptized. In *The First Prayer Book of Edward VI* (1549), the feast was officially called Whitsunday, and this name has continued in the Anglican churches.
·Acts' presentation in light of Old Testament **2**:957h
·Christian language policy pretext **4**:464f
·church year and Jewish rural feasts **4**:601b
·church year development **4**:605a
·East Orthodox belief in man's unity in God **6**:144g
·folk dance in feast and festival **7**:450e
·millennial interpretation of Augustine **12**:202b
·Pentecostal Church's interpretation **14**:30d

Pentecost, Jewish: *see* Shavuot.

Pentecostal Assemblies of Jesus Christ, unitarian "Jesus only" Pentecostal group that arose out of controversies over baptismal ritual within the Pentecostal movement beginning about 1915; merged to form the United Pentecostal Church, Inc., in 1945.
·union with Pentecostal Church, Inc. **14**:33f

Pentecostal Assemblies of the World, Inc., organized in 1914 after many members withdrew from the Assemblies of God during the "Jesus Only" (*q.v.*) controversy. It differs from other Pentecostal groups in that it baptizes in the name of Jesus rather than in the name of the Trinity. In organization it resembles Methodism. Headquarters are in Indianapolis, Ind.; in 1960 it reported 45,000 members.
·Trinitarian views and white withdrawal **14**:33e

Pentecostal Church, Inc., group of whites who, in 1924, broke away from the interracial Pentecostal Assemblies of the World, Inc., to form its own unitarian "Jesus only" organization.
·establishment and Trinitarian views **14**:33f

Pentecostal churches 14:30, a group of Protestant churches originating in the 19th century and teaching that all Christians should seek a post-conversion religious experience called the Baptism with the Holy Spirit. Pentecostalism reflects patterns of faith and practices characteristic of Fundamentalist and Holiness churches. Pentecostals thus hold that a Spirit-baptized believer may receive one or more of the supernatural gifts that were known in the early Church: the ability to prophesy, heal, "speak in tongues," or interpret what is said when someone speaks in an unknown tongue.

The text article covers the origins of Pentecostalism, varieties of American Pentecostalism, Pentecostalism outside the United States, and contemporary developments, teachings, organization, and practices. The article includes an evaluation of Pentecostalism by other Christian churches.

REFERENCES in other text articles:
·charismatic expressions of Holy Spirit **4**:484h
·Christian exorcistic revival **4**:516h
·Holiness churches compared and contrasted **8**:993g
·liturgical spontaneity **4**:496a
·Negro cults' beliefs and influences **12**:942f
·polity development **4**:495b

RELATED ENTRIES in the *Ready Reference and Index: for*
churches and institutions: see Apostolic Overcoming Holy Church of God; Assemblies of God; Church of God in Christ; Churches of God; International Church of the Foursquare Gospel; Pentecostal Assemblies of the World, Inc.; Pentecostal Church of God of America, Inc.; Pentecostal Fellowship of North America; Pentecostal Holiness Church, Inc.; Pentecostal World Conference; United Pentecostal Church, Inc.
distinctive beliefs and practices: "Jesus Only"; Latter Rain revival; tongues, gift of

Pentecostal Church of God of America, Inc., organized in Chicago in 1919, accepts Pentecostal beliefs including divine healing and the Baptism of the Holy Spirit accompanied by the sign of speaking in tongues. It is divided into districts and is governed by district superintendents and district presbyters, with a general superintendent as head of the church. Headquarters and a publishing house are located in Joplin, Mo. In 1967 the church reported 115,000 members. *Major ref.* **14**:33c

Pentecostal Church of the Nazarene: *see* Church of the Nazarene.

Pentecostal Fellowship of North America (PFNA), cooperative organization established in Chicago in 1948 by eight Pentecostal denominations for the purpose of "interdenominational Pentecostal cooperation and fellowship." By 1949 six more denominations had joined the organization. It is governed by a 13-member Board of Administration and a 5-member Executive Committee.

Pentecostal Holiness Church, Inc., organized in Falcon, N.C., in 1911 by the uniting of the Fire-Baptized Holiness Church (organized in 1898 by several Pentecostal associations) and the Pentecostal Holiness Church (organized in 1899). The Tabernacle Pentecostal Church merged into it in 1915. It is basically Methodist in doctrine and policy but expects the premillennial return of Jesus Christ and believes in the necessity of the Baptism of the Holy Spirit accompanied by speaking in tongues (glossolalia). In 1971 there were about 72,000 members in the U.S. Headquarters are at Franklin Springs, Ga. *Major ref.* **14**:33b

Pentecostal Union, later PILLAR OF FIRE, Wesleyan religious body organized in 1901 by Mrs. Alma White.
·Holiness churches' perfectionist emphasis **8**:995b

Pentecostal World Conference, international agency for fellowship and cooperation among Pentecostals. The first meeting was held in Zürich, Switz., in 1947, the second meeting in Paris in 1949, and subsequent meetings have been held every three years. A secretary and committee of five are selected at the conference meeting to serve all members until the next conference.

Pentecost Island, OR RAGA, of the New Hebrides in the southwest Pacific Ocean, 60 mi (100 km) east of Espíritu Santo. Volcanic in origin, it occupies 169 sq mi (438 sq km) and has a central mountain ridge that rises to 3,065 ft (934 m). Many permanent streams flow down the eastern slopes into fertile valleys, where copra and coffee are cultivated. Pentecost is known for its land divers—men who construct high towers from which they dive, suspended only by vines attached to their ankles. Precise planning allows them to survive these plunges. The island has one hospital and two airstrips. Latest census 6,801.
15°42′ S, 168°10′ E

Pentēkostarion, an Eastern Orthodox worship book, used from Easter to the Sunday of the Holy Fathers, that connotes a feeling of joy, over against the penitential mood of the odes of the Triōdion, the service book of worship used during Lent.
·church year in the East **4**:602c
·Eastern Orthodox liturgical cycle **6**:148d

Pentelicus (PENTELIKON), **Mount,** Modern Greek PENDÉLI ÓROS, ancient Greek BRILESSOS or BRILETTOS, mountain range enclosing the Attic plain on its northeast but within Attikí *nomós* (department). The chief summit, about 10 mi (16 km) northeast of Athens, is Kokkinarás (3,638 ft [1,109 m]), which yields white Pentelic marble at Dionysos, on its north slope. In classical times the peak had 25 quarries on the south slope at elevations between 2,500 and 3,300 ft. These provided excellent marble for most of the buildings and sculptures of Athens in the 5th and 4th centuries BC. At the summit was a sanctuary to the goddess Athena.
38°06′ N, 23°54′ E
·Athens' topography **2**:262g

Penthoraceae, family of flowering plants in the order Saxifragales, one genus with three species of perennial herbs native to eastern Asia and eastern North America. All three species have underground stems, toothed leaves, and one-sided flower clusters borne at the branch tips. The Virginian stonecrop (*Penthorum sedoides*) grows to about 0.6 metres (2 feet) tall. It has pale, greenish-yellow flowers, and pale-green leaves that turn bright orange as they mature. Virginian stonecrop is planted as an ornamental at the edges of pools or in shallow water.
·distribution and general features **16**:292g
·general features and classification **16**:301d

penthouse, enclosed area on top of a building. Such a structure may house the top of an elevator shaft, air-conditioning equipment, or the stairs giving access to the roof; it can also provide living or working accommodations. Usually a penthouse is set back from the vertical face of a building, thus providing open spaces or terraces on one or more sides; but in recent practice architects and rental agents have begun to refer to the top floor of any building, regardless of setbacks, as a penthouse. Although the word now connotes glamour, a good view, and a high rental, historically a penthouse was a mere lean-to, or shed, or other small structure attached to a comparatively large building. In medieval times a penthouse, or pentice, was important in siege craft, being the temporary structure that protected besieging forces as they prepared for an attack on the enemy.

Penthouse Theatre (1940), designed by John Ashby Conway at the University of Washington, Seattle.
·arena stage, illus. 11 **18**:248

Penticton, city, southern British Columbia, Canada, between Skaha and Okanagan lakes. First settled in 1865, its name was derived from a Salish Indian word, *phthauntauc* (*pen-hik-ton*) meaning "place to stay forever." Centred in an apple-, peach-, and apricot-growing area, the city's economy depends on tourism, fruit canning and packing, lumber products, construction, transport and storage, and livestock rearing. The Blossom Time Festival in May and the Peach Festival and Square Dance Jamboree in August are annual events. The Peach Bowl convention centre was completed in 1965. Penticton became a district municipality in 1908. Inc. city, 1948. Pop. (1971 prelim.) 17,702.
49°30′ N, 119°35′ W
·map, Canada **3**:716

pentimento, in art, a term derived from the Italian *pentirsi* meaning "to repent" and applied to the reappearance in an oil painting of original elements of drawing or painting that the artist tried to obliterate by overpainting. If the covering pigment becomes transparent, as may happen in the course of years, the ghostly remains of earlier thoughts may show through. Numerous signs of such "repentances," or pentimenti, are found among the thinly painted Dutch panels of the 17th century. One of the most famous examples is a double hat brim in Rembrandt's "Flora" (*c.* 1665; Metropolitan Museum of Art, New York City).

Pentland Firth, strait, between the county of Caithness on the mainland of Scotland and the Orkney Islands (north), connecting the Atlantic Ocean on the west with the North Sea on the east. The strait is about 14 mi (23 km) long and varies between 6 to 8 mi (10 to 13 km) in width. It is notorious for rough seas and navigation made hazardous by rapid tidal currents, treacherous eddies, and such dangerous whirlpools as the Well of Swona and The Swelkie.
58°44′ N, 3°13′ W
·map, United Kingdom **18**:866

Pentland Hills, southeastern Scotland; highest peak is Scald Law (1,898 ft. [579 m]).
55°48′ N, 3°23′ W
·Edinburgh's topography and surroundings **6**:303h

pentlandite, a nickel and iron sulfide mineral, the chief source of nickel. It is nearly always found with pyrrhotite. Typical occurrences are in the highly basic rocks of Bushveld, S.Af.; Bodø, Nor.; and Sudbury, Ont. For chemical formula and detailed physical properties, *see* table under sulfide minerals.
·sulfide mineral properties and occurrences **17**:787f

pentobarbital (drug): *see* barbiturate.

pentode, electronic vacuum tube with five electrodes. Besides the cathode, anode, and control grid of the triode (*q.v.*) and the added screen grid of the tetrode (*q.v.*), there is still another grid (suppressor grid) placed between screen grid and plate and maintained at cathode potential. Thus any electrons emitted from the plate surface by secondary emission are repelled back to the plate. The pentode can be used for almost all purposes for which vacuum tubes are used, including amplification, mixing, oscillation, and pulse generation, and in circuits for timing, control, and counting.

·electronic amplifier development **6**:679d
·electron tube designs and uses **6**:688d; illus.
·radio construction and operation **15**:427g

pentose-phosphate cycle: *see* phosphogluconate pathway.

pentosuria, essential, inborn error of carbohydrate metabolism, characterized by the excessive urinary excretion of L-xylulose, a sugar. The causative agent is a L-xylulose dehydrogenase enzyme. No disabilities are incurred, and no dietary or other measures are necessary. Reducing properties of the urine of affected individuals may lead to confusion with, and unnecessary treatment for, diabetes mellitus, which is not related to pentosuria. The latter condition has been observed almost exclusively in persons of Jewish descent.

pentothal sodium: *see* barbiturate.

Pentremites, extinct genus of stemmed, immobile echinoderms (forms related to the starfish) that is abundant as marine fossils in Mississippian and Pennsylvanian rocks (345,000,000 to 280,000,000 years old), especially in the midcontinent region of North America. The genus is mainly restricted to the Mississippian Period; more than 80 Mississippian species are known. Specimens are frequently well preserved, allowing detailed anatomical and evolutionary studies to be made. The genus is characterized by such distinctive anatomical features as the form and number of openings and the nature of the plates.

Pentremites pyriformis, collected from the Paint Creek Formation at Floraville, Ill.

By courtesy of the Buffalo Museum of Science, Buffalo, N.Y.

Pen-ts'ao kang-mu, the "Great Pharmacopoeia," compilation, AD 1552–78, of approximately 1,000 Chinese treatises, some of great antiquity, on vegetable, animal, and mineral remedies. The work has frequently been revised and reprinted.

·Ming dynasty's herbal contributions **4**:353g
·orientation, contents, and influence **11**:825e
·origin in Taoist research **17**:1042h

Peñuealas, municipality, southern Puerto Rico. Pop. (1980 prelim.) town, 3,471; mun., 18,238.
18°03′ N, 66°43′ W
·area and population table **15**:261

Penuel, or PENIEL, ancient town in Israel, that figures in several Old Testament episodes.

·Gideon's judgeship and Midianite defeat **2**:909h

penumbra (Latin *paene*, "almost"; *umbra*, "shadow"), in astronomy, the partial shadow of a heavenly body cast by the Sun, as compared to the umbra, the total shadow. An observer in the penumbra sees the Sun's disk partially obscured. The term is also used for the outer portion of a sunspot.

·eclipse causes and appearance **6**:188g *passim* to 192c
·radiographic image sharpness control **15**:459g

Penutian languages, major grouping (phylum or superstock) of American Indian languages, spoken along the west coast of North America from British Columbia to central California and central New Mexico. The phylum consists of 15 language families with about 20 languages; the families are Wintun (two languages), Miwok-Costanoan (perhaps five Miwokan languages, plus three extinct Costanoan languages), Sahaptian (two languages), Yakonan (two extinct languages), Yokutsan (three languages), and Maiduan (four languages), plus Klamath-Modoc, Cayuse (extinct), Molale (extinct), Coos, Takelma (extinct), Kalapuya, Chinook (not to be confused with Chinook jargon, a trade language, or lingua franca), Tsimshian, and Zuni, each a family consisting of a single language. All but four of the surviving families are spoken by fewer than 150 persons.

Major languages in the phylum are Zuni, spoken by more than 3,000 persons, in New Mexico; Tsimshian, with about 3,000 speakers, in British Columbia; and the Sahaptian dialects (Klickitat, Umatilla, Wallawalla, Warm Springs, and Yakima), spoken in north central Oregon by more than 1,400 persons.

The Penutian languages are sometimes grouped into a yet larger stock, called either Penutian or Macro-Penutian, that includes several Meso-American Indian languages. The Totonacan, Huave, and Mixe-Zoque language families are often included, and some scholars suggest the inclusion of the large Mayan language family. The U.S. linguist Benjamin L. Whorf proposed to include not only Mixe-Zoque, Huave, Totonacan, and Mayan (including Huastec) but also Uto-Aztecan, another major North and Meso-American language family. This grouping has not been generally accepted.

·North American Indian languages classification table **13**:209; map 210
·North and South American distribution **10**:671g

pen-wu, in the philosophy of the Neo-Taoist Wang Pi, original nonbeing, basic and pure reality, transcending all distinctions and description.

·Taoism, Neo-Taoism, and Neo-Confucianism philosophies **4**:416g *passim* to 418h

Pen-Y-Bont Ar Ogwr (Wales): *see* Bridgend.

Penza, *oblast* (administrative region), western Russian Soviet Federated Socialist Republic, occupies an area of 16,680 sq mi (43,200 sq km) across the western flank of the Volga Upland, which falls gently to the Oka-Don Plain in the extreme west. The *oblast* lies in the zone of forest-steppe. About one-fifth of its surface is in pine or oak forest, mostly in the Sura Basin, but natural vegetation has been widely plowed up, resulting in severe soil erosion. Agriculture, the major economic activity, is dominated by grain, especially winter rye. Industrial crops are less important, and livestock farming is underdeveloped. Engineering, the main industry, is concentrated in Penza city, the *oblast* headquarters, and Kuznetsk; the other cities are small and are mainly concerned with processing food and agricultural products. Timber working is important in the surviving forest areas, and paper is made. Pop. (1970 prelim.) 1,536,000.

Penza, city and administrative centre of Penza *oblast* (region), western Russian Soviet Federated Socialist Republic, at the confluence of the Penza and Sura rivers. The city was founded in 1666 as a major fortress; after 1684 it formed the western end of the Syzran defensive line. It was frequently attacked by the Crimean Tatars, suffering especially in their last assault of 1717. With the settlement of the surrounding lands, Penza became an important agricultural centre. Grain was sent to Moscow, first by the Sura River and, after the 1870s, by rail. The processing of farm products is still a significant economic factor, but it has been surpassed in importance by industries producing machinery, diesel engines, compressors, calculating machines, and bicycles; there are also watchmaking, papermaking, and timber-working industries. The city's tree-lined streets have spread from the hill, on which the fortress originally stood, onto the level Sura floodplain. Penza has teacher-training, polytechnic, engineering, and agricultural institutes, an observatory, and several industrial-research institutions. Pop. (1970 prelim.) 374,000.
53°13′ N, 45°00′ E
·map, Soviet Union **17**:322

Penzance, borough, county of Cornwall, Southwest England, and the country's most westerly town. It overlooks Mounts Bay of the English Channel and has a remarkably equable climate, allowing many subtropical plants to flourish. Early vegetables and flowers are raised locally for the London market and also in the offshore Scilly Islands, with which it is linked by sea and air services. Newlyn, in the borough, is a small fishing port, much frequented by artists. The market charter of Penzance dates from 1332. It was incorporated in 1614, by which time it had become an important fishing port and centre for the local tin mines. Its chief modern function is as a tourist centre. Pop. (1971 prelim.) 19,352.
50°07′ N, 5°33′ W
·map, United Kingdom **18**:866

Penzias, Arno A. (b. April 26, 1933, Munich), U.S. radioastronomer who, with Robert W. Wilson, shared half of the Nobel Prize for Physics in 1978 for their discovery (1965) of cosmic background radiation. The finding provided strong support for the big-bang hypothesis of the origin of the universe.

·cosmic background radiation **18**:1008c

peocilitic texture (mineralogy): *see* poikilitic texture.

peonage, form of involuntary servitude the origins of which have been traced as far back as the Spanish conquest of Mexico, when the conquerors were able to force the poor, especially the Indians, to work for Spanish planters and mine operators. In both the English and Spanish languages, the word peon became synonymous with labourer but was restricted in the U.S. to those workers compelled by contract to pay their creditors in labour. Although the Thirteenth Amendment and congressional legislation prohibited any such involuntary servitude in the United States, the former slaveholding states devised certain legislation, following emancipation, to make labour compulsory. Under these state laws, employers could induce or deceive men into signing contracts for labour to pay their debts or to avoid fines that might be imposed by the courts. A form of peonage exists when prisoners sentenced to hard labour are farmed out to either private or governmental labour camps.

·slavery as form of contract labour **16**:855c
·Spanish colonial causes and conditions **10**:695h

peones, Mexican plantation workers.

·land reform in Mexico to benefit Indians **10**:639e

peony, any plant of the genus *Paeonia* (family Paeoniaceae); there are more than 30 species, known for their large, showy flowers. Most are native to Europe and Asia; the western peony (*Paeonia browni*), however, is found along the Pacific coastal mountains of North America.

Peony (*Paeonia*)
Gilbert H. Wild & Son, Inc.

There are two distinct groups of peonies, the herbaceous and the tree, or moutan, peonies. The herbaceous peonies are perennials that grow to a height of almost one metre (about three feet) and have large, glossy, much-divided leaves that are supported on annual stems produced by fleshy rootstocks. In late spring and early summer they produce large single and double flowers of white, pink, rose, and deep-crimson colour.

The fragrant Chinese *P. lactiflora* and the European common peony (*P. officinalis*) are the familiar garden peonies. With hundreds of hybrids, they produce flowers often tinted with several colours.

The tree peonies have developed from the wild Chinese species *P. suffruticosa*. They are shrubby, with permanent woody stems. The plants sometimes attain a height of 1.2 to 1.8 metres (about 4 to 6 feet); they begin flowering in late spring. The blossoms vary in colour from white to lilac, magenta, violet, rose, and red.

Tree peonies require a hot, dry summer season for best growth, and they can be grafted in late summer or autumn on the roots of herbaceous peonies. A race of hybrids, developed by crossing the tree peony with the yellow Chinese *P. lutea*, has both single and double flowers, sometimes tinged with red. An early-flowering variety of *P. lutea* bears large, butter-yellow flowers on stems about 1.8 metres (6 feet) high.

Peony plants are seldom grown from seeds because they take about two years to germinate.

·plant disease symptoms, illus. **5**:890

people of the book: *see* ahl al-kitāb.

Peoples' Action Party (PAP), major political party of Singapore, founded in 1955 by Lee Kuan Yew.

·Lee Kuan Yew's activities **10**:772d
·Singapore's political environment **16**:788b

People's Anti-Japanese Army, English name of the Philippine organization that conducted the Hukbalahap Rebellion (*q.v.*).

People's Charter (1838), list of grievances that became the basis of the British movement known as Chartism (*q.v.*).

People's Commissariat of Internal Affairs: *see* NKVD.

People's Council (Indonesia): *see* Volksraad.

people's courts, Soviet court of original jurisdiction for minor criminal cases and a large number of civil cases.

·Soviet judicial system in experimental stage **17**:314d

People's Daily (newspaper): *see* Jen-min jih-pao.

People's Democratic Republic of Yemen: *see* Yemen (Aden).

People's Freedom: *see* Narodnaya Volya.

Peoples Friendship University: *see* Patrice Lumumba People's Friendship University.

People's Legislature, German VOLKSKAMMER, the unicameral legislature of the German Democratic Republic.

·citizen participation in government **8**:13g

People's Liberation Army (PLA), Chinese JEN-MIN CHIEH-FANG CHÜN, the official title of the military forces of the People's Republic of China. This name was given to the assorted guerrilla and regular armies that the Chinese Communists had used to oppose the Japanese occupation of China in the period 1937–45 and to the army that defeated the Communists' rivals, the Kuomintang, following the expulsion of the Japanese.

After the Communists won control of the mainland (1949), the PLA began to acquire heavy equipment and technical training for conventional warfare tactics rather than the guerrilla warfare that it had been practicing. It performed adequately in the Korean War (1950–53) and later in the Sino-Indian border dispute (1962).

In the early 1960s, however, when army morale was flagging as a result of the economic dislocations caused by the Great Leap Forward (1958–59), the government decided to move away from a highly specialized army separated from the people and return to the guerrilla model.

The PLA was accordingly indoctrinated in the thought of Mao Tse-tung and became for the most part based among the people, engaging in rural reconstruction work as well as military training. This made the PLA a more effective force against internal disorder or foreign aggression but less so for offensive purposes.

During the Great Proletarian Cultural Revolution (1966–69), in which the Communist Party was purged of many of its leading officials and China underwent a general upheaval, the PLA was the major bulwark for supporters of Mao Tse-tung. In the years immediately after the Cultural Revolution, the army emerged as the major power within the government. In the early 1970s, its influence again declined, but by the later '70s the influence of the army seemed again to be growing; among the members of the new Politburo announced in August 1977, more than half held senior military posts. The PLA on Aug. 1, 1977, celebrated the 50th anniversary of its founding. *Major ref.* **4**:293f

·Chinese Communist Party victory **4**:375h
·Lin's political reform **10**:1014g

People's National Congress (PNC), major political party of Guyana (founded 1955), representing predominantly persons of African descent.

·ethnic group support **8**:511f

People's Party, major Austrian political party, successor in 1945 to the Christian Social Party, founded in the 1890s.

·Austrian political processes **2**:446h

People's Party, political party of Newfoundland, founded in 1907.

·social radicalism in prewar years **12**:1084g

People's Party, Syrian nationalist political party founded in the 1920s.

·Syrian unification demands **17**:956d

People's Party (Turkey): *see* Republican People's Party.

People's Progressive Party (PPP), left-wing political party of Guyana (organized 1950), representing predominantly persons of East Indian descent.

·ethnic group support **8**:511f

People's Representatives, Council of, Socialist government of Germany, established in 1918.

·German Socialist revolution **6**:177b

People's Republics: *see* under countries' names.

People's Socialist Community (Cambodia): *see* Sangkum Reastr Niyum.

People's Union, Flemish VOLKSUNIE (VU), a Flemish nationalist political party of Belgium, which won its first seat in the Chamber of Deputies in the 1954 elections.

·recent popularity trend **2**:823a

People's United Front, Sinhalese MAHAJANA EKSATH PERAMUNA (MEP), a coalition that governed Ceylon (renamed Sri Lanka in 1972) from 1956 to 1959, formed by S.W.R.D. Bandaranaike's Sri Lanka Freedom Party with various smaller political groups, one of them Marxist. Campaigning on a broadly Socialistic platform, with additional promises to make Sinhalese the official national language and to improve the state of Buddhism in Ceylon, the MEP won a landslide victory in the 1956 general election over the United National Party, which had dominated Ceylonese politics since independence (1948). The new government's first step in 1956 was to pass the Sinhala Only Bill, making Sinhalese the official national language. In line with its policy of neutrality in foreign affairs, it terminated Ceylon's defense pact with Britain. It nationalized in 1958 both bus transport and the operation of the port of Colombo. The Marxist segment of the government, unhappy with the small degree of socialization accomplished, defected from the MEP in 1958. The extremist Sinhalese segment of the MEP was unhappy with Bandaranaike for trying to conciliate the Tamil-speaking people of Ceylon, who had been enraged by the Sinhala Only Bill. In addition the government was beset by financial problems because of the heavy burden created by many of its programs, such as nationalization and social welfare. In general, Bandaranaike had difficulties in making good his sweeping campaign promises while trying to conciliate everyone both inside and outside his government. In 1959 Bandaranaike was assassinated, and, soon after, his government fell, resulting in a new general election.

People's Victory Canal, paralleling the Peking–Hangkow Railroad, China. Completed in 1953, it is 30 mi (48 km) long and links the Huang Ho with the Wei Ho at Hsin-ch'iang.

·river system improvement function **8**:1130e; map 1129

People's Will: *see* Narodnaya Volya.

People-to-People Health Foundation, health organization formed in 1958 and responsible for the hospital ship "Hope."

·comprehensive health services **8**:1116f

People Win Through, The (1950), play by U Nu.

·Burmese modern theatre style **17**:246e

Peoria, city, seat of Peoria County, north central Illinois, U.S., on the Illinois River where it widens to form Lake Peoria. With Peoria Heights, West Peoria, Bartonville, East Peoria, Creve Coeur, and Pekin, Peoria forms an urbanized industrial complex.

Named for one of the five Indian tribes in the

Illinois Confederacy, Peoria represents one of the state's oldest settled locations. The French under René Robert Cavelier, sieur de La Salle, built Fort-Crèvecoeur on the bluffs, opposite the present city in 1680, but it was plundered and deserted later that same year. There were later settlements around Lake Peoria by the French, Indians, and Americans. After 1813 the location was known as Ft. Clark, named for the Revolutionary general George Rogers Clark; but when Peoria County was formed in 1825, the community, chosen as the county seat, reverted to the French-Indian name of Peoria. There, on October 16, 1854, Abraham Lincoln denounced slavery in rebuttal to a speech by Stephen Douglas.

Peoria is a major port on the Great-Lakes-to-the-Gulf Waterway and is a trading and shipping centre for a wide agricultural area (corn and livestock). Highly industrialized, its manufactures include earth-moving equipment, trailers, steel, wire, and chemicals. The Caterpillar Tractor Company has its world headquarters there and is the city's largest employer. Distilling and brewing are also major industries. The U.S. Department of Agriculture's Northern Regional Research Laboratory (completed 1940) is nearby. Educational institutions include Bradley University (established as Bradley Polytechnic Institute in 1897) and Illinois Central College (founded 1966). The focal point for Peoria's cultural and recreational activities is Lakeview Park, which contains the Lakeview Centre for the Arts and Sciences, Lakeview Planetarium, Peoria Players Theatre, and Lakeview Swimming Pool and Ice Skating Rink. Inc. town, 1835; city, 1845. Pop. (1980) city, 124,160; metropolitan area (SMSA), 365,864.
40°42′ N, 89°36′ W

·economic base **9**:237a
·map, United States **18**:908

Pepe, Guglielmo (b. Feb. 13, 1783, Squillace, Italy—d. Aug. 8, 1855, Turin), Neapolitan soldier prominent in the Italian Risorgimento and author of valuable eyewitness accounts. After briefly attending a military academy, he enlisted at 16 in the republican army formed in Naples as a result of the French Revolution. He was wounded and taken prisoner by the royalists, but his life was spared because of his youth. In 1800 he fought under Napoleon at Marengo and continued in French service for several years, commanding a brigade in Spain in 1811–13. After the Bourbon restoration in Naples, Pepe accepted a commission in the royal army and helped suppress brigands in Calabria, but when revolution broke out in 1820, he took command of the republican army. Failure of the revolution sent him into exile, mainly in England, where he spent the next several years writing of his experiences, including *A Narrative of the Political and Military Events Which Took Place at Naples in 1820 and 1821* (1821). His memoirs appeared in 1846, but in 1848, following the major revolution of that year, he was once more back in Naples. Sent north to aid in the war against Austria, he was recalled to Naples but instead of returning joined in the defense of Venice. After the city's surrender he went to Paris, where he published his *Narrative of Scenes and Events in Italy, from 1847 to 1849* in two volumes (1850).

Pepel, Atlantic seaport, Northern Province, western Sierra Leone, on Pepel Island, near the mouth of the Sierra Leone River (an estuary formed by the Rokel River and Port Loko Creek). Since 1933 it has exported iron ore transported by rail from the Sierra Leone Development Company's mines at Marampa, 41 mi (66 km) east-northeast. It is the nation's only iron-ore port, enlarged in 1964, and has a loading pier that extends seaward for about half a mile. The local Temne population is also engaged in fishing and rice farming. Latest census 3,793.
8°35′ N, 13°03′ W

peperite (petrology): *see* tuff.

Peperomia, a genus of the family Piperaceae, comprising more than 500 species of tropical and subtropical fleshy herbs, annuals as well as perennials. Some are epiphytic (growing on the branches of trees). The plants are without stems. The leaves, sometimes attractively coloured with veins or spots, are oval, thick, fleshy, and smooth edged. The thick, red stalk of the leaf is fixed to the interior of the leaf. Flowers are minute and densely packed on a slender spike, which is likely to be curved.

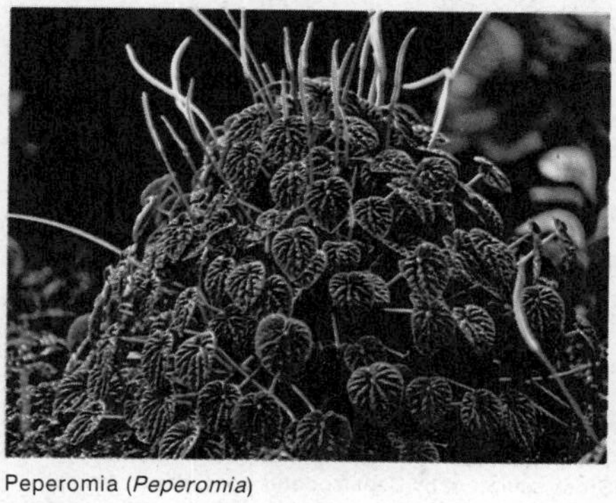

Peperomia (*Peperomia*)
F.K. Anderson—EB Inc.

A few species, particularly *P. argyreia* (sometimes called *P. sandersii* and known commonly as rugby-football plant), are popular houseplants because of their attractive foliage. *P. argyreia*, native to Brazil, grows about 10 to 15 centimetres (4 to 6 inches) tall. Dark-red leafstalks support alternate leaves, which are up to 10 centimetres (4 inches) long and 7.5 centimetres (3 inches) wide. The leaves are handsomely marked with broad, creamy bands parallel to the veins.

P. obtusifolia (sometimes called *P. magnoliifolia*), another popular cultivated species, is also native to the tropics. It lies close to the soil and has wrinkled, reddish stems. The minute flowers are red. The leaves, about 7.5 to 12.5 centimetres (3 to 5 inches) long, have small notches near the tip and are red along the margins. The young leaves and stems of *P. vividispica* are used as food in Central and South America.

·house plants and their care **8**:1120b
·Piperales seed dispersal and structure **14**:467f; illus.

Peperomiaceae, considered a family of flowering plants in some classification schemes but incorporated in the family Piperaceae (order Piperales) in others.

·Piperales classification proposal **14**:467e

Pepi I, 3rd king of the 6th dynasty (*c.* 2345–*c.* 2181 BC) in Egypt whose reign saw the spread of trade and conquest and a growth in the influence of powerful provincials from Upper Egypt.

Pepi was the son of Teti, founder of the 6th dynasty. Before succeeding his father, Pepi had to cope with a usurper whose early success forced Pepi to seek the aid of Upper Egyptian potentates to gain control of the kingdom. Two of Pepi's chief queens were sisters of his vizier, one of the Upper Egyptian potentates; they each bore a son who succeeded to the throne.

Pepi I initiated a policy of intensive penetration of Nubia, the territory south of the First Nile Cataract. Inscriptions record journeys southward early in his reign. Fragments of vessels bearing the King's name were excavated at Kerma, though some scholars believe that the vessels were brought there later. Uni, another Upper Egyptian and a close confidant of the King, recruited troops from Nubia as well as from Egypt in preparation for raids against rebellious Bedouins of the northeastern frontier.

Extensive trade with Lebanon is attested by numerous vessels of Pepi found at Byblos. An Upper Egyptian biography mentions frequent journeys to Punt, on the Somali coast of east Africa. Pepi's courtiers also led quarrying expeditions to various parts of Egypt, and remains of a temple of the King have been found deep in the Nile Delta. Pepi's pyramid complex was built at Ṣaqqārah, southwest of Cairo; its name, MeneferPepi, eventually became attached to Memphis, the capital of Egypt.

Possibly nine years before his death, Pepi named his eldest son, Merenre, co-regent. To commemorate the event, a pair of copper statues was fashioned. Some scholars dispute the 49-year reign generally credited to Pepi, primarily because Old Kingdom reign lengths were calculated by cattle counts, which usually occurred every two years but may on occasion have been annual; for Pepi, 25 cattle counts are attested.

·metalwork sculpture technique **11**:1093c

Pepi II Neferkare, 5th king of the 6th dynasty (*c.* 2345–*c.* 2181 BC) in Egypt, during whose long reign the government became weakened because of internal and external troubles. Late Egyptian tradition states that Pepi II acceded at age six and, along with king lists of the New Kingdom, credits him with a 94-year reign. The highest contemporary texts record his 62nd and 65th years.

Pepi II was a son of Pepi I and was born late in his father's reign. While still very young he succeeded his half brother Merenre, who died at an early age. His mother served as co-regent for a number of years, and the old group of officials serving the royal family maintained the kingdom's stability. Expeditions of trade and conquest to lower Nubia and Punt (the Somali coast of Africa), however, met with resistance, and the signs of external trouble are unmistakable.

Internally, the vizierate passed from the family that had served Pepi's predecessors and descended through a number of other officials. The excessive devotion of resources to funerary endowments drained the country's resources. Further, powerful provincial nobles drew talent away from the capital. Biographies of the era reveal that Pepi had more interest in duties toward the dead than concern for the kingdom. Finally, because of the unusually long reign of the King, Egypt had a senile ruler when it needed vigorous leadership. Those of his children who survived Pepi had brief, ephemeral reigns and failed to cope with the political and economic crises that arose as the 6th dynasty ended.

Pepi's pyramid complex at Ṣaqqārah, across the Nile from Cairo, was among the largest of the 5th and 6th dynasties. Structural weakness, aggravated by an earthquake, later required that a girdle wall be built around the pyramid.

·political and religious fission **6**:468c

Pepin (d. July 8, 810), king of Italy and second son of the Frankish emperor Charlemagne. Given the title of king of Italy in 781, Pepin took part in campaigns against Duke Tassilo III of Bavaria from 787 and led an army against the Avars in 796. His Venetian campaign (809–810) enabled Charlemagne later to come to favourable terms with the Byzantine Empire. As early as 806 Charlemagne, in planning the division of his lands, had decided that on his death Pepin should inherit Italy, Bavaria, and the territory of the Alemanni, but Pepin died four years before his father's death.

·papal crowning as king of the Lombards **4**:45d

Pepin II of Aquitaine (d. after 864, Senlis, Fr.), Carolingian king of Aquitaine. The son of Pepin I of Aquitaine, he gained the throne about 845, after defeating the emperor Charles II the Bald in Angoumois in 844. War soon broke out again, however, and Charles slowly advanced through Aquitaine. Pepin took refuge with Sancho, duke of the Gas-

cons, but in 852 was handed over to Charles, tonsured, and relegated to the monastery of Saint-Médard at Soissons. Escaping in 854, he renewed the struggle, but in 859 the Aquitanians began to abandon him. Thereafter he became a wanderer, sometimes joining Viking raiders, with a band of whom he attacked Toulouse in 864. Captured soon afterward, he died during imprisonment at Senlis.
·Carolingian political decentralization **11**:930d

Pepin II, called PEPIN THE YOUNG, PEPIN OF HERSTAL, OR PEPIN OF HERISTAL (d. Dec. 16, 714, Jupille, near Liège, in present-day Belgium), ruler of the Franks (687–714), the first of the great Frankish mayors of the palace. The son of Begga and Ansegisel, he escaped the massacre of his family, which the ambition of his uncle Grimoald provoked in 662. After the death of the Merovingian king Dagobert II of Austrasia in 679, Pepin established himself as mayor of the palace in that kingdom and defended Austrasian autonomy against Theudoric III of Neustria and Ebroïn, Theudoric's mayor of the palace.

Defeated by Ebroïn in 680 at Lucofao (near Laon), Pepin gained his revenge in 687 at Tertry (near Péronne) and became sole effective ruler of the Franks. He nevertheless retained Theudoric III on the throne and after his death replaced him with three successive Merovingian kings. After several years of warfare Pepin defeated the Frisians on his northeastern border (689) and married his son Grimoald to Theodelind, daughter of the Frisian chief Radbod. He also encouraged Christian missionaries in Bavaria.
·Austrasian expansion and hegemony **11**:928d
·legacy of Frankish rule **4**:61g
·Low Countries intervention and conflicts **11**:133c

Pepin III the Short **14**:35 (d. Sept. 24, 768, Saint-Denis, Fr.), the first king of the Carolingian dynasty and father of Charlemagne.

Abstract of text biography. A son of the mayor of the palace Charles Martel, Pepin became sole ruler of the Franks in 747 and king in 751. He was the first Frankish king to be anointed by the pope (754). During his reign, Pepin engaged in military campaigns in support of the pope and against rebellions in his territory.

REFERENCES in other text articles:
·Boniface and conciliar reform of Franks **3**:32b
·Carolingian seizure of power **4**:44c
·Carolingian usurpation legitimation **11**:929b
·Low Countries political relation **11**:133c
·medieval papacy's hierarchical growth **12**:143e
·papal alliance against the Lombards **9**:1117h
·Schism of 1054 and political background **6**:143b
·support for papal authority **3**:559h

pepino hill, conical hill of residual limestone in a karst region. Pepino hills generally form on relatively flat-lying limestones that are jointed in large rectangles. In an alternating wet and dry climate, high areas become increasingly hard and resistant while low areas are subjected to greater erosion and solution. In some places, such as the Kwangsi area of China, pepino hills may have almost vertical sides and be riddled with caves. Pepino hills develop to greater heights in regions having tropical rainfall; these are generally called mogotes. Other names for such hills are hums and haystack hills.
·Cuban regional topography **5**:350a

peplos, also spelled PEPLUS, a garment worn by Greek women during the early Archaic, Classical, and Hellenistic periods; *i.e.*, up to about AD 300. It consisted of a large, rectangular piece of material folded vertically and hung from the shoulders, with a broad overfold. During the early periods, it was belted around the waist, usually beneath the overfold; if the overfold was long, however, the belt was sometimes placed on top of it, as seen in many statues of Athena. In Hellenistic times, the overfold was belted below the bust. To allow for growing, young girls wore peploses with long overfolds. When worn with other types of dress, the peplos was the outermost garment. Initially, it was made of wool or linen; later, cotton and silk were also used.
·design and wearing method **5**:1021g; illus. 1022

The goddess Eirene wearing a peplos, Roman copy of a Greek sculpture by Cephisodotus the Elder of Athens, marble, 4th century BC; in the Metropolitan Museum of Art, New York City

By courtesy of The Metropolitan Museum of Art, New York, Rogers Fund, 1906

pepo, the characteristic many-seeded fruit of the gourd family (Cucurbitaceae), including cucumber, squash, pumpkin, and melon.
·Cucurbitales form and function **5**:363h
·fruit classification table **16**:482

Pepo, Bencivieni di: *see* Cimabue.

Pepoli, Taddeo de' (d. 1347), lord of Bologna, member of a family that played an important role in the political and economic life of 13th- and 14th-century Bologna.

The Pepoli, wealthy bankers, were leaders of the Guelf (papal) party and helped expel the Ghibelline (imperial) Lambertazzi from the city in 1274. Taddeo's father, Romeo de' Pepoli, ruled the city for several years, but an insurrection forced him to flee with his family, and he died in exile in 1321. Taddeo, who had received a doctorate in law from the University of Bologna, followed his father into banishment, but after six years he returned to Bologna and in 1337 was acclaimed lord of the city, assuming the title of "keeper of peace and justice." Pope Benedict XII later recognized him as papal vicar.

After Taddeo's death, his sons were forced to yield Bologna to the growing power of the Visconti of Milan, and the city fell under the rule of Archbishop Giovanni Visconti in the year 1352.

Unable to recover their political position, the Pepoli became soldiers, scholars, literary men, and jurists. In the 19th century the family was active in the Risorgimento, the movement for Italy's unification.

Peponapis, genus of bees of the order Hymenoptera, class Insecta, phylum Arthropoda.
·Cucurbitales propagation inducers **5**:363d

pepper, true black pepper, *Piper nigrum*, perennial climbing vine of the family Piperaceae indigenous to the Malabar Coast of India, or the hotly pungent spice made from its berries.

One of the earliest spices known, pepper is probably the most widely used spice in the world today. It has a limited usage in medicine as a carminative and as a stimulant of gastric secretions.

In early historic times pepper was widely cultivated in the tropics of Southeast Asia, where it became highly regarded as a condiment. Pepper early became an important article of overland trade between India and Europe. It became a medium of exchange, and tributes were levied in pepper in ancient Greece and Rome. In the Middle Ages the Venetians and Genoese became the main distributors, their virtual monopoly of the trade helping instigate the search for a sea route to the Far East.

The plant is widely cultivated throughout the East Indies. It has been introduced into tropical areas of Africa and of the Western Hemisphere. A woody climber, it may reach heights of 33 feet (10 metres) by means of its aerial roots. Its broad, shiny green leaves are alternately arranged.

The inconspicuous flowers are in dense, slender spikes of about 50 blossoms each. The berrylike fruits, or peppercorns, are nearly globular, about 0.2 inch (5 millimetres) in diameter. They become yellowish red at maturity and bear a single seed. Their odour is penetrating and aromatic; the taste is hot, biting, and very pungent.

The plant requires a long rainy season, fairly high temperatures, and partial shade for best growth. Propagation is usually by stem cuttings, which are set out near a tree or a pole that will serve as a support. Sometimes the plants are interspersed in tea or coffee plantations. Peppers start bearing in two to five years and under good conditions may produce for as long as 40 years.

The berries are picked when they begin to turn red. The collected berries are immersed in boiling water for about 10 minutes, which causes them to turn dark brown or black in an hour. Then they are spread on mats or concrete floors to dry in the sun for three or four days. The whole peppercorns, when ground, yield black pepper.

Black pepper (*Piper nigrum*)

W.H. Hodge

White pepper is obtained from peppercorns from which the outer part of the pericarp has been removed. The outer coating is softened either by keeping the berries in moist heaps for two or three days or by keeping them in sacks submerged in running water for 7 to 15 days, depending on the region. Then the softened outer coating is removed by washing and rubbing or by trampling, and the berries are spread in the sun to dry. Whole white pepper can also be prepared by grinding off the outer coating mechanically. The flavour is less pungent than that of black pepper.

Pepper contains from 1 to 3 percent essential oil that has the aromatic flavour of pepper but not the pungency. The pungent principles are contained in the oleoresin and consist of piperine, $C_{17}H_{19}NO_3$; chavicine, $C_{17}H_{19}NO_3$; piperidine, $(CH_2)_5NH$; and piperettine, $C_{19}H_{21}O_3N$.

Long pepper is prepared from *Piper retrofractum*, native to Java, and *Piper longum*, native to India, chiefly for use in the areas where it is grown. During the Middle Ages it was popular in Europe.

Red, chili, cayenne, and other fleshy peppers are species of the genus *Capsicum* (*q.v.*). The green, red, and yellow peppers are used in seasoning and as a vegetable. The powdered red pepper of commerce is made from dried capsicums.

Various plants called pepper, including the California pepper tree *Schinus molle*, the pepper vine *Ampelopsis arborea*, and the sweet pepper bush *Clethra alnifolia*, are grown as ornamental plants and are not used as spices.

·Ceylonese trade and colonial monopolies **4**:6d
·development of agriculture **1**:325g
·domesticated plant centres of origin **5**:938e
·spice history, use, production, and region of origin **17**:502a; tables 504
·spice production and exportation **14**:467h
·vegetable history, classification, and cultivation **19**:43a; tables 44

pepperbox, pistol developed in late 18th century; contains five or six barrels revolving on a central axis fired individually by a single striker.

·small arms use by military **16**:898b

pepper coral (marine animal): *see* Millepora.

peppered moth (*Biston betularia*), a European moth of the family Geometridae (order Lepidoptera), having speckled black and white wings. It is of significance in exemplifying natural selection through industrial melanism. A dark (melanic) form of the peppered moth, first noticed in Manchester, Eng., in 1848, by 1898 had outnumbered the usual light-coloured moth by 99 to 1. The explanation of this phenomenon is that the dark moth was not as conspicuous to bird predators as the light moth against the black-sooted tree trunks of industrial areas. The difference is genetic and of interest as a striking example of rapid evolutionary change in a localized area.

·coloration adaptations, illus. 2 **4**:925
·genetic changes and industrial melanism **8**:814f
·heterozygous advantage evolution **14**:775c
·industrial melanism and evolution **7**:14g

peppergrass, or PEPPERWORT, common name for about 150 species of annual, biennial, and perennial herbs comprising the genus *Lepidium* of the mustard family (Brassicaceae) and distributed throughout the world. Many, such as *L. perfoliatum*, are lawn and field weeds, but some are useful salad plants. Most species have long taproots,

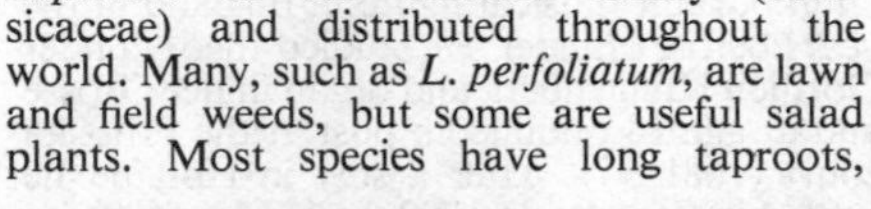

Peppergrass (*Lepidium perfoliatum*)
F.K. Anderson—EB Inc.

broad basal leaves differing from the narrow leaves on the flowering stalks, and spike-like clusters of small, greenish or whitish, four-petalled flowers. Each seed is in a flat, round pod. Garden cress (*L. sativum*), a North African annual, is sometimes cultivated for the flavourful basal leaves of the young plants, which in some forms are golden or as finely cut as parsley. Virginia peppergrass (*L. virginicum*), spread throughout North America, sometimes is known as canary grass because its seed stalks are fed to cage birds. Its leaves are used in salads. Lentejilla, or little lentil (*L. intermedium*), native to Europe but long naturalized in Mexico, is used as a folk medicine. Pepperwort, or field pepper (*L. campestre*), a widespread weed, is native in Europe and naturalized in North America. It has hairy, arrow-like stem leaves and once was marketed as a poison antidote under the name of mithridate pepperwort.

·L. lasiocarpum delayed germination **3**:805b

pepperidge tree: *see* tupelo.

peppermint (*Mentha piperita*), strongly aromatic perennial herb furnishing a widely used flavouring. It has stalked, smooth, dark-green leaves and oblong-obtuse, spikelike clusters of

Peppermint (*Mentha piperita*)
Shunji Watari—EB Inc.

pinkish-lavender flowers, which are dried and used to flavour candy, desserts, beverages, salads, and other foods. Peppermint has a strong, agreeable, sweetish odour, and a warm, pungent taste with a cooling aftertaste. Indigenous to Europe and Asia, it has been naturalized in North America and is found near streams and in other wet sites. It is cultivated in Europe, Asia, and North America for its essential oil. Natural hybridization among wild species has yielded many varieties of peppermint, but only two, the black and the white, are recognized by growers. The former has purplish and the latter green stems. Black peppermint, also called English peppermint or mitcham mint, is extensively grown in the United States. The white variety is less hardy and less productive, but its oil is considered more delicate in odour and obtains a higher price.

Oil of peppermint, a volatile essential oil distilled with steam from the herb, is widely used for flavouring confectionery, chewing gum, dentifrices, and medicines. Pure oil of peppermint is nearly colourless. It consists principally of menthol, $C_{10}H_{20}O$, and menthone, $C_{10}H_{18}O$. Menthol, also called mint camphor or peppermint camphor, has long been used medicinally as a soothing balm in the Eastern as well as the Western part of the world. Oil of Japanese mint is very different from peppermint oil, but is also a rich source of menthol. The name Japanese peppermint is sometimes used for this plant, *Mentha arvensis* variety *piperascens*, but it is not a true peppermint.

peppermint camphor: *see* menthol.

Pepperrell, Sir William (b. June 27, 1696, Kittery, Maine, then a part of Massachusetts —d. July 6, 1759, Kittery), merchant, politician, and soldier who in 1745 commanded

Pepperrell, detail of a portrait by Peter Pelham (1684–1751) after a painting by John Smibert (1688–1751); in the collection of the Massachusetts Historical Society
By courtesy of the Massachusetts Historical Society

land forces that, with a British fleet, captured the French fortress of Louisbourg (in present-day Nova Scotia). For this exploit in King George's War, he was created a baronet (1746), the first man born in one of the 13 colonies to be so honoured. He was also given the rank of lieutenant general in the British Army. For a brief period (1756–57), he was acting governor of Massachusetts.

Pepperrell became prosperous as an associate in his father's mercantile firm and in real estate investments. He served as a member of the Massachusetts General Court and of the Governor's Council and as chief justice of the Court of Common Pleas.

peppershrike (*Cyclarhis*), either of two species of stout-billed tropical American songbirds, constituting the family Cyclarhidae (order Passeriformes), included by some authorities in the vireo family, Vireonidae. Both peppershrikes are olive green above and yellow and white below; they are about 15 centimetres (6 inches) in length. The bill is high and terminally hooked. Peppershrikes are

Peppershrike (*Cyclarhis nigrirostris*)
Painting by H. Jon Janosik

found in open woodland from southern Mexico to Argentina and Paraguay. They feed on large insects and some fruit, taken as they move about in foliage. Their song is a sweet warble, repeated frequently.

pepper tree (*Schinus molle*), small ornamental tree of the cashew family (Anacardiaceae), native to tropical America and cultivated in warm subtropical regions. The long leaves have storage cells that contain a volatile oil. The small white flowers are borne in clusters at the ends of the branches. Each small, pea-like fruit has a hard kernel surrounding one

Pepper tree (*Schinus molle*)

Thase Daniel

seed. The fruits are used in beverages and medicines because of their hot taste and aroma. Pepper tree is a host plant for scale insects that damage orange trees.

pepperwort (plant): *see* peppergrass.

pepsin, the powerful enzyme, or ferment, in gastric juice of the stomach, which digests proteins such as those in meat, eggs, seeds, or dairy products. Enzymes are catalysts that in small quantities speed up biochemical reactions. They are proteins formed by living tissues, and all cells are dependent upon them to speed up the many reactions that otherwise would proceed slowly. Usually, enzymes mix with water to hydrolyze chemical bonds.

Pepsin was first recognized in 1836 by the German physiologist Theodor Schwann. Nearly a century later, in 1930, it was crystallized and its protein nature established by John H. Northrop of the Rockefeller Institute for Medical Research.

Glands in the mucous membrane lining of the stomach make and store pepsin in an inactive form called pepsinogen. Impulses from the vagus nerve and the hormonal secretions of gastrin and secretin stimulate the release of pepsinogen into the stomach, where it is mixed with hydrocholoric acid and rapidly converted to the active pepsin enzyme. Once pepsin is converted, it can act as a catalyst upon other pepsinogen molecules to produce more pepsin; *i.e.*, it is self-accelerating or autocatalytic. The digestive power of pepsin changes with acidity, and it is fastest at the acidity of normal gastric juice (pH 1.5–2.5). In the intestine the gastric acids are neutralized (pH 7), and pepsin is no longer effective.

Proteins, in general, are made up of a number of different amino acids linked together. Only the links between certain pairs of amino acids are opened by pepsin. In the digestive tract this leads to only partial degradation of proteins into smaller units called peptides, which then either are absorbed from the intestine into the bloodstream or are broken down further by pancreatic enzymes. The magnitude of the digestive power of pepsin may be indicated by pointing out that 1 gram (1/30 ounce) of pure pepsin can coagulate (an early step in the digestion) 27,000 litres of milk in an hour at body temperature or can digest thousands of times its weight of other proteins in a similar period. Although pepsin is a protein, it is resistant to its own digestive powers.

Small amounts of pepsin pass from the stomach into the bloodstream. Here, it functions to break down some of the larger, or still partially undigested, fragments of protein that may have been absorbed by the small intestine.

Like other enzymes and proteins, pepsin is a large complex molecule. On a weight scale in which an atom of hydrogen is 1 and ordinary table salt (sodium chloride) is 58, pepsin is 35,000.

Pepsin is prepared commercially from swine stomachs, which contain on the average about one gram of enzyme per stomach. Crude pepsin is used in the leather industry to remove hair and residual tissue from animal hides prior to their being tanned. It is also used in the recovery of silver from discarded movie films by digesting the gelatin layer that holds the silver compound. Another commercial use is in the preparation of peptone (partially digested protein), an important ingredient of growth media for bacteria and related micro-organisms.

·digestion mechanisms in vertebrates **5**:785d
·enzyme qualities and isolation **3**:1004g
·hormonal effects on stomach **6**:814h
·human digestive system anatomy **5**:793b
·immunoglobulin molecule fragmentation **9**:251d; illus.
·pregnancy's effect on gastric function **14**:973e
·protein digestion and gastric secretion **5**:774b
·pure protein identification **15**:95d

pepsinogen, the proenzyme—or precursor—of pepsin. It is an inactive secretion liberated from the gastric glands located in the mucous membrane lining of the lower antrum and pylorus regions of the stomach. The presence of food, hormones, and neuronal stimulation causes release of pepsinogen. Once in the stomach cavity it mixes with another gastric secretion, hydrochloric acid, to form the active protein-reducing enzyme, pepsin. *See* pepsin.

·digestion mechanisms in vertebrates **5**:785e
·protein digestion and gastric secretion **5**:774b

Pepsis: *see* spider wasp.

PEPSU: *see* Patiāla and East Punjab State Union.

peptic esophagitis, inflammation of the esophagus (gullet) by digestive juices that have escaped from the stomach.

·digestive disorder symptoms and treatment **5**:768h
·reflux troubles and results **5**:798b

peptic ulcer, sharply circumscribed, punched-out defect or erosion of tissue in the lining of the stomach or duodenum, produced by the corrosive and digestive action of acid gastric juice. Gastric (stomach) ulcers appear to be caused by failure of the normal mechanisms for protection of the stomach wall: the mucous cells may not secrete an adequate layer of mucus, or gastric acid, though normal or even below normal in quantity, may not be adequately buffered and diluted by swallowed food and by regurgitated intestinal contents. Duodenal ulcers, on the other hand, usually occur in the presence of greater than normal amounts of gastric juice with a high acid concentration. Peptic ulcers occasionally occur in the lower portion of the esophagus, as a result of repeated regurgitation of gastric contents.

Peptic ulcer occurs in 10 to 15 percent of the world's population; men are affected more frequently than women and, except in Japan, duodenal ulcers are more common than gastric. The causes are not completely understood, although many factors have been implicated, including nervous tension, ingestion of certain drugs, such as salicylates and corticoids, and hormonal factors.

The symptoms of gastric and duodenal ulcer are similar, consisting of gnawing, burning, aching, hunger-like pain or discomfort in the mid-upper abdomen, occurring from one to three hours after meals and several hours after retiring. Characteristically, this pain is relieved by ingestion of materials such as food, milk, and baking soda, which dilute and neutralize acid.

Several complicating conditions may occur secondarily to peptic ulcer: obstruction of the stomach outlet, caused by inflammation or scar formation, may cause vomiting; bleeding may occur, leading to weakness and anemia; the intestinal wall may perforate, causing severe localized abdominal pain and peritonitis.

Though peptic ulcer often subsides spontaneously, some relief is provided by medical management, including antacid therapy, antisecretory drugs, and diet and rest control. When complications occur, or when the ulcer fails to heal with medical treatment, surgery may be necessary; a major portion of the stomach is often removed to decrease acid production and thus prevent recurrence.

·dietary cure claim unfounded **13**:425c
·digestive disorders of esophagus and stomach **5**:799a
·emotional causes and effect **5**:788e
·surgical treatment **11**:837g

peptidase (digestion): *see* intestinal juice.

peptide bond, the chemical bond by which α-amino acids, the constituents of proteins, are linked. The carboxyl group ($-COOH$) of one amino acid is joined to the amino group ($-NH_2$) of its neighbour. More than two amino acids joined in this manner are usually termed polypeptides.

·amino-acid linkage in protein **15**:81g
·bacterial proteolytic process **2**:575d
·blood hemoglobin changes in anemia **2**:1138d
·blood transport of protein constituents **2**:1114g
·classification and reaction specificity **6**:899d; table 898
·gene action and protein structure **7**:988a
·inflammatory process chemically linked **9**:561c
·muscle contraction mechanisms **12**:630b

peptizer, in rubber manufacture, an organic sulfur compound that breaks down molecular structure.

·rubber mixing efficiency control **15**:1181c

peptizing agent, substance that promotes formation of a colloid.

·colloid preparation methods **4**:855e

Pepusch, John Christopher, also called JOHANN CHRISTOPH PEPUSCH (b. 1667, Berlin—d. July 20, 1752, London), composer who was an important musical figure in England in the years before Handel. He studied theory under Gottlieb Klingenberg and organ under Grosse and at age 14 obtained a post at the Prussian court (1681–97). After a stay in Holland he settled in England in 1700. In 1712 he became music director to the duke of Chandos. He took a doctorate in music from Oxford in 1713. About this time he became music director at Lincoln's Inn Fields Theatre, for which he wrote several masques and arranged the tunes and composed the overtures for John Gay's *Beggar's Opera* (1728) and its sequel *Polly* (unperformed until 1777). In 1737 he became organist at the Charterhouse. He was in demand as a teacher; William Boyce was among his pupils. He collected a magnificent library of music books and scores. Deeply interested in music of the Renaissance and of ancient Greece and Rome, he had a strong influence on the early development of musical antiquarianism in England; one consequence was the publication of Boyce's anthology *Cathedral Music* (of 16th- and 17th-century England). He helped form the Academy of Ancient Music, which performed works by 16th-century composers, and he edited some works of Corelli. His compositions include cantatas, concerti, and chamber music.

Pepys, Samuel 14:36 (b. Feb. 23, 1633, London—d. May 26, 1703, London), man of letters and naval administrator, celebrated for his diary, which gives a brilliant picture of the social life of his day.

Abstract of text biography. Although born of humble parents, Pepys received a university education at Magdalene College, Cambridge. His career began with a clerkship in 1659. The following year he began his service with the Royal Navy and started his diary, which he was to keep until 1669. By 1673 Pepys had become secretary to the new commission of admiralty and a member of Parliament. His career was interrupted in 1678 by political enemies, but Pepys survived imprisonment in the Tower of London to be appointed adviser to the earl of Dartmouth (1683). He returned to his naval post the next year and became one of the most powerful men in England.

REFERENCES in other text articles:
- autobiographical literary forms **2**:1009g
- blood transfusion descriptions **2**:1143e
- Dryden's plays' popularity **5**:1063f
- ice skating in London during Great Frost **19**:885a
- literary style **10**:1045e
- Newton's mental instability **13**:20b
- pageantry of Lord Mayor criticism **13**:863e
- party game description **4**:245h

Pequot, Algonkian-speaking Indians who lived in the Thames valley, in what is now Connecticut; in the 1600s their population was estimated to be 2,200. Their subsistence was based on the cultivation of maize (corn), hunting, and fishing. The Mohegan (*q.v.*) and the Pequot were jointly ruled by the Pequot chief Sassacus until a rebellion of the subchief Uncas that resulted in Mohegan independence. In 1637 the murder of a trader who had mistreated the Pequot led to war between them and the English colonists (*see* Pequot War). Defeated, some Pequot decided to separate into small bands and abandon the area; many who fled were killed or captured by other Indians or the English; many were sold into slavery in New England or the West Indies, and the Mohegan obtained control of Pequot lands. Those who surrendered were distributed among other tribes, but received such harsh treatment that in 1655 they were placed under the direct control of the colonial government and resettled on the Mystic River. Their numbers declined rapidly, and in the 1970s there were approximately 200 members of the tribe.
- Woodlands Indian culture **6**:169b

Pequot War (1637), slaughter of almost the entire Pequot Indian tribe in southern Connecticut by British colonists seeking revenge for the murder of several white men. Since 1620 most Indians and British settlers in the Massachusetts coastal area had succeeded in living side by side in mutual helpfulness and peaceful trade. Gradually, however, Indian resentment swelled against new colonists who pushed their way westward in a frequently high-handed manner. Most fearful were the Pequots, recently engaged in intertribal warfare and squeezed into the region between Narragansett Bay and the Connecticut River. The tribe had also stirred the ire of the British by limiting its trade to the Dutch.

Following earlier incidents, trouble was sparked in the summer of 1636 by the murder of a Boston trader on Block Island, presumably by a Pequot. A punitive expedition sent by Massachusetts authorities to destroy native villages and crops only aroused the tribe to make a more determined defense of its homeland. Puritan clergymen encouraged violence against the Pequots, whom they regarded as infidels, and the British settlers agreed to take up arms. In a short but vicious war, fought under Capt. John Mason with the aid of Mohegans and Narragansets, the main Pequot fort at Mystic, Conn., was surprised and burned and between 500 and 600 inhabitants were roasted or slaughtered. Escaping survivors were pursued, and the tribe was decimated. As a result of this colonial victory, peace reigned for the next 40 years on the northern frontier, as the entire area was taken over by the white man.

peracid (chemistry): *see* peroxy acid.

Peracini, Jean: *see* Coralli, Jean.

Perahera, Ceylonese Buddhist festival in which a procession moves to the Temple of the Tooth in Kandy.
- kandyan dance street performance **17**:168f

Perak, state (*negeri*), northwestern West Malaysia (Malaya), bordered by Thailand (north), Kelantan and Pahang (east), Selangor (south), the Strait of Malacca (west), and Pinang (formerly Penang) and Kedah (northwest). Its area of 8,110 sq mi (21,004 sq km) includes a large portion of the west coast plains and centres upon the Sungai Perak ("silver river"), which flows 252 mi (406 km) north–south between the Keledang Range to the east and the Bintang Range to the west. An important artery for early Malay settlers, the river turns westward at Telok Anson and meanders through a silting estuary to the Strait of Malacca.

Dutch attempts to control tin exports resulted in a 1765 treaty with the sultan. British influence, which began with an 1818 trade treaty, was extended in 1826, when the Dindings coastal strip and Pangkor Island offshore were ceded to them as bases for pirate suppression. In the Pangkor Treaty (1874), the chiefs accepted a British resident, and Perak became one of the Federated Malay States (1896). The Dindings and Pangkor were returned in 1935 to Perak, which joined the Federation of Malaya after World War II.

Significant in the state's modern economy are the mines of the Kinta Valley (*q.v.*), particularly around the state capital of Ipoh (*q.v.*), which yield most of West Malaysia's tin.

Tasek (Lake) Chenderoh in north central Perak is the site of a hydroelectric dam that supplies power to the valley. Rubber production, paddy (rice) farming, coconut plantations, and fishing are also important. Tobacco is grown as an off-season cash crop in paddy areas. Iron is mined at Ipoh-Tambun, and there are coal deposits at Enggor. Cantonese Chinese predominate in the main towns, while Malays form majorities in agricultural districts such as Kerian, Sungai Manik, and Kampong Changkat. The substantial Indian minority's influx coincided with the rubber boom (early 20th century). Besides Ipoh, other important towns are Kuala Kangsar (the seat of the sultan), Batu Gajah, Kampar, Lumut, Tanjong Rambutan, and Gerik.

While much of the state remains jungle and the ranges are roadless and sparsely inhabited, there is a good network of roads supported by the Malayan Railway along the foothills. Perak is served by the main airport at nearby Pinang and has an airfield at Ipoh for peninsular service. Pop. (1970 prelim.) 1,562,566.
- area and population, table 1 **11**:373
- Malayan history and Muslim influence **11**:366a

Perak War, an unsuccessful attempt by dissident Malay chiefs in Perak to stop the growing economic and political influence of the British. James Birch, the first British resident in Perak, arrived there in November 1874. Birch hoped to have Raja Abdullah accepted as sultan in Upper Perak and to modernize the traditional administrative system (government had been based on personal relationships between the Sultan and the chiefs). Because of rapid and revolutionary administrative changes, especially concerning revenue collection and slavery, the resident soon alienated Abdullah and most chiefs.

The Sultan, at a meeting in July 1875, organized a movement to kill Birch and end foreign influence in Perak. When the resident was in Upper Perak posting new tax proclamations, one of the chiefs, Maharaja Lela, and his men assassinated Birch. An attack on the residency itself failed to materialize. Subsequent British military action crushed weak Malay resistance; the plotters were arrested by mid-1876 and were later tried. Abdullah was deposed as sultan, and the rebel chiefs were severely punished. Thereafter, British residents tended to work through Malay rulers and to avoid sweeping changes.

Peramelidae (marsupial family): *see* bandicoot.

Peramelina, an order of marsupials (superorder Marsupialia).
- classification and general features **11**:545b

Peranabrus scabricollis: *see* shield-backed grasshopper.

Peranakan, in Indonesia, a native-born person of mixed Indonesian and foreign ancestry. There are several kinds of Peranakans in Indonesia, namely Peranakan Chinese, Peranakan Arabs, Peranakan Dutch, and Peranakan Indians. The Peranakan Chinese form the largest and the most important group, and for this reason many scholars use Peranakan to refer to the Chinese group.

Until the end of the 19th century, immigration of Chinese was limited because of difficulties in transportation. Most of those who reached Java, mainly from the southern provinces of China, married indigenous women, usually nominal Muslims or non-Muslims.

In time they formed a stable Peranakan Chinese community. Peranakans partly adopted the indigenous way of life and generally spoke the local native tongue rather than Chinese. Along the northern coast of Java, where most of the Chinese lived, a combination of Bazaar Malay and Hokkien dialect was used as lingua franca, and this language was later known as Bahasa Melaju Tionghoa (Chinese Malay). This community was firmly established by the mid-19th century and had become self-contained with a decline in intermarriage. Peranakan Chinese married among themselves because of a nearly equal sex ratio. New immigrants continued to be rapidly assimilated into the Peranakan community because there was no mass immigration.

In the early 20th century a spectacular increase in Chinese immigrants (including women) in Java, the dynamics of Chinese nationalism, and the development of Chinese medium schools contributed to the shaping of a Totok (Indonesian term for foreign-born people) Chinese community. Unlike the Peranakan Chinese, Totok Chinese were China-born, still spoke a Chinese dialect or Mandarin, and were often strongly China-oriented.

Despite the rapid growth of the Totok community, the Chinese in Java remained overwhelmingly Indonesia-born. In 1930, for example, Indonesia-born Chinese constituted over 79 percent of all the Chinese in Java, and about 53 percent of the total were at least third generation. But they were by no means a homogeneous political group. Before World War II there were three political streams in the Peranakan Chinese community—the Sin Po group, which was China-oriented; the Chung Hwa Hui, which was Dutch East Indies-oriented; and the Partai Tionghoa Indonesia, which was Indonesia-oriented. These three groups were dissolved during the Japanese occupation (1942–45).

Per-Atum (ancient Egyptian city): *see* Pithom.

Peravia, province, southern Dominican Republic, bounded on the south by the Caribbean Sea. The province has an area of 628 sq mi (1,627 sq km) and was created in 1944 from parts of Trujillo and Azua provinces; an older name, Trujillo Valdéz, was changed to Peravia in 1961. Largely mountainous, it is bounded on the north by the Cordillera Central and is crossed in the centre part by the Sierra de Ocoa. The southern coastal plain is semiarid. Peravia is a leading coffee producer and a significant producer of rice and peanuts.

Baní (*q.v.*) is the provincial capital. Pop. (1970 prelim.) 127,587.
·area and population table **5**:945

per bend, also called PARTY PER BEND, in heraldry, a division of the shield.
·heraldic shield design **8**:788e; illus. 789

Percé, city, Bas-Saint-Laurent-Gaspésie region, eastern Quebec province, Canada, on the Gulf of St. Lawrence, at the east end of the Gaspé Peninsula. First visited in 1659 by Bishop François Laval, it has been the site of a Roman Catholic mission since 1670. Percé is now a fishing port and summer resort. Offshore, but connected by a sandbar at low tide, is famed Rocher Percé (Pierced Rock)—a rocky island 290 ft (88 m) high that is pierced by a 60-ft-high arch; it and another tourist attraction, Bonaventure Island (3 mi offshore), are bird sanctuaries. Pop. (1971) 5,617.
48°31′ N, 64°13′ W

perception 14:38, the process whereby sensory stimulation is translated into organized experience.

The text article covers history and such classical problems as sensing and perceiving, temporal (time) relations, and perceiving as synthesizing. Also covered are primary tendencies in perceptual organization, such as Gestalt principles, context effects, and perceptual constancies, and individual differences in perception according to age, sex, culture, expectancies, motives, and conflicts.

REFERENCES in other text articles:
aesthetics
·aesthetic considerations in composition **1**:151g
·affective elements in art perception **2**:49c
·architectural composition effects **1**:1107c
·artistic medium limitations **2**:42c
·drama as mimesis **5**:981d
·music as acoustical phenomenon **12**:665h
·painting space and volume representations **13**:872g; illus. 873
·psychological basis **1**:161d
·theatre audience's perceptual impairment **18**:215b
communication theory
·advertising design communication **1**:108g
·attitude change **4**:1009b
·computer and human ability comparisons **2**:1033g
·overload reaction **15**:42a
·political power dynamics **14**:698b
·porpoise sound discrimination **19**:807e
philosophy
·analysis of mind **12**:224a
·Analytic philosophy approaches **1**:800h
·Berkeley's direct relation theory **2**:846h
·Buddhist metaphysical theory **9**:324f
·Buddhist mysticism and perspective **3**:414h
·Cartesian doctrine and ethics **6**:979e
·empirical scientific study potential **16**:391a
·Epicurean thought process explanation **6**:912a
·Greek and medieval theories **14**:252a *passim* to 257e
·Hobbes's analysis of motion **8**:970g
·Hume's theory of impressions **12**:17a
·Jaina idea of soul's powers and growth **10**:10d
·Kantian analysis of mind and experience **10**:395g
·Kantian themes in psychology **16**:379f
·knowledge and sense experience **6**:926b *passim* to 947f
·Logical Empiricist theories **14**:273a
·Lucretius' view of sense infallibility **11**:174d
·objective reality of cognitive object **15**:539d
·Rationalist de-emphasis as knowledge source **15**:528a
·Renaissance and modern philosophy **14**:263g *passim* to 267e
·resemblance as classification principle **4**:692b *passim* to 693h
·Schopenhauer's theory of knowledge **16**:358g
·sensory awareness as mind attribute **12**:226e
·Ṣūfī controversy in Mughal India **9**:944c
·Whitehead's prehension concept **12**:35c
physiology and psychology
·animal learning definition **10**:731d
·attention as selective awareness **2**:354b
·attitudinal functions and attributes **2**:360g
·bee responses to flower colour patterns **9**:127c
·brainstem mediation mechanisms **12**:1004f
·conceptual and discrimination learning **4**:1062c
·development of precision in children **8**:1141b
·emotional connections **6**:761d
·hallucinations and illusions caused by drugs **8**:557g
·hallucinogenic drug effects **5**:1055a
·human taste in food quality rating **7**:486f
·illusions and environment interpretation **9**:240h
·learning and experience **10**:746h
·linguistic aspects in Whorf's view **16**:507c
·marijuana drug effects **5**:1059a
·memory encoding by perceptual attributes **11**:893b
·physiological and psychological restraints on semantic categories **10**:1000g
·protective coloration in animals **4**:924f
·psychophysiological theories **15**:160a
·retina structure and function **7**:112a
·Rorschach's personality theory **14**:112e
·sense organs specific energy **15**:152d
·sleep deprivation effects **16**:880d
·social and cultural influences **15**:164c
·space perception sensory relationship **17**:378d
·speech and hearing patterns linked **14**:281g
·speech hearing and information theory **10**:1010f
·stimuli filtration in animals **2**:805g
·thinking and stimulus perception **18**:354g
·time awareness and estimation **18**:422c

RELATED ENTRIES in the *Ready Reference and Index*:
constancy phenomenon; psychophysics; sensation

perception of movement 14:45, deals with sensory mechanisms employed by human beings and other animals in orienting to the environment.

The text article points out that visual cues seem most important and are provided by such factors as eye movements, the visual frame of reference, and associated brain mechanisms. Applications in the motion-picture industry and in outdoor advertising are discussed. Consideration also is given to auditory, kinesthetic, and vestibular functions in mediating the perception of movement.

REFERENCES in other text articles:
·disruptive coloration in animals **4**:924f
·distinguishing of external, bodily, voluntary, and involuntary motions **2**:807g
·ear anatomy and equilibrium mechanism **5**:1130b
·ear functions in equilibrium **5**:1132h
·Gestalt perceptual integration theory **14**:42g
·human retina structure and function **7**:105h
·illusions of stationary-object motion **9**:242e
·motion sickness and accelerations **12**:555c
·pitch changes as depth cues **17**:380c
·safety engineering design consideration **16**:141f

perception of space: *see* space perception.

perception of time: *see* time perception.

Perceptron, an experimental computer system equipped to read print and script; and also to be capable of response to spoken commands.
·biological characteristics simulation **2**:1033g

perceptual-motor skills: *see* sensorimotor skills.

Perceval, a hero of Arthurian romance, distinguished by his quality of childlike (often uncouth) innocence, which protected him from worldly temptation and set him apart from other knights in Arthur's fellowship. This quality also links his story with the primitive folktale theme of a great fool or simple hero. In Chrétien de Troyes' poem *Le Conte du Graal* (12th century), Perceval's great adventure was a visit to the castle of the wounded Fisher King, where he saw a mysterious dish (or "grail") but, having previously been scolded for asking too many questions, failed to ask the question that would have healed the Fisher King. Afterward, he set off in search of the Grail and gradually learned the true meaning of chivalry and its close connection with the teachings of the church. In later elaborations of the Grail theme, the pure knight Sir Galahad displaced him as Grail hero, though Perceval continued to play an important part in the quest.

The story of Perceval's spiritual development from simpleton to Grail keeper received its finest treatment in Wolfram von Eschenbach's great 13th-century epic, *Parzival*. This poem was the basis of Wagner's last opera, *Parsifal* (1882). *See also* Grail, Holy.
·literary theme and significance **10**:1102h
·medieval legend of Holy Grail **4**:554c

Perceval, Spencer (b. Nov. 1, 1762, London —d. May 11, 1812, London), lawyer, politician, and British prime minister from 1809 until his assassination in 1812.

Spencer Perceval, detail of an oil painting by G.F. Joseph, 1812; in the National Portrait Gallery, London
By courtesy of the National Portrait Gallery, London

Perceval's rise to power was facilitated through his contacts with William Pitt the Younger. In 1796 he entered Parliament as a member for Northampton. On the formation of the Addington (1st Viscount Sidmouth) government (1801–04), which succeeded that of Pitt, he was appointed solicitor general. From 1802 and through Pitt's second administration (1804–06) he was attorney general. When King George III dismissed William Grenville's ministry in March 1807, Perceval, an ardent opponent of Catholic emancipation, became chancellor of the exchequer and chancellor of the duchy of Lancaster under the 3rd duke of Portland, whom he succeeded as prime minister on Oct. 4, 1809. On May 11, 1812, Perceval was shot in the House of Commons by John Bellingham, a deranged man who had vainly applied to him for redress of a personal complaint against the government.
·cabinet service under Portland **3**:260a
·Palmerston's service as war secretary **13**:936a

perch, either of two species, the common and the yellow perch (*Perca fluviatilis* and *P. flavescens*) of the family Percidae (order Perciformes); the name also is widely, and sometimes confusingly, applied to a variety of other fishes. The common and yellow perches are found, respectively, in the fresh waters of Eurasia and North America. Both are well-known and popular as both food and sport

Yellow perch (*Perca flavescens*)
L.M. Chace—National Audubon Society

fishes. They have two dorsal fins, the first spiny and the second soft-rayed.

Perches are carnivores and inhabit quiet ponds, lakes, streams, and rivers. They spawn in spring, the female at that time laying strings of eggs in the shallows among water plants, branches, and the like. The common, or European, perch is greenish with dark vertical bars on the sides and reddish or orange colouring in the lower fins. It grows to a maximum weight of about three kilograms (six pounds), rarely more. The yellow perch, native to eastern North America and introduced on the Pacific coast, is similar to the European perch but yellower in colour. It grows to about 40 centimetres (15 inches) and 1 kilogram (2.2 pounds).

Other perchlike and perch-named fishes include the surfperch (*q.v.*) and the white perch, a relative of the sea bass (*q.v.*).

·classification and general features **14**:52h; illus. 48

perch, name for various units of measure in U.S. and Great Britain.

·weights and measures, table 5 **19**:734

Perche, district of northern France on the border of Normandie, mainly in the east of the Orne *département*, with extensions into neighbouring *départements*. Formerly a county, it was united to the French crown in 1525. Largely hilly country, the Collines (hills) du Perche, with summits up to 1,000 ft (300 m), it is a district of pastoral farming and dairying, once famous for its breed of draft horses (Percherons). Mortagne-au-Perche and Nogent-le-Rotrou, the chief market towns, were at different times capitals of Perche county.

perched rock, also called MUSHROOM ROCK or PEDESTAL ROCK, boulder balanced on a pinnacle rock, another boulder, or in some other precarious position. Some perched rocks form in place, as where rainwash (and in some cases wind) has removed fine material from around

Near view of a glacial erratic perched on low pedestal of massive granite, Tulare County, California

By courtesy of the U.S. Geological Survey, Washington, D.C.

the boulder. Others may be transported by tectonic forces (involved in deformation of the earth's crust) or by ice (such as erratics, or glacier transports) and let down to an unsettled position. Perched rocks commonly have a hard capping, such as ferruginous duricrust, and they often show crumbling or exudation around their sides.

Percheron, heavy draft-horse breed, originated in the Perche region, France. The breed probably stems from the Flemish great horse of the Middle Ages; modified by Oriental blood to develop a coach-horse type, it was changed again in the 19th century by introduction of draft-type blood to produce animals for heavy farm work. Although a few were imported earlier, Percherons did not become popular in the United States until after 1851. Before mechanization revolutionized farming, Percherons were widespread and influenced U.S. agriculture more than any other draft breed.

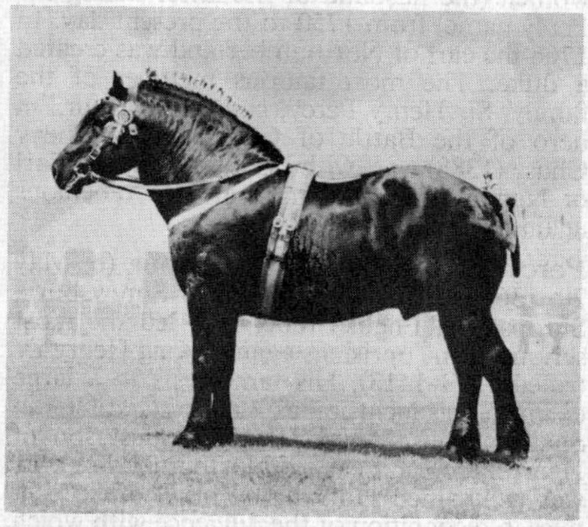

Percheron

Sally Anne Thompson—EB Inc.

Percherons average 16 to 17 hands (64 to 68 inches [163 to 173 centimetres]) high and weigh 1,900 to 2,100 pounds (860 to 950 kilograms). The head is fairly small and clean cut, the neck long, and the body well muscled. Common colours are black and gray. Percherons are agile and energetic for their size and display a mild disposition. The Percheron Horse Association of America and its predecessor organizations date from 1902.

per chevron, also called PARTY PER CHEVRON, in heraldry, division of a shield.

·heraldic shield design **8**:788e; illus. 789

perching, sitting on and holding onto a tree branch or some other precarious site, usually aided, in birds, by adaptations of the foot.

·bay owl's utilization of vertical branches **17**:735h
·Chiroptera skeletal modifications **4**:431d
·mechanism of pigeon, illus. 5 **2**:1057
·passerine foot features **13**:1055c; illus. 1053
·piciform foot specializations **14**:450b
·waterfowl ability and adaptations **1**:943b

perching bird: *see* Passeriformes.

perching duck, any of the species of the tribe Cairinini, family Anatidae (order Anseriformes). They are waterfowl that typically inhabit wet woodlands, nest in holes in trees, and perch on branches by means of their long-clawed toes. The tribe is widely represented, especially in the tropics. Perching ducks are closely akin to dabbling ducks (*q.v.*), which they resemble in feeding habits and, in some species, courtship behaviour; in other respects they are like shelducks. Perching ducks possess a bony knob at the wing bend, and most forms show white wing patches and black wing linings. Drakes are larger than hens and, on the whole, more brightly patterned—sometimes in metallic colours.

Best known among the perching ducks are: the North American wood duck (*Aix sponsa*), or Carolina duck, and its Asian relative, the mandarin duck (*A. galericulata*), both exceptionally colourful; and the Muscovy duck (*Cairina moschata*), of Mexico to Peru and Uruguay. The smallest of waterfowl are the little-known perching ducks of tropical forests; the so-called pygmy geese (*Nettapus* species).

·distinguishing features and classification **1**:947a
·pygmy goose bill adaptations for feeding **1**:945d

perchlorate, any compound formed by replacing the ionizable hydrogen atom of perchloric acid ($HClO_4$) by another positively charged ion, such as potassium K^+) or ammonium (NH_4^+). Perchlorates, which are powerful oxidizing agents, are principally used in explosives and fireworks.

·explosive composition **7**:86a
·formation and chemical properties **8**:569d

perchloric acid, strong fuming liquid acid and oxidizer the salt of which is used in plating and explosives.

·formation and chemical properties **8**:569d

perchloroethylene: *see* tetrachloroethylene.

Perchta (Germanic goddess): *see* Berchta.

Perchten, Austrian Twelfth Night mummers, or masqueraders; their danse-masquerade is part of a complex of related customs. *See* Morris dance; mumming play.

Percidae (fish family): *see* perch; darter; pikeperch.

Percier, Charles (1764–1838), French architect, worked with Pierre Fontaine in designing the Opéra (1794) and the Louvre and Tuileries Palace (1802); with Fontaine, remodelled Malmaison.

·design of Carrousel arch and furniture **13**:1015a
·furniture design in Empire style **7**:802h

Perciformes 14:46, large, diverse order of bony fishes with more than 6,000 species placed in about 150 families. Included among them are some of the most important food and game fishes, such as the tunas, mackerels, marlins, perches, and sea basses.

The text article begins with a section on the general features. It describes economic importance, life cycle, behaviour, and form and function of the perciforms, and includes an annotated classification of the order.

REFERENCES in other text articles:
·Beryciform structural similarity **2**:272a
·classification and characteristics **7**:344f
·commercial importance and feeding **7**:347d *passim* to 350h
·flatfish ancestry and evolution **14**:570b
·poisonous animals, table 6 **14**:612c
·Tetraodontiform evolutionary trends **18**:162e

RELATED ENTRIES in the *Ready Reference and Index: for*

common fishes: see anemone fish; angelfish; archer fish; barracuda; bass; black bass; blenny; bluefish; bonito; butterfish; butterfly fish; cardinal fish; cichlid; climbing perch; cobia; crappie; damselfish; darter; drum; glassfish; goatfish; goby; gourami; grouper; grunt; gunnel; jewfish; labyrinth fish; mackerel; man-of-war fish; marlin; moonfish; Moorish idol; mudskipper; mullet; Nile perch; parrotfish; perch; pikeperch; pilot fish; pompano; porgy; remora; sailfish; sand lance; sea bass; Siamese fighting fish; sleeper; snapper; snook; spearfish; spiny eel; stargazer; sunfish; surfperch; surgeonfish; swordfish; threadfin; tuna; wahoo; weever; wolffish; wrasse; wreckfish

families: Carangidae; Nandidae

percolation, in pharmacology, the process of extracting the soluble constituents of a powdered drug by passage of a liquid through it.

·pharmaceutical preparation methods **14**:197a

percolation, in geology, water movement through rock or soil interstices.

·hydrologic cycle aspects **9**:107b; illus. 103

Percophiidae, family of fishes, order Perciformes.

·classification and general features **14**:55b

Percopsiformes, order of fishes (superorder Paracanthopterygii) including the trout perch, pirate perch, and cave fish (*qq.v.*).

·fish characteristics and classification **7**:344a
·Paracanthopterygii classification and general features **13**:982c; illus. 980

Percopsis (fish): *see* trout-perch.

percussion, medical diagnostic procedure that entails striking the body directly or indirectly with short, sharp taps of a hammer or

finger. Generally ignored by contemporaries of the Austrian physician Leopold Auenbrugger von Auenbrugg, who described it in 1761, the procedure is now routinely employed. The sounds produced by the procedure are helpful in determining the size and position of various internal organs, in revealing the presence of fluid or air in the chest, and in aiding in the diagnosis of pneumonia or pulmonary tuberculosis.
·animal disease diagnostic methods **5**:871f
·Auenbrugger's diagnostic discovery **11**:830h
·physical examination technique **5**:689c

percussion, centre of, the point in a body free to move about a fixed axis at which the body may be squarely struck without jarring the axis.
·percussive tool theory and design **8**:613h

percussion cap, a paper or metal container holding an explosive charge; sometimes used to detonate another charge.
·small arms history of percussion guns **16**:896a

percussion figure, figure formed in a micaceous mineral by a blow from a sharp instrument.
·mica's mineralogical characteristics **12**:94b

percussion instruments 14:58, comprise two distinct groups: (1) idiophones, or instruments whose substance vibrates to produce sound (*e.g.*, bells, cymbals, castanets), and (2) membranophones, emitting sound by the vibration of a stretched membrane (*e.g.*, drums). Both groups are chiefly concerned with delineating or emphasizing rhythm, although many are of definite pitch and can be used for melodic purposes.

The text article classifies the many varieties of idiophones and membranophones. It covers their history and ceremonial and musical use in Europe, America, Asia, and Africa.

REFERENCES in other text articles:
·African types, construction, and music **1**:249g
·Amerindian drums and rattles **1**:664e
·Caribbean steel drum design **3**:906b
·Chinese chung description **11**:1116c
·Islāmic musical instruments **9**:974g
·musical sound production **17**:38c
·Oceanian music developments **13**:458c
·orchestras and ensembles **13**:644b *passim* to 647h
·sequence of instrument evolution **12**:731f
·Southeast Asian types and use **17**:237g

RELATED ENTRIES in the *Ready Reference and Index: for*
bell idiophones: see bell; bell chime; bell founding; carillon; carillon, electronic; handbell
plucked and friction idiophones: glass harmonica; jew's harp; mbira; music box
rattle and scraper idiophones: jingling johnny; rattle; scraper; sistrum
struck idiophones: celesta; chime; glockenspiel; gong; marimba; metallophone; slit drum; steel drum; stone chimes; triangle; tubular bells; tuning fork; vibraphone; xylophone
struck together, or concussion idiophones: bones; castanets; clapper; claves; cymbals
membranophones: bass drum; bongo drums; darabukka; drum; friction drum; kettledrum; mirliton; mrdanga; nakers; snare drum; tablah; taiko; tambourine; tenor drum; timpani; tsuzumi

percussion lock, ignition system in weapons of small-arms type, based on the detonation of an explosive (usually fulminate of mercury) when struck sharply. Invented in 1805, the percussion lock was the predecessor of the percussion cap, which was devised many years later.
·ammunition design history **1**:699f
·small arms history and operation **16**:895h

percussive tool, implement such as ax and hammer which involves violent propulsion to deliver a telling blow.
·hafting and head-weight theory **8**:613f

Percy, the name of a prominent English family, famous in history and ballad for its role in medieval and Tudor times in guarding the English borders against the Scots. Members of the direct male line held the earldom of Northumberland (1377–1537, 1557–1670), and, with the descent passing through two women (the husband of the latter taking the Percy name) from 1750 to the present day. In 1766 the earl of Northumberland was created a duke. The most famous member of the family, Sir Henry Percy, called "Hotspur," a hero of the Battle of Otterburn or Chevy Chase (1388) was, with his father, the 1st Earl of Northumberland, implicated in rebellions against Henry IV.

Percy, Sir Henry, called HOTSPUR (b. May 20, 1364—d. July 21, 1403, near Shrewsbury, Shropshire), English rebel who led the most serious of the uprisings against King Henry IV (ruled 1399–1413). His fame rests to a large extent on his inclusion as a major character in Shakespeare's *Henry IV*. The eldest son of Henry Percy, 1st earl of Northumberland, he was nicknamed Hotspur by his Scottish enemies in recognition of the diligence with which he patrolled the border between England and Scotland. He was captured and ransomed by Scottish invaders in 1388–89, and in 1399 he and his father played a crucial part in helping Henry Bolingbroke (afterward King Henry IV) overthrow King Richard II. Henry IV rewarded Hotspur with lands and offices in northern England and Wales, but the Percys would not be content until they dominated the King. Their stunning victory over the Scots at Homildon (Humbledon) Hill in Durham, in September 1402, contrasted with Henry's fruitless attempts to suppress the Welsh rebel Owen Glendower. Nevertheless, Henry refused to allow Hotspur to ransom the Scottish captives, and he delayed in paying the expenses of Hotspur's border warfare. Hence in 1403 Hotspur and Northumberland decided to depose the King. Hotspur raised a rebellion in Cheshire in July, but Henry intercepted him near Shrewsbury before he could join forces with his father and Glendower; in the ensuing battle Hotspur was killed.

Percy, Thomas (b. April 13, 1729, Bridgnorth, Shropshire—d. Sept. 30, 1811, Dromore, County Down), antiquary scholar and bishop whose collection of ballads *Reliques of Ancient English Poetry* (1765) awakened widespread interest in English and Scottish traditional songs, formerly ignored in literary circles.

Thomas Percy, detail of an engraving by Hawksworth after a painting by Abbott
By courtesy of the trustees of the British Museum; photograph, J.R. Freeman & Co. Ltd.

The basis of Percy's collection was a tattered 15th-century manuscript of ballads (known as the Percy folio) found in the house of a friend when it was about to be used to light a fire. To this nucleus Percy added many other ballads, songs, and romances, supplied by his friends who, at his request, rummaged in libraries, attics, and warehouses for old manuscripts. The judgment with which the ballads were edited, despite some sacrifice of authenticity to readability, influenced concern for original sources and collation of texts. Publication of the *Reliques* inaugurated the "ballad revival," a flood of collections of ancient songs, that proved a source of inspiration to the Romantic poets. Percy was educated at Christ Church, Oxford, and held livings in Northamptonshire, at Easton Maudit (1753) and Wilby (1756). The *Reliques*, dedicated to the Countess of Northumberland, gained him her patronage, and after editing *The Household Book of the Earl of Northumberland in 1512* (1768), a pioneer work of its kind, he became the Earl's chaplain and secretary. In 1778 he acquired the deanery of Carlisle and in 1782 the Irish bishopric of Dromore. Percy's geniality and scholarly interests made him many friends: Samuel Johnson, who encouraged him to edit the *Reliques* and praised his "minute accuracy of enquiry"; the poet William Shenstone, who shared in its planning; the poet Thomas Warton, who ransacked Oxford libraries for comparative texts. With these and with many others, he discussed, by letter, his work and theirs. He has been called "the most knowledgeable man of his age." Translations from Chinese, Hebrew, Spanish, and Icelandic, and the first English version of the Icelandic *Edda* (from Latin, in *Northern Antiquities*, 1770), show his linguistic ability. Above all, his voluminous correspondence, tireless in seeking and generous and perceptive in offering information and advice, confirms his determined pursuit of factual accuracy and places in context the work for which he is principally remembered.

perdesiekte: *see* African horse sickness.

Perdiccas (b. *c.* 365—d. 321 BC), general under Alexander the Great who became regent of the Macedonian empire after Alexander's death (323). Perdiccas served with distinction in Alexander's campaigns, and upon the King's death led the aristocratic party that supported the claim of the unborn child of Roxana (*q.v.*), Alexander's widow, to the succession. After a compromise under which a division of the powers of regency was arranged, Perdiccas exercised a wide authority in Asia as "supreme general" and soon began to act as if he meant to make himself king. This move was strongly resisted by the regional governors, Ptolemy in Egypt, Antigonus in Phrygia, and by Perdiccas' colleagues in the regency, Craterus and Antipater.

In 322 Perdiccas conquered Cappadocia and installed as satrap his most reliable and efficient subordinate, Eumenes of Cardia. Antigonus fled to Europe, where he persuaded Antipater and Craterus that Perdiccas must be destroyed. Leaving Eumenes to hold Asia Minor against Craterus and Antigonus, Perdiccas marched against Ptolemy, but when he failed to ford the Nile he was murdered by mutinous officers.
·Antigonus I's alliance and conquest **1**:990e
·reign and relation to Philip II **14**:225e
·role in Macedonian growth **8**:366g
·role in succession struggle and death **8**:376f
·Seleucus I military relation **16**:503b

Perdix perdix (bird): *see* partridge.

Père Castor (1932), series of children's stories by Paul Faucher.
·educational picture books **4**:240c

Pereda, José María de (b. Feb. 6, 1833, near Santander—d. March 1, 1906, Santander), Spanish writer, the acknowledged leader of the modern Spanish regional novelists, a realist in the tradition of Cervantes and the picaresque writers. Born of a family noted for its fervent Catholicism and its traditionalism, Pereda looked an authentic hidalgo. His first literary effort was the *Escenas montañesas* (1864), starkly realistic sketches of the fisherfolk of Santander and the peasants of the Montaña. There followed other sketches and early novels of pronounced controversial spirit, such as *El buey suelto* (1878), a counterpart to Balzac's thesis in *Petites misères de la vie conjugale; Don Gonzalo González de la Gonzalera* (1879), a satire on the revolution of 1868 and a eulogy of the old patriarchal system of government; and *De tal palo tal astilla* (1880), a protest by a rigid Catholic against the liberal religious tendencies advocated by Benito Pérez Galdós in his novels *Doña Perfecta* and *Gloria*. Except for *Pedro Sánchez* (1883) and *La Montálvez* (1888), all his novels have a Montaña background.

Pereda's best work, one of the finest Spanish novels of the 19th century, was *Sotileza* (1884), an epic of the Santander fisherfolk and a genuine novel of customs. Sotileza, the haughty and enigmatic fishergirl, is a masterpiece of characterization.

Pereda resembles Thomas Hardy in his regionalism and Dickens in his love for the "good old days," but in his virile realism, tinged with a fund of human sympathy, he is thoroughly Castilian. He was not a good psychologist nor a good storyteller, but he possessed the gift of creating human characters, particularly of the humbler variety, and, with his mastery of rich and flexible language, he excels, above all, as a painter of nature, in all its aspects.

·Spanish literature of the 19th century **10**:1202g

Père David's deer (*Elaphurus davidianus*), large, rare Asian deer, family Cervidae (order Artiodactyla). The only member of its genus, it is unknown in nature within historic times. It was probably native to northern China, but it is now found only in zoos, private animal collections, and game reserves.

Père David's deer (*Elaphurus davidianus*)

P. Morris—W.C.I.

The deer is about 1.1 metres (43 inches) tall at the shoulder and is characterized by heavy legs, broad hooves, relatively small ears, and a long, bushy tail. The coat is reddish brown in summer and uniformly grayish brown in winter. The male has long antlers that fork shortly above the base, the front prong branching once and the rear prong extending backward, unbranched. The only known population of this deer in the 19th century was the herd kept for the emperor of China in a game park near Peking. Observations of the deer were made in 1865 by a French missionary, Armand David, and specimens were classified the following year by the French naturalist Henri Milne-Edwards. From 1869 to 1890, several Père David's deer were brought to European zoos. Most of the Chinese herd died in a flood in 1895, and the remaining deer were killed during the Boxer Rebellion (1900). A breeding population was then established at Woburn Abbey, in England, under the care of the Duke of Bedford. The deer bred well in captivity and now survive in zoos and game parks around the world.

·preservation **2**:71d
·preservation from extinction **6**:1049e

Peredvizhniki, English THE WANDERERS, group of Russian painters who in the second half of the 19th century rejected the restrictive and foreign-inspired classicism of the Russian Academy to form a new realist and nationalist art that would serve the common man. Believing that art should be useful, a vehicle for expressing humanitarian and social ideals, they produced realistic portrayals of inspiring or pathetic subjects from Russian middle class and peasant life in a literal, easily understood style. Forming a Society of Wandering Exhibitions in 1870, they organized mobile exhibitions of their works in an effort to bring serious art to the people.

"The Boyarin Morozova," oil painting by Vasily Surikov, one of the Peredvizhniki, 1887; in the State Tretyakov Gallery, Moscow

Novosti Press Agency

The most prominent Russian artists of the 1870s and 1880s, including Ivan Kramskoy, Ilya Repin, Vasily Surikov, Vasily Perov, and Vasily Vereshchagin, belonged to this group. The movement dominated Russian art for nearly 30 years and was the model for the Socialist Realism of the Soviet Union. *Major ref.* **19**:458f

Peregrinatio Etheriae, English PILGRIMAGE OF ETHERIA, an anonymous and incomplete account of travels in the Middle East, written in Latin by a nun from western Europe for her colleagues at home, near the end of the 4th century. It gives important information about religious life and the observances of the church year in the localities visited, which included the chief holy places of the Old and New Testaments in Egypt, Palestine, and Syria. There is a description of the daily and annual liturgical activities in Jerusalem.

Discovered in 1884 in an 11th-century manuscript at Arezzo, Italy, the account was probably written by a Spanish nun called Etheria (Aetheria, Egeria, Eucheria).

peregrine falcon (*Falco peregrinus*), of the family Falconidae, sometimes called duck hawk in the U.S., occurs worldwide, mainly in coastal regions. Bluish-gray above with underparts white to yellowish with black barring, peregrines range from about 33 to 48 centimetres (13 to 19 inches) long. They are strong and fast, flying high and diving at tremendous speeds, striking with clenched talons and killing by impact. The prey includes ducks and shorebirds. Peregrines inhabit rocky open country near water where birds are plentiful. The usual nest is a mere scrape on a ledge, high on a cliff. The usual clutch is two to four reddish-brown eggs. The young fledge in five or six weeks. The peregrine falcon was the first animal to be listed as endangered in the U.S. and in the late 1970s still had that status.

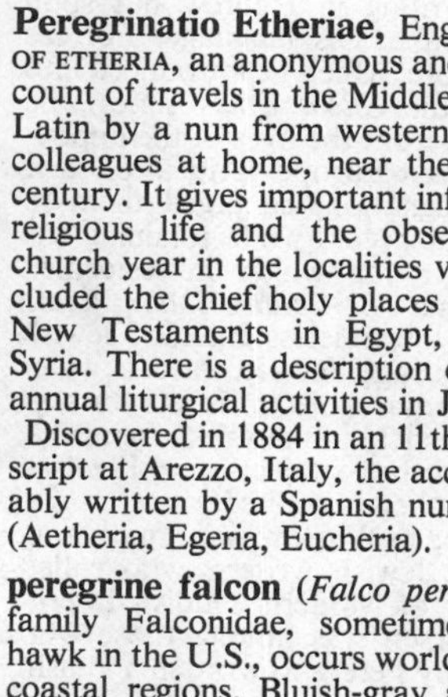

Peregrine falcon (*Falco peregrinus*)

Kenneth W. Fink—Root Resources

·breeding life duration **7**:146d

Peregrinus (pseudonym): *see* Vincent of Lérins, Saint.

peregrinus, plural PEREGRINI, Latin word meaning generally "stranger," or "foreigner," used in Roman law to denote a citizen of a state other than Rome. The word has been anglicized as "peregrine," with the additional meaning of sojourner in any foreign country.

·Roman provincial social differentiation **15**:1109b

Peregrinus de Maricourt, Petrus, French PIERRE LE PÈLERIN DE MARICOURT, also called PETER OF MARICOURT (fl. 13th century), French crusader (his name signifies Peter the Pilgrim from Maricourt) and scholar who rendered the first detailed description of the compass as an instrument of navigation. During the siege of Lucera (in Italy) by Charles of Anjou in August 1269, Peter wrote his letter on the magnet, *Epistola ad Sigerum de Foucaucourt militem de magnete* (commonly known by its short title, *Epistola de magnete*), in which he also wrote of the floating compass as an instrument in common use and described a new pivoted compass in some detail.

The *Epistola* is widely regarded as one of the great works of medieval experimental research and a precursor of modern scientific methodology. Roger Bacon considered Peter to be the greatest experimental scientist of his time, a master of all the technical arts.

·compass documentation and description **4**:1040b
·lodestone experiments and results **6**:540a
·magnetic field discoveries **6**:26h
·magnetism experimental investigation **11**:311c

Peregrinus Proteus (b. AD 100, Parium, in Anatolia—d. 165), Greek Cynic philosopher remembered for his spectacular suicide—he cremated himself on the flames of the Olympic Games in 165. Suspected of murdering his father, he was forced to flee to Palestine, where he became a Christian. His influence in the Christian community led to his arrest. After his release he left Palestine and went to Egypt, where he became a pupil of the Cynic philosopher Agathobulus. He became a wandering preacher and went to Rome and from there to Greece. Lucian, whose account, *Death of Peregrinus*, is the main source of information about Peregrinus, thought of him as an opportunist and exhibitionist.

·Lucian's association and commemoration **11**:173c

Pereira, capital of Risaralda department, west central Colombia, in the western foothills of the Cordillera Central. It was founded in 1863 on the former site of Cartago (*q.v.*) by Remigio Antonio Cañarte and named after Francisco Pereira Gamba, who donated lands for the enterprise. It is a considerable centre for coffee and cattle and has some light manufacturing, mainly textiles. La Laguna del Otún (a fishing and hunting preserve) and El Nevado de Santa Isabel (a ski resort) are nearby. The controversial bronze statue "El Bolívar Desnudo" ("The Naked Bolívar," 1963) by Rodrigo Arenas Betancourt, stands in its own plaza. The cathedral of Nuestra Señora de la Pobreza (Our Lady of the Poor, 1890) and the

Pereira, Colom.
Carl Frank—Photo Researchers

Universidad Tecnológica de Pereira are architectural landmarks. Pop. (1972 est.) city, 221,200; mun., 249,500.
4°49′ N, 75°43′ W
·map, Colombia **4**:866

Pereira, José Maria dos Reis: *see* Régio, José.

Pereira, Nuño Alvares (1360–1431), Portuguese military leader, beatified in 1918 by Pope Benedict XV.
·Portuguese monarchies and wars **14**:867c

Père-Lachaise Cemetery, largest and best known cemetery of Paris.
·Commune fight and famous artists **13**:1018c

Perelman, Chaïm (1912–), Belgian philosopher.
·justice and universalizability **6**:993d

perennial, in botany, a plant that lives for more than two years. The term is usually applied to certain herbaceous (*i.e.*, nonwoody) plants, but all woody plants are also perennials.
·desert root systems and spacing **5**:615e
·fruit production **7**:753h
·life cycle variations in angiosperms **15**:725b
·life-span and life cycle **10**:915e
·plant life-span categories **13**:728d
·responses to cold **5**:959h

perennial stream (hydrology): *see* ephemeral stream.

Pereskia, a cactus genus of about 20 species, family Cactaceae, native to the West Indies, Mexico, Central and South America, especially coastal areas. Known as Barbados or West Indian gooseberry, it is cultivated extensively for hedges, lumber, and its edible fruit. It has large persistent leaves, unlike those of the rest of the family.

P. pititache, the native Mexican species, grows to 10 or 12 metres (about 33 to 40 feet), occasionally 18 metres (about 60 feet). *Pe-*

Pereskia
Werner W. Schulz

reskia may be related to *Phytolacca*, the pokeweed.
·cactus primitive features **3**:575a

Peresvetov, Ivan Semyonovich (fl. 16th century), Russian author and essayist who served in the Muscovite government and advocated the establishment of a strong, centralized autocracy resting upon the support of the lower nobility.

Père Tanquy, Portrait of (1888), painting by Vincent Van Gogh.
·Japanese influence on Van Gogh **8**:232g

Peretti, Felice: *see* Sixtus V.

Peretz, Isaac Leib (b. May 18, 1852, or May 20, 1851, Zamose, Pol.—d. April 3, 1915, Warsaw), prolific writer of poems, short stories, drama, humorous sketches, and satire who was instrumental in raising the standard of Yiddish literature to a high level.

Peretz began writing in Hebrew but soon turned to Yiddish as his language. For his tales of Ḥasidic lore, which he introduced into literature (*e.g.*, the *Silent Souls* series), he drew his material from the lives of the impoverished Jews of east Europe. Critical of their humility and resignation, he urged them to consider temporal needs, while retaining the spiritual grandeur for which he esteemed them. In his drama *The Golden Chain*, Peretz lays stress upon the timeless chain of Jewish culture. To encourage Jews toward a wider knowledge of secular subjects, Peretz for several years wrote articles on physics, chemistry, economics, and other subjects for *Yiddishe Bibliothek*, which he also edited.

The Peretz home in Warsaw was a gathering place for young Jewish writers, who called him the "Father of Modern Yiddish Literature"; Sholem Asch was among those who were persuaded by Peretz to write in Yiddish. During the last ten years of his life, Peretz became the recognized leader of the Yiddishist movement, whose aim—in opposition to the Zionists—was to create a complete cultural and national life for Jewry within the Diaspora with Yiddish as its language.
·contributions to Hebrew literature **10**:1260a
·works, themes, and style **10**:197f

Pereval (The Pass), group of post-Revolutionary Russian writers opposed to the suppression of nonconformist literature and to the concept of enforced writing for the proletariat, ideas that were championed by the Octobrists. They were led by the critic Aleksandr Voronski.

Perey, Marguerite (1909–), French chemist.
·francium discovery **1**:580g

Pereyaslav (PEREJASLAW) **Agreement** (Jan. 18 [Jan. 8, old style], 1654), act undertaken by the *rada* (council) of the Cossack Army in the Ukraine to submit the Ukraine to Russian rule, and the acceptance of this act by emissaries of the Russian tsar Alexis; the agreement precipitated a war between Poland and Russia for control of the Ukraine (1654–67).

The hetman of the Zaporozhie Cossacks, Bohdan Khmelnytsky, had been leading a revolt against Polish rule in the Ukraine since 1648. In October 1653 a Russian *zemsky sobor* ("assembly of the land") approved Khmelnitsky's request that the Tsar form a union between the Ukraine and Russia, and Alexis sent a delegation, headed by V.V. Buturlin, to the Cossacks.

Only after the Cossacks had suffered a disastrous military defeat (December 1653), however, did the *rada* receive the Muscovite delegation at Pereyaslav and formally submit to "the tsar's hand." Two months later (March 1654) the details of the union were negotiated in Moscow. The Cossacks were granted a large degree of autonomy and they, as well as other social groups in the Ukraine, retained all the rights and privileges they had enjoyed under Polish rule. But the unification of the Ukraine with Russia was unacceptable to Poland; a Russo-Polish war (Thirteen Years' War) broke out and ended with the division of the Ukraine between Poland and Russia. *See* Andrusovo, Truce of.
·Alexis Mikhaylovich's conquests **14**:645b

Pereyaslav-Khmelnitsky, town, Kiev *oblast* (administrative region), Ukrainian Soviet Socialist Republic, on the Trubyozh River just above its confluence with the Dnepr. Pereyaslav was first mentioned in 907; in 1654 the Cossacks under Bohdan Khmelnytskiy acknowledged supremacy of the tsars. The small modern town has only local significance. Latest pop. est. 19,000.
50°05′ N, 31°28′ E

Pérez, Antonio (b. 1534, Madrid—d. Nov. 3, 1611, Paris), secretary of Philip II of Spain, who later became a fugitive from Philip's court. Pérez was an illegitimate son of Gonzalo Pérez, secretary of Philip's predecessor, the emperor Charles V. Charming, intelligent, and, through his father, well connected, Pérez quickly rose in Philip's service, becoming the king's secretary (1568) and secretary of several of the royal councils. A long line of historians, dramatists, and novelists have speculated on Pérez's supposed liaison with Doña Ana de Mendoza, the one-eyed princess of Eboli and widow of Philip's favourite, Ruy Gómez de Silva, although it is unlikely that their relationship was more than a political alliance.

The upstart secretary was hated by many of the grandees and by his rivals in the Spanish civil service. The king's favour was unstable, and to safeguard himself, Pérez intrigued with all parties: with Philip II's half brother Don John of Austria and his secretary, Juan de Escovedo, against the king; with the king against Don John; perhaps even with the Netherlands rebels against both. When Don John, then governor-general of the Netherlands, sent Escovedo to Spain in 1577 to plead for his plan to invade England and liberate and marry Mary Stuart, queen of Scots, Pérez feared the exposure of his own intrigues. He persuaded the suspicious king that Escovedo was Don John's evil genius and was plotting treason. The king gave his consent to the murder of Escovedo and Pérez organized his assassination on March 31, 1578.

Philip II never forgave Pérez for having forced his hand. On July 28, 1579, he had Pérez and the princess of Eboli arrested. For eleven years, Pérez remained in prison and all efforts to extract a full confession and all incriminating documents from him failed. In April 1590 he escaped from Madrid to Aragon and placed himself under the protection of the Aragonese courts. Now, for the first time, he accused the king of the murder of Escovedo. Philip thereupon tried to have Pérez handed over to the Inquisition, but the populace of Saragossa twice rioted (May and September 1591) and prevented this move. Philip considered it rebellion and sent a Castilian army into Aragon (October 1591).

Pérez fled to France in November. He spent the remainder of his life at the courts of France and England, carrying on his polemic

against Philip II and contributing to the "black legend" about the king. After Philip II's death (1598), Pérez lost what little influence he had had. He failed to obtain a pardon from Philip III and died in exile. His *Relaciones*, of which there are many editions, was published in 1598.
·Aragon's invasion causes **17**:427b

Pérez, José Joaquín (1800–89), president (1861–71) of Chile.
·liberal–conservative government **4**:256d

Pérez, Manuel Benítez: *see* Cordobés, El.

Pérez de Ayala, Ramón (b. Aug. 9, 1880, Oviedo, Spain—d. Aug. 5, 1962, Madrid), novelist, poet, and critic who was one of the greatest Spanish novelists of the 20th century.
After studying at Jesuit schools in Carrión de los Condes and Gijón, Pérez de Ayala received his law degree from the University of Oviedo, where he was a student of the novelist and critic Leopoldo Alas. During World War I he covered France, Italy, England, South America, and the United States as a correspondent for the Buenos Aires periodical *La prensa*. From 1931 to 1936, he served as the Spanish ambassador to England and afterward voluntarily exiled himself to South America because of the Spanish Civil War (1936–39). He was elected to the Spanish Academy in 1928.
After writing a volume of poetry, *La paz del sendero* (1904; The Peace of the Path"), he produced a series of four novels, *Tinieblas en las cumbres* (1907; "Darkness at the Top"), *AMDG* (1910; *i.e.*, the Jesuit motto "Ad Majorem Dei Gloriam," or "To the Greater Glory of God"), *La Pata de la raposa* (1912; "The Foot of the Fox"), and *Troteras y danzaderas* (1913; "Trotters and Dancers"), dealing with an adolescent's awakening to life. These four novels are in large part autobiographical and somewhat obscured by his rather bitter realism; *AMDG*, for instance, is based upon his painful experiences in Jesuit schools. His *Tres Novelas Poematicas de la vida Española* (1916; "Three Poematic Novellas of Spanish Life"), entitled "Prometeo" ("Prometheus"), "Luz del domingo" ("Light of Sunday"), and "La caida de los limones" ("The Decline of the Lemons"), deal with disillusion and are still marked by the pessimism of his earlier work. His later novels, considered his masterpieces, show a more mature nature. In *Belarmino y Apolonio* (1921; Eng. trans., *Belarmino and Apolonio*, 1971), *Tigre Juan* (1926; "Tiger Juan"), and its sequel, *El curandero de su honra* (1926; "The Honour of The Quack"), he created characters of a more universal nature and gave freer expression to his delightful and wry humour.
Although best known for his novels, Pérez de Ayala also wrote a number of other books: *El sendero innumerable* (1916; "The Innumerable Road") and *El sendero andate* (1921; "Walk the Road"), two volumes of poetry; *Bajo el signo de artemisa* (1924; "Under the Sign of the Mug-Wort") and *El ombligo del mundo* (1924; "The Navel of the World"), collections of short stories; and *Las macares* (1917; "The Masqueraders"), essays on drama.
·novel development and themes **10**:1239d

Pérez de Guzmán, Fernán (b. *c.* 1378—d. *c.* 1460), poet, moralist, and historian, author of the first important work on history and historiography in Spanish, whose historical portraits of his contemporaries have earned him the title of the "Spanish Plutarch."
A member of a distinguished family, a nephew of the poet and historian Pedro López de Ayala, and the uncle of the poet the Marqués de Santillana, Pérez de Guzmán devoted himself to letters after being imprisoned by Alvaro de Luna, a counsellor to King John II of Castile. Although his poetry went through many editions, it is not as a poet that he is chiefly remembered. His fame rests on his *Mar de historias* (1512), a collection of biographies of emperors, philosophers, and saints, and primarily on the third part of this collection, which contains historical portraits of 33 prominent men (and one woman) from the reigns of Henry III to John II (the period 1390 to 1454). He knew many of the people he described, and although the portraits are based on rhetorical models, the prose is clear, economical, and precise, capturing a man's personality in a few pages.
Equally important is the preface to the third part of the *Mar*, in which Pérez de Guzmán does for history what his nephew Santillana did for poetry by providing the first examination in Spanish of the theory of history and the responsibility of the historian, concerning himself with the problems of historical accuracy, the proper prose for a historian, and with the problem of fame as a moral force in history.

Pérez de Hita, Ginés (1544?–?1619), Spanish writer, author of *Historia de los vandos de los Zegries y Abencerrages . . .* (1595–1619), the first Spanish historical novel and the last important collection of Moorish border ballads, the latter punctuating the book's narrative.

Pérez Galdós, Benito (b. May 10, 1843, Las Palmas, Canary Islands—d. Jan. 4, 1920, Madrid), considered by some critics the greatest Spanish novelist since Cervantes. A political and religious liberal who decried the stifling of Spanish intellectual life and the hypocrisies of the ubiquitous and powerful clergy, he thought in national rather than regional terms, although his best work reflected his intimate knowledge of Madrid.
Forsaking the study of law for journalism, Galdós early began to earn his livelihood by writing. His first novel, *La fontana de oro* (1870; "The Fountain of Gold"), along with others of his early works, reflected lines of political thought already evident in his journalism. He began to write a very personal type of historical novel, his *Episodios nacionales*, in 1873. The first series covered Spanish history during the Napoleonic wars, a period neglected by Spanish historians but seen by Galdós as an explanation for the Spain of the 1870s. He perfected a unique mixture of authenticity and fiction in two series of 10 novels each. His contemporary novels, beginning with *Doña Perfecta* (1876), continued the tendentious trends of his earlier works and often had strong theses, but he portrayed Spanish society with great sympathy and insight.

Pérez Galdós, detail of an oil painting by Joaquín Sorolla y Bastida (1863–1923)
By courtesy of the Hispanic Society of America

Galdós knew the works of his European contemporaries. The influence of the literary currents and styles of the day may be seen, for example, in the naturalism of *Lo prohibido* (1884–85) and in his masterpiece, *Fortunata y Jacinta* (4 vols., 1886–87).
In his later novels his fondness for contemporary life and an honest appraisal of it did not stop him from questioning and searching. *Nazarín* (1895) has a Christ-like protagonist, and the central figure of *Misericordia* (1897) is an expression of Galdós' religious humanity. Some of the works Galdós wrote for the theatre were immensely popular, but their success was largely attributable to the political views he presented rather than to their artistic value. His successes were unfortunately matched with equally egregious failures. He began a third series of the *Episodios nacionales* in 1898 and eventually went on to write a fourth and even to start a fifth. His last years showed a decline in mental powers compounded by the blindness that overtook him in 1912.
·Spanish literature of the 19th century **10**:1202h

Pérez Jiménez, Marcos (b. April 25, 1914, Michelena, Venezuela), professional soldier and president of Venezuela whose regime was marked by extravagance, corruption, police oppression, and mounting unemployment.

Pérez Jiménez, 1955
By courtesy of the Library of Congress, Washington, D.C.

A graduate of the Venezuelan Military Academy, Pérez Jiménez began his political career in 1944, participating in the coups d'etat of October 1945 and November 1948. After the second coup he served as a member of the military junta that ruled Venezuela. In December 1952 he became provisional president by designation of the armed forces—an appointment confirmed by the constituent assembly of 1953, which, under his control, elected him to a five-year presidential term (1953–58).
Financed by income from oil royalties, Pérez Jiménez began a vast program of public works, including the construction of highways, hotels, office buildings, factories, and dams. Pérez Jiménez and his associates received a commission from every project. The ubiquitous secret police, the closing of the university, the silencing of the press, rampant inflation, and the jailing of five priests led the church to ally itself with the opposition parties, the dissatisfied workers, and younger military men who felt excluded from the rewards of the administration. After being forced out of office in January 1958, Pérez Jiménez fled to the U.S., reportedly taking with him approximately $200,000,000.
In 1963 Pérez Jiménez was extradited by the U.S. to stand trial for embezzlement of government funds. After serving five years in jail, he was released and went to Spain in August 1968. Elected to the Senate in 1969 *in absentia*, his election was annulled on the grounds that he was not a registered voter in Venezuela. In March 1972 in Madrid he announced his candidacy for president in the forthcoming elections. He returned once more to Caracas in May 1972, but his visit prompted riots in the city, and he returned to Spain again, vowing to continue his candidacy.
·military power and revolt provocation **9**:756h
·Venezuela's liberal majority crushed **19**:70c

perfect gas (physics): *see* gas, perfect.

perfecting machine, OR PERFECTING PRESS, in printing, a double press invented 1818 in

which a sheet of paper is printed on both sides at the same time.
·invention and modification **14**:1055f

perfection, one of the principal notions associated with freedom, notably by Plato and later dialecticians. In general, a philosophical theory that assumes the possibility of knowledge concerning goods that transcend experience finds freedom or perfection in activity done in accordance with those ideals.
·Christian doctrinal conception **4**:490b
·Christian doctrine of progress **4**:488d
·Christian monastic tradition **4**:500d
·Eastern Orthodox humanistic conception **6**:144a *passim* to 145f
·Hindu paths to salvation **8**:889h
·Holiness sanctification doctrine and Wesley **8**:993h *passim* to 995f
·Jaina doctrine of soul and karmic matter **10**:10b
·Luther's concept of salvation as gift **11**:190a
·Mencius on man's innate potential **4**:1093g
·messianistic theme of primal return **11**:1021a
·mokṣa in Indian philosophy **9**:313h
·monastic quest through meditation **12**:336e
·mystical goals and methods **12**:788c
·Paradise and subsequent corruption **16**:201b
·Plato and Aristotle in contrast **14**:254b *passim* to 255b
·Plato's theory of Forms **1**:156c
·postmortem and antemortem salvation **15**:593e
·Protestant justificational criticism **4**:461d
·Sikh path to liberation from saṃsāra **16**:746f
·Ṣūfī principles of purification **9**:945b
·Taoist achievement methods **17**:1053e
·Taoist ideal of the perfect man **17**:1038a

Perfectionists (religious group): *see* Oneida Community.

perfections, Buddhist: *see* pāramitās.

perfective aspect, in grammar, the verb form or forms used to express a single, completed occurrence of a process or action; *e.g.,* "stand up" as opposed to "keep standing up" (imperfective aspect) and "be in a standing position" (stative aspect).
·Indo-European pattern and developments **9**:435d

Perfect Liberty Kyōdan: *see* PL Kyōdan.

perfect number, natural number equal in value to the sum of those natural numbers less than the given number that also divide (with zero remainder) the given number. Thus 6 is the first perfect number, for it is the sum of 1, 2, and 3. There are 24 perfect numbers known. (Computers have been used in the search for perfect numbers.) Although every known perfect number is even, the question of the existence of odd perfect numbers remains an unsolved problem.
·number theory and Mersenne numbers **13**:349f
·number theory principles **13**:358h

per fess, also called PARTY PER FESS, in heraldry, division of the field of a shield into two equal parts by a horizontal line.
·heraldic shield design **8**:788e; illus. 789

perforator, in petroleum extraction, a device resembling a gun for puncturing an oil-well casing at the oil stratum.
·oil well perforation techniques **14**:178h

performance, in law, act of doing that which is required by a contract. The effect of successful performance is to discharge the person bound to do the act from any future contractual liability.

Each party to the contract is bound to perform his promise according to the stipulated terms. In case of any controversy as to the meaning of his promise, the courts have usually decided that he must perform it as the other party reasonably understood it to be. Thus, a preference for the rights of the one who is to receive the benefit of the promise is established.

Attempts to establish hard and fast rules about reasonable interpretations of promises are now discouraged. Although at one time a person would be held to the literal meaning of the contract provisions stating his promise, he is now required to perform the true meaning and intent of the contract, which may not correspond with the fine print. *Major ref.* **5**:127b
·contracts and choice of law **4**:1088e

performance test, in applied psychology, test requiring minimal verbal and maximal motor response; *e.g.,* intelligence tests using a form board, maze, or picture completion.
·test administration and scoring **11**:737c

perfume, product that results from the blending of certain odoriferous substances in appropriate proportions, producing a fragrance pleasing to the sense of smell. The word is derived from the Latin *per fumum,* meaning "through smoke." The art of perfumery was apparently known to the ancient Chinese, Hindus, Egyptians, Israelites, Carthaginians, Arabs, Greeks, and Romans. References to perfumery materials and even perfume formulas are found in the Bible.

Raw materials used in perfumery include natural products, of plant or animal origin, and synthetic materials. Essential oils (*q.v.*), obtained from plant materials, are most often produced by steam distillation, employing a mixture of the plant material and water. Certain delicate oils may be obtained by solvent extraction, a gentle process employing such solvents as petroleum derivatives. This method is also employed to extract waxes and perfume oil, yielding a solid substance called a concrete. Treatment with a second substance, usually alcohol, provides the concentrated flower oil called an absolute. In the extraction method called enfleurage, petals are placed between layers of purified animal fat, which become saturated with flower oil, and alcohol is then used to obtain the absolute. The expression method, used to recover citrus oils from fruit peels, ranges from a traditional procedure of pressing with sponges to mechanical maceration. Specific chemicals used in perfumery may be isolated from the essential oils, usually by distillation, and may sometimes be reprocessed to obtain still other perfumery chemicals.

Certain animal secretions contain odoriferous substances that increase the diffusion and lasting qualities of perfumes. Such substances and some of their constituents act as fixatives, preventing more volatile perfume ingredients from evaporating rapidly. They are usually employed in the form of alcoholic solutions. The animal products include ambergris from the sperm whale, castor (also called castoreum) from the beaver, civet from the civet cat, and musk from the musk deer.

Odour characteristics ranging from floral effects to odours unknown in nature are available with the use of synthetics, man-made aromatic materials built by the combination of chemicals.

Fine perfumes may contain more than 100 ingredients. Each perfume is composed of a top note, the refreshing, volatile odour perceived immediately; a middle note, or modifier, providing full, solid character; and a base note, also called an end note or basic note, which is the most persistent. Perfumes can generally be classified according to one or more identifiable dominant odours. The floral group blends such odours as jasmine, rose, lily of the valley, and gardenia. The spicy blends feature such aromas as carnation, clove, cinnamon, and nutmeg. The woody group is characterized by such odours as vetiver (derived from an aromatic grass called vetiver, or khuskhus), sandalwood, and cedarwood. The mossy family is dominated by an aroma of oak moss. The group known as the Orientals combines woody, mossy, and spicy notes with such sweet odours as vanilla or balsam and is usually accentuated by animal odours such as musk or civet. The herbal group is characterized by such odours as clover and sweet grass. The leather and tobacco group features the aromas of leather, tobacco, and the smokiness of birch tar. The aldehydic group is dominated by odours of aromatic chemicals (aldehydes), usually having a fruity character. Fragrances designed for men are generally classified as citrus, spice, leather, lavender, fern, or woody.

Perfumes designed to be worn are usually in the form of alcoholic solutions. The solutions generally known as perfumes, also called extraits, extracts, or handkerchief perfumes, contain about 10–25 percent perfume concentrates. The terms toilet water and cologne are generally used interchangeably, with such products containing about 2–6 percent perfume concentrate. Originally, eau de cologne was a mixture of citrus oils from such fruits as lemons and oranges, combined with such substances as lavender and neroli (orange-flower oil); toilet waters were less concentrated forms of other types of perfume. Aftershave lotions and splash colognes usually contain about 0.5–2 percent perfume oil. Recent developments include aerosol sprays and highly concentrated bath oils, sometimes called skin perfumes.

Special problems occur in the formulation of perfumes employed to scent soaps, talcums, face powders, deodorants and antiperspirants, and other cosmetic products. The perfume odour may be changed or become unstable in the new medium, or the perfume may change the colour or consistency of the product.

Industrial perfumes are employed to cover up undesirable odours, as in paints and cleaning materials, or to impart a distinctive odour, as in the addition of leather odours to plastics used for furniture coverings and the addition of bread odours to wrapping papers used for breads.
·alcohol odours and fragrances **1**:452g
·civet musk collection and use **3**:935b
·Cologne as production centre **4**:863c
·Dipsacales spikenard importance **5**:816c
·French essence derivation **7**:596d
·grass order aromatic compounds **14**:586c
·ingredients and preparation **5**:197h
·isoprenoid isolation from natural sources **9**:1046a
·Laurales economic importance **10**:709c
·Magnoliales commercial uses **11**:341d *passim* to 342d
·sandal oil's use in fixing fragrances **16**:227d

perfume bottle, a vessel made to hold scent. The earliest example is Egyptian and dates to

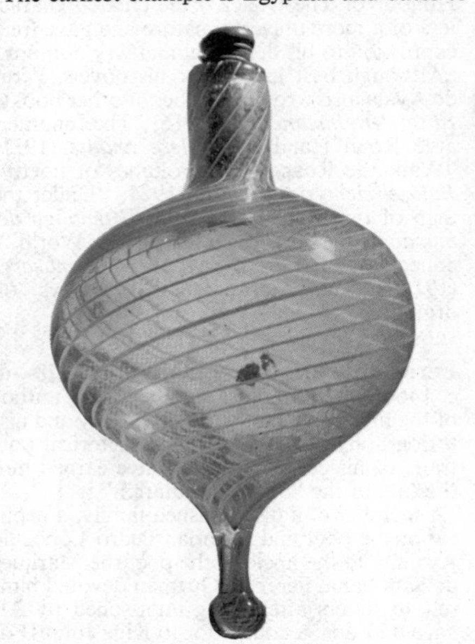

Venetian glass perfume bottle, 16th–17th century; in the Museo Vetrario di Murano, Murano, Italy
electa editrice—Milano

around 1000 BC. The Egyptians used scents lavishly, especially in religious rites; as a result, when they invented glass, it was largely used for perfume vessels. The fashion for perfume spread to Greece, where containers, most of which were of terra-cotta or glass, were made in a variety of shapes and forms such as sandalled feet, birds, animals, and human heads. The Romans, who thought perfumes were aphrodisiacs, used not only molded glass bottles but also blown glass, after its invention at the end of the 1st century BC by Syrian glassmakers. The fashion for perfume declined somewhat with the beginning of Christianity, coinciding with the deterioration of glassmaking.

By the 12th century Philippe-Auguste of France had passed a statute forming the first guild of *parfumeurs*, and by the 13th century Venetian glassmaking had become well established. The perfume bottles produced in Venice were of fine quality, often in various colours simulating precious stones. In the 16th, 17th, and particularly the 18th century, the scent bottle assumed varied and elaborate forms: they were made in gold, silver, copper, glass, porcelain, enamel, or any combination of these materials; 18th-century porcelain perfume bottles were shaped like cats, birds, clowns, and the like; and the varied subject matter of painted enamel bottles included pastoral scenes, chinoiseries, fruits, and flowers.

By the 19th century, classical designs, such as those created by the English pottery ware maker Josiah Wedgwood, came into fashion; but the crafts connected with perfume bottles had deteriorated, and people started collecting old ones.

Perfumes, River of, Vietnamese SONG HUONG, South Vietnam, flows past the city of Hue.
16°33′ N, 107°38′ E
·South Vietnam's urban geography **19**:139c

perfume tree: *see* ylang-ylang.

perfusion, natural flow of fluid through living tissues; also the introduction of fluids into the body for therapeutic purposes.
·blood flow in lung **2**:1133b

Perga, Greek PERGE, modern İHSANIYE, formerly MURTUNA, OR MUITANA, ancient city of Pamphylia, now in Antalya *il* (province), Turkey. It was a centre of native culture and was a seat of the worship of "Queen" Artemis, a purely Anatolian nature goddess.

In Perga the apostles Paul and Barnabus began their first mission in Anatolia (Acts 13:13). A difficult mountain route into Phrygia began at Perga, and Alexander the Great used it for his invasion of the interior. Long the chief city of the district of Pamphylia Secunda, Perga was superseded in Byzantine times by its port, Attaleia. The most notable remains at Perga include a theatre, a stadium, two basilicas, and the agora. Latest census 491.
36°59′ N, 30°48′ E

Pergamino, city, capital of the *partido* of Pergamino, northern Buenos Aires province, Argentina, on a branch of the Río Arrecifes. On the road between Buenos Aires and Córdoba, it was first mentioned in 1626 as an unpopulated spot where a group of Spaniards lost some parchment documents (*pergaminos*). It was settled and became a municipality in 1784.

Collections housed in Pergamino's Museo Pampeano, a national history museum, recall the community's role in the battles of Cepeda (1820); Las Palmitas, the first reaction against dictator Juan Manuel de Rosas, 1829; and Cepeda (1859).

Located at the hub of rail and road networks, including the Pan-American Highway, the city has developed a diverse economy including the processing and distribution of agricultural produce and the manufacture of furniture, metals, and textiles. Pop. (1970 prelim.) 46,557.
33°53′ S, 60°36′ W
·map, Argentina **1**:1136

Pergamum, Greek PERGAMON, modern BERGAMA, in the *il* of Izmir, Tur., an ancient Greek city in Mysia situated 16 miles from the Aegean Sea on a lofty isolated hill on the north side of the broad valley of the Caicus (modern Bakir) River. Pergamum existed at least from the 5th century BC, but it became important only in the Hellenistic Age (323–330 BC), when it served as the residence of the Attalid dynasty. Their fortress and palace stood on the peak of the hill, while the town itself occupied the lower slopes. Under the Roman Empire the city was situated on the plain below.

It had formal autonomy under the Attalids, who, however, interfered in most aspects of civic government. Initially they ruled Pergamum as vassals of the Seleucid Kingdom, but Eumenes I declared himself independent of Antiochus I (263 BC); his nephew and successor, Attalus I (from whom the dynasty received its name), defeated the Galatians and assumed the royal title (241 BC). The original Attalid territory around Pergamum (Mysia) was greatly expanded by 188 BC with the addition of Lydia (excluding most Greek coastal cities), part of Phrygia, Lycaonia, and Pisidia (from 183 BC), all former Seleucid territories. This expansion was accomplished as the result of Eumenes II's alliance with Rome in its conflict with the Seleucid Antiochus III.

When Eumenes' son and second successor, Attalus III, died without an heir, he bequeathed the kingdom to Rome (133). Rome accepted it and set up the province of Asia (129), which included Ionia and the territory of Pergamum, but left the other regions to neighbouring kings, clients of Rome. The kingdom of Pergamum yielded much wealth, especially in agricultural surpluses and silver, first to the Attalid rulers and later to Rome.

The Attalids made the city of Pergamum one of the most important and beautiful of all Greek cities in the Hellenistic Age; it is one of the most outstanding examples of city planning in that period. They built a library excelled only by that at Alexandria, Egypt. The kings after Attalus I collected many works of art from Greece to adorn the city's temples and courtyards, supplementing the many works of sculpture, painting, and decoration commissioned from resident artists. In Roman times, its population was an estimated 200,000. Excavations begun in 1878 under the auspices of the Berlin Museum besides unearthing many artistic treasures have enabled archaeologists to reconstruct the plan of the most important areas of the Hellenistic city. Its monuments included a theatre; the temple to Athena Nicephorus; the great altar of Zeus with its richly decorated frieze, a masterpiece of Hellenistic art. A part of the altar and its surviving reliefs, restored and mounted, now stands in the Pergamon Museum in East Berlin.

The civic structures of the lower city included a large marketplace, a gymnasium, and temples of Hera and Demeter. Roman remains include an amphitheatre, a theatre, and a racetrack. The early Attalids erected the first structures of the upper (royal) city, but the later kings Eumenes II and Attalus III, by their extensive building and rebuilding, were chiefly responsible for the city's great architectural and artistic reputation. After the fall of Rome, Pergamum was ruled by the Byzantines until it passed into Ottoman hands early in the 14th century.
·Anatolian overthrow of Seleucid rule **1**:824h
·ancient water-supply system **19**:648h
·Antiochus III territorial conflicts **1**:993g
·aqueducts of pre-Roman times **1**:1036b
·calligraphic codex form invention **3**:646e
·developments under Hellenistic rule **8**:380e
·Hellenistic libraries **3**:1084e
·Hellenistic sculpture styles **19**:298c; illus.
·humanistic scholarship's development **8**:1172c
·library history and function **10**:857b
·map, Turkey **18**:784
·mosaic art development **12**:466g
·Neoplatonism after Iamblichus **14**:542d
·theatre site, construction, and use **18**:237d

Pergamum altar, Hellenistic altar to Zeus erected between 180 and 160 BC on the acropolis at Pergamum (modern Bergama, Turkey) in commemoration of the victory of Attalus I over the Gauls. The altar is today part of the Staatliche collections in East Berlin and is housed in the Pergamon Museum.

Pergidae, family of sawflies, order Hymenoptera.
·characteristics and classification **9**:132b

pergola, a garden walk or terrace, roofed with an open framework over which plants are trained. Its purpose is to provide a foundation on which climbing plants can be seen to advantage and to give shade. It was known in ancient Egypt and was a common feature of early Renaissance gardens in Italy and subsequently throughout Europe. Pergolas have always been popular in hot climates, and in Mediterranean countries they are frequently covered with vines or ivy. In more northerly

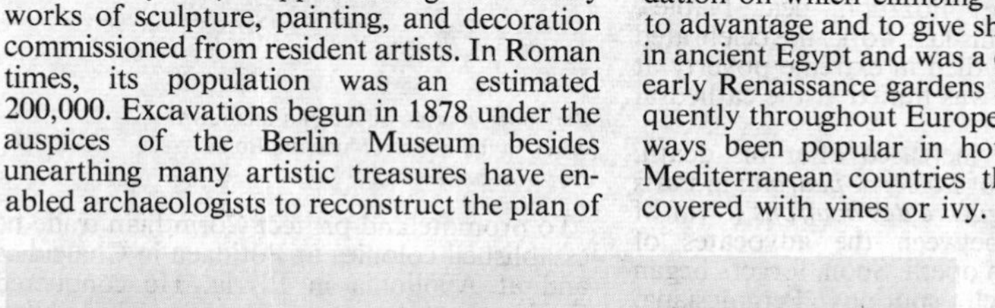

The Greek theatre and part of the terrace in the upper city, Pergamum
By courtesy of Staatliche Museen Preussischer Kulturbesitz, Antikenabteilung, Berlin

Vine covered pergola, wood engraved illustration from Francesco Colonna, the *Hypnerotomachia Poliphili,* Venice, 1499; in the New York Public Library

By courtesy of the New York Public Library, Spencer Collection, Astor, Lennox and Tilden Foundations

countries, where shade is less attractive, they are less common; but they had a marked revival in Great Britain in the early 20th century for the purpose of growing wisteria.

Pergolesi, Giovanni Battista (b. Jan. 4, 1710, Jesi, Italy—d. March 16, 1736, Pozzuoli), composer whose intermezzo *La serva padrona* was one of the most celebrated stage works of the 18th century. His family name was Draghi but having moved to Jesi from Pergola, the family was called Pergolesi, meaning "of Pergola." From 1726 he attended the Conservatorio dei Poveri at Naples, where he earned a high reputation as a violinist. In 1732 he was appointed *maestro di cappella* to the prince of Stigliano at Naples and produced a Neapolitan opera buffa, *Lo frate innammorato*, and a mass (probably his *Mass in F*). Both were well received. In 1733, his opera seria *Il prigionier superbo* was produced. But it was the comic intermezzo *La serva padrona*, inserted between the acts, which achieved success. In 1734 Pergolesi was appointed deputy *maestro di cappella* of Naples, and in May he went to Rome to direct the performance of his *Mass in F*. His subsequent operas met with only occasional success. His health began to fail and in 1736 he left Naples for the Capuchin monastery at Pozzuoli, near Naples, where he finished his last work, the celebrated *Stabat Mater*. He died in extreme poverty at the age of 26 and was buried at the cathedral at Pozzuoli.

Pergolesi's fame increased after his death. The performance of *La serva padrona* in Paris (1752) led to the *guerre des bouffons* ("war of the buffoons") between the advocates of French and Italian opera. Soon, forgers began to produce much spurious Pergolesiana. Among the works of doubtful authenticity ascribed to Pergolesi are the instrumental works used by Stravinsky for his ballet *Pulcinella*, produced in 1920.

Pergolesi's serious style is best illustrated in his *Stabat Mater* and his masses, which demonstrate his ability to handle large choral and instrumental forces.

Perhimpunan Indonesia, English INDONESIAN UNION, an Indonesian students' organization in The Netherlands, formed in the early 1920s, which provided a source of intellectual leadership for the Indonesian nationalist movement. This association originated in 1908 as the Indische Vereeniging (Indies Association), which changed its name to the Indonesische Vereeniging (Indonesian Association) in 1922 as Indonesian nationalism developed. It became known as the Perhimpunan Indonesia in 1924 and was the vanguard of the Indonesian nationalist movement. It advocated national independence, from the Dutch, for Indonesia.

The Perhimpunan Indonesia was the first political organization to use the term Indonesia in its name. It was influenced by socialist ideas and by Gandhi's non-cooperative principle. When the members of this association returned to Indonesia, they were active in study clubs and eventually in political parties. Two prominent figures were Sutan Sjahrir and Mohammad Hatta.

·Sukarno and emerging nationalism **9**:488c

Peri, Jacopo (1561–1633), Florentine singer and the composer of what was probably the first opera, *Dafne* (performed *c.* 1594), a setting of Ottavio Rinuccini's pastoral play.

periaktoi (Greek: "revolving"), ancient theatrical device by which a scene or change of scene was indicated. It was described by Vitruvius in his *De architectura* (*c.* 14 BC) as a revolving triangular prism made of wood, bearing on each of its three sides a different pictured scene. While one scene was presented to the audience, the other two could be changed. Although it was once thought to be a feature of Greek classical drama, it is now believed that it did not originate until the Hellenistic age. The *periaktoi* was revived, notably for the Italian theatre *c.* 1500 and for the 17th-century English stage.

·stage conventions of Greek drama **17**:531d

Periander (d. 586 BC), second tyrant of Corinth, *c.* 627–586, a firm and effective ruler who developed his city's commercial and cultural potential. Reckoned as one of the Seven Wise Men of Greece, he was the supposed author of a collection of maxims in 2,000 verses. Much of the ancient Greek representation of Periander as a cruel despot probably derives from the Corinthian nobility, with whom he dealt harshly.

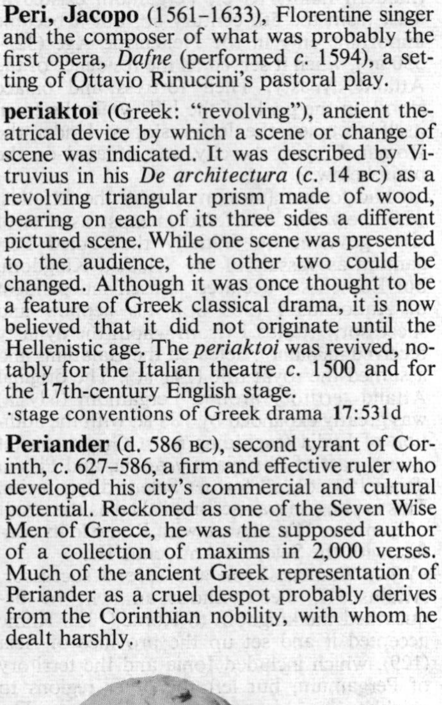

Periander, marble bust by an unknown artist; in the Vatican Museum, Rome

The Mansell Collection

To promote and protect Corinthian trade he established colonies at Potidaea in Chalcidice and at Apollonia in Illyria. He conquered Epidaurus and annexed Corcyra. The *diolkos* ("portage way") across the Isthmus of Corinth was perhaps built during his reign. It appears that the commercial prosperity of Periander's Corinth became so great that the tolls on goods entering her ports accounted for almost all government revenues. Periander cultivated friendly relations with Thrasybulus, tyrant of Miletus, and maintained ties with the kings of Lydia and Egypt. In the cultural sphere he was a patron of art—as evidenced by architectural ruins from this period—and of literature; by his invitation the poet Arion came to the city from Lesbos.

·life and accomplishments **8**:336h

perianth, in botany, the outer part of a flower including the sepals (the outer circle of leaflike scales at the base of a flower) and the petals (corolla), which enclose the reproductive organs of a plant.

·Euphorbiales flower structure **6**:1029c
·Fagales flower development **7**:141h
·reproductive systems in angiosperms **15**:722c

periarteritis nodosa (medicine): *see* polyarteritis nodosa.

periastron, in astronomy, the point nearest a star in an orbit around the star. *Cf.* apastron; *see also* apse.

Peribsen (reigned *c.* 2675 BC), Egyptian king of the 2nd dynasty, who promoted the cult of the god Seth over that of Horus, the god favoured by his predecessors. His tomb was located in Seth's district in Upper Egypt, at Abydos. According to some scholars, Peribsen's ascendancy was accompanied by a violent reaction against the supporters of Horus, but the supremacy of Horus was restored after his death.

pericardial cavity, the cavity that can develop between the epicardium and the other layers of the pericardium (*q.v.*), which is the sac enclosing the heart.

·origins and membranous partitions **6**:753b
·vertebrate heart embryology **4**:631c

pericardial fluid, fluid exuded by membranes of the pericardium, the sac that encloses the heart.

·excesses in inflammatory state **3**:892g
·human cardiovascular system anatomy **3**:876b

pericardial organ, in biology, in decapods (shrimps, lobsters, and crabs), the network of nerve fibres in the sides of the pericardium, from which a hormone is secreted that increases the rate of the heartbeat; the pericardium is the sac that encloses the heart.

·crustacean neurohormonal influence **6**:846g; illus.
·decapod neurohormone secretion **8**:1086c

pericardial tamponade (medicine): *see* cardiac tamponade.

pericarditis, inflammation of the pericardium, the membranous sac that encloses the heart. Acute pericarditis may be associated with any of a number of diseases and conditions, including myocardial infarction (death of a section of heart muscle), uremia (abnormally high levels of urea and other nitrogenous waste products in the blood), allergic disorders, and infections. The infection may be syphilis, rheumatic heart disease, or some other bacterial infection. It may be viral or protozoal; the protozoal organism that causes amebic dysentery, for example, may escape from a liver abscess and invade the pericardium. The infection, finally, may be fungal—infection, for example, with *Histoplasma capsulatum*.

A person with infectious pericarditis experiences pain over the heart and stomach. The pain is sometimes increased during breathing and is relieved by leaning forward. Lying down may accentuate the pain, which may radiate to the left arm, the shoulder, and the neck. The affected person may experience difficulty in breathing and may be weak, anxious, and depressed. His skin may be pale or bluish, and he may be feverish and delirious. The heart and chest sounds and tracings of the heart's electrical activity are characteristic.

Fluid sufficient to interfere with heart action may accumulate in the pericardium. In treatment the accumulation of fluid in the pericardium, called cardiac tamponade, is relieved by drainage of the fluid, and the underlying infection is combatted.

Acute pericarditis may result in the formation of scar tissue that contracts around the heart and interferes with its operation. This condition, called chronic constrictive pericarditis, is corrected by surgical removal of the pericardium.

·acute pericarditis' causes **3**:892g
·causation, symptoms, and treatment **4**:226b
·surgical treatment of chronic constrictive pericarditis **3**:896g

pericardium, the sac that encloses the heart. The sac has two components, a tough outer covering, the fibrous pericardium, and a double inner lining, the serous (moisture-exuding) pericardium. The fibrous pericardium is attached to the inner surface of the breastbone and, at its base, to the muscle fibres and fibrous sheet (the latter is called the central tendon) of the diaphragm, the partition of muscle and membrane that separates the chest and abdominal cavities. The inner layer of the serous pericardium covers the heart, while the outer layer lines the fibrous pericardium. The inferior vena cava, which returns blood to the heart from the lower half of the body, passes through the fibrous pericardium on its way to the heart.

·bivalve circulatory system **2**:1090a; illus.
·cardiac tamponade relation to shock **16**:699h
·cavities of the thorax **2**:1178g
·congenital absence **3**:887e
·embryonic development of vertebrates **5**:636g; illus.
·excretory mechanism of mollusks **7**:47d; illus. 46
·human cardiovascular system anatomy **3**:876a; illus.
·inflammatory diseases processes **3**:892f
·spider circulatory system **1**:1071b; illus. 1070
·surgery of Rehn and Sauerbruch **11**:840c

pericarp, in seed plants, the wall of the matured ovary or fruit. The wall is sometimes thin, as in the pea, but more commonly is composed of three layers: the outer (exocarp), middle (mesocarp), and inner (endocarp) layers. Pericarp tissues may be fleshy, fibrous or stony.

·fruit features and types **16**:481f; table and illus. 482
·palm seeds and ovary walls **1**:1133f

pericentre (astronomy): *see* apse.

perichondritis, inflammation of the perichondrium, the membrane that covers the cartilage of the outer ear. Perichondritis is unusual, but it may result from swimming in contaminated water or from some injury. Perichondritis may also follow a major operation such as radical mastoidectomy, or it may occur as a complication of cauliflower ear. The symptoms include a foul-smelling, greenish-brown discharge from the outer ear canal, tenderness, redness, and a thickening of the outer ear. Permanent deformity can result if the condition is not treated promptly by a physician.

·cause, symptoms, and treatment for ear **5**:1133g

perichondrium, layer of white fibrous tissue that covers a cartilage.

·bone formation mechanisms **16**:829c
·connective tissue growth and matrix secretion **5**:16c

periclase, magnesium oxide mineral (MgO) that occurs as colourless to grayish, glassy, rounded grains; it is a high-temperature metamorphic mineral in marble and in some dolomitic limestones. Occurrences include Monte Somma and Predazzo, Italy; Nordmark and Långban, Swed.; and Crestmore, Calif. For detailed physical properties, *see* table under oxide minerals.

·Earth's mantle mineralogy **16**:764d
·formula and metamorphic occurrence **12**:6h; table 5
·marble and possible mantle occurrence **12**:237a

Pericles 14:68 (b. *c.* 495 BC, Athens—d. 429 BC, Athens), statesman who brought ancient Athenian democracy to its height and nearly established Athens as the leading power in Greece.

Abstract of text biography. Pericles was born into a wealthy Athenian family at the time when the popular vote was first in use as a political weapon. During his early career he saw the cessation of war with other Greek states (451) and Persia (450). Pericles embarked upon a program designed to make Athens the political and cultural focus of Greece. His achievements included the construction of the Acropolis, begun in 447. Pericles was deposed as Athens' general during the war against Sparta in 431 but was returned to office shortly before his death in 429.

REFERENCES in other text articles:
·Cimon's political popularity decline **4**:617g
·Peloponnesian War leadership and strategy **14**:20g
·Socrates in Periclean circle **16**:1001f
·Sophist aid and patronage **17**:11d
·Thucydides' historical evaluation **18**:359h
·views, career, and importance **8**:355d
·visual art of Classical Greece **19**:293g

Pericles, dramatic romance written by Shakespeare, probably first in 1608/09. This version of the widely known medieval story of Apollonius of Tyre (in this instance called Pericles) is based on John Gower's *Confessio amantis* (1390–93) and perhaps on Laurence Twine's *Patterne of Painefull Adventures.* The long and complicated plot essentially deals with the separation of Pericles from his wife Thaisa and daughter Marina, both presumed dead, and his joyful reunion with them 16 years later.

·literature of the Renaissance **10**:1141f
·structure, style, textual problems, and sources **16**:627f

pericline twin, twin law with *b* as the twin axis, occurring in plagioclase feldspars.

·triclinic feldspar crystal structures **7**:214h

pericón, traditional Argentine dance.

·music and dance influences and features **1**:669b

Pericopidae, family of moths, order Lepidoptera.

·classification and general features **10**:830b

pericranium and endocranium, two membranes of periosteum (growth-capable surface of bone) that cover, respectively, the outside and the inside of the cranial cavity. The membranes are continuous through open sutures, fissures, and foramina (holes or canals for the passage of nerves or blood vessels or both). The endocranium is the outer layer of the dura mater (one of three membranes that cover and protect the brain).

Pericrocotus (bird): *see* minivet.

Perictione (fl. 428 BC), mother of Plato.

·Plato's family tree **14**:531f

pericycle, in botany, layer of parenchyma (*q.v.*) cells located between the innermost layer of the cortex (*q.v.*; endodermis) and the central vascular cylinder of a plant root and, in some cases, stem. These unspecialized cells can divide and give rise to lateral, or branch, roots and stems. *See* meristem.

·fern structure and function **7**:241g
·root structure and function **13**:730f; illus. 727
·vascular system development **5**:668b

periderm, a protective tissue in plants that includes cell regions called cork cambium (phellogen), cork (phellem), and cells produced by the phellogen internally (phelloderm) that usually are not distinguishable from cortex cells (outer tissues of stems and roots) except by their occurrence in regular rows. Besides providing protection for stems growing in girth, periderm forms below leaves about to fall.

·development, organization, and function **18**:453a
·stem tissue organization **13**:728b

Peridiscaceae, family of trees, order Violales.

·classification and anatomical features **19**:149g

peridium, outer envelope of the sporophore of many fungi.

·slime mold sporangium structures **16**:885b; illus.

peridot, also called PRECIOUS OLIVINE, gem-quality, transparent green olivine in the forsterite–fayalite series (*q.v.*); it is the birthstone for August (in addition to sardonyx in the U.S.). Gem-quality olivine has been valued for centuries; the deposit on Saint Johns Island in the Red Sea that is mentioned by Pliny in his *Natural History* (AD 70) still produces fine gems. Very large crystals are found in the Mogok district of Burma; peridots from the U.S. are seldom larger than two carats. Yellow-green peridot has been called chrysolite (Greek: "golden stone"); this term, used for various unrelated minerals, has become less common for the gemstone. Peridot is generally faceted with a step cut.

Peridot from St. John's Island, Red Sea

By courtesy of the American Museum of Natural History; photograph, Emil Javorsky—EB Inc.

·gemstone characteristics and value **7**:973c; illus. 975

peridotite, a coarse-grained, dark-coloured, heavy, intrusive igneous rock that contains at least 10 percent olivine, other iron- and magnesia-rich minerals (generally pyroxenes), and not more than 10 percent feldspar. It occurs in four main geologic environments: (1) interlayered with iron-, lime-, and magnesia-rich rocks in the lower parts of tabular-layered igneous complexes or masses; (2) in alpine-type mountain belts as irregular, olivine-rich masses, with or without related gabbro; (3) in volcanic pipes (funnels, more or less oval in cross section, that become narrower with increasing depth) as kimberlite; and (4) as dikes (tabular bodies injected in fissures) and irregular masses with rocks exceptionally rich in potash and soda. The layered complexes are believed to have been formed in place by selective crystallization and crystal settling from a previously intruded fluid or magma; the remaining types seem to have ranged from fluid magmas to semisolid crystal mushes at the time of emplacement. *See also* dunite; kimberlite.

Peridotite is the ultimate source of all chromium ore and naturally occurring diamonds, and of nearly all chrysotile asbestos. It is one of the main host rocks of talc deposits and platinum metals and formerly was a major source of magnesite. Fresh dunite is used in parts of glass furnaces. Nearly all peridotite is more or less altered to serpentine and is cut by many irregular shear surfaces; in warm, humid climates peridotite and serpentine have weathered to soils and related deposits that, though now worked on a relatively small scale, are enormous potential sources of iron, nickel, cobalt, and chromium.

·Earth's mantle composition **9**:221c; table
·high pressure phase transformations and melting **7**:1026g; illus. 1025
·igneous rock classification, table 7 **9**:207
·mantle composition and olivine changes **6**:703f; table 704
·mineralogical composition, illus. 5 **9**:207
·nickel deposition by weathering **13**:71g
·occurrence, origin, and mantle composition **6**:52h; illus. 57
·physical properties **15**:953b; tables

Periegesis, 5th-century-BC geography text by Hecataeus of Miletus.

·Mediterranean area description **8**:821a

Perier, Casimir(-Pierre) (b. Oct. 21, 1777, Grenoble, Fr.—d. May 16, 1832, Paris), French banker and statesman who exercised a decisive influence on the political orientation of the reign of King Louis-Philippe.

Perier was the son of a manufacturer and financier. After service with the staff of the French army in Italy (1798–1801), he returned to France and, together with his brother Antoine-Scipion, founded a new bank. By 1814 he was one of the most important bankers in Paris. In 1817 he opposed the government's policy of relying on foreign banks to finance France's war indemnity. Elected to the Chamber of Deputies in 1817, he sat with the moderate opposition of the left.

After the Revolution of July 1830 that overthrew Charles X and made Louis-Philippe king of the French, Perier was elected president of the Chamber of Deputies. On March 13, 1831, he became president of the council of ministers (premier) and minister of the interior. He set himself to restore order: the National Guard was brought into action against demonstrators in Paris, and later the army put down the silkworkers' insurrection in Lyon (November–December 1831). In foreign affairs he pursued an active policy: a naval squadron was dispatched to Lisbon to force the Portuguese government to compensate French merchants for damages (July 1831); he sent an army to defend Belgium against the Dutch (August 1831); and he ordered the occupation of the Adriatic part of Ancona to check Austrian predominance in the Papal States (February 1832). He faced continual attacks from both left and right, and his authoritarian manner sometimes alienated Louis-Philippe. He died of cholera.

perifovea, in anatomy, ring of tissue in the retina of the eye.

·human eye anatomy **7**:96e

perigee, point nearest the Earth in the orbit of a natural or artificial Earth satellite. The Moon at perigee is about 356,000 kilometres (221,000 miles) distant. *Cf.* apogee; *see also* apse.

·Moon's orbital distance variation **12**:416a
·satellite orbit shapes **17**:360b

periglaciology, study of the large areas of the Earth that were adjacent to but not covered by ice during the glacial periods. Modern representatives of these areas are the sub-Arctic tundra and permafrost regions located in the Northern Hemisphere. All of the conditions derived from such a paleoenvironment can be observed in the geologic record preserved in many areas now free of ice.

·iceberg formation and glacial creep **9**:154f

Pérignon, Dominique-Catherine, marquis de (b. May 31, 1754, Grenade, Fr.—d. Dec. 25, 1818, Paris), general and marshal of France, active during the Revolutionary and Napoleonic wars.

A retired officer of the royal army, Pérignon resumed active service in 1792. Operations against the Spaniards won him the rank of general and, in 1794, command of the Army of the Eastern Pyrenees. As ambassador to Madrid he negotiated the Spanish alliance (1796). While fighting in Italy (1799) he was wounded and taken prisoner by the Russians for 18 months, returning to France to become a senator (1801) and a marshal (1804). He was appointed governor general of Parma (1806) and commander in chief at Naples (1808) and became a count of the Empire in 1811. After Napoleon's abdication he rallied to Louis XVIII, was made a peer and later a commanding officer at Toulouse (1815) and Paris (1816), and was created marquis in 1817.

Périgord, former *pays* (region) of southern France, corresponding to the bulk of the modern *département* of Dordogne, with part of

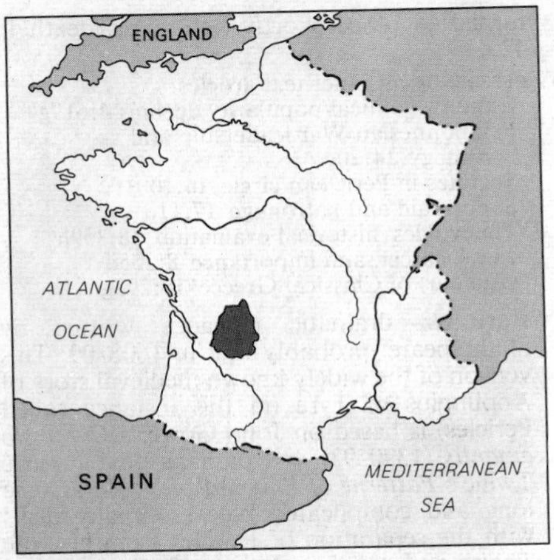

The county of Périgord *c.* 1035

From W. Shepherd, *Historical Atlas*, Harper & Row, Publishers (Barnes & Noble Books), New York; revision Copyright © 1964 by Barnes & Noble, Inc.

Lot-et-Garonne, area of disputed suzerainty between the French and English crowns, particularly during the Hundred Years' War (1337–1453). Originally, the area was inhabited by the Gallic tribe of the Petrocorii, or Petragorici, whose capital became Périgueux. The counts of Périgord later played a part in the troubled affairs of Aquitaine, and, beginning in 1259, control of Périgord was disputed by the French and the English. In 1470 the area was transferred to the House of Albret and subsequently was inherited by the crown of Navarre, whereupon Henry IV united it with the French crown (1607). Under the *ancien régime*, Périgord was included in the province of Guyenne and the *intendance*, or *généralité*, of Bordeaux.

·Revolution and peasant revolts **7**:652e

Perigordian industry, tool tradition of prehistoric men in Upper Paleolithic Europe that followed the Mousterian industry, was contemporary with the Aurignacian, and was succeeded by the Solutrean. Perigordian tools included denticulate (toothed) tools of the type used earlier in the Mousterian tradition and stone knives with one sharp edge and one flat edge, much like modern metal knives. Other Upper Paleolithic tool types are also found in Perigordian culture, including scrapers, borers, burins (woodworking tools rather like chisels), and composite tools; bone implements are relatively uncommon.

The Perigordian has two main stages. The earlier stage, called Châtelperronian, is concentrated in the Périgord region of France but is believed to have originated in southwestern Asia; it is distinguished from contemporary stone tool culture complexes by the presence of backed knives (knives sharpened both on the cutting edge and the back). The later stage is called Gravettian and is found in France, Italy, and into Russia (termed Eastern Gravettian). Gravettian people in the west hunted horses to the near exclusion of the reindeer and bison that other contemporaries hunted; in Russia Gravettians concentrated on mammoths. Both appear to have hunted communally, using stampedes and pitfalls to kill large numbers of animals at one time. Large mammoth bones were used as part of the building material for winter houses; mammoth fat was used to keep fires burning. Gravettian peoples made rather crude, fat "Venus" figurines, used red ochre as pigment, and fashioned jewelry out of shells, animal teeth, and ivory.

·archaeological time scale, illus. 3 **5**:500
·artistic style emphasis and development **17**:702e
·Cro-Magnon man's period of occurrence **5**:289g
·hominid culture and geological period correlation table **8**:1051

Périgueux, town of southwest central France, *préfecture* of the *département* of Dordogne. An episcopal see, it lies on the right bank of the Isle River, east northeast of Bordeaux and southwest of Paris. Originally settled by a Gaulish tribe, the Petrocorii, the town fell to the Romans, who called it Vesuna after a local spring, the Vesone, that became their tutelary deity.

The modern town developed from two nuclei, the Cité and Puy-Saint-Front, which vied with one another until they united in 1251. The Cité, in the southwestern part of the town, occupies the site of Vesuna, subsequently reduced by the barbarians to a small encampment, called the Civitas Petrocorium, from which the names Cité and Périgueux are derived. Puy-Saint-Front, on the east, grew between the 5th and 13th centuries around an abbey sanctuary containing the body of St. Front, Apostle of Périgord and first bishop of Périgueux. The contemporary city spreads west and northwest of Puy-Saint-Front.

Périgueux struggled against the English throughout the Hundred Years' War (1337–1453) and suffered severely under Protestant occupation (1575–81) during the 16th-century Wars of Religion. Given amnesty by Louis XIV in 1654 for its part in the Fronde (a series of civil disturbances, 1648–53), the town then experienced an era of peace. At the time of the French Revolution at the end of the 18th century, it continued as the capital of a *département*, covering the same area as the medieval province of Périgord Blanc. From the July Monarchy (1830) onward many improvements were made, and the town received new impetus under the Second Empire (1852–70) and the Third Republic (1870–1940).

A chief point of cultural interest is the cathedral of Saint-Front, built in the 12th century on the ruins of the abbey, which burned in 1120. One of the largest in southwestern France, it is built in the shape of a Greek cross, topped by five lofty domes and numerous colonnaded turrets. A Romanesque bell tower and cloisters of the 12th, 13th, and 16th centuries adjoin it on the south. Successive restorations, the last ending in 1901, have altered its original character. The Musée du Périgord displays prehistoric and archaeological artifacts of the area, as well as secular and religious art. In the Cité is the 12th-century church of Saint-Étienne, which was the cathedral until 1669. Evidences of early occupation are an arena of the 3rd century AD, a boundary wall of the Roman *civitas* on which is built the Château Barrière (12th–15th century), and the Tour de Vésone, believed to be part of a temple to the goddess Vesuna.

Now one of the most attractive towns in southwestern France, Périgueux is a road and rail junction with connections northwest to Limoges and southwest to Bordeaux. The nearest airport is to the east at Bassilac. Internationally known for its pâté de foie gras, truffles, and wine, Périgueux is also an important hog market. Industries include canneries and plants producing hardware, cutlery, chemicals, textiles, and leather goods. Pop. (1975) 34,779.
45°11′ N, 0°43′ E

·map, France **7**:584

perihelion, point nearest the Sun in the path of a planet, comet, or other object (*e.g.*, a spacecraft) in solar orbit. The Earth at perihelion in early January is about 147,000,000 kilometres (91,341,000 miles) from the Sun. *Cf.* aphelion; *see also* apse.

·Earth climatic changes **4**:740c
·planetary orbit and motion laws **11**:757f
·relativity theory confirmation **15**:586a
·Saturn's distance from Sun **16**:273c

perihelion of Mercury, advance of, in astronomy, continual turning of the major axis of the orbit of the planet Mercury through the plane of the orbit so that its perihelion (point in the orbit closest to the Sun) moves progressively around the Sun. The advance is 9′34″ of arc per century, 43″ more than can be accounted for by the perturbing effects of other planets. The advance was given a reasoned ex-

planation when Einstein pointed out that, according to the general theory of relativity, the gravitational attraction between Mercury and the Sun was changed by their relative velocity; Mercury, the closest planet to the Sun, moves around the Sun faster than any other planet. In 1967 the U.S. physicist Robert H. Dicke postulated that the Sun is flattened at its poles and attributed the advance of Mercury's perihelion, at least in part, to this flattening. The amount of flattening is difficult to measure, so that the relativistic explanation is still the one preferred by most physicists. Advances in the perihelions of other planets are smaller and more difficult to observe.
·investigation and justification **8**:288e
·orbital changes in solar light and heat **11**:916b *passim* to 920c

Perijá, Mountains of, called SERRANÍA DE PERIJÁ in Colombia, SIERRA DE PERIJÁ in Venezuela, a northward extension of the Andean Cordillera Oriental, forming part of the border between Colombia and Venezuela. The range extends for 190 mi (306 km) from the vicinity of Ocaña, Norte de Santander department, Colombia, northward to the Península de la Guajira. Its crest line rises to 12,300 ft (3,750 m) above sea level. Included in the range are the Serranía de los Motilones, the Serranía de Valledupar, and the Montes de Oca. To the west, across the Río César, lies the higher Sierra Nevada de Santa Marta, while to the east stretchs the Maracaibo Lowland of Venezuela.
10°00′ N, 73°00′ W

Perilampidae, family of the order Hymenoptera.
·characteristics and classification **9**:132f

perilla, Asiatic mint plants of the genus *Perilla*, the seeds of which yield a light yellow drying oil. Perilla oil is used along with synthetic resins in the production of varnishes. Perilla oil dries in less time than linseed oil and on drying forms a film that is harder and yellows more than that formed by linseed oil. The paint and varnish industry accounts for the largest usage. Perilla oil also is important in the manufacture of printing inks and linoleum. In the Orient perilla oil is used as an edible oil.

Perilla frutescens
W.H. Hodge

Perilla has been cultivated in China, Korea, Japan, and northern India and is becoming increasingly important. The seeds contain 35 to 45 percent oil.

perilymph, fluid separating the membranous labyrinth from the bony labyrinth in the inner ear.
·production and function in human ear **5**:1122f; illus. 1123

Perim Island, Arabic BARĪM, in the Bab (strait) el-Mandeb off the coast of Yemen (Aden), to which it belongs. A rocky volcanic island, lying just off the southwestern tip of the Arabian Peninsula, Perim is 5 sq mi (13 sq km) in area and rises as high as 214 ft (65 m). It has a harbour on the southwestern shore and an airfield is in the north. Perim was visited by the Portuguese in 1513 and occupied by the French in 1738. The British landed in 1799 but soon left because of a lack of water; they returned in 1857 and established a coaling station. Perim's population expanded greatly thereafter, but declined after the coaling station was abandoned in 1936. The island was incorporated into the British colony of Aden in 1937 and became part of independent Yemen (Aden) in 1967.
12°40′ N, 43°25′ E
·map, Yemen (Aden) **19**:1080

perimysium, connective tissue sheath surrounding a muscle and sending partitions inward that form sheaths for bundles of muscle fibres.
·muscle fibre structure **12**:638d

perinatal mortality, death rate among infants at the time of delivery and in the first week of life.
·childbirth complication rates **13**:1037f

perineum, in anatomy, either the tissues that make up the floor of the pelvis or the area from the anus to the scrotum of the male or the vulva of the female.
·infections and prolapse **5**:802c
·lacerations during childbirth **13**:1039e
·muscle adaptation in human abdomen **12**:637c
·primate genitalia color changes **14**:1025b

perineurium, connective tissue sheath that surrounds a bundle of nerve fibres.
·neuron structure and function **12**:978c

Perino del Vaga, original name PIETRO BONACCORSI (1501–47), Italian painter, was associated with the Raphael circle in Rome and was influential in transmitting the Roman style to Genoa.

Perinthus, modern MARMARAEREGLISI, city, Tekirdag *il* (province), Turkey, on the Sea of Marmara, founded by Samian colonists *c.* 600 BC. It is now a port and grain market. Latest census 1,929.
40°58′ N, 27°57′ E
·Byzantium annexation in AD 196 **9**:1069g

period, for wave motion and vibrations, the time interval between successive waves or vibrations. The period equals the reciprocal of the frequency; for waves, it is also the wavelength divided by the speed.

period, in music, unit of melodic organization made up of several related consecutive phrases. Often the period has two phrases (called, respectively, antecedent and consequent). The implication of finality is usually avoided at the end of the first phrase, and the period ends with a cadence, or point of rest; thus, a period is the expression of a complete musical thought. There is some uncertainty about the lengths of melodies to which the terms phrase and period apply. The use of the terms may vary, but both refer to natural divisions of a melody.

period, in chemistry, a horizontal sequence of elements in the periodic table. The elements, arranged in order of their increasing atomic numbers, are divided into seven periods reflecting periodicities in electronic structure and in their chemical and physical properties. There are three short periods of 2, 8, and 8 elements each; three long periods of 18, 18, and 32 elements; and a further, incomplete, long period containing 19 elements.
The progression of elements along a period represents a systematic assignment of electrons to orbitals or electron shells. A period is completed when all the electron orbitals within a given energy level are filled.
·acidity trends in the periodic table **1**:52g
·chemical element classification **4**:116e
·oxidation state trends of elements **13**:141b
·periodic classification of elements **14**:77b; illus.
·rare-earth comparative chemistry **15**:517f

period, the basic unit of the geological time scale; during these spans of time specific systems of rocks were formed. Originally, the sequential nature of defining periods was a relative one, originating from the superposition of corresponding stratigraphic sequences and the evidence derived from paleontological studies. With the advent of sophisticated radiometric dating methods, absolute ages for various periods can be determined with some degree of confidence.
·geological column and time scale **5**:499d; illus.
·stratigraphy nomenclature **17**:722h; tables 716

periodic function (mathematics): *see* function.

periodicity, biological 14:69, the cyclical, predictable response of an organism to a corresponding environmental cycle.
The text article covers general features, biological rhythms and natural geophysical cycles, the biological clock, and factors affecting biological periodicities.
REFERENCES in other text articles:
·coloration changes in organisms **4**:913a
daily cycles
·bat daily and seasonal cycles **4**:430c *passim* to 431a
·dinoflagellates migration to obtain maximum light **14**:494h
·eye type and daily activity **16**:563g
·group hunting correlation with daily cycle in mongoose relatives **3**:934e
·marine life vertical movement **18**:852a
·plankton vertical movement cycles **1**:1031h
·shrimp daily migration in depth **5**:545d
·sleep in fishes **7**:331g
·sleep movements of leaves and flowers **17**:673g
·sleep-wakefulness alternation **16**:876g
·thermoperiod effects on plants **14**:996e
·disease occurrence in cyclic patterns **5**:840d
disruptions of cycles
·aerospace flight desynchronization **1**:144e
·animal behaviour and weather forecasts **19**:706f
·anteater adaptation to man **6**:299c
·pest control by farm operation timing **14**:143f
·space flight and metabolic periodicity **10**:917a
·vegetable farming variable factors **19**:48b
·zoo reversal of normal animal cycles **19**:1162b
·distribution of organisms as function of time **5**:909c
·lemming migratory behaviour **15**:974f
light-triggered effects
·animal orientation to sun movement **12**:183a
·day length influence on animal pituitary **2**:813a
·human day-length influences **1**:34b
·light's effect on growth patterns **8**:442g
·light's physiological effects **15**:390h
·photoperiodism in plants and animals **14**:352b
·spring community and light intensity **17**:518a
nocturnal activity
·bat behaviour patterns **4**:431a
·eyeshine and protective mechanisms **14**:355e
·rain forest nocturnal animals **10**:344a
·salamander nocturnal and seasonal habits **18**:1086g
reproduction and life-cycles
·animal ovulation influences **15**:714f
·bioluminescent annelid's reproduction **1**:931h
·bug life cycle and factor interactions **8**:846b
·cicada's 17-year life cycle **8**:1037e
·delayed implantation in edentates **6**:300d
·dog estrus in domestication and wild **5**:933f
·dragonfly life cycle and seasons **13**:508e
·hormonal regulation of cyclic sexual activity in mammalian female **8**:1083d
·human menstrual cycle **15**:695a
·insectivore reproduction, dormancy, and other cycles **9**:622d *passim* to 623c
·latitude's effect on falconiform habits and life cycle **7**:145h *passim* to 148c
·lizard breeding and environment **16**:284f

· menstruation's cyclic phases **6**:803e
· palm reproduction and flowering **1**:1132c
· pelecaniform breeding interval **14**:16f
· population fluctuations **14**:831g
· primate birth peak influences **14**:1017c
· rain forest breeding related to food **10**:345a
· reproductive behaviour in palolo worms **15**:684a
· river community's diverse life cycles **15**:891a
· seasonal breeding correlations in carnivores **3**:928d
· seasonality in Lepidoptera generations **10**:821g
· seasonality of short aquatic life cycles **16**:586h
· snake endothermy in dormancy, sleep, and reproduction **16**:559d *passim* to 561g
· social behaviour and sexual cycles **16**:940g
· sooty tern breeding cycle variation **4**:38c
· sponge gemmulation and seasonal changes **14**:850a
· waterfowl life cycle variation from climatic factors **1**:940c

seasonal cycles

· algae population changes **1**:492c
· community time relations **4**:1028d
· conifer growth rhythm **5**:6a
· falconiform predatory behaviour **7**:146f
· frost as limitation of plant growth **7**:749e
· garden plant seasonal features **7**:904a
· innate rhythms in hibernation **5**:965a
· lacustrine seasonal population changes **10**:614e
· mammalian dormancy and migration **11**:404c
· migration regulation techniques **10**:741h
· molting cycle in Charadriiformes **4**:39b
· monotreme hibernation patterns **12**:387b
· oxygen seasonal variation in ponds and protozoan needs **15**:121g
· plant maturation and transition phases **5**:669f
· predatory–prey oscillations **2**:1046d
· regeneration of elk antlers **15**:580e; illus.
· seasonal adaptations of furbearing animals **7**:812a
· tree growth rings **18**:453h
· wood growth ring composition **19**:917d

tidal cycles

· coastal rhythmic activity manifest by tides **4**:806d
· estuary changes in salinity and tides **6**:973d
· fiddler crab tidal patterns **5**:544b

periodic law 14:75, in chemistry, the generalization that there is a recurring pattern in the properties of the elements when they are arranged in order of increasing atomic number (the total number of protons in the atomic nuclei). The relationship is best shown in a periodic table, in which the elements are placed in successive horizontal rows, or periods, of varying length. The elements in each vertical file—usually termed "group"—then show a certain degree of similarity in their chemical and physical properties.

The text article reviews the history of the periodic law and the more important forms of the periodic table. It also reviews the generally accepted picture of the electronic structure of the atom and shows how it leads to periodicity in the properties of the elements.

REFERENCES in other text articles:
· acidity trend in the periodic table **1**:52g
· actinide element comparative chemistry **1**:64g
· atomic concept development **2**:334a
· atomic spectra properties **17**:463e
· atomic weight research **2**:343h
· boron group classification **3**:44a; illus.
· carbon group structural properties **3**:839g
· chemical bonding principles **4**:106e
· chemical bonding theory development **4**:85d
· chemical element classification **4**:116c
· classification and geological occurrence **5**:26a; illus. 25
· electron configuration and reactivity **4**:169g
· electron occupancy of energy levels **6**:667e
· element groupings by properties **4**:173c; illus.
· halogen group chemistry **8**:561d
· hydrogen's two classifications **9**:93c
· Mendeleyev's formulation of periodicity **11**:899g
· metal group properties **11**:1086c
· oxygen group element characteristics **13**:809g; illus. 810
· rare-earths position and properties **15**:515b; illus.
· Seaborg transuranium elements placement theory **16**:442f
· semiconductor group properties **16**:524g
· substitution and antagonism of nutrients within element groups **13**:404g
· superheavy element prediction **18**:682c; illus.
· transition element chemistry **18**:600g; illus.
· zinc group structure and properties **19**:1144a; illus. 1143

RELATED ENTRIES in the *Ready Reference and Index: for*
periodic properties: see electron affinity; electronegativity; ionization potential; oxidation number
allied concepts and classifications: atomic number; chemical symbol; congeners; group; metal; metalloid; nonmetal; octet; period

periodic motion, motion repeated in equal intervals of time, the time of each interval being called the period. Periodic motion is performed, for example, by a rocking chair, a bouncing ball, a vibrating tuning fork, a swing in motion, the Earth in its orbit about the Sun, and a water wave. In each case the interval of time for a repetition, or cycle, of the motion is called a period.

In simple harmonic motion (*see* harmonic motion, simple) the period is the time required to complete one vibration. One period therefore equals the reciprocal of the frequency, or 1/frequency; *e.g.*, a hummingbird's wing that beats with a frequency of 50 per second has a period of .02 second.

When a point moves around a circle with uniform speed, its projection on any line taken as the diameter (*i.e.*, the intersection of a line drawn through the point perpendicular to the diameter) will execute simple harmonic motion. Although the point is moving with constant speed, the projection point will accelerate or decelerate according to whether it is moving toward the centre of the circle or away from it. If the ratio of its displacement distance from the centre to the acceleration is denoted by c, then the period T of a simple harmonic motion is equal to 2π times the square root of c—*i.e.*, $T = 2\pi\sqrt{c}$.

The period (T) of vibration for a weight attached to a stretched spring is equal to 2π times the square root of the weight's mass (m) divided by a constant (k), representing the stiffness of the spring, or $T = 2\pi\sqrt{m/k}$. In a torsional pendulum—*i.e.*, a body suspended on a wire that is free to twist back and forth—the period of vibration is equal to 2π times the square root of the rotational inertia (I) of the body divided by the constant of torsion (K) of the wire, or $T = 2\pi\sqrt{I/K}$. A simple pendulum, such as a bob suspended on a string and swinging through an arc of a few degrees only, will have a period (T) of swing equal to 2π times the square root of the ratio of length (l) to gravity acceleration (g), or $T = 2\pi\sqrt{l/g}$. As may be seen from this last equation, the period is not affected by the mass of the bob so that two simple pendulums of the same length but different masses will have identical periods.

Waves that can be represented by harmonic waves—*i.e.*, sine curves—are periodic. If the wave is propagated with a velocity v and is of wavelength, symbolized by the Greek letter lambda (λ), then the period (T) is equal to wavelength divided by velocity, or $T = \lambda/v$. Because frequency (f) is the reciprocal of the period—*i.e.*, $f = 1/T$—this equation may be written $f = v/\lambda$.

· Hooke's law and equilibrium **19**:667c; illus. 666
· light wave properties **10**:930b
· vibrational harmonic motion principles **19**:99h
· vibratory motion theory **19**:667e
· water wave velocity measurement **19**:658g; table 659

periodic table (chemistry): *see* periodic law.

period–luminosity relationship (astronomy): *see* Cepheid variable.

periodontal membrane, or PERIODONTAL LIGAMENT, fleshy tissue between tooth and tooth socket that holds the tooth in place and enables it to resist the stresses of chewing. The periodontal membrane consists of loose connective tissue supplied with small blood vessels and nerves, and a series of tough, somewhat elastic fibres attached to the tooth cementum and adjacent structures, by which the tooth is suspended in its socket, and the overlying gum is held close to the tooth. It develops from the follicular sac that surrounds the embryonic tooth during growth.
· joint structures and functions **10**:253e
· tooth structure and development **18**:55g; illus. 56

periodontics, dental specialty concerned with the prevention, diagnosis, and treatment of functional and structural diseases of the periodontium, the tissues that surround and support the teeth. Degeneration or inflammation of these tissues can be caused by various systemic or local diseases or by poor oral hygiene. In some cases the cause is not established. Most commonly periodontic diseases are caused by hardened bacteria, called bacterial plaque, which adheres to teeth and destroys tissue. The most prevalent periodontal disease is periodontitis, inflammation of the periodontium; this disease is usually called pyorrhea. If left untreated, periodontitis causes loosening and eventual loss of teeth.
· distinctive features of practice **5**:596b

Periophthalmidae (fish family): *see* mud skipper.

periosteal bone: *see* compact bone.

periosteum, a covering of specialized connective tissue that invests the surfaces of bones. Microscopic examination reveals the periosteum to be composed of two layers, an outer fibrous zone and an internal cellular layer. The inner layer is osteogenic (capable of producing additional bone). The two-layered structure of the periosteum is most obvious during embryonic and postnatal growth when active bone formation is at a maximum. At this time, the osteogenic layer is composed of many osteoblasts, the cells which synthesize new bone. The fibrous layer is present above the cellular region. In the adult the osteoblasts are not so prominent and are difficult to differentiate from other connective tissue cells. They retain their functional capacities, however, and in the event of injury they differentiate to form new bone in the repair process.

The outer fibrous layer is a form of dense connective tissue containing much collagen (a fibrous protein) but few cells. Since nerve endings are present, periosteal damage causes pain. Also found in the fibrous layer are many blood vessels. Branches of the vessels penetrate the bone by passing perpendicularly through Volkmann's canals (after the German physiologist Alfred Volkmann) and by contributing to the longitudinal vessels in haversian systems (*see* osteon). Some of the collagenous fibres of the outer layer of periosteum also turn and penetrate the outer layers of the bone proper. At this point they are known as Sharpey's fibres (for an English anatomist, William Sharpey), and together with the penetrating blood vessels serve to attach the periosteum to the bone.

The periosteum is absent in the regions of long bones that are covered with articular cartilage; *i.e.*, the surfaces that form joints. Periosteum is also absent from those sites where tendons or ligaments are connected to the bone. The patella, or kneecap, has no periosteal covering since it is contained completely within a tendon. The periosteum of the inner surfaces of the flat bones of the skull is somewhat modified since it is fused with the dura mater, the outer layer of connective tissue covering the brain.

The function of the periosteum becomes

most obvious following an injury such as a fracture. The periosteum becomes torn at the site of injury. Periosteal vessels bleed around the traumatized area, and a clot is formed between and around the ends of the bone fragments. Within 48 hours the cells of the osteogenic layer are activated and produce osteoblasts to effect the repair of the bone. The inner layer of periosteum expands to become many cell layers thick, and the cells begin to differentiate and lay down new bone between the ends of the fracture.

·bone development and mechanics **16**:827f
·joints' structural component **10**:253b
·meningeal layers and general features **12**:986g
·synovial joint relationships **10**:254h; illus.

periostracum, outer chitinous (hard and horny) layer to protect the shells of most mollusks and brachiopod from chemical and mechanical wear.

·bivalve shell structure **2**:1089h
·snail shell composition and variations **7**:953e

Peripatetics, students instructed by the Greek philosopher Aristotle in the covered-walk area (*peripatos*) of the Athenian Lyceum; also applied to later students instructed by Aristotle's successors, notably Theophrastus. The name derives from Aristotle's custom of teaching as he strolled with his pupils in the *peripatos*.

·development of Aristotle's views **14**:254e
·history and development **1**:1156c
·logic history from antiquity **11**:59a
·origin of name **1**:1164a

Peripatos (philosophy): *see* Lyceum.

Peripatus (invertebrate): *see* onychophoran.

peripeteia (Greek: "reversal"), the turning point in a drama after which the plot moves steadily to its denouement. It is discussed by Aristotle in the *Poetics* as the shift of the tragic protagonist's fortune from good to bad, which is essential to the plot of a tragedy. It is often an ironic twist, as in Sophocles' *Oedipus Rex* when a messenger brings Oedipus news about his parents that he thinks will cheer him, but the news, instead, slowly brings about the awful recognition that leads to Oedipus' catastrophe. The term is also used for the hero's shift from bad fortune to good in a comedy. *See also* anagnorisis.

·tragedy structure and Aristotelian view **18**:588g

peripheral jet, category of air-cushion vehicle on which experimental work began in the 1950s.

·air-cushion machine propulsion system **1**:392g; illus.

peripheral nervous system, consists of the cranial nerves and spinal nerves (*qq.v.*).

periphrasis, in rhetoric, the expression in a roundabout manner of something that could be said simply. Also called circumlocution, periphrasis is used as a conscious means to embellish language, to express ideas that if said directly would be socially offensive, and for a deliberately comic effect as in, "He brought his enfolded hand into abrupt juxtaposition with his rival's olfactory organ" for "He punched him in the nose." Periphrasis is frequently found in learned academic or professional jargon. Usually it is considered a major stylistic fault.

periphrastic heresy (literary criticism): *see* heresy of paraphrase.

periphyton (biology): *see* Aufwuchs.

Periplaneta americana: *see* cockroach.

Periplus Maris Erythraei ("Circumnavigation of the Erythrean Sea"), anonymous Greek geographical work written in the 1st century AD. It is an important source for the early history of south Arabia, Ethiopia, and the East African coast.

·Ethiopian imperial power **6**:1007c
·Indian–Western trade in ancient times **9**:355e
·Somaliland trade evidence **6**:91b

periscope, optical instrument used in land and sea warfare, submarine navigation, and elsewhere to enable an observer to see his surroundings while remaining under cover, behind armour, or submerged.

A periscope includes two mirrors or reflecting prisms to change the direction of the light coming from the scene observed: the first deflects it down through a vertical tube, the second diverts it horizontally so that the scene can be viewed conveniently. Frequently there is a telescopic optical system that provides magnification, gives as wide an arc of vision as possible, and includes a crossline or reticle pattern to establish the line of sight to the object under observation. There may also be devices for estimating the range and course of the target in military applications and for photographing through the periscope.

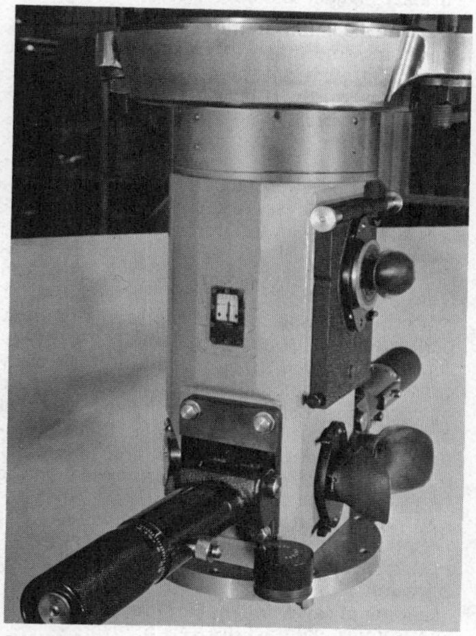

Periscope, eyepiece box and observer's station; handles control rotation about the axis, twist grips provide control of the line-of-sight elevation
By courtesy of Kollmorgen Corp., Northampton, Mass.

The simplest type of periscope consists of a tube at the ends of which are two mirrors, parallel to each other but at 45° to the axis of the tube. This device produces no magnification and does not give a crossline image. The arc of vision is limited by the simple geometry of the tube: the longer or narrower the tube, the smaller the field of view. Periscopes of this type were widely used in World War II in tanks and other armoured vehicles as observation devices for the driver, gunner, and commander. When fitted with a small, auxiliary gunsight telescope, the tank periscope can also be used in pointing and firing the guns. By employing tubes of rectangular cross section, wide, horizontal fields of view can be obtained. The periscopes and their swivel mounts are made as watertight and dusttight as possible. The top mirror assembly or prism may be detachable and readily replaceable with a spare unit if damaged.

·submarine sensor devices and history **17**:752d

perisperm, in botany, nutritive tissue in a seed formed from the nucellus (a female spore-producing structure). It becomes the storage tissue of the developing plant embryo. (*cf.* endosperm).

·angiosperm seed and embryo development **1**:879a
·seed and fruit development **16**:480f

perispore, the covering of a spore.

·fern gametophyte structures, illus. 3 **7**:240

Perissodactyla 14:81, order of hoofed mammals comprising the modern horses, asses, and zebras (family Equidae), tapirs (Tapiridae), rhinoceroses (Rhinocerotidae), and a diverse assemblage of fossil forms placed in about nine families. Perissodactyls are sometimes known collectively as odd-toed ungulates because in advanced forms the weight is carried on the centre toe; in the even-toed ungulates (order Artiodactyla) the weight-bearing hoof consists of both the third and fourth toes.

The text article emphasizes the natural history and structure of modern perissodactyls and includes a fossil history of the order and a complete classification of Recent and fossil families.

REFERENCES in other text articles:
·evolution and mammalian relationships **11**:402a; illus. 414
·fossil record of horse **7**:573d; illus. 572
·horse evolution and domestication **8**:1088b

RELATED ENTRIES in the *Ready Reference and Index:*
ass; Equidae; rhinoceros; tapir; zebra

peristalsis, involuntary movements of the longitudinal and circular muscles, primarily in the digestive tract but occasionally in other hollow tubes of the body, that occur in progressive wavelike contractions. Peristaltic waves occur in the esophagus, stomach, and intestines (*qq.v.*). The waves can be short, local reflexes or long, continuous contractions that travel the whole length of the organ, depending upon their location and what initiates their action. Peristalsis is controlled by the vagus nerve, which usually receives impulses from the muscular walls of an organ. Mechanical expansion of a wall caused by food mass or distention arising from gas pressure can cause peristaltic waves. Both the longitudinal and the circular muscles in an organ's wall are involved in peristalsis. The longitudinal muscle first contracts, and after a slight delay the circular muscle responds similarly; the longitudinal muscle then relaxes, and the circular muscle also relaxes. The combination of these two muscles serves to shorten and squeeze the walls so that the food contents are pushed further along the digestive tract.

In the esophagus, peristaltic waves begin at the upper portion of the tube and travel the whole length pushing food ahead of the wave into the stomach. Particles of food left behind in the esophageal folds initiate secondary peristaltic waves that remove leftover substances. One wave travels the full length of the tube in about nine seconds. Between 10 and 30 centimetres of wall contract at one time. In rapid swallowing, the esophagus remains relaxed until the final swallow, and peristalsis then begins. The peristaltic wave contractions in the esophagus of man are weak compared with those of most other mammals. In cud-chewing animals, such as cows, reverse peristalsis can occur so that the food is brought back from the stomach to the mouth for rechewing.

When the stomach is filled, peristaltic waves are diminished. The presence of fat in a meal can completely stop these movements for a short period until it is diluted with gastric juices or removed from the stomach. Peristaltic waves start as weak contractions at the beginning of the stomach and progressively become stronger as they near the distal stomach regions. The waves help to mix the stomach contents and propel food to the small intestine. Usually, two to three waves are present at one time in different regions of the stomach, and about three waves occur each minute.

Peristaltic waves beginning in the stomach usually continue into the first region of the small intestine, or duodenum. In the small intestine the waves are short, travelling only a few centimetres before ceasing. Their main purpose is to expose food to the intestinal wall for absorption; food is also partially moved by these short waves. Most peristaltic waves begin as local responses to the presence of food particles; waves travelling the whole length of the small intestine are not normal, nor does reverse peristalsis occur in health.

In the large intestine (or colon) the peristaltic wave is continuous and progressive; it advances steadily toward the anal end of the tract pushing waste material in front of the wave at the rate of one to two centimetres per minute. The contractions are usually sustained, keeping the affected segment of the colon closed from five minutes to an hour. Normally three to four times daily, mass contractions occur that move fecal materials from one region of the colon to another. If feces are passed to the rectum and not evacuated from the body, they are returned to the last segment of the colon for longer storage by reverse peristaltic waves. In dogs and cats reverse peristalsis commonly occurs throughout the whole length of the colon so that new waste material is continually mixed with that being stored. Peristaltic waves are particularly important in helping to remove gas from the large intestine and in controlling bacterial growth by mechanically acting as a cleansing agent that dislodges and removes potential colonies of bacteria.

·autonomic system mediation **12**:1038g
·digestion and intestinal motions **5**:776e
·disease-caused interruptions in esophagus and intestines **5**:798c
·intestinal changes during pregnancy **14**:973f
·regulation of intestinal movement **5**:788g
·sperm transport in man **15**:692g
·structural and electrical mechanisms **12**:632c
·swallowing and muscle movements **5**:773a
·ureter structure and function **7**:53b

peristerite (from Greek *peristera*, "pigeon"), iridescent gemstone in the plagioclase (*q.v.*) series of feldspar minerals. The name refers to the resemblance of fine specimens, such as those from Ontario and Quebec, to the often iridescent feathers of a pigeon's neck. In peristerite—usually a form of one of the sodium-rich varieties of plagioclase albite or oligoclase—the sodium aluminosilicate and calcium aluminosilicate that make up the mineral separate and form submicroscopic intergrowths of distinct crystals of the two pure compounds. The iridescence probably arises from diffusion of light by adjoining areas of different optical properties, or from reflection and diffraction of the separating crystals of the two different substances.

·gem characteristics and value **7**:972b
·structure and iridescence **7**:214c; illus.

peristome, in botany, a double row of pointed-toothlike structures encircling the opening of a dry spore capsule of some mosses.

·moss morphology and function **3**:353f; illus. 352
·Nepenthales carnivorous features **12**:961f

perithecium (fungi): *see* ascocarp.

peritoneal cavity, in anatomy, the cavity that can develop between the membrane lining the abdomen and the membrane covering the viscera.

·cancer spreading pathway **3**:766b
·origins and membranous partitions **6**:753b

peritoneum, large membrane in the abdominal cavity that connects and supports internal organs. It is composed of many folds and sacs that pass between or around the various organs. Two folds are of primary concern: the omentum, which hangs in front of the stomach and intestines; and the mesentery, which attaches the small intestine and much of the large intestine to the posterior abdominal cavity.

The omentum and mesentery contain blood vessels, nerves, lymph nodes, varying amounts of fat, elastic fibres for stretching, and protein (collagen) fibres for strength. The omentum is thinner than the mesentery and lacy in appearance. It contains large quantities of fat that serve to keep the organs warm. The mesentery is fan-shaped and well supplied with blood vessels that radiate to the intestines.

The functions of these membranes are to prevent friction between closely packed organs by secreting serum that acts as a lubricant, to help hold the abdominal organs in their proper positions, to separate and unite organs, and to guard as a barrier against infection.

·abdominal structures and disease **2**:1179c; illus.
·arrowworm anatomical structure **4**:18h
·digestive system mesentery origins and fusions **6**:753d
·embryonic origin and development **5**:639h; illus. 632
·human reproductive system structure **15**:694g
·mesenteric attachments in abdomen **2**:1179f; illus.
·urinary bladder anatomy **7**:52h

peritonitis, inflammation of the peritoneum, the membrane that folds on itself to line the abdominal wall on one side and the abdominal organs on the other side. The condition is marked by an accumulation of serum, fibrin, cells, and pus in the peritoneal cavity (between the two folds of the peritoneal membrane) and by abdominal pain and distension, vomiting, and fever. Acute peritonitis is usually secondary to an inflammatory process elsewhere in the body and may be caused by a variety of agents, such as a bacterial invasion from an infected body structure, or blood or other body fluids from a ruptured organ. A perforated gastrointestinal tract, notably a ruptured appendix, is a common primary cause of peritonitis. Peritonitis may be acute or chronic, generalized or localized. Control of the source of inflammation is followed either by remission of the peritoneal inflammation, by the formation of adhesions sealing the two sides of the peritoneal cavity, or by localized abcesses in the peritoneum, which must then be drained. Antibiotic therapy has greatly decreased the incidence of the latter complication.

·abdominal cavity inflammations **2**:1179h
·gastrointestinal tract diseases **5**:769h
·physiological shock causes **16**:701b
·streptococcal septicemic infection **9**:550e

Peritonsillar abcess (medicine): *see* quinsy.

peritrich, any ciliated vase-shaped protozoan of the order Peritrichida (more than 1,000 species), found in both fresh and salt water. Usually nonmotile (sessile), they attach themselves to underwater objects, but a few genera, such as *Telotrochidium*, are free-swimming. In most peritrichs a posterior disk, the scopula, secretes a stalk for attachment. Some primitive forms, such as the genus *Scyphidia*, attach directly to an object with the adhesive secreted by the scopula. Peritrichida, lacking uniform ciliation, have conspicuous rows of cilia (short hairlike processes) around the mouth, and there is a posterior ring of cilia in the free-swimming migratory adults and larvae. Reproduction by longitudinal fission differs from the usual ciliate transverse fission. Some sessile genera (for example, *Vorticella*) are solitary; others (*e.g.*, *Zoothamnium*) form branching colonies.

Peritrich (*Zoothamnium* colony)
J.M. Langham

·protozoan features and classification **15**:129e

periwinkle (plant): *see* Apocynaceae.

periwinkle, any marine snail comprising the family Littorinidae (subclass Prosobranchia of the class Gastropoda) or a similar snail. The shell typically is a fat spiral with a roundish aperture in the first whorl of the shell. Periwinkles, which occur in the intertidal zone, feed on algae.

Periwinkles (*Littorina*)
Jane Burton—Bruce Coleman Ltd.

The genus *Littorina*, abundant on rocky shores worldwide, includes the common periwinkle (*L. littorea*) of northern Europe; it was introduced about 1840 in the region from Nova Scotia to Maryland. Knobby or strongly beaded species are called pricklywinkles. Periwinkles of the family Lacunidae, confined to cold waters, include the common northern lacuna (*Lacuna vincta*). In the southern U.S. any small freshwater snail is likely to be called a periwinkle or pennywinkle.

·coastal life on Atlantic shores illus. **4**:804
·food use, reproduction styles, and effect on coasts **7**:948a *passim* to 952a

Periyapurāṇam (*c.* 1140), 12th book of the Saivasiddhanta sect of Hinduism, compiled by Sekkilar.

·religious theme and influence **17**:141a

Periyār, river and lake in southern Kerala state, India. The river, 140 mi (225 km) long, rises in the Western Ghāts range near the border with Tamil Nadu and flows north to Periyār Lake in Kottayam district. The lake, 12 sq mi (31 sq km) in area, is an artificial reservoir

Logging on the Periyār River, Kerala
Gilbert Leroy—C.I.R.I.

created by damming the river. It lies at an altitude of 2,800 ft (850 m), is ringed by mountain peaks, and is surrounded by a wildlife sanctuary. A tunnel carries water from the lake eastward through the mountains to the Vaigai River in Tamil Nadu where it is used for irrigation.

From the lake the Periyār River flows in a generally northwest direction through the mountains and onto the coastal plain, past Alwaye, emptying into the Arabian Sea at Parūr. Further development of the river was in progress in the early 1970s and included construction of a hydroelectric project and another irrigation dam.

10°12′ N, 76°11′ E

perjury, willful, knowing, and corrupt giving under oath of false testimony regarded as material to the issue or point of inquiry. All elements of the crime are essential for conviction. Criminal intent is required; a person who makes a false statement and then later corrects himself has not committed perjury. The testimony must be material to the issue of inquiry, since perjury on a point not material can be no more than a misdemeanour and may not be punished at all.

The giving of false testimony under oath distinguishes perjury from criminal contempt. The latter is an obstruction of the administration of justice, usually in violation of an order of the court (*see* contempt). Some perjuries that have the effect of obstructing the adjudication of a case may be given increased punishment for that reason. Generally, however, punishment is directed less against the effect of the perjury than against the disregard of the oath itself. Thus, a man who perjures himself numerous times during the adjudication of one case may be convicted of only a single perjury, though his punishment may be increased.

One who knows of another's perjury and does not make his information known to authorities may be convicted of a separate offense of subornation of perjury. This offense covers anyone who is implicated in the perjury.

Perkin, Sir William Henry (b. March 12, 1838, London—d. July 14, 1907, Sudbury, near Harrow, Middlesex), chemist who discovered aniline dyes. In 1853 he entered the Royal College of Chemistry, London, where he studied under August Wilhelm von Hofmann.

While Perkin was working as Hofmann's laboratory assistant, he became inspired by one of his papers and undertook the synthesis of quinine. He obtained a bluish substance with excellent dyeing properties that later became known as aniline purple, Tyrian purple, or mauve. In 1856 he obtained a patent for manufacturing the dye, and the next year, with the aid of his father and his brother Thomas, he set up an aniline manufacturing plant near Harrow.

In 1858 he and B.F. Duppa synthesized glycine in the first laboratory preparation of an amino acid. They synthesized tartaric acid in 1860. Perkin also shared in developing the synthetic red dye alizarin, obtained a patent for the process, and held a monopoly on its manufacture for several years. He discovered the Perkin reaction (1867) and later studied the optical rotation of various substances. On the 50th anniversary of his discovery of mauve he was knighted. He also investigated other dyes, salicyl alcohol, and flavourings, and synthesized the first artificial perfume, coumarin, in 1868. About 1874 he abandoned manufacturing and devoted himself to research.

·dye production development role **18**:43a
·science history and application **16**:374a
·synthetic dye discovery and manufacture **5**:1099g
·synthetic dyestuff discovery **5**:1106h

Perkins, Jacob (1766–1849), U.S. inventor of the horizontal steam engine (1827) that later was successfully developed as the uniflow engine. In 1834 he obtained one of the first patents for a refrigerating machine. His model worked by the expansion of volatile fluids.

·hot-water heating development **8**:710f
·refrigeration equipment development **15**:564b

Perkins, William (1558–1602), English Puritan theologian famous for his powerful and persuasive sermons; his attempt to write a systematic Puritan theology met with some success.

Pērkons, in Latvian, PERKŪNAS in Lithuanian, PERKUNIS in Old Prussian, the Thunderer of Baltic religion, renowned as the guardian of law and order and as a fertility god; the oak, as the tree most often struck by lightning, is sacred to him. Pērkons, a sky deity often confused with Dievs, is related in functions and image to the Slavic Perun, Germanic Thor, and Greek Zeus Keraunos. Often depicted as a vigorous, bearded man holding an ax, Pērkons rides across the sky, striking fire with his two-wheeled chariot, bringing rain to the farmers. In the spring, his lightning purifies the earth and stimulates plant growth. Pērkons also directs his thunderbolts against evil spirits and unjust men and even disciplines the gods: Lithuanian legend recounts that Perkūnas punished the infidelity of Mėnuo, the moon god, by cutting him in two. Thunderbolts—"bullets of Pērkons," found buried in the ground as flint or bronze celts—or any object or man struck by lightning can be used by mortals as protection against devils or as cures for toothache, fever, and fright. Probably the most popular of all Baltic gods, Pērkons is often referred to as *dievaitis*, "little (or dear) god."

·Baltic form of Indo-European archetype **2**:665b
·Slavic parallels **16**:874h

Perkūnas (Baltic deity): *see* Pērkons.

Perl, Joseph (1773–1839), Russian Jewish author.

·satire of superstition and clericalism **10**:323c

Perlak, historic kingdom of northern Sumatra, Indonesia.

·Indonesian introduction of Islām **9**:482e; map 479

Perleidiformes, order of extinct fishes (subclass or infraclass Chondrostei) containing three families that existed from the Lower to the Upper Triassic.

·Chondrosteii classification and general features **4**:438f
·fish characteristics and classification **7**:342c

Perlepe (Yugoslavia): *see* Prilep.

Perlesvaus, early-13th-century romance with Christological overtones.

·themes and Christian allegory **15**:1023e

Perlis, state (*negeri*), northwestern West Malaysia (Malaya), wedged between Thailand and northwestern Kedah State, with a short coastline on the Andaman Sea (southwest). The smallest (307 sq mi [795 sq km]) and most northerly of the Malayan states, it was part of Kedah until 1821. Given sultanate status by Thailand in 1841, Perlis became one of the Unfederated Malay States under British protection when Thai suzerainty ended (1909). After temporary annexation by Thailand in 1943, it again became a British protectorate in 1945 and later joined the Federation of Malaya.

Mainly occupying a closely cultivated and densely settled plain, formed by short streams (from a steep northeastern range) that combine to form the Sungai (River) Perlis, it is one of the country's most productive paddy-(rice-) growing regions. Regular crops of dry paddy are sown, as the coarse alluvium and erratic streams present problems of water shortage for wet farming. Rubber and coconuts are minor crops. Kuala Perlis and Sanglang are small fishing villages with houses built on stilts over water. While Malay paddy farmers are an overwhelming majority, some Chinese are engaged in tin mining in the underground caves and crevices of the northern limestone hills and live in small mining settlements such as Kaki Bukit.

Because of its size, Perlis is not divided into administrative districts. Kangar, the state capital, is a dispersed, open settlement, and the sultan resides at nearby Arau. Roads link the main villages, including Bukit Keteri, Simpang Ampat, and Beseri. At Padang Besar ("big field"), a port of entry, the Malayan Railway crosses into Thailand. Bukit Tengku Lembu is the site of a neolithic burial ground. Pop. (1970 prelim.) 121,062.

·area and population, table 1 **11**:373

perlite, also called PEARLSTONE, a natural glass with concentric cracks such that the rock breaks into small, pearllike bodies. It is formed by rapid cooling of viscous lava or magma. Perlite has a waxy to pearly lustre and is commonly gray or greenish but may be brown, blue, or red.

Some perlites are of intrusive origin (dikes) but others constitute major portions of lava flows. These glassy rocks may grade into nearly completely crystalline volcanic types. Like obsidian, they may contain large crystals (phenocrysts) of quartz, alkali feldspar, plagioclase feldspar, and, in some cases, biotite or hornblende; where phenocrysts are abundant the rock passes into vitrophyre. Crystalline bodies may also abound, and their curved or wavy trains are common evidence of flowage of the viscous molten material.

A rhyolite (*q.v.*), perlite has chemical composition, index of refraction, and specific gravity similar to those of obsidian (*q.v.*). Its water content, however, is considerably higher (generally 3 to 4 percent); much of it is absorbed, subsequent to consolidation, from the sea or wet sediments into which the perlite was intruded.

Devitrification, or conversion of the glass to a microscopically fine crystalline aggregate, is usually initiated spontaneously along cracks or at the surfaces of phenocrysts and crystalline bodies (spherulites). Some minutely crystalline rocks show well-developed perlitic structure and undoubtedly represent completely devitrified perlite. The localization of spherulites along curved and concentric bands in certain glass-free rocks suggests a devitrified perlite with spherulitic growth along the perlitic cracks.

Before about 1950 perlite was virtually unknown in commerce. Since then, however, great deposits have been worked in New Mexico, Nevada, California, and other western states; production outside the U.S. has increased very slowly. When crushed perlite is rapidly heated, the contained water is converted to steam; tiny bubbles are formed within the softened rock, and the perlite is thus expanded up to 20 times its original volume. Because of its very low density, heat-treated perlite is a substitute for sand in lightweight wall plaster and concrete aggregate. The porous nature of perlite makes it the material ideal for heat and sound insulation; other uses include lightweight ceramic products, filters, and fillers.

·classification and fracture mechanism **9**:205c; table 207

perlitic texture (geology): *see* spherulite.

Perlschrift, writing style most widely used for biblical and patristic texts from the end of the 10th century, characterized by plain, neat, rounded letters.

·Greek calligraphy style development **3**:650c

Perm, *oblast* (administrative region), western Russian Soviet Federated Socialist Republic, occupying an area of 62,050 sq mi (160,700 sq km) on the western flank of the central Urals, extending from the crestline in the east across the broad basin of the middle Kama to the

Verkhne Kama Upland in the west. The northwest corner is occupied by the Komi-Permyak national *okrug* (district). Almost the entire *oblast* is thickly forested, with swampy forest, or taiga, of spruce, fir, pine, and birch. Extensive floodplain meadows line the rivers. In 1973, 70 percent of the population was urban, reflecting Perm's position as part of the Urals industrial area. It is exceptionally rich in minerals, notably of salt and potassium along the Kama; these are the basis of the chemical industry of Berezniki, Solikamsk, and Perm city, the administrative centre. Petroleum is extracted along the Kama, in the Sylva and Iren Valleys, and in the south, and is refined in Perm and Krasnokamsk. Chusovoy and Lysva have metallurgical plants, and most cities have engineering industries. The forests supply paper, pulp, and other timber-working industries. Agriculture has a minor role, except for intensive market gardening around the cities. There are several large power stations, notably the Kama hydroelectric plants. Pop. (1973 est.) 2,972,000.

Perm, called MOLOTOV from 1940 to 1957, city and administrative centre of Perm *oblast* (region), western Russian Soviet Federated Socialist Republic, on both banks of the Kama River. In 1723 a copper-smelting works was founded at the village of Yegoshikha (founded 1568), at the junction of the Yegoshikha and Kama rivers. In 1780 the settlement of Yegoshikha became the town of Perm, although another town, Perm the Great (now Cherdyn), had existed 150 mi upstream since the 14th century. The city grew in commercial importance through its position on the navigable Kama and on the Great Siberian Highway, established in 1783, and, later, on the Trans-Siberian Railroad, completed to Yekaterinburg (now Sverdlovsk) in 1878. Modern Perm is still a major focus of communications and is also one of the chief industrial centres of the Urals region. It has a wide range of large-scale engineering industries, a major oil refinery, and a large chemical industry, making fertilizers and dyes. The city's seven institutions of higher education include the A.M. Gorky University, founded in 1918. There are four theatres, a notable art gallery, and a school of ballet. Perm gives its name to the Permian Period (about 225,000,000 to 280,000,000 years ago), which was first identified in the locality. Pop. (1973 est.) 901,000.

58°00′ N, 56°15′ E

·map, Soviet Union **17**:322
·population and resources **17**:336f

permafrost 14:89, permanently frozen earth, with a temperature below 0° C (32° F) continuously for two or more years, estimated to underlie 20 percent of the Earth's land surface and reaching depths of 5,000 feet (1,525 metres) in northern Siberia. The position of the southern boundary of permafrost in the Northern Hemisphere corresponds approximately to the position of the line connecting points whose mean annual air temperature is 0° C.

The text article covers the origin and stability of permafrost, local thickness and ice content, surface manifestations of permafrost and seasonally frozen ground, and problems posed by permafrost.

REFERENCES in other text articles:
·Alaskan mountain location **1**:414d *passim* to 415a
·bog–forest ecotone instability **17**:837d
·distribution, ice forms, and bases **8**:175a
·exploration of frozen ground **7**:82b
·human manipulation and consequences **14**:432b
·hydrologic element role and analysis **9**:114h
·Mackenzie River lowlands formation **11**:266g
·Martian atmosphere and water vapour **11**:524b
·microclimatic freeze–thaw process **12**:117g
·North American soil groupings **13**:190c
·Pleistocene climate evidences **14**:567g
·Pleistocene glaciation and climate **4**:733d
·river-ice freezing and ice jams **9**:168h
·soil composition disadvantage **13**:261c
·tundra climate and geology **18**:733b
·world climates and their distribution **4**:727d
·Yukon industrial growth drawbacks **19**:1109d

RELATED ENTRIES in the *Ready Reference and Index:*
patterned ground; pingo; thermokarst topography

Permalloy, nickel–iron alloy having much higher magnetic permeability than iron alone. It is widely used in such applications as transformer laminations. The proportion of nickel may range from 35 to 90 percent, depending on the properties desired, and is about 78 percent for low-power transformers. An alloy of 50 percent nickel, called Hipernik, is useful for high-power transformers. Heat-treating Permalloy containing 5 percent molybdenum in pure hydrogen yields Supermalloy, with even higher permeability.

·composition and uses **13**:73c
·magnetic material properties **11**:336g; table

Permanent Court of Arbitration, panel of jurists created under the Convention for the Pacific Settlement of International Disputes of 1899. It was succeeded by the Permanent Court of International Justice, created by the League of Nations in 1920, and this in turn was replaced by the International Court of Justice, established by the United Nations after World War II.

·arbitration of international disputes **1**:1077c
·The Hague peace conferences **9**:733e

Permanent Court of International Justice (1920): *see* International Court of Justice.

permanent dentition: *see* dentition, permanent.

Permanent Joint Board on Defense—United States and Canada, created in 1940 after a conference at Ogdensburg, N.Y., between the U.S. president, Franklin D. Roosevelt, and the Canadian prime minister, W.L. Mackenzie King. Its duties are to carry out studies relating to sea, land, and air problems and to consider in the broad sense the defense of the northern half of the Western Hemisphere.

·creation and Canadian significance **3**:745c

permanent wave, a long-lasting hair wave produced by winding hair on curlers; chemicals are applied, sometimes together with heat.

·hair preparations and usage **5**:197g

permanent wilting, wilting point at which a plant will recover only with addition of water to the soil.

·hydrologic element transformations **9**:107g

permanganate, salt or ester of permanganic acid; the salts are deep purple compounds containing the anion formulated MnO_4^-.

·preparation and reactivity **18**:615b

permeability, capacity of a porous material for transmitting a fluid; it is expressed as the velocity with which a fluid of specified viscosity, under the influence of a given pressure, passes through a sample having a certain cross section and thickness. Permeability is dependent on the size and shape of the pores in the substance and, in granular materials such as sedimentary rocks, by the size, shape, and packing arrangement of the grains.

The unit of permeability is the darcy, equivalent to the passage of one cubic centimetre of fluid (having a viscosity of one centipoise) per second through a sample one square centimetre in cross-sectional area driven by a pressure of one atmosphere per centimetre of thickness.

·clay mineral occurrence and effects **4**:705a
·conglomerates, breccias, and tillites **4**:1111c
·drainage systems soil analysis **9**:902f
·groundwater and aquifers **15**:878h
·groundwater geologic factors **8**:435h
·hydraulic conductivity in rocks **15**:963h
·hydrologic transformation processes **9**:110g
·loess textural characteristics **11**:25c
·petroleum development environment **14**:169d
·sedimentary rock properties **16**:468h
·soil properties for engineering **16**:1011g
·soil structure properties **16**:1021h

permeability, magnetic, relative increase or decrease in the resultant magnetic field inside a material compared with the magnetizing field in which the given material is located; or the property of a material that is equal to the magnetic flux density B established within the material by a magnetizing field divided by the magnetic field strength H of the magnetizing field. Magnetic permeability μ (Greek mu) is thus defined as $\mu = B/H$. Magnetic flux density B is a measure of the actual magnetic field within a material considered as a concentration of magnetic field lines, or flux, per unit cross-sectional area. Magnetic field strength H is a measure of the magnetizing field produced by electric current flow in a coil of wire.

In empty, or free, space the magnetic flux density is the same as the magnetizing field because there is no matter to modify the field. In centimetre–gram–second (cgs) units, the permeability B/H of space is dimensionless and has a value of 1. In metre–kilogram–second (mks) units, B and H have different dimensions, and the permeability of free space (special symbol μ_0) is defined as equal to $4\pi \times 10^{-7}$ weber per ampere-metre so that the mks unit of electric current may be the same as the practical unit, the ampere. In the mks system the permeability, B/H, is called the absolute permeability μ of the medium. The relative permeability μ_r is then defined as the ratio μ/μ_0, which is dimensionless and has the same numerical value as the permeability in the cgs system. Thus, the relative permeability of free space, or vacuum, is 1.

Materials may be classified magnetically on the basis of their permeabilities. A diamagnetic material has a constant relative permeability slightly less than 1. When a diamagnetic material, such as bismuth, is placed in a magnetic field, the external field is partly expelled, and the magnetic flux density within it is slightly reduced. A paramagnetic material has a constant relative permeability slightly more than 1. When a paramagnetic material, such as platinum, is placed in a magnetic field, it becomes slightly magnetized in the direction of the external field. A ferromagnetic material, such as iron, does not have a constant relative permeability. As the magnetizing field increases, the relative permeability increases, reaches a maximum, and then decreases. Purified iron and many magnetic alloys have maximum relative permeabilities of 100,000 or more.

·magnetic permeable materials **11**:335h
·magnetism theory and principles **11**:316e
·radio-frequency heating effects **15**:448h

permeability formula, formula used in computing the safety of ships under flooding conditions; the permeability is defined as the ratio of volume of a compartment that can be occupied by water to the total volume.

·ship construction regulations **16**:692d

Përmet, province, southern Albania.

·area and population table **1**:419

Permian languages: *see* Permic languages.

Permian (PERMYAK, PERMIC) **peoples,** Finno-Ugric ethnolinguistic group, composed of the Udmurts (*q.v.*; also called Votyaks) and the Komi (*q.v.*; also called Zyryans). They inhabit the Udmurt A.S.S.R. and the Komi A.S.S.R. of the Russian S.F.S.R.

·origins and present-day representatives **7**:310d

Permian Period 14:96, the geologic period that began about 280,000,000 years ago and lasted about 55,000,000 years; during this final period of the Paleozoic Era, which followed the Upper Carboniferous and preceded the Triassic Period, Permian System rocks were formed.

The text article covers the rocks of the Permian System and also the profound changes that affected every continent: the uplift and deformation of geosynclinal regions that created mountains; the breakup of the ancient continent of Gondwanaland and the drifting apart of the southern continents; and the desert environments that became widespread as the shallow, epicontinental seas (those lying on a continent or continental shelf) withdrew from the continents. Also treated are the Permian climates, wherein the southern continents experienced an extensive and profound period of glaciation at the same time as the northern continents were warm and arid.

The text article covers in detail Permian life, which flourished in marine and terrestrial realms; treated are the invertebrates, vertebrates, and plants that showed increasing adaptive specialization. Also covered is the great decline of many groups that occurred as the period drew to a close, causing the end of the Permian to be regarded as a time of major crisis in the history of life: extinction of many formerly abundant groups occurred for reasons that are not well understood.

REFERENCES in other text articles:
·African marine fossils and continent development 1:182h; map 181
·animal fossil records of major groups 7:558a
·Asian paleogeography 2:153h; map 154
·Australian geological history 2:385h; map 382
·coal and evaporite deposits and orogeny 3:856f
·coal formation and development 4:793a
·conifer geological history 5:7a
·conodont fossil record 5:26g
·continental drift and fossil diversity 13:908h
·coral profusion and reef growth 5:163g
·European features 6:1039d; map 1040
·evaporite mineral deposits 6:1139a
·extrusive igneous rock formation 9:214h
·fish evolutionary trends 7:337e; illus. 339
·geological time scale, illus. 2 5:499
·geologic history, climate, and life 6:14a
·glacial and eolian deposits 16:473c
·glaciation extent and paleogeography 8:164e
·Heteroptera and Homoptera separation 8:850b
·hymenopteran insect possible appearance 9:131f
·Late Permian animal extinctions 18:695a
·plant fossil records of major groups 7:574f
·pollen stratigraphy and evolution 14:740c; illus.
·reptile evolution trends 15:736f; illus.
·South American volcanism and tectonism 17:78c; map 79
·stratigraphic boundary problems 17:723g
·time scale improvement by Murchison 7:1067g
·Upper Paleozoic geology and life 13:921b; map
·varved deposit formation 19:35a

RELATED ENTRIES in the *Ready Reference and Index: for*
depositional basin: see Delaware Basin; Marfa Basin
rock formations: Castile Formation; Coconino Sandstone Formation; Dekkas Volcanic Formation; Dunkard Group; Hermit Shale Formation; Kaibab Limestone Formation; Phosphoria Formation; Salado Formation; Supai Formation; Toroweap Formation
systems: Karroo System; Permian System

Permian System, rocks formed during the Permian Period, which began about 280,000,000 years ago and lasted about 55,000,000 years. Permian rocks have a worldwide distribution and have been divided into an Upper and a Lower Permian Series; each series, in turn, has been further subdivided into regional stages. From this, a composite, international standardized sequence of stages has been determined.
·rock types, distribution, and fossils 14:96a
·Upper Paleozoic stratigraphic units, table 2 13:928

RELATED ENTRIES in the *Ready Reference and Index: for*
Lower Permian Series: see Artinskian Stage; Asselian Stage; Leonardian Stage; Sakmarian Stage; Wolfcampian Stage
Upper Permian Series: Guadalupian Stage; Kazanian Stage; Kungurian Stage; Ochoan Stage; Tartarian Stage

Permic (PERMYAK, PERMIAN) **languages,** division of the Finno-Ugric branch of the Uralic language family, consisting of the Udmurt (Votyak) and Komi (Zyryan) languages. The Permic languages are spoken by nearly 1,000,000 persons along the northern and western reaches of the Ural Mountains in the Soviet Union in and around the Udmurt A.S.S.R. and the Komi A.S.S.R. Udmurt has little dialectal variation, but Komi has many distinctive dialects divided into three major groups: Northern (Zyryan) Komi, Western (Permyak) Komi, and Eastern (Yazva) Komi. Komi has two literary languages, one based on Zyryan and the other on Permyak. Both Udmurt and Komi have flourishing literatures that have developed primarily since the second half of the 19th century, although written records of Komi exist from the 14th century. The Permic languages are of note for their contrast of voiced and voiceless consonants (voiceless *p* contrasts with voiced *b*) generally lacking in the Uralic languages. *See also* Finno-Ugric languages; Komi language; Udmurt language.
·history and location 18:1027a; map 1023

Permic peoples (ethnolinguistic group): *see* Permian peoples.

permittivity, a universal electric constant appearing in the mathematical formulation of two fundamental phenomena, the existence of a physical force between two separated electric charges (*see* Coulomb force), and the modification of the properties of an electric field attending the introduction into it of a dielectric (*see* displacement, electric). Permittivity is a generalized, or large-scale, description of electric behaviour that does not specify detailed features on the atomic dimension.

The permittivity of an insulating, or dielectric, material is commonly symbolized by the Greek letter epsilon, ϵ; the permittivity of a vacuum, or free space, is symbolized ϵ_0; and their ratio ϵ/ϵ_0, called the dielectric constant (*q.v.*), is symbolized by the Greek letter kappa, κ.

In the rationalized metre–kilogram–second (mks) system, the magnitude of the permittivity of a vacuum ϵ_0 is 8.854×10^{-12}. Its units and those of permittivity ϵ are square coulombs per newton square metre. In the mks system, permittivity ϵ and the dimensionless dielectric constant κ are formally distinct and related by the permittivity of free space ϵ_0; $\epsilon = \kappa\epsilon_0$. The magnitude and units of the permittivity of free space in the mks system are a necessary consequence of the laws of physics and of the decision to make the practical electrical units in use, such as volt and ampere, compatible with the mechanical units, such as metre and kilogram. In the centimetre–gram–second (cgs) system, the value of the permittivity of free space ϵ_0 is chosen arbitrarily to be one. Thus, the permittivity ϵ and the dielectric constant κ in the cgs system are identical; both are dimensionless numbers.

Permon, Laure (memoirist): *see* Junot, Laure, duchesse d'Abrantès.

Per-Month (town, Egypt): *see* Hermonthis.

Permoser, Balthasar (1651–1732), artist who became court sculptor at Dresden (1689) and was an outstanding exponent of German Baroque sculpture.
·Baroque sculpture developments 19:430g

permutation, ordered subset selected from a given set, the number of permutations of *n* objects taken *r* at a time being the ratio of *n* factorial (product of the first *n* positive integers) and $(n - r)$ factorial.
·combinatorics theory and method 4:943h
·probability theory and method 14:1105a

permutation, law of, a formula of propositional calculus.
·propositional calculus formula, table 3 11:41

Permyak languages (linguistics): *see* Permic languages.

Permyak peoples (ethnolinguistic group): *see* Permian peoples.

Pernambuco 14:100, state of northeastern Brazil, bounded by the Atlantic Ocean (east), by the states of Alagoas and Bahia (south), by Piauí (west), and by Ceará and Paraíba (north). Its area is 37,947 sq mi (98,281 sq km). The state capital is Recife. Pop. (1970 prelim.) 5,252,590.

The text article covers Pernambuco's history, natural environment, population, administration and social conditions, economy, transportation, and cultural life and institutions.

REFERENCES in other text articles:
·area and population table 3:133
·map, Brazil 3:125
·Recife historical and cultural aspects 15:543b

Pernambuco Abyssal Plain, submarine depression, Atlantic Ocean.
5°00′ S, 25°00′ W
·Atlantic Ocean floor features map 2:299

pernicious anemia, severe, slow-developing disease, characterized by deficiency of red blood cells and often white cells and platelets in the circulation, by associated jaundice from accelerated destruction of red cells in the bone marrow, by lack of gastric juice (achylia gastrica), and by progressive gastrointestinal and neurologic problems. Pernicious anemia is caused by deficiency of vitamin B_{12}, occasionally from dietary lack (*e.g.*, among strict vegetarians) but usually from underproduction of a substance called intrinsic factor, made by parietal cells in the stomach fundus and necessary for absorption of vitamin B_{12} from the food. Lack of vitamin B_{12} leads to disordered production of deoxyribonucleic acid (DNA): in the bone marrow, red-cell production becomes abnormal—the nuclei remain immature, while the surrounding cytoplasm matures normally, eventually becoming overabundant and containing much hemoglobin. Such cells, called megaloblasts, are destroyed in the bone marrow without being freed to the circulation. Some megaloblasts mature to become large red cells, called macrocytes; these reach the circulation but function abnormally and have a reduced life-span. Deficiency of white blood cells (leukopenia) and of platelets (thrombocytopenia) also develops in the circulation. Pernicious anemia may develop after stomach ulcer, cancer, or removal of the stomach; the reason for atrophy of the parietal cells of the stomach fundus, the commonest cause of pernicious anemia, however, is usually not known. Most patients display antibodies against the parietal cells; over 50 percent also show antibodies against intrinsic factor. Pernicious anemia affects males and females equally, is uncommon under age 35, and is commoner in persons with blood group A and in blue-eyed, bulky-framed, light-skinned north Europeans. Symptoms and signs include waxy pallor; fatigue; weakness; shortness of breath; jaundice; smooth, shiny tongue; deficiency of constituents of gastric juice; and progressive neurological problems, such as loss of sensation in fingers and toes, stiffness, incoordination, apathy, and irritability. The administration of vitamin B_{12} by injection produces quick improvement in the anemia; neurological damage is seldom fully reversible.
·blood diseases from B_{12} deficiency 2:1135g
·cause and symptoms 5:860h
·diagnosis with radioactive cobalt 5:694h

·digestive gland atrophy **5**:799g
·treatment before and after 1948 **11**:836a
·vitamin B_{12} secondary deficiency **13**:419h

Pernik, called DIMITROVO from 1949 to 1962, chief town of Pernik *okrŭg* (province), western Bulgaria. The town lies on the Struma River just southwest of Sofia; it is a major industrial, steel, and coal-mining centre and has a ruined Byzantine fortress. Pop. (1971 est.) town, 81,227; *okrŭg*, 181,033.
42°36′ N, 23°02′ W
·area and population table **3**:472
·map, Bulgaria **3**:471

Perninae (bird subfamily): *see* kite.

Perobolinggo (Indonesia): *see* Probolinggo.

Perodicticus potto (primate): *see* potto.

Perognathus (genus of rodent): *see* pocket mouse.

peromelia, congenital absence or malformation of the extremities, of rare occurrence until the thalidomide (*q.v.*) tragedy in the early 1960s. It is caused by errors in segmentation of the embryo in early intrauterine life.

In amelia, one of the rarest of malformations of the extremities, limbs are completely absent. Ectromelia is the absence of one or more extremities. In phocomelia ("seal extremity") the upper part of the limb is extremely underdeveloped or missing, and the lower part is attached directly to the trunk, resembling the flipper of a seal. Hemimelia is a condition in which the upper part of the limb is well formed but the lower part is rudimentary or absent. Sirenomelia ("mermaid extremity") is a severe abnormality in which the legs are fused to a greater or lesser degree and contain malformed bones, the anal and urinary orifices are absent, and the genitals and parts of the intestinal and urinary tracts malformed.

Treatment of major limb malformations involves the fitting of prostheses and special training in their use. Surgery is used with success in relieving minor malformations.
·biological malformation types **11**:379e
·birth defects and incidence **2**:1074f
·bone injury during pregnancy **3**:29d

Peromyscus (genus of rodent): *see* white-footed mouse.

Perón, (María) Eva (Duarte de), *née* IBARGUREN, popularly called EVITA (b. May 7, 1919, Los Toldos, near Buenos Aires—d. July 26, 1952, Buenos Aires), film and radio actress who married Juan Perón (*q.v.*) in 1945 (while he was Argentinian vice president and minister of war) and thereafter, during her husband's first term as president (1946–51), became a powerful though unofficial political leader, revered by the lower economic classes. Regarded as de facto minister of health and of labour, she organized female workers, secured woman suffrage, directed heavy government expenditures on welfare programs, and introduced compulsory religious education into all Argentinian schools. In 1951, although she knew herself to be dying of cancer, she obtained the Peronista Party's nomination for vice president, but the army forced her to withdraw her candidature.
·Fascist policy and movement in Argentina **7**:188d
·marriage and political significance **14**:101h
·political interest and influence **1**:1150a

Perón, Juan (Domingo) 14:101 (b. Oct. 8, 1895, Buenos Aires province, Argentina—d. July 1, 1974, Buenos Aires), president of Argentina (1946–55 and Oct. 12, 1973–July 1, 1974), founder and leader of the Peronista movement.

Abstract of text biography. Born into a lower-middle class creole family, Perón was educated at a military school and served as a military attaché in Italy in the late 1930s. He participated in the military coup of 1943, became vice president and minister of war (1945), and, with the help of his beautiful and popular wife, Eva (*see* Perón, Eva), was elected president of Argentina (1946). His presidency accomplished economic and diplomatic reforms but was marred by graft and the suppression of civil liberties, all opposition being ruthlessly suppressed. Overthrown by a coup in 1955, Perón, in exile, eventually settled in Madrid. In 1973 a revived Peronista movement recalled him to Argentina, and once more he was elected president, with his third wife, María Estela Martínez de Perón, as vice president.

REFERENCES in other text articles:
·economic and social welfare policies and consequences **1**:1140a *passim* to 1143b
·Fascist policy and movement in Argentina **7**:188c
·political position and U.S. conflict **9**:756h
·presidency and continuing influence **1**:1149f

peroneal artery, an artery arising from the posterior tibial artery and having several branches that serve the outside and back of the ankle and deep calf muscles.
·human cardiovascular system anatomy **3**:883c

peroneal nerve, common, also called COMMON FIBULAR NERVE, a general sensory and motor nerve, arising in the sciatic nerve, with branches serving the lower leg and the foot.
·anatomy and functions **12**:1024b

peroneus longus muscle, muscle in the outer part of the calf that functions in various foot movements.
·muscle changes in human evolution **12**:636g

Peronistas, in Argentinian politics, supporters of Juan Perón (*q.v.*), who were an important element in the military clique that seized power in Argentina in June 1943 and who, with Perón as president, ruled Argentina from 1946 to 1955. Peronistas represent many very divergent elements, but the labour unions have always been one of their bastions. During the years in which they were out of power they continued to be a disturbing factor in Argentinian politics. Peronistas again took control of the government in 1973, when they won the presidency, overwhelming numbers in Congress, and all provincial governorships except two. Deep dissension between right-wing and left-wing Peronistas, which had developed before Perón's return to Argentina and which his presence had not alleviated, persisted after his death, and terrorism and violence, with many assassinations, increased.
·origin and continuing influence **1**:1149h *passim* to 1151a
·political significance after Perón **14**:102c

perosis, a disorder of chicks, turkey poults, and young swans, characterized by enlargement of the hock, twisted metatarsi, and slipped tendons; it can be largely eliminated by adding choline to the diet.
·animal feed and manganese deficiency **1**:909c

Perot, Alfred (1863–1925), French physicist.
·spectroscopic interferometer invention **17**:461a

Pérotin, Latin PEROTINUS (d. 1238?, Paris?), composer of sacred polyphonic music believed to have introduced the composition of polyphony in four parts into Western music. Nothing is known of his life, and his identity is not clearly established. He worked probably at the cathedral of Notre-Dame in Paris and his compositions are considered to belong to the Notre-Dame, or Parisian, school, of which he and Leoninus are the only members known by name.

Pérotin's four-part works were revolutionary, since religious music of the 12th century was almost entirely in the form of two-part organum (polyphony in which a plainchant melody is sung against another line of music). In Pérotin's organa the liturgical chant of the tenor is heard against not one voice but against two or three voices that provide highly decorative vocalizations. He is known to have composed two four-part works, "Viderunt" and "Sederunt"; another four-part composition, "Mors," is believed to be his. He also enlarged upon the *Magnus liber organi*, a collection of organa by his predecessor, Léonin, and made innovations in the use of rhythm. "Viderunt" and "Sederunt," musical creations comparable in scope to the cathedrals of Gothic architecture, have both been recorded in modern performance.
·additions to organum form **12**:705d
·counterpoint and rhythmic modes **5**:214a
·motet's form expansion **12**:717a

perovskite, calcium titanate mineral ($CaTiO_3$) that often occurs as brilliant black cubes in basic igneous rocks, in their associated pegmatites, and in metamorphic contact zones. It also occurs in chlorite or talc schists. Occurrences include Germany, Italy, Brazil, Sweden, the Soviet Union, and the U.S. For detailed physical properties, *see* table under oxide minerals.
·upper mantle composition and phase transformation **6**:54a; illus. 53

peroxide, any of a class of chemical compounds in which two oxygen atoms are linked together by a single covalent bond. Several organic and inorganic peroxides are useful as bleaching agents, as initiators (*q.v.*) of polymerization reactions, and in the preparation of hydrogen peroxide (*q.v.*) and other oxygen compounds. The negatively charged peroxide ion (O_2^{2-}) is present in inorganic compounds that may be regarded as salts of the very weak acid hydrogen peroxide; examples are sodium peroxide (Na_2O_2), a bleaching agent, and barium peroxide (BaO_2), formerly used as a source of hydrogen peroxide.

Two categories of peroxides exist in which one or both of the oxygen atoms are covalently linked to atoms other than hydrogen. One category is represented by cumene hydroperoxide, an organic compound used as a polymerization initiator and as a source of phenol and acetone, and peroxysulfuric acid, an inorganic compound used as an oxidizing agent. The other category includes di-*tert*-butyl peroxide and ammonium peroxydisulfate, both used as initiators.
·alkali metal chemistry **1**:582b *passim* to 587e
·alkaline-earth salt preparation **1**:591f
·plastic polymerization activation **14**:519a
·radicals from radiation processes **15**:422g

peroxisome, also spelled PEROXYSOME, also called MICROBODY, or GLYOXYSOME, any of a class of membranous subcellular particles known to occur in mammalian tissues. Peroxisomes contain enzymes (biological catalysts) that facilitate production of hydrogen peroxide and its conversion to oxygen and water.
·cellular oxygen regulation **2**:1040f
·membrane function in cell organelles **11**:879b

peroxy acid, or PERACID, any of a class of chemical compounds in which the atomic group $-O-O-H$ replaces the $-O-H$ group of an oxy acid (a compound in which a hydrogen atom is attached to an oxygen atom by a covalent bond that is easily broken, producing an anion and a hydrogen ion). Examples of peroxy acids are peroxyacetic acid ($CH_3CO-OOH$, related to acetic acid, CH_3CO-OH) and peroxysulfuric acid ($HOSO_2-OOH$ or H_2SO_5, analogous to sulfuric acid, $HOSO_2-OH$ or H_2SO_4).

Peroxy acids usually are prepared by reaction of the oxy acid with hydrogen peroxide; small amounts of sulfuric or other strong acids often are used to accelerate the reaction of weak oxy acids. The peroxy acids are used primarily as oxidizing agents; they readily add oxygen to alkenes to give epoxides and are used to convert ketones to esters and amines to nitro compounds, amine oxides, or nitroso compounds.

Performic, peracetic, and perbenzoic acids are among the important peroxy acids. Performic and peracetic acids are liquids miscible with water; peracetic acid decomposes violently at about 110° C; performic acid explodes on contact with metals and their oxides. Perbenzoic acid is a very volatile solid that turns liquid upon contact with water.
·preparation and utilization **3**:873a

per pale, also called PARTY PER PALE, in heraldry, division of the field of a shield into two equal parts by a vertical line.
·heraldic shield design **8**:788d; illus.

Perpendicular Gothic style, latest of three phases (Early English Gothic style, Decorated Gothic style, and Perpendicular), into which English Gothic architecture is usually divided. Pertaining largely to church construction, it flourished from after 1350 to the end of the 15th century and retained its vitality into the 17th. Perpendicular Gothic is most conspicuously characterized by a predominance of vertical lines in the stone tracery (decorative openwork) of windows and an enlargement of windows to very great proportions, with a concomitant reduction of wall space to a minimum of vertical supports. The vertical

West facade of St. George's Chapel, Windsor, Perpendicular Gothic style, *c.* 1475–1500
A.F. Kersting

tracery lines are crossed by horizontal lines to form rectangular patterns that give an impression of endless repetition; and the colouring of the stained glass is lightened almost to transparency. Structurally, the Perpendicular Gothic style tended toward the elimination of the arching lines characteristic of Gothic architecture (*see* Gothic art). In earlier Gothic churches the nave consisted of three rows of arches—the nave arcade, separating the nave from the side aisles, the triforium arcade, separating the upper nave from galleries above the side aisles, and the clerestory, a row of arched windows at the top of the nave wall—all roughly equal in height. In Perpendicular churches the nave was transformed with the virtual or actual elimination of the triforium and heightening of the other stories into a great vertical expanse, and the typical Gothic pointed vaults were replaced by fan vaults (fan-shaped clusters of tracery-like ribs springing from slender columns or from pendent knobs at the centre of the ceiling), which, when the ceiling was flat and made of timber, were nonfunctional.

The Perpendicular Gothic style was employed in numerous sections of English churches that had been begun in earlier periods, and it also was used for much secular architecture. Perhaps because the entire development of English Gothic architecture had tended toward the perfection of decorative systems rather than structural innovation, the Perpendicular Gothic, though similar in its ornateness to the late French Flamboyant Gothic style, had more integrity and power than the Flamboyant. The Perpendicular Gothic style was so vital that it yielded only slowly to Renaissance ideas in the 16th century, and its effect was felt in building even into the 17th century.

Some of the finest examples of Perpendicular Gothic are the south and west cloisters of Westminster Abbey; the west fronts of Gloucester cathedral, the cathedral at Winchester, and Beverley Minster; St. George's Chapel (*c.* 1475–1500) at Windsor; and King's College Chapel at the University of Cambridge (1446–1515).
·English 15th-century architecture **3**:219h
·Gothic architectural developments **19**:369d
·national and regional art style theory **2**:130d
·stylistic labelling development **2**:124e

perpendicular lines, in geometry, lines that intersect at right angles. The four angles formed by the intersection are all equal.

perpetual motion 14:102, the action of a machine that, once started, would keep going indefinitely and preferably could be used for doing work without drawing on external sources of energy. Such a machine would have to violate the principles of conservation of energy or entropy.

The text article treats the three classes of perpetual-motion machines: those purported to deliver more work than would be required to return them to their initial state; those requiring the complete conversion of heat into mechanical work; and those depending upon the elimination of all nonconservative forces, such as friction and electrical resistance. The article concludes by covering devices actuated by subtle external energy sources, including the Sun and long-lived radioactive isotopes.

REFERENCES in other text articles:
·Earth gradual development contradictions **18**:858g *passim* to 859d
·energy transformation laws **6**:850f
·thermodynamics principles and laws **18**:293a *passim* to 293f

Perpetual Peace, Treaty of (1516), concluded between Switzerland and France.
·Swiss concession of Milan **17**:882d

Perpignan, capital of Pyrénées-Orientales *département*, southeast France, on the Tet River, 8 mi (13 km) west of the Mediterranean Sea, and 19 mi (31 km) north of the Spanish frontier.

Formerly a stronghold town, and once the capital of the old province of Roussillon, it is today a flourishing market centre for the wines, fruit, and vegetables of the rich plain in which it is located. The town walls were dismantled toward the end of the 19th century, but the picturesque Castillet—a 14th- and 15th-century crenellated fort that defended the principal gate—still stands and is now a museum. Nearby are the ancient Loge de Mer, which housed the maritime tribunal, and the 14th- and 15th-century cathedral of Saint-Jean. In the south of the town, the bastions of the great 17th- and 18th-century citadel surround the partially restored medieval palace of the kings of Majorca. Paintings by Catalan primitive artists and by Hyacinthe Rigaud, a native of Perpignan, are in the Rigaud Museum.

After serving as the capital of the counts of Roussillon, Perpignan in 1172 passed to the house of Aragon. James I of Aragon divided his realm between his sons, leaving Roussillon and Majorca to the younger, James, the first of three hereditary kings of Majorca who made the city their capital (1276–1344). Perpignan was heavily fortified during and after the struggle between France and Spain for the province of Roussillon, which became French in 1659, by the Treaty of the Pyrenees. Pop. (1975) 101,198.
42°41′ N, 2°53′ E
·map, France **7**:584

Per-Ramesse: *see* Tanis.

Perrault, Charles (b. Jan. 12, 1628, Paris—d. May 15/16, 1703, Paris), poet, prose writer, and storyteller, a leading member of the Académie Française, and participant in a literary controversy known as the *querelle des anciens et des modernes.* He is best remembered for his collection of fairy stories for children, *Contes de ma mère l'oye* (1697; *The Tales of Mother Goose*, 1729).

Charles Perrault, detail of an oil painting by an unknown French artist, 17th century; in the Musée National de Versailles et des Trianons, Versailles, Fr.
Cliche Musees Nationaux, Paris

A lawyer by training, Perrault first worked as an official in charge of royal buildings. He began to win a literary reputation in about 1660 with some light verse and love poetry and spent the rest of his life in promoting the study of literature and the arts. In 1671 he was elected to the Académie Française, which soon was sharply divided by the "quarrel between the Ancients and the Moderns." Perrault supported the modern view that, as civilization progresses, literature evolves with it and that therefore ancient literature is inevitably more coarse and barbarous than modern literature. His poem *Le Siècle de Louis le Grand* (1687; "The Age of Louis the Great") set such modern writers as Molière and François de Malherbe above the classical authors of Greece and Rome.

Perrault's chief opponent in this controversy was Nicolas Boileau-Despréaux, who on the whole had the better of the argument. Nevertheless, Perrault's stand was a landmark in the eventually successful revolt against the confines of the prevailing tradition.

Perrault's charming fairy stories in *Contes de ma mère l'oye* were written to amuse his children. They include "Little Red Riding Hood," "The Sleeping Beauty," "Puss in Boots," and "Bluebeard," modern versions of half-forgotten folk tales, which Perrault retells in a style that is simple and free from affectation.

Three of Perrault's brothers were also well known in their day: Pierre, who supported his brother's position in the ancient and modern controversy; Claude, a doctor of medicine and an architect, derided by Boileau; and Nicolas, a theologian who preached a form of Jansenism.
·children's literature development **4**:240f
·French literature development **10**:1168h

Perrault, Claude (1613–88), French physician and architect. *See also* Perrault, Charles.
·Louvre palace addition style elements **13**:1009g

Perrault, Pierre (b. 1611?, Paris—d. 1680, Paris), hydrologist whose investigation of the origin of springs was instrumental in establishing the science of hydrology on a quantitative basis. He showed conclusively that precipitation was more than adequate to sustain the flow of rivers; thus he refuted theories traceable as far back as the writings of Plato and Aristotle that invoked some sort of subterranean condensation or return flow of seawater to account for the discharge of water in springs and rivers.

Perrault was not a scientist by profession but had been, in succession, a lawyer, a government administrator, and a writer. In his chief scientific work, *De l'origine des fontaines* (1674; Eng. trans., *On the Origin of Springs*, 1967, by Aurele La Rocque), he presented a study of a substantial section of the Seine River, beginning at its source, northwest of the city of Dijon. His numerical estimates showed that the annual river runoff was only one-sixth of the amount of water falling as rain or snow over the drainage basin in a year.

·hydrological investigations **6**:80d
·hydrologic concepts evolution **9**:103d

Perrers, Alice (d. 1400), mistress of King Edward III of England (ruled 1327–77), exercised great influence at the aging monarch's court from about 1369 until 1376, when she was banished by Parliament.

·Edward III's declining years **3**:213g
·political influence in Edward III's rule **6**:438b

Perret, Auguste (b. Feb. 12, 1874, near Brussels—d. Feb. 25, 1954, Paris), architect notable for his pioneering contributions to the vocabulary of reinforced concrete construction. His father, Claude-Marie Perret, was a stonemason who, after 1881, had a flourishing business as a building contractor in Paris.

Auguste Perret studied architecture at the École des Beaux-Arts, Paris, but left before receiving his diploma to enter his father's business. With his brothers, Gustav and Claude, he built (1903) at 25 rue Franklin, Paris, what was probably the first apartment block designed for reinforced concrete construction. His garage on the rue de Ponthieu (1905) demonstrates how light and open an interior can be when the use of reinforced concrete has minimized the need for structural supports. Through its exposed frame, the garage exhibits Perret's concern for structural honesty. A visible framework was also a notable characteristic of the interior of his Paris Théâtre des Champs-Élysées (1913). He used thin shell roof vaulting for his warehouses in Casablanca (1915), and elegant concrete arches for a clothing factory in Paris (1919).

Publicity resulting from Perret's church of Notre-Dame at Le Raincy (1922–23), near Paris, probably fully established the novel and progressive character of his ideas and the immense structural possibilities of reinforced concrete. Basically a cage of glass, the structure is supported by thin columns. The poured-in-place and precast elements were left as they emerged from the formwork. In later buildings he obtained textural effects by exposing the aggregate.

Church of Notre-Dame, Le Raincy, France, by Auguste and Gustave Perret, 1923, with stained glass by Maurice Denis
GEKS

Among Perret's many notable buildings of the 1920s and 1930s was the École Normale de Musique in Paris (1929), considered by many to be an acoustical masterpiece. After World War II he was appointed chief architect for the reconstruction of Le Havre. Notable Perret buildings there are the Hôtel de Ville and the church of St. Joseph, both designed in 1950 and completed before his death. By that time his ideals were in sharp conflict with those of many of the younger architects who were less interested in the expression of structural systems than in the variety of spacial and sculptural effects made possible by reinforced concrete.

·Le Corbusier association and influence **5**:168d
·modern architecture design innovations **19**:467b

Perreux-sur-Marne, Le (France): *see* Le Perreux-sur-Marne.

Perrin, Ami (d. 1561), Swiss opponent of the French religious Reformer John Calvin at Geneva and leader of the anti-Calvinist Libertines.

A member of a prominent Genevese family, Perrin was associated with the city's anti-Savoyard party (Edidguenots) and commanded a company outfitted against the Duke of Savoy in 1529. Between 1544 and 1555 he stood as one of the most powerful figures in Geneva, serving many times as the city's intercantonial and foreign emissary.

Perrin early embraced the Reformation and championed the cause of Geneva's seminal Reformer, Guillaume Farel. Consequently, he opposed the growth of the Calvinist theocracy, siding with and eventually leading an established party of moderation, the Libertines. In May 1655 an armed rising of his Libertines was resisted by the city's government, and he was condemned to death. He managed to escape to Bern, where, with a few supporters (Fugitifs), he continued a futile opposition in exile.

Perrin, Jean-Baptiste (1870–1942), French physicist who studied the Brownian motion of minute particles suspended in liquids and thereby confirmed the atomic nature of matter. For this achievement he was honoured with the 1926 Nobel Prize for Physics.

Educated at the École Normale Supérieure, Paris, he joined the faculty of the University of Paris (1898) where he became professor of physical chemistry (1910–40). In 1895 he established that cathode rays are negatively charged particles (electrons). Around 1908 he addressed himself to determining the way in which colloidal particles remained suspended in a liquid in defiance of gravity. Through observations of the manner of sedimentation of these particles, he confirmed Einstein's equation for suspension phenomenon, and was also able to estimate the size of atoms and molecules as well as their quantity in a given volume.

Jean-Baptiste Perrin
H. Roger-Viollet

·Brownian movement experiments **3**:333a

Perrine, Charles Dillon (b. July 28, 1867, Steubenville, Ohio—d. June 21, 1951, Villa General Mitre, Argentina), astronomer who discovered the sixth and seventh moons of Jupiter in 1904 and 1905, respectively. He worked at the Lick Observatory in California from 1893 to 1909 and then until his retirement in 1936 was director of the Córdoba Astronomical Observatory in Argentina. His work included counts of extragalactic nebulae and the discovery of 13 comets.

Perron, (Charles) Edgar du (b. Nov. 2, 1899, Meester Cornelis, Java, now Djatinegara, Indon.—d. May 14, 1940, Bergen, Neth.), writer and critic, cofounder with Menno ter Braak of the influential Dutch literary journal *Forum* (1932–35), which aimed to replace superficial elegance of literary style with greater sincerity of literary content. The *Forum* writers resisted National Socialism and the German occupation of The Netherlands.

The son of a Dutch East Indian planter, he returned to Europe in 1921 and lived during exciting times on the Left Bank of Paris, which form the background of his novel *Een voorbereiding* (1927; "A Preparation"). Cosmopolitan in outlook, du Perron did much to counteract Dutch provincialism by publicizing the works of the French writers André Gide and André Malraux. He translated into Dutch Malraux's *Condition humaine* (*Man's Fate*), which had been dedicated to him. His collected essays, *De smalle mens* (1934), deal with the precarious position of the individual in the face of the collective attitudes of left and right. His poems, collected in *Parlando* (1941), are characterized by everyday words and a conversational tone. Shortly before World War II, du Perron spent a few more years in the Dutch East Indies collecting materials for *De man van Lebak* (1937), a critical biography of the great Dutch novelist Multatuli (Eduard Douwes Dekker).

·literary reform movement **10**:1245a

Perronet, Jean(-Rodolphe) (b. Oct. 8, 1708, Suresnes, Fr.—d. Feb. 27, 1794, Paris), civil engineer renowned for his stone-arch bridges, especially the Pont de la Concorde, Paris.

The son of an army officer, Perronet entered the newly formed Corps des Ponts et Chaussées (Bridges and Highways Corps) and so distinguished himself that on the founding, in 1747, of the École des Ponts et Chaussées, the world's first engineering school, he was appointed director.

During construction of a bridge at Mantes in 1763, Perronet made the discovery that the horizontal thrust of a series of elliptical arches was passed along to the abutments at the ends of the bridge. Armed with this knowledge, he carried the stone-arch bridge to its ultimate design form with extremely flat arches that were supported during construction by timbering (falsework) and mounted on very slender piers, which widened the waterway for navigation and reduced scour from the current.

The result was also aesthetically pleasing;

Perronet's Pont de Neuilly has been called the most graceful stone bridge ever built. He was 80 years old when he began the Pont de la Concorde, originally called the Pont Louis XV, in 1787. Despite the outbreak of the French Revolution, he kept the work going, completing it in 1791. His memoirs, published in 1782, give a complete account of his career to that date.
·bridge building in 18th-century France **3**:177c

Perrot, Sir John (b. *c.* 1527, Harroldston, Pembrokeshire—d. September 1592, London), lord deputy of Ireland from 1584 to 1588, who established an English colony in Munster in southwestern Ireland.

Perrot was reputed to be the son of King Henry VIII of England and Mary Berkley, who later married Thomas Perrot of Pembrokeshire. Knighted in 1547, he was appointed president of Munster by Queen Elizabeth I in 1570. After suppressing the Munster rebellion of James (Fitzmaurice) Fitzgerald, he pardoned the rebels and returned to England (1573). In 1584 he was sent back to Ireland as lord deputy. He confiscated vast lands in Munster for plantation by English settlers, but the colonization was poorly organized and executed. He did succeed, however, in bringing the native landowners of Connaught under English law by having them pay the crown a fixed money rent.

Meanwhile, Perrot's tolerance toward Roman Catholics and his plan to convert St. Patrick's Cathedral in Dublin into a university had earned him the enmity of Adam Loftus,

Perrot, engraving by U. Green, 1584
By courtesy of the trustees of the British Museum; photograph, J.R. Freeman & Co. Ltd.

Anglican archbishop of Dublin. In 1588 Loftus had Perrot recalled to England on trumped-up charges of treasonable negotiations with Spain. Perrot was found guilty, but he died in prison before he could be executed.
·Irish administration under Elizabeth I **3**:287e

Perrot, Jules (Joseph) (b. Aug. 18, 1810, Lyons—d. Aug. 24, 1892, Paramé, Fr.), virtuoso dancer and choreographer whose masterpieces of Romantic ballet include *Pas de Quatre* (1845), composed for four of the 19th century's leading ballerinas and frequently revived in the 20th century; Perrot is usually credited with choreographing Giselle's dances in *Giselle* (1841). He studied with Auguste Vestris and Salvatore Viganò, two of the principal exponents of expressive ballet (as opposed to pure or formal ballet). He made his debut in 1830 at the Paris Opéra, where, despite the period's prejudice against male dancers, he was highly applauded for both his classical and his mime dancing. A combination of knee trouble and the professional jealousy of his partner Marie Taglioni led to his resignation in 1835. He then toured Europe (1835–40) as a dancer and choreographer and in Naples was joined by the young ballerina Carlotta Grisi, whom he trained and later married. Perrot again danced in Paris in 1840, but only Grisi was hired to perform at the Opéra. Since he frequently arranged her solos, his choreography is now believed to include that of her title role in *Giselle*, still considered a consummate challenge to a ballerina's artistry; Jean Coralli, however, received all official credit for choreographing Giselle.

From 1842 to 1848 Perrot worked in London, making it an important ballet centre by choreographing such ballets as *Ondine* (1843), *Esmeralda* (1844), and the *Pas de Quatre*,

Jules Perrot, engraving after a drawing
By courtesy of the Bibliotheque de l'Opera, Paris; photograph, Pic

staged for Marie Taglioni, Carlotta Grisi, Lucile Grahn, and Fanny Cerrito. In 1848 Perrot became premier danseur at the Imperial Theatre in St. Petersburg, where he created eight more ballets and revived many others. Some of his ballets, such as *Esmeralda* and *Giselle*, remained in the Russian repertoire long after his departure from St. Petersburg (1859) and eventually became part of the post-Revolution Soviet ballet. On his return to France, Perrot attempted to revive his major works but was unsuccessful, since technical virtuosity had become more popular in western Europe than the expressive and dramatic elements that characterized his ballets.
·choreography's dramatic exploration **4**:453f

Perruzi, Baldassare (1481–1536), Italian painter and architect.
·Mannerist architecture in Rome **15**:1081c

Perry, city, Dallas County, central Iowa, U.S., between the Raccoon River and Beaver Creek. Settled in 1869, it was named for a railroad owner. Perry is an agricultural trade and shipping centre; manufactures include farm machinery and food products. Inc. 1875. Pop. (1980) 7,053.
41°50′ N, 94°06′ W

Perry, city, seat (1893) of Noble County, northern Oklahoma, U.S., north of Oklahoma City. It was founded in 1893 when the Cherokee Outlet (tribal land) was opened for white settlement. Perry is in a farming and oil-producing area, and has flour-milling and dairy-processing plants, and some light industries. The city holds an annual Cherokee Outlet celebration and an annual Shetland pony sale. Inc. 1894. Pop. (1980) 5,796.
36°17′ N, 97°17′ W

Perry, Bliss (b. Nov. 25, 1860, Williamstown, Mass.—d. Feb. 13, 1954, Exeter, N.H.), eminent scholar, professor, and editor, especially noted for his work in U.S. literature. Perry was educated at Williams College, Williamstown, Mass. and the Universities of Berlin and Strassburg (now in France). He taught at Williams (1886–93), Princeton University (1893–1900), and Harvard University (1907–30) and was Harvard lecturer at the University of Paris (1909–10). From 1899 to 1909 he edited the *Atlantic Monthly*. The French government awarded him the Legion of Honor. He edited many volumes, including the works of Edmund Burke, Sir Walter Scott, and Ralph Waldo Emerson, and was general editor (1905–09) of the Cambridge edition of the major American poets. He wrote a number of books, including works on Walt Whitman, John Greenleaf Whittier, Thomas Carlyle, Emerson, and others, as well as novels, short fiction, essays, an autobiography, studies of poetry, and collections of fiction and essays.

Perry, Frederick John (1909–), Wimbledon singles tennis champion, 1934–36.
·tennis championships **18**:133f

Perry, Matthew C(albraith) (b. April 10, 1794, South Kingston, R.I.—d. March 4, 1858, New York City), U.S. naval officer who headed an expedition that forced Japan in 1853–54 to enter into trade and diplomatic relations with the West after more than two centuries of isolation. Through his efforts the United States became an equal power with Britain, France, and Russia in the economic exploitation of East Asia.

Earlier, Perry had served as commanding officer (1837–40) of the first U.S. steamship, the "Fulton"; led a naval squadron to Africa to help suppress the slave trade (1843) in fulfillment of treaty obligations; and successfully commanded naval forces during the Mexican War (1846–48). In March 1852 Pres. Millard Fillmore placed Perry—who was called by his honorary rank of commodore—in charge of a naval expedition to Japan to induce the government to establish diplomatic relations with the U.S. After studying the situation, Perry concluded that Japan's traditional policy of isolation would be altered only if superior naval forces were displayed and if Japanese officials were approached with a "resolute attitude." With two frigates and two sailing vessels, he entered the fortified harbour of Uraga on July 8, 1853—an act widely publicized throughout the world. Calling himself an "admiral," he refused to obey Japanese orders to leave, and sent word that if the government did not delegate a suitable person to receive the documents in his possession, he would deliver them by force if necessary. Although the Japanese had expected Perry's arrival, their defenses were inadequate to resist him, and after a few days of diplomatic sparring they accepted his letter from the President of the United States to the Japanese emperor. Perry apparently did not realize that he was dealing with the shogun—Japan's hereditary military dictator—rather than the figurehead emperor. Perry then reported that he would return the following year for a reply.

In the interim, the Japanese, who were aware of China's recent defeat by the technologically superior Western powers in the Opium War (1839–42), decided to agree to Perry's terms as a way of stalling for time while they im-

Matthew Perry, detail of a Japanese watercolour, *c.* 1853; in Norfolk Museum of Arts and Sciences, Virginia
Collection Norfolk Museum of Arts and Sciences, Virginia

proved their defenses. In February 1854 he reappeared in Edo (modern Tokyo) Bay—this time with nine ships—and on March 31 concluded the first treaty between the two countries. The pact assured better treatment of shipwrecked seamen, permitted U.S. ships to obtain fuel and supplies at two minor ports, arranged for a U.S. consul to reside at Shimoda, and left the way open for the U.S. to acquire further trading privileges in the future. Perry's success demonstrated the Shogun's inability to enforce his country's traditional isolationist policy; the Japanese were soon forced to sign similar treaties with other Western nations. These events contributed to the collapse of the shogunate and ultimately to the modernization of Japan.

As a result of Perry's exploits, his countrymen considered him an authority on the Far East. Through writings and speeches he stressed the danger of British and Russian expansion and urged that the U.S. play a more active role in the Orient. He specifically recommended the acquisition of island bases in the Pacific to assure U.S. military and commercial superiority in the area, but the government was not ready to act on these proposals for roughly half a century.

·Ii Naosuke's role in Japanese treaties **9**:234h

Perry, Oliver Hazard (b. Aug. 20, 1785, South Kingston, R.I.—d. Aug. 23, 1819, at sea), U.S. naval officer who became a national hero when he defeated a British squadron in the Battle of Lake Erie in the War of 1812.

Oliver Hazard Perry, detail from a portrait by an unknown artist
By courtesy of the U.S. Navy

Like his father, Perry entered the naval service. Appointed a midshipman at 14, he served in both the West Indies and the Mediterranean until February 1813, when he was sent to Erie, Pa., to complete the building of a U.S. squadron that would challenge British control of the Great Lakes.

Working diligently all summer to assemble, equip, and man a fleet of 10 small vessels, Perry was ready to engage the enemy by early autumn. For some unexplained reason, the British commander, R.H. Barclay, relaxed the blockade long enough for Perry to cross the Erie bar in water so shallow as to require removing the heaviest guns and ammunition while crossing.

When the battle was joined on September 10, Perry's fleet was greatly superior in short-range firepower but only slightly superior at long range; a light wind prevented him from closing in quickly on Barclay, who commanded six warships. When Perry's flagship, the "Lawrence," was disabled, he transferred to the "Niagara," winning the battle within the next 15 minutes by sailing directly into the British line, firing broadside. In his official report of the British surrender he said, "We have met the enemy and they are ours."

Perry's successful action at Lake Erie helped ensure U.S. control of the Northwest; it also raised him to a position of national eminence and earned him promotion to the rank of captain. He commanded the "Java" in the Mediterranean (1816–17) and a small U.S. fleet sent to the South Atlantic (1819) to bring under control certain vessels that were preying on U.S. shipping out of Buenos Aires and Venezuela. On the return trip he contracted yellow fever and died.

·history of Detroit **5**:620e
·Lake Erie Battle leadership **18**:961a

Perry, Ralph Barton (1876–1957), U.S. Realist philosopher and educator (Harvard, 1902–46), noted for his personalist revision of Pragmatism, his edition of the works of William James, and his revision of Alfred Weber's *History of Philosophy* (1925). His other writings include *The New Realism* (1912), *The Thought and Character of William James* (1935; Pulitzer Prize, 1936), *General Theory of Value* (1926), and *The Humanity of Man* (1956).

·criticism of Idealism **9**:193c
·naturalistic cognitivist meta-ethics **6**:984h
·New Realism movement **15**:541f

Perry, W(illiam) J(ames) (1868–1949), British anthropologist noted for his diffusionist theory of cultural development. Perry believed that Egypt of 4000 BC was the original and sole source of agriculture, pottery, basketry, domestic animals, houses, and towns and that these then spread throughout the world. He explained all cultural differences and similarities by migrations and additions, losses, and combinations of complexes of cultural traits.

·anthropological theory of diffusionism **1**:972a
·cultural evolution and diffusionist theory **4**:659d

Perry Convention (1854): *see* Kanagawa, Treaty of.

Perryville, Battle of (Oct. 8, 1862), a Federal victory over the Confederacy in Kentucky during the U.S. Civil War.

·Civil War strategy and tactics **4**:677c; map 679

per saltire, also called PARTY PER SALTIRE, in heraldry, a type of division of a shield.

·heraldic shield design **8**:788e; illus.

Persarmenia, one of two sections of Armenia created *c.* 390.

·Armenian partition and Persian conflict **18**:1042b

Perse, Saint-John, pseudonym of (MARIE-RENÉ-AUGUSTE-) ALÉXIS SAINT-LÉGER LÉGER (b. May 31, 1887, Saint-Léger-les-Feuilles, Guadeloupe—d. Sept. 20, 1975, Presqu'île-de-Giens, Fr.), French poet and diplomat who was awarded the Nobel Prize for Literature in 1960 "for the soaring flight and evocative imagery of his poetry." He studied at the universities of Bordeaux and Paris and in 1914 entered the diplomatic service. He went to China and was successively consul at Shanghai and secretary at Peking. In 1921 he attended the Washington disarmament conference as an expert on East Asian affairs. He was later secretary (1921–32) to the French statesman Aristide Briand. In 1933 he was appointed secretary general at the Foreign Ministry, with the rank of ambassador. Dismissed from office in 1940, and deprived of French citizenship by the Vichy government, he went to the U.S., where he worked as consultant on French literature in the Library of Congress. He returned to France in 1957.

Saint-John Perse
Harlingue—H. Roger-Viollet

His early poetry, published before his diplomatic career began in earnest, includes *Éloges* (1911; *Éloges, and Other Poems*, 1944), which shows the influence of Symbolism; he later developed a more personal style. The language of his poetry, admired especially by poets for its precision and purity, is difficult, and he made little appeal to the general public. His poetry has been compared to that of Rimbaud. His hypnotic vision is conveyed by a liturgical metre and exotic words. The best known early work is the long poem *Anabase* (1924; Eng. trans., *Anabasis*, by T.S. Eliot, 1930). In the poems written in exile—*Exile* (1942; *Exile, and Other Poems*, 1949), *Vents* (1946; *Winds*, 1953), *Amers* (1957; *Seamarks*, 1958), *Chronique* (1960; bilingual edition in French and English, with the same title, 1961), and *Oiseaux* (1962; *Birds*, 1966)—he achieved a deeply personal note. Some U.S. readers regarded him as an embodiment of the French national spirit: intellectual yet passionate, deeply conscious of the tragedy of life, a man of affairs with an artist's feeling for perfection and symmetry. Among his better known poems translated into English are "I have halted my horse by the tree of the doves" and "Under the bronze leaves a colt was foaled," both from *Anabasis*, and "And you, Seas" from *Seamarks*.

Perse's French publisher issued *Honneur à Saint-John Perse*, an appraisal of his life and work, in 1965, and his collected poetic works were published in Paris in 1972.

·poetic theme and influence **10**:1236c

Persea americana (tree): *see* avocado.

persecution, religious, harassment of individuals or groups because of their religious beliefs. Religious persecutions have affected members of all the major religions and range from restrictions on employment and living quarters to exile and even death by torture. *See also* anti-Semitism.

·Anabaptist uprisings and fall of Münster **11**:906e
·Antiochus IV and Maccabean revolt **10**:310d
·Aurangzeb's religious policies **9**:384f
·Austrian depression of 1873 **2**:469g
·Baptist legal disability in New England **2**:715a
·Bolsheviks and Russian Church **6**:159h
·Book of Daniel's writing stimulus **2**:929a
·Boston's Puritan establishment **3**:55g
·Bunyan imprisoned for religious belief **3**:482a
·Catholic Holy League's leaders and aims **7**:630g
·Christian and Jewish status in Rome **4**:466g
·Christian attitude and Roman policy **4**:469a
·Christian esoteric heresies **4**:529f
·Christian orthodoxy and deviant sects **8**:782c
·Christian positions on dissent **4**:491h
·Christian threat to ancient Rome **4**:538d
·Diocletian's persecution of Christians **5**:71g
·Eusebius of Caesarea under Diocletian **6**:1130c
·expulsion of Jews from Cologne **4**:861f
·Friends under Puritans and Restoration **7**:743e
·Hitler and church relations **8**:119h
·human rights guarantees and protection **8**:1184d
·Islāmic treatment of other religions **9**:912f
·Jesuits' 17th-century suppression **15**:1014c
·Jewish situation in medieval Europe **15**:1007a
·Jezebel's attack on prophets **10**:307b
·Louis XIV's repression of Huguenots **7**:636b
·Mamlūk intolerance in Egypt **6**:491e
·Manichaean history and doctrines **11**:443d
·millennialist growth in spite of Nero **12**:201d
·minority group characteristics and status **12**:261c
·Muḥammad's treatment in Mecca **12**:607b
·Nero's anti-Christian programs **15**:1122a
·North African Donatist controversy **13**:153c
·Paul and Jewish opposition **13**:1091f *passim* to 1093f
·Pius V against heretics and Jews **14**:482a
·Portugal's intolerance of non-Christians **14**:867g

· Portuguese republican government after 1910 **14**:872f
· refugee problems and fostering forces **15**:568c
· religious ghettos of Belfast **13**:239c
· Shaftesbury's anti-Catholic activities **16**:613g
· social effects on early Christianity **4**:463f
· Tokugawa restrictions on foreign sects **10**:110f
· Unitarian repression in Reformation **18**:860c
· witness concept in Catholic Letters **2**:969b

Persephone, Latin PROSERPINA, in Greek religion, daughter of Zeus, the chief god, and Demeter, the goddess of agriculture; she was the wife of Hades, king of the underworld. In the Homeric "Hymn to Demeter," the story is told of how Persephone was gathering flowers

Persephone abducted by Hades, marble sculpture by Gian Lorenzo Bernini, 1621–22; in the Borghese Gallery, Rome
Anderson—Alinari

in the Vale of Nysa when she was seized by Hades and removed to the underworld. Upon learning of the abduction, her mother, Demeter, in her misery, became unconcerned with the harvest or the fruitfulness of the earth, so that widespread famine ensued. Zeus therefore intervened, commanding Hades to release Persephone to her mother. Because Persephone had eaten a single pomegranate seed in the underworld, she could not be completely freed but had to remain one-third of the year with Hades, spending the other two-thirds with her mother.

One of the variants of the name Persephone is Persephassa, which suggests that she was originally a pre-Hellenic goddess of the dead and that her connection with Demeter came later, when she was identified with Kore (Core; Greek: "Maiden"), the young grain goddess and daughter of Demeter. The story that Persephone/Kore spent four months of each year in the underworld was no doubt meant to account for the barren appearance of Greek fields in full summer (after harvest), before their revival in the autumn rains, when they are plowed and sown.

Persephone also appears in the Orphic myth of Zagreus, her son by Zeus, who, as a child, was torn apart by Titans.
· Eleusinian mystery mythology **12**:778h
· literary basis **17**:730d
· seasonal renewal and mythology **8**:405d

Persepolis 14:105, also known as PARSA, modern TAKHT-E JAMSHĪD, the ancient capital of the Achaemenian Empire of Persia, lies 32 miles northeast of Shīrāz, in southwestern Iran.

The text article covers Persepolis' founding in the late 6th or early 5th century BC by Darius I the Great, who made it the Persian capital for part of each year. Alexander the Great sacked the city in 330 BC, making it one of his provincial capitals. It subsequently declined and was abandoned. A number of huge, ruined buildings still stand on the site.

REFERENCES in other text articles:
· Alexander the Great and palace of Xerxes **1**:470d
· architectural structure for ritual use **18**:236d
· architecture of Achaemenian period **19**:270f
· artistry as effectively Persian **9**:837g; maps 834
· bas-relief in the Treasury illus. **5**:491
· Darius I's municipal construction **5**:492b
· destruction by Macedonians **8**:375b
· development and design **18**:1066g
· geographic location map **9**:868
· Persian cultural influence evidence **5**:410d
· Xerxes' construction program **19**:1058a

Perses (Latin: "Persian"), initiatory degree in Mithraism.
· mystery cult initiatory structure **12**:782a

Perseus (b. *c.* 212 BC—d. *c.* 165 BC, Alba Fucens, modern Albe, Italy), the last king of Macedonia (179–168), whose attempts to dominate Greece brought on the final defeat of Macedonia by the Romans, leading to annexation of the region. The elder son of King Philip V of Macedonia, he commanded troops in his father's wars against Rome (199) and Aetolia (189). After three years of intriguing against his brother Demetrius, accusing him of coveting the succession, Perseus in 181 persuaded the King to have Demetrius executed. On succeeding to the throne, Perseus extended his influence in Thrace and Illyria but made special efforts to win over the Greek world. To this end he resumed control of the Delphic Amphictyony, established excellent relations with Rhodes, and encouraged revolution in Aetolia and Thessaly. After subduing a revolt in Dolopia, he aroused widespread alarm in Greece by visiting Delphi with his army. Eumenes II of Pergamum incited Rome against Perseus' allegedly aggressive designs, thus precipitating the Third Macedonian War (171–168). Perseus held off the Romans for three years but in 168 lost the support of Genthius of Illyria, thus exposing his western flank. A Roman army forced him to fight at Pydna (in southern Macedonia), where he was defeated by Lucius Aemilius Paulus. He spent the rest of his life in captivity.
· Antiochus IV military alliance **1**:994g
· defeat by Romans **8**:384h
· reconciliation with Greece **15**:1094d

Perseus, in astronomy, constellation of the northern hemisphere. It contains the famous variable star Algol.
· constellation table **2**:226
· meteors and annual meteor showers **12**:37a; table
· star cluster magnitude **17**:606g

Perseus, in Greek mythology, the slayer of the Gorgon Medusa and the rescuer of Andromeda from a sea monster. Perseus was the son of Zeus and Danaë, the daughter of Acrisius of Argos. As an infant he was cast into the sea in a box with his mother by Acrisius, to whom it had been prophesied that he would be killed by his grandson. After Perseus had grown up on the island of Seriphus, where the box had grounded, King Polydectes of Seriphus, desiring Danaë, tricked Perseus into promising to obtain the head of Medusa, the only mortal among the Gorgons (*q.v.*).

Perseus, protected by Athena, beheads Medusa; metope from a Doric temple at Selinunte, 6th century BC; in the Museo Archeologico Nazionale, Palermo, Sicily
Anderson—Alinari

Aided by Hermes and Athena, Perseus pressed the Graiae, sisters of the Gorgons, into helping him by seizing the one eye and one tooth that the sisters shared and not returning them until they provided him with winged sandals (which enabled him to fly), the helmet of Hades (which conferred invisibility), a curved sword, or sickle, to decapitate Medusa, and a bag in which to conceal the head. (According to another version, the Graiae merely directed him to the Stygian Nymphs, who told him where to find the Gorgons and gave him the bag, sandals, and helmet; Hermes gave him the sword.) Because the gaze of Medusa turned all who looked at her to stone, Perseus guided himself by her reflection in a shield given him by Athena and beheaded Medusa as she slept. He then returned to Seriphus and rescued his mother by turning Polydectes and his supporters to stone at the sight of Medusa's head.

A further legend inserted into Perseus' travels was that of his rescue of the Ethiopian princess Andromeda, when he was on his way home with Medusa's head. Andromeda's mother, Cassiopeia, had claimed to be more beautiful than the sea nymphs, or Nereids (*q.v.*); so Poseidon had punished Ethiopia by flooding it and plaguing it with a sea monster. An oracle informed Andromeda's father, King Cepheus, that the ills would cease if he exposed Andromeda to the monster, which he did. Perseus, passing by, saw Andromeda and fell in love with her. He then turned the monster to stone by showing it Medusa's head and afterward married Andromeda.

Later Perseus gave the Gorgon's head to Athena, who placed it on her shield, and gave his other accoutrements to Hermes. He then took his mother back to her native Argos, where he accidentally struck her father Acrisius dead when throwing the discus, thus fulfilling the prophecy that he would kill his grandfather. He consequently left Argos and founded Mycenae as his capital, becoming the ancestor of the Perseids, among whom was Heracles.

The Perseus legend was a favourite subject in painting and sculpture, both ancient and Renaissance. Sigmund Freud reinterpreted the Gorgon's head in terms of castration, and the English novelist Iris Murdoch used it for modern symbolism in *A Severed Head* (1961).

Perseus spiral arm, region of the Milky Way galaxy near the Sun.
· interstellar matter and blue stars **9**:798a

Pershing, U.S. Army nuclear surface-to-surface missile; length 34.5 feet; weight 10,000 pounds; range is about 400 miles.
· development, range, and deployment **15**:930b; table 932

Pershing, John J(oseph) (b. Sept. 13, 1860, Laclede, Mo.—d. July 15, 1948, Washington, D.C.), army general who commanded the American Expeditionary Force (AEF) in Europe and helped secure an Allied victory in World War I.

Graduating from the United States Military Academy at West Point, N.Y., in 1886, Pershing served in several Indian wars, in the Spanish-American War (1898), as brigadier general in the Philippine Islands (1906–13), and as commander of a punitive raid against the Mexican revolutionary Pancho Villa (1916). He also was a military instructor at the University of Nebraska, Lincoln, and at West Point.

After the United States declared war on Germany (April 1917), Pres. Woodrow Wilson selected Pershing to command the American troops being sent to Europe. In June he submitted a "General Organization Report" recommending an army of 1,000,000 men by 1918 and 3,000,000 by 1919. Though early U.S. planning had not included such a large force, Pershing's recommendations prevailed.

Pershing, 1917

By courtesy of the Library of Congress, Washington, D.C.

By the early part of 1918, U.S. plans called for concentrating an independent army on the Western Front. The exhaustion of the Allies, stemming from military setbacks in 1917, increased Allied dependence on American arms. It also engendered pressure on Pershing to condone the "amalgamation" of small units of his troops with European divisions—an arrangement that he adamantly opposed (though he temporarily released his troops to Marshal Ferdinand Foch, inter-Allied commander, during the German offensive of March–June 1918 that threatened Paris). Pershing also resisted proposals to divert some U.S. troops to secondary theatres, as recommended by the Supreme War Council. These pressures subsided when the Allies assumed the offensive during the summer.

Pershing's army never became entirely self-sufficient, but it conducted two significant operations. In September 1918 the AEF assaulted the Saint-Mihiel salient successfully. Then, at Foch's request, later that month Pershing quickly regrouped his forces for the Meuse-Argonne offensive, despite his original plans to advance toward Metz. Though incomplete preparations and inexperience slowed the operations, the inter-Allied offensive in France destroyed German resistance in early October and precipitated the Armistice in the following month.

Though Pershing's critics exposed some of his operational and logistic errors, nevertheless his creation of the AEF was a remarkable achievement, and he returned home with a sound reputation. In 1919 the rank of general of the armies was conferred upon him—a title created in 1799 for George Washington but never held by him. Pershing's stern bearing and rigid discipline earned him the nickname "Black Jack." Eschewing politics, Pershing remained in the army and served as chief of staff from 1921 until his retirement three years later.

Pershing's memoirs were published as *My Experiences in the World War* (2 vol., 1931).

·Mexican border patrol leadership **18**:985h
·U.S. European command in World War I **19**:958a

Persia, the name used for centuries, mostly in the West, for the kingdom of Iran in southwestern Asia. It originated from a region of southern Iran formerly known as Persis (*q.v.*), alternatively as Pārs or Parsa, modern Fārs (*q.v.*). During the rule of the Persian Achaemenid dynasty (559–330 BC) the ancient Greeks first encountered the inhabitants of Persis on the Iranian Plateau, and the name was extended. The people of Iran have always called their country Iran, Land of the Aryans.

In 1935 the government of Iran requested that the name Iran be used instead of Persia, but in 1949 it announced that it would no longer insist on the usage because of the widespread use of "Persia."

Persia, history of: *see* Iran, history of.

Persian (cat): *see* longhair.

Persian arts: *see* Iran, history of; Islāmic peoples, arts of; Persian literature.

Persian berry, any of several buckthorn berries from southern Europe, Asia Minor, and Iran that are used in textile dyeing.

Persian carpets, general designation referring to rugs and carpets made in Iran. *See also* rugs and carpets.

·design execution and composition **16**:11g
·floor covering origins and types **7**:407d
·Ṣafavid arts under ʿAbbās I **1**:4g
·weaving techniques and materials **17**:1060a

Persian Church: *see* Nestorians.

Persian Cossack Brigade, a cavalry unit founded in Iran in 1879 and modelled after Russian Cossack formations.

The genesis of the Iranian brigade lay in the need for a reliable and well-disciplined fighting force. In 1878 Nāṣer od-Dīn Shāh (ruled 1848–96) asked the Russian government for help in the creation of an Iranian cavalry unit. In 1879 the nucleus of such a force was founded in Tehrān, staffed by active-duty Russian officers under contract to the Iranian government. In its early years the brigade was essentially a ceremonial force, numbering fewer than 1,000 men. But in 1894, with the appointment of Col. V.A. Kosogovsky, the brigade was transformed into an effective fighting force, with a small detachment of artillery and other supporting arms. The brigade was used increasingly as an internal police force and, as a result, became unpopular with Iranian nationalists, who considered it an embodiment of Russian foreign policy and internal despotism.

In June 1908 the brigade, led by Colonel Liakhov and acting under direct orders of Moḥammad ʿAlī Shāh (ruled 1907–09), bombarded the Iranian parliament as part of a plan to undermine constitutional government. In an ensuing civil war (1908–09), the brigade fought on the side of the Shah. During World War I (1914–18) the brigade was expanded into an 8,000-man division and fought with the Russian government against an invading Turkish army and its Iranian allies; the war years saw increasing tensions within the division between the Russian executive officers and the junior Iranian officers. After the Russian Revolution of 1917, the Russian officers of the division were split into "Red" and "White" factions. The Russians departed in 1920, and Col. Reza Khan (who later, in 1925, became shah of Iran) assumed command.

In February 1921 several detachments of the Iranian Cossacks, under Reza Khan's command, carried out a coup d'etat that made Sayyid Zia od-Din Tabataba'i prime minister. Late that year the division was amalgamated with other independent military units, thus forming a unified national army under Reza Khan. Many of the division's Iranian officers rose to positions of prominence.

·Reza Khan's coup d'etat **9**:861a

Persian deer, a fallow deer (*Dama dama mesopotamica*) of western Asia. The maral, an Asiatic red deer, is often called Persian deer also.

Persian gazelle, also called GOITERED GAZELLE, a gazelle (*Gazella subgutturosa*) of Central Asia.

Persian Gulf 14:106, also called ARABIAN GULF, Arabic BAḤR FĀRIS, Persian KHALĪJ-E FĀRS, shallow sea of the Indian Ocean, extending 615 mi (990 km) from the Shaṭṭ al-ʿArab (the mouth of the Tigris and Euphrates rivers) on the northwest to the Strait of Hormuz on the southeast, with a width ranging up to 210 mi. It is bordered by Iran (north, northeast, and east), by the United Arab Emirates and Oman (southeast and south), by Saudi Arabia, Bahrain, and Qatar (southwest and west), and by Iraq and Kuwait (northwest). The Gulf has an area of 92,500 sq mi (240,000 sq km) and is rarely deeper than 300 ft, though it reaches more than 360 ft at its entrance and at isolated localities.

The text article covers the Gulf's physiography, geology, climate, hydrography, economic resources, and prospects for the future. 27°00′ N, 51°00′ E

REFERENCES in other text articles:
·Arabian oil wealth **1**:1051a
·Bahrain's geography and oil supply **2**:594a
·coastal lagoon evaporite deposition **6**:1135h
·gulf development and physiography **8**:485e; table 482

maps
·Asia **2**:148
·Bahrain **2**:594
·Iran **9**:822
·Iraq **9**:875
·Saudi Arabia **16**:279
·Mesopotamian coastal change theory **18**:404h
·saline-flat formation and features **14**:558c
·salt dome composition and size **16**:198h
·skeletal material sedimentation **6**:714e
·United Arab Emirates area and people **18**:862b; map

Persian iris, a bulbous iris (*Iris persica*) native to Asia Minor, often cultivated for its pale lilac-coloured flowers.

Persian (SEHNA) **knot,** type of knot commonly used in weaving of Oriental carpets and rugs.

·Oriental rug knot types **7**:407e; illus.

Persian lamb, a pelt obtained from Karakul (*q.v.*) lambs older than those yielding broadtail; characterized by very silky, tightly curled fur.

·pelt characteristics **7**:811h; table 813

Persian (FĀRSĪ) **language,** member of the Iranian branch of the Indo-Iranian language family; it is the official language of Iran and is widely used in Afghanistan. Written in Arabic characters, modern Persian also has many Arabic loanwords and an extensive literature.

Old Persian, spoken until approximately the 3rd century BC, is attested by numerous inscriptions written in cuneiform, most notable of which is the great monument of Darius I at Bīsitūn (*q.v.*), Iran. The inscriptions at Bīsitūn were generally trilingual—in Old Persian, Elamite, and Akkadian.

Middle Persian, spoken from the 3rd century BC to the 9th century AD, is represented by numerous epigraphic texts of Sāsānian kings written in Aramaic script; there is also a varied literature in Middle Persian embracing both the Zoroastrian and the Manichaean religious traditions. Pahlavi was the name of the official Middle Persian language of the Sāsānian Empire.

Modern Persian grammar is in many ways much simpler than its ancestral forms, having lost most of the inflectional systems of the older varieties of Persian. Other than markers to indicate that nouns and pronouns are direct objects, Modern Persian has no system of case inflections. Possession is shown by addition of a special suffix (called the *ezāfeh*) to the possessed noun. Verbs retain a set of personal endings related to those of other Indo-European languages, but a series of prefixes and infixes (word elements inserted within a word) as well as auxiliary verbs are used instead of a single complex inflectional system to mark tense, mood, voice, and the negative. *Major ref.* **9**:450e

·Afghan branches and distribution **1**:168e
·Arabic contribution and renascence **9**:854f
·dialects and predominance **9**:863c
·English vocabulary borrowings **6**:879b
·history and script invention **9**:836f
·Indo-Iranian languages distribution map **9**:442
·Islāmic literary role **9**:954g
·logogram use **19**:1039a
·Muslim invasions of India **9**:285g
·Seljuqs and Persian cultural autonomy **16**:504g
·theophoric compound personal names **12**:817d
·Turkic culturolinguistic debt **1**:638a

Persian Letters (Montesquieu): *see* Lettres persanes.

Persian literature, body of writings in Modern Persian, the form of the Persian language that emerged by the 9th century, especially in northeast Iran, and became established as the literary form of the Persian language in Iran and northern India. The first writings in Modern Persian were in verse. As prose translations from the Arabic began to be made, rhetorical refinements based on Arab literary conventions, as well as more Arabic words and literary devices, were introduced.
·Indian Muslim literary history **17**:145a
·Islāmic cultural history **9**:933f
·Islāmic folktales **9**:924b
·Islāmic literary role **9**:954g
·Khosrow's secular and religious reign **10**:454a
·Rūmī's mystical poetry **10**:14f
·Sāsānian language and type **9**:850b
·Ṣūfī forms and symbols **9**:944a

Persian melon (variety of muskmelon): *see* Cucumis melo.

Persian Royal Road, pre-Roman road running from Susa, the ancient capital of Persia, across Anatolia to the Aegean Sea, a distance of more than 1,500 miles (2,400 kilometres). Royal messengers, who, according to Herodotus, were stopped by "neither snow, nor rain, nor heat, nor gloom of night," traversed the entire road in nine days, thanks to a system of relays. Normal travel time was about three months. Alexander the Great made use of the Royal Road in his invasion and conquest of the Persian empire. *Major ref.* **15**:892h

Persian Rummy, card game, basically similar to other Rummy games, except that four play as partners using one pack plus four jokers, which count 20 points and may be melded only in groups of jokers. In Persian Rummy, aces count 15 and may be used only as A–K–Q or as a group of aces, not as A–2–3. If all four cards of a rank are melded at once, the value of the meld is doubled. When a player has melded all his cards, the deal ends and his side scores a bonus of 25 points. After stock is exhausted, the discard pile is drawn from until no player is able to make a meld with the exposed card of the discard pile.

Two deals constitute a game. The partnership with the higher total wins the difference between the scores, plus a game bonus of 50.

Persians, Greek PERSAI (472 BC), play by Aeschylus.
·production, themes, and explication **1**:148a

Persichetti, Vincent (b. June 6, 1915, Philadelphia), prolific composer noted for his succinct polyphonic style (based on interwoven melodic lines), forceful rhythms, and generally diatonic (moving stepwise; not atonal or highly chromatic) melodies. Calling himself an "all-round American boy interested mainly in baseball," Persichetti began piano lessons at age 5, studied theory at 8, and produced his first two works at 14. Among his later teachers were the composer Roy Harris and the conductor Fritz Reiner, the latter at the Curtis Institute. In 1942 Persichetti began teaching at the Philadelphia Conservatory, and from 1948 he taught at Juilliard. He also was music editor for the Elkan-Vogel Company.

Among his many published works are several for band and various chamber combinations and the highly regarded *Piano Quintet* (1955). He has written several symphonies and many piano concerti, as well as songs, solo

Persichetti

By courtesy of the Juilliard School, New York; photograph, Clarence E. Premo

sonatas (including one for harpsichord; 1951), ballet music, and a large group of serenades. He is the author of the book *Twentieth-Century Harmony: Creative Aspects and Practice* (1961).

persimmon, globular fruit of trees of the genus *Diospyros* (family Ebenaceae). The Oriental persimmon (*D. kaki*), an important and extensively grown fruit in China and Japan, where it is known as *kaki*, was introduced into France and other Mediterranean countries in the 19th century and grown to a limited extent there. Introduced into the U.S. a little later, it is now grown commercially on a small scale in California and throughout the Gulf states, mainly in home gardens. The fruit, five to eight centimetres (two to three inches) or more in diameter, yellow to red in colour, somewhat resembles a tomato in appearance and is a source of vitamin A and also some vitamin C. Except for such varieties as Fuyu, the fruit tends to be highly astringent until soft-ripe or, as in Japan, until treated with certain gases. The trees will tolerate winter temperatures only to about −18° C (0° F).

Persimmon (*Diospyros virginiana*)

John H. Gerard—National Audubon Society

The native American persimmon (*D. virginiana*) is a small tree, occasionally up to 10 metres (33 feet) in height, and grows from the Gulf states north to central Pennsylvania and central Illinois. The fruit is three to five centimetres (one to two inches) in diameter, usually rather flattened, and dark red to maroon in colour. Most fruits contain several rather large, flattened seeds. As in the Oriental species, the flesh loses its astringency and develops a rich flavour upon softening. Considerable quantities are gathered from the wild and utilized. A number of superior kinds have been named and propagated to a limited extent but are not grown commercially.
·fruit and nut farming, table 5 **7**:766

Persis, Greek form of Old Persian PARSA, modern Fārs (*q.v.*), the southwestern part of Iran. Its name was derived from the Iranian tribe of the Parsua (Parsuash; Parsumash; Persians), who settled there in the 7th century BC. Herodotus lists the leading Persian tribes as the Pasargadae, to which the Achaemenians, the royal family of Persia, belonged; the Maraphii; and the Maspii. It was these three that Cyrus II the Great assembled to approve his plans for his revolt against Astyages, his Median overlord, about 550 BC.

The inhabitants of Persis were considered to be the rulers of the Achaemenian Empire and were exempt from taxation. As the homeland of the Achaemenian dynasty, Persis was closely associated with the monarchy. Cyrus built his capital at Pasargadae, and about 30 miles to the southwest Darius I founded his new capital of Parsa, known to the Greeks as Persepolis, the Persian City.

The history of Persis after the fall of the Achaemenian Empire in 330 BC is obscure. Lying apart from the main stategic and economic highways of Iran, it preserved its ancient culture, language, and religion under the Seleucids and enjoyed considerable autonomy during the Parthian period. In the 3rd century AD its rulers, heirs of the Achaemenian tradition, founded the Sāsānian Empire.
·Greek conquests and Hellenistic kingdoms maps **8**:374

Persius, full name AULUS PERSIUS FLACCUS (b. AD 34, Volaterrae, modern Volterra, Italy—d. 62, Campania), Stoic poet whose Latin satires reached a higher moral tone than any others in classical Latin literature, though they did not attempt the heights of savage indignation later scaled by Juvenal. A pupil and friend of the Stoic philosopher Lucius Annaeus Cornutus and a fellow student of the poet Lucan, who admired all he wrote, Persius discovered his vocation as a satirist through reading the 10th book of Lucilius. He wrote painstakingly, and his book of satires was still incomplete at his premature death. The book, edited by his friends Cornutus and Caesius Bassus, was an immediate success. The six satires, amounting to 650 lines, are in hexameters; but what appears as a prologue, in which Persius (an extremely wealthy man) ironically asserts that he writes to earn his bread, not because he is inspired, is in choliambics. The first satire censures literary tastes of the day, reflecting the decadence of national morals. It contains a description of a poet reciting his own work, an account of literary conversation at a dinner party, and a passage deriding bland mythological writing and languishing style. Here Persius is writing real satire from his own experience; the remaining books are philosophical discussions on themes often handled by Seneca. Satire II discusses what may rightly be asked of the gods; satire III, those who live wrongly though they know the right and those who have not been enlightened by philosophy; satire IV, the necessity of self-knowledge for public men; satire V, the Stoic doctrine of freedom, introducing a dialogue between himself and Cornutus that reveals his affection and respect for his master; and satire VI, dedicated to Bassus, the proper use of money.

Persius is said to have been gentle in disposition, girlishly modest, good-looking, and devoted to his mother, sister, and aunt. To his mother and sister he left a considerable fortune.

person, in law, someone who is capable of having rights and being subject to duties or responsibilities (as opposed to a thing, which is the subject of rights and duties). A person may be an artificial being, such as a corporation.
·cuneiform law approach **5**:369f
·German civil code definition of rights **4**:664d
·Roman legal theory **15**:1057d

persona, in Jungian psychology, the personality the individual projects to others, which is postulated to be at great variance with the authentic self.
·personality and social role **14**:116h

Persona Delusoris, dramatic Latin dialogue of early Middle Ages between Terence and another character.
·Terence's medieval popularity **17**:535d

personal equation, a constant or systematic deviation from an assumed correct observational result depending on the personal qualities of the observer.
·Bessel's corrections observations **2**:870a

personal income (national income accounting): *see* income, personal.

personal income tax: *see* income tax, personal.

personal injury (law): *see* torts, law of.

Personalism, a school of philosophy, usually Idealist, that asserts that the real is the personal; *i.e.*, that the basic features of personality—consciousness, free self-determination, directedness toward ends, self-identity through time, and value retentiveness—make it the paradigm of all reality. In the theistic form that it has often assumed, it has sometimes become specifically Christian, holding that not merely the person but the highest individual instance of personhood—Jesus Christ—is the paradigm.

Personalism is thus in the tradition of the *cogito* of René Descartes ("I think, therefore I am") in holding that, in the subjective flow of lived-through experience, one makes more direct soundings of the real (the metaphysical) than in anything arriving through the tortuous paths of perceptual processes. The word person comes from the Latin *persona*, which referred to the mask worn by an actor and thus to his role. Eventually, it came to mean the dignity of a man among men. The person is thus supreme both in reality (as substance) and in value (as dignity).

There are various kinds of Personalism. Though most Personalists are Idealists, believing that reality is either of, in, or for consciousness, there are also Realistic Personalists, who hold that the natural order, though created by God, is not as such spiritual; and, again, though most Personalists are theists, there are also atheistic Personalists. Among the Idealists there are absolutistic Personalists (*see* absolute Idealism); panpsychistic Personalists (*see* panpsychism); ethical Personalists; and personal Idealists, for whom reality comprises a society of finite persons or an ultimate Person, God.

Though elements of Personalistic thought can be discerned in many of the greatest philosophers of the Western tradition and even in the Orient—as, for example, in Rāmānuja, a 12th-century Hindu theist—Gottfried Wilhelm Leibniz, a famous 17th–18th-century German philosopher and mathematician, is usually singled out as the founder of the movement and George Berkeley, the 18th-century Anglo-Irish churchman and epistomologist, as another of its seminal sources.

Personalism has been strongly represented in France, usually under the name of Spiritualism. Inspired by Maine de Biran, an 18th–19th-century thinker who had taken as primordial the inner experience of acting against a resisting world, Félix Ravaisson-Mollien, a 19th-century philosopher and archaeologist, drew a radical distinction between the spatial world of static necessary law and the world of living individuals, spontaneous, active, and developing. This led in turn to the Personalism of Henri Bergson, a 19th–20th-century intuitionist, who stressed duration as a nonspatial experience in which subjective states both present and past intimately interpenetrate to form the free life of the spiritual person and who posited the élan vital as a cosmic force expressing this life philosophy.

American Personalism matured among 19th–20th-century philosophers of religion, often of the Methodist Church, several of whom had studied in Germany under Rudolf Hermann Lotze, an erudite metaphysician and graduate in medicine.

George Holmes Howison, for example, stressed the autonomy of the free moral person to the point of making him uncreated and eternal and hence free from an infinite Person. Borden Parker Bowne, who made Boston University the citadel of Personalism, was explicitly theistic, holding that men are creatures of God with many dimensions—moral, religious, emotional, logical—each worthy of consideration in its own right and each reflecting the rationality of the Creator. Nature, too, for him, displays the energy and rational purpose of a God who is immanent in it as well as transcendent over it.

Through Bowne's disciples Edgar Brightman and Ralph Tyler Flewelling and many others, Personalism was influential through the mid-20th century, and its impact upon Existentialism and Phenomenology has perpetuated its spirit and many of its insights.
·Idealism emphasizing personhood **9**:192c
·positive and negative individualism **1**:982b
·religious experience issues **15**:647g

personalismo, in Latin America, the practice of glorifying a single leader, with the resulting subordination of the interests of political parties and ideologies and of constitutional government.

Latin American political parties have been often constituted by the personal following of a leader rather than by adherents of certain political beliefs or proponents of certain issues. Thus the popular term for such parties or their members has been often derived from their leaders—*e.g.*, Peronistas (the followers of Juan Perón, Argentine dictator in 1946–55) or Fidelistas (the followers of Fidel Castro, Cuban dictator who came to power in 1959). The archetypical demagogue and focus of *personalismo* in Mexico was Gen. Antonio López de Santa Anna, who dominated Mexican political life between 1821 and 1855. The Dominican Republic and Ecuador in particular have suffered from *personalismo*, but the phenomenon has been rather pervasive throughout Latin American history. *Personalismo* is related to the phenomenon in Latin America called *caudillismo*, by which a government is controlled by dictatorial leaders (caudillos). During and immediately after the Latin American independence movement in the early 19th century, politically unstable conditions led to the widespread emergence of such leaders; thus the period is often referred to as the "age of the caudillos." The flamboyant leader of the independence movement, Simón Bolívar, was the first such ruler (of Gran Colombia, his ephemeral political creation). Although some nations, such as Argentina and Chile, developed more regular forms of constitutional government in the latter 19th century, *caudillismo* remained into the 20th century a common feature of Latin American states and prevailed in some countries as in Argentina, during Perón's regime—as a form of political bossism, whereas in others as outright and brutal military dictatorship—as with the regime of Juan Vicente Gómez in Venezuela (ruled 1908–35). The latter was a ruler in the Venezuelan tradition, following the pattern of such dictators as José Antonio Páez, who controlled the country in 1830–46 and again in 1860–63. Among other well-known caudillos of the 19th century were Juan Manuel de Rosas of Argentina, Francisco Solano López of Paraguay, and Andrés Santa Cruz of Bolivia. In such countries as Argentina and Mexico, during periods of weak central government, regional caudillos operated in their own localities in much the same way as did those on a national scale.
·decentralized power bases **7**:207a
·Ecuadorian political importance **6**:289f
·federalism in Latin America **7**:203e
·monocratic forms in Latin America **14**:717g
·Peru at early independence **14**:134c
·Uruguayan attempts at political stability **18**:1098h

Personalist, The (1920), philosophical quarterly founded by Ralph Taylor Flewelling, a U.S. philosopher.
·Idealism of Personalist school **9**:192c

personality, measurement of 14:108, the identification and quantitative description of distinctive human characteristics for the purpose of predicting the behaviour of people.

The text article covers personality assessment methods (*e.g.*, those employing interviews, rating scales, personality inventories, and inkblot tests). The reliability and validity of such methods are considered.

REFERENCES in other text articles:
·highway safety studies **16**:140d
·human behaviour factors **8**:1149b
·male and female differences **19**:907h
·psychological assessment of behaviour **15**:150a
·social behaviour and test reliability **15**:165a
·testing and measuring methods **11**:735f
·theory development from research data **14**:117c

RELATED ENTRIES in the *Ready Reference and Index:*
Kuder Preference Record; Minnesota Multiphasic Personality Inventory; projective tests; Rorschach Test; Strong Vocational Interest Blank; Thematic Apperception Test

personality, theories of 14:114, efforts to account for the individually unique organization of traits or characteristics within people. Scholarly approaches to the subject tend to be comprehensive, rather than focussing only on the personality traits that give a person social competence and attractiveness.

The text article covers theories of personality types (*e.g.*, those that relate human traits to individual differences in body chemistry); analytic and social theories (*e.g.*, psychoanalysis and those based on the principles of learning). It is suggested that none of these diverse approaches is sufficiently universal to explain all of the complexities of human personality.

REFERENCES in other text articles:
·alienation variants in individuals **1**:574a
·behaviour development of children **8**:1136d
·brain correlates of behaviour **12**:1036e
·Cooley's primary group theory **16**:959f
·cultural conditioning studies **1**:972d
·culture derivation theories **16**:991e
·culture's influence on development **8**:1154c
·dream-sleep stability in various personalities **5**:1013e
·drug abuses and modes of adaptation **5**:1051b
·elderly person's emotional adaptation **13**:548e
·emotion theories and research **6**:757c
·Enlightenment mechanistic psychology **6**:890b
·hallucinations and previous experiences **9**:244e
·humours theory and comic use **7**:134e
·integration of libido, archetype, and religion **15**:596g
·Jung's classification and study **10**:335g
·learning activity use of whole self **6**:409e
·man's self-awareness **1**:982c
·measurement theory and techniques **14**:108b
·memory selectivity as survival mechanism **11**:891c
·modernization's effect on personality **9**:524e
·monkey socialization studies **10**:745d
·motivational theories and history **12**:556g
·persuasion and the ego-defensive man **14**:123d
·philosophical problem of personal identity **12**:232d
·prayer as psychophysical phenomenon **14**:949b
·propaganda psychological appeals **15**:41e
·psychophysiological approaches **15**:163b
·relation to confabulation in paramnesia **11**:890e

religious and mystical theories
·angelic and demonic forces in man **1**:873a
·Buddhist mystical attitudinal goals **3**:414h
·Buddhist philosophical speculation **9**:318f
·Guaraní myth of plant and animal souls **1**:916a
·man's essential nature and afterlife **5**:533g
·religious influences **15**:611g

·sexual behaviour development **16**:596f
·social behaviour and individual traits **15**:165a
·suicide tendency theories **17**:780g
·transfer of training in development **18**:597b
·youth personality development **19**:1091h

RELATED ENTRIES in the *Ready Reference and Index:*
extrovert; imitation; introvert

personality disorder, also called CHARACTER DISORDER, condition marked by persisting patterns of inadequate or antisocial behaviour rather than of predominantly psychological or emotional disturbances that cause suffering and a sense of distress. Persons who always react with undue excitability and ineffectiveness in the presence of minor stress or who regularly display judgment that is not dependable are among those classified as having personality disorders. Such persons have little control over their hostile feelings, are fickle in their relations with others, and are unable to form enduring or satisfactory relationships. Vocationally and socially these persons do poorly, even though they may be of normal or superior intelligence and physically well endowed. Also included in the group with personality disorders are persons who exhibit extreme emotional instability characterized by explosive outbursts of rage upon minor provocation. At times, these personalities may be blustering and threatening; at other times they can be despairing and inaccessible. Two other common forms of personality disorder are seen in persons exhibiting either passive dependence reactions or passive aggressive reactions. The former are generally helpless, indecisive, and clinging. When faced with minor problems, they show anxious and panic-stricken behaviour. In contrast, the passive aggressive person expresses his hostility in stubbornness, procrastination, and inefficiency.

One of the most complex groups of the personality disorders is the category of sociopaths (psychopaths), whose disturbance is characterized chiefly by failure to adapt to prevailing moral and social standards. Persons with sociopathic tendencies act out their hostility on the rest of the world. As a group, they make up the mass of the criminals and delinquent elements of society. Their symptomatology may also include various sexual deviations and drug addiction or alcoholism. Sociopaths generally accept their behaviour as natural, see little reason for or possibility of change, and resist therapy.

·persuasibility among the disturbed **14**:125g
·prison and social deprivation effect **14**:1101h

personality inventory, method of assessing personal attributes by administering various types of questionnaries, usually filled out by the individual himself, containing statements about behaviour and feelings that require a true or false response. Individual scores are evaluated with respect to norms or standards based on the scores of large representative samples.

·behaviour measurement and research **14**:118b
·development, theory, and examples **14**:110c

personality test, an examination designed to reveal an individual's personal characteristics, such as his degree of sociability, self-control, flexibility, tolerance, creativity, leadership capacity, and bias.

·test administration and scoring **11**:737b

personal liberty laws, pre-U.S. Civil War laws passed by Northern state governments to counteract the provisions of the Fugitive Slave Acts and to protect escaped slaves and free Negroes settled in the North. Contravening the Fugitive Slave Act of 1793, which did not provide for trial by jury, Indiana (1824) and Connecticut (1828) enacted laws making jury trials possible upon appeal. In 1840 Vermont and New York granted fugitives the right of jury trial and provided them with attorneys. After 1842, when the Supreme Court ruled that enforcement of the Fugitive Slave Act was a federal function, some Northern state governments passed laws forbidding state authorities to cooperate in the capture and return of fugitives. In the reaction to the Fugitive Slave Act contained in the Compromise of 1850, most Northern states provided further guarantees of jury trial, authorized severe punishment for illegal seizure and perjury against alleged fugitives, and forbade state authorities to recognize claims to fugitives. These laws were cited as a justification for secession by South Carolina in 1860.

personal property (law): *see* real and personal property.

Personal Recollections of Joan of Arc (1895), book by Mark Twain.

·Mark Twain's idealism **18**:807c

personification, figure of speech in which human characteristics are attributed to an abstract quality, animal, or inanimate object, as in "The Moon doth with delight / Look round her when the heavens are bare" (Wordsworth, "Ode: Intimations of Immortality from Recollections of Early Childhood," 1807). Used in European poetry since Homer, personification is a particularly important figure in allegory; for example, the medieval morality play *Everyman* (*c.* 1500) and the Christian prose allegory *Pilgrim's Progress* (1678) by John Bunyan contain characters such as Death, Fellowship, Knowledge, Giant Despair, Sloth, Hypocrisy, and Piety. Personification became almost an automatic mannerism in 18th-century Neoclassical poetry, as in these lines from Thomas Gray's "Elegy Written in a Country Church Yard":

Here rests his head upon the lap of earth
  A youth to Fortune and to Fame unknown:
Fair science frowned not on his humble birth,
  And Melancholy marked him for her own.

·fable use characteristics **7**:133b

personnel administration 14:118, management of employees in working organizations. It includes recruiting, testing, and training; wage and salary administration; promotion, transfer, and discharge of personnel; and the handling of employee benefits and services.

The text article covers these functions as well as the development of personnel administration as a profession.

REFERENCES in other text articles:
·employee security measures **16**:454f
·history of industry's concern for worker **9**:497d
·managerial training, promotion, and transfer **9**:502a
·man-machine system coordination **8**:1168g
·social psychology contributions **15**:166b
·successive-hurdle selection method **11**:734h
·worker replacement problems in science **9**:509b

RELATED ENTRIES in the *Ready Reference and Index:*
bonus; employee association; employee stock ownership; fringe benefits; guaranteed wage plan; pension; profit sharing

personnel carrier, a motor vehicle, usually armoured, for transporting military personnel and their equipment.

·tank designs and use in World War II **17**:1024d; illus. 1022

Persons, Robert: *see* Parsons, Robert.

perspective, method of graphically depicting three-dimensional objects and spatial relationships on a two-dimensional plane or on a plane that is shallower than the original (for example, in flat relief). In contrast to perceptual methods of representing space and volume, which render them as seen at a particular time and from a fixed position and which are characteristic of Chinese and most Western painting since the Renaissançe, are conceptual methods. The pictures of young children and primitives (untrained artists), many of the paintings of cultures such as ancient Egypt and Crete, India, Islām, and pre-Renaissance Europe, as well as the paintings of many modern artists, depict objects and surroundings independently of one another, as they are known to be rather than as they are seen to be, and from the views that best present their most characteristic features; in many Egyptian and Cretan paintings, for example, the head and legs of a figure are shown in profile, while the eye and torso are shown frontally. This system produces not the illusion of depth but the sense that objects and their surroundings have been compressed within a shallow space behind the picture plane.

In Western art, illusions of perceptual volume and space are generally created by use of the linear perspectival system, based on the observations that objects appear to the eye to shrink and parallel lines and planes to converge to infinitely distant vanishing points as they approach the horizon, or viewer's eye level. In Leonardo da Vinci's "Last Supper" (1495–97; Sta. Maria delle Grazie, Milan), for example, all of the perspective lines of the room lead to the vanishing point at the head of Christ. Perceptual space and volume may be simulated on the picture plane by variations on this basic principle, differing according to the number and location of the vanishing points. Instead of one-point (or central) perspective, the artist may use, for instance, angular (or oblique) perspective, which employs two vanishing points.

Another kind of system—parallel perspective combined with a viewpoint from above—is traditional in Chinese painting. When buildings rather than natural contours are painted and it is necessary to show the parallel horizontal lines of the construction, parallel lines are drawn parallel instead of converging, as in linear perspective. Often foliage is used to crop these lines before they extend far enough to cause a building to appear warped.

Linear perspective study for "The Adoration of the Magi," silver point, pen, and bistre heightened with white on prepared ground by Leonardo da Vinci, *c.* 1481; in the Uffizi, Florence

Alinari

Differing in principle from linear perspective and used by both Chinese and European painters, aerial perspective (*q.v.*) is a method of creating the illusion of depth by a modulation of colour.

The early European artist used a perspective that was an individual interpretation of what he saw rather than a fixed mechanical method. At the beginning of the Italian Renaissance, early in the 15th century, the mathematical laws of perspective were discovered by the architect Filippo Brunelleschi, who worked out some of the fundamental principles, including the concept of the vanishing point, which had been known to the Greeks and Romans but had been lost. These principles were applied in painting by Masaccio (for example, in his "Trinity" fresco in Sta. Maria Novella, Florence; *c.* 1427), who within a short period brought about an entirely new approach in painting. A style was soon developed using configurations of architectural exteriors and interiors as the background for religious paintings, which thereby acquired the illusion of great spatial depth. In his seminal *Della pittura* (1436; *On Painting*, 1956), Leon Battista Alberti codified, especially for painters, much of the practical work on the subject that had been carried out by earlier artists; he formulated, for example, the idea that "vision makes a triangle, and from this it is clear that a very distant quantity seems no larger than a point."

Linear perspective dominated Western painting until the end of the 19th century, when Paul Cézanne flattened the conventional Renaissance picture space.

Linear perspective also plays an important part in presentations of ideas for works by architects, engineers, landscape architects, and industrial designers, furnishing an opportunity to view the finished product before it is begun.

·Alberti's impact on Italian art **1**:428e
·Alberti's system realized by Ghiberti **8**:149h
·Bellini's use of line to define form **2**:828f
·Brunelleschi's concept of principles **3**:343f
·Byzantine convention of reversal **4**:519e
·Cézanne's portrayal of space and depth **4**:11d
·distance perception importance **17**:380c
·Donatello's and Ghiberti's techniques **5**:951h
·drafting and pictorial representation **5**:976c; illus. 974
·Egyptian art's portrayal of reality **19**:250b
·El Greco's use of space **8**:306h
·Fra Angelico's spatial illusions **1**:870b
·Giotto's use in Arena Chapel **8**:163c
·Hsia Kuei's atmospheric perspective **8**:1124a; illus. 1123
·illusions and parallel lines **9**:242a
·intarsia work in Renaissance Italy **7**:784h
·landscaping design components and use **7**:886a
·Masaccio's use and development **11**:571d
·Matisse's use of space **11**:700g
·motion-picture techniques and effects **12**:501c; illus.
·photographic lens qualities **14**:307c
·Piero della Francesca's scientific treatises and pictorial space **14**:454b
·Renaissance theory and application **19**:397f
·Roman visual art developments **19**:311a *passim* to 314f
·Sogdian painting technique **3**:1135a
·spatial aspects of painting **13**:872h; illus. 873
·stage and scenery design in Renaissance **18**:243f
·theatrical scene design development **17**:539d *passim* to 540g
·theatrical scenery influence **18**:223b
·wall painting of Classical Greece **19**:295b

Perspex (acrylic plastic): *see* polymethyl methacrylate.

perspiration, in most mammals, water given off by the intact skin, either as vapour by simple evaporation from the epidermis (insensible perspiration) or as sweat, a form of cooling in which liquid actively secreted from sweat glands (*q.v.*) evaporates from the body surface. Sweat glands, although found in the majority of mammals, constitute the primary means of heat dissipation only in certain hoofed animals (orders Artiodactyla and Perissodactyla) and in primates, including man. Their secretion is largely water (usually about 99 per cent), with small amounts of dissolved salts and amino acids.

Eccrine sweat is an important mechanism for temperature control. When the body temperature rises, the sympathetic nervous system stimulates the eccrine sweat glands to secrete water to the skin surface, where it cools the body by evaporation. In extreme conditions, human beings may excrete several litres of such sweat in an hour.

Human eccrine sweat is essentially a dilute sodium chloride solution with trace amounts of other plasma electrolytes. In some cases a reddish pigment may also be present. In a person unused to heavy sweating, the loss of sodium chloride during a period of heavy labour or high temperatures may be great (*see* sodium deficiency), but the efficiency of the gland increases with use, and in acclimatized persons the salt loss is decreased.

The apocrine sweat glands, associated with the presence of hair in human beings (as on the scalp, the armpit, and the genital region), continuously secrete a concentrated fatty sweat into the gland tube. Emotional stress stimulates contraction of the gland, expelling its contents. Skin bacteria break down the fats into unsaturated fatty acids that possess a pungent odour.

·acclimatization to temperature change **1**:33g
·Arctic clothing design and function **1**:1124e
·climatic influence on man **4**:729d
·dehydration and excretion disorders **5**:560c
·human water depletion factor **7**:430b
·humidity control evaporation rate **9**:4f
·secretory stimuli and disease states **16**:849g

persuasion **14**:122, the process by which attitudes or behaviour is influenced by verbal communication.

The text article covers analysis of persuasive communication, theories of persuasion, methods of research, source factors, message factors, channel factors (referring to the modality or medium through which communication is transmitted), receiver factors, destination factors, and inducing resistance to persuasion.

REFERENCES in other text articles:
·advertising design psychology **1**:108d
·Aristotle's divisions and preference **15**:800e
·cognitive dissonance effect **16**:963f
·hypnotic induction and behaviour **9**:135c
·mass communication effects **4**:1009e
·mysticism as social factor **12**:793a
·nonviolent tactics ethical problems **13**:851g
·oratory as one form of appeal **13**:641h
·propaganda goals and methods **15**:36g
·public opinion manipulated by persuasion **15**:210b
·rhetorical stylistic theory **15**:803d

Persuasion (1817), novel by Jane Austen concerning the romance of Anne Elliot and Capt. Frederick Wentworth, who had been engaged to be married when she, succumbing to the "persuasion" of family and friends, broke off the engagement.

·theme and publication **2**:379d

PERT, abbreviation of PROJECT, OR PROGRAM, EVALUATION AND REVIEW TECHNIQUE, a technique for management control employing the critical-path method.

·operations research methodology **13**:600c

Perth, former county, north central Scotland, since the reorganization of 1975 mostly in Perth and Kinross (*q.v.*) district, of Tayside (*q.v.*) region with the remainder in Stirling (*q.v.*) district of Central (*q.v.*) region.

The Highland boundary fault runs across Perth from Alyth in the northeast to Aberfoyle in the southwest, forming a rough boundary between lowland Perth in the southeast and the Grampian highlands in the northwest. Highland Perth, a plateau about 3,000 ft high, rises to Ben More (3,852 ft [1,174 m]), Ben Lawers (3,984 ft), and Schiehallion (3,547 ft); it is much dissected by intensely glaciated valleys often occupied by glacial ribbon lakes (*e.g.*, lochs Rannock, Tummel, Tay, and Earn) and was a Highland centre of ice dispersal during maximum glaciation. Much of lowland Perth lies within the central rift valley of Scotland; it includes the Ochil and Sidlaw hills (1,500–2,000 ft), the vales of Strathmore and Strath Allan, and the Forth plain (100–500 ft), forming a complex, drift-covered, lowland corridor running southwest–northeast. The plain includes the light, fertile fluvioglacial soils of the fruit-growing areas of Strathmore and the Carse of Gowrie. Annual rainfall varies from 60 to 100 in. (1,500 to 2,500 mm) in the Highlands of the southwest to 30 to 35 in. in the drier lowland areas. Spring and summer are usually dry and sunny, but temperatures vary greatly with altitude and position.

The early Pictish inhabitants of Perth were subdued by the Romans, who built many forts (*e.g.*, Inchtuthil), camps, and signal stations (*e.g.*, along Loch Garn). After the Roman withdrawal, the Pictish capital was established first at Abernethy; then at Forteviot, which was sacked by the Norsemen in the 8th century; and then at Scone, where it remained until the 12th century, when it was transferred to the nearby royal burgh (chartered town) of Perth; it was finally moved to Edinburgh in 1452.

Perth's fertile lowlands produce good crops of wheat, sugar beets, and fodder. Large quantities of high-quality seed potatoes are exported. Fruits, particularly raspberries, are intensively cultivated on the low, fertile, riverine lands called carses. Sheep farming predominates on the hills and beef cattle on the foothills. The rivers, especially the Tay, and lochs abound with salmon and trout. The Forestry Commission controls large acreages of woodland, including 17 forests, the largest of which is Rannock Forest (about 45,600 ac, or 18,450 ha). There is a forestry school at Pitlochry. The Tummel-Garry Hydroelectric Scheme of 10 power stations is the largest in Scotland; others include the Breadalbane and Lawers schemes.

Industries include widespread whisky distilling—in Pitlochry, Aberfeldy, and Blackford—and blending and bottling at Perth, which also supports dyeing, linen, and glass industries and acts as the focal market and service centre of the area. Woollens, jute, linen, and tartans are woven in Pitlochry and Aberfeldy. Tourism flourishes, features including winter sports, pony trekking, sailing, and water skiing. Roads radiate mainly from Perth.

Perth, capital, Western Australia, situated on Melville and Perth waters, on the estuary of the Swan River, 12 mi (19 km) above its mouth, which forms the inner harbour of Fremantle (*q.v.*). The city, fifth largest in the nation, is the centre of a metropolitan area in which more than half of the state's population is concentrated. In the early 19th century, the British, suspicious of French and U.S. interest in the Australian west coast, decided to expand settlement and to claim the entire continent. In 1827 Capt. (later Sir) James Stirling arrived to choose a townsite. The following year, Capt. Sir Charles Fremantle took possession of the area and in 1829 a colony, with private financial backing, was declared. It was named after the county of Perth in Scotland, birthplace of Sir George Murray, then secretary of state for the colonies. Proclaimed a city in 1856, it was linked to Adelaide (in South Australia) by telegraph in 1877 and received strong impetus for growth from the discovery (1890) of gold at Coolgardie–Kalgoorlie (374 mi [602 km] east), from the opening of an improved Fremantle harbour (1901), and from the completion of the transcontinental railway in 1917. It became a lord mayoralty in 1929.

Perth is a major industrial centre, with heavy industries concentrated in the suburban zones of Kwinana (*q.v.*), Fremantle, and Welshpool. Diversified manufactures include paint, plaster, printed materials, sheet metal, cement, rubber, tractors, steel, aluminum, and nickel; there are also petroleum refineries and food-processing plants.

The city has an equable climate for eight months of the year, but January and February are uncomfortably hot, and both June and July are cool and damp. The city is accessible via several highways, the transcontinental railway, the port of Fremantle, and the international airport. It was the site of the Commonwealth and Empire Games in 1962. Perth has Anglican and Roman Catholic cathedrals, the University of Western Australia (1911), a technical college and two teachers' training colleges, and several private colleges. Pop. (1974 est.) city, 92,400; metropolitan area, 760,000.

Perth and the Swan River estuary, Western Australia

R. Archibald—Shostal

31°56′ S, 115°50′ E

·Aboriginal tribes location map **2**:425
·map, Australia **2**:400
·map, Australian External Territories **2**:433
·population, economy, and culture **19**:794a

Perth, town, seat of Lanark County, southeastern Ontario, Canada, on the Tay River. Named after the town in Scotland, it was founded in 1816 by Scottish immigrants who were later joined by British-Canadian veterans of the War of 1812. The town, 45 mi (72 km) southwest of Ottawa, has long been an important commercial and administrative centre for the Lanark-Renfrew-Carleton county area, since the construction of the Tay Canal in the 1830s linked it with Montreal and Ottawa (via the Rideau Canal and Ottawa River), though now the canal is used only by pleasure craft. Located in the centre of the Rideau Lakes region, Perth also serves as a summer resort. Manufactures include textiles, shoes, hardware, chemicals, soap, and electrical products. Inc. village, 1850. Pop. (1971) 5,537.
44°54′ N, 76°15′ W

Perth, city, royal burgh (chartered town), and seat of the administrative authority of Perth and Kinross (*q.v.*) district, Tayside region, Scotland, on the right bank of the River Tay.

There is evidence of a Roman settlement on the site of the present city, but the name is probably of Celtic origin (from Abertha, meaning "At the Mouth of the Tay"). Following the conversion of the original British inhabitants to Christianity and the dedication of the first church to St. John the Baptist, Perth also became known as St. John's Town; both names were used until the 17th century.

Perth developed rapidly; it was well established by the 12th century, for it was made a burgh in 1106 and a royal burgh in 1210. Until *c.* 1452 it served as the capital of Scotland, before Edinburgh achieved that status, and was therefore both a frequent royal residence and a centre of government. During the Scottish Wars of Independence, Perth was taken by Edward I of England, who strengthened its fortifications in 1298. It was retaken by Robert I the Bruce in 1313 during the fourth (and most brilliant) of the town's seven sieges. The English, under Edward III, took Perth again in 1335, and it was recaptured by the Scots in 1339. Perth was also the scene of the Battle of the Clans in 1396, described in Sir Walter Scott's *Fair Maid of Perth.* After sufferings from further military episodes in the 17th century, Perth was a Jacobite city during the Scottish uprisings of 1715 and 1745, and the insurgent James, the Old Pretender, was proclaimed king at its market cross.

Little architectural evidence remains of this eventful past, apart from the Church of St. John the Baptist, which was built about 1440 on the site of a church believed to have been built in the time of St. Columba (6th century). The town's friaries have disappeared, as have the castle, palace, and fortress. Notable modern public buildings include St. Ninian's Episcopal Cathedral (1850–90) and Perth prison, originally erected in 1812 to house French prisoners of the Napoleonic Wars.

During the Middle Ages, Perth was a significant river port, but it gradually declined in the face of competition from places farther downstream. Fertilizers are still imported in quantity, and seed potatoes are an export. Perth has long been a centre for dyeing industries, whisky blending and distilling, and the manufacture of twine, jute, and glass. Although the city has always maintained a wide range of industries, it is ultimately dominated by its agricultural hinterland. Its livestock sales (especially the February sales of bulls) are well known in Britain. Pop. (1974 est.) 44,066.
56°24′ N, 3°28′ W

·map, United Kingdom **18**:866

Perth, earls and dukes of, a Scottish title held from 1605 (but with abeyances) by the family of Drummond. The 4th earl supported James VII (James II of England) in exile, and was created by him titular duke of Perth (1690). His immediate descendants were all Jacobites, fighting in the risings of 1715 and 1745. On the death without issue of the 6th duke in 1760, the titular dukedom became extinct. The representation of the earldom passed to a cousin of the 6th duke, James Lundin (afterward Drummond), in whose family it is still held.

Perth Abyssal Plain, submarine feature, Indian Ocean.
29°00′ S, 110°00′ E

·Indian Ocean floor features map **9**:309

Perth Amboy, city and port of entry, Middlesex County, central New Jersey, U.S., at the mouth of the Raritan River, on Raritan Bay at the southern end of Arthur Kill (channel), there bridged to Tottenville, Staten Island, N.Y. Settled in the late 17th century, it was the capital of the East Jersey colony from 1686 to 1702, and after East and West Jersey were united to form New Jersey province it served with Burlington from *c.* 1738 to 1790 as the alternate provincial capital. The last royal governor of the colony was Benjamin Franklin's son William. Perth Amboy was occupied by the British in 1776–77 and was later evacuated when Gen. George Washington seized northern New Jersey.

Industry is well diversified and includes oil refining, electrolytic copper refining, shipbuilding, and the manufacture of ceramics. The original name Amboy is of Indian origin. Later, Perth was added in honour of an early proprietor, the Earl of Perth. Inc. 1718. Pop. (1980) 38,951.
43°31′ N, 74°16′ W

Perth and Kinross, district, Tayside (*q.v.*) region, north central Scotland; created by the reorganization of 1975, it includes the former county of Kinross and most of the former county of Perth (*qq.v.*). The district has an area of 2,022 sq mi (5,237 sq km). Perth is the seat of the district authority. Pop. (1974 est.) 117,911.

Perthes, Jacques Boucher (de Crèvecoeur) de (French archaeologist): *see* Boucher (de Crèvecoeur) de Perthes, Jacques.

perthite, a crystal characteristic or habit of some alkali feldspars in which tiny crystals of sodium-rich feldspar (albite; $NaAlSi_3O_8$) are intimately intergrown with, but distinct from, tiny crystals of potassium-rich feldspar (orthoclase or, less commonly, microcline; $KAlSi_3O_8$). Slow cooling of a homogeneous, molten mixture of sodium and potassium feldspar induces instabilities and results in the separation of tiny crystals of the two phases. In perthite, they sometimes may be seen by the unaided eye; in microperthite, however, they are distinguishable only microscopically, and in cryptoperthite the crystals are so small that the separation can be detected only by X-ray diffraction. Perthite was originally thought to be a single mineral, described at a locality near Perth, Ontario, from which its name is derived.

Perthite from Songo Pond, Maine

B.M. Shaub

·alkali feldspar structures **7**:212f

Pertinax, Publius Helvius (b. Aug. 1, AD 126, Liguria, Italy—d. March 28, 193), Roman emperor from January to March 193. The son of a freed slave, he taught school, then entered the army, commanding units in Syria, in Britain, and on the Danube and the Rhine. He earned distinction during the great invasion by German tribes in 169. Given senatorial rank and command of a legion, he was soon promoted to the consular commands of Moesia, Dacia, and Syria, but under the emperor Commodus (ruled 180–192) he fell from favour, together with the future emperor Septimius Severus, during the ascendancy of the praetorian prefect Perennis. In the last years of Commodus' life, Pertinax

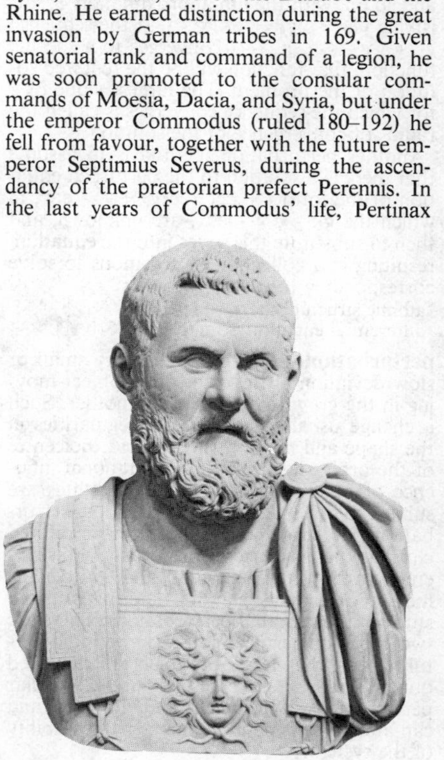

Pertinax, marble bust by an unknown artist; in the Vatican Museum, Rome

Anderson—Mansell

became prefect of the city of Rome, while Severus commanded the armies of the upper Danube. When Commodus was murdered on Dec. 31, 192, the Senate met before dawn and proclaimed Pertinax (then senior marshal of the empire) emperor. He tried to enforce unpopular economies in both civilian and military expenditure and was murdered by a small group of soldiers after less than three months in power. When Severus became emperor later in the year, he decreed divine honours for the slain ruler and took the name Pertinax.
·praetorians' military takeover **15**:1119e

Per Tum (ancient Egyptian city): *see* Pithom.

perturbation, in mathematics, method for solving a problem by comparing it with a similar one for which the solution is known. Usually the solution found in this way is only approximate.

Perturbation is used to find the roots of an algebraic equation that differs slightly from one for which the roots are known. Other examples occur in differential equations. In a physical situation, an unknown quantity is required to satisfy a given differential equation and certain auxiliary conditions that define the values of the unknown quantity at specified times or positions. If the equation or auxiliary conditions are varied slightly, the solution to the problem will also vary slightly.

The process of iteration is one way in which a solution of a perturbed equation can be obtained. Let D represent an operation, such as differentiation, performed on a function, and let $D + \epsilon P$ represent a new operation differing slightly from the first, in which ϵ represents a small constant. Then if f is a solution of the common type of problem $Df = cf$, in which c is a constant, the perturbed problem is that of determining a function g such that $(D + \epsilon P)g = cg$. This last equation can also be written as $(D - c)g = -\epsilon Pg$. Then the function g_1 that satisfies the equation $(D - c)g_1 = -\epsilon Pf$ is called a first approximation to g. The function g_2 that satisfies the equation $(D - c)g_2 = -\epsilon Pg_1$ is called a second approximation to g, and so on, with the nth approximation g_n satisfying $(D - c)g_n = -\epsilon Pg_{n-1}$. If the sequence $g_1, g_2, g_3, \cdots, g_n, \cdots$ converges to a specific function, that function will be the required solution of the problem. The largest value of ϵ for which the sequence converges is called the radius of convergence of the solution.

Another perturbation method is to assume that there is a solution to the perturbed equation of the form $f + \epsilon g_1 + \epsilon^2 g_2 + \ldots$ etc., in which the $g_1, g_2, \cdots$ etc., are unknown, and then to substitute this series into the equation, resulting in a collection of equations to solve corresponding to each power of ϵ.
·atomic structure theory **11**:798f
·differential equation principles **5**:751b

perturbation, in astronomy, a very small or slow deviation in the orbit of an object moving in the gravitational field of another. Such a change usually arises from irregularities in the shape and mass of the body at the centre of the orbit and from the gravitational influence of other bodies. Artificial satellites are subject to both kinds of perturbations. Perturbations in the orbits of planets have offered clues to the existence of previously undiscovered planets; *e.g.,* Neptune and Pluto. The masses of planets can be determined from study of their mutual perturbations. There are two types of perturbations: (1) periodic perturbations, the effects of which are cancelled out at regular intervals of time, and (2) secular perturbations, which increase with time and can after a long period endanger the stability of the system.
·artificial satellite Earth measurements **6**:5d
·celestial coordinates and precession **2**:224h
·cometary orbital changes **4**:972b
·gravity measurement by satellite orbits **6**:21e
·Jupiter satellites and motions **10**:351h
·Neptune discovery and study of Uranus **12**:963c
·Newtonian system confirmations **14**:388d
·planetary motion study **8**:288d
·planetary orbit distortion forces **11**:759d
·Pluto's systematic discovery **14**:580b
·satellite orbital deviations **17**:361b

pertussis: *see* whooping cough.

Pertz, Georg Heinrich (1795–1876), first general editor of the *Monumenta Germaniae Historica* (*q.v.*).

Peru 14:127, republic of South America, astride the Andes Mountains, bounded by Ecuador and Colombia (north), Brazil (east), Bolivia (east and south), Chile (south), and the Pacific Ocean (west).

The text article covers its natural and human landscape, its peoples, the national economy, administration and social conditions, and cultural life and institutions. (For statistical details, *see* p. 897.)

REFERENCES in other text articles:

agriculture, forestry, and fishing
·fishing ground nutrient sources **1**:1031a
·fish population and oceanic upwelling **13**:501h
·fish production and export expansion **7**:500d
·pest control in cotton production **14**:148d

art, archaeology, and architecture
·Baroque architectural developments **19**:420b
·Indian artifact aesthetic evaluation **1**:689d; illus. 690
·jewelry design of Indian culture **10**:181b
·tapestry weaving history and style **17**:1059a; illus.

commerce, industry, and mining
·Buenos Aires trade route **3**:445e
·coal production and reserves, table 5 **4**:781
·copper deposits and production **5**:152a; table 151
·gold production table **8**:239
·iron production, table 1 **9**:894
·petroleum production statistics, table 1 **14**:176
·petroleum reserves of the world table **14**:175
·silver production, table 1 **16**:778
·textile industry development **18**:171g
·tungsten ore production table **18**:737

culture and education
·Indian music in ritual and festival **1**:668g
·Lima cultural institutions **10**:979b
·school growth and literacy comparison **6**:402d

economics, finance, and currency
·gross domestic product by sector **17**:99d; table 98
·gross national debt percentage, table 4 **15**:193
·Inca villages' role in economy **17**:120d
·spice import, export, and value, table 3 **17**:506

government
·armed forces statistics, table 2 **2**:16
·South American political divisions map **17**:98
·Indian relations and heritage **17**:96d

physical geography
·Andes and Altiplano physiography **17**:80g
·Andes origin and physical features **1**:857d; map 856
·Lake Titicaca elevation and geology **18**:461h
·map, South America **17**:77
·mountain geological features **12**:590h
·Permian paleogeography **14**:99b
·sand sheet formations and causes **16**:209d; illus. 210

population and demography
·Christian denominational demography map **4**:459
·Indian population percentages **14**:848b
·urban population percentage growth, table 2 **17**:103

Peru, city, La Salle County, north central Illinois, U.S., adjoining La Salle, on the north bank of the Illinois River, laid out in 1834. Its economy is based on river trade, agriculture, and manufacturing (the chief products being clocks and zinc). St. Bede College was established there in 1899. Illinois Valley Community College (1924) is in nearby La Salle. Inc. city, 1851. Pop. (1980) 10,886.
41°20′ N, 89°08′ W

Peru, city, seat of Miami County, north central Indiana, U.S., on the Wabash River near its juncture with the Mississinewa, midway between South Bend (70 mi [110 km] north) and Indianapolis. Founded in 1826 on the site of a Miami Indian village, it is now a transportation and trading centre for agricultural products. Manufactures include heating equipment, plastics, and items made of paper, wood, and metal. Pioneer, circus, and Indian relics are displayed in the Miami County Historical and Puterbaugh museums. The songwriter Cole Porter was born near Peru. The annual Circus City Festival commemorates Peru's former fame as one of the world's largest circus winter quarters. Grissom Air Force Base and the Mississinewa Reservoir are nearby. Inc. town, 1848; city, 1867. Pop. (1980) 13,764.
40°45′ N, 86°04′ W

Peru, history of 14:134. Home of the advanced Inca civilization, Peru was conquered by Francisco Pizarro in 1531–33 and remained a Spanish colony till 1824.

The text article covers the history of Peru from independence to the present. Freedom from Spain was achieved under Antonio José de Sucre, and a liberal constitution was adopted in 1828. Rivalry among political factions engendered disorder in the early period, resulting often in military rule. Order was finally attained under Gen. Ramón Castilla between 1845 and 1862. Castilla abolished the payment of tribute by the Indians and freed the Negro slaves, although he permitted the importation of thousands of Chinese labourers. He also secured adoption of a constitution that lasted from 1860 until the 1900s.

An abortive invasion by a Spanish naval force (1864–69), a costly program of development, and the War of the Pacific (1879–84), in which Chile decisively defeated Peru and its ally Bolivia in a struggle over control of the nitrate beds in the Atacama Desert, led to virtual bankruptcy. The Peruvian Corporation was formed by Peru's creditors to handle its debt in an orderly manner, and this, together with fairly stable government until 1930, helped restore the economy. Especially beneficial were the two terms of Pres. Augusto Leguía, 1908–12 and 1919–30.

Since 1930, Peru has alternated between military and civilian rule. The Aprista movement (Alianza Popular Revolucionaria Americana), founded by Víctor Raúl Haya de la Torre, established a position that was anti-imperialist, anti-capitalist, and pro-Indian. It galvanized the mass of the people into political activity, but it frequently occasioned a conservative, even military, reaction. Under the presidencies of Manuel Prado, José Bustamante, Gen. Manuel Odría, and Fernando Belaúnde-Terry, economic nationalism came to the fore. A military junta took over in 1968 and furthered that movement. *See also* Andean civilization, history of; Latin America and the Caribbean, colonial.

REFERENCES in other text articles:
·Atacama Desert ownership conflict **2**:255a
·Bolívar and the liberation movement **2**:1207g
·Ecuadorian land dispute in Amazonian area **6**:292e
·Inca culture affected by Conquest **17**:120b
·Lima foundation and development **10**:976f
·military coup d'etat of 1968 **14**:132f

RELATED ENTRIES in the *Ready Reference and Index:*
Civilistas; Gamonalismo; Talambo Affair

Peru, Viceroyalty of, historical political subdivision of Spanish South America.
·colonial political boundaries map **10**:701
·establishment, history, and governmental structure **10**:694b

PERU

Official name: República Peruana (Republic of Peru).
Location: South America.
Form of government: republic.
Official languages: Spanish, Quechua.
Official religion: Roman Catholic.
Area: 496,224 sq mi, 1,285,215 sq km.
Population: (1972 census) 13,538,208; (1975 estimate) 15,839,000.
Capital: Lima.
Monetary unit: 1 sol = 100 centavos.

Demography

Population (1975 estimate): density 31.9 per sq mi, 12.3 per sq km; urban 55.9%, rural 44.1%; male 50.37%, female 49.63%; under 15 44.2%, 15–29 26.8%, 30–44 15.2%, 45–59 8.8%, 60–74 4.0%, 75 and over 0.9%.*
Vital statistics: (1970–75) births per 1,000 population 41.0, deaths per 1,000 population 11.9, natural increase per 1,000 population 29.1; life expectancy at birth—male 53.9, female 57.5; (1970) major causes of death (per 100,000 population)—pneumonia 129.1; senility without mention of psychosis, ill-defined and unknown causes 86.2; enteritis and other diarrheal diseases 75.2; measles 61.4; bronchitis, emphysema, and asthma 40.4; influenza 38.5. *Ethnic composition* (mid-1960s): Mestizo and Indian 88.0%, European 12.0%. *Religious affiliation* (1973 estimate): Roman Catholic 93%, other 7%.

National accounts

Budget (1974). Revenue: 68,560,000,000 soles (income and property taxes 25.0%; import taxes 15.0%; taxes on production and consumption 35.2%, of which, taxes on goods and services 24.9%; extraordinary receipts 9.9%). Expenditures: 98,706,000,000 soles, current, capital, and national debt accounts (current 63.3%, of which, current expenditures on goods and services 43.4 [including salaries 29.4%], transfers to public corporations, and semipublic and private sectors 12.1%; capital expenditures 20.5%, of which, gross capital formation 13.1%; national debt service 16.3%, of which, external 10.0%, internal 6.3%). *Tourism* (1974). Receipts from visitors: U.S. $84,350,000; expenditures by nationals abroad—no data available.

Domestic economy

Gross national product (GNP; at current market prices, 1974): U.S. $10,670,000,000 (U.S. $710 per capita).

Origin of gross domestic product:	1961				1972			
	value in 000,000 soles†	% of total value	labour force 000	% of labour force	value in 000,000 soles‡	% of total value	labour force 000	% of labour force
agriculture, forestry, hunting, fishing	13,760	25.6	1,703.6	52.8	40,593	15.2	1,536.6	40.6
mining, quarrying	3,093	5.8	70.8	2.2	20,398	7.6	52.9	1.4
manufacturing	9,359	17.4	435.0	13.5	66,662	24.9	481.2	12.7
construction	2,144	4.0	110.5	3.4	12,433	4.6	171.0	4.5
electricity, gas, water	346	0.6	9.0	0.3	2,966	1.1	7.2	0.2
transport, storage, communications	2,311	4.3	99.3	3.1	§	...	164.6	4.4
trade	6,665	12.4	276.4	8.6	§	...	399.1	10.5
banking, insurance, real estate	1,561	2.9	20.4	0.6	§	...	45.6	1.2
ownership of dwellings	3,819	7.1	...	...	10,714	4.0	‖	...
public administration, defense	4,796	8.9	175.9	5.5	22,071	8.2	‖	...
services	5,833	10.9	326.0	10.1	91,945§	34.3	664.4‖	17.5
other	...	...	...	...	...	...	264.5¶	7.0
total	53,687	100.0*	3,227.0*	100.0*	267,782	100.0*	3,786.2*	100.0

Production (metric tons except as noted, 1974). Agriculture, forestry, hunting, fishing: sugarcane 9,215,000, corn (maize) 472,000, paddy rice 361,000, potatoes 1,155,000, coffee 42,600, oranges 214,000; livestock (number of live animals): cattle 4,500,000, sheep 17,300,000, pigs 2,300,000, goats 1,950,000; roundwood 6,360,000 cu m♀; fish catch 4,125,337. Mining, quarrying: iron ore 6,220,000; zinc ore 467,000; copper ore 223,000; lead ore 201,000; silver 1,218 kg; petroleum 3,800,000.
Energy (1971): installed electrical capacity 1,797,000 kW, production 5,949,000,000 kWhr (425 kWhr per capita).
Persons economically active: (1972) 3,786,200 (26.2%); (1974) unemployed 195,700.δ

Price and earnings indexes (1970 = 100):	1971	1972	1973	1974	1975
consumer price index□	106.8	114.5	125.4	146.5	181.2
daily earnings index◇	106.7	132.3	162.2	...	...

Land use (1971): total area 128,522,000 ha (forested 67.7%; meadows and pastures 21.4%; agricultural and under permanent cultivation 2.2%; built-on, wasteland, and other 8.7%).

Foreign trade

Imports (1974): U.S. $1,531,060,000 (machinery 28.4%; chemicals and rubber 17.8%, of which, plastics and rubber 6.3%; food 16.2%; metals and metal manufactures 12.3%; mineral products 8.5%; transport equipment 5.1%; paper and paper products 4.8%; instruments 2.9%). *Major import sources:* United States 31.2%, Japan 12.0%, West Germany 10.5%, Ecuador 4.6%, Canada 3.6%, The Netherlands 3.1%.
Exports (1974): U.S. $1,520,600,000 (copper 22.8%; fish meal 13.0%; silver 10.9%; zinc 10.6%; sugar 10.3%; cotton 6.2%; lead 4.4%; iron ore 4.0%; coffee 2.3%). *Major export destinations:* United States 35.7%, Japan 13.5%, West Germany 7.7%, China 4.7%, Argentina 3.4%, Poland 3.2%, Belgium-Luxembourg 3.1%.

Transport and communications

Transport. Railroads: (1973) length 1,521 mi, 2,448 km; (1970) passenger-mi 154,000,000, passenger-km 248,000,000; short ton-mi cargo 418,000,000, metric ton-km cargo 610,000,000. Roads (1974): total length 31,485 mi, 50,670 km (paved 3,117 mi, 5,017 km; gravel and crushed stone 6,190 mi, 9,962 km; earth roads graded and drained 9,157 mi, 14,737 km; unimproved 13,021 mi, 20,954 km). Vehicles (1975): passenger cars 266,910, trucks and buses 139,950. Merchant marine (1975): vessels (100 gross tons and over) 677, total deadweight tonnage 617,070. Air transport: (1973) passenger-mi 251,000,000, passenger-km 404,000,000; short ton-mi cargo 8,600,000, metric ton-km cargo 12,500,000; (1976) airports with scheduled flights 25.
Communications. Daily newspapers: (1973) total number 70; (1970) total circulation 1,660,000,▲ circulation per 1,000 population 122.▲ Radios (1973): total number of receivers 2,001,000 (1 per 7.5 persons). Television (1973): receivers 411,000 (1 per 36 persons). Telephones (1975): 333,346 (1 per 47 persons).

Education and health

Education (1972–73):	schools	teachers	students	student-teacher ratio
primary# (age 6–12)	19,346	73,448	2,648,843	36.1
secondary# (age 12–17)	1,451⊕	26,314	608,905	23.1
vocational, teacher training#	414⊕	8,909	181,120	20.3
higher	121**	11,957	138,935	11.6

College graduates (per 100,000 population, 1971): 40. *Literacy* (1972): total population literate (age 15 and over) 72.5%.
Health: (1972) doctors 8,023 (1 per 1,802 persons); (1972) hospital beds 29,086 (1 per 497 persons); (1970) daily per capita caloric intake 2,310 calories (FAO recommended minimum requirement 2,350 calories).

*Detail does not add to total given because of rounding. †Current prices. ‡1970 prices. §Services includes transport, storage, and communications, trade, and financial services. ‖Services includes ownership of dwellings and public administration. ¶Includes activities not adequately described and those seeking work for the first time. ♀1973. δUrban areas only. □Lima only. ◇Lima and Callao. ▲Circulation refers to 59 dailies. #Includes evening schools. ⊕1970. **1969.

Peru Basin, submarine depression, Pacific Ocean.
15°00′ S, 95°00′ W
·Pacific Ocean floor features map **13**:838

Peru-Chile Trench, also called ATACAMA TRENCH, deep submarine depression in the floor of the eastern Pacific Ocean, near the west coast of South America. It reaches a depth of 25,049 ft (7,635 m) in Richards Deep.
21°00′ S, 72°00′ W
·island arc features and composition **9**:1027f
·Pacific Ocean floor features map **13**:838

Peru Current, also called HUMBOLDT CURRENT, a cold-water current of the southeast Pacific Ocean, with a width of about 900 km (550 mi).

Relatively slow and shallow, it transports only 10,000,000–20,000,000 cu m (350,000,000–700,000,000 cu ft) of water per second. It is an eastern boundary current similar to the California Current of the North Pacific. The West Wind Drift flows east toward South America south of latitude 40° S, and while most of it continues through the Drake Passage around the southern tip of South America to the Atlantic, a shallow stream turns north to parallel the continent as far as latitude 4° S, where it turns west to join the Pacific South Equatorial Current.

As it is a cold current, except at times of the phenomenon known as El Niño Current (*q.v.*), the Peru Current brings fog to the nearby coast but also helps to keep that same coast one of the most intensely arid areas in the world. The cold flow is intensified by upwelling of deep water caused by the combined effects of the drag of surface winds of the Southeast Trades and the Earth's rotation. Upwelling brings abundant nutrients close to the surface and the beneficial effects of sunlight, allowing for rich plankton growth, which makes the waters off Peru, Chile, and Ecuador one of the world's greatest fishing grounds for anchovies and the larger fish (tuna) that feed upon them. Another economic benefit is the guano (used for fertilizer) deposited by the flocks of birds that feed on the anchovies.

The current's alternative name is taken from that of the great German scientist Alexander von Humboldt, who in 1802 took measurements that showed the coldness of the flow in relation to the air above it and the sea around it.

·characteristics and climatic effects **17**:82d
·Chile's climate influenced **4**:247g
·Ecuadorian climate modification **6**:285g
·Galápagos Islands climate peculiarities **7**:827b
·Humboldt scientific study fame **8**:1190e
·Lima's climate influenced **10**:976h
·Pacific southern circulation **13**:842h
·Peruvian climatic effects **14**:127c
·South American coastal climate effect **2**:254h

Perugia, ancient PERUSIA, city, seat of an archbishopric, and capital of Perugia province and Umbria region, in central Italy, north of Rome; it lies on an irregular cluster of hills overlooking the Umbrian and central Tiber valleys and Lago (Lake) Trasimeno. Founded by the Umbrians, it became one of the 12 strongholds of the Etruscan Confederation and belonged to Rome from 310 BC. In AD 592 it became a Lombard duchy; subsequently, it was embroiled in many petty conflicts with neighbouring towns in which it usually took the Guelf, or pro-papal, side. The *condottiere* Braccio Fortebraccio captured it in 1416, and later the rival Oddi and Baglioni families fought there for power before the town became a papal possession in 1540.

Perugia was the centre of the great Umbrian school of painting, which reached its height in the 15th century. It played an active part in the Italian Risorgimento in 1859 and in the following year became part of united Italy.

There are considerable remains of Etruscan

walls with three gateways, as well as the Etruscan nucleus of the well-preserved medieval city enclosed by 13th-century walls, and on the outskirts, the Etruscan *hypogea* (underground burial chambers) of San Manno and of the Volumnii (2nd century BC). In the centre of the city the magnificent square Piazza Quattro Novembre contains the Palazzo dei Priori, or Palazzo Communale (1293–97; extended 1443), housing the National Gallery of Umbria's remarkable collection of paintings and sculpture; the cathedral of S. Lorenzo (1345–1430), in which is the supposed white onyx espousal ring of the Virgin; and the splendid Maggiore Fountain (1278) by Fra Bevignate. Other landmarks include the Collegio del Cambio (1452–57), with a dazzling series of frescoes by Pietro Perugino and his pupils. Particularly notable among the many fine churches are S. Angelo (5th and 6th centuries; on a circular plan); S. Domenico (1305; rebuilt 1632), containing the monumental tomb of Pope Benedict XI; S. Pietro (originally 10th century, often remodelled); S. Severo (15th–18th centuries), with a fresco by Raphael; and S. Bernardino (1457–61). In the former convent of S. Domenico are the state archives and the Etrusco-Roman museum, with an important archaeological collection. The former convent of the Olivetans is the central seat of the university (founded 1307), and the Palazzo Gallenga is the seat of the Italian university for foreigners.

Palazzo dei Priori, Perugia, Italy

Mildred Bernhaut—Photo Researchers

Perugia is an agricultural trade centre noted for its chocolate; its chief economic activities are the food, textile, machine, and pharmaceutical industries. Pop. (1971 prelim.) metropolitan area, 131,843.
43°08′ N, 12°22′ E

·area and population table 1 **9**:1094
·Etruscan stone inscription find **6**:1018d; illus.
·Leo XIII's papal preparation period **10**:807f
·map, Italy **9**:1088
·Renaissance history and culture **15**:663g

Perugia, Lake of (Italy): *see* Trasimeno, Lake.

Perugia, Università degli Studi di, English UNIVERSITY OF PERUGIA, coeducational state institution of higher learning at Perugia, Italy. It was founded in 1200 and recognized as a university in 1308. Among its faculties are law, political science, humanities, education, medicine, and physical sciences.

Perugino 14:136, real name PIETRO DI CRISTOFORO VANNUCCI (b. *c.* 1450, Città della Pieve, near Perugia, Italy—d. February/March 1523, Fontignano, near Perugia), early Renaissance painter whose work is recognized for its compositional clarity, sense of spaciousness, and economy of formal elements. He is also important for his influential role as teacher of Raphael.

Abstract of text biography. Calling himself after the town Perugia, Perugino was employed by Pope Sixtus IV in Rome where he painted frescoes for the Sistine Chapel (1481–82). Upon completion of these frescoes, he returned to Florence, having previously worked in Verrocchio's studio there. After 1500 Perugino's art began to decline and from about 1505 he worked outside Florence, principally in Umbria.

REFERENCE in other text article:
·Botticelli's professional associates **3**:77a

peruke, a man's wig, especially the type popular from the 17th to the early 19th century. Also called a periwig, it was made of

Back view of a squared peruke worn by an effigy of William II, 1725; in the Victoria and Albert Museum, London

By courtesy of the Victoria and Albert Museum, London, Crown copyright

long hair, often with curls on the sides, and drawn back on the nape of the neck. Use of the word peruke probably became widespread in the 16th century when the wearing of wigs became popular. Toward the end of the 16th century and the beginning of the 17th, the peruke was no longer worn as an adornment or to correct nature's defects but rather as a distinctive feature of costume, especially after Louis XIII of France set the fashion in 1624.

Perun, Slavic deity, the heavenly smith, corresponding to the Baltic Pērkons and various other deities of Indo-European peoples.
·attributes, parallels, and importance **16**:874g

Perusia (Italy): *see* Perugia.

Perusia, Battle of (41 BC), Octavian's victory over Antony's brother and wife.
·Octavian's victory in Italy **15**:1106f

Perutz, Max Ferdinand (1914–), Austrian-born chemist who shared the 1962 Nobel Prize for Chemistry with John Cowdery Kendrew for research on the structure of globular proteins, particularly hemoglobin. In 1937 he began his hemoglobin studies at Cambridge University, where he received his doctorate in 1940. He lectured at the Royal Institution, London, before becoming director of the Medical Research Council's molecular biology unit at Cambridge in 1947.

Peruvian-Bolivian Confederation, a transitory union of Peru and Bolivia (1836–39). Bolivia's dictator, Andrés Santa Cruz, conquered Peru after helping to quell an army rebellion against Peruvian president Luís José de Orbegoso in 1835. Santa Cruz then divided Peru into a northern and a southern part with Orbegoso as president in the north and Gen. Ramón Herrera in the south. These states were then joined to Bolivia, of which Gen. José Miguel de Velasco was made president. Santa Cruz assumed the office of "protector" of the confederation, a lifetime and hereditary office. Since he had already proved himself an able administrator in Bolivia, influential Peruvians welcomed his rule.

Great Britain, France, and the United States recognized the confederation, but its South American neighbours feared and opposed the powerful new state that had suddenly been formed. In 1836 fighting broke out between the confederation and Chile, whose relations with independent Peru had already been strained by economic problems centring on rivalry between their ports of Callao (near Lima) and Valparaíso, Chile. In 1837 Santa Cruz' forces defeated an Argentine army sent to topple him.

The Chileans, joined by Peruvians opposed to Santa Cruz, persisted in their fight until, under the command of Gen. Manuel Bulnes, they finally defeated the forces of the confederation at the Battle of Yungay (department of Ancash, Peru) on Jan. 20, 1839. This defeat caused the immediate dissolution of the confederation; Santa Cruz went into exile. Agustín Gammarra assumed the presidency of Peru and tried to subjugate Bolivia to Peru; this attempt ended abruptly with his death on the battlefield in 1841. Both Peru and Bolivia then entered a period of internal disorders.
·Chilean conservative hegemony **4**:255h

Peruvian Corporation, organization established by the Peruvian government in the late 19th century to deal with foreign investment.
·Peruvian development aided **14**:134h

Peruzzi, leading family of medieval Italian financiers whose bankruptcy in the 14th century contributed to the economic depression of the late Middle Ages.

An old Florentine family belonging to the "popular" (democratic) party, the Peruzzi contributed 10 gonfaloniers (chief executives) and 54 priors (members of the governing body) to the republic. Filippo di Amedeo de' Peruzzi was a leader of the Guelf (pro-papal) League in 1260 against the Ghibelline (pro-imperial) leader Farinata degli Uberti and in 1284 was elected prior, a newly created office in which he was one of the first to serve. In their palaces in the Santa Croce quarter of Florence, the Peruzzi entertained many important public figures, including King Robert of Naples in 1310 and the Byzantine emperor John VIII Paleologus in 1439, on the occasion of the church council in Florence that had been convened to reunite the Greek and Latin churches. The Peruzzi Chapel in the church of Sta. Croce was decorated with frescoes by Giotto.

Coming to prominence as bankers *c.* 1275, the Peruzzi soon had branches in most of the important centres of Europe and were second in importance only to the Bardi company. The Florentine chronicler Giovanni Villani was a Peruzzi partner. At the beginning of the Hundred Years War between England and France, they were especially active in Naples, Paris, and London. Beginning in the 1330s, the Peruzzi made large loans to Edward III of England, first in concert with the Bardi company, later by themselves, financing his wars in Scotland and France in return for grants of wool, money, and assignment of customs and taxes. Loans in 1338–39 for the mounting expenses of Edward's wars exhausted both Peruzzi and Bardi resources, and in 1340 Bonifazio di Tommaso de' Peruzzi, head of the company, went to London to deal with the crisis. He died there the following year, according to the family's chronicler, of grief at the impending catastrophe. The two firms, their credits frozen, virtually ceased their loans to the King, who, with little inducement to pay what he owed, in 1342 appointed a commission to examine the companies' accounts. During the next three years members of both companies were arrested for bankruptcy and released only on renunciation of all claims to interest, and the English crown cancelled massive debts to the Peruzzi. At the same time, the King of Naples defaulted on his debts to the two companies, and the King of France exiled them and confiscated their goods.

The disasters abroad brought on panic at home, resulting in 1342 in a movement by the Bardi and Peruzzi and other great banking companies to set up Walter of Brienne, duke of Athens, as ruler of Florence, hoping to control his foreign and financial policies to save their firms from bankruptcy. In 1343, disappointed in their hopes, the bankers ousted the soldier of fortune. When a revolution put the *popolo minuto* (lesser guilds and merchants) in power, the Peruzzi company's bankruptcy followed, heralding the great economic crisis of the mid-14th century.

Peruzzi, Baldassarre (Tommaso) (b. 1481, Siena?, Italy—d. Jan. 6, 1536, Rome), ar-

"Head of the Goddess Ceres," oil painting by Peruzzi; in the Galleria Nazionale, Rome

Photo SASKIA, North Amherst, Mass.

chitect and painter, one of the earliest artists to attempt illusionist architectural painting (*quadratura*), the extension of real architecture into imaginary space. A contemporary of Raphael and Bramante, he began his career as a painter of frescoes in the Cappella S. Giovanni in Siena catherdral. His first architectural work was the Villa Farnesina in Rome (1509–21), and he also assisted in the fresco decoration of this palace. On Raphael's death, in 1520, Peruzzi was appointed one of the architects for St. Peter's in Rome. Among the many edifices attributed to him, the most significant is probably the Palazzo Massimo alle Colonne (*c.* 1535) in Rome.

·High Renaissance and Mannerist designs **19**:385c

Peruzzi Chapel, chapel in Sta. Croce, Florence, containing several frescoes attributed to Giotto.

·Giotto's frescoes and their restoration **8**:163d

Pervomaysk, centre of a *rayon* (district), Nikolayev *oblast* (administrative region), Ukrainian Soviet Socialist Republic, at the confluence of the Sinyukha and Yuzhny Bug rivers. The city, formerly known as Olviopol, was incorporated in 1773 and renamed (literally, First of May, after the international Communist holiday) in 1919. The city is divided by the rivers into three separate parts. It is now an industrial centre, with machine, engineering, food, and furniture industries. Pop. (1970) 59,424.
48°04′ N, 30°52′ E

Pervomaysk, mining town, Voroshilovgrad *oblast* (administrative region), Ukrainian Soviet Socialist Republic, on the Donets Basin coalfield. The town, the name of which means First of May (after the international Communist holiday), was incorporated in 1938, before which it was known as Petromaryevka. Pervomaysk also has electrical-engineering and light industries. Pop. (1970) 45,779.
48°38′ N, 38°33′ E

Pervouralsk, city, Sverdlovsk *oblast* (administrative region), western Russian Soviet Federated Socialist Republic, on the upper Chusovaya River and the railway from Sverdlovsk to Perm. Founded in 1732 as an ironworks, modern Pervouralsk has two steel-pipe factories, one of which is the largest in the U.S.S.R. It also produces mining machinery, chemicals, clothing, and foodstuffs. Iron ore containing vanadium is mined in the vicinity. Pop. (1970) 117,000.
56°54′ N, 59°58′ E

perxenate, chemical formula XeO_6^{4-}, an ion that decomposes in water solution.

·solution and thermal stability **13**:142e

Pesaḥ, also spelled PESACH (Hebrew: Passover), in Judaism, one of three major Pilgrim Festivals, this one commemorating the "passing over," or the sparing, of the firstborn of the Israelites when the Lord "smote the land of Egypt" on the eve of the Exodus (Nisan 14). The Jews had marked their doorposts with the blood of a lamb to signify that they were children of God.

The festival is celebrated for seven days in Israel and by Reform Jews, and for eight days in the Diaspora, though the seven-day period from Nisan 15 to 22 is more properly the festival of "unleavened bread." In the Ashkenazi synagogues, the Song of Solomon (Song of Songs) is read from the Megillot on the sabbath as part of the liturgy. Though the festival is meant to be one of great rejoicing (recalling

"The Seder Meal," illustration for Passover Haggada by Arthur Szyk, 1939

By courtesy of the Jewish Theological Seminary of America, New York, Frank J. Darmstaedter

the greatest event in Jewish history), strict dietary laws (especially against leaven) must be observed, and special prohibitions restrict work at the beginning and end of the celebration.

·Aaron's prominent position **1**:2h
·Chosen People historical perspective **7**:198g
·Christian Easter and Passover **4**:601a
·dietary laws and religious identity **5**:732f
·origin in barley harvest festival **19**:1017b
·practices and concepts through the ages **10**:219f
·ritual dress **15**:635g
·worship in common for group identity **19**:1015a
·Yemenite seder in Israel photo **10**:295b

Pesaro, Roman PISAURUM, capital of Pesaro e Urbino province, in Marche region of northern Italy, a seaport on the Adriatic Sea at the mouth of the Foglia (Pisaurum) River. Destroyed by Witigis the Ostrogoth in 536, the town was rebuilt and fortified by the Byzantine general Belisarius and was one of the five cities of the Maritime Pentapolis under the exarchate of Ravenna. Later disputed between the popes and the Holy Roman emperors, Pesaro came into the hands of the Malatesta family of Rimini *c.* 1285. It was sold in 1445 to the Sforza family, and in 1512, through the influence of Pope Julius II, it went to the pope's nephew Francesco Maria I della Rovere, duke of Urbino. It reverted to the Papal States in 1631. A main point at the Adriatic end of the so-called Gothic line in World War II, Pesaro suffered heavily in the Allied advance of 1944, but many of its old buildings escaped with minor damage. Notable landmarks include the fortress of Rocca Constanza (built 1474–1505 for Constanzo Sforza); the Palazzo Ducale (1450–1510); the cathedral, with a 14th-century facade; and the nearby Villa Imperiale, built (1469–72) for Alessandro Sforza and noted for its fine stucco ceilings, wall paintings, and pavements of majolica (glazed, richly coloured pottery) plates. A new palace, begun in 1530 by Girolamo Genga and his son for Eleonora Gonzaga, was never completed.

The civic museums house the picture gallery and the museum of majolica, with the richest collection in Italy. (Pesaro has been famous for its majolica since 1462.) The Oliveriano Archaeological Museum is important for students of Italian antiquities. The composer Gioacchino Antonio Rossini, a native of Pesaro, left his fortune to found a music school, the Liceo Musicale Rossini, famous for its directors and for the composers who studied there.

Pesaro is a pleasant seaside resort and serves a rich agricultural area; its industries include sulfur refining, boatbuilding, and the manufacture of motorcycles. Pop. (1971 prelim.) metropolitan area, 86,239.
43°54′ N, 12°55′ E

·map, Italy **9**:1088
·province area and population, table 1 **9**:1094

Pesaro Madonna (1519–26), painting by Titian.

·design innovation and influence **18**:458h

Pescadores Islands, Western conventional for Chinese P'ENG-HU LIEH-TAO, Pin-yin romanization PENG-HU LIE-DAO, an archipelago of about 64 small islands, approximately 30 mi (50 km) to the west of the coast of Taiwan, from which they are separated by the Pescadores Channel. Of volcanic origin, many of the islands consist of weathered basalt and are surrounded by coral reefs. They are low-lying, rising mostly about 100–130 ft (30–40 m) above sea level. The highest peak is about 157 ft. The islands have a warm climate, being situated in the path of the warm Kuroshio Current, and the annual temperature range is from 61° F (16° C) to 82° F (28° C). The rain-

Women mending fishnets, Ma-kung, Pescadores Islands, Taiwan

George Holton—Photo Researchers

fall is roughly 35 in. (1,033 mm) annually, almost all of which falls between June to September. For the rest of the year there is a shortage of water, for there are no rivers; in winter the islands are swept by severe winds. The largest islands are P'eng-hu (25 sq mi [64 sq km]), on which more than half of the population lives; Pai-sha; Yü-weng; and Pa-chao. P'eng-hu and Pai-sha are linked by a causeway. The total area of the entire group is only 49 sq mi (127 sq km).

About half of the islands are cultivated, but the soils are poor and the climate harsh; the main crops—sweet potatoes, peanuts (groundnuts), maize (corn), and millet—are those associated with poor hill country in southern China. A large part of the population are fishermen, and the European name Pescadores (Fishermen's Islands) was given to the islands by the Portuguese in the 16th century.

The Pescadores were probably known to the Chinese (under the name Liu-chiu) as early as the 7th century AD. Their name first appears as P'eng-hu (or P'ing-hu) in Chinese sources of the 12th century, and it was at this time that it was probably first settled by Chinese fishermen from Fukien or Chekiang provinces on the mainland. At the beginning of the Ming dynasty (1368–1644) the Chinese government built a fort on P'eng-hu, established a civil government there, and imposed taxes on the fisheries. In 1388, however, the entire population was transported to the mainland. P'eng-hu was then abandoned and became a lair for pirates. Only in the reign of the Ming emperor Wan-li (1573–1620) did Chinese settlers again begin to colonize the islands, first establishing fisheries, and then (in 1625) military colonies. Meanwhile, between 1622 and 1624, the islands had been occupied by the Dutch. At the end of the Ming dynasty, many Fukienese settlers came to the islands to escape the fighting in southeast China, mostly from Chang-chou and Ch'üan-chou. By 1683 there were said to be some 6,000 inhabitants on the islands, who were formally placed under the control of the civil authorities in Taiwan. The population seems to have been organized in bay associations (*ao-she*), numbering 9 in 1693 and 13 in 1727. In 1721 the islands became the base for government punitive action against Chu I-kuei, a rebel on Taiwan.

In the 19th century, when the Western powers began to have designs on Taiwan, the Pescadores again became an important strategic area. They were occupied by the French in 1884–85, and after the Sino-Japanese War of 1894–95 were ceded to Japan, together with Taiwan. Returned to China in 1945, the islands were made a township (*chen*) under Taiwan, and, in 1950, a county (*hsien*) of Taiwan Province.

In the early 1970s the islands remained under the control of the Chinese Nationalist regime on Taiwan; a Chinese Nationalist naval base, Ma-kung, was established on P'eng-hu. In addition to the fishing industry, the working of the islands' phosphate deposits also provided income.

23°20′ N, 119°30′ E

·map, Taiwan **17**:996

·Taiwan area and population table **17**:997

Pescara, capital of Pescara province, Abruzzi region, central Italy, on the Adriatic Sea at the mouth of the Pescara River, east-northeast of Rome. The Roman Aternum, the city was almost destroyed in the barbarian invasions and arose again in the early Middle Ages as Piscaria (*i.e.*, "abounding with fish"). The scene of much fighting throughout its history, it suffered heavy damage in World War II. Since 1927, Castellammare Adriatico, on the north bank of the river, has been part of Pescara. The birthplace (1863) of the poet Gabriele D'Annunzio has been preserved.

Government palace and the Pescara River in Pescara, Italy

Marzari—SCALA, New York

Pescara is a seaside resort and tourist centre on the railway and main road from Bologna to Bari and Brindisi. Fishing and electrical, mechanical, textile, and food-processing industries are important, and there are naval shipyards. Pop. (1971 prelim.) mun., 122,048.

42°28′ N, 14°13′ E

·district area and population, table 1 **9**:1094

·map, Italy **9**:1088

Pescara, Fernando Francesco de Avalos, Marchese di (b. Naples, 1490—d. Dec. 2, 1525, Milan), leader of the forces of Holy Roman emperor Charles V against the French king Francis I. He won an important victory at the Battle of Pavia (1525).

In 1509 Pescara married the poet Vittoria Colonna (later famous as Michelangelo's friend), daughter of the Neapolitan commander Fabrizio Colonna and granddaughter of a famous Renaissance prince, Federico da Montefeltro, duke of Urbino.

A pupil of the soldier of fortune Prospero Colonna, Pescara commanded Spanish forces in Italy in the struggles from 1512 to 1525 between the French on one side and the Spanish and Germans on the other. In 1512 he was wounded at Ravenna, became a prisoner of the French, and was released on the promise not to fight against them again, a promise that was to be broken many times. In subsequent engagements he defeated the Venetians at Vicenza, occupied Padua in 1514, and, once more fighting against the French, took Milan in 1521 and Genoa in 1522. After Prospero Colonna's death in 1523, Pescara became virtual commander of Charles V's troops in Italy, winning a victory at Romagnano (northwest of Milan) in 1524 and, the following year, his greatest battle, at Pavia (south of Milan). There, by a combination of patience and tact, he successfully led his unpaid, ill-fed, and demoralized troops against the French.

After the victory Girolamo Morone, the Milanese chancellor, tried to enlist Pescara in a plot to ally Italy with France against Charles V, offering him the crown of Naples. Pescara at first appeared to give the plan serious consideration—to learn details of the conspiracy, he later claimed. But on Oct. 14, 1525, he arrested Morone, marched on Milan, and forced the Milanese to swear allegiance to the Emperor, demanding the surrender of the citadels of Milan and Cremona (southeast of Milan). The duke of Milan, Francesco Sforza, refused, whereupon Pescara besieged the Castello Sforzesco. He died, however, before the Duke yielded and on his deathbed recommended clemency for Morone.

Pescara River, south central Italy, rises in the Apennines and flows 90 mi (145 km) southwest to enter the Adriatic at Pescara city. It is utilized for hydroelectric power.

42°29′ N, 14°12′ E

·length table of rivers in Apennines **1**:1011

Pescennius Niger Justus, Gaius: *see* Niger, Pescennius.

Pescia, town, Pistoia province, Toscana (Tuscany) region, central Italy, at the base of the Appennino Tosco-Emiliano (Etruscan Apennines) and at the western end of the Nievole River. Its cathedral is notable for an ancient tower, and in the 14th-century church of St. Francis is a picture of St. Francis of Assisi, painted in 1235 by Bonaventura Berlinghieri. There are also several notable paintings in the civic museum.

The town has diverse industries, particularly paper manufacture, which dates from the 15th century. An important distributing centre for local produce, Pescia has an agricultural school and is a busy market in asparagus and flowers. Pop. (1970 est.) 19,684.

43°54′ N, 10°41′ E

·map, Italy **9**:1088

Pescium (Yugoslavia): *see* Peć.

Pesellino, real name FRANCESCO DI STEFANO, also called GIUOCHI (b. 1422, Florence, Italy —d. July 29, 1457, Florence), an artist of the early Renaissance who excelled in the execution of small-scale paintings.

Pesellino was raised by his grandfather, the painter Giuliano il Pesello (1367–1446), and worked as his assistant until Giuliano's death. He then became associated with Fra Filippo Lippi. In 1453 he went into partnership with Piero di Lorenzo di Pratese and during this period began, for the church of the Trinità at Pistoia, the altarpiece now in the National Gallery, London. It was left unfinished at his death.

Pesellino is famous for his *cassone* pictures, intended for the decoration of marriage chests, in which he illustrated old legends or tales in tapestry-like designs. Several of these are in the Gardner Museum, Boston. A number of works by Pesellino may be seen in the National Gallery of Art, Washington, D.C.; the Metropolitan Museum of Art, New York City; and the Museum of Art of Toledo, Ohio.

peshaṭ (Hebrew: "spread out"), the designation for the simple, obvious, literal meaning of a biblical text in the hermeneutical (interpretive) principles and methods used by Jewish rabbis. In the interpretation of the Halakha (the proper way)—*i.e.*, the oral law that was essentially an interpretation of the written law —*peshaṭ* was preferred. Other interpretive principles, however, could be used simultaneously in any given text: *remez* (meaning "hint," in reference to typological or allegorical interpretations); *derash* (meaning "search," in reference to biblical study according to the *middot*, or rules); and *sod* (meaning "secret," or mystical interpretation). The first letters (PRDS) of these four words was first used in medieval Spain as an acronym forming the word PaRaDiSe to designate a theory of four basic interpretive principles: literal, philosophical, inferred, and mystical.

Depending on the needs or preferences of a particular historical period, one of the four principles generally gained a dominant position. During the early scribal and rabbinical period (*c.* 4th century BC–*c.* 2nd century AD), *peshaṭ* was preferred. Later, in the Talmudic period (*c.* 3rd–6th centuries AD), the inferred sense (*derash*) was viewed as more adequately communicating the intent of the divine author of the text—*i.e.*, making the text more relevant by seeking in it ethical and religious implications. Both *remez* and *sod*, which allowed for greater speculation, became favourite interpretive methods of the Kabbalists, Jewish mystics who flourished in Europe and Palestine during the Middle Ages and the early modern period.

Peshāwar, city, district, and division, North-west Frontier Province, Pakistan.

The city (capital of the district, division, and province) lies just west of the Bāra River, a tributary of the Kābul River, near the Khyber Pass. A great centre of transit-caravan trade with Afghanistan and Central Asia, it is connected by the Grand Trunk Road and rail with Lahore, Rāwalpindi, Hyderābād, and Karāchi and by air with Rāwalpindi, Chitrāl, and Kābul, Afg.

Industries include textile and sugar mills,

Mahābat Khān Mosque, Peshāwar, Pak.
Frederic Ohringer from the Nancy Palmer Agency—EB Inc.

fruit canning, and the manufacture of *chappals* (sandals), shoes, leatherwork, glazed pottery, wax and embroidery work, copper utensils, *lungīs* (loincloths), turbans, carpets, ornamental woodwork and furniture, ivory work, knives, and small arms. The ancient Qiṣṣah (Kissa) Khwānī Bāzār (Street of Storytellers) is the meeting place for foreign merchants who deal in dried fruits, woollen products, rugs, carpets, *pūstīns* (sheepskin coats), karakul (lambskin) caps, and Chitrālī *chūghahs* (cloaks).

Gardens and suburbs are outside the old city wall. Historic buildings include: Bālā Ḥissār, a Sikh fort; Gor Khatri, once a Buddhist monastery and later a Hindu temple; the pure white Mahābat Khān Mosque (1630), a monument of Mughal architecture; and Government House. *Qahwah khānahs*, or "coffee houses," are popular.

Constituted a municipality in 1867, the city has three hospitals, a museum (with a large collection of Gandhāran Buddhist relics), an agricultural college, and the University of Peshāwar (founded 1950), with five constituent and 18 affiliated colleges. The Shāhjī-kī Dhērī mounds, to the east, cover ruins of the largest Buddhist *stūpa* in the subcontinent (2nd century AD).

Once the capital of the ancient Kingdom of Gandhāra (*q.v.*), the city was known variously as Paraṣawara and Puruṣapura (Seat of Puruṣ). Also called Begrām, the present name Peshāwar (from *pēsh āwar*, or "frontier town") is ascribed to Akbar, the Mughal emperor of India (1556–1605).

Peshāwar District (area 1,646 sq mi) consists of highly irrigated plains, part of a huge basin drained and irrigated by the Kābul River, and a tract covered by low hills at Cherāt in the southeast. The chief crops are wheat, maize (corn), sugarcane, barley, cotton, and fruit (apples, pears, peaches, pomegranates, and quinces). The inhabitants are mostly Pathans.

Peshāwar Division (area 14,798 sq mi [38,322 sq km]) comprises Mardān, Hazāra, Kohāt (*qq.v.*), Peshāwar districts, with their special attached areas, and the Malakand, Mohmand, Khyber, and Kurram agencies. The Dargai power station has an installed capacity of 20,000 kW and the Warsak, a planned capacity of 240,000 kW. Iron, gypsum, glass sand, barytes, chromite, and marble deposits are abundant.

References to the Peshāwar area occur in early Sanskrit literature and the writings of the classical historians Strabo, Arrian, and the geographer Ptolemy. The Vale of Peshāwar was annexed by the Greco-Bactrian king Eucratides (2nd century BC), and Kaniṣka made Puruṣapura the capital of his Kushan (Kuṣāna) Empire (1st century AD). Buddhism was still dominant in the 5th century AD when Fa-hsien, the Chinese Buddhist monk and traveller, passed through the area. Captured by the Muslims in AD 988, it was by the 16th century in possession of the Afghans, who were nominally dependent on the Mughals. Sikh authority was firmly established by 1834, and the area was under British control from 1849 to 1947. Pop. (1972 prelim.) town, 273,000; district, 1,711,000; division, excluding centrally administered areas, 5,547,000.

·city history, population, and government **13**:255e
·district population density figures **13**:256d
·map, Pakistan **13**:893

Pesherim (Hebrew: "Interpretations"), exegetical works commenting on various biblical works, discovered among the Dead Sea Scrolls.

·content and significance **2**:938d

Peshitta (Syriac: "simple"), the version of the Bible used in the Syrian Christian churches. Written without elaborate critical apparatus (which is the reason for this version being named the Peshitta), this translation is a revision of the Old Syriac version in accordance with Greek textual principles.

Though the term Peshitta appears for the first time in the writings of Moshe bar Kepha, a 9th–early-10th-century bishop of Mosul (present al-Mawṣil, Iraq), evidence for its origins goes back to early 5th-century manuscripts, which are copies of older works. Because of Syrian reactions against Greek influences, the Peshitta was often opposed by the Syrian churches of the East—*i.e.*, the Nestorians, who refused to accept the decrees of the orthodox Council of Ephesus in AD 431 and of Chalcedon in AD 451 and instead stressed the independence of the divine and human persons in Christ that they hold are loosely joined by a moral union; and the Monophysites, who also rejected the decrees of Ephesus and Chalcedon and taught that in the person of Christ there is one divine nature, not a human and a divine nature—for several centuries. The canon of the New Testament of the Peshitta, following the ancient Old Syriac canon, excluded II Peter, II and III John, Jude, and the Revelation to John.

·canonical issues and singularities **2**:889b
·early New Testament Syrian translations **2**:944h

Peshkov, Aleksey Maksimovich: *see* Gorky, Maksim.

Peshtigo, city, Marinette County, northwestern Wisconsin, U.S., on the Peshtigo River. On Oct. 8, 1871, the date of the more famous but less deadly Chicago fire, winds whipped Wisconsin forest fires that had been burning for several days, destroying 1,200,000 ac (500,000 ha); and in a few hours Peshtigo was burned to the ground with 1,152 known deaths. A monument commemorating those who died is in Peshtigo Fire Cemetery. Now a manufacturing community, its chief products are lumber, paper and paper products, and boats. Dairying supplements the economy. The name is derived from the Algonkin Indians, its meaning uncertain. Inc. 1903. Pop. (1980) 2,807.
45°03′ N, 87°45′ W

peshwa, the office of chief minister among the Marāthā people of India. The peshwa, also known as the *mukhya pradhan*, headed the raja Śivajī's (reigned *c.* 1659–80) advisory council, known as the Ashta Pradhan (Council of Eight). After Śivajī's death the council broke up and the office lost its primacy, but it was revived when Śivajī's grandson Shāhū appointed Bālājī Visvanāth Bhat, a Chitpavan Brahmin, as peshwa in 1714. Bālājī's son Bājī Rāo I secured the hereditary succession to the peshwaship; his power was enhanced when Shāhū named him to carry out a decision to expand northward. From Shāhū's death, in 1749, the peshwa Bālājī Bājī Rāo was the virtual ruler of Mahārāshtra. He hoped to succeed the Mughals in Delhi, but after a disastrous defeat at Pānīpat (1761) he became the head of a confederacy of himself and four northern chiefs. Succession disputes from 1772 weakened the peshwa's authority. Defeat by Holkars—the Marāthā rulers of Indore—led Bājī Rāo II to seek British protection by the Treaty of Bassein (1802). Bājī Rāo was deposed after attacking the British in 1818; he died in 1853.

Pesne, Antoine (b. May 23, 1683, Paris—d. Aug. 5, 1757, Berlin), Rococo painter of historical subjects and portraits who was the most important artist in Prussia in the first half of the 18th century. His father, the painter Thomas Pesne, and his maternal great-uncle, Charles de Lafosse, were probably his first teachers. Pesne later studied in Paris, where he was influenced by the leading French portraitists, Hyacinthe Rigaud and Nicolas de Largillière. In Rome and Naples and particularly in Venice, where he studied with Andrea Celesti, Pesne developed a marked colouristic talent.

In 1707 Pesne's full-length portrait of the Prussian ambassador to Venice, von Knyphausen, attracted the attention of Frederick I of Prussia, who appointed him Court portraitist. When Frederick II came of age, Pesne was able to give full scope to his colouristic gifts in mythological and allegorical ceiling paintings and murals, decorating the interiors of the palaces of Rheinsberg, Charlottenburg, Berlin, Potsdam, and Sanssouci. He continued to paint portraits, some of which achieve by their brushwork and brilliant colouring an almost impressionistic effect reminiscent of Renoir. Of special interest are the various representations, in the style of Watteau, of Italian and French dancers and actresses whom Frederick II engaged for the Berlin Opera. These portraits are often cited for their perceptivity in characterization.

·Frederick II portrait illus. **7**:702

peso, monetary unit in a number of Spanish-speaking countries.

·value retention and international role **12**:72b

Pessac, town, southwestern suburb of Bordeaux, Gironde *département*, southwestern France. It was the site of a Gallo-Roman villa of the patrician Pesus. Located in the Graves vineyard district, it is noted for its red wines (Haut-Brion, Pape Clément). The 17th-century château of Haut-Brion, with its famous vineyard, is located there. It has some diversified manufacturing. Latest census 35,343.
44°48′ N, 0°38′ W

Château of Haut-Brion, Pessac, Fr.
Richard Chatagneau

·Le Corbusier house design and rejection **5**:169b

Pessanha, Camilo (b. Sept. 7, 1867, Coimbra, Port.—d. 1926, Macao), the representative in Portuguese poetry of Symbolism at its purest and most genuine and the chief precursor of so-called Modernist poetry. Concluding his studies of law at the university at Coimbra in 1891, he accepted a post two years later as a high school teacher in the Portuguese colony of Macao in China, where he remained, apart from two or three visits home, until his death.

From the beginning, Pessanha assumed Oriental customs, including the opium habit. He learned Cantonese and was one of the last Portuguese men of letters to speak the Chinese language, from which he translated some elegies, *Oito Elegias Chinesas* ("Eight Chinese Elegies"), accompanied by a preface that demonstrates his knowledge of Oriental literature. He also collected Chinese *objets d'art*, which he bequeathed to the Machado de Castro Museum in Coimbra. His writings on China, in particular the *Introdução a um Estudo sobre a Civilização Chinesa* and the *Elegias*, were collected in *China* (1943).

Although he began to write verse in Coimbra, Pessanha was virtually unknown until 1916, when his innovative Symbolist poetry was made known to a new generation in the pages of a progressive review, *Centauro*. It was collected in the volume *Clépsidra* (1920), which became a breviary for the modernist poets. Musical, subtle, penetrated by the mystery of Oriental poetry, Camilo Pessanha is one of the most lyrical of Portuguese poets.

pessimism, the opposite of optimism. Philosophical pessimism is the doctrine, held most notably by the 19th-century German philosopher Arthur Schopenhauer, that this is not the best of all possible worlds, that human life involves substantially more pain than pleasure, and that nature is indifferent to both moral good and evil and to the happiness or unhappiness of its creatures.

·Hardy's view of nature **13**:280h
·millennial dualist thought in Augustine **12**:202a
·Schopenhauer's philosophical theories **16**:358b

Pessoa, Epitácio (da Silva) (1875–1955), Brazilian statesman.

·presidency and economic problems **3**:147b

Pessoa, Fernando António Nogueira (b. June 13, 1888, Lisbon—d. Nov. 30, 1935, Lisbon), the greatest literary figure in Portuguese "modernism," the movement which gave Portuguese literature of the first half of the 20th century its European significance.

In 1934 Pessoa published his first book in Portuguese, *Mensagem*. In addition, all that was known of his work at his death were some booklets of poems in English—a language which Pessoa, who was virtually bilingual, wrote with ease—*Antinous* and *35 Sonnets* (1918) and *Inscriptions* (1920), collected in three volumes under the title *English Poems* (1921); some literary and political manifestoes —*Aviso por Causa da Moral* (1923) and *Interregno* (1928); his editorship of the review *Athena* (1924–25) and his frequent contributions to the avant-garde reviews, especially *Orpheu* (1915), the organ of the modernist movement in which Pessoa, with Mário de Sá-Carneiro and José de Almada Negreiros, was a leading spirit. The posthumous edition of his complete works consists of eight volumes; the poems are grouped under the various names or pseudonyms which the poet employed during his lifetime, each name purporting to represent one of the different personalities which he felt to exist within himself. The most important volumes in the collected edition are *Poesias de Fernando Pessoa* (1942), *Poesias de Álvaro de Campos* (1944), *Poemas de Alberto Caeiro* (1946) and *Odes de Ricardo Reis* (1946), in addition to the *Mensagem* of 1934. Examples of his prose writings as a critic and thinker of a paradoxical spirit can be found in the collection entitled *Páginas de Doutrina Estética* (1946). A good selection of his work, with an introduction, is in A. Casais Monteiro, *Fernando Pessoa* (1945).

·poetic style and impact **10**:1240b

Pest, *megye* (county), north central Hungary, extends southward from the Budapest area to near the Tisza River and has an area of 2,468 sq mi (6,393 sq km). The *megye* is very much oriented toward Budapest, the national capital and *megye* seat, which is a county in its own right.

After Budapest, the principal industrial communities are Érd, Vác, Cegléd, and Nagykőrös, and Dunakeszi.

Market garden vegetables, fruits, pigs, and poultry are the main farm products, and there is a high crop value yield per acre and per capita, especially sugar peas and tomatoes. Pop. (1970 prelim.) 869,864.

·area and population table **9**:25
·map, Hungary **9**:22

pest, animal or plant judged as a threat to man or to his interests.

·barnacle fouling problem **5**:312d
·bear damage to corn and fruit **3**:930c
·beetle larval and adult habits **4**:829f
·controls, ecology, and results **14**:139a
·crabs and shrimp as destructive **5**:543b
·insect status due to human context **9**:610b
·Lepidoptera characteristics and habits **10**:820b
·Lepidopteran examples, illus., **10**:Lepidoptera, Plates II and III
·mole direct and indirect damage **9**:622b
·passerine urban and agricultural damage **13**:1053a
·predator–prey oscillations **14**:835a
·raccoons damage of crops and waterfowl **3**:931d
·snails and slugs **7**:948e
·tick and mite habits and disease **1**:20a
·wolverine and other weasel relatives **3**:933b

Pestalozzi, Johann Heinrich **14**:138 (b. Jan. 12, 1746, Zürich—d. Feb. 17, 1827, Brugg, Switz.), educational reformer, was among the first to stress the need for better popular education.

Abstract of text biography. Active in social and political reform during his student days, Pestalozzi earned the reputation as champion of the underprivileged early in life. In 1774 he established an orphanage at which he attempted to teach neglected children to become self-reliant; the experiment failed, and Pestalozzi in a period of despair wrote *The Evening Hours of a Hermit* (1780), which contained the key to his philosophy. His four-volume novel, *Leonard and Gertrude* (1781–87), publicized his ideas on social, moral, and political reform and was widely read.

In 1805 Pestalozzi founded his boarding school at Yverdon near Neuchâtel; it flourished for 20 years and was attended by students from all over Europe and visited by many important figures. The institute served as an experimental basis for his principles of intellectual education, which were elaborated in *How Gertrude Teaches Her Children* (1801); it stressed the importance of accurate observation of actual objects as the basis for clear and accurate thinking. He established an industrial school for the poor, but it existed for only two years.

REFERENCES in other text articles:
·naturalistic theory of learning **13**:1100d
·object teaching method initiation **18**:5g
·pedagogy, philosophy, and influence **6**:359f

Pestalozzianism, pedagogical doctrines of Swiss educator Johann Heinrich Pestalozzi (1746–1827) stressing that instruction should proceed from the familiar to the new, incorporate the performance of concrete arts and the experience of actual emotional responses, and be paced to follow the gradual unfolding of the child's development. Although his ideas may sound commonplace today, they were revolutionary in his day, when rote learning and iron discipline ruled the classroom.

Pestalozzi's curriculum emphasized group rather than individual recitation and focussed on such participatory activities as drawing, writing, singing, physical exercise, model making, collecting, map making, and field trips. Among Pestalozzi's innovations were making allowances for individual pupil differences, ability groupings, and formal teacher training as part of a scientific approach to education.

pest control **14**:139, the regulation of population size of a plant or an animal species considered to conflict economically or medically with human welfare and interests. Pests may be controlled by biological, chemical, or cultural (environmental) means, or by a combination of methods known as integrated control.

The text article includes principles, methods, and evaluation of each type of pest control.

REFERENCES in other text articles:
·agricultural protection measures **1**:353e
·agricultural science fields of study **1**:323e
·agricultural uses and history **1**:344f
·airplane use in agriculture **7**:403h
·alkaloid protection of plants **1**:597d
·arsenic use in agriculture **13**:132a
·barnacle fouling problems **4**:641f
·beetles as useful predators **4**:829e
·biological and insecticide methods **9**:610d
·birds as threat to man **2**:1053g
·bugs preying on injurious organisms **8**:845h
·canid predator control tactics **3**:929c
·cats as mousers **3**:936g
·cereal crop protection measures **3**:1161b
·climatic influence on crops **4**:728h
·collembolan response to various measures **1**:1024g
·cotton insect damage **7**:273f
·dog internal and external parasites **5**:934a
·environmental effect of pesticides **5**:43f
·falconiform predation benefits to man **7**:148g
·food crop losses in developing nations **7**:500a
·forestry practices in tree protection **7**:532a
·fruit farming techniques **7**:763h; illus. 764
·garden plant disease prevention **7**:906g
·genet, mongoose, and others as mousers **3**:935c
·genetic resistance to insecticides **8**:814e
·gull reduction of crop damage **4**:33h
·honeybee diseases and colony damage **2**:794b
·hormone function in insects **14**:439e
·horticulture methods **8**:1110h
·house plant insect pests **8**:1122b
·hunting control of varmints and game **8**:500d
·infectious disease control methods **9**:547c
·insect population natural regulation **8**:1036f
·international monitoring needs **5**:59f
·lady beetle use for scale suppression **2**:1046f
·lagomorph control by myxomatosis **10**:588f
·lead insecticide production **10**:730e
·marine fouling control **16**:679a
·natural predators versus pesticides **2**:1046f
·orchid symbiosis with protective ants **13**:655a
·orthopteran pests and hormone study **13**:743d
·parasitic hymenopteran importance **9**:130a
·parasitic hymenopteran uses **9**:126h
·pheromones and insect control **4**:182f
·pigeon crop damage and remedial action **4**:932f
·plant disease control methods **5**:883g
·pollution analysis instrumentation **9**:642b
·population number regulation **14**:825e
·prairie dog burrow damage **15**:971c
·radiation control of screwworm fly **15**:455b
·rhythmic variation and susceptibility **14**:69h
·rodent control by weasel relatives **3**:933b
·Siphonaptera infestation prevention methods **16**:809b
·skunk population decline **3**:932b
·slug control by ashes **7**:953b
·sugarcane biological and chemical protections **17**:771c
·synthetic mimicking of insect juvenile hormone in insecticides **8**:1086a
·technology's impact on environment **18**:22d
·termite prevention and extermination **9**:1050c
·tobacco resistance and fumigation **18**:465a
·vegetable farming technology **19**:50g
·waterfowl crop damage **1**:939g
·white-pine rust eradication **16**:295a

RELATED ENTRIES in the *Ready Reference and Index:*
biological control; chemosterilant; fumigant; fungicide; insecticide; miticide; pesticide; rodenticide

Peste, La (1947), translated THE PLAGUE (1948), novel by Camus.

·symbolism and rejection of nihilism **3**:712f

Pestel, Pavel Ivanovich (1793–1826), a leader of the first Russian revolutionaries, the Decembrists, was head of the secret Southern Society. He planned to overthrow the Russian autocracy and found a centralized republic, but was arrested just before the Decembrist uprising (December 1825) and executed a few months later.

·Pan-Slavic nationalist doctrine **16**:60e

Pesthouse of Jaffa, The, translation of BONAPARTE VISITANT LES PESTIFÉRÉS DE JAFFA (1804), painting by A.J. Gros.

·Romantic rendering of history **19**:456d

Pesti, Gábor, 16th-century Hungarian humanist.
·literature of the Renaissance **10**:1145b

pesticide, any toxic substance used to kill animals or plants that cause economic damage to crop or ornamental plants or are hazardous to the health of domestic animals or man. All pesticides interfere with normal metabolic processes in the pest organism and often are classified according to the type of organism they are principally intended to control.
·agricultural uses and history **1**:344f
·arsenic use in agriculture **13**:132a
·biotic interaction and natural balance **2**:1046g
·cancer causation **3**:764c
·clay mineral industrial uses **4**:706c
·ecological effects of use **6**:199f
·environmental effect and conservation **5**:43e
·horticultural pest control **8**:1111b
·industrial environment risks **9**:529f
·international monitoring needs **5**:59f
·plant disease-causing agents **5**:886d
·pollution analysis instrumentation **9**:642b
·pollution causation factor **1**:361b
·soil organism population and pest control **16**:1014c
·tin compound manufacture and use **18**:432b
·toxicity rating and effects **14**:618f; table 619
·water and land pollution **14**:754c
RELATED ENTRIES in the *Ready Reference and Index:*
fumigant; fungicide; herbicide; insecticide; miticide; rodenticide

Pesti Hirlap, liberal Hungarian newspaper edited by Lajos Kossuth in 1841; it attained the second largest circulation in the country by 1937.

pestle, an implement, usually club-shaped, for pounding or grinding substances, especially in a mortar.
·percussive tool theory and design **8**:613f

Pestsäule, Baroque statue erected in Vienna in thanksgiving for the end of the plague that struck the city in 1679.
·style and purpose **19**:116c

pet 14:149, any animal kept by man as a source of companionship and pleasure. The term includes a wide range of vertebrates and a few invertebrates.

The text article reviews briefly the history and rationale of pet keeping and surveys the types of pets most frequently seen. Sources of supply, legal restrictions, and disease problems are mentioned briefly.
REFERENCES in other text articles:
·birds for ornament and recreation **2**:1053f
·cat domestication and care **3**:997a
·cats as mousers **3**:936g
·crocodilian adaptability to captivity **5**:287h
·dog domestication, traits, puppy raising, and recognized breeds **5**:929d
·economic importance of dogs **3**:929b
·genet, mongoose, and others as mousers **3**:935c
·hobby methods and rationale **8**:979b
·passerines importance as cage birds **13**:1052f
·raccoon and relatives' mischievousness **3**:930h
·snake importations and collection **16**:560a

Peta, also known as SUKARELA TENTARA PEMBELA TANAH AIR, Indonesian volunteer defense force created in 1943.
·Indonesian training under Japanese **9**:488h

Petacci, Claretta (d. 1945), Mussolini's mistress.
·death with Mussolini **12**:752e

Petah Tiqwa, city, west central Israel, on the Plain of Sharon, east-northeast of Tel Aviv-Yafo and part of that city's metropolitan area. Situated in the valley of Achor near the Yarqon River, the city takes its name (meaning "door of hope") from the biblical allusion in Hos. 2:15: ". . . and make the valley of Achor a door of hope." Petah Tiqwa was the first village (founded 1878) in the modern Jewish settlement of Palestine and is known as 'Em ha-Moshavot (Hebrew: "mother of villages"). Because the village was founded in a swampy, malarial area, the settlers first planted eucalyptus trees for drainage. They then turned to truck and citrus farming; the first orange groves in modern Palestine were there. With the growth of Tel Aviv, much of the agricultural land was converted to suburban residential and industrial use. Petah Tiqwa was incorporated as a city in 1937. Manufacturing includes canned fruits, oils and soaps, textiles, and agricultural machinery.

About 5 mi (8 km) east-northeast of Petah Tiqwa is the tell (mound) of Aphek, an ancient Canaanite city, mentioned in Egyptian texts as early as the 18th century BC. In the Bible, Aphek was the site of the rout of the Israelites by the Philistines (I Sam. 4). Later Herod the Great, king of Judaea, built the city of Antipatris on the site (*c.* 20 BC). Pop. (1970 est.) 83,200.
32°05′ N, 34°53′ E

Pétain, Philippe 14:152 (b. April 24, 1856, Cauchy-à-la-Tour, Fr.—d. July 23, 1951, Île d'Yeu), general, was a French national hero for his victory at the Battle of Verdun in World War I and was chief of state of the French government at Vichy in World War II.

Abstract of text biography. Pétain was educated at Saint-Cyr and served as a second lieutenant in an Alpine regiment. As a professor at the War College he advocated tactical theories based upon defense rather than attack. Because his theories were unpopular with the French high command, his advancement was slow. He was finally made a general when he was 58 years old. After his successful defense of Verdun in 1916, he became a national hero. In 1918 he was made a marshal of France and was subsequently appointed to the highest military offices. Named premier in the hour of France's defeat in 1940, the aged Pétain negotiated an armistice with Nazi Germany and until 1944 headed the Fascist-oriented Vichy government of unoccupied France. Discredited as a collaborationist, he was imprisoned after the war.
REFERENCES in other text articles:
·de Gaulle's association and dispute **7**:962g
·North African invasion resistance **19**:984b
·Vichy government policy **7**:674d
·World War I offensives **19**:954b
·World War I tactics at Champagne **19**:580h

Petalichthyida, order of extinct jawed fishes of the class Placodermi represented by the Devonian genera *Lunaspis* and *Macropetalichthys.* The petalichthyids, like the related arthrodires, were armoured fishes, but their bony head and body shields were not connected by ball-and-socket joints. *Macropetalichthys* had extensive head shields, thoracic plates, and a pair of shoulder spines. In *Lunaspis* the portion of the body behind the armour was covered by large scales.

Possible relatives of the petalichthyids, such as the genera *Stensiöella* and *Pseudopetalichthys,* may have represented a transitional stage between the placoderms and sharks.
·classification and general features **14**:489h
·traits, behaviour, and classification **14**:488f

Petaling Jaya, town, Selangor state, Malaysia. Pop. (1970 prelim.) 106,141.
3°07′ N, 101°39′ E
·Malaysian rarity of urban planning **11**:370b

Petalión, Gulf of, Greek KÓLPOS PETALIÓN, broad inlet of the Aegean Sea between Attikí and southern Euboea (Évvoia) *nomoi* (departments), Greece, some 20 mi (32 km) broad at its entrance below Nisís (island) Megálo. It contains two groups of islands administered by Euboea *nomós:* the Petali (Petalioí), which includes Megálo, Xeró, and four islets; and the Stíra islands, which lie opposite the Marathon peninsula. North of the marble quarries of Mt. Pentelicus on the Attica side, the agricultural plain of Marathon opens to the northwest.
37°59′ N, 24°02′ E

Petaluma, city, Sonoma County, western California, U.S., at the head of navigation on the Petaluma River. Founded in 1852, it derived its name from the Rancho Petaluma (Miwok Indian *pe'ta,* "flat"; *lu'ma,* "back"). The poultry and egg industry, dairying, and wine making are foremost commercial activities, supplemented by light manufactures (notably processing machinery and fishing tackle). Nearby is the Petaluma Adobe State Historical Monument (1836; restored home of Mexican general Guadalupe Vallejo). Inc. town, 1858; city, 1884. Pop. (1980) 33,834.
38°14′ N, 122°39′ W

Petare, city, northwestern Miranda state, in the central highlands of northern Venezuela. Formerly a commercial centre in a fertile agricultural area producing coffee, cacao, and sugarcane, the city has become a residential suburb of the national capital and is now a part of the Caracas metropolitan area. Cardboard is manufactured in the city. Expressways lead from Petare to downtown Caracas, approximately 10 mi (16 km) to the west-northwest. Pop. (1971) 225,419.
10°29′ N, 66°49′ W
·map, Venezuela **19**:60

petasos, also spelled PETASUS, a wide-brimmed hat with a conical crown worn in ancient Greece. The petasos worn by men had a rather low crown, while that worn by women

Man wearing a petasos, terracotta sculpture from Tanagra, Greece, early 5th century BC; in the British Museum
By courtesy of the trustees of the British Museum

had a tall one. A hat used for travelling, the petasos was made of felt or straw and had a chin strap, so that when not in use it could be hung down the back. The winged hat of the god Hermes was also called a petasos.

Petauridae, family of terrestrial and arboreal marsupials, order Diprotodonta (superorder Marsupialia).
·classification and general features **11**:545d; illus. 539

Petaurus (marsupial genus): *see* glider.

Petavatthu (Pāli: "Tales of Ghosts"), one of the 15 divisions of the *Khuddhaka Nikāya,* itself the fifth of five sections of the *Sutta Piṭaka,* a Buddhist sacred scripture.
·Buddhist sacred text description **3**:434d

petechia, in medicine, a tiny, circular, dark red spot in the skin caused by the rupture of a blood vessel.
·causative diseases and disorders **3**:900b

petechial fever, an acute or subacute toxemic state in horses commonly secondary to an infectious disease and characterized by dropsical swelling of the legs, abdomen, and head, and by small purple hemorrhages in these swellings and in the mucous membranes.
·infectious diseases of animals, table 2 **5**:867

petechiasis, in medicine, the presence of petechiae over large areas of the body.
·associated diseases and disorders **3**:900b

Petén Itzá, Lake, Spanish LAGO PETÉN ITZÁ, central El Petén department, northern Guatemala. A depression in the low limestone plateau, it measures about 15 mi (24 km) from east to west, 2 mi (3 km) from north to south, and is 165 ft (50 m) deep; its area is 40 sq mi (100 sq km). Once the stronghold of the Maya Itzá Indians, who were not conquered by the Spanish until 1697, the shores of the lake are now dotted with modern towns: Flores, the departmental capital, which lies on an island in the southwestern portion of the lake; San Benito, in the southwest; and San Andrés, on the northwestern shore. Much of the surrounding land is covered by dense tropical rain forest; but there is some cultivation of cacao, sugarcane, grains, and tropical fruits around Flores.
16°58′ N, 89°50′ W
·map, Guatemala **8**:454

Peter (ruled 927–969), king of Bulgaria.
·Old Church Slavonic revision **16**:869b

Peter, king of Hungary, reigned 1038–41 and 1044–46.
·Árpád dynastic conflicts **9**:31a

Peter I the Great, of Russia 14:157 (b. June 9 [May 30, old style], 1672, Moscow—d. Feb. 8 [Jan. 28, O.S.], 1725, St. Petersburg, now Leningrad), tsar and emperor of Russia and one of his country's greatest statesmen and reformers.

Abstract of text biography. Proclaimed tsar in 1682, Peter assumed control of the government in 1689 and embarked on his policy to secure access for Russia to the Baltic and Black Seas, engaging in a war with Ottoman Turkey (1695–96) and in the Great Northern War with Sweden (1700–21). Peter's most far-reaching accomplishment was to draw Russia further into the European sphere. After touring western Europe himself (1697–98), he transferred the capital to St. Petersburg on the Baltic coast, introduced Western technology, and completely overhauled the Russian government and military system, further increasing the power of the monarchy at the expense of the nobles and the Orthodox Church.

REFERENCES in other text articles:
·Arctic explorations and mapping program **1**:1119a
·Byzantine formal theological schools **6**:145g
·Church reforms on Protestant model **6**:157f
·comparison to Catherine the Great **3**:1005c
·diplomatic and military ambitions **6**:1095c; map 1097
·Great Northern War tactics **8**:96b
·Leningrad's founding and first building **10**:799a
·Livonian and Estonian acquisition **2**:672e
·Livonian annexation and Polish alliance **14**:645g
·Moscow's development under rule **12**:477h
·reign and historical assessment **16**:49g; maps
·state utilitarian school development **6**:355d
·Swedish–Russian relations **4**:58c
·Voltaire's favourable evaluation **19**:513b
·Westernization and school development **6**:331h

Peter I (1068–1104), king of Aragon from June 1094. From the Moors of Saragossa he conquered Huesca in 1096 and Barbastro in 1100.

Peter I, known to Spanish tradition as PETER THE CRUEL (1334–69), king of Castile from 1350. His right to the throne was challenged by his half brother, Henry of Trastámara, who was backed by France and Aragon. Deposed by the French in 1366, Peter was restored with English help the following year, but was finally defeated and slain by Henry at the Battle of Monteil (March 23, 1369). Castilian historians favourable to the house of Trastámara depicted Peter as a harsh and unprincipled tyrant.
·Ibn Khaldūn's early political career **9**:148c
·Sevillian architectural enrichment **16**:581d

Peter I (1329–69), French sovereign of the Latin kingdom of Cyprus from 1359, is sometimes credited with having led the last serious attempt to regain Palestine for Christendom from the Muslims, although his crusading operations did not in fact take place in the Holy Land. In 1361 he captured two Ottoman Turkish strongholds in Asia Minor, and the next year he went to Western Europe to gather military and naval forces for a new crusade. The capture of Alexandria on Oct. 10, 1365, and the subsequent looting of that Egyptian city, were the chief accomplishments of his expedition. While trying to assemble another army, he was murdered on Cyprus by one of his own knights.
·Alexandria conquest expedition **5**:309g
·Cypriot appeal to Christian Europe **5**:407g

Peter I (b. July 11 [June 29, old style], 1844, Belgrade—d. Aug. 16, 1921, Topčider, near Belgrade), king of Serbia from 1903, the first strictly constitutional monarch of his country. In 1918 he became the first king of the Serbs, Croats, and Slovenes (Yugoslavia).

Born the third son of the reigning Prince Alexander Karađorđević (1842–58), Peter became heir to the throne on the death of his brother Svetozar (1847). After his father was forced to abdicate (1858), Peter lived in exile for the next 45 years. Educated in France, mainly at military schools, such as the prestigious Saint-Cyr, he served as a lieutenant in the French Army during the Franco-Prussian War and was decorated with the Cross of the Legion of Honour for heroism. When the Serbs of Hercegovina revolted against the Turks in 1877, Peter organized a party of volunteers to assist them. Afterward he became an honorary senator in Montenegro (1883) and improved his dynastic ties by marrying Zorka, the first child of Prince Nicholas of Montenegro (1883).

In 1903 the Serbian king Alexander Obrenović V (1889–1903) was assassinated, ending the Obrenović dynasty, and Peter was elected king of Serbia. His reputation as a liberal (he translated John Stuart Mill's essay *On Liberty* into Serbian in 1868) and his strong advocacy of constitutional government helped improve the political situation at home and win recognition abroad. Incapacitated by age and poor health, Peter named his heir, Prince Alexander, to be regent on June 24, 1914. During World War I, after the defeat of Serbia by the Central Powers (Germany and Austria) in 1915, he took part in the retreat to the Adriatic, being carried in a litter. At the end of World War I he returned to Belgrade, where he was proclaimed king of the Serbs, Croats, and Slovenes (Dec. 1, 1918).

Peter I, Montenegrin PETROVIĆ NJEGOŠ (b. *c.* 1747, Njegoš, Montenegro, now in Yugoslavia—d. Oct. 30 [Oct. 18, old style], 1830, Cetinje, Montenegro), the Great Vladika, or prince-bishop, of Montenegro from 1782 to 1830, who won full independence of his country from the Turks.

As successor to his saintly but inept uncle Sava, Peter became the reigning prince in theocratic Montenegro in 1782 and was consecrated bishop two years later. To cement relations with Russia, always a potential ally against the Turks, he visited Russia that same year. On his return he found his land was being overrun by the forces of the Pasha of Scutari. Uniting his warlike clans, he drove the invaders out. War with the Turks flared up periodically, sometimes with, and sometimes without, a powerful ally, such as Russia or Austria. In 1796 a second invasion by the Pasha of Scutari led to a series of brilliant victories over the Turks, with Peter leading his men. The Pasha was captured and beheaded, and by a treaty in 1799 Sultan Selim III was forced to recognize the independence of Montenegro. New territories were added, including Brda, recently settled by Serbs from Herzegovina, which was to double the size of Montenegro during Peter's reign.

During the Napoleonic Wars Montenegro became involved in the struggle between the Great Powers. When by the Treaty of Pressburg with Austria (1804) the French took over Dalmatia, Peter allied himself first with the Russians until 1807 and then with the British in 1813 to maintain Montenegrin occupation of the town and fjord of Kotor. After the French left in 1813, the territory was annexed by Peter (October 1813), and Kotor became his capital for a year. At the Congress of Vienna (1815), however, the land was returned to Austria. In Peter's last years as ruler he was involved in more wars with the Turks (1819 and 1821) and in settling blood feuds among his montaineers; his efforts further enhanced his reputation as a just prince.

Peter I of Dreux, called MAUCLERC (b. 1190—d. 1250, at sea en route to France), duke or count of Brittany from 1213 to 1237, French prince of the Capetian dynasty, who by skillful diplomacy maintained himself in a position of national and international importance.

Peter was married, by his cousin King Philip II Augustus of France, to Alix, heiress to Brittany. On the death of Alix's half-brother, Philip received Peter's homage for Brittany and transferred the province to him, whereupon Peter assumed the title of duke, though he was considered merely a count by the French. He energetically asserted his authority over the Breton lands, annexing new fiefs to the ducal domain. With the help of the Frenchman Raoul, bishop of Quimper, he introduced into Brittany the usages of the Capetian chancery; he sought the support of the towns, granting a number of charters of privileges.

When Alix died (1221), Peter retained control of Brittany as guardian for his son John I. As John would inherit control of his mother's lands upon reaching his majority, Peter adopted a policy of risky and opportunistic alliances in order to secure lands and concessions in his own right: he extorted concessions from the French regency in 1227 by means of rebellion; and he transferred his allegiance from the French to the English king in 1229 until 1234. When John came of age (1237), Peter had to renounce Brittany and henceforth was merely count of Braine.

Peter was called Mauclerc (Bad Clerk) either because his early training for the church was abortive or because he quarreled continually with the episcopate. As a result he spent much of his life under excommunication and was persuaded to go on a crusade (1239–40), an effective penance for his conduct. In 1248 he went to Egypt on another crusade. Wounded in battle, he died on his way home.
·revolt against the monarchy **11**:118h

Peter I Range, Russian PETRA PERVOGO KHREBET, branch spur of the Pamir-Alai mountain system, in the Tadzhik Soviet Socialist Republic.
39°00′ N, 71°00′ E
·glacier inclusion in Pamir system **13**:938f

Peter II (b. Oct. 23 [Oct. 12, old style], 1715—d. Jan. 29 [Jan. 18, O.S.], 1730, Moscow), emperor of Russia from 1727 to 1730. Grandson of Peter I the Great (ruled 1682–1725), Peter II was named heir to the Russian throne by Catherine I (ruled 1725–27) and was crowned at the age of 11 (May 18 [May 7, O.S.], 1727).

Because Catherine had named the Supreme Privy Council to act as regent for the youth, Aleksandr D. Menshikov, who had been a close adviser to both Peter I and Catherine I and had become the most prominent member of the council, dominated the first months of Peter's reign. Menshikov installed the young emperor in his own household and arranged for his daughter and Peter to become betrothed. Peter, however, did not welcome the domineering kindness of his guardian and turned to the Dolgorukys, an old aristocratic family. In September 1727 the Dolgoruky family arrested Menshikov, exiled him to Siberia, and replaced him as the dominant political figures in Russia. They subsequently moved Peter's capital from St. Petersburg (modern Leningrad) to Moscow (1728) and prepared for Peter's marriage to Princess Yekaterina Alekseyevna Dolgorukaya (1729). On the day set for the wedding, however, Peter II died of smallpox.

·Dolgoruky's political domination **16**:52f

Peter II (1174–1213), king of Aragon from April 1196. In 1204 Peter had himself crowned by Pope Innocent III in Rome and declared his kingdom a feudatory of the Holy See. He took part in the important victory over the Moors at Las Navas de Tolosa in 1212.

·Crusade alliance **10**:20h
·papal crusade against the Albigenses **17**:409d

Peter II, originally PETAR PETROVIĆ (b. Sept. 6, 1923, Belgrade—d. Nov. 3, 1970, Los Angeles), the last king of Yugoslavia. The son of Alexander I, who was assassinated during a visit to France on Oct. 10, 1934, Peter became titular king at 11, but the actual rule was in the hands of a regent, his uncle Prince Paul. After Paul was deposed by a coup of officers led by Gen. Dušan Simović on March 27, 1941, Peter ruled for a few weeks until Axis troops invaded. He then fled into exile in London, where he led an émigré government. In 1944 he married Princess Alexandra of Greece, and, after the Yugoslav monarchy was abolished by Tito in 1945, he settled in the U.S. He wrote *A King's Heritage* (1955) and worked in public relations in New York.

Peter II (b. Nov. 13 [Nov. 1, old style], 1813, Njegoš, Montenegro—d. Oct. 31 [Oct. 19, O.S.], 1851, Cetinje, Montenegro, now in Yugoslavia), the *vladika* or prince-bishop of Montenegro from 1830 to 1851, renowned as an enlightened ruler, an intrepid warrior, and especially as a poet. His principal works were "The Ray of the Microcosm," "The False Tsar Stephen the Small," and "The Mountain Garland."

On succeeding his uncle Peter I, he took the title of Peter II rather than his own Christian name of Rado. As part of the tradition of theocratic Montenegro, Peter was consecrated bishop in 1833 (the practice was discontinued by his successor). While maintaining his lands in wars against the hereditary enemy, the Turks, Peter II conducted reforms that were financed in part by an annual subsidy from Tsar Nicholas I of Russia. Schools were founded, and the first printing press was installed at Cetinje, the capital. Peter strengthened his government by eliminating the office of civil governor, which had been held on a hereditary basis by the Radonić family, and by transferring the power of local chieftains to a senate of 12 leading chiefs, meeting in Cetinje under his supervision.

Peter III, originally KARL PETER ULRICH, DUKE OF HOLSTEIN-GOTTORP (b. Feb. 21, 1728, Kiel, Holstein-Gottorp, now in West Germany—d. July 17 [July 6, old style], 1762, Ropsha, near St. Petersburg, modern Leningrad), emperor of Russia from Jan. 5, 1762 (Dec. 25, 1761, O.S.) to July 9 (June 28, O.S.), 1762. Son of Anna, one of Peter I the Great's daughters, and Charles Frederick, duke of Holstein-Gottorp, the young duke was brought to Russia by his aunt Elizabeth shortly after she became empress of Russia (Dec. 5–6, 1741). Renamed Peter Fyodorovich, he was received into the Russian Orthodox Church (Nov. 18 [Nov. 7, O.S.], 1742) and proclaimed the heir to the Russian throne. On Aug. 21, 1745, he married Sophie Frederike Auguste, a princess from Anhalt-Zerbst, in Germany, who took the name Catherine Alekseyevna.

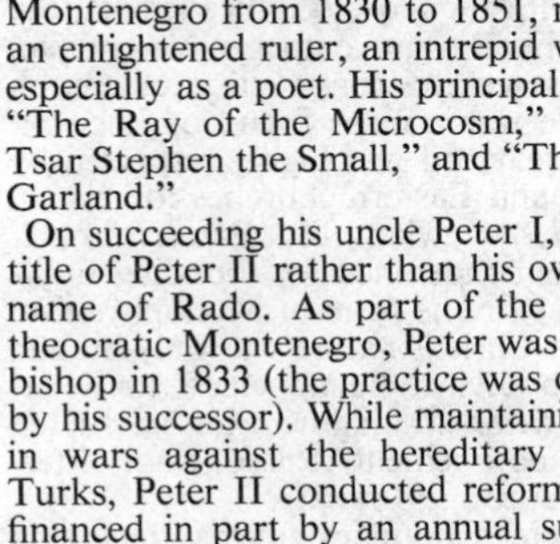

Peter III, emperor of Russia, detail of an engraving by Johann Stenglin (1715–70) after a painting by G.C. Grooth; in the collection of Mrs. Merriweather Post, Hillwood, Va.

By courtesy of Mrs. Merriweather Post, Hillwood, Va.

Peter, who was mentally feeble and extremely pro-Prussian, not only alienated the affections of his wife soon after their marriage but also failed to gain the favour of politically powerful court cliques. His popularity diminished further after he succeeded Elizabeth and, reversing her foreign policy, made peace with Prussia and withdrew from the Seven Years' War (1756–63), formed an alliance with Prussia, and prepared to engage Russia in a war against Denmark to help his native Holstein gain control of Schleswig. Even when he relieved the gentry of their obligation to serve the state (March 1, 1762), he did not gain supporters. When he offended the Russian Orthodox Church by trying to force it to adopt Lutheran religious practices and also alienated the imperial guards by making their service requirements more severe and threatening to disband them, Catherine, who suspected that he was planning to divorce her, conspired with her lover Grigory Grigoryevich Orlov and other members of the guard to overthrow him.

On July 9 (June 28, O.S.), 1762, Catherine, with the approval of the guard, the senate, and the church, became Catherine II, empress of Russia. Peter, who was at his residence at Oranienbaum, near St. Petersburg, formally abdicated on July 10 (June 29, O.S.); he was arrested and taken to the village of Ropsha, where, while in the custody of one of the conspirators, Aleksey Grigoryevich Orlov, he was killed in a brawl.

·Danish fear of his policies **16**:320e
·diplomatic ambitions **6**:1097d
·Frederick the Great admiration and aid **7**:705a
·incompetence and dethronement **16**:53h
·life, reign, and assassination **3**:1005h
·Russian policy in Seven Years' War **16**:578a
·Seven Year's War diplomacy **2**:459e
·Seven Years' War peace **8**:98b

Peter III the Great (1239–1285), king of Aragon from July 1276 and of Sicily from 1282. Known for his great stature and physical strength, Peter, by making good his claim to the throne of Sicily, inaugurated four centuries of Spanish rule over the island. At home he repelled a French invasion (1285), but was forced by the nobles and towns to diminish the rights of the crown.

·Palermo's growth under his rule **13**:930g
·Sicilian choice as ruler and its result **7**:619c
·Sicily's conquest and papal action **17**:412e
·territorial acquisitions **10**:21d

Peter IV the Ceremonius (1319–87), king of Aragon from January 1336. In 1343 and 1344 he re-incorporated the Balearic Islands and Roussillon into his realm and in 1348 crushed the Aragonese nobles who challenged his authority. From 1356 to 1366 he was involved, as an ally of France, in a war with Castile in support of the claims of Henry of Trastamara to the Castilian throne; he thereafter maintained neutrality between France and England, the two contending powers in the Hundred Years' War.

·Majorca's reconquest and noble threat **17**:412g

Peter, Acts of, an apocryphal (noncanonical) work of the New Testament, composed in Greek *c.* AD 150–200.

·Apocrypha literary form and dramatic content **2**:973g

Peter, Apocalypse of, also called REVELATION TO PETER, an apocryphal (noncanonical and unauthentic) Christian writing dating from the first half of the 2nd century AD. The unknown author, who claimed to be Peter the Apostle, relied on the canonical Gospels and on Revelation to John to construct a conversation between himself and Jesus regarding events at the end of the world. Unlike Revelation to John, however, the *Apocalypse of Peter* dwells on eternal rewards and punishments. The graphic account of the torments to be borne by sinful men was apparently borrowed from Orphic and Pythagorean religious texts, thereby introducing pagan ideas of heaven and hell into Christian literature. The most complete extant version (in Ethiopic) was discovered in 1910.

Peter, Gospel of, an apocryphal (noncanonical and unauthentic) Christian writing of the mid-2nd century AD, the extant portion of which covers the condemnation, crucifixion, and Resurrection of Jesus. Because the work reflects the view that Christ's body had only the appearance of reality, Serapion, bishop of Antioch *c.* AD 190, believed it was written by a member of the heretical Docetist sect. Modern scholars are more inclined to attribute it to a Syrian Christian Gnostic because the Gospel does not view the crucifixion as an act of atonement. It contains, however, no extensive mythological or cosmological speculations characteristic of most Gnostic sects. Possibly to convince non-Christians of the truth of the Resurrection, the *Gospel of Peter* goes beyond the four canonical Gospels in claiming that Roman soldiers and Jewish officials witnessed the event.

·content and pseudonymous authorship **2**:969f

Peter (PETERS), **Hugh** (b. 1598, Fowey, Cornwall—d. Oct. 16, 1660, London), English Independent minister, army preacher, and propagandist during the Civil War and Commonwealth. Educated at Trinity College, Cambridge, he was ordained priest in the Anglican Church in 1623. He went to London in 1626 and was appointed preacher at St. Sepulchre's, but his unorthodox views led to the suspension of his preaching licence in 1627. He was in Holland from 1629 to 1635 when he returned to England and sailed to Massachusetts where he succeeded Roger Williams as preacher at Salem in December 1636. He played a leading part in the colony's affairs and helped in the founding of Connecticut. Peter returned to England in 1641 as an agent for Massachusetts but after the Irish Insurrection (October 1641) he went to Ireland as chaplain to a company of adventurers under Alexander, Lord Forbes, which fought against the Irish rebels (June–September 1642). As chaplain to the New Model Army, Peter preached during the campaigns of 1645 and 1646.

He accompanied Oliver Cromwell to Ireland in 1649 and was present at the fall of Wexford. Appointed chaplain to the council of state (1650), he preached at Whitehall continually during the Commonwealth and Protectorate, but his protests against the Dutch War (1652–54) brought him a reprimand from Parliament. During the later years of the Protectorate, his part in civil and military affairs was less prominent. At the Restoration in 1660 he was specially exempted from the Act of Indemnity and at his trial in October 1660 was found guilty of abetting the execution of Charles I. He was executed at Charing Cross.

Peter's works included sermons, accounts of battles and sieges, and tracts on legal, economic, and social reforms.

Peter, letters of, two New Testament writings attributed to the foremost of Jesus' twelve Apostles but probably written during the 2nd century.

The first letter, addressed to persecuted Christians living in five regions of Asia Minor, exhorts the readers to emulate the suffering Christ in their distress, remembering that after his Passion and death Jesus rose from the dead and is now in glory. The Christians are urged to repay evil with goodness and to love one another and are cautioned to safeguard their reputation as good citizens of high morality, thereby removing all doubt about the injustice of their sufferings. The question of authorship has not been solved to the satisfaction of scholars. Whereas the fluent Greek style and certain historical references seem to argue against Petrine authorship, the description of a primitive church organization, for example, seems to indicate an early composition, with the actual writing perhaps done by a secretary or spokesman for Peter.

The second letter is principally concerned with the Second Coming of Jesus. The author attributes the apparent delay to God's patience in allowing time for universal redemption and notes that in the sight of God 1,000 years are like one day. The writer also warns against false teachers, whose conduct is as immoral as their words are deceptive. They, and those who follow them, says the writer, will be destroyed in a great conflagration that will precede "new heavens and a new earth in which righteousness dwells" (3:13). Though the author explicitly identifies himself as Peter, numerous textual difficulties as early as the 3rd century created doubts about the actual authorship, which have been reinforced by subsequent scholarship. *Major ref.* **2**:969f
·Peter's life **14**:153e *passim* to 157a

Peterborough, town, southeast South Australia, at the south end of the Flinders Range, north of Adelaide. Established in 1880, it was originally known as Petersburg, which was changed to the present, less Germanic form during World War I. It became a municipality in 1887. The town, a major rail junction, is served by four rail systems that carry heavy traffic in both passengers and freight (principally grain and livestock). Ore trains bound for Port Pirie from Broken Hill also pass through Peterborough, which has large railway repair shops. Pop. (1976 prelim.) 2,760.
32°58′ S, 138°50′ E
·map, Australia **2**:401

Peterborough, city, seat of Peterborough County, southeastern Ontario, Canada, on the Otonabee River. In 1821, Adam Scott founded a sawmill and grist mill at the site, which became known as Scott's Plains. In 1825 nearly 2,000 Irish immigrants settled there, and the town and county were renamed for the group's director, Peter Robinson. Peterborough, 70 mi (110 km) northeast of Toronto, became a commercial and manufacturing centre of the surrounding area and a tourist centre for the Kawartha Lakes region.

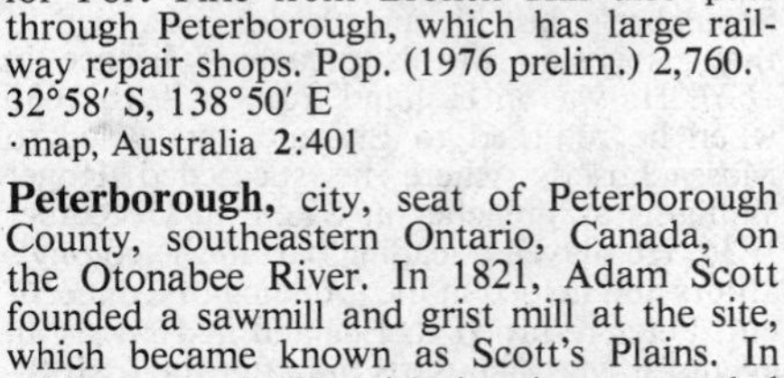

Lift lock on the canalized Otonabee River at Peterborough, Ont.
Shostal

Canalization of the Otonabee as part of the Trent Canal system provided direct communication with Lake Ontario and Georgian Bay by means of the world's highest (65 ft. [20 m]) hydraulic lift lock (1904). Manufactures include electrical appliances and machinery, canoes, boats and marine equipment, hardware, lumber, watches, and cereals and other food products. The city is the site of Trent University (founded 1963), Sir Sandford Fleming College of Applied Arts and Technology, and Peterborough's Teachers' College. Inc. 1905. Pop. (1976) 59,683.
44°18′ N, 78°19′ W
·map, Canada **3**:717

Peterborough, former (until 1973) municipal borough in Cambridgeshire, England. Before 1974 it was in the county of Huntingdon and Peterborough; after 1974, it became a district of Cambridgeshire. The Soke of Peterborough (from Market Deeping, in Lincolnshire, in the north to Peterborough itself in the south), an ancient administrative entity, was a separate county from 1884 to 1965. Within the soke, north of the River Nen (or Nene), lay the Liberty of Peterborough, originally under the jurisdiction of the abbot of the monastery. In the northwest corner of the soke is a great Elizabethan mansion, Burghley House.

The town itself, the seat of a bishop, is an important industrial and agricultural centre on the western edge of the region of reclaimed swampland known as the Fens and also on the River Nen, navigable from there to the North Sea by ships of 500 tons. In the city centre is St. Peter's Cathedral, built mainly of limestone, begun in 1118 and consecrated in 1238. It is an important example of the Late Norman style. The fine Early English west front suffered from changes in builders' plans, and the Perpendicular style porch (1375) increases the somewhat discordant effect. The flanking turrets have Decorated and Perpendicular style spires and pinnacles. The painted ceiling (*c.* 1220) of the nave is impressive, and the lozenge patterns contain several curious figures. The Hedda Stone, an interesting example of Saxon sculpture (*c.* 800), is a block of black stone with figures of the apostles in relief. There is some fine stained glass (1862) by the noted artist William Morris.

The outer gate, built at the end of the 12th century and greatly altered in the early 14th century, connects the cathedral precinct with the market place. Victorian buildings include the Abbot's Gate (early 14th century) with the Knights' Chamber above, St. Thomas' Chapel (*c.* 1330), Priory Gate (early 16th century), and the 13th-century infirmary. Apart from the cathedral, Peterborough has few interesting architectural features. The parish Church of St. John the Baptist in the market place (1407) is in Perpendicular style.

Nearby are Thorpe Hall (1653–56) and St. Botolph's Church (1263) at Longthorpe, where 14th-century Longthorpe Hall has fine wall paintings of the same period. A Benedictine abbey was founded by Peada, king of Mercia (one of the early Anglo-Saxon kingdoms), at the village of Medeshamstede in 655. It was destroyed by the Danes in 870 and then rebuilt, only to be sacked in the 11th century by Hereward the Wake, leader of an Anglo-Saxon revolt against the Norman Conquest of 1066. The monastery and much of the town were also destroyed by fire in 1116. The town became a borough in the 12th century and a city in 1541 after the monastery had been dissolved and the monastery church had become a cathedral (the interior of which was badly damaged by Parliamentarian soldiers in 1643, during the English Civil War). Economically, Peterborough was an important weaving and wool-combing centre in the 14th century. When the Fens were reclaimed, Peterborough grew as a market centre. After it had become a railway junction in the mid-19th century, many industries were established, including the making of diesel engines, steam turbines, pumps and electrical appliances, fruit and vegetable canning, and sugar-beet processing.

In the 1930s a major reconstruction scheme was carried out in the centre, and a town hall and municipal buildings were built in Priestgate. Educational institutions include King's School and Deacon's School. Peterborough, officially designated an "expanded town," was growing rapidly in the early 1970s. Pop. (1973 est.) mun. borough 72,270; (1978 est.) district 125,700.
52°35′ N, 0°15′ W
·map, United Kingdom **18**:867

Peterborough, or PETERBORO, town (township), Hillsboro County, southern New Hampshire, U.S., at the confluence of the Contoocook and Nubanusit rivers. The site was permanently settled in 1749 and named after Charles Mordaunt, 3rd earl of Peterborough. The town became well known after the establishment of the MacDowell Colony there by Marian Nevins, the wife of music composer Edward MacDowell, following his death in 1908. The colony attracted numerous composers and writers, including Stephen Vincent Benét, Willa Cather, and Thornton Wilder. Tourism and some light manufacturing (textiles, baskets) are the economic mainstays. The Sharon Arts Center in the town is run by the League of New Hampshire Arts and Crafts. Inc. 1760. Pop. (1980) 4,895.
42°53′ N, 71°57′ W

Peter Chrysologus, Saint (b. *c.* 400/406, Imola, Italy—d. *c.* 450, Imola), archbishop of Ravenna, Italy, whose orthodox discourses earned him the title of doctor of the church. About 433 he became archbishop of Ravenna, where, with the aid of Galla Placidia, the mother of the Roman emperor Valentinian III, he promoted the construction of church buildings. He was a close friend of Pope St. Leo I the Great and was highly respected by the Western and Eastern churches for his orthodoxy. In 448 when the Eastern monk Eutyches was condemned for founding Eutychianism, an extreme form of Monophysitism teaching that Christ's nature was only human and not also divine, he appealed to Peter, whose reply withheld judgment but instructed Eutyches to be obedient to Leo. Soon afterward Peter retired to Imola.

Many of Peter's homilies survive, including the letter to Eutyches. In the standard collection of 176 sermons made in the 8th century, however, several are unauthentic. His short sermons stress the fundamental Christian doctrines and the duties of Christian life in keeping with the needs and ideals of the times. The title Chrysologus ("Golden Orator") came later, probably to create a Western counterpart to the Eastern patriarch St. John Chrysostom. Peter was declared a doctor of the church by Pope Benedict XIII in 1729, and his feast day is December 4. G. Gann's *Saint Peter Chrysologus: Selected Sermons* appeared in 1953.
·Annunciation sermons **4**:603e

Peter Claver, Saint, Spanish PEDRO CLAVER (b. 1581, Verdu, Spain—d. Sept. 4, 1654, Cartagena, Colom.), Jesuit missionary to South America who, in dedicating his life to the aid of Negro slaves, earned the title of apostle of the Negroes. He entered the Society of Jesus in 1602 and eight years later was sent to Cartagena, where he was ordained in 1616. The miserable condition of the slaves aboard ship and in the pens of Cartagena, South America's chief slave market, caused Peter to declare himself "the slave of the Negroes forever." Accompanied by interpreters and carrying food and medicines, he boarded every incoming slave ship and visited the pens, where he nursed the sick and taught religion. Despite strong official opposition, Peter persevered for 38 years, baptizing an estimated 300,000 slaves. He was canonized in 1888 by Pope Leo XIII, who in 1896 proclaimed him patron of all Roman Catholic missions to Negroes. His feast day is September 9. Arnold Lunn's *Saint in the Slave Trade* appeared in 1935.

Peter des Rivaux (b. *c.* 1190, Poitou—d. 1262), one of the Poitevin administrators who dominated the government of young King Henry III of England (*q.v.*) from 1232 to 1234; Peter failed in his efforts to create an all-powerful central administration. His father (or uncle), Peter des Roches (bishop of Winchester, 1205–38), became tutor to Henry upon the King's accession. Peter des Rivaux served as a king's clerk from 1218 to 1223 but was exiled from England when Henry threw off the tutelage of Peter des Roches in 1227. Returning to England under Henry's protection in 1230, Peter des Rivaux was appointed treasurer of the household in June 1232.

After Henry stripped the powerful Hubert de Burgh, the last of the great justiciars, of his authority (July–November 1232), Peter des Rivaux took over the machinery of government and immediately initiated a reorganization of the financial and administrative system. These innovations, if fully executed, would have made Henry the richest and most powerful monarch in Europe, but the English barons, led by Edmund Rich, archbishop of Canterbury, forced Henry to dismiss Peter and the other Poitevins in 1234. Peter served as baron of the exchequer again in 1253 and keeper of the wardrobe in 1257–58, but he never regained his former power.

Peter des Roches (d. June 1238, Farnham, Hampshire), native of Poitou, in France, and diplomat, soldier, and administrator, one of the ablest statesmen of his time. He enjoyed a brilliant but checkered career, largely in England in the service of the kings John and Henry III (*q.v.*). As bishop of Winchester from 1205 to 1238, he organized and added to the financial resources of his see.

He held ecclesiastical appointments in Touraine and Poitou and afterward went to England, where King John influenced his election to the see of Winchester. He remained in England and retained his see throughout the interdict (1208–13), filling several administrative and military roles. He became chief justiciar in 1214 but was unpopular and was replaced in June 1215. He supported John loyally during the war with the barons and was one of his executors.

Peter crowned Henry III and was his tutor until 1227. As the most influential Poitevin in the country, he headed that group of alien officials and soldiers who suffered political defeat at the hands of the justiciar, Hubert de Burgh, in 1223–24. He accompanied the crusade led (1228–29) by the emperor Frederick II and reached Jerusalem. In 1230 he helped to reconcile Frederick with Pope Gregory IX and in 1231 negotiated a truce between Henry III and the French. On his return to England in 1231, he influenced Henry III to promote his son (or nephew) Peter des Rivaux to numerous posts and brought about Hubert's fall in 1232. The administrative methods he advocated, however, led to baronial opposition in 1233, and in 1234 Henry III dismissed Peter from favour and Peter des Rivaux from office.

Peter Grimes (1945), opera by Benjamin Britten, with libretto by Montague Slater.

·opera development **13**:592h
·regional characteristics of story **6**:872a

Peterhead, seaport, most easterly town in Scotland, in Banff and Buchan district, Grampian region (until 1975 in Buchan district, county of Aberdeen). The town, built of locally quarried red granite, was founded in 1593, and the Peterhead estate eventually was acquired in the 18th century by the Merchant Maiden Hospital of Edinburgh. The town developed as a port and, during the 18th century, as a spa. By the early 19th century Peterhead was also the chief centre of the British whaling industry, but this activity declined with the rise of the herring fisheries to their early 20th-century peak. Peterhead remains an important herring fishing port, but fishing for whiting is assuming greater significance. Fish and food-processing plants and some light engineering are the main industries, along with some export trade in oats, potatoes, and local beef. Pop. (1974 est.) 14,994.
57°30′ N, 1°49′ W

·map, United Kingdom **18**:866

Peterhof (Russian S.F.S.R.): *see* Petrodvorets.

Peter Lombard, Latin PETRUS LOMBARDUS (b. *c.* 1100, Novara, Lombardy—d. Aug. 21/22, 1160, Paris), bishop of Paris whose *Four Books of Sentences* (*Sententiarum libri IV*) was the standard theological text of the Middle Ages. After early schooling at Bologna, Italy, he went to France to study at Reims and then at Paris. From 1136 to 1150 he taught theology in the school of Notre Dame, Paris, where in 1144–45 he became a canon. He was present at the Council of Reims (1148) that assembled to examine the writings of the French theologian Gilbert de La Porrée. In June 1159 he was consecrated bishop of Paris and died the following year.

Although he wrote sermons, letters, and commentaries on Holy Scripture, Lombard's *Four Books of Sentences* (1148–51) established his reputation and subsequent fame, earning him the title of *Magister Sententiarum* ("Master of the *Sentences*"). The *Sentences*, a collection of teachings of the Church Fathers and opinions of medieval masters arranged as a systematic treatise, marked the culmination of a long tradition of theological pedagogy, and until the 16th century it was the official textbook in the universities. Hundreds of scholars, including Thomas Aquinas, wrote commentaries on it.

Book I of the *Sentences* discusses God, the Trinity, divine guidance, evil, predestination; book II, angels, demons, the fall of man, grace, sin; book III, the incarnation of Jesus Christ, the redemption of sins, virtues, the Ten Commandments; book IV, the sacraments and the four last things—death, judgment, hell, and heaven. While Lombard showed originality in choosing and arranging his texts, in utilizing different currents of thought, and in avoiding extremes, of special importance to medieval theologians was his clarification of the theology of the sacraments. He asserted that there are seven of these and that a sacrament is not merely a "visible sign of invisible grace" (after Augustine of Hippo) but also the "cause of the grace it signifies." In ethical matters, he decreed that a man's actions are judged good or bad according to their cause and intention, except those acts that are evil by nature.

Lombard's teachings were opposed during his lifetime and after his death. Later theologians have rejected a number of his views, but he has never been regarded as unorthodox, and efforts to have his works condemned were unsuccessful. The fourth Lateran Council (1215) approved his teaching on the Trinity and prefaced a profession of faith with the words, "We believe with Peter Lombard. . . ." His collected works are in J.-P. Migne, *Patrologia Latina*, vol. 191–192. The best edition of the *Four Books of Sentences* (no English translation) is considered to be that of the Franciscans of the College of St. Bonaventura (near Florence), *Libri quattuor sententiarum* (2 vol., 1916). E.F. Rogers' *Peter Lombard and the Sacramental System* appeared in 1917.

·dialectic approach to theology **15**:1004h
·Scholastic Augustinianism
dissemination **16**:355d

Peterloo Massacre, also called MANCHESTER MASSACRE, in English history, the name given in bitter derision (after Waterloo) to the brutal dispersal by hussars and yeomanry of a radical meeting held on Aug. 16, 1819, on St. Peter's Fields in Manchester. The "massacre" attests to the profound fears of the privileged classes of the imminence of Jacobin revolution in England in the years after the Napoleonic Wars. To radicals and reformers Peterloo came to symbolize government callousness and tyranny.

The meeting was the culmination of a series of political rallies held in 1819, a year of industrial depression and high food prices. It was intended to be a great demonstration of discontent, and its political object was parliamentary reform. About 60,000 persons attended the rally, including a high proportion of women and children. None was armed and their behaviour was wholly peaceable. The magistrates, nervous before the event, were alarmed by the size and mood of the crowd, and ordered the Manchester yeomanry to arrest the speakers immediately after the meeting had begun.

The untrained yeomanry did not confine themselves to seizing the leaders but, wielding sabres, made a general attack on the crowd. The chairman of the bench of magistrates thereupon ordered the 15th Hussars and the Cheshire Volunteers to join the attack; in 10 minutes the place was cleared except for bodies. The numbers of killed and wounded were disputed; probably about 500 people were injured and 11 killed. The news of Peterloo shocked opponents of the government throughout the country, but the government did not repudiate the magistrates.

Petermann Ranges, mountains extending for 200 mi (320 km) from Western Australia southeastward into the Northern Territory. A continuation of the granite and gneiss formations of the Musgrave Ranges to the southeast, the Petermanns rise to a height of 3,800 ft (1,158 m). Explored (1874) by Ernest Giles, the mountains were named after August Petermann, a German geographer. The eastern section lies within the Petermann Aboriginal Reserve. To the east is the Ayers Rock-Mount Olga National Park.
25°00′ S, 129°46′ E

Peter Martyr, name commonly used in English for (1) that Peter who was killed in 1252 by the Cathari (*see* Peter Martyr, Saint); (2) Peter Martyr d'Anghiera, who was an Italian historian (*see* Anghiera, Pietro Martire d'); (3) Peter Martyr Vermigli, who was one of the greatest Italian Reformers and a leading exponent of the Reformed doctrine of the sacraments (*see* Vermigli, Pietro Martire).

Peter Martyr, Saint, also called PETER OF VERONA (b. 1205?, Verona, Italy—d. April 6, 1252, near Milan), inquisitor, vigorous preacher, and religious founder who, for his militant reformation, was assassinated by the neo-Manichaean sect, the Cathari. His parents were members of the Cathari, and there was some family opposition to Peter's studying at the University of Bologna. There he befriended Dominic (Domingo de Guzmán), whose religious order, the Order of Friars Preachers, he entered about 1221.

Peter gained his initial reputation as preacher in Lombardy, where eventually he was forbidden to preach because of spurious moral charges made against him. After receiving what he regarded as divine inspiration, he resumed his evangelization with such fervour that Pope Gregory IX appointed him general inquisitor about 1232. In this capacity he preached against the Cathari throughout northern and central Italy.

According to a 14th-century work ascribed to Peter of Todi, who was prior general of the Servite order from 1314 to 1344, Peter Martyr helped the Seven Holy Founders to establish the Servites during the 1240s. Peter himself influenced and founded various confraternities to combat heresies. He served as prior of the Italian Dominican centres of Asti in 1240, of Piacenza in 1241, and of Como in 1251, the year that Pope Innocent IV named him papal inquisitor.

While returning to Milan from a preaching mission at Como, Peter and his companion, the friar Dominic, were attacked by Cathari, who bludgeoned Peter with an ax. According to pious tradition, he wrote on the ground *Credo in Deum* ("I believe in God") with his own blood before being fatally stabbed in the heart. Dominic died a few days later. Peter was canonized by Innocent in the following year and was subsequently named patron of inquisitors. He was buried in the church of Sant' Eustorgio, Milan, and his feast day is April 29. In 1952 appeared two biographies (in Italian), by R. Francisco and by G. Ederle.

Peter Nolasco, Saint, French PIERRE NOLASQUE (b. *c.* 1182, probably Barcelona—d. Dec. 25?, 1249/56, Barcelona), founder of the order of Our Lady of Ransom (Mercedarians, or Nolascans), a religious institute originally designed to ransom Christian captives from the Moors; today, the Mercedarians, whose numbers have declined, are engaged mostly in hospital work. Peter dedicated himself to helping the poor. In Spain, where the Moors held many Christian slaves gained from struggles between the Moorish and the Christian kingdoms there, he ransomed them with funds from his inheritance and from contributions. Between 1218 and 1234, he founded his order at Barcelona. Peter is said to have gone twice to Africa to redeem Christian slaves there. He resigned his offices of master general and ransomer some years before his death.

Peter was canonized in 1628 by Pope Urban VIII. When his cause for canonization was being considered in Rome, there was presented a notarial act, the *documento de los sellos* ("document of the seals"), declaring that the Blessed Virgin Mary came to Peter in a vision and instructed him to found his order. The *documento* has since been proved to be a forgery. His feast day is January 28. P.N. Pérez' *San Pedro Nolasco, fundador de la orden de la Merced* appeared in 1915.

Peter of Albano (1257–1315), Italian professor of medicine at Padua.
·Aristotelianism and Averroism **1**:1159g

Peter of Alcántara, Saint, original name PEDRO GARAVITO (b. 1499, Alcántara, Spain—d. Oct. 18, 1562, Arenas), Franciscan mystic who founded an austere form of Franciscan life known as the Alcantarines or Discalced (*i.e.,* barefooted) Friars Minor. Of noble birth, he entered the Franciscan Order at Alcántara in 1515 and was ordained priest in 1524. As a friar, Peter emphasized the penitential aspects of the life of St. Francis of Assisi, founder of the Franciscans. He then wrote special instructions for his disciples and in Spain and Portugal founded convents that were unique for their isolation and discomfort. From his first friary at El Pedroso, Spain, his friars spread to Italy, Germany, and France.

Peter had spirited correspondence with SS. Francis Borgia, Louis of Granada, and especially with the mystical writer Teresa of Avila, whom he aided in her reform of the Carmelite nuns and whose autobiography is one of the best sources of his life. Peter's *Tratado de la oración y meditación* (*Treatise on Prayer and Meditation*) has been translated into numerous languages (Eng. trans., 1926). He was canonized in 1669 by Pope Clement IX, and his feast day is October 18; he is the patron saint of Brazil.

Peter of Blois (*c.* 1135–*c.* 1212), English Humanist author and poet whose collection of his own letters (written partly in his own name and partly in the names of illustrious persons) made him famous throughout the Middle Ages.

Peter of Castelnau, French PIERRE DE CASTELNAU (b. Château-Neuf, Montpellier, Fr.—d. Jan. 14, 1208, near Saint-Gilles, now in Belgium), Cistercian martyr, apostolic legate, and inquisitor against the Albigenses, most particularly the Cathari (heretical Christian sect in southern France), whose assassination led to the Albigensian Crusade. He became an archdeacon in 1199 and in 1202 joined the Cistercian order.

In 1207 Pope Innocent III appointed Peter as apostolic legate and inquisitor to lead an expedition against the Albigenses and particularly to obtain the recantation of Count Raymond VI (*q.v.*) of Toulouse, who was indifferent to the heresy spreading over his domain. Having urged him from 1205 to stamp out the heretics, Peter now excommunicated Raymond, placing the Languedoc region under interdict, which aroused grave opposition. Peter's campaign on behalf of Innocent ended in disaster. He was assassinated, supposedly at Raymond's instigation, and in response to this act Innocent launched the Albigensian Crusade, a holy war in which Toulouse was ravaged and its inhabitants, Cathar and non-Cathar alike, were massacred.

Peter's relics were enshrined in the church of Saint-Gilles, and his feast day is March 5. He is venerated as a martyr in the dioceses of the Midi, in France.

Peter of Colechurch, 13th-century English curate who built the Old London Bridge.
·London Bridge construction **3**:176g; illus.

Peter of Courtenay (d. ?1219), briefly Latin emperor of Constantinople, the son of Peter of Courtenay (died 1183) and a grandson of the French king Louis VI, obtained the counties of Auxerre and Tonnerre by his first marriage. He later took Yolande (died 1219), sister of Baldwin I and Henry of Flanders, first and second Latin emperors of Constantinople, as his second wife; she brought him the marquessate of Nevers. Chosen successor to Henry of Flanders when Henry died without sons in 1216, Peter was consecrated emperor in S. Lorenzo Fuori le Mura, Rome, by Pope Honorius III on April 9, 1217. Accompanied by an army and a papal legate, he subsequently embarked at Brindisi on ships furnished by the Venetians, for whom he tried to conquer Durazzo (now Durrës, Alb.) from Theodore Ducas, Greek despot of Epirus. Failing in that enterprise, Peter set out overland toward Thessalonica (Thessaloníki). In the mountains near Elbasan he was taken by Theodore and died, probably by assassination, after an imprisonment of at least two years.

Peter of Savoy, in Italian PIETRO II, CONTE DI SAVOIA, called THE LITTLE CHARLEMAGNE (b. between 1203 and 1213, Susa, Italy—d. May 15?, 1268, Pierre-Châtel, Fr.), influential Savoyard adviser to King Henry III of England (ruled 1216–72). Peter was the son of Thomas I, count of Savoy, and Margaret, daughter of William I, count of Geneva. Although he obtained preferments in the church, Peter renounced clerical status *c.* 1234 upon inheriting the counties of Bugey and Vaud (now in Switzerland). He acquired more territory by marrying his cousin Agnes, heiress of Faucigny, and through diplomacy and war he expanded his dominions. His niece Eleanor of Provence married Henry III in 1236, and four years later the King invited Peter to England, where he became a trusted royal counsellor.

Henry used Peter's influence in Savoy to promote his own ambitions in Italy. In 1258 Peter backed the reforms imposed on Henry by the barons, and he became a member of the reforming council of 15. Nevertheless, after 1260 Peter supported Henry against the extreme reformer Simon de Montfort. After inheriting the county of Savoy in 1263, Peter left England to dislodge a rival claimant. Although he never returned, he continued to aid Henry from afar.

Peter of Spain (pope): *see* John XXI.

Peter of Tarentaise: *see* Innocent V.

Peter of Verona, Saint: *see* Peter Martyr, Saint.

Peter Pan (first performed 1904), dramatic fantasy for children by the British author Sir James Barrie, relating the adventures of the Darling children in the Never-Never Land of the fairy Tinker Bell and Peter Pan, a boy who refuses to grow up. After encountering Indians, pirates, and memorable characters such as Captain Hook, the children return to their former life, leaving Peter to his eternal boyhood. In 1911 Barrie published the story under the title *Peter and Wendy.* It has often been revived as a play, as, for example, the Broadway musical version of 1950 with score by Leonard Bernstein.
·dramatic style of children's plays **5**:987h

Battle of Peter Pan (Maude Adams) and Captain Hook (Ernest Lawford), Act V, *Peter Pan,* New York, 1905
Museum of the City of New York, Theatre and Music Collection

Peters, Carl (b. Sept. 27, 1856, Neuhaus-an-der-Elbe, now in East Germany—d. Sept. 10, 1918, Bad Harzburg, now in West Germany), explorer who advanced the establishment of the German East African protectorate of Tanganyika, now a part of Tanzania. After visiting London to study British principles of colonization, he founded the Society for German Colonization in 1884 and later that year, in the Usambara Mountains area of present-day northeastern Tanzania, made a number of contracts with chiefs who surrendered their territories to him. He later helped to extend the German sphere of influence and established the German East Africa Company, which obtained an imperial charter in 1885. He reached Uganda in 1890 and concluded a treaty with the king, but without the support

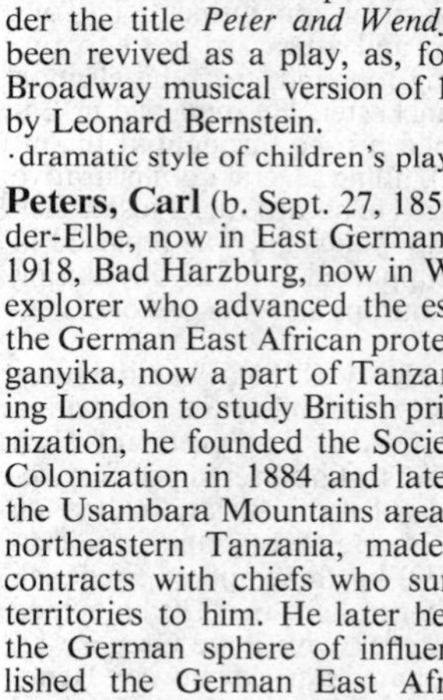

Peters, oil painting by Herbert Sidney, 1912
Historia-Photo

of the German government. This treaty was declared void, for an agreement had been reached between Germany and Great Britain by which Uganda was left in the British sphere. He became imperial high commissioner for Kilimanjaro in 1891 but was deprived of his commission in 1897 for misuse of official power in his treatment of the Africans. From 1899 to 1901 he explored regions along the Zambezi River with a view to commercial exploitation and described his discovery of ancient cities and gold mines in *Im Goldland des Altertums* (*The Eldorado of the Ancients*, both 1902). He also published *Die deutsche Emin Pasha Expedition*, (*New Light on Dark Africa*, both 1891), among other works.

Peters, Lenrie (b. 1932, Bathurst, Gambia), physician, novelist, and among West Africa's most important poets, whose medical background gives his poetry a scientific perspective.

Educated at Bathurst, Freetown (Sierra Leone) and at Trinity College, Cambridge, where he earned a medical degree in 1959, with further studies in surgery, he broadcast on several British Broadcasting Corporation programs (and chaired its *Africa Forum*) before returning to Gambia.

His novel *The Second Round* (1965) is semi-autobiographical in its story of the disillusionment and alienation of a young doctor returning from England to Freetown after completing his medical studies and finding his home unsettled and unsettling, the people there having rejected all traditional values without substituting anything positive. The doctor drifts among acquaintances for a time but finally seeks some meaning by working in an isolated upcountry hospital.

Peters' poetry (*Poems*, 1964; *Satellites*, 1967; and in several anthologies) is less pessimistic, characterized by a hope that good will prevail and by a sense of discovery. Some of his poems, however, tell of an estrangement similar to that in *The Second Round*. In style he follows European conventions, although he concentrates upon African themes and images.

·style and publication **1**:240g

Petersburg, city, seat (1839) of Menard County, central Illinois, U.S., on the Sangamon River, 20 mi (32 km) northwest of Springfield. The area was settled *c.* 1820, and in 1826 a plat for Petersburg surveyed by Abraham Lincoln was recorded. In a hillside cemetery near the city, which is on the Lincoln Heritage Trail, is the grave of Lincoln's fiancée, Ann Rutledge, whose headstone is inscribed with an epitaph written by the poet and novelist Edgar Lee Masters, a native son. The boyhood home of Masters, who is buried in the same cemetery, is maintained as a museum. The county courthouse has a display of Lincoln papers. Lincoln's New Salem State Park is just to the south.

The city's economy is basically agricultural with corn (maize), wheat, and soybeans being the chief crops. Inc. 1841. Pop. (1980) 2,419.
40°01′ N, 89°51′ W

Petersburg, city, in, but independent of, Dinwiddie County, southeast Virginia, U.S., on the Appomattox River (bridged), south of Richmond. In 1646, Ft. Henry was built at the falls of the Appomattox, the site of the present city. The name (earlier, Peter's Point and Peter's Town) reputedly honours Maj. Peter Jones, who became commander of the fort in 1675. In 1733 Col. William Byrd II surveyed the site, but it was not until 1748 that an act of the colonial legislature established the town. During the American Revolution it was captured by British troops under William Phillips and Benedict Arnold (April 25, 1781). On May 20, Cornwallis arrived with his army to prepare for the campaign that was to end with his surrender at Yorktown.

In 1784 Petersburg, Blandford, Pocahontas, and Ravenscroft were combined and incorporated as Petersburg. It was the scene of bitter fighting in the Civil War (*see* Petersburg Campaign).

The city's industrial output includes cigarettes, textiles, wood products, and writing implements. It is the seat of Richard Bland (junior) College (1961), Virginia State College (1882), and John Tyler Community College (1967). Historic sites include Petersburg National Battlefield (scene of the "Battle of the Crater"), Old Blandford Church and Cemetery with 30,000 Confederate graves, and Center Hill Mansion Museum (1823). Ft. Lee, U.S. Army quartermaster training command, is nearby. Inc. city, 1850. Pop. (1980) city, 41,055; Petersburg–Colonial Heights–Hopewell metropolitan area (SMSA), 129,296.
37°13′ N, 77°24′ W

·map, United States **18**:908

Petersburg Campaign, a series of military operations in southern Virginia, 1864–65, during the final months of the U.S. Civil War, culminating in the defeat of the South. Petersburg, an important rail centre 20 miles southeast of Richmond, was a strategic point for the defense of the Confederate capital. In June 1864 the Union Army began a siege of the two cities, with both sides rapidly constructing 35-mile-long fortifications. In a series of battles that summer, Federal losses were heavy, but by the end of August, Gen. Ulysses S. Grant had crossed the Petersburg-Weldon Railroad; he captured Ft. Harrison on September 29. By year's end, however, Gen. Robert E. Lee still held Richmond and Petersburg. But due to Confederate disasters elsewhere, Southern railroads had broken down or been destroyed.

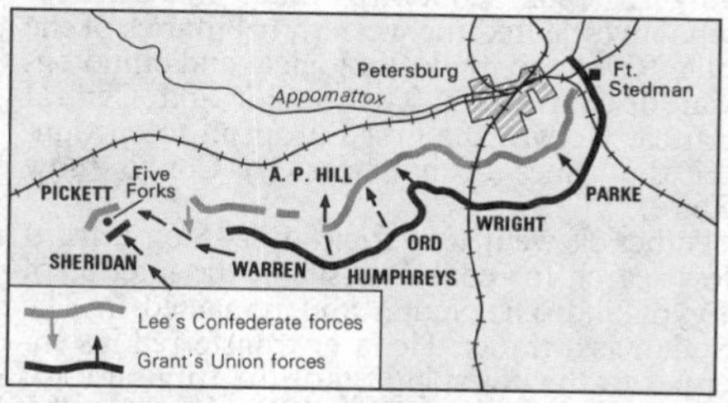

The Petersburg Campaign, Federal attacks on April 1–2, 1865

From *A Dictionary of Battles* by David Eggenberger, Copyright © 1967 by David Eggenberger, reprinted with permission of the publisher, Thomas Y. Crowell Company Inc.

Thus the Confederates were ill-fed to the point of physical exhaustion, and the lack of draft animals and cavalry mounts nearly immobilized the troops. Hunger, exposure, and the apparent hopelessness of further resistance led to increasing desertion, especially among recent conscripts. In March 1865 the Confederates were driven back at the Battle of Ft. Stedman, leaving Lee with 50,000 troops as opposed to Grant's 120,000. Soon after, Grant crushed a main Southern force under Gen. George E. Pickett and Gen. Fitzhugh Lee at the Battle of Five Forks (April 1); the next day the defenders were driven back within the Petersburg inner defenses. Lee immediately informed Pres. Jefferson Davis that the two cities could no longer be held, and the evacuation was carried out that night. After Lee's plan to join with Gen. Joseph E. Johnston was thwarted, he surrendered to General Grant on April 9 at Appomattox Court House.

·Grant strategy and siege activity **4**:678h; map 679

·Lee's strategy and surrender resignation **10**:771e

Peterson, Oscar (b. Aug. 15, 1925, Montreal), Canadian Jazz pianist and singer. After playing with a popular Canadian orchestra, Peterson went to the United States in 1949, where he appeared in a Norman Granz concert at Carnegie Hall. He toured with the "Jazz at the Philharmonic" throughout the 1950s, leading a trio with Ray Brown (bass) and Irving Ashby (guitar), later succeeded by Barney Kessel and Herb Ellis. In the late 1950s, after Ellis left the trio, Peterson substituted drums (Ed Thigpen) for guitar and continued to develop his own personal style in the tradition of swing and bop (having been at first influenced by Art Tatum and Earl Hines, among others). In the mid-1960s Louis Hayes replaced Thigpen and Sam Jones replaced Ray Brown. Peterson was also heard as a singer in the manner of Nat Cole from the early 1950s. His own compositions include *Hallelujah Time*, *Children's Tune*, *The Smudge*, *Lovers' Promenade*, and *Canadiana Suite*.

Peterson, Roger Tory (b. Aug. 28, 1908, Jamestown, N.Y.), ornithologist, author, conservationist, and wildlife artist whose field books on birds, beginning with *A Field Guide to the Birds* (1934, rev. ed. 1942), did much in the United States and Europe to stimulate public interest in bird study. The "Peterson Field Guide Series" includes his own books on birds of western North America (1954, rev. 1961), of Britain and Europe (with British ornithologists Guy Mountfort and P.A.D. Hollum; 1954, rev. ed. 1966), and of Mexico (1973) and on the wild flowers of eastern North America (with Margaret McHenney; 1968), as well as a number of guides by other authors.

Peterson started drawing birds while in high school and studied at the Art Student's League, New York (1927–29), and the National Academy of Design, New York (1929–31). In painting for the field guides, he stressed those features of each species that would aid the reader in identifying it in the field. In addition to the field guides, he wrote many popular books of a more general nature, among them *Birds Over America* (1948), *Wildlife in Color* (1951), *Wild America* (1955), *The Birds* (1963), *The World of Birds* (with James Fisher; 1964). He received the Brewster Medal of the American Ornithologists' Union (1944), the John Burroughs Medal of the John Burroughs Memorial Association (1951), the gold medal of the New York Zoological Society (1961), the Allen Medal of the Laboratory of Ornithology, Cornell University (1967), and the Audubon Medal of the National Audubon Society (1971).

Peterson was an officer of many ornithological and conservation organizations, including the American Ornithologists' Union, National Audubon Society, and International Committee for Bird Preservation.

Peter the Apostle, Saint 14:153 (d. *c.* AD 64, Rome), recognized in the early Christian Church as the leader of the disciples of Jesus Christ and by the Roman Catholic Church as the first of its unbroken succession of popes.

Peter, a fisherman, was called to be a disciple of Jesus at the beginning of his ministry, probably in Galilee. Though untrained in the Mosaic Law and apparently a slow learner, he was a mature and capable leader when entrusted with responsibility. Originally known as Simeon, or Simōn, he received from Jesus the name Cephas (*i.e.*, "Rock," hence Peter, from the Latin *petrus*), and he assumed the position of spokesman and leader among the disciples. An important but controversial passage in the New Testament (Matt. 16:16–19) records Peter's confession of faith in Jesus, followed by his naming and receiving of authority. Peter denied knowing Jesus when he was arrested but later grieved over this act. According to Paul, it was to Peter that the resurrected Christ first appeared.

Peter emerged immediately after Jesus' death as the leader of the earliest church, and he dominated the community for approximately 15 years after the Resurrection. Imprisoned about AD 44, he miraculously escaped and then departed from Jerusalem. The later work of Peter is not clear, although it seems that he assumed a missionary role. At the Jerusalem Council (AD 49 or 50) it was decided that Paul's mission should be to the Gentiles and

Peter's to the Jews. According to tradition, Peter was the first bishop of Antioch.

Peter's residence, martyrdom, and burial at Rome are among the most complicated and controversial problems encountered in the study of the New Testament and the early church.

TEXT BIOGRAPHY covers:
The man and his position among the disciples **14**:153e
Incidents important in interpretations of Peter 154e
The position of Peter in the Apostolic Church 155b
Tradition of Peter in Rome 156a
Later traditions about Peter 157a

REFERENCES in other text articles:
· Mark Gospel authorship association **2**:951d
· papacy and apostolic succession **13**:955g
· papal authority theories **13**:960d
· Peter epistles' authorship and content **2**:969f
· position among twelve Apostles **4**:535g
· primitive Christian traditions in Acts **2**:957d
· St. John and Jesus' intimates **10**:241b

Peter the Great (1895–1923), U.S. Standardbred, founder of one of two dominant male lines of trotting horses. (Axworthy founded the other.) Sired by Pilot Medium out of Santos, Peter the Great was a descendant of Happy Medium, a son of Hambletonian. After three seasons (1897–99), in which he raced only a few times but performed well, he was retired to stud.

Peter the Great Bay, Russian ZALIV PETRA VELIKOGO, inlet, Sea of Japan, northwest Pacific Ocean, in the maritime territory of the Soviet Union. Extending 115 mi (185 km) from the mouth of the Tumen River (on the Soviet–Chinese border) northeast across to Cape Povorotny, the bay is 55 mi long. In the north, the port of Vladivostok is situated on the Murav'yyov-Amursky Peninsula between Amur and Ussuri bays. The town of Posyet is on Posyeto Bay (southwest). The functioning of these harbours is severely limited by the freezing of the bay from early December to mid-April. Formerly (from 1855) known as Victoria Bay, the inlet was renamed (1859) to honour Czar Peter I the Great.
42°40′ N, 132°00′ E

Peter the Hermit, sometimes called PETER THE LITTLE and PETER OF AMIENS (b. *c.* 1050, probably Amiens, Fr.—d. July 8, 1115, Huy, now in Belgium), ascetic, monastic founder, crusader, and enormously influential preacher, is considered one of the chief stimulators in the launching of the First Crusade. He reputedly visited the Holy Land *c.* 1093.

When Pope Urban II proclaimed the Crusade at the Council of Clermont in November 1095, Peter began his preaching. He travelled from Berry (region in central France) across Champagne and down the Meuse Valley to Cologne, where he arrived in April 1096. His eloquence attracted thousands. Leaving Cologne in May, Peter led his enthusiastic followers across Europe to Constantinople (now Istanbul), where in late July he joined forces with more contingents. On August 5–6 the crusaders advanced to Nicomedia (modern Izmir, Tur.). Unable to maintain discipline, Peter soon returned to Constantinople to seek help from the Byzantine emperor, Alexius I. In his absence most of his army was annihilated (October 21) by the Turks. He waited in Constantinople until the princely expeditions from western Europe were finally assembled there (May 1097) and accompanied them southeastward across Anatolia. In Antioch (now Antakya, Tur.) he became discouraged by the hardships attending the crusaders' siege in October and was dissuaded only with difficulty from abandoning the enterprise (January 1098).

At last having reached Jerusalem, Peter was appointed almoner of the Christian army in spring 1099. He preached a sermon on the Mount of Olives shortly before the storming of Jerusalem in July, and he conducted processions there in August. He returned to Europe in 1100, becoming prior of the Augustinian monastery of Neufmoutier, at Huy, which he founded, and died there. Y. Le Febvre's *Pierre l'Ermite et la croisade* appeared in 1946.

· Crusades instigation and leadership **5**:299e

Peter the Venerable, also known as BLESSED PETER OF MONTBOISSIER (b. *c.* 1092, Montboissier, Auvergne, France—d. Dec. 25, 1156, Cluny, Burgundy), outstanding French abbot of Cluny whose spiritual, intellectual, and financial reforms restored Cluny to its high place among the religious establishments of Europe. He joined St. Bernard of Clairvaux in supporting Pope Innocent II, thereby weakening the position of the antipope, Anacletus II. After Peter Abelard's teachings had been condemned at the Council of Sens (1140), Peter received him at Cluny and reconciled him with St. Bernard and with the Pope. He also tried to convert the Crusades into nonviolent missionary ventures; ordered the first Latin translation of the Qur'ān so that it might be refuted; and was papal ambassador to Aquitaine, Italy, and England. He wrote hymns and poems in addition to theological tracts and left about 200 letters of considerable historiographical interest. Although Peter has not been canonized, his cult received papal approval in 1862; his feast day is December 29.

Petherick, John (b. 1813, Glamorgan—d. July 15, 1882, London), trader and explorer who investigated the western tributaries of the Nile River and made zoological and ethnological discoveries in The Sudan and Central Africa. He was the first European to encounter the tribes of northeastern Congo (now Zaire).

Petherick went to Africa in 1845 on a fruitless search for coal deposits in the interior of Egypt and The Sudan and remained in The Sudan as a trader. He later transferred his energies to the investigation of the tributaries of the Nile, which run through the southern Sudan, notably the Baḥr-al-Ghazāl (Gazelle River). In 1853 he reached the borders of the Zande nation (in Zaire). Following the publication of his accounts of his travels, *Egypt, the Soudan and Central Africa* (1861), the Royal Geographical Society appointed him to meet John H. Speke and James A. Grant on their return from discovering the source of the Nile, but while carrying out further investigations in the Zande, Petherick misjudged Speke's arrival and missed him.

Pethick-Lawrence, Frederick William Pethick-Lawrence, 1st Baron, originally FREDERICK WILLIAM LAWRENCE (b. Dec. 28, 1871, London—d. Sept. 10, 1961, London), a leader of the woman suffrage movement in Great Britain during the first two decades of the 20th century; he later served (1945–47) as secretary of state for India and Burma.

In 1901 Lawrence married Emmeline Pethick, a fellow social worker in the East End of London, and added her family name to his own. Together they assailed their nation's prosecution of the South African War (1899–1902) and then became leaders in the agitation for woman suffrage. Pethick-Lawrence spent nearly all his considerable inheritance paying suffragettes' fines; and in 1912, after a demonstration in London, he served a few months in jail.

A Socialist and Labour Party member, he defeated Winston Churchill, at that time a Liberal, in the 1923 election to the House of Commons from West Leicester. In James Ramsay MacDonald's second Labour ministry (1929–31) he was financial secretary to the Treasury. As secretary of state for India and Burma (August 1945–April 1947) in the Labour government of Clement Richard (afterward 1st Earl) Attlee, he was unable to reconcile Jawaharlal Nehru and Mohammed Ali Jinnah, respectively leaders of the Hindus and Muslims in India. He was created a baron in 1945. His autobiography, *Fate Has Been Kind*, was published in 1943 and *Pethick-Lawrence*, by Vera Mary Brittain, in 1963.

petiole (botany): *see* leaf.

Pétion, Alexandre Sabès (b. April 2, 1770, Port-au-Prince, Haiti—d. March 29, 1818, Port-au-Prince), Haitian liberator and president remembered by the Haitian people for his liberal rule and by South Americans for his support of Simon Bolívar during the struggle for independence from Spain.

The son of a wealthy French colonist and a mulatto, Pétion served in the French colonial army before the French Revolution and then joined, first, the revolutionary troops of Toussaint-louverture and, later, those of the mulatto general André Rigaud. Fleeing to France after Toussaint defeated Rigaud, who had set up a mulatto state in the southern provinces, Pétion returned in 1802 with the French army sent to reconquer the colony but then became one of the first Haitian officers to revolt against France. In 1806 he was a leader in the revolt against the rule of Jean-Jacques Dessalines, who had played a principal role in 1803 in ousting the French. When, after Dessalines' death, Henry Christophe set up a separate state in northern Haiti, Pétion was elected president of southern Haiti in 1807. He was re-elected in 1811 and made president for life in 1816.

Influenced by ideals of French liberalism, Pétion divided the large plantations into small lots, giving one to each of his soldiers. Freed from the burden of producing a surplus for the plantation owners, the people produced only enough for their own needs, and the resulting slowdown in the economy led to galloping inflation. Pétion's regime was also marked by continual struggles with Christophe and with dissident generals in his own country.

· mulatto revolt leadership **8**:551c

Pétion de Villeneuve, Jérôme (b. Jan. 3, 1756, Chartres, Fr.—d. 1794, near Saint-Émilion), politician of the French Revolution who was at first a close associate, and later a bitter enemy, of the Jacobin leader Robespierre.

The son of a lawyer of Chartres, Pétion practiced as an advocate before accepting a seat with the bourgeois Third Estate at the States General of 1789. When the Third Estate obtained control of the States General (which became the National Assembly) and set about abolishing France's feudal institutions, Pétion and Robespierre led the small minority of deputies who pressed for enfranchisement of the lower classes and other far-reaching democratic reforms. The National Assembly dissolved itself on Sept. 30, 1791, and in November Pétion was elected mayor of Paris. Without breaking with Robespierre, he formed ties with the Girondins, the moderate bourgeois-democrats who opposed Robespierre in the newly formed Legislative Assembly.

When the Girondins organized a popular demonstration against King Louis XVI in Paris on June 20, 1792, Pétion made only half-hearted efforts to preserve order. Louis retaliated by suspending him from office on July 12, but the Legislative Assembly reinstated the mayor on August 3. Nevertheless, during the Paris insurrection that overthrew the monarchy on August 10, Pétion avoided committing himself to the Revolutionary cause.

In September 1792, Pétion was elected the first president of the National Convention, which succeeded the Legislative Assembly. Jealous of Robespierre's pre-eminence among the Montagnards (as the Jacobins of the Convention were called), Pétion joined the Girondins, and on June 2, 1793, he and 28 other Girondin leaders were expelled from the Convention in a Montagnard coup d'etat. Escaping arrest, Pétion made his way to the vicinity of Saint-Émilion, where he and another prominent Girondin, François Buzot, committed suicide. Their bodies were discovered on June 18, 1794.

Pétionville, eastern suburb of Port-au-Prince, Ouest *département*, southern Haiti, on the northern hills of the Massif de la Selle. Named for Alexandre-Sabès Pétion, a mulatto who fought in Haiti's wars for independence in the early 19th century and was later president of the southern kingdom, it is primarily a residential and resort area. It is linked to Port-au-Prince, the national capital, by a winding toll road, the proceeds of which were intended to finance Duvalierville, a model city, now defunct. Pop. (1971) 28,860.
·map, Haiti **8**:547

Petipa, Marius (b. March 11, 1819, Marseilles, France—d. June 2, 1910, Gurzuf, Russia), dancer and choreographer who worked for nearly 60 years at the Mariinsky Theatre in St. Petersburg and had a profound influence on modern classical Russian ballet. He directed many of the greatest artists in Russian ballet and developed ballets that retain an important position in Soviet dance repertoire. Petipa and his brother Lucien (later principal dancer at the Paris Opéra) received their early training from their father, Jean, a ballet master long active in Brussels. After Marius' debut in Nantes, France, in 1838, he danced in Belgium, France, and the United States (he appeared in New York in 1839) before accepting an engagement in Spain, where he gathered material for ballets later produced in Russia. He established a reputation as a talented pantomime artist and one of the outstanding dancers of his day.

Petipa, 1869
Novosti Press Agency

He made his initial appearance at the St. Petersburg Mariinsky Theatre in 1847 in *Paquita* and staged his first original ballet, *Un Mariage sous la régence* ("A Regency Marriage") there in 1858. For his wife, the ballerina Mariya Surovshchikova, he created *Le Marché des innocents* (1859; "The Children's March"). His first outstanding success was *La fille du pharaon* (1862; "The Pharaoh's Daughter"). Later, after becoming choreographer in 1862 and chief choreographer in 1869, he produced more than 60 ballets, working from carefully detailed plans that became the basis of modern classical ballet in Russia. He collaborated with Tchaikovsky on *The Nutcracker* (*Casse Noisette*, choreographed by his assistant Lev Ivanov) and *The Sleeping Beauty* and presented versions of *Swan Lake*, *Raymonda*, and *Giselle* that have been revived frequently.
After the death of his first wife, Petipa married another dancer, Lyubov Leonidovna.
·choreographic principles **4**:453h
·choreographic rule in Russia **2**:650h
·contribution to ballet **5**:465c

Petit, Alexis-Thérèse (1791–1820), French physicist.
·heat capacities and atomic weights **8**:701c

Petit, Roland (b. Jan. 13, 1924, Villemomble, Fr.), dancer and choreographer whose dramatic ballets combined fantasy with elements of contemporary realism. Trained at

Roland Petit partnering Danielle Jossy in "Maldoror"
Serge Lido

the Paris Opéra Ballet school, he joined the company in 1940 but left in 1944 to create and perform his own works at the Théâtre Sarah Bernhardt, in Paris. In 1945 Petit was instrumental in creating Les Ballets des Champs-Elysées, where he remained as principal dancer, ballet master, and choreographer until 1947. In 1948 he formed the Ballets de Paris de Roland Petit (1948–50, 1953–54, 1955, and 1958), which made several tours of Europe and the U.S. Dancers who rose to prominence in his companies include Jean Babilée, Colette Marchand, Leslie Caron, and Renée ("Zizi") Jeanmaire, whom he married in 1954.
Petit believed ballet was capable of more than simply preserving the classical works or creating new ballets within the classical tradition; he wanted to transform ballet into a fully contemporary medium, particularly by portraying emotions or characters that were individual rather than stylized. His choreography was often angular or acrobatic and was considered theatrical in its use of mime dance, occasional singing, and props such as cigarettes and telephones. His works included the realistic ballet *Les Forains* (1945; "The Strolling Players"), a study of indigent circus performers; the imaginative creation *La Croqueuse de diamants* (1950; "The Diamond Cruncher"), whose heroine eats the gems her associates steal; and *L'Oeuf à la coque* (1949; "The Soft-Boiled Egg"), in which the leading female dancer hatches from an egg in hell. *Carmen* (1949) was one of Petit's most popular ballets; the choreography was passionate and erotic, and Jeanmaire became famous for her interpretation of the title role. *Le Jeune Homme et la mort* (1946; "The Young Man and Death") and *Les Demoiselles de la nuit* (1948; "The Ladies of Midnight") were among his other notable ballets.
Petit staged several music hall revues for his wife and choreographed the dances for the films *Hans Christian Andersen* (1952), *The Glass Slipper* (1955), *Daddy Long Legs* (1955), *Anything Goes* (1956), and others. The ballet film *Black Tights* (1962) consisted of Petit's works *La Croqueuse de diamants*, *Cyrano de Bergerac*, *A Merry Mourning* (originally presented in 1953 as *Deuil en 24 heures*, "A 24-Hour Mourning"), and *Carmen*. Petit also staged several of his ballets for Sadler's Wells Ballet (now the Royal Ballet) and for the Royal Danish Ballet.
·choreographic innovations **4**:454g

Petit Chose, Le (1868), autobiographical novel by Alphonse Daudet.
·theme based on real-life experiences **5**:514b

Petitcodiac River, in southeast New Brunswick, Canada. About 60 mi (97 km) long, the river flows northeast and east, and then south through a wide estuary (20 mi long) to Shepody Bay, an inlet of Chignecto Bay, and the northern extremity of the Bay of Fundy. A tidal bore or wave, 3–6 ft (1–2 m) high at its crest, surges upward from the Bay of Fundy towards Moncton.
45°50′ N, 64°33′ W
·Bay of Fundy tidal bore **7**:780h
·tidal bore characteristics **19**:654g

Petite Idole (1920), novel by Sarah Bernhardt.
·autobiographical element in plot **2**:863d

petit feu, in ceramics, term referring to an overglaze or low temperature glaze.
·pottery glazing techniques **14**:896g

petition, form of prayer in which something is requested.
·prayer elements and rationales **14**:949f

petition, written instrument directed to some individual, official, legislative body, or court in order to redress a grievance or to request the granting of a favour. Petitions are also used to collect signatures to enable a candidate to get on a ballot or to put an issue before the electorate. They are also used to pressure representatives and deputies to vote in a certain way.
Most governments allow citizens to petition in some form for redress of grievances, and, indeed, in many countries it is an established right. The history of its growth has been wide and varied. In England the right of petitioning the crown was recognized indirectly as early as the Magna Carta (1215) and reaffirmed in the Bill of Rights of 1689. At first, petitions to the crown appear to have been for the redress of private and local grievances. Moreover, in Parliament many statutes were drawn up from the petitions from Commons to the crown and the latter's answers. Although the right to petition Parliament itself is not mentioned in the Bill of Rights, it is a convention of the constitution. In modern times, the presentation of public petitions plays little effective part in parliamentary affairs because most fail to conform to very strict tests of technical validity.
In the United States the right to petition was recognized during the Revolution and formalized in the First Amendment of the Constitution. Now both Congress and the various state legislatures have well-defined procedures for receiving and acting upon materials of this kind. Although the rules are not as stringent as those in England, individual officials often have wide discretion in interpreting the validity of petitions.
In France the petitions of the people and the National Assembly played a significant role throughout the Revolution.

petition of right, legal petition asserting a right against the English crown, the most notable example being the Petition of Right of 1628, which Parliament sent to Charles I complaining of a series of breaches of law. The term also referred to the procedure by which a subject could sue the crown, until it was abolished in 1947.
At common law the crown, or the sovereign in his official capacity, could not be sued in the king's courts. Since the king was, historically, the supreme lord of those courts, administering justice in them between his subjects, he was not subject to their jurisdiction. Hence it became a practice, whenever a subject's real or personal property had come into the possession of the king or his servants without legal right, for the subject to petition the

king in council for its restoration. The king then might or might not, at his discretion, refer the suppliant's petition to one of his courts, usually to the old Court of Exchequer, with a writ directing the judges to do what was just (*fiat justitia*). In the late 19th century, the tasks of deciding whether there was cause for action and of issuing the *fiat justitia* were left, respectively, to the attorney general and the home secretary.

Although judgment was given in the ordinary manner, the execution of the judgment presented certain difficulties because the courts could not decree execution against the crown and its servants. By the end of the 19th century, judgments in favour of the suppliant were certified by the court to the treasury with the stipulation that they be satisfied out of public funds. In 1947 a new pattern for remedies against the crown was established, doing away with the petition of right.

·Charles I's acceptance of terms **3**:241h
·Charles I's unwilling formal consent **4**:53b
·Coke's limits on royal prerogative **4**:826d

petitio principii, also called BEGGING THE QUESTION OR CIRCULAR ARGUMENT, in logic, fallacious argument in which part or all of the conclusion is assumed in one or more of the premises.

·fallacies in argumentation **15**:803f

Petit Journal, Le, French newspaper bought by Émile de Girardin in 1872.

·newspaper publishing history **15**:242a

petit jury, also called TRIAL JURY, COMMON JURY, OR TRAVERSE JURY, a group chosen from the citizenry of a district to try a question of fact. It is the standard jury used in civil and criminal trials—at the request of either party to a civil action and only at the defendant's request in a criminal action. It is distinguished from the grand jury (*q.v.*), which formulates accusations, whereas the petit jury tests the accuracy of such accusations by standards of proof.

Generally, the petit jury's function is to deliberate questions of fact, questions of law being left to the trial judge; however, the distinction is often blurred. The petit jury has less discretion than is often imagined. The trial judge supervises it, rules on what evidence it may view and on what laws are applicable, and sometimes directs its verdict. If he deems that the jury has grossly ignored the weight of the evidence, he can set aside their verdict.

Although petit juries in England and the United States have historically contained 12 members, there is no uniform number. Numerical requirements for a valid verdict vary (*e.g.*, unanimity in America, a majority in Scotland and Italy, two-thirds in Portugal), as do subject areas of operation. In the United States, for example, juvenile defendants may not request a jury, and in England juries have been eliminated from civil cases. Outside England and the United States the petit jury is declining. In nations having civil rather than common law, the jury, where found, is only used for criminal trials. Germany and France have a mixed tribunal of judges and jurors, and Japan abolished its petit jury in 1943 after a brief experimental period for civil cases.

Scholars disagree on the time and place of the trial jury's birth. Some suggest that King Alfred the Great of England initiated the institution in the 9th century. Others trace it to the Norman Conquest of England (1066). The petit jury emerged as a distinct form when the Articles of Visitation in England (1194) separated accusatory and trial juries—the grand and petit juries of today.

The future of the petit jury is uncertain. Even in England and the United States it is hotly debated. Proponents argue that the trial jury is a bulwark against tyranny, being drawn from the populace at large. Detractors insist the system is inconvenient and clumsy and that modern legal complexities are beyond most petit jurors. Court backlogs continue to underscore the need for greater efficiency in the administration of justice.

·constitutional right to jury trial **10**:361b
·English medieval legal institutions **3**:205d
·jury history and use **10**:360g

petit mal (French: "little sickness"), type of epilepsy characterized by episodes of brief unresponsiveness. They generally last less than 15 seconds each and usually occur many times in a day—sometimes several hundred times. No involuntary movement or falling occurs (as in grand mal, *q.v.*). After the short interruption of consciousness, the individual is mentally clear and able to continue what he was doing before. Petit mal occurs mainly in children and does not appear initially after age 20; it tends to disappear before or during early adult life. Each short absence is accompanied by an electroencephalogram pattern in which "spike and wave" discharges recur three times a second. At times petit mal can be nearly continuous, and the person may continue his activities in a clouded, partially responsive state for minutes or hours. *See also* epilepsy.

·causation, incidence, and treatment **12**:1055g

Petitot, Jean (b. July 12, 1607, Geneva, Switz.—d. April 3, 1691, Vevey, Switz.), painter who was the first great miniature portraitist in enamel. The son of sculptor Faulle Petitot, he was apprenticed to a Swiss jeweller from 1622 to 1626. About 1633 he went to France, where he probably became the pupil of Jean and Henri Toutin, the originators of the art of painting miniature portraits in enamel. By 1637 Petitot had arrived in England, where he was patronized by Charles I and his court. Only a few miniatures are known from this period, and all are copies of portraits by the court painter Sir Anthony Van Dyck (1599–1641).

Portrait of an unknown lady, painted enamel miniature by Jean Petitot; in the Musée Condé, Chantilly, Fr.
Giraudon

Petitot had high expectations of his stay in England, but after the outbreak of the Civil War he returned to France. For many years he enjoyed the patronage of Louis XIV (1638–1715) and his courtiers. He executed many portraits of the king, his family, and the most celebrated figures in his entourage; most were based upon paintings by fashionable artists. Petitot worked in partnership with Jacques Bordier until the latter's death in 1684. When the Edict of Nantes, a document of religious freedom, was revoked in 1685, Petitot, as a Protestant, was imprisoned. Worn out by fever and old age, he signed a recantation and was freed. In 1687 he was allowed to return to Geneva and was received back into the Reformed Church.

Although priority in the discovery of the art of painting enamel miniature portraits belongs to the Toutins, it was Petitot who raised the art to a level never surpassed. While relying primarily on original portraits by others, he was able to preserve to a remarkable degree the character of the work he was transforming into a small, jewel-like roundel. The most important collections of his works are in the Victoria and Albert Museum, London, and the Louvre, Paris. His style, much imitated in his own time, called into being a vast number of 18th- and 19th-century copies or imitations.

His son Jean Louis Petitot (1653–after 1699) painted portrait enamels in a style closely resembling that of his father.

petit point, form of canvas embroidery similar to gros point, or cross-stitch (*q.v.*), embroidery but even finer because of the small scale.

Petit point embroidered box, English, *c.* 1670; in the Royal Scottish Museum, Edinburgh

By courtesy of the Royal Scottish Museum, Edinburgh; photograph, Tom Scott

The squareness and regularity of the outlines of the forms represented is less apparent at ordinary viewing distance. The stitch used—also called petit point or tent stitch—is worked either in diagonal or horizontal rows across the intersection of the canvas threads. The thread is carried back from stitch to stitch in a uniform manner to ensure that the pull of the thread at the front is consistent.

Petit point was widely used in France in the 17th and early 18th centuries, particularly for pole screens and upholstery covering.

Petit porcelain, a French hard-paste porcelain produced by Jacob Petit (b. 1796). Petit worked at the porcelain factory at Sèvres as a painter. With his brother Mardochée he bought a porcelain factory in Fontainebleau in 1830, finally settling in Paris in 1863.

The wares he made were of a purely ornamental character; *e.g.*, vases, statuettes, clocks. The high-quality porcelain may have been fired in Limoges. The usual colours are pale pink, light green, mauve, black, and gold. The shapes are idiosyncratic interpretations of

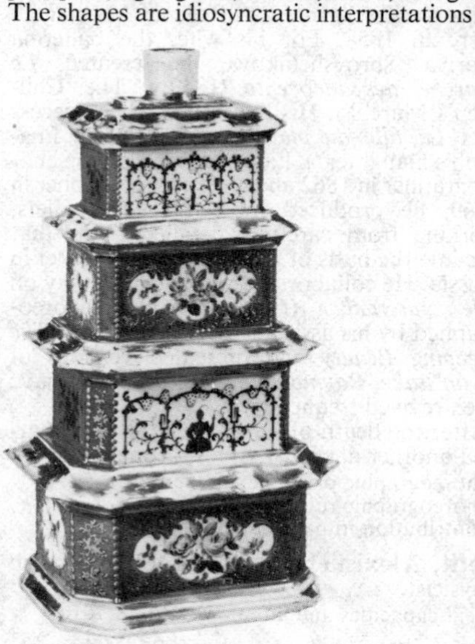

Petit porcelain tea jar from Jacob Petit's factory at Fontainebleau, Fr., *c.* 1840; in the Victoria and Albert Museum, London

By courtesy of the Victoria and Albert Museum, London

Louis XV-style porcelain (perhaps influenced by Capodimonte ware of the 18th century) typical of the taste of the Louis-Philippe period for the neo-Rococo. Impressed or in blue, the mark for Petit porcelain is JP.

Petit Prince, Le (1943), English translation THE LITTLE PRINCE (1943), fairy tale in the form of a mystical parable by the French author Antoine de Saint-Exupéry, drawn from his personal experiences as an aviator. The story centres on a pilot's encounter with a simple but wise young person in the African desert, and the tale embodies a profound understanding of the values important in human life. A musical play based on the story was filmed in 1974.

·work's audience and appeal **4**:241a

Petit-Saint-Bernard, Col du (France–Italy): *see* Little Saint Bernard Pass.

Petit Soldat, Le (1960), English title THE LITTLE SOLDIER, motion picture directed by Jean-Luc Godard.

·theme and message **8**:221g

Petit Testament, Le, also known as LE LAIS, English THE LEGACY, poem by François Villon.

·structure, style, and themes **19**:147c

Petit Théâtre, puppet theatre founded in Paris in the late 19th century by Henri Signoret.

·design and audience composition **15**:294g

Petlyura, Symon (b. May 17 [May 5, old style], 1879, Poltava, Russia, now in Ukrainian S.S.R.—d. May 25, 1926, Paris), non-Bolshevik Socialist leader of the Ukraine's unsuccessful fight for independence after the Russian Revolutions of 1917.

One of the founders of the Ukrainian Social-Democratic Workers' Party in 1905, Petlyura published the Socialist weekly newspapers *Slovo* (1905–09; "The Word") in Kiev and *Ukrainskaya Zhizn* (1912–14; "Ukrainian Life") in Moscow before the onset of World War I, when he became an officer in the Russian Army (1914). After the imperial government of Russia was overthrown by the February Revolution (1917), he joined the Ukrainian Central Rada ("council"), which proclaimed the Ukraine to be an autonomous republic (June 1917); and in July he was appointed minister of war of the newly formed government.

Soon thereafter, however, the Germans occupied the Ukraine, established a puppet government, and forced Petlyura and his colleagues into inactivity. When the Germans withdrew at the end of the war, he assumed a leading role in the Ukraine's movement for independence, heading the five-member directorate of the Rada, becoming *ataman* (commander in chief) of the Ukrainian Army, and seizing power from the Germans' puppet regime.

Petlyura's government then had to confront hostile Soviet Russian armies as well as forces of the anti-Bolshevik White Russians, both of which wanted the Ukraine to remain Russian territory. When the White armies, which had occupied the Ukraine and replaced Petlyura's government at the end of 1918, withdrew in the autumn of 1919, the Ukraine fell under Soviet authority.

To overthrow the Soviet regime, Petlyura concluded a treaty of alliance with Józef Piłsudski, head of the Polish state, in April 1920 and supported the Poles in their war against Soviet Russia (Russo-Polish War of 1919–20). Although the Poles repulsed the Soviet Army, they were unable to secure independence for the Ukraine when they concluded the Treaty of Riga with the Bolsheviks (March 18, 1921).

The Ukraine subsequently remained under Soviet control, and Petlyura, after spending some months in Warsaw, moved with his government to Paris, where, several years later, he was fatally shot by Shalom Shvartsbard, in revenge for the deaths of Jews during pogroms staged by members of Petlyura's army.

PETN, abbreviation of PENTAERYTHRITOL TETRANITRATE, a highly explosive organic compound belonging to the same chemical family as nitroglycerin; that is, the nitric acid esters of polyalcohols.

PETN was first prepared in 1891, but it was not introduced as an explosive until after World War I. It is used by itself in detonators and detonating fuses (Primacord) and in a mixture, called pentolite, with an equal amount of trinitrotoluene (TNT), developed during World War II, in grenades and projectiles.

PETN is a colourless, crystalline material that is generally stored and shipped as a mixture with water. It is less sensitive than nitroglycerin but is easily detonated. Valued for its shattering force and efficiency, PETN is the least stable of the common military explosives but retains its properties on storage for longer periods than nitroglycerin or cellulose nitrate (nitrocellulose) does.

PETN is also used in medicine as a heart stimulant.

·ignition primer and advantages **7**:87e

Peto, John Frederick (b. May 21, 1854, Philadelphia—d. Nov. 23, 1907, Island Heights, N.J.), still-life painter who, though influenced by the style and subject matter of the better known trompe l'oeil (fool-the-eye) still-life painter William Harnett, developed a distinctive mode of expression. Biographical information on Peto is meagre, and few of his works were signed or dated. He may have been a student at the Philadelphia Academy of Fine Arts. From 1879 to 1886 he con-

"Old Time Letter Rack," oil on canvas by John Frederick Peto, 1894; in the Museum of Modern Art, New York City

By courtesy of the Museum of Modern Art, New York, gift of Nelson A. Rockefeller

tributed irregularly to academy exhibitions. He knew Harnett, and possibly they were close friends. Peto and Harnett painted many of the same subjects—money, books, violins, and guns. A favourite subject of both, but particularly of Peto, was the letter rack in which a group of tapes tacked to a vertical surface held letters and other objects. Such pictures were done both early and late in Peto's career, the late ones, such as "Old Reminiscences" (Phillips Collection, Washington, D.C.), being stronger in abstract composition. Characteristically, Peto chose common, everyday objects as his subjects. He used colour in a soft, radiant way reminiscent of the 17th-century Dutch painter Jan Vermeer. Although he created illusionistic effects, he was much less interested in them than Harnett was; and he also had much greater interest than did Harnett in light and shade, which he often used dramatically.

From 1875 to 1889 Peto worked in Philadelphia and, from 1889 to his death, in the village of Island Heights. Most of his works date from the second period. Because he was unknown and away from the world of art, his works were often represented as Harnett's.

Petőfi, Sándor, pseudonym of ALEXANDER PETROVICS (b. Jan. 1, 1823, Kiskőrös, Hung.—d. July 31, 1849, Segesvár), one of the greatest Hungarian poets and a revolutionary who symbolizes to his countrymen their desire for freedom. Petőfi had an eventful youth; he studied at eight different schools, joined for a short time a group of strolling players, and enlisted as a private soldier, but because of ill health was soon dismissed from the army. He travelled extensively in Hungary, mostly on foot. As a schoolboy he displayed a keen interest in the stage and in literature, and his first poem was published in 1842. After years of vicissitudes, in 1844, on the recommendation of Mihály Vörösmarty, then the leading Hungarian poet, he became an assistant editor of the literary periodical *Pesti Divatlap*. His first volume of poetry, *Versek*, appeared in the same year and made him famous at once, though the tone of his poems scandalized many. In 1847 he married Julia Szendrey, who inspired his best love poems.

Petőfi played a leading role in the literary life of the period preceding the outbreak of the Hungarian Revolution of 1848. After 1847, together with Mór Jókai, he edited the magazine *Életképek*. A fervent partisan of the French Revolution, an admirer of Pierre-Jean de Béranger and Hégésippe Moreau, he castigated the social conditions of his country, attacking the privileges of the nobles and the monarchy. Politically he was an extreme radical, an inspired agitator, but he was lacking in experience and failed to obtain a seat in the Diet. His poems were glowing with political passion, and one of them, "Talpra magyar" ("Rise, Hungarian"), written on the eve of the revolution, became its anthem. During the revolution he became the aide-de-camp of Gen. Jozef Bem, then head of the Transylvanian army, who had great affection for the somewhat unsoldierly but enthusiastic poet. Petőfi disappeared during the Battle of Segesvár, July 31, 1849. People refused to believe in his death and for many decades hoped to see him return.

Petőfi's poetry brought about a revolution in Hungarian literature. Opposed to the fashionable literary conventions and mannerisms, he introduced a direct, unpretentious style and a clear, unornamented construction adapted from national folk songs. This simplicity was the more arresting as it was used to reveal subtle emotions and political or philosophical ideas. His poetry is characterized by realism, humour, and descriptive power and imbued with a peculiar vigour. Of his epic poems the *János vitéz* (1845), an entrancing fairy tale, is the most popular. Petőfi's popularity has never diminished in Hungary, and were it not for the barrier of language his name would probably take its place with those of Burns and Heine in world literature.

A critical edition of Petőfi's works by B. Varjas Béla was published in six volumes, 1948–56.

·Hungarian 19th-century literature **10**:1214e

Petoskey, resort city, seat (1853) of Emmet County, Michigan, U.S., on Little Traverse Bay of Lake Michigan. Settled in 1852 and named for the Ottawa chief Pet-o-sega, it was the site of an Indian mission and school. Originally a lumber town, it has turned to tourism and small manufacturing. Petoskey State Park is nearby, and the Petoskey Winter Sports Festival is an annual event. North Central Michigan Junior College (1958) is there. Inc. village, 1879; city, 1895. Pop. (1980) 6,097.

45°22′ N, 84°57′ W

·map, United States **18**:909

Petra, Arabic BAṬRĀ, an ancient city, centre of an Arab kingdom in Hellenistic and Roman times; its ruins are in Maʿān *muḥāfaẓah* (governorate), Jordan. The city was built on a terrace, pierced from east to west by the Wādī Mūsā (the Valley of Moses)—one of the places where, according to tradition, the Israelite leader Moses struck a rock and water gushed forth. The valley is enclosed by sandstone cliffs veined with shades of red and purple varying to pale yellow; and for this reason Petra is often called the "rose-red city."

The Nabataean rock-cut temple of al-Khaznah at Petra

Brian Brake—Rapho Guillumette

The Greek name Petra (Rock) probably replaced the biblical name Sela. The site is usually approached from the east by a narrow gorge known as the Sik (Wādī as-Sīk), one and a fourth miles long. Remains from the Paleolithic and the Neolithic periods have been discovered at Petra, but little is known about the site up to *c.* 312 BC, when the Nabataeans, an Arab tribe, occupied it and made it the capital of their kingdom. Under their rule, the city prospered as a centre of the spice trade.

When the Nabataeans were defeated by the Romans in AD 106, Petra became part of the Roman province of Arabia but continued to flourish until changing trade routes caused its gradual commercial decline. After the Islāmic invasion in the 7th century, it disappeared from history until it was finally rediscovered by the Swiss traveller John Lewis Burckhardt in 1812.

Excavations from 1958 onward on behalf of the British School of Archaeology in Jerusalem and the American School of Oriental Research have added considerably to knowledge of pre-Roman Petra. Al-Khaznah, one of the many rock-cut monuments, has an impressive columned facade and probably dates from the 2nd century AD. The most noteworthy features of Petra are the tombs, often with elaborate facades and now used as dwelling places.
·art of ancient Near East **19**:272d

Petracha (king of Siam): *see* Bedraja.

Petrachevsky circle, group of Russian Socialists who met secretly to read forbidden Socialist literature and to discuss political issues. Among the group were Mikhail Vasilyevich (Butashevich) Petrachevsky, the poet Aleksey Pleshcheyev, and the novelist Dostoyevsky. Arrested in 1849, they were sentenced to death but were reprieved and sentenced instead to exile or to military service.

Petrakis, Harry Mark (b. June 5, 1923, St. Louis, Mo.), novelist and short-story writer whose exuberant and sensitive works deal with the lives of Greek immigrants in urban America. Petrakis attended the University of Illinois in 1940–41 and in 1970 was McGuffey Visiting Lecturer at Ohio University. His novels and stories concern Greek-Americans and are usually set in Chicago. They include *Lion at My Heart* (1959); *The Odyssey of Kostas Volakis* (1963); *Pericles on 31st Street* (1965); *The Founder's Touch* (1965); *A Dream of Kings* (1966); *The Waves of Night* (1969); and *Stelmark* (1970). Though sometimes repetitious in characterization and somewhat sentimental, his fiction is warm and compassionate in its account of the immigrant's reaction to the urban world.

Petra Pervogo Khrebet (mountains, Tadzhik S.S.R.): *see* Peter I Range.

Petrarch 14:161, full name FRANCESCO PETRARCA (b. July 20, 1304, Arezzo, Italy—d. July 18/19, 1374, Arqua, near Padua), scholar, poet, and Humanist whose poems addressed to Laura, an idealized beloved, were the impulse for the Renaissance flowering of lyric poetry in Italy, France, Spain, and England.

Abstract of text biography. Petrarch's inquiring mind and love of classical authors led him to travel, visiting men of learning and searching monastic libraries for classical manuscripts. He was recognized as the greatest scholar of his age. He recognized in the past the nutriment of the present and asserted the continuity of classical culture and the Christian message. In doing so he paved the way for the attitudes of the Renaissance.

REFERENCES in other text articles:
·Boccaccio's friendship and career **2**:1173g *passim* to 1176b
·contribution to Italian literature **10**:1121d
·historiographic researches **8**:951h
·library history and function **10**:858b
·Renaissance classical revival **6**:887f
·Renaissance scholarship and literature **15**:660f
·translation and syllabic metre use **15**:71a

Petra Velikogo, Zaliv (inlet, Sea of Japan): *see* Peter the Great Bay.

Petre, Sir Edward (b. 1631, London—d. May 15, 1699, Watten, Flanders), Jesuit, favourite of King James II of Great Britain. Educated in France, he entered the Society of Jesus in 1652 and took orders in 1671, when he returned to England. In 1679 he succeeded to the family baronetcy and estates and was appointed vice provincial of the English Jesuits but was imprisoned for suspected complicity in the "Popish Plot" (an alleged conspiracy to massacre Protestants, murder the King, and burn London). Released in 1680 by the influence of James (then duke of York), he was later blamed for the King's more extreme policies. James made him clerk to the closet (1686) and a member of the Privy Council (1687). Late in 1688 Petre fled abroad.

Petre, engraving by an unknown artist

By courtesy of the trustees of the British Museum; photograph, J.R. Freeman & Co. Ltd.

petrel, name for a number of seabirds of the order Procellariiformes and particularly applied to certain members of the family Procellariidae; members of the Hydrobatidae are increasingly called storm petrels (*q.v.*); those of the Pelecanoididae are usually called diving petrels (*q.v.*).

Among the procellariid petrels, some two dozen species of the genera *Pterodroma* and *Bulweria* are called gadfly petrels because their flight is more fluttering than that of most typical shearwaters (*q.v.; Puffinus*). Certain heavy-bodied petrels are known as fulmars (*q.v.*; especially *Fulmarus*) and one, *Macronectes giganteus*, is called both giant fulmar and giant petrel.

Gadfly petrels nest in loose colonies on islands in the tropical and subtropical regions of the major oceans. A single egg (rarely two) is laid on the soil surface or in a burrow or crevice. The chick is tended by both parents and deserted about a week before it has its flight plumage; it completes its development on stored fat. During the nonbreeding season, these birds, like most other shearwaters, roam the open ocean, feeding on squid and small fish.

Most gadfly petrels are dark above and light beneath, with long wings and short, wedge-shaped tails, and are difficult to tell apart.

The following are some of the better known species.

Bermuda petrel: *see* cahow (below).

Black-capped petrel, or diablotin (*Pterodroma hasitata*): length 35–40 cm (14–15½ in.); breeds in interior mountains of Hispaniola; rare, long believed extinct but now known to number at least several thousand.

Bonin petrel (*P. hypoleuca*): 30 cm (11¾ in.); breeds on Leeward, Bonin, and Volcano Islands, in the tropical Pacific.

Cahow (*P. cahow;* sometimes considered a race of *P. hasitata*): 35 cm; breeds on a few islets off Bermuda; long thought extinct but population now believed to number several hundred individuals, still perilously low and endangered by DDT residues in their food.

Dark-rumped petrel (*P. phaeopygia*), also called Hawaiian petrel: 40 cm; breeds on the larger Hawaiian and Galápagos Islands.

Diablotin: see black-capped petrel, above; name also applied to certain species of *Puffinus*.

Phoenix petrel (*P. alba*): 32 cm (12½ in.); breeds on Marquesas, Tuamotu, Tonga, and several other tropical Pacific archipelagos.

Several other procellariids are also called petrels. Among them are the pintado petrel, or Cape pigeon (*Daption capensis*), a sub-Antarctic species about 40 cm long, marked with bold patches of black and white. The snow petrel (*Pagodroma nivea*), 35 cm, a pure white species, and the Antarctic petrel (*Thalassoica antarctica*), a 42 cm (16¼ in.) brown-and-white-pied species, are rarely seen outside Antarctic waters.
·defenses against predation **1**:299d
·migration and feeding behaviour **1**:959a
·traits, behaviour, and classification **15**:15d; illus. 17

Petrel, British sounding rocket; has payload of 30 pounds, reaches altitude of 95 miles.
·payload and altitude, table 5 **15**:941

Petri, Laurentius (1499–1573), Swedish churchman. He was appointed the first Protestant archbishop of Uppsala in 1531 and held this office until his death. His influence was very great, although he was less dynamic and forceful than his brother Olaus (*see:* Petri, Olaus). The Swedish Bible of 1541, for which he was principally responsible, was as important for Swedish life and literature as Luther's German translation was for the German-speaking peoples. His *kyrkoordning* (church order) of 1571 defined the practice of the church, particularly its relation to government, and went far toward establishing the independence of the church from the crown which has been characteristic of most of its history.
·literature of the Renaissance **10**:1144f

Petri, Olaus (b. 1493, Örebro, Swed.—d. 1552, Stockholm), churchman who, with his brother Laurentius, played a decisive role in the reformation of the Swedish church. He studied at Wittenberg (1516–18) and absorbed the reformed teaching of Luther and Melanchthon. When Gustavus Vasa was crowned king in 1523, Olaus had already attracted attention and criticism by his preaching. The Roman Catholic hierarchy were hostile to the king, who became a supporter of

the reformed teaching. Laurentius Andreae, secretary and later chancellor to the king, was a friend of Olaus Petri, who preached the coronation sermon. Olaus rose in prominence and served briefly as chancellor (1531). Later he opposed the autocratic policy of the king, and both he and Andreae fell from favour and were condemned to death in 1540, the sentence being remitted for a heavy fine. Later he regained favour and was appointed pastor of Storkyrkan church in Stockholm. Olaus provided most of the literature for the Swedish Reformation movement, including a Swedish New Testament, hymnbook, church manual, the Swedish liturgy, and many homiletical and polemical writings. His *Chronicle* is an important historical document.
·literature of the Renaissance **10**:1144f

Petrie, Sir (William Matthew) Flinders **14**:164 (b. June 3, 1853, Charlton, near Greenwich, London—d. July 28, 1942, Jerusalem), archaeologist and Egyptologist who made valuable contributions to the techniques and methods of field excavation and invented a sequence dating method for historical reconstruction.

Abstract of text biography. Petrie published *Inductive Metrology, or the Recovery of Ancient Measures from the Monuments* in 1877 and *Stonehenge: Plans, Description, and Theories* in 1880. In that year he began his many excavations in Egypt and Palestine with surveys and excavations of the Great Pyramid of Giza. He found fragments of a colossal statue of Ramses II during the excavation of the Temple of Tanis in 1884. He first applied his principle of sequence dating in Palestine in 1890. His suggestion that chronology could be established by potsherds was doubted by many of his contemporaries; it is now routine procedure. In 1892 he was appointed Edwards professor of Egyptology at University College, London, and in 1894 founded the Egyptian Research Account (later known as the British School of Archaeology). He published *Methods and Aims in Archaeology* in 1904 and *The Formation of the Alphabet* in 1912. He was knighted in 1923.

REFERENCES in other text articles:
·archaeological dating technique **1**:1081h
·archaeological development in Egypt **6**:462h

Petrified Forest National Park, in eastern Arizona, U.S., 18 mi (29 km) east of Holbrook. Established as a national monument in 1906 and as a national park in 1962, it occupies an area of 147 sq mi (381 sq km). There are extensive exhibits of petrified wood in several "forest" areas. The park includes the inaccessible Black Forest in the Painted Desert (*q.v.*), a badlands region of colourful wind-

Natural bridge in the Blue Mesa section of the Petrified Forest National Park, Ariz.
David Muench—EB Inc.

eroded hills near the north entrance, where Pilot Rock (6,235 ft [1,900 m]), the park's highest point, is located. Other sections (Blue Mesa, Jasper, Crystal, and Rainbow forests) are mostly filled with fossilized leaves, plants and broken logs. Other features include petroglyphs (such as Newspaper Rock) and ancient Indian Pueblo ruins, notably the Puerco Indian Ruin (just south of the Painted Desert) and the Rainbow Forest Museum near the south entrance.

The park's elevation ranges from 5,300 to Pilot Rock's 6,235 ft, and annual precipitation is less than 10 in. (250 mm), primary factors in determining the type of plant and animal life. Many of the plants are small and inconspicuous, but they include some that blossom in spring—yuccas, mariposa lilies, and cacti—and others that provide summer flowers—asters, rabbit brush, and sunflowers. Wildlife includes coyotes, bobcats, antelopes, rattlesnakes, lizards, and a variety of birds, notably the horned lark, rock wren, and phoebe.
·ancient conifer species **5**:7e

petrified wood, a fossil formed by mineral replacement of natural wood fibres, usually by silica (silicon dioxide, SiO_2). The petrified forests of the western United States are silicified wood, the tree tissues having been replaced by chalcedony (cryptocrystalline

Petrified wood from (top left) Coal City, Ill.; (top right) Holbrook, Ariz.; (bottom left) Clover Creek, Lincoln City, Idaho; (bottom right) Arizona
By courtesy of the Field Museum of Natural History, Chicago, and Joseph and Helen Guetterman collection; photograph, John H. Gerard—EB Inc.

quartz). Often this replacement is so accurate that the internal structure as well as the external shape is faithfully represented; sometimes even the cell structure may be determined.
·ancient theories **6**:76h

Petrine theory, the basis of Roman Catholic doctrine on papal primacy, resting partly on Christ's bestowing the "keys of the Kingdom" on Peter (the first pope, according to Catholic tradition), and partly on Christ's words: "And I tell you, you are Peter [Greek *Petros*], and on this rock [Greek *petra*] I will build my church" (Matt. 16:18).
·papal primacy theory and
development **13**:960d

petrochemicals, chemicals derived from a starting raw material obtained from petroleum and used for a variety of commercial purposes; they cover the whole range of aliphatic, aromatic, and naphthenic organic chemicals, as well as carbon black and such inorganic materials as sulfur and ammonia. Many of these same chemicals are also obtainable from other sources, such as coal, coke, and vegetable products.

The largest outlets for petrochemical raw materials are in the manufacture of plastics, man-made fibres, synthetic rubbers, detergents, nitrogen fertilizers, insecticides, and solvents. Such diverse industries as food processing and automobile, textile, and paint manufacturing use petrochemicals. In building construction they are used in protective and decorative coatings, flooring, adhesives, electrical equipment, tiles and fixtures, panels and laminations, piping, and moisture barriers. *Major ref.* **14**:180d
·automated processing with computers **2**:508b
·cracking's influence on development **18**:46c
·dye-making industry consumption **5**:1100c
·industrial environment hazards **9**:529a
·natural gas condensate distillation **12**:862d
·petroleum consumption needs and
trends **14**:165f
·Texas production in national
percentage **18**:167e

Petrodvorets, formerly PETERHOF, city, Leningrad *oblast*, northwestern Russian Soviet Federated Socialist Republic, on the shore of the Gulf of Finland, west of the city of Leningrad. The town grew up around the palace and gardens built for Peter I in 1721. The palace (designed by Alexandre Le Blond, enlarged by Bartolomeo Rastrelli in 1752) and its gardens, fountains, and pavilions were destroyed during World War II but have been restored. Pop. (1970) 43,136.
59°53′ N, 29°54′ E
·parks, architecture, and restoration **10**:802g

The Grand Cascade in the gardens of the restored imperial palace, Petrodvorets, Russian S.F.S.R.
Valerie J. Edessis—EB Inc.

Petr of Aspelt, 14th-century archbishop and adviser to John of Luxembourg, king of Bohemia.
·Bohemian monarchical decline **2**:1187d

Petrograd: *see* Leningrad.

Petrograd Soviet of Workers' and Soldiers' Deputies, unofficial governing body that was formed in Petrograd (now Leningrad) in the first days of the February Revolution in Russia (1917) and represented the city's factory workers and military regiments; dominated by Socialists, the Petrograd Soviet, which became increasingly radical, rivalled the authority of the Provisional Government until the October Revolution, when the Bolsheviks seized power and the soviets became the ruling organs in Russia.
·authority surrender to Provisional
Government and Lenin's use **10**:794g
passim to 795f
·call for insurrection **19**:958b
·founding, composition, and authority **16**:68a

petrographic microscope, instrument used to examine rocks in thin sections or crystal fragments emersed in oils; it is the principal tool of petrography and optical mineralogy. The petrographic microscope is distinguished from an ordinary microscope principally by the inclusion of special Nicol prisms of Iceland spar (optically satisfactory calcite) that permit the observer to view specimens in plane-polarized light (light vibrating in a single plane). This makes it possible to determine a large number of optical properties and, in effect, to identify minerals.
·mineralogy use **7**:1054f

petrography: *see* petrology, igneous and metamorphic.

Petroica multicolor (bird): *see* robin.

Petrokrepost, formerly SHLISSELBURG, town, Leningrad *oblast* (administrative region), northwestern Russian Soviet Federated Socialist Republic, at the effluence of the Neva River from Lake Ladoga, east of Leningrad city. Founded as Oreshek in 1323 by the Republic of Novgorod, it was captured in the early 17th century by the Swedes, who built the fortress of Noteburg. Taken by Peter I the Great in 1702, the town was renamed Shlisselburg and the fortress became important in the protection of St. Petersburg (now Leningrad). Renamed Petrokrepost in 1944, the town is a shipbuilding and repair centre on the White Sea–Baltic Waterway. Pop. (latest census) 7,100.
59°57′ N, 31°02′ E

petrol: *see* gasoline.

Petrolândia, town, south central Pernambuco state, northeastern Brazil, located on the left (east) bank of the São Francisco River, at the borders of Bahia, Pernambuco, and Alagoas states.

It was known as Jatobá until 1939 and as Itaparica from 1939 until 1943. Petrolândia is the western terminus of the railroad leading from Piranhas, in Alagoas, around the Cachoeira (falls) de Paulo Afonso. A hydroelectric plant and lignite (brown-coal) deposits are located near the town, which is also an agricultural centre. Highways from Recife, Maceió, Aracaju, and other coastal settlements converge upon Petrolândia. Pop. (1970) 4,181.
9°05′ S, 38°18′ W

petrolatum, also called PETROLEUM JELLY, translucent, yellowish to amber or white, unctuous substance having almost no odour or taste. It is derived from petroleum and is used principally as a protective dressing or ointment and as a substitute for fats in cosmetics and other ointments. It is also used in many types of polishes and in lubricating greases, rust preventives, and modelling clay.

Petrolatum is obtained by dewaxing heavy lubricating-oil stocks. It has a melting-point range from 38° to 54° C (100° to 130° F).

Chemically, petrolatum is a mixture of hydrocarbons, chiefly of the methane series.

petroleum 14:164, complex mixture of hydrocarbons that occurs in the Earth in liquid, gaseous, or solid forms. Petroleum is generally understood, however, as the liquid form, more properly called crude oil.

The text article covers the history of man's use of petroleum, its physical and chemical characteristics, its origins (including the organic source materials and creation of source beds), its migration and accumulation, and its world occurrence and distribution.

REFERENCES in other text articles:
·agricultural potentials and progress **1**:366a
·anaerobic bituminization **13**:536f
·animal-feed products 7:484a
·chemical synthesis model **4**:163b
·clay mineral industrial uses **4**:706e
·commodity trade importance **4**:997f
·conservation need and practice **5**:50d
·diesel engine fueling **5**:726h *passim* to 728c
·dye manufacturing processes and materials **5**:1099a
·element sources and origin problem **6**:708b
·energy source development **6**:854e
·formation from organic matter in shales **16**:634g
geographic regions of occurrence
·African distribution and barrel measure **1**:198f
·Arabian Desert oil discoveries **1**:1056d
·Asian reserves **2**:171g
·Atlantic oil field exploitation **2**:303c
·Australian deposits **2**:396h; illus.
·California production record **3**:617e
·Canadian estimated reserves in Alberta **1**:425f
·Egypt's production and interests **6**:453g
·European reserves **6**:1050c; illus. 1053
·India's coastal exploration **9**:291e
·Iran's production and reserves **9**:825c
·Louisiana location and development **11**:127g
·Mackenzie River area reserves **11**:267b
·Mashriq cultural effects of capital **11**:577g
·Montana resource discoveries and use **12**:399b
·North American fuel deposits **13**:193b; map 198
·North Sea discovery **3**:282a
·Northwest Passage's commercial significance **13**:257f
·Ohio's oil and gas resources **13**:519e
·Pacific areas of occurrence **13**:844a
·Persian Gulf reserves **14**:107f
·Red Sea's natural resource variety **15**:545e
·Saudi Arabian wealth effects **9**:150f
·Tunisian production and economic role **18**:747h
·U.S. resource areas and energy production **18**:931e *passim* to 933f
·Venezuelan deposits and importance **19**:64h
·hydrocarbon sources **9**:83h
·internal-combustion engine and 1900s refining development **18**:40g
·kerosine advantages as jet fuel **10**:159e
·lubricant's desirable properties **11**:170b
·marine research and geology **18**:844g
·natural gas use in oil production **12**:861h
·occurrence, prospecting, and extraction **14**:175h
·oceanic shipment costs **13**:501e
·paleogeography and marine origin of oil **13**:908f
·refining development and processes **14**:180d
·salt dome traps **6**:1133a
·sandstone economic importance **16**:216d
·sedimentary facies and oil deposits **16**:459b
·subsurface accumulation and flow **8**:438f; fig. 439
·thiol content nuisance factor **13**:708c
·urban pollutant concentration and effects **18**:1050c

RELATED ENTRIES in the *Ready Reference and Index: for*
components: see asphalt; bitumen; crude oil
occurrence: oil or gas field; petroleum dike; pitch lake; tar sands; trap, petroleum
scientific study: anticlinal theory; API gravity scale; flash point; formation factor; water, oilfield

petroleum and gas extraction 14:175, methods by which subterranean deposits of petroleum and natural gas are located and exploited and the means by which crude oil and gas are transported and stored.

The text article covers the nature and occurrence of petroleum; the history of petroleum production; and the methods used to locate petroleum and natural gas deposits, to drill and complete oil and gas wells, and to recover, transport, and store these fossil fuels.

REFERENCES in other text articles:
·Alagoas economy and resources **1**:408h
·Alaskan pipeline construction dispute **1**:410b
·Austrian resources and production **2**:444h
·borehole condensate recovery methods **12**:861h
·Caspian Sea location and removal **3**:982c
·Chinese pond gas collection **1**:903b
·clay mineral industrial uses **4**:706a
·conservation need and practice **5**:50d
·coral forms of economic value **5**:162f
·Drake's oil strike and importance **18**:40g
·Dubai underwater storage **18**:862h
·exploration for oil resources **7**:79h
·explosives in blasting oil wells **7**:85b
·Gulf of Mexico production **12**:78g
·isotopic tracing of oil rock formation **15**:454e
·Libya oil industry **10**:879h
·man as a physiographic agent **14**:431g
·materials-handling systems **11**:615g
·Mexican reserves and location **12**:72e
·natural gas distribution and storage **7**:923d
·North Sea's reserves and production **13**:249c; illus. 250
·oceanic production and deposits **13**:502g
·oil shale processing and uses **13**:535h
·rare-earth industrial uses **15**:525h
·rocket use in oil drilling **15**:942e
·Sahara desert resources **16**:150h; map 148
·sedimentary facies and oil and gas reserves **16**:459b
·Suez Canal traffic and pipelines **17**:767c
·telemetric pipeline control **18**:80a; illus.
·underground petroleum storage **18**:764b

RELATED ENTRIES in the *Ready Reference and Index:*
casing, well; derrick; drilling mud; offshore drilling; pipeline; well logging

petroleum dike, veinlike or dikelike deposit of solid petroleum compounds at the Earth's surface. Such deposits are thought to be fossil petroleum seepages from which the light gaseous and liquid compounds have been removed, leaving the solid residue.
·surface occurrences **14**:172e

Petroleum Exporting Countries, Organization of (OPEC), multinational body established to coordinate the petroleum policies of its members and to provide the member states with technical and economic aid. The organization was formally constituted in January 1961 by Iran, Iraq, Kuwait, Saudi Arabia, and Venezuela. Members admitted since OPEC was founded include Qatar (1961), Indonesia and Libya (1962), Abu Dhabi (1967; membership transferred to the United Arab Emirates in 1974), Algeria (1969), Nigeria (1971), Ecuador (1973), and Gabon (1975). The headquarters of OPEC, initially in Geneva, were moved to Vienna in 1965.

In 1964 the OPEC Economic Commission was created to assist the organization in establishing international petroleum prices. The OPEC Special Fund, created in 1976, provides financial assistance to developing nations that are not members of the organization.

petroleum geology: *see* economic geology.

petroleum jelly: *see* petrolatum.

petroleum nut, common name in the Philippines for the fruit of *Pittosporum resiniferum* (order Saxifragales).
·description and chemical composition **16**:294e

petroleum province: *see* oil or gas field.

petroleum refining 14:180, separation of crude oil into various components, purifying them, and blending them into useful products.

The text article covers the physical techniques of petroleum refining by separation of its component parts, the chemical refining methods that alter molecular structure, the purification processes, petroleum products and their uses, and refinery plants and facilities.

REFERENCES in other text articles:
·African resource development **1**:210d
·alkane reforming to aromatic compounds **9**:91a
·automobile fuelling requirements **2**:521a
·catalysis use in gasoline reforming **3**:1003f
·chemical industry interaction **4**:126a
·clay mineral industrial uses **4**:706e
·diesel fuel composition and rating **5**:728c
·emulsion principles and properties **4**:856d
·fluid properties and characteristics **16**:1052a
·fuel oil grades and steam generation **17**:628b
·gas product handling and uses **7**:924c
·Houdry process use of gas turbines **18**:775h
·industrial process instrumentation **9**:635c
·ion exchange and cracking catalysis **9**:803c
·kerosine advantages as jet fuel **10**:159e
·lubricant processing **11**:170b
·Mendeleyev's criticism of oil industry **11**:900f
·oil lamp development importance **10**:958a
·plastic materials from coal and oil **14**:517g
·platinum as gasoline-making catalyst **14**:530g
·Russian proportion of fuel production **16**:94e
·technological developments **18**:46c
·transition metal catalysts **18**:608e

RELATED ENTRIES in the *Ready Reference and Index: for*
products of refining: see fuel oil; gas oil; gasoline; kerosine; liquefied petroleum gas; microcrystalline wax; naphtha; paraffin; petrolatum; petroleum wax
other related entries: alkylation; cracking; petrochemicals; reforming; Standard Oil Company of Ohio; stripping

petroleum wax, any wax obtained from petroleum, including paraffin, microcrystalline wax, and petrolatum (petroleum jelly). Animal and vegetable waxes are generally higher in cost, of varying chemical constitution, and uncertain availability compared to the petroleum products. About 90 percent of the waxes used during the early 1970s were derived from petroleum. *See also* microcrystalline wax; paraffin; petrolatum.

Petrolina, city, southwestern Pernambuco state, northeastern Brazil. It lies on the left (north) bank of the São Francisco River, just across from Juàzeiro, in Bahia, with which it is linked by ferry and railroad bridge (completed in 1951). Petrolina is the southern terminus of a railroad running northwestward for approximately 100 mi (160 km) to Paulistana, in Piauí. The principal goods shipped from Petrolina are cotton, tobacco, and sugar. The city is also accessible by highway and by air. Pop. (1970 prelim.) 37,801.
9°24′ S, 40°30′ W
·map, Brazil **3**:124

petrology, experimental, study of rocks by means of laboratory synthesis. The goal of experimental petrology is to establish chemical and physical conditions under which all possible mineral assemblages can be obtained, thus allowing the petrologist to ascertain the conditions under which the rocks found in nature had been formed. When the limiting conditions for the existence of each mineral assemblage are established, the petrologist will be better able to decipher the thermal, depth, and chemical history of the Earth and its components.

Common rocks may be synthesized by placing proper proportions of the major chemical components together in a reaction vessel and promoting the reaction with heat or the presence of water or both. High experimental pressures can simulate inner Earth conditions; maximum pressure presently obtainable in the laboratory is 30 kilobars, which is equivalent to about a 90-kilometre (55-mile) depth in the Earth. Mineral assemblages that come to equilibrium at different temperatures will be different, and certain of the mineral products will have compositions that depend on the temperature. Changes in the pressures at the equilibrium point will also change the resulting mineralogy; in like manner, certain changes in chemical components and component amounts will produce alterations in final mineral compositions.
·Bowen's pioneering contributions **3**:85g
·origin as a science **6**:85g

petrology, igneous and metamorphic, scientific discipline that is concerned with all aspects of igneous rocks—those derived by the cooling and crystallization of silicate melts —and metamorphic rocks—those derived by the alteration of any pre-existing rock by changes in temperature and/or pressure. The goals of petrologic studies may include the description and classification of rocks, their occurrence and distribution, and their origins in terms of the physicochemical conditions of formation. Petrology includes the subdisciplines of experimental petrology, which is devoted to the study of silicate systems at high temperatures and pressures, and petrography, which is the study of rocks in thin section by means of a petrographic microscope (one that employs polarized light that vibrates in a single plane).

Field study is also an essential method of igneous and metamorphic petrology; careful mapping and sampling of rock units provides information on regional gradations of rock types and on rock associations that are unavailable by other means.
·Bowen's pioneering contributions **3**:85g
·Darwin's deformation theory of rocks **5**:493d
·early rock crystallization studies **9**:201b

Petromus typicus (rodent): *see* rock rat.

Petromyzonidae (aquatic animal): *see* lamprey.

Petronia petronia, species of rock sparrow, family Ploceidae, order Passeriformes, class Aves.
·population competitive exclusion **14**:837h

Petronius, Gaius, 1st-century Roman prefect of Egypt.
·Egyptian military occupation **15**:1110b

Petronius Arbiter 14:189, full name probably TITUS PETRONIUS NIGER (d. AD 66), reputed author of the *Satyricon*, a portrait of society of the 1st century, considered to be the first western European novel.

Abstract of text biography. Few facts are known about this close friend of the emperor Nero, who appointed him *arbiter elegantiae* ("director of elegance"). He incurred the enmity of Nero's guard, Tigellinus, who denounced Petronius as one of those implicated in a plot of 65 to assassinate the Emperor. In the hours leading up to Petronius' drawn out death by suicide, he spent the time chatting with friends and in other light diversions. In his will, instead of customary legacies, he detailed Nero's sexual perversions.

REFERENCE in other text article:
·novel development out of Roman prose **13**:277b

Petronius Maximus: *see* Maximus, Petronius.

Petropavlovsk, city and administrative centre of Severo-Kazakhstan *oblast* (region), Kazakh Soviet Socialist Republic, on the Ishim River in the centre of the Ishim Steppe region. The second oldest *oblast* centre in northern Kazakhstan after Pavlodar, it was founded as a Russian fort in 1752 and soon became an important centre of trade between Russia and Central Asia and the Kazakh steppes. The Trans-Siberian Railroad reached Petropavlovsk in 1896, and by 1917 the population was nearly 50,000. Petropavlovsk now has some notable industrial undertakings and accounts for nine-tenths of the industrial output of the *oblast*. It is also important as the junction of the Trans-Siberian and Trans-Kazakhstan railroads. The city has a theatre, a television station, and a teacher-training institute. Pop. (1970 prelim.) 173,000.
54°54′ N, 69°06′ E
·Kazakh S.S.R. settlement patterns **10**:408f
·map, Soviet Union **17**:322

Petropavlovsk-Kamchatsky, port and administrative centre of Kamchatka *oblast* (region), far eastern Russian Soviet Federated Socialist Republic, on the landlocked Avachinskaya Gulf on the Pacific coast of the Kamchatka Peninsula. The city was founded in 1740 during V.J. Bering's Second Kamchatka Expedition. In 1854, during the Crimean War, an Anglo-French attack on Petropavlovsk was repulsed. The modern city is a fishing centre and has fish-processing, canmaking, net-making, and ship-repairing industries. Pop. (1970 prelim.) 154,000.
53°01′ N, 158°39′ E

Petrópolis, city, north of the city of Rio de Janeiro, Brazil, in Rio de Janeiro state, situated in a valley at 2,667 ft (813 m) above sea level, in the Serra da Estrêla (or Serra dos Órgãos). The city was founded in 1845 by Bavarian immigrants under the sponsorship of Dom Pedro II, the Brazilian emperor for whom it was named. The Emperor was attracted by the site's relatively cool climate and held court there during the warmer months. His possessions, along with those of Dom Pedro I and João VI of Portugal, remain in the ornate royal palace, now the Museum of the Empire. Petrópolis served as the state capital from 1894 until 1903. A treaty with Bolivia was signed there in 1903 for an exchange of lands and a Brazilian commitment to construct the Madeira–Mamoré Railway.

The cathedral at Petrópolis, Braz.
Walter Aguiar—EB Inc.

The city has diversified industries and is the seat of the Catholic University of Petrópolis (1961). Rich farmlands are nearby. Pop. (1970prelim.) 116,080.
22°31′ S, 43°10′ W
·map, Brazil **3**:124

Petrópolis, Treaty of (1903), pact signed at Petrópolis, Braz., by which Bolivia sold Brazil the rubber-producing territory (now Acre) on their common border.
·Bolivian–Brazilian territorial settlement **3**:11e
·Brazilian acquisition of Acre territory **1**:58b

Petrosaurus mearnsi, species of banded rock lizard of the class Reptilia.
·body size and egg size **15**:728d

Petroşeni, town, Hunedoara district (*judeţ*), west central Romania. Founded in the 17th century, it is the principal town of the upper Jiu Valley coalfield (output in the late 1960s, 5,000,000–6,000,000 tons of low-grade bituminous coal annually). It is the administrative headquarters for a group of nearby mining centres, including Lupeni, Petrila, and Vulcan, and the new town of Uricani at the foot of Mount Retezat. Petroşeni manufactures coal byproducts and is the site of a state mining institute. It is also the cultural centre for the coalfield area, having a state theatre and a school of fine arts. Pop. (1970 est.) city, 39,706; municipal area, 141,338.
45°25′ N, 23°22′ E
·map, Romania **15**:1048

Petrosyan, Tigran Vartanovich (b. June 17, 1929, Tbilisi, Georgian S.S.R.), chess master, won the world championship from Mikhail Botvinnik in 1963, defended it successfully against Boris Spassky in 1966, and was defeated by Spassky in 1969. Petrosyan's play, subtle and tirelessly patient, was designed to weaken an opponent's position gradually rather than to crush it at a single blow. Against masters of comparable strength he played a great many drawn games.

He was educated at Yerevan Teachers' College in the Armenian S.S.R. and continued postgraduate study in philosophy there after becoming world chess champion.

petrous bone, a portion of the temporal bone that is extremely hard and that encloses the inner ear.
·labyrinth of internal ear **16**:814g
·structure and function in human ear **5**:1132g

Petrov, Vladimir Mikhaylovich and Yevdokiya Alekseyevna (respectively b. Feb. 15, 1907, Larikha, Siberia; b. 1914, Lipki, Russ.), staff officers of the Soviet embassy in Canberra, applied for political asylum in Australia in April 1954 and supplied documents exposing Soviet espionage in that country. Petrov (whose original name was Afanasy Mikhaylovich Shorokhov) and his wife had been in Canberra for three years when, fearing punishment as a supposed adherent of the Beria faction, Petrov defected. Mrs. Petrov, while being forcibly escorted back to the Soviet Union, was freed by Australian police during an airplane stop at Darwin. The Soviet Union immediately broke off diplomatic relations with Australia. The Petrovs later testified before a royal commission appointed to investigate Soviet espionage. In 1956 they became citizens of Australia and published a joint autobiography, *Empire of Fear* (1956).

Petrov, Yevgeny (Petrovich), pseudonym of YEVGENY PETROVICH KATAYEV (b. Dec. 13 [Nov. 30, old style], 1903, Odessa, Ukraine—d. July 2, 1942, Sevastopol), Soviet satirist and humorist best known for his collaboration with Ilya Ilf (*q.v.*).

Brought up in Odessa, Petrov became associated with the southern school of writers. He met Ilf while working on the staff of the humorous periodical *Train Whistle* in Moscow. The two soon formed a literary partnership, and for the party newspaper *Pravda* they produced a number of satiric short stories. Perhaps their best known works are the humorous adventure novels *Dvenadtsat stulyev* (1928; *The Twelve Chairs*, 1961) and *Zolotoy telyonok* (1931; *The Little Golden Calf*, 1962).

Ilf and Petrov travelled to the United States in 1936, gathering material for a satirical novel, *Odnoetazhnaya Amerika* (1936; "One-Storyed America"). Shortly after their return, Ilf fell ill and died. Petrov continued to edit humorous magazines. During World War II he was a correspondent at the front and was killed during the defense of Sevastopol.

Petrović, Petar: *see* Peter II.

Petrovics, Alexander: *see* Petőfi, Sándor.

Petrozavodsk, capital of the Karelian Autonomous Soviet Socialist Republic, in the northwestern Russian Soviet Federated Socialist Republic, lies on the western shore of Lake Onega, south of the Shuya River outflow. The city was founded in 1703 by Peter the Great as an ironworks to supply ordnance to his new capital, St. Petersburg. Its modern industries include engineering and timber working. The many scientific and educational establishments include a university, a teacher-training institute, and a branch of the Academy of Sciences of the U.S.S.R. Pop. (1976 est.) 216,000.
61°47′ N, 34°20′ E
·map, Soviet Union **17**:322

Petrucci, Ottaviano dei (b. 1466, Fossombrone, near Ancona, Italy—d. 1539, Venice), music printer whose collection of chansons, *Harmonice Musices Odhecaton A* (1501), was the first polyphonic music printed from movable type. Petrucci went to Venice in 1490, holding music printing monopolies there from 1498 to 1511 and later at Fossombrone. In 1536, at the request of the Venetian Senate, he returned to Venice. His 61 music publications contain masses, motets, chansons, and *frottole* by the foremost composers of the 15th and early 16th centuries, among them Josquin des Prez, Jean d'Okeghem, and Loyset Compère. He also published the first book of printed lute music, Francesco Spinaccino's *Intabolatura de lauto* (1507).

Petrucci, Pandolfo (b. *c.* 1452, Siena, Italy—d. May 21, 1512, San Quirico), merchant and politician who succeeded in gaining supreme power over Siena. Although an absolute and tyrannical ruler, he greatly augmented the artistic splendour of his native city.

Exiled from Siena as a partisan of the Nove faction, Petrucci returned in 1487 and took advantage of the struggles among political factions. Having married Aurella Borghese, daughter of one of the most powerful men in the city, Petrucci entered public office, acquiring so much authority and wealth that he became the despot of Siena with the title of *signore* (lord). Petrucci's ambition, however, alienated even Niccolò Borghese, whom Petrucci later assassinated (July 1500).

As head of state, Petrucci consolidated his power by surrounding himself with supporters whose loyalty was guaranteed by the income they received from certain public lands. Yet the authoritarian and arbitrary Petrucci stopped the sale of public offices, secured economic advantages for the city, reformed the monetary system, and protected arts and letters.

Involved in the political struggle between France and Spain on the Italian peninsula, Petrucci was implicated in a plot against the powerful Cesare Borgia. He fled from Siena in January 1503 but was returned in March through the intervention of Louis XII of France. After the death of Cesare in 1507, Petrucci became more powerful than ever. By secret accords he allied himself with the Spanish and Pope Julius II against the French shortly before his death.
·power seizure and dictatorship **16**:733g

Petrus Aureoli, also PETRUS AUREOLUS, English PETER AUREOL, French PIERRE AURIOL, ORIOL, or D'ORIOL (b. *c.* 1280, near Gourdon, Fr.—d. 1322, Avignon/Aix), churchman, philosopher, and critical thinker, called *Doctor facundus* ("eloquent teacher"), important as a forerunner to William of Ockham. Petrus may have become a Franciscan at Gourdon before 1300; he was in Paris (1304) to study, possibly under John Duns Scotus. He became lector at Bologna (1312), Toulouse (1314–15), and Paris (1316–18). Provincial of his order for Aquitaine *c.* 1320, he was nominated archbishop of Aix-en-Provence and consecrated in 1321 by Pope John XXII, to whom he had dedicated *c.* 1316 his *Commentariorum in primum librum Sententiarum* (2 vol., 1596–1605; "Commentary on the First Book of Sentences").

Criticizing Duns Scotus and St. Thomas Aquinas' theory of knowledge, Petrus promoted an individualistic empiricism (*i.e.*, the attitude of the mind that emphasizes the part played by experience in knowledge against that played by reasoning), supported by a doctrine of universals, or general words that can be applied to more than one particular thing; this doctrine is partly Nominalistic (denying the absolute reality of universal essences) and partly conceptualistic (acknowledging universals as existing only in the mind). According to Petrus, knowledge is appearance of objects: man knows what exists by direct impressions, more or less clearly, but without intermediaries; forms, essences, and universals are fictions. Although some of his philosophical theories are individual, he generally conforms to the dictum subsequently known as "Ockham's razor"—*i.e.*, that entities are not to be multiplied beyond necessity. Essentially, Petrus anticipated the conceptualism that Ockham developed more fully.

Petrus' works include *Tractatus de paupertate* (1311; "Treatise on Poverty"), the unfinished *Tractatus de principiis naturae* (4 vol.; "Treatise on the Principles of Nature"), and *Tractatus de conceptione beatae Mariae Virginis* (1314/15; "Treatise on the Conception of the Blessed Mary the Virgin"). In 1319 he wrote his popular *Compendium . . . totius Scripturae* ("Compendium . . . of the Whole Scripture").

Petrus wrote two versions of the commentary on the *Sentences*; E.M. Buytaert's critical edition (2 vol.) of the first version appeared in 1952–56.

Petrus de Vinea: *see* Pietro della Vigna.

Petrushka, Russian puppet character similar to the western European Punch (*q.v.*).

Petrushka, ballet in four acts with music by Igor Stravinsky. The original production had scenery and costumes designed by Alexandre Benois and choreography by Michel Fokine. The story is based on the traditional Slavic legend of the puppet Petrushka, the eternal clown who acts and dances in satirical comedies. The ballet was first performed by Sergey Diaghilev's Ballets Russes at the Théâtre du Châtelet, Paris, on June 13, 1911, and was revised by Stravinsky in 1947.
·choreography and music **12**:696d
·Diaghilev's artistic influence **5**:683f
·Stravinsky's score **17**:729g

Pétrus Ky, also known as TRUONG VINH KY and JEAN-BAPTISTE PÉTRUS (b. Dec. 6, 1837, Vinh Long province, Vietnam—d. 1898), Vietnamese scholar whose literary works served as a bridge between his civilization and that of the West. He helped popularize the romanized script of the Vietnamese language, Quocngu.

Pétrus Ky was born into a Roman Catholic family, and in 1848 he attended a mission college in Cambodia; three years later he studied at the Catholic college in Penang (now Pinang, Malaysia), established by French missionaries, and decided to enter the priesthood. Having studied French, Latin, and Greek, Pétrus Ky was designated by the missionaries as their most competent interpreter, and so his future was redirected. In 1863 he went with the statesman Phan Thanh Gian as an interpreter on a diplomatic mission to France. Pétrus Ky saw the great cultural differences between the Vietnamese and the French, and he stayed in Europe until 1865, visiting England, Spain, Italy, and Egypt, while compiling a Vietnamese–French dictionary.

In 1867–74 Pétrus Ky taught Oriental languages in Saigon and wrote prolifically in the French-sponsored Vietnamese language newspaper *Gia-Dinh Bao*. In 1876 he visited northern Vietnam (Tonkin in French usage) and prepared a confidential report on political conditions there, urging a French advance into this still uncolonized region. In 1886 Gov. Gen. Paul Bert designated Pétrus Ky as the teacher of French to the emperor Dong Kanh at the court of Hue.

Pétrus Ky assumed responsibility for translating not only the French language but also Western attitudes and philosophies for the Vietnamese. He was a prolific writer on many diverse subjects; among his publications are *Thanh suy bi tho'i phu* (1883; "Whims of Destiny"), *Phong hoa dieu hanh* (1885; "Morals and Deeds"), *Grammaire de la langue annamite* (1867; "Grammar of the Vietnamese Language"), *Petit cours de géographie de la Basse-Cochinchine* (1875; "Handbook of the Geography of Lower Cochinchina"), *Cours d'histoire annamite* (1875–77; "Course of Vietnamese History"), and *Histoire d'Annam* ("History of Vietnam"), the first significant history of Vietnam written in a European language and following European historiographic models.

Petrus Lombardus: *see* Peter Lombard.

Petsuchos (Egyptian sacred crocodile): *see in* Sebek.

Pettazzoni, Raffaele (b. Feb. 3, 1883, Persiceto, Italy—d. Dec. 8, 1959, Rome), historian of religions, a founder and president (1950–59) of the International Association for the History of Religions. His original comparative method is shown in many works, among them his studies *La confessione dei peccati* (3 vol., 1929–35; "The Confession of Sins")

and *L'essere supremo nelle religioni primitive* (1957; "The Supreme Being in Primitive Religions").
·divinized sky in monotheism development **15**:626e
·mythological creation tale significance **12**:799h

Pettengill, Gordon (1926–), U.S. astronomer.
·Mercury rotation study with radar **11**:918g

Petterman Glacier, glacier in Greenland, the largest in the Northern Hemisphere. 81°00′ N, 62°00′ W
·size, location, and iceberg production **9**:155c

Petterssen, Sverre (b. Feb. 19, 1898, Hadsel, Nor.—d. Dec. 31, 1974, London), meteorologist who specialized in both dynamic meteorology, concerned with atmospheric motions and the forces creating them, and synoptic meteorology, which uses charts and weather observations for the identification, study, and forecasting of weather.

Petterssen was a meteorologist with the Norwegian Meteorological Service (1924–31), advancing to regional director (1931–39). He went to the Massachusetts Institute of Technology, Cambridge, in 1939, becoming professor and chairman of the meteorology department (1940–42) and writing *Weather Analysis and Forecasting* (1940) and *Introduction to Meteorology* (1941). He served with the British Air Ministry during World War II and then returned to the Norwegian Meteorological Institute, Oslo. Back in the United States, he joined the weather service of the Air Force (1948–52) and became professor of meteorology at the University of Chicago (1952–63), chairman of meteorology (1959–61), and chairman of geophysical science (1961–63). He was co-author, with W.C. Jacobs and B.C. Haynes, of *Meteorology of the Arctic* (1956).

petticoat, in modern usage, an underskirt worn by women. The term petycote (probably derived from the Old French *petite cote*, "little coat") appeared in literature from the 15th century in reference to a kind of padded waistcoat, or undercoat, worn for warmth over the shirt by men. The petticoat developed as a piece of woman's apparel—a skirt worn under an overgown—at the end of the Middle Ages. By the beginning of the 16th century, the overgown had an inverted V opening, and the petticoat, now visible, was brocaded or embroidered. In the 17th century, the outer skirt was looped up prominently, showing the petticoat underneath. In the early 19th century, women wore many petticoats, bound together, to show the great fullness of the skirt. By the 1850s, however, these voluminous petticoats had been abandoned for the more comfortable crinoline (*q.v.*). Around 1900, when skirts became less full, the petticoat was visible only when a woman lifted her dress—as when crossing the street. Thereafter, petticoats became increasingly unimportant as part of a woman's visible attire.

Woman being helped on with her petticoat, detail of "Choristoa," oil painting by José Gutierrez Solana; in the Museo de Arte Moderno, Barcelona
Archivo Mas, Barcelona

Pettijohn, Francis John (b. June 20, 1904, Waterford, Wis.), geologist known for his fundamental synthesis of knowledge of sedimentary rocks.

Pettijohn was a member of the faculty of the University of Chicago from 1929 until 1952, when he became professor at Johns Hopkins University, Baltimore, where he served as chairman of the geology department (1963–68). He was also a member of the U.S. Geological Survey (1943–53) and a consultant for the Shell Development Company (1953–63). His work includes research on the environments of deposition of Precambrian sedimentary rocks (those older than 570,000,000 years), the resistance to weathering of common rock-forming minerals, and the discovery of Precambrian glacial sediments in Michigan. He wrote *Manual of Sedimentary Petrography* with William C. Krumbein (1938), *Sedimentary Rocks* (1949), and, with P.E. Potter, *Paleocurrents and Basin Analysis* (1963) and *Atlas and Glossary of Primary Sedimentary Structures* (1964).

Pettit, Bob, full name ROBERT E. LEE PETTIT (b. Dec. 2, 1932, Baton Rouge, La.), professional basketball player, first to score 20,000 points in the National Basketball Association (NBA). A graceful 6-foot 9-inch athlete, he was considered to be the first really agile player of extraordinary height in professional basketball.

After graduation from Louisiana State University, Baton Rouge, Pettit played NBA ball for 11 seasons (1954–65) with the Hawks, a team representing Milwaukee, Wis., during the 1954–55 season and St. Louis, Mo., afterward. In each season but his last, he led the Hawks in scoring and rebounding. Twice (1955–56 and 1958–59) he was the NBA scoring champion. On Nov. 22, 1961, he set an NBA single-game record by scoring 19 free throws without missing. In 792 NBA regular season games, Pettit scored 20,880 points (average 26.4 points a game) and captured 12,851 rebounds. For 88 championship playoff games his totals were 2,240 points (25.5 average) and 1,304 rebounds.

Pettit, Edison (1890–1962), U.S. astronomer.
·infrared astronomy development **9**:581c

Pettitot, Jean, 17th-century craftsman in enamel.
·enamelwork tradition of the Renaissance **6**:777c

Petty, Sir William (b. May 26, 1623, Romsey, Hampshire—d. Dec. 16, 1687, London), political economist and statistician whose main contribution to political economy, *Treatise of Taxes and Contributions* (1662), considered the role of the state in the economy and touched on the labour theory of value. As a young man, Petty abandoned a life at sea to take up the study of medicine at the universities of Leiden, Paris, and Oxford. He was successively a physician, professor of anatomy at Oxford, professor of music in London, inventor, surveyor, and landowner in Ireland, and member of Parliament.

A protagonist of the empirical scientific doctrines of the newly established Royal Society, of which he was a founder, Petty was one of the originators of political arithmetic, which he defined as the art of reasoning by figures upon things relating to government. His *Essays in Political Arithmetick and Political Survey or Anatomy of Ireland* (1672) presented population estimates and rough calculations of social income. His ideas on monetary theory and policy were developed in *Verbum Sapienti* (1665) and in *Quantulumcunque Concerning Money, 1682* (1695).

Petty, detail of a portrait attributed to Isaac Fuller, *c.* 1649–51; in the National Portrait Gallery, London
By courtesy of the National Portrait Gallery, London

His most significant work, however, is his *Treatise on Taxes*. Petty favoured giving free rein to the natural forces of individual self-interest. Unlike liberals after Adam Smith, however, Petty considered the maintenance of a high level of employment by monetary and fiscal policies and by public works to be a duty of the state. In the *Treatise*, he also argued that the labour necessary for production was the main determinant of exchange value.
·dyestuff and dyeing chemistry **5**:1106d
·health statistics history **8**:695h
·vocational education ideas **6**:351e

Petty-Fitzmaurice, Henry Charles Keith, 5th marquess of Lansdowne: *see* Lansdowne, Henry Charles Keith Petty-Fitzmaurice, 5th marquess of.

petty morrel (plant): *see* spikenard.

petty officer, in some navies, an enlisted rate corresponding to that of a noncommissioned officer in the army—*i.e.*, a corporal or higher. In the United States Navy a petty officer third class is the lowest noncommissioned rate, followed by petty officer second class, petty officer first class, and chief petty officer, with occasionally one or two higher rates (such as senior chief petty officer).

Pétursson, Hallgrímur (b. 1614, Hólar, Ice.—d. 1674, Ferstikla), Lutheran pastor and greatest religious poet of Iceland. Though he came from a good family, he lived an errant life; as a boy he ran away to Copenhagen and became a blacksmith's apprentice. Through the influence of Bishop Brynjólfur Sveinsson he was later enrolled in the Danish Frúar Skóli (Our Lady's School), where he was exposed to a Latin Humanist education. In 1636 he was entrusted with the re-Christianizing of a party of Icelanders who had been held captive by Algerian pirates for nine years. Among them was a 38-year-old woman, Gudridur Símonardóttir, who bore a child by Hallgrímur and later married him. Returning to Iceland, Hallgrímur worked for a time as a labourer and a fisherman but eventually became a parson at Saurbær (1651–69). In an age marked by poverty, famine, sickness, misgovernment, and crushing taxation in Iceland, he contracted leprosy and out of this misery produced his *Passiusálmar* ("Hymns on the Passion"), which ranks among the best religious poetry of the world. The first hymn

begins with the Agony in the Garden, the 50th closes with the guards posted at Christ's tomb. In each hymn the poet merges his personal suffering with that of Christ. The effect of the Passion Hymns in bolstering the morale of a desperate people was attested to by their immediate widespread popularity. First printed in 1666 and for the 64th time in 1957, they remain the most cherished devotional songs of the Icelanders. They are still sung in homes and recited over the radio during Lent, and one is the traditional dirge for funerals. The Hallgrimskirkja, a memorial church built in the poet's honour at Saurbær, is one of the largest and finest churches in Iceland.
·Icelandic literature development **10**:1161f

Petworth, small market town, county of West Sussex, England, adjoining the great park of Petworth House (owned by the National Trust, a British conservation group). The associated manor house, largely rebuilt 1688–96 by Charles Seymour, the 6th duke of Somerset, contains a noted English picture and wood-carving collection. Pop. (1971) 2,455.
50°59′ N, 0°38′ W

Petzholdt, Julius (1812–91), librarian of the Royal Library, Dresden, Germany.
·bibliographic guide compilation **2**:979e

petzite, silver gold telluride, a mineral.
·sulfide mineral ore association **17**:787h

Petzolt, Hans, 17th-century German craftsman.
·Diana Cup illus. **11**:1106

Petzval, Józeph Miksa (1807–1891), Hungarian mathematician.
·lens aberration studies **13**:615d

Peuerbach (PURBACH), **Georg von** (1423–61), Austrian mathematician and astronomer who is credited with early use of the sines in trigonometry in the West; compiled a table of sines.
·history of calculatory device and table **11**:650a

Peugeot, French automobile company manufacturing small sedans; named for Armand Peugeot, late-19th-century French automobile pioneer, who began making cars with the Daimler engine in 1890.
·auto industry growth in Europe **2**:530a

Peul language: *see* Fulani language.

Peutinger Table, copy of a Roman map, made in 1265 by a monk of Colmar (Alsace) on 12 sheets of parchment. Eleven sheets are now in the Nationalbibliothek in Vienna. The dimensions are 268 by 13⅓ inches (6.82 by 0.34 metres). The copy was found by Conradus Celtis in 1494 and bequeathed by him to his friend Konrad Peutinger (1465–1547) of Augsburg.

The shape of the map, an elongated rectangle, causes a grave deformation of the Roman world, the distances from north to south being compressed and those from east to west being unduly extended. The map is in six colours—black, red, green, yellow, blue, and rose. Opinions have differed as to how closely the lost original depended on Roman itineraries and world maps. The table goes beyond the frontiers of the Roman Empire to the east. *See also* itinerarium.

Pevensey, village, county of East Sussex, southeastern England. Once an English Channel port, it now lies a mile inland; from the 13th century on, silting-up brought about its economic decline, and it ceased to be a borough in 1833. The remains of the walls and towers of the Roman Anderida (*c.* 250), a fort, rank among the best extant examples of Roman building in England. After the Norman Conquest (1066) another castle was built within the Roman walls. The gatehouse, towers, and inner courtyard walls were added in the 13th century. Latest census 2,151.
50°49′ N, 0°20′ E

Ruins of Pevensey Castle, in East Sussex
A.F. Kersting

Pevsner, Antoine (b. Jan. 18, 1886, Orël, Russia—d. April 12, 1962, Paris), sculptor and painter who—like his brother, Naum Gabo—advanced the constructivist style, which employs such materials as metal, glass, and wire and eschews mass in favour of space intervals and a sense of movement.

Pevsner studied art in Kiev, went to Paris in 1911 and 1913, and in 1915 joined his brother Naum in Oslo, where they experimented in art that would be "capable of utilizing emptiness and liberating us from the compact mass." The brothers returned to Russia after the Revolution, and Pevsner became a professor at Moscow's school of fine arts. They soon saw experimentation in art give way to political manipulation. In 1920 they issued a "realist manifesto" of constructivism, championing their form of art, which they exhibited that year, and the artist's right to seek reality and truth autonomously. Pevsner became an émigré after he was sent to Berlin with the first Russian art exhibition (1922). A naturalized Frenchman by 1930, he was cofounder and later honorary president of the Réalités Nouvelles group of exhibiting artists.

Synthesizing plastic arts, painting, sculpture, and architecture, Pevsner's work is characterized by precision and spatial intervals.

pew, originally used to describe a raised and enclosed place in a church designed for an ecclesiastical dignitary or officer but later extended to include special seating in the body of the church for distinguished laity and, finally, to include all church seating. In its early stages, the pew was meant for standing in and was close in conception to a pulpit; but in its second phase of development, it became an elaborate wooden structure, shut off from the main body of the nave, with seats, praying benches, and other accessories. Such pews were owned by individuals or institutions and appeared both in wills and in legal actions. In its final and more generalized context, a pew consisted of a long, backed, oak or pine bench with a fixed kneeling board. The upright ends were squared off or terminated in a finial or other carved ornament.

pewee, also spelled PEEWEE, any of eight species of birds of the genus *Contopus* (family Tyrannidae, order Passeriformes), is named for its call, which is monotonously repeated from an open perch. In North America a sad, clear "pee-oo-wee" announces the presence of the eastern wood pewee (*C. virens*), a blurry "peeurrr," the western wood pewee (*C. sordidulus*). Some authorities consider the western form to be a race of *C. virens*. Both forms are plain birds, about 14 centimetres (6 inches) long, that resemble the eastern phoebe; the two forms differ from the eastern phoebe, however, in being browner and more slender and in having two distinct whitish wing bars.

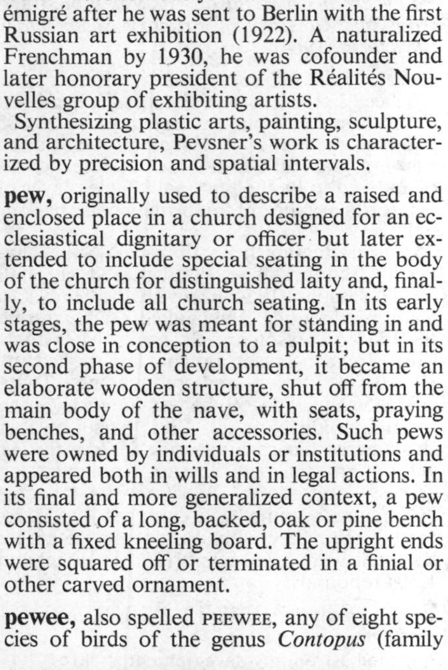
Eastern wood pewee (*Contopus virens*)
Thase Daniel

Wood pewees winter chiefly in northern South America. Other pewees are found in Central and South America.

pewter, tin-based alloy first used nearly 2,000 years ago by the ancient Orientals and Romans. Old pewter has a dark satin sheen; the surface is darkened with age because of its lead content.

Modern pewter is tin hardened with antimony and copper. The best grades have no lead. The surface may have a crisp, bright finish or a soft, satin sheen. Modern pewter resists tarnish, retaining its colour and finish indefinitely.
·furniture decoration use **7**:782h
·history, production, and use **18**:431c; table
·history techniques and products **11**:1107e; illus.
·metalwork of 16th-century Germany, illus., **11**:Metalwork, Plate IV

Peyer's patches, nodes of lymphatic cells that aggregate together to become bundles or patches and occur usually only in the lowest portion (ileum) of the small intestine, named for the 17th-century Swiss anatomist Hans Conrad Peyer.

Peyer's patches are round or oval, varying from 0.3 to 0.8 inch (8 to 20 millimetres) in length, and are located in the mucous membrane lining of the intestine opposite the point at which the mesentery (a membrane supporting the intestines) is attached to the external wall surface. They can be seen by the naked eye as elongated thickened areas, and their surface is free of the usual projections (villi) or depressions (crypts of Lieberkühn).

Usually there are only 30 to 40 patches in each individual. In young adults, however, they may be more numerous, and as an individual ages they tend to become less prominent. The function of the Peyer's patches is to collect and transport fat that has been absorbed by the intestinal wall and emulsified into a milky fluid, which is called chyle. The chyle is transported from the lymph nodes to the main lymphatic vessels, which are situated in deeper tissue layers. In typhoid fever, these patches may become sites of inflammation, in which case they may develop into ulcerations, hemorrhages, or perforations.
·human digestive system anatomy **5**:794d
·intestinal lymphatics and lymph nodules **11**:210d

peyote, two species of the cactus genus *Lophophora*, family Cactaceae, native to North America.

Peyote, well-known for its hallucinogenic effects, has at least 28 alkaloids, the principal one of which is mescaline (*q.v.*). Peyote figures prominently in old religious rituals of certain Indian tribes. As dried "mescal buttons" or as live plants from dealers, its sale, use, or possession is now prohibited by law in some places.

It is found only on limestone soils of the Chihuahuan Desert of southern Texas, in the United States, and northern Mexico.

Averaging about eight centimetres (three inches) wide and five centimetres (two inches) tall, the body of the peyote cactus is soft and frequently blue green.

The more common species, *L. williamsii*, has pink to white flowers in summer, the fruit ripening the following year. *L. diffusa*, more

Peyote (*Lophophora williamsii*)

Dennis E. Anderson

primitive, grows in a small area in the state of Querétaro, Mexico. Its flowers are white to yellow, and the body is not bluish.

·drug use, experiences, and active principle **5**:1048g
·hallucinogenic and sacramental uses **8**:558g
·religious use in Mexico **14**:200d

peyotism, officially NATIVE AMERICAN CHURCH, the most widespread indigenous religious movement among North American Indians and one of the most influential forms of Pan-Indianism. The term peyote derives from the Nahuatl name *peyotl* for a cactus. The tops of the plants contain mescaline, an alkaloid drug that has hallucinogenic effects. It was used in Mexico in pre-Columbian times to induce supernatural visions and as a medicine. From the mid-19th century, use of peyote extended north into the Great Plains of the U.S., and probably first developed into a distinct peyote religion about 1885 among the Kiowa and Comanche of Oklahoma. After 1891 it spread rapidly as far north as Canada and is now practiced among more than 50 tribes. Statistics are uncertain, but reports suggest nearly a fifth of the Navajo in 1951 practiced the peyote religion (despite strong tribal council opposition) and one-third of Oklahoma Indians in 1965. The Native American Church claimed over 200,000 adherents in the 1960s, a figure that is most likely exaggerated.

The various forms of peyotist beliefs combine Indian and Christian elements in differing degrees. Thus, among the Teton, the Cross Fire group uses the Bible and sermons, which are rejected by the Half Moon followers, who, however, teach a similar Christian morality. In general peyotist doctrine consists of belief in one supreme God (the Great Spirit), who deals with men through various spirits. These include the traditional waterbird or thunderbird spirits that carry prayers to God. In many tribes peyote itself is personified as Peyote Spirit, considered to be either God's equivalent for the Indians to his Jesus for the whites, or Jesus himself. In some tribes Jesus is regarded as an Indian culture hero returned, as an intercessor with God or as a guardian spirit who has turned to the Indians after being killed by the whites. Peyote, eaten in the ritual context, enables the individual to commune with God and the spirits (including those of the departed) in contemplation and vision and so to receive from them spiritual power, guidance, reproof, and healing.

The rite characteristically, but not always, takes place in a tepee around a crescent-shaped, earthen altar mound and a sacred fire. The all-night ceremony usually commences about 8 PM Saturday and is led by a peyote "chief." The services include prayer, singing, sacramental eating of peyote, water rites, and contemplation, and concludes with a communion breakfast on Sunday morning. The way of life is called the Peyote Road and enjoins brotherly love, family care, self-support through steady work, and avoidance of alcohol.

Peyotism has been much persecuted. Although peyote was banned by government agents in 1888 and later by 15 states, Congress, backed by the Bureau of Indian Affairs, the churches, and some Indian groups, resisted repeated attempts from 1916 to 1937 to have its use prohibited. In self-defense, peyote groups sought incorporation under state laws —first in Oklahoma as the First-born Church of Jesus Christ in 1914, then as the Native American Church in 1918, and by 1960 in some further 11 states. In the 1960s appeals by peyotists in the name of constitutional freedom of religion were supported by anthropologists and others and upheld in several state supreme courts.

·Christian-influenced tribal cults **18**:702d
·Great Basin peyote rituals **13**:207d
·hallucinogenic sacrament **8**:558g
·Mexican dance style and occurrence **1**:675b
·musical influences and instrument use **1**:664d *passim* to 664g
·new tribal cults characteristics **18**:700d
·Oklahoma official recognition **13**:543h

Arapaho peyote ceremony, watercolour by Carl Sweezy, *c.* 1930–40; in the collection of the University of Oklahoma Library

By courtesy of the Western History Collections, University of Oklahoma Library

·origin and U.S.–Mexican song difference **1**:668b
·Plains Indian religious practices **13**:227c
·religious use of peyote **14**:200e *passim* to 203a

Pezizales: *see* cup fungus.

Pezophaps solitaria (bird): *see* dodo.

Pezoporus wallicus, species of ground parrot, family Psittacide, order Psittaciformes.

·traits, behaviour, and classification **15**:139g

Pezza, Michele: *see* Diavolo, Fra.

Pfaff, Johann Friedrich (b. Dec. 22, 1765, Stuttgart, now in West Germany—d. April 21, 1825, Halle), mathematician who proposed the first general method of integrating partial differential equations of the first order.

Pfaff was professor of mathematics at the University of Helstedt from 1788 until 1810, when he was appointed professor of mathematics at the University of Halle.

Pfaff made notable contributions to calculus, the theory of series, and the solution of differential equations. He completed his work on the general method of partial differential equation integration in 1814–15. The term Pfaffian problem was originated in his honour. Among his published works are *Disquisitiones analyticae* (1797; "Analytic Works"), and *Observationes ad Euleri institutiones calculi integralis* ("Observations of Eulerian Methods of the Integral Calculus").

Pfann, William Gardner (1917–), U.S. physical metallurgist; worked on crystal growth.

·zone levelling development **19**:1160c

Pfeffer, Wilhelm (Friedrich Philipp) (b. March 9, 1845, Grebenstein, now in West

Pfeffer

Archiv fur Kunst und Geschichte

Germany—d. Jan. 31, 1920, Leipzig), botanist whose work on osmotic pressure made him a pioneer in the study of modern plant physiology.

After earning his Ph.D. from the University of Göttingen in 1865 Pfeffer continued his studies at the universities of Marburg and Bonn. He then held teaching positions at Bonn (1873), Basel (1877), Tübingen (1878), and Leipzig (1877), where he remained until his death. Pfeffer's work on cell metabolism led to his pioneer work in 1877 in devising a semi-permeable membrane that he used to study osmosis. He developed a method for measuring osmotic pressure and showed that pressure depended on the size of the molecules too large to pass through the membrane. Pfeffer was then able to measure the size of giant molecules. His findings were published in *Osmotische Untersuchungen, Studien sur Zellmechanik* (1877; "Osmotic Research Studies on Cell Mechanics"). His best publication, however, is *Pflanzenphysiologie. Ein Handbuch des Stoffwechsels und Kraftwechsels in der Pflanse* (1881), standard handbook on plant physiology. The English edition, *Physiology of Plants*, was published in the early 1900s.

Pfefferkorn, Johannes (Joseph) (1469–1524), German controversialist—a converted

Jew—opponent of Jewish literature, whose dispute with the humanist and Hebraist Johannes Reuchlin was a European *cause célèbre* in the early 16th century.

Pfitzner, Hans (Erich) (b. May 5, 1869, Moscow—d. May 22, 1949, Salzburg), composer who upheld traditional ideals during the post-Wagnerian era. Pfitzner was a pupil at Frankfurt of Iwan Knorr. Between 1892 and 1934 he held posts as teacher and conductor in several German towns, including Strassburg, where he was director of the conservatory and of the opera. His operas include *Der arme Heinrich* (Mainz, 1895), *Die Rose vom Liebesgarten* (Eberfeld, 1901), and *Palestrina* (Munich, 1917), the last being his best-known work. His works were widely played in Germany but made little impression in other countries.
·opera in conservative idiom **13**:591f

Pfleiderer, Otto (1839–1908), German Protestant theologian and religious historian.
·religion's essence and classification **15**:630g

Pflimlin, Pierre (1907–), French statesman.
·Algerian crisis and resignation **7**:678e

Pflüger, Eduard Friedrich Wilhelm (1829–1910), German physiologist.
·physiological publications in Germany **14**:436h

PFNA: *see* Pentecostal Fellowship of North America.

Pforzheim, city, Baden-Württemberg *Land* (state), southwestern West Germany, on the northern edge of the Schwarzwald (Black Forest), where the Nagold and Würm rivers join the Enz, northwest of Stuttgart. A Roman settlement (Porta Hercyniae), chartered *c.* 1195, it was occasionally the residence of the margraves of Baden-Baden and Baden-Durlach. The Humanist Johann Reuchlin was born there (1455), and its medieval Latin school was famous. The city was sacked during the Thirty Years' War (1618–48) and the War of the Grand Alliance (1689–97) and was virtually destroyed during World War II. It has been rebuilt with broad thoroughfares and open spaces along the rivers. Notable buildings include the castle-church of St. Michael (13th–15th centuries), the Franciscan Barfüsserkirche (13th century), and the Reuchlin House (containing both history and jewelry museums). Pforzheim has been the centre of the German jewelry and watch industry since the 18th century and has schools for precious metalworking, watchmaking, and mechanics. Other manufactures include machinery, radio and television apparatus, and paper. Pop. (1970 est.) 90,800.
48°52′ N, 8°42′ E
·map, Federal Republic of Germany **8**:46

Pfund series (physics): *see* spectral line series.

Pfyffer, Ludwig (b. 1524—d. May 17, 1594, Luzern), military leader, spokesman for Roman Catholic interests in the cantons and probably the most important Swiss political figure in the latter half of the 16th century, whose nickname was "King of the Swiss."

For many years an active and intrepid warrior in the service of France, Pfyffer won fame for safely leading the royal family of Charles IX from Meaux to Paris while under Huguenot attack (1567). Elected chief magistrate for Luzern in 1570—which office he continued to occupy until his death—he made that city the centre of Catholic Counter-Reformation activity in Switzerland. His Golden (or Borromean) League (1586)—the alliance of the seven Catholic cantons for furtherance of religious interests—nearly led to the destruction of the Swiss Confederation and precipitated the division of the canton of Appenzell along religious lines. Pfyffer established close relations with the Holy League of Philip II of Spain and Henri, duc de Guise, and concluded a Swiss alliance with Spain (1587) against the accession of Henry of Navarre (Henry IV) to the French throne. He also acquired a substantial fortune from foreign pensions and as a supplier of mercenaries to the pope.
·Golden League and Appenzell partition **17**:883f

PGA: *see* Professional Golfers' Association of America.

PGR: *see* psychogalvanic reflex.

pH, in chemistry, a quantitative measure of the acidity or basicity of liquid solutions. A pH value of 7 corresponds to the hydrogen ion concentration of neutral water (ions are atoms that have gained or lost one or more electrons). A solution with a pH value less than 7 is considered acidic. A solution with a pH value greater than 7 is considered basic. If the pH value is exactly 7, such as a solution of sodium chloride in water, it is called neutral.

The measurement was originally used by the Danish biochemist S.P.L. Sørensen to represent the hydrogen ion concentration, expressed in equivalents per litre, of an aqueous solution: $pH = \log 1/[H^+]$. The expression provides a convenient scale for the large range of values of the hydrogen ion concentration encountered in experimental work.

Because of uncertainty about the physical significance of the hydrogen ion concentration, the current adopted definition of the pH is an operational one—*i.e.*, it is based on a method of measurement. The National Bureau of Standards has defined pH values in terms of the electromotive force existing between certain standard electrodes in specified solutions. To find the pH of a test solution, the electromotive force, *E*, generated is measured by placing two standard electrodes (usually a glass electrode and a calomel electrode) into the test solution. The pH at 25° C (77° F) is obtained from the expression $pH_x = [(E_x - E_s)/.05916] + pH_s$. Here, pH_s and E_s are values for a standard solution using the same electrodes. The electromotive force as used in the equation is given in volts.
·acid–base equilibria of buffers **1**:51b; illus.
·agricultural production requirements **1**:351h
·blood buffers and carbon dioxide level **2**:1112f
·chemical monitoring instrumentation **9**:635d
·clay mineral formation **4**:705f
·conductivity and ionization measurement **6**:683b
·definition and freshwater buffering **7**:733f
·definition and phase diagram use **7**:1030d; illus. 2 1031
·digestive enzyme activity **5**:775c
·disease causes and internal balance **5**:844a
·duricrust formation and ionic solubility **5**:1091f
·effect on flower coloration **4**:917d
·enzyme reaction variables **6**:901c
·glass electrode reaction and pH error **8**:210h
·hemoglobin gas-transport capability **15**:758h; illus. 759
·hot springs progressive values factors **8**:133d
·human blood variable **7**:429g
·lake water acidity balance and changes **10**:605a
·meat hardening and deterioration **11**:747b
·ocean acidity and sediment formation **13**:477f; illus. 479
·protozoan distribution and growth **15**:121h
·rare-earth chemical properties **15**:519e
·soil acidity and alkalinity control **8**:1110c
·tissue culture's limiting factors **18**:440f
·vegetable farming soil requirements **19**:48g
·water ionization characteristics **19**:636g
·wine making and regulation of acidity **19**:876f

Phacelia, a genus of 200 species of blue- or white-flowering herbs, native to North America and Andean South America and including several species of garden flowers. It belongs to the family Hydrophyllaceae. Native to dry slopes of Southern California, *P. campanularia* bears blue, five-lobed blooms in loose sprays over the dark-green, toothed, oval leaves, on plants 23 centimetres (9 inches) tall.

Phacelia
F.K. Anderson—EB Inc.

From similar areas, the closely related California bluebell, or wild Canterbury bell (*P. whitlavia*), has urn-shaped blooms.

Phacellaria, in botany, genus of the family Santalaceae, order Santalales.
·sandalwood plant comparison **16**:228a

Phacochoerus aethiopicus: *see* warthog.

Phacops, genus of extinct trilobites found as fossils in Silurian and Devonian rocks (between 430,000,000 and 345,000,000 years old) in Europe and North America. *Phacops* is a common and easily recognizable form, with its rounded rather than angular outline, globose head region, and large compound eyes. A common form is the species *Phacops rana*.

Phacops rana milleri, collected in Sylvania, Ohio
By courtesy of the Buffalo Museum of Science, Buffalo, New York

Phaedo, also known as PHAEDON (b. *c.* 417 BC, Elis, now Iliá, Greece), philosopher, founder of a Socratic school of philosophy at Elis on the Peloponnese and author of works on dialectics and ethics.

Born of an aristocratic family, Phaedo was made a prisoner in the war with Sparta (400–399 BC) and was sold as a slave. Bought and freed by an Athenian who was a friend of Socrates, Phaedo became Socrates' disciple. Plato named one of his dialogues after him. After Socrates' death, Phaedo returned to Elis and established his school.

Many dialogues were attributed to Phaedo, but only the *Zopyrus* and *Simon* have survived.

Phaedo, one of the dialogues of Plato, reporting the last hours of Socrates' life, named for Phaedo of Elis. This work puts forth the Platonic theory of literally innate ideas, or Forms, which cannot be perceived by the senses but are acquired by the soul before its union with the body. Also in *Phaedo* are discussions of the dualism in man—the soul and the body, divinity and mortality—and Plato's theory of immortality of the soul.
·biographical literature development **2**:1011a
·concepts and innate ideas **6**:769g
·dualistic ontology of Platonism **5**:1067b
·nous and theory of Forms **6**:931d
·Plato's metaphysical doctrines **14**:533e
·Socrates' life and teachings **16**:1001g
·soul's liberation at death **12**:18g

Phaedra (Greek mythology): *see in* Hippolytus.

Phaedrus (b. *c.* 15 BC, Thrace—d. *c.* AD 50, Italy), Roman fabulist, the first writer to Latinize whole books of fables, producing free versions in iambic metre of Greek prose fables then circulating under the name of Aesop.

A slave by birth, Phaedrus went to Italy early in life, became a freedman in the emperor Augustus' household, and received the usual education in Greek and Latin authors.

The poets Ennius, Lucilius, and Horace had introduced fables into their poems, but Phaedrus elevated the form into an independent genre. His style is animated and marked by brevity and clear and simple language. His fables include such favourites as "The Fox and the Sour Grapes," "The Wolf and the Lamb," "The Lion's Share," "The Two Wallets," and "The Pearl in the Dung-Heap." His work became extremely popular in the Middle Ages, when numerous prose and poetic versions of his tales appeared in Europe and Britain. A collection called *Romulus* was the basis of most of them; Phaedrus' identity having been lost, some scholars assumed that Romulus was the author.

In the early 18th century a manuscript was discovered at Parma that contained 64 fables of Phaedrus, of which 30 were new. Another manuscript was later found in the Vatican and published in 1831. Later research identified 30 more fables as written in the iambics of Phaedrus.
·literary works **7**:135d

Phaedrus, one of the dialogues of Plato, named for the philosopher Phaedrus of Athens. The central theme of the dialogue is the foundation of scientific rhetoric on logic and the scientific study of human passions. The mind is presented as having both appetitive and higher desires and the additional capacity of reason, which controls, directs, and adjudicates the desires. In this work Plato also extols the virtues of art and discusses the psychology of love.
·mind's immateriality and properties **12**:230c
·Plato's attitude toward art **2**:53h
·Plato's view of love **14**:535f
·rhetorical theory development **15**:800c
·supreme being idea from change concept **18**:265h

Phaenias (Greek philosopher): *see* Phanias.

Phaenicophaeus, a genus of cuckoo, the malcoha (*q.v.*).

Phaenomena (Greek: "Phenomena"), poem describing the characteristics of the stars, written *c.* 270 BC by Aratus (*q.v.*).
·Hellenistic astronomy popularity **6**:326a
·star and constellation description **2**:225g

Phaeophyta: *see* brown algae.

Phaestus, Greek PHAESTOS, ancient city of Crete, on the western end of the southern plain (Mesára), about 3.5 miles from the sea. The site was occupied from the 4th millennium BC, and its importance grew in the Early and Middle Bronze ages (*c.* 3000–*c.* 1600 BC). In the latter period its palace was first built and later remodelled. In the Late Bronze Age, about 1400, it was destroyed in the earthquake that also destroyed Knossos and other sites on Crete. It was reoccupied in the final phase of the Late Bronze Age (13th century BC) and was widely known in Classical and Hellenistic times (*c.* 6th–1st century BC) until neighbouring Gortyn eclipsed it under the Roman Empire.
·excavations and findings **1**:118a; map 112
·Minoan civilization sites **5**:252h
·Minoan palace architecture **19**:274h

Phaethon (Greek: Shining, or Radiant), in Greek mythology, the son of the sun god, Helios, and the heroine Clymene. Taunted with illegitimacy, he appealed to his father, who swore to prove his paternity by giving him whatever he wanted. Phaethon asked to be allowed to drive the chariot of the sun through the heavens for a single day. Helios, bound by his oath, had to let him make the attempt. Phaethon set off but was entirely unable to control the horses of the sun chariot, which came too near to the earth and began to scorch it. To prevent further damage, Zeus hurled a thunderbolt at Phaethon, who fell to the earth at the mouth of the Eridanus, a river later identified as the Po. Phaethon's sisters, who had yoked the horses to the chariot, were then transformed into poplars and their tears into amber.

Phaethontidae: *see* tropic bird.

Phaethornis, species of hummingbird (*q.v.*).

phaeton, light, open, four-wheeled, doorless carriage, popular in the 19th century. It usually contained two seats, with a folding top for the front seat, and had large wheels.

Phaeton, *c.* 1770; in the Science Museum, London
By courtesy of the Science Museum, London, lent by Sir John Lionel Armytage

The most spectacular phaeton was the English four-wheeled high-flyer, the body of which consisted of a light seat for two, resting atop two great crossed springs and reached by ladder. A curved iron stay attached the springs to the axles. Much more reasonably constructed and graceful phaetons were the mail stanhope, spider, and tilbury phaetons. The mail phaeton, used chiefly to convey passengers with luggage, met incoming stagecoaches. The spider phaeton, of U.S. origin, was a light vehicle made for gentlemen drivers. The stanhope and tilbury phaetons were also fashionable carriages, both used at horse shows.
·carriage use as sporting vehicle **19**:524b

phage (virus): *see* bacteriophage.

Phag-mo-gru, Tibetan monastic order that in the 14th century liberated Tibet from Mongol control and re-established centralized native rule in the country for the first time in 500 years. A monastery of the Bra'-rgyud-pa Buddhist sect, the Phag-mo-gru had begun to extend its power over the surrounding countryside in the 13th century at a time when the country was being governed by a series of lamas from the Sa-skya monastery residing at the Mongol (Yüan) court in China. The death of the great emperor Kublai Khan in 1294 marked the beginning of the decline of Mongol power; the Phag-mo-gru, under its lama Byang-chub rgyal-mtshan, soon began to actively dispute the Sa-skya lama. By 1358 Byang-chub rgyal-mtshan had liberated all of central Tibet, eradicating Mongol control over the country. Byang-chub rgyal-mtshan and the Phag-mo-gru leaders who succeeded him assumed the title of Gong-ma and divided Tibet into districts governed by centrally appointed officials. During the next 100 years in which the Phag-mo-gru was dominant, a semblance of central authority was re-established in the country. In the middle of the 15th century, however, the Phag-mo-gru rule was gradually usurped by the Rin-spung family, who had previously been ministers to the Gong-ma.
·Tibetan relations with Mongols **18**:380b

phagocytosis, process by which living cells ingest or engulf other cells or particles. The phagocytic cell may be a free-living, one-celled organism, such as an amoeba, or one of the body cells, such as a leukocyte (white blood cell). The particles commonly phagocytized include bacteria, tissue cells (usually dead), protozoa, various dust particles, pigments, and other minute foreign bodies. In the simpler forms of animal life, such as amoebae and sponges, phagocytosis is a means of feeding; in higher animals phagocytosis is chiefly a defensive reaction against infection.

In man and in vertebrates generally, the most effective phagocytic cells are the macrophages (large phagocytic cells) and the granular leukocytes (small phagocytic cells). The macrophages occur especially in the liver, spleen, and lymph nodes, in which their function is to free the blood and lymph of bacteria and other particles. Macrophages are also found in all tissues as wandering amoeboid cells, and a cell related to the macrophage is found in the blood. The smaller type of phagocyte (granular leukocyte) is carried along by the circulating blood until it reaches an area of infection, in which it crawls through the blood vessel wall, being directed toward the invading bacteria by means of substances given off by the bacteria. This directed movement is known as chemotaxis.

Before phagocytosis is accomplished, the phagocyte and particle must adhere to each other, and whether this is possible depends largely on the chemical nature of the surface of the particle. On less virulent bacteria, ordinary proteins from the blood form a surface film to which leukocytes adhere, and phagocytosis follows. Virulent bacteria are ingested with more difficulty. Leukocytes, instead of adhering to them, succeed only in pushing them away. If, however, the leukocytes succeed in pushing them against a firm surface, such as the lining of a blood vessel, the bacteria may not be able to slip away and are ingested. This process is known as surface phagocytosis. Other virulent bacteria may not be phagocytized until their surfaces are coated with peculiar globulins (proteins) formed by the body in response to the presence of that kind of bacterium. Such globulins are called antibodies, and antibodies are of great importance in establishing immunity of the body to diseases.

The manner in which a phagocytic cell ingests a particle varies somewhat with the size of the particle. Small particles, such as bacteria or minute grains of charcoal, seem to be ingested in an instant. At one moment they appear through the microscope to be adherent to the surface of the phagocyte; at another moment they are inside it. Larger objects, such as clumps of bacteria or tissue cells, are phagocytized by a more prolonged response of the leukocyte. The cell flows around the object until it has been completely engulfed.

The results of phagocytosis are digestion and destruction of the particle by means of enzymes inside the phagocyte. If the particle is indigestible, however, as is a grain of carbon, it eventually may be ejected by the phagocyte. Also, ingested living organisms, such as tubercle bacilli, may be resistant to the intracellular digestive enzymes and not only survive but multiply within the phagocyte. In moving about, the phagocyte may then carry such bacteria into other parts of the body and therefore actually assist in the spread of disease instead, as is more usual, of defending the body against infection. *See also* pinocytosis.
Major ref. **5**:845a
·animal tissue functions **18**:444h
·blood cell removal by engulfment **2**:1117f
·cell membrane functional mechanisms **3**:1049f
·connective tissue macrophage property **5**:15b
·echinoderm blood cell functions **2**:1124c
·excretion of particulate wastes **6**:720d
·immunological processes **9**:248d
·inflammatory process and leukocyte function **9**:559f
·joint cellular components **10**:256a
·leukocyte adaptations and functions **3**:1062b
·lymph nodes and defense **11**:211e
·macrophage activity in delayed allergy **1**:609d
·protozoan feeding behaviour **5**:781d; illus.
·RES role in body defenses **15**:782f
·reticuloendothelial cell function **15**:780c

phagosome, a digestive vacuole created during endocytosis.
·cell membrane functional mechanisms **3**:1049g

phagostimulant, taste or odour that induces an animal to feed.
·chemoreception role in food selection **4**:176f

phagotrophism, ability of certain slime molds to feed on small particles by engulfing them.
·slime mold feeding behaviour **16**:890c

'Phags-pa (b. 1235—d. 1280), Tibetan scholar-monk who set up a Buddhist theocracy in Tibet. After Mongol suzerainty was established in his country, 'Phags-pa, a member of the Sa-skya-pa school of Buddhism, based at the Sa-skya monastery and noted for its emphasis on scholarship, accompanied his uncle, the Sa-skya lama, on a visit to Mongolia in 1247. 'Phags-pa later succeeded his uncle as lama and came to have great influence with Kublai Khan, founder (1279) of the Yüan dynasty of China, to whom he became adviser. With Kublai he worked out the relation of Tibet to China as a personal bond between the lama as priest and the emperor as patron (*yon-mchod*). With Kublai also he developed the "dual principle" of the parity of power and dignity of church and state in political matters. 'Phags-pa also invented an alphabet for the Mongol language.
·Mongol political and religious policy **10**:543e
·Sa-skya-pa development **3**:388d
·Tibet's relationship to Mongols **18**:380a
·Yüan dynasty's adoption of Buddhism **4**:344a

Phagwāra, city, Kapūrthala district, Punjab state, northern India, southeast of Jullundur, with which it is connected by the Grand Trunk Road. It is a commercial and light industrial centre in the Bist Doāb region; cotton textiles are a major product. It was part of the former princely state of Kapūrthala. In the early 1970s it was classified as the centre of an urban agglomeration; its suburbs include Mohalla Gobindpura and Kotrani. It is served by a railway to Nawāshankar. Pop. (1971) 50,863.
31°14′ N, 75°46′ E

Phainias (Greek philosopher): *see* Phanias.

Phainopepla nitens, bird species of the family Bombycillidae (*q.v.*).

phala (Sanskrit: "fruit"), though its primary meaning is indeed "fruit," as that of a tree, an important term in Indian philosophy that is frequently used to mean the fruit or consequence of a particular action (*karman*). The almost universally held conviction among Indian philosophers that this life is but one in a chain of lives (*saṃsāra*) and that human class, nature, dispositions, and character are the result of deeds in a previous life underlies the significance of both *phala* and *karman*. The moral energy of man's past deeds is conserved and automatically fructifies in the circumstances of a future life.

Phalaborwa, also spelled PALABORA, town and mining centre, Letaba district, northern Transvaal, S.Af., 6 mi (9 km) north of the Olifants River, 63 mi (104 km) east of Tzaneen. The town is located on a site of ancient iron and copper mining works dating, on archaeological evidence, to the 8th century AD.

Modern copper mining begun *c.* 1904 proved unsuccessful because of the lack of transportation. Large deposits of phosphates, discovered in 1951, formed the economic basis for development. A 31-mi (50-km) railway spur was built to Hoedspruit, and the modern township was established by 1957. In 1965 the Palabora Mining Company began large-scale mining and processing of copper. Pop. (1976 est.) 12,000.
23°55′ S, 31°13′ E

Phalacridae, family of shining flower beetles of the order Coleoptera.
·traits and classification **4**:835h

Phalacrocoracidae: *see* cormorant.

Phalaenopsis: *see* moth orchid.

Phalaenoptilus nuttallii (bird): *see* poorwill.

phalangeal cell, also called CELL OF DEITERS, in anatomy, one of the supporting cells for the outer hair cells of the organ of Corti of the inner ear.
·structure and function in human ear **5**:1124a

phalanger, general name for about 45 species of Australasian marsupial mammals of the family Phalangeridae. They are called possums in Australia and Tasmania. The cuscus, glider (flying possum), and koala (*qq.v.*) belong to this family. The greater glider, the

Golden brush-tailed possum (*Trichosurus*)
Warren Garst—Tom Stack and Associates

koala, and ring-tailed possums—species having cheek pouches and the molar teeth adapted to chewing leaves—are sometimes separated as the family Phascolarctidae.

Phalangers are arboreal: the clawless innermost hind digit and, sometimes, the first and second digits of the forefoot are opposable, making it possible for the animal to grasp branches. The second and third digits of the hindfoot are united. The tail is long and often prehensile. The pouch opens forward (except in the koala); there are usually two to four teats. The first incisor tooth is long and stout; the side teeth are tiny. The pelage often is woolly, and many species are striped. Total length ranges from 12 to 120 centimetres (5 to 47 inches).

Phalangers are native to forests of Australia, Tasmania, New Guinea, and islands west to Celebes and east to the Solomons. All are herbivorous; some also eat insects and small vertebrates. Phalangers are active chiefly at night. Most bear their young—usually two or three—in tree hollows and unused birds' nests; a few build leafy nests of their own.

Several species are endangered: they are the prey of snakes and cats, and certain species are trapped for their fur. Adelaide chinchilla is the fur of the brush-tailed possum (*Trichosurus vulpecula*), the most widely distributed Australian and Tasmanian marsupial, which has also been introduced into New Zealand. It looks rather like a squirrel.

Ring-tailed possums—the 17 species of the genus *Pseudocheirus* of New Guinea to Tasmania—usually carry their tails in a circle at the tip. The three dormouse possums, or mundardas (*Cercartetus*), and the three pygmy possums (*Eudromicia*) store fat in the tail and become torpid at times. Striped phalangers, also called striped possums (*Dactylonax palpator* and the three species of *Dactylopsila*), are chiefly New Guinean; they have the fourth digit of the front foot elongated to serve as a probe for grubs in rotten wood. The long-snouted phalanger, or honey possum (*Tarsipes spenserae*), also called noolbenger, has an extended muzzle and only 22 teeth—fewest among marsupials. It uses its bristle-tipped tongue to take nectar from flowers.
·traits, behaviour, and classification **11**:540d *passim* to 543g; illus.

phalanges (sing. phalanx), tubular bones of fingers and toes (digits). In man, the thumb (pollex) and big toe (hallux) each contain two phalanges; the remaining digits each contain three. These bones articulate between themselves and with the metacarpal (hand) and metatarsal (foot) bones by ellipsoidal joints. The terminal phalanges, at the tips of the digits, carry a nail. *See also* digit.
·bird modification and feather attachment **2**:1057c
·evolution of vertebrate forelimb, illus. 1 **7**:9
·joint and bone relationships **10**:256f
·skeletal comparison of human extremities **16**:818c; illus. 1 813
·skeletal variations in vertebrates **16**:826d; illus.

Phalangida (arthropod): *see* harvestman.

phalanx, tactical formation consisting of heavily armed infantry standing shoulder to shoulder in files normally eight men deep. The use of the formation, developed by the ancient Greeks and maintained throughout their history, apparently spread throughout Greece during the 7th century BC. The Greek hoplites who manned the phalanx were armoured infantrymen, each armed with a long pike and a double-edged sword. The pikes formed a barrier to cavalry attack, although the phalanx was somewhat vulnerable to archers, either mounted or on foot.

Since the phalanx held in solid ranks and was divided only into the centre and wings, there was generally little need for an officer corps; the whole line advanced in step to the sound of the flute. The Spartans, however, did train officers to manoeuvre the phalanx. *See also* hoplite.
·ancient Greek military practices **8**:335e
·Macedonian army tactics **8**:367c
·military tactics in history **19**:572e *passim* to 577b; illus. 574

Phalaris (d. *c.* 554 BC), tyrant of Acragas (modern Agrigento), Sicily, notorious for his cruelty. He is alleged to have roasted his victims alive in a bronze bull, their shrieks representing the animal's bellowing. A statue of a bull of some kind seems to have existed, but the facts surrounding its use have been embellished. For example, the supposed inventor of the bull, Perilaus, or Perillus, was said to have been the first man executed in it.

After assuming the responsibility for building the temple of Zeus Atabyrios, in the citadel at Acragas, Phalaris armed his workers and seized power. Under his rule Acragas seems to have prospered and to have expanded its territory. The splendid layout of the city probably belongs to his time. Eventually Phalaris was overthrown by Telemachus, the ancestor of Theron (tyrant *c.* 488–472). It is said that the deposed tyrant was burned to death in his own bronze bull.

Contrary to the legends that stress the cruelty of Phalaris, he was represented by the sophists of the Roman Empire as a humane and cultured man. The well-known 148 *Epistles of Phalaris* were proved by the great English Classical scholar Richard Bentley, in his *Dissertation upon the Epistles of Phalaris* (1699), to have been written much later by a sophist or rhetorician, possibly Adrianus of Tyre (died *c.* AD 193).

phalarope (Greek: "coot-foot"), shorebird with lobed toes, adapted to swimming. There are three species, which comprise the family Phalaropodidae (order Charadriiformes). They are lightly built, slim-necked birds, about 20 to 25 centimetres (8 to 10 inches) long. Phalaropes are noted for complete sexual reversal. Females, larger and more brightly coloured than males, fight for nesting territories and do the courting; males undertake all nesting duties and lead the young southward in autumn after the females have departed.

Wilson's phalarope (*Steganopus tricolor*)
Alice B. Kessler

Phalaropes are marked with red and soft gray in summer; in winter they are quite plain. Breeding around the Arctic Circle are the red phalarope (*Phalaropus fulicarius*), called gray phalarope in Britain, and the northern phalarope (*Lobipes lobatus*), called red-necked phalarope in Britain. Both species winter on tropical oceans, where they are known as sea snipe. Wilson's phalarope (*Steganopus tricolor*) breeds in interior western North America and migrates chiefly to the Argentine pampas.

·characteristics and classification **4**:41g; illus. 39
·reproductive behaviour pattern **15**:688a

Phalaropodidae (bird): *see* phalarope.

Phalium (marine snail): *see* helmet shell.

Phallales (fungi): *see* stinkhorn.

phallic cult, widely distributed religious activity that involves sexuality or that utilizes the symbolism of the male or female sexual organs. The term phallic cult, or phallism, is a broad title, within which a number of distinctions can be made.

The most important forms of sexual rituals are those in which intercourse is believed to promote fertility, those that release a flood of creative energy by breaking boundaries and by returning a culture to the state of primeval and powerful chaos (*e.g.*, the orgy during New Year festivals), or those in which sexual intercourse symbolizes the bringing together of opposites (*e.g.*, alchemy or Tantrism, a Hindu esoteric meditation system).

In other traditions objects of adoration are representations of the sexual organs (*e.g.*, the phallus borne in Dionysiac processions in Greece and Rome; the male *liṅga* and female *yoni* in India) or deities with prominent genitals (*e.g.*, Priapus in Greece). In these instances, the powers of creativity that the sexual organ represents, rather than the organ itself, are worshipped.

The most difficult class of phallic symbols are those that do not directly represent the sexual organs in facsimiles. Though there is no doubt that objects such as figs and cowrie shells may serve as phallic objects, scholars have repudiated such interpretations of all objects bearing some resemblance to sexual organs.

There is no evidence that any cult is pre-eminently phallic.

·fire-making in primitive cultures **12**:883b
·Hindu liṅga veneration of Vīraśaivas **8**:895g
·Indonesian Śaivite symbology **9**:478b
·Śaivite Liṅgāyat doctrines **8**:916d
·Tantric influence in Hinduism **9**:364f

phallic stage, in psychoanalytic theory, beginning of the early genital stage (*q.v.*), when the child first seeks determinedly to impress his masculinity or her femininity on the parent of the opposite sex. Freud designated the phallic and genital stages as clearly delineated phases.

·behaviour development of children **8**:1137a

phallic symbol, representation of the penis as a symbol of fertility and of the generative principle; there are also corresponding female symbols. *See also* phallic cult.

Phallostethidae, family of small saltwater and brackish-water fishes of the order Atheriniformes, found in southeastern Asia and the Philippines.

·classification, features, and sexuality **2**:274a

phallus, in anatomy, organ rudiment that develops into the penis or clitoris in the later embryo.

·human embryogeny in male and female **15**:691f

Phalodi, town, Jodhpur district, Rājasthān state, India. The town is connected by road and rail with Jodhpur and is a trade centre for camels, sheep, hides, and salt. Local manufactures include metal utensils, camel's-hair mats, and pottery. Located in the Great Indian Desert (Thar Desert), Phalodi is an old caravan centre, believed to have been founded in the 15th century. Architectural monuments include a fort and palaces. Just north lies the Phalodi salt source, a large saline depression of the desert. Camels are bred nearby. Pop. (1971) 17,379.
27°08′ N, 72°22′ E

phāmsāna, type of North Indian temple spire (śikhara; *q.v.*) that is rectilinear in outline and composed of horizontal slabs capped by a bell-shaped element called the *ghaṇṭā*.

·construction and regional use **17**:175h

Pham van Bong (Buddhist monk): *see* Tri Quang.

Phanariote, term applied to principal Greek families of the Phanar, the Greek quarter of Constantinople (Istanbul), whose members, as administrators in the civil bureaucracy, exercised great influence in the Ottoman Empire in the 18th century. Some members of these families, which had acquired great wealth and influence during the 17th century, abandoned their traditional careers in commerce to enter the bureaucracy of the Ottoman Empire. From 1669 until 1821 Phanariotes served as dragomans (interpreters who also acted as foreign affairs advisers) to the Sublime Porte and to foreign embassies. They were also appointed *hospodars* of the Danubian principalities, Moldavia and Walachia (vassal states of the Ottoman Empire), during the period 1711–1821, which is, therefore, known as the Phanariote period in Romanian history. Phanariotes also dominated the administration of the Eastern Orthodox Church and frequently intervened in the selection of prelates, including the Patriarch of Constantinople. Leading families were the Argyropoulos, Cantacuzino, Mavrokordátos, and Ypsilantis.

·Bucharest under Greek rule **3**:363c
·episcopal control under Ottomans **6**:156b
·Ottoman imperial collapse **2**:622g

Phan Boi Chau, also called PHAN GIAI SAN, PHAN SAO NAM, PHAN THI HAN, or HAI THU, originally PHAN VAN SAN (b. 1867, Nghe An province, northern Vietnam—d. Oct. 29, 1940, Hue), dominant personality of early Vietnamese resistance movements, whose impassioned writings and tireless schemes for independence earned him the reverence of his people as one of Vietnam's greatest patriots.

Phan Boi Chau was the son of a poor scholar, who stressed education and preparation for the mandarin examinations, the only means to success in the traditional bureaucracy. By the time he received his doctorate in 1900, Phan Boi Chau had become a firm nationalist.

In 1903 he wrote *Luu cau huyet le tan thu* ("Ryukyu's Bitter Tears"), an allegory equating Japan's bitterness at the loss of the Ryukyu Islands with the Vietnamese loss of independence. With fellow revolutionaries he formed the Duy Tan Hoi (Reformation Society; *see* Duy Tan) in 1904 and secured the active support of Prince Cuong De (*q.v.*), thus presenting to the people an alliance of royalty and resistance.

In 1905 Phan Boi Chau moved his resistance movement to Japan, and in 1906 he met the Chinese revolutionary Sun Yat-sen. His plans to place Cuong De on the throne of Vietnam resulted in a meeting in 1906 with the Prince and the Vietnamese reformer Phan Chau Trinh. A Franco-Japanese understanding forced Phan Boi Chau, the Vietnamese students he had brought to Japan, and Cuong De to leave Japan in 1908–09. By 1912 Phan Boi Chau had reluctantly given up his monarchist scheme. He reorganized the resistance movement in Canton, China, under the name Viet Nam Quang Phuc Hoi (Vietnam Restoration Society). The organization launched a plan to assassinate the French governor general of Indochina, but the plan failed. Phan Boi Chau was imprisoned in Canton from 1914 to 1917; during his confinement he wrote *Nguc trung thu* ("Prison Notes"), a short autobiography.

Upon his release, Phan Boi Chau studied Marxist doctrine and resumed his resistance to the French. In June 1925 he was seized and taken to Hanoi, but hundreds of Vietnamese protested against his arrest. The French pardoned him and offered him a civil service position that he refused.

Phan Boi Chau lived out his later years in quiet retirement at Hue, under French surveillance. He wrote a second autobiography, replete with directives for future revolutionaries, and several volumes of poetry. Among his other works are *Viet Nam vong quoc su* (1906; "History of the Loss of Vietnam"), renowned as Vietnam's first revolutionary history book, and *Hau Tran dat su* ("Strange Story of the Latter Tran"), a historical novel with political implications.

·Vietnamese nationalist leadership **19**:127f

Phan Chau (CHU) **Trinh** (b. 1872, Tay Loc, Vietnam—d. March 24, 1926, Saigon), nationalist leader and reformer who played a vital role in the movement for Vietnamese independence and who was the leading proponent of a reformist program that joined the aims of expelling the French and of restructuring Vietnamese society.

Trained in military skills by his father, Phan Chau Trinh fought in 1885 against French forces that were searching for the fugitive rebel king Ham Nghi, the symbol of the resistance. In an encounter with the French, his father was killed, possibly by a member of a nationalist–royalist organization who thought him a traitor. Thereafter, Phan Chau Trinh would not associate with any plans to oppose the French that involved a monarchist symbol.

Phan Chau Trinh resumed his education in 1887, studying the Chinese classics in preparation for the mandarin examinations, which he passed in 1900. By 1906 he had come to view the mandarin bureaucracy and the Vietnamese monarchy as symbols of a backwardness that would forever prevent technological progress and the development of an autonomous state. That year he went to Japan, where he discussed plans for overthrowing the French regime with another Vietnamese nationalist, Phan Boi Chau. Phan Chau Trinh argued for the gradual development of an autonomous state by laying firm foundations in economic and industrial development. His primary goal was modernization, from which he believed a Vietnamese democratic republic would follow.

Returning to Vietnam, Phan Chau Trinh started small business enterprises and spread propaganda encouraging the development of local industries and a modern education for all Vietnamese. Gaining a large following, he tried to persuade the French to undertake major reforms, and he urged replacing the mandarin civil service system with vocational schools and commercial firms. He asked wealthy Vietnamese to develop national commerce through personal investments.

Greatly influenced by the writings of Jean-Jacques Rousseau and Montesquieu, Phan Chau Trinh began by appealing in vain to French colonialists in terms of their own revolutionary tradition. In 1908 he was seized in Hanoi during a series of arrests of anti-colonialist agitators. He maintained a silent protest through a hunger strike while awaiting trial at Hue. After a trial in a joint mandarin and French court, he was sentenced in May 1908 to life imprisonment on Poulo Condore (now Con Son). He was pardoned and released in 1911, however, apparently to work with the colonial regime for modernization. Subsidized by the French, he went to Paris; he was again imprisoned early in World War I, this time for draft evasion and pro-German leanings. He was released in 1915 but received no more subsidies from the French. Phan Chau Trinh returned to Vietnam in 1924 and died of tuberculosis in 1926. He was mourned by Vietnamese of all classes in a national funeral ceremony that lasted a week.

A complete biography of Phan Chau Trinh is available only in Vietnamese. Nguyen Ba The's *Phan Chau Trinh, 1872–1926* (1956) gives details of his life as well as his writings and speeches. An excellent critical assessment of Phan Chau Trinh's writings and his influence on Vietnam's historical development is given in David Marr's *Vietnamese Anticolonialism* (1971).

Phan Dinh Phung (b. 1847, Ha Tinh province, Vietnam—d. Dec. 28, 1895?, Nghe Tinh province), Vietnamese government official who opposed French expansion in Vietnam and became a leader of the nationalist resistance movement.

Phan was a mandarin at the court of the Vietnamese emperor Tu Duc. After Tu Duc's death in 1883, Phan opposed the succession of the Emperor's nephew Ham Nghi. Ham Nghi ascended the throne in 1884, however, and Phan was condemned to death by his enemies at court; the sentence was later commuted to banishment. Ham Nghi became the youthful figurehead leader of an unsuccessful rebellion against the French in 1885.

By 1894 Phan led another rebellion that failed because of inadequate support from the scholar–gentry class. Phan and his fellow revolutionaries were forced to retreat to the mountains of Nghe Tinh province. In July 1895 the French sent 3,000 troops to Nghe Tinh, but Phan's resistance movement held out for several months. At the end of the year, Phan died of dysentery, and the remainder of his followers were caught and executed.

·Vietnamese resistance to France **19**:127e

phaneritic (PHANEROCRYSTALLINE) **texture,** descriptive term for igneous rocks in which the constituents are distinctly crystalline and are visible megascopically. Some authors distinguish rocks on the basis of the percentage of phaneritic minerals they contain; thus, a rock in which more than half of the constituents are phaneritic may be called a phanerite. Phaneritic rocks typically form at depth in the crust of the Earth; *i.e.*, they are plutonic. The constituents of volcanic rocks often cannot be distinguished megascopically, and such rocks are called aphanitic. Whether a rock is phaneritic or aphanitic depends on a complex interplay of chemistry and the conditions under which crystallization occurs. In general, crystals in plutonic rocks grow for a greater length of time.

·igneous rock characteristics **9**:203e; illus.; table 207

phanerophyte, plant life form in which woody plants survive an annual unfavourable season by well-protected buds borne above 25 centimetres (10 inches) from soil level. *Cf.* hydrophyte; geophyte.

·plant life form categories, table 2 **18**:147
·plant stratification and growth **4**:1027h

Phaneropleuridae, family of extinct fish of the order Dipnoi.

·classification and fossil record **5**:815c

Phanerozoic Eon, span of geologic time from the end of the Cryptozoic Eon, the eon of hidden life, about 570,000,000 years ago to the present. The Phanerozoic Eon, the eon of visible life, is divided into three major spans of time on the basis of characteristic assemblages of life-forms: the Paleozoic, Mesozoic, and Cenozoic eras. Although life clearly originated at some time, probably quite early, in the Cryptozoic Eon, not until the Phanerozoic did a rapid expansion and evolution of forms occur and fill the various ecological niches available. The key to this great Phanerozoic expansion appears to lie in the development of plants able to carry out the photosynthetic process and thus release free oxygen into the atmosphere. Before this time, the Earth's atmosphere contained negligible amounts of free oxygen, and animals, in which energy transfers involving the process of respiration are critical, were unable to develop. During the Phanerozoic, the Earth gradually assumed its present configuration and physical features through such processes as continental drift, mountain building, and continental glaciation. Thus, although the Phanerozoic Eon represents only about the last one-eighth of time since the crust of the Earth formed, its importance far exceeds its relatively short duration.

·Earth geologic history **6**:8c
·fossil record **7**:557c
·time scale chronological history **7**:1066c

Phanerozonia (order of starfishes): *see* starfish.

Phangnga, administrative headquarters of Phangnga province (*changwat*), southern Thailand. It lies near the west coast on a major road and is a tin-mining centre. The province (area 1,580 sq mi [4,100 sq km]) has a coastline on the Indian Ocean and embraces a number of offshore islands. The main towns, on the coastal road, include Khok Kloi and Thai Muang. Pop. (1970) town, 21,865; province, 135,101.

8°28′ N, 98°32′ E

·map, Thailand **18**:199
·province area and population table **18**:202

Phanias, also spelled PHAENIAS, OR PHAINIAS (fl. *c.* 320 BC), Greek philosopher of Eresus on the island of Lesbos, a pupil of Aristotle and a friend of Theophrastus, whom he joined in the Peripatetic School. He is mentioned as the author of works on logic, in which he probably followed Aristotle's doctrine; he also wrote, as Theophrastus did, on botany; and there are remains of works by him on poets, on the Socratic philosophers, and on history. His *Prytaneis of Eresus* was a history in which events in the Greek world in general were included, the chronology being determined by the series of successive magistrates of his native place. In his *Tyrants of Sicily* he seems to have dealt with Western history against a pan-Hellenic background.

Phan Khoi (b. 1888?, Quang Nam province, southern Vietnam—d. 1958, Hanoi), intellectual leader who inspired a North Vietnamese variety of the Chinese Hundred Flowers Campaign, in which scholars were permitted to criticize the Communist regime, but for which he himself was ultimately persecuted by the Communist Party.

Phan Khoi was a dedicated nationalist who in his youth followed the patriot Phan Chau Trinh in working for social and political reforms in Vietnam. When Vietnam was divided in 1954, Phan Khoi chose to remain under the Communist government in the north, becoming North Vietnam's most illustrious intellectual. He was the editor of *Nhan Van* ("Humanism") and *Giai Pham Mua Xuan* ("Beautiful Flowers of the Spring"), two radical literary reviews that took advantage of the liberalizing proclamation of Mao Tse-tung, of China, to offer stringent criticisms of the Hanoi regime. Phan Khoi accused the Communist Party of corruption, attacked alleged anti-intellectualism of the Vietnam People's Army, and voiced other complaints.

"Art is a private sphere," he wrote, "Politics should not encroach upon it." The criticisms, however, were more than the government could endure. The liberalization policy ended, and Phan Khoi was imprisoned on charges of "deviationism."

Phantasien über die Kunst, für Freunde der Kunst (1799; "Fantasies on Art, for Friends of Art"), book by Wilhelm Heinrich Wackenroder (*q.v.*) and Ludwig Tieck.

·German romanticism **19**:455e
·Schopenhauer's metaphysical theory **16**:358c

Phan Thanh Gian(g) (b. *c.* 1803, Ben Tre province, southern Vietnam—d. Aug. 4, 1867, Vinh Long), Vietnamese government official and diplomat whose conservatism and strict adherence to the political and ethical tenets of Confucianism contributed to the French conquest of Vietnam.

The son of a low-ranking administrative employee, Phan Thanh Gian was outstanding in state examinations and won a doctoral degree—the first awarded in Cochinchina (southern Vietnam)—and a position close to Emperor Minh Mang. At the imperial court he progressed rapidly through the scholarly ranks, becoming a mandarin of the second order and a counsellor of the Emperor. Following Confucian principles strictly, he informed his sovereign of errors and shortcomings in imperial edicts and practices, thus incurring imperial displeasure. Minh Mang deprived him of his titles and demoted him to fight as a common soldier in the region of Quang Nam, in central Vietnam.

On the battlefield, Phan Thanh Gian marched in the front lines and provided an example of courage and discipline. His behaviour won him the respect and admiration of officers as well as his fellows, and Minh Mang recalled him to court. Under succeeding rulers he was named to the highest governmental positions.

When the Vietnamese sovereigns began the persecution of Christian missionaries, France invaded southern Vietnam and by 1862 had captured Saigon, Bien Hoa, and Vinh Long. By treaty, Phan Thanh Gian surrendered Gia Dinh and Dinh Thong (present-day My Tho), in the hope that the French would stay out of the rest of Vietnam. The French thus controlled the richest parts of Cochinchina—its three easternmost provinces.

In 1863 Phan Thanh Gian went to Paris and proposed a new treaty by which France would halt all future colonization efforts in Vietnam and give back the three provinces in return for commercial settlements and land around Saigon, My Tho, and Mui Vung Tau (Cap Saint-Jacques), the promise of yearly tribute, and the provision that all Cochinchina be declared a French protectorate. The terms were approved by France and, although the emperor Tu Duc later reneged on some points and added further modifications that favoured the Vietnamese, the treaty was signed in 1864. The following year, however, France declared that it would respect only the terms of the original treaty. Phan Thanh Gian was dismayed, feeling that he had failed and had betrayed his people. He feared the influence of Western civilization and distrusted European technology. When the French seized lands that had been under his own personal protection in 1867, he committed suicide.

Phan Thiet, seaport and seat of Bin Thuan province, southern South Vietnam. On the South China Sea, it is at the head of a broad crescent bay, 112 mi (180 km) east-northeast of Saigon. Originally a fishing village, it gained resort facilities under the French colonial administration. It is one of South Vietnam's most important fishing ports and fish processing and marketing centres; it is headquarters of the Vietnamese fishing cooperatives, and there is a considerable brick- and tile-making industry. A vital activity is the manufacture of *nuoc mam*, the national condiment derived from certain types of fermented fish. There are hospitals and a commercial airport. Pop. (1971 est.) 76,652.
10°56′ N, 108°06′ E
·map, South Vietnam **19**:141

phantom limb, illusion experienced by amputees that involves sensations felt in limbs that are actually missing. The phantom limb itself often seems to be embedded in the stump.
·causative mechanism and treatment **12**:1040a
·pain from neurogenic source **13**:866f

phantom midge, any insect of the subfamily Chaoboridae, order Diptera, similar in appearance to the mosquito. The common name for this group is derived from the fact that the larvae are almost transparent. Their antennae are modified into grasping organs. The larvae, found in pools, often destroy mosquito larvae. The adults do not bite.

Phao Sriyanond, also spelled PHAO SRIYANON or PHAO SRIYANAOND (b. March 1, 1910, Siam, now Thailand—d. Nov. 21, 1960, Geneva), director general of the Thai government national police, who as one of a powerful triumvirate, with Pibul Songgram and Sarit Thanarat, built up a formidable armed force in an unsuccessful attempt to assert his individual authority.

Of Thai-Burmese ancestry, Phao Sriyanond joined in the coup of 1947 that restored Pibul Songgram; he held various ministries in the new regime and was given command of the national police force. In a purge of Thailand's Communists in 1952–53, he directed his police to destroy the Chinese population. His reputation was marred by charges of widespread corruption among police officials, who were accused of opium smuggling and profiteering in national commercial enterprises.

Throughout the early 1950s he and Sarit Thanarat became more powerful than Pibul Songgram, and the rivalry between Thanarat and Sriyanond led in 1957 to a bloodless coup that forced Sriyanond into exile.

Phapitreron, genus of brown fruit doves, family Columbidae, order Columbiformes.
·adaptations for arboreal habitats **4**:933h

Phaps histrionica, species of flock pigeon, family Columbidae, order Columbiformes.
·habitat distinct from feeding grounds **4**:935f

pharaoh, Greek form derived from a Hebrew version of the Egyptian word meaning "great house," signifying the royal palace, an epithet applied in the New Kingdom and after, as a title of respect, to the Egyptian king himself. In the 22nd dynasty the title was added to the king's personal name. In official documents the full titulary of the Egyptian king contained five names. The first and oldest identified him as the incarnation of the falcon god, Horus;

Royal cartouche of the pharaoh Sesostris I, from Karnak; in the Egyptian Museum, Cairo
Hirmer Fotoarchiv, Munchen

it was often written inside a square called *serekh*, depicting the facade of the archaic palace. The second name, "two ladies," placed him under the protection of Nekhbet and Buto, the vulture and uraeus (snake) goddesses of Upper and Lower Egypt; the third, "golden Horus," signified perhaps originally "Horus victorious over his enemies." The last two names, written within a ring, or cartouche, are generally referred to as the praenomen and nomen, and were the names most commonly used; the praenomen, preceded by the hieroglyph meaning "king of Upper and Lower Egypt," usually contained a reference to the king's unique relationship with the sun god, Re, while the fifth, or nomen, was preceded by the hieroglyph for "son of Re," or by that for "lord of the two lands." The last name was given him at birth, the rest at his coronation.
·administration of Egyptian law **6**:502a
·early administration concepts **6**:461b
·Egyptian art's ideologic role **19**:250a
·magical and religious attributes **11**:298f
·New Kingdom bureaucracy **6**:477d
·sacred ancestry and ma'at preservation **7**:199d
·sacred status **16**:119c *passim* to 122c
·salvific attributes and functions **16**:202h

Pharaoh (card game): *see* Faro.

Pharaoh's chicken (Old World vulture): *see* vulture.

Pharisees, a Jewish religious party that flourished during the latter part of the Second Temple period. Their insistence on the binding force of oral tradition ("the unwritten Torah") still remains a basic tenet of Jewish theological thought. When the Mishna (the first constituent part of the Talmud) was compiled about AD 200, it incorporated the teachings of the Pharisees on Jewish law.

Though the Pharisees do not appear in history until early in the 2nd century BC, they were, in fact, spiritual descendants of the Hasideans (*q.v.*), who were noted for their piety, their earnest prayer, and their careful observance of the commandments and the sabbath. Preserving this religious heritage, the Pharisees strove to imbue the daily lives of the Jewish people with a sense of God. By interpreting the Law of Moses in the context of changing situations, the Pharisees provided clear-cut norms for virtually every moment of life. This practice led to accusations (reflected in New Testament accounts) that the Pharisees insisted on the letter of the law and a formalistic legalism that killed the spirit. Nonetheless, the personal austerity and the deep religious spirit of the Pharisees won a wide following among the common people, who also felt great enmity toward the pagan Roman rulers.

Whereas the priestly Sadducees maintained the Temple of Jerusalem and taught that the written Torah was the only source of revelation, the Pharisees invoked the "entire Torah" (both oral tradition and the first five books of the Bible) while instructing in the synagogue. Working from this broader base, they professed belief in an immortal soul, personal resurrection, divine punishment of sin, free will reconciled with predestination, and the existence of angelic spirits. These beliefs formed a common bond with Christians against the Sadducees.

With the destruction of Jerusalem in AD 70, the Pharisees quickly disappeared from history, but their theology lived on. Modern rabbinic scholars, like Talmudic scholars before them, view the Pharisees with admiration and gratitude as the preservers and transmitters of normative Jewish religious traditions.
·beliefs and practices in Jesus' time **10**:147c
·early Christian religious environment **4**:533g
·economic factors **15**:607d
·Halakhic orientation and ideal **10**:294b
·Hasmonean period religious disputes **17**:950a
·Johanan ben Zakkai's position **10**:229d
·Josephus' literary career **10**:277g
·Law interpretation and eschatological belief **2**:946e
·mysticism's status in normative Judaism **10**:184c
·origins, beliefs, and position **10**:310f
·prophecy as phenomenon of past **15**:65b
·Torah and exegetical tradition **10**:286h
·Torah interpretation **3**:1084b

pharmaceuticals, production of 14:191, the manufacture of drugs for use in medicine, an important industry that produces a wide range of compounds.

The text article covers the history of pharmaceutical preparations from ancient civilizations to modern times, then briefly the classification of pharmaceutical products. The main part of the article is divided into three sections: (1) raw materials and their processing; (2) preparation of dosage forms; and (3) worldwide pharmaceutical production.

REFERENCES in other text articles:
·algae use in drug preparation **1**:489e
·aluminum compound medical uses **1**:644d
·antibiotic research and development **11**:833e
·chemical industry development **4**:128f
·drug development in the 20th century **18**:47g
·iron compounds medical uses **9**:898d
·marine pharmacological products **7**:350g
·mercuric compound uses **11**:923a
·opium derivatives and medical use **13**:963f
·Rutales medicinal plants **16**:103c
·tranquillizers' chemical properties and history **18**:595a

Pharmacichthyidae, extinct family of fishes of the order Lampridiformes, class Actinopterygii, phylum Chordata.
·classification of extinct family **2**:273c

pharmacological cults 14:199, more or less organized groups in past and contemporary history that have used drugs for various religious purposes.

The text article covers the types of drugs used and their effects, the goals of practitioners; the history of drug use in religions; pharmacological cults in the 20th century; and religious considerations.

REFERENCES in other text articles:
· American Indian guardian revelation **1**:660d
· American Indian spiritual contact **14**:1043a
· Great Basin Indian peyote sect **13**:207d
· Inca divinatory and religious narcotics **9**:261b
· Iranian ancient religious ritual **9**:837a
· mushrooms, peyote, and cocaine in Americas **5**:1048h
· mystical experiments through the ages **12**:788b
· Native American Church and peyote **8**:558g
· religious experience preparation **15**:650d
· Scythian use of hempseed **16**:440c
· South American forest culture practices **17**:124a

pharmacology, the science of drugs, chemical agents that affect living processes. It encompasses various specialized subdivisions: chemotherapy, the study of anti-infective agents; psychopharmacology, the study of drugs that affect psychological or behavioral functions; and pharmacogenetics, the study of the influence of hereditary factors in drug response.

General pharmacology, or pharmacodynamics, attempts to establish the mechanism of drug action. Other disciplines associated with pharmacology include the preparation and dispensing of drugs (pharmacy); the application of drugs in treating disease (therapeutics or pharmacotherapy); and the study of drug poisoning (toxicology).
· comparison to toxicology **14**:617h
· drug components and actions **5**:1041a
· pharmacy's development and scope **14**:203c
· therapeutic uses of drugs **18**:278g

Pharmacopoea Internationalis (INTERNATIONAL PHARMACOPOEIA), a catalog of official drugs published under the auspices of the World Health Organization of the United Nations.
· pharmacy's worldwide standardization **14**:204a

pharmacopoeia, a book published by a government, or otherwise under official sanction, to provide, for a specific political area, standards of identity, quality, and strength for the medicinals representing the best practice and teaching of medicine. The primary function of a pharmacopoeia is to describe each drug on the approved list such that the drug, whenever dispensed, meets the standards of quality and strength established for it. The provisions of the pharmacopoeia in force (*i.e.*, the one that is "official") are binding upon all who produce drugs and those who dispense them.

The oldest record in the form of a pharmacopoeia is a stone tablet of ancient Babylonia (*c.* 1700 BC). The first true pharmacopoeia in Europe was the Florentine *Nuovo Receptaris* (1498). The Danish pharmacopoeia (established 1772) is the oldest in continued existence.

The task of compiling most pharmacopoeias is carried out without compensation by experts in the professions of medicine, chemistry, and pharmacy at the request of the agency undertaking the compilation, usually that responsible for matters of public welfare. Most programs are financed from government funds, but the *British Pharmacopoeia* and the *United States Pharmacopeia* are written by private, nonprofit organizations with the sanction of their respective governments. The proceeds of their sale support the revision. Most countries not having a national pharmacopoeia have adopted one of another nation (or nations), or in some cases the international pharmacopoeia.

Pharmacopoeial standards form the basis for law enforcement on drug quality. Enforcement the standards is generally a function of a separate agency, but there are exceptions, notably in Canada.

International and intranational differences result in variations in the strength and quality of drugs, causing confusion for both travellers and medical practitioners. Travellers benefit especially from uniform drug standards; a diabetic, for example, who travels must depend largely upon local sources for the insulin that makes the difference for him between good health and dangerous illness. Insulin is prepared from the pancreatic glands of cattle, and its potency must be standardized by assays on rabbits or mice. Furthermore, it deteriorates if not kept cold. The acceptance of uniform pharmacopoeial standards have made good insulin available almost everywhere.

Efforts to eliminate international differences in drug standards date from 1865, but the first practical move was made in 1902 when the Belgian government sponsored an international conference in Brussels that produced the Brussels agreement of 1906, in which were proposed uniform nomenclature and standards of strength for many important drugs. A second conference in 1925 further established uniformity in pharmacopoeial standards. These agreements, limited in scope, applied to only a few of the drugs in use.

The problem became more acute with the increase in international travel and in international trade in medicinal products after 1925, and received the attention of the Health Organization of the League of Nations, which created a Technical Commission of Pharmacopoeial Experts. The original seven-member group undertook to prepare an international pharmacopoeia, but this was interrupted when the League went out of existence. The work was resumed almost immediately upon creation in 1948 of the World Health Organization (WHO), a specialized agency of the United Nations. The Expert Committee on the International Pharmacopoeia and Pharmaceutical Preparations compiled the first volume of the *Pharmacopoea Internationalis* for publication in 1951. Complementary volumes and supplements have been added since that time.

The *Pharmacopoea Internationalis* was put forward by WHO only as a recommendation aimed at minimizing or eliminating entirely variations among national pharmacopoeial standards. Some nations among those without their own pharmacopoeia have made the international pharmacopoeia official within their borders.

The four Scandinavian countries and Iceland provided a notable example of international cooperation toward uniformity in drug standards. They formed the Scandinavian Pharmacopoeial Council, which laid the foundation for publication of a single pharmacopoeia in four languages (Danish, Finnish, Norwegian, and Swedish) that supersedes the existing national pharmacopoeias of those countries as the binding authority on the identity, quality, and strength of drugs.
· first publication in Nuremberg in 1546 **14**:191c

pharmacosiderite, hydrated iron arsenate mineral $[Fe_3(AsO_4)_2(OH)_3 \cdot 5H_2O]$ that forms olive-green to honey-yellow, yellowish-brown, and brown, transparent to translucent, striated cubes. It usually occurs as a weathering product of arsenic-rich minerals, as in Cornwall; Saxony (E.Ger.) and Bavaria (W.Ger.); and Utah. For detailed physical properties, *see* table under arsenate minerals.

pharmacy 14:203, the science and art that deals with the collection, preparation, and standardization of drugs and is concerned with the cultivation of plants used as drugs, the synthesis of chemical compounds having medicinal value, and the analysis and standardization of medicines. Pharmacists prepare and dispense the medications prescribed by physicians, dentists, and veterinarians.

The text article reviews the historical development of pharmacy, describes modern education in pharmaceutical science, briefly surveys the laws regulating the practice of pharmacy, alludes to various national and international organizations concerned with pharmaceutical interests, and considers the scope of pharmaceutical research.

REFERENCES in other text articles:
· alchemy, medicine, and immortality **1**:432g
· drug development in the 20th century **18**:47g

pharmakos, in Greek religion, a human scapegoat used in certain state rituals. In Athens, for example, a man and a woman were selected as scapegoats each year. At the festival of the Thargelia in May or June, they were feasted, led round the town, beaten with green twigs, and driven out or killed with stones. The custom was meant to rid the place annually of ill luck.

Pharnabazus (fl. late 5th and early 4th centuries BC), Persian soldier and statesman, hereditary satrap of Dascylium under Darius II and Artaxerxes II. Pharnabazus was an outstanding military and naval commander in Persia's wars against Athens and Sparta. In the war with Athens, beginning in 413 BC, he supported Spartan operations in the Hellespont. When war broke out with Sparta in 400 BC, he persuaded Artaxerxes to organize a naval counterstroke, and in 394 the Persian navy, jointly commanded by Pharnabazus and the Athenian admiral Conon, completely destroyed the Spartan fleet off Cnidus and gained the mastery of the Aegean. When in 388 the revival of Athenian imperialist ambitions led Artaxerxes to enter into an alliance with Sparta, Pharnabazus, as the chief opponent of Sparta, was recalled with honour from his command. In 385 and 373 he commanded unsuccessful invasions of Egypt.

Pharnaces II, Anatolian king of Pontus (63–47 BC) and son of Mithradates VI Eupator.
· Caesar's military conquests in Anatolia **3**:578h
· Mithradates VI's military career **12**:288e

Pharnacia (Turkey): *see* Giresun.

Pharnacia (insect): *see* walkingstick.

Pharos of Alexandria, one of the Seven Wonders of the World; it was the most fa-

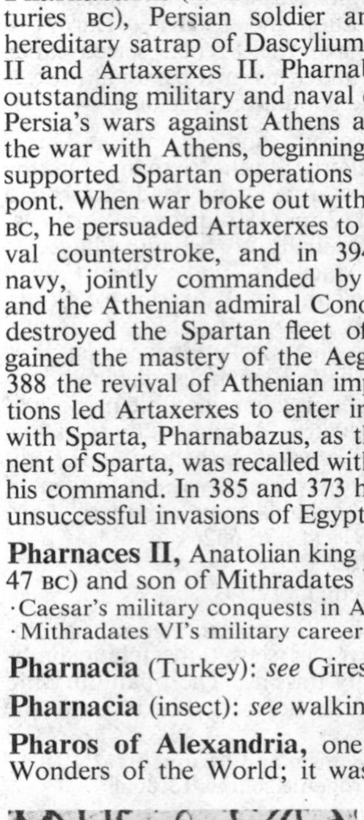

Pharos of Alexandria, Egypt, detail of a mosaic in St. Mark's church, Venice, late 13th century

Douglas B. Hague

mous lighthouse in antiquity. A technological triumph and the archetype of every modern lighthouse, it was built by Sostratus of Cnidus for Ptolemy II of Egypt about 280 BC on the island of Pharos in the harbour of Alexandria. It was said to be over 440 feet (135 metres) high and built in three stages, all sloping slightly inward; the lowest was square, the next octagonal, and the top cylindrical. A broad spiral ramp led to the top, where a fire burned at night. The lighthouse was surmounted by a huge statue, probably representing either Alexander the Great or Ptolemy I Soter in the form of the sun god Helios. Though it was well-known earlier, the Pharos does not appear in any list of wonders until the 6th century AD (the earliest list gives the walls of Babylon instead). In the Middle Ages the Arabs replaced the beacon with a small mosque. The Pharos was still standing in the 12th century, although by 1477 the Mamlūk sultan Qā'it Bāy was able to build a fort from its ruins.

·ancient harbour construction **18**:652c
·construction and later history **1**:481a
·lighthouses of antiquity **10**:952a
·visual art of ancient Greece **19**:298b

Pharr, city, Hidalgo County, southern Texas, U.S., in the lower Rio Grande Valley. It is part of a group of small cities (including McAllen, San Juan, and Edinburg) with mixed farm–oil–gas economies. Settled in the 1900s, it developed as a shipping and processing point for an irrigated agricultural area producing citrus fruits, cotton, and vegetables. Since the 1930s the economy has been broadened by the discovery of natural gas and oil. A recycling plant making propane, diesel fuel, and kerosene from natural gas is in operation within the city. Inc. 1916. Pop. (1980) 21,381.
26°12′ N, 98°11′ W

Pharsalia (AD 39–65), epic by Lucan.
·epic poetry themes and tradition **6**:909h

Pharsalus, Battle of (48 BC), the decisive engagement in the ancient Roman civil war between Julius Caesar and Pompey. After Caesar had been defeated by Pompey at Dyrrhachium in 48 BC, both armies departed and again made contact somewhere near what is today Fársala, Greece. After several days of manoeuvring, Pompey finally offered Caesar battle (August 9 by the uncorrected Roman calendar; June 6, Julian). Caesar had approximately 22,000 men; Pompey possibly had as many as 45,000. Pompey massed the main force of his cavalry on his left infantry wing, hoping to outflank and overpower Caesar's right wing, which was made up of a mixed band of cavalry and infantry. Caesar, however, foresaw the defeat of his right wing and had stationed behind it about 2,000 of his best legionnaires. In the ensuing battle, Pompey's cavalry drove back Caesar's cavalry, only to find itself faced by the advancing corps of select men using their *pila* as stabbing spears rather than as javelins. Confused by the unusual infantry attack, Pompey's cavalry turned and fled. The victorious legionnaires then began to outflank the left wing of Pompey's infantry; at the same time Caesar's third division, which had been held in reserve, was ordered to attack. Pompey's legions broke, and he himself fled to Larissa.

·Antonius' military appointment **1**:1000a
·Pompey's defeat in Greece **15**:1105h
·Pompey's impact and flight **14**:795b

Pharus, genus of grasses of the family Poaceae, order Poales.
·leaf blade structure **14**:585c

pharyngeal, a fricative consonant produced by constriction of the walls of the pharynx. It is characteristic of Arabic and other Hamito-Semitic languages.
·phonetic articulatory description **14**:277c

pharyngeal plexus, in anatomy, a nerve network of branches of the vagus and glossopharyngeal nerves and fibres from the superior cervical sympathetic ganglion.
·anatomic relationships and functions **12**:1020h

pharyngitis, inflammation and infection of the pharynx (throat), usually as a result of infections with bacteria or viruses. A streptococcal infection of the throat may be a complication arising from a common cold. Many viral infections closely mimic the symptoms of a streptococcal infection. The symptoms of pharyngitis caused by streptococci are generally redness and swelling of the throat, a pustulant fluid on the tonsils or discharged from the mouth, extreme soreness of the throat that is felt during swallowing, swelling of lymph nodes, and a slight fever; sometimes in children there are abdominal pain, nausea, headache, and irritability. Within approximately three days the fever leaves; the other symptoms may persist for another two to three days. Treatment is with antibiotics.

Viral pharyngitis infections also occur. They can produce raised whitish to yellow lesions in the pharynx that are surrounded by reddened tissue. They cause fever, headache, and sore throat that lasts for four to 14 days. Lymphatic tissue in the pharynx may also become involved.

A number of other infectious diseases may cause pharyngitis, including tuberculosis, syphilis, diphtheria, and meningitis.
·digestive system affected by infection **5**:797g

Pharyngobdellida, order of leeches of the class Hirudinea, phylum Annelida.
·characteristics and classification **1**:936h; illus. 935

pharyno-esophageal junction (anatomy): *see* esophageal sphincter, upper.

pharynx (Greek: "throat"), a conical-shaped passageway leading from the oral and nasal cavities in the head to the esophagus and larynx. In man it is about 5 inches (13 centimetres) long, narrowing from 2 inches at the base of the skull to 1 inch at its junction with the esophagus. The pharynx chamber serves both respiratory and digestive functions. Thick fibres of muscle and connective tissue attach the pharynx to the base of the skull and surrounding structures. Both circular and longitudinal muscles occur in the walls of this organ; the circular muscles form constrictions that help push food to the esophagus and prevent air from being swallowed, while the longitudinal fibres lift the walls of the pharynx during swallowing.

The pharynx consists of three main divisions. The anterior portion is the nasal pharynx, the back section of the nasal cavity. The nasal pharynx connects to the second region, the oral pharynx, by means of a passage called an isthmus. The oral pharynx begins at the back of the mouth cavity and continues down the throat to the epiglottis, a flap of tissue that covers the air passage to the lungs and that channels food to the esophagus. The oral passage accommodates both air and food; it is lined with tissue of stratified epithelial cells durable enough to withstand food abrasion. Triangular-shaped recesses in the walls of this region house the palatine tonsils, two masses of lymphatic tissue prone to infection. The isthmus connecting the oral and nasal regions is extremely beneficial to man. It allows him to breathe through either the nose or the mouth and, when medically necessary, allows food to be passed to the esophagus by nasal tubes. The third region is the laryngeal pharynx, which begins at the epiglottis and leads down to the esophagus. Its function is to regulate the passage of air to the lungs and food to the esophagus. It is lined with the same type of stratified epithelium as the oral pharynx.

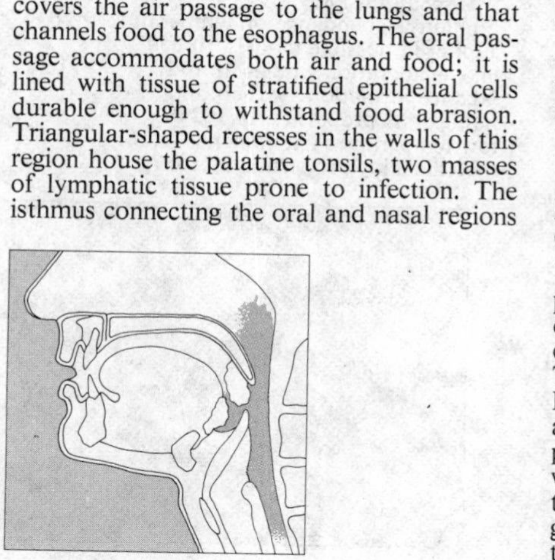
Pharynx
Drawing by Charles Joslin

The act of swallowing food, the pharynx's main digestive function, is very complex and rapid. The medulla of the brain controls the muscles involved, and once food reaches the back of the mouth swallowing occurs automatically and cannot be stopped voluntarily. Food is passed from the oral pharynx to the esophagus in about one second. During that second many things occur spontaneously: the nasal pharynx is closed off by the walls of the isthmus; the walls of the oral pharynx rise to accept food; respiration stops while the larynx and air passage (glottis) are closed off; the epiglottis slants downward directing food toward the esophagus; and circular muscles help propel food to the esophageal opening. Animals and children can be made to swallow pills by placing them back far enough in the mouth cavity so that the swallowing reflex occurs.

Two small tubes (eustachian tubes) connect the middle ears to the pharynx and allow air pressure on the eardrum to be equalized. Head colds sometimes inflame these tubes causing earaches and hearing difficulties. Other medical afflictions associated with the pharynx include tonsillitis, cancer, and various types of throat paralyses caused by polio, diphtheria, rabies, or nervous system injuries.

comparative zoology
·annelid worm anatomy, illus. 1 and 3 **1**:928
·cyclostome anatomy and respiration **15**:755g
·eel swallowing and respiration **1**:899g
·embryonic development and derivatives **5**:639e
·platyhelminth feeding adaptations **14**:549e
·vertebrate digestive system comparisons **5**:787e

human anatomy, physiology, and disease
·Ascaris musculature, illus. 5 **12**:641
·cranial nerve distributions **12**:1020c; illus. 1017
·digestive disorder symptoms **5**:768a
·digestive system anatomy **5**:791h
·diseases of digestive tract **5**:796f
·embryology of the head **6**:753c
·glossopharyngeal nerve disorders **12**:1049b
·muscle movements in swallowing **5**:772g
·neural basis of swallowing **12**:1038g
·respiratory pathway anatomy **15**:764a; illus.
·vocal apparatus anatomy **17**:479b

Phascolarctidae (marsupial family): *see* koala; phalanger.

Phascolomyidae (marsupial family): *see* wombat.

Phascolonus, genus of fossil giant wombat, family Phascolomyidae, order Diprotodonta (superorder Marsupialia).
·body features and classification **11**:544d

Phascolosomatidae, family of peanutworms (phylum Sipuncula).
·classification and features of family **16**:810e

phase, in astronomy, the varying appearance of a celestial body as different amounts of its disk are seen to be illuminated by the Sun. The Moon displays four main phases: New, First Quarter, Full, and Last Quarter. Earth, as seen from the Moon, shows the same phases in opposite order; *e.g.*, Earth is full when the Moon is new. Planets more distant than Earth is from the Sun display only full or gibbous (over half but not entirely full) phases to an observer on the Earth; *i.e.*, are always seen with more than half of their apparent disks in sunlight. Mercury and Venus, closer

to the Sun than Earth is, show full cycles of phases like the Moon's.
· lunar myths and folk traditions **12**:880g

phase, in thermodynamics, a chemically and physically uniform or homogeneous quantity of matter that can be separated mechanically from a non-homogeneous mixture and that may consist of a single substance or of a mixture of substances. The three fundamental phases of matter are solid, liquid, and gas (vapour), but others are considered to exist, including crystalline, colloidal, glassy, amorphous, and plasma phases.

Matter is considered to form one homogeneous phase if its atomic or molecular dispersion is uniform; *e.g.*, a glass of water containing dissolved salt, sugar, bicarbonate of soda, and a dye constitutes only a single liquid phase. If hundreds of grains of sand were added, all the grains together would constitute only a single additional (solid) phase.

The different phases of a pure substance bear a fixed relationship to one another in terms of temperature and pressure. Thus, if the pressure on some liquids is raised, they will freeze at a higher temperature. This relationship is extremely important in industrial as well as scientific work (*see* phase diagram).
· gel structure and molecular weight **12**:321c
· molecular structure determinants **12**:315d
· solid state properties and theory **16**:1032d
· thermodynamics and geochemical systems **7**:1023c
· thermodynamics concepts and laws **18**:292a
· thermodynamics systems and principles **18**:299b

phase, in wave motion, the fraction of a period (*i.e.*, the time required to complete a full

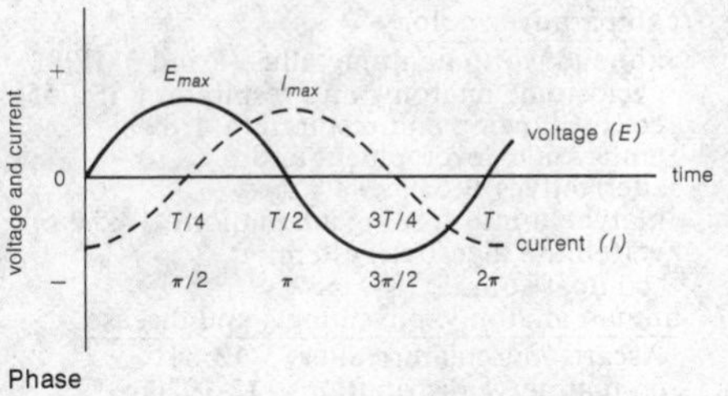

cycle) that a point completes after last passing through the reference, or zero, position. For example, the reference position for the hands of a clock is at the numeral 12, and the minute hand has a period of one hour. At a quarter past the hour the minute hand has a phase of one-quarter period, having passed through a phase angle of 90°, or $\pi/2$ radians. In this example the motion of the minute hand is a uniform circular motion, but the concept of phase also applies to simple harmonic motion such as that experienced by waves and vibrating bodies.

If the position y of a point or particle changes according to a simple harmonic law, then it will change in time t according to the product of the amplitude, or maximum displacement, r, of the particle and a sine or cosine function composed of its angular speed, symbolized by the Greek letter omega (ω), the time t, and what is called the epoch angle, symbolized by the Greek letter epsilon (ϵ): $y = r \sin(\omega t + \epsilon)$. The angle $(\omega t + \epsilon)$ is called the phase angle at time t, which at zero time is equal to ϵ. Phase, itself, is a fractional value—that is, the ratio of elapsed time t to the period T, or t/T—and is equal to the ratio of the phase angle to the angle of the complete cycle, 360°, or 2π radians. Thus, phase for uniform circular or harmonic motion has the value $(\omega t + \epsilon)/2\pi$. Applying this expression to the example of the moving minute hand cited above, ϵ is zero (zero phase angle at zero time), angular speed is 2π radians per hour, and time t is ¼ hour, giving a phase of ¼.

When comparing the phases of two or more periodic motions, such as waves, the motions are said to be in phase when corresponding points reach maximum or minimum displacements simultaneously. If the crests of two waves pass the same point or line at the same time, then they are in phase for that position; however, if the crest of one and the trough of the other pass at the same time, the phase angles differ by 180°, or π radians, and the waves are said to be of opposite phase. Two periodic motions represented by the equations $y_1 = r_1 \sin(\omega_1 t + \epsilon_1)$ and $y_2 = r_2 \sin(\omega_2 t + \epsilon_2)$ have a phase-angle difference $(\omega_2 t + \epsilon_2) - (\omega_1 t + \epsilon_1)$, or $(\omega_2 - \omega_1)t + (\epsilon_2 - \epsilon_1)$. At zero time, or if the angular speeds ω_1 and ω_2 are identical, the phase-angle difference is $(\epsilon_2 - \epsilon_1)$ and the phase difference is $(\epsilon_2 - \epsilon_1)/2\pi$.

One important use of the measurement of phase difference is in alternating-current technology. In the Figure, two waves are shown that represent the voltage (E) and the current (I) in an alternating-current (ac) circuit with pure inductance. The difference in phase angle $(\epsilon_E - \epsilon_I)$ is 90°, and the phase difference is 90°/360° = ¼; the current is said to lag one-quarter cycle behind in phase. This lag may also be seen from the diagram: the voltage has already completed one-quarter cycle by the time the current has reached zero. In ac power transmission, the terms multiphase and polyphase refer to two or more circuits out of phase with one another. In a two-phase system, there are two currents with a phase difference of 90°; in a three-phase system, the currents differ in phase by 120°.
· cross array and radio interferometer **18**:102h

phase changes and equilibria 14:204, the interconversions that take place between solid, liquid, and gaseous forms of matter. Many substances can exist as a gas, a liquid, and one or more solid forms; others cannot be liquefied or vaporized without undergoing reversible or irreversible transformations into different materials.

The text article covers the restrictions upon the numbers of phases, components, and degrees of freedom of a material system and separately treats systems made up of one, two, or three components. *See also* gaseous state; liquid state; solid state of matter.

REFERENCES in other text articles:
· carbonate mineral polymorphism **3**:838b
· chemical analysis separation principles **4**:79a
· chemical kinetics and thermodynamics **4**:140e
· chemical separation methods **4**:156h
· cooling and reheating steel **17**:660f
· crystallization and growth processes **5**:334h
· emulsion principles and properties **4**:857a
· gas condensation process **7**:915f
· glass and crystal formation comparison **8**:207b; illus.
· graywacke diagenesis and mineral content **8**:297g
· heat transfer and vaporization **8**:708g
· high pressure effects on phase changes **8**:868d; illus. 869
· humidity dependence on temperature **9**:2b
· Jupiter in possible models **10**:350f
· lake evaporation studies **10**:611f
· lake-ice formation **9**:166b; illus.
· liquid state properties **10**:1024b
· low-temperature phenomena **11**:161g
· metallic alloy properties **11**:1087g
· metallurgical vacuum-induction melting **11**:1069e
· meteorite impact and rock melting **12**:53c
· molecular structure determinants **12**:315d
· oceanic air-sea transport **13**:492c
· ore deposit formation conditions **13**:666h
· organic compound reaction principles **4**:112c
· petroleum fractional distillation **14**:181e
· rock metamorphism principles **15**:949d
· solid state properties and bonding **16**:1033c
· solution transport properties **16**:1051h
· thermodynamics principles and systems **18**:299a; illus.
· water vapour in snow and ice formation **16**:910g *passim* to 914d
· zone melting principles **19**:1158e

RELATED ENTRIES in the *Ready Reference and Index: for*
equilibrium temperatures and pressure: see boiling point; critical point; freezing point; melting point; phase diagram
phase changes: condensation; fusion, thermal; phase; sublimation; vaporization; vapour
other related entries: latent heat; phase rule, Gibbs; vapour pressure

phase diagram, empirically derived graph showing the limiting conditions for solid, liquid, and gaseous phases (states) of a single substance or of a mixture of substances while undergoing changes in pressure and temperature or in some other combination of variables, such as solubility and temperature. The Figure shows a typical phase diagram for a one-component system (*i.e.*, one consisting of a single pure substance), the curves having been obtained from measurements made at various pressures and temperatures. At any point in the areas separated by the curves, the pressure and temperature allow only one phase (solid, liquid, or gas) to exist, and changes in temperature and pressure, up to the points on the curves, will not alter this phase. At any point on the curves, the temperature and pressure allow two phases to exist in equilibrium: solid–liquid, solid–vapour, or liquid–vapour. For example, the line drawn for the variation with temperature of vapour pressure for the liquid is the boundary between liquid and vapour; only vapour can exist on the low-pressure, high-temperature side of the line, while the substance must be liquid on the high-pressure, low-temperature side; liquid and vapour exist together at temperatures and pressures corresponding to points on the line; at the place where this line vanishes, called the critical point, the liquid and its vapour become indistinguishable. Along the line between liquid and solid the melting temperatures for different pressures can be found. The junction of the three curves, called the triple point, represents the unique conditions under which all three phases exist in equilibrium together. A phase diagram for two components usually shows melting curves on a temperature–composition diagram.

Phase diagrams are specific for each substance and mixture. Complex mixtures may require three-dimensional phase diagrams, which can be represented in two dimensions through use of perspective. Phase diagrams are widely used in studies of mineral equilibria in connection with the conditions of formation of rocks and minerals within the Earth. They also are invaluable when designing industrial

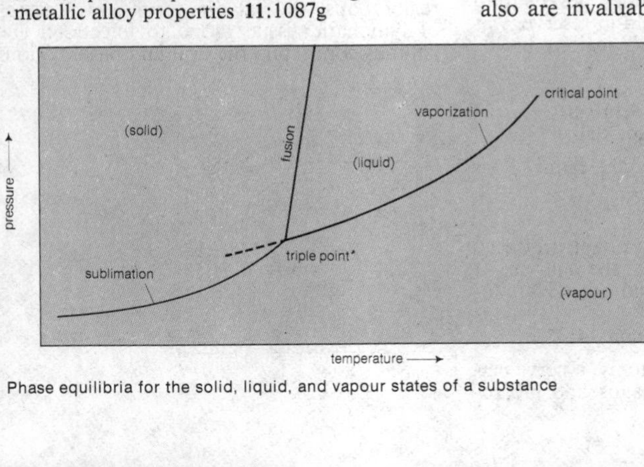

Phase equilibria for the solid, liquid, and vapour states of a substance

equipment and seeking optimum conditions for manufacturing processes, and in determining the purity of substances.
·equilibrium system properties **14**:205h; illus. 206
·geochemical equilibrium representations **7**:1023d; illus. 1022
·liquid state phase changes **10**:1024h; illus.
·phase equilibria diagrams **14**:206c
·thermodynamics system properties **18**:299e

phase distortion (electronics): *see* distortion.

phaseolus: *see* bean.

phase rule, Gibbs, law relating variables of a system in equilibrium, deduced by the U.S. physicist J. Willard Gibbs in his papers on thermodynamics (1875–78). Systems in equilibrium are generally considered to be isolated from their environment in some kind of closed container, but geological systems can often be considered to obey the phase rule. The variables are: the number of phases P (states or forms of matter; *i.e.*, solid, liquid, and gas not necessarily of a single chemical component), the number of chemical components C (pure compounds or elements), and the number of degrees of freedom F of intensive variables, such as temperature, pressure, and percentage composition, which can be altered without affecting the equilibrium. The phase rule states that $F = C - P + 2$. Thus, for a one-component system with one phase, the number of degrees of freedom is two, and any temperature and pressure, within limits, can be attained. With one component and two phases —liquid and vapour, for example—only one degree of freedom exists, and there is one pressure for each temperature. For one component and three phases (*e.g.*, ice floating in water with water vapour above it, in a closed container), there is no degree of freedom, and temperature and pressure are both fixed at what is called the triple point (*see* phase diagram).

In multicomponent systems, the number of components to be counted may be less than the total number if some are in chemical equilibrium with one another. For example, a monomer (simple molecule) in equilibrium with its dimer (two molecules chemically bonded) would count as a single component.
·equilibrium system properties **14**:205g
·geochemical equilibrium relationships **7**:1023f
·liquid state properties **10**:1024g
·rock metamorphism and chemical equilibrium **15**:949d
·thermodynamics systems and principles **18**:299a

phase velocity (physics): *see* wave velocity.

Phasi, Isaac ben Jacob al-: *see* Alfasi, Isaac ben Jacob.

Phasianidae (bird family): *see* jungle fowl; partridge; peacock; pheasant; quail.

phasic muscle, one of two broad groups of muscles distinguished by the rates at which they contract: phasic contraction is typically brief and rapid, and tonic contraction is prolonged and slow. The same muscle may be phasic at one time, tonic at another.
·muscle function and rapid movement **12**:638e; illus. 639

Phasmida, order of insects containing the walkingstick and the leaf insect (*qq.v.*).
·Insecta classification and traits **9**:620e; illus. 609
·orthopteran classification and features **13**:748g

Phasmidia, also called SECERNENTEA, subclass of the invertebrate class Nematoda, phylum Aschelminthes.
·classification and general features **2**:142h

Phat Song (philosopher): *see* Huynh Phu So.

Phatthalung, also spelled PHATALUNG, administrative headquarters of Phatthalung province (*changwat*), southwestern Thailand. It lies on the Bangkok–Singapore rail line. The province, with an area of 1,252 sq mi (3,269 sq km), occupies a fertile plain planted largely in rice and coconuts. Fishing is a major activity near Thale (lake) Luang. Latest pop. est. town, 12,322; (1970 prelim.) province, 298,000.
7°38′ N, 100°04′ E
·map, Thailand **18**:198
·province area and population table **18**:202

Phaulkon, Constantine (b. 1647, Cephalonia, Greece—d. June 5, 1688, Ayutthaya, Thailand), soldier of fortune who became one of the most daring and prominent figures in the history of 17th-century European expansion in Southeast Asia. He used his friendship with the King of Siam to climb to a position of high authority in the Siamese government, shaping policy according to his own interests.

Phaulkon signed on an English merchant ship in Greece at 12 and sailed to Siam (now Thailand). He learned Siamese quickly, and this ability, combined with his knowledge of Portuguese, Malay, French, and English, rendered him invaluable as an interpreter, in which capacity he served with the English East India Company in the years 1670–78. He then offered his services to the Siamese court and cultivated a friendship with King Narai (Narayana) of Siam.

Phaulkon rose quickly from interpreter to personal adviser to the King and soon became director of Siamese foreign policy.

With the assistance of Phaulkon, who spoke to King Narai on their behalf, French Roman Catholics were able to establish a mission in Siam. Phaulkon corresponded with Jean-Baptiste Colbert, minister of Louis XIV of France, and devised a scheme to gain a foothold for France in Siam. He encouraged the Dutch and Portuguese as well. Though the English also tried to win his favour, Phaulkon disliked his former English masters and refused to grant them special concessions. British fortunes were thus doomed in Siam. One result of these involvements was the accumulation of a great personal fortune for Phaulkon as he rose to become Narai's chief minister.

Phaulkon's ambitions and his dynamic rise to power were viewed with suspicion by Siamese court officials and lesser ministers, who were jealous of his relationship with the King. Narai, however, became even more dependent upon Phaulkon. When Phaulkon was knighted and made a count by the French in return for aiding French interests in Siam, the Siamese became alarmed and prepared to undermine his authority.

In 1688 King Narai became seriously ill and was unable to protect Phaulkon. With France ready to seize the country, the Siamese, under the leadership of General Bedraja (P'etraja), ordered Phaulkon's execution. Following Phaulkon's death, there was a rapid decline of foreign involvement in Siam.
·Thai expulsion of French **16**:721c

Phaulkon-Tachard conspiracy, an attempt to establish French control over Thailand (Siam) in the 1680s, in which Constantine Phaulkon, a high-level royal adviser to Thailand's King Narai, cooperated with Gui Tachard, a French Jesuit missionary.

A Greek by birth, Phaulkon had worked with the British East India Company in Java, and then entered the service of the Siamese king, rising to the position of virtual prime minister.

Tachard, who arrived at Ayutthaya, the Siamese capital, in 1685, hoped to convert the Thais to Christianity and to extend French influence and enlisted Phaulkon's aid for these purposes. After negotiations between the two men, a treaty was drafted in December 1685, granting France numerous trading privileges and allowing troops to be stationed in the town of Singora (Songkhla). A joint Franco-Thai delegation then journeyed to France to have the treaty finalized. The French king, Louis XIV, presented additional demands to Narai's ambassadors and in 1687 sent an armed French expedition to Thailand to secure acceptance of his terms, which included French garrisons at the strategic cities of Bangkok and Mergui. Narai became suspicious of French designs, and to placate him Phaulkon engaged the French garrison troops as mercenaries in the service of Thailand. The final treaty was then ratified by Narai, and Tachard returned to France to begin recruitment of Jesuit and other personnel to strengthen the French presence in Thailand.

In March 1688, King Narai became seriously ill. Phaulkon, isolated without the King's support, was overthrown and executed by an anti-French faction at the Siamese court; and the French garrisons were expelled from the country.

The effect of the Phaulkon-Tachard conspiracy was to reverse a policy of openness to foreigners encouraged by previous Siamese kings. Bedraja (Phetraja), Narai's successor, adopted an isolationist policy with respect to Europeans that was pursued into the mid-19th century.

Phayre, Arthur Purves (b. May 7, 1812, Shrewsbury, Shropshire—d. Dec. 14, 1885, Bray, County Wicklow), the first British commissioner in Burma, who made a novel attempt to spread European education through traditional Burmese institutions.

Educated at the Shrewsbury School in England, Phayre joined the army in India in 1828. He was an army officer in Moulmein in the province of Tenasserim, Burma; in 1846 he was appointed assistant to the commissioner of the province. In 1849 he was made commissioner of Arakan, where he learned to speak fluent Burmese.

After the Second Anglo-Burmese War (1852), Phayre became commissioner of Pegu (Lower Burma) and played a major role in the relations between the government of India and the new king Mindon Min. He served as interpreter for Mindon's mission to Calcutta in 1854 and the following year headed a return mission to the Burmese capital, Amarapura. Although no treaty was signed, Phayre and the Burmese king came to an understanding that prevented the outbreak of further war. In 1862, when Phayre was made commissioner for the entire province of British Burma (including Arakan, Tenasserim, and Pegu), he concluded a commercial treaty with Mindon to facilitate trade between Lower and Upper Burma and to establish a British representative at the capital. Five years later Phayre left Burma; after serving for a few years as governor of Mauritius, he retired to Bray. Phayre was a renowned scholar of Burmese culture and history; he wrote the first standard *History of Burma* (1883). His effort to introduce modern education into Burma using Buddhist monastic schools as a foundation was ultimately unsuccessful.

Phazania (Africa): *see* Fezzan.

pheasant, any member of the family Phasianidae (order Galliformes), that is larger than a quail or partridge. Most pheasants—some 50 species in about 16 genera of the subfamily Phasianinae—are long-tailed birds of open woodlands and fields, where they feed in small flocks. All have hoarse calls and a variety of other notes. The males of most species are strikingly coloured. A male pheasant—pugnacious in breeding season—has one or more leg spurs and may have fleshy ornaments on the face. Courting males sometimes fight to the death in the presence of hens, who seem utterly indifferent to the commotion.

Centre of distribution of pheasants is China to Malaysia. Several species have been naturalized elsewhere, and many are prized as ornamentals in zoos and private collections. A number of species have been brought to the verge of extinction by hunting.

The common pheasant (*Phasianus colchicus*) has 20–30 races ranging across Asia. Birds

Pheasant: (top) common (*Phasianus colchicus*), (bottom) Lady Amherst's (*Chrysolophus amherstiae*)

(Top) H. Reinhard—Bruce Coleman Inc., (bottom) K.W. Fink—Bruce Coleman Inc.

naturalized elsewhere are mixtures of races, with the gray-rumped ringneck (or Chinese) strain usually dominating.

The pheasant prefers grain fields near brushy cover. The male, about 90 centimetres (35 inches) long, with streaming, narrow, cross-barred tail, has a brown back and coppery breast, purplish-green neck, and two small ear tufts; his entire body is speckled and barred. He collects a harem of about three brownish, relatively short-tailed hens. The grassy nest contains about 10 eggs, which hatch in three to four weeks.

The green pheasant, or *kiji* (*P. versicolor*), of Japan, is mainly metallic green. It is sensitive to earth tremors unfelt by man and calls in concert when a quake impends.

The argus pheasants, of southeastern Asia, carry long feathers covered with "eyes." Two distinct types are known: the crested argus, or ocellated pheasants (*Rheinardia*), and the great argus (*Argusianus*). The great argus of Malaya, Sumatra, and Borneo (*A. argus*) can attain a length of 2 metres (6½ feet). During display the large "eyes" seem to revolve as the bird quivers.

Ornamental pheasants have been kept for centuries and are represented in collections throughout the world. Best known ornamentals in the west are two species of ruffed pheasants: Lady Amherst's (*Chrysolophus amherstiae*) and the golden pheasant (*C. pictus*).

Several pheasants are of exceptional coloration. Such are the monals, or Impeyan pheasants, of south central Asia. The male Himalayan Impeyan (*Lophophorus impejanus*) has metallic green head and throat, coppery nape and neck, green-gold mantle, purplish wings, white back, orangish tail, and black underparts; the hen is streaked brown.

The male tragopans, or horned pheasants (*Tragopan* species), of Asia also, are among the world's most colourful birds. They show a bright apron of flesh under the bill during courtship and short fleshy horns. The white-spotted plumage may be mainly red, yellow, or gray.

·distribution-limiting factors **5**:910g
·traits, behaviour, and classification **7**:854a

pheasant's-eye, common name for *Adonis annua*, an annual herbaceous (nonwoody) plant of the buttercup family (Ranunculaceae) native to Europe. It is 20 to 40 centimetres (8 to 16 inches) tall and is noted for its small, bright-scarlet flowers.

Phebus (1331–91): *see* Foix, Gaston III, comte de.

Phèdre (first performed 1677), English translation PHEDRA (1776), the last play written for public performance by Jean Racine, often judged his finest tragedy. Its intricately balanced plot, principally based on plays by Euripides (*Hippolytus*, 428 BC) and Seneca (*Phaedra*), presents the disaster evoked by the unrequited, uncontrolled passion of Phèdre for her step-son Hippolyte.

In the play, Phèdre (encouraged by her nurse-confidante Oenone and by reports that her husband Thésée has died on his travels) reveals her long-hidden love to Hippolyte. Repulsed, she has her honour protected by Oenone, who tells Thésée on his return that Hippolyte has attempted adultery. The furious Thésée banishes and curses his son. Finally he learns the truth, which is corroborated by the suicides of first Oenone and then Phèdre, but only after Neptune's monster (evoked by Thésée's curse) has killed Hippolyte.

·Bernhardt's passionate quality **2**:863a
·French use of alexandrine line **15**:71a
·moral struggle and classical norms **18**:585b
·poetic justice and character of Phèdre **18**:589g
·Racine's artistic development **15**:358g

Pheidole: *see* ant.

Pheidon (fl. probably early 7th century BC), king of Argos, Greece, who made his city an important power in the Peloponnese. Herodotus implies that Pheidon flourished about 600 BC, but at this time Corinth and Sicyon, not the Argives, were in the ascendance. Although some later writers assigned Pheidon to the 8th century BC, most modern scholars place him in the early 7th century. He was said to have been the tenth successor to Temenus, the founder of Argos, and ruler of a region (including Sicyon and Epidamnus) in the northeast Peloponnese. Pheidon united this region—the "lot of Temenus," marched across the Peloponnese and seized Olympia (perhaps in 672 or 668).

The system of standard measures instituted by Pheidon remained in effect in the Peloponnese long after his death; it was also employed in Athens before the reforms of Solon (6th century BC). The statement of the 4th-century Greek historian Ephorus that Pheidon was the first to coin silver money cannot be correct, for the beginning of coinage in mainland Greece is now generally ascribed to the late 7th century. In general the King used his royal power more effectively than was usual in an age when the aristocracy was in control. The Argive recovery that he instigated did not last long against the alliance of Sparta and Elis, and the northeastern cities were soon independent under their own tyrants.

·life and accomplishments **8**:336b

phellem (botany): *see* cork.

Phellineaceae, plant family of the order Celastrales.

·classification and general features **3**:1039c

phelonion (vestment): *see* chasuble.

Phelps, William Lyon (b. Jan. 2, 1865, New Haven, Conn.—d. Aug. 21, 1943, New Haven), scholar and critic who did much to popularize the teaching of contemporary literature. He attended Yale (B.A. 1887, Ph.D. 1891) and Harvard (M.A. 1891), taught at

Phelps, detail of an oil painting by Jere Raymond Wickwire, 1926; in the Yale University Art Gallery

By courtesy of the Yale University Art Gallery, bequest of William Lyon Phelps

Harvard for a year, and then returned to Yale, where he was for 41 years a member of the English department, and Lampson professor from 1901 until his retirement in 1933. For years his students voted him Yale's most inspiring professor and thronged to his classes on contemporary drama. In 1895 he taught the first U.S. college course in the modern novel. Both in this course and in his *Essays on Russian Novelists* (1911), Phelps was influential in introducing Russian novelists to U.S. readers. He was a popular lecturer and critic, and his literary essays in *Scribner's Magazine* and other periodicals and his syndicated newspaper column, "A Daily Thought," brought him an audience estimated in the millions. His numerous books were devoted chiefly to English literature, notably *The Beginnings of the English Romantic Movement* (1893). His *Autobiography with Letters* was published in 1939.

Pheme (Greek mythology): *see* Fama.

phenacetin (drug): *see* acetophenetidin.

Phenacodus, extinct genus of primitive mammals known from early Eocene deposits (the Eocene Epoch began 54,000,000 years ago and lasted 16,000,000 years). Though too late in time to have been the ancestral form from which the hoofed mammals evolved, *Phenacodus* represents a late-surviving form that retained many of the primitive traits that

Phenacodus, restoration painting by Charles R. Knight, 1898

By courtesy of the American Museum of Natural History, New York

a common ancestor must have possessed. In terms of structure and dentition, *Phenacodus* appears to be intermediate between the early carnivores and the early herbivores. Though the canine teeth are large and well developed, the cheek teeth were at least partly adapted to a plant diet.

·fossil mammals and evolution, illus. 13 **7**:573

Phenacolemuridae, family of the suborder Plesiadapoidea, order Primates.
·classification and fossil record **14**:1028f

phenacyl chloride: *see* chloroacetophenone, alpha-.

phenakite, rare mineral, beryllium silicate, $BeSiO_4$, used as a gemstone; its name alludes to its deceptive quartzlike appearance (Greek *phenax,* "deceiver"). Phenakite has long been known from the emerald and chrysoberyl mine on the Takovaya River, near Sverdlovsk, in the Urals, U.S.S.R., where large crystals occur in mica schist. It also occurs in the granite of the Ilmen Mountains in the Urals and of the Pikes Peak region in Colorado. Other notable localities include Kragerø, Nor., and San Miguel de Piricicaba, Braz. For detailed physical properties, *see* table under silicate minerals.

Phenakite on feldspar from Minas Gerais state, Brazil
By courtesy of the Field Museum of Natural History, Chicago; photograph, John H. Gerard—EB Inc.

For gem purposes the stone is brilliant cut; *i.e.,* with numerous facets. It is often colourless and glassy but may be wine yellow, pale rose or brown. Its indices of refraction are higher than those of quartz, beryl, or topaz; it is consequently rather brilliant and may sometimes be mistaken for diamond. Nevertheless, it is not in general use, and fine examples are seldom seen outside private or museum collections.

Phenakospermum (plant): *see* Strelitziaceae.

phenazocine, synthetic narcotic drug and the first analgesic of a new structural type introduced in the 1960s. Phenazocine belongs to the benzomorphan series, a group of organic compounds with similarities to both morphine (which has benzomorphan at its nucleus) and the narcotic antagonists (which have an extension of the molecule at the piperidine nitrogen atom). Investigated during a search for a potent, nonaddicting analgesic, phenazocine is about four times as potent as morphine, and addiction appears to develop more slowly than does addiction to morphine.

Phenazocine, administered by intramuscular injection in the form of the hydrobromide salt ($C_{22}H_{28}BrNO$), is available in solution and sometimes marketed under the trade name Prinadol.

Phenazocine hydrobromide occurs as white crystals or powder.

phenelzine, synthetic drug of the monoamine-oxidase inhibitor type, used to treat mental depression. Like other monoamine-oxidase inhibitor drugs, phenelzine prevents the enzymatic breakdown of norepinephrine, the brain-neurotransmitter substance concerned with emotional stimulation. It does so by inhibiting the enzyme monoamine oxidase (MAO), which normally breaks down norepinephrine at nerve endings. Phenelzine is administered orally. The onset of action is delayed, the effects of the drug developing slowly over the first two weeks of therapy. As with other monoamine-oxidase inhibitor drugs, liver damage is a possible side effect.
·characteristics and action **17**:693g

phengite, muscovite variety with aluminum substitution for magnesium and silicon.
·formation at high pressure **16**:761g

Phenix City, city, seat (1935) of Russell County, eastern Alabama, U.S., port of Chattahoochee River, opposite Columbus, Ga. Incorporated in 1883 as Brownville, it was renamed Phenix City in 1889 for the old Phoenix Mills in Columbus. In 1923 it annexed Girard (settled 1820, inc. 1890). Manufactures include paperboard, bricks, and textiles. The last Civil War battle east of the Mississippi was fought there (April 16, 1865). Ft. Benning (a military reservation) and the remains of Ft. Mitchell (erected in 1813 during the Creek Wars) are nearby. Pop. (1980) 26,928.
32°29′ N, 85°01′ W
·map, United States **18**:908

phenobarbital, barbiturate drug that became available in 1912, is used in medicine as a sedative, hypnotic, and anticonvulsant. *See* barbiturate.
·toxicity rating for drugs, table 2 **14**:619

phenocryst (geology): *see* porphyritic texture.

phenogenetics, also known as DEVELOPMENTAL GENETICS, the part of genetics that deals with the mechanisms of development and the differentiation of certain qualities controlled by genes.
·gene expression and metabolism **8**:808d

phenol, any of a family of organic compounds characterized by the attachment of at least one hydroxyl (OH) group to a carbon atom forming part of the benzene ring or any other substance of the aromatic series. *see* alcohols, phenols, and ethers.

phenol coefficient, a figure representing the disinfectant quality of an antiseptic or germicide in relation to that of phenol, which is used as a standard, or control. The phenol coefficient of a chemical is found by adding micro-organisms to several samples of various concentrations of the chemical and to samples of phenol for a known period of time. The action of the chemicals is stopped before samples are removed from each solution and added to a suitable liquid growth medium. The sample in which no visible microbial growth occurs is considered the end-point sample for the chemical. An end-point concentration is recorded for phenol as well. Then a ratio is determined, comparing the concentrations of the two end-point samples.
·antiseptic and germicide types **1**:996d

phenol–formaldehyde resin, synthetic resin based on phenol, used in many industrial applications as an electrical insulator, in molding and casting operations, as an adhesive, and in paints and baked enamel coatings. Phenol–formaldehyde resins are indispensable in manufacturing chemical equipment, machine and instrument housings, bottle closures, and many machine and electrical components.

The production method for manufacturing this plastic was devised in 1909 by L.H. Baekeland in the United States, and the name Bakelite is a registered trademark of the Union Carbide Corporation. It displaced celluloid for nearly all applications early in the 20th century.

Phenol–formaldehyde resin is made by reacting phenol found in coal tar, with an aldehyde, formaldehyde, a derivative of methyl alcohol, obtained either synthetically or by the distillation of wood.
·Bauhaus use in furniture construction **7**:805c
·chemical composition and importance **18**:47d
·colloidal polymer synthesis **4**:859c
·phenol reaction characteristics **1**:457d
·polymer discovery and development **14**:765f

phenolic resin, any of various usually thermosetting resins of high mechanical strength and electrical resistance; made by condensation of a phenol with an aldehyde.
·paint binder use and composition **13**:890b

phenolphthalein, an organic dye of the phthalein family seldom used as a dye but widely employed as an acid–base indicator and as a laxative.

The colourless form of phenolphthalein that exists in acidic solution is converted by alkali to an anionic form (with a negative charge) that also is colourless. Further alkali produces the bluish-red form, which is a doubly charged anion. In very strongly alkaline solutions, the chromophoric (colour-producing) system is disrupted, and the triply charged anion is colourless.

Phenolphthalein, which is closely related to the triphenylmethane dyes, was discovered in 1871 by the German chemist Adolf von Baeyer, who prepared it by fusing phenol and phthalic anhydride in the presence of sulfuric acid or zinc chloride, the procedure still employed.
·acidity change as indicator in titrations **5**:1104g

phenolsulfonphthalein test, or PSP TEST, clinical procedure for the estimation of overall blood flow through the kidney. A specific dose of the PSP dye is injected intravenously, and its recovery in the urine is measured at successive time intervals. The recovery value at 15 minutes after injection (normally about 35 percent) is the most significant diagnostically, since even a damaged kidney may be able to remove the PSP dye from circulation after a longer time interval. PSP excretion is decreased in most chronic kidney diseases and may be increased in some liver disorders.

phenomenalism, a philosophical theory of perception and the external world. Its essential tenet is that propositions about material objects are reducible to propositions about actual and possible sensations, or sense data, or appearances. According to the phenomenalists, a material object is not a mysterious something "behind" the appearances that men experience in sensation. If it were, the material world would be unknowable; indeed, the term matter itself would be unintelligible unless it somehow could be defined by reference to sense experiences. In speaking about a material object, then, reference must be made to a very large group or system of many different possibilities of sensation. Whether actualized or not, these possibilities continue during a certain period of time. When the object is observed, some of these possibilities are actualized, though not all of them. So long as it is unobserved, none of them is actualized. In this way, the phenomenalist claims, an "empirical cash value" can be given to the concept of matter by analyzing it in terms of sensations.

Some philosophers have raised the objection against phenomenalism that, if these hypothetical propositions play such an important role in the phenomenalist analysis—analyzing all material-object expressions in terms of actual and possible sense experiences—it nonetheless remains difficult for him to avoid using material-object expressions in his "if . . . then" clauses; and this would make his analysis circular. A second and even more important objection is that it is very difficult to believe that categorical propositions about material objects (*e.g.,* "There is a fire in the next room") can be analyzed without remainder into sets of hypotheticals or if . . . then clauses; *i.e.,* that a statement about what there actually is can be reduced to a set of statements about what there would be if certain (nonexistent) conditions were to be fulfilled.
·alternatives to epistemic dualism **6**:946e
·Berkeley on substance and quality **14**:267c
·Humean impression and idea **6**:941b
·immaterialist theory of physical bodies **12**:231a
·Japanese relationship to Absolute **10**:104f

·knowledge of physical objects **6**:927f
·objectivity of science concepts **16**:390e
·Phenomenology's critique and methods **14**:211a
·progression from Berkeley and Locke **6**:769c
·Realist rejection of object-sensation equation **15**:540a

Phénoménologie de la perception (1945), English PHENOMENOLOGY OF PERCEPTION (1962), work by Maurice Merleau-Ponty.
·probability and human situation **7**:77g

Phenomenology 14:210, a school of philosophy that arose at the turn of the 20th century with the work of Edmund Husserl. Its primary objective has been to take a fresh approach to concretely experienced phenomena through the direct investigation of the data of consciousness—without theories about their causal explanation and as free as possible from unexamined presuppositions—and to attempt to describe them as faithfully as possible. By carefully exploring examples, one can thus fathom the essential structures and relationships of phenomena.

The text article covers the characteristics of Phenomenology in contrast with other movements. It deals with the origin and development of Husserl's Phenomenology: its basic principles, including antipsychologism, antinaturalism, and antihistoricism; and its basic method and basic concepts. The article covers later developments of Phenomenology: the Phenomenology of essences; Martin Heidegger's hermeneutic Phenomenology; and the phenomenologies of Eugen Fink and Ludwig Landgrebe. It concludes by reviewing the dissemination of Phenomenology into France, Germany, other European countries, and the United States; its influence on other disciplines; and its possible future.

REFERENCES in other text articles:
·branches of Continental philosophy **14**:273e
·Christian doctrine of creation **4**:559h
·communication models and argumentation **15**:799b
·ethics theory development **6**:978g
·Existential analysis of Being **7**:75b
·Heidegger divergence from Husserl **8**:739c
·Husserlian thought development **9**:67e
·influence on study of religion **15**:614d
·Japanese Buddhist philosophies **10**:104b
·Jaspers' psychiatric theory **10**:116b
·Kantianism criticism **10**:397h
·Marcel's Existentialist metaphysics **11**:489c
·metaphysics and ontology **12**:34b
·philosophical psychology development **15**:154b
·religions classification methods **15**:632h
·religious study applicability **15**:603b
·sacred experience and religious study **16**:123b
·Sartre's use of method **16**:256g
·static typology in religious study **15**:623e

RELATED ENTRIES in the *Ready Reference and Index:*
intentionality; life-world; psychology, phenomenological; reduction, eidetic; reduction, phenomenological

Phenomenology of Mind, The (1910), German PHÄNOMENOLOGIE DES GEISTES (1807), work by G.W.F. Hegel.
·consciousness and the spirit **8**:730a
·revisions of Schelling's philosophy **16**:340d

phenomenon, in philosophy, any object, fact, or occurrence perceived or observed. In general, phenomena are the objects of the senses (*e.g.*, sights and sounds) as contrasted with what is apprehended by the intellect. The Greek verb *phainesthai* ("to seem," or "to appear") does not indicate whether the thing perceived is other than what it appears to be. Thus in Aristotle's ethics "the apparent good" is what seems good to a man, whether or not it really is good. Later Greek philosophers distinguished observed facts (phenomena) from theories devised to explain them. This usage is still current.

In modern philosophy the word is sometimes used for what is immediately apprehended by the senses before any judgment is made; it has, however, never become a technical term, many philosophers preferring sense-datum or some such expression—though they commonly accept the cognate forms phenomenalism and phenomenology. In English translations of Kant, "phenomenon" is often used to translate *Erscheinung* ("appearance"), his term for the immediate object of sensory intuition, the bare datum that becomes an object only when interpreted through the categories of substance and cause. Kant contrasted it to the noumenon, or thing-in-itself, to which the categories do not apply. *See also* appearance.
·Buddhist thought in China **4**:418e
·conditioned nature for Kant **10**:391f
·Greek and medieval theories **14**:252a *passim* to 257e
·perception according to various philosophies **6**:927a *passim* to 946c
·Phenomenology's concepts and methods **14**:210e
·Platonist and Rationalist metaphysics **12**:11a *passim* to 21f
·Sophist antilogic and Plato **17**:11h

Phenomenon of Man, The (1959), French LE PHÉNOMÈNE HUMAIN (1938–40), work by Pierre Teilhard de Chardin.
·mystical leadership in mental evolution **12**:793c

phenothiazine, anthelmintic, or worming agent, used in veterinary medicine. Phenothiazine is an organic compound effective against a broad range of parasites in cattle, horses, poultry, sheep, and swine. Highly toxic, it is not recommended for human use and is not effective in dogs and cats. Many popular tranquillizing drugs, classed as phenothiazines, are derivatives of phenothiazine.

The chemical formula for phenothiazine is $C_{12}H_9NS$.
·psychiatric treatment usage **15**:143b
·tranquillizers and psychosis treatment **18**:595b
·tranquillizer side effects **5**:1058b

phenotype, all the observable characteristics of an organism, such as shape, size, colour, and behaviour, that result from the action of its total genetic inheritance with the environment. "Phenotype" also refers to the general form and appearance of the majority of individuals comprising a group or a species, the so-called normal individuals. This average phenotype may be produced by different genotypes as a result of various gene substitutions, gene combinations, or mutations. Environmental conditions may favour the expression of certain potentials common to all the individuals. The phenotype may change constantly throughout the life of an individual because of environmental changes and the physiological and morphological changes associated with aging.

Different biological and physical backgrounds influence development of inherited traits (for example, size is affected by available food supply) and alter expression by similar genotypes (for example, twins maturing in dissimilar families). All inherited possibilities in the genotype are not expressed in the phenotype, because some are the result of latent, recessive, or inhibited genes.
·animal breeding assessment and use **1**:903h
·genetic and environmental interactions **7**:12e
·genetic and nongenetic modification **14**:774d
·human behaviour and heredity **8**:1146c
·racial distribution **14**:841e *passim* to 847f
·racial typing by physical traits **15**:351c

phenylalanine, an amino acid present in common proteins. It is one of three aromatic amino acids (the others, tryptophan and tyrosine), so called because the molecule contains a benzene ring (within the dotted line; *see* figure). Human hemoglobin (the oxygen-carrying pigment of red blood cells) is one of the richest sources, yielding 9.6 percent by weight. First isolated in 1881 from lupine seedlings, phenylalanine is one of several so-called essential amino acids for fowls and mammals; *i.e.*, they cannot synthesize it and require dietary sources. Inability to metabolize it in human beings is called phenylketonuria.

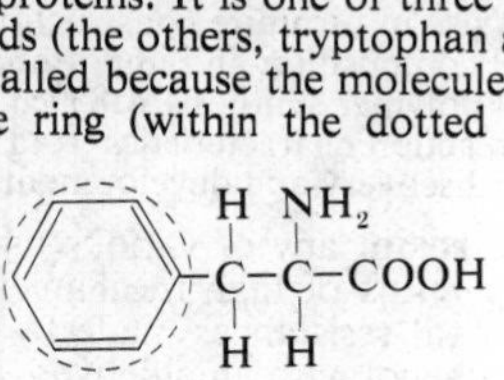

phenylalanine

·cereal and soybean content levels, tables 7 and 13 **3**:1160
·genetic code triplets, table 2 **7**:990
·human genetic metabolism error **7**:1000e
·nutrient needs and alternative source **13**:406g; table 405
phenalanine hydroxylase
·hereditary disease, table 1 **6**:897
·metabolic deficiency in PKU **11**:1053c; table 1052
·urine content in phenylketonuria **7**:41g
·structure and light absorption **15**:82f; illus. 83

phenylamine (chemistry): *see* aniline.

phenylcarbinol (chemistry): *see* benzyl alcohol.

phenylketonuria (PKU), also called PHENYLPYRUVIC OLIGOPHRENIA, hereditary inability of the body to metabolize normally the amino acid phenylalanine. Phenylalanine is normally converted to tyrosine, another amino acid, by a specific organic catalyst, or enzyme, called phenylalanine hydroxylase. This enzyme is not active in persons who have phenylketonuria. As a result of this metabolic block, a high level of phenylalanine is observed in blood plasma, cerebrospinal fluid, and urine. Abnormal metabolic products of phenylalanine can also be detected in the urine. In the tissues, the excess amino acid and its abnormal metabolites interfere with various metabolic processes. The central nervous system, notably, is affected; impairment of some aspect of nerve cell function manifests itself by mental retardation, epileptic seizures, and abnormal brain wave patterns. The mechanism of injury is not known. The first behavioral signs of nerve cell damage are usually evident in an affected child at the age of four to six months. The retention of phenylalanine in body tissues also inhibits the course of tyrosine metabolism and leads specifically to a decrease in the formation of a product of tyrosine, melanin, the pigment found in the skin, hair, and eye. This may explain why persons with phenylketonuria generally have blond hair, blue eyes, and fair skin.

The disorder is transmitted by an autosomal recessive gene; two unaffected carriers of the trait who mate and have four children can expect, on the basis of chance, one child who is phenylketonuric, two children who are unaffected but are carriers, and one completely normal child. Reliable tests are available to detect carriers as well as infants who have the disorder. Approximately one in 10,000 newborn infants show abnormally high plasma phenylalanine levels; of these, about two-thirds have the classic form of phenylketonuria, which, if untreated, causes severe mental retardation. In the treatment of the disorder, a lifelong diet low in phenylalanine is effective in controlling the body level of this amino acid. *Major ref.* **11**:1052c; table
·brain development effect **12**:995h
·causation and symptoms **5**:861c
·diagnosis in newborn **7**:996c
·dietary therapy **13**:415g
·enzyme abnormality, table 1 **6**:897
·gene abnormalities **7**:982f
·genetic mechanism and consequences **7**:1000e
·incidence frequency in racial groups **15**:354e
·neurological evaluation **12**:1044g; table
·urine content in metabolic diseases **7**:41g

phenyl methyl ketone (chemistry): *see* acetophenone.

phenylpyruvic acid, a derivative of pyruvic acid (*q.v.*).

phenylpyruvic oligophrenia (metabolic disorder): *see* phenylketonuria.

phenylthiocarbamide tasting, a genetically controlled ability to taste phenylthiocarbamide (PTC) and a number of related substances, all of which have some antithyroid activity. PTC-tasting ability is a simple genetic trait governed by a pair of alleles, dominant *T* for tasting and recessive *t* for nontasting. Persons with genotypes *TT* and *Tt* are tasters and persons with genotype *tt* are nontasters; there appears to be hormonal mediation of the tasting ability, however, since women are more often taste sensitive in this regard than are men. It has been suggested that PTC tasting may be related to the genetically determined level of dithiotyrosine in the saliva.

PTC-tasting ability is not particularly useful, it would seem, since PTC does not occur in food, but some substances related to PTC do occur in food items. As for the utility of being able to taste PTC, it appears that nontasters of PTC may have a higher than average rate of goitre, a disease of the thyroid gland sometimes associated with lack of iodine; since PTC and related compounds contain iodine, there may be a selective advantage of some kind for tasters or nontasters in different environments. It has also been suggested that tasters may have more food aversions than nontasters, a disadvantage in situations of food scarcity.

The chief reason for interest in tasting ability, however, is that the frequency of tasters varies from population to population and from race to race. Difference in PTC-taster frequency is of use to the physical anthropologist, as are the observed differences in BAIB excretion (*see* aminoisobutyric acid, beta-, excretion) and blood group distribution in the determination of relationships between population groupings.

·innate human sensory factors **8**:1147e
·racial typing through genetics **15**:353c
·sensory reception and taste blindness **16**:553a

pheochromocytoma, a chromaffin tumour, sometimes referred to as chromaffinoma, most often nonmalignant, causing abnormally high blood pressure because of hypersecretion of adrenaline and noradrenaline (*q.v.*). Usually the tumour is in the medullary cells of the adrenal gland but may occur elsewhere; *e.g.*, in the chromaffin tissues of the ganglions of the nervous system.

The hypertension may be persistent or periodic. Patients with persistent hypertension usually are afflicted with a constant headache, are thin and nervous, and have high blood sugar and an elevated basal metabolic rate. With the paroxysmal attacks, which last from one-half to three-quarters of an hour, the headache is much more intense and is accompanied by sweating, pallor, and tremor. Satisfactory treatment for both types has been attained with medication.

·causation and symptoms **5**:860a
·familial occurrence **3**:765e
·incidence and treatment **6**:832d
·pregnancy affected by adrenal tumour **14**:979e

Pherecydes of Syros (fl. *c.* 550 BC), Greek mythographer and cosmogonist traditionally associated with the Seven Wise Men of Greece (especially Thales); he is credited with originating metempsychosis, a doctrine that holds the human soul to be immortal, passing into another body, either human or animal, after death. He is also known as the author of *Heptamychos*, a work, extant in fragments only, describing the origin of the world. Pherecydes was characterized by Aristotle as a theologian who mixed philosophy and myth. Tradition says that he was the teacher of Pythagoras. He is not to be confused with Pherecydes of Athens, a genealogist who lived about a century later.

pheromone, any chemical used in intraspecific communication between animals. Widespread among insects, fishes, and mammals but unknown among birds, these chemicals may be secreted by special glands or incorporated in other products, such as urine. They may be shed freely into the environment, as are the sex attractants of many moths, or placed in carefully chosen locations, such as the scent trails laid down by ants and the territorial markings of many mammals.

·aggressive behaviour of insect colonies **1**:299a
·barnacle mating behaviour **4**:642b
·chemoreception and mating behaviour of crabs **4**:180b
·chemoreception in insect courtship **4**:182d
·evolutionary precursors and associated behaviours **4**:1019c
·fire ant odour trails **4**:1016d; illus. 1013
·hymenopteran behaviour **9**:131c
·insect social behaviour regulation **8**:1086b
·lepidopteran mating behaviour **10**:822f
·orchid imitations of insect sex lures **13**:654d
·orthopteran courtship behaviour **13**:745a
·ostariophysian communication mechanism **13**:761g

queen substance
·bee colony activity regulation **9**:131d
·sex attractants in honeybee **8**:1086b
·social behaviour patterns in ants **16**:939b
·reproductive behaviour mechanism **15**:680d *passim* to 683d
·sensory reception in insects **16**:547f
·sexual attractants of insects **9**:612d
·starfish egg-shedding control **6**:845g
·termite caste system regulation **9**:1050g

Pherosophus: *see* ground beetle.

Phet Buri, province (*changwat*), southwestern Thailand, located in the northern portion of the Malay Peninsula. The hilly region occupies an area of 2,454 sq mi (6,357 sq km) and lies between Burma (west) and the Gulf of Thailand (east). It has a coastline 57 mi (91 km) long and is drained by the navigable Mae Nam Phet Buri (Phet Buri River). Rice is grown on irrigated land in the east; and there are coconut, melon, and palm-sugar plantations. Apart from the provincial capital of Phet Buri, the main towns are Samut Songkhram, Khao Yoi, and Cha-am.

Stūpa, Phet Buri town, Thailand
Rene Burri—Magnum

Near the mouth of the Mae Nam Phet Buri, the capital is located on the southern railway. Before the sea route around the Malay Peninsula was developed, the town was on an overland trade route from Europe and India to continental Southeast Asia. There are neighbouring ruins of old Brahmin and Buddhist temples and caves; Khao Luang cave is a Buddhist shrine. Both King Mongkut and his son, Chulalongkorn, built palaces in Phet Buri town. Haad Chao Samran, a popular beach, is nearby. Latest pop. est. town, 11,687; (1970 prelim.) province, 278,000.

·area and population table **18**:202
·map, Thailand **18**:198

Phetchabun, also spelled PETCHABUN, administrative headquarters of Phetchabun province (*changwat*), central Thailand, on the Mae Nam (river) Pa Sak. It is a commercial centre trading in rice, tobacco, and teak and served as the Thai capital under the Japanese (1944–45). The province (area 4,310 sq mi [11,166 sq km]) includes part of Thung Salaeng Luang National Park. Apart from Phetchabun town, the main population centres are Phu Khieo and Chon Daen. Latest pop. est. town, 6,277; (1970 prelim.) province, 513,000.
16°24′ N, 101°11′ E

·map, Thailand **18**:198
·province area and population table **18**:202

Phetchabun, Thiu Khao, in central Thailand, is a southern extension of the Doi (mountains) Luang Phra Bang Range. Heavily forested, it runs north–south, forming the western rim of the Khorat Plateau, and rises to 5,840 ft (1,780 m).
16°20′ N, 100°55′ E

Pheucticus ludovicianus (bird): *see* grosbeak.

phi (Asian religious spirits): *see* nat.

Phichit, administrative headquarters of Phichit province (*changwat*), west central Thailand, is on the Mae Nam (river) Nan and the Bangkok–Chiang Mai railroad. It is a commercial centre for an agricultural region.

The province occupies a lowland area of 1,750 sq mi (4,530 sq km), well drained by the Yom and Nan rivers. Main towns include Taphan-Hin and Ban Bung Na Rang. Latest pop. est. town, 12,109; (1970 prelim.) province, 440,000.
16°24′ N, 100°21′ E

·map, Thailand **18**:198
·province area and population table **18**:202

Phidias (fl. *c.* 490–430 BC), Athenian sculptor, one of the most outstanding of all sculptors, who directed the construction, and probably the design, of the marble sculptures of the Parthenon. It is said of Phidias that he alone had seen the exact image of the gods and that he revealed it to man. He established forever general conceptions of Zeus and Athena.

Little is known about Phidias' life. When Pericles rose to power in 449, he initiated a great building program in Athens and placed Phidias in charge of all artistic undertakings. Among other works for which Phidias is famous are three monuments to Athena on the Athenian Acropolis (the Athena Promachos, the Lemnian Athena, and the colossal Athena Parthenos for the Parthenon) and the colossal seated Zeus for the temple of Zeus at Olympia; none of these survives in the original.

The first of Phidias' monuments to Athena, the bronze Athena Promachos, was one of his earliest works. It was placed on the Athenian Acropolis *c.* 456. According to the preserved inscription, it measured about 30 feet high. At the time, it was the largest statue yet erected in Athens.

The so-called Lemnian Athena was dedicated as a thank offering by Athenian colonists who were sent to Lemnos between 451 and 448. A head of Athena in Bologna and two statues of Athena in Dresden are thought to be copies, in marble, of Phidias' original work in bronze.

The colossal statue of the Athena Parthenos, which Phidias made for the Parthenon, was completed and dedicated in 438. The original work was made of gold and ivory and stood some 38 feet high. The goddess stood erect, wearing a tunic, aegis, and helmet and holding a Nike (goddess of Victory) in her extended right hand and a spear in her left. A decorated shield and a serpent were by her side. Several copies have been identified from this description; among them are the Varakion, a Roman copy of *c.* AD 130 (now in the National Archaeological Museum of Athens), and a Hellenistic copy, from *c.* 160 BC made for the main hall of the royal library at Pergamum (now in the Staatliche Museen Preussischer Kulturbesitz in Berlin).

Like the Athena Parthenos, Phidias' Zeus for the Temple of Zeus at Olympia was of gold and ivory. The ancient writers considered it to be Phidias' masterpiece. Zeus was seated on a throne, holding a Nike in his right hand, a sceptre in his left. His flesh was of ivory, his drapery of gold. The throneback rose above his head. Everything surrounding the figure, including the statues and paintings (by Panaenos), was richy decorated. The Olympian Zeus was about seven times life size (or 42 feet) and occupied the full height of the temple.

Phidias' last years remain a mystery. Pericles' enemies accused him of stealing gold from the statue of the Athena Parthenos in 432, but he was able to disprove the charge. They then accused him of impiety (for including portraits of Pericles and himself on the shield of Athena on the Athena Parthenos), and he was thrown into prison. Until recently, it was thought that Phidias died in prison shortly thereafter; now it is believed that he was exiled to Elis, where he worked on the Olympian Zeus. A "workroom," thought to be Phidias' has been found in Olympia. It contains a number of terra-cotta molds believed to have been used for the drapery of the Olympian Zeus.

Phidias was also responsible for the marble sculptures that adorned the Parthenon. Since several of these fragments are extant, they are reliable surviving indications of Phidias' style. Most of these remains (the Elgin Marbles), are now in the British Museum.

Several other sculptures have been attributed to Phidias, but none with certainty. All are now lost. Among the most plausible of these attributions are the Amazon at Ephesus, possibly reproduced in the Amazon Mattei of the Vatican; the Apollo Parnopius erected on the Acropolis and possibly reflected in the Kassel Apollo; and the Anadumenus of Olympia, possibly reproduced on the Farnese Diadumenus of the British Museum.

The Varakion, a Roman marble copy (*c.* AD 130) of the colossal gold and ivory statue of the Athena Parthenos by Phidias (438 BC); in the National Archaeological Museum, Athens

Alinari

From these works one can gain some idea of Phidias' style. Quiet stances, serene expressions, and a certain majesty of conception characterize his single figures; even when movement is represented in some of his reliefs, a monumental quality is imparted. Though the construction of the human body is perfectly understood, its rendering is restrained and harmonized. In other words, Phidias may be called the initiator of the idealistic, classical style that distinguishes Greek art in the later 5th and the 4th centuries. And this idealistic quality—expressed in restrained modelling and in elevation of spirit—is still considered typical of Greek art.

Phidias was also a painter, an engraver, and a worker in embossed metalware.

·Acropolis construction and enrichment **2**:266e
·Classical Greek sculpture **19**:294g; illus.
·Greek artisans' social status **2**:97d
·Greek religious statuary **8**:410d
·Olympian statue of Zeus **13**:565c

Phi function (mathematics): *see* Euler Phi function.

Phigalia, also called PHIALIA, in Greece, an ancient city on the Neda River in southwest

Temple of Apollo Epikourios, Phigalia

Alison Frantz

Arcadia; the site of the Temple of Apollo Epikourio (the Helper). Pausanias, Greek geographer of the 2nd century AD, called the temple the finest in the Peloponnese after that of Artemis at Tegea; it is also the best preserved temple in Greece after the Parthenon and the Temple of Hephaestus at Athens.

Although Greek historical writing mentions little about Phigalia, Pausanias described some of its religious peculiarities and occult practices, which probably existed elsewhere in Arcadia. Its gods included horseheaded Black Demeter, whose sanctuary was a cave, and the fishtailed Artemis Eurynome.

Philadelphia (Jordan): *see* Amman.

Philadelphia, city, seat of Neshoba County, east central Mississippi, U.S., seat of the Mississippi Choctaw Indian Reservation. It was settled on an old Indian site, Aloon Looanshaw, following the Treaty of Dancing Rabbit Creek (1830). The Choctaw Indian Agency was established in 1918, and more than 3,000 Indians live nearby. In 1964 the city received national attention when three civil rights workers, murdered during a voter-registration drive, were found buried nearby. The city is an agricultural-trade centre (cattle, cotton, corn) with some light manufactures (textiles, electric motors, lumber products). The Choctaw Indian Fair is an annual summer event. Inc. 1906. Pop. (1980) 6,434.
32°46′ N, 89°07′ W

Philadelphia 14:215, city and port, coextensive with Philadelphia County, southeastern Pennsylvania, U.S., at the confluence of the Delaware and Schuylkill rivers. It lies in the centre of the urban corridor of the Atlantic Seaboard and is the fourth largest city in the U.S. Pop. (1980) city, 1,688,210 (38% black); metropolitan area (SMSA), 4,716,818.

The text article, after a brief survey of the city, covers its history and contemporary features such as its physical layout, people, economy, government, services, and cultural life and institutions.
39°57′ N, 75°07′ W

REFERENCES in other text articles:
·city layout **18**:1081f
·coins and modern mint operation **4**:823g
history
·British capture and Washington's defeat **19**:615a
·colonial and U.S. expansion maps **18**:950 *passim* to 969
·Delaware historical, economic, and cultural connections **5**:567b
·Franklin social and cultural activities **7**:694e
·interior design in colonial period **9**:720h; illus. 721
·Pennsylvania early development role **14**:26b
·Revolutionary War activities **19**:604a
·map, United States **18**:908
·New Jersey economic association **12**:1097a
·political and cultural roles **14**:28f

Philadelphia Academy (1751), school in Philadelphia, forerunner of the University of Pennsylvania.
·academy initiation and Latin School comparison **6**:357h

Philadelphia Aurora, U.S. newspaper published in Philadelphia; founded 1790.
·newspaper publishing history **15**:239e

Philadelphia Baptist Association, formed in 1707, embracing five churches in Pennsylvania, New Jersey, and Delaware.
·establishment and missionary activity **2**:714g

Philadelphia Centennial Exposition, fair celebrating first 100 years of U.S. independence; opened May 10, 1876.
·Edison's idea for electric light bulb **6**:309h

Philadelphia chair, also called WINDSOR CHAIR, a wooden chair of stick construction having a spindle back, turned raking legs, and usually a saddle seat.
·origin, development, and variations **7**:788c

Philadelphia chromosome, chromosome (*q.v.*) associated with chronic granulocytic leukemia, one of the cancers of the blood-forming tissues.
·cancer cell types **3**:765f
·diagnosis by tissue culture **18**:442d

Philadelphia Yearly Meeting, major legislative and administrative body in Philadelphia Society of Friends, founded in 1681.
·Quaker support of Evangelicalism **7**:744b

Philadelphia Zoo, in full PHILADELPHIA ZOOLOGICAL GARDENS, the first zoo in the United States, opened in Philadelphia in 1874 with an animal inventory of several hundred native and exotic specimens. It was begun and continues to be operated by the Zoological Society of Philadelphia, founded in 1859. After the American Civil War, a 17-hectare (42-acre) plot was selected in Fairmount Park, an architect was sent to study the London Zoo, and an animal collector began gathering specimens. During 1876, when the Centennial Exposition was celebrated in Philadelphia, the zoo had 677,630 visitors, a record not exceeded for 75 years. The Philadelphia Zoo established the first zoo laboratory (1901) and the first children's zoo (1938) in America. It has excellent cat and waterfowl collections and is famous for the longevity records of its animals. It has about 1,200 specimens of 485 species. Annual attendance is about 1,260,000.

Philadelphus (plant): *see* Hydrangeaceae.

Philadelphus, Attalus II (king of Pergamum): *see* Attalus II Philadelphus.

Philadelphus, Ptolemy II (king of Egypt): *see* Ptolemy II Philadelphus.

Philae, Arabic JARĪZAT FĪLAH, known locally as QAṢR ANAS AL-WUJŪD, after a hero of *The Arabian Nights' Entertainments*, island of the Nile situated just above the First Cataract

Temple of Isis (left) and the unfinished peristyle pavilion called the Kiosk of Trajan, late Ptolemic and imperial Roman periods, Philae Island, in the Nile near Aswān, Egypt

Ewing Galloway

and the old Aswān Dam and 7 mi (11 km) south-southwest of Aswān town. Its ancient Egyptian name was P-aaleq; the Coptic-derived name Pilak (End or Remote Place) probably refers to its marking the boundary with Nubia. The present name is Greek. Before its gradual submergence in the successively heightened reservoir, created by the Aswān Dam in 1902 and 1907, the alluvium-covered crystalline granite rock of Philae, measuring 1,500 by 480 ft (460 by 150 m), had always been above the highest Nile floodings. Accordingly, it attracted a number of ancient temple and shrine builders, earning the still current name of Jazīrat al-Birba (Temple Island).

From early Egyptian times the island was sacred to the goddess Isis; the earliest buildings known are those of Nectanebo II (Nektharehbe), last king of the 30th dynasty (380–343 BC). His temple to Isis was rebuilt into the present complex of structures by Ptolemy II Philadelphus and his successor, Ptolemy III Euergetes. Its decorations, dating from the period of the Roman emperors Augustus and Tiberius (27 BC to AD 37), were, however, never completed. The temple continued to flourish during Roman times and was not closed until the reign of Justinian (AD 527–565), even though since 378 there had been an edict of Theodosius I banning worship of Osiris and Isis. The priests of Isis had obtained great powers in Upper Egypt, probably because they held gold mines at Wadi Alaki and controlled the terminus of the caravan route at Kubban.

Other small temples or shrines dedicated to Egyptian deities include a temple to Imhotep and one to Hathor, and chapels to Osiris, Horus, and Nephthys. There is also a pavilion built by the Roman emperor Trajan (reigned AD 98–117) and dedicated to Isis and Horus, as well as two Coptic churches. All these structures were thoroughly explored and reinforced (1895–96) before being partially flooded behind the old Aswān Dam. In 1907 a careful inspection revealed that salts were damaging sandstone inscriptions. When the temples re-emerged after 1970 with the completion of the High Dam upstream, it was found that considerable damage had been done to the shrines.

24°01′ N, 32°53′ E

·map, Egypt **6**:447

·temple architecture under the Ptolemies **19**:257c

Philaemon (worm): *see* leech.

Philaenus leucophthalmus (insect): *see* froghopper.

Philagathus, Joannes (antipope): *see* John XVI.

Philanisus plebius, a species of caddisfly of the order Trichoptera.

·Trichopteran inhabiting intertidal zone **18**:709c

philanthropic foundation, legal and social instrument for applying private wealth to public purposes. Although charitable endowments have existed since ancient times, the modern foundation is predominantly a 20th-century United States phenomenon. It is a large, autonomous organization formed to support research or public service in such fields as education, science, medicine, public health, and social welfare. It may be an operating foundation with a service and research staff, but it is usually a grant-making organization. Its legal form may be that of a charitable trust or a nonprofit corporation. An individual may endow a foundation by bequest or by a gift made during his lifetime; a business firm or a family may create and support a foundation through continued giving.

In ancient Egypt, Greece, and Rome, a foundation was usually a single-purpose perpetuity supporting an academy, library, or local charity. The typical medieval European foundation was an ecclesiastical perpetuity operating a monastery, almshouse, orphanage, or school. During the Renaissance, merchants created numerous special foundations for educational and local charitable purposes, notably for poor relief; but these perpetuities drew increased criticism after 1750 for their mismanagement, obsolescence of purpose, or palliative character. The 18th-century economists Adam Smith in England and Anne-Robert-Jacques Turgot in France were among their early critics.

Although foundations or charitable trusts with narrow, local purposes have survived, they are overshadowed by large foundations possessing broad purposes and flexibility of action. Among the first of these in the United States was the Smithsonian Institution, created by bequest of the English scientist James Smithson "for the increase and diffusion of knowledge among men"; an act of Congress formally created the institution in 1846. In 1867 the Peabody Fund was founded in the United States to promote education in the South; its creator was George Peabody, an American who had become a wealthy banker in England. As business fortunes and organized philanthropy developed, other general foundations were created, notably by Andrew Carnegie and John D. Rockefeller, Jr., after 1900. Carnegie's gifts and bequests, exceeding $330,000,000, mainly went to endow several foundations, including the Carnegie Corporation of New York, the Carnegie Endowment for International Peace, and many other trusts and perpetuities in America and Europe. Three generations of Rockefellers would give well over $1,000,000,000 to philanthropy, endowing a number of foundations, including the Rockefeller Foundation.

As a result of the publicity and success attending these foundations, many others appeared in the United States; a number also appeared in Canada and Great Britain, and a few also in the continental countries of Europe. After 1914 the United States also witnessed a substantial growth of community foundations and after 1940 a wave of personal, family, and company-sponsored foundations. The Ford Foundation, established in 1936, was the major example of the family-sponsored foundation; its multi-billion-dollar endowment has made it the largest foundation in the world. It has made grants to existing organizations and to a number of autonomous funds of its own creation, including the Fund for the Advancement of Education (1951), Fund for Adult Education (1951), Fund for the Republic (1952), and National Merit Scholarship Corporation (1955). In 1954 it established the Center for Advanced Study in the Behavioral Sciences at Stanford, Calif. It also funds technical assistance and other development programs in Asia, Latin America, and Africa.

Among the world's wealthiest charitable foundations may also be included the Russell Sage Foundation (1907), The Commonwealth Fund (1918), Twentieth Century Fund, Inc. (1919), The Duke Endowment (1924), John Simon Guggenheim Memorial Foundation (1925), Danforth Foundation (1927), W.K. Kellogg Foundation (1930), Alfred P. Sloan Foundation (1934), Lilly Endowment, Inc. (1937), and John A. Hartford Foundation, Inc. (incorporated 1942).

·museum founding and financing **12**:652b

Philanthropinum, late-18th-century school founded in Dessau, Germany, by the educator Johann Bernhard Basedow. Aiming to foster in its students a humanitarian world view, an awareness of the community of interest among men, it taught rich and poor boys together regardless of religious or class distinctions. The school had many enthusiastic supporters, among them the philosophers Kant, Lessing, and Moses Mendelssohn, and its influence spread to neighbouring countries, particularly Switzerland.

Basedow believed in state rather than religious control of education and in a pragmatic approach to teaching. He stressed modern rather than classical languages, teaching them through conversation and games. Scientific subjects such as natural history, anatomy, and physics, and practical ones such as carpentry were emphasized; and the students made field trips to studios, farms, mines, and the shops of artisans. Physical education was given an important place in the curriculum; through such activities as open-air games and races, wrestling, and swimming, upper class boys were released from the artificialities and conventionalities that formerly had been part of their training. Further, in an age when schools were noted for their harsh discipline, Basedow held that school could be so pleasant and absorbing that punishment would be virtually unnecessary.

One important offshoot of the Philanthropist movement was the beginning of a children's literature in German. *Robinson der Jüngere* (1779; "The Young Robinson") by J.H. Campe, an associate of Basedow, was the earliest children's book in German and was followed by a flood of stories and books of instruction written expressly for children.

·location and duration **6**:354g

Philaret (b. FYODOR NIKITICH ROMANOV, *c.* 1553—d. Oct. 11, 1633, Moscow), Russian Orthodox patriarch of Moscow and father of the first Romanov tsar. During the rule (1584–98) of his cousin, Tsar Theodore I Rurik, he served in the military campaign against the Swedes in 1590 and later (1593–94) conducted diplomatic negotiations with them. After Theodore's death, Philaret was banished to a monastery by Boris Godunov (ruled 1598–1605). On Godunov's overthrow by the first False Dmitry in 1605, Philaret was released and made metropolitan, or archbishop, of Rostov. In 1610 he was imprisoned by the Poles while attempting to arrange the accession of Prince Władysław of Poland to the Russian throne, but he was freed in 1619 after the election of his son Michael as tsar. Philaret was made patriarch of Moscow in the same year.

Exercising both ecclesiastical and political rule in Russia, Philaret reformed the church administration, instituted a program of establishing a divinity college in each diocese, and established libraries to upgrade theological scholarship. In a Moscow synod he decreed that all Latin Christians coming into the Russian Orthodox Church would require rebaptism. His ecclesiastical policy strove to minimize the influence of the Roman Catholic Church among Russian and Polish bishops. In addition to further developing the Russian liturgical books, Philaret also sponsored social legislation to stabilize the peasant farmers, reformed the tax structure, and reorganized the military.

·role in the Thirty Years' War **18**:340a

Philaret (b. VASILY MIKHAYLOVICH DROZDOV, Dec. 26, 1782, Kolomna, near Moscow—d. Nov. 19, 1867, Moscow), Russian Orthodox theologian and metropolitan, or archbishop, of Moscow whose scholarship, oratory, and administrative ability made him the leading Russian churchman of the 19th century.

A monk and lecturer at Trinity Monastery near Moscow, Philaret was named, in 1808, professor of philosophy and theology, and subsequently rector, at St. Petersburg's (modern Leningrad) Ecclesiastical Academy. Rising rapidly in his church career, he became a member of the Holy Synod in 1818 after serving with numerous ecclesiastical reform commissions, was named archbishop of Tver (modern Kalinin) in 1819, and in 1821 was transferred to Moscow. An activist, Philaret quickly established himself as a power in church and state. Considered as charismatic by the Russian Orthodox, he served as the final authority in theological and legal questions, his decisions eventually being published in 1905 with the title "Views and Comments."

By 1858, having overcome extended opposition, Philaret successfully directed the translation of the Slavonic Bible and basic liturgical prayers into modern Russian. His chief theological work was the "Christian Catechism of the Orthodox Catholic Eastern Greco-Russian Church," treating the 4th-century Nicene Creed, the theology of prayer, and the Mosaic Law. First published in 1823, Philaret's "Catechism" was subjected to several revisions to expunge its Lutheran influences, but after 1839 it exercised widespread influence on 19th-century Russian theology.

Philargos, Petros (antipope): *see* Alexander V.

Philastre, Paul-Louis-Félix (b. Feb. 7, 1837, Brussels—d. Sept. 11, 1902, Buyat-Beayeau, Fr.), diplomat in the formative years of colonialism in French Indochina who played a crucial role in mitigating relations between the European colonialists and the French administration, on the one hand, and the indigenous population and its royal court at Hue, in central Vietnam; he was considered generally sympathetic to the Vietnamese.

Philastre was graduated from France's naval school in 1857 and signed onto the "Avalanche," bound for China. He arrived in Cochinchina, now in South Vietnam, in 1861 and was named inspector of indigenous affairs in January 1863 at My Tho, a Mekong Delta village. Two years after his appointment as chief of native law (June 1868), he was taken ill and returned to France.

During the Franco-German War and the Paris Commune, Philastre commanded an artillery regiment in the defense of Paris. He returned to Saigon in 1873 and was promoted to inspector of native affairs under Adm. Marie-Jules Dupré.

An avid imperialist, Dupré had been seeking official recognition from the Vietnamese emperor Tu Duc of French holdings in three western provinces formally ceded to France in an 1862 treaty that Tu Duc had reneged upon. Meanwhile, in the summer of 1873 the profiteering trader Jean Dupuis, eager to secure northern Vietnam for trade with China, attacked Hanoi. Dupré then sent an expedition north under Francis Garnier, ostensibly to suppress Dupuis' bold move. Garnier, however, with Dupré's approval, joined forces with the trader and laid claim to Hanoi. But Dupré had meanwhile received word from France officially condemning the whole affair, and he commissioned Philastre as ambassador to try to win concessions from Emperor Tu Duc.

Philastre was poorly received at Hue by Tu Duc, who asked him to go north to resolve matters with the French forces there. At Hanoi, feeling that the Vietnamese had been wronged, he acted contrary to Dupré's implicit directives and, while presenting himself as Dupré's representative, ordered a cease-fire. Arriving shortly after Garnier had been killed in battle, Philastre was able to assert his authority. He laid the foundations of the treaty of 1874, under which Tu Duc at last bowed to the French conquest of the south. Thereafter he served as representative of the protectorate of Cambodia (1876) and as chargé d'affaires at Hue 1877–79. Because of the debilitating climate, he returned to France (1880) and taught mathematics at Cannes and Nice (1882–94).

Briefly discredited because of his countercoup in the Dupuis-Garnier affair, which delayed French expansion into the north of Indochina for a decade, Philastre won the acclaim of later French writers for his honesty and for the respect he showed for the people and traditions of Vietnam.

philately, also called STAMP COLLECTING, the hobby of collecting and studying postage stamps. The term philately was coined in 1865 by a Frenchman, M.G. Herpin, who invented it from the Greek *philos*, "love," *a*, "negative," *telein*, "to tax"; the postage stamp permitted the letter to come free of charge to the recipient, rendering it untaxed.

The first postage stamps were put on sale on May 1, 1840, in England. The earliest reference to stamp collecting is an advertisement in *The Times* of London in 1841 placed by "a young lady, being desirous of covering her dressing-room with cancelled postage stamps."

The first lists of stamps were issued in 1861 by Oscar Berger-Levrault in Strasbourg and Alfred Potiquet in Paris. In England, Frederick Booty, J.E. Gray, and Mount Brown all issued catalogs in 1862; Brown's third edition (1866) listed 2,400 varieties, inclusive of what is now termed postal stationery or envelopes, wrappers, and letter sheets, as well as many local issues. The standard modern catalogs (*e.g.*, Yvert and Tellier in France, Michel's in Germany, Gibbons' in Great Britain, and Scott or Minkus in the United States) exclude this latter material, and yet the total number of listings, including minor varieties, reaches more than 100,000.

Specialization. Because of the sheer bulk, not to mention the prohibitive expense, of a general collection, most collectors turn to more or less limited fields. They may collect only the stamps of one country, for example, or of one continent or of one period. Others specialize in collections of certain kinds of stamps; some collect only one issue and study it thoroughly, others may collect only revenue stamps or postal stationery. Those interested purely in stamp designs may collect art or religion on stamps, or flowers, fish, bridges, etc.; this sort of collecting is called topical or thematic.

The collection of postal markings, both on stamped and pre-stamp covers, is a form of specialization; collecting of precancelled stamps is another. Meters (machines that print a postal frank on the envelope) have given rise to yet another specialized form. Telegraph stamps or Christmas seals are also collected by some specialists.

Famous collections. Many famous collections of the past have been dispersed and absorbed by others; some have been sold at auction, bringing total prices of several million dollars. The unique one-cent British Guiana magenta of 1856 was sold by private negotiation for a price reputed to be more than $50,000. In 1970 it was sold again at auction for $280,000.

One of the outstanding collections in Europe—especially rich in British and colonial issues—was formed principally by King George V, a famed philatelist, and passed on to those who succeeded him as the British monarch. The Thomas K. Tapling collection, bequeathed to the British Museum, may well be the finest in public hands. The Smithsonian Institution collection at Washington, D.C., stresses U.S. stamps. The postal museums of many European capitals have outstanding collections, such as those at Berlin, at The Hague, and at Stockholm; the last received the Hans Lagerlof (New York) collection.

Societies. Clubs or societies of collectors are to be found in most cities of the world, with national and international societies to bind them together. Many of the prominent national societies, as the Royal Philatelic Society of London and the American Philatelic Society, were formed in the 19th century. The International Philatelic Federation, formed in 1926, had more than 40 member national organizations by the 1970s. Many specialist societies have also sprung up, notably since 1945. One of the most important activities of stamp clubs is the holding of exhibitions from time to time. International, national, and regional societies hold regular exhibitions, offering valuable awards to outstanding collections.

BIBLIOGRAPHY. Winthrop S. Boggs, *The Foundations of Philately* (1955); Richard M. Cabeen, *Standard Handbook of Stamp Collecting* (1957); Barbara R. Mueller, *Common Sense Philately* (1956); R.J. Sutton, *The Stamp Collector's Encyclopaedia*, 6th ed. (1970).

·Falkland Islands stamps **7**:154e
·hobby development and specialization **8**:977a

Philby, Harold Adrian Russell, called "KIM" PHILBY (b. Jan. 1, 1912, Ambāla, India), British intelligence officer until 1951 and one of the most successful Soviet spies of the Cold War period. While a student at Cambridge, Philby became a Communist and in 1933 a Soviet agent. In 1940 Guy Burgess, a British secret agent who was himself a Soviet spy, recruited Philby into the secret service. By 1949 Philby had risen to become first secretary of the British embassy in Washington, D.C., and was in charge of liaison with the U.S. in security matters. Philby fled to Russia in 1963 and subsequently published a book, *My Silent War* (1968), detailing his exploits. By his own account he had revealed to the U.S.S.R. an Allied plan to send armed bands into Albania in 1950, thereby assuring their defeat; had warned two Russian spies in the British diplomatic service, Burgess and Donald Maclean, who then escaped to Russia in 1951; and had transmitted information about the Central Intelligence Agency during his residence in Washington (1949–51) as liaison officer between the British and U.S. intelligence services.

Philby, H(arry) St. John (Bridger) (1885–1960), British explorer and Arabist, one of the great explorers of Arabia, and one of the three Europeans who (independently of one another) crossed the Empty Quarter before automobile travel in the desert was feasible. He later became a Muslim and an adviser to King Ibn Saʿūd of Saudi Arabia.
·councillor of Ibn Saʿūd **1**:1056c

Philco Corporation, U.S. company manufacturing radios, television sets, and electronic equipment; acquired by Ford Motor Company in 1961.
·auto industry product diversification **2**:532d

Philemon (b. *c.* 368 BC, Syracuse, Sicily—d. *c.* 264 BC), poet of the Athenian New Comedy, elder contemporary and successful rival of Menander, noted for his neatly contrived plots, vivid description, dramatic surprises, and platitudinous moralizing. By 328 he was producing plays in Athens, where he eventually became a citizen; he also worked in Alexandria, Egypt, for a time. Of 97 comedies some 60 titles survive in Greek fragments and Latin adaptations.

Philemon, Letter of Paul to, a brief New Testament letter written by Paul the Apostle to a wealthy Christian of Colossae, Asia Minor, on behalf of Onesimus, Philemon's former slave. Paul, writing from prison, expresses affection for the newly converted Onesimus and asks that he be received in the same spirit that would mark Paul's own arrival, even though Onesimus may be guilty of previous failings. While passing no judgment on slavery itself, Paul exhorts Philemon to manifest true Christian love that removes barriers between slaves and free men. The letter was probably composed in Rome about AD 61 and carried by messengers who were entrusted to deliver at the same time Paul's letter to the Colossians.
·identity of Onesimus and epistle's canonicity **2**:967b
·manumission concern **2**:958e
·Paul's activities in prison **13**:1093f

Philemon and Baucis, in Greek mythology, a pious Phrygian couple who hospitably received Zeus and Hermes when their richer neighbours turned away the two gods, who were disguised as wayfarers. As a reward, they were saved from a flood that drowned the rest of the country; their cottage was turned into a temple, and at their own request they became priest and priestess of it. Long after, they ended their lives at the same moment, being turned into trees. Similar stories are given in the *Märchen* ("fairy tales") of the Grimm brothers.

Philepittidae, bird family, order Passeriformes, comprising asities and false sunbirds. *See* asity; false sunbird.

Philes, Manuel (fl. 13th/14th century), Byzantine court poet from Ephesus. He lived in Constantinople under the emperors Michael VIII Palaeologus and Andronicus I and II, was acquainted with the chief persons of his day, and travelled widely. His poems include verses on church festivals, works of art, and animals, as well as dialogues and occasional pieces. Their literary quality is not high, but they have historical and social interest.

Philesiaceae, a family of boxlily of the order Liliales.
·general features and classification **10**:975d

Philesturnus carunculatus (bird): *see* saddleback.

Philetaerus (b. *c.* 343 BC, Tios, in Paphlagonia, a region of northern Anatolia—d. 263), founder (reigned 282–263) of the Attalid dynasty, a line of rulers of a powerful kingdom of Pergamum, in northwest Anatolia, in the 3rd and 2nd centuries BC. Philetaerus initiated the policies that made Pergamum a leading centre of Greek civilization in the East. His father, Attalus, was either Greek or Macedonian, and his mother, Boa, came from Paphlagonia. Philetaerus served under Antigonus I Monophthalmus, successor to Alexander the Great in Phrygia, in northern Anatolia, until 302, when he deserted to Antigonus' rival, Lysimachus, ruler of Thrace. Lysimachus made him guardian of the fortress of Pergamum with its treasure of some 9,000 talents. In 282 Philetaerus transferred his allegiance to Seleucus I, the successor to Alexander the Great in Syria, who allowed him a far larger measure of independence than he had hitherto enjoyed.

The territory Philetaerus controlled was as yet quite small—no more than Pergamum and its environs—and it was largely of necessity that he curried favour with the first Seleucid kings. His gifts to the temples at Delphi, Greece, and on the island of Delos, in the Aegean Sea, secured for his family some prestige outside of Anatolia. When, after the death of Seleucus I in 280, the Seleucid grip on Asia Minor slackened, Philetaerus found a chance to increase the area under his control. He probably came to rule the whole of Mysia (region of which Pergamum is a part), and before his death in 263 he had abandoned the Seleucids in favour of a tie with Egypt.

Philetaerus was reportedly a eunuch; he adopted one of his nephews, Eumenes, as his heir and successor.

Philetairus socius (bird): *see* social weaver.

Philetas of Cos (b. *c.* 330 BC—d. *c.* 270 BC), Greek poet and grammarian from the Aegean island of Cos, regarded as the founder of the Hellenistic school of poetry, which flourished in Alexandria after *c.* 323 BC. He is reputed to have been the tutor of Ptolemy II and the poet Theocritus. The Roman poets Propertius and Ovid mention him as their model, but only fragments of his work have survived. His most important poem appears to have been the *Demeter*, an elegy narrating the wanderings of the goddess of the Earth, Demeter. He also compiled a dictionary of rare words from Homer, the Greek dialects, and other sources.

Philharmonic Society, nationalist organization in Romania founded in 1833.
·Revolution of 1848 **2**:627b

Philharmonic Society of London, music organization of 19th-century London, after 1912 title changed to Royal Philharmonic Society of London.
·Beethoven's popularity in Britain **2**:798h

Philibert, Emmanuel: *see* Emmanuel Philibert.

Philibert of Orange-Châlon (b. 1502, France—d. Aug. 3, 1530, Florence), prince of Orange, count of Franche-Comté (now in France) and of Brabant in the Low Countries, stadholder of the Dutch provinces of Holland, Zeeland, and Utrecht, who united the French lands of the house of Orange-Châlon with territory in the Burgundian Netherlands; his possessions became the nucleus of the lands of the House of Orange-Nassau, the present rulers of the Kingdom of The Netherlands.

Last prince of the Burgundian house of Châlon, Philibert joined the service of the Holy Roman emperor Charles V to regain his lands in Orange (now in France) that King Francis I of France had seized. For his successful direction of the siege of Fuenterrabia (Spain) in 1523, the Emperor granted him the duchy of Brabant and the office of stadholder (chief executive) of Holland, Zeeland, and Utrecht. Charles V also forced Francis I to return Orange to its prince (1526). Appointed viceroy of Naples in 1528, Philibert died at the siege of Florence. Childless, he had bequeathed his hereditary estates to his nephew, René of Nassau, who became prince of Orange.

Philidor, André, original family name DANICAN, nicknamed "L'AÎNÉ" (b. *c.* 1647—d. Aug. 11, 1730, Dreux, Fr.), musician and composer, an outstanding member of a large and important family of musicians long connected with the French court. The first recorded representatives of the family were Michel Danican (died *c.* 1659), upon whom the nickname Philidor (the name of a famous Italian musician) was bestowed by Louis XIII as a complimentary reference to his skill, and André's father Jean (died 1679), who, like Michel, played various instruments in the Grande Écurie, the king's band.

André and his brothers, Jacques, called "le Cadet" (died 1708), and Alexandre, whose birth and death dates are unknown, also played in the royal band. André distinguished himself as a performer in Louis XIV's chamber and chapel and composed several divertissements, or opéra ballets, for royal entertainment, as well as marches, fanfares and similar music. Further, as keeper of the royal music library from 1684, he collected hundreds of volumes of dances, operas, sacred music, songs, marches, and other music from the time of Henry III onward; a large part of this invaluable collection survives.

André and Jacques each had children who carried on the family tradition, the most important being André's son François-André Philidor (*q.v.*), noted as a composer and chess player. Another son of André, Michel, whose birth and death dates are unknown, a drummer in the Grande Écurie, is said to have worked with the instrument builder Jean Hotteterre (*q.v.*) in the invention of the oboe.

Philidor, François-André, original family name DANICAN (b. Sept. 7, 1726, Dreux, Fr.—d. Aug. 24, 1795, London), composer whose operas were successful and widely known in his day and who was a famous and remarkable Chess player. The last member of a large and prominent musical family (*see* Philidor, André), François-André was thoroughly trained in music, but at age 18 he turned entirely to Chess competition throughout Europe. He was particularly well received in England, where he published a book on Chess and eventually received a pension from the London Chess Club. In 1754 he returned to Paris and set about composing highly popular operas, such as *Sancho Pança dans son isle* (1762) and *Tom Jones* (1765), as well as other dramatic and sacred music. He continued composing and playing Chess for the remainder of his life, travelling regularly to London.
·development of modern Chess **4**:198b

Philidota (mammal order): *see* pangolin.

Philikí Etaireía (Greek: Friendly Brotherhood), Greek revolutionary secret society founded by merchants in Odessa in 1814 to overthrow Ottoman rule in southeastern Europe and to establish an independent Greek state. The society's claim of Russian support and the romance of its commitment (each member swore "irreconcilable hatred against the tyrants of my country") brought thousands into its ranks. Though some recruits believed that the society was secretly directed by the Russian emperor's foreign secretary—the Greek Ioánnis, Count Kapodístrias—it was Alexander Ypsilantis, an officer in the Russian Army, who accepted the leadership in 1820. Having planned uprisings in the Danubian principalities as well as in the Peloponnese and the Greek islands, Ypsilantis launched the revolt in the spring of 1821. The Romanian peasants did not join his forces, however; the Russian emperor Alexander I repudiated him, and the Turks quickly defeated him. The venture resulted primarily in bringing an end to Greek Phanariote rule in Moldavia and Wallachia.
·Vladimirescu Uprising of 1821 **2**:625h
·Ypsilantis' leadership and strategy **2**:625c

Philinoglossacea, order of slugs of the class Gastropoda.
·characteristics and classification **7**:956c

Philip (fl. 8th century, Italy), antipope during July 768. Temporal rulers coveted the papal throne following the death (767) of Pope St. Paul I and Toto, duke of Nepi, had his brother Constantine II, a layman, elected pope. The Lombard king Desiderius then sent troops to Rome, killing Toto and deposing Constantine. Backed by some Romans, the Lombards, *c.* July 31, 768, secretly set Philip up as Pope. Philip had been a monk in the monastery of St. Vito. He was ejected, however, and Stephen III (IV) was elected pope on Aug. 1, 768. Philip retired to his monastery, and nothing more is known about him.

Philip, also known as PHILIP OF SWABIA (b. 1178—d. June 21, 1208, Bamberg, now in West Germany), German Hohenstaufen king whose rivalry for the German crown involved him in a decade of warfare with the Welf Otto IV.

Philip of Swabia, sculpture, *c.* 1207; in the St. Ulrich Museum, Regensburg, W.Ger.

By courtesy of the St. Ulrich Museum; photograph, Foto Marburg

The youngest son of the Holy Roman emperor Frederick I Barbarossa, Philip was destined for the church. After serving as provost of the cathedral at Aachen, he was, in 1190 or 1191, elected bishop of Würzburg. Shortly after the death of his brother Frederick (1191), however, he abandoned his ecclesiastical career. Another brother, the Holy Roman emperor Henry VI, made him duke of Tuscany in 1195 and duke of Swabia in 1196. In May 1197 he married Irene, daughter of the Byzantine emperor Isaac II Angelus.

At Henry VI's death in September 1197, his son, the future emperor Frederick II, was only two years old, and the German princes were unwilling to accept him as king. The princes favourable to the Hohenstaufens elected Philip German king in March 1198. The opposing party, led by Archbishop Adolf of Cologne, elected Otto, a son of Henry the Lion of Brunswick of the rival Welf dynasty, king in June of that year: Otto was crowned at Aachen, the proper place for the ceremony, by Archbishop Adolf. Philip's coronation, by another prelate, did not take place until September 1198 at Mainz.

In the ensuing civil war the Hohenstaufen cause prospered at first. In 1201, however, Pope Innocent III recognized Otto as king and excommunicated Philip. Philip's fortunes were only restored in 1204, by a series of defections from Otto's side, culminating in that of Adolf of Cologne himself. In June 1205, Adolf crowned Philip at Aachen.

The city of Cologne, which, notwithstanding its archbishop, had sided with Otto, was captured in January 1207, and Otto's cause seemed lost. Late in 1207, however, when Philip offered to give Otto one of his daughters in marriage and to enfeoff him with either the duchy of Swabia or the kingdom of Arles. Otto, buoyed by hopes of financial, if not military, support from the kings of England and Denmark, rejected the offer. Nevertheless, a truce was arranged that lasted until June of the following year.

In 1208 Pope Innocent recognized Philip as king and promised to crown him emperor. Philip, who had mobilized his army at Bamberg in order to move against Otto, was waiting for the truce to expire when he was murdered by Otto of Wittelsbach, count palatine of Bavaria, to whom he had refused to give one of his daughters in marriage.

A brave man, Philip was praised by contemporaries for his mildness and generosity. The diversion of the Fourth Crusade to Constantinople is assumed by some authorities to have been prompted by him in the interests of his brother-in-law, the Byzantine emperor Alexius IV.
·Innocent III and the German crisis **9**:605h

Philip (b. 20 BC—d. AD 34), son of Herod I the Great, ruled ably as tetrarch over the former northeastern quarter of his father's kingdom of Judaea.

When the Roman emperor Augustus adjusted Herod's will, Philip was assigned to the region east of the Sea of Galilee, in modern northern Israel, Lebanon, and southern Syria. In AD 6, he may have joined in charging his half-brother of misgoverning Judaea, but with little benefit to himself, for Judaea then became a Roman province.

Of his father's inheritance his was the poorest share, but he ruled it well. Because he had few Jewish subjects, he pursued a policy of Hellenization. His coins bore the Emperor's image and he rebuilt a town, Beth-saida (on the northern shore of the Sea of Galilee), renaming it Julias in honour of the Emperor's daughter. Near the source of the Jordan he founded another town and allowed it a large degree of self-government, on the Greek pattern.

Philip was less extravagant a ruler than any of his brothers. He avoided prolonged trips to Rome, instead spending much time touring his territory and devoting his time to his subjects. Late in his reign he married Salome, the daughter of Herodias, who was her mother's tool in securing from Herod Antipas the execution of John the Baptist.
·last Seleucid defeat **16**:501d

Philip, (1720–65), duke of Parma, reigned 1748–65.
·Bourbon influence in Italy **3**:82d

Philip I (b. 1052—d. July 29/30, 1108, Melun, Fr.), king of France who came to the throne at a time when the Capetian monarchy was extremely weak but who succeeded in enlarging the royal treasury by a policy of devious alliances, the sale of his neutrality in the quarrels of powerful vassals, and the practice of simony on an enormous scale.

Philip was the elder son of Henry I of France by his second wife, Anne of Kiev. Crowned at Reims in May 1059, he became sole king on his father's death in 1060. His minority ending in 1066, he immediately displayed a talent for skillful manoeuvre and in 1068 obtained from Fulk IV of Réchin the county of Gâtinais as the price of his neutrality in the struggle between Fulk and his brother for the heritage of Anjou. Philip thus secured a territorial link between his possessions in Sens and the lands of the royal domain around Paris, Melun, and Orléans. In 1070 he took advantage of a similar dynastic conflict to attach the town of Corbie to the royal domain. His major efforts, however, were directed toward Normandy, in which from 1076 he supported Robert II Curthose, the ineffectual duke of Normandy, first against his father, King William I of England, then against his brother, William II. Philip's true goal was to prevent the emergence of a rival power in Normandy, for he was willing to abandon Robert whenever it seemed possible that he might become dangerous.

Because of his firm determination to retain control over all ecclesiastical appointments, Philip was eventually drawn into conflict with the papacy. This conflict was exacerbated when in 1092 Philip abducted Fulk IV of Réchin's wife, Bertrada de Montfort. He next demanded the annulment of his marriage with his wife Bertha, and of Fulk's with Bertrada; before long he had found a complaisant bishop, and the King and Bertrada went through a marriage ceremony of dubious legality. Pope Urban II and later his successor Paschal II repeatedly excommunicated Philip, and not until 1104, after Philip and the papacy had settled some of their political differences, did Paschal II turn a blind eye to his relations with Bertrada. By this time Louis VI, Philip's son by Bertha, had taken over the administration of the kingdom, Philip having been rendered inactive by his extreme obesity.
·Bohemond I's marriage tie **2**:1201h

Philip I the Handsome (b. July 22, 1478, Bruges, now in Belgium—d. Sept. 25, 1506, Burgos, Spain), king of Castile for less than a month before his death and the founder of the Habsburg dynasty in Spain.

Philip was the son of the future Holy Roman emperor Maximilian I of Habsburg and Mary of Burgundy. At his mother's death (1482) he succeeded to her Netherlands dominions, with Maximilian acting as regent for him during his minority. When Philip became of age, his interest in the Netherlands soon became subordinated to his hopes for the Spanish succession. In 1496 Philip was married to Joan the Mad, daughter of Ferdinand II the Catholic of Aragon and Isabella I the Catholic of Castile; Joan later inherited the crown of Castile. From January 1502 to March 1503 Philip and Joan lived in Spain and received homage as prospective heirs to the kingdoms of Aragon and Castile. Isabella died in 1504 leaving the crown of Castile to Joan. Philip was recognized as king consort. Because Joan was in the Netherlands at the time, Ferdinand, in accordance with Isabella's will, acted as regent.

Philip soon began to oppose his father-in-law, who was unwilling to give up his control of Castile, and in early 1506 sailed to Spain to claim his wife's inheritance. On his voyage his ships had to take shelter in England, where King Henry VII forced him to agree to two treaties, the first of which secured English support for Philip's Castilian rights. The second (April 30, 1506), the *Intercursus Malus*, was a trade agreement disadvantageous to the Netherlands. In Castile, Philip, backed by the nobility, soon raised a strong army. He negotiated Ferdinand's withdrawal June 27, 1506. By that time Joan's mental condition had deteriorated further, and Philip assumed sole control. He was in the process of organizing his administration when he was stricken with a fever and died. His son Charles I of Spain (the Holy Roman emperor Charles V) became king of Aragon and Castile on Ferdinand's death in 1516, thus firmly establishing the dynasty that was to govern Spain for nearly two centuries.
·diplomatic and military goals **6**:1083d
·Ferdinand II's succession in Castile **17**:423h
·Habsburgs and the Spanish throne **2**:453e
·imperial succession of Habsburgs, table **8**:531
·Low Countries centralized administration **11**:140a

Philip I (king of Portugal): *see* Philip II of Spain.

Philip II Augustus, of France 14:221 (b. Aug. 21, 1165, Paris—d. July 14, 1223, Mantes), first great Capetian king of medieval France, destroyed the Angevin Empire of the kings of England.

Abstract of text biography. Son of Louis VII, Philip assumed the throne in 1179. His generally successful campaign (begun in 1187) to gain control of English possessions in France was interrupted by participation in the Third Crusade (1190–91). Philip acquired northeastern territory as well as the Plantagenet lands in the west; he also began the extension of Capetian power into Languedoc. Internally, he maintained control of the nobility and won the support of the clergy and the towns. His administrative changes further strengthened his dynasty.

REFERENCES in other text articles:
·chancellor power reaction **5**:812b
·Crusades expeditionary leadership **5**:305b
·English relations and conflicts **3**:208g
·French expansion and consolidation **7**:615h
·Innocent III and conflicts with England **9**:606b
·John's alliance and opposition **10**:236h
·Low Countries political relation **11**:136c
·marriage and Plantagenet opposition **7**:618g
·rivalry with Richard I of England **15**:827c

Philip II of Macedonia 14:225 (b. 382 BC —d. 336 BC, Asia Minor), king who unified his nation and made it supreme in Greece, laying the foundations for the great expansion accomplished by his son Alexander the Great.

Abstract of text biography. The son of Amyntas III, Philip gained the throne upon the death of his brother, Perdiccas III, in 359. He restored internal peace to Macedonia and by 339 had gained control of Greece by military and diplomatic means. He organized the Greek states into the League of Corinth (337) for a war against Persia but was assassinated before he could begin it.

REFERENCES in other text articles:
·Alexander's youth and early battles **1**:468h
·Aristotle's relationship and tutoring of son **1**:1162g
·Demosthenes' Philippics opposition **5**:579a
·Istanbul under siege **9**:1069f
·Macedonian rise and Greek unification **8**:365f *passim* to 369c
·military tactics of Macedonians **19**:574c
·Persian blunder and loss of Greece **9**:836d

Philip II (king of Portugal): *see* Philip III (king of Spain).

Philip II of Spain 14:227, ruled Portugal as PHILIP I (b. May 21, 1527, Valladolid, Spain—d. Sept. 13, 1598, El Escorial, outside Madrid), champion of the Roman Catholic Counter-Reformation and king of Spain during the period of its greatest power and influence.

Abstract of text biography. The son of Holy Roman emperor Charles V and Isabella of Portugal, Philip was trained as a youth for his future position. He became king of Spain and the Spanish empire in 1556 while in the Netherlands. After his return in 1559, he never left the Iberian Peninsula. Philip conducted his 42-year reign from Madrid and El Escorial (which he built, 1563–84). He inherited the throne of Portugal in 1580. Philip's position as a defender of Catholicism helped provoke rebellion in the Netherlands (1568–1609) and Granada (1568–70) and contributed to Spanish involvement in wars with the Ottoman Empire (1571–78) and England (1588–1604). Despite some setbacks Philip died leaving Spain still at the height of its power.

REFERENCES in other text articles:
·Charles V marriage plans and abdication **4**:50d
·colonial office distribution **10**:694f
·Counter-Reformation leadership **15**:1012a
·El Greco's commissions for king **8**:307g
·Elizabeth I's reign and courtships **6**:726c
·English diplomacy and wars **3**:225h
·Escorial construction and style **19**:393c
·Francis Drake's role in Spain's defeat **5**:978f
·French Catholic Holy League support **7**:630g
·Habsburg external and internal weaknesses **8**:532d; table
·Henry IV military opposition **8**:774a
·heresy suppression and Inquisition **14**:482e
·interior design national influence **9**:714e; illus.
·Mary I's marriage and Catholic restoration **11**:564b
·Milanese and Sicilian administration **9**:1150e
·military and diplomatic ambitions **6**:1087d
·Netherlands repressive rule **11**:140d
·Netherlands revolt against Spain **7**:180f
·political and economic policies **17**:425h *passim* to 428g
·Portugal and Spain united under monarch **14**:868b
·Portuguese power loss **4**:882g
·Renaissance conflicts significance **15**:667f
·Spanish control of Milan **12**:191d
·Titian portrait and mythological series **18**:459g *passim* to 461a
·William the Silent's political relation **19**:833e

Philip III, also called PHILIP THE BOLD (b. April 3, 1245, Poissy, Fr.—d. Oct. 5, 1285, Perpignan), king of France (1270–85), in whose reign the power of the monarchy was enlarged and the royal domain extended, though his foreign policy and military ventures were largely unsuccessful.

Philip, the second son of Louis IX of France (Saint Louis), became heir to the throne on the death of his elder brother Louis (1260). Accompanying his father's crusade against Tunis in 1270, he was in Africa when Louis IX died. He was annointed king at Reims in 1271.

Philip continued his father's highly successful administration by keeping in office his able and experienced household clerks. Mathieu de Vendôme, abbot of Saint-Denis, whom Louis IX had left as regent in France, remained in control of the government. The death in 1271 of Alphonse of Poitiers and his wife, heiress of Toulouse, enabled Philip early in his reign to annex their vast holdings to the royal domain. Nevertheless, in 1279 he was obliged to cede the county of Agenais to Edward I of England. In 1274 Henry I, king of Navarre and count of Champagne, died, leaving as his heiress his infant daughter Joan, already betrothed to a son of Edward I of England. Philip succeeded, however, in securing her betrothal to his own son, with the agreement that Philip should rule Navarre for Joan until her majority. The regency led to the eventual union of the crowns of France and Navarre. In addition Philip over the years made numerous small territorial acquisitions.

Philip III of France, coronation, illustration from *Les Grandes Chroniques de France*, c. 1400; in the Bibliothèque Nationale, Paris (MS. Fr. 2608)

By courtesy of the Bibliotheque Nationale, Paris

Philip was less successful militarily. In 1276 he declared war to support the claims of his nephews as heirs in Castile. But diplomatic pressures and suggestions of treachery prompted the King to disperse the huge French army assembled on the French side of the Pyrenees. In 1284, at the instigation of Pope Martin IV, Philip launched a campaign against Peter III of Aragon, as part of the War of the Sicilian Vespers, in which the Aragonese opposed the Anjou rulers of Sicily. Philip crossed the Pyrenees with his army in May 1285, but the atrocities perpetrated by his forces provoked a guerrilla uprising. After a meaningless victory at Gerona Philip was forced to retreat. He died of fever on the way home.

·Aragon campaign failure **7**:619c
·Edward I's challenge in Gascony **6**:436a
·negation of 1259 Treaty of Paris **9**:15h

Philip III (king of Portugal): *see* Philip IV (king of Spain).

Philip III, ruled Portugal as PHILIP II (b. April 14, 1578, Madrid—d. March 31, 1621, Madrid), king of Spain whose reign (1598–1621) was characterized by a successful peaceful foreign policy in western Europe and internally by the expulsion of the Moriscos (Christians of Moorish ancestry) and government by the King's favourites.

Philip III of Spain, detail of a portrait by D. Velázquez (1599–1660); in the Prado, Madrid

By courtesy of the Museo del Prado, Madrid

Philip was the son of Philip II of Spain by his fourth consort, his niece Anna of Austria. Though pious, benevolent, and highly virtuous in private conduct, Philip, after he became king (Sept. 13, 1598), showed himself to be indolent and indifferent to his responsibilities. His father revealed his disappointment when he remarked that his son was unfit to govern the kingdoms God had given him and would instead be governed by them. In April 1599 the new king married his Habsburg cousin the Austrian archduchess Margaret.

From the beginning, Philip placed affairs entirely in the hands of a favourite, Francisco Gómez de Sandoval y Rojas, marqués de Denia, later the duke of Lerma—the first in a line of royal favourites who governed 17th-century Spain. Philip's government continued a policy of hostility to the Turks, and in Italy it faced the rivalry of the Republic of Venice and the Duchy of Savoy. In the rest of western Europe, however, a Spanish policy of conciliation ruled. Peace in the West enabled the government to deal with the internal problem of the Moriscos; and on April 9, 1609, the decision was made for their expulsion, which caused serious economic and demographic difficulties in certain areas. The peace was brought to an end by the outbreak (1618) of the Thirty Years' War in which Philip gave his unconditional support to the Holy Roman emperor Ferdinand II and the Catholic German princes.

Remote from his subjects, Philip spent huge sums on court entertainments and neglected Spain's growing economic problems, which were to reach crisis proportions in the follow-

ing reign. Having resided in Valladolid in the first years of his reign, he eventually fixed his court in Madrid. After a visit to Portugal (1619), he suffered the first attack of an illness that two years later brought about his death.
·diplomatic and military ambitions **6**:1089h
·imperial succession of Habsburgs, table 2 **8**:532
·political indecision and incompetence **17**:428g
·Portuguese reforms neglected by Spain **14**:869e
·renunciation of German claims **8**:91h
·Rubens' diplomatic–artistic success **16**:2b

Philip IV the Fair, of France **14**:223 (b. 1268, Fontainebleau, Fr.—d. Nov. 29, 1314, Fontainebleau), one of the greatest kings of France's Capetian dynasty, established his authority in ecclesiastical matters over the papacy and instituted important reforms in government.

Abstract of text biography. Philip's early years were spent in the troubled, suspicious atmosphere of the royal court. He gained the throne in 1285, continued the policy of administrative reform, and waged war with England (1294–1303) and Flanders (1302–05). The central feature of his reign, Philip's conflict of power with the papacy, began in 1296 and ended with the transfer of the papal Curia to Avignon, Fr., during the reign of Pope Clement V (1305–14). In 1306, Philip expelled all Jews from France and in 1307 quashed the crusading order of Knights Templars. His final years were marked with insurrection in Flanders and unrest in France.

REFERENCES in other text articles:
·Alba's devious statecraft **1**:416f
·Boniface VIII's papal supremacy conflict **3**:33a
·confiscation of Guienne from English **9**:16a
·Edward I's challenge in Gascony **6**:436a
·foreign policy and domestic rule **7**:617f
·German friendship treaty **8**:79c
·kidnapping and death of Boniface VIII **4**:592d
·stock exchange and brokerage history **16**:449d
·taxation of church property **5**:1084a
·taxation of the clergy **9**:1134a

Philip IV, ruled Portugal as PHILIP III (b. April 8, 1605, Valladolid, Spain—d. Sept. 17, 1665, Madrid), king of Spain (1621–65) during its decline as a great world power. Succeeding his father, Philip III of Spain, in 1621, Philip gave effective control of the government to a

Philip IV of Spain, detail of a portrait by Diego Velázquez (1599–1660); in the National Gallery, London

By courtesy of the National Gallery, London

chief minister (*valido*), the Conde-Duque de Olivares, who involved the country in a series of disastrous wars in an attempt to preserve Spanish dominance in Europe. Philip dismissed Olivares in 1643 and replaced him with Don Luis Méndez de Haro, who remained in office until his death in 1661. Thereafter the King had no *valido*, but frequently relied on the advice of a nun and mystic, Maria de Ágreda, who corresponded with him on both spiritual matters and affairs of state. By the end of his reign Spain, weakened by military reverses and economic and social distress, had become a second class power.

Philip's first wife was Elizabeth (Spanish, Isabel), daughter of Henry IV of France; after her death in 1644, he married Maria Anna (Mariana), daughter of the Holy Roman emperor Ferdinand III. A poet and patron of the arts, Philip was the friend and patron of the painter Velázquez, many of whose works portray Philip and members of his court.
·decadence and decline **17**:429h
·imperial succession of Habsburgs, table 2 **8**:532
·Louis XIV marriage negotiations **6**:1091d
·Olivares' personal and political position **13**:560b
·Rubens British diplomatic mission **16**:3d
·Thirty Years' War role **18**:335d
·Velázquez' relationship and work **19**:54e

Philip V, also called PHILIP THE TALL (b. *c.* 1293—d. Jan. 3, 1322), king of France and Navarre from 1316, largely succeeded in restoring the royal power to what it had been under Louis X.

Philip V of France, detail of a Latin manuscript, early 14th century; in the Bibliothèque Nationale, Paris (MS. Latin 5286)

By courtesy of the Bibliotheque Nationale, Paris

Philip was the second son of King Philip IV, who made him count of Poitiers in 1311. His elder brother, King Louis X, died in 1316, leaving an infant daughter Joan by his adulterous first wife, and a pregnant widow, Clémence of Hungary. Philip hastened to Paris, won the support of the officers of the crown and of the bourgeoisie, and was recognized as regent until the unborn child reached its majority. Upon the death of the child in November 1316, five days after its birth, Philip, disregarding the rights of the infant Joan, declared himself king. Anointed at Reims in January 1317, Philip quickly moved to consolidate his position, and on February 2 an assembly of barons, prelates, Parisian bourgeois, and doctors of the University of Paris recognized him as king, enunciating the principle that Joan, as a woman, could not succeed to the throne of France. Shortly thereafter the death of Philip's only son made Philip's major opponent, his brother, the future Charles IV, heir presumptive to the throne, and so the two were reconciled. The partisans of the infant Joan came to terms with Philip in March 1318. The count of Flanders, who had been for two years on the brink of declaring war, finally did homage to Philip in April 1320, and the danger of civil war was over.

Anxious to ensure peace and order as a means to the prosperity of the kingdom, Philip established a system of local militias under officers responsible to the crown; he also increased the efficiency of government machinery at all levels and checked the abuses of local officials. Yet he could do little against the Pastoureaux, marauding bands of religious enthusiasts, and his ordinance of June 1321 against the lepers, who were alleged to be conspiring with the Moors for the ruin of Christendom, resulted in severe persecutions.
·English and French dispute over Guienne **9**:16b

Philip V (b. 238—d. 179 BC, Amphipolis, Macedonia), king of Macedonia from 221 to 179, whose attempt to extend Macedonian influence throughout Greece resulted in his defeat by Rome. His career is significant mainly as an episode in Rome's expansion. The son of Demetrius II and his wife Phthia (Chryseis), the young prince was adopted, after his father's death in 229, by his half cousin Antigonus Doson, who took the throne. Philip succeeded upon Antigonus' death (summer 221). Philip soon won renown by supporting the Hellenic League in its war against Sparta, Aetolia, and Elis (220–217). In 215 Philip, allied with Hannibal, the Carthaginian general who was invading Italy (Second Punic War), attacked the Roman client states in Illyria and initiated ten years of inconclusive warfare against Rome (First Macedonian War). The Romans countered his moves by an alliance with the Greek cities of the Aetolian League, but Philip effectively aided his allies. When the Romans withdrew in 207, he forced an independent settlement upon Aetolia (206) and concluded the war with Rome on favourable terms (Peace of Phoenice, 205).

Philip then turned to the east. He plotted against Rhodes and in 203–202 conspired with Antiochus III of Syria to plunder the possessions of the Egyptian king Ptolemy V. But the people of Rhodes and Pergamum defeated Philip at sea off Chios (201) and so exaggerated reports of his aggression that Rome decided to declare war (Second Macedonian War, 200–196). The Roman campaigns in Macedonia (199) and Thessaly (198) shook Philip's position in Greece, and in 197 the Romans decisively defeated him at Cynoscephalae in Thessaly.

The terms of the peace confined Philip to Macedonia; he had to surrender 1,000 talents indemnity and most of his fleet and deposit hostages, including his younger son, Demetrius, at Rome. Until 189 Philip aided Rome against her enemies on the Greek peninsula. As a reward his tribute was remitted and his son restored (190).

Philip devoted the last decade of his life to consolidating his kingdom. He reorganized finances, transplanted populations, reopened mines, and issued central and local currencies. But neighbouring states constantly and successfully accused him at Rome. Becoming convinced that Rome intended to destroy him, he extended his authority into the Balkans in three campaigns (184, 183, 181). In 179, while pursuing a scheme for directing the Bastarnae against the Dardanians, Philip died. He had been a fine soldier and a popular king whose plans for expansion lacked consistent aims and achieved only temporary success. F.W. Walbank's *Philip V of Macedonia* (1940) is the standard biography.
·Antiochus III military alliance **1**:993h
·Carthage alliance and war on Rome **15**:1093a
·Punic Wars and Roman power struggles **15**:279f
·role in the Social War **8**:383h

Philip V (b. Dec. 19, 1683, Versailles, Fr.—d. July 9, 1746, Madrid), king of Spain from

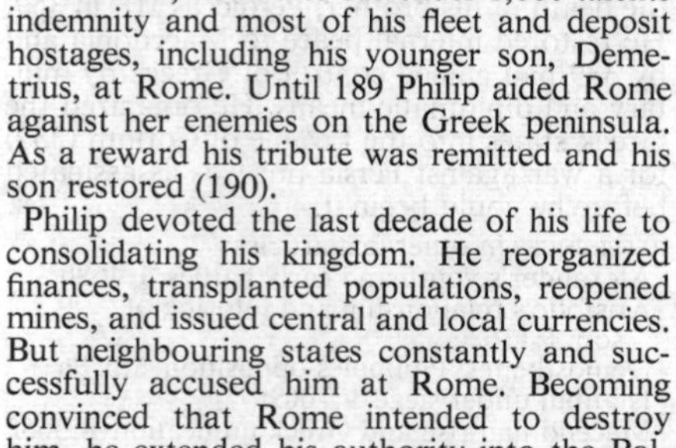

Philip V of Spain, detail of a portrait by Louis-Michel Van Loo (1707–71); in the Prado, Madrid

By courtesy of the Museo del Prado, Madrid

1700 (except for a brief period from January to August 1724) and founder of the Bourbon dynasty in Spain. During his reign Spain regained much of its former influence in international affairs. He was a son of the dauphin Louis (son of Louis XIV of France) and of Marie Anne, daughter of Ferdinand, elector of Bavaria. Philip's whole career was influenced by the fact that he was a grandson of Louis XIV of France and a great grandson of Philip IV, king of Spain. Philip held the title of duc d'Anjou until 1700, when he emerged as a person of political importance. In that year Charles II, the last Habsburg king of Spain, who died without issue, left Philip all his possessions (Spain, Spanish America, the Spanish Netherlands, and parts of Italy). The refusal of Louis XIV to exclude Philip from the line of succession to the French throne resulted in the War of the Spanish Succession. The Treaty of Utrecht, signed in 1713, deprived Philip of the Spanish Netherlands and of the Italian possessions of the Spanish Habsburgs, but left him the throne of Spain and Spanish America.

During the first 13 years of Philip's reign France had a dominant influence on the Spanish court, and the French ambassador had a place on the inmost council of state. After the death of his first wife (María Luisa of Savoy) in 1714, Philip came under the influence of his second wife, Princess Isabella Farnese, who was the niece and stepdaughter of the duke of Parma. Because of Isabella's desire to secure territories in Italy for her sons, Spain became embroiled in conflict with Austria, Great Britain, France, and the United Provinces, but managed to secure the succession of Philip and Isabella's oldest son, Don Carlos (later Charles III of Spain), to the duchy of Parma. Philip abdicated from the Spanish throne in January 1724 in favour of his oldest son, Luis, but was persuaded to become king again after Luis died of smallpox in August 1724. Philip's reign is noted primarily for the governmental and economic reforms instituted by his French and Italian advisers.

Philip had few intimate friends; his chief interests were religion, hunting, and music. During the last years of his reign he often lapsed into periods of insanity, and his wife largely controlled public affairs.

·diplomatic and military goals **6**:1094e
·French and Spanish Bourbon connection **3**:80g
·Madrid building program **11**:288h
·Spanish Bourbon dynasty establishment **11**:123c
·Spanish Succession War origins **17**:433b
·War of Spanish Succession and Barcelona **2**:720c

Philip VI (b. 1293—d. Aug. 22, 1350, near Paris), first French king of the Valois dynasty. Reigning at the outbreak of the Hundred Years' War (1337–1453), he had no means of imposing on his country the measures necessary for the maintenance of his monarchical power, though he continued the efforts of the 13th century Capetians toward the centralization of the administration in Paris. To raise taxes for war, he was obliged to make concessions to the nobility, the clergy, and the bourgeoisie; hence his reign witnessed the important development of the political power of the estates. The bourgeoisie, profiting from the king's power, proved grateful and loyal; but among the clergy and nobility a movement for reform of finances took root.

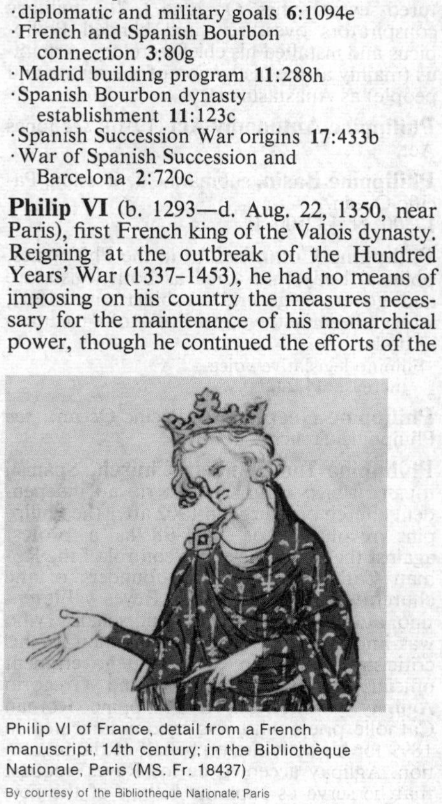

Philip VI of France, detail from a French manuscript, 14th century; in the Bibliothèque Nationale, Paris (MS. Fr. 18437)

By courtesy of the Bibliotheque Nationale, Paris

The elder son of Charles of Valois, Philip was first cousin to the brothers Louis X, Philip V, and Charles IV, the last Capetian kings of the direct line. On the death of Charles IV in 1328, Philip, in the face of opposition from the partisans of the claim of Edward III of England, assumed the regency until the end of the pregnancy of Charles IV's widow. When the widow produced a daughter, who therefore could not succeed to the throne, Philip became king and was crowned at Reims in May 1328.

After the outbreak of a revolt in Flanders in August of that year, the count of Flanders appealed to Philip, whose knights butchered thousands of rebellious Flemings at the battle of Cassel. When shortly thereafter Robert of Artois, who had helped Philip to win the crown, claimed the countship of Artois against a member of the royal family, Philip was forced to institute judicial proceedings against Robert, who became his bitter enemy. In 1334 Robert went to England and began to foment trouble between Edward III and Philip, hastening the deterioration of Anglo-French relations, which in 1337 led to the outbreak of the Hundred Years' War. Military operations were at first restricted. In 1340, however, France suffered a grave defeat in the naval Battle of Sluys. Meanwhile, the internal situation had worsened, as a result of resentment over the preponderant influence of the nominees of the powerful Duke of Burgundy in the king's council. A serious crisis resulted in 1343 and forced Philip to summon to Paris the estates of the kingdom, which took some measures to appease public opinion and to relieve the burdens of administration. France's devastating defeat by the English at Crécy (1346) gave rise to another crisis. To conciliate opponents, the government was obliged to entrust finances to three abbots. A new meeting of the estates in November 1347 again forced the King to recast his council. The spread of the Black Death in 1348 and 1349, however, overshadowed all political questions. When Philip died, he left France divided by war and plague, although by purchase he had made some important additions to the territory of the kingdom.

·Flemish revolt, tax, and English war **7**:622h
·Hundred Years' War causal factors **9**:16d

Philip, King (American Indian): *see* Metacom.

Philip, Acts of, apocryphal (noncanonical) book of the New Testament.

·Apocrypha literary form and dramatic content **2**:973g

Philip, duke of Edinburgh: *see* Edinburgh, Prince Philip, duke of.

Philip, Gospel of, an early Christian writing composed about the end of the 2nd century AD and generally considered to be apocryphal (unauthentic). It is but one of many such writings that circulated in the early church and were rediscovered in modern times. A 5th-century Coptic version is extant, but the original Greek is lost. Though the author shows familiarity with many canonical books of the New Testament, his heterodox views seem to classify him as belonging to the heretical Valentinians (*q.v.*). The writer, for example, uses such standard Gnostic terms as "spiritual" and "material" to distinguish those who possessed *gnōsis* ("esoteric knowledge") and those who did not. Salvation, moreover, is said to come from Christ through the redeeming *gnōsis*, and the crucifixion of Jesus is not equated with atonement for the sins of mankind. The *Gospel of Philip* also enumerates "bridal chamber" among the sacraments, a specifically Valentinian doctrine that views the Saviour as the bridegroom of Sophia (Wisdom), one of the emanations of God.

Philip, John (b. April 14, 1775, Kirkcaldy, Fife—d. Aug. 27, 1851, Hankey, now in South Africa), controversial missionary in South Africa who championed the rights of the Africans against the European settlers.

In 1818, at the invitation of the London Missionary Society, Philip left his congregation in Aberdeen, where he had served since 1804, to investigate the conditions at mission stations in South Africa. His findings led to a condemnation of the colonists for their harsh treatment of the Hottentots. Subsequently appointed the first superintendent for the missions of the society, Philip devoted the rest of his life to promoting the cause of the native races. Unpopular among the settlers and ignored by local authorities, he aroused philanthropic sentiment at home with his lecture tour in 1826 and his *Researches in South Africa* (1828). Supported by influential friends, among them William Wilberforce, who had secured abolition of the British slave trade, Philip secured the enactment by the British government of an ordinance bestowing equal rights for all the natives in South Africa in 1828. With the backing of public opinion in Britain, Philip hoped to create a series of native states to the north and east of Cape Colony, but in the end colonial expansion prevailed.

Opinion regarding Philip is still strongly divided. To his admirers, he is a high-minded, far-sighted humanitarian who did much to promote the welfare and education of the natives. His many white detractors in South Africa see him as an arbitrary mischief-maker who used false evidence and political intrigue to gain his ends.

Philipon, Charles (b. April 19, 1806, Lyon, Fr.—d. Jan. 25, 1862, Paris), caricaturist, lithographer, and liberal journalist who made caricatures a regular journalistic feature. He settled in Paris in 1823, took to lithography, and began to draw caricatures for a living. He

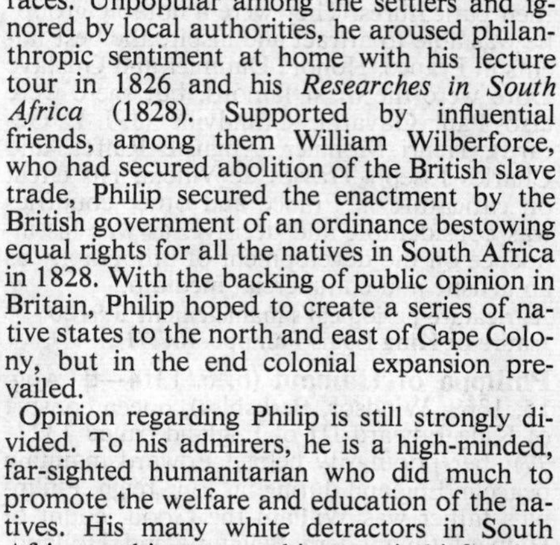

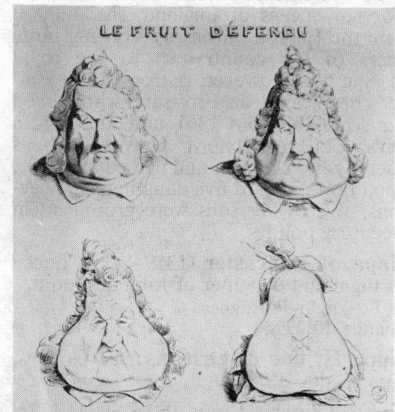

"La Poire," caricature of Louis-Philippe by Charles Philipon, first half of the 19th century; in the Musée Carnavalet, Paris

Giraudon

was an excellent draftsman with a fertile and irrepressible sense of satire. Moreover, he had vigorous political opinions, an enterprising spirit, and boundless energy. In 1830 he published a journal of political satire, *La Caricature.* Its career was brief and turbulent; after an avalanche of legal actions, it was suppressed in 1834. Meanwhile, in 1832, Philipon had produced a daily paper (with a new caricature every day) called *Le Charivari*. This was founded with the intent of holding up to good-natured ridicule the foibles of society. Ten years later *Le Charivari* was to become godfather to *Punch*, subtitled *The London Charivari*. In 1838 *La Caricature* made a cautious reappearance under the title of *La Caricature Provisoire*, but its success was such that, before long, the adjective *provisoire* was discarded. His next publication of importance, *Le Journal pour Rire* (later *Le Journal Amusant*), appeared in 1849 in the form of large newspaper sheets filled with woodcuts. Besides these journals, Philipon issued many occasional publications, such as *Le Musée Philipon*, *Le Robert Macaire*, *Les Physiologies*, and numerous political brochures.

As an artist, his best-known invention was a drawing that depicted the gradual transformation of Louis-Philippe into the shape of a pear. *La Poire* became the common symbol of the King, and all Philipon's artists used it in their caricatures. They were a notable group: he was able to attract and inspire the best talents in France. Honoré Daumier and Gustave Doré were the most famous, but there were also Paul Gavarni, Grandville (J.-I.-I. Gérard), Henri Monnier, Auguste Raffet, and Charles-Joseph Traviès de Villers. His effect on caricature in France and other countries was considerable and decisive, as was his influence on the development of lithography as an artistic and commercial medium.

·caricature periodical's management **3**:912b
·satire of King Louis-Philippe **16**:271g

Philippa of Hainaut (b. *c.* 1314—d. Aug. 15, 1369, Windsor, Berkshire), queen consort of King Edward III of England (ruled 1327–77); her popularity helped Edward maintain peace in England during his long reign. Philippa's father was William the Good, count of Hainaut (in modern Belgium) and Holland, and her mother, Jeanne de Valois, was the granddaughter of King Philip III of France. She was married to Edward in October 1327, nine months after he ascended the throne. Accompanying him on his expeditions to Scotland (1333) and Flanders (1338–40), she won universal respect for her gentleness and compassion. In 1347 she interceded and saved the lives of six burghers of Calais, Fr., whom Edward had threatened to execute. Unlike earlier foreign queens of England, she did not alienate the English barons by bringing large numbers of her countrymen to the royal court. She was, however, patron to the Hainauter chronicler Jean Froissart, who served as her secretary from 1361 until her death. Queen's College, Oxford University, was founded by her chaplain and named after her. Philippa bore Edward five daughters and seven sons; five of her sons were prominent in 14th-century politics.

Philippa of Lancaster (1359–1415), queen of Portugal and daughter of John of Gaunt.
·John I's Anglo–Portuguese alliance **10**:239g

Philippe II, duc d' Orléans: *see* Orléans, Phillipe II, duc d'.

Philippe, Charles-Louis (b. Aug. 4, 1874, Cérilly, Fr.—d. Dec. 21, 1909, Paris), writer of novels that describe from personal experience the sufferings of the poor. The son of a shoemaker, he was ambitious to become an army officer but was refused entry to the École Polytechnique in 1894 because of his puny physique. He finally found employment in the Paris municipal service as a shop inspector.

His novels either describe the Paris poor or are set in his native province of Bourbonnais. Of the first group, the most notable is *Bubu de Montparnasse* (1901; English trans., 1952), which tells the story of a young prostitute's relationship with her procurer, and with a young intellectual who tries to save her. The novels of rural poverty include *La Mère et l'enfant* (1900), in which he tenderly recalls his own childhood; *Le Père perdrix* (1902; title page 1903), the story of an old blacksmith, reduced by illness to indigence, and of a young engineer who loses his job because of his independent outlook; and the unfinished *Charles Blanchard* (1913), an evocation of the unhappy childhood of the author's father.

Charles-Louis Philippe
Harlingue—H. Roger-Viollet

Philippe's novels are distinguished by pity for the social outcast and by his power to depict the sufferings of the poor. Although his style can seem cloying, at its best it conveys emotional intensity through its simplicity and sincerity.

Philippe le Hardi: *see* Philip the Bold.

Philippeville (Algeria): *see* Skikda.

Philippi, modern FÍLIPPOI, in the department (*nomós*) of Dráma, Greece, a hill town overlooking the coastal plain and the bay at Neopolis (Kavála). Philip II of Macedon fortified this old Thasian settlement in 356 BC to control neighbouring gold mines.

In the Battle of Philippi in 42 BC Mark Antony and Octavian (later the emperor Augustus) here defeated Brutus and Cassius. Cassius committed suicide when his camp was overrun by Antony, unaware that Brutus had just inflicted the same loss on Octavian. Three weeks later (October 23), after losing a second engagement, Brutus, too, killed himself, in despair over the lost republican cause.

The Letter of Paul to the Philippians was addressed to Christian converts here whom he had visited in his second and third missionary journeys. Many ruins, especially of the imperial epoch, are spread over the site.

·Antonius' political and military redress **1**:1000b
·Brutus' and Cassius' deaths **15**:1106e
·early Christianity in Europe **13**:1091h; map 1092
·Horace's role **8**:1072b
·Philip of Macedonia's conquest **14**:226a

Philippi, Battle of (June 3, 1861), early U.S. Civil War clash, in what is now West Virginia, in which Union forces were victorious.

Philippians, Letter of Paul to the, one of the New Testament Pauline writings, composed in prison (probably at Rome about AD 62) and addressed to the Christian congregation established by Paul in Macedonia. Apprehensive that his execution was close at hand, yet hoping somehow to visit the Philippians again, Paul explains that he was imprisoned for preaching the gospel of Christ. Though he welcomes death for Jesus' sake, he is equally anxious to continue his apostolate. Paul exhorts his readers to remain steadfast in their faith and to imitate the humility of Christ, who "emptied himself" and "became obedient unto death, even death on a cross" (2:7–8). Exegetes generally believe that this much-quoted passage was taken from an early Christian hymn. Paul further urges the Philippians to work out their "own salvation with fear and trembling" (2:12), words often cited by theologians in discussing the role of free will in gaining personal salvation.

·apocalyptic millenarian aspects **12**:201d
·composite form **2**:958d
·Paul's concern for the early churches **13**:1091h
·rearrangement of letter fragments for clarity **2**:963a

Philippics, orations delivered by the Athenian statesman Demosthenes denouncing Philip II of Macedon as an enemy of the Greeks and urging resistance to him.

·content and effect **8**:367h
·Demosthenes' Macedonian opposition **5**:579a

Philippicus Bardanes, originally known as VARDAN (b. Armenia—d. after 713), Byzantine emperor whose brief reign (711–713) was marked by his quarrels with the papacy and his ineffectiveness in defending the empire from Bulgar and Arab invaders.

Philippicus was the son of the patrician Nicephorus of Pergamum (modern Bergama, western Turkey). His original name, Vardan, of Armenian extraction, may have been derived from that of his mother. Emperor Tiberius III Apsimar (ruled 698–705) exiled Vardan to the Ionian island of Cephalonia for his pretensions to the throne, but in 711 Tiberius' rival, Justinian II, recalled him and sent him to Cherson (in the Crimea) to suppress a revolt. Instead, he made common cause with Cherson and was proclaimed emperor under the Greek name of Philippicus. He sailed to Constantinople, gained the throne, and had Justinian and his family killed.

Philippicus was an advocate of the Monothelite heresy, the belief in a single will of Christ. Even before entering Constantinople, he had ordered the picture of the Third Council of Constantinople (which had condemned Monothelitism in 680) to be removed from the palace and the names of those the council had condemned restored. Patriarch Cyrus refused to support the new policy and was deposed and replaced by the more compliant deacon John early in 712. Pope Constantine therefore refused to recognize the new emperor.

In foreign policy, Philippicus' reign was disastrous. The Bulgarians besieged Constantinople in 712, and in 712–713 the Arabs captured several cities. On June 3, 713, military conspirators overthrew and blinded Philippicus and installed his chief secretary, Artemius (mainly at the instigation of the senate and people) as Anastasius II.

Philippine Autonomy Act (1916): *see* Jones Act.

Philippine Basin, submarine depression, Pacific Ocean.
17°00′ N, 132°00′ E

Philippine Commission, in the Philippines, political body that acted as both legislature and governor general's cabinet until 1907, when it became the upper house of a bicameral body.

·Filipino legislative voice increase **14**:242f

Philippine Deep (North Pacific Ocean): *see* Philippine Trench.

Philippine Independent Church, Spanish IGLESIA FILIPINA INDEPENDIENTE, an independent church organized in 1902 after the Philippine revolution of 1896–98 as a protest against the Spanish clergy's control of the Roman Catholic Church. Co-founders of the church were Isabelo de los Reyes y Florentino, author, labour leader, and senator, who was imprisoned during the revolution for his criticism of Spanish clergy and government officials in the Philippines, and Gregorio Aglipay y Labayán, a Philippine Roman Catholic priest who was excommunicated in 1899 for his activities on behalf of the revolution. Aglipay accepted de los Reyes' request that he serve as supreme bishop of the new church in 1903, a position he held until his death in 1940.

The church continued to follow Roman Catholic forms of worship, but for many years doctrine was strongly influenced by Unitarianism. A schism developed in 1946, and a unitarian faction left the church. Under Isabelo de los Reyes, Jr., elected bishop in 1946, the church adopted in 1947 a new declaration of faith and articles of religion that were Trinitarian. The Protestant Episcopal Church in the U.S.A. consecrated three bishops of the Philippine Independent Church in 1948, and the two churches entered into a close association. In 1961 the church was accepted into full communion with the Church of England and the Old Catholic churches.

In the 1960s an inclusive membership of 2,050,000 was reported by the church.

·formation and history **13**:553f

Philippine Insurrection, a war between the United States and Filipino revolutionaries from 1899 to 1902; the insurrection may be seen as a continuation of the Philippine Revolution against Spanish rule. The Treaty of Paris (1898) transferred Philippine sovereignty from Spain to the United States but was not recognized by Filipino leaders, whose troops were in actual control of the entire archipelago except the capital city of Manila. Although an end to the insurrection was declared in 1902, sporadic fighting continued for several years thereafter.

Commo. George Dewey defeated the Spanish fleet in Manila Bay on the morning of May 1, 1898, but could not occupy Manila until ground troops arrived three months later. On August 13 Manila fell after a bloodless "battle." Spanish Governor Fermín Jáudenes had secretly arranged a surrender after a mock show of resistance to salvage his honour. With American troops in possession of the city and Filipino insurgents controlling the rest of the country, conflict was inevitable.

The war began with shooting on the outskirts of Manila on the night of February 4, 1899. Throughout the spring of 1899, American troops pushed north into the central Luzon Plain, and by the end of that year Filipino general Emilio Aguinaldo retreated into the inaccessible northern mountains. The period of conventional battles ended, but insurgent leaders in many provinces continued bitter guerrilla warfare.

Fighting flared up with increased bitterness on the island of Samar in 1901. Gen. Jacob F. Smith, enraged by a guerrilla massacre of U.S. troops, launched a retaliatory campaign of such indiscriminate ferocity that he was subsequently court-martialled and forced to retire.

After 1902 the American civil government regarded the remaining guerrillas as mere bandits, though the fighting continued. About 1,000 guerrillas under Simeón Ola were not defeated until late 1903, and in Batangas province, south of Manila, troops commanded by Macario Sakay resisted capture until as late as 1906.

The last organized resistance to U.S. power took place on Samar from 1904 to 1906. There, the rebels' tactic of burning pacified villages contributed to their own defeat. America was now in undisputed control of the Philippines and retained possession of the islands until 1946.

·causes, duration, and outcome **14**:242d

Philippine languages, the aboriginal languages of the Philippine Islands. Consisting of about 75 70 separate languages, they belong to the Indonesian branch of the Austronesian family and are subdivided into two main subgroups—the central (or Mesophilippine) division and the northern (or Cordilleran) division—with a number of other member languages forming smaller groups or remaining unclassified. The most important languages in the central division are Tagalog (a standardized form of which, Pilipino, is the official national language) and Cebuano; the most important in the northern division is Ilocano.

·morphological and phonological systems **2**:489a

Philippine Revolution (1896–98), a Filipino independence struggle that, after more than 300 years of Spanish colonial rule, exposed the weakness of Spanish administration but failed to evict Spaniards from the islands. The Spanish–American War brought Spain's rule in the Philippines to a close in 1898 but precipitated a bloody war between Filipino revolutionaries and the U.S. Army.

Numerous quasi-religious uprisings had punctuated the long era of Spanish sovereignty over the Philippines, but none possessed sufficient coordination to oust the Europeans. During the 19th century, however, an educated Filipino middle class emerged and with it a desire for Philippine independence. Opposition before 1872 was primarily confined to the Filipino clergy, who resented the Spanish monopoly of power within the Roman Catholic Church in the islands. In that year the abortive Cavite Mutiny served as an excuse for renewed Spanish repression. The martyrdom of three Filipino priests—José Burgos, Mariano Gómez, and Jacinto Zamora—for allegedly conspiring with the rebels at Cavite sparked a wave of anti-Spanish sentiment.

Reform-minded Filipinos took refuge in Europe, where they carried on a literary campaign known as the Propaganda Movement. Dr. José Rizal quickly emerged as the leading Propagandist. His novel *Noli me tangere* (*The Social Cancer;* 1887) exposed the corruption of Manila Spanish society and stimulated the movement for independence.

By 1892 it became obvious that Spain was unwilling to reform its colonial government. Andres Bonifacio, a self-educated warehouse clerk, organized a secret revolutionary society, the Katipunan, in Manila. Membership grew to an estimated 100,000 by August 1896, when the Spaniards discovered its existence. Bonifacio immediately issued a call for armed rebellion. The Spanish then arrested Rizal, who had advocated reform but never condoned the revolution. Rizal's public execution, on Dec. 30, 1896, so enraged and united Filipinos as to make permanent retention of power by Spain clearly impossible.

In March 1897 leadership of the revolution passed to a young general, Emilio Aguinaldo, who had Bonifacio shot for alleged sedition. Aguinaldo proved incapable of militarily defeating the Spanish troops, who were augmented by Filipino mercenaries. In the later months of 1897, Aguinaldo's revolutionary army was pushed into the mountains southeast of Manila. Their situation was becoming untenable.

On Dec. 15, 1897, the pact of Biak-na-Bato was proclaimed. Though its precise terms have been a matter of impassioned debate ever since, the pact brought a temporary end to the Philippine Revolution. Aguinaldo and other revolutionary leaders accepted exile in Hong Kong and 400,000 pesos, plus Spanish promises of substantial governmental reforms, in return for laying down their arms.

Neither side executed the terms of the pact in good faith. Aguinaldo used the money to purchase arms in Hong Kong, and the Spanish reneged on the promised reforms. After the U.S. Navy commodore George Dewey annihilated the Spanish fleet in Manila Bay on May 1, 1898, Aguinaldo immediately returned to the Philippines and began the revolution anew. Now the Filipinos were faced with a more powerful enemy in the United States, which assumed title to the Philippines as a result of the Spanish defeat. Aguinaldo was captured in 1901 and subsequently appealed to Filipinos to cease fighting and accept American sovereignty.

·leadership and U.S. intervention complication **14**:242b

Philippines 14:231, a republic comprising an archipelago of about 7,100 islands and islets in the southwest Pacific Ocean, about 500 mi (800 km) off the Southeast Asian mainland. The island group is bounded on the east by the Philippine Sea, on the south by the Celebes Sea, and on the west and north by the South China Sea. (For statistical details, *see* pp. 946–947.)

The text article covers the relief and drainage of the Philippine Islands as well as their climate, vegetation, animal life, landscape under human settlement, people and population, national economy, transport system, administration, social conditions, cultural life and institutions, and prospects for the future.

REFERENCES in other text articles:

agriculture, forestry, and fishing
·abaca production and consumption **7**:282b
·fish and seaweed cultivation **7**:348d
·armed forces statistics, table 2 **2**:16
·artistic and architectural history **17**:270f; illus. 271
·Christian denominational demography map **4**:459
commerce, industry, and mining
·chromium production table **4**:571
·coal production and reserves, table 5 **4**:781
·copper production, table 2 **5**:151
·gold production table **8**:239
culture and education
·cuisine variety and menu **7**:945b
·educational planning and progress **6**:405b
·linguistic profile **2**:488b; map 485
·literature, music, and performing arts **17**:234b
·Southeast Asian socioreligious patterns **17**:222g
·theatre and dance forms **17**:249d; illus.
economics, finance, and currency
·gross national debt percentage table 4 **15**:193
·income elasticity for various food expenditures, table 6 **5**:106
·property taxation practices **15**:61c
·spice import, export, and value, table 3 **17**:506
government
·land reform of 1963 **10**:640f
·Manila's trade and Philippine banking **11**:450f
·U.S. economic, military, and cultural interaction **14**:244e
·newspaper publishing statistics table **15**:237
physical geography
·Asian physical and human geography **2**:159f
·map, Asia **2**:148
·monsoon climatic variation **12**:390h
·rain forest varieties, characteristics, and locations **10**:337f; map 1
population and demography
·urban population ratio table **16**:26
·Southeast Asian cultural inclusion **17**:230g

Philippines, history of the 14:240. The Philippine archipelago was the only area in Southeast Asia that became subject to Western colonialism before it had developed either a centralized government or an advanced elite culture.

The text article covers the way of life of the early tribal inhabitants of the islands and the coming of the Spanish in 1521. In 1571 the Spanish city of Manila was founded. Over the next 300 years, Spanish economic and political control was extended throughout the islands and many of the people were converted to Catholicism. During the Spanish-American War of 1898, U.S. forces aided members of the Philippine independence movement against Spanish rule, but in 1899–1901 they suppressed the new republic and the U.S. took control of the country. The U.S. allowed the Philippines a measure of self-government in the Tydings–McDuffie Act of 1934, which provided for a 10-year commonwealth period to be followed by independence. Japan occupied the Philippines during World War II. The U.S. returned in 1944, and independence was granted two years later. in the decades that followed, successive governments maintained close ties with the U.S., and the islands were troubled by repeated internal conflicts.

REFERENCES in other text articles:
- armour use by Moros **2**:29f
- Asian colonialism **2**:178d
- education aims and colonial contributions **6**:405a
- literature influences and nationalism **17**:236g
- MacArthur World War II Pacific operations **11**:220d
- Magellan's voyages and death **11**:293c
- Manila's history **11**:448c
- Philippine Independent Church **13**:553f
- socio-religious organization **17**:227g
- Theodore Roosevelt Pacific power concern **15**:1143g
- U.S. acquisitions in Asia **18**:982c
- World War II invasions **19**:989g; map 990

RELATED ENTRIES in the *Ready Reference and Index: for*
pre-Spanish institutions: see barangay; Kalantiyaw, Code of
Spanish relations: Cavite Mutiny; Manila galleons; Philippine Revolution
United States relations: Bell Trade Act; Friar Lands Question; Hare-Hawes-Cutting Act; Jones Act; Moro Wars; Philippine Insurrection; Spooner Amendment; Tydings-McDuffie Act; Wood-Forbes Mission
other: Hukbalahap Rebellion; Sakdal Uprising

Philippine Sea, section of the western North Pacific, lying east and north of the Philippines. The floor of this portion of the ocean is formed into a structural basin by a series of geologic folds and faults that protrude above the surface in the form of bordering island arcs. The Philippine islands of Luzon, Samar, and Mindanao are on the southwest; Palau, Yap, and Ulithi (of the Carolines) on the southeast; the Marianas, including Guam, Saipan, and Tinian, on the east; the Bonin and Volcano islands (Iwo Jima) on the northeast; the Japanese islands of Honshu, Shikoku, and Kyushu on the north; the Ryukyu Islands (Okinawa) on the northwest; and Taiwan (Formosa) in the extreme west. They surround an area measuring 1,800 mi (2,900 km) north–south by 1,500 mi east-west and occupying a total surface area of 40,000 sq mi (1,000,000 sq km), or about 3 percent of the entire Pacific region. This basin, with a general depth of 19,700 ft (6,000 m), plunges to its greatest depths in trenches to the east of the island arcs. The deepest is the 34,440-ft (10,497-m) Philippine Trench. Numerous seamounts rise from the basin floor, some of them volcanic with their peaks, often flat (called tablemounts, or guyots), capped with coral. The warm Pacific North Equatorial Current flows westward across the southern part of the sea. On meeting the Philippines, the current divides; part swings north near Luzon to form the Kuroshio of which some will return to the sea as the Kuroshio Countercurrent, and part swings south as the Pacific Equatorial Countercurrent. These currents, together with areas near reefs, ridges, and seamounts, are the sites of fishing grounds. The sea is a breeding place of hurricanes and typhoons, the storms becoming particularly strong in September.

maps
- Japan **10**:37
- Philippines **14**:233
- Trust Territory of the Pacific Islands **13**:832

Philippine Sea, Battle of the (June 19–20, 1944), U.S. victory over Japan in World War II.
- Japanese naval and air losses **19**:1004g; map 990

Philippine Trade Act of 1946: *see* Bell Trade Act.

Philippine Trench, also called PHILIPPINE DEEP, MINDANAO TRENCH, or MINDANAO DEEP, a submarine depression in the Philippine Sea section of the western North Pacific Ocean bordering the east coast of the island of Mindanao. The abyss, which reaches the second greatest depth known in any ocean, was first plumbed in 1927 by the German ship "Emden." The 34,120-ft (10,400-m) reading obtained at that time was the first indication of the actual near-record depth. In 1945 the USS "Cape Johnson" recorded a sounding of 34,440 ft (10,497 m); this was thought to have been slightly exceeded by the 34,578-ft (10,540-m) sounding originally made by the Danish "Galathea" in 1951, but that sounding was later corrected to 33,677 ft (10,265 m). Later soundings reported to exceed these have been found to be instrumentation errors.
9°00′ N, 127°00′ E
- oceanic trench formation **13**:435c
- Pacific Ocean floor features map **13**:840

Philippopoli (Bulgaria): *see* Plovdiv.

Philippsburg, town, Baden-Württemberg *Land* (state), West Germany, on the Saalbach River where it enters an arm of the Rhine. Originally a fortress, it was frequently besieged and captured during the wars of the 17th and 18th centuries. Pop. (1970) 5,563.
49°14′ N 8°27′ E
- capture by French in Thirty Years' War **18**:777d
- Vauban's siege tactics in 1688 **19**:38f

Philippus, Lucius Marcius (fl. 1st century BC), Roman statesman.
- Drusus' opposition to reform plans **15**:1102g

Philippus, Marcus Julius: *see* Philip the Arabian.

Philippus, Quintus Marcius (fl. 2nd century BC), Roman statesman.
- Rhodes in the Third Macedonian War **15**:1094f

Philips, Ambrose (b. Oct. 9, 1674, Shrewsbury, Shropshire—d. June 1/2, 1749, London), poet and playwright whose *Pastorals* (1710), written while he was a fellow of St. John's College, Cambridge, won immediate praise from leading men of letters, including Sir Richard Steele, Joseph Addison, and even Alexander Pope (who later attacked him in his satires). His adulatory verses ("Dimpley damsel, sweetly smiling") won Philips the nickname "Namby-Pamby." *The Distrest Mother* (1712), his adaptation of Jean Racine's *Andromaque*, was a success. The *Pastorals* were parodied by John Gay in *The Shepherd's Week* (1714).

Philips, John (1676–1709), English poet and writer, best known for his brilliant parody of John Milton's style in *The Splendid Shilling* (1705). *Blenheim* (1705) was written in answer to Joseph Addison's poem *The Campaign* (1705). Philips' *Cyder* (1708), one of the earliest 18th-century didactic poems, is modelled on the *Georgics* of Virgil.

Philips, Katherine (1632–64), English poet called the Matchless Orinda, the central figure in a romantic literary circle in Cardigan in Wales, wrote lyrics that represent a transition from courtly poetry to the Augustan Restoration style.

Philips, Obbe (*c.* 1500–68), Dutch religious leader who founded an independent Anabaptist sect, the Obbenites (*q.v.*).
- Menno Simons' baptism **11**:906g

Philips, Peter (b. 1561—d. 1628, Brussels), English composer of madrigals, motets, and keyboard music of considerable reputation in his lifetime. He was a Roman Catholic, and in

PHILIPPINES

Official name: Republika n̄g Pilipinas, Republic of the Philippines.
Location: southeastern Asia.
Form of government: republic.
Official languages: Pilipino, English.
Official religion: none.
Area: 115,830 sq mi, 300,000 sq km.
Population: (1970 census) 36,684,486; (1977 estimate) 45,028,000.
Capital: Manila.
Monetary unit: 1 peso = 100 centavos.

For the Philippines flag, *see* Addenda, Volume X, page 1057. For comparative statistics, *see* Volume X, page 910 ff.

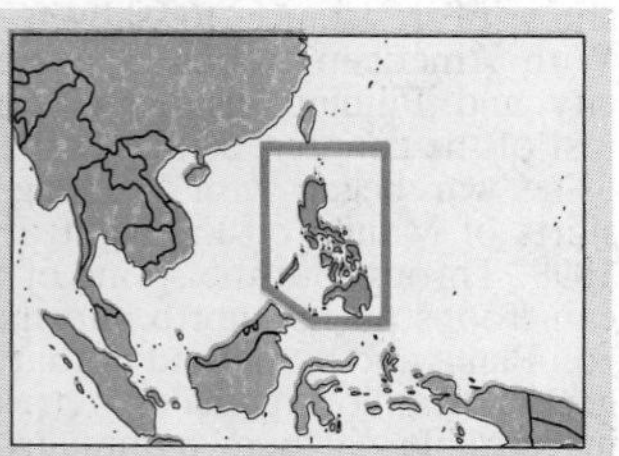

Demography

Population: (1977 estimate) density 388.2 per sq mi, 150.1 per sq km; (1970) urban 31.8%, rural 68.2%; (1975) male 49.96%, female 50.04%; (1975) under 15 years 43.2%, 15–29 28.7%, 30–44 14.9%, 45–49 8.6%, 60–74 3.8%, 75 and over 0.8%.
Vital statistics: (1970–75) births per 1,000 population 43.8, deaths per 1,000 population 10.5, natural increase per 1,000 population 33.3; (1970–75) life expectancy at birth—male 56.9, female 60.0; (1974) major causes of death (per 100,000 population)—infectious and parasitic diseases 154.9, of which tuberculosis 74.8; diseases of the respiratory system 151.5, of which pneumonia 110.7; diseases of the circulatory system 91.7; ill-defined conditions 75; accidents, poisonings, and violence, including motor vehicle accidents 37.6; endocrine, nutritional, and metabolic diseases 33.2; malignant neoplasms, including neoplasms of lymphatic and hematopoietic tissues 31.4; diseases of the digestive system 25.6.
Ethnic composition (1970): Tagalog 24.5%, Cebuano 24.1%, Ilocano 11.3%, Hiligaynon (Ilongo) 10.2%, Bicolano 6.8%, Waray-Waray 4.8%, other 18.3%. *Religious affiliation* (1970): Roman Catholic 85.0%, Islām 4.3%, Aglipayan 3.9%, Protestant 3.1%, Iglesia ni Kristo 1.3%, others, including Buddhists, 1.8%, none 0.7%.*

National accounts

Budget (1976): Revenue: 17,327,100,000 pesos (import duties 26.0%, income taxes 20.9%, excise taxes 11.5%, export duties 5.9%, other receipts 13.7%). Expenditures: 22,399,000,000 pesos (transportation and communications 16.1%, agriculture and natural resources 15.3%, other social services 14.4%, other economic services 13.3%, national defense 12.3%, education 9.6%). *Total national debt* (1976): 18,869,000,000 pesos. *Tourism* (1975): receipts from visitors, U.S. $155,217,232.

Domestic economy

Gross national product (GNP; at current market prices, 1976): U.S. $17,810,000,000 (U.S. $410 per capita).

Origin of gross domestic product (at current market prices):	1965				1975			
	value in 000,000 pesos	% of total value	labour force	% of labour force	value in 000,000 pesos	% of total value	labour force	% of labour force
agriculture, forestry, hunting, fishing	6,017	27.4	6,052,000	52.7	31,482	27.7	7,881,000	52.0
mining, quarrying	232	1.1	28,000	0.2	1,743	1.5	57,000	0.4
manufacturing	3,400	15.5	1,221,000	10.6	21,984	19.4	1,720,000	11.3
construction	758	3.4	299,000	2.6	2,728	2.4	503,000	3.3
electricity, gas, water	†	...	22,000	0.2	583	0.5	49,000	0.3
transport, storage, communications	781†	3.6	367,000	3.2	2,405	2.1	515,000	3.4
trade	2,914‡	13.3	1,120,000	9.7	8,162	7.2	} 1,660,000	10.9
banking, insurance, real estate	‡	...	...	...	4,590	4.0	}	
ownership of dwellings	§	...	...	...	2,762	2.4	...	...
public administration, defense	§	...	...	...	§	...	...	...
services	4,571§	20.8	1,426,000	12.4	12,937§	11.4	2,467,000	16.3
other	3,290	15.0	956,000	8.3	24,145	21.3	308,000	2.0
total	21,963	100.0*	11,491,000	100.0*	113,521	100.0*	15,161,000	100.0*

1582 he left England for Italy, where he became organist of the English College in Rome. In 1585 he entered the service of Lord Thomas Paget, with whom he travelled extensively. After Paget's death in 1590 Philips went to Antwerp. In 1597 he moved to Brussels, becoming organist of the royal chapel of the archduke Albert of Austria. In 1593 he was accused by the Dutch authorities of planning the murder of Queen Elizabeth I, but after imprisonment and trial he was released. He probably took holy orders, for in 1610 he was appointed to a canonry.

Philips published volumes of his own madrigals, to Italian texts, in 1596, 1598, and 1603. Eight volumes of his church music were published between 1612 and 1633. A posthumously published volume of masses is lost. Many of his compositions appeared in contemporary collections, including Thomas Morley's *First Book of Consort Lessons* (1599) and the *Fitzwilliam Virginal Book*, which contains 19 keyboard pieces by him. Philips' style reveals Italian and Dutch as well as English traits; J.P. Sweelinck was a powerful influence, and his firm polyphonic passages are at times reminiscent of William Byrd.

Philip the Apostle, Saint (b. Bethsaida of Galilee—d. traditionally Hierapolis, in modern Turkey; fl. 1st century), one of the Twelve. Mentioned only by name in the Apostle lists of the Synoptic Gospels, he is a frequent character in the Gospel According to John, according to which in 1:43–51 he came from Bethsaida, answered Christ's call ("Follow me"), and was instrumental in the call of St. Nathanael (probably Bartholomew the Apostle), whom he brought to Jesus.

At the time of his call, Philip seemingly belonged to a group influenced by St. John the Baptist. He participated in the miracle of the loaves and fishes (John 6:5–9), accounting for his symbol in medieval art of loaves. With St. Andrew the Apostle, he brought word to Jesus that certain Greeks had asked to see him (John 12:21–22). In John 14:8–9, Philip asked Jesus to reveal the Father, receiving the answer, "Have I been with you so long, and yet you do not know me, Philip? He who has seen me has seen the Father."

Nothing more is known about him from the New Testament. In later legends he was often confused with St. Philip the Evangelist (Philip the Deacon), one of the seven deacons of the early church (Acts 6:5). His apostolate was supposedly in the territory of Scythia, an ancient Eurasian area, partly in the U.S.S.R. He died of natural causes according to one tradition but according to another, of crucifixion, accounting for his other medieval symbol of a tall cross. His feast day in the Western Church, commemorated with the Apostle St. James the Less, was transferred in 1955 from May 1 to May 11. In the Eastern Church it is November 14. The *Acts of Philip* are apocryphal and probably date from the 3rd/4th century.

Philip the Arabian, Latin name in full MARCUS JULIUS PHILIPPUS (d. AD 249), Roman emperor from 244 to 249. A member of a distinguished equestrian family of Arab descent, he was praetorian prefect when the emperor Gordian III was killed in a mutiny (perhaps with Philip's connivance). Philip became emperor and quickly concluded a peace ending a war with Persia. After undertaking a series of campaigns against the Goths and other tribes on the Danube, he returned to Rome to celebrate in 248 the 1,000th anniversary of the founding of the city. Philip then faced a series of revolts by provincial army commanders, the last of whom, Decius, killed and succeeded him in the autumn of 249. Christian writers

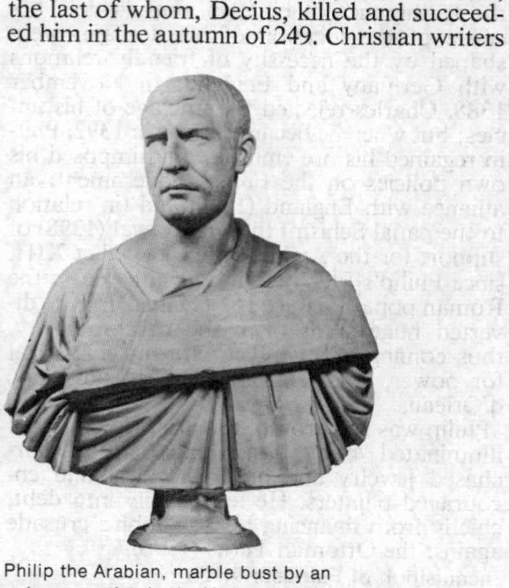

Philip the Arabian, marble bust by an unknown artist; in the Vatican Museum

The Mansell Collection

of the 4th century and later regarded Philip as the first Christian emperor; whether he was or not is unclear, but it is certain he did not adopt Christianity openly.

Philip the Bold (b. Jan. 17, 1342, Pontoise, now in France—d. April 27, 1404, Halle, now in Belgium), duke of Burgundy and the youngest son of the French king John II the Good. One of the most powerful men of his day in France, he was for a time regent for his nephew Charles VI; and when Charles went insane, he became virtual ruler of France.

Philip the Bold, detail of a sculpture by Claus Sluter, 14th century; portal of the Chartreuse de Champmol, Dijon

Lauros—Giraudon

John II's grant of the duchy of Burgundy to Philip did not become effective until June 1364, when the new king, Philip's brother Charles V, confirmed it. Philip and Charles supported each other's policies. The duke's marriage (June 1369) to Margaret of Flanders was arranged by Charles to prevent her from marrying an English prince. In 1384, Philip and his wife inherited Flanders, Artois, Rethel, Nevers, Franche-Comté, and some lands in Champagne. By purchase and skillful alliance he also secured several holdings in the Netherlands. In 1386 his domains had become so extensive that he arranged separate administrations at Lille and Dijon for his northern and southern territories.

During the minority of their nephew Charles VI, Philip and his brothers shared the government of France and the spoils of power. Philip

Production (metric tons except as noted). Agriculture, forestry, hunting, fishing (1970–71): rice 5,343,000, maize (corn) 2,005,000, sugarcane 15,481,000, centrifugal sugar 2,207,000, copra 1,822,000, abaca 133,000, pigs 6,600,000 head,¶ buffaloes 4,430,000 head,¶ cattle 1,650,000 head,¶ roundwood 10,700,000 cu m,♀ sawnwood 765,000 cu m,♀ fish catch 1,086,000,♂ coconuts 8,000,000,000 nuts,□ bananas 760,000,□ sweet potatoes and yams 706,000.□ Mining, quarrying (1970): copper concentrates 160,000, gold 18,747 kg. Manufacturing (1971): cement 2,447,000,♀ sugar 1,927,000,♀ cotton yarn 41,400, rubber tires 780,000, cotton fabrics 145,000,000 m,♀ cigarettes 39,671,000,000 sticks,♀ wheat flour 418,800, caustic soda 37,320. Construction (permits issued, 1969): residential 1,668,300 sq m, nonresidential 1,247,000 sq m.

Energy (1969): installed electrical capacity 2,036,000 kW, production 7,800,000,000 kW-hr (210 kW-hr per capita).

Persons economically active (1969): 12,046,000 (32.4%), unemployed 812,000 (6.7%).

Price and earnings indexes (1963 = 100):	1964	1965	1966	1967	1968	1969	1970	1971
consumer price index	108.2	111.0	117.9	124.6	125.0	126.9	148.8	177.1
daily earnings index	100.9	108.0	115.9	121.3	135.0	141.4	156.9	...

Land use (1970): forested 53.0%; agricultural and under permanent cultivation 29.9%; meadows and pastures 4.7%; built-on, wasteland, and other 12.4%.

Foreign trade

Imports (1970): U.S. $1,090,100,000 (nonelectrical machinery 21.6%, base metals 13.2%, mineral fuels and lubricants 10.9%, transport equipment 9.7%, electrical machinery 5.4%, explosives 4.6%, textile fibres 3.7%, cereals 3.0%, dairy products 3.0%, textile yarns and fabrics 2.2%). *Major import sources:* Japan 31.6%, United States 28.9%, West Germany 5.9%, Australia 4.6%, United Kingdom 4.3%, Malaysia and Singapore 2.8%, Indonesia 2.4%, Netherlands 2.0%.

Exports (1970): U.S. $1,061,700,000 (logs and lumber 23.5%, sugar 17.7%, copper concentrates 17.4%, coconut oil 9.0%, copra 7.5%, canned pineapple 2.0%, plywood 1.9%, desiccated coconut 1.8%, abaca 1.4%). *Major export destinations:* United States 41.5%, Japan 39.6%, Netherlands 4.1%, West Germany 1.9%, Taiwan 1.8%, Hong Kong 1.1%, United Kingdom 1.0%.

Transport and communication

Transport. Railroads: (1968) length 822 mi, 1,323 km; (1970) passenger mi 283,000,000, passenger km 455,000,000; short ton-mi cargo 32,000,000, metric ton-km cargo 47,000,000. Roads (1971): total length 45,691 mi, 73,532 km (paved 9,679 mi, 15,577 km; gravel and crushed stone 23,771 mi, 38,255 km; earth, graded and drained 12,241 mi, 19,700 km). Vehicles (1970): passenger cars 279,172, trucks and buses 179,445. Merchant marine (1970): vessels (over 1,000 gross tons) 167, total deadweight tonnage 1,270,000. Air transport: (1970) passenger mi 904,466,000, passenger km 1,455,600,000; short ton-mi cargo 17,976,000, metric ton-km cargo 26,244,000; (1971) airports with scheduled flights 33.

Communication. Daily newspapers (1970): total number 19, circulation per 1,000 population 24, total circulation 890,532. Radios (1968): total number of receivers 1,633,000 (1 per 22 persons). Television (1971): receivers 421,000 (1 per 90 persons); broadcasting stations 18. Telephones (1971): 309,922 (1 per 122 persons).

Education and health

Education (1969–70):	schools	teachers	students	student–teacher ratio
primary (age 7 to 13)	1,758	228,179	6,720,737	29.5
secondary (age 13 to 17)	2,098	51,349	1,501,917	29.2
vocational, teacher training	672	1,915	87,322	45.6
higher	600	24,589	583,382	23.7

College graduates (per 100,000 population, 1967): 274. *Literacy* (1970): total population literate (10 and over) 20,937,511 (83.4%), males literate 10,387,316 (84.6%), females literate 10,550,195 (82.2%).

Health: (1967) doctors 24,921 (1 per 1,390 persons); (1969) hospital beds 43,492 (1 per 822 persons); (1969) daily per capita caloric intake 2,040 calories (FAO recommended minimum requirement 2,270 calories).

*Percentages do not add to 100.0 because of rounding. †Transport, storage, communication includes electricity, gas, water. ‡Trade includes banking, insurance, real estate. §Services includes ownership of dwellings, public administration, defense. ‖Figures do not add to total given because of rounding. ¶1969–70. ♀1970. ♂1971. □1969.

did not hesitate to involve the government in the furtherance of his own aims, which, because of the location of his domain, were shaped by the necessity of friendly relations with Germany and England. In November 1388, Charles rejected the tutelage of his uncles; but when he became insane in 1392, Philip regained his pre-eminence and imposed his own policies on the French government: an alliance with England (1396) and (in relation to the papal Schism) the withdrawal (1398) of support for the Avignon pope Benedict XIII, since Philip's Flemish subjects adhered to the Roman pope Boniface IX. He furthermore diverted huge sums from the royal treasury, thus coming into conflict with his chief rival for power, Charles VI's brother Louis, duc d'Orléans.

Philip was a patron of the arts. He collected illuminated books and manuscripts, purchased jewelry and precious cloth, and encouraged painters. He fell heavily into debt, chiefly from financing his son John's crusade against the Ottoman Turks (1396).

·acquisition of Flanders **9**:18h
·Burgundian crusade and son's education **10**:243d
·Burgundian territorial expansion **3**:498d
·Flemish policy and English plan **7**:624d
·Low Countries political relation **11**:139f
·patronage of Claus Sluter **16**:893a

Philip the Evangelist, Saint, also known as PHILIP THE DEACON (b. Caesarea? [Qīsārya, modern Israel]; fl. 1st century), in the early church, one of the seven deacons appointed to tend the Christians of Jerusalem, thereby enabling the Apostles to freely conduct their missions. His energetic preaching, however, earned him the title of Philip the Evangelist and led him to minister successfully in Samaria (in modern Israel), where he converted, among others, the famous magician Simon Magus (Acts 8:9–13). Later, on the road from Jerusalem to Gaza, he instructed and baptized a court official from Ethiopia.

Philip's missionary journey ended at Caesarea (Acts 8), where he raised his four daughters, reputed to be prophets, and where, *c.* AD 58, he entertained the Apostle St. Paul and his companions on their last journey to Jerusalem (Acts 21:8). According to Greek tradition, he became bishop of Tralles (modern Aydin, Tur.). His feast day is June 6.

Philip the Good, duke of Burgundy 14:229 (b. July 31, 1396, Dijon, Burgundy, now in France—d. June 15, 1467, Bruges, now in Belgium), most important of the Valois dukes of Burgundy and true founder of the Burgundian state that rivalled France in the 15th century.

Abstract of text biography. Philip was made duke in 1419 and soon exhibited his primary concern for the welfare of his realm. He allied himself variously with England and France and conquered several neighbouring kingdoms (1420–43). Philip was an enthusiastic patron of the arts, employing painters such as Jan van Eyck. He created (1430) the Toison d'Or (Golden Fleece), a noble order that catered to his sense of pageantry.

REFERENCES in other text articles:
·Armagnac conflict **3**:498e
·civil war and Charles VII's settlement **7**:624h
·efforts to control French crown **9**:19g
·Jan van Eyck service **7**:89g
·Louis XI's sojourn and observation **11**:120h
·Low Countries territory acquisition **11**:139g

Philip the Magnanimous, landgrave of Hesse 14:230 (b. Nov. 13, 1504, Marburg, Hesse, now in West Germany—d. March 31, 1567, Cassel, Hesse), father of political Protestantism and champion of the independence of German princes against the Holy Roman emperor Charles V.

Abstract of text biography. The son of Landgrave William II, Philip became landgrave in 1518 and carried out reforms in administration and foreign affairs. Converted to the doctrines of Martin Luther (1524), Philip made Hesse a Protestant authoritarian state. He established (1531) the Schmalkaldic League of German Protestant states, which became a centre of Protestant politics and agitation against the Catholic Habsburgs. Philip's power was lost with the collapse of the league (1546–47) and his imprisonment by Charles V (1547–52). Released, he saw the Emperor defeated and Lutherans guaranteed equality with Catholics in the Peace of Augsburg (1555).

REFERENCES in other text articles:
·arrangement of reformist reconciliation **11**:194h
·Bucer's defense of bigamous union **3**:362a
·Protestantism reconciliation efforts **19**:1179f
·Swiss alliance attempt **8**:89d
·Zwingli's proposed Protestant union **17**:883a

Philistines, a people of Aegean origin who settled on the southern coast of Palestine in the 12th century BC shortly before the arrival of the Israelites. According to biblical tradition (Deut. 2:23; Jer. 47:4; etc.), they came from Caphtor (possibly Crete). They are mentioned in Egyptian records as *prst*, one of the Peoples of the Sea that invaded Egypt during the eighth year of Ramses III (*c.* 1190) after ravaging Anatolia, Cyprus, and Syria. Repulsed by the Egyptians, they occupied the coastal plain of Palestine from Joppa (modern Yafo) to the Gaza Strip. The area contained the five cities (the Pentapolis) of the Philistine confederacy (Gaza, Ashkelon [Ascalon], Ashdod, Gath, and Ekron) and was known as Philistia or the Land of the Philistines. It was from this designation that the whole of the country was later called Palestine by the Greeks.

The Philistines expanded into neighbouring areas and soon came into conflict with the Israelites, a struggle represented by the Samson saga (Judg. 14–16). With their superior arms and military organization the Philistines were able (*c.* 1050) to occupy part of the Judaean hill country. They were finally defeated by the Israelite king David (10th century), and thereafter their history was that of individual cities rather than of a people.

In the early part of the 7th century, Gaza, Ashkelon, Ekron, Ashdod, and probably Gath were vassals of the Assyrian rulers; but during the second half of that century the cities became Egyptian vassals. With the conquests of the Babylonian king Nebuchadrezzar II (604–562) in Syria and Palestine, the Philistine cities became part of the Neo-Babylonian Empire. In later times they came under the control of Persia, Greece, and Rome.

There are no documents in the Philistine language, which was probably replaced by Canaanite, Aramaic, and, later, Greek. Nor is much known of the Philistine religion, since all their gods mentioned in biblical and other sources have Semitic names and were probably borrowed from the conquered Canaanites. Until their defeat by David, the Philistine cities were ruled by *seranim*, "lords," who acted in council for the common good of the nation. After their defeat, the *seranim* were replaced by kings.

The Philistines long held a monopoly on smithing iron, a skill probably acquired in Anatolia. At sites occupied by the Philistines at an early period, a distinctive type of pottery, a variety of the 13th-century Mycenaean styles, has been found.

The use of the term Philistine for a person deficient in liberal culture and whose chief interests are material, prosaic, and commonplace arose in the mid-19th century. In the early 19th century, German students applied the epithet *Philister* to those who had not received a university training and who were therefore considered uncultured. The term was popularized by English writers, especially Matthew Arnold who employed it (1869) in *Culture and Anarchy*. It is now often used of those who oppose innovations in the arts.

·David's early military exploits **5**:517g
·government and cultural history **17**:941f
·Hebrew centralization for defense **10**:305e
·Israelite toleration of Canaanites in Judges **2**:909c
·Judaean commercial rivalry **16**:1044e
·military encounter with Israelites **2**:910h
·North African cities under Greek rule **13**:149h
·Old Testament basis in history **2**:896e
·Pentapolis government and culture **17**:941f
·religious forms and worship of Dagon **17**:967e
·Saul's victory, kingship, and collapse **16**:281f

Philistus (b. *c.* 430 BC, Syracuse, Sicily—d. 356), Greek historian of Sicily who helped Dionysius I to seize power in 405 and then became his right-hand man and commander of the citadel until he was exiled (386/385) for reasons now obscure.

Recalled after 20 years by Dionysius II at the time of Plato's first visit to his court, Philistus held high command first in the Adriatic and later at home in the civil war and died on active service. During his exile, spent mostly in Epirus, he began his history, which ultimately totalled 13 books, 7 on Sicilian affairs before 405, 4 on the reign of Dionysius I, and 2 on the early years of Dionysius II (367–363). It was continued by the Syracusan Athanas. His history clearly became a standard work, used by Ephorus in his Sicilian sections and also by Timaeus and Plutarch, writers who disliked his pro-monarchical viewpoint.

·Thucydides' historical substantiation **18**:360f

Phillip, Arthur (b. Oct. 11, 1738, London—d. Aug. 31, 1814, Bath), British admiral whose convict settlement established at Sydney in 1788 was the first permanent European colony on the Australian continent.

Phillip joined the British Navy in 1755, retired in 1763 to farm for 13 years in England, then served with the Portuguese Navy against Spain (1776) and with the British Navy against France (1778). In 1786 he was assigned the duty of founding a British convict settlement in New South Wales, and the following year he set sail with 11 ships.

Arthur Phillip, detail from an oil painting by F. Wheatley, 1786; in the National Portrait Gallery, London

By courtesy of the National Portrait Gallery, London

The first governor of New South Wales, Phillip struggled with rebellious convicts and troops and—until the middle of 1790—with the threat of famine; but he successfully created a permanent community. Despite his conciliatory policy toward the native Aborigines, he failed to establish peace between the settlers and the natives. He returned to England in 1792 because of poor health, but he saw further action at sea (1796–98) and was promoted to admiral in 1814.

·first Australian settlement and government **2**:413h
·Sydney discovery and settlement **17**:888c

Phillip Island, astride the entrance to Western Port (bay) on the south coast of Victoria, Australia, southeast of Melbourne. About 14 mi (23 km) long and 6 mi (10 km) at its widest, the island occupies 40 sq mi (100 sq km) and rises to 360 ft (110 m). Discovered in 1798 by the English explorer George Bass, it was originally called Grant Island, after Lieut.

James Grant, who landed there in 1801, and renamed in honour of Capt. Arthur Phillip, first governor of New South Wales. Sealers and whalers were in residence by 1802. It was proclaimed a shire in 1928. The island, the main town of which is Cowes, supports stock grazing and chicory cultivation and is a growing resort and retirement centre. It is the site of a koala bear sanctuary, seal, muttonbird, and fairy penguin rookeries, and a geological formation known as the Giant's Pipe Organ. The island is bridged to San Remo, on the east (mainland) shore of Western Port. Pop. (1971 prelim.) 11,691.
38°29′ S, 145°14′ E

Phillips, Horatio Frederick (1845–1912), English aviator pioneer.
·airplane wing design **7**:385c

Phillips, John, 17th-century bishop of Sodor and Man, also translated *The Book of Common Prayer* into Manx in 1630.
·Manx literature development **10**:1180g

Phillips, John (1800–1874), English geologist.
·Carboniferous System definition **3**:852g

Phillips, Sir Richard (1767–1840), British author, bookseller, and publisher.
·one-volume encyclopaedia trade **6**:784d

Phillips, Stephen (b. July 28, 1864, Summertown, Oxford—d. Dec. 9, 1915, Deal, Kent), actor and poet who was briefly successful as a playwright. Educated at Trinity College School, Stratford-on-Avon, and at

Stephen Phillips, watercolor by Percy Anderson, 1902; in the National Portrait Gallery, London
By courtesy of the National Portrait Gallery, London

King's School, Peterborough, he joined F.R. Benson's company in 1885. His *Poems* (1897) was followed by several verse dramas, including *Herod* (1901), *Ulysses* (1902), and *Nero* (1906). Phillips was compared to Shakespeare for *Paolo and Francesca* (1900), but his reputation soon declined and he died in poverty.

Phillips, Thomas (1770–1845), English painter of portraits and historical subjects.
·Grey portrait illus. **8**:425
·Ricardo portrait illus. **15**:825

Phillips, Wendell (b. Nov. 29, 1811, Boston—d. Feb. 2, 1884, Boston), Abolitionist crusader whose oratorical eloquence helped fire the anti-slavery cause throughout the antebellum period of United States history. Sacrificing social status and a prospective political career, the wealthy young Harvard Law School graduate joined the anti-slavery movement soon after opening a law office in Boston. In 1837 he married Ann Terry Greene, a fervent disciple of Abolitionist leader William Lloyd Garrison, and she never ceased to encourage and support her husband in his work. Phillips became a close associate of Garrison, lecturing for anti-slavery societies, writing pamphlets and editorials for the *Liberator*, and contributing financially to the Abolition Movement.

His reputation as an orator was established at Faneuil Hall, Boston (Dec. 8, 1837), at a

Wendell Phillips
By courtesy of the Library of Congress, Washington, D.C.

meeting called to protest the murder of Abolitionist Elijah Lovejoy at Alton, Ill., the previous month. When Phillips spontaneously delivered a stirring and passionate denunciation of the mob action against the martyred editor, he was recognized as one of the most brilliant orators of his day, introducing a direct and colloquial manner of speaking to the U.S. public platform.

As a reform crusader, Phillips allied himself with Garrison in refusing to link Abolition with political action; together they condemned the federal Constitution for its compromises over slavery and advocated national disunion rather than continued association with the slave states. During the Civil War (1861–65) he assailed Pres. Abraham Lincoln's reluctance to uproot slavery at once, and after the Emancipation Proclamation (January 1863) he threw his support to full civil liberties for freedmen. In 1865 he became president of the American Anti-slavery Society after Garrison resigned.

After the Civil War, Phillips also devoted himself to temperance, women's rights, universal suffrage, and the Greenback Party (a minor political movement). He was an unsuccessful Massachusetts gubernatorial candidate of the Labor Reform and Prohibition parties in 1870. He continued to lecture on the Lyceum circuits until the 1880s.

BIBLIOGRAPHY. Oscar Sherwin, *Prophet of Liberty* (1958); Lorenzo Sears, *Wendell Phillips* (1909).

Phillips, William (1731?–1781), British major general, a subordinate commander under Gen. John Burgoyne at the Battle of Saratoga (1777) in the U.S. War of Independence. A prisoner after Saratoga, he was exchanged for a Continental general and later served in Virginia.

Phillips, William (1775–1829), English geologist.
·time scale and Carboniferous period **7**:1067d

Phillips Academy, in Andover, Mass., private college preparatory school (grades 9–12) for boys. Founded in 1778 by Samuel Phillips, then lieutenant governor of Massachusetts, it is the oldest incorporated academy in the U.S. The school is commonly called Phillips Andover, or simply Andover, to distinguish it from Phillips Exeter Academy.

Phillipsburg, town, Warren County, New Jersey, U.S., on the Delaware River. Its twin city, Easton, Pa., is across the river, and together they comprise a commercial hub of an otherwise agricultural region. The site was a Delaware Indian settlement called Chintewink. The town was named either for the Indian chief Philip or for William Phillips, who settled there in 1735. It developed after completion of the Morris Canal (1832), the coming of the Central Railroad of New Jersey (1852), and the introduction of the Bessemer steel process by Peter Cooper (1856). Manufacturing is diversified. Inc. 1861. Pop. (1980) 16,647.
40°42′ N, 75°12′ W

Phillips Collection, museum containing an outstanding small collection of late-19th- and 20th-century American and European painting that was founded in 1918 by Duncan Phillips. It is housed in Phillips' residence in Washington, D.C.

Phillips' curve, graphic representation of the economic relationship between the rate of unemployment (or the rate of change of unemployment) and the rate of change of money wages. It indicates that wages tend to rise faster when unemployment is low. In his original article (1958), A.W. Phillips plotted the unemployment rates and the rates of change of money wages for the U.K. from 1861 to 1957. He found that, except for the years of unusually large and rapid increases in import prices, the rate of change in money wages could be explained by the level of unemployment. As economic theory would predict, in times with low unemployment rates

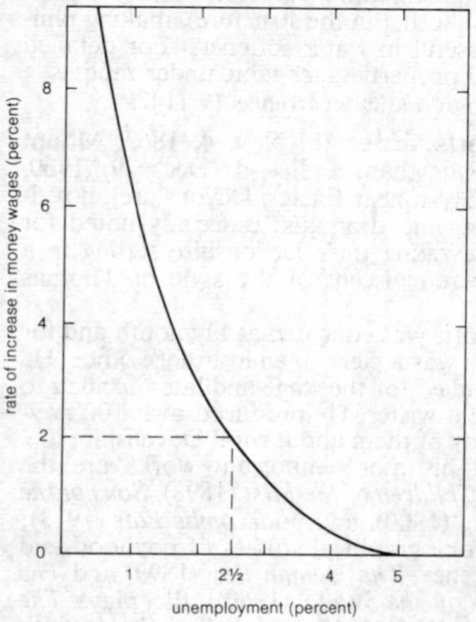

Phillips' curve
From *Economica* (1958)

employers are more likely to bid wages up in an effort to lure the higher quality employees away from their competitors. When unemployment rates are high, such bidding is unnecessary and the rate of change in money wages is lower. This analysis has been used by economists of other countries, with varying degrees of accuracy and success, to examine the inverse relationship between price stability and levels of unemployment.
·cost-push inflation theory **9**:567b
·full employment and price instability **7**:327c

Phillips Exeter Academy, in Exeter, N.H., private college preparatory school (grades 9–12) for boys. It was founded in 1781 by John Phillips, a local merchant and uncle of the Samuel Phillips who three years earlier had founded Phillips Academy in Andover, Mass. The school was richly endowed in 1931 by philanthropist Edward S. Harkness.

Phillipsia, genus of extinct trilobites uncommonly found as fossils in Mississippian to Per-

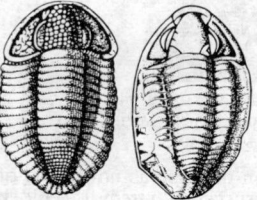

Phillipsia
Reprinted from H. Shimer and R. Shrock, *Fossil Index of North America*, by permission of the M.I.T. Press, Cambridge, Massachusetts, Copyright 1944 by the Massachusetts Institute of Technology, Copyright renewed 1972 by the Massachusetts Institute of Technology

mian rocks (345,000,000 to 225,000,000 years old) in Europe, North America, and the East Indies. One of the last known trilobite genera, *Phillipsia* is characterized by a relatively large head region and a large posterior region. Some forms are characterized by an unusual development of small surface nodes.

phillipsite, a hydrated calcium, sodium, and potassium aluminosilicate mineral, $(\frac{1}{2}Ca,Na,K)_3Al_3Si_5O_{16}\cdot 6H_2O$, in the zeolite family. It typically is found as brittle white crystals filling cavities and fissures in basalt and in phonolite lava, occurring near Rome; on Sicily; in Victoria, Australia; and in Germany. Phillipsite's molecular structure is a framework containing four- and eight-membered rings of linked silicate tetrahedra (four oxygen atoms arranged at the points of a triangular pyramid about a central silicon atom); this structure gives phillipsite cation-exchange properties (dissolved sodium, potassium, calcium, and magnesium readily replacing one another in the structure), making phillipsite useful in water softeners. For detailed physical properties, *see* table under zeolites.
·dehydration and occurrence **19**:1142a

Phillpotts, Eden (b. Nov. 4, 1862, Mount Abu, Rājasthān, India—d. Dec. 29, 1960, Broad Clyst, near Exeter, Devonshire), novelist, poet, and dramatist especially noted for novels evoking their Devonshire setting in a manner reminiscent of the style of Thomas Hardy.

Phillpotts was educated at Plymouth and for 10 years was a clerk in an insurance office. He then studied for the stage and later decided to become a writer. He produced over 100 novels, many of them about rural Devonshire life. Among his more important works are the novels *Children of the Mist* (1898), *Sons of the Morning* (1900), and *Widecombe Fair* (1913); the autobiographical studies of boyhood and adolescence, *The Human Boy* (1899) and *The Waters of the Walla* (1950); the plays *The Farmer's Wife* (1917) and *Yellow Sands* (with his daughter Adelaide, 1926); and the poetry collections *The Iscariot* (1912), *Brother Beast* (1928), and *The Enchanted Wood* (1948). He also wrote *One Thing and Another* (1954), a collection of poems and essays.

Phillpotts, Henry (b. May 6, 1778, Bridgwater, Somersetshire—d. Sept. 18, 1869, Torquay, Devonshire), Church of England bishop of Exeter (from 1830), represented the conservative High Church wing of the Oxford Movement and emphasized liturgical forms of worship, episcopal government, monastic life,

Henry Phillpotts, engraving by D.J. Pound (19th century) after a photograph
Radio Times Hulton Picture Library

and early Christian doctrine as normative of orthodoxy. His unsuccessful attempt to block (1847–51) the pastoral appointment of George C. Gorham because of his Calvinistic view of baptism gave rise to one of the most famous ecclesiastical law suits in the 19th century, and agitated High Church feeling against Parliament's intervention in religious questions. He actively supported Tory politics, opposing social reform and religious toleration.

Phillyrea (shrub): *see* mock privet.

Philocrates, Peace of, concluded between Athens and Philip II of Macedonia (April 346 BC).
·content and importance **8**:368c
·Demosthenes' part in treaty negotiation **5**:579c

Philoctetes, Greek legendary hero who played a decisive part in the final stages of the Trojan War. He (or his father, Poeas) had been bequeathed the bow and arrows of the Greek hero Heracles in return for lighting his funeral pyre; Philoctetes thus became a famous archer. En route for Troy he was incapacitated by a snakebite and was left behind. After a seer revealed that Troy could be taken only with the aid of Heracles' bow and arrows, the Greek warriors Odysseus and Diomedes went to Philoctetes and persuaded him to accompany them to Troy. There he was healed of his wound and killed Paris (son of Priam, king of Troy), thus paving the way for the city's fall. He subsequently returned home but wandered as a colonist to southern Italy, where he ultimately died in battle.

The theme of this story was used by the ancient Greek writer Sophocles in his *Philoctetes.*

Philodemus (b. *c.* 110 BC, Gadara, Syria—d. *c.* 35 BC, Herculaneum, Italy), Greek poet and Epicurean philosopher who did much to spread Epicureanism to Rome.

After studying under the Epicurean Zeno of Sidon at Athens, he moved to Rome *c.* 75 BC and became the mentor of the Roman aristocrat Lucius Calpurnius Piso, who invited Philodemus to live in his villa at Herculaneum, near Naples. In the ruins of that villa were found fragments of Philodemus' writings. He was known for his theory of art, which contradicted classical doctrines of aesthetics. His fame rests largely, however, on his love epigrams in the Palatine Anthology, allusions to which are found in works by the later Roman poets Virgil, Ovid, and Horace.
·Epicurean works in Herculaneum Papyri **6**:912f

Philodendron (plant genus): *see* Arales.

Philodendron pertusum, juvenile stage of the Swiss cheese plant, *Monstera deliciosa*, of the family Araceae.
·house plants and their care **8**:1119g

Philohela minor (bird): *see* woodcock.

Philo Judaeus: *see* Philo of Alexandria.

Philokalia (Greek: "Love of the Good, the Beautiful"), a prose anthology of Greek monastic texts that was part of a movement for spiritual renewal in Eastern monasticism and Orthodox devotional life in general. Compiled by the Greek monk Nikodimos and Makarios, the bishop of Corinth, the *Philokalia* was first published in Venice in 1782 and gathered the unpublished writings of all major Hesychasts (hermits) of the Christian East, from Evagrius Ponticus to Gregory Palamas.

The *Philokalia* is concerned with "inner asceticism," not merely outward obedience to one's superior or the practice of physical austerities. Inner asceticism means, above all, daily recollection of death and judgment, together with perpetual remembrance of God as omnipresent and omnipotent, and ceaseless prayer. It is through this compilation that the tradition of the "prayer of the mind," or Jesus prayer, uttered in a particular bodily position with a special way of breathing, became better known and gained new followers among Orthodox as well as Western Christians.

The *Philokalia* had great success in the Slavic countries, especially Russia, and a Church Slavonic version appeared in 1793 in St. Petersburg under the title of *Dobrotoliubie.* It was translated by the *starets* (spiritual leader) Paissy Velitchkovsky, who introduced a neo-Hesychast spiritual renewal into Russian and Moldavian monasticism. Whereas in Greece the *Philokalia* apparently had little influence outside certain schools of monasticism (although attempts were made to reach a wider public with new editions in 1867 and 1957), the Church Slavonic version became through the influence of the *startsy* one of the favourite spiritual books of all classes of Russian laity during the 19th century. In 1877 Theophan Zatvornik (Theophane the Recluse), the former bishop of Tambov, compiled a Russian version in five volumes, which altered the selection of extracts in a way that had been characteristic for Russian monasticism since the time of Nil Sorsky in the 16th century.

Philolaus (fl. *c.* 475 BC), philosopher of the Pythagorean School, named after the Greek thinker Pythagoras (fl. *c.* 530 BC). He was born either at Tarentum or, according to the 3rd-century-AD Greek historian Diogenes Laërtius, at Croton, in southern Italy. When, after the death of Pythagoras, dissension was prevalent in Italian cities, Philolaus, according to some accounts, fled first to Lucania and then to Thebes, in Greece. He later returned to Italy, where he may have been a teacher of the Greek thinker Archytas.

Philolaus was a student of the celebrated number theory of Pythagoras, who stressed the importance of numerical groupings. He was particularly interested in the properties inherent in the decad, the sum of the first four numbers. The successor of Plato as head of the Greek Academy, the philosopher Speusippus, is reported to have reproduced the doctrine of the first four numbers from a book by Philolaus. Only fragments of his works survive, however, and the belief that Philolaus was the first systematizer of Pythagoreanism is widely disputed.

Pythagoras probably knew the construction of three of the regular solids in geometry, and his disciple Empedocles is stated to have been the first who maintained that four elements compose the universe. Philolaus, combining these ideas, held that the elementary nature of bodies depends on their form. Thus, he assigned the tetrahedron to fire, the octahedron to air, the icosahedron to water, and the cube to earth. To the dodecahedron he assigned a fifth element, ether, or the pure air that surrounds the universe. Also attracted by the Pythagorean notion of opposites, Philolaus believed that the health of an animate body consists in a balance between heat and cold. Regarding the soul as a "mixture and harmony" of the bodily parts, he also assumed a substantial soul the existence of which in the body amounts to an exile brought about by sin.

A Pythagorean system of astronomy is also sometimes attributed to Philolaus. At its centre is a great fire in which is situated the force that directs the movement of the universe. The Earth's revolution around the fire was apparently believed to occur on its own axis during the period of a day and a night, or 24 hours. Such a system remarkably anticipates modern astronomy as it originated in the work of Nicolaus Copernicus, a Polish astronomer.

Before the *Timaeus* of Plato, it had been held to be impossible that the astronomy and the physics credited to Philolaus could be valid. Some critics have even asserted that the man himself was an invention of Plato, while others believe that his works were forgeries by the 4th-century-BC philosopher Speusippus; descriptions of Philolaus' views by ancient writers thus need to be examined with caution.

philology, in British usage, an old term for comparative linguistics and historical linguistics, the study of the evolution and interrelations of languages and of language change. In American and continental usage, it usually refers to the study of written texts. Comparative philology, now usually called comparative linguistics, became a significant field of study in the 19th century. The principles and methods of comparative philology were used to establish language families on the basis of linguistic relationships.

For further information, *see also* comparative method; linguistics, diachronic; linguistics, historical; and Neogrammarians.

·dictionary development since Webster **5**:716g
·exegetical uses and misuses **7**:61b
·grammar-study developments after 1800 **8**:268d
·humanistic scholarship's relationship **8**:1170c
·Indo-European contributions in 1800s **10**:993g
·Italic language reconstruction **9**:1075c
·Mommsen artistic approach **12**:334b
·Müller's application to religious study **15**:617f
·Nietzsche as classical scholar **13**:77c
·relationship to linguistics **10**:992f
·Renaissance humanist developments **8**:1176b
·textual criticism methodology **18**:189c
·writing's basis in linguistics **19**:1041a

Philomachus pugnax (bird): *see* ruff.

Philometer (king of Syria): *see* Demetrius III.

Philometor (king of Egypt): *see* Ptolemy VI Philometor.

Philometor Euergetes, Attalus III (king of Pergamum): *see* Attalus III Philometor Euergetes.

Philon of Byzantium, 1st-century-BC scientist.

·thermometer development **8**:701g

Philo of Alexandria **14**:245 (b. between 15 and 10 BC, Alexandria, Egypt—d. Alexandria), a Greek-speaking Jewish philosopher and theologian whose attempt to synthesize revealed faith and philosophical reason foreshadowed later developments in Christian theology.

Abstract of text biography. Philo's fame derives from his writings, which consist of scriptural essays and homilies, philosophical and religious essays, and essays on contemporary subjects. His philosophy was influenced by Aristotle, the Neo-Pythagoreans, the Cynics, the Stoics, and especially Plato. In theology he was the first to distinguish between the knowability of God's existence and the unknowability of his essence and to expound on the mystic love of God that God has implanted in man and through which man becomes Godlike.

REFERENCES in other text articles:

·Bible in Neoplatonic terms **7**:65d
·biblical literature and Platonism **15**:1121h
·Christian, Jewish, and Greek Logos **4**:478f
·Christian adaptation of Logos theology **4**:468a
·Christian philosophical borrowing **4**:460b
·duality of soul and self in man **15**:153a
·Greek influence on Jewish philosophy **10**:208d
·Hellenism in Judaism and in Saint Paul **4**:535f *passim* to 536g
·Platonic influence **14**:540b
·prophecy, Judaism, and divine power **15**:65d
·reality of divine ideas **15**:540h
·scriptural interpretation **3**:1084b
·Torah and Greek thought reconciled **10**:311h *passim* to 313g

Philo of Byblos, 2nd-century-AD chronicler who compiled information on the religions along the coast of Palestine.

·Mediterranean religious studies **17**:968h

Philopoemen (b. *c.* 252 BC, Megalopolis, Arcadia—d. 182 BC, Messene), general of the Achaean League whose principal fame lay in his restoration of Achaean military efficiency. He was trained to a career of arms by the Academic philosophers Ecdelus and Demophanes. After spending 11 years as a mercenary leader in Crete, he returned to Achaea and was elected federal cavalry commander for 210/209, when his reorganized cavalry defeated the Aetolians on the Elean frontier. As general of the confederation for 208/207 he introduced heavier Macedonian armour and phalanx tactics and crushed the Spartans under Machanidas at Mantineia (207). General again in 206/205 and 201/200, he expelled Nabis of Sparta from Messene and routed him at Tegea. In a fourth generalship (193/192) he failed against Nabis by sea but almost annihilated his army near Gythium. The Roman general Flamininus prevented his taking Sparta, but on Nabis' assassination (192) Philopoemen incorporated it in the confederation. Henceforth he dominated Achaean policy, but, when Messene rebelled, he was taken in a skirmish and given poison (182). Plutarch relates his life.

·Achaean League control **15**:1094a

Philoponus, John, also known as JOHN THE GRAMMARIAN (fl. 6th century), Greek Christian philosopher, theologian, and literary scholar whose writings expressed an independent Christian synthesis of classical Hellenistic thought, which in translation contributed to Syriac and Arabic cultures and to medieval Western thought. As a theologian, he proposed certain esoteric views on the Christian doctrine of the Trinity and the nature of Christ.

A native of Alexandria, Egypt, and a student there of the celebrated Aristotelian commentator Ammonius Hermiae, Philoponus interpreted Aristotle critically in the light of Neoplatonic Idealism and Christian theology; thus, he identified Aristotle's concept of the first cause with the Christian notion of a personal God; arguing for the Christian doctrine of creation, he composed a treatise, now lost, "On the Eternity of the World," contradicting the 5th-century Neoplatonist Proclus.

Possibly Philoponus' Christianization of Aristotelian doctrine allowed the Alexandrian academy to continue despite criticism from the church. Among his notable commentaries are those on Aristotle's *Metaphysics*, the logical treatises of the *Organon*, the tract on *Physics*, the three books of *De anima* ("On the Soul"), and *De generatione animalium* ("On the Generation of Animals"). In philosophical theology Philoponus produced his major work, *Diaitētēs ē peri henōseōs* ("Mediator, or Concerning Union"), in which he discusses the Trinity and Christology. Because he held that every nature necessarily is individualized, he concluded that in Christ only one nature was possible, the divine. Although such a theological position appeared to be heretical Monophysitism, Philoponus approximated the orthodox teaching by explaining that though Christ's humanity was devoid of personhood, it was not dissolved by its fundamental union with the divinity. This view disconcerted the strict Monophysites, who had considered Philoponus one of them. Moreover, he had written a tract on Christ's bodily resurrection from the dead, unusual for its distinction between the earthly and glorified bodies. Claiming that his Christology was traditional, Philoponus criticized the doctrinal statements of Pope Leo I (440–461) and the Council of Chalcedon (451); ironically, he was consequently censured by the third Council of Constantinople (681) for his alleged Monophysitism.

Applying Philoponus' principle that every nature is individualized to his conclusion that the Trinity comprises three individual expressions of the divinity, the inferred tritheism is only verbal; nowhere does he say there are three gods. Because the Neoplatonists attempted to reduce all reality to absolute unity, however, he termed them pantheists. Philoponus' Christological and Trinitarian doctrines show the influence of another of his theories—that the whole is not simply the sum of its parts; outside the reality of the total object, component parts are purely fictitious.

In order to defend the Christian dogma of personal immortality, Philoponus broke with the common Aristotelian and Stoic interpretation of a single universal mind operative in all men and taught that each person possesses an individual intellect. Among his other original contributions to Western thought was his development of Aristotle's kinetic theory of motion (the principle that nothing moves except that it be moved by an external force), by affirming that velocity is directly proportional to the excess of force to resistance. Philoponus' two treatises on grammar were later revised in lexicon form and received wide recognition during the Middle Ages.

·influence on Jewish philosophy **10**:209b

Philopotamidae, family of caddisflies of the order Trichoptera.

·classification and characteristics **18**:710d

Philopteridae, family of lice of the order Phthiraptera.

·classification and description **14**:376a

Philorheithridae, family of caddisflies of the order Trichoptera.

·classification and basic features **18**:710g

Philosophe, Le (1743), treatise by Dumarsais.

·content and significance **10**:1170g

philosopher-kings, concept developed by Plato in his dialogue *Republic*, in which he asserted that the ideal state would be headed by an aristocracy of philosophers, men prepared through long intellectual discipline and governing through personal insight.

·function within ideal state **14**:686a
·shaping of idea **8**:371e

philosopher's stone, an unknown substance sought by alchemists for its supposed ability to transform base metals into gold. The stone, also referred to as the "tincture," or the "powder" (Greek *xērion*, which passed through Latin into Arabic as *elixir*), was allied to an elixir of life, believed by alchemists to be a liquid derived from it. Inasmuch as alchemy was concerned not only with the search for a method of upgrading less valuable metals but also of perfecting the human soul, the philosopher's stone was thought to cure illnesses, prolong life, and bring about spiritual revitalization.

The philosopher's stone, described variously, was sometimes said to be a common substance, found everywhere but unrecognized and unappreciated. The quest for the stone encouraged alchemists of the medieval period (and as late as the end of the 17th century) to examine in their laboratories numerous substances and their interactions on one another. Thus, the quest provided a body of knowledge that led ultimately to the sciences of chemistry, metallurgy, and pharmacology.

The process by which it was hoped common metals such as iron, lead, tin, and copper could be turned into the more valuable metals —*e.g.*, silver and gold—involved heating the base material in a characteristic pear-shaped glass crucible (called the vase of Hermes or the philosopher's egg). Colour changes were carefully watched—black indicating the death of the old material preparatory to its revitalization; white, the colour required for change into silver; and red, the highest stage, the colour required for change into gold.

Philosopher's Stone, The (1958), translation of PARAS PATHAR, film by Satyajit Ray.

·Satyajit Ray's satirical films **15**:538b

Philosophes, literary men, scientists, and thinkers of 18th-century France who were united, in spite of divergent personal views, in their conviction in the supremacy and efficacy of human reason. Inspired by the philosophic thought of René Descartes, the Skepticism of the Libertins, or freethinkers, and the popularization of science by Bernard de Fontenelle, they expressed concern for social, economic, and political reform, occasioned by sectarian dissensions within the church, the weakening of the absolute monarchy, and the ruinous wars that had occurred toward the end of Louis XIV's reign. In the early part of the

18th century, the movement was dominated by Voltaire and Montesquieu, but that restrained phase became more volatile in the second half of the century. Diderot, Rousseau, Georges-Louis Leclerc de Buffon, Étienne Bonnot de Condillac, Anne-Robert-Jacques Turgot, and the Marquis de Condorcet were among the Philosophes who thrust their energies into the *Encyclopédie*, the great intellectual achievement of the century.
·atheism in the Enlightenment **2**:259e
·British contributions to Enlightenment **3**:262h
·d'Alembert and rationalist spirit **1**:464f *passim* to 465f
·Deist and atheistic views **5**:563a
·Diderot's intellectual friendships **5**:723e
·French intellectual situation in 18th century **15**:1172c
·French literature development **10**:1171e
·French national education theory **6**:354h
·Montesquieu's support and its result **12**:402h
·orientation and representatives **19**:512g
·revolutionary impact evaluation **7**:643e
·science popular appeal **16**:372d

Philosophes français du XIXe siècle, Les (1857), translated as FRENCH PHILOSOPHERS OF THE 19TH CENTURY, work by Hippolyte Taine.
·French Positivism developmente, 1857 **17**:992h

Philosophiae Naturalis Principia Mathematica, English translation MATHEMATICAL PRINCIPLES OF NATURAL PHILOSOPHY, work published in 1687 by Sir Isaac Newton; it is his principal work and constitutes one of the fundamental treatises in physical science. The *Principia* set forth Newton's theories on motion and explained for the first time the way in which a single mathematical law could account for the movement of planetary bodies, objects on Earth, the tides, and other natural phenomena. *See also* Newton, Sir Isaac.
·background, content, and influence **13**:18c
·biological sciences development **2**:1021h
·content and impact **8**:286h
·Earth's figure deductions **6**:2e
·Halley's contributions and publication **8**:556c
·hypotheses in science methodology **16**:378h
·impact on Enlightenment philosophy **14**:266d
·mathematics history from antiquity **11**:643g
·nerve impulse speculation **2**:1034g
·science history and philosophy **16**:371b
·scientific revolution culmination **14**:387b *passim* to 388c

philosophical anthropology: *see* anthropology, philosophical.

Philosophical Commentaries (1944), also published as COMMONPLACE BOOK OF OCCASIONAL METAPHYSICAL THOUGHTS (1871), notebooks written by George Berkeley in 1707–08.
·Berkeley's philosophic ideas **2**:846h

Philosophical Essays Concerning Human Understanding (1748), revision entitled INQUIRY CONCERNING HUMAN UNDERSTANDING (1758), book by David Hume.
·Hume's principles of human knowledgeme) **8**:1192f

Philosophical Fragments, full title PHILOSOPHICAL FRAGMENTS, OR A FRAGMENT OF PHILOSOPHY (1936), translation of PHILOSOPHISKE SMULER, ELLER EN SMULE PHILOSOPHI (1844), by the 19th-century Danish philosopher Søren Kierkegaard, discusses the implications for faith as decision making based on the historicity of Christianity.
·attack on Rationalism **6**:937c
·theme and anti-Hegelian intent **10**:466c

Philosophical Investigations (1953), original German PHILOSOPHISCHE UNTERSUCHUNGEN (1953), by Ludwig Wittgenstein.
·doctrines and influence **19**:903a
·later thought of Wittgenstein **1**:805a
·philosophy as language critique **14**:273c
·revision of logic theory **6**:945a

Philosophical Transactions, a journal of the Royal Society of London that since its first volume appeared in 1665–66 has contained many important scientific articles.
·biological sciences development **2**:1020f
·Leeuwenhoek's scientific discoveries **10**:773d
·magazine publishing history **15**:247h
·soft drink development **16**:1010b

Philosophical View of Reform, A (written 1819, published, 1920), prose work by Percy Shelley.
·theme of practical reform **16**:663d

Philosophie (1932), English translation PHILOSOPHY, 1969), work by Karl Jaspers.
·human choice as constrained by destiny **7**:76e

Philosophie als strenge Wiessenschaft, published in 1910 in *Logos*, English translation PHILOSOPHY AS RIGOROUS SCIENCE in *Phenomenology and the Crisis of Philosophy* (1965), essay by Edmund Husserl.
·critique of naturalism and historicism **14**:211f

Philosophie de l'art (1865; "Philosophy of Art"), work by French philosopher Hippolyte Taine.
·aesthetic theory of art forms **1**:156g

Philosophische Briefe über Dogmatismus und Kritizismus (1796; "Philosophical Letters on Dogmatism and Criticism"), book by Friedrich Schelling.
·intuition and the Absolute **16**:339f

Philosophische Untersuchungen (Wittgenstein): *see* Philosophical Investigations.

philosophy. An academic discipline and itself the name of a concept studied by that discipline, aspects of which are treated under philosophy, history of Western. *See* also Buddhist philosophy; Chinese philosophy; Christian philosophy; Indian philosophy; Islāmic theology and philosophy; Japanese philosophy; and Jewish philosophy.

philosophy, first, in Aristotle's philosophy, the study of Being, metaphysical principles, and first causes.
·origin of term **12**:10f

philosophy, history of Western **14**:247, the history of efforts of Western man to reflect deeply in a rational, methodical, and systematic way upon those aspects of experience that are of greatest concern to man. It traces the vicissitudes of certain basic oppositions: between monists, dualists, and pluralists; Materialists and Idealists; Nominalists and Realists; Rationalists and Empiricists; Utilitarians, self-realizationists, and proponents of duty; partisans of logic and partisans of emotion.

The text article provides a synoptic view of the history of philosophy in the West; relates philosophic ideas and movements to their historical backgrounds and to the cultural situations of their time; and clarifies philosophy's changing conception of its own definition, its function, and its unique task.

TEXT ARTICLE covers:
Philosophy in the Western tradition **14**:248a
General consideration of the history 249c
The Pre-Socratic philosophers 250e
Socrates, Plato, and Aristotle 253a
Stoics, Epicureans, and Skeptics 255a
Neo-Pythagoreans and Neoplatonists 256d
Early medieval philosophy 257b
Transition to Scholasticism 258d
The age of the schoolmen 259a
Philosophy in the late Middle Ages 260d
The Renaissance through the Enlightenment 261d
Rise of Empiricism and Rationalism 263h
Classical British Empiricism 266f
Nonepistemological movements 267e
Critical examination of reason in Kant 268g
German Idealism of Fichte, Schelling, and Hegel 269f
Positivism and social theory in Comte, Mill, and Marx 270d
Individual philosophies of Bergson, Dewey, Whitehead 272a
Marxist, Analytic, and continental philosophy 272e

REFERENCES in other text articles:
·aesthetics theories and development **1**:150a
·analogical approach to prehistory **14**:984g
·Analytic philosophy trends **1**:799f
·astrological history from ancient times **2**:220a
·atheism's intellectual development **2**:258g
·belief systems at inception of Christianity **2**:947e
·Berkeley's life and ideas **2**:846g
·Bruno's life and thought **3**:345g
·Carnap's career and Logical Positivism **3**:925b
·Cartesianism and modern philosophy **3**:968b *passim* to 970c
·censorship in Greece, Rome, and Europe **3**:1084c
·Chinese philosophical reconstruction **4**:420e
<u>Christian philosophy themes and history</u> **4**:555a
·Abelard's career and major works **1**:10c
·Anselm of Canterbury's life and works **1**:937g
·Aquinas' development and conclusion **18**:345g
·attitudes and contributions **4**:514b
·Augustine's studies and contributions **2**:365b
·development of Greek ideas **4**:460b
·dogmatic concerns **4**:476a
·medieval application to theology **15**:1004h
·medieval intellectual traditions **12**:163f
·millennial thought in early church, Augustine, and post-Enlightenment **12**:201g
·Nestorian contributions from *c.* AD 500 **6**:138h
·Protestantism's development in 1600s **15**:113e
·relationship to Hellenism **4**:467h
·Scholasticism roots and development **16**:352e
·use of pagan philosophies **13**:1080c
·classification theories and reality **4**:693g
·conflict model importance **16**:992d
·cosmologies since 6th century BC **18**:1007a
·Croce's liberalism in Fascist Italy **5**:285c
·Deist doctrines and development **5**:561g
·Descartes' intellectual development **5**:598e
·Dewey's contribution and Chicago School **5**:680h
<u>educational philosophy</u> **6**:409g
·medieval higher education content **6**:336d
·19th-century German educational theory **6**:361d
·Empiricism and rejection of Rationalism **6**:768d
·Enlightenment in France **7**:643h
·Enlightenment thought and belief **6**:887d
<u>epistemology methods and history</u> **6**:931c
·Marcel existentialist phenomenology **11**:488g
·perception's epistemological aspects **14**:38g
·phenomenology origins and impact **9**:68b
·phenomenology's methods and influence **14**:210e
·ethical analysis and development **6**:976f
·Fichte and German Idealism **7**:289f
·Francis Bacon's thought and major works **2**:563h
·Frege mathematical innovation impact **7**:712b
<u>Greece and pre-Christian Rome</u>
·approaches in classical Athens **8**:360f
·Archaic Greeks' contribution **8**:333e
·Christian, Jewish, and Greek Logos **4**:478e
·Christian dogmatic adaptations **4**:476a
·Christian philosophical indebtedness **4**:467h
·Cicero's intermediate and lingual roles **4**:610a
·dualism of classical Greece **5**:1066g
·Eleatic school and its rivals **6**:525d
·Epicurean cosmology and ethics **6**:911a
·Greek contribution in the 4th century BC **8**:372e
·Greek philosophy in Hellenistic Judaism **10**:311g
·Greek rationalistic pantheist systems **13**:951e
·Hellenistic teaching profession and organization **6**:326d
·Jewish borrowing of doctrines of man **10**:289b
·millenarian view undermined in church **12**:201g
·Pericles' philosophy associations **14**:67b
·Philo of Alexandria influenced **14**:246e
·Plato's philosophical foundations **14**:531e
·Socratic teachings as foundation **16**:1001c
·Greek and Roman literature development **10**:1093d
·group behaviour philosophy development **16**:961b
·Haeckel's monist and evolutionary theories **8**:541h

· Hegelianism's development and criticism **8**:732g
· Hegel's dialectical system **8**:728e
· Heidegger Existentialism development **8**:738g
· historiography's origin in Greece **8**:946c
· humanistic scholarship's role **8**:1170f
· Hume's skeptical Empiricism **8**:1191h
· ideology and idea system development **9**:194a
· impact on 19th-century thought **6**:1072f
· Indian similarities and differences **9**:313e
Islāmic interactions **9**:1022d
· Avicenna's influence from 12th century **2**:541c
· Byzantine influence on Islāmic thought **15**:67a
· Greek influence on Judeo–Arabic culture **10**:318h
· James's pragmatic theory formulation **10**:28h
· Jaspers' existential humanism **10**:115e
Jewish philosophical thought **10**:208b
· Islāmic influences **10**:185b
· Jewish contributions since 19th century **10**:325b
· Jewish medieval anthropology **10**:290e
· Maimonides contribution and life **11**:352g
· Philo as pre-Gnostic, pre-Neoplatonic **10**:313f
· Philo of Alexandria's contribution **14**:245c
· Kantianism's influence and status **10**:395a
· Kierkegaardian renaissance **10**:467e
language concepts from antiquity **10**:993b
· grammar study in Greece and later **8**:266g
· linguistic theories and investigations **10**:1012f
· semantic theories from 19th century **16**:507a
· Leśniewski's contributions to logic **10**:832g
· logic history from antiquity **11**:56c
· Lucretius' explication of atomism **11**:173g
· man and nature relationship concepts **1**:918c
· Materialism and related theories **11**:612a
· mathematics history from antiquity **11**:641c
· measurement theory development **11**:740a
· Nietzsche's life and works **13**:76h
· pacifism from ancient Greece to present **13**:847d *passim* to 849f
political philosophy concerns **14**:702d
· constitution and government theories **5**:93d
· revolution theories in ancient times **15**:787c
· Western law's analysis and history **10**:715f *passim* to 720d
· Rationalism in fields of philosophy **15**:527g
· Realist currents in Western thought **15**:540h
religious systems and investigations **15**:598d
· Christian, Jewish, and pagan Logos **4**:478e
· religions classification in 1900s **15**:629h
· religion study **15**:622b
· religious experience controversies **15**:647d
· studies and systematizations **15**:615a
· theology's origins in ancient Greece **18**:274a
· 20th-century concerns **15**:602g
· Renaissance Humanist tradition **15**:665a
· rivalry of movements in Roman Empire **4**:536f
· Santayana's naturalism **16**:230c
· Schelling's career and philosophy **16**:339c
· Schopenhauer's philosophical theories **16**:358b
science philosophy **16**:375h
· biological theories and development **2**:1026a
· biology's early records and theories **2**:1017c
· Copernican and Ptolemaic systems of astronomy **5**:145h
· Saint-Simon's scientific doctrines **16**:176b
· science development and meaning **16**:366d
· secular agnosticism roots **1**:312c
· skepticism's challenge to accepted views **16**:830c
· social science development influence **16**:980h
· Spencer's evolutionist optimism **17**:492b
· Stoicism in ancient and modern thought **17**:698b
· Taine's scientific methodology **17**:992d
· tragic drama's ethical nature **18**:580h
· Utilitarianism's roots and modern trends **19**:1a
· Vico's life and cultural theory **19**:103d
· Voltaire's expression of secular goals **19**:513c
· Wittgenstein's two periods **19**:901e

RELATED ENTRIES in the *Ready Reference and Index: for*
classical schools: see Alexandrists; Cynics; Cyrenaics; Megarian School of philosophy; Peripatetics
fields of study: axiology; common sense, philosophy of; epistemic logic
metaphysics: God, knowledge of; God, nature of; immanence
methodology: eristic; synthesis
philosophic positions: categorical imperative; determinism; dualism, mind–body; instrumentalism; Nominalism; pluralism and monism; pre-established harmony; relativism, ethical
other: category; free will; truth value

Philosophy as Rigorous Science, published in *Phenomenology and the Crisis of Philosophy* (1965), translation of PHILOSOPHIE ALS STRENGE WISSENSCHAFT, published in 1910 in *Logos*, essay by Edmund Husserl.
· critique of naturalism and historicism **14**:211f

Philosophy of Rhetoric, The (1776), a work by George Campbell.
· intellectual susceptibility to passions **15**:802a

Philosophy of Right, The (1942), original German NATURRECHT UND STAATSWISSENSCHAFT IM GRUNDRISSE (1821), changed to GRUNDLINIEN DER PHILOSOPHIE DES RECHTS (1833), by G.W.F. Hegel.
· human will and law **8**:731b

Philosophy of the Inductive Sciences, Founded upon Their History, The (1840), by William Whewell, English philosopher; later expanded to three separate books, *History of Scientific Ideas* (2 vol., 1858), *Novum Organon Renovatum* (1858), and *On the Philosophy of Discovery* (1860).
· Mill's fusion of induction and deduction **12**:198d

Philosophy of the Revolution (1954), work by Gamal Abdel Nasser.
· Arab and Islāmic unity **12**:845a

Philostorgius (b. *c.* AD 368, Borissus, Asia Minor, near modern Kayseri, Tur.—d. *c.* 433, probably Constantinople, modern Istanbul), Byzantine historian, partisan of the Arian sect, a Christian heresy asserting the inferiority of Christ to God the father. His church history, preserved in part, was the most extensive collection of Arian source texts assembled in a single work and furnished valuable data on the history, personalities, and intellectual milieu of theological controversy in the early church.

Son of a staunch Arian, Philostorgius from the age of 20 studied in Constantinople and became a follower of Eunomius of Cyzicus, a leading exponent of extreme Arianism. This branch of the heresy stressed an absolute monotheism and thus interpreted the Christian Trinity as a hierarchy of persons: only the Father is perfect God; the Son, and Christ, are inferior creatures.

Between 425 and 433 (during the reign of Emperor Theodosius II), Philostorgius wrote his church history in 12 books, after visiting Arian communities throughout the Eastern empire. The work, covering the period 300 to 425, was intended to continue the monumental *Ecclesiastical History* by the 4th-century chronicler Eusebius of Caesarea. In reality it constituted an apology for the radical Arian school. Beyond fragmentary references by Byzantine historians from the 9th to the 13th century, it has survived only in a summary and commentary in the *Bibliotheca* ("The Library," or annotated bibliography) of Photius, the 9th-century scholarly patriarch of Constantinople. Although he acclaimed Philostorgius' style and diction, Photius charged him with obscurity and bias, particularly in his laudatory treatment of Eunomius and other Arian spokesmen and in his condemnation of orthodox theologians and emperors. Philostorgius refrained from attacking directly the celebrated orthodox leaders Gregory Nazianzene and Basil of Caesarea; he admitted the cogency of some of their refutations of heterodox Trinitarian theology but chided them for their criticism of his mentor, Eunomius. The *History* appealed to the cultured Greek because of its Arian emphasis on the rational intelligibility of Christian revelation. It also depicts the Arian response to the pagan accusation that Christianity influenced the political misfortunes of the Greco-Roman empire and civilization. Philostorgius countered that the lamentable collapse of classical culture into barbarism verified Christian apocalyptic teaching, or the predictions and signs portending the end of the world and the second coming of Christ.

Byzantine chronicles mention an apology for Christianity, written against the 3rd-century Neoplatonist Porphyry, but this tract has been lost. An English translation of *The Ecclesiastical History of Philostorgius as Epitomized by Photius* was done by E. Walford (1851). A critical edition of the Greek text, with a valuable biography and analysis, was compiled by Joseph Bidez in the series *Die Griechischen Christlichen Schrifsteller, der ersten drei Jahrhunderte*, vol. 21 ("The Greek Christian Writers" 1913).

Philostratus, the name of at least three members of a family of ancient Greek writers. They are often confused, and the attribution of certain works among them is controversial.

Flavius Philostratus (b. *c.* AD 170—d. *c.* 245), called "the Athenian," studied at Athens, and some time after 202 entered the circle of the philosophical Syrian empress of Rome, Julia Domna, whom he probably accompanied on her travels. On her death he settled in Tyre. He wrote the *Gymnasticus* (a treatise dealing with athletic contests); a life of the Pythagorean philosopher Apollonius of Tyana; *Bioi sophiston* (*Lives of the Sophists*), treating both the Classical Sophists of the 5th century BC and later philosophers and rhetoricians; a discourse on nature and law; and the epistles ("Love Letters") of which one forms the basis of Ben Jonson's "Drink to Me Only with Thine Eyes." He may have written the *Heroicus*.

Philostratus (b. *c.* AD 190), called "the Lemnian," son-in-law of Flavius Philostratus, was the author of a letter to Aspasius of Ravenna and of the first series of the *Imagines* in two books, discussing 65 real or imaginary paintings on mythological themes in a portico at Naples. They are an important source for the knowledge of Hellenistic art and roused the enthusiasm of Goethe, but they are not now regarded as providing serious artistic criticism.

Philostratus, called "the Younger," grandson of Philostratus the Lemnian, wrote a second series of *Imagines* in the 3rd century AD.
· sainthood of Apollonius of Tyana **16**:165b

Philotheus Coccinus (b. *c.* 1300, Salonika, now Thessaloníki, Greece—d. 1379, Constantinople, modern Istanbul), theologian, monk, and patriarch of Constantinople, a leading protagonist of Byzantine quietist mysticism and principal opponent of the Greek Orthodox movement for union with the Roman church.

Born of a Jewish mother, Philotheus became a monk and then abbot of the Great Laura on Mt. Athos, Greece. He soon began promoting Hesychasm, the contemplative prayer method developed by the Athonite monk Gregory Palamas, who had integrated meditation, bodily posture, and mystical experience. In 1347 Philotheus was named bishop of Heraclea, near Constantinople, but spent most of his time at the imperial capital; when his cathedral city was sacked by the Genoese in 1352, he sent a consolatory letter to his people from Constantinople.

A protégé of the emperor John VI Cantacuzenus, whose son Matthew he agreed to crown, Philotheus was appointed patriarch of Constantinople in November 1353. He was imprisoned, however, and charged with treason by the anti-Hesychast, unionist faction that deposed Cantacuzenus and restored the emperor John V Palaeologus in 1354. Reappointed patriarch in 1364, Philotheus continued to oppose the efforts of John V and the Orthodox group to negotiate with the popes Urban V and Gregory XI. Asserting his patriarchal authority, he fostered the Hesychast cause by canonizing Gregory Palamas and acclaiming him a doctor of the Greek Orthodox Church at the synod of 1368. Through an independent ecclesiastical policy, moreover, Philotheus consolidated the Orthodox Serbs, Bulgarians, and Russians with the Greek patriarchate to counter the growing menace of the Ottoman Turks. Concommitantly, he implemented, sometimes indecorously, his theory of Constantinople's patriarchal supremacy over the entire Eastern Church, if not over Rome itself. This concept of church government, which he expressed by repressing the Byzantine Romans and frustrating any reconciliation with the West, had a lasting influence on the development of the Orthodox churches.

Philotheus' most notable work was his *Hagioritic Tome* at Mt. Athos *c.* 1339, the definitive doctrinal apology for Hesychast prayer according to the principles of Gregory Palamas. At that time he also wrote two tracts against the Orthodox theologian Gregorios Akindynos, a severe critic of Palamas. He supplemented the tracts with 14 *Kephalaia* ("chapters") denouncing as heretical the antimysticism of Akindynos and the monk Barlaam the Calabrian. The 15 *Antirrhētika* ("diatribes") of *c.* 1354, against the anti-Hesychast historian Nicephorus Gregoras are Philotheus' most imposing polemics. His hagiographical writings include the lives of Germanus the monk and Gregory Palamas, intended to extoll Hesychast ideals and to prevent Gregoras' writings from affecting the Orthodox liturgy. Addresses honouring St. Thomas the Apostle and the 4th-century Greek Church father John Chrysostom, liturgical verse and hymns, and a precis of the divine liturgy are prominent in Philotheus' extensive literary production. Much of his exegetical writings, including commentaries on the Psalms and on the Gospels, as well as his patriarchal decrees and protocol papers remain unedited. Some of his works appear in *Patrologia Graeca*, ed. J.-P. Migne, vol. 151, 152, and 154 (1866).

Philoxenus of Mabbug, Syriac AKHSĒNĀYĀ (b. *c.* 440, Tahal, East Syria, near modern Kirkūk, Iraq—d. *c.* 523, Gangra, Black Sea coast, near modern Samsun, Tur.), Syrian bishop, theologian, and classical author, leader of the Jacobite Monophysite church, a heterodox group teaching a single, divine nature in Christ, subsuming his humanity. He also contributed significantly to Syriac literary heritage, particularly with the Philoxenian New Testament based on the original Greek text.

A student at the school of Edessa, now Urfa, Tur., Philoxenus rejected the Nestorian doctrine of Christ that posited in him an autonomous human nature conjoined to the divinity simply by a moral bond. Subscribing to the moderate form of Christology as expressed by the spokesman for orthodoxy, Cyril of Alexandria, he accented the dynamic hegemony of Christ's divinity over his humanity. Because of his zeal in expounding the Monophysite cause and labelling as heretical other Christological doctrines proposed by traditional theologians, especially the canonical teaching of the Council of Chalcedon (451), he was expelled from Edessa by the Orthodox patriarch of Antioch. Responding to a denunciation of his doctrine by orthodox churchmen before the Byzantine emperor Zeno, Philoxenus submitted a statement of belief *c.* 482 that satisfied orthodox requirements. With the support of Peter the Fuller, Monophysite patriarch of Antioch, he was named bishop of Mabbug-Hierapolis, near modern Aleppo, Syria, in 485.

Investigated by Flavian II, orthodox successor to Peter the Fuller, Philoxenus was condemned as a heretic by Macedonius, patriarch of Constantinople. Supported, however, by the new emperor, Anastasius I, Philoxenus undertook a campaign to replace Orthodox bishops with Monophysite churchmen. Although bested in a theological dispute at the Synod of Sidon, Lebanon, in 511, the following year he influenced the nomination of a colleague, the eminent Monophysite Severus, to be patriarch of Antioch. At the accession of the Orthodox emperor Justin I, Philoxenus was exiled to Philippopolis, now Plovdiv, Bulg., where he continued his polemical and ascetical writings during the rigours of captivity. It is possible he died violently.

Philoxenus collaborated in a Syriac version of the New Testament *c.* 508 with Polycarp of Hierapolis, his chorepiscopus ("auxiliary bishop"). Together with the celebrated Peshitta, an early Syriac Bible text, the Philoxenian New Testament, as it is called, served as the principal scriptural source for Syriac Christianity for two centuries.

The doctrinal writings of Philoxenus show a nominal rather than the strict Monophysitism developed during the early 5th century and denounced at the Council of Chalcedon. With Cyril of Alexandria, he inclined toward an emphasis on Christ's essentially pervasive divinity that reduced his humanity to irrelevance. He opposed the blatant dualism (separate human and divine personalities) in Christ as taught by Nestorian extremists. For his original contribution to elucidating the complex Christological question, he was acclaimed a saint and doctor of the Jacobite church.

Philoxenus' principal works in Christology have been edited with a Latin translation by A. Vaschalde, *Philoxeni Mabbugensis Tractatus tres de Trinitate et Incarnatione* (1907; "Three Treatises of Philoxenus of Mabbug on the Trinity and the Incarnation"). *The Discourses of Philoxenus*, a collection of 13 addresses on the Christian life, were edited and translated by Sir Ernest Alfred Thompson Wallis Budge (2 vol., 1894). Additional writings were edited in part by J. Lebon (1930).

·Monophysitism and Bible translation **13**:1084e
·mosaic imitation of Battle of Issus **12**:467c

Philya inflata, a species of treehopper of the order Homoptera.

·sexual dimorphism **8**:1038f

Philydraceae, plant family of the order Liliales.

·general features and classification **10**:975h

Phimai, village, Nakhon Ratchasima province (*changwat*), eastern Thailand, on the Mae Nam (river) Mun. It is the site of the ruins of a Khmer temple dating from the 11th to the 12th century. Latest pop. est. 2,569.

·Khmer temple art and Tantrism **17**:256d

phimosis, in medicine, a condition in which the foreskin of the penis is too tight to be drawn back over the glans, or the analogous condition of a hooded clitoris.

·cause, effects, and treatment **15**:697b

Phineus (Greek mythology): *see* Argonauts.

phin nam tao, musical instrument of Cambodia, plucked monochord used as accompaniment to songs.

·Cambodian rural musical tradition **17**:239g

Phiomia, a genus of extinct elephant of the order Proboscidea.

·body traits and distribution **15**:3h

Phiomorpha, a suborder of rodents of the order Rodentia.

·classification and general features **15**:979f

Phiomyidae, family of extinct rodents of the order Rodentia.

·classification and general features **15**:979g

phi phenomenon, visual illusion in which stationary objects appear to move, commonly experienced in viewing motion pictures, which create their illusion of motion by projecting successive static images rapidly enough to transcend the threshold at which they can be perceived separately. It was named and described in 1912 by Max Wertheimer, founder of Gestalt psychology.

Phippsia algida, species of high Alpine grass of the order Poales.

·structural diversity and habitat **14**:585c

Phips (PHIPPS), **Sir William** (1651–95), British colonial governor in Massachusetts.

·Quebec invasion attempt **15**:336f

Phitsanulok, also spelled PHISANULAUK, province (*changwat*), north central Thailand, with an area of 3,729 sq mi (9,659 sq km); its short northeastern border adjoins Laos. The eastern portion of the province, around the towns of Nakhon Thai and Wang Thong, is isolated and underdeveloped. Population is concentrated in the west, a region drained by the Mae Nam Nan (Nan River) and the Mae Nam Yom; this area is the site of the major towns of Phitsanulok (the provincial capital) and Phrom Phiram. Rice is the main crop, and there are a number of rice mills. Thung Salaeng Luang National Park and the Wang Nong Ann Waterfall are local attractions.

Phitsanulok town is located on the Mae Nam Nan and the Bangkok–Chiengmai railroad. It is also served by an airport and by roads north to Sukhothai and west to Tak. The commercial centre in the southern part of town deals in rice, cotton, and tobacco. The old walled city dates to the 13th century, and from 1350 to 1767 it was second in size and importance to the national capital of Phra Nakhon Si Ayutthaya. The Wat Phra Si Rattana Mahathat houses the Phra Buddha Jinaraj, an early bronze figure famed for its beauty. Latest pop. est. town, 40,521; (1970 prelim.) province, 492,000.

Phiz: *see* Browne, Hablot Knight.

Phlaeothripidae, family of thrips of the order Thysanoptera.

·classification and distribution **18**:369a

Phlaocyon, small, extinct carnivore found in North America Miocene deposits. It resembled the members of the raccoon family (Procyonidae) in dental features, but was possibly more closely related to the dogs (Canidae).

phlebitis, inflammation of the wall of a vein; it may result from infection or trauma or may follow a surgical operation or childbirth. Indications of phlebitis include localized pain, swelling, redness, and heat over the inflamed vein. The condition may last for years, and formation of blood clots may be a complication. *See* thrombophlebitis.

·characteristics treatment **3**:899f
·Virchow's demonstration of cause **19**:150h

phlebothrombosis, formation of a blood clot in a vein that is not inflamed. Inactivity, such as bed rest during convalescence, can lead to the condition, which frequently progresses to thrombophlebitis (*q.v.*), in which the clot adherent to the wall of the vein is accompanied by inflammation of the vessel.

·diagnosis of cardiovascular disease **5**:687c

Phlebotomidae: *see* sand fly.

phlebotomus fever: *see* pappataci fever.

Phleger corer, undersea drilling device used to obtain samples from the sea bottom.

·design and operation **18**:851b

phlegmasia alba dolens (medicine): *see* milk leg.

phlegmatic temperament: *see* humour.

Phlegyas, in Greek mythology, son of the war god, Ares, and who, as their king, gave his name to the savage Phlegyae in Thessaly; they were also associated with central Greece and the Peloponnese. His daughter Coronis, seduced by the god Apollo, gave birth to Asclepius, the god of medicine. Phlegyas, in revenge for the seduction, set fire to the Temple of Apollo at Delphi and was killed by the god.

Phleum pratense (grass): *see* timothy.

phloem, the tissues in plants that conduct foods made in the leaves to all other parts of the plant. Phloem is composed of specialized cells called sieve-tube cells, companion cells, phloem fibres, and phloem parenchyma cells. Primary phloem is formed by the apical meristems (zones of new cell production) of root and shoot tips; it may be either protophloem, the cells of which are matured before elongation (during growth) of the area in which it lies, or metaphloem, the cells of which mature after elongation. Sieve tubes of protophloem are unable to stretch with the elongating tissues and are torn and destroyed as the plant ages. The other cell types in the phloem may be converted to fibres. The later maturing metaphloem is not destroyed and may function during the rest of the plant's life in nonwoody species but is replaced by secondary phloem in woody flowering plants. Secondary phloem is formed by the vascular cambium which produces new cells that add to the thickness of stems and roots.

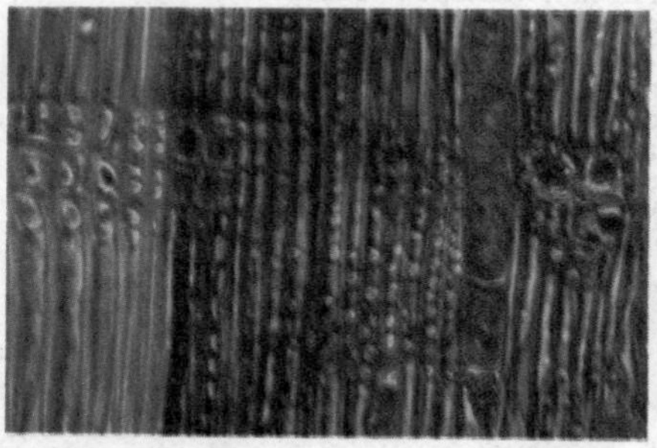

Longitudinal section through xylem (pink) and phloem (blue green), small circles within the phloem are the sieve areas of the sieve cells, and the dark red areas in the phloem are phloem parenchyma cells
J.M. Langham

Sieve tubes, which are columns of sieve-tube cells having perforated areas in their lateral or end walls, provide the wide channels in which food substances travel. Phloem parenchyma cells, called transfer cells and border parenchyma cells, are located near the finest branches and terminations of sieve tubes in leaf veinlets, where they also function in the translocation of foods. Phloem fibres are flexible long cells that make up the so-called soft fibres (*e.g.*, flax and hemp) of commerce. *See also* cambium; sieve tube; vascular bundle. *Major ref.* **18**:451h
·angiosperm-gymnosperm comparison **1**:879b
·conifer root form and function **5**:4g
·fern stem structure, illus. 4 7:241
·integumentary system, illus. 1 **9**:665
·Laurales vascular system **10**:709e
·organ structure and function **13**:727e; illus.
·plant internal transport **14**:500g; illus. 502
·tree growth and internal structure **18**:691c; illus.
·vascular system development **5**:667c

Phloeomys: *see* cloud rat.

phlogiston, in early chemical theory, the hypothetical principle of fire, of which every combustible substance was in part composed. In this view, the phenomena of burning, now called oxidation, are caused by the liberation of phlogiston with the dephlogisticated substance left as an ash or residue.

The German chemist Johann Joachim Becher in 1669 set forth his view that substances contained three kinds of earth, which he called the vitrifiable, the mercurial, and the combustible. He supposed that, when a substance burned, combustible earth (Latin *terra pinguis*, literally "fat earth") was liberated. Thus, wood was a combination of phlogiston and wood ashes. To this hypothetical substance the German chemist Georg Ernst Stahl, at about the beginning of the 18th century, applied the name phlogiston (from Greek, meaning "burned"). Stahl believed that the corrosion of metals in air (*e.g.*, the rusting of iron) was also a form of combustion, so that when a metal was converted to its calx, or metallic ash (its oxide, in modern terms), phlogiston was lost. Therefore, metals were composed of calx and phlogiston. The function of air was merely to carry away the liberated phlogiston.

The major objection to the theory, that the ash of organic substances weighed less than the original while the calx was heavier than the metal, was of little significance to Stahl, who thought of phlogiston as a more or less immaterial "principle" rather than an actual substance. As chemistry advanced and chemists applied quantitative measurements more frequently, such a view became untenable. Phlogiston was considered a true substance, and much effort was expended in accounting for the changes in weight observed. Some workers thought phlogiston had a negative weight. When hydrogen, very light in weight and extremely flammable, was discovered, some thought that it was pure phlogiston.

The phlogiston theory was overthrown by the French chemist Antoine Lavoisier between 1770 and 1790. He studied the gain or loss of weight when tin, lead, phosphorus, and sulfur underwent reactions of oxidation or reduction (deoxidation); and he showed that the newly discovered element oxygen was always involved. Although a number of chemists—notably Joseph Priestley, one of the discoverers of oxygen—tried to retain some form of the phlogiston theory, by 1800 practically everyone recognized the correctness of Lavoisier's oxygen theory.
·chemical reaction theory development **4**:143d
·combustion and flame theory development **4**:954f
·combustion limitation **8**:703b
·explanation of chemical change **14**:390f
·formulation and discredit **8**:703a
·Priestley's experiments in combustion **14**:1013h
·redox concept's historical origins **13**:804b
·Stahl's development and importance **17**:566b

phlogopite, OR BROWN MICA, a silicate mineral, basic aluminosilicate of potassium, magnesium, and iron, that is a member of the common mica group. When it contains only small amounts of iron, it is economically important as an electrical insulator. Phlogopite occurs typically as a metamorphic product (*e.g.*, in crystalline metamorphosed limestones), and it also occurs in ultrabasic igneous rocks. Phlogopite forms a chemical substitution series with biotite, from which it is arbitrarily distinguished by a magnesium-to-iron ratio greater than 2:1. For detailed physical properties, *see* table under micas.

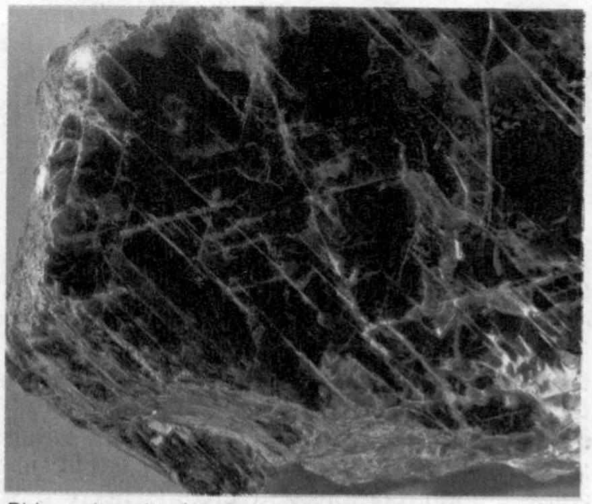

Phlogopite mica from Warwick, N.Y.
By courtesy of the Field Museum of Natural History, Chicago; photograph, John H Gerard—EB Inc.

The name phlogopite also is used for an end-member molecule making up a large part of the mineral. Its chemical composition is $K_2Mg_6(Si_6Al_2O_{20})(OH)_4$.
·characteristics, occurrence, and synthesis **12**:93c; tables
·dehydration reactions at high temperature and pressure **7**:1024g; illus. 1025
·formula and metamorphic minerals table **12**:5
·trioctahedral crystal structure **16**:761d

Phlox, a genus of about 65 species of plants belonging to the family Polemoniaceae, ad-

Moss pink (*Phlox subulata*)
Russ Kinne—Photo Researchers

mired both in gardens and in the wilds for the clustered heads of flowers. All species but one from northeast Asia are native to North America. *Phlox* is herbaceous, usually with oval or linear leaves, often stalkless; it has heads of massed tubular flowers with five flaring lobes.

Summer phlox (*P. paniculata*) sometimes reaches over 1½ metres (5 feet), on straight, stiff stems topped by reddish-purple to white, fragrant, large, flat flower heads. It is a long-lived perennial native in eastern North America, in rich, moist soils. Annual phlox (*P. drummondii*), a 45-centimetre (1½-foot), branching plant with usually reddish-purple blooms, is native to southwestern North America. It has given rise to many cultivated forms with petals of two colours and starlike shape. Blue phlox (*P. divaricata*), native in woodlands of eastern and central North America, is a spring-flowering perennial growing to 45 centimetres, with blue to white flower clusters. Perennial phlox (*P. pilosa*), about the same height, bears red-purple flowers on hairy plants in summer in upland woods and prairies of central North America.

Moss pink, or creeping phlox (*Phlox subulata*), a low, evergreen mat covered in early spring with blue, purple, pink, or white massed blooms, is native to sandy soil and rocky ledges in eastern North America. Often grown as garden perennials, moss pinks creep along the soil, branching freely.

phlyakes, farces adopted from Greek Middle Comedy plays and especially popular in southern Italy in the 4th and 3rd centuries BC. Known principally from vase paintings, these burlesques of tragedy, myth, and daily life received literary form in the works of Rhinthon, Sciras, and Sopater, and later were incorporated in the *fabula Atellana*, native Italian farces that were popular in republican and early imperial Rome.
·mime and pantomime in ancient Greece **12**:211b; illus.
·theatre design in ancient Rome **17**:532c

Phnom Aural, mountain of central Cambodia.
12°02′ N, 104°10′ E
·Cambodia's geographic features **3**:675c

Phnom Bakheng, site of Yásodharapura, royal capital of the ancient kingdom of Angkor in Cambodia.
·Angkor's adaptations for cosmic symbols **1**:886a
·development and design **18**:1068c

Phnom Penh, Cambodian PHNUM PÉNH, also spelled PNOM PENH OR PHOM PENH, capital and chief city of Cambodia (Khmer Republic), at the confluence of the Basăk (Bassac), Sab (Sap), and Mekong river systems. It was founded in 1434 to succeed Angkor Thom as the capital but was abandoned several times before being re-established in 1865 by King

Norodom. Surrounded by, but independent of, Kândal province (*khêt*), the city functions as a processing centre, with textiles, brewing, distilling, and rice milling. Its chief assets, however, are cultural. Institutions of higher learning include the Université Nationale de Phnom Penh (founded in 1956 as the Université Royale Khmère), with its schools of engineering, fine arts, technology, and agricultural sciences, the latter at Chamcar Daung, a suburb. There is also the Université Royale de Sciences Agronomiques and the Lycée Agricole de Prek Leap. The picturesque city is built around the royal palace and Preah Morokot Pagoda, the latter famous for its floor of silver tiles. The European quarter, in the northern sector, stands at the foot of the high Phnom Penh (Penh Hill), atop which is a pagoda housing the ashes of the legendary Lady Penh, whose discovery of a bronze Buddha there inspired the settlement bearing her name. The royal palace compound includes the royal palace (1919), the Musée du Palais Royal, and the Veal Mien (Royal Plain), on which the national congress meets twice a year. The Jayavarman VII Art Museum has a display of Khmer jewels, and the Musée National displays Khmer art and historical documents. Other institutions include the independent Buddhist University and institutes for Buddhist and Pāli studies. A world-famous attraction is the Royal Ballet, until recent decades restricted to performances before Cambodian royalty. Its authentically bejewelled dancing girls give mimed versions of ancient Buddhist and Hindu legends. There is also a national theatre.

The Royal Palace at Phnom Penh, Cambodia
M. Mattson—Shostal

Although 180 mi (290 km) from the sea, Phnom Penh is a major port of the Mekong Valley, linked to the South China Sea by the Hau Giang channel of the Mekong Delta. It trades in dried fish, corn (maize), cotton, and pepper. The capital has steamer service to Saigon and to several river towns of Cambodia and is linked by railway to Thailand via Poŭthĭsăt (Pursat) and Bătdâmbâng (Battambang). The railway was extended to the deep-water port of Kâmpóng Saôm (formerly Sihanoukville), on the Gulf of Thailand, to the southwest, and also by the more circuitous Khmer-American Friendship Highway. The international airport in Pochentong has daily flights to Bangkok, Saigon, and Hong Kong and to Siĕmréab (Siem Reap), location of Cambodia's ancient Khmer ruins of Angkor Thom and Angkor Wat. Pop. (1971 est.) 479,300.
11°33′ N, 104°55′ E

·Khmer's new capital establishment **3**:686d
·map, Cambodia **3**:676
·Mekong River physical geography **11**:860g; map 861
·urban location, area, and population **3**:675h; table 678

phobia, or ANXIETY HYSTERIA, an extreme, irrational fear of a specific object or situation, traditionally classified as a type of psychoneurosis (neurosis), or relatively mild psychiatric disorder. Phobias are thought to be learned emotional responses. It is generally held that phobias occur when fear produced by an original threatening situation is transferred to other similar situations, with the original fear often repressed or forgotten. An excessive, unreasoning fear of water, for example, may be based on a childhood experience of almost drowning that has been completely forgotten. Different types of behaviour therapy are often successful in overcoming phobias. In such therapy, learned anxiety is experienced under either nonthreatening or rewarding conditions until it is extinguished.

Although psychiatrists classify phobias as a single type of neurosis, hundreds of words have been coined to specify the nature of the fear by prefixing "phobia" with the Greek word for the object feared. Among the more common examples are acrophobia, fear of high places; claustrophobia, fear of closed places; nyctophobia, fear of the dark; ochlophobia, fear of crowds; xenophobia, fear of strangers; and zoophobia, fear of animals.

·theories of origin, therapeutic approaches, and common types **15**:168h; table 169

Phobos (Greek god): *see* Ares.

Phobos (astronomy): *see* Mars satellites.

Phoca: *see* harbour seal; harp seal; ringed seal.

Phocaea, modern FOÇA, ancient Ionian city on the northern promontory of the İzmir Körfezi (gulf), İzmir *il* (province), Turkey; it was the mother city of several Greek colonies. The Phocaeans arrived in Anatolia perhaps as late as the 10th century BC, and, lacking arable land, established colonies in the Dardanelles at Lampsacus, on the Black Sea at Amisus (Samsun), and in the Crimea. In the Mediterranean, they colonized as far west as Massilia (Marseille) and Emporion (Ampurias in northeastern Spain). Besieged by the Persians about 545 BC, most of the citizens chose emigration rather than submission. In 190 BC, allied with the Seleucids against Rome and Pergamum, the Phocaeans so savagely repelled the Roman forces that the praetor Lucius Aemilius Regillus was obliged to withdraw his men and entreat the citizens not to take the war so seriously; his infuriated troops took advantage of the truce to sack the city. After participating in an uprising against Roman rule in 132 BC, Phocaea was sentenced to destruction but was reprieved through the intercession of its daughter city Massilia. Latest census 2,953.
38°39′ N, 26°46′ E

·growth and importance in Archaic Period **8**:346b; map 326

Phocas (d. 610), Thracian centurion who was Byzantine emperor from 602 to 610. Following an army rebellion against the emperor Maurice in 602, Phocas was sent to Constantinople as spokesman. There he took advantage of revolts in the capital to get himself chosen emperor in place of Maurice, who, together with his son, was executed. Phocas enjoyed good relations with eRome, his recognition of the primacy of the pope in matters of religion winning him praise from Pope Gregory I. Having made peace with the Avars (604), agreeing to pay them an increased annual tribute, he had to face the avenging forces of Maurice's ally, Khosrow II, under whom the Persians moved into Asia Minor, reaching the Bosphorus by 608. Phocas' persecution of a Christian sect, the Monophysites, and of the Jews brought him the hatred of the eastern provinces, and in the capital he grew increasingly tyrannical. Fear of the Persians, together with general discontent, led to an appeal to the exarch of Carthage, who in 610 sent an expedition under his son Heraclius; the latter had Phocas executed and was himself proclaimed emperor on Oct. 5, 610.

·Gregory I's religio-political conflicts **8**:416a
·Heraclius' seizure of power **8**:781g
·rise to power and later reign **3**:556c

Phocas, Bardas, 10th-century Byzantine general and father of Nicephorus II Phocas.

·Arab defeats in the East **13**:64f

Phocas, Nicephorus II: *see* Nicephorus II Phocas.

Phocidae, family of mammals of the order Carnivora, suborder Pinnipedia, including the true, or earless, seals; (*see* seal).

·characteristics, diving behaviour, and breeding **3**:937f; illus. 941a

Phocion (b. *c.* 402 BC—d. 318), Athenian statesman and general, an opponent of the anti-Macedonian party of Demosthenes, and virtual ruler of Athens between 322 and 318. Phocion was a pupil of Plato and in later life a close friend of the Platonic philosopher Xenocrates. He distinguished himself in the naval battle of Naxos (376) and, either *c.* 350 or 344/343, served the Achaemenian king Artaxerxes III as a mercenary commander. According to Plutarch, the Athenians elected him general 45 times.

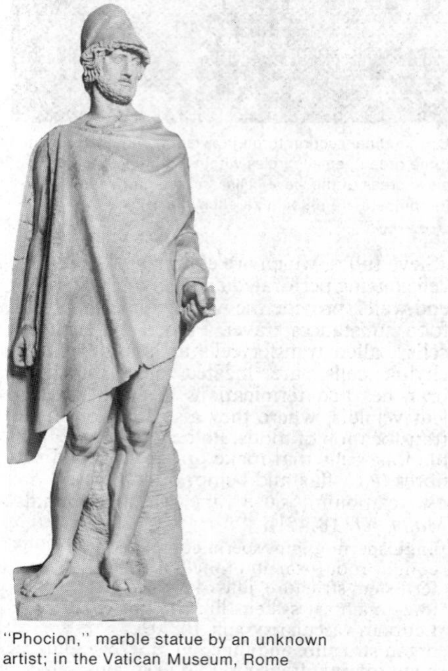

"Phocion," marble statue by an unknown artist; in the Vatican Museum, Rome
Anderson—Mansell

In 348 he saved the Athenian force operating in Euboea by his victory at Tamynae. He assisted Megara and Byzantium against Philip II of Macedon but defended Philip's supporter, the orator Aeschines, in 343. Phocion opposed the Lamian War (323) that followed the death of Alexander the Great, though he led the defense against a Macedonian raid. The defeat of Athens in the war and the subsequent restriction of democracy in the city established Phocion as the dominant political figure.

He ruled Athens with great moderation but in 319 failed to prevent the Macedonian seizure of Piraeus, the city's port. Upon the restoration of democracy in the spring of 318, he was deposed. He fled to the Macedonian regent Polyperchon but was sent back to Athens, tried for treason, and executed. Shortly afterward the Athenians decreed a public burial and a statue in his honour.

Phocis, Modern Greek FOKÍS, district of ancient central Greece, bounded on the west by Ozolian Locris and Doris, on the north by Opuntian Locris, on the east by Boeotia, and on the south by the Gulf of Corinth. It corresponds to the southeastern portions of present Fthiótis and Phocis *nomoi* (departments), whose capitals are Lamía and Amphissa (*qq.v.*), respectively. The massive ridge of Parnassus (8,061 ft [2,457 m]) traverses the heart of the ancient region. Between Parnassus and the range of Kallídhromon (1,650–5,000 ft [500–1,500 m]), which forms the northern frontier, is the narrow, fertile valley of the principal river, the Cephissus (Kifisós or Sarandapótamos), along which lay most of the Phocian settlements: Amphicaea (modern Amfíklia), Tithoréa, Elatea (Elátia), Hyampolis (Bogdhánou), Abae (Éxarkhos), and Daulis (Dhávlia). South of Parnassus the small plains of Crisa (around modern Itéa) and Anticyra are separated by Mt. Cirphis. The economy of Phocis traditionally includes wheat, olives, and grapes, but livestock raising is now the principal activity.

Its early history is obscure; Phocis was mainly pastoral and the population was thought to be of the Aeolians, one of the earliest Greek-speaking peoples in the peninsula. Before the 6th century BC, however, Boeotians and Thessalians encroached on their territory. Traditionally, the Phocians controlled the sanctuary of Delphi, but about 590 BC a coalition of Greek states proclaimed a sacred war, destroyed the city of Crisa, and put the sanctuary under the control of a council administered jointly by neighbouring communities. The irresolute conduct of the Phocians contributed to the Greek defeat by Persia at Thermopylae (480); at Plataea they were on the Persian side. In 449 or 448 the Spartans expelled the Phocians from Delphi but with the help of their new ally, Athens, they soon recaptured it. When Athenian land power declined, Phocis wavered again and became an ally of Sparta in the Peloponnesian War (431–404 BC).

In the 4th century Phocis was constantly endangered by Boeotian aggression. During the Corinthian War (395–387) Phocis helped Sparta to invade Boeotia, but afterward it submitted to the growing power of Thebes. Phocians took part in the Theban Epaminondas' campaigns in the Peloponnese (370–366) but not in the successful campaign of Mantineia (362). In return for this negligence the Thebans secured a penal decree against them (for religious offenses). The Phocians retaliated by seizing Delphi, which they looted to finance mercenaries for an invasion of Boeotia and Thessaly; they were driven out of Delphi by Philip II of Macedon, who split their towns into villages and exacted an indemnity (346). In 338 they fought unsuccessfully against Philip at Chaeronea.

During the 3rd century Phocis passed under the control of Macedonia and was annexed to the Aetolian League in 196. The Roman emperor Augustus enrolled Phocis in the new Achaean League. The league was last heard of under the emperor Trajan (reigned AD 98–117).

·growth and importance in Archaic Period **8**:345f
·role in Philip of Macedonia's victory **8**:367e
·Tartessos' loans and Carthage's war **17**:402c

Phocoenoides: *see* porpoise.

phocomelia (birth defect): *see* peromelia.

Phocus, in Greek mythology, the son of Aeacus, king of Aegina, and the Nereid Psamathe who had assumed the likeness of a seal (Greek *phoce*) in trying to escape Aeacus' embraces. Peleus and Telamon, Aeacus' legitimate sons, resented Phocus' superior athletic prowess. At the instigation of their mother, Endeis, they plotted his death, drawing lots to decide which should destroy him. The lot fell on Telamon, who murdered Phocus, feigning an accident. Aeacus, however, discovered the truth and banished both his sons.

Phocus, Nicephorus II: *see* Nicephorus II Phocas.

Phocylides (fl. *c.* 540 BC), Greek gnomic poet (*i.e.*, writer of pithy moral aphorisms) from Miletus, on the coast of Asia Minor. He is mentioned by the orator Isocrates as the author of "admonitions" (*hypothēkai*), of which a few fragments have survived by quotation. Almost all of them are in hexameters and begin "This too is Phocylides'. . . ."

Phodilus badius: *see* bay owl.

phoebe (*Sayornis*), any of three species of New World birds of the family Tyrannidae (order Passeriformes). In North America the best known species is the eastern phoebe, (*S. phoebe*), 18 centimetres (7½ inches) long, plain brownish gray above and paler below.

Eastern phoebe (*Sayornis phoebe*)

John Hennessy—National Audubon Society

Its call is a brisk "fee-bee" uttered over and over. It makes a mossy nest, strengthened with mud, on a ledge, often under a bridge. In the open country of western North America is Say's phoebe, (*S. saya*) a slightly larger bird with buff-hued underparts. The most widely distributed is the black phoebe (*S. nigricans*), occurring from the southwestern United States to Argentina; dark above with a contrasting white belly. All phoebes have the habit of twitching their tails when perching.

Phoebe, one of the ten satellites of Saturn.
·Saturn's satellite characteristics **16**:275b; table

Phoebe Island (Pacific Ocean): *see* Baker Island.

Phoebetria (bird): *see* albatross.

Phoebus (god): *see* Apollo.

Phoebus (1331–91): *see* Foix, Gaston III, comte de.

Phoenicia, ancient name given to a region corresponding to modern Lebanon with adjoining parts of modern Syria and Israel. The chief cities (excluding colonies) were Gebal (Greek Byblos, modern Jubayl); Sidon (modern Ṣaydā); Tsor (Greek Tyros, modern Tyre, Arabic Ṣūr); and Berot (Greek Berytos, modern Beirut).

It is not certain what the Phoenicians called themselves in their own language; it appears to have been Kenaʿani (Akkadian Kinahna), "Canaanites." In Hebrew the word *kenaʿani* has the secondary meaning of "merchant," a term that well characterizes the Phoenicians.

The Phoenicians probably arrived in the area about 3000 BC. Nothing is known of their original homeland, though some traditions place it in the region of the Persian Gulf.

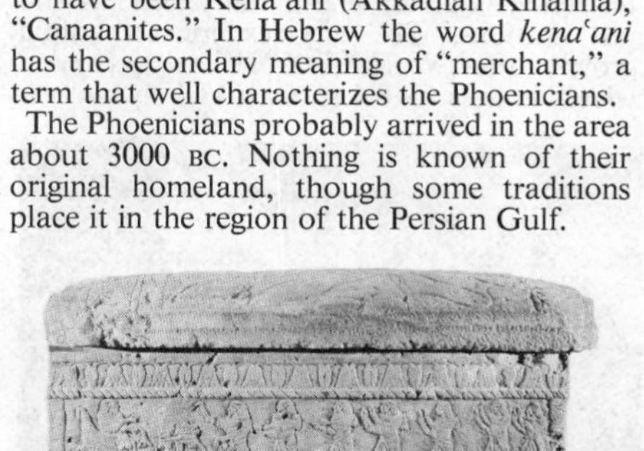

Carved limestone sarcophagus of Ahiram bearing a Phoenician inscription, 11th century BC; in the Musée National, Beirut

By courtesy of the National Museum of Lebanon, Beirut

At Byblos, commercial and religious connections with Egypt are attested from the Egyptian 4th dynasty (*c.* 2613–*c.* 2494); extensive trade was certainly carried on by the 16th century, and the Egyptians soon established suzerainty over much of Phoenicia. The 14th century, however, was one of much political unrest, and Egypt eventually lost its hold over the area. Beginning in the 9th century, the independence of Phoenicia was increasingly threatened by the advance of Assyria, the kings of which several times exacted tribute and took control of parts or all of Phoenicia.

In 538 Phoenicia passed under the rule of the Persians, The country was later taken by Alexander the Great and in 64 BC was incorporated into the Roman province of Syria; Aradus, Sidon, and Tyre, however, retained self-government.

The oldest form of Phoenician government seems to have been kingship—limited by the power of the wealthy merchant families. Federation of the cities on a large scale never seems to have occurred.

The Phoenicians were well-known to their contemporaries as sea-traders and colonizers, and, by the 2nd millennium, they had already extended their influence along the coast of the Levant by a series of settlements, including Joppa (Jaffa, modern Yafo), Dor, Acre, and Ugarit. Colonization of areas in North Africa (*e.g.*, Carthage), Anatolia, and Cyprus also occurred at an early date. Several smaller Phoenician settlements were planted as stepping stones along the route to Spain and its mineral wealth. Phoenician exports included cedar and pine wood, fine linen from Tyre, Byblos, and Berytos, cloths dyed with the famous Tyrian purple (made from the snail *Murex*), embroideries from Sidon, wine, metalwork and glass, glazed faience, salt, and dried fish. In addition, the Phoenicians conducted an important transit trade.

Phoenician glass vessels from Camirus (left) and from Tharros (right) inlaid with threads of different colours; in the British Museum

By courtesy of the trustees of the British Museum

In the artistic products of Phoenicia, Egyptian motifs and ideas were mingled with those of Mesopotamia, the Aegean, and Syria. Though little survives of Phoenician sculpture in the round, relief sculpture is much more abundant. The earliest major work of Phoenician sculpture to survive was found at Byblos; it was the limestone sarcophagus of Ahiram, king of Byblos at the end of the 11th century.

Ivory and wood carving became Phoenician specialties, and Phoenician goldsmiths' and metalsmiths' work was also well-known. Glassblowing was probably invented in the coastal area of Phoenicia in the 1st century or earlier.

Although the Phoenicians used cuneiform (Mesopotamian writing), they also produced a script of their own. The Phoenician alphabetic script of 22 letters was used at Byblos as early as the 15th century. This method of writing, later adopted by the Greeks, is the ancestor of the modern western alphabet. It was the

Phoenicians' most remarkable and distinctive contribution to human arts and civilization.

The religion of the Phoenicians was inspired by the powers and processes of nature. Many of the gods they worshipped, however, were localized, and are now known only under their local names. A pantheon was presided over by the father of the gods, El; Asherah of the Sea was his wife and their mother. Of his family, the goddess Astarte (Ashtart) was the principal figure.

·African voyages of exploration **1**:206c
·Barcelona's founding **2**:720a
·colonization in Spain **17**:402c
·cultural origins and history **17**:942h; map 943
·Cyprus colonization **5**:406d
·Egyptian 18th-dynasty commercial ties **6**:473d
·gods and religious practices **17**:966f
·Greek conquests and Hellenistic kingdoms maps **8**:374
·irrigation knowledge and dissemination **9**:899h
·Italian colony conflicts with Greeks **8**:346c
·jewelry-making development **10**:169b
·Judaean military alliance **16**:1044e
·Lisbon's foundation legend **10**:1029h
·Maltese contact evidence **11**:391g
·merchant ship design **16**:677e; illus.
·North African trade and settlements **13**:146e
·numerals and numeral systems **11**:647b
·Palermo's settlement **13**:930b
·Red Sea explorations **15**:546a
·Rhodian sea law of general average **4**:988a
·sailing ship and navigational history **16**:157c
·Sardinian settlement and history **16**:245a
·Seleucids' rule and trade **16**:501e; map
·ship design developments **18**:651d
·ship design history **12**:885d
·silverwork stylistic origins **11**:1102h
·visual art history of Syro-Palestine **19**:265c
·weights and measures system source **19**:728f

Phoenician alphabet, writing system that developed out of the North Semitic alphabet and was spread over the Mediterranean area by Phoenician traders. It was the probable ancestor of the Greek alphabet and hence of all Western alphabets. The earliest Phoenician inscription that has survived is the Ahiram epitaph at Byblos in Phoenicia (present-day Lebanon), dating probably from the 11th century BC and written in the North Semitic alphabet. The Phoenician alphabet gradually developed from this North Semitic prototype and was in use until about the 1st century BC in Phoenicia proper. Phoenician colonial scripts, variants of the mainland Phoenician alphabet, are classified as Cypro-Phoenician (10th–2nd century BC) and Sardinian (*c.* 9th century BC) varieties. A third variety of the colonial Phoenician script evolved into the Punic and neo-Punic alphabets of Carthage, which continued to be written until about the 3rd century AD. Punic was a monumental script and neo-Punic a cursive form.

The Phoenician alphabet (called a syllabary by some) in all its variants changed from its North Semitic ancestor only in external form —the shapes of the letters varied a little in mainland Phoenician and a good deal in Punic and neo-Punic. The alphabet remained, however, essentially a Semitic alphabet of 22 letters, written from right to left, with only consonants represented and phonetic values unchanged from the North Semitic script. *See also* Semitic alphabet, North.

·North African inscriptions **13**:153h
·origins and spread **1**:619g; illus. 620
·Semitic calligraphy development **3**:661g
·transmission to the West **17**:944g
·writing development and origins **19**:1036g; table 1035

Phoenician language, Semitic language of the Northern Central (often called Northwestern) group, spoken in ancient times on the coast of Syria and Palestine in Tyre, Sidon, Byblos, and neighbouring towns. Phoenician is very close to Hebrew and Moabite, with which it forms a Canaanite subgroup of the Northern Central Semitic languages. The earliest Phoenician inscription deciphered dates probably from the 11th century BC; the latest inscription from Phoenicia proper is from the 1st century BC, when the language was gradually being superseded by Aramaic.

In addition to being used in Phoenicia, the language spread to many of its colonies. In one, the North African city of Carthage, a later stage of the language, known as Punic, became the language of the Carthaginian Empire. Punic was influenced throughout its history by the language of the Berbers; it continued to be used by North African peasants until the 6th century AD.

Phoenician words are found in abundance in classical literature as well as in Egyptian, Akkadian, and Hebrew writings. The language is written with a 22-character alphabet that does not indicate vowels.

·North African language traditions **13**:153h
·relationships, writing, and phonology **8**:592d

Phoenicopteridae (bird family): *see* flamingo.

Phoeniculidae (bird family): *see* wood hoopoe.

Phoenicurus (bird genus): *see* redstart.

Phoenix, in Greek mythology, son of Amyntor, king of Thessalian Hellas. After a quarrel Amyntor cursed him with childlessness, and Phoenix escaped to Peleus, king of the Myrmidons in Thessaly, who made him responsible for the upbringing of his son Achilles. Phoenix accompanied the young Achilles to Troy and was one of the envoys who tried to reconcile him with Agamemnon, chief commander of the Greek forces, after Agamemnon and Achilles had quarrelled.

In another version of the story, Amyntor blinded his son, whose sight was later restored by Chiron.

Phoenix, city, capital (since 1889) of Arizona, U.S., and seat (1871) of Maricopa County, which is coextensive with its metropolitan area, in the south central part of the state. On the Salt River, it occupies a semi-arid, saucer-shaped valley, surrounded by mountains, near the Tonto National Forest. In 1867 Jack Swilling visited the area and organized an irrigation company; canals and harvests followed, and a village was founded. An associate of Swilling, Darrel Duppa, was impressed by evidences of prehistoric culture, the Hohokam; like the legendary phoenix—which, consumed by fire, sprang anew from its ashes—Duppa predicted, the Salt River city would be born from the ancient Indian ruins.

Phoenix developed as the commercial focus of the extensive Salt River irrigation projects, fed from the Roosevelt and other dams. Diversified manufacturing (almost nonexistent before 1940) has become the chief source of income, augmented by agriculture, mining, timbering, tourism, and military airfields and test stations. The city experienced rapid growth after World War II and expanded widely in area (248.4 sq mi [643.4 sq km]); it embraces the Desert Botanical Gardens and Papago Park. The original state capitol building is constructed of native tufa in Neoclassic style. Phoenix Civic Plaza Center is a six-square-block convention centre. Educational institutions include Phoenix College (1920), Grand Canyon College (1949), Arizona Bible College (1947), Thunderbird Graduate School (1946), Southwestern College (1960), and Maricopa County Junior College (1968). Arizona State University is at nearby Tempe. Annual events are the Copper Bowl parade and football game, the World's Championship Rodeo, and the Arizona State Fair. The city is the home of many types of professional sports. Inc. 1881. Pop. (1960) city, 439,170; metropolitan area (SMSA), 663,510; (1970) city, 581,562 (4.8% black); SMSA, 967,522; (1980) city, 789,703 (4.9% black); SMSA, 1,508,030.
33°27′ N, 112°05′ W

·map, United States **18**:908
·population, economics, and culture **2**:2e

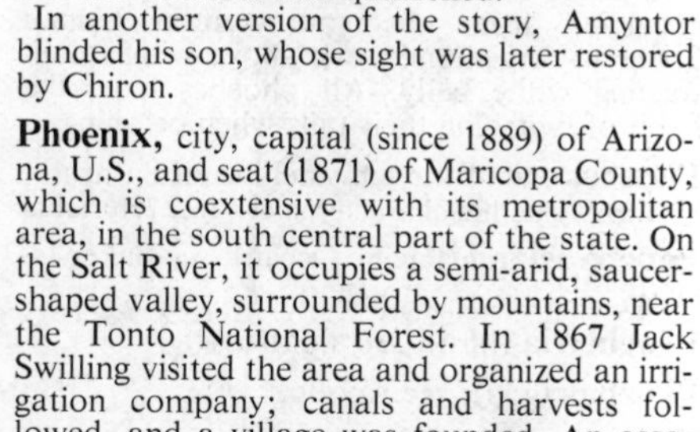

Capitol building, Phoenix, Ariz.
Markow Photography

phoenix, a fabulous bird connected with the worship of the sun, especially in ancient Egypt and in classical antiquity. The phoenix was said to be as large as an eagle, with brilliant scarlet and gold plumage and a melodious cry. Only one phoenix existed at any time, and it was very long-lived—no ancient authority gave it a life-span of less than 500 years. As its end approached, the phoenix fashioned a nest of aromatic boughs and spices, set it on fire, and was consumed in the flames. From the pyre miraculously sprang a new phoenix, which, after embalming its father's ashes in an egg of myrrh, flew with them to Heliopolis ("City of the Sun") in Egypt, where it deposited them on the altar in the temple of the Egyptian sun god, Re. A variant of the story made the dying phoenix fly to Heliopolis and immolate itself in the fire burning on the altar, a young phoenix rising from the flames.

The *bennu*, a heron, was traditionally associated with sun worship in Egypt, appearing on monuments as a symbol of the rising sun and of the life after death. But despite the common religious associations, the phoenix as described in literature did not at all resemble a heron in appearance, and its home was not in Egypt but nearer the rising sun (normally in Arabia or India, where spices for the nest and egg were plentiful). Probably the phoenix story originated in the Orient and was assimilated to Egyptian sun worship by the priests of Heliopolis. The adaptation of the myth to an Egyptian environment helped to bring about the connection between the phoenix and the palm tree (also called *phoinix* in Greek), which was long associated with sun worship in Egypt.

The Egyptians associated the phoenix with immortality, and that symbolism had a widespread appeal in late antiquity. The phoenix was compared to undying Rome, and it appears on the coinage of the late Roman Empire as a symbol of the Eternal City. It was also widely interpreted as an allegory of resurrection and life after death—ideas which also appealed to emergent Christianity.

In Islāmic mythology, the phoenix was identified with the *ʿanqāʾ* (Persian *sīmorgh*), a huge, mysterious bird (probably a heron) that was originally created by God with all perfections but had thereafter become a plague and was killed.

In Chinese mythology, the appearance of a phoenix (*feng-huang*; *q.v.*) presaged a momentous event.

·Chinese symbolic lore **4**:414g
·heraldic shield design **8**:789d
·mystery cult iconographic remains **12**:784g

Phoenix, U.S. steamboat built by John Stevens in 1807.

·steamship development importance **18**:654d

Phoenix, U.S. air-to-air missile.

·design characteristics, table 4 **15**:934

Phoenix and the Turtle, The (1601), poem by William Shakespeare.
·obscure allusions and style **16**:619g

Phoenix dactylifera (plant): *see* date palm.

Phoenix Islands, group of uninhabited coral atolls in the west central Pacific Ocean, 1,650 mi (2,650 km) southwest of Hawaii. The group comprises Phoenix, Sydney (Manra), McKean, Gardner (Nikumaroro), Birnie, Hull (Orona), Canton, and Enderbury atolls. The first six, with a total land area of 5 sq mi (14 sq km), are part of the Gilbert and Ellice Islands, a British crown colony. Canton and Enderbury atolls (*qq.v.*) are under a joint U.S.–British administration. All are low, sandy atolls, which were discovered in the 19th century by American whaling ships. Several also were worked for their limited supplies of guano. The islands, annexed by Britain (1889), were joined to the Gilbert and Ellice colony in 1937.
·map, Pacific Islands **2**:433

Phoenix Park, recreational area of Dublin, containing the former viceregal residence.
·pattern and use **5**:1074g

Phoenix Park murders, assassination by stabbing on May 6, 1882, in Dublin, of the chief secretary of Ireland, Lord Frederick Cavendish, and his under secretary, T.H. Burke. The Chief Secretary had arrived in Dublin only that day and was walking in the city's Phoenix Park in the evening when set upon by members of a nationalist secret society, the Invincibles.

The event occurred just after Charles Stewart Parnell, leader of the Irish Home Rule party in the British House of Commons, was released from Kilmainham jail, Dublin, where he had been confined for his violent speeches against the Land Act (1881), which was considered insufficiently generous to Irish tenants. The result of the assassinations was a revulsion against terrorism. Parnell, who in the Kilmainham Treaty had just compromised with the British government over the land question, was consequently able to subordinate the Irish National League, a nationalist organization, to the Home Rule Party in Parliament. The Kilmainham Treaty was not jeopardized by the murders, as was feared.

Phoenixville, borough, Chester County, southeastern Pennsylvania, U.S., on the Schuylkill River between French and Pickering creeks, west of Philadelphia. The site was originally settled in 1720 by the Rev. Francis Buckwalter, a German refugee, and the town was founded (1731) by his followers. It marked the most westerly point reached by the British in Pennsylvania during the American Revolution. The steel industry dates from 1783. In 1856 John Griffen, superintendent of the Phoenix Iron Works, turned out the first Griffen gun (a light cannon), later used by the Federal Army during the Civil War. Steel remains economically important. Light manufactures include textiles, paper and rubber products, abrasives, and chemicals. Inc. 1849. Pop. (1980) 14,165.
40°08′ N, 75°31′ W

Pholadidae (mollusk family): *see* piddock.

Pholcidae, family of daddy longlegs spiders of the order Araneida.
·classification and general features **1**:1073a

Pholidae (fish family): *see* gunnel.

Pholidichthyidae, family of leopard-eel blenny of the order Perciformes.
·classification and general features **14**:56c

Pholidophoriformes, order of extinct fishes (subclass or infraclass Holostei) that existed from the Middle Triassic to the Lower Cretaceous. Members lived in both marine and fresh water.
·classification and general features **8**:1013a; illus. 1011

Pholidopleuriformes, extinct order of fishes (subclass or infraclass Chondrostei) that existed during the Triassic Period. The members of the single family were widely distributed in both marine and fresh water.
·classification and general features **4**:438g

Pholiota (fungus): *see* Agaricales.

Pholisma arenarium, a species of parasitic flowering plants of the order Polemoniales.
·plant structure illus. **14**:659

Phom Penh (Cambodia): *see* Phnom Penh.

phon (loudness unit): *see* loudness.

phoneme, in linguistics, smallest unit of speech distinguishing one word (or word element) from another, as the sound *p* in "tap," which separates that word from "tab," "tag," and "tan." A phoneme actually represents a set of similar speech sounds, called allophones (*q.v.*), which function as a single sound; for example, the *p* of "pat," "spat," and "tap" differ slightly phonetically, but that difference, determined by context, has no significance in English. In some languages, where the variant sounds of *p* can change meaning, they are classified as separate phonemes; *e.g.* in Thai aspirated *p* (pronounced with an accompanying puff of air) and unaspirated *p* are distinguished. Phonemes are based on spoken rather than written language and may be recorded with special symbols, like those of the International Phonetic Alphabet (*q.v.*). In transcription, linguists conventionally place phonemes between slash marks: /p/. Often, such features as pitch, stress, and juncture (pauses) are phonemic in a language, notably in tone languages such as Chinese and Thai. *See also* phonemics; phonological change; phonology.
·alphabet's basis in phonology **19**:1036h; table 1037
·diachronic theories and considerations **10**:1007d
·phonetics of meaningful utterances **14**:280b
·Prague school distinctive features **10**:1006b
·stratificational concepts of analysis **10**:1004h
·structuralist synchronic analysis **10**:996e

phonemics, in linguistics, a study of the phoneme, the smallest meaningful speech unit, and the classification of phonemes in the entire sound system of a language. Phonemics is not concerned with the production or description of all speech sounds (phonetics) nor, according to some linguists, with historical sound change. *See also* phoneme; phonology.
·generative grammar concepts **10**:1003h
·phonetics in reference to grammar **14**:279h
·structuralist synchronic analysis **10**:996e

phonetics 14:275, the study and classification of speech sounds and the analysis of their production and distinguishing characteristics.

The text article deals with standards of pronunciation; articulatory phonetics, acoustic phonetics; phonology, the study of the sound patterns that occur within languages; phonetic transcription; experimental work in phonetics; and the history of phonetics.

REFERENCES in other text articles:
·dictionary sound symbols **5**:720c
·Indo-European differentiation concepts **9**:432c
·linguistic developments of 19th century **10**:994f
·linguistic principles of sound change **10**:1006h
·physiological survey of articulation **10**:648f
·scope and principles of study **10**:644f
·sound production methods **17**:29e
·speech sound classification **17**:484b
·structural synchronic linguistic study **10**:996c
·writing's correspondence to language **19**:1037c

RELATED ENTRIES in the *Ready Reference and Index: for*
articulation, manners of: see affricate; articulation; aspirate; click; flap; fricative; lateral consonant; liquid; nasal consonant; resonant; retroflex consonant; sibilant; sonorant; stop; trill; voiced sounds
articulation, points of: alveolar consonant; articulation; bilabial consonant; dental consonant; glottal stop; labiodental consonant; palatal consonant; velar consonant
historical phonology: dissimilation; etymology; Grimm's law; laryngeal theory; linguistics, historical; metathesis; phonological change; umlaut; Verner's law
phonological studies: acoustic phonetics; articulation; International Phonetic Alphabet; morphophonemics; phonemics; phonology
secondary articulation: glottalization; palatalization; rounding; velarization
suprasegmentals: intonation; pitch; stress; suprasegmental; whisper
other: International Phonetic Association

Phong Dinh, province (*tinh*) of the flat Mekong Delta region of southern South Vietnam. It is bounded on the northeast by the Song Hau Giang (Bassac River), a major branch and mouth of the Mekong, on whose left bank is situated the provincial seat and independent municipality of Can Tho (*q.v.*). Acquired in the 18th century from the Khmer (Cambodian) kingdom by the Annamese lords of Hue, almost all of the alluvial, 617-sq-mi (1,597-sq-km) region is subject to the annual summer monsoonal flooding of the Mekong, which is controlled by levees and canals along which grow betel palms and cocoa trees. Rice grown from seedling transplants on submerged land is harvested in the more deeply inundated northwest and seeded varieties elsewhere. Industries include timber cutting, rice mills, sawmills, and brick- and tile-making. The principal inland waterways include one linking Can Tho with Vi Thanh, capital of Chuong Thien province, and another linking Phung Hiep with Khan Hung, capital of Ba Xuyen province. Can Tho, the seat of a national university (1956), is linked by highway to Khan Hung and to Saigon, 116 mi (187 km) to the northwest by highway via ferries across the Song Hau Giang and Song So Chien channels of the Mekong. It has two airports, the major one Binh Thuy, northwest of the city. Pop. (1971 est.) 377,159.
·area and population table **19**:142

Phong Saly, town and province (*khoueng*), the northernmost in Laos, situated between Yunnan Province, China, and North Vietnam. It was a trouble spot for the colonial French, who fought Chinese bandits there during World War I. Under French military administration until 1947, the mountainous province, 6,100 sq mi (15,800 sq km) in area, in 1962 became a refuge for Pathet Lao insurgents, who used the Nam Hou Valley to launch attacks on the royal capital, Luang Prabang, 125 air mi (200 km) south of the provincial seat. The Khmu of the Lao-Theng (Mountain Mon-Khmer) group are numerous in the east, while Lolo (Laotian Houo-Ni) of Chinese origin occupy the central and northern hills, interspersed with tribal Black Tai (Tai Dam). The river valleys are occupied by valley Lao, who raise rice and corn (maize). The province has unexploited anthracite and copper deposits, the latter north of Phong Saly town, a small market centre served by the port of Hat Sa on the Nam Hou (Hou River) and linked by road to Chiang-ch'eng, China. Pop. (latest est.) town, 3,000; (1971 est.) province, 121,000.
·map, Laos **10**:674

phonocardiography, obtaining a graphic record, or phonocardiogram, of the sounds and murmurs produced by the heart and associated great vessels.

The phonocardiogram is obtained either by intracardiac phonocatheterization (the introduction of a small tubular instrument with a small sound pickup in the tip into one of the heart chambers) or by acoustic pickup with a chest microphone. The phonocardiogram usually supplements the information obtained by listening to body sounds with a stethoscope (*see* auscultation) and is of special diagnostic value when recorded simultaneously with the electrical properties of the heart (*see* electrocardiography) and pulse rate.

Phonofilm, system used in the 1920s to provide sound synchronized with motion pictures, employing a sound track photographically recorded on the film by a beam of light modulated by the sound waves. The sound was reproduced during projection by directing a beam of light through the sound track onto a photocell the response of which was electronically amplified.
·cinema sound era origins **12**:527a
·De Forest's development and exposition **5**:553f
·motion picture sound beginnings **12**:541h

phonogram, representation of a word in a language in writing with the understanding that it is to be read for its sound value and not necessarily for its meaning; thus, if English words were represented by such a writing system, the picture of a can might represent the verb "can."
·ambiguity in interpetation of hieroglyphics **8**:854e

phonograph, instrument for reproducing sounds by means of the vibration of a stylus, or needle, following a groove on a rotating disc or cylinder. The device is sometimes called a record player. Though experimental mechanisms of this type appeared as early as 1857, general credit for invention of the phonograph belongs to the United States inventor Thomas Edison (1877).

All modern phonographs have certain components in common: a turntable (*q.v.*) that spins the record; a stylus that tracks a groove in the record; a pickup that converts the mechanical movements of the stylus into electrical impulses; an amplifier that builds up these electrical impulses; and a loudspeaker (*q.v.*) that converts the amplified signals back into sound. Some phonographs are also equipped with a record changer (*q.v.*). Phonographs capable of high-quality reproduction of sound are called high-fidelity sound systems (*q.v.*); those that utilize two independent channels of information are designated stereophonic, and four-channel systems are called quadraphonic. *Major ref.* **17**:51g *passim* to 60b
·acoustic operation theory **17**:32c
·Edison's conception and development **6**:309g
·electric motor design **6**:612d
·electronic pickup of sound wave **6**:682f
·invention, development, and importance **12**:692c
·motion picture sound recording **12**:541h
·non-written communication, table 1 **19**:1033
·oral folk tradition supplanted **7**:468a
·piezoelectric pickup mountings **14**:462c; illus.

phonolite (from Greek *phone* "sound," *lithos* "stone"), group of extrusive igneous rocks (lavas) rich in nepheline and potash feldspar. The name is a Greek rendition of the German *Klingstein*, referring to fine-grained compact lavas that split into thin, tough plates and give out a ringing sound when struck.

The most important constituent of phonolite is alkali feldspar, either sanidine or anorthoclase, which forms not only the bulk of the groundmass (matrix), but most of the large crystals (phenocrysts) in porphyritic varieties. Nepheline rarely appears in large crystals but may occur either interstitially or in well-formed microphenocrysts. The principal dark-coloured (mafic; ferromagnesian) mineral is pyroxene: aegirine or titaniferous augite. Pyroxene phenocrysts occur as euhedral (well-formed) crystals; in the groundmass, pyroxene occurs characteristically as slender needles, often abundant enough to colour the rock green. An alkaline amphibole nearly always occurs as phenocrysts; barkevikite, riebeckite, or arfvedsonite are typical. Feldspathoids other than nepheline may be present as accessory minerals; the commonest are nosean, sodalite, and leucite. Glass has been reported occasionally but only in small amounts.

Most phonolites are of Tertiary or Recent age and therefore formed within the last 65,000,000 years; but excellent examples occur at several localities in the Carboniferous strata of Scotland and Brazil, which means that they are about 300,000,000 years old. Tertiary or Recent phonolites are common in Europe, as in the former province of Auvergne, France; the Eifel plateau and the Laacher See, West Germany; Czechoslovakia; and the Mediterranean area (chiefly in Italy). They also occur at Cripple Creek, Colo., and the Black Hills, South Dakota; Devil's Tower, Wyoming, is variously described as tinguaite or phonolite, depending on whether it is considered a volcanic plug or a flow.

Leucite phonolites are perhaps best known from the vicinity of Naples. Apachite, from the Apache Mountains, Texas, is an amphibole phonolite. Kenyite, from Mt. Kenya, in East Africa, is rich in olivine. The phonolite of Olbrück, W.Ger., a rather popular local building stone, is said to contain about 15 percent nosean and 8 percent leucite. Phonolite trachytes occur on St. Helena and a number of other volcanic islands.
·igneous rock classification **9**:206f; table 207
·mineralogical composition table **9**:221
·origin and chemical composition **9**:218d; table 214

phonological change, alteration in the sounds or in the sound system of a language during the course of its development. *Major ref.* **10**:1006h
·Armenian radical changes of Indo-European **2**:24a
·High German consonant shift **8**:23g; table
·Italic language reconstruction **9**:1075c

phonology, study of the sound patterns that occur within languages. Some linguists include phonetics, the study of the production and description of speech sounds, within the study of phonology. Diachronic (historical) phonology examines and constructs theories about the changes and modifications in speech sounds and sound systems over a period of time. For example, it is concerned with the process by which the English words "sea" and "see," once pronounced with different vowel sounds (as indicated by the modern spelling), have come to be pronounced alike today. Descriptive (synchronic) phonology investigates sounds at a single stage in the development of a language, to discover the sound patterns that can occur. For example, in English, *nt* and *dm* can appear within or at the end of words ("rent," "admit") but not at the beginning. *See also* phonemics. *Major ref.* **10**:996c
·African distinguishing characteristics **1**:220g
·phonetic variation within utterances **14**:280a
·pidgin language simplification **14**:453a
·Prague school features analysis **10**:1006a
·Sino-Tibetan classification importance **16**:799h
·system and function in language **10**:644f

phonon, any energy packet associated with the vibration of atoms about their rest positions in crystals and some liquids. Sound waves in solids and the vibrations associated with heat in a solid are understood as groups of phonons.

Experimental studies of the amount of heat required to increase the temperature of solids show that each phonon is quantized—that is, the vibrational energy of each atom is proportional to its discrete frequency of vibration. Materials at room temperature contain few high-frequency phonons, because the large energies needed to create such vibrations are not available. Lower frequency phonons, such as those corresponding to sound waves, are much more common.

Phonons, which produce periodic displacements of the atoms of a solid from their regularly spaced positions, affect the conduction of heat and electricity through a material. The interactions of phonons with each other and with entities such as electrons and photons account for many phenomena observable in solids, including superconductivity. *Major ref.* **6**:577g
·acoustic radiation theory **17**:27d
·atomic theory of Mössbauer effect **12**:492h
·crystal system energy states **11**:307b
·glass ultraviolet spectroscopy **8**:209f
·ionic crystal vibration and heat conduction **9**:807c
·metals theory and properties **11**:1091e
·solid state structure and properties **16**:1036c

phonoreception, or HEARING, the perception and discrimination of sound energy. Sound is ubiquitous and contains much information about the environment, and so the ability to perceive sound, especially in air, is an important attribute of most terrestrial animals. At the lowest frequencies of sound, particularly in water, the pressure changes involved may be so slow that it is more convenient to consider their perception as mechanoreception.

Invertebrate animals depend on a variety of structures for hearing; apparently, however, only arthropods are able to hear sounds in the range of human hearing (15 to 20,000 Hertz). Some insects are known to detect sounds of up to at least 100,000 Hertz.

Many arthropods have tactile hairs that are stimulated by sound energy, in addition to other forms of energy. Certain roaches and crickets possess cercal organs (tufts of hairs supplied with nerves) that are located at the tip of the abdomen and are sensitive to a wide range of sound frequencies. Tympanal organs, found on the abdomen, thorax, or first legs of certain members of the insect orders Orthoptera (crickets), Homoptera (cicadas), and Lepidoptera (moths), consist of a membrane at the body surface or in a trachea (respiratory tubule). Changes in the tension of the tympanal membrane induced by impinging sound waves are sensed by chordotonal, or scolophore, organs, highly specialized nervous structures that record tension changes in a variety of situations in the insect body.

The hearing apparatus of vertebrate animals is surprisingly uniform, considering the range of body types and habitats of vertebrates. In the evolution from jawless fishes to mammals and birds, the ear has become progressively more complex and increasingly able to discriminate sound frequencies. The structure is complicated by the presence of three semicircular canals (*q.v.*), which function in the determination of the animal's position changes. The basic sound-sensitive structures of the fish ear are the sacculus, utriculus, and lagena, interconnecting, fluid-filled cavities derived from the lateral line system (*q.v.*). In amphibians the ear is basically like that of fishes, except that frogs have an additional cavity, the air-filled middle ear, with a membrane, the eardrum, or tympanic membrane, lying at the skin surface and connected to the inner ear by a small bone, the columella. In reptiles the lagena is somewhat elongated (the start of a true cochlea, or inner ear), and the eardrum is withdrawn into the head. Snakes have lost the middle ear and the external opening but have retained the columella; they hear airborne sound poorly but are highly sensitive to vibrations of the ground.

The ear of birds is basically reptilian, but the cochlea is longer and more sensitive. Pitch discrimination is far more acute in birds, many of which perceive frequencies well above the range of human hearing.

The mammalian ear is characterized by a coiled cochlea, the number of turns varying from one-quarter (in the duck-billed platypus, *Ornithorhynchus anatinus*) to nearly four (in the guinea pig, *Cavia porcellus*). This fluid-filled spiral contains the nerve endings that react to the mechanical energy of sound waves.

A projecting external ear, or pinna, is present in nearly all terrestrial mammals but lacking in cetaceans and phocid seals and reduced or lacking in many burrowing mammals. Sounds reaching it are reflected into the meatus, a duct leading to the tympanic membrane. In the middle ear, sound is transmitted from the tympanic membrane to the cochlea by three minute bones, the ossicles; it loses considerable amplitude but gains pressure.

Many land mammals have upper hearing limits well above that of man; cetaceans and bats, which orient by echolocation (*q.v.*), perceive sounds of at least 100,000 Hertz.

·arthropod nervous systems **12**:981d
·Chiroptera echolocation mechanism **4**:432d
·dog frequency range **5**:930g
·insect hearing anatomy and abilities **17**:40h; illus. 41
·movement perception methods **14**:46b
·orthopteran sense of sound detection **13**:747g
·ostariophysian communication mechanism **13**:761d
·shark sensitivity to stimuli **16**:496c
·sound reception in animals **17**:39c
·tarpons' special swim bladder modifications **6**:730a
·whale sound reception **19**:808g

Phony War, journalistic term given to the inactivity in World War II from the collapse of Poland in September 1939 until the Nazi offensive against France in the spring of 1940.
·German naval campaigns **19**:981d

phoqca, Inca unit of measurement equal to 26 quarts.
·Inca measurement system **1**:853g

Phoradendron (plant genus): *see* mistletoe.

phorate, a systemic insecticide used in pest control.
·systemic pesticide use **14**:141d

phoresy, the transportation of a minute parasite, such as a mite or a feather louse (Mallophaga), by a larger, more mobile parasite (*e.g.*, a hippoboscid fly) of the same host, enabling the smaller parasite to colonize new host individuals. Feather lice accomplish phoresy by clinging to the body hairs of blood-sucking flies.
·arachnid modes of transportation **1**:1063c
·mites and arthropod hosts **1**:21a

Phoridae: *see* humpbacked fly.

Phormia regina: *see* blow fly.

phorminx (musical instrument): *see* kithara.

Phormio (161 BC), play by Terence.
·Terence's career as dramatist **18**:143a

Phormion (d. *c.* 428 BC), brilliant Athenian admiral who won several engagements before and during the Peloponnesian War. He was one of the generals leading reinforcements to the siege of Samos in 440. He assisted the Acarnanians and Amphilochians against Ambracia, which resulted in an Acarnanian alliance useful to Athens. In 432–31 he headed the siege of Potidaea and was sent (432) with 20 ships to block the entrance to the Gulf of Corinth, where, in 429, he defeated 47 Peloponnesian ships that were advancing to reinforce the Spartan Cnemus' campaign in Acarnania; in a second battle he routed Cnemus' 77-vessel fleet.
·Athenian Peloponnesian War victories **14**:21h

phormium, common name for *Phormium tenax*, a plant of the agave family (Agavaceae), and for its fibre, belonging to the group called leaf fibres (*q.v.*), obtained from plant leaves.

The plant is native to New Zealand, where the fibre, sometimes called New Zealand "hemp" or "flax," has been used since ancient times for cordage, fabrics, and baskets. Grown in southern Ireland, mainly as an ornamental since 1798, the plant was later introduced to parts of Europe; and commercial plantings were started in St. Helena, the Azores, Australia, southern Africa, and Japan. In the 1930s cultivation was established in the South American countries of Brazil (where the plant is called formio), Chile, and Argentina.

The plant is composed of about 8 to 12 shoots growing from a central rootstock. Each shoot bears at least five dark-green, lance-shaped leaves arranged in fanlike form. The leaves, tapering to a point from a base 2 inches (5 centimetres) wide, are about 3–14 feet (0.9–4.2 metres) long, with smooth, hard outer surfaces and undersides marked with a middle rib. The flower stalk grows from the plant centre to a height of 12–15 feet (3.6–4.5 metres) and bears bunches of yellow flowers, each about 1.5 inches (3.8 centimetres) long. The numerous black seeds are flat and shiny.

Crops, adaptable to various soils, grow best in well-drained, loose, moderately rich soil and in temperate climates with moderate rainfall. Plants are propagated from shoots of mature roots (rhizomes) or sometimes from seed and are spaced 4–6 feet (1.2–1.8 metres) apart. The first leaves are ready for harvesting four to six years after planting, and additional leaves can be taken at intervals of one to four years thereafter. At each harvest three to four outer leaves are taken from each shoot. They are cut off by hand, 6–8 inches (15–20 centimetres) above the point at which they grow from the stalk, since lower cutting would free the red-coloured plant juice, staining the fibre.

In commercial processing the leaves, sorted according to quality and length, are subjected to machine decortication, a crushing and scraping process that frees the fibre. The decorticated fibre strands are washed, then sun-dried to promote bleaching and bring out lustre. Phormium, creamy white when carefully processed, is flexible, with fair strength and good lustre, and is resistant to damage in saltwater. It is used in twines and ropes and also made into bagging fabrics and such items as mats and shoe soles. In 1968 world production was about 6,500 metric tons, much of it used locally.
·fibre cultivation, location, and use **7**:283c
·rope making and plant fibre preparation **15**:1145h

Phoroneus, in Greek legend, an early king of Argos and the son of Inachus. (Inachus, according to one tradition, was the earliest of all Hellenic rulers, but sometimes he was identified as simply a river god. Thus, Phoroneus was considered the first mortal king.) Traditionally Phoroneus and two river gods had to decide between the sea god, Poseidon, and Hera, the goddess of marriage and the wife of Zeus, as the deity of the land. They chose Hera, and Poseidon took his vengeance by depriving the Argos region of water.

Phoronida 14:283, a phylum of invertebrate marine animals with an elongated, nonsegmented body from 0.5 to 25 centimetres in length. The approximately 16 known species occur mostly in the intertidal zone or in shallow waters in the temperate zone.

The text article covers natural history, form and function, evolution, and classification.

REFERENCE in other text article:
·circulatory system anatomy **4**:623f

Phoronis, genus of marine invertebrate of the phylum Phoronida.
·phoronid structure and tentacles **14**:283h; illus.

Phororhacidae, a fossil family of birds of the order Gruiformes.
·classification and fossil record **8**:448h

phororhacoids, common name of fossil birds of the family Phororhacidae, order Gruiformes.
·bird fossil record and evolution **2**:1060f

Phororhacos (bird genus): *see* Diatryma.

Phort Lairge (Ireland): *see* Waterford.

phosgene, also known as CARBONYL CHLORIDE, a colourless, chemically reactive, highly toxic gas having an odour like that of musty hay, used in making organic chemicals, dyestuffs, polycarbonate resins, and isocyanates for making polyurethane resins. It first came into prominence during World War I, when it was used, either alone or mixed with chlorine, against troops. Inhalation causes severe lung injury, the full effects appearing several hours after exposure.

First prepared in 1811, phosgene is manufactured by the reaction of carbon monoxide and chlorine in the presence of a catalyst. It can be formed by the decomposition of chlorinated hydrocarbons; *e.g.*, when carbon tetrachloride (*q.v.*) is used as a fire extinguisher. Gaseous phosgene, which has a density about three and one-half times that of air, liquefies at a temperature of 8.2° C (46.8° F); it is usually stored and transported as the liquid under pressure in steel cylinders or as a solution in toluene. With water, phosgene reacts to form carbon dioxide and hydrochloric acid.
·formation from carbon tetrachloride **7**:321e
·industrial environment hazards **9**:529c
·infrared analyzer measurement table **9**:635
·production and uses **7**:927g

phosphagen, a compound found in muscle. It contains phosphorus in a chemical entity called phosphoryl, which is transferred to adenosine diphosphate (ADP) to form adenosine triphosphate (ATP).
·muscle contraction metabolism **12**:627f

phosphate, any of numerous chemical compounds related to phosphoric acid (H_3PO_4). One group of these derivatives is composed of salts containing the phosphate ion (PO_4^{3-}), the hydrogen phosphate ion (HPO_4^{2-}), or the dihydrogen phosphate ion ($H_2PO_4^-$), and positively charged ions such as those of sodium or calcium; a second group is composed of esters, in which the hydrogen atoms of phosphoric acid have been replaced by organic combining groups such as ethyl (C_2H_5) or phenyl (C_6H_5).
·Alpine Lakes' algae and eutrophication **1**:632d
·Arabian Sea fish kills **1**:1060f
·biological energy exchanges **11**:1023b
·bone affected by kidney disease **3**:25d
·bone formation and dissolution **3**:21c
·enzyme reaction mechanisms **6**:900b; illus. 899
·fluid and electrolyte disorders in humans **5**:843g; table
·glass types and uses **8**:208e
·hormonal influences on metabolism **6**:814c
·ionic buffering action in the plasma **2**:1115f
·muscle contraction metabolism **12**:627e
·parathormone influence on removal **8**:1080b
·renal tubular absorption **7**:38f; table
·toxin reaction site and effect, table 4 **14**:622

phosphate minerals 14:284, major source of phosphate fertilizers and phosphorus for industrial use. More than 200 minerals containing up to 5 percent phosphorus are known; many are rare, however, and most minable phosphorus is found in the apatite series of calcium phosphates. Other phosphate minerals are sources of thorium (monazite), rare earths (monazite, xenotime), and uranium (torbernite, autunite). Some are also used as gemstones (turquoise, apatite, variscite).

Phosphate minerals may be classified as anhydrous, as hydrous with hydroxyl or halogen, or as hydrous with water and hydroxyl or halogen. The structure is based on the orthophosphate ion composed of four oxygen atoms at the corners of a tetrahedron, around a central phosphorus atom. Structurally and chemically related are the arsenate minerals and the vanadate minerals.

The text article covers the structure, composition, occurrence, and distribution of the phosphate minerals. *See* separate titles listed in the Table (*see* pp. 962–963).

REFERENCES in other text articles:
·acid and fertilizer production **1**:594a
·African distribution and tonnage **1**:200f
·chemically deposited sediments **16**:461b
·concentration in marine skeletons **6**:715c; table 714
·conservation and resource renewability **5**:46f
·continental shelf deposits **13**:503b

·Florida mining economic significance **7**:427b
·intrusive igneous rock minerals **9**:220g
·Morocco's reserves and significance **12**:449b
·phosphorite types and composition **14**:288h
·silviculture's use as fertilizer **7**:530h
·superphosphate fertilizer production **3**:586c
·turquoise gem characteristics **7**:976a

phosphate rock (geology): *see* phosphorites.

phosphatide (biochemistry): *see* phospholipid.

phosphene, sensation of seeing light when none enters the eye, which occurs after external pressure is applied to the eyeball or following adaptation of the eyes to a darkened area. *Cf.* after-image.
·visual reception and pressure **16**:547g

phosphine, also called HYDROGEN PHOSPHIDE, a colourless, flammable, extremely toxic gas, with a disagreeable, garlic-like odour. Phosphine (PH_3) is formed by the action of a strong base or hot water on white phosphorus. It is used as a starting material in the synthesis of some organic phosphorus compounds, for the preparation of phosphonium chlorides, and as a doping agent for solid-state electronic components.
·organic derivatives and nomenclature **13**:704a
·production, properties, and reactions **13**:130b

phosphofructokinase, enzyme (biological catalyst) that is important in cells in regulating the process of fermentation (*q.v.*), by which one molecule of the simple sugar glucose is broken down to two molecules of the compound pyruvic acid. Phosphofructokinase is a so-called regulatory enzyme of fermentation (*see* allosteric control). The enzyme not only catalyzes a specific reaction—the formation of fructose-1,6-diphosphate and adenosine diphosphate (ADP) from fructose-6-phosphate and adenosine triphosphate (ATP)—but its activity is sensitive to the ATP/ADP ratio in the cell. ATP and ADP are called modulators of the enzyme's activity. They bind to the enzyme at a site (modulator or effector site) other than the one at which catalytic activity occurs (active site).

Phosphofructokinase thus requires ATP as a substrate (the ATP occupies the active site), but ATP is also a modulator of activity. If its concentration becomes higher than is required to saturate the active site of the enzyme, the rate of the reaction decreases. This occurs because the excess ATP occupies the effector site of the enzyme. It thus acts as a negative, or inhibitory, modulator, and the enzyme is inactive; *i.e.*, ATP acts as a feedback inhibitor (*see* feedback inhibition). If, on the other hand, the concentration of ADP in the cell is high, the activity of the enzyme is enhanced, and the rate of the reaction increases (positive modulation). Such regulation ensures that no substance is over- or underproduced.
·muscle contraction metabolism **12**:628c
·muscle weakness in glycogen disease **12**:635a
·regulation of metabolism **11**:1047h

phosphogluconate pathway, also called PENTOSE-PHOSPHATE CYCLE, a cyclic series of reactions in which glucose-6-phosphate is oxidized by nicotinamide adenine dinucleotide phosphate, resulting in the formation of pentose phosphate and the release of carbon dioxide.
·carbohydrate catabolism reactions **11**:1028e; illus. 1029

phosphoglyceric acid, in biological systems, an intermediate chemical compound in the metabolism of carbohydrates. It is also a product of photosynthesis formed from ribulose diphosphate and carbon dioxide.
·carbohydrates and photosynthesis **3**:824a

phospholipid, also called PHOSPHATIDE, any member of a class of complex, fatlike, phosphorus-containing substances that play structural and metabolic roles in living cells. The phospholipids, with the sphingolipids, or glycolipids, and the lipoproteins, make up a group sometimes called compound lipids, as distinguished from the neutral, or simple, lipids (fats and waxes) and from other fat-soluble cell components, mostly isoprenoids and steroids.

In the molecular structure of phospholipids, phosphoric acid is combined with two alcoholic constituents, one of which imparts water-solubility. The other either confers fat-solubility by its own structure or, in the phosphoglycerides, serves as a link to still other components, such as fatty acids, that bestow that property.

Phosphate minerals

name formula	colour	lustre	Mohs hardness	specific gravity	habit or form	fracture or cleavage	refractive indices	crystal system space group	remarks
amblygonite (Li, Na)$AlPO_4$(F, OH)	white to creamy white; slightly tinted	vitreous to greasy	5½–6	3.0–3.1	large, translucent, cleavable masses; small transparent crystals	one perfect and one good cleavage	ambl mont α = 1.578–1.611 β = 1.595–1.619 γ = 1.598–1.633	triclinic $P\bar{1}$	forms solid solution series with montebrasite which has a greater percentage of OH than F
apatite									
carbonate-apatite $Ca_{10}(PO_4)_6CO_3 \cdot H_2O$	variable, greens predominating	vitreous	5	2.9–3.2	prismatic or thick tabular crystals; coarse granular to compact massive; nodular concretions	conchoidal to uneven fracture	n = 1.63–1.67	hexagonal $C\frac{6_3}{m}$	often fluorescent in ultraviolet light, cathode rays, or X-rays; phosphorescent; sometimes strongly thermoluminescent
chlorapatite $Ca_5(PO_4)_3Cl$									
fluorapatite $Ca_5(PO_4)_3F$									
hydroxylapatite $Ca_5(PO_4)_3OH$									
autunite $Ca(UO_2)_2(PO_4)_2 \cdot$ $10–12H_2O$	lemon yellow to sulfur yellow; greenish yellow to pale green	vitreous to pearly	2–2½	3.1–3.2	thin tabular crystals; flaky aggregates; crusts	one perfect, micalike cleavage	α = 1.553 β = 1.575 γ = 1.577	tetragonal $I\frac{4}{m}mm$	fluoresces yellowish green under ultraviolet light
brushite $CaHPO_4 \cdot 2H_2O$	colourless to pale yellow	vitreous or pearly	2½	2.3	transparent to translucent efflorescences or minute crystals	two perfect cleavages	α = 1.539 β = 1.546 γ = 1.551	monoclinic A2	piezoelectric
collophane (massive apatite)	grayish white; yellowish; brown	weakly vitreous to dull	3–4	2.5–2.9	cryptocrystalline massive; hornlike concretions and nodules		n = 1.59–1.61		
lazulite $MgAl_2(PO_4)_2(OH)_2$	azure blue or sky blue; bluish white, bluish green; deep blue	vitreous	5½–6	3.1–3.4	crystals; compact masses; grains	two cleavages; uneven to splintery fracture	lazul scorz α = 1.604–1.639 β = 1.626–1.670 γ = 1.637–1.680	monoclinic $P\frac{2_1}{n}$	forms solid solution series with scorzalite in which Fe replaces Mg in the crystal structure
monazite (Ce, La)PO_4	yellowish brown or reddish brown to brown	usually resinous or waxy; sometimes vitreous or adamantine	5–5½	4.6–5.4; usually 5.0–5.2	translucent, small, flattened crystals	one distinct cleavage	α = 1.79–1.80 β = 1.79–1.80 γ = 1.84–1.85	monoclinic $P\frac{2_1}{n}$	moderately paramagnetic
pyromorphite $Pb_5(PO_4)_3Cl$	olive green; yellow; gray; brown to orange	resinous to subadamantine	3½–4	7.0	barrel-shaped prisms; globular, kidney-shaped, or grape-like masses	uneven to subconchoidal fracture	ϵ = 2.030–2.031 ω = 2.041–2.144	hexagonal $C\frac{6_3}{m}$	forms solid solution series with mimetite in which As replaces P in the crystal structure
torbernite $Cu(UO_2)_2(PO_4)_2 \cdot$ $8–12H_2O$	various shades of green	vitreous to subadamantine	2–2½	3.2	tabular crystals; micalike masses	one perfect, platy cleavage	ϵ = 1.582 ω = 1.592	tetragonal $I\frac{4}{m}mm$	water content depends on temperature and humidity

Lecithin (phosphatidyl choline), in which choline is bound to phosphoric acid, and the cephalins (phosphatidylethanolamine and phosphatidylserine) comprise the bulk of the total lipids in plant and animal cells, lecithin being the most abundant. (It occurs in only a few bacteria.) Nerve tissue has a high phosphoglyceride content: in beef brain, 40 percent of the white matter and 25 percent of the gray matter are phosphoglycerides, cephalins accounting for 55 percent, lecithin for 25 percent; the other 20 percent consists of other lipid materials—sphingomyelins (*see* sphingolipid).

Other phosphoglycerides include plasmalogens, present in brain and heart and apparently of limited occurrence in nonanimal tissues; phosphoinositides, present in brain; and cardiolipin, initially isolated from heart.

Commercial phosphoglycerides from oils such as corn (maize) and soybean oils may be dried (commercially, the products are called lecithin) and used as emulsifiers in such products as margarine, chocolate, and emulsion paints. *Major ref.* **10**:1020c

- ·biosynthesis and functions **11**:1041c
- ·blood clotting activation **2**:1108f
- ·chloroplast composition and functions **14**:369h
- ·choline metabolism functions **19**:492a
- ·digestion and absorption of fats **5**:779b
- ·lecithin importance for gallstone formation **5**:802h
- ·lecithin structure and properties **10**:1020d
- ·membrane lipid composition **11**:876f
- ·nerve impulses and membrane potential **12**:974g
- ·nutrient needs of organisms **13**:405f
- ·oil refining process **13**:529f
- ·plasma concentrations and composition **2**:1115c

phosphor, solid material that emits light, or luminesces, when exposed to radiation such as ultraviolet light or an electron beam. Hundreds of thousands of phosphors have been synthesized, each one having its own characteristic colour of emission and period of time that light is emitted after excitation ceases. When certain phosphors luminesce from electron excitation, the process is called electroluminescence (*q.v.*), and these phosphors are used in the production of radar and television screens. Phosphors excited by ultraviolet, visible, and infrared light are used principally in the so-called fluorescent lamps employed for general illumination.

- ·Becquerel discovery of radioluminescence **2**:790h
- ·colour television use **15**:526c
- ·oscilloscope and picture tubes **6**:690c
- ·television picture tube construction **18**:115e
- ·types and production **11**:180f
- ·types and radiation detection uses **15**:397d

phosphor bronze: *see* bronze.

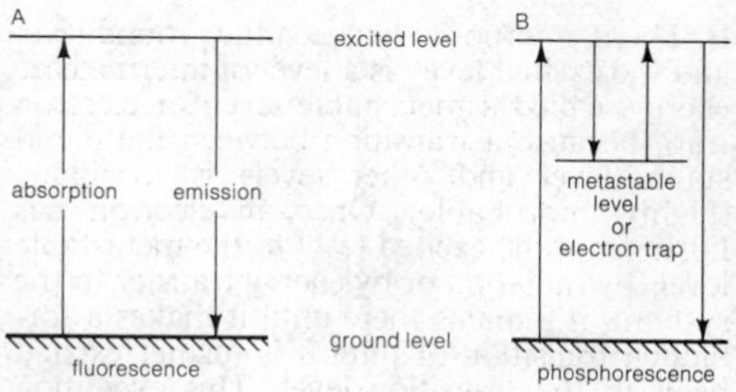

Phosphorescence

phosphorescence, emission of light from a substance exposed to radiation and persisting as an afterglow after the radiation has been removed. Unlike fluorescence, in which the absorbed light is spontaneously emitted about 10^{-8} second after excitation, phosphorescence requires additional excitation to produce radiation and may last from about 10^{-3} second to days or years, depending on the circumstances.

To understand the difference between phosphorescence and fluorescence it is helpful to refer to the energy level diagrams in the Figure, in which the relative distance of a line, or level, above a base line (the ground level) denotes the energy of an electron occupying that level. In A, representing fluorescence, an electron is raised from the ground level to an excited level by a light photon or other radiation. Transition of the electron back to the ground level can occur spontaneously with radiation of the same energy as that which was absorbed. According to electromagnetic theory, the return is almost coincident, occurring within 10^{-8} second or so. The case for phosphorescence is illustrated in the Figure by

Phosphate minerals (continued)

name formula	colour	lustre	Mohs hardness	specific gravity	habit or form	fracture or cleavage	refractive indices	crystal system space group	remarks
triphylite $LiFePO_4$	bluish or greenish gray (triphylite); clove brown, honey yellow, or salmon (lithiophilite)	vitreous to subresinous	4–5	3.3–3.6 not varying linearly with composition	transparent to translucent cleavable or compact massive	one perfect cleavage	triph lith α = 1.694–1.669 β = 1.695–1.673 γ = 1.700–1.682	orthorhombic Pmnb	forms solid solution series with lithiophilite in which Mn replaces Fe in the molecular structure; structure similar to olivine
triplite $(Mn, Fe, Mg, Ca)_2PO_4(F, OH)$	dark brown; flesh red; salmon pink	vitreous to resinous	5–5½	3.5–3.9	massive	one good cleavage	α = 1.643–1.696 β = 1.647–1.704 γ = 1.668–1.713	monoclinic $I\frac{2}{m}$	
turquoise $CuAl_6(PO_4)_4(OH)_8 \cdot 4H_2O$	blue to various shades of green; greenish to yellowish gray	waxy	5–6	2.6–2.8	opaque, dense, cryptocrystalline to fine granular massive	one perfect and one good cleavage	α = 1.61 β = 1.62 γ = 1.65	triclinic $P\bar{1}$	forms solid solution series with chalcosiderite in which Fe replaces Al in the molecular structure
variscite $AlPO_4 \cdot 2H_2O$	yellowish green, pale to emerald green, bluish green or colourless (variscite); peach-blossom red, carmine, violet (strengite)	vitreous to faintly waxy	3½–4½	2.2–2.5	fine-grained, round or grape-like aggregates, nodules, veins, or crusts	one good cleavage	varis stren α = 1.563–1.707 β = 1.588–1.719 γ = 1.594–1.741	orthorhombic Pcab	forms solid solution series with strengite in which Fe replaces Al in the molecular structure; both variscite and strengite have monoclinic forms
vivianite $Fe_3(PO_4)_2 \cdot 8H_2O$	colourless when fresh, darkening to deep blue or bluish black	vitreous	1½–2	2.7	rounded prismatic crystals; kidney-shaped, tubelike, or globular masses; concretions	one perfect cleavage	α = 1.579–1.616 β = 1.602–1.656 γ = 1.629–1.675	monoclinic $C\frac{2}{m}$	
wavellite $Al_3(PO_4)_2(OH)_3 \cdot 5H_2O$	greenish white; green to yellow	vitreous	3½–4	2.4	translucent, hemispherical, or globular aggregates	one perfect and one good cleavage	α = 1.520–1.535 β = 1.526–1.543 γ = 1.545–1.561	orthorhombic Pcmm	
xenotime YPO_4	yellowish brown to reddish brown; flesh red, grayish white, pale yellow, or greenish	vitreous	4–5	4.4–5.1	small prismatic crystals; coarse radial aggregates; rosettes	uneven to splintery fracture	ϵ = 1.816–1.827 ω = 1.721–1.720	tetragonal $I\frac{4}{a}md$	moderately paramagnetic; similar in appearance and identical in form and structure to zircon, but softer

B. There, interposed between the ground level and the excited level, is a level of intermediate energy, called a metastable level, or electron trap, because a transition between the metastable level and other levels is forbidden (highly improbable). Once an electron has fallen from the excited level to the metastable level (by radiation or by energy transfer to the system), it remains there until it makes a forbidden transition or until it is further excited back to the transition level. This excitation may come about through thermal agitation of the neighbouring atoms or molecules (called thermoluminescence) or through optical (*e.g.*, infrared) stimulation. The time spent in the metastable level, or electron trap, determines the length of time that phosphorescence persists.

- Becquerel discovery of radioluminescence **2**:790h
- biological emission of stored light **2**:1028a
- electron energy transition **11**:182d
- fluorescence
  - cancer research application **3**:770c
  - coloration mechanisms in animals **4**:918c
  - electromagnetic radiation generation **16**:1043h
  - electron energy transition **11**:182d
  - electron excitation in ionic crystal **6**:670a
  - fluorescence microscope characteristics **12**:134a
  - light quantum theory **10**:947d
  - material crack testing **11**:630c
  - metal testing under ultraviolet light **11**:1077g
  - mineral X-ray spectroscopic analysis **11**:1065e
  - molecular spectra emission **17**:471b
  - phosphorescence comparison **11**:179e
  - photosynthetic electron flow studies **14**:368e
  - radiation detection methods **15**:393g
  - ultraviolet radiation detection **6**:652e
  - X-ray secondary emissions **19**:1058f
- fluorescence comparison **11**:179e
- mass spectrometer detection system **11**:607a
- molecular activation principles **15**:409d
- photochemical reaction rates **14**:293h

phosphorescence, marine, heatless light generated chemically by marine plants and animals. Bioluminescence is exhibited by a wide variety of oceanic organisms, from bacteria to large squids and fish. The light is emitted when a flavin pigment, luciferin, is oxidized in the presence of luciferase, an enzyme also produced by the organism. The light produced is usually blue-green, near the point in the spectrum of maximum transmission for seawater and most visible for many deep-sea organisms. Most of the homogeneous phosphorescence of the sea, the glowing wakes, is caused by the presence of blooming phytoplankton, notably the microscopic dinoflagellate *Noctiluca miliaris*, as well as some jellyfish. Many small crustaceans, such as the *Cypridina hilgendorfii*, which is 3 to 4 millimetres (about ⅙ inch) long, also emit phosphorescence when disturbed. Many squids emit luminous clouds when threatened. Some species of fish possess distinctive arrays of light-emitting organs or flash lights at regular intervals, permitting individuals to form or maintain schools. Some deep-sea fish, notably the angler fish, possess lights in or near the mouth with which to attract and illuminate prey.

Phosphorescent Bay, a bay in Puerto Rico in which there occur displays of luminescence by marine organisms.

- bioluminescent marine organisms **2**:1028h

Phosphoria Formation, rock formation that occurs in northeastern Utah, eastern Idaho, western and southwestern Montana, and Wyoming; it was named for exposures studied in the type locality of Phosphoria Gulch, near Meade Peak, Idaho. It is an Upper Permian formation that is part of the Guadalupian Stage (the Permian Period began about 280,000,000 years ago and lasted about 55,000,000 years) and typically consists of a basal, black phosphatic shale that is succeeded by a cherty limestone; in some areas, however, it intertongues with red shales. The Phosphoria deposits were laid down on the Permian continental shelf in a shallow sea where circulation was restricted. The phosphate-rich beds are extensively quarried for use in chemicals and fertilizers.

phosphoric acid, also called ORTHOPHOSPHORIC ACID, the most important oxygen acid of phosphorus, used to make phosphate salts for fertilizers and detergents. It is also used in dental cements, in the preparation of albumin derivatives, and in the sugar and textile industries. It serves as an acidic, fruitlike flavouring in food products.

Pure phosphoric acid (H_3PO_4) is a crystalline solid (melting point 42.35° C, or 108.2° F); in less concentrated form it is a colourless syrupy liquid. The crude acid is prepared from phosphate rock, while acid of higher purity is made from white phosphorus.

Phosphoric acid forms three classes of salts corresponding to replacement of one, two, or three hydrogen atoms. Among the important phosphate salts are: sodium dihydrogen phosphate (NaH_2PO_4), used for control of hydrogen ion concentration (acidity) of solutions; disodium hydrogen phosphate (Na_2HPO_4), used in water treatment as a precipitant for polyvalent metals; trisodium phosphate (Na_3PO_4), used in soaps and detergents; calcium dihydrogen phosphate or calcium superphosphate ($Ca[H_2PO_4]_2$), a major fertilizer ingredient; calcium monohydrogen phosphate ($CaHPO_4$), used as a conditioning agent for salts and sugars.

Phosphoric acid molecules interact under suitable conditions, often at high temperatures, to form larger molecules (usually with loss of water). Thus, diphosphoric, or pyrophosphoric, acid ($H_4P_2O_7$) is formed from two molecules of phosphoric acid, less one molecule of water. It is the simplest of a homologous series of long chain molecules called polyphosphoric acids, with the general formula $H(HPO_3)_nOH$, in which $n = 2,3,4, \ldots$. Metaphosphoric acids, $(HPO_3)_n$, in which $n = 3,4,5, \ldots$, are another class of polymeric phosphoric acids. The known metaphosphoric acids are characterized by cyclic molecular structures. The term metaphosphoric acid is used also to refer to a viscous, sticky substance, which is a mixture of both long chain and ring forms of $(HPO_3)_n$. The various polymeric forms of phosphoric acid are also prepared by hydration of phosphorus oxides.

- chemical industry fertilizer production **4**:133g
- hydrogen bonding and polymerization **13**:130f
- inorganic sulfur-containing acids **13**:713f
- pH and composition graph **1**:51
- phosphate ester formation **13**:702g; table

phosphoric anhydride: *see* phosphorus pentoxide.

phosphorites 14:288, minable deposits of phosphorus-containing rocks; most natural phosphorus occurs in minerals of the apatite family of calcium phosphates. Nearly all phosphate fertilizer and phosphorus for industrial use is obtained from phosphorites.

The text article covers the principal types of phosphate deposits, including (in order of size and world importance) marine phosphorites, igneous apatite deposits, residual phosphorites, phosphatized rock, river pebble, and guano. In addition, the article treats in detail the phosphate deposits in the United States and briefly those in other countries.

REFERENCES in other text articles:

- composition and classification **16**:466c; illus.
- continental shelf deposits **13**:503b
- Permian rock distribution **14**:96c
- phosphorus production and use **4**:133f; illus.
- world mineral production table **12**:247

Phosphoros (mythology): *see* Lucifer.

phosphorous acid, also called ORTHOPHOSPHOROUS ACID, one of several oxygen acids of phosphorus; used as reducing agent in chemical analysis. It is a white or yellowish crystalline substance (melting point about 73° C, or 163° F) with a garlic-like taste. An unstable compound that readily absorbs moisture, it is converted to phosphoric acid (H_3PO_4) in the presence of oxygen or when heated above 180° C (360° F). Phosphorous acid (H_3PO_3) forms salts called phosphites, also used as reducing agents. Phosphorous acid is prepared by dissolving tetraphosphorus hexoxide (P_4O_6) or phosphorus trichloride (PCl_3) in water.

- phosphorus pentoxide reaction in water **13**:130f

phosphorus (from Greek *phōsphoros*, "light-bearing"), symbol P, nonmetallic chemical element of the nitrogen family (Group Va of the periodic table). Ordinarily a colourless, semitransparent, soft, waxy solid that glows in the dark, it takes fire spontaneously upon exposure to air and forms dense white fumes of the oxide; it is essential to plant and animal life. Phosphorus was first prepared in elemental form in 1669 by a German alchemist, Hennig Brand, from a residue of evaporated urine.

Phosphorus is present in the fluids within cells of living tissues as the phosphate ion, PO_4^{3-}, one of the most important mineral constituents needed for cellular activity. The genes, which direct heredity and other cellular functions and are found in the nucleus of each cell, are molecules of DNA (deoxyribonucleic acid), which all contain phosphorus. Cells store the energy obtained from nutrients in molecules of adenosine triphosphate (ATP). Calcium phosphate is the principal inorganic constituent of teeth and bones.

Not found free in nature except in a few meteorites, phosphorus occurs in compounds that are widely distributed in many rocks, minerals, plants, and animals. Ranking 12th in abundance among the elements in the Earth's crust, phosphorus composes approximately 0.12 percent of the crust in the form of minerals such as apatite, wavellite, and vivianite, in which it always occurs as the phosphate ion. The chief commercial source is phosphate rock, an impure massive form of carbonate-bearing apatite.

Elemental phosphorus is prepared industrially in electric furnaces in which phosphate rock, coke, and silica pebble are continuously charged and heated until they are chemically converted into phosphorus vapour, carbon monoxide gas, and a calcium silicate slag. The stream of gas is cooled to condense the phosphorus to the liquid and eventually to the solid form, which is stored under water to prevent spontaneous ignition.

The element has about ten forms (allotropes) that occur within three major categories: white, red, and black. White phosphorus has two allotropes: the alpha form, which is stable at ordinary temperatures, has a density of 1.82 grams per cubic centimetre and a cubic crystal structure; the beta form, which is stable below −78° C (−108° F), has a density of 1.88 grams per cubic centimetre and a hexagonal crystal structure. White phosphorus, usually slightly yellow because of the presence of impurities, is extremely soluble in carbon disulfide and almost insoluble in water. It is poisonous. Exposure to sunlight or to heat converts white phosphorus to red, which neither phosphoresces nor spontaneously burns in air. Black phosphorus, which is flaky like graphite, is made by subjecting white phosphorus to high pressures or by keeping it at temperatures near 300° C (570° F) for several days in the presence of a small amount of mercury and a seed crystal of black phosphorus. Black phosphorus is chemically the least reactive form, and white is by far the most reactive.

Much of the white phosphorus produced is burned to phosphorus pentoxide, which is treated with water to make phosphoric acid. A little phosphoric acid is used in some soft drinks, but most is used to make fertilizers and other chemicals. White phosphorus also is converted to phosphorus sulfides, chlorides, and oxides, which in turn are utilized in the manufacture of organic chemicals and matches. White phosphorus has been used for military purposes as a source of smoke and to fill mortar shells, artillery shells, and grenades. Red phosphorus is used in preparing the striking surface for safety matches.

Phosphorus reacts with many metals and metalloids to form phosphides and with hydrogen to yield the very poisonous gas phosphine, PH_3. The usual oxidation state of the element is +3 or +5, as exhibited, for example, in the trichloride, PCl_3, and the pentachloride, PCl_5. Phosphorus pentoxide (a name derived from the empirical formula P_2O_5 although the correct molecular formula is P_4O_{10}) has an extremely great attraction for water, making it one of the most effective drying agents known. Phosphorus atoms can bond directly with carbon atoms in forming a large number of organic phosphorus compounds, among which are some nerve gases and biocides. Phosphoric acid, H_3PO_4 (orthophosphoric acid), is one of the most important compounds of the element. Its salts contain the phosphate ion, PO_4^{3-}, more carefully referred to as the orthophosphate ion, because several other phosphate ions are known. All naturally occurring phosphorus is the stable isotope, phosphorus-31. Radioactive phosphorus-32 has a half-life of 14.3 days; it is a useful tracer in studies of the life cycles of plants and animals.

atomic number	15
atomic weight	30.9738
melting point (white)	44.1° C (111.4° F)
boiling point (white)	280° C (536° F)
density (white)	1.82 g/cc at 20° C (68° F)
oxidation states	−3, +3, +5
electron configuration	$1s^2 2s^2 2p^6 3s^2 3p^3$

·agricultural practices and adversaries **1**:362b
·agricultural production requirements **1**:350e
·animal feed and mineral supplements **1**:909b
·aquatic productivity factors **1**:1030a
·atomic weight and number table **2**:345
·Bessemer's steel production difficulty **2**:871b
·bone mediation of body fluid levels **3**:21a
·calcium phosphide production and uses **3**:586b
·chemical warfare in weapons history **19**:695a
·chondrite meteorite oxidation degree **12**:44f
·concentration in marine skeletons **6**:715c
·deficiency's effect on plant colour **4**:917b
·element abundance, table 6 **17**:602
·endocrine system disorders **6**:821b
·fertilizer industry and soil nutrition **4**:133c
·geochemical abundances and dispersal by marine organisms **6**:709e; tables 702
·human body component **7**:433e
·isotopes in fertilizer and medical research **15**:453g *passim* to 454h
·Lavoisier combustion theory development **10**:714c
·life origin and materials **10**:902a; table 900
·Montana resources and economy **12**:399a
·muscle contraction metabolism **12**:627e
·nitrogen group comparative chemistry **13**:120h; table 121
·n-type semiconductor composition **15**:427g
·organic compound classes **13**:701a
·organic halogen compound preparation **13**:685g
·organic qualitative and quantitative analysis **4**:80f
·phosphorite deposit economic importance **14**:288h
·polymeric compound structures **4**:105a
·pregnant woman's mineral need **14**:976c
·pressure effects on polymorphism **8**:870f
·production, properties, and reactions **13**:129a; table 122
·radiation-induced mutation **12**:755b
·radiation therapy for bone disease **18**:286d
·reactivity and occurrence in minerals **14**:284a
·solar abundances, table 2 **17**:803
·steel acid Bessemer process problem **11**:1067c
·steel production problems and solution **18**:42b
·steel refining techniques **17**:640b
·stereoisomeric compound formation **9**:1042b
·vitamin D regulation of bone growth **13**:410c
·white phosphorous Bern conference prohibitions **8**:699f

phosphorus compounds, organic: *see* organic phosphorus compounds.

phosphorus cycle, in biology, the process by which phosphorus, a mineral essential for plant and animal life, is circulated through the biosphere, or living world, and returned to an inorganic state for recycling. Phosphorus occurs in nature in the form of salts called phosphates. Plants take up the phosphates and introduce them into terrestrial and shallow-water food chains. Decomposition of dead organic matter returns the phosphorus to the soil, where it may re-enter the food chain or become part of sedimentary rock. Much phosphorus is lost to deep-sea sediments by erosion of phosphorus-containing rock and excretion by marine animals. Upwelling from the deeps returns some phosphorus to the photosynthetic zone, where it is consumed by shallow-water organisms; it may then be returned to land by terrestrial fish eaters, mainly as guano deposited by marine birds. In general, however, there is an overall loss of phosphorus to the ocean deeps.

·biosphere eutrophication, illus. 5 **2**:1043

phosphorus deficiency, condition in which an organism does not receive an adequate supply of phosphorus, a mineral vitally important to the normal metabolism of numerous compounds and (in solution) an acid that, with sulfur, must be neutralized by the base-forming ions of sodium, potassium, calcium, and magnesium. About 70 percent of retained phosphorus combines with calcium in bone and tooth structure, while nitrogen combines with most of the remaining 30 percent to metabolize fats and carbohydrates. Phosphorus is the principal element in the structure of the nucleus and cytoplasm of all tissue cells. In addition, this mineral probably has the power to regulate hydrogen ion concentration and vitamin absorption in living tissues. It is also a universally distributed component of skeletal, nerve, and muscle tissues.

Deficiencies relating to the ratio of phosphorus to calcium may cause bone diseases such as rickets in children and osteoporosis or osteomalacia in adults. Sometimes an improper ratio causes bone fragility and tetany (severe muscle spasms in fingers and toes), but it remains questionable as a factor in dental caries (decay).

Dietary sources of phosphorus include milk products, egg yolk, fresh foods, legumes, nuts, and whole grains.

phosphorus pentafluoride, a dense, colourless, gaseous compound, PF_5, prepared by heating phosphorus pentachloride with calcium fluoride; it has been used as a catalyst for polymerization reactions.

·electron orbital and bond formation **13**:123a
·structure and chemical properties **13**:131a

phosphorus pentoxide, also called PHOSPHORIC ANHYDRIDE and DIPHOSPHORUS PENTOXIDE, a soft white powder, or colourless crystalline solid, obtained when phosphorus is burned in excess air; its true molecular composition is P_4O_{10}, not P_2O_5, as suggested by its name. It is corrosive to skin, eyes, and mucous membranes. Absorbing moisture from air, it hydrolyzes to metaphosphoric, pyrophosphoric, or orthophosphoric acid, depending on reaction conditions and the amount of water absorbed. It is used in chemical analysis as a dehydrating agent and in organic synthesis as a condensing agent.

·crustal and upper mantle abundances, tables 1 and 2 **5**:120

phosphorylation, the addition of a phosphoryl group (PO_3^{2-}) to an organic compound. The process by which much of the energy in foods is conserved and made available to the cell is called oxidative phosphorylation (*see* respiration, cellular). The process by which green plants convert light energy to chemical energy is called photophosphorylation (*see* photosynthesis).

·biological energy transduction **11**:1036a; illus.
·organophosphorus biological role **13**:703f
·photosynthetic mechanism **14**:371b

Photian Schism, a 9th-century-AD controversy between Eastern and Western Christianity that was precipitated by the opposition of the Roman Pope to the appointment by the Byzantine emperor Michael III of the lay scholar Photius to the patriarchate of Constantinople, and also involved Eastern and Western ecclesiastical jurisdictional rights in the Bulgarian Church as well a doctrinal dispute over the *Filioque* ("and from the Son") clause that had been added to the Nicene Creed by the Latin Church.

·Church factions and diplomatic failures **4**:544d
·creedal disputes and reconciliation **6**:153h
·Photius' relations with Rome **14**:290e

photic zone, the surface layer of the ocean that receives sunlight. There are also three subzones. The uppermost 80 metres (260 feet) or more of the ocean, which is sufficiently illuminated to permit photosynthesis by phytoplankton and plants, is called the euphotic zone. Sunlight insufficient for photosynthesis illuminates the disphotic zone, which extends from the base of the euphotic zone down to depths of about 200 metres. The thicknesses of the photic and euphotic zones vary with the intensity of sunlight as a function of season and latitude and with the degree of water turbidity. The bottommost (aphotic) zone is the region of perpetual darkness that lies beneath the photic zone and includes most of the ocean waters.

·Arabian Sea nutrient concentrations **1**:1060f
·conditions and life forms **13**:498c; illus. 485
·marine life and photosynthesis **7**:346g
·plankton life importance **2**:302g

Photinus, genus of North American firefly belonging to the beetle family Lampyridae. *See* firefly.

·mimicry of light signals by predator **12**:217d; illus.

Photisarath, also spelled PHOTHISARA or P'OT'ISARAT, also known as PHOTISARA-RAJA NORINTHARAJ (b. 1501—d. 1547), ruler of the Laotian kingdom of Lan Xang (Lan Chang) in 1520–47, whose territorial acquisitions resulted in a series of insurrections and wars that determined the character of Southeast Asian history for the remainder of the 16th century.

Photisarath, described in historical annals as an especially pious Buddhist, was the chief promulgator of Buddhism in ancient Laos, and his efforts helped the religion gain in popularity among his people. After receiving his education in a monastery, he was ordained as a monk in 1525 but left the order to assume the reins of government. He constructed many new monasteries and magnificent temples and spread Buddhism by royal decree.

Photisarath then married a princess from Chiengmai (now in northern Thailand), and when his father-in-law, the ruler of Chiengmai, died without male issue, he laid claim to that principality and placed his son and successor, Sethathirath I, on the throne of Chiengmai. The defense of Chiengmai as part of Lan Xang embroiled the kingdom in wars for more than two generations with the surrounding states, some with equally legitimate claims to the Chiengmai sovereignty.

In 1547 Photisarath suffered an accident while hunting wild elephants; he died a few days later and was succeeded by Sethathirath I.

·Laotian struggles with Burma and Siam **10**:677f

Photius 14:290 (b. *c.* 820, Constantinople—d. 891, Bordi, Armenia), patriarch of Constantinople (858–867 and 877–886), defender of the autonomous traditions of his church against Rome and leading figure of the 9th-century Byzantine renascence.

Abstract of text biography. Photius began his career as professor of philosophy at the Imperial Academy. He was elected patriarch of Constantinople while still a layman (858) and rapidly promoted through all the necessary ecclesiastical orders. He was subsequently in conflict with Pope Nicholas I over the rights of his church. Photius was deposed in 867 but returned as patriarch 10 years later. He resigned in 886, perhaps voluntarily.

REFERENCES in other text articles:
·Aristotelianism in Byzantine Renaissance **1**:1157b
·Basil I's influence in church struggle **2**:748e
·Byzantine historiographic losses **8**:950g
·canon law sources in Eastern councils **3**:774b
·Constantinopolitan pre-eminence thesis **4**:469f
·faction and schism **4**:544d
·Filioque disputes with Frankish papacy **6**:153h
·missionary and diplomatic activities **3**:560b

photoautotroph, a green plant or photosynthetic bacterium capable of utilizing energy from sunlight.
·life dependency on sunlight **10**:896b

Photoblepharon, genus of Indonesian fish of the order Beryciformes.
·bioluminescence and symbiotic bacteria **2**:1030g; illus. 1029

photocathode, an element of a phototube that emits electrons when struck by light, making possible the flow of electric current through the device. A substance often used for photocathodes is a partially oxidized silver–cesium alloy.
·design and scintillation counter use **15**:396f
·television camera tube operation **18**:112c

photocell: *see* photoelectric cell.

photochemical equivalence law, a fundamental principle relating to chemical reactions induced by light, which states that for every quantum of radiation that is absorbed, one molecule of the substance reacts. A quantum is a unit of electromagnetic radiation with energy equal to the product of a constant (Planck's constant, h) and the frequency of the radiation, symbolized by the Greek letter nu (ν). In chemistry, the quantitative measure of substances is expressed in terms of gram moles, one gram mole comprising 6.0225×10^{23} (Avogadro's number) molecules. Thus, the photochemical equivalence law is restated as: for every mole of a substance that reacts 6.0225×10^{23} quanta of light are absorbed.

The photochemical equivalence law applies to the part of a light-induced reaction that is referred to as the primary process; that is, the initial chemical change that results directly from the absorption of light. In most photochemical reactions the primary process is usually followed by so-called secondary processes that are normal interactions between reactants not requiring absorption of light. As a result such reactions do not appear to obey the one quantum–one molecule reactant relationship. The law is further restricted to conventional photochemical processes using light sources with moderate intensities; high-intensity light sources such as those used in flash photolysis and in laser experiments are known to cause so-called biphotonic processes; *i.e.*, the absorption by a molecule of a substance of two photons of light.

The photochemical equivalence law is also sometimes called the Stark–Einstein law after the German-born physicists Johannes Stark and Albert Einstein, who independently formulated the law between 1908 and 1913.

photochemical reactions 14:291, chemical processes initiated by the absorption of visible, ultraviolet, or infrared radiation. The most important photochemical process for living systems is photosynthesis, the production by green plants of carbohydrates from carbon dioxide and water. Vision in animals depends on photochemical reactions that occur in the eye, and reactions of this kind are involved in photography, bleaching of laundry and tanning of the skin by sunlight, and in numerous processes used in the chemical industry.

The text article, after a brief survey of the kinds of photochemical reactions, treats the photochemical process, including terms employed in its description, and primary and secondary steps following the absorption of electromagnetic energy; experimental methods used in studying photochemical reactions, including means of illuminating the sample, monitoring the reaction, and determining mechanisms of the reactions; applications of photochemical reactions in chemical synthesis; and the role of these reactions in atmospheric pollution.

REFERENCES in other text articles:
·aeronomy theory and research **2**:325c
·alkane poly-substitution reaction **9**:84d
·aryl halide preparation **13**:689g *passim* to 690g
·atmospheric dissociation and ionization **2**:308h *passim* to 312a
·atmospheric oxygen development **13**:477c
·carbene production techniques **3**:821d
·catalytic chain reaction **3**:1001e
·free radical reaction mechanism **15**:422e
·geochemical processes in primeval atmosphere **6**:711c
·Herschel's interest and success **8**:827b
·light initiated chemical reactions **15**:416c
·mass spectrometric ionization processes **11**:606e
·nerve impulses and birefringence **12**:973a
·photographic image formation **14**:335b
·photoionization laws and principles **15**:410g
·photon activation energy **4**:144f
·photon radiation absorption **6**:655e
·photosynthetic energy conversion **2**:1038g
·photosynthetic rates and mechanisms **14**:367b; illus.
·proto-ocean oxygen production **13**:487c
·radiation properties of light **15**:400d
·rhodopsin light absorption in eye **7**:109b
·semiconductor photoelectric mechanisms **16**:527d
·visual pigment functional mechanisms **14**:363f

RELATED ENTRIES in the *Ready Reference and Index:*
actinometer, chemical; photolysis; photosensitization

photocoagulation, in medicine, the alteration of tissues by beams of intense light to control bleeding.
·eye disease treatment **7**:123e

photocollography (printing): *see* collotype.

photocomposition, also known as PHOTOTYPESETTING or FILMSETTING, method of assembling or setting type by photographing characters on film that, when developed, serve as a basis for making the printing surface. The characters are developed as photographic positives on film or paper from a negative master containing all the characters; the film, carrying the completed text, is then used for making a plate (for letterpress, gravure, or lithographic printing) by a photomechanical process.

Most photocomposing machines automatically select and position the negative of the desired character so that its image is projected on a roll of unexposed film, which is then exposed at high speed. Different sizes of type can be obtained by varying the projection scale. A keyboard similar to a typewriter controls the operation.

Perhaps the most important innovation in typesetting since the development of movable type, photocomposition eliminates metal casting and the depth of the matrix. The page it reproduces is indistinguishable from one printed from metal type. Typesetting by photography was proposed as early as 1866. The Hungarian engineer Eugene Porzolt designed the first photocomposing machine in 1894, but machines such as the Fotosetter did not become available commercially until the 1950s. By the 1960s it was being combined with the digital computer, which prepared tapes and controlled machines in high-speed photocomposition operations. *See also* typesetting machines.
·present-day machines and methods **14**:1062e
·printing development role **18**:52e
·prospects for increasing importance **14**:1073d

photoconductivity, increase in the ability of a material to allow an electric current to flow in it when struck by light, frequently used to detect and measure the amount of light, as in light meters used by photographers.

Many crystals, including those made from the chemical elements silicon and germanium, are poor current conductors because their electrons are unable to move freely within the material when an electrical voltage is applied. Light directed on such materials is absorbed by some electrons, however, freeing them to pass more easily from one atom to the next, when a voltage is applied. In contrast, good conductors such as metals have an abundance of free current carrying electrons even when not struck by light.

When materials such as silicon and germanium are removed from the light, they again exhibit low electrical conductivity because the freed electrons return to their more tightly bound relation. The time required for the reduction to normal conductivity is called the lifetime of a free current carrier and varies widely from one type of crystal to another.

To excite an electron into its freely conducting condition, light must supply a definite amount of energy. For silicon, all visible light and some infrared has sufficient energy for this excitation. In this light range, the number of free or conduction electrons increases with the brightness of the light.
·electron and charged hole production **14**:298f
·electronic cell production **6**:682c
·electrophotographic processes **14**:342b
·phosphor electron excitation **11**:184e
·selenium electrical properties **13**:817g
·semiconductor behaviour and theory **16**:523a
·Vidicon camera tube operation **18**:112g

photocopying machine, device for producing copies of drawings or written material by the use of light, heat, chemicals, or electrostatic charges. Photographic devices most commonly use either diffusion transfer or dye line processes. In the diffusion transfer process, the master copy is made by typing, drawing, or printing on a translucent paper or cloth sheet; it is then placed upon sensitized negative paper and exposed to light. The negative is then placed in contact with a sheet of positive transfer paper and fed into a developer. When these two sheets are peeled apart the image is transferred to the positive paper. The dye line process requires a translucent original and uses only one sheet of sensitized paper, but the principle is similar. The dry dye line process uses ammonia fumes rather than liquid to develop the image, obviating problems of paper shrinkage.

In the commercial application of heat or infrared copying methods, sometimes called thermography, special copy paper and the original copy are placed in contact with each other and passed through a machine where they are exposed to infrared or heat rays. The original copy absorbs the rays in areas darkened by print, line drawings, or illustrations, thereby making the same impressions on the heat-sensitive surface of the copy paper.

Xerography as a means of copying is based on the principles of electrostatics and thus differs from other methods that use chemicals or heat rays. A flexible method, it will copy anything written, printed, typed, or drawn. It requires the preparation of a xerographic photoconductive insulating layer on a conductive support, such as selenium on a sheet of aluminum. This layer is given an electrical charge, exposed, and then sprinkled with powder. Negatively charged powder adheres

to the positively charged image to be copied. A sheet of ordinary paper is placed over the plate and charged positively. The copy paper attracts powder from the plate, forming a direct positive image. This paper is then heated briefly to form a permanent print.
·cancer diagnosis convenience **3**:769a
·image production chemistry **14**:342b
·map compilation in reduction stage **11**:480c
·office duplicating and copying machines **13**:510d
·printing technique and importance **18**:52e

Photocorynus spiniceps, species of angler fish of the order Lophiiformes; the males are minute and remain permanently attached to females as parasites.
·parasitic male as adjunct to female **16**:589d

photocyte, in vertebrate physiology, special light-producing cells found in certain fishes.
·bioluminescent cells in fish **2**:1030h

photodiode, light-sensitive diode (*q.v.*). *See also* photoelectric cell.
·construction, operation, and use **16**:519b
·spectra detection methods **17**:461e

photodisintegration, also called PHOTOTRANSMUTATION, in physics, nuclear reaction in which the absorption of high-energy electromagnetic radiation (a gamma-ray photon) causes the absorbing nucleus to change to another species by ejecting a subatomic particle, such as a proton, neutron, or alpha particle. An isotope of magnesium, for example, magnesium-25, upon absorbing a photon of sufficient energy emits a proton and becomes sodium-24. Photodisintegration differs from the nuclear reaction photofission in which a nucleus upon absorbing a photon splits into two fragments of nearly equal mass.

photodissociation, fragmentation of compounds into neutral atoms or molecules by the action of light.
·light energy absorption principles **14**:293c

photodynamism, the conversion of certain substances in the animal skin into other substances by the action of light. Many of the resultant compounds produce disorders of the skin. The original compound may be present in normal skin; it may be derived from certain foods; it may result from an inherited biochemical defect; or it may be a combination of the preceding.

photoelasticity, the property of some transparent materials, such as glass or plastic, while under stress, to become doubly refracting (*i.e.*, a ray of light will split into two rays at entry). When photoelastic materials are subjected to pressure, internal strains develop that can be observed in polarized light; *i.e.*, light vibrating normally in two planes, which has had one plane of vibration removed by passing through a substance called a polarizer. Two polarizers that are crossed ordinarily do not transmit light, but if a stressed material is placed between them and if the principal axis of the stress is not parallel to this plane of polarization, some light will be transmitted in the form of coloured fringes. Stresses in opaque mechanical structures can be analyzed by making models in plastic and studying the fringe pattern under polarized light, which may be either white (a mixture of all wavelengths) or a single wavelength. A photoelastic model under stress is shown in the photograph. *See* refraction, double.

Photoelastic stress pattern of a ring in diametral compression
By courtesy of Dr. W.M. Murray, Massachusetts Institute of Technology, Cambridge

·cold-cathode electron emission process **6**:688a; illus.
·waterfall recession and crest stresses **19**:642h

photoelectric cell, also called ELECTRIC EYE, PHOTOCELL, or PHOTOTUBE, an electron tube with a photosensitive cathode that emits electrons when illuminated, and an anode for collecting the emitted electrons. Various cathode materials are sensitive to specific spectral regions, such as ultraviolet, infrared, or visible light. The voltage between the anode and cathode causes no current in darkness because no electrons are emitted, but illumination excites electrons that are attracted to the anode, producing current proportional to the intensity of the illumination. These tubes are used in control systems, where interrupting a beam of light by an object, as the body or an arm, brings about the desired operation, as the opening of a door. The tubes are also used in photometry, to measure light intensities, and in spectroscopy.
·astronomical photometry methods **14**:348c
·camera photoelectric systems **14**:332d
·electron emission process and uses **6**:688a; illus.
·electronic tubes and TV transmission **6**:679h
·electro-optics and image detectors **13**:605e
·industrial measurement instrumentation **9**:638h
·meteorological instruments **12**:56d
·motion picture light measurement **12**:547f
·motion picture optical recording **12**:541h
·phototypesetter designs and function **14**:1062h
·printing quality control **14**:1068e
·smoke detection device operation **7**:316e
·solar cell uses and efficiency **2**:769c; table
·star studies with photomultiplier tube **18**:104c
·television systems development **18**:106b

photoelectric effect **14**:296, the interaction of electromagnetic radiation with matter resulting in a dissociation of that matter into electrically charged particles. The simplest example occurs when light shines on a piece of metal and releases electrons.

The text article covers the history of the photoelectric effect from the time it was first observed in the 19th century; photoemission, which explains the theory in terms of quantum mechanics; photoconductivity, the phenomenon of a change in electrical conductivity that many materials exhibit when irradiated; the photovoltaic effect, the generation of an electromotive force due to radiation absorption; the Auger effect, in which certain orbital electrons are released from an atom; the Compton effect, the process whereby a photon shares its energy with an electron; the photonuclear effect, which results in the emission of a neutron or proton from an atomic nucleus; and applications, such as to photocells for exposure meters, semiconductors, solar cells for energy conversion, and television-camera tubes.

REFERENCES in other text articles:
·astronomical photometry methods **14**:347g
·aurora causes and spectral features **2**:375d
·Einstein explanation origin **6**:511e
·Einstein's theory development **6**:653g
·electromagnetic radiation absorption **15**:404e
·electronics and vacuum tube development **6**:678f
·electron surface emission processes **6**:671f
·electrophotographic processes **14**:342b
·gamma ray matter interactions **15**:439g
·implications of discovery **14**:390d
·industrial measurement instrumentation **9**:638h
·ionosphere formation process **9**:810h
·light quantum theory **10**:947a
·light theory development **2**:335d
·luminescence wavelength changes **11**:180b
·metal surface phenomena **11**:1091h
·photochemical reaction theory development **14**:292c
·photochromic hologram recording **8**:1009g
·photomultiplier tube for star study **18**:104c
·photon concept development **11**:795c
·physical constant measurement methods **5**:77b
·semiconductor behaviour research **16**:527c
·smoke detection device operation **7**:316e
·solid state electron emission **16**:1040d
·spectra detection methods **17**:461e
·television camera tube operation **18**:111d
·X-ray particle properties **19**:1060b

RELATED ENTRIES in the *Ready Reference and Index:*
photoconductivity; photoionization; photovoltaic effect; work function, electronic

photoelectric scanner, astronomical device combining the spectroscope and phototube.
·stellar magnitude and spectral type **18**:104d

photoelectron (physics): *see* photo-ionization.

photoemission (physics): *see* photoelectric effect.

photoengraving **14**:300, photochemical techniques for producing a printing plate. The term engraving is also used for the process of creating a work of art by etching and for producing decoration by mechanical incision of a design on a surface. For engraving as the process of creating a work of art, *see* printmaking.

The text article is concerned only with engraving as part of the printing process. It summarizes the history of the techniques developed in the 19th and 20th centuries and describes modern plate making from photography with process camera through plate coating and exposing, etching, finishing, blocking, and proofing; it also explains colour reproduction techniques and such special engraving techniques as intaglio and gravure.

REFERENCES in other text articles:
·application to rotogravure **14**:1056g
·integrated circuitry fabrication **9**:663b
·motion-picture processing machine **12**:548a; illus.
·printmaking technique and history **14**:1083d
·rotogravure plates and press **14**:1069f

photofission, in physics, splitting of an atomic nucleus into two fragments of nearly equal mass when induced by absorption of electromagnetic radiation. It most commonly occurs in heavy nuclei, as in those of uranium or thorium, upon their bombardment by high-energy gamma rays in the 10,000,000 to 20,000,000 electron-volt range. The term is a contraction of photon fission, a photon being the quantum unit of electromagnetic radiation.

Photofission differs from photodisintegration (phototransmutation), a nuclear reaction in which an incident photon, upon being absorbed by a target nucleus, does not cause fission but triggers the emission of neutrons, protons, or alpha particles.
·photonuclear effects **14**:299g

photofluorography, the photography of image produced on a fluroescent screen by X-rays.
·radiologic methodology and applications **15**:462e

photogenic drawing, photographic process invented by W.H.F. Talbot.
·early photographic processes **14**:309g

photogeology, scientific discipline that is concerned with the geological interpretation of aerial photographs. Photogrammetry, the body of knowledge pertaining to the determination of accurate measurements, is utilized in conjunction with knowledge of rocks, soils, vegetation, landforms, and structure to make these interpretations and, quite commonly, to produce a geological or special purpose map from the aerial photographs.

photogrammetry, the use of photographs for measurements in map making and surveying. As early as 1851 the French inventor Aimé Laussedat perceived the possibilities of the application of the newly invented camera to mapping. Laussedat was handicapped by the narrow lenses and imperfections of his equipment, and not for another 50 years was the technique employed with success. In the decade before World War I, terrestrial photogrammetry, as it came to be known later, was widely used; the war introduced the far more effective aerial photogrammetry. From the air, large areas can be photographed quickly with overlapping pictures, and blind areas, hidden from terrestrial cameras, are minimized. Plotting machines and other techniques are used to overcome the complications caused by the lack of known base lines. A wide variety of accurate maps can now be made from aerial photographs, vastly simplifying the problem of mapping inaccessible areas of the world.
·building survey techniques **2**:58g
·map-making techniques **17**:833a
·stereoscopic technique and applications **14**:344c

photographic emulsion, nuclear, radiation detector generally in the form of a glass plate thinly coated with a transparent medium containing a silver halide compound. Passage of charged subatomic particles are recorded in the emulsion in the same way ordinary black and white photographic film records a picture. After photographic developing, a permanent record of the paths of the charged particles remains and may be observed through a microscope. Nuclear emulsions are used especially in cosmic ray research and in high-energy nuclear physics for counting the number of particles in a beam of radiation and for identifying the kind and energy of charged particles, especially those resulting from nuclear reactions involving atomic nuclei of the emulsion itself. Radioactivity itself was discovered in 1896 by its effect on a photographic plate.
·cosmic ray visual detectors **5**:201e

photographic memory: *see* eidetic image.

Photographic Society, founded in London in 1853 and later known as the ROYAL PHOTOGRAPHIC SOCIETY.
·Newton's principles of Fine Art **14**:312d

photographic-stencil method: *see* stencilling.

photography, making a picture of an object by means of a system of lenses and a light-sensitive plate or film. The plate or film may be of cellulose acetate, glass, or other transparent material coated with an emulsion of a halide (or salt) of silver, such as silver bromide or silver chloride. After exposure to light for a certain time period, the film is placed in a chemical developer solution that yields fine black silver particles. The particles cluster where light was strongest on the film, producing a reverse, or negative, image of the light and shadow of the object photographed. The particles are chemically fixed on the negative by washing in a fixer, frequently a solution of sodium thiosulfate called hypo. Other chemicals dissolve the unexposed silver salts, which are washed out with water.

An accurate positive image, or photograph, is made on special sensitized paper by placing the finished negative over the paper and exposing it to light. The lightest portions of the negative transmit the most light, and darker portions screen out more light, so that the negative image is reversed on the print. Fixing and washing of this positive image are performed as for the negative.

The name photography, from Greek *phōtos*, "light," and *graphein*, "to draw," was first used by Sir John Herschel in 1839, replacing the names heliography and sun drawing used by Joseph-Nicéphore Niepce.
·aerial reconnaissance devices **19**:599d
·camera invention and motion pictures **12**:511h
·criminology type variation **14**:675c
·lightning flash studies **10**:969e
·magazines and photojournalism **15**:253g
·mapping techniques and advantages **11**:475b
·microform varieties and library use **10**:872f
·ocean charting and position fixing **9**:98h
·photocopying machines and processes **13**:511d
·photogrammetric development, instrumentation, and innovations **11**:482a
·radiation ionization applications **15**:410d
·reconnaissance aircraft methods **1**:384e
·ship designing applications **16**:694e
·spectra recording methods **17**:461e
·steel quality control **17**:655g
·weather observation and forecasting **19**:698f
·X-ray detection methods **19**:1063c

Photography, a Pictorial Art, title of lecture by Peter Henry Emerson delivered at a meeting of the Camera Club of London in 1886.
·views on aesthetics of photography **14**:316d

photography, art of 14:306, concerns visual communication and expression based on the production of a permanent record of an image by the combined action of light and chemical processing.

TEXT ARTICLE covers:
Lenses **14**:307c
Cameras 307f
Controls in exposure and processing 308c
The pioneers 309b
Developments to World War I 310c
Developments since World War I 318e

REFERENCES in other text articles:
·advertising design development **1**:110e
·amateur participation and diversity **8**:975d
·animation potentialities **1**:919a; illus.
·artistic aspects of training **2**:96d
·camera origins and invention **12**:511h
·Cartier-Bresson's photographic imagery **3**:971d
·cinematic directing and technique **5**:829c
·classification as medium **2**:84c
·motion picture beginnings **12**:540b
·motion picture techniques and style **12**:497c
·photoengraving history and technology **14**:301a *passim* to 306c
·photographic technology development **14**:328d
·printmaking technique assimilation **14**:1084h; illus.
·Steichen's influence and technique **17**:665c
·Stieglitz' art photography exploration **17**:690d

RELATED ENTRIES in the *Ready Reference and Index:*
carte-de-visite; Fotoform; Group f.64; Linked Ring; photomontage; Photo-Secession Group; vortograph

photography, celestial, began with a daguerrotype (the earliest kind of practical photograph) of the Moon, made by the chemist John William Draper of New York City on March 23, 1840. He used an exposure of 20 minutes. Probably the first photograph of a star was a daguerrotype of Vega taken at Harvard College Observatory on July 17, 1850. Because of the poor sensitivity of the daguerrotype process there was little success in stellar photography until the invention of the collodion plate process used in the 1850s. Photographs of the planets were made during the 19th century but showed less detail than could be seen by direct observation. In the 20th century, photography has made it possible to map the Moon in detail and to study, particularly by comparing photographs taken in light of different colours, the surfaces and atmospheres of the planets. The advantages of photography to the astronomer include the making of a permanent record of whatever is observed and the discovery, through time exposures, of objects and details too dim to be seen directly. Automatic cameras are used to record meteors (*see* meteoritics). From spacecraft, close-range photographs have been made of the Moon, the Earth, and other planets. Aboard unmanned craft the film is developed automatically, and the information it contains is sent by radio to Earth where it is used to reproduce the photograph. Photometry, the precise measurement of light, generally by electrical means, has now replaced photography for many astronomical purposes.
·astronomical photometry methods **14**:347f
·astronomical research methods **2**:254b
·dark nebulae and star cluster studies **7**:834h
·external galaxy studies **7**:828e *passim* to 832a
·first solar eclipse photograph **6**:192g
·life detection on other planets **10**:906e; illus.
·mapping of sky with telescope **2**:224a
·Martian observation and mapping **11**:520f
·Mercury surface feature photography **11**:917d
·meteor velocity and height observation **12**:38a
·nebula research techniques **12**:927d
·Pluto's systematic discovery **14**:580c
·Schmidt telescope in star survey **18**:99g
·spectroscopy techniques and equipment **2**:236a
·star maps and catalogues **2**:230c
·stellar parallax measurement **13**:995g
·telescope and stellar astronomy **18**:103g
·time-lapse technique **14**:345c

photography, colour, is accomplished by either of two basic methods. In the additive processes, now seldom used, the subject is photographically separated into its blue, green, and red components (three-colour process), and negative images are used to combine blue, green, and red light to reproduce the subject with the same proportions of colours as in the original. In subtractive processes, positives are made in colours complementary (yellow, magenta, and cyan) to negative images photographed by blue, green, and red light; the three positive layers superimposed on each other reproduce the colours present in the original subject.
·azomethine dye characteristics **5**:1104h
·colour film and development **14**:329h
·colour processing technique and use **14**:309a
·electromechanical colour separation **14**:303a
·holographic colour recording **8**:1008g
·mapping of coastal features **11**:482e
·motion picture colour separation **12**:542b
·printing plate production **14**:304b

photography, infrared, making a picture of an object with film sensitive to invisible infrared radiation instead of to ordinary light. Hot objects emit infrared rays and may be photographed in the dark, showing details of temperature distribution over the surface. Distant objects may be photographed with improved clarity because infrared light is not scattered as much by atmospheric haze as is ordinary light. The technique is widely used in astronomy; nebulae and stars that are invisible because of haze may be photographed by infrared photography. It has been applied to detect irregularities in treated and dyed textiles; to decipher old or altered documents; in aerial photography to observe pollution in streams and lakes and to detect diseased trees in a forest; and, militarily, to distinguish green paint from foliage, revealing camouflage, as chlorophyll is transparent to infrared radiation.
·effects on images **14**:308d

photography, technology of 14:328, production of visible images of objects through the action of light on light-sensitive materials, using various mechanical devices, and physical and chemical techniques.

TEXT ARTICLE covers:
History and basic technology **14**:328d
Cameras and lenses 330d
The photographic process 335a
Polaroid photography 341b
Special photosensitive systems 342a
Special techniques and applied photography 342h
The photograph industry 345g

REFERENCES in other text articles:
·camera idea origins and invention **12**:511h
·Cartier-Bresson's use of Leica **3**:971g
·dye use in development and colour **5**:1104h
·film image production theory **9**:809f
·holography principles and techniques **8**:1007e

·lens design and optical considerations **13**:604c
·motion-picture equipment
  development **12**:542b *passim* to 555a
·photochemical reaction mechanisms **16**:527d
·photoengraving history and
  technology **14**:301a *passim* to 306c
·printing methods development **14**:1056g
·radiation effects in photography **15**:401a
·radiographic film and development **15**:459f
·recent camera and film developments **18**:52e
·rotogravure and other printing
  methods **14**:1069f *passim* to 1073d
·silver in commercial application **16**:777e
·silver recovery in film development **14**:754g
·spectroheliography and related studies **17**:799f
·technique development in the 1800s **18**:44f

RELATED ENTRIES in the *Ready Reference and Index: for*
auxiliary photographic equipment: see enlarger, photographic; exposure meter; filter, light
cameras and their components: camera obscura; camera, photographic; film, photographic; lens, photographic; range finder; shutter, photographic; viewfinder
photographic techniques: calotype; Clayden effect; daguerreotype; dry plate; photography; photography, colour; photography, infrared; photography, ultraviolet; wet collodion process

photography, ultraviolet, making a photograph of an object illuminated with ultraviolet rather than ordinary visible light. In the direct method, a plate or film sensitive to ultraviolet light is exposed to the ultraviolet rays reflected off the object. In the fluorescence method, the ultraviolet light induces fluorescence, or the production of visible light, in the object, and this fluorescent light provides the illumination for the photograph.

Ultraviolet light increases the resolution of a microscope, and, because of the selective absorption of ultraviolet by the specimen, details of structure in a living specimen may be differentiated, making killing and staining unnecessary and giving a more informative picture.

Ultraviolet photography, with its capability of detecting characteristic fluorescences, serves as a tool for identifying paintings, ceramics, grades of paper, and erasures in documents.

Because of the excessive scattering of the short wavelengths of ultraviolet by the atmosphere, ultraviolet photography is not adapted to landscape photography; such photos appear blurred and show no shadows. *Major ref.* **14**:344e

photo-ionization, ejection of an electron, or unit negative charge, from an atom that has been struck by light. The residual charged atom is a positive ion. The pulse of light energy (photon) that is absorbed disappears completely; part of the energy (ionization energy) strips the electron from the atom, and the rest is converted into energy of motion of the removed electron. The large-scale removal of electrons by light from many atoms grouped closely, as in a solid, is called the photoelectric effect.
·aeronomy theory and research **2**:326d
·atmospheric photo-ionization
  mechanisms **2**:311e
·interplanetary hydrogen reactions **9**:787c
·ionosphere formation process **9**:810h
·light energy absorption principles **14**:293b
·photomultiplier tube principles **15**:396f
·photon energy transfer principles **15**:404e
·photovoltaic effect **14**:299b
·silver compound ionization **14**:335b
·X-ray ejection properties **19**:1058h

photoluminescence, emission of light from a substance as a result of absorption of electromagnetic radiation; such a substance is called a phosphor, and the emitted light usually has a longer wavelength than the incident radiation. *Major ref.* **11**:180b
·electromagnetic radiation generation **16**:1043h

photolysis, the term generally applied to the chemical process by which molecules are broken down into smaller units through the use of light. Light is an intense source of energy; hence, the cleavage of chemical bonds, which is the basic process involved in photolysis, often is effected by absorption of light.

The best known example of a photolytic process is the experimental technique known as flash photolysis, employed in the study of short-lived chemical intermediates formed in many photochemical reactions. The technique, developed by the English chemists R.G.W. Norrish and George Porter in 1949, consists of subjecting a gas or liquid to an intense burst of light lasting a few microseconds or milliseconds, followed by a second, generally less intense flash. The first flash dissociates the absorbing compound into short-lived molecular fragments and the second flash provides a means for their identification by spectrophotometry. The method is a valuable tool for the identification of transient chemical intermediates and hence for the study of mechanisms of fast chemical reactions.
·carbene formation from diazo
  compounds **3**:821e
·oxygen production from water molecules
  2:316g; table 318
·photochemical reaction theory
  development **14**:291f
·radical production by radiation **15**:422f

photometry, the science of measuring visible light. The human eye is not uniformly sensitive to radiant energy of all wavelengths but responds most to green light and not at all to wavelengths longer than red and shorter than violet. An arbitrary unit, the lumen, which measures the visual effect of a light source (*see* luminous intensity), is used for the fundamental photometric unit. Photometry is distinguished from radiometry, the science of measuring radiant energy throughout the entire electromagnetic spectrum, from the shortest cosmic rays to the longest electrical waves, in the nonsubjective unit of power, the watt.

The lumen is basic to describing the intensity of light emitted by a point source or the brightness of a surface. It is also employed for measuring the amount of light falling (per unit of time) on a given surface, called illumination. A host of photometric terms is in common use; not all are consistent with one another. No international agreement on a complete set of photometric units has been achieved.
·astronomical photometry **14**:346h
·light measuring devices **10**:965c
·photographic light measurement
  systems **14**:332f
·radiometric analysis principles and
  methods **4**:82h
·radiometric study of geological
  forms **7**:1058d
·spectra analysis methods **17**:475h

photometry, astronomical **14**:346, a branch of astronomy dealing with the measurement and study of the brightness of celestial objects. Modern astronomical photometry more often deals with the measurement of brightness in restricted wavelength (that is, colour regions) than with the measurement of total radiation emitted at all wavelengths of light. It is used in determining the physical properties of stars and other celestial objects.

The text article covers the origin of the magnitude scale (in antiquity); some forerunners of the precisely defined modern colour systems of magnitudes; internationally established colour systems using, generally, three or more colour regions or wavelength bands; special programs, such as magnitude estimates of extended objects (galaxies, some star clusters, and nebulae); and the production of light curves of variable stars.

REFERENCES in other text articles:
·catalogues of stellar magnitudes **2**:230e
·colour index determination **17**:587h
·infrared source detection **9**:582b
·luminosity range in cluster galaxies **18**:1014h
·lunar surface studies **12**:425g
·magnitude, spectra, and distance **7**:835f
·Michelson star diameter measurement **12**:104c
·Pluto's brightness variability **14**:581b
·research techniques and applications **2**:247b
·stellar spectroscopic parallax **13**:996f
·telescopic star magnitude studies **18**:104c
·X-ray and optical radiation
  correlation **19**:1065d

RELATED ENTRIES in the *Ready Reference and Index:*
albedo; light curve; limb darkening; magnitude; seeing; UBV system

photomicrography, photography of objects under a microscope. Opaque objects such as metal and stone may be ground smooth and etched chemically to show their structure and photographed by reflected light with a metallurgical microscope. Biological materials may be killed, dyed so that their structure can be seen, and mounted on glass slides for photographing by transmitted light using ordinary light microscopes; or, by using ultraviolet, infrared, electron, or X-ray microscopes, sharp photographs can be made of living, unstained specimens.

Cinephotomicrography, taking motion pictures of magnified objects, is useful in studying organism growth, colloidal movement, and chemical reactions.
·camera and lens design **14**:344a

photomontage, a pictorial composition made up of parts of different photographs. Photomontages may be made by pasting parts of prints together, by making multiple exposures on a single negative, or by printing superimposed negatives in a single print. The

Study for a composition picture by Henry Peach Robinson, *c.* 1860

By courtesy of the Gernsheim Collection, the University of Texas at Austin

first photomontage was Oscar G. Rejlander's "The Two Ways of Life" (1857), composed of more than 30 negatives. Photomontages became popular in the 19th century. Such 20th-century graphic artists as George Grosz and László Moholy-Nagy used the technique, and Robert Rauschenberg incorporated photomontage into his paintings by the silk-screen process. Contemporary photographers continue to make photomontages, but the technique is now used primarily in advertising design. Photomontage has much in common with collage. *Major ref.* **14**:321f; illus.
·advertising design developments **1**:111a

photomosaic, in mapmaking, technique of assembling pieces of aerial photographs.
·distortion correction in photomapping **11**:482f

photomultiplier tube, electron multiplier tube that utilizes the multiplication of electrons by secondary emission to measure low light intensities. It is useful in television camera tubes, in astronomy to measure intensity of faint stars, and in nuclear studies to detect and measure minute flashes of light. The tube utilizes a photosensitive cathode, that is, a cathode that emits electrons when light strikes it, followed by a series of additional electrodes, or dynodes, each at a successively higher positive potential so that it will attract electrons given off by the previous dynode.

The first dynode is made to emit several electrons by each electron striking it; similarly, each electron from the first dynode causes the second dynode to emit several electrons, leading to an increase, or multiplication, of electrons at each dynode until the final dynode is reached. Total amplification may reach 1,000,000, with nine dynodes customarily employed.

·astronomical photometry methods **14**:348f
·cosmic ray detector principles **5**:201c
·design and scintillation counter use **15**:396f
·electron surface emission processes **6**:671g
·luminescent process in fluoroscope **11**:180c
·mass spectrometer detection system **11**:607a
·photoelectric devices and uses **14**:300a
·spectra detection methods **17**:461f
·stellar magnitude measurements **18**:104d
·television photo amplification **6**:689h; illus. 690
·X-ray detection methods **19**:1063e

photon, a quantum, or minute energy packet of electromagnetic radiation. The concept originated (1905) in Albert Einstein's explanation of the photoelectric effect, in which he proposed the physical existence of discrete energy packets during the transmission of light. Earlier (1900) Max Planck had prepared the way for the concept by explaining that heat radiation is emitted and absorbed in distinct units, or quanta. The concept came into general use after Arthur Compton demostrated (1923) the corpuscular nature of X-rays. The term photon (from Greek *phōs*, *phōtos*, "light"), however, was not used until 1926. The energy of a photon, $h\nu$ (h is Planck's constant and ν is the frequency), depends on radiation frequency; there are photons of all energies from high-energy gamma and X-rays, through visible light, to low-energy infrared. All photons travel at the speed of light. Considered among the subatomic particles, photons are bosons, having no electric charge or rest mass and one unit of spin; they are field particles, or carriers of the electromagnetic field.

·chemical reaction activation energy **4**:144e
·cosmic cascade showers **5**:207g
·electromagnetic wave interaction **4**:172g
·electron–positron production **6**:668c; illus.
·energy laws and principles **6**:853a
·galactic X-ray emission processes **19**:1064f
·ionic crystal radiation absorption **9**:808h
·ionization process in mass spectrometer **11**:606b
·ionosphere formation process **9**:810h
·light aberration on wave hypothesis **10**:950c; illus.
·light composition and behaviour **15**:401d
·light quantum theory **10**:946h
·luminescence activation process **11**:183d
·nebular gas energy emission **12**:929c
·nuclear interactions and spin **5**:35f; table 34
·nuclear interaction with radiation **13**:344f
·photoemission process and energy **14**:297c
·photosynthetic efficiency and light waves **14**:367e
·physical constant measurement theory **5**:75f
·physics principles and research **14**:426d
·probability theory of cascade shower **14**:1113b
·quantum electrodynamics theory **14**:421b
·quantum theory development **11**:794g
·quantum theory of light beams **14**:292c
·radiation detection methods **15**:392e
·relativity theory applications **15**:587h
·semiconductor luminescence mechanisms **16**:527f
·solid state interaction properties **16**:1042c
·spectra emission principles **17**:457d
·subatomic particle properties **13**:1022f; tables 1024
·theoretical formulation and properties **6**:653g
·visual pigment absorption capacities **14**:363f
·X-ray particle properties **19**:1058g

Photon-Lumitype, a series of phototypesetting machines.

·construction, operation, and speed **14**:1064b; illus.

photoperiodism **14**:352, the functional or behavioral response of an organism to changes of duration in daily, seasonal, or yearly cycles of light and darkness. Common examples of photoperiodism include flowering in plants, breeding in animals, and migration in birds.

The text article covers photoperiodism in both plants and animals.

REFERENCES in other text articles:
·acclimatization to temperature change **1**:33a
·agricultural needs and adjustments **1**:358e
·animal day length mechanism **2**:813a
·animal orientation to daylight rhythm **12**:183a
·animal ovulation influences **15**:714f
·animal reproductive cycle control **16**:591b
·biological clock-setting cues and daylength results in animals and plants **14**:69d
·bird mating mechanisms **18**:447h
·conifer production efficiency **5**:6a
·dormancy induction mechanisms **5**:959d
·external control of echinoderm feeding **6**:181a
·falconiform life cycle **7**:145h
·forest community response to change **7**:538c
·grape maturation and sunlight **19**:876g
·light control of plant processes **8**:1108f
·light's effect on growth patterns **8**:442f
·lizard reproduction response **16**:84f
·phytochrome forms and functions **4**:920c
·pigeon reproductive regulation **4**:934h
·pineal body's endocrine gland function **12**:983g
·plankton vertical migration **1**:1031h
·plant development regulation **5**:669g
·pupal diapause in insects **9**:612b
·reproductive physiology of angiosperms **15**:725c
·seasonal adaptations of furbearing animals **7**:812a
·spring community and light intensity **17**:518a
·tropical plants' varied light response **7**:907d
·vegetable farming variables **19**:48b
·waterfowl breeding cycle **1**:944a
·zoological use in aviaries **19**:1162c

photophone, a device whereby a sound signal is transmitted by causing it to modulate a beam of visible or infrared light that is received by a photoelectric cell and reconverted into sound.

·invention and design **2**:827g

photophore, light organ found in certain bioluminescent animals. Photophores are glandular in origin and produce light by a chemical reaction. Photophores vary in size and form but often contain such structures as lenses, reflecting layers, and filters in addition to the light-producing material. The light is emitted when the animal is stimulated in some way.

·cephalopod bioluminescence **3**:1150g
·courtship signals in fireflies **4**:926h
·crustacean luminous features **5**:316c
·decapod patterns and uses **5**:545d
·derivation and possible function **9**:669a
·light-emitting organ structure **2**:1028g
·salmoniform structures and functions **16**:190c

photopigment, in physiology, pigments found in photoreceptors that absorb light. The variety of the pigments determines the number of colours that can be distinguished.

·sensory-reception theory and processes **16**:546d

photopolymer, in chemistry, light-sensitive, polymerized material used in nonphotographic holography.

·hologram image recording **8**:1009f

photoprotein, in biochemistry, protein that can give off light when oxidized. Such a system occurs in *Aequorea*, a luminescent jellyfish; the single organic chemical aequorin requires calcium or strontium ions for luminescence to occur. *Cf.* luciferin.

·bioluminescent chemical reactions **2**:1032b

photoreception **14**:353, the perception of light by an organism through the conversion of light energy to electrochemical energy. Most animals have specialized organs for the perception of light, ranging from the simple structures (eyespots) of one-celled organisms to the complex eyes of arthropods and vertebrates.

The text article surveys the structure, optics, physiology, and biochemistry of photoreceptors, with special emphasis on the eyes of invertebrate animals.

REFERENCES in other text articles:
comparative botany and zoology
·algae eyespot function and morphology **1**:494b
·animal tissue comparisons **18**:447a
·colour vision in honeybees and pollinating birds **14**:745b
·communication channel function of vision **4**:1012e
·Darwin's study of plant adaptation **5**:494h
·deep-sea life vitamin balance **13**:500b
·embryonic brain vesicles and details of eye formation **5**:633f; illus. 631
·hormone control in plants **12**:975h
·lower limit for retina cells **7**:545g
·optical changes in stimulated nerves **12**:973a
·plant and animal responses **14**:352b
·plant germination mechanisms **5**:663f
·sensory-reception theory and processes **16**:545h
·stereotyped responses **17**:675a
·visual response in animals **10**:735e; illus.
invertebrate
·arachnid simple eye variations **1**:1063d
·Araneida rhabdom function **1**:1070f
·arrowworm eye structure **4**:18g
·bee vision and flower characteristics **9**:131b
·Daphnia response to light variations **3**:115a
·homopteran eye comparison **8**:1040b
·insect colour vision and quality **9**:612h
·insect mosaic visual image **9**:618a
·protozoan light-reception structures **15**:125c
·sexual dimorphism in bee vision **9**:127c
vertebrate
·Chiroptera visual specializations **4**:434e
·dog sight limitations **5**:930h
·fish eye and seeing abilities **7**:336b
·horse's eye placement and vision **8**:1089e
·human eye anatomy and function **7**:95f
·neurological tests of optic nerve **12**:1042b
·optic nerve disorders **12**:1048d
·owl sensitivity and eye structure **17**:736b
·primate eye variations **14**:1024c
·processing of stimuli by frog retina **2**:806f
·reptile vision correlations **15**:734g
·salmoniform structural variations **16**:190a
·sensory reception classification **16**:547e
·shark eye pigments **4**:921d
·shark sensitivity to stimuli **16**:496c
·visual effects of retinal damage **7**:120g
·whale sight variations **19**:808g

RELATED ENTRIES in the *Ready Reference and Index:*
eye, invertebrate; eyespot; visual pigment

photorecovery, the restoration to the normal state, by the action of visible light, of the deoxyribonucleic acid composing the hereditary material in animal skin cells and plant epidermal cells damaged by exposure to ultraviolet light. The phenomenon is also called photoreactivation, especially in micro-organisms. The failure of cells to repair such damage, in individuals with certain biochemical disorders, leads to serious skin problems.

·repair of radiation damage **15**:390b

photorepair, opening of bonds between dimers (chemical bonds between neighbouring pyrimidines) by shortwave visible light which restores the original state of DNA before mutational changes occur.

·radiation-induced mutation reversal **12**:755f

Photo-Secession Group, the first important group of U.S. photographers that worked to get photography accepted as an art form. Led by Alfred Stieglitz (1864–1946), the group also included Edward Steichen (1879–1973), Clarence H. White (1871–1925), Gertrude Käsebier (1852–1934), and Alvin Langdon Coburn (1882–). These photographers broke away from the New York Camera Club in 1902 and began the practice of manipulating negatives and printing paper to approximate the effects of drawings, etchings, and oil paintings.

The Photo-Secession Group actively promoted its ideas. It published the important quarterly *Camera Work*, edited by Stieglitz, who also opened the Little Gallery (also known as the Photo-Secession Gallery and "291" from its address on Fifth Avenue), providing the group with a place to exhibit their work. In 1910 the Photo-Secession sponsored an international show of over 500 photographs by its members or photographers whose aims were similar to its own. Held in the Albright-Knox Art Gallery in Buffalo, it was the first time that an entire U.S. museum was given over to the exhibition of photographs. The show was a sensation and encouraged acceptance of photography as an art form.

By 1910, however, the members of the Photo-Secession had become divided. Some continued to manipulate their negatives and prints to achieve nonphotographic effects, while others came to feel that such manipulation destroyed tone and texture and was inappropriate to photography. Torn by this division, the group soon dissolved.

·photography as an artistic concern **14**:318a
·Steichen's promotion of photography as art **17**:665d
·Stieglitz' art photography promotion **17**:691a

photosensitivity, intolerance to light. It is basic to the photographic process, in which it is chemically induced. Evidence of it appears in many persons, especially blond and redheaded, whose skin is reddened by relatively brief exposure to sunlight because they do not experience such protective responses as thickening of the skin and tanning. It may be brought on by such diseases as lupus erythematosus, porphyria, and liver disease and also by many drugs and dyestuffs.

·biomedical models, table 1 **5**:866
·photodynamic sensitizing substances **15**:390f
·skin response to drugs **16**:849a

photosensitization, the process of initiating a reaction through the use of a substance capable of absorbing light and transferring the energy to the desired reactants. The technique is commonly employed in photochemical work, particularly for reactions requiring light sources of certain wavelengths that are not readily available. A commonly used sensitizer is mercury, which absorbs radiation at 1849 and 2537 angstroms; these are the wavelengths of light produced in high-intensity mercury lamps. Also used as sensitizers are cadmium; some of the noble gases, particularly xenon; zinc; benzophenone; and a large number of organic dyes.

In a typical photosensitized reaction, as in the photodecomposition of ethylene to acetylene and hydrogen, a mixture of mercury vapour and ethylene is irradiated with a mercury lamp. The mercury atoms absorb the light energy, there being a suitable electronic transition in the atom that corresponds to the energy of the incident light. In colliding with ethylene molecules, the mercury atoms transfer the energy and are in turn deactivated to their initial energy state. The excited ethylene molecules subsequently undergo decomposition. Another mode of photosensitization observed in many reactions involves direct participation of the sensitizer in the reaction itself.

·discovery as basis of printing methods **14**:1056g
·photochemical energy transfer **14**:294f
·photoconductivity theory **14**:298g
·rotogravure and other printing methods **14**:1069f *passim* to 1071d

photosphere, the visible surface of the Sun, about 400 kilometres (250 miles) thick, from which is emitted most of the Sun's light that reaches the Earth directly. Light generated deeper in the Sun cannot get out without absorption and re-emission. Temperatures in the Sun's photosphere range from about 10,000° K (18,000° F) at the bottom to 4,400° K (8,000° F) at the top; density is about $1/1,000$ that of air at the surface of the Earth. Sunspots are photospheric phenomena.

Large-scale images of the photosphere show a granular structure. Each grain or cell is a mass of hot gas several hundred kilometres in diameter; each rises from inside the Sun, radiates energy, and sinks back within a few minutes to be replaced by others in a constantly changing pattern, shown particularly well in time-lapse motion pictures of the Sun.

·appearance and physical basis **17**:801; illus.
·screening during eclipse **6**:192d
·solar abundances, table 2 **17**:803
·spectroscopic research methods **2**:238a
·stellar radiation emission **2**:251f

photosynthesis **14**:365, in green plants, the conversion—in the presence of light—of water, carbon dioxide, and minerals into oxygen and various organic compounds.

The text article includes sections on the importance, evolution, and overall reaction of photosynthesis; factors that influence the rate; the energy efficiency of the process; and ways of studying it. The role of chloroplasts is dealt with, and a detailed explanation of photosynthesis concludes the article.

REFERENCES in other text articles:
·agricultural needs and adjustments **1**:358d
·algae contribution to biosphere **1**:487b
·algae light requirements **1**:493b
·aquatic ecosystem productivity factors **1**:1029h
·aquatic–terrestrial productivity ratio **1**:1035a
·biochemical study of nutritional needs **2**:995d
·biological carbon concentration **6**:713e
·biosphere energy dynamics **2**:1038g; illus. 1039
·botany research history **3**:65g
·Cambrian fauna and atmospheric effect **3**:691h
·carbohydrate production and use **3**:824a
·chlorophyll types and properties **4**:919a
·conifer production factors **5**:5h
·desert plant modifications **5**:617b
·energy production in plants and animals **14**:437f
·evolution of autotrophic plants **7**:18b
·evolution of early life and plastids **14**:377f
·forest production of organic matter **7**:541h
·geochemical processes in primeval atmosphere **6**:711b
·gymnosperm stem features **8**:522b
·isotopic study of oxidation process **15**:453h
·lake conditions and occurrence **10**:612g
·lichen independence of environment **10**:884e
·life cycle of plants **10**:896b
·light control of plant processes **8**:1108e
·magnesium role in light reaction **1**:593f
·metabolic synthesis in autotrophs **4**:1028f
·nutrient intake mechanisms in plants **5**:781b
·nutrient metabolic types and evolution **13**:401g; table 402
·oil shales' biogenic origin **13**:536f
·oxygen production from water molecules **2**:316h; table 318
·plankton productivity **14**:495h
·plant internal transport roles **14**:501a
·Priestley's study of light and air **14**:1014b
·radiation's biological effects **15**:414g
·reduction reaction significance **13**:805f
·seawater biochemical cycles **9**:124h
·seawater oxygen production **13**:486c
·soil organisms and carbon utilization **16**:1015d; illus. 1017
·transition metal biological functions **18**:609d

phototransistor, type of transistor (*q.v.*) that is sensitive to light.

·construction and operation **16**:521c
·electronic photoconductivity devices **6**:682d

phototransmutation (physics): *see* photodisintegration.

phototroph (biology): *see* nutritional type.

phototropism (biology): *see* tropism.

phototube: *see* photoelectric cell.

phototypesetting: *see* photocomposition.

photovoltaic effect, process in which two dissimilar materials pressed into tight contact act as an electric cell when struck by light or other radiant energy. If the free ends of the two materials are connected by a wire, an electric current flows. This current can be used to measure the brightness of the incident light or to power an electrical circuit, as in the modern solar battery.

A solar battery is a combination of many individual photovoltaic cells. One composed of two different types of silicon crystals can supply 170 watts of electric power per square metre (16 watts per square foot) of the contact area between the two materials when struck by sunlight outside the Earth's atmosphere. This ability represents an efficiency of 14 percent in the conversion of the Sun's light energy into electrical energy. A germanium photovoltaic battery produces a voltage of one-half volt when illuminated.

Light striking such crystals as silicon or germanium, in which electrons are usually not free to move from atom to atom within the crystal, provides the energy needed to free some electrons from their bound condition. Free electrons cross the junction between two dissimilar crystals more easily in one direction than in the other, giving one side of the junction a negative charge and, therefore, a negative voltage with respect to the other side, just as one electrode of a battery has a negative voltage with respect to the other. The photovoltaic battery can continue to provide voltage and current as long as light continues to fall on the two materials. The ability to provide current is greater when the battery is struck by brighter light.

·electronic cell production **6**:682c
·ionization and current generation **14**:299b

Photuris, genus of the insect family Lampyridae (order Coleoptera). *See* firefly.

Photuris versicolor, a species of firefly of the order Coleoptera.

·predatory subterfuge, illus. 2 **12**:217

Phoxinus (fish genus): *see* minnow; dace.

Phra (Egyptian god): *see* Re.

Phra Aphaimani, poetic romance by Thai 18th century writer Sunthon Phu.

·Thai court poetry decline **17**:235d

Phraaspa, old Parthian town alleged to be the birthplace of Zoroaster.

·development and design **18**:1066h

Phraates I, Parthian king, reigned *c.* 176–171 BC.

·Parthian expansion and succession **9**:842c

Phraates II, Parthian PRDTY II, New Persian FARHĀD II (d. 128 BC), king of Parthia in ancient Persia (reigned *c.* 138–128 BC), the son and successor of Mithradates I. Phraates was attacked in 130 by the Seleucid Antiochus VII Sidetes, who after initial successes was defeated and killed during 129 in Media. With his defeat, Seleucid dominion over the countries east of the Euphrates River was finally ended. During these wars great changes had taken place in eastern Persia, into which two powerful nomadic tribes, the Sacae and the Tochari, had forced their way. Phraates advanced against them, pressing into service Greek prisoners from the army of Antiochus; but when the Greeks deserted him in battle, Phraates was defeated and slain. He was succeeded by his uncle Artabanus II.

·Parthian victory over Macedonians **9**:842h

Phraates III, Parthian PRDTY, New Persian FARHAD (d. *c.* 57 BC), king of Parthia in ancient Persia (reigned 70–58/57 BC); he was the son and successor of Sanatruces (Sinatruces). On his accession, the Roman general Lucullus was preparing to attack King Tigranes I of Armenia, who had wrested several vassal states from the Parthian kingdom. Phraates declined to assist Tigranes against the Romans; instead he made an alliance with the Roman general Pompey and invaded Armenia (66 BC). Pompey at first abandoned all of Mesopotamia to Phraates, but later he reversed his stand and occupied the Parthian vassal states of Gordyene and Osroëne. Before Phraates could take any action, he was murdered by his two sons, Orodes II and Mithradates III.

·Roman treachery and defeat **9**:843e

Phraates IV, Parthian PRDTY, New Persian FARHAD (d. 2 BC), king of Parthia in ancient Persia (reigned *c.* 37–2 BC); he murdered his father, Orodes II, and his brothers to secure the throne. In 36 the Romans under Mark Antony attacked Parthia, penetrating through Armenia into Media Atropatene. Phraates, however, defeated Antony, who retreated with heavy losses. In 34 Phraates' vassal king in Media made an alliance with Antony; but when Antony later withdrew, the Parthians reoccupied Media. A revolt soon broke out in Parthia, and Tiridates II of Armenia drove Phraates from the throne, forcing him to take refuge with the Sacae nomads. In 30, however, Phraates was able to regain power, and Tiridates fled to the Romans with the son of Phraates as a hostage.

Phraates IV, coin, 1st century BC; in the British Museum

By courtesy of the trustees of the British Museum; photograph, J.R. Freeman & Co. Ltd.

The emperor Augustus made peace with Phraates and returned his son. Armenia and Osroëne were recognized as Roman dependencies. Augustus also sent Phraates an Italian concubine named Musa. On her advice, Phraates sent four of his sons to Rome, where they remained as hostages of Augustus. Phraates was later poisoned by Musa, who then ruled jointly with her son Phraates V.

·Parthian royal succession struggle **9**:844b

Phraates V, or PHRAATACES, Parthian PRDTY (d. *c.* AD 4), king of Parthia in ancient Persia (reigned *c.* 2 BC–*c.* AD 4); he was the son and successor of Phraates IV. His mother, Musa, secured the throne for him by murdering his father. The two were later married (AD 2) and ruled jointly. Under Phraates, war with Rome threatened to break out over the control of Armenia. When the Roman emperor Augustus sent his adopted son Gaius Caesar to invade Parthia, the Parthians preferred to conclude a treaty (AD 1), by which Armenia was recognized as being in the Roman sphere. Together with his mother, Phraates was later slain or driven into Syria.

·Parthian Oedipal event **9**:844e

Phra Chedi Sam Ong (Thailand): *see* Three Pagodas Pass.

Phrae, administrative headquarters of Phrae province (*changwat*), northern Thailand, lies south of the Doi (mountain) Luang Phra Bang Range on the Mae Nam (river) Yom, in a rice-growing region. It is also a commercial centre for teak. Phrae province has an area of 2,257 sq mi (5,847 sq km). Latest pop. est. town, 17,410; (1970 prelim.) province, 365,000. 18°07′ N, 100°11′ E

·area and population table **18**:202
·map, Thailand **18**:198

Phragmipedium (orchid): *see* lady's slipper.

Phragmites, genus of widely distributed reedlike grasses.

·marsh types and characteristic flora **17**:839c

phragmocone, in belemnites and other mollusks, a cone internally divided by a series of septa and perforated by a partly calcareous median tube of skin.

·belemnite cephalopods, illus. 5 **3**:1153

phragmoplast, in biology, the name given to the spindle when it assumes a barrel shape during mitosis.

·mitotic processes and structures **3**:1055f

Phra Nakhon, or PHRA NAKORN, province (*changwat*) of south central Thailand, encompassing Bangkok, the nation's capital and largest city. Thailand's most populous and most densely populated province, it occupies an area of 598 sq mi (1,549 sq km). It lies on the east bank of the Mae Nam Chao Phraya (Chao Phraya River), in the heart of Thailand's canal-ribbed rice-producing area. The province also produces most of the nation's fruits and vegetables.

Industry and government, as well as commerce and educational institutions, are concentrated in Phra Nakhon, which is the hub of Thailand's rail, air, and highway networks. Bangkok International (Don Muang) Airport, north of Bangkok, is one of the largest and busiest international airports in Southeast Asia. Khlong Toei Harbour is a flourishing river and ocean port, and Nong Chok and Bang Khen are major service towns. Pop. (1970 prelim.) 2,132,000.

·area and population table **18**:202

Phra Nakhon Si Ayutthaya, also called AYUTTHAYA, AYUDHYA, AYUTHIA, and PHRA-NAKHORN SRI-AYUTHA, province (*changwat*) and former Thai capital, central Thailand. The province lies immediately north of Bangkok and Phra Makhon *changwat*.

The town was founded by Ramathibodi I *c.* 1350 on an island formed by the Mae Nam (river) Lop Buri at the mouth of the Mae Nam Pa Sak and intersected by many canals. Political Thailand (Siam) is said to date from its founding, for the kingdom became one of the most powerful states in Southeast Asia. It claimed allegiance from all of present-day Thailand, except Chiang Mai province in the far north, and Burma from Moulmein southward. Often referred to as Krung Kao ("ancient capital"), the town flourished for more than 400 years with extensive political and commercial ties. A wealth of architecture, art, and literature survived its sack in 1767 by invading Burmese; the seat of government was moved 45 mi (72 km) south to Bangkok.

The modern town, set quietly among its magnificent ruins, is now the administrative headquarters for Phra Nakhon Si Ayutthaya province and is linked by road, rail, and river with Bangkok. It is the site of Ayuthaya Agricultural College, and is a commercial centre for an intensive rice-growing area. Secondary crops include corn (maize), tobacco, and sesame.

Ayutthaya's busiest "street" is a waterway, a large floating market crowded with houseboats and shop boats. Tourism is a major source of income, and visitors frequent the town's numerous shrines and temples. At the Chao Sam Phraya National Museum bronze images of Buddha date from the foundation of the capital, and its Thai Pavilion holds relics of Buddha. The Phra Sri Sanpet monastery served as the royal chapel, and the Chedi Sri Suriyothai is a memorial to a famous queen, Sri Suriyothai, who died trying to save her husband during a 1563 battle with the Burmese. Phra Monkal Borpitr contains one of the world's largest seated Buddhas, a bronzed image that was built by King Ekathotsarat early in the 17th century.

Phra Nakhon Si Ayutthaya province has an area of 958 sq mi (2,480 sq km), well irrigated by the wide, central portion of the Mae Nam (river) Chao Phraya system. Like the provincial headquarters, its major towns are riverine and include Sena, Bang Ban, and Maha Rat. The former royal summer palace is at Bang Pa-in. Pop. (latest est.) town, 39,291; (1970 prelim.) province, 421,000. *Major ref.* **16**:719f

·Buddhist influence of Khmers **3**:412e
·Burmese tribal kingdom formation **3**:512e
·Malayan history and conquests **11**:365f
·map, Thailand **18**:198
·Siamese ancient capital and significance **2**:684e

Phra Naret (king of Siam): *see* Naresuan.

Phraortes, Iranian FRAVARTISH (d. 653 BC), a name used by the 5th-century BC Greek historian Herodotus for the king of Media from 675 to 653 BC, apparently in reference to Khshathrita (Assyrian Kashtariti). Phraortes was originally a village chief of Kar Kashi but later subjugated the Persians and a number of other Asian peoples, eventually forming an anti-Assyrian coalition of Medes and Cimmerians. In his attack on Assyria, however, he was defeated and killed in battle.

Another Phraortes was a usurper who reigned for a short time in Media during a rebellion against the Achaemenian king Darius I in 522 BC. Darius' rock inscription at Bīsitūn relates that "a man of the name of Fravartish [*i.e.*, Phraortes], a Mede, rebelled in Media and spoke to the people thus 'I am Khshathrita, of the family of Uvakhshtra [Cyaxares].'" After a short reign this king was defeated and executed at Ecbatana, the Median capital. The deception of the usurper Phraortes probably led to Herodotus' mistake about the name of the earlier king.

·Herodotus' and Assyrian records **9**:832g

Phra Prang Sam Yot, temple located at Lop Buri, Thailand.

·Khmer architectural style **17**:256d

phrase, division of a musical line.

·structural organization of melody **12**:725c

phratry, a term used by anthropologists to designate a cluster of sibs, clans, or kinship groups claiming common unilineal descent that have grouped together, either because they share a belief in a common ancestor or because even though the sibs or clans are actually unrelated by blood, they have adopted common ceremonial and kinship practices, such as exogamy (*i.e.*, the custom of marrying outside one's group). The term phratry also must refer to three or more groups constituting a tribal society. (With only two such groupings, the society takes on features of dual organization, and the groups are termed moieties.)

A description of the phratry in relation to sib and moiety is useful. A sib, as has been noted, is a group of unilineal descent groups, either matrilineal or patrilineal, whose members claim a common ancestor, even if the latter cannot be traced. (Some anthropologists, particularly in Europe, use the word clan instead of sib.) The next order of magnitude in social groupings above the lineage (*q.v.*) and the sib is the phratry, a group of sibs banded together for common practical or ceremonial purpose or because of kinship claims. Finally comes the moiety, one of two exhaustive divisions of a society, each moiety containing a number of sibs and possibly of phratries. If three or more phratries are not further distributed into moieties, however, relationships between members of different phratries will not take on the characteristics of dual organization, which appear only when a society is divided into two moieties. *See also* dual organization; clan.

·Ancient Greece's social units **8**:334g
·Hopi Indian kinship grouping **17**:307a
·Plains Indian kinship groups **13**:225b

Phraya Taksin (Siamese king): *see* Taksin.

phreatophyte, plant that lives in dry regions along streams or in areas with a shallow water table. These plants (*e.g.*, mesquite, cottonwood, tamarisk) have very deep roots that absorb enough water for them to live.

·groundwater utilization and importance **8**:437a; table
·individuals and characteristics **8**:278c

phrenic nerve, branch of the cervical plexus, found in both sides of the neck and chest. It is composed of sensory and motor nerve fibres and innervates several visceral structures, especially the diaphragm (*q.v.*).
·anatomic interrelationships **12**:1023c
·diaphragm paralysis **15**:778a
·human liver anatomy **10**:1268h
·nerve impulse phenomena, illus. 1 **12**:968

phrenic veins, inferior, in anatomy, blood vessels that carry blood from various viscera to the inferior vena cava.
·human cardiovascular system anatomy **3**:885a

phrenology, analysis of the contours of the skull to determine a person's dispositions, characteristics, and talents. Franz Joseph Gall (1758–1828), a Viennese doctor, introduced the notion that the physical formation of the skull was directly related to such things as intellectual capacity, religious beliefs, and propensity to crime. His disciple Johann Kaspar Spurzheim (1776–1832), did much to foster popular interest in phrenology. Lectures on phrenology were banned in Vienna from 1802,

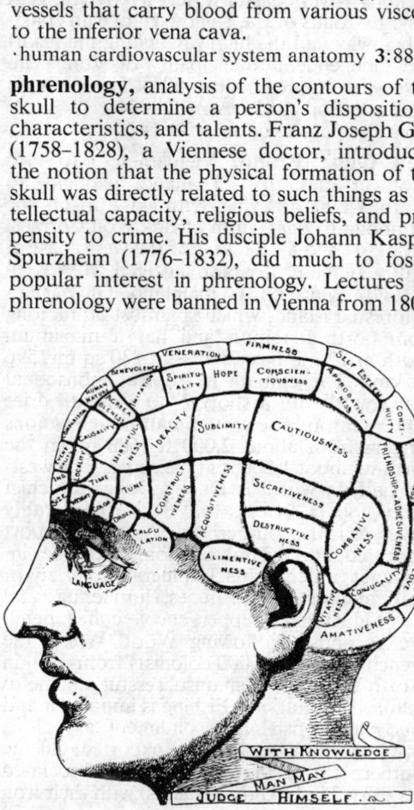

Phrenological diagram, 1893
Radio Times Hulton Picture Library

chiefly because Gall's doctrines implied elements of determinism, which the regime in Austria found disturbing. In modern times, phrenology has given way to more scientific methods of discerning personality.
·history of medicine before 1900 **11**:831c

Phrixothrix, a genus of railroad worm, or glowworm, of the order Coleoptera.
·bioluminescence in each body segment **2**:1031c

Phrixus (Greek mythology): *see* Argonauts.

Phrom River, stream of central Thailand. 16°27′ N, 102°18′ E
·Mekong River area hydroelectric project **11**:862g

Phryganeidae, family of caddisfly of the order Trichoptera.
·classification criteria **18**:710f

Phryganopsychidae, family of caddisfly of the order Trichoptera.
·classification criteria **18**:710f

Phrygia, ancient district in west central Anatolia, named after a people the Greeks called Phryges, who dominated Asia Minor between the Hittite collapse (13th century BC) and the Lydian ascendancy (7th century BC). The Phrygians, perhaps of Thracian origin, settled in northwestern Anatolia late in the 2nd millennium. Upon the disintegration of the Hittite kingdom they moved into the central highlands, founding their capital at Gordium and an important religious centre at "Midas City" (modern Yazılıkaya).

Between the 12th and 9th centuries Phrygia formed the western part of a loose confederation of peoples (identified as "Mushki" in Assyrian records) that dominated the entire Anatolian peninsula. This early civilization borrowed heavily from the Hittites, whom they had replaced, and established a system of roads later utilized by the Persians. About 730 the Assyrians detached the eastern part of the confederation, and the locus of power shifted to Phrygia proper under the rule of the legendary king Midas.

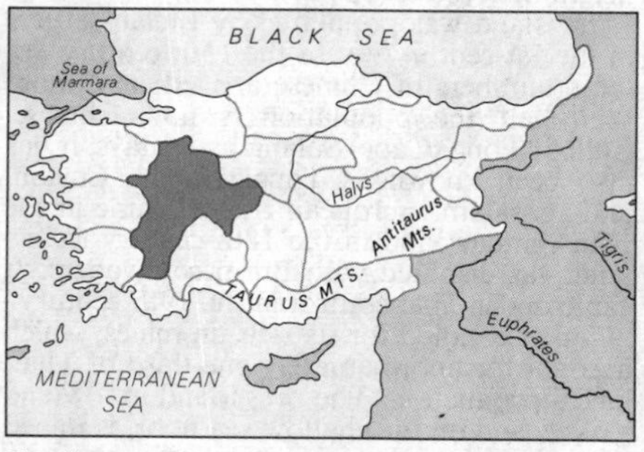

The district of Phrygia under the Roman Empire
From W. Shepherd, *Historical Atlas*, Harper & Row, Publishers (Barnes & Noble Books), New York; revision copyright © 1964 by Barnes & Noble, Inc.

Midas' kingdom came to an abrupt end (*c.* 700) with the invasions of the Cimmerians, a trans-Caucasian people who burned Gordium and transferred the hegemony of western Anatolia to the Lydians. After the Cimmerian invasion Phrygia lingered as a geographical expression under the successive rulers of Anatolia; its people were valued as slaves by the Greeks. The Phrygians excelled in metalwork and wood carving and are said to have originated the art of embroidery. Some magnificently carved stone tombs and shrines were uncovered after World War II by American archaeologists. Among the various Phrygian religious practices, the cult of the Great Mother (Cybele) predominated and was passed on to the Greeks.

The Phrygian cap, a soft conical headdress worn by the ancient Phrygians, symbolized the setting free of Greek and Roman slaves and, after the French Revolution, has been identified with the liberty cap.
·Anatolian independent invasion **1**:830f
·Anatolian religion and Cybele cult **2**:192h
·Assyrian territorial conflicts **11**:984f
·Boğazköy post-Hittite settlements **2**:1182h
·Greek conquests and Hellenistic kingdoms maps **8**:374
·origins, culture, and significance **1**:819f; maps
·sepulchral epigraphic comparison **6**:922h
·visual art of Anatolia **19**:267e; illus. 269

Phrygian cap, soft felt or wool conically shaped headdress fitting closely around the head and characterized by a pointed crown that curls forward. It originated in the ancient country of Phrygia in Asia Minor and is represented in ancient Greek art as the type of headdress worn by Orientals. In Rome the Phrygian cap was worn by emancipated slaves as a symbol of their freedom. During the 11th and 12th centuries it was again extensively used.

Youth wearing a Phrygian cap, marble, Roman copy of a Greek original, 4th century BC; in the Fitzwilliam Museum, Cambridge, Eng.
By permission of the Syndics of the Fitzwilliam Museum, Cambridge, Eng.

The Phrygian cap once more became the emblem of liberty in the 18th century during the French Revolution, when it was adopted by the Revolutionaries as "the red cap of liberty." It continues to be associated with the national allegorical figure of Liberté.

Phrygian language, ancient language spoken in north central Asia Minor north and east of Lydia. Texts occur in two alphabets corresponding to two separate time periods: Old Phrygian texts in an early Greek alphabet, dating from *c.* 730–450 BC, and New Phrygian texts (most of them sepulchral inscriptions) in the Greek alphabet from the 1st and 2nd centuries AD. Phrygian is believed by most scholars to be an Indo-European language somehow connected to Greek or Armenian.
·aboriginality according to Herodotus **10**:643g
·alphabetic inscriptions research **1**:832h
·Anatolian affiliations **1**:830f
·epigraphic inscription study **1**:838b
·Indo-European grammatical character **1**:833h

Phrygian mode, musical mode having the scale pattern E–F–G–A–B–C–D–E. The Phrygian mode was the third of the eight medieval church modes. In that context, Phrygian mode, or Mode III, implies a general range from the E below middle C to the E above, with melodies normally having the lower E as the *finalis*, or final note, and C as the *tenor*, or reciting note.

In ancient Greek music, Phrygian referred to the scale pattern, or octave species, conventionally represented in modern writings as D–D.
·history, construction, and use **12**:296a

Phrymaceae, family of herbs of the order Lamiales.
·classification and general features **10**:622e

Phryma leptostachya, a species of lopseed of the order Lamiales.
·Lamiales distribution features **10**:619h

Phryne (Greek: Toad), nickname of the Athenian courtesan MUESARETE (fl. 4th century BC), the model for Appelles' picture of Aphrodite Anadyomene (Rising from the Sea), and also probably for the statue of the Cnidian Aphrodite by Praxiteles, her lover.

Phrynichida: *see* tailless whip scorpion.

Phrynichus, the name of three important ancient Athenians and one Bithynian.

One Athenian tragic poet (flourished *c.* 500 BC), was an older contemporary of Aeschylus, and the earliest tragedian of whose work some conception can be formed. His first victory was probably about 510, and he was probably the first to introduce the female mask; *i.e.*, women characters, into his plays. The extant fragments are too meagre to be revealing: the titles *Danaides* and *Aegyptii* indicate the same theme as an Aeschylean trilogy, and the *Alcestis* anticipates Euripides. After the fall of Miletus in 494 he produced the *Capture of Miletus*, which so harrowed Athenian feelings that he was fined; in 476 his *Phoenissae*, in which news of the battle of Salamis comes to the Persian court, proved a more acceptable subject and won the first prize.

A second Phrynichus, an Athenian poet of the Old Comedy (fl. *c.* 420 BC), a contemporary of Aristophanes, began producing in 430 and won two victories. His most clearly recognizable subjects show an odd parallelism with Aristophanes: his *Monotropos* ("The Solitary"), which rejected contemporary civilization, was placed third when the *Birds* was second, in 414, and his *Muses* second to the *Frogs* in 405.

Phrynichus Arabius, of Bithynia (2nd century AD), grammarian and rhetorician, produced *Sophistike Paraskeue* ("A Grounding in Sophistic"), of which a few fragments and a summary by Photius survive, and an *Attikistes*, extant in an abridged form, called the *Ekloge* ("Selected Atticisms"). He is critical not only of contemporary deviations from the best Old Attic usage but also of what he considers the lapses of his Attic models themselves. In spite of some mistaken pedantry his judgments are often acute and learned, and a useful commentary on the language of his own day.

An Athenian general called Phrynichus (fl. 5th century BC), fought in the Peloponnesian War. He took a leading part in establishing the oligarchy of the Four Hundred at Athens in 411 BC, and, according to Thucydides, was assassinated in the same year.

Phrynomerus: *see* narrow-mouthed toad.

Phrynosoma (lizard): *see* horned toad.

Phthah (Egyptian religion): *see* Ptah.

phthalic acid, in chemistry, any of three isomeric acids $C_8H_6O_4$ obtained by oxidation of various benzene derivatives.

·alkyd plastics production and uses **14**:512g

phthalocyanine dyes, a series of organic dyestuffs and pigments noted for their high stability when exposed to light, heat, acids, and alkalies. Most of the members of the series are bright blue or green in colour; they are primarily used in inks, enamels, and paints.

·manufacturing processes and raw materials **5**:1102a
·synthetic dyestuff development **5**:1107g
·usage and high quality **13**:889c

phthanite (geology): *see* chert and flint.

Phthiraptera 14:373, order of insects including the chewing or biting lice (Mallophaga) and the sucking lice (Anoplura). These small wingless insects are parasites on birds and mammals and may transmit diseases.

The text article covers general features, natural history, and form and function and includes an annotated classification of the order.

REFERENCE in other text article:
·dog infestations and treatment **5**:934b

RELATED ENTRIES in the *Ready Reference and Index:*
bird louse; chewing louse; human louse; louse; pubic louse; sucking louse

Phthirus pubis: *see* pubic louse.

phthisis: *see* tuberculosis.

Phu Bon, province (*tinh*), central highlands of South Vietnam. Somewhat isolated, its main northwest–southeast-trending valley, cut by the Song (river) Da Rang and its tributaries, is flanked by high hills of the Chaîne Annamitique (Annamite Mountains) rising to about 3,300 ft (1,000 m). The 1,850-sq-mi (4,785-sq-km) province is occupied predominantly by non-Vietnamese peoples; Hroy and Krung tribes of the Cham (Austronesian) family are found both north and south of the Song Da Rang, and Mon-Khmer-speaking Bahnar are chiefly north of the stream. Economic activities are limited, the tribes practicing shifting cultivation and raising valley and upland rice. Hau Bon (Che Reo), the provincial seat, sits on the south bank of the Song Da Rang just below the confluence of the Ia (river) Ayun and Song Ba. It is linked to Tuy Hoa on the coast and to My Thach in Pleiku province by an unpaved secondary road, which generally follows the Song Da Rang and Ia Ayun valleys. It has a hospital and an all-weather commercial airport. Pop. (1971 est.) 69,765.

·area and population table **19**:142

Phuket, island province (*changwat*), southwestern Thailand, in the Andaman Sea, off the west coast of peninsular Thailand. Its area of 309 sq mi (801 sq km) is mostly level land but is dotted with isolated hills that reach a height of 1,700 ft (520 m).

The island was populated by Indian settlers in the 1st century BC. In the 15th century AD, large numbers of Chinese arrived; and more than half the population is now Chinese. Called Ujong (Cape) Salang by Malays, it has also been known as Tongka, Junk Ceylon, and Jonsalam. European traders came in the 16th century; and in the 18th century the island was disputed with Burmese invaders. It came under Thai control in the 19th century.

Phuket is noted for its rich tin mines, which account for approximately one-third of Thailand's production. The ore, found in lowland gravels and on the shallow sea floor, is mined by river and ocean boat dredges and pumps.

The island is reached by ferry from Phangnga province, north across a narrow strait. A road links the major settlements of Thalang, Phuket (the provincial capital), and Ban Rawai.

Phuket city, located in the southeastern portion of the island, is the main Thai port and commercial centre on the Andaman Sea. Its harbour exports tin, rubber, charcoal, lumber, and fish products south to Malaysia and Singapore and north to Burma. Rice and manufactures are imported. The city is served by an airfield. Pop. (latest est.) city, 34,744; (1970 prelim.) province, 100,000.

·area and population table **18**:202
·map, Thailand **18**:198

Phūlbani, town and district, central Orissa state, India. The district, also called Baudh-Khondmals, is 4,278 sq mi (11,081 sq km) in area and consists of a plain in the north, across which the Mahānadi River flows, and the Khondmal and Balliguda highlands in the south, part of which is cultivated by the Khond tribes. The district's main products are rice, oilseeds, and timber, though irrigation works have been built, and such cash crops as jute and cotton are being tried.

The town, the district headquarters, is relatively modern despite its small size. The only other town of any size, Baudh, lies on the Mahānadi River. It is notable for its huge 11th-century image of the Buddha. Gandharadi, just northwest, has twin temples built in the 9th century. Pop. (1971 prelim.) district, 619,924; town, 10,612.

Phuntsholing, town of Bhutan.
26°52′ N, 89°26′ E
·market centre growth **2**:877b; map

Phuoc Long, province (*tinh*), South Vietnam. Bordering on Cambodia (Khmer Republic) and embracing the southernmost extremity of the central highlands, it drains to the South China Sea, principally by the Rach (river) Be, or Song (river) Be, also known as Ap Son Thuy. Straddling a portion of the border of the old Annamite kingdom (north) and the provinces of Cochinchina (south), the 2,046-sq-mi (5,299-sq-km) province is highest in the extreme northwest where hills of the Plateau du Mnong, inhabited by the Stieng, a Mon-Khmer-speaking tribe, rise to 1,565 ft (477 m). The principal products of the province include rubber and rice, the latter harvested chiefly in the lower central districts. There is also laterite, used in road building. Phuoc Binh, the provincial seat, has a hospital and airport but is served only by secondary and unpaved roads, the main highway passing several miles to the south. Pop. (1971 est.) 47,210.

·area and population table **19**:142
·map, South Vietnam **19**:140

Phuoc Tuy, province (*tinh*), South China Sea coast, southern South Vietnam. Embracing, rolling, and dissected plains in the north, it is quite flat on the coast; in the western districts outliers of the Chaîne Annamitique (Annamite Mountains) rise to 1,654 ft (504 m) and are inhabited by Mon-Khmer-speaking Chrau. Economic activities of the 851-sq-mi (2,203-sq-km) province include rubber, lowland rice, and coastal salt pans. The provincial seat, Phuoc Le, a northern terminus of the Mekong River coastal waterway system, is at the crossroads of the Saigon–Ham Tan coastal highway and the highway linking the resort and independent municipality of Vung Tau (*q.v.*) with Xuan Loc, capital of Long Khanh province. Pop. (1971 est.) 124,844.

·area and population table **19**:142

Phu Quoc Island, Vietnamese DAO PHU QUOC, in the Gulf of Thailand, belonging to South Vietnam. Lying 7 mi (11 km) off the Cambodian coast south of Bok Koŭ (formerly Bokor) and 43 mi west of the west coast of South Vietnam, it is administered from Kien Giang province on the mainland. The partially forested island, which is almost 30 mi long from north to south and has a maximum width of 17 mi, has an area of 230 sq mi (596 sq km). The climate is tropical monsoonal year round with a short 2- to 3-month drier winter season. The eastern half has elevations ranging from about 2,000 ft (600 m) in the north to about 1,200 ft in the south. The western half, in which is Duong Dong, the chief town (pop. [1971 est.] 16,073), is considerably lower, as is the southern tip, where the airport is located, at An Thoi. Economic activities include jet (a dense, black mineral, a variety of coal) and anthracite mines, lumbering, and the production of pepper, cocoa, coffee, betel, and coconuts. Following World War I the French imported 3,000 colonists from Tonkin (North Vietnam) in an unsuccessful scheme to establish plantations. Fishing is important and *nuoc mam*, a fish-sauce condiment, as well as copra and tortoise shells are exported. Off the southern tip of the island lie the associated Îles d'An Thoi (Anthoi Islands) with their iron deposits.
10°13′ N, 104°00′ E
·map, South Vietnam **19**:140

phur-bu (Tibetan: "peg" or "nail"), a ritual dagger used in the Tantric (esoteric) rites of

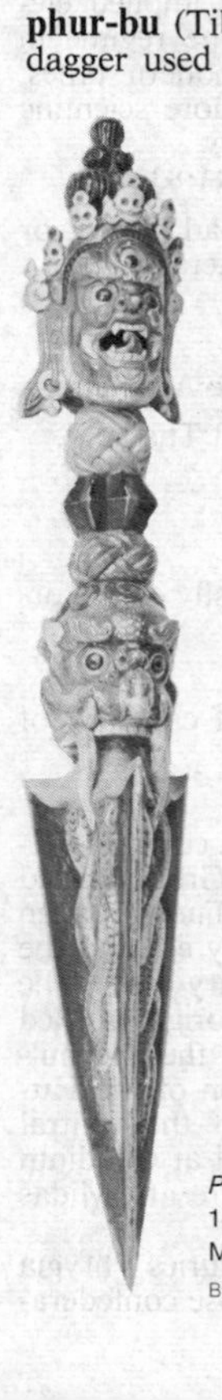

Phur-bu (magic dagger), painted wood, *c.* 1800; in the Newark (New Jersey) Museum
By courtesy of the Newark Museum, New Jersey

Tibetan Buddhism to exorcise evil. The dagger has a three-sided blade and a hilt that terminates in the head of Hayagrīva (Tibetan Rta-mgrin), the fierce protective deity identified by a horse's head in the headdress. Other symbols characteristically used to ornament the *phur-bu* are the knots of immortality, head of a *makara* (crocodile-like creature), and entwined serpents.
·ritual expelling and protective devices **3**:1177h

Phu Yen, province (*tinh*), central South Vietnam. Facing the South China Sea in the east, in the west it borders on the Plateau du Kontum where hills of the Chaîne Annamitique (Annamite Mountains) prevail. There are also hills in the north. The 2,020-sq-mi (5,233-sq-km) province is drained by the Song (river) Da Rang and a secondary coastal valley is drained by the Song Ky Lo, along which titanium deposits have been found. The provincial seat, Tuy Hoa, is near the mouth of the Song Da Rang, 69 mi (111 km) south of Qui Nhon. The Tuy Hoa district, irrigated by a dam across the river, chiefly produces and processes sugarcane, although rice is also harvested there and in other coastal areas. Nine miles north of Tuy Hoa there are commercial clay deposits, while 26 mi north is the fishing port of Song Cau surrounded by an agricultural district. Other coastal industries include several salt pans and a resort behind the Mui (point) Ke Ga (Cap [cape] Varella). Tuy Hoa is linked to Saigon and Hue by the coastal railway and is served by a hospital and commercial airport. While its ruined Cham tower is a vivid reminder of the Champa (*q.v.*) past, ethnically the city and province are almost wholly Vietnamese. Pop. (1971 est.) 334,184.
·area and population table **19**:142

Phya Taksin (Siamese king): *see* Taksin.

phycobiont, algal member of a lichen.
·lichens as associations of algae and fungi **10**:882e

phycocolloids, any of several polysaccharide hydrocolloids from brown or red seaweeds.
·extraction and commercial uses **7**:351a

phycoerythrin, a biological red pigment found in cell sap of red algae, protein in nature.
·properties and occurrence in plants **4**:920a

Phyfe, Duncan (b. DUNCAN FIFE, 1768, near Loch Fannich, Ross and Cromarty—d. Aug. 16, 1854, New York City), furniture designer, a leading exponent of the Neoclassical style, sometimes considered the greatest of all American cabinetmakers.

The Fife family went to the U.S. in 1784, settling in Albany, N.Y., where he worked as an apprentice cabinetmaker and eventually opened his own shop. In 1792 he moved to New York City (changing his name to Phyfe *c.* 1793). Two years later he was listed as a cabinetmaker in the *New York Directory and Register*. His first shop was located on Broad Street, whence he later moved to Fulton Street. In later years he employed more than 100 carvers and cabinetmakers. One of the first U.S. cabinetmakers to successfully use the factory method of manufacturing furniture, in 1837 he took two of his sons, Michael and James, into partnership. After the death of Michael (1840), the firm name was changed to Duncan Phyfe and Son. In 1847 the business was sold and Duncan retired.

Although Phyfe did not originate a new furniture style, he interpreted fashionable European styles in a manner so distinguished by grace and excellent proportions that he became a major spokesman for Neoclassicism in the U.S. He produced America's most highly individual Neoclassical furniture, using a unique combination of motifs. About 1800 his workshop was executing delicate furniture in the Sheraton, Regency, and French Directoire styles; by 1825, as taste changed, his pieces transpired into the Empire style. His Sheraton chairs, tables, and sofas often had delicate, reeded legs; and his Empire pieces, massive claw feet. His furniture, with its low relief carvings in the manner of the great English Neoclassicist Robert Adam, was decorated with typical period ornaments—harps, lyres, acanthus leaves, bow knots, and lion masks—and generally was made of high-quality mahogany; often he executed suites for fashionable New Yorkers.

The patronage of John Jacob Astor, Anglo-American tycoon and philanthropist, helped make Phyfe's furniture popular. His prices were high for the time, and he achieved considerable popularity in the South. At his death, his fortune was estimated to have been almost $500,000.

Interest in Phyfe's furniture was revived in 1922 when the Metropolitan Museum of Art, New York City, organized a comprehensive exhibition of his work.
·furniture design stylistic influences **7**:802h; illus. 804

phyi-mchod, in Tibetan Buddhist ceremonies, the seven offerings of external worship, presented before the tranquil deities. They are basically the seven ways of honouring a distinguished guest—by offering water for drinking, water for washing, flowers, incense, lamps, perfume, and food (the sacrificial cake *gtorma*). In the regular, daily attendance on the deities, the seven offerings are often represented by seven small bowls filled with water, though special ceremonies and festivals require the full offerings.

The *phyi-mchod* are distinguished from the *nang-mchod*, or offerings of internal worship, also called offerings of the five senses (*q.v.*).

For honouring the wrathful Tantric deities, the presentations are six in number—a cemetery flower, incense of singed flesh, lamp burning human fat (or substitute), scent of bile, blood (usually symbolized by red water), and human flesh (symbolically made from parched barley flour and butter realistically coloured and modelled).

phylactery, Greek PHYLAKTERION, Hebrew TEFILLIN, in Jewish religious practice, a small, black-leather, cube-shaped case containing four Torah texts written on parchment, which, in accordance with Deut. 6:8 (and similar statements in Deut. 11:18 and Ex. 13:9, 16), are to be worn by male Jews of 13 years and older as constant reminders of God and the obligation to keep the Law during daily life. They are not used on sabbaths and festivals, for these days themselves make one mindful of God and his Law. Such outward signs are common, and ancient Jews wore amulets and signs, perhaps originally tattooed. Phylacteries, however, have a purely religious significance.

According to rabbinic regulations, phylacteries are worn on the left arm facing the heart and on the forehead at the morning service (except on the sabbath and festivals) and at the afternoon service on the Ninth of Av.

Worshiper putting on phylacteries
Irving Herzberg, Brooklyn, N.Y.

The bands of the *tefillin* are knotted to represent the letters *daleth*, *yod*, and *shin*, which taken together form the divine name Shaddai. The hand phylactery (*tefillin shel yad*) has one compartment with the texts written on a single parchment; the head phylactery (*tefillin shel rosh*) has four compartments, each with one text. The extracts are Ex. 13:1–10, 11–16; Deut. 6:4–9, 11:13–21. Reform Jews interpret the biblical commandment in a figurative sense and, hence, do not wear phylacteries. Because of rabbinic controversies over the exact sequence of the four scriptural passages, very pious Jews wear two pairs of phylacteries.
·design and ceremonial use **15**:635d
·Israeli soldiers at prayer illus. **10**:327
·manner of wearing **3**:1179c
·synagogue worship concepts and practice **10**:295f

phylactolaemate, any member of the class Phylactolaemata of the invertebrate phylum Bryozoa. The class is found in freshwater all over the world and includes about 12 genera (*e.g.*, *Cristatella*, *Pectinatella*, *Plumatella*).

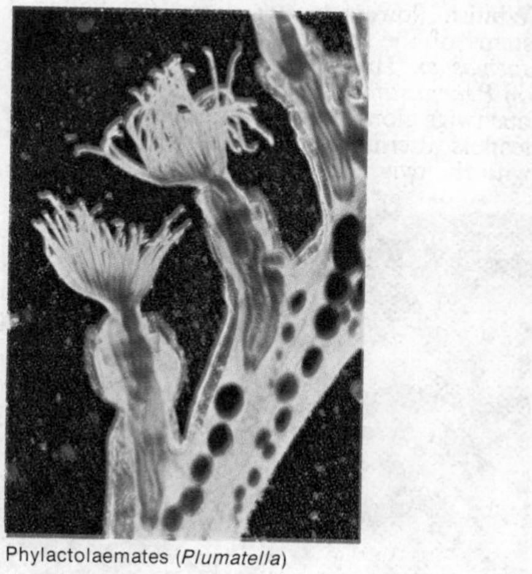

Phylactolaemates (*Plumatella*)
J. Clegg—Tourist Photo Library Ltd.

The individuals (zooids) that comprise a phylactolaemate colony are cylindrical in shape. The lophophore, a tentacle-bearing structure at the tip of the body is horseshoe-shaped; the tentacles are used during feeding.
·characteristics and classification **3**:355d; illus.

phyle (pl. phylae), the largest political subgroup of all Dorian and most Ionian Greek city-states in antiquity. Phylae were kinship groups embracing all citizens, corporations with their own officials and priests, and local units for administrative and military purposes. Sometimes the phylae of a state would be altered after a change in the form of government or makeup of the body of citizens. The original phylae of Athens were the Geleontes, Hopletes, Argadeis, and Aegicoreis (found sometimes in other Ionian states also).

At Athens the old phylae, which were dominated by the nobles and excluded a large number of new citizens, were supplanted by ten new phylae in Cleisthenes' political reorganization (508/507 BC). They were, in their official order, Erechtheis, Aegeis, Pandionis, Leontis, Acamantis, Oeneis, Cecropis, Hippothontis, Aeantis, and Antiochis. Enrollment depended upon residence when the reform was instituted; thereafter membership was transmitted by descent. The governmental organs and personnel of the Athenian democracy were based on the phylae: the nine archons (magistrates) plus their secretary, the ten *stratēgoi* ("generals"), and others were each chosen from a specific phyle; each of the 10

Prytaneis (executive committees) of the Boule (Council) of 500 represented a phyle; the 10 regiments of hoplites and 10 cavalry detachments were each drawn from a particular phyle. In dramatic competitions at festivals each phyle was represented by a *choros* and a *chorēgos* ("producer"). In the Hellenistic and Roman periods some new phylae were added to honour certain rulers; altogether their number usually did not exceed 12.

The original three Doric phylae at Sparta were supplanted by five local phylae (*c.* 8th century BC) that elected the five ephors (magistrates) and from which the five *lochoi* (regiments) of the Spartan army were recruited.

·Ancient Greece's political units **8**:334g

phyletism, Eastern Christian ecclesiastical principle by which separate autonomous or autocephalous churches were created for each Christian nationality or language group.

·Bulgarian 19th-century schism **6**:159a

Phyllanthus, a genus of flowering plants of the family Euphorbiaceae that contains among its 600 species some of ornamental value and others with interesting botanical adaptations. Some have flattened, green stems, called phyllodes, that function as leaves. Whitish flowers cluster along the flattened stems of the West Indian seaside laurel (*P. speciosus*). There are similar reddish blooms on *P. angustifolius*. Other species have deciduous twigs along which small leaves resembling leaflets alternate; the leaflets are shed along with the twig.

Otaheite gooseberry (*Cicca acida*)
W.H. Hodge

Species best showing this shedding adaptation have been shifted from *Phyllanthus* to two other genera, *Cicca* and *Emblica*, though many less known *Phyllanthus* species have the same adaptation. Otaheite gooseberry (*Cicca acida* or *C. disticha*, formerly *P. acidus*) is a small Indian tree bearing dangling clusters of light-yellow or green, vertically ribbed, acid-sour fruits, nearly 2 centimetres (0.8 inch) in diameter; the fruit is used for making preserves. The long, deciduous twigs are lined with rows of sharp-pointed, alternating leaves. Because of its even more feathery leaf-bearing twigs, each with about 100 tiny alternating leaves, the emblic, or myrobalan (*Emblica officinalis*, formerly *P. emblica*), gives the impression of a hemlock. Its acid-tasting yellow or reddish fruits are prescribed in traditional Indian medicine as a tonic. The leaves and bark contain tannin, utilized for tanning and as a colour concentrator in dyeing. The dried fruit has been used as ink, hair dye, and detergent. The delicately branched Polynesian shrub, snowbush (*Breynia nivosa*, formerly *P. nivosus*) is widely grown in the tropical gardens and as a greenhouse plant in the north for its gracefully slender branches and delicate green and white leaves (pink and red in *B. nivosa* variety *roseopicta*).

phyllarenite, sandstone type deposited rapidly in tectonic regions.

·sandstone bedding structure **16**:215h; illus.

phyllid, leaflike appendage characteristic of the gametophytic (sexual) generation of mosses.

·liverwort form and structure **8**:780e
·moss morphology and development **3**:353d

Phylliidae: *see* leaf insect.

phyllite, fine-grained metamorphic rock formed by the reconstitution of fine-grained, parent sedimentary rocks, typically a mudstone or shale. Phyllite has a marked fissility (a tendency to split into sheets or slabs), due to the parallel alignment of platy minerals; it may have a sheen on its surfaces due to tiny plates of micas. Its grain size is larger than that of slate but smaller than that of schist.

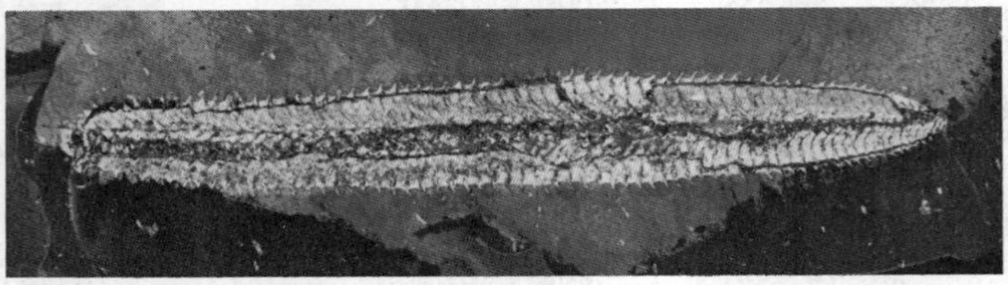

Phyllograptus
By courtesy of the trustees of the British Museum (Natural History); photograph, Imitor

Phyllite is formed by relatively low-grade metamorphic conditions in the lower part of the greenschist facies. Parent rocks may be only partially reconstituted so that some of the original mineralogy and sedimentary bedding are preserved. Depending upon the direction of the stresses applied during metamorphism, phyllite sheets may parallel or crosscut the original bedding; in some rocks, two stages of deformation, called pre-crystalline and post-crystalline deformations, can be distinguished on the basis of two orientations of definable surfaces in the rock. Pre-crystalline surfaces have slaty cleavage, or flow cleavage, whereas post-crystalline surfaces have false, fracture, or strain-slip cleavage. Such terms can be used only when the type of deformation and its relation to time can be determined.

·minerals and texture **12**:4a; illus.

Phyllobates: *see* arrow-poison frog.

Phylloceras, extinct genus of cephalopods (animals related to modern squid, octopus, and nautilus) the fossils of which are widespread in Triassic to Cretaceous (225,000,000- to 65,000,000-year-old) marine rocks. The external shell is a compressed spiral, small and rather smooth. The surfaces between the successive chambers of the shell are complexly convoluted in a series of lobes and troughs, with secondary crenulations distinctively superimposed on the main pattern.

Phylloceratina, extinct suborder of Mesozoic ammonites.

·extinction survivals and new evolutions **7**:562c

phylloclade, flattened photosynthetic stem, *e.g.*, stems of the genus *Phyllanthus*.

·Phyllanthus stem and branch function **6**:1028a

Phyllocladus asplenifolius: *see* celery-top pine.

Phyllocystis, genus of fossil invertebrate of the phylum Echinodermata.

·extinct echinoderm, illus. 4 **6**:184

phyllode, in botany, a flattened leaflike stalk of a leaf.

·leaf climatic adaptations **13**:730b

Phyllodocemorpha, order of worms of the class Polychaeta (phylum Annelida).

·characteristics and classification **1**:936a; illus. 935

Phyllodontidae, family of extinct fish of the order Elopiformes.

·classification and general features **6**:731a

Phylloglossum, a plant genus of the order Lycopodiales, contains only one species, *P. drummondii*, native to Australia and New Zealand. It is believed to be very old because of its high number of chromosomes. *Phylloglossum* has a bulblike underground base, a few spike-shaped, succulent leaves, and one stalk bearing a cluster of spore capsules. The plant is three to five centimetres (one to two inches) tall. It dies to the ground during the dry season and reappears with the return of the rains.

Phyllograptus, extinct genus of graptolites, small colonial marine animals related to the primitive chordates, readily distinguished by its characteristic leaflike form and structure. Various species of *Phyllograptus* are excellent guide or index fossils for Ordovician rocks and time (the Ordovician Period began 500,000,000 years ago and lasted 70,000,000 years) and allow the correlation of sometimes widely separated rock units.

Phyllolepida, an order of extinct fishes of the class Placodermi.

·traits, behaviour, and classification **14**:488f

phyllonite: *see* cataclastic rocks.

Phyllonoma, a genus of shrubs of the order Saxifragales.

·folk medicine preparation **16**:293g

Phyllonomaceae, also called DULONGIACEAE, a family of trees and shrubs of the order Saxifragales.

·general features and classification **16**:300f

Phyllophaga: *see* June beetle.

Phyllorhynchus: *see* leaf-nosed snake.

Phylloscopus collybita (bird): *see* chiffchaff.

phyllosilicates, formerly DISILICATES, compounds with structures that have silicate tetrahedrons (a central silicon atom surrounded by four oxygen atoms at the corners of a tetrahedron) arranged in sheets. Examples are talc and mica. Three of the oxygen atoms of each tetrahedron are shared with other tetrahedrons, but no two tetrahedrons have more than one oxygen atom in common; each tetrahedron, therefore, is linked to three others. The silicon atoms are arranged at the corners of hexagons, and the unshared oxygen atoms are commonly oriented on the same side of the sheet. Because these are capable of forming chemical bonds with other metal atoms, the silicate sheets are interleaved with layers of other elements. The various layers are stacked to form a grouping with the unshared oxygen atoms toward the centre, and these groups are held together by the weak van der Waal's forces; this gives the phyllosilicates their distinct cleavage parallel to the layers. Phyllosilicates have chemical formulas that contain silicon (Si) and oxygen (O) in some multiple of Si_2O_5.

·mica crystal structures **12**:94f

Phyllostomatidae, family of about 130 species of tropical and subtropical bats known collectively as American leaf-nosed, or spear-nosed, bats; native to the New World from the United States to Argentina. Phyllostomatid bats are found in habitats ranging from forests to deserts. Their features vary, but most species are broad-winged and have a simple, spear-shaped structure, the nose leaf, on the muzzle. Coloration of the fur ranges within and among the species from gray, pale brown, and dark brown to orange, red, yellow, or whitish; some forms, such as the tent-

American false vampire bat (*Vampyrum spectrum*) carrying a mouse
Nina Leen, *Life* © Time Inc.

building, or yellow-eared, bat (*Uroderma bilobatum*), have striped faces. Phyllostomatid bats are 4 to 13.5 centimetres (1½–5⅓ inches) without the tail, which may be absent or to 5.5 centimetres long. The largest member of the family, and the largest of any American bats, is the tropical American false vampire bat (*Vampyrum spectrum*); it is 12.5–13.5 centimetres long with a wingspan of 90 centimetres or more.

The diet of phyllostomatid bats varies. Many, such as the naked-backed bats (*Pteronotus*), are insect eaters; some larger forms, such as the tropical American false vampire, are carnivorous. Many other species feed on fruit, nectar, or pollen; among these are the long-tongued (*Glossophaga*) and brown-flower (*Erophylla*) bats, which have specialized long snouts and tongues for feeding.

Phyllostomatid bats usually live in groups; some, such as the mustache bats (*Chilonycteris*), form colonies of tens of thousands. Roosting sites include caves, tree hollows, buildings, and the undersides of bridges. The tent-building bat and the small fruit-eating *Artibeus cinereus watsoni* are the only bats that create shelters; they roost on the undersides of palm leaves after biting across the leaves to make their ends hang downward.

·classification and general features **4**:435f

Phyllostylon brasiliensis, species of San Domingo boxwood or West Indian boxwood of the order Urticales.

·features and economic importance **18**:1090a

Phylloxera vitifoliae (insect): *see* grape phylloxera.

Phylloxeridae, family of insects of the order Homoptera.

·general features and classification **8**:1042a

phylogenetic tree, or DENDROGRAM, a diagram showing interrelations of a group of organisms connected by a common ancestral form. The ancestor is in the tree "trunk"; organisms that have arisen from it are placed at the ends of tree "branches." The distance of one group from the other groups indicates the degree of relationship; *i.e.*, closely related groups are located on branches close to one another. Phylogenetic trees, although speculative, provide a convenient method for studying phylogenetic relationships.

·biological classification development **4**:685g

phylogeny 14:376, the evolutionary history of a group of organisms.

The text article covers the basis of phylogeny, the early stages of phylogeny (chemical evolution and probable main lines of descent), major trends in the phylogeny of plants and animals, and some phylogenetic generalizations.

REFERENCES in other text articles:

comparative biology

·behavioral evolution and genetics **2**:804b
·behavioral similarities and assessments **4**:1019e
·biological classification construction **4**:689b
·evolutionary kinship and antibody study **7**:996a
·genetic mutation in evolution **12**:756a
·gruiform egg protein analysis **8**:449b
·Haeckel's evolutionary interpretations **8**:541h
·lice as indices of host taxonomy **14**:375e
·Pleistocene organism and habitat change **14**:568c
·Upper Paleozoic plants and animals **13**:926a

invertebrate animals

·annelid probable relationships, illus. 5 **1**:935
·arrowworm lack of linkage with other animals **4**:19a
·arthropod origin and group problems **2**:70c
·beetle evolution and evidence **4**:833f
·cephalopod shell and life-style changes **3**:1152g *passim* to 1153f
·conflicting evidence on decapods **5**:549b
·echinoderm classification and revisions **6**:185h
·flatworm relation to comb jellies **5**:348d
·fly larvae characteristics **5**:820g; illus.
·homopteran evolutionary relationships **8**:1041f
·hymenopteran insect ancestry **9**:131f
·insect ancestors and major groups **9**:618d; illus.
·insect descent problems **1**:1023h
·molluscan prototype anatomy and relations to other phyla **12**:328c; illus.

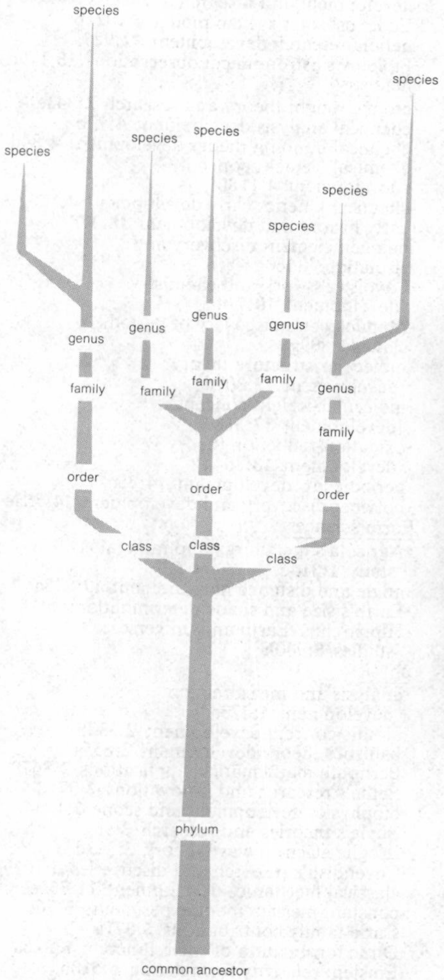

Phylogenetic tree

·phoronid unique classification **14**:283c
·protozoan origin and polyphyly **15**:127b
·scorpion derivation from eurypterids **16**:402h

plants

·algae procaryote–eucaryote transition **1**:495d
·angiosperm evolution from gymnosperms **1**:880h
·convergences in orchids **13**:655b
·Cornales order origin **5**:176g
·lichen symbiosis evolution **10**:887c

vertebrate animals

·Atheriniforms and rise of like orders **2**:271h
·carnivore derivation and major lines **3**:939h; illus. 941
·crocodilian relation to birds **5**:288g
·Edentata living and extinct forms **6**:301d
·hominid fossil record interpretations **8**:1023b
·human evolution and speciations **11**:419a
·insectivore ancestry and relations **9**:627c *passim* to 628a
·primate ancestry and evolution **14**:1025h
·reptile ancestors and descendants **15**:739b; illus. 736
·sloth and anteater ancestries **6**:303d
·snake ancestry and habitat **16**:565f
·speech as recent acquisition of man **17**:478c
·waterfowl ancestry and diversification **1**:946c

RELATED ENTRIES in the *Ready Reference and Index:*
adaptive radiation; cephalization; cosmozoic theory; Deuterostomia; eucaryote; morphogenesis; ontogeny; phylogenetic tree; procaryote; Protostomia; spontaneous generation; vestigial structure

phylum (biology): *see* taxon.

phylum, in linguistics, group of languages or families of languages. The distinction between *phylum* and *family* is relative and not observed uniformly by all linguists; but usually, of the two terms, phylum denotes a group of languages that, though demonstrably related, have fewer cognates and phonetic similarities and, in general, more obscure ties. A phylum, as noted, can consist of two or more families of languages.

·definition and linguistic usage **10**:663c

Phymatidae (insect family): *see* ambush bug.

Physalia (marine animal): *see* Portuguese man-of-war.

Physalis, a genus of about 100 species (family Solanaceae, *q.v.*) of small herbs noted for

Ground cherry (*Physalis alkekengi*)
G.E. Hyde from the Natural History Photographic Agency—EB Inc.

their inflated, baglike calyx (fused sepals), which encloses a fleshy berry and often becomes bright orange red at maturity. The berries of some are edible, and the plants accordingly go by names such as ground cherry; winter cherry; strawberry, or gooseberry, tomato; and husk tomato. Chinese lantern plant is a name alluding to the showy bladder-like calyx of the mature fruit.

Physarales, order of slime molds (class Myxomycetes, *q.v.*) with dark brown or black spores (reproductive bodies). The members of this group are widely distributed and occupy a variety of habitats.
·mycota classification and features **12**:765e
·slime mold classification and general features **16**:891g

Physarum polycephalum, species of slime mold of the class Myxomycetes.
·slime mold cytoplasmic streaming **16**:886f

Physcomitrium: *see* urn moss.

Physcon (king of Egypt): *see* Ptolemy VIII Euergetes II.

Physeter catodon: *see* sperm whale.

Physica (treatise by Aristotle): *see Physics.*

Physica et Mystica, Engish NATURAL AND MYSTICAL THINGS, 3rd-century BC treatise by Bolos of Mende; details the making of gold and silver.
·alchemical recipe book **1**:433e

physical chemistry, a branch of chemistry which deals with the application of physical methods and theories to the study of chemical systems.
·chemistry divisions and disciplines **4**:166h

physical conditioning: *see* exercise and physical conditioning.

physical education, training in hygiene, calisthenics, and athletics.
·early Roman purpose and program **6**:327b
·Hellenistic organization and decline **6**:325c
·Nazi school curriculum role **6**:376a
·Vittorino Rambaldoni's youth concern **6**:344e

physical examination, inspection of an individual's body to assess the state of his health. In conducting the examination, the physician makes use of his trained senses of sight, touch, and hearing (*see* palpation; percussion; auscultation) to determine whether or not the various body organs are healthy. Instruments most frequently used include those that help in listening to body sounds (*see* stethoscope), those that extend the visual examination to the body interior (*see* endoscopy), and those used to obtain body measurements such as blood pressure (*see* sphygmomanometer). The physical examination may be extended into a more comprehensive medical checkup that includes appropriate laboratory tests of body fluids and tissues (*see* blood analysis; urinalysis; biopsy), together with X-ray and other techniques aimed at providing information on the structure and function of specific body organs (*see* electrocardiography; electroencephalography; electromyography).
·animal disease diagnostic methods **5**:871g
·coronary artery disease detection **3**:888e
·diagnosis of nervous system disorders **12**:1041d
·diagnostic procedures and problems **5**:688d

physical geology, scientific discipline that is concerned with all aspects of the Earth's structure, composition, physical properties, constituent rocks and minerals, and surficial features. Accordingly, physical geology is essentially a superdiscipline that overlaps geophysics, geochemistry, mineralogy, petrology, structural geology, and geomorphology, among others.

physicalism, in philosophy, a thesis of Logical Positivism, directly opposed to metaphysics; it maintains that an ideal syntactical language can be constructed to explain all scientific facts (of whatever level) in terms of the language of physical science. It was espoused by the Vienna Circle, a group of unusually illustrious scholars—philosophers, scientists, and mathematicians—who regularly met in Vienna between World Wars I and II to discuss the philosophy of meaning and truth. Physicalism was propagated chiefly by Otto Neurath (1882–1945), an erudite Marxian sociologist, and Rudolf Carnap (1891–1970), a top-ranking philosopher of science and language. Its implication that all of science (including psychology) is reductively one is vigorously defended in the *International Encyclopedia of Unified Science*, edited by Neurath. An exception is made for the purely formal sciences of mathematics and logic. Some critics see special problems in so reducing biology, but even those who regard biology as merely a dialect of physical science hesitate to include societal facts such as moral systems and behavioral choices.
·Carnap's derivation and interpretation **3**:926a
·criticisms of validity **12**:33g *passim* to 34g
·experiential referent as science ground **14**:880g
·Materialism and nuclear physics **11**:611b

physical medicine: *see* physical therapy.

physical sciences, history of 14:384, covers astronomy, physics, chemistry, and allied sciences from antiquity to modern times.
The text article divides the history of physical sciences into the following sections: ancient science, science in the Middle Ages, the scientific revolution (15th, 16th, and 17th centuries), the 18th century to the present, concluding with 20th-century trends. Each age is linked to the next by continuing coverage of the inquiries into the same or comparable problems.

REFERENCES in other text articles:
astronomy
·astronomical maps and catalogues **2**:225e
·astronomical photometry development **14**:347b
·astronomical spectroscopy development **2**:234h
·Brahe's contributions **3**:103b
·Copernican theories **5**:145b
·cosmic ray study and apparatus **5**:200d
·development and research **2**:246d
·Eudoxus' solar system model **6**:1021b
·nebula research development **12**:927a
·Ptolemy's astronomical observations **15**:179d
chemistry
·atomic weight theory and research **2**:343e
·chemical analysis development **4**:77b
·chemical bonding theory development **4**:84d
·chemical element concept development **4**:118b
·chemical kinetics early development **4**:138g
·early history and development **18**:37f
·halogen element discovery and isolation **8**:560g
·Lavoisier's work and chemistry development **10**:714c
·Mendeleyev's discovery of periodic law **11**:899g
·molecular structure theory development **12**:309d
·molecular-weight concept development **12**:318d
·oxidation-reduction theory development **13**:804a
·periodic law development **14**:75c
·polymer discovery and development **14**:765e
Earth sciences
·Agricola's metallurgy and mineralogy study **1**:314e
·angle and distance measurement **17**:828a
·Earth's size and shape determinations **6**:1f
·Hipparchus' Earth and universe studies **8**:940h
physics
·analysis and measurement development **1**:773a
·atomic concept development **2**:332h
·ballistics theory development **2**:655a
·Bernoulli mathematical applications **2**:867f
·Bethe's research and innovations **2**:871d
·biophysics development and scope **2**:1034e
·Boyle's theories and research **3**:96g
·Broglie electron wave theory **3**:323d
·Cavendish's research and discoveries **3**:1019c
·classical mechanics development **11**:762e
·constant measurement experiments **5**:76c
·Curie family contributions **5**:371a
·Dirac formulation of wave function **5**:826a
·Einstein relativity formulation **6**:510h
·electricity theory development **6**:539h
·electromagnetic theory development **6**:645e
·fluid mechanics development **11**:780c
·Galileo's discoveries and methods **7**:851d
·Galvani's pioneering electrophysiology **7**:859f
·gas particle theory development **7**:918h
·Gay-Lussac's research and innovations **7**:968a
·gravitational theory development **8**:286h
·Helmholtz' classical mechanics work **8**:751g
·Huygens' work and contributions **9**:74g
·Kelvin's theories and inventions **10**:414d
·light theory development **10**:928g
·luminescence concept development **11**:179b
·magnetic-resonance development **11**:306a
·magnetism theory development **11**:311b
·Maxwell and electromagnetic theory of light **11**:718g
·measurement theory development and use **11**:740b
·Michelson–Morley experiment **12**:104b
·Newton's effect on classical mechanics **13**:16g
·nuclear fission discovery **13**:324e
·particle accelerator development **1**:23h
·photoemission theory development **14**:297a
·quantum theory development **11**:793c
·radio theory and experimentation **15**:426c
·Rayleigh's diverse research **15**:538d
·relativity theory development **15**:581h
·Rutherford's atomic structure studies **16**:106g
·sound wave theory development **17**:19f
·spectroscopy principles development **17**:457g
·subatomic particle theory development **13**:1022e
·superconductivity discovery and research **17**:811h
·thermal theory development **8**:700h
·thermodynamics theory development **18**:290g
·thermoelectric effect discovery **18**:315h
·Thomson's atomic structure research **18**:348h
·wave motion theory development **19**:665d

physical theories, mathematical aspects of 14:392, deals with some fundamental aspects of nine subdivisions of theoretical physics.

TEXT ARTICLE covers:
Mechanics of particles and systems **14**:392e
Fluid mechanics 396b
Mechanics of solids 398h
Statistical mechanics 402b
Electromagnetic theory 408c
Relativity theory 410e
Riemannian geometry 414a
Quantum mechanics 416c
Dimensional analysis 422a

REFERENCES in other text articles:
·atmospheric dynamics basic principles **2**:323d
·Bernoulli calculus development and use **2**:867h
·Cayley space–time relativity and mechanics problem basis **3**:1033e
·chemical bonding and quantum mechanics **4**:88d
·chemical kinetics theory and analysis **4**:138f
·classical and quantum mechanics **11**:793g
·complex analysis fundamentals **1**:730f
·conservation laws and symmetry **5**:33c
·Copernican theories of astronomy **5**:146b
·differential equation principles **5**:736f
·dimensional analysis application to measurements in classical physics **11**:740f *passim* to 742g
·Einstein relativity equation **6**:511e
·electromagnetic radiation theory **6**:657e
·Euler's contribution and influence **6**:1027d
·Fourier impact on mathematical physics **7**:577b
·Gauss's celestial orbit calculations **7**:966h
·gravitational measurement and study **8**:288e
·Hamilton's discoveries and influence **8**:588e
·Hilbert's contributions and influence **8**:872g
·hydrologic systems research methods **9**:119g
·information theory entropy formula **9**:576b
inverse-square law
·electromagnetic radiation intensity **6**:648h
·lighting intensity measurement **10**:964d
·magnetic force principles **11**:313d
·Priestley's electrical experiments **14**:1013c
·PSI produced by energy not obeying law **13**:1004c
·sound wave propagation **17**:21a
·landform entropy probability theory **10**:625b
·Laplace and theory of gravitation **10**:680g
·mathematics history from antiquity **11**:645e

·molecular-weight determination **12**:318d
·Newton's optics and classical mechanics **13**:18a
·physical constant measurement theory **5**:75f
·physics principles and research **14**:428c
·probability theory and method **14**:1109f
·real analysis basis and applications **1**:779b
·relativity theory calculations **15**:583d
·Riemann space influence on relativity **15**:840b
·tidal forces and tide prediction **18**:384d
·transition metal ligand-field theory **18**:610c
·vector and tensor analysis principles **1**:791c
·von Neumann quantum-mechanical system **12**:1067b
·wave motion equations **19**:667c

RELATED ENTRIES in the *Ready Reference and Index: for*
classical mechanics: see d'Alembert's principle; equilibrium, mechanical; inertia; interaction, fundamental; momentum; Newton's laws of motion; reference frame; scalar; vector
dimensional analysis: centimetre-gram-second system; constant; dimension; metre-kilogram-second system; parameter
electromagnetic theory: electromagnetic field; electromagnetic wave; Maxwell's equations; Poynting vector
fluid mechanics: Archimedes' principle; Bernoulli's theorem; laminar flow; Mach number; Pascal's principle; Reynolds number; turbulent flow
mechanics of solids: bulk modulus; elastic limit; Hooke's law; shear modulus; strain; stress; tensile strength; tensor; Young's modulus
quantum mechanics: Bose–Einstein statistics; complementarity principle; de Broglie wave; eigenvalue; Fermi–Dirac statistics; operator; Planck's radiation law; Schrodinger equation; uncertainty principle
relativity: equivalence principle; fourth dimension; Lorentz transformations; relativistic mass; Riemannian geometry; space-time; tensor field; time dilation; unified field theory; vector field
statistical mechanics: degree of freedom; distribution function; Gaussian distribution; kinetic theory of gases; macroscopic state; Maxwell–Boltzmann statistics; mean free path
thermodynamics: canonical ensemble; closed system; enthalpy; entropy; free energy; Hamiltonian; Lagrangian; path; reversible process; thermodynamics, laws of

physical therapy, the treatment of bodily ailment by the application of physical agents such as heat and exercise. This specialized medical service is aimed at rehabilitating persons disabled by pain or ailments affecting the motor functions of the body. Physical therapy is one means employed to assist these patients to return to a comfortable and productive life, often despite the persistence of a medical problem. For centuries man used such natural physical agents as hot springs and sunlight to treat his ailments, but the development of physical therapy as a specialized medical service took place largely after World War I. Two forces influenced its growth, epidemic poliomyelitis and the world wars, both of which created large numbers of young, seriously handicapped persons. Physical therapy then became available for the treatment of patients with such diverse problems as fractures, burns, tuberculosis, painful backs, strokes, and nerve injuries. Physical therapy is closely associated with orthopedic surgery, but it is also prescribed by physicians and surgeons in all branches of medicine. Physicians who specialize in physical medicine are called physiatrists.

The objectives of physical therapy may be summarized as follows: relief of pain; improvement or maintenance of functions such as strength and mobility; training in the most effective method of performing essential activities; and testing of function in various areas. Tests cover such fields as muscle strength, degree of joint mobility, breathing capacity, and muscular coordination.

The means most commonly employed include heat, massage, exercise, electrical currents, and functional training.

Heat is used generally to stimulate circulation and relieve pain in the area treated. It may be applied by infrared lamps, shortwave radiation, or diathermy currents; hot moist compresses or immersion in hot water; application of melted paraffin wax; or by ultrasound.

Massage is used primarily to aid circulation and relieve local pain or muscle spasm. It is usually applied by the therapist's hands alone, although swirling water or mechanical devices may be employed. The most common massage strokes are stroking and kneading of the tissues. The lubricant applied to the skin usually is a neutral substance such as mineral oil.

Exercise, the most varied and widely used of all physical treatments, is usually designed to do one or more of three things: increase the amount of motion in a joint, increase the strength in a muscle, or train a muscle to contract and relax in useful coordination with other muscles. Exercises may be simple or complex, performed actively by the patient or passively with the therapist carrying the part through the motion. Such passive motion may be useful in improving mobility in a joint, but strengthening or training of a muscle can be accomplished only through its active contraction by the patient. Various exercise equipment is used; and treatment may be given with the patient immersed in warm water. While a patient is still confined to bed after illness or injury, exercises may be begun to prevent stiffness or weakness. As he improves, the exercises become more complex and strenuous, until the damaged parts are capable of meeting the demands of daily activity. In addition to its obvious use following stiffness or paralysis, exercise may be used to improve the breathing of patients with lung disorders, assist circulation, relax overly tense muscles, and correct faulty posture.

Electrical currents of very low strength may be applied through the skin to superficial muscles, causing them to contract spontaneously. This therapy may help train weakened muscles and also test the status of nerves supplying those muscles. Electrical currents are applied to assist the penetration of the skin by certain medicines and for numerous other purposes.

Functional training teaches the patient how, in spite of a handicapping ailment, to carry out most safely and effectively the activities of his daily life. This training may mean learning to use crutches, a brace, or an artificial arm; or it may involve working out and practicing the best way for a mother with one hand to do her housework or for a workman with a stiff leg to board the factory bus. Such training often requires long hours of practice; it may be facilitated by use of assistive devices that make it easier to fasten buttons, hold a fork, or dial a telephone.

Other treatments such as ultraviolet radiation and cold applications are also used. Therapeutic use of X-rays is considered a separate specialty and not a physical therapy procedure.

physical weathering, or MECHANICAL WEATHERING, disintegration of rocks at or near the Earth's surface that involves a breakdown of the rock into particles, with no decay of any of the minerals. This type of weathering commonly occurs in association with chemical decay of the rock. Frost action is one of the most important processes of physical weathering. Water lodged in numerous cracks in a rock may expand by freezing and thus exert a pressure sufficient to widen the fissure in which it rests. Repeated freezing and thawing causes many rocks to break down into slabs and plates; if the water is interstitial, the rock is broken down into granules. Similar interstitial crystallization of salts such as sodium chloride and gypsum is also cited as a cause of rock disintegration, particularly in arid regions. Other processes of mechanical weathering include the force produced by plant roots, which penetrate and widen fractures, and the action of burrowing animals.

Several theories of the causes of mechanical weathering are now not very widely accepted. For example, thermal expansion and contraction long was considered a cause of rock disintegration, particularly in the tropical deserts, where great extremes of temperature are experienced; most of the field evidence, however, is contrary to the theoretical predictions. Similar doubts concern the interpretation of sheet structure, thick slabs of rock developed in crystalline and sedimentary rocks. These slabs were accepted for many years as a manifestation of offloading, or pressure release, at the Earth's surface, but considerable evidence again suggests that the offloading hypothesis is not everywhere applicable.
·frost action and cirque formation **8**:169c

physics 14:424, scientific discipline that is concerned with energy and matter and their interactions with one another.

The text article examines the traditionally organized branches of classical and modern physics and describes the subject matter of each. The branches covered are mechanics, (classical, quantum, and relativistic), thermodynamics and heat, electricity and magnetism, optics, atomic physics, and the physics of subatomic particles. The methodology of physics research is reviewed, and the separate roles of the experimentalist and theoretician are examined. The relationship of physics to other disciplines and to society is considered. The article concludes with a summary of the exchange of information in physics.

REFERENCES in other text articles:
·Aristotelian philosophic inquiry **1**:1169e
·Aristotle's first and second philosophy **12**:10f
·atmospheric science basic principles **2**:320a
·atomic concept development **2**:333b
·biophysics source discipline **2**:1034e
·chemical bonding theory development **4**:85d
·Chrysippus and Stoic thought **17**:699c
·classical mechanics principles **11**:762a
·classification of non-perceptual objects **4**:692d *passim* to 693e
·colloid study development **4**:855a
·Curie family role in development **5**:371a
·electromagnet research applications **11**:338h
·field theory classification **7**:293d
·Heisenberg and quantum mechanics **8**:745g *passim* to 746f
·history and relation to other sciences **14**:384b *passim* to 391e
·Kant's analysis of ground **10**:390g *passim* to 393g
·logics of physical application **11**:35b
·Materialist theory of matter **11**:611b *passim* to 614c
·mathematical concepts and formulations **14**:392b
·molecular structure theory development **12**:309d
·particle accelerator development **1**:23e
·philosophical concepts and theory **12**:866a
·philosophy of science as related field **16**:375h *passim* to 382h
·physical constant measurement theory **5**:75c
·physiological factors in perception **14**:38h
·Positivist theories and methodology **14**:878c *passim* to 880h
·quantum theory development **11**:793c
·Renaissance natural philosophy **14**:263b *passim* to 264h
·science history and philosophy **16**:366h
·theory validation in various forms **16**:388f
·thermodynamics principles and theory **18**:290b
·time in contemporary theories **18**:417f
·universality of composition of matter **18**:1013e
·value of Plato's theories **14**:254d
·Whitehead's philosophy of science **19**:817e
·Wren's experiment and Newton's laws **19**:1021c

Physics, translation of PHYSICA, one of the 47 principal works that constitute the main body of existing writings of Aristotle (*q.v.*). In the *Physics* and in his other scientific treatises Aristotle rejected the Platonic view of the real world as something outside the world of man's senses and thus laid the basis for rational investigation of all natural phenomena.

- ·Aristotelian influence on other schools **1**:1157a
- ·first and second philosophy **12**:10g
- ·philosophies of science and nature **16**:377d
- ·physical sciences and metaphysics **1**:1167g

physics, Stoic, one of the three branches of philosophy—along with logic and ethics—according to the Stoics, in which the essential rationality of the cosmos, and—as opposed to the discrete atoms of the Epicureans—the continuity of matter were stressed and in which that single rational entity, the world, was conceptualized as a continuum—an idea still persisting in the field theory of today.

The Stoics spoke of the "whole," all that is real—the sum of the corporeal and the incorporeal, outside of which is the infinite void. The world itself is without void and is finite and spherical, on every side tending toward its centre, and is perfectly one. The Stoics (unlike the Epicureans) left room in their theories for the role of Divine Providence, later developed by Poseidonius (2nd–1st century BC) into an elaborate theory of cosmic symphony, in which all of the forces of the world act together in concert.

The complicated details of Stoic physics involved eclectic borrowings from Platonic, Aristotelian, and other sources. The Stoa (4th–3rd century BC) claimed that they went back for their main inspiration to one of the Pre-Socratics, to Heracleitus, a 6th–5th century BC cryptic and caustic sage of Ephesus, just as the Epicureans had returned to the Atomists. Thus, the *logos* and the cosmic fire, both Heracleitian concepts, played important roles in their physics.

Most Stoics believed in a periodic total conflagration of the world, with God first forming it and then taking it back and forming it again, in an unending series. God is, therefore, the *Logos*, or the active principle, and also fire; and he contains the active forms of all things in himself. These forms, called *logoi spermatikoi*, were like material seeds, from which everything comes into being.

Although the basic orientation of the Stoics was deterministic, most of them held that man is free in that he can become aware of the true nature of things and see them as the necessary working out of God's life, his body, and will. Man can, therefore, welcome all things gratefully, for Providence ordered all things for the best.

Physics Abstracts, a semimonthly publication of summaries of articles, reviews, and books related to physics, published by the Institution of Electrical Engineers (London) in cooperation with the American Institute of Physics (New York). Indexes appear semiannually and cumulative indexes at five-year intervals.

Physics and Politics (1872), a work by Walter Bagehot.

- ·political sociology influenced **2**:585a

Physiocratic school, 18th-century school of economic thought generally regarded as the first scientific school of economics. It is best understood as a reaction against the policies of the mercantilists, who had believed that national strength and security depended more on manufacturing and trade than on the products of the soil. The Physiocrats regarded land, or agriculture, as the source of all wealth because they believed that only agriculture produced a clear surplus over the costs of production. Other forms of production merely changed the products of agriculture into consumable form; workers engaged in nonagricultural trades added only the value of their labour to the product and were regarded as the sterile class. Agricultural products ought to be sold at high prices and manufactured products at low prices because a rise in agricultural income would mean a rise in net product (an increase in national prosperity). In addition to the productive (farming) and sterile (nonfarming and nonmining) classes, the Physiocrats recognized the landowners as a legitimate class entitled to rent on their lands, because they or their ancestors were the first ones to clear it and prepare it for farming. In this sense, the Physiocratic school accepted the prerevolutionary structure of society.

The founder of the Physiocratic school was François Quesnay, court physician to Louis XV. His crowning work was the *Tableau économique* (1758), the first schematic portrayal of an entire economy. The term physiocracy denotes the rule of nature; their famous phrase *laissez faire, laissez passer* ("let it be, let it go") reflected their belief that natural economic laws should prevail. The Physiocrats attacked mercantilism because of its mass of economic regulations.

Because they believed that only agriculture yielded a net surplus, the Physiocrats favoured the imposition of an *impôt unique*, or single tax, directly on the net product that accrued to the landowners and the elimination of all the other taxes that had become so burdensome to the entire French economy.

Anne-Robert-Jacques Turgot became minister of finance in 1774 and began to effect some of the reforms suggested by Physiocratic thought. As a result of some of these he was removed by the King in 1776 when the landed class strongly objected to his policies. With this, the influence of the Physiocrats ended.

- ·Adam Smith and French reformers **16**:905e
- ·mercantilism and free trade **4**:888g
- ·political economy theory **16**:984g
- ·property taxation as revenue resource **15**:59h
- ·Quesnay's laissez-faire philosophy **6**:893g
- ·Turgot's travels and economic ideas **18**:781f

physiognomy, the systematic relation of psychological characteristics to facial features or body structure. Since many efforts to specify such relationships have been discredited, the term physiognomy commonly connotes pseudoscience or charlatanry on the level of fortune-telling or palmistry. While this disreputable word is scorned among scientists, there is ample evidence that a number of facial and bodily characteristics are definite correlates of psychological function. Familiar examples in medical practice include distinctive physiognomic signs observed in forms of mental deficiency, abnormal psychosexual behaviour, and emotional disturbance (*e.g.*, cretinism; hydrocephalus; hermaphroditism; Addison's disease; pellagra; hyperthyroidism).

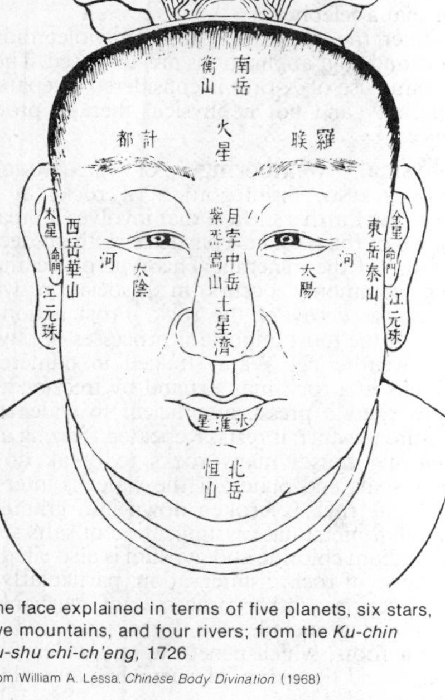

The face explained in terms of five planets, six stars, five mountains, and four rivers; from the *Ku-chin t'u-shu chi-ch'eng*, 1726

From William A. Lessa, *Chinese Body Divination* (1968)

Aristotle wrote the earliest known systematic treatise on physiognomy; the chief basis of his work was analogical. People with facial features resembling particular animals were thought to have analogous temperaments; *e.g.*, a bulldog jaw signified tenacity.

In the 18th and 19th centuries J.K. Lavater of Switzerland and C. Lombroso of Italy were influential proponents of similar physiognomic notions that failed to survive empirical scrutiny. The British investigator Sir Charles Goring published a monumental study that found the Lombrosian system of criminological physiognomy to be fallacious. H.L. Hollingworth of the U.S. summarized many experiments and found little relation between physiognomic measurements and psychological traits; D.G. Paterson, also of the U.S., in 1930 published an evaluation of studies made during the preceding 40 years that revealed a consistent trend of negative results.

Body build as a subdivision of physiognomy has persisted from the time of the ancient Greek physician Hippocrates (flourished 400 BC), and the medical significance of differences in body build has been established. The German psychiatrist E. Kretschmer in the 1920s developed a morphological basis for psychiatric diagnosis; similar findings were reported for normal people in the 1940s by W.H. Sheldon of the U.S. and co-workers. In neither case are the correlations sufficiently high to be especially useful in psychological diagnosis. However, physiognomic aspects of human character and personality continue slowly to yield to codisciplinary study involving human genetics, biochemistry, and psychology. For example, genetic bases have been established for mongolian idiocy (characterized by typical eyelid folds) and the syndrome of dwarfism and mental retardation known as galactosemia.

BIBLIOGRAPHY. J.K. Lavater, *Essays on Physiognomy*, trans. by T. Holcroft, 4 vol. (1804); Aristotle, *History of Animals and a Treatise on Physiognomy*, trans. by T. Taylor (1809); D.G. Paterson, *Physique and Intellect* (1930); W.H. Sheldon, S.S. Stevens, and W.B. Tucker, *Varieties of Human Physique*, reprint (1963); H. Asano, *Faces Never Lie* (1964).

physiographic effects of man 14:429, changes of the Earth's landscape brought about directly or indirectly by man and his activities as these influence natural processes.

The text article treats the rise of man's influence—from his discovery of fire, through agrarian development, to the building of cities, harbours, and other engineering works. The article also deals with modern man, delineating his activities in terms of their direct and indirect effects on the Earth.

REFERENCES in other text articles:

- ·African vegetation and animal life **1**:195f *passim* to 197c
- ·beaches and effects of technology **2**:779g
- ·Berlin hills built of bombing rubble **2**:851h
- ·biosphere exploitation and management **2**:1042h
- ·Caspian sea level and constructions **3**:981h
- ·desert expansion causes **5**:614h
- ·English landscape transformation **6**:867g
- ·estuary sediment deposits affected **6**:970g
- ·floodplain alluviation **15**:885b
- ·grassland environmental control **8**:285d
- ·lake formation and resultant problems **10**:610e
- ·North American European colonization **13**:194f
- ·Northern Ireland's lack of forests **13**:238c
- ·Pacific Coast environmental problems **13**:825g
- ·pollution and urban and global climate **18**:1045f
- ·primitive and European cultural impact **5**:42b
- ·river environment manipulation **7**:437g
- ·sediment yield variations and reservoirs **16**:476d; illus. 477
- ·South American deforestation **17**:88d
- ·strip mining environmental effects **5**:51a; illus.

· United Kingdom vegetation destruction **18**:872c
· water balance changes **19**:648d

physiographic effects of tectonism **14**:433, role played by the Earth's crustal movements in the formation of large-scale landscape features.

The text article provides a general review of the several modern theories regarding the role of tectonism in physiographic change, including sections on recent tectonic movements; dynamics of the Earth's surface features; the large relief forms that emerge as a result of the interaction of tectonic forces and denudational processes; and tectonism of the ocean floor.

REFERENCES in other text articles:
· African rift valleys **15**:842b
· alluvial fan evolution theory **1**:616g
· Arabian peninsula separation **1**:1052a
· Asian platforms and mountains **2**:147e
· Canadian Shield formation **3**:713g
· Caucasus Mountains origin **3**:1016c
· continental elevation and climates **4**:741b
· continental island formation **13**:826f
· Death Valley faulting and mountains **5**:539d
· estuary basin formation **6**:969h
· European and Asian landscape **6**:45c
· geosyncline deformation **6**:10e
· graywacke and geosyncline deformation **8**:299d
· Hercynian orogeny world extent **3**:858d
· Indian Ocean bottom structure **9**:310e
· island arc and landform theories **9**:1026c
· Lake Baikal bay formation and springs **2**:596b
· landform evolution theories **10**:624f
· mountain formation methods **12**:588d
· mountain origin and tectonic belts **12**:578h; illus.
· Mt. Everest's geological formation **6**:1139h
· new global tectonics concept **9**:1030b
· oceanic ridge origin **13**:473d
· ocean valley formation by faulting **3**:790f
· Ordovician deformation and sediments **13**:657d
· Pacific Coast Range formation **13**:825a
· Pacific geologic history **13**:837e
· Permian forces on Appalachian and Ural Mountains **14**:99c
· Pyrenees height, passes, and rivers **15**:315f
· river systems' evolution **15**:887f
· rock formation and composition **9**:218d
· Rocky Mountain formation and faults **15**:964h *passim* to 968c
· Ross Sea coastal feature development **15**:1161g
· sea-floor spreading processes **16**:446f
· sea-level changes and crust deformation **8**:1002c
· stream alteration and basin formation **8**:434c
· Tertiary mountain building and volcanoes **3**:1080d
· waterfall association with faulting **19**:640h

physiological clock (biology): *see* biological rhythm.

physiological dead space, in anatomy, the total space within the respiratory system filled with gases that are unable to take part in the oxygen and carbon dioxide exchange occurring between the circulating blood and lung tissues during breathing; it is the space included in the airways (nose, throat, windpipe, and bronchi) plus the total space in the lung formed by tissues that do not partake in gas exchanges.
· significance in ventilation **15**:749d

physiological psychology: *see* psychology, physiological.

Physiological Society, a British scientific society founded in 1876.
· Foster's influence on organization **14**:436g

Physiologie du mariage, La (1829), novel by Honoré de Balzac.
· theme and attitude toward women **2**:680d

Physiologus, 2nd-century-AD Greek bestiary.
· mythic and moral objectives **1**:916d

physiology **14**:435, the study of the activities and functions of living matter.

The text article covers historical background, scope, societies and publications, and prospects.

REFERENCES in other text articles:
· Bernard's experimental medicine beliefs **2**:859d
· biological sciences classification **2**:1014g
· biophysics source disciplines **2**:1034h
· botany methodology **3**:67d
· Cartesian mechanistic analysis **3**:968e
· chemotherapy history and importance **4**:188g
· diagnosis foundations **5**:684f
· disease classification systems **5**:863b
· early foundations in science and art **16**:981c
· Galen's experiments and theories **7**:849g
· Galvani's muscle and nerve studies **7**:859g
· life defined physiologically **10**:893d
· mechanist–vitalist debate **16**:380a
· Oriental medicine's history **11**:824b
· pragmatic reductionism in sciences **16**:389b
· respiratory systems experimentation **15**:751b
· science history and philosophy **16**:366h
· scientific progress in the 19th century **11**:831e
· theoretic and methodologic history **19**:1165e
· Wren's experiment with narcotics **19**:1021d

physiotherapy: *see* physical therapy.

physis, in Greek philosophy, the source of growth or change inherent in or construed as nature.
· Sophist theory of natural law **12**:863f

Physoclisti, former ordinal name for fishes with closed swim bladders, now used as a discriptive term for such fishes.
· buoyancy system and processes **14**:995d; illus.

physogastry, enlargement of the abdomen of termite queen (order Isoptera) due to development of the ovaries and fat bodies.
· termite queen egg-laying capacity **9**:1051c

physostome, name sometimes used for bony fishes whose swim bladder, called a physostomous swim bladder, is connected with the digestive system.
· buoyancy system and processes **14**:995c; illus.
· swim-bladder and water depth sensitivity **11**:804h

Phytamastigophorea (protozoan): *see* phytoflagellate.

Phytelephas, a genus of ivorypalm of the order Arecales.
· palm inflorescence and flower size **1**:1133c

Phyteuma (plant): *see* rampion.

phytochemistry, a branch of chemistry which deals with the study of the chemical composition and properties of plants.
· botany study approaches **3**:69a

phytochrome, name given to a system of protein pigments in the cytoplasm of the cells of green plants. They are not associated with photosynthesis but with light absorption that affects plant growth and development.
· botanical research and discoveries **3**:67b
· growth regulation factors **8**:442f
· light absorption reversibility **14**:352g
· properties and occurrence in plants **4**:920a

phytoflagellate, any plantlike member of the protozoan class Phytamastigophorea. Many phytoflagellates contain the pigment chlorophyll and various accessory pigments. Species without chlorophyll are similar in form to related chlorophyll-bearing species. Phytoflagellates may obtain nutrients by photosynthesis, by absorption through the body surface, or by ingestion of food particles. For some of the more important members of this class, *see Euglena*; *Holomastigotoides*; trichomonad; *Chlamydomonas*; *Volvox*; chloromonad; dinoflagellate; cryptomonad; and chrysomonad.
· protozoan features and classification **15**:120d

phytohemagglutinin, an extract of the red bean (*Phaseolus vulgaris*). It can induce growth and division of small lymphocytes, certain primitive white blood cells in humans.
· Fabales therapeutic importance **7**:130h
· lymphocytes and growth stimulation **11**:210c

phytol, an organic compound occurring as part of the chlorophyll molecule which makes plants green and is used in the manufacture of synthetic vitamins E and K_1. Its molecular structure ($C_{20}H_{40}O$) is that of an alcohol with an attached diterpene group (a molecule consisting of C_5H_8 units). The pure compound is an oily liquid that boils at about 203°–204° C (397°–399° F).

Phytol was first obtained by hydrolysis (decomposition by water) of chlorophyll in 1909 by the German chemist Richard Wilstätter. Its structure was determined in 1928 by the German chemist F.G. Fischer, who also synthesized the compound from farnesol, an alcohol of similar structure but containing one less C_5H_8 unit.

Conversion of phytol to α-tocopherol, the most potent of the E vitamins essential for reproduction in rats, was reported from three laboratories in 1938 and has been applied in commercial manufacture. A synthesis of phytonadione, or vitamin K_1, was developed in 1939.

Phytol may be obtained in the process of separating chlorophyll from alfalfa. In some applications phytol has been replaced by its synthetic equivalent, isophytol.
· formula and use in chlorophyll synthesis **9**:1048h

phytolaccaceae (tropical herb): *see* poke.

Phytolacca dioica, a species of ombu (herbaceous trees of South America) of the order Caryophyllales.
· tree growth features **18**:689c

Phytophaga destructor: *see* Hessian fly.

Phytophthora infestans, a species of fungus (phylum Mycota) that causes late blight of potatoes.
· potato blight transmission and control **5**:890c

phytoplankton, a flora of freely floating minute organisms that drift with water currents. Like land vegetation, phytoplankton uses carbon dioxide, releases oxygen, and converts minerals to a form animals can use. In fresh water, large numbers of green algae often colour lakes and ponds, and blue-green algae may affect the taste of drinking water.

Oceanic phytoplankton is the primary food source, directly or indirectly, of all sea organisms. Composed of groups with siliceous skeletons, such as diatoms, dinoflagellates, and coccolithophores, phytoplankton varies seasonally in amount, increasing in spring and fall with favourable light, temperature, and minerals.
· algae distribution and ecological effects **1**:491d
· Alpine Lakes' algae and eutrophication **1**:632d
· Arctic Ocean food chain **1**:1122g
· Beaufort Sea mass and diversity **2**:782a
· Black Sea diminishing population **2**:1098d
· coastal area production akin to energy use **4**:807a
· coral locale optimum conditions **5**:164c
· ecological and commerical importance **7**:347b *passim* to 349e
· oceanic form and function **1**:1031f
· oxygen source for astronauts **14**:494c
· petroleum occurrence and composition **14**:168a
· pigment synthesis and effect on animals **4**:915e
· polar biotic interactions **14**:655h *passim* to 657c

phytosaur, extinct heavily armoured, semiaquatic reptile restricted to the Late Triassic (the Triassic Period began 225,000,000 years ago and lasted 35,000,000 years). Although they were not ancestral to the crocodiles, in many ways the phytosaurs resembled the modern crocodiles and probably had similar habits. The long and pointed skull was armed with numerous sharp teeth; it is probable that the phytosaurs preyed largely upon fish that were caught in the streams and rivers that the

reptiles inhabited. The nostrils in the phytosaurs were set in a mound high on the skull near the eyes, an adaptive feature related to an aquatic existence that allowed the animal to open its mouth underwater without breathing in any water. The body and tail were elongated; the hindlimbs, better developed than the forelimbs, indicated that the phytosaurs descended from bipedal reptilian ancestors and reverted to a quadrupedal pose. Phytosaurs also were well able to move about on land. Phytosaurian fossils occur in North America, Europe, and India, but their remains have not been found in the southern continents. Familiar genera of phytosaurs include *Rutiodon* and *Phytosaurus*, the genus that gives its name to the group as a whole. *Rutiodon* was more than 3 metres (10 feet) long; its skull alone was about 1 metre (3.5 feet) long and was armed with many sharp teeth.
·reptile evolution and classification **15**:737a

Phytotoma (bird): *see* plantcutter.

phytotoxin: *see* toxin.

Phyu, 16th-century Burmese poetess.
·Burmese court literary style **17**:234g

pi, Greek letter π used as a symbol for the ratio of a circle's circumference to its diameter. This number is independent of the size of the circle; it is transcendental and has the approximate decimal expansion 3.1416.
·Archimedes' treatise on the circle **1**:1088e
·Babylonian mathematics **11**:640g
·real analysis principles **1**:773e

pi, Chinese jade carved in the form of a flat disc with a hole in the center. The earliest examples, which are unornamented, date from the Neolithic Period (*c.* 3000–1500 BC); later examples, from the Shang (*c.* 1766–*c.* 1122 BC) and Chou (*c.* 1122–221 BC) dynasties, have increasingly elaborate surface embellishment, especially in the late Chou (*c.* 600–221 BC), when the *pi* appears in combination with other forms. The *pi* may have been a symbol of heaven or of the Sun. *See also* Chinese jade, art of.
·Chinese ritual art, illus., **19**:Visual Arts, East Asian, Plate I
·origin and purposes **19**:181a

pia-arachnoid (anatomy): *see* pia mater.

Piacenza, capital of Piacenza province, in the Emilia-Romagna region of northern Italy, on the south bank of the Po River just below the mouth of the Trebia, southeast of Milan. It was founded as the Roman colony of Placentia in 218 BC, the same year it gave protection to the remnants of Scipio's Roman army after the Battle of the Trebia. After being besieged unsuccessfully by the Carthaginian general Hasdrubal in 207 BC and sacked by the Gauls in 200, it was restored and reinforced. In 187 BC it became the terminus of the Via Aemilia, the great arterial road to Ariminum (Rimini), and was later the focus of other major Roman roads. After the barbarian invasions, Piacenza was governed by its bishops from 997 to 1035. It became a free commune in the 12th century and a leading member of the Lombard league of towns in opposition to the emperor Frederick I Barbarossa. Despite political vicissitudes, it prospered from its control of river and road traffic. A long period of struggle between the Visconti and Sforza families, alternating with papal and French rule, was concluded in 1545 by the creation by Pope Paul III of the hereditary duchy of Parma and Piacenza for his son Pier Luigi Farnese. For the subsequent history of Piacenza, *see* Parma and Piacenza, Duchy of.

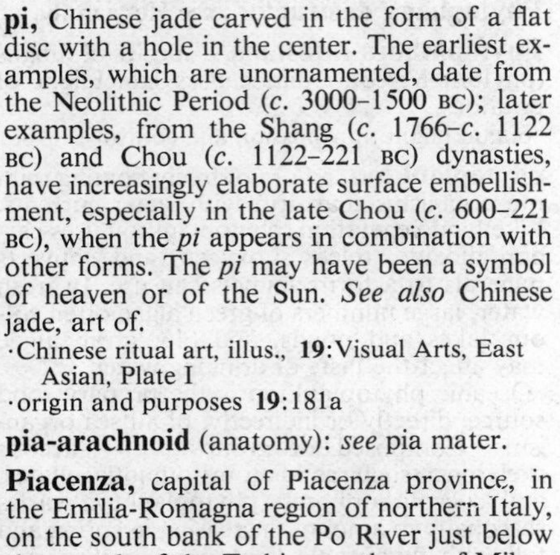

Marconi Square, Piacenza, Italy
Photo Research International

No Roman monuments survive, but the rectangular street plan in the centre of the city is Roman. The brick cathedral (1122–1253) is a fine example of Lombard Romanesque style. Other noteworthy medieval churches are the former cathedral of S. Antonino, incorporating an 11th-century facade and elements of the 13th- and 14th-century construction; the restored S. Savino (consecrated 1107), with unusual 12th-century floor mosaics; S. Francesco (begun 1278); S. Sisto (1499–1511), the original home of Raphael's painting "Sistine Madonna"; and Sta. Maria di Campagna (1522–28), with frescoes by Pordenone. Notable palaces include the Palazzo Comunale (begun 1281) and the grandiose Palazzo Farnese, begun in 1558 for Margaret of Austria and never completed. Two bronze equestrian statues (1612–29) of dukes Alessandro and Ranuccio I Farnese by Franceso Mochi stand in the main square.

Piacenza is a rail and road centre on the main routes from Milan to Bologna. It is a long-established centre for cereal growing and viticulture and has a number of rapidly developing light industries, including the manufacture of chemicals, office furniture, and buttons. Pop. (1979 est.) mun., 109,095.
45°01′ N, 9°40′ E
·Etruscan language epigraphic records **6**:1018d
·map, Italy **9**:1088
·province area and population, table 1 **9**:1094

Piacenza, Domenico da, 15th-century Italian dancing master who wrote an early dance manual.
·social dance treatise content **14**:801b
·Western dance first manual **5**:460a

Piacenzan Stage, lowermost major division of Pliocene rocks and time (the Pliocene Epoch began about 7,000,000 years ago and lasted about 4,500,000 years). The Piacenzan Stage, named for the exposures in the Piacenza region of Italy, is composed of characteristic blue marls that contain a distinctive fauna; it precedes the Astian Stage and follows the Miocene Epoch. The Piacenzan also is known by the term Plaisancian, the French name for the Piacenzan region.

Pia Desideria (Latin: "Pious Desires"), religious work by Philipp Jakob Spener, published in 1675. An English translation was published under same title in 1964.
·Protestant Pietist phase **15**:113b

piaffe, in horsemanship, movement consisting of a collected trot executed in place.
·haute école airs of Lipizzaner horses **15**:838f; illus. 839

Piaget, Jean (b. Aug. 9, 1896, Neuchâtel, Switz.—d. Sept. 16, 1980, Geneva), psychologist and a leading investigator of thought processes, especially among children. At the age of 10 he published an article on his observations of an albino sparrow, and by 15 his publications on mollusks made him known to international specialists. After he obtained his doctorate in science at the University of Neuchâtel (1918), his biological training, together with an intense interest in logic and epistemology, or theory of knowledge, led him into psychology.

During two years of research at the Sorbonne, Piaget began to explore why children fail in tests of reasoning. His resulting article brought him the directorship of the Institut J.J. Rousseau, Geneva. He was professor of psychology at the University of Geneva from 1929, and in 1955 he became the director of the International Centre of Genetic Epistemology at Geneva. In addition to many articles and monographs, he wrote some 30 books, including *Le Langage et la pensée chez l'enfant* (1923; *The Language and Thought of the Child*, 1926), *Le Jugement et le raisonnement chez l'enfant* (1924; *Judgement and Reasoning in the Child*, 1928), *La Naissance de l'intelligence chez l'enfant* (1948; *The Origins of Intelligence in Children*, 1952), and *Mémoire et intelligence* (with Bärbel Inhelder, 1968; *Memory and Intelligence*, 1973).

Piaget's description of the development of cognitive abilities is held in high professional repute. Adopting an earlier view that thinking arises in situations that cannot be handled by automatic, learned performances and reflexes, Piaget then suggested that thinking is a refined, flexible, trial-and-error process. He traced four stages in the development of children's thinking. The first, or sensorimotor stage, occurs in the first two years of life and is characterized by an empirical, largely nonverbal intelligence. The child, experimenting with objects and connecting newer experiences with older ones, can be said to be learning from experience. In the second, or pre-operational level, from two years to seven, objects of the child's perceptions come to be represented by words, which he now manipulates experimentally in his mind as he had previously experimented physically with concrete objects. In stage three, from age 7 to 12, his first logical operations occur, and he classifies objects by their similarities and differences. In the last stage, from 12 and into adulthood, the individual begins experimenting with formal logical operations, and thinking becomes a more flexible kind of experimentation. Piaget's later work attempted to describe the interaction between cognitive and emotional factors in his postulated four stages of thought development.
·attention in children **2**:355b
·behaviour development of children **8**:1136e
·concept formation by young children **4**:1063e
·intellectual development stages **14**:992b
·intelligence and epistemology **9**:679d
·learning theories in education **13**:1100e *passim* to 1101e
·logic and psychological theorizing **11**:77a
·philosophical aspects of studies **16**:377a
·Rationalist view of experience theory **15**:528a
·thought process and origin of reasoning **18**:352f
·thought process theory development **6**:375b
·time perception ability development **18**:423g

Piaggia, Carlo (b. Jan. 4, 1827, Lucca, Italy —d. Jan. 17, 1882, Karkawj, now in The Sudan), explorer who discovered Lake Kyoga (in Uganda) and investigated the Upper (southern) Nile River system. Piaggia had no formal education. He was, however, an acute observer who collected a wealth of information about the geography, natural history, and ethnology of northeastern Africa. He made the first ethnological study of the Zande peoples in the southern Sudan and northeastern Zaire.

Piaggia first entered the interior of Africa in 1856 to collect specimens of rare animals in the Egyptian Sudan (now The Sudan). In 1860–61 he again accompanied naturalists to the Egyptian Sudan, reaching the basin of the Baḥr-al-Ghazāl (Gazelle River) and the borders of the Zande nation. He was intrigued by the Zande peoples and undertook an expedition among them (1863–65), returning with a mass of ethnographical data. In 1871 he explored the Ethiopian highlands and circumnavigated Lake Tana. On another expedition to explore the Upper Nile (1875), he searched for a river passage between the Nile and the great lakes of East Africa; it was during this journey that he discovered Lake Kyoga (1876). He died while on an exploration of the Blue Nile.

pia mater, in anatomy, innermost of three membranes enclosing the brain and spinal cord.
·brain and spinal cord types **12**:999b; illus.
·meningeal layers and general features **12**:986g
·nervous system origins and development **6**:750f

Pian He (China): *see* Pien Canal.

Piankh, 20th-dynasty (1200–1085 BC) Egyptian high priest.
·accession to priesthood and Kush battle **6**:477d

Piankhi (fl. 8th century BC), king of Kush (Cush, in the Sudan; *c.* 751–716) who invaded Egypt from the south and ended the petty kingdoms of the 23rd dynasty (*c.* 817–*c.* 730 BC) in Lower Egypt. According to Egyptian tradition, his brother Shabako founded the 25th dynasty, but Piankhi laid the foundations.

The kingdom of Kush, of which Piankhi was ruler, emerged out of the Egyptianized population of the Sudan near Jabal Barkal, between the Third and Fourth Nile cataracts. The cult of the Egyptian god Amon Re was strongly entrenched among the Kushites, and a threat by Tefnakhte, a Libyan chieftain of the Delta, to Amon's homeland in Upper Egypt provoked Piankhi to move northward. Following a ritual visit to Thebes, Piankhi's forces met the Libyans' river fleet and defeated it. They then vanquished a land army near Heracleopolis, in Middle Egypt, and advanced to take Hermopolis, another Middle Egyptian stronghold of the Libyans, and Memphis, Egypt's ancient capital. Piankhi received the submission of several Delta potentates and, later, of the last representative of the 23rd dynasty. He then invaded the Delta, where more local rulers surrendered. Finally, Tefnakhte sent a message of submission, and Piankhi sent an emissary to obtain his oath of fealty. After some final submissions by holdouts, Piankhi sailed home to Jabal Barkal with the spoils of his venture. He remained in his capital and was buried there; the great stela recounting his deeds also was found there and is dated in the 21st year of his reign.
·Egypt's defeat and occupation **13**:109f
·Libyan–Kushite competition for Egypt **6**:479g
·Memphis siege and conquest of Egypt **11**:896g

piano, or PIANOFORTE, keyboard instrument in which tone is produced by struck strings. The vibration of the strings is transmitted to a soundboard by means of a bridge over which the strings are stretched; the soundboard amplifies the sound and affects its tone quality. The hammers that strike the strings are affixed to a mechanism resting on the far ends of the keys; hammer and mechanism comprise the "action." The function of the mechanism is to accelerate the motion of the hammer, catch it as it rebounds from the strings, and hold it in position for the next attack. Modern hammers are covered with felt; earlier, various kinds of leather were used. The modern piano has a cast-iron frame capable of withstanding the tremendous tension of the strings; early pianos had only wood frames and thus could only be lightly strung. Modern pianos are therefore much louder than were those of the 18th century, and this increase in loudness was necessitated in part by the large size of 19th-century concert halls. Of the three pedals found on most pianos, the damper pedal on the far right lifts all the felt dampers above the strings, allowing them all to vibrate freely; the far-left pedal shifts the keyboard and action sideways to enable the hammer to strike only one of the two or three unison strings of each tenor and treble key (the bass notes are only single-strung); the middle pedal usually holds up the dampers only of those keys depressed when the pedal is depressed.

Double-action pianoforte built by Bartolomeo Cristofori in 1720; in the Metropolitan Museum of Art, New York City

By courtesy of the Metropolitan Museum of Art, New York, the Crosby Brown Collection of Musical Instruments, 1889

The piano was apparently invented by Bartolomeo Cristofori (*q.v.*) in Florence *c.* 1709. It began to become widely popular in the mid-18th century, and thereafter it attracted many of the great European composers and was the medium for salon music, chamber music, concerti, song accompaniments, and other music. Built in various shapes and sizes, the piano has undergone continued development, and modern pianos differ in sound quality and touch from early ones. For development of piano designs other than the normal wing-shaped grand piano, *see* square piano; upright piano. *See also* barrel piano; player piano.
·art song accompaniment **19**:499f
·Beethoven's sonata style **2**:800f
·Brahms's style and accomplishment **3**:107b
·chamber ensemble instrumentation **4**:22c
·Chopin's style and technique **4**:439c
·concerto literature pre-eminence **4**:1070g
·design, operation, and development **10**:442g
·forerunner in principles of dulcimer **12**:732c
·interdependence of parts in chamber ensemble **4**:24h
·Mozart's pianistic innovations **12**:602h
·octave representation on keyboard **17**:37a; illus.
·Romantic forms and styles **12**:714a
·sound produced by striking strings **17**:38d
·tuning, construction, and zither classification **17**:739e *passim* to 741f
·value as ensemble instrument **13**:645a
·varying jazz styles **10**:123f

Pianola: *see* player piano.

piano nobile, in architecture, main floor of a Renaissance building. In the typical *palazzo*, or palace, erected by an Italian prince of the Renaissance, the main reception rooms were in an upper story, usually the story immediately above the basement or ground floor. These rooms had higher ceilings than the rooms on the other floors of the palace and were more elegantly decorated. Often a grand exterior staircase or two led from ground level up to the *piano nobile*, which means "noble floor" in Italian. The term is also used in reference to the main floors of similarly constructed buildings of the English Palladian style of the 18th century and of those built in Great Britain and the United States during the Renaissance revival of the mid- and late 19th century.

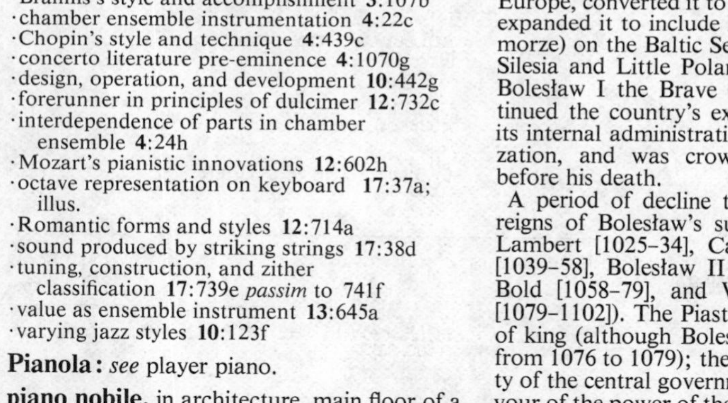

Piano nobile of Kedleston Hall near Derby Eng., designed by Robert Adam in the 1760s

A.F. Kersting

Pianosa Island, Italian ISOLA PIANOSA, ancient PLANASIA, island of the Arcipelago Toscano, in the Tyrrhenian Sea, part of Livorno (Leghorn) province, Italy, just south of the island of Elba. It has an area of 6 sq mi (16 sq km) and is, as its name indicates, flat, with its highest point only about 90 ft (27 m) above sea level. In Roman history it figures as the place of banishment of Agrippa Postumus, grandson of the emperor Augustus. It suffered from the depredations of the Turks in the 16th century. In 1856 an agricultural penal colony was established there. Latest census 878.
42°35′ N, 10°04′ E
·map, Italy **9**:1088

Piast dynasty, first ruling family of Poland. According to a 12th-century legend, when Prince Popiel of Gnesen (now Gniezno) died in the second half of the 9th century, he was succeeded by Siemowit, the son of the Prince's plowman, Piast, thus founding a dynasty that ruled the Polish lands until 1370. (The name Piast was not applied to the dynasty until the 17th century.) By 963 Mieszko I (ruled *c.* 963–992), probably the fourth prince of the Piast line, was ruling a highly developed, if somewhat isolated, political community in the territories later known as Great Poland and possibly also in Mazovia. Mieszko brought his state into closer association with western Europe, converted it to Christianity (966), and expanded it to include Pomerania (Polish Pomorze) on the Baltic Sea (967–990) as well as Silesia and Little Poland (989–992). His son Bolesław I the Brave (ruled 992–1025) continued the country's expansion, strengthened its internal administration and church organization, and was crowned its king shortly before his death.

A period of decline then set in during the reigns of Bolesław's successors (Mieszko II Lambert [1025–34], Casimir I the Restorer [1039–58], Bolesław II the Generous or the Bold [1058–79], and Władysław I Herman [1079–1102]). The Piast princes lost their title of king (although Bolesław II held it briefly, from 1076 to 1079); they allowed the authority of the central government to diminish in favour of the power of the regional nobility, and they engaged the state in numerous struggles that resulted in a territorial loss. Only after Bolesław III the Wry-Mouthed (ruled 1102–38) succeeded to the throne and exiled his brother and co-ruler Zbigniew (1107) did Poland's boundaries reach those of Mieszko I's domain (by 1125). But Bolesław failed to regain the title of king as well as to reverse the decentralizing tendencies that were undermining the unity of his state. Therefore, in order to avoid future internal conflict based on regional rivalry and to retain unity among the Piast lands, Bolesław divided Poland among his sons. Each of the territorial subdivisions—defined by 1166 as Silesia, Great Poland, Mazovia, and Sandomierz—was to be held as the hereditary domain of one of Bolesław's sons. The senior member of the entire dynasty was also to acquire temporary possession of Cracow and Pomerania and rule as grand prince over the entire loosely federated state of Poland.

The new arrangement, however, stimulated more divisiveness; the power of the grand prince of Cracow declined after the reigns of Casimir II the Just (1177–94) and Leszek the White (1202–27). For the next 150 years Poland suffered from increasing disunity and disintegration, aggravated by dynastic struggles and civil wars, foreign intervention and invasion, and the secession and conquest of its border regions.

Nevertheless, throughout this period of political division, the Piast lands retained their common church structure, language, and economy, all of which provided a basis for various princes to try to reunify the Polish kingdom. The first attempts failed; they were made by the Silesian princes Henry I and Henry II in the 1230s and by the prince of Great Poland Przemysł II (ruled at Cracow 1279–96; crowned king of Poland 1295). But after Wenceslas II (Polish Wacław) of Bohemia gained control of two-thirds of the Polish lands and became king of Poland (1300–05), Władysław I the Short (Łokietek), a grandson of Conrad of Mazovia, gained support from the gentry, the leading clergy, and some members of the upper nobility, won control of Sandomir and Cracow (by 1306), and, with the aid of Hungary and the Pope, became the ruler of Great Poland and also king of Poland (1320). Władysław I strengthened Poland substantially by forming close alliances, through the marriages of his children, with both Hungary and Lithuania.

His son Casimir III the Great assumed the throne of the restored Polish kingdom (1333) and further improved its position by coming to terms with his two major enemies, Bohemia and the Teutonic Knights. He accepted Poland's loss of Silesia and Pomerania, annexed Galicia, and regained Mazovia (1349). Casimir also consolidated his rule over the state by improving its economy and military and civil administrations, codifying the laws of Great and Little Poland, and founding a university at Cracow (1364).

Casimir's death, however, brought an end to his line of the Piast dynasty. Having developed the newly reunified Piast lands into a stable, prosperous, and powerful nation, he left his kingdom to his sister's son, Louis I of Hungary. After ruling from 1370 to 1382, Louis was succeeded by his daughter Jadwiga and her husband Jogaila (Władysław II Jagiełło), the grand duke of Lithuania and founder of the Jagiellon dynasty in Poland.

·Casimir III's reign and accomplishments **3**:978b
·Polish national development **14**:638c

Piatra Neamţ, capital, northern Neamţ district (*judeţ*), northeastern Romania, north of Bucharest. In the valley of the Bistriţa, it is surrounded by the Cozla, Petricica, and Cer-

The Piast dynasty

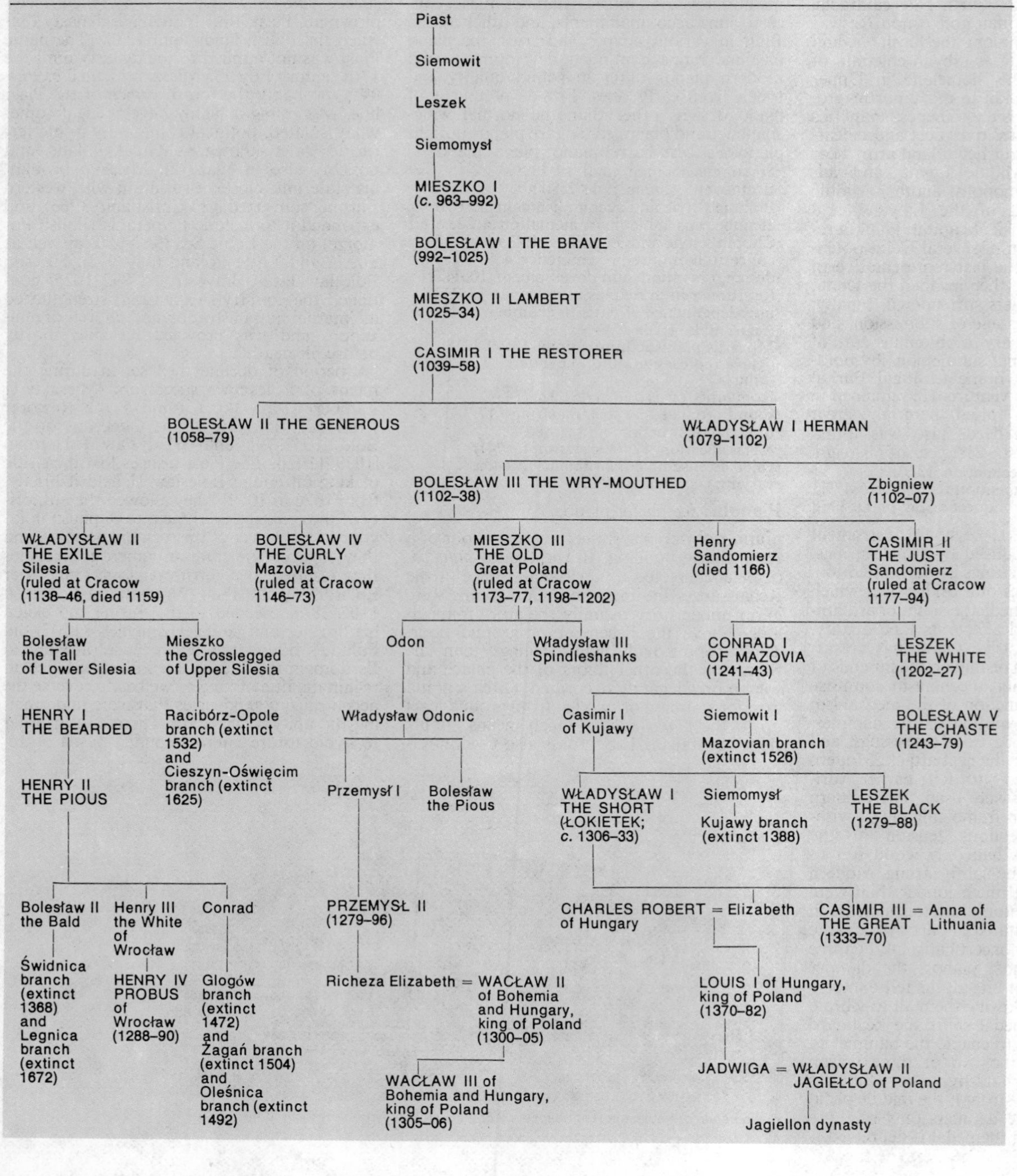

negura mountains. It was first documented in the 15th century as Piatra lui Crăciun, or Camena, a market town where fairs were held. Stephen (Ştefan) the Great of Moldavia built the church of Sf. Ion (St. John) in 1497–98, a classic example of ornate Moldavian architecture. There is a state theatre, a regional natural-science museum, and an archaeological museum of Neolithic pottery. Industries include a fertilizer plant, a pulp and paper mill, and several food-processing plants. Southeast of the town, in the Bistriţa Valley, are two large factories, producing synthetic fibre and nitrogenous fertilizer. The Bistriţa Monastery, founded at the beginning of the 15th century by Prince Alexander (Alexandru) the Good and rebuilt in 1554 by Prince Alexander Lăpuşneanu, is 5 mi (8 km) west of Piatra Neamţ. Pop. (1970 est.) 53,630.
46°56′ N, 26°22′ E
·map, Romania **15**:1048

Piauí 14:440, state of northeastern Brazil, bordered by the states of Ceará and Pernambuco (east), by Bahia and Goiás (south), by Maranhão (west), and by the Atlantic Ocean (north). Its area of 96,886 sq mi (250,934 sq km) is less than 3 percent of Brazil's total. The state capital is Teresina. Pop. (1970 prelim.) 1,734,865.

The text article covers the state's geography, climate, population, and transport system.

REFERENCES in other text articles:
·area and population table **3**:133
·map, Brazil **3**:124

Piave River, Italian FIUME PIAVE, in northeastern Italy, rises on the slopes of Monte Peralba in the Carnic Alps near the Austrian frontier and flows southward to the Belluno basin and its gorge at Feltre, where it turns southeast to meander across the Venetian plain, reaching the Adriatic Sea at Cortellazzo, northeast of Venice. The river is 137 mi (220 km) long, with a drainage basin of 1,580 sq mi (4,092 sq km). The variations in its flow are extreme; during late summer most of the Piave's lower course is a great bed of dry gravel. Until about 1500 the mouth of the Piave was farther south, near Treporti on the lagoon of Venice. After several changes the river mouth settled near Caorle until a disastrous flood in 1683, when it shifted to its present outlet. In 1966, swollen by rains, the river burst its dikes in a major flood. Its upper valley has major hydroelectric stations at Pieve di Cadore and Fadalto, while downstream its waters are used extensively for irrigation. Occasional navigation by barges extends only about 20 mi inland. In World War I the Piave became the main line of Italian defense after the Austrian breakthrough at Caporetto in 1917. Despite concerted Austrian attacks in 1918, the line held, and the Austrians were decisively defeated at the Battle of Vittorio Veneto at the end of October 1918.
45°32′ N, 12°44′ E
·map, Italy **9**:1088

Piaya: *see* cuckoo.

Piazza Armerina, town and episcopal see, Enna province, central Sicily, Italy, west-southwest of Catania. Among the many historic monuments are the 17th-century cathedral, with a 14th-century campanile, the Baroque palace of Trigona della Floresta, the church of San Rocco (1613), the Civic Museum, the 14th-century four-sided castle, and the well-preserved remains of the Roman villa of Casale. The Norman Count Roger, associated with the foundation of the town in the 11th century, is said to have received from Pope Nicholas II the Byzantine statue of Madonna delle Vittorie (Our Lady of Victories) in the cathedral, which is borne through the streets on the Feast of the Assumption. There are sulfur mines in the neighbourhood, and nougat is produced in the town. Pop. (1970 est.) 22,372.
37°23′ N, 14°22′ E
·map, Italy **9**:1088

Piazza Tales, The (1856), collection of short stories by Herman Melville.
·Hawthorne's literary influence **8**:680b

Piazzetta, Giovanni Battista (b. Feb. 13, 1682, Venice—d. April 28, 1754, Venice), painter, illustrator, and designer who was one of the outstanding Venetian artists of the 18th century. His art evolved from Italian Baroque traditions of the 17th century to a Rococo manner in his mature style. He began his career in the studio of his father, Giacomo, a wood-carver. Soon after assisting the latter to carve the still-surviving bookcases of the library of SS. Giovanni e Paolo at Venice, he abandoned the family profession and began to study painting under Antonio Molinari.

"Fortune teller," oil painting by Piazzetta, 1740; in the Accademia, Venice
Alinari

About 1703 he went to Bologna, where he worked in the studio of G.M. Crespi. He was back in Venice by 1711 and continued to work there until his death. From Molinari, and the study of Bolognese painting (especially Guercino's work), he learned the heavily shadowed manner that he henceforth adopted; Crespi probably awakened his interest in genre painting. The Caravaggesque lighting effects at which he aimed have become emphasized with time, for his olive-gray and brown colours have darkened and the deep-red ground on which he invariably painted has become more prominent.

Little is known of the dating of Piazzetta's works, especially those of his youth. "St. James Led to Martyrdom" (S. Stae, Venice) is dated about 1717; at this period he was a powerful influence on the young Giambattista Tiepolo, who was to become the most famous Venetian painter of the 18th century. About 1725–27 he undertook his only ceiling painting, the "Glorification of St. Dominic" for the Chapel of the Sacrament in SS. Giovanni e Paolo, in which the reverse influence of the now mature Tiepolo on Piazzetta is apparent. The "Ecstasy of St. Francis" (Pinacoteca Civica, Vicenza), perhaps his finest religious work, dates from about 1732, and some three years later he was commissioned to execute an "Assumption" for the elector of Cologne (museum, Lille). The celebrated "Fortune Teller" (Accademia, Venice) is dated 1740. "The Pastoral" (Art Institute of Chicago) and the "Idyll by the Seashore" (Wallraf-Richartz Museum, Cologne, copy in Dublin), both in the same Rococo-pastoral vein, must have been painted about the same time or a little before. In his last years he carried out a number of large-scale decorations with subjects taken from classical history.

In 1727 Piazzetta had been elected a member of the Bolognese Accademia Clementina, and on the foundation of the Venetian Academy in 1750 he was made its first director and teacher of drawing from the nude. He produced many works for private patrons, especially half-lengths of single saints, biblical subjects, and studies of peasants, soldiers, or adolescents, and a few portraits. He was a very slow worker and in spite of his popularity was compelled to produce innumerable drawings for sale to eke out a penurious existence for his large family. He also carried out many designs for book illustrations, mostly for his friend, the publisher G.B. Albrizzi, the edition of T. Tasso's *Gerusalemme liberata* (1745) being among the finest illustrated books of the 18th century.

Piazzi, Giuseppe (b. July 16, 1746, Ponte di Valtellina, Italy—d. July 22, 1826, Naples), astronomer who discovered (Jan. 1, 1801) and named the first minor planet, Ceres. He had become a Theatine monk *c.* 1764, a professor of theology in Rome in 1779, and in 1780 was appointed professor of higher mathematics at the Academy of Palermo. Later, with the aid of the viceroy of Sicily, he founded the Observatory of Palermo. There he produced his great catalog of the positions of 7,646 stars and demonstrated that most stars are in motion relative to the Sun. There also he discovered Ceres and the high proper motion of the important double star 61 Cygni.
·minor planet discoveries **14**:491g

pi bond, in chemistry, a cohesive interaction between two atoms and a pair of electrons that occupy an orbital (*q.v.*) located in two regions roughly parallel to the line determined by the two atoms. A pair of atoms may be connected by one or by two pi bonds only if a sigma bond (*q.v.*) also exists between them; in the molecule of nitrogen (N_2), for example, the triple bond between the two nitrogen atoms comprises a sigma bond and two pi bonds.
·alkene double bond geometry **9**:85c
·carbanion bonding and resonance structure **3**:818d
·coordination compound bond structure **5**:137e
·heterocycle structure and aromaticity **8**:833h
·organic halogen compound properties **13**:684a
·phosphorus–oxygen bonds and reactivity **13**:701h
·quantum-mechanical analysis **4**:92g
·transition element structure **18**:604a; illus.

Pibor River, southeastern Sudan, flows about 200 mi (320 km) north to join the Baro, forming the Sobat River.
8°26′ N, 33°13′ E
·Nile flood and river physiography **13**:106f; map 103

Pibul (PIBUN) **Songgram, Luang** (b. July 14, 1897, near Bangkok—d. June 12, 1964, Tokyo), field marshal and premier of Thailand in 1938–44 and 1948–57. Pibul was most closely associated with Thailand's pro-Japa-

Pibul Songgram, 1957
Popperfoto

nese policies during World War II and with a long succession of military governments.

After studying at a military school in France, Pibul returned to Thailand (then Siam) in 1927 to become a captain in the army. In 1932 he participated in the bloodless revolution that abolished the absolute monarchy and forced King Prajadhipok (Rama VII) to grant a constitution. Acting as minister of defense and deputy commander in chief, Pibul, with a young lawyer, Pridi Phanomyong, controlled the government until 1938. When the moderate premier, Phya Bahol, resigned, Pibul established a military government, the forerunner of similar regimes in Burma, Indonesia, and Cambodia.

Pibul modelled his state along fascist lines, styling himself "the leader" and calling for the establishment of a "Greater Thai State" to include Laos, the Shan States, and even the Tai minority regions of China's Yunnan Province, as well as Siam (the term Thailand was substituted for Siam in 1939). Extremely pro-Japanese, he signed a pact with Japan in 1940 and declared war on the United States and Great Britain on Jan. 25, 1942. His domestic policies were similar to those of Japan at that time. Education was strictly controlled, Buddhism was promoted as a kind of patriotic state religion, and Christians suffered discrimination. Because Thailand, although technically an ally of Japan, was treated as a vassal state, a large, antifascist Free Thai Movement developed. Pibul's government collapsed in July 1944, and power passed to Pridi Phanomyong.

After the war Pibul retired, but the civilian government could not maintain control; and, after the mysterious death of King Ananda Mahidol in June 1946, Pibul returned to power in 1948 on a wave of anti-Communist feeling. In 1954 Pibul allied Thailand to the West in the cold war by helping to establish the South East Asia Treaty Organization (SEATO), with its headquarters in Bangkok. After a brief experiment with democracy in 1956 and 1957, when political parties were allowed and the ban on freedom of speech was lifted, he was ousted in 1957 by colleagues who were tired of the corruption and inefficiency of his government. He then fled to Tokyo, where he lived until his death.

pic, also called PIK, PICKI, and DIRAA, any of various units of length used in Mediterranean countries, as Greece, Turkey, Egypt, Algeria, and Cyprus; equal to between 18 and 30 inches.

·weights and measures, table 5 **19**:734

Picabia, Francis (b. Jan. 22, 1879, Paris—d. Nov. 30, 1953, Paris), painter, illustrator, designer, writer, and editor whose successive involvement with the Cubist, Dadaist, and Surrealist movements reflected the rapidly shifting currents of early 20th-century art. After studying at the École des Beaux-Arts and the École des Arts Décoratifs, Picabia worked for nearly six years in an Impressionist mode akin to that of Alfred Sisley. In 1911 he became a member of the Section d'Or ("Golden Section"), a Cubist group that met at the studio of Jacques Villon. Also in 1911 he met the artist Marcel Duchamp, and Picabia's rejection of the unemotional themes of Cubism for intricate still lifes and symbolic figures is thought to have resulted from this association. For these Orphic, or colour-orchestrated, paintings, Picabia gradually adopted proto-Dadaist names; *e.g.*, "I See Again in Memory My Dear Udnie" (1913; Museum of Modern Art, New York City) and "Catch as Catch Can" (1913; Philadelphia Museum of Art).

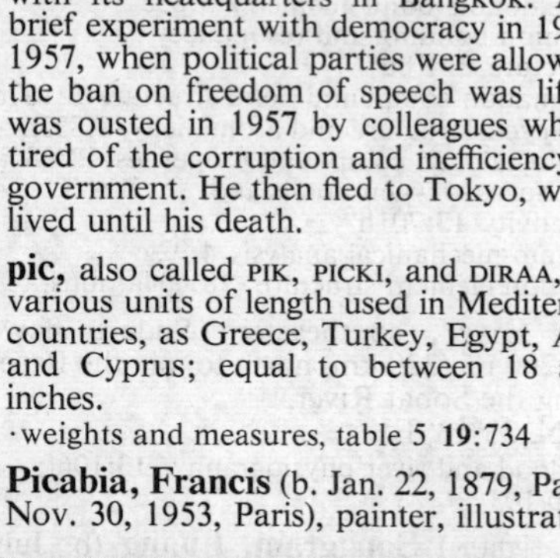

Untitled oil on canvas by Francis Picabia, 1920s; in the Solomon R. Guggenheim Museum Collection, New York City

The Solomon R. Guggenheim Museum, New York City, gift of Mr. and Mrs. Andrew Fuller, New York; permission S.P.A.D.E.M. 1973 by French Reproduction Rights, Inc.

In 1913 he was in New York, where he exhibited at the Armory Show and at Alfred Stieglitz's Photo-Secession Gallery. He contributed to the proto-Dadaist review *291* and also to Stieglitz's magazine, *Camera Work*, where he promulgated Amorphism, a satire on current art trends. In 1917 Picabia and the wealthy poet-scholar-collector, Walter Arensberg, launched the periodical *391*, a continuation of *291*. With Marcel Duchamp, Marius de Zayas, and Man Ray, he was part of a Dada-like group of European artists living in New York. His insolent, mocking "Universal Prostitution" (1916–19; Yale University Art Gallery) dates from this time.

In 1917 Picabia returned to Europe and he was active as a Dadaist in Barcelona, Paris, and Zürich, where he collaborated in 1918 with Tristan Tzara on the fourth and fifth issues of the magazine *Dada*. In Paris in 1920 he began to publish a review called *Cannibale*.

Picabia's changing styles reflected his involvement with the major art movements of his time. His early Cubist paintings—closer to Fernand Léger than to Picasso—are richly coloured and have the appearance of closely fitted, highly polished metallic shapes. As he moved away from Cubism toward Orphism, the colours and shapes became softer until, about 1916, he began to concentrate on the satiric, mechanistic contrivances of Dadaism. After 1927 Picabia rejected the total abstraction that had occupied him for so many years for paintings based on the human figure—superimposed, transparent, linear forms.

Picabia was deeply involved in writing as well as painting. Among his many literary works, *Poèmes et dessins de la fille née sans mère* (1918) is generally considered the most important.

·Stieglitz' American art promotion **17**:691b
·stylistic evolution with Duchamp **5**:1078h

picador, in bullfighting, mounted *torero* who prods the bull with a lance in order to weaken the neck and shoulder muscles.

·bullfighting history and function **3**:476d

Pica pica (bird): *see* magpie.

Picard, (Charles-) Émile (b. July 24, 1856, Paris—d. Dec. 11, 1941, Paris), mathematician whose theories did much to advance research into analysis, algebraic geometry, and mechanics. He became a lecturer at the University of Paris in 1878 and a professor at the University of Toulouse the following year. From 1881 to 1898 he held various posts with the University of Toulouse and the École Normale Supérieure, Paris, and in 1898 he was appointed professor at the University of Paris. In 1917 he was elected permanent secretary for the mathematical sciences in the Académie des Sciences, Paris.

Picard worked on quadratic forms, on Fuchsian and Abelian functions, and on the allied theories of discontinuous and continuous groups of transformation and discovered hyperfuchsian and hyperabelian functions. His work led to a study of the algebraic manifold now known as the Picard variety, which plays a fundamental role in algebraic geometry. In 1879 he proved the theorem known by his name, that an integral function of the complex variable takes every finite value, with one possible exception. His theorem became the starting point for many important studies in the theory of complex functions.

Émile Picard

H. Roger-Viollet

Picard introduced a new means of proving the existence of solutions to differential equations: the method of successive approximations. His method proved so useful that for ordinary differential equations it replaced the Cauchy-Lipschitz method. He also created a theory of linear differential equations, later extended by his pupil Ernest Vessiot, analogous to the Galois theory of algebraic equations.

Inspired by Niels H. Abel of Norway and Bernhard Riemann of Germany, Picard's study of the integrals attached to algebraic surfaces and the related topological questions developed into an important part of algebraic geometry, with varied applications to topology and function theory. His research was expounded in the treatise he published with Georges Simart, *Théorie des fonctions algébriques de deux variables indépendantes*, 2 vol. (1897, 1906; "Theory of Algebraic Functions of Two Independent Variables"). His studies of harmonic vibrations, coupled with the contributions of Hermann Schwarz of Germany and Henri Poincaré of France, marked the beginning of the theory of integral equations.

Picard, Jean (b. July 21, 1620, La Flèche, Fr.—d. July 12, 1682, Paris), astronomer who first accurately measured the length of a degree of a meridian (longitude line) and from that computed the size of the Earth. Picard became professor of astronomy at the Collège de France, Paris, in 1655. His measurement of the Earth was used by Sir Isaac Newton to verify his theory of gravitation. In 1671 Picard went to the observatory of the noted 16th-century Danish astronomer Tycho Brahe at Hven Island, Sweden, to determine its exact location so that Brahe's observations could be more precisely compared with those made elsewhere. He brought back copies of the originals of Brahe's principal work. Picard is also given credit for the introduction of telescopic sights and the use of pendulum clocks as contributions to greater precision in astronomical observations. In 1675 he made the first recorded observation of barometric light, the light that appears in the vacuum above the mercury in a barometer when the barometer is moved about. In 1679 Picard founded and became editor of *La Connaissance des temps ou des mouvements célestes* ("Knowledge of Time or the Celestial Motions"), the first national astronomical ephemeris, or collection of tables giving the positions of celestial bodies at regular intervals.

·Earth's arc measurement **6**:2d

Picard, Leo (b. June 3, 1900, Wangen, now in W.Ger.), Israeli geologist known for his regional studies of the geology of Israel. He was a professor and head of the department of geology at the Hebrew University (Jerusalem) from 1934 until 1963, when he became a geological adviser to the Israeli government and to several oil companies. He served as the director of the Geological Survey of Israel in 1950–54. His work includes studies of the area's hydrology, paleontology, and structural geology.

Picardy, French PICARDIE, region of northern France lying between Normandy and the historic Netherlands and north of Île-de-France and Champagne; its core forms the modern *département* of Somme and the northern part of Aisne. Since Picardy was never unified in the feudal period, its boundaries are disputable. Linguistically, Picardy extended beyond its geographic boundaries to Artois, Cambrésis, Tournésis, and parts of Flanders and Hainaut; ecclesiastically, it embraced not only the medieval dioceses of Amiens, Noyon, and Laon but also the northern parts of those of Beauvais and of Soissons. The province of Picardy from the 16th century to the end of the *ancien régime* comprised the Somme Basin from Saint-Quentin to the Channel, the basins of the Serre and of the upper Oise, and Montreuil on the Canche beyond the Authie.

The *gouvernement* of Picardy in 1789

Occupied by the Salian Franks in the 5th century, Picardy, divided in the feudal period, encompassed six countships: Boulogne, Montreuil, Ponthieu, Amiénois, Vermandois, and Laonnois. Philip II Augustus gradually united Amiénois and Vermandois to his domain (from 1185), but Ponthieu was held by the English as a fief almost continuously from 1279 to 1360 and then as an outright possession till 1369. The dukes of Burgundy acquired Ponthieu, the Somme towns, and Montdidier under the Treaty of Arras in 1435. Reconquered for France by Louis XI in 1477, Picardy was thereafter a frontier area invaded frequently from the Habsburg Netherlands until the French acquisition of Artois and southern Hainaut in 1659.

·area and population table **7**:594
·map, France **7**:584
·World War I German tactics **19**:580g

picaresque novel, early form of novel, usually a first-person narrative, relating the adventures of a *pícaro*, or rogue, as he drifts, in his effort to survive, from place to place and from one social milieu to another. In its episodic structure the picaresque novel resembles the long, rambling romances of chivalry, to which it provides a realistic counterpart. Unlike the idealistic knight-errant hero, the picaroon hero is cynical; his wits are sharpened by hunger, and the ends he serves are his own. Though amoral, he is not a villain. Actually, he is a conformist who learns his tricks from the respectable members of a society that excludes him.

The type originated in Spain with *Lazarillo de Tormes* (1554; doubtfully attributed to Diego Hurtado de Mendoza). Lazarillo begins his career as a guide to a cruel and cunning blind man. His next master is a penurious priest who starves him; the next is a fine nobleman who dines on crusts that Lazarillo begs on the street; the next is a dealer in papal indulgences and performer of "miracles"; the next is a chaplain who sells water. Lazarillo finds content at the end with a slight rise in status to a level of respectability that allows him to commit crimes with impunity.

Lazarillo became one of the most widely read books of its time and established the genre, which remained viable from 1550 to 1750. Numerous Spanish successors followed it, the best known being Mateo Aleman's *Guzmán de Alfarache* (1599) and Francisco Gómez de Quevedo's *Vida del Buscón* (1626; "The Life of a Scoundrel"). In *La picara Justina* (1605; Francisco López de Úbeda), a woman picaroon deceives lovers as the pícaro does masters.

In Germany the type was represented by Grimmelshausen's *Simplicissimus* (1669). In England it was naturalized with Thomas Nashe's *Unfortunate Traveller, or, the Life of Jacke Wilton* (1594). The female picaroon was revived in Defoe's *Moll Flanders* (1722), and the classic tradition continued with Henry Fielding's *Jonathan Wild* (1725) and Tobias Smollett's *Roderick Random* (1748), *Peregrine Pickle* (1751), and *Ferdinand, Count Fathom* (1753). The outstanding French example is Alain René Lesage's *Gil Blas* (1715–35), which preserves a Spanish setting and borrows incidents from forgotten Spanish novels but portrays a gentler, more humanized picaroon.

In the mid-18th century, the growth of the dramatic realistic novel with its tight sequence of cause and effect and its greater development of character brought the decline of the picaresque, which came to be considered not a novel at all. In comparison to the new novel, its chronological structure seemed primitive, and it lacked any unifying principle other than its central character, who, with the exception of Simplicissimus, never changed. It was also found lacking in moral insight and probability. The picaroon's fortunes might rise or fall, but it was by chance rather than just deserts, and he was as likely to be booted or beaten for an honest deed as he was to profit by a false trick.

Still, many elements of the picaresque tradition survived in the well-made novel. The opportunity for social satire provided by the rogue's rapid changes of milieu, the realistic language and detail, the acceptance of the demi-world, and, above all, the advantages of the point of view of an "outsider" were often successfully incorporated into the new novel. Resemblances to the picaresque tradition are evident in Fielding's *Joseph Andrews* (1742) and *Tom Jones* (1749), Gogol's *Dead Souls* (1842–52), Thomas Mann's *Confessions of Felix Krull* (1954), and Saul Bellow's *Adventures of Augie March* (1953). Some critics have seen in the mid-20th-century revolt against the dramatic novel a return to the formless, additive structure of the picaresque.

·literature of the Renaissance **10**:1136e
·novel plot types and characteristics **13**:278a
·Spain's Siglo de Oro satirical themes **17**:428c

Picasso, Pablo (Ruiz y) 14:440 (b. Oct. 25, 1881, Málaga, Spain—d. April 8, 1973, Mougins, Fr.), painter, sculptor, printmaker, ceramicist, and stage designer, the greatest and most influential artist of the 20th century and the creator (with Georges Braque) of Cubism (*q.v.*).

Abstract of text biography. Even Picasso's earliest drawings (*c.* 1890), executed when he was about nine years old, showed exceptional talent. When the family moved to Barcelona in October 1895, Picasso attended La Lonja, the school of fine arts there (1896), and the Real Academia de Bellas Artes de San Fernando in Madrid (1897). In October 1900 he made the first of three visits to Paris, where he established himself finally in April 1904. During the intensely creative years 1899–1905, Picasso's style varied considerably. At the start, he used strong colours (1900–01). Then he painted predominantly in blue (the so-called Blue Period; late 1901–spring 1904). Until mid-1901 his principal subjects were lively scenes of popular and bourgeois life (cabarets, racecourses, dance halls, etc.); toward the end of 1901, however, Picasso's world became that of the suffering victims of society: prostitutes, beggars, drunkards, etc. In 1904 his gloom lifted, and he looked freshly at humanity with tenderness and admiration and adopted warmer colours and a more harmonious, classical style of draftsmanship; during this Rose Period, his favourite subjects were dancers and acrobats, particularly the Harlequin figure of the commedia dell'arte.

Between the end of 1906 and the spring of 1907, influenced by the paintings of Paul Cézanne, by Greco-Iberian art, and by African sculpture, Picasso discovered that if he disregarded the conventional means used for creating an illusion of reality, such as one-point perspective, chiaroscuro, and the erosion of form and colour by light, he could represent things more realistically by conceptual procedures. He put this to the test in "Les Demoiselles d'Avignon" (Museum of Modern Art, New York City); the painting represented the beginning of Cubism, a new pictorial language that Picasso was to continue elaborating and perfecting until 1925. In 1908 Picasso and Georges Braque began to work along parallel courses, and in close friendship. Simultaneously with the development of his Cubist style, in 1915, Picasso began to work in the opposite direction, depicting figures of a subtly detached classicism—linear, sculptural, and monumental.

After 1925 Picasso began to invent emotionally charged pictorial formulations of bodies and heads, whose dislocations give rise to double images and pictorial metaphors. A private Surrealist vocabulary of powerful symbols (*e.g.*, the Minotaur) emerged to express personal dilemmas and distress. Picasso's interest in sculpture, dormant since 1905, revived at this time.

The outbreak of the Spanish Civil War in 1936 inspired the great and harrowing painting "Guernica" (1937; Museum of Modern Art, New York City), the first reference in his work to political events. In 1944 Picasso joined the Communist Party, and in 1949 his "Dove" lithograph was adopted as the symbol of the World Peace Congress. In the postwar years much of Picasso's work centred on the themes of war and peace and man's right to leisure and peaceful relaxation. After 1955 the theme of the artist and his magic powers assumed great importance in his work.

Picasso's powerful inventive gifts led him to work in many fields. He produced (1917–24) some famous decors for Diaghilev's Russian ballet company (*e.g.*, *Parade*, *Le Tricorne*, *Pulcinella*). He also made significant technical innovations in lithography and linocutting and produced a great quantity of painted pottery.

REFERENCES in other text articles:
·animated film innovation in visual arts **1**:919a
·banquet in honour of Henri
Rousseau **15**:1169h
·Braque's friendship and collaboration **3**:118h
·Gauguin's primitivism influence **7**:959e
·grotesque portrayal of life's joy **4**:966c
·line drawing artistry **5**:1009f; illus. 1001
·modern visual art history **19**:477h
·Stieglitz' modern art promotion in
U.S. **17**:691b
·20th-century European printmaking
14:1094h; illus. 1078

Picathartes (bird): *see* rockfowl.

Picault, Lazare, French captain who explored the Seychelles in 1742 and 1744.

·Seychelles exploration **16**:611c

Picayune, city, Pearl River County, southeastern Mississippi, U.S. Settled in 1811 as Hobolochitto (originally a Choctaw Indian

town), it was renamed (1884) after the *Daily Picayune*, a New Orleans newspaper owned by Eliza Poitevent Nicholson. Her birthplace, the Hermitage, is an antebellum house on the Hobolochitto River. Located in an extensive tung-oil region, it has the nation's largest tung mill. Other manufactures include wood products, naval stores, and metal products. The Mississippi Test Operations (MTO), U.S. rocket testing site, is nearby. Inc. 1906. Pop. (1980) 10,361.
30°26′ N, 89°41′ W

Piccadilly Circus, famous entertainment centre and traffic hub in the West End of London, where several main streets—including Piccadilly, Regent and Shaftesbury Avenue—meet. The circus contains a fountain with a statue, popularly called "Eros," in memory of the 7th Earl of Shaftesbury.
·attractions and architectural features **11**:105b

Piccadilly weepers, alternately called MUTTON CHOPS, DUNDREARYS, BURNSIDES, OR SIDEBURNS, name for whiskers popular in the 19th century.
·period of popularity and name origin **5**:1032a

Piccard family 14:445, Swiss family of scholars, scientists, and explorers who are noted for their contributions to science and public affairs. Most noted are the twins Auguste and Jean-Félix (b. Jan. 28, 1884, Basel, Switz.—d. respectively March 24, 1962, Lausanne, Switz., and Jan. 28, 1963, Minneapolis, Minn.), who explored both the upper stratosphere and the depths of the sea in ships of their own design.

Abstract of text biography. Important members of the Piccard family in the early 19th century include Rodolphe Piccard (1807–88), painter to the court of Russia, and his brother Jules-François, who prepared plates for the official map of Switzerland. The twins Auguste and Jean-Félix were sons of Jules-François. Auguste studied physics at the Swiss Federal Institute of Technology in Zürich and remained at the institute after receiving his doctorate. He became interested in balloon ascents for experimental purposes. In 1922 he accepted the chair for applied physics at the Free University of Brussels. In 1930 he built a balloon to study cosmic rays. In 1932 he developed a new cabin design for balloons, and began to include radio equipment on them. He completed a bathyscaphe in 1948, but the first trial dive was unsuccessful.

Jean-Félix Piccard studied chemistry at the Swiss Federal Institute of Technology and taught at Munich and Lausanne after receiving his doctorate. In 1926 he became research instructor at the Massachusetts Institute of Technology and in 1936 was appointed professor of aeronautical engineering at the University of Minnesota.

Jacques Piccard (b. July 28, 1922), son of Auguste, built a bathyscaphe that competed in 1953 with a French bathyscaphe and descended 3,150 metres (10,330 feet) into the Mediterranean Sea.

REFERENCES in other text articles:
·Auguste's use of balloons in atmospheric research **7**:402h
Jacques Piccard
·discovery of life at ocean depths **18**:844b
·investigation of Atlantic depths **2**:303g
·submarine atmosphere control system **10**:924c

Piccinino, Niccolò (b. 1386, Perugia, Italy—d. 1444, Milan), soldier of fortune who played an important role in the 15th-century wars of the Visconti of Milan against Venice, Florence, and the Pope.

A butcher's son, Piccinino began his career as a weaver but seized the chance to enlist as a page in the service of a nobleman of the Romagna, the region south of Venice. In spite of his small stature, he managed to become a soldier, eventually joining the forces of the *condottiere* (commander of mercenary soldiers) Braccio da Montone, whose daughter he married. When Braccio was killed in battle (1424), Piccinino took over command of his company, and the following year, with the young soldier of fortune Francesco Sforza, he entered the employ of Duke Filippo Maria Visconti of Milan. After brief service against Venice and Florence, he was dispatched to fight Pope Eugene IV (1434), helping to drive him out of Rome. In 1438 Piccinino, battling the Venetians at Lake Garda, faced Sforza, now the Venetian captain general. After destroying a Venetian fleet on the lake, Piccinino was surrounded by the enemy and barely escaped—according to one story, concealed in a sack.

Invading Tuscany in 1440, Piccinino suffered a crushing defeat by the Florentines at Anghiari near Florence, leading his Visconti employer to sue for peace. The following year Piccinino, so ill that he could hardly ride a horse, had a last confrontation with Sforza, who was now fighting for the Pope and King Alfonso of Naples, in the Marches in east central Italy. After a preliminary setback, Piccinino was summoned to Milan; as soon as he left, Sforza attacked, capturing Piccinino's son Francesco and inflicting a decisive defeat. Piccinino died a few days after receiving the news, a frustrated man. Though an able soldier, he achieved none of the power and status of such *condottieri* as Francesco Sforza.

Piccinni, Niccolò (b. Jan. 16, 1728, Bari, Italy—d. May 7, 1800, Passy, Fr.), one of the outstanding opera composers of the Neapolitan school, who wrote in both the comic and

Piccinni, engraving by J.F. Schröter
By courtesy of the Royal College of Music, London

the serious styles, but who, in the century following his death, was chiefly remembered as the rival of Gluck. He studied in Naples, where he produced several operas. The masterpiece of his early years was the opera buffa (comic opera) *La buona figliuola*, or *La cecchina* (1760), on a libretto by Goldoni based on Richardson's novel *Pamela*. It was written in the new style, later epitomized in the operas of Mozart, that incorporated serious or sentimental subject matter into the flexible musical style of the older, farcical, opera buffa.

In 1776 he was invited to Paris by supporters of the Italian operatic style, who opposed the opera reforms of Gluck. Piccinni was thus drawn into a continuation of the earlier controversy between supporters of Italian and French opera, the "Guerre des Buffons." Although Piccinni admired Gluck's operas, and steadfastly refused to encourage his own partisans, the warring factions nevertheless created a rivalry. Each composer's work was compared unfavourably with that of the other, although their aims were quite dissimilar: Piccinni maintained the traditional sequence of arias and recitatives, whereas Gluck was laying the foundations of an operatic reform. At the height of the controversy, both composers were commissioned to write operas on the subject *Iphigénie en Tauride*. Gluck's famous opera was given in 1779, Piccinni's, in 1781. After Gluck's departure from Paris in 1779, Piccinni continued to produce operas but was deprived of his post at the École Royale de Musique in 1789, during the Revolution. He then returned to Naples but went to Paris again in 1798 before retiring to Passy.
·Gluck assailed by Piccinists **8**:213e
·influence of Gluck opera reform **13**:583a

piccolo, in full FLAUTO PICCOLO (Italian: "small flute"), highest pitched woodwind instrument of orchestras and military bands. It is a small transverse (horizontally played) flute of conical or cylindrical bore fitted with

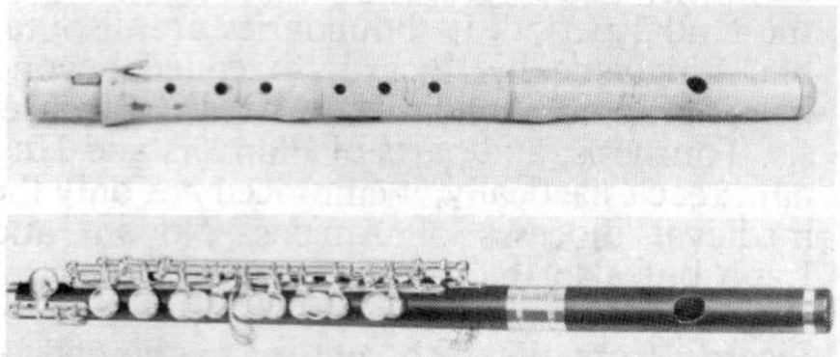

(Top) One-keyed English piccolo, in the Pitt Rivers Museum, Oxford; (bottom) contemporary wood piccolo
By courtesy of (top) the Pitt Rivers Museum, Oxford, (bottom) the Conn Corp.

Böhm system keywork and sounds an octave higher than the ordinary concert flute. Its compass extends three octaves upward from the second D above middle C. Its orchestral use dates from the late 18th century, when it replaced the flageolet (also called *flauto piccolo*). A six-keyed piccolo in D♭ was formerly used in military bands to facilitate playing in flat keys.

Piccolomini, noble family prominent in Sienese politics from the 12th century as leaders of the Guelf (papal) party and as operators of a banking firm with branches in France and England as well as in Italy.

Tracing their origins, according to family legend, to the Etruscan king Porsenna, the Piccolomini by the 12th century played an important role in the aristocratic consular commune of Siena. In the 13th century the family reached its commercial apogee, despite being twice banished from their native city, a Ghibelline (imperial) party stronghold. They managed to escape the economic crisis of the 14th century, thanks to large investments in land, and in 1458 were named counts palatine by the Holy Roman emperor Frederick III. The family included soldiers, prelates, literary men, and two popes—Enea Silvio, who became Pius II (1458–64), and his nephew Francesco, who was Pius III (1503).

Piccolomini, Alessandro (1508–78), Italian writer who produced the first book of printed star charts.
·printed star charts and lettering **2**:227h

Piccolomini, Ottavio, Prince (b. Nov. 11, 1599, Florence—d. Aug. 11, 1656, Vienna),

Ottavio Piccolomini, an anonymous engraving, *c.* 1640
Archiv fur Kunst und Geschichte

general and diplomat in the service of the House of Habsburg during the Thirty Years' War (1618–48) and one of the imperial generalissimo Albrecht von Wallenstein's most trusted lieutenants. His skills both on the battlefield (Thionville, 1639) and at the conference table (Congress of Nürnberg, 1649) made him an invaluable servant of the Austrian and Spanish crowns.

Born into a noble Tuscan family, Piccolomini entered the Habsburg service in 1616. After campaigning in Bohemia and Hungary (from 1618), he returned to Italy in 1623 as a volunteer in Spanish pay. In 1627, Piccolomini began his association with Wallenstein, whose bodyguard he soon commanded. From 1627–29, he was used on a number of the generalissimo's diplomatic missions and, after the outbreak of the War of the Mantuan Succession, in which Austria opposed France, he went to Italy with both military and diplomatic powers (1629). Two years later, however, he was forced to sign an unfavourable peace in order to give Austria a free hand against the Swedes in the north.

After his return to Germany, Piccolomini, who was instrumental in Wallenstein's reinstatement as generalissimo and almost turned the Battle of Lützen (November 1632) into an imperial victory, became increasingly disillusioned when his superior bequeathed favours and promotions on other men. He played a leading role with the Austrian general Matthias von Gallas in the generals' conspiracy that toppled and assassinated Wallenstein on Feb. 25, 1634. Although emperor Ferdinand II rewarded Piccolomini richly, he gave the supreme command to Gallas. After the victory at Nördlingen (Sept. 6, 1634), which freed Bavaria, Piccolomini returned to the Spanish service and campaigned against the French in the Netherlands (1635–39), winning the spectacular victory of Thionville (June 1639), for which he was created duke of Amalfi. He then re-entered the Austrian Army, but after his defeat at the second Battle of Breitenfeld (November 1642), he again returned to the Spanish service in the Netherlands. Finally, in May 1648, the emperor Ferdinand III named him commander in chief, and Piccolomini thus conducted the last campaign of the Thirty Years' War. The next year he served as head of the imperial delegation to the Congress of Nürnberg, which negotiated issues left unsettled by the Peace of Westphalia (1648). Named a prince of the realm (1650), he died in the Austrian capital six years later.

·role in Thirty Years' War **18**:340b
·Wallenstein conspiracy betrayal **19**:532f

Piccolo San Bernardino, Colle Del (France–Italy): *see* Little Saint Bernard Pass.

Picenes, Early Iron Age inhabitants of the Adriatic coast of Italy from Rimini to the Sangro River. Their burial rite was inhumation. The dead were laid on the side, knees drawn up (a position common among primitive people), in a simple trench. Men and women dressed in wool; men wore armour, weapons, and ornaments of bronze or iron; women had numerous fibulae, torques, bracelets, girdles, and ornamental pendants. They had two main centres, one at Novilara in the north, and another around Belmonte and Fermo farther south. The Picenes traded with the Greeks as early as the 7th century BC, but there is little evidence of trade with Etruria, except at the inland site of Fabriano. The evidence suggests that Picenes were primitive, warlike, with little artistic ability of their own, but wealthy enough to sustain a flourishing trade. In 268 BC their territory was annexed by Rome.

·eastern Italic peoples' civilization **9**:1084b
·funerary art of Italic Iron Age **19**:281d
·Hadrian's ancestry confusion **8**:538h

Pichegru, (Jean-) Charles (b. Feb. 16, 1761, near Arbois, Fr.—d. April 5, 1804, Paris), general of the French Revolutionary Wars who played a leading role in the conquest of the Austrian Netherlands and Holland (1794–95); he subsequently ruined his reputation by conspiring with counterrevolutionaries (1795) and against the French dictator Napoleon Bonaparte (1804).

Born into a peasant family, Pichegru taught mathematics at the military academy at Brienne before he joined an artillery regiment in 1780. He was sergeant major at the outbreak of the Revolution in 1789, and in 1792 he became lieutenant colonel of a volunteer battalion formed to defend France from Austro-Prussian invaders. Appointed commander of the Army of the Rhine in October 1793, he helped Gen. Lazare Hoche drive the Austro-Prussian armies from the Alsace in December. Nevertheless, Pichegru was jealous of Hoche. By convincing the government that Hoche was a traitor, he managed to have his rival imprisoned (March 1794). Pichegru was given command of the 150,000-man Army of the North.

In April 1794, Pichegru and Gen. Jean-Baptiste Jourdan, commander of the Army of the Moselle, launched an invasion of the Austrian Netherlands. Pichegru defeated the enemy at Tourcoing on May 18 and captured Antwerp on July 27. In the autumn he marched northward into the Dutch Netherlands, capturing Amsterdam in January 1795. Returning to Paris, he was hailed as a saviour of his country. Although he was appointed commander of the armies of the Rhine and Moselle in mid-1795, he had already begun to turn against France's republican regime. He initiated secret contacts with agents of French émigrés (nobles in exile) in August and then withheld support from Jourdan's unsuccessful campaign in Germany (September–October).

Pichegru, portrait by C.H. Hodges (1764–1837)

H. Roger-Viollet

In March 1796, Pichegru resigned his commission. Elected president of the Council of Five Hundred (the lower chamber of the legislature) in May 1797, he sided with the royalist deputies. Nevertheless, word of his previous treasonable contacts reached Paris; when the royalists were expelled from the government in the coup d'etat of 18 Fructidor (Sept. 4, 1797), Pichegru was arrested and deported to the Guianas. Escaping from the islands, he made his way to Germany, then to England. In January 1804, he secretly entered France and began plotting to overthrow Bonaparte's military regime. Arrested in Paris on February 28, he was found strangled with his cravat in Temple prison on April 5; it is not known whether he was murdered or committed suicide.

·Holland invasion campaign **7**:721g

pichhwāi, cloth hanging used as a backdrop for images worshipped in temples of the Hindu Vallabhācārya sect, who are ardent devotees of the god Kṛṣṇa. *Pichhwāi*s, which form a part of the temple decor, are frequently changed according to the day, the season, and the occasion. Some are fairly large and are made from such costly fabrics as velvet and brocade, while others are smaller and are made of cotton cloth decorated with embroidery or painting. In the 18th century the decoration consisted mainly of landscapes with small animal and human figures; later, large human figures began to predominate. Among the main themes are episodes from the life of Kṛṣṇa, such as the lifting of Mt. Govardhana, the stealing of the clothes of the bathing milkmaids, and the divine dance. Representations

Detail of a *pichhwāi* showing landscape and female figures, from Andhra Pradesh, 18th century; in the Prince of Wales Museum of Western India, Bombay

M. Chandra

of rituals and festivals are also found. Although *pichhwāi*s were painted at several centres in Rājasthān, Gujarāt, and the Deccan, the main centre of manufacture has been and still is Nathdwāra, near Udaipur in Rājasthān.

pichi: *see* armadillo.

pichiciago: *see* armadillo.

Pi-chieh, city, Kweichow province, China. Pop. (1970 est.) 10,000–50,000.
27°18′ N, 105°16′ E

·population and industry **10**:559f

Pichincha, province of north central highland Ecuador, with a small lowland fringe (west), covering a total area of 5,976 sq mi (15,478 sq km). The provincial capital, Quito (*q.v.*), also the national capital, has made it a focal point of Ecuadorian history and political life.

In the early 15th century, the Quitu Indians, original inhabitants of the area, were conquered by the Cara Indians. These last were soon supplanted by the Incas, who, from their Peruvian centre, swept through central Ecuador at about the same time as the landfall of Columbus. The Inca emperor Huayna Capac (died *c.* 1525) established Quito as an important governmental and military outpost, and

Sheep grazing in a valley of the Andean plateau, Pichincha province, Ecuador

Bjorn Bolstad—Photo Researchers

his followers settled the territory now composing Pichincha province. Later, the province was the site of a decisive battle in the Latin American wars of independence. *See* Pichincha, Battle of.

Most of the population is concentrated in the more temperate valleys of the high Andean plateau. Although agriculture and cattle raising are the main occupations, thriving industries (concentrated mainly in Quito), including textile mills and food-processing plants, contribute to the economy. The province produces cereals, potatoes, sugarcane, cacao, coffee, and rice. Its forests are sources of fine woods and there are copper deposits. Tourism is a growing economic factor. Pop. (1971 est.) 876,200.
0°10′ S, 78°40′ W
·area and population table **6**:288
·map, Ecuador **6**:286

Pichincha, Battle of (May 24, 1822), in the Latin American wars of independence, a victory by South American rebels, commanded by Antonio José de Sucre, over the Spanish royalists on the lower slopes of Cerro Pichincha, an Andean volcano. It enabled the rebels to occupy nearby Quito, Ecuador, the following day. Simón Bolívar, leader of the revolutionary forces in northern South America, was acclaimed liberator, and Ecuador was joined to the newly formed but transitory Republic of Gran Colombia.
·Ecuadorian independence achieved **6**:291c

Picidae, bird family of the order Piciformes: woodpeckers, piculets, and wrynecks. The 210 species occur worldwide except in Madagascar, Australia, and the remote Pacific islands.

Eurasian wryneck (*Jynx torquilla*)
Eric Hosking—National Audubon Society

Most are specialized for gleaning insects from tree bark, usually by boring with their bills; some also eat nuts, fruits, and sap; and a few gather ants and grubs from the ground.
·classification and general features **14**:451g

RELATED ENTRIES in the *Ready Reference and Index:*
flicker; ivory-billed woodpecker; piculet; sapsucker; woodpecker; wryneck

Piciformes 14:447, bird order that contains the woodpeckers, toucans, barbets, and allies. The 370 species are rather solitary in woods and brushlands.

The text article covers natural history and form and function and includes an annotated classification of the order.

REFERENCE in other text article:
·mutualism of African honeyguide and honey badger **3**:932b

RELATED ENTRIES in the *Ready Reference and Index:*
barbet; flicker; honey guide; ivory-billed woodpecker; jacamar; Picidae; piculet; puffbird; sapsucker; tinkerbird; toucan; toucanet; woodpecker

pick, or SHOT, in weaving, an individual length of weft extending from one edge of the cloth to the other.
·textile industry weaving techniques **18**:176e; illus. 177

Pick, Frank (1878–1941), British industrial designer.
·definition of good design **9**:512h

pickaback plant: *see* Saxifragaceae.

pickerel, North American pike (*q.v.*) distinguished from the related muskellunge and northern pike by its smaller size, completely scaled cheeks and gill covers, and banded or chainlike markings. The chain pickerel (*Esox niger*) grows to about 0.6 metres (2 feet) and a weight of about 1.4 kilograms (3 pounds). The barred pickerel (*E. americanus*) and the grass pickerel (*E. vermiculatus*) are smaller species reaching a maximum weight of about 0.5 kilograms.

pickerel frog (*Rana palustris*), dark-spotted frog, family Ranidae, found in eastern North

Pickerel frog (*Rana palustris*)
Leonard Lee Rue III

America, usually in such areas as meadows, cool streams, and sphagnum bogs. The pickerel frog is about 5 to 7.5 centimetres (2 to 3 inches) long and has lengthwise rows of squarish spots on its golden or brownish skin. When it leaps it reveals the orange or yellow on the inner surfaces of its hindlegs. The skin secretions, which protect this frog from snakes, are reported also to be toxic to other frogs.

pickerelweed, common name for four genera of aquatic plants comprising the family Pontederiaceae, especially those of the genus *Pontederia*. Most species are perennials, native primarily to tropical America. They have creeping rootstocks, fibrous roots, and leaves in clusters at the base of the plant or borne on branched stems. The fruit is a capsule containing many seeds, or a one-seeded winged structure. Plants of the genus *Pontederia*, about five species of perennials, have spikes of bluish-purple flowers at the top of a one-leaved stem, clusters of lance- or heart-shaped leaves at the base, and thick rootstocks. Pickerelweed (*P. cordata*) is common in shallow lakes and muddy shores in eastern North America. It is sometimes cultivated as an ornamental garden pool or aquarium plant. Water hyacinth (*Eichhornia*) and mud plantain (*Heteranthera*) are other widely distributed genera of the family.

Pickering, Edward Charles (b. July 19, 1846, Boston—d. Feb. 3, 1919, Cambridge, Mass.), U.S. physicist and astronomer who introduced the use of the meridian photometer to measure the magnitude of stars and established the *Harvard Photometry* (1884), the first great photometric catalog. In 1867 Pickering became professor of physics at the Massachusetts Institute of Technology, Cambridge, where he established the first U.S. laboratory in which students were instructed by actual handling of laboratory instruments and measurements. In 1876 he was appointed professor of astronomy and director of the Harvard College Observatory.

He invented the meridian photometer, which utilized a calcite prism to juxtapose the image

Edward Charles Pickering
By courtesy of Harvard College Observatory and the Niels Bohr Library, American Institute of Physics, New York

of a star with one of the pole stars to compare their relative brightnesses, and used it to compile his catalog. After the Arequipa Observatory was established in Peru in 1891, it became possible to include measurements made of the stars throughout the Southern Hemisphere within the scope of the work of the Harvard College Observatory. Under Pickering this work included photometry, a scale of photographic magnitude, a system of classification of variable stars, and a system of stellar spectroscopy (study of light from stars separated according to wavelength) that was for many years universally adopted and later used as a basis for modifications.

Pickering, Timothy (b. July 17, 1745, Salem, Mass.—d. Jan. 29, 1829, Salem), American Revolutionary officer and Federalist politician who served (1770–1800) with distinction in the first two U.S. Cabinets. During the war, he served in several capacities under Gen. George Washington, among them quartermaster general (1780–85). In 1786, after taking up residence in Philadelphia, he helped resolve the dispute with Connecticut settlers over claims to Pennsylvania's Wyoming Valley and helped develop the town of Wilkes-Barre.

In Washington's administration Pickering served as Indian commissioner (1790–95), postmaster general (1791–95), secretary of war (1795), and secretary of state from August 1795 until May 12, 1800, when he was dismissed from office by Pres. John Adams after a policy dispute.

Timothy Pickering, pastel drawing by Charles Fevret de Saint-Mémin (1770–1852); in the Museum of Fine Arts, Boston
By courtesy of the Museum of Fine Arts, Boston, Frederick Brown Fund

During the administrations of Jefferson and Madison, Pickering led the Federalist opposition in Congress, serving as senator from Massachusetts (1803–11) and as a member of the House of Representatives (1813–17). Remaining friendly to England and fearing the power of Napoleon, he bitterly opposed the War of 1812. After his retirement from Congress, he devoted himself to agricultural experimentation and education.

Pickering, William Hayward (b. Dec. 24, 1910, Wellington, N.Z.), engineer, physicist, and head of the team that developed Explorer

1, the first U.S. satellite. He joined the staff of the California Institute of Technology, Pasadena, in 1936. Working under the U.S. physicist Robert A. Millikan, Pickering developed cosmic-radiation-detection gear for high-altitude balloon flights. In 1944 he became a section chief of the Jet Propulsion Laboratory, where he developed the first telemetry system used in U.S. rockets. He was manager of the Corporal rocket project, which brought about important early advances in guidance and communication techniques.

In 1951 Pickering became chief of the division of guided-missile electronics and three years later was appointed director of the Jet Propulsion Laboratory. He was in charge of the development of the Explorer 1 satellite and the modification of the Jupiter C launch vehicle. Among other important projects of the laboratory were the Ranger spacecraft for unmanned flights to the Moon, the Mariner spacecraft for survey flights to Venus and Mars, and numerous other unmanned probes into the solar system.

Pickering, William Henry (b. Feb. 15, 1858, Boston—d. Jan. 17, 1938, Mandeville, Jam.), U.S. astronomer who discovered Phoebe, the ninth satellite of Saturn. In 1891 he joined his brother Edward in establishing the Arequipa station of the Harvard Observatory in Peru. He returned to the U.S. in 1893 and the next year erected the observatory and telescope at Flagstaff, Ariz., for the noted U.S. astronomer Percival Lowell. In 1900 he established a station for the Harvard Observatory at Mandeville.

William Henry Pickering

By courtesy of the Lick Observatory Archives, Santa Cruz, Calif.

He discovered Phoebe in 1899 and noted that it revolves around Saturn in the opposite direction (retrograde) from that of Saturn's other satellites. His announcement in 1905 of a tenth satellite, which he named Themis, is generally discounted, for it was never observed again. The tenth satellite (Janus) that was discovered in 1967 is probably not the same one, for its orbit is the innermost of all Saturn's moons, whereas Pickering's Themis was supposed to lie between Titan and Hyperion. In 1919 Pickering also predicted the existence of, and gave a position for, the planet Pluto.

pickeringite (mineral): *see* halotrichite.

Pickersgill, H(enry) W(illiam) (1782–1875), English portraitist whose subjects included many prominent men of his time.
·Bentham oil painting illus. **2**:838
·Herschel portrait illus. **8**:825
·Richard Owen portrait illus. **13**:800

Pickett, George Edward (b. Jan. 25, 1825, Richmond, Va.—d. July 30, 1875, Norfolk), U.S. and Confederate Army officer, known for Pickett's Charge at the Battle of Gettysburg. After graduating from the U.S. Military Academy at West Point (1846), last in a 59-member class, he served with distinction in the Mexican War (1846–47). He resigned his commission in June 1861 and entered the Confederate Army, in which he was made brigadier general in February 1862. Pickett rose to ma-

George Edward Pickett

By courtesy of the Library of Congress, Washington, D.C.

jor general in October and was given command of a Virginia division. At the Battle of Fredricksburg he commanded the centre of Lee's line but saw little action. Hostilities then shifted to Pennsylvania.

At Gettysburg (July 3, 1863) three brigades of Pickett's division (4,300 men) constituted somewhat less than half the force in the climactic attack known as Pickett's Charge. The attack was actually under the command of Gen. James Longstreet. Its bloodily disastrous repulse is often considered the turning point of the U.S. Civil War. Pickett's conduct at this time has been adversely criticized. He was even charged by some with cowardice. Such charges are refuted, however, by Lee's retention of him in divisional command throughout the Virginia Campaign of 1864. Eight days before the surrender at Appomattox (April 9, 1865), Pickett's division was almost destroyed at Five Forks while he was attending a shad bake.

After the war he worked in an insurance business in Norfolk, Va.

Pickett, Joseph (b. 1848, New Hope, Pa.—d. 1918, New Hope), primitivist or folk painter known for his naïve depictions of town and landscape around his native New Hope, Pa. After a life as a carpenter, shipbuilder, carny, and storekeeper, Joseph Pickett began painting when he was about 65. Self-taught, his works exemplify an untrained artist's detailed interest in local landscape and history, portrayed with straightforward disregard of perspective but with full sense of colour and flat pattern design; *e.g.*, "Manchester Valley" (*c.* 1914–18; Museum of Modern Art, New York City). Pickett's works were not discovered by the art critics and public until the 1930s.

Pickford, Mary, original name GLADYS MARY SMITH (b. April 9, 1893, Toronto, Ont.), motion-picture actress, "America's sweetheart" of the silent screen, and one of the first film stars. At the height of her career, she was one of the richest and most famous women in the United States. She made her first stage ap-

Mary Pickford

By courtesy of United Artists Corp. and the Museum of Modern Art, Film Stills Archive, New York

pearance in a Toronto stock company at the age of five. At eight, she went on tour and within ten years was playing on Broadway under her real name, Gladys Mary Smith.

Mary Pickford began working as a motion-picture extra at D.W. Griffith's Biograph Studio, starring in his 1909 film *The Lonely Villa*. By 1913 she had turned permanently to the screen, rising to first rank with Adolph Zukor's Famous Players Company. She is famous for films such as *Tess of the Storm Country* (1914), *Pollyanna* (1920), *Rebecca of Sunnybrook Farm* (1917), and *Poor Little Rich Girl* (1917).

Miss Pickford was not only America's symbol of sweetness and innocence but also a shrewd businesswoman. In 1919 she was primarily instrumental in forming the United Artists Corporation with two actors, Charlie Chaplin and Douglas Fairbanks, and the director D.W. Griffith.

She married Owen Moore, a fellow actor at Griffith's Biograph Studio, in 1911 (divorced, 1919); Douglas Fairbanks in 1920 (divorced, 1936); and actor Charles (Buddy) Rogers in 1937.

Miss Pickford retired from motion pictures in the early 1930s.

pickling (probably from Dutch *pekel*, "brine, preserved in brine"), soaking in a solution, usually acidic or saline, but sometimes alcoholic, to condition or preserve.

In the food industry, pickling is commonly used to preserve and enhance the flavour of fruits, eggs, fish, meat (particularly pork), and meat products. Pickling is essential in countries where distribution of refrigerated and frozen fish, meat, and produce has not been well developed.

Metals and alloys are pickled in acid solutions to cleanse, brighten, and smooth their surfaces, usually preparatory to further processing. Iron and steel for electroplating must be cleansed of oxides by pickling in sulfuric or hydrochloric acid. Metal rods are pickled before drawing into wire. Mints pickle metal blanks before impressing them with the coin design.

Some other pickling processes are the curing of certain leathers in a sulfuric acid-and-salt pickle and the pickling of paintings to simulate antique appearance. The preservation of biological specimens in alcohol is also called pickling.
·aluminum chemical etching process **1**:648d
·cable wire manufacturing processes **15**:1149b
·electroplate precleaning process **6**:692c
·food preservation technology **7**:494a; table 493
·leather manufacturing and storage preparation **10**:761g
·rolling mill operation **17**:654e
·steelmaking by-product methods **11**:624a
·vegetable processing techniques and specifications **19**:47b; table

Pick's disease, condition marked by progressive impairment of intellect and judgment, caused by atrophic changes of the cerebral cortex.
·brain changes in psychoses **15**:178a
·causation, course, and incidence **12**:1051h

Pickstone, Sir Ernest John, 2nd Baronet Benn: *see* Benn, Sir Ernest John Pickstone, 2nd Baronet.

pickup, in electronics, device that converts some form of intelligence, as a scene, a sound, or a temperature, into corresponding electrical signals. Thus a phonograph pickup converts vibrations caused by variations in a record groove into an electrical signal. Television cameras and microphones are pickups. Different pickup designs use choices of a number of known principles for converting the intelligence to electrical signals, such as the piezoelectric effect in certain crystals, variable resistance, variable capacity, variable magnet-

ic-flux cutting, variable magnetic reluctance, and photoelectric effects.
·electronic sound transducer **6**:682f
·piezoelectric phonograph pickup **14**:462c; illus.

pickwickian syndrome, a complex of respiratory and circulatory symptoms that seem to be associated with some cases of extreme obesity. The name of this disease originates from the red-faced, fat boy depicted in Charles Dickens' *Pickwick Papers*, who showed some of the same traits. (Extreme obesity is medically classified as body weight of 325 pounds [147 kilograms] or more.) The main symptoms are breathlessness on exertion and drowsiness. There may also be a bluish tint to the skin, increased heart beats, high blood pressure with dilation of the vessels, enlargement of the liver, and an abnormally high number of red blood cells. The effect upon the system seems to be diminished total lung volume, decreased lung compression and expansion, more airway resistance during breathing, and less air actually utilized by the body. The oxygen saturation level of the blood is as much as 80 percent less than the normal amount, and carbon dioxide levels are high in the bloodstream.

The factors causing this syndrome are not clear, but obesity seems to be a predominant factor. Obesity causes an increased work load, which always places stress on the heart. With a low oxygen level and high blood pressure, heart and lung failure eventually ensue. The abundance of fat in the chest muscles and diaphragm (the muscular partition between the chest and the abdominal cavity) has been blamed for the reduced ability to expand and contract the lungs; some authorities think that merely the added body weight on the chest restricts the respiratory movements. The treatment is directed toward loss of weight.
·sleep theories and research **16**:881g

Pickwick Papers, The, novel by the 19th-century English author Charles Dickens. Entitled *The Posthumous Papers of the Pickwick Club*, the work was first published (1836–37) serially under the pseudonym Boz.
·picaresque novel tradition **13**:285g
·serialization, popularity, and comedy **5**:706h
·Wellerism word game origins **19**:926h

Pico della Mirandola, Giovanni, Conte (b. Feb. 24, 1463, Mirandola, near Ferrara, Italy—d. Nov. 17, 1494, Florence), scholar and Platonist philosopher whose *De hominis dignitate oratio* ("Oration on the Dignity of Man"), a characteristic Renaissance work composed in 1486, reflected his syncretistic method of taking the best elements from other philosophies and combining them in his own work.

His father, Giovanni Francesco Pico, prince of the small territory of Mirandola, provided for his precocious child's thorough Humanistic education at home. Pico then studied canon law at Bologna and Aristotelian philosophy at Padua, and visited Paris and Florence, where he learned Hebrew, Aramaic, and Arabic. At Florence he met Marsilio Ficino, a leading Renaissance Platonist philosopher.

Introduced to the Hebrew Kabbala, Pico became the first Christian scholar to use Kabbalistic doctrine in support of Christian theology. In 1486, planning to defend 900 theses he had drawn from diverse Greek, Hebrew, Arabic, and Latin writers, he invited scholars from all of Europe to Rome for a public disputation. For the occasion he composed his celebrated *Oratio*. A papal commission, however, denounced 13 of the theses as heretical, and the assembly was forbidden by Pope Innocent VIII.

Despite his ensuing *Apologia* for the theses, Pico found it prudent to flee to France, where he was arrested. After a brief imprisonment he settled in Florence, where he became associat-

Pico della Mirandola, detail of a portrait by an unknown artist, late 15th century; in the Uffizi, Florence
Alinari

ed with the Platonic Academy, under the protection of the Florentine prince Lorenzo de' Medici. Except for short trips to Ferrara, Pico spent the rest of his life there. He was absolved from the charge of heresy by Pope Alexander VI in 1492. Toward the end of his life he came under the influence of the strictly orthodox Girolamo Savonarola, martyr and enemy of Lorenzo.

Pico's early death, at the age of 31, prevented him from constructing a complete philosophical system, but his writings contain ideas that subsequently became influential. Against the Venetian Humanist Ermolao Barbaro he defended positive aspects of medieval Scholasticism, and he collected favourable features from numerous other schools and philosophers. His emphasis on human dignity revolved around the element of free will, by which man can determine his own place in the world and his own nature. This view contradicted more orthodox teachings that man was a limited being who occupied a particular place in a universal hierarchy.

Pico's unfinished treatise against enemies of the church includes a discussion of the deficiencies of astrology. Though this critique was religious rather than scientific in its foundation, it influenced the 17th-century scientist Johannes Kepler, whose studies of planetary movements underlie modern astronomy. Pico's other works include an exposition of Genesis under the title *Heptaplus* (Greek *hepta*, "seven"), indicating his seven points of argument, and a synoptic treatment of Plato and Aristotle, of which the completed work *De ente et uno* is a portion. Pico's works were first collected in *Commentationes Joannis Pici Mirandulae* (1495–96); E. Garin began a modern edition in 1942.
·Humanism in Oratio **14**:262e
·Renaissance Christian tradition **15**:665c
·Renaissance Humanistic scholarship **8**:1176c

Picoides (bird): *see* woodpecker.

Pico Island, Portuguese ILHA DO PICO, part of the Portuguese Azores archipelago in the North Atlantic Ocean and administratively within Horta district. Separated from the Ilha do Faial by the Canal (channel) do Faial, it has an area of 163 sq mi (433 sq km) and is dominated by the Ponta do Pico volcano,

Ships off the coast of Pico Island, detail of "A Whaling Voyage Round the World," tempera panorama by Russell-Purrington, 1846; in the Whaling Museum, New Bedford, Mass.
By courtesy of the Whaling Museum, New Bedford, Mass.

highest in the Azores (7,713 ft [2,351 m]). Its economy is basically agricultural, dairying being the most important activity, followed by cattle raising and vine cultivation. Whaling is still practiced in small boats without mechanical aids. Lajes and São Roque do Pico are the island's two urban centres. Pop. (1970 prelim.) 18,014.
38°28′ N, 28°20′ W
·map, Portugal **14**:857

Pico Rivera, city, Los Angeles County, southwestern California, U.S., between the Rio Hondo and San Gabriel rivers, southeastern suburb of Los Angeles. It originated as two communities growing oranges and avocados, Pico (named for Pío Pico, the last Mexican governor of California) and Rivera. Rapid urbanization occurred after World War II with planned industrial sites occupied by plants of the Ford Motor Company, the Parke, Davis Company, and other national firms. The two communities were joined by incorporation in 1958. Pop. (1950) about 18,000; (1980) 53,459.
33°58′ N, 118°07′ W

picornavirus, a large group of the smallest known viruses, "pico" referring to small size and "rna" referring to the type of nucleic acid core. This group includes enteroviruses, which attack the vertebrate intestinal tract and often invade the central nervous system as well; rhinoviruses, which infect the tissues in the vertebrate nose; and foot-and-mouth disease (doubtful). Among the enteroviruses are polioviruses, ECHO viruses (*e*nteric, *c*ytopathogenic, *h*uman, *o*rphan), and Coxsackie viruses. ECHO viruses cause fever with rash and meningitis. Coxsackie viruses cause sore throat or fever with chest or abdominal pains. The virus particle lacks an envelope, is cubical, from 20 to 30 nanometres (nm; 1 nm=10^{-9} metre) across, is covered with subunits called capsomeres, and contains ribonucleic acid (RNA).
·diseases of laboratory animals, table 8 **5**:876

picot (fabric design): *see* brides.

Picquart, Georges (1854–1914), French army officer, produced important evidence for the defense in the Dreyfus case. Picquart was minister of war (1905–09).

Picquigny, Truce of (Aug. 29, 1475), pact by which Edward IV of England agreed to withdraw his invading army from France in exchange for gold and a yearly pension.
·Edward IV's alliance defection **4**:61e
·Edward IV's invasion of France **6**:439a
·Hundred Years' War conclusion **9**:21b

picric acid, or 2,4,6-TRINITROPHENOL, pale yellow, odourless crystalline solid that has been used as a military explosive, as a yellow dye, and as an antiseptic. Its chemical formula is $HOC_6H_2(NO_2)_3$. Picric acid (Greek *pikros*, "bitter") was so named by J.-B.-A. Dumas, a 19th-century French chemist, because of the extremely bitter taste of its yellow aqueous solution; yellow scales, plates, or needles can be crystallized from the solution, depending on the concentration. It melts at 122°–123° C (251.5°–253.4° F) and sublimes with slow heat, but with rapid heat it explodes. Percussion also can cause it to explode.

Picric acid was first obtained in 1771 by Peter Woulfe, a British chemist, by treating indigo with nitric acid. It was used as a yellow dye, initially for silk, beginning in 1849.

As an explosive, picric acid was formerly of great importance. The French began using it from 1886 as a bursting charge for shells under the name of melinite. In 1888 Great Britain began using it under the name of lyddite, and in Japan it was called *shimose*. By the time of the Russo-Japanese War, picric acid was the most widely used military explosive. Its highly corrosive action on the metal surfaces of shells was a disadvantage, and after World War I its use declined.

Ammonium picrate, one of the salts of picric acid, is used in modern armour-piercing shells because it is insensitive enough to withstand the severe shock of penetration before detonating.

Picric acid has antiseptic and astringent properties and is used medically incorporated in a surface anesthetic ointment or solution, and in burn ointments. It is a blood poison and has toxic vapours.

As a chemical reagent, picric acid is much stronger than phenol; it decomposes carbonates and may be titrated with bases. In a basic medium, lead acetate produces a bright yellow precipitate, lead picrate.

·explosives as war weapons **7**:88g
·phenol's industrial consumption **1**:457g

picrite, intrusive igneous rock of ultrabasic (very silica-poor) composition that is composed largely of olivine and augite and is somewhat similar to peridotite. Picrites are dark, heavy rocks and contain a small but variable amount of plagioclase feldspar; hornblende and biotite may also be present. Picrites usually occur in sills (tabular bodies inserted while molten between other rocks) or sheets, but, unlike peridotites, seldom in large plutonic masses. Varieties include augite-, enstatite-, and hornblende-picrite. The term picrite-basalt is reserved for feldspar-poor basalts rich in olivine.

The minerals in picrite are very frequently decomposed. Serpentine partially or wholly replaces olivine, and hornblende, talc, and chlorite appear as secondary products after the mineral. Augite passes into hornblende or chlorite, and the essential feldspar is often represented by epidote, prehnite, and white mica. In some picrites, as in the peridotites, a lustre mottling is produced by the inclusion of unoriented grains of olivine within large crystals of augite or hornblende.

Many picrites clearly possess alkaline affinities. Thus, the augite picrites of Scotland and Moravia, central Czechoslovakia, contain interstitial analcime and are closely related to the teschenites with which they are associated. Other picrites are more clearly calc-alkaline and are associated with diorites or diabases; the hornblende picrites of Caernarvon and Anglesey, Wales, are of this type. Picrites accompany diabases in the Devonian rocks of the Fichtelgebirge (in West Germany) and Nassau, as well as Cornwall and Devon.

Picrodendron baccaturn, a species of bittertree of the order Euphorbiales.

·plant structure illus. **6**:1029

picromerite, hydrous magnesium potassium sulfate, an evaporate mineral.

·evaporite mineralogy and composition **6**:1134f; table

Pictet de Rochemont, Charles (b. Sept. 21, 1755, Geneva—d. Dec. 28, 1824, Lancy, Switz.), statesman, writer, and diplomat who prepared the declaration of Switzerland's permanent neutrality ratified by the great powers in November 1815.

After serving in the French Army, Pictet settled in Geneva in 1789 and reorganized the militia. He was arrested during the Reign of Terror (1794) in Geneva following the French Revolution and subsequently was imprisoned. With the re-establishment of the Republic of Geneva after the retreat of Napoleon's armies (1813), he resumed political activity, taking part in the provisional government created in December 1813.

In January 1814 Pictet argued on behalf of Geneva's independence and union with the Swiss Confederation before the allied sovereigns at Basel and later obtained recognition of his canton's independence in the Treaties of Paris (May 1814). In October 1814 he was delegated to the Congress of Vienna, where he helped secure Geneva's attachment to the reconstructed Swiss Confederation; and at the Paris peace conference (August–November 1815) that followed Napoleon's defeat at Waterloo, he served as representative of the whole confederation. He personally redrafted the act that was accepted as the basis of permanent Swiss neutrality by the powers on Nov. 20, 1815. His last diplomatic mission—to Turin (January–March 1816)—secured a rectification of the Swiss–Sardinian frontier (Treaty of Turin, March 1816). A man of letters, he helped edit the *Bibliothèque britannique* (the *Bibliothèque universelle* after 1815) and wrote works in politics and agronomy.

Picti (people): *see* Picts.

Pictish language, spoken by the Picts in northern Scotland and replaced by Gaelic after the union in the 9th century of the Pictish kingdom with the rest of Scotland. Knowledge concerning the Pictish language is derived from place names, the names in medieval works such as the *Pictish Chronicle* and the writings of Bede, inscriptions from the Pictish areas of Britain, statements about the language by medieval writers who wrote while the language was still in use, and names from northern Scotland found in classical works.

Although there has been considerable controversy among scholars concerning the possible relationship of Pictish to other languages, most leading scholars consider the language to be a survival of the pre-Celtic inhabitants of Britain. It is apparently unrelated to any other language.

The name Pictish has also been used sometimes to designate a Celtic language (one more closely related to Gaulish and Brythonic than to Goidelic) that was spoken in the same area as the non-Indo-European Pictish language during the period from *c.* 100 BC until both languages were replaced by Gaelic.

·ogham discoveries in Scotland **1**:626a; table 625

pictography, human expression and communication by means of pictures and drawings that have a communicative aim. These pictures and drawings (called pictographs) are usually considered to be a forerunner of true writing and are characterized by stereotyped execution and by omission of all details not necessary for the expression of the communication. (Pictographs that are drawn or painted on rocks are known as petrograms; those that are incised or carved on rocks are called petroglyphs.) A pictograph that stands for an individual idea or meaning is called an ideogram; if a pictograph stands for an individual word, it is called a logogram (*q.v.*). Pictographs are also used as memory aids. Various North American Indian tribes used pictographs both as ideograms and as memory aids.

·Aztec system limitations and use **1**:663a
·Elamite use of logogram **19**:267h
·hieroglyph theories and methods **8**:853c; illus. 856
·writing development and systems **19**:1034d
·writing systems evolution **10**:658h

Picton, town, seat of Prince Edward County, southeastern Ontario, Canada, on Lake Ontario's Bay of Quinte. Founded in 1786 by United Empire Loyalists led by Andrew and Henry Johnson, the town was known as Hallowell before being renamed in honour of Sir Thomas Picton, a British major general in the Napoleonic Wars. Picton, 16 mi (26 km) southeast of Belleville, is the commercial centre of the county; its deepwater port on Picton Bay, an arm of the Bay of Quinte, handles iron-ore shipments from mines near Marmora, 40 mi northwest. Industries include fruit and vegetable canning, textile and lumber milling, and dairying. A large army base and several provincial parks are nearby. Inc. 1837. Pop. (1971 prelim.) 4,860.
44°00′ N, 77°08′ W

Picton, borough and port of Marlborough County, northeast South Island, New Zealand, on Waitohi Bay (Picton Harbour), a southwest extension of Queen Charlotte Sound. In 1848 a Maori *pa* (fortified settlement) on this site was occupied by Gov. Sir George Grey (1845–53) and Francis Dillon Bell, of the New Zealand Company. They proceeded to lay out the village of Newton. From 1861 to 1865 the village (renamed in 1859 to honour Sir Thomas Picton, a commander under the Duke of Wellington in the Peninsular War) served as the capital of Marlborough Province. In 1864 its population increased for a time as the result of a gold strike on the Wakamarina River (west). Sir Edward Stafford, prime minister of New Zealand, was then waging an unsuccessful campaign to have the town designated as the national capital. It was made a borough in 1876. Picton is the northern terminus of the South Island Main Trunk Railway from Christchurch (218 mi [351 km] southwest) and is the principal outlet for the Marlborough district, having regular cargo and rail and car ferry service to Wellington, 40 mi west across Cook Strait. Its deepwater port exports wool, grain, and fruit. Other industries are meat freezing, fish packing and curing, general engineering, and small boatbuilding. Picton serves as the centre of a holiday resort area based on the many inlets along this coast. Pop. (1970 est.) 2,700.
41°16′ S, 174°00′ E

·map, New Zealand **13**:44

Picton, Sir Thomas (b. August 1758, Poyston, Pembrokeshire—d. June 18, 1815, at the Battle of Waterloo), British lieutenant general prominent in the French Revolutionary and Napoleonic wars. He took part in the capture of the West Indies islands of St. Lucia and St. Vincent (1796) and of Trinidad (1797), of which he became governor. Accused of tyranny (1803), he resigned, was found guilty in 1806, but was vindicated at a second trial in 1808.

Picton, detail of a painting by M.A. Shee (1769–1850); in the National Portrait Gallery, London

By courtesy of the National Portrait Gallery, London

Picton was appointed to the command of the 3rd division of Wellington's army in Portugal in 1810 but was sent home because of illness in 1812. Knighted in 1813, he returned to Spain and served till the end of the war there. He was commander of the 5th division at Waterloo.

Pictor, Quintus Fabius: *see* Fabius Pictor, Quintus.

Pictorial Effect in Photography (1869), book on photography by Henry Peach Robinson.

·rules for photographers **14**:312h

Pictou, chief town, Pictou county, northern Nova Scotia, Canada, just northwest of New Glasgow, on Pictou Harbour, facing Northumberland Strait. The site, a former Micmac Indian village, was settled in 1767 by six families from Maryland and Pennsylvania. They were joined in 1773 by a group of Highlanders from Scotland. The community was named (1790) from an Indian word *piktook* ("bubbling water"). It has developed one of Canada's largest lobster fisheries and holds a lobster carnival each July. Lumbering and coal

mining are also well established; other industries include foundries, canneries, and the production of biscuits and confectionery. During World War II, steel merchant ships were built in the shipyard. Pictou Academy was founded in 1816. Inc. 1874. Pop. (1971 prelim.) 4,247.
45°41′ N, 62°43′ W

Picts, Latin PICTI (painted), Irish CRUITHIN, Welsh PRYDYN, a Scottish people who forged their own kingdom before uniting in AD 843 with the rest of Scotland under Kenneth I MacAlpin. They are first mentioned in AD 297, and their name, in both native and Latin forms, may refer to their custom of body tatooing. After 367 their raids upon Roman Britain became increasingly fierce. The Pictish kingdom, which in the 8th century extended from Caithness to Fife, is notable for the stylized but vigorous beauty of its carved memorial stones and crosses. The round stone towers known as brochs, or "Pictish towers," and the underground stone houses called weems, or "Picts' houses," however, both predate this kingdom. Christianity penetrated the area in the late 6th century.
·medieval migrations map **12**:140
·Scotland's early peoples and cultures **3**:233d

Pictured Rocks, cliff formations of red Cambrian sandstone, extending east of Munising for about 15 mi (24 km) along the southern shore of Lake Superior in Alger County, Michigan, U.S. Rising 150–200 ft (46–61 m) above the shoreline, the cliffs are multicoloured and form intricate designs, caves, and columns carved by wind and wave action. Named as the dwelling place of the gods of thunder and lightning in Longfellow's poem *The Song of Hiawatha*, the area was created a national lakeshore by the U.S. Congress in 1966 and includes 65,000 ac (26,000 ha) of surrounding forest.
46°26′ N, 86°37′ W

Picture of Dorian Gray, The (1891), Oscar Wilde's only novel, a moral fantasy about a handsome young man, Dorian Gray, who has his portrait done by the artist Basil Hallward. Through Hallward, Dorian becomes acquainted with Lord Henry Wotton and is tempted into a life of vice in which he progressively degrades himself. But it is the portrait, rather than the model, that takes the marks of age and sin. Later, Dorian murders Hallward and stabs the painting. He is found aged and hideous, dead of a stab wound to the heart, while the portrait has returned to its original appearance.
·Irish novel tradition **13**:291a
·sources, aesthetics, and criticism **19**:824d

Picturephone, telephone installation that permits transmission of images of user as well as voice; introduced by Bell Telephone System in 1964.
·development and applications **18**:122d

Picture Post, British illustrated newspaper, started by Sir Edward Hulton in 1938; closed in 1957.
·magazine publishing history **15**:253g

Pictures at an Exhibition, collection of descriptive piano pieces composed in 1874 by the Russian Modest Mussorgsky. Each of the pieces was inspired by a picture Mussorgsky had seen at a commemorative posthumous exhibition of the works of V.A. Hartmann, a minor Russian painter and architect. The work is usually heard in the orchestral arrangement by Maurice Ravel.
·suite style form **12**:727h

picture tube, also called KINESCOPE, a cathode-ray tube containing a screen of luminescent material on which are produced visible images, such as television pictures or oscillograph curves.
·operation principles and design **18**:115d; illus.

picture-winged fly: *see* otitid fly.

picul, any of various units of weight used in China and Southeast Asia.
·weights and measures, table 5 **19**:734

piculet, name for about 29 species of small, stub-tailed birds related to the woodpeckers and constituting the subfamily Picumniae, family Picidae (order Piciformes). Nearly all are restricted to Central and South America; there are three species in eastern Asia and one in western Africa. Piculets, 9–14 centimetres (3½–5½ inches) long, are mottled gray-green to brown above, often with salt-and-pepper head, and are white below, with spots or bars.

White-scaled piculet (*Picumnus albosquamatus*)
Painting by Murrell Butler

They climb like nuthatches, looking for insects, and are able to perch crosswise on branches. Though small-billed, piculets dig nest holes in soft wood. The most widely distributed New World species is the white-barred piculet (*Picumnus cirratus*), found from the Guianas to Argentina. The Chinese piculet (*P. innominatus*), brown and yellow, drums on dry bamboo.
·traits, behaviour, and classification **14**:447a; illus.

Picumnus (bird): *see* piculet.

Picunche, Araucanian Indians of middle Chile who were conquered by the Spanish in the 16th century.
·Spanish Conquest and results **17**:120d

Picus, in Roman mythology, ancient Roman woodpecker, sacred to the god Mars. It was widely reverenced in ancient Italy and developed into a minor god. Picus was an agricultural deity associated particularly with the fertilization of the soil with manure. The woodpecker was also an important bird in augury.

Later rationalizations made Picas an early king of Italy. The Roman poet Virgil, for instance, made him son of Saturn, father of Faunus, and grandfather of Latinus. His bride, Circe, for reasons of unrequited love, changed him into a woodpecker. As son of Saturn he later came to be identified with Zeus. His earliest representations were as a wooden pillar mounted with the image of a woodpecker. In more sophisticated form Picas is a youth carved of marble with a woodpecker on his head. In zoology *Picus* is a genus of woodpecker (*q.v.*).

Picus viridis (bird): *see* woodpecker.

Pidal, Ramón Menéndez: *see* Menéndez Pidal, Ramón.

Piddington, Henry, 19th-century British ship captain, investigated revolving storms affecting the Bay of Bengal and the Arabian Sea.
·cyclone name source **6**:84g

piddock, common name for marine bivalve mollusks of the family Pholadidae (Adesmoidea). Worldwide in distribution, they are specially adapted for boring into rock, shells, peat, hard clay, or mud. Most species occur in the intertidal zone; a few in deeper water.

One end of each of the two valves is armed with rows of serrated cutting edges for boring. Some species drill to a depth only slightly more than the length of the shell. Others, with extensible siphons, may bore to depths several times the length of the shell. The siphons of many deep borers are protected by tough plates. Like most bivalves, piddocks feed on minute organisms in the water.

The great piddock (*Zirfaea crispata*), which attains lengths of up to eight centimetres (about three inches) and has an oblong shell that is grayish white or rusty in colour, occurs on both sides of the Atlantic Ocean. Found from the intertidal zone to depths of 75 metres (250 feet), *Z. crispata* bores into limestone and wood.

The wood piddock (*Martesia striata*), up to 2.5 centimetres long and grayish white in colour, commonly occurs in waterlogged timbers cast up on the beach and ranges from North Carolina to Brazil. *M. pusilla* and *M. cuneiformis* have similar habits and distribution. Smith's martesia (*M. smithi*), which resembles a fat gray pea, bores into rocks and mollusk shells in the Atlantic from New York to the Gulf of Mexico.

The flat-topped piddock (*Penitella penita*), from the Arctic Ocean to Lower California, bores into hard clay, sandstone, and cement, sometimes damaging man-made structures. Some *Penitella* and *Diplothyra* species bore into the shells of other mollusks, particularly oysters and abalone.

Pholas dactylus, which bores into gneiss—a very hard rock—is luminescent. At one time it was highly esteemed in Europe as food. *Pholas chiloensis*, found on the Pacific coast of South America, is eaten locally.
·bioluminescence mechanism **2**:1032c
·luminescent chemical reaction **11**:179d

Pidgeon process, in metallurgy, a thermal process of obtaining magnesium developed in Canada in 1941; utilizes ferrosilicon and calcined dolomite.
·magnesium reduction processes **11**:303d; illus.

pidgin 14:452, a language with a greatly reduced grammar and vocabulary, often based on a western European language. Pidgins usually arise as methods of communication between groups that have no language in common and in some instances later become established first or second languages of one of the groups involved. Some examples of pidgins are Chinese pidgin English, Haitian French Creole, and Melanesian Pidgin English.

The text article covers pidgin, creole, and lingua franca; the origin of pidgins and their survival as spoken languages; phonology, morphology, and vocabulary of English-based pidgins; and the various spelling systems and the modern functions of pidgin.

REFERENCES in other text articles:
·commercial communication function **9**:742a
·status and use as language **10**:647f

RELATED ENTRIES in the *Ready Reference and Index: for*
pidgins and creoles: see Chinese Pidgin English; Gullah; Haitian Creole; Louisiana Creole; Melanesian Pidgin; Papiamento; Sranantonga
other: creole; lingua franca

Pidurutalagala, highest mountain peak in Sri Lanka (Ceylon). Located in the Piduru Ridges, about 60 mi (97 km) east of Colombo, it rises to 8,281 ft (2,524 m).
7°00′ N, 80°46′ E
·map, Sri Lanka **17**:520

pidyon ha-ben (Hebrew: "redemption of the son"), Jewish ceremony in which the father redeems his wife's firstborn son by offering to a *cohen* (a male Jew descended from the first priest, Aaron) the equivalent of five silver shekels (ancient coins). The ceremony, which normally takes place 30 days after the child's birth, dates from Old Testament times, when the firstborn sons of the Israelites were spared from death on the first Passover (Ex. 12). These children subsequently belonged to God in a special way and would have constituted the Jewish priesthood had not the Levites been substituted in their place. *Pidyon ha-ben* thus commemorates a historical event, for the father ritually gives money to a *cohen* in order to keep his son. If the father is a *cohen* or if either parent is related to the tribe of Levi, such children already belong to God by reason of heredity, and no redemption is required.

In rabbinic law, the firstborn son may not actually have been the first, since the law does not apply to stillbirths, cesarean deliveries, and malformed offspring. *Pidyon ha-ben* also acknowledges the general law that, in the broadest sense, all "firstfruits" (including grain, animals, and fruit) rightfully belong to God.

pièce bien faite (theatre): *see* well-made play.

pièce croisée, 17th-century genre of French keyboard music played only on double manual harpsichords because of continually crossing musical lines in the same range.
·harpsichord playing method **10**:440a

piece mold, sculpture mold of a statue made in a number of separate parts used for producing more than one cast from a soft or rigid original.
·sculpture casting techniques **16**:430f

pie-crested cuckoo: *see* cuckoo.

pie crust, paste for pies, the pastry shell of a pie.
·baking preparation and ingredients **2**:605b

piecrust table, a light table on a tripod stand, in common use for tea and similar occasions beginning in the latter half of the 18th century. The name is derived from a raised scallop pattern that decorates the rim of the table and gives it the appearance of the outside, notched edge of a pie crust. The term did not become common until the 19th century.

Mahogany piecrust table, English, mid-18th century; in the Victoria and Albert Museum, London
By courtesy of the Victoria and Albert Museum, London

pied-billed grebe (bird): *see* grebe.

pied goose: *see* magpie goose.

Piedigrotta, in full FESTIVAL OF OUR LADY OF PIEDIGROTTA, annual festival of Naples.
·decline of tradition **12**:827h

Piedmont, Italian PIEMONTE, region, northwestern Italy, comprises the provinces of Alessandria, Asti, Cuneo, Novara, Torino, and Vercelli, with an area of 9,807 sq mi (25,399 sq km). Surrounded to the south, west, and north by the vast arc of the Appennino Ligure and the Maritime, Cottian, Graian, and Pennine Alps, the core of the region is the Po Valley, open to the east and consisting of some of the best farmlands in Italy. The name piedmont ("at the foot of a mountain") has become a term generally applied to such a region. South of the Po are the low and intensively cultivated hills of Monferrato and of Langhe. In the foothills of the Alps are lakes Maggiore and Orta. The Po and its tributaries, the Dora Baltea, Dora Riparia, Sesia, Tanaro, and Scrivia, provide ample water for agriculture.

In Roman times Piedmont was important because its passes connected Italy with the transalpine provinces of the empire. After periods of Lombard and Frankish rule, the House of Savoy emerged as the most important feudatory of northwest Italy. This dynasty first became powerful as successor to the marquesses of Ivrea and of Torino (Turin), but after 1400 Savoy's control of both slopes of the Alps, ruling over what is now French Savoie and over Piedmont, gave it undisputed sovereignty over much of the region. After 1700 practically all of Piedmont passed under Savoyard domination, and the addition of Sardinia and its territories provided still wider interests. During the Risorgimento (movement for Italian independence), Piedmont led the attempts of 1848, 1859, and 1866 to unite all Italy; and Victor Emmanuel II, originally king of Piedmont and Sardinia, became modern Italy's first king in 1861.

The Alpine arc of Piedmont plays a vital part in the power production of the region and of northern Italy as a whole; its hydroelectric plants supply energy for industry, transportation, and domestic use. The forests provide lumber; the Alpine and sub-Alpine meadows afford excellent pasture for cattle as the base of a prosperous dairy industry. The lowlands produce wheat and rice, vegetables and fruit, milk and cheese; the hills south of the Po are noted for some of Italy's highest quality wines, both of the sparkling (Asti) and still (Barbera) variety. Piedmont forms part of the great industrial triangle of north Italy (Torino–Genoa–Milan), and manufactures are widely diversified. Turin (*q.v.*), the capital, largest city, and leading industrial centre, is the site of one of the largest automobile plants in Europe, as well as of printing, textile, and machine industries. Ivrea (*q.v.*), northeast of Torino, is the headquarters of one of Europe's leading makers of office machinery. Textiles, chemicals, and glass are among the other important Piedmontese industries. The principal rail connection between France and Italy, the Torino–Col du Mont Cenis (Mt. Cenis Tunnel)–Paris line, passes through Piedmont, while to the north the Simplon Tunnel leads to Switzerland. An excellent network of roads and expressways ties all parts of the region closely together; Genoa, easily reached from Piedmont, is its port. Development projects in the 1970's included an all-weather road between France and Italy, passing through a long tunnel under Mont Blanc, thence through the Valle d'Aosta to Torino and Milan. Pop. (1971 prelim.) 4,461,527.
·area, population, and cultural influences **9**:1092d; table 1094
·Crimean War and Austrian war results **3**:1029h *passim* to 1032g
·cuisine ingredients and method **7**:946a
·diplomacy and wars from 1856 to 1914 **6**:1107f
·map, Italy **9**:1088
·Mazzini independence activity **11**:726f
·Pius IX and Italian nationalism **14**:483f
·post-Napoleonic government and history **9**:1158c

piedmont (landform): *see* bajada.

piedmont glacier, ice stream that has emerged from a mountain valley and spread out over a relatively flat plain. A piedmont glacier differs from an ice sheet in the manner of origin. If the valley glacier does not maintain the ice supply, the piedmont glacier will disappear. The Malaspina and Bering glaciers in Alaska are of this type, and each covers about 4,000 square kilometres (1,500 square miles).

piedmontite (mineral): *see* epidote.

Piedmont Province, geographical region in the eastern U.S., between the Appalachian Mountains (west) and the Atlantic Coastal Plain (east). It comprises a relatively low rolling plateau cut by many streams and is a fertile agricultural region.
·Alabama geographic features **1**:406a
·Appalachian mountain-building process **13**:181c
·Delaware landform feature significance **5**:568b
·Georgia's physiographic features **7**:1128f
·location and productivity **18**:907d; map 906
·North Carolina location and features **13**:231c
·Pennsylvania division features **14**:26f
·sediment yield variation factors **16**:477c
·South Carolina landform features **17**:212b

Piedmont–Sardinia, Kingdom of: *see* Savoy, House of.

Piedras Negras, city, northeastern Coahuila state, northeastern Mexico. It lies at 722 ft (220 m) above sea level on the Rio Grande (Río Bravo del Norte), just across from Eagle Pass, Texas, U.S., with which it is connected by two bridges. Founded in 1849, it was renamed Ciudad Porfirio Díaz in 1888; after that dictator's downfall, the original name was restored. Much of the city's prosperity is due to its function as a customs station and an international highway, railroad, and airline hub 840 mi (1,350 km) north by west of Mexico City. Piedras Negras is also the commercial and manufacturing centre for the agricultural hinterland, in which cotton and corn (maize) are cultivated and cattle are raised. Coal, silver, gold, and zinc are mined nearby. Industries in the city include zinc smelters, a cement plant, flour and textile mills, a lard factory, and sawmills. Its principal exports are cattle, sheep, hides, wheat, and bran. A superhighway to Mexico City was opened in 1958. Pop. (1970) 41,033.
28°42′ N, 100°31′ W

Piegan (people): *see* Blackfoot.

Pielinen, Lake, Finnish PIELISJÄRVI, located in Pohjois-Karjalan *lääni* (Pohjois-Karjala province), eastern Finland, near the U.S.S.R. border. The lake is approximately 60 mi (100 km) long between the town of Nurmes and the village of Uimaharju and ranges from 1 to 25 mi in width. Lake Pielinen has many islands and is drained southward into the large Saimaa lake system by the Pielisjoki (river). It is surrounded by dense forests, particularly on its scenic and rugged western shore, capped by Koli hill, which rises to a height of 1,141 ft (348 m) and is the centre of an important winter sports area. There is no passenger-ship service on the lake. Apart from Nurmes, the town of Lieksa on the eastern shore and the village of Juuka on the western shore are the only major settlements on the lake.
63°15′ N, 29°40′ E
·map, Finland **7**:304

Pieman River, northwest Tasmania, Australia, formed near Tullah by the confluence of the Rivers Macintosh (flowing 22 mi [35 km] southwest from the Central Plateau) and Murchison (flowing 23 mi northwest). The 65-mi mainstream, fed by the Huskisson and Stanley rivers, then flows generally west to its estuary, which also receives the Donaldson, Whyte, and Savage rivers at Belton Bay on the Indian Ocean. The river was named for an infamous convict, Alexander Pierce (Jimmy the Pieman), who was recaptured at its mouth after escaping from the Macquarie Harbour penal colony. It was the scene of some gold and tin mining during the 1870s and 1890s. After 1965, the development of iron-ore mining on the Savage and increased copper-min-

ing activity at nearby Mount Lyell provided impetus to the harnessing of the Pieman's hydropower potential. There is a small timber industry based at the port of Corinna (on the estuary).
41°40′ S, 144°55′ E

Piemonte (Italy): *see* Piedmont.

Pien Canal, Wade-Giles romanization PIEN HO, Pin-yin romanization PIAN HE, runs through Honan, Anhwei, and Kiangsu provinces (*sheng*) of China. In medieval times the name Pien Ho was given to several different canals that connected the Huang Ho, which is north of Cheng-chou (Honan), with the Huai Ho (river), and thus, via the old-established Shan-yang-tu Canal from Huai-an (Kiangsu) to the Yangtze River (Ch'ang Chiang) at Yang-chou (Kiangsu). The terrain in this region is so flat and the drainage system so impermanent that no major engineering works were involved, apart from the manpower needed to excavate new channels. The canals made considerable use of existing waterways, which were widened, linked, and canalized.

The eastern section of the canal, from the Huang Ho to the region of modern K'ai-feng (Honan), was constructed as early as Han times (206 BC–AD 220), possibly before, and was known as the Lang-tang Ch'ü. The Han Canal, known in later times as the Old Pien Canal, ran southeast from K'ai-feng as far as modern Shang-ch'iu (Honan), then ran eastward to pass through the gap in the southward spur of the Shantung Hills at modern Süchow in Kiangsu Province. Here it joined the Ssu Shui (river), which flows into the Huai above Ch'ing-chiang (Kiangsu).

The New Pien Canal was built in 605 by the Emperor Sui Yang Ti of the Sui dynasty (581–618). It followed the old canal as far as Shang-ch'iu (Honan) but then flowed southeastward through Yung-ch'eng (Honan) and Su-hsien (Anhwei) to Ssu-hung (Kiangsu), where it joined the Huai above the Hung-tse Hu (lake) in Kiangsu, which was very much smaller in the 7th century. The New Pien Canal was constructed on a much larger scale than its predecessors. The whole length of the canal was followed by a post road and lined with willow trees; the canal itself had regular anchorages and guard stations. A million *corvée* (forced) labourers were mustered for its construction and worked under terrible conditions, leaving a legacy of disaffection with the Sui government. In 610, with the construction of a further canal, the Yung-chi Ch'ü, joining the Huang Ho to the region of modern Peking, there was a direct transport link from the Yangtze Basin to the north of the North China Plain.

Increasingly dependent upon revenue and grain supplies from the Huai and Yangtze region, the T'ang dynasty (618–907) developed this system still further during the 8th century. Under the Sung (960–1126), when the capital was moved to K'ai-feng the canal became even more important; and by the 11th century the volume of traffic was probably about three times that of T'ang times.

In the early 12th century, however, with the division of China between the Juchen (1122–1234) in the north and the Southern Sung (1126–1279) in the south, the canal was abandoned. When, under the Mongols (1279–1368) and the Ming dynasty (1368–1644), the unity of the empire was restored, the political centre was transferred to Peking (known to the Mongols as Ta-tu) and a totally new north-south canal—the Grand Canal (Yün Ho)—was built. The old east-west link between the Huang Ho and the Huai Ho lost its importance.

In the late 1960s, however, a New Pien Canal was constructed, as a part of the water-conservancy scheme for the Huai Ho Basin. The New Pien Canal scheme was initiated in 1966 and completed in 1970, with 450,000 labourers working on it four successive years. Altogether some 155 mi (250 km) long, it takes the canalized upper waters of the Tuo and Kuo rivers, via the canalized course of the Sui dynasty New Pien Canal, through a new channel 85 mi long, roughly following the course of the T'ang-period Pien Canal, through Ling-pi (Anhwei), Ssu-hsien, and Ssu-hung, and thus into the Hung-tse Hu. Although primarily designed as a flood-control scheme, the canal also provides transport facilities for the area on the borders of Honan, Anhwei, and Kiangsu, and is used for extensive irrigation in some 14 counties.

Pien-ching, city in China that was an operations base during the Five Dynasties period (907–960) and became the capital of the Northern Sung.
·original architecture accounts **19**:192f

Pieniny, small mountain range northeast of Zakopane, Pol.
49°27′ N, 20°25′ E
·Western Carpathian Mountains
structure **3**:949f

p'ien wen ("parallel prose"), Chinese literary genre characterized by antithetic construction and balanced tonal patterns without use of rhyme.
·pattern and characteristics **10**:1051e

piepoudre court, OR PIEPOWDER COURT, lowest and most expeditious of the courts of justice known to the ancient common law of England; it was generally constituted by merchants and dealt with fair trading. The name is derived from the dusty feet of the participants (from French *pied poudré*, "dusty foot"), for the courts were often held outdoors.

The court decided summarily and on the spot disputes arising in fairs and markets. Its civil jurisdiction extended to all matters of contract arising within the district of the fair or market. These cases were mostly trade disputes; hence, the decisions were based upon the law as it was interpreted by the local merchants (*see* law merchant). Its criminal jurisdiction extended to all offenses committed at the particular fair where the court was held.

Pier, province in southwestern Albania. The capital is Fier.
·area and population table **1**:419

pier (marine architecture): *see* dock.

pier, in building construction, vertical load-bearing member such as an intermediate support for adjacent ends of two bridge spans. In foundations for large buildings, piers are usually cylindrical concrete shafts, cast in prepared holes, or in the form of caissons, which are sunk into position. They serve the same purpose as piles but are not installed by hammers and, if based on a stable substrate, will support a greater load than a pile.

Especially adapted to large construction jobs, pier shafts have been excavated to depths greater than 100 feet (30 metres) at widths of over 6 feet (2 metres). Piers may be more economical than footings even in small jobs if substrate conditions are favourable.
·bridge construction history **3**:175b; illus.
·foundations and building construction **3**:458b
·pile-cylinder bridge foundations **3**:190b

Pierce, Franklin (b. Nov. 23, 1804, Hillsboro, N.H.—d. Oct. 8, 1869, Concord), 14th president of the United States (1853–57); he failed to deal effectively with the corroding sectional controversy over slavery in the decade preceding the U.S. Civil War (1861–65). An attorney and the son of a governor of New Hampshire, Pierce entered political life there as a Democrat, serving in the state legislature (1829–33), the U.S. House of Representatives (1833–37), and the Senate (1837–42). He became a devoted supporter of Pres. Andrew Jackson but was continually overshadowed by a galaxy of older and more prominent men on the national scene. Resigning from the Senate for personal reasons, he

Franklin Pierce
By courtesy of the Library of Congress, Washington, D.C.

returned to Concord, where he resumed his law practice and also served as federal district attorney.

Except for a brief stint as an officer in the Mexican War (1846–48), Pierce remained out of the public eye until the Democratic nominating convention of 1852, at which a deadlock developed among the leading presidential contenders. Pierce's name was entered as a compromise candidate. Almost unknown nationally, he unexpectedly won both the nomination and the election (Nathaniel Hawthorne wrote a campaign biography of him). The campaign was dominated by controversy over the slavery issue. Pierce reflected the views of the party's Eastern element, which opposed the divisive effects of anti-slavery agitation and generally tried to placate Southern opinion. Thus in the selection of his Cabinet, as in both domestic and foreign policy, he represented a coalition of Southern planters and Northern businessmen.

Internationally, Pierce promoted the extension of U.S. territorial and commercial interests. In an effort to buy Cuba, he ordered the U.S. minister to Spain, Pierre Soulé, to try to secure the influence of European financiers upon the Spanish government. The resulting diplomatic statement, the Ostend Manifesto (October 1854), was interpreted by the public as a call to wrest Cuba from Spain by force if necessary. The ensuing controversy forced the administration to disclaim responsibility for the document and to recall Soulé. Pierce's administration also effected a reorganization of the diplomatic and consular service and the creation of the U.S. Court of Claims.

Among Pierce's domestic policies were preparations for a transcontinental railroad and the opening up of the Northwest for settlement. In order to open the way for a southerly route to California, almost 30,000 square miles (80,000 square kilometres) of territory were acquired from Mexico (1853; the Gadsden Purchase) for $10,000,000. Mainly to stimulate migration to the Northwest and to facilitate the construction of a central route to the Pacific, the Kansas–Nebraska Act was enacted in 1854 and received the President's sanction. This measure opened two new territories for settlement and provided resolution of the slavery question by popular sovereignty (local option). The indignation aroused by the act, which included repeal of the Missouri Compromise of 1820 (prohibiting slavery in the territories north of latitude 36° 30′), and the resultant violent conflict over slavery in the territories were the main causes of the rise of the Republican Party in the mid-1850s. Pierce's ineptness in handling the Kansas struggle made him unacceptable as a candidate for a second term. Except for a three-year European tour, he spent the rest of his life uneventfully in Concord.
·Hawthorne's friendship and career **8**:679g

Pierce, John Robinson (b. March 27, 1910, Des Moines, Iowa), communications engineer, scientist, and father of the communications satellite. Pierce began working for Bell Telephone Laboratories, Inc., New York, in 1936. He improved the travelling-wave tube, which is used as a broad-band amplifier of microwaves, and designed a new electrostatically focussed electron multiplier tube, used as a sensitive radiation detector. His Pierce electron gun produces high-density electron beams. During World War II, in collaboration with J.O. McNally and W.G. Shepherd, Pierce developed the low-voltage reflex klystron oscillator that was almost universally used in U.S. radar receivers.

In 1952 Pierce became director of electronics research at the New Jersey division of Bell Laboratories at Murray Hill. Two years later he began work on the theory of communications satellites. Although he wrote numerous papers detailing the advantages of using satellites to relay radio communications to all parts of the Earth, his ideas were largely ignored. Seeing the opportunity offered by the Echo balloon satellite for studying space phenomena, he persuaded the National Aeronautics and Space Administration (NASA) to convert the 100-foot (30-metre) aluminized sphere into a radio-wave reflector. Echo I was launched on Aug. 12, 1960. The success of the communications experiments carried out with Echo I provided the impetus to develop Telstar, a satellite designed to amplify signals from one Earth station and relay the signals back to another Earth station. These early satellites marked the beginning of efficient worldwide radio and television communication.

Pierce retired from Bell Laboratories in 1971 and became professor of engineering at California Institute of Technology, Pasadena. He began writing science fiction in high school and later published stories under the pseudonym J.J. Coupling. This literary genre greatly influenced his career, for in one of his stories he forecast the advent of communications satellites. His nonfiction works include *Traveling-wave Tubes* (1950) and *Symbols, Signals and Noise* (1961).

·satellite communication development **16**:261g

pierced work, in metalwork, general term for perforations in metals for decorative or functional effect or both; the French term for

Pierced work silver cake basket, by Samuel Courtauld, London, 1751; in the Folger's Coffee Collection of Antique English Silver

By courtesy of the Procter and Gamble Company

such work is ajouré. Both hand-operated and mechanical tools such as saws, drills, chisels, and punches are used. The principal present-day exponents of this ancient technique are perhaps Asiatic Indian craftsmen, for whom complicated pierced objects are commonplace and traditional. In European metalwork—apart from its functional and decorative use on handles, lids, covers, finials, and the like—pierced work is most often associated with such articles as locks and keys, iron and steel caskets, and guns, as well as with jewelry and other small objects. In the 18th century, however, it enjoyed a period of great popularity, when certain pieces of domestic silver—for example, cake baskets, sugar basins, and coasters—consisted almost entirely of intricate pierced-work patterns. A new tool was developed in order to pierce Sheffield plate (*q.v.*) in this manner.

·pottery-making decorative techniques **14**:895c

Piería, department, Macedonia, Greece.

·area and population table **8**:318

Pieridae, in zoology, cosmopolitan family of butterflies (order Lepidoptera) containing over 1,000 species. Its members are divided into the whites, sulphurs (or yellows), and orange-tips because of unique pigmentation, a byproduct of the uric acid wastes. Adults have a wingspan of 37 to 63 millimetres (1½ to 2½ inches) and usually have white or yellow wings with black marginal markings. Sexual dimorphism and seasonal dimorphism in pattern and colour occur in many species.

White butterfly (*Pieris brassicae*)

Chr. Lederer—Bavaria-Verlag

Many of the green, slender larvae are pests. The majority are covered with a short down, or pile. The pupae are attached to a twig by a posterior spine and held secure by a girdle of silk.

One of the most common whites in North America is the European cabbage butterfly (*Pierisrapae*), whose larva is an important economic pest, attacking cabbage and related plants. It was introduced into North America about 1860.

The orange-tips (so called because most species have an orange spot on the top of the forewings) have whitish wings with black markings and green marbling on the underside. The larvae feed on plants in the mustard family.

The sulphurs, or yellows, are generally bright yellow or orange in colour. Some species have two colour patterns; *e.g., Colias eurytheme* is usually orange with black wing margins, but some females are white. The larvae feed on clover and may seriously damage crops.

·classification and general features **10**:830d
·coloration pigments and protective uses **4**:913e
·mimicry and warning systems **12**:214d
·sulphur butterfly eggs and aggregation, illus., **10**: Lepidoptera, Plates I and III

Pieris, in botany, genus of about 10 species of evergreen, white-flowered shrubs and small

Pieris (*Pieris*)

Valerie Finnis

trees (heath family: Ericaceae) native to eastern Asia and eastern North America. *Pieris* is also a genus of the butterfly family Pieridae (*q.v.*).

The leaves are usually alternate, broad, leathery, lance-shaped, and toothed. The flowers, which are cylindrical or urn-shaped, have a five-lobed calyx (the sepals, collectively) and grow in a terminal or axillary (*i.e.*, from the leaf axil) cluster.

Several species of *Pieris*, including *P. floribunda*, *P. japonica*, and *P. taiwanensis*, are cultivated as ornamentals.

Pierleone, Pietro: *see* Anacletus II.

Piero della Francesca 14:454 (b. *c.* 1420, Sansepolcro, Italy—d. Oct. 12, 1492, Sansepolcro), fully recognized only in the 20th century as one of the most important Italian Renaissance artists. Late in his life and in the following generation he was known chiefly for his scientific contributions. His reticent and disciplined art had little influence on his contemporaries.

Abstract of text biography. Piero's working association with Domenico Veneziano in Florence (1439) laid the foundations of his style, bringing him into contact with the work of key artists and thinkers of the early Renaissance, including Donatello, Brunelleschi, Masaccio and Alberti. Between withdrawals to Sansepolcro, Piero worked successively in Ferrara for the d'Estes (*c.* 1448); Rimini, for Sigismondo Malatesta (1451); Arezzo (intermittently, 1452 onward; fresco cycle, S. Francesco, completed 1466); the Vatican (1459); and, most importantly, Urbino (late 1450s–72/74). In Urbino, at the highly cultured court of Count (later Duke) Federico da Montefeltro, Piero undertook the best known of his mature works. These included the famous diptych portrait of Count Federico and his consort (1465; Uffizi, Florence).

Piero spent his last two decades in Sansepolcro, abandoning painting to write painting and mathematical treatises in the manner of Alberti and the ancient Greeks.

REFERENCES in other text articles:
·Bellini's use of composition and colour **2**:828g
·"Flagellation of Christ," oil on wood, illus., **19**:Visual Arts, Western, Plate IX
·Florentine training and style **19**:399a
·Resurrezione illus. **4**:481

Piero di Cosimo, real name PIERO DI LORENZO (b. 1462, Florence—d. 1521, Florence), Renaissance painter noted for his eccentric character and his fanciful mythological paintings. His name derives from that of his master, Cosimo Rosselli, whom he assisted (1481) in the frescoes "Crossing of the Red Sea" and "Sermon on the Mount" in the Sistine Chapel in the Vatican. There he saw the frescoes of Sandro Botticelli and Domenico Ghirlandaio, whose styles dominate his early "Story of Jason" (1486; National Gallery of South Africa, Capetown, S.Af.). In "The Visitation with Two Saints" (*c.* 1487; National Gallery of Art, Washington, D.C.), the permanent influence of the enamel-like colours of Hugo van der Goes' "Portinari Altarpiece" is first visible.

Piero's mature style is exemplified by his mythological paintings, which exhibit a bizarre, romantic fantasy found in no other Renaissance artist. Many of these paintings are based on Vitruvius's account of the evolution of man. They are filled with fantastic hybrid forms of men and animals engaged in revels ("The Discovery of Wine," *c.* 1500; Fogg Art Museum, Cambridge, Mass.) or in fighting ("Battle of the Centaurs and the Lapiths," 1486; National Gallery, London). Others show early man learning to use fire ("A Forest Fire," *c.* 1487; Ashmolean Museum, Oxford) and tools ("Vulcan and Aeolus," *c.* 1486; National Gallery of Canada, Ottawa). The multitude of firm, glossy-skinned nudes in these paintings show Piero's interest in Luca Signorelli's work. But, while "The Discovery of Honey" (*c.* 1500; Worcester Art Museum, Worcester, Mass.) retains Signorelli's figure types, its forms are more softly modelled and its light is warmer, showing Piero's mastery of the new technique of oil painting. In the "Rescue of Andromeda" (*c.* 1515; Uffizi, Florence), Piero adopts Leonardo da Vinci's *sfumato* (smoky light and shade) to achieve a new lush, atmospheric effect.

Piero painted several portraits, of which the best known is the memorial bust of Simonetta Vespucci (*c.* 1498; Musée Condé, Chantilly), mistress of Giuliano de' Medici. Simonetta is partly nude, and her rhythmic profile is accentuated by the black cloud placed behind it. She wears a gold necklace, around which two snakes coil, possibly an allusion to her consumptive death. Contemplation of death is probably the theme of the famous "Death of Procris" (*c.* 1490–1500; National Gallery, London). The softly undulating contour of the dead Procris and the apprehensive satyr kneeling beside her are viewed against a distant river emptying into the sea. Procris's dog at her feet and three dark hounds on the barren beach heighten the effect of melancholy and desolation.

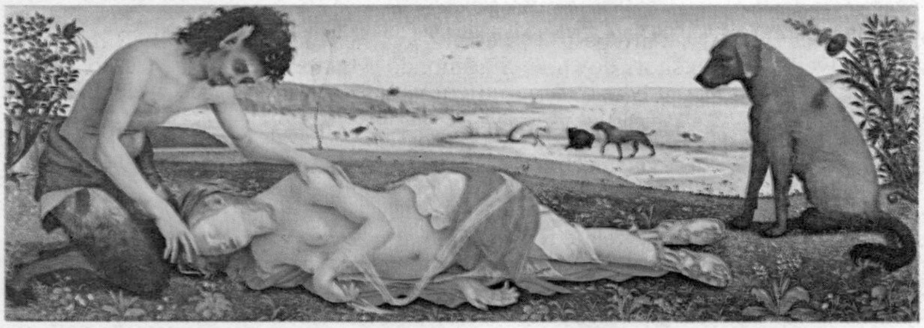

"The Death of Procris," panel painting by Piero di Cosimo, *c.* 1500; in the National Gallery, London

By courtesy of the trustees of the National Gallery, London; photograph, J.R. Freeman & Co. Ltd.

Piero's art reflects his bizarre, misanthropic personality. He belonged to no school of painting. Instead, he borrowed from many artists, incorporating elements of their style into his own idiosyncratic manner. He painted many works to please only himself (an unusual practice for the time) and declared that he often found inspiration for his paintings in the stains on walls.

·jewelry of the period in paintings **10**:173e; illus.

Piero di Giovanni: *see* Lorenzo Monaco.

Pierozzi, Antonio: *see* Antoninus, Saint.

Pierre (in personal names): *see* under Peter.

Pierre [locally pronounced peer], capital of South Dakota, U.S., seat (1880) of Hughes County, on the Missouri River, in the geographical centre of the state. Before 1800 the capital of the Arikara Indian nation was located on its site. Founded in June 1880 as the western terminus of the Chicago and North Western Railway, it was first known as Mahto (Sioux: Bear), but was renamed in December 1880 for Pierre Chouteau, French fur trader. Growth was spurred by its position as a railhead for the mining industry and as a trade centre for a large area, including three Indian reservations and prosperous farming and cattle country. In 1889, when South Dakota became a state, Pierre was named the temporary capital; in elections in 1890 and 1904 it was chosen the permanent capital. The capitol building (1905–10) is on a 30-ac (12-ha) tract overlooking the Missouri River, which includes a war memorial building housing the State Historical Society and Museum (1930), the governor's mansion (1936), state office building (1951), state highway building (1955), and a 7-ac artesian-fed lake. The Oahe

The capitol building, Pierre, S.D.

E.P.A. Inc.—EB Inc.

Dam (1948–62), a power, irrigation, and flood-control project 5 mi north of Pierre, has impounded a 200-mi (320-km) lake along the Missouri River.

Fort Pierre, across the river, was the fur-trade capital of the Northwest from 1817 to *c.* 1867. A monument there marks the place where Louis and François Vérendrye buried a lead plate in 1743 claiming the region for France.

Pierre is the trade centre for a large diversified agricultural area. Lakes created by the Missouri Basin Development Plan form the basis of a large tourist industry. The Farm Island State Recreation Area is 4 mi east. Inc. city, 1883. Pop. (1980) 11,973.
44°22′ N, 100°21′ W

·map, United States **18**:908
·population and location **17**:214f

Pierre (1852), novel by Herman Melville.
·publication and lack of success **11**:874f

Pierrefonds, city, Montréal region, southern Quebec province, Canada, on the Rivière des Prairies, at the west end of Île de Montréal, opposite Île Bizard. Established as the "municipality of the Parish of Sainte-Geneviève" in 1845, it received its present name upon being incorporated as a town in 1958. Pierrefonds is now primarily a western residential suburb of Montreal, having grown rapidly with the post-World-War II spread of the metropolitan area. Inc. city, 1963. Pop. (1951) 1,322; (1961) 12,171; (1971) 33,010.
45°27′ N, 73°55′ W

Pierre Shale Formation, division of Upper Cretaceous rocks in the U.S. (the Cretaceous Period began about 136,000,000 years ago and lasted about 71,000,000 years). Named for exposures studied near old Ft. Pierre, South Dakota, the Pierre Shale occurs in South Dakota, Colorado, Minnesota, New Mexico, Wyoming, and Nebraska. In South Dakota the Pierre Shale Formation underlies the Fox Hills Sandstone and overlies the Niobrara Limestone Formation. The Pierre consists of about 600 metres (2,000 feet) of dark-gray shale, some sandstone, and many layers of bentonite (altered volcanic-ash falls that look and feel much like soapy clays). In some regions the Pierre Shale may be as little as 200 metres (650 feet) thick. The fossil Cretaceous sea turtle *Archelon*, the largest turtle that ever lived, has been found in South Dakota. *Archelon* was about 3.3 metres (11 feet) long and about 3.7 metres (12 feet) across the flippers.

·annual sediment yield, table 2 **16**:478

Pierrot (theatrical character): *see* Pedrolino.

pier table, a narrow table designed to stand underneath a pier glass (a mirror filling the space between two adjacent windows), forming a decorative unit with it. Often, though not invariably, it had a marble top, and it was usually decorated to match the surroundings.

Piesmatidae, a family of insects of the order Heteroptera.

·vectors of plant viruses, characteristics, and classification **8**:846a

Piešťany, Hungarian PÖSTYÉN, town, Západoslovensky *kraj* (Western Slovakia region), Czechoslovakia, occupies an island in the Váh River, about 40 mi (64 km) northeast of Bratislava. It is a Carpathian health resort, known since the Middle Ages for its warm sulfur springs and mud baths. Latest pop. est. 14,367.
48°36′ N, 17°50′ E

·Carpathian Mountains health resorts **3**:950h
·map, Czechoslovakia **5**:412

Pietà, as a theme in Christian art, depiction of the Virgin Mary supporting the body of the dead Christ. Some representations of the Pietà include St. John the Apostle, St. Mary Magdalene, and sometimes other figures on either side of the Virgin; but the great majority show only the two figures of Mary and her Son. The theme, which has no literary source but grew out of the theme of the lamentation (*q.v.*) over Christ's body, first appeared in the early 14th century in Germany. It soon spread to France and enjoyed great popularity in northern Europe in the 14th and 15th centuries; it came late to Italy, however, and never had great importance in Italian art, remaining primarily a Franco-German theme.

The Pietà was widely represented in both painting and sculpture, being one of the most poignant visual expressions of current popular concern with the emotional aspects of the lives of Christ and the Virgin.

The format of the Virgin bearing the body of Christ on her knees was standard until the 16th century, when, influenced by the Renaissance concern with logic and proportions, artists usually depicted Christ lying at the Vir-

"Pietà," marble sculpture by Michelangelo, 1499; in St. Peter's, Rome (photo taken before the sculpture was damaged in 1972)

SCALA, New York

gin's feet, with only his head propped against her knees. This form was adopted by Italian Baroque art and was passed on to Spain, Flanders, and Holland. The theme of the Pietà found its most delicate and psychologically penetrating expression in France; in Spain it was treated with the greatest depth of emotion.

Most religious art suffered a decline after the 17th century, but, because of its special emotional appeal, the Pietà continued to be a vital theme through the 19th century.

·Botticelli's thematic and stylistic significance **3**:77e
·Del Sarto work's style and mood **1**:866e
·Ghirlandajo work's approximate dating and subject **8**:150e
Michelangelo
·chaste features of the Virgin **12**:98d
·commission, composition, and tone **19**:409b
·form and analysis of Florentine Pietà **12**:100c; illus. 97
·Perugino work's composition and perspective **14**:137e
·Titian work's composition and colour effects **18**:460c

Pietarsaari (Finland): *see* Jakobstad.

Pietas, in Roman religion, personification of a respectful and faithful attachment to gods, country, and relatives, especially parents. Pietas had a sanctuary at Rome and was often represented on coins as a matron casting incense upon an altar, sometimes accompanied by a stork, the symbol of filial piety.

Pietermaritzburg, popularly MARITZBURG, capital of Natal Province, Republic of South Africa, in a valley between the Umsindusi River and Dorp Spruit. Founded in 1839 by Boers from the Cape after a victory over the Zulus, it was named to honour their dead leaders Piet Retief and Gerrit Maritz. The British took control in 1843 and built Ft. Napier (now a historical monument). Pietermaritzburg became a city in 1853 and achieved capital status in 1856. Known as the "City of Flowers" for its parks and botanical gardens, the city includes a campus of the University of Natal (1909), teachers' training and technical colleges, the Natal Museum, and the Voortrekker Museum (housed in the Church of the Vow; 1839). A model native village is nearby in the Mountain Rise area. Many residents commute to Durban via the excellent highway. Pietermaritzburg is the heart of an industrial complex; manufactures include furniture, aluminum ware, and wattle extract. The city is a gateway to Natal's game reserves and mountain resorts. Pop. metropolitan area (1970 prelim.) 158,921 (29% white).
29°37′ S, 30°16′ E

·map, South Africa **17**:62
·population, education, agriculture, and culture **12**:846d *passim* to 847e

Pietersburg, plain of northeast Transvaal, South Africa.

·Transvaal infertile land areas **18**:685e

Pieterz, Barent: *see* Fabritius, Barent.

Pieterzoon, Pieter: *see* Hein, Piet.

Pietism 14:455, an influential religious reform movement that began in German Lutheranism in the 17th century. Emphasizing personal faith in protest against secularization in the church, Pietism soon spread to other countries and during its history expanded its emphases to include social and educational concerns.

The text article covers the nature and significance of Pietism, its history from its pre-17th-century roots to the 20th century, and its theology, practices, and institutions. The article concludes with an assessment of the influence of Pietism in the 20th century.

REFERENCES in other text articles:
·Brethren churches background **3**:156h
·Christian love ethic personalization **4**:526b
·German educational reform basis **6**:352g
·German movement characteristics **17**:566d
·Greenland missions in 18th century **16**:321g
·Holiness church sympathies **8**:995h
·Lutheran trends after orthodox movement **11**:197f
·Moravian Church development of beliefs **12**:435f
·Protestantism, theology, and devotion **15**:113b
·Protestant reaction to intellectualization **15**:100e
·Protestant re-institution of monasticism in 19th century **15**:117b
·Ritschl ethical doctrine opposition **15**:863c
·Zinzendorf's German ecumenism **19**:1155b

RELATED ENTRIES in the *Ready Reference and Index:*
Amana Society; Bishop Hill; Evangelical Covenant Church of America; Rijnsburger Collegiants

Pietra, Don, 16th-century Italian monk.

·bookkeeping history and methods **3**:37e

Pietra del paragone, La (1812), translation THE TOUCHSTONE, opera by Gioacchino Rossini.

·La Scala's first production **15**:1160b

pietra dura, the designation applied to any of the hard stones used in *commesso* (*q.v.*) work, an art that flourished in Florence particularly in the late 16th and 17th centuries and involved the fashioning of highly illusionistic pictures out of cut-to-shape pieces of coloured stone. The term *pietra dura* ("hard stone") signifies the requisite hardness and durability of the materials used in this work, officially describing those stones that fall between the sixth and tenth degrees of Mohs scale of hardness; that is, between feldspar and a diamond. The most commonly used of these hard stones were quartzes, chalcedonies, agates, jaspers, granites, porphyries, and petrified woods, all of which are variable in hue and together provide an almost limitless range of colour. Lapis lazuli, a semihard stone of brilliant blue, was the only stone regularly used in *commesso* work that does not fall into the *pietra dura* classification.

·Italian Baroque furniture decoration **7**:799h
·sculptural handling processes **16**:425a

Pietrasanta, centre of a district known as Versilia, Lucca province, Toscana (Tuscany) region, central Italy, at the foot of the Alpi Apuane (mountains) just southeast of Carrara. Its piazza is surrounded by fine buildings including the cathedral of S. Martino and the church of S. Agostino (a baptistery with a medieval font), both dating from the 14th century, and the remains of the Rocca, a 12th-century citadel. Pietrasanta was strategically situated on the German Gothic Line in World War II and saw heavy fighting. Agricultural activities, tourism, and the quarrying and processing of marble are the principal industries of the town. Pop. (1970 est.) 25,552.
43°57′ N, 10°14′ E

Pietro II Orseolo (ruled 991–1008), doge of Venice.

·territorial and economic expansion **9**:1122f

Pietro da Cortona, originally PIETRO BERRETTINI, (b. Nov. 1, 1596, Cortona, Italy—d. May 16, 1669, Rome), architect, painter, and decorator, an outstanding exponent of Baroque. He studied in Rome from *c.* 1612 under the minor Florentine painters Andrea Commodi and Baccio Ciarpi and was influenced by the Antique and the work of Raphel. The most important of his earliest paintings were three frescoes (1624–26) in Sta. Bibiana, Rome. In the 1620s he designed the Villa del Pigneto near Rome and possibly another villa at Castel Fusano, both for his patrons, the Sacchetti family.

His fame reached its climax in the 1630s with the church of SS. Luca e Martina (1635–50) and the ceiling fresco of *Allegory of Divine Providence* (1633–39) in the Barberini Palace. The design of SS. Luca e Martina derives more from Florentine than Roman sources, resulting in a different type of Baroque from that of either Bernini or Borromini. The ceiling, conceived as a painted glorification of the Barberini pope, Urban VIII, is treated illusionistically. Its strong colour and steep perspective recall Veronese, whose work Cortona may have seen in Venice in 1637.

Church of Sta. Maria della Pace, Rome, by Pietro da Cortona
Anderson—Alinari

Also in 1637 he visited Florence, where he began painting the frescoes representing the Four Ages for Grand Duke Ferdinando II of Tuscany in the Pitti Palace. In 1640 he returned to finish these and paint the ceilings of a suite of apartments in the palace named after the planets. He treated the entire surface as a single spatial unit adding a wealth of real stucco decoration, partly gilt, beneath. He returned to Rome in 1647, where he painted frescoes in Sta. Maria in Vallicella and the ceiling of the long gallery of the Pamphili Palace in Piazza Navona (1651–54) for Innocent X. His chief architectural works of this period were the facades of Sta. Maria della Pace (1656–57)—perhaps his most ingenious conception—and Sta. Maria in Via Lata (1658–62). He also produced designs for the modernization of the Pitti Palace and the east front of the Louvre in Paris (1664). He painted religious and mythological easel pictures throughout his life. From 1634–38 he was head of the Academy of St. Luke, Rome. Despite a correspondence in feeling between his architecture and his painting, there is little physical connection between them and he never decorated one of his own churches.

·Baroque architectural developments **19**:415d
·Baroque stylistic characteristics **2**:133g

Pietro della Vigna, also known as PETRUS DE VINEA (b. *c.* 1190, Capua, Italy—d. 1249, Pisa?), chief minister of the Holy Roman emperor Frederick II, distinguished as jurist, poet, and man of letters whose sudden fall from power and tragic death captured the imagination of poets and chroniclers, including Dante. Pietro was a brilliant representative of a rising class of government functionaries created by the Emperor outside the feudal hierarchy.

Born in the mainland part of the Kingdom of Sicily to a poor family (his parents were said to have been beggars), he studied law at Bologna, apparently at the expense of that city. In 1221 the Archbishop of Palermo presented him to Frederick, who made him a court notary. From 1225 to 1234, he served as a judge in the Magna Curia (high court) of Sicily, in which role he became the principal author of the Constitutions of Melfi (1231), a legal code that systematized Norman law, superimposing the new Hohenstaufen absolutism. The code was written in the elegant Latin style for which Pietro became famous.

An exponent of the rhetorical *ars dictaminis* ("craft of composition"), Pietro influenced the literary form of Frederick's letters and public documents and, through them, the rhetoric of European courts. As a poet, writing in both Latin and Italian, he played a part in the development of the *dolce stil nuovo* ("sweet new style").

From 1230 on, Pietro was Frederick's closest adviser and most trusted ambassador. He undertook repeated missions to the popes Gregory IX and Innocent IV and in 1234 travelled to England to arrange a marriage between Frederick and Isabella, who was the sister of Henry III.

The Emperor's collaborator and instrument in every important act of his reign, Pietro reached the apogee of his power in 1246, when he was appointed prothonotary (chief court official) and logothete (chancellor) of the Kingdom of Sicily.

In 1249, however, Pietro was accused of plotting to poison the Emperor. Arrested at Cremona, he was carried in chains from city to city until, finally, he was blinded at San Miniato, near Florence.

It is not certain whether he died there, from the injury, or near Pisa, by suicide. The question of the guilt of the man who, according to Dante, "held both keys of Frederick's heart," preoccupied contemporary writers, most of whom absolved him.

·Sicilian court's intellectual climate **7**:701b

Pietro di Candia, Italian form of the original name of the antipope Alexander V (*q.v.*).

Pietrosul, highest peak (7,556 ft [2,303 m]) in the Rodna Massif of Romania.
47°36′ N, 24°38′ E
·Inner Eastern Carpathians' elevations **3**:949g
·map, Romania **15**:1049

piezoelectric devices 14:461, devices containing crystals that convert mechanical energy into electrical energy when a stress is applied, and, conversely, electrical energy into mechanical energy when a voltage is applied. These two properties are useful in transducers, stable oscillators, and wave filters.

The text article covers the history of piezoelectric devices, quartz as a piezoelectric crystal, piezoelectric transducers (including measurements and applications of resonant devices), the application of freely vibrating crystals (including frequency control, wave filters, and light modulators), and specialized applications of piezoelectric devices.

REFERENCES in other text articles:
·electroacoustic sound sources **17**:30c
·electronic pickup of sound wave **6**:682f
·oscillator types and circuitry **6**:686b
·phono pickup with crystal **17**:54g
·pressure-type crystal microphone **17**:57h
·quartz-crystal clockwork design **4**:746g
·radio transmission oscillators **15**:428d
·semiconductor operation principles **16**:528g
·sonar transducers and electric fields **17**:4d
·telemetry transducer operation **18**:80d
·transducer construction and operation **18**:840g

RELATED ENTRIES in the *Ready Reference and Index:*
filter, band-pass; modulator, light; piezoelectricity; quartz; Rochelle salt; transducer

piezoelectricity, appearance of positive electric charge on one side of certain nonconducting crystals and negative charge on the opposite side when the crystals are subjected to mechanical pressure. The pressure on an electrically neutral crystal polarizes it by slightly separating the centre of positive charge from that of the negative charge in those crystals not having a centre of structural symmetry; equal and unlike charges on opposite faces of the crystal result.

This charge separation may be described as a resultant electric field and may be detected by an appropriate voltmeter as a potential difference, or voltage, between the opposite crystal faces.

This occurrence, also called the piezoelectric effect, has a converse. The converse piezoelectric effect is the production of a mechanical deformation in a crystal across which an electric field or a potential difference is applied. A reversal of the field reverses the direction of the mechanical deformation. Alternating electric fields produce alternating mechanical vibrations of the same frequency. A piezoelectric material, such as a thin slab of quartz, can convert a high-frequency alternating electric signal to an ultrasonic wave of the same frequency. Or by the direct piezoelectric effect, such a crystal can convert a mechanical vibration, such as sound, into a corresponding electrical signal (alternating voltage).

The converse piezoelectric effect is somewhat similar to electrostriction (*q.v.*), a more general effect, common to all nonconducting crystals, usually much weaker than the converse piezoelectric effect and not characterized by reversed deformation when the electric field is reversed. *Major ref.* **6**:602f
·bone collagen property due to force **3**:21f
·discovery by Curies **5**:371b
·forced vibration of quartz **19**:101a
·mineral properties and quartz **12**:240c
·polarization structure **6**:560b
·quartz properties and uses **16**:752g
·wood electrical properties **19**:921b

piezomagnetism, weak ferromagnetism produced in antiferromagnetic materials by the application of external stress.
·ferromagnetization process **7**:251h

pig, wild or domestic swine, a mammal of the Suidae family. In Britain, the term refers to all domestic swine; in the United States, to younger swine weighing less than 120 pounds (50 kilograms), others being called hogs. Pigs are stout-bodied, short-legged, omnivorous mammals, with thick skins usually coated

Yorkshire Large White boar
J.C. Allen and Son

with short bristles. Their hooves have two functional and two nonfunctional digits. There are three basic types of domestic pigs: large-framed lard types with a comparatively thick layer of fat and carcasses usually weighing at least 220 pounds (100 kilograms); smaller bacon types with carcasses of about 150 pounds (70 kilograms); and pork types with carcasses averaging around 100 pounds.

China probably has the largest domestic pig population of any country in the world, but scientific breeding was concentrated in Europe and the U.S. Denmark produced the Landrace breed, raised for its excellent bacon. In the United Kingdom the Yorkshire Large White, the world's most popular breed, originated in the 18th century. In the United States, government experiment stations have produced breeds such as the Beltsville, Maryland, Minnesota, and Montana. Both Japan and the Soviet Union are endeavouring to breed leaner hogs, partly with the help of imported breeds. *Major ref.* **10**:1281g
·agricultural research in breeding **1**:342h
·breeding procedures and relevant traits **1**:904d
·classification and general features **2**:79e
·development of agriculture **1**:325f
·diseases of animals, tables 2 and 3 **5**:868
·domesticated animal origins **5**:940f
·food productivity worldwide increase **7**:500c
·housing and sheltering methods **7**:176d
·infectious diseases of animals **9**:537e
·leading world producers **11**:746b
·leather and hide utilization by man **10**:760c
·Melanesian domestication and use **11**:865g
·traits, behaviour, and classification **2**:70f
·ungulate digital suppression **16**:826g; illus.
·Vietnamese use as manure supply **19**:134b

RELATED ENTRIES in the *Ready Reference and Index:*
babirusa; boar; bush pig; Suidae; swine; warthog; wild pig

Breeds of domesticated pig

name and type	distribution	appearance	characteristics
Beltsville No. 1 and No. 2 (meat)	both developed in U.S.	No. 1 is black; No. 2 is red	both raised for meat
Berkshire (meat)	U.K., Japan, Australia, N.Z., South America	medium sized, colour mostly black	raised for pork and bacon in different areas
Chester White (lard)	developed Chester County, Pa.	large and white with pinkish skin	quiet disposition; sows prolific
Duroc, or Duroc-Jersey (lard)	North and South America	medium length body; drooping ears	½ Jersey Red, ½ Duroc
Hampshire (meat)	U.S. breed	medium weight, long body, black colour	active, alert, a good grazer
Hereford (lard)	developed U.S., about 1900	medium size; light to dark red colour	raised for lard
Landrace (meat)	north and central Europe and U.S.	medium size; white in colour	several breeds; raised for bacon
Maryland No. 1 (meat)	developed U.S., 1941	medium size; black and white spotted	about 60% Landrace, 40% Berkshire
Minnesota No. 1, No. 2, and No. 3	developed U.S.	various colours	all meat breeds
Montana No. 1 (meat)	developed U.S., 1930s	slightly curved back, trim jowls	combination of Landrace and Hampshire
Palouse (meat)	developed U.S., 1945	white, medium sized	⅔ Landrace, ⅓ Chester White
Poland China (meat)	developed U.S.	mostly black; white legs, nose, tail	developed from Russian, Byfield, Big China hogs
Spotted Poland China (meat)	developed U.S.	mostly white except for black legs	sometimes called Spots
Tamworth (meat)	U.S., U.K., N.Z., Australia, Canada	large, various colours	used for crossbreeding; raised for bacon
Yorkshire Large White (meat)	worldwide distribution	white colour	a bacon breed; sows are prolific

Pigafetta, Antonio (1491–1534), Italian traveller.

·Magellan's voyage description **11**:293e

Pigalle, Jean-Baptiste (b. Jan. 26, 1714, Paris—d. Aug. 21, 1785, Paris), unofficial court sculptor to Louis XV of France after 1750, foreshadowed Neoclassicism but followed a highly personal realism. Of a family of master carpenters, he began training as a sculptor at age eight with Robert Le Lorrain, later studied with Jean-Baptiste Lemoyne, from about 1734, and finally at the Académie Royale. He was accepted for study in 1736 at the French Academy at Rome but lacked financial support. He walked from Paris, endured illness and poverty, and finally won a prize from the Accademia di S. Luca. After returning to Paris by way of Lyon, Pigalle worked for local churches.

He enjoyed the patronage of the Comte d'Argenson, of Madame de Pompadour, and also of King Louis XV. He was received by the Académie Royale after he presented to it a model of his "Mercure" in 1744. Louis commissioned both the "Mercure" and a "Venus" to be done life size in marble for presentation to Frederick II of Prussia in 1749. Pigalle was appointed a professor at the Académie Royale in 1752.

Pigalle was popular for his portraits as well as for smaller decorative, sentimental pieces. His royal portraits and monuments were destroyed during the Revolution. The base of the royal monument at Reims, however, survived. A notable part of it, perhaps his greatest surviving work, is his "Citizen," a self-portrait. His realism showed itself shockingly in the tomb of the Duc d'Harcourt (1769–76; Paris, Notre-Dame), which has a repulsive cadaver thrusting from the sarcophagus. His masterpiece of realism, however, is his nude larger-than-life Voltaire (1770–76; Paris, Palais de l'Institut de France).

pigeon, domestic (*Columba livia*), perhaps the first bird tamed by man. The domestic pigeon belongs to the order Columbiformes. Figurines, mosaics, and coins have portrayed it since at least 4500 BC (Mesopotamia). From Egyptian times the pigeon has been important as food. Its military and commercial role as messenger is very old. Today it is an important laboratory animal, especially in endocrinology and genetics.

Throwbacks among modern domestic pigeons indicate a common ancestor, the rock dove. This tendency is clearly seen in street pigeons in cities everywhere. Many are white, reddish, or checkered like some of their cousins in racing-pigeon lofts, but most are somewhat narrow-bodied and broad-billed replicas of the blue-gray ancestral form. Street pigeons nest year-round, on buildings and beneath bridges, where they may be a nuisance with their droppings and transmission of disease. These hardy birds may live 35 years.

The three main kinds of domestic pigeons are fliers, fancy breeds raised chiefly for show, and utility breeds, which produce squabs for meat—nestlings taken when 25 to 30 days old and weighing 350 to 700 grams (¾ to 1½ pounds). Utility breeds are known as dual-purpose birds if they are bred to exhibition standards.

Domestic pigeon (*Columba livia*)

Lilyan Simmons—EB Inc.

Pigeon-raising is a worldwide hobby (and business). National preferences are evident; *e.g.*, in England for birds of highly standardized appearance and bearing ("form pigeons"), in Germany for birds that have unusual markings ("colour pigeons"), in Belgium for racing pigeons, and in the U.S. for dual-purpose breeds. Hundreds of varieties of complicated lineage represent centuries of development.

·allergic response of human lungs **15**:773c
·feeding behaviour and threat displays **4**:935b; illus.
·pet ownership responsibility **14**:150f
·squab production **10**:1287a
·Venetian art destruction **19**:73h

pigeon, passenger: *see* passenger pigeon.

pigeon and dove, imprecise names for birds of the family Columbidae, order Columbiformes. Smaller forms, especially those with long tails, usually are called doves; larger forms with short tails usually are called pigeons, except that the white domestic pigeon is symbolically the "dove of peace." For the domestic pigeon, *see* pigeon, domestic.

(Top) Mourning dove (*Zenaidura macroura*), (bottom) turtle dove (*Streptopelia turtur*)

(Top) Alvin E. Staffan—National Audubon Society; (bottom) Stephen Dalton—EB Inc.

Pigeons occur worldwide except in the coldest regions and the most remote islands. Nearly 300 species are known; two-thirds of them occur in tropical southeastern Asia, Australia, and western Pacific islands, but the family also has many members in Africa and South America and a few in temperate Eurasia and North America. All members of the family suck liquids, rather than sip and swallow as in other birds, and all feed their young "pigeon's milk," the sloughed-off crop lining of both parents, stimulated by the hormone prolactin. The nestling obtains the "milk" by poking its bill down the parent's throat.

The 40 to 50 genera may be classified in 4 to 6 subfamilies, as follows:

Columbinae—typical pigeons; about 175 species in 30 genera; worldwide in temperate to tropical regions. Seed and fruit eaters, highly gregarious at times, in trees or on the ground; mainly soft gray or brown, often with reddish tints; some have iridescent patches or black-and-white markings on neck, wings, or tail. Major kinds are wood pigeons, rock doves, and street pigeons (*Columba*); turtledoves and ringdoves (*Streptopelia*); spot-winged, emerald, and bronze-winged doves of the Old World; and the American and Old World mourning, ground, and quail doves.

Gourinae—crowned pigeons; three species in one genus; New Guinea. Largest members of the family, with lacy crests and abundant tail-feathering; fruit eaters.

Didunculinae—tooth-billed pigeon; Samoa.

Treroninae—fruit pigeons; about 115 species in 10 genera; Africa, southeastern Asia, Australia, nearby islands. Many are highly coloured. Major kinds are green pigeons (*Treron*), fruit doves (*Ptilinopus*), and imperial, or nutmeg, pigeons (*Ducula*). *Major ref.* **4**:931h

·attack and defensive threat patterns **1**:296d
·pet ownership inconveniences **14**:150f

pigeon

·concept formation ability **10**:738c *passim* to 740h
·flight motion of wings **11**:23e; illus.
·hearing range experiment **17**:48e
·longevity comparison, table 1 **10**:913
·milk production mechanism **18**:450g
·psittacosis and disease transmission **9**:539a
·respiration volume and functions **15**:758c
·skeleton with near wing raised, illus. 3 **2**:1056
·thermoreceptive areas of mouth **18**:330h
·wild and domestic courtship and hormonal triggering **2**:809e

pigeon flying, use for sport or communication of the homing pigeon, a specialized variety developed through selective crossbreeding and training for maximum distance and speed in directed flight.

The earliest record of the domestication of pigeons is from the 5th Egyptian dynasty (*c.* 2494–*c.* 2345 BC). The Sultan of Baghdad established a pigeon post system in 1150. Messages were attached to the pigeon's leg or back by means of specially designed capsules. Genghis Khan used such a system as his conquests spread. Pigeons were widely used for messenger service during the Revolution of 1848 in France. In 1849 pigeons were used to carry messages during interruptions in telegraphic service between Berlin and Brussels. Pigeons were also used as emergency message carriers in war well into the 20th century.

Belgium is credited as the home of pigeon racing as a sport. In 1818 the first long-distance race of over 100 miles was held, while in 1820 a race took place between Paris and Liège and, in 1823, from London to Belgium. The sport gained prominence in the late 1800s in Great Britain, the United States, and France. Nowhere, however, did it match the popularity enjoyed in Belgium, where nearly every village had a Société Colombophile (pigeon club). The annual Belgian Concours National, a race of about 750 kilometres (470 miles) from Toulouse to Brussels, was inaugurated in 1881; during the same year the first regular races in Great Britain—from Exeter, Plymouth, and Penzance to London—took place.

Racers are trained, by repeated practice, to return to their home loft when released at various distances and to enter the loft through the trapdoors.

At the start of a race, competing birds are banded; they are then liberated together by a starter who records the time of release. The birds ascend rapidly, become oriented, and head directly toward their lofts.

As the birds enter their home lofts, the band is removed from the leg and placed in a timing device that indicates the time of arrival. The distance of the pigeon's flight is divided by the time consumed to determine which pigeon has made the fastest speed. A bird is not considered to have arrived "home" until actually through the trap of its loft. Pigeons have been known to cover distances of several thousand miles in returning home, and some have attained average speeds of better than 90 miles per hour (145 kilometres per hour) in races.

Two books on the subject are Carl A. Naether's *Book of the Racing Pigeon* (1950) and A.N. Hutton's *Pigeon Racing* (1955). *See also* sporting record.

pigeon guillemot (bird): *see* guillemot.

pigeon hawk: *see* merlin.

pigeonite, silicate mineral in the pyroxene family that occurs only in quickly chilled rocks, such as those formed from lava. It is considered to be intermediate between clinoenstatite and diopside. Inverted pigeonite (pigeonite with orthorhombic instead of monoclinic symmetry) commonly occurs in plutonic rocks, particularly gabbros. For detailed physical properties, *see* pyroxenes.
·composition and basalt crystallization trends **16**:760a; illus. 759
·silicate chain structure **15**:319d; photomicrograph 320a

pigeon orchid: *see* Dendrobium.

Pigeon River, rises on the Blue Ridge Mountains in Pisgah National Forest, western North Carolina, U.S. It flows northward past Canton and Clyde, continues on around the eastern side of the Great Smoky Mountains National Park, where it is dammed to form Waterville Lake, and on into eastern Tennessee to join the French Broad River near Douglas Reservoir in west Cocke County, after a course of 100 mi (160 km).
36°00′ N, 83°11′ W

pigeon shooting, the 19th-century sport of shooting at pigeons released from box traps. It evolved into the modern sports of trapshooting and skeet shooting through the substitution of clay disks for birds.
·shotguns and skills **8**:501b
·target-shooting sports history **16**:705b

pigeon's milk, or CROP-MILK, whitish fluid with cheese-like particles, produced from the glandular crop lining in both sexes of pigeons and doves (Columbidae), and used to feed the young.
·pigeon composition and hormonal control **4**:932a *passim* to 934g
·production and use **2**:813d
·prolactin influence on production **8**:1075f

Pigeon's Ranch, battle of: *see* La Glorieta Pass, Battle of.

pigeon wheat, also called HAIR-CAP MOSS, common name for the genus *Polytrichum* (order Bryales) with over 100 species; it often forms large mats in peat bogs, old fields, and areas with high soil acidity. About ten species are found in North America. The most widely distributed species is *P. commune*, which often attains a height of 15 centimetres (6 inches) or more, and may form large tussocks or wide beds, especially in peat bogs. The reddish-brown or dark-green phyllids (leaves), often 12 millimetres (⅖ inch) long, have sheathed bases and pointed tips.

Male and female reproductive organs are borne on separate plants. The top of the male shoot forms a flowerlike structure each year, and elongation of the shoot results in a series of "flowers" over a period of several years. Each capsule (spore case) has a light-brown, hoodlike covering (calyptra) fringed with long hairs and resembles a wheat grain. The capsules of *P. commune* are box shaped, and a prominent white membrane that covers the "mouth" can be seen after the lid falls. Pigeon wheat often grows from underground rhizoids (filaments). It has been used in stuffing bedding, and in the manufacture of brooms, dusters, and baskets.
·economic value **3**:352d
·life-span and age indicator **10**:915a
·reproductive system comparisons **15**:718e

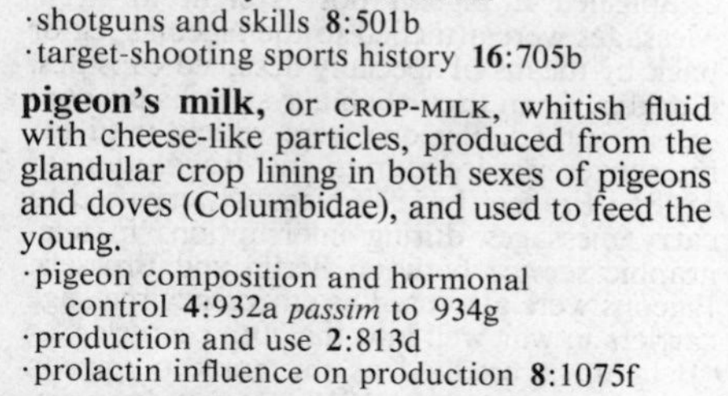

Pigeon wheat (*Polytrichum commune*)
Hugh Spencer

pig-footed bandicoot (marsupial): *see* bandicoot.

Piggot, Charles Snowdon (b. June 5, 1892, Sewanee, Tenn.), geophysicist known for his study of the Earth's radioactivity and its employment in determining the age of rocks.

Piggot was an investigator at the Geophysical Laboratory of the Carnegie Institution (1924–48) and executive director of the committee of geophysical science of the National Research and Development Board from 1946 until his retirement in 1949. He measured the radioactivity of rocks found in deep-sea drillings, made determinations of geological time, and studied radium distribution in the Earth.

Piggott, Lester (Keith) (b. Nov. 5, 1935, Wantage, Berkshire), one of the world's leading jockeys in Thoroughbred flat racing, British riding champion in 1960 and from 1964 through 1971. Born to parents whose families had long been associated with the turf, he rode in his first race at the age of 12. He won the Derby at Epsom (Surrey) on six occasions (1954, 1957, 1960, 1968, 1970, 1972) and also scored numerous triumphs in the St. Leger (6 times), the 2,000 Guineas, the Ascot Gold Cup, and other major British races. In addition, he rode successfully in French flat races and in British steeplechases. In 1968 and 1969 he won the Washington, D.C., International, a flat race.
·horse racing achievements **8**:1099a

piggyback (freight transport), arrangement whereby truck trailers loaded with freight are placed on railroad flat cars for shipment over relatively long distances. This procedure can be cheaper than hauling the trailer behind a truck for long distances.
·flatcar design variations **15**:486f
·materials-handling systems **11**:618e

pig iron, crude cast iron taken directly from the blast furnace and placed in molds.
·blast-furnace and electric-furnace smelting **11**:1066e
·by-products in steel production **11**:623h
·European production 1870–1965 map **6**:238
·industrial limitations **6**:230h
·production and name derivation **17**:638e
·production and transport in steel mill **17**:642e; table 662

pigment, substance that imparts colour, including black or white, to other materials. For chemical aspects, *see* dyestuffs and pigments; for industrial aspects, *see* dyes and dyeing; for biological aspects, *see* pigmentation.

pigment, respiratory: *see* respiration and respiratory systems.

pigmentation, an increase, decrease, or absence of colour in the skin, eyes, or hair, the main pigment in these structures being melanin. Extraneous skin pigment may be introduced as a tattoo. Certain drugs and chemicals and even foods may also induce local or generalized changes in either skin or hair. *Major ref.* **4**:914c
·aging and waste product accumulation **1**:305d
·animal colour pattern, illus., **4**:Coloration, Biological, Plate I
·animal lung disease **5**:870h
·Cactales and Caryophyllales features **3**:575e
·Caryophyllales unique features **3**:974d
human
·albinism and tyrosinase synthesis **11**:1054c
·climatic influences **4**:728h
·endocrine system disorders **6**:830c
·eye colour variations **7**:95d
·eyelid incidence and function **7**:92h
·genetic absence of pigments **7**:999h
·genetic regulation of skin colour **8**:804f
·melanocytes and pigmentation changes **16**:847h
·obsolete racial typing criteria **15**:351c
·physical characteristics of human races **14**:841e
·pregnancy skin colour changes **14**:975b
·skin cell sites and function **9**:668b; illus.

pigment migration, movement of pigment particles in specialized animal cells, as in the eyes of many nocturnal animals. It enables them to change the sensitivity of the eye to various levels of light. Pigment migration in the skin of certain amphibians and reptiles enables them to change colour within a narrow range.
·Exner's dark adaptation experiments **14**:358h

Pignatelli, Antonio: *see* Innocent XII.

Pignatelli, Giovanni Battista, 16th-century Italian equestrian.
·horsemanship and early riding schools **15**:836a

Pigneau de Béhaine, Pierre-Joseph-Georges (b. Nov. 2, 1741, Origny-Sainte-Benoîte, Fr.—d. Oct. 9, 1799, Qui Nhon, Annam, now central Vietnam), Roman Catholic missionary who paved the way for French colonization of Indochina.

Pigneau de Béhaine left France in 1765, telling his family that he was going to Cádiz, Spain, with the Société des Missions Étrangères, the French Society of Foreign Missions; instead, he went to Southeast Asia to establish a seminary school in southern Cochinchina (now part of South Vietnam). A military dispute in Cochinchina delayed his arrival at Ha Tien, near the Cambodian frontier, until 1767. He remained there for two years, preparing Vietnamese pupils for the priesthood, until the seminary was destroyed in a Siamese invasion. After spending two months in jail, he escaped to Malacca with several of his students. He re-established the school in Pondichéry (Pondicherry), French India. He was made a bishop in 1770, and about that time he left India and returned to Macao, where he compiled a dictionary and wrote a catechism in Vietnamese.

In 1774–75 Pigneau de Béhaine made his way back to Cochinchina via Cambodia. He remained at Ha Tien until 1777, when the rebel nationalist Tay Son brothers overthrew the reigning Nguyen dynasty and orphaned the young heir apparent, Prince Nguyen Anh, who fled to him for protection. Two years later Pigneau de Béhaine spirited the Prince away to comparative safety on a nearby French-held island. His action won him the enduring gratitude of Nguyen Anh, who became the emperor Gia Long. The Bishop returned to France in 1787 and persuaded King Louis XVI to sign a treaty with the Vietnamese prince, but he was unsuccessful in his attempts to obtain armaments and troops to reinstate his protégé. Undaunted, he returned to India, where he won support from French merchants for Nguyen Anh's cause. With their help, Nguyen Anh overcame the rebels, united the country, and was installed as Emperor Gia Long in 1802.

Pigneau de Béhaine, in the position of foreign minister, helped the Emperor organize his domain. He pleaded with the Vatican for greater tolerance of ancestor worship, but he was never able to convince Gia Long to do much more than grudgingly allow Christian missionary work in Vietnam to continue during his lifetime.

After long suffering with dysentery, Pigneau de Béhaine died on a journey to Nha Trang and was buried with military honours at Saigon.

pignolia (nut): *see* pine.

Pigot, George Pigot, Baron (b. May 4, 1719, London—d. May 11, 1777, Madras), wealthy British East India merchant and governor of Madras, southern India.

Baron Pigot, oil painting by George Willison, 1777; in the National Portrait Gallery, London
By courtesy of the National Portrait Gallery, London

At 17 Pigot entered the East India Company service, becoming governor and commander in chief of Madras in 1755. He stoutly defended Madras against the French in 1758–59, and after the capture of Pondicherry (a former French enclave on the southeast coast) by Lieut. Col. (afterward Sir) Eyre Coote in 1761, Pigot occupied the town on behalf of the Company. He returned to England in 1763 with a fortune of £400,000 and was given a baronetcy the following year. Member of Parliament for Wallingford (1765–68) and Bridgnorth (1768–77), he was created an Irish peer as Baron Pigot in 1766.

Returning to Madras in 1775 as governor, Pigot tried to suppress widespread corruption in the public service, but in so doing created enemies. A majority of his council, backed by the East India trader Paul Benfield, opposed Pigot because of his proposed restoration of the raja (ruler) of Tanjore (or Thanjāvūr, now a town in Tamil Nadu state). Pigot suspended two members of the council and ordered the arrest of the commandant, Sir Robert Fletcher. Government was then taken over by the majority of the council, and Pigot was imprisoned. From London, the court of directors ordered the restoration of Pigot to his post followed by his resignation; but he died before the order arrived. Parliament discussed the case in 1779, and four of those responsible for his arrest were tried and fined £1,000 each.

Pigot, Robert (1720–1796), British officer largely responsible for the defeat of the North American colonists at the Battle of Bunker Hill (June 17, 1775), during the U.S. War of Independence.

Pigott, Richard (*c.* 1828–89), Irish journalist and forger of a letter to *The Times* published in 1887.

·Parnell reaction to forgery attempt **13**:1021h

Pigou, Arthur Cecil (b. Nov. 18, 1877, Ryde, Isle of Wight, in the English Channel—d. March 7, 1959, Cambridge, Cambridgeshire), one of the most eminent British economists of the 20th century, noted for his studies in welfare economics.

Educated at King's College, Cambridge, Pigou succeeded Alfred Marshall in the Cambridge chair of political economy in 1908. It was primarily through his efforts that Marshall's ideas were disseminated and provided the leading theoretical basis for what subsequently became known as the Cambridge school of economics.

Pigou's most significant and influential work was *The Economics of Welfare* (1920), in which he sought to explore the effects of economic activity upon the total welfare of society and its various groups and classes. Pigou applied his powers of economic analysis to a number of other problems, including tariff policy, unemployment, and public finance. He also served on the Royal Commission on Income Tax (1919–20) and on two committees on the currency (1918–19; 1924–25).

·business cycles and exogenous theories **3**:538h

pigpen: *see* hog house.

pigskin, leather manufactured from the skin of swine, used to make such items as shoes, wallets, and bookbindings. *See* leather and hides.

Pig War, tariff conflict, between Serbia and Austria-Hungary (March 1906–June 1909), so named because during it the export of live Serbian pigs to Austria-Hungary was prohibited. In 1903 Serbia, regenerated with the accession of a new king that year, threatened Austria-Hungary in the Balkans, and the Austro-Serb commercial treaty was running out. Renewal negotiations foundered, for Serbia wanted to reduce its economic dependence on Austria, which took 80 to 90 percent of all exports and supplied 50 to 60 percent of all imports. In January 1904 Serbia placed a munitions order with a French firm rather than the usual Austrian one; and a Serbo-Bulgarian customs union (Aug. 4, 1905) ruined the trade negotiations between Austria-Hungary and Serbia. On March 1, 1906, the "Pig War" started with the closing of the frontier to trade. As a result, Serbia found fresh markets, foreign trade increased by 10,000,000 dinars, credits for slaughterhouses and canning plants were obtained from France, and imports were arranged from Germany. Serbian hostility to Austria-Hungary had increased; and a need for a trade outlet to the Adriatic Sea developed, sharpening Serbia's nationalist ambitions with regard to Bosnia.

·Habsburg economic pressure **2**:473a

pigweed (*Amaranthus*), coarse, often weedy and annual herbs of the order Caryophyllales.

·seed type and germination mechanism **5**:960d

Přídoli Beds: *see* Budňany Limestone.

Pijao, extinct Indian people of the southern highlands of Colombia. The Pijao spoke a language of the Chibchan family, related to that of the Páez (*q.v.*), their neighbours to the south. They were agriculturalists, raising corn (maize), sweet manioc (yuca), beans, potatoes, and many fruits; they also hunted and fished. They lived in settlements of several families in houses built of wood and plastered with mud and clay. They made pottery, wove cotton, worked stone, and smelted and worked gold and copper. They generally wore no clothing except palm-leaf hats, though they painted the body and adorned it with feathers and sometimes gold ornaments. They deformed the skulls of their infants by tying boards against them. They were also cannibals who devoured their slain enemies. The Pijao worshipped idols and believed that the dead were reincarnated as animals. They refused to make peace with the Spaniards and were completely annihilated by the mid-17th century.

·geographic distribution and socioeconomic structure **17**:117h; map

Pijnacker, Adriaen, 18th-century Dutch potter at Delft.

·Delft dorée and Delft noir work **14**:911e

pik, also called PIC, PICKI, and DIRAA, any of various units of length used in Mediterranean countries, as Greece, Turkey, Egypt, Algeria, and Cyprus; equal to between 18 and 30 inches.

·weights and measures, table 5 **19**:734

pika, also called LITTLE CHIEF HARE, MOUSE HARE, WHISTLING HARE, or PIPING HARE, small, essentially tailless, rabbitlike mammal found in parts of western North America and in Asia and eastern Europe. The names rock rabbit and cony (coney) are sometimes ambiguously applied to these animals as well as to the unrelated hyrax (*q.v.*).

Pikas belong to the genus *Ochotona*, the family Ochotonidae, and the order Lagomorpha. Their ears are rounded rather than elongated; their brownish or reddish fur is soft, long, and thick. Pikas are about 15 to 30 centimetres (6–12 inches) long and weigh about 125 to 440 grams (4–14 ounces).

Pika (*Ochotona princeps*)
Kenneth W. Fink—Root Resources

Most pikas live in rocky, mountainous areas, but, in Asia, some species inhabit burrows in forests and even in desert areas. Pikas do not seem to hibernate. During the summer and autumn months, pikas "harvest" vegetation, which they dry in the sun. This hay, stored under rocks or in other protected places, provides a source of food during the winter. Pikas bear several litters of two to six naked young in the spring and summer months. The gestation period is about one month.

·distribution pattern **5**:910a
·lagomorph morphology and classification **10**:588d

pike, voracious freshwater fish, family Esocidae, caught both commercially and for sport. It is recognized by the elongate body, small scales, long head, shovellike snout, and large mouth armed with strong teeth. The dorsal and anal fins are far back on the tail.

The northern pike (*Esox lucius*) of North America, Europe, and northern Asia has pale, bean-shaped spots on the body and lacks scales on the lower parts of the gill covers. It is a fairly common and prized gamefish with a maximum size and weight of about 1.4 metres (4½ feet) and 21 kilograms (46 pounds). The muskellunge and pickerel (*qq.v.*) are North American pikes similar in habit to the northern pike.

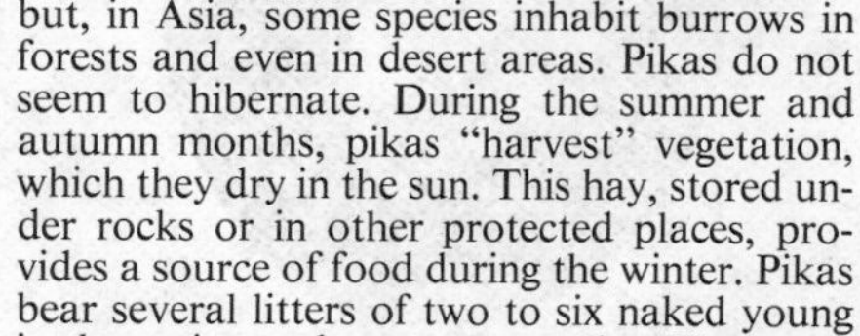

Northern pike (*Esox lucius*)
Russ Kinne—Photo Researchers

Solitary hunters, pikes, pickerel, and muskellunge lie motionless in the water or lurk in a clump of weeds. As a victim comes within reach, they make a sudden rapid lunge and seize the prey. They usually eat small fishes, insects, and aquatic invertebrates, but larger forms also take waterfowl and small mammals. They spawn in weedy shallows from late winter through spring.

Pikes are of the order Salmoniformes. Walleyed pikes are not true pikes; they are members of the perch order (Perciformes). *See* pikeperch.

·freshwater fish commercial importance **7**:349g
·oxygen consumption, table 1 **15**:751
·traits, behaviour, and classification **16**:185f

pike, ancient and medieval infantry weapon, was a long, metal-pointed spear with heavy wooden shaft 10 to 20 feet (3 to 6 metres) long. The pike disappeared from land warfare with introduction of the bayonet, though it was retained as a naval boarding weapon through the 19th century.

·Spanish use in military tactics **19**:577g

Pike, Kenneth L(ee) (1912–), U.S. linguist and anthropologist noted for his extensive studies of the aboriginal languages of such countries as Mexico, Guatemala, Peru, Ecuador, Ghana, Nigeria, the Philippines, and New Guinea. He has been especially associated with research in phonemics and in what he has termed tagmemics (*q.v.*).

·tagmemic analysis development **10**:996a

Pike, Zebulon Montgomery (b. Jan. 5, 1779, Lamberton, N.J.—d. April 27, 1813, York, now Toronto, Ont.), U.S. army officer

Pike, portrait by C.W. Peale, 1792; in the Independence National Historical Park collection, Philadelphia

By courtesy of the Independence National Historical Park, Philadelphia

and explorer for whom Pikes Peak in Colorado was named. In 1805, under orders from Gen. James Wilkinson, Pike, then an army lieutenant, led a 20-man exploring party to the headwaters of the Mississippi with instructions to discover the source of that stream, negotiate peace treaties with Indian tribes, and assert the legal claim of the United States to the area. Pike travelled 2,000 miles by boat and on foot from St. Louis, Mo., to Leech and Sandy lakes, in northern Minnesota. He erroneously identified Leech Lake as the river's source.

In July 1806 Pike was dispatched to the Southwest to explore the Arkansas and Red rivers and to obtain information about the adjacent Spanish territory. Near the site of present-day Pueblo, Colo., Pike erected a post and, after trying unsuccessfully to scale the mountain peak later named for him, proceeded southward until his party reached the vast tableland of northern New Mexico, where they were apprehended by Spanish officials on the charge of illegal entry into New Mexico. Pike's maps, notes, and papers, some of which were recovered a century later by the historian Herbert E. Bolton, were seized. The Americans were escorted across Texas to the Spanish-American border at Natchitoches, La., where on July 1, 1807, they were released.

Pike's report on Santa Fe, with information noting particularly the military weakness of the capital and the lucrativeness of the overland trade with Mexico, stimulated the expansionist movement into Texas. Pike served in the War of 1812, attaining the rank of brigadier general. He was killed in action during the attack on York.

BIBLIOGRAPHY. Eliott Coues (ed.), *The Expeditions of Zebulon Montgomery Pike*, 3 vol. (1895); W.E. Hollon, *The Lost Pathfinder, Zebulon Montgomery Pike* (1949).

·Kansas early explorations **10**:383b

pikeman, foot soldier armed with a pike (*q.v.*).

·bayonets and history of muskets **19**:685a

·small arms and history of bayonet **16**:894h

pikeperch, any of several freshwater food and game fishes of the family Percidae (order

Pikeperch (*Stizostedion lucioperca*)

Painted especially for *Encyclopædia* Britannica by Tom Dolan, under the supervision of Loren P. Woods, Chicago Natural History Museum

Perciformes), found in Europe and North America. Although more elongated and slender than perches, pikeperches have the two dorsal fins characteristic of the family. They are, like perches, carnivorous and, as adults, feed largely on other fishes.

The European pikeperch, or zander (*Stizostedion*, or *Lucioperca*, *lucioperca*) is found in lakes and rivers of eastern, central, and (where introduced) western Europe. It is greenish or grayish, usually with darker markings, and generally attains a length and weight of 50–66 centimetres (20–26 inches) and 3 kilograms (6.6 pounds).

The North American pikeperches include the walleye (*S. vitreum*), of clear, cool lakes and rivers, and the sauger (*S. canadense*), of lakes and rather silty rivers. Both are darkly mottled fishes native to eastern North America. The sauger, the smaller of the two, does not usually exceed a length and weight of about 30 cm (11¾ in) and 1 kg (2.2 lb). The walleye rarely weighs more than 4.5 kg (10 lb) and has a maximum length and weight of about 90 cm (35½ in) and 11 kg (24 lb).

·freshwater fish commercial importance **7**:349g

Pikes Peak, in the front range of the Rocky Mountains in El Paso County, Colorado, U.S., 10 mi (16 km) west of Colorado Springs.

Pikes Peak above Gateway Rocks, Colorado

David Muench—EB Inc.

Although it ranks 32nd in altitude (14,110 ft [4,301 m]) among Colorado peaks, it is widely known by reason of its commanding location and easy accessibility. On the edge of the Great Plains, it is isolated from other peaks; to the southwest is the famous Cripple Creek gold district. Ascent to the summit (a fairly level area of about 60 ac [24 ha]) may be easily accomplished by trail, by cog railway (8.75 mi), or by automobile toll road (18 mi). An average snowfall of about 9½ ft on the northern slope and 14 ft on the southern provides skiing facilities. Colorado Springs draws its main water supply from Pikes Peak Watershed. The timberline is between 11,400 and 12,000 ft; above it rises nearly 2,500 ft of bare granite. The view from the summit is said to have inspired Katharine Lee Bates to write "America the Beautiful" in 1893.

The Peak was discovered in November 1806, by Lieut. Zebulon Pike (*q.v.*), who abandoned his attempt to climb it because of snow and inadequate clothing. It was climbed by Edwin James, J. Verplank, and Z. Wilson of Maj. Stephen Long's expedition on July 14–15, 1820—the first recorded ascent of a 14,000-ft peak in the U.S. Long named the mountain for James, but common usage had bestowed Pike's name upon it by 1859, when it became the focal point of a gold rush.

38°51′ N, 105°03′ W

·map, United States **18**:908

·mountaineering record and data table **12**:585

Pikesville (Maryland, U.S.): *see* Baltimore County.

piki (nut): *see* souari nut.

Piła, German SCHNEIDEMÜHL, town, northern Poznań *województwo* (province), west central Poland, on the Gwda River. Its economic growth has been steady since World War II. Industries include lumber mills, railroad workshops, and potato-processing facilities. The town lies on the Berlin–Gdańsk (Danzig) rail line.

First chronicled in the 15th century, Piła received town rights in 1512. It passed to Prussia (1772) and was returned to Poland in 1945. About 80 percent of Piła was destroyed during World War II. Pop. (1970 prelim.) 43,800.

53°10′ N, 16°44′ E

·map, Poland **14**:626

Pilar, capital, Ñeembucú department, southwestern Paraguay. It lies on the east bank of the Paraguay River across from the mouth of the Arrogo (river) Bermejo. Founded in 1778, the settlement was originally known as Ñeembucú. The city is now an important river port handling the agricultural products of the fertile area between the Paraguay and Paraná rivers; it is also a manufacturing centre, with sawmills, distilleries, and textile mills. A road leads eastward from Pilar to the Asunción–Encarnación highway. Latest pop. est. 6,300.

26°52′ S, 58°23′ W

·map, Paraguay **13**:986

pilaster, in classical architecture, shallow rectangular column that projects slightly beyond the wall into which it is built and conforms precisely to the order or style of the adjacent columns. The anta of ancient Greece was the direct ancestor of the Roman pilaster. The anta, however, which served a structural purpose as the terminus of the sidewall of a temple, never had to conform in style to the temple columns. In ancient Roman architecture the pilaster gradually became more and more decorative rather than structural, as it served to break up an empty expanse of wall. The fourth-story wall of the Colosseum, the great amphitheater built in Rome during the 1st century AD, contains examples of the Roman use of pilasters. In Renaissance architecture, beginning in Italy and spreading to France and England, pilasters were extremely popu-

Pilasters in the Pazzi Chapel, Sta. Croce, Florence, by Filippo Brunelleschi, ?1442–60's

Foto Marburg

lar scattered all over the walls, both interior and exterior, as were also the designs of the later Neoclassical periods.
·furniture adaptation and period use **7**:793c

Pilate, Pontius (d. after AD 36), Roman procurator of Judaea who condemned Jesus Christ to be crucified.

A Roman equestrian (knight) of the Samnite clan of the Pontii (hence his name Pontius), Pilate was appointed procurator of Judaea (AD 26) through the intervention of Sejanus, a favourite of the Roman emperor Tiberius. Protected by Sejanus, he incurred the enmity of the Jews by insulting their religious sensibilities, as when he hung worship images of the Emperor throughout Jerusalem and had coins bearing pagan religious symbols minted. After Sejanus' fall (31), Pilate was exposed to sharper criticism from the Jews, who may have capitalized on his vulnerability by obtaining a legal death sentence on Jesus (John 19:12). The Samaritans reported him to Vitellius, Legate of Syria, after he had attacked them on Mt. Gerizim (AD 36). He was then ordered back to Rome to stand trial for cruelty and oppression, particularly on the charge that he executed men without proper trial. According to an uncertain 4th-century tradition, Pilate killed himself on orders from Emperor Caligula in AD 39.

Various legends stressing Pilate's efforts to release Jesus, whom he considered innocent but whom he condemned in order to escape accusation of disloyalty to the Emperor, made him almost a hero in some Christian traditions; in the Ethiopian (Coptic) Church he is venerated as a saint. In Jewish tradition he is the anti-Semitic prototype.
·historical depiction of role in Passion **10**:153f

Pilâtre de Rozier, Jean-François (1756–85), French physicist and aeronaut.
·balloon flight history **12**:410g

Pilbara, or PILBARRA, a district of northwest Western Australia, extending south from the De Grey River to the Fortescue River and up to 450 mi (720 km) inland; it occupies an area of 32,000 sq mi (83,000 sq km) and averages 1,000 ft (300 m) in elevation. Gold, discovered there in 1883, led to the declaration of the Pilbara (1888) and West Pilbara (1895) goldfields. Tin was found in 1899, and deposits of copper, talc, manganese, silver, beryllium, and columbite have also been worked. There

Iron ore mine at Mt. Newman, (Ophthalmia Range) in Pilbara, Western Australia
By courtesy of the Australian News and Information Bureau

still remain valuable deposits of asbestos at Wittenoom Gorge in the Hamersley Range and tantalite at Wodgina. Iron-ore reserves, previously earmarked for domestic use, are now developed primarily for export to Japan. One of the principal mines is Mt. Goldsworthy, from which ore is shipped by rail northward to Port Hedland. The Pilbara forms a statistical division and also supports sheep stations.

Pilbara Nucleus, geological feature, Australia.
·formation and composition **2**:384e

pilchard (fish): *see* sardine.

Pilcher, Percy Sinclair (b. January 1866—d. Oct. 2, 1899, Leicestershire), British engineer, aviation pioneer, and glider experimenter. He began the study of heavier-than-air flight in 1895 under the influence of Otto Lilienthal, whom he twice visited in Germany.

In 1895 Pilcher built his first glider, the "Bat," which he then modified after Lilienthal's ideas and on which he made many successful glides. His second machine, the "Beetle," was also built in 1895, and his third, the "Gull," in 1896. It was with his fourth glider, the "Hawk" (1896), that Pilcher achieved his most productive flying. It was a monoplane, with rear fin and tail plane, and wheeled undercarriage, controlled in the Lilienthal manner of swinging the torso and legs from a hanging position between the wings.

He then turned his attention to the problem of powered flying. He had almost completed his first powered machine—for which he had also built the engine—when on Sept. 30, 1899, the "Hawk" broke up in the air when Pilcher was gliding in it at Stanford Park, near Market Harborough. He died of his injuries two days later.

Pilcomayo River, Spanish RÍO PILCOMAYO, chief western tributary stream of the Paraguay River, south central South America, rises in the eastern Andes Mountains (in Bolivia) and flows in a southeasterly direction through the Gran Chaco plains of Paraguay to join the Paraguay River opposite Asunción, after a course of 700 mi (1,125 km). Its lower course (about 410 mi), used for navigation by small craft, is much braided and shifts direction with each flood season. The Pilcomayo (Guaraní "River of the Birds") forms part of the international border (delimited in 1945) between Formosa Province, Argentina, and Paraguay.
25°21′ S, 57°42′ W

pile (nuclear engineering): *see* reactor.

pile, in textiles, the surface of a cloth composed of an infinite number of loops of warp threads, or else of an infinite number of free ends of either warp or weft (filling) threads that stand erect from the foundation or ground structure of the cloth (*see* weaving). In looped pile, the loops are uncut; in cut pile, the same or similar loops are cut, either in the loom during weaving or by a special machine after the cloth leaves the loom.

Velvet is a short-pile fabric and plush a long-pile fabric, both of which have pile formed by warp threads. Velveteen is fabric with pile formed of weft or filling threads that have been cut.

Among the loop-pile fabrics are Brussels tapestry, imitation Brussels carpeting, and Moquettes. In some cases the surfaces of carpets, such as Wilton and Axminster, are formed of cut pile; in others, both looped (uncut pile) and cut pile appear on the surface of the same fabric. Imitation furs are pile fabrics. The surfaces of pile fabrics may have decorative designs appearing in both kinds of pile and in several colours.
·method, appearance, and use **18**:181a
·rug and carpet styles and types **7**:406b

pile, in building construction, a postlike foundation member used from prehistoric times. In modern civil engineering, piles of timber, steel, or concrete are driven into the ground to support a structure; bridge piers may be supported on groups of large diameter piles. On unstable soils, piles are indispensable building supports, and may also be used on stable ground when exceptionally large structural loads are involved. Piles are driven into the ground by pile drivers (machines consisting usually of a high frame with appliances for raising and dropping a pile hammer or for supporting and guiding a stream or air hammer).
·bridge construction trends **3**:190b
·bridge pier construction history **3**:175b
·foundations and building construction **3**:458b; illus.
·harbours and sea works engineering **8**:635e
·permafrost and frost heaving **14**:95a
·steam hammer uses **17**:632h
·types, engineering principle, and usage **16**:1012e

Pilea (plant): *see* Urticaceae.

piles (medicine): *see* hemorrhoids.

Pileta Cave, La, prehistoric archaeological site in Spain.
·cave painting style correlations **17**:705d

pileus, a close-fitting, brimless hat worn by the ancient Romans and copied from the Greek sailor's hat, *pilos*. In Roman times the

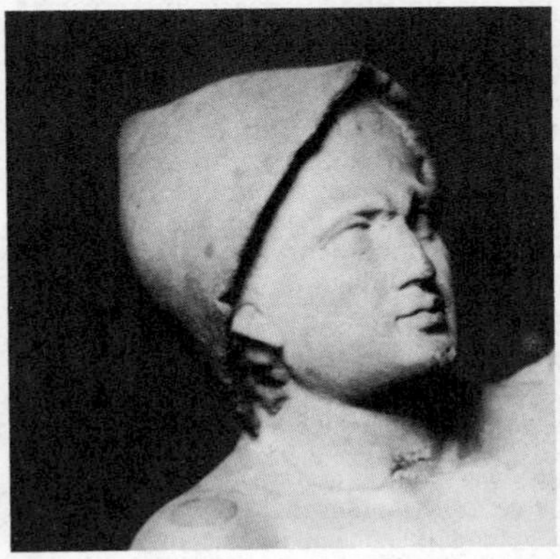

Man wearing a pileus, detail of a Greco-Roman statue; in the Mansell Collection
The Mansell Collection

head was generally uncovered, but commoners and freed slaves sometimes wore the felt pileus. The hat was again popular during the Renaissance, especially in Italy, when it was square or rounded and made of black or red velvet or felt. The zucchetto (*q.v.*), which developed from the pileus, is worn by some orders of clergy and by monks.

Pilgrim, The (1923), film written and directed by Charlie Chaplin.
·plot and technique **12**:521d

pilgrimage, journey to a sacred spot undertaken for religious motives. Muslims, for example, travel to Mecca, Christians to various shrines, and Sikhs to *gurdwārās* ("temples").
·Jain shrines and ceremonies **10**:11f; illus. 12
·medieval travel methods **18**:650e
·miracles and sacred places **12**:271g
·practice's origin **5**:536a
·saint shrines and folk practices **16**:166h
·Sikh sacred gurdwārās **16**:746h
·symbolic and ritualistic practices **17**:904h
·Tokugawa period Shintō practices **10**:77b

pilgrimage, Buddhist, though not required for followers of the religion, attracts Buddhists in large numbers to centres and shrines associated with the Buddha or his disciples. Paramount among these are the four sites associated with the four great events of the Buddha's life: (1) Lumbinī (the modern village of Rummindei in Nepal); an Aśokan pillar and a small temple mark the site of the Buddha's birthplace; (2) Bodh Gayā (near modern Gayā, in Bihār state, India); promenande railings dating from the 1st century BC and the Mahābodhi temple, a restoration of earlier restorations of a structure probably erected in the 2nd century AD, indicate the continuity of worship at the site of the Buddha's enlightenment; (3) The Deer Park (Isipatana) at Sārnāth (near modern Vārānasi, Uttar Pradesh, India); an Aśokan pillar and a *stūpa* (commemorative monument) denote the place where the Buddha preached his first sermon, *Dhammacakkapavattana Sutta* ("Setting in Motion the Wheel of the Law"); and (4) Kuśinagara (east of modern Gorakhpur, Uttar Pradesh, India); a *stūpa* and a shrine commemorate the site of the Buddha's *parinirvāṇa*, or death.

Also of great attraction to Buddhist pilgrims in India are the ruins of Nālandā, the great medieval centre of religious learning; Rājagṛha (modern Rājgīr), the site of the Buddha's first monastery; Śrāvastī, where he spent 24 rainy seasons; and Sāñchī, where the relics of two noted disciples are enshrined.

Highly venerated for the relics believed to be preserved there are the Temple of the Tooth at Kandy, Ceylon, and the Shwe Dagon pagoda at Rangoon, Burma.

Among Mahāyāna Buddhists, gratitude for the teaching of the way is extended to founders of sects. Thus, in Japan, in addition to visits to the famous Buddha images preserved at Kamakura and Nara, pilgrims gather before the image of Shinran, founder of the Shin sect (Jōdo Shinshū) at Hongan-ji. Popular in China are the mountain shrines dedicated to the *bodhisattvas* (Buddhas-to-be), such as the temple of O-mei Shan (mountain) in Szechwan Province, honouring the *bodhisattva* of happiness, Samantabhadra.

·Buddhist sites and relics **3**:394c

pilgrimage, Christian, journey to a saint's shrine or other sacred place, undertaken for a variety of motives: to gain supernatural help; as an act of thanksgiving or penance; for the sake of devotion. Records indicate that pilgrimages were made to Jerusalem as early as the 2nd century; and excavations in the 1940s at St. Peter's Basilica in Rome unearthed a 2nd-century memorial to the Apostle with numerous scratched inscriptions of the 2nd and 3rd centuries, evidencing acts of piety. The Roman liturgical calendar of the year AD 354 lists 29 local sanctuaries of the saints at which the faithful gathered annually. The travel memoir of Etheria (*c.* AD 400), a Spanish nun, testified to a system of guides and lodgings for those visiting the Palestinian holy sites. In Britain, Bede, the Venerable (died 735), a church historian, catalogued visits to graves of several saints from the 5th to the 8th century.

The medieval pilgrim began his journey with a blessing by a priest. His garb was recognizable, and on his return trip he would wear on his hat the badge of the shrine visited. Along the way he would find hospices set up specifically for pilgrims. The chief attractions for pilgrims in medieval times were the Holy Land, Santiago de Compostela in Spain, and Rome; but there were hundreds of pilgrim resorts of more local reputation, including the tombs of St. Francis (died 1226) in Assisi, Italy; of St. Martin (died 397) in Tours, Fr.; of St. Boniface (died 754) in Fulda, Ger.; of Thomas Becket (died 1170) at Canterbury, Eng.; and of St. Patrick at Downpatrick, Ire.

Not all churchmen approved entirely of pilgrimages. Some warned against excesses and questioned the value of the practice, while others questioned the authenticity of some of the relics.

Though many medieval centres still attract Roman Catholic pilgrims, the more recent shrines of St. Francis Xavier (died 1552) in Goa, India; of the Shroud of Turin (1578) at Turin, Italy; of St. Anne de Beaupré (1658) in Canada; of St. Jean-Baptiste-Marie Vianney (died 1859) at Ars and of St. Thérèse de Lisieux (died 1897) at Lisieux, both in France; and the Marian centres of Our Lady of Guadalupe (1531) in Mexico, of La Salette (1846) and Lourdes (1858) in France, and of Fátima (1917) in Portugal have grown steadily in importance.

Members of the Eastern Orthodox faith commonly make pilgrimages to celebrated monasteries to ask for spiritual and practical help from the holy men (*startsy*).

The attitude of the 16th-century Protestant Reformers found expression in 1530 in the Augsburg Confession, which portrayed pilgrimages as "childish and useless works." Although modern Protestants may visit such places as Martin Luther's grave at Wittenberg or the Wesleyan Memorial at Epworth, Lincolnshire, such visits are not regarded as devotional acts.

·Christian Jewish heritage **4**:499g
·Crusades' religious motivations **5**:298g
·European coastal religious traditions **6**:1065c
·medieval European popularity **15**:1003d
·medieval religious environment **12**:161h
·popular Christianity in late Empire **4**:541e

pilgrimage, Hindu: *see* tīrthayātrā.

pilgrimage, Muslim: *see* ḥajj; ʿumrah.

Pilgrimage of Grace (1536), a rising in the northern counties of England, the only overt immediate discontent shown against the Reformation legislation of King Henry VIII. Part of the resentment was caused by attempts, especially under Henry's minister Thomas Cromwell, to increase government control in the north; there was an element of agrarian opposition to enclosures for pasture; and there was a religious element, aroused especially by the dissolution of the monasteries, then in progress. The arrival of commissioners sent by Cromwell to collect a financial subsidy and to dissolve the smaller monasteries triggered the rising. In Louth in Lincolnshire there were riots on October 1, and commissioners were attacked. The rebels occupied Lincoln, demanding an end to the dissolution, revenge on Cromwell, and the dismissal of heretical bishops. But Henry refused to treat with men in arms against him (although professing their loyalty), and the Lincolnshire movement collapsed on October 19. Meanwhile, a more serious rising had begun in Yorkshire, led by Robert Aske, a country gentleman and lawyer. Aske took York and by October 24 was supported by about 30,000 armed men and by magnates such as Edward Lee, archbishop of York, and Thomas Darcy, Baron Darcy of Templehurst. The government had insufficient troops in the area, but on October 27, at Doncaster Bridge, Thomas Howard, the 3rd duke of Norfolk, temporized with Aske, playing for time until adequate forces could be assembled. At a council at Pontefract on December 2, the rebels drew up their demands, similar to those of the Lincolnshire men but including a return of England to papal obedience and the summoning of a Parliament free from royal influence. To these Norfolk, on December 6, made vague promises and offered a full pardon, whereupon Aske naïvely assumed he had gained his objectives and persuaded his followers to disperse. Sporadic riots in January and February 1537 enabled the government to deal with the troubles piecemeal; about 220–250 men were executed, including Darcy and Aske. The pilgrimage achieved nothing and received no support from other parts of the country.

·domestic opposition to Reformation **3**:224b

pilgrim badge, plaque or hat badge sold in the Middle Ages to devout visitors at places of pilgrimage.

·origins, appearance, and remains **11**:1108c

pilgrim bottle, vessel with a body varying from an almost full circle, flattened, to a pear shape, with a shortish neck, spreading foot and, generally, two loops on the shoulders through which either a chain or cord was passed to maintain the stopper in place.

Pilgrim bottles date to ancient Roman times in the West and to 7th-century China in the East. They were made in a wide range of materials, including earthenware, porcelain, silver, and glass, and possibly also in more perishable materials such as leather. Originally, these vessels may have been carried by travellers on their journeys; but the ones that have survived are so sumptuous that their function was probably purely ornamental, or, if they were used, it must have been—as in the case of some of the travelling tea or coffee sets in Meissen—exclusively by the very wealthy. Pottery pilgrim bottles are found in China from the T'ang dynasty (618–907), possibly imitations of even earlier metal prototypes dating as far back as the Chou dynasty (*c.* 1122–221 BC). In 16th-century Europe, metal pilgrim bottles—generally of silver or silver gilt and probably of Chinese inspiration—were made mainly in Augsburg, Ger.; they were also made in coloured glass (generally green) with ormolu (*q.v.*), or gilded brass mounts in Augsburg. Along with the Chinese blue-and-white Ming (1368–1644) pilgrim bottles, the most famous are the pear-shaped stoneware bottles made at Meissen by Johann Friedrich Böttger.

Porcelain pilgrim bottle, Ch'ing dynasty, Yung-cheng period (1723–35); Percival David Collection

By courtesy of the Percival David Foundation of Chinese Art

Pilgrim Fathers, in U.S. colonial history, settlers of Plymouth (*q.v.*), Mass., the first permanent colony in New England (1620). Of the 102 colonists, 35 were members of the English Separatist Church (the left wing of Puritanism) who had earlier fled to Leyden, the Netherlands, to escape persecution at home. Seeking a more abundant life along with religious freedom, the Separatists negotiated with a London stock company to finance a pilgrimage to America. Approximately two-thirds of those making the trip aboard the "Mayflower" (*q.v.*) were non-Separatists, hired to protect the company's interests; these included John Alden and Myles Standish.

These first settlers, initially referred to as the Old Comers and later as the Forefathers, did not become known as the Pilgrim Fathers until two centuries after their arrival. A responsive chord was struck with the discovery of a manuscript of Gov. William Bradford referring to the "saints" who had left Holland as "pilgrimes." At a commemorative bicentennial celebration in 1820, orator Daniel Webster used the phrase Pilgrim Fathers, and the term became common usage thereafter.

·covenant concept in secular state **5**:230a
·health problems and mortality rate **8**:695e
·Massachusetts religious background role **11**:592e
·Plymouth colony landing and settlement **11**:590h
·Plymouth settlement and control **18**:948c
·Protestant antiestablishmentarianism in England **15**:111d
·Puritan reaction to Canons of 1604 **3**:240d

Pilgrim Festivals, Hebrew SHALOSH REGELIM, in Judaism, the three occasions on which male Israelites were required to go to Jerusalem to offer sacrifice at the Temple and bring offerings of their produce from the fields. In the synagogue liturgy, special Psalms (called collectively Hallel) are read and prayers are

recited that vary with the nature of the festival. Thus, the Song of Solomon is read on Pesaḥ (Passover), the Book of Ruth on Shavuot (Feast of Weeks), and Ecclesiastes on Sukkot (Feast of Tabernacles).
·practices and concepts through the ages **10**:219f

Pilgrim Holiness Church: *see* Wesleyan Church.

Pilgrim's Progress, religious allegory by the English writer John Bunyan, a symbolic vision of the good man's pilgrimage through life, at one time second only to the Bible in popularity. Part I (1678), in which Christian travels from the City of Destruction to the Celestial City, is presented as a dream. Carrying his burden of sin on his back and the Bible in his hand, Christian sets off in uncertain light, having no directions but the word of Evangelist, to find the Wicket Gate that is the entrance to salvation. He passes through such dangers as the Slough of Despond, the Valley of the Shadow of Death, and Vanity Fair before he arrives at the Delectable Mountains. On the way he is helped and hindered by various companions, but at last he safely crosses the River of Death to the Celestial City. Christian's anguished struggle toward salvation, though it dominates Part I, does not totally eclipse other, contrasting, qualities. Written in homely, yet dignified biblical prose, the work has some of the qualities of a folk tale; and in its humour and realistic portrayals of Mr. Worldly Wiseman, Faithful, Hopeful, Pliant, and Obstinate, it anticipates the 18th-century novel. In Part II (1684), which deals with the effort of Christian's wife and sons to join him, the psychological intensity is relaxed and the capacity for humour and realistic observation becomes more evident. Christian's family has a somewhat easier time because Christian has smoothed the way, and even such companions as Mrs. Much-afraid and Mr. Ready-to-halt manage to complete the journey.
·allegory of Christian life **3**:482f
·literary style and theme **10**:1151c
·Puritan belief expression **3**:480h
·Puritanism in children's literature **4**:232b
·structure and interpretation **15**:799f

Pilgrims' Way, name popularly applied to the North Downs trackway in southern England. It is a famous prehistoric route between the English Channel and the chalk heartland of prehistoric Britain in Wessex and survives often as roads used for light traffic or bridle paths, marked Pilgrims' Way in the British Ordnance Survey maps. Both a ridgeway and a lower terrace way beneath the chalk escarpment can be traced. Such tracks were not fixed ways but shifted seasonally with changing ground conditions. The name, though not attested before the 18th century, was given further currency by the Anglo-French poet Hilaire Belloc. In *The Old Road* (1904), he posited a continuous prehistoric track between Winchester and Canterbury revived by pilgrims journeying to St. Thomas Becket's shrine. Possibly pilgrims did use it, although the London–Canterbury road celebrated earlier by the medieval poet Chaucer was the frequented route. Belloc's "Pilgrims' Way," however, does not coincide with the prehistoric trackway west of the Hog's Back in Surrey.

Pīlībhīt, administrative headquarters, Pīlībhīt district, Uttar Pradesh state, northern India, northeast of Bareilly, on a tributary of the Rāmganga River. It is a rail junction and is linked with Bareilly by road. Sugar processing is the largest industry, and there is an active trade in agricultural products, both locally and with Nepal. On the town's western outskirts is a large 18th-century mosque built by Ḥāfiz Raḥmāt Khān, the town's founder.

Pīlībhīt district, 1,351 sq mi (3,500 sq km) in area, lies on the Ganges Plain near the Himalayan foothills and adjoins Nepal on the northeast. It is watered by the Sārda Canal and by tributaries of the Ganges River. There are forests in the east. The most productive land and the greatest population density are in the district's extreme south. Crops include rice, wheat, gram, barley, and sugarcane. Pop. (1971 prelim.) town, 68,380; district, 751,948.
·map, India **9**:278

pili nut, the nut of any tree of the genus *Canarium*, particularly the edible nut of the Philippine tree *Canarium ovatum*.
·fruit and nut farming, table 1 **7**:755

Pílion, Óros (Greece): *see* Pelion, Mount.

Pilipino language, a standardized form of Tagalog, spoken in many parts of Luzon, which was adopted as the national language of the Philippines upon achieving independence in 1946. The name Pilipino was made official in 1959, by decree.
·establishment as national language **2**:488c

Pilkington, Francis (d. 1638, Chester, England), composer of lute songs and madrigals. He took a bachelor of music degree from Oxford in 1595, became a cantor at Chester cathedral in 1602, and a minor canon in 1612. His *First Book of Ayres* (1605) contains 21 songs for four voices or for solo voice and lute and a *Pavin for Lute and Bass Viol.* He published sets of madrigals in 1613 and 1624. Though not of the first rank, they are pleasing and well constructed. Particularly known is the madrigal "O softly singing lute," for six voices. He also composed a number of attractive lute solos.

pill, small globular or oval medicinal preparation, sometimes coated, to be swallowed whole.
·pharmaceutical preparation methods **14**:197f

Pillai, Vetanayakam (1824–89), Indian Tamil novelist.
·literary style and inspiration **17**:149a

pillar and scroll shelf clock, a wooden shelf clock mass-produced in the U.S. from the second decade of the 19th century onward. The rectangular case is topped by a scroll broken in the centre by an ornament such as an urn; on either side of the case is a vertical pillar, each of which is topped by the same kind of ornament that breaks the scroll.

Pillar and scroll shelf clock by Eli Terry, 1816; in the Shelburne Museum, Vermont
By courtesy of the Shelburne Museum, Vermont

These clocks usually had a 30-hour wooden movement, using oak plates, laurelwood pillars, and black cherry wood gears, though these were later supplanted by brass around 1840, when that metal became cheaper. The clocks are usually associated with the name of Eli Terry (1772–1852), who gave them their definitive form.

pillar-and-stall, technique of underground mining for coal.
·coal mining techniques **4**:774b

Pillar carpets, Chinese carpets designed so that when wrapped around a pillar the edges will fit together to form a continuous pattern.
·design and composition **16**:22d; illus. 23

pillar cell, in anatomy, an elongated cell in the spiral organ of the inner ear.
·structure and function in human ear **5**:1124a; illus. 1123

Pillared Hall, Mauryan building excavated at Kumrahar, in Bihār, India.
·Kumrahar's archaeological excavations **13**:1076f

Pillar of Fire, originally PENTECOSTAL UNION, Wesleyan religious body organized in 1901 by Mrs. Alma White.
·Holiness churches and perfectionist emphasis **8**:995a

Pillars of Islām: *see* arkān al-Islām.

Pillars of Society (1937), translation of SAMFUNDETS STØTTER (published and performed 1877), the first social-problem play of the Norwegian dramatist Henrik Ibsen. It is the story of Karsten Bernick, a highly respected town leader, who attempts to conceal his past misdeeds by sending the sole witness to them to sea on a rotten ship. When Bernick discovers that his only son, Olaf, has run away from home and is a stowaway on the same ship, he confesses his crime in time to prevent tragedy.
·Ibsen's social satire and reputation **9**:153a
·realistic mode departures **18**:229d

pill bug, any member of the families Armadillidiidae and Armadillidae (order Isopoda), terrestrial crustaceans that roll into a ball when disturbed. Like the sow bug (*q.v.*), it is sometimes called the wood louse. For mollusks also known as pill bugs, *see* chiton.

Pill bugs (*Armadillidium vulgare*)
E.S. Ross

The common pill bug *Armadillidium vulgare* (family Armadillidiidae) is about 17 millimetres (7/10 inch) long. The gray body, with its platelike segments, somewhat resembles a miniature armadillo, an armoured mammal that also curls into a ball when disturbed. *A. vulgare* occurs in dry, sunny places, in leaf litter, and on the edges of wooded areas. Originally found in Europe, it now occurs worldwide. *A. nasatum*, native to northern Europe, has been introduced into North America. *Armadillo officinalis* (family Armadillidae), which attains lengths of 19 millimetres (3/4 inch), is native to southern Europe.
·body plan, illus. 2 **5**:312
·reproductive system anatomy **15**:704g

Pillement, Jean (1728–1808), French painter.
·chinoiserie tapestry tradition **17**:1064c; illus.

Pillersdorf constitution (1848), liberal constitution of Austria.
·Austria's reaction to revolution **2**:464f

pilli, Aztec noble social class.
·Aztec societal structure **11**:952f

Pillnitz, Declaration of (1791), Habsburg and Prussian declaration threatening the use of force against revolutionary France.
·Prussian and Austrian threat to France **7**:652f

Pillow Book, or MAKURA-NO-SŌSHI (*c.* 1000), title of a book of reminiscences and impressions by the 11th-century Japanese court lady,

Sei Shōnagon (*q.v.*). Whether the title was generic and whether Sei Shōnagon herself used it, is not known, but other diaries of the Heian period (794–1185) indicate that such journals may have been kept by both men and women in their sleeping quarters, hence the name. The entries in *Makura-no-sōshi*, although some are dated, are not in chronological order but are rather divided under such headings as "Amusing Things" and "Vexatious Things." The "Pillow Book" belongs to the genre of *zuihitsu* ("random jottings"). A complete English translation of *Makura-no-sōshi* appeared in 1967 (*The Pillow Book of Sei Shōnagon*). *See also* Yoshida Kenkō, author of *Tsurezuregusa*, a 14th-century example of this genre.
·comic overtones **10**:1068a

pillow lace: *see* bobbin lace.

pillow structure, descriptive term for some lavas, particularly those with a basaltic composition, that have formed a series of sacklike, balloon-like, or bolster-shaped bodies up to several feet in diameter with an ellipsoidal outline in cross section. The actual formation of pillow structure has seldom, if ever, been observed, but the most widely accepted explanation of origin is that it forms during the emplacement of lavas under water. Blebs of lava may separate from the front edge of a flow and then solidify as individual masses; in some cases complete separation will not occur, and the pillows will be connected by necks. The outer surfaces of the pillows usually are glassy, showing rapid cooling, and the inner portions may be crowded with gas bubbles trapped by the glassy shell.
·formation and occurrence **9**:205h
·formation theories and structure **19**:507c
·Precambrian volcanism and rock types **14**:956e
·sedimentary deformation structures **16**:470f; illus.

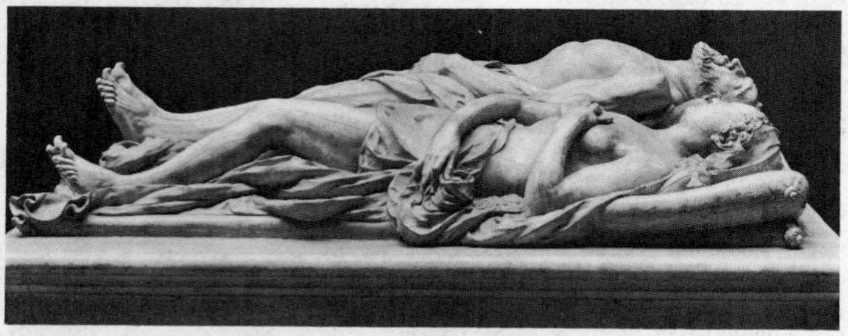

Gisant of Catherine de Médicis and Henry II by Pilon, 1563–70; in the church of Saint-Denis, Paris
J.E. Bulloz

Pillsbury, Harry Nelson (1872–1906), U.S. chess player.
·modern chess development **4**:198e

Pilnyak, Boris (Andreyevich), last name originally VOGAU (b. 1894, Mozhaisk, Russia—d. 1938?), Soviet writer of Symbolist novels and stories, prominent in the 1920s.

Pilnyak spent his childhood in provincial towns near Moscow, in Saratov, and in a village on the Volga river. He attended high school in Nizhny Novgorod and a commercial institute in Moscow. In his autobiography he stated that he began writing at the age of nine, but it was the publication of his novel *Goly god* (1922; Eng. trans., *The Naked Year*, 1928) that brought him popularity. This book was a panorama of the Revolution and Civil War, seen through a series of flashbacks and close-ups encompassing all levels of society. The fragmentary, chaotic style of construction matched the tone and character of the times he portrayed.

Pilnyak's style and ideas did not harmonize with the dominant Communist point of view. He was not himself a Communist, and his doubts were often visible in his stories and novels. In the late 1920s he was strongly criticized. Attempting to meet Soviet literary demands, he wrote *Volga vpadayet v Kaspiyskoye more* (1930; Eng. trans., *The Volga Flows into the Caspian Sea*, 1931). The novel succeeded in some respects, but the author's sympathy seemed to be with the Asiatic past as much as with the Communist future. His ambivalence did not escape the authorities; his work was branded as reactionary, and he was forced to recant. During the 1930s he disappeared, and after 1937 his name was not mentioned in the press. He is thought to have died about 1938.

Pilon, Germain (b. 1535, Paris—d. Feb. 3, 1590, Paris), one of the greatest French sculptors of the late 16th century. His work, principally monumental tombs, is a transitional link between the Gothic tradition and sculpture of the Baroque period.

A sculptor's son, Pilon was employed at 20 on the decoration of the tomb of King Francis I at Saint-Denis. His earlier work shows an Italian influence, but eventually he developed a more distinctively French expression, achieved by fusing elements from classical art, Gothic sculpture, and Michelangelo with the Fontainebleau adaptation of Mannerism, a development in art characterized by subjective conceptions, studied elegance, and virtuoso artifice. His monument for the heart of King Henry II (*c.* 1561), perhaps following a design by the Italian sculptor Francesco Primaticcio, consists of three marble Graces of great elegance supporting an urn. For the tomb of Henry II and Catherine de Médicis at Saint-Denis (1563–70), also designed by Primaticcio, Pilon created four bronze corner figures and, above, the kneeling figures of the King and Queen in bronze. Most important, however, are the seminude, marble gisants, or figures of the royal pair recumbent in death. Considered by some to be his most sublime achievement, the gisants are a Renaissance idealization of a Gothic convention and possess a depth of emotion that Pilon perhaps never again attained.

Sculptor royal from 1568, Pilon enjoyed a successful career as a portraitist, his most celebrated work in the genre being the kneeling figure of René de Birague (1583–85; Louvre). Appointed controller of the mint in 1572, in 1575 he brought eminence to French medal casting with a distinguished series of bronze medallions.

Pilon, Jean-Guy (1930–), Canadian poet.
·literary themes and works **10**:1229c

Pílos (Greece): *see* Pylos.

Pilot, The (1823), novel by James Fenimore Cooper, the first of his sea stories.
·sea novel popularity and influence **5**:133g

pilotage: *see* navigation.

pilotaxitic texture, descriptive term for igneous rocks consisting of a felted mass of microlites (tiny crystals) suspended in an entirely crystalline groundmass. In contrast, hyalopilitic texture has a groundmass composed of glass. Volcanic rocks display this texture, which indicates rapid cooling after extrusion and during flow on the surface. The loss of volatiles, due to a pressure decrease and an increase in the viscosity of the rock magma, hinders the growth of crystals. Lath-shaped microlites of plagioclase may be arranged in parallel lines that indicate flow of the rock while it was partially crystallized. When there is no preferred orientation of the plagioclase laths, the term felty may be used to describe the texture. Andesites and trachytes commonly are pilotaxitic.

pilot fish (*Naucrates ductor*), widely distributed marine fish of the family Carangidae

Pilot fish (*Naucrates ductor*)
Painting by Gilbert Emerson

(order Perciformes) noted for associating with ships and large fishes, especially sharks. The pilot fish, found in the open sea throughout warm and tropical waters, is elongated and has a forked tail, a lengthwise keel on each side of the tail base, and a few small spines in front of the dorsal and anal fins. It grows to a length of about 60 centimetres (2 feet) and is distinctively marked with 5 to 7 vertical dark bands on a bluish body. It is carnivorous and is thought to follow sharks and ships to feed on parasites and leftover scraps of food.
·feeding dependence on larger fish **2**:1049e

pilot whale, also known as BLACKFISH or CAA'ING WHALE (*Globicephala*), slender whale of the dolphin family Delphinidae, found in all oceans of the world except the Arctic and Antarctic. One to three species, all more or less similar, are recognized, depending on the authority. They are *G. melaena*, *G. macrorhyncha*, and *G. scammoni*. The pilot whale is also known as caa'ing whale because of a roaring sound it makes when stranded. It is black, usually with a lighter splash on the throat and chest, and has a round, bulging forehead; a short, beaklike snout; and slender, pointed flippers. Its length is usually about 4 to 6 metres (13 to 20 feet); males are larger than females.

The pilot whale is highly gregarious and lives

Pilot whale (*Globicephala melaena*) performing at Marineland of Florida
Appel Color Photography with Marineland of Florida

in schools, sometimes of hundreds or thousands of individuals. It feeds mainly on squid. In some areas it is hunted for meat and oil and in the Faeroe Islands is captured in schools, the hunters frightening and driving them ashore. It has been kept in oceanaria and has been trained to perform.
·social behaviour patterns **19**:806a

Piloty, Karl von (b. Oct. 1, 1826, Munich—d. July 21, 1886, Munich), the foremost representative of the realistic school of painting in Germany.

Piloty was the son of Ferdinand Piloty (died 1895), the noted lithographer. His picture of "Seni at the Dead Body of Wallenstein" (1855) gained for the young painter the membership of the Munich Academy, where he became professor. He executed a number of mural paintings for the royal palace in Munich, and for Baron von Schach he painted the celebrated "Discovery of America." In 1874 he was appointed keeper of the Munich Academy and was later ennobled by the King of Bavaria. Piloty was a successful teacher, many of his pupils becoming distinguished painters.

pilpul (biblical exegesis): *see* middot.

Pilsen (Czechoslovakia): *see* Plzeň.

Piłsudski, Józef Klemens 14:464 (b. Dec. 5, 1867, Żułów, Russian Poland, now in Lithuanian S.S.R.—d. May 12, 1935, Warsaw), statesman whose efforts were instrumental in the re-establishment of the Polish state in the 20th century.

Abstract of text biography. The second son of a poor Polish nobleman, Piłsudski opposed imperial Russian rule as a youth. He was arrested in 1887 and banished to Siberia (1887–92). Arrested again (1900–01), he escaped and later travelled to Japan to plead for aid in a Polish revolution. Piłsudski returned to Poland and continued to fight for independence, helping guarantee the re-creation of Poland in 1918. He was chief of state from 1918 to 1922 and led the Polish Army in the Russo-Polish War (1919–20). Returning to power in a coup d'etat (1926), he dominated the executive branch of the government as minister of war from 1926 to 1935 and as prime minister from October 1926 to June 1928 and August to December 1930.

REFERENCES in other text articles:
·Austro-German concessions **19**:963b
·Polish Socialist Party split **14**:650a *passim* to 651e
·Vilnius liberation movement **2**:674b

Piltdown man (*Eoanthropus dawsoni*), name given to supposed fossil remains of primitive man, discovered in 1912 but later proved to be fraudulent. The forgery was sufficiently convincing to generate scholarly controversy that lasted about 40 years. Apparently fossilized fragments of cranium and jawbone were found in a gravel formation at Barkham Manor, on Piltdown Common near Lewes, Eng. Together with these were fossil remains of extinct animals, which supported an early Pleistocene dating of the site, and worked implements of bone and flint, the latter attributable to a very early human culture (pre-Abbevillian). In 1926 the gravels were found to be much less ancient than supposed, and in 1953 and 1954, as an outcome of later discoveries of fossil man and intensive re-examination, the remains were shown to be skillfully disguised fragments of a quite modern human cranium and an ape (orangutan) jaw fraudulently introduced into the shallow gravels, as were the implements and animal bones.

Piltdown "man" was distinct from *Pithecanthropus* (Java man), Neanderthal, and modern man in combining a large modern-looking brain case, devoid of marked eyebrow ridges, with a chimpanzee-like jaw, molars worn to a flatness expected in a human, and a canine tooth worn in a way never found in modern apes.

As long as the remains were accorded a high antiquity, Piltdown man seemed a feasible alternative to *Pithecanthropus* (then known only from scanty remains) as an ancestor for modern man. From 1930, more finds of *Pithecanthropus*, the discoveries of the more primitive *Australopithecus*, and further examples of Neanderthal man left Piltdown man completely isolated in the evolutionary sequence.

Analyses in 1953–54 showed that the jaw and cranium contained different amounts of fluorine, nitrogen, uranium, organic carbon, and organic water, these differences all indicating that the jaw was of relatively recent date and the cranium somewhat older; carbon-14 dating in 1959 confirmed these conclusions. Chemical tests revealed that the fragments had been deliberately stained, some with chromium and others with acid iron sulfate solution—neither of which occur in the region—and that although the associated remains were of genuine extinct animals, they were not of British provenance. X-rays demonstrated that the molar teeth (probably of an orangutan) had undergone artificial abrasion to simulate the human mode of flat wear.

The outcome of this exposure was to clarify the human sequence of evolution by removing the greatest anomaly in the fossil record. At the same time, a series of valuable new tests were developed for paleontological study.

For scientific papers dealing with all aspects of the exposure, see *Bulletin of the British Museum* (*Natural History*), vol. 2, no. 3 and 6. For an account of the finds at Piltdown and for a discussion of the authorship of the deception and the tests carried out, see J.S. Weiner, *The Piltdown Forgery* (1955).

P'i-lu-che-na (Buddhism): *see* Vairocana.

pilus, one of the thin hairlike structures that cover some plants.
·bacterial structures **2**:573g; illus.

Pima, North American Indians who call themselves the "River People," as opposed to the Papago (*q.v.*), who call themselves "Desert People," and who traditionally lived along the Gila and Salt rivers in Arizona in what was the core area of the prehistoric Hohokam culture (*q.v.*). The Pima, who speak a Uto-Aztecan language, are usually considered to be the descendants of the Hohokam, although this remains to be proved. Like their presumed ancestors, the Pima were sedentary farmers who lived in one-room houses and utilized the rivers for irrigation. Some hunting and gathering were done to supplement the diet; but in drought years, which occurred on the average of one year in five, the crops of maize and other vegetables would fail, and hunting and gathering became the sole mode of subsistence. During these dry years jackrabbits and mesquite beans were the dietary staples.

The intensive farming of the Pima made possible larger villages than were feasible for their neighbours and relatives, the Papago. With larger communities came a stronger and more complex political organization. In early Spanish times the Pima possessed a strong tribal organization, with a tribal chief elected by the chiefs of the various villages. The tribal chief attained his status through his personal qualities rather than through birth, and this was true of local chiefs also. The village chief, aided by a council of all adult males, had the responsibilities of directing the communal irrigation projects and of protecting the village against alien tribes, notably the Apache. Planting and harvesting of crops were handled as a cooperative venture.

From the time of their earliest recorded contacts with whites, the Pima have been regarded as friendly Indians. At the time of the California Gold Rush (1849–50), the Pima often sold food to white gold seekers and provided them with an escort through Apache territory. During the Apache wars (1861–86) numbers of Pima served as scouts for the U.S. Army. Such close contacts with white culture resulted in disintegration of aboriginal Pima culture.

In the 1970s the Pima numbered about 7,500 and were mostly concentrated on the Gila River and Salt River reservations in Arizona.
·American Indian local races **15**:349b
·habitation and cultural patterns **17**:305g; map
·numbers and habitation area **13**:245e; map 246

Pima cotton, a cotton with fibre of exceptional strength and firmness developed in the southwestern U.S. by selection and breeding of Egyptian cottons.
·group description and location **7**:274d

Piman languages, Uto-Aztecan language group of the Sonoran division, including Papago, Pima, Nevome or Lower Pima, Tepecano, Northern Tepehuán, and Southern Tepehuán, spoken in northern Mexico and in Arizona, U.S., by more than 13,000 speakers.
·Meso-American languages table **11**:958b; map 957

Pimelodidae, family of fishes, order Siluriformes.
·classification and general features **13**:762a

Pimenta dioica, species of plant (order Myrtales).
·economic importance and commercial uses **12**:773g

pimento: *see* allspice.

Pimephales (fish): *see* minnow.

pi meson (physics): *see* meson.

pimiento, any of various mild peppers of the genus *Capsicum*, having distinctive flavour but lacking pungency, so-named from the Spanish word for pepper. These include European paprikas, which provide the paprika of commerce, a powdered, red condiment.

Pimiko: *see* Himiko.

"Pima *Ki*," photograph by Edward Curtis, 1907; from *The North American Indian*

By courtesy of the Newberry Library, Chicago, Ayer Collection

pimpernel, common name for any plant of the genus *Anagallis* (family Primulaceae), which comprises about 30 species of low, annual, biennial, or perennial herbs mostly native to western Europe.

Most species are prostrate in habit. The plant has leaves that are opposite or in whorls and small, solitary flowers that are short-stalked and bell-shaped. The five-lobed corolla (structure formed by the petals) is red, pink, or blue.

The scarlet pimpernel (*A. arvensis*), also called poor-man's weatherglass, is an annual native to Europe, Asia, and North America. It grows 6 to 30 centimetres (2¼–12 inches) tall and has red, pink, or blue flowers.

Pimpinella anisum (herb): *see* anise.

pimple, common name for a small, circumscribed, solid elevation of the skin that may be filled with pus (pustule) or may not (papule).
·disease causes and defense mechanisms **5**:846g

pin, peg or bolt used for fastening or support. In mechanical and civil engineering, machine parts and structural fasteners are called pins; but the term is most commonly used for the small, pointed and headed piece of stiff wire used to secure clothing or papers.

Bronze pins 2 to 8 inches (5 to 20 centimetres) long with gold heads or decorative gold bands have been found in ancient Egyptian tombs. The Greeks and Romans used pins or brooches similar to the safety pin for fastening their clothing. In medieval Europe, skewers of wood, bone, ivory, silver, gold, or brass were used, elaborately fashioned for persons of wealth and simply made of wood for poor people. By the end of the 15th century, the manufacture of pins from drawn, iron wire was well established, particularly in France.

Pinmaking machines were introduced early in the 19th century. In New York John Ireland Howe founded a successful factory with his improved machines, while in Birmingham, Eng., Daniel Foote-Taylen profitably applied the pinmaking patents of Lemuel W. Wright. Subsequently many pinmaking machines were developed, including devices for thrusting finished pins through crimped papers. Modern machines are completely automatic.

Pina, Rui de (*c.* 1440–*c.* 1523), Portuguese historian.
·literature of the Renaissance **10**:1137c

pinacate bug: *see* darkling beetle.

Pinaceae, pine family of conifers, 10 genera of trees (rarely shrubs) native to north temperate regions. Fir (*Abies*), *Keteleeria*, *Cathaya*, Douglas fir (*Pseudotsuga*), hemlock (*Tsuga*), spruce (*Picea*), golden larch (*Pseudolarix*), larch or tamarack (*Larix*), cedar (*Cedrus*), and pine (*Pinus*) contain many species that are sources of timber, paper pulp, oils, and resins. Some are cultivated as ornamentals. Both male and female reproductive structures are borne on the same plant. The needlelike leaves are solitary, in bundles, or on specialized short branches. The pollen-bearing male cones are solitary or clustered and have many spirally arranged scales, each bearing two pollen sacs. The compound, seed-bearing female cones also have many spirally arranged scales. Each scale is free from the bract below it and bears two inverted ovules on its upper side. In members of the genus *Pinus*, the bract disappears as the cones mature. Only one of the many embryos that form survives to maturity.
·conifer fossil record **5**:7g
·conifer taxonomic features **5**:8g

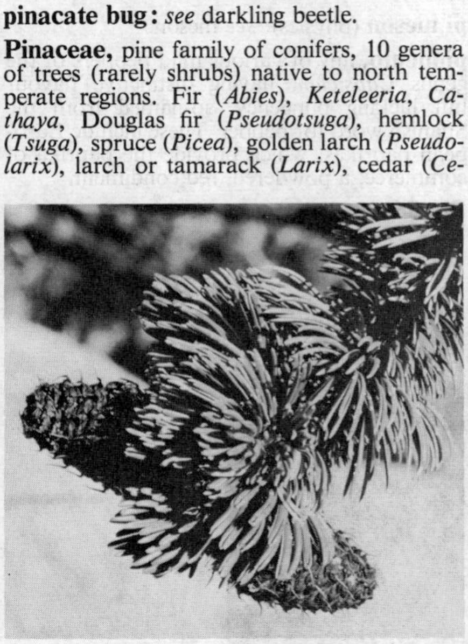
Seed-bearing female cones of bristlecone pine (*Pinus aristata*)
Grant Heilman—EB Inc.

pinacocyte, in zoology, any of various types of large flattened granule-containing cells found in certain sponges (phylum Porifera). Exopinacocytes form a layer on the body surface; endopinacocytes line canals within the sponge; and basipinacocytes are in contact with the surface to which the sponge is attached.
·muscle mechanisms in sponges **12**:641e
·sponge adaptation for canal lining **14**:851h; illus. 852

pinacoid (crystallography): *see* form, crystal.

pinacol, tetramethylethylene glycol, 2,3-dimethyl-2,3-butanediol, $(CH_3)_2C(OH)C(OH)(CH_3)_2$, provided an important example of molecular rearrangement in an elimination reaction when, at Göttingen, the German chemist Rudolph Fittig first observed (about 1860) what has come to be called the pinacolone reaction: pinacol eliminates water when it is heated with a mineral acid and is converted to a ketone pinacolone, $(CH_3)_3CCOCH_3$, which has a different carbon skeleton than pinacol. The structure of pinacolone was established in 1873 by the Russian chemist Aleksandr Butlerov. Some commercial interest was shown in pinacol during World War II in Germany because it is possible by catalytic dehydration to convert it into 2,3-dimethyl-1,3-butadiene (also called di-isopropenyl), from which synthetic rubber can be made. Pinacol is prepared by the bimolecular reduction of acetone by amalgamated magnesium.

pinacolyl methylphosphonofluoridate (SOMAN), highly toxic organic phosphorus compound, one of the so-called nerve gases developed for use as a chemical warfare agent.

Pinakotheke, wing of the Propylaea (5th century BC), entryway to the Acropolis in Athens.
·history and architecture **2**:264e

Pinang, formerly PENANG, state (*negeri*), West Malaysia (Malaya), comprising Pulau (island) Pinang (formerly Penang) off the northwestern coast of the Malay Peninsula and Province Wellesley on the mainland. The total area is 399 sq mi (1,033 sq km).

Pulau Pinang ("betel nut"; 113 sq mi) has a mountainous interior and narrow coastal plains, most extensive in the northeast, where Malaysia's first port, Pinang (Georgetown), uses the sheltered harbourage of Penang Strait (width 2 to 10 mi [3 to 16 km]), which separates it from Province Wellesley.

The island's strategic location in the northern part of the Strait of Malacca led Capt. Francis Light of the East India Company to found a British colony there in 1786. The British occupation was made legal in 1791 by a treaty with the sultan of Kedah; the mainland area was added in 1800. In 1826 Penang combined with Malacca and Singapore to form the Straits Settlements (*q.v.*); it joined the Federation of Malaya in 1948. The island, called Prince of Wales Island until after 1867, flourished commercially, attracting a population of Chinese, Indians, Sumatrans, and Burmese.

While the state is predominantly Chinese in character, a sizable number of Malays are engaged in paddy (rice) farming and fishing, particularly toward Balik Pulau in the southwest. Vegetables and fruit are grown for the urban market, and there are small rubber holdings in the foothills. A 75-mi coast road encircles the island, which has an international airport at Bayan Lepas on its southeastern corner. Penang Hill (2,723 ft [830 m]), a resort, is reached by a mile-long funicular railway. Pulau Jerejak (Jerejak Island), off the southeastern coast, is the site of a leprosarium and tuberculosis settlement.

Province Wellesley is bounded by the states of Kedah (north and east) and Perak (south); it is continuous with the west Kedah Plain on one side and the tin and rubber belt on the other. In contrast with Pulau Pinang, it is predominantly Malay in character. Subsistence rice is grown and rubber is exported. Its shallow streams, often flanked by nipa-palm swamps, impede overland transport. A heavy northern current tends to silt piers and harbours, hindering coastal approaches. Despite these drawbacks, north–south road and rail facilities and a major highway link with the east coast of the peninsula have made Province Wellesley the hub of land and sea transport for Pinang's international trade. The main towns are Perai (formerly Prai), the terminus of a branch of the Malayan railway, and Butterworth (*q.v.*), the main ferry point for Pinang. Bukit Mertajam is an important inland commercial centre. Ancient Sanskrit inscriptions were discovered at Cherok Tekum. Pop. (1978 est.) 903,189.
·map, Malaysia **11**:371

Pinang, also called PENANG OR GEORGETOWN, leading port of Malaysia and capital of Pinang (formerly Penang) state, on a small triangular plain sheltered to the west by a central mountain range, in northeastern Pulau Pinang (Pinang Island). Its sheltered harbour is separated from the west coast mainland by a 3-mi (5-km) channel through which international shipping approaches from the north to avoid the many shallows of the southern route.

Wharf scene in Pinang harbour, Malaysia
Jack Fields—Photo Researchers

The town, founded in 1786 by Capt. Francis Light of the British East India Company, flourished as a port of call for shipping on the India–China run and became the capital and commercial centre of the Straits Settlements (*q.v.*). Fort Cornwallis (a former British naval base), St. George's Church (1817), and the Esplanade recall its colonial past. As a thriving entrepôt (distribution centre), Penang attracted Chinese (mainly Hokkien and Cantonese) and Indian traders. Although Chinese culture predominated, there is a sizable Malay minority; serious race riots erupted in 1967.

Industries in the southern suburbs include tin smelting, rice and coconut-oil milling, and the manufacture of soap and articles of rattan and bamboo. Most of the mainland exports are ferried or brought by lighter from the smaller ports of Butterworth and Perai (formerly Prai). With the development of the east–west highway, the bulk of the peninsula's cargo, previously channelled through the east coast ports, now moves through Pinang. Major exports include tin, rubber, and copra. The gov-

ernor's residence is in Georgetown. The Science University of Malaysia is at Minden Barracks, on the outskirts. The Snake Temple has hundreds of snakes secreted among altars and rafters. Ban Hood Pagoda, the Pagoda of 10,000 Buddhas, is there. Pop. (1970) city, 270,019; metropolitan area, 332,128.
5°24′ N, 100°19′ E
·Malaysian urban characteristics **11**:370b; illus. 369
·map, Malaysia **11**:371

pinang (nut): *see* betel.

Pinar del Río, province, western Cuba, formed chiefly of low mountain ranges, including the Sierra de los Órganos and the Sierra del Rosario. The territory has an area of about 5,200 sq mi (13,500 sq km). The sandy soils of the southern plain produce some of the world's best tobacco, and the pine forests have been exploited heavily. Copper has been mined at Matahambre since 1913. The province also produces sugarcane, rice, pineapples, coffee, and livestock. Railroads and highways traverse much of it, passing through the capital city, Pinar del Río. Pop. (1970) 547,288.
·area and population table **5**:352
·map, Cuba **5**:351

Pinar del Río, capital, Pinar del Río province, western Cuba. Founded in 1775, the city is situated in hilly pinelands at an elevation of about 200 ft (60 m) above sea level, near the base of the Sierra de los Órganos. In 1800 it was officially named Nueva Filipina and was made capital of the western jurisdiction of Cuba. Its importance dates from about 1830, when the tobacco industry of the Vuelta Abajo region was developed. With the completion of the railroad from Havana came the development of Pinar del Río as a commercial centre for the hinterland, which yields tobacco, sugarcane, rice, pineapples, coffee, and livestock. Industrial activity centres on the manufacture of cigars, cigarettes, and furniture. Pinar del Río is also the western terminus of the central highway. Pop. (1970) 75,485.
22°25′ N, 83°42′ W
·map, Cuba **5**:351

pincer (zoology): *see* chela.

pincers, an instrument used for gripping objects.
·gripping tool development **8**:622d

Pinchback, Pinckney Benton Stewart (b. May 10, 1837, Macon, Ga.—d. Dec. 21, 1921, Washington, D.C.), black freedman who fought for the North in the U.S. Civil War and played a leading role in Louisiana politics during Reconstruction (1865–77).

Pinchback
By courtesy of the Library of Congress, Washington, D.C.

Pinchback was one of 10 children born to Maj. William Pinchback, a white Mississippi planter, and a slave named Eliza Stewart, whom the father subsequently freed. He was educated at a Cincinnati, Ohio, school. When the father died in 1848, the family fled to Ohio after being warned that white relatives might attempt to disinherit and re-enslave them.

Destitute at 12 years of age, Pinchback worked his way up to steward on the steamboats plying the Mississippi, Missouri, and Red rivers. The eight years he spent in this hard-drinking, hard-gambling, rough-and-tumble world forged him into a shrewd and aggressive man. When war broke out between the states, he went to Federal-held New Orleans, where he raised a company of black volunteers for the North. When he encountered racial discrimination in the service, he resigned his captain's commission. Later, however, he applied for another commission in a company of Negro cavalry but was refused on the grounds that only noncommissioned status was open to Negroes.

Returning to the South after the war, Pinchback became a delegate to the convention that established a new constitution and civil government for Louisiana. He was elected to the state senate in 1868 and then was named its president *pro tempore;* as such he became lieutenant governor upon the death of the incumbent in 1871. He also had gone into business as a commission merchant and acquired control of the New Orleans *Louisianian*, which advocated freedmen's rights.

In 1872 Pinchback was declared elected as Republican congressman-at-large, but his Democratic opponent contested the election and won the seat. A year later he was elected to the U.S. Senate, but after a three-year battle he was again refused the seat amid charges and countercharges of fraud and election irregularities—although some observers said it was the colour of his skin that counted against him. He was appointed to his last office in 1882 as surveyor of customs in New Orleans.

At the age of 50 he determined to take up a new profession and entered Straight College, New Orleans, to study law; he was subsequently admitted to the bar. Disillusioned with the outcome of Reconstruction and the return to power of the traditional white hierarchy, he moved to Washington, D.C., where he practiced law until his death.

pinch effect, the self-constriction of a cylinder of current-carrying plasma. When an electric current is passed through a gaseous plasma, a magnetic field is set up that tends to force the current-carrying particles together. This force can compress the plasma, so that it is heated as well as confined, but such a self-pinched plasma cylinder is unstable and will quickly develop kinks (kink instability) or break up into a series of lumps resembling a string of sausages (sausage instability). The pinch effect, therefore, must be augmented with other magnetic-field configurations to produce a stable magnetic bottle.
·magnetic field effects on plasmas **14**:508c
·nuclear fusion plasma control **13**:312c; illus.

Pincher Creek, town, southern Alberta, Canada, on Pincher Creek, a tributary of the Oldman River. Settlement dates from 1878, when the North West Mounted Police established a post at the site. The name stems from the finding in 1875 of a pair of pincers (locally pinchers) that had been lost by prospectors in 1861. Lumbering, farming, and production of oil and gas are basic economic activities. Beauvais Lake Provincial Park and Waterton Lakes National Park are nearby. Inc. village, 1898; town, 1906. Pop. (1971) 3,227.
49°29′ N, 113°57′ W

Pincherle, Alberto: *see* Moravia, Alberto.

pinching bug: *see* stag beetle.

Pinchot, Gifford (b. Aug. 11, 1865, Simsbury, Conn.—d. Oct. 4, 1946, New York City), pioneer of U.S. forestry and conservation and public official. He graduated from Yale in 1889 and studied at the École Nationale Forestière in Nancy, Fr., and in Switzerland, Germany, and Austria. Upon his return home in 1892, he began the first systematic forestry work in the United States at Biltmore, the estate of George W. Vanderbilt in North Carolina. In 1896 he was made a member of the National Forest Commission of the National Academy of Sciences, which worked out the plan of U.S. forest reserves, and in 1897 he became confidential forest agent to the Secretary of the Interior. In 1898 he was appointed chief of the Division, later Bureau, of Forestry and then the Forest Service (created 1905) in the Department of Agriculture, which office he held under McKinley, Roosevelt, and Taft until 1910. During his administration the entire forest service system and administrative machinery were built up, and Pinchot's enthusiasm and promotional work did much for the conservation movement in general. He founded the Yale School of Forestry at New Haven, Conn., as well as the Yale Summer School of Forestry at Milford, Pa., and in 1903 became professor of forestry at Yale. With Theodore Roosevelt, Pinchot helped to found the Bull Moose Party in 1912.

Pinchot
By courtesy of Yale University Archives, Yale University Library

Pinchot's autobiography, *Breaking New Ground*, was published posthumously in 1947.
·Theodore Roosevelt's conservation campaign **15**:1143c

Pinckney, Charles (b. Oct. 26, 1757, Charleston, S.C.—d. Oct. 29, 1824), U.S. founding father, political leader, and diplomat whose proposals for a new government—called the Pinckney plan—were largely incorporated into the federal Constitution drawn up in 1787. During the Revolution, Pinckney was captured and held prisoner by the British. Serving in the Continental Congress for three years (1784–87), he opposed abandonment to Spain of the right of navigation on the Mississippi River, supported a more effective revenue system, and played a leading role in calling a national convention to revise and strengthen the Articles of Confederation.

As a South Carolina delegate to the Constitutional Convention at Philadelphia, he served as a member of the procedures committee and participated frequently in debates. He is best remembered, however, for the detailed plan of government that he submitted to the convention. Although the original draft of the Pinckney plan was not preserved, it is known to have contained 31 or 32 provisions that were incorporated into the new Constitution. Pinckney probably had as large a share in determining the style, form, and content of the document as any one person. At home he supported ratification, presided over the convention that remodelled the South Carolina Constitution in 1790, and as governor (1789–92) guided the adjustment between the state and federal governments.

Pinckney began his political career as a Federalist but in 1791 transferred his allegiance to the Jeffersonian Republican Party, the forerunner of the Democratic Party. He served in the state legislature (1792–96, 1810–14), as governor (1796–98, 1806–08), U.S. senator (1798–1801), and representative (1819–21). He supported amendments to the state constitution that gave greater representation to the back country and extended suffrage to all white men. By opposing Federalist policies, especially in 1798, he estranged two politically active cousins, Charles Cotesworth Pinckney and Thomas Pinckney. Reflecting his Southern background, he bitterly assailed the proposed restrictions on slavery contained in the Missouri Compromise of 1820.

His fidelity to his party was rewarded by appointment as U.S. minister to Spain (1801–05), where he negotiated an agreement providing for a joint tribunal to settle spoliation claims (arising from the seizure of a ship's papers when confiscated for suspected smuggling, carrying contraband of war, or being an enemy ship) and the restoration to U.S. shippers of the right of deposit (temporary storage of goods) at the port of New Orleans. He also won Spain's reluctant consent to Napoleon's sale of Louisiana to the U.S., but the incorporation of part of western Florida into a U.S. customs district precluded the desired cession of Florida to the U.S. and the successful settlement of shipping claims.

Pinckney, Charles Cotesworth (b. Feb. 25, 1746, Charleston, S.C.—d. Aug. 16, 1825, Charleston), U.S. soldier, statesman, and diplomat who participated in the XYZ affair, an unsavory diplomatic incident with France in 1798. Pinckney entered public service in 1769 as a member of the South Carolina Assembly. He served in the first South Carolina Provincial Congress (1775) and later in both houses of the South Carolina legislature.

Charles C. Pinckney, detail of an oil painting on wood by John Trumbull, 1791; in the Yale University Art Gallery
By courtesy of the Yale University Art Gallery

During the American Revolution he was an aide to Gen. George Washington at Brandywine and Germantown, Pa. (both 1777), and later commanded a regiment at Savannah, Ga.; he was promoted to brigadier general in 1783. He took part in the Constitutional Convention of 1787, along with his cousin Charles Pinckney.

Pinckney was appointed minister to France (1796) but was refused recognition by the French Directory and left Paris for Amsterdam. He returned to Paris the following year as a member of a commission that included John Marshall and Elbridge Gerry. When one of the group of French negotiators (later referred to in the correspondence as "X,Y, and Z") suggested that the U.S. representatives offer a gift, Pinckney is said to have replied, "No! No! Not a sixpence!" No treaty was negotiated and an undeclared war with France ensued. Upon his return home Pinckney was made a major general.

An unsuccessful Federalist candidate for vice president in 1800 and for president in 1804 and 1808, Pinckney spent his later years in law practice.

Pinckney, Thomas (b. Oct. 23, 1750, Charleston, S.C.—d. Nov. 2, 1828, Charleston), U.S. soldier, politician, and diplomat who negotiated the Treaty of San Lorenzo (Oct. 27, 1795) with Spain. After military service in the Revolutionary War, Pinckney, a younger brother of the diplomat Charles Cotesworth Pinckney, turned to law and politics. He served as governor of South Carolina (1787–89) and as president of the state convention that ratified the U.S. Constitution. As U.S. minister to Great Britain (1792–96) and envoy extraordinary to Spain in 1795, he negotiated the Treaty of San Lorenzo, or Pinckney's Treaty (*q.v.*).

Thomas Pinckney, portrait by John Trumbull, 1791; in the Yale University Art Gallery
By courtesy of the Yale University Art Gallery

Pinckney was the unsuccessful Federalist candidate for vice president in 1796. John Adams, a Federalist, won the presidency, but his running mate, Pinckney, lost, under the electoral system then prevailing, to the Republican candidate, Thomas Jefferson. Pinckney was a member of the U.S. House of Representatives (1797–1801) and a major general in the War of 1812. A frequent contributor to the *Southern Agriculturist*, he served from 1825 until his death as president general of the Society of the Cincinnati, an organization of Continental Army veterans.

Pinckney's Treaty, also known as the TREATY OF SAN LORENZO (Oct. 27, 1795), between Spain and the U.S., fixed the southern boundary of the U.S. at 31° N latitude and established commercial arrangements favourable to the U.S. United States citizens were accorded free navigation of the Mississippi River through Spanish territory. The treaty granted Americans the privilege of tax-free deposit (temporary storage of goods) at New Orleans. Each side agreed to restrain Indians within its borders from attacks on the other, and there were provisions respecting freedom of the seas. The treaty was negotiated by Thomas Pinckney for the U.S. and Manuel de Godoy for Spain.

Pinctada: *see* oyster.

pincushion cactus, about 30 to 60 species (depending on the authority) of the genus *Coryphantha*, family Cactaceae. Pincushion also refers to the straight-spined species of the genus *Mammillaria* (*q.v.*).

Coryphantha species are native to western North America and central Mexico, with one species in Cuba. Globose to cylindroid, with tubercules (protuberances) not connected into ribs, they range in size from *C. minima* of Texas, about 1¼ centimetres (½ inch) in height and diameter, to large Mexican species such as *C. calipensis*, which reach about 60 centimetres (2 feet) in length and 8 centimetres (about 3 inches) in diameter. A groove on the top of the tubercule, connecting the growing points, is characteristic of the genus and distinguishes it from *Mammillaria*.

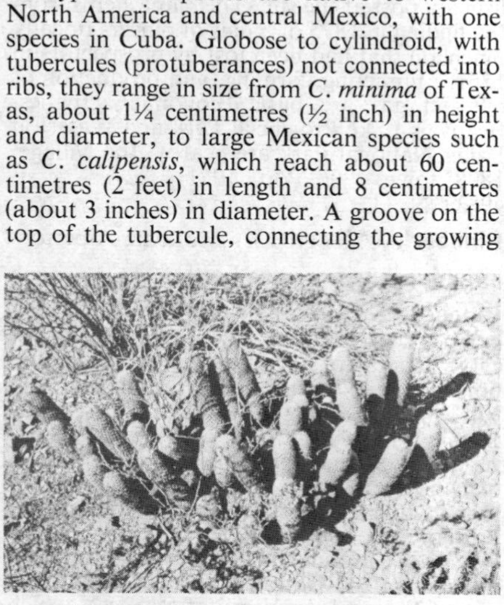

Pincushion cactus (*Coryphantha erecta*)
Edward F. Anderson

C. vivipara (including its varieties) is almost as cold resistant as the prickly pears (*see* Opuntia). It ranges from Alberta and Manitoba, in Canada, to Oklahoma and California, in the U.S.

Coryphantha species have large flowers for the size of the plant. They are in shades of lavender, rose purple, pink, orange, yellow, and white. Fruits of the genus are green, red, or yellowish edible berries.

Neobesseya and *Escobaria* are usually considered subgenera of *Coryphantha*.

pincushion flower: *see* scabious.

piṇḍa (Hinduism): *see* gotra.

Pindar 14:465 (b. 518/522 BC, Cynoscephalae, Boeotia, central Greece—d. after 446, probably *c.* 438 BC), the greatest of the Greek choral lyricists, master of *epinicia* (odes celebrating an athletic victory). His poetry includes choral lyrics of unsurpassed splendour and sustained nobility. The choral lyric itself had little future by his time; tragedy absorbed what was most vital in the tradition, and Pindar had no worthy successors.

Abstract of text biography. Few details are known of his life. An aristocrat, born near Thebes, he studied at neighbouring Athens. His early work, including religious hymns in honour of the gods, has not survived. His masterpieces were the *epinicia*, of which 44 are known, celebrating victories achieved in the Pythian, Olympic, Isthmian, and Nemean games. These were commissioned by various aristocratic families. In 476 he went to Sicily, where he remained for probably two years at Hieron's court and at that of Theron of Acragas.

REFERENCES in other text articles:
·Homeric epic framework **8**:1171e
·literary style and contributions **10**:1091g
·style and life **8**:351h

Pindar, Peter, pen name of JOHN WOLCOT (baptized May 9, 1738, Dodbrooke, Devonshire—d. Jan. 14, 1819, London), writer of a running commentary in satirical verse on society, politics, and personalities, 1778–1817. Although he lacked the depth of the great satirists, he was a master of verse caricature (shown especially in his scurrilous lampoons of George III in *The Lousiad, an Heroi-Comic Poem*, 1785–95; *Ode Upon Ode or a Peep at St. James's or New Year's Day*, 1787; and *The Royal Visit to Exeter*, 1795, a tour de force of Devon dialect humour) and in the virtuosity of his doggerel rhymes. His other targets included James Boswell, author of *The Life of Samuel Johnson LL.D.*, and the painter Benjamin West. With some knowledge of art, he was at his best in attacks on painters: he first became famous with his *Lyric Odes to the Royal Academicians* (1782–85).

After studying medicine at Aberdeen, Wolcot went to Jamaica as physician to the governor in 1767. He was ordained in 1769 but then forsook the church. He returned to England, practicing medicine in Cornwall, in 1772, and settled in London in 1781. Despite blindness, he continued to write to the end of his life, producing more than 70 satirical works and some other poems. He was buried at his own request "close to the author of *Hudibras*," the 17th-century satirist Samuel Butler, in St. Paul's Covent Garden, London.

·Aeschylus's style and theme comparison **1**:148d
·eclipse theme in 9th paean **6**:195h
·Horace's influence by Greeks **8**:1073f

Pindari, name for an irregular horseman and plunderer, first applied to foragers attached to Muslim armies in India who were allowed to plunder in lieu of pay. The word is Marathi and probably derives from two words, meaning "bundle of grass" and "who takes."

The Pindaris followed the Marāthā bands who raided Mughal territory from the late 17th century. With the collapse of the Mughal

Empire in the 18th century, these camp followers organized themselves into groups, each usually attached to one of the leading Marāthā chiefs. But as those chiefs themselves grew weak at the end of the century, the Pindaris became largely a law unto themselves and conducted raids from hideouts in central India. The majority of their leaders were Muslims, but they recruited from all classes.

After the regular forces of the Marāthās had been broken up by the British in the campaigns of 1803–04, the Pindaris made their headquarters in Mālwa, under the tacit protection of the rulers of Gwalior and Indore. They usually assembled in November to set forth over British-held territory in search of plunder. In one such raid on the Masulipatam coast they plundered 339 villages, killing and wounding 682 persons, torturing 3,600, and carrying off much valuable property. In 1808–09 they plundered Gujarāt and, in 1812, Mirzāpur. In 1814 their strength was reckoned at 25,000 to 30,000 horsemen, half well armed.

At last their practices became intolerable, and in 1816 the British organized the campaign known as the Pindari War (1817–18). The Pindaris were surrounded on all sides by an army of 120,000 men and 300 guns, which converged upon them from Bengal, the Deccan, and Gujarāt under the supreme command of the governor general Warren Hastings. The Pindaris' protectors in Gwalior were overawed and signed a treaty (1817) against the Pindaris. Their other allies against the British took up arms but were separately defeated. The Pindaris themselves offered little resistance; most of the leaders surrendered and their followers dispersed.

·plundering and British suppression **9**:392a

Pindaric ode, ceremonious poem by or in the manner of Pindar, a Greek professional lyrist of the 5th century BC. Pindar employed the triadic structure of Stesichorus (7th and 6th centuries BC), consisting of a strophe (two or more lines repeated as a unit) followed by a metrically harmonious antistrophe, concluding with a summary line (called an epode) in a different metre. These three parts corresponded to the movement of the chorus to one side of the stage, then to the other, and their pause midstage to deliver the epode.

Although fragments of Pindar's poems in all of the classical choral forms are extant, it is the collection of four books of epinician odes (*q.v.*) that has influenced poets of the Western world since their publication by Aldus Manutius in 1513. Each of the books is devoted to one of the great series of Greek classical games: the Olympian, Pythian, Isthmian, and Nemean. Celebrating the victory of a winner with a performance of choral chant and dance, these epicinian odes are elaborately complex, rich in metaphor and intensely emotive language. They reveal Pindar's sense of vocation as a poet dedicated to preserving and interpreting great deeds and their divine values. The metaphors, myths, and gnomic sayings that ornament the odes are often difficult to grasp because of the rapid shifts of thought and the sacrifice of syntax to achieving uniform poetic colour.

With the publication of Pierre de Ronsard's four books of French *Odes* (1550), the Pindaric ode became established in the vernacular languages. True Pindaric odes were written in England by Thomas Gray in 1757, "The Progress of Poesy" and "The Bard." Abraham Cowley's *Pindarique Odes* (1656), however, introduced a looser version known as Pindarics. These are irregular rhymed odes in which the length of line and stanza are capriciously varied so as to suggest, but not to reproduce, the style and manner of Pindar. These spurious Pindarics compose some of the greatest odes in the English language, including John Dryden's "Alexander's Feast" (1697), William Wordsworth's "Ode: Intimations of Immortality from Recollections of Early Childhood," Percy Bysshe Shelley's "Ode to the West Wind," Alfred Lord Tennyson's "Ode on the Death of the Duke of Wellington," and John Keats's "Ode on a Grecian Urn."

Pindemonte, Giovanni (b. Dec. 4, 1751, Verona, Italy—d. Jan. 23, 1812, Verona), poet, dramatist, and politician who was popular in his time for several successful tragic dramas but remembered primarily as the older brother of Ippolito Pindemonte, noted pre-Romantic poet and translator of the *Odyssey*.

Of noble birth, Giovanni Pindemonte held high government offices in Venice and Milan but also spent many years in exile. He wrote lyric poetry, and his tragedies were extremely successful in his day and praised by the French writers Madame de Staël and Stendhal. Among the best known were *I baccanali* ("The Bacchanalia"), *Lucio Quinzio Cincinnato*, and *Ginevra di Scozia*, all of which show the influence of the classics, Shakespeare, and his contemporary, the Italian poet, Vittorio Alfieri. Pindemonte's *Poesie e lettere* was edited in 1883.

Pindemonte, Ippolito (b. Nov. 13, 1753, Verona, Italy—d. Nov. 18, 1828, Verona), prose writer, translator, and poet remembered for his gentle, melancholy, pre-Romantic lyrics and particularly for his highly prized translation of the *Odyssey*.

Born into a noble and cultivated family, Ippolito Pindemonte was educated at a college in Modena and during the early part of his life travelled in Europe. He published a volume of Arcadian verse, *Le stanze* (1779), and a sequence of gentle and sad lyrics, called *Poesie campestri* (1788; "Rural Poetry"). Both showed a sensitivity to nature and the influence of the contemporary English poets Thomas Gray and Edward Young. A stay in Paris inspired the poem "La Francia" (1789) and a prose satire on political conditions in Europe, *Abaritte* (1790). Disillusioned by the French Revolution's Reign of Terror, Pindemonte left for London, Berlin, and Vienna. On his return to Italy his *Prose campestri* was published (1794), a companion volume to the earlier poetry.

In 1805 Pindemonte began his translation of the *Odyssey*, an effort that occupied nearly 15 years. It was published as *Odissea* (1822; modern ed., *L'Odissea*, 1928). His close friend Ugo Foscolo dedicated his major work, the patriotic poem "I sepolcri" (1807), to Pindemonte, who also wrote a poem of the same name. Pindemonte also wrote two tragedies and some moralistic letters and sermons. His *Poesie originali* was edited by A. Torri in 1858.

Pindus Mountains, Modern Greek PÍNDHOS ÓROS, principal range and backbone of mainland Greece, trending north-northwest–south-southeast from Albania to central Greece north of the Peloponnese.

In antiquity, the name Pindus applied to ranges south of the Aracynthus (Zygós) Pass west of Thessaly. Occasionally the Pindus is said to extend into Albania and to include the Tymphrestos (Timfristós) massif and even the Gióna massif north of Amphissa in Phocis (Fokís) *nomós* (department). The highest point of the range is 8,651 ft (2,637 m) in the Smólikas massif, near the Albanian border.

Mt. Tymphrestos in the southern Pindus range, Greece

Anthony J. Huxley—EB Inc.

An extension of the calcareous Dinaric range of the Balkans, the core of the Pindus appears to comprise metamorphic and volcanic rocks: schists, serpentines, granite, and jasper. The northern parts, less elevated, have folded Balkan characteristics. Lacking uniformity, the Pindus consists largely of a series of small ranges separated by transverse valleys eroded from limestones that on the eastern slopes often are overlain by geologically younger sandy and marl deposits. The result is often wild, precipitous slopes that afford few passes; the principal one is the Métsovan gap (4,800 ft [1,450 m]), a historic defile that carries the highway from the Epirus to Thessaly.

The southern limits of the Pindus are generally considered to be the Tymphrestos Mountains northeast of Karpenísion. From the Albanian border, the local massifs are the Grámmos and Vóïon, Tímfi, Smolias, Lingos, Lákmos (the latter rising at Peristéri to 7,529 ft [2,295 m]), and the Athamánon, between the Árakhthos and Achelous rivers, rising at Tzoumérka to 8,100 ft (2,469 m).

Forested with oak, fir, beech, and pine, the Pindus creates a barrier for the westerly weather fronts, which puts the Thessalian plain to the east in a rain shadow. The mountains, snowcapped in winter, receive heavy rainfall that feeds such rivers as the Achelous and Mégdhova on the western slopes and the Piniós and Sperkhiós on the eastern.

39°49′ N, 21°14′ E

·formation and physiographic features **8**:312e
·map, Greece **8**:314

pine, common name for over 100 species of ornamental and timber evergreen conifers of the genus *Pinus* (family Pinaceae), distributed throughout the world, but native primarily to north temperate regions. The greatest number of species is found in eastern and southeastern Asia and in the Mexican and Central American highlands, both centres of evolution for pines.

Red pine (*Pinus resinosa*)

Alvin E. Staffan from National Audubon Society

Young trees are usually conical, with whorls of horizontal branches; older trees may have round, flat, or spreading crowns. Most species have thick, rough, furrowed bark. Pine trees can tolerate drought but require full sunlight and clean air for good growth and reproduction.

Pines have two types of branches, long shoots and short shoots, and three types of leaves, primordial, scale, and adult. Seedling plants bear the lance-shaped, spirally arranged primordial leaves; the triangular-scale

White pine (*Pinus strobus*)
Grant Heilman—EB Inc.

leaves, also lance-shaped, are borne on the long shoots of older trees. Both long and short shoots develop in the axils of the deciduous scale leaves. The needlelike, photosynthetic adult leaves, with two to many resin canals, are borne in fascicles (bundles) of two to five (rarely, up to eight or solitary) at the tip of each short shoot; they remain on the tree 2 to 17 years.

Male cones are covered with many fertile scales, each of which bears two pollen sacs. Female cones, borne on the same tree, have several spirally arranged bracts (modified leaves), each of which is located below a scale with two ovules (potential seeds). In spring or early summer the pollen sacs release pollen through longitudinal slits; each grain has two air bladders for wind dispersal. The scales on the female cones open to receive the pollen and then close; actual fertilization takes place late the following spring. After fertilization, the woody female cone develops over a two-year to three-year period. In some species, the cones open at maturity and the seeds are released; in others the cones remain closed for several years till they are opened by rotting, by food-seeking animals, or by fire. In some pines the scale bearing the nutlike seed may be expanded to form a wing for airborne dispersal.

Pines are softwoods, but commercially they may be designated as soft pines or hard pines. Soft pines, such as white, sugar, and piñon pines, have relatively soft timber, needles in bundles of five (rarely, one to four), stalked cones with scales lacking prickles, and little resin. Their wood is close-grained, with thin, nearly white sapwood; the sheaths of the leaf clusters are deciduous, and the leaves contain a single fibrovascular bundle. Hard pines, such as Scots, Corsican, and loblolly pines, have relatively hard timber, needles in bundles of two or three (rarely five to eight), cone scales with prickles, and large amounts of resin. Their wood is coarse-grained and usually dark coloured, with pale, often thick sapwood; the sheaths of the leaf clusters are persistent, and the leaves have two fibrovascular bundles.

The chief value of pines is in the construction and paper products industries, but they are also sources of turpentine, rosin, oils, and wood tars (naval stores); longleaf, slash, cluster, and Chir pines are cut for these materials. Charcoal, lampblack, and fuel gases are distillation by-products. Pine-leaf oil, used medicinally, is a distillation product of the leaves. Edible pine seeds are sold commercially as pine nuts, or pignons, produced by stone, Armand, Siberian, piñon, Torrey, Coulter, and digger pines. Many species of pines are cultivated as ornamentals including black, white, Himalayan, and stone pines; others such as Scots, Corsican, cluster, and knobcone pines are planted in reforestation projects or for windbreaks.

Pines are susceptible to several fungal diseases, among them white-pine blister rust, and are attacked by many insects, such as sawflies, weevils, bark beetles, and tip moths. Pine forests often suffer severe fire damage, being very combustible because of their high resin content.

Many botanists consider the genus *Pinus* to contain two subgenera, separated primarily by the number of fibrovascular bundles in the needles: *Haploxylon*, or soft, pines have one fibrovascular bundle; *Diploxylon*, or hard, pines have two.

Many pines have both lumber trade names and several common names. Numerous trees commonly called pines are not true pines but belong to other genera in the family Pinaceae or to other families of conifers.

·age and tissues **10**:915a; table 914
·bristlecone and screw pine characteristics, illus., **18**: Tree, Plates I and II
·climatic influence on vegetation **4**:728e
·conifer global distribution **5**:1f
·economic importance **8**:518d; illus. 520
·embryo formation and early nutrition **5**:662f; illus. 663
·forestry and importance of conifers **7**:528h
·fossil plants and eras, illus. 14 **7**:575
·geographical distribution in forests **7**:539h
·mountain vegetation, illus. 2 **4**:1033
·pignolia culinary uses and composition **7**:758d; tables 755
·pollen dispersal data **14**:737e
·P. ponderosa needles and cones, illus. 1 **5**:2
·reproductive system comparisons **15**:721e
·rubber colouring and pine tar **15**:1180h
·tall oil production and uses **13**:528a
·taxonomic features of conifers **5**:8g

Pine, Robert Edge (1730–88), British painter.

·Garrick oil painting illus. **7**:911

pineal gland, also called PINEAL BODY or EPIPHYSIS CEREBRI, an endocrine gland of uncertain function found in vertebrate animals; it develops from the roof of the diencephalon, a section of the brain. In some lower vertebrates it has a well-developed eyelike structure; in others, though not organized as an eye, it functions as a light receptor. The apparent endocrine function of the gland is to elaborate the hormone melatonin, which causes the concentration of melanin (any of various black or brown pigments) in pigment cells (melanophores).

·anatomy, size changes, and hormonal activity **6**:815h; illus. 800
·autonomic nerve supply **12**:1030b
·contents and autonomic influences **12**:1037h
·embryonic orgin and vertebrate types **6**:841d
·evolution and secretory function **8**:1085c
·human anatomy, illus. 5 and 14 **12**:1001
·innervation and response to light **12**:453e
·light's physiological effects **15**:391a
·pigment production control **16**:848a
·structure, function, and diseases **6**:838e
·structure and attributed functions **12**:983g

pineal sand, also called ACERVULUS CEREBRI or BRAIN SAND, minute accumulations of calcareous material in the brain.

·age relationship and composition **6**:816a

pineapple (*Ananas comosus*), a fruit-bearing plant of the family Bromeliaceae, native to tropical and subtropical America but introduced elsewhere.

The pineapple plant resembles the agave or some yuccas in general appearance. It has from 30 to 40 stiff, succulent leaves closely spaced in a rosette on a thick, fleshy stem. With commercial varieties, a determinate inflorescence forms about 15 to 20 months after planting on a flower stalk 100–150 millimetres (4–6 inches) in length. The originally separate lavender flowers, together with their bracts, each attached to a central axis core, become fleshy and fuse to form the pineapple fruit, which ripens five to six months after flowering begins. Fruits of commercial varieties range from one to two kilograms (two to four pounds) in weight. Earliest written references to pineapple are by Columbus, Gonzalo Fernández de Oviedo y Valdés, and Sir Walter Raleigh, who found pineapple growing in the West Indies, where it was used for food and wine making.

The Portuguese were apparently responsible for early dissemination of the pineapple. They introduced it to Saint Helena shortly after they discovered that island in 1502. Soon after, they carried it to Africa and by about 1550 to India. Before the end of the 16th century, cultivation of the plant had spread over most of the tropical areas of the world, including some of the islands of the South Pacific.

Pineapple (*Ananas comosus*)
By courtesy of Dole Company

When pineapple is cultivated on plantations, an asphalt-impregnated mulch paper is first laid on well-tilled soil in rows, with the edges covered to anchor the strips of paper. The pineapple propagating pieces are inserted through the paper into the soil, so spaced as to give a population of 15,000–20,000 plants per acre. In many areas, the soil is fumigated to kill parasitic nematodes on the roots of the pineapple plants.

Total world production of pineapples for all purposes ordinarily averages about 3,900,000 tons annually, of which an estimated 28 percent is produced in the Hawaiian Islands. Other areas of substantial production include Brazil, Mexico, the Philippines, Cuba, and Taiwan. Hawaii also produces approximately 60 percent of the world's total supply of canned pineapple products, practically all sold in the U.S. Other areas that market substantial quantities of canned pineapple products in the U.S. are the Philippines, Puerto Rico, and Taiwan. Pineapple canned in Australia, Malaysia, and South Africa is exported principally to Great Britain. Except in those countries where it is grown, trade in fresh pineapple is limited.

·development of agriculture **1**:330c
·domesticated plant origin **5**:938e
·fruit farming economics **7**:752d; tables 754
·growth habit **3**:323h; illus. 324
·Hawaiian production **8**:676e

Pineau, Nicolas (b. Oct. 8, 1684, Paris—d. April 24, 1754), French wood-carver and in-

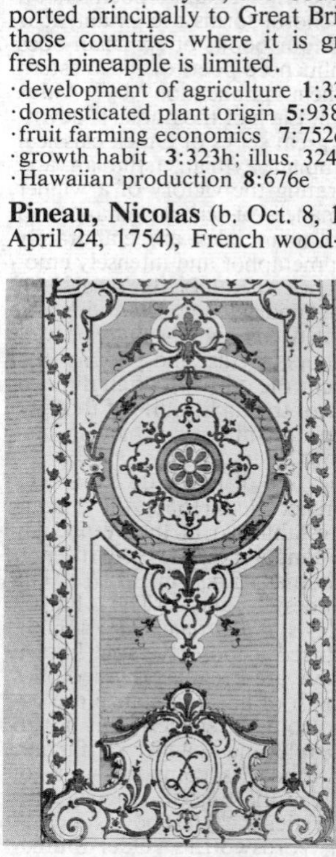

Etching of a design for a counterpane by Pineau, *c.* 1740
By courtesy of the Victoria and Albert Museum, London

terior designer, a leader in the development of interior decorating in the light, asymmetric, lavishly decorated Rococo style.

After study with the architects François Mansart and Germain Boffrand, Pineau began his career as a carver of woodwork. His father, Jean-Baptiste Pineau, was a sculptor in wood, and his son, Dominique (1718–86), also became a wood sculptor.

One of a group of French artisans visiting the newly established city of St. Petersburg (now Leningrad) in 1716 at the invitation of Peter the Great, Pineau remained in Russia until about 1728, carving the Tsar's cabinet in the Peterhof palace and also serving as an architect and interior designer. Returning to Paris, he became an important designer, launching the vogue for Rococo rooms in private dwellings.

Pineau's works are characterized by shallow recesses with rounded corners and ornamentation employing shell motifs, leafy scrolls, and classical busts in medallions. Later interior designers and architects were influenced by his engravings.

Pine Bluff, city, seat (1832) of Jefferson County, central Arkansas, U.S., on high bluffs overlooking the Arkansas River. Settled in 1819 as Mount Marie, it was renamed for its forest of giant pines in 1832. It was the scene of a Civil War engagement (Oct. 25, 1863) when a Confederate force under Gen. John S. Marmaduke was repulsed by a Federal brigade under Gen. Powell Clayton. The city is an industrial, rail, and market centre and a river port with slack-water harbour facilities. Cotton, paper, lumber, and archery supplies are basic to its economy. It is the seat of Arkansas Agricultural, Mechanical and Normal College (1873) and a vocational technical school. Pine Bluff Arsenal (15,000 ac [6,100 ha]) includes chemical and biological warfare laboratories. Inc. town, 1839; city, 1846. Pop. (1980) 56,576.
34°13′ N, 92°01′ W
·map, United States **18**:908

Pine Creek, town, in northwestern central Northern Territory, Australia. Named after a stream (part of the Daly River system), it was founded during an 1871–74 gold rush but subsequently declined almost to a ghost town. It revived, however, with iron-ore mining developments to the east at Frances Creek, to which it is connected by a spur of the North Australia Railway. The mine has been exporting ore to Japan since 1967. Pine Creek, which has an airfield and is on the Stuart Highway to Darwin (152 mi [245 km] northwest), also serves beef-cattle stations. Pop. (1971 prelim.) 215.
13°49′ S, 131°49′ E
·map, Australia **2**:400

Pine Falls, village, southeastern Manitoba, Canada, on the Winnipeg River. It originated around a paper mill built in 1925, and the arrival of a railroad branch line from Winnipeg (60 mi [100 km] southwest) in 1926 spurred its development. The site, within Fort Alexander Indian Reserve, was leased from the Department of Indian Affairs, and the Manitoba Pulp and Paper Company, which planned the village, is the administrator and chief employer of the community. Pine Falls is now a service centre for a lumbering and trapping region. Immediately to the east is Manitoba Hydro's Pine Falls power plant, which supplies electricity to metropolitan Winnipeg. Latest census 1,233.
50°35′ N, 96°15′ W

Pinega River, Soviet Union, flows 484 mi (779 km) into the northern Dvina.
64°08′ N, 41°54′ E
·Northern Dvina river system **5**:1096d

Pinel, Philippe (b. April 20, 1745, Saint-André, Tarn, Fr.—d. Oct. 25, 1826, Paris), physician and a founder of psychiatry who pioneered in the humane treatment of the mentally ill. Arriving in Paris (1778), he supported himself for a number of years by translating scientific and medical works and by teaching mathematics. During that period he also began visiting privately confined mental patients and writing articles on his observations. In 1792 he became the chief physician at the Paris asylum for men, Bicêtre, and made his first bold reform by unchaining patients, many of whom had been restrained for 30 to 40 years. He performed the same mercy for the female inmates of Salpêtrière when he became the director there in 1794.

Pinel, engraving by Pierre-Roch Vigneron (1789–1872)
Giraudon

Shunning the long-popular equation of mental illness with demoniacal possession, Pinel regarded mental illness as the result of excessive exposure to social and psychological stresses and, in some measure, of heredity and physiological damage. He distinguished various psychoses and described, among other phenomena, hallucination, withdrawal, and a variety of other symptoms. In its time, his *Nosographie philosophique* (1798; "Philosophical Classification of Diseases") contained probably the most simple and accurate description of mental illnesses.

Pinel did away with treatments such as bleeding, purging, and blistering and favoured a therapy that included close and friendly contact with the patient, discussion of personal difficulties, and a program of purposeful activities. His *Traité médico-philosophique sur l'aliénation mentale ou la manie* (1801; "Medico-Philosophical Treatise on Mental Alienation or Mania") details his psychologically orientated approach and is one of the classics of psychiatry. Largely through his efforts, France became a leading nation in the more enlightened treatment of the mentally ill.

Pinellas Park, city, Pinellas County, west Florida, U.S., near Old Tampa Bay, just northwest of St. Petersburg. A settlement called Pinellas was established on the site around 1864, deriving its name from what was thought to be a Spanish word for "pine trees." In 1910, Pinellas Farms and the Florida Association divided tracts for agricultural and real-estate development. A post office was opened in 1911, and "Park" was added to Pinellas when it became a centre for citrus, flowers, and vegetables. It remained a small agricultural community until after World War II, when it developed primarily as a residential community, with retail businesses, tourism, and light manufacturing adding to the city. Inc. town, 1915; city, 1959. Pop. (1970) 22,287; (1980) 32,811.
27°51′ N, 82°43′ W

Pinelli cable, an oil-filled, paper-insulated cable for transmitting electric current.
·design and operation **6**:629c

Pine Mountain, ridge on the Cumberland Plateau (section of the Appalachian Mountains, U.S.), extends for 125 mi (200 km) across southeast Kentucky, along the Virginia border, and into northern Tennessee. With average heights of 2,100 to 2,800 ft (640 to 850 m), the ridge rises to Big Black Mountain (4,145 ft), the highest point in Kentucky. A scenic highway crosses a section of the wooded ridge, which is partly within a division of the Jefferson National Forest.
36°55′ N, 83°20′ W

pine mouse: *see* vole.

pinene, alpha-, a colourless liquid occurring as a major component of the essential oil of pine trees and used as a chemical raw material. It is an organic compound belonging to the terpene series (organic compounds containing two C_5H_8 units) and has a molecular formula $C_{10}H_{16}$.

The principal source of α-pinene is turpentine obtained in the sulfate process for making paper. It is isolated by distillation and treated with hypochlorites or adsorbents to lower the sulfur content and to improve the odour. The commercial product is 90–95 percent pure and contains a small amount of antioxidant.

Large amounts of α-pinene are converted to synthetic pine oil or to camphene, which is chlorinated to toxaphene, an insecticide, or treated with acetic acid to form isobornyl acetate, a perfume with a pine-needle aroma and an intermediate in synthetic camphor manufacture.

Pure α-pinene melts at −50° C (−58° F) and boils at 156° C (313° F); its density is 0.8595 grams per millilitre (20° C, or 68° F). It is not soluble in water, but is soluble in common organic solvents.

pine oil, essential oil consisting of a colourless to light-amber liquid of characteristic odour obtained from pine trees or a synthetic oil having a similar aroma and other properties. Pine oil is used as a solvent for gums, resins, and other substances. It has germicidal properties and is used medically as a main constituent of general disinfectants. It is also used in deodorants, insecticides, detergents, liquid soaps, wetting and emulsifying agents, wax preparations, antifoaming agents, in textile scouring, and in the flotation process for refining lead and zinc ores.

Pitch-soaked wood of the pine tree, principally *Pinus palustris* but also certain other species of Pinaceae, is subjected to steam distillation, solvent extraction followed by steam distillation, or destructive distillation to obtain the pine oil, which boils at 200°–220° C.

A variety of similar pine oils are obtained by distillation of cones and needles of various species of pines or by the extraction from the stumps using solvents and steam. Synthetic pine oil is produced by hydration of terpene hydrocarbons forming terpene alcohols.

Chemically, pine oils consist principally of cyclic terpene alcohols and are used in the manufacture of terpin chemicals. Pine oil is insoluble in water but dissolves in alcohol and other organic solvents.
·antiseptic properties and uses, table 2 **1**:997

Pinero, Sir Arthur Wing (b. May 24, 1855, London—d. Nov. 23, 1934, London), a leading playwright of the late Victorian and Edwardian eras in England who made an important contribution toward the creation of a self-respecting theatre by helping to found a "social" drama that drew a fashionable audience. His later work, in a serious vein, gained something from the spirit of Realism that swept the European theatre toward the end of the 19th century, when plays began again to deal with genuine problems of society and the individual. It is his farces, however—literate, superbly constructed, with a precise, clockwork inevitability of plot and a brilliant use of coincidence—that have proved to be of permanent theatrical value. They remain excellent entertainment and are still frequently played, whereas his serious work seems too embedded in the thought and style of his day to warrant regular revival. Pinero abandoned legal studies to become an actor; and, though still a young man, he played older character parts for the leading theatre company headed by Henry Irving. His first play, *£200 a Year*, was produced in 1877. His best farces, such as

Pinero, detail of an oil painting by J. Mordecai, 1891; in the National Portrait Gallery, London

By courtesy of the National Portrait Gallery, London

The Magistrate (1885), *The Schoolmistress* (1886), and *Dandy Dick* (1887), were written for the Royal Court Theatre in London. Pinero was at the same time studying serious drama by adapting plays from the French (including *The Iron Master*, 1884; and *Mayfair*, 1885) and also mining a profitable vein of sentiment of his own, as in *The Squire* (1881) and *Sweet Lavender* (1888). The two elements fused in *The Profligate* (1889) and—most sensationally—in *The Second Mrs. Tanqueray* (1893), which established Pinero as an important playwright. This was the first of several plays depicting women battling with their situation in society, and they included *The Notorious Mrs. Ebbsmith* (1895), *Iris* (1901), and *Letty* (1903). These plays not only created good parts for actresses but also demanded sympathy for women, who were judged by a stricter moral code than were men in Victorian society. In a less serious vein, *Trelawney of the "Wells"* (written for the Royal Court Theatre and produced in 1898) portrayed theatrical company life in the old style of the 1860s—already then a vanishing tradition—and *The Gay Lord Quex* (1899) was about a theatrical rake of no placeable period but great panache. Of Pinero's numerous later plays, *The Enchanted Cottage* (1922), a curious and fantastic piece somewhat in the vein of his contemporary Sir James M. Barrie, remains the most popular. Many of the others are considered laboured and without the breath of theatrical life. There is a good biography of Pinero by W.D. Dunkel (1941).

Pinerolo, town, Torino province, Piemonte (Piedmont) region, northwestern Italy, at the entrance to the Valle del Chisone, at the foot of the Alps, southwest of Torino (Turin). First mentioned in 996 as a possession of Torino, it belonged to the nearby Abbey of Sta. Maria in 1078. Under the House of Savoy from 1246, it was the capital (1295–1418) of the princes of Acaia, a subsidiary line. Occupied by the French in 1536–74, 1631–96, and 1801–14, its fortress was used during the 17th century as a state prison for such political prisoners as the Duc de Lauzun, enemy of Louis XIV's mistress Mme de Montespan; Nicolas Fouquet, Louis's embezzling finance minister; and the mysterious "Man in the Iron Mask," whose story is best known from one of the 19th-century three musketeers novels of Alexandre Dumas. It became a bishop's see in 1748.

Notable buildings include the 15th–16th-century S. Donato's Cathedral (founded 1044), the Church of S. Maurizio (1334–1490; restored), the palace of the princes of Acaia (1318; later modernized), and remains of the old fortifications.

Pinerolo is a rail junction with textile, metal, chemical, printing, and food industries. Pop. (1971 prelim.) mun., 39,411.
44°53′ N, 7°21′ E
·map, Italy **9**:1088

Pines, Isle of (Cuba): *see* Isle of Pines.

Pines, Isle of (New Caledonia): *see* Pins, Île des.

pine snake: *see* bull snake.

Pinetti, also called CHEVALIER PINETTI (b. GIUSEPPE PINETTI DE WILDALLE, 1750, Orbitello, Italy—d. 1800, Russia), conjurer who founded the classical school of magic, characterized by elaborate tricks and the use of mechanical devices (suitable, as a rule, for stage performance only). While touring Europe in the 1780s, he introduced the second-sight trick (the apparent transference of thought from the magician to his assistant), automata, and escape tricks, including chain releases and escape from the "thumb tie." He used elaborate stage apparatus and draped tables, with trapdoors operated by offstage assistants.

Pineville, city, seat of Bell County, southeastern Kentucky, U.S., on the Cumberland River, in the Cumberland Mountains. It was settled in 1799 after the Kentucky legislature appropriated funds (1797) for erecting a tollgate on the Wilderness Road from Cumberland Gap at the Narrows, a gap in nearby Pine Mountain. The city is a resort centre and shipping point for lumber and coal. A natural amphitheatre in Pine Mountain State Park, just south, is the site of the annual (May) Mountain Laurel Festival, one of the state's most important events. Pop. (1980) 2,599.
36°46′ N, 83°42′ W

Pineville, city, Rapides Parish, central Louisiana, U.S., on the Red River, opposite Alexandria, its sister city. Settled in the early 18th century, it was incorporated as a town in 1878 and as a city in 1947. An industrial centre, its manufactures include machinery and soap, paper, and wood products. It is the seat of Louisiana College (Baptist, 1906). A national cemetery and veterans' hospital are also located there. Camp Beauregard, at which army troops were trained during World War II, is nearby. Pop. (1980) 12,034.
31°19′ N, 92°26′ W

pine weevil, common name for important wood-boring beetles of the family Curculionidae (order Coleoptera). The white pine weevil (*Pissodes strobi*) of North America kills the central growth shoot of white pine trees, forcing one of the side shoots to take over the upward growth of the tree. This results in bends in the tree trunk and reduces its value as lumber.

Piney Woods, physiographic region in southern Mississippi.
·physical and social character **12**:276h

pin fastener, in machine construction, a steel pin, usually cylindrical, that can keep machine parts in proper alignment or fasten them together. The illustration shows several types of pin fasteners in common use.

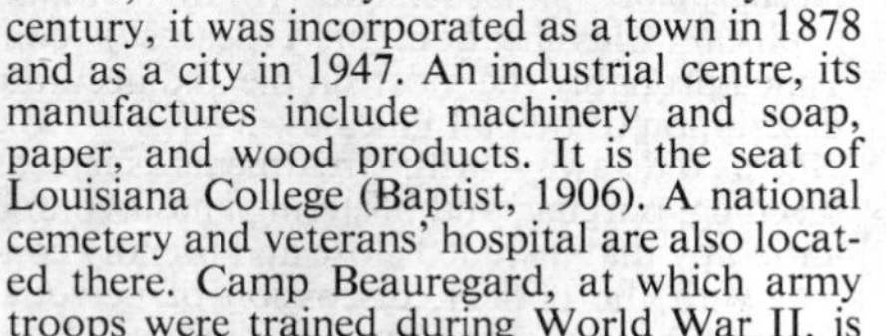

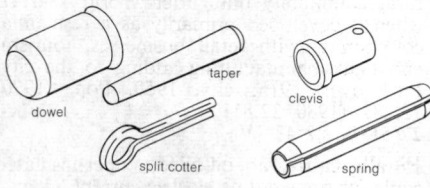

Several types of pin fasteners

Hardened and precisely shaped dowel pins are used to keep machine components in accurate alignment; they are also used as location guides for adjacent machine parts and to keep the two sections of a punch and die in alignment.

The taper pin provides a cheap, convenient method of fixing the hub of a gear or a pulley to a shaft. The pin is driven into a tapered hole that extends radially through the hub and shaft.

The split cotter pin is used to prevent nuts from turning on bolts and to keep loosely fitting pins in place. The head of the nut has radial slots that are aligned with one of the radial holes in the bolt. The pin is a loose fit in the hole and is kept in place by spreading the ends. The clevis pin is a fastening device with a flange at one end and is kept in place by a cotter pin inserted through a hole in the other end.

The spring pin is a split tube with a slightly larger diameter than the hole into which it is placed. The pin is compressed when driven into the hole and exerts a spring pressure against the wall of the hole that creates a frictional locking grip. These pins can be removed and re-used without appreciable loss of effectiveness; they are widely used for attaching lightly loaded pulleys and gears to shafts.

Groove pins are solid pins with longitudinal grooves produced by upsetting the metal so that it interferes with the hole when the pin is driven in. The pin can thus be used to fasten two components together.

P'ing, king of the Chou dynasty, fl. 771 BC.
·Lo-yang foundation and growth **11**:165a

Ping, Mae Nam, in northwestern Thailand, is one of the headstreams of the Mae Nam (river) Chao Phraya. It rises on the Thailand–Burma border in the Daen Lao Range and flows south-southeast and is largely navigable. The Mae Nam Wang is its main tributary. At Pak Nam Pho it joins the combined Nan-Yom to form the Chao Phraya after a course of 367 mi (590 km). Important towns on its banks are Chiang Mai, Tak, Phisai, and Kamphaeng Phet.
15°40′ N, 100°09′ E

Piṅgali Sūranna, 16th-century Indian poet.
·verse novel style **17**:141f

P'ing-ch'iao (China): *see* Hsin-yang.

pin gear, also called LANTERN PINION, a gear pinion having cylindrical bars instead of teeth inserted at their ends in two parallel disks.
·design and construction **11**:236g

Pingelap, atoll, Caroline Islands, Trust Territory of the Pacific. Pop. (1970) 849.
6°15′ N, 160°40′ E
·Micronesian Ponapean cultural link **12**:122d

Pingeyrar, medieval Icelandic monastery.
·literary contribution in Middle Ages **10**:1118g

Ping Fa (Sun Tzu): *see* Art of War, The.

P'ing-hsiang, Pin-yin romanization PINGXIANG, city lying in western Kiangsi Province (*sheng*), China. It is a county- (*hsien-*) level municipality in the I-ch'un Area (*ti-ch'ü*). Situated on the borders of Hunan Province in the midst of the Wu-kung Shan (mountain range) on the upper waters of the Lu Shui (river), on what has always been a major route between Ch'ang-sha (Hunan Province) and Nan-ch'ang (Kiangsi), the county was established in AD 267 and has existed ever since, usually being dependent on Yüan-chou (modern I-ch'un). For a brief period (1295–1367) it was an independent prefecture.

Its modern importance began with the discovery of rich coal deposits there at the end of the 19th century by German experts employed by the Han-yang Iron Works in Hupeh Province, which was urgently seeking a source of coking coal. A railway was built during 1903–05 to transport the coal, and coke ovens were installed in the city. By 1909 production had reached about 500,000 tons and during World War I reached almost 1,000,000 tons annually. The depressed market for iron in the postwar years, however, led to the decline and eventual closing of the ironworks, so

that demand for P'ing-hsiang coal and coke fell dramatically, the mines closing down for a time in 1925–26. In the 1930s production was only about 20 percent of what it had been during the peak period. After much neglect and destruction during World War II, the mines were modernized in the 1950s and by the 1970s had again become a major mining centre with an annual output of more than 5,000,000 tons. In the late 1950s large iron and steel industry, producing pig iron and ingot steel, was established. P'ing-hsiang also has a ceramic industry. Latest pop. est. 27,000.
27°37′ N, 113°51′ E

P'ing-hsiang, Pin-yin romanization PING-XIANG, city in the southwest of the Kwangsi Chuang Autonomous Region (*tzu-chih-ch'ü*), China. The city is an autonomous subprovincial-level municipality (*shih*) on the border of North Vietnam in the southwest of the Nanning Area (*ti-ch'ü*). Until 1951 it was an insignificant town. Founded as a military outpost under the name P'ing-hsiang during the Sung dynasties (960–1279), under the Ming dynasty (1368–1644) it became a county (*hsien*), later a prefecture (*fu*); it was, however, little more than an administrative outpost among non-Chinese tribesmen. The Ch'ing dynasty (1644–1911) made it a subprefecture, but in 1949 it still had no more than 300 households.

P'ing-hsiang's modern growth stemmed from the railway from Nan-ning, which provides a through route from central China to North Vietnam, crossing the border a few miles to the south at Yu-i-kuan. Construction of this line was begun in 1938 by the French, who completed it as far as Ning-ming; but, following the Japanese occupation of Nan-ning, work was abandoned in 1943–44, and much of the track was dismantled. The line was finally completed in 1951 and linked with the North Vietnamese rail system in 1955. After this, P'ing-hsiang rapidly grew into a commercial centre for international trade with North Vietnam; it also developed some small-scale industries. A considerable part of Sino-Vietnamese trade passes through P'ing-hsiang because the rail link is superior to the older line that runs through Yunnan Province and also provides a direct route to Wu-han as well as connections to Kweichow and Szechwan provinces and to the Canton area. Latest pop. est. 7,000.
22°09′ N, 106°43′ E
·coal and coke production **10**:461a
·railway network statistics **4**:285h
·urban border role and trade **10**:551g

Ping Hsin (Pure in Heart), literary name of HSIEH WAN-YING (b. Oct. 5, 1900, Min-hou, Fukien Province, China), writer of sentimental stories and poems that enjoyed great popularity in the early 1920s. Ping Hsin studied the Chinese Classics and began writing traditional Chinese stories as a child, but her conversion to Christianity and her attendance at an American school in Peking soon bestowed a didactic and Western influence on her literary efforts. The short stories and poems that Ping Hsin published during her college years at Yen-ch'ing University—lyrical pieces about childhood and nature—won her instant fame and a grant to study at Wellesley College in the United States, where she received an M.A. degree in 1926. She wrote little after this time, but became very active in cultural affairs under the Communist government.

P'ing-Liang, Pin-yin romanization PING-LIANG, town, eastern Kansu Province (*sheng*), north central China, near the Ningsia Hui and Shensi borders. Economic activities include wool and tobacco processing and agriculture. Pop. (1970 est) 50,000–100,000.
35°27′ N, 107°10′ E
·map, China **4**:262
·seasonal precipitation pattern **10**:388a

pingo, dome-shaped hill formed in a permafrost area when the hydrostatic pressure of freezing groundwater causes the upheaval of a layer of frozen ground. Pingos may be up to 90 metres (300 feet) high and over 800 metres (½ mile) across and are usually circular or oval. The core, which may be only slightly smaller than the pingo itself, consists of a lens of clear, injected ice. Modern pingos occur in the continental tundras and are generally restricted to latitudes of 65° to 75° N. Rupture of the overlying material at the top of the pingo exposes the ice to melting and may create a smaller crater and lake. Two types are recognized, the open-system pingo and the closed-system pingo.

Ibyuk pingo near Tuktoyaktuk in the Mackenzie River Delta, N.W.T.; it is 140 feet high

J. Ross Mackay

The open-system pingo forms in regions of discontinuous or thin permafrost. Artesian pressure builds up under the permafrost layer, and as the water rises, pushing up the overlying material, it freezes in a lens shape. This type of pingo usually occurs in the alluvial material of a mountainous or hilly area.

The closed-system pingo forms in a shallow lake when advancing permafrost generates hydrostatic pressure under the lake basin. The confined mass of saturated soil freezes, pushing the overlying material upward as it expands.

Scars of former pingos have been found in areas near the edges of former Pleistocene ice sheets. Because pingos form under specific conditions, they serve as good indicators of climatic change.
·formation and characteristics **8**:176b
·permafrost composition and ground ice **14**:92c

Ping-Pong: *see* table tennis.

Ping-Pong diplomacy, diplomatic contacts between the People's Republic of China and the United States beginning in 1971, following a Chinese invitation to the U.S. table-tennis team to visit China; these contacts led to a 1972 rapprochement between the two powers.
·China's invitations and intentions **4**:402c

Ping-qiao (China): *see* Hsin-yang.

P'ing Ti (8 BC–AD 6), last emperor of China's Former Han dynasty. P'ing Ti was placed on the throne in 1 BC by the powerful minister Wang Mang, whose daughter he married five years later. Though proof is lacking, it has been claimed that P'ing Ti was poisoned by his father-in-law. In any case, P'ing Ti's death allowed Wang to assume the title of regent to a child emperor; in AD 8, Wang finally set aside the Han dynasty altogether and established himself as emperor of the Hsin dynasty.
·Han court intrigue and death **4**:310h
·Wang Mang's imperial support and control **19**:537d

P'ing-tung Hsien, county of Taiwan.
·area and population table **17**:997

pinguecula, yellowish nodule in the conjunctiva at the front of the eye, usually but not always on the nasal side. It occurs in elderly persons and is thought to represent degeneration in the conjunctiva as a result of exposure to wind and dust. The condition does not require medical or surgical treatment.

pinguin (plant): *see* Bromeliaceae.

Pinguinus impennis (bird): *see* great auk.

Ping-xiang (China): *see* P'ing-hsiang.

pinhole camera, photographic camera that has a very small aperture and has no lens.
·images and optimum hole size **13**:609c

Pin Hole Cave, archaeological site in Derbyshire, England.

Pin-hsien, Pin-yin romanization BIN-XIAN, city in Heilungkiang Province (*sheng*), China, situated on the eastern outskirts of Harbin in the Sung-hua-chiang Area (*ti-ch'ü*). It is the communications centre of a prosperous and productive agricultural district, which supplies a large part of the foodstuff, particularly grain and vegetables, consumed in Harbin. In addition to its importance as a collecting and commercial centre, it has also developed some light industry, consisting principally of food processing, light engineering, the production of bricks and tiles, and woodworking. Pop. (1970 est.) 10,000-50,000.
45°44′ N, 127°27′ E

Pinicola enucleator (bird): *see* grosbeak.

Pinilla, Gustavo Rojas: *see* Rojas Pinilla, Gustavo.

pinion, a gear with a small number of teeth designed to mesh with a larger wheel or rack.
·gear and speed ratios **11**:236h; illus. 237

Piniós (PENEUS) **River,** Greek PINIÓS POTAMÓS, principal stream of Thessaly, Greece, rising in the Óros (mountains) Lákmos of the Pindus Mountains (*q.v.*) just east of Métsovon in Tríkala *nomós* (department); it is navigable in its lower course. In prehistoric times the Piniós formed a great lake before it broke through the Vale of Tempe. It now flows 127 mi (205 km) through the mountains and plains of Thessaly, thrusting itself through the Vale of Tempe between the Olympus and Ossa massifs and debouching at the entrance to the Thermaïkós Kólpos (gulf) of the western Aegean Sea. Entering the western Thessalian plain, it receives the Enipévs and immediately winds through the saddle of low hills between the Zarkou Mountains on the north and the Mavrovoúni outliers that divide the Thessalian plain into two distinct parts. Other tributaries include the Lithaíos and the Titarísios.
39°54′ N, 22°45′ E
·map, Greece **8**:314

pinite, or PINITOL, sugary substance extracted from the sugar pine, used by American Indians as food and medicine.
·sources and uses **5**:6e

Pinjarra, Battle of (Oct. 28, 1834), a clash between Aborigines and a force of European soldiers, police, and settlers near the Western Australian settlement of Pinjarra (also Pinjarrup); it led to the disorganization of the area's Aboriginal population. From the establishment of a European settlement in the region in 1829, relations between the natives and the colonists were strained. The murders of several Europeans—especially the April 1834 killing of a young soldier—prompted the colony's governor, Sir James Stirling (1831–39), to mount a punitive expedition against the local Aborigines. On Oct. 28, 1934, the European force, numbering 24 in all, encountered a group of approximately 80 Aborigines near Pinjarra. In the ensuing battle, one European and at least 15 Aborigines were killed. The area's Aborigines scattered as a result of this clash, but the claims of Western Australian colonists that this disorganization of the Aborigines significantly contributed to the colony's development are doubtful.

Pinjor Zone (geology): *see* Siwalik Series.

pink (plant): *see* Caryophyllaceae.

pink bollworm: *see* gelechiid moth.

Pinkerton, Allan (b. Aug. 25, 1819, Glasgow—d. July 1, 1884, Chicago), detective and

founder of a famous U.S. private-detective agency. After emigrating to Illinois in 1842, Pinkerton began his career by capturing a gang of counterfeiters; he was appointed deputy sheriff of Kane County, Illinois (1846), and then of Cook County (which includes the city of Chicago). He resigned from the Chicago police force (1850) to organize the Pinkerton National Detective Agency, which specialized in railway theft cases. In 1861, working for the North during the Civil War under the name E.J. Allen, he headed an organization that obtained military information in the Southern states. After the war he resumed management of the Pinkerton Agency, which then assisted in breaking up the Molly Maguires, an organization of coal miners supposedly engaged in terrorism, and helped oppose the labour unions during strikes in 1877. Pinkerton wrote *The Molly Maguires and the Detective* (1877), *The Spy of the Rebellion* (1883), and *Thirty Years a Detective* (1884).
·security service development **16**:453e

pinkeye (medicine): *see* conjunctivitis.

pinkeye (veterinary medicine): *see* bovine infectious keratoconjunctivitis.

Pinkney, William (b. March 17, 1764, Annapolis, Md.—d. Feb. 25, 1822, Washington, D.C.), statesman and diplomat, considered one of the foremost lawyers of his day. A member of the Maryland convention that ratified the federal Constitution in 1788, he voted against ratification. He served in the Maryland state legislature (1788–92; 1795) and on the state's Executive Council (1792–95). From 1796 to 1804 he represented the U.S. as a commissioner to negotiate an agreement with Great Britain concerning American maritime losses, and he served as U.S. minister to Great Britain from 1807 to 1811.

Pinkney was attorney general of the U.S. (1811–14) in Pres. James Madison's administration, served in the House of Representatives (1815–16), and was minister to Russia (1816–18). From 1819 to 1822 he was a member of the U.S. Senate, where he became a champion of the slave states. He successfully argued many important cases before the Supreme Court, including *McCulloch* v. *Maryland* (1819), in which the power of Congress to charter the Bank of the United States was upheld.

pink salmon, also called HUMPBACK SALMON (*Oncorhynchus gorbuscha*), North Pacific food fish, family Salmonidae, weighing about 2

Pink salmon (*Oncorhynchus gorbuscha*)

Painted especially for *Encyclopaedia Britannica* by Tom Dolan, under the supervision of Loren P. Woods, Chicago Natural History Museum

kilograms (4½ pounds) and marked with large, irregular spots. It often spawns on tidal flats, the young entering the sea immediately after hatching. The alternative name humpback salmon refers to the hump that develops on the back of the breeding male. *See also* salmon.
·reproductive behaviour and migration **16**:187f

pinna (anatomy): *see* auricle of the ear.

pinnacle, in architecture, vertical ornament of pyramidal or conical shape, crowning a buttress, spire, or other architectural member. A pinnacle is distinguished from a finial (*q.v.*) by its greater size and complexity and from a tower or spire (*q.v.*) by its smaller size and subordinate architectural role. A tower may be decorated with pinnacles, each one capped by a finial.

Pinnacles on the flying buttresses and parapet of the cathedral of Milan, *c.* 1385-1485

A.F. Kersting

Simple pinnacles were used on Romanesque churches, especially to mask the abrupt transition from square tower to polygonal spire; but they were far more prominent in developed Gothic architecture and decoration, in which they were used to give vertical emphasis and to break up hard outlines. They appeared at every major corner of a building, flanked gables, and decorated parapets and buttresses. Some of the most striking pinnacles crown the piers of flying buttresses, on which, although primarily decorative, they enhance the stability of the buttresses by their additional weight and thereby help to counteract the lateral thrust of the vault. The early 14th-century buttress pinnacles around the choir of Notre-Dame at Paris and the magnificent 80-foot (24-metre) pinnacles at Reims cathedral (13th century) are representative examples. In England, pinnacles were especially developed in the Decorated style and played an important part in tower design.

In the 18th, 19th, and 20th centuries, pinnacles were often used in eclectic architecture. Notable examples include, in England, Horace Walpole's Strawberry Hill (1747; Twickenham, now in the London borough of Richmond upon Thames); the Houses of Parliament (begun 1840; London); and, in the United States, the Woolworth Building in New York City (1913).

pinnacle, in geology, needle-shaped landform. Pinnacles are particularly well represented in southern Libya and other parts of the southern Sahara.

Pinnacles National Monument, in west central California, U.S., in the Gabilan Range, 35 mi (56 km) north of King City. Established in 1908, it is an area (23 sq mi [60 sq km]) of spirelike rock formations 500 to 1,200 ft (150 to 365 m) high, caverns, and other volcanic features that were formed during the Tertiary Period. A foot trail leads to the highest point, North Chalone Peak (3,305 ft). Annual rainfall, mainly in winter and spring, amounts to about 15 in. (380 mm), and summer and autumn are hot and dry. Wildfire, now suppressed by man with some success, was an important factor in shaping the shrub vegetation—mainly dry, leathery chaparral, although Digger pine has become established and spring wildflowers are abundant. Small, dull-coloured mammals (foxes, bobcats, rodents, rabbits) match the dwarf forest of the locality.

Pinneberg, town, Schleswig-Holstein *Land* (state), northeastern West Germany, on the Pinnau River, just northwest of Hamburg. A district centre (*Kreisstadt*) and the seat of a district court, the town is interspersed with woodlands and gardens. It is a centre of rose cultivation, with an annual rose festival. There are various light industries. Pop. (1974 est.) 37,100.
53°40′ N, 9°47′ E
·map, Federal Republic of Germany **8**:47

Pinnipedia, suborder of aquatic, fin-footed mammals in the order Carnivora, often considered a separate order. It contains three existing families: Odobenidae (*see* walrus) and Phocidae and Otariidae (*see* seal). *Major ref.* **3**:937f *passim* to 943e
·Arctic Ocean animal life **1**:1122h

Pinnotheres (genus of decapods): *see* pea crab.

pinnule, a thin single-celled unit on the tentacles of beardworms that acts as a filter for incoming food.
·gutless filter feeding in beardworms **14**:604a

pin oak (*Quercus palustris*), North American ornamental and timber tree belonging to the red oak group of the genus *Quercus* of the beech family (Fagaceae), found on bottomlands and moist upland soils in the eastern and central U.S. Usually about 27 metres tall but occasionally reaching 36 metres, the tree has a broad, pyramidal crown and drooping lower branches. Spurlike, slender branchlets stand out like pins on the trunk and larger limbs. The elliptical, glossy green leaves are about 12 centimetres long; they have five to seven deeply cut lobes and turn scarlet in autumn. The dark-brown acorns are enclosed at the base in a thin, shallow cup.

The northern pin oak (*Q. ellipsoidalis*) also has pinlike branchlets but usually occurs on upland sites that are dry. Its ellipse-shaped acorns are nearly half enclosed in a scaly cup. The leaves become yellow or pale brown in autumn, often with purple blotches.

Pinochet (Ugarte), Augusto (b. Nov. 11, 1915, Valparaíso, Chile), leader of the military junta that overthrew the government of Pres. Salvador Allende of Chile in September 1973. A graduate of the military academy in Santiago (1936), Pinochet was a career military officer who received the commission of brigadier general in 1968. He served as chief of staff of the army (1972) and three times as commander in chief of the armed forces (1972–73). Before the coup d'etat Pinochet appeared to be an apolitical army officer and had been chosen by Allende as his military strong man apparently because of his neutrality.

Pinochle, card game, in which points are scored for holding and declaring certain combinations of cards and for taking certain cards in tricks. It is generally thought to be of German origin but was virtually unknown in Europe long after it had been introduced into the United States by European immigrants, who developed the game and its variants by combining features of Bezique and Skat. The "modern" versions of the game became popular in the 1860s.

In the original two-hand game, two 24-card packs (A–K–Q–J–10–9 of each suit) are used, and each player is dealt 12 cards, three at a time. The next card is turned face up to establish the trump suit, and the remainder are placed face down as the stockpile. The nondealer leads any card to the first trick. While stock remains, his opponent need not follow suit; he may play to the trick any card in his hand. A trick—one card from each player—is won by the highest card of the suit led or by a trump; if identical cards are played, leader wins. In play, the 10 ranks as the second highest card in all suits. The winner of a trick may meld (German *melden*, "to announce"— *i.e.*, declare by placing face up on the table) any one of the specified scoring combinations of the game:

Sequence or flush (A, K, Q, J, 10 in trumps)	150
Royal marriage (K, Q in trumps)	40
Marriage (K, Q in any other suit)	20
Four aces, one in each suit ("Hundred Aces")	100
Four Kings, one in each suit ("Eighty kings")	80
Four queens, one in each suit ("Sixty queens")	60
Four knaves, one in each suit ("Forty jacks")	40
Pinochle (♤ Q and ◇ J)	40
Dix, lowest trump	10

Only one meld may be made in a turn. For each meld, at least one card must be taken from the hand and placed on the table. The same meld may be repeated only with entirely different cards from those used previously. As in Bezique, a meld from which a card is played cannot be re-formed. In Pinochle, however, cards can be added to an existing meld to form a higher-value meld, which then can be scored; *e.g.*, the A-J-10 may be added to a previous royal marriage (K-Q of trumps) for an additional score for the trump sequence.

After the winner of a trick has a chance to meld, each player draws the top card of the stock, the winner drawing first and then leading to the next trick, either from his hand or from one of his melds already on the table. When stock is exhausted, each player takes his tabled melds into his hand; in the play to ensuing tricks, leader's opponent must follow suit if able. Nonleader must "go over"—*i.e.*, play a higher card—only when a trump is led. When won in a trick an ace counts 11; a 10, 10; a king, 4; a queen, 3; a knave, 2; a 9, nothing. Some follow a simpler method: aces and 10s, 10 each; kings and queens, 5 each; other cards, nothing.

The lowest trump, 9 in Pinochle, is called dix (pronounced deece) and has a special role and value. If the card turned to establish trump is a dix (9), dealer scores 10. The winner of a trick may also exchange a dix for the trump card or may merely show the dix and score 10.

The game is won by the first player to reach 1,000. A player may call himself out in the middle of the play, and if his score, including his melds and tricks in the current deal, equals 1,000, he wins the game even though his opponent has a higher score; but if he has less than 1,000 he loses the game. If both sides pass 1,000 without calling out, game becomes 1,250 points, and so on.

The variants, Auction Pinochle and Partnership Pinochle, have become more popular than the original two-hand game. In Auction Pinochle, three players bid for the right to meld and name the trump suit; the two low-bidding players then join in a temporary partnership to try to prevent the high bidder from fulfilling his contract. In Partnership Pinochle, four play in partnerships of two against two, the partners being seated alternately. Partnerships score jointly, although a player may not combine his cards with those of his partner to form a meld. In Partnership Auction Pinochle, an even more popular offshoot of these two variants, players bid the number of points that they think their side can score in melds and tricks, and the highest bidder melds and names trump. The high-bidding side must fulfill its contract to score, otherwise, the amount of its bid is subtracted from its running score. The opposing side scores whatever points it makes in tricks.

·card game history and strategy **3**:904a

Pinochle Rummy (card game): *see* Five-Hundred Rum.

pinocytosis, a process by which particles or, more commonly, liquid droplets are ingested by living cells. Rather than passing as individual molecules through the cell membrane without disrupting it, the droplet first becomes bound or adsorbed on the cell membrane, which then invaginates (forms a pocket) and pinches off to form a vesicle, or vacuole, in the cytoplasm. It is believed that a vesicle may carry extracellular fluid to the opposite side of the cell, where it undergoes reverse pinocytosis. A droplet of fluid could thus be transported through the cell without disturbing its cytoplasm. Alternatively, intracellular digestion of the vacuole wall would permit the droplet to mix with the cytoplasm. *See also* phagocytosis.

·cell membrane functional mechanisms **3**:1049f
·membrane function in transport **11**:884e
·protozoan feeding behaviour **5**:781d; illus.
·protozoan feeding mechanisms **15**:126e
·tissue culture's contributions **18**:441f

Piño Hachado Pass, in the Andes on the Argentine–Chile border, traversed by a road connecting Las Lajas, Arg., and Lonquimay, Chile.
38°39′ S, 70°54′ W
·Andes location and elevation **1**:857b

pinpricked pictures, in the visual arts, pictures, often of great complexity, produced by pricking holes through paper to achieve a lacelike effect. Possibly deriving from the cartoon techniques of the early Renaissance, it became a fashionable hobby for ladies in the late 18th and 19th centuries, largely because it could be created very easily with the spiked wheel used by dressmakers to trace a pattern on cloth.

Pinpricked picture of a woman and children, English, *c.* 1780; in the Victoria and Albert Museum, London

By courtesy of the Victoria and Albert Museum, London

Pins, Île des, English ISLE OF PINES, also called KUNIE ISLAND, in the southwest Pacific Ocean, within the French overseas territory of New Caledonia (Nouvelle-Calédonie). With an area of 59 sq mi (152 sq km), it is forested with pinelike coniferous trees of the genus *Araucaria* (hence its name) and is rugged, rising to Nga Peak (870 ft [265 m]). The island was once a penal colony but by the 1970s had a growing tourist trade, as it lies only 60 mi southeast of Nouméa, which is on the trans-Pacific air route. Exports include shrimp and oysters. The main town and administrative centre is Vao, on the south coast. Pop. (1974 prelim.) 1,159.
22°37′ S, 167°30′ E

Pinsk, city, Brest *oblast* (administrative region), Belorussian Soviet Socialist Republic, at the confluence of the Pina and Pripyat rivers. It was first mentioned in 1097 and was the seat of a Russian princedom. It passed under Lithuanian rule (13th–16th centuries), then Polish (1569–1793), Russian (1793–World War I), Polish again (1920–39), then Soviet (with German occupation during 1941–44). At the eastern end of the Dneprovsko-Bugsky Kanal, Pinsk is a significant river port. There are timber-working industries, metalworking, manufacture of artificial leather, and shipbuilding and repair yards. Pop. (1973 est.) 73,000.
52°07′ N, 26°04′ E

Pinsker, Leo (b. JUDAH LEIB PINSKER, 1821, Tomaszów, Russian Poland—d. Dec. 21, 1891, Odessa, now in Ukrainian S.S.R.), physician, polemicist, and pioneer Jewish nationalist, a precursor of Theodor Herzl (1860–1904) and other major political Zionists.

While conducting the practice of medicine in Odessa, Pinsker maintained a deep interest in Jewish community affairs. He joined the Society for the Promotion of Culture Among the Jews, an assimilationist organization founded in 1863. As a means of integrating Jews into Russian society, he advocated secular education for Jews and the translation of the Bible and Hebrew prayer books into Russian. A pogrom in Odessa in 1871 shook but did not destroy his beliefs; in 1881, however, another severe pogrom broke out in Odessa, not only ignored but even abetted by the government and defended by the press. His assimilationist beliefs were shattered, and he turned to nationalism as a solution for Jewish suffering.

In 1882 Pinsker anonymously published in German an incisive, embittered, and impassioned pamphlet, "Auto-Emanzipation. Ein Mahnruf an seine Stammesgenossen. Von einem russischen Juden" ("Self-Emancipation. A Warning Addressed to His Brethren. By a Russian Jew"; Eng. trans., *Auto-Emancipation*, 1884), which provoked strong reactions, both critical and commendatory, from Jewish leaders. In the pamphlet he contended that the nations in which the Jews lived as minorities would never allow them to be assimilated, and the only restorative for Jewish dignity and spiritual health lay in a Jewish homeland, not necessarily to be established in Palestine.

Pinsker's authorship was soon discovered, and a newly formed Zionist group, Ḥibbat Ẕiyyon (Love of Zion), made him one of its leaders. In 1884 he convened the Kattowitz (Katowice, Pol.) Conference, which established a permanent committee with headquarters in Odessa. Although Ḥibbat Ẕiyyon (later Ḥovevei Ẕiyyon, Lovers of Zion) was crippled by lack of funds, it did establish a few colonies in Palestine and founded the Society for the Support of Jewish Agriculturists and Handicraftsmen in Syria and Palestine.

pint, any of various units of capacity equal to one-half quart.
·weights and measures, table 4 **19**:732

Pinta, one of the three ships with which Columbus sailed to the New World.
·Columbus' first voyage **4**:938f

pinta, chronic skin disease characterized by initial papular lesions followed after several years by white, blue, brown, or red patches on the extremities and horny overgrowths on the soles and palms.

Pinta, Isla, English PINTA ISLAND, also ABINGDON ISLAND, one of the northernmost of the Galápagos Islands, in the eastern Pacific Ocean, 600 mi (965 km) west of Ecuador, which administers the Galápagos. With an area of 20 sq mi (52 sq km), it is uninhabited.
0°35′ N, 90°44′ W
·map, Ecuador **6**:286

Pinter, Harold (b. Oct. 10, 1930, London), playwright who achieved international renown as one of the most complex and challenging post-World War II dramatists. His plays are English in their use of understatement, small talk, reticence—and even silence—to convey the substance of a character's thought, which often lies several layers beneath, and contradicts, his speech. He is perhaps more universally of his age, however, in his emphasis on the radical instability of modern man, deprived of every certainty, including clarity about who he and others are and why they do what they do. The "meaning" of his plays, therefore, cannot be explained in a conventional sense.

The son of a Jewish tailor, Pinter grew up in London's East End in a working-class area with a large immigrant population and was exposed early to the violence that is a brooding presence in his plays. As a child during World War II, he was evacuated more than once, but lived in London during some of the worst of the bombing. He was confirmed in his insecurity after the war by encounters with Fascist toughs who considered the carrying of books evidence of Communist leanings.

Granted a scholarship to study acting at the Royal Academy of Dramatic Art, Pinter left after two terms; called up for National Service at 18, he declared himself a conscientious objector. Having given no religious reasons for his refusal to serve, he underwent two court trials and was eventually fined. In 1950 his poems began to appear in *Poetry London*, and the next year he resumed acting classes at the Central School of Speech Training and Dramatic Art London.

Pinter toured Ireland with an acting company in 1951–52 (a period he writes of in his memoir, *Mac*, 1968), and from 1954 to 1957 acted under the name David Baron in provincial repertory theatres. In 1956 he married an actress, Vivien Merchant, who became an accomplished interpreter of his plays. *The Room* (performed 1957), was his first play, a one-act drama that established the mood of comic menace that was to figure largely in his early plays. His first full-length play, *The Birthday Party* (1958, filmed 1968), puzzled the London audiences and lasted only a week, but later it was televised and revived successfully on the stage.

Pinter's reputation was secured by his second full-length play, *The Caretaker* (1960, filmed 1963), in which a former mental patient brings a tramp to the house he shares with his brother. The play's blend of realism and mystery, and its extraordinarily accurate rendering of actual speech, indicated to critics that Pinter was more than just another practitioner of the currently popular Theatre of the Absurd. *The Homecoming* (1965) focusses on the return to his East End London home of a man who has become a university professor in the U.S. and brings his wife to meet his family.

A lighter, more tranquil play was *Old Times* (1971), in which a husband, his wife, and her woman friend relive episodes of their past and in so doing highlight unsuspected insecurities in the couple's present relationship.

Pinter also is the author of many short plays and of radio and television drama. Among his notable screenplays, all based on the novels of others, are *The Servant* (1962), *Accident* (1967), and *The Go-Between* (1971).

·absurdist themes, sources, and humour **18**:232e
·direction of his own plays **5**:828d
·English theatre development **10**:1222f
·popular and high dramatic coordination **14**:807a

Pinto (Spanish: Painted), a spotted horse; the pinto has also been called paint, particoloured, pied, piebald, calico, and skewbald. The Indian ponies of western U.S. were often pintos, and the type was often considered of poor quality. The pure-breed associations usually refuse to register horses with pin-

Sorrel and white Pinto
Margie Spence

to colouring. The colour does not determine the type of horse, however, and many fine Pintos have been developed. The Pinto Horse Association, organized in 1956, recognizes colour patterns called overo (white spreading irregularly up from the belly, mixed with a darker colour) and tobiano (white spreading down from the back in smooth, clean-cut patterns).

Pinto, Fernão Mendes (b. *c.* 1510, Montemor-o-Velho, Port.—d. July 8, 1583, Almada, near Lisbon), adventurer and author of the *Peregrinaçam* (1614, "Peregrination"), a literary masterpiece depicting the impression made on a European by Asian civilization, notably that of China, in the 16th century. He went to India in 1537 and later claimed to have travelled, fought, and traded in almost every part of Asia during the next 21 years and also to have experienced drastic reversals of fortune, having been made "13 times a prisoner and 17 a slave." In China, for example, he was convicted of plundering royal tombs and, as punishment, had his thumbs severed and was sentenced to a year of hard labour on construction of the Great Wall. The *Peregrinaçam* was written after Pinto's return to Portugal in 1558. He settled in Almada, married, and received a pension from King Philip. The work describes the sights and sounds of China in colourful detail and includes vivid impressions of clamorous festivals and the fascinating floating markets of Nanking. To date, there is no good critical edition in any language. Existing editions appear in G. Le Gentil's *Fernão Mendes Pinto. Un précurseur de l'exotisme au XVIe siècle* (1947, "Fernão Mendes Pinto. A Precursor of the 16-Century Exoticism") and M. S. Collins' *The Grand Peregrination* (1949).

pintor de su deshonra, El (*c.* 1645), Spanish play by Calderón de la Barca.
·Calderón's works and style **3**:594a

pin tumbler, or EGYPTIAN LOCK, the part of a cylinder lock that, in conjunction with others, prevents motion unless the proper key is used.
·design, construction, and use **11**:10b; illus.

Pinturicchio (b. BERNARDINO DI BETTO DI BIAGO; *c.* 1454, Perugia, Italy—d. Dec. 11, 1513, Siena, Italy), early Renaissance painter of Umbria, known for the highly decorative style of his frescoes. He was associated with the Umbrian artist Perugino by 1481, whose influence on him was permanent. It is generally agreed that Pinturicchio assisted Perugino on some of the frescoes ("Journey of Moses" and the "Baptism of Christ") in the Sistine Chapel in the Vatican (1481/82). In the 1480s, he worked in the Bufalini Chapel in Sta. Maria in Aracoeli and also in Sta. Maria del Popolo (both in Rome).

Pinturicchio's most important work of this period was the decoration of the suite of six rooms in the Vatican known as the Appartamento Borgia for Pope Alexander VI between 1492 and 1494. In these frescoes he retains Perugino's figure types but lacks his clarity of conception. Instead, Pinturicchio relies on brilliant, often jarring colours, gilding, and ancient Roman ornamental motifs to achieve a highly decorative style.

Pinturicchio's last major works were the ten scenes from the life of Pope Pius II painted (1503–08) in fresco in the Piccolomini Library

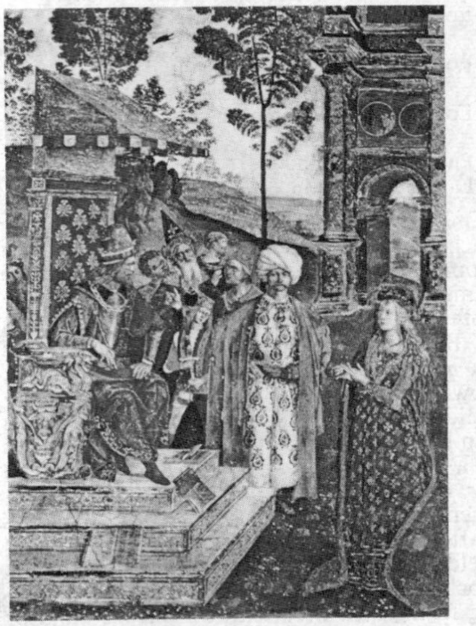

Detail of "The Dispute of St. Catherine," fresco by Pinturicchio, 1492–94; in the Borgia Apartment of the Vatican
SCALA, New York

of Siena cathedral. The compositions are generally considered to be unimaginative, and the figures are often placed and posed by rote.
·Alexander VI fresco detail illus. **1**:468a

Pinus (tree genus): *see* pine.

Pinus aristata: *see* bristlecone pine.

Pinus pinea, species of European stone pine, family Pinaceae, a gymnosperm.
·economic uses **7**:758d

pinworm, also called SEAT WORM or THREADWORM (*Enterobius* [*Oxyuris*] *vermicularis*), a white worm of the class Oxyuroidea (phylum Aschelminthes). Pinworms occur only in the Northern Hemisphere and are common human intestinal parasites, especially in children. They are also known to occur in other vertebrates.

Male pinworms are 2 to 5 millimetres (about 0.08 to 0.2 inch) long and are rarely seen; females range in length from 8 to 13 millimetres (0.3 to 0.5 inch). The long tails of the worms give them a pinlike appearance.

Pinworms usually occur in the large intestine but sometimes are found in the small intestine, the stomach, or farther up the gastrointestinal tract. After being fertilized by the

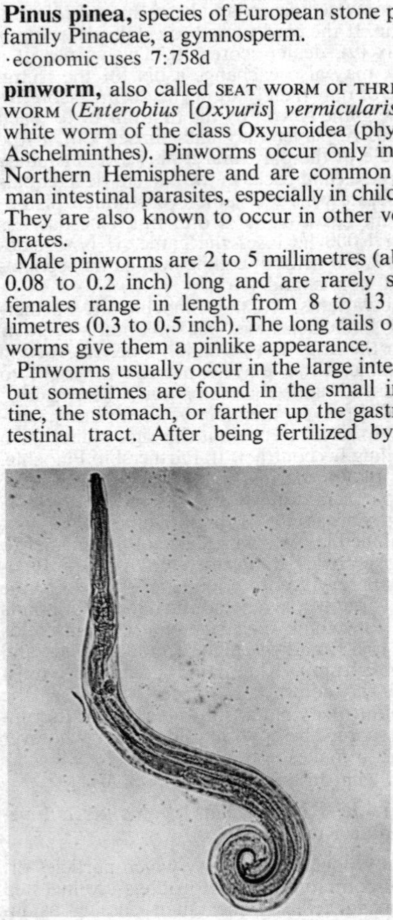

Pinworm (*Enterobius vermicularis*)
Walter Dawn

male, the female travels to the anus, deposits the eggs on the skin near the anal opening, and usually dies. Movements of the worm on the skin cause itching. Eggs, transferred beneath the fingernails by scratching, are passed to the mouth, from which the eggs or larvae make their way to the intestine. The life cycle requires 15 to 43 days.
·general features, behaviour, evolution, and classification **2**:138b

Pinxton porcelain, English porcelain produced in Derbyshire in 1796–1813. The factory was established by John Coke (who had lived in Dresden) with the help of William Billingsley, who had worked as a painter at Derby. Billingsley remained at Pinxton until

Pinxton porcelain goblet by William Billingsley, Derbyshire, Eng., *c.* 1800; in the Victoria and Albert Museum, London

By courtesy of the Victoria and Albert Museum, London; photograph, EB Inc.

1801, concentrating on the production of the porcelain rather than its decoration as at Derby. He made a ware that contained bone ash, was granular yet transparent, and had a brilliant glaze. Pinxton produced only domestic and tableware. In 1804 the factory was taken over by John Cutts, but the wares produced thereafter were inferior.

Pin-yang, triple-cave temple at Lung-men (*see* Lung-men caves), China, begun in 505.
·Buddhist art style **11**:165d
·Buddhist cave sculpture and style **19**:185f; illus. 186

Pinyin, system of romanization for the Chinese language, based on the pronunciation of the Peking (or Northern Mandarin) dialect. Pinyin was formally adopted in 1958 as a means of aiding the spread of standard (Mandarin) Chinese throughout China. Although the Pinyin romanization of most sounds is clear to a speaker of English, the phonetic values of some letters, such as *q* and *x*, differ from those of English usage. In 1979 numerous non-Chinese periodicals adopted Pinyin as standard usage.
·phonemic notations **16**:801d; table 802

Pinzón, Martín Alonso and Vicente Yáñez (respectively b. *c.* 1441, Palos, Spain—d. 1493, Palos; b. *c.* 1460?, Palos—d. *c.*

Martín Alonso Pinzón, detail of a portrait by an unknown artist; in the Museo Naval, Madrid

Archivo Mas, Barcelona

1523?), brothers from a family of Spanish shipowners and navigators who were associated with Christopher Columbus in his maiden voyage to America.

Martín, part owner of the "Pinta" and "Niña," helped prepare and man them for the expedition of 1492 and commanded the "Pinta," on which his brother Francisco was pilot. His suggestion to change course on October 7 brought the fleet to a landfall in the Bahamas on October 12. Near Cuba, however, he left the fleet, searching for the land of gold and spices. When he rejoined Columbus a few months later, he blamed harsh weather for his disappearance. Returning with the fleet to Spain, he left Columbus once again, hoping to be the first to arrive back. Columbus reached Spain first, however, and Martín is remembered only for his disloyalty.

Vicente commanded the "Niña" in 1492–93 and remained with Columbus throughout the expedition. One of the most successful and capable Spanish explorers in his own right, he sailed early in 1500 across the Atlantic to the southwest and landed on the Brazilian coast at Cabo (cape) de Santo Agostinho. He probably rounded Cabo Sâo Roque and then turned north, discovered the Amazon Estuary, and went as far as the present Costa Rica. He was made governor of his newly discovered lands but did not take possession. In 1508, commissioned by the Spanish crown to discover a passage to the Spice Islands, he sailed with Juan Díaz de Solís along the coast of Central America. Historians are not sure whether he discovered Honduras and Yucatán or went southward to Venezuela and Brazil. Trouble developed with de Solís, and they returned to Spain in August 1509. No records exist of Vicente after 1523.
·Columbus' voyages **4**:938d *passim* to 940b
·French Guiana exploration and Vicente Yáñez Pinzón **7**:714f
·Spanish exploration of Brazil **3**:144e

Pinzón (DUNCAN) **Island,** one of the Galápagos Islands, in the eastern Pacific Ocean, about 600 mi (965 km) west of Ecuador. It has an area of about 7 sq mi (18 sq km) and is flanked on the west by five small islets known as Guy Fawkes Island. The relief is made up of cactus-studded littoral and several volcanic craters, the highest rising to 1,300 ft (400 m). Originally named for Sir Anthony Dean (Deane), an English shipbuilder, the island was renamed in the 18th century to honour the English admiral Viscount Duncan. The official Ecuadorian name is Isla Pinzón. It has a large marine tortoise reserve, as well as a seal rookery, but no human population.
0°36′ S, 90°40′ W
·map, Ecuador **6**:286

Pioche Shale Formation, Lower Cambrian rocks that occur in the House Range of western Utah and the Pioche region of eastern Nevada (the Cambrian Period began about 570,000,000 years ago and lasted about 70,000,000 years). The Pioche Formation underlies the Middle Cambrian Lyndon Formation and overlies the Prospect Mountain Quartzite. It was named by C.D. Walcott in 1908 for exposures seen in the type locality of Pioche, Nev. The Pioche Shale consists of about 340 metres (1,120 feet) of yellow or brown shales and interbedded limestones and is characterized by a Lower Cambrian fossil fauna typified by the trilobite genus *Olenellus*.

Piombino, town, Livorno province, in the Tuscany region of central Italy, at the tip of the Piombino promontory below Monte Massoncello, opposite the island of Elba. Once a possession of the archbishops of Pisa, it was declared a princedom in 1594 and was variously owned or occupied before becoming part of the kingdom of Italy in 1861. Nearby Populonia has Etruscan, Roman, and medieval remains. An old seaport with significant shipping traffic, Piombino has ironworks and steelworks and provides ship service to Elba;

Iron works at Piombino, Italy

S.E. Hedin—Ostman Agency

it is connected by branch railway with Campiglia Marittima on the main Rome–Genoa line. Pop. (1978 est.) mun., 40,023.
42°55′ N, 10°32′ E
·map, Italy **9**:1088

Piombo, Sebastiano del (Italian painter): *see* Sebastiano del Piombo.

pion (physics): *see* meson.

Pioneer, series of unmanned U.S. interplanetary probes. In 1960 Pioneer 5 made important measurements of cosmic-ray intensity in space. Pioneers 10 and 11 passed near Jupiter in December 1973 and 1974, respectively, and Pioneer 11 reached to within 13,300 mi (21,400 km) of Saturn in September 1979. They were expected to leave the Solar System and each carried a plaque with drawings of human beings and an astronomical map showing its place of origin.

Pioneer Venus 1 and 2 encountered Venus in December 1978; the former was an orbiter, and segments of the latter crashed on the planet.
·Jupiter flight path and launching **17**:375a; illus. 374
·launching and arrival dates **16**:1030b

Pioneer, submarine built in 1862 for the Confederate States by Horace L. Hunley.
·Confederate submarines built by Hunley **17**:748a

Pioneers (Soviet youth organization): *see* All-Union Leninist Communist League of Youth.

Pioneers of France in the New World (1865), work by Francis Parkman, first of seven in his series *France and England in North America*.
·theme and series initiation **13**:1020a

pioneer species, in an ecological system, organisms that thrive soon after a bare or disturbed area has an opportunity for recovery but that decline to zero as waves of replacement species arrive.
·ecosystem establishment dynamics **18**:147d

Piophilidae (fly family): *see* skipper.

Piotrków, *województwo* (province), central Poland; until 1975 part of Łódź *województwo*. With an area of 2,418 sq mi (6,262 sq km), it is bounded by the provinces of Łódź to the northwest, Skierniewice to the northeast, Radom to the east, Kielce to the southeast, Częstochowa to the southwest, and Sieradz to the west. Piotrków Trybunalski, a manufacturing centre and the provincial capital, lies 30 mi (50 km) south of the city of Łódź. Other major industrial towns in the *województwo* include Tomaszów Mazowiecki and Radomsko.

The province, drained by the Pilica and Widowka rivers, has rich alluvial soil. Agriculture is the main economic activity, with rye, wheat, and potatoes the principal crops. The textile industry is an extension of the textile mills centred around Łódź. Major roads and the Warsaw–Katowice rail line connect Piotrków Trybunalski with other provincial capitals. Pop. (1979 est.) 181,600.

Piotrków Trybunalski, capital of Piotrkowskie *województwo* (province; until 1975 part of Łódź *województwo*), central Poland. Pop. (1979 est.) 68,900.
51°25′ N, 19°42′ E
·map, Poland **14**:626

Piozzi, Hester Lynch, *née* SALUSBURY, best known as MRS. THRALE (b. Jan. 27, 1740, Bodvel, Carnarvonshire, Wales—d. May 2, 1821, Clifton, Bristol), writer and friend of Samuel Johnson. In 1763 she married a wealthy brewer named Henry Thrale. In January 1765 Samuel Johnson was brought to dinner, and the next year, following a severe illness, Johnson spent most of the summer in the country with the Thrales. Gradually, he became part of the family circle.

In 1781 Thrale died, and his wife was left a wealthy widow. To everyone's dismay, she fell in love with her daughter's music master, Gabriel Piozzi, an Italian singer and composer, married him in 1784 and set off for Italy on a honeymoon. Dr. Johnson openly disapproved. The resulting estrangement saddened his last months of life.

When news reached her of Johnson's death, she hastily compiled and sent back to England copy for *Anecdotes of the late Samuel Johnson, LL.D., during the last Twenty Years of his Life* (1786), which thrust her into open rivalry with James Boswell. The breach was further widened when, after her return to England in 1787, she brought out a two-volume edition of *Letters to and from the late Samuel Johnson, LL.D.* (1788). Although less accurate in some details than Boswell's, her accounts show other aspects of Johnson's character, especially the more human and affectionate side of his nature.

Piozzi, drawing by George Dance, 1793; in the National Portrait Gallery, London
By courtesy of the National Portrait Gallery, London

When many old friends remained aloof, Mrs. Piozzi drew around her a new artistic circle, the central figure being the actress Sarah Siddons. Her pen remained active, and thousands of her entertaining, gossipy letters have survived. The standard authorities remain J.L. Clifford's *Hester Lynch Piozzi* (*Mrs. Thrale*) (1941); and *Thraliana* (her journal kept sporadically between 1776 and 1809), ed. by K.C. Balderston, 2 vol. (1942).
·attitude toward Goldsmith **8**:240e
·Johnson's friendship **10**:249e *passim* to 251d

p'i-p'a, short-necked Chinese lute prominent in Chinese opera orchestras and as a solo instrument. Ultimately of West Asian origin (*see* 'ūd), it was known in China by the 2nd century AD. It has a shallow, pear-shaped body with a wooden belly and, sometimes, two crescent-shaped sound holes. There are

Woman playing a *p'i-p'a,* detail from 18th-century silk painting; in the Náprstkovo Muzeum Asijských, Prague
By courtesy of the Naprstkovo Muzeum Asijskych, Prague

four convex frets on the neck and six to 13 frets on the belly. The four silk strings run from a fastener on the belly to conical tuning pegs in the sides of the bent-back pegbox. They are plucked with a plectrum while the instrument is held vertically on the thigh. A common tuning (relative pitch) is c–f–g–c′ (top note around middle C).

There are several varieties of *p'i-p'a* in China, and closely related instruments are also found in Vietnam and Korea. The *p'i-p'a* reached Japan at least by the 8th century AD, the Japanese form of the instrument, the *biwa*, also existing in several varieties.
·construction, classification, and use in ballad genre **17**:739h *passim* to 746c
·influence on samisen playing method **12**:687b
·narrative music revival **12**:689b
·solo instrumental popularity **12**:676f

pipa, unit of measure used in Portugal that equals 500 litres.
·weights and measures, table 5 **19**:734

pipal: *see* Bo tree.

Pipa pipa: *see* Surinam toad.

pipe, in music, specifically, the three-holed flute played with a tabor drum (*see* pipe and tabor); generically, aereophonic (wind) instruments consisting of pipes, either flutes or reed pipes (as a clarinet), and also the reed and flue pipes of organs.

A pipe's pitch depends on its length, a long pipe having a low pitch. Pipes stopped at one end sound an octave lower than open pipes of equal length. Additional notes are obtained by using fingerholes to alter the length of the air column enclosed by the pipe or by vigorously overblowing, forcing the air column to vibrate in segments and sound overtones (harmonics) of the fundamental pitch.

In reed pipes and organ reed pipes a vibrating reed causes the column of air in the pipe to vibrate. In flutes and organ flue pipes a stream of air passing a sharp edge sets up vibrations in the pipe's air column. *See also* flute; fipple flute; reed instruments.
·African wind instruments **1**:249d
·organ pipes **13**:677d
·wind instruments **19**:848b *passim* to 859

pipe, in steel production, shrinkage cavity formed in the head of a steel ingot during solidification.
·ingot-casting methods **17**:651b

pipe, in mineralogy, deep, vertical body of ore that is cylindrical or funnel-shaped.
·ore deposit shapes and formation **13**:664f

pipe, tobacco, hollow bowl used for smoking tobacco; it is equipped with a hollow stem through which smoke is drawn into the mouth. The bowl can be made of any number of materials such as clay, corncob, meerschaum (a mineral composed of magnesia, silica, and water), and, most importantly, briar-wood, the roots of a species of heather. *See also* tobacco smoking.
·Hopewell culture artifact illus. **1**:682
·Melanesian materials **11**:866b
·tobacco processing and health hazards **18**:466g

pipe and tabor, three-holed whistle flute played with a small snare drum. The player holds the pipe with the left hand, stopping the holes with the thumb, first, and second fingers; the other two fingers support the instrument. A scale is obtained by overblowing, using the second to the fourth harmonics; the gaps between the harmonics are filled by uncovering the finger holes. The tabor, suspended from the player's left wrist or elbow, is beaten with the right hand to provide rhythmic accompaniment.

Pipe and tabor player, detail from the Luttrell Psalter, early 14th century; in the British Museum (Add. 42130)
By courtesy of the trustees of the British Museum

Mention of the pipe and tabor first occurs in the Middle Ages, as an ensemble providing music for court dances. By the 17th century it began to decline, surviving primarily as a folk instrument. In Provence and Spain the tradition of playing remains unbroken. In England, where pipe and tabor playing was associated with the Morris dancers, the 20th-century renewal of interest in English folk music stimulated a revival.
·tabor survival in Western Europe **14**:64c

pipe dance, North American Indian ritual.
·gestural symbolism **1**:671f

pipefish, common name for over 150 species of elongated fishes allied to the sea horses,

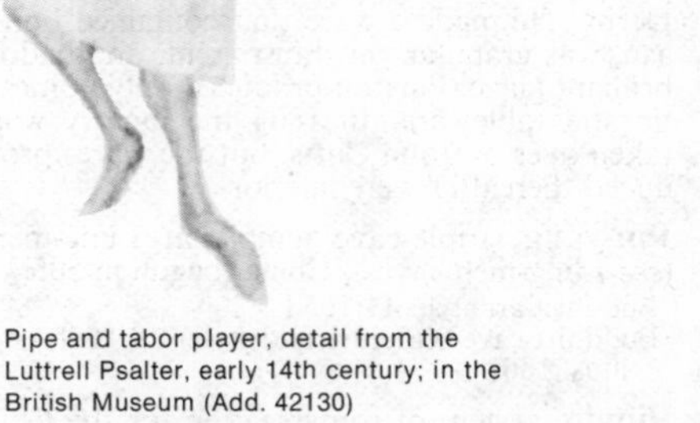

Banded pipefish (*Dunkerocampus caulleryi*)
Douglas Faulkner

in the family Syngnathidae (order Gasterosteiformes). Pipefishes are very slender, long-bodied fishes covered, like sea horses, with rings of bony armour. They have long, tubular snouts and small mouths, a single dorsal fin, and, usually, a small tail fin. Depending on the species, they may range in length from about 2.5 to 50 centimetres (1–20 inches).

Pipefishes, found in warm regions, are primarily marine, although some live in or enter freshwater. They are weak, slow swimmers and usually live in beds of seaweed, eelgrass, or other aquatic plants among which they can feed and hide. They feed by sucking their prey (small aquatic organisms) rapidly into their mouths. Their reproductive behaviour, like that of sea horses, is distinctive in that the male, not the female, carries the fertilized eggs until they hatch. Among pipefishes, the eggs may be stuck to the surface of the body, embedded in a spongy area, or carried in a brood pouch. The brood pouch is derived from lengthwise folds of skin and, depending on the species, affords varying degrees of coverage for the incubating eggs.

Related to the pipefishes are the ghost pipefishes of the family Solenostomidae. These are small, rare, Indo-Pacific fishes with long snouts and enlarged fins. They also brood their eggs, but in this instance the female carries them in a brood pouch formed by the union of the ventral fins.

·classification and general features **7**:939f; illus. 938
·traits, behaviour, and evolution **7**:938d

pipe jacking, method of excavating a tunnel.
·tunnelling methods **18**:756c; illus.

pipeline, line of pipe connected to pumps, valves, and control devices for conveying liquids, gases, or slurries (finely divided solids suspended in a liquid). Pipeline sizes vary from the 2-inch (5-centimetre) diameter lines in oil-well gathering systems to 48-inch (122-centimetre) lines for carrying petroleum from producing areas to large consumer centres; a few even larger lines are used to transport large volumes of water. Pipelines are welded into continuous lengths and usually placed underground. Since corrosion, potentially causing dangerous leakage, is a major problem, the lines are coated with protective materials such as asphalted felt. Pumping stations are located at intervals along the pipelines to help move petroleum or other materials over long distances. In the early 1970s the longest pipelines were for petroleum; one in North America ran 1,700 miles, while under construction in the Soviet Union was a line 2,760 miles (4,440 kilometres), from Aleksandrovsk on the Ob River to the Pacific coast port of Nakhodka.

·aqueducts and various pipe materials **1**:1036b
·Canadian transportation distinction **3**:727h
·coal transportation and practicability **4**:780e
·corrosion prevention methods **11**:1077c
·flexibility and workability of lead pipe **10**:729f
·gasoline supply in World War II **11**:82b
·gas turbine use in gas transport **18**:776a
·gas versus oil pipeline in cold climate **7**:924a
·iron transportation by slurry pipeline **9**:895g
·irrigation water delivery systems **9**:901f
·isotope tracing of leak and obstruction **15**:454d
·lead pipe development **10**:727h
·materials-handling systems **11**:615g
·natural gas transportation **12**:862f
·petroleum transportation systems **14**:188g
·plastic filament winding process **14**:525a
·plumbing and building construction **3**:464h
·plumbing system design and construction **14**:575c; illus.
·product transport capabilities **18**:658b
·size and use in petroleum transport **14**:179h
·Soviet Union gas and oil transport **17**:348e
·Suez Canal closing **17**:768e
·surveying of construction routes **17**:834f
·telemetric monitoring and control **18**:80a; illus.
·thermoelectric corrosion prevention **18**:319d
·timber floor construction **3**:955e
·tin production and use **18**:429a
·types and production methods **17**:654f; illus.
·United Kingdom transportation systems **18**:884b
·water supply and conveyance systems **19**:651a

pipe organ, refers informally to the organ, to distinguish it from 19th- and 20th-century instruments such as the harmonium (reed organ) and the electronic organ, both of which lack pipes and utilize distinct acoustical principles. *See* organ.

Bruckner Organ (pipe organ), 18th century; in the church of the abbey of Sankt Florian, Austria
Toni Schneiders

·construction and tone production **13**:676b; illus. 677

Piper, Carl, Count (b. July 29, 1647, Stockholm—d. May 29, 1716, Nöteborg, now Pakhisaari, Fin.), Swedish statesman who served as King Charles XII's leading minister during the Northern War (1700–21).

Piper was of lesser noble background. He became an official in the Swedish chancellry's department of home affairs under King Charles XI but reached the heights of Swedish government in 1697, when the newly crowned Charles XII raised him to a countship and appointed him to the council of state.

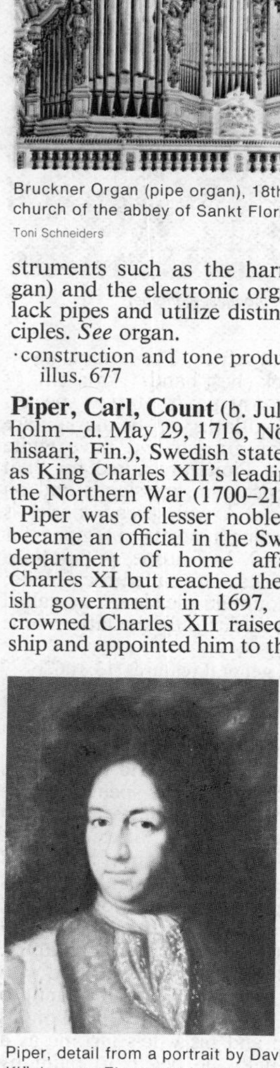

Piper, detail from a portrait by David Klöcker von Ehrenstrahl (1629–98); in Gripsholm Castle, Sweden
By courtesy of the Svenska Portrattarkivet, Stockholm

Piper was the only high councillor to accompany Charles in the field during the Northern War. While he approved, along with the other field advisers, a decision to invade Russia, Piper later strongly opposed Charles's determination to remain there following early setbacks.

Piper was captured during the Battle of Poltava (July 1709), and he remained a prisoner of the Russians until his death in 1716. Charles XII's repeated efforts to win the freedom of his trusted adviser through prisoner exchanges were all in vain.

Piperaceae, the pepper family, commercially important particularly because of *Piper nigrum*, the source of black pepper. The family comprises about 10 genera, of which 2, *Piper* (about 1,000 species) and *Peperomia* (*q.v.*; over 500 species), are the most important. The plants grow as herbs, vines, shrubs, and trees and are widely distributed throughout the tropics and subtropics.

The leaves of Piperaceae, which have a pungent flavour, grow singly. The numerous flowers, lacking sepals and petals, are crowded in dense spikes. *Piper* species are mostly shrubs, woody vines, and small trees. Many are used in medicines and in food and beverages as spices and seasonings. *P. cubeba*, of particular importance in Southeast Asia, is the source of cubeb, used in various medicines and for flavouring cigarettes and bitters. In the Orient the leaves of the betel (*q.v.*) pepper, *P. betle*, are widely chewed with slices of betel nut and lime. An intoxicating drink of Polynesia, variously known as kava, kawakawa, aiva, and yagona, is made from the root of *P. methysticum*. *Peperomia* species mostly grow as low herbs. Several are cultivated for their attractive foliage. The young leaves and stems of *P. vividispica* are used as food in Central and South America.

·classification and general features **14**:468f; illus. 467
·pepper production and exportation **14**:467h; illus.
·religious cult use **14**:200g

Piperales 14:467, an order of flowering plants containing two families—Piperaceae (the pepper family) and Saururaceae (the lizard's-tail family)—and about 3,000 species of largely tropical herbs. In some classification systems a third family, Chloranthaceae, is included; in others, the family Peperomiaceae is included.

The text article covers general features and economic importance of the Piperales and includes an annotated classification of the order.

REFERENCE in other text article:
·angiosperm features and classification **1**:882e
RELATED ENTRIES in the *Ready Reference and Index:*
lizard's-tail; Peperomia; Piperaceae

piperazine, also called DIETHYLENE DIAMINE or HEXAHYDROPYRAZINE, anthelmintic drug (worming agent) effective against intestinal roundworm infection in man and domestic animals (including poultry) and against pinworm infection in man. It is administered orally, usually as the citrate salt. Its action causes worms to be eliminated with normal stool. The chemical formula is $C_4H_{10}N_2$.
·roundworm infection treatment **4**:189f

piperine, an organic compound classed either with the lipid family (a group consisting of fats and fatlike substances) or with the alkaloids, a family of nitrogenous compounds with marked physiological properties. It is one of the sharp-tasting constituents of the fruit of the pepper vine (*Piper nigrum*).

Piperine, the oldest known of the pungent acid amides, comprises approximately 5–9 percent of commercial black or white pepper. It was first isolated in 1820, and its chemical constitution was established by laboratory syntheses in 1882 and 1894. The pure compound is a colourless solid, practically insoluble in water and neutrals, that melts at 130°–132.5° C (266°–271° F). It is tasteless at first but has a burning aftertaste.

The sharp flavour of freshly ground pepper is attributed to the compound chavicine, a geometrical isomer (having the same molecular formula but differing in structure) of piperine. The loss of pungency of ground pepper on storage is associated with slow transformation of chavicine into piperine.

Pipe Rolls, or GREAT ROLLS OF THE EXCHEQUER, the oldest and longest series of English public records and a valuable source for the financial and administrative history of medieval England. Apart from an isolated survival from 1130, they begin in 1156 and continue with few breaks until 1832. Their name probably derives from the fact that the sheepskin rolls, when stored in their presses, resemble a stack of pipes.

The rolls contain the yearly accounts of the sheriffs (and sometimes other royal officials) for each county. Royal income from feudal dues, judicial fees, and other sources is balanced against the expenses of the crown's officers, providing a basis for the calculation of the king's revenue. Yet such calculations can only be approximate, for even in the 12th century, by no means all of the king's income passed through the Exchequer (treasury). As new accounting offices were set up to handle new sources of revenue, the Exchequer accounts diminished in importance. In 1883 a Pipe Roll Society was founded and by the 1970s had published all the rolls up to and including that for 1214.

Pipestem State Park, protected area in southeastern West Virginia.
·West Virginia recreation centres **19**:803d

Pipestone, city, seat of Pipestone County, southwestern Minnesota, U.S., on Coteau des Prairies. Laid out in 1876, it developed with the coming of the railroads (1879–84), was incorporated (1901), and is the business centre for a mixed farming area. Population in 1980 was 4,887.

Pipestone National Monument (283 ac [115 ha]), immediately northwest, was established in 1937. It has quarries of a reddish-coloured stone that was used by Plains Indians to make ceremonial peace pipes (*see* sacred pipe). The site, considered sacred, was long fought over before being declared neutral ground. The stone (named catlinite for George Catlin, the artist, who visited there in 1836) is reserved for the Indians who quarry it under special permits issued by the National Park Service. Longfellow popularized the quarries in *The Song of Hiawatha*, and the city stages an annual Hiawatha pageant.
43°60′ N, 96°19′ W
·Indian use of rock **12**:257d

pipe vine (plant): *see* Dutchman's-pipe.

pipewort (plant): *see* Eriocaulales.

pipe wrench, a tool with an adjustable jaw for turning pipe collars.
·wrench design history **8**:622f

pi phat, musical ensemble accompanying theatre performances in Thailand, Laos, and Cambodia.
·Southeast Asian style and function **17**:237e

Pipidae, family of South American and African frogs, including the Surinam toad and clawed frog (*qq.v.*).
·classification and general features **1**:1008f

Pipilo erythrophthalmus (bird): *see* towhee.

Pipils (people): *see* Yaqui and Mayo.

piping, in geology, fluvial process that creates subsurface channels and hollows in easily erodible alluvial sediments, particularly in arid and semiarid regions.
·desert wash formation process **5**:611a; illus.
·gully formation **15**:887b

Pipiolos and Pelucones (Spanish: "novices" or "greenhorns," and "bigwigs," respectively), the two political partisan groups active in Chilean politics for about a century after national independence was achieved in the 1820s. The Pipiolos were liberals and the Pelucones conservatives. Between 1830 and 1861 the Pelucones were ascendant. Between 1861 and 1891 both groups realigned and splintered; the liberal coalitions acquired the upper hand and used their strength to gradually reduce executive in favour of congressional power. By the 1890s both liberals and conservatives represented mostly wealthy, vested interests, and after 1900 they were challenged by new middle and working class parties.

pipistrelle (*Pipistrellus*), any of about 40 to 50 species of bats, family Vespertilionidae, found in almost all parts of the world. Pipistrelles are grayish, brown, reddish, or black bats about 3.5–10 centimetres (1.4–4 inches) long without the 2.5–6-centimetre tail. Erratic fliers, they appear before most other bats in the evening and sometimes fly about even during the day. Representatives include *P. pipistrellus* of Eurasia and the eastern (*P. subflavus*) and western (*P. hesperus*) pipistrelles of North America.

pipit, any of the 30-odd species of the genus *Anthus*, family Motacillidae (order Passeriformes) and the golden pipit (*Tmetothylacus tenellus*) of Africa. The latter is a yellow bird with black chest band. (For a bird of similar name, *see* Ant pipit.) *Anthus* species, sometimes called titlarks or fieldlarks, are streaked brown or grayish and have white outer tail feathers. Pipits are noted for "tail pumping." They occur in grasslands and on beaches, worldwide. A widespread species is *A. spinoletta*, breeding in northern regions (far south in mountains). In Europe, populations nesting along seacoasts are called rock pipits; those found in mountain meadows are called water pipits; in America only the latter name is used.
·classification and general features **13**:1062b

Richard's pipit (*Anthus novaeseelandiae*)
M.F. Soper—Bruce Coleman Inc.

Pippin, Horace (b. Feb. 22, 1888, West Chester, Pa.—d. July 6, 1946, West Chester), folk painter known for his primitivist depictions of American Negro life and the horrors of war. Pippin's childhood was spent in Goshen, N.Y., a town that sometimes appears in his paintings. There he drew horses at the local racetrack and, to the despair of his school teachers, preferred drawing to writing. He was variously employed as an ironworker, junk dealer, porter, mover, and packer, until World War I when he served in the infantry. He was wounded in 1918 and discharged with a paralyzed right arm and classified as unfit to work. He settled in West Chester living on his disability pension and his wife's income as a laundress. Eventually he began to paint by burning a design into a lap-held wood panel with a red hot poker and then filling in the outlined areas with paint. By supporting his right wrist with his left hand, he was able to paint at an easel.

"John Brown Going to His Hanging," oil painting by Pippin, *c.* 1942; in the Pennsylvania Academy of the Fine Arts, Philadelphia
By courtesy of the Pennsylvania Academy of the Fine Arts, Philadelphia

His first large canvas was an eloquent protest against war, "End of the War: Starting Home" (1931–34), which was followed by other antiwar pictures, such as "Shell Holes and Observation Balloon" and the many versions of "Holy Mountain."

His most popular themes centred on the American Negro, such as his series entitled "Cabin in the Cotton," and his paintings of episodes in the life of the antislavery leader John Brown. After the art world discovered Pippin in 1937, these pictures particularly brought him wide acclaim as the greatest Negro painter of his time. Pippin also executed portraits and biblical subjects.

His early works are characterized by their heavy impasto and restricted use of colour, which was applied with attention to tonal variation. His later works are more precisely painted and are distinguished for their use of bold colour.

Pipridae (bird): *see* manakin.

pipsissewa, common name for certain evergreen, herbaceous (*i.e.*, nonwoody) plants of the genus *Chimaphila* (family Pyrolaceae), especially *C. umbellata* and *C. maculata*. The former, sometimes also called prince's pine, love-in-winter, and wintergreen (*q.v.*), occurs in North America from Canada to Mexico and in Europe and Japan. *C. maculata*, sometimes called striped pipsissewa, rheumatism root, dragon's tongue, and spotted wintergreen, occurs in North America from Canada to southern United States. The name pipsissewa derives from a Cree Indian word referring to the diuretic properties of the leaves when eaten.

Pipsissewa (*Chimaphila umbellata*)
Mary W. Ferguson

Pipsissewas are woodland plants with leathery leaves and five-petalled, fragrant, pink or white flowers that grow in a sparse, terminal cluster. They arise from rhizomes (underground stems). Though difficult to cultivate, they are sometimes grown in gardens.

Chimaphila maculata grows 10–25 centimetres (4–10 inches) tall; the stem is more or less prostrate. The lance-shaped leaves are 2.5–7.5 centimetres long and have white spots along the veins. The nodding flowers are about 2.5 centimetres across. *C. umbellata* grows 12–30 centimetres tall. The leaves are somewhat broader than those of *C. maculata* and are not spotted. The flowers are about 2 centimetres across and appear throughout the summer.

Pipunculidae, family of big-headed flies, order Diptera.
·classification and features **5**:824b

Piqua, city, Miami County, western Ohio, U.S., on the Great Miami River. The original Shawnee village of Piqua near modern Springfield, Ohio, was destroyed by George Rogers Clark and his Kentucky volunteers in 1780. The Indians then moved to the present site, where they established two settlements, Upper and Lower Piqua. In 1794 Gen. "Mad Anthony" Wayne built Ft. Piqua near Upper Piqua, and from there the famous Indian chief Tecumseh departed in 1796 for the headwaters of the Whitewater in Indiana. A town called Washington was subsequently laid out on the site in 1807. Renamed Piqua in 1816, it developed as a flatboat river port trading in corn, flour, bacon, and flax and was incorporated in 1823. The completion of the Miami and Erie Canal (1836) and the arrival of the railroads (1850s) gave impetus to its growth as a manufacturing community. The city's Archaeology Museum (founded 1961) displays artifacts representing five prehistoric Indian cultures of the area. Inc. city, 1850. Pop. (1980) 20,480.
40°09′ N, 84°15′ W

Piqueria (plant): *see* Asteraceae.

Piquet, a game of cards, probably a development of Roufa, a game mentioned by the Italian poet Francesco Berni in 1526. The Spanish name of the game was Cientos (Latin *centum*, "a hundred"). Piquet was played in England under the name of Cent, probably as early as 1550, but is not much played today.

Piquet is essentially a game for two players, although there are variants for three and four. A pack of 32 cards is used, ranking: A (high), K, Q, J, 10, 9, 8, 7. Twelve cards are dealt to each player, 2 or 3 at a time. The remaining 8 cards, the stock, are spread face down. If either player holds carte blanche (a hand with no court card), he announces it and scores 10 points. Players may then discard and draw from the stock to improve their hands.

After the draw, players compare their holdings in each of three classes of scoring combinations. The classes are point, sequence, and set, and are scored in that order. Only one player may score in each class.

Point is the longest suit or, if the long suits in both hands are equal in length, the highest total count in those suits, reckoning ace as 11, court cards 10 each, and other cards their pip values. Whoever has the better point scores one for each card in the suit. A tie scores for neither.

A sequence is three or more cards of the same suit in consecutive rank: tierce for sequence of three, quart for four, quint for five, etc. The longest sequence is "good," and the holder may also score any additional sequences he holds. Between equal-length sequences, that of higher rank is good. Tierce scores 3, quart 4; quint or better scores 10, plus one for each card. If there is a tie for best sequence, no sequences are scored.

Sets are 3 of a kind (trio) or 4 of a kind (quatorze) of rank 10 or higher. A quatorze, counting 14, is good against a trio, counting 3. Between equal-length sets, that of higher rank wins. The player with the highest set may count it and any additional set he holds.

Upon completion of the declarations, play begins, the nondealer making the first lead. Each lead requires the other to follow suit if able. The trick is won by the higher card of the suit led. (There is no trump suit.) The winner of a trick leads to the next. For each lead he makes and each trick he wins on an adverse lead, the player scores one point. The last trick counts one extra point. The winner of a majority of the 12 tricks scores 10 points. If he wins all the tricks he scores 40 for capot.

If by declared combinations a player reaches 30 or more points before his opponent scores a point, he adds 60 to his score for repique. If he reaches 30 in declaring and play (excluding capot) before his opponent scores, he adds 30 for pique.

In the early Piquet au Cent, a game was continued by alternate deals until one player reached 100 points. This game was superseded by Rubicon Piquet, in which a game is six deals. The winner receives a bonus of 100 for game, plus the difference of the final totals. If the loser fails to reach 100 (even if the winner also is below 100), he is rubiconed, and the winner takes 100 plus the sum of the final totals. Some players prefer a short game of four deals, the first and last counting double.
·history and strategy **3**:904a

piqué work, decorative technique, usually employed on tortoiseshell, in which inlaid designs are created by means of small gold or silver pins. The art reached its highest point in 17th- and 18th-century France, particularly for the decoration of small tortoiseshell articles such as combs, patch boxes, and snuff boxes. By an adroit arrangement of the gold and silver pins, by placing them in small or large clusters, effects of light and shade could be created in the design. In the finest French work, the pins are placed so close to each other and with such accuracy that they appear to form a continuous line. Decorative motifs include chinoiserie (reflecting Chinese influence) scenes, geometric designs, and arabesques. In England, where the craft had been brought by the Huguenots at the end of the 17th century, Matthew Boulton in 1770 developed factory methods of producing piqué panels. Many of his designs show the influence of the Neoclassical designer Robert Adam. During the 19th century, piqué was widely employed for small tortoiseshell jewelry, much of it after 1872 being made by machine in Birmingham, Eng.

Piquillacta, Inca archaeological site in the Cuzco Valley, Peru.
·pre-Incan cultural characteristics **1**:845d; map 840

pīr (Islāmic mystical teacher): *see* shaykh.

Piracicaba, city, in the highlands of east central São Paulo state, Brazil, at 1,772 ft (540 m) above sea level on the Rio Tietê. Formerly called Santo Antônio de Piracicaba and Vila Nova da Constituição, the settlement was given town status in 1821 and made the seat of a municipality in 1856. The city is in the centre of the state's main sugarcane-producing area; cotton, rice, coffee, and other crops are also cultivated. In addition to sugar refineries, the city has distilleries, food-processing factories, and machinery plants. One of the state's chief agricultural colleges is nearby. Piracicaba is linked by road, rail, and air to São Paulo, the state capital, 85 mi (137 km) southeast. Pop. (1970 prelim.) 125,490.
22°43′ S, 47°38′ W
·map, Brazil **3**:124

Piracicaba Braz. showing the Agricultural College (centre)
Plessner International

piracy, any robbery or other violent action, for private ends and without authorization by public authority, committed on the seas or in the air outside the normal jurisdiction of any state. Because piracy has been regarded as an offense against the law of nations, the public vessels of any state have been permitted to seize a pirate ship, to bring it into port, to try the crew (regardless of their nationality or domicile), and, if found guilty, to punish them and to confiscate the ship.

A key point in a definition of piracy according to international law is that the act takes place outside the normal jurisdiction of a state, without state authority, and that the intent is private, not political. Thus, although acts of unlawful warfare, acts of insurgents and revolutionists, mutiny, and slave trading have been defined as piracy by national laws of various countries or by special treaties, they are not, in most cases, piracy by the law of nations.

Piracy has occurred in all stages of history. In the ancient Mediterranean, piracy was often closely related to maritime commerce, and the Phoenicians appear to have engaged in both, as did the Greeks, Romans, and Carthaginians. In the Middle Ages, Vikings from the north and Moors from the south also engaged in piracy. At the conclusion of European wars during the Renaissance and after, naval vessels would be laid up and their crews disbanded. From among these men, pirates recruited their crews. A common source of piracy, for instance, was the privateer, a privately owned and armed ship commissioned by a government to make reprisals, to gain reparation for specified offenses in time of peace, or to prey upon the enemy in time of war, with the right of the officers and crew to share in prize money from captured vessels. The temptation was great to continue this profitable business after the war without authorization. During the Elizabethan wars with Spain in the late 16th century, treasure-laden Spanish galleons proceeding from Mexico into the Caribbean were a natural target for privateers, and the line between privateering and piracy became difficult to draw.

From the 16th to the 18th centuries, after the weakening of Turkish rule had resulted in the virtual independence of the Barbary States of North Africa, piracy became common in the Mediterranean. Morocco, Algiers, Tunis, and Tripoli so tolerated or even organized piracy that they came to be called pirate states. In the early 19th century they were suppressed by successive actions of American, British, and French forces.

The increased size of merchant vessels, the improved naval patrolling of most ocean highways, the regular administration of most islands and land areas of the world, and the general recognition by governments of piracy as an international offense resulted in a great decline in piracy in the 19th and 20th centuries. Piracy has, however, occurred in the 20th century in the South China Sea, and the practice of hijacking ships or airplanes has developed into a new form of piracy. In the 1960s and early 1970s, airplanes flying within or from the United States were sometimes hijacked by persons on board, often for unauthorized flights to Cuba. In each case the hijacker with threats of force compelled the pilot to change his course; the intent might be political or private or the result of a desire for publicity by a deranged mind. Such incidents presented great danger to passengers and crew (a few were killed) and proved difficult to police. Legislation was enacted for punishment of hijacking of airplanes as an offense analogous to piracy.
·air laws concerning seizure of aircraft **1**:398c
·Bahamian raids and retaliation **2**:591c
·Berber gains for Ottoman Empire **13**:160b
·Dutch naval wars on privateering **18**:716e
·Etruscan maritime activity **9**:1080h
·fraudulence in the arts **2**:89f
·Geneva Convention of 1958 **1**:398b
·Haitian plantation settlements **8**:550h
·Havana attack and destruction **8**:668f
·Jamaican historical significance **10**:17e
·legal definition **9**:748c
·New York colonial history **13**:30d
·Spanish colonial vulnerability **10**:697c

Piraeus, Modern Greek PIRAIÉVS, the port of Athens and largest port in Greece, on Órmos Fálirou (Phaleron Bay), southwest of the metropolis by highway. The main harbour, Kántharos (ancient Cantharus), is embraced on the west by the small Ietionía peninsula, on the south by the main Áyion Óros (Akti) peninsula (the Peraïki sector of the port), and on the east by Munychia (modern Kastélla), its highest point. The port has been rebuilt since the bombings of World War II. Its many new factories are mainly engineering and chemical support industries and shipyards. It is the terminal station for all the main Greek railways and is linked to Athens by electric railway and superhighway.

The harbour at Piraeus, the port of Athens on the Saronic Gulf

K. Honkanen—Ostman Agency

In the 7th and 6th centuries BC the Athenians used Phaleron Bay for mooring, since the present port was separated from the mainland by marshes. The Athenian statesman Themistocles persuaded his colleagues (*c.* 493) to fortify Piraeus for the new Athenian fleet. Soon after 460 the long walls from the base of Munychia to Athens were built. The modern street pattern approximates the grid laid out at that time. In 86 BC the Roman conspirator Sulla destroyed the city, and it was insignificant from that time until its revival in the 19th century. In 1854–59, following the Crimean War, Piraeus was occupied by the Anglo-French fleet to forestall disturbances.

Bronze and marble statues of the 6th to 4th centuries BC that had been awaiting shipment to Rome when Sulla burned the town were found in 1959. Traces of the long wall foundations of "ship houses" surrounding Zea and Munychia and of a Hellenistic theatre remain. There is a Naval Academy and an Archaeological Museum, with statuary and pottery from both the Greek and Roman periods. Pop. (1971) 187,458.

37°57′ N, 23°38′ E

·department area and population table **8**:318
·importance during the Athenian Empire
  8:356d; map 326
·map, Greece **8**:314
·Themistocles' initial support **18**:270b

piragua (boat): *see* pirogue.

Pi-Ramesse (Egypt): *see* Tanis.

Pirandello, Luigi 14:469 (b. June 28, 1867, Agrigento, Sicily—d. Dec. 10, 1936, Rome), playwright, novelist, and short-story writer, winner of the 1934 Nobel Prize for Literature. With his invention of the "theatre within the theatre" (in *Six Characters in Search of an Author*), he became an important innovator in modern drama.

Abstract of text biography. Although he was the son of a sulfur merchant who destined him for commerce, Pirandello's desire for study and for liberty took him, in 1887, to the University of Rome and thence to Bonn, where in 1891 he gained his doctorate in philology. His marriage in 1894 to the daughter of a wealthy sulfur merchant enabled him to settle in Rome as a writer; but in 1903 a disaster overtook the family fortunes, and he had to earn his living by teaching and writing. His wife's subsequent mental illness coloured his outlook and provided themes—such as the dislocation of personality—already perceptible in his early short stories.

The success of Pirandello's drama *Così è (se vi pare)* in 1917 was the beginning of the series of dramatic successes that were to make him world famous in the 1920s. His two greatest plays are considered to be *Sei personaggi in cerca d'autore* (1921; *Six Characters in Search of an Author*) and *Enrico IV* (1922; *Henry IV*). Of his novels the most successful were *Il fu Mattia Pascal* (1904), *I vecchi e i giovani* (1913), and *Uno, nessuno e centomila* (1925–26; *One, None and a Hundred Thousand*, 1933). Many of his more than 50 plays were dramatized versions of his short stories. He also wrote *L'umorismo* (1908), a study in humour and in the principles of his art.

REFERENCES in other text articles:
·Italian literary role and influence **10**:1237g
·Italian novel **13**:294h
·technique and mood of
  work **9**:1111d
·theatre function and philosophy of
  man **18**:231b
·tragicomedy and the grotesque **4**:964g

Piranesi, Giambattista (b. Oct. 4, 1720, Mestre, Italy—d. Nov. 9, 1778, Rome), Italian draftsman and etcher known for his popular prints of Roman ruins.

Piranesi studied perspective and stage design in Venice and learned etching from Guiseppe Vasi and Felice Polanzani in Rome (1740–44). In the late 1740s he began a series of 135 *Vedute di Roma* ("Views of Rome"), dramatizing Classical and contemporary Roman sites. His most famous series of plates was *Carceri d'invenzione* (*c.* 1745, 2nd ed. 1760; "Imaginary Prisons"), combining romantic fantasy and architectural landscape. His later works include *Le Antichità romane*, etchings of Roman ruins (1748), views of the Greek temples at Paestum (1777–78), and a book of eccentric designs for interior decoration (1769). His major architectural work was the rebuilding of the church of Sta. Maria del Priorato on the Aventine Hill (1764–65).

A prolific etcher, Piranesi created more than 1,000 plates. His unparalleled accuracy and his imaginative evocation of a structure's dramatic and romantic grandeur made these prints the most original and impressive representations of architecture to be found in Western art.

·architectural etchings **14**:1091b; illus.
·Neoclassical architectural
  developments **19**:437a
·Robert Adam's acquaintance **1**:72f
·Roman artistic beautification **15**:1077a
·Roman drawings **5**:1009a; illus. 1007
·scene design in classical motif **17**:540h

"Veduta di Piazza Cavello," drawing from the series *Vedute di Roma* by Piranesi, *c.* 1748–60; in the British Museum

By courtesy of the trustees of the British Museum; photograph, J.R. Freeman & Co. Ltd.